BUTTERWORTH
COMPETITION LA
HANDBOOK

BUTTERWORTHS COMPETITION LAW HANDBOOK

Twenty-seventh edition

EDITED BY

Antonio F. Bavasso, JD, PhD (Solicitor and Avvocato),
Partner, Simpson Thacher & Bartlett LLP
Visiting Professor and Director of the Jevons Institute for Competition Law and Economics at University College London

ASSISTED BY

Anna Battersby,
BA (Hons) (Wits) (Solicitor),
Associate, Simpson Thacher & Bartlett LLP

Members of the LexisNexis® Group worldwide

United Kingdom	RELX (UK) Limited trading as LexisNexis®, 1–3 Strand, London WC2N 5JR
LNUK Global Partners	LexisNexis® encompasses authoritative legal publishing brands dating back to the 19th century including: Butterworths® in the United Kingdom, Canada and the Asia-Pacific region; Les Editions du Juris Classeur in France; and Matthew Bender® worldwide. Details of LexisNexis® locations worldwide can be found at **www.lexisnexis.com**

Published by LexisNexis®

This is a Butterworths® title

A CIP Catalogue record for this book is available from the British Library.

ISBN for this volume: 978 1 4743 1791 7

Printed and bound by CPI Group (UK) Ltd, Croydon, CR0 4YY.

Visit LexisNexis at www.lexisnexis.co.uk

PREFACE

The first year after the end of the Brexit transition period has continued to see major developments in UK and EU antitrust policy and enforcement. The Competition and Markets Authority and European Commission are in the process of adapting current rules to make them 'fit for purpose', particularly for fast-moving digital markets. Ground-breaking new regimes are under development in both jurisdictions. Both authorities continue to streamline procedures and update materials to reflect recent practice and experience.

In the UK, a number of possible reforms are on the horizon. The UK government has consulted on wide-ranging proposed reforms to the competition regime including significant changes to the merger control thresholds, amendments to the markets regime to give the CMA greater flexibility and powers, expanding the territorial scope of its rules on anti-competitive conduct, and incentivising leniency applications. Meanwhile the CMA has consulted on proposed amendments to its settlement procedures for Competition Act 1998 cases. The proposals aim to ensure that any settlement normally brings finality to the investigation. Links to these consultations can be found in the Appendix.

Earlier in the year, the CMA overhauled its 2010 mergers assessment guidance (see Part 3.C.1), most notably revising its approach to market definition and adding new sections on potential and dynamic competition, two-sided platforms and the assessment of evidence. Other updates reflect the CMA's current best practice, including a revised test for the failing firm defence. The CMA also issued new guidance on reporting, investigation and enforcement of potential breaches of merger and market investigation remedies. This guidance codifies its existing approach to actual or potential breaches of final undertakings and orders put in place to address concerns identified in merger, monopoly and market investigations (see Part 3.A).

On the antitrust side, while the CMA has recommended that the government replace the retained EU block exemption regulation on vertical agreements with a new UK Vertical Agreements Block Exemption Order when it expires on 31 May 2022, the Commission's new rules on vertical agreements are in near final form. Both the EU and UK proposals see a softening of the rules in areas such as online sales restrictions (for example, dual pricing) and increased flexibility for selective distribution models, but a tightening of provisions relating to "most favoured nation" clauses. The Commission has also consulted on proposed adjustments to the block exemptions relating to horizontal co-operation agreements and is likely to propose new rules in 2022. Again, links to these materials are included in the Appendix.

The hotly anticipated National Security and Investment Act 2021 will come into force on 4 January 2022, with a "call-in" power allowing the government to review any relevant deals that closed on or after 12 November 2021. The Act drastically expands the government's powers to scrutinise investment on national security grounds, through a requirement for mandatory notification of transactions in certain sensitive sectors – with the 'call-in' power applying to an extremely wide range of deals involving both UK and foreign targets active across all sectors of the UK economy, with no turnover or market share thresholds. These rules supersede the 2020 threshold reductions (together with similar amendments made in 2018) and takes national security screening outside the scope of the UK merger control regime altogether. While the government is keen to stress that the UK remains open to investment and that most transactions will be cleared without any intervention, the resulting regulatory burden created by the new regime is set to have a significant impact on acquirers looking to invest in the UK. The Act and accompanying statutory instruments are included in Parts 1 and 2 – while relevant BEIS guidance is included in Part 3.E. At the time of going to print, additional guidance on submitting a notification and the government's approach to compliance and enforcement is expected to be published before the Act comes into force.

With the impact of the COVID-19 pandemic having been partially mitigated by vaccination programmes, some of the temporary measures adopted by the UK authorities and in Brussels have been revoked or modified. In the UK, most of the exclusion orders adopted in 2020 to ensure that, on a temporary basis, certain types of cooperation arrangements (such as coordination between health service providers to share facilities or jointly purchase goods/services) did not fall foul of UK antitrust rules, have been revoked – though the government has adopted two additional exclusion orders in 2021 (see Part 8.A). In the EU, the Commission's Temporary Framework for State aid measures to support the economy during the outbreak has been amended for the sixth time and extended until 30 June 2022 (see Part 8.C).

In both the EU and UK, new regimes to regulate key players in the digital economy have been proposed. In the EU, a new Digital Markets Act proposes to place special obligations on digital "gatekeepers" to prevent them from imposing unfair conditions on businesses and consumers, and ensuring the openness of important digital services. Under the UK proposals, an enforceable code of conduct aimed to ensure fair trading, open choices and trust and transparency would be imposed on firms with "strategic market status." A standalone merger regime would also apply to such firms. The Commission has also published a proposed regulation to tackle the possible distortive effects of foreign subsidies. The Appendix contains links to all of these materials.

In the EU, in order to tackle a possible enforcement gap in relation to "killer acquisitions" of entities housing nascent innovations without legislative changes, the Commission has revised its guidelines on the referral of merger cases by Member States to encourage referrals from EU national competition authorities in certain circumstances, even where those authorities have no jurisdiction to review the deals at national level (see Part 4.F.2). Under the new guidelines, the Commission accepted France's request to review gene sequencing company Illumina's acquisition of Grail, a small cancer-testing company with no activities in Europe. Illumina appealed the Commission's decision to the General Court and closed the deal despite the Commission's ongoing investigation, making it a test case for the Commission's revised approach. The Commission has imposed interim measures on Illumina for gun-jumping in the meantime and is expected to issue a fine.

The Commission has also launched an impact assessment to explore policy options for further simplification of merger review procedures as well as further streamlining the existing simplified procedure to speed up reviews. Any resulting changes to guidance will likely be in next year's edition of the Handbook.

There have been no major EU antitrust developments although, as mentioned above, a new set of vertical rules and guidelines is to be expected for 2022. In State aid, this edition of the Handbook now contains a revised consolidated version of the General Block Exemption Regulation, reflecting amendments to widen its scope to cover aid granted through national funds for projects also supported under certain EU centrally-managed programmes, as well as aid to support the twin transition to a green and digital economy that will, at the same time, help the recovery from the effects of the coronavirus pandemic (see Part 5.A). The Commission has issued new guidelines on the enforcement of State aid rules by national courts aimed to encourage closer cooperation between the Commission and national courts, while BEIS has issued guidance on the UK's international subsidy control commitments (both in Part 5.A). Also included are revised guidelines on regional State aid and State aid relating to important projects of common European interest (both of which apply from 1 January 2021 – see Part 5.C.3 and Part 5.C.8 respectively). Part 7.B now includes Commission guidance on the withdrawal of the UK and EU Rules in the field of State aid.

The Commission has consulted on revised draft State aid guidelines relating to risk finance investments, energy and environmental protection, research and development and innovation, short-term export credit insurance and broadband networks. The current guidelines are due to expire on 31 December 2021 but, at the time of going to print, the revised guidelines had not been published. The Commission has also conducted a further targeted review of the General Block Exemption Regulation relating to the green and digital transition and has consulted on a draft revised *de minimis* Regulation for aid in the agriculture and fishery sectors. The draft materials are all available in the Appendix.

This Handbook follows the standard Butterworths Handbooks style, with amendments made by new legislation incorporated into the text of existing legislation. Details of the provenance of changes are given in the NOTES which include, where appropriate, details of any savings and transitional provisions in the implementing legislation. Commencement information is given at provision level for Acts and statutory instruments in cases where the provision came into force within the last 3 years, or where it is not yet in force for all or some purposes. If no commencement information is given at provision level then the provision in question was brought into force for all purposes before 1 November 2018. Commencement information is given in relation to amendments where those amendments come into force on or after IP completion day (31 December 2020), or where the commencement date of the amendment has not yet been appointed.

In the text:

- an ellipsis (. . .) indicates that text has been repealed or revoked (or is outside the scope of this Handbook);
- square brackets denote text that has been inserted or substituted;
- italicised text is prospectively repealed or substituted, or repealed subject to savings (in the case of prospective substitutions the 'new' text is set out in the notes).

This Handbook is up to date to 1 November 2021; though later changes have been incorporated where possible. In particular, this edition also includes the following:

- New Regulations made under the National Security and Investment Act 2021 (National Security and Investment Act 2021 (Monetary Penalties) (Turnover of a Business) Regulations 2021; National Security and Investment Act 2021 (Notifiable Acquisition) (Specification of Qualifying Entities) Regulations 2021; National Security and Investment Act 2021 (Procedure for Service) Regulations 2021; National Security and Investment Act 2021 (Prescribed Form and Content of Notices and Validation Applications) Regulations 2021) (see Part 2.G);
- New BEIS guidance on the 2021 Act relating to notifiable acquisitions, and Section 3 Statements. As well as updated general guidance relating to the new rules (see Part 3.E);
- New Commission guidelines on state aid to promote the execution of important projects of common European interest (see Part 5.C);
- The sixth amendment to the Temporary Framework for State aid measures to support the economy in the current COVID-19 outbreak (see Part 8.C).

Antonio Bavasso and Anna Battersby
25 November 2021

CONTENTS

B. COMPETITION ACT 1998 INVESTIGATIONS AND CARTELS

1. General

2. Sector Specific

(i) General

(ii) Communications

(iii) Energy

(iv) Water

(v) Financial Services

(vi) Transport

(vii) Healthcare

PART 4 EU & RETAINED EU MATERIALS

A. GENERAL

B. COOPERATION AGREEMENTS

F. CONCENTRATIONS

1. General

2. Procedure

B. TEMPORARY RULES ESTABLISHED IN RESPONSE TO THE ECONOMIC AND FINANCIAL CRISIS

C. HORIZONTAL RULES

1. Training Aid

2. Employment Aid

3. Regional Aid

4. Research and Development and Innovation Aid

5. Environmental Aid

6. Risk Capital Aid

7. Rescue and Restructuring Aid

8. Projects of Common European Interest

D. SECTOR-SPECIFIC RULES

1. Audiovisual Production

2. Broadcasting

3. Broadband

4. Transport

5. Electricity (Stranded Costs)

6. Postal Services

7. Steel

8. Coal

9. Agriculture

10. Fisheries

E. SPECIFIC AID INSTRUMENTS

1. State Guarantees

2. Export Credit Insurance

3. Tax Rulings

4. State-Owned Enterprises

F. SERVICES OF GENERAL ECONOMIC INTEREST

PART 6 UK AND EU COURT MATERIALS

A. UK COURTS

B. EU COURTS

PART 7 BREXIT-RELATED MATERIALS

A. UK Legislation

B. Other materials

PART 1
STATUTES

FAIR TRADING ACT 1973

(1973 c 41)

ARRANGEMENT OF SECTIONS

PART IX
AMENDMENTS OF RESTRICTIVE TRADE PRACTICES ACTS

PART XII
MISCELLANEOUS AND SUPPLEMENTARY PROVISIONS

SCHEDULES

An Act to provide for the appointment of a Director General of Fair Trading and of a Consumer Protection Advisory Committee, and to confer on the Director General and the Committee so appointed, on the Secretary of State, on the Restrictive Practices Court and on certain other courts new functions for the protection of consumers; to make provisions, in substitution for the Monopolies and Restrictive Practices (Inquiry and Control) Act 1948 and the Monopolies and Mergers Act 1965, for the matters dealt with in those Acts and related matters, including restrictive labour practices; to amend the Restrictive Trade Practices Act 1956 and the Restrictive Trade Practices Act 1968, to make provision for extending the said Act of 1956 to agreements relating to services, and to transfer to the Director General of Fair Trading the functions of the Registrar of Restrictive Trading Agreements; to make provision with respect to pyramid selling and similar trading schemes; to make new provision in place of section 30(2) to (4) of the Trade Descriptions Act 1968; and for purposes connected with those matters

[25 July 1973]

NOTES

Disclosure of information

Information held by a public authority in connection with the exercise of any function it has under Parts I, III–VIII, XI of this Act is "specified information" for the purposes of the Enterprise Act 2002, Pt 9 (ss 237–247 and Schs 14, 15), and can be disclosed in the United Kingdom and, except in the case of information obtained under Pts IV–VI of this Act, overseas; see ss 238, 241, 243 of, and Schs 14, 15 to, that Act at **[1.417]**, **[1.420]**, **[1.423]**, **[1.443]**, **[1.444]**.

Regulatory Functions

By the Legislative and Regulatory Reform (Regulatory Functions) Order 2007, SI 2007/3544, art 2, Schedule, Pts 3, 6 (made under the Legislative and Regulatory Reform Act 2006, s 24(2)), any regulatory function under or by virtue of this Act (including any regulatory function conferred by subordinate legislation made thereunder), so far as exercisable by local authorities, is a function to which ss 21 and 22 of the 2006 Act apply (ie, the principle that regulatory activities should be carried out in a way which is transparent, accountable, proportionate and consistent; and should be targeted only at cases in which action is needed) (subject to arts 3, 4 of that order).

Part I (ss 1–12) (Introductory)

Ss 1, 2 concerned the establishment of the office of the Director General of Fair Trading and the functions of the Director. They were repealed by the Enterprise Act 2002, s 278(2), Sch 26 (for transitional provisions in relation to the pensions, etc, of former Directors, and the effect of the transfer of the functions of the Director to the OFT, see Sch 24, paras 2, 6 to the 2002 Act at **[1.445]**; s 3 repealed by the Enterprise Act 2002, ss 10(1)(a), 278(2), Sch 26; s 4 repealed by the Competition Act 1998, s 74(1), (3), Sch 12, para 1(1), (2), Sch 14, Pt I.

S 5 (Principal functions of Commission) was repealed by the Enterprise Act 2002 and Media Mergers (Consequential Amendments) Order 2003, SI 2003/3180, art 2, Schedule, para 1(1), (2), subject to transitional provisions and savings contained in art 3 of that Order in relation to (a) a transfer of a newspaper or of newspaper assets which was made before 29 December 2003; (b) a proposed transfer of a newspaper or of newspaper assets in relation to which an application for the consent of the Secretary of State under s 58 of this Act was made before that date; and (c) the making by the Secretary of State of references under the Water Industry Act 1991, s 32 (duty to refer merger of water or sewerage undertakings) or any references so made.

Ss 6–12 were repealed by the Enterprise Act 2002, ss 9, 278(2), Sch 26; for savings in relation to the application of s 6 (Monopoly situation in relation to supply of goods), see the Enterprise Act 2002 (Commencement No 3, Transitional and Transitory Provisions and Savings) Order 2003, SI 2003/1397, art 11 (savings in relation to specified Telecommunication Regulations).

Part II (ss 13–33) (References to the Consumer Protection Advisory Committee)

Repealed by a combination of the Enterprise Act 2002 and the Consumer Protection from Unfair Trading Regulations 2008, SI 2008/1277. In so far as the 2008 Regulations provided for savings and transitional provisions in connection with the repeal of certain provisions in this Part, they are outside the scope of this work.

Part III (ss 34–43) (Additional functions of the Director for protection of consumers)

Ss 34–42 were repealed by the Enterprise Act 2002, s 278, Sch 25, para 5(1), (3), Sch 26; s 43 was repealed by the Legal Aid Act 1974, s 42(1), Sch 5, Pt I, the Legal Aid (Scotland) Act 1986, s 45(3), Sch 5, and the Legal Aid, Advice, and Assistance (Northern Ireland) Order 1981, SI 1981/228, Sch 4. For savings see the Enterprise Act 2002 (Commencement No 3, Transitional and Transitory Provisions and Savings) Order 2003, SI 2003/1397, art 7, which provides that where any proceedings were commenced under Part III of this Act before the 20 June 2003 then those proceedings shall not be affected by the repeal of Part III but may be continued until they are finally determined (including any appeals that may be brought) and the Court may make any order that it could have made on the application had Part III not been repealed.

Pt IV (ss 44–56G) (Functions of Director and Commission in relation to monopoly situations and uncompetitive practices)

Repealed by the Enterprise Act 2002, s 278(2), Sch 26.

Pt V (ss 57–77) (Mergers)

Ss 57–62 were repealed by the Communications Act 2003, ss 373, 406, Sch 19.

Ss 63–75K, 76 were repealed by the Enterprise Act 2002, s 278(2), Sch 26. For transitional provisions and savings (including an exception in relation the merger of water and sewerage undertakers), see Sch 24, paras 13, 15–19 to that Act at **[1.445]**, and the Enterprise Act 2002 (Commencement No 3, Transitional and Transitory Provisions and Savings) Order 2003, SI 2003/1397, arts 3, 4. See also, the Enterprise Act 2002 (Commencement No 7 and Transitional Provisions and Savings) Order 2004, SI 2004/3233 (which commences the Enterprise Act 2002 in relation to water mergers, subject to transitional provisions and savings regarding anticipated and completed mergers).

S 77 was repealed by the Enterprise Act 2002 and Media Mergers (Consequential Amendments) Order 2003, SI 2003/3180, art 2, Schedule, para 1(1), (3) (subject to transitional provisions and savings contained in art 3 of that Order as noted above).

Pt VI (ss 78–80) (References to Commission other than monopoly and merger references)

Repealed by the Enterprise Act 2002, ss 208, 278(2), Sch 26, subject to transitional provisions and savings in relation to the merger of water and sewerage undertakers, as noted above.

Pt VII (ss 81–83) (Provisions Relating to References to Advisory Committee or to Commission)

S 81 was repealed by the Enterprise Act 2002, s 278(2), Sch 26, subject to transitional provisions and savings in relation to the merger of water and sewerage undertakers, as noted above; ss 82, 83 were repealed by the Enterprise Act 2002 and Media Mergers (Consequential Amendments) Order 2003, SI 2003/3180, art 2, Schedule, para 1(1), (4), (5), subject to transitional provisions and savings contained in art 3 of that Order as noted above.

Part VIII (84–93B) (Additional Provisions Relating to References to Commission)

Ss 84, 86, 88–93A were repealed by the Enterprise Act 2002, s 278(2), Sch 26, subject to transitional provisions and savings in relation to the merger of water and sewerage undertakers, as noted above; ss 85, 87 were repealed by the Enterprise Act 2002 and Media Mergers (Consequential Amendments) Order 2003, SI 2003/3180, art 2, Schedule, para 1(1), (6), (7), subject to transitional provisions and savings contained in art 3 of that Order as noted above; s 93B was repealed by the Civil Aviation Act 2012, s 76(4), Sch 9, para 1.

PART IX AMENDMENTS OF RESTRICTIVE TRADE PRACTICES ACTS

[1.1]

94 Transfer of functions of Registrar to Director

(1) Subject to the transitional provisions having effect by virtue of section 139 of this Act, the functions of the Registrar of Restrictive Trading Agreements are hereby transferred to the Director . . .

(2) . . .

NOTES

Sub-s (1): words omitted repealed by the Statute Law (Repeals) Act 2004.

Sub-s (2): repealed by the Resale Prices Act 1976, s 29, Sch 3, Pt I.

The Director: ie, the Director General of Fair Trading. The Enterprise Act 2002, s 2(1) provided that, as from the coming into force of that section (on 1 April 2003), the functions of the Director General of Fair Trading, his property, rights and liabilities were transferred to the Office of Fair Trading. Accordingly, (by virtue of s 2(2), (3) of the 2002 Act) the office of the Director was abolished, and any reference to the Director in any enactment, instrument or other document passed or made before the commencement of s 2(1) had, in so far as was necessary, effect as if it were a reference to the Office of Fair Trading. For transitional provisions in connection with the transfer, see Sch 24, para 6 to the 2002 Act at **[1.445]**. Section 2 of the 2002 Act was repealed by the Enterprise and Regulatory Reform Act 2013, s 26(3), Sch 5, Pt 4, para 229. As to the subsequent abolition of the OFT, see the Enterprise and Regulatory Reform Act 2013, s 26 at **[1.447]**.

95–123 *(Ss 95–106, ss 107–117 (Pt X) repealed and consolidated by the Restrictive Trade Practices Act 1976 (the 1976 Act was subsequently repealed by the Competition Act 1998); ss 118–123 (Pt XI) (pyramid selling and similar trading schemes) outside the scope of this work.)*

PART XII MISCELLANEOUS AND SUPPLEMENTARY PROVISIONS

124–128 *(Ss 124, 125 repealed by the Enterprise Act 2002, s 278(2), Sch 26; s 126 repealed by the Patents Act 1977, s 132(7), Sch 6; s 127 inserts the Agricultural Marketing Act 1958, s 19A; s 128 repealed and consolidated by the Restrictive Trade Practices Act 1976.))*

[1.2]

129 Time-limit for prosecutions

(1) No prosecution for an offence under this Act shall be commenced after the expiration of three years from the commission of the offence or one year from its discovery by the prosecutor, whichever is the earlier.

(2) Notwithstanding anything in [section 127(1) of the Magistrates' Courts Act 1980], a magistrates' court may try an information for an offence under this Act if the information was laid within twelve months from the commission of the offence.
(3) Notwithstanding anything in [section 136 of the Criminal Procedure (Scotland) Act 1995], summary proceedings in Scotland for an offence under this Act may be commenced within twelve months from the commission of the offence, and [subsection (3) of the said section 136] shall apply for the purposes of this subsection as it applies for the purposes of that section.
(4) In the application of this section to Northern Ireland, for the references in subsection (2) to [section 127(1) of the Magistrates' Courts Act 1980], and to the trial and laying of an information there shall be substituted respectively references to [Article 19(1) of the Magistrates' Courts (Northern Ireland) Order 1981] and to the hearing and determination and making of a complaint [and as if in that subsection for the words "an offence under this Act" there were substituted the words "an offence under section 30(1) . . . of this Act"].

NOTES

Sub-s (2): words in square brackets substituted by the Magistrates' Courts Act 1980, s 154, Sch 7, para 118.

Sub-s (3): words in square brackets substituted by the Criminal Procedure (Consequential Provisions) (Scotland) Act 1995, s 5, Sch 4, para 9.

Sub-s (4): words in first pair of square brackets substituted by the Magistrates' Courts Act 1980, s 154, Sch 7, para 118. Words in second pair of square brackets substituted by the Magistrates' Courts (Northern Ireland) Order 1981, SI 1981/1675, art 170(2), Sch 6, Pt I. Words in final pair of square brackets added by the Criminal Justice (Northern Ireland) Order 1980, SI 1980/704, art 12, Sch 1, Pt II. Words omitted repealed by the Enterprise Act 2002, s 278(2), Sch 26 (for savings in relation the merger of water and sewerage undertakers, see the Enterprise Act 2002 (Commencement No 3, Transitional and Transitory Provisions and Savings) Order 2003, SI 2003/1397, art 3, and the Enterprise Act 2002 (Commencement No 7 and Transitional Provisions and Savings) Order 2004, SI 2004/3233, arts 3–5).

130, 131 *(Repealed by the Enterprise Act 2002, s 278(2), Sch 26.)*

[1.3]
132 Offences by bodies corporate

(1) Where an offence under . . . , . . . , ... [section 93B] or Part XI of this Act, which has been committed by a body corporate, is proved to have been committed with the consent or connivance of, or to be attributable to any neglect on the part of, any director, manager, secretary or other similar officer of the body corporate, or any person who was purporting to act in any such capacity, he as well as the body corporate shall be guilty of that offence and be liable to be proceeded against and punished accordingly.
(2) Where the affairs of a body corporate are managed by its members, subsection (1) of this section shall apply in relation to the acts and defaults of a member in connection with his functions of management as if he were a director of the body corporate.

NOTES

Sub-s (1): first words omitted repealed by the Consumer Protection from Unfair Trading Regulations 2008, SI 2008/1277, reg 30(3), Sch 4, Pt 1. Second words omitted repealed by the Enterprise Act 2002, s 278(2), Sch 26 (for savings in relation the merger of water and sewerage undertakers, see the Enterprise Act 2002 (Commencement No 3, Transitional and Transitory Provisions and Savings) Order 2003, SI 2003/1397, art 3, and the Enterprise Act 2002 (Commencement No 7 and Transitional Provisions and Savings) Order 2004, SI 2004/3233, arts 3–5). Third words omitted repealed by the Enterprise Act 2002 and Media Mergers (Consequential Amendments) Order 2003, SI 2003/3180, art 2, Schedule, para 1(1), (9) (subject to transitional provisions and savings contained in art 3 of that Order as noted in the introductory note to this Act). Words in square brackets inserted by the Companies Act 1989, s 153, Sch 20, para 17.

133 *(Repealed by the Enterprise Act 2002, ss 247(b), 278(2), Sch 26.)*

[1.4]
134 Provisions as to orders

(1) Any statutory instrument whereby any order is made under any of the preceding provisions of this Act, other than a provision which requires a draft of the order to be laid before Parliament before making the order, or whereby any regulations are made under this Act, shall be subject to annulment in pursuance of a resolution of either House of Parliament.
(2) Any power conferred by any provision of this Act to make an order by statutory instrument shall include power to revoke or vary the order by a subsequent order made under that provision.

[1.5]
135 Financial provisions

(1) The Secretary of State shall pay all remuneration, allowances or other sums payable under this Act to or in respect of persons who are or have been members of the Advisory Committee . . . , and shall defray—
 (a) . . .
 (b) to such amount as the Secretary of State with the approval of the Minister for the Civil Service may determine, all other expenses duly incurred by the Advisory Committee . . .
(2) There shall be defrayed out of moneys provided by Parliament—
 (a) all expenses incurred by the Secretary of State in consequence of the provisions of this Act;
 (b) any expenses incurred in consequence of those provisions by any other Minister of the Crown or government department, not being a Minister or department of the Government of Northern Ireland;
 (c) the remuneration of, and any travelling or other allowances payable under this Act to, the Director and any staff of the Director, any other sums payable under this Act to or in respect of the Director, and any expenses duly incurred by the Director or by any of his staff in consequence of the provisions [of this or any other Act];
 (d) any increase attributable to this Act in the sums payable out of moneys so provided under the Superannuation Act 1972.

(3) . . .

NOTES

Sub-s (1): words omitted repealed by the Competition Act 1998, s 74(1), (3), Sch 12, para 1(1), (15), Sch 14, Pt I.

Sub-s (2): words in square brackets in para (c) inserted by the Competition Act 1980, s 32(2).

Sub-s (3): repealed by the Northern Ireland (Modification of Enactments—No 1) Order 1973, SI 1973/2163, art 14(2), Sch 6.

Minister for the Civil Service: the functions of the Minister for the Civil Service were transferred to the Treasury by the Transfer of Functions (Civil Service and Treasury) Order 1981, SI 1981/1670. Note, however, that subsequent orders have transferred certain functions back to the Minister.

The Director: see the note "The Director" to s 94 at **[1.1]**.

136 (*Repealed by the Statute Law (Repeals) Act 1977.*)

[1.6]

137 General interpretation provisions

(1) In this Act—

"the Act of 1948" means the Monopolies and Restrictive Practices (Inquiry and Control) Act 1948;

. . .

"the Act of 1965" means the Monopolies and Mergers Act 1965;

. . .

"contract of employment" means a contract of service or of apprenticeship, whether it is express or implied, and (if it is express) whether it is oral or in writing;

"scale" (where the reference is to the scale on which any services are, or are to be, made available, supplied or obtained) means scale measured in terms of money or money's worth or in any other manner.

(2) Except in so far as the context otherwise requires, in this Act, . . . , the following expressions have the meanings hereby assigned to them respectively, that is to say—

. . .

"agreement" means any agreement or arrangement, in whatever way and in whatever form it is made, and whether it is, or is intended to be, legally enforceable or not;

"business" includes a professional practice and includes any other undertaking which is carried on for gain or reward or which is an undertaking in the course of which goods or services are supplied otherwise than free of charge;

. . .

. . .

. . .

"consumer" (subject to subsection (6) of this section) means any person who is either—

(a) a person to whom goods are or are sought to be supplied (whether by way of sale or otherwise) in the course of a business carried on by the person supplying or seeking to supply them, or

(b) a person for whom services are or are sought to be supplied in the course of a business carried on by the person supplying or seeking to supply them,

and who does not receive or seek to receive the goods or services in the course of a business carried on by him;

"the Director" means the Director General of Fair Trading;

"enactment" includes an enactment of the Parliament of Northern Ireland;

"goods" includes buildings and other structures, and also includes ships, aircraft and hovercraft, . . . ;

. . .

. . .

"merger situation qualifying for investigation" has the meaning assigned to it by section 64(8) of this Act;

"Minister" includes a government department but shall not by virtue of this provision be taken to include the [Competition and Markets Authority], and, except where the contrary is expressly provided, does not include any Minister or department of the Government of Northern Ireland;

. . .

. . .

"practice" means any practice, whether adopted in pursuance of an agreement or otherwise;

. . .

. . .

"supply", in relation to the supply of goods, includes supply by way of sale, lease, hire or hire-purchase, and, in relation to buildings or other structures, includes the construction of them by a person for another person;

. . .

. . .

(3) In the provisions of this Act . . . "the supply of services" does not include the rendering of any services under a contract of employment but, . . .

(a) includes the undertaking and performance for gain or reward of engagements (whether professional or other) for any matter other than the supply of goods, and

(b) includes both the rendering of services to order and the provision of services by making them available to potential users; [and

(c) includes the making of arrangements for a person to put or keep on land a caravan (within the meaning of Part I of the Caravan Sites and Control of Development Act 1960) other than arrangements by virtue of which the person may occupy the caravan as his only or main residence;] [and

(d) includes the making of arrangements for the use by public service vehicles (within the meaning of the Public Passenger Vehicles Act 1981) of a parking place which is used as a point at which passengers on services provided by means of such vehicles may be taken up or set down;] [and

(e) includes the making of arrangements permitting use of the tunnel system (within the meaning of the Channel Tunnel Act 1987) by a person operating services for the carriage of passengers or goods by rail;] [and

[(f) includes the making of arrangements, by means of such an agreement as is mentioned in [paragraph 17 of Schedule 3A to the Communications Act 2003 (the electronic communications code)], for the sharing of the use of any electronic communications apparatus; and]]

[(g) includes the supply of network services and station services, within the meaning of Part I of the Railways Act 1993;]

and any reference in those provisions to services supplied or to be supplied, or to services provided or to be provided, shall be construed accordingly.

[(3A) The Secretary of State may by order made by statutory instrument—

(a) provide that "the supply of services" in the provisions of this Act is to include, or to cease to include, any activity specified in the order which consists in, or in making arrangements in connection with, permitting the use of land; and

(b) for that purpose, amend or repeal any of paragraphs (c), (d), (e) or (g) of subsection (3) above.

(3B) No order under subsection (3A) above is to be made unless a draft of the order has been laid before Parliament and approved by a resolution of each House of Parliament.

(3C) The provisions of Schedule 9 to this Act apply in the case of a draft of any such order as they apply in the case of a draft of an order to which section 91(1) above applies.]

(4) . . .

(5) For the purposes of the provisions of this Act . . . , any two bodies corporate are to be treated as interconnected if one of them is a body corporate of which the other is a subsidiary (within the meaning of [section 1159 of the Companies Act 2006]) or if both of them are subsidiaries (within the meaning of that section) of one and the same body corporate; and in those provisions "interconnected bodies corporate" shall be construed accordingly, and "group of interconnected bodies corporate" means a group consisting of two or more bodies corporate all of whom are interconnected with each other.

(6) For the purposes of the application of any provision of this Act in relation to goods or services of a particular description or to which a particular practice applies, "consumers" means persons who are consumers (as defined by subsection (2) of this section) in relation to goods or services of that description or in relation to goods or services to which that practice applies.

(7) . . .

(8) Except in so far as the context otherwise requires, any reference in this Act to an enactment shall be construed as a reference to that enactment as amended or extended by or under any other enactment, including this Act.

NOTES

Sub-s (1): definition "the Act of 1964" (omitted) repealed by the Resale Prices Act 1976, s 29, Sch 3, Pt I. Definition "the Act of 1968" (omitted) repealed by the Restrictive Trade Practices Act 1976, s 44, Sch 6. Definition "the Act of 1976" (omitted) repealed by the Competition Act 1998 (Transitional, Consequential and Supplemental Provisions) Order 2000, SI 2000/311, art 9(1), (6). Definition "assignment" (omitted) repealed by the Enterprise Act 2002 and Media Mergers (Consequential Amendments) Order 2003, SI 2003/3180, art 2, Schedule, para 1(1), (10)(a) (subject to transitional provisions and savings contained in art 3 of that Order as noted in the introductory note to this Act).

Sub-s (2): first words omitted repealed by the Restrictive Trade Practices Act 1976, s 44, Sch 6. Definitions "the Advisory Committee" (omitted) and "the Director" (in italics) repealed by the Enterprise Act 2002, s 278(2), Sch 26 (as from a day to be appointed in the case of the definition "the Director"). Definitions "commercial activities in the United Kingdom", "complex monopoly situation", "group", "merger reference", "monopoly reference", "monopoly situation", "newspaper merger reference", "price", "produce", "uncompetitive practices", and "worker" (all omitted) repealed by SI 2003/3180, art 2, Schedule, para 1(1), (10)(b) (subject to transitional provisions and savings contained in art 3 of that Order as noted in the introductory note to this Act). Words omitted from the definition "goods" repealed by the Electricity Act 1989, s 112(4), Sch 18. Definition "the Commission" (omitted) repealed, and words in square brackets in the definition "Minister" substituted, by the Enterprise and Regulatory Reform Act 2013 (Competition) (Consequential, Transitional and Saving Provisions) Order 2014, SI 2014/892, art 2, Sch 1, Pt 2, para 28, subject to transitional provisions as noted to the Enterprise Act 2002, s 8A at **[1.187]**.

Sub-s (3): words omitted repealed by the Restrictive Trade Practices Act 1976, s 44, Sch 6. Para (c) and the word immediately preceding it inserted by the Competition Act 1980, s 23. Para (d) and the word immediately preceding it inserted by the Transport Act 1985, s 116(1). Para (e) and the word immediately preceding it inserted by the Channel Tunnel Act 1987, s 33(10). Para (f) and the word immediately preceding it inserted by the Broadcasting Act 1990, s 192(1). Para (f) subsequently substituted by the Communications Act 2003, s 406(1), Sch 17, para 44, and words in square brackets in that paragraph substituted by the Digital Economy Act 2017, s 4(10), Sch 3, Pt 2, para 9. Para (g) and the word immediately preceding it inserted by the Railways Act 1993, s 66(4).

Sub-ss (3A)–(3C): inserted by the Competition Act 1998, s 68.

Sub-s (4): repealed by the Electricity Act 1989, s 112(4), Sch 18.

Sub-s (5): words omitted repealed by the Restrictive Trade Practices Act 1976, s 44, Sch 6. Words in square brackets substituted by the Companies Act 2006 (Consequential Amendments, Transitional Provisions and Savings) Order 2009, SI 2009/1941, art 2(1), Sch 1, para 26.

Sub-s (7): repealed by SI 2003/3180, art 2, Schedule, para 1(1), (10)(c) (subject to transitional provisions and savings contained in art 3 of that Order as noted in the introductory note to this Act).

The Director: see the note "The Director" to s 94 at **[1.1]**.

Monopolies and Mergers Act 1965; Monopolies and Restrictive Practices (Inquiry and Control) Act 1948: repealed by s 139(1) of, and Sch 13 to, this Act.

[1.7]

138 Supplementary interpretation provisions

(1) This section applies to the following provisions of this Act, that is to say, section 2(4), . . . , section 137(6), and the definition of "consumer" contained in section 137(2).

(2) For the purposes of any provisions to which this section applies it is immaterial whether any person supplying goods or services has a place of business in the United Kingdom or not.
(3) For the purposes of any provisions to which this section applies any goods or services supplied wholly or partly outside the United Kingdom, if they are supplied in accordance with arrangements made in the United Kingdom, whether made orally or by one or more documents delivered in the United Kingdom or by correspondence posted from and to addresses in the United Kingdom, shall be treated as goods supplied to, or services supplied for, persons in the United Kingdom.
(4) In relation to the supply of goods under a hire-purchase agreement, a credit-sale agreement or a conditional sale agreement, the person conducting any antecedent negotiations, as well as the owner or seller, shall for the purposes of any provisions to which this section applies be treated as a person supplying or seeking to supply the goods.
[(5) In subsection (4) of this section, the following expressions have the meanings given by, or referred to in, section 189 of the Consumer Credit Act 1974—

"antecedent negotiations",
"conditional sale agreement",
"credit-sale agreement",
"hire-purchase agreement".]

(6) In any provisions to which this section applies—
(a) any reference to a person to or for whom goods or services are supplied shall be construed as including a reference to any guarantor of such a person, and
(b) any reference to the terms or conditions on or subject to which goods or services are supplied shall be construed as including a reference to the terms or conditions on or subject to which any person undertakes to act as such a guarantor;

and in this subsection "guarantor", in relation to a person to or for whom goods or services are supplied, includes a person who undertakes to indemnify the supplier of the goods or services against any loss which he may incur in respect of the supply of the goods or services to or for that person.
(7) For the purposes of any provisions to which this section applies goods or services supplied by a person carrying on a business shall be taken to be supplied in the course of that business if payment for the supply of the goods or services is made or (whether under a contract or by virtue of an enactment or otherwise) is required to be made.

NOTES

Sub-s (1): words omitted repealed by the Enterprise Act 2002, s 278(2), Sch 26 (for savings in relation the merger of water and sewerage undertakers, see the Enterprise Act 2002 (Commencement No 3, Transitional and Transitory Provisions and Savings) Order 2003, SI 2003/1397, art 3, and the Enterprise Act 2002 (Commencement No 7 and Transitional Provisions and Savings) Order 2004, SI 2004/3233, arts 3–5).

Sub-s (5): substituted by the Consumer Credit Act 1974, s 192(3)(a), Sch 4, Pt I, para 37.

[1.8]
139 Amendments, repeals and transitional provisions
(1) Subject to the transitional provisions and savings contained in Schedule 11 to this Act—
(a) the enactments specified in Schedule 12 to this Act shall have effect subject to the amendments specified in that Schedule (being minor amendments or amendments consequential upon the preceding provisions of this Act), and
(b) the enactments specified in Schedule 13 to this Act are hereby repealed to the extent specified in the third column of that Schedule.
(2) The provisions of Schedule 11 to this Act shall have effect for the purposes of this Act.

[1.9]
140 Short title, citation, commencement and extent
(1) This Act may be cited as the Fair Trading Act 1973.
(2), (3) . . .
(4) Where any provision of this Act, other than a provision contained in Schedule 11, refers to the commencement of this Act, it shall be construed as referring to the day appointed under this section for the coming into operation of that provision.
(5) This Act extends to Northern Ireland.

NOTES

Sub-s (2): repealed by the Restrictive Trade Practices Act 1976, s 44, Sch 6.

Sub-s (3): repealed by the Statute Law (Repeals) Act 2004.

Commencement orders were made under this section but have lapsed on the repeal of sub-s (3) (the enabling power). The effect of those orders was to bring into force certain provisions of this Act on 14 September 1973 and the remainder on 1 November 1973.

SCHEDULES

SCHEDULES 1–10

(Sch 1 repealed by the Enterprise Act 2002, s 278(2), Sch 26 (for transitional provisions, see Sch 24, paras 2, 6 to the 2002 Act at **[1.445]**; *Sch 2 repealed by the Enterprise Act 2002, ss 10(1)(a), 278(2), Sch 26; Sch 3 repealed by the Competition Act 1998, s 74(1), (3), Sch 12, para 1(1), (2), Sch 14, Pt I (paras 6, 8, 9 have continuing effect in respect of any pension, allowance, gratuity or sum by way of compensation in respect of which a determination has been made prior to 1 April 1999 (see SI 1999/506, art 5); Sch 4, Sch 5, Pt I repealed by the Enterprise Act 2002, s 278(2), Sch 26; Sch 5, Pt II repealed by the Telecommunications Act 1984, s 109(6), Sch 7, Pt I; Sch 6 repealed by the Enterprise Act 2002, s 278(2), Sch 26; Sch 7 repealed by the Enterprise Act 2002, s 278(2), Sch 26 (for transitional*

provisions, see Sch 24, paras 14–19 to the 2002 Act at **[1.445]**)*; Schs 8, 9 repealed by the Enterprise Act 2002, s 278(2), Sch 26 (for transitional provisions and savings (including an exception in relation the merger of water and sewerage undertakers), see Sch 24, paras 13, 15–19 to that Act at* **[1.445]**, *the Enterprise Act 2002 (Commencement No 3, Transitional and Transitory Provisions and Savings) Order 2003, SI 2003/1397, arts 3, 4, and the Enterprise Act 2002 (Commencement No 7 and Transitional Provisions and Savings) Order 2004, SI 2004/3233, arts 3–5); Sch 10 repealed by the Restrictive Trade Practices Act 1976, s 44, Sch 6.)*

SCHEDULE 11
TRANSITIONAL PROVISIONS AND SAVINGS

Sections 139, 140

General provisions

[1.10]

1. (1) Subject to the following provisions of this Schedule, in so far as anything done under an enactment repealed by this Act could have been done under a corresponding provision of this Act, it shall not be invalidated by the repeal but shall have effect as if done under that provision.

(2) In relation to the Commission (by whichever of the names mentioned in section 4(1) of this Act it was for the time being called) sub-paragraph (1) of this paragraph applies, in particular, to any appointment of a member of the Commission (including any appointment, or extension of the term of service, of a chairman or deputy chairman of the Commission) or of any of the staff of the Commission, any reference made to the Commission, any proceedings or report of the Commission on such a reference, and any order made in consequence of any such report.

(3) A provision of this Act shall, for the purposes of this Schedule, be regarded as corresponding to an enactment repealed by this Act if (notwithstanding that it differs, whether to a small extent or substantially, from that enactment) it fulfils in this Act a purpose similar to that which that enactment fulfilled in the repealed enactments; and any reference in this Schedule to provisions of the repealed enactments corresponding to any provisions of this Act shall be construed accordingly.

(4) In this Schedule "the repealed enactments" means the enactments repealed by this Act, and "the commencement of this Act", where that expression occurs in any provision of this Schedule—

- (a) if the same day is appointed under section 140 of this Act for the repeal of all those enactments, means the day so appointed, or
- (b) if different days are appointed under that section for the repeal of different enactments, means such day as may be specified for the purposes of this sub-paragraph in an order made by the Secretary of State by statutory instrument;

and different days may be so specified in relation to different provisions of this Schedule.

2. For the purposes of the operation of paragraph 1 of this Schedule, anything done by or in relation to the Board of Trade shall be treated as having been done by or in relation to the Secretary of State, whether apart from this paragraph it would fall to be so treated or not.

3. Without prejudice to any express amendment made by this Act, where an Act (whether passed before, or in the same Session as, this Act) or any document refers, either expressly or by implication, to an enactment repealed by this Act, the reference shall, except where the context otherwise requires, be construed as, or as including, a reference to any corresponding provision of this Act.

4. Where any period of time specified in an enactment repealed by this Act is current at the commencement of this Act, and there is a corresponding provision in this Act, this Act shall have effect as if that corresponding provision had been in force when that period began to run.

5. Without prejudice to paragraph 1 of this Schedule, any reference in this Act (whether express or implied) to a thing done or required or authorised to be done, or omitted to be done, or to an event which has occurred, under or for the purposes of or by reference to or in contravention of any provisions of this Act shall, except where the context otherwise requires, be construed as including a reference to the corresponding thing done or required or authorised to be done, or omitted, or to the corresponding event which occurred, as the case may be, under or for the purposes of or by reference to or in contravention of any corresponding provisions of the repealed enactments.

6. Nothing in this Act shall affect the repealed enactments in their operation in relation to offences committed before the commencement of this Act.

Reference made to Commission before commencement of Act

7. (1) Any reference made to the Commission under the repealed enactments, and any report of the Commission made before the commencement of this Act on any such reference, shall have effect in accordance with paragraph 1 of this Schedule if made in accordance with such of the repealed enactments as were applicable to it, and shall so have effect notwithstanding that the reference or report was not made in accordance with the corresponding provisions of this Act.

(2) In the case of any such reference on which the Commission have not made their report before the commencement of this Act—

- (a) any proceedings of the Commission on that reference after the commencement of this Act shall be conducted in accordance with the repealed enactments as if they had not been repealed, and
- (b) any report of the Commission on that reference shall be made in accordance with those enactments and not in accordance with any corresponding provisions of this Act;

but nothing in this sub-paragraph shall be construed as excluding the operation of any provisions of this Act relating to any functions of the Director in relation to the Commission, to the transmission to the Director of copies of reports of the Commission, or to any other action authorised or required to be taken in relation to or in consequence of a report made by the Commission.

(3) In particular, but without prejudice to the generality of the preceding sub-paragraphs, any reference, proceedings or report to which either of those sub-paragraphs applies shall have effect, or shall be conducted or made, as mentioned in that sub-paragraph notwithstanding that the reference or report related or relates to the question whether conditions to which the Act of 1948 applied prevailed or prevail, and not to the existence or possible existence of a monopoly situation within the meaning of this Act.

(4) For the purposes of the operation of sub-paragraph (2) of this paragraph in relation to a report made by the Commission after the commencement of this Act, section 29(1) of the Act of 1956 (whereby conditions to which the Act of 1948 applied were not to be considered to prevail by reason of any agreement to which Part I of the Act of 1956 applied) shall be construed as if section 6(1) of the Act of 1956 had been originally enacted as amended by section 95 of this Act.

Report of Commission made before 5th August 1965

8. An order made under section 56 of this Act in consequence of a report made by the Commission before the commencement of the Act of 1965 shall not exercise any of the powers specified in Part II of Schedule 8 to this Act; and accordingly the powers conferred by section 89 of this Act shall not be exercisable in consequence of any such report.

Undertaking given in consequence of report on reference made under repealed enactments

9. (1) This paragraph applies to any undertaking given to a Minister which is certified by the Secretary of State to have been given in relation to matters dealt with in a report made by the Commission on a reference under section 2 of the Act of 1948 or on a reference under section 6 of the Act of 1965 and which either—

(a) was given before the commencement of this Act, or

(b) is given after the commencement of this Act in a case where no request under subsection (1) of section 88 of this Act has been made to the Director to carry out consultations in accordance with that subsection.

(2) A copy of any certificate given by the Secretary of State under the preceding sub-paragraph shall be furnished to the Director and the Minister to whom any such undertaking was or is given shall furnish particulars of it to the Director.

(3) Subsection (4) of section 88 of this Act shall have effect in relation to any undertaking to which this paragraph applies as if—

(a) it were an undertaking of which particulars have been furnished to the Director under subsection (2) of that section, and

(b) any reference in subsection (4) of that section to the report of the Director were a reference to a report made by the Commission as mentioned in sub-paragraph (1) of this paragraph.

(4) The preceding provisions of this paragraph shall have effect without prejudice—

(a) to the duty of the Commission under section 86 of this Act to transmit to the Director copies of reports which were made by the Commission before the commencement of this Act and which, by virtue of paragraphs 1 and 7 of this Schedule, have effect as if made under this Act, or

(b) to any duty of the Director, where requested by the appropriate Minister or Ministers to do so with respect to any such report, to carry out such consultations as are mentioned in section 88(1) of this Act.

Functions of Director in relation to orders made under Acts of 1948 and 1965

10. Subsection (5) of section 88 of this Act shall have effect in relation to any order which was made under section 10 of the Act of 1948 or under section 3 or section 6 of the Act of 1965 and which, by virtue of paragraph 1 of this Schedule, has effect as if made under this Act, as that subsection has effect in relation to orders made under this Act in the circumstances specified in that subsection.

Provisions consequential upon transfer of functions from Registrar to Director

11. (1) Except as provided by paragraph 15 of this Schedule, in relation to any time after the commencement of this Act, anything which has before the commencement of this Act been done by or in relation to the Registrar shall have effect as if it had been done by or in relation to the Director.

(2) Sub-paragraph (1) of this paragraph applies, in particular, to any regulations made by the Registrar, any register kept or document issued by the Registrar, any particulars furnished to the Registrar, and any application to or proceedings before . . . any . . . court, tribunal or authority, made or instituted by or against the Registrar or to which the Registrar was otherwise a party; and any such proceedings, if pending at the commencement of this Act, may accordingly be continued by or against the Director, or with the Director being otherwise treated as a party to them, as the circumstances may require, and for the purpose of so continuing them anything done by or in relation to the Registrar in connection with any such proceedings shall be treated as having been done by or in relation to the Director.

(3) In this Schedule "the Registrar" means the Registrar of Restrictive Trading Agreements.

12, 13. . . .

Pension benefits

14. The repeal by this Act of the following enactments, that is to say, Part II of Schedule 1 to the Act of 1965 and section 3(4)(d) of the Superannuation (Miscellaneous Provisions) Act 1967, shall not affect the operation of those enactments in relation to any person who was appointed to be chairman or deputy chairman of the Commission before the commencement of this Act; and, in relation to any such person, a recommendation made under paragraph 5 of that Schedule shall have effect whether made before or after the commencement of this Act.

15. (1) The repeal by this Act of subsections (7) and (8) of section 1 of the Act of 1956 shall not affect the operation of those subsections in relation to any person who was appointed to be the Registrar before the commencement of this Act; and, in relation to any such person, a determination made under subsection (7) of that section shall have effect whether made before or after the commencement of this Act.

(2) Paragraph 11 of this Schedule shall not have effect for the purposes of the operation of subsection (7) or subsection (8) of section 1 of the Act of 1956 in accordance with the preceding sub-paragraph.

Trade Descriptions Act 1968, s 30

16. The repeal by this Act of subsections (2) to (4) of section 30 of the Trade Descriptions Act 1968 shall not affect the operation of those subsections in their application to any case where a notice under subsection (2) of that section, or a certificate under subsection (4) of that section or a document purporting to be such a certificate, has been given or issued before the commencement of this Act; and the duty imposed by section 130(1) of this Act shall not apply where such a notice has been so given.

NOTES

Para 11: words omitted from sub-para (2) repealed by the Competition Act 1998 (Consequential Provisions) Order 2013, SI 2013/294, art 2, Schedule.

Paras 12, 13: repealed and consolidated by the Restrictive Trade Practices Act 1976, s 44, Sch 6 (now repealed).

Savings: see the Enterprise Act 2002 (Commencement No 3, Transitional and Transitory Provisions and Savings) Order 2003, SI 2003/1397, art 6 which provides that the commencement of the amendments and repeals in the Enterprise Act 2002, Schs 25, 26 relating to this Act shall not have effect in relation to (a) any orders which by virtue of para 1 of this Schedule have effect as if made under this Act, or (b) undertakings to which para 9 of this Schedule applies.

The Director: see the note "The Director" to s 94 at **[1.1]**.

Act of 1948: the Monopolies and Restrictive Practices (Inquiry and Control) Act 1948: repealed by s 139(1) of, and Sch 13 to, this Act.

Act of 1956: the Restrictive Trade Practices Act 1956: repealed by the Restrictive Practices Court Act 1976, s 11, Schedule, the Restrictive Trade Practices Act 1976, s 44, Sch 6, and the Resale Prices Act 1976, s 29, Sch 3.

Act of 1965: the Monopolies and Mergers Act 1965: repealed by s 139(1) of, and Sch 13 to, this Act.

Superannuation (Miscellaneous Provisions) Act 1967, s 3(4)(d); Trade Descriptions Act 1968, s 30(2)–(4): repealed by s 139(1) of, and Sch 13 to, this Act.

SCHEDULES 12, 13

(Sch 12, in so far as unrepealed, contains miscellaneous amendments; Sch 13 contains repeals.)

COMPETITION ACT 1980

(1980 c 21)

ARRANGEMENT OF SECTIONS

An Act to abolish the Price Commission; to make provision for the control of anti-competitive practices in the supply and acquisition of goods and the supply and securing of services; to provide for references of certain public bodies and other persons to the Monopolies and Mergers Commission; to provide for the investigation of prices and charges by the Director General of Fair Trading; to provide for the making of grants to certain bodies; to amend and provide for the amendment of the Fair Trading Act 1973; to make amendments with respect to the Restrictive Trade Practices Act 1976; to repeal the remaining provisions of the Counter-Inflation Act 1973; and for purposes connected therewith

[3 April 1980]

NOTES

Disclosure of information: information which comes to a public authority in connection with the exercise of any function it has under or by virtue of this Act is "specified information" for the purposes of the Enterprise Act 2002, s 238; see s 238(1) of, and Sch 14 to, that Act at **[1.417]**, **[1.443]**. A public authority which holds information to which s 237 of the 2002 Act applies (general restriction on disclosure) may disclose that information to any other person for the purpose of facilitating the exercise by that person of any function he has under or by virtue of this Act and the 2002 Act; see s 241(3) of, and Sch 15 to, the 2002 Act at **[1.420]**, **[1.444]**. As to the disclosure of information to an overseas authority, see s 243 of, and Sch 14 to, the 2002 Act at **[1.423]**, **[1.443]**.

1–10 *(S 1 repealed by the Statute Law (Repeals) Act 1989; ss 2–10 repealed by the Competition Act 1998, ss 17, 74(3), Sch 14, Pt I, subject to transitional provisions and savings in relation to undertakings accepted by the Director under ss 4 or 9 of this Act (see Sch 13, Pt VI, para 43 to the 1998 Act at* **[1.162]***).)*

Further references and investigations

[1.11]

11 References of public bodies and certain other persons to the [CMA]

(1) The Secretary of State may at any time refer to the [CMA] any question relating to—

(a) the efficiency and costs of, [or]

(b) the service provided by, . . .

(c) . . .

a person falling within subsection (3) below and specified in the reference, including any question whether, in relation to a matter falling within [paragraph (a) or (b)] above, the person is pursuing a course of conduct which operates against the public interest.

(2) . . .

(3) The persons referred to in subsection (1) above are—

(a) any body corporate—

(i) which supplies goods or services by way of business,

(ii) the affairs of which are managed by its members, and

(iii) the members of which hold office as such by virtue of their appointment to that or another office by a Minister under any enactment; or

[(aa) any publicly owned railway company, within the meaning of the Railways Act 1993, which supplies network services or station services, within the meaning of Part I of that Act; or]

[(b) any person (not falling within paragraph (a) above) who provides in Northern Ireland a bus service within the meaning of section 14 of the Finance Act (Northern Ireland) 1966; or]

[(bb) any person who provides a railway passenger service in pursuance of an agreement entered into by Transport for London or any of its subsidiaries (within the meaning of the Greater London Authority Act 1999) by virtue of section 156(2) or (3) of the Greater London Authority Act 1999; or]

[(c) the [Environment Agency];] or

[(ca) Scottish water;]

[(cc) . . .]

(d) any board administering a scheme under the Agricultural Marketing Act 1958 [or the Agricultural Marketing (Northern Ireland) Order 1982]; or

(e) any body corporate with a statutory duty to promote and assist the maintenance and development of the efficient supply of any goods or services by a body falling within paragraphs (a) to (d) above; or

(f) any subsidiary, within the meaning of [section 1159 of the Companies Act 2006], of a body falling within paragraphs (a) to (e) above.

(4) The Secretary of State may by order exclude from subsection (3)(b) [or (bb)] above persons of such descriptions as may be specified in the order.

(5) No question concerning a person falling within subsection (3)(b) [or (bb)] above or a subsidiary of a body falling within [either of those paragraphs] may be referred to the [CMA] under this section unless it relates to the carriage of passengers by the person or, as the case may be, the subsidiary.

(6) The Secretary of State may at any time by notice given to the [CMA] vary a reference under this section.

(7) On making a reference under this section or on varying such a reference under subsection (6) above the Secretary of State shall arrange for the reference or, as the case may be, the variation to be published in such manner as he considers most suitable for bringing it to the attention of persons who in his opinion would be affected by it or be likely to have an interest in it.

(8) On a reference under this section the [CMA] shall investigate and report on any question referred to them but shall exclude from their investigation and report consideration of—

(a) any question relating to the appropriateness of any financial obligations or guidance as to financial objectives (however expressed) imposed on or given to the person in question by or under any enactment, or otherwise by a Minister; . . .

(b) . . .

[(9), (9A)] . . .

(10) A report of the [CMA] on a reference under this section shall be made to the Secretary of State and shall state, with reasons, the conclusions of the [CMA] with respect to any question referred to them and, where the [CMA] conclude that the person specified in the reference is pursuing a course of conduct which operates against the public interest, the report may include recommendations as to what action (if any) should be taken by the person for the purpose of remedying or preventing what the [CMA] consider are the adverse effects of that course of conduct.

[(10A) The functions of the CMA with respect to a reference under this section (including functions under sections 109 to 115 of the Enterprise Act 2002, as applied by section 11B) are to be carried out on behalf of the CMA by a group constituted for the purpose by the chair of the CMA under Schedule 4 to the Enterprise and Regulatory Reform Act 2013.]

(11) In this section "Minister" includes a Northern Ireland department and the head of such a department.

NOTES

In the section heading and sub-ss (1), (5), (6), (8), (10), references to the "CMA" substituted by the Enterprise and Regulatory Reform Act 2013, s 26(4), Sch 6, Pt 1, paras 1, 2(1), (2), (4). For various transitional provisions (including those relating to the abolition of the OFT and the Competition Commission, existing references to those bodies and provisions relating to continuity), see the Enterprise and Regulatory Reform Act 2013 (Commencement No 6, Transitional Provisions and Savings) Order 2014, SI 2014/416, Schedule at **[2.13]**. This section is also amended as follows:

Sub-s (1): word in square brackets in para (a) inserted, para (c) and the word immediately preceding it repealed, and words in final pair of square brackets substituted, by the Enterprise Act 2002, s 278, Sch 25, para 10(1), (2)(a), Sch 26.

Sub-s (2): repealed by the Enterprise Act 2002, s 278, Sch 25, para 10(1), (2)(b).

Sub-s (3): para (aa) inserted by the Railways Act 1993, s 152(1), Sch 12, para 12(1). Para (b) substituted by the Transport Act 1985, s 114(1). Para (bb) inserted by the London Regional Transport Act 1984, s 71(3)(a), Sch 6, para 15, and substituted by the Transport for London (Consequential Provisions) Order 2003, SI 2003/1615, art 2, Sch 1, Pt 1, para 6. Para (c) substituted by the Water Act 1989, s 190(1), Sch 25, para 59(1), and words in square brackets in that paragraph substituted by the Environment Act 1995 (Consequential Amendments) Regulations 1996, SI 1996/593, reg 2, Sch 1. Para (ca) inserted by the Water Industry (Scotland) Act 2002 (Consequential Modifications) Order 2004, SI 2004/1822, art 2, Schedule, Pt 1, para 10. Para (cc) inserted, in relation to Scotland only, by the Local Government etc (Scotland) Act 1994, s 72, and repealed by the Water Industry (Scotland) Act 2002, s 71, Sch 7, para 10. Words in square brackets in para (d) substituted by the Agricultural Marketing (Northern Ireland) Order 1982, SI 1982/1080, art 46, Schs 8, 9. Words in square brackets in para (f) substituted by the Companies Act 2006 (Consequential Amendments, Transitional Provisions and Savings) Order 2009, SI 2009/1941, art 2(1), Sch 1, para 42(a).

Sub-s (4): words in square brackets inserted by the London Regional Transport Act 1984, s 71(3)(a), Sch 6, para 15.

Sub-s (5): words in first pair of square brackets inserted, and words in second pair of square brackets substituted, by the London Regional Transport Act 1984, s 71(3)(a), Sch 6, para 15.

Sub-s (8): words omitted repealed by the Competition Act 1998, s 74(1), (3), Sch 12, para 4(1), (2), Sch 14, Pt I, subject to transitional provisions and savings in Sch 13, Pt V, para 40 of the 1998 Act at **[1.161]**.

Sub-ss (9), (9A): substituted, for the original sub-s (9), by the Competition Act 1998, s 74(1), Sch 12, para 4(1), (3), and subsequently repealed by the Enterprise Act 2002, s 278, Sch 25, para 10(1), (2)(b), Sch 26.

Sub-s (10A): inserted by the Enterprise and Regulatory Reform Act 2013, s 26(4), Sch 6, Pt 1, paras 1, 2(1), (3), subject to transitional provisions in SI 2014/416 as noted above.

References under sub-s (1): as to the duty of the Office of Rail and Road to disclose information and provide assistance to a CMA group in carrying out an investigation on certain references under this section, see the Railways Act 1993, s 67.

Ministers of the Crown, etc: the Enterprise Act 2002, Sch 25, para 10(10) provides that for the purposes of the Scotland Act 1998, the amendments made by Sch 25, para 10(1)–(9) to that Act (including the amendments made to this section) shall be taken to be pre-commencement enactments within the meaning of the 1998 Act; references to a Minister of the Crown should be construed accordingly.

[1.12]

[11A References under section 11: time-limits

(1) Every reference under section 11 above shall specify a period (not longer than six months beginning with the date of the reference) within which a report on the reference is to be made.

(2) A report of the [CMA] on a reference under section 11 above shall not have effect (and no action shall be taken in relation to it under section 12 below) unless the report is made before the end of the period specified in the reference or such further period (if any) as may be allowed by the Secretary of State under subsection (3) below.

(3) The Secretary of State may, if he has received representations on the subject from the [CMA] and is satisfied that there are special reasons why the report cannot be made within the period specified in the reference, extend that period by no more than three months.

(4) No more than one extension is possible under subsection (3) above in relation to the same reference.

(5) The Secretary of State shall publish any extension made by him under subsection (3) above in such manner as he considers most suitable for bringing it to the attention of persons who in his opinion would be affected by it or be likely to have an interest in it.]

NOTES

Inserted, together with ss 11B–11D, by the Enterprise Act 2002, s 278(1), Sch 25, para 10(3).

Sub-ss (2), (3): references to the "CMA" substituted by the Enterprise and Regulatory Reform Act 2013, s 26(4), Sch 6, Pt 1, paras 1, 3. For various transitional provisions (including those relating to the abolition of the OFT and the Competition Commission, existing references to those bodies and provisions relating to continuity), see the Enterprise and Regulatory Reform Act 2013 (Commencement No 6, Transitional Provisions and Savings) Order 2014, SI 2014/416, Schedule at **[2.13]**.

Ministers of the Crown, etc: see the note to s 11 at **[1.11]**.

[1.13]

[11B References under section 11: powers of investigation and penalties

(1) The following sections of Part 3 of the Enterprise Act 2002 shall apply, with the modifications mentioned in subsections [(1A) to] (3) below, for the purposes of references under section 11 above as they apply for the purposes of references under that Part—

(a) section 109 (attendance of witnesses and production of documents etc);
(b) section 110 (enforcement of powers under section 109: general);
[(ba) section 110A (restriction on powers to impose penalties under section 110);]
(c) section 111 (penalties);
(d) section 112 (penalties: main procedural requirements);
(e) section 113 (payments and interest by instalments);
(f) section 114 (appeals in relation to penalties);
(g) section 115 (recovery of penalties); and
(h) section 116 (statement of policy).

[(1A) Section 109 shall in its application by virtue of subsection (1) above, have effect as if—

(a) in subsection (A1), for paragraphs (a) and (b) there were substituted—

"(a) assisting the CMA in carrying out any functions, including enforcement functions, in connection with a reference under section 11 of the Competition Act 1980 (the "1980 Act") (references of public bodies and certain other persons to the CMA);

(b) assisting the Secretary of State in carrying out any functions, including enforcement functions, in connection with an order under section 11D of that Act (interim orders) or section 12 of that Act (orders following report under section 11 of that Act).", and

(b) in subsection (8A), for paragraphs (a) and (b) there were substituted—

"(a) in relation to the CMA, functions conferred by virtue of section 87 on the CMA by orders under section 11D or 12 of the 1980 Act;

(b) in relation to the Secretary of State—

(i) functions conferred by virtue of section 87 on the Secretary of State by orders under section 11D or 12 of the 1980 Act;

(ii) the functions of the Secretary of State in relation to the variation or revocation of orders under section 11D or 12 of the 1980 Act.".]

(2) Section 110 shall, in its application by virtue of subsection (1) above, have effect as if—

(a) subsection (2) were omitted;

(b) . . .

(c) in subsection (9) the words from "or section" to "section 65(3))" were omitted.

[(2A) Section 110A shall, in its application by virtue of subsection (1) above, have effect as if for subsections (5) to (8) there were substituted—

"(5) Where the section 109 power is exercised for the purpose mentioned in subsection (A1)(a) of that section, in connection with a reference under section 11 of the 1980 Act, the relevant day is the day when the report of the CMA on the reference concerned is laid before both Houses of Parliament.

(6) Where the section 109 power is exercised for the purpose mentioned in subsection (A1)(b) of that section, in connection with an order under section 11D of the 1980 Act (interim orders) or section 12 of that Act (orders following report under section 11 of that Act), the relevant day is the day when the Secretary of State makes the order concerned or decides not to make an order under section 11D or 12 of that Act, as the case may be.".]

[(3) Section 111(5)(b) shall, in its application by virtue of subsection (1) above, have effect as if for sub-paragraph (ii) there were substituted—

"(ii) if earlier, the day on which the report of the CMA on the reference concerned is made or, if no such report is made within the period permitted for that purpose, the latest day on which the report may be made within the permitted period.".]

NOTES

Inserted as noted to s 11A at **[1.12]**.

All amendments to this section were made by the Enterprise and Regulatory Reform Act 2013 (Competition) (Consequential, Transitional and Saving Provisions) Order 2014, SI 2014/892, art 2, Sch 1, Pt 2, paras 35, 36 (note that the amendments do not apply in relation to any notice given before 1 April 2014 under section 109 of the 2002 Act as applied by this section (see Sch 2, para 2 to that Order)).

Ministers of the Crown, etc: see the note to s 11 at **[1.11]**.

[1.14]

[11C References under section 11: further supplementary provisions

(1) Section 117 of the Enterprise Act 2002 (false or misleading information) shall apply in relation to functions under this Act as it applies in relation to functions under Part 3 of that Act but as if, in subsections (1)(a) and (2)[—

(a) the words ", OFCOM or the Secretary of State" were omitted, and

(b) for the words "their functions" there were substituted "its functions".]

(2) Section 125 of the Enterprise Act 2002 (offences by bodies corporate) shall apply for the purposes of this Act as it applies for the purposes of Part 3 of that Act.

(3) For the purposes of section 12 below, a conclusion contained in a report of the [CMA] is to be disregarded if the conclusion is not that of at least two-thirds of the members of the group constituted [by the chair of the CMA for the purpose of carrying out the functions of the CMA with respect to the reference].]

NOTES

Inserted as noted to s 11A at **[1.12]**.

Sub-ss (1), (3): words in square brackets substituted by the Enterprise and Regulatory Reform Act 2013, s 26(4), Sch 6, Pt 1, paras 1, 4. For various transitional provisions (including those relating to the abolition of the OFT and the Competition Commission, existing references to those bodies and provisions relating to continuity), see the Enterprise and Regulatory Reform Act 2013 (Commencement No 6, Transitional Provisions and Savings) Order 2014, SI 2014/416, Schedule at **[2.13]**.

Ministers of the Crown, etc: see the note to s 11 at **[1.11]**.

[1.15]

[11D Interim orders

(1) Subsection (2) below applies where, in the circumstances specified in subsection (1) of section 12 below, the Secretary of State has under consideration the making of an order under subsection (5) of that section.

(2) The Secretary of State may by order, for the purpose of preventing pre-emptive action—

(a) prohibit or restrict the doing of things which the Secretary of State considers would constitute pre-emptive action;
(b) impose on any person concerned obligations as to the carrying on of any activities or the safeguarding of any assets;
(c) provide for the carrying on of any activities or the safeguarding of any assets either by the appointment of a person to conduct or supervise the conduct of any activities (on such terms and with such powers as may be specified or described in the order) or in any other manner;
(d) do anything which may be done by virtue of paragraph 19 of Schedule 8 to the Enterprise Act 2002 (information powers).

(3) An order under this section shall come into force at such time as is determined by or under the order.

(4) An order under this section shall, if it has not previously ceased to be in force, cease to be in force on the making of the order under section 12(5) below or (as the case may be) on the making of the decision not to make such an order.

(5) The Secretary of State shall publish any decision made by him not to make an order under section 12(5) below in such manner as he considers most suitable for bringing it to the attention of persons who in his opinion would be affected by it or would be likely to have an interest in it.

(6) The Secretary of State shall, as soon as reasonably practicable, consider any representations received by him in relation to varying or revoking an order under this section.

(7) The following provisions of Part 3 of the Enterprise Act 2002 shall apply in relation to orders under this section as they apply in relation to orders under paragraph 2 of Schedule 7 to that Act—
(a) section 86(2) and (3) (enforcement orders: general provisions);
(b) section 87 (delegated power of directions); . . .
(c) section 94(1) to (5), (8) and (9) (rights to enforce orders) [and
(d) section 94A (interim orders: penalties)].

(8) In this section "pre-emptive action" means action which might impede the making of an order under section 12(5) below.]

NOTES

Inserted as noted to s 11A at **[1.12]**.

Sub-s (7): word omitted from para (b) repealed, and para (d) (and the preceding word) inserted, by the Enterprise and Regulatory Reform Act 2013 (Competition) (Consequential, Transitional and Saving Provisions) Order 2014, SI 2014/892, art 2, Sch 1, Pt 2, paras 35, 37.

Ministers of the Crown, etc: see the note to s 11 at **[1.11]**.

[1.16]

12 Orders following report under section 11

(1) This section applies where a report of the [CMA] on a reference under section 11 above concludes that the person specified in the reference is pursuing a course of conduct which operates against the public interest.

(2) If it appears to the Secretary of State that any other Minister has functions directly relating to the person specified in the reference or, in the case of a reference only concerning the activities of the person in a part of the United Kingdom, functions directly relating to the person in respect of his activities in that part, he shall send a copy of the report of the [CMA] on the reference to that Minister; and in subsection (3) below "the relevant Minister" means—
(a) in a case where it appears to the Secretary of State that any Minister (including himself) has such functions, that Minister, and
(b) in a case where it appears to the Secretary of State that no Minister has such functions, the Secretary of State.

(3) If—
(a) the relevant Minister considers it appropriate for the purpose of remedying or preventing what he considers are the adverse effects of the course of conduct specified in the report of the [CMA] as operating against the public interest, and
(b) the person specified in the reference does not fall within paragraph (d) of section 11(3) above and is not a subsidiary of a body falling within that paragraph,

he may by order direct the person to prepare within such time, if any, as may be specified in the order a plan for remedying or preventing such of those effects as are so specified; but where there is more than one relevant Minister no such order shall be made except by all the relevant Ministers acting jointly and where none of the relevant Ministers is the Secretary of State no such order shall be made except after consultation with him.

(4) It shall be the duty of a person to whom a direction is given under subsection (3) above to prepare such a plan as is mentioned in that subsection and to send a copy of that plan to the Minister or Ministers by whom the order containing the direction was made who shall lay it before Parliament; and, in a case where the plan involves the use by a body of its powers in relation to any subsidiary within the meaning of [section 1159 of the Companies Act 2006], the plan shall specify the manner in which the body proposes using those powers.

(5) Whether or not an order has been or may be made under subsection (3) above, the Secretary of State may, if he considers it appropriate for the purpose of remedying or preventing what he considers are the adverse effects of the course of conduct specified in the report of the [CMA] as operating against the public interest, [make an order under this subsection].

[(5A) An order under subsection (5) above may contain anything permitted by Schedule 8 to the Enterprise Act 2002, except paragraphs 8, 13 and 14 of that Schedule.

(5B) An order under subsection (5) above shall come into force at such time as is determined by or under the order.]

[(6) The following provisions of Part 3 of the Enterprise Act 2002 shall apply in relation to orders under subsection (5) above as they apply in relation to orders under paragraph 11 of Schedule 7 to that Act—
(a) section 86(2) and (3) (enforcement orders: general provisions);
(b) section 87 (delegated power of directions);
(c) section 88 (contents of certain enforcement orders);
(d) section 94(1) to (5), (8) and (9) (rights to enforce orders); and

(e) Schedule 10 (procedural requirements for orders).

(7) The Secretary of State shall publish any decision made by him to dispense with the requirements of Schedule 10 to the Enterprise Act 2002 as applied by subsection (6) above; and shall do so in such manner as he considers most suitable for bringing the decision to the attention of persons who in his opinion would be affected by it or be likely to have an interest in it.]

NOTES

Sub-ss (1)–(3): references to the "CMA" substituted by the Enterprise and Regulatory Reform Act 2013, s 26(4), Sch 6, Pt 1, paras 1, 5. For various transitional provisions (including those relating to the abolition of the OFT and the Competition Commission, existing references to those bodies and provisions relating to continuity), see the Enterprise and Regulatory Reform Act 2013 (Commencement No 6, Transitional Provisions and Savings) Order 2014, SI 2014/416, Schedule at **[2.13]**.

Sub-s (4): words in square brackets substituted by the Companies Act 2006 (Consequential Amendments, Transitional Provisions and Savings) Order 2009, SI 2009/1941, art 2(1), Sch 1, para 42(b).

Sub-s (5): word in first pair of square brackets substituted by the Enterprise and Regulatory Reform Act 2013, s 26(4), Sch 6, Pt 1, paras 1, 5, subject to transitional provisions in SI 2014/416 as noted above. Words in second pair of square brackets substituted by the Enterprise Act 2002, s 278(1), Sch 25, para 10(4)(a).

Sub-ss (5A), (5B): inserted by the Enterprise Act 2002, s 278(1), Sch 25, para 10(4)(b).

Sub-ss (6), (7): substituted, for the original sub-s (6), by the Enterprise Act 2002, s 278(1), Sch 25, para 10(4)(c).

Ministers of the Crown, etc: see the note to s 11 at **[1.11]**.

13 (*Repealed by the Enterprise Act 2002, ss 9, 278(2), Sch 26.*)

Patents and agricultural schemes

14 (*Repealed by the Copyright, Designs and Patents Act 1988, s 303(2), Sch 8.*)

[1.17]

15 Agricultural schemes: special provisions

(1) . . .

(2) The Secretary of State shall not—

(a), (b) . . .

(c) make or vary a reference under section 11 above,

in a case where the person to whom or to whose conduct or activities the investigation or reference relates falls within section 11(3)(d) above unless he has first consulted the relevant Minister.

(3), (4) . . .

(5) In this section "the relevant Minister" means—

(a) in the case of a board administering a scheme under the said Act of 1958, the Minister who would have power to make an order under section 19 of that Act in relation to that board or the board administering that scheme, and

(b) in the case of a board administering a scheme under [the said Order of 1982], the Department of Agriculture for Northern Ireland.

NOTES

Sub-s (1): repealed by the Enterprise Act 2002 and Media Mergers (Consequential Amendments) Order 2003, SI 2003/3180, art 2, Schedule, para 3.

Sub-s (2): para (a) repealed by the Deregulation and Contracting Out Act 1994, s 81(1), Sch 17. Para (b) repealed by the Competition Act 1998, s 74(1), (3), Sch 12, para 4(1), (5), Sch 14, Pt I.

Sub-ss (3), (4): repealed by the Competition Act 1998, s 74(1), (3), Sch 12, para 4(1), (5), Sch 14, Pt I.

Sub-s (5): words in square brackets substituted by the Agricultural Marketing (Northern Ireland) Order 1982, SI 1982/1080, art 46(1), Schs 8, 9.

Act of 1958: ie, the Agricultural Marketing Act 1958.

Order of 1982: ie, the Agricultural Marketing (Northern Ireland) Order 1982, SI 1982/1080.

General provisions about references and investigations

[1.18]

16 General provisions as to reports

(1) . . .

(2) For the purposes of the law relating to defamation, absolute privilege shall attach to any report of the [CMA] . . . under this Act.

[(3) . . .]

NOTES

Sub-s (1): repealed by the Enterprise Act 2002, s 278, Sch 25, para 10(5)(a), Sch 26.

Sub-s (2): reference to the "CMA" substituted by the Enterprise and Regulatory Reform Act 2013, s 26(4), Sch 6, Pt 1, paras 1, 6; for various transitional provisions (including those relating to the abolition of the OFT and the Competition Commission, existing references to those bodies and provisions relating to continuity), see the Enterprise and Regulatory Reform Act 2013 (Commencement No 6, Transitional Provisions and Savings) Order 2014, SI 2014/416, Schedule at **[2.13]**. Words omitted repealed by the Enterprise Act 2002, s 278, Sch 25, para 10(5)(b), Sch 26.

Sub-s (3): originally added by the Deregulation and Contracting Out Act 1994, s 39, Sch 11, para 4(1), (5). Subsequently repealed by the Competition Act 1998, s 74(1), (3), Sch 12, para 4(1), (6), Sch 14, Pt I.

Ministers of the Crown, etc: see the note to s 11 at **[1.11]**.

[1.19]

17 Laying before Parliament and publication of reports

(1) Subject to subsection (2) below, the Secretary of State shall lay a copy of any report made to him under section . . . 11(10) . . . above before each House of Parliament and shall arrange for the report to be published in such manner as appears to him appropriate.

(2) The Secretary of State shall not lay a copy of a report made to him under section . . . 11(10) above before either House of Parliament unless at least twenty-four hours before doing so he has transmitted to every person specified in the reference a copy of the report in the form in which it is laid (or by virtue of subsection (3) below is treated as being laid) before each House of Parliament.

(3) If a report made to him under section . . . 11(10) . . . above is presented by command of Her Majesty to either House of Parliament otherwise than at or during the time of a sitting of that House, the presentation of the report shall for the purposes of this section be treated as the laying of a copy of it before that House by the Secretary of State.

(4) If it appears to the Secretary of State that the publication of any matter in a report made to him under section . . . 11(10) . . . above would be [inappropriate], he shall exclude that matter from the copies of the report as laid before Parliament and from the report as published under this section.

[(5) In deciding what is inappropriate for the purposes of subsection (4) the Secretary of State shall have regard to the considerations mentioned in section 244 of the Enterprise Act 2002.]

(6) Any reference in [section] 12 above to a report of the [CMA] shall be construed as a reference to the report in the form in which copies of it are laid (or by virtue of subsection (3) of this section are treated as having been laid) before each House of Parliament under this section.

NOTES

Sub-ss (1), (3): first words omitted repealed by the Competition Act 1998, s 74(1), (3), Sch 12, para 4(1), (7)(a), (b), Sch 14, Pt I. Second words omitted repealed by the Enterprise Act 2002, s 278, Sch 25, para 10(6)(a), Sch 26.

Sub-s (2): word omitted repealed by the Competition Act 1998, s 74(1), (3), Sch 12, para 4(1), (7)(b), Sch 14, Pt I.

Sub-s (4): first word omitted repealed by the Competition Act 1998, s 74(1), (3), Sch 12, para 4(1), (7)(a), (b), Sch 14, Pt I. Second words omitted repealed, and word in square brackets substituted, by the Enterprise Act 2002, s 278, Sch 25, para 10(6)(a), (b), Sch 26.

Sub-s (5): substituted by the Enterprise Act 2002, s 278(1), Sch 25, para 10(6)(c).

Sub-s (6): word in first pair of square brackets substituted by the Competition Act 1998, s 74(1), Sch 12, para 4(1), (7)(c). Reference to the "CMA" substituted by the Enterprise and Regulatory Reform Act 2013, s 26(4), Sch 6, Pt 1, paras 1, 7 (for various transitional provisions (including those relating to the abolition of the OFT and the Competition Commission, existing references to those bodies and provisions relating to continuity), see the Enterprise and Regulatory Reform Act 2013 (Commencement No 6, Transitional Provisions and Savings) Order 2014, SI 2014/416, Schedule at **[2.13]**).

Ministers of the Crown, etc: see the note to s 11 at **[1.11]**.

18–30 *(Ss 18, 20, 21, 24 repealed by the Enterprise Act 2002, s 278, Sch 25, para 10(7), Sch 26; s 19 partly repealed by the Enterprise Act 2002, ss 247(f), 278(2), Sch 26, the Agricultural Marketing (Northern Ireland) Order 1982, SI 1982/1080, art 46(2), Sch 9, and the Statute Law (Repeals) Act 1993 and, in so far as still in force, amends enactments outside the scope of this work; ss 22, 25–30 repealed by the Competition Act 1998, s 74(1), (3), Sch 12, para 4(1), (11), (13), Sch 14, Pt I, subject to transitional provisions and savings in Sch 13, Pt VI, para 44 to the 1998 Act at* **[1.162]**; *s 23 amends the Fair Trading Act 1973, s 137(3) at* **[1.6]**.)

Supplementary

[1.20]

31 Orders and regulations

(1) Any power of the Secretary of State to make orders . . . under this Act shall be exercisable by statutory instrument.

(2) . . .

(3) Any statutory instrument containing . . . an order under section . . . 11(4)[, 11D] or 12(3) or (5) above[, or section 111(4) or (6) or 114(3)(b) or (4)(b) of the Enterprise Act 2002 as applied by section 11B(1)(c) or (f) above,] shall be subject to annulment in pursuance of a resolution of either House of Parliament.

(4) . . .

[(5) Any power of the Secretary of State to make an order under this Act—

(a) may be exercised so as to make different provision for different cases or different purposes; and

(b) includes power to make such incidental, supplementary, consequential, transitory, transitional or saving provision as the Secretary of State considers appropriate.]

NOTES

Sub-s (1): words omitted repealed by the Enterprise Act 2002, s 278, Sch 25, para 10(8)(a), Sch 26.

Sub-s (2): repealed by the Competition Act 1998, s 74(1), (3), Sch 12, para 4(1), (14)(a), Sch 14, Pt I.

Sub-s (3): first words omitted repealed, and words in square brackets inserted, by the Enterprise Act 2002, s 278, Sch 25, para 10(8)(b), Sch 26. Second word omitted repealed by the Competition Act 1998, s 74(1), (3), Sch 12, para 4(1), (14)(b), Sch 14, Pt I.

Sub-s (4): repealed by the Enterprise Act 2002, s 278, Sch 25, para 10(8)(c), Sch 26.

Sub-s (5): added by the Enterprise Act 2002, s 278(1), Sch 25, para 10(8)(d).

Ministers of the Crown, etc: see the note to s 11 at **[1.11]**.

[1.21]

32 Financial provisions

(1) There shall be defrayed out of moneys provided by Parliament—

(a) any expenses incurred by the Secretary of State in consequence of the provisions of this Act; and

(b) any increase attributable to this Act in the sums payable out of moneys so provided under any other Act.

(2) (*Amends the Fair Trading Act 1973, s 135(2)(c) at* **[1.5]**).

[1.22]

33 Short title, interpretation, repeals, commencement and extent

(1) This Act may be cited as the Competition Act 1980.

[(2) Unless the context otherwise requires, in this Act "Minister" includes a government department and the following expressions shall have the same meanings as they have in Part 3 of the Enterprise Act 2002—

"business"
["the CMA"]
"enactment"
"goods"
"services"
"supply (in relation to the supply of goods)"
"the supply of services".]

(3), (4) . . .

(5) This Act shall come into operation on such day as the Secretary of State may by order appoint, and different days may be so appointed for different provisions and for different purposes.

(6) An order under this section appointing a day for the coming into operation of any provision of Schedule 2 to this Act may contain such savings with respect to the operation of that provision and such incidental and transitional provisions as appear to the Secretary of State to be appropriate.

(7) Any reference in any provision of this Act to the appointed day shall be construed as a reference to the day appointed or, as the case may require, first appointed under this section for the coming into operation of that provision.

(8) This Act extends to Northern Ireland.

NOTES

Sub-s (2): substituted by the Enterprise Act 2002, s 278(1), Sch 25, para 10(9). Words in square brackets substituted by the Enterprise and Regulatory Reform Act 2013, s 26(4), Sch 6, Pt 1, paras 1, 8; for various transitional provisions (including those relating to the abolition of the OFT and the Competition Commission, existing references to those bodies and provisions relating to continuity), see the Enterprise and Regulatory Reform Act 2013 (Commencement No 6, Transitional Provisions and Savings) Order 2014, SI 2014/416, Schedule at **[2.13]**.

Sub-ss (3), (4): repealed by the Competition Act 1998, s 74(1), (3), Sch 12, para 4(1), (15)(b), Sch 14, Pt I.

Ministers of the Crown, etc: see the note to s 11 at **[1.11]**.

Orders: the Competition Act 1980 (Commencement No 1) Order 1980, SI 1980/497; the Competition Act 1980 (Commencement No 2) Order 1980, SI 1980/978.

SCHEDULES 1, 2

(Sch 1 repealed by the Statute Law (Repeals) Act 1989; Sch 2 contains repeals to enactments that are outside the scope of this work.)

COMPANY DIRECTORS DISQUALIFICATION ACT 1986

(1986 c 46)

ARRANGEMENT OF SECTIONS

Disqualification for competition infringements

Miscellaneous and general

An Act to consolidate certain enactments relating to the disqualification of persons from being directors of companies, and from being otherwise concerned with a company's affairs

[25 July 1986]

NOTES

Only the provisions of this Act most relevant to competition law are reproduced; provisions omitted are not annotated.

References to the "European Community", "Community", etc: see the Treaty of Lisbon (Changes in Terminology) Order 2011, SI 2011/1043, arts 3, 4, 6 which provide as follows—

3 Application

(1) The amendments made by this Part apply to provisions contained in—

(a) an Act of Parliament,
(b) an Act of the Scottish Parliament, or
(c) an instrument made under an Act of Parliament or an Act of the Scottish Parliament (or both).

(2) The amendments made by this Part do not apply to—

(a) an instrument falling within article 8(1),
(b) an Order in Council mentioned in section 24(5)(c), (e) or (g) of the Interpretation Act 1978 (Northern Ireland legislation),
(c) the European Communities Act 1972,
(d) the Interpretation Act 1978,
(e) the European Union (Amendment) Act 2008,
(f) the title of an Act or statutory instrument,
(g) a reference to the title of an Act or statutory instrument,
(h) a reference to the title of an item of European Community legislation, or
(i) a reference to a term defined in an item of European Community legislation.

(3) The amendments made by this Part do not apply to a reference that relates only to things done before 1 December 2009 (the date on which the Treaty of Lisbon entered into force) and do not affect any other reference in its application to things done before that date.

4 European Community—European Union

(1) For references to the European Communities or to the European Community or the European Coal and Steel Community (including references to "the Communities", "the Community", "the EC" or "the EEC") substitute references to the European Union.

(2) Paragraph (1) does not apply to—
(a) the use of "Community", "EC" or "EEC" as an adjective (but see article 6);
(b) a reference that forms part of a reference to a treaty (but see article 5).

6 "Community"

(1) In the following terms (which were defined by the European Communities Act 1972 as it had effect before the passing of the European Union (Amendment) Act 2008) for the word "Community" substitute "EU"—
(a) Community treaties,
(b) Community customs duty,
(c) Community institution,
(d) Community instrument,
(e) Community obligation, and
(f) enforceable Community right.

(2) In the following terms, and in those terms preceded by the word "European", for "Community", or as the case may be "European Community", substitute "EU"—
(a) Community law,
(b) Community legislation, and
(c) Community provision.

(3) Where the term mentioned in paragraph (1) or (2) is preceded by the word "a", for "a" substitute "an".

(4) Paragraphs (1) to (3) do not apply where the term mentioned in paragraph (1) or (2) forms part of a reference to a treaty.

(5) Paragraph (2) does not apply to the term "specified Community provision" where used in an enactment containing a definition of that term.".

Disclosure of information

A public authority which holds information to which s 237 of the Enterprise Act 2002 applies (general restriction on disclosure) may disclose that information to any other person for the purpose of facilitating the exercise by that person of any function he has under or by virtue of this Act and the 2002 Act; see s 241(3) of, and Sch 15 to, the 2002 Act at **[1.420]**, **[1.444]**.

[Disqualification for competition infringements

[1.23]

9A Competition disqualification order

(1) The court must make a disqualification order against a person if the following two conditions are satisfied in relation to him.

(2) The first condition is that an undertaking which is a company of which he is a director commits a breach of competition law.

(3) The second condition is that the court considers that his conduct as a director makes him unfit to be concerned in the management of a company.

(4) An undertaking commits a breach of competition law if it engages in conduct which infringes [either of the following]—
(a) the Chapter 1 prohibition (within the meaning of the Competition Act 1998) (prohibition on agreements, etc preventing, restricting or distorting competition);
(b) the Chapter 2 prohibition (within the meaning of that Act) (prohibition on abuse of a dominant position);
(c) [Article 101 of the Treaty on the Functioning of the European Union] (prohibition on agreements, etc preventing, restricting or distorting competition);
(d) [Article 102] of that Treaty (prohibition on abuse of a dominant position).

(5) For the purpose of deciding under subsection (3) whether a person is unfit to be concerned in the management of a company the court—
(a) must have regard to whether subsection (6) applies to him;
(b) may have regard to his conduct as a director of a company in connection with any other breach of competition law;
(c) must not have regard to the matters mentioned in Schedule 1.

(6) This subsection applies to a person if as a director of the company—
(a) his conduct contributed to the breach of competition law mentioned in subsection (2);
(b) his conduct did not contribute to the breach but he had reasonable grounds to suspect that the conduct of the undertaking constituted the breach and he took no steps to prevent it;

(c) he did not know but ought to have known that the conduct of the undertaking constituted the breach.

(7) For the purposes of subsection (6)(a) it is immaterial whether the person knew that the conduct of the undertaking constituted the breach.

(8) For the purposes of subsection (4)(a) *or (c)* references to the conduct of an undertaking are references to its conduct taken with the conduct of one or more other undertakings.

(9) The maximum period of disqualification under this section is 15 years.

(10) An application under this section for a disqualification order may be made by the [Competition and Markets Authority] or by a specified regulator.

(11) [Section 60A of the Competition Act 1998 (certain principles etc to be considered or applied from IP completion day] applies in relation to any question arising by virtue of subsection (4)(a) or (b) above as it applies in relation to any question arising under Part 1 of that Act.]

NOTES

Inserted, together with the preceding heading and ss 9B–9E, by the Enterprise Act 2002, s 204(1), (2).

Sub-s (4): the words in the first pair of square brackets were substituted (for the original words "either of the following"), and paras (c) and (d) were repealed, by the Competition (Amendment etc) (EU Exit) Regulations 2019, SI 2019/93, reg 60, Sch 1, para 1(1), (2), as from IP completion day (as defined in the European Union (Withdrawal Agreement) Act 2020, s 39) (for transitional provisions and savings in relation to the operation of the 2019 Regulations, see Sch 4 to those Regulations at **[7.69]** et seq, and see, in particular, Sch 4, Pt 8 to the 2019 Regulations at **[7.77]**). Words in square brackets in paras (c), (d) substituted by the Treaty of Lisbon (Changes in Terminology or Numbering) Order 2012, SI 2012/1809, art 3, Schedule, Pt 1

Sub-s (8): words in italics repealed by SI 2019/93, reg 60, Sch 1, para 1(1), (3), as from IP completion day (as defined in the European Union (Withdrawal Agreement) Act 2020, s 39) (for transitional provisions and savings in relation to the operation of the 2019 Regulations, etc, see the first note relating to those Regulations above).

Sub-s (10): words in square brackets substituted by the Enterprise and Regulatory Reform Act 2013 (Competition) (Consequential, Transitional and Saving Provisions) Order 2014, SI 2014/892, art 2, Sch 1, Pt 2, paras 52, 53(b), subject to transitional provisions as noted to the Enterprise Act 2002, s 8A at **[1.187]**.

Sub-s (11): the words square brackets were substituted (for the original words "Section 60 of the Competition Act 1998 (c 41) (consistent treatment of questions arising under United Kingdom and Community law)") by SI 2019/93, reg 60, Sch 1, para 1(1), (4), as from IP completion day (as defined in the European Union (Withdrawal Agreement) Act 2020, s 39) (for transitional provisions and savings in relation to the operation of the 2019 Regulations, etc, see the first note relating to those Regulations above). Note that Sch 1, para 1(4) to the 2019 Regulations was amended by the Competition (Amendment etc) (EU Exit) Regulations 2020, SI 2020/1343, reg 13, with effect from immediately before IP completion day; and the effect of that amendment has been incorporated in the text set out above.

References to the European Community and related expressions: see the note "References to "the European Community", "Community", etc" in the introductory notes to this Act.

[1.24]

[9B Competition undertakings

(1) This section applies if—

(a) the [Competition and Markets Authority] or a specified regulator thinks that in relation to any person an undertaking which is a company of which he is a director has committed or is committing a breach of competition law,

(b) the [Competition and Markets Authority] or the specified regulator thinks that the conduct of the person as a director makes him unfit to be concerned in the management of a company, and

(c) the person offers to give the [Competition and Markets Authority] or the specified regulator (as the case may be) a disqualification undertaking.

(2) The [Competition and Markets Authority] or the specified regulator (as the case may be) may accept a disqualification undertaking from the person instead of applying for or proceeding with an application for a disqualification order.

(3) A disqualification undertaking is an undertaking by a person that for the period specified in the undertaking he will not—

(a) be a director of a company;

(b) act as receiver of a company's property;

(c) in any way, whether directly or indirectly, be concerned or take part in the promotion, formation or management of a company;

(d) act as an insolvency practitioner.

(4) But a disqualification undertaking may provide that a prohibition falling within subsection (3)(a) to (c) does not apply if the person obtains the leave of the court.

(5) The maximum period which may be specified in a disqualification undertaking is 15 years.

(6) If a disqualification undertaking is accepted from a person who is already subject to a disqualification undertaking under this Act or to a disqualification order the periods specified in those undertakings or the undertaking and the order (as the case may be) run concurrently.

(7) Subsections (4) to (8) of section 9A apply for the purposes of this section as they apply for the purposes of that section but in the application of subsection (5) of that section the reference to the court must be construed as a reference to the [Competition and Markets Authority] or a specified regulator (as the case may be).]

NOTES

Inserted as noted to s 9A at **[1.23]**.

Sub-ss (1), (2), (7): words in square brackets substituted by the Enterprise and Regulatory Reform Act 2013 (Competition) (Consequential, Transitional and Saving Provisions) Order 2014, SI 2014/892, art 2, Sch 1, Pt 2, paras 52, 53(c), subject to transitional provisions as noted to the Enterprise Act 2002, s 8A at **[1.187]**.

[1.25]

[9C Competition investigations

(1) If the [Competition and Markets Authority] or a specified regulator has reasonable grounds for suspecting that a breach of competition law has occurred it or he (as the case may be) may carry out an investigation for the purpose of deciding whether to make an application under section 9A for a disqualification order.

(2) For the purposes of such an investigation sections 26 to 30 of the Competition Act 1998 (c 41) apply to the OFT and the specified regulators as they apply to the [Competition and Markets Authority] for the purposes of an investigation under section 25 of that Act.

(3) Subsection (4) applies if as a result of an investigation under this section the [Competition and Markets Authority] or a specified regulator proposes to apply under section 9A for a disqualification order.

(4) Before making the application the [Competition and Markets Authority] or regulator (as the case may be) must—

- (a) give notice to the person likely to be affected by the application, and
- (b) give that person an opportunity to make representations.]

NOTES

Inserted as noted to s 9A at **[1.23]**.

Words in square brackets substituted by the Enterprise and Regulatory Reform Act 2013 (Competition) (Consequential, Transitional and Saving Provisions) Order 2014, SI 2014/892, art 2, Sch 1, Pt 2, paras 52, 53(c), subject to transitional provisions as noted to the Enterprise Act 2002, s 8A at **[1.187]**.

[1.26]

[9D Co-ordination

(1) The Secretary of State may make regulations for the purpose of co-ordinating the performance of functions under sections 9A to 9C (relevant functions) which are exercisable concurrently by two or more persons.

(2) Section 54(5) to (7) of the Competition Act 1998 (c 41) applies to regulations made under this section as it applies to regulations made under that section and for that purpose in that section—

- (a) references to Part 1 functions must be read as references to relevant functions;
- (b) references to a regulator must be read as references to a specified regulator;
- [(ba) the reference in subsection (6A)(b) to notice under section 31(1) of the Competition Act 1998 that the regulator proposes to make a decision within the meaning given by section 31(2) of that Act is to be read as notice under section 9C(4) that the specified regulator proposes to apply under section 9A for a disqualification order;]
- (c) a competent person also includes any of the specified regulators.

(3) The power to make regulations under this section must be exercised by statutory instrument subject to annulment in pursuance of a resolution of either House of Parliament.

(4) Such a statutory instrument may—

- (a) contain such incidental, supplemental, consequential and transitional provision as the Secretary of State thinks appropriate;
- (b) make different provision for different cases.]

NOTES

Inserted as noted to s 9A at **[1.23]**.

Sub-s (2): para (ba) inserted by the Enterprise and Regulatory Reform Act 2013 (Competition) (Consequential, Transitional and Saving Provisions) Order 2014, SI 2014/892, art 2, Sch 1, Pt 2, paras 52, 54, subject to transitional provisions as noted to the Enterprise Act 2002, s 8A at **[1.187]**.

[1.27]

[9E Interpretation

(1) This section applies for the purposes of sections 9A to 9D.

(2) Each of the following is a specified regulator for the purposes of a breach of competition law in relation to a matter in respect of which he or it has a function—

- [(a) the Office of Communications;]
- (b) the Gas and Electricity Markets Authority;
- [(c) the Water Services Regulation Authority;]
- (d) [the Office of Rail and Road];
- (e) the Civil Aviation Authority;
- [(f) Monitor];
- [(g) the Payment Systems Regulator established under section 40 of the Financial Services (Banking Reform) Act 2013];
- [(h) the Financial Conduct Authority].

(3) The court is the High Court or (in Scotland) the Court of Session.

(4) Conduct includes omission.

(5) Director includes shadow director.]

NOTES

Inserted as noted to s 9A at **[1.23]**.

Sub-s (2): para (a) substituted by the Communications Act 2003, s 406, Sch 17, para 83. Para (c) substituted by the Water Act 2003, s 101(1), Sch 7, Pt 2, para 25. Words in square brackets in para (d) substituted by the Office of Rail Regulation (Change of Name) Regulations 2015, SI 2015/1682, reg 2(2), Schedule, Pt 1, para 4(h). Para (f) added by the Health and Social Care Act 2012, s 74(4). Para (g) added by the Financial Services (Banking Reform) Act 2013, s 67(1). Para (h) added by s 129 of, and Sch 8, Pt 2, para 8 to, the 2013 Act.

Miscellaneous and general

[1.28]

24 Extent

(1) This Act extends to England and Wales and to Scotland.

[(2) Subsections (1) to (2A) of section 11 also extend to Northern Ireland.]

NOTES

Sub-s (2): substituted by the Small Business, Enterprise and Employment Act 2015, s 113(2).

[1.29]

25 Commencement

This Act comes into force simultaneously with the Insolvency Act 1986.

NOTES

The Insolvency Act 1986 came into force on 29 December 1986.

[1.30]

26 Citation

This Act may be cited as the Company Directors Disqualification Act 1986.

WATER INDUSTRY ACT 1991

(1991 c 56)

ARRANGEMENT OF SECTIONS

PART II
APPOINTMENT AND REGULATION OF UNDERTAKERS

CHAPTER III PROTECTION OF CUSTOMERS ETC

Provisions with respect to competition

An Act to consolidate enactments relating to the supply of water and the provision of sewerage services, with amendments to give effect to recommendations of the Law Commission

[25 July 1991]

NOTES

Only the provisions of this Act most relevant to competition law are reproduced; provisions omitted are not annotated. By virtue of s 223 of this Act (not reproduced) the provisions included in this Handbook apply to England and Wales only.

As to the transfer of certain functions of the Secretary of State under this Act to the National Assembly for Wales (now the Senedd Cymru), in so far as those functions are exercisable in relation to Wales, see the National Assembly for Wales (Transfer of Functions) Order 1999, SI 1999/672, art 2, Sch 1.

See the Isles of Scilly (Application of Water Legislation) Order 2019, SI 2019/1259, art 4, which provides that this Act applies to the Isles of Scilly as it applies to the rest of England.

PART II APPOINTMENT AND REGULATION OF UNDERTAKERS

CHAPTER III PROTECTION OF CUSTOMERS ETC

Provisions with respect to competition

[1.31]

31 Functions of [Authority] with respect to competition

(1) . . .

[(2) The functions to which subsection (2A) below applies shall be concurrent functions of [the Authority] and the [CMA].

(2A) This subsection applies to the functions of the [CMA] under Part 4 of the 2002 Act (other than sections 166[, 171 and 174E]) so far as [those functions—

(a) are exercisable by the CMA Board (within the meaning of Schedule 4 to the Enterprise and Regulatory Reform Act 2013), and

(b) relate to] commercial activities connected with the supply of water or the provision of sewerage services.]

[(3) [The Authority] shall be entitled to exercise, concurrently with the [CMA], the functions of the [CMA] under the provisions of Part 1 of the Competition Act 1998 (other than sections 31D(1) to (6), 38(1) to (6)[, 40B(1) to (4)] and 51), so far as relating to—

(a) agreements, decisions or concerted practices of the kind mentioned in section 2(1) of that Act,

(b) conduct of the kind mentioned in section 18(1) of that Act, [or]

[(c) transferred EU anti-trust commitments or transferred EU anti-trust directions (as defined in section 40ZA of that Act),]

which relate to commercial activities connected with the supply of water or securing a supply of water or with the provision or securing of sewerage services.]

[(4) So far as necessary for the purposes of, or in connection with, subsections (2) and (2A) [above—

(a) references] in Part 4 of the 2002 Act to the [CMA] (including references in provisions of that Act applied by that Part) shall be construed as including references to [the Authority] (except in sections 166[, 171 and 174E] of that Act and in any other provision of that Act where the context otherwise [requires);

(b) references in that Part to section 5 of the 2002 Act are to be construed as including references to section 27(1) and (2) of this Act].]

[(4ZA) Section 130A of the 2002 Act is to have effect in its application in relation to the Authority by virtue of subsections (2) and (2A)—

(a) as if for subsection (1) of that section there were substituted—

"(1) Where the Water Services Regulation Authority—

(a) is proposing to carry out its functions under section 27(1) and (2) of the Water Industry Act 1991 in relation to a matter for the purposes mentioned in subsection (2), and

(b) considers that the matter is one in respect of which it would be appropriate for the Authority to exercise its powers under section 174 (investigation) in connection with deciding whether to make a reference under section 131,

the Authority must publish a notice under this section (referred to in this Part as a "market study notice").", and

(b) as if in subsection (2)(a) of that section, for "the acquisition or supply of goods or services of one or more than one description in the United Kingdom" there were substituted "commercial activities connected with the supply of water or the provision of sewerage services (within the meaning given by section 219(1) of the Water Industry Act 1991)".]

[(4A) So far as necessary for the purposes of, or in connection with, the provisions of subsection (3) above, references in Part I of the Competition Act 1998 to [the CMA] are to be read as including a reference to [the Authority] ([except in sections 31D(1) to (6), 38(1) to (6)][, 40B(1) to (4)], 51, 52(6) and (8) and 54 of that Act and in any other provision of that Act where the context otherwise requires).]

[(5) Before the [CMA] or [the Authority] first exercises in relation to any matter functions which are exercisable concurrently by virtue of subsection (2) above, that person shall consult the other.

(6) Neither the [CMA] nor [the Authority] shall exercise in relation to any matter functions which are exercisable concurrently by virtue of subsection (2) above if functions which are so exercisable have been exercised in relation to that matter by the other.]

(7) It shall be the duty of [the Authority], for the purpose of assisting [a CMA group] in carrying out an investigation on a [market investigation reference made by the Authority (under section 131 of the 2002 Act)] by virtue of subsection (2) . . . above, to give to the [group]—

(a) any information which is in his possession and which relates to matters falling within the scope of the investigation, and which is either requested by the [group] for that purpose or is information which in his opinion it would be appropriate for that purpose to give to the [group] without any such request; and

(b) any other assistance which the [group] may require, and which it is within his power to give, in relation to any such matters;

and the [group] shall, for the purposes of carrying out any such investigation, take into account any information given to them for that purpose under this subsection.

[(7A) In subsection (7) "CMA group" has the same meaning as in Schedule 4 to the Enterprise and Regulatory Reform Act 2013.]

(8) If any question arises as to whether subsection (2) or (3) above [. . .] applies to any particular case, that question shall be referred to and determined by the Secretary of State; and no objection shall be taken to anything done under—

(a) [Part 4 of the 2002 Act]; or

[(b) Part I of the Competition Act 1998 ([other than sections 31D(1) to (6), 38(1) to (6)][, 40B(1) to (4)] and 51),]

by or in relation to [the Authority] on the ground that it should have been done by or in relation to [the CMA].

[(8A) Section 117 of the 2002 Act (offences of supplying false or misleading information) as applied by section 180 of that Act shall have effect so far as relating to functions exercisable by [the Authority] by virtue of subsection (2) above as if the references in section 117(1)(a) and (2) to the [CMA] included references to [the Authority].]

(9) . . .

NOTES

Section heading: word in square brackets substituted by virtue of the Water Act 2003, s 36(2).

References to "CMA" and "the CMA" in square brackets in each place they occur substituted by the Enterprise and Regulatory Reform Act 2013 (Competition) (Consequential, Transitional and Saving Provisions) Order 2014, SI 2014/892, art 2, Sch 1, Pt 2, paras 73, 84(1), (2), (3)(a), (4), (5)(b), (7), (8), (11), (12), subject to transitional provisions as noted to the Enterprise Act 2002, s 8A at **[1.187]**.

Words "the Authority" in square brackets in each place they occur substituted by virtue of the Water Act 2003, s 36(2).

Other amendments to this section are as follows:

Sub-s (1): repealed by the Enterprise Act 2002, s 278, Sch 25, para 25(1), (8)(a), Sch 26.

Sub-s (2): substituted together with sub-s (2A), for the original sub-s (2), by the Enterprise Act 2002, s 168(9), Sch 9, Pt 2, para 19(1), (2).

Sub-s (2A): substituted as noted to sub-s (2) above. Words in second and third pairs of square brackets substituted by SI 2014/892, art 2, Sch 1, Pt 2, paras 73, 84(1), (3)(b), (c), subject to transitional provisions as noted above.

Sub-s (3) was substituted by SI 2004/1261, reg 5, Sch 2, para 4(1), (2)(a); and is subsequently amended as follows:

Words ", 40B(1) to (4)" in square brackets inserted by the Enterprise and Regulatory Reform Act 2013, s 57, Sch 15, paras 4, 5.

The word "or" in square brackets at the end of para (b) was inserted, and para (c) was substituted (for the original paras (c) and (d)), by the Competition (Amendment etc) (EU Exit) Regulations 2019, SI 2019/93, reg 60, Sch 1, para 4, as from IP completion day (as defined in the European Union (Withdrawal Agreement) Act 2020, s 39) (for transitional provisions and savings in relation to the operation of the 2019 Regulations, see Sch 4 to those Regulations at **[7.69]** et seq). Note that Sch 1, para 4 to the 2019 Regulations was amended by the Competition (Amendment etc) (EU Exit) Regulations 2020, SI 2020/1343, reg 16, with effect from immediately before IP completion day; and the effect of those amendments has been incorporated in the text set out above. Note also that paras (c) and (d) (as amended by SI 2012/1809, art 3(1), Schedule, Pt 1) previously read as follows—

"(c) agreements, decisions or concerted practices of the kind mentioned in [Article 101(1) of the Treaty on the Functioning of the European Union], or

(d) conduct which amounts to abuse of the kind mentioned in [Article 102 of the Treaty on the Functioning of the European Union],".

Sub-s (4): substituted by the Enterprise Act 2002, s 168(9), Sch 9, Pt 2, para 19(1), (3). Words in square brackets substituted by SI 2014/892, art 2, Sch 1, Pt 2, paras 73, 84(1), (5), subject to transitional provisions as noted above.

Sub-s (4ZA): inserted by SI 2014/892, art 2, Sch 1, Pt 2, paras 73, 84(1), (6), subject to transitional provisions as noted above.

Sub-s (4A): inserted by the Competition Act 1998, s 54(2), Sch 10, para 5(8). Words in third pair of square brackets substituted by SI 2004/1261, reg 5, Sch 2, para 4(1), (2)(b). Words in fourth pair of square brackets inserted by the Enterprise and Regulatory Reform Act 2013, s 57, Sch 15, paras 4, 5.

Sub-ss (5), (6): substituted by the Enterprise Act 2002, s 168(9), Sch 9, Pt 2, para 19(1), (4).

Sub-s (7): other words in square brackets substituted by SI 2014/892, art 2, Sch 1, Pt 2, paras 73, 84(1), (9), subject to transitional provisions as noted above. Words omitted repealed by the Competition Act 1998, ss 54(2), 74(3), Sch 10, para 5(11), Sch 14, Pt I.

Sub-s (7A): inserted by SI 2014/892, art 2, Sch 1, Pt 2, paras 73, 84(1), (10), subject to transitional provisions as noted above.

Sub-s (8): words omitted originally inserted by the Deregulation and Contracting Out Act 1994, s 7(2), Sch 2, para 10(4), and subsequently repealed by the Enterprise Act 2002, ss 168(9), 278(2), Sch 9, Pt 2, para 19(1), (5)(a), Sch 26. Words in square brackets in para (a) substituted by the Enterprise Act 2002, s 168(9), Sch 9, Pt 2, para 19(1), (5)(b). Para (b) substituted by the Competition Act 1998, s 54(2), Sch 10, para 5(12). Words in first pair of square brackets in para (b) substituted by SI 2004/1261, reg 5, Sch 2, para 4(1), (2)(c). Words in second pair of square brackets in para (b) substituted by the Enterprise and Regulatory Reform Act 2013, s 57, Sch 15, paras 4, 5.

Sub-s (8A): inserted by the Competition Act 1998, s 54(3), Sch 10, para 13(8), and substituted by the Enterprise Act 2002, s 168(9), Sch 9, Pt 2, para 19(1), (6).

Sub-s (9): repealed by the Enterprise Act 2002, ss 168(9), 278(2), Sch 9, Pt 2, para 19(1), (7), Sch 26.

[1.32]

[32 Duty to refer merger of water or sewerage undertaking

[Subject to sections 33 and 33A below,] it shall be the duty of the [CMA to make a reference to its chair for the constitution of a group under Schedule 4 to the Enterprise and Regulatory Reform Act 2013 if the CMA believes] that it is or may be the case—

(a) that arrangements are in progress which, if carried into effect, will result in a merger of any two or more water enterprises; or

(b) that such a merger has taken place otherwise than as a result of the carrying into effect of arrangements that have been the subject of a reference by virtue of paragraph (a) above.]

NOTES

Substituted by the Enterprise Act 2002, s 70(1).

Words in first pair of square brackets substituted by the Water Act 2014, s 14(1).

Words in second pair of square brackets substituted by the Enterprise and Regulatory Reform Act 2013 (Competition) (Consequential, Transitional and Saving Provisions) Order 2014, SI 2014/892, art 2, Sch 1, Pt 2, paras 73, 85, subject to transitional provisions as noted to the Enterprise Act 2002, s 8A at **[1.187]**.

[1.33]

33 Exclusion of small mergers from duty to make reference

(1) The [CMA] shall not make a merger reference under section 32 above in respect of any actual or prospective merger of two or more water enterprises if it appears to the [CMA]—

(a) that the value of the turnover of the water enterprise being taken over does not exceed or, as the case may be, would not exceed £10 million; or

(b) that the only water enterprises already belonging to the person making the take over are enterprises each of which has a turnover the value of which does not exceed or, as the case may be, would not exceed £10 million.

(2) For the purposes of subsection (1)(a) above, the value of the turnover of the water enterprise being taken over shall be determined by taking the total value of the turnover of the water enterprises ceasing to be distinct enterprises and deducting—

(a) the turnover of any water enterprise continuing to be carried on under the same ownership and control; or

(b) if there is no water enterprise continuing to be carried on under the same ownership and control, the turnover which, of all the turnovers concerned, is the turnover of the highest value.

(3) For the purposes of subsection (1)(b) above—

(a) every water enterprise ceasing to be a distinct enterprise and whose turnover is to be deducted by virtue of subsection (2)(a) or (b) above shall be treated as a water enterprise belonging to the person making the take over; and

(b) water enterprises shall be treated as separate enterprises so far as they are carried on by different companies holding appointments under Chapter 1 of this Part.

(4) For the purposes of this section the turnover of a water enterprise shall be determined in accordance with such provisions as may be specified in regulations made by the Secretary of State.

(5) Regulations under subsection (4) above may, in particular, make provision as to—

(a) the amounts which are, or which are not, to be treated as comprising an enterprise's turnover; and

(b) the date or dates by reference to which an enterprise's turnover is to be determined.

(6) Regulations under subsection (4) above may, in particular, make provision enabling the Secretary of State or the [CMA] to determine matters of a description specified in the regulations (including any of the matters mentioned in paragraphs (a) and (b) of subsection (5) above).

[(6A) The CMA must—

(a) keep under review the conditions set out in subsection (1)(a) and (b), and

(b) from time to time advise the Secretary of State as to whether the conditions in subsection (1)(a) and (b), and the sums mentioned in those paragraphs, are still appropriate.]

(7) The Secretary of State may by regulations amend subsection (1) above so as—

(a) to alter the sum for the time being mentioned in paragraph (a) of that subsection or otherwise to modify the condition set out in that paragraph; or

(b) to alter the sum for the time being mentioned in paragraph (b) of that subsection or otherwise to modify the condition set out in that paragraph.

(8) Regulations under subsection (7) above—

(a) shall not make any modifications in relation to mergers on or before the coming into force of the regulations; and

(b) may, in particular, include supplemental, consequential or transitional provision amending or repealing any provision of this section.

(9) References in this section to enterprises being carried on under the same ownership and control shall be construed in accordance with Part 3 of the 2002 Act.]

NOTES

Substituted by the Enterprise Act 2002, s 70(1).

Sub-ss (1), (6): references to "CMA" in square brackets substituted by the Enterprise and Regulatory Reform Act 2013 (Competition) (Consequential, Transitional and Saving Provisions) Order 2014, SI 2014/892, art 2, Sch 1, Pt 2, paras 73, 86, subject to transitional provisions as noted to the Enterprise Act 2002, s 8A at **[1.187]**.

Sub-s (6A): inserted by the Water Act 2014, s 15.

Regulations: the Water Mergers (Determination of Turnover) Regulations 2004, SI 2004/3206; the Isles of Scilly (Application of Water Legislation) Order 2020, SI 2020/214.

[1.34]

[33A Exceptions to duty to make reference

(1) The CMA may decide not to make a merger reference under section 32 as regards a case falling within section 32(a) if it believes that—

(a) the arrangements concerned are not sufficiently far advanced, or are not sufficiently likely to proceed, to justify the making of a merger reference;

(b) the prospective merger is not likely to prejudice the ability of the Authority, in carrying out its functions by virtue of this Act, to make comparisons between water enterprises; or

(c) the prospective merger is likely to prejudice that ability, but the prejudice in question is outweighed by relevant customer benefits relating to the merger.

(2) The CMA may decide not to make a merger reference under section 32 as regards a case falling within section 32(b) if it believes that—

(a) the merger has not prejudiced and is not likely to prejudice the ability of the Authority, in carrying out its functions by virtue of this Act, to make comparisons between water enterprises; or

(b) the merger has prejudiced or is likely to prejudice that ability, but the prejudice in question is outweighed by relevant customer benefits relating to the merger.

(3) Before forming a view as to the matters in subsection (1)(b) or (c) or (2)(a) or (b), the CMA must—

(a) request the Authority to give an opinion under section 33B, and

(b) consider that opinion.

(4) The CMA may not make a merger reference under section 32 if—

(a) it is considering whether to accept an undertaking under section 33D instead of making such a reference; or

(b) it is prevented by section 74 of the Enterprise Act 2002 (effect of accepting an undertaking in lieu), in a case where that section as applied by paragraph 1 of Schedule 4ZA may have effect to prevent such a merger reference.

(5) In this section "relevant customer benefit" has the meaning given by paragraph 7 of Schedule 4ZA.]

NOTES

Inserted, together with ss 33B, 33C, by the Water Act 2014, s 14(2).

[1.35]

[33B Opinion of the Authority

(1) Where the CMA makes a request under section 33A(3), the Authority must give its opinion on—

(a) whether and to what extent the actual or prospective merger has prejudiced or is likely to prejudice the Authority's ability, in carrying out its functions by virtue of this Act, to make comparisons between water enterprises, and

(b) where it forms the view that the actual or prospective merger has prejudiced or is likely to prejudice that ability, whether the prejudice in question is outweighed by any relevant customer benefits relating to the merger.

(2) In forming an opinion on the matters in subsection (1), the Authority must apply the methods set out in the statement under section 33C that has effect when the request under section 33A(3) is made.

(3) In this section "relevant customer benefit" has the meaning given by paragraph 7 of Schedule 4ZA, except that references in paragraph 7 to what the CMA believes are to be read for the purposes of this section as references to what the Authority believes.]

NOTES

Inserted as noted to s 33A at **[1.34]**.

[1.36]

[33C Statement of methods

(1) The Authority must prepare and keep under review a statement of the methods to be applied in forming an opinion on the matters in section 33B(1).

(2) The statement must in particular set out—

(a) the criteria to be used for assessing the effect of any particular water enterprise ceasing to be a distinct enterprise on the Authority's ability, in carrying out its functions by virtue of this Act, to make comparisons between water enterprises;

(b) the relative weight to be given to the criteria.

(3) Before preparing or altering the statement, the Authority must consult—

(a) the Secretary of State,

(b) the Welsh Ministers,

(c) the CMA, and

(d) relevant undertakers.

(4) The Authority must from time to time publish the statement as it has effect for the time being.]

NOTES

Inserted as noted to s 33A at **[1.34]**.

[1.37]

[33D Undertakings in lieu of a merger reference

(1) If the CMA considers that it is under a duty to make a merger reference under section 32, it may instead of making such a reference accept undertakings to take such action as it thinks appropriate from such of the parties concerned in the actual or prospective merger as it considers appropriate.

(2) The power under subsection (1) is to be exercised for the purpose of remedying, mitigating or preventing the prejudicial effect on the Authority's ability, in carrying out its functions by virtue of this Act, to make comparisons between water enterprises that the actual or prospective merger has had, may have had or may be likely to have.

(3) In forming a view for the purposes of subsection (1) as to whether it is under a duty to make a merger reference under section 32, the CMA—

(a) is to disregard the effect of section 33A(4)(a), but

(b) is to take into account the powers under section 33A(1) and (2) to decide not to make a merger reference.

(4) In proceeding under subsection (1), the CMA must, in particular, have regard to the need to achieve as comprehensive a solution as is reasonable and practicable to the prejudicial effect on the Authority's ability, in carrying out its functions by virtue of this Act, to make comparisons between water enterprises.

(5) In proceeding under subsection (1), the CMA may, in particular, have regard to the effect of any action on any relevant customer benefits in relation to the actual or prospective merger.

(6) Before deciding whether or not to accept an undertaking under this section, the CMA must—

(a) request the Authority to give its opinion on the effect of the undertakings offered, and

(b) consider the Authority's opinion.

(7) Where the CMA makes a request under subsection (6), the Authority must give its opinion on the effect of the undertakings offered.

(8) An undertaking under this section—

(a) comes into force when accepted;

(b) may be varied or superseded by another undertaking under this section;

(c) may be released by the CMA.

(9) An undertaking under this section ceases to be in force if an order under section 75 or 76 of the Enterprise Act 2002 (powers to make an order where an undertaking is not fulfilled) is made, in a case where that provision of the Enterprise Act 2002 as applied by paragraph 1 of Schedule 4ZA may have effect in relation to such an undertaking.

(10) The CMA must consider any representations received by it in relation to varying or releasing an undertaking under this section as soon as reasonably practicable.

(11) In this section "relevant customer benefit" has the meaning given by paragraph 7 of Schedule 4ZA, except that references in paragraph 7 to what the CMA believes are to be read for the purposes of subsection (7) as references to what the Authority believes.]

NOTES

Inserted by the Water Act 2014, s 14(3).

[1.38]

[34 Application of provisions of Enterprise Act 2002

The provisions of Schedule 4ZA to this Act shall have effect with respect to mergers of water enterprises.]

NOTES

Substituted by the Enterprise Act 2002, s 70(1).

[1.39]

35 Construction of merger provisions

(1) In this Chapter (including Schedule 4ZA)—

"enterprise" has the same meaning as in Part 3 of the 2002 Act; and

"water enterprise" means an enterprise carried on by a [relevant undertaker].

(2) References in this Chapter (including Schedule 4ZA), in relation to any two or more enterprises, to the merger of those enterprises are references to those enterprises ceasing, within the meaning of Part 3 of the 2002 Act, to be distinct enterprises; and sections 27 and 29 of that Act and any provision made under section 34 of that Act (time at which enterprises cease to be distinct) shall have effect for the purposes of this Chapter (including Schedule 4ZA) as they have effect for the purposes of that Part.

(3) Nothing in sections 32 to 34 above (including Schedule 4ZA) shall prejudice any power of the [CMA] or the Secretary of State, in a case in which, or to any extent to which, the [CMA] is not required to make a reference under section 32 above, to make a reference under Part 3 of the 2002 Act in respect of any actual or prospective merger of two or more water enterprises.

(4) Where two or more enterprises have merged or will merge as part of transactions or arrangements which also involve an actual or prospective merger of two or more water enterprises, Part 3 of the 2002 Act shall apply in relation to the actual or prospective merger of the enterprises concerned excluding the water enterprises; and references in that Part to the creation of a relevant merger situation shall be construed accordingly.

(5) Subject to subsections (3) and (4), Part 3 of the 2002 Act shall not apply in a case in which the [CMA] is required to make a reference under section 32 above except as applied by virtue of Schedule 4ZA.]

NOTES

Substituted by the Enterprise Act 2002, s 70(1).

Sub-s (1): words in square brackets in the definition "water enterprise" substituted by the Water Act 2003, s 101(1), Sch 7, Pt 2, para 27(1), (2).

Sub-ss (3), (5): references to "CMA" in square brackets substituted by the Enterprise and Regulatory Reform Act 2013 (Competition) (Consequential, Transitional and Saving Provisions) Order 2014, SI 2014/892, art 2, Sch 1, Pt 2, paras 73, 87, subject to transitional provisions as noted to the Enterprise Act 2002, s 8A at **[1.187]**.

SCHEDULES

[SCHEDULE 4ZA
APPLICATION OF PROVISIONS OF ENTERPRISE ACT 2002 TO MERGERS OF WATER ENTERPRISES

Section 34

[1.40]

1. Part 3 of the 2002 Act (and any other provisions of that Act so far as relating to that Part) shall apply, with such prescribed modifications as the Secretary of State considers to be necessary or expedient, in relation to water mergers and merger references under section 32 of this Act as it applies in relation to relevant merger situations and references under Part 3 of that Act.

2. The modifications made by virtue of paragraph 1 above shall include modifications to give effect to paragraphs [2A to 6] below.

[2A. Where a reference is made to the chair of the CMA under section 32 for the constitution of a group under Schedule 4 to the Enterprise and Regulatory Reform Act 2013, the functions of the CMA in relation to the matter are to be carried out on behalf of the CMA by the group so constituted in any case where those functions would be carried out by a group so constituted in relation to a reference under Part 3 of that Act.]

3. (1) The first questions to be decided by the [CMA] on a merger reference under section 32(a) of this Act shall be—

(a) whether arrangements are in progress which, if carried into effect, will result in a water merger; and

(b) if so, whether that merger may be expected to prejudice the ability of [the Authority], in carrying out [its] functions by virtue of this Act, to make comparisons between different water enterprises.

(2) The first questions to be decided by the [CMA] on a merger reference under section 32(b) of this Act shall be—

(a) whether a water merger has taken place; and

(b) if so, whether that merger has prejudiced, or may be expected to prejudice, the ability of [the Authority], in carrying out [its] functions by virtue of this Act, to make comparisons between different water enterprises.

(3) Any decision of the [CMA] on a merger reference under section 32(a) of this Act that arrangements are in progress which, if carried into effect, will result in a water merger shall be treated as a decision that no arrangements are in progress which, if carried into effect, will result in a water merger if the decision is not that of at least two-thirds of the members of the group constituted in connection with the reference [under Schedule 4 to the Enterprise and Regulatory Reform Act 2013].

(4) Any decision of the [CMA] on a merger reference under section 32(a) of this Act that a water merger may be expected to prejudice the ability of [the Authority], in carrying out [its] functions by virtue of this Act, to make comparisons between different water enterprises shall be treated as a decision that the water merger may be expected

not to prejudice that ability of [the Authority] if the decision is not that of at least two-thirds of the members of the group constituted in connection with the reference [under Schedule 4 to the Enterprise and Regulatory Reform Act 2013].

(5) Any decision of the [CMA] on a merger reference under section 32(b) of this Act that a water merger has taken place shall be treated as a decision that no water merger has taken place if the decision is not that of at least two-thirds of the members of the group constituted in connection with the reference [under Schedule 4 to the Enterprise and Regulatory Reform Act 2013].

(6) Any decision of the [CMA] on a merger reference under section 32(b) of this Act that a water merger has prejudiced, or may be expected to prejudice, the ability of [the Authority], in carrying out [its] functions by virtue of this Act, to make comparisons between different water enterprises shall be treated as a decision that the water merger has not prejudiced, or may be expected not to prejudice, that ability of [the Authority] if the decision is not that of at least two-thirds of the members of the group constituted in connection with the reference [under Schedule 4 to the Enterprise and Regulatory Reform Act 2013].

4. (1) In deciding, on a merger reference under section 32(a) of this Act whether to take action for the purpose of remedying, mitigating or preventing the prejudice to [the Authority] or any adverse effect which may be expected to result from the prejudice to [the Authority] and, if so, what action should be taken, the [CMA] may, in particular, have regard to the effect of any such action on any relevant customer benefits in relation to the merger concerned provided that—

- (a) a consideration of those benefits would not prevent a solution to the prejudice concerned; or
- (b) the benefits which may be expected to accrue are substantially more important than the prejudice concerned.

(2) In deciding, on a merger reference under section 32(b) of this Act whether to take action for the purpose of remedying, mitigating or preventing the prejudice to [the Authority] or any adverse effect which has resulted from, or may be expected to result from, the prejudice to [the Authority] and, if so, what action should be taken, the [CMA] may, in particular, have regard to the effect of any such action on any relevant customer benefits in relation to the merger concerned provided that—

- (a) a consideration of those benefits would not prevent a solution to the prejudice concerned; or
- (b) the benefits which have accrued, or may be expected to accrue, are substantially more important than the prejudice concerned.

(3) This paragraph is without prejudice to the power of the Secretary of State to provide in regulations made under paragraph 1 above for other matters to which the [CMA] may or must have regard in deciding the questions as mentioned in sub-paragraph (1) or (2) above (including matters which are to take priority over the effect of action on relevant customer benefits).

5. (1) No enforcement action shall be taken on a merger reference under section 32(b) of this Act in respect of an actual merger unless the reference was made within the period of four months beginning with whichever is the later of—

- (a) the day on which the merger took place; and
- (b) the day on which the material facts about the transactions which resulted in the merger first came to the attention of the [CMA] or were made public (within the meaning given by section 24(3) of the 2002 Act).

(2) This paragraph is without prejudice to the power of the Secretary of State to provide in regulations made under paragraph 1 above for extensions of the four month period; and, if any such provision is made in such regulations, the provision which is to be made in regulations under paragraph 1 above by virtue of sub-paragraph (1) above or paragraph 6 below may be adjusted accordingly.

6. If, on a merger reference under section 32(b) of this Act, the [CMA] are satisfied that the reference was not made within the period of four months mentioned in paragraph 5 above, its report on the reference shall state that fact.

7. (1) For the purposes of this Schedule a benefit is a relevant customer benefit if—

- (a) it is a benefit to relevant customers in the form of—
  - (i) lower prices, higher quality or greater choice of goods or services in any market in the United Kingdom; or
  - (ii) greater innovation in relation to such goods or services; and
- (b) the [CMA] believes—
  - (i) in the case of a merger reference under section 32(a) of this Act, as mentioned in sub-paragraph (2) below; and
  - (ii) in the case of a merger reference under section 32(b) of this Act, as mentioned in sub-paragraph (3) below.

(2) The belief, in the case of a merger reference under section 32(a) of this Act, is that—

- (a) the benefit may be expected to accrue within a reasonable period as a result of the merger concerned; and
- (b) the benefit is unlikely to accrue without the merger concerned or a similar prejudice to [the Authority].

(3) The belief, in the case of a merger reference under section 32(b) of this Act is that—

- (a) the benefit has accrued as a result of the merger concerned or may be expected to accrue within a reasonable period as a result of the merger concerned; and
- (b) the benefit was, or is, unlikely to accrue without the merger concerned or a similar prejudice to [the Authority].

(4) In sub-paragraph (1) above "relevant customers" means—

- (a) customers of any person carrying on an enterprise which, in the merger concerned, has ceased to be, or (as the case may be) will cease to be, a distinct enterprise;
- (b) customers of such customers; and
- (c) any other customers in a chain of customers beginning with the customers mentioned in paragraph (a);

and in this sub-paragraph "customers" includes future customers.

8. In this Schedule—

"customers", "goods", "market in the United Kingdom", "services" and "relevant merger situation" have the same meanings as in Part 3 of the 2002 Act; and

"water merger" means a merger of any two or more water enterprises.]

NOTES

Inserted by the Enterprise Act 2002, s 70(2), Sch 6.

References to the "CMA" in each paces they occur substituted by the Enterprise and Regulatory Reform Act 2013 (Competition) (Consequential, Transitional and Saving Provisions) Order 2014, SI 2014/892, art 2, Sch 1, Pt 2, paras 73, 93(1), (4)–(7), subject to transitional provisions as noted to the Enterprise Act 2002, s 8A at **[1.187]**. This Schedule is also amended as follows—

Para 2: words in square brackets substituted by SI 2014/892, art 2, Sch 1, Pt 2, paras 73, 93(1), (2), subject to transitional provisions as noted above.

Para 2A: inserted by SI 2014/892, art 2, Sch 1, Pt 2, paras 73, 93(1), (3), subject to transitional provisions as noted above.

Para 3: words "the Authority" and "its" in square brackets in each place they occur substituted by virtue of the Water Act 2003, s 36(2).

Paras 4, 7: words "the Authority" in square brackets in each place they occur substituted by virtue of the Water Act 2003, s 36(2).

Regulations: the Water Mergers (Modification of Enactments) Regulations 2004, SI 2004/3202; the Water Mergers (Miscellaneous Amendments) Regulations 2015, SI 2015/1936; the Isles of Scilly (Application of Water Legislation) Order 2020, SI 2020/214.

COMPETITION ACT 1998

(1998 c 41)

ARRANGEMENT OF SECTIONS

PART I COMPETITION

CHAPTER I AGREEMENTS

Introduction

The prohibition

Excluded agreements

Exemptions

CHAPTER II ABUSE OF DOMINANT POSITION

The prohibition

Excluded cases

CHAPTER III INVESTIGATION AND ENFORCEMENT

Investigations

An Act to make provision about competition and the abuse of a dominant position in the market; to confer powers in relation to investigations conducted in connection with [Article 81 or 82] of the treaty establishing the European Community; to amend the Fair Trading Act 1973 in relation to information which may be required in connection with investigations under that Act; to make provision with respect to the meaning of "supply of services" in the Fair Trading Act 1973; and for connected purposes

[9 November 1998]

NOTES

The words in square brackets in the long title to this Act were substituted by the Competition Act 1998 and Other Enactments (Amendment) Regulations 2004, SI 2004/1261, reg 4, Sch 1, para 1. Articles 81 and 82 of the Treaty establishing the European Community were subsequently replaced by Articles 101 and 102 of the Treaty on the Functioning of the EU. References in this work to the original Articles should be construed accordingly.

Director General of Fair Trading. The Enterprise Act 2002, s 2(1) provided that, as from the coming into force of that section (on 1 April 2003), the functions of the Director General of Fair Trading, his property, rights and liabilities were transferred to the Office of Fair Trading. Accordingly, (by virtue of s 2(2), (3) of the 2002 Act) the office of the Director was abolished, and amendments were made to this Act by the 2002 Act to take account of this (see Sch 25, para 38). Section 2 of the 2002 Act was repealed by the Enterprise and Regulatory Reform Act 2013, s 26(3), Sch 5, Pt 4, para 229. As to the subsequent abolition of the OFT, see the Enterprise and Regulatory Reform Act 2013, s 26 at **[1.446]**.

References to the "European Community", "Community", etc. See the Treaty of Lisbon (Changes in Terminology) Order 2011, SI 2011/1043, which provides (with effect from 22 April 2011): (1) that for references to the "European Communities" or to the "European Community" (including references to "the Communities", "the Community", "the EC" or "the EEC") substitute references to the European Union; and (2) that "EU" should be substituted for the word "Community" (subject to certain exceptions) in references to "Community treaties", "Community customs duty", "Community institution", "Community instrument", "Community obligation", "enforceable Community right", "Community law", "Community legislation", and "Community provision". Also, where such a term is preceded by the word "a", for "a" substitute "an". For more details see arts 3, 4, 6 of the 2011 Order as set out in the introductory notes to the Company Directors Disqualification Act 1986 preceding **[1.23]**.

Disclosure of information. Information which comes to a public authority in connection with the exercise of any function it has under or by virtue of this Act is "specified information" for the purposes of the Enterprise Act 2002, s 238; see s 238(1) of, and Sch 14 to, that Act at **[1.417]**, **[1.443]**. A public authority which holds information to which s 237 of the 2002 Act applies (general restriction on disclosure) may disclose that information to any other person for the purpose of facilitating the exercise by that person of any function he has under or by virtue of this Act and the 2002 Act; see s 241(3) of, and Sch 15 to, the 2002 Act at **[1.420]**, **[1.444]**. As to the disclosure of information to an overseas authority, see s 243 of, and Sch 14 to, the 2002 Act at **[1.423]**, **[1.443]**.

See also the list of consultations and draft documents in the Appendix at **[A1]**.

PART I COMPETITION

NOTES

Sectoral regulators: certain functions of the CMA under this Part are exercisable concurrently with various sectoral regulators; ie—

(i) the CMA shall exercise its functions under this Part (other than ss 31D(1)–(6), 38(1)–(6), 40B(1)–(4) and 51) concurrently with the Office of Rail and Road in so far as relating to (a) agreements, decisions or concerted practices of the kind mentioned in s 2(1) of this Act; (b) conduct of the kind mentioned in s 18(1) of this Act; (c) transferred EU anti-trust commitments or transferred EU anti-trust directions (as defined in section 40ZA of this Act), and which relate to the supply of services relating to railways (see the Railways Act 1993, s 67(3));

(ii) the CMA shall exercise its functions under this Part (other than ss 31D(1)–(6), 38(1)–(6), 40B(1)–(4) and 51) concurrently with the Office of Communications (OFCOM) in so far as relating to (a) agreements, decisions or concerted practices of the kind mentioned in s 2(1) of this Act; (b) conduct of the kind mentioned in s 18(1) of this Act; (c) transferred EU anti-trust commitments or transferred EU anti-trust directions (as defined in section 40ZA of this Act), and which relate to activities connected with communication matters (see the Communications Act 2003, s 371(1), (2));

(iii) the CMA shall exercise its functions under this Part (other than ss 31D(1)–(6), 38(1)–(6), 40B(1)–(4) and 51) concurrently with the Gas and Electricity Markets Authority in so far as relating to (a) agreements, decisions or concerted practices of the kind mentioned in s 2(1) of this Act; (b) conduct of the kind mentioned in s 18(1) of this Act; (c) transferred EU anti-trust commitments or transferred EU anti-trust directions (as defined in section 40ZA of this Act), and which relate to the supply (etc) of gas to any premises and ancillary matters (see the Gas Act 1986, s 36A(3));

(iv) the CMA shall exercise its functions under this Part (other than ss 31D(1)–(6), 38(1)–(6), 40B(1)–(4) and 51) concurrently with the Gas and Electricity Markets Authority in so far as relating to (a) agreements, decisions or concerted practices of the kind mentioned in s 2(1) of this Act; (b) conduct of the kind mentioned in s 18(1) of this Act; (c) transferred EU anti-trust commitments or transferred EU anti-trust directions (as defined in section 40ZA of this Act), and which relate to commercial activities connected with the generation, transmission or supply of electricity or the use of electricity interconnectors (see the Electricity Act 1989, s 43(3));

(v) the CMA shall exercise its functions under this Part (other than ss 31D(1)–(6), 38(1)–(6), 40B(1)–(4) and 51) concurrently with the Water Services Regulation Authority in so far as relating to (a) agreements, decisions or concerted practices of the kind mentioned in s 2(1) of this Act; (b) conduct of the kind mentioned in s 18(1) of this Act; (c) transferred EU anti-trust commitments or transferred EU anti-trust directions (as defined in section 40ZA of this Act), and which relate to commercial activities connected with the supply of water or securing a supply of water or with the provision or securing of sewerage services (see the Water Industry Act 1991, s 31(3));

(vi) the CMA shall exercise its functions under this Part (other than ss 31D(1)–(6), 38(1)–(6), 40B(1)–(4) and 51) concurrently with the Civil Aviation Authority in so far as relating to (a) agreements, decisions or concerted practices of the kind mentioned in s 2(1) of this Act, (b) conduct of the kind mentioned in s 18(1) of this Act, (c) transferred EU anti-trust commitments or transferred EU anti-trust directions (as defined in section 40ZA of this Act), and which relate to (i) the supply of air traffic services (see the Transport Act 2000, s 86(3)), or (ii) the provision of airport operation services (see the Civil Aviation Act 2012, s 62(2), (3)).

(vii) the CMA shall exercise its functions under this Part (other than ss 31D(1)–(6), 38(1)–(6), 40B(1)–(4) and 51) concurrently with Monitor in so far as relating to (a) agreements, decisions or concerted practices of the kind mentioned in s 2(1) of this Act, (b) conduct of the kind mentioned in s 18(1) of this Act, (c) transferred EU anti-trust commitments or transferred EU anti-trust directions (as defined in section 40ZA of this Act), and which concern the provision of health care services in England (see the Health and Social Care Act 2012, 72(2)).

(viii) the CMA shall exercise its functions under this Part (other than ss 31D(1)–(6), 38(1)–(6), 40B(1)–(4) and 51) concurrently with the Payment Systems Regulator in so far as relating to (a) agreements, decisions or concerted practices of the kind mentioned in s 2(1) of this Act, (b) conduct of the kind mentioned in s 18(1) of this Act, (c) transferred EU anti-trust commitments or transferred EU anti-trust directions (as defined in section 40ZA of this Act), and which relate to participation in payment systems (see the Financial Services (Banking Reform) Act 2013, 61(1)–(3)).

(ix) the CMA shall exercise its functions under this Part (other than ss 31D(1)–(6), 38(1)–(6), 40B(1)–(4) and 51) concurrently with the FCA in so far as relating to (a) agreements, decisions or concerted practices of the kind mentioned in s 2(1) of this Act, (b) conduct of the kind mentioned in s 18(1) of this Act, (c) transferred EU anti-trust commitments or transferred EU anti-trust directions (as defined in section 40ZA of this Act), and which relate to the provision of financial services or relate to the provision of claims management services in Great Britain (see the Financial Services and Markets Act 2000, s 234J).

Accordingly (and by virtue of the Railways Act 1993, 67(3A), the Communications Act 2003, s 371(3), the Gas Act 1986, s 36A(3A), the Electricity Act 1989, s 43(3A), the Water Industry Act 1991, s 31(4A), the Transport Act 2000, s 86(4), the Civil Aviation Act 2012, s 62(4), the Health and Social Care Act 2012, 72(3), the Financial Services (Banking Reform) Act 2013, 61(4), and the Financial Services and Markets Act 2000, s 234J(4)), references in this Part (other than in the ss 31D(1)–(6), 38(1)–(6), 40B(1)–(4), 51, 52(6), (8), 54, and where the context otherwise requires) to the CMA shall, in so far as is necessary for the purposes of, or in connection with the concurrent exercise of functions, be construed as including references to the appropriate sectoral regulator.

Note that the Competition (Amendment etc) (EU Exit) Regulations 2019, SI 2019/93, reg 63, Sch 1 amended all of the provisions listed in paragraphs (i) to (ix) above to remove references to agreements, decisions or concerted practices of the kind mentioned in Article 101(1) of the Treaty on the Functioning of the European Union, and conduct which amounts to abuse of the kind mentioned in Article 102 of the TFEU (as from IP completion day (as defined in the European Union (Withdrawal Agreement) Act 2020, s 39)). Such references were replaced with references to transferred EU anti-trust commitments or transferred EU anti-trust directions (as defined in section 40ZA of this Act).

For the power of the Secretary of State to make a sectoral regulator order so as to remove all the functions of sectoral regulator under this Part of this Act that are exercisable concurrently by the regulator and the Competition and Markets Authority, see the Enterprise and Regulatory Reform Act 2013, ss 52, 53 at **[1.451]**, **[1.452]**.

For the duty of the Competition and Markets Authority to prepare a report containing an assessment of how the arrangements for co-operation between the Authority and the sectoral regulators in respect of functions which are exercisable concurrently by the Authority and one or more of the regulators under this Part of this Act have operated during each financial year, see the Enterprise and Regulatory Reform Act 2013, Sch 4, Pt 1, para 16 at **[1.460]**.

CHAPTER I AGREEMENTS

Introduction

[1.41]

1 Enactments replaced

The following shall cease to have effect—

(a) the Restrictive Practices Court Act 1976 (c 33),
(b) the Restrictive Trade Practices Act 1976 (c 34),
(c) the Resale Prices Act 1976 (c 53), and
(d) the Restrictive Trade Practices Act 1977 (c 19).

The prohibition

[1.42]

2 Agreements etc preventing, restricting or distorting competition

(1) Subject to section 3, agreements between undertakings, decisions by associations of undertakings or concerted practices which—

(a) may affect trade within the United Kingdom, and

(b) have as their object or effect the prevention, restriction or distortion of competition within the United Kingdom,

are prohibited unless they are exempt in accordance with the provisions of this Part.

(2) Subsection (1) applies, in particular, to agreements, decisions or practices which—

(a) directly or indirectly fix purchase or selling prices or any other trading conditions;

(b) limit or control production, markets, technical development or investment;

(c) share markets or sources of supply;

(d) apply dissimilar conditions to equivalent transactions with other trading parties, thereby placing them at a competitive disadvantage;

(e) make the conclusion of contracts subject to acceptance by the other parties of supplementary obligations which, by their nature or according to commercial usage, have no connection with the subject of such contracts.

(3) Subsection (1) applies only if the agreement, decision or practice is, or is intended to be, implemented in the United Kingdom.

(4) Any agreement or decision which is prohibited by subsection (1) is void.

(5) A provision of this Part which is expressed to apply to, or in relation to, an agreement is to be read as applying equally to, or in relation to, a decision by an association of undertakings or a concerted practice (but with any necessary modifications).

(6) Subsection (5) does not apply where the context otherwise requires.

(7) In this section "the United Kingdom" means, in relation to an agreement which operates or is intended to operate only in a part of the United Kingdom, that part.

(8) The prohibition imposed by subsection (1) is referred to in this Act as "the Chapter I prohibition".

Excluded agreements

[1.43]

3 Excluded agreements

(1) The Chapter I prohibition does not apply in any of the cases in which it is excluded by or as a result of—

(a) Schedule 1 (mergers and concentrations);

(b) Schedule 2 (competition scrutiny under other enactments);

(c) Schedule 3 (planning obligations and other general exclusions); . . .

(d) . . .

(2) The Secretary of State may at any time by order amend Schedule 1, with respect to the Chapter I prohibition, by—

(a) providing for one or more additional exclusions; or

(b) amending or removing any provision (whether or not it has been added by an order under this subsection).

(3) The Secretary of State may at any time by order amend Schedule 3, with respect to the Chapter I prohibition, by—

(a) providing for one or more additional exclusions; or

(b) amending or removing any provision—

(i) added by an order under this subsection; or

(ii) included in paragraph 1, 2, 8 or 9 of Schedule 3.

(4) The power under subsection (3) to provide for an additional exclusion may be exercised only if it appears to the Secretary of State that agreements which fall within the additional exclusion—

(a) do not in general have an adverse effect on competition, or

(b) are, in general, best considered under Chapter II or [the Enterprise Act 2002].

(5) An order under subsection (2)(a) or (3)(a) may include provision (similar to that made with respect to any other exclusion provided by the relevant Schedule) for the exclusion concerned to cease to apply to a particular agreement.

(6) Schedule 3 also gives the Secretary of State power to exclude agreements from the Chapter I prohibition in certain circumstances.

NOTES

Sub-s (1): para (d) and the word immediately preceding it repealed by the Enterprise Act 2002, ss 207, 278(2), Sch 26 (subject to savings in Sch 24, para 20 to that Act at **[1.445]**).

Sub-s (4): words in square brackets substituted by the Enterprise Act 2002, s 278(1), Sch 25, para 38(1), (2) (for savings in relation to the merger of water and sewerage undertakers, see the Enterprise Act 2002 (Commencement No 3, Transitional and Transitory Provisions and Savings) Order 2003, SI 2003/1397, art 3, and the Enterprise Act 2002 (Commencement No 7 and Transitional Provisions and Savings) Order 2004, SI 2004/3233, arts 3–5).

Exemptions

4, 5 (*Repealed by the Competition Act 1998 and Other Enactments (Amendment) Regulations 2004, SI 2004/1261, reg 4, Sch 1, paras 2, 3 (for savings and transitional provisions see regs 6, 8, 10 of those Regulations at* **[2.6]**, **[2.8]**, **[2.10]**).)

[1.44]

6 Block exemptions

(1) If agreements which fall within a particular category of agreement are, in the opinion of the [CMA], likely to be [exempt agreements], the [CMA] may recommend that the Secretary of State make an order specifying that category for the purposes of this section.

(2) The Secretary of State may make an order ("a block exemption order") giving effect to such a recommendation—

(a) in the form in which the recommendation is made; or

(b) subject to such modifications as he considers appropriate.

(3) An agreement which falls within a category specified in a block exemption order is exempt from the Chapter I prohibition.

(4) An exemption under this section is referred to in this Part as a block exemption.

(5) A block exemption order may impose conditions or obligations subject to which a block exemption is to have effect.

(6) A block exemption order may provide—

(a) that breach of a condition imposed by the order has the effect of cancelling the block exemption in respect of an agreement;

(b) that if there is a failure to comply with an obligation imposed by the order, the [CMA] may, by notice in writing, cancel the block exemption in respect of the agreement;

(c) that if the [CMA] considers that a particular agreement is not [an exempt agreement], [it] may cancel the block exemption in respect of that agreement.

(7) A block exemption order may provide that the order is to cease to have effect at the end of a specified period.

[(8) In this section—

"exempt agreement" means an agreement which is exempt from the Chapter I prohibition as a result of section 9; and

"specified" means specified in a block exemption order.]

NOTES

References to the "CMA" substituted by the Enterprise and Regulatory Reform Act 2013, s 26(3), Sch 5, Pt 1, paras 1, 2. For various transitional provisions (including those relating to the abolition of the OFT and the Competition Commission, existing references to those bodies and provisions relating to continuity), see the Enterprise and Regulatory Reform Act 2013 (Commencement No 6, Transitional Provisions and Savings) Order 2014, SI 2014/416, Schedule at **[2.13]**. This section is also amended as follows:

Sub-s (1): words in second pair of square brackets substituted by the Competition Act 1998 and other enactments (Amendment) Regulations 2004, SI 2004/1261, reg 4, Sch 1, para 4(1), (2).

Sub-s (6): words in second pair of square brackets in para (c) substituted by SI 2004/1261, reg 4, Sch 1, para 4(1), (3). Word in third pair of square brackets in para (c) substituted by the Enterprise Act 2002, s 278, Sch 25, para 38.

Sub-s (8): substituted by SI 2004/1261, reg 4, Sch 1, para 4(1), (4).

Orders: the Competition Act 1998 (Public Transport Ticketing Schemes Block Exemption) Order 2001, SI 2001/319; the Competition Act 1998 (Public Transport Ticketing Schemes Block Exemption) (Amendment) Order 2005, SI 2005/3347; the Competition Act 1998 (Public Transport Ticketing Schemes Block Exemption) (Amendment) Order 2011, SI 2011/227; the Competition Act 1998 (Public Transport Ticketing Schemes Block Exemption) (Amendment) Order 2016, SI 2016/126.

7 (*Repealed by the Competition Act 1998 and Other Enactments (Amendment) Regulations 2004, SI 2004/1261, reg 4, Sch 1, para 5.*)

[1.45]

8 Block exemptions: procedure

(1) Before making a recommendation under section 6(1), the [CMA] must—

(a) publish details of [its] proposed recommendation in such a way as [it] thinks most suitable for bringing it to the attention of those likely to be affected; and

(b) consider any representations about it which are made to [it].

(2) If the Secretary of State proposes to give effect to such a recommendation subject to modifications, he must inform the [CMA] of the proposed modifications and take into account any comments made by the [CMA].

(3) If, in the opinion of the [CMA], it is appropriate to vary or revoke a block exemption order [it] may make a recommendation to that effect to the Secretary of State.

(4) Subsection (1) also applies to any proposed recommendation under subsection (3).

(5) Before exercising his power to vary or revoke a block exemption order (in a case where there has been no recommendation under subsection (3)), the Secretary of State must—

(a) inform the [CMA] of the proposed variation or revocation; and

(b) take into account any comments made by the [CMA].

(6) A block exemption order may provide for a block exemption to have effect from a date earlier than that on which the order is made.

NOTES

References to the "CMA" substituted by the Enterprise and Regulatory Reform Act 2013, s 26(3), Sch 5, Pt 1, paras 1, 3. For various transitional provisions (including those relating to the abolition of the OFT and the Competition Commission, existing references to those bodies and provisions relating to continuity), see the Enterprise and Regulatory Reform Act 2013 (Commencement No 6, Transitional Provisions and Savings) Order 2014, SI 2014/416, Schedule at **[2.13]**. This section is also amended as follows:

Sub-s (1): words in second, third and fourth pairs of square brackets substituted by the Enterprise Act 2002, s 278, Sch 25, para 38.

Sub-s (3): word in second pair of square brackets substituted by the Enterprise Act 2002, s 278, Sch 25, para 38.

Orders: the Competition Act 1998 (Public Transport Ticketing Schemes Block Exemption) Order 2001, SI 2001/319; the Competition Act 1998 (Public Transport Ticketing Schemes Block Exemption) (Amendment) Order 2005, SI 2005/3347.

[1.46]

9 [Exempt Agreements]

[(1)] [An agreement is exempt from the Chapter I prohibition if it]—

(a) contributes to—

(i) improving production or distribution, or

(ii) promoting technical or economic progress,

while allowing consumers a fair share of the resulting benefit; [and]

(b) does not—

(i) impose on the undertakings concerned restrictions which are not indispensable to the attainment of those objectives; or

(ii) afford the undertakings concerned the possibility of eliminating competition in respect of a substantial part of the products in question.

[(2) In any proceedings in which it is alleged that the Chapter I prohibition is being or has been infringed by an agreement, any undertaking or association of undertakings claiming the benefit of subsection (1) shall bear the burden of proving that the conditions of that subsection are satisfied.]

NOTES

The section heading was substituted, sub-s (1) was renumbered as such, the words in square brackets in that subsection were substituted, and sub-s (2) was added, by the Competition Act 1998 and Other Enactments (Amendment) Regulations 2004, SI 2004/1261, reg 4, Sch 1, para 6.

[1.47]

10 [Retained exemptions]

[(A1) An agreement is exempt from the Chapter I prohibition if it falls within a category of agreements specified as exempt in a retained block exemption regulation.]

(1) An agreement is exempt from the Chapter I prohibition if it is exempt from the Community prohibition—

(a) by virtue of a Regulation, [or

(b) because of a decision of the Commission under Article 10 of the EC Competition Regulation].

(2) An agreement is exempt from the Chapter I prohibition if it does not affect trade between Member States but otherwise falls within a category of agreement which is exempt from the Community prohibition by virtue of a Regulation.

(3) An exemption from the Chapter I prohibition under this section is referred to in this Part as a [retained exemption].

(4) A [retained exemption]—

(a) takes effect on the date on which the relevant exemption from the Community prohibition takes effect or, in the case of a parallel exemption under subsection (2), would take effect if the agreement in question affected trade between Member States; and

(b) ceases to have effect—

(i) if the relevant [retained block exemption regulation] ceases to have effect; or

(ii) on being cancelled by virtue of subsection (5) or (7).

(5) In such circumstances and manner as may be specified in rules made under section 51, the [CMA] may—

(a) impose conditions or obligations subject to which a [retained exemption] is to have effect [in respect of an agreement];

(b) vary or remove any such condition or obligation;

(c) impose one or more additional conditions or obligations;

(d) cancel the exemption [in respect of an agreement].

(6) In such circumstances as may be specified in rules made under section 51, the date from which cancellation of an exemption is to take effect may be earlier than the date on which notice of cancellation is given.

(7) Breach of a condition imposed by the [CMA] has the effect of cancelling the exemption.

(8) In exercising [its] powers under this section, the [CMA] may require any person who is a party to the agreement in question to give [it] such information as [it] may require.

(9) For the purpose of this section references to an agreement being exempt from the Community prohibition are to be read as including references to the prohibition being inapplicable to the agreement by virtue of a Regulation [other than the EC Competition Regulation] or a decision by the Commission.

(10) In this section—

"the Community prohibition" means the prohibition contained in—

[(a) [Article 101(1)];]

(b) any corresponding provision replacing, or otherwise derived from, that provision;

(c) such other Regulation as the Secretary of State may by order specify; and

"Regulation" means a Regulation adopted by the Commission or by the Council.

(11) This section has effect in relation to the prohibition contained in paragraph 1 of Article 53 of the EEA Agreement (and the EFTA Surveillance Authority) as it has effect in relation to the Community prohibition (and the Commission) subject to any modifications which the Secretary of State may by order prescribe.

[(12) In this Part, "retained block exemption regulation" means the following regulations as amended from time to time—

(a) Council Regulation (EC) 169/2009 applying rules of competition to transport by rail, road and inland waterway;

(b) Commission Regulation (EC) 906/2009 on the application of Article 81(3) of the Treaty to certain categories of agreements, decisions and concerted practices between liner shipping companies (consortia);

(c) Commission Regulation (EU) 330/2010 on the application of Article 101(3) of the Treaty on the Functioning of the European Union to categories of vertical agreements and concerted practices;

(d) Commission Regulation (EU) 461/2010 on the application of Article 101(3) of the Treaty on the Functioning of the European Union to categories of vertical agreements and concerted practices in the motor vehicle sector;
(e) Commission Regulation (EU) 1217/2010 on the application of Article 101(3) of the Treaty on the Functioning of the European Union to certain categories of research and development agreements;
(f) Commission Regulation (EU) 1218/2010 on the application of Article 101(3) of the Treaty on the Functioning of the European Union to certain categories of specialisation agreements;
(g) Commission Regulation (EU) 316/2014 on the application of Article 101(3) of the Treaty on the Functioning of the European Union to categories of technology transfer agreements.]

NOTES

References to the "CMA" substituted by the Enterprise and Regulatory Reform Act 2013, s 26(3), Sch 5, Pt 1, paras 1, 4. For various transitional provisions (including those relating to the abolition of the OFT and the Competition Commission, existing references to those bodies and provisions relating to continuity), see the Enterprise and Regulatory Reform Act 2013 (Commencement No 6, Transitional Provisions and Savings) Order 2014, SI 2014/416, Schedule at **[2.13]**. This section is also amended as follows:

Section heading: the words in square brackets were substituted (for the original words "Parallel exemptions") by the Competition (Amendment etc) (EU Exit) Regulations 2019, SI 2019/93, regs 2, 3(1), (2), as from IP completion day (as defined in the European Union (Withdrawal Agreement) Act 2020, s 39) (for transitional provisions and savings in relation to the operation of the 2019 Regulations, see Sch 4 to those Regulations at **[7.69]** et seq and, in particular, Sch 4, Pt 2 to the 2019 Regulations at **[7.70]**).

Sub-s (A1): inserted by SI 2019/93, regs 2, 3(1), (3), as from IP completion day (as defined in the European Union (Withdrawal Agreement) Act 2020, s 39) (for transitional provisions and savings see the first note relating to the 2019 Regulations above).

Sub-s (1): para (b) and the word immediately preceding it substituted (for the original paras (b), (c)) by the Competition Act 1998 and Other Enactments (Amendment) Regulations 2004, SI 2004/1261, reg 4, Sch 1, para 7(1), (2) (for savings and transitional provisions see reg 7 of those Regulations at **[2.7]**). This subsection was repealed by SI 2019/93, regs 2, 3(1), (4), as from IP completion day (as defined in the European Union (Withdrawal Agreement) Act 2020, s 39) (for transitional provisions and savings see the first note relating to the 2019 Regulations above).

Sub-s (2): repealed by SI 2019/93, regs 2, 3(1), (4), as from IP completion day (as defined in the European Union (Withdrawal Agreement) Act 2020, s 39) (for transitional provisions and savings see the first note relating to the 2019 Regulations above).

Sub-s (3): the words in square brackets were substituted (for the original words "parallel exemption") by SI 2019/93, regs 2, 3(1), (5), as from IP completion day (as defined in the European Union (Withdrawal Agreement) Act 2020, s 39) (for transitional provisions and savings see the first note relating to the 2019 Regulations above).

Sub-s (4): the words in the first pair of square brackets were substituted (for the original words "parallel exemption"), para (a) was repealed, and the words in square brackets in sub-para (b)(i) were substituted (for the original words "exemption from the Community prohibition"), by SI 2019/93, regs 2, 3(1), (6), as from IP completion day (as defined in the European Union (Withdrawal Agreement) Act 2020, s 39) (for transitional provisions and savings see the first note relating to the 2019 Regulations above).

Sub-s (5): the words in the second pair of square brackets were substituted (for the original words "parallel exemption"), and the words in the third and final pairs of square brackets were inserted, by SI 2019/93, regs 2, 3(1), (7), as from IP completion day (as defined in the European Union (Withdrawal Agreement) Act 2020, s 39) (for transitional provisions and savings see the first note relating to the 2019 Regulations above).

Sub-s (8): words in first, third and fourth pairs of square brackets substituted by the Enterprise Act 2002, s 278, Sch 25, para 38.

Sub-s (9): words in square brackets inserted by SI 2004/1261, reg 4, Sch 1, para 7(1), (3). This subsection was repealed by SI 2019/93, regs 2, 3(1), (8), as from IP completion day (as defined in the European Union (Withdrawal Agreement) Act 2020, s 39) (for transitional provisions and savings see the first note relating to the 2019 Regulations above).

Sub-s (10): in definition "the Community prohibition" para (a) was substituted by SI 2004/1261, reg 4, Sch 1, para 7(1), (4). Words in square brackets in that paragraph substituted by the Treaty of Lisbon (Changes in Terminology or Numbering) Order 2012, SI 2012/1809, art 3(1), Schedule, Pt 1. This subsection was repealed by SI 2019/93, regs 2, 3(1), (8), as from IP completion day (as defined in the European Union (Withdrawal Agreement) Act 2020, s 39) (for transitional provisions and savings see the first note relating to the 2019 Regulations above).

Sub-s (11): repealed by SI 2019/93, regs 2, 3(1), (8), as from IP completion day (as defined in the European Union (Withdrawal Agreement) Act 2020, s 39) (for transitional provisions and savings see the first note relating to the 2019 Regulations above).

Sub-s (12): added by SI 2019/93, regs 2, 3(1), (9), as from IP completion day (as defined in the European Union (Withdrawal Agreement) Act 2020, s 39) (for transitional provisions and savings see the first note relating to the 2019 Regulations above).

References to the European Community and related expressions: see the note "References to "the European Community", "Community", etc" in the introductory notes to this Act.

[1.48]

[10A Power to vary etc retained block exemption regulations

(1) The Secretary of State may by regulations vary or revoke a retained block exemption regulation.

(2) In exercising the power under subsection (1), the Secretary of State must have regard to the conditions specified in section 9(1) for exemption from the Chapter 1 prohibition.

(3) If, in the opinion of the CMA, it is appropriate to vary or revoke a retained block exemption regulation, the CMA may make a recommendation to that effect to the Secretary of State.

(4) Before making a recommendation under subsection (3), the CMA must—
(a) publish details of its proposed recommendation in such a way as it thinks most suitable for bringing it to the attention of those likely to be affected; and
(b) consider any representations about it which are made to it.

(5) Before exercising the power to vary or revoke a retained block exemption regulation (in a case where there has been no recommendation under subsection (3)), the Secretary of State must—
(a) inform the CMA of the proposed variation or revocation; and

(b) take into account any comments made by the CMA.]

NOTES

Commencement: IP completion day (as defined in the European Union (Withdrawal Agreement) Act 2020, s 39).

Inserted by the Competition (Amendment etc) (EU Exit) Regulations 2019, SI 2019/93, regs 2, 4, as from IP completion day (as defined in the European Union (Withdrawal Agreement) Act 2020, s 39) (for transitional provisions and savings in relation to the operation of the 2019 Regulations, see Sch 4 to those Regulations at **[7.69]** et seq and, in particular, Sch 4, Pt 2 to the 2019 Regulations at **[7.70]**).

[1.49]

11 Exemption for certain other agreements

(1) The fact that a ruling may be given by virtue of [Article 104] of the Treaty on the question whether or not agreements of a particular kind are prohibited by [Article 101(1)] does not prevent such agreements from being subject to the Chapter I prohibition.

(2) But the Secretary of State may by regulations make such provision as he considers appropriate for the purpose of granting an exemption from the Chapter I prohibition, in prescribed circumstances, in respect of such agreements.

(3) An exemption from the Chapter I prohibition by virtue of regulations under this section is referred to in this Part as a section 11 exemption.

NOTES

Repealed by the Competition (Amendment etc) (EU Exit) Regulations 2019, SI 2019/93, regs 2, 5, as from IP completion day (as defined in the European Union (Withdrawal Agreement) Act 2020, s 39) (for transitional provisions and savings in relation to the operation of the 2019 Regulations, see Sch 4 to those Regulations at **[7.69]** et seq and, in particular, Sch 4, Pt 2 to the 2019 Regulations at **[7.70]**).

Sub-s (1): words in square brackets substituted by the Treaty of Lisbon (Changes in Terminology or Numbering) Order 2012, SI 2012/1809, art 3(1), Schedule, Pt 1.

Regulations: the Competition Act 1998 (Section 11 Exemption) Regulations 2001, SI 2001/2993 at **[2.74]**.

12–16 (*Repealed by the Competition Act 1998 and Other Enactments (Amendment) Regulations 2004, SI 2004/1261, reg 4, Sch 1, para 9 (for savings and transitional provisions in relation to ss 13, 14 see reg 9 of those Regulations at* **[2.9]**.)

CHAPTER II ABUSE OF DOMINANT POSITION

17 (*Repeals the Competition Act 1980, ss 2–10.*)

The prohibition

[1.50]

18 Abuse of dominant position

(1) Subject to section 19, any conduct on the part of one or more undertakings which amounts to the abuse of a dominant position in a market is prohibited if it may affect trade within the United Kingdom.

(2) Conduct may, in particular, constitute such an abuse if it consists in—

(a) directly or indirectly imposing unfair purchase or selling prices or other unfair trading conditions;

(b) limiting production, markets or technical development to the prejudice of consumers;

(c) applying dissimilar conditions to equivalent transactions with other trading parties, thereby placing them at a competitive disadvantage;

(d) making the conclusion of contracts subject to acceptance by the other parties of supplementary obligations which, by their nature or according to commercial usage, have no connection with the subject of the contracts.

(3) In this section—

"dominant position" means a dominant position within the United Kingdom; and "the United Kingdom" means the United Kingdom or any part of it.

(4) The prohibition imposed by subsection (1) is referred to in this Act as "the Chapter II prohibition".

Excluded cases

[1.51]

19 Excluded cases

(1) The Chapter II prohibition does not apply in any of the cases in which it is excluded by or as a result of—

(a) Schedule 1 (mergers and concentrations); or

(b) Schedule 3 (general exclusions).

(2) The Secretary of State may at any time by order amend Schedule 1, with respect to the Chapter II prohibition, by—

(a) providing for one or more additional exclusions; or

(b) amending or removing any provision (whether or not it has been added by an order under this subsection).

(3) The Secretary of State may at any time by order amend paragraph 8 of Schedule 3 with respect to the Chapter II prohibition.

(4) Schedule 3 also gives the Secretary of State power to provide that the Chapter II prohibition is not to apply in certain circumstances.

20–24 (*Repealed by the Competition Act 1998 and Other Enactments (Amendment) Regulations 2004, SI 2004/1261, reg 4, Sch 1, para 9.*)

CHAPTER III INVESTIGATION AND ENFORCEMENT

Investigations

[1.52]

[25 Power of [CMA] to investigate

(1) In any of the following cases, the [CMA] may conduct an investigation.

(2) The first case is where there are reasonable grounds for suspecting that there is an agreement which—

(a) may affect trade within the United Kingdom; and

(b) has as its object or effect the prevention, restriction or distortion of competition within the United Kingdom.

(3) The second case is where there are reasonable grounds for suspecting that there is an agreement which—

(a) may affect trade between Member States; and

(b) has as its object or effect the prevention, restriction or distortion of competition within the Community.

(4) The third case is where there are reasonable grounds for suspecting that the Chapter II prohibition has been infringed.

(5) The fourth case is where there are reasonable grounds for suspecting that the prohibition in [Article 102] has been infringed.

(6) The fifth case is where there are reasonable grounds for suspecting that, at some time in the past, there was an agreement which at that time—

(a) may have affected trade within the United Kingdom; and

(b) had as its object or effect the prevention, restriction or distortion of competition within the United Kingdom.

(7) The sixth case is where there are reasonable grounds for suspecting that, at some time in the past, there was an agreement which at that time—

(a) may have affected trade between Member States; and

(b) had as its object or effect the prevention, restriction or distortion of competition within the Community.

(8) Subsection (2) does not permit an investigation to be conducted in relation to an agreement if the [CMA]—

(a) considers that the agreement is exempt from the Chapter I prohibition as a result of a block exemption or a [retained exemption]; and

(b) does not have reasonable grounds for suspecting that the circumstances may be such that it could exercise its power to cancel the exemption.

(9) Subsection (3) does not permit an investigation to be conducted if the [CMA]—

(a) considers that the agreement is an agreement to which the prohibition in [Article 101(1)] is inapplicable by virtue of a regulation of the Commission ("the relevant regulation"); and

(b) does not have reasonable grounds for suspecting that the conditions set out in Article 29(2) of the EC Competition Regulation for the withdrawal of the benefit of the relevant regulation may be satisfied in respect of that agreement.

(10) Subsection (6) does not permit an investigation to be conducted in relation to any agreement if the [CMA] considers that, at the time in question, the agreement was exempt from the Chapter I prohibition as a result of a block exemption or a [retained exemption].

(11) Subsection (7) does not permit an investigation to be conducted in relation to any agreement if the [CMA] considers that, at the time in question, the agreement was an agreement to which the prohibition in [Article 101(1)] was inapplicable by virtue of a regulation of the Commission.

(12) It is immaterial for the purposes of subsection (6) *or (7)* whether the agreement in question remains in existence.]

NOTES

Substituted by the Competition Act 1998 and other enactments (Amendment) Regulations 2004, SI 2004/1261, reg 4, Sch 1, para 10.

References to the "CMA" substituted by the Enterprise and Regulatory Reform Act 2013, s 26(3), Sch 5, Pt 1, paras 1, 5. For various transitional provisions (including those relating to the abolition of the OFT and the Competition Commission, existing references to those bodies and provisions relating to continuity), see the Enterprise and Regulatory Reform Act 2013 (Commencement No 6, Transitional Provisions and Savings) Order 2014, SI 2014/416, Schedule at **[2.13]**.

This section is also amended as follows:

Sub-ss (3), (5), (7), (9), (11): repealed by the Competition (Amendment etc) (EU Exit) Regulations 2019, SI 2019/93, regs 2, 6(1), (2), (4), (6), as from IP completion day (as defined in the European Union (Withdrawal Agreement) Act 2020, s 39) (for transitional provisions and savings in relation to the operation of the 2019 Regulations, see Sch 4 to those Regulations at **[7.69]** et seq and, in particular, Sch 4, Pt 3 to the 2019 Regulations at **[7.71]**). The other words in square brackets in sub-ss (5), (9), (11) were substituted by the Treaty of Lisbon (Changes in Terminology or Numbering) Order 2012, SI 2012/1809, art 3(1), Schedule, Pt 1.

Sub-ss (8), (10): the words "retained exemption" in square brackets were substituted (for the original words "parallel exemption") by SI 2019/93, regs 2, 6(1), (3), (5), as from IP completion day (as defined in the European Union (Withdrawal Agreement) Act 2020, s 39) (for transitional provisions and savings see the first note relating to the 2019 Regulations above).

Sub-s (12): words in italics repealed by SI 2019/93, regs 2, 6(1), (7), as from IP completion day (as defined in the European Union (Withdrawal Agreement) Act 2020, s 39) (for transitional provisions and savings see the first note relating to the 2019 Regulations above).

References to the European Community and related expressions: see the note "References to "the European Community", "Community", etc" in the introductory notes to this Act.

[1.53]

[25A Power of CMA to publish notice of investigation

(1) Where the CMA decides to conduct an investigation it may publish a notice which may, in particular—

(a) state its decision to do so;

(b) indicate which of [subsections (2), (4) and (6)] of section 25 the investigation falls under;

(c) summarise the matter being investigated;

(d) identify any undertaking whose activities are being investigated as part of the investigation;

(e) identify the market which is or was affected by the matter being investigated.

(2) Section 57 does not apply to a notice under subsection (1) to the extent that it includes information other than information mentioned in that subsection.

(3) Subsection (4) applies if—

(a) the CMA has published a notice under subsection (1) which identifies an undertaking whose activities are being investigated, and

(b) the CMA subsequently decides (without making a decision within the meaning given by section 31(2)) to terminate the investigation of the activities of the undertaking so identified.

(4) The CMA must publish a notice stating that the activities of the undertaking in question are no longer being investigated.]

NOTES

Inserted by the Enterprise and Regulatory Reform Act 2013, s 42(1), (2). For various transitional provisions (including those relating to the abolition of the OFT and the Competition Commission, existing references to those bodies and provisions relating to continuity), see the Enterprise and Regulatory Reform Act 2013 (Commencement No 6, Transitional Provisions and Savings) Order 2014, SI 2014/416, Schedule at **[2.13]**.

Sub-s (1): the words in square brackets were substituted (for the original words "subsections (2) to (7)") by the Competition (Amendment etc) (EU Exit) Regulations 2019, SI 2019/93, regs 2, 7, as from IP completion day (as defined in the European Union (Withdrawal Agreement) Act 2020, s 39) (for transitional provisions and savings in relation to the operation of the 2019 Regulations, see Sch 4 to those Regulations at **[7.69]** et seq and, in particular, Sch 4, Pt 3 to the 2019 Regulations at **[7.71]**).

[1.54]

26 [Investigations: powers to require documents and information]

(1) For the purposes of an investigation . . . , the [CMA] may require any person to produce to [it] a specified document, or to provide [it] with specified information, which [it] considers relates to any matter relevant to the investigation.

(2) The power conferred by subsection (1) is to be exercised by a notice in writing.

(3) A notice under subsection (2) must indicate—

(a) the subject matter and purpose of the investigation; and

(b) the nature of the offences created by sections [43 and] 44.

(4) In subsection (1) "specified" means—

(a) specified, or described, in the notice; or

(b) falling within a category which is specified, or described, in the notice.

(5) The [CMA] may also specify in the notice—

(a) the time and place at which any document is to be produced or any information is to be provided;

(b) the manner and form in which it is to be produced or provided.

(6) The power under this section to require a person to produce a document includes power—

(a) if the document is produced—

(i) to take copies of it or extracts from it;

(ii) to require him, or any person who is a present or past officer of his, or is or was at any time employed by him, to provide an explanation of the document;

(b) if the document is not produced, to require him to state, to the best of his knowledge and belief, where it is.

NOTES

References to the "CMA" substituted by the Enterprise and Regulatory Reform Act 2013, s 26(3), Sch 5, Pt 1, paras 1, 6. For various transitional provisions (including those relating to the abolition of the OFT and the Competition Commission, existing references to those bodies and provisions relating to continuity), see the Enterprise and Regulatory Reform Act 2013 (Commencement No 6, Transitional Provisions and Savings) Order 2014, SI 2014/416, Schedule at **[2.13]**. This section is also amended as follows:

Section heading substituted by the Enterprise and Regulatory Reform Act 2013, s 39(1), (3), subject to transitional provisions in SI 2014/416 as noted above.

Sub-s (1): words omitted repealed by the Competition Act 1998 and other enactments (Amendment) Regulations 2004, SI 2004/1261, reg 4, Sch 1, para 11. Words in second, third and fourth pairs of square brackets substituted by the Enterprise Act 2002, s 278, Sch 25, para 38.

Sub-s (3): words in square brackets substituted by the Enterprise and Regulatory Reform Act 2013, s 57, Sch 15, paras 8, 9, subject to transitional provisions in SI 2014/416 as noted above.

[1.55]

[26A Investigations: power to ask questions

(1) For the purposes of an investigation, the CMA may give notice to an individual who has a connection with a relevant undertaking requiring the individual to answer questions with respect to any matter relevant to the investigation—

(a) at a place specified in the notice, and

(b) either at a time so specified or on receipt of the notice.

(2) The CMA must give a copy of the notice under subsection (1) to each relevant undertaking with which the individual has a current connection at the time the notice is given to the individual.

(3) The CMA must take such steps as are reasonable in all the circumstances to comply with the requirement under subsection (2) before the time at which the individual is required to answer questions.

(4) Where the CMA does not comply with the requirement under subsection (2) before the time mentioned in subsection (3), it must comply with that requirement as soon as practicable after that time.

(5) A notice under subsection (1) must be in writing and must indicate—

(a) the subject matter and purpose of the investigation, and

(b) the nature of the offence created by section 44.

(6) For the purposes of this section—

(a) an individual has a connection with an undertaking if he or she is or was—
   (i) concerned in the management or control of the undertaking, or
   (ii) employed by, or otherwise working for, the undertaking, and
(b) an individual has a current connection with an undertaking if, at the time in question, he or she is so concerned, is so employed or is so otherwise working.

(7) In this section, a "relevant undertaking" means an undertaking whose activities are being investigated as part of the investigation in question.]

NOTES

Inserted by the Enterprise and Regulatory Reform Act 2013, s 39(1), (2). For various transitional provisions (including those relating to the abolition of the OFT and the Competition Commission, existing references to those bodies and provisions relating to continuity), see the Enterprise and Regulatory Reform Act 2013 (Commencement No 6, Transitional Provisions and Savings) Order 2014, SI 2014/416, Schedule at **[2.13]**.

[1.56]

27 [Power to enter business premises without a warrant]

(1) Any officer of the [CMA] who is authorised in writing by the [CMA] to do so ("an investigating officer") may enter [any business premises] in connection with an investigation . . .

(2) No investigating officer is to enter any premises in the exercise of his powers under this section unless he has given to the occupier of the premises a written notice which—
(a) gives at least two working days' notice of the intended entry;
(b) indicates the subject matter and purpose of the investigation; and
(c) indicates the nature of the offences created by sections 42 to 44.

(3) Subsection (2) does not apply—
(a) if the [CMA] has a reasonable suspicion that the premises are, or have been, occupied by—
   (i) a party to an agreement which [it] is investigating under [section 25]; or
   (ii) an undertaking the conduct of which [it] is investigating under [section 25]; or
(b) if the investigating officer has taken all such steps as are reasonably practicable to give notice but has not been able to do so.

(4) In a case falling within subsection (3), the power of entry conferred by subsection (1) is to be exercised by the investigating officer on production of—
(a) evidence of his authorisation; and
(b) a document containing the information referred to in subsection (2)(b) and (c).

(5) An investigating officer entering any premises under this section may—
(a) take with him such equipment as appears to him to be necessary;
(b) require any person on the premises—
   (i) to produce any document which he considers relates to any matter relevant to the investigation; and
   (ii) if the document is produced, to provide an explanation of it;
(c) require any person to state, to the best of his knowledge and belief, where any such document is to be found;
(d) take copies of, or extracts from, any document which is produced;
(e) require any information which is [stored in any electronic form] and is accessible from the premises and which the investigating officer considers relates to any matter relevant to the investigation, to be produced in a form—
   (i) in which it can be taken away, and
   (ii) in which it is visible and legible [or from which it can readily be produced in a visible and legible form];
[(f) take any steps which appear to be necessary for the purpose of preserving or preventing interference with any document which he considers relates to any matter relevant to the investigation].

[(6) In this section "business premises" means premises (or any part of premises) not used as a dwelling.]

NOTES

References to the "CMA" substituted by the Enterprise and Regulatory Reform Act 2013, s 26(3), Sch 5, Pt 1, paras 1, 7. For various transitional provisions (including those relating to the abolition of the OFT and the Competition Commission, existing references to those bodies and provisions relating to continuity), see the Enterprise and Regulatory Reform Act 2013 (Commencement No 6, Transitional Provisions and Savings) Order 2014, SI 2014/416, Schedule at **[2.13]**. This section is also amended as follows—

Section heading: substituted by the Competition Act 1998 and Other Enactments (Amendment) Regulations 2004, SI 2004/1261, reg 4, Sch 1, para 12(1), (6).

Sub-s (1): words in final pair of square brackets substituted, and words omitted repealed, by SI 2004/1261, reg 4, Sch 1, para 12(1), (2).

Sub-s (3): words in second and fourth pairs of square brackets substituted by the Enterprise Act 2002, s 278, Sch 25, para 38. Words "section 25" in both places that they occur substituted by SI 2004/1261, reg 4, Sch 1, para 12(1), (3).

Sub-s (5): words in first pair of square brackets in para (e) substituted, and words in second pair of square brackets in that paragraph added, by the Criminal Justice and Police Act 2001, s 70, Sch 2, Pt 2, para 21; para (f) added by SI 2004/1261, reg 4, Sch 1, para 12(1), (4).

Sub-s (6): added by SI 2004/1261, reg 4, Sch 1, para 12(1), (5).

[1.57]

28 [Power to enter business premises under a warrant]

(1) [On an application made to it by the CMA, the court or the Tribunal may issue a warrant if it is satisfied that]—
(a) there are reasonable grounds for suspecting that there are on [any business premises] documents—
   (i) the production of which has been required under section 26 or 27; and
   (ii) which have not been produced as required;
(b) there are reasonable grounds for suspecting that—

(i) there are on [any business premises] documents which the [CMA] has power under section 26 to require to be produced; and
(ii) if the documents were required to be produced, they would not be produced but would be concealed, removed, tampered with or destroyed; or

(c) an investigating officer has attempted to enter premises in the exercise of his powers under section 27 but has been unable to do so and that there are reasonable grounds for suspecting that there are on the premises documents the production of which could have been required under that section.

(2) A warrant under this section shall authorise a named officer of the [CMA], and any other of [the [CMA's] officers whom the [CMA]] has authorised in writing to accompany the named officer—

(a) to enter the premises specified in the warrant, using such force as is reasonably necessary for the purpose;
(b) to search the premises and take copies of, or extracts from, any document appearing to be of a kind in respect of which the application under subsection (1) was granted ("the relevant kind");
(c) to take possession of any documents appearing to be of the relevant kind if—
  (i) such action appears to be necessary for preserving the documents or preventing interference with them; or
  (ii) it is not reasonably practicable to take copies of the documents on the premises;
(d) to take any other steps which appear to be necessary for the purpose mentioned in paragraph (c)(i);
(e) to require any person to provide an explanation of any document appearing to be of the relevant kind or to state, to the best of his knowledge and belief, where it may be found;
(f) to require any information which is [stored in any electronic form] and is accessible from the premises and which the named officer considers relates to any matter relevant to the investigation, to be produced in a form—
  (i) in which it can be taken away, and
  (ii) in which it is visible and legible [or from which it can readily be produced in a visible and legible form].

(3) If, in the case of a warrant under subsection (1)(b), [the court or (as the case may be) the Tribunal] is satisfied that it is reasonable to suspect that there are also on the premises other documents relating to the investigation concerned, the warrant shall also authorise action mentioned in subsection (2) to be taken in relation to any such document.

[(3A) A warrant under this section may authorise persons specified in the warrant to accompany the named officer who is executing it.]

(4) Any person entering premises by virtue of a warrant under this section may take with him such equipment as appears to him to be necessary.

(5) On leaving any premises which he has entered by virtue of a warrant under this section, the named officer must, if the premises are unoccupied or the occupier is temporarily absent, leave them as effectively secured as he found them.

(6) A warrant under this section continues in force until the end of the period of one month beginning with the day on which it is issued.

(7) Any document of which possession is taken under subsection (2)(c) may be retained for a period of three months.

[(7A) An application for a warrant under this section must be made—

(a) in the case of an application to the court, in accordance with rules of court;
(b) in the case of an application to the Tribunal, in accordance with Tribunal rules.]

[(8) In this section "business premises" has the same meaning as in section 27.]

NOTES

Section heading: substituted by the Competition Act 1998 and Other Enactments (Amendment) Regulations 2004, SI 2004/1261, reg 4, Sch 1, para 13(1), (4).

Sub-s (1) is amended as follows:

Words in first pair of square brackets substituted by the Enterprise and Regulatory Reform Act 2013, s 41, Sch 13, paras 1, 2(1), (2). For various transitional provisions (including those relating to the abolition of the OFT and the Competition Commission, existing references to those bodies and provisions relating to continuity), see the Enterprise and Regulatory Reform Act 2013 (Commencement No 6, Transitional Provisions and Savings) Order 2014, SI 2014/416, Schedule at **[2.13]**.

Words "any business premises" in square brackets substituted by SI 2004/1261, reg 4, Sch 1, para 13(1), (2)(a).

Reference to the "CMA" substituted by the Enterprise and Regulatory Reform Act 2013, s 26(3), Sch 5, Pt 1, paras 1, 8(1), (2), subject to transitional provisions in SI 2014/416 as noted above.

Sub-s (2) is amended as follows:

References to "CMA" and "CMA's" substituted by the Enterprise and Regulatory Reform Act 2013, s 26(3), Sch 5, Pt 1, paras 1, 8(1), (3), subject to transitional provisions in SI 2014/416 as noted above.

Words in second (outer) pair of square brackets substituted by the Enterprise Act 2002, s 278(1), Sch 25, para 38.

In para (f), words in first and second pairs of square brackets substituted and inserted respectively, by the Criminal Justice and Police Act 2001, s 70, Sch 2, Pt 2, para 21.

Sub-s (3): words in square brackets substituted by the Enterprise and Regulatory Reform Act 2013, s 41, Sch 13, paras 1, 2(1), (3), subject to transitional provisions in SI 2014/416 as noted above.

Sub-s (3A): inserted by the Enterprise Act 2002, s 203(1), (2).

Sub-s (7A): inserted by the Enterprise and Regulatory Reform Act 2013, s 41, Sch 13, paras 1, 2(1), (4), subject to transitional provisions in SI 2014/416 as noted above.

Sub-s (8): added by SI 2004/1261, reg 4, Sch 1, para 13(1), (3).

Search the premises, etc: the powers of seizure conferred by sub-s (2) are powers to which the Criminal Justice and Police Act 2001, s 50 apply (additional powers of seizure from premises); see s 50(5) of, and Sch 1, Pt 1, para 67 to, that Act. Section 50 of the 2001 Act reads as follows—

"50 Additional powers of seizure from premises

(1) Where—

(a) a person who is lawfully on any premises finds anything on those premises that he has reasonable grounds for believing may be or may contain something for which he is authorised to search on those premises,

(b) a power of seizure to which this section applies or the power conferred by subsection (2) would entitle him, if he found it, to seize whatever it is that he has grounds for believing that thing to be or to contain, and
(c) in all the circumstances, it is not reasonably practicable for it to be determined, on those premises—
(i) whether what he has found is something that he is entitled to seize, or
(ii) the extent to which what he has found contains something that he is entitled to seize,
that person's powers of seizure shall include power under this section to seize so much of what he has found as it is necessary to remove from the premises to enable that to be determined.

(2) Where—
(a) a person who is lawfully on any premises finds anything on those premises ("the seizable property") which he would be entitled to seize but for its being comprised in something else that he has (apart from this subsection) no power to seize,
(b) the power under which that person would have power to seize the seizable property is a power to which this section applies, and
(c) in all the circumstances it is not reasonably practicable for the seizable property to be separated, on those premises, from that in which it is comprised,

that person's powers of seizure shall include power under this section to seize both the seizable property and that from which it is not reasonably practicable to separate it.

(3) The factors to be taken into account in considering, for the purposes of this section, whether or not it is reasonably practicable on particular premises for something to be determined, or for something to be separated from something else, shall be confined to the following—
(a) how long it would take to carry out the determination or separation on those premises;
(b) the number of persons that would be required to carry out that determination or separation on those premises within a reasonable period;
(c) whether the determination or separation would (or would if carried out on those premises) involve damage to property;
(d) the apparatus or equipment that it would be necessary or appropriate to use for the carrying out of the determination or separation; and
(e) in the case of separation, whether the separation—
(i) would be likely, or
(ii) if carried out by the only means that are reasonably practicable on those premises, would be likely,
to prejudice the use of some or all of the separated seizable property for a purpose for which something seized under the power in question is capable of being used.

(4) Section 19(6) of the 1984 Act and Article 21(6) of the Police and Criminal Evidence (Northern Ireland) Order 1989 (SI 1989/1341 (NI 12)) (powers of seizure not to include power to seize anything that a person has reasonable grounds for believing is legally privileged) shall not apply to the power of seizure conferred by subsection (2).

(5) This section applies to each of the powers of seizure specified in Part 1 of Schedule 1.

(6) Without prejudice to any power conferred by this section to take a copy of any document, nothing in this section, so far as it has effect by reference to the power to take copies of documents under section 28(2)(b) of the Competition Act 1998 (c 41), shall be taken to confer any power to seize any document.".

The Criminal Justice and Police Act 2001, ss 54 (obligation to return items subject to legal privilege), 59 (application to appropriate judicial authority), 62 (use of inextricably linked property), also apply to the powers of seizure conferred by sub-s (2) of this section.

[1.58]

[28A Power to enter domestic premises under a warrant

(1) [On an application made to it by the CMA, the court or the Tribunal may issue a warrant if it is satisfied that]—
(a) there are reasonable grounds for suspecting that there are on any domestic premises documents—
(i) the production of which has been required under section 26; and
(ii) which have not been produced as required; or
(b) there are reasonable grounds for suspecting that—
(i) there are on any domestic premises documents which the [CMA] has power under section 26 to require to be produced; and
(ii) if the documents were required to be produced, they would not be produced but would be concealed, removed, tampered with or destroyed.

(2) A warrant under this section shall authorise a named officer of the [CMA], and any other of its officers whom the [CMA] has authorised in writing to accompany the named officer—
(a) to enter the premises specified in the warrant, using such force as is reasonably necessary for the purpose;
(b) to search the premises and take copies of, or extracts from, any document appearing to be of a kind in respect of which the application under subsection (1) was granted ("the relevant kind");
(c) to take possession of any documents appearing to be of the relevant kind if—
(i) such action appears to be necessary for preserving the documents or preventing interference with them; or
(ii) it is not reasonably practicable to take copies of the documents on the premises;
(d) to take any other steps which appear to be necessary for the purpose mentioned in paragraph (c)(i);
(e) to require any person to provide an explanation of any document appearing to be of the relevant kind or to state, to the best of his knowledge and belief, where it may be found;
(f) to require any information which is stored in any electronic form and is accessible from the premises and which the named officer considers relates to any matter relevant to the investigation, to be produced in a form—
(i) in which it can be taken away, and
(ii) in which it is visible and legible or from which it can readily be produced in a visible and legible form.

(3) If, in the case of a warrant under subsection (1)(b), [the court or (as the case may be) the Tribunal] is satisfied that it is reasonable to suspect that there are also on the premises other documents relating to the investigation concerned, the warrant shall also authorise action mentioned in subsection (2) to be taken in relation to any such document.

(4) A warrant under this section may authorise persons specified in the warrant to accompany the named officer who is executing it.

(5) Any person entering premises by virtue of a warrant under this section may take with him such equipment as appears to him to be necessary.

(6) On leaving any premises which he has entered by virtue of a warrant under this section, the named officer must, if the premises are unoccupied or the occupier is temporarily absent, leave them as effectively secured as he found them.

(7) A warrant under this section continues in force until the end of the period of one month beginning with the day on which it is issued.

(8) Any document of which possession is taken under subsection (2)(c) may be retained for a period of three months.

[(8A) An application for a warrant under this section must be made—

(a) in the case of an application to the court, in accordance with rules of court;

(b) in the case of an application to the Tribunal, in accordance with Tribunal rules.]

(9) In this section, "domestic premises" means premises (or any part of premises) that are used as a dwelling and are—

(a) premises also used in connection with the affairs of an undertaking or association of undertakings; or

(b) premises where documents relating to the affairs of an undertaking or association of undertakings are kept.]

NOTES

Inserted by the Competition Act 1998 and Other Enactments (Amendment) Regulations 2004, SI 2004/1261, reg 4, Sch 1, para 14.

Sub-s (1): words in square brackets substituted by the Enterprise and Regulatory Reform Act 2013, ss 26(3), 41, Sch 5, Pt 1, paras 1, 9, Sch 13, paras 1, 3(1), (4). For various transitional provisions (including those relating to the abolition of the OFT and the Competition Commission, existing references to those bodies and provisions relating to continuity), see the Enterprise and Regulatory Reform Act 2013 (Commencement No 6, Transitional Provisions and Savings) Order 2014, SI 2014/416, Schedule at **[2.13]**.

Sub-s (2): references to the "CMA" substituted by the Enterprise and Regulatory Reform Act 2013, s 26(3), Sch 5, Pt 1, paras 1, 9, subject to transitional provisions in SI 2014/416 as noted above.

Sub-s (3): words in square brackets substituted by the Enterprise and Regulatory Reform Act 2013, s 41, Sch 13, paras 1, 3(1), (3), subject to transitional provisions in SI 2014/416 as noted above.

Sub-s (8A): inserted by the Enterprise and Regulatory Reform Act 2013, s 41, Sch 13, paras 1, 3(1), (4), subject to transitional provisions in SI 2014/416 as noted above.

[1.59]

29 Entry of premises under warrant: supplementary

(1) A warrant issued under section 28 [or 28A] must indicate—

(a) the subject matter and purpose of the investigation;

(b) the nature of the offences created by sections 42 to 44.

(2) The powers conferred by section 28 [or 28A] are to be exercised on production of a warrant issued under that section.

(3) If there is no one at the premises when the named officer proposes to execute such a warrant he must, before executing it—

(a) take such steps as are reasonable in all the circumstances to inform the occupier of the intended entry; and

(b) if the occupier is informed, afford him or his legal or other representative a reasonable opportunity to be present when the warrant is executed.

(4) If the named officer is unable to inform the occupier of the intended entry he must, when executing the warrant, leave a copy of it in a prominent place on the premises.

(5) In this section—

"named officer" means the officer named in the warrant; and

"occupier", in relation to any premises, means a person whom the named officer reasonably believes is the occupier of those premises.

NOTES

Sub-ss (1), (2): words in square brackets inserted by the Competition Act 1998 and Other Enactments (Amendment) Regulations 2004, SI 2004/1261, reg 4, Sch 1, para 15.

[1.60]

30 Privileged communications

(1) A person shall not be required, under any provision of this Part, to produce or disclose a privileged communication.

(2) "Privileged communication" means a communication—

(a) between a professional legal adviser and his client, or

(b) made in connection with, or in contemplation of, legal proceedings and for the purposes of those proceedings,

which in proceedings in the High Court would be protected from disclosure on grounds of legal professional privilege.

(3) In the application of this section to Scotland—

(a) references to the High Court are to be read as references to the Court of Session; and

(b) the reference to legal professional privilege is to be read as a reference to confidentiality of communications.

[1.61]

[30A Use of statements in prosecution

[(1)] A statement made by a person in response to a requirement imposed by virtue of any of sections [sections 26, 27 to 28A and 40ZD] may not be used in evidence against him on a prosecution for an offence under section 188 of the Enterprise Act 2002 unless, in the proceedings—

(a) in giving evidence, he makes a statement inconsistent with it, and
(b) evidence relating to it is adduced, or a question relating to it is asked, by him or on his behalf.

[(2) A statement by an individual in response to a requirement imposed by virtue of section 26A (a "section 26A statement") may only be used in evidence against the individual—

(a) on a prosecution for an offence under section 44, or
(b) on a prosecution for some other offence in a case falling within subsection (3).

(3) A prosecution falls within this subsection if, in the proceedings—

(a) in giving evidence, the individual makes a statement inconsistent with the section 26A statement, and
(b) evidence relating to the section 26A statement is adduced, or a question relating to it is asked, by or on behalf of the individual.

(4) A section 26A statement may not be used in evidence against an undertaking with which the individual who gave the statement has a connection on a prosecution for an offence unless the prosecution is for an offence under section 44.

(5) For the purposes of subsection (4), an individual has a connection with an undertaking if he or she is or was—

(a) concerned in the management or control of the undertaking, or
(b) employed by, or otherwise working for, the undertaking.]]

NOTES

Inserted by the Enterprise Act 2002, s 198.

Sub-s (1) numbered as such, and sub-ss (2)–(5) added, by the Enterprise and Regulatory Reform Act 2013, s 39. For various transitional provisions (including those relating to the abolition of the OFT and the Competition Commission, existing references to those bodies and provisions relating to continuity), see the Enterprise and Regulatory Reform Act 2013 (Commencement No 6, Transitional Provisions and Savings) Order 2014, SI 2014/416, Schedule at **[2.13]**.

The words in square brackets in sub-s (1) were substituted (for the original words sections 26 and 27 to 28A) by the Competition (Amendment etc) (EU Exit) Regulations 2019, SI 2019/93, reg 7A, as from IP completion day (as defined in the European Union (Withdrawal Agreement) Act 2020, s 39) (for transitional provisions and savings in relation to the operation of the 2019 Regulations, see Sch 4 to those Regulations at **[7.69]** et seq and, in particular, Sch 4, Pt 3 to the 2019 Regulations at **[7.71]**). Note that reg 7A of the 2019 Regulations was inserted by the Competition (Amendment etc) (EU Exit) Regulations 2020, SI 2020/1343, reg 3, with effect from immediately before IP completion day.

[1.62]

[31 Decisions following an investigation

(1) If as a result of an investigation the [CMA] proposes to make a decision, the [CMA] must—

(a) give written notice to the person (or persons) likely to be affected by the proposed decision; and
(b) give that person (or those persons) an opportunity to make representations.

(2) For the purposes of this section and sections 31A and 31B "decision" means a decision of the [CMA]—

(a) that the Chapter I prohibition has been infringed; [or]
(b) that the Chapter II prohibition has been infringed;
(c) that the prohibition in [Article 101(1)] has been infringed; or
(d) that the prohibition in [Article 102] has been infringed.]

NOTES

Substituted by the Competition Act 1998 and Other Enactments (Amendment) Regulations 2004, SI 2004/1261, reg 4, Sch 1, para 17.

References to the "CMA" substituted by the Enterprise and Regulatory Reform Act 2013, s 26(3), Sch 5, Pt 1, paras 1, 10. For various transitional provisions (including those relating to the abolition of the OFT and the Competition Commission, existing references to those bodies and provisions relating to continuity), see the Enterprise and Regulatory Reform Act 2013 (Commencement No 6, Transitional Provisions and Savings) Order 2014, SI 2014/416, Schedule at **[2.13]**.

The word in square brackets in sub-s (2)(a) was inserted, and sub-s (2)(c) and (d) were repealed, by the Competition (Amendment etc) (EU Exit) Regulations 2019, SI 2019/93, regs 2, 8, as from IP completion day (as defined in the European Union (Withdrawal Agreement) Act 2020, s 39) (for transitional provisions and savings in relation to the operation of the 2019 Regulations, see Sch 4 to those Regulations at **[7.69]** et seq and, in particular, Sch 4, Pt 3 to the 2019 Regulations at **[7.71]**).

The words in square brackets in sub-s (2)(c), (d) were substituted by the Treaty of Lisbon (Changes in Terminology or Numbering) Order 2012, SI 2012/1809, art 3(1), Schedule, Pt 1.

[1.63]

[31A Commitments

(1) Subsection (2) applies in a case where the [CMA] has begun an investigation under section 25 but has not made a decision (within the meaning given by section 31(2)).

(2) For the purposes of addressing the competition concerns it has identified, the [CMA] may accept from such person (or persons) concerned as it considers appropriate commitments to take such action (or refrain from taking such action) as it considers appropriate.

(3) At any time when commitments are in force the [CMA] may accept from the person (or persons) who gave the commitments—

(a) a variation of them if it is satisfied that the commitments as varied will address its current competition concerns;
(b) commitments in substitution for them if it is satisfied that the new commitments will address its current competition concerns.

(4) Commitments under this section—

(a) shall come into force when accepted; and
(b) may be released by the [CMA] where—
  (i) it is requested to do so by the person (or persons) who gave the commitments; or
  (ii) it has reasonable grounds for believing that the competition concerns referred to in subsection (2) or (3) no longer arise.

(5) The provisions of Schedule 6A to this Act shall have effect with respect to procedural requirements for the acceptance, variation and release of commitments under this section.]

NOTES

Inserted, together with ss 31B–31E, by the Competition Act 1998 and Other Enactments (Amendment) Regulations 2004, SI 2004/1261, reg 4, Sch 1, para 18.

References to the "CMA" substituted by the Enterprise and Regulatory Reform Act 2013, s 26(3), Sch 5, Pt 1, paras 1, 11. For various transitional provisions (including those relating to the abolition of the OFT and the Competition Commission, existing references to those bodies and provisions relating to continuity), see the Enterprise and Regulatory Reform Act 2013 (Commencement No 6, Transitional Provisions and Savings) Order 2014, SI 2014/416, Schedule at **[2.13]**.

[1.64]

[31B Effect of commitments under section 31A

(1) Subsection (2) applies if the [CMA] has accepted commitments under section 31A (and has not released them).

(2) In such a case, the [CMA] shall not—
(a) continue the investigation,
(b) make a decision (within the meaning of section 31(2)), or
(c) give a direction under section 35,

in relation to the agreement or conduct which was the subject of the investigation (but this subsection is subject to subsections (3) and (4)).

(3) Nothing in subsection (2) prevents the [CMA] from taking any action in relation to competition concerns which are not addressed by commitments accepted by it.

(4) Subsection (2) also does not prevent the [CMA] from continuing the investigation, making a decision, or giving a direction where—
(a) it has reasonable grounds for believing that there has been a material change of circumstances since the commitments were accepted;
(b) it has reasonable grounds for suspecting that a person has failed to adhere to one or more of the terms of the commitments; or
(c) it has reasonable grounds for suspecting that information which led it to accept the commitments was incomplete, false or misleading in a material particular.

(5) If, pursuant to subsection (4), the [CMA] makes a decision or gives a direction the commitments are to be treated as released from the date of that decision or direction.]

NOTES

Inserted as noted to s 31A at **[1.63]**.

References to the "CMA" substituted by the Enterprise and Regulatory Reform Act 2013, s 26(3), Sch 5, Pt 1, paras 1, 12. For various transitional provisions (including those relating to the abolition of the OFT and the Competition Commission, existing references to those bodies and provisions relating to continuity), see the Enterprise and Regulatory Reform Act 2013 (Commencement No 6, Transitional Provisions and Savings) Order 2014, SI 2014/416, Schedule at **[2.13]**.

[1.65]

[31C Review of commitments

(1) Where the [CMA] is reviewing or has reviewed the effectiveness of commitments accepted under section 31A it must, if requested to do so by the Secretary of State, prepare a report of its findings.

(2) The [CMA] must—
(a) give any report prepared by it under subsection (1) to the Secretary of State; and
(b) publish the report.]

NOTES

Inserted as noted to s 31A at **[1.63]**.

References to the "CMA" substituted by the Enterprise and Regulatory Reform Act 2013, s 26(3), Sch 5, Pt 1, paras 1, 13. For various transitional provisions (including those relating to the abolition of the OFT and the Competition Commission, existing references to those bodies and provisions relating to continuity), see the Enterprise and Regulatory Reform Act 2013 (Commencement No 6, Transitional Provisions and Savings) Order 2014, SI 2014/416, Schedule at **[2.13]**.

[1.66]

[31D Guidance

(1) The [CMA] must prepare and publish guidance as to the circumstances in which it may be appropriate to accept commitments under section 31A.

(2) The [CMA] may at any time alter the guidance.

(3) If the guidance is altered, the [CMA] must publish it as altered.

(4) No guidance is to be published under this section without the approval of the Secretary of State.

(5) The [CMA] may, after consulting the Secretary of State, choose how it publishes its guidance.

(6) If the [CMA] is preparing or altering guidance under this section it must consult such persons as it considers appropriate.

(7) If the proposed guidance or alteration relates to a matter in respect of which a regulator exercises concurrent jurisdiction, those consulted must include that regulator.

(8) When exercising its discretion to accept commitments under section 31A, the [CMA] must have regard to the guidance for the time being in force under this section.]

NOTES

Inserted as noted to s 31A at **[1.63]**.

References to the "CMA" substituted by the Enterprise and Regulatory Reform Act 2013, s 26(3), Sch 5, Pt 1, paras 1, 14. For various transitional provisions (including those relating to the abolition of the OFT and the Competition Commission, existing references to those bodies and provisions relating to continuity), see the Enterprise and Regulatory Reform Act 2013 (Commencement No 6, Transitional Provisions and Savings) Order 2014, SI 2014/416, Schedule at **[2.13]**.

[1.67]

[31E Enforcement of commitments

(1) If a person from whom the [CMA] has accepted commitments fails without reasonable excuse to adhere to the commitments (and has not been released from them), the [CMA] may apply to the court for an order—

(a) requiring the defaulter to make good his default within a time specified in the order; or

(b) if the commitments relate to anything to be done in the management or administration of an undertaking, requiring the undertaking or any of its officers to do it.

(2) An order of the court under subsection (1) may provide for all the costs of, or incidental to, the application for the order to be borne by—

(a) the person in default; or

(b) any officer of an undertaking who is responsible for the default.

(3) In the application of subsection (2) to Scotland, the reference to "costs" is to be read as a reference to "expenses".]

NOTES

Inserted as noted to s 31A at **[1.63]**.

Sub-s (1): references to the "CMA" substituted by the Enterprise and Regulatory Reform Act 2013, s 26(3), Sch 5, Pt 1, paras 1, 15. For various transitional provisions (including those relating to the abolition of the OFT and the Competition Commission, existing references to those bodies and provisions relating to continuity), see the Enterprise and Regulatory Reform Act 2013 (Commencement No 6, Transitional Provisions and Savings) Order 2014, SI 2014/416, Schedule at **[2.13]**.

[1.68]

[31F Power for Secretary of State to impose time-limits on investigations etc

(1) The Secretary of State may by order impose time-limits in relation to—

(a) the conduct by the CMA of investigations or investigations of a description specified in the order;

(b) the making by the CMA of decisions (within the meaning given by section 31(2)) as a result of investigations or investigations of such a description.

(2) Before making an order under subsection (1), the Secretary of State must consult the CMA and such other persons as the Secretary of State considers appropriate.]

NOTES

Inserted by the Enterprise and Regulatory Reform Act 2013, s 45.

Enforcement

[1.69]

32 Directions in relation to agreements

(1) If the [CMA] has made a decision that an agreement infringes the Chapter I prohibition [*or that it infringes the prohibition in [Article 101(1)]*], [it] may give to such person or persons as [it] considers appropriate such directions as [it] considers appropriate to bring the infringement to an end.

(2) . . .

(3) A direction under this section may, in particular, include provision—

(a) requiring the parties to the agreement to modify the agreement; or

(b) requiring them to terminate the agreement.

(4) A direction under this section must be given in writing.

NOTES

Sub-s (1): reference to the "CMA" substituted by the Enterprise Act 2002, s 278, Sch 25, para 38) by the Enterprise and Regulatory Reform Act 2013, s 26(3), Sch 5, Pt 1, paras 1, 16 (for various transitional provisions (including those relating to the abolition of the OFT and the Competition Commission, existing references to those bodies and provisions relating to continuity), see the Enterprise and Regulatory Reform Act 2013 (Commencement No 6, Transitional Provisions and Savings) Order 2014, SI 2014/416, Schedule at **[2.13]**). Words in second (outer) pair of square brackets inserted by the Competition Act 1998 and Other Enactments (Amendment) Regulations 2004, SI 2004/1261, reg 4, Sch 1, para 19(1), (2). Words in third (inner) pair of square brackets substituted by the Treaty of Lisbon (Changes in Terminology or Numbering) Order 2012, SI 2012/1809, art 3(1), Schedule, Pt 1. Word "it" in square brackets (in each place that it occurs) substituted by the Enterprise Act 2002, s 278, Sch 25, para 38. The words in italics were repealed by the Competition (Amendment etc) (EU Exit) Regulations 2019, SI 2019/93, regs 2, 9, as from IP completion day (as defined in the European Union (Withdrawal Agreement) Act 2020, s 39) (for transitional provisions and savings in relation to the operation of the 2019 Regulations, see Sch 4 to those Regulations at **[7.69]** et seq and, in particular, Sch 4, Pt 3 to the 2019 Regulations at **[7.71]**).

Sub-s (2): repealed by SI 2004/1261, reg 4, Sch 1, para 19(1), (3).

[1.70]

33 Directions in relation to conduct

(1) If the [CMA] has made a decision that conduct infringes the Chapter II prohibition [*or that it infringes the prohibition in [Article 102]*], [it] may give to such person or persons as [it] considers appropriate such directions as [it] considers appropriate to bring the infringement to an end.

(2) . . .

(3) A direction under this section may, in particular, include provision—

(a) requiring the person concerned to modify the conduct in question; or

(b) requiring him to cease that conduct.

(4) A direction under this section must be given in writing.

NOTES

Sub-s (1): reference to the "CMA" substituted by the Enterprise and Regulatory Reform Act 2013, s 26(3), Sch 5, Pt 1, paras 1, 17 (for various transitional provisions (including those relating to the abolition of the OFT and the Competition Commission, existing references to those bodies and provisions relating to continuity), see the Enterprise and Regulatory Reform Act 2013 (Commencement No 6, Transitional Provisions and Savings) Order 2014, SI 2014/416, Schedule at **[2.13]**). Words in second (outer) pair of square brackets inserted by the Competition Act 1998 and Other Enactments (Amendment) Regulations 2004, SI 2004/1261, reg 4, Sch 1, para 20(1), (2). Words in third (inner) pair of square brackets substituted by the Treaty of Lisbon (Changes in Terminology or Numbering) Order 2012, SI 2012/1809, art 3(1), Schedule, Pt 1. Word "it" in square brackets (in each place that it occurs) substituted by the Enterprise Act 2002, s 278, Sch 25, para 38. The words in italics were repealed by the Competition (Amendment etc) (EU Exit) Regulations 2019, SI 2019/93, regs 2, 10, as from IP completion day (as defined in the European Union (Withdrawal Agreement) Act 2020, s 39) (for transitional provisions and savings in relation to the operation of the 2019 Regulations, see Sch 4 to those Regulations at **[7.69]** et seq and, in particular, Sch 4, Pt 3 to the 2019 Regulations at **[7.71]**).

Sub-s (2): repealed by SI 2004/1261, reg 4, Sch 1, para 20(1), (3).

[1.71]

34 Enforcement of directions

(1) If a person fails, without reasonable excuse, to comply with a direction under section 32 or 33, the [CMA] may apply to the court for an order—

(a) requiring the defaulter to make good his default within a time specified in the order; or

(b) if the direction related to anything to be done in the management or administration of an undertaking, requiring the undertaking or any of its officers to do it.

(2) An order of the court under subsection (1) may provide for all of the costs of, or incidental to, the application for the order to be borne by—

(a) the person in default; or

(b) any officer of an undertaking who is responsible for the default.

(3) In the application of subsection (2) to Scotland, the reference to "costs" is to be read as a reference to "expenses".

NOTES

Sub-s (1): reference to the "CMA" substituted by the Enterprise and Regulatory Reform Act 2013, s 26(3), Sch 5, Pt 1, paras 1, 18. For various transitional provisions (including those relating to the abolition of the OFT and the Competition Commission, existing references to those bodies and provisions relating to continuity), see the Enterprise and Regulatory Reform Act 2013 (Commencement No 6, Transitional Provisions and Savings) Order 2014, SI 2014/416, Schedule at **[2.13]**.

[1.72]

35 Interim measures

[(1) Subject to [subsection (8)], this section applies if the [CMA] has begun an investigation under section 25 and not completed it (but only applies so long as the [CMA] has power under section 25 to conduct that investigation).]

(2) If the [CMA] considers that it is necessary for [it] to act under this section as a matter of urgency for the purpose—

(a) of preventing [significant damage] to a particular person or category of person, or

(b) of protecting the public interest,

[it] may give such directions as [it] considers appropriate for that purpose.

(3) Before giving a direction under this section, the [CMA] must—

(a) give written notice to the person (or persons) to whom [it] proposes to give the direction; and

(b) give that person (or each of them) an opportunity to make representations.

(4) A notice under subsection (3) must indicate the nature of the direction which the [CMA] is proposing to give and [its] reasons for wishing to give it.

[(5) A direction given under this section may if the circumstances permit be replaced by—

(a) a direction under section 32 or (as appropriate) section 33, or

(b) commitments accepted under section 31A,

but, subject to that, has effect while this section applies.]

(6) In the [cases mentioned in [section 25(2) and (6)]], sections 32(3) and 34 also apply to directions given under this section.

(7) In the [cases mentioned in [section 25(4)]], sections 33(3) and 34 also apply to directions given under this section.

[(8) In the case of an investigation conducted by virtue of section 25(2) or (6), this section does not apply if a person has produced evidence to the [CMA] in connection with the investigation that satisfies it on the balance of probabilities that, in the event of it reaching the basic infringement conclusion, it would also reach the conclusion that the suspected agreement is exempt from the Chapter I prohibition as a result of section 9(1); and in this subsection "the basic infringement conclusion" is the conclusion that there is an agreement which—

(a) may affect trade within the United Kingdom, and

(b) has as its object or effect the prevention, restriction or distortion of competition within the United Kingdom.

(9) In the case of an investigation conducted by virtue of section 25(3) or (7), this section does not apply if a person has produced evidence to the [CMA] in connection with the investigation that satisfies it on the balance of probabilities that, in the event of it reaching the basic infringement conclusion, it would also reach the conclusion that the suspected agreement is an agreement to which the prohibition in [Article 101(1)] is inapplicable because the agreement satisfies the conditions in [Article 101(3)]; and in this subsection "the basic infringement conclusion" is the conclusion that there is an agreement which—

(a) *may affect trade between Member States, and*
(b) *has as its object or effect the prevention, restriction or distortion of competition within the Community.]*

NOTES

References to the "CMA" substituted by the Enterprise and Regulatory Reform Act 2013, s 26(3), Sch 5, Pt 1, paras 1, 19.

For various transitional provisions (including those relating to the abolition of the OFT and the Competition Commission, existing references to those bodies and provisions relating to continuity), see the Enterprise and Regulatory Reform Act 2013 (Commencement No 6, Transitional Provisions and Savings) Order 2014, SI 2014/416, Schedule at **[2.13]**. This section is also amended as follows:

Sub-s (1): substituted by the Competition Act 1998 and Other Enactments (Amendment) Regulations 2004, SI 2004/1261, reg 4, Sch 1, para 21(1), (2). The words in the first pair of square brackets were substituted (for the original words "subsections (8) and (9))" by the Competition (Amendment etc) (EU Exit) Regulations 2019, SI 2019/93, regs 2, 11(a), as from IP completion day (as defined in the European Union (Withdrawal Agreement) Act 2020, s 39) (for transitional provisions and savings in relation to the operation of the 2019 Regulations, see Sch 4 to those Regulations at **[7.69]** et seq and, in particular, Sch 4, Pt 3 to the 2019 Regulations at **[7.71]**).

Sub-s (2): word "it" in square brackets (in each place that it occurs) substituted by the Enterprise Act 2002, s 278, Sch 25, para 38. Words in square brackets in para (a) substituted by the Enterprise and Regulatory Reform Act 2013, s 43, subject to transitional provisions in SI 2014/416 as noted above.

Sub-ss (3), (4): word in second pair of square brackets substituted by the Enterprise Act 2002, s 278, Sch 25, para 38.

Sub-s (5): substituted by SI 2004/1261, reg 4, Sch 1, para 21(1), (3).

Sub-s (6): words in first (outer) pair of square brackets substituted by SI 2004/1261, reg 4, Sch 1, para 21(1), (4). The words in the second (inner) pair of square brackets were substituted (for the original words "section 25(2), (3), (6) and (7)") by SI 2019/93, regs 2, 11(b), as from IP completion day (as defined in the European Union (Withdrawal Agreement) Act 2020, s 39) (for transitional provisions and savings see the first note relating to the 2019 Regulations above).

Sub-s (7): words in first (outer) pair of square brackets substituted by SI 2004/1261, reg 4, Sch 1, para 21(1), (5). The words in the second (inner) pair of square brackets were substituted (for the original words "section 25(4) and (5)") by SI 2019/93, regs 2, 11(c), as from IP completion day (as defined in the European Union (Withdrawal Agreement) Act 2020, s 39) (for transitional provisions and savings see the first note relating to the 2019 Regulations above).

Sub-s (8): added by SI 2004/1261, reg 4, Sch 1, para 21(1), (6).

Sub-s (9): added by SI 2004/1261, reg 4, Sch 1, para 21(1), (6). Words in second and third pairs of square brackets substituted by the Treaty of Lisbon (Changes in Terminology or Numbering) Order 2012, SI 2012/1809, art 3(1), Schedule, Pt 1 This subsection was repealed by SI 2019/93, regs 2, 11(d), as from IP completion day (as defined in the European Union (Withdrawal Agreement) Act 2020, s 39) (for transitional provisions and savings see the first note relating to the 2019 Regulations above).

References to the European Community and related expressions: see the note "References to "the European Community", "Community", etc" in the introductory notes to this Act.

[1.73]

36 [Penalties]

(1) On making a decision that an agreement has infringed the Chapter I prohibition [*or that it has infringed the prohibition in [Article 101(1)]*], the [CMA] may require an undertaking which is a party to the agreement to pay [the [CMA]] a penalty in respect of the infringement.

(2) On making a decision that conduct has infringed the Chapter II prohibition [*or that it has infringed the prohibition in [Article 102]*], the [CMA] may require the undertaking concerned to pay [the [CMA]] a penalty in respect of the infringement.

(3) The [CMA] may impose a penalty on an undertaking under subsection (1) or (2) only if [the [CMA]] is satisfied that the infringement has been committed intentionally or negligently by the undertaking.

(4) Subsection (1) is subject to section 39 and does not apply [in relation to a decision that an agreement has infringed the Chapter I prohibition] if the [CMA] is satisfied that the undertaking acted on the reasonable assumption that that section gave it immunity in respect of the agreement.

(5) Subsection (2) is subject to section 40 and does not apply [in relation to a decision that conduct has infringed the Chapter II prohibition] if the [CMA] is satisfied that the undertaking acted on the reasonable assumption that that section gave it immunity in respect of the conduct.

(6) Notice of a penalty under this section must—
 (a) be in writing; and
 (b) specify the date before which the penalty is required to be paid.

(7) The date specified must not be earlier than the end of the period within which an appeal against the notice may be brought under section 46.

[(7A) In fixing a penalty under this section the CMA must have regard to—
 (a) the seriousness of the infringement concerned, and
 (b) the desirability of deterring both the undertaking on whom the penalty is imposed and others from—
  (i) entering into agreements which infringe the Chapter 1 prohibition *or the prohibition in Article 81(1)*, or
  (ii) engaging in conduct which infringes the Chapter 2 prohibition *or the prohibition in Article 82*.]

(8) No penalty fixed by the [CMA] under this section may exceed 10% of the turnover of the undertaking (determined in accordance with such provisions as may be specified in an order made by the Secretary of State).

(9) Any sums received by the [CMA] under this section are to be paid into the Consolidated Fund.

NOTES

References to the "CMA" substituted by the Enterprise and Regulatory Reform Act 2013, s 26(3), Sch 5, Pt 1, paras 1, 20.

For various transitional provisions (including those relating to the abolition of the OFT and the Competition Commission, existing references to those bodies and provisions relating to continuity), see the Enterprise and Regulatory Reform Act 2013 (Commencement No 6, Transitional Provisions and Savings) Order 2014, SI 2014/416, Schedule at **[2.13]**. This section is also amended as follows:

Section heading: substituted by the Competition Act 1998 and Other Enactments (Amendment) Regulations 2004, SI 2004/1261, reg 4, Sch 1, para 22(1), (6).

Sub-ss (1), (2): words in first (outer) pair of square brackets inserted by SI 2004/1261, reg 4, Sch 1, para 22(1)–(3). Words in second (inner) pair of square brackets substituted by the Treaty of Lisbon (Changes in Terminology or Numbering) Order 2012, SI 2012/1809, art 3(1), Schedule, Pt 1. Words in italics repealed by the Competition (Amendment etc) (EU Exit) Regulations 2019, SI 2019/93, regs 2, 12, as from IP completion day (as defined in the European Union (Withdrawal Agreement) Act 2020, s 39) (for transitional provisions and savings in relation to the operation of the 2019 Regulations, see Sch 4 to those Regulations at **[7.69]** et seq and, in particular, Sch 4, Pt 3 to the 2019 Regulations at **[7.71]**).

Sub-ss (4), (5): words in first pair of square brackets inserted by SI 2004/1261, reg 4, Sch 1, para 22(1), (4), (5).

Sub-s (7A): inserted by the Enterprise and Regulatory Reform Act 2013, s 44(1), (2), subject to transitional provisions in SI 2014/416 as noted above (references to Articles 81 and 82 should now be read as references as Articles 101 and 102). Words in italics repealed by SI 2019/93, regs 2, 12, as from IP completion day (as defined in the European Union (Withdrawal Agreement) Act 2020, s 39) (for transitional provisions and savings see the first note relating to the 2019 Regulations above).

Orders: the Competition Act 1998 (Determination of Turnover for Penalties) Order 2000, SI 2000/309 at **[2.31]**; the Competition Act 1998 (Determination of Turnover for Penalties) (Amendment) Order 2004, SI 2004/1259.

[1.74]

37 Recovery of penalties

(1) If the specified date in a penalty notice has passed and—

(a) the period during which an appeal against the imposition, or amount, of the penalty may be made has expired without an appeal having been made, or

(b) such an appeal has been made and determined,

the [CMA] may recover from the undertaking, as a civil debt due to [the [CMA]], any amount payable under the penalty notice which remains outstanding.

(2) In this section—

"penalty notice" means a notice given under section 36; and "specified date" means the date specified in the penalty notice.

NOTES

Sub-s (1): references to the "CMA" substituted by the Enterprise and Regulatory Reform Act 2013, s 26(3), Sch 5, Pt 1, paras 1, 21. For various transitional provisions (including those relating to the abolition of the OFT and the Competition Commission, existing references to those bodies and provisions relating to continuity), see the Enterprise and Regulatory Reform Act 2013 (Commencement No 6, Transitional Provisions and Savings) Order 2014, SI 2014/416, Schedule at **[2.13]**.

[1.75]

38 The appropriate level of a penalty

(1) The [CMA] must prepare and publish guidance as to the appropriate amount of any penalty under this Part [in respect of an infringement of [the Chapter 1 prohibition or the Chapter 2 prohibition].

[(1A) The guidance must include provision about the circumstances in which, in determining [such a penalty], the [CMA] may take into account effects in another Member State of the agreement or conduct concerned.]

(2) The [CMA] may at any time alter the guidance.

(3) If the guidance is altered, the [CMA] must publish it as altered.

(4) No guidance is to be published under this section without the approval of the Secretary of State.

(5) The [CMA] may, after consulting the Secretary of State, choose how [it] publishes [its] guidance.

(6) If the [CMA] is preparing or altering guidance under this section [it] must consult such persons as [it] considers appropriate.

(7) If the proposed guidance or alteration relates to a matter in respect of which a regulator exercises concurrent jurisdiction, those consulted must include that regulator.

(8) When setting the amount of a penalty under this Part [in respect of an infringement of a kind mentioned in subsection (1)], the [CMA] [and the Tribunal] must have regard to the guidance for the time being in force under this section.

(9) If a penalty or a fine has been imposed by the Commission, or by a court or other body in another Member State, in respect of an agreement or conduct, the [CMA], [the Tribunal] or the appropriate court must take that penalty or fine into account when setting the amount of a penalty under this Part in relation to that agreement or conduct.

(10) In subsection (9) "the appropriate court" means—

(a) in relation to England and Wales, the Court of Appeal;

(b) in relation to Scotland, the Court of Session;

(c) in relation to Northern Ireland, the Court of Appeal in Northern Ireland;

[(d) the Supreme Court].

NOTES

References to the "CMA" substituted by the Enterprise and Regulatory Reform Act 2013, s 26(3), Sch 5, Pt 1, paras 1, 22. For various transitional provisions (including those relating to the abolition of the OFT and the Competition Commission, existing references to those bodies and provisions relating to continuity), see the Enterprise and Regulatory Reform Act 2013 (Commencement No 6, Transitional Provisions and Savings) Order 2014, SI 2014/416, Schedule at **[2.13]**. This section is also amended as follows:

Sub-s (1): words in second (outer) pair of square brackets inserted by the Enterprise and Regulatory Reform Act 2013, s 40(1), (3), (4), subject to transitional provisions in SI 2014/416 as noted above (references to Articles 81 and 82 should be read as references as Articles 101 and 102). Words in third (inner) pair of square brackets substituted (for the original words "the Chapter 1 prohibition, the Chapter 2 prohibition, the prohibition in Article 81(1) or the prohibition in Article 82") by the Competition (Amendment etc) (EU Exit) Regulations 2019, SI 2019/93, regs 2, 13(a), as from IP completion day (as defined in the European Union (Withdrawal Agreement) Act 2020, s 39) (for transitional provisions and savings in relation to the operation of the 2019 Regulations, see Sch 4 to those Regulations at **[7.69]** et seq and, in particular, Sch 4, Pt 3 to the 2019 Regulations at **[7.71]**).

Sub-s (1A): inserted by the Competition Act 1998 and Other Enactments (Amendment) Regulations 2004, SI 2004/1261, reg 4, Sch 1, para 23. Words in first pair of square brackets substituted by the Enterprise and Regulatory Reform Act 2013, s 40(1), (3), (5), subject to transitional provisions in SI 2014/416 as noted above. This subsection was repealed by SI 2019/93, regs 2, 13(b), as from IP completion day (as defined in the European Union (Withdrawal Agreement) Act 2020, s 39) (for transitional provisions and savings see the first note relating to the 2019 Regulations above).

Sub-ss (5), (6): words in second and third pairs of square brackets substituted by the Enterprise Act 2002, s 278, Sch 25, para 38.

Sub-s (8): words in first and third pairs of square brackets inserted by the Enterprise and Regulatory Reform Act 2013, ss 40(1), (3), (6), 44(1), (3), subject to transitional provisions in SI 2014/416 as noted above.

Sub-s (9): words in second pair of square brackets substituted by the Enterprise and Regulatory Reform Act 2013, s 57, Sch 15, paras 8, 10, subject to transitional provisions in SI 2014/416 as noted above. This subsection was repealed by SI 2019/93, regs 2, 13(c), as from IP completion day (as defined in the European Union (Withdrawal Agreement) Act 2020, s 39) (for transitional provisions and savings see the first note relating to the 2019 Regulations above).

Sub-s (10): para (d) substituted by the Constitutional Reform Act 2005, s 40(4), Sch 9, Pt 1, para 65(1), (2). This subsection was repealed by SI 2019/93, regs 2, 13(c), as from IP completion day (as defined in the European Union (Withdrawal Agreement) Act 2020, s 39) (for transitional provisions and savings see the first note relating to the 2019 Regulations above).

[1.76]

39 [Limited immunity in relation to Chapter I prohibition]

(1) In this section "small agreement" means an agreement—

(a) which falls within a category prescribed for the purposes of this section; but

(b) is not a price fixing agreement.

(2) The criteria by reference to which a category of agreement is prescribed may, in particular, include—

(a) the combined turnover of the parties to the agreement (determined in accordance with prescribed provisions);

(b) the share of the market affected by the agreement (determined in that way).

(3) A party to a small agreement is immune from the effect of section 36(1) [so far as that provision relates to decisions about infringement of the Chapter I prohibition]; but the [CMA] may withdraw that immunity under subsection (4).

(4) If the [CMA] has investigated a small agreement, [it] may make a decision withdrawing the immunity given by subsection (3) if, as a result of [its] investigation, [it] considers that the agreement is likely to infringe the Chapter I prohibition.

(5) The [CMA] must give each of the parties in respect of which immunity is withdrawn written notice of [its] decision to withdraw the immunity.

(6) A decision under subsection (4) takes effect on such date ("the withdrawal date") as may be specified in the decision.

(7) The withdrawal date must be a date after the date on which the decision is made.

(8) In determining the withdrawal date, the [CMA] must have regard to the amount of time which the parties are likely to require in order to secure that there is no further infringement of the Chapter I prohibition with respect to the agreement.

(9) In subsection (1) "price fixing agreement" means an agreement which has as its object or effect, or one of its objects or effects, restricting the freedom of a party to the agreement to determine the price to be charged (otherwise than as between that party and another party to the agreement) for the product, service or other matter to which the agreement relates.

NOTES

References to the "CMA" substituted by the Enterprise and Regulatory Reform Act 2013, s 26(3), Sch 5, Pt 1, paras 1, 23. For various transitional provisions (including those relating to the abolition of the OFT and the Competition Commission, existing references to those bodies and provisions relating to continuity), see the Enterprise and Regulatory Reform Act 2013 (Commencement No 6, Transitional Provisions and Savings) Order 2014, SI 2014/416, Schedule at **[2.13]**. This section is also amended as follows:

Section heading: substituted by the Competition Act 1998 and Other Enactments (Amendment) Regulations 2004, SI 2004/1261, reg 4, Sch 1, para 24(1), (3).

Sub-s (3): words in first pair of square brackets inserted by SI 2004/1261, reg 4, Sch 1, para 24(1), (2).

Sub-s (4): words in second, third and fourth pairs of square brackets substituted by the Enterprise Act 2002, s 278, Sch 25, para 38.

Sub-s (5): word in second pair of square brackets substituted by the Enterprise Act 2002, s 278, Sch 25, para 38.

Regulations: the Competition Act 1998 (Small Agreements and Conduct of Minor Significance) Regulations 2000, SI 2000/262 at **[2.25]**.

[1.77]

40 Limited immunity in relation to the Chapter II prohibition

(1) In this section "conduct of minor significance" means conduct which falls within a category prescribed for the purposes of this section.

(2) The criteria by reference to which a category is prescribed may, in particular, include—

(a) the turnover of the person whose conduct it is (determined in accordance with prescribed provisions);

(b) the share of the market affected by the conduct (determined in that way).

(3) A person is immune from the effect of section 36(2)[, so far as that provision relates to decisions about infringement of the Chapter II prohibition,] if his conduct is conduct of minor significance; but the [CMA] may withdraw that immunity under subsection (4).

(4) If the [CMA] has investigated conduct of minor significance, [it] may make a decision withdrawing the immunity given by subsection (3) if, as a result of [its] investigation, [it] considers that the conduct is likely to infringe the Chapter II prohibition.

(5) The [CMA] must give the person, or persons, whose immunity has been withdrawn written notice of [its] decision to withdraw the immunity.

(6) A decision under subsection (4) takes effect on such date ("the withdrawal date") as may be specified in the decision.

(7) The withdrawal date must be a date after the date on which the decision is made.
(8) In determining the withdrawal date, the [CMA] must have regard to the amount of time which the person or persons affected are likely to require in order to secure that there is no further infringement of the Chapter II prohibition.

NOTES

References to the "CMA" substituted by the Enterprise and Regulatory Reform Act 2013, s 26(3), Sch 5, Pt 1, paras 1, 24. For various transitional provisions (including those relating to the abolition of the OFT and the Competition Commission, existing references to those bodies and provisions relating to continuity), see the Enterprise and Regulatory Reform Act 2013 (Commencement No 6, Transitional Provisions and Savings) Order 2014, SI 2014/416, Schedule at **[2.13]**. This section is also amended as follows:

Sub-s (3): words in first pair of square brackets inserted by the Competition Act 1998 and Other Enactments (Amendment) Regulations 2004, SI 2004/1261, reg 4, Sch 1, para 25.

Sub-s (4): words in second, third and fourth pairs of square brackets substituted by the Enterprise Act 2002, s 278, Sch 25, para 38.

Sub-s (5): word in second pair of square brackets substituted by the Enterprise Act 2002, s 278, Sch 25, para 38.

Regulations: the Competition Act 1998 (Small Agreements and Conduct of Minor Significance) Regulations 2000, SI 2000/262 at **[2.25]**.

[Transferred EU anti-trust commitments and transferred EU anti-trust directions

[1.78]
40ZA Interpretation

(1) In this section and in sections 40ZB and 40ZD "transferred EU anti-trust commitments" means EU anti-trust commitments—
- (a) which are the subject of an Article 95(2) commitments transfer decision (and, where those commitments are modified by, or as contemplated by, that decision, or by a later Article 95(2) commitments transfer decision, means those commitments as so modified), and
- (b) which have not been wholly waived or substituted by the European Commission.

(2) In this section—

"Article 95(2) commitments transfer decision" means an instrument issued by the European Commission in accordance with Article 95(2) of the EU withdrawal agreement transferring responsibility for the monitoring and enforcement of EU anti-trust commitments to the CMA;

"EU anti-trust commitments" means commitments contained, pursuant to Article 9(1) of Regulation 1/2003, in a decision adopted by the European Commission under that Regulation.

(3) In this section and in sections 40ZC and 40ZD a "transferred EU anti-trust direction" means an EU anti-trust direction—
- (a) which is the subject of an Article 95(2) direction transfer decision (and, where that direction is modified by, or as contemplated by, that decision, or by a later Article 95(2) direction transfer decision, means that direction as so modified), and
- (b) which has not been wholly revoked by the European Commission.

(4) In this section—

"Article 95(2) direction transfer decision" means an instrument issued by the European Commission in accordance with Article 95(2) of the EU withdrawal agreement transferring responsibility for the monitoring and enforcement of an EU anti-trust direction to the CMA;

"EU anti-trust direction" means a direction given pursuant to Article 7(1) of Regulation 1/2003 in a decision adopted by the European Commission under that Regulation;

"Regulation 1/2003" means Council Regulation (EC) No 1/2003 of 16 December 2002 on the implementation of the rules on competition laid down in Articles 81 and 82 of the Treaty.

(5) So far as the context permits or requires, transferred EU anti-trust commitments and transferred EU anti-trust directions are to be treated for the purposes of this section and sections 40ZB to 40ZD as if—
- (a) any reference to the area of the European Union or of the European Economic Area included the United Kingdom;
- (b) any reference to the internal market included the United Kingdom;
- (c) any reference to a member State included the United Kingdom;
- (d) any reference to a party to the EEA agreement included the United Kingdom.

(6) Subsection (5) is subject to any different provision made by the Article 95(2) commitments transfer decision or Article 95(2) direction transfer decision in question.]

NOTES

Commencement: IP completion day (as defined in the European Union (Withdrawal Agreement) Act 2020, s 39).

Sections 40ZA–40ZD were inserted, together with the preceding heading, by the Competition (Amendment etc) (EU Exit) Regulations 2019, SI 2019/93, reg 13A, as from IP completion day (as defined in the European Union (Withdrawal Agreement) Act 2020, s 39) (for transitional provisions and savings in relation to the operation of the 2019 Regulations, see Sch 4 to those Regulations at **[7.69]** et seq and, in particular, Sch 4, Pt 3 to the 2019 Regulations at **[7.71]**). Note that reg 13A of the 2019 Regulations was inserted by the Competition (Amendment etc) (EU Exit) Regulations 2020, SI 2020/1343, reg 4, with effect from immediately before IP completion day.

[1.79]
[40ZB Transferred EU anti-trust commitments

(1) The CMA has the function of monitoring compliance with transferred EU anti-trust commitments.
(2) If a person who is bound by transferred EU anti-trust commitments fails, without reasonable excuse, to adhere to those commitments, the CMA may apply to the court for an order—
- (a) requiring the defaulter to make good the default within a time specified in the order; or

(b) if any of the transferred EU anti-trust commitments relate to anything to be done in the management or administration of an undertaking, requiring the undertaking or any of its officers to do it.

(3) An order of the court under subsection (2) may provide for all of the costs of, or incidental to, the application for the order to be borne by—

(a) the person in default; or

(b) any officer of an undertaking who is responsible for the default.

(4) In the application of subsection (3) to Scotland, the reference to "costs" is to be read as a reference to "expenses".

(5) In this section, "transferred EU anti-trust commitments" has the meaning given by section 40ZA(1).]

NOTES

Commencement: IP completion day (as defined in the European Union (Withdrawal Agreement) Act 2020, s 39).

Inserted as noted to s 40ZA at **[1.78]**.

[1.80]

[40ZC Transferred EU anti-trust directions

(1) The CMA has the function of monitoring compliance with transferred EU anti-trust directions.

(2) If a person fails, without reasonable excuse, to comply with a transferred EU anti-trust direction, the CMA may apply to the court for an order—

(a) requiring the defaulter to make good the default within a time specified in the order; or

(b) if the transferred EU anti-trust direction related to anything to be done in the management or administration of an undertaking, requiring the undertaking or any of its officers to do it.

(3) An order of the court under subsection (2) may provide for all of the costs of, or incidental to, the application for the order to be borne by—

(a) the person in default; or

(b) any officer of an undertaking who is responsible for the default.

(4) In the application of subsection (3) to Scotland, the reference to "costs" is to be read as a reference to "expenses".

(5) In this section, "transferred EU anti-trust direction" has the meaning given by section 40ZA(3)].

NOTES

Commencement: IP completion day (as defined in the European Union (Withdrawal Agreement) Act 2020, s 39).

Inserted as noted to s 40ZA at **[1.78]**.

[1.81]

[40ZD Information relating to transferred EU anti-trust commitments and transferred EU anti-trust directions

(1) The CMA may require any person to produce to the CMA a specified document, or to provide the CMA with specified information, for the purposes of assisting the CMA—

(a) to monitor compliance with transferred EU anti-trust commitments, or

(b) to decide whether to make an application under section 40ZB(2) in respect of those transferred EU anti-trust commitments.

(2) The CMA may require any person to produce to the CMA a specified document, or to provide the CMA with specified information, for the purposes of assisting the CMA—

(a) to monitor compliance with a transferred EU anti-trust direction, or

(b) to decide whether to make an application under section 40ZC(2) in respect of a transferred EU anti-trust direction.

(3) The powers conferred by subsections (1) and (2) are to be exercised by a notice in writing which indicates the subject matter and purpose of the demand (including identifying the transferred EU anti-trust commitments or transferred EU anti-trust direction in question).

(4) The CMA may also specify in the notice—

(a) the time and place at which any document is to be produced or any information is to be provided;

(b) the manner and form in which it is to be produced or provided.

(5) The power under this section to require a person to produce a document includes power—

(a) if the document is produced—

(i) to take copies of it or extracts from it;

(ii) to require that person, or any person who is a present or past officer of, or is or was at any time employed by, that person, to provide an explanation of the document;

(b) if the document is not produced, to require that person to state, to the best of their knowledge and belief, where it is.

(6) In this section—

"specified" means—

(a) specified, or described, in the notice under subsection (3), or

(b) falling within a category which is specified, or described, in that notice;

"transferred EU anti-trust commitments" has the meaning given by section 40ZA(1);

"transferred EU anti-trust direction" has the meaning given by section 40ZA(3).]

NOTES

Commencement: IP completion day (as defined in the European Union (Withdrawal Agreement) Act 2020, s 39).

Inserted as noted to s 40ZA at **[1.78]**.

[Civil sanctions

[1.82]

40A Penalties: failure to comply with requirements

(1) Where the CMA considers that a person has, without reasonable excuse, failed to comply with a requirement imposed on the person under section 26, 26A, 27, [28, 28A or 40ZD], it may impose a penalty of such amount as it considers appropriate.

(2) The amount may be—

(a) a fixed amount,

(b) an amount calculated by reference to a daily rate, or

(c) a combination of a fixed amount and an amount calculated by reference to a daily rate.

(3) A penalty imposed under subsection (1) must not—

(a) in the case of a fixed amount, exceed such amount as the Secretary of State may by order specify;

(b) in the case of an amount calculated by reference to a daily rate, exceed such amount per day as the Secretary of State may so specify;

(c) in the case of a fixed amount and an amount calculated by reference to a daily rate, exceed such fixed amount and such amount per day as the Secretary of State may so specify.

(4) The fixed amount specified for the purposes of subsection (3)(a) or (c) may not exceed £30,000.

(5) The amount per day specified for the purposes of subsection (3)(b) or (c) may not exceed £15,000.

(6) In imposing a penalty by reference to a daily rate—

(a) no account is to be taken of any days before the service of the notice under section 112 of the Enterprise Act 2002 (as applied by subsection (9)) on the person concerned, and

(b) unless the CMA determines an earlier date (whether before or after the penalty is imposed), the amount payable ceases to accumulate at the beginning of the earliest of the days mentioned in subsection (7).

(7) The days are—

(a) the day on which the requirement concerned is satisfied;

(b) the day on which the CMA makes a decision (within the meaning given by section 31(2)) or terminates the investigation in question without making such a decision;

(c) if the Secretary of State has made an order under section 31F(1)(b) imposing a time-limit on the making of such a decision, the latest day on which such a decision may be made as a result of the investigation in question.

(8) Before making an order under subsection (3), the Secretary of State must consult the CMA and such other persons as the Secretary of State considers appropriate.

(9) Sections 112 to 115 of the Enterprise Act 2002 (supplementary provisions about penalties) apply in relation to a penalty imposed under subsection (1) as they apply in relation to a penalty imposed under section 110(1) of that Act.]

NOTES

Inserted, together with the preceding heading and s 40B, by the Enterprise and Regulatory Reform Act 2013, s 40(1), (2). For various transitional provisions (including those relating to the abolition of the OFT and the Competition Commission, existing references to those bodies and provisions relating to continuity), see the Enterprise and Regulatory Reform Act 2013 (Commencement No 6, Transitional Provisions and Savings) Order 2014, SI 2014/416, Schedule at **[2.13]**.

Sub-s (1): words in square brackets substituted (for the original words "28 or 28A") by the Competition (Amendment etc) (EU Exit) Regulations 2019, SI 2019/93, reg 13B, as from IP completion day (as defined in the European Union (Withdrawal Agreement) Act 2020, s 39) (for transitional provisions and savings in relation to the operation of the 2019 Regulations, see Sch 4 to those Regulations at **[7.69]** et seq and, in particular, Sch 4, Pt 3 to the 2019 Regulations at **[7.71]**). Note that reg 13B of the 2019 Regulations was inserted by the Competition (Amendment etc) (EU Exit) Regulations 2020, SI 2020/1343, reg 4, with effect from immediately before IP completion day.

Orders: the Competition and Markets Authority (Penalties) Order 2014, SI 2014/559 at **[2.61]**.

[1.83]

[40B Statement of policy on penalties

(1) The CMA must prepare and publish a statement of policy in relation to the use of its powers under section 40A.

(2) The CMA must, in particular, include a statement about the considerations relevant to the determination of the nature and amount of any penalty imposed under section 40A.

(3) The CMA may revise its statement of policy and, where it does so, it must publish the revised statement.

(4) The CMA must consult such persons as it considers appropriate when preparing or revising its statement of policy.

(5) If the proposed statement of policy or revision relates to a matter in respect of which a regulator exercises concurrent jurisdiction, those consulted must include that regulator.

(6) In deciding whether and, if so, how to proceed under section 40A, the CMA must have regard to the statement of policy which was most recently published under this section at the time when the failure concerned occurred.]

NOTES

Inserted as noted to s 40A at **[1.82]**.

Offences

41 (*Repealed by the Competition Act 1998 and Other Enactments (Amendment) Regulations 2004, SI 2004/1261, reg 4, Sch 1, para 26.*)

[1.84]

42 Offences

(1)–(4) . . .

(5) A person is guilty of an offence if he intentionally obstructs an officer acting in the exercise of his powers under section 27.

(6) A person guilty of an offence under subsection . . . (5) is liable—

(a) on summary conviction, to a fine not exceeding the statutory maximum;
(b) on conviction on indictment, to a fine.

(7) A person who intentionally obstructs an officer in the exercise of his powers under a warrant issued under [section 28 or 28A] is guilty of an offence and liable—

(a) on summary conviction, to a fine not exceeding the statutory maximum;
(b) on conviction on indictment, to imprisonment for a term not exceeding two years or to a fine or to both.

NOTES

Sub-ss (1)–(4): repealed by the Enterprise and Regulatory Reform Act 2013, s 40(1), (7), (8). For various transitional provisions (including those relating to the abolition of the OFT and the Competition Commission, existing references to those bodies and provisions relating to continuity), see the Enterprise and Regulatory Reform Act 2013 (Commencement No 6, Transitional Provisions and Savings) Order 2014, SI 2014/416, Schedule at **[2.13]**.

Sub-s (6): words omitted repealed by the Enterprise and Regulatory Reform Act 2013, s 40(1), (7), (9), subject to transitional provisions in SI 2014/416 as noted above.

Sub-s (7): words in square brackets substituted by SI 2004/1261, reg 4, Sch 1, para 27(1), (3).

[1.85]

43 Destroying or falsifying documents

(1) A person is guilty of an offence if, having been required to produce a document under section 26, 27[, 28 or 28A]—

(a) he intentionally or recklessly destroys or otherwise disposes of it, falsifies it or conceals it, or
(b) he causes or permits its destruction, disposal, falsification or concealment.

(2) A person guilty of an offence under subsection (1) is liable—

(a) on summary conviction, to a fine not exceeding the statutory maximum;
(b) on conviction on indictment, to imprisonment for a term not exceeding two years or to a fine or to both.

NOTES

Sub-s (1): words in square brackets substituted by the Competition Act 1998 and Other Enactments (Amendment) Regulations 2004, SI 2004/1261, reg 4, Sch 1, para 28.

[1.86]

44 False or misleading information

(1) If information is provided by a person to the [CMA] in connection with any function of the [CMA] under this Part, that person is guilty of an offence if—

(a) the information is false or misleading in a material particular, and
(b) he knows that it is or is reckless as to whether it is.

(2) A person who—

(a) provides any information to another person, knowing the information to be false or misleading in a material particular, or
(b) recklessly provides any information to another person which is false or misleading in a material particular,

knowing that the information is to be used for the purpose of providing information to the [CMA] in connection with any of [its] functions under this Part, is guilty of an offence.

(3) A person guilty of an offence under this section is liable—

(a) on summary conviction, to a fine not exceeding the statutory maximum;
(b) on conviction on indictment, to imprisonment for a term not exceeding two years or to a fine or to both.

NOTES

References to the "CMA" substituted by the Enterprise and Regulatory Reform Act 2013, s 26(3), Sch 5, Pt 1, paras 1, 25. For various transitional provisions (including those relating to the abolition of the OFT and the Competition Commission, existing references to those bodies and provisions relating to continuity), see the Enterprise and Regulatory Reform Act 2013 (Commencement No 6, Transitional Provisions and Savings) Order 2014, SI 2014/416, Schedule at **[2.13]**. This section is also amended as follows:

Sub-s (2): word in second pair of square brackets substituted by the Enterprise Act 2002, s 278, Sch 25, para 38.

CHAPTER IV [APPEALS BEFORE THE TRIBUNAL AND PROCEEDINGS AND SETTLEMENTS RELATING TO INFRINGEMENTS OF COMPETITION LAW]

NOTES

Chapter heading: substituted by the Claims in respect of Loss or Damage arising from Competition Infringements (Competition Act 1998 and Other Enactments (Amendment)) Regulations 2017, SI 2017/385, reg 2, Sch 1, paras 1, 2.

. . .

45 *(Repealed, together with the preceding heading, by the Enterprise and Regulatory Reform Act 2013, s 26(3), Sch 5, Pt 3, paras 218, 220. For various transitional provisions (including those relating to the abolition of the OFT and the Competition Commission, existing references to those bodies and provisions relating to continuity), see the Enterprise and Regulatory Reform Act 2013 (Commencement No 6, Transitional Provisions and Savings) Order 2014, SI 2014/416, Schedule at* **[2.13]**.*)*

[Appeals before the Tribunal]

NOTES

The heading above was substituted by the Claims in respect of Loss or Damage arising from Competition Infringements (Competition Act 1998 and Other Enactments (Amendment)) Regulations 2017, SI 2017/385, reg 3, Sch 2, paras 1, 2.

[1.87]

46 Appealable decisions

(1) Any party to an agreement in respect of which the [CMA] has made a decision may appeal to [the Tribunal] against, or with respect to, the decision.

(2) Any person in respect of whose conduct the [CMA] has made a decision may appeal to [the Tribunal] against, or with respect to, the decision.

[(3) In this section "decision" means a decision of the [CMA]—

(a) as to whether the Chapter I prohibition has been infringed,

(b) as to whether the prohibition in [Article 101(1)] has been infringed,

(c) as to whether the Chapter II prohibition has been infringed,

(d) as to whether the prohibition in [Article 102] has been infringed,

(e) cancelling a block or [retained exemption],

(f) withdrawing the benefit of a regulation of the Commission pursuant to Article 29(2) of the EC Competition Regulation,

(g) not releasing commitments pursuant to a request made under section 31A(4)(b)(i),

(h) releasing commitments under section 31A(4)(b)(ii),

(i) as to the imposition of any penalty under section 36 or as to the amount of any such penalty,

and includes a direction under section 32, 33 or 35 and such other decisions under this Part as may be prescribed.]

(4) Except in the case of an appeal against the imposition, or the amount, of a penalty, the making of an appeal under this section does not suspend the effect of the decision to which the appeal relates.

(5) Part I of Schedule 8 makes further provision about appeals.

NOTES

References to the "CMA" substituted by the Enterprise and Regulatory Reform Act 2013, s 26(3), Sch 5, Pt 1, paras 1, 26. For various transitional provisions (including those relating to the abolition of the OFT and the Competition Commission, existing references to those bodies and provisions relating to continuity), see the Enterprise and Regulatory Reform Act 2013 (Commencement No 6, Transitional Provisions and Savings) Order 2014, SI 2014/416, Schedule at **[2.13]**. This section is also amended as follows:

Sub-ss (1), (2): words in second pair of square brackets substituted by the Enterprise Act 2002, s 21, Sch 5, paras 1, 2(a); subject to transitional provisions as noted below.

Sub-s (3): substituted by the Competition Act 1998 and Other Enactments (Amendment) Regulations 2004, SI 2004/1261, reg 4, Sch 1, para 29 (for savings and transitional provisions see reg 8 of those Regulations at **[2.8]**). Words in square brackets in paras (b), (d) substituted by the Treaty of Lisbon (Changes in Terminology or Numbering) Order 2012, SI 2012/1809, art 3(1), Schedule, Pt 1. Paras (b), (d) and (f) were repealed, and the words in square brackets in para (e) were substituted (for the original words "parallel exemption"), by the Competition (Amendment etc) (EU Exit) Regulations 2019, SI 2019/93, regs 2, 14, as from IP completion day (as defined in the European Union (Withdrawal Agreement) Act 2020, s 39) (for transitional provisions and savings in relation to the operation of the 2019 Regulations, see Sch 4 to those Regulations at **[7.69]** et seq).

Transitional provisions: for transitional provisions in relation to the constitution, etc, of the Tribunal, see the Enterprise Act 2002, Sch 24, paras 7–11 at **[1.445]**; and for transitional provisions in connection with an appeal made to the Competition Commission under ss 46 or 47 of this Act which has not been finally determined before 1 April 2003, see the Enterprise Act 2002 (Commencement No 2, Transitional and Transitory Provisions) Order 2003, SI 2003/766, art 3.

Regulations: the Competition Act 1998 (Appealable Decisions and Revocation of Notification of Excluded Agreements) Regulations 2004, SI 2004/1078 at **[2.1]**.

[1.88]

[47 Third party appeals

[(1) A person who does not fall within section 46(1) or (2) may appeal to the Tribunal with respect to—

(a) a decision falling within [paragraph (a), (c) or (e)] of section 46(3);

(b) a decision falling within paragraph (g) of section 46(3);

(c) a decision of the [CMA] to accept or release commitments under section 31A, or to accept a variation of such commitments other than a variation which is not material in any respect;

(d) a decision of the [CMA] to make directions under section 35;

(e) a decision of the [CMA] not to make directions under section 35; or

(f) such other decision of the [CMA] under this Part as may be prescribed.]

(2) A person may make an appeal under subsection (1) only if the Tribunal considers that he has a sufficient interest in the decision with respect to which the appeal is made, or that he represents persons who have such an interest.

(3) The making of an appeal under this section does not suspend the effect of the decision to which the appeal relates.]

NOTES

Substituted by the Enterprise Act 2002, s 17 (for transitional provisions, see the note to s 46 at **[1.87]**, and the Enterprise Act 2002 (Commencement No 3, Transitional and Transitory Provisions and Savings) Order 2003, SI 2003/1397, art 5).

Sub-s (1): substituted by the Competition Act 1998 and Other Enactments (Amendment) Regulations 2004, SI 2004/1261, reg 4, Sch 1, para 30 (for savings and transitional provisions see reg 8 of those Regulations at **[2.8]**). References to the "CMA" substituted by the Enterprise and Regulatory Reform Act 2013, s 26(3), Sch 5, Pt 1, paras 1, 27 (for various transitional provisions (including those relating to the abolition of the OFT and the Competition Commission, existing references to those bodies and provisions relating to continuity), see the Enterprise and Regulatory Reform Act 2013 (Commencement No 6, Transitional Provisions and Savings) Order 2014, SI 2014/416, Schedule at **[2.13]**). The words in square brackets in para (a) were substituted (for the original words "paragraph (a) to (f)") by the Competition (Amendment etc) (EU Exit) Regulations 2019, SI 2019/93, regs 2, 15, as from IP completion day (as defined in the European Union (Withdrawal Agreement) Act 2020, s 39) (for transitional provisions and savings in relation to the operation of the 2019 Regulations, see Sch 4 to those Regulations at **[7.69]** et seq).

Regulations: the Competition Act 1998 (Appealable Decisions and Revocation of Notification of Excluded Agreements) Regulations 2004, SI 2004/1078 at **[2.1]**.

[Claims for loss or damage: proceedings before the Tribunal]

NOTES

The heading above was inserted by the Claims in respect of Loss or Damage arising from Competition Infringements (Competition Act 1998 and Other Enactments (Amendment)) Regulations 2017, SI 2017/385, reg 3, Sch 2, paras 1, 3.

[1.89]

[47A Proceedings before the Tribunal: claims for damages etc

(1) A person may make a claim to which this section applies in proceedings before the Tribunal, subject to the provisions of this Act and Tribunal rules.

(2) This section applies to a claim of a kind specified in subsection (3) which a person who has suffered loss or damage may make in civil proceedings brought in any part of the United Kingdom in respect of an infringement decision or an alleged infringement of—

(a) the Chapter I prohibition, [or]
(b) the Chapter II prohibition,
(c) the prohibition in Article 101(1), or
(d) the prohibition in Article 102.

(3) The claims are—

(a) a claim for damages;
(b) any other claim for a sum of money;
(c) in proceedings in England and Wales or Northern Ireland, a claim for an injunction.

(4) For the purpose of identifying claims which may be made in civil proceedings, any limitation rules or rules relating to prescription that would apply in such proceedings are to be disregarded.

(5) The right to make a claim in proceedings under this section does not affect the right to bring any other proceedings in respect of the claim.

[(6) In this Part (except in section 49C) "infringement decision" means—

(a) a decision of the CMA that the Chapter I prohibition or the Chapter II prohibition has been infringed, or
(b) a decision of the Tribunal on an appeal from the decision of the CMA that the Chapter I prohibition or the Chapter II prohibition has been infringed.]

NOTES

Inserted by the Enterprise Act 2002, s 18(1).

Subsequently substituted by the Consumer Rights Act 2015, s 80, Sch 8, Pt 1, paras 1, 4, with effect in relation to claims arising before 1 October 2015 as it applies to claims arising after that date.

The word in square brackets in sub-s (2)(a) was inserted, sub-s (2)(c) and (d) were repealed, and sub-s (6) was substituted, by the Competition (Amendment etc) (EU Exit) Regulations 2019, SI 2019/93, regs 2, 16, as from IP completion day (as defined in the European Union (Withdrawal Agreement) Act 2020, s 39) (for transitional provisions and savings in relation to the operation of the 2019 Regulations, see Sch 4 to those Regulations at **[7.69]** et seq). The original sub-s (6) read as follows—

"(6) In this Part (except in section 49C) "infringement decision" means—

(a) a decision of the CMA that the Chapter I prohibition, the Chapter II prohibition, the prohibition in Article 101(1) or the prohibition in Article 102 has been infringed,
(b) a decision of the Tribunal on an appeal from a decision of the CMA that the Chapter I prohibition, the Chapter II prohibition, the prohibition in Article 101(1) or the prohibition in Article 102 has been infringed, or
(c) a decision of the Commission that the prohibition in Article 101(1) or the prohibition in Article 102 has been infringed.".

[1.90]

[47B Collective proceedings before the Tribunal

(1) Subject to the provisions of this Act and Tribunal rules, proceedings may be brought before the Tribunal combining two or more claims to which section 47A applies ("collective proceedings").

(2) Collective proceedings must be commenced by a person who proposes to be the representative in those proceedings.

(3) The following points apply in relation to claims in collective proceedings—

(a) it is not a requirement that all of the claims should be against all of the defendants to the proceedings,
(b) the proceedings may combine claims which have been made in proceedings under section 47A and claims which have not, and
(c) a claim which has been made in proceedings under section 47A may be continued in collective proceedings only with the consent of the person who made that claim.

(4) Collective proceedings may be continued only if the Tribunal makes a collective proceedings order.

(5) The Tribunal may make a collective proceedings order only—

(a) if it considers that the person who brought the proceedings is a person who, if the order were made, the Tribunal could authorise to act as the representative in those proceedings in accordance with subsection (8), and
(b) in respect of claims which are eligible for inclusion in collective proceedings.

(6) Claims are eligible for inclusion in collective proceedings only if the Tribunal considers that they raise the same, similar or related issues of fact or law and are suitable to be brought in collective proceedings.

(7) A collective proceedings order must include the following matters—

(a) authorisation of the person who brought the proceedings to act as the representative in those proceedings,
(b) description of a class of persons whose claims are eligible for inclusion in the proceedings, and
(c) specification of the proceedings as opt-in collective proceedings or opt-out collective proceedings (see subsections (10) and (11)).

(8) The Tribunal may authorise a person to act as the representative in collective proceedings—

(a) whether or not that person is a person falling within the class of persons described in the collective proceedings order for those proceedings (a "class member"), but

(b) only if the Tribunal considers that it is just and reasonable for that person to act as a representative in those proceedings.

(9) The Tribunal may vary or revoke a collective proceedings order at any time.

(10) "Opt-in collective proceedings" are collective proceedings which are brought on behalf of each class member who opts in by notifying the representative, in a manner and by a time specified, that the claim should be included in the collective proceedings.

(11) "Opt-out collective proceedings" are collective proceedings which are brought on behalf of each class member except—

(a) any class member who opts out by notifying the representative, in a manner and by a time specified, that the claim should not be included in the collective proceedings, and

(b) any class member who—

(i) is not domiciled in the United Kingdom at a time specified, and

(ii) does not, in a manner and by a time specified, opt in by notifying the representative that the claim should be included in the collective proceedings.

(12) Where the Tribunal gives a judgment or makes an order in collective proceedings, the judgment or order is binding on all represented persons, except as otherwise specified.

(13) The right to make a claim in collective proceedings does not affect the right to bring any other proceedings in respect of the claim.

(14) In this section and in section 47C, "specified" means specified in a direction made by the Tribunal.]

NOTES

Inserted by the Enterprise Act 2002, s 19.

Subsequently substituted by the Consumer Rights Act 2015, s 80, Sch 8, Pt 1, paras 1, 5, with effect in relation to claims arising before 1 October 2015 as it applies to claims arising after that date.

Note that the Specified Body (Consumer Claims) Order 2005, SI 2005/2365 was made under subsection (9) of this section prior to its substitution as noted above. That Order specified the Consumers' Association as a body able to bring a claim to which s 47A applies.

[1.91]

[47C Collective proceedings: damages and costs

(1) . . .

(2) The Tribunal may make an award of damages in collective proceedings without undertaking an assessment of the amount of damages recoverable in respect of the claim of each represented person.

(3) Where the Tribunal makes an award of damages in opt-out collective proceedings, the Tribunal must make an order providing for the damages to be paid on behalf of the represented persons to—

(a) the representative, or

(b) such person other than a represented person as the Tribunal thinks fit.

(4) Where the Tribunal makes an award of damages in opt-in collective proceedings, the Tribunal may make an order as described in subsection (3).

(5) Subject to subsection (6), where the Tribunal makes an award of damages in opt-out collective proceedings, any damages not claimed by the represented persons within a specified period must be paid to the charity for the time being prescribed by order made by the Lord Chancellor under section 194(8) of the Legal Services Act 2007.

(6) In a case within subsection (5) the Tribunal may order that all or part of any damages not claimed by the represented persons within a specified period is instead to be paid to the representative in respect of all or part of the costs or expenses incurred by the representative in connection with the proceedings.

(7) The Secretary of State may by order amend subsection (5) so as to substitute a different charity for the one for the time being specified in that subsection.

(8) A damages-based agreement is unenforceable if it relates to opt-out collective proceedings.

(9) In this section—

(a) "charity" means a body, or the trustees of a trust, established for charitable purposes only;

(b) "damages" (except in the term "exemplary damages") includes any sum of money which may be awarded by the Tribunal in collective proceedings (other than costs or expenses);

(c) "damages-based agreement" has the meaning given in section 58AA(3) of the Courts and Legal Services Act 1990.]

NOTES

Inserted by the Consumer Rights Act 2015, s 80, Sch 8, Pt 1, paras 1, 6.

Sub-s (1): repealed by the Claims in respect of Loss or Damage arising from Competition Infringements (Competition Act 1998 and Other Enactments (Amendment)) Regulations 2017, SI 2017/385, reg 3, Sch 2, paras 1, 4(1). Note that Sch 2, para 4(2) to the 2017 Regulations provides that sub-s (1) "continues to apply in relation to collective proceedings to the extent that paragraph 36 of Schedule 8A to this Act does not apply to them (see Part 10 of that Schedule) (and see the further saving in paragraph 10 of this Schedule)".

[1.92]

[47D Proceedings under section 47A or collective proceedings: injunctions etc

(1) An injunction granted by the Tribunal in proceedings under section 47A or in collective proceedings—

(a) has the same effect as an injunction granted by the High Court, and

(b) is enforceable as if it were an injunction granted by the High Court.

(2) In deciding whether to grant an injunction in proceedings under section 47A or in collective proceedings, the Tribunal must—

(a) in proceedings in England and Wales, apply the principles which the High Court would apply in deciding whether to grant an injunction under section 37(1) of the Senior Courts Act 1981, and

(b) in proceedings in Northern Ireland, apply the principles that the High Court would apply in deciding whether to grant an injunction.

(3) Subsection (2) is subject to Tribunal rules which make provision of the kind mentioned in paragraph 15A(3) of Schedule 4 to the Enterprise Act 2002 (undertakings as to damages in relation to claims subject to the fast-track procedure).]

NOTES

Inserted by the Consumer Rights Act 2015, s 80, Sch 8, Pt 1, paras 1, 7.

47E (*Inserted by the Consumer Rights Act 2015, s 80, Sch 8, Pt 1, paras 1, 8, except in relation to claims arising before 1 October 2015. Subsequently repealed by the Claims in respect of Loss or Damage arising from Competition Infringements (Competition Act 1998 and Other Enactments (Amendment)) Regulations 2017, SI 2017/385, reg 3, Sch 2, paras 1, 5(1). Note that Sch 2, para 5(2) to the 2017 Regulations provides that this section "continues to apply in respect of claims to which section 47A of this Act applies to the extent that Part 5 of Schedule 8A to this Act does not apply to them (see Part 10 of that Schedule)".*)

[Further provision about claims in respect of loss or damage before a court or the Tribunal

[1.93]

47F Further provision about claims in respect of loss or damage before a court or the Tribunal

Schedule 8A makes further provision about claims in respect of loss or damage before a court or the Tribunal.]

NOTES

Inserted, together with the preceding heading, by the Claims in respect of Loss or Damage arising from Competition Infringements (Competition Act 1998 and Other Enactments (Amendment)) Regulations 2017, SI 2017/385, reg 2, Sch 1, paras 1, 3.

[Further appeals from the Tribunal]

NOTES

The above heading was inserted by the Claims in respect of Loss or Damage arising from Competition Infringements (Competition Act 1998 and Other Enactments (Amendment)) Regulations 2017, SI 2017/385, reg 3, Sch 2 paras 1, 6.

48 (*Repealed by the Enterprise Act 2002, ss 21, 278(2), Sch 5, paras 1, 3, Sch 26.*)

[1.94]

[49 Further appeals [from the Tribunal]

(1) An appeal lies to the appropriate court—

(a) from a decision of the Tribunal as to the amount of a penalty under section 36; [and]

(b) . . .

(c) on a point of law arising from any other decision of the Tribunal on an appeal under section 46 or 47.

[(1A) An appeal lies to the appropriate court on a point of law arising from a decision of the Tribunal in proceedings under section 47A or in collective proceedings—

(a) as to the award of damages or other sum (other than a decision on costs or expenses), or

(b) as to the grant of an injunction.

(1B) An appeal lies to the appropriate court from a decision of the Tribunal in proceedings under section 47A or in collective proceedings as to the amount of an award of damages or other sum (other than the amount of costs or expenses).

(1C) An appeal under subsection (1A) arising from a decision in respect of a stand-alone claim may include consideration of a point of law arising from a finding of the Tribunal as to an infringement of a prohibition listed in section 47A(2).

(1D) In subsection (1C) "a stand-alone claim" is a claim—

(a) in respect of an alleged infringement of a prohibition listed in section 47A(2), and

(b) made in proceedings under section 47A or included in collective proceedings.]

(2) An appeal under this section—

(a) [except as provided by subsection (2A),] may be brought by a party to the proceedings before the Tribunal or by a person who has a sufficient interest in the matter; and

(b) requires the permission of the Tribunal or the appropriate court.

[(2A) An appeal from a decision of the Tribunal in respect of a claim included in collective proceedings may be brought only by the representative in those proceedings or by a defendant to that claim.]

(3) In this section "the appropriate court" means the Court of Appeal or, in the case of an appeal from Tribunal proceedings in Scotland, the Court of Session.]

NOTES

Substituted by the Enterprise Act 2002, s 21, Sch 5, paras 1, 4 (for transitional provisions, see the note to s 46 at **[1.87]**).

Section heading: words in square brackets inserted by the Claims in respect of Loss or Damage arising from Competition Infringements (Competition Act 1998 and Other Enactments (Amendment)) Regulations 2017, SI 2017/385, reg 3, Sch 2, paras 1, 7.

Sub-s (1): word in square brackets in para (a) inserted, and para (b) repealed, by the Consumer Rights Act 2015, s 80, Sch 8, Pt 1, paras 1, 9(1), (2).

Sub-ss (1A)–(1D), (2A): inserted by the Consumer Rights Act 2015, s 80, Sch 8, Pt 1, paras 1, 9(1), (3), (5).

Sub-s (2): words in square brackets in para (a) inserted by the Consumer Rights Act 2015, s 80, Sch 8, Pt 1, paras 1, 9(1), (4).

[Settlements relating to infringements of competition law

[1.95]

49A Collective settlements: where a collective proceedings order has been made

(1) The Tribunal may, in accordance with this section and Tribunal rules, make an order approving the settlement of claims in collective proceedings (a "collective settlement") where—

(a) a collective proceedings order has been made in respect of the claims, and

(b) the Tribunal has specified that the proceedings are opt-out collective proceedings.

(2) An application for approval of a proposed collective settlement must be made to the Tribunal by the representative and the defendant in the collective proceedings.

(3) The representative and the defendant must provide agreed details of the claims to be settled by the proposed collective settlement and the proposed terms of that settlement.

(4) Where there is more than one defendant in the collective proceedings, "defendant" in subsections (2) and (3) means such of the defendants as wish to be bound by the proposed collective settlement.

(5) The Tribunal may make an order approving a proposed collective settlement only if satisfied that its terms are just and reasonable.

(6) On the date on which the Tribunal approves a collective settlement—

(a) if the period within which persons may opt out of or (in the case of persons not domiciled in the United Kingdom) opt in to the collective proceedings has expired, subsections (8) and (10) apply so as to determine the persons bound by the settlement;

(b) if that period has not yet expired, subsections (9) and (10) apply so as to determine the persons bound by the settlement.

(7) If the period within which persons may opt out of the collective proceedings expires on a different date from the period within which persons not domiciled in the United Kingdom may opt in to the collective proceedings, the references in subsection (6) to the expiry of a period are to the expiry of whichever of those periods expires later.

(8) Where this subsection applies, a collective settlement approved by the Tribunal is binding on all persons falling within the class of persons described in the collective proceedings order who—

(a) were domiciled in the United Kingdom at the time specified for the purposes of determining domicile in relation to the collective proceedings (see section 47B(11)(b)(i)) and did not opt out of those proceedings, or

(b) opted in to the collective proceedings.

(9) Where this subsection applies, a collective settlement approved by the Tribunal is binding on all persons falling within the class of persons described in the collective proceedings order.

(10) But a collective settlement is not binding on a person who—

(a) opts out by notifying the representative, in a manner and by a time specified, that the claim should not be included in the collective settlement, or

(b) is not domiciled in the United Kingdom at a time specified, and does not, in a manner and by a time specified, opt in by notifying the representative that the claim should be included in the collective settlement.

(11) This section does not affect a person's right to offer to settle opt-in collective proceedings.

(12) In this section and in section 49B, "specified" means specified in a direction made by the Tribunal.]

NOTES

Inserted, together with preceding cross-heading, by the Consumer Rights Act 2015, s 80, Sch 8, Pt 1, paras 1, 10, with effect in relation to claims arising before 1 October 2015 as it applies to claims arising after that date.

[1.96]

[49B Collective settlements: where a collective proceedings order has not been made

(1) The Tribunal may, in accordance with this section and Tribunal rules, make an order approving the settlement of claims (a "collective settlement") where—

(a) a collective proceedings order has not been made in respect of the claims, but

(b) if collective proceedings were brought, the claims could be made at the commencement of the proceedings (disregarding any limitation or prescriptive period applicable to a claim in collective proceedings).

(2) An application for approval of a proposed collective settlement must be made to the Tribunal by—

(a) a person who proposes to be the settlement representative in relation to the collective settlement, and

(b) the person who, if collective proceedings were brought in respect of the claims, would be a defendant in those proceedings (or, where more than one person would be a defendant in those proceedings, such of those persons as wish to be bound by the proposed collective settlement).

(3) The persons applying to the Tribunal under subsection (2) must provide agreed details of the claims to be settled by the proposed collective settlement and the proposed terms of that settlement.

(4) The Tribunal may make an order approving a proposed collective settlement (see subsection (8)) only if it first makes a collective settlement order.

(5) The Tribunal may make a collective settlement order only—

(a) if it considers that the person described in subsection (2)(a) is a person who, if the order were made, the Tribunal could authorise to act as the settlement representative in relation to the collective settlement in accordance with subsection (7), and

(b) in respect of claims which, if collective proceedings were brought, would be eligible for inclusion in the proceedings (see section 47B(6)).

(6) A collective settlement order must include the following matters—

(a) authorisation of the person described in subsection (2)(a) to act as the settlement representative in relation to the collective settlement, and

(b) description of a class of persons whose claims fall within subsection (5)(b).

(7) The Tribunal may authorise a person to act as the settlement representative in relation to a collective settlement—

(a) whether or not that person is a person falling within the class of persons described in the collective settlement order for that settlement, but

(b) only if the Tribunal considers that it is just and reasonable for that person to act as the settlement representative in relation to that settlement.

(8) Where the Tribunal has made a collective settlement order, it may make an order approving a proposed collective settlement only if satisfied that its terms are just and reasonable.

(9) A collective settlement approved by the Tribunal is binding on all persons falling within the class of persons described in the collective settlement order.

(10) But a collective settlement is not binding on a person who—

(a) opts out by notifying the settlement representative, in a manner and by a time specified, that the claim should not be included in the collective settlement, or

(b) is not domiciled in the United Kingdom at a time specified, and does not, in a manner and by a time specified, opt in by notifying the settlement representative that the claim should be included in the collective settlement.

(11) In this section, "settlement representative" means a person who is authorised by a collective settlement order to act in relation to a collective settlement.]

NOTES

Inserted by the Consumer Rights Act 2015, s 80, Sch 8, Pt 1, paras 1, 11, with effect in relation to claims arising before 1 October 2015 as it applies to claims arising after that date.

[1.97]

[49C Approval of redress schemes by the CMA

(1) A person may apply to the CMA for approval of a redress scheme.

(2) The CMA may consider an application before the infringement decision to which the redress scheme relates has been made, but may approve the scheme only—

(a) after that decision has been made, or

(b) in the case of a decision of the CMA, at the same time as that decision is made.

(3) In deciding whether to approve a redress scheme, the CMA may take into account the amount or value of compensation offered under the scheme.

(4) The CMA may approve a redress scheme under subsection (2)(b) subject to a condition or conditions requiring the provision of further information about the operation of the scheme (including about the amount or value of compensation to be offered under the scheme or how this will be determined).

(5) If the CMA approves a redress scheme subject to such a condition, it may—

(a) approve the scheme subject to other conditions;

(b) withdraw approval from the scheme if any conditions imposed under subsection (4) or paragraph (a) are not met;

(c) approve a redress scheme as a replacement for the original scheme (but may not approve that scheme subject to conditions).

(6) An approved scheme may not be varied by the CMA or the compensating party.

(7) But, where the CMA approves a redress scheme subject to a condition of the kind mentioned in subsection (4), subsection (6) does not prevent further information provided in accordance with the condition from forming part of the terms of the scheme.

(8) The Secretary of State may make regulations relating to the approval of redress schemes, and the regulations may in particular—

(a) make provision as to the procedure governing an application for approval of a redress scheme, including the information to be provided with the application;

(b) provide that the CMA may approve a redress scheme only if it has been devised according to a process specified in the regulations;

(c) provide that the CMA may approve a redress scheme only if it is in a form, or contains terms, specified in the regulations (which may include terms requiring a settlement agreement under the scheme to be in a form, or contain terms, specified in the regulations);

(d) provide that the CMA may approve a redress scheme only if (so far as the CMA can judge from facts known to it) the scheme is intended to be administered in a manner specified in the regulations;

(e) describe factors which the CMA may or must take into account, or may not take into account, in deciding whether to approve a redress scheme.

(9) The CMA must publish guidance with regard to—

(a) applications for approval of redress schemes,

(b) the approval of redress schemes, and

(c) the enforcement of approved schemes, and in particular as to the criteria which the CMA intends to adopt in deciding whether to bring proceedings under section 49E(4).

(10) Guidance under subsection (9) must be approved by the Secretary of State before it is published.

(11) In this section and sections 49D and 49E—

"approved scheme" means a redress scheme approved by the CMA,

"compensating party" means a person offering compensation under an approved scheme,

["infringement decision" means a decision of the CMA that the Chapter I prohibition or the Chapter II prohibition has been infringed,] and

"redress scheme" means a scheme under which a person offers compensation in consequence of an infringement decision made in respect of that person.

(12) For the purposes of this section and section 49E, "compensation"—

(a) may be monetary or non-monetary, and

(b) may be offered to persons who have not suffered a loss as a result of the infringement decision to which the redress scheme relates.]

NOTES

Inserted, together with ss 49D, 49E, by the Consumer Rights Act 2015, s 80, Sch 8, Pt 1, paras 1, 12.

Sub-s (11): the definition "infringement decision" (excluding the word "and" at the end) was substituted by the Competition (Amendment etc) (EU Exit) Regulations 2019, SI 2019/93, regs 2, 17, as from IP completion day (as defined in the European Union (Withdrawal Agreement) Act 2020, s 39) (for transitional provisions and savings in relation to the operation of the 2019 Regulations, see Sch 4 to those Regulations at **[7.69]** et seq). The original definition read as follows—

""infringement decision" means—

(a) a decision of the CMA that the Chapter I prohibition, the Chapter II prohibition, the prohibition in Article 101(1) or the prohibition in Article 102 has been infringed, or
(b) decision of the Commission that the prohibition in Article 101(1) or the prohibition in Article 102 has been infringed,".

Regulations: the Competition Act 1998 (Redress Scheme) Regulations 2015, SI 2015/1587 at **[2.66]**.

[1.98]

[49D Redress schemes: recovery of costs

(1) The CMA may require a person making an application for approval of a redress scheme to pay some or all of the CMA's reasonable costs relating to the application.
(2) A requirement to pay costs is imposed by giving that person written notice specifying—
(a) the amount to be paid,
(b) how that amount has been calculated, and
(c) by when that amount must be paid.
(3) A person required to pay costs under this section may appeal to the Tribunal against the amount.
(4) Where costs required to be paid under this section relate to an approved scheme, the CMA may withdraw approval from that scheme if the costs have not been paid by the date specified in accordance with subsection (2)(c).
(5) Costs required to be paid under this section are recoverable by the CMA as a debt.]

NOTES

Inserted as noted to s 49C at **[1.97]**.

[1.99]

[49E Enforcement of approved schemes

(1) A compensating party is under a duty to comply with the terms of an approved scheme ("the duty").
(2) The duty is owed to any person entitled to compensation under the terms of the approved scheme.
(3) Where such a person suffers loss or damage as a result of a breach of the duty, the person may bring civil proceedings before the court for damages, an injunction or interdict or any other appropriate relief or remedy.
(4) Where the CMA considers that the compensating party is in breach of the duty, the CMA may bring civil proceedings before the court for an injunction or interdict or any other appropriate relief or remedy.
(5) Subsection (4) is without prejudice to any right that a person has to bring proceedings under subsection (3).
(6) In any proceedings brought under subsection (3) or (4), it is a defence for the compensating party to show that it took all reasonable steps to comply with the duty.
(7) Where the CMA considers that it is no longer appropriate for the compensating party to be subject to the duty, the CMA may give notice in writing to that party stating that it is released from the duty.
(8) Where a person has entered into a settlement agreement with the compensating party, that agreement remains enforceable notwithstanding the release of the compensating party under subsection (7) from the duty.
(9) In this section "the court" means—
(a) in England and Wales, the High Court or the county court,
(b) in Northern Ireland, the High Court or a county court,
(c) in Scotland, the Court of Session or the sheriff.]

NOTES

Inserted as noted to s 49C at **[1.97]**.

CHAPTER V MISCELLANEOUS

Vertical agreements and land agreements

[1.100]

50 Vertical agreements and land agreements

(1) The Secretary of State may by order provide for any provision of this Part to apply in relation to—
(a) vertical agreements, or
(b) land agreements,
with such modifications as may be prescribed.
(2) An order may, in particular, provide for exclusions or exemptions, or otherwise provide for prescribed provisions not to apply, in relation to—
(a) vertical agreements, or land agreements, in general; or
(b) vertical agreements, or land agreements, of any prescribed description.
(3) An order may empower the [CMA] to give directions to the effect that in prescribed circumstances an exclusion, exemption or modification is not to apply (or is to apply in a particular way) in relation to an individual agreement.
(4) Subsections (2) and (3) are not to be read as limiting the powers conferred by section 71.
(5) In this section—
"land agreement" and "vertical agreement" have such meaning as may be prescribed; and
"prescribed" means prescribed by an order.

NOTES

Sub-s (3): reference to the "CMA" substituted by the Enterprise and Regulatory Reform Act 2013, s 26(3), Sch 5, Pt 1, paras 1, 29. For various transitional provisions (including those relating to the abolition of the OFT and the Competition Commission, existing references to those bodies and provisions relating to continuity), see the Enterprise and Regulatory Reform Act 2013 (Commencement No 6, Transitional Provisions and Savings) Order 2014, SI 2014/416, Schedule at **[2.13]**.

Orders: the Competition Act 1998 (Land Agreements Exclusion Revocation) Order 2010, SI 2010/1709 at **[2.77]**.

[CMA's] rules, guidance and fees

[1.101]

51 Rules

(1) The [CMA] may make such rules about procedural and other matters in connection with the carrying into effect of the provisions of this Part as [it] considers appropriate.

(2) Schedule 9 makes further provision about rules made under this section but is not to be taken as restricting the [CMA's] powers under this section.

(3) If the [CMA] is preparing rules under this section [it] must consult such persons as [it] considers appropriate.

(4) If the proposed rules relate to a matter in respect of which a regulator exercises concurrent jurisdiction, those consulted must include that regulator.

(5) No rule made by the [CMA] is to come into operation until it has been approved by an order made by the Secretary of State.

(6) The Secretary of State may approve any rule made by the [CMA]—

(a) in the form in which it is submitted; or

(b) subject to such modifications as he considers appropriate.

(7) If the Secretary of State proposes to approve a rule subject to modifications he must inform the [CMA] of the proposed modifications and take into account any comments made by the [CMA].

(8) Subsections (5) to (7) apply also to any alteration of the rules made by the [CMA].

(9) The Secretary of State may, after consulting the [CMA], by order vary or revoke any rules made under this section.

(10) If the Secretary of State considers that rules should be made under this section with respect to a particular matter he may direct the [CMA] to exercise [its] powers under this section and make rules about that matter.

NOTES

In this section and in the preceding heading, the references to "CMA" and "CMA's" were substituted by the Enterprise and Regulatory Reform Act 2013, s 26(3), Sch 5, Pt 1, paras 1, 30, 31. For various transitional provisions (including those relating to the abolition of the OFT and the Competition Commission, existing references to those bodies and provisions relating to continuity), see the Enterprise and Regulatory Reform Act 2013 (Commencement No 6, Transitional Provisions and Savings) Order 2014, SI 2014/416, Schedule at **[2.13]**.

The words "it" and "its" in square brackets (in every place that they occur) were substituted by the Enterprise Act 2002, s 278, Sch 25, para 38.

Rules: the Competition Act 1998 (Competition and Markets Authority's Rules) Order 2014, SI 2014/458 at **[2.14]**.

[1.102]

52 Advice and information

(1) [The CMA] must prepare and publish general advice and information about—

(a) the application of the Chapter I prohibition and the Chapter II prohibition, and

(b) the enforcement of those prohibitions.

[(1A) [The CMA] must prepare and publish general advice and information about—

(a) the application of the prohibitions in [Article 101(1) and Article 102]; and

(b) the enforcement by it of those prohibitions.]

(2) The [CMA] may at any time publish revised, or new, advice or information.

(3) Advice and information published under this section must be prepared with a view to—

(a) explaining provisions of this Part to persons who are likely to be affected by them; and

(b) indicating how the [CMA] expects such provisions to operate.

(4) Advice (or information) published by virtue of subsection (3)(b) may include advice (or information) about the factors which the [CMA] may take into account in considering whether, and if so how, to exercise a power conferred on [it] by Chapter I, II or III.

(5) Any advice or information published by the [CMA] under this section is to be published in such form and in such manner as [it] considers appropriate.

(6) If the [CMA] is preparing any advice or information under this section [it] must consult such persons as [it] considers appropriate.

(7) If the proposed advice or information relates to a matter in respect of which a regulator exercises concurrent jurisdiction, those consulted must include that regulator.

(8) In preparing any advice or information under this section about a matter in respect of which he may exercise functions under this Part, a regulator must consult—

(a) the [CMA];

(b) the other regulators; and

(c) such other persons as he considers appropriate.

NOTES

The references to the "CMA" were substituted by the Enterprise and Regulatory Reform Act 2013, s 26(3), Sch 5, Pt 1, paras 1, 32(1), (4). For various transitional provisions (including those relating to the abolition of the OFT and the Competition Commission, existing references to those bodies and provisions relating to continuity), see the Enterprise and Regulatory Reform Act 2013 (Commencement No 6, Transitional Provisions and Savings) Order 2014, SI 2014/416, Schedule at **[2.13]**. This section is also amended as follows:

Sub-s (1): words in square brackets substituted by the Enterprise and Regulatory Reform Act 2013, s 26(3), Sch 5, Pt 1, paras 1, 32(1), (2), subject to transitional provisions in SI 2014/416 as noted above.

Sub-s (1A): inserted by the Competition Act 1998 and Other Enactments (Amendment) Regulations 2004, SI 2004/1261, reg 4, Sch 1, para 31. Words in first pair of square brackets substituted by the Enterprise and Regulatory Reform Act 2013, s 26(3), Sch 5, Pt 1, paras 1, 32(1), (3), subject to transitional provisions in SI 2014/416 as noted above. Words in second pair of square brackets substituted by the Treaty of Lisbon (Changes in Terminology or Numbering) Order 2012, SI 2012/1809, art 3(1), Schedule, Pt 1. This subsection was repealed by the Competition (Amendment etc) (EU Exit) Regulations 2019, SI

2019/93, regs 2, 18, as from IP completion day (as defined in the European Union (Withdrawal Agreement) Act 2020, s 39) (for transitional provisions and savings in relation to the operation of the 2019 Regulations, see Sch 4 to those Regulations at **[7.69]** et seq).

Sub-s (4)–(6): word "it" in square brackets (in each place that it occurs) substituted by the Enterprise Act 2002, s 278, Sch 25, para 38.

---

53 *(Repealed by the Competition Act 1998 and Other Enactments (Amendment) Regulations 2004, SI 2004/1261, reg 4, Sch 1, para 32.)*

Regulators

[1.103]

54 Regulators

(1) In this Part "regulator" means[—

[(a) the Office of Communications;]

(b) the Gas and Electricity Markets Authority;

(c) . . .

[(d) the Water Services Regulation Authority;]

(e) [the Office of Rail and Road];

[(f) the Northern Ireland Authority for Utility Regulation;]

(g) the Civil Aviation Authority][; . . .

(h) Monitor];

[(i) the Payment Systems Regulator established under section 40 of the Financial Services (Banking Reform) Act 2013;]

[(j) the Financial Conduct Authority].

(2) Parts II and III of Schedule 10 provide for functions of the [CMA] under this Part to be exercisable concurrently by regulators.

(3) Parts IV and V of Schedule 10 make minor and consequential amendments in connection with the regulators' competition functions.

(4) The Secretary of State may make regulations for the purpose of co-ordinating the performance of functions under this Part ("Part I functions") which are exercisable concurrently by two or more competent persons as a result of [any enactment (including any subordinate legislation) whenever passed or made].

(5) The regulations may, in particular, make provision—

(a) as to the procedure to be followed by competent persons when determining who is to exercise Part I functions in a particular case;

(b) as to the steps which must be taken before a competent person exercises, in a particular case, such Part I functions as may be prescribed;

(c) as to the procedure for determining, in a particular case, questions arising as to which competent person is to exercise Part I functions in respect of the case;

(d) for Part I functions in a particular case to be exercised jointly—

(i) by the [CMA] and one or more regulators, or

(ii) by two or more regulators,

and as to the procedure to be followed in such cases;

(e) as to the circumstances in which the exercise by a competent person of such Part I functions as may be prescribed is to preclude the exercise of such functions by another such person;

(f) for cases in respect of which Part I functions are being, or have been, exercised by a competent person to be transferred to another such person;

(g) for the person ("A") exercising Part I functions in a particular case—

(i) to appoint another competent person ("B") to exercise Part I functions on A's behalf in relation to the case; or

(ii) to appoint officers of B (with B's consent) to act as officers of A in relation to the case;

(h) for notification as to who is exercising Part I functions in respect of a particular case.

(6) Provision made by virtue of subsection (5)(c) may[—

(a) prescribe circumstances in which the CMA may decide that, in a particular case, it is to exercise Part 1 functions in respect of the case rather than a regulator;

(b)] provide for questions to be referred to and determined by the Secretary of State[, the CMA] or by such other person as may be prescribed.

[(6A) Where the regulations make provision as mentioned in subsection (6)(a), they must—

(a) include provision requiring the CMA to consult the regulator concerned before making a decision that the CMA is to exercise Part 1 functions in respect of a particular case, and

(b) provide that, in a case where a regulator has given notice under section 31(1) that it proposes to make a decision (within the meaning given by section 31(2)), the CMA may only decide that it is to exercise Part 1 functions in respect of the case rather than the regulator if the regulator consents.]

[(6B) The Secretary of State may by regulations make provision requiring arrangements to be made for the sharing of information between competent persons in connection with concurrent cases.

(6C) For the purposes of subsection (6B), "a concurrent case" is a case in respect of which—

(a) the CMA considers that Part 1 functions are, or (but for provision made under subsection (5)(e)) would be, exercisable by both it and any regulator;

(b) any regulator considers that Part 1 functions are, or (but for provision made under subsection (5)(e)) would be, exercisable by it.]

(7) "Competent person" means the [CMA] or any of the regulators.

[(8) In this section, "subordinate legislation" has the same meaning as in section 21(1) of the Interpretation Act 1978 (c 30) and includes an instrument made under—

(a) an Act of the Scottish Parliament;
(b) Northern Ireland legislation.]

NOTES

Sub-s (1) is amended as follows:

Paras (a)–(g) substituted by the Enterprise Act 2002, s 278(1), Sch 25, para 38(41)(a).

Para (a) further substituted by the Communications Act 2003, s 371(5)(a).

Para (c) repealed by the Enterprise and Regulatory Reform Act 2013, s 57, Sch 15, paras 8, 11(a). For various transitional provisions (including those relating to the abolition of the OFT and the Competition Commission, existing references to those bodies and provisions relating to continuity), see the Enterprise and Regulatory Reform Act 2013 (Commencement No 6, Transitional Provisions and Savings) Order 2014, SI 2014/416, Schedule at **[2.13]**.

Pare (d) further substituted by the Water Act 2003, s 101(1), Sch 7, Pt 2, para 32(1), (2).

Words in square brackets in para (e) substituted by the Office of Rail Regulation (Change of Name) Regulations 2015, SI 2015/1682, reg 2(2), Schedule, Pt 1, para 4(m).

Para (f) substituted by the Enterprise and Regulatory Reform Act 2013, s 57, Sch 15, paras 8, 11(b), subject to transitional provisions in SI 2014/416 as noted above.

Word omitted from para (g) repealed by the Financial Services (Banking Reform) Act 2013, ss 67(2).

Para (h) (and the preceding word) added, by the Health and Social Care Act 2012, s 74(5).

Paras (i), (j) added by the Financial Services (Banking Reform) Act 2013, ss 67(2), 129, Sch 8, Pt 2, para 9.

Sub-ss (2), (5), (7): references to the "CMA" substituted by the Enterprise and Regulatory Reform Act 2013, s 26(3), Sch 5, Pt 1, paras 1, 33, subject to transitional provisions in SI 2014/416 as noted above.

Sub-s (4): words in square brackets substituted by the Competition Act 1998 and Other Enactments (Amendment) Regulations 2004, SI 2004/1261, reg 4, Sch 1, para 33(1), (2).

Sub-s (6): words in square brackets inserted by the Enterprise and Regulatory Reform Act 2013, s 51(1), (2).

Sub-ss (6A)–(6C): inserted by the Enterprise and Regulatory Reform Act 2013, s 51(1), (3), (4).

Sub-s (8): added by SI 2004/1261, reg 4, Sch 1, para 33(1), (3).

Regulations: the Competition Act 1998 (Concurrency) Regulations 2014, SI 2014/536 at **[2.47]**.

Confidentiality and immunity from defamation

55, 56 *(Repealed by the Enterprise Act 2002, ss 247(j), 278(2), Sch 26.)*

[1.104]

57 Defamation

For the purposes of the law relating to defamation, absolute privilege attaches to any advice, guidance, notice or direction given, or decision made, by the [CMA] in the exercise of any of [its] functions under this Part.

NOTES

Reference to the "CMA" substituted by the Enterprise and Regulatory Reform Act 2013, s 26(3), Sch 5, Pt 1, paras 1, 34. For various transitional provisions (including those relating to the abolition of the OFT and the Competition Commission, existing references to those bodies and provisions relating to continuity), see the Enterprise and Regulatory Reform Act 2013 (Commencement No 6, Transitional Provisions and Savings) Order 2014, SI 2014/416, Schedule at **[2.13]**.

Word "its" in square brackets substituted by the Enterprise Act 2002, s 278, Sch 25, para 38.

Findings of fact by [CMA]

[1.105]

58 Findings of fact by [CMA]

(1) Unless the court [or the Tribunal] directs . . . , [a CMA's] finding which is relevant to an issue arising in Part I proceedings is binding on the parties if—

(a) the time for bringing an appeal [under section 46 or 47] in respect of the finding has expired and the relevant party has not brought such an appeal; or
(b) the decision of [the Tribunal] on such an appeal has confirmed the finding.

(2) In this section—

["[a CMA's] finding" means a finding of fact made by the [CMA] in the course of conducting an investigation;]

["Part I proceedings" means proceedings brought otherwise than by the [CMA]—

[(za) in respect of an infringement decision; [or]]
(a) in respect of an alleged infringement of the Chapter I prohibition or of the Chapter II prohibition; *or*
(b) in respect of an alleged infringement of the prohibitions in [Article 101(1) or Article 102];]

"relevant party" means—

(a) in relation to the Chapter I prohibition [*or the prohibition in [Article 101(1)]*], a party to the agreement which [has been found to have infringed the prohibition or is alleged to have infringed the prohibition (as the case may be)]; and
(b) in relation to the Chapter II prohibition [*or the prohibition in [Article 102]*], the undertaking whose conduct [has been found to have infringed the prohibition or is alleged to have infringed the prohibition (as the case may be)].

(3) Rules of court [or Tribunal rules] may make provision in respect of assistance to be given by the [CMA] to the court [or the Tribunal] in Part I proceedings.

[(4) In this section "the court" means—

(a) in England and Wales or Northern Ireland, the High Court,
(b) in Scotland, the Court of Session or the sheriff.]

NOTES

In the section heading, the preceding cross-heading and sub-s (3), the references to the "CMA" were substituted by the Enterprise and Regulatory Reform Act 2013, s 26(3), Sch 5, Pt 1, paras 1, 35, 36(1), (4), (5). For various transitional provisions (including those relating to the abolition of the OFT and the Competition Commission, existing references to those bodies and provisions relating to continuity), see the Enterprise and Regulatory Reform Act 2013 (Commencement No 6, Transitional Provisions and Savings) Order 2014, SI 2014/416, Schedule at **[2.13]**. This section is also amended as follows:

Sub-s (1): words in first pair of square brackets inserted by the Consumer Rights Act 2015, s 80, Sch 8, Pt 1, paras 1, 13(1), (2). Words omitted repealed by the Competition Act 1998 and Other Enactments (Amendment) Regulations 2004, SI 2004/1261, reg 4, Sch 1, para 34(1), (2). Words in second pair of square brackets substituted by the Enterprise and Regulatory Reform Act 2013, s 26(3), Sch 5, Pt 1, paras 1, 36(1), (2), subject to transitional provisions in SI 2014/416 as noted above. Words in third pair of square brackets inserted, and words in fourth pair of square brackets substituted, by the Enterprise Act 2002, ss 21, 27, 83(1), Sch 5, paras 1, 5, Sch 25, para 38(1), (43)(b).

Sub-s (2) is amended as follows:

References to "a CMA's" and "CMA" substituted by the Enterprise and Regulatory Reform Act 2013, s 26(3), Sch 5, Pt 1, paras 1, 36(1), (3), subject to transitional provisions in SI 2014/416 as noted above.

Definitions "a CMA's finding" and "Part I proceedings" substituted, and words in first (outer) and third (outer) pairs of square brackets in the definition "relevant party" inserted, by SI 2004/1261, reg 4, Sch 1, para 34(1), (3).

The words "Article 101(1) or Article 102" in square brackets in the definition "Part I proceedings", and the words "Article 101(1)" and "Article 102" in square brackets in the definition "relevant party" were substituted by the Treaty of Lisbon (Changes in Terminology or Numbering) Order 2012, SI 2012/1809, art 3(1), Schedule, Pt 1.

In the definition "Part I proceedings" para (za) was inserted, and in the definition "relevant party" the final words in square brackets in paras (a), (b) were inserted, by the Consumer Rights Act 2015, s 80, Sch 8, Pt 1, paras 1, 13(1), (3).

The word "or" in square brackets in para (za) of the definition "Part I proceedings" was inserted, para (b) of that definition and the word "or" in italics immediately preceding it were repealed, and the words in italics in the definition "relevant party" were repealed, by the Competition (Amendment etc) (EU Exit) Regulations 2019, SI 2019/93, regs 2, 19, as from IP completion day (as defined in the European Union (Withdrawal Agreement) Act 2020, s 39) (for transitional provisions and savings in relation to the operation of the 2019 Regulations, see Sch 4 to those Regulations at **[7.69]** et seq).

Sub-s (3): words in first and third pairs of square brackets inserted by the Consumer Rights Act 2015, s 80, Sch 8, Pt 1, paras 1, 13(1), (4).

Sub-s (4): added by the Consumer Rights Act 2015, s 80, Sch 8, Pt 1, paras 1, 13(1), (5).

[Findings of infringements

[1.106]

[58A Infringement decisions

(1) This section applies to a claim in respect of an infringement decision which is brought in proceedings—
  (a) before the court, or
  (b) before the Tribunal under section 47A or 47B.

(2) The court or the Tribunal is bound by the infringement decision once it has become final.

(3) An infringement decision specified in section 47A(6)(a) or (b) becomes final—
  (a) when the time for appealing against that decision expires without an appeal having been brought; [or
  (b) where an appeal has been brought against the decision, when—
    (i) the appeal and any further appeal in relation to the decision has been decided or has otherwise ended, and
    (ii) the time for appealing against the result of the appeal or further appeal has expired without another appeal having been brought.]

(4) An infringement decision specified in section 47A(6)(c) becomes final—
  (a) when the time for appealing against that decision in the European Court expires without an appeal having been brought; or
  [(b) where such an appeal has been brought against the decision, when—
    (i) the appeal and any further appeal in the European Court in relation to the decision has been decided or has otherwise ended, and
    (ii) the time for appealing against the result of the appeal or further appeal in the European Court has expired without another appeal having been brought.]

(5) This section applies to the extent that the court or the Tribunal would not otherwise be bound by the infringement decision in question.

(6) In this section "the court" means—
  (a) in England and Wales or Northern Ireland, the High Court,
  (b) in Scotland, the Court of Session or the sheriff.]

NOTES

Inserted, together with the preceding heading, by the Enterprise Act 2002, s 20(1).

Substituted by the Consumer Rights Act 2015, s 80, Sch 8, Pt 1, paras 1, 14, except in relation to decisions made before 1 October 2015.

Sub-s (3): para (b) (and the preceding word) were substituted (for the original paras (b)–(d)) by the Claims in respect of Loss or Damage arising from Competition Infringements (Competition Act 1998 and Other Enactments (Amendment)) Regulations 2017, SI 2017/385, reg 3, Sch 2 paras 1, 8(1), (2), (4). Note that this amendment applies only in relation to a claim in respect of an infringement decision in relation to which the first proceedings before a court or the Tribunal began on or after 9 March 2017.

Sub-s (4): repealed by the Competition (Amendment etc) (EU Exit) Regulations 2019, SI 2019/93, regs 2, 20, as from IP completion day (as defined in the European Union (Withdrawal Agreement) Act 2020, s 39) (for transitional provisions and savings in relation to the operation of the 2019 Regulations, see Sch 4 to those Regulations at **[7.69]** et seq). Para (b) was previously substituted by SI 2017/385, reg 3, Sch 2 paras 1, 8(1), (3), (4) (note that this amendment applies only in relation to a claim in respect of an infringement decision in relation to which the first proceedings before a court or the Tribunal began on or after 9 March 2017).

Interpretation and governing principles

[1.107]

59 [Interpretation of Part 1]

(1) In this Part—

["agreement" is to be read with section 2(5) and (6);]

. . .

[*"Article 101(1)" means Article 101(1) of the Treaty;*
"Article 101(3)" means Article 101(3) of the Treaty;
"Article 102" means Article 102 of the Treaty;]
"block exemption" has the meaning given in section 6(4);
"block exemption order" has the meaning given in section 6(2);
"the Chapter I prohibition" has the meaning given in section 2(8);
"the Chapter II prohibition" has the meaning given in section 18(4);
["class member" has the meaning given in section 47B(8)(a);]
["the CMA" means the Competition and Markets Authority;]
["collective proceedings" has the meaning given in section 47B(1);]
["collective proceedings order" means an order made by the Tribunal authorising the continuance of collective proceedings;]
"the Commission" . . . means the European Commission;
"the Council" means the Council of the European Union;
"the court", except in sections [49E,] 58[, 58A] and [60A] [and Schedule 8A] and the expression "European Court", means—

(a) in England and Wales, the High Court;
(b) in Scotland, the Court of Session; and
(c) in Northern Ireland, the High Court;

. . .
"document" includes information recorded in any form;
"the EEA Agreement" means the Agreement on the European Economic Area signed at Oporto on 2nd May 1992 as it has effect for the time being;
"the European Court" means the Court of Justice of the European Communities and includes the [General Court];
[*"the EC Competition Regulation" means Council Regulation (EC) No 1/2003 of 16th December 2002 on the implementation of the rules on competition laid down in Articles 81 and 82 of the Treaty;*]
. . .
"information" includes estimates and forecasts;
["infringement decision", except in section 49C, has the meaning given in section 47A(6);]
["injunction" includes an interim injunction;]
"investigating officer" has the meaning given in section 27(1);
["investigation" means an investigation under section 25;]
"Minister of the Crown" has the same meaning as in the Ministers of the Crown Act 1975;
["OFCOM" means the Office of Communications;]
"officer", in relation to a body corporate, includes a director, manager or secretary and, in relation to a partnership in Scotland, includes a partner;
["opt-in collective proceedings" has the meaning given in section 47B(10);]
["opt-out collective proceedings" has the meaning given in section 47B(11);]
. . .
"parallel exemption" has the meaning given in section 10(3);
"person", in addition to the meaning given by the Interpretation Act 1978, includes any undertaking;
["premises" includes any land or means of transport;]
"prescribed" means prescribed by regulations made by the Secretary of State;
"regulator" has the meaning given by section 54;
["representative" means a person who is authorised by a collective proceedings order to bring collective proceedings;]
["represented person" means a class member who—

(a) has opted in to opt-in collective proceedings,
(b) was domiciled in the United Kingdom at the time specified for the purposes of determining domicile (see section 47B(11)(b)(i)) and has not opted out of opt-out collective proceedings, or
(c) has opted in to opt-out collective proceedings;]

["retained block exemption regulation" has the meaning given in section 10(12);]
["retained exemption" has the meaning given in section 10(3);]
"section 11 exemption" has the meaning given in section 11(3); and
[*"the Treaty" means the treaty on the Functioning of the European Union;*]
["the Tribunal" means the Competition Appeal Tribunal;
"Tribunal rules" means rules under section 15 of the Enterprise Act 2002];
["working day" means a day which is not—

(a) Saturday,
(b) Sunday,
(c) Christmas Day,
(d) Good Friday, or
(e) a day which is a bank holiday under the Banking and Financial Dealings Act 1971 (c 80) in any part of the United Kingdom].

[(1A) In this Part, in respect of proceedings in Scotland, ["claimant" is to be read as "pursuer" and] "defendant" is to be read as "defender".

(1B) Sections 41, 42, 45 and 46 of the Civil Jurisdiction and Judgments Act 1982 apply for the purpose of determining whether a person is regarded as "domiciled in the United Kingdom" for the purposes of this Part.]

(2) The fact that to a limited extent the Chapter I prohibition does not apply to an agreement, because of an exclusion provided by or under this Part or any other enactment, does not require those provisions of the agreement to which the exclusion relates to be disregarded when considering whether the agreement infringes the prohibition for other reasons.

(3) For the purposes of this Part, the power to require information, in relation to information recorded otherwise than in a legible form, includes power to require a copy of it in a legible form.

(4) Any power conferred on the [CMA] by this Part to require information includes power to require any document which [it] believes may contain that information.

NOTES

Section heading: substituted by the Competition Act 1998 and other enactments (Amendment) Regulations 2004, SI 2004/1261, reg 4, Sch 1, para 35(1), (3).

Sub-s (1) is amended as follows:

Definition "agreement" inserted by SI 2004/1261, reg 4, Sch 1, para 35(1), (2)(a).

Definition "appeal tribunal" (omitted) repealed by the Enterprise Act 2002, ss 21, 278(2), Sch 5, paras 1, 6(a), Sch 26.

Definitions "Article 101(1)", "Article 101(3)", "Article 102", and "the Treaty" substituted by the Treaty of Lisbon (Changes in Terminology or Numbering) Order 2012, SI 2012/1809, art 3(1), Schedule, Pt 1. These definitions were repealed by the Competition (Amendment etc) (EU Exit) Regulations 2019, SI 2019/93, regs 2, 21, as from IP completion day (as defined in the European Union (Withdrawal Agreement) Act 2020, s 39) (for transitional provisions and savings in relation to the operation of the 2019 Regulations, see Sch 4 to those Regulations at **[7.69]** et seq).

Definitions "class member", "collective proceedings", "collective proceedings order", "infringement decision", "injunction", "opt-in collective proceedings", "opt-out collective proceedings", "representative", and "represented person" inserted by the Consumer Rights Act 2015, s 80, Sch 8, Pt 1, paras 1, 15(1), (2).

Definition "the CMA" inserted by the Enterprise and Regulatory Reform Act 2013, s 26(3), Sch 5, Pt 1, paras 1, 38(1), (2)(a).

Words omitted from the definition "the Commission" repealed by the Enterprise and Regulatory Reform Act 2013, s 26(3), Sch 5, Pt 3, paras 218, 221. For various transitional provisions (including those relating to the abolition of the OFT and the Competition Commission, existing references to those bodies and provisions relating to continuity), see the Enterprise and Regulatory Reform Act 2013 (Commencement No 6, Transitional Provisions and Savings) Order 2014, SI 2014/416, Schedule at **[2.13]**. This definition was repealed by SI 2019/93, regs 2, 21, as from IP completion day (as defined in the European Union (Withdrawal Agreement) Act 2020, s 39) (for transitional provisions and savings in relation to the operation of the 2019 Regulations, see Sch 4 to those Regulations at **[7.69]** et seq).

Definitions "the Council", "the EEA Agreement", "parallel exemption", and "section 11 exemption" repealed by SI 2019/93, regs 2, 21, as from IP completion day (as defined in the European Union (Withdrawal Agreement) Act 2020, s 39) (for transitional provisions and savings in relation to the operation of the 2019 Regulations, see Sch 4 to those Regulations at **[7.69]** et seq).

First figure in square brackets in the definition "the court" inserted by the Consumer Rights Act 2015, s 80, Sch 8, Pt 1, paras 1, 15(1), (3). Second figure in square brackets in that definition inserted by the Enterprise Act 2002, s 20(3). The figure "60A" in square brackets was substituted (for the original figure "60") by SI 2019/93, regs 2, 21, as from IP completion day (as defined in the European Union (Withdrawal Agreement) Act 2020, s 39) (for transitional provisions and savings in relation to the operation of the 2019 Regulations, see Sch 4 to those Regulations at **[7.69]** et seq). Words "and Schedule 8A" in square brackets inserted by the Claims in respect of Loss or Damage arising from Competition Infringements (Competition Act 1998 and Other Enactments (Amendment)) Regulations 2017, SI 2017/385, reg 3, Sch 2 paras 1, 9(1), (2).

Definition "the Director" (omitted) repealed by the Enterprise Act 2002, s 278, Sch 25, para 38(1), (44)(a), Sch 26.

Words in square brackets in the definition "the European Court" substituted by SI 2012/1809, art 3(1), Schedule, Pt 1. This definition was repealed by SI 2019/93, regs 2, 21, as from IP completion day (as defined in the European Union (Withdrawal Agreement) Act 2020, s 39) (for transitional provisions and savings in relation to the operation of the 2019 Regulations, see Sch 4 to those Regulations at **[7.69]** et seq).

Definition "the EC Competition Regulation" inserted by SI 2004/1261, reg 4, Sch 1, para 35(1), (2)(d). This definition was repealed by SI 2019/93, regs 2, 21, as from IP completion day (as defined in the European Union (Withdrawal Agreement) Act 2020, s 39) (for transitional provisions and savings in relation to the operation of the 2019 Regulations, see Sch 4 to those Regulations at **[7.69]** et seq).

Definition "individual exemption" (omitted) repealed by SI 2004/1261, reg 4, Sch 1, para 35(1), (2)(e).

Definition "investigation" inserted by SI 2004/1261, reg 4, Sch 1, para 35(1), (2)(f).

Definition "OFCOM" inserted by the Communications Act 2003, s 371(7).

Definition "the OFT" (omitted) originally inserted by the Enterprise Act 2002, s 278(1), Sch 25, para 38(1), (44)(a), and subsequently repealed by the Enterprise and Regulatory Reform Act 2013, s 26(3), Sch 5, Pt 1, paras 1, 38(1), (2)(b), subject to transitional provisions in SI 2014/416 as noted above.

Definition "premises" substituted by SI 2004/1261, reg 4, Sch 1, para 35(1), (2)(g).

Definitions "retained block exemption regulation" and "retained exemption" inserted by SI 2019/93, regs 2, 21, as from IP completion day (as defined in the European Union (Withdrawal Agreement) Act 2020, s 39) (for transitional provisions and savings in relation to the operation of the 2019 Regulations, see Sch 4 to those Regulations at **[7.69]** et seq).

Definitions "the Tribunal" and "Tribunal rules" inserted by the Enterprise Act 2002, s 21, Sch 5, paras 1, 6(b).

Definition "working day" inserted by SI 2004/1261, reg 4, Sch 1, para 35(1), (2)(h).

Sub-ss (1A), (1B): inserted by the Consumer Rights Act 2015, s 80, Sch 8, Pt 1, paras 1, 15(1), (4). Words in square brackets in sub-s (1A) inserted by SI 2017/385, reg 3, Sch 2 paras 1, 9(1), (3).

Sub-s (4): reference to "CMA" substituted by the Enterprise and Regulatory Reform Act 2013, s 26(3), Sch 5, Pt 1, paras 1, 38(1), (3), subject to transitional provisions in SI 2014/416 as noted above; word "it" in square brackets substituted by the Enterprise Act 2002, s 278, Sch 25, para 38.

References to the European Community and related expressions: see the note "References to "the European Community", "Community", etc" in the introductory notes to this Act.

[1.108]
60 Principles to be applied in determining questions

(1) The purpose of this section is to ensure that so far as is possible (having regard to any relevant differences between the provisions concerned), questions arising under this Part in relation to competition within the United Kingdom are dealt with in a manner which is consistent with the treatment of corresponding questions arising in Community law in relation to competition within the Community.

(2) At any time when the court determines a question arising under this Part, it must act (so far as is compatible with the provisions of this Part and whether or not it would otherwise be required to do so) with a view to securing that there is no inconsistency between—

(a) the principles applied, and decision reached, by the court in determining that question; and

(b) the principles laid down by the Treaty and the European Court, and any relevant decision of that Court, as applicable at that time in determining any corresponding question arising in Community law.

(3) The court must, in addition, have regard to any relevant decision or statement of the Commission.

(4) Subsections (2) and (3) also apply to—

(a) the [CMA]; and

(b) any person acting on behalf of the [CMA], in connection with any matter arising under this Part.

(5) In subsections (2) and (3), "court" means any court or tribunal.

(6) In subsections (2)(b) and (3), "decision" includes a decision as to—

(a) the interpretation of any provision of Community law;

(b) the civil liability of an undertaking for harm caused by its infringement of Community law.

NOTES

This section was repealed by the Competition (Amendment etc) (EU Exit) Regulations 2019, SI 2019/93, regs 2, 22, as from IP completion day (as defined in the European Union (Withdrawal Agreement) Act 2020, s 39) (for transitional provisions and savings in relation to the operation of the 2019 Regulations, see Sch 4 to those Regulations at **[7.69]** et seq).

Sub-s (4): references to "CMA" substituted by the Enterprise and Regulatory Reform Act 2013, s 26(3), Sch 5, Pt 1, paras 1, 39. For various transitional provisions (including those relating to the abolition of the OFT and the Competition Commission, existing references to those bodies and provisions relating to continuity), see the Enterprise and Regulatory Reform Act 2013 (Commencement No 6, Transitional Provisions and Savings) Order 2014, SI 2014/416, Schedule at **[2.13]**.

References to the European Community and related expressions: see the note "References to "the European Community", "Community", etc" in the introductory notes to this Act.

[1.109]
[60A Certain principles etc to be considered or applied from IP completion day

(1) This section applies when one of the following persons determines a question arising under this Part in relation to competition within the United Kingdom—

(a) a court or tribunal;

(b) the CMA;

(c) a person acting on behalf of the CMA in connection with a matter arising under this Part.

(2) The person must act (so far as is compatible with the provisions of this Part) with a view to securing that there is no inconsistency between—

(a) the principles that it applies, and the decision that it reaches, in determining the question, and

(b) the principles laid down by the Treaty on the Functioning of the European Union and the European Court before IP completion day, and any relevant decision made by that Court before IP completion day, so far as applicable immediately before IP completion day in determining any corresponding question arising in EU law,

subject to subsections (4) to (7).

(3) The person must, in addition, have regard to any relevant decision or statement of the European Commission made before IP completion day and not withdrawn.

(4) Subsection (2) does not require the person to secure that there is no inconsistency with a principle or decision referred to in subsection (2)(b) so far as the principle or decision is excluded from the law of England and Wales, Scotland and Northern Ireland on or after IP completion day.

(5) For the purposes of subsection (4), a principle or decision is to be treated as not excluded from the law of England and Wales, Scotland and Northern Ireland if it is excluded only by virtue of an exclusion or revocation in the Competition (Amendment etc) (EU Exit) Regulations 2019.

(6) Subsection (2) does not apply so far as the person is bound by a principle laid down by, or a decision of, a court or tribunal in England and Wales, Scotland or Northern Ireland that requires the person to act otherwise.

(7) Subsection (2) does not apply if the person thinks that it is appropriate to act otherwise in the light of one or more of the following—

(a) differences between the provisions of this Part under consideration and the corresponding provisions of EU law as those provisions of EU law had effect immediately before IP completion day;

(b) differences between markets in the United Kingdom and markets in the European Union;

(c) developments in forms of economic activity since the time when the principle or decision referred to in subsection (2)(b) was laid down or made;

(d) generally accepted principles of competition analysis or the generally accepted application of such principles;

(e) a principle laid down, or decision made, by the European Court on or after IP completion day;

(f) the particular circumstances under consideration.

(8) In subsection (2)(b), the reference to principles laid down before IP completion day is a reference to such principles as they have effect in EU law immediately before IP completion day, disregarding the effect of principles laid down, and decisions made, by the European Court on or after IP completion day.

(9) In this section, references to a decision of the European Court or the European Commission include a decision as to—

(a) the interpretation of a provision of EU law;

(b) the civil liability of an undertaking for harm caused by its infringement of EU law.]

NOTES

Commencement: IP completion day (as defined in the European Union (Withdrawal Agreement) Act 2020, s 39).

This section was inserted by the Competition (Amendment etc) (EU Exit) Regulations 2019, SI 2019/93, regs 2, 23, as from IP completion day (as defined in the European Union (Withdrawal Agreement) Act 2020, s 39) (for transitional provisions and savings in relation to the operation of the 2019 Regulations, see Sch 4 to those Regulations at **[7.69]** et seq). Note that reg 23 of the 2019 Regulations was amended by the Competition (Amendment etc) (EU Exit) Regulations 2020, SI 2020/1343, reg 5, with effect from immediately before IP completion day; and the effect of the amendments has been incorporated in the text set out above.

[PART 2 INSPECTIONS UNDER ARTICLES 20, 21 AND 22(2)

[1.110]

61 Interpretation of Part 2

In this Part—

"Article 20 inspection" means an inspection ordered by a decision of the Commission under Article 20(4) of the EC Competition Regulation which is not an Article 22(2) inspection;

"Article 21 inspection" means an inspection ordered by a decision of the Commission under Article 21 of the EC Competition Regulation;

"Article 22(2) inspection" means an inspection requested by the Commission under Article 22(2) of the EC Competition Regulation;

"books and records" includes books and records stored on any medium;

["the CMA" means the Competition and Markets Authority;]

"the Commission" means the European Commission;

"the EC Competition Regulation" means Council Regulation (EC) No 1/2003 of 16th December 2002 on the implementation of the rules on competition laid down in Articles 81 and 82 of the Treaty;

. . .

"premises" includes any land or means of transport;

["the Treaty" means the treaty on the Functioning of the European Union];

["the Tribunal" means the Competition Appeal Tribunal;

"Tribunal rules" means rules under section 15 of the Enterprise Act 2002].]

NOTES

This section, and the preceding Part heading, were substituted by the Competition Act 1998 and other enactments (Amendment) Regulations 2004, SI 2004/1261, reg 4, Sch 1, para 36.

Part 2 (ss 61–65B) was repealed by the Competition (Amendment etc) (EU Exit) Regulations 2019, SI 2019/93, regs 2, 24, as from IP completion day (as defined in the European Union (Withdrawal Agreement) Act 2020, s 39) (for transitional provisions and savings in relation to the operation of the 2019 Regulations, see Sch 4 to those Regulations at **[7.69]** et seq and, in particular, Sch 4, Pt 4 to the 2019 Regulations at **[7.72]**).

Definition "the CMA" inserted, and definition "the OFT" (omitted) repealed, by the Enterprise and Regulatory Reform Act 2013, s 26(3), Sch 5, Pt 1, paras 1, 40. For various transitional provisions (including those relating to the abolition of the OFT and the Competition Commission, existing references to those bodies and provisions relating to continuity), see the Enterprise and Regulatory Reform Act 2013 (Commencement No 6, Transitional Provisions and Savings) Order 2014, SI 2014/416, Schedule at **[2.13]**.

Definition "the Treaty" substituted by the Treaty of Lisbon (Changes in Terminology or Numbering) Order 2012, SI 2012/1809, art 3(1), Schedule, Pt 1.

Definitions "the Tribunal" and "Tribunal rules" inserted by the Enterprise and Regulatory Reform Act 2013, s 41, Sch 13, paras 1, 4, subject to transitional provisions in SI 2014/416 as noted above.

[1.111]

62 [Power to enter business premises under a warrant: Article 20 inspections]

(1) [On an application made to it by the CMA, the High Court or the Tribunal must issue a warrant if it is satisfied that]—

[(a) the Commission has ordered an Article 20 inspection;

(b) the Article 20 inspection is being, or is likely to be, obstructed; and

(c) the measures that would be authorised by the warrant are neither arbitrary nor excessive having regard to the subject matter of the Article 20 inspection].

(2) [An Article 20 inspection] is being obstructed if—

(a) [a Commission official], exercising his power in accordance with [Article 20(3) of the EC Competition Regulation], has attempted to enter [any business premises] but has been unable to do so; and

(b) there are reasonable grounds for suspecting that there are [on any business premises] books or records . . . which the Commission official has power to examine.

(3) [An Article 20 inspection] is also being obstructed if there are reasonable grounds for suspecting that there are [on any business premises] books or records . . . —

(a) the production of which has been required by [a Commission official] exercising his power in accordance with [Article 20(3) of the EC Competition Regulation]; and

(b) which have not been produced as required.

(4) [An Article 20 inspection] is likely to be obstructed if—

(a) . . .

(b) there are reasonable grounds for suspecting that there are [on any business premises] books or records . . . which [a Commission official] has power to examine; and

(c) *there are also reasonable grounds for suspecting that, if the Commission official attempted to exercise his power to examine any of the books or records, they would not be produced but would be concealed, removed, tampered with or destroyed.*

[(5) A warrant under this section shall authorise a named officer of the [CMA] and any other [CMA] officer, or Commission official, accompanying the named officer—

(a) *to enter any business premises specified in the warrant using such force as is reasonably necessary for the purpose;*

(b) *to search for books and records which a Commission official has power to examine, using such force as is reasonably necessary for the purpose;*

(c) *to take or obtain copies of or extracts from such books and records;*

(d) *to seal the premises, any part of the premises or any books or records which a Commission official has power to seal, for the period and to the extent necessary for the inspection.]*

[(5A) A warrant under this section may authorise persons specified in the warrant to accompany the named officer who is executing it.]

(6) Any person entering any premises by virtue of a warrant under this section may take with him such equipment as appears to him to be necessary.

(7) On leaving any premises entered by virtue of the warrant the named officer must, if the premises are unoccupied or the occupier is temporarily absent, leave them as effectively secured as he found them.

(8) A warrant under this section continues in force until the end of the period of one month beginning with the day on which it is issued.

[(8A) An application for a warrant under this section must be made—

(a) *in the case of an application to the High Court, in accordance with rules of court;*

(b) *in the case of an application to the Tribunal, in accordance with Tribunal rules.]*

(9) In the application of this section to Scotland, references to the High Court are to be read as references to the Court of Session.

[(10) In this section—

"business premises" means any premises of an undertaking or association of undertakings which a Commission official has under Article 20 of the EC Competition Regulation power to enter in the course of the Article 20 inspection;

"Commission official" means any of the persons authorised by the Commission to conduct the Article 20 inspection; and

"[CMA] officer" means any officer of the [CMA] whom the [CMA] has authorised in writing to accompany the named officer.

(11) In subsection (10), the reference in the definition of "business premises" to Article 20 of the EC Competition Regulation does not include a reference to that Article as applied by Article 21 of that Regulation.]

NOTES

Part 2 (ss 61–65B) was repealed by the Competition (Amendment etc) (EU Exit) Regulations 2019, SI 2019/93, regs 2, 24, as from IP completion day (as defined in the European Union (Withdrawal Agreement) Act 2020, s 39) (for transitional provisions and savings in relation to the operation of the 2019 Regulations, see Sch 4 to those Regulations at **[7.69]** et seq and, in particular, Sch 4, Pt 4 to the 2019 Regulations at **[7.72]**).

Section heading: substituted by the Competition Act 1998 and other enactments (Amendment) Regulations 2004, SI 2004/1261, reg 4, Sch 1, para 37(1), (8).

Sub-s (1) is amended as follows:

Words in first pair of square brackets substituted by the Enterprise and Regulatory Reform Act 2013, s 41, Sch 13, paras 1, 5(1), (2). For various transitional provisions (including those relating to the abolition of the OFT and the Competition Commission, existing references to those bodies and provisions relating to continuity), see the Enterprise and Regulatory Reform Act 2013 (Commencement No 6, Transitional Provisions and Savings) Order 2014, SI 2014/416, Schedule at **[2.13]**.

Paras (a)–(c) substituted by SI 2004/1261, reg 4, Sch 1, para 37(1), (2)(b).

Sub-s (2): words in first, second, third and fourth pairs of square brackets substituted, words in fifth pair of square brackets inserted, and words omitted repealed, by SI 2004/1261, reg 4, Sch 1, para 37(1), (3).

Sub-s (3): words in first, third and fourth pairs of square brackets substituted, words in second pair of square brackets inserted, and words omitted repealed, by SI 2004/1261, reg 4, Sch 1, para 37(1), (4).

Sub-s (4): words in first and third pairs of square brackets substituted, para (a) and words omitted from para (b) repealed, and words in second pair of square brackets inserted, by SI 2004/1261, reg 4, Sch 1, para 37(1), (5).

Sub-s (5): substituted by SI 2004/1261, reg 4, Sch 1, para 37(1), (6). References to "CMA" substituted by the Enterprise and Regulatory Reform Act 2013, s 26(3), Sch 5, Pt 1, paras 1, 41, subject to transitional provisions in SI 2014/416 as noted above

Sub-s (5A): inserted by the Enterprise Act 2002, s 203(1), (3).

Sub-s (8A): inserted by the Enterprise and Regulatory Reform Act 2013, s 41, Sch 13, paras 1, 5(1), (3), subject to transitional provisions in SI 2014/416 as noted above.

Sub-ss (10), (11): added by SI 2004/1261, reg 4, Sch 1, para 37(1), (7). In sub-s (10), references to the "CMA" substituted by the Enterprise and Regulatory Reform Act 2013, s 26(3), Sch 5, Pt 1, paras 1, 41, subject to transitional provisions in SI 2014/416 as noted above.

[1.112]

[62A Power to enter non-business premises under a warrant: Article 21 inspections

(1) [On an application made to it by the CMA, the High Court or the Tribunal must issue a warrant if it is satisfied that]—

(a) *the Commission has ordered an Article 21 inspection; and*

(b) *the measures that would be authorised by the warrant are neither arbitrary nor excessive having regard in particular to the matters mentioned in subsection (2).*

(2) Those matters are—

(a) *the seriousness of the suspected infringement of [Article 101(1) or 102] of the Treaty;*

(b) the importance of the evidence sought;

(c) the involvement of the undertaking or association of undertakings concerned; and

(d) whether it is reasonably likely that business books and records relating to the subject matter of the Article 21 inspection are kept on the non-business premises that would be specified in the warrant.

(3) A warrant under this section shall authorise a named officer of the [CMA] and any other [CMA] officer, or Commission official, accompanying the named officer to enter any non-business premises specified in the warrant.

(4) A warrant under this section may authorise a named officer of the [CMA] and any other [CMA] officer, or Commission official, accompanying the named officer to search for books or records which a Commission official has power to examine.

(5) A warrant under this section may authorise a named officer of the [CMA] and any other [CMA] officer, or Commission official, accompanying the named officer to take or obtain copies of books or records of which a Commission official has power to take or obtain copies.

(6) A warrant granted under this section may authorise the use, for either or both of the purposes mentioned in subsections (3) and (4), of such force as is reasonably necessary.

(7) A warrant under this section may authorise persons specified in the warrant to accompany the named officer who is executing it.

(8) Any person entering any premises by virtue of a warrant under this section may take with him such equipment as appears to him to be necessary.

(9) On leaving any premises entered by virtue of a warrant the named officer must, if the premises are unoccupied or the occupier is temporarily absent, leave them as effectively secured as he found them.

(10) A warrant under this section continues in force until the end of the period of one month beginning with the day on which it is issued.

[(10A) An application for a warrant under this section must be made—

(a) in the case of an application to the High Court, in accordance with rules of court;

(b) in the case of an application to the Tribunal, in accordance with Tribunal rules.]

(11) In the application of this section to Scotland, references to the High Court are to be read as references to the Court of Session.

(12) In this section—

"non-business premises" means any premises to which a decision of the Commission ordering the Article 21 inspection relates;

"Commission official" means any of the persons authorised by the Commission to conduct the Article 21 inspection; and

"[CMA] officer" means any officer of the [CMA] whom the [CMA] has authorised in writing to accompany the named officer.]

NOTES

This section was inserted by the Competition Act 1998 and Other Enactments (Amendment) Regulations 2004, SI 2004/1261, reg 4, Sch 1, para 38.

Part 2 (ss 61–65B) was repealed by the Competition (Amendment etc) (EU Exit) Regulations 2019, SI 2019/93, regs 2, 24, as from IP completion day (as defined in the European Union (Withdrawal Agreement) Act 2020, s 39) (for transitional provisions and savings in relation to the operation of the 2019 Regulations, see Sch 4 to those Regulations at **[7.69]** et seq and, in particular, Sch 4, Pt 4 to the 2019 Regulations at **[7.72]**).

Sub-s (1): words in square brackets substituted by the Enterprise and Regulatory Reform Act 2013, s 41, Sch 13, paras 1, 6(1), (2). For various transitional provisions (including those relating to the abolition of the OFT and the Competition Commission, existing references to those bodies and provisions relating to continuity), see the Enterprise and Regulatory Reform Act 2013 (Commencement No 6, Transitional Provisions and Savings) Order 2014, SI 2014/416, Schedule at **[2.13]**.

Sub-s (2): words in square brackets in para (a) substituted by the Treaty of Lisbon (Changes in Terminology or Numbering) Order 2012, SI 2012/1809, art 3(1), Schedule, Pt 1.

Sub-ss (3)–(5), (12): references to the "CMA" substituted by the Enterprise and Regulatory Reform Act 2013, s 26(3), Sch 5, Pt 1, paras 1, 42, subject to transitional provisions in SI 2014/416 as noted above.

Sub-s (10A): inserted by the Enterprise and Regulatory Reform Act 2013, s 41, Sch 13, paras 1, 6(1), (3), subject to transitional provisions in SI 2014/416 as noted above.

[1.113]

[62B Powers when conducting an Article 22(2) inspection

(1) For the purposes of an Article 22(2) inspection, an authorised officer of the [CMA] has the powers specified in Article 20(2) of the EC Competition Regulation.

(2) For the purposes of this section and section 63—

"authorised officer of the [CMA]" means any officer of the [CMA] to whom an authorisation has been given; and

"authorisation" means an authorisation given in writing by the [CMA] for the purposes of the Article 22(2) inspection which—

(i) identifies the officer;

(ii) indicates the subject matter and purpose of the inspection; and

(iii) draws attention to any penalties which a person may incur under the EC Competition Regulation in connection with the inspection.]

NOTES

This section was inserted by the Competition Act 1998 and Other Enactments (Amendment) Regulations 2004, SI 2004/1261, reg 4, Sch 1, para 39.

Part 2 (ss 61–65B) was repealed by the Competition (Amendment etc) (EU Exit) Regulations 2019, SI 2019/93, regs 2, 24, as from IP completion day (as defined in the European Union (Withdrawal Agreement) Act 2020, s 39) (for transitional provisions and savings in relation to the operation of the 2019 Regulations, see Sch 4 to those Regulations at **[7.69]** et seq and, in particular, Sch 4, Pt 4 to the 2019 Regulations at **[7.72]**).

References to the "CMA" substituted by the Enterprise and Regulatory Reform Act 2013, s 26(3), Sch 5, Pt 1, paras 1, 43. For various transitional provisions (including those relating to the abolition of the OFT and the Competition Commission, existing references to those bodies and provisions relating to continuity), see the Enterprise and Regulatory Reform Act 2013 (Commencement No 6, Transitional Provisions and Savings) Order 2014, SI 2014/416, Schedule at **[2.13]**.

[1.114]

63 [Power to enter business premises under a warrant: Article 22(2) inspections]

(1) [On an application made to it by the CMA, the High Court or the Tribunal must issue a warrant if it is satisfied that]—

[(a) the Commission has requested the [CMA] to conduct an Article 22(2) inspection which the Commission has ordered by a decision under Article 20(4) of the EC Competition Regulation;

(b) the Article 22(2) inspection is being, or is likely to be, obstructed; and

(c) the measures that would be authorised by the warrant are neither arbitrary nor excessive having regard to the subject matter of the Article 22(2) inspection].

(2) [An Article 22(2) inspection] is being obstructed if—

(a) an authorised officer of the [CMA] has attempted to enter [any business] premises but has been unable to do so;

(b) the officer has produced his authorisation to the undertaking, or association of undertakings, concerned; and

(c) there are reasonable grounds for suspecting that there are [on any business premises] books or records . . . which the officer has power to examine.

(3) [An Article 22(2) inspection] is also being obstructed if—

(a) there are reasonable grounds for suspecting that there are [on any business premises] books or records . . . which an authorised officer of the [CMA] has power to examine;

(b) the officer has produced his authorisation to the undertaking, or association of undertakings, and has required production of the books or records; and

(c) the books and records have not been produced as required.

(4) [An Article 22(2) inspection] is likely to be obstructed if—

(a) there are reasonable grounds for suspecting that there are [on any business premises] books or records . . . which an authorised officer of the [CMA] has power to examine; and

(b) there are also reasonable grounds for suspecting that, if the officer attempted to exercise his power to examine any of the books or records, they would not be produced but would be concealed, removed, tampered with or destroyed.

[(5) A warrant under this section shall authorise a named authorised officer of the [CMA] and any other authorised officer of the [CMA], or Commission official, accompanying the named authorised officer—

(a) to enter any business premises specified in the warrant using such force as is reasonably necessary for the purpose;

(b) to search for books and records which an authorised officer of the [CMA] has power to examine, using such force as is reasonably necessary for the purpose;

(c) to take or obtain copies of or extracts from such books and records; and

(d) to seal the premises, any part of the premises or any books or records which an authorised officer of the [CMA] has power to seal, for the period and to the extent necessary for the inspection.]

[(5A) A warrant under this section may authorise persons specified in the warrant to accompany the named authorised officer who is executing it.]

(6) Any person entering any premises by virtue of a warrant under this section may take with him such equipment as appears to him to be necessary.

(7) On leaving any premises which he has entered by virtue of the warrant the [named authorised officer] must, if the premises are unoccupied or the occupier is temporarily absent, leave them as effectively secured as he found them.

(8) A warrant under this section continues in force until the end of the period of one month beginning with the day on which it is issued.

[(8A) An application for a warrant under this section must be made—

(a) in the case of an application to the High Court, in accordance with rules of court;

(b) in the case of an application to the Tribunal, in accordance with Tribunal rules.]

(9) In the application of this section to Scotland, references to the High Court are to be read as references to the Court of Session.

[(10) In this section—

"business premises" means any premises of an undertaking or association of undertakings which an authorised officer of the [CMA] has power to enter in the course of the Article 22(2) inspection;

"Commission official" means any person authorised by the Commission to assist with the Article 22(2) inspection.]

NOTES

Part 2 (ss 61–65B) was repealed by the Competition (Amendment etc) (EU Exit) Regulations 2019, SI 2019/93, regs 2, 24, as from IP completion day (as defined in the European Union (Withdrawal Agreement) Act 2020, s 39) (for transitional provisions and savings in relation to the operation of the 2019 Regulations, see Sch 4 to those Regulations at **[7.69]** et seq and, in particular, Sch 4, Pt 4 to the 2019 Regulations at **[7.72]**).

Section heading: substituted by the Competition Act 1998 and other enactments (Amendment) Regulations 2004, SI 2004/1261, reg 4, Sch 1, para 40(1), (9).

Sub-s (1): words in first pair of square brackets substituted, and reference to "CMA" substituted, by the Enterprise and Regulatory Reform Act 2013, ss 26(3), 41, Sch 5, Pt 1, paras 1, 44, Sch 13, paras 1, 7(1), (2) (for various transitional provisions (including those relating to the abolition of the OFT and the Competition Commission, existing references to those bodies and provisions relating to continuity), see the Enterprise and Regulatory Reform Act 2013 (Commencement No 6, Transitional Provisions and Savings) Order 2014, SI 2014/416, Schedule at **[2.13]**). Paras (a)–(c) substituted by SI 2004/1261, reg 4, Sch 1, para 40(1), (2)(b).

Sub-s (2): words in first pair of square brackets substituted, words in third and fourth pairs of square brackets inserted, and words omitted repealed, by SI 2004/1261, reg 4, Sch 1, para 40(1), (3); reference to the "CMA" substituted by the Enterprise and Regulatory Reform Act 2013, s 26(3), Sch 5, Pt 1, paras 1, 44, subject to transitional provisions in SI 2014/416 as noted above.

Sub-ss (3), (4): words in first pair of square brackets substituted, words in second pair of square brackets inserted, and word omitted repealed, by SI 2004/1261, reg 4, Sch 1, para 40(1), (4), (5); references to the "CMA" substituted by the Enterprise and Regulatory Reform Act 2013, s 26(3), Sch 5, Pt 1, paras 1, 44, subject to transitional provisions in SI 2014/416 as noted above.

Sub-s (5): substituted by SI 2004/1261, reg 4, Sch 1, para 40(1), (6); references to the "CMA" substituted by the Enterprise and Regulatory Reform Act 2013, s 26(3), Sch 5, Pt 1, paras 1, 44, subject to transitional provisions in SI 2014/416 as noted above.

Sub-s (5A): inserted by the Enterprise Act 2002, s 203(1), (4).

Sub-s (7): words in square brackets substituted by SI 2004/1261, reg 4, Sch 1, para 40(1), (7).

Sub-s (8A): inserted by the Enterprise and Regulatory Reform Act 2013, s 41, Sch 13, paras 1, 7(1), (3), subject to transitional provisions in SI 2014/416 as noted above.

Sub-s (10): added by SI 2004/1261, reg 4, Sch 1, para 40(1), (8); reference to the "CMA" substituted by the Enterprise and Regulatory Reform Act 2013, s 26(3), Sch 5, Pt 1, paras 1, 44, subject to transitional provisions in SI 2014/416 as noted above.

[1.115]

64 Entry of premises under sections 62[, 62A] and 63: supplementary

(1) A warrant issued under section 62[, 62A] or 63 must indicate—

(a) the subject matter and purpose of the [inspection];

(b) the nature of the offence created by section 65.

(2) The powers conferred by section 62[, 62A] or 63 are to be exercised on production of a warrant issued under that section.

(3) If there is no one at the premises when the named officer proposes to execute such a warrant he must, before executing it—

(a) take such steps as are reasonable in all the circumstances to inform the occupier of the intended entry; and

(b) if the occupier is informed, afford him or his legal or other representative a reasonable opportunity to be present when the warrant is executed.

(4) If the named officer is unable to inform the occupier of the intended entry he must, when executing the warrant, leave a copy of it in a prominent place on the premises.

(5) In this section—

["named officer" means—

(a) for the purposes of a warrant issued under section 62 or 62A, the officer named in the warrant; and

(b) for the purposes of a warrant issued under section 63, the authorised officer named in the warrant;]

"occupier", in relation to any premises, means a person whom the named officer reasonably believes is the occupier of those premises.

NOTES

Part 2 (ss 61–65B) was repealed by the Competition (Amendment etc) (EU Exit) Regulations 2019, SI 2019/93, regs 2, 24, as from IP completion day (as defined in the European Union (Withdrawal Agreement) Act 2020, s 39) (for transitional provisions and savings in relation to the operation of the 2019 Regulations, see Sch 4 to those Regulations at **[7.69]** et seq and, in particular, Sch 4, Pt 4 to the 2019 Regulations at **[7.72]**).

All amendments to this section were made by the Competition Act 1998 and other enactments (Amendment) Regulations 2004, SI 2004/1261, reg 4, Sch 1, para 41.

[1.116]

65 Offences

(1) A person is guilty of an offence if he intentionally obstructs any person in the exercise of his powers under a warrant issued under section 62[, 62A] or 63.

(2) A person guilty of an offence under subsection (1) is liable—

(a) on summary conviction, to a fine not exceeding the statutory maximum;

(b) on conviction on indictment, to imprisonment for a term not exceeding two years or to a fine or to both.

NOTES

Part 2 (ss 61–65B) was repealed by the Competition (Amendment etc) (EU Exit) Regulations 2019, SI 2019/93, regs 2, 24, as from IP completion day (as defined in the European Union (Withdrawal Agreement) Act 2020, s 39) (for transitional provisions and savings in relation to the operation of the 2019 Regulations, see Sch 4 to those Regulations at **[7.69]** et seq and, in particular, Sch 4, Pt 4 to the 2019 Regulations at **[7.72]**).

Sub-s (1): figure in square brackets inserted by the Competition Act 1998 and other enactments (Amendment) Regulations 2004, SI 2004/1261, reg 4, Sch 1, para 42.

[1.117]

[65A Privileged communications: Article 22(2) inspections

(1) A person shall not be required, by virtue of any provision of section 62B or 63, to produce or disclose a privileged communication.

(2) "Privileged communication" means a communication—

(a) between a professional legal adviser and his client, or

(b) made in connection with, or in contemplation of, legal proceedings and for the purposes of those proceedings, which in proceedings in the High Court would be protected from disclosure on grounds of legal professional privilege.

(3) In the application of this section to Scotland—

(a) the reference to the High Court is to be read as a reference to the Court of Session; and

(b) the reference to legal professional privilege is to be read as a reference to confidentiality of communications.]

NOTES

This section was inserted, together with s 65B, by the Competition Act 1998 and Other Enactments (Amendment) Regulations 2004, SI 2004/1261, reg 4, Sch 1, para 43.

Part 2 (ss 61–65B) was repealed by the Competition (Amendment etc) (EU Exit) Regulations 2019, SI 2019/93, regs 2, 24, as from IP completion day (as defined in the European Union (Withdrawal Agreement) Act 2020, s 39) (for transitional provisions and savings in relation to the operation of the 2019 Regulations, see Sch 4 to those Regulations at **[7.69]** et seq and, in particular, Sch 4, Pt 4 to the 2019 Regulations at **[7.72]**).

[1.118]

[65B Use of statements in prosecution: Article 22(2) inspections

A statement made by a person in response to a requirement imposed by virtue of section 62B or 63 may not be used in evidence against him on a prosecution for an offence under section 188 of the Enterprise Act 2002 unless, in the proceedings—

(a) in giving evidence, he makes a statement inconsistent with it, and

(b) evidence relating to it is adduced, or a question relating to it is asked, by him or on his behalf.]

NOTES

Inserted as noted to s 65A at **[1.117]**.

Part 2 (ss 61–65B) was repealed by the Competition (Amendment etc) (EU Exit) Regulations 2019, SI 2019/93, regs 2, 24, as from IP completion day (as defined in the European Union (Withdrawal Agreement) Act 2020, s 39) (for transitional provisions and savings in relation to the operation of the 2019 Regulations, see Sch 4 to those Regulations at **[7.69]** et seq and, in particular, Sch 4, Pt 4 to the 2019 Regulations at **[7.72]**).

[PART 2A ARTICLE 22(1) INVESTIGATIONS

[1.119]

65C Interpretation of Part 2A

(1) In this Part—

"Article 22(1) investigation" means an investigation conducted by the [CMA] on behalf and for the account of a competition authority of another Member State pursuant to Article 22(1) of the EC Competition Regulation;

"the Commission" means the European Commission;

"competition authority of another Member State" means a competition authority designated as such under Article 35 of the EC Competition Regulation by a Member State other than the United Kingdom;

"the EC Competition Regulation" means Council Regulation (EC) No 1/2003 of 16th December 2002 on the implementation of the rules on competition laid down in Articles 81 and 82 of the Treaty; and

"investigating officer" has the meaning given in section 65F(1).

(2) In this Part, the following expressions have the same meanings as in Part 1—

"[Article 101(1)]";
"[Article 102]";
["the CMA";]
"the court";
"document";
"information";
"officer";
. . .
"person";
"premises"
"the Treaty";
["the Tribunal";
"Tribunal rules";] and
"working day".

(3) For the purposes of this Part, the power to require information, in relation to information recorded otherwise than in a legible form, includes power to require a copy of it in a legible form.

(4) Any power conferred on the [CMA] by this Part to require information includes power to require any document which it believes may contain that information.]

NOTES

Part 2A (ss 65C–65N) was inserted by the Competition Act 1998 and Other Enactments (Amendment) Regulations 2004, SI 2004/1261, reg 4, Sch 1, para 44.

Part 2A was subsequently repealed by the Competition (Amendment etc) (EU Exit) Regulations 2019, SI 2019/93, regs 2, 24, as from IP completion day (as defined in the European Union (Withdrawal Agreement) Act 2020, s 39) (for transitional provisions and savings in relation to the operation of the 2019 Regulations, see Sch 4 to those Regulations at **[7.69]** et seq and, in particular, Sch 4, Pt 4 to the 2019 Regulations at **[7.72]**).

Sub-ss (1), (4): references to the "CMA" substituted by the Enterprise and Regulatory Reform Act 2013, s 26(3), Sch 5, Pt 1, paras 1, 45(1), (2), (4). For various transitional provisions (including those relating to the abolition of the OFT and the Competition Commission, existing references to those bodies and provisions relating to continuity), see the Enterprise and Regulatory Reform Act 2013 (Commencement No 6, Transitional Provisions and Savings) Order 2014, SI 2014/416, Schedule at **[2.13]**.

Sub-s (2): words in first and second pairs of square brackets substituted by the Treaty of Lisbon (Changes in Terminology or Numbering) Order 2012, SI 2012/1809, art 3(1), Schedule, Pt 1. Words in third, fourth and final pairs of square brackets inserted, and words omitted repealed, by the Enterprise and Regulatory Reform Act 2013, s 26(3), Sch 5, Pt 1, paras 1, 45(1), (3), (4), subject to transitional provisions in SI 2014/416 as noted above.

[1.120]

[65D Power to conduct an Article 22(1) investigation

(1) In any of the following cases, the [CMA] may conduct an Article 22(1) investigation.

(2) The first case is where there are reasonable grounds for suspecting that there is an agreement which—

(a) may affect trade between Member States; and

(b) has as its object or effect the prevention, restriction or distortion of competition within the Community.

(3) The second case is where there are reasonable grounds for suspecting that the prohibition in [Article 102] has been infringed.

(4) The third case is where there are reasonable grounds for suspecting that, at some time in the past, there was an agreement which at that time—

(a) may have affected trade between Member States; and

(b) had as its object or effect the prevention, restriction or distortion of competition within the Community.

(5) It is immaterial for the purposes of subsection (4) whether the agreement in question remains in existence.

(6) A provision of this Part which is expressed to apply to, or in relation to, an agreement is to be read as applying equally to, or in relation to, a decision by an association of undertakings or a concerted practice.]

NOTES

Part 2A was as noted to s 65C at **[1.119]**.

Part 2A was subsequently repealed by the Competition (Amendment etc) (EU Exit) Regulations 2019, SI 2019/93, regs 2, 24, as from IP completion day (as defined in the European Union (Withdrawal Agreement) Act 2020, s 39) (for transitional provisions and savings in relation to the operation of the 2019 Regulations, see Sch 4 to those Regulations at **[7.69]** et seq and, in particular, Sch 4, Pt 4 to the 2019 Regulations at **[7.72]**).

Sub-s (1): reference to the "CMA" substituted by the Enterprise and Regulatory Reform Act 2013, s 26(3), Sch 5, Pt 1, paras 1, 46. For various transitional provisions (including those relating to the abolition of the OFT and the Competition Commission, existing references to those bodies and provisions relating to continuity), see the Enterprise and Regulatory Reform Act 2013 (Commencement No 6, Transitional Provisions and Savings) Order 2014, SI 2014/416, Schedule at **[2.13]**.

Sub-s (3): words in square brackets substituted by the Treaty of Lisbon (Changes in Terminology or Numbering) Order 2012, SI 2012/1809, art 3(1), Schedule, Pt 1.

References to the European Community and related expressions: see the note "References to "the European Community", "Community", etc" in the introductory notes to this Act.

[1.121]

[65E Powers when conducting Article 22(1) investigations

(1) For the purposes of an Article 22(1) investigation, the [CMA] may require any person to produce to it a specified document, or to provide it with specified information, which it considers relates to any matter relevant to the investigation.

(2) The power conferred by subsection (1) is to be exercised by a notice in writing.

(3) A notice under subsection (2) must indicate—

(a) the subject matter and purpose of the Article 22(1) investigation; and

(b) the nature of the offences created by sections 65L to 65N.

(4) In subsection (1) "specified" means—

(a) specified, or described, in the notice; or

(b) falling within a category which is specified, or described, in the notice.

(5) The [CMA] may also specify in the notice—

(a) the time and place at which any document is to be produced or any information is to be provided;

(b) the manner and form in which it is to be produced or provided.

(6) The power under this section to require a person to produce a document includes power—

(a) if the document is produced—

(i) to take copies of it or extracts from it;

(ii) to require him, or any person who is a present or past officer of his, or is or was at any time employed by him, to provide an explanation of the document;

(b) if the document is not produced, to require him to state, to the best of his knowledge and belief, where it is.]

NOTES

Part 2A was as noted to s 65C at **[1.119]**.

Part 2A was subsequently repealed by the Competition (Amendment etc) (EU Exit) Regulations 2019, SI 2019/93, regs 2, 24, as from IP completion day (as defined in the European Union (Withdrawal Agreement) Act 2020, s 39) (for transitional provisions and savings in relation to the operation of the 2019 Regulations, see Sch 4 to those Regulations at **[7.69]** et seq and, in particular, Sch 4, Pt 4 to the 2019 Regulations at **[7.72]**).

Sub-ss (1), (5): references to the "CMA" substituted by the Enterprise and Regulatory Reform Act 2013, s 26(3), Sch 5, Pt 1, paras 1, 47. For various transitional provisions (including those relating to the abolition of the OFT and the Competition Commission, existing references to those bodies and provisions relating to continuity), see the Enterprise and Regulatory Reform Act 2013 (Commencement No 6, Transitional Provisions and Savings) Order 2014, SI 2014/416, Schedule at **[2.13]**.

[1.122]

[65F Power to enter business premises without a warrant

(1) Any officer of the [CMA] who is authorised in writing by the [CMA] to do so ("an investigating officer") may enter any business premises in connection with an Article 22(1) investigation.

(2) No investigating officer is to enter any premises in the exercise of his powers under this section unless he has given to the occupier of the premises a written notice which—

(a) gives at least two working days' notice of the intended entry;

(b) indicates the subject matter and purpose of the Article 22(1) investigation; and

(c) indicates the nature of the offences created by sections 65L to 65N.

(3) Subsection (2) does not apply—

(a) if the [CMA] has a reasonable suspicion that the premises are, or have been, occupied by—

(i) a party to an agreement which it is investigating under section 65D; or

(ii) an undertaking the conduct of which it is investigating under section 65D; or

(b) if the investigating officer has taken all such steps as are reasonably practicable to give notice but has not been able to do so.

(4) In a case falling within subsection (3), the power of entry conferred by subsection (1) is to be exercised by the investigating officer on production of—

(a) evidence of his authorisation; and

(b) a document containing the information referred to in subsection (2)(b) and (c).

(5) An investigating officer entering any premises under this section may—

(a) take with him such equipment as appears to him to be necessary;

(b) require any person on the premises—

(i) to produce any document which he considers relates to any matter relevant to the investigation; and

(ii) if the document is produced, to provide an explanation of it;

(c) require any person to state, to the best of his knowledge and belief, where any such document is to be found;

(d) take copies of, or extracts from, any document which is produced;

(e) require any information which is stored in any electronic form and is accessible from the premises and which the investigating officer considers relates to any matter relevant to the investigation, to be produced in a form—

(i) in which it can be taken away, and

(ii) in which it is visible and legible or from which it can readily be produced in a visible and legible form;

(f) take any steps which appear to be necessary for the purpose of preserving or preventing interference with any document which he consider relates to any matter relevant to the investigation.

(6) In this section "business premises" means premises (or any part of premises) not used as a dwelling.]

NOTES

Part 2A was as noted to s 65C at **[1.119]**.

Part 2A was subsequently repealed by the Competition (Amendment etc) (EU Exit) Regulations 2019, SI 2019/93, regs 2, 24, as from IP completion day (as defined in the European Union (Withdrawal Agreement) Act 2020, s 39) (for transitional provisions and savings in relation to the operation of the 2019 Regulations, see Sch 4 to those Regulations at **[7.69]** et seq and, in particular, Sch 4, Pt 4 to the 2019 Regulations at **[7.72]**).

Sub-ss (1), (3): references to the "CMA" substituted by the Enterprise and Regulatory Reform Act 2013, s 26(3), Sch 5, Pt 1, paras 1, 48. For various transitional provisions (including those relating to the abolition of the OFT and the Competition Commission, existing references to those bodies and provisions relating to continuity), see the Enterprise and Regulatory Reform Act 2013 (Commencement No 6, Transitional Provisions and Savings) Order 2014, SI 2014/416, Schedule at **[2.13]**.

[1.123]

[65G Power to enter business premises under a warrant

(1) [On an application made to it by the CMA, the court or the Tribunal may issue a warrant if it is satisfied that]—

(a) there are reasonable grounds for suspecting that there are on any business premises documents—

(i) the production of which has been required under section 65E or 65F; and

(ii) which have not been produced as required;

(b) there are reasonable grounds for suspecting that—

(i) there are on any business premises documents which the [CMA] has power under section 65E to require to be produced; and

(ii) if the documents were required to be produced, they would not be produced but would be concealed, removed, tampered with or destroyed; or

(c) an investigating officer has attempted to enter premises in the exercise of his powers under section 65F but has been unable to do so and that there are reasonable grounds for suspecting that there are on the premises documents the production of which could have been required under that section.

(2) A warrant under this section shall authorise a named officer of the [CMA] and any other of its officers whom the [CMA] has authorised in writing to accompany the named officer—

(a) to enter the premises specified in the warrant, using such force as is reasonably necessary for the purpose;

(b) to search the premises and take copies of, or extracts from, any document appearing to be of a kind in respect of which the application under subsection (1) was granted ("the relevant kind");

(c) to take possession of any documents appearing to be of the relevant kind if—

(i) such action appears to be necessary for preserving the documents or preventing interference with them; or

(ii) it is not reasonably practicable to take copies of the documents on the premises;

(d) to take any other steps which appear to be necessary for the purpose mentioned in paragraph (c)(i);

(e) to require any person to provide an explanation of any document appearing to be of the relevant kind or to state, to the best of his knowledge and belief, where it may be found;

(f) to require any information which is stored in any electronic form and is accessible from the premises and which the named officer considers relates to any matter relevant to the Article 22(1) investigation, to be produced in a form—

(i) in which it can be taken away, and

(ii) in which it is visible and legible or from which it can readily be produced in a visible and legible form.

(3) If, in the case of a warrant under subsection (1)(b), [the court or (as the case may be) the Tribunal] is satisfied that it is reasonable to suspect that there are also on the premises other documents relating to the Article 22(1) investigation concerned, the warrant shall also authorise action mentioned in subsection (2) to be taken in relation to any such document.

(4) A warrant under this section may authorise persons specified in the warrant to accompany the named officer who is executing it.

(5) Any person entering premises by virtue of a warrant under this section may take with him such equipment as appears to him to be necessary.

(6) On leaving any premises which he has entered by virtue of a warrant under this section, the named officer must, if the premises are unoccupied or the occupier is temporarily absent, leave them as effectively secured as he found them.

(7) A warrant under this section continues in force until the end of the period of one month beginning with the day on which it is issued.

(8) Any document of which possession is taken under subsection (2)(c) may be retained for a period of three months.

[(8A) An application for a warrant under this section must be made—

- *(a) in the case of an application to the court, in accordance with rules of court;*
- *(b) in the case of an application to the Tribunal, in accordance with Tribunal rules.]*

(9) In this section "business premises" has the same meaning as in section 65F.]

NOTES

Part 2A was as noted to s 65C at **[1.119]**.

Part 2A was subsequently repealed by the Competition (Amendment etc) (EU Exit) Regulations 2019, SI 2019/93, regs 2, 24, as from IP completion day (as defined in the European Union (Withdrawal Agreement) Act 2020, s 39) (for transitional provisions and savings in relation to the operation of the 2019 Regulations, see Sch 4 to those Regulations at **[7.69]** et seq and, in particular, Sch 4, Pt 4 to the 2019 Regulations at **[7.72]**).

Words in first pair of square brackets in sub-s (1) substituted, words in square brackets in sub-s (3) substituted, and sub-s (8A) inserted, by the Enterprise and Regulatory Reform Act 2013, s 41, Sch 13, paras 1, 9. For various transitional provisions (including those relating to the abolition of the OFT and the Competition Commission, existing references to those bodies and provisions relating to continuity), see the Enterprise and Regulatory Reform Act 2013 (Commencement No 6, Transitional Provisions and Savings) Order 2014, SI 2014/416, Schedule at **[2.13]**.

References to the "CMA" in sub-ss (1)(b)(i), (2) substituted by the Enterprise and Regulatory Reform Act 2013, s 26(3), Sch 5, Pt 1, paras 1, 49, subject to transitional provisions in SI 2014/416 as noted above.

[1.124]

[65H Power to enter domestic premises under a warrant

(1) [On an application made to it by the CMA, the court or the Tribunal may issue a warrant if it is satisfied that]—

- *(a) there are reasonable grounds for suspecting that there are on any domestic premises documents—*
  - *(i) the production of which has been required under section 65E; and*
  - *(ii) which have not been produced as required; or*
- *(b) there are reasonable grounds for suspecting that—*
  - *(i) there are on any domestic premises documents which the [CMA] has power under section 65E to require to be produced; and*
  - *(ii) if the documents were required to be produced, they would not be produced but would be concealed, removed, tampered with or destroyed.*

(2) A warrant under this section shall authorise a named officer of the [CMA], and any other of its officers whom the [CMA] has authorised in writing to accompany the named officer—

- *(a) to enter the premises specified in the warrant, using such force as is reasonably necessary for the purpose;*
- *(b) to search the premises and take copies of, or extracts from, any document appearing to be of a kind in respect of which the application under subsection (1) was granted ("the relevant kind");*
- *(c) to take possession of any documents appearing to be of the relevant kind if—*
  - *(i) such action appears to be necessary for preserving the documents or preventing interference with them; or*
  - *(ii) it is not reasonably practicable to take copies of the documents on the premises;*
- *(d) to take any other steps which appear to be necessary for the purpose mentioned in paragraph (c)(i);*
- *(e) to require any person to provide an explanation of any document appearing to be of the relevant kind or to state, to the best of his knowledge or belief, where it may be found;*
- *(f) to require any information which is stored in any electronic form and is accessible from the premises and which the named officer considers relates to any matter relevant to the investigation, to be produced in a form—*
  - *(i) in which it can be taken away; and*
  - *(ii) in which it is visible and legible or from which it can readily be produced in a visible and legible form.*

(3) If, in the case of a warrant under subsection (1)(b), [the court or (as the case may be) the Tribunal] is satisfied that it is reasonable to suspect that there are also on the premises other documents relating to the investigation concerned, the warrant shall also authorise action mentioned in subsection (2) to be taken in relation to any such document.

(4) A warrant under this section may authorise persons specified in the warrant to accompany the named officer who is executing it.

(5) Any person entering premises by virtue of a warrant under this section may take with him such equipment as appears to him to be necessary.

(6) On leaving any premises which he has entered by virtue of a warrant under this section, the named officer must, if the premises are unoccupied or the occupier is temporarily absent, leave them as effectively secured as he found them.

(7) A warrant under this section continues in force until the end of the period of one month beginning with the day on which it is issued.

(8) Any document of which possession is taken under subsection (2)(c) may be retained for a period of three months.

[(8A) An application for a warrant under this section must be made—

(a) in the case of an application to the court, in accordance with rules of court;

(b) in the case of an application to the Tribunal, in accordance with Tribunal rules.]

(9) In this section, "domestic premises" means premises (or any part of premises) that are used as a dwelling and are—

(a) premises also used in connection with the affairs of an undertaking or association of undertakings; or

(b) premises where documents relating to the affairs of an undertaking or association of undertakings are kept.]

NOTES

Part 2A was as noted to s 65C at **[1.119]**.

Part 2A was subsequently repealed by the Competition (Amendment etc) (EU Exit) Regulations 2019, SI 2019/93, regs 2, 24, as from IP completion day (as defined in the European Union (Withdrawal Agreement) Act 2020, s 39) (for transitional provisions and savings in relation to the operation of the 2019 Regulations, see Sch 4 to those Regulations at **[7.69]** et seq and, in particular, Sch 4, Pt 4 to the 2019 Regulations at **[7.72]**).

Words in first pair of square brackets in sub-s (1) substituted, words in square brackets in sub-s (3) substituted, and sub-s (8A) inserted, by the Enterprise and Regulatory Reform Act 2013, s 41, Sch 13, paras 1, 10. For various transitional provisions (including those relating to the abolition of the OFT and the Competition Commission, existing references to those bodies and provisions relating to continuity), see the Enterprise and Regulatory Reform Act 2013 (Commencement No 6, Transitional Provisions and Savings) Order 2014, SI 2014/416, Schedule at **[2.13]**.

References to the "CMA" in sub-ss (1)(b)(i), (2) substituted by the Enterprise and Regulatory Reform Act 2013, s 26(3), Sch 5, Pt 1, paras 1, 50, subject to transitional provisions in SI 2014/416 as noted above.

[1.125]

[65I Entry of premises under a warrant: supplementary

(1) A warrant issued under section 65G or 65H must indicate—

(a) the subject matter of the Article 22(1) investigation;

(b) the nature of the offences created by sections 65L to 65N.

(2) The powers conferred by section 65G or 65H are to be exercised on production of a warrant issued under that section.

(3) If there is no one at the premises when the named officer proposes to execute such a warrant he must, before executing it—

(a) take such steps as are reasonable in all the circumstances to inform the occupier of the intended entry; and

(b) if the occupier is informed, afford him or his legal or other representative a reasonable opportunity to be present when the warrant is executed.

(4) If the named officer is unable to inform the occupier of the intended entry he must, when executing the warrant, leave a copy of it in a prominent place on the premises.

(5) In this section—

"named officer" means the officer named in the warrant; and

"occupier", in relation to any premises, means a person whom the named officer reasonably believes is the occupier of those premises.]

NOTES

Part 2A was as noted to s 65C at **[1.119]**.

Part 2A was subsequently repealed by the Competition (Amendment etc) (EU Exit) Regulations 2019, SI 2019/93, regs 2, 24, as from IP completion day (as defined in the European Union (Withdrawal Agreement) Act 2020, s 39) (for transitional provisions and savings in relation to the operation of the 2019 Regulations, see Sch 4 to those Regulations at **[7.69]** et seq and, in particular, Sch 4, Pt 4 to the 2019 Regulations at **[7.72]**).

[1.126]

[65J Privileged communications

(1) A person shall not be required, under any provision of this Part, to produce or disclose a privileged communication.

(2) "Privileged communication" means a communication—

(a) between a professional legal adviser and his client, or

(b) made in connection with, or in contemplation of, legal proceedings and for the purposes of those proceedings,

which in proceedings in the High Court would be protected from disclosure on grounds of legal professional privilege.

(3) In the application of this section to Scotland—

(a) the reference to the High Court is to be read as a reference to the Court of Session; and

(b) the reference to legal professional privilege is to be read as a reference to confidentiality of communications.]

NOTES

Part 2A was as noted to s 65C at **[1.119]**.

Part 2A was subsequently repealed by the Competition (Amendment etc) (EU Exit) Regulations 2019, SI 2019/93, regs 2, 24, as from IP completion day (as defined in the European Union (Withdrawal Agreement) Act 2020, s 39) (for transitional provisions and savings in relation to the operation of the 2019 Regulations, see Sch 4 to those Regulations at **[7.69]** et seq and, in particular, Sch 4, Pt 4 to the 2019 Regulations at **[7.72]**).

[1.127]

[65K Use of statements in prosecution

A statement made by a person in response to a requirement imposed by virtue of any of sections 65E to 65H may not be used in evidence against him on a prosecution for an offence under section 188 of the Enterprise Act 2002 unless, in the proceedings—

(a) in giving evidence, he makes a statement inconsistent with it, and

(b) evidence relating to it is adduced, or a question relating to it is asked, by him or on his behalf.]

NOTES

Part 2A was as noted to s 65C at **[1.119]**.

Part 2A was subsequently repealed by the Competition (Amendment etc) (EU Exit) Regulations 2019, SI 2019/93, regs 2, 24, as from IP completion day (as defined in the European Union (Withdrawal Agreement) Act 2020, s 39) (for transitional provisions and savings in relation to the operation of the 2019 Regulations, see Sch 4 to those Regulations at **[7.69]** et seq and, in particular, Sch 4, Pt 4 to the 2019 Regulations at **[7.72]**).

[1.128]

[65L Offences

(1) A person is guilty of an offence if he fails to comply with a requirement imposed on him under section 65E, 65F, 65G or 65H.

(2) If a person is charged with an offence under subsection (1) in respect of a requirement to produce a document, it is a defence for him to prove—

(a) that the document was not in his possession or under his control; and

(b) that it was not reasonably practicable for him to comply with the requirement.

(3) If a person is charged with an offence under subsection (1) in respect of a requirement—

(a) to provide information,

(b) to provide an explanation of a document, or

(c) to state where a document is to be found,

it is a defence for him to prove that he had a reasonable excuse for failing to comply with the requirement.

(4) Failure to comply with a requirement imposed under section 65E or 65F is not an offence if the person imposing the requirement has failed to act in accordance with that section.

(5) A person is guilty of an offence if he intentionally obstructs an officer acting in the exercise of his powers under section 65F.

(6) A person guilty of an offence under subsection (1) or (5) is liable—

(a) on summary conviction, to a fine not exceeding the statutory maximum;

(b) on conviction on indictment, to a fine.

(7) A person who intentionally obstructs an officer in the exercise of his powers under a warrant issued under section 65G or 65H is guilty of an offence and liable—

(a) on summary conviction, to a fine not exceeding the statutory maximum;

(b) on conviction on indictment, to imprisonment for a term not exceeding two years or to a fine or to both.]

NOTES

Part 2A was as noted to s 65C at **[1.119]**.

Part 2A was subsequently repealed by the Competition (Amendment etc) (EU Exit) Regulations 2019, SI 2019/93, regs 2, 24, as from IP completion day (as defined in the European Union (Withdrawal Agreement) Act 2020, s 39) (for transitional provisions and savings in relation to the operation of the 2019 Regulations, see Sch 4 to those Regulations at **[7.69]** et seq and, in particular, Sch 4, Pt 4 to the 2019 Regulations at **[7.72]**).

[1.129]

[65M Destroying or falsifying documents

(1) A person is guilty of an offence if, having been required to produce a document under section 65E, 65F, 65G or 65H—

(a) he intentionally or recklessly destroys or otherwise disposes of it, falsifies it or conceals it, or

(b) he causes or permits its destruction, disposal, falsification or concealment.

(2) A person guilty of an offence under subsection (1) is liable—

(a) on summary conviction, to a fine not exceeding the statutory maximum;

(b) on conviction on indictment, to imprisonment for a term not exceeding two years or to a fine or to both.]

NOTES

Part 2A was as noted to s 65C at **[1.119]**.

Part 2A was subsequently repealed by the Competition (Amendment etc) (EU Exit) Regulations 2019, SI 2019/93, regs 2, 24, as from IP completion day (as defined in the European Union (Withdrawal Agreement) Act 2020, s 39) (for transitional provisions and savings in relation to the operation of the 2019 Regulations, see Sch 4 to those Regulations at **[7.69]** et seq and, in particular, Sch 4, Pt 4 to the 2019 Regulations at **[7.72]**).

[1.130]

[65N False or misleading information

(1) If information is provided by a person to the [CMA] in connection with any function of the [CMA] under this Part, that person is guilty of an offence if—

(a) the information is false or misleading in a material particular; and

(b) he knows that it is or is reckless as to whether it is.

(2) A person who—

(a) provides any information to another person, knowing the information to be false or misleading in a material particular, or

(b) recklessly provides any information to another person which is false or misleading in a material particular, knowing that the information is to be used for the purpose of providing information to the [CMA] in connection with any of its functions under this Part, is guilty of an offence.

(3) A person guilty of an offence under this section is liable—

(a) on summary conviction, to a fine not exceeding the statutory maximum;

(b) on conviction on indictment, to imprisonment for a term not exceeding two years or to a fine or to both.]

NOTES

Part 2A was as noted to s 65C at **[1.119]**.

Part 2A was subsequently repealed by the Competition (Amendment etc) (EU Exit) Regulations 2019, SI 2019/93, regs 2, 24, as from IP completion day (as defined in the European Union (Withdrawal Agreement) Act 2020, s 39) (for transitional provisions and savings in relation to the operation of the 2019 Regulations, see Sch 4 to those Regulations at **[7.69]** et seq and, in particular, Sch 4, Pt 4 to the 2019 Regulations at **[7.72]**).

References to the "CMA" substituted by the Enterprise and Regulatory Reform Act 2013, s 26(3), Sch 5, Pt 1, paras 1, 51. For various transitional provisions (including those relating to the abolition of the OFT and the Competition Commission, existing references to those bodies and provisions relating to continuity), see the Enterprise and Regulatory Reform Act 2013 (Commencement No 6, Transitional Provisions and Savings) Order 2014, SI 2014/416, Schedule at **[2.13]**.

PART III MONOPOLIES

66–69 (*Ss 66, 67 repealed by the Enterprise Act 2002, s 278(2), Sch 26; s 68 inserts s 137(3A)–(3C) of the Fair Trading Act 1973 at* **[1.6]**; *s 69 amended s 83 of the 1973 Act (repealed).*)

PART IV SUPPLEMENTAL AND TRANSITIONAL

70 (*Repeals the Patents Act 1977, ss 44, 45.*)

[1.131]

71 Regulations, orders and rules

(1) Any power to make regulations or orders which is conferred by this Act is exercisable by statutory instrument.

(2) The power to make rules which is conferred by section 48 is exercisable by statutory instrument.

(3) Any statutory instrument made under this Act may—

(a) contain such incidental, supplemental, consequential and transitional provision as the Secretary of State considers appropriate; and

(b) make different provision for different cases.

(4) No order is to be made under—

(a) section 3,

(b) section 19,

(c) section 36(8),

[(ca) section 45(8),]

[(cb) section 47C(7),]

(d) section 50, or

(e) paragraph 6(3) of Schedule 4,

unless a draft of the order has been laid before Parliament and approved by a resolution of each House.

(5) Any statutory instrument made under this Act, apart from one made—

(a) under any of the provisions mentioned in subsection (4), or

(b) under section 76(3),

shall be subject to annulment by a resolution of either House of Parliament.

NOTES

Sub-s (4): para (ca) inserted by the Enterprise Act 2002, s 278(1), Sch 25, para 38(1), (49). Para (cb) inserted by the Consumer Rights Act 2015, s 80, Sch 8, Pt 1, paras 1, 16.

[1.132]

72 Offences by bodies corporate etc

(1) This section applies to an offence under any of sections 42 to 44, [*65 or 65L to 65N*].

(2) If an offence committed by a body corporate is proved—

(a) to have been committed with the consent or connivance of an officer, or

(b) to be attributable to any neglect on his part,

the officer as well as the body corporate is guilty of the offence and liable to be proceeded against and punished accordingly.

(3) In subsection (2) "officer", in relation to a body corporate, means a director, manager, secretary or other similar officer of the body, or a person purporting to act in any such capacity.

(4) If the affairs of a body corporate are managed by its members, subsection (2) applies in relation to the acts and defaults of a member in connection with his functions of management as if he were a director of the body corporate.

(5) If an offence committed by a partnership in Scotland is proved—

(a) to have been committed with the consent or connivance of a partner, or

(b) to be attributable to any neglect on his part,

the partner as well as the partnership is guilty of the offence and liable to be proceeded against and punished accordingly.

(6) In subsection (5) "partner" includes a person purporting to act as a partner.

NOTES

Sub-s (1): words in square brackets originally substituted by the Competition Act 1998 and Other Enactments (Amendment) Regulations 2004, SI 2004/1261, reg 4, Sch 1, para 45. These words were repealed by the Competition (Amendment etc) (EU Exit) Regulations 2019, SI 2019/93, regs 2, 25, as from IP completion day (as defined in the European Union (Withdrawal Agreement) Act 2020, s 39) (for transitional provisions and savings in relation to the operation of the 2019 Regulations, see Sch 4 to those Regulations at **[7.69]** et seq).

[1.133]

73 Crown application

(1) Any provision made by or under this Act binds the Crown except that—

(a) the Crown is not criminally liable as a result of any such provision;
(b) the Crown is not liable for any penalty under any such provision; and
(c) nothing in this Act affects Her Majesty in her private capacity.

(2) Subsection (1)(a) does not affect the application of any provision of this Act in relation to persons in the public service of the Crown.

(3) Subsection (1)(c) is to be interpreted as if section 38(3) of the Crown Proceedings Act 1947 (interpretation of references in that Act to Her Majesty in her private capacity) were contained in this Act.

[(4) If an investigation is conducted under section 25 *or 65D* in respect of an agreement where none of the parties is the Crown or a person in the public service of the Crown, or in respect of conduct otherwise than by the Crown or such a person—

(a) the power conferred by section 27 *or (as the case may be) section 65F* may not be exercised in relation to land which is occupied by a government department, or otherwise for purposes of the Crown, without the written consent of the appropriate person; and
(b) [sections 28 and 28A do not apply] in relation to land so occupied.]

(5) In any case in which consent is required under subsection (4), the person who is the appropriate person in relation to that case is to be determined in accordance with regulations made by the Secretary of State.

(6) Sections 62[, 62A] and 63 do not apply in relation to land which is occupied by a government department, or otherwise for purposes of the Crown, unless the matter being investigated is [an agreement to which the Crown or a person in the service of the Crown is a party, or conduct by the Crown or such a person].

[(6A) In [subsection (4)]) "agreement" includes a suspected agreement and is to be read as applying equally to, or in relation to, a decision by an association of undertakings or a concerted practice; and "conduct" includes suspected conduct.]

(7) . . .

(8) If the Secretary of State certifies that it appears to him to be in the interests of national security that the powers of entry—

(a) conferred by section 27 [*or 65F*], or
(b) that may be conferred by a warrant under [section 28 or 28A],

should not be exercisable in relation to premises held or used by or on behalf of the Crown and which are specified in the certificate, those powers are not exercisable in relation to those premises.

(9) Any amendment, repeal or revocation made by this Act binds the Crown to the extent that the enactment amended, repealed or revoked binds the Crown.

NOTES

Other than noted bellow, all amendments to this section were made by the Competition Act 1998 and Other Enactments (Amendment) Regulations 2004, SI 2004/1261, reg 4, Sch 1, para 46.

The following amendments were made by the Competition (Amendment etc) (EU Exit) Regulations 2019, SI 2019/93, regs 2, 26, as from IP completion day (as defined in the European Union (Withdrawal Agreement) Act 2020, s 39) (for transitional provisions and savings in relation to the operation of the 2019 Regulations, see Sch 4 to those Regulations at **[7.69]** et seq)—

In subsection (4)—
(a) the words "or 65D" in italics were repealed;
(b) in paragraph (a), the words "or (as the case may be) section 65F" in italics were repealed;
(c) in paragraph (b), the words "sections 28 and 28A do not apply" in square brackets were substituted (for the original words "none of sections 28, 28A, 65G and 65H applies").

Subsection (6) was repealed.

In subsection (6A), the words "subsection (4)" in square brackets were substituted (for the original words "subsections (4) and (6)");

In subsection (8)—
(a) in paragraph (a), the words "or 65F" in italics were repealed;
(b) in paragraph (b), the words "section 28 or 28A" in square brackets were substituted (for the original words "section 28, 28A, 62, 62A, 63, 65G or 65H".

Regulations: the Competition Act 1998 (Definition of Appropriate Person) Regulations 1999, SI 1999/2282 at **[2.23]**.

[1.134]

74 Amendments, transitional provisions, savings and repeals

(1) The minor and consequential amendments set out in Schedule 12 are to have effect.

(2) The transitional provisions and savings set out in Schedule 13 are to have effect.

(3) The enactments set out in Schedule 14 are repealed.

[1.135]

75 Consequential and supplementary provision

(1) The Secretary of State may by order make such incidental, consequential, transitional or supplemental provision as he thinks necessary or expedient for the general purposes, or any particular purpose, of this Act or in consequence of any of its provisions or for giving full effect to it.

(2) An order under subsection (1) may, in particular, make provision—

(a) for enabling any person by whom any powers will become exercisable, on a date specified by or under this Act, by virtue of any provision made by or under this Act to take before that date any steps which are necessary as a preliminary to the exercise of those powers;
(b) for making savings, or additional savings, from the effect of any repeal made by or under this Act.

(3) Amendments made under this section shall be in addition, and without prejudice, to those made by or under any other provision of this Act.

(4) No other provision of this Act restricts the powers conferred by this section.

NOTES

Orders: the Judicial Pensions (Qualifying Judicial Offices) (President of the Competition Commission Appeal Tribunals) Order 1999, SI 1999/2283; the Competition Act 1998 (Transitional, Consequential and Supplemental Provisions) Order 2000, SI 2000/311; the Competition Act 1998 (Consequential and Supplemental Provisions) Order 2000, SI 2000/2031; the Competition Act 1998 (Public Transport Ticketing Schemes Block Exemption) Order 2001, SI 2001/319; the Competition Act 1998 (Consequential Provisions) Order 2013, SI 2013/294 (which provides for repeals and revocations consequential on the coming into force (on 10 March 2013) of provisions of this Act repealing the Restrictive Practices Court Act 1976).

[1.136]

[75A Rules in relation to Part 2 and Part 2A

(1) The [CMA] may make such rules about procedural and other matters in connection with the carrying into effect of the provisions of Parts 2 and 2A as it considers appropriate.

(2) If the [CMA] is preparing rules under this section it must consult such persons as it considers appropriate.

(3) No rule made by the [CMA] is to come into operation until it has been approved by an order made by the Secretary of State.

(4) The Secretary of State may approve any rule made by the [CMA]—

(a) in the form in which it is submitted; or

(b) subject to such modifications as he considers appropriate.

(5) If the Secretary of State proposes to approve a rule subject to modifications he must inform the [CMA] of the proposed modifications and take into account any comments made by the [CMA].

(6) Subsections (3) to (5) apply also to any alteration of the rules made by the [CMA].

(7) The Secretary of State may, after consulting the [CMA], by order vary or revoke any rules made under this section.

(8) If the Secretary of State considers that rules should be made under this section with respect to a particular matter he may direct the [CMA] to exercise its powers under this section and make rules about that matter.]

NOTES

Inserted by the Competition Act 1998 and other enactments (Amendment) Regulations 2004, SI 2004/1261, reg 4, Sch 1, para 47.

Repealed by the Competition (Amendment etc) (EU Exit) Regulations 2019, SI 2019/93, regs 2, 27, as from IP completion day (as defined in the European Union (Withdrawal Agreement) Act 2020, s 39) (for transitional provisions and savings in relation to the operation of the 2019 Regulations, see Sch 4 to those Regulations at **[7.69]** et seq and, in particular, Sch 4, Pt 4 to the 2019 Regulations at **[7.72]**).

References to the "CMA" substituted by the Enterprise and Regulatory Reform Act 2013, s 26(3), Sch 5, Pt 1, paras 1, 52. For various transitional provisions (including those relating to the abolition of the OFT and the Competition Commission, existing references to those bodies and provisions relating to continuity), see the Enterprise and Regulatory Reform Act 2013 (Commencement No 6, Transitional Provisions and Savings) Order 2014, SI 2014/416, Schedule at **[2.13]**.

Rules: the Competition Act 1998 (Competition and Markets Authority's Rules) Order 2014, SI 2014/458 at **[2.14]**.

[1.137]

76 Short title, commencement and extent

(1) This Act may be cited as the Competition Act 1998.

(2) Sections 71 and 75 and this section and paragraphs 1 to 7 and 35 of Schedule 13 come into force on the passing of this Act.

(3) The other provisions of this Act come into force on such day as the Secretary of State may by order appoint; and different days may be appointed for different purposes.

(4) This Act extends to Northern Ireland.

NOTES

Orders: the Competition Act 1998 (Commencement No 1) Order 1998, SI 1998/2750; the Competition Act 1998 (Commencement No 2) Order 1998, SI 1998/3166; the Competition Act 1998 (Commencement No 3) Order 1999, SI 1999/505; the Competition Act 1998 (Commencement No 4) Order 1999, SI 1999/2859; the Competition Act 1998 (Commencement No 5) Order 2000, SI 2000/344; the Competition Act 1998 (Commencement No 6) Order 2013, SI 2013/284.

SCHEDULES

SCHEDULE 1
EXCLUSIONS: MERGERS AND CONCENTRATIONS

Sections 3(1)(a) and 19(1)(a)

PART I MERGERS

Enterprises ceasing to be distinct: the Chapter I prohibition

[1.138]

1. (1) To the extent to which an agreement (either on its own or when taken together with another agreement) results, or if carried out would result, in any two enterprises ceasing to be distinct enterprises for the purposes of [Part 3 of the Enterprise Act 2002 ("the 2002 Act")], the Chapter I prohibition does not apply to the agreement.

(2) The exclusion provided by sub-paragraph (1) extends to any provision directly related and necessary to the implementation of the merger provisions.

(3) In sub-paragraph (2) "merger provisions" means the provisions of the agreement which cause, or if carried out would cause, the agreement to have the result mentioned in sub-paragraph (1).

(4) [Section 26 of the 2002 Act] applies for the purposes of this paragraph as if—

(a) in subsection (3) (circumstances in which a person or group of persons may be treated as having control of an enterprise), and

(b) in subsection (4) (circumstances in which a person or group of persons may be treated as bringing an enterprise under their control),

for "may" there were substituted "must".

Enterprises ceasing to be distinct: the Chapter II prohibition

2. (1) To the extent to which conduct (either on its own or when taken together with other conduct)—

(a) results in any two enterprises ceasing to be distinct enterprises for the purposes of [Part 3 of the 2002 Act]), or

(b) is directly related and necessary to the attainment of the result mentioned in paragraph (a),

the Chapter II prohibition does not apply to that conduct.

(2) [Section 26 of the 2002 Act] applies for the purposes of this paragraph as it applies for the purposes of paragraph 1.

. . .

3. . . .

Withdrawal of the paragraph 1 exclusion

4. (1) The exclusion provided by paragraph 1 does not apply to a particular agreement if the [CMA] gives a direction under this paragraph to that effect.

(2) If the [CMA] is considering whether to give a direction under this paragraph, [it] may by notice in writing require any party to the agreement in question to give [the [CMA]] such information in connection with the agreement as [it] may require.

(3) The [CMA] may give a direction under this paragraph only as provided in sub-paragraph (4) or (5).

(4) If at the end of such period as may be specified in rules under section 51 a person has failed, without reasonable excuse, to comply with a requirement imposed under sub-paragraph (2), the [CMA] may give a direction under this paragraph.

(5) The [CMA] may also give a direction under this paragraph if—

[(a) it considers that the agreement will, if not excluded, infringe the Chapter I prohibition; and]

(b) the agreement is not a protected agreement.

(6) . . .

(7) A direction under this paragraph—

(a) must be in writing;

(b) may be made so as to have effect from a date specified in the direction (which may not be earlier than the date on which it is given).

Protected agreements

5. An agreement is a protected agreement for the purposes of paragraph 4 if—

[(a) the [CMA] or (as the case may be) the Secretary of State has published its or his decision not to make a reference . . . under section 22, 33, 45 or 62 of the 2002 Act in connection with the agreement;

(b) the [CMA] or (as the case may be) the Secretary of State has made a reference . . . under section 22, 33, 45 or 62 of the 2002 Act in connection with the agreement and [the CMA] has found that the agreement has given rise to, or would if carried out give rise to, a relevant merger situation or (as the case may be) a special merger situation;

(c) the agreement does not fall within paragraph (a) or (b) but has given rise to, or would if carried out give rise to, enterprises to which it relates being regarded under section 26 of the 2002 Act as ceasing to be distinct enterprises (otherwise than as the result of subsection (3) or (4)(b) of that section); or

(d) the [CMA] has made a reference . . . under section 32 of the Water Industry Act 1991 in connection with the agreement and [the CMA] has found that the agreement has given rise to, or would if carried out give rise to, a merger of any two or more water enterprises of the kind to which that section applies].

NOTES

Para 1: words in square brackets sub-paras (1), (4) substituted by the Enterprise Act 2002, s 278(1), Sch 25, para 38(1), (50)(a) (for savings in relation the merger of water and sewerage undertakers, see the Enterprise Act 2002 (Commencement No 3, Transitional and Transitory Provisions and Savings) Order 2003, SI 2003/1397, art 3, and the Enterprise Act 2002 (Commencement No 7 and Transitional Provisions and Savings) Order 2004, SI 2004/3233, arts 3–5).

Para 2: words in square brackets sub-paras (1)(a), (2) substituted by the Enterprise Act 2002, s 278(1), Sch 25, para 38(1), (50)(b) (for savings see the para 1 note above).

Para 3: repealed by the Communications Act 2003, s 406(7), Sch 19(1).

Para 4: references to the "CMA" substituted by the Enterprise and Regulatory Reform Act 2013, s 26(3), Sch 5, Pt 1, paras 1, 53(1), (2) (for various transitional provisions (including those relating to the abolition of the OFT and the Competition Commission, existing references to those bodies and provisions relating to continuity), see the Enterprise and Regulatory Reform Act 2013 (Commencement No 6, Transitional Provisions and Savings) Order 2014, SI 2014/416, Schedule at **[2.13]**). The words "it" in square brackets (in all places that it occurs) was substituted by the Enterprise Act 2002, s 278(1), Sch 25, para 38(1), (50)(c) (for savings see the para 1 note above). Sub-para (5)(a) was substituted, and sub-para (6) was repealed, by the Competition Act 1998 and Other Enactments (Amendment) Regulations 2004, SI 2004/1261, reg 4, Sch 1, para 48(1), (2).

Para 5: sub-paras (a)–(d) substituted by the Enterprise Act 2002, s 278(1), Sch 25, para 38(1), (50)(d). In sub-paras (a), (b), (d), the references to the "CMA" were substituted, the words omitted from those sub-paras were repealed, and the words "the CMA" in square brackets in sub-paras (b), (d) were substituted, by the Enterprise and Regulatory Reform Act 2013, ss 26(3), 57, Sch 5, Pt 1, paras 1, 53(1), (3), Sch 15, paras 8, 12, subject to transitional provisions in SI 2014/416 as noted to para 4 above.

Modification: by virtue of the Enterprise Act 2002 (Protection of Legitimate Interests) Order 2003, SI 2003/1592, Sch 4, para 15(1)(a), (b), the following modifications of this Part of this Schedule apply: (a) in para 5(a), (b) above a reference to the Enterprise Act, s 62 includes a reference to art 5 of the 2003 Order; and (b) in para 5(b) above a reference to a "special merger situation" includes a reference to a "European relevant merger situation". Note that s 68 of the Enterprise Act 2002 (under which the 2003 Order was made) was repealed by the Competition (Amendment etc) (EU Exit) Regulations 2019, SI 2019/93, regs 32, 47, as from IP completion day (as defined in the European Union (Withdrawal Agreement) Act 2020, s 39). See, however, Sch 4, Pt 7, paras 25–27 to the 2019 Regulations (at **[7.76]**) which provides for the continued application of the 2003 Order in the circumstances specified in those paragraphs.

PART II CONCENTRATIONS SUBJECT TO EC CONTROLS

[1.139]

6. (1) To the extent to which an agreement (either on its own or when taken together with another agreement) gives rise to, or would if carried out give rise to, a concentration, the Chapter I prohibition does not apply to the agreement if the Merger Regulation gives the Commission exclusive jurisdiction in the matter.

(2) To the extent to which conduct (either on its own or when taken together with other conduct) gives rise to, or would if pursued give rise to, a concentration, the Chapter II prohibition does not apply to the conduct if the Merger Regulation gives the Commission exclusive jurisdiction in the matter.

(3) In this paragraph—

"concentration" means a concentration with a Community dimension within the meaning of Articles 1 and 3 of the Merger Regulation; and

["Merger Regulation" means Council Regulation (EC) No 139/2004 of 20th January 2004 on the control of concentrations between undertakings].

NOTES

This Part was repealed by the Competition (Amendment etc) (EU Exit) Regulations 2019, SI 2019/93, regs 2, 28, as from IP completion day (as defined in the European Union (Withdrawal Agreement) Act 2020, s 39) (for transitional provisions and savings in connection with all amendments made by the 2019 Regulations, see Sch 4 to those Regulations at **[7.69]** et seq). Note also that the Merger Regulation was repealed, in its application to the UK, by Sch 3, para 1 to the 2019 Regulations, as from IP completion day.

Para 6: in sub-para (3), the definition "Merger Regulation" was substituted by the EC Merger Control (Consequential Amendments) Regulations 2004, SI 2004/1079, reg 2, Schedule, para 1.

References to the European Community and related expressions: see the note "References to "the European Community", "Community", etc" in the introductory notes to this Act.

SCHEDULE 2

(Sch 2, Pt I repealed by the Financial Services Act 2012, s 114(2), Sch 19; Sch 2, Pts II, IV repealed by the Competition Act 1998 and Other Enactments (Amendment) Regulations 2004, SI 2004/1261, reg 4, Sch 1, para 49; Sch 2, Pt III (Broadcasting) amends the Broadcasting Act 1990 and further provides (in para 5) that the Chapter I prohibition does not apply in respect of any networking arrangements under the 1990 Act to the extent that they (a) have been approved for the purposes of licence conditions imposed under section 291 of the Communications Act 2003; or (b) are arrangements that have been considered under Schedule 4 to the Broadcasting Act 1990 and fall to be treated as so approved; nor does that prohibition apply in respect of things done with a view to arrangements being entered into or approved to the extent that those things have effect for purposes that are directly related to, and necessary for compliance with, conditions so imposed. Furthermore, OFCOM must publish a list of the networking arrangements which in their opinion are excluded from the Chapter I prohibition by virtue of the above.)

SCHEDULE 3
GENERAL EXCLUSIONS

Sections 3(1)(c) and 19(1)(b)

Planning obligations

[1.140]

1. (1) The Chapter I prohibition does not apply to an agreement—

(a) to the extent to which it is a planning obligation;

(b) which is made under section 75 (agreements regulating development or use of land) or 246 (agreements relating to Crown land) of the Town and Country Planning (Scotland) Act 1997; or

(c) which is made under Article 40 of the Planning (Northern Ireland) Order 1991.

(2) In sub-paragraph (1)(a), "planning obligation" means—

(a) a planning obligation for the purposes of section 106 of the Town and Country Planning Act 1990; or

(b) a planning obligation for the purposes of section 299A of that Act.

. . .

2. . . .

EEA Regulated Markets

3. (1) The Chapter I prohibition does not apply to an agreement for the constitution of an EEA regulated market to the extent to which the agreement relates to any of the rules made, or guidance issued, by that market.

(2) The Chapter I prohibition does not apply to a decision made by an EEA regulated market, to the extent to which the decision relates to any of the market's regulating provisions.

(3) The Chapter I prohibition does not apply to—

(a) any practices of an EEA regulated market; or

(b) any practices which are trading practices in relation to an EEA regulated market.

(4) The Chapter I prohibition does not apply to an agreement the parties to which are or include—

(a) an EEA regulated market, or

(b) a person who is subject to the rules of that market,

to the extent to which the agreement consists of provisions the inclusion of which is required or contemplated by the regulating provisions of that market.

(5) In this paragraph—

"EEA regulated market" is a market which—

(a) is listed by an EEA State other than the United Kingdom pursuant to [[Article 56 of Directive 2014/65/EU of the European Parliament and of the Council of 15 May 2014] on markets in financial instruments]; and

(b) operates without any requirement that a person dealing on the market should have a physical presence in the EEA State from which any trading facilities are provided or on any trading floor that the market may have;

"EEA State" means a State which is a contracting party to the EEA Agreement;

"regulating provisions", in relation to an EEA regulated market, means—

(a) rules made, or guidance issued, by that market,

(b) practices of that market, or

(c) practices which, in relation to that market, are trading practices;

"trading practices", in relation to an EEA regulated market, means practices of persons who are subject to the rules made by that market, and—

(a) which relate to business in respect of which those persons are subject to the rules of that market, and which are required or contemplated by those rules or by guidance issued by that market; or

(b) which are otherwise attributable to the conduct of that market as such.

Services of general economic interest etc

4. Neither the Chapter I prohibition nor the Chapter II prohibition applies to an undertaking entrusted with the operation of services of general economic interest or having the character of a revenue-producing monopoly in so far as the prohibition would obstruct the performance, in law or in fact, of the particular tasks assigned to that undertaking.

Compliance with legal requirements

5. (1) The Chapter I prohibition does not apply to an agreement to the extent to which it is made in order to comply with a legal requirement.

(2) The Chapter II prohibition does not apply to conduct to the extent to which it is engaged in an order to comply with a legal requirement.

(3) In this paragraph "legal requirement" means a requirement—

(a) imposed by or under any enactment in force in the United Kingdom;

[(b) imposed by or under the EU withdrawal agreement or the EEA EFTA separation agreement and having legal effect in the United Kingdom without further enactment (and in this paragraph, "EEA EFTA separation agreement" has the same meaning as in the European Union (Withdrawal Agreement) Act 2020 (see section 39(1) of that Act));]

(c) imposed by or under the law in force in another Member State and having legal effect in the United Kingdom.

Avoidance of conflict with international obligations

6. (1) If the Secretary of State is satisfied that, in order to avoid a conflict between provisions of this Part and an international obligation of the United Kingdom, it would be appropriate for the Chapter I prohibition not to apply to—

(a) a particular agreement, or

(b) any agreement of a particular description,

he may by order exclude the agreement, or agreements of that description, from the Chapter I prohibition.

(2) An order under sub-paragraph (1) may make provision for the exclusion of the agreement or agreements to which the order applies, or of such of them as may be specified, only in specified circumstances.

(3) An order under sub-paragraph (1) may also provide that the Chapter I prohibition is to be deemed never to have applied in relation to the agreement or agreements, or in relation to such of them as may be specified.

(4) If the Secretary of State is satisfied that, in order to avoid a conflict between provisions of this Part and an international obligation of the United Kingdom, it would be appropriate for the Chapter II prohibition not to apply in particular circumstances, he may by order provide for it not to apply in such circumstances as may be specified.

(5) An order under sub-paragraph (4) may provide that the Chapter II prohibition is to be deemed never to have applied in relation to specified conduct.

(6) An international arrangement relating to civil aviation and designated by an order made by the Secretary of State is to be treated as an international obligation for the purposes of this paragraph.

(7) In this paragraph and paragraph 7 "specified" means specified in the order.

Public policy

7. (1) If the Secretary of State is satisfied that there are exceptional and compelling reasons of public policy why the Chapter I prohibition ought not to apply to—

(a) a particular agreement, or

(b) any agreement of a particular description,

he may by order exclude the agreement, or agreements of that description, from the Chapter I prohibition.

(2) An order under sub-paragraph (1) may make provision for the exclusion of the agreement or agreements to which the order applies, or of such of them as may be specified, only in specified circumstances.

(3) An order under sub-paragraph (1) may also provide that the Chapter I prohibition is to be deemed never to have applied in relation to the agreement or agreements, or in relation to such of them as may be specified.

(4) If the Secretary of State is satisfied that there are exceptional and compelling reasons of public policy why the Chapter II prohibition ought not to apply in particular circumstances, he may by order provide for it not to apply in such circumstances as may be specified.

(5) An order under sub-paragraph (4) may provide that the Chapter II prohibition is to be deemed never to have applied in relation to specified conduct.

Coal and steel

8. (1) The Chapter I prohibition does not apply to an agreement which relates to a coal or steel product to the extent to which the ECSC Treaty gives the Commission exclusive jurisdiction in the matter.

(2) Sub-paragraph (1) ceases to have effect on the date on which the ECSC Treaty expires ("the expiry date").

(3) The Chapter II prohibition does not apply to conduct which relates to a coal or steel product to the extent to which the ECSC Treaty gives the Commission exclusive jurisdiction in the matter.

(4) Sub-paragraph (3) ceases to have effect on the expiry date.

(5) In this paragraph—

"coal or steel product" means any product of a kind listed in Annex I to the ECSC Treaty; and "ECSC Treaty" means the Treaty establishing the European Coal and Steel Community.

Agricultural products

9. *(1) The Chapter I prohibition does not apply to an agreement to the extent to which it relates to production of or trade in an agricultural product and—*

- *(a) forms an integral part of a national market organisation;*
- *(b) is necessary for the attainment of the objectives set out in [Article 39 of the Treaty on the Functioning of the European Union]; or*
- *(c) is an agreement of farmers or farmers' associations (or associations of such associations) belonging to a single member State which concerns—*
  - *(i) the production or sale of agricultural products, or*
  - *(ii) the use of joint facilities for the storage, treatment or processing of agricultural products,*

  and under which there is no obligation to charge identical prices.

(2) If the Commission determines that an agreement does not fulfil the conditions specified by the provision for agricultural products for exclusion from [Article 101(1)], the exclusion provided by this paragraph ("the agriculture exclusion") is to be treated as ceasing to apply to the agreement on the date of the decision.

(3) The *agriculture exclusion* does not apply to a particular agreement if the [CMA] gives a direction under this paragraph to that effect.

(4) If the [CMA] is considering whether to give a direction under this paragraph, [it] may by notice in writing require any party to the agreement in question to give [the [CMA]] such information in connection with the agreement as [it] may require.

(5) The [CMA] may give a direction under this paragraph only as provided in sub-paragraph (6) or (7).

(6) If at the end of such period as may be specified in rules under section 51 a person has failed, without reasonable excuse, to comply with a requirement imposed under sub-paragraph (4), the [CMA] may give a direction under this paragraph.

(7) The [CMA] may also give a direction under this paragraph if [it] considers that an agreement (whether or not [it] considers that it infringes the Chapter I prohibition) is likely, or is intended, substantially and unjustifiably to prevent, restrict or distort competition in relation to an agricultural product.

(8) A direction under this paragraph—

- (a) must be in writing;
- (b) may be made so as to have effect from a date specified in the direction (which may not be earlier than the date on which it is given).

(9) In this paragraph—

"agricultural product" means any product of a kind listed in [Annex I] to the Treaty; and

"provision for agricultural products" means Council Regulation (EEC) No 26/62 of 4th April 1962 applying certain rules of competition to production of and trade in agricultural products.

[10. (1) The Chapter 1 prohibition does not apply to an agreement to the extent that it is an agreement between the members of a recognised interbranch organisation that has the object of carrying out one or more specified activities, provided that the condition in sub-paragraph (2) is also met.

This exclusion is referred to in this paragraph as the "RIBO exclusion".

(2) The condition in this sub-paragraph is that the organisation has notified the agreement to the CMA and provided all further details required by the CMA, and—

- (a) the CMA has decided that it is appropriate for the RIBO exclusion to apply, or
- (b) within two months of the CMA receiving all the details it requires, the CMA has not decided that it is inappropriate for the RIBO exclusion to apply.

(3) In deciding whether it is appropriate for the RIBO exclusion to apply, the CMA must consider whether the benefit of the agreement to the specified activities of the recognised interbranch organisation outweighs any prevention, restriction or distortion of competition within the United Kingdom as a result of the agreement.

(4) The CMA may at any time give a direction to the effect that the RIBO exclusion no longer applies to a particular agreement.

(5) Sub-paragraphs (4) to (8) of paragraph 9 apply to a direction under this paragraph as they apply to a direction under paragraph 9.

(6) In this paragraph—

"recognised interbranch organisation" means an organisation of agricultural businesses recognised under section 30 of the Agriculture Act 2020;

"specified activities" means the activities specified in regulations under section 30(6)(e) of that Act.]

NOTES

Para 2: repealed by the Competition Act 1998 and Other Enactments (Amendment) Regulations 2004, SI 2004/1261, reg 4, Sch 1, para 50(a).

Para 3: words in first (outer) pair of square brackets in para (a) of the definition "EEA regulated market" in sub-para (5) substituted by the Financial Services and Markets Act 2000 (Markets in Financial Instruments) Regulations 2007, SI 2007/126, reg 3(6), Sch 6, Pt 1, para 13. Words in second (inner) pair of square brackets in that paragraph substituted by the Financial Services and Markets Act 2000 (Markets in Financial Instruments) Regulations 2017, SI 2017/701, reg 50(3), Sch 4, para 5. This paragraph was repealed by the Competition (Amendment etc) (EU Exit) Regulations 2019, SI 2019/93, regs 2, 29, as from IP completion day (as defined in the European Union (Withdrawal Agreement) Act 2020, s 39) (for transitional provisions and savings in relation to the operation of the 2019 Regulations, see Sch 4 to those Regulations at **[7.69]** et seq).

Para 5: sub-para (3)(b) was substituted, and sub-para (3)(c) was repealed by SI 2019/93, regs 2, 29, as from IP completion day (as defined in the European Union (Withdrawal Agreement) Act 2020, s 39) (for transitional provisions and savings in relation to the operation of the 2019 Regulations, see Sch 4 to those Regulations at **[7.69]** et seq). Note that reg 29 of the 2019 Regulations was amended by the Competition (Amendment etc) (EU Exit) Regulations 2020, SI 2020/1343, reg 6, with effect from immediately before IP completion day; and the effect of that amendment has been incorporated in the text set out above. Note also that the original sub-para (3)(b) read as follows—

"(b) imposed by or under the Treaty or the EEA Agreement and having legal effect in the United Kingdom without further enactment; or".

Para 9 is amended as follows:

Words in square brackets in sub-paras (1)(b) and (2) substituted by the Treaty of Lisbon (Changes in Terminology or Numbering) Order 2012, SI 2012/1809, art 3(1), Schedule, Pt 1.

Sub-para (1) is substituted (as follows), and sub-para (2) is repealed, by the Agriculture Act 2020, s 31, Sch 2, para 2(1)–(3), as from a day to be appointed—

"(1) The Chapter 1 prohibition does not apply to an agreement to the extent that it is an agreement between the members of—

(a) a recognised producer organisation ("PO"), or
(b) a recognised association of producer organisations ("APO"),

for the PO or APO (as the case may be) to carry out one or more of the activities mentioned in sub-paragraph (1A) on behalf of its members (for all or part of their total production), provided that Conditions A and B are also met.

This exclusion is referred to in this paragraph as the "RPO exclusion".

(1A) The activities are—

(a) planning production;
(b) optimising production costs;
(c) concentrating supply;
(d) placing products on the market;
(e) negotiating supply contracts.

(1B) Condition A is that—

(a) in the case of a PO, the PO concentrates supply and places the products of its members on the market, whether or not there is a transfer of ownership of agricultural products by the producers to the PO, or
(b) in the case of an APO, the APO concentrates supply and places the products of the members of the POs it represents on the market, whether or not there is a transfer of ownership of agricultural products by the producers to the APO or to any of the POs the APO represents.

(1C) Condition B is that—

(a) in the case of a PO, none of the producers concerned are members of any other PO as regards the products covered by the activities mentioned in sub-paragraph (1A) to which the agreement relates, or
(b) in the case of an APO, none of the producers concerned are members of a PO that is a member of any other APO as regards the products covered by the activities mentioned in sub-paragraph (1A) to which the agreement relates.

(1D) But the Secretary of State may decide that the RPO exclusion applies if Condition B is not met, if—

(a) every producer which is a member of more than one PO holds distinct production units located in different geographical areas, and
(b) the Secretary of State considers that it is appropriate in all the circumstances for the RPO exclusion to apply.

(1E) If the Secretary of State is considering whether to make a decision under sub-paragraph (1D), the Secretary of State may by notice in writing require any party to the agreement in question to give the Secretary of State such information in connection with the agreement as the Secretary of State may require.".

For the words in italics in sub-para (3) there are substituted the words "RPO exclusion" by the Agriculture Act 2020, s 31, Sch 2, para 2(1), (4), as from a day to be appointed.

References to the "CMA" substituted by the Enterprise and Regulatory Reform Act 2013, s 26(3), Sch 5, Pt 1, paras 1, 55 (for various transitional provisions (including those relating to the abolition of the OFT and the Competition Commission, existing references to those bodies and provisions relating to continuity), see the Enterprise and Regulatory Reform Act 2013 (Commencement No 6, Transitional Provisions and Savings) Order 2014, SI 2014/416, Schedule at **[2.13]**).

Word "it" in square brackets in every place that it occurs in sub-paras (4), (7), substituted by the Enterprise Act 2002, s 278(1), Sch 25, para 38.

Words in square brackets in the definition "agricultural product" in sub-para (9) substituted by SI 2004/1261, reg 4, Sch 1, para 50(b).

Sub-para (9) is substituted by the Agriculture Act 2020, s 31, Sch 2, para 2(1), (5), as from a day to be appointed, as follows—

"(9) In this paragraph—

"agricultural product" means a product that falls within a sector mentioned in Schedule 1 to the Agriculture Act 2020;

"recognised association of producer organisations" means an association recognised under section 30 of that Act;
"recognised producer organisation" means a producer organisation recognised under section 30 of that Act.".

Para 10: added by the Agriculture Act 2020, s 31, Sch 2, para 3, as from a day to be appointed.

See also the Agriculture Act 2020, ss 31, 32 which provides that the Secretary of State may, by Regulations, make further provision about recognised organisations (ie, recognised producer organisations, recognised associations of producer organisations, and recognised interbranch organisations).

Restrictive Trade Practices Act 1976: repealed by s 74 of, and Sch 14, Pt I to, this Act.

References to the European Community and related expressions: see the note "References to "the European Community", "Community", etc" in the introductory notes to this Act.

Orders: the Competition Act 1998 (Public Policy Exclusion) Order 2006, SI 2006/605 (which excludes from the Chapter I prohibition any agreement where the purpose of the agreement is to enable the parties to provide or receive maintenance and repair services for surface warships, and the agreement does not have as its object or effect the prevention, restriction or distortion of competition within the UK except in relation to the market for maintenance and repair of surface warships); the Competition Act 1998 (Public Policy Exclusion) Order 2008, SI 2008/1820 (which excludes from the Chapter I prohibition any agreements concerning any part of a Core Competence between the Secretary of State and a Submarine Enterprise Collaboration Participant, or between two or more Submarine Enterprise Collaboration Participants, or between one or more Submarine Enterprise Collaboration Participants and any other person in order to give effect to a joint buying agreement, and the agreement does not have as its object or effect the prevention, restriction or distortion of competition within the UK except to the extent that it concerns the exercise of any part of a Core Competence by a Submarine Enterprise Collaboration Participant); the Competition Act 1998 (Public Policy Exclusion) (Revocation) Order 2011, SI 2011/2886 (which revoked the Competition Act 1998 (Public Policy Exclusion) Order 2007, SI 2007/1896, which excluded agreements between two or more members of the Team Complex Weapons ("Team CW") or between a member of Team CW and any other person together with conduct by a member of Team CW, which had as their purpose of protecting the essential security interests of the UK from the prohibitions contained in Chapters I and II); the Competition Act 1998 (Public Policy Exclusion) Order 2012, SI 2012/710 (which excludes from the Chapter I prohibition an agreement between the Secretary of State for Energy and Climate Change and representatives of the petroleum supply industry concerning the supply of fuel in an emergency. It also excludes from the prohibition certain arrangements implementing that agreement); the Competition Act 1998 (Coronavirus) (Public Policy Exclusions) (Amendment and Revocation) Order 2020, SI 2020/933 at **[8.10]**; the Competition Act 1998 (Coronavirus) (Public Policy Exclusions) (Revocations) Order, SI 2021/773 at **[8.11]**; the Competition Act 1998 (Football Broadcasting Rights) (Public Policy Exclusion) Order 2021, SI 2021/1148 at **[8.12]**.

Note also that the following Regulations which were made under this Schedule in connection with the Coronavirus pandemic have subsequently been revoked: the Competition Act 1998 (Health Services for Patients in England) (Coronavirus) (Public Policy Exclusion) Order 2020, SI 2020/368; the Competition Act 1998 (Groceries) (Coronavirus) (Public Policy Exclusion) Order 2020, SI 2020/369; the Competition Act 1998 (Solent Maritime Crossings) (Coronavirus) (Public Policy Exclusion) Order 2020, SI 2020/370; the Competition Act 1998 (Health Services for Patients in Wales) (Coronavirus) (Public Policy Exclusion) Order 2020, SI 2020/435; the Competition Act 1998 (Dairy Produce) (Coronavirus) (Public Policy Exclusion) Order 2020, SI 2020/481; the Competition Act 1998 (Groceries) (Public Policy Exclusion) Order 2020, SI 2020/1568.

SCHEDULES 4–6

(Sch 4 repealed by the Enterprise Act 2002, ss 207, 278(2), Sch 26, subject to savings in relation to designation orders made under that Schedule (see Sch 24, para 20 to the 2002 Act at ***[1.445]****). Schs 5, 6 repealed by the Competition Act 1998 and Other Enactments (Amendment) Regulations 2004, SI 2004/1261, reg 4, Sch 1, para 51.)*

[SCHEDULE 6A
COMMITMENTS

Section 31A

PART 1 PROCEDURAL REQUIREMENTS FOR THE ACCEPTANCE AND VARIATION OF COMMITMENTS

[1.141]

1. Paragraph 2 applies where the [CMA] proposes to—

(a) accept any commitments under section 31A; or

(b) accept any variation of such commitments other than a variation which is not material in any respect.

2. (1) Before accepting the commitments or variation, the [CMA] must—

(a) give notice under this paragraph; and

(b) consider any representations made in accordance with the notice and not withdrawn.

(2) A notice under this paragraph must state—

(a) that the [CMA] proposes to accept the commitments or variation;

(b) the purpose of the commitments or variation and the way in which the commitments or variation would meet the [CMA's] competition concerns;

(c) any other facts which the [CMA] considers are relevant to the acceptance or variation of the commitments; and

(d) the period within which representations may be made in relation to the proposed commitments or variation.

(3) The period stated for the purposes of sub-paragraph (2)(d) must be at least 11 working days starting with the date the notice is given or, if that date is not a working day, with the date of the first working day after that date.

3. (1) The [CMA] must not accept the commitments or variation of which notice has been given under paragraph 2(1) with modifications unless it—

(a) gives notice under this paragraph of the proposed modifications; and

(b) considers any representations made in accordance with the notice and not withdrawn.

(2) A notice under this paragraph must state—

(a) the proposed modifications;

(b) the reasons for them; and
(c) the period within which representations may be made in relation to the proposed modifications.

(3) The period stated for the purposes of sub-paragraph (2)(c) must be at least 6 working days starting with the date the notice is given or, if that date is not a working day, with the date of the first working day after that date.

4. If, after giving notice under paragraph 2 or 3 the [CMA] decides—
(a) not to accept the commitments or variation concerned, and
(b) not to proceed by virtue of paragraph 5 or 6,
the [CMA] must give notice that it has so decided.

5. The requirements of paragraph 3 shall not apply if the [CMA]—
(a) has already given notice under paragraph 2 but not under paragraph 3; and
(b) considers that the modifications which are now being proposed are not material in any respect.

6. The requirements of paragraph 3 shall not apply if the [CMA]—
(a) has already given notices under paragraphs 2 and 3; and
(b) considers that the further modifications which are now being proposed are not material in any respect or do not differ in any material respect from the modifications in relation to which notice was last given under paragraph 3.

7. As soon as practicable after accepting commitments or a variation under section 31A the [CMA] must publish the commitments or the variation in such manner as the [CMA] considers appropriate.

8. A notice under paragraph 2 or 3 shall be given by—
(a) sending a copy of the notice to such person or persons as the [CMA] considers appropriate for the purpose of bringing the matter to which it relates to the attention of those likely to be affected by it; or
(b) publishing the notice in such manner as the [CMA] considers appropriate for the purpose of bringing the matter to which it relates to the attention of those likely to be affected by it.]

NOTES

Inserted by the Competition Act 1998 and other Enactments (Amendment) Regulations 2004, SI 2004/1261, reg 4, Sch 1, para 52.

References to the "CMA" and the "CMA's" substituted by the Enterprise and Regulatory Reform Act 2013, s 26(3), Sch 5, Pt 1, paras 1, 56. For various transitional provisions (including those relating to the abolition of the OFT and the Competition Commission, existing references to those bodies and provisions relating to continuity), see the Enterprise and Regulatory Reform Act 2013 (Commencement No 6, Transitional Provisions and Savings) Order 2014, SI 2014/416, Schedule at **[2.13]**.

[PART 2 PROCEDURAL REQUIREMENTS FOR THE RELEASE OF COMMITMENTS

[1.142]

10. Paragraph 11 applies where the [CMA] proposes to release any commitments under section 31A.

11. (1) Before releasing the commitments, the [CMA] must—
(a) give notice under this paragraph;
(b) send a copy of the notice to the person (or persons) who gave the commitments; and
(c) consider any representations made in accordance with the notice and not withdrawn.

(2) A notice under this paragraph must state—
(a) the fact that a release is proposed;
(b) the reasons for it; and
(c) the period within which representations may be made in relation to the proposed release.

(3) The period stated for the purposes of sub-paragraph (2)(c) must be at least 11 working days starting with the date the notice is given or, if that date is not a working day, with the date of the first working day after that date.

12. If after giving notice under paragraph 11 the [CMA] decides not to proceed with the release, it must—
(a) give notice that it has so decided; and
(b) send a copy of the notice to the person (or persons) who gave the commitments.

13. As soon as practicable after releasing the commitments, the [CMA] must—
(a) publish the release in such manner as it considers appropriate; and
(b) send a copy of the release to the person (or persons) who gave the commitments.

14. A notice under paragraph 11 or 12 shall be given by—
(a) sending a copy of the notice to such other person or persons as the [CMA] considers appropriate for the purpose of bringing the matter to which it relates to the attention of those likely to be affected by it; or
(b) publishing the notice in such manner as the [CMA] considers appropriate for the purpose of bringing the matter to which it relates to the attention of those likely to be affected by it.]

NOTES

Inserted by the Competition Act 1998 and other enactments (Amendment) Regulations 2004, SI 2004/1261, reg 4, Sch 1, para 52.

References to the "CMA" substituted by the Enterprise and Regulatory Reform Act 2013, s 26(3), Sch 5, Pt 1, paras 1, 56. For various transitional provisions (including those relating to the abolition of the OFT and the Competition Commission, existing references to those bodies and provisions relating to continuity), see the Enterprise and Regulatory Reform Act 2013 (Commencement No 6, Transitional Provisions and Savings) Order 2014, SI 2014/416, Schedule at **[2.13]**.

SCHEDULES 7, 7A

(Schs 7 and 7A were repealed by the Enterprise and Regulatory Reform Act 2013, s 26(3), Sch 5, Pt 3, paras 218, 222,

223. For various transitional provisions (including those relating to the abolition of the OFT and the Competition Commission, existing references to those bodies and provisions relating to continuity), see the Enterprise and Regulatory Reform Act 2013 (Commencement No 6, Transitional Provisions and Savings) Order 2014, SI 2014/416, Schedule at **[2.13]**.)

SCHEDULE 8
APPEALS

Sections 46(5) and 48(4)

PART I GENERAL

. . .

[1.143]

1. . . .

General procedure

2. (1) An appeal to the [Tribunal under section [46, 47 or 49D(3)] must be made by sending a notice of appeal to it] within the specified period.

(2) The notice of appeal must set out the grounds of appeal in sufficient detail to indicate—

- (a) under which provision of this Act the appeal is brought;
- (b) to what extent (if any) the appellant contends that the decision against, or with respect to which, the appeal is brought was based on an error of fact or was wrong in law; and
- (c) to what extent (if any) the appellant is appealing against the [[CMA's] exercise of its] discretion in making the disputed decision.

(3) The [Tribunal] may give an appellant leave to amend the grounds of appeal identified in the notice of appeal.

[(4) In this paragraph references to the Tribunal are to the Tribunal as constituted (in accordance with section 14 of the Enterprise Act 2002) for the purposes of the proceedings in question.

(5) Nothing in this paragraph restricts the power under section 15 of the Enterprise Act 2002 (Tribunal rules) to make provision as to the manner of instituting proceedings before the Tribunal.]

Decisions of the [Tribunal]

3. [(A1) This paragraph applies to any appeal under section 46 or 47 other than—

- (a) an appeal under section 46 against, or with respect to, a decision of the kind specified in subsection (3)(g) or (h) of that section, and
- (b) an appeal under section 47(1)(b) or (c).]

(1) The [Tribunal] must determine the appeal on the merits by reference to the grounds of appeal set out in the notice of appeal.

(2) The [Tribunal] may confirm or set aside the decision which is the subject of the appeal, or any part of it, and may—

- (a) remit the matter to the [CMA],
- (b) impose or revoke, or vary the amount of, a penalty,
- (c) . . .
- (d) give such directions, or take such other steps, as the [CMA] could [itself] have given or taken, or
- (e) make any other decision which the [CMA] could [itself] have made.

(3) Any decision of the [Tribunal] on an appeal has the same effect, and may be enforced in the same manner, as a decision of the [CMA].

(4) If the [Tribunal] confirms the decision which is the subject of the appeal it may nevertheless set aside any finding of fact on which the decision was based.

[3A. (1) This paragraph applies to—

- (a) any appeal under section 46 against, or with respect to, a decision of the kind specified in subsection (3)(g) or (h) of that section, and
- (b) any appeal under section 47(1)(b) or (c).

(2) The Tribunal must, by reference to the grounds of appeal set out in the notice of appeal, determine the appeal by applying the same principles as would be applied by a court on an application for judicial review.

(3) The Tribunal may—

- (a) dismiss the appeal or quash the whole or part of the decision to which it relates; and
- (b) where it quashes the whole or part of that decision, remit the matter back to the [CMA] with a direction to reconsider and make a new decision in accordance with the ruling of the Tribunal.]

[3B. (1) This paragraph applies to an appeal under section 49D(3).

(2) The Tribunal must determine the appeal on the merits by reference to the grounds of appeal set out in the notice of appeal.

(3) The Tribunal may—

- (a) approve the amount of costs which is the subject of the appeal, or
- (b) impose a requirement to pay costs of a different amount.

(4) The Tribunal may also give such directions, or take such other steps, as the CMA could itself have given or taken.

(5) A requirement imposed by the Tribunal under sub-paragraph (3)(b) has the same effect, and may be enforced in the same manner, as a requirement imposed by the CMA under section 49D.]

4. . . .

NOTES

Paras 1, 4: repealed by the Enterprise Act 2002, ss 21, 278(2), Sch 5, paras 1, 8(1), (2), (5), Sch 26.

Para 2: words in first (outer) pair of square brackets in sub-para (1) substituted, words in square brackets in sub-paras (2)(c), (3) substituted, and sub-paras (4), (5) added, by the Enterprise Act 2002, ss 21, 278(1), Sch 5, paras 1, 8(1), (3), Sch 25, para 38(1), (54)(b). Reference to the "CMA's" in sub-para (2)(c) substituted by the Enterprise and Regulatory Reform Act 2013, s 26(3), Sch 5, Pt 1, paras 1, 57(1), (2) (for various transitional provisions (including those relating to the abolition of the OFT and the Competition Commission, existing references to those bodies and provisions relating to continuity), see the Enterprise and Regulatory Reform Act 2013 (Commencement No 6, Transitional Provisions and Savings) Order 2014, SI 2014/416, Schedule at **[2.13]**); words in second (inner) pair of square brackets in sub-para (1) substituted by the Consumer Rights Act 2015, s 80, Sch 8, Pt 1, paras 1, 17(1), (2).

Para 3: sub-para (A1) inserted, and sub-para (2)(c) repealed, by the Competition Act 1998 and Other Enactments (Amendment) Regulations 2004, SI 2004/1261, reg 4, Sch 1, para 53(1)–(3) (for savings and transitional provisions see reg 8 of those Regulations at **[2.8]**). Words "Tribunal" and "itself" in square brackets substituted by the Enterprise Act 2002, ss 21, 278(1), Sch 5, paras 1, 8(1), (4), Sch 25, para 38(1), (54)(c). References to the "CMA" substituted by the Enterprise and Regulatory Reform Act 2013, s 26(3), Sch 5, Pt 1, paras 1, 57(1), (3), subject to transitional provisions in SI 2014/416 as noted above.

Para 3A: inserted by SI 2004/1261, reg 4, Sch 1, para 53(1), (4) (for savings and transitional provisions see reg 8 of those Regulations at **[2.8]**). Reference to the "CMA" in sub-para (3)(b) substituted by the Enterprise and Regulatory Reform Act 2013, s 26(3), Sch 5, Pt 1, paras 1, 57(1) (4), subject to transitional provisions in SI 2014/416 as noted above.

Para 3B: inserted by the Consumer Rights Act 2015, s 80, Sch 8, Pt 1, paras 1, 17(1), (3).

Transitional provisions: for transitional provisions in relation to the constitution, etc, of the Tribunal, see the Enterprise Act 2002, Sch 24, paras 7–11 at **[1.445]**, and for transitional provisions in connection with existing appeals, see the Enterprise Act 2002 (Commencement No 2, Transitional and Transitory Provisions) Order 2003, SI 2003/766, art 3.

(Sch 8, Pt II repealed by the Enterprise Act 2002, ss 21, 278(2), Sch 5, paras 1, 8(1), (5), Sch 26.)

[SCHEDULE 8A
FURTHER PROVISION ABOUT CLAIMS IN RESPECT OF LOSS OR DAMAGE BEFORE A COURT OR THE TRIBUNAL

Section 47F

PART 1 INTERPRETATION

[1.144]

1. This Part of this Schedule contains definitions and other provisions about interpretation which apply for the purposes of this Schedule.

Competition law etc

2. (1) "Competition law" means—
- (a) the Chapter I prohibition, [and]
- (b) the Chapter II prohibition,
- *(c) the prohibition in Article 101(1), and*
- *(d) the prohibition in Article 102.*

(2) "Competition claim" means a claim in respect of loss or damage arising from an infringement of competition law (whatever the legal basis of the claim) which is made by or on behalf of—
- (a) the person who suffered the loss or damage, or
- (b) a person who has acquired that person's right to make the claim (whether by operation of law or otherwise).

(3) "Competition damages claim" means a competition claim to the extent that it is a claim for damages.

(4) "Competition proceedings" means proceedings before a court or the Tribunal to the extent that they relate to a competition claim.

(5) Where the context requires, references to an infringement of competition law and to loss or damage (however expressed) include an alleged infringement and alleged loss or damage.

Competition authority etc

3. (1) "Competition authority" means—
- (a) the CMA, [and]
- (b) a regulator, so far as it exercises functions under Part 1 of this Act concurrently with the CMA,
- *(c) the Commission, and*
- *(d) a member State competition authority.*

(2) A "member State competition authority" means an authority designated by a member State other than the United Kingdom, under Article 35 of the EC Competition Regulation, as being responsible for the application of Article 101 and Article 102 of the Treaty.

(3) "Investigation materials", in relation to a competition authority, means—
- (a) information prepared by a person (other than a competition authority) for the purpose of an investigation by the competition authority into an infringement of competition law;
- (b) information sent by the competition authority, during the course of such an investigation, to an undertaking which is the subject of the investigation;
- (c) a settlement submission which has been withdrawn.

(4) [Section 58A(3) applies] for the purposes of determining when a decision of the [the CMA or a regulator] becomes "final".

(5) A decision of a member State competition authority becomes "final"—
- *(a) when the time for appealing against it expires without an appeal having been brought, or*

(b) where an appeal has been brought against the decision, when—
(i) the appeal and any further appeal in relation to the decision has been decided or has otherwise ended, and
(ii) the time for appealing against the result of the appeal or further appeal has expired without another appeal having been brought.

(6) Where the law of a member State other than the United Kingdom requires or enables a member State competition authority to bring proceedings before a court of the member State in relation to an infringement of Article 101(1) or Article 102, rather than making a decision itself in relation to the infringement—
(a) references to an investigation by a competition authority into an infringement of competition law include such proceedings brought by the member State competition authority;
(b) references to a competition authority closing an investigation include the termination of such proceedings by the member State competition authority or by another person, except where the competition authority's investigation of the infringement continues after the proceedings terminate;
(c) references to a decision of a competition authority include a decision of a court in such proceedings;
(d) sub-paragraph (5) applies in relation to a decision of a court in such proceedings as it applies in relation to a decision of a member State competition authority.

Cartels

4. (1) "Cartel" means an agreement or concerted practice between two or more competitors aimed at—
(a) co-ordinating their competitive behaviour in a market, or
(b) otherwise influencing competition in a market,
through practices such as (but not limited to) those listed in sub-paragraph (2).

(2) Those practices are—
(a) fixing or co-ordinating purchase or selling prices or other trading conditions, including in relation to intellectual property rights,
(b) allocating production or sales quotas, and
(c) sharing markets and customers, including bid-rigging, restrictions of imports or exports or anti-competitive actions against other competitors.

(3) "Cartel leniency programme" means a programme operated by a competition authority under which—
(a) an undertaking that has participated in a cartel may provide the competition authority with information about the cartel and the undertaking's involvement in it, and
(b) if it does so voluntarily and independently of the other cartel members, the competition authority may give the undertaking immunity from, or a reduction in, a financial penalty which would otherwise be payable by the undertaking for its participation in the cartel.

(4) "Cartel leniency statement" means a set of information provided, orally or in writing, to a competition authority by or on behalf of a person which—
(a) consists of information about a cartel and the person's role in relation to the cartel,
(b) is provided voluntarily, and
(c) is provided specifically for the purposes of the competition authority's cartel leniency programme,
excluding any pre-existing information.

(5) For the purposes of sub-paragraph (4)—
(a) "pre-existing information" means information that exists irrespective of a competition authority's investigations, and
(b) the fact that information is in a competition authority's file does not prevent it from being pre-existing information.

(6) References to a cartel leniency statement include—
(a) a part of a cartel leniency statement,
(b) a quotation from a cartel leniency statement,
(c) all or part of a record of a cartel leniency statement, and
(d) a copy of all or part of a cartel leniency statement or of a record of such a statement.

(7) On the application of a claimant in competition proceedings, a court or the Tribunal may, in accordance with procedural rules, determine whether information is a cartel leniency statement.

(8) For the purposes of making a determination under sub-paragraph (7), the court or the Tribunal may—
(a) take evidence from the author of the document, and
(b) obtain assistance from a competition authority,
but may not obtain assistance from anyone else.

Settlement submission to a competition authority

5. (1) "Settlement submission" means a statement made, orally or in writing, to a competition authority by or on behalf of an undertaking—
(a) which states—
(i) that the undertaking accepts that it has infringed competition law, or
(ii) that the undertaking does not accept that it has infringed competition law but will not dispute a decision of the competition authority that it has done so,
(b) which is made voluntarily, and
(c) which is made for the sole purpose of allowing the competition authority to follow a simplified or expedited procedure in connection with the infringement.

(2) References to a settlement submission include—
(a) a part of a settlement submission,
(b) a quotation from a settlement submission,

(c) all or part of a record of a settlement submission, and
(d) a copy of all or part of a settlement submission or of a record of such a submission.

(3) On the application of a claimant in competition proceedings, a court or the Tribunal may, in accordance with procedural rules, determine whether a document is a settlement submission.

(4) For the purposes of making a determination under sub-paragraph (3), the court or the Tribunal may—
(a) take evidence from the author of the document, and
(b) obtain assistance from a competition authority,
but may not obtain assistance from anyone else.

Consensual dispute resolution process

6. (1) "Consensual dispute resolution process" means arbitration, mediation or any other process enabling parties to a dispute to resolve it out of court.

(2) A dispute is resolved "out of court" even if the process involves a court or the Tribunal approving what the parties agree or declaring their agreement binding.

Other definitions

7. (1) "Court" means—
(a) the High Court or the Court of Appeal in England and Wales,
(b) the sheriff or the Court of Session,
(c) the High Court or the Court of Appeal in Northern Ireland, or
(d) the Supreme Court,
except in paragraphs 3(6) and 35.

(2) "Damages" includes any sum of money (other than costs or expenses) which may be awarded in respect of a competition claim.

(3) "Procedural rules" means—
(a) in relation to proceedings before a court, rules of court, and
(b) in relation to proceedings before the Tribunal, Tribunal rules.

(4) "Undertaking" includes an association of undertakings.]

NOTES

Inserted by the Claims in respect of Loss or Damage arising from Competition Infringements (Competition Act 1998 and Other Enactments (Amendment)) Regulations 2017, SI 2017/385, reg 2, Sch 1 paras 1, 4.

This Part was amended (as follows) by the Competition (Amendment etc) (EU Exit) Regulations 2019, SI 2019/93, regs 2, 30, as from IP completion day (as defined in the European Union (Withdrawal Agreement) Act 2020, s 39) (for transitional provisions and savings in relation to the operation of the 2019 Regulations, see Sch 4 to those Regulations at **[7.69]** et seq)—

The word in square brackets in para 2(1)(a) and 3(1)(a) was inserted.

Paras 2(1)(c), (d) were repealed.

Paras 3(1)(c), (d) and (2), (5) and (6) were repealed.

In Para 3(4) the words "Section 58A(3) applies" in square brackets were substituted (for the original words "Subsections (3) and (4) of section 58A apply"), and the words "the CMA or a regulator" in square brackets were substituted (for the original words "the CMA, a regulator or the Commission").

[PART 2 PASSING ON

Overcharges and underpayments

[1.145]

8. For the purposes of this Part of this Schedule—
(a) there is an overcharge as a result of an infringement of competition law if, when a product or service is acquired directly from the infringer, the price actually paid exceeds the price that would have been paid in the absence of the infringement, and
(b) there is an underpayment as a result of an infringement of competition law if, when a product or service is provided directly to the infringer, the price actually paid is less than the amount that would have been paid in the absence of the infringement.

Burden of proof where an overcharge is passed on to an indirect purchaser

9. (1) Sub-paragraph (2) applies where—
(a) there is an overcharge as a result of an infringement of competition law, and
(b) a competition claim is made in respect of loss or damage which—
(i) arises, directly or indirectly, from the overcharge, and
(ii) was suffered by a person who acquired a product or service indirectly from the infringer ("the injured person").

(2) The claimant is to be treated as having proved that the overcharge was passed on to the claimant if the claimant proves that—
(a) the defendant infringed competition law,
(b) as a result of the infringement, there was an overcharge when a person acquired a product or service directly from the defendant, and
(c) the claimant subsequently acquired—
(i) the product or service mentioned in paragraph (b), or
(ii) a product or service derived from or containing the product or service mentioned in paragraph (b).

(3) Sub-paragraph (2) does not apply if the defendant proves that the overcharge, or part of it, was not passed on to the claimant.

(4) Where the claimant is not the injured person, the following are to be read as references to the injured person—
(a) the second reference to the claimant in the opening words of sub-paragraph (2), and

(b) the references to the claimant in sub-paragraphs (2)(c) and (3).

(5) Where the defendant is not the infringer, the references in sub-paragraph (2)(a) and (b) to the defendant are to be read as references to the infringer.

Burden of proof where an underpayment is passed on to an indirect provider

10. (1) Sub-paragraph (2) applies where—

(a) there is an underpayment as a result of an infringement of competition law, and

(b) a competition claim is made in respect of loss or damage which—

(i) arises, directly or indirectly, from the underpayment, and

(ii) was suffered by a person who provided a product or service indirectly to the infringer ("the injured person").

(2) The claimant is to be treated as having proved that the underpayment was passed on to the claimant if the claimant proves that—

(a) the defendant infringed competition law,

(b) as a result of the infringement, there was an underpayment when a person provided a product or service directly to the defendant, and

(c) the product or service mentioned in paragraph (b)—

(i) was provided to the person by the claimant, or

(ii) contained or was derived from a product or service provided by the claimant.

(3) Sub-paragraph (2) does not apply if the defendant proves that the underpayment, or part of it, was not passed on to the claimant.

(4) Where the claimant is not the injured person, the following are to be read as references to the injured person—

(a) the second reference to the claimant in the opening words of sub-paragraph (2), and

(b) the references to the claimant in sub-paragraphs (2)(c) and (3).

(5) Where the defendant is not the infringer, the references in sub-paragraph (2)(a) and (b) to the defendant are to be read as references to the infringer.

Burden of proof where an overcharge or underpayment is passed on by the claimant

11. (1) This paragraph applies where—

(a) there is an overcharge or underpayment as a result of an infringement of competition law,

(b) a person makes a competition claim in respect of loss or damage which arises, directly or indirectly, from the overcharge or underpayment, and

(c) in its defence, the defendant claims that the claimant passed on all or part of the overcharge or underpayment to another person.

(2) The defendant has the burden of proving—

(a) that the claimant passed on the overcharge or underpayment, and

(b) the extent to which the claimant did so.

(3) Where the competition claim is made by someone other than the person who suffered the loss or damage ("the injured person"), the references in sub-paragraphs (1)(c) and (2) to the claimant are to be read as references to the injured person.]

NOTES

Inserted by the Claims in respect of Loss or Damage arising from Competition Infringements (Competition Act 1998 and Other Enactments (Amendment)) Regulations 2017, SI 2017/385, reg 2, Sch 1 paras 1, 4.

[PART 3 SMALL AND MEDIUM-SIZED ENTERPRISES

Liability of small and medium-sized enterprises

[1.146]

12. (1) Sub-paragraph (3) applies where—

(a) an undertaking participated in an infringement of competition law with one or more other undertakings,

(b) throughout the period of the infringement, the undertaking's share of the relevant market (or, if there was more than one, each relevant market) was less than 5%,

(c) but for this paragraph, the undertaking's liability to pay damages in respect of the infringement (whatever the legal basis of the liability) would irretrievably jeopardise its economic viability and cause its assets to lose all their value, and

(d) the undertaking is a small or medium-sized enterprise.

(2) Sub-paragraph (3) does not apply where—

(a) the undertaking led the infringement,

(b) the undertaking coerced one or more of the other undertakings to participate in the infringement, or

(c) the undertaking has previously been found to have infringed competition law.

(3) The undertaking is not liable (either alone or jointly) to pay damages in respect of loss or damage suffered by a person as a result of the infringement of competition law (whatever the legal basis of the liability) except where—

(a) the person acquired a product or service that was the object of the infringement directly or indirectly from the undertaking, or

(b) the person acquired a product or service containing or derived from a product or service that was the object of the infringement indirectly from the undertaking.

(4) The reference in sub-paragraph (1)(c) to the effect of the undertaking's liability to pay damages is to its effect taking account of the undertaking's other liabilities.

(5) In this paragraph "small or medium-sized enterprise" means a small or medium-sized enterprise as defined in the Annex to Commission Recommendation (EC) No 2003/361 of 6 May 2003 [("the SME Annex"), subject to sub-paragraph (6)].

[(6) For the purposes of this paragraph, the SME Annex has effect as if—
- (a) in Article 2(1), for "EUR 50 million and/or an annual balance sheet total not exceeding EUR 43 million" there were substituted "£44,000,000 and/or an annual balance sheet total not exceeding £38,000,000";
- (b) in Article 2(2), for "EUR 10 million" there were substituted "£8,800,000";
- (c) in Article 2(3), for "EUR 2 million" there were substituted "£1,750,000";
- (d) in Article 3(2)(a), for "EUR 1 250 000" there were substituted "£1,100,000";
- (e) in Article 3(2)(d), for "EUR 10 million" there were substituted "£8,800,000";
- (f) in Article 3(5), for "by national or Community rules" there were substituted "under the law of the United Kingdom (or any part of it)";
- (g) in Article 5(b), for "national law" there were substituted "the law of the United Kingdom (or any part of it)".]]

NOTES

Inserted by the Claims in respect of Loss or Damage arising from Competition Infringements (Competition Act 1998 and Other Enactments (Amendment)) Regulations 2017, SI 2017/385, reg 2, Sch 1 paras 1, 4.

The words in square brackets in sub-para (5), and all of sub-para (6), were inserted by the Competition (Amendment etc) (EU Exit) Regulations 2019, SI 2019/93, regs 2, 30, as from IP completion day (as defined in the European Union (Withdrawal Agreement) Act 2020, s 39) (for transitional provisions and savings in relation to the operation of the 2019 Regulations, see Sch 4 to those Regulations at **[7.69]** et seq).

[PART 4 CARTELS

Presumption that cartels cause harm

[1.147]

13. For the purposes of competition proceedings, it is to be presumed, unless the contrary is proved, that a cartel causes loss or damage.

Immunity recipients

14. (1) Paragraphs 15 and 16 apply where—
- (a) undertakings have infringed the Chapter I prohibition *or the prohibition in Article 101(1)* by participating in a cartel, and
- (b) in respect of its participation in the infringement (the "cartel infringement"), an undertaking has been granted immunity from financial penalties under a cartel leniency programme.

(2) The undertaking mentioned in sub-paragraph (1)(b) is referred to in paragraphs 15 and 16 as "an immunity recipient".

Liability of immunity recipients

15. An immunity recipient is not liable (either alone or jointly) to pay damages in respect of loss or damage suffered by a person as a result of the cartel infringement (whatever the legal basis of the liability) except where—
- (a) the person acquired a product or service that was the object of the cartel infringement directly or indirectly from the immunity recipient,
- (b) the person acquired a product or service containing or derived from a product or service that was the object of the cartel infringement indirectly from the immunity recipient,
- (c) the person provided a product or service that was the object of the cartel infringement directly or indirectly to the immunity recipient,
- (d) a product or service that was the object of the cartel infringement contained or was derived from a product or service provided by the person, or
- (e) the person is unable to obtain full compensation for the loss or damage from other undertakings involved in the cartel infringement.

Contribution between participants in cartels

16. (1) Sub-paragraph (2) applies in relation to proceedings to recover contribution under section 1 of the Civil Liability (Contribution) Act 1978 or section 3(2) of the Law Reform (Miscellaneous Provisions) (Scotland) Act 1940 where contribution is to be recovered—
- (a) in respect of loss or damage suffered by a person as a result of a cartel infringement, and
- (b) from a person who is an immunity recipient in relation to the cartel infringement.

(2) The amount of contribution that the immunity recipient may be required to pay may not exceed the amount of the loss or damage the immunity recipient caused to—
- (a) persons who acquired products or services that were the object of the cartel infringement directly or indirectly from the immunity recipient,
- (b) persons who acquired products or services containing or derived from products or services that were the object of the cartel infringement indirectly from the immunity recipient,
- (c) persons who provided products or services that were the object of the cartel infringement directly or indirectly to the immunity recipient, and
- (d) persons who provided—
  - (i) products or services that were subsequently contained in products or services that were the object of the cartel infringement, or
  - (ii) products or services from which products or services that were the object of the cartel infringement were subsequently derived.

(3) The following have effect subject to sub-paragraph (2)—
- (a) section 2(1) of the Civil Liability (Contribution) Act 1978 (assessment of contribution);

(b) section 3(2) of the Law Reform (Miscellaneous Provisions) (Scotland) Act 1940 (contribution among joint wrongdoers).]

NOTES

Inserted by the Claims in respect of Loss or Damage arising from Competition Infringements (Competition Act 1998 and Other Enactments (Amendment)) Regulations 2017, SI 2017/385, reg 2, Sch 1 paras 1, 4.

Para 14: the words in italics in sub-para (1) were repealed by the Competition (Amendment etc) (EU Exit) Regulations 2019, SI 2019/93, regs 2, 30, as from IP completion day (as defined in the European Union (Withdrawal Agreement) Act 2020, s 39) (for transitional provisions and savings in relation to the operation of the 2019 Regulations, see Sch 4 to those Regulations at **[7.69]** et seq).

[PART 5 LIMITATION AND PRESCRIPTIVE PERIODS

Time limits for bringing competition proceedings

[1.148]

17. (1) Under the law of England and Wales and the law of Northern Ireland, proceedings in respect of a competition claim may not be brought before a court or the Tribunal after the end of the limitation period for the claim determined in accordance with this Part of this Schedule.

(2) Under the law of Scotland—

(a) proceedings in respect of a competition claim may not be brought before a court or the Tribunal after the end of the prescriptive period for the claim determined in accordance with this Part of this Schedule, and

(b) accordingly, an obligation in respect of the loss or damage that is the subject of the claim is extinguished,

except where the subsistence of the obligation in relation to which the claim is made was relevantly acknowledged before the end of that period.

(3) Section 6 of the Prescription and Limitation (Scotland) Act 1973 (extinction of obligations by prescriptive periods of 5 years) does not apply in relation to an obligation described in sub-paragraph (2).

(4) The following provisions of the Prescription and Limitation (Scotland) Act 1973 apply for the purposes of, or in relation to, sub-paragraph (2) as they apply for the purposes of, or in relation to, section 6 of that Act—

(a) section 10 (relevant acknowledgment);

(b) section 13 (prohibition of contracting out);

(c) section 14(1)(c) and (d) (computation of prescriptive periods).

Length of limitation or prescriptive period

18. (1) The limitation period is 6 years.

(2) The prescriptive period is 5 years.

(3) But see—

(a) the provision in paragraphs 20 to 25 for the running of the period to be suspended in certain circumstances, and

(b) paragraph 23(5), which extends the period in certain circumstances.

Beginning of limitation or prescriptive period

19. (1) The limitation or prescriptive period for a competition claim against an infringer begins with the later of—

(a) the day on which the infringement of competition law that is the subject of the claim ceases, and

(b) the claimant's day of knowledge.

(2) "The claimant's day of knowledge" is the day on which the claimant first knows or could reasonably be expected to know—

(a) of the infringer's behaviour,

(b) that the behaviour constitutes an infringement of competition law,

(c) that the claimant has suffered loss or damage arising from that infringement, and

(d) the identity of the infringer.

(3) Where the claimant has acquired the right to make the competition claim from another person (whether by operation of law or otherwise)—

(a) the reference in sub-paragraph (2) to the day on which the claimant first knows or could reasonably be expected to know something is to be read as a reference to the first day on which either the claimant or a person in whom the cause of action was previously vested first knows or could reasonably be expected to know it, and

(b) the reference to the claimant in sub-paragraph (2)(c) is to be read as a reference to the injured person.

(4) In sub-paragraph (3), "injured person", in relation to a competition claim, means a person who suffered the loss or damage that is the subject of the claim.

(5) Where a person ("P") has acquired an infringer's liability in respect of an infringement of competition law from another person (whether by operation of law or otherwise)—

(a) the reference to an infringer in sub-paragraph (1) is to be read as a reference to P, but

(b) the references to the infringer in sub-paragraph (2) are to be read as references to the original infringer.

(6) The references in sub-paragraphs (2) and (3) to a person knowing something are to a person having sufficient knowledge of it to bring competition proceedings.

(7) This paragraph has effect subject to the provision in paragraphs 20 to 25, which defers the beginning of the limitation or prescriptive period in certain circumstances.

Effect of disability on beginning of limitation period: England and Wales and Northern Ireland

20. (1) This paragraph applies if the claimant in relation to a competition claim is under a disability on the day on which, but for this paragraph, the limitation period for the claim would begin.

(2) In England and Wales and Northern Ireland, the limitation period for the claim begins with the earlier of—

(a) the day on which the claimant ceases to be under a disability, and

(b) the day on which the claimant dies.

(3) Where—

(a) the claimant has acquired the right to make the competition claim from another person (whether by operation of law or otherwise), and

(b) but for this paragraph, the limitation period would begin on the day specified in paragraph 19(2),

the references to the claimant in sub-paragraphs (1) and (2) of this paragraph are to be read as references to the person by reference to whose knowledge that day would fall to be determined in accordance with paragraph 19(3).

(4) In England and Wales, references in this paragraph to a person being "under a disability" have the same meaning as in the Limitation Act 1980 (see section 38(2) of that Act).

(5) In Northern Ireland, references in this paragraph to a person being "under a disability" have the same meaning as in the Limitation (Northern Ireland) Order 1989 (SI 1989/1339 (NI 11)) (see article 47 of that Order).

Suspension during investigation by competition authority

21. (1) Where a competition authority investigates an infringement of competition law, the period of the investigation is not to be counted when calculating whether the limitation or prescriptive period for a competition claim in respect of loss or damage arising from the infringement has expired.

(2) The period of an investigation by a competition authority begins when the competition authority takes the first formal step in the investigation.

(3) The period of an investigation by a competition authority ends—

(a) if the competition authority makes a decision in relation to the infringement as a result of the investigation, at the end of the period of one year beginning with the day on which the decision becomes final, and

(b) otherwise, at the end of the period of one year beginning with the day on which the competition authority closes the investigation.

Suspension during consensual dispute resolution process

22. (1) This paragraph applies where—

(a) a dispute arising from an infringement of competition law is the subject of a consensual dispute resolution process,

(b) a competition claim is made which arises from the dispute, and

(c) the claimant and the defendant participated in the consensual dispute resolution process.

(2) The period of the consensual dispute resolution process is not to be counted when calculating whether the limitation or prescriptive period for the claim expired.

(3) The period of a consensual dispute resolution process in relation to a dispute begins with the first day on which either of the following occurs—

(a) the claimant and the defendant (with or without others) enter into an agreement to engage in the process in respect of the dispute, or

(b) the claimant and the defendant submit the dispute to the person who is to run the process.

(4) The period of a consensual dispute resolution process ends with the first day on which one of the following occurs—

(a) the claimant and the defendant reach an agreement to resolve the dispute;

(b) where the process is the subject of an agreement or rules, the process comes to an end in accordance with the agreement or rules;

(c) the claimant or defendant notifies the other that it has withdrawn from the process;

(d) the claimant or the defendant asks the other to confirm that it wishes to continue with the process and does not receive a response within the period of 14 days beginning with the day on which the request is made;

(e) the claimant and the defendant are notified that the person to whom they submitted the dispute refuses to deal with it;

(f) the claimant and defendant are notified that the person running the process cannot continue to act in relation to the dispute and fail to agree to submit the dispute to another person within the period of 14 days beginning with the day on which they are notified.

(5) Where the competition claim is made in collective proceedings, the references to the claimant in sub-paragraphs (1)(c), (3) and (4) are to be read as references to the claimant or the representative.

(6) Where the claimant has acquired the right to make the competition claim from another person (whether by operation of law or otherwise), the references to the claimant in sub-paragraphs (1)(c), (3), (4) and (5) are to be read as references to the claimant or a person in whom the cause of action was previously vested.

(7) Where the defendant has acquired the infringer's liability in respect of the infringement of competition law from another person (whether by operation of law or otherwise), the references to the defendant in sub-paragraphs (1)(c), (3) and (4) are to be read as references to the defendant or a person who has previously held the liability.

Suspension during collective proceedings

23. (1) Where a competition claim is made in collective proceedings at the commencement of those proceedings ("the section 47B claim"), this paragraph applies for the purpose of determining the limitation or prescriptive period for the claim if it is subsequently made in proceedings under section 47A.

(2) The period of the collective proceedings is not to be counted when calculating whether the limitation or prescriptive period has expired.

(3) The period of collective proceedings begins with the day on which the collective proceedings are commenced.

(4) The period of collective proceedings ends with the first day on which one of the following occurs—

(a) the Tribunal declines to make a collective proceedings order in respect of the collective proceedings;

(b) the Tribunal makes a collective proceedings order in respect of the proceedings, but the order does not provide that the section 47B claim is eligible for inclusion in the proceedings;
(c) the Tribunal rejects the section 47B claim;
(d) in the case of opt-in collective proceedings, the period within which a person may choose to have the section 47B claim included in the proceedings expires without the person having done so;
(e) in the case of opt-out collective proceedings—
 (i) a person domiciled in the United Kingdom chooses (within the period in which such a choice may be made) to have the section 47B claim excluded from the collective proceedings, or
 (ii) the period within which a person not domiciled in the United Kingdom may choose to have the section 47B claim included in the collective proceedings expires without the person having done so;
(f) the section 47B claim is withdrawn;
(g) the Tribunal revokes the collective proceedings order in respect of the collective proceedings;
(h) the Tribunal varies the collective proceedings order in such a way that the section 47B claim is no longer included in the collective proceedings;
(i) the section 47B claim is settled with or without the Tribunal's approval;
(j) the section 47B claim is dismissed, discontinued or otherwise disposed of without an adjudication on the merits.

(5) Where—
(a) there is a period of collective proceedings in relation to a competition claim, and
(b) but for this sub-paragraph, the limitation or prescriptive period would expire before the end of the period of 6 months beginning with the day after the day on which the period of collective proceedings ends,

the limitation or prescriptive period for the claim is to be treated as expiring at the end of that 6 month period.

Suspension of prescriptive period during period of disability: Scotland

24. (1) This paragraph applies if the injured person in relation to a competition claim is under legal disability for a period at any time.

(2) In Scotland, the period during which the injured person is under legal disability is not to be counted when calculating whether the prescriptive period for the claim has expired.

(3) References in this paragraph to a person being "under legal disability" have the same meaning as in the Prescription and Limitation (Scotland) Act 1973 (see section 15(1) of that Act).

(4) In this paragraph, "injured person", in relation to a competition claim, means a person who suffered the loss or damages that is the subject of the claim.

Continuity of limitation or prescriptive period

25. For the purposes of calculating whether the limitation or prescriptive period for a competition claim has expired, a period described in paragraph 21, 22, 23 or 24 is not to be regarded as separating the time immediately before it from the time immediately after it.

New claims in pending actions: England and Wales and Northern Ireland

26. (1) In section 35 of the Limitation Act 1980 (new claims in pending actions)—
(a) subsection (1) applies for the purposes of this Part of this Schedule as it applies for the purposes of that Act, and
(b) subsections (3) to (8) apply in relation to a competition claim that is a new claim and to competition proceedings as they apply in relation to other new claims and proceedings.

(2) In Article 73 of the Limitation (Northern Ireland) Order 1989 (SI 1989/1339 (NI 11)) (new claims in pending actions)—
(a) paragraph (1) applies for the purposes of this Part of this Schedule as it applies for the purposes of that Order, and
(b) paragraphs (2) to (7) apply in relation to a competition claim that is a new claim and to competition proceedings as they apply in relation to other new claims and proceedings.]

NOTES

Inserted by the Claims in respect of Loss or Damage arising from Competition Infringements (Competition Act 1998 and Other Enactments (Amendment)) Regulations 2017, SI 2017/385, reg 2, Sch 1 paras 1, 4.

[PART 6 DISCLOSURE ETC

Disclosure orders

[1.149]

27. (1) For the purposes of this Part of this Schedule (and subject to sub-paragraph (2)), a court or the Tribunal makes a disclosure order in respect of something if—
(a) in England and Wales or Northern Ireland, it orders its disclosure or production in accordance with procedural rules, or
(b) in Scotland, it grants commission and diligence for its recovery or makes an order in respect of it under section 1 of the Administration of Justice (Scotland) Act 1972 (inspection of documents etc).

(2) A court or the Tribunal does not make a disclosure order in respect of something if it does something described in sub-paragraph (1) for the purposes of enabling a court or the Tribunal to determine whether it is a cartel leniency statement or a settlement submission.

Restriction in relation to settlement submissions and cartel leniency statements

28. For the purposes of competition proceedings, a court or the Tribunal must not make a disclosure order in respect of—
(a) a settlement submission which has not been withdrawn, or

(b) a cartel leniency statement (whether or not it has been withdrawn).

Restriction in relation to investigation materials

29. For the purposes of competition proceedings, a court or the Tribunal must not make a disclosure order in respect of a competition authority's investigation materials before the day on which the competition authority closes the investigation to which those materials relate.

Restriction in relation to material in a competition authority's file

30. (1) For the purposes of competition proceedings, a court or the Tribunal must not make a disclosure order addressed to a competition authority in respect of documents or information included in a competition authority's file.

(2) Sub-paragraph (1) does not apply where the court or the Tribunal making the order is satisfied that no-one else is reasonably able to provide the documents or information.

Power of High Court in Northern Ireland to order disclosure etc by non-parties

31. (1) On the application of a party to competition proceedings, where it appears to the High Court in Northern Ireland that evidence relevant to the proceedings is likely to be in the possession, custody or power of a person who is not a party to the proceedings, the court may order the person—

(a) to disclose whether such evidence is in the person's possession, custody or power, and

(b) if it is, to produce it—

(i) to the applicant, or

(ii) on such conditions as may be specified in the order, to the applicant's legal adviser or other professional adviser.

(2) An order under sub-paragraph (1) must not be made if the court considers that compliance with it would be likely to be injurious to the public interest.

(3) Rules of court may make provision specifying circumstances in which a court may or may not make an order under sub-paragraph (1).

(4) The power under sub-paragraph (3) includes power to make incidental, supplementary and consequential provision.

(5) Sub-paragraph (1) is without prejudice to the exercise by the High Court in Northern Ireland of any power to make orders which is exercisable apart from this paragraph.]

NOTES

Inserted by the Claims in respect of Loss or Damage arising from Competition Infringements (Competition Act 1998 and Other Enactments (Amendment)) Regulations 2017, SI 2017/385, reg 2, Sch 1 paras 1, 4.

[PART 7 USE OF EVIDENCE

Cartel leniency statements and settlement submissions

[1.150]

32. (1) A settlement submission which has not been withdrawn is not admissible in evidence in competition proceedings.

(2) A cartel leniency statement is not admissible in evidence in competition proceedings (whether or not it has been withdrawn).

(3) The prohibitions in sub-paragraphs (1) and (2) do not apply if a party to the proceedings obtained the submission or statement—

(a) lawfully, and

(b) otherwise than from a competition authority's file.

Investigation materials

33. (1) A competition authority's investigation materials are not admissible in evidence in competition proceedings at any time before the competition authority has closed the investigation to which those materials relate.

(2) The prohibition in sub-paragraph (1) does not apply if a party to the proceedings obtained the materials—

(a) lawfully, and

(b) otherwise than from a competition authority's file.

Material obtained from a competition authority's file

34. Documents or information obtained by a person ("P") from a competition authority's file are admissible in evidence in competition proceedings only where—

(a) the proceedings relate, entirely or partly, to a competition claim made by P or by a person who has acquired P's right to make the claim (whether by operation of law or otherwise), and

(b) none of the prohibitions in paragraphs 32 and 33 applies.

Decisions of member State competition authorities

35. *(1) For the purposes of competition proceedings, a final decision of a member State competition authority or review court that there has been an infringement of Article 101(1) or Article 102 by an undertaking is prima facie evidence of the infringement.*

(2) "Review court" means a court of a member State other than the United Kingdom which—

(a) hears appeals in connection with a decision of a competition authority of the member State that there has been an infringement of Article 101(1) or Article 102, or

(b) reviews judgments made by another court of the member State in connection with such decisions,

and paragraph 3(5) (when a decision becomes final) applies in relation to a decision of a review court as it applies in relation to a decision of a member State competition authority.]

NOTES

Inserted by the Claims in respect of Loss or Damage arising from Competition Infringements (Competition Act 1998 and Other Enactments (Amendment)) Regulations 2017, SI 2017/385, reg 2, Sch 1 paras 1, 4.

Para 35: repealed by the Competition (Amendment etc) (EU Exit) Regulations 2019, SI 2019/93, regs 2, 30, as from IP completion day (as defined in the European Union (Withdrawal Agreement) Act 2020, s 39) (for transitional provisions and savings in relation to the operation of the 2019 Regulations, see Sch 4 to those Regulations at **[7.69]** et seq).

[PART 8 EXEMPLARY DAMAGES

Exemplary damages

[1.151]

36. A court or the Tribunal may not award exemplary damages in competition proceedings.]

NOTES

Inserted by the Claims in respect of Loss or Damage arising from Competition Infringements (Competition Act 1998 and Other Enactments (Amendment)) Regulations 2017, SI 2017/385, reg 2, Sch 1 paras 1, 4.

[PART 9 CONTRIBUTION AND CONSENSUAL SETTLEMENTS

Consensual settlement

[1.152]

37. In this Part of this Schedule, "consensual settlement" means an agreement relating to a dispute about loss or damage arising from an infringement of competition law which—

(a) is reached through a consensual dispute resolution process,

(b) is made between—

(i) an infringer or a person who has acquired an infringer's liability in respect of the infringement (whether by operation of law or otherwise) ("the settling infringer"), and

(ii) a person who suffered the loss or damage or a person who has acquired such a person's right to make a claim in respect of the loss or damage (whether by operation of law or otherwise) ("the settling complainant"), and

(c) entirely resolves the dispute between the settling infringer and the settling complainant.

Assessment of contribution

38. (1) This paragraph applies in relation to proceedings to recover contribution under section 1 of the Civil Liability (Contribution) Act 1978 or section 3(2) of the Law Reform (Miscellaneous Provisions) (Scotland) Act 1940 where contribution is to be recovered in respect of loss or damage suffered by a person as a result of an infringement of competition law.

(2) The amount of contribution that one person liable in respect of the loss or damage may recover from another must be determined in the light of their relative responsibility for the whole of the loss or damage caused by the infringement.

(3) The determination of that amount must take into account any damages paid by the other person in respect of the loss or damage in accordance with a consensual settlement.

(4) The following have effect subject to this paragraph—

(a) section 2(1) of the Civil Liability (Contribution) Act 1978 (assessment of contribution);

(b) section 3(2) of the Law Reform (Miscellaneous Provisions) (Scotland) Act 1940 (contribution among joint wrongdoers).

Effect of consensual settlement on the amount of a claim

39. (1) Where loss or damage arising from an infringement of competition law is the subject of—

(a) a consensual settlement, and

(b) a competition damages claim by the settling complainant,

the amount of the settling complainant's claim is reduced by the settling infringer's share of the loss or damage.

(2) Sub-paragraph (1) has effect regardless of the terms of the consensual settlement.

Effect of consensual settlement for the settling infringer

40. (1) Where loss or damage arising from an infringement of competition law is the subject of a consensual settlement, the settling complainant ceases to have a right of action against the settling infringer in respect of the loss or damage.

(2) Sub-paragraph (1) has effect regardless of the terms of the consensual settlement.

(3) Sub-paragraphs (1) and (2) do not apply where—

(a) an undertaking other than the settling infringer is liable to pay damages to the settling complainant in respect of loss or damage which arises from the infringement,

(b) that undertaking is (or, if there is more than one, those undertakings are) unable to pay damages corresponding to the outstanding amount of the settling complainant's claim, and

(c) the settling infringer's liability for that amount is not expressly excluded by the terms of the consensual settlement.

Effect of consensual settlement on contribution between defendants

41. (1) Where—

(a) loss or damage arising from an infringement of competition law is the subject of a consensual settlement,

(b) it is also the subject of a competition damages claim by the settling complainant, and

(c) an undertaking other than the settling infringer is liable to pay damages to the settling complainant in respect of the loss or damage that is the subject of the claim, that undertaking may not recover contribution from the settling infringer in respect of the loss or damage under section 1 of the Civil Liability (Contribution) Act 1978 or section 3(2) of the Law Reform (Miscellaneous Provisions) (Scotland) Act 1940.

(2) Sub-paragraph (1) has effect regardless of the terms of the consensual settlement.

(3) The following have effect subject to this paragraph—

(a) section 1 of the Civil Liability (Contribution) Act 1978;

(b) section 3(2) of the Law Reform (Miscellaneous Provisions) (Scotland) Act 1940.]

NOTES

Inserted by the Claims in respect of Loss or Damage arising from Competition Infringements (Competition Act 1998 and Other Enactments (Amendment)) Regulations 2017, SI 2017/385, reg 2, Sch 1 paras 1, 4.

[PART 10 APPLICATION

[1.153]

42. (1) Parts 2 to 5, 8 and 9 of this Schedule apply in relation to competition claims, competition proceedings, claims for contribution arising from competition claims and proceedings relating to such claims only to the extent that the claims and proceedings relate to loss or damage suffered on or after the relevant day as a result of an infringement of competition law that takes place on or after that day.

(2) Where an infringement of competition law takes place over a period of 2 or more days it is to be taken for the purposes of sub-paragraph (1) to have taken place on the first of those days

43. The following provisions of this Schedule apply only in relation to proceedings on a competition claim in relation to which the first proceedings before a court or the Tribunal began on or after the relevant day—

(a) paragraphs 4(7) and (8) and 5(3) and (4);

(b) Parts 6 and 7.

44. In this Part of this Schedule "the relevant day" means the day on which the Claims in respect of Loss or Damage arising from Competition Infringements (Competition Act 1998 and Other Enactments (Amendment)) Regulations 2017 come into force.]

NOTES

Inserted by the Claims in respect of Loss or Damage arising from Competition Infringements (Competition Act 1998 and Other Enactments (Amendment)) Regulations 2017, SI 2017/385, reg 2, Sch 1 paras 1, 4.

SCHEDULE 9
[CMA'S] RULES

Section 51(2)

General

[1.154]

[1. In this Schedule "rules" means rules made by the [CMA] under section 51.]

[Delegation of functions

[1A. (1) Rules may provide for the exercise of a function of the CMA under this Part on its behalf—

(a) by one or more members of the CMA Board (see Part 2 of Schedule 4 to the Enterprise and Regulatory Reform Act 2013);

(b) by one or more members of the CMA panel (see Part 3 of that Schedule to that Act);

(c) by one or more members of staff of the CMA;

(d) jointly by one or more of the persons mentioned in paragraph (a), (b) or (c).

(2) Sub-paragraph (1) does not apply in relation to any function prescribed in regulations made under section 7(1) of the Civil Aviation Act 1982 (power for Secretary of State to prescribe certain functions of the Civil Aviation Authority which must not be performed on its behalf by any other person).]

2–4. . . .

Decisions

5. (1) Rules may make provision as to—

(a) the form and manner in which notice of any decision is to be given;

(b) the person or persons to whom the notice is to be given;

(c) the manner in which the [CMA] is to publish a decision;

[(d) the procedure to be followed if—

(i) the [CMA] takes further action with respect to an agreement after having decided that it does not infringe the Chapter I prohibition; [or]

(ii) the [CMA] takes further action with respect to an agreement after having decided that it does not infringe the prohibition in [Article 101(1)];

(iii) the [CMA] takes further action with respect to conduct after having decided that it does not infringe the Chapter II prohibition; *or*

(iv) the [CMA] takes further action with respect to conduct after having decided that it does not infringe the prohibition in [Article 102]].

[(2) In this paragraph "decision" means a decision of the [CMA]—

(a) as to whether or not an agreement has infringed the Chapter I prohibition; [or]

(b) as to whether or not an agreement has infringed the prohibition in [Article 101(1)];

(c) as to whether or not conduct has infringed the Chapter II prohibition; *or*

(d) as to whether or not conduct has infringed the prohibition in [Article 102].]

6, 7. . . .

Block exemptions

[**8.** Rules may make provision as to—

(a) the procedure to be followed by the [CMA] if it cancels a block exemption;

(b) the procedure to be followed by the [CMA] if it withdraws the benefit of a regulation of the Commission pursuant to Article 29(2) of the EC Competition Regulation.]

[Retained exemptions]

9. Rules may make provision as to—

(a) the circumstances in which the [CMA] may—
  (i) impose conditions or obligations in relation to a [retained exemption],
  (ii) vary or remove any such conditions or obligations,
  (iii) impose additional conditions or obligations, or
  (iv) cancel the exemption;

(b) as to the procedure to be followed by the [CMA] if [it] is acting under section 10(5);

(c) the form and manner in which notice of a decision to take any of the steps in sub-paragraph (a) is to be given;

(d) the circumstances in which an exemption may be cancelled with retrospective effect.

Section 11 exemptions

10. *Rules may, with respect to any exemption provided by regulations made under section 11, make provision similar to that made with respect to parallel exemptions by section 10 or by rules under paragraph 9.*

Directions withdrawing exclusions

11. Rules may make provision as to the factors which the [CMA] may take into account when [it] is determining the date on which a direction given under paragraph 4(1) of Schedule 1 or paragraph . . . 9(3) of Schedule 3 is to have effect.

Disclosure of information

12. (1) Rules may make provision as to the circumstances in which the [CMA] is to be required, before disclosing information given to [it] by a third party in connection with the exercise of any of the [CMA's] functions under Part I, to give notice, and an opportunity to make representations, to the third party.

(2) In relation to the agreement (or conduct) concerned, "third party" means a person who is not a party to the agreement (or who has not engaged in the conduct).

Applications under section 47

13. Rules may make provision as to—

(a) the period within which an application under section 47(1) must be made;

(b) the procedure to be followed by the [CMA] in dealing with the application;

(c) the person or persons to whom notice of the [CMA's] response to the application is to be given.

[Oral hearings: procedure

13A. (1) Rules may make provision as to the procedure to be followed by the CMA in holding oral hearings as part of an investigation.

(2) Rules may, in particular, make provision as to the appointment of a person mentioned in sub-paragraph (3) who has not been involved in the investigation in question to—

(a) chair an oral hearing, and

(b) prepare a report following the hearing and give it to the person who is to exercise on behalf of the CMA its function of making a decision (within the meaning given by section 31(2)) as a result of the investigation.

(3) The persons are—

(a) a member of the CMA Board;

(b) a member of the CMA panel;

(c) a member of staff of the CMA.

(4) The report must—

(a) contain an assessment of the fairness of the procedure followed in holding the oral hearing, and

(b) identify any other concerns about the fairness of the procedure followed in the investigation which have been brought to the attention of the person preparing the report.]

[Procedural complaints

13B. (1) Rules may make provision as to arrangements to be made by the CMA for dealing with complaints about the conduct by the CMA of an investigation.

(2) Rules may, in particular, make provision as to—

(a) the appointment of a person mentioned in sub-paragraph (3) who has not been involved in the investigation in question to consider any such complaint;

(b) the time-table for the consideration of any such complaint.

(3) The persons are—

(a) a member of the CMA Board;

(b) a member of the CMA panel;

(c) a member of staff of the CMA.]

[Settling cases

13C. Rules may make provision as to the procedure to be followed in a case where, during an investigation, one or more persons notify the CMA that they accept that there has been an infringement of a kind to which the investigation relates.]

Enforcement

14. Rules may make provision as to the procedure to be followed when the [CMA] takes action under any of sections [32 to 40] with respect to the enforcement of the provisions of this Part.

NOTES

References to the "CMA" and the "CMA's" substituted by the Enterprise and Regulatory Reform Act 2013, s 26(3), Sch 5, Pt 1, paras 1, 58. For various transitional provisions (including those relating to the abolition of the OFT and the Competition Commission, existing references to those bodies and provisions relating to continuity), see the Enterprise and Regulatory Reform Act 2013 (Commencement No 6, Transitional Provisions and Savings) Order 2014, SI 2014/416, Schedule at **[2.13]**. This Schedule is also amended as follows:

Para 1: substituted by the Competition Act 1998 and other enactments (Amendment) Regulations 2004, SI 2004/1261, reg 4, Sch 1, para 54(1), (2), (7).

Para 1A: inserted by the Enterprise and Regulatory Reform Act 2013, s 42(1), (3), (4), subject to transitional provisions in SI 2014/416 as noted above.

Paras 2–4, 6, 7: repealed by SI 2004/1261, reg 4, Sch 1, paras 54(1), (3), (6) (for savings and transitional provisions in relation to para 6, see reg 10 of those Regulations at **[2.10]**).

Para 5: sub-paras (1)(d), (2) substituted by SI 2004/1261, reg 4, Sch 1, paras 54(1), (4), (5). Words "Article 101(1)" and "Article 102" in square brackets substituted by the Treaty of Lisbon (Changes in Terminology or Numbering) Order 2012, SI 2012/1809, art 3(1), Schedule, Pt 1. The word "or" in square brackets in sub-para (1)(d)(i) and (2)(a) was inserted, and all words in italics in sub-paras (1) and (2) were repealed, by the Competition (Amendment etc) (EU Exit) Regulations 2019, SI 2019/93, regs 2, 31, as from IP completion day (as defined in the European Union (Withdrawal Agreement) Act 2020, s 39) (for transitional provisions and savings in relation to the operation of the 2019 Regulations, see Sch 4 to those Regulations at **[7.69]** et seq).

Para 8: substituted by SI 2004/1261, reg 4, Sch 1, para 54(1), (2), (7). Sub-para (b) was repealed by SI 2019/93, regs 2, 31, as from IP completion day (as defined in the European Union (Withdrawal Agreement) Act 2020, s 39) (for transitional provisions and savings in relation to the operation of the 2019 Regulations, see Sch 4 to those Regulations at **[7.69]** et seq).

Para 9: word in second pair of square brackets in sub-para (b) substituted by the Enterprise Act 2002, s 278, Sch 25, para 38. The heading before para 9 was substituted (for the original heading "Parallel exemptions"), and the words in square brackets in sub-para (a)(i) were substituted (for the original words "retained exemption"), by SI 2019/93, regs 2, 31, as from IP completion day (as defined in the European Union (Withdrawal Agreement) Act 2020, s 39) (for transitional provisions and savings in relation to the operation of the 2019 Regulations, see Sch 4 to those Regulations at **[7.69]** et seq).

Para 10: repealed by SI 2019/93, regs 2, 31, as from IP completion day (as defined in the European Union (Withdrawal Agreement) Act 2020, s 39) (for transitional provisions and savings in relation to the operation of the 2019 Regulations, see Sch 4 to those Regulations at **[7.69]** et seq).

Paras 11, 12: word in second pair of square brackets substituted by the Enterprise Act 2002, s 278, Sch 25, para 38. Words omitted repealed by SI 2004/1261, reg 4, Sch 1, para 54(1), (8).

Paras 13A–13C: inserted by the Enterprise and Regulatory Reform Act 2013, s 42(3), (5)–(7), subject to transitional provisions in SI 2014/416 as noted above.

Para 14: words in second pair of square brackets substituted by SI 2004/1261, reg 4, Sch 1, para 54(1), (9).

SCHEDULE 10
REGULATORS

Sections 54 and 66(5)

(Sch 10, Pt I repealed by the Enterprise Act 2002, s 278(2), Sch 26.)

PART II THE PROHIBITIONS

[1.155]

2. . . .

Gas

3. (1) In consequence of the repeal by this Act of provisions of the Competition Act 1980, the functions transferred by subsection (3) of section 36A of the Gas Act 1986 (functions with respect to competition) are no longer exercisable by the Director General of Gas Supply.

(2)–(11) . . .

Electricity

4. (1) In consequence of the repeal by this Act of provisions of the Competition Act 1980, the functions transferred by subsection (3) of section 43 of the Electricity Act 1989 (functions with respect to competition) are no longer exercisable by the Director General of Electricity Supply.

(2)–(9) . . .

Water

5. (1) In consequence of the repeal by this Act of provisions of the Competition Act 1980, the functions exercisable by virtue of subsection (3) of section 31 of the Water Industry Act 1991 (functions of Director with respect to competition) are no longer exercisable by the Director General of Water Services.

(2)–(13) . . .

Railways

6. (1) In consequence of the repeal by this Act of provisions of the Competition Act 1980, the functions transferred by subsection (3) of section 67 of the Railways Act 1993 (respective functions of the Regulator and the Director etc) are no longer exercisable by the Rail Regulator.

(2)–(9) . . .

NOTES

Para 2: repealed by a combination of the Communications Act 2003, s 406(7), Sch 19, and the Enterprise Act 2002, s 278(2), Sch 26.

Para 3: sub-paras (2)–(11) amend the Gas Act 1986, ss 4, 36A; repealed in part by the Utilities Act 2000, s 108, Sch 8, and the Enterprise Act 2002, s 278(2), Sch 26.

Para 4: sub-paras (2)–(9) amend the Electricity Act 1989, ss 3, 43; repealed in part by the Utilities Act 2000, s 108, Sch 8, and the Enterprise Act 2002, s 278(2), Sch 26.

Para 5: sub-paras (2)–(13) amend the Water Industry Act 1991, ss 2, 31; repealed in part by the Enterprise Act 2002, s 278(2), Sch 26, and the Water Act 2003, s 101, Sch 7, Pt 2, para 32(1), (4)(a), Sch 9, Pt 3.

Para 6: sub-paras (2)–(9) amend the Railways Act 1993, ss 4, 67; repealed in part by the Enterprise Act 2002, s 278(2), Sch 26.

Director General of Gas Supply and the Director General of Electricity Supply: the functions, etc, of the Director General of Gas Supply and the Director General of Electricity Supply were transferred to the Gas and Electricity Markets Authority on 20 December 2000 (see the Utilities Act 2000, s 3(2)).

The Rail Regulator: the functions, etc, of the Rail Regulator were transferred to the Office of Rail Regulation on 5 July 2004. See now the Office of Rail Regulation (Change of Name) Regulations 2015, SI 2015/1682 which renamed the Office of Rail Regulation as the Office of Rail and Road.

Director General of Water Services: the functions, etc, of the Director General of Water Services were transferred to the Water Services Regulation Authority on 1 April 2006 (see the Water Act 2003, s 36(1)).

The Director: ie, the Director General of Fair Trading. See further the note to Sch 13, Pt I to this Act at **[1.157]**.

PART III THE PROHIBITIONS: NORTHERN IRELAND

Electricity

[1.156]

7. (1) In consequence of the repeal by this Act of provisions of the Competition Act 1980, the functions transferred by paragraph (3) of Article 46 of the Electricity (Northern Ireland) Order 1992 (functions with respect to competition) are no longer exercisable by the Director General of Electricity Supply for Northern Ireland.

(2)–(9) . . .

Gas

8. (1) In consequence of the repeal by this Act of provisions of the Competition Act 1980, the functions transferred by paragraph (3) of Article 23 of the Gas (Northern Ireland) Order 1996 (functions with respect to competition) are no longer exercisable by the Director General of Gas for Northern Ireland.

(2)–(11) . . .

NOTES

Para 7: sub-paras (2)–(9) amend the Electricity (Northern Ireland) Order 1992, SI 1992/231 (NI 1), arts 6, 46; repealed in part by the Enterprise Act 2002, s 278(2), Sch 26, and the Energy (Northern Ireland) Order 2003, SI 2003/419, art 65, Sch 5.

Para 8: sub-paras (2)–(11) amend the Gas (Northern Ireland) Order 1996, SI 1996/275 (NI 2), arts 5, 23; repealed in part by the Enterprise Act 2002, s 278(2), Sch 26, and the Energy (Northern Ireland) Order 2003, SI 2003/419, art 65, Sch 5.

(Sch 10, Pt IV (Utilities: minor and consequential amendments), Sch 10, Pt V (Minor and consequential amendments: Northern Ireland) outside the scope of this work.)

SCHEDULES 11 AND 12

(Sch 11 repealed by the Enterprise Act 2002, ss 247(j), 278(2), Sch 26; Sch 12 (Minor and consequential amendments) in so far as relevant to this work, these have been incorporated where appropriate.)

SCHEDULE 13
TRANSITIONAL PROVISIONS AND SAVINGS

Section 74(2)

PART I GENERAL

Interpretation

[1.157]

1. (1) In this Schedule—

"RPA" means the Resale Prices Act 1976;
"RTPA" means the Restrictive Trade Practices Act 1976;
"continuing proceedings" has the meaning given by paragraph 15;
"the Court" means the Restrictive Practices Court;
"Director" means the Director General of Fair Trading;
"document" includes information recorded in any form;
"enactment date" means the date on which this Act is passed;
"information" includes estimates and forecasts;

"interim period" means the period beginning on the enactment date and ending immediately before the starting date;
"prescribed" means prescribed by an order made by the Secretary of State;
"regulator" means any person mentioned in paragraphs (a) to (g) of paragraph 1 of Schedule 10 [and the Civil Aviation Authority];
"starting date" means the date on which section 2 comes into force;
"transitional period" means the transitional period provided for in Chapters III and IV of Part IV of this Schedule.

(2) Sections 30, 44, 51, 53, 55, 56, 57 and 59(3) and (4) and paragraph 12 of Schedule 9 ("the applied provisions") apply for the purposes of this Schedule as they apply for the purposes of Part I of this Act.

(3) Section 2(5) applies for the purposes of any provisions of this Schedule which are concerned with the operation of the Chapter I prohibition as it applies for the purposes of Part I of this Act.

(4) In relation to any of the matters in respect of which a regulator may exercise powers as a result of paragraph 35(1), the applied provisions are to have effect as if references to the Director included references to the regulator.

(5) The fact that to a limited extent the Chapter I prohibition does not apply to an agreement, because a transitional period is provided by virtue of this Schedule, does not require those provisions of the agreement in respect of which there is a transitional period to be disregarded when considering whether the agreement infringes the prohibition for other reasons.

General power to make transitional provision and savings

2. (1) Nothing in this Schedule affects the power of the Secretary of State under section 75 to make transitional provisions or savings.

(2) An order under that section may modify any provision made by this Schedule.

Advice and information

3. (1) The Director may publish advice and information explaining provisions of this Schedule to persons who are likely to be affected by them.

(2) Any advice or information published by the Director under this paragraph is to be published in such form and manner as he considers appropriate.

NOTES

Para 1: in sub-para (1) words in square brackets in the definition "regulator" inserted by the Transport Act 2000, s 97, Sch 8, Pt IV, para 16(1), (2).

The Director General of Fair Trading: the Enterprise Act 2002, s 2(1) provided that, as from the coming into force of that section (on 1 April 2003), the functions of the Director General of Fair Trading, his property, rights and liabilities were transferred to the Office of Fair Trading. Accordingly, (by virtue of s 2(2), (3) of the 2002 Act) the office of the Director was abolished, and any reference to the Director in any enactment, instrument or other document passed or made before the commencement of s 2(1) was to, in so far as was necessary, have effect as if it were a reference to the Office of Fair Trading. For transitional provisions in connection with the transfer, see Sch 24, para 6 to the 2002 Act at **[1.445]**. Section 2 of the 2002 Act was repealed by the Enterprise and Regulatory Reform Act 2013, s 26(3), Sch 5, Pt 4, para 229. As to the subsequent abolition of the OFT, see the Enterprise and Regulatory Reform Act 2013, s 26 at **[1.446]**.

PART II DURING THE INTERIM PERIOD

Block exemptions

[1.158]

4. (1) The Secretary of State may, at any time during the interim period, make one or more orders for the purpose of providing block exemptions which are effective on the starting date.

(2) An order under this paragraph has effect as if properly made under section 6.

Certain agreements to be non-notifiable agreements

5. An agreement which—
- (a) is made during the interim period, and
- (b) satisfies the conditions set out in paragraphs (a), (c) and (d) of section 27A(1) of the RTPA,

is to be treated as a non-notifiable agreement for the purposes of RTPA.

Application of RTPA during the interim period

6. In relation to agreements made during the interim period—
- (a) the Director is no longer under the duty to take proceedings imposed by section 1(2)(c) of the RTPA but may continue to do so;
- (b) section 21 of that Act has effect as if subsections (1) and (2) were omitted; and
- (c) section 35(1) of that Act has effect as if the words "or within such further time as the Director may, upon application made within that time, allow" were omitted.

Guidance

7. (1) Sub-paragraphs (2) to (4) apply in relation to agreements made during the interim period.

(2) An application may be made to the Director in anticipation of the coming into force of section 13 in accordance with directions given by the Director and such an application is to have effect on and after the starting date as if properly made under section 13.

(3) The Director may, in response to such an application—
- (a) give guidance in anticipation of the coming into force of section 2; or
- (b) on and after the starting date, give guidance under section 15 as if the application had been properly made under section 13.

(4) Any guidance so given is to have effect on and after the starting date as if properly given under section 15.

NOTES

The Director: see the note "The Director General of Fair Trading" to Pt I of this Schedule at **[1.157]**.

PART III ON THE STARTING DATE

Applications which fall

[1.159]

8. (1) Proceedings in respect of an application which is made to the Court under any of the provisions mentioned in sub-paragraph (2), but which is not determined before the starting date, cease on that date.

(2) The provisions are—

(a) sections 2(2), 35(3), 37(1) and 40(1) of the RTPA and paragraph 5 of Schedule 4 to that Act;

(b) section 4(1) of the RTPA so far as the application relates to an order under section 2(2) of that Act; and

(c) section 25(2) of the RPA.

(3) The power of the Court to make an order for costs in relation to any proceedings is not affected by anything in this paragraph or by the repeals made by section 1.

Orders and approvals which fall

9. (1) An order in force immediately before the starting date under—

(a) section 2(2), 29(1), 30(1), 33(4), 35(3) or 37(1) of the RTPA; or

(b) section 25(2) of the RPA,

ceases to have effect on that date.

(2) An approval in force immediately before the starting date under section 32 of the RTPA ceases to have effect on that date.

PART IV ON AND AFTER THE STARTING DATE

CHAPTER I GENERAL

Duty of Director to maintain register etc

[1.160]

10. (1) This paragraph applies even though the relevant provisions of the RTPA are repealed by this Act.

(2) The Director is to continue on and after the starting date to be under the duty imposed by section 1(2)(a) of the RTPA to maintain a register in respect of agreements—

(a) particulars of which are, on the starting date, entered or filed on the register;

(b) which fall within sub-paragraph (4);

(c) which immediately before the starting date are the subject of proceedings under the RTPA which do not cease on that date by virtue of this Schedule; or

(d) in relation to which a court gives directions to the Director after the starting date in the course of proceedings in which a question arises as to whether an agreement was, before that date—

(i) one to which the RTPA applied;

(ii) subject to registration under that Act;

(iii) a non-notifiable agreement for the purposes of that Act.

(3) The Director is to continue on and after the starting date to be under the duties imposed by section 1(2)(a) and (b) of the RTPA of compiling a register of agreements and entering or filing certain particulars in the register, but only in respect of agreements of a kind referred to in paragraph (b), (c) or (d) of sub-paragraph (2).

(4) An agreement falls within this sub-paragraph if—

(a) it is subject to registration under the RTPA but—

(i) is not a non-notifiable agreement within the meaning of section 27A of the RTPA, or

(ii) is not one to which paragraph 5 applies;

(b) particulars of the agreement have been provided to the Director before the starting date; and

(c) as at the starting date no entry or filing has been made in the register in respect of the agreement.

(5) Sections 23 and 27 of the RTPA are to apply after the starting date in respect of the register subject to such modifications, if any, as may be prescribed.

(6) In sub-paragraph (2)(d) "court" means—

(a) the High Court;

(b) the Court of Appeal;

(c) the Court of Session;

(d) the High Court or Court of Appeal in Northern Ireland; or

[(e) the Supreme Court].

RTPA section 3 applications

11. (1) Even though section 3 of the RTPA is repealed by this Act, its provisions (and so far as necessary that Act) are to continue to apply, with such modifications (if any) as may be prescribed—

(a) in relation to a continuing application under that section; or

(b) so as to allow an application to be made under that section on or after the starting date in respect of a continuing application under section 1(3) of the RTPA.

(2) "Continuing application" means an application made, but not determined, before the starting date.

RTPA section 26 applications

12. (1) Even though section 26 of the RTPA is repealed by this Act, its provisions (and so far as necessary that Act) are to continue to apply, with such modifications (if any) as may be prescribed, in relation to an application which is made under that section, but not determined, before the starting date.

(2) If an application under section 26 is determined on or after the starting date, this Schedule has effect in relation to the agreement concerned as if the application had been determined immediately before that date.

Right to bring civil proceedings

13. (1) Even though section 35 of the RTPA is repealed by this Act, its provisions (and so far as necessary that Act) are to continue to apply in respect of a person who, immediately before the starting date, has a right by virtue of section 27ZA or 35(2) of that Act to bring civil proceedings in respect of an agreement (but only so far as that right relates to any period before the starting date or, where there are continuing proceedings, the determination of the proceedings).

(2) Even though section 25 of the RPA is repealed by this Act, the provisions of that section (and so far as necessary that Act) are to continue to apply in respect of a person who, immediately before the starting date, has a right by virtue of subsection (3) of that section to bring civil proceedings (but only so far as that right relates to any period before the starting date or, where there are continuing proceedings, the determination of the proceedings).

CHAPTER II CONTINUING PROCEEDINGS

The general rule

14. (1) The Chapter I prohibition does not apply to an agreement at any time when the agreement is the subject of continuing proceedings under the RTPA.

(2) The Chapter I prohibition does not apply to an agreement relating to goods which are the subject of continuing proceedings under section 16 or 17 of the RPA to the extent to which the agreement consists of exempt provisions.

(3) In sub-paragraph (2) "exempt provisions" means those provisions of the agreement which would, disregarding section 14 of the RPA, be—

(a) void as a result of section 9(1) of the RPA; or
(b) unlawful as a result of section 9(2) or II of the RPA.

(4) If the Chapter I prohibition does not apply to an agreement because of this paragraph, the provisions of, or made under, the RTPA or the RPA are to continue to have effect in relation to the agreement.

(5) The repeals made by section 1 do not affect—

(a) continuing proceedings; or
(b) proceedings of the kind referred to in paragraph 11 or 12 of this Schedule which are continuing after the starting date.

Meaning of "continuing proceedings"

15. (1) For the purposes of this Schedule "continuing proceedings" means proceedings in respect of an application made to the Court under the RTPA or the RPA, but not determined, before the starting date.

(2) But proceedings under section 3 or 26 of the RTPA to which paragraph 11 or 12 applies are not continuing proceedings.

(3) The question whether (for the purposes of Part III, or this Part, of this Schedule) an application has been determined is to be decided in accordance with sub-paragraphs (4) and (5).

(4) If an appeal against the decision on the application is brought, the application is not determined until—

(a) the appeal is disposed of or withdrawn; or
(b) if as a result of the appeal the case is referred back to the Court—
    (i) the expiry of the period within which an appeal ("the further appeal") in respect of the Court's decision on that reference could have been brought had this Act not been passed; or
    (ii) if later, the date on which the further appeal is disposed of or withdrawn.

(5) Otherwise, the application is not determined until the expiry of the period within which any party to the application would have been able to bring an appeal against the decision on the application had this Act not been passed.

RTPA section 4 proceedings

16. Proceedings on an application for an order under section 4 of the RTPA are also continuing proceedings if—

(a) leave to make the application is applied for before the starting date but the proceedings in respect of that application for leave are not determined before that date; or
(b) leave to make an application for an order under that section is granted before the starting date but the application itself is not made before that date.

RPA section 16 or 17 proceedings

17. Proceedings on an application for an order under section 16 or 17 of the RPA are also continuing proceedings if—

(a) leave to make the application is applied for before the starting date but the proceedings in respect of that application for leave are not determined before that date; or
(b) leave to make an application for an order under section 16 or 17 of the RPA is granted before the starting date, but the application itself is not made before that date.

Continuing proceedings which are discontinued

18. (1) On an application made jointly to the Court by all the parties to any continuing proceedings, the Court must, if it is satisfied that the parties wish it to do so, discontinue the proceedings.

(2) If, on an application under sub-paragraph (1) or for any other reason, the Court orders the proceedings to be discontinued, this Schedule has effect (subject to paragraphs 21 and 22) from the date on which the proceedings are discontinued as if they had never been instituted.

CHAPTER III THE TRANSITIONAL PERIOD

The general rule

19. (1) Except where this Chapter or Chapter IV provides otherwise, there is a transitional period, beginning on the starting date and lasting for one year, for any agreement made before the starting date.

(2) The Chapter I prohibition does not apply to an agreement to the extent to which there is a transitional period for the agreement.

(3) The Secretary of State may by regulations provide for sections 13 to 16 and Schedule 5 to apply with such modifications (if any) as may be specified in the regulations, in respect of applications to the Director about agreements for which there is a transitional period.

Cases for which there is no transitional period

20. (1) There is no transitional period for an agreement to the extent to which, immediately before the starting date, it is—

(a) void under section 2(1) or 35(1)(a) of the RTPA;
(b) the subject of an order under section 2(2) or 35(3) of the RTPA; or
(c) unlawful under section 1, 2 or 11 of the RPA or void under section 9 of that Act.

(2) There is no transitional period for an agreement to the extent to which, before the starting date, a person has acted unlawfully for the purposes of section 27ZA(2) or (3) of the RTPA in respect of the agreement.

(3) There is no transitional period for an agreement to which paragraph 25(4) applies.

(4) There is no transitional period for—

(a) an agreement in respect of which there are continuing proceedings, or
(b) an agreement relating to goods in respect of which there are continuing proceedings,

to the extent to which the agreement is, when the proceedings are determined, void or unlawful.

Continuing proceedings under the RTPA

21. In the case of an agreement which is the subject of continuing proceedings under the RTPA, the transitional period begins—

(a) if the proceedings are discontinued, on the date of discontinuance;
(b) otherwise, when the proceedings are determined.

Continuing proceedings under the RPA

22. (1) In the case of an agreement relating to goods which are the subject of continuing proceedings under the RPA, the transitional period for the exempt provisions of the agreement begins—

(a) if the proceedings are discontinued, on the date of discontinuance;
(b) otherwise, when the proceedings are determined.

(2) In sub-paragraph (1) "exempt provisions" has the meaning given by paragraph 14(3).

Provisions not contrary to public interest

23. (1) To the extent to which an agreement contains provisions which, immediately before the starting date, are provisions which the Court has found not to be contrary to the public interest, the transitional period lasts for five years.

(2) Sub-paragraph (1) is subject to paragraph 20(4).

(3) To the extent to which an agreement which on the starting date is the subject of continuing proceedings is, when the proceedings are determined, found by the Court not to be contrary to the public interest, the transitional period lasts for five years.

Goods

24. (1) In the case of an agreement relating to goods which, immediately before the starting date, are exempt under section 14 of the RPA, there is a transitional period for the agreement to the extent to which it consists of exempt provisions.

(2) Sub-paragraph (1) is subject to paragraph 20(4).

(3) In the case of an agreement relating to goods—

(a) which on the starting date are the subject of continuing proceedings, and
(b) which, when the proceedings are determined, are found to be exempt under section 14 of the RPA,

there is a transitional period for the agreement, to the extent to which it consists of exempt provisions.

(4) In each case, the transitional period lasts for five years.

(5) In sub-paragraphs (1) and (3) "exempt provisions" means those provisions of the agreement which would, disregarding section 14 of the RPA, be—

(a) void as a result of section 9(1) of the RPA; or
(b) unlawful as a result of section 9(2) or 11 of the RPA.

Transitional period for certain agreements

25. (1) This paragraph applies to agreements—

(a) which are subject to registration under the RTPA but which—
 (i) are not non-notifiable agreements within the meaning of section 27A of the RTPA, or
 (ii) are not agreements to which paragraph 5 applies; and

(b) in respect of which the time for furnishing relevant particulars as required by or under the RTPA expires on or after the starting date.

(2) "Relevant particulars" means—

(a) particulars which are required to be furnished by virtue of section 24 of the RTPA; or

(b) particulars of any variation of an agreement which are required to be furnished by virtue of sections 24 and 27 of the RTPA.

(3) There is a transitional period of one year for an agreement to which this paragraph applies if—

(a) relevant particulars are furnished before the starting date; and

(b) no person has acted unlawfully (for the purposes of section 27ZA(2) or (3) of the RTPA) in respect of the agreement.

(4) If relevant particulars are not furnished by the starting date, section 35(1)(a) of the RTPA does not apply in relation to the agreement (unless sub-paragraph (5) applies).

(5) This sub-paragraph applies if a person falling within section 27ZA(2) or (3) of the RTPA has acted unlawfully for the purposes of those subsections in respect of the agreement.

Special cases

26. (1) In the case of an agreement in respect of which—

(a) . . .

(b) a direction under section 194A(3) of the Broadcasting Act 1990 ("the 1990 Act") is in force immediately before the starting date,

the transitional period lasts for five years.

(2) . . .

(3) Sub-paragraphs (1) . . . do not affect the power of—

(a) . . .

(b) the Secretary of State to make a declaration under section 194A of the 1990 Act (as amended by Schedule 2 to this Act),

in respect of an agreement for which there is a transitional period.

CHAPTER IV THE UTILITIES

General

27. In this Chapter "the relevant period" means the period beginning with the starting date and ending immediately before the fifth anniversary of that date.

Electricity

28. (1) For an agreement to which, immediately before the starting date, the RTPA does not apply by virtue of a section 100 order, there is a transitional period—

(a) beginning on the starting date; and

(b) ending at the end of the relevant period.

(2) For an agreement which is made at any time after the starting date and to which, had the RTPA not been repealed, that Act would not at the time at which the agreement is made have applied by virtue of a section 100 order, there is a transitional period—

(a) beginning on the date on which the agreement is made; and

(b) ending at the end of the relevant period.

(3) For an agreement (whether made before or after the starting date) which, during the relevant period, is varied at any time in such a way that it becomes an agreement which, had the RTPA not been repealed, would at that time have been one to which that Act did not apply by virtue of a section 100 order, there is a transitional period—

(a) beginning on the date on which the variation is made; and

(b) ending at the end of the relevant period.

(4) If an agreement for which there is a transitional period as a result of sub-paragraph (1), (2) or (3) is varied during the relevant period, the transitional period for the agreement continues if, had the RTPA not been repealed, the agreement would have continued to be one to which that Act did not apply by virtue of a section 100 order.

(5) But if an agreement for which there is a transitional period as a result of sub-paragraph (1), (2) or (3) ceases to be one to which, had it not been repealed, the RTPA would not have applied by virtue of a section 100 order, the transitional period ends on the date on which the agreement so ceases.

(6) Sub-paragraph (3) is subject to paragraph 20.

(7) In this paragraph and paragraph 29—

"section 100 order" means an order made under section 100 of the Electricity Act 1989; and expressions which are also used in Part I of the Electricity Act 1989 have the same meaning as in that Part.

Electricity: power to make transitional orders

29. (1) There is a transitional period for an agreement (whether made before or after the starting date) relating to the generation, transmission or supply of electricity which—

(a) is specified, or is of a description specified, in an order ("a transitional order") made by the Secretary of State (whether before or after the making of the agreement but before the end of the relevant period); and

(b) satisfies such conditions as may be specified in the order.

(2) A transitional order may make provision as to when the transitional period in respect of such an agreement is to start or to be deemed to have started.

(3) The transitional period for such an agreement ends at the end of the relevant period.

(4) But if the agreement—

(a) ceases to be one to which a transitional order applies, or

(b) ceases to satisfy one or more of the conditions specified in the transitional order,

the transitional period ends on the date on which the agreement so ceases.

(5) Before making a transitional order, the Secretary of State must consult [the Gas and Electricity Markets Authority] and the Director.

(6) The conditions specified in a transitional order may include conditions which refer any matter to the Secretary of State for determination after such consultation as may be so specified.

(7) In the application of this paragraph to Northern Ireland, the reference in sub-paragraph (5) to the Director General of Electricity Supply is to be read as a reference to the Director General of Electricity Supply for Northern Ireland.

Gas

30. (1) For an agreement to which, immediately before the starting date, the RTPA does not apply by virtue of section 62 or a section 62 order, there is a transitional period—

(a) beginning on the starting date; and

(b) ending at the end of the relevant period.

(2) For an agreement which is made at any time after the starting date and to which, had the RTPA not been repealed, that Act would not at the time at which the agreement is made have applied by virtue of section 62 or a section 62 order, there is a transitional period—

(a) beginning on the date on which the agreement is made; and

(b) ending at the end of the relevant period.

(3) For an agreement (whether made before or after the starting date) which, during the relevant period, is varied at any time in such a way that it becomes an agreement which, had the RTPA not been repealed, would at that time have been one to which that Act did not apply by virtue of section 62 or a section 62 order, there is a transitional period—

(a) beginning on the date on which the variation is made; and

(b) ending at the end of the relevant period.

(4) If an agreement for which there is a transitional period as a result of sub-paragraph (1), (2) or (3) is varied during the relevant period, the transitional period for the agreement continues if, had the RTPA not been repealed, the agreement would have continued to be one to which that Act did not apply by virtue of section 62 or a section 62 order.

(5) But if an agreement for which there is a transitional period as a result of sub-paragraph (1), (2) or (3) ceases to be one to which, had it not been repealed, the RTPA would not have applied by virtue of section 62 or a section 62 order, the transitional period ends on the date on which the agreement so ceases.

(6) Sub-paragraph (3) also applies in relation to a modification which is treated as an agreement made on or after 28th November 1985 by virtue of section 62(4).

(7) Sub-paragraph (3) is subject to paragraph 20.

(8) In this paragraph and paragraph 31—

"section 62" means section 62 of the Gas Act 1986;

"section 62 order" means an order made under section 62.

Gas: power to make transitional orders

31. (1) There is a transitional period for an agreement of a description falling within section 62(2)(a) and (b) or section 62(2A)(a) and (b) which—

(a) is specified, or is of a description specified, in an order ("a transitional order") made by the Secretary of State (whether before or after the making of the agreement but before the end of the relevant period); and

(b) satisfies such conditions as may be specified in the order.

(2) A transitional order may make provision as to when the transitional period in respect of such an agreement is to start or to be deemed to have started.

(3) The transitional period for such an agreement ends at the end of the relevant period.

(4) But if the agreement—

(a) ceases to be one to which a transitional order applies, or

(b) ceases to satisfy one or more of the conditions specified in the transitional order,

the transitional period ends on the date when the agreement so ceases.

(5) Before making a transitional order, the Secretary of State must consult [the Gas and Electricity Markets Authority] and the Director.

(6) The conditions specified in a transitional order may include—

(a) conditions which are to be satisfied in relation to a time before the coming into force of this paragraph;

(b) conditions which refer any matter (which may be the general question whether the Chapter I prohibition should apply to a particular agreement) to the Secretary of State, the Director or [the Gas and Electricity Markets Authority] for determination after such consultation as may be so specified.

Gas: Northern Ireland

32. (1) For an agreement to which, immediately before the starting date, the RTPA does not apply by virtue of an Article 41 order, there is a transitional period—

(a) beginning on the starting date; and

(b) ending at the end of the relevant period.

(2) For an agreement which is made at any time after the starting date and to which, had the RTPA not been repealed, that Act would not at the time at which the agreement is made have applied by virtue of an Article 41 order, there is a transitional period—

(a) beginning on the date on which the agreement is made; and

(b) ending at the end of the relevant period.

(3) For an agreement (whether made before or after the starting date) which, during the relevant period, is varied at any time in such a way that it becomes an agreement which, had the RTPA not been repealed, would at that time have been one to which that Act did not apply by virtue of an Article 41 order, there is a transitional period—

(a) beginning on the date on which the variation is made; and

(b) ending at the end of the relevant period.

(4) If an agreement for which there is a transitional period as a result of sub-paragraph (1), (2) or (3) is varied during the relevant period, the transitional period for the agreement continues if, had the RTPA not been repealed, the agreement would have continued to be one to which that Act did not apply by virtue of an Article 41 order.

(5) But if an agreement for which there is a transitional period as a result of sub-paragraph (1), (2) or (3) ceases to be one to which, had it not been repealed, the RTPA would not have applied by virtue of an Article 41 order, the transitional period ends on the date on which the agreement so ceases.

(6) Sub-paragraph (3) is subject to paragraph 20.

(7) In this paragraph and paragraph 33— "Article 41 order" means an order under Article 41 of the Gas (Northern Ireland) Order 1996; "Department" means the Department of Economic Development.

Gas: Northern Ireland—power to make transitional orders

33. (1) There is a transitional period for an agreement of a description falling within Article 41(1) which—

(a) is specified, or is of a description specified, in an order ("a transitional order") made by the Department (whether before or after the making of the agreement but before the end of the relevant period); and

(b) satisfies such conditions as may be specified in the order.

(2) A transitional order may make provision as to when the transitional period in respect of such an agreement is to start or to be deemed to have started.

(3) The transitional period for such an agreement ends at the end of the relevant period.

(4) But if the agreement—

(a) ceases to be one to which a transitional order applies, or

(b) ceases to satisfy one or more of the conditions specified in the transitional order,

the transitional period ends on the date when the agreement so ceases.

(5) Before making a transitional order, the Department must consult the Director General of Gas for Northern Ireland and the Director.

(6) The conditions specified in a transitional order may include conditions which refer any matter (which may be the general question whether the Chapter I prohibition should apply to a particular agreement) to the Department for determination after such consultation as may be so specified.

Railways

34. (1) In this paragraph—

"section 131" means section 131 of the Railways Act 1993 ("the 1993 Act");

"section 131 agreement" means an agreement—

(a) to which the RTPA does not apply immediately before the starting date by virtue of section 131(1); or

(b) in respect of which a direction under section 131(3) is in force immediately before that date;

"non-exempt agreement" means an agreement relating to the provision of railway services (whether made before or after the starting date) which is not a section 131 agreement; and

"railway services" has the meaning given by section 82 of the 1993 Act.

(2) For a section 131 agreement there is a transitional period of five years.

(3) There is a transitional period for a non-exempt agreement to the extent to which the agreement is at any time before the end of the relevant period required or approved—

(a) by the Secretary of State or the Rail Regulator in pursuance of any function assigned or transferred to him under or by virtue of any provision of the 1993 Act;

(b) by or under any agreement the making of which is required or approved by the Secretary of State or the Rail Regulator in the exercise of any such function; or

(c) by or under a licence granted under Part I of the 1993 Act.

(4) The transitional period conferred by sub-paragraph (3)—

(a) is to be taken to have begun on the starting date; and

(b) ends at the end of the relevant period.

(5) Sub-paragraph (3) is subject to paragraph 20.

(6) Any variation of a section 131 agreement on or after the starting date is to be treated, for the purposes of this paragraph, as a separate non-exempt agreement.

The regulators

35. (1) Subject to sub-paragraph (3), each of the regulators may exercise, in respect of sectoral matters and concurrently with the Director, the functions of the Director under paragraph 3, 7, 19(3), 36, 37, 38 or 39.

(2) In sub-paragraph (1) "sectoral matters" means—

(a) . . .

(b) in the case of [the Gas and Electricity Markets Authority], the matters referred to in section 36A(3) and (4) of the Gas Act 1986;

(c) in the case of [the Gas and Electricity Markets Authority], the matters referred to in section 43(3) of the Electricity Act 1989;

(d) in the case of the Director General of Electricity Supply for Northern Ireland, the matters referred to in Article 46(3) of the Electricity (Northern Ireland) Order 1992;
(e) in the case of the [Water Services Regulation Authority], the matters referred to in section 31(3) of the Water Industry Act 1991;
(f) in the case of the Rail Regulator, the matters referred to in section 67(3) of the Railways Act 1993;
(g) in the case of the Director General of Gas for Northern Ireland, the matters referred to in Article 23(3) of the Gas (Northern Ireland) Order 1996;
[(h) in the case of the Civil Aviation Authority, the supply of air traffic services within the meaning given by section 98 of the Transport Act 2000.]

(3) The power to give directions in paragraph 7(2) is exercisable by the Director only but if the Director is preparing directions which relate to a matter in respect of which a regulator exercises concurrent jurisdiction, he must consult that regulator.

(4) Consultations conducted by the Director before the enactment date, with a view to preparing directions which have effect on or after that date, are to be taken to satisfy sub-paragraph (3).

(5) References to enactments in sub-paragraph (2) are to the enactments as amended by or under this Act.

CHAPTER V EXTENDING THE TRANSITIONAL PERIOD

36. (1) A party to an agreement for which there is a transitional period may apply to the Director, not less than three months before the end of the period, for the period to be extended.

(2) The Director may (on his own initiative or on an application under sub-paragraph (1))—
(a) extend a one-year transitional period by not more than twelve months;
(b) extend a transitional period of any period other than one year by not more than six months.

(3) An application under sub-paragraph (1) must—
(a) be in such form as may be specified; and
(b) include such documents and information as may be specified.

(4) If the Director extends the transitional period under this paragraph, he must give notice in such form, and to such persons, as may be specified.

(5) The Director may not extend a transitional period more than once.

(6) In this paragraph—
"person" has the same meaning as in Part I; and
"specified" means specified in rules made by the Director under section 51.

CHAPTER VI TERMINATING THE TRANSITIONAL PERIOD

General

37. (1) Subject to sub-paragraph (2), the Director may by a direction in writing terminate the transitional period for an agreement, but only in accordance with paragraph 38.

(2) The Director may not terminate the transitional period, nor exercise any of the powers in paragraph 38, in respect of an agreement which is excluded from the Chapter I prohibition by virtue of any of the provisions of Part I of this Act other than paragraph 1 of Schedule 1 or paragraph 2 or 9 of Schedule 3 [or the Competition Act 1998 (Land and Vertical Agreements Exclusion) Order 2000].

Circumstances in which the Director may terminate the transitional period

38. (1) If the Director is considering whether to give a direction under paragraph 37 ("a direction"), he may in writing require any party to the agreement concerned to give him such information in connection with that agreement as he may require.

(2) If at the end of such period as may be specified in rules made under section 51, a person has failed, without reasonable excuse, to comply with a requirement imposed under sub-paragraph (1), the Director may give a direction.

(3) The Director may also give a direction if he considers—
(a) that the agreement would, but for the transitional period or a relevant exclusion, infringe the Chapter I prohibition; and
(b) that he would not be likely to grant the agreement an unconditional individual exemption.

(4) For the purposes of sub-paragraph (3) an individual exemption is unconditional if no conditions or obligations are imposed in respect of it under section 4(3)(a).

(5) In this paragraph—
"person" has the same meaning as in Part I;
"relevant exclusion" means an exclusion under paragraph 1 of Schedule 1 or paragraph 2 or 9 of Schedule 3 [or the Competition Act 1998 (Land and Vertical Agreements Exclusion) Order 2000].

Procedural requirements on giving a paragraph 37 direction

39. (1) The Director must specify in a direction under paragraph 37 ("a direction") the date on which it is to have effect (which must not be less than 28 days after the direction is given).

(2) Copies of the direction must be given to—
(a) each of the parties concerned, and
(b) the Secretary of State,
not less than 28 days before the date on which the direction is to have effect.

(3) In relation to an agreement to which a direction applies, the transitional period (if it has not already ended) ends on the date specified in the direction unless, before that date, the direction is revoked by the Director or the Secretary of State.

(4) If a direction is revoked, the Director may give a further direction in respect of the same agreement only if he is satisfied that there has been a material change of circumstance since the revocation.

(5) If, as a result of paragraph 24(1) or (3), there is a transitional period in respect of provisions of an agreement relating to goods—

(a) which immediately before the starting date are exempt under section 14 of the RPA, or

(b) which, when continuing proceedings are determined, are found to be exempt under section 14 of the RPA,

the period is not affected by paragraph 37 or 38.

NOTES

Commencement: 9 November 1998 (para 35); 11 January 1999 (paras 10(5), 19(3), paras 11, 12(1), certain purposes); 1 March 2000 (paras 10(1)–(4), (6), 12(2), 13–18, 19(1), (2), 20–34, 36–39, para 12(1) remaining purposes); to be appointed (para 11 otherwise). Note that para 11 is only in force for the purpose of prescribing modifications to the Restrictive Trade Practices Act 1976 (and that the 1976 Act is now repealed).

Para 10: sub-para (6)(e) substituted by the Constitutional Reform Act 2005, s 40(4), Sch 9, Pt 1, para 65(1), (5).

Para 26: words omitted repealed by the Financial Services Act 2012, s 114(2), Sch 19.

Paras 29, 31: words in square brackets substituted by virtue of the Utilities Act 2000, s 3(2).

Para 35: sub-para (2)(a) repealed by the Communications Act 2003, s 406(7), Sch 19. Words in square brackets in sub-paras (b), (c) substituted by virtue of the Utilities Act 2000, s 3(2). Words in square brackets in sub-para (2)(e) substituted by the Water Act 2003, s 101(1), Sch 7, Pt 2, para 32(1), (5). Sub-para (2)(h) added by the Transport Act 2000, s 97, Sch 8, Pt IV, para 16(1), (3).

Para 37: words in square brackets in sub-para (2) added by the Competition Act 1998 (Transitional, Consequential and Supplemental Provisions) Order 2000, SI 2000/311, art 2.

Para 38: words in square brackets in sub-para (5) inserted by the Competition Act 1998 (Consequential and Supplemental Provisions) Order 2000, SI 2000/2031, art 2.

The Director: see the note "The Director General of Fair Trading" to Pt I of this Schedule at **[1.157]**.

Director General of Gas Supply and the Director General of Electricity Supply: the functions of the Director General of Gas Supply and the Director General of Electricity Supply were, on 20 December 2000, transferred to the Gas and Electricity Markets Authority by virtue of the Utilities Act 2000, s 3(2). References in this Schedule to either of those Directors should be construed accordingly.

The Rail Regulator: the Railways and Transport Safety Act 2003, s 16 provides that, as from the coming into force of that section (on 5 July 2004), the functions, property, rights and liabilities, etc, of the Rail Regulator are transferred to the Office of Rail Regulation. Schedule 3, para 4 to that Act further provides that references in any enactment, instrument or other document to the Rail Regulator shall, so far as necessary or appropriate in consequence of s 16, be treated after commencement as a reference to the Office of Rail Regulation. See now the Office of Rail Regulation (Change of Name) Regulations 2015, SI 2015/1682 which renamed the Office of Rail Regulation as the Office of Rail and Road.

RPA: ie, the Resale Prices Act 1976; repealed by ss 1(c), 74(3) of, and Sch 14, Pt I to, this Act.

RTPA: ie, the Restrictive Trade Practices Act 1976; repealed by ss 1(b), 74(3) of, and Sch 14, Pt I to, this Act.

Financial Services Act 1986, s 127: repealed.

Railways Act 1993, s 131: repealed by ss 54(3), 74(3) of, and Sch 10, Pt IV, para 15(1), (8), Sch 14, Pt I to, this Act.

Competition Act 1998 (Land and Vertical Agreements Exclusion) Order 2000: revoked by the Competition Act 1998 (Land Agreements Exclusion and Revocation) Order 2004, SI 2004/1260 (the 2004 Order was revoked by the Competition Act 1998 (Land Agreements Exclusion Revocation) Order 2010 SI 2010/1709).

Regulations: the Competition Act 1998 (Appealable Decisions and Revocation of Notification of Excluded Agreements) Regulations 2004, SI 2004/1078 at **[2.1]**.

PART V THE FAIR TRADING ACT 1973

References to the Monopolies and Mergers Commission

[1.161]

40. (1) If, on the date on which the repeal by this Act of a provision mentioned in sub-paragraph (2) comes into force, the Monopolies and Mergers Commission has not completed a reference which was made to it before that date, continued consideration of the reference may include consideration of a question which could not have been considered if the provision had not been repealed.

(2) The provisions are—

(a) sections 10(2), 54(5) and 78(3) and paragraph 3(1) and (2) of Schedule 8 to the Fair Trading Act 1973 (c 41);

(b) section 11(8)(b) of the Competition Act 1980 (c 21);

(c) section 14(2) of the Telecommunications Act 1984 (c 12);

(d) section 45(3) of the Airports Act 1986 (c 31);

(e) section 25(2) of the Gas Act 1986 (c 44);

(f) section 13(2) of the Electricity Act 1989 (c 29);

(g) section 15(2) of the Water Industry Act 1991 (c 56);

(h) article 16(2) of the Electricity (Northern Ireland) Order 1992;

(i) section 14(2) of the Railways Act 1993 (c 43);

(j) article 36(3) of the Airports (Northern Ireland) Order 1994;

(k) article 16(2) of the Gas (Northern Ireland) Order 1996.

Orders under Schedule 8

41. (1) In this paragraph—

"the 1973 Act" means the Fair Trading Act 1973;

"agreement" means an agreement entered into before the date on which the repeal of the limiting provisions comes into force;

"the order" means an order under section 56 or 73 of the 1973 Act;

"the limiting provisions" means sub-paragraph (1) or (2) of paragraph 3 of Schedule 8 to the 1973 Act (limit on power to make orders under paragraph 1 or 2 of that Schedule) and includes any provision of the order included because of either of those sub-paragraphs; and

"transitional period" means the period which—
(a) begins on the day on which the repeal of the limiting provisions comes into force; and
(b) ends on the first anniversary of the starting date.

(2) Sub-paragraph (3) applies to any agreement to the extent to which it would have been unlawful (in accordance with the provisions of the order) but for the limiting provisions.

(3) As from the end of the transitional period, the order is to have effect in relation to the agreement as if the limiting provisions had never had effect.

Part III of the Act

42. (1) The repeals made by section 1 do not affect any proceedings in respect of an application which is made to the Court under Part III of the Fair Trading Act 1973, but is not determined, before the starting date.

(2) The question whether (for the purposes of sub-paragraph (1)) an application has been determined is to be decided in accordance with sub-paragraphs (3) and (4).

(3) If an appeal against the decision on the application is brought, the application is not determined until—
(a) the appeal is disposed of or withdrawn; or
(b) if as a result of the appeal the case is referred back to the Court—
  (i) the expiry of the period within which an appeal ("the further appeal") in respect of the Court's decision on that reference could have been brought had this Act not been passed; or
  (ii) if later, the date on which the further appeal is disposed of or withdrawn.

(4) Otherwise, the application is not determined until the expiry of the period within which any party to the application would have been able to bring an appeal against the decision on the application had this Act not been passed.

(5) Any amendment made by Schedule 12 to this Act which substitutes references to a relevant Court for references to the Court is not to affect proceedings of the kind referred to in sub-paragraph (1).

NOTES

Monopolies and Mergers Commission: the Monopolies and Mergers Commission was dissolved by s 45(3) of this Act (repealed), which also transferred the functions of the Monopolies and Mergers Commission to the Competition Commission. As to the subsequent abolition of the Competition Commission, see the Enterprise and Regulatory Reform Act 2013, s 26 at **[1.447]**

Airports Act 1986, Competition Act 1980, Electricity Act 1989, Fair Trading Act 1973, Gas Act 1986, Railways Act 1993, Telecommunications Act 1984, Water Industry Act 1991: the provisions of these Acts mentioned in para 40 above are all repealed by this Act.

PART VI THE COMPETITION ACT 1980

Undertakings

[1.162]

43. (1) Subject to sub-paragraph (2), an undertaking accepted by the Director under section 4 or 9 of the Competition Act 1980 ceases to have effect on the coming into force of the repeal by this Act of that section.

(2) If the undertaking relates to an agreement which on the starting date is the subject of continuing proceedings, the undertaking continues to have effect for the purposes of section 29 of the Competition Act 1980 until the proceedings are determined.

Application of sections 25 and 26

44. The repeals made by section 1 do not affect—
(a) the operation of section 25 of the Competition Act 1980 in relation to an application under section 1(3) of the RTPA which is made before the starting date;
(b) an application under section 26 of the Competition Act 1980 which is made before the starting date.

NOTES

The Director: see the note "The Director General of Fair Trading" to Pt I of this Schedule at **[1.157]**.
RTPA: ie, the Restrictive Trade Practices Act 1976; repealed by ss 1(b), 74(3) of, and Sch 14, Pt I to, this Act.
Competition Act 1980: ss 4, 9, 25, 26, 29 of that Act are all repealed by this Act.

PART VII MISCELLANEOUS

Disclosure of information

[1.163]

45. (1) Section 55 of this Act applies in relation to information which, immediately before the starting date, is subject to section 41 of the RTPA as it applies in relation to information obtained under or as a result of Part I.

(2) But section 55 does not apply to any disclosure of information of the kind referred to in sub-paragraph (1) if the disclosure is made—
(a) for the purpose of facilitating the performance of functions of a designated person under the Control of Misleading Advertisements Regulations 1988; or
(b) for the purposes of any proceedings before the Court or of any other legal proceedings under the RTPA or the Fair Trading Act 1973 or the Control of Misleading Advertisements Regulations 1988.

(3) Section 56 applies in relation to information of the kind referred to in sub-paragraph (1) if particulars containing the information have been entered or filed on the special section of the register maintained by the Director under, or as a result of, section 27 of the RTPA or paragraph 10 of this Schedule.

(4) Section 55 has effect, in relation to the matters as to which section 41(2) of the RTPA had effect, as if it contained a provision similar to section 41(2).

The Court

46. If it appears to the Lord Chancellor that a person who ceases to be a non-judicial member of the Court as a result of this Act should receive compensation for loss of office, he may pay to him out of moneys provided by Parliament such sum as he may with the approval of the Treasury determine.

NOTES

The Director: see the note "The Director General of Fair Trading" to Pt I of this Schedule at **[1.157]**.

RTPA: ie, the Restrictive Trade Practices Act 1976; repealed by ss 1(b), 74(3) of, and Sch 14, Pt I to, this Act.

SCHEDULE 14

(*Sch 14 contains repeals and revocations and, in so far as relevant to this work, they have been incorporated at the appropriate place.*)

FINANCIAL SERVICES AND MARKETS ACT 2000

(2000 c 8)

ARRANGEMENT OF SECTIONS

PART 1A
THE REGULATORS

CHAPTER 1 THE FINANCIAL CONDUCT AUTHORITY

The FCA's general duties

An Act to make provision about the regulation of financial services and markets; to provide for the transfer of certain statutory functions relating to building societies, friendly societies, industrial and provident societies and certain other mutual societies; and for connected purposes

[14 June 2000]

NOTES

Only the provisions of this Act most relevant to competition law are reproduced; provisions omitted are not annotated. All of the provisions reproduced here were either substituted or inserted by the Financial Services Act 2012 and the Financial Services (Banking Reform) Act 2013. By virtue of s 430 (Extent) the provisions reproduced here apply to the whole of the UK.

Disclosure of information: information which comes to a public authority in connection with the exercise of any function it has under or by virtue of Chapter 4 of Part 9A is "specified information" for the purposes of the Enterprise Act 2002, s 238; see s 238(1) of, and Sch 14 to, that Act at **[1.417]**, **[1.443]**. A public authority which holds information to which s 237 of the 2002 Act applies (general restriction on disclosure) may disclose that information to any other person for the purpose of facilitating the exercise by that person of any function he has under or by virtue of this Act and the 2002 Act; see s 241(3) of, and Sch 15 to, the 2002 Act at **[1.420]**, **[1.444]**. As to the disclosure of information to an overseas authority, see s 243 of, and Sch 14 to, the 2002 Act at **[1.423]**, **[1.443]**.

[PART 1A THE REGULATORS

NOTES

Transitional provisions: For transitional provisions in relation to the commencement of this Part, see the Financial Services Act 2012 (Transitional Provisions) (Miscellaneous Provisions) Order 2013, SI 2013/442. Part 2 of that Order contains transitional provisions in respect of the Financial Conduct Authority and the Prudential Regulation Authority. Article 2 makes provision in respect of the board of the Financial Services Authority (which is renamed as the Financial Conduct Authority by FSMA 2000 (as amended by the 2012 Act)). Article 3 makes provision in respect of the FCA's first annual report, and article 4 makes provision in respect of the PRA's first annual report. Articles 5 and 6 make provision in respect of the Consumer and Practitioner Panels. Article 7 makes provision in respect of references to "consumers" in certain provisions of this Act, including s 1G *post*.

[CHAPTER 1 THE FINANCIAL CONDUCT AUTHORITY

The FCA's general duties

[1.164]

1B The FCA's general duties

(1) In discharging its general functions the FCA must, so far as is reasonably possible, act in a way which—

- (a) is compatible with its strategic objective, and
- (b) advances one or more of its operational objectives.

(2) The FCA's strategic objective is: ensuring that the relevant markets (see section 1F) function well.

(3) The FCA's operational objectives are—

- (a) the consumer protection objective (see section 1C);
- (b) the integrity objective (see section 1D);
- (c) the competition objective (see section 1E).

(4) The FCA must, so far as is compatible with acting in a way which advances the consumer protection objective or the integrity objective, discharge its general functions in a way which promotes effective competition in the interests of consumers.

(5) In discharging its general functions the FCA must have regard to—

- (a) the regulatory principles in section 3B, and
- (b) the importance of taking action intended to minimise the extent to which it is possible for a business carried on—
  - (i) by an authorised person or a recognised investment exchange, or
  - (ii) in contravention of the general prohibition,

  to be used for a purpose connected with financial crime.

(6) For the purposes of this Chapter, the FCA's general functions are—

- (a) its function of making rules under this Act (considered as a whole),
- [(aa) its function of making technical standards in accordance with Chapter 2A of Part 9A;]
- (b) its function of preparing and issuing codes under this Act (considered as a whole),
- (c) its functions in relation to the giving of general guidance under this Act (considered as a whole), and
- (d) its function of determining the general policy and principles by reference to which it performs particular functions under this Act.

(7) Except to the extent that an order under section 50 of the Financial Services Act 2012 (orders relating to mutual societies functions) so provides, the FCA's general functions do not include functions that are transferred functions within the meaning of section 52 of that Act.

[(7A) . . .]

(8) "General guidance" has the meaning given in section 139B(5).]

NOTES

This section was substituted (together with the rest of Part 1A (ie, ss 1A–1T, 2A–2O, 3A–3S) for the original Part I (ss 1–18)) by the Financial Services Act 2012, s 6(1) (for transitional provisions and savings in relation to the transfer of the FSA's functions, property, rights and liabilities, see s 119 of, and Schs 20, 21 to, the 2012 Act).

Sub-s (6): para (aa) inserted by the Financial Regulators' Powers (Technical Standards etc) (Amendment etc) (EU Exit) Regulations 2018, SI 2018/1115, reg 7(1), (3).

Sub-s (7A): inserted by the Pension Schemes Act 2015, s 47, Sch 3, paras 1, 3. Repealed by the Financial Guidance and Claims Act 2018, s 25, Sch 3, paras 5, 7.

[1.165]

[1E The competition objective

(1) The competition objective is: promoting effective competition in the interests of consumers in the markets for—

(a) regulated financial services, or

(b) services provided by a recognised investment exchange in carrying on regulated activities in respect of which it is by virtue of section 285(2) exempt from the general prohibition.

(2) The matters to which the FCA may have regard in considering the effectiveness of competition in the market for any services mentioned in subsection (1) include—

(a) the needs of different consumers who use or may use those services, including their need for information that enables them to make informed choices,

(b) the ease with which consumers who may wish to use those services, including consumers in areas affected by social or economic deprivation, can access them,

(c) the ease with which consumers who obtain those services can change the person from whom they obtain them,

(d) the ease with which new entrants can enter the market, and

(e) how far competition is encouraging innovation.]

NOTES

Substituted as noted to s 1B at **[1.164]**.

[Interpretation of terms used in relation to FCA's general duties

[1.166]

[1G Meaning of "consumer"

(1) In sections 1B to 1E "consumers" means persons . . . —

(a) [who] use, have used or may use—

(i) regulated financial services, or

(ii) services that are provided by persons other than authorised persons but are provided in carrying on regulated activities,

(b) [who] have relevant rights or interests in relation to any of those services,

(c) [who] have invested, or may invest, in financial instruments, . . .

(d) [who] have relevant rights or interests in relation to financial instruments[, . . .

(e) [who] have rights, interests or obligations that are affected by the level of a regulated benchmark][; or

(f) in respect of whom a person carries on an activity which is specified in article 89G of the Financial Services and Markets Act 2000 (Regulated Activities) Order 2001 (seeking out etc claims) whether that activity, as carried on by that person, is a regulated activity, or is, by reason of an exclusion provided for under the 2001 Order or the 2000 Act, not a regulated activity].

(2) A person ("P") has a "relevant right or interest" in relation to any services within subsection (1)(a) if P has a right or interest—

(a) which is derived from, or is otherwise attributable to, the use of the services by others, or

(b) which may be adversely affected by the use of the services by persons acting on P's behalf or in a fiduciary capacity in relation to P.

(3) If a person is providing a service within subsection (1)(a) as trustee, the persons who are, have been or may be beneficiaries of the trust are to be treated as persons who use, have used or may use the service.

(4) A person who deals with another person ("B") in the course of B providing a service within subsection (1)(a) is to be treated as using the service.

(5) A person ("P") has a "relevant right or interest" in relation to any financial instrument if P has—

(a) a right or interest which is derived from, or is otherwise attributable to, investment in the instrument by others, or

(b) a right or interest which may be adversely affected by the investment in the instrument by persons acting on P's behalf or in a fiduciary capacity in relation to P.]

NOTES

Substituted as noted to s 1B at **[1.164]**.

Sub-s (1): first word omitted and word omitted from para (d) repealed, words in square brackets in paras (a)–(e) inserted, and para (f) and the preceding word added, by the Financial Services and Markets Act 2000 (Claims Management Activity) Order 2018, SI 2018/1253, art 91(1), (2). The word omitted from para (c) was repealed, and para (e) (and the word immediately preceding it) was inserted, by the Financial Services and Markets Act 2000 (Regulated Activities) (Amendment) Order 2013, SI 2013/655, art 3(1), (2).

Note: the definition of "consumers" is extended for the purposes of this section by the Financial Services and Markets Act 2000 (Regulated Activities) (Amendment) (No 2) Order 2013, SI 2013/1881, art 65. See also as to the meaning of "consumers", art 89E of the Financial Services and Markets Act 2000 (Regulated Activities) Order 2001, SI 2001/544 and art 89 of the Financial Services and Markets Act 2000 (Claims Management Activity) Order 2018, SI 2018/1253.

[CHAPTER 2 THE PRUDENTIAL REGULATION AUTHORITY

[The PRA's general duties

[1.167]

2B The PRA's general objective

(1) In discharging its general functions the PRA must, so far as is reasonably possible, act in a way which advances its general objective.

(2) The PRA's general objective is: promoting the safety and soundness of PRA-authorised persons.

(3) That objective is to be advanced primarily by—

(a) seeking to ensure that the business of PRA-authorised persons is carried on in a way which avoids any adverse effect on the stability of the UK financial system, . . .

(b) seeking to minimise the adverse effect that the failure of a PRA-authorised person could be expected to have on the stability of the UK financial system[, and

(c) discharging its general functions in relation to the matters mentioned in subsection (4A) in a way that seeks to—

(i) ensure that the business of ring-fenced bodies is carried on in a way that avoids any adverse effect on the continuity of the provision in the United Kingdom of core services,

(ii) ensure that the business of ring-fenced bodies is protected from risks (arising in the United Kingdom or elsewhere) that could adversely affect the continuity of the provision in the United Kingdom of core services, and

(iii) minimise the risk that the failure of a ring-fenced body or of a member of a ring-fenced body's group could affect the continuity of the provision in the United Kingdom of core services].

(4) The adverse effects mentioned in [subsection (3)(a) and (b)] may, in particular, result from the disruption of the continuity of financial services.

[(4A) The matters referred to in subsection (3)(c) are—

(a) Part 9B (ring-fencing);

(b) ring-fenced bodies (see section 142A);

(c) any body corporate incorporated in the United Kingdom that has a ring-fenced body as a member of its group;

(d) applications under Part 4A which, if granted, would result, or would be capable of resulting, in a person becoming a ring-fenced body.]

(5) In this Act "PRA-authorised person" means an authorised person who has permission—

(a) given under Part 4A, or

(b) resulting from any other provision of this Act,

to carry on regulated activities that consist of or include one or more PRA-regulated activities (see section 22A).

(6) Subsection (1) is subject to sections 2C and 2D.]

NOTES

Substituted as noted to s 1B at **[1.164]**.

The word omitted from sub-s (3)(a) was repealed, sub-s (3)(c) (and the word preceding it) was inserted, the words in square brackets in sub-s (4) were substituted, and sub-s (4A) was inserted, by the Financial Services (Banking Reform) Act 2013, s 1(1)–(4).

[1.168]

[2H Secondary competition objective and duty to have regard to regulatory principles

(1) When discharging its general functions in a way that advances its objectives (see section 2F), the PRA must so far as is reasonably possible act in a way which, as a secondary objective, facilitates effective competition in the markets for services provided by PRA-authorised persons in carrying on regulated activities.

(2) In discharging its general functions, the PRA must also have regard to the regulatory principles in section 3B.]

NOTES

Substituted as noted to s 1B at **[1.164]**.

Further substituted by the Financial Services (Banking Reform) Act 2013, s 130(1).

[PART 9A RULES AND GUIDANCE

CHAPTER 4 COMPETITION SCRUTINY

NOTES

This Chapter applies to the Payment Systems Regulator's practices and regulating provisions in relation to payment systems as it applies to the FCA's practices and regulating provisions within the meaning of this Chapter; see the Financial Services (Banking Reform) Act 2013, s 107 at **[1.483]**.

[1.169]

140A Interpretation

(1) In this Chapter—

["the CMA" means the Competition and Markets Authority.]

"market in the United Kingdom" includes—

(a) so far as it operates in the United Kingdom or a part of the United Kingdom, any market which operates there and in another country or territory or in a part of another country or territory, and

(b) any market which operates only in a part of the United Kingdom;

. . .

"practices", in relation to each regulator, means practices adopted by that regulator in the exercise of functions under this Act;

"regulating provisions" means—

(a) in relation to the FCA, any—

(i) rules of the FCA;

(ii) general guidance (as defined by section 139B(5) [. . .]);

(iii), (iv) . . .

[(v), (vi) . . .]

(b) in relation to the PRA, any—

(i) rules of the PRA;

(ii), (iii) . . .

(2) . . .

(3) For the purposes of this Chapter, any reference to a feature of a market in the United Kingdom for goods or services is to be read as a reference to—

(a) the structure of the market concerned or any aspect of that structure,
(b) any conduct (whether or not in the market concerned) of one or more than one person who supplies or acquires goods or services in the market concerned, or
(c) any conduct relating to the market concerned of customers of any person who supplies or acquires goods or services.

(4) In subsection (3) "conduct" includes any failure to act (whether or not intentional) and any other unintentional conduct.]

NOTES

This section was substituted (together with the rest of Part 9A (ie, ss 137A–137T, 138A–138O, 139A, 139B, 140A–140H, 141A) for the original Part X (ss 138–164)) by the Financial Services Act 2012, s 24(1).

Sub-s (1) is amended as follows:

Definition "the CMA" inserted, and definition "the OFT" (omitted) repealed, by the Enterprise and Regulatory Reform Act 2013 (Competition) (Consequential, Transitional and Saving Provisions) Order 2014, SI 2014/892, art 2, Sch 1, Pt 2, paras 120, 121(1), (2), subject to transitional provisions as noted to the Enterprise Act 2002, s 8A at **[1.187]**.

The words in square brackets in sub-para (a)(ii) of the definition "regulating provisions" were originally inserted, and sub-para (a)(v), (vi) of that definition were originally inserted, by the Pension Schemes Act 2015, s 47, Sch 3, paras 1, 10. All of these words were repealed by the Financial Guidance and Claims Act 2018, s 25, Sch 3, paras 5, 17.

Para (a)(iv) of the definition "regulating provisions" was repealed by the Financial Services and Markets Act 2000 (Market Abuse) Regulations 2016, SI 2016/680, reg 10(1), (7).

The other words omitted from the definition "regulating provisions" were repealed by the Financial Services (Banking Reform) Act 2013, s 35, Sch 3, para 10.

Sub-s (2): repealed by SI 2014/892, art 2, Sch 1, Pt 2, paras 120, 121(1), (3), subject to transitional provisions as noted above.

[1.170]

[140B Advice about effect of regulating provision or practice

(1) In this Chapter, any reference to the giving of "section 140B advice" to a regulator is to be read in accordance with this section.

[(2) The CMA gives "section 140B advice" to a regulator if—
(a) it gives advice to the regulator under section 7 of the Enterprise Act 2002 (provision of competition advice to Ministers etc) and the advice states that in the opinion of the CMA one or more of the things mentioned in subsection (4) may cause, or contribute to, the effect mentioned in subsection (5), or might be expected to do so in the future;
(b) a report published by it under section 136 of the Enterprise Act 2002 (investigations and reports on market investigation reference) contains—
  (i) a decision that one or more of the things mentioned in subsection (4) may cause, or contribute to, the effect mentioned in subsection (5), and
  (ii) a recommendation that any action should be taken by that regulator.]

(3) . . .

(4) Those things are—
(a) a regulating provision or practice of the regulator,
(b) two or more regulating provisions or practices (of that regulator or of both regulators) taken together,
(c) a particular combination of regulating provision or practices (of that regulator or of both regulators), or
(d) a feature, or combination of features, of [one or more markets] in the United Kingdom that could be dealt with by regulating provision or practices (of that regulator or of both regulators).

(5) That effect is the prevention, restriction or distortion of competition in connection with the supply or acquisition of any goods or services in the United Kingdom or a part of the United Kingdom.]

NOTES

Substituted as noted to s 140A at **[1.169]**.

Sub-s (2) substituted, sub-s (3) repealed, and words in square brackets in sub-s (4)(d) substituted, by the Enterprise and Regulatory Reform Act 2013 (Competition) (Consequential, Transitional and Saving Provisions) Order 2014, SI 2014/892, art 2, Sch 1, Pt 2, paras 120, 122, subject to transitional provisions as noted to the Enterprise Act 2002, s 8A at **[1.187]**.

[1.171]

[140C Consultation with regulator

Before giving section 140B advice, [the CMA] must consult the regulator to which the advice is to be given.]

NOTES

Substituted as noted to s 140A at **[1.169]**.

Words in square brackets substituted by the Enterprise and Regulatory Reform Act 2013 (Competition) (Consequential, Transitional and Saving Provisions) Order 2014, SI 2014/892, art 2, Sch 1, Pt 2, paras 120, 123, subject to transitional provisions as noted to the Enterprise Act 2002, s 8A at **[1.187]**.

[1.172]

[140D Investigation powers of [CMA]

[(1)] Where the [CMA] is deciding whether to exercise its power under section 7 of the Enterprise Act 2002 to give advice which, if given, would be section 140B advice, section 174 of that Act has effect as if—

[(a) for subsection (1) there were substituted—

> "(1) For the purposes of this section, a permitted purpose is assisting the CMA in deciding whether to exercise its power under section 7 to give advice which for the purposes of Chapter 4 of Part 9A of the Financial Services and Markets Act 2000 would be section 140B advice.", and

(b) subsection (9A) were omitted.]

[(2) Where the CMA has exercised any of its powers under section 174 of the Enterprise Act 2002, as applied by subsection (1), section 174B of that Act has effect as if, after subsection (9), there were inserted—

"(10) Where the section 174 power is exercised for the purpose of assisting the CMA in deciding whether to exercise its power under section 7 to give advice which for the purposes of Chapter 4 of Part 9A of the Financial Services and Markets Act 2000 would be section 140B advice, the relevant day is the day when the CMA publishes that advice.".]]

NOTES

Substituted as noted to s 140A at **[1.169]**.

Sub-s (1) was numbered as such, sub-s (2) was added, and all other words in square brackets were substituted, by the Enterprise and Regulatory Reform Act 2013 (Competition) (Consequential, Transitional and Saving Provisions) Order 2014, SI 2014/892, art 2, Sch 1, Pt 2, paras 120, 124, subject to transitional provisions as noted to the Enterprise Act 2002, s 8A at **[1.187]**. See also Sch 2, para 4 to the 2014 Order which provides that these amendments do not apply in relation to any notice given before 1 April 2014 under s 174 of the Enterprise Act 2002 Act as applied by this Act.

[1.173]

[140E Publication by CMA of section 140B advice

Where the giving of advice under section 7 of the Enterprise Act 2002 to either regulator constitutes the giving of section 140B advice, the CMA must publish that advice in such manner as it thinks fit.]

NOTES

Originally substituted as noted to s 140A at **[1.169]**.

Further substituted by the Enterprise and Regulatory Reform Act 2013 (Competition) (Consequential, Transitional and Saving Provisions) Order 2014, SI 2014/892, art 2, Sch 1, Pt 2, paras 120, 125, subject to transitional provisions as noted to the Enterprise Act 2002, s 8A at **[1.187]**.

[1.174]

[140F Duty of [CMA] to send report to regulator

(1) Where the publication of a report of the [CMA] under section 142 of the Enterprise Act 2002 constitutes the giving of section 140B advice to either regulator, the [CMA] must give a copy of the report to that regulator.

(2) The day on which the copy is given is the day on which the regulator is to be taken to receive the section 140B advice.]

NOTES

Substituted as noted to s 140A at **[1.169]**.

References to the "CMA" substituted by the Enterprise and Regulatory Reform Act 2013 (Competition) (Consequential, Transitional and Saving Provisions) Order 2014, SI 2014/892, art 2, Sch 1, Pt 2, paras 120, 126, subject to transitional provisions as noted to the Enterprise Act 2002, s 8A at **[1.187]**.

[1.175]

[140G Duty of regulator to publish response

(1) A regulator must, within 90 days after the day on which it receives section 140B advice, publish a response stating how it proposes to deal with the advice and in particular—

(a) whether it has decided to take any action, or to take no action, in response to the advice,

(b) if it has decided to take action, what action it proposes to take, and

(c) its reasons for its proposals.

(2) Publication is to be in such manner as the regulator thinks fit.]

NOTES

Substituted as noted to s 140A at **[1.169]**.

[1.176]

[140H Role of the Treasury

(1) This section applies where—

(a) [the CMA] has given section 140B advice and the regulator has published a response under section 140G, and

(b) the [CMA] remains of the opinion that one or more of the things mentioned in section 140B(4) may cause or contribute to, the effect mentioned in section 140B(5).

(2) The [CMA] may refer the section 140B advice to the Treasury by sending the Treasury—

(a) a copy of the section 140B advice and of the response, and

(b) a request to consider the advice and the response.

(3) In referring the section 140B advice, the [CMA] may give advice to the Treasury as to what action, if any, ought to be taken by the regulator.

(4) If section 140B advice is referred to them, the Treasury may give a direction to the regulator to which the advice was given requiring the regulator to take such action as may be specified in the direction.

(5) In considering whether to give a direction and, if so, what action to specify, the Treasury must have regard to—

(a) any advice the [CMA] has given under subsection (3),

(b) any action which the section 140B advice suggests that the regulator should take, and

(c) the response of the regulator to the section 140B advice.

(6) The direction may not require the regulator to do anything that it has no power to do, but the existence of the direction is relevant to the exercise of any discretion conferred on the regulator.

(7) Before giving a direction under this section, the Treasury must consult the regulator to which it is to be given.

(8) If the Treasury give a direction under this section they must—

(a) publish in such manner as they think fit a statement giving details of the direction and of their reasons for giving it, and

(b) lay a copy of the statement before Parliament.]

NOTES

Substituted as noted to s 140A at **[1.169]**.

All words in square brackets were substituted by the Enterprise and Regulatory Reform Act 2013 (Competition) (Consequential, Transitional and Saving Provisions) Order 2014, SI 2014/892, art 2, Sch 1, Pt 2, paras 120, 127, subject to transitional provisions as noted to the Enterprise Act 2002, s 8A at **[1.187]**.

[PART 16A CONSUMER PROTECTION AND COMPETITION

Competition

234H (*Inserted by the Financial Services Act 2012, s 43. Repealed by the Financial Services (Banking Reform) Act 2013, s 129, Sch 8, Pt 1, paras 1, 2.*)

[1.177]

[234I The FCA's functions under Part 4 of the Enterprise Act 2002

(1) The functions to which this subsection applies ("the concurrent functions") are to be concurrent functions of the FCA and the Competition and Markets Authority (referred to in this Part as "the CMA").

(2) Subsection (1) applies to the functions of the CMA under Part 4 of the Enterprise Act 2002 (market investigations), so far as those functions—

- (a) are exercisable by the CMA Board (within the meaning of Schedule 4 to the Enterprise and Regulatory Reform Act 2013), and
- (b) relate to the provision of financial services [or to the provision of claims management services in Great Britain].

(3) But subsection (1) does not apply to functions under the following sections of the Enterprise Act 2002—

section 166 (duty to maintain register of undertakings and orders);
section 171 (duty to publish guidance).

(4) So far as is necessary for the purposes of, or in connection with, subsections (1) and (2)—

- (a) references in Part 4 of the Enterprise Act 2002 to the CMA (including references in provisions of that Act applied by that Part) are to be read as including references to the FCA, and
- (b) references in that Part to section 5 of that Act are to be read as including references to section 234M of this Act.

(5) But subsection (4) does not apply—

- (a) in relation to section 166 or 171 of that Act, or
- (b) where the context otherwise requires.

(6) Section 130A of the Enterprise Act 2002 has effect in relation to the FCA by virtue of subsections (1) and (2) as if—

- (a) in subsection (2)(a) of that section, the reference to the acquisition or supply of goods or services of one or more than one description in the United Kingdom were a reference to the acquisition or provision in the United Kingdom of financial services [or in Great Britain of claims management services], and
- (b) in subsection (2)(b) of that section, the reference to the extent to which steps can and should be taken were a reference to the extent to which steps that might include steps under Part 4 of that Act can and should be taken.

(7) Before the CMA or the FCA first exercises any of the concurrent functions in relation to any matter, it must consult the other.

(8) Neither the CMA nor the FCA may exercise any of the concurrent functions in relation to any matter if any of those functions have been exercised in relation to that matter by the other.]

NOTES

Inserted, together with ss 234J–234O, by the Financial Services (Banking Reform) Act 2013, s 129, Sch 8, Pt 1, paras 1, 3.

Sub-ss (2), (6): words in square brackets inserted by the Financial Guidance and Claims Act 2018, s 27(1), (7).

[1.178]

[234J The FCA's functions under the Competition Act 1998

(1) The functions to which this subsection applies are to be concurrent functions of the FCA and the CMA.

(2) Subsection (1) applies to the functions of the CMA under the provisions of Part 1 of the Competition Act 1998, so far as relating to any of the following that relate to the provision of financial services [or relate to the provision of claims management services in Great Britain]—

- (a) agreements, decisions or concerted practices of the kind mentioned in section 2(1) of that Act,
- (b) conduct of the kind mentioned in section 18(1) of that Act, [and]
- [(c) transferred EU anti-trust commitments or transferred EU anti-trust directions (as defined in section 40ZA of that Act)].

(3) But subsection (1) does not apply to functions under the following provisions of that Act—

section 31D(1) to (6) (duty to publish guidance);
section 38(1) to (6) (duty to publish guidance about penalties);
section 40B(1) to (4) (duty to publish statement of policy on penalties);
section 51 (rules).

(4) So far as necessary for the purposes of, or in connection with, the provisions of subsections (1) and (2), references to the CMA in Part 1 of the Competition Act 1998 are to be read as including references to the FCA.

(5) But subsection (4) does not apply—

- (a) in relation to sections 31D(1) to (6), 38(1) to (6), 40B(1) to (4), 51, 52(6) and (8) and 54 of that Act, or
- (b) where the context otherwise requires.]

NOTES

Inserted as noted to s 234I at **[1.177]**.

Sub-s (2) is amended as follows:

Words in first pair of square brackets inserted by the Financial Guidance and Claims Act 2018, s 27(1), (8).

Word in square brackets in para (b) inserted, and para (c) substituted (for the original paras (c) and (d)), by the Competition (Amendment etc) (EU Exit) Regulations 2019, SI 2019/93, reg 60, Sch 1, para 8, as from IP completion day (as defined in the European Union (Withdrawal Agreement) Act 2020, s 39) (for transitional provisions and savings in relation to the operation of the 2019 Regulations, see Sch 4 to those Regulations at **[7.69]** et seq). Note that Sch 1, para 8 to the 2019 Regulations was amended by the Competition (Amendment etc) (EU Exit) Regulations 2020, SI 2020/1343, reg 20, with effect from immediately before IP completion day; and the effect of those amendments has been incorporated in the text set out above. Note also that the original paras (c) and (d) read as follows—

"(c) agreements, decisions or concerted practices of the kind mentioned in Article 101(1) of the Treaty on the Functioning of the European Union, and

(d) conduct which amounts to abuse of the kind mentioned in Article 102 of the Treaty on the Functioning of the European Union.".

[1.179]

[234K Duty to consider exercise of powers under Competition Act 1998

(1) Before exercising a power listed in subsection (3), the FCA must consider whether it would be more appropriate to proceed under the Competition Act 1998.

(2) The FCA must not exercise such a power if it considers that it would be more appropriate to proceed under the Competition Act 1998.

(3) Those powers are—

(a) the power under section 55J(2) to vary or cancel a Part 4A permission;

(b) the power under section 55L to impose a requirement on an authorised person with a Part 4A permission, or to vary a requirement imposed under that section;

(c) the power to take action under section 88E;

(d) the power to take action under section 89U;

(e) the power to give a direction under section 192C;

(f) . . .]

NOTES

Inserted as noted to s 234I at **[1.177]**.

Sub-s (3): para (f) repealed by the EEA Passport Rights (Amendment, etc, and Transitional Provisions) (EU Exit) Regulations 2018, SI 2018/1149, reg 3, Schedule, Pt 1, paras 1, 17, as from IP completion day (as defined in the European Union (Withdrawal Agreement) Act 2020, s 39).

[1.180]

[234L Provision of information and assistance to a CMA group

(1) For the purpose of assisting a CMA group in carrying out a relevant investigation, the FCA must give the CMA group—

(a) any relevant information which the FCA has in its possession, and

(b) any other assistance which the CMA group may reasonably require in relation to any matters falling within the scope of the investigation.

(2) A "relevant investigation" is an investigation carried out on a reference made by the FCA under section 131 of the Enterprise Act 2002 by virtue of section 234I.

(3) "Relevant information", in relation to a relevant investigation, is information—

(a) which relates to matters falling within the scope of the investigation, and

(b) which—

(i) is requested by the CMA group for the purpose of the investigation, or

(ii) in the FCA's opinion, it would be appropriate to give to the CMA group for that purpose.

(4) A CMA group, in carrying out a relevant investigation, must take into account any information given to it under this section.

(5) In this section "CMA group" has the same meaning as in Schedule 4 to the Enterprise and Regulatory Reform Act 2013.]

NOTES

Inserted as noted to s 234I at **[1.177]**.

[1.181]

[234M Function of keeping market under review

(1) For the purpose of the functions conferred on it by sections 234I to 234L the FCA is to have the function of keeping under review the market for financial services [and the market in Great Britain for claims management services].

(2) The function conferred by subsection (1) is to be carried out with a view to (among other things) ensuring that the FCA has sufficient information to take informed decisions and to carry out its other functions effectively.]

NOTES

Inserted as noted to s 234I at **[1.177]**.

Sub-s (1): words in square brackets inserted by the Financial Guidance and Claims Act 2018, s 27(1), (9).

[1.182]

[234N Exclusion of general duties

(1) Section 1B (the FCA's general duties) does not apply in relation to anything done by the FCA in the carrying out of its functions by virtue of sections 234I to 234L.

(2) But in the carrying out of any functions by virtue of sections 234I to 234L, the FCA may have regard to any of the matters in respect of which a duty is imposed by section 1B if it is a matter to which the CMA is entitled to have regard in the carrying out of those functions.]

NOTES

Inserted as noted to s 234I at **[1.177]**.

[1.183]

[234O Supplementary provision

(1) If any question arises as to whether, by virtue of section 234I or 234J, any functions fall to be, or are capable of being, carried out by the FCA in relation to any particular case, that question is to be referred to, and determined by, the Treasury.

(2) No objection is to be taken to anything done under the Competition Act 1998 or Part 4 of the Enterprise Act 2002 by or in relation to the FCA on the ground that it should have been done by or in relation to the CMA.]

NOTES

Inserted as noted to s 234I at **[1.177]**.

ENTERPRISE ACT 2002

(2002 c 40)

ARRANGEMENT OF SECTIONS

PART 1
THE OFFICE OF FAIR TRADING

General functions of the CMA

Miscellaneous

PART 2
THE COMPETITION APPEAL TRIBUNAL

The Competition Appeal Tribunal

PART 3
MERGERS

CHAPTER 1 DUTY TO MAKE REFERENCES

Duty to make references: completed mergers

Duty to make references: anticipated mergers

Supplementary provision: time-limits for decisions about references

Cases referred by European Commission under EC Merger Regulation

Determination of references

CHAPTER 2 PUBLIC INTEREST CASES

Power to make references

Cases referred by European Commission under the EC Merger Regulation

Reports on references

Decisions of the Secretary of State

Other

CHAPTER 3 OTHER SPECIAL CASES

Special public interest cases

European mergers

CHAPTER 4 ENFORCEMENT

Powers exercisable before references under section 22 or 33

Interim restrictions and powers

Final powers

Public interest and special public interest cases

Undertakings and orders: general provisions

Enforcement functions of CMA

Other

Transferred EU merger commitments

CHAPTER 5 SUPPLEMENTARY

Merger notices

General duties in relation to references

Information and publicity requirements

CHAPTER 2 PUBLIC INTEREST CASES

Intervention notices

Intervention notices under section 139(1)

Intervention notices under section 139(2)

Other

CHAPTER 3 ENFORCEMENT

Undertakings and orders

Undertakings and orders: monitoring, consultation and advice

Supplementary

CHAPTER 4 SUPPLEMENTARY

Regulated markets

Consultation, information and publicity

Investigation powers

SCHEDULES

Establish and provide for the functions of the Office of Fair Trading, the Competition Appeal Tribunal and the Competition Service; to make provision about mergers and market structures and conduct; to amend the constitution and functions of the Competition Commission; to create an offence for those entering into certain anti-competitive agreements; to provide for the disqualification of directors of companies engaging in certain anti-competitive practices; to make other provision about competition law; to amend the law relating to the protection of the collective interests of consumers; to make further provision about the disclosure of information obtained under competition and consumer legislation; to amend the Insolvency Act 1986 and make other provision about insolvency; and for connected purposes

[7 November 2002]

NOTES

See also the list of consultations and draft documents in the Appendix at **[A1]**.

References to the "European Community", "Community", etc: see the Treaty of Lisbon (Changes in Terminology) Order 2011, SI 2011/1043, which provides (with effect from 22 April 2011): (1) that for references to the "European Communities" or to the "European Community" (including references to "the Communities", "the Community", "the EC" or "the EEC") substitute references to the European Union; and (2) that "EU" should be substituted for the word "Community" (subject to certain exceptions) in references to "Community treaties", "Community customs duty", "Community institution", "Community instrument", "Community obligation", "enforceable Community right", "Community law", "Community legislation", and "Community provision". Also, where such a term is preceded by the word "a", for "a" substitute "an". For more details, see arts 3, 4, 6 of the 2011 Order as set out in the introductory notes to the Company Directors Disqualification Act 1986 preceding **[1.23]**.

PART 1 [GENERAL FUNCTIONS OF THE CMA]

NOTES

Words in square brackets in the Part heading substituted by the Enterprise and Regulatory Reform Act 2013, s 26(3), Sch 5, Pt 2, paras 59, 65. For various transitional provisions (including those relating to the abolition of the OFT and the Competition Commission, existing references to those bodies and provisions relating to continuity), see the Enterprise and Regulatory Reform Act 2013 (Commencement No 6, Transitional Provisions and Savings) Order 2014, SI 2014/416, Schedule at **[2.13]**.

. . .

1–4 *(Ss 1–4 repealed, together with the preceding heading, by the Enterprise and Regulatory Reform Act 2013, s 26(3), Sch 5, Pt 4, para 229. For various transitional provisions (including those relating to the abolition of the OFT and the Competition Commission, existing references to those bodies and provisions relating to continuity), see the Enterprise and Regulatory Reform Act 2013 (Commencement No 6, Transitional Provisions and Savings) Order 2014, SI 2014/416, Schedule at* **[2.13]**.)

General functions of [the CMA]

NOTES

Words in square brackets in the preceding heading substituted by the Enterprise and Regulatory Reform Act 2013, s 26(3), Sch 5, Pt 2, paras 59, 60(1), (3). For various transitional provisions (including those relating to the abolition of the OFT and the Competition Commission, existing references to those bodies and provisions relating to continuity), see the Enterprise and Regulatory Reform Act 2013 (Commencement No 6, Transitional Provisions and Savings) Order 2014, SI 2014/416, Schedule at **[2.13]**.

[1.184]

5 Acquisition of information etc

(1) The [CMA] has the function of obtaining, compiling and keeping under review information about matters relating to the carrying out of its functions.

(2) That function is to be carried out with a view to (among other things) ensuring that the [CMA] has sufficient information to take informed decisions and to carry out its other functions effectively.

(3) In carrying out that function the [CMA] may carry out, commission or support (financially or otherwise) research.

NOTES

References to the "CMA" substituted by the Enterprise and Regulatory Reform Act 2013, s 26(3), Sch 5, Pt 2, paras 59, 60(1), (2). For various transitional provisions (including those relating to the abolition of the OFT and the Competition Commission, existing references to those bodies and provisions relating to continuity), see the Enterprise and Regulatory Reform Act 2013 (Commencement No 6, Transitional Provisions and Savings) Order 2014, SI 2014/416, Schedule at **[2.13]**.

[1.185]

6 Provision of information etc to the public

(1) The [CMA] has the function of—

(a) making the public aware of the ways in which competition may benefit consumers in, and the economy of, the United Kingdom; and

(b) giving information or advice in respect of matters relating to any of its functions to the public.

(2) In carrying out those functions the [CMA] may—

(a) publish educational materials or carry out other educational activities; or

(b) support (financially or otherwise) the carrying out by others of such activities or the provision by others of information or advice.

NOTES

References to the "CMA" substituted by the Enterprise and Regulatory Reform Act 2013, s 26(3), Sch 5, Pt 2, paras 59, 61. For various transitional provisions (including those relating to the abolition of the OFT and the Competition Commission, existing references to those bodies and provisions relating to continuity), see the Enterprise and Regulatory Reform Act 2013 (Commencement No 6, Transitional Provisions and Savings) Order 2014, SI 2014/416, Schedule at **[2.13]**.

Sectoral regulators: before publishing under this section, the CMA is under a duty to consult with the various sectoral regulators about matters falling within the remit of those regulators; see the Gas Act 1986, s 35(3A), the Electricity Act 1989, s 48(3), the Water Industry Act 1991, s 201(4), the Railways Act 1993, s 71(3), and the Transport Act 2000, s 90(6).

[1.186]

7 Provision of information and advice to Ministers etc

(1) The [CMA] has the function of—

(a) making proposals, or

(b) giving other information or advice,

on matters relating to any of its functions to any Minister of the Crown or other public authority (including proposals, information or advice as to any aspect of the law or a proposed change in the law).

[(1A) The CMA may, in particular, carry out the function under subsection (1)(a) by making a proposal in the form of a recommendation to a Minister of the Crown about the potential effect of a proposal for Westminster legislation on competition within any market or markets in the United Kingdom for goods or services

(1B) The CMA must publish such a recommendation in such manner as the CMA considers appropriate for bringing the subject matter of the recommendation to the attention of those likely to be affected by it.]

(2) A Minister of the Crown may request the [CMA] to make proposals or give other information or advice on any matter relating to any of its functions; and the [CMA] shall, so far as is reasonably practicable and consistent with its other functions, comply with the request.

[(3) In this section—

"market in the United Kingdom" includes—

(a) so far as it operates in the United Kingdom or a part of the United Kingdom, any market which operates there and in another country or territory or in a part of another country or territory; and

(b) any market which operates only in a part of the United Kingdom;

and the reference to a market for goods or services includes a reference to a market for goods and services; and

"Westminster legislation" means—

(a) an Act of Parliament, or

(b) subordinate legislation (within the meaning given by section 21 of the Interpretation Act 1978).]

NOTES

Sub-ss (1), (2): references to the "CMA" substituted by the Enterprise and Regulatory Reform Act 2013, s 26(3), Sch 5, Pt 2, paras 59, 62. For various transitional provisions (including those relating to the abolition of the OFT and the Competition Commission, existing references to those bodies and provisions relating to continuity), see the Enterprise and Regulatory Reform Act 2013 (Commencement No 6, Transitional Provisions and Savings) Order 2014, SI 2014/416, Schedule at **[2.13]**.

Sub-ss (1A), (1B), (3): inserted and added respectively by the Small Business, Enterprise and Employment Act 2015, s 37.

8 (*Repealed by the Enterprise and Regulatory Reform Act 2013, s 26(3), Sch 5, Pt 2, paras 59, 63. For various transitional provisions (including those relating to the abolition of the OFT and the Competition Commission, existing references to those bodies and provisions relating to continuity), see the Enterprise and Regulatory Reform Act 2013 (Commencement No 6, Transitional Provisions and Savings) Order 2014, SI 2014/416, Schedule at* **[2.13]**.)

[1.187]

[8A Exclusion of public consumer advice scheme

The [CMA] may not under this Part support a public consumer advice scheme, where that support of a scheme consists of providing, or securing the provision of, an arrangement for giving advice without charge to individual consumers on matters personal to them.]

NOTES

Inserted by the Public Bodies (The Office of Fair Trading Transfer of Consumer Advice Scheme Function and Modification of Enforcement Functions) Order 2013, SI 2013/783, art 3.

Reference to the "CMA" substituted by the Enterprise and Regulatory Reform Act 2013 (Competition) (Consequential, Transitional and Saving Provisions) Order 2014, SI 2014/892, art 2, Sch 1, Pt 1, paras 1, 2, subject to transitional provisions in relation to the abolition of the OFT and the Competition Commission and the continuity of functions, etc, in art 3 of the 2014 Order as noted below.

Transitional provisions: the Enterprise and Regulatory Reform Act 2013 (Competition) (Consequential, Transitional and Saving Provisions) Order 2014, SI 2014/892, art 3, provides as follows—

"3 Continuity of functions

(1) Anything which, immediately before the commencement date, is in the process of being done by or in relation to the transferor may, so far as it relates to a relevant function, be continued by or in relation to the transferee.

(2) Anything done (or having effect as if done) by or in relation to the transferor for the purposes of or in connection with a relevant function is, if in force or effective immediately before the commencement date, to have effect as if done by or in relation to the transferee so far as that is required for continuing its effect on or after the commencement date.

(3) In the application of paragraph (1) or (2)—

(a) any reference made before the commencement date under section 32 of the Water Industry Act 1991 to the Commission is to be treated, so far as provided by those paragraphs, as a reference under that section to the chair of the CMA for the constitution of a CMA group,

(b) where any functions exercisable immediately before the commencement date by a Commission group are to be exercisable on or after that date by a CMA group—

(i) any person who, immediately before the commencement date, is a member of the Commission group is to be treated, on or after that date, as a member of the CMA group concerned if the person is a member of the CMA panel,

(ii) any person who, immediately before the commencement date, is the chairman of the Commission group is to be treated, on or after that date, as the chair of the CMA group if the person is a member of the CMA panel, and

(iii) the persons treated as mentioned in paragraph (i) or (ii) are to be treated, on or after the commencement date, as if they have been constituted in accordance with Part 3 of Schedule 4 to the Act as the chair and other members of the CMA group (and that Part applies accordingly in relation to the operation of the group), and

(c) an authorisation given (whether by warrant or otherwise) before the commencement date, so far as it authorises a named member, or member of staff, of the OFT or the Commission, continues to authorise that individual (but no other) on or after the commencement date if, and only if, the individual is a member, or (as the case may be, a member of staff, of the CMA.

(4) Paragraphs (1) to (3)—

(a) do not apply in relation to any matter dealt with by a transfer scheme under section 27 of the Act or by any other transitional provision made by virtue of the Act; and

(b) do not apply so as to convert an appointment as a member of the OFT or the Commission into an appointment as a member of the CMA.

(5) Any enactment, instrument or other document passed or made before the commencement date is to have effect, so far as necessary for the purposes of or in consequence of its continued effect by virtue of Schedule 2, as if any references (however expressed) to the transferor were references to the transferee.

(6) Any enactment, instrument or other document passed or made before the commencement date is to have effect, so far as necessary for the purposes of or in consequence of—

(a) anything transferred from the transferor to the transferee by virtue of this Order or Part 3 or 4 of the Act, or

(b) the abolition of the OFT or the Commission,

as if any references (however expressed) to the transferor were references to the transferee

(7) The repeals of section 45(4) of the Competition Act 1998 and section 2(3) of the Enterprise Act 2002 by Parts 3 and 4 of Schedule 5 to the Act do not apply so far as those sections create references to the transferor to which paragraph (5) or (6) above are capable of applying.

(8) The abolition of the OFT or the Commission does not affect the validity of anything done (or having effect as if done) by or in relation to the transferor before the commencement date.

(9) In this article—

"CMA Board" has the same meaning as in Schedule 4 to the Act (see Part 2 of that Schedule);

"CMA group" means a group constituted in accordance with Part 3 of Schedule 4 to the Act;

"CMA panel" has the same meaning as in Schedule 4 to the Act (see Part 3 of that Schedule);

"commencement date" means 1st April 2014;

"Commission group" means a group constituted under any enactment to perform functions of the Commission;

"relevant function" means any function of the transferor which is transferred to the transferee by this Order;

"transferee" means the CMA, the CMA Board, a CMA group, the chair of the CMA or another member of the CMA or (as the case may be) a member of staff of the CMA;

"transferor" means the OFT, the Commission, a Commission group, the chairman of the OFT or Commission, another member of the OFT or Commission, or a member of staff of the OFT or the Commission;

and references in this article to things done include references to things omitted to be done.

(10) Schedule 2 (which makes further transitional provision in relation to amendments in Schedule 1 to the investigation powers of the CMA) has effect.".

Miscellaneous

9, 10 *(S 9 repeals the Fair Trading Act 1973, s 12, and the Competition Act 1980, s 13; s 10(1) repeals the Fair Trading Act 1973, ss 3, 13–22, Sch 2; s 10(2)–(4) repealed by the Consumer Protection from Unfair Trading Regulations 2008, SI 2008/1277, reg 30(1), (3), Sch 2, Pt 1, paras 68, 69, Sch 4, Pt 1.)*

[1.188]

11 Super-complaints to [CMA]

(1) This section applies where a designated consumer body makes a complaint to the [CMA] that any feature, or combination of features, of a market in the United Kingdom for goods or services is or appears to be significantly harming the interests of consumers.

(2) The [CMA] must, within 90 days after the day on which it receives the complaint, publish a response stating how it proposes to deal with the complaint, and in particular—

(a) whether it has decided to take any action, or to take no action, in response to the complaint, and

(b) if it has decided to take action, what action it proposes to take.

(3) The response must state the [CMA's] reasons for its proposals.

(4) The Secretary of State may by order amend subsection (2) by substituting any period for the period for the time being specified there.

(5) "Designated consumer body" means a body designated by the Secretary of State by order.

(6) The Secretary of State—

(a) may designate a body only if it appears to him to represent the interests of consumers of any description, and

(b) must publish (and may from time to time vary) other criteria to be applied by him in determining whether to make or revoke a designation.

(7) The [CMA]—

(a) must issue guidance as to the presentation by the complainant of a reasoned case for the complaint, and

(b) may issue such other guidance as appears to it to be appropriate for the purposes of this section.

(8) An order under this section—

(a) shall be made by statutory instrument, and

(b) shall be subject to annulment in pursuance of a resolution of either House of Parliament.

(9) In this section—

(a) references to a feature of a market in the United Kingdom for goods or services have the same meaning as if contained in Part 4, and

(b) "consumer" means an individual who is a consumer within the meaning of that Part.

NOTES

References to the "CMA" and the "CMA's" substituted by the Enterprise and Regulatory Reform Act 2013, s 26(3), Sch 5, Pt 2, paras 59, 64. For various transitional provisions (including those relating to the abolition of the OFT and the Competition Commission, existing references to those bodies and provisions relating to continuity), see the Enterprise and Regulatory Reform Act 2013 (Commencement No 6, Transitional Provisions and Savings) Order 2014, SI 2014/416, Schedule at **[2.13]**.

Orders: the Enterprise Act 2002 (Bodies Designated to make Super-complaints) Order 2004, SI 2004/1517 at **[2.39]**; the Enterprise Act 2002 (Bodies Designated to make Super-complaints) (Amendment) Order 2009, SI 2009/2079.

PART 2 THE COMPETITION APPEAL TRIBUNAL

The Competition Appeal Tribunal

[1.189]

12 The Competition Appeal Tribunal

(1) There shall be a tribunal, to be called the Competition Appeal Tribunal (in this Part referred to as "the Tribunal").

(2) The Tribunal shall consist of—

(a) a person appointed by the Lord Chancellor to preside over the Tribunal (in this Part referred to as "the President");

[(aa) such judges as are nominated from time to time by the Lord Chief Justice of England and Wales from the High Court of England and Wales;

(ab) such judges as are nominated from time to time by the Lord President of the Court of Session from the judges of the Court of Session;

(ac) such judges as are nominated from time to time by the Lord Chief Justice of Northern Ireland from the High Court in Northern Ireland;]

(b) members appointed by the Lord Chancellor to form a panel of chairmen; and

(c) members appointed by the Secretary of State to form a panel of ordinary members.

(3) The Tribunal shall have a Registrar appointed by the Secretary of State.

(4) The expenses of the Tribunal shall be paid by the Competition Service.

(5) Schedule 2 (which makes further provision about the Tribunal) has effect.

NOTES

Sub-s (2): paras (aa)–(ac) inserted by the Consumer Rights Act 2015, s 82(1).

Appointed: in connection with an appointment under sub-s (2)(a) or (b), see the Constitutional Reform Act 2005, ss 85–88 (by virtue of s 85(1)(c) of, Sch 14 to, that Act).

[1.190]

13 The Competition Service

(1) There shall be a body corporate called the Competition Service (in this Part referred to as "the Service").

(2) The purpose of the Service is to fund, and provide support services to, the Competition Appeal Tribunal.

(3) In subsection (2) "support services" includes the provision of staff, accommodation and equipment and any other services which facilitate the carrying out by the Tribunal of its functions.

(4) The activities of the Service are not carried out on behalf of the Crown (and its property is not to be regarded as held on behalf of the Crown).
(5) The Secretary of State shall pay to the Service such sums as he considers appropriate to enable it to fund the activities of the Tribunal and to carry out its other activities.
(6) Schedule 3 (which makes further provision about the Service) has effect.

NOTES

For the power of a Minister to abolish, by order, the Competition Service, see the Public Bodies Act 2011, s 1, Sch 1.

[1.191]
14 Constitution of Tribunal for particular proceedings and its decisions
(1) For the purposes of any proceedings before it[, including proceedings relating to the approval of a collective settlement under section 49A or 49B of the 1998 Act,] the Tribunal shall consist of a chairman and two other members.
[(1A) But in the case of proceedings relating to a claim under section 47A of the 1998 Act which is subject to the fast-track procedure (as described in Tribunal rules), the Tribunal may consist of a chairman only.]
(2) The chairman must be the President[, a judge within any of paragraphs (aa) to (ac) of section 12(2)] or a member of the panel of chairmen.
(3) The other members may be chosen from [the judges within paragraphs (aa) to (ac) of section 12(2),] the panel of chairmen or the panel of ordinary members.
(4) If the members of the Tribunal as constituted in accordance with this section are unable to agree on any decision, the decision is to be taken by majority vote.
(5) This section has effect subject to [paragraphs 10A(1)(a) and 18] of Schedule 4 (consequences of a member of the Tribunal being unable to continue after the proceedings have begun to be heard).
(6) Part 1 of Schedule 4 (which makes further provision about the decisions of the Tribunal and their enforcement) has effect.

NOTES

Sub-s (1): words in square brackets inserted by the Consumer Rights Act 2015, s 81, Sch 8, Pt 2, paras 18, 19(1), (2).
Sub-s (1A): inserted by the Consumer Rights Act 2015, s 81, Sch 8, Pt 2, paras 18, 19(1), (3).
Sub-s (2): words in square brackets inserted by the Consumer Rights Act 2015, s 82(2)(a).
Sub-s (3): words in square brackets substituted by the Consumer Rights Act 2015, s 82(2)(b).
Sub-s (5): words in square brackets substituted by the Enterprise and Regulatory Reform Act 2013, s 48(6). For various transitional provisions (including those relating to the abolition of the OFT and the Competition Commission, existing references to those bodies and provisions relating to continuity), see the Enterprise and Regulatory Reform Act 2013 (Commencement No 6, Transitional Provisions and Savings) Order 2014, SI 2014/416, Schedule at **[2.13]**.

[1.192]
15 Tribunal rules
(1) The Secretary of State may, after consulting the President and such other persons as he considers appropriate, make rules (in this Part referred to as "Tribunal rules") with respect to proceedings before the Tribunal[, including proceedings relating to the approval of a collective settlement under section 49A or 49B of the 1998 Act].
(2) Tribunal rules may make provision with respect to matters incidental to or consequential upon appeals provided for by or under any Act to the Court of Appeal or the Court of Session in relation to a decision of the Tribunal.
(3) Tribunal rules may—

(a) specify qualifications for appointment as Registrar;
(b) confer functions on the President or the Registrar in relation to proceedings before the Tribunal; and
(c) contain incidental, supplemental, consequential or transitional provision.

(4) The power to make Tribunal rules is exercisable by statutory instrument subject to annulment in pursuance of a resolution of either House of Parliament.
(5) Part 2 of Schedule 4 (which makes further provision about the rules) has effect, but without prejudice to the generality of subsection (1).

NOTES

Sub-s (1): words in square brackets inserted by the Consumer Rights Act 2015, s 81, Sch 8, Pt 2, paras 18, 20.
Rules: the Competition Appeal Tribunal Rules 2015, SI 2015/1648 at **[6.8]**. Note also that the Competition Appeal Tribunal Rules 2003, SI 2003/1372 (at **[6.1]**) were also made under this section, and revoked in relation to cases beginning on or after 1 October 2015, by the 2015 Rules.

[1.193]
16 Transfers of certain proceedings to and from Tribunal
(1) The Lord Chancellor may by regulations—

(a) make provision enabling the court—
  (i) to transfer to the Tribunal for its determination so much of any proceedings before the court as relates to an infringement issue; and
  (ii) to give effect to the determination of that issue by the Tribunal; and
(b) make such incidental, supplementary, consequential, transitional or saving provision as the Lord Chancellor may consider appropriate.

(2) The power to make regulations under subsection (1) is exercisable by statutory instrument subject to annulment in pursuance of a resolution of either House of Parliament.
(3) Rules of court may prescribe the procedure to be followed in connection with a transfer mentioned in subsection (1).
(4) The court may transfer to the Tribunal, in accordance with rules of court, so much of any proceedings before it as relates to a claim to which section 47A of the 1998 Act applies.

(5) Rules of court may make provision in connection with the transfer from the Tribunal to the [court of all or any part of] a claim made in proceedings under section 47A of the 1998 Act.

(6) In this section—

"the court" means—

(a) the High Court [or the county court]; or

(b) the Court of Session or a sheriff court; and

["infringement issue" means any question relating to whether or not an infringement of the Chapter I prohibition or the Chapter II prohibition has been or is being committed;

but otherwise any terms used in this section and Part 1 of the 1998 Act have the same meaning as they have in that Part.]

NOTES

Sub-s (5): words in square brackets substituted by the Consumer Rights Act 2015, s 81, Sch 8, Pt 2, paras 18, 21.

Sub-s (6): words in square brackets in the definition "the court" substituted by the Crime and Courts Act 2013, s 17(5), Sch 9, Pt 3, para 81(a).The definition "infringement issue" was substituted by the Competition (Amendment etc) (EU Exit) Regulations 2019, SI 2019/93, regs 32, 33, as from IP completion day (as defined in the European Union (Withdrawal Agreement) Act 2020, s 39) (for transitional provisions and savings in relation to the operation of the 2019 Regulations, see Sch 4 to those Regulations at **[7.69]**et seq). The original definition (as amended by the Treaty of Lisbon (Changes in Terminology or Numbering) Order 2012, SI 2012/1809, art 3(1), Schedule, Pt 1) read as follows—

"infringement issue" means any question relating to whether or not an infringement of—

(a) the Chapter I prohibition or the Chapter II prohibition; or

(b) [Article 101 or 102] of the Treaty,

has been or is being committed;".

Regulations: the Section 16 Enterprise Act 2002 Regulations 2015, SI 2015/1643 at **[2.185]**.

Rules: the Act of Sederunt (Ordinary Cause Rules) Amendment (Competition Appeal Tribunal) 2004, SSI 2004/350.

17–21 (*S 17 substitutes the Competition Act 1998, s 47, at* **[1.88]**; *s 18 inserts s 47A of the 1998 Act, at* **[1.89]**; *s 19 inserts s 47B of the 1998 Act, at* **[1.90]**; *s 20 inserts s 58A of the 1998 Act, at* **[1.106]**, *except in relation to decisions made before the commencement of s 20, and amends 59(1) of that Act at* **[1.107]**; *s 21 introduces Sch 5 to this Act (further amendments of the 1998 Act).*)

PART 3 MERGERS

NOTES

For general savings and transitional provisions with regard to the operation of this Part (ie, ss 22–130, Schs 6–8, Sch 9, Pt 1, Sch 10), see Sch 24, para 13 to this Act at **[1.445]**, and the Enterprise Act 2002 (Commencement No 3, Transitional and Transitory Provisions and Savings) Order 2003, SI 2003/1397, art 4.

For savings and transitional provisions in connection with the application of this Part to water and sewerage undertakers, see the Enterprise Act 2002 (Commencement No 3, Transitional and Transitory Provisions and Savings) Order 2003, SI 2003/1397, art 3, and the Enterprise Act 2002 (Commencement No 7 and Transitional Provisions and Savings) Order 2004, SI 2004/3233, arts 3–5. As to the application of this Part in relation to such mergers, see the Water Industry Act 1991, ss 32–35, Sch 4ZA (at **[1.31]** et seq), and the Water Mergers (Modification of Enactments) Regulations 2004, SI 2004/3202 (at **[2.127]** et seq). See also the Water Services etc (Scotland) Act 2005 (Consequential Provisions and Modifications) Order 2005, SI 2005/3172.

The merger regime contained in this Act did not, by virtue of s 69, apply to newspaper mergers. As such, the provisions relating to such mergers in the Fair Trading Act 1973 continued to have effect. Section 69 of this Act, and ss 57–62 of the 1973 Act, were repealed by the Communications Act 2003, as from 29 December 2003 (subject to transitional provisions contained in Sch 18, paras 59–62 to that Act, as to which, see the introductory note to the Fair Trading Act 1973). As to the duty of OFCOM to review the operation of the provisions of this Part of this Act (in so far as they relate to intervention by the Secretary of State in connection with newspapers or other media enterprises), see the Communications Act 2003, s 391.

Public interest cases: where the Secretary of State has reasonable grounds for suspecting that it is or may be the case that a relevant merger situation has been created, he may, where the provisions of s 42(1) *post* are satisfied, give an intervention notice to the CMA if he believes that it is or may be the case that one or more public interest consideration is relevant to a consideration of the relevant merger situation (see s 42(1), (2) *post*). In such a case, the provisions of ss 23–30 (read together with s 34) apply, with modifications, for the purposes of deciding whether a relevant merger situation has been created; see s 42(5), (6) *post*.

Special public interest cases: where the Secretary of State has reasonable grounds for suspecting that it is or may be the case that a special merger situation has been created, he may give a special intervention notice to the CMA if he believes that it is or may be the case that one or more than one consideration specified in s 58 *post* is relevant to a consideration of the special merger situation (see s 59(1), (2) *post*). In such a case, the provisions of ss 23–30 (read together with s 34) apply, with modifications, for the purposes of deciding whether a relevant merger situation has been created; see s 59(5), (6) *post*.

Intervention to protect legitimate interests (European intervention notices): see 67(1), (2) *post*. Note that s 67 of this Act was repealed by the Competition (Amendment etc) (EU Exit) Regulations 2019, SI 2019/93, regs 32, 37, as from IP completion day (as defined in the European Union (Withdrawal Agreement) Act 2020, s 39) (for transitional provisions and savings in relation to the operation of the 2019 Regulations, see Sch 4 to those Regulations at **[7.69]** et seq and, in particular, Sch 4, Pt 7 to the 2019 Regulations at **[7.76]**). See also the Enterprise Act 2002 (Protection of Legitimate Interests) Order 2003, SI 2003/1592 at **[2.103]** et seq. Note that s 68 of the Enterprise Act 2002 (under which the 2003 Order was made) was also repealed by the Competition (Amendment etc) (EU Exit) Regulations 2019, SI 2019/93, regs 32, 47, as from IP completion day. See, however, Sch 4, Pt 7, paras 25–27 to the 2019 Regulations (at **[7.76]**) which provides for the continued application of the 2003 Order in the circumstances specified in those paragraphs.

CHAPTER 1 DUTY TO MAKE REFERENCES

Duty to make references: completed mergers

[1.194]

22 Duty to make references in relation to completed mergers

(1) [The CMA shall, subject to subsections (2) and (3), make a reference to its chair for the constitution of a group under Schedule 4 to the Enterprise and Regulatory Reform Act 2013 if the CMA believes that it is or may be the case that]—

(a) a relevant merger situation has been created; and

(b) the creation of that situation has resulted, or may be expected to result, in a substantial lessening of competition within any market or markets in the United Kingdom for goods or services.

(2) The [CMA] may decide not to make a reference under this section if it believes that—

(a) the market concerned is not, or the markets concerned are not, of sufficient importance to justify the making of a reference . . . ; or

(b) any relevant customer benefits in relation to the creation of the relevant merger situation concerned outweigh the substantial lessening of competition concerned and any adverse effects of the substantial lessening of competition concerned.

(3) No reference shall be made under this section if—

[(za) the period within which the CMA is required by section 34ZA to decide whether the duty to make the reference applies has expired without such a decision having been made;]

(a) the making of the reference is prevented by section . . . 74(1) . . . or paragraph 4 of Schedule 7;

(b) the [CMA] is considering whether to accept undertakings under section 73 instead of making such a reference;

(c) the relevant merger situation concerned is being, or has been, dealt with in connection with a reference made under section 33; [or]

(d) a notice under section 42(2) is in force in relation to the matter or the matter to which such a notice relates has been finally determined under Chapter 2 otherwise than in circumstances in which a notice is then given to the [CMA] under section 56(1); . . .

(e) the European Commission is considering a request made, in relation to the matter concerned, by the United Kingdom (whether alone or with others) under article [22(1) of the EC Merger Regulation], is proceeding with the matter in pursuance of such a request or has dealt with the matter in pursuance of such a request[; or

(f) subject to subsection (3A), a reasoned submission requesting referral to the European Commission has been submitted to the European Commission under article 4(5) of the EC Merger Regulation].

[(3A) Subsection (3)(f) shall cease to apply if the [CMA] is informed that a Member State competent to examine the concentration under its national competition law has, within the time permitted by Article 4(5) of the EC Merger Regulation, expressed its disagreement as regards the request to refer the case to the European Commission; and this subsection shall be construed in accordance with that Regulation.]

(4) A reference under this section shall, in particular, specify—

(a) the enactment under which it is made; and

(b) the date on which it is made.

(5) The references in this section to the creation of a relevant merger situation shall be construed in accordance with section 23, the reference in subsection (2) of this section to relevant customer benefits shall be construed in accordance with section 30 and the reference in subsection (3) of this section to a matter to which a notice under section 42(2) relates being finally determined under Chapter 2 shall be construed in accordance with section 43(4) and (5).

(6) In this Part "market in the United Kingdom" includes—

(a) so far as it operates in the United Kingdom or a part of the United Kingdom, any market which operates there and in another country or territory or in a part of another country or territory; and

(b) any market which operates only in a part of the United Kingdom;

and references to a market for goods or services include references to a market for goods and services.

(7) In this Part "the decision-making authority" means—

(a) in the case of a reference or possible reference under this section or section 33, [the CMA]; and

(b) in the case of a notice or possible notice under section 42(2) or 59(2) or a reference or possible reference under section 45 or 62, [the CMA] or (as the case may be) the Secretary of State.

NOTES

Sub-s (1): words in square brackets substituted by the Enterprise and Regulatory Reform Act 2013, s 26(3), Sch 5, Pt 2, paras 59, 67(1), (2). For various transitional provisions (including those relating to the abolition of the OFT and the Competition Commission, existing references to those bodies and provisions relating to continuity), see the Enterprise and Regulatory Reform Act 2013 (Commencement No 6, Transitional Provisions and Savings) Order 2014, SI 2014/416, Schedule at **[2.13]**.

Sub-s (2): reference to the "CMA" substituted, and words omitted repealed, by the Enterprise and Regulatory Reform Act 2013, s 26(3), Sch 5, Pt 2, paras 59, 67(1), (3), subject to transitional provisions in SI 2014/416 as noted above.

Sub-s (3): para (za) inserted, second words omitted from para (a) repealed, and references to the "CMA" in paras (b) and (d) substituted, by the Enterprise and Regulatory Reform Act 2013, ss 26(3), 32(2), Sch 5, Pt 2, paras 59, 67(1), (4), Sch 8, paras 1, 2, subject to transitional provisions in SI 2014/416 as noted above. First figure omitted from para (a) repealed by the Communications Act 2003, s 406(7), Sch 19. Word omitted from the end of para (d) repealed, words in square brackets in para (e) substituted, and para (f) and the word immediately preceding it added, by the EC Merger Control (Consequential Amendments) Regulations 2004, SI 2004/1079, Schedule, para 2(1)–(3). The word "or" in square brackets in para (c) was inserted, and paras (e) and (f) were repealed, by the Competition (Amendment etc) (EU Exit) Regulations 2019, SI 2019/93, regs 32, 33(1), (2), as from IP completion day (as defined in the European Union (Withdrawal Agreement) Act 2020, s 39) (for transitional provisions and savings in relation to the operation of the 2019 Regulations, see Sch 4 to those Regulations at **[7.69]** et seq and, in particular, Sch 4, Pt 7 to the 2019 Regulations at **[7.76]**).

Sub-s (3A): inserted by SI 2004/1079, reg 2, Schedule, para 2(1), (4). Reference to the "CMA" substituted by the Enterprise and Regulatory Reform Act 2013, s 26(3), Sch 5, Pt 2, paras 59, 67(1), (4), subject to transitional provisions in SI 2014/416 as noted above. This subsection was repealed by SI 2019/93, regs 32, 33(1), (3), as from IP completion day (as defined in the European Union (Withdrawal Agreement) Act 2020, s 39) (for transitional provisions and savings see the first note relating to the 2019 Regulations above).

Sub-s (7): words in square brackets in paras (a), (b) substituted by the Enterprise and Regulatory Reform Act 2013, s 26(3), Sch 5, Pt 2, paras 59, 67(1), (5), subject to transitional provisions in SI 2014/416 as noted above.

[1.195]

23 Relevant merger situations

(1) For the purposes of this Part, a relevant merger situation has been created if—

(a) two or more enterprises have ceased to be distinct enterprises at a time or in circumstances falling within section 24; and

[(b) the value of the turnover in the United Kingdom of the enterprise being taken over exceeds—

(i) £70 million; or

(ii) £1 million, where the value of the turnover does not exceed £70 million and in the course of the enterprises ceasing to be distinct, a person or group of persons has brought a relevant enterprise (within the meaning of either subsection (2) or (3) of section 23A) under the ownership or control of the person or group].

(2) For the purposes of this Part, a relevant merger situation has also been created if—

(a) two or more enterprises have ceased to be distinct enterprises at a time or in circumstances falling within section 24; and

[(b) the share of supply test is met.]

[(2A) The share of supply test is met if—

(a) as a result of the enterprises ceasing to be distinct enterprises, one or both of the conditions mentioned in subsections (3) and (4) below prevails or prevails to a greater extent; or

(b) in the course of the enterprises ceasing to be distinct a person or group of persons has brought a relevant enterprise under the ownership or control of the person or group and one or both of the conditions mentioned in subsections (4A) and (4B) below was satisfied in relation to the relevant enterprise before it ceased to be a distinct enterprise.]

(3) The condition mentioned in this subsection is that, in relation to the supply of goods of any description, at least one-quarter of all the goods of that description which are supplied in the United Kingdom, or in a substantial part of the United Kingdom—

(a) are supplied by one and the same person or are supplied to one and the same person; or

(b) are supplied by the persons by whom the enterprises concerned are carried on, or are supplied to those persons.

(4) The condition mentioned in this subsection is that, in relation to the supply of services of any description, the supply of services of that description in the United Kingdom, or in a substantial part of the United Kingdom, is to the extent of at least one-quarter—

(a) supply by one and the same person, or supply for one and the same person; or

(b) supply by the persons by whom the enterprises concerned are carried on, or supply for those persons.

[(4A) The condition mentioned in this subsection is that, in relation to the supply of goods of any description—

(a) at least one-quarter of all goods of that description which were supplied in the United Kingdom, or in a substantial part of the United Kingdom, were supplied by or to the person or persons by whom the enterprise was carried on, and

(b) that supply was made in connection with activities of the enterprise by virtue of which it was a relevant enterprise.

(4B) The condition mentioned in this subsection is that, in relation to the supply of services of any description—

(a) the supply of services of that description in the United Kingdom, or in a substantial part of the United Kingdom, was to the extent of at least one-quarter of all the services of that description, supply by or for the person or persons by whom the enterprise is carried on, and

(b) that supply was made in connection with activities of the enterprise by virtue of which it was a relevant enterprise.]

(5) For the purpose of deciding whether the proportion of one-quarter mentioned in subsection *(3)[, (4), (4A) or (4B)]* is fulfilled with respect to goods or (as the case may be) services of any description, the decision-making authority shall apply such criterion (whether value, cost, price, quantity, capacity, number of workers employed or some other criterion, of whatever nature), or such combination of criteria, as the decision-making authority considers appropriate.

(6) References in subsections *(3)[, (4), (4A) and (4B)]* to the supply of goods or (as the case may be) services shall, in relation to goods or services of any description which are the subject of different forms of supply, be construed in whichever of the following ways the decision-making authority considers appropriate—

(a) as references to any of those forms of supply taken separately;

(b) as references to all those forms of supply taken together; or

(c) as references to any of those forms of supply taken in groups.

(7) For the purposes of subsection (6) the decision-making authority may treat goods or services as being the subject of different forms of supply whenever—

(a) the transactions concerned differ as to their nature, their parties, their terms or their surrounding circumstances; and

(b) the difference is one which, in the opinion of the decision-making authority, ought for the purposes of that subsection to be treated as a material difference.

(8) The criteria for deciding when goods or services can be treated, for the purposes of this section, as goods or services of a separate description shall be such as in any particular case the decision-making authority considers appropriate in the circumstances of that case.

(9) For the purposes of this Chapter, the question whether a relevant merger situation has been created shall be determined as at—

(a) in the case of a reference which is treated as having been made under section 22 by virtue of section 37(2), such time as the [CMA] may determine; and

(b) in any other case, immediately before the time when the reference has been, or is to be, made.

[(10) Subsections (2) to (4) of section 26 apply for the purposes of this section as they apply for the purposes of that section.]

NOTES

Sub-s (1) is amended as follows:

Para (b) substituted by the Enterprise Act 2002 (Turnover Test) (Amendment) Order 2020, SI 2020/763, art 2. Note that this amendment applies only in relation to cases where enterprises cease to be distinct after 21 July 2020 (and note also that it takes effect immediately after the commencement of the Enterprise Act 2002 (Share of Supply) (Amendment) Order 2020, SI 2020/748). The original text (as amended by the Enterprise Act 2002 (Turnover Test) (Amendment) Order 2018, SI 2018/593, art 2) read as follows—

"(b) the value of the turnover in the United Kingdom of the enterprise being taken over exceeds[—

(i) £1 million, if in the course of the enterprises ceasing to be distinct, a person or group of persons has brought a relevant enterprise (see section 23A) under the ownership or control of the person or group; or

(ii) £70 million, in any other case].".

This subsection is substituted by the National Security and Investment Act 2021, s 58, Sch 2, para 2(2), as from a day to be appointed, as follows—

"(1) For the purposes of this Part, a relevant merger situation has been created if—

(a) two or more enterprises have ceased to be distinct enterprises at a time or in circumstances falling within section 24; and

(b) the value of the turnover in the United Kingdom of the enterprise being taken over exceeds £70 million.".

Sub-s (2) is amended as follows:

Para (b) substituted by the Enterprise Act 2002 (Share of Supply Test) (Amendment) Order 2018, SI 2018/578, art 3(1), (2), in relation to cases where enterprises cease to be distinct after 11 June 2018.

This subsection is substituted by the National Security and Investment Act 2021, s 58, Sch 2, para 2(2), as from a day to be appointed, as follows—

"(2) For the purposes of this Part, a relevant merger situation has also been created if—

(a) two or more enterprises have ceased to be distinct enterprises at a time or in circumstances falling within section 24; and

(b) as a result, one or both of the conditions mentioned in subsections (3) and (4) below prevails or prevails to a greater extent.".

Sub-ss (2A), (4A), (4B): inserted by SI 2018/578, art 3(3), (4), in relation to cases where enterprises cease to be distinct after 11 June 2018. These subsections are repealed by the National Security and Investment Act 2021, s 58, Sch 2, para 2(3), as from a day to be appointed.

Sub-s (5): words in square brackets substituted by SI 2018/578, art 3(5), in relation to cases where enterprises cease to be distinct after 11 June 2018. For the words in italics there are substituted the words "(3) or (4)" by the National Security and Investment Act 2021, s 58, Sch 2, para 2(4), as from a day to be appointed.

Sub-s (6): words in square brackets substituted by SI 2018/578, art 3(6), in relation to cases where enterprises cease to be distinct after 11 June 2018. For the words in italics there are substituted the words "(3) and (4)" by the National Security and Investment Act 2021, s 58, Sch 2, para 2(5), as from a day to be appointed.

Sub-s (9): word in square brackets substituted by the Enterprise and Regulatory Reform Act 2013, s 26(3), Sch 5, Pt 2, paras 59, 68. For various transitional provisions (including those relating to the abolition of the OFT and the Competition Commission, existing references to those bodies and provisions relating to continuity), see the Enterprise and Regulatory Reform Act 2013 (Commencement No 6, Transitional Provisions and Savings) Order 2014, SI 2014/416, Schedule at **[2.13]**.

Sub-s (10): added by SI 2018/578, art 3(10), in relation to cases where enterprises cease to be distinct after 11 June 2018. This subsection is repealed by the National Security and Investment Act 2021, s 58, Sch 2, para 2(6), as from a day to be appointed.

[1.196]

[23A ***Relevant enterprises***

(1) In section 23 "relevant enterprise" means an enterprise falling within subsection (2) or (3).

(2) An enterprise falls within this subsection if its activities consist in or include—

(a) developing or producing restricted goods;

(b) holding information (including but not limited to information comprised in software and documents such as blueprints, manuals, diagrams and designs) that—

(i) is capable of use in connection with the development or production of restricted goods; and

(ii) is responsible for achieving or exceeding the performance levels, characteristics or functions of the restricted goods that are specified in the relevant export control legislation;

(c) owning, creating or supplying intellectual property relating to the functional capability of—

(i) computer processing units;

(ii) the instruction set architecture for such units;

(iii) computer code that provides low level control for such units;

(d) designing, maintaining or providing support for the secure provisioning or management of—

(i) roots of trust of computer processing units;

(ii) computer code that provides low level control for such units;

(e) research into—

(i) quantum computing or simulation;

(ii) quantum imaging, sensing, timing or navigation;
(iii) quantum communications; or
(iv) quantum resistant cryptography;

(f) developing or producing anything designed for use in—
(i) quantum computing or simulation;
(ii) quantum imaging, sensing, timing or navigation;
(iii) quantum communications; or
(iv) quantum resistant cryptography;

(g) supplying services employing—
(i) quantum computing or simulation;
(ii) quantum imaging, sensing, timing or navigation;
(iii) quantum communications; or
(iv) quantum resistant cryptography.

(3) An enterprise falls within this subsection if its activities consist in or include—

(a) developing or producing—
(i) advanced materials; or
(ii) any product where cryptographic authentication is its primary function;

(b) owning, creating or supplying intellectual property relating to the functional capability of advanced materials;

(c) research into—
(i) artificial intelligence;
(ii) cryptographic authentication; or
(iii) advanced materials;

(d) developing or producing anything designed for use in artificial intelligence;

(e) supplying services employing—
(i) artificial intelligence; or
(ii) cryptographic authentication;

(f) developing or producing anything designed as an enabler;

(g) providing know-how about or the use of enablers.

(4) In this section—

"advanced materials" means—

(a) any materials that are capable of modifying (including in real time) the appearance, detectability, traceability or identification of any object to a human or to sensors within the range 1.5e13 Hz up to and including ultraviolet;

(b) any alloys that are formed by chemical or electrochemical reduction of feedstocks in the solid state;

(c) any manufacturing processes that are involved in the solid state formation of alloys in or into crude or semi-fabricated forms, or powders for additive manufacturing, where "additive manufacturing" means a process of joining materials to make parts from three-dimensional model data; or

(d) any metamaterials that do not include—
(i) fibre-reinforced plastics in structural components, products or coatings with completely random dispersion of pigment or other filler; or
(ii) any packaged device components that are designed for civil application;

"artificial intelligence" means technology enabling the programming or training of a device or software to use or process external data (independent of any further input or programming) to carry out or undertake (with a view to achieving complex, specific tasks)—

(a) automated data analysis or automated decision making; or

(b) analogous processing and use of data or information;

"cryptographic authentication" means the method of verifying—

(a) the identity of a person, user, process or device; or

(b) the origin or content of a message, data or information, by means of electronic communication, where the method of verification has been encrypted or subject to other analogous application, to protect the authenticity, confidentiality and integrity of the matters set out in paragraphs (a) and (b);

"enabler" means any material or process which is not an advanced material but is used in the manufacture of an advanced material;

"feedstock" means a metal, polymer, ceramic or other material used to supply the manufacturing process used to produce an advanced material;

"intellectual property" means—

(a) any patent, trade mark, registered design, copyright or design right,

(b) any right under the law of a country or territory outside the United Kingdom corresponding to, or similar to, a right within paragraph (a); or

(c) any information or technique not protected by a right within paragraph (a) or (b) but having industrial, commercial or other economic value;

"metamaterial" means a composite material in which the constituents are designed and spatially arranged through a rational design-led approach to change the manner in which electromagnetic, acoustic or vibrational energy interacts with the material, in order to achieve a property or performance that is not possible naturally and includes a metasurface and for this purpose "composite material" means a solid material formed from two or more constituents and "constituent" includes a region containing a vacuum, gas or liquid;

"metasurface" means a two-dimensional form of metamaterial which includes one or more layers of material that are intentionally patterned or textured (irrespective of whether they are periodic or not) through a rational design-led approach;

"quantum communications" means—

(a) *the transmission of information, utilising the properties of quantum mechanics, in particular superposition or entanglement, and*

(b) *includes the establishment of cryptographic keys and the generation of true random numbers using a quantum physical process;*

"quantum computing or simulation" means the study, simulation or realisation of systems that utilise certain properties of quantum mechanics, in particular superposition or entanglement, to process information, run algorithms or perform operations on data;

"quantum imaging" means utilising certain properties of quantum mechanics, in particular superposition or entanglement, to create images of objects with a resolution or other imaging criteria that is beyond what is possible in non-quantum optics;

"quantum navigation" means utilising certain properties of quantum mechanics, including measurements of suspensions of atoms or ions, to establish the location or movement of objects with a resolution or sensitivity that is beyond what is possible in non-quantum devices or systems;

"quantum resistant cryptography" means methods of securing information or data being transmitted or stored, including by non-quantum means, with a view to resisting attack by a quantum computer;

"quantum sensing" means utilising certain properties of quantum mechanics, including measurements of suspensions of atoms or ions, to determine a property or rate of change in the property of an object, or the effect of an object on a measurable quantity, with a resolution or sensitivity that is beyond what is possible in non-quantum devices or systems;

"quantum timing" means utilising certain properties of quantum mechanics, including measurements of suspensions of atoms or ions, to provide a timing signal with a resolution or sensitivity that is beyond what is possible in non-quantum devices or systems; "relevant export control legislation" means—

(a) *Schedules 2 and 3 to the Export Control Order 2008;*

(b) *the Schedule to the Export of Radioactive Sources (Control) Order 2006;*

(c) *Annex I to Council Regulation (EC) No 428/2009;*

"restricted goods" means goods, software or information the export or transfer of which is controlled by virtue of their being specified in the relevant export control legislation but excluding any goods, software or information which are controlled only to the extent that they are prohibited from being exported or transferred to one country only;

"roots of trust" means—

(a) *hardware, firmware, or software components that are inherently trusted to perform critical security functions, and*

(b) *includes cryptographic key material bound to a device that can identify the device or verify a digital signature to authenticate a remote entity.]*

NOTES

Commencement: 21 July 2020.

Inserted by the Enterprise Act 2002 (Share of Supply Test) (Amendment) Order 2018, SI 2018/578, arts 2, 4, in relation to cases where enterprises cease to be distinct after 11 June 2018.

Substituted by the Enterprise Act 2002 (Share of Supply) (Amendment) Order 2020, SI 2020/748, arts 2, 3. Note that this amendment applies only in relation to cases where enterprises cease to be distinct after 21 July 2020. The original text read as follows—

"23A Relevant enterprises

(1) In section 23 "relevant enterprise" means an enterprise the activities of which consist in or include—

(a) developing or producing restricted goods;

(b) holding information (including but not limited to information comprised in software and documents such as blueprints, manuals, diagrams and designs) that—

(i) is capable of use in connection with the development or production of restricted goods; and

(ii) is responsible for achieving or exceeding the performance levels, characteristics or functions of the restricted goods that are specified in the relevant export control legislation;

(c) owning, creating or supplying intellectual property relating to the functional capability of—

(i) computer processing units;

(ii) the instruction set architecture for such units;

(iii) computer code that provides low level control for such units;

(d) designing, maintaining or providing support for the secure provisioning or management of—

(i) roots of trust of computer processing units;

(ii) computer code that provides low level control for such units;

(e) research into—

(i) quantum computing or simulation;

(ii) quantum imaging, sensing, timing or navigation;

(iii) quantum communications; or

(iv) quantum resistant cryptography;

(f) developing or producing anything designed for use in—

(i) quantum computing or simulation;

(ii) quantum imaging, sensing, timing or navigation;

(iii) quantum communications; or

(iv) quantum resistant cryptography;

(g) developing or producing anything designed for use in—supplying services employing—

(i) quantum computing or simulation;

(ii) quantum imaging, sensing, timing or navigation;

(iii) quantum communications; or

(iv) quantum resistant cryptography;

(2) In this section—

"intellectual property" means—

(a) any patent, trade mark, registered design, copyright or design right,
(b) any right under the law of a country or territory outside the United Kingdom corresponding to, or similar to, a right within paragraph (a), or
(c) any information or technique not protected by a right within paragraph (a) or (b) but having industrial, commercial or other economic value;

"quantum communications"—
(a) means the transmission of information, utilising the properties of quantum mechanics, in particular superposition or entanglement, and
(b) includes the establishment of cryptographic keys and the generation of true random numbers using a quantum physical process;

"quantum computing or simulation" means the study, simulation or realisation of systems that utilise certain properties of quantum mechanics, in particular superposition or entanglement, to process information, run algorithms or perform operations on data;

"quantum imaging" means utilising certain properties of quantum mechanics, in particular superposition or entanglement, to create images of objects with a resolution or other imaging criteria that is beyond what is possible in non-quantum optics;

"quantum navigation" means utilising certain properties of quantum mechanics, including measurements of suspensions of atoms or ions, to establish the location or movement of objects with a resolution or sensitivity that is beyond what is possible in non-quantum devices or systems;

"quantum resistant cryptography" means methods of securing information or data being transmitted or stored, including by non-quantum means, with a view to resisting attack by a quantum computer;

"quantum sensing" means utilising certain properties of quantum mechanics, including measurements of suspensions of atoms or ions, to determine a property or rate of change in the property of an object, or the effect of an object on a measurable quantity, with a resolution or sensitivity that is beyond what is possible in non-quantum devices or systems;

"quantum timing" means utilising certain properties of quantum mechanics, including measurements of suspensions of atoms or ions, to provide a timing signal with a resolution or sensitivity that is beyond what is possible in non-quantum devices or systems;

"relevant export control legislation" means—
(a) Schedules 2 and 3 to the Export Control Order 2008;
(b) the Schedule to the Export of Radioactive Sources (Control) Order 2006;
(c) Annex I to Council Regulation (EC) No 428/2009;

"restricted goods" means goods, software or information the export or transfer of which is controlled by virtue of their being specified in the relevant export control legislation but excluding any goods, software or information which are controlled only to the extent that they are prohibited from being exported or transferred to one country only;

"roots of trust"—
(a) means hardware, firmware, or software components that are inherently trusted to perform critical security functions, and
(b) includes cryptographic key material bound to a device that can identify the device or verify a digital signature to authenticate a remote entity.".

This section is repealed by the National Security and Investment Act 2021, s 58, Sch 2, para 3, as from a day to be appointed.

[1.197]

24 Time-limits and prior notice

(1) For the purposes of section 23 two or more enterprises have ceased to be distinct enterprises at a time or in circumstances falling within this section if—
(a) the two or more enterprises ceased to be distinct enterprises before the day on which the reference relating to them is to be made and did so not more than four months before that day; or
(b) notice of material facts about the arrangements or transactions under or in consequence of which the enterprises have ceased to be distinct enterprises has not been given in accordance with subsection (2).

(2) Notice of material facts is given in accordance with this subsection if—
(a) it is given to the [CMA] prior to the entering into of the arrangements or transactions concerned or the facts are made public prior to the entering into of those arrangements or transactions; or
(b) it is given to the [CMA], or the facts are made public, more than four months before the day on which the reference is to be made.

(3) In this section—
"made public" means so publicised as to be generally known or readily ascertainable; and "notice" includes notice which is not in writing.

NOTES

Sub-s (2): references to the "CMA" substituted by the Enterprise and Regulatory Reform Act 2013, s 26(3), Sch 5, Pt 2, paras 59, 69. For various transitional provisions (including those relating to the abolition of the OFT and the Competition Commission, existing references to those bodies and provisions relating to continuity), see the Enterprise and Regulatory Reform Act 2013 (Commencement No 6, Transitional Provisions and Savings) Order 2014, SI 2014/416, Schedule at **[2.13]**.

[1.198]

25 Extension of time-limits

(1) The [CMA] and the persons carrying on the enterprises which have or may have ceased to be distinct enterprises may agree to extend by no more than 20 days the four month period mentioned in section 24(1)(a) or (2)(b).

(2) The [CMA] may by notice to the persons carrying on the enterprises which have or may have ceased to be distinct enterprises extend the four month period mentioned in section 24(1)(a) or (2)(b) if it considers that any of those persons [has failed (with or without a reasonable excuse) to comply with any requirement of a notice under section 109].

[(3) An extension under subsection (2) shall come into force when notice of the extension is given and end—

(a) when the person concerned provides the information or documents to the satisfaction of the CMA or (as the case may be) appears as a witness in accordance with the requirements of the CMA; or

(b) if earlier, the CMA cancels the extension.]

(4) The [CMA] may by notice to the persons carrying on the enterprises which have or may have ceased to be distinct enterprises extend the four month period mentioned in section 24(1)(a) or (2)(b) if it is seeking undertakings from any of those persons under section 73.

(5) An extension under subsection (4) shall be for the period beginning with the receipt of the notice under that subsection and ending with the earliest of the following events—

(a) the giving of the undertakings concerned;

(b) the expiry of the period of 10 days beginning with the first day after the receipt by the [CMA] of a notice from the person who has been given a notice under subsection (4) and from whom the undertakings are being sought stating that he does not intend to give the undertakings; or

(c) the cancellation by the [CMA] of the extension.

(6) The [CMA] may by notice to the persons carrying on the enterprises which have or may have ceased to be distinct enterprises extend the four month period mentioned in section 24(1)(a) or (2)(b) if the European Commission is considering a request made, in relation to the matter concerned, by the United Kingdom (whether alone or with others) under article [22(1) of the EC Merger Regulation] (but is not yet proceeding with the matter in pursuance of such a request).

(7) An extension under subsection (6) shall be for the period beginning with the receipt of the notice under that subsection and ending with the receipt of a notice under subsection (8).

(8) The [CMA] shall, in connection with any notice given by it under subsection (6), by notice inform the persons carrying on the enterprises which have or may have ceased to be distinct enterprises of the completion by the European Commission of its consideration of the request of the United Kingdom.

(9) Subject to subsections (10) and (11), where the four month period mentioned in section 24(1)(a) or (2)(b) is extended or further extended by virtue of this section in relation to a particular case, any reference to that period in section 24 or the preceding provisions of this section shall have effect in relation to that case as if it were a reference to a period equivalent to the aggregate of the period being extended and the period of the extension (whether or not those periods overlap in time).

(10) Subsection (11) applies where—

(a) the four month period mentioned in section 24(1)(a) or (2)(b) is further extended;

(b) the further extension and at least one previous extension is made under one or more of [subsections (2) and (4)]; and

(c) the same days or fractions of days are included in or comprise the further extension and are included in or comprise at least one such previous extension.

(11) In calculating the period of the further extension, any days or fractions of days of the kind mentioned in subsection (10)(c) shall be disregarded.

(12) No more than one extension is possible under subsection (1).

NOTES

References to the "CMA" substituted by the Enterprise and Regulatory Reform Act 2013, s 26(3), Sch 5, Pt 2, paras 59, 70. For various transitional provisions (including those relating to the abolition of the OFT and the Competition Commission, existing references to those bodies and provisions relating to continuity), see the Enterprise and Regulatory Reform Act 2013 (Commencement No 6, Transitional Provisions and Savings) Order 2014, SI 2014/416, Schedule at **[2.13]**. This section is also amended as follows:

Sub-s (2): words in second pair of square brackets substituted by the Enterprise and Regulatory Reform Act 2013, s 57, Sch 15, paras 15, 16(1), (2), subject to transitional provisions in SI 2014/416 as noted above.

Sub-s (3): substituted by the Enterprise and Regulatory Reform Act 2013, s 57, Sch 15, paras 15, 16(1), (3), subject to transitional provisions in SI 2014/416 as noted above.

Sub-s (6): words in square brackets substituted by the EC Merger Control (Consequential Amendments) Regulations 2004, SI 2004/1079, reg 2, Schedule, para 2(1), (5). This subsection was repealed by the Competition (Amendment etc) (EU Exit) Regulations 2019, SI 2019/93, regs 32, 35(a), as from IP completion day (as defined in the European Union (Withdrawal Agreement) Act 2020, s 39) (for transitional provisions and savings in relation to the operation of the 2019 Regulations, see Sch 4 to those Regulations at **[7.69]** et seq and, in particular, Sch 4, Pt 7 to the 2019 Regulations at **[7.76]**).

Sub-ss (7), (8): repealed by SI 2019/93, regs 32, 35(a), as from IP completion day (as defined in the European Union (Withdrawal Agreement) Act 2020, s 39) (for transitional provisions and savings see the first note relating to the 2019 Regulations above).

Sub-s (10): the words in square brackets were substituted (for the original words "subsections (2), (4) and (6)") by SI 2019/93, regs 32, 35(b), as from IP completion day (as defined in the European Union (Withdrawal Agreement) Act 2020, s 39) (for transitional provisions and savings see the first note relating to the 2019 Regulations above).

[1.199]

26 Enterprises ceasing to be distinct enterprises

(1) For the purposes of this Part any two enterprises cease to be distinct enterprises if they are brought under common ownership or common control (whether or not the business to which either of them formerly belonged continues to be carried on under the same or different ownership or control).

(2) Enterprises shall, in particular, be treated as being under common control if they are—

(a) enterprises of interconnected bodies corporate;

(b) enterprises carried on by two or more bodies corporate of which one and the same person or group of persons has control; or

(c) an enterprise carried on by a body corporate and an enterprise carried on by a person or group of persons having control of that body corporate.

(3) A person or group of persons able, directly or indirectly, to control or materially to influence the policy of a body corporate, or the policy of any person in carrying on an enterprise but without having a controlling interest in that body corporate or in that enterprise, may, for the purposes of subsections (1) and (2), be treated as having control of it.

(4) For the purposes of subsection (1), in so far as it relates to bringing two or more enterprises under common control, a person or group of persons may be treated as bringing an enterprise under his or their control if—

(a) being already able to control or materially to influence the policy of the person carrying on the enterprise, that person or group of persons acquires a controlling interest in the enterprise or, in the case of an enterprise carried on by a body corporate, acquires a controlling interest in that body corporate; or

(b) being already able materially to influence the policy of the person carrying on the enterprise, that person or group of persons becomes able to control that policy.

[1.200]

27 Time when enterprises cease to be distinct

(1) Subsection (2) applies in relation to any arrangements or transaction—

(a) not having immediate effect or having immediate effect only in part; but

(b) under or in consequence of which any two enterprises cease to be distinct enterprises.

(2) The time when the parties to any such arrangements or transaction become bound to such extent as will result, on effect being given to their obligations, in the enterprises ceasing to be distinct enterprises shall be taken to be the time at which the two enterprises cease to be distinct enterprises.

(3) In accordance with subsections (1) and (2) (but without prejudice to the generality of those subsections) for the purpose of determining the time at which any two enterprises cease to be distinct enterprises no account shall be taken of any option or other conditional right until the option is exercised or the condition is satisfied.

(4) Subsections (1) to (3) are subject to subsections (5) to (8) and section 29.

(5) The decision-making authority may, for the purposes of a reference, treat successive events to which this subsection applies as having occurred simultaneously on the date on which the latest of them occurred.

(6) Subsection (5) applies to successive events—

(a) which occur within a period of two years under or in consequence of the same arrangements or transaction, or successive arrangements or transactions between the same parties or interests; and

(b) by virtue of each of which, under or in consequence of the arrangements or the transaction or transactions concerned, any enterprises cease as between themselves to be distinct enterprises.

(7) The decision-making authority may, for the purposes of subsections (5) and (6), treat such arrangements or transactions as the decision-making authority considers appropriate as arrangements or transactions between the same interests.

(8) In deciding whether it is appropriate to treat arrangements or transactions as arrangements or transactions between the same interests the decision-making authority shall, in particular, have regard to the persons substantially concerned in the arrangements or transactions concerned.

[1.201]

28 Turnover test

(1) For the purposes of section 23 the value of the turnover in the United Kingdom of the enterprise being taken over shall be determined by taking the total value of the turnover in the United Kingdom of the enterprises which cease to be distinct enterprises and deducting—

(a) the turnover in the United Kingdom of any enterprise which continues to be carried on under the same ownership and control; or

(b) if no enterprise continues to be carried on under the same ownership and control, the turnover in the United Kingdom which, of all the turnovers concerned, is the turnover of the highest value.

(2) For the purposes of this Part (other than section 121(4)(c)(ii)) the turnover in the United Kingdom of an enterprise shall be determined in accordance with such provisions as may be specified in an order made by the Secretary of State.

(3) An order under subsection (2) may, in particular, make provision as to—

(a) the amounts which are, or which are not, to be treated as comprising an enterprise's turnover;

(b) the date or dates by reference to which an enterprise's turnover is to be determined;

(c) the connection with the United Kingdom by virtue of which an enterprise's turnover is turnover in the United Kingdom.

(4) An order under subsection (2) may, in particular, make provision enabling the decision-making authority to determine matters of a description specified in the order (including any of the matters mentioned in paragraphs (a) to (c) of subsection (3)).

(5) The [CMA] shall—

(a) keep under review the sum for the time being mentioned in section 23(1)(b); and

(b) from time to time advise the Secretary of State as to whether the sum is still appropriate.

(6) The Secretary of State may by order amend section 23(1)(b) so as to alter the sum for the time being mentioned there.

NOTES

Sub-s (5): references to the "CMA" substituted by the Enterprise and Regulatory Reform Act 2013, s 26(3), Sch 5, Pt 2, paras 59, 71. For various transitional provisions (including those relating to the abolition of the OFT and the Competition Commission, existing references to those bodies and provisions relating to continuity), see the Enterprise and Regulatory Reform Act 2013 (Commencement No 6, Transitional Provisions and Savings) Order 2014, SI 2014/416, Schedule at **[2.13]**.

Orders: the Enterprise Act 2002 (Merger Fees and Determination of Turnover) Order 2003, SI 2003/1370 at **[2.92]**; the Enterprise Act 2002 (Merger Fees and Determination of Turnover) (Amendment) Order 2004, SI 2004/3204; the Enterprise Act 2002 (Turnover Test) (Amendment) Order 2018, SI 2018/593 (revoked by the National Security and Investment Act 2021, s 58, Sch 2, para 11, as from a day to be appointed); the Enterprise Act 2002 (Turnover Test) (Amendment) Order 2020, SI 2020/763 (revoked by the National Security and Investment Act 2021, s 58, Sch 2, para 11, as from a day to be appointed).

[1.202]

29 Obtaining control by stages

(1) Where an enterprise is brought under the control of a person or group of persons in the course of two or more transactions (in this section a "series of transactions") to which subsection (2) applies, those transactions may, if the decision-making authority considers it appropriate, be treated for the purposes of a reference as having occurred simultaneously on the date on which the latest of them occurred.

(2) This subsection applies to—

(a) any transaction which—

(i) enables that person or group of persons directly or indirectly to control or materially to influence the policy of any person carrying on the enterprise;

(ii) enables that person or group of persons to do so to a greater degree; or

(iii) is a step (whether direct or indirect) towards enabling that person or group of persons to do so; and

(b) any transaction by virtue of which that person or group of persons acquires a controlling interest in the enterprise or, where the enterprise is carried on by a body corporate, in that body corporate.

(3) Where a series of transactions includes a transaction falling within subsection (2)(b), any transaction occurring after the occurrence of that transaction is to be disregarded for the purposes of subsection (1).

(4) Where the period within which a series of transactions occurs exceeds two years, the transactions that may be treated as mentioned in subsection (1) are any of those transactions that occur within a period of two years.

(5) Sections 26(2) to (4) and 127(1), (2) and (4) to (6) shall apply for the purposes of this section to determine—

(a) whether an enterprise is brought under the control of a person or group of persons; and

(b) whether a transaction is one to which subsection (2) applies;

as they apply for the purposes of section 26 to determine whether enterprises are brought under common control.

(6) In determining for the purposes of this section the time at which any transaction occurs, no account shall be taken of any option or other conditional right until the option is exercised or the condition is satisfied.

[1.203]

30 Relevant customer benefits

(1) For the purposes of this Part a benefit is a relevant customer benefit if—

(a) it is a benefit to relevant customers in the form of—

(i) lower prices, higher quality or greater choice of goods or services in any market in the United Kingdom (whether or not the market or markets in which the substantial lessening of competition concerned has, or may have, occurred or (as the case may be) may occur); or

(ii) greater innovation in relation to such goods or services; and

(b) the decision-making authority believes—

(i) in the case of a reference or possible reference under section 22 or 45(2), as mentioned in subsection (2); and

(ii) in the case of a reference or possible reference under section 33 or 45(4), as mentioned in subsection (3).

(2) The belief, in the case of a reference or possible reference under section 22 or section 45(2), is that—

(a) the benefit has accrued as a result of the creation of the relevant merger situation concerned or may be expected to accrue within a reasonable period as a result of the creation of that situation; and

(b) the benefit was, or is, unlikely to accrue without the creation of that situation or a similar lessening of competition.

(3) The belief, in the case of a reference or possible reference under section 33 or 45(4), is that—

(a) the benefit may be expected to accrue within a reasonable period as a result of the creation of the relevant merger situation concerned; and

(b) the benefit is unlikely to accrue without the creation of that situation or a similar lessening of competition.

(4) In subsection (1) "relevant customers" means—

(a) customers of any person carrying on an enterprise which, in the creation of the relevant merger situation concerned, has ceased to be, or (as the case may be) will cease to be, a distinct enterprise;

(b) customers of such customers; and

(c) any other customers in a chain of customers beginning with the customers mentioned in paragraph (a);

and in this subsection "customers" includes future customers.

31 (*Repealed by the Enterprise and Regulatory Reform Act 2013, s 57, Sch 15, paras 15, 17. For various transitional provisions (including those relating to the abolition of the OFT and the Competition Commission, existing references to those bodies and provisions relating to continuity), see the Enterprise and Regulatory Reform Act 2013 (Commencement No 6, Transitional Provisions and Savings) Order 2014, SI 2014/416, Schedule at* **[2.13]**.)

[1.204]

32 Supplementary provision for purposes of [section 25]

(1)–(3) . . .

(4) In determining for the purposes of section 25(1) or (5)(b) . . . any period which is expressed in the enactment concerned as a period of days or number of days no account shall be taken of—

(a) Saturday, Sunday, Good Friday and Christmas Day; and

(b) any day which is a bank holiday in England and Wales.

NOTES

Words in square brackets in the section heading substituted, sub-ss (1)–(3) repealed, and words omitted from sub-s (4) repealed, by the Enterprise and Regulatory Reform Act 2013, s 57, Sch 15, paras 15, 18. For various transitional provisions (including those relating to the abolition of the OFT and the Competition Commission, existing references to those bodies and provisions relating to continuity), see the Enterprise and Regulatory Reform Act 2013 (Commencement No 6, Transitional Provisions and Savings) Order 2014, SI 2014/416, Schedule at **[2.13]**.

Duty to make references: anticipated mergers

[1.205]

33 Duty to make references in relation to anticipated mergers

(1) [The CMA shall, subject to subsections (2) and (3), make a reference to its chair for the constitution of a group under Schedule 4 to the Enterprise and Regulatory Reform Act 2013 if the CMA believes that it is or may be the case that]—

(a) arrangements are in progress or in contemplation which, if carried into effect, will result in the creation of a relevant merger situation; and

(b) the creation of that situation may be expected to result in a substantial lessening of competition within any market or markets in the United Kingdom for goods or services.

(2) The [CMA] may decide not to make a reference under this section if it believes that—

(a) the market concerned is not, or the markets concerned are not, of sufficient importance to justify the making of a reference . . . ;

(b) the arrangements concerned are not sufficiently far advanced, or are not sufficiently likely to proceed, to justify the making of a reference . . . ; or

(c) any relevant customer benefits in relation to the creation of the relevant merger situation concerned outweigh the substantial lessening of competition concerned and any adverse effects of the substantial lessening of competition concerned.

(3) No reference shall be made under this section if—

[(za) the period within which the CMA is required by section 34ZA to decide whether the duty to make the reference applies has expired without such a decision having been made;]

(a) the making of the reference is prevented by section . . . 74(1) . . . or paragraph 4 of Schedule 7;

(b) the [CMA] is considering whether to accept undertakings under section 73 instead of making such a reference;

(c) the arrangements concerned are being, or have been, dealt with in connection with a reference made under section 22; [or]

(d) a notice under section 42(2) is in force in relation to the matter or the matter to which such a notice relates has been finally determined under Chapter 2 otherwise than in circumstances in which a notice is then given to the [CMA] under section 56(1); . . .

(e) the European Commission is considering a request made, in relation to the matter concerned, by the United Kingdom (whether alone or with others) under article [22(1) of the EC Merger Regulation], is proceeding with the matter in pursuance of such a request or has dealt with the matter in pursuance of such a request[; or

(f) subject to subsection (3A), a reasoned submission requesting referral to the European Commission has been submitted to the European Commission under article 4(5) of the EC Merger Regulation].

[(3A) Section 33(3)(f) shall cease to apply if the [CMA] is informed that a Member State competent to examine the concentration under its national competition law has, within the time permitted by Article 4(5) of the EC Merger Regulation, expressed its disagreement as regards the request to refer the case to the European Commission; and this subsection shall be construed in accordance with that Regulation.]

(4) A reference under this section shall, in particular, specify—

(a) the enactment under which it is made; and

(b) the date on which it is made.

NOTES

Sub-s (1): words in square brackets substituted by the Enterprise and Regulatory Reform Act 2013, s 26(3), Sch 5, Pt 2, paras 59, 72(1), (2). For various transitional provisions (including those relating to the abolition of the OFT and the Competition Commission, existing references to those bodies and provisions relating to continuity), see the Enterprise and Regulatory Reform Act 2013 (Commencement No 6, Transitional Provisions and Savings) Order 2014, SI 2014/416, Schedule at **[2.13]**.

Sub-s (2): reference to the "CMA" substituted, and words omitted repealed, by the Enterprise and Regulatory Reform Act 2013, s 26(3), Sch 5, Pt 2, paras 59, 72(1), (3), subject to transitional provisions in SI 2014/416 as noted above.

Sub-s (3): para (za) inserted, second words omitted from para (a) repealed, and references to the "CMA" in paras (b) and (d) substituted, by the Enterprise and Regulatory Reform Act 2013, ss 26(3), 32(2), Sch 5, Pt 2, paras 59, 72(1), (4), Sch 8, paras 1, 3, subject to transitional provisions in SI 2014/416 as noted above. First figure omitted from para (a) repealed by the Communications Act 2003, s 406(7), Sch 19. Word omitted from the end of para (d) repealed, words in square brackets in para (e) substituted, and para (f) and the word immediately preceding it added, by the EC Merger Control (Consequential Amendments) Regulations 2004, SI 2004/1079, Schedule, para 2(1), (6), (7). The word "or" in square brackets in para (c) was inserted, and paras (e) and (f) were repealed, by the Competition (Amendment etc) (EU Exit) Regulations 2019, SI 2019/93, regs 32, 36(1), (2), as from IP completion day (as defined in the European Union (Withdrawal Agreement) Act 2020, s 39) (for transitional provisions and savings in relation to the operation of the 2019 Regulations, see Sch 4 to those Regulations at **[7.69]** et seq and, in particular, Sch 4, Pt 7 to the 2019 Regulations at **[7.76]**).

Sub-s (3A): inserted by SI 2004/1079, reg 2, Schedule, para 2(1), (8). Reference to the "CMA" substituted by the Enterprise and Regulatory Reform Act 2013, s 26(3), Sch 5, Pt 2, paras 59, 72(1), (4), subject to transitional provisions in SI 2014/416 as noted above. This subsection was repealed by SI 2019/93, regs 32, 36(1), (3), as from IP completion day (as defined in the European Union (Withdrawal Agreement) Act 2020, s 39) (for transitional provisions and savings see the first note relating to the 2019 Regulations above).

[1.206]

34 Supplementary provision in relation to anticipated mergers

(1) The Secretary of State may by order make such provision as he considers appropriate about the operation of sections 27 and 29 in relation to—

(a) references under this Part which relate to arrangements which are in progress or in contemplation; or

(b) notices under section 42(2) [or 59(2)] which relate to such arrangements.

(2) An order under subsection (1) may, in particular—

(a) provide for sections 27(5) to (8) and 29 to apply with modifications in relation to such references or notices or in relation to particular descriptions of such references or notices;
(b) enable particular descriptions of events, arrangements or transactions which have already occurred—
(i) to be taken into account for the purposes of deciding whether to make such references or such references of a particular description or whether to give such notices or such notices of a particular description;
(ii) to be dealt with under such references or such references of a particular description or under such notices or such notices of a particular description.

NOTES

Sub-s (1): the words in square brackets were substituted (for the original words ", 59(2) or 67(2)") by the Competition (Amendment etc) (EU Exit) Regulations 2019, SI 2019/93, regs 32, 37, as from IP completion day (as defined in the European Union (Withdrawal Agreement) Act 2020, s 39) (for transitional provisions and savings in relation to the operation of the 2019 Regulations, see Sch 4 to those Regulations at **[7.69]** et seq).

Orders: the Enterprise Act 2002 (Anticipated Mergers) Order 2003, SI 2003/1595 at **[2.123]**.

[Supplementary provision: time-limits for decisions about references

[1.207]

34ZA Time-limits for decisions about references

(1) In carrying out its function of deciding whether to make a reference under section 22 or 33, the CMA shall, within the initial period—
(a) decide whether the duty to make a reference under the section applies (taking account of the power under section 22(2) or (as the case may be) 33(2) and the operation of section 22(3) or (as the case may be) 33(3)); and
(b) inform the persons carrying on the enterprises concerned by notice of the decision and of the reasons for it.

(2) Nothing in this section prevents the CMA from making a reference under section 22 or 33 in the event that—
(a) it decides that the duty to make a reference does not apply because it is considering whether to accept undertakings under section 73; but
(b) no such undertakings are offered or accepted.

(3) In this section—

"the initial period" means (subject to any extension under section 34ZB) the period of 40 working days beginning with—
(a) where the CMA is carrying out its function in consequence of the giving of a merger notice under section 96, the first working day after the day on which the CMA gives notice under section 96(2A) to the person who gave the merger notice, and
(b) in any other case, the first working day after the day on which the CMA informs the persons carrying on the enterprises concerned by notice that it has sufficient information to enable it to begin an investigation for the purposes of deciding whether to make a reference;

"working day" means any day which is not—
(a) a Saturday, a Sunday, Good Friday or Christmas Day, or
(b) a day which is a bank holiday in England and Wales.

(4) For the purposes of paragraph (a) in the definition of "initial period" in subsection (3), the CMA is carrying out its function in consequence of the giving of a merger notice under section 96 if it is considering whether to make a reference under section 22 or 33 in relation to—
(a) arrangements of which notice is given in the merger notice or arrangements which do not differ from them in any material respect, or
(b) the creation of any relevant merger situation which is, or may be, created in consequence of carrying such arrangements into effect.

(5) Nothing in this section applies where section 34A(2) or 46A(2) applies (duties where case referred by the European Commission).]

NOTES

Inserted, together with the preceding heading and ss 34ZB, 34ZC, by the Enterprise and Regulatory Reform Act 2013, s 32(2), Sch 8, paras 1, 4. For various transitional provisions (including those relating to the abolition of the OFT and the Competition Commission, existing references to those bodies and provisions relating to continuity), see the Enterprise and Regulatory Reform Act 2013 (Commencement No 6, Transitional Provisions and Savings) Order 2014, SI 2014/416, Schedule at **[2.13]**.

Sub-s (5): repealed by the Competition (Amendment etc) (EU Exit) Regulations 2019, SI 2019/93, regs 32, 38, as from IP completion day (as defined in the European Union (Withdrawal Agreement) Act 2020, s 39) (for transitional provisions and savings in relation to the operation of the 2019 Regulations, see Sch 4 to those Regulations at **[7.69]** et seq and, in particular, Sch 4, Pt 7 to the 2019 Regulations at **[7.76]**).

[1.208]

[34ZB Extension of time-limits

(1) The CMA may extend the initial period mentioned in section 34ZA(1) if it considers that a relevant person has failed (with or without a reasonable excuse) to comply with any requirement of a notice under section 109 in relation to the case in question.

(2) In subsection (1), "relevant person" means—
(a) any person carrying on any of the enterprises concerned;
(b) any person who (whether alone or as a member of a group) owns or has control of any such person; or
(c) any officer, employee or agent of any person mentioned in paragraph (a) or (b).

(3) For the purposes of subsection (2), a person or group of persons able, directly or indirectly, to control or materially to influence the policy of a body of persons corporate or unincorporate, but without having a controlling interest in that body of persons, may be treated as having control of it.

(4) Where an intervention notice is in force in relation to the matter concerned, the CMA may extend the initial period by no more than 20 working days.

(5) The CMA may by notice extend the initial period if the European Commission is considering a request made, in relation to the matter concerned, by the United Kingdom (whether alone or with others) under article 22(1) of the EC Merger Regulation (but is not yet proceeding with the matter in pursuance of such a request).

(6) An extension under subsection (1) or (4) comes into force when published under section 107.

(7) An extension under subsection (1) continues in force until—

(a) the person concerned provides the information or documents to the satisfaction of the CMA or (as the case may be) appears as a witness in accordance with the requirements of the CMA; or

(b) the CMA publishes its decision to cancel the extension.

(8) An extension under subsection (5) shall be for the period which—

(a) begins when notice is given under that subsection, and

(b) ends when the CMA gives notice of the completion by the European Commission of its consideration of the request of the United Kingdom.

(9) In this section, "working day" has the same meaning as in section 34ZA.]

NOTES

Inserted as noted to s 34ZA at **[1.207]**.

Sub-ss (5), (8): repealed by the Competition (Amendment etc) (EU Exit) Regulations 2019, SI 2019/93, regs 32, 39, as from IP completion day (as defined in the European Union (Withdrawal Agreement) Act 2020, s 39) (for transitional provisions and savings in relation to the operation of the 2019 Regulations, see Sch 4 to those Regulations at **[7.69]** et seq and, in particular, Sch 4, Pt 7 to the 2019 Regulations at **[7.76]**).

[1.209]

[34ZC Sections 34ZA and 34ZB: supplementary

(1) An extension of the period mentioned in section 34ZA(1) may be made under each of [subsections (1) or (4)] of section 34ZB.

(2) No more than one extension is possible under section 34ZB(4).

(3) Where a period is extended or further extended under [section 34ZB(1) or (4)], the period as extended or (as the case may be) further extended shall, subject to subsections (4) and (5), be calculated by taking the period being extended and adding to it the period of the extension (whether or not those periods overlap in time).

(4) Subsection (5) applies where—

(a) the period mentioned in section 34ZA(1) is further extended;

(b) the further extension and at least one previous extension is made under [subsection (1)] of section 34ZB; and

(c) the same days or fractions of days are included in or comprise the further extension and are included in or comprise at least one such previous extension.

(5) In calculating the period of the further extension, any days or fractions of days of the kind mentioned in subsection (4)(c) are to be disregarded.

(6) The Secretary of State may by order do either or both of the following—

(a) amend section 34ZA so as to alter the period of 40 working days mentioned in subsection (3) of that section or any period for the time being mentioned in that subsection in substitution for that period;

(b) amend section 34ZB so as to alter the period of 20 working days mentioned in subsection (4) of that section or any period for the time being mentioned in that subsection in substitution for that period.

(7) But no alteration may be made by virtue of subsection (6) which results in—

(a) the period for the time being mentioned in section 34ZA(3) exceeding 40 working days; or

(b) the period for the time being mentioned in section 34ZB(4) exceeding 20 working days.

(8) Before making an order under subsection (6), the Secretary of State shall consult the CMA and such other persons as the Secretary of State considers appropriate.

(9) In this section, "working day" has the same meaning as in section 34ZA.]

NOTES

Inserted as noted to s 34ZA at **[1.207]**.

The words in square brackets in sub-s (1) were substituted (for the original words "subsections (1), (4) or (5)"), the words in square brackets in sub-s (3) were substituted (for the original words "section 34ZB(1), (4) or (5)"), and the words in square brackets in sub-s (4) were substituted (for the original words "one or more of subsections (1) and (5)"), by the Competition (Amendment etc) (EU Exit) Regulations 2019, SI 2019/93, regs 32, 40, as from IP completion day (as defined in the European Union (Withdrawal Agreement) Act 2020, s 39) (for transitional provisions and savings in relation to the operation of the 2019 Regulations, see Sch 4 to those Regulations at **[7.69]** et seq and, in particular, Sch 4, Pt 7 to the 2019 Regulations at **[7.76]**).

[Cases referred by European Commission under EC Merger Regulation

[1.210]

34A Duty of [CMA] where case referred by the European Commission

(1) Subsection (2) applies if the European Commission has by a decision referred the whole or part of a case to the [CMA] under Article 4(4) or 9 of the EC Merger Regulation, or is deemed to have taken such a decision, unless an intervention notice is in force in relation to that case.

(2) Before the end of the preliminary assessment period, the [CMA] shall—

(a) decide whether to make a reference . . . under section 22 or 33; and

(b) inform the persons carrying on the enterprises concerned by notice of that decision and of the reasons for it.

(3) The [CMA] may, for the purposes of subsection (2), decide not to make a reference on the basis that it is considering whether to seek or accept undertakings under section 73 instead of making a reference; but a decision taken on that basis does not prevent the [CMA] from making a reference under section 22 or 33 in the event of no such undertakings being offered or accepted.

(4) In this section—

"the preliminary assessment period" means, subject to subsection (5), the period of 45 working days beginning with the day after the day on which the decision of the European Commission to refer the case is taken (or is deemed to have been taken); and

"working day" means any day which is not—

(a) a Saturday;
(b) a Sunday; or
(c) a day which is a European Commission holiday (as published in the Official Journal of the European Communities before the beginning of the year in which it occurs).

[(5) The CMA may extend the preliminary assessment period if it considers that any of the persons carrying on the enterprises concerned has failed (whether with or without reasonable excuse) to comply with any requirement of a notice under section 109.]

[(6) An extension under subsection (5) shall come into force when published under section 107.

(6A) An extension under subsection (5) shall continue in force until—

(a) the person concerned provides the information or documents to the satisfaction of the CMA or (as the case may be) appears as a witness in accordance with the requirements of the CMA; or
(b) the CMA publishes its decision to cancel the extension.]

(7) . . .]

NOTES

Inserted, together with the preceding heading and s 34B, by the EC Merger Control (Consequential Amendments) Regulations 2004, SI 2004/1079, reg 2, Schedule, para 2(1), (9).

This section, and the preceding heading, were repealed by the Competition (Amendment etc) (EU Exit) Regulations 2019, SI 2019/93, regs 32, 41, as from IP completion day (as defined in the European Union (Withdrawal Agreement) Act 2020, s 39) (for transitional provisions and savings in relation to the operation of the 2019 Regulations, see Sch 4 to those Regulations at **[7.69]** et seq and, in particular, Sch 4, Pt 7 to the 2019 Regulations at **[7.76]**).

Section heading, sub-ss (1), (3): references to the "CMA" substituted by the Enterprise and Regulatory Reform Act 2013, s 26(3), Sch 5, Pt 2, paras 59, 73(1), (2), (4), (5). For various transitional provisions (including those relating to the abolition of the OFT and the Competition Commission, existing references to those bodies and provisions relating to continuity), see the Enterprise and Regulatory Reform Act 2013 (Commencement No 6, Transitional Provisions and Savings) Order 2014, SI 2014/416, Schedule at **[2.13]**. This section is also amended as follows:

Sub-s (2): reference to the "CMA" substituted, and words omitted from para (a) repealed, by the Enterprise and Regulatory Reform Act 2013, s 26(3), Sch 5, Pt 2, paras 59, 73(1), (3), subject to transitional provisions in SI 2014/416 as noted above.

Sub-ss (5), (6), (6A) substituted (for original sub-ss (5), (6)), and sub-s (7) repealed, by the Enterprise and Regulatory Reform Act 2013, s 57, Sch 15, paras 15, 19, subject to transitional provisions in SI 2014/416 as noted above.

References to the European Community and related expressions: see the note "References to "the European Community", "Community", etc" in the introductory notes to this Act.

34B *(Originally inserted as noted to s 34A ante, and repealed by the Enterprise and Regulatory Reform Act 2013, s 57, Sch 15, paras 15, 20. For various transitional provisions (including those relating to the abolition of the OFT and the Competition Commission, existing references to those bodies and provisions relating to continuity), see the Enterprise and Regulatory Reform Act 2013 (Commencement No 6, Transitional Provisions and Savings) Order 2014, SI 2014/416, Schedule at* **[2.13]**.)

Determination of references

[1.211]

[34C Functions to be exercised by CMA groups

(1) Where a reference is made to the chair of the CMA under section 22 or 33 for the constitution of a group under Schedule 4 to the Enterprise and Regulatory Reform Act 2013, the functions of the CMA under or by virtue of the following provisions of this Part in relation to the matter concerned are to be carried out on behalf of the CMA by the group so constituted—

(a) sections 35 to 41B, except for sections 35(6) and (7), 36(5) and (6) and 37(6);
(b) where a reference is treated by virtue of section 37(2) as having been made under section 22, section 23(9)(a);
(c) section 76, as it applies in relation to orders under section 83, and sections 77, 78 and 80 to 84;
(d) section 87, so far as relating to an enforcement order made on behalf of the CMA by the group;
(e) sections 92(4), 94 and 94A, so far as relating to an enforcement undertaking or enforcement order made on behalf of the CMA by the group;
(f) section 104, so far as relating to a decision mentioned in paragraph (a)(iii) of the definition of relevant decision in subsection (6) of that section;
(g) section 107, so far as relating to anything done on behalf of the CMA by the group;
(h) section 109, where the permitted purpose in question relates to a function that (by virtue of this section) is being or is to be carried out on behalf of the CMA by the group;
(i) sections 110 to 115, so far as relating to a notice given under section 109 on behalf of the CMA by the group;
(j) section 120(5)(b), so far as relating to a decision of the group;
(k) Schedule 10, so far as relating to an enforcement undertaking or enforcement order which the group is considering accepting or making, or which the group has accepted or made, on behalf of the CMA.

(2) The functions of the CMA under section 95(4) in relation to the matter concerned may be carried out on behalf of the CMA by the group.

(3) Nothing in subsection (1) prevents the CMA Board from exercising a function of the CMA under or by virtue of the following provisions of this Part where the group constituted as mentioned in subsection (1) has ceased to exist—

(a) section 76 and Schedule 10, so far as relating to the making of an order under section 76 in relation to an order under section 83;
(b) section 83 and Schedule 10, so far as relating to the making of an order under section 83;

(c) sections 76 (as it applies in relation to an order under section 83), 80 to 84 and Schedule 10, so far as relating to the variation, supersession or release of enforcement undertakings or the variation or revocation of enforcement orders;
(d) section 87;
(e) sections 92(4) and 94.]

NOTES

Inserted by the Enterprise and Regulatory Reform Act 2013, s 26(3), Sch 5, Pt 2, paras 59, 74. For various transitional provisions (including those relating to the abolition of the OFT and the Competition Commission, existing references to those bodies and provisions relating to continuity), see the Enterprise and Regulatory Reform Act 2013 (Commencement No 6, Transitional Provisions and Savings) Order 2014, SI 2014/416, Schedule at **[2.13]**.

[1.212]

35 Questions to be decided in relation to completed mergers

(1) Subject to subsections (6) and (7) and section 127(3), the [CMA] shall, on a reference under section 22, decide the following questions—
(a) whether a relevant merger situation has been created; and
(b) if so, whether the creation of that situation has resulted, or may be expected to result, in a substantial lessening of competition within any market or markets in the United Kingdom for goods or services.

(2) For the purposes of this Part there is an anti-competitive outcome if—
(a) a relevant merger situation has been created and the creation of that situation has resulted, or may be expected to result, in a substantial lessening of competition within any market or markets in the United Kingdom for goods or services; or
(b) arrangements are in progress or in contemplation which, if carried into effect, will result in the creation of a relevant merger situation and the creation of that situation may be expected to result in a substantial lessening of competition within any market or markets in the United Kingdom for goods or services.

(3) The [CMA] shall, if it has decided on a reference under section 22 that there is an anti-competitive outcome (within the meaning given by subsection (2)(a)), decide the following additional questions—
(a) whether action should be taken by it under section 41(2) for the purpose of remedying, mitigating or preventing the substantial lessening of competition concerned or any adverse effect which has resulted from, or may be expected to result from, the substantial lessening of competition;
(b) whether it should recommend the taking of action by others for the purpose of remedying, mitigating or preventing the substantial lessening of competition concerned or any adverse effect which has resulted from, or may be expected to result from, the substantial lessening of competition; and
(c) in either case, if action should be taken, what action should be taken and what is to be remedied, mitigated or prevented.

(4) In deciding the questions mentioned in subsection (3) the [CMA] shall, in particular, have regard to the need to achieve as comprehensive a solution as is reasonable and practicable to the substantial lessening of competition and any adverse effects resulting from it.

(5) In deciding the questions mentioned in subsection (3) the [CMA] may, in particular, have regard to the effect of any action on any relevant customer benefits in relation to the creation of the relevant merger situation concerned.

(6) In relation to the question whether a relevant merger situation has been created, a reference under section 22 may be framed so as to require the [CMA] to exclude from consideration—
(a) subsection (1) of section 23;
(b) subsection (2) of that section; or
(c) one of those subsections if the [CMA] finds that the other is satisfied.

(7) In relation to the question whether*[, for the purposes of section 23(2)(b), the share of supply test is met]*, a reference under section 22 may be framed so as to require the [CMA] to confine its investigation to the supply of goods or services in a part of the United Kingdom specified in the reference.

NOTES

References to the "CMA" substituted by the Enterprise and Regulatory Reform Act 2013, s 26(3), Sch 5, Pt 2, paras 59, 75. For various transitional provisions (including those relating to the abolition of the OFT and the Competition Commission, existing references to those bodies and provisions relating to continuity), see the Enterprise and Regulatory Reform Act 2013 (Commencement No 6, Transitional Provisions and Savings) Order 2014, SI 2014/416, Schedule at **[2.13]**. This section is also amended as follows:

Sub-s (7): words in first pair of square brackets substituted by the Enterprise Act 2002 (Share of Supply Test) (Amendment) Order 2018, SI 2018/578, arts 2, 5(1), in relation to cases where enterprises cease to be distinct after 11 June 2018. These words are subsequently substituted (with the words "any such result as is mentioned in section 23(2)(b) has arisen") by the National Security and Investment Act 2021, s 58, Sch 2, para 4, as from a day to be appointed.

[1.213]

36 Questions to be decided in relation to anticipated mergers

(1) Subject to subsections (5) and (6) and section 127(3), the [CMA] shall, on a reference under section 33, decide the following questions—
(a) whether arrangements are in progress or in contemplation which, if carried into effect, will result in the creation of a relevant merger situation; and
(b) if so, whether the creation of that situation may be expected to result in a substantial lessening of competition within any market or markets in the United Kingdom for goods or services.

(2) The [CMA] shall, if it has decided on a reference under section 33 that there is an anti-competitive outcome (within the meaning given by section 35(2)(b)), decide the following additional questions—
(a) whether action should be taken by it under section 41(2) for the purpose of remedying, mitigating or preventing the substantial lessening of competition concerned or any adverse effect which may be expected to result from the substantial lessening of competition;

(b) whether it should recommend the taking of action by others for the purpose of remedying, mitigating or preventing the substantial lessening of competition concerned or any adverse effect which may be expected to result from the substantial lessening of competition; and
(c) in either case, if action should be taken, what action should be taken and what is to be remedied, mitigated or prevented.

(3) In deciding the questions mentioned in subsection (2) the [CMA] shall, in particular, have regard to the need to achieve as comprehensive a solution as is reasonable and practicable to the substantial lessening of competition and any adverse effects resulting from it.

(4) In deciding the questions mentioned in subsection (2) the [CMA] may, in particular, have regard to the effect of any action on any relevant customer benefits in relation to the creation of the relevant merger situation concerned.

(5) In relation to the question whether a relevant merger situation will be created, a reference under section 33 may be framed so as to require the [CMA] to exclude from consideration—
(a) subsection (1) of section 23;
(b) subsection (2) of that section; or
(c) one of those subsections if the [CMA] finds that the other is satisfied.

(6) In relation to the question whether*[, for the purposes of section 23(2)(b), the share of supply test will be met]*, a reference under section 33 may be framed so as to require the [CMA] to confine its investigation to the supply of goods or services in a part of the United Kingdom specified in the reference.

NOTES

References to the "CMA" substituted by the Enterprise and Regulatory Reform Act 2013, s 26(3), Sch 5, Pt 2, paras 59, 76. For various transitional provisions (including those relating to the abolition of the OFT and the Competition Commission, existing references to those bodies and provisions relating to continuity), see the Enterprise and Regulatory Reform Act 2013 (Commencement No 6, Transitional Provisions and Savings) Order 2014, SI 2014/416, Schedule at **[2.13]**. This section is also amended as follows:

Sub-s (6): words in first pair of square brackets substituted by the Enterprise Act 2002 (Share of Supply Test) (Amendment) Order 2018, SI 2018/578, arts 2, 5(2), in relation to cases where enterprises cease to be distinct after 11 June 2018. These words are subsequently substituted (with the words "any such result as is mentioned in section 23(2)(b) will arise") by the National Security and Investment Act 2021, s 58, Sch 2, para 5, as from a day to be appointed.

[1.214]

37 Cancellation and variation of references under section 22 or 33

(1) The [CMA] shall cancel a reference under section 33 if it considers that the proposal to make arrangements of the kind mentioned in the reference has been abandoned.

(2) The [CMA] may, if it considers that doing so is justified by the facts (including events occurring on or after the making of the reference concerned), treat a reference made under section 22 or 33 as if it had been made under section 33 or (as the case may be) 22; and, in such cases, references in this Part to references under those sections shall, so far as may be necessary, be construed accordingly.

(3) Where, by virtue of subsection (2), the [CMA] treats a reference made under section 22 or 33 as if it had been made under section 33 or (as the case may be) 22, sections 77 to 81 shall, in particular, apply as if the reference had been made under section 33 or (as the case may be) 22 instead of under section 22 or 33.

(4) Subsection (5) applies in relation to any undertaking accepted under section 80, or any order made under section 81, which is in force immediately before the [CMA], by virtue of subsection (2), treats a reference made under section 22 or 33 as if it had been made under section 33 or (as the case may be) 22.

(5) The undertaking or order shall, so far as applicable, continue in force as if—
(a) in the case of an undertaking or order which relates to a reference made under section 22, accepted or made in relation to a reference made under section 33; and
(b) in the case of an undertaking or order which relates to a reference made under section 33, accepted or made in relation to a reference made under section 22;

and the undertaking or order concerned may be varied, superseded, released or revoked accordingly.

(6) The [CMA] may at any time vary a reference under section 22 or 33.

(7), (8) . . .

(9) No variation by the [CMA] under this section shall be capable of altering the period permitted by section 39 within which the report of the [CMA] under section 38 is to be prepared and published.

NOTES

References to the "CMA" substituted, and sub-ss (7), (8) repealed, by the Enterprise and Regulatory Reform Act 2013, s 26(3), Sch 5, Pt 2, paras 59, 77. For various transitional provisions (including those relating to the abolition of the OFT and the Competition Commission, existing references to those bodies and provisions relating to continuity), see the Enterprise and Regulatory Reform Act 2013 (Commencement No 6, Transitional Provisions and Savings) Order 2014, SI 2014/416, Schedule at **[2.13]**.

[1.215]

38 Investigations and reports on references under section 22 or 33

(1) The [CMA] shall prepare and publish a report on a reference under section 22 or 33 within the period permitted by section 39.

(2) The report shall, in particular, contain—
(a) the decisions of the [CMA] on the questions which it is required to answer by virtue of section 35 or (as the case may be) 36;
(b) its reasons for its decisions; and
(c) such information as the [CMA] considers appropriate for facilitating a proper understanding of those questions and of its reasons for its decisions.

(3) The [CMA] shall carry out such investigations as it considers appropriate for the purposes of preparing a report under this section.

(4) . . .

NOTES

References to the "CMA" substituted, and sub-s (4) repealed, by the Enterprise and Regulatory Reform Act 2013, s 26(3), Sch 5, Pt 2, paras 59, 78. For various transitional provisions (including those relating to the abolition of the OFT and the Competition Commission, existing references to those bodies and provisions relating to continuity), see the Enterprise and Regulatory Reform Act 2013 (Commencement No 6, Transitional Provisions and Savings) Order 2014, SI 2014/416, Schedule at **[2.13]**.

[1.216]

39 Time-limits for investigations and reports

(1) The [CMA] shall prepare and publish its report under section 38 within the period of 24 weeks beginning with the date of the reference concerned.

(2) . . .

(3) The [CMA] may extend, by no more than 8 weeks, the period within which a report under section 38 is to be prepared and published if it considers that there are special reasons why the report cannot be prepared and published within that period.

(4) The [CMA] may extend the period within which a report under section 38 is to be prepared and published if it considers that a relevant person has failed (whether with or without a reasonable excuse) to comply with any requirement of a notice under section 109.

(5) In [this section] "relevant person" means—

(a) any person carrying on any of the enterprises concerned;

(b) any person who (whether alone or as a member of a group) owns or has control of any such person; or

(c) any officer, employee or agent of any person mentioned in paragraph (a) or (b).

(6) For the purposes of subsection (5) a person or group of persons able, directly or indirectly, to control or materially to influence the policy of a body of persons corporate or unincorporate, but without having a controlling interest in that body of persons, may be treated as having control of it.

(7) An extension under subsection (3) or (4) shall come into force when published under section 107.

(8) An extension under subsection (4) shall continue in force until—

(a) the person concerned provides the information or documents to the satisfaction of the [CMA] or (as the case may be) appears as a witness in accordance with the requirements of the [CMA]; or

(b) the [CMA] publishes its decision to cancel the extension.

[(8A) In the case of a report on a reference under section 33, the CMA may provide that a specified period of no more than 3 weeks is to be disregarded for the purposes of any time-limit for the preparation and publication of the report which applies by virtue of this section if—

(a) a relevant person has so requested before the end of the period of 3 weeks beginning with the date of the reference concerned; and

(b) the CMA reasonably believes that the arrangements in question might be abandoned.

(8B) If the CMA exercises the power under subsection (8A), the CMA shall publish a notice to that effect.]

(9) References in this Part to the date of a reference shall be construed as references to the date specified in the reference as the date on which it is made.

(10) This section is subject to section 40.

NOTES

In sub-ss (1), (3), (4), (8), the references to the "CMA" were substituted by the Enterprise and Regulatory Reform Act 2013, s 26(3), Sch 5, Pt 2, paras 59, 79. For various transitional provisions (including those relating to the abolition of the OFT and the Competition Commission, existing references to those bodies and provisions relating to continuity), see the Enterprise and Regulatory Reform Act 2013 (Commencement No 6, Transitional Provisions and Savings) Order 2014, SI 2014/416, Schedule at **[2.13]**.

Sub-s (2) repealed by the EC Merger Control (Consequential Amendments) Regulations 2004, SI 2004/1079, reg 2, Schedule, para 2(1), (10).

Words in square brackets in sub-s (5) substituted, and sub-ss (8A), (8B) inserted, by the Enterprise and Regulatory Reform Act 2013, s 32(2), Sch 8, paras 1, 5, subject to transitional provisions in SI 2014/416 as noted above.

[1.217]

40 Section 39: supplementary

(1), (2) . . .

(3) A period extended under subsection (3) of section 39 may also be extended under subsection (4) of that section and a period extended under subsection (4) of that section may also be extended under subsection (3) of that section.

(4) No more than one extension is possible under section 39(3).

(5) Where a period within which a report under section 38 is to be prepared and published is extended or further extended under section 39(3) or (4), the period as extended or (as the case may be) further extended shall, subject to subsections (6) and (7), be calculated by taking the period being extended and adding to it the period of the extension (whether or not those periods overlap in time).

(6) Subsection (7) applies where—

(a) the period within which the report under section 38 is to be prepared and published is further extended;

(b) the further extension and at least one previous extension is made under section 39(4); and

(c) the same days or fractions of days are included in or comprise the further extension and are included in or comprise at least one such previous extension.

(7) In calculating the period of the further extension, any days or fractions of days of the kind mentioned in subsection (6)(c) shall be disregarded.

(8) The Secretary of State may by order amend section 39 so as to alter any one or more of the following periods—

(a) the period of 24 weeks mentioned in subsection (1) of that section or any period for the time being mentioned in that subsection in substitution for that period;

(b) . . .

(c) the period of 8 weeks mentioned in subsection (3) of that section or any period for the time being mentioned in that subsection in substitution for that period.

(9) No alteration shall be made by virtue of subsection (8) which results in the period for the time being mentioned in subsection (1) . . . of section 39 exceeding 24 weeks or the period for the time being mentioned in subsection (3) of that section exceeding 8 weeks.

(10) An order under subsection (8) shall not affect any period of time within which the [CMA] is under a duty to prepare and publish its report under section 38 in relation to a reference under section 22 or 33 if the [CMA] is already under that duty in relation to that reference when the order is made.

(11) Before making an order under subsection (8) the Secretary of State shall consult the [CMA] and such other persons as he considers appropriate.

(12) The Secretary of State may make regulations for the purposes of section 39(8).

(13) The regulations may, in particular—

(a) provide for the time at which information or documents are to be treated as provided (including the time at which they are to be treated as provided to the satisfaction of the [CMA] for the purposes of section 39(8));

(b) provide for the time at which a person is to be treated as appearing as a witness (including the time at which he is to be treated as appearing as a witness in accordance with the requirements of the [CMA] for the purposes of section 39(8));

(c) provide for the persons carrying on the enterprises which have or may have ceased to be, or may cease to be, distinct enterprises to be informed, in circumstances in which section 39(8) applies, of the fact that—

(i) the [CMA] is satisfied as to the provision of the information or documents required by it; or

(ii) the person concerned has appeared as a witness in accordance with the requirements of the [CMA];

(d) provide for the persons carrying on the enterprises which have or may have ceased to be, or may cease to be, distinct enterprises to be informed, in circumstances in which section 39(8) applies, of the time at which the [CMA] is to be treated as satisfied as mentioned in paragraph (c)(i) above or the person concerned is to be treated as having appeared as mentioned in paragraph (c)(ii) above.

NOTES

Sub-ss (1), (2): repealed by the EC Merger Control (Consequential Amendments) Regulations 2004, SI 2004/1079, reg 2, Schedule, para 2(1), (11)(a).

Sub-s (8): para (b) repealed by SI 2004/1079, reg 2, Schedule, para 2(1), (11)(a).

Sub-s (9): words omitted repealed by SI 2004/1079, reg 2, Schedule, para 2(1), (11)(b).

Sub-ss (10), (11), (13): references to the "CMA" substituted by the Enterprise and Regulatory Reform Act 2013, s 26(3), Sch 5, Pt 2, paras 59, 80. For various transitional provisions (including those relating to the abolition of the OFT and the Competition Commission, existing references to those bodies and provisions relating to continuity), see the Enterprise and Regulatory Reform Act 2013 (Commencement No 6, Transitional Provisions and Savings) Order 2014, SI 2014/416, Schedule at **[2.13]**.

[1.218]

41 Duty to remedy effects of completed or anticipated mergers

(1) Subsection (2) applies where a report of the [CMA] has been prepared and published under section 38 within the period permitted by section 39 and contains the decision that there is an anti-competitive outcome.

(2) The [CMA] shall take such action under section 82 or 84 as it considers to be reasonable and practicable—

(a) to remedy, mitigate or prevent the substantial lessening of competition concerned; and

(b) to remedy, mitigate or prevent any adverse effects which have resulted from, or may be expected to result from, the substantial lessening of competition.

(3) The decision of the [CMA] under subsection (2) shall be consistent with its decisions as included in its report by virtue of section 35(3) or (as the case may be) 36(2) unless there has been a material change of circumstances since the preparation of the report or the [CMA] otherwise has a special reason for deciding differently.

(4) In making a decision under subsection (2), the [CMA] shall, in particular, have regard to the need to achieve as comprehensive a solution as is reasonable and practicable to the substantial lessening of competition and any adverse effects resulting from it.

(5) In making a decision under subsection (2), the [CMA] may, in particular, have regard to the effect of any action on any relevant customer benefits in relation to the creation of the relevant merger situation concerned.

NOTES

References to the "CMA" substituted by the Enterprise and Regulatory Reform Act 2013, s 26(3), Sch 5, Pt 2, paras 59, 81. For various transitional provisions (including those relating to the abolition of the OFT and the Competition Commission, existing references to those bodies and provisions relating to continuity), see the Enterprise and Regulatory Reform Act 2013 (Commencement No 6, Transitional Provisions and Savings) Order 2014, SI 2014/416, Schedule at **[2.13]**.

[1.219]

[41A Time-limit for discharging duty under section 41

(1) The CMA shall discharge its duty under section 41(2) within the period of 12 weeks beginning with the date on which it publishes the report concerned under section 38.

(2) The CMA may extend, by no more than 6 weeks, the period within which its duty under section 41(2) shall be discharged if it considers that there are special reasons for doing so.

(3) The CMA may extend the period within which its duty under section 41(2) shall be discharged if it considers that a relevant person has failed (whether with or without reasonable excuse) to comply with any requirement of a notice under section 109 which is given in relation to the reference.

(4) In subsection (3), "relevant person" means—

(a) any person carrying on any of the enterprises concerned;

(b) any person who (whether alone or as a member of a group) owns or has control of any such person; or
(c) any officer, employee or agent of any person mentioned in paragraph (a) or (b).

(5) For the purposes of subsection (4), a person or group of persons able, directly or indirectly, to control or materially to influence the policy of a body of persons corporate or unincorporate, but without having a controlling interest in that body of persons, may be treated as having control of it.

(6) An extension under subsection (2) or (3) comes into force when published under section 107.

(7) An extension under subsection (3) continues in force until—

(a) the person concerned provides the information or documents to the satisfaction of the CMA or (as the case may be) appears as a witness in accordance with the requirements of the CMA; or
(b) the CMA publishes its decision to cancel the extension.]

NOTES

Inserted, together with s 41B, by the Enterprise and Regulatory Reform Act 2013, s 32(2), Sch 8, paras 1, 6. For various transitional provisions (including those relating to the abolition of the OFT and the Competition Commission, existing references to those bodies and provisions relating to continuity), see the Enterprise and Regulatory Reform Act 2013 (Commencement No 6, Transitional Provisions and Savings) Order 2014, SI 2014/416, Schedule at **[2.13]**.

[1.220]

[41B Section 41A: supplementary

(1) A period extended under section 41A(2) may also be extended under section 41A(3), and a period extended under section 41A(3) may also be extended under section 41A(2).

(2) No more than one extension is possible under section 41A(2).

(3) Where a period is extended or further extended under section 41A(2) or (3), the period as extended or (as the case may be) further extended is, subject to subsections (4) and (5), to be calculated by taking the period being extended and adding to it the period of the extension (whether or not those periods overlap in time).

(4) Subsection (5) applies where—

(a) the period within which the CMA must discharge its duty under section 41(2) is further extended;
(b) the further extension and at least one previous extension is made under section 41A(3); and
(c) the same days or fractions of days are included in or comprise the further extension and are included in or comprise at least one such previous extension.

(5) In calculating the period of the further extension, any days or fractions of days of the kind mentioned in subsection (4)(c) are to be disregarded.

(6) The Secretary of State may by order amend section 41A so as to alter either or both of the following periods—

(a) the period of 12 weeks mentioned in subsection (1) of that section or any period for the time being mentioned in that subsection in substitution for that period;
(b) the period of 6 weeks mentioned in subsection (2) of that section or any period for the time being mentioned in that subsection in substitution for that period.

(7) But no alteration may be made by virtue of subsection (6) which results in—

(a) the period for the time being mentioned in section 41A(1) exceeding 12 weeks; or
(b) the period for the time being mentioned in section 41A(2) exceeding 6 weeks.

(8) Before making an order under subsection (6) the Secretary of State shall consult the CMA and such other persons as the Secretary of State considers appropriate.]

NOTES

Inserted as noted to s 41A at **[1.219]**.

CHAPTER 2 PUBLIC INTEREST CASES

Power to make references

[1.221]

42 Intervention by Secretary of State in certain public interest cases

(1) Subsection (2) applies where—

(a) the Secretary of State has reasonable grounds for suspecting that it is or may be the case that a relevant merger situation has been created or that arrangements are in progress or in contemplation which, if carried into effect, will result in the creation of a relevant merger situation;
(b) no reference under section 22 or 33 has been made in relation to the relevant merger situation concerned;
(c) no decision has been made not to make such a reference (other than a decision made by virtue of subsection (2)(b) of section 33 or a decision to accept undertakings under section 73 instead of making such a reference); and
(d) no reference is prevented from being made under section 22 or 33 by virtue of—
  (i) [section 22(3)(za) or (a)] or (as the case may be) [33(3)(za) or (a)]; *or*
  (ii) Community law or anything done under or in accordance with it.

(2) The Secretary of State may give a notice to the [CMA] (in this Part "an intervention notice") if he believes that it is or may be the case that one or more than one public interest consideration is relevant to a consideration of the relevant merger situation concerned.

(3) For the purposes of this Part a public interest consideration is a consideration which, at the time of the giving of the intervention notice concerned, is specified in section 58 or is not so specified but, in the opinion of the Secretary of State, ought to be so specified.

(4) No more than one intervention notice shall be given under subsection (2) in relation to the same relevant merger situation.

(5) For the purposes of deciding whether a relevant merger situation has been created or whether arrangements are in progress or in contemplation which, if carried into effect, will result in the creation of a relevant merger situation, sections 23 [to 30] (read together with section 34) shall apply for the purposes of this Chapter as they do for the purposes of Chapter 1 but subject to subsection (6).

(6) In their application by virtue of subsection (5) sections 23 [to 30] shall have effect as if—

(a) for paragraph (a) of section 23(9) there were substituted—

"(a) in relation to the giving of an intervention notice, the time when the notice is given;

(aa) in relation to the making of a report by the [CMA] under section 44, the time of the making of the report;

(ab) in the case of a reference which is treated as having been made under section 45(2) or (3) by virtue of section 49(1), such time as the [CMA] may determine; and";

(b) the references to the [CMA] in [section 25(1) to (3), *(6) and (8)*] included references to the Secretary of State;

(c) the references to the [CMA] in section 25(4) and (5) were references to the Secretary of State;

(d) the reference in section 25(4) to section 73 were a reference to paragraph 3 of Schedule 7;

(e) after section 25(5) there were inserted—

"(5A) The Secretary of State may by notice to the persons carrying on the enterprises which have or may have ceased to be distinct enterprises extend the four month period mentioned in section 24(1)(a) or (2)(b) if, by virtue of section 46(5) or paragraph 3(6) of Schedule 7, he decides to delay a decision as to whether to make a reference under section 45.

(5B) An extension under subsection (5A) shall be for the period of the delay.";

(f) in section 25(10)(b) [for "and (4)" there were substituted ", (4) and (5A)"];

(g) the reference in section 25(12) to one extension were a reference to one extension by the [CMA] and one extension by the Secretary of State;

(h) the powers to extend time-limits under section 25 as applied by subsection (5) above . . . were not exercisable by the [CMA] or the Secretary of State before the giving of an intervention notice but the existing time-limits [by virtue of section 24 (as so applied)] in relation to possible references under section 22 or 33 were applicable for the purposes of the giving of that notice;

(i) the existing time-limits [by virtue of section 24 (as so applied)] in relation to possible references under section 22 or 33 (except for extensions under section 25(4)) remained applicable on and after the giving of an intervention notice as if any extensions were made under section 25 as applied by subsection (5) above but subject to further alteration by the [CMA] or the Secretary of State under section 25 as so applied;

(j) . . .

(k) in the case of the giving of intervention notices, the references in sections 23 [to 30] to the making of a reference or a reference were, so far as necessary, references to the giving of an intervention notice or an intervention notice; . . .

(l) . . .

(7) Where the Secretary of State has given an intervention notice mentioning a public interest consideration which, at that time, is not finalised, he shall, as soon as practicable, take such action as is within his power to ensure that it is finalised.

(8) For the purposes of this Part a public interest consideration is finalised if—

(a) it is specified in section 58 otherwise than by virtue of an order under subsection (3) of that section; or

(b) it is specified in that section by virtue of an order under subsection (3) of that section and the order providing for it to be so specified has been laid before, and approved by, Parliament in accordance with subsection (7) of section 124 and within the period mentioned in that subsection.

NOTES

Sub-s (1): the words in the first pair of square brackets in sub-para (d)(i) were substituted (for the original words "section 22(3)(za), (a) or (e)"), the words in the second pair of square brackets in sub-para (d)(i) were substituted (for the original words "33(3)(za), (a) or (e)"), and sub-para (d)(ii) and the preceding word were repealed, by the Competition (Amendment etc) (EU Exit) Regulations 2019, SI 2019/93, regs 32, 42(1), (2), as from IP completion day (as defined in the European Union (Withdrawal Agreement) Act 2020, s 39) (for transitional provisions and savings in relation to the operation of the 2019 Regulations, see Sch 4 to those Regulations at **[7.69]** et seq and, in particular, Sch 4, Pt 7 to the 2019 Regulations at **[7.76]**).

Sub-s (2): reference to the "CMA" substituted by the Enterprise and Regulatory Reform Act 2013, s 26(3), Sch 5, Pt 2, paras 59, 82(1), (2), subject to transitional provisions in SI 2014/416 as noted above.

Sub-s (5): words in square brackets substituted by the Enterprise and Regulatory Reform Act 2013, s 57, Sch 15, paras 15, 21(1), (3) (for various transitional provisions (including those relating to the abolition of the OFT and the Competition Commission, existing references to those bodies and provisions relating to continuity), see the Enterprise and Regulatory Reform Act 2013 (Commencement No 6, Transitional Provisions and Savings) Order 2014, SI 2014/416, Schedule at **[2.13]**).

Sub-s (6): the words "by virtue of section 24 (as so applied)" in square brackets in paras (h), (i) were inserted, the words omitted were repealed, and all other words in square brackets were substituted, by the Enterprise and Regulatory Reform Act 2013, ss 26(3), 57, Sch 5, Pt 2, paras 59, 82(1), (3), Sch 15, paras 15, 21(1), (4)–(10), subject to transitional provisions as noted above. The words in italics in para (b) were repealed, and the words in square brackets in para (f) were substituted (for the original words "after the word "(4)" there were inserted ", (5A)""), by SI 2019/93, regs 32, 42(1), (2), as from IP completion day (as defined in the European Union (Withdrawal Agreement) Act 2020, s 39) (for transitional provisions and savings see the first note relating to the 2019 Regulations above).

References to the European Community and related expressions: see the note "References to "the European Community", "Community", etc" in the introductory notes to this Act.

[1.222]

43 Intervention notices under section 42

(1) An intervention notice shall state—

(a) the relevant merger situation concerned;

(b) the public interest consideration or considerations which are, or may be, relevant to a consideration of the relevant merger situation concerned; and

(c) where any public interest consideration concerned is not finalised, the proposed timetable for finalising it.

(2) Where the Secretary of State believes that it is or may be the case that two or more public interest considerations are relevant to a consideration of the relevant merger situation concerned, he may decide not to mention in the intervention notice such of those considerations as he considers appropriate.

(3) An intervention notice shall come into force when it is given and shall cease to be in force when the matter to which it relates is finally determined under this Chapter.

(4) For the purposes of this Part, a matter to which an intervention notice relates is finally determined under this Chapter if—

(a) the time within which the [CMA] [or (if relevant) OFCOM] is to report to the Secretary of State under section 44 [or (as the case may be) 44A] has expired and no such report has been made;

(b) the Secretary of State decides to accept an undertaking or group of undertakings under paragraph 3 of Schedule 7 instead of making a reference under section 45;

(c) the Secretary of State otherwise decides not to make a reference under that section;

(d) the [CMA] cancels such a reference under section 48(1) or 53(1);

(e) the time within which the [CMA] is to prepare a report under section 50 and give it to the Secretary of State has expired and no such report has been prepared and given to the Secretary of State;

(f) the time within which the Secretary of State is to make and publish a decision under section 54(2) has expired and no such decision has been made and published;

(g) the Secretary of State decides under section 54(2) to make no finding at all in the matter;

(h) the Secretary of State otherwise decides under section 54(2) not to make an adverse public interest finding;

(i) the Secretary of State decides under section 54(2) to make an adverse public interest finding but decides neither to accept an undertaking under paragraph 9 of Schedule 7 nor to make an order under paragraph 11 of that Schedule; or

(j) the Secretary of State decides under section 54(2) to make an adverse public interest finding and accepts an undertaking under paragraph 9 of Schedule 7 or makes an order under paragraph 11 of that Schedule.

(5) For the purposes of this Part the time when a matter to which an intervention notice relates is finally determined under this Chapter is—

(a) in a case falling within subsection (4)(a), (e) or (f), the expiry of the time concerned;

(b) in a case falling within subsection (4)(b), the acceptance of the undertaking or group of undertakings concerned;

(c) in a case falling within subsection (4)(c), (d), (g) or (h), the making of the decision concerned;

(d) in a case falling within subsection (4)(i), the making of the decision neither to accept an undertaking under paragraph 9 of Schedule 7 nor to make an order under paragraph 11 of that Schedule; and

(e) in a case falling within subsection (4)(j), the acceptance of the undertaking concerned or (as the case may be) the making of the order concerned.

[(6) In this Part "OFCOM" means the Office of Communications.]

NOTES

References to the "CMA" in sub-s (4) substituted by the Enterprise and Regulatory Reform Act 2013, s 26(3), Sch 5, Pt 2, paras 59, 83. For various transitional provisions (including those relating to the abolition of the OFT and the Competition Commission, existing references to those bodies and provisions relating to continuity), see the Enterprise and Regulatory Reform Act 2013 (Commencement No 6, Transitional Provisions and Savings) Order 2014, SI 2014/416, Schedule at **[2.13]**.

The words "or (if relevant) OFCOM" and "or (as the case may be) 44A" in sub-s (4) were inserted, and sub-s (6) was added, by the Communications Act 2003, s 389(1), Sch 16, para 8.

[1.223]

44 Investigation and report by [CMA]

(1) Subsection (2) applies where the Secretary of State has given an intervention notice in relation to a relevant merger situation.

(2) The [CMA] shall, within such period as the Secretary of State may require, give a report to the Secretary of State in relation to the case.

(3) The report shall contain—

(a) advice from the [CMA] on the considerations relevant to the making of a reference under section 22 or 33 which are also relevant to the Secretary of State's decision as to whether to make a reference under section 45; and

(b) a summary of any representations about the case which have been received by the [CMA] and which relate to any public interest consideration mentioned in the intervention notice concerned [(other than a media public interest consideration)] and which is or may be relevant to the Secretary of State's decision as to whether to make a reference under section 45.

(4) The report shall, in particular, include decisions as to whether the [CMA] believes that it is, or may be, the case that—

(a) a relevant merger situation has been created or arrangements are in progress or in contemplation which, if carried into effect, will result in the creation of a relevant merger situation;

(b) the creation of that situation has resulted, or may be expected to result, in a substantial lessening of competition within any market or markets in the United Kingdom for goods or services;

(c) the market or markets concerned would not be of sufficient importance to justify the making of a reference . . . under section 22 or 33;

(d) in the case of arrangements which are in progress or in contemplation, the arrangements are not sufficiently far advanced, or not sufficiently likely to proceed, to justify the making of such a reference;

(e) any relevant customer benefits in relation to the creation of the relevant merger situation concerned outweigh the substantial lessening of competition and any adverse effects of the substantial lessening of competition; or

(f) it would be appropriate to deal with the matter (disregarding any public interest considerations mentioned in the intervention notice concerned) by way of undertakings under paragraph 3 of Schedule 7.

(5) If the [CMA] believes that it is or may be the case that it would be appropriate to deal with the matter (disregarding any public interest considerations mentioned in the intervention notice concerned) by way of undertakings under paragraph 3 of Schedule 7, the report shall contain descriptions of the undertakings which the [CMA] believes are, or may be, appropriate.

[(5A) The report may, in particular, contain a summary of any representations about the case which have been received by the [CMA] and which relate to any media public interest consideration mentioned in the intervention notice concerned and which is or may be relevant to the Secretary of State's decision as to whether to make a reference under section 45.]

(6) The report may, in particular, include advice and recommendations on any public interest consideration mentioned in the intervention notice concerned and which is or may be relevant to the Secretary of State's decision as to whether to make a reference under section 45.

(7) The [CMA] shall carry out such investigations as it considers appropriate for the purposes of producing a report under this section.

[(8) In this Part "media public interest consideration" means any consideration which, at the time of the giving of the intervention notice concerned—

(a) is specified in section 58(2A) to (2C); or

(b) in the opinion of the Secretary of State, is concerned with broadcasting or newspapers and ought to be specified in section 58.

(9) In this Part "broadcasting" means the provision of services the provision of which—

(a) is required to be licensed under Part 1 or 3 of the Broadcasting Act 1990 or Part 1 or 2 of the Broadcasting Act 1996; or

(b) would be required to be so licensed if provided by a person subject to licensing under the Part in question.

(10) In this Part "newspaper" means a daily, Sunday or local (other than daily or Sunday) newspaper circulating wholly or mainly in the United Kingdom or in a part of the United Kingdom.

(11) The Secretary of State may by order amend subsections (9) and (10).]

NOTES

References to the "CMA" substituted, and words omitted from sub-s (4)(c) repealed, by the Enterprise and Regulatory Reform Act 2013, s 26(3), Sch 5, Pt 2, paras 59, 84. For various transitional provisions (including those relating to the abolition of the OFT and the Competition Commission, existing references to those bodies and provisions relating to continuity), see the Enterprise and Regulatory Reform Act 2013 (Commencement No 6, Transitional Provisions and Savings) Order 2014, SI 2014/416, Schedule at **[2.13]**.

The words "(other than a media public interest consideration)" in square brackets in sub-s (3) were inserted, and sub-ss (5A), (8)–(11) were inserted and added respectively, by the Communications Act 2003, s 376.

[1.224]

[44A Additional investigation and report by OFCOM: media mergers

(1) Subsection (2) applies where—

(a) the Secretary of State has given an intervention notice in relation to a relevant merger situation; and

(b) the intervention notice mentions any media public interest consideration.

(2) OFCOM shall, within such period as the Secretary of State may require, give a report to the Secretary of State on the effect of the consideration or considerations concerned on the case.

(3) The report shall contain—

(a) advice and recommendations on any media public interest consideration mentioned in the intervention notice concerned and which is or may be relevant to the Secretary of State's decision as to whether to make a reference under section 45; and

(b) a summary of any representations about the case which have been received by OFCOM and which relate to any such consideration.

(4) OFCOM shall carry out such investigations as they consider appropriate for the purposes of producing a report under this section.]

NOTES

Inserted by the Communications Act 2003, s 377.

[1.225]

45 Power of Secretary of State to refer matter to [CMA]

(1) Subsections (2) to (5) apply where the Secretary of State—

(a) has given an intervention notice in relation to a relevant merger situation; and

(b) has received a report of the [CMA] under section 44[, and any report of OFCOM which is required by virtue of section 44A,] in relation to the matter.

(2) The Secretary of State may make a reference [to the chair of the CMA for the constitution of a group under Schedule 4 to the Enterprise and Regulatory Reform Act 2013] if he believes that it is or may be the case that—

(a) a relevant merger situation has been created;

(b) the creation of that situation has resulted, or may be expected to result, in a substantial lessening of competition within any market or markets in the United Kingdom for goods or services;

(c) one or more than one public interest consideration mentioned in the intervention notice is relevant to a consideration of the relevant merger situation concerned; and

(d) taking account only of the substantial lessening of competition and the relevant public interest consideration or considerations concerned, the creation of that situation operates or may be expected to operate against the public interest.

(3) The Secretary of State may make a reference [to the chair of the CMA for the constitution of a group under Schedule 4 to the Enterprise and Regulatory Reform Act 2013] if he believes that it is or may be the case that—

(a) a relevant merger situation has been created;

(b) the creation of that situation has not resulted, and may be expected not to result, in a substantial lessening of competition within any market or markets in the United Kingdom for goods or services;

(c) one or more than one public interest consideration mentioned in the intervention notice is relevant to a consideration of the relevant merger situation concerned; and

(d) taking account only of the relevant public interest consideration or considerations concerned, the creation of that situation operates or may be expected to operate against the public interest.

(4) The Secretary of State may make a reference [to the chair of the CMA for the constitution of a group under Schedule 4 to the Enterprise and Regulatory Reform Act 2013] if he believes that it is or may be the case that—

(a) arrangements are in progress or in contemplation which, if carried into effect, will result in the creation of a relevant merger situation;

(b) the creation of that situation may be expected to result in a substantial lessening of competition within any market or markets in the United Kingdom for goods or services;

(c) one or more than one public interest consideration mentioned in the intervention notice is relevant to a consideration of the relevant merger situation concerned; and

(d) taking account only of the substantial lessening of competition and the relevant public interest consideration or considerations concerned, the creation of the relevant merger situation may be expected to operate against the public interest.

(5) The Secretary of State may make a reference [to the chair of the CMA for the constitution of a group under Schedule 4 to the Enterprise and Regulatory Reform Act 2013] if he believes that it is or may be the case that—

(a) arrangements are in progress or in contemplation which, if carried into effect, will result in the creation of a relevant merger situation;

(b) the creation of that situation may be expected not to result in a substantial lessening of competition within any market or markets in the United Kingdom for goods or services;

(c) one or more than one public interest consideration mentioned in the intervention notice is relevant to a consideration of the relevant merger situation concerned; and

(d) taking account only of the relevant public interest consideration or considerations concerned, the creation of the relevant merger situation may be expected to operate against the public interest.

(6) For the purposes of this Chapter any anti-competitive outcome shall be treated as being adverse to the public interest unless it is justified by one or more than one public interest consideration which is relevant.

(7) This section is subject to section 46.

NOTES

All words in square brackets in this section were substituted by the Enterprise and Regulatory Reform Act 2013, s 26(3), Sch 5, Pt 2, paras 59, 85. For various transitional provisions (including those relating to the abolition of the OFT and the Competition Commission, existing references to those bodies and provisions relating to continuity), see the Enterprise and Regulatory Reform Act 2013 (Commencement No 6, Transitional Provisions and Savings) Order 2014, SI 2014/416, Schedule at **[2.13]**.

[1.226]

46 References under section 45: supplementary

(1) No reference shall be made under section 45 if—

(a) the making of the reference is prevented by section . . . 74(1) . . . or paragraph 4 of Schedule 7; . . .

(b) the European Commission is considering a request made, in relation to the matter concerned, by the United Kingdom (whether alone or with others) under article [22(1) of the EC Merger Regulation], is proceeding with the matter in pursuance of such a request or has dealt with the matter in pursuance of such a request[; or

(c) subject to subsection (1A), a reasoned submission requesting referral to the European Commission has been submitted to the European Commission under article 4(5) of the EC Merger Regulation].

[(1A) Subsection (1)(c) shall cease to apply if the Secretary of State is informed that a Member State competent to examine the concentration under its national competition law has, within the time permitted by Article 4(5) of the EC Merger Regulation, expressed its disagreement as regards the request to refer the case to the European Commission; and this subsection shall be construed in accordance with that Regulation.]

(2) The Secretary of State, in deciding whether to make a reference under section 45, shall accept the decisions of the [CMA] included in its report by virtue of subsection (4) of section 44 and any descriptions of undertakings as mentioned in subsection (5) of that section.

(3) Where the decision to make a reference under section 45 is made at any time on or after the end of the period of 24 weeks beginning with the giving of the intervention notice concerned, the Secretary of State shall, in deciding whether to make such a reference, disregard any public interest consideration which is mentioned in the intervention notice but which has not been finalised before the end of that period.

(4) Subject to subsection (5), where the decision to make a reference under section 45(2) or (4) is made at any time before the end of the period of 24 weeks beginning with the giving of the intervention notice concerned, the Secretary of State shall, in deciding whether to make such a reference, disregard any public interest consideration which is mentioned in the intervention notice but which has not been finalised if its effect would be to prevent, or to help to prevent, an anti-competitive outcome from being adverse to the public interest.

(5) The Secretary of State may, if he believes that there is a realistic prospect of the public interest consideration mentioned in subsection (4) being finalised within the period of 24 weeks beginning with the giving of the intervention notice concerned, delay deciding whether to make the reference concerned until the public interest consideration is finalised or, if earlier, the period expires.

(6) A reference under section 45 shall, in particular, specify—

(a) the subsection of that section under which it is made;

(b) the date on which it is made; and

(c) the public interest consideration or considerations mentioned in the intervention notice concerned which the Secretary of State is not under a duty to disregard by virtue of subsection (3) above and which he believes are or may be relevant to a consideration of the relevant merger situation concerned.

NOTES

Sub-s (1): first figure omitted from para (a) repealed by the Communications Act 2003, s 406(7), Sch 19. Second words omitted from para (a) repealed by the Enterprise and Regulatory Reform Act 2013, s 57, Sch 15, paras 15, 22 (for various transitional provisions (including those relating to the abolition of the OFT and the Competition Commission, existing references to those bodies and provisions relating to continuity), see the Enterprise and Regulatory Reform Act 2013 (Commencement No 6, Transitional Provisions and Savings) Order 2014, SI 2014/416, Schedule at **[2.13]**). Final word omitted from para (a) repealed, words in square brackets in para (b) substituted, and para (c) and the word immediately preceding it added, by the EC Merger Control (Consequential Amendments) Regulations 2004, SI 2004/1079, reg 2, Schedule, para 2(1), (12), (13). Paras (b) and (c) were repealed by the Competition (Amendment etc) (EU Exit) Regulations 2019, SI 2019/93, regs 32, 43, as from IP completion day (as defined in the European Union (Withdrawal Agreement) Act 2020, s 39) (for transitional provisions and savings in relation to the operation of the 2019 Regulations, see Sch 4 to those Regulations at **[7.69]** et seq).

Sub-s (1A): inserted by SI 2004/1079, reg 2, Schedule, para 2(1), (14). This subsection was repealed by SI 2019/93, regs 32, 43, as from IP completion day (as defined in the European Union (Withdrawal Agreement) Act 2020, s 39) (for transitional provisions and savings see the first note relating to the 2019 Regulations above).

Sub-s (2): reference to the "CMA" substituted by the Enterprise and Regulatory Reform Act 2013, s 26(3), Sch 5, Pt 2, paras 59, 86, subject to transitional provisions in SI 2014/416 as noted above.

[Cases referred by European Commission under the EC Merger Regulation

[1.227]

46A Cases referred by the European Commission where intervention notice is in force

(1) Subsection (2) applies if the European Commission has by a decision referred the whole or part of a case to the [CMA] under Article 4(4) or 9 of the EC Merger Regulation, or is deemed to have taken such a decision, and an intervention notice is in force in relation to that case.

(2) Before the end of the preliminary assessment period, the Secretary of State shall—

(a) decide whether to make a reference . . . under section 45; and

(b) inform the persons carrying on the enterprises concerned by notice of that decision and of the reasons for it.

(3) The Secretary of State may, for the purposes of subsection (2), decide not to make a reference on the basis that he is considering whether to seek or accept undertakings under paragraph 3 of Schedule 7 instead of making a reference; but a decision taken on that basis does not prevent the Secretary of State from making a reference under section 45 in the event of no such undertakings being offered or accepted.

(4) In this section—

"the preliminary assessment period" means, subject to section 46B, the period of 45 working days beginning with the day after the day on which the decision of the European Commission to refer the case is taken (or is deemed to have been taken); and

"working day" means any day which is not—

(a) a Saturday;

(b) a Sunday; or

(c) a day which is a European Commission holiday (as published in the Official Journal of the European Communities before the beginning of the year in which it occurs).]

NOTES

Inserted, together with the preceding heading and ss 46B, 46C, by the EC Merger Control (Consequential Amendments) Regulations 2004, SI 2004/1079, reg 2, Schedule, para 2(1), (15).

This section and the preceding heading were repealed by the Competition (Amendment etc) (EU Exit) Regulations 2019, SI 2019/93, regs 32, 44, as from IP completion day (as defined in the European Union (Withdrawal Agreement) Act 2020, s 39) (for transitional provisions and savings in relation to the operation of the 2019 Regulations, see Sch 4 to those Regulations at **[7.69]** et seq and, in particular, Sch 4, Pt 7 to the 2019 Regulations at **[7.76]**).

Reference to the "CMA" in sub-s (1) substituted, and words omitted from sub-s (2) repealed, by the Enterprise and Regulatory Reform Act 2013, s 26(3), Sch 5, Pt 2, paras 59, 87. For various transitional provisions (including those relating to the abolition of the OFT and the Competition Commission, existing references to those bodies and provisions relating to continuity), see the Enterprise and Regulatory Reform Act 2013 (Commencement No 6, Transitional Provisions and Savings) Order 2014, SI 2014/416, Schedule at **[2.13]**.

References to the European Community and related expressions: see the note "References to "the European Community", "Community", etc" in the introductory notes to this Act.

[1.228]

[46B Extension of preliminary assessment period

[(1) The CMA may extend the preliminary assessment period for the purposes of section 46A if it considers that any of the persons carrying on the enterprises concerned has failed (whether with or without reasonable excuse) to comply with any requirement of a notice under section 109.]

(2) . . .

[(3) An extension under subsection (1) shall come into force when published under section 107.

(3A) An extension under subsection (1) shall continue in force until—

(a) the person concerned provides the information or documents to the satisfaction of the CMA or (as the case may be) appears as a witness in accordance with the requirements of the CMA; or

(b) the CMA publishes its decision to cancel the extension.]

(4) . . .]

NOTES

Inserted as noted to s 46A at **[1.227]**.

This section was repealed by the Competition (Amendment etc) (EU Exit) Regulations 2019, SI 2019/93, regs 32, 44, as from IP completion day (as defined in the European Union (Withdrawal Agreement) Act 2020, s 39) (for transitional provisions and savings in relation to the operation of the 2019 Regulations, see Sch 4 to those Regulations at **[7.69]** et seq and, in particular, Sch 4, Pt 7 to the 2019 Regulations at **[7.76]**).

Sub-s (1) substituted, sub-ss (2), (4) repealed and sub-ss (3), (3A) substituted (for the original sub-s (3)), by the Enterprise and Regulatory Reform Act 2013, s 57, Sch 15, paras 15, 23. For various transitional provisions (including those relating to the abolition of the OFT and the Competition Commission, existing references to those bodies and provisions relating to continuity), see the Enterprise and Regulatory Reform Act 2013 (Commencement No 6, Transitional Provisions and Savings) Order 2014, SI 2014/416, Schedule at **[2.13]**.

46C *(Originally inserted as noted to s 46A ante, and repealed by the Enterprise and Regulatory Reform Act 2013, s 57, Sch 15, paras 15, 24. For various transitional provisions (including those relating to the abolition of the OFT and the Competition Commission, existing references to those bodies and provisions relating to continuity), see the Enterprise and Regulatory Reform Act 2013 (Commencement No 6, Transitional Provisions and Savings) Order 2014, SI 2014/416, Schedule at* **[2.13]**.*)*

Reports on references

[1.229]

[46D Functions to be exercised by CMA groups

Where a reference is made to the chair of the CMA under section 45 for the constitution of a group under Schedule 4 to the Enterprise and Regulatory Reform Act 2013, the functions of the CMA under or by virtue of the following provisions of this Part in relation to the matter concerned are to be carried out on behalf of the CMA by the group so constituted—

(a) sections 47 to 53;
(b) where a reference is treated by virtue of section 49(1) as having been made under section 45(2) or (3), section 23(9)(ab) (as it has effect by virtue of section 42(6));
(c) sections 104, so far as relating to any decision mentioned in paragraph (a)(iii) of the definition of relevant decision in subsection (6) of that section, and 104A;
(d) section 107, so far as relating to anything done on behalf of the CMA by the group;
(e) section 109, where the permitted purpose relates to a function that (by virtue of this section) is being or is to be carried out on behalf of the CMA by the group;
(f) sections 110 to 115, so far as relating to a notice given under section 109 on behalf of the CMA by the group;
(g) section 118(4);
(h) section 120(5)(b), so far as relating to a decision of the group.]

NOTES

Inserted by the Enterprise and Regulatory Reform Act 2013, s 26(3), Sch 5, Pt 2, paras 59, 88. For various transitional provisions (including those relating to the abolition of the OFT and the Competition Commission, existing references to those bodies and provisions relating to continuity), see the Enterprise and Regulatory Reform Act 2013 (Commencement No 6, Transitional Provisions and Savings) Order 2014, SI 2014/416, Schedule at **[2.13]**.

[1.230]

47 Questions to be decided on references under section 45

(1) The [CMA] shall, on a reference under section 45(2) or (3), decide whether a relevant merger situation has been created.

(2) If the [CMA] decides that such a situation has been created, it shall, on a reference under section 45(2), decide the following additional questions—

(a) whether the creation of that situation has resulted, or may be expected to result, in a substantial lessening of competition within any market or markets in the United Kingdom for goods or services; and
(b) whether, taking account only of any substantial lessening of competition and the admissible public interest consideration or considerations concerned, the creation of that situation operates or may be expected to operate against the public interest.

(3) If the [CMA] decides that a relevant merger situation has been created, it shall, on a reference under section 45(3), decide whether, taking account only of the admissible public interest consideration or considerations concerned, the creation of that situation operates or may be expected to operate against the public interest.

(4) The [CMA] shall, on a reference under section 45(4) or (5), decide whether arrangements are in progress or in contemplation which, if carried into effect, will result in the creation of a relevant merger situation.

(5) If the [CMA] decides that such arrangements are in progress or in contemplation, it shall, on a reference under section 45(4), decide the following additional questions—

(a) whether the creation of that situation may be expected to result in a substantial lessening of competition within any market or markets in the United Kingdom for goods or services; and
(b) whether, taking account only of any substantial lessening of competition and the admissible public interest consideration or considerations concerned, the creation of that situation may be expected to operate against the public interest.

(6) If the [CMA] decides that arrangements are in progress or in contemplation which, if carried into effect, will result in the creation of a relevant merger situation, it shall, on a reference under section 45(5), decide whether, taking account only of the admissible public interest consideration or considerations concerned, the creation of that situation may be expected to operate against the public interest.

(7) The [CMA] shall, if it has decided on a reference under section 45 that the creation of a relevant merger situation operates or may be expected to operate against the public interest, decide the following additional questions—

(a) whether action should be taken by the Secretary of State under section 55 for the purpose of remedying, mitigating or preventing any of the effects adverse to the public interest which have resulted from, or may be expected to result from, the creation of the relevant merger situation;

(b) whether the [CMA] should recommend the taking of other action by the Secretary of State or action by persons other than itself and the Secretary of State for the purpose of remedying, mitigating or preventing any of the effects adverse to the public interest which have resulted from, or may be expected to result from, the creation of the relevant merger situation; and

(c) in either case, if action should be taken, what action should be taken and what is to be remedied, mitigated or prevented.

(8) Where the [CMA] has decided by virtue of subsection (2)(a) or (5)(a) that there is or will be a substantial lessening of competition within any market or markets in the United Kingdom for goods or services, it shall also decide separately the following questions (on the assumption that it is proceeding as mentioned in section 56(6))—

(a) whether action should be taken by it under section 41 for the purpose of remedying, mitigating or preventing the substantial lessening of competition concerned or any adverse effect which has resulted from, or may be expected to result from, the substantial lessening of competition;

(b) whether the [CMA] should recommend the taking of action by other persons for the purpose of remedying, mitigating or preventing the substantial lessening of competition concerned or any adverse effect which has resulted from, or may be expected to result from, the substantial lessening of competition; and

(c) in either case, if action should be taken, what action should be taken and what is to be remedied, mitigated or prevented.

(9) In deciding the questions mentioned in subsections (7) and (8) the [CMA] shall, in particular, have regard to the need to achieve as comprehensive a solution as is reasonable and practicable to—

(a) the adverse effects to the public interest; or

(b) (as the case may be) the substantial lessening of competition and any adverse effects resulting from it.

(10) In deciding the questions mentioned in subsections (7) and (8) in a case where it has decided by virtue of subsection (2)(a) or (5)(a) that there is or will be a substantial lessening of competition, the [CMA] may, in particular, have regard to the effect of any action on any relevant customer benefits in relation to the creation of the relevant merger situation concerned.

(11) In this section "admissible public interest consideration" means any public interest consideration which is specified in the reference under section 45 and which the [CMA] is not under a duty to disregard.

NOTES

References to the "CMA" substituted by the Enterprise and Regulatory Reform Act 2013, s 26(3), Sch 5, Pt 2, paras 59, 89. For various transitional provisions (including those relating to the abolition of the OFT and the Competition Commission, existing references to those bodies and provisions relating to continuity), see the Enterprise and Regulatory Reform Act 2013 (Commencement No 6, Transitional Provisions and Savings) Order 2014, SI 2014/416, Schedule at **[2.13]**.

[1.231]

48 Cases where references or certain questions need not be decided

(1) The [CMA] shall cancel a reference under section 45(4) or (5) if it considers that the proposal to make arrangements of the kind mentioned in that reference has been abandoned.

(2) In relation to the question whether a relevant merger situation has been created or the question whether a relevant merger situation will be created, a reference under section 45 may be framed so as to require the [CMA] to exclude from consideration—

(a) subsection (1) of section 23;

(b) subsection (2) of that section; or

(c) one of those subsections if the [CMA] finds that the other is satisfied.

(3) In relation to the question whether*[, for the purposes of section 23(2)(b), the share of supply test is or will be met]*, a reference under section 45 may be framed so as to require the [CMA] to confine its investigation to the supply of goods or services in a part of the United Kingdom specified in the reference.

NOTES

References to the "CMA" substituted by the Enterprise and Regulatory Reform Act 2013, s 26(3), Sch 5, Pt 2, paras 59, 90. For various transitional provisions (including those relating to the abolition of the OFT and the Competition Commission, existing references to those bodies and provisions relating to continuity), see the Enterprise and Regulatory Reform Act 2013 (Commencement No 6, Transitional Provisions and Savings) Order 2014, SI 2014/416, Schedule at **[2.13]**. This section is also amended as follows:

Sub-s (3): words in first pair of square brackets substituted by the Enterprise Act 2002 (Share of Supply Test) (Amendment) Order 2018, SI 2018/578, arts 2, 5(3), in relation to cases where enterprises cease to be distinct after 11 June 2018. These words are substituted (with the words "any such result as is mentioned in section 23(2)(b) has arisen or the question whether any such result will arise") by the National Security and Investment Act 2021, s 58, Sch 2, para 6, as from a day to be appointed.

[1.232]

49 Variation of references under section 45

(1) The [CMA] may, if it considers that doing so is justified by the facts (including events occurring on or after the making of the reference concerned), treat—

(a) a reference made under subsection (2) or (3) of section 45 as if it had been made under subsection (4) or (as the case may be) (5) of that section; or

(b) a reference made under subsection (4) or (5) of section 45 as if it had been made under subsection (2) or (as the case may be) (3) of that section;

and, in such cases, references in this Part to references under those enactments shall, so far as may be necessary, be construed accordingly.

(2) Where, by virtue of subsection (1), the [CMA] treats a reference made under subsection (2) or (3) of section 45 as if it had been made under subsection (4) or (as the case may be) (5) of that section, paragraphs . . . 2, 7 and 8 of Schedule 7 shall, in particular, apply as if the reference had been made under subsection (4) or (as the case may be) (5) of that section instead of under subsection (2) or (3) of that section.
(3) Where, by virtue of subsection (1), the [CMA] treats a reference made under subsection (4) or (5) of section 45 as if it had been made under subsection (2) or (as the case may be) (3) of that section, paragraphs . . . 2, 7 and 8 of Schedule 7 shall, in particular, apply as if the reference had been made under subsection (2) or (as the case may be) (3) of that section instead of under subsection (4) or (5) of that section.
(4) Subsection (5) applies in relation to . . . any order made under paragraph 2 of [Schedule 7], which is in force immediately before the [CMA], by virtue of subsection (1), treats a reference as mentioned in subsection (1).
(5) The . . . order shall, so far as applicable, continue in force as if—

- (a) in the case of an . . . order which relates to a reference under subsection (2) or (3) of section 45, . . . made in relation to a reference made under subsection (4) or (as the case may be) (5) of that section; and
- (b) in the case of an . . . order which relates to a reference made under subsection (4) or (5) of that section, . . . made in relation to a reference made under subsection (2) or (as the case may be) (3) of that section;

and the . . . order concerned may be varied . . . revoked accordingly.
(6) The Secretary of State may at any time vary a reference under section 45.
(7) The Secretary of State shall consult the [CMA] before varying any such reference.
(8) Subsection (7) shall not apply if the [CMA] has requested the variation concerned.
(9) No variation by the Secretary of State under this section shall be capable of altering the public interest consideration or considerations specified in the reference or the period permitted by section 51 within which the report of the [CMA] under section 50 is to be prepared and given to the Secretary of State.

NOTES

References to the "CMA" in sub-ss (1)–(4), (7)–(9) substituted by the Enterprise and Regulatory Reform Act 2013, s 26(3), Sch 5, Pt 2, paras 59, 91. For various transitional provisions (including those relating to the abolition of the OFT and the Competition Commission, existing references to those bodies and provisions relating to continuity), see the Enterprise and Regulatory Reform Act 2013 (Commencement No 6, Transitional Provisions and Savings) Order 2014, SI 2014/416, Schedule at **[2.13]**.

Figures omitted from sub-ss (2), (3) repealed by the Enterprise and Regulatory Reform Act 2013, s 57, Sch 15, paras 15, 25(1)–(3), subject to transitional provisions in SI 2014/416 as noted above.

In sub-s (4), words omitted repealed, and words in first pair of square brackets substituted, by the Enterprise and Regulatory Reform Act 2013, s 57, Sch 15, paras 15, 25(1), (4), subject to transitional provisions in SI 2014/416 as noted above.

Words omitted from sub-s (5) repealed by the Enterprise and Regulatory Reform Act 2013, s 57, Sch 15, paras 15, 25(1), (5), subject to transitional provisions in SI 2014/416 as noted above,.

[1.233]
50 Investigations and reports on references under section 45

(1) The [CMA] shall prepare a report on a reference under section 45 and give it to the Secretary of State within the period permitted by section 51.
(2) The report shall, in particular, contain—

- (a) the decisions of the [CMA] on the questions which it is required to answer by virtue of section 47;
- (b) its reasons for its decisions; and
- (c) such information as the [CMA] considers appropriate for facilitating a proper understanding of those questions and of its reasons for its decisions.

[(2A) Where the report relates to a reference under section 45 which has been made after a report of OFCOM under section 44A, the [CMA] shall give a copy of its report (whether or not published) to OFCOM.]
(3) The [CMA] shall carry out such investigations as it considers appropriate for the purpose of producing a report under this section.

NOTES

References to the "CMA" substituted by the Enterprise and Regulatory Reform Act 2013, s 26(3), Sch 5, Pt 2, paras 59, 92. For various transitional provisions (including those relating to the abolition of the OFT and the Competition Commission, existing references to those bodies and provisions relating to continuity), see the Enterprise and Regulatory Reform Act 2013 (Commencement No 6, Transitional Provisions and Savings) Order 2014, SI 2014/416, Schedule at **[2.13]**.

Sub-s (2A) was inserted by the Communications Act 2003, s 389(1), Sch 16, para 10.

[1.234]
51 Time-limits for investigations and reports by [CMA]

(1) The [CMA] shall prepare its report under section 50 and give it to the Secretary of State under that section within the period of 24 weeks beginning with the date of the reference concerned.
(2) . . .
(3) The [CMA] may extend, by no more than 8 weeks, the period within which a report under section 50 is to be prepared and given to the Secretary of State if it considers that there are special reasons why the report cannot be prepared and given to the Secretary of State within that period.
(4) The [CMA] may extend the period within which a report under section 50 is to be prepared and given to the Secretary of State if it considers that a relevant person has failed (whether with or without a reasonable excuse) to comply with any requirement of a notice under section 109.
(5) In subsection (4) "relevant person" means—

- (a) any person carrying on any of the enterprises concerned;
- (b) any person who (whether alone or as a member of a group) owns or has control of any such person; or
- (c) any officer, employee or agent of any person mentioned in paragraph (a) or (b).

(6) For the purposes of subsection (5) a person or group of persons able, directly or indirectly, to control or materially to influence the policy of a body of persons corporate or unincorporate, but without having a controlling interest in that body of persons, may be treated as having control of it.

(7) An extension under subsection (3) or (4) shall come into force when published under section 107.

(8) An extension under subsection (4) shall continue in force until—

(a) the person concerned provides the information or documents to the satisfaction of the [CMA] or (as the case may be) appears as a witness in accordance with the requirements of the [CMA]; or

(b) the [CMA] publishes its decision to cancel the extension.

(9) This section is subject to sections 52 and 53.

NOTES

References to the "CMA" substituted by the Enterprise and Regulatory Reform Act 2013, s 26(3), Sch 5, Pt 2, paras 59, 93. For various transitional provisions (including those relating to the abolition of the OFT and the Competition Commission, existing references to those bodies and provisions relating to continuity), see the Enterprise and Regulatory Reform Act 2013 (Commencement No 6, Transitional Provisions and Savings) Order 2014, SI 2014/416, Schedule at **[2.13]**.

Sub-s (2) was repealed by the EC Merger Control (Consequential Amendments) Regulations 2004, SI 2004/1079, reg 2, Schedule, para 2(1), (16).

[1.235]

52 Section 51: supplementary

(1), (2) . . .

(3) A period extended under subsection (3) of section 51 may also be extended under subsection (4) of that section and a period extended under subsection (4) of that section may also be extended under subsection (3) of that section.

(4) No more than one extension is possible under section 51(3).

(5) Where a period within which a report under section 50 is to be prepared and given to the Secretary of State is extended or further extended under section 51(3) or (4), the period as extended or (as the case may be) further extended shall, subject to subsections (6) and (7), be calculated by taking the period being extended and adding to it the period of the extension (whether or not those periods overlap in time).

(6) Subsection (7) applies where—

(a) the period within which the report under section 50 is to be prepared and given to the Secretary of State is further extended;

(b) the further extension and at least one previous extension is made under section 51(4); and

(c) the same days or fractions of days are included in or comprise the further extension and are included in or comprise at least one such previous extension.

(7) In calculating the period of the further extension, any days or fractions of days of the kind mentioned in subsection (6)(c) shall be disregarded.

(8) The Secretary of State may by order amend section 51 so as to alter any one or more of the following periods—

(a) the period of 24 weeks mentioned in subsection (1) of that section or any period for the time being mentioned in that subsection in substitution for that period;

(b) . . .

(c) the period of 8 weeks mentioned in subsection (3) of that section or any period for the time being mentioned in that subsection in substitution for that period.

(9) No alteration shall be made by virtue of subsection (8) which results in the period for the time being mentioned in subsection (1) . . . of section 51 exceeding 24 weeks or the period for the time being mentioned in subsection (3) of that section exceeding 8 weeks.

(10) An order under subsection (8) shall not affect any period of time within which the [CMA] is under a duty to prepare and give to the Secretary of State its report under section 50 in relation to a reference under section 45 if the [CMA] is already under that duty in relation to that reference when the order is made.

(11) Before making an order under subsection (8) the Secretary of State shall consult the [CMA] and such other persons as he considers appropriate.

(12) The Secretary of State may make regulations for the purposes of section 51(8).

(13) The regulations may, in particular—

(a) provide for the time at which information or documents are to be treated as provided (including the time at which they are to be treated as provided to the satisfaction of the [CMA] for the purposes of section 51(8));

(b) provide for the time at which a person is to be treated as appearing as a witness (including the time at which he is to be treated as appearing as a witness in accordance with the requirements of the [CMA] for the purposes of section 51(8));

(c) provide for the persons carrying on the enterprises which have or may have ceased to be, or may cease to be, distinct enterprises to be informed, in circumstances in which section 51(8) applies, of the fact that—

(i) the [CMA] is satisfied as to the provision of the information or documents required by it; or

(ii) the person concerned has appeared as a witness in accordance with the requirements of the [CMA];

(d) provide for the persons carrying on the enterprises which have or may have ceased to be, or may cease to be, distinct enterprises to be informed, in circumstances in which section 51(8) applies, of the time at which the [CMA] is to be treated as satisfied as mentioned in paragraph (c)(i) above or the person concerned is to be treated as having appeared as mentioned in paragraph (c)(ii) above.

NOTES

Sub-ss (1), (2): repealed by the EC Merger Control (Consequential Amendments) Regulations 2004, SI 2004/1079, reg 2, Schedule, para 2(1), (17)(a).

Sub-s (8): para (b) repealed by SI 2004/1079, reg 2, Schedule, para 2(1), (17)(a).

Sub-s (9): words omitted repealed by SI 2004/1079, reg 2, Schedule, para 2(1), (17)(b).

Sub-ss (10), (11), (13): references to the "CMA" substituted by the Enterprise and Regulatory Reform Act 2013, s 26(3), Sch 5, Pt 2, paras 59, 94. For various transitional provisions (including those relating to the abolition of the OFT and

the Competition Commission, existing references to those bodies and provisions relating to continuity), see the Enterprise and Regulatory Reform Act 2013 (Commencement No 6, Transitional Provisions and Savings) Order 2014, SI 2014/416, Schedule at **[2.13]**.

[1.236]

53 Restrictions on action where public interest considerations not finalised

(1) The [CMA] shall cancel a reference under section 45 if—

(a) the intervention notice concerned mentions a public interest consideration which was not finalised on the giving of that notice or public interest considerations which, at that time, were not finalised;

(b) no other public interest consideration is mentioned in the notice;

(c) at least 24 weeks has elapsed since the giving of the notice; and

(d) the public interest consideration mentioned in the notice has not been finalised within that period of 24 weeks or (as the case may be) none of the public interest considerations mentioned in the notice has been finalised within that period of 24 weeks.

(2) Where a reference . . . under section 45 specifies a public interest consideration which has not been finalised before the making of the reference, the [CMA] shall not give its report to the Secretary of State under section 50 in relation to that reference unless—

(a) the period of 24 weeks beginning with the giving of the intervention notice concerned has expired; [or]

(b) the public interest consideration concerned has been finalised; . . .

(c) . . .

(3) The [CMA] shall, in reporting on any of the questions mentioned in section 47(2)(b), (3), (5)(b), (6) and (7), disregard any public interest consideration which has not been finalised before the giving of the report.

(4) The [CMA] shall, in reporting on any of the questions mentioned in section 47(2)(b), (3), (5)(b), (6) and (7), disregard any public interest consideration which was not finalised on the giving of the intervention notice concerned and has not been finalised within the period of 24 weeks beginning with the giving of the notice concerned.

(5) Subsections (1) to (4) are without prejudice to the power of the [CMA] to carry out investigations in relation to any public interest consideration to which it might be able to have regard in its report.

NOTES

References to the "CMA" substituted, and first words omitted from sub-s (2) repealed, by the Enterprise and Regulatory Reform Act 2013, s 26(3), Sch 5, Pt 2, paras 59, 95. For various transitional provisions (including those relating to the abolition of the OFT and the Competition Commission, existing references to those bodies and provisions relating to continuity), see the Enterprise and Regulatory Reform Act 2013 (Commencement No 6, Transitional Provisions and Savings) Order 2014, SI 2014/416, Schedule at **[2.13]**.

Word "or" in square brackets in sub-s (2)(a) inserted, and sub-s (2)(c) (and the word immediately preceding it) repealed, by the EC Merger Control (Consequential Amendments) Regulations 2004, SI 2004/1079, reg 2, Schedule, para 2(1), (18).

Decisions of the Secretary of State

[1.237]

54 Decision of Secretary of State in public interest cases

(1) Subsection (2) applies where the Secretary of State has received a report of the [CMA] under section 50 in relation to a relevant merger situation.

(2) The Secretary of State shall decide whether to make an adverse public interest finding in relation to the relevant merger situation and whether to make no finding at all in the matter.

(3) For the purposes of this Part the Secretary of State makes an adverse public interest finding in relation to a relevant merger situation if, in relation to that situation, he decides—

(a) in connection with a reference . . . under subsection (2) of section 45, that it is the case as mentioned in paragraphs (a) to (d) of that subsection or subsection (3) of that section;

(b) in connection with a reference . . . under subsection (3) of that section, that it is the case as mentioned in paragraphs (a) to (d) of that subsection;

(c) in connection with a reference . . . under subsection (4) of that section, that it is the case as mentioned in paragraphs (a) to (d) of that subsection or subsection (5) of that section; and

(d) in connection with a reference . . . under subsection (5) of that section, that it is the case as mentioned in paragraphs (a) to (d) of that subsection.

(4) The Secretary of State may make no finding at all in the matter only if he decides that there is no public interest consideration which is relevant to a consideration of the relevant merger situation concerned.

(5) The Secretary of State shall make and publish his decision under subsection (2) within the period of 30 days beginning with the receipt of the report of the [CMA] under section 50.

(6) In making a decision under subsections (2) to (4), the Secretary of State shall disregard any public interest consideration not specified in the reference under section 45 and any public interest consideration disregarded by the [CMA] for the purposes of its report.

(7) In deciding whether to make an adverse public interest finding under subsection (2), the Secretary of State shall accept—

(a) in connection with a reference . . . under section 45(2) or (4), the decision of the report [of the CMA] under section 50 as to whether there is an anti-competitive outcome; and

(b) in connection with a reference . . . under section 45(3) or (5)—

(i) the decision of the report [of the CMA] under section 50 as to whether a relevant merger situation has been created or (as the case may be) arrangements are in progress or in contemplation which, if carried into effect, will result in the creation of a relevant merger situation; and

(ii) the decision of the report of the [CMA] under section 44 as to the absence of a substantial lessening of competition.

(8) In determining for the purposes of subsection (5) the period of 30 days no account shall be taken of—

(a) Saturday, Sunday, Good Friday and Christmas Day; and

(b) any day which is a bank holiday in England and Wales.

NOTES

Words in square brackets substituted, and words omitted repealed, by the Enterprise and Regulatory Reform Act 2013, s 26(3), Sch 5, Pt 2, paras 59, 96. For various transitional provisions (including those relating to the abolition of the OFT and the Competition Commission, existing references to those bodies and provisions relating to continuity), see the Enterprise and Regulatory Reform Act 2013 (Commencement No 6, Transitional Provisions and Savings) Order 2014, SI 2014/416, Schedule at **[2.13]**.

[1.238]

55 Enforcement action by Secretary of State

(1) Subsection (2) applies where the Secretary of State has decided under subsection (2) of section 54 within the period required by subsection (5) of that section to make an adverse public interest finding in relation to a relevant merger situation and has published his decision within the period so required.

(2) The Secretary of State may take such action under paragraph 9 or 11 of Schedule 7 as he considers to be reasonable and practicable to remedy, mitigate or prevent any of the effects adverse to the public interest which have resulted from, or may be expected to result from, the creation of the relevant merger situation concerned.

(3) In making a decision under subsection (2) the Secretary of State shall, in particular, have regard to the report of the [CMA] under section 50.

(4) In making a decision under subsection (2) in any case of a substantial lessening of competition, the Secretary of State may, in particular, have regard to the effect of any action on any relevant customer benefits in relation to the creation of the relevant merger situation concerned.

NOTES

Sub-s (3): reference to the "CMA" substituted by the Enterprise and Regulatory Reform Act 2013, s 26(3), Sch 5, Pt 2, paras 59, 97. For various transitional provisions (including those relating to the abolition of the OFT and the Competition Commission, existing references to those bodies and provisions relating to continuity), see the Enterprise and Regulatory Reform Act 2013 (Commencement No 6, Transitional Provisions and Savings) Order 2014, SI 2014/416, Schedule at **[2.13]**.

Other

[1.239]

56 Competition cases where intervention on public interest grounds ceases

(1) Where the Secretary of State decides not to make a reference under section 45 on the ground that no public interest consideration to which he is able to have regard is relevant to a consideration of the relevant merger situation concerned, he shall by notice require the [CMA] to deal with the matter otherwise than under this Chapter.

(2) Where a notice is given to the [CMA] in the circumstances mentioned in subsection (1), the [CMA] shall decide whether to make a reference under section 22 or 33; and any time-limits in relation to the Secretary of State's decision whether to make a reference under section 45 (including any remaining powers of extension) shall apply in relation to the decision of the [CMA] whether to make a reference under section 22 or 33.

(3) Where the [CMA] cancels under section 53(1) a reference under section 45 and the [its report] under section 44 contains the decision that it is or may be the case that there is an anti-competitive outcome in relation to the relevant merger situation concerned, the [CMA] shall proceed under this Part as if a reference under section 22 or (as the case may be) 33 had been made . . . .

(4) In proceeding by virtue of subsection (3) to prepare and publish a report under section 38, the [CMA] shall proceed as if—

(a) the reference under section 22 or 33 had been made at the same time as the reference under section 45;

(b) the timetable for preparing and giving its report under section 50 (including any remaining powers of extension and as extended by an additional period of 20 days) were the timetable for preparing and publishing its report under section 38; and

(c) in relation to the question whether a relevant merger situation has been created or the question whether arrangements are in progress or in contemplation which, if carried into effect, will result in the creation of a relevant merger situation, the [CMA] were confined to the questions on the subject to be investigated by it under section 47.

(5) In determining the period of 20 days mentioned in subsection (4) no account shall be taken of—

(a) Saturday, Sunday, Good Friday and Christmas Day; and

(b) any day which is a bank holiday in England and Wales.

(6) Where the Secretary of State decides under section 54(2) to make no finding at all in the matter in connection with a reference under section 45(2) or (4), the [CMA] shall proceed under this Part as if a reference under section 22 or (as the case may be) 33 had been made . . . instead of a reference under section 45 and as if its report to the Secretary of State under section 50 had been prepared and published by it under section 38 within the period permitted by section 39.

(7) In relation to proceedings by virtue of subsection (6), the reference in section 41(3) to decisions of the [CMA] as included in its report by virtue of section 35(3) or 36(2) shall be construed as a reference to decisions which were included in the report of the [CMA] by virtue of section 47(8).

(8) Where the [CMA] becomes under a duty to proceed as mentioned in subsection (3) or (6)[—

(a)] references in this Part to references under sections 22 and 33 shall, so far as may be necessary, be construed accordingly; and, in particular, sections 77 to 81 shall apply as if a reference has been made . . . under section 22 or (as the case may be) 33[; and

(b) for the purposes of section 34C, the group constituted in consequence of the reference under section 45 is to be treated as if it were constituted in consequence of a reference under section 22 or (as the case may be) 33].

NOTES

Words in square brackets substituted (except for the words in the second and third pairs of square brackets in sub-s (8) which are inserted) and words omitted repealed, by the Enterprise and Regulatory Reform Act 2013, s 26(3), Sch 5, Pt 2, paras 59, 98.

For various transitional provisions (including those relating to the abolition of the OFT and the Competition Commission, existing references to those bodies and provisions relating to continuity), see the Enterprise and Regulatory Reform Act 2013 (Commencement No 6, Transitional Provisions and Savings) Order 2014, SI 2014/416, Schedule at **[2.13]**.

[1.240]

57 Duties of [CMA and OFCOM] to inform Secretary of State

(1) The [CMA] shall, in considering whether to make a reference under section 22 or 33, bring to the attention of the Secretary of State any case which it believes raises any consideration specified in section 58 unless it believes that the Secretary of State would consider any such consideration immaterial in the context of the particular case.

(2) The [CMA and OFCOM] shall bring to the attention of the Secretary of State any representations about exercising his powers under section 58(3) which have been made to the [CMA or (as the case may be) OFCOM].

NOTES

Words in square brackets substituted by the Enterprise and Regulatory Reform Act 2013, s 26(3), Sch 5, Pt 2, paras 59, 99.

For various transitional provisions (including those relating to the abolition of the OFT and the Competition Commission, existing references to those bodies and provisions relating to continuity), see the Enterprise and Regulatory Reform Act 2013 (Commencement No 6, Transitional Provisions and Savings) Order 2014, SI 2014/416, Schedule at **[2.13]**.

[1.241]

58 Specified considerations

(1) The interests of national security are specified in this section.

(2) In subsection (1) "national security" includes public security; and in this subsection "public security" has the same meaning as in article [21(4) of the EC Merger Regulation].

[(2A) The need for—

(a) accurate presentation of news; and

(b) free expression of opinion;

in newspapers is specified in this section.

(2B) The need for, to the extent that it is reasonable and practicable, a sufficient plurality of views in newspapers in each market for newspapers in the United Kingdom or a part of the United Kingdom is specified in this section.

(2C) The following are specified in this section—

(a) the need, in relation to every different audience in the United Kingdom or in a particular area or locality of the United Kingdom, for there to be a sufficient plurality of persons with control of the media enterprises serving that audience;

(b) the need for the availability throughout the United Kingdom of a wide range of broadcasting which (taken as a whole) is both of high quality and calculated to appeal to a wide variety of tastes and interests; and

(c) the need for persons carrying on media enterprises, and for those with control of such enterprises, to have a genuine commitment to the attainment in relation to broadcasting of the standards objectives set out in section 319 of the Communications Act 2003.]

[(2D) The interest of maintaining the stability of the UK financial system is specified in this section *(other than for the purposes of sections 67 and 68 or references made, or deemed to be made, by the European Commission to the OFT under article 4(4) or 9 of the EC Merger Regulation)*.]

[(2E) The need to maintain in the United Kingdom the capability to combat, and to mitigate the effects of, public health emergencies is specified in this section.]

(3) The Secretary of State may by order modify this section for the purpose of specifying in this section a new consideration or removing or amending any consideration which is for the time being specified in this section.

(4) An order under this section may, in particular—

(a) provide for a consideration to be specified in this section for a particular purpose or purposes or for all purposes;

(b) apply in relation to cases under consideration by the [CMA, OFCOM] or the Secretary of State before the making of the order as well as cases under consideration on or after the making of the order.

NOTES

Sub-s (1): repealed by the National Security and Investment Act 2021, s 58, Sch 2, para 7, as from a day to be appointed.

Sub-s (2): words in square brackets substituted by the EC Merger Control (Consequential Amendments) Regulations 2004, SI 2004/1079, reg 2, Schedule, para 2(1), (19). The words "; and in this subsection "public security" has the same meaning as in article [21(4) of the EC Merger Regulation]" were repealed by the Competition (Amendment etc) (EU Exit) Regulations 2019, SI 2019/93, regs 32, 45, as from IP completion day (as defined in the European Union (Withdrawal Agreement) Act 2020, s 39) (for transitional provisions and savings in relation to the operation of the 2019 Regulations, see Sch 4 to those Regulations at **[7.69]** et seq). This subsection is repealed by the National Security and Investment Act 2021, s 58, Sch 2, para 7, as from a day to be appointed.

Sub-ss (2A)–(2C): inserted by the Communications Act 2003, s 375(1).

Sub-s (2D): inserted by the Enterprise Act 2002 (Specification of Additional Section 58 Consideration) Order 2008, SI 2008/2645, art 2. Words in italics repealed by SI 2019/93, regs 32, 45, as from IP completion day (as defined in the European Union (Withdrawal Agreement) Act 2020, s 39) (for transitional provisions and savings in relation to the operation of the 2019 Regulations, see Sch 4 to those Regulations at **[7.69]** et seq).

Sub-s (2E): inserted by the Enterprise Act 2002 (Specification of Additional Section 58 Consideration) Order 2020, SI 2020/627, art 2.

Sub-s (4): words in square brackets in para (b) substituted by the Enterprise and Regulatory Reform Act 2013, s 26(3), Sch 5, Pt 2, paras 59, 100. For various transitional provisions (including those relating to the abolition of the OFT and

the Competition Commission, existing references to those bodies and provisions relating to continuity), see the Enterprise and Regulatory Reform Act 2013 (Commencement No 6, Transitional Provisions and Savings) Order 2014, SI 2014/416, Schedule at **[2.13]**.

Orders: the Enterprise Act 2002 (Specification of Additional Section 58 Consideration) Order 2008, SI 2008/2645 (which amends this section and ss 129, 130, Sch 8 *post*); the Enterprise Act 2002 (Specification of Additional Section 58 Consideration) Order 2020, SI 2020/627 (which amends this section and Sch 8 *post*, and the Enterprise Act 2002 (Protection of Legitimate Interests) Order 2003).

[1.242]

[58A Construction of consideration specified in section 58(2C)

(1) For the purposes of section 58 and this section an enterprise is a media enterprise if it consists in or involves broadcasting.

(2) In the case of a merger situation in which at least one of the enterprises ceasing to be distinct consists in or involves broadcasting, the references in section 58(2C)(a) or this section to media enterprises include references to newspaper enterprises.

(3) In this Part "newspaper enterprise" means an enterprise consisting in or involving the supply of newspapers.

(4) Wherever in a merger situation two media enterprises serving the same audience cease to be distinct, the number of such enterprises serving that audience shall be assumed to be more immediately before they cease to be distinct than it is afterwards.

(5) For the purposes of section 58, where two or more media enterprises—

(a) would fall to be treated as under common ownership or common control for the purposes of section 26, or

(b) are otherwise in the same ownership or under the same control,

they shall be treated (subject to subsection (4)) as all under the control of only one person.

(6) A reference in section 58 or this section to an audience shall be construed in relation to a media enterprise in whichever of the following ways the decision-making authority considers appropriate—

(a) as a reference to any one of the audiences served by that enterprise, taking them separately;

(b) as a reference to all the audiences served by that enterprise, taking them together;

(c) as a reference to a number of those audiences taken together in such group as the decision-making authority considers appropriate; or

(d) as a reference to a part of anything that could be taken to be an audience under any of paragraphs (a) to (c) above.

(7) The criteria for deciding who can be treated for the purposes of this section as comprised in an audience, or as comprised in an audience served by a particular service—

(a) shall be such as the decision-making authority considers appropriate in the circumstances of the case; and

(b) may allow for persons to be treated as members of an audience if they are only potentially members of it.

(8) In this section "audience" includes readership.

(9) The power under subsection (3) of section 58 to modify that section includes power to modify this section.]

NOTES

Inserted by the Communications Act 2003, s 375(2).

CHAPTER 3 OTHER SPECIAL CASES

Special public interest cases

[1.243]

59 Intervention by Secretary of State in special public interest cases

(1) Subsection (2) applies where the Secretary of State has reasonable grounds for suspecting that it is or may be the case that a special merger situation has been created or arrangements are in progress or in contemplation which, if carried into effect, will result in the creation of a special merger situation.

(2) The Secretary of State may give a notice to the [CMA] (in this Part "a special intervention notice") if he believes that it is or may be the case that one or more than one consideration specified in section 58 is relevant to a consideration of the special merger situation concerned.

[(3) For the purposes of this Part a special merger situation has been created if—

(a) the condition mentioned in subsection (3A) is satisfied; and

(b) immediately before the enterprises concerned ceased to be distinct—

(i) the conditions mentioned in subsection (3B) were satisfied;

(ii) the condition mentioned in subsection (3C) was satisfied; or

(iii) the condition mentioned in subsection (3D) was satisfied.

(3A) The condition mentioned in this subsection is that—

(a) no relevant merger situation has been created because of section 23(1)(b) and (2)(b); but

(b) a relevant merger situation would have been created if those enactments were disregarded.

(3B) The conditions mentioned in this subsection are that—

(a) at least one of the enterprises concerned was carried on in the United Kingdom or by or under the control of a body corporate incorporated in the United Kingdom; and

(b) a person carrying on one or more of the enterprises concerned was a relevant government contractor.

(3C) The condition mentioned in this subsection is that, in relation to the supply of newspapers of any description, at least one-quarter of all the newspapers of that description which were supplied in the United Kingdom, or in a substantial part of the United Kingdom, were supplied by the person or persons by whom one of the enterprises concerned was carried on.

(3D) The condition mentioned in this subsection is that, in relation to the provision of broadcasting of any description, at least one-quarter of all broadcasting of that description provided in the United Kingdom, or in a substantial part of the United Kingdom, was provided by the person or persons by whom one of the enterprises concerned was carried on.]

(5) For the purposes of deciding whether a relevant merger situation has been created or whether arrangements are in progress or in contemplation which, if carried into effect, will result in the creation of a relevant merger situation, sections 23 [to 30] (read together with section 34) shall apply for the purposes of this Chapter as they do for the purposes of Chapter 1 but subject to subsection (6).

(6) In their application by virtue of subsection (5) sections 23 [to 30] shall have effect as if—

(a) for paragraph (a) of section 23(9) there were substituted—

"(a) in relation to the giving of a special intervention notice, the time when the notice is given;

(aa) in relation to the making of a report by the [CMA] under section 61, the time of the making of the report;

(ab) in the case of a reference which is treated as having been made under section 62(2) by virtue of section 64(2), such time as the [CMA] may determine; and";

(b) the references to the [CMA] in section 24(2)(a) and (b) included references to the Secretary of State;

(c) the references to the [CMA] in [section 25(1) to (3), *(6) and (8)*] included references to the Secretary of State;

(d) the references to the [CMA] in section 25(4) and (5) were references to the Secretary of State;

(e) the reference in section 25(4) to section 73 were a reference to paragraph 3 of Schedule 7;

(f) the reference in section 25(12) to one extension were a reference to one extension by the [CMA] and one extension by the Secretary of State;

(g) the powers to extend time-limits under section 25 as applied by subsection (5) above . . . were not exercisable by the [CMA] or the Secretary of State before the giving of a special intervention notice;

(h) . . .

(i) in the case of the giving of special intervention notices, the references in sections 23 [to 30] to the making of a reference or a reference were, so far as necessary, references to the giving of a special intervention notice or a special intervention notice; . . .

(j) . . .

[(6A) The Secretary of State may by order amend the conditions mentioned in subsection (3)(b)(ii) and (iii).]

(7) No more than one special intervention notice shall be given under subsection (2) in relation to the same special merger situation.

(8) In this section "relevant government contractor" means—

(a) a government contractor—

(i) who has been notified by or on behalf of the Secretary of State of information, documents or other articles relating to defence and of a confidential nature which the government contractor or an employee of his may hold or receive in connection with being such a contractor; and

(ii) whose notification has not been revoked by or on behalf of the Secretary of State; or

(b) a former government contractor who was so notified when he was a government contractor and whose notification has not been revoked by or on behalf of the Secretary of State.

(9) In this section—

"defence" has the same meaning as in section 2 of the Official Secrets Act 1989 (c 6); and

"government contractor" has the same meaning as in the Act of 1989 and includes any sub-contractor of a government contractor, any sub-contractor of that sub-contractor and any other sub-contractor in a chain of sub-contractors which begins with the sub-contractor of the government contractor.

NOTES

Sub-s (2): reference to the "CMA" substituted by the Enterprise and Regulatory Reform Act 2013, s 26(3), Sch 5, Pt 2, paras 59, 101(1), (2). For various transitional provisions (including those relating to the abolition of the OFT and the Competition Commission, existing references to those bodies and provisions relating to continuity), see the Enterprise and Regulatory Reform Act 2013 (Commencement No 6, Transitional Provisions and Savings) Order 2014, SI 2014/416, Schedule at **[2.13]**.

Sub-ss (3), (3A)–(3D): substituted, for sub-ss (3), (4) as originally enacted, by the Communications Act 2003, s 378(1). Sub-ss (3)(b)(i) and (3B) are repealed by the National Security and Investment Act 2021, s 58, Sch 2, para 8, as from a day to be appointed.

Sub-s (5): words in square brackets substituted by the Enterprise and Regulatory Reform Act 2013, s 57, Sch 15, paras 15, 26(1), (2), subject to transitional provisions in SI 2014/416 as noted above.

Sub-s (6): words in square brackets substituted, and words omitted repealed, by the Enterprise and Regulatory Reform Act 2013, ss 26(3), 57, Sch 5, Pt 2, paras 59, 101(1), (3), Sch 15, paras 15, 26(1), (3)–(8), subject to transitional provisions in SI 2014/416 as noted above. Words in italics in para (c) repealed by the Competition (Amendment etc) (EU Exit) Regulations 2019, SI 2019/93, regs 32, 46, as from IP completion day (as defined in the European Union (Withdrawal Agreement) Act 2020, s 39) (for transitional provisions and savings in relation to the operation of the 2019 Regulations, see Sch 4 to those Regulations at **[7.69]** et seq).

Sub-s (6A): inserted by the Communications Act 2003, s 378(2).

Sub-ss (8), (9): repealed by the National Security and Investment Act 2021, s 58, Sch 2, para 8, as from a day to be appointed.

[1.244]

[59A Construction of conditions in section 59(3C) and (3D)

(1) For the purpose of deciding whether the proportion of one-quarter mentioned in section 59(3C) or (3D) is fulfilled with respect to—

(a) newspapers of any description, or

(b) broadcasting of any description,

the decision-making authority shall apply such criterion (whether value, cost, price, quantity, capacity, number of workers employed or some other criterion, of whatever nature), or such combination of criteria, as the decision-making authority considers appropriate.

(2) References in section 59(3C) to the supply of newspapers shall, in relation to newspapers of any description which are the subject of different forms of supply, be construed in whichever of the following ways the decision-making authority considers appropriate—

(a) as references to any of those forms of supply taken separately;

(b) as references to all those forms of supply taken together; or

(c) as references to any of those forms of supply taken in groups.

(3) For the purposes of subsection (2) the decision-making authority may treat newspapers as being the subject of different forms of supply whenever—

(a) the transactions concerned differ as to their nature, their parties, their terms or their surrounding circumstances; and

(b) the difference is one which, in the opinion of the decision-making authority, ought for the purposes of that subsection to be treated as a material difference.

(4) References in section 59(3D) to the provision of broadcasting shall, in relation to broadcasting of any description which is the subject of different forms of provision, be construed in whichever of the following ways the decision-making authority considers appropriate—

(a) as references to any of those forms of provision taken separately;

(b) as references to all those forms of provision taken together; or

(c) as references to any of those forms of provision taken in groups.

(5) For the purposes of subsection (4) the decision-making authority may treat broadcasting as being the subject of different forms of provision whenever—

(a) the transactions concerned differ as to their nature, their parties, their terms or their surrounding circumstances; and

(b) the difference is one which, in the opinion of the decision-making authority, ought for the purposes of that subsection to be treated as a material difference.

(6) The criteria for deciding when newspapers or broadcasting can be treated, for the purposes of section 59, as newspapers or broadcasting of a separate description shall be such as in any particular case the decision-making authority considers appropriate in the circumstances of that case.

(7) In section 59 and this section "provision" and cognate expressions have the same meaning in relation to broadcasting as in Part 3 of the Communications Act 2003; but this subsection is subject to subsections (4) and (5) of this section.]

NOTES

Inserted by the Communications Act 2003, s 378(3).

[1.245]

60 Special intervention notices under section 59

(1) A special intervention notice shall state—

(a) the special merger situation concerned; and

(b) the consideration specified in section 58 or considerations so specified which are, or may be, relevant to the special merger situation concerned.

(2) Where the Secretary of State believes that it is or may be the case that two or more considerations specified in section 58 are relevant to a consideration of the special merger situation concerned, he may decide not to mention in the special intervention notice such of those considerations as he considers appropriate.

(3) A special intervention notice shall come into force when it is given and shall cease to be in force when the matter to which it relates is finally determined under this Chapter.

(4) For the purposes of this Part, a matter to which a special intervention notice relates is finally determined under this Chapter if—

(a) the time within which the [CMA] [or (if relevant) OFCOM] is to report to the Secretary of State under section 61 [or (as the case may be) 61A] has expired and no such report has been made;

(b) the Secretary of State decides to accept an undertaking or group of undertakings under paragraph 3 of Schedule 7 instead of making a reference under section 62;

(c) the Secretary of State otherwise decides not to make a reference under that section;

(d) the [CMA] cancels such a reference under section 64(1);

(e) the time within which the [CMA] is to prepare a report under section 65 and give it to the Secretary of State has expired and no such report has been prepared and given to the Secretary of State;

(f) the time within which the Secretary of State is to make and publish a decision under section 66(2) has expired and no such decision has been made and published;

(g) the Secretary of State decides under subsection (2) of section 66 otherwise than as mentioned in subsection (5) of that section;

(h) the Secretary of State decides under subsection (2) of section 66 as mentioned in subsection (5) of that section but decides neither to accept an undertaking under paragraph 9 of Schedule 7 nor to make an order under paragraph 11 of that Schedule; or

(i) the Secretary of State decides under subsection (2) of section 66 as mentioned in subsection (5) of that section and accepts an undertaking under paragraph 9 of Schedule 7 or makes an order under paragraph 11 of that Schedule.

(5) For the purposes of this Part the time when a matter to which a special intervention notice relates is finally determined under this Chapter is—

(a) in a case falling within subsection (4)(a), (e) or (f), the expiry of the time concerned;

(b) in a case falling within subsection (4)(b), the acceptance of the undertaking or group of undertakings concerned;

(c) in a case falling within subsection (4)(c), (d) or (g), the making of the decision concerned;

(d) in a case falling within subsection (4)(h), the making of the decision neither to accept an undertaking under paragraph 9 of Schedule 7 nor to make an order under paragraph 11 of that Schedule; and
(e) in a case falling within subsection (4)(i), the acceptance of the undertaking concerned or (as the case may be) the making of the order concerned.

NOTES

Sub-s (4): references to the "CMA" substituted by the Enterprise and Regulatory Reform Act 2013, s 26(3), Sch 5, Pt 2, paras 59, 102 (for various transitional provisions (including those relating to the abolition of the OFT and the Competition Commission, existing references to those bodies and provisions relating to continuity), see the Enterprise and Regulatory Reform Act 2013 (Commencement No 6, Transitional Provisions and Savings) Order 2014, SI 2014/416, Schedule at **[2.13]**). Words in second and third pairs of square brackets in para (a) inserted by the Communications Act 2003, s 389(1), Sch 16, para 13.

[1.246]

61 Initial investigation and report by [CMA]

(1) Subsection (2) applies where the Secretary of State has given a special intervention notice in relation to a special merger situation.

(2) The [CMA] shall, within such period as the Secretary of State may require, give a report to the Secretary of State in relation to the case.

(3) The report shall contain—
(a) advice from the [CMA] on the considerations relevant to the making of a reference under section 22 or 33 which are also relevant to the Secretary of State's decision as to whether to make a reference under section 62; and
(b) a summary of any representations about the case which have been received by the [CMA] and which relate to any consideration mentioned in the special intervention notice concerned [(other than a consideration which, at the time of the giving of the notice, was specified in section 58(2A) to (2C))] and which is or may be relevant to the Secretary of State's decision as to whether to make a reference under section 62.

(4) The report shall include a decision as to whether the [CMA] believes (disregarding section [59(3B)(b)]) that it is, or may be, the case that a special merger situation has been created or (as the case may be) arrangements are in progress or in contemplation which, if carried into effect, will result in the creation of a special merger situation.

[(4A) The report may, in particular, contain a summary of any representations about the case which have been received by the [CMA] and which relate to any consideration which—
(a) is mentioned in the special intervention notice concerned and, at the time of the giving of that notice, was specified in section 58(2A) to (2C); and
(b) is or may be relevant to the Secretary of State's decision as to whether to make a reference under section 62.]

(5) The report may, in particular, include advice and recommendations on any consideration mentioned in the special intervention notice concerned and which is or may be relevant to the Secretary of State's decision as to whether to make a reference under section 62.

(6) The [CMA] shall carry out such investigations as it considers appropriate for the purposes of producing a report under this section.

NOTES

References to the "CMA" substituted by the Enterprise and Regulatory Reform Act 2013, s 26(3), Sch 5, Pt 2, paras 59, 103. For various transitional provisions (including those relating to the abolition of the OFT and the Competition Commission, existing references to those bodies and provisions relating to continuity), see the Enterprise and Regulatory Reform Act 2013 (Commencement No 6, Transitional Provisions and Savings) Order 2014, SI 2014/416, Schedule at **[2.13]**.

The words in second pair of square brackets in sub-s (3)(b) were inserted, the figure "59(3B)(b)" in square brackets in sub-s (4) was substituted, and sub-s (4A) was inserted, by the Communications Act 2003, s 379.

[1.247]

[61A Additional investigation and report by OFCOM: certain media mergers

(1) Subsection (2) applies where—
(a) the Secretary of State has given a special intervention notice in relation to a special merger situation; and
(b) the special intervention notice mentions any consideration which, at the time of the giving of the notice, was specified in section 58(2A) to (2C).

(2) OFCOM shall, within such period as the Secretary of State may require, give a report to the Secretary of State on the effect of the consideration or considerations concerned on the case.

(3) The report shall contain—
(a) advice and recommendations on any consideration which—
(i) is mentioned in the special intervention notice concerned and, at the time of the giving of that notice, was specified in section 58(2A) to (2C); and
(ii) is or may be relevant to the Secretary of State's decision as to whether to make a reference under section 62; and
(b) a summary of any representations about the case which have been received by OFCOM and which relate to any such consideration.

(4) OFCOM shall carry out such investigations as they consider appropriate for the purposes of producing a report under this section.]

NOTES

Inserted by the Communications Act 2003, s 380.

[1.248]

62 Power of Secretary of State to refer the matter

(1) Subsection (2) applies where the Secretary of State—

(a) has given a special intervention notice in relation to a special merger situation; and
(b) has received a report of the [CMA] under section 61[, and any report of OFCOM which is required by virtue of section 61A,] in relation to the matter.

(2) The Secretary of State may make a reference [to the chair of the CMA for the constitution of a group under Schedule 4 to the Enterprise and Regulatory Reform Act 2013] if he believes that it is or may be the case that—
(a) a special merger situation has been created;
(b) one or more than one consideration mentioned in the special intervention notice is relevant to a consideration of the special merger situation concerned; and
(c) taking account only of the relevant consideration or considerations concerned, the creation of that situation operates or may be expected to operate against the public interest.

(3) The Secretary of State may make a reference [to the chair of the CMA for the constitution of a group under Schedule 4 to the Enterprise and Regulatory Reform Act 2013] if he believes that it is or may be the case that—
(a) arrangements are in progress or in contemplation which, if carried into effect, will result in the creation of a special merger situation;
(b) one or more than one consideration mentioned in the special intervention notice is relevant to a consideration of the special merger situation concerned; and
(c) taking account only of the relevant consideration or considerations concerned, the creation of that situation may be expected to operate against the public interest.

(4) No reference shall be made under this section if the making of the reference is prevented by . . . paragraph 4 of Schedule 7.

(5) The Secretary of State, in deciding whether to make a reference under this section, shall accept the decision of the [CMA] included in its report under section 61 by virtue of subsection (4) of that section.

(6) A reference under this section shall, in particular, specify—
(a) the subsection of this section under which it is made;
(b) the date on which it is made; and
(c) the consideration or considerations mentioned in the special intervention notice which the Secretary of State believes are, or may be, relevant to a consideration of the special merger situation concerned.

NOTES

References to the "CMA" in sub-ss (1), (5) substituted, and words in square brackets in sub-ss (2), (3) substituted, by the Enterprise and Regulatory Reform Act 2013, s 26(3), Sch 5, Pt 2, paras 59, 104. For various transitional provisions (including those relating to the abolition of the OFT and the Competition Commission, existing references to those bodies and provisions relating to continuity), see the Enterprise and Regulatory Reform Act 2013 (Commencement No 6, Transitional Provisions and Savings) Order 2014, SI 2014/416, Schedule at **[2.13]**.

The words in second pair of square brackets in sub-s (1)(b) were inserted, and the words omitted from sub-s (4) were repealed, by the Communications Act 2003, ss 389(1), 406(7), Sch 16, para 14, Sch 19.

[1.249]

[62A Functions to be exercised by CMA groups

Where a reference is made to the chair of the CMA under section 62 for the constitution of a group under Schedule 4 to the Enterprise and Regulatory Reform Act 2013, the functions of the CMA under or by virtue of the following provisions of this Part in relation to the matter concerned are to be carried out on behalf of the CMA by the group so constituted—
(a) sections 63 to 65;
(b) where a reference is treated by virtue of section 64(2) as having been made under section 62(2), section 23(9)(ab) (as it has effect by virtue of section 59(6));
(c) sections 104, so far as relating to any decision mentioned in paragraph (a)(iii) of the definition of relevant decision in subsection (6) of that section, and 104A;
(d) section 107, so far as relating to anything done on behalf of the CMA by the group;
(e) section 109, where the permitted purpose relates to a function that (by virtue of this section) is being or is to be carried out on behalf of the CMA by the group;
(f) sections 110 to 115, so far as relating to a notice given under section 109 on behalf of the CMA by the group;
(g) section 118(4);
(h) section 120(5)(b), so far as relating to a decision of the group.]

NOTES

Inserted by the Enterprise and Regulatory Reform Act 2013, s 26(3), Sch 5, Pt 2, paras 59, 105. For various transitional provisions (including those relating to the abolition of the OFT and the Competition Commission, existing references to those bodies and provisions relating to continuity), see the Enterprise and Regulatory Reform Act 2013 (Commencement No 6, Transitional Provisions and Savings) Order 2014, SI 2014/416, Schedule at **[2.13]**.

[1.250]

63 Questions to be decided on references under section 62

(1) The [CMA] shall, on a reference under section 62(2), decide whether a special merger situation has been created.

(2) The [CMA] shall, on a reference under section 62(3), decide whether arrangements are in progress or in contemplation which, if carried into effect, will result in the creation of a special merger situation.

(3) If the [CMA] decides that a special merger situation has been created or that arrangements are in progress or in contemplation which, if carried into effect, will result in the creation of a special merger situation, it shall, on a reference under section 62, decide whether, taking account only of the consideration or considerations mentioned in the reference, the creation of that situation operates or may be expected to operate against the public interest.

(4) The [CMA] shall, if it has decided on a reference under section 62 that the creation of a special merger situation operates or may be expected to operate against the public interest, decide the following additional questions—

(a) whether action should be taken by the Secretary of State under section 66 for the purpose of remedying, mitigating or preventing any of the effects adverse to the public interest which have resulted from, or may be expected to result from, the creation of the special merger situation concerned;

(b) whether the [CMA] should recommend the taking of other action by the Secretary of State or action by persons other than itself and the Secretary of State for the purpose of remedying, mitigating or preventing any of the effects adverse to the public interest which have resulted from, or may be expected to result from, the creation of the special merger situation concerned; and

(c) in either case, if action should be taken, what action should be taken and what is to be remedied, mitigated or prevented.

NOTES

References to the "CMA" substituted by the Enterprise and Regulatory Reform Act 2013, s 26(3), Sch 5, Pt 2, paras 59, 106.

For various transitional provisions (including those relating to the abolition of the OFT and the Competition Commission, existing references to those bodies and provisions relating to continuity), see the Enterprise and Regulatory Reform Act 2013 (Commencement No 6, Transitional Provisions and Savings) Order 2014, SI 2014/416, Schedule at **[2.13]**.

[1.251]

64 Cancellation and variation of references under section 62

(1) The [CMA] shall cancel a reference under section 62(3) if it considers that the proposal to make arrangements of the kind mentioned in that reference has been abandoned.

(2) The [CMA] may, if it considers that doing so is justified by the facts (including events occurring on or after the making of the reference concerned), treat a reference made under subsection (2) or (3) of section 62 as if it had been made under subsection (3) or (as the case may be) (2) of that section; and, in such cases, references in this Part to references under those enactments shall, so far as may be necessary, be construed accordingly.

(3) Where, by virtue of subsection (2), the [CMA] treats a reference made under subsection (2) or (3) of section 62 as if it had been made under subsection (3) or (as the case may be) (2) of that section, paragraphs . . . 2, 7 and 8 of Schedule 7 shall, in particular, apply as if the reference had been made under subsection (3) or (as the case may be) (2) of that section instead of under subsection (2) or (3) of that section.

(4) Subsection (5) applies in relation to . . . any order made under paragraph 2 of [Schedule 7], which is in force immediately before the [CMA], by virtue of subsection (2), treats a reference made under subsection (2) or (3) of section 62 as if it had been made under subsection (3) or (as the case may be) (2) of that section.

(5) The . . . order shall, so far as applicable, continue in force as if—

(a) in the case of an . . . order which relates to a reference under subsection (2) of section 62, . . . made in relation to a reference made under subsection (3) of that section; and

(b) in the case of an . . . order which relates to a reference made under subsection (3) of that section, . . . made in relation to a reference made under subsection (2) of that section;

and the . . . order concerned may be varied . . . or revoked accordingly.

(6) The Secretary of State may at any time vary a reference under section 62.

(7) The Secretary of State shall consult the [CMA] before varying any such reference.

(8) Subsection (7) shall not apply if the [CMA] has requested the variation concerned.

(9) No variation by the Secretary of State under this section shall be capable of altering the consideration or considerations specified in the reference or the period permitted by virtue of section 65 within which the report of the [CMA] under that section is to be prepared and given to the Secretary of State.

NOTES

References to the "CMA" substituted by the Enterprise and Regulatory Reform Act 2013, s 26(3), Sch 5, Pt 2, paras 59, 107.

For various transitional provisions (including those relating to the abolition of the OFT and the Competition Commission, existing references to those bodies and provisions relating to continuity), see the Enterprise and Regulatory Reform Act 2013 (Commencement No 6, Transitional Provisions and Savings) Order 2014, SI 2014/416, Schedule at **[2.13]**.

Figure omitted from sub-s (3) repealed by the Enterprise and Regulatory Reform Act 2013, s 57, Sch 15, paras 15, 27(1), (2), subject to transitional provisions in SI 2014/416 as noted above.

In sub-s (4), words omitted repealed, and words in first pair of square brackets substituted, by the Enterprise and Regulatory Reform Act 2013, s 57, Sch 15, paras 15, 27(1), (3), subject to transitional provisions in SI 2014/416 as noted above.

Words omitted from sub-s (5) repealed by the Enterprise and Regulatory Reform Act 2013, s 57, Sch 15, paras 15, 27(1), (4), subject to transitional provisions in SI 2014/416 as noted above.

[1.252]

65 Investigations and reports on references under section 62

(1) The [CMA] shall prepare a report on a reference under section 62 and give it to the Secretary of State within the period permitted by virtue of this section.

(2) The report shall, in particular, contain—

(a) the decisions of the [CMA] on the questions which it is required to answer by virtue of section 63;

(b) its reasons for its decisions; and

(c) such information as the [CMA] considers appropriate for facilitating a proper understanding of those questions and of its reasons for its decisions.

[(2A) Where the report relates to a reference under section 62 which has been made after a report of OFCOM under section 61A, the [CMA] shall give a copy of its report (whether or not published) to OFCOM.]

(3) Sections 51 and 52 (but not section 53) shall apply for the purposes of a report under this section as they apply for the purposes of a report under section 50.

(4) The [CMA] shall carry out such investigations as it considers appropriate for the purpose of producing a report under this section.

NOTES

References to the "CMA" substituted by the Enterprise and Regulatory Reform Act 2013, s 26(3), Sch 5, Pt 2, paras 59, 108.

For various transitional provisions (including those relating to the abolition of the OFT and the Competition Commission, existing references to those bodies and provisions relating to continuity), see the Enterprise and Regulatory Reform Act 2013 (Commencement No 6, Transitional Provisions and Savings) Order 2014, SI 2014/416, Schedule at **[2.13]**.

Sub-s (2A) was inserted by the Communications Act 2003, s 389(1), Sch 16, para 15.

[1.253]

66 Decision and enforcement action by Secretary of State

(1) Subsection (2) applies where the Secretary of State has received a report of the [CMA] under section 65 in relation to a special merger situation.

(2) The Secretary of State shall, in connection with a reference under section 62(2) or (3), decide the questions which the [CMA] is required to decide by virtue of section 63(1) to (3).

(3) The Secretary of State shall make and publish his decision under subsection (2) within the period of 30 days beginning with the receipt of the report of the [CMA] under section 65; and subsection (8) of section 54 shall apply for the purposes of this subsection as it applies for the purposes of subsection (5) of that section.

(4) In making his decisions under subsection (2), the Secretary of State shall accept the decisions of the report of the [CMA] under section 65 as to whether a special merger situation has been created or whether arrangements are in progress or in contemplation which, if carried into effect, will result in the creation of a special merger situation.

(5) Subsection (6) applies where the Secretary of State has decided under subsection (2) that—

(a) a special merger situation has been created or arrangements are in progress or in contemplation which, if carried into effect, will result in the creation of a special merger situation;

(b) at least one consideration which is mentioned in the special intervention notice concerned is relevant to a consideration of the special merger situation concerned; and

(c) taking account only of the relevant consideration or considerations concerned, the creation of that situation operates or may be expected to operate against the public interest;

and has so decided, and published his decision, within the period required by subsection (3).

(6) The Secretary of State may take such action under paragraph 9 or 11 of Schedule 7 as he considers to be reasonable and practicable to remedy, mitigate or prevent any of the effects adverse to the public interest which have resulted from, or may be expected to result from, the creation of the special merger situation concerned.

(7) In making a decision under subsection (6), the Secretary of State shall, in particular, have regard to the report of the [CMA] under section 65.

NOTES

References to the "CMA" substituted by the Enterprise and Regulatory Reform Act 2013, s 26(3), Sch 5, Pt 2, paras 59, 109.

For various transitional provisions (including those relating to the abolition of the OFT and the Competition Commission, existing references to those bodies and provisions relating to continuity), see the Enterprise and Regulatory Reform Act 2013 (Commencement No 6, Transitional Provisions and Savings) Order 2014, SI 2014/416, Schedule at **[2.13]**.

European mergers

[1.254]

67 Intervention to protect legitimate interests

(1) Subsection (2) applies where—

(a) the Secretary of State has reasonable grounds for suspecting that it is or may be the case that—

(i) a relevant merger situation has been created or that arrangements are in progress or in contemplation which, if carried into effect, will result in the creation of a relevant merger situation; and

(ii) a concentration with a Community dimension (within the meaning of the [EC Merger Regulation]), or a part of such a concentration, has thereby arisen or will thereby arise;

(b) a reference . . . is prevented from being made under [section 22 or 33] in relation to the relevant merger situation concerned [(whether or not there would otherwise have been a duty to make such a reference)] by virtue of Community law or anything done under or in accordance with it; and

(c) the Secretary of State is considering whether to take appropriate measures to protect legitimate interests as permitted by article [21(4) of the EC Merger Regulation].

(2) The Secretary of State may give a notice to the [CMA] (in this section "a European intervention notice") if he believes that it is or may be the case that one or more than one public interest consideration is relevant to a consideration of the relevant merger situation concerned.

(3) A European intervention notice shall state—

(a) the relevant merger situation concerned;

(b) the public interest consideration or considerations which are, or may be, relevant to a consideration of the relevant merger situation concerned; and

(c) where any public interest consideration concerned is not finalised, the proposed timetable for finalising it.

(4) Where the Secretary of State believes that it is or may be the case that two or more public interest considerations are relevant to a consideration of the relevant merger situation concerned, he may decide not to mention in the intervention notice such of those considerations as he considers appropriate.

(5) No more than one European intervention notice shall be given under subsection (2) in relation to the same relevant merger situation.

(6) Where the Secretary of State has given a European intervention notice mentioning a public interest consideration which, at that time, is not finalised, he shall, as soon as practicable, take such action as is within his power to ensure that it is finalised.

(7) For the purposes of deciding whether a relevant merger situation has been created or whether arrangements are in progress or in contemplation which, if carried into effect, will result in the creation of a relevant merger situation, sections 23 [to 30] (read together with section 34) shall apply for the purposes of this section as they do for the purposes of Chapter 1 but subject to subsection (8).

(8) In their application by virtue of subsection (7) sections 23 [to 30] shall have effect as if—

(a) references in those sections to the decision-making authority were references to the Secretary of State;

(b) for paragraphs (a) and (b) of section 23(9) there were substituted ", in relation to the giving of a European intervention notice, the time when the notice is given";

(c) the references to the [CMA] in section 24(2)(a) and (b) included references to the Secretary of State;

(d) [section 25] were omitted; and

(e) the references in sections 23 to 29 to the making of a reference or a reference were, so far as necessary, references to the giving of a European intervention notice or a European intervention notice.

(9) Section 42(3) shall, in its application to this section and section 68, have effect as if for the words "intervention notice" there were substituted "European intervention notice".

NOTES

This section, and the preceding heading, were repealed by the Competition (Amendment etc) (EU Exit) Regulations 2019, SI 2019/93, regs 32, 47, as from IP completion day (as defined in the European Union (Withdrawal Agreement) Act 2020, s 39) (for transitional provisions and savings in relation to the operation of the 2019 Regulations, see Sch 4 to those Regulations at **[7.69]** et seq and, in particular, Sch 4, Pt 7 to the 2019 Regulations at **[7.76]**).

Sub-s (1): words in square brackets in sub-paras (a)(ii), (c) substituted by the EC Merger Control (Consequential Amendments) Regulations 2004, SI 2004/1079, reg 2, Schedule, para 2(1), (20). Words omitted from para (b) repealed, words in first pair of square brackets in that paragraph substituted, and words in second pair of square brackets inserted, by the Communications Act 2003, ss 389(1), 406(7), Sch 16, para 16, Sch 19.

Sub-s (2): reference to the "CMA" substituted by the Enterprise and Regulatory Reform Act 2013, s 26(3), Sch 5, Pt 2, paras 59, 110. For various transitional provisions (including those relating to the abolition of the OFT and the Competition Commission, existing references to those bodies and provisions relating to continuity), see the Enterprise and Regulatory Reform Act 2013 (Commencement No 6, Transitional Provisions and Savings) Order 2014, SI 2014/416, Schedule at **[2.13]**.

Sub-s (7): words in square brackets substituted by the Enterprise and Regulatory Reform Act 2013, s 57, Sch 15, paras 15, 28(1), (2), subject to transitional provisions in SI 2014/416 as noted above.

Sub-s (8): words in first pair of square brackets substituted, reference to the "CMA" in para (c) substituted, and words in square brackets in para (d) substituted, by the Enterprise and Regulatory Reform Act 2013, ss 26(3), 57, Sch 5, Pt 2, paras 59, 110, Sch 15, paras 15, 28(1), (3), (4), subject to transitional provisions in SI 2014/416 as noted above.

References to the European Community and related expressions: see the note "References to "the European Community", "Community", etc" in the introductory notes to this Act.

[1.255]

68 Scheme for protecting legitimate interests

(1) The Secretary of State may by order provide for the taking of action, where a European intervention notice has been given, to remedy, mitigate or prevent effects adverse to the public interest which have resulted from, or may be expected to result from, the creation of a European relevant merger situation.

(2) In subsection (1) "European relevant merger situation" means a relevant merger situation—

(a) which has been created or will be created if arrangements which are in progress or in contemplation are carried into effect;

(b) by virtue of which a concentration with a Community dimension (within the meaning of the [EC Merger Regulation]), or a part of such a concentration, has arisen or will arise; and

(c) in relation to which a reference . . . was prevented from being made under [section 22 or 33 (whether or not there would otherwise have been a duty to make such a reference)] by virtue of Community law or anything done under or in accordance with it.

(3) Provision made under subsection (1) shall include provision ensuring that considerations which are not public interest considerations mentioned in the European intervention notice concerned may not be taken into account in determining whether anything operates, or may be expected to operate, against the public interest.

(4) Provision made under subsection (1) shall include provision—

(a) applying with modifications sections 23 [to 30] for the purposes of deciding for the purposes of this section whether a relevant merger situation has been created or whether arrangements are in progress or in contemplation which, if carried into effect, will result in the creation of a relevant merger situation;

(b) requiring the [CMA] to make a report to the Secretary of State before a reference is made;

(c) enabling the Secretary of State to make a reference [to the chair of the CMA for the constitution of a group under Schedule 4 to the Enterprise and Regulatory Reform Act 2013];

(d) requiring [the CMA, acting through a group so constituted,] to investigate and report to the Secretary of State on such a reference;

(e) enabling the taking of interim and final enforcement action.

(5) An order under this section may include provision (including provision for the creation of offences and penalties, the payment of fees and the delegation of functions) corresponding to any provision made in, or in connection with, this Part in relation to intervention notices or special intervention notices and the cases to which they relate.

(6) In this section "European intervention notice" has the same meaning as in section 67.

NOTES

This section was repealed by the Competition (Amendment etc) (EU Exit) Regulations 2019, SI 2019/93, regs 32, 47, as from IP completion day (as defined in the European Union (Withdrawal Agreement) Act 2020, s 39) (for transitional provisions and savings in relation to the operation of the 2019 Regulations, see Sch 4 to those Regulations at **[7.69]** et seq and, in particular, Sch 4, Pt 7 to the 2019 Regulations at **[7.76]**).

Sub-s (2): words in square brackets in para (b) substituted by the EC Merger Control (Consequential Amendments) Regulations 2004, SI 2004/1079, reg 2, Schedule, para 2(1), (21). Words omitted from para (c) repealed, and words in square brackets in that paragraph substituted, by the Communications Act 2003, s 389(1), 406(7), Sch 16, para 17, Sch 19.

Sub-s (4): words in square brackets substituted by the Enterprise and Regulatory Reform Act 2013, ss 26(3), 57, Sch 5, Pt 2, paras 59, 111, Sch 15, paras 15, 29. For various transitional provisions (including those relating to the abolition of the OFT and the Competition Commission, existing references to those bodies and provisions relating to continuity), see the Enterprise and Regulatory Reform Act 2013 (Commencement No 6, Transitional Provisions and Savings) Order 2014, SI 2014/416, Schedule at **[2.13]**.

References to the European Community and related expressions: see the note "References to "the European Community", "Community", etc" in the introductory notes to this Act.

Orders: the Enterprise Act 2002 (Protection of Legitimate Interests) Order 2003, SI 2003/1592 at **[2.103]**; the Enterprise Act 2002 (Protection of Legitimate Interests) (Amendment) Order 2014, SI 2014/891 at **[2.179]**. Note that this section was repealed by the Competition (Amendment etc) (EU Exit) Regulations 2019, SI 2019/93, regs 32, 47, as from IP completion day (as noted above). See, however, Sch 4, Pt 7, paras 25–27 to the 2019 Regulations (at **[7.76]**) which provides for the continued application of the 2003 Order in the circumstances specified in those paragraphs.

69, 70 *(S 69 (disapplication of this Part in relation to newspaper mergers) was repealed by the Communications Act 2003, ss 374, 406(7), Sch 19 (for transitional provisions and savings in relation to (a) a transfer of a newspaper or of newspaper assets which was made before 29 December 2003; or (b) a proposed transfer of a newspaper or of newspaper assets in relation to which an application for the consent of the Secretary of State under the Fair Trading Act 1973, s 58 was made before that date, see Sch 18, paras 59–62 to that Act); s 70 substitutes the Water Industry Act 1991, ss 32–35, and inserts Sch 4ZA to that Act (outside the scope of this work).)*

CHAPTER 4 ENFORCEMENT

Powers exercisable before references under section 22 or 33

71 *(Repealed by the Enterprise and Regulatory Reform Act 2013, s 30(1). For various transitional provisions (including those relating to the abolition of the OFT and the Competition Commission, existing references to those bodies and provisions relating to continuity), see the Enterprise and Regulatory Reform Act 2013 (Commencement No 6, Transitional Provisions and Savings) Order 2014, SI 2014/416, Schedule at* **[2.13]**.)

[1.256]

72 Initial enforcement orders: [completed or anticipated mergers]

[(1) Subsection (2) applies where—

(a) the CMA is considering whether to make a reference under section 22 or 33; and

(b) the CMA has reasonable grounds for suspecting that it is or may be the case that two or more enterprises have ceased to be distinct or that arrangements are in progress or in contemplation which, if carried into effect, will result in two or more enterprises ceasing to be distinct.]

(2) The [CMA] may by order, for the purpose of preventing pre-emptive action—

(a) prohibit or restrict the doing of things which the [CMA] considers would constitute pre-emptive action;

(b) impose on any person concerned obligations as to the carrying on of any activities or the safeguarding of any assets;

(c) provide for the carrying on of any activities or the safeguarding of any assets either by the appointment of a person to conduct or supervise the conduct of any activities (on such terms and with such powers as may be specified or described in the order) or in any other manner;

(d) do anything which may be done by virtue of paragraph 19 of Schedule 8.

(3) . . .

[(3A) Subsection (3B) applies where—

(a) subsection (1)(a) and (b) applies; and

(b) the CMA also has reasonable grounds for suspecting that pre-emptive action has or may have been taken.

(3B) The CMA may by order, for the purpose of restoring the position to what it would have been had the pre-emptive action not been taken or otherwise for the purpose of mitigating its effects—

(a) do anything mentioned in subsection (2)(b) to (d);

(b) impose such other obligations, prohibitions or restrictions as it considers appropriate for that purpose.]

[(3C) A person may, with the consent of the CMA, take action or action of a particular description where the action would otherwise constitute a contravention of an order under this section.]

(4) An order under this section—

(a) shall come into force at such time as is determined by or under the order; and

(b) may be varied or revoked by another order.

(5) . . .

(6) An order under this section shall, if it has not previously ceased to be in force and if it is not adopted under . . . paragraph 2 of Schedule 7, cease to be in force—

(a) where the [CMA] has decided to make the reference concerned under section 22 [or 33][—

(i) if the CMA accepts an undertaking under section 80 or makes an order under section 81, on the acceptance of the undertaking or the making of the order, and

(ii) otherwise on the final determination of the reference concerned;]

(b) where the [CMA] has decided to accept an undertaking under section 73 instead of making that reference, on the acceptance of that undertaking;

(c) where an intervention notice is in force, at the end of the period of 7 days beginning with the giving of that notice; and

(d) where the [CMA] has otherwise decided not to make the reference concerned under section 22 [or 33], on the making of that decision.

(7) The [CMA] shall, as soon as reasonably practicable, consider any representations received by it in relation to varying or revoking an order under this section.

[(8) In this section "pre-emptive action" means action which might prejudice the reference concerned or impede the taking of any action under this Part which may be justified by the CMA's decisions on the reference.]

NOTES

Section heading: words in square brackets substituted by the Enterprise and Regulatory Reform Act 2013, s 30(2), (9). For various transitional provisions (including those relating to the abolition of the OFT and the Competition Commission, existing references to those bodies and provisions relating to continuity), see the Enterprise and Regulatory Reform Act 2013 (Commencement No 6, Transitional Provisions and Savings) Order 2014, SI 2014/416, Schedule at **[2.13]**.

Sub-s (1): substituted by the Enterprise and Regulatory Reform Act 2013, s 30(2), (3), subject to transitional provisions in SI 2014/416 as noted above.

Sub-ss (2), (7): references to the "CMA" substituted by the Enterprise and Regulatory Reform Act 2013, s 26(3), Sch 5, Pt 2, paras 59, 112, subject to transitional provisions in SI 2014/416 as noted above.

Sub-s (3): repealed by the Enterprise and Regulatory Reform Act 2013, s 30(2), (4), subject to transitional provisions in SI 2014/416 as noted above.

Sub-ss (3A)–(3C): inserted by the Enterprise and Regulatory Reform Act 2013, s 30(2), (5), (6), subject to transitional provisions in SI 2014/416 as noted above.

Sub-s (5): repealed by the Enterprise and Regulatory Reform Act 2013, s 30(10), Sch 7, paras 1, 5(1), (2), subject to transitional provisions in SI 2014/416 as noted above.

Sub-s (6): words omitted repealed, references to the "CMA" in paras (a), (b), (d) substituted, words "or 33" in square brackets in paras (a), (d) inserted, and words in third pair of square brackets in para (a) substituted, by the Enterprise and Regulatory Reform Act 2013, ss 26(3), 30(2), (7), (10), Sch 5, Pt 2, paras 59, 112, Sch 7, paras 1, 5(1), (3), subject to transitional provisions in SI 2014/416 as noted above.

Sub-s (8): added by the Enterprise and Regulatory Reform Act 2013, s 30(2), (8), subject to transitional provisions in SI 2014/416 as noted above.

[1.257]

73 Undertakings in lieu of references under section 22 or 33

(1) Subsection (2) applies if the [CMA] considers that it is under a duty to make a reference under section 22 or 33 (disregarding the operation of section 22(3)(b) or (as the case may be) 33(3)(b) but taking account of the power of the [CMA] under section 22(2) or (as the case may be) 33(2) to decide not to make such a reference).

(2) The [CMA] may, instead of making such a reference and for the purpose of remedying, mitigating or preventing the substantial lessening of competition concerned or any adverse effect which has or may have resulted from it or may be expected to result from it, accept from such of the parties concerned as it considers appropriate undertakings to take such action as it considers appropriate.

(3) In proceeding under subsection (2), the [CMA] shall, in particular, have regard to the need to achieve as comprehensive a solution as is reasonable and practicable to the substantial lessening of competition and any adverse effects resulting from it.

(4) In proceeding under subsection (2), the [CMA] may, in particular, have regard to the effect of any action on any relevant customer benefits in relation to the creation of the relevant merger situation concerned.

(5) An undertaking under this section—

(a) shall come into force when accepted;

(b) may be varied or superseded by another undertaking; and

(c) may be released by the [CMA].

(6) An undertaking under this section which is in force in relation to a relevant merger situation shall cease to be in force if an order comes into force under section 75 or 76 in relation to that undertaking.

(7) The [CMA] shall, as soon as reasonably practicable, consider any representations received by it in relation to varying or releasing an undertaking under this section.

NOTES

References to the "CMA" substituted by the Enterprise and Regulatory Reform Act 2013, s 26(3), Sch 5, Pt 2, paras 59, 113. For various transitional provisions (including those relating to the abolition of the OFT and the Competition Commission, existing references to those bodies and provisions relating to continuity), see the Enterprise and Regulatory Reform Act 2013 (Commencement No 6, Transitional Provisions and Savings) Order 2014, SI 2014/416, Schedule at **[2.13]**.

[1.258]

[73A Time-limits for consideration of undertakings

(1) A party concerned who wishes to offer an undertaking to the CMA for the purposes of section 73(2) must do so before the end of the period of 5 working days beginning with—

(a) the day after the CMA gives the person the notice required by section 34ZA(1)(b); *or*

(b) in a case where subsection (2) of section 34A applies, the day after the CMA gives the person the notice required by paragraph (b) of that subsection.

(2) If an undertaking is offered for those purposes, the CMA shall, before the end of the period of 10 working days beginning with the day mentioned in subsection (1)—

(a) decide whether there are reasonable grounds for believing that the undertaking or a modified version of it might be accepted by the CMA under section 73(2), and

(b) if it considers that it might be, give notice to the person who offered the undertaking that it is considering it.

(3) If such a notice is given, the CMA shall decide whether to accept the undertaking before the end of the period of 50 working days beginning with the day mentioned in subsection (1).

(4) The CMA may extend the period mentioned in subsection (3), by no more than 40 working days, if it considers that there are special reasons for doing so.

(5) The CMA shall prepare and publish guidance in relation to the exercise of its power under subsection (4).

(6) The CMA may revise any such guidance and, where it does so, shall publish the revised statement.

(7) The CMA may extend the period mentioned in subsection (3) if it considers that a relevant person has failed (with or without reasonable excuse) to comply with any requirement of a notice given under section 109 in relation to the case in question.

(8) In subsection (7), "relevant person" means—

(a) any person carrying on any of the enterprises concerned;

(b) any person who (whether alone or as a member of a group) owns or has control of any such person; or

(c) any officer, employee or agent of any person mentioned in paragraph (a) or (b).

(9) For the purposes of subsection (8), a person or group of persons able, directly or indirectly, to control or materially influence the policy of a body of persons corporate or unincorporate, but without having a controlling interest in that body of persons, may be treated as having control of it.

(10) An extension under subsection (4) or (7) comes into force when published under section 107.

(11) An extension under subsection (7) continues in force until—

(a) the person concerned provides the information or documents to the satisfaction of the CMA or (as the case may be) appears as a witness in accordance with the requirements of the CMA; or

(b) the CMA publishes its decision to cancel the extension.

(12) In this section and section 73B, "working day" means any day which is not—

(a) a Saturday, a Sunday, Good Friday or Christmas Day, or

(b) a day which is a bank holiday in England and Wales.]

NOTES

Inserted by the Enterprise and Regulatory Reform Act 2013, s 32(2), s 32(2), Sch 8, paras 1, 7. For various transitional provisions (including those relating to the abolition of the OFT and the Competition Commission, existing references to those bodies and provisions relating to continuity), see the Enterprise and Regulatory Reform Act 2013 (Commencement No 6, Transitional Provisions and Savings) Order 2014, SI 2014/416, Schedule at **[2.13]**.

Sub-s (1): para (b) and the preceding word were repealed by the Competition (Amendment etc) (EU Exit) Regulations 2019, SI 2019/93, regs 32, 48, as from IP completion day (as defined in the European Union (Withdrawal Agreement) Act 2020, s 39) (for transitional provisions and savings in relation to the operation of the 2019 Regulations, see Sch 4 to those Regulations at **[7.69]** et seq and, in particular, Sch 4, Pt 7 to the 2019 Regulations at **[7.76]**).

[1.259]

[73B Section 73A: supplementary

(1) A period extended under section 73A(4) may also be extended under section 73A(7), and a period extended under section 73A(7) may also be extended under section 73A(4).

(2) No more than one extension is possible under section 73A(4).

(3) Where a period is extended or further extended under section 73A(4) or (7), the period as extended or (as the case may be) further extended is, subject to subsections (4) and (5), to be calculated by taking the period being extended and adding to it the period of the extension (whether or not those periods overlap in time).

(4) Subsection (5) applies where—

(a) the period within which the CMA must discharge its duty under section 73A(3) is further extended,

(b) the further extension and at least one previous extension is made under section 73A(7), and

(c) the same days or fractions of days are included in or comprise the further extension and are included in or comprise at least one such previous extension.

(5) In calculating the period of the further extension, any days or fractions of days of the kind mentioned in subsection (4)(c) are to be disregarded.

(6) The Secretary of State may by order amend section 73A so as to alter one or more of the periods for the time being mentioned in the section.

(7) But no alteration may be made by virtue of subsection (6) which results in—

(a) the period mentioned in section 73A(1) exceeding 5 working days;

(b) the period mentioned in section 73A(2) exceeding 10 working days;

(c) the period mentioned in section 73A(3) exceeding 50 working days;

(d) the period mentioned in section 73A(4) exceeding 40 working days.

(8) Before making an order under subsection (6) the Secretary of State shall consult the CMA and such other persons as the Secretary of State considers appropriate.]

NOTES

Inserted by the Enterprise and Regulatory Reform Act 2013, s 32(2), s 32(2), Sch 8, paras 1, 7. For various transitional provisions (including those relating to the abolition of the OFT and the Competition Commission, existing references to those bodies and provisions relating to continuity), see the Enterprise and Regulatory Reform Act 2013 (Commencement No 6, Transitional Provisions and Savings) Order 2014, SI 2014/416, Schedule at **[2.13]**.

[1.260]

74 Effect of undertakings under section 73

(1) The relevant authority shall not make a reference under section 22, 33 or 45 in relation to the creation of a relevant merger situation if—

(a) the [CMA] has accepted an undertaking or group of undertakings under section 73; and

(b) the relevant merger situation is the situation by reference to which the undertaking or group of undertakings was accepted.

(2) Subsection (1) does not prevent the making of a reference if material facts about relevant arrangements or transactions, or relevant proposed arrangements or transactions, were not notified (whether in writing or otherwise) to the [CMA] or made public before any undertaking concerned was accepted.

(3) For the purposes of subsection (2) arrangements or transactions, or proposed arrangements or transactions, are relevant if they are the ones in consequence of which the enterprises concerned ceased or may have ceased, or may cease, to be distinct enterprises.

(4) In subsection (2) "made public" means so publicised as to be generally known or readily ascertainable.

(5) In this section "relevant authority" means—

(a) in relation to a possible reference under section 22 or 33, the [CMA]; and

(b) in relation to a possible reference under section 45, the Secretary of State.

NOTES

References to the "CMA" substituted by the Enterprise and Regulatory Reform Act 2013, s 26(3), Sch 5, Pt 2, paras 59, 114. For various transitional provisions (including those relating to the abolition of the OFT and the Competition Commission, existing references to those bodies and provisions relating to continuity), see the Enterprise and Regulatory Reform Act 2013 (Commencement No 6, Transitional Provisions and Savings) Order 2014, SI 2014/416, Schedule at **[2.13]**.

[1.261]

75 Order-making power where undertakings under section 73 not fulfilled etc

(1) Subsection (2) applies where the [CMA] considers that—

(a) an undertaking accepted by it under section 73 has not been, is not being or will not be fulfilled; or

(b) in relation to an undertaking accepted by it under that section, information which was false or misleading in a material respect was given to the [CMA] by the person giving the undertaking before the [CMA] decided to accept the undertaking.

(2) The [CMA] may, for any of the purposes mentioned in section 73(2), make an order under this section.

(3) Subsections (3) and (4) of section 73 shall apply for the purposes of subsection (2) above as they apply for the purposes of subsection (2) of that section.

(4) An order under this section may contain—

(a) anything permitted by Schedule 8; and

(b) such supplementary, consequential or incidental provision as the [CMA] considers appropriate.

(5) An order under this section—

(a) shall come into force at such time as is determined by or under the order;

(b) may contain provision which is different from the provision contained in the undertaking concerned; and

(c) may be varied or revoked by another order.

(6) The [CMA] shall, as soon as reasonably practicable, consider any representations received by it in relation to varying or revoking an order under this section.

NOTES

References to the "CMA" substituted by the Enterprise and Regulatory Reform Act 2013, s 26(3), Sch 5, Pt 2, paras 59, 115. For various transitional provisions (including those relating to the abolition of the OFT and the Competition Commission, existing references to those bodies and provisions relating to continuity), see the Enterprise and Regulatory Reform Act 2013 (Commencement No 6, Transitional Provisions and Savings) Order 2014, SI 2014/416, Schedule at **[2.13]**.

Revocation or modification of licence conditions, etc under certain sectoral enactments: an order under this section may also provide for the revocation or modification of licence conditions, etc, for certain regulated industries; see: (a) the Gas Act 1986, s 27(1); (b) the Electricity Act 1989, s 15(1); (c) the Broadcasting Act 1990(1), s 193; (d) the Water Industry Act 1991, s 17(1); (e) the Railways Act 1993, s 16(1); (f) the Transport Act 2000, s 19(1).

[1.262]

76 Supplementary interim order-making power

(1) Subsection (2) applies where—

(a) the [CMA] has the power to make an order under section 75 in relation to a particular undertaking and intends to make such an order; or

(b) the [CMA] has the power to make an order under section 83 in relation to a particular undertaking and intends to make such an order.

(2) The [CMA], for the purpose of preventing any action which might prejudice the making of that order, make an order under this section.

(3) No order shall be made under subsection (2) unless the [CMA] has reasonable grounds for suspecting that it is or may be the case that action which might prejudice the making of the order under section 75 or (as the case may be) 83 is in progress or in contemplation.

(4) An order under subsection (2) may—

(a) prohibit or restrict the doing of things which the [CMA] considers would prejudice the making of the order under section 75 or (as the case may be) 83;

(b) impose on any person concerned obligations as to the carrying on of any activities or the safeguarding of any assets;

(c) provide for the carrying on of any activities or the safeguarding of any assets either by the appointment of a person to conduct or supervise the conduct of any activities (on such terms and with such powers as may be specified or described in the order) or in any other manner;

(d) do anything which may be done by virtue of paragraph 19 of Schedule 8.

(5) An order under this section—

(a) shall come into force at such time as is determined by or under the order; and

(b) may be varied or revoked by another order.

(6) An order under this section shall, if it has not previously ceased to be in force, cease to be in force on—

(a) the coming into force of an order under section 75 or (as the case may be) 83 in relation to the undertaking concerned; or

(b) the making of the decision not to proceed with such an order.

(7) The [CMA] shall, as soon as reasonably practicable, consider any representations received by it in relation to varying or revoking an order under this section.

NOTES

References to the "CMA" substituted by the Enterprise and Regulatory Reform Act 2013, s 26(3), Sch 5, Pt 2, paras 59, 116. For various transitional provisions (including those relating to the abolition of the OFT and the Competition Commission, existing references to those bodies and provisions relating to continuity), see the Enterprise and Regulatory Reform Act 2013 (Commencement No 6, Transitional Provisions and Savings) Order 2014, SI 2014/416, Schedule at **[2.13]**.

Interim restrictions and powers

[1.263]

77 Restrictions on certain dealings: completed mergers

(1) Subsections (2) and (3) apply where—

(a) a reference has been made under section 22 but not finally determined; and

(b) no undertakings under section . . . 80 are in force in relation to the relevant merger situation concerned and no orders under section 72 or 81 are in force in relation to that situation.

(2) No relevant person shall, without the consent of the [CMA]—

(a) complete any outstanding matters in connection with any arrangements which have resulted in the enterprises concerned ceasing to be distinct enterprises;

(b) make any further arrangements in consequence of that result (other than arrangements which reverse that result); or

(c) transfer the ownership or control of any enterprises to which the reference relates.

(3) No relevant person shall, without the consent of the [CMA], assist in any of the activities mentioned in paragraphs (a) to (c) of subsection (2).

(4) The prohibitions in subsections (2) and (3) do not apply in relation to anything which the person concerned is required to do by virtue of any enactment.

(5) The consent of the [CMA] under subsection (2) or (3)—

(a) may be general or special;

(b) may be revoked by the [CMA]; and

(c) shall be published in such manner as the [CMA] considers appropriate for the purpose of bringing it to the attention of any person entitled to the benefit of it.

(6) Paragraph (c) of subsection (5) shall not apply if the [CMA] considers that publication is not necessary for the purpose mentioned in that paragraph.

(7) Subsections (2) and (3) shall apply to a person's conduct outside the United Kingdom if (and only if) he is—

(a) a United Kingdom national;

(b) a body incorporated under the law of the United Kingdom or of any part of the United Kingdom; or

(c) a person carrying on business in the United Kingdom.

(8) In this section "relevant person" means—

(a) any person who carries on any enterprise to which the reference relates or who has control of any such enterprise;

(b) any subsidiary of any person falling within paragraph (a); or

(c) any person associated with any person falling within paragraph (a) or any subsidiary of any person so associated.

NOTES

Words omitted from sub-s (1)(b) repealed, and references to the "CMA" substituted, by the Enterprise and Regulatory Reform Act 2013, ss 26(3), 57, Sch 5, Pt 2, paras 59, 117, Sch 15, paras 15, 30. For various transitional provisions (including those relating to the abolition of the OFT and the Competition Commission, existing references to those bodies and provisions relating to continuity), see the Enterprise and Regulatory Reform Act 2013 (Commencement No 6, Transitional Provisions and Savings) Order 2014, SI 2014/416, Schedule at **[2.13]**.

[1.264]

78 Restrictions on certain share dealings: anticipated mergers

(1) Subsection (2) applies where—

(a) a reference has been made under section 33; and

(b) no undertakings under section 80 are in force in relation to the relevant merger situation concerned and no orders under [section 72 or 81] are in force in relation to that situation.

(2) No relevant person shall, without the consent of the [CMA], directly or indirectly acquire during the relevant period an interest in shares in a company if any enterprise to which the reference relates is carried on by or under the control of that company.

(3) The consent of the [CMA] under subsection (2)—

(a) may be general or special;

(b) may be revoked by the [CMA]; and

(c) shall be published in such manner as the [CMA] considers appropriate for bringing it to the attention of any person entitled to the benefit of it.

(4) Paragraph (c) of subsection (3) shall not apply if the [CMA] considers that publication is not necessary for the purpose mentioned in that paragraph.

(5) Subsection (2) shall apply to a person's conduct outside the United Kingdom if (and only if) he is—

(a) a United Kingdom national;

(b) a body incorporated under the law of the United Kingdom or of any part of the United Kingdom; or

(c) a person carrying on business in the United Kingdom.

(6) In this section and section 79—

"company" includes any body corporate;

"relevant period" means the period beginning with the making of the reference concerned and ending when the reference is finally determined;

"relevant person" means—

(a) any person who carries on any enterprise to which the reference relates or who has control of any such enterprise;

(b) any subsidiary of any person falling within paragraph (a); or

(c) any person associated with any person falling within paragraph (a) or any subsidiary of any person so associated; and

"share" means share in the capital of a company, and includes stock.

NOTES

Sub-s (1): words in square brackets in para (b) substituted by the Enterprise and Regulatory Reform Act 2013, s 57, Sch 15, paras 15, 31. For various transitional provisions (including those relating to the abolition of the OFT and the Competition Commission, existing references to those bodies and provisions relating to continuity), see the Enterprise and Regulatory Reform Act 2013 (Commencement No 6, Transitional Provisions and Savings) Order 2014, SI 2014/416, Schedule at **[2.13]**.

Sub-ss (2)–(4): references to the "CMA" substituted by the Enterprise and Regulatory Reform Act 2013, s 26(3), Sch 5, Pt 2, paras 59, 118, subject to transitional provisions in SI 2014/416 as noted above.

[1.265]

79 Sections 77 and 78: further interpretation provisions

(1) For the purposes of this Part a reference under section 22 or 33 is finally determined if—

(a) the reference is cancelled under section 37(1);

(b) the time within which the [CMA] is to prepare and publish a report under section 38 in relation to the reference has expired and no such report has been prepared and published;

(c) the report of the [CMA] under section 38 contains the decision that there is not an anti-competitive outcome;

(d) the report of the [CMA] under section 38 contains the decision that there is an anti-competitive outcome and the [CMA] has decided under section 41(2) neither to accept an undertaking under section 82 nor to make an order under section 84; or

(e) the report of the [CMA] under section 38 contains the decision that there is an anti-competitive outcome and the [CMA] has decided under section 41(2) to accept an undertaking under section 82 or to make an order under section 84.

(2) For the purposes of this Part the time when a reference under section 22 or 33 is finally determined is—

(a) in a case falling within subsection (1)(a), the making of the decision concerned;

(b) in a case falling within subsection (1)(b), the expiry of the time concerned;

(c) in a case falling within subsection (1)(c), the publication of the report;

(d) in a case falling within subsection (1)(d), the making of the decision under section 41(2); and

(e) in a case falling within subsection (1)(e), the acceptance of the undertaking concerned or (as the case may be) the making of the order concerned.

(3) For the purposes of section 78 and subject to subsection (4) below, the circumstances in which a person acquires an interest in shares include those where—

(a) he enters into a contract to acquire the shares (whether or not for cash);

(b) he is not the registered holder but acquires the right to exercise, or to control the exercise of, any right conferred by the holding of the shares; or

(c) he—

(i) acquires a right to call for delivery of the shares to himself or to his order or to acquire an interest in the shares; or

(ii) assumes an obligation to acquire such an interest.

(4) The circumstances in which a person acquires an interest in shares for the purposes of section 78 do not include those where he acquires an interest in pursuance of an obligation assumed before the publication by the [CMA] of the reference concerned.

(5) The circumstances in which a person acquires a right mentioned in subsection (3)—

(a) include those where he acquires a right, or assumes an obligation, whose exercise or fulfilment would give him that right; but

(b) do not include those where he is appointed as proxy to vote at a specified meeting of a company or of any class of its members or at any adjournment of the meeting or he is appointed by a corporation to act as its representative at any meeting of the company or of any class of its members.

(6) References to rights and obligations in subsections (3) to (5) include conditional rights and conditional obligations.

(7) References in sections 77 and 78 to a person carrying on or having control of any enterprise includes a group of persons carrying on or having control of an enterprise and any member of such a group.

(8) Sections 26(2) to (4) and 127(1), (2) and (4) to (6) shall apply for the purposes of sections 77 and 78 to determine whether any person or group of persons has control of any enterprise and whether persons are associated as they apply for the purposes of section 26 to determine whether enterprises are brought under common control.

(9) [Section 1159 of, and Schedule 6 to, the Companies Act 2006] shall apply for the purposes of sections 77 and 78 to determine whether a company is a subsidiary of an individual or of a group of persons as they apply to determine whether it is a subsidiary of a company; and references to a subsidiary in [paragraph 8 of Schedule 6] as so applied shall be construed accordingly.

NOTES

Sub-ss (1), (4): references to "CMA" substituted by the Enterprise and Regulatory Reform Act 2013, s 26(3), Sch 5, Pt 2, paras 59, 119. For various transitional provisions (including those relating to the abolition of the OFT and the Competition Commission, existing references to those bodies and provisions relating to continuity), see the Enterprise and Regulatory Reform Act 2013 (Commencement No 6, Transitional Provisions and Savings) Order 2014, SI 2014/416, Schedule at **[2.13]**.

Sub-s (9): words in square brackets substituted by the Companies Act 2006 (Consequential Amendments, Transitional Provisions and Savings) Order 2009, SI 2009/1941, art 2(1), Sch 1, para 199(1), (2).

[1.266]

80 Interim undertakings

(1) [Subsections (2) and (2A)]) apply where a reference under section 22 or 33 has been made but is not finally determined.

(2) The [CMA] may, for the purpose of preventing pre-emptive action, accept from such of the parties concerned as it considers appropriate undertakings to take such action as it considers appropriate.

[(2A) Where the CMA has reasonable grounds for suspecting that pre-emptive action has or may have been taken, it may, for the purpose of restoring the position to what it would have been had the action not been taken or otherwise for the purpose of mitigating its effects, accept from such of the parties concerned as it considers appropriate undertakings to take such action as it considers appropriate.]

[(2B) A person may, with the consent of the CMA, take action or action of a particular description where the action would otherwise constitute a contravention of an undertaking under this section.]

(3), (4) . . .

(5) [An undertaking] under this section—

(a) shall come into force when accepted;

(b) may be varied or superseded by another undertaking; and

(c) may be released by the [CMA].

(6) . . .

(7) An undertaking which is in force under this section in relation to a reference under section 22 or 33 shall cease to be in force if an order under section 81 comes into force in relation to that reference.

(8) An undertaking under this section shall, if it has not previously ceased to be in force, cease to be in force when the reference under section 22 or 33 is finally determined.

(9) The [CMA] shall, as soon as reasonably practicable, consider any representations received by it in relation to varying or releasing an undertaking under this section.

(10) In this section and section 81 "pre-emptive action" means action which might prejudice the reference concerned or impede the taking of any action under this Part which may be justified by the [CMA's] decisions on the reference.

NOTES

References to the "CMA" and the "CMA's" substituted by the Enterprise and Regulatory Reform Act 2013, s 26(3), Sch 5, Pt 2, paras 59, 120. For various transitional provisions (including those relating to the abolition of the OFT and the Competition Commission, existing references to those bodies and provisions relating to continuity), see the Enterprise and Regulatory Reform Act 2013 (Commencement No 6, Transitional Provisions and Savings) Order 2014, SI 2014/416, Schedule at **[2.13]**. This section is also amended as follows:

Sub-s (1): words in square brackets substituted by the Enterprise and Regulatory Reform Act 2013, s 30(10), Sch 7, paras 1, 2(1), (2), subject to transitional provisions in SI 2014/416 as noted above.

Sub-ss (2A), (2B): inserted by the Enterprise and Regulatory Reform Act 2013, s 30(10), Sch 7, paras 1, 2(1), (3), (4), subject to transitional provisions in SI 2014/416 as noted above.

Sub-ss (3), (4), (6): repealed by the Enterprise and Regulatory Reform Act 2013, s 30(10), Sch 7, paras 1, 2(1), (5), (7), subject to transitional provisions in SI 2014/416 as noted above.

Sub-s (5): words in first pair of square brackets substituted by the Enterprise and Regulatory Reform Act 2013, s 30(10), Sch 7, paras 1, 2(1), (6), subject to transitional provisions in SI 2014/416 as noted above.

[1.267]

81 Interim orders

(1) [Subsections (2) and (2A)] apply where a reference has been made under section 22 or 33 but is not finally determined.

(2) The [CMA] may by order, for the purpose of preventing pre-emptive action—

(a) prohibit or restrict the doing of things which the [CMA] considers would constitute pre-emptive action;

(b) impose on any person concerned obligations as to the carrying on of any activities or the safeguarding of any assets;

(c) provide for the carrying on of any activities or the safeguarding of any assets either by the appointment of a person to conduct or supervise the conduct of any activities (on such terms and with such powers as may be specified or described in the order) or in any other manner;

(d) do anything which may be done by virtue of paragraph 19 of Schedule 8.

[(2A) Where the CMA has reasonable grounds for suspecting that pre-emptive action has or may have been taken, it may by order, for the purpose of restoring the position to what it would have been had the action not been taken or otherwise for the purpose of mitigating its effects—

(a) do anything mentioned in subsection (2)(b) to (d);

(b) impose such other obligations, prohibitions or restrictions as it considers appropriate for that purpose.]

[(2B) A person may, with the consent of the CMA, take action or action of a particular description where the action would otherwise constitute a contravention of an order under this section.]

(3), (4) . . .

(5) [An order] under this section—

(a) shall come into force at such time as is determined by or under the order; and

(b) may be varied or revoked by another order.

(6) . . .

(7) An order which is in force under this section in relation to a reference under section 22 or 33 shall cease to be in force if an undertaking under section 80 comes into force in relation to that reference.

(8) An order under this section shall, if it has not previously ceased to be in force, cease to be in force when the reference under section 22 or 33 is finally determined.

(9) The [CMA] shall, as soon as reasonably practicable, consider any representations received by it in relation to varying or revoking an order under this section.

NOTES

Sub-ss (1), (5): words in square brackets substituted by the Enterprise and Regulatory Reform Act 2013, s 30(10), Sch 7, paras 1, 3(1), (2), (6). For various transitional provisions (including those relating to the abolition of the OFT and the Competition Commission, existing references to those bodies and provisions relating to continuity), see the Enterprise and Regulatory Reform Act 2013 (Commencement No 6, Transitional Provisions and Savings) Order 2014, SI 2014/416, Schedule at **[2.13]**.

Sub-ss (2), (9): references to "CMA" substituted by the Enterprise and Regulatory Reform Act 2013, s 26(3), Sch 5, Pt 2, paras 59, 121, subject to transitional provisions in SI 2014/416 as noted above.

Sub-ss (2A), (2B): inserted by the Enterprise and Regulatory Reform Act 2013, s 30(10), Sch 7, paras 1, 3(1), (3), (4), subject to transitional provisions in SI 2014/416 as noted above.

Sub-ss (3), (4), (6): repealed by the Enterprise and Regulatory Reform Act 2013, s 30(10), Sch 7, paras 1, 3(1), (5), (7), subject to transitional provisions in SI 2014/416 as noted above.

Final powers

[1.268]

82 Final undertakings

(1) The [CMA] may, in accordance with section 41, accept, from such persons as it considers appropriate, undertakings to take action specified or described in the undertakings.

(2) An undertaking under this section—

(a) shall come into force when accepted;

(b) may be varied or superseded by another undertaking; and

(c) may be released by the [CMA].

(3) An undertaking which is in force under this section in relation to a reference under section 22 or 33 shall cease to be in force if an order under section 76(1)(b) or 83 comes into force in relation to the subject-matter of the undertaking.

(4) No undertaking shall be accepted under this section in relation to a reference under section 22 or 33 if an order has been made under—

(a) section 76(1)(b) or 83 in relation to the subject-matter of the undertaking; or

(b) section 84 in relation to that reference.

(5) The [CMA] shall, as soon as reasonably practicable, consider any representations received by it in relation to varying or releasing an undertaking under this section.

NOTES

References to the "CMA" substituted by the Enterprise and Regulatory Reform Act 2013, s 26(3), Sch 5, Pt 2, paras 59, 122. For various transitional provisions (including those relating to the abolition of the OFT and the Competition Commission, existing references to those bodies and provisions relating to continuity), see the Enterprise and Regulatory Reform Act 2013 (Commencement No 6, Transitional Provisions and Savings) Order 2014, SI 2014/416, Schedule at **[2.13]**.

[1.269]

83 Order-making power where final undertakings not fulfilled

(1) Subsection (2) applies where the [CMA] considers that—

(a) an undertaking accepted by it under section 82 has not been, is not being or will not be fulfilled; or

(b) in relation to an undertaking accepted by it under that section, information which was false or misleading in a material respect was given to the [CMA] by the person giving the undertaking before the [CMA decided] to accept the undertaking.

(2) The [CMA] may, for any of the purposes mentioned in section 41(2), make an order under this section.

(3) Subsections (3) to (5) of section 41 shall apply for the purposes of subsection (2) above as they apply for the purposes of subsection (2) of that section.

(4) An order under this section may contain—

(a) anything permitted by Schedule 8; and

(b) such supplementary, consequential or incidental provision as the [CMA] considers appropriate.

(5) An order under this section—

(a) shall come into force at such time as is determined by or under the order;

(b) may contain provision which is different from the provision contained in the undertaking concerned; and

(c) may be varied or revoked by another order.

(6) . . .

NOTES

Sub-s (1): words in square brackets substituted by the Enterprise and Regulatory Reform Act 2013, s 26(3), Sch 5, Pt 2, paras 59, 123(1)–(3). For various transitional provisions (including those relating to the abolition of the OFT and the Competition Commission, existing references to those bodies and provisions relating to continuity), see the Enterprise and Regulatory Reform Act 2013 (Commencement No 6, Transitional Provisions and Savings) Order 2014, SI 2014/416, Schedule at **[2.13]**.

Sub-ss (2), (4): references to the "CMA" substituted by the Enterprise and Regulatory Reform Act 2013, s 26(3), Sch 5, Pt 2, paras 59, 123(1), (4), subject to transitional provisions in SI 2014/416 as noted above.

Sub-s (6): repealed by the Enterprise and Regulatory Reform Act 2013, s 26(3), Sch 5, Pt 2, paras 59, 123(1), (5), subject to transitional provisions in SI 2014/416 as noted above.

Revocation or modification of licence conditions, etc under certain sectoral enactments: an order under this section may also provide for the revocation or modification of licence conditions, etc, for certain regulated industries; see: (a) the Gas Act 1986, s 27(1); (b) the Electricity Act 1989, s 15(1); (c) the Broadcasting Act 1990(1), s 193; (d) the Water Industry Act 1991, s 17(1); (e) the Railways Act 1993, s 16(1); (f) the Transport Act 2000, s 19(1).

[1.270]

84 Final orders

(1) The [CMA] may, in accordance with section 41, make an order under this section.

(2) An order under this section may contain—

(a) anything permitted by Schedule 8; and

(b) such supplementary, consequential or incidental provision as the [CMA] considers appropriate.

(3) An order under this section—

(a) shall come into force at such time as is determined by or under the order; and

(b) may be varied or revoked by another order.

(4) . . .

(5) No order shall be made under this section in relation to a reference under section 22 or 33 if an undertaking has been accepted under section 82 in relation to that reference.

NOTES

Sub-ss (1), (2): references to the "CMA" substituted by the Enterprise and Regulatory Reform Act 2013, s 26(3), Sch 5, Pt 2, paras 59, 124(1), (2). For various transitional provisions (including those relating to the abolition of the OFT and the Competition Commission, existing references to those bodies and provisions relating to continuity), see the Enterprise and Regulatory Reform Act 2013 (Commencement No 6, Transitional Provisions and Savings) Order 2014, SI 2014/416, Schedule at **[2.13]**.

Sub-s (4): repealed by the Enterprise and Regulatory Reform Act 2013, s 26(3), Sch 5, Pt 2, paras 59, 124(1), (3), subject to transitional provisions in SI 2014/416 as noted above.

Revocation or modification of licence conditions, etc under certain sectoral enactments: an order under this section may also provide for the revocation or modification of licence conditions, etc, for certain regulated industries; see: (a) the Gas Act 1986, s 27(1); (b) the Electricity Act 1989, s 15(1); (c) the Broadcasting Act 1990(1), s 193; (d) the Water Industry Act 1991, s 17(1); (e) the Railways Act 1993, s 16(1); (f) the Transport Act 2000, s 19(1).

Public interest and special public interest cases

[1.271]

85 Enforcement regime for public interest and special public interest cases

(1) Schedule 7 (which provides for the enforcement regime in public interest and special public interest cases) shall have effect.

(2) The [CMA] may advise the Secretary of State in relation to the taking by him of enforcement action under Schedule 7.

NOTES

Sub-s (2): reference to the "CMA" substituted by the Enterprise and Regulatory Reform Act 2013, s 26(3), Sch 5, Pt 2, paras 59, 125. For various transitional provisions (including those relating to the abolition of the OFT and the Competition Commission, existing references to those bodies and provisions relating to continuity), see the Enterprise and Regulatory Reform Act 2013 (Commencement No 6, Transitional Provisions and Savings) Order 2014, SI 2014/416, Schedule at **[2.13]**.

Undertakings and orders: general provisions

[1.272]

86 Enforcement orders: general provisions

(1) An enforcement order may extend to a person's conduct outside the United Kingdom if (and only if) he is—
- (a) a United Kingdom national;
- (b) a body incorporated under the law of the United Kingdom or of any part of the United Kingdom; or
- (c) a person carrying on business in the United Kingdom.

(2) Nothing in an enforcement order shall have effect so as to—
- (a) cancel or modify conditions in licences granted—
  - (i) under a patent granted under the Patents Act 1977 (c 37) or a European patent (UK) (within the meaning of the Act of 1977); or
  - (ii) in respect of a design registered under the Registered Designs Act 1949 (c 88);

  by the proprietor of the patent or design; or
- (b) require an entry to be made in the register of patents or the register of designs to the effect that licences under such a patent or such a design are to be available as of right.

(3) An enforcement order may prohibit the performance of an agreement already in existence when the order is made.

(4) Schedule 8 (which provides for the contents of certain enforcement orders) shall have effect.

(5) Part 1 of Schedule 9 (which enables certain enforcement orders to modify licence conditions etc in regulated markets) shall have effect.

(6) In this Part "enforcement order" means an order made under section 72, 75, 76, 81, 83 or 84 or under paragraph 2, 5, 6, 10 or 11 of Schedule 7.

NOTES

Orders: the Public Interest Merger Reference (Mettis Aerospace Ltd) (Pre-emptive Action) Order 2019, SI 2019/1515; the Public Interest Merger Reference (Cobham Ultra Acquisitions Ltd and Ultra Electronics Holdings plc) (Pre-emptive Action) Order 2021, SI 2021/944; the Public Interest Merger Reference (Perpetuus Advanced Materials plc) (Pre-emptive Action) Order 2021, SI 2021/993.

[1.273]

87 Delegated power of directions

(1) An enforcement order may authorise the person making the order to give directions falling within subsection (2) to—
- (a) a person specified in the directions; or
- (b) the holder for the time being of an office so specified in any body of persons corporate or unincorporate.

(2) Directions fall within this subsection if they are directions—
- (a) to take such action as may be specified or described in the directions for the purpose of carrying out, or ensuring compliance with, the enforcement order concerned; or
- (b) to do, or refrain from doing, anything so specified or described which the person might be required by that order to do or refrain from doing.

(3) An enforcement order may authorise the person making the order to vary or revoke any directions so given.

(4) The court may by order require any person who has failed to comply with directions given by virtue of this section to comply with them, or otherwise remedy his failure, within such time as may be specified in the order.

(5) Where the directions related to anything done in the management or administration of a body of persons corporate or unincorporate, the court may by order require the body of persons concerned or any officer of it to comply with the directions, or otherwise remedy the failure to comply with them, within such time as may be specified in the order.
(6) An order under subsection (4) or (5) shall be made on the application of the person authorised by virtue of this section to give the directions concerned.
(7) An order under subsection (4) or (5) may provide for all the costs or expenses of, or incidental to, the application for the order to be met by any person in default or by any officers of a body of persons corporate or unincorporate who are responsible for its default.
(8) In this section "the court" means—
(a) in relation to England and Wales or Northern Ireland, the High Court; and
(b) in relation to Scotland, the Court of Session.

NOTES

Orders: the Public Interest Merger Reference (Mettis Aerospace Ltd) (Pre-emptive Action) Order 2019, SI 2019/1515; the Public Interest Merger Reference (Cobham Ultra Acquisitions Ltd and Ultra Electronics Holdings plc) (Pre-emptive Action) Order 2021, SI 2021/944; the Public Interest Merger Reference (Perpetuus Advanced Materials plc) (Pre-emptive Action) Order 2021, SI 2021/993.

[1.274]
88 Contents of certain enforcement orders
(1) This section applies in relation to any order under section 75, 83 or 84 or under paragraph 5, 10 or 11 of Schedule 7.
(2) The order or any explanatory material accompanying the order shall state—
(a) the actions that the persons or description of persons to whom the order is addressed must do or (as the case may be) refrain from doing;
(b) the date on which the order comes into force;
(c) the possible consequences of not complying with the order; and
(d) the section of this Part under which a review can be sought in relation to the order.

[1.275]
89 Subject-matter of undertakings
(1) The provision which may be contained in an enforcement undertaking is not limited to the provision which is permitted by Schedule 8.
(2) In this Part "enforcement undertaking" means an undertaking under section . . . 73, 80 or 82 or under paragraph . . . 3 or 9 of Schedule 7.

NOTES

Sub-s (2): figures omitted repealed by the Enterprise and Regulatory Reform Act 2013, s 57, Sch 15, paras 15, 32. For various transitional provisions (including those relating to the abolition of the OFT and the Competition Commission, existing references to those bodies and provisions relating to continuity), see the Enterprise and Regulatory Reform Act 2013 (Commencement No 6, Transitional Provisions and Savings) Order 2014, SI 2014/416, Schedule at **[2.13]**.

[1.276]
90 Procedural requirements for certain undertakings and orders
Schedule 10 (which provides for the procedure for accepting certain enforcement undertakings and making certain enforcement orders and for their termination) shall have effect.

[1.277]
91 Register of undertakings and orders
(1) The [CMA] shall compile and maintain a register for the purposes of this Part.
(2) The register shall be kept in such form as the [CMA] considers appropriate.
(3) The [CMA] shall ensure that the following matters are entered in the register—
(a) the provisions of any enforcement undertaking accepted under this Part;
(b) the provisions of any enforcement order made under this Part;
(c) the details of any variation, release or revocation of such an undertaking or order; and
(d) the details of any consent given by the [CMA] under section 77(2) or (3) or 78(2) or by the Secretary of State under paragraph 7(2) or (3) or 8(2) of Schedule 7.
(4) The duty in subsection (3) does not extend to anything of which the [CMA] is unaware.
(5) The [Secretary of State] shall inform the [CMA] of any matters which are to be included in the register by virtue of subsection (3) and which relate to enforcement undertakings accepted [by the Secretary of State], enforcement orders made [by the Secretary of State] or consents given [by the Secretary of State].
(6) The [CMA] shall ensure that the contents of the register are available to the public—
(a) during (as a minimum) such hours as may be specified in an order made by the Secretary of State; and
(b) subject to such reasonable fees (if any) as the [CMA] may determine.
(7) If requested by any person to do so and subject to such reasonable fees (if any) as the [CMA] may determine, the [CMA] shall supply the person concerned with a copy (certified to be true) of the register or of an extract from it.

NOTES

References to the "CMA" substituted, and words in first and final pairs of square brackets in sub-s (5) substituted, by the Enterprise and Regulatory Reform Act 2013, s 26(3), Sch 5, Pt 2, paras 59, 126. For various transitional provisions (including those relating to the abolition of the OFT and the Competition Commission, existing references to those bodies and provisions relating to continuity), see the Enterprise and Regulatory Reform Act 2013 (Commencement No 6, Transitional Provisions and Savings) Order 2014, SI 2014/416, Schedule at **[2.13]**.

Orders: the CMA Registers of Undertakings and Orders (Available Hours) Order 2014, SI 2014/558 at **[2.59]**.

Enforcement functions of [CMA]

[1.278]

92 Duty of [CMA] to monitor undertakings and orders

(1) The [CMA] shall keep under review—

(a) the carrying out of any enforcement undertaking or any enforcement order; and

(b) compliance with the prohibitions in sections 77(2) and (3) and 78(2) and in paragraphs 7(2) and (3) and 8(2) of Schedule 7.

(2) The [CMA] shall, in particular, from time to time consider—

(a) whether an enforcement undertaking or enforcement order has been or is being complied with;

(b) whether, by reason of any change of circumstances, an enforcement undertaking is no longer appropriate and—

(i) one or more of the parties to it can be released from it; or

(ii) it needs to be varied or to be superseded by a new enforcement undertaking; and

(c) whether, by reason of any change of circumstances, an enforcement order is no longer appropriate and needs to be varied or revoked.

(3) The [CMA] shall give . . . the Secretary of State such advice as it considers appropriate in relation to—

(a) any possible variation or release by . . . the Secretary of State of an enforcement undertaking accepted by . . . him;

(b) any possible new enforcement undertaking to be accepted by . . . the Secretary of State so as to supersede another enforcement undertaking given to . . . the Secretary of State;

(c) any possible variation or revocation by . . . the Secretary of State of an enforcement order made by . . . the Secretary of State;

(d) any possible enforcement undertaking to be accepted by . . . the Secretary of State instead of an enforcement order or any possible enforcement order to be made by . . . the Secretary of State instead of an enforcement undertaking;

(e) the enforcement by virtue of section 94(6) to (8) of any enforcement undertaking or enforcement order; or

(f) the enforcement by virtue of section 95(4) and (5) of the prohibitions in sections 77(2) and (3) and 78(2) and in paragraphs 7(2) and (3) and 8(2) of Schedule 7.

(4) The [CMA] shall take such action as it considers appropriate in relation to—

(a) any possible variation or release by it of an enforcement undertaking accepted by it;

(b) any possible new enforcement undertaking to be accepted by it so as to supersede another enforcement undertaking given to it;

(c) any possible variation or revocation by it of an enforcement order made by it;

(d) any possible enforcement undertaking to be accepted by it instead of an enforcement order or any possible enforcement order to be made by it instead of an enforcement undertaking;

(e) the enforcement by it by virtue of section 94(6) of any enforcement undertaking or enforcement order; or

(f) the enforcement by it by virtue of section 95(4) and (5) of the prohibitions in sections 77(2) and (3) and 78(2) and in paragraphs 7(2) and (3) and 8(2) of Schedule 7.

(5) The [CMA] shall keep under review the effectiveness of enforcement undertakings accepted under this Part and enforcement orders made under this Part.

(6) The [CMA] shall, whenever requested to do so by the Secretary of State and otherwise from time to time, prepare a report of its findings under subsection (5).

(7) The [CMA] shall—

(a) . . .

(b) give a copy of [any report prepared by it under subsection (6)] to the Secretary of State; and

(c) publish the report.

NOTES

References to the "CMA" (including in the section heading and preceding cross-heading) substituted, words omitted from sub-s (3) repealed, sub-s (7)(a) repealed, and words in square brackets in sub-s (7)(b) substituted, by the Enterprise and Regulatory Reform Act 2013, s 26(3), Sch 5, Pt 2, paras 59, 127, 128. For various transitional provisions (including those relating to the abolition of the OFT and the Competition Commission, existing references to those bodies and provisions relating to continuity), see the Enterprise and Regulatory Reform Act 2013 (Commencement No 6, Transitional Provisions and Savings) Order 2014, SI 2014/416, Schedule at **[2.13]**.

[1.279]

93 Further role of [CMA] in relation to undertakings and orders

(1) Subsections (2) and (3) apply where—

(a) . . .

(b) the Secretary of State is considering whether to accept undertakings under paragraph . . . 3 or 9 of Schedule 7.

(2) [The Secretary of State] may require the [CMA] to consult with such persons as the [Secretary of State] considers appropriate with a view to discovering whether they will offer undertakings which the [Secretary of State] would be prepared to accept under . . . paragraph . . . 3 or 9 of Schedule 7.

(3) The [Secretary of State] may require the [CMA] to report to the [Secretary of State] on the outcome of the [CMA's] consultations within such period as the [Secretary of State] may require.

(4) A report under subsection (3) shall, in particular, contain advice from the [CMA] as to whether any undertakings offered should be accepted by the [Secretary of State] under . . . paragraph . . . 3 or 9 of Schedule 7.

(5) The powers conferred on the relevant authority by subsections (1) to (4) are without prejudice to the power of the relevant authority to consult the persons concerned itself.

(6) If asked by the [Secretary of State] for advice in relation to the taking of enforcement action (whether or not by way of undertaking) in a particular case, the [CMA] shall give such advice as it considers appropriate.

NOTES

Words in square brackets substituted, and words omitted repealed, by the Enterprise and Regulatory Reform Act 2013, ss 26(3), 57, Sch 5, Pt 2, paras 59, 129, Sch 15, paras 15, 33. For various transitional provisions (including those relating to the abolition of the OFT and the Competition Commission, existing references to those bodies and provisions relating to continuity), see the Enterprise and Regulatory Reform Act 2013 (Commencement No 6, Transitional Provisions and Savings) Order 2014, SI 2014/416, Schedule at **[2.13]**.

Note that the references to the "relevant authority" in subsection (5) of this section were not substituted with references to the "Secretary of State" by the 2013 Act.

Other

[1.280]

94 Rights to enforce undertakings and orders

(1) This section applies to any enforcement undertaking or enforcement order.

(2) Any person to whom such an undertaking or order relates shall have a duty to comply with it.

(3) The duty shall be owed to any person who may be affected by a contravention of the undertaking or (as the case may be) order.

(4) Any breach of the duty which causes such a person to sustain loss or damage shall be actionable by him.

(5) In any proceedings brought under subsection (4) against a person to whom an enforcement undertaking or an enforcement order relates it shall be a defence for that person to show that he took all reasonable steps and exercised all due diligence to avoid contravening the undertaking or (as the case may be) order.

(6) Compliance with an enforcement undertaking or an enforcement order shall also be enforceable by civil proceedings brought by the [CMA] for an injunction or for interdict or for any other appropriate relief or remedy.

(7) . . .

(8) Compliance with an undertaking under paragraph . . . 3 or 9 of Schedule 7, an order made by the Secretary of State under paragraph 2 of that Schedule or an order under paragraph 5, 6, 10 or 11 of that Schedule, shall also be enforceable by civil proceedings brought by the Secretary of State for an injunction or for interdict or for any other appropriate relief or remedy.

(9) Subsections (6) to (8) shall not prejudice any right that a person may have by virtue of subsection (4) to bring civil proceedings for contravention or apprehended contravention of an enforcement undertaking or an enforcement order.

NOTES

Sub-s (6): reference to the "CMA" substituted by the Enterprise and Regulatory Reform Act 2013, s 26(3), Sch 5, Pt 2, paras 59, 130(1), (2). For various transitional provisions (including those relating to the abolition of the OFT and the Competition Commission, existing references to those bodies and provisions relating to continuity), see the Enterprise and Regulatory Reform Act 2013 (Commencement No 6, Transitional Provisions and Savings) Order 2014, SI 2014/416, Schedule at **[2.13]**.

Sub-s (7): repealed by the Enterprise and Regulatory Reform Act 2013, s 26(3), Sch 5, Pt 2, paras 59, 130(1), (3), subject to transitional provisions in SI 2014/416 as noted above.

Sub-s (8): figure omitted repealed by the Enterprise and Regulatory Reform Act 2013, s 57, Sch 15, paras 15, 34, subject to transitional provisions in SI 2014/416 as noted above.

[1.281]

[94A Interim undertakings and orders under this Part: penalties

(1) Where the appropriate authority considers that a person has, without reasonable excuse, failed to comply with an interim measure, it may impose a penalty of such fixed amount as it considers appropriate.

(2) A penalty imposed under subsection (1) shall not exceed 5% of the total value of the turnover (both in and outside the United Kingdom) of the enterprises owned or controlled by the person on whom it is imposed.

(3) For the purposes of subsection (2), the Secretary of State may by order make provision for determining—

(a) when an enterprise is to be treated as controlled by a person; and

(b) the turnover (both in and outside the United Kingdom) of an enterprise.

(4) An order under subsection (3)(b) may, in particular, make provision as to—

(a) the amounts which are, or which are not, to be treated as comprising an enterprise's turnover;

(b) the date or dates by reference to which an enterprise's turnover is to be determined.

(5) An order under subsection (3) may, in particular, make provision enabling the appropriate authority to determine matters of a description specified in the order (including any of the matters mentioned in paragraphs (a) and (b) of subsection (4)).

(6) The Secretary of State may by order amend subsection (2) so as to alter the percentage for the time being mentioned there to any percentage not exceeding 5%.

(7) Sections 112 to 115 apply in relation to a penalty imposed under subsection (1) as they apply in relation to a penalty of a fixed amount imposed under section 110(1), with the modification that any reference in those provisions to the CMA is to be read as a reference to the person who imposed the penalty under this section.

(8) In this section—

"interim measure" means—

(a) an undertaking under section 80; or

(b) an order under section 72 or 81 or paragraph 2 of Schedule 7;

"appropriate authority" means—

(a) in relation to an interim measure which is an order made by the Secretary of State under paragraph 2 of Schedule 7, the Secretary of State;

(b) in relation to any other interim measure, the CMA.]

NOTES

Inserted, together with s 94B, by the Enterprise and Regulatory Reform Act 2013, s 31(1). For various transitional provisions (including those relating to the abolition of the OFT and the Competition Commission, existing references to those bodies and provisions relating to continuity), see the Enterprise and Regulatory Reform Act 2013 (Commencement No 6, Transitional Provisions and Savings) Order 2014, SI 2014/416, Schedule at **[2.13]**.

Orders: the Enterprise Act 2002 (Mergers) (Interim Measures: Financial Penalties) (Determination of Control and Turnover) Order 2014, SI 2014/533 at **[2.175]**.

[1.282]

[94B Statement of policy in relation to powers under sections 94 and 94A

(1) The CMA shall prepare and publish a statement of policy in relation to the use of its powers under—

(a) section 94, insofar as they relate to interim measures; and

(b) section 94A.

(2) The CMA shall, in particular, include a statement about the considerations relevant to the determination of the amount of any penalty imposed under section 94A.

(3) The CMA may revise its statement of policy and, where it does so, it shall publish the revised statement.

(4) The CMA shall consult the Secretary of State and such other persons as it considers appropriate when preparing or revising its statement of policy.

(5) A statement or revised statement of policy may not be published under this section unless the Secretary of State approves the statement.

(6) In this section, "interim measure" has the same meaning as in section 94A.]

NOTES

Inserted as noted to s 94A at **[1.281]**.

[1.283]

95 Rights to enforce statutory restrictions

(1) The obligation to comply with section 77(2) or (3) or 78(2) or paragraph 7(2) or (3) or 8(2) of Schedule 7 shall be a duty owed to any person who may be affected by a contravention of the enactment concerned.

(2) Any breach of the duty which causes such a person to sustain loss or damage shall be actionable by him.

(3) In any proceedings brought under subsection (2) against a person who has an obligation to comply with section 77(2) or (3) or 78(2) or paragraph 7(2) or (3) or 8(2) of Schedule 7 it shall be a defence for that person to show that he took all reasonable steps and exercised all due diligence to avoid contravening the enactment concerned.

(4) Compliance with section 77(2) or (3) or 78(2) shall also be enforceable by civil proceedings brought by the [CMA] for an injunction or for interdict or for any other appropriate relief or remedy.

(5) Compliance with paragraph 7(2) or (3) or 8(2) of Schedule 7 shall also be enforceable by civil proceedings brought by the [CMA] or the Secretary of State for an injunction or for interdict or for any other appropriate relief or remedy.

(6) Subsections (4) and (5) shall not prejudice any right that a person may have by virtue of subsection (2) to bring civil proceedings for contravention or apprehended contravention of section 77(2) or (3) or 78(2) or paragraph 7(2) or (3) or 8(2) of Schedule 7.

NOTES

Sub-ss (4), (5): references to "CMA" substituted by the Enterprise and Regulatory Reform Act 2013, s 26(3), Sch 5, Pt 2, paras 59, 131. For various transitional provisions (including those relating to the abolition of the OFT and the Competition Commission, existing references to those bodies and provisions relating to continuity), see the Enterprise and Regulatory Reform Act 2013 (Commencement No 6, Transitional Provisions and Savings) Order 2014, SI 2014/416, Schedule at **[2.13]**.

[Transferred EU merger commitments

[1.284]

95A Transferred EU merger commitments

(1) The CMA must—

(a) monitor compliance with transferred EU merger commitments; and

(b) take such action (if any) under subsection (3) or section 95B as it considers appropriate.

(2) Any person to whom transferred EU merger commitments relate has a duty to comply with those commitments.

(3) Compliance with transferred EU merger commitments is enforceable by civil proceedings brought by the CMA for an injunction or for interdict or for any other appropriate relief or remedy.

(4) The rights of the CMA under subsection (3) are not affected by any provisions of transferred EU merger commitments which provide for disputes relating to compliance with the commitments to be resolved by arbitration.

(5) The CMA must ensure that the provisions of transferred EU merger commitments are entered and kept up to date in the register referred to in section 91.

(6) In this Part "transferred EU merger commitments" means EU merger commitments—

(a) which are the subject of an Article 95(2) transfer decision (and, where those commitments are modified by, or as contemplated by, that decision or by a later Article 95(2) transfer decision, means those commitments as so modified); and

(b) which have not been waived or substituted by the European Commission.

(7) In this section—

"Article 95(2) transfer decision" means an instrument issued by the European Commission in accordance with Article 95(2) of the EU withdrawal agreement transferring responsibility for the monitoring and enforcement of EU merger commitments to the CMA;

"EU merger commitments" means commitments attached to a decision adopted by the European Commission under Article 6(1)(b) and (2) or 8(2) of Council Regulation (EC) No 139/2004 of 20 January 2004 on the control of concentrations between undertakings.

(8) So far as the context permits or requires, transferred EU merger commitments are to be treated for the purposes of this Part as if—

(a) any reference to the area of the European Union or of the European Economic Area included the United Kingdom;

(b) any reference to the internal market included the United Kingdom;

(c) any reference to a member State included the United Kingdom;

(d) any reference to a party to the EEA agreement included the United Kingdom.

(9) Subsection (8) is subject to any different provision made by the Article 95(2) transfer decision in question.]

NOTES

Commencement: IP completion day (as defined in the European Union (Withdrawal Agreement) Act 2020, s 39).

Sections 95A, 95B were inserted, together with the preceding heading, by the Competition (Amendment etc) (EU Exit) Regulations 2019, SI 2019/93, reg 48A, as from IP completion day (as defined in the European Union (Withdrawal Agreement) Act 2020, s 39) (for transitional provisions and savings in relation to the operation of the 2019 Regulations, see Sch 4 to those Regulations at **[7.69]** et seq). Note that reg 48A of the 2019 Regulations was inserted by the Competition (Amendment etc) (EU Exit) Regulations 2020, SI 2020/1343, reg 8, with effect from immediately before IP completion day.

[1.285]

[95B Power of directions in connection with transferred EU merger commitments

(1) The CMA may give directions falling within subsection (2) to—

(a) a person specified in the directions; or

(b) the holder for the time being of an office so specified in any body of persons corporate or unincorporate.

(2) Directions fall within this subsection if they are directions—

(a) to take such action as may be specified or described in the directions for the purpose of carrying out, or ensuring compliance with, transferred EU merger commitments; or

(b) to do, or refrain from doing, anything so specified or described which the person is required by transferred EU merger commitments to do or refrain from doing.

(3) The CMA may vary or revoke any directions so given.

(4) Directions under this section may extend to a person's conduct outside the United Kingdom if (and only if) the person is—

(a) a person bound by the transferred EU merger commitments concerned;

(b) a United Kingdom national;

(c) a body incorporated under the law of the United Kingdom or of any part of the United Kingdom; or

(d) a person carrying on business in the United Kingdom.

(5) The court may by order require any person who has failed to comply with directions given under this section to comply with them, or otherwise remedy the failure, within such time as may be specified in the order.

(6) Where the directions related to anything done in the management or administration of a body of persons corporate or unincorporate, the court may by order require the body of persons concerned or any officer of it to comply with the directions, or otherwise remedy the failure to comply with them, within such time as may be specified in the order.

(7) An order under subsection (5) or (6) may only be made on the application of the CMA.

(8) An order under subsection (5) or (6) may provide for all the costs or expenses of, or incidental to, the application for the order to be met by any person in default or by any officers of a body of persons corporate or unincorporate who are responsible for its default.

(9) In this section "the court" means—

(a) in relation to England and Wales or Northern Ireland, the High Court; and

(b) in relation to Scotland, the Court of Session.]

NOTES

Commencement: IP completion day (as defined in the European Union (Withdrawal Agreement) Act 2020, s 39).

Inserted as noted to s 95A at **[1.284]**.

CHAPTER 5 SUPPLEMENTARY

Merger notices

[1.286]

96 Merger notices

(1) A person authorised to do so by regulations under section 101 may give notice to the [CMA] [of arrangements or proposed arrangements which might have resulted or might result in the creation of a relevant merger situation].

(2) Any such notice (in this Part a "merger notice")—

(a) shall be in the prescribed form;

[(aa) shall contain the prescribed information;] and

(b) shall state that the existence of the proposal has been made public.

[(2A) Where the CMA is satisfied that a merger notice meets the requirements of subsection (2), it shall give notice to that effect to the person who gave the merger notice.]

(3), (4) . . .

(5) In this section and sections 99(5)(c) and 100(1)(c) "prescribed" means prescribed by the [CMA] by notice having effect for the time being and published in the London, Edinburgh and Belfast Gazettes.

(6) In this Part "notified arrangements" means arrangements of which notice is given under subsection (1) above or arrangements not differing from them in any material respect.

NOTES

References to the "CMA" in sub-ss (1), (5) substituted by the Enterprise and Regulatory Reform Act 2013, s 26(3), Sch 5, Pt 2, paras 59, 132. For various transitional provisions (including those relating to the abolition of the OFT and the Competition Commission, existing references to those bodies and provisions relating to continuity), see the Enterprise and Regulatory Reform Act 2013 (Commencement No 6, Transitional Provisions and Savings) Order 2014, SI 2014/416, Schedule at **[2.13]**.

Words in second pair of square brackets in sub-s (1) substituted, sub-ss (2)(aa) and (2A) inserted, and sub-ss (3) and (4) repealed, by the Enterprise and Regulatory Reform Act 2013, s 32(2), Sch 8, paras 1, 8, subject to transitional provisions in SI 2014/416 as noted above.

97, 98 (*Repealed by the Enterprise and Regulatory Reform Act 2013, s 32(2), Sch 8, paras 1, 9. For various transitional provisions (including those relating to the abolition of the OFT and the Competition Commission, existing references to those bodies and provisions relating to continuity), see the Enterprise and Regulatory Reform Act 2013 (Commencement No 6, Transitional Provisions and Savings) Order 2014, SI 2014/416, Schedule at* **[2.13]**.)

[1.287]

99 Certain functions of [CMA] in relation to merger notices

(1) The [CMA] shall, so far as practicable and when [the initial period (within the meaning of section 34ZA) begins in relation to the merger notice], take such action as the [CMA] considers appropriate to bring—

(a) the existence of the proposal;

(b) the fact that the merger notice has been given; and

(c) the date on which the period for considering the notice may expire;

to the attention of those whom the [CMA] considers would be affected if the arrangements were carried into effect.

(2)–(4) . . .

(5) The [CMA] may, at any time before the end of [the initial period (within the meaning of section 34ZA) in relation to a merger notice], reject the notice if—

(a) the [CMA] suspects that any information given in respect of the notified arrangements (whether in the merger notice or otherwise) by the person who gave the notice or any connected person is in any material respect false or misleading;

(b) the [CMA] suspects that it is not proposed to carry the notified arrangements into effect; [or]

(c) any prescribed information is not given in the merger notice [or the person who gave the merger notice has failed (with or without a reasonable excuse) to comply with any requirement of a notice under section 109 in relation to the case concerned]; *or*

(d) the [CMA] considers that the notified arrangements are, or if carried into effect would result in, a concentration with a Community dimension within the meaning of the [EC Merger Regulation].

(6) In this section and section 100 "connected person", in relation to the person who gave a merger notice, means—

(a) any person who, for the purposes of section 127, is associated with him; or

(b) any subsidiary of the person who gave the merger notice or of any person so associated with him.

NOTES

Except as noted below, all words in square brackets were substituted, and sub-ss (2)–(4) were repealed, by the Enterprise and Regulatory Reform Act 2013, ss 26(3), 32(2), 57, Sch 5, Pt 2, paras 49, 133, Sch 8, paras 1, 10, Sch 15, paras 15, 35. For various transitional provisions (including those relating to the abolition of the OFT and the Competition Commission, existing references to those bodies and provisions relating to continuity), see the Enterprise and Regulatory Reform Act 2013 (Commencement No 6, Transitional Provisions and Savings) Order 2014, SI 2014/416, Schedule at **[2.13]**.

The word "or" in square brackets in sub-s (5)(b) was inserted, and sub-s (5)(d) and the preceding word were repealed, by the Competition (Amendment etc) (EU Exit) Regulations 2019, SI 2019/93, regs 32, 59, as from IP completion day (as defined in the European Union (Withdrawal Agreement) Act 2020, s 39) (for transitional provisions and savings in relation to the operation of the 2019 Regulations, see Sch 4 to those Regulations at **[7.69]** et seq).

The words "EC Merger Regulation" in square brackets in sub-s (5)(d) substituted by the EC Merger Control (Consequential Amendments) Regulations 2004, SI 2004/1079, reg 2, Schedule, para 2(1), (23).

References to the European Community and related expressions: see the note "References to "the European Community", "Community", etc" in the introductory notes to this Act.

[1.288]

100 Exceptions to protection given by merger notices

(1) [Sections 22(3)(za) and 33(3)(za) do not] prevent any reference being made [under section 22 or (as the case may be) 33] if—

(a) before the end of [the initial period (within the meaning of section 34ZA) in relation to the merger notice], the [CMA] rejects the notice under section 99(5);

(b) . . .

(c) any information (whether prescribed information or not) that—

(i) is, or ought to be, known to the person who gave the merger notice or any connected person; and

(ii) is material to the notified arrangements;

is not disclosed to the [CMA] . . . ;

(d) at any time after the merger notice is given but before the enterprises to which the notified arrangements relate cease to be distinct from each other, any of those enterprises ceases to be distinct from any enterprise other than an enterprise to which those arrangements relate;

(e) the six months beginning with the end of [the initial period (within the meaning of section 34ZA) in relation to the merger notice] expires without the enterprises to which the notified arrangements relate ceasing to be distinct from each other;

(f) the merger notice is withdrawn; or

(g) any information given in respect of the notified arrangements (whether in the merger notice or otherwise) by the person who gave the notice or any connected person is in any material respect false or misleading.

(2) Subsection (3) applies where—

(a) two or more transactions which have occurred, or, if any arrangements are carried into effect, will occur, may be treated for the purposes of a reference under [section 22 or 33] as having occurred simultaneously on a particular date; and

(b) [sections 22(3)(za) and 33(3)(za) do not] prevent such a reference in relation to the last of those transactions.

(3) [Sections 22(3)(za) and 33(3)(za) do not] prevent such a reference in relation to any of those transactions which actually occurred less than six months before—

(a) that date; or

(b) the actual occurrence of another of those transactions in relation to which such a reference may be made (whether or not by virtue of this subsection).

(4) In determining for the purposes of subsections (2) and (3) the time at which any transaction actually occurred, no account shall be taken of any option or other conditional right until the option is exercised or the condition is satisfied.

(5) In this section references to the enterprises to which the notified arrangements relate are references to those enterprises that would have ceased to be distinct from one another if the arrangements mentioned in the merger notice concerned had been carried into effect at the time when the notice was given.

NOTES

Sub-ss (1)–(3): words in square brackets substituted, and words omitted repealed, by the Enterprise and Regulatory Reform Act 2013, ss 26(3), 32(2), Sch 5, Pt 2, paras 59, 134, Sch 8, paras 1, 11. For various transitional provisions (including those relating to the abolition of the OFT and the Competition Commission, existing references to those bodies and provisions relating to continuity), see the Enterprise and Regulatory Reform Act 2013 (Commencement No 6, Transitional Provisions and Savings) Order 2014, SI 2014/416, Schedule at **[2.13]**.

[1.289]

101 Merger notices: regulations

(1) The Secretary of State may make regulations for the purposes of sections 96 to 100.

(2) The regulations may, in particular—

(a) provide for . . . section 100(1)(e) to apply as if any reference to a period of days or months were a reference to a period specified in the regulations for the purposes of the enactment concerned;

(b) provide for the manner in which any merger notice is authorised or required to be rejected or withdrawn, and the time at which any merger notice is to be treated as received or rejected;

(c)–(f) . . .

(g) provide for the time at which any fee is to be treated as paid;

(h) provide that a person is, or is not, to be treated, in such circumstances as may be specified in the regulations, as acting on behalf of a person authorised by regulations under this section to give a merger notice or a person who has given such a notice.

NOTES

Sub-s (2): words omitted from para (a) repealed, and paras (c)–(f) repealed, by the Enterprise and Regulatory Reform Act 2013, s 32(2), Sch 8, paras 1, 12. For various transitional provisions (including those relating to the abolition of the OFT and the Competition Commission, existing references to those bodies and provisions relating to continuity), see the Enterprise and Regulatory Reform Act 2013 (Commencement No 6, Transitional Provisions and Savings) Order 2014, SI 2014/416, Schedule at **[2.13]**.

Regulations: the Enterprise Act 2002 (Merger Prenotification) Regulations 2003, SI 2003/1369 at **[2.84]**.

[1.290]

102 Power to modify sections 97 to 101

The Secretary of State may, for the purposes of determining the effect of giving a merger notice and the action which may be or is to be taken by any person in connection with such a notice, by order modify sections 97 to 101.

General duties in relation to references

[1.291]

103 Duty of expedition in relation to references

(1) [In making any decision for the purposes of its functions of making and determining references under this Part, the CMA] shall have regard, with a view to the prevention or removal of uncertainty, to the need for making a decision as soon as reasonably practicable.

(2) In deciding whether to make a reference under section 45 or 62 the Secretary of State shall have regard, with a view to the prevention or removal of uncertainty, to the need for making a decision as soon as reasonably practicable.

NOTES

Sub-s (1): words in square brackets substituted by the Enterprise and Regulatory Reform Act 2013, s 32(1). For various transitional provisions (including those relating to the abolition of the OFT and the Competition Commission, existing references to those bodies and provisions relating to continuity), see the Enterprise and Regulatory Reform Act 2013 (Commencement No 6, Transitional Provisions and Savings) Order 2014, SI 2014/416, Schedule at **[2.13]**.

[1.292]

104 Certain duties of relevant authorities to consult

(1) Subsection (2) applies where the relevant authority is proposing to make a relevant decision in a way which the relevant authority considers is likely to be adverse to the interests of a relevant party.

(2) The relevant authority shall, so far as practicable, consult that party about what is proposed before making that decision.

(3) In consulting the party concerned, the relevant authority shall, so far as practicable, give the reasons of the relevant authority for the proposed decision.

(4) In considering what is practicable for the purposes of this section the relevant authority shall, in particular, have regard to—

(a) any restrictions imposed by any timetable for making the decision; and

(b) any need to keep what is proposed, or the reasons for it, confidential.

(5) The duty under this section shall not apply in relation to the making of any decision so far as particular provision is made elsewhere by virtue of this Part for consultation before the making of that decision.

(6) In this section—

"the relevant authority" means the [CMA] or the Secretary of State;

"relevant decision" means—

(a) in the case of the [CMA], any decision by the [CMA]—

(i) as to whether to make a reference under section 22 or 33 or accept undertakings under section 73 instead of making such a reference; or

(ii) to vary under section 37 such a reference; [or

(iii) on the questions mentioned in section 35(1) or (3), 36(1) or (2), 47 or 63;]

(b) . . .

(c) in the case of the Secretary of State, any decision by the Secretary of State—

(i) as to whether to make a reference under section 45 or 62; or

(ii) to vary under section 49 or (as the case may be) 64 such a reference; and

"relevant party" means any person who appears to the relevant authority to control enterprises which are the subject of the reference or possible reference concerned.

NOTES

Sub-s (6): words in square brackets substituted or inserted, and words omitted repealed, by the Enterprise and Regulatory Reform Act 2013, s 26(3), Sch 5, Pt 2, paras 59, 135. For various transitional provisions (including those relating to the abolition of the OFT and the Competition Commission, existing references to those bodies and provisions relating to continuity), see the Enterprise and Regulatory Reform Act 2013 (Commencement No 6, Transitional Provisions and Savings) Order 2014, SI 2014/416, Schedule at **[2.13]**.

[1.293]

[104A Public consultation in relation to media mergers

(1) Subsection (2) applies where the [CMA]—

(a) is preparing—

(i) a report under section 50 on a reference which specifies a media public interest consideration; or

(ii) a report under section 65 on a reference which specifies a consideration specified in section 58(2A) to (2C); and

(b) is not under a duty to disregard the consideration concerned.

(2) The [CMA] shall have regard (among other things) to the need to consult the public so far as they might be affected by the creation of the relevant merger situation or special merger situation concerned and so far as such consultation is practicable.

(3) Any consultation of the kind mentioned in subsection (2) may be undertaken by the [CMA] by consulting such representative sample of the public or section of the public concerned as the [CMA] considers appropriate.]

NOTES

Inserted by the Communications Act 2003, s 381.

References to the "CMA" substituted by the Enterprise and Regulatory Reform Act 2013, s 26(3), Sch 5, Pt 2, paras 59, 136. For various transitional provisions (including those relating to the abolition of the OFT and the Competition Commission, existing references to those bodies and provisions relating to continuity), see the Enterprise and Regulatory Reform Act 2013 (Commencement No 6, Transitional Provisions and Savings) Order 2014, SI 2014/416, Schedule at **[2.13]**.

Information and publicity requirements

[1.294]

105 General information duties of [CMA]

(1) Where the [CMA] decides to investigate a matter so as to enable it to decide whether to make a reference under section 22 or 33, or so as to make a report under section 44 or 61, it shall, so far as practicable, take such action as it considers appropriate to bring information about the investigation to the attention of those whom it considers might be affected by the creation of the relevant merger situation concerned or (as the case may be) the special merger situation concerned.

[(1A) Where OFCOM decide to investigate a matter so as to make a report under section 44A or 61A, they shall, so far as practicable, take such action as they consider appropriate to bring information about the investigation to the attention of those who they consider might be affected by the creation of the relevant merger situation concerned or (as the case may be) the special merger situation concerned.]

(2) [Subsections (1) and (1A) do] not apply in relation to arrangements which might result in the creation of a relevant merger situation if a merger notice has been given in relation to those arrangements under section 96.

(3) The [CMA] shall give . . . [OFCOM]—

(a) such information in its possession as . . . [OFCOM] may reasonably require to enable . . . [OFCOM] to carry out its functions under this Part; and

(b) any other assistance which the . . . [OFCOM] may reasonably require for the purpose of assisting it in carrying out its functions under this Part and which it is within the power of the [CMA] to give.

[(3A) OFCOM shall give the [CMA]—

(a) such information in their possession as the [CMA] may reasonably require to enable the [CMA] to carry out its functions under this Part; and

(b) any other assistance which the [CMA] may reasonably require for the purpose of assisting it in carrying out its functions under this Part and which it is within the power of OFCOM to give.]

(4) The [CMA] shall give [OFCOM] any information in its possession which has not been requested by [OFCOM] but which, in the opinion of the [CMA], would be appropriate to give to . . . [OFCOM] for the purpose of assisting it in carrying out its functions under this Part.

[(4A) OFCOM shall give the [CMA] any information in their possession which has not been requested by the [CMA] but which, in the opinion of OFCOM, would be appropriate to give to the [CMA] for the purpose of assisting it in carrying out its functions under this Part.]

(5) The [CMA and OFCOM] shall give the Secretary of State—

- (a) such information in their possession as the Secretary of State may by direction reasonably require to enable him to carry out his functions under this Part; and
- (b) any other assistance which the Secretary of State may by direction reasonably require for the purpose of assisting him in carrying out his functions under this Part and which it is within the power of the [CMA or (as the case may be) OFCOM] to give.

(6) The [CMA] [and OFCOM] shall give the Secretary of State any information in [their] possession which has not been requested by the Secretary of State but which, in the opinion of the [CMA] [or (as the case may be) OFCOM], would be appropriate to give to the Secretary of State for the purpose of assisting him in carrying out his functions under this Part.

(7) The [CMA] shall have regard to any information given to it under subsection [(3A) or (4A)]; and the Secretary of State shall have regard to any information given to him under subsection (5) or (6).

[(7A) OFCOM shall have regard to any information given to them under subsection (3) or (4) . . .]

(8) Any direction given under subsection (5)—

- (a) shall be in writing; and
- (b) may be varied or revoked by a subsequent direction.

NOTES

Section heading, sub-s (1), (4A) references to the "CMA" substituted by the Enterprise and Regulatory Reform Act 2013, s 26(3), Sch 5, Pt 2, paras 59, 137(1), (2), (11). For various transitional provisions (including those relating to the abolition of the OFT and the Competition Commission, existing references to those bodies and provisions relating to continuity), see the Enterprise and Regulatory Reform Act 2013 (Commencement No 6, Transitional Provisions and Savings) Order 2014, SI 2014/416, Schedule at **[2.13]**.

Sub-s (1A): inserted by the Communications Act 2003, s 382(1), (2).

Sub-s (2): words in square brackets substituted by the Communications Act 2003, s 382(1), (3).

Sub-s (3): references to the "CMA" substituted, and words omitted repealed, by the Enterprise and Regulatory Reform Act 2013, s 26(3), Sch 5, Pt 2, paras 59, 137(1), (3), subject to transitional provisions in SI 2014/416 as noted above. References to "OFCOM" in square brackets inserted by the Communications Act 2003, s 382(1), (4).

Sub-s (3A): inserted by the Communications Act 2003, s 382(1), (5). References to the "CMA" substituted by the Enterprise and Regulatory Reform Act 2013, s 26(3), Sch 5, Pt 2, paras 59, 137(1), (4), subject to transitional provisions in SI 2014/416 as noted above.

Sub-s (4): words in square brackets substituted, and words omitted repealed, by the Enterprise and Regulatory Reform Act 2013, s 26(3), Sch 5, Pt 2, paras 59, 137(1), (5), subject to transitional provisions in SI 2014/416 as noted above.

Sub-s (4A): inserted by the Communications Act 2003, s 382(1), (7). References to the "CMA" substituted by the Enterprise and Regulatory Reform Act 2013, s 26(3), Sch 5, Pt 2, paras 59, 137(1), (6), subject to transitional provisions in SI 2014/416 as noted above.

Sub-ss (5), (7): words in square brackets substituted by the Enterprise and Regulatory Reform Act 2013, s 26(3), Sch 5, Pt 2, paras 59, 137(1), (7), (9), subject to transitional provisions in SI 2014/416 as noted above.

Sub-s (6): words in first and fourth pairs of square brackets substituted by the Enterprise and Regulatory Reform Act 2013, s 26(3), Sch 5, Pt 2, paras 59, 137(1), (8), subject to transitional provisions in SI 2014/416 as noted above. Words in second and fifth pairs of square brackets inserted, and word in third pair of square brackets substituted, by the Communications Act 2003, s 382(1), (9).

Sub-s (7A): inserted by the Communications Act 2003, s 382(1), (11). Words omitted repealed by the Enterprise and Regulatory Reform Act 2013, s 26(3), Sch 5, Pt 2, paras 59, 137(1), (10), subject to transitional provisions in SI 2014/416 as noted above.

[1.295]

106 Advice and information about references under sections 22 and 33

(1) . . . [The CMA] shall prepare and publish general advice and information about[—

- (a) the making and consideration by it of references under section 22 or 33, and
- (b) the way in which relevant customer benefits may affect the taking of enforcement action in relation to such references.]

(2) The [CMA] may at any time publish revised, or new, advice or information.

(3) . . .

(4) . . .

(5) Advice and information published under this section shall be prepared with a view to—

- (a) explaining relevant provisions of this Part to persons who are likely to be affected by them; and
- (b) indicating how the [CMA] expects such provisions to operate.

(6) Advice (or information) published by virtue of subsection (1) . . . may include advice (or information) about the factors which the [CMA] may take into account in considering whether, and if so how, to exercise a function conferred by this Part.

(7) Any advice or information published by the [CMA] under this section shall be published in such manner as the [CMA] considers appropriate.

(8) In preparing any advice or information under this section, the [CMA shall consult such persons] as it considers appropriate.

(9) . . .

NOTES

Words omitted repealed, and words in square brackets substituted, by the Enterprise and Regulatory Reform Act 2013, s 26(3), Sch 5, Pt 2, paras 59, 138. For various transitional provisions (including those relating to the abolition of the OFT and the Competition Commission, existing references to those bodies and provisions relating to continuity), see the Enterprise and Regulatory Reform Act 2013 (Commencement No 6, Transitional Provisions and Savings) Order 2014, SI 2014/416, Schedule at **[2.13]**.

[1.296]

[106A Advice and information in relation to media mergers

(1) The Secretary of State may prepare and publish general advice and information about the considerations specified in section 58(2A) to (2C).

(2) The Secretary of State may at any time publish revised, or new, advice or information.

(3) Advice or information published under this section shall be prepared with a view to—

(a) explaining the considerations specified in section 58(2A) to (2C) to persons who are likely to be affected by them; and

(b) indicating how the Secretary of State expects this Part to operate in relation to such considerations.

(4) Any advice or information published by the Secretary of State under this section shall be published in such manner as the Secretary of State considers appropriate.

(5) In preparing any advice or information under this section, the Secretary of State shall consult the [CMA, OFCOM] and such other persons as he considers appropriate.]

NOTES

Inserted by the Communications Act 2003, s 383.

Sub-s (5): words in square brackets substituted by the Enterprise and Regulatory Reform Act 2013, s 26(3), Sch 5, Pt 2, paras 59, 139. For various transitional provisions (including those relating to the abolition of the OFT and the Competition Commission, existing references to those bodies and provisions relating to continuity), see the Enterprise and Regulatory Reform Act 2013 (Commencement No 6, Transitional Provisions and Savings) Order 2014, SI 2014/416, Schedule at **[2.13]**.

[1.297]

[106B General advisory functions of OFCOM

(1) OFCOM may, in connection with any case on which they are required to give a report by virtue of section 44A or 61A, give such advice as they consider appropriate to the Secretary of State in relation to—

(a) any report made in such a case by the [CMA] under section 50 or 65; and

(b) the taking by the Secretary of State of enforcement action under Schedule 7.

(2) OFCOM may, if requested to do so by the Secretary of State, give such other advice as they consider appropriate to the Secretary of State in connection with any case on which they are required to give a report by virtue of section 44A or 61A.

(3) OFCOM shall publish any advice given by them under this section but advice given by them in relation to a report of the [CMA] under section 50 or 65 or related enforcement action shall not be published before the report itself is published.]

NOTES

Inserted by the Communications Act 2003, s 384.

Sub-ss (1), (3): references to the "CMA" substituted by the Enterprise and Regulatory Reform Act 2013, s 26(3), Sch 5, Pt 2, paras 59, 140. For various transitional provisions (including those relating to the abolition of the OFT and the Competition Commission, existing references to those bodies and provisions relating to continuity), see the Enterprise and Regulatory Reform Act 2013 (Commencement No 6, Transitional Provisions and Savings) Order 2014, SI 2014/416, Schedule at **[2.13]**.

[1.298]

107 Further publicity requirements

(1) The [CMA] shall publish—

[(a) any decision made by it that the duty to make a reference under section 22 or 33 applies and any such reference made by it;

(aa) any decision made by it that the duty to make such a reference does not apply (other than a decision made by virtue of subsection (2)(b) of section 33);]

[(ab) any notice given by it as mentioned in paragraph (b) of the definition of "initial period" in section 34ZA(3);

(ac) any extension by it under section 34ZB of the initial period;

(ad) any decision made by it to cancel an extension as mentioned in section 34ZB(7)(b);

(ae) any extension by it under section 34A of the preliminary assessment period;

(af) any decision made by it to cancel an extension as mentioned in section 34A(6A)(b);.

(ag) any extension by it under section 46B of the preliminary assessment period;

(ah) any decision made by it to cancel an extension as mentioned in section 46B(3A)(b);]

(b) any variation made by it under section 37 of a reference under section 22 or 33;

(c) such information as it considers appropriate about any decision made by it under section 57(1) to bring a case to the attention of the Secretary of State;

(d) . . .

(e) any enforcement order made by it under section 72 . . . or paragraph 2 of Schedule 7;

[(ea) any notice given by it under section 73A(2)(b);

(eb) any extension by it under section 73A of the period for considering whether to accept an undertaking under section 73;

(ec) any decision made by it to cancel an extension as mentioned in section 73A(11)(b);]

(f) any variation, release or revocation of [an order mentioned in paragraph (e)];
(g) . . .
(h) . . . [; and
(i) any decision made by it to cancel an extension as mentioned in section 73A(11)(b);]

(2) The [CMA shall also] publish—
(a) any cancellation by it under section 37(1) of a reference under section 33;
(b) any decision made by it under section 37(2) to treat a reference made under section 22 or 33 as if it had been made under section 32 or (as the case may be) 22;
(c) any extension by it under section 39 of the period within which a report under section 38 is to be prepared and published;
(d) any decision made by it to cancel an extension as mentioned in section 39(8)(b);
(e) any decision made by it under section 41(2) neither to accept an undertaking under section 82 nor to make an order under section 84;
[(ea) any extension by it under section 41A of the period within which its duty under section 41(2) is to be discharged;
(eb) any decision made by it to cancel an extension as mentioned in section 41A(7)(b);]
(f) any decision made by it that there has been a material change of circumstances as mentioned in subsection (3) of section 41 or there is another special reason as mentioned in that subsection of that section;
(g) any cancellation by it under section 48(1) or 53(1) of a reference under section 45 or any cancellation by it under section 64(1) of a reference under section 62;
(h) any decision made by it under section 49(1) to treat—
  (i) a reference made under subsection (2) or (3) of section 45 as if it had been made under subsection (4) or (as the case may be) (5) of that section; or
  (ii) a reference made under subsection (4) or (5) of section 45 as if it had been made under subsection (2) or (as the case may be) (3) of that section;
(i) any extension by it under section 51 of the period within which a report under section 50 is to be prepared and published;
(j) any decision made by it under section 51(8)(b) to cancel such an extension;
(k) any extension by it under section 51 as applied by section 65(3) of the period within which a report under section 65 is to be prepared and published;
(l) any decision made by it under section 51(8)(b) as applied by section 65(3) to cancel such an extension;
(m) any decision made by it under section 64(2) to treat a reference made under subsection (2) or (3) of section 62 as if it had been made under subsection (3) or (as the case may be) (2) of that section;
(n) any decision made by it as mentioned in section 76(6)(b);
(o) any enforcement order made by it under section 76 or 81;
(p) any enforcement undertaking accepted by it under section 80;
(q) any variation, release or revocation of such an order or undertaking; and
(r) any decision made by it to dispense with the requirements of Schedule 10.

(3) The Secretary of State shall publish—
(a) any intervention notice or special intervention notice given by him;
(b) any report of the [CMA] under section 44 or 61 which has been received by him;
[(ba) any report of OFCOM under section 44A or 61A which has been received by him;]
(c) any reference made by him under section 45 or 62 or any decision made by him not to make such a reference;
(d) any variation made by him under section 49 of a reference under section 45 or under section 64 of a reference under section 62;
(e) any report of the [CMA] under section 50 or 65 which has been received by him;
(f) any decision made by him neither to accept an undertaking under paragraph 9 of Schedule 7 nor to make an order under paragraph 11 of that Schedule;
(g) any notice given by him under section 56(1);
(h), (i) . . .
(j) any decision made by him as mentioned in paragraph 6(6)(b) of Schedule 7; and
(k) any decision made by him to dispense with the requirements of Schedule 10.

(4) Where any person is under a duty by virtue of subsection (1), (2) or (3) to publish the result of any action taken by that person or any decision made by that person, the person concerned shall, subject to subsections (5) and (6), also publish that person's reasons for the action concerned or (as the case may be) the decision concerned.

(5) Such reasons need not, if it is not reasonably practicable to do so, be published at the same time as the result of the action concerned or (as the case may be) as the decision concerned.

(6) Subsections (4) and (5) shall not apply in relation to any information published under subsection (1)(c).

(7) The Secretary of State shall publish his reasons for—
(a) any decision made by him under section 54(2) or 66(2); or
(b) any decision to make an order under section 58(3) or vary or revoke such an order.

(8) Such reasons may be published after—
(a) in the case of subsection (7)(a), the publication of the decision concerned; and
(b) in the case of subsection (7)(b), the making of the order or of the variation or revocation;

if it is not reasonably practicable to publish them at the same time as the publication of the decision or (as the case may be) the making of the order or variation or revocation.

(9) The Secretary of State shall publish—
(a) the report of the [CMA] under section 44[, and any report of OFCOM under section 44A,] in relation to a matter no later than publication of his decision as to whether to make a reference under section 45 in relation to that matter; and
(b) the report of the [CMA] under section 50 in relation to a matter no later than publication of his decision under section 54(2) in relation to that matter.

(10) The Secretary of State shall publish—

(a) the report of the [CMA] under section 61[, and any report of OFCOM under section 61A,] in relation to a matter no later than publication of his decision as to whether to make a reference under section 62 in relation to that matter; and

(b) the report of the [CMA] under section 65 in relation to a matter no later than publication of his decision under section 66(2) in relation to that matter.

(11) Where the Secretary of State has decided under section 55(2) or 66(6) to accept an undertaking under paragraph 9 of Schedule 7 or to make an order under paragraph 11 of that Schedule, he shall (after the acceptance of the undertaking or (as the case may be) the making of the order) lay details of his decision and his reasons for it, and the [CMA's] report under section 50 or (as the case may be) 65, before each House of Parliament.

NOTES

Sub-s (1): words in square brackets substituted or inserted, and words omitted repealed, by the Enterprise and Regulatory Reform Act 2013, ss 26(3), 57, Sch 5, Pt 2, paras 59, 141(1), (2), Sch 15, paras 15, 36(1)–(7) (for various transitional provisions (including those relating to the abolition of the OFT and the Competition Commission, existing references to those bodies and provisions relating to continuity), see the Enterprise and Regulatory Reform Act 2013 (Commencement No 6, Transitional Provisions and Savings) Order 2014, SI 2014/416, Schedule at **[2.13]**). Paras (ae), (af), (ag) and (ah) were repealed by the Competition (Amendment etc) (EU Exit) Regulations 2019, SI 2019/93, regs 32, 50, as from IP completion day (as defined in the European Union (Withdrawal Agreement) Act 2020, s 39) (for transitional provisions and savings in relation to the operation of the 2019 Regulations, see Sch 4 to those Regulations at **[7.69]** et seq and, in particular, Sch 4, Pt 7 to the 2019 Regulations at **[7.76]**).

Sub-s (2): words in first pair of square brackets substituted, and paras (ea), (eb) inserted, by the Enterprise and Regulatory Reform Act 2013, ss 26(3), 57, Sch 5, Pt 2, paras 59, 141(1), (3), Sch 15, paras 15, 36(1), (8), subject to transitional provisions in SI 2014/416 as noted above.

Sub-s (3): para (ba) inserted by the Communications Act 2003, s 389(1), Sch 16, para 18(1), (2); references to the "CMA" in paras (b), (e) substituted, and paras (h), (i) repealed, by the Enterprise and Regulatory Reform Act 2013, ss 26(3), 57, Sch 5, Pt 2, paras 59, 141(1), (4), Sch 15, paras 15, 36(1), (9), subject to transitional provisions in SI 2014/416 as noted above.

Sub-ss (9), (10): references to the "CMA" substituted by the Enterprise and Regulatory Reform Act 2013, s 26(3), Sch 5, Pt 2, paras 59, 141(1), (5), (6), subject to transitional provisions in SI 2014/416 as noted above; words in second pair of square brackets in para (a) inserted by the Communications Act 2003, s 389(1), Sch 16, para 18(1), (3), (4).

Sub-s (11): word in square brackets substituted by the Enterprise and Regulatory Reform Act 2013, s 26(3), Sch 5, Pt 2, paras 59, 141(1), (7), subject to transitional provisions in SI 2014/416 as noted above.

[1.299]

108 Defamation

For the purposes of the law relating to defamation, absolute privilege attaches to any advice, guidance, notice or direction given, or decision or report made, by the [CMA, OFCOM] or the Secretary of State in the exercise of any of their functions under this Part.

NOTES

Words in square brackets substituted by the Enterprise and Regulatory Reform Act 2013, s 26(3), Sch 5, Pt 2, paras 59, 142. For various transitional provisions (including those relating to the abolition of the OFT and the Competition Commission, existing references to those bodies and provisions relating to continuity), see the Enterprise and Regulatory Reform Act 2013 (Commencement No 6, Transitional Provisions and Savings) Order 2014, SI 2014/416, Schedule at **[2.13]**.

Investigation powers

[1.300]

109 Attendance of witnesses and production of documents etc

[(A1) For the purposes of this section, the permitted purposes are the following—

(a) assisting the CMA in carrying out any functions, including enforcement functions, exercisable by it under or by virtue of this Part in connection with a matter that is or has been the subject of a reference or possible reference under section 22 or 33;

(b) assisting the CMA or the Secretary of State in carrying out any functions, including enforcement functions, of the CMA or (as the case may be) the Secretary of State under or by virtue of this Part in connection with a matter that is or has been the subject of a reference or possible reference under section 45 or 62.]

(1) [The CMA may, for a permitted purpose,] give notice to any person requiring him—

(a) to attend at a time and place specified in the notice; and

(b) to give evidence to the [CMA] or a person nominated by the [CMA] for the purpose.

(2) [The CMA may, for a permitted purpose,] give notice to any person requiring him—

(a) to produce any documents which—

(i) are specified or described in the notice, or fall within a category of document which is specified or described in the notice; and

(ii) are in that person's custody or under his control; and

(b) to produce them at a time and place so specified and to a person so specified.

(3) [The CMA may, for a permitted purpose,] give notice to any person who carries on any business requiring him—

(a) to supply to [the CMA] such estimates, forecasts, returns or other information as may be specified or described in the notice; and

(b) to supply it at a time and place, and in a form and manner, so specified and to a person so specified.

(4) A notice under this section shall[—

(a) specify the permitted purpose for which the notice is given, including the function or functions in question; and

(b)] include information about the possible consequences of not complying with the notice.

(5) [The CMA, or any person nominated by it for the purpose, may for a permitted purpose] take evidence on oath, and for that purpose may administer oaths.

(6) The person to whom any document is produced in accordance with a notice under this section may, [for a permitted purpose] copy the document so produced.

(7) No person shall be required under this section—

- (a) to give any evidence or produce any documents which he could not be compelled to give or produce in civil proceedings before the court; or
- (b) to supply any information which he could not be compelled to supply in evidence in such proceedings.

(8) No person shall be required, in compliance with a notice under this section, to go more than 10 miles from his place of residence unless his necessary travelling expenses are paid or offered to him.

[(8A) In subsection (A1), "enforcement functions" means—

- (a) in relation to the CMA—
  - (i) functions conferred by virtue of section 87 on the CMA by enforcement orders;
  - (ii) functions of the CMA in relation to the variation, supersession or release of enforcement undertakings or the variation or revocation of enforcement orders;
  - (iii) functions of the CMA under or by virtue of section 75, 76, 83 or 92 in relation to enforcement undertakings or enforcement orders;
- (b) in relation to the Secretary of State—
  - (i) functions conferred by virtue of section 87 on the Secretary of State by enforcement orders;
  - (ii) functions of the Secretary of State in relation to the variation, supersession or release of enforcement undertakings or the variation or revocation of enforcement orders;
  - (iii) functions of the Secretary of State under or by virtue of paragraph 5, 6 or 10 of Schedule 7 in relation to enforcement undertakings or enforcement orders.]

(9) Any reference in this section to the production of a document includes a reference to the production of a legible and intelligible copy of information recorded otherwise than in legible form.

(10) In this section "the court" means—

- (a) in relation to England and Wales or Northern Ireland, the High Court; and
- (b) in relation to Scotland, the Court of Session.

NOTES

Sub-s (A1): inserted by the Enterprise and Regulatory Reform Act 2013, s 29(1), (2), (9) (for various transitional provisions (including those relating to the abolition of the OFT and the Competition Commission, existing references to those bodies and provisions relating to continuity), see the Enterprise and Regulatory Reform Act 2013 (Commencement No 6, Transitional Provisions and Savings) Order 2014, SI 2014/416, Schedule at **[2.13]**).

Sub-s (1): words in first pair of square brackets substituted by the Enterprise and Regulatory Reform Act 2013, s 29(1), (3), subject to transitional provisions in SI 2014/416 as noted above. References to the "CMA" in para (b) substituted by the Enterprise and Regulatory Reform Act 2013 (Competition) (Consequential, Transitional and Saving Provisions) Order 2014, SI 2014/892, art 2, Sch 1, Pt 1, paras 1, 3, subject to transitional provisions as noted to s 8A at **[1.187]**.

Sub-s (2), (5), (6): words in square brackets substituted by the Enterprise and Regulatory Reform Act 2013, s 29(1), (4), (7), (8), subject to transitional provisions in SI 2014/416 as noted above.

Sub-s (3): words in square brackets substituted by the Enterprise and Regulatory Reform Act 2013, ss 26(3), 29(1), (5), Sch 5, Pt 2, paras 59, 143, subject to transitional provisions in SI 2014/416 as noted above.

Sub-s (4): words in square brackets inserted by the Enterprise and Regulatory Reform Act 2013, s 29(1), (6), subject to transitional provisions in SI 2014/416 as noted above.

Sub-s (8A): inserted by the Enterprise and Regulatory Reform Act 2013, s 29(1), (2), (9) (for various transitional provisions (including those relating to the abolition of the OFT and the Competition Commission, existing references to those bodies and provisions relating to continuity), see the Enterprise and Regulatory Reform Act 2013 (Commencement No 6, Transitional Provisions and Savings) Order 2014, SI 2014/416, Schedule at **[2.13]**).

[1.301]

[109A Transferred EU merger commitments: witnesses, documents etc

Any power exercisable by the CMA under section 109 for "permitted purposes" (as mentioned in subsection (A1) of that section) is also exercisable by the CMA under that section for the purposes of assisting the CMA in carrying out any of its functions under or by virtue of section 95A(1) or 95B.]

NOTES

Commencement: IP completion day (as defined in the European Union (Withdrawal Agreement) Act 2020, s 39).

Inserted by the Competition (Amendment etc) (EU Exit) Regulations 2019, SI 2019/93, reg 50A, as from IP completion day (as defined in the European Union (Withdrawal Agreement) Act 2020, s 39) (for transitional provisions and savings in relation to the operation of the 2019 Regulations, see Sch 4 to those Regulations at **[7.69]** et seq). Note that reg 50A of the 2019 Regulations was inserted by the Competition (Amendment etc) (EU Exit) Regulations 2020, SI 2020/1343, reg 9, with effect from immediately before IP completion day.

[1.302]

110 Enforcement of powers under section 109: general

(1) Where the [CMA] considers that a person has, without reasonable excuse, failed to comply with any requirement of a notice under section 109, it may impose a penalty in accordance with section 111.

(2) The [CMA] may proceed (whether at the same time or at different times) under subsection (1) and section 39(4) or (as the case may be) 51(4) (including that enactment as applied by section 65(3)) in relation to the same failure.

(3) Where the [CMA] considers that a person has intentionally obstructed or delayed another person in the exercise of his powers under section 109(6), it may impose a penalty in accordance with section 111.

(4) . . .

(5) A person, subject to subsection (6), commits an offence if he intentionally alters, suppresses or destroys any document which he has been required to produce by a notice under section 109.

(6) A person does not commit an offence under subsection (5) in relation to any act which constitutes a failure to comply with a notice under section 109 if the [CMA] has proceeded against that person under subsection (1) above in relation to that failure.

(7) A person who commits an offence under subsection (5) shall be liable—

(a) on summary conviction, to a fine not exceeding the statutory maximum;

(b) on conviction on indictment, to imprisonment for a term not exceeding two years or to a fine or to both.

(8) The [CMA] shall not proceed against a person under subsection (1) in relation to an act which constitutes an offence under subsection (5) if that person has been found guilty of that offence.

(9) In deciding whether and, if so, how to proceed under subsection (1) or (3) or section 39(4) or 51(4) (including that enactment as applied by section 65(3)), the [CMA] shall have regard to the statement of policy which was most recently published under section 116 at the time when the failure concerned or (as the case may be) the obstruction or delay concerned occurred.

(10) The reference in this section to the production of a document includes a reference to the production of a legible and intelligible copy of information recorded otherwise than in legible form; and the reference to suppressing a document includes a reference to destroying the means of reproducing information recorded otherwise than in legible form.

NOTES

References to the "CMA" substituted by the Enterprise and Regulatory Reform Act 2013, s 26(3), Sch 5, Pt 2, paras 59, 144. For various transitional provisions (including those relating to the abolition of the OFT and the Competition Commission, existing references to those bodies and provisions relating to continuity), see the Enterprise and Regulatory Reform Act 2013 (Commencement No 6, Transitional Provisions and Savings) Order 2014, SI 2014/416, Schedule at **[2.13]**.

Sub-s (4): repealed by the Enterprise and Regulatory Reform Act 2013, s 29(1), (10), subject to transitional provisions in SI 2014/416 as noted above.

[1.303]

[110A Restriction on powers to impose penalties under section 110

(1) No penalty shall be imposed by virtue of section 110(1) or (3) if more than 4 weeks have passed since the day which is the relevant day in the case in question; but this subsection shall not apply in relation to any variation or substitution of the penalty which is permitted by virtue of this Part.

(2) In the following provisions of this section, "the section 109 power" means the power under section 109 to which the failure or (as the case may be) the obstruction or delay in question relates.

(3) Where the section 109 power is exercised in connection with an enforcement function (within the meaning of that section), the relevant day is the day when the enforcement undertaking concerned is superseded or released or (as the case may be) the enforcement order concerned is revoked.

(4) Except where subsection (3) applies, the relevant day is the day determined in accordance with the following provisions of this section.

(5) Where the section 109 power is exercised for the purpose mentioned in section 109(A1)(a) in connection with a matter that is the subject of a possible reference under section 22 or 33, the relevant day is the day when the CMA finally decides whether to make the reference.

(6) Where the section 109 power is exercised for the purpose mentioned in section 109(A1)(a) in connection with a matter that is the subject of a reference under section 22 or 33, the relevant day is the day when the reference is finally determined (see section 79).

(7) Where the section 109 power is exercised for the purpose mentioned in section 109(A1)(b) in connection with a matter that is the subject of a possible reference under section 45 or 62, the relevant day is the day when the Secretary of State finally decides whether to make the reference.

(8) Where the section 109 power is exercised for the purpose mentioned in section 109(A1)(b) in connection with a matter that is the subject of a reference under section 45 or 62, the relevant day is the day when the reference is finally determined.

[(9) Where the section 109 power is exercised for the purposes of assisting the CMA in carrying out any of its functions under or by virtue of section 95A(1) or 95B (see section 109A), the relevant day is the day when the transferred EU merger commitments concerned are waived or substituted by the European Commission.]]

NOTES

Inserted by the Enterprise and Regulatory Reform Act 2013, s 29(11). For various transitional provisions (including those relating to the abolition of the OFT and the Competition Commission, existing references to those bodies and provisions relating to continuity), see the Enterprise and Regulatory Reform Act 2013 (Commencement No 6, Transitional Provisions and Savings) Order 2014, SI 2014/416, Schedule at **[2.13]**.

Sub-s (9): inserted by the Competition (Amendment etc) (EU Exit) Regulations 2019, SI 2019/93, reg 50B, as from IP completion day (as defined in the European Union (Withdrawal Agreement) Act 2020, s 39) (for transitional provisions and savings in relation to the operation of the 2019 Regulations, see Sch 4 to those Regulations at **[7.69]** et seq). Note that reg 50B of the 2019 Regulations was inserted by the Competition (Amendment etc) (EU Exit) Regulations 2020, SI 2020/1343, reg 9, with effect from immediately before IP completion day.

[1.304]

[110B Section 110A: supplementary provision

(1) For the purpose of section 110A(5), the CMA finally decides whether to make a reference under section 22 or 33 if—

(a) the CMA decides that the duty to make such a reference applies;

(b) the CMA accepts an undertaking under section 73;

(c) the CMA decides not to make such a reference (otherwise than because it has accepted an undertaking under section 73);

(d) the initial period for the purposes of section 34ZA expires without the CMA having complied with the duty under subsection (1) of that section;

(e) *the preliminary assessment period for the purposes of section 34A expires without the CMA having complied with the duty under subsection (2) of that section;*

(f) the period permitted by section 73A for the CMA to make a decision required by subsection (2)(a) or (3) of that section expires without the CMA having made the decision.

(2) For the purpose of section 110A(5), the time when the CMA finally decides whether to make a reference under section 22 or 33 is—

(a) in a case falling within subsection (1)(a), the making of the decision that the duty to make such a reference applies;

(b) in a case falling within subsection (1)(b), the acceptance of the undertaking;

(c) in a case falling within subsection (1)(c), the making of the decision not to make the reference;

(d) in a case falling within subsection (1)(d), the expiry of the initial period;

(e) *in a case falling within subsection (1)(e), the expiry of the preliminary assessment period;*

(f) in a case falling within subsection (1)(f), the expiry of the period in question.

(3) For the purpose of section 110A(7), the Secretary of State finally decides whether to make a reference under section 45 or 62 if—

(a) the Secretary of State makes such a reference;

(b) the Secretary of State accepts an undertaking under paragraph 3 of Schedule 7;

(c) the Secretary of State decides not to make such a reference (otherwise than because of the acceptance of an undertaking under paragraph 3 of Schedule 7);

(d) *the preliminary assessment period for the purposes of section 46A expires without the CMA having complied with the duty under subsection (2) of that section.*

(4) For the purpose of section 110A(7), the time when the Secretary of State finally decides whether to make a reference under section 45 or 62 is—

(a) in a case falling within subsection (3)(a), the making of the reference;

(b) in a case falling within subsection (3)(b), the acceptance of the undertaking;

(c) in a case falling within subsection (3)(c), the making of the decision not to make the reference;

(d) *in a case falling within subsection (3)(d), the expiry of the preliminary assessment period.*

(5) Paragraph 7(8) to (10) of Schedule 7 applies for deciding if and when a reference under section 45(2) or (3) or 62(2) is finally determined for the purpose of section 110A(8) as it applies for deciding those questions for the purpose of paragraph 7 of Schedule 7.

(6) Paragraph 8(7) to (9) of Schedule 7 applies for deciding if and when a reference under section 45(4) or (5) or 62(3) is finally determined for the purpose of section 110A(8) as it applies for deciding those questions for the purpose of the definition of "relevant period" in paragraph 8(6) of that Schedule.]

NOTES

Inserted by the Enterprise and Regulatory Reform Act 2013, s 29(11). For various transitional provisions (including those relating to the abolition of the OFT and the Competition Commission, existing references to those bodies and provisions relating to continuity), see the Enterprise and Regulatory Reform Act 2013 (Commencement No 6, Transitional Provisions and Savings) Order 2014, SI 2014/416, Schedule at **[2.13]**.

Sub-ss (1)(e), (2)(e), (3)(d) and (4)(d) were repealed by the Competition (Amendment etc) (EU Exit) Regulations 2019, SI 2019/93, regs 32, 51, as from IP completion day (as defined in the European Union (Withdrawal Agreement) Act 2020, s 39) (for transitional provisions and savings in relation to the operation of the 2019 Regulations, see Sch 4 to those Regulations at **[7.69]** et seq and, in particular, Sch 4, Pt 7 to the 2019 Regulations at **[7.76]**).

[1.305]

111 Penalties

(1) A penalty imposed under section 110(1) or (3) shall be of such amount as the [CMA] considers appropriate.

(2) The amount may, in the case of a penalty imposed under section 110(1), be a fixed amount, an amount calculated by reference to a daily rate or a combination of a fixed amount and an amount calculated by reference to a daily rate.

(3) The amount shall, in the case of a penalty imposed under section 110(3), be a fixed amount.

(4) No penalty imposed under section 110(1) shall—

(a) in the case of a fixed amount, exceed such amount as the Secretary of State may by order specify;

(b) in the case of an amount calculated by reference to a daily rate, exceed such amount per day as the Secretary of State may so specify; and

(c) in the case of a fixed amount and an amount calculated by reference to a daily rate, exceed such fixed amount and such amount per day as the Secretary of State may so specify.

(5) In imposing a penalty by reference to a daily rate—

(a) no account shall be taken of any days before the service of the notice under section 112 on the person concerned; and

(b) unless the [CMA] determines an earlier date (whether before or after the penalty is imposed), the amount payable shall cease to accumulate at the beginning of—

(i) the day on which the requirement of the notice concerned under section 109 is satisfied . . . ; or

(ii) if earlier, [the day which is the relevant day in the case in question for the purposes of section 110A].

(6) No penalty imposed under section 110(3) shall exceed such amount as the Secretary of State may by order specify.

(7) An order under subsection (4) or (6) shall not specify—

(a) in the case of a fixed amount, an amount exceeding £30,000;

(b) in the case of an amount calculated by reference to a daily rate, an amount per day exceeding £15,000; and

(c) in the case of a fixed amount and an amount calculated by reference to a daily rate, a fixed amount exceeding £30,000 and an amount per day exceeding £15,000.

(8) Before making an order under subsection (4) or (6) the Secretary of State shall consult the [CMA] and such other persons as he considers appropriate.

NOTES

Sub-ss (1), (8): references to "CMA" substituted by the Enterprise and Regulatory Reform Act 2013, s 26(3), Sch 5, Pt 2, paras 59, 145. For various transitional provisions (including those relating to the abolition of the OFT and the Competition Commission, existing references to those bodies and provisions relating to continuity), see the Enterprise and Regulatory Reform Act 2013 (Commencement No 6, Transitional Provisions and Savings) Order 2014, SI 2014/416, Schedule at **[2.13]**.

Sub-s (5): reference to the "CMA" in first pair of square brackets substituted, words omitted from sub-para (b)(i) repealed, and words in square brackets in sub-para (b)(ii) substituted, by the Enterprise and Regulatory Reform Act 2013, ss 26(3), 29(1), (12), Sch 5, Pt 2, paras 59, 145, subject to transitional provisions in SI 2014/416 as noted above.

Orders: the Competition and Markets Authority (Penalties) Order 2014, SI 2014/559 at **[2.61]**.

[1.306]

112 Penalties: main procedural requirements

(1) As soon as practicable after imposing a penalty under section 110(1) or (3), the [CMA] shall give notice of the penalty.

(2) The notice shall state—

(a) that the [CMA] has imposed a penalty on the person concerned;

(b) whether the penalty is of a fixed amount, of an amount calculated by reference to a daily rate or of both a fixed amount and an amount calculated by reference to a daily rate;

(c) the amount or amounts concerned and, in the case of an amount calculated by reference to a daily rate, the day on which the amount first starts to accumulate and the day or days on which it might cease to accumulate;

(d) the failure or (as the case may be) the obstruction or delay which the [CMA] considers gave it the power to impose the penalty;

(e) any other facts which the [CMA] considers justify the imposition of a penalty and the amount or amounts of the penalty;

(f) the manner in which, and place at which, the penalty is required to be paid to the [CMA];

(g) the date or dates, no earlier than the end of the relevant period beginning with the date of service of the notice on the person concerned, by which the penalty or (as the case may be) different portions of it are required to be paid;

(h) that the penalty or (as the case may be) different portions of it may be paid earlier than the date or dates by which it or they are required to be paid; and

(i) that the person concerned has the right to apply under subsection (3) below or to appeal under section 114 and the main details of those rights.

(3) The person against whom the penalty was imposed may, within 14 days of the date of service on him of a notice under subsection (1), apply to the [CMA] for it to specify a different date or (as the case may be) different dates by which the penalty or (as the case may be) different portions of it are to be paid.

(4) A notice under this section shall be given by—

(a) serving a copy of the notice on the person on whom the penalty was imposed; and

(b) publishing the notice.

(5) In this section "relevant period" means the period of 28 days mentioned in subsection (3) of section 114 or, if another period is specified by the Secretary of State under that subsection, that period.

NOTES

References to the "CMA" substituted by the Enterprise and Regulatory Reform Act 2013, s 26(3), Sch 5, Pt 2, paras 59, 146. For various transitional provisions (including those relating to the abolition of the OFT and the Competition Commission, existing references to those bodies and provisions relating to continuity), see the Enterprise and Regulatory Reform Act 2013 (Commencement No 6, Transitional Provisions and Savings) Order 2014, SI 2014/416, Schedule at **[2.13]**.

[1.307]

113 Payments and interest by instalments

(1) If the whole or any portion of a penalty is not paid by the date by which it is required to be paid, the unpaid balance from time to time shall carry interest at the rate for the time being specified in section 17 of the Judgments Act 1838 (c 110).

(2) Where an application has been made under section 112(3), the penalty shall not be required to be paid until the application has been determined, withdrawn or otherwise dealt with.

(3) If a portion of a penalty has not been paid by the date required for it, the [CMA] may, where it considers it appropriate to do so, require so much of the penalty as has not already been paid (and is capable of being paid immediately) to be paid immediately.

(4) Any sums received by the [CMA] in or towards the payment of a penalty, or interest on a penalty, shall be paid into the Consolidated Fund.

NOTES

Sub-ss (3), (4): references to the "CMA" substituted by the Enterprise and Regulatory Reform Act 2013, s 26(3), Sch 5, Pt 2, paras 59, 147. For various transitional provisions (including those relating to the abolition of the OFT and the Competition Commission, existing references to those bodies and provisions relating to continuity), see the Enterprise and Regulatory Reform Act 2013 (Commencement No 6, Transitional Provisions and Savings) Order 2014, SI 2014/416, Schedule at **[2.13]**.

[1.308]

114 Appeals in relation to penalties

(1) This section applies if a person on whom a penalty is imposed under section 110(1) or (3) is aggrieved by—

(a) the imposition or nature of the penalty;

(b) the amount or amounts of the penalty; or

(c) the date by which the penalty is required to be paid or (as the case may be) the different dates by which portions of the penalty are required to be paid.

(2) The person aggrieved may apply to the Competition Appeal Tribunal.

(3) If a copy of the notice under section 112(1) was served on the person on whom the penalty was imposed, the application to the Competition Appeal Tribunal shall, subject to subsection (4), be made within—

(a) the period of 28 days starting with the day on which the copy was served on the person concerned; or

(b) such other period as the Secretary of State may by order specify.

(4) If the application relates to a decision of the [CMA] on an application by the person on whom the penalty was imposed under section 112(3), the application to the Competition Appeal Tribunal shall be made within—

(a) the period of 28 days starting with the day on which the person concerned is notified of the decision; or

(b) such other period as the Secretary of State may by order specify.

(5) On an application under this section, the Competition Appeal Tribunal may—

(a) quash the penalty;

(b) substitute a penalty of a different nature or of such lesser amount or amounts as the Competition Appeal Tribunal considers appropriate; or

(c) in a case falling within subsection (1)(c), substitute for the date or dates imposed by the [CMA] an alternative date or dates;

if it considers it appropriate to do so.

(6) The Competition Appeal Tribunal shall not substitute a penalty of a different nature under subsection (5)(b) unless it considers that the person on whom the penalty is imposed will, or is likely to, pay less under the substituted penalty than he would have paid under the original penalty.

(7) Where an application has been made under this section—

(a) the penalty shall not be required to be paid until the application has been determined, withdrawn or otherwise dealt with; and

(b) the [CMA] may agree to reduce the amount or amounts of the penalty in settlement of the application.

(8) Where the Competition Appeal Tribunal substitutes a penalty of a different nature or of a lesser amount or amounts it may require the payment of interest on the substituted penalty at such rate or rates, and from such date or dates, as it considers appropriate.

(9) Where the Competition Appeal Tribunal specifies as a date by which the penalty, or a portion of the penalty, is to be paid a date before the determination of the application under this section it may require the payment of interest on the penalty, or portion, from that date at such rate as it considers appropriate.

(10) An appeal lies to the appropriate court—

(a) on a point of law arising from a decision of the Tribunal in proceedings under this section; or

(b) from a decision of the Tribunal in such proceedings as to the amount or amounts of a penalty.

(11) An appeal under subsection (10)—

(a) may be brought by a party to the proceedings before the Tribunal; and

(b) requires the permission of the Tribunal or the appropriate court.

(12) In this section "the appropriate court" means the Court of Appeal or, in the case of Tribunal proceedings in Scotland, the Court of Session.

NOTES

Sub-ss (4), (5), (7): references to the "CMA" substituted by the Enterprise and Regulatory Reform Act 2013, s 26(3), Sch 5, Pt 2, paras 59, 148. For various transitional provisions (including those relating to the abolition of the OFT and the Competition Commission, existing references to those bodies and provisions relating to continuity), see the Enterprise and Regulatory Reform Act 2013 (Commencement No 6, Transitional Provisions and Savings) Order 2014, SI 2014/416, Schedule at **[2.13]**.

[1.309]

115 Recovery of penalties

Where a penalty imposed under section 110(1) or (3), or any portion of such a penalty, has not been paid by the date on which it is required to be paid and—

(a) no application relating to the penalty has been made under section 114 during the period within which such an application may be made, or

(b) any such application which has been made has been determined, withdrawn or otherwise dealt with,

the [CMA] may recover from the person on whom the penalty was imposed any of the penalty and any interest which has not been paid; and in England and Wales and Northern Ireland such penalty and interest may be recovered as a civil debt due to the [CMA].

NOTES

References to the "CMA" substituted by the Enterprise and Regulatory Reform Act 2013, s 26(3), Sch 5, Pt 2, paras 59, 149. For various transitional provisions (including those relating to the abolition of the OFT and the Competition Commission, existing references to those bodies and provisions relating to continuity), see the Enterprise and Regulatory Reform Act 2013 (Commencement No 6, Transitional Provisions and Savings) Order 2014, SI 2014/416, Schedule at **[2.13]**.

[1.310]

116 Statement of policy

(1) The [CMA] shall prepare and publish a statement of policy in relation to the enforcement of notices under section 109.

(2) The statement shall, in particular, include a statement about the considerations relevant to the determination of the nature and amount of any penalty imposed under section 110(1) or (3).

(3) The [CMA] may revise its statement of policy and, where it does so, it shall publish the revised statement.

(4) The [CMA] shall consult such persons as it considers appropriate when preparing or revising its statement of policy.

NOTES

References to the "CMA" substituted by the Enterprise and Regulatory Reform Act 2013, s 26(3), Sch 5, Pt 2, paras 59, 150. For various transitional provisions (including those relating to the abolition of the OFT and the Competition Commission, existing references to those bodies and provisions relating to continuity), see the Enterprise and Regulatory Reform Act 2013 (Commencement No 6, Transitional Provisions and Savings) Order 2014, SI 2014/416, Schedule at **[2.13]**.

[1.311]

117 False or misleading information

(1) A person commits an offence if—

(a) he supplies any information to the [CMA, OFCOM] or the Secretary of State in connection with any of their functions under this Part;

(b) the information is false or misleading in a material respect; and

(c) he knows that it is false or misleading in a material respect or is reckless as to whether it is false or misleading in a material respect.

(2) A person commits an offence if he—

(a) supplies any information to another person which he knows to be false or misleading in a material respect; or

(b) recklessly supplies any information to another person which is false or misleading in a material respect;

knowing that the information is to be used for the purpose of supplying information to the [CMA, OFCOM] or the Secretary of State in connection with any of their functions under this Part

(3) A person who commits an offence under subsection (1) or (2) shall be liable—

(a) on summary conviction, to a fine not exceeding the statutory maximum;

(b) on conviction on indictment, to imprisonment for a term not exceeding two years or to a fine or to both.

NOTES

Sub-ss (1), (2): words in square brackets substituted by the Enterprise and Regulatory Reform Act 2013, s 26(3), Sch 5, Pt 2, paras 59, 151. For various transitional provisions (including those relating to the abolition of the OFT and the Competition Commission, existing references to those bodies and provisions relating to continuity), see the Enterprise and Regulatory Reform Act 2013 (Commencement No 6, Transitional Provisions and Savings) Order 2014, SI 2014/416, Schedule at **[2.13]**.

Sectoral regulators: certain functions of the CMA under Part 4 of this Act are exercisable concurrently with various sectoral regulators and, in so far as those functions are to be exercised concurrently, this section has effect as if references to the CMA included those sectoral regulators (for details of the relevant statutory provisions, see the note preceding s 131 at **[1.328]**).

See also, the EEC Merger Control (Distinct Market Investigations) Regulations 1990, SI 1990/1715 (as amended) which confer investigative powers upon the CMA for the purpose of furnishing information to the European Commission under the Merger Regulation. Article 5 of the Regulations (at **[2.83]**) provides that this section has effect as if those Regulations were contained in Part 3 of this Act. Note that the 1990 Regulations were revoked by the Competition (Amendment etc) (EU Exit) Regulations 2019, SI 2019/93, reg 61, Sch 2, Pt 3, para 9, as from IP completion day (as defined in the European Union (Withdrawal Agreement) Act 2020, s 39). For transitional provisions and savings in relation to the operation of the 2019 Regulations, see Sch 4 to those Regulations at **[7.69]** et seq and see, in particular, Sch 4, Pt 7, para 35B to the 2019 Regulations at **[7.76]**.

Reports

[1.312]

118 Excisions from reports

(1) Subsection (2) applies where the Secretary of State is under a duty to publish—

(a) a report of the [CMA] under section 44 or 61;

[(aa) a report of OFCOM under section 44A or 61A;] or

(b) a report of the [CMA] under section 50 or 65.

(2) The Secretary of State may exclude a matter from the report concerned if he considers that publication of the matter would be inappropriate.

(3) In deciding what is inappropriate for the purposes of subsection (2) the Secretary of State shall have regard to the considerations mentioned in section 244.

(4) The body which has prepared the report shall advise the Secretary of State as to the matters (if any) which it considers should be excluded by him under subsection (2).

(5) References in sections 38(4) and 107(11) to the giving or laying of a report of the [CMA] shall be construed as references to the giving or laying of the report as published.

NOTES

References to the "CMA" substituted by the Enterprise and Regulatory Reform Act 2013, s 26(3), Sch 5, Pt 2, paras 59, 152. For various transitional provisions (including those relating to the abolition of the OFT and the Competition Commission, existing references to those bodies and provisions relating to continuity), see the Enterprise and Regulatory Reform Act 2013 (Commencement No 6, Transitional Provisions and Savings) Order 2014, SI 2014/416, Schedule at **[2.13]**.

Para (aa) of sub-s (1) was inserted by the Communications Act 2003, s 389(1), Sch 16, para 21.

[1.313]

119 Minority reports of [CMA]

(1) Subsection (2) applies where, on a reference to the [CMA] under this Part, a member of a group constituted in connection with the reference . . . , disagrees with any decisions contained in the report of the [CMA] under this Part as the decisions of the [CMA].

(2) The report shall, if the member so wishes, include a statement of his disagreement and of his reasons for disagreeing.

NOTES

References to the "CMA" substituted, and words omitted from sub-s (1) repealed, by the Enterprise and Regulatory Reform Act 2013, s 26(3), Sch 5, Pt 2, paras 59, 153. For various transitional provisions (including those relating to the abolition of the

OFT and the Competition Commission, existing references to those bodies and provisions relating to continuity), see the Enterprise and Regulatory Reform Act 2013 (Commencement No 6, Transitional Provisions and Savings) Order 2014, SI 2014/416, Schedule at **[2.13]**.

[Further provision about media mergers

[1.314]

119A Other general functions of OFCOM in relation to this Part

(1) OFCOM have the function of obtaining, compiling and keeping under review information about matters relating to the carrying out of their functions under this Part.

(2) That function is to be carried out with a view to (among other things) ensuring that OFCOM have sufficient information to take informed decisions and to carry out their other functions effectively.

(3) In carrying out that function OFCOM may carry out, commission or support (financially or otherwise) research.

(4) Section 3 of the Communications Act 2003 (general duties of OFCOM) shall not apply in relation to functions of OFCOM under this Part.]

NOTES

Inserted, together with the preceding heading, by the Communications Act 2003, s 385.

[1.315]

[119B Monitoring role for [CMA] in relation to media mergers

(1) The [CMA] has the function of obtaining, compiling and keeping under review information about matters which may be relevant to the Secretary of State in deciding whether to give a special intervention notice mentioning a consideration specified in section 58(2A) to (2C).

(2) That function is to be carried out with a view to (among other things) ensuring that the Secretary of State is aware of cases where, in the opinion of the [CMA], he might wish to consider giving such a notice.

(3) That function does not extend to obtaining, compiling or keeping under review information with a view to carrying out a detailed analysis in each case of the operation in relation to that case of the consideration specified in section 58(2A) to (2C).]

NOTES

Inserted by the Communications Act 2003, s 386.

References to the "CMA" substituted by the Enterprise and Regulatory Reform Act 2013, s 26(3), Sch 5, Pt 2, paras 59, 154. For various transitional provisions (including those relating to the abolition of the OFT and the Competition Commission, existing references to those bodies and provisions relating to continuity), see the Enterprise and Regulatory Reform Act 2013 (Commencement No 6, Transitional Provisions and Savings) Order 2014, SI 2014/416, Schedule at **[2.13]**.

Miscellaneous

[1.316]

120 Review of decisions under Part 3

(1) Any person aggrieved by a decision [mentioned in subsection (1A)] may apply to the Competition Appeal Tribunal for a review of that decision.

[(1A) The decisions are—

(a) a decision of the CMA, OFCOM or the Secretary of State under this Part in connection with a reference or possible reference in relation to a relevant merger situation or a special merger situation;

(b) a decision of the CMA under this Part in connection with transferred EU merger commitments.]

(2) For this purpose "decision"—

(a) does not include a decision to impose a penalty under [section 94A(1) or 110(1) or (3)]; but

(b) includes a failure to take a decision permitted or required by this Part in connection with a reference or possible reference [or transferred EU merger commitments].

(3) Except in so far as a direction to the contrary is given by the Competition Appeal Tribunal, the effect of the decision is not suspended by reason of the making of the application.

(4) In determining such an application the Competition Appeal Tribunal shall apply the same principles as would be applied by a court on an application for judicial review.

(5) The Competition Appeal Tribunal may—

(a) dismiss the application or quash the whole or part of the decision to which it relates; and

(b) where it quashes the whole or part of that decision, refer the matter back to the original decision maker with a direction to reconsider and make a new decision in accordance with the ruling of the Competition Appeal Tribunal.

(6) An appeal lies on any point of law arising from a decision of the Competition Appeal Tribunal under this section to the appropriate court.

(7) An appeal under subsection (6) requires the permission of the Tribunal or the appropriate court.

(8) In this section—

"the appropriate court" means the Court of Appeal or, in the case of Tribunal proceedings in Scotland, the Court of Session; and

"Tribunal rules" has the meaning given by section 15(1).

NOTES

Sub-s (1): words in square brackets substituted (for the original words "of the [CMA], [OFCOM,] [or the Secretary of State] under this Part in connection with a reference or possible reference in relation to a relevant merger situation or a special merger situation") by the Competition (Amendment etc) (EU Exit) Regulations 2019, SI 2019/93, reg 51A(2), as from IP completion day (as defined in the European Union (Withdrawal Agreement) Act 2020, s 39) (for transitional provisions and savings in relation to the operation of the 2019 Regulations, see Sch 4 to those Regulations at **[7.69]** et seq). Note that reg 51A of the 2019 Regulations was inserted by the Competition (Amendment etc) (EU Exit) Regulations 2020, SI 2020/1343, reg 10, with effect from immediately before IP completion day. Note also that the original words as set out above are reproduced as amended by the Enterprise and Regulatory Reform Act 2013, s 26(3), Sch 5, Pt 2, paras 59, 155, and the Communications Act 2003, s 389(1), Sch 16, para 22.

Sub-s (1A): inserted by the Competition (Amendment etc) (EU Exit) Regulations 2019, SI 2019/93, reg 51A(3), as from IP completion day (as defined in the European Union (Withdrawal Agreement) Act 2020, s 39) (for transitional provisions and savings in relation to the operation of the 2019 Regulations, see Sch 4 to those Regulations at **[7.69]** et seq). Note that reg 51A of the 2019 Regulations was inserted by the Competition (Amendment etc) (EU Exit) Regulations 2020, SI 2020/1343, reg 10, with effect from immediately before IP completion day.

Sub-s (2): words in square brackets in para (a) substituted by the Enterprise and Regulatory Reform Act 2013, s 31(2), subject to transitional provisions in SI 2014/416 as noted above. Words in square brackets in para (b) inserted by the Competition (Amendment etc) (EU Exit) Regulations 2019, SI 2019/93, reg 51A(4), as from IP completion day (as defined in the European Union (Withdrawal Agreement) Act 2020, s 39) (for transitional provisions and savings in relation to the operation of the 2019 Regulations, see Sch 4 to those Regulations at **[7.69]** et seq). Note that reg 51A of the 2019 Regulations was inserted by the Competition (Amendment etc) (EU Exit) Regulations 2020, SI 2020/1343, reg 10, with effect from immediately before IP completion day.

[1.317]
121 Fees

(1) The Secretary of State may by order require the payment to him or the [CMA of] such fees as may be prescribed by the order in connection with the exercise by the Secretary of State, the [CMA and OFCOM] of their functions under or by virtue of this Part . . . and sections 32 to 34 of, and Schedule 4ZA to, the Water Industry Act 1991 (c 56).

(2) An order under this section may, in particular, provide for fees to be payable—

(a) in respect of a merger notice; [or]

(b) . . .

(c) on the occurrence of any event specified in the order.

(3) The events that may be specified in an order under this section by virtue of subsection (2)(c) include, in particular—

(a) the decision by the [CMA] in relation to a possible reference under section 22 or 33 that it is or may be the case that a relevant merger situation has been created or (as the case may be) that arrangements are in progress or in contemplation which, if carried into effect, will result in the creation of a relevant merger situation;

(b) the decision by the Secretary of State in relation to a possible reference under section 45 that it is or may be the case that a relevant merger situation has been created or (as the case may be) that arrangements are in progress or in contemplation which, if carried into effect, will result in the creation of a relevant merger situation;

(c) the decision by the Secretary of State in relation to a possible reference under section 62 that—

(i) it is or may be the case that a special merger situation has been created or (as the case may be) that arrangements are in progress or in contemplation which, if carried into effect, will result in the creation of a special merger situation; and

(ii) one or more than one consideration mentioned in the special intervention notice is relevant to a consideration of the special merger situation concerned; and

(d) the decision by the [CMA] in relation to a possible reference under section 32 of the Act of 1991 that it is or may be the case that arrangements are in progress which, if carried into effect, will result in a merger of any two or more water enterprises or that such a merger has taken place otherwise than as a result of the carrying into effect of arrangements that have been the subject of a reference by virtue of paragraph (a) of that section.

(4) An order under this section may, in particular, contain provision—

(a) for ascertaining the persons by whom fees are payable;

(b) specifying whether any fee is payable to the Secretary of State or the [CMA];

(c) for the amount of any fee to be calculated by reference to matters which may include—

(i) . . .

(ii) . . . the value of the turnover of the enterprises concerned;

(d) as to the time when any fee is to be paid; and

(e) for the repayment by the Secretary of State or the [CMA] of the whole or part of any fee in specified circumstances.

(5) For the purposes of subsection (4)(c)(ii) the turnover of an enterprise shall be determined in accordance with such provisions as may be specified in an order under this section.

(6) Provision made by virtue of subsection (5) may, in particular, include provision—

(a) as to the amounts which are, or which are not, to be treated as comprising an enterprise's turnover;

(b) as to the date or dates by reference to which an enterprise's turnover is to be determined;

(c) restricting the turnover to be taken into consideration to turnover which has a connection of a particular description with the United Kingdom.

(7) An order under this section may, in particular, in connection with provisions of the kind mentioned in subsection (5) make provision enabling the Secretary of State or the [CMA] to determine matters of a description specified in the order (including any of the matters mentioned in paragraphs (a) to (c) of subsection (6)).

(8) In determining the amount of any fees to be prescribed by an order under this section, the Secretary of State may take into account all costs incurred by him and by the [CMA in] respect of the exercise by him, the [CMA and OFCOM] of their respective functions under or by virtue of this Part . . . and sections 32 to 34 of, and Schedule 4ZA to, the Act of 1991.

(9) Fees paid to the Secretary of State or the [CMA] under this section shall be paid into the Consolidated Fund.

(10) . . .

Part 1 Statutes

NOTES

Sub-s (1): words in square brackets substituted by the Enterprise and Regulatory Reform Act 2013, s 26(3), Sch 5, Pt 2, paras 59, 156(1), (2) (for various transitional provisions (including those relating to the abolition of the OFT and the Competition Commission, existing references to those bodies and provisions relating to continuity), see the Enterprise and Regulatory Reform Act 2013 (Commencement No 6, Transitional Provisions and Savings) Order 2014, SI 2014/416, Schedule at **[2.13]**). Words omitted repealed by the Communications Act 2003, ss 389(1), 406(7), Sch 16, para 23(1), (2)(b), Sch 19.

Sub-s (2): word in square brackets in para (a) inserted, and para (b) repealed, by the Communications Act 2003, ss 389(1), 406(7), Sch 16, para 23(1), (3), Sch 19.

Sub-ss (3), (7), (9): references to the "CMA" substituted by the Enterprise and Regulatory Reform Act 2013, s 26(3), Sch 5, Pt 2, paras 59, 156(1), (3), (5), subject to transitional provisions in SI 2014/416 as noted above.

Sub-s (4): references to the "CMA" substituted by the Enterprise and Regulatory Reform Act 2013, s 26(3), Sch 5, Pt 2, paras 59, 156(1), (3), subject to transitional provisions in SI 2014/416 as noted above. Words omitted from para (c) repealed by the Communications Act 2003, ss 389(1), 406(7), Sch 16, para 23(1), (4), Sch 19.

Sub-s (8): words in square brackets substituted by the Enterprise and Regulatory Reform Act 2013, s 26(3), Sch 5, Pt 2, paras 59, 156(1), (4), subject to transitional provisions in SI 2014/416 as noted above. Words omitted repealed by the Communications Act 2003, ss 389(1), 406(7), Sch 16, para 23(1), (5)(b), Sch 19.

Sub-s (10): repealed by the Communications Act 2003, ss 389(1), 406(7), Sch 16, para 23(1), (6), Sch 19.

Orders: the Enterprise Act 2002 (Merger Fees and Determination of Turnover) Order 2003, SI 2003/1370 at **[2.92]**; the Enterprise Act 2002 (Merger Fees and Determination of Turnover) (Amendment) Order 2004, SI 2004/3204; the Enterprise Act 2002 (Merger Fees) (Amendment) Order 2009, SI 2009/2396; the Enterprise Act 2002 (Merger Fees) (Amendment and Revocation) Order 2012, SI 2012/1878; the Enterprise Act 2002 (Merger Fees and Determination of Turnover) (Amendment) Order 2014, SI 2014/534; the Water Mergers (Miscellaneous Amendments) Regulations 2015, SI 2015/1936.

[1.318]

122 Primacy of [EU] law

(1) Advice and information published by virtue of section 106(1) . . . shall include such advice and information about the effect of [EU] law, and anything done under or in accordance with it, on the provisions of this Part as the [CMA] considers appropriate.

(2) Advice and information published by the [CMA] by virtue of section 106(1) shall, in particular, include advice and information about the circumstances in which the duties of the [CMA] under sections 22 and 33 do not apply as a result of the [EC Merger Regulation] or anything done under or in accordance with them.

(3) The duty or power to make a reference under section 22 or 45(2) or (3), and the power to give an intervention notice under section 42, shall apply in a case in which the relevant enterprises ceased to be distinct enterprises at a time or in circumstances not falling within section 24 if the condition mentioned in subsection (4) is satisfied.

(4) The condition mentioned in this subsection is that, because of the [EC Merger Regulation] or anything done under or in accordance with them, the reference, or (as the case may be) the reference under section 22 to which the intervention notice relates, could not have been made earlier than 4 months before the date on which it is to be made.

(5) Where the duty or power to make a reference under section 22 or 45(2) or (3), or the power to give an intervention notice under section 42, applies as mentioned in subsection (3), references in this Part to the creation of a relevant merger situation shall be construed accordingly.

NOTES

This section was repealed by the Competition (Amendment etc) (EU Exit) Regulations 2019, SI 2019/93, regs 32, 52, as from IP completion day (as defined in the European Union (Withdrawal Agreement) Act 2020, s 39) (for transitional provisions and savings in relation to the operation of the 2019 Regulations, see Sch 4 to those Regulations at **[7.69]** et seq and, in particular, Sch 4, Pt 7 to the 2019 Regulations at **[7.76]**).

Section heading: "EU" in square brackets substituted by the Treaty of Lisbon (Changes in Terminology) Order 2011, SI 2011/1043, art 6(2)(a).

Sub-s (1): words omitted repealed, and words in second pair of square brackets substituted, by the Enterprise and Regulatory Reform Act 2013, s 26(3), Sch 5, Pt 2, paras 59, 157(1), (2) (for various transitional provisions (including those relating to the abolition of the OFT and the Competition Commission, existing references to those bodies and provisions relating to continuity), see the Enterprise and Regulatory Reform Act 2013 (Commencement No 6, Transitional Provisions and Savings) Order 2014, SI 2014/416, Schedule at **[2.13]**). "EU" in first pair of square brackets substituted by SI 2011/1043, art 6(2)(a).

Sub-s (2): references to the "CMA" substituted by the Enterprise and Regulatory Reform Act 2013, s 26(3), Sch 5, Pt 2, paras 59, 157(1), (3), subject to transitional provisions in SI 2014/416 as noted above. Words in final pair of square brackets substituted by the EC Merger Control (Consequential Amendments) Regulations 2004, SI 2004/1079, reg 2, Schedule, para 2(1), (24).

Sub-s (4): words in square brackets substituted by SI 2004/1079, reg 2, Schedule, para 2(1), (24).

References to the European Community and related expressions: see the note "References to "the European Community", "Community", etc" in the introductory notes to this Act.

[1.319]

123 Power to alter share of supply test

(1) The Secretary of State may by order amend or replace the conditions which determine for the purposes of this Part whether a relevant merger situation has been created.

(2) The Secretary of State shall not exercise his power under subsection (1)—

(a) to amend or replace the conditions mentioned in paragraphs (a) and (b) of subsection (1) of section 23;

(b) to amend or replace the condition mentioned in paragraph (a) of subsection (2) of that section.

(3) In exercising his power under subsection (1) to amend or replace the condition mentioned in paragraph (b) of subsection (2) of section 23 or any condition which for the time being applies instead of it, the Secretary of State shall, in particular, have regard to the desirability of ensuring that any amended or new condition continues to operate by reference to the degree of commercial strength which results from the enterprises concerned having ceased to be distinct.

(4) Before making an order under this section the Secretary of State shall consult the [CMA].

(5) An order under this section may provide for the delegation of functions to the decision-making authority.

NOTES

Sub-s (4): reference to the "CMA" substituted by the Enterprise and Regulatory Reform Act 2013, s 26(3), Sch 5, Pt 2, paras 59, 158. For various transitional provisions (including those relating to the abolition of the OFT and the Competition Commission, existing references to those bodies and provisions relating to continuity), see the Enterprise and Regulatory Reform Act 2013 (Commencement No 6, Transitional Provisions and Savings) Order 2014, SI 2014/416, Schedule at **[2.13]**.

Orders: the Enterprise Act 2002 (Share of Supply Test) (Amendment) Order 2018, SI 2018/578; the Enterprise Act 2002 (Share of Supply) (Amendment) Order 2020, SI 2020/748 (revoked by the National Security and Investment Act 2021, s 58, Sch 2, para 11, as from a day to be appointed).

Other

[1.320]

124 Orders and regulations under Part 3

(1) Any power of the Secretary of State to make an order or regulations under this Part shall be exercisable by statutory instrument.

(2) Any power of the Secretary of State to make an order or regulations under this Part—

(a) may be exercised so as to make different provision for different cases or different purposes; and

(b) includes power to make such incidental, supplementary, consequential, transitory, transitional or saving provision as the Secretary of State considers appropriate.

(3) The power of the Secretary of State under section 34[, 59(6A)] or 123 (including that power as extended by subsection (2) above) may be exercised by modifying any enactment comprised in or made under this Act, or any other enactment.

(4) The power of the Secretary of State under section [34ZC(6),] 40(8), [41B(6),] [44(11),] 52(8) (including that enactment as applied by section 65(3)), 58(3), *68*[, 73B(6),] [, 94A(6)] or 102 as extended by subsection (2) above may be exercised by modifying any enactment comprised in or made under this Act, or any other enactment.

(5) An order made by the Secretary of State under section 28 (including that enactment as applied by section 42(5)[and 59(5)]), [34ZC(6),] 40(8), [41B(6),] 52(8) (including that enactment as applied by section 65(3)), [73B(6),] [94A(3) or (6),] 111(4) or (6), 114(3)(b) or (4)(b) or 121 or Schedule 7 shall be subject to annulment in pursuance of a resolution of either House of Parliament.

(6) No order shall be made by the Secretary of State under section 34, [44(11), 59(6A),] *68*, 102, 123 or 128(6) unless a draft of it has been laid before, and approved by a resolution of, each House of Parliament.

(7) An order made by the Secretary of State under section 58(3) shall be laid before Parliament after being made and shall cease to have effect unless approved, within the period of 28 days beginning with the day on which it is made, by a resolution of each House of Parliament.

(8) In calculating the period of 28 days mentioned in subsection (7), no account shall be taken of any time during which Parliament is dissolved or prorogued or during which both Houses are adjourned for more than four days.

(9) If an order made by the Secretary of State ceases to have effect by virtue of subsection (7), any modification made by it of an enactment is repealed (and the previous enactment revived) but without prejudice to the validity of anything done in connection with that modification before the order ceased to have effect and without prejudice to the making of a new order.

(10) If, apart from this subsection, an order made by the Secretary of State under section 58(3) would be treated for the purposes of the standing orders of either House of Parliament as a hybrid instrument, it shall proceed in that House as if it were not such an instrument.

NOTES

Sub-s (3): figure ", 59(6A)" in square brackets inserted by the Communications Act 2003, s 389(1), Sch 16, para 24(1), (2).

Sub-s (4): figures "34ZC(6),", "41B(6),", ", 73B(6)," and ", 94A(6)" in square brackets inserted by the Enterprise and Regulatory Reform Act 2013, ss 31(3)(a), 32(2), Sch 8, paras 1, 13(1), (2) (for various transitional provisions (including those relating to the abolition of the OFT and the Competition Commission, existing references to those bodies and provisions relating to continuity), see the Enterprise and Regulatory Reform Act 2013 (Commencement No 6, Transitional Provisions and Savings) Order 2014, SI 2014/416, Schedule at **[2.13]**). Figure "44(11)," in square brackets inserted by the Communications Act 2003, s 389(1), Sch 16, para 24(1), (3). The figure ", 68" in italics was repealed by the Competition (Amendment etc) (EU Exit) Regulations 2019, SI 2019/93, regs 32, 53(1), (2), as from IP completion day (as defined in the European Union (Withdrawal Agreement) Act 2020, s 39) (for transitional provisions and savings in relation to the operation of the 2019 Regulations, see Sch 4 to those Regulations at **[7.69]** et seq).

Sub-s (5): figures "34ZC(6),", "41B(6)," and "73B(6)," in square brackets, and words "94A(3) or (6)," in square brackets, inserted by the Enterprise and Regulatory Reform Act 2013, ss 31(3)(b), 32(2), Sch 8, paras 1, 13(1), (3), subject to transitional provisions in SI 2014/416 as noted above. The words "and 59(5)" in square brackets were substituted (for the original words ", 59(5) and 67(7)") by SI 2019/93, regs 32, 53(1), (3), as from IP completion day (as defined in the European Union (Withdrawal Agreement) Act 2020, s 39) (for transitional provisions and savings in relation to the operation of the 2019 Regulations, etc, see the first note relating to those Regulations above).

Sub-s (6): figures "44(11), 59(6A)," in square brackets inserted by the Communications Act 2003, s 389(1), Sch 16, para 24(1), (4). The figure "68," in italics was repealed by SI 2019/93, regs 32, 53(1), (4), as from IP completion day (as defined in the European Union (Withdrawal Agreement) Act 2020, s 39) (for transitional provisions and savings in relation to the operation of the 2019 Regulations, etc, see the first note relating to those Regulations above).

[1.321]

125 Offences by bodies corporate

(1) Where an offence under this Part committed by a body corporate is proved to have been committed with the consent or connivance of, or to be attributable to any neglect on the part of—

(a) a director, manager, secretary or other similar officer of the body corporate, or

(b) a person purporting to act in such a capacity,

he as well as the body corporate commits the offence and shall be liable to be proceeded against and punished accordingly.

(2) Where the affairs of a body corporate are managed by its members, subsection (1) applies in relation to the acts and defaults of a member in connection with his functions of management as if he were a director of the body corporate.

(3) Where an offence under this Part is committed by a Scottish partnership and is proved to have been committed with the consent or connivance of a partner, or to be attributable to any neglect on the part of a partner, he as well as the partnership commits the offence and shall be liable to be proceeded against and punished accordingly.

(4) In subsection (3) "partner" includes a person purporting to act as a partner.

[1.322]

126 Service of documents

(1) Any document required or authorised by virtue of this Part to be served on any person may be served—

- (a) by delivering it to him or by leaving it at his proper address or by sending it by post to him at that address;
- (b) if the person is a body corporate other than a limited liability partnership, by serving it in accordance with paragraph (a) on the secretary of the body;
- (c) if the person is a limited liability partnership, by serving it in accordance with paragraph (a) on a member of the partnership; or
- (d) if the person is a partnership, by serving it in accordance with paragraph (a) on a partner or a person having the control or management of the partnership business.

(2) For the purposes of this section and section 7 of the Interpretation Act 1978 (c 30) (service of documents by post) in its application to this section, the proper address of any person on whom a document is to be served shall be his last known address, except that—

- (a) in the case of service on a body corporate (other than a limited liability partnership) or its secretary, it shall be the address of the registered or principal office of the body;
- (b) in the case of service on a limited liability partnership or a member of the partnership, it shall be the address of the registered or principal office of the partnership;
- (c) in the case of service on a partnership or a partner or a person having the control or management of a partnership business, it shall be the address of the principal office of the partnership.

(3) For the purposes of subsection (2) the principal office of a company constituted under the law of a country or territory outside the United Kingdom or of a partnership carrying on business outside the United Kingdom is its principal office within the United Kingdom.

(4) Subsection (5) applies if a person to be served under this Part with any document by another has specified to that other an address within the United Kingdom other than his proper address (as determined under subsection (2)) as the one at which he or someone on his behalf will accept documents of the same description as that document.

(5) In relation to that document, that address shall be treated as his proper address for the purposes of this section and section 7 of the Interpretation Act 1978 in its application to this section, instead of that determined under subsection (2).

(6) Any notice in writing or other document required or authorised by virtue of this Part to be served on any person may be served on that person by transmitting the text of the notice or other document to him by means of [an electronic communications network] or by other means but while in electronic form provided the text is received by that person in legible form and is capable of being used for subsequent reference.

(7) This section does not apply to any document if rules of court make provision about its service.

(8) In this section references to serving include references to similar expressions (such as giving or sending).

NOTES

Sub-s (6): words in square brackets substituted by the Communications Act 2003, s 406(1), Sch 17, para 174(1), (2).

[1.323]

127 Associated persons

(1) Associated persons, and any bodies corporate which they or any of them control, shall be treated as one person—

- (a) for the purpose of deciding under section 26 whether any two enterprises have been brought under common ownership or common control;
- [(aa) for the purposes of section 58(2C); and]
- (b) for the purpose of determining what activities are carried on by way of business by any one person so far as that question arises in connection with paragraph 13(2) of Schedule 8.

(2) Subsection (1) shall not exclude from section 26 any case which would otherwise fall within that section.

(3) A reference under section 22, 33, 45 or 62 (whether or not made by virtue of this section) may be framed so as to exclude from consideration, either altogether or for a specified purpose or to a specified extent, any matter which, apart from this section, would not have been taken into account on that reference.

(4) For the purposes of this section—

- (a) any individual and that individual's spouse or partner and any relative, or spouse[, civil partner] or partner of a relative, of that individual or of that individual's spouse[, civil partner] or partner;
- (b) any person in his capacity as trustee of a settlement and the settlor or grantor and any person associated with the settlor or grantor;
- (c) persons carrying on business in partnership and the spouse[, civil partner] or partner and relatives of any of them; or
- (d) two or more persons acting together to secure or exercise control of a body of persons corporate or unincorporate or to secure control of any enterprise or assets,

shall be regarded as associated with one another.

(5) The reference in subsection (1) to bodies corporate which associated persons control shall be construed in accordance with section 26(3) and (4).

(6) In this section "relative" means a brother, sister, uncle, aunt, nephew, niece, lineal ancestor or descendant (the stepchild of any person, or anyone adopted by a person, whether legally or otherwise, as his child being regarded as a relative or taken into account to trace a relationship in the same way as that person's child); and references to a spouse[, civil partner] or partner shall include a former spouse[, civil partner] or partner.

NOTES

Sub-s (1): para (aa) substituted for the original word "and" at the end of para (a) by the Communications Act 2003, s 375(3).

Sub-ss (4), (6): words in square brackets inserted by the Civil Partnership Act 2004, s 261(1), Sch 27, para 168.

Step-child: this includes relationships arising through civil partnerships; see the Civil Partnership Act 2004, ss 246, 247, Sch 21.

[1.324]

128 Supply of services and market for services etc

(1) References in this Part to the supply of services shall be construed in accordance with this section; and references in this Part to a market for services and other related expressions shall be construed accordingly.

(2) The supply of services does not include the provision of services under a contract of service or of apprenticeship whether it is express or implied and (if it is express) whether it is oral or in writing.

(3) The supply of services includes—

(a) performing for gain or reward any activity other than the supply of goods;

(b) rendering services to order;

(c) the provision of services by making them available to potential users.

(4) The supply of services includes making arrangements for the use of computer software or for granting access to data stored in any form which is not readily accessible.

(5) The supply of services includes making arrangements by means of a relevant agreement [(within the meaning of paragraph 17 of Schedule 3A to the Communications Act 2003 (the electronic communications code)) for sharing the use of electronic communications apparatus].

(6) The supply of services includes permitting or making arrangements to permit the use of land in such circumstances as the Secretary of State may by order specify.

NOTES

Sub-s (5): words in square brackets substituted by the Digital Economy Act 2017, s 4(10), Sch 3, Pt 2, paras 42, 43.

Orders: the Enterprise Act 2002 (Supply of Services) Order 2003, SI 2003/1594, which specifies the circumstances in which permitting or making arrangements to permit the use of land will be regarded as a supply of services for the purposes of Parts 3, 4 and 8 of this Act. The arrangements specified for the purposes of Parts 3, 4 and 8 relate to permitting the use of caravan sites and car parks. Additional arrangements specified for the purposes only of Parts 3 and 4 relate to the use of bus stations, the Channel Tunnel System and railway stations and networks.

[1.325]

129 Other interpretation provisions

(1) In this Part, unless the context otherwise requires—

"action" includes omission; and references to the taking of action include references to refraining from action;

"agreement" means any agreement or arrangement, in whatever way and whatever form it is made, and whether it is, or is intended to be, legally enforceable or not;

"business" includes a professional practice and includes any other undertaking which is carried on for gain or reward or which is an undertaking in the course of which goods or services are supplied otherwise than free of charge;

"change of circumstances" includes any discovery that information has been supplied which is false or misleading in a material respect;

"Community law" means—

(a) all the rights, powers, liabilities, obligations and restrictions from time to time created or arising by or under the Community Treaties; and

(b) all the remedies and procedures from time to time provided for by or under the Community Treaties;

"consumer" means any person who is—

(a) a person to whom goods are or are sought to be supplied (whether by way of sale or otherwise) in the course of a business carried on by the person supplying or seeking to supply them; or

(b) a person for whom services are or are sought to be supplied in the course of a business carried on by the person supplying or seeking to supply them;

and who does not receive or seek to receive the goods or services in the course of a business carried on by him;

"customer" includes a customer who is not a consumer;

["the EC Merger Regulation" means Council Regulation (EC) No 139/2004 of 20th January 2004 on the control of concentrations between undertakings;]

"enactment" includes an Act of the Scottish Parliament, Northern Ireland legislation and an enactment comprised in subordinate legislation, and includes an enactment whenever passed or made;

"enterprise" means the activities, or part of the activities, of a business;

. . .

"goods" includes buildings and other structures, and also includes ships, aircraft and hovercraft;

"modify" includes amend or repeal;

"notice" means notice in writing;

"price" includes any charge or fee (however described);

"subordinate legislation" has the same meaning as in the Interpretation Act 1978 (c 30) and also includes an instrument made under an Act of the Scottish Parliament and an instrument made under Northern Ireland legislation;

"subsidiary" has the meaning given by [section 1159 of the Companies Act 2006];

"supply", in relation to the supply of goods, includes supply by way of sale, lease, hire or hire-purchase, and, in relation to buildings or other structures, includes the construction of them by a person for another person;

["the UK financial system" means the financial system in the United Kingdom;] and

"United Kingdom national" means an individual who is—

(a) a British citizen, a British overseas territories citizen, a British National (Overseas) or a British Overseas citizen;

(b) a person who under the British Nationality Act 1981 (c 61) is a British subject; or

(c) a British protected person within the meaning of that Act.

(2) For the purposes of this Part any two bodies corporate are interconnected if—

(a) one of them is a body corporate of which the other is a subsidiary; or

(b) both of them are subsidiaries of one and the same body corporate;

and in this Part "interconnected bodies corporate" shall be construed accordingly and "group of interconnected bodies corporate" means a group consisting of two or more bodies corporate all of whom are interconnected with each other.

(3) References in this Part to a person carrying on business include references to a person carrying on business in partnership with one or more other persons.

(4) Any duty to publish which is imposed on a person by this Part shall, unless the context otherwise requires, be construed as a duty on that person to publish in such manner as he considers appropriate for the purpose of bringing the matter concerned to the attention of those likely to be affected by it.

NOTES

Sub-s (1) is amended as follows:

The definitions in italics were repealed by the Competition (Amendment etc) (EU Exit) Regulations 2019, SI 2019/93, regs 32, 54, as from IP completion day (as defined in the European Union (Withdrawal Agreement) Act 2020, s 39) (for transitional provisions and savings in relation to the operation of the 2019 Regulations, see Sch 4 to those Regulations at **[7.69]** et seq). The definition "the EC Merger Regulation" was originally inserted by the EC Merger Control (Consequential Amendments) Regulations 2004, SI 2004/1079, reg 2, Schedule, para 2(1), (25).

Definition "the European Merger Regulations" (omitted) repealed by SI 2004/1079, reg 2, Schedule, para 2(1), (25).

Words in square brackets in the definition "subsidiary" substituted by the Companies Act 2006 (Consequential Amendments, Transitional Provisions and Savings) Order 2009, SI 2009/1941, art 2(1), Sch 1, para 199(1), (3).

Definition "the UK financial system" inserted by the Enterprise Act 2002 (Specification of Additional Section 58 Consideration) Order 2008, SI 2008/2645, art 3(1).

References to the European Community and related expressions: see the note "References to "the European Community", "Community", etc" in the introductory notes to this Act.

[1.326]

130 Index of defined expressions

In this Part, the expressions listed in the left-hand column have the meaning given by, or are to be interpreted in accordance with, the provisions listed in the right-hand column.

Expression	***Provision of this Act***
Action (and the taking of action)	Section 129(1)
Adverse public interest finding	Section 54(3)
Agreement	Section 129(1)
Anti-competitive outcome	Section 35(2)
[Broadcasting	Section 44(9)]
Business (and carrying on business)	Section 129(1) and (3)
Change of circumstances	Section 129(1)
[The CMA	Section 273]
. . .	. . .
Community law	*Section 129(1)*
Consumer	Section 129(1)
Customer	Section 129(1)
Date of reference	Section 39(9)
The decision-making authority	Section 22(7)
[*EC Merger Regulation*	*Section 129(1)*]
Enactment	Section 129(1)
Enforcement order	Section 86(6)
Enforcement undertaking	Section 89(2)
Enterprise	Section 129(1)
Enterprises ceasing to be distinct	Section 26(1)
. . .	. . .
Final determination of matter to which intervention notice relates	Section 43(4) and (5)
Final determination of matter to which special intervention notice relates	Section 60(4) and (5)

Expression	*Provision of this Act*
Final determination of reference under section 22 or 33	Section 79(1) and (2)
Goods	Section 129(1)
Interconnected bodies corporate (and a group of interconnected bodies corporate)	Section 129(2)
Intervention notice	Section 42(2)
Market for goods or services	Section 22(6)
Market in the United Kingdom	Section 22(6)
[Media public interest consideration	Section 44(8)]
Merger notice	Section 96(2)
Modify	Section 129(1)
[Newspaper	Section 44(10)
Newspaper enterprise	Section 58A(3)]
Notice	Section 129(1)
Notified arrangements	Section 96(6)
[OFCOM	Section 43(6)]
. . .	. . .
Orders under section 81	Section 81(6)
Orders under paragraph 2 of Schedule 7	Paragraph 2(7) of Schedule 7
The period for considering a merger notice	Sections 97 and 98
Price	Section 129(1)
Public interest consideration	[Section 42(3)]
Public interest consideration being finalised	Section 42(8)
Publish	Section 129(4)
References under section 22, 33, 45 or 62	Sections 37(2), 49(1), 56(8) and 64(2)
Relevant customer benefit	Section 30
Relevant merger situation	Section 23 (as read with other enactments)
Reports of the [CMA]	Section 118(5)
Special intervention notice	Section 59(2)
Special merger situation	Section 59(3)
Subordinate legislation	Section 129(1)
Subsidiary	Section 129(1)
Supply (in relation to the supply of goods)	Section 129(1)
The supply of services (and a market for services etc)	Section 128
[Transferred EU merger commitments	Section 95A(6)]
The turnover in the United Kingdom of an enterprise	Section 28(2)
[The UK financial system	Section 129(1)]
Undertakings under section 80	Section 80(6)
. . .	. . .
United Kingdom national	Section 129(1)

NOTES

Entries "Broadcasting", "Media public interest consideration", "Newspaper", "Newspaper enterprise", and "OFCOM" inserted by the Communications Act 2003, s 389, Sch 16, para 25.

Entry "The CMA" inserted, entries "The Commission", "The OFT" and "Undertakings under paragraph 1 of Schedule 7" (omitted) repealed, and in the entry "Reports of the CMA", reference to the "CMA" substituted, by the Enterprise and Regulatory Reform Act 2013, ss 26(3), 57, Sch 5, Pt 2, paras 59, 159, Sch 15, paras 15, 37. For various transitional provisions (including those relating to the abolition of the OFT and the Competition Commission, existing references to those bodies and provisions relating to continuity), see the Enterprise and Regulatory Reform Act 2013 (Commencement No 6, Transitional Provisions and Savings) Order 2014, SI 2014/416, Schedule at **[2.13]**.

The entries in italics were repealed, the words in square brackets in the entry "Public interest consideration" were substituted (for the original words "Sections 42(3) and 67(9)", and the entry "Transferred EU merger commitments" was inserted, by the Competition (Amendment etc) (EU Exit) Regulations 2019, SI 2019/93, regs 32, 55, as from IP completion day (as defined in the European Union (Withdrawal Agreement) Act 2020, s 39) (for transitional provisions and savings in relation to the operation of the 2019 Regulations, see Sch 4 to those Regulations at **[7.69]** et seq). Note that reg 55 of the 2019 Regulations was amended by the Competition (Amendment etc) (EU Exit) Regulations 2020, SI 2020/1343, reg 11, with effect from immediately before IP completion day; and the effect of that amendment has been incorporated in the text set out above. The entry "EC Merger Regulation" was originally inserted by the EC Merger Control (Consequential Amendments) Regulations 2004, SI 2004/1079, reg 2, Schedule, para 2(1), (26).

Entry "European Merger Regulations" (omitted) repealed by SI 2004/1079, reg 2, Schedule, para 2(1), (26).

Entry "The UK financial system" inserted by the Enterprise Act 2002 (Specification of Additional Section 58 Consideration) Order 2008, SI 2008/2645, art 3(2).

References to the European Community and related expressions: see the note "References to "the European Community", "Community", etc" in the introductory notes to this Act.

PART 4 [MARKET STUDIES AND] MARKET INVESTIGATIONS

NOTES

Words in square brackets in the Part heading inserted by the Enterprise and Regulatory Reform Act 2013, s 38, Sch 12, paras 7, 8. For various transitional provisions (including those relating to the abolition of the OFT and the Competition Commission, existing references to those bodies and provisions relating to continuity), see the Enterprise and Regulatory Reform Act 2013 (Commencement No 6, Transitional Provisions and Savings) Order 2014, SI 2014/416, Schedule at **[2.13]**.

Sectoral regulators: certain functions of the CMA under this Part are exercisable concurrently with various sectoral regulators; ie—

(i) the CMA shall exercise its functions under this Part (other than ss 166, 171, 174E) concurrently with the Office of Rail and Road in so far as relating to the supply of services relating to railways (see the Railways Act 1993, s 67(2), (2A));

(ii) the CMA shall exercise its functions under this Part (other than ss 166, 171, 174E) concurrently with the Gas and Electricity Markets Authority in so far as relating to commercial activities connected with the supply, conveyance (etc) of gas to any premises and ancillary matters (see the Gas Act 1986, s 36A(2), (2A));

(iii) the CMA shall exercise its functions under this Part (other than ss 166, 171, 174E) concurrently with the Gas and Electricity Markets Authority in so far as relating to commercial activities connected with the generation, transmission or supply of electricity or the use of electricity interconnectors (see the Electricity Act 1989, s 43(2), (2A));

(iv) the CMA shall exercise its functions under this Part (other than ss 166, 171, 174E) concurrently with the Water Services Regulation Authority in so far as relating to commercial activities connected with the supply of water or the provision of sewerage services (see the Water Industry Act 1991, s 31(2), (2A));

(v) the CMA shall exercise its functions under this Part (other than ss 166, 171, 174E) concurrently with the Office of Communications in so far as relating to commercial activities connected with communications matters (see the Communications Act 2003, s 370(1), (2));

(vi) the CMA shall exercise its functions under this Part (other than ss 166, 171, 174E) concurrently with the Civil Aviation Authority in so far as they relate to (i) the supply of air traffic services (see the Transport Act 2000, s 86(1), (2)) and (ii) the provision of airport operation services (see the Civil Aviation Act 2012, ss 60, 61).

(vii) the CMA shall exercise its functions under this Part (other than ss 166, 171, 174E) concurrently with Monitor in so far as they relate to the provision of health care services in England (see the Health and Social Care Act 2012, ss 73, 74).

(viii) the CMA shall exercise its functions under this Part (other than ss 166, 171) concurrently with the Payment Systems Regulator in so far as they relate to participation in payment systems (see the Financial Services (Banking Reform) Act 2013, s 59).

(ix) the CMA shall exercise its functions under this Part (other than ss 166, 171) concurrently with the FCA in so far as they relate to the provision of financial services, or relate to the provision of claims management services in Great Britain (see the Financial Services and Markets Act 2000, s 234I).

Accordingly (and by virtue of the Railways Act 1993, s 67(2B), the Gas Act 1986, s 36A(2B), the Electricity Act 1989, s 43(2B), the Water Industry Act 1991, s 31(4), the Communications Act 2003, s 370(3), the Transport Act 2000, s 86(4), the Civil Aviation Act 2012, s 60(3), the Health and Social Care Act 2012, s 73(3), the Financial Services (Banking Reform) Act 2013, s 59(4), and the Financial Services and Markets Act 2000, s 234I(4)) references in this Part (other than in the sections noted above or where the context otherwise requires) to the CMA shall, in so far as is necessary for the purposes of, or in connection with the concurrent exercise of functions, be construed as including references to the appropriate sectoral regulator.

For the power of the Secretary of State to make a sectoral regulator order so as to remove all the functions of sectoral regulator under this Part of this Act that are exercisable concurrently by the regulator and the Competition and Markets Authority, see the Enterprise and Regulatory Reform Act 2013, ss 52, 53 at **[1.451]**, **[1.452]**.

For the duty of the Competition and Markets Authority to prepare a report containing an assessment of how the arrangements for co-operation between the Authority and the sectoral regulators in respect of functions which are exercisable concurrently by the Authority and one or more of the regulators under this Part of this Act have operated during each financial year, see the Enterprise and Regulatory Reform Act 2013, Sch 4, Pt 1, para 16 at **[1.460]**.

CHAPTER 1 [MARKET STUDIES AND] MARKET INVESTIGATION REFERENCES

NOTES

Words in square brackets in the Chapter heading inserted by the Enterprise and Regulatory Reform Act 2013, s 38, Sch 12, paras 7, 9. For various transitional provisions (including those relating to the abolition of the OFT and the Competition Commission, existing references to those bodies and provisions relating to continuity), see the Enterprise and Regulatory Reform Act 2013 (Commencement No 6, Transitional Provisions and Savings) Order 2014, SI 2014/416, Schedule at **[2.13]**.

[Market studies

[1.327]

130A Duty to publish market study notice

(1) Where the CMA is proposing to carry out its functions under section 5 in relation to a matter for the purposes mentioned in subsection (2), the CMA must publish a notice under this section (referred to in this Part as a "market study notice").

(2) The purposes are—

(a) to consider the extent to which a matter in relation to the acquisition or supply of goods or services of one or more than one description in the United Kingdom has or may have effects adverse to the interests of consumers; and

(b) to assess the extent to which steps can and should be taken to remedy, mitigate or prevent any such adverse effects.

(3) A market study notice shall, in particular, specify—

(a) the matter in relation to which the CMA is proposing to carry out its functions under section 5;

(b) the period during which representations may be made to the CMA in relation to the matter; and

(c) the dates by which the CMA is required to comply with the requirements imposed on it by sections 131A and 131B.]

NOTES

Inserted, together with the preceding heading, by the Enterprise and Regulatory Reform Act 2013, s 38, Sch 12, para 1. For various transitional provisions (including those relating to the abolition of the OFT and the Competition Commission, existing references to those bodies and provisions relating to continuity), see the Enterprise and Regulatory Reform Act 2013 (Commencement No 6, Transitional Provisions and Savings) Order 2014, SI 2014/416, Schedule at **[2.13]**.

Making of references

[1.328]

131 Power of [CMA] to make references

(1) [The CMA may, subject to subsection (4), make a reference to its chair for the constitution of a group under Schedule 4 to the Enterprise and Regulatory Reform Act 2013 if the CMA] has reasonable grounds for suspecting that any feature, or combination of features, of a market in the United Kingdom for goods or services prevents, restricts or distorts competition in connection with the supply or acquisition of any goods or services in the United Kingdom or a part of the United Kingdom.

(2) For the purposes of this Part any reference to a feature of a market in the United Kingdom for goods or services shall be construed as a reference to—

(a) the structure of the market concerned or any aspect of that structure;

(b) any conduct (whether or not in the market concerned) of one or more than one person who supplies or acquires goods or services in the market concerned; or

(c) any conduct relating to the market concerned of customers of any person who supplies or acquires goods or services.

[(2A) In a case where the feature or each of the features concerned falls within subsection (2)(b) or (c), a reference under subsection (1) may be made in relation to more than one market in the United Kingdom for goods or services.]

(3) In subsection (2) "conduct" includes any failure to act (whether or not intentional) and any other unintentional conduct.

(4) No reference shall be made under this section if—

(a) the making of the reference is prevented by [section 156(A1) or (1)]; or

(b) a reference has been made under section 132 [or 140A(6)] in relation to the same matter but has not been finally determined.

(5) References in this Part to a market investigation reference being finally determined shall be construed in accordance with section 183(3) to (6).

(6) In this Part—

["cross-market reference" means a reference under this section which falls within subsection (2A) or a reference under section 132 which falls within subsection (3A) of that section (and see section 140A);]

"market in the United Kingdom" includes—

(a) so far as it operates in the United Kingdom or a part of the United Kingdom, any market which operates there and in another country or territory or in a part of another country or territory; and

(b) any market which operates only in a part of the United Kingdom;

"market investigation reference" means a reference under this section or section 132 [or 140A(6)];

["ordinary reference" means a reference under this section or section 132 which is not a cross-market reference (and see section 140A);]

and references to a market for goods or services include references to a market for goods and services.

NOTES

Section heading: reference to the "CMA" substituted by the Enterprise and Regulatory Reform Act 2013, s 26(3), Sch 5, Pt 2, paras 59, 163(1), (3). For various transitional provisions (including those relating to the abolition of the OFT and the Competition Commission, existing references to those bodies and provisions relating to continuity), see the Enterprise and Regulatory Reform Act 2013 (Commencement No 6, Transitional Provisions and Savings) Order 2014, SI 2014/416, Schedule at **[2.13]**.

Sub-s (1): words in square brackets substituted by the Enterprise and Regulatory Reform Act 2013, s 26(3), Sch 5, Pt 2, paras 59, 163(1), (2), subject to transitional provisions in SI 2014/416 as noted above.

Sub-s (2A): inserted by the Enterprise and Regulatory Reform Act 2013, s 33(1), (2), subject to transitional provisions in SI 2014/416 as noted above.

Sub-s (4): words in square brackets in para (a) substituted, and words in square brackets in para (b) inserted by the Enterprise and Regulatory Reform Act 2013, ss 33(1), (3), 35(10), Sch 10, paras 1, 2(1), (2), subject to transitional provisions in SI 2014/416 as noted above.

Sub-s (6): definitions "cross-market reference" and "ordinary reference" inserted, and words in square brackets in definition "market investigation reference" inserted, by the Enterprise and Regulatory Reform Act 2013, s 33(1), (4), 35(10), Sch 10, paras 1, 2(1), (3), subject to transitional provisions in SI 2014/416 as noted above.

[1.329]

[131A Decisions about references under section 131: consultation

(1) This section applies to a case where the CMA has published a market study notice and—

(a) the CMA is proposing to make a reference under section 131 in relation to the matter specified in the notice; or

(b) a representation has been made to the CMA within the period specified in the notice under section 130A(3)(b) to the effect that such a reference should be made but the CMA is proposing not to make such a reference.

(2) The CMA shall—

(a) publish notice of the proposal concerned; and

(b) consult the relevant persons about the proposal, in such manner as it considers practicable, before deciding whether to make a reference.

(3) The CMA may, for the purposes of subsection (1), ignore any representation which it considers to be frivolous or vexatious.

(4) For the purposes of subsection (2), a person is a "relevant person" if the CMA considers that its decision whether to make a reference is likely to have a substantial impact on the person's interests.

(5) In consulting a person for the purposes of this section, the CMA shall, so far as practicable, give its reasons for the proposal.

(6) In considering what is practicable for the purposes of this section, the CMA shall, in particular, have regard to—

(a) the restrictions imposed by the time-table for making the decision (see section 131B); and

(b) any need to keep what is proposed, or the reasons for it, confidential.]

NOTES

Inserted, together with the ss 131B, 131C, by the Enterprise and Regulatory Reform Act 2013, s 38, Sch 12, para 2. For various transitional provisions (including those relating to the abolition of the OFT and the Competition Commission, existing references to those bodies and provisions relating to continuity), see the Enterprise and Regulatory Reform Act 2013 (Commencement No 6, Transitional Provisions and Savings) Order 2014, SI 2014/416, Schedule at **[2.13]**.

[1.330]

[131B Market studies and the making of decisions to refer: time-limits

(1) Where the CMA has published a market study notice in a case to which section 131A applies, the CMA shall, within the period of 6 months beginning with the date on which it publishes the notice—

(a) publish the notice under section 131A(2)(a); and

(b) begin the process of consultation under section 131A(2)(b) (but the CMA need not complete the process within that period).

(2) Subsection (3) applies where—

(a) the CMA has published a market study notice;

(b) no representation has been made to the CMA within the period specified in the notice under section 130A(3)(b) to the effect that a reference under section 131 should be made in relation to the matter specified in the notice; and

(c) the CMA has decided not to make such a reference.

(3) The CMA shall, within the period of 6 months beginning with the date on which it publishes the market study notice, publish notice of the decision not to make a reference.

(4) Where the CMA has published a market study notice it shall, within the period of 12 months beginning with the date on which it publishes the notice, prepare and publish a report (referred to in this Part as a "market study report") which sets out—

(a) the findings of the CMA in relation to the matter specified in the notice; and

(b) the action (if any) which the CMA proposes to take in relation to the matter.

(5) In a case to which section 131A applies, the market study report shall, in particular, contain—

(a) the decision of the CMA to make a reference under section 131 in relation to the matter specified in the market study notice, the decision to accept an undertaking under section 154 instead of making such a reference or (as the case may be) the decision otherwise not to make such a reference;

(b) the CMA's reasons for the decision; and

(c) such information as the CMA considers appropriate for facilitating a proper understanding of its reasons for the decision.

(6) Where a market study report contains a decision of the CMA to make a reference under section 131 in relation to a matter, the CMA shall, at the same time as it publishes the report, make the reference.

(7) This section is subject to section 140A (duty of Secretary of State to refer in public interest intervention cases).]

NOTES

Inserted as noted to s 131A at **[1.329]**.

[1.331]

[131C Time-limits under section 131B: supplementary

(1) The Secretary of State may by order amend section 131B so as to alter one or more of the following periods—

(a) the period of 6 months mentioned in subsection (1) or (3) or any period for the time being mentioned in either of those subsections in substitution for that period;

(b) the period of 12 months mentioned in subsection (4) or any period for the time being there mentioned in substitution for that period.

(2) But no alteration may be made by virtue of subsection (1) which results in—

(a) the period for the time being mentioned in subsection (1) or (3) exceeding 6 months; or

(b) the period for the time being mentioned in subsection (4) exceeding 12 months.

(3) Before making an order under this section the Secretary of State shall consult the CMA and such other persons as the Secretary of State considers appropriate.]

NOTES

Inserted as noted to s 131A at **[1.329]**.

[1.332]

132 Ministerial power to make references

(1) Subsection (3) applies where, in relation to any goods or services[—

(a)] the appropriate Minister is not satisfied with a decision of the [CMA] not to make a reference under section 131[; and

(b) in a case in which the CMA has published a market study notice under section 130A, the period permitted by section 131B for the preparation and publication by the CMA of the market study report has expired].

(2) Subsection (3) also applies where, in relation to any goods or services, the appropriate Minister—

(a) has brought to the attention of the [CMA] information which the appropriate Minister considers to be relevant to the question of whether the [CMA] should make a reference under section 131; but

(b) is not satisfied that the [CMA] will decide, within such period as the appropriate Minister considers to be reasonable, whether [to publish a market study notice in relation to the matter concerned].

(3) The appropriate Minister may, subject to subsection (4), make a reference to the [chair of the CMA for the constitution of a group under Schedule 4 to the Enterprise and Regulatory Reform Act 2013] if he has reasonable grounds for suspecting that any feature, or combination of features, of a market in the United Kingdom for goods or services prevents, restricts or distorts competition in connection with the supply or acquisition of any goods or services in the United Kingdom or a part of the United Kingdom.

[(3A) In a case where the feature or each of the features concerned falls within section 131(2)(b) or (c), a reference under subsection (3) may be made in relation to more than one market in the United Kingdom for goods or services.]

(4) No reference shall be made under this section if[—

(a)] the making of the reference is prevented by [section 156(A1) or (1)][; or

(b) a reference has been made under section 140A(6) in relation to the same matter but has not been finally determined].

(5) In this Part "the appropriate Minister" means—

(a) the Secretary of State; . . .

(b) the Secretary of State and one or more than one other Minister of the Crown acting jointly;

[(c) the Scottish Ministers and the Secretary of State acting jointly; or;

(d) the Scottish Ministers, the Secretary of State and one or more than one other Minister of the Crown, acting jointly].

NOTES

Sub-s (1): para (a) numbered as such, para (b) inserted, and reference to the "CMA" substituted, by the Enterprise and Regulatory Reform Act 2013, ss 26(3), 38, Sch 5, Pt 2, paras 59, 164(1), (2), Sch 12, paras 7, 10(1), (2). For various transitional provisions (including those relating to the abolition of the OFT and the Competition Commission, existing references to those bodies and provisions relating to continuity), see the Enterprise and Regulatory Reform Act 2013 (Commencement No 6, Transitional Provisions and Savings) Order 2014, SI 2014/416, Schedule at **[2.13]**.

Sub-s (2): references to the "CMA" substituted, and words in final pair of square brackets substituted, by the Enterprise and Regulatory Reform Act 2013, ss 26(3), 38, Sch 5, Pt 2, paras 59, 164(1), (2), Sch 12, paras 7, 10(1), (3), subject to transitional provisions in SI 2014/416 as noted above.

Sub-s (3): words in square brackets substituted by the Enterprise and Regulatory Reform Act 2013, s 26(3), Sch 5, Pt 2, paras 59, 164(1), (3), subject to transitional provisions in SI 2014/416 as noted above.

Sub-s (3A): inserted by the Enterprise and Regulatory Reform Act 2013, s 34(1), (2), subject to transitional provisions in SI 2014/416 as noted above.

Sub-s (4): para (a) designated as such, para (b) inserted, and words in square brackets in para (a) substituted, by the Enterprise and Regulatory Reform Act 2013, ss 34(1), (3), 35(10), Sch 10, paras 1, 3, subject to transitional provisions in SI 2014/416 as noted above.

Sub-s (5): word omitted from para (a) repealed, and paras (c), (d) inserted, by the Scotland Act 2016, s 63.

[1.333]

133 Contents of references

(1) A market investigation reference shall, in particular, specify—

(a) the enactment under which it is made;

(b) the date on which it is made; . . .

(c) [in the case of an ordinary reference,] the description of goods or services to which the feature or combination of features concerned relates[; and

(d) in the case of a cross-market reference, the feature or features concerned and the descriptions of goods or services to which it or they relate.]

(2) A market investigation reference may be framed so as to require the [group constituted by the chair of the CMA in respect of the reference] to confine its investigation into the effects of features of markets in the United Kingdom for goods or services of a description specified in the reference to the effects of features of such of those markets as exist in connection with—

(a) a supply [or, in the case of a cross-market reference, supplies], of a description specified in the reference, of the goods or services concerned; or

(b) an acquisition [or, in the case of a cross-market reference, acquisitions], of a description specified in the reference, of the goods or services concerned.

(3) A description of the kind mentioned in subsection (2)(a) or (b) may, in particular, be by reference to—

(a) the place where the goods or services are supplied or acquired; or

(b) the persons by or to whom they are supplied or by or from whom they are acquired.

NOTES

Sub-s (1): the word omitted from para (b) was repealed, the words in square brackets in para (c) were added, and para (d) and the preceding word were added, by the Enterprise and Regulatory Reform Act 2013, s 34(4), Sch 9, paras 1, 2(1), (2). For various transitional provisions (including those relating to the abolition of the OFT and the Competition Commission, existing references to those bodies and provisions relating to continuity), see the Enterprise and Regulatory Reform Act 2013 (Commencement No 6, Transitional Provisions and Savings) Order 2014, SI 2014/416, Schedule at **[2.13]**.

Sub-s (2): words in first pair of square brackets substituted, and words in square brackets in paras (a), (b) inserted, by the Enterprise and Regulatory Reform Act 2013, s 26(3), 34(4), Sch 5, Pt 2, paras 59, 165, Sch 9, paras 1, 2(1), (3), subject to transitional provisions in SI 2014/416 as noted above.

Determination of references

[1.334]

[133A Functions to be exercised by CMA groups

(1) Where a reference is made to the chair of the CMA under section 131, 132 or 140A for the constitution of a group under Schedule 4 to the Enterprise and Regulatory Reform Act 2013, the functions of the CMA under or by virtue of the following provisions of this Part in relation to the matter concerned are to be carried out on behalf of the CMA by the group so constituted—

(a) sections 134 to 138B, except for section 135(1);
(b) sections 140B to 145, 148, 148A and 151;
(c) sections 157 and 158;
(d) section 159;
(e) section 160, except for subsection (6) of that section;
(f) section 161, except for subsection (5) of that section;
(g) section 162(4), so far as relating to an enforcement undertaking or enforcement order made on behalf of the CMA by the group;
(h) section 164(2)(b), so far as relating to an enforcement order made on behalf of the CMA by the group;
(i) section 167, so far as relating to an enforcement undertaking or enforcement order made on behalf of the CMA by the group;
(j) section 168;
(k) section 169, so far as relating to a decision mentioned in paragraph (a)(iii) of the definition of relevant decision in subsection (6) of that section;
(l) section 172, so far as relating to anything done on behalf of the CMA by the group;
(m) section 174, where the permitted purpose in question relates to a function that (by virtue of this section) is being or is to be carried out on behalf of the CMA by the group;
(n) sections 174A to 174D, so far as relating to a notice given under section 174 on behalf of the CMA by the group;
(o) section 179(5)(b), so far as relating to a decision of the group;
(p) Schedule 10, so far as relating to an enforcement undertaking or enforcement order which the group is considering accepting or making, or which the group has accepted or made, on behalf of the CMA.

(2) Nothing in subsection (1) prevents the CMA Board from carrying out a function of the CMA under or by virtue of the following provisions of this Part where the group constituted as mentioned in subsection (1) has ceased to exist—

(a) section 160 and Schedule 10, so far as relating to the making of an order under section 160;
(b) sections 159 to 161 and Schedule 10, so far as relating to the variation, supersession or release of enforcement undertakings or the variation or revocation of enforcement orders;
(c) section 162(4);
(d) section 164(2)(b);
(e) section 167.]

NOTES

Inserted by the Enterprise and Regulatory Reform Act 2013, s 26(3), Sch 5, Pt 2, paras 59, 166. For various transitional provisions (including those relating to the abolition of the OFT and the Competition Commission, existing references to those bodies and provisions relating to continuity), see the Enterprise and Regulatory Reform Act 2013 (Commencement No 6, Transitional Provisions and Savings) Order 2014, SI 2014/416, Schedule at **[2.13]**.

[1.335]

134 Questions to be decided on market investigation references

(1) The [CMA] shall, on [an ordinary] reference, decide whether any feature, or combination of features, of each relevant market prevents, restricts or distorts competition in connection with the supply or acquisition of any goods or services in the United Kingdom or a part of the United Kingdom.

[(1A) The CMA shall, on a cross-market reference, decide in relation to each feature and each combination of the features specified in the reference, whether the feature or combination of features, as it relates to goods or services of one or more than one of the descriptions so specified, prevents, restricts or distorts competition in connection with the supply or acquisition of any goods or services in the United Kingdom or a part of the United Kingdom.]

(2) For the purposes of this Part, in relation to [an ordinary] reference, there is an adverse effect on competition if any feature, or combination of features, of a relevant market prevents, restricts or distorts competition in connection with the supply or acquisition of any goods or services in the United Kingdom or a part of the United Kingdom.

[(2A) For the purposes of this Part, in relation to a cross-market reference, there is an adverse effect on competition if a feature or a combination of the features specified in the reference, as that feature or combination of features relates to goods or services of one or more than one of the descriptions so specified, prevents, restricts or distorts competition in connection with the supply or acquisition of any goods or services in the United Kingdom or a part of the United Kingdom.]

(3) In subsections (1) and (2) "relevant market" means—

(a) in the case of subsection (2) so far as it applies in connection with a possible reference, a market in the United Kingdom—
  (i) for goods or services of a description to be specified in the reference; and
  (ii) which would not be excluded from investigation by virtue of section 133(2); and

(b) in any other case, a market in the United Kingdom—
  (i) for goods or services of a description specified in the reference concerned; and
  (ii) which is not excluded from investigation by virtue of section 133(2).

(4) The [CMA] shall, if it has decided on a market investigation reference that there is an adverse effect on competition, decide the following additional questions—

(a) whether action should be taken by it under section 138 for the purpose of remedying, mitigating or preventing the adverse effect on competition concerned or any detrimental effect on customers so far as it has resulted from, or may be expected to result from, the adverse effect on competition;

(b) whether it should recommend the taking of action by others for the purpose of remedying, mitigating or preventing the adverse effect on competition concerned or any detrimental effect on customers so far as it has resulted from, or may be expected to result from, the adverse effect on competition; and

(c) in either case, if action should be taken, what action should be taken and what is to be remedied, mitigated or prevented.

(5) For the purposes of this Part, in relation to a market investigation reference, there is a detrimental effect on customers if there is a detrimental effect on customers or future customers in the form of—

(a) higher prices, lower quality or less choice of goods or services in any market in the United Kingdom (whether or not the market [or markets] to which the feature or features concerned relate); or

(b) less innovation in relation to such goods or services.

(6) In deciding the questions mentioned in subsection (4), the [CMA] shall, in particular, have regard to the need to achieve as comprehensive a solution as is reasonable and practicable to the adverse effect on competition and any detrimental effects on customers so far as resulting from the adverse effect on competition.

(7) In deciding the questions mentioned in subsection (4), the [CMA] may, in particular, have regard to the effect of any action on any relevant customer benefits of the feature or features of the market [or markets] concerned.

(8) For the purposes of this Part a benefit is a relevant customer benefit of a feature or features of a market if—

(a) it is a benefit to customers or future customers in the form of—
  (i) lower prices, higher quality or greater choice of goods or services in any market in the United Kingdom (whether or not the market [or markets] to which the feature or features concerned relate); or
  (ii) greater innovation in relation to such goods or services; and

(b) the [CMA or (as the case may be) the Secretary of State] believes that—
  (i) the benefit has accrued as a result (whether wholly or partly) of the feature or features concerned or may be expected to accrue within a reasonable period as a result (whether wholly or partly) of that feature or those features; and
  (ii) the benefit was, or is, unlikely to accrue without the feature or features concerned.

NOTES

References to the "CMA" in sub-ss (1), (4), (6), (7) substituted, and words in square brackets in sub-s (8)(b) substituted, by the Enterprise and Regulatory Reform Act 2013, s 26(3), Sch 5, Pt 2, paras 59, 167. For various transitional provisions (including those relating to the abolition of the OFT and the Competition Commission, existing references to those bodies and provisions relating to continuity), see the Enterprise and Regulatory Reform Act 2013 (Commencement No 6, Transitional Provisions and Savings) Order 2014, SI 2014/416, Schedule at **[2.13]**.

Words "an ordinary" in square brackets in sub-ss (1), (2) substituted, sub-ss (1A), (2A) inserted, and words "or markets" in sub-ss (5)(a), (7), (8)(a) inserted, by the Enterprise and Regulatory Reform Act 2013, s 34(4), Sch 9, paras 1, 3, subject to transitional provisions in SI 2014/416 as noted above.

[1.336]

135 Variation of market investigation references

(1) The [CMA] or (as the case may be) the appropriate Minister may at any time vary a market investigation reference made [by it under section 131 or (as the case may be) by the appropriate Minister under section 132].

(2) The . . . appropriate Minister shall consult the [CMA] before varying any such reference [made by him].

(3) Subsection (2) shall not apply if the [CMA] has requested the variation concerned.

(4) . . .

NOTES

All words in square brackets were substituted or inserted, and the words omitted were repealed, by the Enterprise and Regulatory Reform Act 2013, ss 26(3), 35(1), 38, Sch 5, Pt 2, paras 59, 168, Sch 10, paras 1, 4, Sch 12, paras 7, 11. For various transitional provisions (including those relating to the abolition of the OFT and the Competition Commission, existing references to those bodies and provisions relating to continuity), see the Enterprise and Regulatory Reform Act 2013 (Commencement No 6, Transitional Provisions and Savings) Order 2014, SI 2014/416, Schedule at **[2.13]**.

[1.337]

136 Investigations and reports on market investigation references

(1) The [CMA] shall prepare and publish a report on a market investigation reference within the period permitted by section 137.

(2) The report shall, in particular, contain—

(a) the decisions of the [CMA] on the questions which it is required to answer by virtue of section 134;

(b) its reasons for its decisions; and

(c) such information as the [CMA] considers appropriate for facilitating a proper understanding of those questions and of its reasons for its decisions.

(3) The [CMA] shall carry out such investigations as it considers appropriate for the purposes of preparing a report under this section.

[(4) Where a reference has been made by the appropriate Minister under section 132 the CMA shall, at the same time as the report under this section is published, give it to the appropriate Minister.]

(5) Where a reference has been made by the [CMA] under section 131 or by the appropriate Minister under section 132 in circumstances in which a reference could have been made by a relevant sectoral regulator under section 131 as it has effect by virtue of a relevant sectoral enactment, the [CMA] shall, at the same time as the report under this section is published, give a copy of it to the relevant sectoral regulator concerned.

(6) . . .

(7) In this Part "relevant sectoral enactment" means—

(a) . . .

(b) in relation to the Gas and Electricity Markets Authority, section 36A of the Gas Act 1986 (c 44) or (as the case may be) section 43 of the Electricity Act 1989 (c 29);

(c) in relation to [the Water Services Regulation Authority], section 31 of the Water Industry Act 1991 (c 56);

(d) . . .

(e) in relation to [the Office of Rail and Road], section 67 of the Railways Act 1993 (c 43);

[(ea) in relation to the Financial Conduct Authority, section 234J of the Financial Services and Markets Act 2000;]

(f) . . .

(g) in relation to the Civil Aviation Authority, section 86 of the Transport Act 2000 (c 38) [or section 60 of the Civil Aviation Act 2012];

[(h) in relation to the Office of Communications, sections 370 and 371 of the Communications Act 2003];

[(h) in relation to the Northern Ireland Authority for Utility Regulation, Article 46 of the Electricity (Northern Ireland) Order 1992, Article 23 of the Gas (Northern Ireland) Order 1996 or Article 29 of the Water and Sewerage Services (Northern Ireland) Order 2006];

[(i) in relation to Monitor, section 73 of the Health and Social Care Act 2012];

[(j) in relation to the Payment Systems Regulator, section 59 of the Financial Services (Banking Reform) Act 2013].

(8) In this Part "relevant sectoral regulator" means . . . the Gas and Electricity Markets Authority, [the Water Services Regulation Authority], . . . , [the Office of Rail and Road], [the Financial Conduct Authority,] . . . [the Civil Aviation Authority or the Office of [Communications,]] [the Northern Ireland Authority for Utility Regulation][, Monitor or the Payment Systems Regulator.]

(9) The Secretary of State may by order modify subsection (7) or (8).

[(10) In this section "the Payment Systems Regulator" means the body established under section 40 of the Financial Services (Banking Reform) Act 2013.]

NOTES

Sub-ss (1)–(3), (5): references to the "CMA" substituted by the Enterprise and Regulatory Reform Act 2013, s 26(3), Sch 5, Pt 2, paras 59, 169(1), (2), (4). For various transitional provisions (including those relating to the abolition of the OFT and the Competition Commission, existing references to those bodies and provisions relating to continuity), see the Enterprise and Regulatory Reform Act 2013 (Commencement No 6, Transitional Provisions and Savings) Order 2014, SI 2014/416, Schedule at **[2.13]**.

Sub-s (4): substituted by the Enterprise and Regulatory Reform Act 2013, s 26(3), Sch 5, Pt 2, paras 59, 169(1), (3), subject to transitional provisions in SI 2014/416 as noted above.

Sub-s (6): repealed by the Enterprise and Regulatory Reform Act 2013, s 26(3), Sch 5, Pt 2, paras 59, 169(1), (5), subject to transitional provisions in SI 2014/416 as noted above.

Sub-s (7) is amended as follows:

Para (a) repealed, and first para (h) inserted, by the Communications Act 2003, s 406(1), (7), Sch 17, para 174(1), (4)(a), Sch 19.

Words in square brackets in para (c) substituted by the Water Act 2003, s 101(1), Sch 7, Pt 2, para 36(1), (2).

Paras (d), (f) repealed, and second para (h) inserted, by the Water and Sewerage Services (Northern Ireland) Order 2006, SI 2006/3336, art 308, Sch 12, para 46(1), Sch 13.

Words in square brackets in para (e) substituted by the Office of Rail Regulation (Change of Name) Regulations 2015, SI 2015/1682, reg 2(2), Schedule, Pt 1, para 4(q)(i).

Para (ea) inserted by the Financial Services (Banking Reform) Act 2013, s 129, Sch 8, Pt 2, para 10(1), (2).

Words in square brackets in para (g) inserted by the Civil Aviation Act 2012, s 61(11).

Para (i) added by the Health and Social Care Act 2012, s 74(6)(a).

Para (j) inserted by the Financial Services (Banking Reform) Act 2013, s 67(3)(a).

Sub-s (8) is amended as follows:

First words omitted repealed, and words ", the Civil Aviation Authority or the Office of Communications" in square brackets substituted, by the Communications Act 2003, s 406(7), Sch 19(1).

Words "the Water Services Regulation Authority" in square brackets substituted by the Water Act 2003, s 101(1), Sch 7, Pt 2, para 36(1), (2).

Second and third words omitted repealed, and words "or the Northern Ireland Authority for Utility Regulation" in square brackets inserted, by SI 2006/3336, art 308, Sch 12, para 46(2), Sch 13.

Words "the Office of Rail and Road" in square brackets substituted by the Office of Rail Regulation (Change of Name) Regulations 2015, SI 2015/1682, reg 2(2), Schedule, Pt 1, para 4(q)(i).

Words "the Financial Conduct Authority," in square brackets inserted by the Financial Services (Banking Reform) Act 2013, s 129, Sch 8, Pt 2, para 10(1), (3).

Word "Communications," in square brackets substituted by the Health and Social Care Act 2012, s 74(6)(b).

Words ", Monitor or the Payment Systems Regulator" in square brackets substituted by the Financial Services (Banking Reform) Act 2013, s 67(3)(b).

Sub-s (10): added by the Financial Services (Banking Reform) Act 2013, s 67(3)(c).

[1.338]

137 Time-limits for market investigations and reports

(1) The [CMA] shall prepare and publish its report under section 136 within the period of [18 months] beginning with the date of the market investigation reference concerned.

(2) Subsection (1) is subject to section 151(3) and (5).

[(2A) The CMA may extend, by no more than 6 months, the period within which its report under section 136 is to be prepared and published if it considers that there are special reasons for doing so.
(2B) An extension under subsection (2A) shall come into force when published under section 172.
(2C) No more than one extension is possible under subsection (2A).]
[(3) The Secretary of State may by order amend this section so as to alter one or more of the following periods—
 (a) the period of 18 months mentioned in subsection (1) or any period for the time being there mentioned in substitution for that period;
 (b) the period of 6 months mentioned in subsection (2A) or any period for the time being there mentioned in substitution for that period.
(4) But no alteration shall be made by virtue of subsection (3) which results in—
 (a) the period for the time being mentioned in subsection (1) exceeding 18 months; or
 (b) the period for the time being mentioned in subsection (2A) exceeding 6 months.].
(5) An order under subsection (3) shall not affect any period of time within which the [CMA] is under a duty to prepare and publish its report under section 136 in relation to a market investigation reference if the [CMA] is already under that duty in relation to that reference when the order is made.
(6) Before making an order under subsection (3) the Secretary of State shall consult the [CMA] and such other persons as he considers appropriate.
(7) References in this Part to the date of a market investigation reference shall be construed as references to the date specified in the reference as the date on which it is made.

NOTES

References to "CMA" in sub-ss (1), (5), (6) substituted by the Enterprise and Regulatory Reform Act 2013, s 26(3), Sch 5, Pt 2, paras 59, 170. For various transitional provisions (including those relating to the abolition of the OFT and the Competition Commission, existing references to those bodies and provisions relating to continuity), see the Enterprise and Regulatory Reform Act 2013 (Commencement No 6, Transitional Provisions and Savings) Order 2014, SI 2014/416, Schedule at **[2.13]**.

Words in second pair of square brackets in sub-s (1) substituted, sub-ss (2A)–(2C) inserted, and sub-ss (3), (4) substituted, by the Enterprise and Regulatory Reform Act 2013, s 38, Sch 12, para 3, subject to transitional provisions in SI 2014/416 as noted above.

[1.339]
138 Duty to remedy adverse effects

(1) Subsection (2) applies where a report of the [CMA] has been prepared and published under section 136 within the period permitted by section 137 and contains the decision that there is one or more than one adverse effect on competition.
(2) The [CMA] shall, [within the period permitted by section 138A,] in relation to each adverse effect on competition, take such action under section 159 or 161 as it considers to be reasonable and practicable—
 (a) to remedy, mitigate or prevent the adverse effect on competition concerned; and
 (b) to remedy, mitigate or prevent any detrimental effects on customers so far as they have resulted from, or may be expected to result from, the adverse effect on competition.
(3) The decisions of the [CMA] under subsection (2) shall be consistent with its decisions as included in its report by virtue of section 134(4) unless there has been a material change of circumstances since the preparation of the report or the [CMA] otherwise has a special reason for deciding differently.
(4) In making a decision under subsection (2), the [CMA] shall, in particular, have regard to the need to achieve as comprehensive a solution as is reasonable and practicable to the adverse effect on competition concerned and any detrimental effects on customers so far as resulting from the adverse effect on competition.
(5) In making a decision under subsection (2), the [CMA] may, in particular, have regard to the effect of any action on any relevant customer benefits of the feature or features of the market [or markets] concerned.
(6) The [CMA] shall take no action under subsection (2) to remedy, mitigate or prevent any detrimental effect on customers so far as it may be expected to result from the adverse effect on competition concerned if—
 (a) no detrimental effect on customers has resulted from the adverse effect on competition; and
 (b) the adverse effect on competition is not being remedied, mitigated or prevented.

NOTES

References to the "CMA" substituted by the Enterprise and Regulatory Reform Act 2013, s 26(3), Sch 5, Pt 2, paras 59, 171. For various transitional provisions (including those relating to the abolition of the OFT and the Competition Commission, existing references to those bodies and provisions relating to continuity), see the Enterprise and Regulatory Reform Act 2013 (Commencement No 6, Transitional Provisions and Savings) Order 2014, SI 2014/416, Schedule at **[2.13]**.

Words in second pair of square brackets in sub-s (2) inserted by the Enterprise and Regulatory Reform Act 2013, s 38, Sch 12, para 4, subject to transitional provisions in SI 2014/416 as noted above.

Words in second pair of square brackets in sub-s (5) inserted by the Enterprise and Regulatory Reform Act 2013, s 34(4), Sch 9, paras 1, 4, subject to transitional provisions in SI 2014/416 as noted above.

[1.340]
[138A Time-limits for discharging duty under section 138

(1) The CMA shall discharge its duty under section 138(2) within the period of 6 months beginning with the date on which it publishes the report concerned under section 136.
(2) The CMA may extend, by no more than 4 months, the period within which its duty under section 138(2) is required to be discharged if it considers that there are special reasons for doing so.
(3) The CMA may extend the period within which its duty under section 138(2) is required to be discharged if it considers that—
 (a) a person has failed (whether with or without reasonable excuse) to comply with any requirement of a notice under section 174 which was given in relation to the reference; and
 (b) the failure is preventing the CMA from properly discharging its duty under section 138(2).

(4) An extension under subsection (2) or (3) shall come into force when published under section 172.
(5) An extension under subsection (3) continues in force until—
(a) the person concerned provides the information or documents to the satisfaction of the CMA or (as the case may be) appears as a witness in accordance with the requirements of the CMA; or
(b) the CMA publishes its decision to cancel the extension.]

NOTES

Inserted, together with s 138B, by the Enterprise and Regulatory Reform Act 2013, s 38, Sch 12, para 5. For various transitional provisions (including those relating to the abolition of the OFT and the Competition Commission, existing references to those bodies and provisions relating to continuity), see the Enterprise and Regulatory Reform Act 2013 (Commencement No 6, Transitional Provisions and Savings) Order 2014, SI 2014/416, Schedule at **[2.13]**.

[1.341]
[138B Section 138A: supplementary
(1) A period extended under section 138A(2) may also be extended under section 138A(3), and a period extended under section 138A(3) may also be extended under section 138A(2).
(2) No more than one extension is possible under section 138A(2).
(3) Where a period is extended or further extended under section 138A(2) or (3), the period as extended or (as the case may be) further extended shall, subject to subsections (4) and (5), be calculated by taking the period being extended and adding to it the period of the extension (whether or not those periods overlap in time).
(4) Subsection (5) applies where—
(a) the period within which the CMA shall discharge its duty under section 138(2) is further extended;
(b) the further extension and at least one previous extension is made under section 138A(3); and
(c) the same days or fractions of days are included in or comprise the further extension and are included in or comprise at least one such previous extension.
(5) In calculating the period of the further extension, any days or fractions of days of the kind mentioned in subsection (4)(c) shall be disregarded.
(6) The Secretary of State may by order amend section 138A so as to alter one or more of the following periods—
(a) the period of 6 months mentioned in subsection (1) or any period for the time being there mentioned in substitution for that period;
(b) the period of 4 months mentioned in subsection (2) or any period for the time being there mentioned in substitution for that period.
(7) But no alteration shall be made by virtue of subsection (6) which results in—
(a) the period for the time being mentioned in section 138A(1) exceeding 6 months; or
(b) the period for the time being mentioned in section 138A(2) exceeding 4 months.
(8) Before making an order under subsection (6) the Secretary of State shall consult the CMA and such other persons as the Secretary of State considers appropriate.]

NOTES

Inserted as noted to s 138A at **[1.340]**.

CHAPTER 2 PUBLIC INTEREST CASES

Intervention notices

[1.342]
139 Public interest intervention by Secretary of State
[(A1) This section applies where—
(a) the CMA has published a market study notice in relation to a matter; or
(b) the CMA has begun the process of consultation under section 169 in respect of a decision of the kind mentioned in subsection (6)(a)(i) of that section.
(1) The Secretary of State may, within the permitted period, give a notice to the CMA if the Secretary of State believes that it is or may be the case that one or more than one public interest consideration is relevant to the matter.
(1A) For the purposes of subsection (1), the permitted period, in a case to which this section applies by virtue of paragraph (a) of subsection (A1), is the period beginning with the publication of the market study notice and ending with—
(a) the acceptance by the CMA of an undertaking under section 154 instead of the making of a reference under section 131 in relation to the matter;
(b) the publication of notice of the fact that the CMA has otherwise decided not to make such a reference in relation to the matter;
(c) the making of such a reference in relation to the matter; or
(d) in a case where the period permitted by section 131B for the preparation and publication by the CMA of the market study report in relation to the matter has expired and no such report has been prepared or published, the end of that period.
(1B) For the purposes of subsection (1), the permitted period, in a case to which this section applies by virtue of paragraph (b) of subsection (A1), is the period beginning with the date on which the CMA begins the process of consultation concerned and ending with—
(a) the acceptance by the CMA of an undertaking under section 154 instead of the making of a reference under section 131 in relation to the matter concerned;
(b) the publication of notice of the fact that the CMA has otherwise decided not to make such a reference in relation to the matter; or
(c) the making of such a reference in relation to the matter.]
(2) The Secretary of State may[, within the permitted period,] give a notice to the [CMA] if—
(a) the [CMA] is considering whether to accept—

(i) an undertaking under section 154 instead of making a reference under section 131 [in relation to the matter]; or

(ii) an undertaking varying or superseding any such undertaking;

(b) the [CMA] has published a notice under section 155(1) or (4); and

(c) the Secretary of State believes that it is or may be the case that one or more than one public interest consideration is relevant to the [proposal to accept the undertaking].

[(2A) For the purposes of subsection (2), the permitted period is—

(a) where the CMA publishes a notice under section 155(1), the period within which representations may be made in relation to the proposed undertaking (as to which, see section 155(2)(f));

(b) where the CMA publishes a notice under section 155(4), the period within which representations may be made in relation to the proposed modifications to the proposed undertaking (as to which, see section 155(5)(c)).]

(3) In this Part "intervention notice" means a notice under subsection (1) or (2).

[(4) No more than one intervention notice shall be given under subsection (1) in relation to the same matter.

(4A) An intervention notice shall not be given under subsection (2) in relation to a proposal to accept an undertaking if the proposal relates to a matter in respect of which an intervention notice under subsection (1) has already been given.

(4B) No more than one intervention notice shall be given under subsection (2) in relation to the same proposed undertaking or in relation to proposed undertakings which do not differ from each other in any material respect.]

[(4C) In this section, a reference to the acceptance of an undertaking shall, in a case where the CMA has accepted a group of undertakings under section 154, be treated as a reference to the acceptance of the last undertaking in the group; but undertakings which vary, supersede or revoke earlier undertakings shall be disregarded for the purposes of this section.]

(5) For the purposes of this Part a public interest consideration is a consideration which, at the time of the giving of the intervention notice concerned, is specified in section 153 or is not so specified but, in the opinion of the Secretary of State, ought to be so specified.

(6) Where the Secretary of State has given an intervention notice mentioning a public interest consideration which, at that time, is not finalised, he shall, as soon as practicable, take such action as is within his power to ensure that it is finalised.

(7) For the purposes of this Part a public interest consideration is finalised if—

(a) it is specified in section 153 otherwise than by virtue of an order under subsection (3) of that section; or

(b) it is specified in that section by virtue of an order under subsection (3) of that section and the order providing for it to be so specified has been laid before, and approved by, Parliament in accordance with subsection (6) of section 181 and within the period mentioned in that subsection.

NOTES

Sub-ss (A1), (1), (1A), (1B): substituted (for the original sub-s (1)) by the Enterprise and Regulatory Reform Act 2013, s 35(1)–(3). For various transitional provisions (including those relating to the abolition of the OFT and the Competition Commission, existing references to those bodies and provisions relating to continuity), see the Enterprise and Regulatory Reform Act 2013 (Commencement No 6, Transitional Provisions and Savings) Order 2014, SI 2014/416, Schedule at **[2.13]**.

Sub-s (2): words in first pair of square brackets inserted, words in square brackets in sub-para (a)(i) inserted, words in square brackets in para (c) substituted, and references to the "CMA" substituted, by the Enterprise and Regulatory Reform Act 2013, ss 26(3), 35(1), (2), (4), Sch 5, Pt 2, paras 59, 172, subject to transitional provisions in SI 2014/416 as noted above.

Sub-ss (2A), (4C): inserted by the Enterprise and Regulatory Reform Act 2013, s 35(1), (5), (7), subject to transitional provisions in SI 2014/416 as noted above.

Sub-ss (4), (4A), (4B): substituted (for the original sub-s (4)) by the Enterprise and Regulatory Reform Act 2013, s 35(1), (2), (6), subject to transitional provisions in SI 2014/416 as noted above.

Intervention notices under section 139(1)

[1.343]

140 Intervention notices under section 139(1)

(1) An intervention notice under section 139(1) shall state—

[(a) the matter to which the market study notice or (as the case may be) the consultation under section 169 concerned relates;

(b) the date of publication of that notice or (as the case may be) on which the process of consultation began;]

(c) the public interest consideration or considerations which are, or may be, relevant to the [matter]; and

(d) where any public interest consideration concerned is not finalised, the proposed timetable for finalising it.

(2) Where the Secretary of State believes that it is or may be the case that two or more public interest considerations are relevant to the [matter], he may decide not to mention in the intervention notice such of those considerations as he considers appropriate.

(3) The Secretary of State may at any time revoke an intervention notice which has been given under section 139(1) and which is in force.

(4) An intervention notice under section 139(1) shall come into force when it is given and shall cease to be in force when the matter to which it relates is finally determined under this Chapter.

[(4A) An intervention notice under section 139(1) shall also cease to be in force if—

(a) it mentions a public interest consideration which was not finalised on the giving of the notice or public interest considerations which, at that time, were not finalised;

(b) no other public interest consideration is mentioned in the notice;

(c) at least 24 weeks has elapsed since the giving of the notice;

(d) the public interest consideration mentioned in the notice has not been finalised within that period of 24 weeks or (as the case may be) none of the public interest considerations mentioned in the notice has been finalised within that period of 24 weeks; and

(e) the Secretary of State has not, by the end of that period of 24 weeks, made a reference under section 140A in relation to the matter.

(4B) Subsection (4D) applies in a case where—

(a) an intervention notice ceases to be in force in accordance with subsection (4A);

(b) the CMA has, before the time at which the notice ceases to be in force, prepared a market study report in relation to the matter within the period permitted by section 131B(4) and given it to the Secretary of State in accordance with section 140A(3)(b); and

(c) the report contains the decision of the CMA that it should make a reference in relation to the matter concerned under section 131.

(4C) Subsection (4D) also applies in a case where—

(a) an intervention notice ceases to be in force in accordance with subsection (4A); and

(b) the CMA has, before the time at which the notice ceases to be in force—

(i) decided that it should make an ordinary reference or a cross-market reference under section 131 in relation to the matter concerned; and

(ii) given a document containing its decision, the reasons for it and such information as the CMA considers appropriate for facilitating a proper understanding of the reasons for its decision to the Secretary of State in accordance with section 140A(3)(c).

(4D) In a case to which this subsection applies—

(a) the CMA shall, as soon as reasonably practicable, make a reference in relation to the matter under section 131; and

(b) the reference is to be treated for the purposes of this Part as having been made in accordance with the requirements imposed by this Part.]

(5) For the purposes of subsection (4) a matter to which an intervention notice under section 139(1) relates is finally determined under this Chapter if—

[(za) the CMA accepts an undertaking under section 154 instead of making a reference under section 131 in relation to the matter;

(zb) the CMA publishes notice that it has otherwise decided not to make a reference under section 131 in relation to the matter;

(zc) the period permitted for the preparation by the CMA of the market study report in relation to the matter and for the report to be published under section 131B(4) or (as the case may be) given to the Secretary of State under section 140A(3) has expired and no such report has been so prepared or no such action has been taken;

(zd) the Secretary of State makes a reference under section 140A(5) in relation to the matter;]

(a) the period permitted by section 144 for the preparation of the report of the [CMA] under section 142 and for action to be taken in relation to it under section 143(1) or (3) [or (as the case may be) 143A(2) or (3)] has expired and no such report has been so prepared or no such action has been taken;

(b) the [CMA] decides under section 145(1) to terminate its investigation;

(c) the report of the [CMA] has been prepared under section 142 and published under section 143(1) [or (as the case may be) 143A(2)] within the period permitted by section 144;

(d) the Secretary of State fails to make and publish a decision under subsection (2) of section 146 within the period required by subsection (3) of that section [or (as the case may be) fails to make and publish a decision under subsection (2) of section 146A within the period required by subsection (6) of that section];

(e) the Secretary of State decides under section 146(2) that no eligible public interest consideration is relevant [or (as the case may be) decides under section 146A(2) to make no finding at all in relation to the matter];

(f) the Secretary of State decides under section 147(2) [or (as the case may be) 147A(2)] neither to accept an undertaking under section 159 nor to make an order under section 161;

(g) the Secretary of State accepts an undertaking under section 159 or makes an order under section 161; or

(h) the Secretary of State decides to revoke the intervention notice concerned.

(6) For the purposes of subsections (4) and (5) the time when a matter to which an intervention notice under section 139(1) relates is finally determined under this Chapter is—

[(za) in a case falling within subsection (5)(za), the acceptance of the undertaking concerned;

(zb) in a case falling within subsection (5)(zb), the publication of the notice concerned;]

(a) in a case falling within subsection (5)[(zc),] (a) or (d), the expiry of the period concerned;

[(aa) in a case falling within subsection (5)(zd), the making of the reference concerned;]

(b) in a case falling within subsection (5)(b), (e), (f) or (h), the making of the decision concerned;

(c) in a case falling within subsection (5)(c), the publication of the report concerned; and

(d) in a case falling within subsection (5)(g), the acceptance of the undertaking concerned or (as the case may be) the making of the order concerned.

[(6A) In subsection (6)(za) the reference to the acceptance of the undertaking concerned shall, in a case where the CMA has accepted a group of undertakings under section 154, be treated as a reference to the acceptance of the last undertaking in the group; but undertakings which vary, supersede or revoke earlier undertakings shall be disregarded for the purposes of subsections (5)(za) and (6)(za).]

(7) In subsection (6)(d) the reference to the acceptance of the undertaking concerned or the making of the order concerned shall, in a case where the enforcement action under section 147(2) [or (as the case may be) 147A(2)] involves the acceptance of a group of undertakings, the making of a group of orders or the acceptance and making of a group of undertakings and orders, be treated as a reference to the acceptance or making of the last undertaking or order in the group; but undertakings or orders which vary, supersede or revoke earlier undertakings or orders shall be disregarded for the purposes of subsections (5)(g) and (6)(d).

NOTES

Sub-s (1): paras (a), (b) substituted, and word in square brackets in para (c) substituted, by the Enterprise and Regulatory Reform Act 2013, s 35(10), Sch 10, paras 1, 5(1), (2). For various transitional provisions (including those relating to the abolition of the OFT and the Competition Commission, existing references to those bodies and provisions relating to continuity), see the Enterprise and Regulatory Reform Act 2013 (Commencement No 6, Transitional Provisions and Savings) Order 2014, SI 2014/416, Schedule at **[2.13]**.

Sub-s (2): word in square brackets substituted by the Enterprise and Regulatory Reform Act 2013, s 35(10), Sch 10, paras 1, 5(1), (3), subject to transitional provisions in SI 2014/416 as noted above.

Sub-ss (4A)–(4D), (6A): inserted by the Enterprise and Regulatory Reform Act 2013, s 35(10), Sch 10, paras 1, 5(1), (4), (7), subject to transitional provisions in SI 2014/416 as noted above.

Sub-s (5): references to the "CMA" substituted, and all other words in square brackets inserted, by the Enterprise and Regulatory Reform Act 2013, ss 26(3), 35(10), Sch 5, Pt 2, paras 59, 173, Sch 10, paras 1, 5(1), (5), subject to transitional provisions in SI 2014/416 as noted above.

Sub-ss (6), (7): words in square brackets inserted by the Enterprise and Regulatory Reform Act 2013, s 35(10), Sch 10, paras 1, 5(1), (6), (8), subject to transitional provisions in SI 2014/416 as noted above.

[1.344]

[140A Section 139(1) intervention notices: Secretary of State's duty to refer

(1) This section applies where—

(a) the CMA has prepared a market study report in relation to a matter within the period permitted by section 131B(4);

(b) an intervention notice under section 139(1) is in force in relation to the matter at the time when the CMA would (but for this section) be required to publish the report; and

(c) the report contains the decision of the CMA that it should make an ordinary reference or a cross-market reference in relation to the matter under section 131.

(2) This section also applies where—

(a) the CMA has conducted a consultation under section 169 in respect of a decision of the kind mentioned in subsection (6)(a)(i) of that section;

(b) the CMA has decided that it should make an ordinary reference or a cross-market reference in relation to the matter concerned under section 131; and

(c) an intervention notice under section 139(1) is in force in relation to the matter at the time when the CMA makes that decision.

(3) The CMA—

(a) shall not exercise the power under section 131 to refer the matter;

(b) in a case falling within subsection (1), shall not publish the market study report under section 131B(4) and shall instead, within the period mentioned in section 131B(4), give the report to the Secretary of State; and

(c) in a case falling within subsection (2), shall give to the Secretary of State a document containing—

(i) its decision and the reasons for its decision; and

(ii) such information as the CMA considers appropriate for facilitating a proper understanding of the reasons for its decision.

(4) The Secretary of State shall decide whether any public interest consideration which was mentioned in the intervention notice is relevant to the matter in question.

(5) Where the Secretary of State decides that there is no relevant public interest consideration—

(a) the Secretary of State shall (in accordance with the CMA's decision) make a reference in relation to the matter to the chair of the CMA for the constitution of a group under Schedule 4 to the Enterprise and Regulatory Reform Act 2013; and

(b) the reference is to be treated for the purposes of this Part as an ordinary reference or (as the case may be) a cross-market reference made under section 131 in accordance with the requirements imposed by this Part.

(6) Where the Secretary of State decides that there is one or more than one relevant public interest consideration, the Secretary of State shall (in accordance with the CMA's decision) make a reference in relation to the matter to the chair of the CMA for the constitution of a group under Schedule 4 to the Enterprise and Regulatory Reform Act 2013.

(7) The Secretary of State shall specify in a reference made under subsection (6)—

(a) the relevant public interest consideration or considerations; and

(b) whether the reference is a restricted PI reference or a full PI reference (as to which, see sections 141 and 141A respectively).

(8) Where the Secretary of State makes a full PI reference under subsection (6), the reference shall also specify whether the Secretary of State proposes to appoint a public interest expert under section 141B.

(9) For the purposes of this Part, a reference under subsection (6) is to be treated—

(a) in a case where the decision of the CMA was that it should make an ordinary reference, as an ordinary reference;

(b) in a case where the decision of the CMA was that it should make a cross-market reference, as a cross-market reference.

(10) In a case falling within subsection (1), the Secretary of State shall publish the market study report concerned at the same time as the Secretary of State makes a reference under this section.

(11) In a case falling within subsection (2), the Secretary of State shall publish the document given to the Secretary of State by the CMA under subsection (3)(c), at the same time as the Secretary of State makes a reference under this section.

(12) In this Part—

"full PI reference" means a reference made by the Secretary of State under subsection (6) which specifies that it is a full PI reference;

"restricted PI reference" means a reference made by the Secretary of State under subsection (6) which specifies that it is a restricted PI reference.]

NOTES

Inserted by the Enterprise and Regulatory Reform Act 2013, s 35(1), (8). For various transitional provisions (including those relating to the abolition of the OFT and the Competition Commission, existing references to those bodies and provisions relating to continuity), see the Enterprise and Regulatory Reform Act 2013 (Commencement No 6, Transitional Provisions and Savings) Order 2014, SI 2014/416, Schedule at **[2.13]**.

[1.345]

[140B Variation of restricted PI references and full PI references

(1) The Secretary of State may at any time vary a restricted PI reference or a full PI reference.

(2) The Secretary of State shall consult the CMA before varying any such reference.

(3) But subsection (2) does not apply if the CMA requested the variation concerned.

(4) No variation under this section is capable of altering the public interest consideration or considerations specified in the reference.]

NOTES

Inserted by the Enterprise and Regulatory Reform Act 2013, s 35(10), Sch 10, paras 1, 6. For various transitional provisions (including those relating to the abolition of the OFT and the Competition Commission, existing references to those bodies and provisions relating to continuity), see the Enterprise and Regulatory Reform Act 2013 (Commencement No 6, Transitional Provisions and Savings) Order 2014, SI 2014/416, Schedule at **[2.13]**.

[1.346]

141 [Restricted PI references: questions to be decided by CMA]

[(1) This section applies where the Secretary of State makes a restricted PI reference.]

(2) The [CMA] shall[, on an ordinary reference,] decide whether any feature, or combination of features, of each relevant market (within the meaning given by section 134(3)) prevents, restricts or distorts competition in connection with the supply or acquisition of any goods or services in the United Kingdom or a part of the United Kingdom.

[(2A) The CMA shall, on a cross-market reference, decide in relation to each feature and each combination of the features specified in the reference, whether the feature or combination of features, as it relates to goods or services of one or more than one of the descriptions so specified, prevents, restricts or distorts competition in connection with the supply or acquisition of any goods or services in the United Kingdom or a part of the United Kingdom.]

(3) The [CMA] shall, if it has decided that there is an adverse effect on competition, decide the following additional questions—

- (a) whether action should be taken by the Secretary of State under section 147 for the purpose of remedying, mitigating or preventing the adverse effect on competition concerned or any detrimental effect on customers so far as it has resulted from, or may be expected to result from, the adverse effect on competition;
- (b) whether the [CMA] should recommend the taking of other action by the Secretary of State or action by persons other than itself and the Secretary of State for the purpose of remedying, mitigating or preventing the adverse effect on competition concerned or any detrimental effect on customers so far as it has resulted from, or may be expected to result from, the adverse effect on competition; and
- (c) in either case, if action should be taken, what action should be taken and what is to be remedied, mitigated or prevented.

(4) The [CMA] shall, if it has decided that there is an adverse effect on competition, also decide separately the following questions (on the assumption that it is proceeding as mentioned in section 148(1))—

- (a) whether action should be taken by it under section 138 for the purpose of remedying, mitigating or preventing the adverse effect on competition concerned or any detrimental effect on customers so far as it has resulted from, or may be expected to result from, the adverse effect on competition;
- (b) whether the [CMA] should recommend the taking of action by other persons for the purpose of remedying, mitigating or preventing the adverse effect on competition concerned or any detrimental effect on customers so far as it has resulted from, or may be expected to result from, the adverse effect on competition; and
- (c) in either case, if action should be taken, what action should be taken and what is to be remedied, mitigated or prevented.

(5) In deciding the questions mentioned in subsections (3) and (4), the [CMA] shall, in particular, have regard to the need to achieve as comprehensive a solution as is reasonable and practicable to the adverse effect on competition concerned and any detrimental effects on customers so far as resulting from the adverse effect on competition.

(6) In deciding the questions mentioned in subsections (3) and (4), the [CMA] may, in particular, have regard to the effect of any action on any relevant customer benefits of the feature or features of the market [or markets] concerned.

NOTES

Section heading: words in square brackets substituted by the Enterprise and Regulatory Reform Act 2013, s 35(10), Sch 10, paras 1, 7(1), (3). For various transitional provisions (including those relating to the abolition of the OFT and the Competition Commission, existing references to those bodies and provisions relating to continuity), see the Enterprise and Regulatory Reform Act 2013 (Commencement No 6, Transitional Provisions and Savings) Order 2014, SI 2014/416, Schedule at **[2.13]**.

Sub-s (1): substituted by the Enterprise and Regulatory Reform Act 2013, s 35(10), Sch 10, paras 1, 7(1), (2), subject to transitional provisions in SI 2014/416 as noted above.

Sub-s (2): reference to the "CMA" substituted, and words in second pair of square brackets inserted, by the Enterprise and Regulatory Reform Act 2013, ss 26(3), 34(4), Sch 5, Pt 2, paras 59, 174, Sch 9, paras 1, 5(1), (2), subject to transitional provisions in SI 2014/416 as noted above.

Sub-s (2A): inserted by the Enterprise and Regulatory Reform Act 2013, s 34(4), Sch 9, paras 1, 5(1), (3), subject to transitional provisions in SI 2014/416 as noted above.

Sub-ss (3)–(5): references to the "CMA" substituted by the Enterprise and Regulatory Reform Act 2013, s 26(3), Sch 5, Pt 2, paras 59, 174, subject to transitional provisions in SI 2014/416 as noted above.

Sub-s (6): reference to the "CMA" substituted, and words in second pair of square brackets inserted, by the Enterprise and Regulatory Reform Act 2013, ss 26(3), 34(4), Sch 5, Pt 2, paras 59, 174, Sch 9, paras 1, 5(1), (4), subject to transitional provisions in SI 2014/416 as noted above.

[1.347]

[141A Full PI references: questions to be decided by CMA

(1) This section applies where the Secretary of State makes a full PI reference.

(2) The CMA shall, on an ordinary reference, decide whether any feature, or combination of features, of each relevant market (within the meaning given by section 134(3)) prevents, restricts or distorts competition in connection with the supply or acquisition of any goods or services in the United Kingdom or a part of the United Kingdom.

(3) The CMA shall, on a cross-market reference, decide in relation to each feature and each combination of the features specified in the reference, whether the feature or combination of features, as it relates to goods or services of one or more than one of the descriptions so specified, prevents, restricts or distorts competition in connection with the supply or acquisition of any goods or services in the United Kingdom or a part of the United Kingdom.

(4) The CMA shall, if it has decided that there is an adverse effect on competition, decide whether, taking account only of any adverse effect on competition and the admissible public interest consideration or considerations concerned, any feature or combination of features which gave rise to an adverse effect on competition operates or may be expected to operate against the public interest.

(5) The CMA shall, if it has decided that any such feature or combination of features operates or may be expected to operate against the public interest, also decide separately the following additional questions—

(a) whether action should be taken by the Secretary of State under section 147A for the purpose of remedying, mitigating or preventing any of the effects adverse to the public interest concerned;

(b) whether the CMA should recommend the taking of other action by the Secretary of State, or action by persons other than itself and the Secretary of State, for the purpose of remedying, mitigating or preventing any of the effects adverse to the public interest concerned; and

(c) in either case, if action should be taken, what action should be taken and what is to be remedied, mitigated or prevented.

(6) The CMA shall, if it has decided that there is an adverse effect on competition, also decide separately the following questions (on the assumption that it is proceeding as mentioned in section 148A(2))—

(a) whether action should be taken by it under section 138 for the purpose of remedying, mitigating or preventing the adverse effect on competition concerned or any detrimental effect on customers so far as it has resulted from, or may be expected to result from, the adverse effect on competition;

(b) whether the CMA should recommend the taking of action by other persons for the purpose of remedying, mitigating or preventing the adverse effect on competition concerned or any detrimental effect on customers so far as it has resulted from, or may be expected to result from, the adverse effect on competition; and

(c) in either case, if action should be taken, what action should be taken and what is to be remedied, mitigated or prevented.

(7) In a case where the Secretary of State has appointed a public interest expert under section 141B in relation to a full PI reference, the CMA shall, in deciding the questions mentioned in subsections (4) and (5), have regard, in particular, to the views of the expert.

(8) In deciding the questions mentioned in subsection (5), the CMA shall, in particular, have regard to—

(a) the need to achieve as comprehensive a solution as is reasonable and practicable to the effects adverse to the public interest concerned; and

(b) any detrimental effects on customers so far as resulting from those effects.

(9) In deciding the questions mentioned in subsection (6), the CMA shall, in particular, have regard to—

(a) the need to achieve as comprehensive a solution as is reasonable and practicable to the adverse effect on competition concerned; and

(b) any detrimental effects on customers so far as resulting from it.

(10) In deciding the questions mentioned in subsections (5) and (6), the CMA may, in particular, have regard to the effect of any action on any relevant customer benefits of the feature or features of the market or markets concerned.

(11) In this section, "admissible public interest consideration" means any public interest consideration specified in the reference concerned and which the CMA is not under a duty to disregard.

NOTES

Inserted, together with s 141B, by the Enterprise and Regulatory Reform Act 2013, s 35(1), (9). For various transitional provisions (including those relating to the abolition of the OFT and the Competition Commission, existing references to those bodies and provisions relating to continuity), see the Enterprise and Regulatory Reform Act 2013 (Commencement No 6, Transitional Provisions and Savings) Order 2014, SI 2014/416, Schedule at **[2.13]**.

[1.348]

[141B Full PI references: power of Secretary of State to appoint expert

(1) This section applies where the Secretary of State makes a full PI reference.

(2) The Secretary of State may appoint one or more than one person to advise the CMA on the questions mentioned in subsections (4) and (5) of section 141A in relation to the reference.

(3) A person so appointed shall be a person who appears to the Secretary of State to have particular knowledge of, or expertise in, matters relating to a public interest consideration specified in the reference.

(4) Each person so appointed is referred to in this Part as a "public interest expert".

(5) The terms and conditions of appointment of a public interest expert (including, in particular, as to remuneration) are to be determined by the Secretary of State.

(6) Any appointment of a public interest expert under this section shall be made within the period of 2 months beginning with the date of the reference concerned.

(7) Before appointing a public interest expert the Secretary of State shall consult the chair of the CMA.]

NOTES

Inserted as noted to s 141A at **[1.347]**.

[1.349]

142 Investigations and reports by [CMA]

(1) [Where the Secretary of State makes a restricted PI reference or a full PI reference, the CMA] shall prepare a report on the reference and take action in relation to it under section 143(1) or (3) [or (as the case may be) 143A(2) or (3)] within the period permitted by section 144.

(2) The report shall, in particular, contain—

(a) the decisions of the [CMA] on the questions which it is required to answer by virtue of section 141 [or (as the case may be) 141A];

(b) its reasons for its decisions; . . .

(c) such information as the [CMA] considers appropriate for facilitating a proper understanding of those questions and of its reasons for its decisions[; and

(d) in the case of a report in relation to a full PI reference in respect of which the Secretary of State appointed a public interest expert, a summary of the views of the expert.]

[(2A) A summary of the views of a public interest expert in a report under this section shall be approved by the expert before action is taken in relation to the report under section 143A(2) or (3).]

(3) The [CMA] shall carry out such investigations as it considers appropriate for the purposes of preparing a report under this section.

NOTES

References to the "CMA" substituted by the Enterprise and Regulatory Reform Act 2013, s 26(3), Sch 5, Pt 2, paras 59, 175. For various transitional provisions (including those relating to the abolition of the OFT and the Competition Commission, existing references to those bodies and provisions relating to continuity), see the Enterprise and Regulatory Reform Act 2013 (Commencement No 6, Transitional Provisions and Savings) Order 2014, SI 2014/416, Schedule at **[2.13]**.

In sub-s (1), words in first pair of square brackets substituted, and words in second pair of square brackets inserted, by the Enterprise and Regulatory Reform Act 2013, s 35(10), Sch 10, paras 1, 8(1), (2), subject to transitional provisions in SI 2014/416 as noted above.

The other words in square brackets in sub-s (2)(a) were inserted, the word omitted from sub-s (2)(b) was repealed, sub-s (2)(d) and the preceding word were inserted, and sub-s (2A) was inserted, by the Enterprise and Regulatory Reform Act 2013, s 35(10), Sch 10, paras 1, 8(1), (3), (4), subject to transitional provisions in SI 2014/416 as noted above.

[1.350]

143 [Restricted PI references: publication etc of reports of CMA]

[(A1) This section applies in relation to a report prepared under section 142 in respect of a restricted PI reference.]

(1) The [CMA] shall publish [the report] if it contains—

(a) the decision of the [CMA] that there is no adverse effect on competition; or

(b) the decisions of the [CMA] that there is one or more than one adverse effect on competition but, on the question mentioned in section 141(4)(a) and in relation to each adverse effect on competition, that no action should be taken by it.

(2) . . .

(3) Where [the report] contains the decisions of the [CMA] that there is one or more than one adverse effect on competition and, on the question mentioned in section 141(4)(a) and in relation to at least one such adverse effect, that action should be taken by it, the [CMA] shall give the report to the Secretary of State.

(4) The Secretary of State shall publish, no later than publication of his decision under section 146(2) in relation to the case, a report of the [CMA] given to him under subsection (3) and not required to be published by virtue of section 148(2).

(5)–(8) . . .

NOTES

All amendments to this section were made by the Enterprise and Regulatory Reform Act 2013, ss 26(3), 35(10), Sch 5, Pt 2, paras 59, 176, Sch 10, paras 1, 9. For various transitional provisions (including those relating to the abolition of the OFT and the Competition Commission, existing references to those bodies and provisions relating to continuity), see the Enterprise and Regulatory Reform Act 2013 (Commencement No 6, Transitional Provisions and Savings) Order 2014, SI 2014/416, Schedule at **[2.13]**.

[1.351]

[143A Full PI references: publication etc of reports of CMA

(1) This section applies in relation to a report prepared under section 142 in respect of a full PI reference.

(2) The CMA shall publish the report if it contains—

(a) the decision of the CMA that there is no adverse effect on competition;

(b) the decision of the CMA that there is an adverse effect on competition but that the feature or combination of features which gave rise to it does not operate and may not be expected to operate against the public interest; or

(c) the decisions of the CMA that there is one or more than one adverse effect on competition and that one or more than one of the features or combinations of features which gave rise to an adverse effect on competition operates or may be expected to operate against the public interest but, on the question mentioned in section 141A(5)(a), and in relation to each effect adverse to the public interest concerned, that no action should be taken by the Secretary of State.

(3) The CMA shall give the report to the Secretary of State if it contains the decisions of the CMA—

(a) that there is one or more than one adverse effect on competition and that one or more than one of the features or combinations of features which gave rise to an adverse effect on competition operates or may be expected to operate against the public interest; and

(b) in relation to at least one effect adverse to the public interest concerned, that action should be taken by the Secretary of State.

(4) The Secretary of State shall publish, no later than publication of the Secretary of State's decision under section 146A(2) in relation to the case, a report of the CMA given to the Secretary of State under subsection (3) and not required to be published by virtue of section 148A(3).]

NOTES

Inserted by the Enterprise and Regulatory Reform Act 2013, s 35(10), Sch 10, paras 1, 10. For various transitional provisions (including those relating to the abolition of the OFT and the Competition Commission, existing references to those bodies and provisions relating to continuity), see the Enterprise and Regulatory Reform Act 2013 (Commencement No 6, Transitional Provisions and Savings) Order 2014, SI 2014/416, Schedule at **[2.13]**.

[1.352]

144 Time-limits for investigations and reports: Part 4

(1) The [CMA] shall, within the period of [18 months] beginning with [the relevant date], prepare its report under section 142 and [publish it under section 143(1) or 143A(2) or (as the case may be) give it to the Secretary of State in accordance with section 143(3) or 143A(3)].

[(1A) For the purposes of subsection (1), the "relevant date" is—

(a) in the case of a report in relation to a restricted PI reference or to a full PI reference which specifies that the Secretary of State does not propose to appoint a public interest expert, the date of the reference;

(b) in the case of a report in relation to a full PI reference which specifies that the Secretary of State proposes to appoint a public interest expert, the earliest of the following—

(i) the date of the appointment of the expert;

(ii) the date on which the Secretary of State gives notice to the CMA that the Secretary of State no longer intends to appoint such an expert;

(iii) the end of the period of 2 months beginning with the date of the reference.]

[(1B) The CMA may extend, by no more than 6 months, the period within which its report under section 142 is to be prepared and action is to be taken in relation to it under section 143(1) or (3) or (as the case may be) 143A(2) or (3) if it considers that there are special reasons for doing so.

(1C) An extension under subsection (1B) shall come into force when published under section 172.

(1D) No more than one extension is possible under subsection (1B).]

(2) The Secretary of State may by order amend[—

(a)] subsection (1) so as to alter the period of [18 months] mentioned in that subsection or any period for the time being mentioned in that subsection in substitution for that period;

[(b) subsection (1B) so as to alter the period of 6 months mentioned in that subsection or any period for the time being mentioned in that subsection in substitution for that period].

(3) No alteration shall be made by virtue of subsection (2) which results in[—

(a)] the period for the time being mentioned in subsection (1) exceeding [18 months][; or

(b) the period for the time being mentioned in subsection (1B) exceeding 6 months].

(4) An order under subsection (2) shall not affect any period of time within which, in relation to a market investigation reference, the [CMA] is under a duty to prepare its report under section 142 and take action in relation to it under section 143(1) or (3) [or (as the case may be) 143A(2) or (3)] if the [CMA] is already under that duty in relation to that reference when the order is made.

(5) Before making an order under subsection (2) the Secretary of State shall consult the [CMA] and such other persons as he considers appropriate.

NOTES

Sub-s (1): words in square brackets substituted by the Enterprise and Regulatory Reform Act 2013, ss 26(3), 35(10), 38, Sch 5, Pt 2, paras 59, 177, Sch 10, paras 1, 11(1), (2), Sch 12, para 6(1), (2). For various transitional provisions (including those relating to the abolition of the OFT and the Competition Commission, existing references to those bodies and provisions relating to continuity), see the Enterprise and Regulatory Reform Act 2013 (Commencement No 6, Transitional Provisions and Savings) Order 2014, SI 2014/416, Schedule at **[2.13]**.

Sub-s (1A): inserted by the Enterprise and Regulatory Reform Act 2013, s 35(10), Sch 10, paras 1, 11(1), (3), subject to transitional provisions in SI 2014/416 as noted above.

Sub-ss (1B)–(1D): inserted by the Enterprise and Regulatory Reform Act 2013, s 38, Sch 12, para 6(1), (3), subject to transitional provisions in SI 2014/416 as noted above.

Sub-ss (2), (3): words "18 months" in square brackets substituted, and other words in square brackets inserted, by the Enterprise and Regulatory Reform Act 2013, s 38, Sch 12, para 6(1), (4), (5), subject to transitional provisions in SI 2014/416 as noted above.

Sub-s (4): references to the "CMA" substituted, and words in second pair of square brackets inserted, by the Enterprise and Regulatory Reform Act 2013, s 26(3), 35(10), Sch 5, Pt 2, paras 59, 177, Sch 10, paras 1, 11(1), (4), subject to transitional provisions in SI 2014/416 as noted above.

Sub-s (5): reference to the "CMA" substituted by the Enterprise and Regulatory Reform Act 2013, s 26(3), Sch 5, Pt 2, paras 59, 177, subject to transitional provisions in SI 2014/416 as noted above.

[1.353]

145 Restrictions where public interest considerations not finalised: Part 4

(1) The [CMA] shall terminate its investigation under section 142 if—

(a) the intervention notice concerned mentions a public interest consideration which was not finalised on the giving of that notice or public interest considerations which, at that time, were not finalised;

(b) no other public interest consideration is mentioned in the notice;

(c) at least 24 weeks has elapsed since the giving of the notice; and

(d) the public interest consideration mentioned in the notice has not been finalised within that period of 24 weeks or (as the case may be) none of the public interest considerations mentioned in the notice has been finalised within that period of 24 weeks.

(2) Where the intervention notice concerned mentions a public interest consideration which is not finalised on the giving of the notice, the [CMA] shall not give its report under section 142 to the Secretary of State in accordance with section 143(3) [or (as the case may be) 143A(3)] unless the period of 24 weeks beginning with the giving of the intervention notice concerned has expired or the public interest consideration concerned has been finalised.

(3) The [CMA] shall, in reporting on any of the questions mentioned in section 141(3) [or (as the case may be) 141A(4) and (5)], disregard any public interest consideration which has not been finalised before the giving of the report.

(4) The [CMA] shall, in reporting on any of the questions mentioned in section 141(3) [or (as the case may be) 141A(4) and (5)], disregard any public interest consideration which was not finalised on the giving of the intervention notice concerned and has not been finalised within the period of 24 weeks beginning with the giving of the notice concerned.

(5) Subsections (1) to (4) are without prejudice to the power of the [CMA] to carry out investigations in relation to any public interest consideration to which it might be able to have regard in its report.

NOTES

References to the "CMA" substituted, and other words in square brackets in sub-ss (2), (3), (4) inserted, by the Enterprise and Regulatory Reform Act 2013, s 26(3), 35(10), Sch 5, Pt 2, paras 59, 178, Sch 10, paras 1, 12. For various transitional provisions (including those relating to the abolition of the OFT and the Competition Commission, existing references to those bodies and provisions relating to continuity), see the Enterprise and Regulatory Reform Act 2013 (Commencement No 6, Transitional Provisions and Savings) Order 2014, SI 2014/416, Schedule at **[2.13]**.

[1.354]

146 [Restricted PI references:] decision of Secretary of State

(1) Subsection (2) applies where the Secretary of State has received a [report of the CMA in relation to a restricted PI reference] which—

- (a) has been prepared under section 142;
- (b) contains the decisions that there is one or more than one adverse effect on competition and, on the question mentioned in section 141(4)(a) and in relation to at least one such adverse effect, that action should be taken by it; and
- (c) has been given to the Secretary of State as required by section 143(3).

(2) The Secretary of State shall decide whether—

- (a) any eligible public interest consideration is relevant; or
- (b) any eligible public interest considerations are relevant;

to any action which is mentioned in the report by virtue of section 141(4)(a) and (c) and which the [CMA] should take for the purpose of remedying, mitigating or preventing any adverse effect on competition concerned or any detrimental effect on customers so far as it has resulted or may be expected to result from any adverse effect on competition.

(3) The Secretary of State shall make and publish his decision under subsection (2) within the period of 90 days beginning with the receipt of the report of the [CMA] under section 142.

(4) In this section "eligible public interest consideration" means a public interest consideration which—

- (a) was mentioned in the intervention notice concerned; and
- (b) was not disregarded by the [CMA] for the purposes of its report under section 142.

NOTES

Section heading: words in square brackets inserted by the Enterprise and Regulatory Reform Act 2013, s 35(10), Sch 10, paras 1, 13(1), (3). For various transitional provisions (including those relating to the abolition of the OFT and the Competition Commission, existing references to those bodies and provisions relating to continuity), see the Enterprise and Regulatory Reform Act 2013 (Commencement No 6, Transitional Provisions and Savings) Order 2014, SI 2014/416, Schedule at **[2.13]**.

Sub-s (1); words in square brackets substituted by the Enterprise and Regulatory Reform Act 2013, s 35(10), Sch 10, paras 1, 13(1), (2), subject to transitional provisions in SI 2014/416 as noted above.

Sub-ss (2)–(4): references to the "CMA" substituted by the Enterprise and Regulatory Reform Act 2013, s 26(3), Sch 5, Pt 2, paras 59, 179, subject to transitional provisions in SI 2014/416 as noted above.

[1.355]

[146A Full PI references: decision of Secretary of State

(1) Subsection (2) applies where the Secretary of State has received a report of the CMA in relation to a full PI reference which—

- (a) has been prepared under section 142;
- (b) contains the decisions of the CMA that there is one or more than one adverse effect on competition and that one or more than one of the features or combinations of features that gave rise to an adverse effect on competition operates or may be expected to operate against the public interest and that, in relation to at least one effect adverse to the public interest concerned, action should be taken by the Secretary of State; and
- (c) has been given to the Secretary of State as required by section 143A(3).

(2) The Secretary of State shall decide whether to make an adverse public interest finding in relation to the matter and whether to make no finding at all in the matter.

(3) For the purposes of this Part, the Secretary of State makes an adverse public interest finding in relation to a matter if, in relation to that matter, the Secretary of State decides—

- (a) that there is an adverse effect on competition;
- (b) that there is one or more than one admissible public interest consideration which is relevant to the matter; and
- (c) taking account only of any adverse effect on competition and any relevant admissible public interest consideration or considerations, that any feature or combination of features which gave rise to an adverse effect on competition operates or may be expected to operate against the public interest.

(4) The Secretary of State may make no finding at all in a matter only if the Secretary of State decides that there is no admissible public interest consideration which is relevant to a consideration of the matter concerned.
(5) In deciding whether to make an adverse public interest finding under subsection (2), the Secretary of State shall accept the decision of the CMA as to whether there is an adverse effect on competition in relation to the matter.
(6) The Secretary of State shall make and publish the decision under subsection (2) within the period of 90 days beginning with the receipt of the report of the CMA under section 142.
(7) In this section "admissible public interest consideration" means a public interest consideration which—
(a) was mentioned in the intervention notice concerned; and
(b) was not disregarded by the CMA for the purposes of its report under section 142.]

NOTES

Inserted by the Enterprise and Regulatory Reform Act 2013, s 35(10), Sch 10, paras 1, 14. For various transitional provisions (including those relating to the abolition of the OFT and the Competition Commission, existing references to those bodies and provisions relating to continuity), see the Enterprise and Regulatory Reform Act 2013 (Commencement No 6, Transitional Provisions and Savings) Order 2014, SI 2014/416, Schedule at **[2.13]**.

[1.356]
147 [Restricted PI references:] remedial action by Secretary of State
(1) Subsection (2) applies where the Secretary of State—
(a) has decided under subsection (2) of section 146 within the period required by subsection (3) of that section that an eligible public interest consideration is relevant as mentioned in subsection (2) of that section or eligible public interest considerations are so relevant; and
(b) has published his decision within the period required by subsection (3) of that section.
(2) The Secretary of State may, in relation to any adverse effect on competition identified in the report concerned, take such action under section 159 or 161 as he considers to be—
(a) reasonable and practicable—
(i) to remedy, mitigate or prevent the adverse effect on competition concerned; or
(ii) to remedy, mitigate or prevent any detrimental effect on customers so far as it has resulted from, or may be expected to result from, the adverse effect on competition; and
(b) appropriate in the light of the eligible public interest consideration concerned or (as the case may be) the eligible public interest considerations concerned.
(3) In making a decision under subsection (2), the Secretary of State shall, in particular, have regard to—
(a) the need to achieve as comprehensive a solution as is reasonable and practicable to the adverse effect on competition concerned and any detrimental effects on customers so far as resulting from the adverse effect on competition; and
(b) the report of the [CMA] under section 142.
(4) In having regard by virtue of subsection (3) to the report of the [CMA] under section 142, the Secretary of State shall not challenge the decision of the [CMA] contained in the report that there is one or more than one adverse effect on competition.
(5) In making a decision under subsection (2), the Secretary of State may, in particular, have regard to the effect of any action on any relevant customer benefits of the feature or features of the market [or markets] concerned.
(6) The Secretary of State shall take no action under subsection (2) to remedy, mitigate or prevent any detrimental effect on customers so far as it may be expected to result from the adverse effect on competition concerned if—
(a) no detrimental effect on customers has resulted from the adverse effect on competition; and
(b) the adverse effect on competition is not being remedied, mitigated or prevented.
(7) In this section "eligible public interest consideration" has the same meaning as in section 146.

NOTES

Section heading: words in square brackets inserted by the Enterprise and Regulatory Reform Act 2013, s 35(10), Sch 10, paras 1, 15 For various transitional provisions (including those relating to the abolition of the OFT and the Competition Commission, existing references to those bodies and provisions relating to continuity), see the Enterprise and Regulatory Reform Act 2013 (Commencement No 6, Transitional Provisions and Savings) Order 2014, SI 2014/416, Schedule at **[2.13]**.

Sub-ss (3), (4): references to "CMA" substituted by the Enterprise and Regulatory Reform Act 2013, s 26(3), Sch 5, Pt 2, paras 59, 180, subject to transitional provisions in SI 2014/416 as noted above.

Sub-s (5): words in square brackets inserted by the Enterprise and Regulatory Reform Act 2013, s 34(4), Sch 9, paras 1, 6, subject to transitional provisions in SI 2014/416 as noted above.

[1.357]
[147A Full PI references: remedial action by Secretary of State
(1) Subsection (2) applies where the Secretary of State has decided under subsection (2) of section 146A within the period required by subsection (6) of that section to make an adverse public interest finding in relation to a matter and has published the decision within the period so required.
(2) The Secretary of State may take such action under section 159 or 161 as the Secretary of State considers to be reasonable and practicable to remedy, mitigate or prevent any of the effects adverse to the public interest which have resulted from, or may be expected to result from, the features or combinations of features in question.
(3) In making a decision under subsection (2), the Secretary of State shall, in particular, have regard to the report of the CMA under section 142.
(4) In making a decision under subsection (2), the Secretary of State may, in particular, have regard to—
(a) the need to achieve as comprehensive a solution as is reasonable and practicable to the effects adverse to the public interest concerned; and
(b) any detrimental effects on customers so far as resulting from those effects.]

NOTES

Inserted by the Enterprise and Regulatory Reform Act 2013, s 35(10), Sch 10, paras 1, 16. For various transitional provisions (including those relating to the abolition of the OFT and the Competition Commission, existing references to those bodies and provisions relating to continuity), see the Enterprise and Regulatory Reform Act 2013 (Commencement No 6, Transitional Provisions and Savings) Order 2014, SI 2014/416, Schedule at **[2.13]**.

[1.358]

148 [Restricted PI references: reversion of the matter to CMA]

(1) If—

(a) the Secretary of State fails to make and publish his decision under subsection (2) of section 146 within the period required by subsection (3) of that section; or

(b) the Secretary of State decides that no eligible public interest consideration is relevant as mentioned in subsection (2) of that section;

the [CMA] shall proceed under section 138 as if the report had been prepared and published under section 136 within the period permitted by section 137.

(2) The [CMA] shall publish the report which has been prepared by it under section 142 (if still unpublished) as soon as it becomes able to proceed by virtue of subsection (1).

(3)–(5) . . .

(6) In relation to proceedings by virtue of subsection (1), the reference in section 138(3) to decisions of the [CMA] included in its report by virtue of section 134(4) shall be construed as a reference to decisions which were included in the report of the [CMA] by virtue of section 141(4).

(7) Where the [CMA], in proceeding by virtue of subsection (1), intends to proceed in a way which is not consistent with its decisions as included in its report by virtue of section 141(4), it shall not so proceed without the consent of the Secretary of State.

(8) The Secretary of State shall not withhold his consent under subsection (7) unless he believes that the proposed alternative way of proceeding will operate against the public interest.

(9) For the purposes of subsection (8) a proposed alternative way of proceeding will operate against the public interest only if any eligible public interest consideration or considerations outweigh the considerations which have led the [CMA] to propose proceeding in that way.

(10) In deciding whether to withhold his consent under subsection (7), the Secretary of State shall accept the [CMA's] view of what, if the only relevant consideration were how to remedy, mitigate or prevent the adverse effect on competition concerned or any detrimental effect on customers so far as resulting from the adverse effect on competition, would be the most appropriate way to proceed.

(11) In this section "eligible public interest consideration" has the same meaning as in section 146.

NOTES

Section heading substituted by the Enterprise and Regulatory Reform Act 2013, s 35(10), Sch 10, paras 1, 17(1), (3). For various transitional provisions (including those relating to the abolition of the OFT and the Competition Commission, existing references to those bodies and provisions relating to continuity), see the Enterprise and Regulatory Reform Act 2013 (Commencement No 6, Transitional Provisions and Savings) Order 2014, SI 2014/416, Schedule at **[2.13]**.

The references to the "CMA" and the "CMA's" were substituted by the Enterprise and Regulatory Reform Act 2013, s 26(3), Sch 5, Pt 2, paras 59, 181, subject to transitional provisions in SI 2014/416 as noted above.

Sub-ss (3)–(5) were repealed by the Enterprise and Regulatory Reform Act 2013, s 35(10), Sch 10, paras 1, 17(1), (2), subject to transitional provisions in SI 2014/416 as noted above.

[1.359]

[148A Full PI references: reversion of the matter to CMA

(1) This section applies if—

(a) the Secretary of State decides under section 146A(2) to make no finding at all in the matter; or

(b) the Secretary of State fails to make and publish the decision under subsection (2) of section 146A within the period required by subsection (6) of that section.

(2) The CMA shall proceed under section 138 as if—

(a) a reference under section 131 had been made (in accordance with the requirements imposed by this Part) instead of a full PI reference; and

(b) its report had been prepared and published under section 136 within the period permitted by section 137.

(3) The CMA shall publish the report which has been prepared by it under section 142 (if still unpublished) as soon as it becomes able to proceed by virtue of subsection (2).

(4) In relation to proceedings by virtue of subsection (2), the reference in section 138(3) to decisions of the CMA included in its report by virtue of section 134(4) is to be construed as a reference to decisions which were included in the report of the CMA by virtue of section 141A(6).

(5) Where the CMA becomes under a duty to proceed as mentioned in subsection (2), references in this Part to a reference under section 131, so far as necessary, are to be construed accordingly.

(6) Where the CMA, in proceeding by virtue of subsection (2), intends to proceed in a way which is not consistent with its decisions as included in its report by virtue of section 141A(6), it shall not so proceed without the consent of the Secretary of State.

(7) The Secretary of State shall not withhold consent under subsection (6) unless the Secretary of State believes that the proposed alternative way of proceeding will operate against the public interest.

(8) For the purposes of subsection (7) a proposed alternative way of proceeding will operate against the public interest only if any admissible public interest consideration or considerations outweigh the considerations which have led the CMA to propose proceeding in that way.

(9) In deciding whether to withhold consent under subsection (6), the Secretary of State shall accept the CMA's view of what, if the only relevant consideration were how to remedy, mitigate or prevent the adverse effect on competition concerned or any detrimental effect on customers so far as resulting from the adverse effect on competition, would be the most appropriate way to proceed.

(10) In this section "admissible public interest consideration" has the same meaning as in section 146A.]

NOTES

Inserted by the Enterprise and Regulatory Reform Act 2013, s 35(10), Sch 10, paras 1, 18. For various transitional provisions (including those relating to the abolition of the OFT and the Competition Commission, existing references to those bodies and provisions relating to continuity), see the Enterprise and Regulatory Reform Act 2013 (Commencement No 6, Transitional Provisions and Savings) Order 2014, SI 2014/416, Schedule at **[2.13]**.

Intervention notices under section 139(2)

[1.360]

149 Intervention notices under section 139(2)

(1) An intervention notice under section 139(2) shall state—

(a) the proposed undertaking which may be accepted by the [CMA];

(b) the notice under section 155(1) or (4);

(c) the public interest consideration or considerations which are, or may be, relevant to the [proposal to accept the undertaking]; and

(d) where any public interest consideration concerned is not finalised, the proposed timetable for finalising it.

(2) Where the Secretary of State believes that it is or may be the case that two or more public interest considerations are relevant to the [proposal to accept the undertaking], he may decide not to mention in the intervention notice such of those considerations as he considers appropriate.

(3) The Secretary of State may at any time revoke an intervention notice which has been given under section 139(2) and which is in force.

(4) An intervention notice under section 139(2) shall come into force when it is given and shall cease to be in force on the occurrence of any of the events mentioned in subsection (5).

(5) The events are—

(a) the acceptance by the [CMA] with the consent of the Secretary of State of an undertaking which is the same as the proposed undertaking mentioned in the intervention notice by virtue of subsection (1)(a) or which does not differ from it in any material respect;

(b) the decision of the [CMA] to proceed neither with the proposed undertaking mentioned in the intervention notice by virtue of subsection (1)(a) nor a proposed undertaking which does not differ from it in any material respect; or

(c) the decision of the Secretary of State to revoke the intervention notice concerned.

NOTES

Sub-ss (1), (2): words in square brackets substituted by the Enterprise and Regulatory Reform Act 2013, ss 26(3), 35(10), Sch 5, Pt 2, paras 59, 182, Sch 10, paras 1, 19. For various transitional provisions (including those relating to the abolition of the OFT and the Competition Commission, existing references to those bodies and provisions relating to continuity), see the Enterprise and Regulatory Reform Act 2013 (Commencement No 6, Transitional Provisions and Savings) Order 2014, SI 2014/416, Schedule at **[2.13]**.

Sub-s (5): references to the "CMA" substituted by the Enterprise and Regulatory Reform Act 2013, s 26(3), Sch 5, Pt 2, paras 59, 182, subject to transitional provisions in SI 2014/416 as noted above.

[1.361]

150 Power of veto of Secretary of State

[(A1) Where an intervention notice under subsection 139(1) is in force, the CMA shall not, without the consent of the Secretary of State, accept any proposed undertaking under section 154 in relation to the matter concerned.]

(1) Where an intervention notice under section 139(2) is in force, the [CMA] shall not, without the consent of the Secretary of State, accept the proposed undertaking concerned or a proposed undertaking which does not differ from it in any material respect.

(2) The Secretary of State shall withhold his consent if he believes that it is or may be the case that the proposed undertaking will, if accepted, operate against the public interest.

(3) For the purposes of subsection (2) a proposed undertaking will, if accepted, operate against the public interest only if any public interest consideration which is mentioned in the intervention notice concerned and has been finalised, or any public interest considerations which are so mentioned and have been finalised, outweigh the considerations which have led the [CMA] to propose accepting the undertaking.

(4) In making his decision under subsection (2) the Secretary of State shall accept the [CMA's] view of what undertakings, if the only relevant consideration were how to remedy, mitigate or prevent the adverse effect on competition concerned or any detrimental effect on customers so far as resulting from the adverse effect on competition, would be most appropriate.

(5) Where a public interest consideration which is mentioned in the intervention notice concerned is not finalised on the giving of the notice, the Secretary of State shall not make his decision as to whether to give his consent under this section before—

(a) the end of the period of 24 weeks beginning with the giving of the intervention notice; or

(b) if earlier, the date on which the public interest consideration concerned has been finalised.

(6) Subject to subsections (2) to (5), the Secretary of State shall not withhold his consent under this section.

NOTES

Sub-s (A1): inserted by the Enterprise and Regulatory Reform Act 2013, s 35(10), Sch 10, paras 1, 20. For various transitional provisions (including those relating to the abolition of the OFT and the Competition Commission, existing

Part 1 Statutes

references to those bodies and provisions relating to continuity), see the Enterprise and Regulatory Reform Act 2013 (Commencement No 6, Transitional Provisions and Savings) Order 2014, SI 2014/416, Schedule at **[2.13]**.

References to the "CMA" and the "CMA's" substituted by the Enterprise and Regulatory Reform Act 2013, s 26(3), Sch 5, Pt 2, paras 59, 183, subject to transitional provisions in SI 2014/416 as noted above.

Other

[1.362]

151 [Public interest intervention cases: interaction with general procedure]

[(1) Sections 134(1), (1A), (4), (6) and (7), 136(1) to (6), 137(1) to (6), 138 and 138A do not apply in relation to a restricted PI reference or a full PI reference.]

(2) Where the Secretary of State revokes an intervention notice which has been given under section 139(1) [at a time after the Secretary of State has made a restricted PI reference or a full PI reference, the CMA shall proceed as if the reference concerned had instead been made under section 131 (in accordance with the requirements imposed by this Part)].

(3) Where the [CMA] is proceeding by virtue of subsection (2), the period within which the [CMA] shall prepare and publish its report under section 136 shall be extended by an additional period of 20 days.

(4) Where the [CMA] terminates its investigation under section 145(1)[, the CMA shall proceed as if the restricted PI reference or (as the case may be) the full PI reference concerned had instead been made by the CMA under section 131 (in accordance with the requirements imposed by this Part)].

(5) Where the [CMA] is proceeding by virtue of subsection (4), the period within which the [CMA] shall prepare and publish its report under section 136 shall be extended by an additional period of 20 days.

(6) In determining the period of 20 days mentioned in subsection (3) or (5) no account shall be taken of—

(a) Saturday, Sunday, Good Friday and Christmas Day; and

(b) any day which is a bank holiday in England and Wales.

NOTES

All words in square brackets in this section were substituted by the Enterprise and Regulatory Reform Act 2013, ss 26(3), 35(10), Sch 5, Pt 2, paras 59, 184, Sch 10, paras 1, 21. For various transitional provisions (including those relating to the abolition of the OFT and the Competition Commission, existing references to those bodies and provisions relating to continuity), see the Enterprise and Regulatory Reform Act 2013 (Commencement No 6, Transitional Provisions and Savings) Order 2014, SI 2014/416, Schedule at **[2.13]**.

[1.363]

152 Certain duties of [CMA]

(1) The [CMA] shall, in considering whether to make a reference under section 131, bring to the attention of the Secretary of State any case which it believes raises any consideration specified in section 153 unless it believes that the Secretary of State would consider any such consideration immaterial in the context of the particular case.

(2) . . .

(3) The [CMA] shall bring to the attention of the Secretary of State any representations about exercising his power under section 153(3) which have been made to the [CMA].

NOTES

Reference to the "CMA" substituted by the Enterprise and Regulatory Reform Act 2013, s 26(3), Sch 5, Pt 2, paras 59, 185. For various transitional provisions (including those relating to the abolition of the OFT and the Competition Commission, existing references to those bodies and provisions relating to continuity), see the Enterprise and Regulatory Reform Act 2013 (Commencement No 6, Transitional Provisions and Savings) Order 2014, SI 2014/416, Schedule at **[2.13]**.

Sub-s (2): repealed by the Enterprise and Regulatory Reform Act 2013, s 35(10), Sch 10, paras 1, 22, subject to transitional provisions in SI 2014/416 as noted above.

[1.364]

153 Specified considerations: Part 4

(1) The interests of national security are specified in this section.

(2) In subsection (1) "national security" includes public security; and in this subsection "public security" has the same meaning as in article [21(4) of Council Regulation (EC) No 139/2004 of 20th January 2004 on the control of concentrations between undertakings].

(3) The Secretary of State may by order modify this section for the purpose of specifying in this section a new consideration or removing or amending any consideration which is for the time being specified in this section.

(4) An order under this section may apply in relation to cases under consideration by the [CMA], [by the Secretary of State or], by the appropriate Minister (other than the Secretary of State acting alone) . . . before the making of the order as well as cases under consideration on or after the making of the order.

NOTES

Sub-s (2): the words from "; and in this subsection" to the end of sub-s (2) were repealed by the Competition (Amendment etc) (EU Exit) Regulations 2019, SI 2019/93, regs 32, 56, as from IP completion day (as defined in the European Union (Withdrawal Agreement) Act 2020, s 39) (for transitional provisions and savings in relation to the operation of the 2019 Regulations, see Sch 4 to those Regulations at **[7.69]** et seq). The words in square brackets were previously substituted by the EC Merger Control (Consequential Amendments) Regulations 2004, SI 2004/1079, reg 2, Schedule, para 2(1), (27). This subsection is repealed by the National Security and Investment Act 2021, s 58, Sch 2, para 9, as from a day to be appointed.

Sub-s (4): words in square brackets substituted, and words omitted repealed, by the Enterprise and Regulatory Reform Act 2013, s 26(3), Sch 5, Pt 2, paras 59, 186. For various transitional provisions (including those relating to the abolition of the OFT and the Competition Commission, existing references to those bodies and provisions relating to continuity), see the Enterprise and Regulatory Reform Act 2013 (Commencement No 6, Transitional Provisions and Savings) Order 2014, SI 2014/416, Schedule at **[2.13]**.

CHAPTER 3 ENFORCEMENT

Undertakings and orders

[1.365]

154 Undertakings in lieu of market investigation references

(1) Subsection (2) applies if the [CMA] considers that it has the power to make a reference under section 131 and otherwise intends to make such a reference.

(2) The [CMA] may, instead of making such a reference and for the purpose of remedying, mitigating or preventing—

(a) any adverse effect on competition concerned; or

(b) any detrimental effect on customers so far as it has resulted from, or may be expected to result from, the adverse effect on competition;

accept, from such persons as it considers appropriate, undertakings to take such action as it considers appropriate.

(3) In proceeding under subsection (2), the [CMA] shall, in particular, have regard to the need to achieve as comprehensive a solution as is reasonable and practicable to the adverse effect on competition concerned and any detrimental effects on customers so far as resulting from the adverse effect on competition.

(4) In proceeding under subsection (2), the [CMA] may, in particular, have regard to the effect of any action on any relevant customer benefits of the feature or features of the market [or markets] concerned.

(5) The [CMA] shall take no action under subsection (2) to remedy, mitigate or prevent any detrimental effect on customers so far as it may be expected to result from the adverse effect on competition concerned if—

(a) no detrimental effect on customers has resulted from the adverse effect on competition; and

(b) the adverse effect on competition is not being remedied, mitigated or prevented.

(6) An undertaking under this section—

(a) shall come into force when accepted;

(b) may be varied or superseded by another undertaking; and

(c) may be released by the [CMA].

(7) The [CMA] shall, as soon as reasonably practicable, consider any representations received by it in relation to varying or releasing an undertaking under this section.

(8) This section is subject to sections 150 and 155.

NOTES

References to the "CMA" substituted, and words "or markets" in square brackets in sub-s (4) inserted, by the Enterprise and Regulatory Reform Act 2013, ss 26(3), 34(4), Sch 5, Pt 2, paras 59, 187, Sch 9, paras 1, 7. For various transitional provisions (including those relating to the abolition of the OFT and the Competition Commission, existing references to those bodies and provisions relating to continuity), see the Enterprise and Regulatory Reform Act 2013 (Commencement No 6, Transitional Provisions and Savings) Order 2014, SI 2014/416, Schedule at **[2.13]**.

[1.366]

155 Undertakings in lieu: procedural requirements

(1) Before accepting an undertaking under section 154 (other than an undertaking under that section which varies an undertaking under that section but not in any material respect), the [CMA] shall—

(a) publish notice of the proposed undertaking; and

(b) consider any representations made in accordance with the notice and not withdrawn.

(2) A notice under subsection (1) shall state—

(a) that the [CMA] proposes to accept the undertaking;

(b) the purpose and effect of the undertaking;

(c) the situation that the undertaking is seeking to deal with;

(d) any other facts which the [CMA] considers justify the acceptance of the undertaking;

(e) a means of gaining access to an accurate version of the proposed undertaking at all reasonable times; and

(f) the period (not less than 15 days starting with the date of publication of the notice) within which representations may be made in relation to the proposed undertaking.

(3) The matters to be included in a notice under subsection (1) by virtue of subsection (2) shall, in particular, include—

(a) the terms of the reference under section 131 which the [CMA] considers that it has power to make and which it otherwise intends to make [or (but for the effect of section 140A(3)) it would have had power to make and which it would otherwise have intended to make]; and

(b) the adverse effect on competition, and any detrimental effect on customers so far as resulting from the adverse effect on competition, which the [CMA] has identified.

(4) The [CMA] shall not accept the undertaking with modifications unless it—

(a) publishes notice of the proposed modifications; and

(b) considers any representations made in accordance with the notice and not withdrawn.

(5) A notice under subsection (4) shall state—

(a) the proposed modifications;

(b) the reasons for them; and

(c) the period (not less than 7 days starting with the date of the publication of the notice under subsection (4)) within which representations may be made in relation to the proposed modifications.

(6) If, after publishing notice under subsection (1) or (4), the [CMA] decides—

(a) not to accept the undertaking concerned; and

(b) not to proceed by virtue of subsection (8) or (9);

it shall publish notice of that decision.

(7) As soon as practicable after accepting an undertaking to which this section applies, the [CMA] shall—

(a) serve a copy of the undertaking on any person by whom it is given; and

(b) publish the undertaking.

(8) The requirements of subsection (4) (and those of subsection (1)) shall not apply if the [CMA]—
(a) has already published notice under subsection (1) but not subsection (4) in relation to the proposed undertaking; and
(b) considers that the modifications which are now being proposed are not material in any respect.

(9) The requirements of subsection (4) (and those of subsection (1)) shall not apply if the [CMA]—
(a) has already published notice under subsections (1) and (4) in relation to the matter concerned; and
(b) considers that the further modifications which are now being proposed do not differ in any material respect from the modifications in relation to which notice was last given under subsection (4).

(10) Paragraphs 6 to 8 (but not paragraph 9) of Schedule 10 (procedural requirements before terminating undertakings) shall apply in relation to the proposed release of undertakings under section 154 (other than in connection with accepting an undertaking under that section which varies or supersedes an undertaking under that section) as they apply in relation to the proposed release of undertakings under section 73.

NOTES

References to the "CMA" substituted by the Enterprise and Regulatory Reform Act 2013, s 26(3), Sch 5, Pt 2, paras 59, 188. For various transitional provisions (including those relating to the abolition of the OFT and the Competition Commission, existing references to those bodies and provisions relating to continuity), see the Enterprise and Regulatory Reform Act 2013 (Commencement No 6, Transitional Provisions and Savings) Order 2014, SI 2014/416, Schedule at **[2.13]**.

Words in second pair of square brackets in sub-s (3)(a) inserted by the Enterprise and Regulatory Reform Act 2013, s 35(10), Sch 10, paras 1, 23, subject to transitional provisions in SI 2014/416 as noted above.

[1.367]

156 Effect of undertakings under section 154

[(A1) No market investigation reference shall be made by the CMA or the appropriate Minister in relation to any feature, or combination of features, of a market in the United Kingdom for goods or services if—
(a) the CMA has accepted an undertaking or group of undertakings under section 154 within the previous 12 months;
(b) the feature or combination of features to which the undertaking or group of undertakings relates is the same as the feature or combination of features to which the reference would relate; and
(c) the goods or services to which the undertaking or group of undertakings relates are of the same description as the goods or services to which the reference would relate.]

(1) No [ordinary] reference shall be made by the [CMA] or the appropriate Minister in relation to any feature, or combination of features, of a market in the United Kingdom for goods or services if—
(a) the [CMA] has[, instead of making an ordinary reference,] accepted an undertaking or group of undertakings under section 154 within the previous 12 months; and
(b) the goods or services to which the undertaking or group of undertakings relates are of the same description as the goods or services to which [the reference would relate].

(2) [Subsections (A1) and (1) do] not prevent the making of a market investigation reference if—
(a) the [CMA] considers that any undertaking concerned has been breached and has given notice of that fact to the person responsible for giving the undertaking; or
(b) the person responsible for giving any undertaking concerned supplied, in connection with the matter, information to the [CMA] which was false or misleading in a material respect.

[(3) The expiry of the period mentioned in section 131B(4) does not prevent the making of a market investigation reference if the CMA has accepted an undertaking or group of undertakings under section 154 and—
(a) the CMA considers that any undertaking concerned has been breached and has given notice of that fact to the person responsible for giving the undertaking; or
(b) the person responsible for giving any undertaking concerned supplied, in connection with the matter, information to the OFT which was false or misleading in a material respect.]

NOTES

Sub-s (A1): inserted by the Enterprise and Regulatory Reform Act 2013, s 34(4), Sch 9, paras 1, 8(1), (2). For various transitional provisions (including those relating to the abolition of the OFT and the Competition Commission, existing references to those bodies and provisions relating to continuity), see the Enterprise and Regulatory Reform Act 2013 (Commencement No 6, Transitional Provisions and Savings) Order 2014, SI 2014/416, Schedule at **[2.13]**.

Sub-s (1): the words ", instead of making an ordinary reference," in square brackets were inserted, and the other words in square brackets were substituted, by the Enterprise and Regulatory Reform Act 2013, ss 26(3), 34(4), Sch 5, Pt 2, paras 59, 189, Sch 9, paras 1, 8(1), (3), subject to transitional provisions in SI 2014/416 as noted above.

Sub-s (2): words in square brackets substituted by the Enterprise and Regulatory Reform Act 2013, ss 26(3), 34(4), Sch 5, Pt 2, paras 59, 189, Sch 9, paras 1, 8(1), (4), subject to transitional provisions in SI 2014/416 as noted above.

Sub-s (3): added by the Enterprise and Regulatory Reform Act 2013, s 38, Sch 12, paras 7, 12, subject to transitional provisions in SI 2014/416 as noted above.

[1.368]

157 Interim undertakings: Part 4

(1) Subsection (2) applies where—
(a) a market investigation reference has been made;
(b) a report has been published under section 136 within the period permitted by section 137 or (as the case may be) a report prepared under section 142 and given to the Secretary of State under section 143(3) [or (as the case may be) 143A(3)] within the period permitted by section 144 has been published; and
(c) the market investigation reference concerned is not finally determined.

(2) The relevant authority may, for the purpose of preventing pre-emptive action, accept, from such persons as the relevant authority considers appropriate, undertakings to take such action as the relevant authority considers appropriate.

[(2A) Subsection (2B) applies where—

(a) subsection (1)(a) to (c) applies; and
(b) the relevant authority has reasonable grounds for suspecting that pre-emptive action has or may have been taken.

(2B) The relevant authority may, for the purpose of restoring the position to what it would have been had the pre-emptive action not been taken or otherwise for the purpose of mitigating its effects, accept, from such persons as the relevant authority considers appropriate, undertakings to take such action as the relevant authority considers appropriate.]

[(2C) A person may, with the consent of the relevant authority, take action of a particular description where the action would otherwise constitute a contravention of an undertaking accepted under this section.]

(3) An undertaking under this section—
(a) shall come into force when accepted;
(b) may be varied or superseded by another undertaking; and
(c) may be released by the relevant authority.

(4) An undertaking under this section shall, if it has not previously ceased to be in force, cease to be in force when the market investigation reference is finally determined.

(5) The relevant authority shall, as soon as reasonably practicable, consider any representations received by the relevant authority in relation to varying or releasing an undertaking under this section.

(6) In this section and section 158—

"pre-emptive action" means action which might impede the taking of any action under section 138(2)[, 147(2) or (as the case may be) 147A(2)] in relation to the market investigation reference concerned; and

["the relevant authority" means—
(a) in the case of a restricted PI reference or a full PI reference, the Secretary of State;
(b) in any other case, the CMA.]

NOTES

Sub-s (1): words in square brackets in para (b) inserted by the Enterprise and Regulatory Reform Act 2013, s 35(10), Sch 10, paras 1, 24(1), (2). For various transitional provisions (including those relating to the abolition of the OFT and the Competition Commission, existing references to those bodies and provisions relating to continuity), see the Enterprise and Regulatory Reform Act 2013 (Commencement No 6, Transitional Provisions and Savings) Order 2014, SI 2014/416, Schedule at **[2.13]**.

Sub-ss (2A)–(2C): inserted by the Enterprise and Regulatory Reform Act 2013, s 37(1)–(3), subject to transitional provisions in SI 2014/416 as noted above.

Sub-s (6): words in square brackets in definition "pre-emptive action" substituted, and definition "relevant authority" substituted, by the Enterprise and Regulatory Reform Act 2013, s 35(10), Sch 10, paras 1, 24(1), (3), subject to transitional provisions in SI 2014/416 as noted above.

[1.369]

158 Interim orders: Part 4

(1) Subsection (2) applies where—
(a) a market investigation reference has been made;
(b) a report has been published under section 136 within the period permitted by section 137 or (as the case may be) a report prepared under section 142 and given to the Secretary of State under section 143(3) [or (as the case may be) 143A(3)] within the period permitted by section 144 has been published; and
(c) the market investigation reference concerned is not finally determined.

(2) The relevant authority may by order, for the purpose of preventing pre-emptive action—
(a) prohibit or restrict the doing of things which the relevant authority considers would constitute pre-emptive action;
(b) impose on any person concerned obligations as to the carrying on of any activities or the safeguarding of any assets;
(c) provide for the carrying on of any activities or the safeguarding of any assets either by the appointment of a person to conduct or supervise the conduct of any activities (on such terms and with such powers as may be specified or described in the order) or in any other manner;
(d) do anything which may be done by virtue of paragraph 19 of Schedule 8.

[(2A) Subsection (2B) applies where—
(a) subsection (1)(a) to (c) applies; and
(b) the relevant authority has reasonable grounds for suspecting that pre-emptive action has or may have been taken.

(2B) The relevant authority may by order, for the purpose of restoring the position to what it would have been had the pre-emptive action not been taken or otherwise for the purpose of mitigating its effects—
(a) do anything mentioned in subsection (2)(b) to (d);
(b) impose such other obligations, prohibitions or restrictions as it considers appropriate for that purpose.]

[(2C) A person may, with the consent of the relevant authority, take action of a particular description where the action would otherwise constitute a contravention of an order under this section.]

(3) An order under this section—
(a) shall come into force at such time as is determined by or under the order; and
(b) may be varied or revoked by another order.

(4) An order under this section shall, if it has not previously ceased to be in force, cease to be in force when the market investigation reference is finally determined.

(5) The relevant authority shall, as soon as reasonably practicable, consider any representations received by the relevant authority in relation to varying or revoking an order under this section.

NOTES

Sub-s (1): words in square brackets in para (b) inserted by the Enterprise and Regulatory Reform Act 2013, s 35(10), Sch 10, paras 1, 25. For various transitional provisions (including those relating to the abolition of the OFT and

the Competition Commission, existing references to those bodies and provisions relating to continuity), see the Enterprise and Regulatory Reform Act 2013 (Commencement No 6, Transitional Provisions and Savings) Order 2014, SI 2014/416, Schedule at **[2.13]**.

Sub-ss (2A)–(2C): inserted by the Enterprise and Regulatory Reform Act 2013, s 37(1), (4), (5), subject to transitional provisions in SI 2014/416 as noted above.

[1.370]
159 Final undertakings: Part 4

(1) The [CMA] may, in accordance with section 138, accept, from such persons as it considers appropriate, undertakings to take action specified or described in the undertakings.
(2) The Secretary of State may, in accordance with section 147 [or (as the case may be) 147A], accept, from such persons as he considers appropriate, undertakings to take action specified or described in the undertakings.
(3) An undertaking under this section shall come into force when accepted.
(4) An undertaking under subsection (1) or (2) may be varied or superseded by another undertaking under that subsection.
(5) An undertaking under subsection (1) may be released by the [CMA] and an undertaking under subsection (2) may be released by the Secretary of State.
(6) The [CMA] or (as the case may be) the Secretary of State shall, as soon as reasonably practicable, consider any representations received by it or (as the case may be) him in relation to varying or releasing an undertaking under this section.

NOTES

Sub-ss (1), (5), (6): references to the "CMA" substituted by the Enterprise and Regulatory Reform Act 2013, s 26(3), Sch 5, Pt 2, paras 59, 190. For various transitional provisions (including those relating to the abolition of the OFT and the Competition Commission, existing references to those bodies and provisions relating to continuity), see the Enterprise and Regulatory Reform Act 2013 (Commencement No 6, Transitional Provisions and Savings) Order 2014, SI 2014/416, Schedule at **[2.13]**.

Sub-s (2): words in square brackets inserted by the Enterprise and Regulatory Reform Act 2013, s 35(10), Sch 10, paras 1, 26, subject to transitional provisions in SI 2014/416 as noted above.

[1.371]
160 Order-making power where final undertakings not fulfilled: Part 4

(1) Subsection (2) applies where the relevant authority considers that—
  (a) an undertaking accepted by the relevant authority under section 159 has not been, is not being or will not be fulfilled; or
  (b) in relation to an undertaking accepted by the relevant authority under that section, information which was false or misleading in a material respect was given to [a relevant person] by the person giving the undertaking before the relevant authority decided to accept the undertaking.
[(1A) In subsection (1), a "relevant person" means—
  (a) in a case where the relevant authority is the CMA, the CMA;
  (b) in a case where the relevant authority is the Secretary of State, the Secretary of State or the CMA.]
(2) The relevant authority may, for any of the purposes mentioned in section 138(2)[, 147(2) or (as the case may be) 147A(2)], make an order under this section.
(3) Subsections (3) to (6) of section 138 [or 147 or (as the case may be) subsections (3) and (4) of section 147A] shall apply for the purposes of subsection (2) above as they apply for the purposes of that section.
(4) An order under this section may contain—
  (a) anything permitted by Schedule 8; and
  (b) such supplementary, consequential or incidental provision as the relevant authority considers appropriate.
(5) An order under this section—
  (a) shall come into force at such time as is determined by or under the order;
  (b) may contain provision which is different from the provision contained in the undertaking concerned; and
  (c) may be varied or revoked by another order.
(6) [The Secretary of State shall not vary or revoke an order made by him under this section unless the CMA] advises that such a variation or revocation is appropriate by reason of a change of circumstances.
(7) In this section "the relevant authority" means—
  (a) in the case of an undertaking accepted under section 159 by the [CMA], the [CMA]; and
  (b) in the case of an undertaking accepted under that section by the Secretary of State, the Secretary of State.

NOTES

Sub-s (1): words in square brackets in para (b) substituted by the Enterprise and Regulatory Reform Act 2013, s 26(3), Sch 5, Pt 2, paras 59, 191(1), (2). For various transitional provisions (including those relating to the abolition of the OFT and the Competition Commission, existing references to those bodies and provisions relating to continuity), see the Enterprise and Regulatory Reform Act 2013 (Commencement No 6, Transitional Provisions and Savings) Order 2014, SI 2014/416, Schedule at **[2.13]**.

Sub-s (1A): inserted by the Enterprise and Regulatory Reform Act 2013, s 26(3), Sch 5, Pt 2, paras 59, 191(1), (3), subject to transitional provisions in SI 2014/416 as noted above.

Sub-ss (2), (3): words in square brackets substituted by the Enterprise and Regulatory Reform Act 2013, s 35(10), Sch 10, paras 1, 27, subject to transitional provisions in SI 2014/416 as noted above.

Sub-ss (6), (7): words in square brackets substituted by the Enterprise and Regulatory Reform Act 2013, s 26(3), Sch 5, Pt 2, paras 59, 191(1), (4), (5), subject to transitional provisions in SI 2014/416 as noted above.

Revocation or modification of licence conditions, etc under certain sectoral enactments: an order under this section or s 161 may also provide for the revocation or modification of licence conditions, etc, for certain regulated industries; see: (a) the Gas Act 1986, s 27(1); (b) the Electricity Act 1989, s 15(1); (c) the Broadcasting Act 1990(1), s 193; (d) the Water Industry Act 1991, s 17(1); (e) the Railways Act 1993, s 16(1); (f) the Transport Act 2000, s 19(1).

[1.372]

161 Final orders: Part 4

(1) The [CMA] may, in accordance with section 138, make an order under this section.

(2) The Secretary of State may, in accordance with section 147 [or (as the case may be) 147A], make an order under this section.

(3) An order under this section may contain—

(a) anything permitted by Schedule 8; and

(b) such supplementary, consequential or incidental provision as the person making it considers appropriate.

(4) An order under this section—

(a) shall come into force at such time as is determined by or under the order; and

(b) may be varied or revoked by another order.

(5) [The Secretary of State shall not vary or revoke an order made by him under this section unless the CMA] advises that such a variation or revocation is appropriate by reason of a change of circumstances.

NOTES

Sub-s (1): reference to the "CMA" substituted by the Enterprise and Regulatory Reform Act 2013, s 26(3), Sch 5, Pt 2, paras 59, 192(1), (2). For various transitional provisions (including those relating to the abolition of the OFT and the Competition Commission, existing references to those bodies and provisions relating to continuity), see the Enterprise and Regulatory Reform Act 2013 (Commencement No 6, Transitional Provisions and Savings) Order 2014, SI 2014/416, Schedule at **[2.13]**.

Sub-s (2): words in square brackets inserted by the Enterprise and Regulatory Reform Act 2013, s 35(10), Sch 10, paras 1, 28, subject to transitional provisions in SI 2014/416 as noted above.

Sub-s (5): words in square brackets substituted by the Enterprise and Regulatory Reform Act 2013, s 26(3), Sch 5, Pt 2, paras 59, 192(1), (3), subject to transitional provisions in SI 2014/416 as noted above.

Revocation or modification of licence conditions, etc under certain sectoral enactments: see the note to s 160 at **[1.371]**.

[Undertakings and orders: monitoring, consultation and advice]

NOTES

The above heading was substituted by the Enterprise and Regulatory Reform Act 2013, s 26(3), Sch 5, Pt 2, paras 59, 193. For various transitional provisions (including those relating to the abolition of the OFT and the Competition Commission, existing references to those bodies and provisions relating to continuity), see the Enterprise and Regulatory Reform Act 2013 (Commencement No 6, Transitional Provisions and Savings) Order 2014, SI 2014/416, Schedule at **[2.13]**.

[1.373]

162 Duty of [CMA] to monitor undertakings and orders: Part 4

(1) The [CMA] shall keep under review the carrying out of any enforcement undertaking or any enforcement order.

(2) The [CMA] shall, in particular, from time to time consider—

(a) whether an enforcement undertaking or enforcement order has been or is being complied with;

(b) whether, by reason of any change of circumstances, an enforcement undertaking is no longer appropriate and—

(i) one or more of the parties to it can be released from it; or

(ii) it needs to be varied or to be superseded by a new enforcement undertaking; and

(c) whether, by reason of any change of circumstances, an enforcement order is no longer appropriate and needs to be varied or revoked.

(3) The [CMA] shall give . . . the Secretary of State such advice as it considers appropriate in relation to—

(a) any possible variation or release by . . . the Secretary of State of an enforcement undertaking accepted by . . . him;

(b) any possible new enforcement undertaking to be accepted by . . . the Secretary of State so as to supersede another enforcement undertaking given to . . . the Secretary of State;

(c) any possible variation or revocation by . . . the Secretary of State of an enforcement order made by . . . the Secretary of State;

(d) any possible enforcement undertaking to be accepted by . . . the Secretary of State instead of an enforcement order or any possible enforcement order to be made by . . . the Secretary of State instead of an enforcement undertaking; or

(e) the enforcement by virtue of section [167(6) and (7)] of any enforcement undertaking or enforcement order.

(4) The [CMA] shall take such action as it considers appropriate in relation to—

(a) any possible variation or release by it of an undertaking accepted by it under section 154;

(b) any possible new undertaking to be accepted by it under section 154 so as to supersede another undertaking given to it under that section;

[(ba) any possible variation or release by it of an enforcement undertaking accepted by it;

(bb) any possible new enforcement undertaking to be accepted by it so as to supersede another enforcement undertaking given to it;

(bc) any possible variation or revocation by it of an enforcement order made by it;

(bd) any possible enforcement undertaking to be accepted by it instead of an enforcement order or any possible enforcement order to be made by it instead of an enforcement undertaking;] or

(c) the enforcement by it by virtue of section 167(6) of any enforcement undertaking or enforcement order.

(5) The [CMA] shall keep under review the effectiveness of enforcement undertakings accepted under this Part and enforcement orders made under this Part.

(6) The [CMA] shall, whenever requested to do so by the Secretary of State and otherwise from time to time, prepare a report of its findings under subsection (5).

(7) The [CMA] shall—

(a) . . .

(b) give a copy of [any report prepared by it under subsection (6)] to the Secretary of State; and

(c) publish the report.

(8) In this Part—

"enforcement order" means an order made under section 158, 160 or 161; and

"enforcement undertaking" means an undertaking accepted under section 154, 157 or 159.

NOTES

All amendments to this section were made by the Enterprise and Regulatory Reform Act 2013, s 26(3), Sch 5, Pt 2, paras 59, 194. For various transitional provisions (including those relating to the abolition of the OFT and the Competition Commission, existing references to those bodies and provisions relating to continuity), see the Enterprise and Regulatory Reform Act 2013 (Commencement No 6, Transitional Provisions and Savings) Order 2014, SI 2014/416, Schedule at **[2.13]**.

[1.374]

163 [Role of CMA in relation to undertakings and orders in public interest cases: Part 4]

(1) Subsections (2) and (3) apply where . . . the Secretary of State . . . is considering whether to accept undertakings under section 157 or 159.

(2) The [Secretary of State] may require the [CMA] to consult with such persons as the [Secretary of State] considers appropriate with a view to discovering whether they will offer undertakings which the relevant authority would be prepared to accept under section 157 or (as the case may be) 159.

(3) The [Secretary of State] may require the [CMA] to report to the [Secretary of State] on the outcome of the [CMA's] consultations within such period as the [Secretary of State] may require.

(4) A report under subsection (3) shall, in particular, contain advice from the [CMA] as to whether any undertakings offered should be accepted by the [Secretary of State] under section 157 or (as the case may be) 159.

(5) The powers conferred on the [Secretary of State] by subsections (1) to (4) are without prejudice to the power of the [Secretary of State] to consult the persons concerned . . . .

(6) If asked by the [Secretary of State] for advice in relation to the taking of enforcement action (whether or not by way of undertakings) in a particular case, the [CMA] shall give such advice as it considers appropriate.

NOTES

All amendments to this section were made by the Enterprise and Regulatory Reform Act 2013, s 26(3), Sch 5, Pt 2, paras 59, 195. For various transitional provisions (including those relating to the abolition of the OFT and the Competition Commission, existing references to those bodies and provisions relating to continuity), see the Enterprise and Regulatory Reform Act 2013 (Commencement No 6, Transitional Provisions and Savings) Order 2014, SI 2014/416, Schedule at **[2.13]**.

Supplementary

[1.375]

164 Enforcement undertakings and orders under this Part: general provisions

(1) The provision which may be contained in an enforcement undertaking is not limited to the provision which is permitted by Schedule 8.

(2) The following enactments in Part 3 shall apply in relation to enforcement orders under this Part as they apply in relation to enforcement orders under that Part—

(a) section 86(1) to (5) (enforcement orders: general provisions); and

(b) section 87 (power of directions conferred by enforcement order).

(3) An enforcement order under section 160 or 161 or any explanatory material accompanying the order shall state—

(a) the actions that the persons or description of persons to whom the order is addressed must do or (as the case may be) refrain from doing;

(b) the date on which the order comes into force;

(c) the possible consequences of not complying with the order; and

(d) the section of this Part under which a review can be sought in relation to the order.

[1.376]

165 Procedural requirements for certain undertakings and orders: Part 4

Schedule 10 (procedural requirements for certain undertakings and orders), other than paragraph 9 of that Schedule, shall apply in relation to undertakings under section 159 and orders under section 160 or 161 as it applies in relation to undertakings under section 82 and orders under section 83 or 84.

[1.377]

166 Register of undertakings and orders: Part 4

(1) The [CMA] shall compile and maintain a register for the purposes of this Part.

(2) The register shall be kept in such form as the [CMA] considers appropriate.

(3) The [CMA] shall ensure that the following matters are entered in the register—

(a) the provisions of any enforcement undertaking accepted by virtue of this Part . . . ;

(b) the provisions of any enforcement order made by virtue of this Part . . . ; and

(c) the details of any variation, release or revocation of such an undertaking or order.

(4) The duty in subsection (3) does not extend to anything of which the [CMA] is unaware.

(5) The . . . Secretary of State and any relevant sectoral regulator shall inform the [CMA] of any matters which are to be included in the register by virtue of subsection (3) and which relate to enforcement undertakings accepted by them or enforcement orders made by them.

(6) The [CMA] shall ensure that the contents of the register are available to the public—

(a) during (as a minimum) such hours as may be specified in an order made by the Secretary of State; and

(b) subject to such reasonable fees (if any) as the [CMA] may determine.

(7) If requested by any person to do so and subject to such reasonable fees (if any) as the [CMA] may determine, the [CMA] shall supply the person concerned with a copy (certified to be true) of the register or of an extract from it.

NOTES

All amendments to this section were made by the Enterprise and Regulatory Reform Act 2013, s 26(3), Sch 5, Pt 2, paras 59, 196. For various transitional provisions (including those relating to the abolition of the OFT and the Competition Commission, existing references to those bodies and provisions relating to continuity), see the Enterprise and Regulatory Reform Act 2013 (Commencement No 6, Transitional Provisions and Savings) Order 2014, SI 2014/416, Schedule at **[2.13]**.

Note that the 2013 Act actually provides (in Sch 5, para 196(3)(b)) that the words "(whether by the Commission, the Secretary of State or a relevant sectoral regulator)" should be repealed from sub-s (3)(a); it is assumed that this is an error and that the intention is to repeal the words "(whether by the OFT, the Commission, the Secretary of State or a relevant sectoral regulator)".

Orders: the CMA Registers of Undertakings and Orders (Available Hours) Order 2014, SI 2014/558 at **[2.59]**.

[1.378]

167 Rights to enforce undertakings and orders under this Part

(1) This section applies to any enforcement undertaking or enforcement order.

(2) Any person to whom such an undertaking or order relates shall have a duty to comply with it.

(3) The duty shall be owed to any person who may be affected by a contravention of the undertaking or (as the case may be) order.

(4) Any breach of the duty which causes such a person to sustain loss or damage shall be actionable by him.

(5) In any proceedings brought under subsection (4) against a person to whom an enforcement undertaking or enforcement order relates it shall be a defence for that person to show that he took all reasonable steps and exercised all due diligence to avoid contravening the undertaking or (as the case may be) order.

(6) Compliance with an enforcement undertaking or an enforcement order shall also be enforceable by civil proceedings brought by the [CMA] for an injunction or for interdict or for any other appropriate relief or remedy.

(7) Compliance with an undertaking accepted [by the Secretary of State] under section 157 or 159, or an order [made by the Secretary of State] under section 158, 160 or 161, shall also be enforceable by civil proceedings brought by the [Secretary of State] for an injunction or for interdict or for any other appropriate relief or remedy.

(8) . . .

(9) Subsections [(6) and (7)] shall not prejudice any right that a person may have by virtue of subsection (4) to bring civil proceedings for contravention or apprehended contravention of an enforcement undertaking or an enforcement order.

NOTES

The words in square brackets in sub-ss (6), (7) and (9) were substituted or inserted, and sub-s (8) was repealed, by the Enterprise and Regulatory Reform Act 2013, s 26(3), Sch 5, Pt 2, paras 59, 197. For various transitional provisions (including those relating to the abolition of the OFT and the Competition Commission, existing references to those bodies and provisions relating to continuity), see the Enterprise and Regulatory Reform Act 2013 (Commencement No 6, Transitional Provisions and Savings) Order 2014, SI 2014/416, Schedule at **[2.13]**.

CHAPTER 4 SUPPLEMENTARY

Regulated markets

[1.379]

168 Regulated markets

(1) Subsection (2) applies where the [CMA] or the Secretary of State is considering for the purposes of this Part whether relevant action would be reasonable and practicable for the purpose of remedying, mitigating or preventing an adverse effect on competition or any detrimental effect on customers so far as resulting from such an effect.

(2) The [CMA] or (as the case may be) the Secretary of State shall, in deciding whether such action would be reasonable and practicable, have regard to the relevant statutory functions of the sectoral regulator concerned.

(3) In this section "relevant action" means—

(a), (b) . . .

(c) modifying the conditions of a licence granted under section 7[, 7A or 7AB] of the Gas Act 1986 (c 44);

(d) modifying the conditions of a licence granted under section 6 of the Electricity Act 1989 (c 29);

(e) modifying networking arrangements (within the meaning given by [section 290 of the Communications Act 2003]);

(f) modifying the conditions of a company's appointment under Chapter 1 of Part 2 of the Water Industry Act 1991 (c 56);

[(ff) modifying the conditions of a licence granted under Chapter 1A of Part 2 of the Act of 1991 or modifying the terms and conditions of an agreement under section 66D [or 117E] of that Act;]

(g) modifying the conditions of a licence granted under article 10 of the Electricity (Northern Ireland) Order 1992 (SI 1992/231 (NI 1));

(h) modifying the conditions of a licence granted under section 8 of the Railways Act 1993 (c 43);

[(hh) modifying the conditions of a SNRP issued pursuant to the Railways Infrastructure (Access, Management and Licensing of Railway Undertakings) Regulations (Northern Ireland) 2005;]

(i) modifying an access agreement (within the meaning given by section 83(1) of the Act of 1993) or a franchise agreement (within the meaning given by section 23(3) of that Act);

(j) modifying conditions in force under Part 4 of the Airports (Northern Ireland) Order 1994 (SI 1994/426 (NI 1)) other than any conditions imposed or modified in pursuance of article 40(3) or (4) of that Order;

(k) modifying the conditions of a licence granted under article 8 of the Gas (Northern Ireland) Order 1996 (SI 1996/275 (NI 2));

(l) . . .

(m) modifying the conditions of a licence granted under section 5 of the Transport Act 2000 (c 38);

[(n) modifying the conditions of a company's appointment under Chapter I of Part III of the Water and Sewerage Services (Northern Ireland) Order 2006];
[(o) modifying regulatory conditions imposed under Part 3 of the Postal Services Act 2011];
[(p) modifying the conditions of a licence issued under section 87 of the Health and Social Care Act 2012];
[(q) modifying the conditions of a licence granted under Chapter 1 of Part 1 of the Civil Aviation Act 2012].

(4) In this section "relevant statutory functions" means—

(a), (b) . . .
(c) in relation to any licence granted under section 7[, 7A or 7AB] of the Gas Act 1986 (c 44), the objectives and duties of the Gas and Electricity Markets Authority under section 4AA and 4AB(2) of that Act;
(d) in relation to any licence granted under section 6 of the Electricity Act 1989 (c 29), the objectives and duties of the Gas and Electricity Markets Authority under section 3A and 3B(2) of that Act;
[(e) in relation to any networking arrangements (within the meaning given by section 290 of the Communications Act 2003), the duty of the Office of Communications under subsection (1) of section 3 of that Act to secure the matters mentioned in subsection (2)(c) of that section;]
(f) in relation to a company's appointment under Chapter 1 of Part 2 of the Water Industry Act 1991 (c 56), the duties of [the Water Services Regulation Authority] under section 2 of that Act;
[(ff) in relation to a licence granted under Chapter 1A of Part 2 of the Act of 1991 or an agreement under section 66D [or 117E] of that Act, the duties of the Authority under section 2 of that Act or under that section and section 66D [or 117E] of that Act (as the case may be);]
(g) in relation to any licence granted under article 10 of the Electricity (Northern Ireland) Order 1992 (SI 1992/231 (NI 1)), the duty of the Director General of Electricity Supply for Northern Ireland under article 6 of that Order;
(h) in relation to any licence granted under section 8 of the Railways Act 1993 (c 43) . . . the duties of [the Office of Rail and Road] under section 4 of that Act;
[(hh) in relation to a SNRP issued pursuant to the Railways Infrastructure (Access, Management and Licensing of Railway Undertakings) Regulations (Northern Ireland) 2005 where none of the conditions of the SNRP relate to consumer protection, the duties of the Department for Regional Development under regulation 36 of those Regulations;]
(i) . . .
(j) in relation to any access agreement (within the meaning given by section 83(1) of the Act of 1993), the duties of [the Office of Rail and Road] under section 4 of the Act of 1993;
(k) in relation to any franchise agreement (within the meaning given by section 23(3) of the Act of 1993), the duties of the [Secretary of State, the Scottish Ministers and the National Assembly for Wales under section 4 of the Act of 1993];
(l) in relation to conditions in force under Part 4 of the Airports (Northern Ireland) Order 1994 (SI 1994/426 (NI 1)) other than any conditions imposed or modified in pursuance of article 40(3) or (4) of that Order, the duties of the Civil Aviation Authority under article 30(2) and (3) of that Order;
(m) in relation to any licence granted under article 8 of the Gas (Northern Ireland) Order 1996 (SI 1996/275 (NI 2)), the duties of the Director General of Gas for Northern Ireland under article 5 of that Order;
(n) . . .
(o) in relation to any licence granted under section 5 of the Transport Act 2000, the duties of the Civil Aviation Authority under section 87 of that Act;
[(p) in relation to a company's appointment under Chapter I of Part III of the Water and Sewerage Services (Northern Ireland) Order 2006, the duties of the Northern Ireland Authority for Utility Regulation under Article 6 of that Order];
[(q) in relation to regulatory conditions imposed under Part 3 of the Postal Services Act 2011, the duty of the Office of Communications under section 29 of that Act];
[(r) in relation to any licence issued under section 87 of the Health and Social Care Act 2012, the duties of Monitor under sections 62 and 66 of that Act];
[(s) in relation to a licence granted under Chapter 1 of Part 1 of the Civil Aviation Act 2012, the duties of the Civil Aviation Authority under section 1 of that Act].

(5) In this section "sectoral regulator" means—

(a) the Civil Aviation Authority;
[(b) the Northern Ireland Authority for Utility Regulation;]
(d) . . .
[(e) the Water Services Regulation Authority;]
(f) the Gas and Electricity Markets Authority;
[(g) the Office of Communications;]
(h) . . .
(i) [the Office of Rail and Road]; . . .
[(ia) [Monitor;]
[(j) the Secretary of State;
(k) the Scottish Ministers; or
(l) the National Assembly for Wales].

(6) Subsection (7) applies where the [CMA] or the Secretary of State is considering for the purposes of this Part whether modifying the conditions of a licence granted under section 7[, 7A or 7AB] of the Gas Act 1986 (c 44) or section 6 of the Electricity Act 1989 (c 29) would be reasonable and practicable for the purpose of remedying, mitigating or preventing an adverse effect on competition or any detrimental effect on customers so far as resulting from such an effect.

(7) The [CMA] or (as the case may be) the Secretary of State may, in deciding whether modifying the conditions of such a licence would be reasonable and practicable, have regard to those matters to which the Gas and Electricity Markets Authority may have regard by virtue of section 4AA(4) of the Act of 1986 or (as the case may be) section 3A(4) of the Act of 1989.

(8) The Secretary of State may by order modify subsection (3), (4), (5), (6) or (7).

(9) Part 2 of Schedule 9 (which makes provision for functions under this Part to be exercisable by various sectoral regulators) shall have effect.

NOTES

Sub-ss (1), (2), (6), (7): references to "CMA" substituted by the Enterprise and Regulatory Reform Act 2013, s 26(3), Sch 5, Pt 2, paras 59, 198. For various transitional provisions (including those relating to the abolition of the OFT and the Competition Commission, existing references to those bodies and provisions relating to continuity), see the Enterprise and Regulatory Reform Act 2013 (Commencement No 6, Transitional Provisions and Savings) Order 2014, SI 2014/416, Schedule at **[2.13]**.

Sub-s (3) is amended as follows:

Para (a) repealed by the Communications Act 2003, s 406(7), Sch 19(1).

Para (b) repealed by the Civil Aviation Act 2012, s 76, Sch 9, paras 13, 14(1), (2).

Words in square brackets in para (c) substituted by the Electricity and Gas (Smart Meters Licensable Activity) Order 2012, SI 2012/2400, art 31.

Words in square brackets in para (e) substituted by the Communications Act 2003, s 406(1), Sch 17, para 174(1), (5)(a).

Para (ff) inserted by the Water Act 2003, s 101(1), Sch 8, para 55(1), (2)(a). Words in square brackets inserted by the Water Act 2014, s 56, Sch 7, paras 128, 129(1), (2).

Para (hh) inserted by the Railways Infrastructure (Access, Management and Licensing of Railway Undertakings) Regulations (Northern Ireland) 2005, SR 2005/537, reg 45, Sch 5, para 4(a).

Para (l) repealed, and para (o) inserted, by the Postal Services Act 2011, s 91, Sch 12, Pt 3, para 164.

Para (n) inserted by the Water and Sewerage Services (Northern Ireland) Order 2006, SI 2006/3336, art 308(1), Sch 12, para 46(3).

Para (p) inserted by the Health and Social Care Act 2012, s 74(7)(a).

Para (q) inserted by the Civil Aviation Act 2012, s 76, Sch 9, paras 13, 14(1), (2).

Sub-s (4) is amended as follows:

Para (a) repealed by the Communications Act 2003, s 406(7), Sch 19(1).

Para (b) repealed by the Civil Aviation Act 2012, s 76, Sch 9, paras 13, 14(1), (3).

Words in square brackets in para (c) substituted by SI 2012/2400, art 31.

Para (e) substituted by the Communications Act 2003, s 406(1), Sch 17, para 174(1), (5)(b).

Words in square brackets in para (f) substituted by the Water Act 2003, s 101(1), Sch 7, Pt 2, para 36(1), (3)(a).

Para (ff) added by the Water Act 2003, s 101(1), Sch 8, para 55(1), (2)(b). Words in square brackets inserted by the Water Act 2014, s 56, Sch 7, paras 128, 129(1), (3).

Words omitted from para (h) repealed by the Railways Act 2005, s 59(1), (6), Sch 12, para 18(1), (2)(a), Sch 13, Pt 1. Words in square brackets substituted by the Office of Rail Regulation (Change of Name) Regulations 2015, SI 2015/1682, reg 2(2), Schedule, Pt 1, para 4(q)(ii).

Para (hh) inserted by the Railways Infrastructure (Access, Management and Licensing of Railway Undertakings) Regulations (Northern Ireland) 2005, SR 2005/537, reg 45, Sch 5, para 4(b).

Para (i) repealed by the Railways Act 2005, s 59(1), (6), Sch 12, para 18(1), (2)(b), Sch 13, Pt 1.

Words in square brackets in para (j) substituted by SI 2015/1682, reg 2(2), Schedule, Pt 1, para 4(q)(ii).

Words in square brackets in para (k) substituted by the Railways Act 2005, s 59(1), Sch 12, para 18(1), (2)(c).

Para (n) repealed, and para (q) inserted, by the Postal Services Act 2011, s 91, Sch 12, Pt 3, para 164.

Para (p) inserted by the Water and Sewerage Services (Northern Ireland) Order 2006, SI 2006/3336, art 308(1), Sch 12, para 46(4).

Para (r) inserted by the Health and Social Care Act 2012, s 74(7)(b).

Para (s) inserted by the Civil Aviation Act 2012, s 76, Sch 9, paras 13, 14(1), (3).

Sub-s (5) is amended as follows:

Para (b) substituted, for original paras (b), (c), by the Water and Sewerage Services (Northern Ireland) Order 2006, SI 2006/3336, art 308(1), Sch 12, para 46(5).

Para (d) repealed by the Communications Act 2003, s 406(7), Sch 19(1).

Para (e) substituted by the Water Act 2003, s 101(1), Sch 7, Pt 2, para 36(1), (3)(b).

Para (g) substituted by the Communications Act 2003, s 406(1), Sch 17, para 174(1), (5)(c).

Para (h) repealed by the Postal Services Act 2011, s 91, Sch 12, Pt 3, para 164.

Words in square brackets in para (i) substituted by SI 2015/1682, reg 2(2), Schedule, Pt 1, para 4(q)(ii). Word omitted from that paragraph repealed by the Railways Act 2005, s 59(6), Sch 13, Pt 1 (in relation to England, Scotland and Wales), and by the Railways Infrastructure (Access, Management and Licensing of Railway Undertakings) Regulations (Northern Ireland) 2005, SR 2005/537, reg 45, Sch 5, para 4(c)(i) (in relation to Northern Ireland).

Para (ia) inserted by the Health and Social Care Act 2012, s 74(7)(c).

Paras (j)–(l) substituted, for original para (j), by the Railways Act 2005, s 59(1), Sch 12, para 18(1), (3) (in relation to England, Scotland and Wales). For a corresponding amendment in relation to Northern Ireland, see SR 2005/537, reg 45, Sch 5, para 4(c).

National Assembly for Wales: see further, in relation to the renaming of the National Assembly for Wales as the Senedd Cymru or the Welsh Parliament, the Senedd and Elections (Wales) Act 2020. See also ss 3–9 of the 2020 Act in relation to the renaming of Acts of the National Assembly for Wales, Members of the National Assembly for Wales, etc.

Consultation, information and publicity

[1.380]

169 Certain duties of relevant authorities to consult: Part 4

(1) Subsection (2) applies where the relevant authority is proposing to make a relevant decision in a way which the relevant authority considers is likely to have a substantial impact on the interests of any person.

(2) The relevant authority shall, so far as practicable, consult that person about what is proposed before making that decision.

(3) In consulting the person concerned, the relevant authority shall, so far as practicable, give the reasons of the relevant authority for the proposed decision.

(4) In considering what is practicable for the purposes of this section the relevant authority shall, in particular, have regard to—

(a) any restrictions imposed by any timetable for making the decision; and

(b) any need to keep what is proposed, or the reasons for it, confidential.

(5) The duty under this section shall not apply in relation to the making of any decision so far as particular provision is made elsewhere by virtue of this Part for consultation before the making of that decision.

(6) In this section—

"the relevant authority" means the [CMA, the appropriate Minister] [or the Secretary of State]; and

"relevant decision" means—

(a) in the case of the [CMA], any decision by the [CMA]—

[(i) to make a reference under section 131 in a case where the CMA has not published a market study notice under section 130A in relation to the matter concerned;

(ia) as to whether to accept undertakings under section 154 instead of making any reference under section 131;]

(ii) to vary under section 135 such a reference; [or

(iii) on the questions mentioned in section 134, 141 or 141A; and]

(b) in the case of the appropriate Minister [(other than the Secretary of State acting alone)], any decision by the appropriate Minister—

(i) . . . to make a reference under section 132; or

(ii) to vary under section 135 such a reference; . . .

[(ba) in the case of the Secretary of State, any decision by the Secretary of State—

(i) to make a reference under section 132;

(ii) to vary under section 135 such a reference;

(iii) in a case where the Secretary of State is required to make a reference under section 140A, whether to make a reference under subsection (5) or (6) of that section; or

(iv) to vary under section 140B a reference made under section 140A(6).]

(c) . . .

NOTES

Sub-s (6): all amendments were made by the Enterprise and Regulatory Reform Act 2013, ss 26(3), 35(10), 38 Sch 5, Pt 2, paras 59, 199, Sch 10, paras 1, 29, Sch 12, paras 7, 13. For various transitional provisions (including those relating to the abolition of the OFT and the Competition Commission, existing references to those bodies and provisions relating to continuity), see the Enterprise and Regulatory Reform Act 2013 (Commencement No 6, Transitional Provisions and Savings) Order 2014, SI 2014/416, Schedule at **[2.13]**.

[1.381]

170 General information duties

(1), (2) . . .

(3) The [CMA] shall give the Secretary of State or the appropriate Minister so far as he is not the Secretary of State acting alone—

(a) such information in [its possession] as the Secretary of State or (as the case may be) the appropriate Minister concerned may by direction reasonably require to enable him to carry out his functions under this Part; and

(b) any other assistance which the Secretary of State or (as the case may be) the appropriate Minister concerned may by direction reasonably require for the purpose of assisting him in carrying out his functions under this Part and which it is within the power of the [CMA] to give.

(4) The [CMA] shall give the Secretary of State or the appropriate Minister so far as he is not the Secretary of State acting alone any information in its possession which has not been requested by the Secretary of State or (as the case may be) the appropriate Minister concerned but which, in the opinion of the [CMA], would be appropriate to give to the Secretary of State or (as the case may be) the appropriate Minister concerned for the purpose of assisting him in carrying out his functions under this Part.

(5) [The Secretary of State] or (as the case may be) the appropriate Minister concerned shall have regard to any information given to him under subsection (3) or (4).

(6) Any direction given under subsection (3)—

(a) shall be in writing; and

(b) may be varied or revoked by a subsequent direction.

NOTES

All amendments to this section were made by the Enterprise and Regulatory Reform Act 2013, s 26(3), Sch 5, Pt 2, paras 59, 200(1), (2). For various transitional provisions (including those relating to the abolition of the OFT and the Competition Commission, existing references to those bodies and provisions relating to continuity), see the Enterprise and Regulatory Reform Act 2013 (Commencement No 6, Transitional Provisions and Savings) Order 2014, SI 2014/416, Schedule at **[2.13]**.

[1.382]

171 Advice and information: Part 4

(1) . . . [The CMA] shall prepare and publish general advice and information about[—

(a) the making and consideration by it of market investigation references, and

(b) the way in which relevant customer benefits may affect the taking of enforcement action in relation to such references.]

(2) The [CMA] may at any time publish revised, or new, advice or information.

(3), (4) . . .
(5) Advice and information published under this section shall be prepared with a view to—
(a) explaining relevant provisions of this Part to persons who are likely to be affected by them; and
(b) indicating how the [CMA] expects such provisions to operate.
(6) Advice and information published by virtue of subsection (1) . . . shall include such advice and information about the effect of Community law, and anything done under or in accordance with it, on the provisions of this Part as the [CMA] considers appropriate.
(7) Advice (or information) published by virtue of subsection (1) . . . may include advice (or information) about the factors which the [CMA] may take into account in considering whether, and if so how, to exercise a function conferred by this Part.
(8) Any advice or information published by the [CMA] under this section shall be published in such manner as the [CMA] considers appropriate.
(9) In preparing any advice or information under this section, the [CMA shall consult such persons] as it considers appropriate.
(10) . . .
(11) In this section "Community law" means—
(a) all the rights, powers, liabilities, obligations and restrictions from time to time created or arising by or under the Community Treaties; and
(b) all the remedies and procedures from time to time provided for by or under the Community Treaties.

NOTES

Except as noted below, all amendments to this section were made by the Enterprise and Regulatory Reform Act 2013, s 26(3), Sch 5, Pt 2, paras 59, 201. For various transitional provisions (including those relating to the abolition of the OFT and the Competition Commission, existing references to those bodies and provisions relating to continuity), see the Enterprise and Regulatory Reform Act 2013 (Commencement No 6, Transitional Provisions and Savings) Order 2014, SI 2014/416, Schedule at **[2.13]**.

Sub-ss (6) and (11) were repealed by the Competition (Amendment etc) (EU Exit) Regulations 2019, SI 2019/93, regs 32, 57, as from IP completion day (as defined in the European Union (Withdrawal Agreement) Act 2020, s 39) (for transitional provisions and savings in relation to the operation of the 2019 Regulations, see Sch 4 to those Regulations at **[7.69]** et seq).

References to the European Community and related expressions: see the note "References to "the European Community", "Community", etc" in the introductory notes to this Act.

[1.383]

172 Further publicity requirements: Part 4

(1) The [CMA] shall publish—
(a) any reference made by it under section 131[, other than a reference treated as so made by virtue of section 140A(5)(b)];
[(aa) any decision not to make a reference under section 131 following a consultation in relation to the matter concerned under section 169;]
(b) any variation made by it under section 135 of a reference under section 131;
(c) any decision of a kind mentioned in section 149(5)(b); and
(d) such information as it considers appropriate about any decision made by it under section 152(1) to bring a case to the attention of the Secretary of State.
(2) The [CMA shall also] publish—
[(za) any extension by it under section 137 of the period within which a report under section 136 is to be prepared and published;
(zb) any extension by it under section 138A of the period within which its duty under section 138(2) is to be discharged;]
(a) any decision made by it under section 138(2) neither to accept an undertaking under section 159 nor to make an order under section 161;
(b) any decision made by it that there has been a material change of circumstances as mentioned in section 138(3) or there is another special reason as mentioned in that section;
[(ba) any extension by it under section 144 of the period within which a report under section 142 is to be prepared and action is to be taken in relation to it;]
(c) any termination under section 145(1) of an investigation by it;
(d) . . .
(e) any enforcement undertaking accepted by it under section 157;
(f) any enforcement order made by it under section 158; and
(g) any variation, release or revocation of such an undertaking or order.
(3) The Secretary of State shall publish—
(a) any reference made by him under section 132;
(b) any variation made by him under section 135 of a reference under section 132;
(c) any intervention notice given by him;
(d) any decision made by him to revoke such a notice;
[(da) any reference made by him under section 140A(5) or (6);
(db) any variation made by him under section 140B of a reference under section 140A(6);]
(e) any decision made by him under section 147(2) [or (as the case may be) 147A(2)] neither to accept an undertaking under section 159 nor to make an order under section 161;
(f) any enforcement undertaking accepted by him under section 157;
(g) any variation or release of such an undertaking; and
(h) any direction given by him under section 170(3) in connection with the exercise by him of his functions under section 132(3).
(4) The appropriate Minister (other than the Secretary of State acting alone) shall publish—

(a) any reference made by him under section 132;
(b) any variation made by him under section 135 of a reference under section 132; and
(c) any direction given by him under section 170(3) in connection with the exercise by him of his functions under section 132(3).

(5) Where any person is under an obligation by virtue of subsection (1), (2), (3) or (4) to publish the result of any action taken by that person or any decision made by that person, the person concerned shall, subject to subsections (6) and (7), also publish that person's reasons for the action concerned or (as the case may be) the decision concerned.

(6) Such reasons need not, if it is not reasonably practicable to do so, be published at the same time as the result of the action concerned or (as the case may be) as the decision concerned.

(7) Subsections (5) and (6) shall not apply in relation to any case falling within subsection (1)(d) . . . .

[(7A) Subsection (6) shall not apply in relation to any case falling within subsection (1)(a) [or (3)(da)].]

(8) The Secretary of State shall publish his reasons for—
(a) any decision made by him under section 146(2) [or 146A(2)]; or
(b) any decision to make an order under section 153(3) or vary or revoke such an order.

(9) Such reasons may be published after—
(a) in the case of subsection (8)(a), the publication of the decision concerned; and
(b) in the case of subsection (8)(b), the making of the order or of the variation or revocation;

if it is not reasonably practicable to publish them at the same time as the publication of the decision or (as the case may be) the making of the order or variation or revocation.

(10) Where the Secretary of State has decided under section 147(2) [or 147A(2)] to accept an undertaking under section 159 or to make an order under section 161, he shall (after the acceptance of the undertaking or (as the case may be) the making of the order) lay details of his decision and his reasons for it, and the [CMA's] report under section 142, before each House of Parliament.

NOTES

All amendments to this section were made by the Enterprise and Regulatory Reform Act 2013, ss 26(3), 35(10), 38, Sch 5, Pt 2, paras 59, 202, Sch 10, paras 1, 30, Sch 12, paras 7, 14. For various transitional provisions (including those relating to the abolition of the OFT and the Competition Commission, existing references to those bodies and provisions relating to continuity), see the Enterprise and Regulatory Reform Act 2013 (Commencement No 6, Transitional Provisions and Savings) Order 2014, SI 2014/416, Schedule at **[2.13]**.

[1.384]

173 Defamation: Part 4

For the purposes of the law relating to defamation, absolute privilege attaches to any advice, guidance, notice or direction given, or decision or report made, by the [CMA], [by the Secretary of State or] by the appropriate Minister (other than the Secretary of State acting alone) . . . in the exercise of any of their functions under this Part.

NOTES

Words in square brackets substituted, and words omitted repealed, by the Enterprise and Regulatory Reform Act 2013, s 26(3), Sch 5, Pt 2, paras 59, 203. For various transitional provisions (including those relating to the abolition of the OFT and the Competition Commission, existing references to those bodies and provisions relating to continuity), see the Enterprise and Regulatory Reform Act 2013 (Commencement No 6, Transitional Provisions and Savings) Order 2014, SI 2014/416, Schedule at **[2.13]**.

Investigation powers

[1.385]

174 [Attendance of witnesses and production of documents etc]

[(1) For the purposes of this section, the permitted purposes are the following—
(a) assisting the CMA in carrying out its functions under section 5 in relation to a matter in a case where it has published a market study notice;
(b) assisting the CMA in carrying out any functions, including enforcement functions, exercisable by it under or by virtue of this Part in connection with a matter that is or has been the subject of a reference under section 131 or 132 or possible reference under section 131;
(c) assisting the CMA or the Secretary of State in carrying out any functions, including enforcement functions, of the CMA or (as the case may be) the Secretary of State under or by virtue of this Part in connection with a matter that is or has been the subject of a reference under section 140A(6) or possible reference under section 140A(5) or (6).

(2) The CMA may exercise any of the powers in subsections (3) to (5) for a permitted purpose.]

(3) The [CMA] may give notice to any person requiring him—
(a) to attend at a time and place specified in the notice; and
(b) to give evidence to the [CMA] or a person nominated by the [CMA] for the purpose.

(4) The [CMA] may give notice to any person requiring him—
(a) to produce any documents which—
 (i) are specified or described in the notice, or fall within a category of document which is specified or described in the notice; and
 (ii) are in that person's custody or under his control; and
(b) to produce them at a time and place so specified and to a person so specified.

(5) The [CMA] may give notice to any person who carries on any business requiring him—
(a) to supply to the [CMA] such estimates, forecasts, returns or other information as may be specified or described in the notice; and
(b) to supply it at a time and place, and in a form and manner, so specified and to a person so specified.

(6) A notice under this section shall[—
(a) specify the permitted purpose for which the notice is given, including the function or functions in question; and

(b)] include information about the possible consequences of not complying with the notice.

[(6A) The CMA or any person nominated by it for the purpose may, for a permitted purpose, take evidence on oath and for that purpose may administer oaths.]

(7) The person to whom any document is produced in accordance with a notice under this section may, for [a permitted purpose], copy the document so produced.

(8) No person shall be required under this section—

(a) to give any evidence or produce any documents which he could not be compelled to give or produce in civil proceedings before the court; or

(b) to supply any information which he could not be compelled to supply in evidence in such proceedings.

(9) No person shall be required, in compliance with a notice under this section, to go more than 10 miles from his place of residence unless his necessary travelling expenses are paid or offered to him.

[(9A) In subsection (1), "enforcement functions" means—

(a) in relation to the CMA—

(i) functions conferred by virtue of section 164(2)(b) on the CMA by enforcement orders;

(ii) functions of the CMA in relation to the variation, supersession or release of enforcement undertakings or the variation or revocation of enforcement orders;

(iii) functions of the CMA under or by virtue of section 160 or 162 in relation to enforcement undertakings or enforcement orders;

(b) in relation to the Secretary of State—

(i) functions conferred by virtue of section 164(2)(b) on the Secretary of State by enforcement orders;

(ii) functions of the Secretary of State in relation to the variation, supersession or release of enforcement undertakings or the variation or revocation of enforcement orders;

(iii) functions of the Secretary of State under or by virtue of section 160 in relation to enforcement undertakings or enforcement orders.]

(10) Any reference in this section to the production of a document includes a reference to the production of a legible and intelligible copy of information recorded otherwise than in legible form.

(11) In this section "the court" means—

(a) in relation to England and Wales or Northern Ireland, the High Court; and

(b) in relation to Scotland, the Court of Session.

NOTES

Section heading, sub-ss (1), (2): substituted by the Enterprise and Regulatory Reform Act 2013, s 36(1), (2), (7). For various transitional provisions (including those relating to the abolition of the OFT and the Competition Commission, existing references to those bodies and provisions relating to continuity), see the Enterprise and Regulatory Reform Act 2013 (Commencement No 6, Transitional Provisions and Savings) Order 2014, SI 2014/416, Schedule at **[2.13]**.

Sub-ss (3)–(5): references to the "CMA" substituted by the Enterprise and Regulatory Reform Act 2013, s 26(3), Sch 5, Pt 2, paras 59, 204, subject to transitional provisions in SI 2014/416 as noted above.

Sub-s (6): words in square brackets inserted by the Enterprise and Regulatory Reform Act 2013, s 36(1), (3), subject to transitional provisions in SI 2014/416 as noted above.

Sub-ss (6A), (9A): inserted by the Enterprise and Regulatory Reform Act 2013, s 36(1), (4), (6), subject to transitional provisions in SI 2014/416 as noted above.

Sub-s (7): words in square brackets substituted by the Enterprise and Regulatory Reform Act 2013, s 36(1), (5), subject to transitional provisions in SI 2014/416 as noted above.

[1.386]

[174A Enforcement of powers under section 174: general

(1) Where the CMA considers that a person has, without reasonable excuse, failed to comply with any requirement of a notice under section 174, it may impose a penalty in accordance with section 174D.

(2) The CMA may proceed (whether at the same time or at different times) under subsection (1) and section 138A(3) in relation to the same failure.

(3) Where the CMA considers that a person has intentionally obstructed or delayed another person in the exercise of its powers under section 174(7), it may impose a penalty in accordance with section 174D.

(4) A person commits an offence if the person intentionally alters, suppresses or destroys any document which the person has been required to produce by a notice under section 174.

(5) But a person does not commit an offence under subsection (4) in relation to any act which constitutes a failure to comply with a notice under section 174 if the CMA has proceeded against the person under subsection (1) in relation to that failure.

(6) A person who commits an offence under subsection (4) is liable—

(a) on summary conviction, to a fine not exceeding the statutory maximum;

(b) on conviction on indictment, to imprisonment for a term not exceeding 2 years or to a fine or to both.

(7) The CMA shall not proceed against a person under subsection (1) in relation to an act which constitutes an offence under subsection (4) if that person has been found guilty of that offence.

(8) In deciding whether and, if so, how to proceed under subsection (1) or (3) or section 138A(3), the CMA shall have regard to the statement of policy which was most recently published under section 174E at the time the failure or (as the case may be) the obstruction or delay concerned occurred.

(9) In this section—

(a) the reference to the production of a document includes a reference to the production of a legible and intelligible copy of information recorded otherwise than in legible form; and

(b) the reference to suppressing a document includes a reference to destroying the means of reproducing information recorded otherwise than in legible form.]

NOTES

Inserted, together with ss 174B–174E, by the Enterprise and Regulatory Reform Act 2013, s 36(8), Sch 11, para 1. For various transitional provisions (including those relating to the abolition of the OFT and the Competition Commission, existing references to those bodies and provisions relating to continuity), see the Enterprise and Regulatory Reform Act 2013 (Commencement No 6, Transitional Provisions and Savings) Order 2014, SI 2014/416, Schedule at **[2.13]**.

[1.387]

[174B Restriction on powers to impose penalties under section 174A

(1) No penalty shall be imposed by virtue of section 174A(1) or (3) if more than 4 weeks have passed since the day which is the relevant day in the case in question; but this subsection shall not apply in relation to any variation or substitution of the penalty which is permitted by virtue of this Part.

(2) In the following provisions of this section, "the section 174 power" means the power under section 174 to which the failure or (as the case may be) the obstruction or delay in question relates.

(3) Where the section 174 power is exercised for the purpose mentioned in section 174(1)(a), the relevant day is the day when the CMA finally concludes the carrying out of its section 5 functions.

(4) Where the section 174 power is exercised in connection with an enforcement function (within the meaning of that section), the relevant day is the day when the enforcement undertaking concerned is superseded or released or (as the case may be) the enforcement order concerned is revoked.

(5) Except where subsection (3) or (4) applies, the relevant day is the day determined in accordance with the following provisions of this section.

(6) Where the section 174 power is exercised for the purpose mentioned in section 174(1)(b) in connection with a matter that is the subject of a possible reference under section 131, the relevant day is the day when the CMA finally decides whether to make the reference.

(7) Where the section 174 power is exercised for the purpose mentioned in section 174(1)(b) in connection with a matter that is the subject of a reference under section 131 or 132, the relevant day is the day when the reference is finally determined (see section 183).

(8) Where the section 174 power is exercised for the purpose mentioned in section 174(1)(c) in connection with a matter that is the subject of a possible reference under section 140A(5) or (6), the relevant day is the day when the Secretary of State makes the reference.

(9) Where the section 174 power is exercised for the purpose mentioned in section 174(1)(c) in connection with a matter that is the subject of a reference under section 140A(6), the relevant day is the day when the reference is finally determined (see section 183).]

NOTES

Inserted as noted to s 174A at **[1.386]**.

[1.388]

[174C Section 174B: supplementary provision

(1) For the purpose of section 174B(3), the CMA finally concludes the carrying out of its section 5 functions if—

(a) the CMA publishes the market study report under section 131B(4) or (as the case may be) gives it to the Secretary of State under section 140A(3)(b); or

(b) the period permitted for the preparation by the CMA of the market study report and for the report to be published under section 131B(4) or (as the case may be) given to the Secretary of State under section 140A(3)(b) expires and no such report has been so prepared or no such action has been taken.

(2) For the purpose of section 174B(3), the time when the CMA finally concludes the carrying out of its section 5 functions is—

(a) in a case falling within subsection (1)(a), the publication of the report or (as the case may be) the giving of it to the Secretary of State;

(b) in a case falling within subsection (1)(b), the expiry of the period concerned.

(3) For the purpose of section 174B(6), the CMA finally decides whether to make a reference under section 131 if—

(a) the CMA makes such a reference;

(b) the CMA accepts an undertaking under section 154 instead of making such a reference;

(c) the CMA publishes notice that it has otherwise decided not to make such a reference; or

(d) the period permitted for the preparation by the CMA of a market study report in relation to the matter and for the report to be published under section 131B(4) has expired and no such report has been so prepared or published.

(4) For the purpose of section 174B(6), the time when the CMA finally decides whether to make a reference under section 131 is—

(a) in a case falling within subsection (3)(a), the making of the reference;

(b) in a case falling within subsection (3)(b), the acceptance of the undertaking concerned;

(c) in a case falling within subsection (3)(c), the publication of the notice concerned;

(d) in a case falling within subsection (3)(d), the expiry of the period concerned.

(5) In subsection (4)(b) the reference to the acceptance of the undertaking concerned shall, in a case where the CMA has accepted a group of undertakings under section 154, be treated as a reference to the acceptance of the last undertaking in the group; but undertakings which vary, supersede or revoke earlier undertakings shall be disregarded for the purposes of subsections (3)(b) and (4)(b).]

NOTES

Inserted as noted to s 174A at **[1.386]**.

[1.389]

[174D Penalties

(1) A penalty imposed under section 174A(1) or (3) shall be of such amount as the CMA considers appropriate.

(2) In the case of a penalty imposed under section 174A(1), the amount may be—

(a) a fixed amount;

(b) an amount calculated by reference to a daily rate; or

(c) a combination of a fixed amount and an amount calculated by reference to a daily rate.

(3) In the case of a penalty imposed under section 174A(3), the amount shall be a fixed amount.

(4) A penalty imposed under section 174A(1) shall not—

(a) in the case of a fixed amount, exceed such amount as the Secretary of State may by order specify;

(b) in the case of an amount calculated by reference to a daily rate, exceed such amount per day as the Secretary of State may so specify; and

(c) in the case of a fixed amount and an amount calculated by reference to a daily rate, exceed such fixed amount and such amount per day as the Secretary of State may so specify.

(5) A penalty imposed under section 174A(3) shall not exceed such amount as the Secretary of State may by order specify.

(6) An order under subsection (4) or (5) shall not specify—

(a) in the case of a fixed amount, an amount exceeding £30,000;

(b) in the case of an amount calculated by reference to a daily rate, an amount per day exceeding £15,000; and

(c) in the case of a fixed amount and an amount calculated by reference to a daily rate, a fixed amount exceeding £30,000 and an amount per day exceeding £15,000.

(7) Before making an order under subsection (4) or (5), the Secretary of State shall consult—

(a) the CMA; and

(b) such other persons as the Secretary of State considers appropriate.

(8) In imposing a penalty by reference to a daily rate—

(a) no account is to be taken of any days before the service on the person concerned of notice of the penalty under section 112 (as applied by subsection (10)); and

(b) unless the CMA determines an earlier date (whether before or after the penalty is imposed), the amount payable ceases to accumulate at the beginning of the earliest of the days mentioned in subsection (9).

(9) Those days are—

(a) the day on which the requirement of the notice concerned under section 174 is satisfied;

(b) the day which is the relevant day in the case in question for the purposes of section 174B.

(10) Sections 112 to 115 apply in relation to a penalty imposed under section 174A(1) or (3) as they apply in relation to a penalty imposed under section 110(1) or (3).]

NOTES

Inserted as noted to s 174A at **[1.386]**.

Orders: the Competition and Markets Authority (Penalties) Order 2014, SI 2014/559 at **[2.61]**.

[1.390]

[174E Statement of policy on penalties

(1) The CMA shall prepare and publish a statement of policy in relation to the enforcement of notices given under section 174.

(2) The statement shall, in particular, include a statement about the considerations relevant to the determination of the nature and amount of any penalty imposed under section 174A(1) or (3).

(3) The CMA may revise its statement of policy and, where it does so, it shall publish the revised statement.

(4) The CMA shall consult such persons as it considers appropriate when preparing or revising its statement of policy.]

NOTES

Inserted as noted to s 174A at **[1.386]**.

175, 176 (*Repealed by the Enterprise and Regulatory Reform Act 2013, s 36(8), Sch 11, paras 2–4. For various transitional provisions (including those relating to the abolition of the OFT and the Competition Commission, existing references to those bodies and provisions relating to continuity), see the Enterprise and Regulatory Reform Act 2013 (Commencement No 6, Transitional Provisions and Savings) Order 2014, SI 2014/416, Schedule at* **[2.13]**.)

Reports

[1.391]

177 Excisions from reports: Part 4

(1) Subsection (2) applies where the Secretary of State is under a duty to publish a report of the [CMA] under section 142.

(2) The Secretary of State may exclude a matter from the report if he considers that publication of the matter would be inappropriate.

(3) In deciding what is inappropriate for the purposes of subsection (2) the Secretary of State shall have regard to the considerations mentioned in section 244.

(4) The [CMA] shall advise the Secretary of State as to the matters (if any) which it considers should be excluded by him under subsection (2).

(5) References in sections 136(4) to (6) . . . and 172(10) to the giving or laying of a report of the [CMA] shall be construed as references to the giving or laying of the report as published.

NOTES

References to the "CMA" substituted, and words omitted from sub-s (5) repealed, by the Enterprise and Regulatory Reform Act 2013, s 26(3), 35(10), Sch 5, Pt 2, paras 59, 205, Sch 10, paras 1, 31. For various transitional provisions (including those relating to the abolition of the OFT and the Competition Commission, existing references to those bodies and provisions relating to continuity), see the Enterprise and Regulatory Reform Act 2013 (Commencement No 6, Transitional Provisions and Savings) Order 2014, SI 2014/416, Schedule at **[2.13]**.

[1.392]

178 Minority reports of [CMA]: Part 4

(1) Subsection (2) applies where, on a market investigation reference, a member of a group constituted in connection with the reference . . . , disagrees with any decisions contained in the report of the [CMA] under this Part as the decisions of the [CMA].

(2) The report shall, if the member so wishes, include a statement of his disagreement and of his reasons for disagreeing.

NOTES

References to the "CMA" substituted, and words omitted from sub-s (1) repealed, by the Enterprise and Regulatory Reform Act 2013, s 26(3), Sch 5, Pt 2, paras 59, 206. For various transitional provisions (including those relating to the abolition of the OFT and the Competition Commission, existing references to those bodies and provisions relating to continuity), see the Enterprise and Regulatory Reform Act 2013 (Commencement No 6, Transitional Provisions and Savings) Order 2014, SI 2014/416, Schedule at **[2.13]**.

Other

[1.393]

179 Review of decisions under Part 4

(1) Any person aggrieved by a decision of the [CMA], the appropriate Minister [or the Secretary of State] in connection with a reference or possible reference under this Part may apply to the Competition Appeal Tribunal for a review of that decision.

(2) For this purpose "decision"—

[(za) does not include a decision whether to carry out functions under section 5 in a case where the CMA is, or would have been, required to publish a market study notice (see section 130A(1));]

(a) does not include a decision to impose a penalty under [section 174A(1) or (3)]; but

(b) includes a failure to take a decision permitted or required by this Part in connection with a reference or possible reference.

(3) Except in so far as a direction to the contrary is given by the Competition Appeal Tribunal, the effect of the decision is not suspended by reason of the making of the application.

(4) In determining such an application the Competition Appeal Tribunal shall apply the same principles as would be applied by a court on an application for judicial review.

(5) The Competition Appeal Tribunal may—

(a) dismiss the application or quash the whole or part of the decision to which it relates; and

(b) where it quashes the whole or part of that decision, refer the matter back to the original decision maker with a direction to reconsider and make a new decision in accordance with the ruling of the Competition Appeal Tribunal.

(6) An appeal lies on any point of law arising from a decision of the Competition Appeal Tribunal under this section to the appropriate court.

(7) An appeal under subsection (6) requires the permission of the Tribunal or the appropriate court.

(8) In this section—

"the appropriate court" means the Court of Appeal or, in the case of Tribunal proceedings in Scotland, the Court of Session; and

"Tribunal rules" has the meaning given by section 15(1).

NOTES

Sub-s (1): words in square brackets substituted by the Enterprise and Regulatory Reform Act 2013, s 26(3), Sch 5, Pt 2, paras 59, 207. For various transitional provisions (including those relating to the abolition of the OFT and the Competition Commission, existing references to those bodies and provisions relating to continuity), see the Enterprise and Regulatory Reform Act 2013 (Commencement No 6, Transitional Provisions and Savings) Order 2014, SI 2014/416, Schedule at **[2.13]**.

Sub-s (2): para (za) inserted, and words in square brackets in para (a) substituted, by the Enterprise and Regulatory Reform Act 2013, ss 36(8), 38, Sch 11, paras 2, 5, Sch 12, paras 7, 15, subject to transitional provisions in SI 2014/416 as noted above.

[1.394]

180 Offences

(1) Sections 117 (false or misleading information) and 125 (offences by bodies corporate) shall apply, with the modifications mentioned in subsection (2) below, for the purposes of this Part as they apply for the purposes of Part 3.

(2) Section 117 shall, in its application by virtue of subsection (1) above, have effect as if references to the Secretary of State included references to the appropriate Minister so far as he is not the Secretary of State acting alone [and as if the references to OFCOM were omitted].

NOTES

Sub-s (2): words in square brackets added by the Communications Act 2003, s 389(1), Sch 16, para 26.

[1.395]

181 Orders under Part 4

(1) Any power of the Secretary of State to make an order under this Part shall be exercisable by statutory instrument.

(2) Any power of the Secretary of State to make an order under this Part—

(a) may be exercised so as to make different provision for different cases or different purposes;

(b) includes power to make such incidental, supplementary, consequential, transitory, transitional or saving provision as the Secretary of State considers appropriate.

(3) The power of the Secretary of State under section [131C(1), 136(9), 137(3), 138B(6)], 144(2), 153(3) or 168(8) as extended by subsection (2) above may be exercised by modifying any enactment comprised in or made under this Act, or any other enactment.

(4) An order made by the Secretary of State under section [131C(1), 137(3), 138B(6)], 144(2), 158, 160[, 161, 174D(4) or (5), or under section 114(3)(b) or (4)(b) as applied by section 174D], shall be subject to annulment in pursuance of a resolution of either House of Parliament.

(5) No order shall be made by the Secretary of State under section 136(9) or 168(8), or section 128(6) as applied by section 183(2), unless a draft of it has been laid before, and approved by a resolution of, each House of Parliament.

(6) An order made by the Secretary of State under section 153(3) shall be laid before Parliament after being made and shall cease to have effect unless approved, within the period of 28 days beginning with the day on which it is made, by a resolution of each House of Parliament.

(7) In calculating the period of 28 days mentioned in subsection (6), no account shall be taken of any time during which Parliament is dissolved or prorogued or during which both Houses are adjourned for more than four days.

(8) If an order made by the Secretary of State ceases to have effect by virtue of subsection (6), any modification made by it of an enactment is repealed (and the previous enactment revived) but without prejudice to the validity of anything done in connection with that modification before the order ceased to have effect and without prejudice to the making of a new order.

(9) If, apart from this subsection, an order made by the Secretary of State under section 153(3) would be treated for the purposes of the standing orders of either House of Parliament as a hybrid instrument, it shall proceed in that House as if it were not such an instrument.

(10) References in this section to an order made under this Part include references to an order made under section . . . 114(3)(b) or (4)(b) as applied by section [174D] and an order made under section 128(6) as applied by section 183(2).

NOTES

Sub-ss (3), (4): figures and words in square brackets substituted by the Enterprise and Regulatory Reform Act 2013, ss 36(8), 38, Sch 11, paras 2, 6(1), (2), Sch 12, paras 7, 16. For various transitional provisions (including those relating to the abolition of the OFT and the Competition Commission, existing references to those bodies and provisions relating to continuity), see the Enterprise and Regulatory Reform Act 2013 (Commencement No 6, Transitional Provisions and Savings) Order 2014, SI 2014/416, Schedule at **[2.13]**.

Sub-s (10): words omitted repealed, and figure in square brackets substituted, by the Enterprise and Regulatory Reform Act 2013, s 36(8), Sch 11, paras 2, 6(1), (3), subject to transitional provisions in SI 2014/416 as noted above.

[1.396]

182 Service of documents: Part 4

Section 126 shall apply for the purposes of this Part as it applies for the purposes of Part 3.

[1.397]

183 Interpretation: Part 4

(1) In this Part, unless the context otherwise requires—

"action" includes omission; and references to the taking of action include references to refraining from action;

"business" includes a professional practice and includes any other undertaking which is carried on for gain or reward or which is an undertaking in the course of which goods or services are supplied otherwise than free of charge;

"change of circumstances" includes any discovery that information has been supplied which is false or misleading in a material respect;

"consumer" means any person who is—

(a) a person to whom goods are or are sought to be supplied (whether by way of sale or otherwise) in the course of a business carried on by the person supplying or seeking to supply them; or

(b) a person for whom services are or are sought to be supplied in the course of a business carried on by the person supplying or seeking to supply them;

and who does not receive or seek to receive the goods or services in the course of a business carried on by him;

"customer" includes a customer who is not a consumer;

"enactment" includes an Act of the Scottish Parliament, Northern Ireland legislation and an enactment comprised in subordinate legislation, and includes an enactment whenever passed or made;

"goods" includes buildings and other structures, and also includes ships, aircraft and hovercraft;

"Minister of the Crown" means the holder of an office in Her Majesty's Government in the United Kingdom and includes the Treasury;

"modify" includes amend or repeal;

"notice" means notice in writing;

"subordinate legislation" has the same meaning as in the Interpretation Act 1978 (c 30) and also includes an instrument made under an Act of the Scottish Parliament and an instrument made under Northern Ireland legislation; and

"supply", in relation to the supply of goods, includes supply by way of sale, lease, hire or hire-purchase, and, in relation to buildings or other structures, includes the construction of them by a person for another person.

(2) Sections 127(1)(b) and (4) to (6) and 128 shall apply for the purposes of this Part as they apply for the purposes of Part 3.

(3) For the purposes of this Part a market investigation reference is finally determined if—

(a) [where the reference is made under section 131 or 132—]

(i) the period permitted by section 137 for preparing and publishing a report under section 136 has expired and no such report has been prepared and published;

(ii) such a report has been prepared and published within the period permitted by section 137 and contains the decision that there is no adverse effect on competition;

(iii) the [CMA] has decided under section 138(2) neither to accept undertakings under section 159 nor to make an order under section 161; or

(iv) the [CMA] has accepted an undertaking under section 159 or made an order under section 161;

(b) [where the reference is a restricted PI reference or a full PI reference—]

(i) the period permitted by section 144 for the preparation of the report of the [CMA] under section 142 and for action to be taken in relation to it under section 143(1) or (3) [or (as the case may be) 143A(2) or (3)] has expired while the intervention notice is still in force and no such report has been so prepared or no such action has been taken;

(ii) the [CMA] has terminated under section 145(1) its investigation and the reference is finally determined under paragraph (a) above . . . ;

(iii) the report of the [CMA] has been prepared under section 142 and published under section 143(1) [or (as the case may be) 143A(2)] within the period permitted by section 144;

(iv) the intervention notice was revoked and the reference is finally determined under paragraph (a) above . . . ;

[(v) the Secretary of State has failed to make and publish a decision under subsection (2) of section 146 within the period permitted by subsection (3) of that section or (as the case may be) under subsection (2) of section 146A within the period permitted by subsection (6) of that section and the reference is finally determined under paragraph (a) above;]

(vi) the Secretary of State has decided under section 146(2) that no eligible public interest consideration is relevant and the reference is finally determined under paragraph (a) above . . . ;

[(via) the Secretary of State has made no finding at all under section 146A(2) and the reference is finally determined under paragraph (a) above;]

(vii) the Secretary of State has decided under 146(2) that a public interest consideration is relevant but has decided under section 147(2) neither to accept an undertaking under section 159 nor to make an order under section 161; . . .

[(viia) the Secretary of State has made an adverse public interest finding under section 146A(2) but has decided under section 147A(2) neither to accept an undertaking under section 159 nor to make an order under section 161;]

(viii) the Secretary of State has decided under section 146(2) that a public interest consideration is relevant and has accepted an undertaking under section 159 or made an order under section 161[; or

(ix) the Secretary of State has made an adverse public interest finding under section 146A(2) and has accepted an undertaking under section 159 or made an order under section 161].

(4) For the purposes of this Part the time when a market investigation reference is finally determined is—

(a) in a case falling within subsection (3)(a)(i) or (b)(i), the expiry of the time concerned;

(b) in a case falling within subsection (3)(a)(ii) or (b)(iii), the publication of the report;

(c) in a case falling within subsection (3)(a)(iv) or (b)(viii) [or (ix)], the acceptance of the undertaking concerned or (as the case may be) the making of the order concerned; and

(d) in any other case, the making of the decision or last decision concerned or the taking of the action concerned.

(5) The references in subsection (4) to subsections (3)(a)(i), (ii) and (iv) include those enactments as applied by subsection (3)(b)(ii), (iv), (v)[, (vi) or (via)].

(6) In subsection (4)(c) the reference to the acceptance of the undertaking concerned or the making of the order concerned shall, in a case where the enforcement action concerned involves the acceptance of a group of undertakings, the making of a group of orders or the acceptance and making of a group of undertakings and orders, be treated as a reference to the acceptance or making of the last undertaking or order in the group; but undertakings or orders which vary, supersede or revoke earlier undertakings or orders shall be disregarded for the purposes of subsections (3)(a)(iv) and (b)(viii) [and (ix)] and (4)(c).

(7) Any duty to publish which is imposed on a person by this Part shall, unless the context otherwise requires, be construed as a duty on that person to publish in such manner as that person considers appropriate for the purpose of bringing the matter concerned to the attention of those likely to be affected by it.

NOTES

Sub-s (3): all amendments were made by the Enterprise and Regulatory Reform Act 2013, ss 26(3), 35(10), Sch 5, Pt 2, paras 59, 208, Sch 10, paras 1, 32(1)–(3). For various transitional provisions (including those relating to the abolition of the OFT and the Competition Commission, existing references to those bodies and provisions relating to continuity), see the Enterprise and Regulatory Reform Act 2013 (Commencement No 6, Transitional Provisions and Savings) Order 2014, SI 2014/416, Schedule at **[2.13]**.

Sub-ss (4), (6): words in square brackets inserted by the Enterprise and Regulatory Reform Act 2013, s 35(10), Sch 10, paras 1, 32(1), (4), (6), subject to transitional provisions in SI 2014/416 as noted above.

Sub-s (5): words in square brackets substituted by the Enterprise and Regulatory Reform Act 2013, s 35(10), Sch 10, paras 1, 32(1), (5), subject to transitional provisions in SI 2014/416 as noted above.

[1.398]

184 Index of defined expressions: Part 4

In this Part, the expressions listed in the left-hand column have the meaning given by, or are to be interpreted in accordance with, the provisions listed in the right-hand column.

Expression	*Provision of this Act*
Action (and the taking of action)	Section 183(1)
Adverse effect on competition	Section 134(2) [and (2A)]
[Adverse public interest finding	Section 146A(3)]
Appropriate Minister	Section 132(5)
Business	Section 183(1)
[The CMA	Section 273]

Expression	*Provision of this Act*
Change of circumstances	Section 183(1)
. . .	
Consumer	Section 183(1)
[Cross-market reference	Section 131(6)]
Customer	Section 183(1)
Date of market investigation reference	Section 137(7)
Detrimental effect on customers	Section 134(5)
Enactment	Section 183(1)
Enforcement order	Section 162(8)
Enforcement undertaking	Section 162(8)
Feature of a market	Section 131(2)
Final determination of market investigation reference	Section 183(3) to (6)
[Full PI reference	Section 140A(12)]
Goods	Section 183(1)
Intervention notice	Section 139(3)
Market for goods or services	Section 131(6)
Market in the United Kingdom	Section 131(6)
Market investigation reference	Section 131(6)
[Market study notice	Section 130A(1)]
[Market study report	Section 131B(4)]
Minister of the Crown	Section 183(1)
Modify	Section 183(1)
Notice	Section 183(1)
. . .	. . .
[Ordinary reference	Section 131(6)]
Public interest consideration	Section 139(5)
Public interest consideration being finalised	Section 139(7)
[Public interest expert	Section 141B(4)]
Publish	Section 183(7)
Relevant customer benefit	Section 134(8)
Relevant sectoral enactment	Section 136(7)
Relevant sectoral regulator	Section 136(8)
Reports of the [CMA]	Section 177(5)
[Restricted PI reference	Section 140A(12)]
Subordinate legislation	Section 183(1)
Supply (in relation to the supply of goods)	Section 183(1)
The supply of services (and a market for services etc)	Section 183(2)

NOTES

Words in square brackets in the entry "Adverse effect on competition" inserted, and entries "Cross-market reference" and "Ordinary reference" inserted, by the Enterprise and Regulatory Reform Act 2013, s 34(4), Sch 9, paras 1, 9. For various transitional provisions (including those relating to the abolition of the OFT and the Competition Commission, existing references to those bodies and provisions relating to continuity), see the Enterprise and Regulatory Reform Act 2013 (Commencement No 6, Transitional Provisions and Savings) Order 2014, SI 2014/416, Schedule at **[2.13]**.

Entries, "Adverse public interest finding", "Full PI reference", "Public interest expert", and "Restricted PI reference" inserted by the Enterprise and Regulatory Reform Act 2013, s 35(10), Sch 10, paras 1, 33, subject to transitional provisions in SI 2014/416 as noted above.

Entry "The CMA" inserted, entries "The Commission" and "The OFT" (omitted) repealed, and reference to "CMA" in square brackets in the entry "Reports of the CMA" substituted, by the Enterprise and Regulatory Reform Act 2013, s 26(3), Sch 5, Pt 2, paras 59, 209, subject to transitional provisions in SI 2014/416 as noted above.

Entries "Market study notice" and "Market study report" inserted by the Enterprise and Regulatory Reform Act 2013, s 38, Sch 12, paras 7, 17, subject to transitional provisions in SI 2014/416 as noted above.

185–187 *(Ss 185–187 (Part 5) introduced Schs 11, 12 to this Act (amendments to the Competition Act 1998) and made other amendments to the Competition Act 1998. Pt 5 was repealed by the Enterprise and Regulatory Reform Act 2013, s 26(3), Sch 5, Pt 3, paras 224, 225. For various transitional provisions (including those relating to the abolition of the OFT and the Competition Commission, existing references to those bodies and provisions relating to continuity),* *see the Enterprise and Regulatory Reform Act 2013 (Commencement No 6, Transitional Provisions and Savings) Order 2014, SI 2014/416, Schedule at* **[2.13]**.)

PART 6 CARTEL OFFENCE

Cartel offence

[1.399]

188 Cartel offence

(1) An individual is guilty of an offence if he . . . agrees with one or more other persons to make or implement, or to cause to be made or implemented, arrangements of the following kind relating to at least two undertakings (A and B).

(2) The arrangements must be ones which, if operating as the parties to the agreement intend, would—

(a) directly or indirectly fix a price for the supply by A in the United Kingdom (otherwise than to B) of a product or service,

(b) limit or prevent supply by A in the United Kingdom of a product or service,

(c) limit or prevent production by A in the United Kingdom of a product,

(d) divide between A and B the supply in the United Kingdom of a product or service to a customer or customers,

(e) divide between A and B customers for the supply in the United Kingdom of a product or service, or

(f) be bid-rigging arrangements.

(3) Unless subsection (2)(d), (e) or (f) applies, the arrangements must also be ones which, if operating as the parties to the agreement intend, would—

(a) directly or indirectly fix a price for the supply by B in the United Kingdom (otherwise than to A) of a product or service,

(b) limit or prevent supply by B in the United Kingdom of a product or service, or

(c) limit or prevent production by B in the United Kingdom of a product.

(4) In subsections (2)(a) to (d) and (3), references to supply or production are to supply or production in the appropriate circumstances (for which see section 189).

(5) "Bid-rigging arrangements" are arrangements under which, in response to a request for bids for the supply of a product or service in the United Kingdom, or for the production of a product in the United Kingdom—

(a) A but not B may make a bid, or

(b) A and B may each make a bid but, in one case or both, only a bid arrived at in accordance with the arrangements.

(6) . . .

(7) "Undertaking" has the same meaning as in Part 1 of the 1998 Act.

[(8) This section is subject to section 188A.]

NOTES

Word omitted from sub-s (1) repealed, sub-s (6) repealed, and sub-s (8) added, by the Enterprise and Regulatory Reform Act 2013, s 47(1)–(4), subject to s 47(8) thereof, which provides that these amendments apply only in relation to agreements falling within section 188(1) of the 2002 Act which are made after 1 April 2014 and relate to arrangements made or to be made after that date. See also, for various transitional provisions, the Enterprise and Regulatory Reform Act 2013 (Commencement No 6, Transitional Provisions and Savings) Order 2014, SI 2014/416, Schedule at **[2.13]**.

[1.400]

[188A Circumstances in which cartel offence not committed

(1) An individual does not commit an offence under section 188(1) if, under the arrangements—

(a) in a case where the arrangements would (operating as the parties intend) affect the supply in the United Kingdom of a product or service, customers would be given relevant information about the arrangements before they enter into agreements for the supply to them of the product or service so affected,

(b) in the case of bid-rigging arrangements, the person requesting bids would be given relevant information about them at or before the time when a bid is made, or

(c) in any case, relevant information about the arrangements would be published, before the arrangements are implemented, in the manner specified at the time of the making of the agreement in an order made by the Secretary of State.

(2) In subsection (1), "relevant information" means—

(a) the names of the undertakings to which the arrangements relate,

(b) a description of the nature of the arrangements which is sufficient to show why they are or might be arrangements of the kind to which section 188(1) applies,

(c) the products or services to which they relate, and

(d) such other information as may be specified in an order made by the Secretary of State.

(3) An individual does not commit an offence under section 188(1) if the agreement is made in order to comply with a legal requirement.

(4) In subsection (3), "legal requirement" has the same meaning as in paragraph 5 of Schedule 3 to the Competition Act 1998.

(5) A power to make an order under this section—

(a) is exercisable by statutory instrument,

(b) may be exercised so as to make different provision for different cases or different purposes, and

(c) includes power to make such incidental, supplementary, consequential, transitory, transitional or saving provision as the Secretary of State considers appropriate.

(6) A statutory instrument containing an order under this section is subject to annulment in pursuance of a resolution of either House of Parliament.]

NOTES

Inserted by the Enterprise and Regulatory Reform Act 2013, s 47(1), (5), subject to s 47(8) thereof, which provides that this insertion applies only in relation to agreements falling within section 188(1) of the 2002 Act which are made after 1 April 2014 and relate to arrangements made or to be made after that date. See also, for various transitional provisions, the Enterprise and Regulatory Reform Act 2013 (Commencement No 6, Transitional Provisions and Savings) Order 2014, SI 2014/416, Schedule at **[2.13]**.

Orders: the Enterprise Act 2002 (Publishing of Relevant Information under section 188A) Order 2014, SI 2014/535 at **[2.45]**.

[1.401]

[188B Defences to commission of cartel offence

(1) In a case where the arrangements would (operating as the parties intend) affect the supply in the United Kingdom of a product or service, it is a defence for an individual charged with an offence under section 188(1) to show that, at the time of the making of the agreement, he or she did not intend that the nature of the arrangements would be concealed from customers at all times before they enter into agreements for the supply to them of the product or service.

(2) It is a defence for an individual charged with an offence under section 188(1) to show that, at the time of the making of the agreement, he or she did not intend that the nature of the arrangements would be concealed from the CMA.

(3) It is a defence for an individual charged with an offence under section 188(1) to show that, before the making of the agreement, he or she took reasonable steps to ensure that the nature of the arrangements would be disclosed to professional legal advisers for the purposes of obtaining advice about them before their making or (as the case may be) their implementation.]

NOTES

Inserted by the Enterprise and Regulatory Reform Act 2013, s 47(1), (6), subject to s 47(8) thereof, which provides that this insertion applies only in relation to agreements falling within section 188(1) of the 2002 Act which are made after 1 April 2014 and relate to arrangements made or to be made after that date. See also, for various transitional provisions, the Enterprise and Regulatory Reform Act 2013 (Commencement No 6, Transitional Provisions and Savings) Order 2014, SI 2014/416, Schedule at **[2.13]**.

[1.402]

189 Cartel offence: supplementary

(1) For section 188(2)(a), the appropriate circumstances are that A's supply of the product or service would be at a level in the supply chain at which the product or service would at the same time be supplied by B in the United Kingdom.

(2) For section 188(2)(b), the appropriate circumstances are that A's supply of the product or service would be at a level in the supply chain—

(a) at which the product or service would at the same time be supplied by B in the United Kingdom, or
(b) at which supply by B in the United Kingdom of the product or service would be limited or prevented by the arrangements.

(3) For section 188(2)(c), the appropriate circumstances are that A's production of the product would be at a level in the production chain—

(a) at which the product would at the same time be produced by B in the United Kingdom, or
(b) at which production by B in the United Kingdom of the product would be limited or prevented by the arrangements.

(4) For section 188(2)(d), the appropriate circumstances are that A's supply of the product or service would be at the same level in the supply chain as B's.

(5) For section 188(3)(a), the appropriate circumstances are that B's supply of the product or service would be at a level in the supply chain at which the product or service would at the same time be supplied by A in the United Kingdom.

(6) For section 188(3)(b), the appropriate circumstances are that B's supply of the product or service would be at a level in the supply chain—

(a) at which the product or service would at the same time be supplied by A in the United Kingdom, or
(b) at which supply by A in the United Kingdom of the product or service would be limited or prevented by the arrangements.

(7) For section 188(3)(c), the appropriate circumstances are that B's production of the product would be at a level in the production chain—

(a) at which the product would at the same time be produced by A in the United Kingdom, or
(b) at which production by A in the United Kingdom of the product would be limited or prevented by the arrangements.

[1.403]

190 Cartel offence: penalty and prosecution

(1) A person guilty of an offence under section 188 is liable—

(a) on conviction on indictment, to imprisonment for a term not exceeding five years or to a fine, or to both;
(b) on summary conviction, to imprisonment for a term not exceeding six months or to a fine not exceeding the statutory maximum, or to both.

(2) In England and Wales and Northern Ireland, proceedings for an offence under section 188 may be instituted only—

(a) by the Director of the Serious Fraud Office, or
(b) by or with the consent of the [CMA].

(3) No proceedings may be brought for an offence under section 188 in respect of an agreement outside the United Kingdom, unless it has been implemented in whole or in part in the United Kingdom.
(4) Where, for the purpose of the investigation or prosecution of offences under section 188, the [CMA] gives a person written notice under this subsection, no proceedings for an offence under section 188 that falls within a description specified in the notice may be brought against that person in England and Wales or Northern Ireland except in circumstances specified in the notice.

NOTES

Sub-ss (2), (4): references to the "CMA" substituted by the Enterprise and Regulatory Reform Act 2013, s 26(3), Sch 5, Pt 2, paras 59, 210. For various transitional provisions (including those relating to the abolition of the OFT and the Competition Commission, existing references to those bodies and provisions relating to continuity), see the Enterprise and Regulatory Reform Act 2013 (Commencement No 6, Transitional Provisions and Savings) Order 2014, SI 2014/416, Schedule at **[2.13]**.

[1.404]
[190A Cartel offence: prosecution guidance

(1) The CMA must prepare and publish guidance on the principles to be applied in determining, in any case, whether proceedings for an offence under section 188(1) should be instituted.
(2) The CMA may at any time issue revised or new guidance.
(3) Guidance published by the CMA under this section is to be published in such manner as it considers appropriate.
(4) In preparing guidance under this section the CMA must consult—
(a) the Director of the Serious Fraud Office;
(b) the Lord Advocate; and
(c) such other persons as it considers appropriate.]

NOTES

Inserted by the Enterprise and Regulatory Reform Act 2013, s 47(1), (7). For various transitional provisions (including those relating to the abolition of the OFT and the Competition Commission, existing references to those bodies and provisions relating to continuity), see the Enterprise and Regulatory Reform Act 2013 (Commencement No 6, Transitional Provisions and Savings) Order 2014, SI 2014/416, Schedule at **[2.13]**.

191 (*Repealed by the Extradition Act 2003, ss 219(1), 220, Sch 3, paras 1, 14, Sch 4 (except in relation to any request for extradition, whether made under the Extradition Act 1989 or the Backing of Warrants (Republic of Ireland) Act 1965 or otherwise, which is received by the relevant authority in the United Kingdom, and an extradition made from or to the United Kingdom on or before 31 December 2003).*)

Criminal investigations by [CMA]

NOTES

Note that neither the Enterprise and Regulatory Reform Act 2013 nor the Enterprise and Regulatory Reform Act 2013 (Competition) (Consequential, Transitional and Saving Provisions) Order 2014, SI 2014/892 substitute the original reference to the OFT with a reference to the CMA in the above heading. It is assumed that this is an oversight, and the amendment has been made above.

[1.405]
192 Investigation of offences under section 188

(1) The [CMA] may conduct an investigation if there are reasonable grounds for suspecting that an offence under section 188 has been committed.
(2) The powers of the [CMA] under sections 193 and 194 are exercisable, but only for the purposes of an investigation under subsection (1), in any case where it appears to the [CMA] that there is good reason to exercise them for the purpose of investigating the affairs, or any aspect of the affairs, of any person ("the person under investigation").

NOTES

References to the "CMA" substituted by the Enterprise and Regulatory Reform Act 2013, s 26(3), Sch 5, Pt 2, paras 59, 211. For various transitional provisions (including those relating to the abolition of the OFT and the Competition Commission, existing references to those bodies and provisions relating to continuity), see the Enterprise and Regulatory Reform Act 2013 (Commencement No 6, Transitional Provisions and Savings) Order 2014, SI 2014/416, Schedule at **[2.13]**.

[1.406]
193 Powers when conducting an investigation

(1) The [CMA] may by notice in writing require the person under investigation, or any other person who it has reason to believe has relevant information, to answer questions, or otherwise provide information, with respect to any matter relevant to the investigation at a specified place and either at a specified time or forthwith.
(2) The [CMA] may by notice in writing require the person under investigation, or any other person, to produce, at a specified place and either at a specified time or forthwith, specified documents, or documents of a specified description, which appear to the [CMA] to relate to any matter relevant to the investigation.
(3) If any such documents are produced, the [CMA] may—
(a) take copies or extracts from them;
(b) require the person producing them to provide an explanation of any of them.
(4) If any such documents are not produced, the [CMA] may require the person who was required to produce them to state, to the best of his knowledge and belief, where they are.
(5) A notice under subsection (1) or (2) must indicate—
(a) the subject matter and purpose of the investigation; and
(b) the nature of the offences created by section 201.

NOTES

Sub-ss (1)–(4): references to the "CMA" substituted by the Enterprise and Regulatory Reform Act 2013, s 26(3), Sch 5, Pt 2, paras 59, 212. For various transitional provisions (including those relating to the abolition of the OFT and the Competition Commission, existing references to those bodies and provisions relating to continuity), see the Enterprise and Regulatory Reform Act 2013 (Commencement No 6, Transitional Provisions and Savings) Order 2014, SI 2014/416, Schedule at **[2.13]**.

[1.407]

194 Power to enter premises under a warrant

(1) [On an application made to it by the CMA or, in Scotland, the procurator fiscal, the appropriate body may issue a warrant if it is satisfied] that there are reasonable grounds for believing—

(a) that there are on any premises documents which the [CMA] has power under section 193 to require to be produced for the purposes of an investigation; and

(b) that—

(i) a person has failed to comply with a requirement under that section to produce the documents;

(ii) it is not practicable to serve a notice under that section in relation to them; or

(iii) the service of such a notice in relation to them might seriously prejudice the investigation.

[(1A) In subsection (1), "appropriate body" means—

(a) in England and Wales and Northern Ireland, the High Court or the Competition Appeal Tribunal;

(b) in Scotland, the sheriff.]

(2) A warrant under this section shall authorise a named officer of the [CMA], and any other officers of the [CMA] whom the [CMA] has authorised in writing to accompany the named officer—

(a) to enter the premises, using such force as is reasonably necessary for the purpose;

(b) to search the premises and—

(i) take possession of any documents appearing to be of the relevant kind, or

(ii) take, in relation to any documents appearing to be of the relevant kind, any other steps which may appear to be necessary for preserving them or preventing interference with them;

(c) to require any person to provide an explanation of any document appearing to be of the relevant kind or to state, to the best of his knowledge and belief, where it may be found;

(d) to require any information which is stored in any electronic form and is accessible from the premises and which the named officer considers relates to any matter relevant to the investigation, to be produced in a form—

(i) in which it can be taken away, and

(ii) in which it is visible and legible or from which it can readily be produced in a visible and legible form.

(3) Documents are of the relevant kind if they are of a kind in respect of which the application under subsection (1) was granted.

(4) A warrant under this section may authorise persons specified in the warrant to accompany the named officer who is executing it.

[(4A) An application for a warrant under this section must be made—

(a) in the case of an application to the High Court or the sheriff, in accordance with rules of court;

(b) in the case of an application to the Competition Appeal Tribunal, in accordance with rules made under section 15.]

(5) (*Inserts the Criminal Justice and Police Act 2001, Sch 1, Pt 1, para 73B.*)

NOTES

Sub-s (1): words in square brackets substituted by the Enterprise and Regulatory Reform Act 2013, ss 26(3), 48(1), (2), Sch 5, Pt 2, paras 59, 213. For various transitional provisions (including those relating to the abolition of the OFT and the Competition Commission, existing references to those bodies and provisions relating to continuity), see the Enterprise and Regulatory Reform Act 2013 (Commencement No 6, Transitional Provisions and Savings) Order 2014, SI 2014/416, Schedule at **[2.13]**.

Sub-ss (1A), (4A): inserted by the Enterprise and Regulatory Reform Act 2013, s 48(1), (3), (4), subject to transitional provisions in SI 2014/416 as noted above.

Sub-s (2): references to the "CMA" substituted by the Enterprise and Regulatory Reform Act 2013, s 26(3), Sch 5, Pt 2, paras 59, 213, subject to transitional provisions in SI 2014/416 as noted above.

Seize and detain documents, etc: the powers of seizure conferred by sub-s (2) are powers to which the Criminal Justice and Police Act 2001, s 50 apply (additional powers of seizure from premises); see s 50(5) of, and Sch 1, Pt 1, para 73B to, that Act. See also the notes to the Competition Act 1998, s 28 (at **[1.57]**) for the full text of s 50 of the 2001 Act.

[1.408]

195 Exercise of powers by authorised person

(1) The [CMA] may authorise any competent person who is not an officer of the [CMA] to exercise on its behalf all or any of the powers conferred by section 193 or 194.

(2) No such authority may be granted except for the purpose of investigating the affairs, or any aspect of the affairs, of a person specified in the authority.

(3) No person is bound to comply with any requirement imposed by a person exercising powers by virtue of any authority granted under this section unless he has, if required to do so, produced evidence of his authority.

NOTES

Sub-s (1): references to the "CMA" substituted by the Enterprise and Regulatory Reform Act 2013, s 26(3), Sch 5, Pt 2, paras 59, 214. For various transitional provisions (including those relating to the abolition of the OFT and the Competition Commission, existing references to those bodies and provisions relating to continuity), see the Enterprise and

Regulatory Reform Act 2013 (Commencement No 6, Transitional Provisions and Savings) Order 2014, SI 2014/416, Schedule at **[2.13]**.

[1.409]
196 Privileged information etc

(1) A person may not under section 193 or 194 be required to disclose any information or produce any document which he would be entitled to refuse to disclose or produce on grounds of legal professional privilege in proceedings in the High Court, except that a lawyer may be required to provide the name and address of his client.

(2) A person may not under section 193 or 194 be required to disclose any information or produce any document in respect of which he owes an obligation of confidence by virtue of carrying on any banking business unless—

(a) the person to whom the obligation of confidence is owed consents to the disclosure or production; or

(b) the [CMA] has authorised the making of the requirement.

(3) In the application of this section to Scotland, the reference in subsection (1)—

(a) to proceedings in the High Court is to be read as a reference to legal proceedings generally; and

(b) to an entitlement on grounds of legal professional privilege is to be read as a reference to an entitlement by virtue of any rule of law whereby—

(i) communications between a professional legal adviser and his client, or

(ii) communications made in connection with or in contemplation of legal proceedings and for the purposes of those proceedings,

are in such proceedings protected from disclosure on the ground of confidentiality.

NOTES

Sub-s (2): reference to the "CMA" substituted by the Enterprise and Regulatory Reform Act 2013, s 26(3), Sch 5, Pt 2, paras 59, 215. For various transitional provisions (including those relating to the abolition of the OFT and the Competition Commission, existing references to those bodies and provisions relating to continuity), see the Enterprise and Regulatory Reform Act 2013 (Commencement No 6, Transitional Provisions and Savings) Order 2014, SI 2014/416, Schedule at **[2.13]**.

[1.410]
197 Restriction on use of statements in court

(1) A statement by a person in response to a requirement imposed by virtue of section 193 or 194 may only be used in evidence against him—

(a) on a prosecution for an offence under section 201(2); or

(b) on a prosecution for some other offence where in giving evidence he makes a statement inconsistent with it.

(2) However, the statement may not be used against that person by virtue of paragraph (b) of subsection (1) unless evidence relating to it is adduced, or a question relating to it is asked, by or on behalf of that person in the proceedings arising out of the prosecution.

198–200 *(S 198 inserts the Competition Act 1998, s 30A, at* **[1.61]***; s 199 amends the Regulation of Investigatory Powers Act 2000; s 200 amends the Police Act 1997.)*

[1.411]
201 Offences

(1) Any person who without reasonable excuse fails to comply with a requirement imposed on him under section 193 or 194 is guilty of an offence and liable on summary conviction to imprisonment for a term not exceeding six months or to a fine not exceeding level 5 on the standard scale or to both.

(2) A person who, in purported compliance with a requirement under section 193 or 194—

(a) makes a statement which he knows to be false or misleading in a material particular; or

(b) recklessly makes a statement which is false or misleading in a material particular,

is guilty of an offence.

(3) A person guilty of an offence under subsection (2) is liable—

(a) on conviction on indictment, to imprisonment for a term not exceeding two years or to a fine or to both; and

(b) on summary conviction, to imprisonment for a term not exceeding six months or to a fine not exceeding the statutory maximum, or to both.

(4) Where any person—

(a) knows or suspects that an investigation by the Serious Fraud Office or the [CMA] into an offence under section 188 is being or is likely to be carried out; and

(b) falsifies, conceals, destroys or otherwise disposes of, or causes or permits the falsification, concealment, destruction or disposal of documents which he knows or suspects are or would be relevant to such an investigation,

he is guilty of an offence unless he proves that he had no intention of concealing the facts disclosed by the documents from the persons carrying out such an investigation.

(5) A person guilty of an offence under subsection (4) is liable—

(a) on conviction on indictment, to imprisonment for a term not exceeding 5 years or to a fine or to both; and

(b) on summary conviction, to imprisonment for a term not exceeding six months or to a fine not exceeding the statutory maximum, or to both.

(6) A person who intentionally obstructs a person in the exercise of his powers under a warrant issued under section 194 is guilty of an offence and liable—

(a) on conviction on indictment, to imprisonment for a term not exceeding 2 years or to a fine or to both; and

(b) on summary conviction, to a fine not exceeding the statutory maximum.

NOTES

Sub-s (4): reference to the "CMA" substituted by the Enterprise and Regulatory Reform Act 2013, s 26(3), Sch 5, Pt 2, paras 59, 216. For various transitional provisions (including those relating to the abolition of the OFT and

the Competition Commission, existing references to those bodies and provisions relating to continuity), see the Enterprise and Regulatory Reform Act 2013 (Commencement No 6, Transitional Provisions and Savings) Order 2014, SI 2014/416, Schedule at **[2.13]**.

[1.412]

202 Interpretation of sections 192 to 201

In sections 192 to 201—

"documents" includes information recorded in any form and, in relation to information recorded otherwise than in a form in which it is visible and legible, references to its production include references to producing it in a form in which it is visible and legible or from which it can readily be produced in a visible and legible form;

"person under investigation" has the meaning given in section 192(2).

PART 7 MISCELLANEOUS COMPETITION PROVISIONS

203, 204 *(S 203 amends the Competition Act 1998, ss 28, 62, 63, at* **[1.57]**, **[1.111]**, **[1.114]**; *s 204 inserts the Company Directors Disqualification Act 1986, ss 9A–9E at* **[1.23]**–**[1.27]**, *and amends ss 1, 8A, 16, 17, 18 of that Act).)*

Miscellaneous

[1.413]

205 Super-complaints to regulators other than [CMA]

(1) The Secretary of State may by order provide that section 11 is to apply to complaints made to a specified regulator in relation to a market of a specified description as it applies to complaints made to the [CMA], with such modifications as may be specified.

(2) An order under this section—

(a) shall be made by statutory instrument, and

(b) shall be subject to annulment in pursuance of a resolution of either House of Parliament.

(3) In this section—

"regulator" has the meaning given in section 54(1) of the 1998 Act; and

"specified" means specified in the order.

NOTES

References to the "CMA" substituted by the Enterprise and Regulatory Reform Act 2013 (Competition) (Consequential, Transitional and Saving Provisions) Order 2014, SI 2014/892, art 2, Sch 1, Pt 1, paras 1, 4, subject to transitional provisions as noted to s 8A at **[1.187]**.

Orders: the Enterprise Act 2002 (Super-complaints to Regulators) Order 2003, SI 2003/1368 at **[2.36]**; the Enterprise Act 2002 (Water Services Regulation Authority) Order 2006, SI 2006/522.

[1.414]

206 Power to modify Schedule 8

(1) The Secretary of State may by order made by statutory instrument modify Schedule 8.

(2) An order under this section may make—

(a) different provision for different cases or different purposes;

(b) such incidental, supplementary, consequential, transitory, transitional or saving provision as the Secretary of State considers appropriate.

(3) An order under this section may, in particular, modify that Schedule in its application by virtue of Part 3 of this Act, in its application by virtue of Part 4 of this Act, in its application by virtue of any other enactment (whether by virtue of Part 4 of this Act as applied by that enactment or otherwise) or in its application by virtue of every enactment that applies it.

(4) An order under this section as extended by subsection (2) may modify any enactment comprised in or made under this Act, or any other enactment.

(5) No order shall be made under this section unless a draft of it has been laid before, and approved by a resolution of, each House of Parliament.

(6) No modification of Schedule 8 in its application by virtue of Part 3 of this Act shall be made by an order under this section if the modification relates to a relevant merger situation or (as the case may be) a special merger situation which has been created before the coming into force of the order.

(7) No modification shall be made by an order under this section of Schedule 8 in its application in relation to references made under section 22, 33, 45 or 62 before the coming into force of the order.

(8) No modification shall be made by an order under this section of Schedule 8 in its application in relation to references made under section 131 or 132 before the coming into force of the order (including references made under section 131 as applied by another enactment).

(9) Before making an order under this section, the Secretary of State shall consult the [CMA].

(10) Expressions used in this section which are also used in Part 3 of this Act have the same meaning in this section as in that Part.

NOTES

Sub-s (9): reference to the "CMA" substituted by the Enterprise and Regulatory Reform Act 2013 (Competition) (Consequential, Transitional and Saving Provisions) Order 2014, SI 2014/892, art 2, Sch 1, Pt 1, paras 1, 5, subject to transitional provisions as noted to s 8A at **[1.187]**.

207, 208 *(S 207 repeals the Competition Act 1998, s 3(1)(d), Sch 4; s 208 repeals the Fair Trading Act 1973, ss 78–80.)*

[1.415]

209 Reform of [EU competition law]

(1) The Secretary of State may by regulations make such modifications of the 1998 Act as he considers appropriate for the purpose of eliminating or reducing any differences between—

(a) the domestic provisions of the 1998 Act, and

(b) [EU competition law],

which result (or would otherwise result) from a relevant Community instrument made after the passing of this Act.

(2) In subsection (1)—

"the domestic provisions of the 1998 Act" means the provisions of the 1998 Act so far as they do not implement or give effect to a relevant Community instrument;

"[EU competition law]" includes any Act or subordinate legislation so far as it implements or gives effect to a relevant Community instrument;

"relevant Community instrument" means a regulation or directive under [Article 103 of the Treaty on the Functioning of the European Union].

(3) The Secretary of State may by regulations repeal or otherwise modify any provision of an Act (other than the 1998 Act) which excludes any matter from the Chapter I prohibition or the Chapter II prohibition (within the meaning of Part 1 of the 1998 Act).

(4) The power under subsection (3) may not be exercised—

(a) before the power under subsection (1) has been exercised; or

(b) so as to extend the scope of any exclusion that is not being removed by the regulations.

(5) Regulations under this section may—

(a) confer power to make subordinate legislation;

(b) make such consequential, supplementary, incidental, transitory, transitional or saving provision as the Secretary of State considers appropriate (including provision modifying any Act or subordinate legislation); and

(c) make different provision for different cases or circumstances.

(6) The power to make regulations under this section is exercisable by statutory instrument.

(7) No regulations may be made under this section unless a draft of them has been laid before and approved by a resolution of each House of Parliament.

(8) Paragraph 1(1)(c) of Schedule 2 to the European Communities Act 1972 (c 68) (restriction on powers to legislate) shall not apply to regulations which implement or give effect to a relevant Community instrument made after the passing of this Act.

NOTES

This section was repealed by the Competition (Amendment etc) (EU Exit) Regulations 2019, SI 2019/93, regs 32, 58, as from IP completion day (as defined in the European Union (Withdrawal Agreement) Act 2020, s 39) (for transitional provisions and savings in relation to the operation of the 2019 Regulations, see Sch 4 to those Regulations at **[7.69]** et seq and, in particular, Sch 4, Pt 7 to the 2019 Regulations at **[7.76]**).

Words in square brackets substituted by the Treaty of Lisbon (Changes in Terminology or Numbering) Order 2012, SI 2012/1809, art 3(1), Schedule, Pt 1.

References to the European Community and related expressions: see the note "References to "the European Community", "Community", etc" in the introductory notes to this Act.

Regulations: the Competition Act 1998 and other enactments (Amendment) Regulations 2004, SI 2004/1261 at **[2.3]**; the Claims in respect of Loss or Damage arising from Competition Infringements (Competition Act 1998 and Other Enactments (Amendment)) Regulations 2017, SI 2017/385.

210–236 *((Pt 8: Enforcement of certain consumer legislation) outside the scope of this work.)*

PART 9 INFORMATION

NOTES

See also the EEC Merger Control (Distinct Market Investigations) Regulations 1990, SI 1990/1715, art 5 at **[2.83]** (this Part to have effect as if the 1990 Regulations were contained in Part 3 of this Act). Note that the 1990 Regulations were revoked by the Competition (Amendment etc) (EU Exit) Regulations 2019, SI 2019/93, reg 61, Sch 2, Pt 3, para 9, as from IP completion day (as defined in the European Union (Withdrawal Agreement) Act 2020, s 39). For transitional provisions and savings in relation to the operation of the 2019 Regulations, see Sch 4 to those Regulations at **[7.69]** et seq and see, in particular, Sch 4, Pt 7, para 35B to the 2019 Regulations at **[7.76]**.

Restrictions on disclosure

[1.416]

237 General restriction

(1) This section applies to specified information which relates to—

(a) the affairs of an individual;

(b) any business of an undertaking.

(2) Such information must not be disclosed—

(a) during the lifetime of the individual, or

(b) while the undertaking continues in existence, unless the disclosure is permitted under this Part.

(3) But subsection (2) does not prevent the disclosure of any information if the information has on an earlier occasion been disclosed to the public in circumstances which do not contravene—

(a) that subsection;

(b) any other enactment or rule of law prohibiting or restricting the disclosure of the information.

(4) Nothing in this Part authorises a disclosure of information which contravenes [the data protection legislation].

(5) Nothing in this Part affects the Competition Appeal Tribunal.

(6) This Part (except section 244) does not affect any power or duty to disclose information which exists apart from this Part.

[(7) In this section, "the data protection legislation" has the same meaning as in the Data Protection Act 2018 (see section 3 of that Act).]

NOTES

Sub-s (4): words in square brackets substituted by the Data Protection Act 2018, s 211(1)(a), Sch 19, Pt 1, para 86(1), (2).

Sub-s (7): added by the Data Protection Act 2018, s 211(1)(a), Sch 19, Pt 1, para 86(1), (3).

[1.417]

238 Information

(1) Information is specified information if it comes to a public authority in connection with the exercise of any function it has under or by virtue of—

(a) Part 1, 3, 4, 6, 7 or 8;
(b) an enactment specified in Schedule 14;
(c) such subordinate legislation as the Secretary of State may by order specify for the purposes of this subsection.

(2) It is immaterial whether information comes to a public authority before or after the passing of this Act.

(3) Public authority (except in the expression "overseas public authority") must be construed in accordance with section 6 of the Human Rights Act 1998 (c 42).

(4) In subsection (1) the reference to an enactment includes a reference to an enactment contained in—

(a) an Act of the Scottish Parliament;
(b) Northern Ireland legislation;
(c) subordinate legislation.

(5) The Secretary of State may by order amend Schedule 14.

(6) The power to make an order under subsection (5) includes power to add, vary or remove a reference to any provision of—

(a) an Act of the Scottish Parliament;
(b) Northern Ireland legislation.

(7) An order under this section must be made by statutory instrument subject to annulment in pursuance of a resolution of either House of Parliament.

(8) This section applies for the purposes of this Part.

NOTES

Orders: the Enterprise Act 2002 (Part 9 Restrictions on Disclosure of Information) (Amendment and Specification) Order 2003, SI 2003/1400; the Enterprise Act 2002 (Part 9 Restrictions on Disclosure of Information) (Amendment and Specification) (No 2) Order 2003, SI 2003/2580; the Enterprise Act 2002 (Part 9 Restrictions on Disclosure of Information) (Specification) Order 2004, SI 2004/693; the Enterprise Act 2002 (Part 9 Restrictions on Disclosure of Information) (Amendment and Specification) Order 2007, SI 2007/2977.

The Enterprise Act 2002 (Part 9 Restrictions on Disclosure of Information) (Amendment and Specification) Order 2003, SI 2003/1400, art 5, Sch 3 (as amended) provides that the following subordinate legislation is specified for the purposes of sub-s (1) above—

— Crystal Glass (Descriptions) Regulations 1973

— Textile Products (Indications of Fibre Content) Regulations 1986 (Editorial note: the 1986 Regulations were revoked and replaced by the Textile Products (Labelling and Fibre Composition) Regulations 2012)

— Footwear (Indication of Composition) Labelling Regulations 1995

— General Product Safety Regulations 2005

— Consumer Protection from Unfair Trading Regulations 2008

— Cancellation of Contracts made in a Consumer's Home or Place of Work etc Regulations 2008 (Editorial note: the 2008 Regulations are superseded, in relation to contracts entered into on or after 13 June 2014, by the Consumer Contracts (Information, Cancellation and Additional Charges) Regulations 2013)

— Business Protection from Misleading Marketing Regulations 2008

— Timeshare, Holiday Products, Resale and Exchange Contracts Regulations 2010

— Regulation 55 of the Simple Pressure Vessels (Safety) Regulations 2016 (in so far as information comes to a public authority enforcing those regulations in respect of vessels for private use or consumption)

— Package Travel and Linked Travel Arrangements Regulations 2018.

The Enterprise Act 2002 (Part 9 Restrictions on Disclosure of Information) (Specification) Order 2004, SI 2004/693, art 2, Sch 1 (as amended) provides that the following subordinate legislation is specified for the purposes of sub-s (1) above—

— Household Appliances (Noise Emission) Regulations 1990

— Supply of Machinery (Safety) Regulations 1992 (Editorial note: the 1992 Regulations were revoked and replaced by the Supply of Machinery (Safety) Regulations 2008)

— Lifts Regulations 1997 (Editorial note: the 1997 Regulations were revoked and replaced (subject to savings) by the Lifts Regulations 2016)

— Recreational Craft Regulations 2004 insofar as not revoked by the Recreational Craft Regulations 2017

— Supply of Machinery (Safety) Regulations 2008

— Batteries and Accumulators (Placing on the Market) Regulations 2008

— Restriction of the Use of Certain Hazardous Substances in Electrical and Electronic Equipment Regulations 2012

— Cosmetic Products Enforcement Regulations 2013

— Packaging (Essential Requirements) Regulations 2015

— Pressure Equipment (Safety) Regulations 2016

— Electromagnetic Compatibility Regulations 2016

— Radio Equipment Regulations 2017

— Recreational Craft Regulations 2017

— Non-Road Mobile Machinery (Type-Approval and Emission of Gaseous and Particulate Pollutants) Regulations 2018

— Personal Protective Equipment (Enforcement) Regulations 2018.

The Enterprise Act 2002 (Part 9 Restrictions on Disclosure of Information) (Amendment and Specification) Order 2007, SI 2007/2977, art 3 provides that the following subordinate legislation is specified for the purposes of sub-s (1) above—

— Unfair Terms in Consumer Contracts Regulations 1999 (Editorial note: the 1999 Regulations were revoked (subject to savings) by the Consumer Rights Act 2015).

Specified information: the Consumers, Estate Agents and Redress Act 2007, s 29(3) provides that information obtained by Citizens Advice or Citizens Advice Scotland under or by virtue of the Gas Act 1986, Pt 1, the Electricity Act 1989, Pt 1, and the Utilities Act 2000, and information obtained by the consumer advocacy bodies under or by virtue of the Postal Services Act 2011, is "specified information" for the purposes of this Part.

Permitted disclosure

[1.418]
239 Consent

(1) This Part does not prohibit the disclosure by a public authority of information held by it to any other person if it obtains each required consent.

(2) If the information was obtained by the authority from a person who had the information lawfully and the authority knows the identity of that person the consent of that person is required.

(3) If the information relates to the affairs of an individual the consent of the individual is required.

(4) If the information relates to the business of an undertaking the consent of the person for the time being carrying on the business is required.

(5) For the purposes of subsection (4) consent may be given—

(a) in the case of a company by a director, secretary or other officer of the company;

(b) in the case of a partnership by a partner;

(c) in the case of an unincorporated body or association by a person concerned in the management or control of the body or association.

[1.419]
240 Community obligations

This Part does not prohibit the disclosure of information held by a public authority to another person if the disclosure is required for the purpose of a Community obligation.

NOTES

This section was repealed by the Competition (Amendment etc) (EU Exit) Regulations 2019, SI 2019/93, regs 32, 59, as from IP completion day (as defined in the European Union (Withdrawal Agreement) Act 2020, s 39) (for transitional provisions and savings in relation to the operation of the 2019 Regulations, see Sch 4 to those Regulations at **[7.69]** et seq and, in particular, Sch 4, Pt 7 to the 2019 Regulations at **[7.76]**).

References to the European Community and related expressions: see the note "References to "the European Community", "Community", etc" in the introductory notes to this Act.

[1.420]
241 Statutory functions

(1) A public authority which holds information to which section 237 applies may disclose that information for the purpose of facilitating the exercise by the authority of any function it has under or by virtue of this Act or any other enactment.

(2) If information is disclosed under subsection (1) so that it is not made available to the public it must not be further disclosed by a person to whom it is so disclosed other than with the agreement of the public authority for the purpose mentioned in that subsection.

[(2A) Information disclosed under subsection (1) so that it is not made available to the public must not be used by the person to whom it is disclosed for any purpose other than that mentioned in subsection (1).]

(3) A public authority which holds information to which section 237 applies may disclose that information to any other person for the purpose of facilitating the exercise by that person of any function he has under or by virtue of—

(a) this Act;

(b) an enactment specified in Schedule 15;

(c) such subordinate legislation as the Secretary of State may by order specify for the purposes of this subsection.

(4) Information disclosed under subsection (3) must not be used by the person to whom it is disclosed for any purpose other than a purpose relating to a function mentioned in that subsection.

(5) In subsection (1) the reference to an enactment includes a reference to an enactment contained in—

(a) an Act of the Scottish Parliament;

(b) Northern Ireland legislation;

(c) subordinate legislation.

(6) The Secretary of State may by order amend Schedule 15.

(7) The power to make an order under subsection (6) includes power to add, vary or remove a reference to any provision of—

(a) an Act of the Scottish Parliament;

(b) Northern Ireland legislation.

(8) An order under this section must be made by statutory instrument subject to annulment in pursuance of a resolution of either House of Parliament.

NOTES

Sub-s (2A): inserted by the Enterprise and Regulatory Reform Act 2013, s 55. For various transitional provisions (including those relating to the abolition of the OFT and the Competition Commission, existing references to those bodies and provisions relating to continuity), see the Enterprise and Regulatory Reform Act 2013 (Commencement No 6, Transitional Provisions and Savings) Order 2014, SI 2014/416, Schedule at **[2.13]**.

Orders: the Enterprise Act 2002 (Part 9 Restrictions on Disclosure of Information) (Amendment and Specification) Order 2003, SI 2003/1400; the Enterprise Act 2002 (Part 9 Restrictions on Disclosure of Information) (Specification) Order 2004, SI 2004/693; the Enterprise Act 2002 (Part 9 Restrictions on Disclosure of Information) (Amendment) Order 2006, SI 2006/2909; the Enterprise Act 2002 (Part 9 Restrictions on Disclosure of Information) (Amendment and Specification) Order 2007, SI 2007/2977; the Enterprise Act 2002 (Part 9 Restrictions on Disclosure of Information) (Specification)

Order 2013, SI 2013/1808; the Enterprise Act 2002 (Part 9 Restrictions on Disclosure of Information) (Amendment) Order 2014, SI 2014/2807; the Enterprise Act 2002 (Part 9 Restrictions on Disclosure of Information) (Specification) Order 2018, SI 2018/104.

The Enterprise Act 2002 (Part 9 Restrictions on Disclosure of Information) (Amendment and Specification) Order 2003, SI 2003/1400, art 6, Sch 4 (as amended) provides that the following subordinate legislation is specified for the purposes of sub-s (3) above—

— Crystal Glass (Descriptions) Regulations 1973

— Measuring Container Bottles (EEC Requirements) Regulations 1977

— Textile Products (Indications of Fibre Content) Regulations 1986 (Editorial note: the 1986 Regulations were revoked and replaced by the Textile Products (Labelling and Fibre Composition) Regulations 2012)

— Insolvency Rules (Northern Ireland) 1991

— Licensing of Air Carriers Regulations 1992 (Editorial note: the 1992 Regulations were revoked by the Operation of Air Services Regulations 2009)

— Footwear (Indication of Composition) Labelling Regulations 1995

— Open-Ended Investment Companies (Investment Companies with Variable Capital) Regulations (Northern Ireland) 1997

— Railways Regulations 1998 (Editorial note: the 1998 Regulations were revoked by the Railways Infrastructure (Access and Management) Regulations 2005 which were also subsequently revoked by the Railways (Access, Management and Licensing of Railway Undertakings) Regulations 2016)

— Unfair Terms in Consumer Contracts Regulations 1999 (Editorial note: the 1999 Regulations were revoked (subject to savings) by the Consumer Rights Act 2015)

— Consumer Protection (Distance Selling) Regulations 2000 (Editorial note: the 2000 Regulations were superseded, in relation to contracts entered into on or after 13 June 2014, by the Consumer Contracts (Information, Cancellation and Additional Charges) Regulations 2013)

— Open-Ended Investment Companies Regulations 2001

— Transport (Scotland) Act 2001 (Conditions attached to PSV Operator's Licence and Competition Test for Exercise of Bus Functions) Order 2001

— General Product Safety Regulations 2005

— Parts 2 and 3 of the Railways and Other Guided Transport Systems (Safety) Regulations 2006

— Consumer Protection from Unfair Trading Regulations 2008

— Business Protection from Misleading Marketing Regulations 2008

— Cancellation of Contracts made in a Consumer's Home or Place of Work etc Regulations 2008 (Editorial note: the 2008 Regulations were superseded, in relation to contracts entered into on or after 13 June 2014, by the Consumer Contracts (Information, Cancellation and Additional Charges) Regulations 2013)

— Timeshare, Holiday Products, Resale and Exchange Contracts Regulations 2010

— Regulation 55 of the Simple Pressure Vessels (Safety) Regulations 2016 (in so far as information is disclosed to a public authority enforcing those regulations in respect of vessels for private use or consumption)

— Insolvency (England and Wales) Rules 2016

— Package Travel and Linked Travel Arrangements Regulations 2018.

The Enterprise Act 2002 (Part 9 Restrictions on Disclosure of Information) (Specification) Order 2013, SI 2013/1808, art 2 provides that the following subordinate legislation is specified for the purposes of sub-s (3) above—

— Green Deal Framework (Disclosure, Acknowledgment, Redress etc) Regulations 2012.

The Enterprise Act 2002 (Part 9 Restrictions on Disclosure of Information) (Specification) Order 2018, SI 2018/104, art 2 provides that the following subordinate legislation is specified for the purposes of sub-s (3)(c) above—

— Electricity and Gas (Market Integrity and Transparency) (Enforcement etc) Regulations 2013

— Electricity and Gas (Market Integrity and Transparency) (Criminal Sanctions) Regulations 2015.

As to the subordinate legislation specified for the purposes of sub-s (3) by the Enterprise Act 2002 (Part 9 Restrictions on Disclosure of Information) (Specification) Order 2004, SI 2004/693, art 2, Sch 1, see the note to s 238 at **[1.417]**.

[1.421]

[241A Civil proceedings

(1) A public authority which holds prescribed information to which section 237 applies may disclose that information to any person—

(a) for the purposes of, or in connection with, prescribed civil proceedings (including prospective proceedings) in the United Kingdom or elsewhere, or

(b) for the purposes of obtaining legal advice in relation to such proceedings, or

(c) otherwise for the purposes of establishing, enforcing or defending legal rights that are or may be the subject of such proceedings.

(2) Subsection (1) does not apply to—

(a) information which comes to a public authority in connection with an investigation under Part 4, 5 or 6 of the 1973 Act or under section 11 of the Competition Act 1980;

(b) . . .

(c) information which comes to a public authority in connection with an investigation under Part 3 or 4 or section 174 of this Act;

(d) information which comes to a public authority in connection with an investigation under the Competition Act 1998 (c 41).

(3) In subsection (1) "prescribed" means prescribed by order of the Secretary of State.

(4) An order under this section—

(a) may prescribe information, or civil proceedings, for the purposes of this section by reference to such factors as appear to the Secretary of State to be appropriate;

(b) may prescribe for the purposes of this section all information, or civil proceedings, or all information or civil proceedings not falling within one or more specified exceptions;

(c) must be made by statutory instrument subject to annulment in pursuance of a resolution of either House of Parliament.

(5) Information disclosed under this section must not be used by the person to whom it is disclosed for any purpose other than those specified in subsection (1).]

NOTES

Inserted by the Companies Act 2006, s 1281.

Sub-s (2): para (b) repealed by the Financial Services Act 2012, s 114(2), Sch 19.

Orders: the Enterprise Act 2002 (Disclosure of Information for Civil Proceedings etc) Order 2007, SI 2007/2193 at **[2.42]**.

[1.422]

242 Criminal proceedings

(1) A public authority which holds information to which section 237 applies may disclose that information to any person—

- (a) in connection with the investigation of any criminal offence in any part of the United Kingdom;
- (b) for the purposes of any criminal proceedings there;
- (c) for the purpose of any decision whether to start or bring to an end such an investigation or proceedings.

(2) Information disclosed under this section must not be used by the person to whom it is disclosed for any purpose other than that for which it is disclosed.

(3) A public authority must not make a disclosure under this section unless it is satisfied that the making of the disclosure is proportionate to what is sought to be achieved by it.

[1.423]

243 Overseas disclosures

(1) A public authority which holds information to which section 237 applies (the discloser) may disclose that information to an overseas public authority for the purpose mentioned in subsection (2).

(2) The purpose is facilitating the exercise by the overseas public authority of any function which it has relating to—

- (a) carrying out investigations in connection with the enforcement of any relevant legislation by means of civil proceedings;
- (b) bringing civil proceedings for the enforcement of such legislation or the conduct of such proceedings;
- (c) the investigation of crime;
- (d) bringing criminal proceedings or the conduct of such proceedings;
- (e) deciding whether to start or bring to an end such investigations or proceedings.

(3) But subsection (1) does not apply to any of the following—

- (a) information which is held by a person who is designated by virtue of section 213(4) as a designated enforcer for the purposes of Part 8;
- (b) information which comes to a public authority in connection with an investigation under Part 4, 5 or 6 of the 1973 Act or under section 11 of the Competition Act 1980 (c 21);
- (c) . . .
- (d) information which comes to a public authority in connection with an investigation under Part *3 or* 4 or section 174 of this Act.

(4) The Secretary of State may direct that a disclosure permitted by this section must not be made if he thinks that in connection with any matter in respect of which the disclosure could be made it is more appropriate—

- (a) if any investigation is to be carried out, that it is carried out by an authority in the United Kingdom or in another specified country or territory;
- (b) if any proceedings are to be brought, that they are brought in a court in the United Kingdom or in another specified country or territory.

(5) The Secretary of State must take such steps as he thinks are appropriate to bring a direction under subsection (4) to the attention of persons likely to be affected by it.

(6) In deciding whether to disclose information under this section a public authority must have regard in particular to the following considerations—

- (a) whether the matter in respect of which the disclosure is sought is sufficiently serious to justify making the disclosure;
- (b) whether the law of the country or territory to whose authority the disclosure would be made provides appropriate protection against self-incrimination in criminal proceedings;
- (c) whether the law of that country or territory provides appropriate protection in relation to the storage and disclosure of personal data;
- (d) whether there are arrangements in place for the provision of mutual assistance as between the United Kingdom and that country or territory in relation to the disclosure of information of the kind to which section 237 applies.

(7) Protection is appropriate if it provides protection in relation to the matter in question which corresponds to that so provided in any part of the United Kingdom.

(8) The Secretary of State may by order—

- (a) modify the list of considerations in subsection (6);
- (b) add to those considerations;
- (c) remove any of those considerations.

(9) An order under subsection (8) must be made by statutory instrument subject to annulment in pursuance of a resolution of either House of Parliament.

(10) Information disclosed under this section—

- (a) may be disclosed subject to the condition that it must not be further disclosed without the agreement of the discloser, and
- (b) must not otherwise be used by the overseas public authority to which it is disclosed for any purpose other than that for which it is first disclosed.

(11) An overseas public authority is a person or body in any country or territory outside the United Kingdom which appears to the discloser to exercise functions of a public nature in relation to any of the matters mentioned in paragraphs (a) to (e) of subsection (2).

(12) Relevant legislation is—

(a) this Act, any enactment specified in Schedule 14 and such subordinate legislation as is specified by order for the purposes of section 238(1);
(b) any enactment or subordinate legislation specified in an order under section 211(2);
(c) any enactment or subordinate legislation specified in [Schedule 13];
(d) legislation in any country or territory outside the United Kingdom which appears to the discloser to make provision corresponding to this Act or to any such enactment or subordinate legislation.

NOTES

Sub-s (3) is amended as follows:

Para (c) repealed by the Financial Services Act 2012, s 114(2), Sch 19.

The words "3 or" in italics in para (d) were repealed by the National Security and Investment Act 2021, s 59, as from 1 July 2021. See also the National Security and Investment Act 2021 (Commencement No 1 and Transitional Provision) Regulations 2021, SI 2021/788, reg 3 which provides that this amendment applies only to information which comes to a public authority on or after 1 July 2021 in connection with an investigation under Part 3 of this Act.

Sub-s (12): the words in square brackets in para (c) were substituted by the Consumer Protection (Enforcement) (Amendment etc) (EU Exit) Regulations 2019, SI 2019/203, reg 3(1), (19), as from IP completion day (as defined in the European Union (Withdrawal Agreement) Act 2020, s 39).

[1.424]

244 Specified information: considerations relevant to disclosure

(1) A public authority must have regard to the following considerations before disclosing any specified information (within the meaning of section 238(1)).

(2) The first consideration is the need to exclude from disclosure (so far as practicable) any information whose disclosure the authority thinks is contrary to the public interest.

(3) The second consideration is the need to exclude from disclosure (so far as practicable)—
(a) commercial information whose disclosure the authority thinks might significantly harm the legitimate business interests of the undertaking to which it relates, or
(b) information relating to the private affairs of an individual whose disclosure the authority thinks might significantly harm the individual's interests.

(4) The third consideration is the extent to which the disclosure of the information mentioned in subsection (3)(a) or (b) is necessary for the purpose for which the authority is permitted to make the disclosure.

Offences

[1.425]

245 Offences

(1) A person commits an offence if he discloses information to which section 237 applies in contravention of section 237(2).

(2) A person commits an offence if he discloses information in contravention of a direction given under section 243(4).

(3) A person commits an offence if he uses information disclosed to him under this Part for a purpose which is not permitted under this Part.

(4) A person who commits an offence under this section is liable—
(a) on summary conviction to imprisonment for a term not exceeding three months or to a fine not exceeding the statutory maximum or to both;
(b) on conviction on indictment to imprisonment for a term not exceeding two years or to a fine or to both.

General

[1.426]

246 Subordinate legislation

In this Part "subordinate legislation" has the same meaning as in section 21(1) of the Interpretation Act 1978 (c 30) and includes an instrument made under—
(a) an Act of the Scottish Parliament;
(b) Northern Ireland legislation.

247–272 (*S 247 repeals the Trade Descriptions Act 1968, s 28(5), (5A), the Fair Trading Act 1973, s 30(3), 133, the Prices Act 1974, Schedule, para 12, the Consumer Credit Act 1974, s 174, the Estate Agents Act 1979, s 10, the Competition Act 1980, s 19(1)–(3), (4)(c), (d), (f), (5), (6), the Consumer Protection Act 1987, s 38, the Property Misdescriptions Act 1991, Schedule, para 7, the Timeshare Act 1992, Sch 2, para 5, the Competition Act 1998, ss 55, 56, Sch 11, and the Financial Services and Markets Act 2000, s 351(1)–(3), (7), Sch 19. Ss 248–272 (Part 10: Insolvency) outside the scope of this work.*)

PART 11 SUPPLEMENTARY

[1.427]

273 Interpretation

In this Act—

"the 1973 Act" means the Fair Trading Act 1973 (c 41);

"the 1998 Act" means the Competition Act 1998 (c 41);

["the CMA" means the Competition and Markets Authority;]

"the Director" means the Director General of Fair Trading; and

. . .

NOTES

Definition "CMA" substituted, and definition "the OFT" (omitted) repealed, by the Enterprise and Regulatory Reform Act 2013, s 26(3), Sch 5, Pt 2, paras 59, 217. For various transitional provisions (including those relating to the abolition of the OFT and the Competition Commission, existing references to those bodies and provisions relating to continuity), see the Enterprise and Regulatory Reform Act 2013 (Commencement No 6, Transitional Provisions and Savings) Order 2014, SI 2014/416, Schedule at **[2.13]**.

[1.428]

274 Provision of financial assistance for consumer purposes

The Secretary of State may give financial assistance to any person for the purpose of assisting—

(a) activities which the Secretary of State considers are of benefit to consumers; or

(b) the provision of—

(i) advice or information about consumer matters;

(ii) educational materials relating to consumer matters; or

(iii) advice or information to the Secretary of State in connection with the formulation of policy in respect of consumer matters.

[1.429]

275 Financial provision

There shall be paid out of money provided by Parliament—

(a) any expenditure incurred by the OFT, the Secretary of State, any other Minister of the Crown or a government department by virtue of this Act; and

(b) any increase attributable to this Act in the sums payable out of money so provided by virtue of any other Act.

[1.430]

276 Transitional or transitory provision and savings

(1) Schedule 24 (which makes transitional and transitory provisions and savings) has effect.

(2) The Secretary of State may by order made by statutory instrument make such transitional or transitory provisions and savings as he considers appropriate in connection with the coming into force of any provision of this Act.

(3) An order under subsection (2) may modify any Act or subordinate legislation.

(4) Schedule 24 does not restrict the power under subsection (2) to make other transitional or transitory provisions and savings.

NOTES

Orders: the Enterprise Act 2002 (Commencement No 2, Transitional and Transitory Provisions) Order 2003, SI 2003/766; the Enterprise Act 2002 (Commencement No 3, Transitional and Transitory Provisions and Savings) Order 2003, SI 2003/1397; the Enterprise Act 2002 (Part 8 Designated Enforcers: Criteria for Designation, Designation of Public Bodies as Designated Enforcers and Transitional Provisions) Order 2003, SI 2003/1399; the Enterprise Act 2002 (Commencement No 4 and Transitional Provisions and Savings) Order 2003, SI 2003/2093; the Enterprise Act 2002 (Transitional Provisions) (Insolvency) Order 2003, SI 2003/2332; the Enterprise Act 2002 (Commencement No 7 and Transitional Provisions and Savings) Order 2004, SI 2004/3233.

[1.431]

277 Power to make consequential amendments etc

(1) The Secretary of State may by order make such supplementary, incidental or consequential provision as he thinks appropriate—

(a) for the general purposes, or any particular purpose, of this Act; or

(b) in consequence of any provision made by or under this Act or for giving full effect to it.

(2) An order under this section may—

(a) modify any Act or subordinate legislation (including this Act);

(b) make incidental, supplementary, consequential, transitional, transitory or saving provision.

(3) The power to make an order under this section is exercisable by statutory instrument subject to annulment in pursuance of a resolution of either House of Parliament.

(4) The power conferred by this section is not restricted by any other provision of this Act.

NOTES

Orders: the Enterprise Act 2002 (Consequential and Supplemental Provisions) Order 2003, SI 2003/1398; the Enterprise Act 2002 (Part 9 Restrictions on Disclosure of Information) (Amendment and Specification) Order 2003, SI 2003/1400; the Enterprise Act 2002 (Insolvency) Order 2003, SI 2003/2096; the Enterprise Act 2002 and Media Mergers (Consequential Amendments) Order 2003, SI 2003/3180; the Enterprise Act 2002 (Part 9 Restrictions on Disclosure of Information) (Specification) Order 2004, SI 2004/693; the Enterprise Act 2002 (Insolvency) Order 2004, SI 2004/2312; the Enterprise Act 2002 (Judicial Pensions and Retirement Act 1993) (Consequential Amendment) Order 2005, SI 2005/53; the Enterprise Act 2002 (Enforcement Undertakings) Order 2006, SI 2006/354; the Enterprise Act 2002 (Enforcement Undertakings and Orders) Order 2006, SI 2006/355; the Insolvency (Scotland) Amendment Order 2006, SI 2006/735; the Enterprise Act 2002 (Enforcement Undertakings) (No 2) Order 2006, SI 2006/3095; the Enterprise Act 2002 (Part 8) (Designation of the Financial Conduct Authority as a Designated Enforcer) Order 2013, SI 2013/478; the Co-operative and Community Benefit Societies (Administration) (Amendment) Order 2021, SI 2021/1048.

278 (*Introduces Sch 25 (minor and consequential amendments) and Sch 26 (repeals and revocations).*)

[1.432]

279 Commencement

The preceding provisions of this Act shall come into force on such day as the Secretary of State may by order made by statutory instrument appoint; and different days may be appointed for different purposes.

NOTES

Orders: the Enterprise Act 2002 (Commencement No 1) Order 2003, SI 2003/765; the Enterprise Act 2002 (Commencement No 2, Transitional and Transitory Provisions) Order 2003, SI 2003/766; the Enterprise Act 2002 (Commencement No 3, Transitional and Transitory Provisions and Savings) Order 2003, SI 2003/1397; the Enterprise Act 2002 (Commencement No 4 and Transitional Provisions and Savings) Order 2003, SI 2003/2093; the Enterprise Act 2002 (Commencement No 5 and

Amendment) Order 2003, SI 2003/3340; the Enterprise Act 2002 (Commencement No 6) Order 2004, SI 2004/1866; the Enterprise Act 2002 (Commencement No 7 and Transitional Provisions and Savings) Order 2004, SI 2004/3233.

[1.433]

280 Extent

(1) Sections 256 to 265, 267, 269 and 272 extend only to England and Wales.

(2) Sections 204, 248 to 255 and 270 extend only to England and Wales and Scotland (but subsection (3) of section 415A as inserted by section 270 extends only to England and Wales).

(3) Any other modifications by this Act of an enactment have the same extent as the enactment being modified.

(4) Otherwise, this Act extends to England and Wales, Scotland and Northern Ireland.

[1.434]

281 Short title

This Act may be cited as the Enterprise Act 2002.

SCHEDULES

SCHEDULE 1

(*Sch 1 (The Office of Fair Trading) was repealed by the Enterprise and Regulatory Reform Act 2013, s 26(3), Sch 5, Pt 4, para 229. For various transitional provisions (including those relating to the abolition of the OFT and the Competition Commission, existing references to those bodies and provisions relating to continuity), see the Enterprise and Regulatory Reform Act 2013 (Commencement No 6, Transitional Provisions and Savings) Order 2014, SI 2014/416, Schedule at* **[2.13]**.)

SCHEDULE 2
THE COMPETITION APPEAL TRIBUNAL

Section 12

Appointment, etc of President and chairmen

[1.435]

1. (1) A person is not eligible for appointment as President unless—

[(a) he satisfies the judicial-appointment eligibility condition on a 7-year basis;]

(b) he is an advocate or solicitor in Scotland of at least [7] years' standing; or

(c) he is a member of the Bar of Northern Ireland or [solicitor of the Court of Judicature of Northern Ireland] of at least [7] years' standing;

and he appears to the Lord Chancellor to have appropriate experience and knowledge of competition law and practice.

(2) A person is not eligible for appointment as a chairman unless—

[(a) he satisfies the judicial-appointment eligibility condition on a 5-year basis;]

(b) he is an advocate or solicitor in Scotland of at least [5] years' standing; or

(c) he is a member of the Bar of Northern Ireland or [solicitor of the Court of Judicature of Northern Ireland] of at least [5] years' standing;

and he appears to the Lord Chancellor to have appropriate experience and knowledge (either of competition law and practice or any other relevant law and practice).

(3) Before appointing an advocate or solicitor in Scotland under this paragraph, the Lord Chancellor must consult the Lord President of the Court of Session.

(4) . . .

2. (1) The members appointed as President or as chairmen shall hold and vacate office in accordance with their terms of appointment, subject to the following provisions.

(2) A person may not be a chairman for more than 8 years (but this does not prevent a temporary re-appointment for the purpose of continuing to act as a member of the Tribunal as constituted for the purposes of any proceedings instituted before the end of his term of office).

(3) The President and the chairmen may resign their offices by notice in writing to the Lord Chancellor.

(4) The Lord Chancellor may remove a person from office as President or chairman on the ground of incapacity or misbehaviour.

[(5) The Lord Chancellor may remove a person from office as President under sub-paragraph (4) only with the concurrence of all of the following—

(a) the Lord Chief Justice of England and Wales;

(b) the Lord President of the Court of Session;

(c) the Lord Chief Justice of Northern Ireland.

(6) The Lord Chancellor may remove a person from office as chairman under sub-paragraph (4) only with the concurrence of the appropriate senior judge.

(7) The appropriate senior judge is the Lord Chief Justice of England and Wales, unless—

(a) the person to be removed exercises functions wholly or mainly in Scotland, in which case it is the Lord President of the Court of Session, or

(b) the person to be removed exercises functions wholly or mainly in Northern Ireland, in which case it is the Lord Chief Justice of Northern Ireland.]

3. If the President is absent or otherwise unable to act the Lord Chancellor may appoint as acting President any person qualified for appointment as a chairman.

Appointment, etc of ordinary members

4. (1) Ordinary members shall hold and vacate office in accordance with their terms of appointment, subject to the following provisions.

(2) A person may not be an ordinary member for more than 8 years (but this does not prevent a temporary re-appointment for the purpose of continuing to act as a member of the Tribunal as constituted for the purposes of any proceedings instituted before the end of his term of office).

(3) An ordinary member may resign his office by notice in writing to the Secretary of State.

(4) The Secretary of State may remove a person from office as an ordinary member on the ground of incapacity or misbehaviour.

Remuneration etc for members

5. (1) The Competition Service shall pay to the President, the chairmen and the ordinary members such remuneration (whether by way of salaries or fees), and such allowances, as the Secretary of State may determine.

(2) The Competition Service shall, if required to do so by the Secretary of State—

- (a) pay such pension, allowances or gratuities as may be determined by the Secretary of State to or in respect of a person who holds or has held office as President, a chairman or an ordinary member; or
- (b) make such payments as may be so determined towards provision for the payment of a pension, allowance or gratuities to or in respect of such a person.

Compensation for loss of office

6. If, where any person ceases to hold office as President, a chairman or ordinary member, the Secretary of State determines that there are special circumstances which make it right that he should receive compensation, the Competition Service shall pay to him such amount by way of compensation as the Secretary of State may determine.

Staff, accommodation and property

7. Any staff, office accommodation or equipment required for the Tribunal shall be provided by the Competition Service.

Miscellaneous

8. The President must arrange such training for members of the Tribunal as he considers appropriate.

9. In this Schedule "chairman" and "ordinary member" mean respectively a member of the panel of chairmen, or a member of the panel of ordinary members, appointed under section 12.

10, 11. (*Amend the House of Commons Disqualification Act 1975, Sch 1, and the Northern Ireland Assembly Disqualification Act 1975, Sch 1.*)

NOTES

Para 1 is amended as follows:

Sub-para (1)(a) substituted, and figures in square brackets in sub-paras (1)(b), (c) substituted, by the Tribunals, Courts and Enforcement Act 2007, s 50, Sch 10, Pt 1, para 36(1), (2), subject to transitional provisions in the Tribunals, Courts and Enforcement Act 2007 (Commencement No 5 and Transitional Provisions) Order 2008, SI 2008/1653, arts 3, 4 relating to processes to select a person for appointment to an office or other position that began before 31 July 2008.

Words in square brackets in sub-paras (1)(c), (2)(c) substituted by the Constitutional Reform Act 2005, s 59(5), Sch 11, Pt 3, para 5.

Sub-para (2)(a) substituted, and numbers in square brackets in sub-paras (2)(b), (c) substituted, by the Tribunals, Courts and Enforcement Act 2007, s 50, Sch 10, Pt 1, para 36(1), (3)(a), (b), subject to transitional provisions as noted above.

Sub-para (4) repealed by the Tribunals, Courts and Enforcement Act 2007, s 146, Sch 23, Pt 2.

Para 2: sub-paras (5)–(7) added by the Constitutional Reform Act 2005, s 15(1), Sch 4, Pt 1, paras 304, 307.

SCHEDULE 3
THE COMPETITION SERVICE

Section 13

PART 1 CONSTITUTION ETC

Membership of the Service

[1.436]

1. (1) The Service shall consist of—

- (a) the President of the Competition Appeal Tribunal;
- (b) the Registrar of the Competition Appeal Tribunal; and
- (c) one or more appointed members.

(2) An appointed member shall be appointed by the Secretary of State after consulting the President.

Chairman of Service

2. (1) Subject to sub-paragraph (2), the members shall choose one of their number to be chairman of the Service.

(2) The Secretary of State shall designate one of the members to be the first chairman of the Service for such period as the Secretary of State may determine.

Appointed members

3. An appointed member shall hold and vacate office in accordance with the terms of his appointment (and is eligible for re-appointment).

Allowances, etc for members

4. (1) The Service shall pay—

(a) such travelling and other allowances to its members, and

(b) such remuneration to any appointed member,

as may be determined by the Secretary of State.

(2) The Service shall, if required to do so by the Secretary of State—

(a) pay such pension, allowances or gratuities as may be determined by the Secretary of State to or in respect of a person who holds or has held office as an appointed member; or

(b) make such payments as may be so determined towards provision for the payment of a pension, allowances or gratuities to or in respect of such a person.

5. If, where any person ceases to hold office as an appointed member, the Secretary of State determines that there are special circumstances which make it right that he should receive compensation, the Service shall pay to him such amount by way of compensation as the Secretary of State may determine.

Staff

6. (1) The Service may, with the approval of the Secretary of State as to numbers and terms and conditions of service, appoint such staff as it may determine.

(2) The persons to whom section 1 of the Superannuation Act 1972 (c 11) (persons to or in respect of whom benefits may be provided by schemes under that section) applies shall include the staff of the Service.

(3) The Service shall pay to the Minister for the Civil Service, at such times as he may direct, such sums as he may determine in respect of any increase attributable to sub-paragraph (2) in the sums payable out of money provided by Parliament under the Superannuation Act 1972.

Procedure

7. (1) The Service may regulate its own procedure (including quorum).

(2) The validity of anything done by the Service is not affected by a vacancy among its members or by a defect in the appointment of a member.

8. (1) The application of the seal of the Service shall be authenticated by the signature of—

(a) any member; or

(b) some other person who has been authorised for that purpose by the Service, whether generally or specially.

(2) Sub-paragraph (1) does not apply in relation to any document which is, or is to be, signed in accordance with the law of Scotland.

9. A document purporting to be duly executed under the seal of the Service, or signed on its behalf, shall be received in evidence and, unless the contrary is proved, be taken to be so executed or signed.

The Service's powers

10. The Service has power to do anything which is calculated to facilitate, or is conducive or incidental to, the performance of its functions.

Accounts

11. (1) The Service shall keep proper accounts and proper records in relation to its accounts.

(2) In performing that duty the Service shall, in addition to accounts and records relating to its own activities (including the services provided to the Tribunal), keep separate accounts and separate records in relation to the activities of the Tribunal.

12. (1) The Service shall—

(a) prepare a statement of accounts in respect of each of its financial years; and

(b) prepare a statement of accounts for the Tribunal for each of its financial years.

(2) The Service must send copies of the accounts required by sub-paragraph (1) to the Secretary of State and to the Comptroller and Auditor General before the end of August following the financial year to which they relate.

(3) Those accounts must comply with any directions given by the Secretary of State with the approval of the Treasury as to—

(a) the information to be contained in them;

(b) the manner in which that information is to be presented; and

(c) the methods and principles according to which they are to be prepared.

(4) The Comptroller and Auditor General shall—

(a) examine, certify and report on each statement of accounts received by him; and

(b) lay copies of each statement before Parliament.

(5) In this paragraph "financial year" means the period of 12 months ending with 31st March.

NOTES

For the power of a Minister to abolish, by order, the Competition Service, see the Public Bodies Act 2011, s 1, Sch 1.

(Sch 3, Pt 2 was repealed by the Enterprise and Regulatory Reform Act 2013, s 26(3), Sch 5, Pt 3, paras 224, 226 (for various transitional provisions (including those relating to the abolition of the OFT and the Competition Commission, existing references to those bodies and provisions relating to continuity), see the Enterprise and Regulatory Reform Act 2013 (Commencement No 6, Transitional Provisions and Savings) Order 2014, SI 2014/416, Schedule at **[2.13]***). Sch 3, Pt 3 amends the House of Commons Disqualification Act 1975, Sch 1, and the Northern Ireland Assembly Disqualification Act 1975, Sch 1.)*

SCHEDULE 4
TRIBUNAL: PROCEDURE

Sections 14 and 15

PART 1 GENERAL

Decisions of the Tribunal

[1.437]

1. (1) A decision of the Tribunal in any proceedings before it must—

[(a) state the reasons for the decision;

(aa) state whether the decision was unanimous or taken by a majority or, where proceedings are heard by a chairman only, state that fact;]

(b) be recorded in a document signed and dated by the chairman of the Tribunal dealing with the proceedings.

(2) In preparing that document the Tribunal shall have regard to the need for excluding, so far as practicable—

(a) information the disclosure of which would in its opinion be contrary to the public interest;

(b) commercial information the disclosure of which would or might, in its opinion, significantly harm the legitimate business interests of the undertaking to which it relates;

(c) information relating to the private affairs of an individual the disclosure of which would, or might, in its opinion, significantly harm his interests.

(3) But the Tribunal shall also have regard to the extent to which any disclosure mentioned in sub-paragraph (2) is necessary for the purpose of explaining the reasons for the decision.

(4) The President shall make such arrangements for the publication of the decisions of the Tribunal as he considers appropriate.

[Enforcement of injunctions in England and Wales and Northern Ireland

1A. (1) Where a person ("A") fails to comply with an injunction granted by the Tribunal in proceedings under section 47A or 47B of the 1998 Act, the Tribunal may certify the matter to the High Court.

(2) The High Court may enquire into the matter.

(3) If, after hearing any witnesses who may be produced against or on behalf of A, and any statement made by or on behalf of A, the High Court is satisfied that A would have been in contempt of court if the injunction had been granted by the High Court, the High Court may deal with A as if A were in contempt.]

Enforcement of decisions in Great Britain

2. If a decision of the Tribunal is registered in England and Wales in accordance with rules of court or any practice direction—

(a) payment of damages which are awarded by the decision;

(b) costs or expenses awarded by the decision; and

(c) any direction given as a result of the decision,

may be enforced by the High Court as if the damages, costs or expenses were an amount due in pursuance of a judgment or order of the High Court, or as if the direction were an order of the High Court.

3. If a decision of the Tribunal awards damages, costs or expenses, or results in any direction being given, the decision may be recorded for execution in the Books of Council and Session and shall be enforceable accordingly.

4. Subject to rules of court or any practice direction, a decision of the Tribunal may be registered or recorded for execution—

(a) for the purpose of enforcing a direction given as a result of the decision, by the Registrar of the Tribunal or a person who was a party to the proceedings;

(b) for the purpose of enforcing a decision to award damages, costs or expenses (other than a decision to which paragraph (c) applies), by the person to whom the sum concerned was awarded; and

(c) for the purpose of enforcing a decision to award damages which is the subject of an order under section [47C(3) or (4)] of the 1998 Act, by the [representative in the proceedings under section 47B of that Act].

Enforcement of decisions in Northern Ireland

5. (1) A decision of the Tribunal may be enforced in Northern Ireland with the leave of the High Court in Northern Ireland—

(a) in the case of a direction given as a result of the decision, by the Registrar of the Tribunal or a person who was a party to the proceedings;

(b) for the purpose of enforcing a decision to award damages, costs or expenses (other than a decision to which paragraph (c) applies), by the person to whom the sum concerned was awarded; and

(c) for the purpose of enforcing a decision to award damages which is the subject of an order under section [47C(3) or (4)] of the 1998 Act, by the [representative in the proceedings under section 47B of that Act].

(2) For the purpose of enforcing in Northern Ireland a decision to award damages, costs or expenses—

(a) payment may be enforced as if the damages, costs or expenses were an amount due in pursuance of a judgment or order of the High Court in Northern Ireland; and

(b) a sum equal to the amount of damages, costs or expenses shall be deemed to be payable under a money judgment within the meaning of Article 2(2) of the Judgments Enforcement (Northern Ireland) Order 1981 (SI 1981/226 (NI 6)) (and the provisions of that Order apply accordingly).

(3) For the purpose of enforcing in Northern Ireland a direction given as a result of a decision of the Tribunal, the direction may be enforced as if it were an order of the High Court in Northern Ireland.

Miscellaneous

6. A decision of the Tribunal in proceedings under section 47B of the 1998 Act which—

[(a) awards damages to a person in respect of a claim made or continued on behalf of that person (but is not the subject of an order under section 47C(3) or (4) of that Act); or]

(b) awards costs or expenses to [a person] in respect of proceedings in respect of a claim made under section 47A of that Act prior to its being continued on [behalf of that person] in the proceedings under section 47B,

may only be enforced by the [person] concerned with the permission of the High Court or Court of Session.

7. An award of costs or expenses against a [representative] in proceedings under section 47B of the 1998 Act may not be enforced against any [person] on whose behalf a claim was made or continued in those proceedings.

8. In this Part of this Schedule any reference to damages includes a reference to any sum of money (other than costs or expenses) which may be awarded in respect of a claim made under section 47A of the 1998 Act or included in proceedings under section 47B of that Act.

NOTES

Para 1: sub-paras (1)(a), (aa) substituted (for the original sub-para (1)(a)), by the Consumer Rights Act 2015, s 81, Sch 8, Pt 2, paras 18, 22, 23.

Para 1A: inserted by the Consumer Rights Act 2015, s 81, Sch 8, Pt 2, paras 18, 22, 24.

Paras 4, 5: words and figures in square brackets substituted by the Consumer Rights Act 2015, s 81, Sch 8, Pt 2, paras 18, 22, 25.

Paras 6, 7: words in square brackets substituted by the Consumer Rights Act 2015, s 81, Sch 8, Pt 2, paras 18, 22, 26, 27.

PART 2 TRIBUNAL RULES

General

[1.438]

9. [(1)] In this Schedule "the Tribunal", in relation to any proceedings before it, means the Tribunal as constituted (in accordance with section 14) for the purposes of those proceedings.

[(2) In this Schedule, where a paragraph is capable of applying to proceedings relating to the approval of a collective settlement under section 49A or 49B of the 1998 Act, any reference in that paragraph to "proceedings" includes a reference to those proceedings.]

10. Tribunal rules may make different provision for different kinds of proceedings.

[10A. (1) Tribunal rules may make provision as to proceedings on an application for a warrant under section 194 of this Act or section 28, 28A, 62, 62A, 63, 65G or 65H of the 1998 Act, including provision—

(a) for the Tribunal dealing with the proceedings to consist only of the President or a member of the panel of chairmen;

(b) as to the manner in which the proceedings are to be conducted, including provision—

(i) for such applications to be determined without a hearing;

(ii) in cases where there is a hearing, for it to be held in private if the Tribunal considers it appropriate because it is considering information of a kind mentioned in paragraph 1(2);

(c) as to the persons entitled to be heard in such proceedings (where there is a hearing);

(d) for requiring persons to attend to give evidence and produce documents, and for authorising the administration of oaths to witnesses;

(e) as to the evidence which may be required or admitted and the extent to which it should be oral or written;

(f) allowing the Tribunal to fix time-limits with respect to any aspect of the proceedings and to extend any time-limit (before or after its expiry).

(2) Paragraphs 2 to 8, and 11 to 17, of this Schedule do not apply in relation to the institution or conduct of proceedings for a warrant mentioned in sub-paragraph (1).]

Institution of proceedings

11. (1) Tribunal rules may make provision as to the period within which and the manner in which proceedings are to be brought.

(2) That provision may, in particular—

[(a) make further provision as to procedural aspects of the operation of the limitation or prescriptive periods in relation to claims which may be made in proceedings under section 47A of the 1998 Act, as set out in [paragraph 23 of Schedule 8A to that Act];]

(b) provide for the Tribunal to extend the period in which any particular proceedings may be brought; and

(c) provide for the form, contents, amendment and acknowledgement of the documents by which proceedings are to be instituted.

12. Tribunal rules may provide for the Tribunal to reject any proceedings (other than proceedings under section 47A or 47B of the 1998 Act) if it considers that—

(a) the person instituting them does not have a sufficient interest in the decision with respect to which the proceedings are brought; or

(b) the document by which he institutes them discloses no valid grounds for bringing them.

[13. (1) Tribunal rules may provide for the Tribunal—

(a) to reject a claim made under section 47A of the 1998 Act or a section 47B claim if it considers that there are no reasonable grounds for making it;

(b) to reject a section 47B claim if—

(i) the Tribunal declines to make a collective proceedings order in respect of the proceedings under section 47B of the 1998 Act,

(ii) the Tribunal makes a collective proceedings order in respect of the proceedings, but the order does not provide that the claim in question is eligible for inclusion in the proceedings,
(iii) the Tribunal revokes the collective proceedings order in respect of the proceedings, or
(iv) the Tribunal varies the collective proceedings order in such a way that the claim in question is no longer included in the proceedings;

(c) to reject a section 47B claim if the claim had been previously made in proceedings under section 47A of the 1998 Act by a person who has not consented to its being continued in proceedings under section 47B of that Act.

(2) In this paragraph, "a section 47B claim" means a claim made in proceedings under section 47B of the 1998 Act at the commencement of those proceedings.]

14. Tribunal rules may provide for the Tribunal to reject any proceedings if it is satisfied that the person instituting the proceedings has habitually and persistently and without any reasonable ground—

(a) instituted vexatious proceedings (whether against the same person or against different persons); or
(b) made vexatious applications in any proceedings.

15. Tribunal rules must ensure that no proceedings are rejected without giving the parties the opportunity to be heard.

[Fast-track procedure

15A. (1) Tribunal rules may make provision in relation to a fast-track procedure for claims made in proceedings under section 47A of the 1998 Act, including describing the factors relevant to determining whether a claim is suitable to be dealt with according to that procedure.

(2) Tribunal rules may make different provision for claims in proceedings under section 47A of the 1998 Act which are and which are not subject to the fast-track procedure.

(3) Tribunal rules may, in particular, provide for the Tribunal to—

(a) grant an interim injunction on a claim in proceedings under section 47A of the 1998 Act which is subject to the fast-track procedure to a person who has not given an undertaking as to damages, or
(b) impose a cap on the amount that a person may be required to pay under an undertaking as to damages given on the granting of such an interim injunction.

(4) In sub-paragraph (3) "an undertaking as to damages" means an undertaking to pay damages which a person sustains as a result of the interim injunction and which the Tribunal considers the person to whom the injunction is granted should pay.

Collective proceedings

15B. (1) Tribunal rules may make provision in relation to collective proceedings under section 47B of the 1998 Act.

(2) Rules under sub-paragraph (1) must in particular make provision as to the following matters—

(a) the procedure governing an application for a collective proceedings order;
(b) the factors which the Tribunal must take into account in deciding whether a claim is suitable to be brought in collective proceedings (but rules need not make provision in connection with the determination as to whether claims raise the same, similar or related issues of fact or law);
(c) the factors which the Tribunal must take into account in deciding whether to authorise a person to act as a representative in collective proceedings;
(d) the procedure by which the Tribunal is to reach a decision as to whether to make a collective proceedings order;
(e) the procedure by which a person may opt in or opt out of collective proceedings;
(f) the factors which the Tribunal must take into account in deciding whether to vary or revoke a collective proceedings order;
(g) the assessment of damages in collective proceedings;
(h) the payment of damages in collective proceedings, including the procedure for publicising an award of damages;
(i) the effect of judgments and orders in collective proceedings.

Collective settlements

15C. (1) Tribunal rules may make provision in relation to collective settlements under sections 49A and 49B of the 1998 Act.

(2) Rules under sub-paragraph (1) must in particular make provision as to the following matters—

(a) the procedure governing an application for approval of a proposed collective settlement;
(b) where section 49B applies, the factors which the Tribunal must take into account in deciding whether to make a collective settlement order (but rules need not make provision in connection with the determination as to whether claims raise the same, similar or related issues of fact or law);
(c) where section 49B applies, the factors which the Tribunal must take into account in deciding whether to authorise a person to act as a settlement representative in relation to a collective settlement;
(d) where section 49B applies, the procedure by which the Tribunal is to reach a decision as to whether to make a collective settlement order;
(e) the factors which the Tribunal must take into account in deciding whether to approve a proposed collective settlement;
(f) the procedure by which the Tribunal is to reach a decision as to whether to approve a collective settlement;
(g) the procedure by which a person may opt in or opt out of a collective settlement;
(h) the payment of compensation under a collective settlement, including the procedure for publicising a compensation award.]

Pre-hearing reviews and preliminary matters

16. (1) Tribunal rules may make provision for the carrying out by the Tribunal of a preliminary consideration of proceedings (a "pre-hearing review").

(2) That provision may include—

(a) provision enabling such powers to be exercised on a pre-hearing review as may be specified in the rules;

(b) provision for security and supplemental provision relating to security.

(3) For the purposes of sub-paragraph (2)(b)—

(a) "provision for security" means provision authorising the Tribunal, in specified circumstances, to order a party to the proceedings, if he wishes to continue to participate in them, to pay a deposit not exceeding such sum as may be specified or calculated in a specified manner; and

(b) "supplemental provision", in relation to security, means provision as to—

(i) the manner in which the amount of a deposit is to be determined;

(ii) the consequences of non-payment of a deposit;

(iii) the circumstances in which the deposit, or any part of it, may be refunded to the person who paid it or paid to another party to the proceedings.

Conduct of the hearing

17. (1) Tribunal rules may make provision—

(a) as to the manner in which proceedings are to be conducted, including provision for any hearing to be held in private if the Tribunal considers it appropriate because it is considering information of a kind mentioned in paragraph 1(2);

(b) as to the persons entitled to appear on behalf of the parties;

(c) for requiring persons to attend to give evidence and produce documents, and for authorising the administration of oaths to witnesses;

(d) as to the evidence which may be required or admitted and the extent to which it should be oral or written;

(e) allowing the Tribunal to fix time limits with respect to any aspect of proceedings and to extend any time limit (before or after its expiry);

(f) enabling the Tribunal, on the application of any party or on its own initiative, to order—

(i) the disclosure between, or the production by, the parties of documents or classes of documents; or

(ii) such recovery or inspection of documents as might be ordered by a sheriff;

(g) for the appointment of experts for the purposes of proceedings;

(h) for the award of costs or expenses, including allowances payable to persons in connection with attendance before the Tribunal;

[(ha) allowing the Tribunal to order payments in respect of the representation of a party to proceedings under section 47A or 47B of the 1998 Act, where the representation by a legal representative was provided free of charge;]

(i) for taxing or otherwise settling any costs or expenses awarded by the Tribunal or for the enforcement of any order awarding costs or expenses.

(2) Rules under sub-paragraph (1)(h) may provide, in relation to a claim made under section 47A of the 1998 Act which is continued on behalf of [a person] in proceedings under section 47B of that Act, for costs or expenses to be awarded to or against [that person] in respect of proceedings on that claim which took place before it was included in the proceedings under section 47B of that Act.

[(2A) Rules under sub-paragraph (1)(h) may provide for costs or expenses to be awarded to or against a person on whose behalf a claim is made or continued in proceedings under section 47B of the 1998 Act in respect of an application in the proceedings made by that person (where that application is not made by the representative in the proceedings on that person's behalf).]

(3) Otherwise Tribunal rules may not provide for costs or expenses to be awarded to or against [a person] on whose behalf a claim is made or continued in proceedings under section 47B of the 1998 Act.

(4) Tribunal rules may make provision enabling the Tribunal to refer any matter arising in any proceedings (other than proceedings under section 47A or 47B of the 1998 Act) back to the authority that made the decision to which the proceedings relate, if it appears that the matter has not been adequately investigated.

(5) A person who without reasonable excuse fails to comply with—

(a) any requirement imposed by virtue of sub-paragraph (1)(c); or

(b) any requirement with respect to the disclosure, production, recovery or inspection of documents which is imposed by virtue of sub-paragraph (1)(f),

is guilty of an offence and liable on summary conviction to a fine not exceeding level 3 on the standard scale.

Quorum

18. (1) Tribunal rules may make provision as to the consequences of a member of the Tribunal being unable to continue after part of any proceedings have been heard.

(2) The rules may allow the Tribunal to consist of the remaining members for the rest of the proceedings.

(3) The rules may enable the President, if it is the chairman of the Tribunal who is unable to continue—

(a) to appoint either of the remaining members to chair the Tribunal; and

(b) if that person is not [a judge within any of paragraphs (aa) to (ac) of section 12(2) or] a member of the panel of chairmen, to appoint himself or some other suitably qualified person to attend the proceedings and advise the remaining members on any questions of law arising.

(4) For the purpose of sub-paragraph (3) a person is "suitably qualified" if he is, or is qualified for appointment as, a member of the panel of chairmen.

Interest

19. (1) Tribunal rules may make provision allowing the Tribunal to order that interest is payable on any sum awarded by the Tribunal or on any fees ordered to be paid under paragraph 20.

(2) That provision may include provision—

(a) as to the circumstances in which such an order may be made;

(b) as to the manner in which, and the periods in respect of which, interest is to be calculated and paid.

Fees

20. (1) Tribunal rules may provide—

(a) for fees to be chargeable in respect of specified costs of proceedings; and

(b) for the amount of such costs to be determined by the Tribunal.

(2) Any sums received in respect of such fees shall be paid into the Consolidated Fund.

[Stay or sist of proceedings

20A. (1) In relation to proceedings in England and Wales or Northern Ireland under section 47A or 47B of the 1998 Act, Tribunal rules may make provision as to the stay of the proceedings, including as to—

(a) the circumstances in which a stay may be ordered or removed at the request of a party to the proceedings,

(b) the circumstances in which the proceedings may be stayed at the instance of the Tribunal, and

(c) the procedure to be followed.

(2) In relation to proceedings in Scotland under section 47A or 47B of the 1998 Act, Tribunal rules may make provision as to the sist of the proceedings, including as to—

(a) the circumstances in which a sist may be granted or recalled at the request of a party to the proceedings,

(b) the circumstances in which the proceedings may be sisted at the instance of the Tribunal, and

(c) the procedure to be followed.

(3) Rules under sub-paragraph (1) or (2) may in particular make provision in relation to the stay or sist of proceedings under section 47A or 47B which relate to a claim in respect of an infringement decision (as defined in section 47A(6)) which has not become final (see section 58A of the 1998 Act).]

Withdrawal of proceedings

21. (1) Tribunal rules may make provision—

(a) preventing a party who has instituted proceedings from withdrawing them without the permission of the Tribunal or, in specified circumstances, the President or the Registrar;

(b) for the Tribunal to grant permission to withdraw proceedings on such conditions as it considers appropriate;

(c) enabling the Tribunal to publish any decision which it would have made in any proceedings, had the proceedings not been withdrawn;

(d) as to the effect of withdrawal of proceedings; and

(e) as to the procedure to be followed if parties to proceedings agree to settle.

(2) Tribunal rules may make, in relation to a claim included in proceedings under section 47B of the 1998 Act, any provision which may be made under sub-paragraph (1) in relation to the whole proceedings.

[Injunctions

21A. Tribunal rules may make provision in relation to the grant of injunctions (including interim injunctions) in proceedings under section 47A or 47B of the 1998 Act.]

Interim orders

22. (1) Tribunal rules may provide for the Tribunal to make an order, on an interim basis—

(a) suspending the effect of any decision which is the subject matter of proceedings before it;

(b) in the case of an appeal under section 46 or 47 of the 1998 Act, varying the conditions or obligations attached to an exemption;

(c) granting any remedy which the Tribunal would have had power to grant in its final decision.

(2) Tribunal rules may also make provision giving the Tribunal powers similar to those given to the [CMA] by section 35 of the 1998 Act.

Miscellaneous

23. (1) Tribunal rules may make provision enabling the Tribunal to decide where to sit for the purposes of, or of any part of, any proceedings before it.

(2) Tribunal rules may make provision enabling the Tribunal to decide that any proceedings before it are to be treated, for purposes connected with—

(a) any appeal from a decision of the Tribunal made in those proceedings; and

(b) any other matter connected with those proceedings,

as proceedings in England and Wales, Scotland or Northern Ireland (regardless of the decision made for the purposes of sub-paragraph (1)).

(3) For the purposes of sub-paragraph (2), Tribunal rules may provide for each claim made or continued on behalf of [a person] in proceedings under section 47B of the 1998 Act to be treated as separate proceedings.

24. Tribunal rules may make provision—

(a) for a person who is not a party to be joined in any proceedings;

(b) for hearing a person who is not a party where, in any proceedings, it is proposed to make an order or give a direction in relation to that person;

(c) for proceedings to be consolidated on such terms as the Tribunal thinks appropriate in such circumstances as may be specified.

25. Tribunal rules may make provision for the Tribunal to transfer [all or any part of] a claim made in proceedings under section 47A of the 1998 Act to—

(a) the High Court or [the county court in England and Wales or the High Court or a county court in] Northern Ireland; or

(b) the Court of Session or a sheriff court in Scotland.

26. Tribunal rules may make provision in connection with the transfer of any proceedings from a court mentioned in paragraph 25 to the Tribunal under section 16.

NOTES

Para 9: sub-para (1) numbered as such, and sub-para (2) added, by the Consumer Rights Act 2015, s 81, Sch 8, Pt 2, paras 18, 22, 28.

Para 10A: inserted by the Enterprise and Regulatory Reform Act 2013, s 48(5). For various transitional provisions (including those relating to the abolition of the OFT and the Competition Commission, existing references to those bodies and provisions relating to continuity), see the Enterprise and Regulatory Reform Act 2013 (Commencement No 6, Transitional Provisions and Savings) Order 2014, SI 2014/416, Schedule at **[2.13]**.

Para 11: sub-para (2)(a) substituted by the Consumer Rights Act 2015, s 81, Sch 8, Pt 2, paras 18, 22, 29. Words in square brackets in sub-para (2)(a) substituted by the Claims in respect of Loss or Damage arising from Competition Infringements (Competition Act 1998 and Other Enactments (Amendment)) Regulations 2017, SI 2017/385, reg 3, Sch 2, paras 1, 11(1).

Para 13: substituted by the Consumer Rights Act 2015, s 81, Sch 8, Pt 2, paras 18, 22, 30.

Paras 15A–15C: inserted by the Consumer Rights Act 2015, s 81, Sch 8, Pt 2, paras 18, 22, 31.

Para 17: sub-paras (1)(ha), (2A) inserted, and words in square brackets in sub-paras (2), (3) substituted, by the Consumer Rights Act 2015, s 81, Sch 8, Pt 2, paras 18, 22, 32.

Para 18: words in square brackets in sub-para (3)(b) inserted by the Consumer Rights Act 2015, s 82(3).

Paras 20A, 21A: inserted by the Consumer Rights Act 2015, s 81, Sch 8, Pt 2, paras 18, 22, 33, 34.

Para 22: reference to the "CMA" in sub-para (2) substituted by the Enterprise and Regulatory Reform Act 2013, s 26(3), Sch 5, Pt 2, paras 59, 66, subject to transitional provisions in SI 2014/416 as noted above.

Para 23: words in square brackets in sub-para (3) substituted by the Consumer Rights Act 2015, s 81, Sch 8, Pt 2, paras 18, 22, 35.

Para 25: words in first pair of square brackets inserted by the Consumer Rights Act 2015, s 81, Sch 8, Pt 2, paras 18, 22, 36. Words in square brackets in sub-para (a) substituted by the Crime and Courts Act 2013, s 17(5), Sch 9, Pt 3, para 81(d).

Rules: the Competition Appeal Tribunal Rules 2015, SI 2015/1648 at **[6.8]**.

SCHEDULES 5 AND 6

(Sch 5 amends the Competition Act 1998, Pt I, at **[1.41]***, et seq; Sch 6 inserts the Water Industry Act 1991, Sch 4ZA at* **[1.40]***.)*

SCHEDULE 7
ENFORCEMENT REGIME FOR PUBLIC INTEREST AND SPECIAL PUBLIC INTEREST CASES

Section 85

Pre-emptive undertakings and orders

[1.439]

1. . . .

2. (1) Sub-paragraph (2) applies where an intervention notice or special intervention notice is in force.

(2) The Secretary of State or the [CMA] may by order, for the purpose of preventing pre-emptive action—

(a) prohibit or restrict the doing of things which the Secretary of State or (as the case may be) the [CMA] considers would constitute pre-emptive action;

(b) impose on any person concerned obligations as to the carrying on of any activities or the safeguarding of any assets;

(c) provide for the carrying on of any activities or the safeguarding of any assets either by the appointment of a person to conduct or supervise the conduct of any activities (on such terms and with such powers as may be specified or described in the order) or in any other manner;

(d) do anything which may be done by virtue of paragraph 19 of Schedule 8.

[(2A) Sub-paragraph (2B) applies where—

(a) an intervention notice or special intervention notice is in force, and

(b) the Secretary of State or the CMA has reasonable grounds for suspecting that pre-emptive action has or may have been taken.

(2B) The Secretary of State or (as the case may be) the CMA may by order, for the purpose of restoring the position to what it would have been had the pre-emptive action not been taken or otherwise for the purpose of mitigating its effects—

(a) do anything mentioned in sub-paragraph (2)(b) to (d);

(b) impose such other obligations, prohibitions or restrictions as it considers appropriate for that purpose.]

[(2C) A person may, with the consent of the Secretary of State or (as the case may be) the CMA, take action or action of a particular description where the action would otherwise constitute a contravention of an order under this paragraph by the Secretary of State or (as the case may be) the CMA.]

(3) Sub-paragraph (4) applies where an intervention notice is in force.

(4) The Secretary of State . . . may, for the purpose of preventing pre-emptive action, adopt an order made [by the CMA] under section 72 if the order is still in force when the Secretary of State . . . adopts it.

(5) An order adopted under sub-paragraph (4)—

(a) shall continue in force, in accordance with its terms, when adopted; and

(b) may be varied or revoked by an order under this paragraph.

(6) Any other order under this paragraph—

(a) shall come into force at such time as is determined by or under the order; and

(b) may be varied or revoked by another order.

(7) References in this Part to orders under this paragraph shall, unless the context otherwise requires, include references to orders adopted under this paragraph; and references to the making of orders under this paragraph shall be construed accordingly.

(8) An order which is in force under this paragraph in relation to a reference or possible reference under section 45 or (as the case may be) 62 shall cease to be in force if an undertaking under paragraph . . . 3 comes into force in relation to that reference.

(9) An order under this paragraph shall, if it has not previously ceased to be in force, cease to be in force when the intervention notice concerned or (as the case may be) special intervention notice concerned ceases to be in force.

(10) No order shall be made by the Secretary of State or the [CMA] under this paragraph before the making of a reference under section 45 or (as the case may be) 62 unless[—

(a) the Secretary of State or (as the case may be) the CMA has reasonable grounds for suspecting that it is or may be the case that two or more enterprises have ceased to be distinct or that arrangements are in progress or in contemplation which, if carried into effect, will result in two or more enterprises ceasing to be distinct; or

(b) the order relates to a special merger situation which has been, or may have been, created.]

(11) The Secretary of State or (as the case may be) the [CMA] shall, as soon as reasonably practicable, consider any representations received by that person in relation to varying or revoking an order under this paragraph.

[(12) In this paragraph "pre-emptive action" means action which might prejudice the reference or possible reference concerned under section 45 or (as the case may be) 62 or impede the taking of any action under this Part which may be justified by the Secretary of State's decisions on the reference.]

Undertakings in lieu of reference under section 45 or 62

3. (1) Sub-paragraph (2) applies if the Secretary of State has power to make a reference to the Commission under section 45 or 62 and otherwise intends to make such a reference.

(2) The Secretary of State may, instead of making such a reference and for the purpose of remedying, mitigating or preventing any of the effects adverse to the public interest which have or may have resulted, or which may be expected to result, from the creation of the relevant merger situation concerned or (as the case may be) the special merger situation concerned, accept from such of the parties concerned as he considers appropriate undertakings to take such action as he considers appropriate.

(3) In proceeding under sub-paragraph (2), the Secretary of State shall, in particular—

(a) accept the decisions of the [CMA] included in its report under section 44 so far as they relate to the matters mentioned in subsections (4) and (5) of that section; or

(b) (as the case may be) accept the decisions of the [CMA] included in its report under section 61 so far as they relate to the matters mentioned in subsections (3)(a) and (4) of that section.

(4) In proceeding under sub-paragraph (2) in relation to an anti-competitive outcome, the Secretary of State may, in particular, have regard to the effect of any action on any relevant customer benefits in relation to the creation of the relevant merger situation concerned.

(5) No undertaking shall be accepted by the Secretary of State under this paragraph in connection with a possible reference under section 45 if a public interest consideration mentioned in the intervention notice concerned has not been finalised and the period of 24 weeks beginning with the giving of that notice has not expired.

(6) The Secretary of State may delay making a decision as to whether to accept any such undertaking (and any related decision as to whether to make a reference under section 45) if he considers that there is a realistic prospect of the public interest consideration being finalised within the period of 24 weeks beginning with the giving of the intervention notice concerned.

(7) A delay under sub-paragraph (6) shall not extend beyond—

(a) the time when the public interest consideration is finalised; or

(b) if earlier, the expiry of the period of 24 weeks mentioned in that sub-paragraph.

(8) An undertaking under this paragraph—

(a) shall come into force when accepted;

(b) may be varied or superseded by another undertaking; or

(c) may be released by the Secretary of State.

(9) An undertaking under this paragraph which is in force in relation to a relevant merger situation or (as the case may be) a special merger situation shall cease to be in force if an order comes into force under paragraph 5 or 6 in relation to that undertaking.

(10) The Secretary of State shall, as soon as reasonably practicable, consider any representations received by him in relation to varying or releasing an undertaking under this section.

4. (1) The relevant authority shall not make a reference under section 22, 33 or 45 in relation to the creation of a relevant merger situation or (as the case may be) a reference under section 62 in relation to the creation of a special merger situation if—

(a) the Secretary of State has accepted an undertaking or group of undertakings under paragraph 3; and

(b) the relevant merger situation or (as the case may be) the special merger situation is the situation by reference to which the undertaking or group of undertakings was accepted.

(2) In sub-paragraph (1) "the relevant authority" means—

(a) in relation to a possible reference under section 22 or 33, the [CMA]; and

(b) in relation to a possible reference under section 45 or 62, the Secretary of State.

(3) Sub-paragraph (1) does not prevent the making of a reference if material facts about relevant arrangements or transactions, or relevant proposed arrangements or transactions, were not notified (whether in writing or otherwise) to the Secretary of State or the [CMA] or made public before any undertaking concerned was accepted.

(4) For the purposes of sub-paragraph (3) arrangements or transactions, or proposed arrangements or transactions, are relevant if they are the ones in consequence of which the enterprises concerned ceased or may have ceased, or may cease, to be distinct enterprises.

(5) In sub-paragraph (3) "made public" means so publicised as to be generally known or readily ascertainable.

5. (1) Sub-paragraph (2) applies where the Secretary of State considers that—

(a) an undertaking accepted by him under paragraph 3 has not been, is not being or will not be fulfilled; or

(b) in relation to an undertaking accepted by him under that paragraph, information which was false or misleading in a material respect was given to him or the [CMA] by the person giving the undertaking before he decided to accept the undertaking.

(2) The Secretary of State may, for any of the purposes mentioned in paragraph 3(2), make an order under this paragraph.

(3) Sub-paragraphs (3) and (4) of paragraph 3 shall apply for the purposes of sub-paragraph (2) above as they apply for the purposes of sub-paragraph (2) of that paragraph.

(4) An order under this paragraph may contain—

(a) anything permitted by Schedule 8; and

(b) such supplementary, consequential or incidental provision as the Secretary of State considers appropriate.

(5) An order under this paragraph

(a) shall come into force at such time as is determined by or under the order; and

(b) may contain provision which is different from the provision contained in the undertaking concerned.

(6) No order shall be varied or revoked under this paragraph unless the [CMA] advises that such a variation or revocation is appropriate by reason of a change of circumstances.

6. (1) Sub-paragraph (2) applies where—

(a) the Secretary of State has the power to make an order under paragraph 5 in relation to a particular undertaking and intends to make such an order; or

(b) the Secretary of State has the power to make an order under paragraph 10 in relation to a particular undertaking and intends to make such an order.

(2) The Secretary of State may, for the purpose of preventing any action which might prejudice the making of that order, make an order under this paragraph.

(3) No order shall be made under sub-paragraph (2) unless the Secretary of State has reasonable grounds for suspecting that it is or may be the case that action which might prejudice the making of the order under paragraph 5 or (as the case may be) 10 is in progress or in contemplation.

(4) An order under sub-paragraph (2) may—

(a) prohibit or restrict the doing of things which the Secretary of State considers would prejudice the making of the order under paragraph 5 or 10;

(b) impose on any person concerned obligations as to the carrying on of any activities or the safeguarding of any assets;

(c) provide for the carrying on of any activities or the safeguarding of any assets either by the appointment of a person to conduct or supervise the conduct of any activities (on such terms and with such powers as may be specified or described in the order) or in any other manner;

(d) do anything which may be done by virtue of paragraph 19 of Schedule 8.

(5) An order under this paragraph shall come into force at such time as is determined by or under the order.

(6) An order under this paragraph shall, if it has not previously ceased to be in force, cease to be in force on—

(a) the coming into force of an order under paragraph 5 or (as the case may be) 10 in relation to the undertaking concerned; or

(b) the making of the decision not to proceed with such an order.

(7) The Secretary of State shall, as soon as reasonably practicable, consider any representations received by him in relation to varying or revoking an order under this paragraph.

Statutory restrictions following reference under section 45 or 62

7. (1) Sub-paragraphs (2) and (3) apply where—

(a) a reference has been made under section 45(2) or (3) or 62(2) but not finally determined; and

[(b) no orders under paragraph 2 are in force in relation to the relevant merger situation concerned or (as the case may be) the special merger situation concerned.]

(2) No relevant person shall, without the consent of the Secretary of State—

(a) complete any outstanding matters in connection with any arrangements which have resulted in the enterprises concerned ceasing to be distinct enterprises;

(b) make any further arrangements in consequence of that result (other than arrangements which reverse that result); or

(c) transfer the ownership or control of any enterprises to which the reference relates.

(3) No relevant person shall, without the consent of the Secretary of State, assist in any of the activities mentioned in paragraphs (a) to (c) of sub-paragraph (2).

(4) The prohibitions in sub-paragraphs (2) and (3) do not apply in relation to anything which the person concerned is required to do by virtue of any enactment.

(5) The consent of the Secretary of State under sub-paragraph (2) or (3)—

(a) may be general or specific;
(b) may be revoked by the Secretary of State; and
(c) shall be published in such manner as the Secretary of State considers appropriate for bringing it to the attention of any person entitled to the benefit of it.

(6) Paragraph (c) of sub-paragraph (5) shall not apply if the Secretary of State considers that publication is not necessary for the purpose mentioned in that paragraph.

(7) Sub-paragraphs (2) and (3) shall apply to a person's conduct outside the United Kingdom if (and only if) he is—
(a) a United Kingdom national;
(b) a body incorporated under the law of the United Kingdom or of any part of the United Kingdom; or
(c) a person carrying on business in the United Kingdom.

(8) For the purpose of this paragraph a reference under section 45(2) or (3) is finally determined if—
(a) the time within which the [CMA] is to prepare a report under section 50 in relation to the reference and give it to the Secretary of State has expired and no such report has been so prepared and given;
(b) the [CMA] decides to cancel the reference under section 53(1);
(c) the time within which the Secretary of State is to make and publish a decision under section 54(2) has expired and no such decision has been made and published;
(d) the Secretary of State decides under section 54(2) to make no finding at all in the matter;
(e) the Secretary of State otherwise decides under section 54(2) not to make an adverse public interest finding;
(f) the Secretary of State decides under section 54(2) to make an adverse public interest finding but decides neither to accept an undertaking under paragraph 9 of this Schedule nor to make an order under paragraph 11 of this Schedule; or
(g) the Secretary of State decides under section 54(2) to make an adverse public interest finding and accepts an undertaking under paragraph 9 of this Schedule or makes an order under paragraph 11 of this Schedule.

(9) For the purpose of this paragraph a reference under section 62(2) is finally determined if—
(a) the time within which the [CMA] is to prepare a report under section 65 in relation to the reference and give it to the Secretary of State has expired and no such report has been so prepared and given;
(b) the time within which the Secretary of State is to make and publish a decision under section 66(2) has expired and no such decision has been made and published;
(c) the Secretary of State decides under subsection (2) of section 66 otherwise than as mentioned in subsection (5) of that section;
(d) the Secretary of State decides under subsection (2) of section 66 as mentioned in subsection (5) of that section but decides neither to accept an undertaking under paragraph 9 of this Schedule nor to make an order under paragraph 11 of this Schedule; or
(e) the Secretary of State decides under subsection (2) of section 66 as mentioned in subsection (5) of that section and accepts an undertaking under paragraph 9 of this Schedule or makes an order under paragraph 11 of this Schedule.

(10) For the purposes of this paragraph the time when a reference under section 45(2) or (3) or (as the case may be) 62(2) is finally determined is—
(a) in a case falling within sub-paragraph (8)(a) or (c) or (as the case may be) (9)(a) or (b), the expiry of the time concerned;
(b) in a case falling within sub-paragraph (8)(b), (d) or (e) or (as the case may be) (9)(c), the making of the decision concerned;
(c) in a case falling within sub-paragraph (8)(f) or (as the case may be) (9)(d), the making of the decision neither to accept an undertaking under paragraph 9 of this Schedule nor to make an order under paragraph 11 of this Schedule; and
(d) in a case falling within sub-paragraph (8)(g) or (as the case may be) (9)(e), the acceptance of the undertaking concerned or (as the case may be) the making of the order concerned.

(11) In this paragraph "relevant person" means—
(a) any person who carries on any enterprise to which the reference relates or who has control of any such enterprise;
(b) any subsidiary of any person falling within paragraph (a); or
(c) any person associated with any person falling within paragraph (a) or any subsidiary of any person so associated.

8. (1) Sub-paragraph (2) applies where—
(a) a reference has been made under section 45(4) or (5) or 62(3); and
[(b) no orders under paragraph 2 are in force in relation to the relevant merger situation concerned or (as the case may be) the special merger situation concerned.]

(2) No relevant person shall, without the consent of the Secretary of State, directly or indirectly acquire during the relevant period an interest in shares in a company if any enterprise to which the reference relates is carried on by or under the control of that company.

(3) The consent of the Secretary of State under sub-paragraph (2)—
(a) may be general or specific;
(b) may be revoked by the Secretary of State; and
(c) shall be published in such manner as the Secretary of State considers appropriate for bringing it to the attention of any person entitled to the benefit of it.

(4) Paragraph (c) of sub-paragraph (3) shall not apply if the Secretary of State considers that publication is not necessary for the purpose mentioned in that paragraph.

(5) Sub-paragraph (2) shall apply to a person's conduct outside the United Kingdom if (and only if) he is—
(a) a United Kingdom national;

(b) a body incorporated under the law of the United Kingdom or of any part of the United Kingdom; or
(c) a person carrying on business in the United Kingdom.

(6) In this paragraph—

"company" includes any body corporate;

"relevant period" means the period beginning with the publication of the decision of the Secretary of State to make the reference concerned and ending when the reference is finally determined;

"relevant person" means—

(a) any person who carries on any enterprise to which the reference relates or who has control of any such enterprise;
(b) any subsidiary of any person falling within paragraph (a); or
(c) any person associated with any person falling within paragraph (a) or any subsidiary of any person so associated; and

"share" means share in the capital of a company, and includes stock.

(7) For the purposes of the definition of "relevant period" in sub-paragraph (6), a reference under section 45(4) or (5) is finally determined if—

(a) the [CMA] cancels the reference under section 48(1) or 53(1);
(b) the time within which the [CMA] is to prepare a report under section 50 in relation to the reference and give it to the Secretary of State has expired and no such report has been so prepared and given;
(c) the time within which the Secretary of State is to make and publish a decision under section 54(2) has expired and no such decision has been made and published;
(d) the Secretary of State decides under section 54(2) to make no finding at all in the matter;
(e) the Secretary of State otherwise decides under section 54(2) not to make an adverse public interest finding;
(f) the Secretary of State decides under section 54(2) to make an adverse public interest finding but decides neither to accept an undertaking under paragraph 9 of this Schedule nor to make an order under paragraph 11 of this Schedule; or
(g) the Secretary of State decides under section 54(2) to make an adverse public interest finding and accepts an undertaking under paragraph 9 of this Schedule or makes an order under paragraph 11 of this Schedule.

(8) For the purposes of the definition of "relevant period" in sub-paragraph (6), a reference under section 62(3) is finally determined if—

(a) the [CMA] cancels the reference under section 64(1);
(b) the time within which the [CMA] is to prepare a report under section 65 in relation to the reference and give it to the Secretary of State has expired and no such report has been so prepared and given;
(c) the time within which the Secretary of State is to make and publish a decision under section 66(2) has expired and no such decision has been made and published;
(d) the Secretary of State decides under subsection (2) of section 66 otherwise than as mentioned in subsection (5) of that section;
(e) the Secretary of State decides under subsection (2) of section 66 as mentioned in subsection (5) of that section but decides neither to accept an undertaking under paragraph 9 of this Schedule nor to make an order under paragraph 11 of this Schedule; or
(f) the Secretary of State decides under subsection (2) of section 66 as mentioned in subsection (5) of that section and accepts an undertaking under paragraph 9 of this Schedule or makes an order under paragraph 11 of this Schedule.

(9) For the purposes of the definition of "relevant period" in sub-paragraph (6) above, the time when a reference under section 45(4) or (5) or (as the case may be) 62(3) is finally determined is—

(a) in a case falling within sub-paragraph (7)(a), (d) or (e) or (as the case may be) (8)(a) or (d), the making of the decision concerned;
(b) in a case falling within sub-paragraph (7)(b) or (c) or (as the case may be) (8)(b) or (c), the expiry of the time concerned;
(c) in a case falling within sub-paragraph (7)(f) or (as the case may be) (8)(e), the making of the decision neither to accept an undertaking under paragraph 9 of this Schedule nor to make an order under paragraph 11 of this Schedule; and
(d) in a case falling within sub-paragraph (7)(g) or (as the case may be) (8)(f), the acceptance of the undertaking concerned or (as the case may be) the making of the order concerned.

(10) Section 79 shall apply for the purposes of paragraph 7 and this paragraph in relation to a reference under section 45 or 62 as it applies for the purposes of sections 77 and 78 in relation to a reference under section 22 or 33.

(11) In its application by virtue of sub-paragraph (10) section 79 shall have effect as if—

(a) subsections (1) and (2) were omitted; and
(b) for the reference in subsection (4) to the [CMA] there were substituted a reference to the Secretary of State.

Final undertakings and orders

9. (1) The Secretary of State may, in accordance with section 55 or (as the case may be) 66(5) to (7), accept, from such persons as he considers appropriate, undertakings to take action specified or described in the undertakings.

(2) An undertaking under this paragraph—

(a) shall come into force when accepted;
(b) may be varied or superseded by another undertaking; and
(c) may be released by the Secretary of State.

(3) An undertaking which is in force under this paragraph in relation to a reference under section 45 or 62 shall cease to be in force if an order under paragraph 6(1)(b) or 10 comes into force in relation to the subject-matter of the undertaking.

(4) No undertaking shall be accepted under this paragraph in relation to a reference under section 45 or 62 if an order has been made under—

(a) paragraph 6(1)(b) or 10 in relation to the subject-matter of the undertaking; or

(b) paragraph 11 in relation to that reference.

(5) The Secretary of State shall, as soon as reasonably practicable, consider any representations received by him in relation to varying or releasing an undertaking under this section.

10. (1) Sub-paragraph (2) applies where the Secretary of State considers that—

(a) an undertaking accepted by him under paragraph 9 has not been, is not being or will not be fulfilled; or

(b) in relation to an undertaking accepted by him under that paragraph, information which was false or misleading in a material respect was given to him or the [CMA] by the person giving the undertaking before he decided to accept the undertaking.

(2) The Secretary of State may, for any purpose mentioned in section 55(2) or (as the case may be) 66(6), make an order under this paragraph.

(3) Subsections (3) and (4) of section 55 or (as the case may be) subsection (7) of section 66 shall apply for the purposes of sub-paragraph (2) above as they or it applies for the purposes of section 55(2) or (as the case may be) 66(6).

(4) An order under this paragraph may contain—

(a) anything permitted by Schedule 8; and

(b) such supplementary, consequential or incidental provision as the Secretary of State considers appropriate.

(5) An order under this paragraph—

(a) shall come into force at such time as is determined by or under the order; and

(b) may contain provision which is different from the provision contained in the undertaking concerned.

(6) No order shall be varied or revoked under this paragraph unless the [CMA] advises that such a variation or revocation is appropriate by reason of a change of circumstances.

11. (1) The Secretary of State may, in accordance with section 55 or (as the case may be) 66(5) to (7), make an order under this paragraph.

(2) An order under this paragraph may contain—

(a) anything permitted by Schedule 8; and

(b) such supplementary, consequential or incidental provision as the Secretary of State considers appropriate.

(3) An order under this paragraph shall come into force at such time as is determined by or under the order.

(4) No order shall be made under this paragraph in relation to a reference under section 45 or (as the case may be) 62 if an undertaking has been accepted under paragraph 9 in relation to that reference.

(5) No order shall be varied or revoked under this paragraph unless the [CMA] advises that such a variation or revocation is appropriate by reason of a change of circumstances.

NOTES

Para 1: repealed by the Enterprise and Regulatory Reform Act 2013, s 30(10), Sch 7, paras 1, 4(1), (2). For various transitional provisions (including those relating to the abolition of the OFT and the Competition Commission, existing references to those bodies and provisions relating to continuity), see the Enterprise and Regulatory Reform Act 2013 (Commencement No 6, Transitional Provisions and Savings) Order 2014, SI 2014/416, Schedule at **[2.13]**.

Para 2 is amended as follows (subject to transitional provisions in SI 2014/416 as noted to para 1 above):

References to the "CMA" in sub-paras (2), (10), (11) substituted by the Enterprise and Regulatory Reform Act 2013, s 26(3), Sch 5, Pt 2, paras 59, 160(1), (2).

Sub-paras (2A)–(2C) inserted by the Enterprise and Regulatory Reform Act 2013, s 30(10), Sch 7, paras 1, 4(1), (3), (4).

In sub-para (4), words omitted repealed, and words in square brackets substituted, by the Enterprise and Regulatory Reform Act 2013, s 30(10), Sch 7, paras 1, 4(1), (5).

Words omitted from sub-para (8) repealed by the Enterprise and Regulatory Reform Act 2013, s 30(10), Sch 7, paras 1, 4(1), (6).

Words in second pair of square brackets in sub-para (10) substituted by the Enterprise and Regulatory Reform Act 2013, s 30(10), Sch 7, paras 1, 4(1), (7).

Sub-para (12) inserted by the Enterprise and Regulatory Reform Act 2013, s 30(10), Sch 7, paras 1, 4(1), (8).

Paras 3–5, 10, 11: references to the "CMA" substituted by the Enterprise and Regulatory Reform Act 2013, s 26(3), Sch 5, Pt 2, paras 59, 160(1), (3)–(5), (8), (9), and subject to transitional provisions in SI 2014/416 as noted to para 1 above.

Paras 7, 8: sub-para (1)(b) substituted, and references to the "CMA" substituted, by the Enterprise and Regulatory Reform Act 2013, ss 26(3), 57, Sch 5, Pt 2, paras 59, 160(1), (6), Sch 15, paras 15, 38 and subject to transitional provisions in SI 2014/416 as noted to para 1 above.

Revocation or modification of licence conditions, etc under certain sectoral enactments: an order under this Schedule may also provide for the revocation or modification of licence conditions, etc, for certain regulated industries; see: (a) the Gas Act 1986, s 27(1); (b) the Electricity Act 1989, s 15(1); (c) the Broadcasting Act 1990(1), s 193; (d) the Water Industry Act 1991, s 17(1); (e) the Railways Act 1993, s 16(1); (f) the Transport Act 2000, s 19(1).

Orders: the Public Interest Merger Reference (Mettis Aerospace Ltd) (Pre-emptive Action) Order 2019, SI 2019/1515; the Public Interest Merger Reference (Cobham Ultra Acquisitions Ltd and Ultra Electronics Holdings plc) (Pre-emptive Action) Order 2021, SI 2021/944; the Public Interest Merger Reference (Perpetuus Advanced Materials plc) (Pre-emptive Action) Order 2021, SI 2021/993.

SCHEDULE 8
PROVISION THAT MAY BE CONTAINED IN CERTAIN ENFORCEMENT ORDERS

Section 86(4)

Introductory

[1.440]

1. This Schedule applies in relation to such orders, and to such extent, as is provided by this Part and Part 4 and any other enactment; and references in this Schedule to an order shall be construed accordingly.

General restrictions on conduct

2. (1) An order may—

(a) prohibit the making or performance of an agreement;

(b) require any party to an agreement to terminate the agreement.

(2) An order made by virtue of sub-paragraph (1) shall not—

(a) prohibit the making or performance of; or

(b) require any person to terminate,

an agreement so far as, if made, the agreement would relate, or (as the case may be) so far as the agreement relates, to the terms and conditions of employment of any workers or to the physical conditions in which any workers are required to work.

3. (1) An order may prohibit the withholding from any person of—

(a) any goods or services;

(b) any orders for any such goods or services.

(2) References in sub-paragraph (1) to withholding include references to—

(a) agreeing or threatening to withhold; and

(b) procuring others to withhold or to agree or threaten to withhold.

4. An order may prohibit requiring as a condition of the supply of goods or services to any person—

(a) the buying of any goods;

(b) the making of any payment in respect of services other than the goods or services supplied;

(c) the doing of any other such matter or the refraining from doing anything mentioned in paragraph (a) or (b) or any other such matter.

5. An order may prohibit—

(a) discrimination between persons in the prices charged for goods or services;

(b) anything which the relevant authority considers to be such discrimination;

(c) procuring others to do anything which is such discrimination or which the relevant authority considers to be such discrimination.

6. An order may prohibit—

(a) giving, or agreeing to give in other ways, any preference in respect of the supply of goods or services or in respect of the giving of orders for goods or services;

(b) giving, or agreeing to give in other ways, anything which the relevant authority considers to be a preference in respect of the supply of goods or services or in respect of the giving of orders for goods or services;

(c) procuring others to do anything mentioned in paragraph (a) or (b).

7. An order may prohibit—

(a) charging, for goods or services supplied, prices differing from those in any published list or notification;

(b) doing anything which the relevant authority considers to be charging such prices.

8. (1) An order may regulate the prices to be charged for any goods or services.

(2) No order shall be made by virtue of sub-paragraph (1) unless the relevant report in relation to the matter concerned identifies the prices charged for the goods or services as requiring remedial action.

(3) In this paragraph "the relevant report" means the report of the [CMA] which is required by the enactment concerned before an order can be made under this Schedule.

9. An order may prohibit the exercise of any right to vote exercisable by virtue of the holding of any shares, stock or securities.

General obligations to be performed

10. (1) An order may require a person to supply goods or services or to do anything which the relevant authority considers appropriate to facilitate the provision of goods or services.

(2) An order may require a person who is supplying, or is to supply, goods or services to supply such goods or services to a particular standard or in a particular manner or to do anything which the relevant authority considers appropriate to facilitate the provision of such goods or services to that standard or in that manner.

11. An order may require any activities to be carried on separately from any other activities.

Acquisitions and divisions

12. (1) An order may prohibit or restrict—

(a) the acquisition by any person of the whole or part of the undertaking or assets of another person's business;

(b) the doing of anything which will or may result in two or more bodies corporate becoming interconnected bodies corporate.

(2) An order may require that if—

(a) an acquisition of the kind mentioned in sub-paragraph (1)(a) is made; or

(b) anything is done which results in two or more bodies corporate becoming interconnected bodies corporate;

the persons concerned or any of them shall observe any prohibitions or restrictions imposed by or under the order.

(3) This paragraph shall also apply to any result consisting in two or more enterprises ceasing to be distinct enterprises (other than any result consisting in two or more bodies corporate becoming interconnected bodies corporate).

13. (1) An order may provide for—

(a) the division of any business (whether by the sale of any part of the undertaking or assets or otherwise);

(b) the division of any group of interconnected bodies corporate.

(2) For the purposes of sub-paragraph (1)(a) all the activities carried on by way of business by any one person or by any two or more interconnected bodies corporate may be treated as a single business.

(3) An order made by virtue of this paragraph may contain such provision as the relevant authority considers appropriate to effect or take account of the division, including, in particular, provision as to—

(a) the transfer or creation of property, rights, liabilities or obligations;

(b) the number of persons to whom the property, rights, liabilities or obligations are to be transferred or in whom they are to be vested;

(c) the time within which the property, rights, liabilities or obligations are to be transferred or vested;

(d) the adjustment of contracts (whether by discharge or reduction of any liability or obligation or otherwise);

(e) the creation, allotment, surrender or cancellation of any shares, stock or securities;

(f) the formation or winding up of any company or other body of persons corporate or unincorporate;

(g) the amendment of the [articles] or other instruments regulating any such company or other body of persons;

(h) the extent to which, and the circumstances in which, provisions of the order affecting a company or other body of persons corporate or unincorporate in its share capital, constitution or other matters may be altered by the company or other body of persons concerned;

(i) the registration of the order under any enactment by a company or other body of persons corporate or unincorporate which is affected by it as mentioned in paragraph (h);

(j) the continuation, with any necessary change of parties, of any legal proceedings;

(k) the approval by the relevant authority or another person of anything required by virtue of the order to be done or of any person to whom anything is to be transferred, or in whom anything is to be vested, by virtue of the order; or

(l) the appointment of trustees or other persons to do anything on behalf of another person which is required of that person by virtue of the order or to monitor the doing by that person of any such thing.

14. The references in paragraph 13 to the division of a business as mentioned in sub-paragraph (1)(a) of that paragraph shall, in the case of an order under section 75, 83, 84, 160 or 161, or an order under paragraph 5, 10 or 11 of Schedule 7, be construed as including references to the separation, by the sale of any part of any undertaking or assets concerned or other means, of enterprises which are under common control (within the meaning of section 26) otherwise than by reason of their being enterprises of interconnected bodies corporate.

Supply and publication of information

15. . . .

16. An order may prohibit any person from notifying (whether by publication or otherwise) to persons supplying goods or services prices recommended or suggested as appropriate to be charged by those persons for those goods or services.

17. (1) An order may require a person supplying goods or services to publish [or otherwise notify]—

(a) accounting information in relation to the supply of the goods or services;

(b) information in relation to the quantities of goods or services supplied;

(c) information in relation to the geographical areas in which they are supplied;

[(d) information in relation to prices of the goods or services supplied;

(e) such other information in relation to the goods or services supplied as the relevant authority considers appropriate].

[(1A) An order may prohibit the publication or other notification of information falling within sub-paragraph (1)(a) to (e) by a person supplying goods or services.]

(2) In sub-paragraph (1) "accounting information", in relation to a supply of goods or services, means information as to—

(a) the costs of the supply, including fixed costs and overheads;

(b) the manner in which fixed costs and overheads are calculated and apportioned for accounting purposes of the supplier; and

(c) the income attributable to the supply.

18. An order made by virtue of paragraph . . . 17 may provide for the manner in which information is to be published or otherwise notified.

19. An order may—

(a) require any person to supply information to the relevant authority;

(b) where the [CMA] is not the relevant authority, require any person to supply information to the [CMA];

(c) provide for the publication, by the person who has received information by virtue of paragraph (a) or (b), of that information.

National security

20. (1) An order may make such provision as the person making the order considers to be appropriate in the interests of national security *(within the meaning of section 58(1))*.

(2) Such provision may, in particular, include provision requiring a person to do, or not to do, particular things.

[Newspaper mergers

20A. (1) This paragraph applies in relation to any order—

(a) which is to be made following the giving of—

(i) an intervention notice which mentions a newspaper public interest consideration;

(ii) an intervention notice which mentions any other media public interest consideration in relation to a relevant merger situation in which one of the enterprises ceasing to be distinct is a newspaper enterprise;

(iii) a special intervention notice which mentions a consideration specified in section 58(2A) or (2B); or

(iv) a special intervention notice which, in relation to a special merger situation in which one of the enterprises ceasing to be distinct is a newspaper enterprise, mentions a consideration specified in section 58(2C); and

(b) to which the consideration concerned is still relevant.

(2) The order may make such provision as the person making the order considers to be appropriate in all circumstances of the case.

(3) Such provision may, in particular, include provision requiring a person to do, or not to do, particular things.

(4) Provision made by virtue of this paragraph may, in particular, include provision—

(a) altering the constitution of a body corporate (whether in connection with the appointment of directors, the establishment of an editorial board or otherwise);

(b) requiring the agreement of the relevant authority or another person before the taking of particular action (including the appointment or dismissal of an editor, journalists or directors or acting as a shadow director);

(c) attaching conditions to the operation of a newspaper;

(d) prohibiting consultation or co-operation between subsidiaries.

(5) In this paragraph "newspaper public interest consideration" means a media public interest consideration other than one which is such a consideration—

(a) by virtue of section 58(2C); or

(b) by virtue of having been, in the opinion of the Secretary of State, concerned with broadcasting and a consideration that ought to have been specified in section 58.

(6) This paragraph is without prejudice to the operation of the other paragraphs of this Schedule in relation to the order concerned.]

[Maintaining the stability of the UK financial system

20B. (1) This paragraph applies for the purposes of a relevant order under paragraph 5, 10 or 11 of Schedule 7 (enforcement orders in cases relating to the stability of the UK financial system) but not for any other purposes of Part 3 or 4 or any other enactment.

(2) The order may make such provision as the person making the order considers to be appropriate in the interest of maintaining the stability of the UK financial system.

(3) Such provision may, in particular, include provision requiring a person to do, or not to do, particular things.

(4) This paragraph is without prejudice to the operation of the other paragraphs of this Schedule in relation to the order.

(5) In this paragraph "relevant order" means an order—

(a) which is to be made following the giving of an intervention notice or special intervention notice which mentions the consideration specified in section 58(2D) (including, in the case of a notice given before the consideration was so specified, an intervention notice which mentions the consideration as a consideration which ought to be specified in section 58); and

(b) to which the consideration is still relevant.]

[Maintaining the capability to combat etc public health emergencies

20BA. (1) This paragraph applies for the purposes of a relevant order under paragraph 5, 10 or 11 of Schedule 7 (enforcement orders in cases relating to maintaining the capability to combat etc public health emergencies) but not for any other purposes of this Part or Part 4 or any other enactment.

(2) The order may make such provision as the person making the order considers to be appropriate for the purpose of maintaining in the United Kingdom the capability to combat, or to mitigate the effects of, public health emergencies.

(3) Such provision may, in particular, include provision requiring a person to do, or not to do, particular things.

(4) This paragraph is without prejudice to the operation of the other paragraphs of this Schedule in relation to the order.

(5) In this paragraph "relevant order" means an order—

(a) which is to be made following the giving of an intervention notice or special intervention notice which mentions the consideration specified in section 58(2E); and

(b) to which the consideration is still relevant.]

[Monitoring of compliance and determination of disputes

20C. (1) An order may provide for the appointment of one or more than one person (referred to in this paragraph as an "appointee") by the relevant authority or by such other persons as may be specified or described in the order to—

(a) monitor compliance with such terms of the order as are so specified or described or terms of any directions given under the order;

(b) determine any dispute between persons who are subject to the order about what is required by any such terms.

(2) An order made by virtue of this paragraph must make provision as to the terms of an appointee's appointment.

(3) A determination made by virtue of an order under this paragraph is binding on—

(a) any person who is subject to the order;

(b) the relevant authority; and

(c) in the case where the relevant authority is the Secretary of State, the CMA.]

Supplementary

21. (1) An order, as well as making provision in relation to all cases to which it may extend, may make provision in relation to—

(a) those cases subject to specified exceptions; or

(b) any particular case or class of case.

(2) An order may, in relation to the cases in relation to which it applies, make the full provision which may be made by it or any less provision (whether by way of exception or otherwise).

(3) An order may make provision for matters to be determined under the order.

(4) An order may—

(a) make different provision for different cases or classes of case or different purposes;

(b) make such transitional, transitory or saving provision as the person making it considers appropriate.

22. (1) An order which may prohibit the doing of anything (or the refraining from doing anything) may in particular by virtue of paragraph 21(2) prohibit the doing of that thing (or the refraining from doing of it) except to such extent and in such circumstances as may be provided by or under the order.

(2) Any such order may, in particular, prohibit the doing of that thing (or the refraining from doing of it)—

(a) without the agreement of the relevant authority or another person; or

(b) by or in relation to a person who has not been approved by the relevant authority or another person.

Interpretation

23. References in this Schedule to the notification of prices or other information are not limited to the notification in writing of prices or other information.

24. In this Schedule "the relevant authority" means—

(a) . . .

(b) in the case of an order to be made by the [CMA], the [CMA]; and

(c) in the case of an order to be made by the Secretary of State, the Secretary of State.

NOTES

Para 8: reference to the "CMA" in sub-para (3) substituted by the Enterprise and Regulatory Reform Act 2013, s 26(3), Sch 5, Pt 2, paras 59, 161(1), (2). For various transitional provisions (including those relating to the abolition of the OFT and the Competition Commission, existing references to those bodies and provisions relating to continuity), see the Enterprise and Regulatory Reform Act 2013 (Commencement No 6, Transitional Provisions and Savings) Order 2014, SI 2014/416, Schedule at **[2.13]**.

Para 13: word in square brackets in sub-para (3)(g) substituted by the Companies Act 2006 (Consequential Amendments, Transitional Provisions and Savings) Order 2009, SI 2009/1941, art 2(1), Sch 1, para 199(1), (5).

Para 15: repealed by the Enterprise and Regulatory Reform Act 2013, s 50(1), (2), subject to transitional provisions in SI 2014/416 as noted above.

Para 17: words in first pair of square brackets in sub-para (1) inserted, sub-paras (1)(d), (e) inserted, and sub-para (1A) inserted, by the Enterprise and Regulatory Reform Act 2013, s 50(1), (3)–(5), subject to transitional provisions in SI 2014/416 as noted above.

Para 18: words omitted repealed by the Enterprise and Regulatory Reform Act 2013, s 50(1), (6), subject to transitional provisions in SI 2014/416 as noted above.

Para 19: references to the "CMA" substituted by the Enterprise and Regulatory Reform Act 2013, s 26(3), Sch 5, Pt 2, paras 59, 161(1), (3), subject to transitional provisions in SI 2014/416 as noted above.

Para 20: the words "(within the meaning of section 58(1))" in italics in sub-para (1) are repealed by the National Security and Investment Act 2021, s 58, Sch 2, para 10, as from a day to be appointed.

Para 20A: inserted, together with preceding heading, by the Communications Act 2003, s 387.

Para 20B: inserted, together with preceding heading, by the Enterprise Act 2002 (Specification of Additional Section 58 Consideration) Order 2008, SI 2008/2645, art 4.

Para 20BA: inserted, together with preceding heading, by the Enterprise Act 2002 (Specification of Additional Section 58 Consideration) Order 2020, SI 2020/627, art 3.

Para 20C: inserted, together with preceding heading, by the Enterprise and Regulatory Reform Act 2013, s 49, subject to transitional provisions in SI 2014/416 as noted above.

Para 24: sub-para (a) repealed, and references to the "CMA" in sub-para (b) substituted, by the Enterprise and Regulatory Reform Act 2013, s 26(3), Sch 5, Pt 2, paras 59, 161(1), (4), subject to transitional provisions in SI 2014/416 as noted above.

SCHEDULE 9

(Sch 9 (amendments of sectoral enactments) outside the scope of this work.)

SCHEDULE 10
PROCEDURAL REQUIREMENTS FOR CERTAIN ENFORCEMENT UNDERTAKINGS AND ORDERS

Section 90

Requirements for accepting undertakings and making orders

[1.441]

1. Paragraph 2 applies in relation to—

(a) any undertaking under section 73 or 82 or paragraph 3 or 9 of Schedule 7 (other than an undertaking under the enactment concerned which varies an undertaking under that enactment but not in any material respect); and

(b) any order under section 75, 83 or 84 or paragraph 5, 10 or 11 of Schedule 7 (other than an order under the enactment concerned which is a revoking order of the kind dealt with by paragraphs 6 to 8 below).

2. (1) Before accepting an undertaking to which this paragraph applies or making an order to which this paragraph applies, [the CMA] or (as the case may be) the Secretary of State (in this Schedule "the relevant authority") shall—

(a) give notice of the proposed undertaking or (as the case may be) order; and

(b) consider any representations made in accordance with the notice and not withdrawn.

(2) A notice under sub-paragraph (1) shall state—

(a) that the relevant authority proposes to accept the undertaking or (as the case may be) make the order;

(b) the purpose and effect of the undertaking or (as the case may be) order;

(c) the situation that the undertaking or (as the case may be) order is seeking to deal with;

(d) any other facts which the relevant authority considers justify the acceptance of the undertaking or (as the case may be) the making of the order;

(e) a means of gaining access to an accurate version of the proposed undertaking or (as the case may be) order at all reasonable times; and

(f) the period (not less than 15 days starting with the date of publication of the notice in the case of an undertaking and not less than 30 days starting with that date in the case of an order) within which representations may be made in relation to the proposed undertaking or (as the case may be) order.

(3) A notice under sub-paragraph (1) shall be given by—

(a) in the case of a proposed order, serving on any person identified in the order as a person on whom a copy of the order should be served a copy of the notice and a copy of the proposed order; and

(b) in every case, publishing the notice.

(4) The relevant authority shall not accept the undertaking with modifications or (as the case may be) make the order with modifications unless the relevant authority—

(a) gives notice of the proposed modifications; and

(b) considers any representations made in accordance with the notice and not withdrawn.

(5) A notice under sub-paragraph (4) shall state—

(a) the proposed modifications;

(b) the reasons for them; and

(c) the period (not less than 7 days starting with the date of the publication of the notice under sub-paragraph (4)) within which representations may be made in relation to the proposed modifications.

(6) A notice under sub-paragraph (4) shall be given by—

(a) in the case of a proposed order, serving a copy of the notice on any person identified in the order as a person on whom a copy of the order should be served; and

(b) in every case, publishing the notice.

3. (1) If, after giving notice under paragraph 2(1) or (4), the relevant authority decides—

(a) not to accept the undertaking concerned or (as the case may be) make the order concerned; and

(b) not to proceed by virtue of paragraph 5;

the relevant authority shall give notice of that decision.

(2) A notice under sub-paragraph (1) shall be given by—

(a) in the case of a proposed order, serving a copy of the notice on any person identified in the order as a person on whom a copy of the order should be served; and

(b) in every case, publishing the notice.

4. As soon as practicable after accepting an undertaking to which paragraph 2 applies or (as the case may be) making an order to which that paragraph applies, the relevant authority shall (except in the case of an order which is a statutory instrument)—

(a) serve a copy of the undertaking on any person by whom it is given or (as the case may be) serve a copy of the order on any person identified in the order as a person on whom a copy of the order should be served; and

(b) publish the undertaking or (as the case may be) the order.

5. (1) The requirements of paragraph 2(4) (and those of paragraph 2(1)) shall not apply if the relevant authority—

(a) has already given notice under paragraph 2(1) but not paragraph 2(4) in relation to the proposed undertaking or order; and

(b) considers that the modifications which are now being proposed are not material in any respect.

(2) The requirements of paragraph 2(4) (and those of paragraph 2(1)) shall not apply if the relevant authority—

(a) has already given notice under paragraphs 2(1) and (4) in relation to the matter concerned; and

(b) considers that the further modifications which are now being proposed do not differ in any material respect from the modifications in relation to which notice was last given under paragraph 2(4).

Termination of undertakings[, commitments] and orders

6. Paragraph 7 applies where the relevant authority is proposing to—

(a) release any undertaking under section 73 or 82 or paragraph 3 or 9 of Schedule 7 (other than in connection with accepting an undertaking under the enactment concerned which varies or supersedes an undertaking under that enactment); or

(b) revoke any order under section 75, 83 or 84 or paragraph 5, 10 or 11 of Schedule 7 (other than in connection with making an order under the enactment concerned which varies or supersedes an order under that enactment).

7. (1) Before releasing an undertaking to which this paragraph applies or (as the case may be) revoking an order to which this paragraph applies, the relevant authority shall—

(a) give notice of the proposed release or (as the case may be) revocation; and
(b) consider any representations made in accordance with the notice and not withdrawn.

(2) A notice under sub-paragraph (1) shall state—
(a) the fact that a release or (as the case may be) revocation is proposed;
(b) the reasons for it; and
(c) the period (not less than 15 days starting with the date of publication of the notice in the case of an undertaking and not less than 30 days starting with that date in the case of an order) within which representations may be made in relation to the proposed release or (as the case may be) revocation.

(3) If after giving notice under sub-paragraph (1) the relevant authority decides not to proceed with the release or (as the case may be) the revocation, the relevant authority shall give notice of that decision.

(4) A notice under sub-paragraph (1) or (3) shall be given by—
(a) serving a copy of the notice on the person who gave the undertaking which is being released or (as the case may be) on any person identified in the order being revoked as a person on whom a copy of the order should be served; and
(b) publishing the notice.

8. As soon as practicable after releasing the undertaking or making the revoking order, the relevant authority shall (except in the case of an order which is a statutory instrument)—
(a) serve a copy of the release of the undertaking on the person who gave the undertaking or (as the case may be) serve a copy of the revoking order on any person identified in the order being revoked as a person on whom a copy of that order should be served; and
(b) publish the release or (as the case may be) the revoking order.

Power to dispense with the requirements of the Schedule

9. The relevant authority may dispense with any or all of the requirements of this Schedule if the relevant authority considers that the relevant authority has special reasons for doing so.

NOTES

The words "the CMA" in square brackets in para 2 were substituted by the Enterprise and Regulatory Reform Act 2013, s 26(3), Sch 5, Pt 2, paras 59, 162. For various transitional provisions (including those relating to the abolition of the OFT and the Competition Commission, existing references to those bodies and provisions relating to continuity), see the Enterprise and Regulatory Reform Act 2013 (Commencement No 6, Transitional Provisions and Savings) Order 2014, SI 2014/416, Schedule at **[2.13]**.

SCHEDULES 11, 12

(Schs 11, 12 amended the Competition Act 1998 Sch 7 and inserted Sch 7A, and were repealed by the Enterprise and Regulatory Reform Act 2013, s 26(3), Sch 5, Pt 3, paras 224, 227, 228, subject to transitional provisions in the Enterprise and Regulatory Reform Act 2013 (Commencement No 6, Transitional Provisions and Savings) Order 2014, SI 2014/416, Schedule at **[2.13]**.)

[SCHEDULE 13
LISTED ENACTMENTS

Sections 210 and 243(12)(c)

[1.442]

1. Sections 9 to 11 of the Supply of Goods (Implied Terms) Act 1973, to the extent that those sections continue to apply to a contract for a trader to supply goods to a consumer by virtue of the saving made, in connection with their amendment by the Consumer Rights Act 2015, by article 6 of the Consumer Rights Act 2015 (Commencement No 3, Transitional Provisions, Savings and Consequential Amendments) Order 2015.

2. The Consumer Credit Act 1974 and secondary legislation made under that Act excluding requirements relating to consumer hire agreements.

3. Sections 6(2), 7(1), 7(2), 20(2), 21 and 27(2) of the Unfair Contract Terms Act 1977, to the extent that those sections remain in force, or continue to apply to a consumer contract, by virtue of the saving made, in connection with their repeal or disapplication by the Consumer Rights Act 2015, by article 6 of the Consumer Rights Act 2015 (Commencement No 3, Transitional Provisions, Savings and Consequential Amendments) Order 2015.

4. Sections 13 to 15, 15B, 20 and 32 of the Sale of Goods Act 1979, to the extent that those sections continue to apply to a contract for a trader to supply goods to a consumer by virtue of the saving made, in connection with their amendment by the Consumer Rights Act 2015, by article 6 of the Consumer Rights Act 2015 (Commencement No 3, Transitional Provisions, Savings and Consequential Amendments) Order 2015.

5. Sections 48A to 48F of the Sale of Goods Act 1979, to the extent that those sections remain in force by virtue of the saving made, in connection with their repeal by the Consumer Rights Act 2015, by article 6 of the Consumer Rights Act 2015 (Commencement No 3, Transitional Provisions, Savings and Consequential Amendments) Order 2015.

6. Sections 3 to 5, 11C to 11E and 13 of the Supply of Goods and Services Act 1982, and any rule of law in Scotland which provides comparable protection to section 13, to the extent that those sections continue to apply to a contract for a trader to supply goods or, in the case of section 13, a contract for a trader to supply a service, to a consumer by virtue of the saving made, in connection with their amendment by the Consumer Rights Act 2015, by article 6 of the Consumer Rights Act 2015 (Commencement No 3, Transitional Provisions, Savings and Consequential Amendments) Order 2015.

7. Sections 11M to 11S of the Supply of Goods and Services Act 1982 to the extent that those sections remain in force by virtue of the saving made, in connection with their repeal by the Consumer Rights Act 2015, by article 6 of the Consumer Rights Act 2015 (Commencement No 3, Transitional Provisions, Savings and Consequential Amendments) Order 2015.

8. The Package Travel, Package Holidays and Package Tours Regulations 1992, to the extent that those Regulations remain in force by virtue of the saving made, in connection with their revocation, by regulation 37(2) of the Package Travel and Linked Travel Arrangements Regulations 2018.

9. The Unfair Terms in Consumer Contracts Regulations 1999, to the extent that those Regulations remain in force by virtue of the saving made, in connection with their revocation by the Consumer Rights Act 2015, by article 6 of the Consumer Rights Act 2015 (Commencement No 3, Transitional Provisions, Savings and Consequential Amendments) Order 2015.

9A. Rules made under sections 137A, 137R and 137T of the Financial Services and Markets Act 2000 which give effect to Articles 10, 11, 13 to 18 and 21 to 23, Chapter 10 and Annexes I and II of Directive 2014/17/EU of the European Parliament and of the Council of 4 February 2014 on credit agreements for consumers relating to residential immovable property and amending Directives 2008/48/EC and 2013/36/EU and Regulation (EU) No 1093/2010.

10. The Consumer Protection (Distance Selling) Regulations 2000, to the extent that those Regulations remain in force for contracts entered into prior to their disapplication by virtue of regulation 2(a) of the Consumer Contracts (Information, Cancellation and Additional Charges) Regulations 2013.

10A. Sections 319, 321, 322, 325, 368F, 368G and 368H of the Communications Act 2003.

11. Regulations 6, 7, 8, 9 and 11 of the Electronic Commerce (EC Directive) Regulations 2002.

12. Regulation 15 of the Sale and Supply of Goods to Consumers Regulations 2002, to the extent that regulation 15 remains in force by virtue of the saving made, in connection with its revocation by the Consumer Rights Act 2015, by article 6 of the Consumer Rights Act 2015 (Commencement No 3, Transitional Provisions, Savings and Consequential Amendments) Order 2015.

13. Regulations 19 to 26, 30 and 32 of the Privacy and Electronic Communications (EC Directive) Regulations 2003.

14. The Price Marking Order 2004.

15. Regulation (EC) No 261/2004 of the European Parliament and of the Council of 11 February 2004 establishing common rules on compensation and assistance to air passengers in the event of denied boarding and of cancellation or long delay of flights.

16. The Financial Services (Distance Marketing) Regulations 2004 and rules corresponding to any provisions of those Regulations made by the Financial Conduct Authority or a designated professional body within the meaning of section 326(2) of the Financial Services and Markets Act 2000.

17. The Price Marking Order (Northern Ireland) 2004.

18. The Civil Aviation (Denied Boarding, Compensation and Assistance) Regulations 2005.

18A. Regulation (EC) No 1107/2006 of the European Parliament and of the Council of 5 July 2006 concerning the rights of disabled persons and persons with reduced mobility when travelling by air.

18B. Regulation (EC) No 1371/2007 of the European Parliament and of the Council of 23 October 2007 on rail passengers' rights and obligations.

18C. Regulations 2, 4, 13, 15 and 18 of the Business Protection from Misleading Marketing Regulations 2008.

19. The Consumer Protection from Unfair Trading Regulations 2008.

20. The Cancellation of Contracts made in a Consumer's Home or Place of Work etc Regulations 2008, to the extent that those Regulations remain in force for contracts entered into prior to their disapplication by regulation 2(b) of the Consumer Contracts (Information, Cancellation and Additional Charges) Regulations 2013.

20A. Article 23 of Regulation (EC) No 1008/2008 of the European Parliament and of the Council of 24 September 2008 on common rules for the operation of air services in the Community.

21. The Provision of Services Regulations 2009.

21A. The Rail Passengers' Rights and Obligations Regulations 2010.

21B. Regulation (EU) No 1177/2010 of the European Parliament and of the Council of 24 November 2010 concerning the rights of passengers when travelling by sea and inland waterway and amending Regulation (EC) No 2006/2004.

22. The Timeshare, Holiday Products, Resale and Exchange Contracts Regulations 2010.

22A. Regulation (EU) No 181/2011 of the European Parliament and of the Council of 16 February 2011 concerning the rights of passengers in bus and coach transport and amending Regulation (EC) No 2006/2004.

23. Chapters 1 and 2 of Part 14 of the Human Medicines Regulations 2012.

24. Regulations 4 and 6A to 10 of the Consumer Rights (Payment Surcharges) Regulations 2012.

24A. The Merchant Shipping (Passengers' Rights) Regulations 2013.

24B. The Operation of Air Services in the Community (Pricing etc) Regulations 2013.

24C. The Rights of Passengers in Bus and Coach Transport (Exemptions and Enforcement) Regulations 2013.

25. The Consumer Contracts (Information, Cancellation and Additional Charges) Regulations 2013.

25A. The Bus and Coach Passengers Rights and Obligations (Designation and Enforcement) Regulations (Northern Ireland) 2014.

25B. The Bus and Coach Passengers Rights and Obligations (Designation of Terminals, Tour Operators and Enforcement) Regulations (Northern Ireland) 2014.

25C. The Civil Aviation (Access to Air Travel for Disabled Persons and Persons with Reduced Mobility) Regulations 2014.

26. Regulation 19(1) and (2) of the Alternative Dispute Resolution for Consumer Disputes (Competent Authorities and Information) Regulations 2015.

27. Sections 2, 3, 5, 9 to 15, 19, 23, 24, 28 to 32, 36(3) and (4), 37, 38, 42, 50, 54, 58, 59, 61 to 64, 67 to 70, 72 to 74 of, and Schedules 2 and 3 and Part 3 of Schedule 5 to, the Consumer Rights Act 2015.

28. Article 10(4) of Regulation (EU) 2015/751 of the European Parliament and of the Council of 29 April 2015 on interchange fees for card-based payment transactions.

28A. Parts 2 and 3 and regulations 18, 19, 20(1), 20(3) to 20(5), 21 to 25, 27(2) and 27(3) of, and Schedules 1 to 6 to, the Payment Accounts Regulations 2015.

28B. The Rail Passengers Rights and Obligations (Designation and Enforcement) Regulations (Northern Ireland) 2017.

29. The Package Travel and Linked Travel Arrangements Regulations 2018.]

NOTES

Commencement: IP completion day (as defined in the European Union (Withdrawal Agreement) Act 2020, s 39).

This Schedule was substituted by the Consumer Protection (Enforcement) (Amendment etc) (EU Exit) Regulations 2019, SI 2019/203, reg 3(20), as from IP completion day (as defined in the European Union (Withdrawal Agreement) Act 2020, s 39). Note that reg 3(20) of the 2019 Regulations was amended by the Consumer Protection (Enforcement) (Amendment etc) (EU Exit) Regulations 2020, SI 2020/1347 (with effect from immediately before IP completion day); and the effect of the amendments has been incorporated in the text set out above.

SCHEDULE 14
SPECIFIED FUNCTIONS

Sections 238 and 243

[1.443]

Trade Descriptions Act 1968 (c 29).

[Parts 1, . . . , 3, 4, 5, 6, 7, 8 and 11 of the Fair Trading Act 1973 (c 41).]

[Hallmarking Act 1973 (c 43).]

Prices Act 1974 (c 24).

Consumer Credit Act 1974 (c 39).

[Customs and Excise Management Act 1979 (c 12).]

Estate Agents Act 1979 (c 38).

Competition Act 1980 (c 21).

[Video Recordings Act 1984 (c 39).]

Consumer Protection Act 1987 (c 43).

[Consumer Protection (Northern Ireland) Order 1987 (SI 1987/2049 (NI 20)).]

[Copyright, Designs and Patents Act 1988 (c 48).]

. . .

. . .

[Clean Air Act 1993 (c 11).]

[Value Added Tax Act 1994 (c 23).]

[Trade Marks Act 1994 (c 26).]

Competition Act 1998 (c 41).

[Chapter 4 of Part 9A] of the Financial Services and Markets Act 2000 (c 8).

An order made under section 95 of that Act.

[Fireworks Act 2003 (c 22).]

[. . .]

[Consumers, Estate Agents and Redress Act 2007.]

[Groceries Code Adjudicator Act 2013.]

[Parts 3 and 4 of the Enterprise and Regulatory Reform Act 2013.]

[Chapter 5 of Part 3 of the Consumer Rights Act 2015.]

[Schedule 3 to the Consumer Rights Act 2015.]

[Paragraph 13(2), (3) or (7) of Schedule 5 to the Consumer Rights Act 2015.]

[Part 4 of the Small Business, Enterprise and Employment Act 2015.]

[Part 4 of the United Kingdom Internal Market Act 2020.]

NOTES

Entry relating to the "Fair Trading Act 1973" substituted, and entries relating to the "Hallmarking Act 1973", the "Video Recordings Act 1984", the "Consumer Protection (Northern Ireland) Order 1987", the "Copyright, Designs and Patents Act 1988", the "Clean Air Act 1993", and the "Trade Marks Act 1994" inserted, by the Enterprise Act 2002 (Part 9 Restrictions on Disclosure of Information) (Amendment and Specification) Order 2003, SI 2003/1400, art 3, Sch 1.

Figure omitted from entry relating to the "Fair Trading Act 1973" repealed by the Consumer Protection from Unfair Trading Regulations 2008, SI 2008/1277, reg 30(3), Sch 4, Pt 1.

Entries relating to the "Customs and Excise Management Act 1979" and the "Value Added Tax Act 1994" inserted by the Enterprise Act 2002 (Part 9 Restrictions on Disclosure of Information) (Amendment and Specification) (No 2) Order 2003, SI 2003/2580, art 3, Sch 1.

Entry relating to "Property Misdescriptions Act 1991" (omitted) repealed by the Property Misdescriptions Act 1991 (Repeal) Order 2013, SI 2013/1575, art 3, Schedule, Pt 1, paras 8, 10.

Entry relating to the "Timeshare Act 1992" (omitted) repealed by the Timeshare, Holiday Products, Resale and Exchange Contracts Regulations 2010, SI 2010/2960, reg 36(3), (5), Sch 6, para 3(1), (3), Sch 8, Pt 1.

Words in square brackets in the entry relating to the "Financial Services and Markets Act 2000" substituted by the Financial Services Act 2012, s 114(1), Sch 18, Pt 2, para 95(1), (3).

Entry relating to the "Fireworks Act 2003" inserted by the Fireworks Act 2003, s 12(3).

Entry relating to the "Compensation Act 2006" (omitted) originally inserted by the Enterprise Act 2002 (Part 9 Restrictions on Disclosure of Information) (Amendment and Specification) Order 2007, SI 2007/2977, art 2(1), (2), and subsequently repealed by the Financial Services and Markets Act 2000 (Claims Management Activity) Order 2018, SI 2018/1253, art 92(a).

Entry relating to the "Consumers, Estate Agents and Redress Act 2007" inserted by the Consumers, Estate Agents and Redress Act 2007, s 29(1).

Entry relating to the "Groceries Code Adjudicator Act 2013" inserted by the Groceries Code Adjudicator Act 2013, s 21(4).

Entry relating to the "Enterprise and Regulatory Reform Act 2013" inserted by the Enterprise and Regulatory Reform Act 2013 (Competition) (Consequential, Transitional and Saving Provisions) Order 2014, SI 2014/892, art 2, Sch 1, Pt 1, paras 1, 17, subject to transitional provisions as noted to s 8A at **[1.187]**.

Entries relating to "Chapter 5 of Part 3 of the Consumer Rights Act 2015" and "Schedule 3 to the Consumer Rights Act 2015" inserted by the Consumer Rights Act 2015 (Consequential Amendments) Order 2015, SI 2015/1726, art 2, Schedule, Pt 1, paras 2, 3.

Entry relating to "Paragraph 13(2), (3) or (7) of Schedule 5 to the Consumer Rights Act 2015" inserted by the Consumer Rights Act 2015, s 77(2), Sch 6, paras 67, 81.

Entry relating to "Part 4 of the Small Business, Enterprise and Employment Act 2015" inserted by the Small Business, Enterprise and Employment Act 2015, s 41(4), Sch 1, Pt 3, para 26.

Entry relating to "Part 4 of the United Kingdom Internal Market Act 2020" inserted by the United Kingdom Internal Market Act 2020, s 41(10), as from 14 June 2021.

See also the EEC Merger Control (Distinct Market Investigations) Regulations 1990, SI 1990/1715, art 5 at **[2.83]** (Part 9 of this Act to have effect as if the 1990 Regulations were contained in Part 3 of this Act). Note that the 1990 Regulations were revoked by the Competition (Amendment etc) (EU Exit) Regulations 2019, SI 2019/93, reg 61, Sch 2, Pt 3, para 9, as from IP completion day (as defined in the European Union (Withdrawal Agreement) Act 2020, s 39). For transitional provisions and savings in relation to the operation of the 2019 Regulations, see Sch 4 to those Regulations at **[7.69]** et seq and see, in particular, Sch 4, Pt 7, para 35B to the 2019 Regulations at **[7.76]**.

Fair Trading Act 1973: most of this Act has now been repealed: see further the 1973 Act at **[1.1]**.

SCHEDULE 15
ENACTMENTS CONFERRING FUNCTIONS

Section 241

[1.444]

Gun Barrel Proof Act 1868 (c cxiii).

Gun Barrel Proof Act 1950 (c iii).

Trade Descriptions Act 1968.

Unsolicited Goods and Services Act 1971 (c 30).

Fair Trading Act 1973.

Hallmarking Act 1973 (c 43).

Prices Act 1974.

[the relevant statutory provisions within the meaning of Part I of the Health and Safety at Work etc Act 1974 (c 37).]

Consumer Credit Act 1974.

[Unsolicited Goods and Services (Northern Ireland) Order 1976 (SI 1976/57 (NI 1)).]

Gun Barrel Proof Act 1978 (c 9).

[the relevant statutory provisions within the meaning of the Health and Safety at Work (Northern Ireland) Order 1978 (SI 1978/1039 (NI 9)).]

Estate Agents Act 1979.

Competition Act 1980.

[Weights and Measures (Northern Ireland) Order 1981 (SI 1981/231 (NI 10)).]

National Audit Act 1983 (c 44).

Telecommunications Act 1984 (c 12).

[Video Recordings Act 1984 (c 39).]

. . .

Weights and Measures Act 1985 (c 72).

Airports Act 1986 (c 31).

Gas Act 1986 (c 44).

[Insolvency Act 1986 (c 45).]

[Company Directors Disqualification Act 1986 (c 46).]

Financial Services Act 1986 (c 60).

[. . .]

Consumer Protection Act 1987 (c 43).

[Consumer Protection (Northern Ireland) Order 1987 (SI 1987/2049 (NI 20)).]

[Banking Act 1987 (c 22).]

[Education Reform Act 1988 (c 40).]

Copyright, Designs and Patents Act 1988 (c 48).

[Education (Unrecognised Degrees) (Northern Ireland) Order 1988 (SI 1988/1989 (NI 22)).]

Water Act 1989 (c 15).

Electricity Act 1989 (c 29).

[Companies Act 1989 (c 40).]

[. . .]

[Insolvency (Northern Ireland) Order 1989 (SI 1989/2405 (NI 19)).]

[. . .]

[Companies No 2 (Northern Ireland) Order 1990 (SI 1990/1504 (NI 10)).]

Courts and Legal Services Act 1990 (c 41).

Broadcasting Act 1990 (c 42).

. . .

Water Industry Act 1991 (c 56).

Water Resources Act 1991 (c 57).

. . .

Land Drainage Act 1991 (c 59).

[Water Consolidation (Consequential Provisions) Act 1991 (c 60).]

. . .

[Electricity (Northern Ireland) Order 1992 (SI 1992/231 (NI 1)).]

[Clean Air Act 1993 (c 11).]

Railways Act 1993 (c 43).

Coal Industry Act 1994 (c 21).

Trade Marks Act 1994 (c 26).

[Part IV of the Airports (Northern Ireland) Order 1994 (SI 1994/426 (NI 1)).]

Gas Act 1995 (c 45).

Broadcasting Act 1996 (c 55).

[Gas (Northern Ireland) Order 1996 (SI 1996/275 (NI 2)).]

Competition Act 1998 (c 41).

Financial Services and Markets Act 2000 (c 8).

Government Resources and Accounts Act 2000 (c 20).

Postal Services Act 2000 (c 26).

Utilities Act 2000 (c 27).

[Transport Act 2000 (c 38).]

[Company Directors Disqualification (Northern Ireland) Order 2002 (SI 2002/3150 (NI 4)).]

[Communications Act 2003 (c 21).]

[Fireworks Act 2003 (c 22).]

[Water Act 2003 (c 37).]

[Railways Act 2005 (c 14).]

[Gambling Act 2005 (c 19).]

[. . .

Wireless Telegraphy Act 2006 (c 36).]

[Water and Sewerage Services (Northern Ireland) Order 2006.]

[Consumers, Estate Agents and Redress Act 2007.]

[the Companies Acts (as defined in section 2 of the Companies Act 2006).]

[Postal Services Act 2011.]

[Airport Charges Regulations 2011.]

[Electronic Money Regulations 2011.]

[Civil Aviation Act 2012.]

[Consumer Rights (Payment Surcharges) Regulations 2012.]

[Health and Social Care Act 2012.]

[Groceries Code Adjudicator Act 2013.]

[Parts 3 and 4 of the Enterprise and Regulatory Reform Act 2013.]

[Financial Services (Banking Reform) Act 2013.]

[the relevant statutory provisions within the meaning of Part 3 of the Energy Act 2013 (c 32).]

[Water Act 2014.]

[Chapter 5 of Part 3 of the Consumer Rights Act 2015.]

[Schedule 3 to the Consumer Rights Act 2015.]

[Part 4 of the Small Business, Enterprise and Employment Act 2015.]

[Payment Card Interchange Fee Regulations 2015.]

[Payment Services Regulations 2017.]

NOTES

Entry relating to "Property Misdescriptions Act 1991" (omitted) repealed by the Property Misdescriptions Act 1991 (Repeal) Order 2013, SI 2013/1575, art 3, Schedule, Pt 1, paras 8, 11.

Entry relating to the "Statutory Water Companies Act 1991" (omitted) repealed by the Deregulation Act 2015, s 107, Sch 23, Pt 5, para 28(6).

Entry relating to the "Timeshare Act 1992" (omitted) repealed by the Timeshare, Holiday Products, Resale and Exchange Contracts Regulations 2010, SI 2010/2960, reg 36(3), (5), Sch 6, para 3(1), (4), Sch 8, Pt 1.

Entry relating to the "Transport Act 2000" substituted by the Enterprise Act 2002 (Part 9 Restrictions on Disclosure of Information) (Amendment and Specification) Order 2003, SI 2003/1400, art 4, Sch 2, paras 1, 17.

Entry relating to the "Communications Act 2003" inserted by the Communications Act 2003, s 406(1), Sch 17, para 174(1), (7).

Entry relating to the "Fireworks Act 2003" inserted by the Fireworks Act 2003, s 12(3).

Entry relating to the "Water Act 2003" inserted by the Water Act 2003, s 101(1), Sch 7, Pt 2, para 36(1), (4).

Entry relating to the "Railways Act 2005" inserted by the Railways Act 2005, s 59(1), Sch 12, para 18(1), (4).

Entries relating to the "Companies Act 1985" and the "Companies (Northern Ireland) Order 1986" (omitted) repealed, and entry relating to "the Companies Acts (as defined in section 2 of the Companies Act 2006)" inserted, by the Companies Act 2006 (Commencement No 3, Consequential Amendments, Transitional Provisions and Savings) Order 2007, SI 2007/2194, art 10(1), (2), Sch 4, Pt 3, para 98.

Entries relating to the "Companies (Northern Ireland) Order 1989" and the "Companies (Northern Ireland) Order 1990" (omitted) repealed by the Companies Act 2006 (Consequential Amendments, Transitional Provisions and Savings) Order 2009, SI 2009/1941, art 2(1), Sch 1, para 199(1), (6).

Entry relating to the "Gambling Act 2005" inserted by the Enterprise Act 2002 (Part 9 Restrictions on Disclosure of Information) (Amendment) Order 2006, SI 2006/2909, art 2.

Entry relating to the "Compensation Act 2006" (omitted) originally inserted by the Enterprise Act 2002 (Part 9 Restrictions on Disclosure of Information) (Amendment and Specification) Order 2007, SI 2007/2977, art 2(1), (3), and subsequently repealed by the Financial Services and Markets Act 2000 (Claims Management Activity) Order 2018, SI 2018/1253, art 92(b).

Entry relating to the "Wireless Telegraphy Act 2006" inserted by SI 2007/2977, art 2(1), (3).

Entry relating to the "Water and Sewerage Services (Northern Ireland) Order 2006" inserted by the Water and Sewerage Services (Northern Ireland) Order 2006, SI 2006/3336, art 308(1), Sch 12, para 46(6).

Entry relating to the "Consumers, Estate Agents and Redress Act 2007" inserted by the Consumers, Estate Agents and Redress Act 2007, s 29(2).

Entry relating to "Postal Services Act 2011" inserted by the Postal Services Act 2011, s 91(1), (2), Sch 12, Pt 3, paras 163, 166.

Entry relating to the "Airport Charges Regulations 2011" inserted by the Airport Charges Regulations 2011, SI 2011/2491, reg 31, Sch 3, para 6.

Entry relating to the "Electronic Money Regulations 2011" inserted by the Payment Services Regulations 2017, SI 2017/752, reg 156, Sch 8, Pt 1, para 3(b)(i).

Entry relating to the "Civil Aviation Act 2012" inserted by the Civil Aviation Act 2012, s 76(4), Sch 9, paras 13, 15.

Entry relating to the "Consumer Rights (Payment Surcharges) Regulations 2012" inserted by SI 2017/752, reg 156, Sch 8, Pt 1, para 3(b)(ii)7.

Entry relating to the "Health and Social Care Act 2012" inserted by the Enterprise and Regulatory Reform Act 2013, s 57, Sch 15, paras 15, 39.

Entry relating to the "Groceries Code Adjudicator Act 2013" inserted by the Groceries Code Adjudicator Act 2013, s 21(4).

Entry relating to the "Enterprise and Regulatory Reform Act 2013" inserted by the Enterprise and Regulatory Reform Act 2013 (Competition) (Consequential, Transitional and Saving Provisions) Order 2014, SI 2014/892, art 2, Sch 1, Pt 1, paras 1, 17, subject to transitional provisions as noted to s 8A at **[1.187]**.

Entry relating to the "Energy Act 2013" inserted by the Energy Act 2013 (Office for Nuclear Regulation) (Consequential Amendments, Transitional Provisions and Savings) Order 2014, SI 2014/469, art 6(1), Sch 2, para 22.

Entry relating to the "Financial Services (Banking Reform) Act 2013" inserted by the Enterprise Act 2002 (Part 9 Restrictions on Disclosure of Information) (Amendment) Order 2014, SI 2014/2807, art 2.

Entry relating to "Water Act 2014" inserted by the Water Act 2014 (Consequential Amendments etc) Order 2017, SI 2017/506, art 14.

Entry relating to "Chapter 5 of Part 3 of the Consumer Rights Act 2015" inserted by the Consumer Rights Act 2015 (Consequential Amendments) Order 2015, SI 2015/1726, art 2, Schedule, Pt 1, paras 2, 4.

Entry relating to "Schedule 3 to the Consumer Rights Act 2015" inserted by the Consumer Rights Act 2015, s 75, Sch 4, para 35.

Entry relating to the "Small Business, Enterprise and Employment Act 2015" inserted by the Small Business, Enterprise and Employment Act 2015, s 41(4), Sch 1, Pt 3, para 26.

Entry relating to the "Payment Card Interchange Fee Regulations 2015" inserted by the Payment Card Interchange Fee Regulations 2015, SI 2015/1911, reg 18(1), (3).

Entry relating to the "Payment Services Regulations 2017." inserted by SI 2017/752, reg 156, Sch 8, Pt 1, para 3(b)(iii).

Other entries in square brackets inserted by SI 2003/1400, art 4, Sch 2, paras 1–16, 18.

See also the EEC Merger Control (Distinct Market Investigations) Regulations 1990, SI 1990/1715, art 5 at **[2.83]** (Part 9 of this Act to have effect as if the 1990 Regulations were contained in Part 3 of this Act). Note that the 1990 Regulations were revoked by the Competition (Amendment etc) (EU Exit) Regulations 2019, SI 2019/93, reg 61, Sch 2, Pt 3, para 9, as from IP completion day (as defined in the European Union (Withdrawal Agreement) Act 2020, s 39). For transitional provisions and savings in relation to the operation of the 2019 Regulations, see Sch 4 to those Regulations at **[7.69]** et seq and see, in particular, Sch 4, Pt 7, para 35B to the 2019 Regulations at **[7.76]**..

Financial Services Act 1986; Banking Act 1987: repealed by SI 2001/3949.

SCHEDULES 16–23

(Schs 16–23 (insolvency provisions) outside the scope of this work.)

SCHEDULE 24
TRANSITIONAL AND TRANSITORY PROVISIONS AND SAVINGS

Section 276

[1.445]

1. . . .

Pensions etc of former Directors

2. In the case of any such person who has held the office of the Director as may be determined by the Secretary of State with the approval of the Minister for the Civil Service—

(a) such pension, allowance or gratuity shall be paid to or in respect of him on his retirement or death, or

(b) such contributions or payments shall be paid towards provision for such a pension, allowance or gratuity,

as may be so determined.

3–5. . . .

Effect of transfers under section 2

6. (1) In this paragraph—

"commencement" means the commencement of section 2(1);

"transferred" means transferred by section 2(1).

(2) Anything which—

(a) has been done by or in relation to the Director for the purposes of or in connection with anything transferred; and

(b) is in effect immediately before commencement, shall be treated as if done by or in relation to the OFT.

(3) Anything (including legal proceedings) which—

(a) relates to anything transferred; and

(b) is in the process of being done by or in relation to the Director immediately before it is transferred,

may be continued by or in relation to the OFT.

(4) Nothing in section 2 or this paragraph affects the validity of anything done by or in relation to the Director before commencement.

First President and Registrar of the Competition Appeal Tribunal

7. The person who is President of the Competition Commission Appeal Tribunals (under paragraph 4 of Schedule 7 to the 1998 Act) immediately before the commencement of section 12 is on that date to become the President of the Competition Appeal Tribunal as if duly appointed under that section, on the same terms.

8. The person who is Registrar of Appeal Tribunals (under paragraph 5 of Schedule 8 to the 1998 Act) immediately before the commencement of section 12 is on that date to become the Registrar of the Competition Appeal Tribunal as if duly appointed under that section, on the same terms.

9. Any person who is a member of the Competition Commission appeal panel (but not a member of the panel of chairmen) immediately before the commencement of section 12 is on that date to become a member of the Competition Appeal Tribunal, on such terms and for such a period as the Secretary of State may determine.

10. Any member of the Competition Commission appeal panel who is, immediately before the commencement of section 12, a member of the panel of chairmen under paragraph 26 of Schedule 7 to the 1998 Act is on that date to become a chairman of the Competition Appeal Tribunal, on such terms and for such a period as the Lord Chancellor may determine.

11. Nothing in paragraph 7, 8, 9 or 10 applies to any person who, before the commencement of section 12, gives notice to the Secretary of State stating that he does not wish that paragraph to apply to him.

Tribunal rules

12. (1) Any rules made under section 48 of the 1998 Act which are in force immediately before the commencement of section 15 above shall be treated after that commencement as having been made under section 15.

(2) The Secretary of State may treat any consultation carried out with the President of the Competition Commission Appeal Tribunals (before the appointment of the President of the Competition Appeal Tribunal) as being as effective for the purposes of section 15(1) as if it had been carried out with the President of the Competition Appeal Tribunal.

Merger references

13. (1) Subject to paragraphs 15 to 18, the old law shall continue to apply where—

(a) two or more enterprises have ceased to be distinct enterprises (within the meaning of Part 5 of the 1973 Act); and

(b) the cessation has occurred before the appointed day.

(2) Subject to sub-paragraphs (3), (4) and (5) and paragraphs 15 to 18, the old law shall continue to apply in relation to any relevant arrangements which were in progress or in contemplation before the appointed day and are in progress or in contemplation on that day and (if events so require) the actual results of those arrangements where, before the appointed day—

(a) a merger notice was given, and not rejected under section 75B(7) of the 1973 Act or withdrawn, in relation to the arrangements;

(b) no merger notice was so given but, in relation to the arrangements—

(i) a reference was made under section 75 of the 1973 Act;

(ii) undertakings were accepted under section 75G of that Act; or

(iii) a decision was made by the Secretary of State neither to make a reference under section 75 of that Act nor to accept undertakings under section 75G of that Act; or

(c) a merger notice was so given, was rejected under section 75B(7) of the 1973 Act or withdrawn, paragraph (a) does not apply in relation to a different merger notice given in relation to the arrangements and, in relation to the arrangements, paragraph (b)(i), (ii) or (iii) applies.

(3) Subject to sub-paragraph (8), the new law shall, in a case of the kind mentioned in sub-paragraph (2)(a), apply in relation to any relevant arrangements and (if events so require) the actual results of those arrangements if, on or after the appointed day, a merger notice is rejected under section 75B(7) of the 1973 Act or withdrawn in relation to the arrangements.

(4) Subject to sub-paragraph (8), the new law shall, in a case of the kind mentioned in sub-paragraph (2)(a), apply in relation to any relevant arrangements and (if events so require) the actual results of those arrangements if—

(a) the making of a reference under section 64 or 75 of the 1973 Act in relation to those arrangements and (if events so require) the actual results of those arrangements was, immediately before the appointed day and by virtue of section 75C(1)(c), (e) or (g) of that Act, not prevented;

(b) the period for considering the merger notice has expired (whether before, on or after the appointed day); and

(c) no reference has been made under section 64 or 75 of the 1973 Act and no undertakings have been accepted under section 75G of that Act.

(5) Subject to sub-paragraph (8), the new law shall, in a case of the kind mentioned in sub-paragraph (2)(a), apply in relation to any relevant arrangements and (if events so require) the actual results of those arrangements if—

(a) the making of a reference under section 64 or 75 of the 1973 Act in relation to those arrangements and (if events so require) the actual results of those arrangements becomes, on or after the appointed day and by virtue of section 75C(1)(b), (c), (d), (e) or (g) of that Act, not prevented;

(b) the period for considering the merger notice has expired (whether before, on or after the appointed day); and

(c) no reference has been made under section 64 or 75 of the 1973 Act and no undertakings have been accepted under section 75G of that Act.

(6) Subject to sub-paragraph (8), the new law shall apply in relation to relevant arrangements and (if events so require) the actual results of those arrangements if—

(a) the arrangements were in progress or in contemplation before the appointed day and are in progress or in contemplation on that day;

(b) before the appointed day and in relation to the arrangements—

(i) no reference was made under section 75 of the 1973 Act;

(ii) no undertakings were accepted under section 75G of that Act; and

(iii) a decision neither to make a reference under section 75 of that Act nor to accept undertakings under section 75G of that Act was not made by the Secretary of State; and

(c) no merger notice was given to the Director or the OFT before that day in relation to the arrangements.

(7) Subject to sub-paragraph (8), the new law shall, in a case of the kind mentioned in sub-paragraph (2)(c) (excluding the words from "and" to the end), apply in relation to any relevant arrangements and (if events so require) the actual results of those arrangements if, in relation to the arrangements, sub-paragraph (2)(b)(i), (ii) and (iii) do not apply.

(8) Subject to paragraphs 15 to 18, the old law shall continue to apply in relation to concentrations with a Community dimension (within the meaning of the European Merger Regulations) notified before the appointed day to the European Commission under article 4 of those Regulations.

(9) In this paragraph references to relevant arrangements which are in progress or in contemplation on the appointed day include references to the actual results of those arrangements if the arrangements were in progress or in contemplation immediately before the appointed day and have, at the beginning of the appointed day, resulted in two or more enterprises ceasing to be distinct enterprises (within the meaning of Part 5 of the 1973 Act).

(10) In this paragraph—

"the European Merger Regulations" has the meaning given by section 129(1);

"merger notice" means a notice under section 75A(1) of the 1973 Act;

"the new law" means Part 3 of this Act and any related provision of law (including, in particular, any modification made under section 276(2) to that Part or any such provision);

"the old law" means sections 64 to 75K of the 1973 Act and any related provision of law (including, in particular, any modification made under section 276(2) to those sections or any such provision); and

"relevant arrangements" means arrangements which might result in two or more enterprises ceasing to be distinct enterprises (within the meaning of Part 5 of the 1973 Act).

Monopoly references

14. (1) Subject to paragraphs 15 to 18, the old law shall continue to apply in relation to any monopoly reference made before the appointed day under section 50 or 51 of the 1973 Act.

(2) No person has to comply on or after the appointed day with a requirement imposed before that day under section 44 of the 1973 Act.

(3) In this paragraph—

"monopoly reference" has the meaning given by section 5(3) of the 1973 Act; and

"the old law" means Part 4 of the 1973 Act and any related provision of law (including, in particular, any modification made under section 276(2) to that Part or any such provision).

Enforcement undertakings and orders

15. (1) Section 94(1) to (6) shall apply in relation to any undertaking—

(a) accepted (whether before, on or after the appointed day) by a Minister of the Crown—

(i) in pursuance of a proposal under section 56A of the 1973 Act; or

(ii) under section 56F, 75G or 88 of that Act; and

(b) of a description specified in an order made by the Secretary of State under this paragraph;

as it applies in relation to enforcement undertakings under Part 3.

(2) Section 94(1) to (6) shall apply in relation to any order made by a Minister of the Crown under section 56, 73, 74, 75K or 89 of the 1973 Act (whether before, on or after the appointed day) and of a description specified in an order made by the Secretary of State under this paragraph as it applies in relation to enforcement orders under Part 3.

[(2A) Subject to sub-paragraph (3), the functions of the CMA under section 94(6) as applied by virtue of sub-paragraph (1) or (2) are to be carried out on its behalf by the CMA Board (within the meaning of Schedule 4 to the Enterprise and Regulatory Reform Act 2013).]

(3) Compliance with—

(a) an undertaking accepted by a Minister of the Crown under section 88 of the 1973 Act (whether before, on or after the appointed day) and of a description specified in an order made by the Secretary of State under this paragraph; or

(b) an order made by a Minister of the Crown under section 56, 73, 74 or 89 of the 1973 Act (whether before, on or after the appointed day) and of a description specified in an order made by the Secretary of State under this paragraph;

shall also be enforceable by civil proceedings brought by [a group constituted for the purpose by the chair of the CMA under Schedule 4 to the Enterprise and Regulatory Reform Act 2013] for an injunction or for interdict or for any other appropriate relief or remedy.

(4) Sub-paragraph (3) and section 94(6) as applied by virtue of sub-paragraph (1) or (2) shall not prejudice any right that a person may have by virtue of section 94(4) as so applied to bring civil proceedings for contravention or apprehended contravention of an undertaking or order.

(5) Sections 93 and 93A of the 1973 Act shall accordingly cease to apply in relation to undertakings and orders to which sub-paragraphs (1) to (3) above apply.

16. (1) Sub-paragraph (2) applies to any undertaking—

(a) accepted (whether before, on or after the appointed day) by a Minister of the Crown—

(i) in pursuance of a proposal under section 56A of the 1973 Act; or

(ii) under section 56F, 75G or 88 of that Act; and

(b) of a description specified in an order made by the Secretary of State under this paragraph.

(2) An undertaking to which this sub-paragraph applies may be—

(a) superseded by a new undertaking accepted by the [CMA] under this paragraph;

(b) varied by an undertaking accepted by the [CMA] under this paragraph; or

(c) released by the [CMA].

(3) Subject to sub-paragraph (4) and any provision made under section 276(2), the power of the [CMA] under this paragraph to supersede, vary or release an undertaking is exercisable in the same circumstances, and on the same terms and conditions, as the power of the Minister concerned to supersede, vary or release the undertaking would be exercisable under the 1973 Act.

(4) The duty under section 75J(b) of the 1973 Act to give advice shall be a duty of the [CMA] to consider what action (if any) it should take.

(5) Where the [CMA] has the power by virtue of this paragraph to supersede, vary or release an undertaking accepted by a Minister of the Crown—

(a) in pursuance of a proposal under section 56A of the 1973 Act; or

(b) under section 56F, 75G or 88 of that Act;

the Minister concerned shall accordingly cease to have the power under that Act to supersede, vary or release the undertaking.

[(6) The functions of the CMA under this paragraph are to be carried out on its behalf—

(a) in the case of an undertaking accepted in pursuance of a proposal under section 56A of the 1973 Act or an undertaking under section 56F or 75G of that Act, by the CMA Board (within the meaning of Schedule 4 to the Enterprise and Regulatory Reform Act 2013), and

(b) in the case of an undertaking accepted under section 88 of that Act, by a group constituted for the purpose by the chair of the CMA under Schedule 4 to the Enterprise and Regulatory Reform Act 2013.]

17. (1) Any order made by a Minister of the Crown under section 56, 73, 74 or 89 of the 1973 Act (whether before, on or after the appointed day) and of a description specified in an order made by the Secretary of State under this paragraph may be varied or revoked by an order made by the [CMA] under this paragraph.

(2) Any order made by a Minister of the Crown under section 75K of the 1973 Act (whether before, on or after the appointed day) and of a description specified in an order made by the Secretary of State under this paragraph may be varied or revoked by an order made by the [CMA] under this paragraph.

(3) Subject to sub-paragraph (4) and any provision made under section 276(2), the power of the [CMA] to make an order under [sub-paragraphs (1) and (2)] is exercisable in the same circumstances, and on the same terms and conditions, as the power of the Minister concerned to make a corresponding varying or revoking order under the 1973 Act would be exercisable.

(4) The power of the [CMA] to make an order [sub-paragraphs (1) and (2)] shall not be exercisable by statutory instrument and shall not be subject to the requirements of section 134(1) of the 1973 Act.

(5) Where the [CMA] has the power by virtue of this paragraph to vary or revoke an order made by a Minister of the Crown under section 56, 73, 74, 75K or 89 of the 1973 Act, the Minister concerned shall accordingly cease to have the power to do so under that Act.

[(6) The functions of the CMA under this paragraph are to be carried out on its behalf—

(a) in the case of an order under sub-paragraph (1), by a group constituted for the purpose by the chair of the CMA under Schedule 4 to the Enterprise and Regulatory Reform Act 2013, and

(b) in the case of an order under sub-paragraph (2), by the CMA Board (within the meaning of Schedule 4 to the Enterprise and Regulatory Reform Act 2013).]

18. (1) Section 94(1) to (6) shall apply in relation to undertakings accepted under paragraph 16 and orders made under paragraph 17 as it applies in relation to enforcement undertakings and enforcement orders under Part 3.

[(1A) Subject to sub-paragraph (2), the functions of the CMA under section 94(6) as applied by virtue of sub-paragraph (1) are to be carried out on its behalf by the CMA Board (within the meaning of Schedule 4 to the Enterprise and Regulatory Reform Act 2013).]

(2) Compliance with an undertaking accepted by [a group constituted by the chair of the CMA under Schedule 4 to the Enterprise and Regulatory Reform Act 2013 ("CMA group")] under paragraph 16 or an order made by [a CMA group] under paragraph 17 shall also be enforceable by civil proceedings brought by [a CMA group] for an injunction or for interdict or for any other appropriate relief or remedy.

(3) Sub-paragraph (2) and section 94(6) as applied by virtue of sub-paragraph (1) shall not prejudice any right that a person may have by virtue of section 94(4) as so applied to bring civil proceedings for contravention or apprehended contravention of an undertaking or order.

Paragraphs 13 to 18: supplementary provision

19. (1) In paragraphs 13 to 18 "the appointed day" means such day as the Secretary of State may by order made by statutory instrument appoint; and different days may be appointed for different purposes.

(2) An order made by the Secretary of State under paragraph 15, 16 or 17—

(a) may make different provision for different purposes; and

(b) shall be made by statutory instrument which shall be subject to annulment in pursuance of a resolution of either House of Parliament.

Designation orders under Schedule 4 to the 1998 Act

20. (1) Subject to sub-paragraph (2), the repeals made by section 207 do not affect—

(a) the operation of Schedule 4 to the 1998 Act in relation to any application for designation of a professional rule which is made before the commencement date;

(b) the operation of section 3(1)(d) of and Schedule 4 to the 1998 Act in relation to any designation effected by an order made before the commencement date or on an application mentioned in paragraph (a).

(2) No designation order (whenever made) shall have any effect in relation to any period of time after the end of the transitional period.

(3) Subject to sub-paragraph (2) a designation order may be made after the end of the transitional period on an application mentioned in sub-paragraph (1)(a).

(4) For the purposes of this paragraph—

"commencement date" means the day on which section 207 comes into force;

"designation" means designation under paragraph 2 of Schedule 4 to the 1998 Act; and

"the transitional period" means the period of three months beginning with the commencement date.

Proceedings under Part 3 of the 1973 Act

21. . . .

Supplementary

22. Any provision made by any of paragraphs 1 to 21 shall not apply if, and to the extent that, an order under section 276(2) makes alternative provision or provides for it not to apply.

NOTES

Paras 1, 3–5: repealed by the Enterprise and Regulatory Reform Act 2013 (Competition) (Consequential, Transitional and Saving Provisions) Order 2014, SI 2014/892, art 2, Sch 1, Pt 1, paras 1, 18(1), (2), subject to transitional provisions as noted to s 8A at **[1.187]**.

Para 15: sub-para (2A) inserted, and words in square brackets in sub-para (3) substituted, by SI 2014/892, art 2, Sch 1, Pt 1, paras 1, 18(1), (3), subject to transitional provisions as noted to s 8A at **[1.187]**.

Para 16: references to the "CMA" substituted, and sub-para (6) substituted, by SI 2014/892, art 2, Sch 1, Pt 1, paras 1, 18(1), (4), subject to transitional provisions as noted to s 8A at **[1.187]**.

Para 17: words in square brackets substituted, and sub-para (6) added, by SI 2014/892, art 2, Sch 1, Pt 1, paras 1, 18(1), (5), subject to transitional provisions as noted to s 8A at **[1.187]**.

Para 18: sub-para (1A) inserted, and words in square brackets in sub-para (2) substituted, by SI 2014/892, art 2, Sch 1, Pt 1, paras 1, 18(1), (6), subject to transitional provisions as noted to s 8A at **[1.187]**.

Para 21: repealed by the Competition Act 1998 (Consequential Provisions) Order 2013, SI 2013/294, art 2, Schedule.

References to the European Community and related expressions: see the note "References to "the European Community", "Community", etc" in the introductory notes to this Act.

Orders: the Enterprise Act 2002 (Commencement No 3, Transitional and Transitory Provisions and Savings) Order 2003, SI 2003/1397 (made under para 19(1) and appointing 20 June 2003 for the purposes of paras 13–18 above); the Enterprise Act 2002 (Enforcement Undertakings and Orders) Order 2004, SI 2004/2181 (made under paras 15(1)–(3), 16(1), 17(1)); the Enterprise Act 2002 (Enforcement Undertakings) Order 2006, SI 2006/354 (made under paras 15(1), 16(1)); the Enterprise Act 2002 (Enforcement Undertakings and Orders) Order 2006, SI 2006/355 (made under paras 15(1)–(3), 16(1), 17(1)); the Enterprise Act 2002 (Enforcement Undertakings) (No 2) Order 2006, SI 2006/3095 (made under paras 15(1), (3), 16(1)).

SCHEDULES 25, 26

(Sch 25 contains minor and consequential amendments. Sch26 contains repeals and revocations. In so far as these are relevant to this work, they have been incorporated at the appropriate place.)

ENTERPRISE AND REGULATORY REFORM ACT 2013

(2013 c 24)

ARRANGEMENT OF SECTIONS

SCHEDULES

An Act to make provision about the UK Green Investment Bank; to make provision about employment law; to establish and make provision about the Competition and Markets Authority and to abolish the Competition Commission and the Office of Fair Trading; to amend the Competition Act 1998 and the Enterprise Act 2002; to make provision for the reduction of legislative burdens; to make provision about copyright and rights in performances; to make provision about payments to company directors; to make provision about redress schemes relating to lettings agency work and property management work; to make provision about the supply of customer data; to make provision for the protection of essential supplies in cases of insolvency; to make provision about certain bodies established by Royal Charter; to amend section 9(5) of the Equality Act 2010; and for connected purposes

[25th April 2013]

NOTES

Only the provisions of this Act most relevant to competition law are reproduced; provisions omitted are not annotated.

PART 3 THE COMPETITION AND MARKETS AUTHORITY

NOTES

For various transitional provisions (including those relating to the abolition of the OFT and the Competition Commission, existing references to those bodies and provisions relating to continuity), see the Enterprise and Regulatory Reform Act 2013 (Commencement No 6, Transitional Provisions and Savings) Order 2014, SI 2014/416, Schedule at **[2.13]**.

[1.446]

25 The Competition and Markets Authority

(1) There is to be a body corporate known as the Competition and Markets Authority.

(2) In this Part that body is referred to as "the CMA".

(3) The CMA must seek to promote competition, both within and outside the United Kingdom, for the benefit of consumers.

(4) Schedule 4 (which makes provision about the CMA) has effect.

[1.447]

26 Abolition of the Competition Commission and the OFT

(1) The Competition Commission is abolished.

(2) The Office of Fair Trading is abolished.

(3) Schedule 5 (which amends the Competition Act 1998 and the Enterprise Act 2002 to make provision for the transfer of certain functions from the Competition Commission and the Office of Fair Trading to the CMA and to make other minor and consequential amendments) has effect.

(4) Schedule 6 (which amends other enactments to make provision for the transfer of certain functions from the Competition Commission and the Office of Fair Trading to the CMA) has effect.

[1.448]

27 Transfer schemes

(1) The Secretary of State may make one or more transfer schemes in connection with—

(a) the establishment of the CMA under this Act,

(b) the transfer of functions under or by virtue of this Act from the Competition Commission or the Office of Fair Trading to the CMA, or

(c) the abolition of that Commission or that Office under this Act.

(2) A transfer scheme is a scheme for the transfer of property, rights and liabilities of the Competition Commission or the Office of Fair Trading to—

(a) the CMA, or

(b) a Minister of the Crown (as defined by section 8 of the Ministers of the Crown Act 1975).

(3) The things that may be transferred under a transfer scheme include—

(a) property, rights and liabilities that could not otherwise be transferred;

(b) property acquired, and rights and liabilities arising, after the making of the scheme.

(4) A transfer scheme may make consequential, supplementary, incidental or transitional provision and may in particular—

(a) create rights, or impose liabilities, in relation to property or rights transferred;

(b) make provision about the continuing effect of things done by the transferor in respect of anything transferred;

(c) make provision about the continuation of things (including legal proceedings) in the process of being done by, on behalf of, or in relation to the transferor in respect of anything transferred;

(d) make provision for references to the transferor in an instrument or other document in respect of anything transferred to be treated as references to the transferee;

(e) make provision for the shared ownership or use of property;

(f) make provision that is the same as or similar to the TUPE regulations.

(5) A transfer scheme may provide—

(a) for the scheme to be modified by agreement after it comes into effect;

(b) for modifications to have effect from the date when the scheme first came into effect.

(6) For the purposes of this section—

(a) an individual who holds employment in the civil service is to be treated as employed by virtue of a contract of employment, and

(b) the terms of the individual's employment in the civil service are to be regarded as constituting the terms of the contract of employment.

(7) In this section—

"civil service" means the civil service of the State;

"TUPE regulations" means the Transfer of Undertakings (Protection of Employment) Regulations 2006 (SI 2006/246);

references to rights and liabilities include rights and liabilities relating to a contract of employment;

references to the transfer of property include references to the grant of a lease.

[1.449]

28 Transitional provision: consultation

(1) This section applies in relation to a provision of this Act under or by virtue of which the CMA has a function of consulting another person in preparing rules, statements of policy, guidance or general advice or information.

(2) At any time before the provision comes into force, the Office of Fair Trading or the Competition Commission or both bodies acting jointly—

(a) may carry out any consultation that the CMA would have power to carry out after the provision comes into force, and

(b) for that purpose, may prepare drafts of any documents to which the consultation relates.

(3) At any time after the provision comes into force, the CMA may elect to treat any consultation carried out or other thing done under subsection (2) by the Office of Fair Trading or the Competition Commission (or by both bodies acting jointly) as carried out or done by the CMA.

(4) The Secretary of State may direct the Office of Fair Trading or the Competition Commission, or both of them acting jointly, to exercise a power conferred by subsection (2).

PART 4 COMPETITION REFORM

29–38 *(Ss 29–32 (Chapter 1—Mergers) and ss 33–38 (Chapter 2—Markets) contain amendments to Parts 3 and 4 of the Enterprise Act 2002 (which have been incorporated in the appropriate place) and introduce Schs 7–12 to this Act (further amendments in relation to markets and mergers).)*

CHAPTER 3 ANTI-TRUST

39–45 *(Ss 39–45 contain amendments to Part 1 of the Competition Act 1998 (which have been incorporated in the appropriate place (see* **[1.194]** *et seq)) and introduce Sch 13 to this Act (which amends the 1998 Act to extend the powers under that Act to issue warrants to the CAT).)*

Miscellaneous

[1.450]

46 Review of operation of Part 1 of 1998 Act

(1) The Secretary of State must—

(a) review the operation of Part 1 of the 1998 Act, and

(b) prepare and publish a report on the outcome of the review.

(2) The report must be published before the end of the period of 5 years beginning with the day on which Part 1 of Schedule 5 (which transfers the functions of the Office of Fair Trading under Part 1 of the 1998 Act to the Competition and Markets Authority) comes into force.

(3) The Secretary of State must lay the report before Parliament.

47, 48 *(Ss 47, 48 (Chapter 4—Cartels) contain amendments to Part 6 of the Enterprise Act 2002 (which have been incorporated in the appropriate place (see* **[1.399]** *et seq)).)*

CHAPTER 5 MISCELLANEOUS

49, 50 *(Ss 49, 50 amend the Enterprise Act 2002, Sch 8 at* **[1.440]**.*)*

Concurrency

51 *(S 51 amends the Competition Act 1998, s 54 at, and introduces Sch 14 to this Act (which makes provision governing the relationship between the powers of regulators under the 1998 Act and those under sector-specific legislation).)*

[1.451]

52 Power to remove concurrent competition functions of sectoral regulators

(1) The Secretary of State may make a sectoral regulator order if the Secretary of State considers that it is appropriate to do so for the purpose of promoting competition, within any market or markets in the United Kingdom, for the benefit of consumers.

(2) A sectoral regulator order is an order that amends one or more enactments so as to remove from a sectoral regulator either or both of the following—

(a) all the functions of the regulator under Part 1 of the 1998 Act that are exercisable concurrently by the regulator and the Competition and Markets Authority ("the CMA") or that would be so exercisable but for provision made by virtue of section 54(5)(e) of that Act;

(b) all the functions of the regulator under Part 4 of the 2002 Act that are exercisable concurrently by the regulator and the CMA.

(3) A sectoral regulator order may make such other amendments of any enactment as the Secretary of State considers appropriate in consequence of the removal of the functions.

(4) Each of the following is a sectoral regulator—
(a) the Office of Communications;
(b) the Gas and Electricity Markets Authority;
(c) the Water Services Regulation Authority;
(d) [the Office of Rail and Road]
(e) the Northern Ireland Authority for Utility Regulation;
(f) the Civil Aviation Authority;
[(g) the Payment Systems Regulator established under section 40 of the Financial Services (Banking Reform) Act 2013];
[(h) the Financial Conduct Authority].
(5) A sectoral regulator order may include transitional, transitory or saving provision.
(6) A statutory instrument containing a sectoral regulator order is not to be made unless a draft of the instrument has been laid before, and approved by a resolution of, each House of Parliament.
(7) In this section—
"amend" includes repeal or revoke;
"enactment" includes—
(a) an enactment contained in subordinate legislation (within the meaning of the Interpretation Act 1978),
(b) an enactment contained in, or in an instrument made under, an Act of the Scottish Parliament,
(c) an enactment contained in, or in an instrument made under, a Measure or Act of the National Assembly for Wales, and
(d) an enactment contained in, or in an instrument made under, Northern Ireland legislation.
(8) The references to the CMA in subsection (2) are to be read, in relation to any time before the commencement of section 25(3), as references to the Office of Fair Trading.

NOTES

Sub-s (4): words in square brackets in para (d) substituted by the Office of Rail Regulation (Change of Name) Regulations 2015, SI 2015/1682, reg 2(2), Schedule, Pt 1, para 4(v)(i). Paras (g), (h) inserted by the Financial Services (Banking Reform) Act 2013, ss 67(4), 129, Sch 8, Pt 2, para 11.

National Assembly for Wales: see further, in relation to the renaming of the National Assembly for Wales as the Senedd Cymru or the Welsh Parliament, the Government of Wales 2006, s 150A (as amended by the Senedd and Elections (Wales) Act 2020, s 9, Sch 1, para 2(1), (7)).

[1.452]

53 Orders under section 52: procedural requirements

(1) If the Secretary of State proposes to make a sectoral regulator order, the Secretary of State must carry out the first stage consultation.
(2) The first stage consultation is consultation with—
(a) the regulator whose functions would be removed by the order,
(b) the Competition and Markets Authority,
(c) where the regulator is [the Office of Rail and Road], the Scottish Ministers,
(d) where the regulator is the Northern Ireland Authority for Utility Regulation, the Department of Enterprise, Trade and Investment in Northern Ireland and the Department for Regional Development in Northern Ireland, and
(e) where the regulator is the Water Services Regulation Authority, the Welsh Ministers.
(3) If (following the first stage consultation) the Secretary of State still proposes to make a sectoral regulator order, the Secretary of State must carry out the second stage consultation.
(4) The second stage consultation is consultation with—
(a) the persons consulted at the first stage,
(b) any bodies who appear to the Secretary of State to represent the interests of persons in respect of whom the functions that would be removed by the order are exercisable ("regulated providers"),
(c) any bodies who appear to the Secretary of State to represent the interests of persons who use the services supplied by regulated providers, and
(d) such other persons as the Secretary of State considers appropriate.
(5) The Secretary of State must give the following information to each of the persons consulted as part of the first stage or second stage consultation—
(a) an explanation as to whether the Secretary of State is proposing to remove the functions of the regulator mentioned in subsection (2)(a) of section 52, the functions of the regulator mentioned in subsection (2)(b) of that section or both sets of functions;
(b) the reasons why the Secretary of State considers it appropriate to make the order.
(6) The reference to the Competition and Markets Authority in subsection (2) is to be read, in relation to any time before the commencement of section 25(3), as a reference to the Office of Fair Trading.
(7) In this section, "sectoral regulator order" has the same meaning as in section 52.

NOTES

Sub-s (2): words in square brackets in para (c) substituted by the Office of Rail Regulation (Change of Name) Regulations 2015, SI 2015/1682, reg 2(2), Schedule, Pt 1, para 4(v)(ii).

Miscellaneous

54, 55 *(S 54 inserts the Communications Act 2003, s 193A; s 55 amends the Enterprise Act 2002, s 241.)*

[1.453]

56 Review of certain provisions of Chapters 1 and 2

(1) The Secretary of State must, before the end of each review period—

(a) carry out a review of the provisions of this Part mentioned in subsection (2), and
(b) prepare and publish a report setting out the conclusions of the review.

(2) The provisions of this Part are—
(a) sections 29 and 36 and Schedule 11 (investigation powers: mergers and markets),
(b) section 30 and Schedule 7 (interim measures and pre-emptive action: mergers), and
(c) sections 32 and 38 and Schedules 8 and 12 (time-limits etc: mergers and markets).

(3) The report must in particular—
(a) set out the objectives intended to be achieved by the provisions,
(b) assess the extent to which those objectives have been achieved, and
(c) assess whether those objectives remain appropriate and, if so, the extent to which they could be achieved in another way which imposed less regulation.

(4) The Secretary of State must lay the report before Parliament.

(5) Each of the following is a review period for the purposes of this section—
(a) the period of 5 years beginning with the first day on which any of the provisions mentioned in subsection (2) comes into force (whether wholly or partly), and
(b) each successive period of 5 years.

57, 58 (*S 57 introduces Sch 15 to this Act (which makes minor and consequential amendments related to this Part); s 58 provides for interpretation.*)

PART 6 MISCELLANEOUS AND GENERAL

General

[1.454]

99 Consequential amendments, repeals and revocations

(1) The Secretary of State may by order made by statutory instrument make such provision as the Secretary of State considers appropriate in consequence of this Act.

(2) The power conferred by subsection (1) includes power—
(a) to make transitional, transitory or saving provision;
(b) to amend, repeal, revoke or otherwise modify any provision made by or under an enactment (including any enactment passed or made in the same Session as this Act).

(3) An order under subsection (1) which makes provision for the transfer of a function from the Competition Commission or the Office of Fair Trading to the Competition and Markets Authority in consequence of Part 3 of this Act may make such modifications to the function as the Secretary of State considers appropriate in consequence of the transfer.

(4) The modifications mentioned in subsection (3) may, in particular, alter the circumstances in which, or the conditions under which, the function is exercisable.

(5) A statutory instrument containing (whether alone or with other provision) an order under this section which amends, repeals or revokes any provision of primary legislation is not to be made unless a draft of the instrument has been laid before, and approved by a resolution of, each House of Parliament.

(6) A statutory instrument containing an order under this section which does not amend, repeal or revoke any provision of primary legislation is subject to annulment in pursuance of a resolution of either House of Parliament.

(7) In this section—
"enactment" includes an Act of the Scottish Parliament, a Measure or Act of the National Assembly for Wales and Northern Ireland legislation;
"primary legislation" means—
(a) an Act of Parliament,
(b) an Act of the Scottish Parliament,
(c) a Measure or Act of the National Assembly for Wales, and
(d) Northern Ireland legislation.

NOTES

National Assembly for Wales: see further, in relation to the renaming of the National Assembly for Wales as the Senedd Cymru or the Welsh Parliament, the Senedd and Elections (Wales) Act 2020. See also ss 3–9 of the 2020 Act in relation to the renaming of Acts of the National Assembly for Wales, Members of the National Assembly for Wales, etc.

Orders: the Enterprise and Regulatory Reform Act 2013 (Competition and Markets Authority) (Consequential Amendments) Order 2013, SI 2013/2268 (which contains a consequential amendment to the National Assembly for Wales (Disqualification) Order 2010 necessitated by the establishment of the CMA); the Enterprise and Regulatory Reform Act 2013 (Competition) (Consequential, Transitional and Saving Provisions) (No 2) Order 2014, SI 2014/549 at **[2.19]**; the Enterprise and Regulatory Reform Act 2013 (Competition) (Consequential, Transitional and Saving Provisions) Order 2014, SI 2014/892.

Note: other Orders made under this section concerning areas of law that are outside the scope of this work (eg, planning and insolvency) are not listed.

[1.455]

100 Transitional, transitory or saving provision

The Secretary of State may by order made by statutory instrument make such transitional, transitory or saving provision as the Secretary of State considers appropriate in connection with the coming into force of any provision of this Act.

NOTES

Orders: the Enterprise and Regulatory Reform Act 2013 (Commencement No 3, Transitional Provisions and Savings) Order 2013, SI 2013/2227; the Enterprise and Regulatory Reform Act 2013 (Commencement No 6, Transitional Provisions and Savings) Order 2014, SI 2014/416 at **[2.11]**.

Note: other Orders made under this section concerning areas of law that are outside the scope of this work are not listed.

[1.456]

101 Financial provision

There is to be paid out of money provided by Parliament—

(a) any expenditure incurred under or by virtue of this Act by the Secretary of State or the Competition and Markets Authority, and

(b) any increase attributable to this Act in the sums payable under any other Act out of money so provided

[1.457]

102 Extent

(1), (2) *(Outside the scope of this work).*

(3) Part 3 extends to England and Wales, Scotland and Northern Ireland, except as follows—

(a) paragraphs 15 to 44, 69 to 84 and 101 to 107 of Schedule 6 extend only to England and Wales and Scotland;

(b) paragraphs 52 to 68, 96, 108 to 123 and 127 to 139 of that Schedule extend only to England and Wales;

(c) paragraphs 9 to 14, 45 to 51, 171 to 180 and 192 to 209 of that Schedule extend only to Scotland;

(d) paragraphs 149 to 170 and 181 to 191 of that Schedule extend only to Northern Ireland.

(4) Part 4 extends to England and Wales, Scotland and Northern Ireland, except as follows—

(a) paragraphs 1 to 7 and 11 to 14 of Schedule 14 and paragraphs 2, 3, 7, 13 and 41 of Schedule 15, extend only to England and Wales and Scotland;

(b) paragraphs 8 to 10 and 20 to 22 of Schedule 14, and paragraphs 4 to 6 and 47 to 49 of Schedule 15, extend only to England and Wales;

(c) paragraphs 23 to 29 of Schedule 14, and paragraphs 53 to 55 of Schedule 15, extend only to Northern Ireland.

(5)–(8) *(Outside the scope of this work).*

[1.458]

103 Commencement

(1) The following provisions come into force on the day on which this Act is passed—

(a), (b) *(outside the scope of this work);*

(c) section 28;

(d) sections 52 and 53;

(e)–(g) *(outside the scope of this work);*

(h) sections 98 to 104;

(i) any other provision so far as is necessary for enabling the exercise on or after the day on which this Act is passed of any power (arising under or by virtue of that provision) to make provision by regulations, rules or order made by statutory instrument.

(2) *(Outside the scope of this work).*

(3) Except as provided by subsections (1) and (2), the provisions of this Act come into force on such day as the Secretary of State may by order made by statutory instrument appoint.

(4) An order under subsection (3) may appoint different days for different purposes.

NOTES

Orders: (i) the Enterprise and Regulatory Reform Act 2013 (Commencement No 3, Transitional Provisions and Savings) Order 2013, SI 2013/2227. Article 2(a), (j), (k) and (l) of the Order commences s 25 of this Act (and provisions in Sch 4) on 1 October 2013 to allow the creation of the Competition and Markets Authority. Article 2(b) brings into force (on the same date) s 27 which allows the Secretary of State to make transfer schemes in connection with the establishment of the CMA, the transfer of functions under or by virtue of this Act from the Competition Commission and the Office of Fair Trading to the CMA. Article 3 makes transitional provision to allow members of the Competition Commission who are immediately prior to its abolition on a panel constituted under any enactment through which the functions of the Commission are being performed to become a CMA member for the purposes of allowing the CMA to complete the functions formerly performed by the Competition Commission; (ii) the Enterprise and Regulatory Reform Act 2013 (Commencement No 6, Transitional Provisions and Savings) Order 2014, SI 2014/416 at **[2.11]**.

Note: other Orders made under this section concerning areas of law that are outside the scope of this work are not listed.

[1.459]

104 Short title

This Act may be cited as the Enterprise and Regulatory Reform Act 2013.

SCHEDULES

SCHEDULE 4
THE COMPETITION AND MARKETS AUTHORITY

Section 25(4)

PART 1 GENERAL

Membership

[1.460]

1. (1) The CMA is to consist of—

(a) a person appointed by the Secretary of State to chair the CMA and the CMA Board (the "chair"), and

(b) other persons appointed by the Secretary of State [as follows]—

(i) [persons appointed to membership of] the CMA Board (see Part 2);

(ii) [persons appointed to membership of] the CMA panel (see Part 3);

(iii) [persons appointed to membership of] both the CMA Board and the CMA panel;

[(iv) a person (the "OIM panel chair") appointed to chair the Office for the Internal Market panel and to membership of the CMA Board;

(v) other persons appointed to membership of the Office for the Internal Market panel ("the OIM panel") (see Part 3A)].

(2) The Secretary of State must consult the chair before making an appointment under sub-paragraph (1)(b).

[(2A) In making appointments under paragraphs (iv) and (v) of sub-paragraph (1)(b), the Secretary of State must have regard to the desirability of securing that—

(a) a variety of skills, knowledge and experience is available among the members of the OIM panel, and

(b) there is an appropriate balance among the members of that panel of persons who have skills, knowledge or experience relating to the operation of the United Kingdom internal market in different parts of the United Kingdom.

(2B) Before making an appointment under paragraph (iv) or (v) of sub-paragraph (1)(b), the Secretary of State must seek the consent of—

(a) the Scottish Ministers,

(b) the Welsh Ministers, and

(c) the Department for the Economy in Northern Ireland.

(2C) Sub-paragraph (2D) applies if consent to an appointment is not given by any of those authorities within the period of one month beginning with the day on which it is sought from that authority.

(2D) In that event the Secretary of State—

(a) may make the appointment without the consent of the authority or authorities concerned, and

(b) must, if the appointment is made, inform each authority which did not give consent of the reasons for the decision to proceed with the appointment.]

(3) At least five of the members appointed under sub-paragraph (1)(b) must be appointed to membership of the CMA Board.

(4) At least one of the members appointed under sub-paragraph (1)(b) must be appointed to membership of the CMA Board and to membership of the CMA panel.

(5) Of the persons appointed to membership of the CMA Board under sub-paragraph (1)(b), no more than half may be members of staff of the CMA.

(6) In this Schedule, references to members of the CMA are to persons appointed under sub-paragraph (1).

(7) A person holding office as a member of the Competition Appeal Tribunal is ineligible for appointment under this paragraph.

Terms and conditions

2. (1) The members of the CMA are to hold and vacate office in accordance with the terms and conditions of their appointments.

(2) Those terms and conditions are to be determined by the Secretary of State.

Term of appointment

3. (1) Appointment to membership of the CMA Board under paragraph 1(1)(b) is to be for a term of not more than five years.

(2) Appointment to membership of the CMA panel under paragraph 1(1)(b) is to be for a term of not more than eight years.

[(2A) Appointment to membership of the OIM panel under paragraph 1(1)(b) is to be for a term of not more than eight years.]

(3) Appointment as the chair is to be for a term of not more than five years.

[(4) Where at the beginning of a person's term of appointment to membership of the CMA panel the person has already begun (and continues) to hold office as a member of the OIM panel, the term of the person's appointment to membership of the CMA panel is to be treated for the purposes of sub-paragraph (2) as beginning when the person's term of appointment to membership of the OIM panel began.

(5) Where at the beginning of a person's term of appointment to membership of the OIM panel the person has already begun (and continues) to hold office as a member of the CMA panel, the term of the person's appointment to membership of the OIM panel is to be treated for the purposes of sub-paragraph (2A) as beginning when the person's term of appointment to membership of the CMA panel began.]

Re-appointment

4. (1) A person who has been appointed to membership of the CMA panel may be re-appointed to membership of the CMA panel only for the purpose of continuing to act as a member of a group constituted under paragraph 36 before the expiry of his or her term of office.

[(1A) A person who has been appointed to membership of the OIM panel may be re-appointed to membership of the OIM panel only for the purpose of continuing to act as a member of a group constituted under paragraph 58B before the expiry of the person's term of office.]

(2) Subject to [sub-paragraphs (1) and (1A)], a person's previous appointment under paragraph 1 does not affect eligibility for a subsequent appointment under that paragraph.

Remuneration etc of members

5. (1) The CMA must pay to its members such remuneration, allowances and expenses as the Secretary of State may determine.

(2) The CMA must pay or make provision for the payment of such pension, allowances or gratuities as the Secretary of State may determine to or in respect of a current or former member.

(3) If a person ceases to hold an office to which he or she has been appointed under paragraph 1, and the Secretary of State decides that there are special circumstances which mean that the person should be compensated, the CMA must pay compensation to the person of such amount as the Secretary of State may determine.

Resignation

6. (1) The chair may at any time resign from membership of the CMA by giving written notice to this effect to the Secretary of State.

(2) A person who is a member [of one, but not more than one, of the CMA Board, the CMA panel and the OIM panel,] may at any time resign from membership of the CMA by giving written notice to this effect to the Secretary of State.

(3) A person who is a member of both the CMA Board and the CMA panel [or both the CMA panel and the OIM panel] may at any time, by giving written notice to this effect to the Secretary of State—

[(a) resign from one of those memberships (without resigning from the other), or]

(b) resign from membership of the CMA.

[(4) The OIM panel chair may at any time resign from membership of the CMA by giving written notice to this effect to the Secretary of State (and may not resign from the OIM panel, or any other office to which the person is appointed by virtue of paragraph 1(1)(b)(iv), except in accordance with this sub-paragraph).]

Termination of membership

7. The Secretary of State may at any time remove a person from office as a member of the CMA on any of the following grounds—

(a) incapacity;

(b) misbehaviour;

(c) failure to carry out his or her duties.

Status

8. The CMA is to perform its functions on behalf of the Crown.

Chief executive and other staff

9. (1) The CMA is to have a chief executive appointed by the Secretary of State (the "chief executive").

(2) The chief executive may also be a member of the CMA, but must not be—

(a) the chair, . . .

(b) a member of the CMA panel[, or

(c) a member of the OIM panel].

(3) Before appointing the chief executive, the Secretary of State must consult the chair.

(4) The appointment—

(a) is to be for a term of not more than five years;

(b) subject to that, is to be on such terms and conditions as the Secretary of State considers fit.

(5) The chief executive holds that office as a member of the staff of the CMA.

(6) A previous appointment as chief executive does not affect a person's eligibility for re-appointment.

10. (1) The CMA may appoint other members of staff.

(2) A person appointed as a member of the CMA's staff under sub-paragraph (1) may also be a member of the CMA, but must not be—

(a) the chair, or

(b) a member of the CMA panel [or the OIM panel].

(3) The following are to be determined by the CMA with the approval of the Minister for the Civil Service—

(a) the number of members of staff appointed under sub-paragraph (1);

(b) their conditions of service.

11. A person holding office as a member of the Competition Appeal Tribunal is ineligible for appointment under paragraph 9 or 10.

Annual plan

12. (1) The CMA must prepare an annual plan for each financial year.

(2) The plan must—

(a) set out the CMA's main objectives for the year and indicate the relative priorities of each of those objectives;

(b) provide a summary of the proposed allocation of the CMA's financial resources to the activities to be carried on in connection with those objectives.

(3) The CMA must arrange for the plan to be laid before[—

(a) Parliament,

(b) the Scottish Parliament,

(c) Senedd Cymru, and

(d) the Northern Ireland Assembly].

(4) The CMA must publish the plan, in whatever way it considers appropriate, before the start of the financial year in question.

13. (1) Before finalising an annual plan, the CMA must draw up proposals for it.

(2) The CMA must arrange for the proposals to be laid before[—

(a) Parliament,

(b) the Scottish Parliament,

(c) Senedd Cymru, and

(d) the Northern Ireland Assembly].

(3) The CMA must—

(a) publish the proposals in whatever way it considers appropriate, and

(b) make arrangements to consult with the public about them.

(4) Arrangements made under sub-paragraph (3)(b) may provide for consultation with the public to be effected in whatever way the CMA considers appropriate.

Performance report

14. (1) As soon as practicable after the end of each financial year, the CMA must prepare and send to the Secretary of State an annual report on its activities and performance during the year.

(2) The report must include—

(a) a survey of developments, during the year, in matters relating to the CMA's functions;

(b) an assessment of the extent to which the CMA's objectives for the year, as set out in the plan published under paragraph 12, have been met;

(c) a summary of the significant decisions, investigations or other activities made or carried out by the CMA during the year;

(d) a summary of the allocation of the CMA's financial resources to its various activities during the year;

(e) an assessment of the CMA's performance and practices, during the year, in relation to its enforcement functions.

(3) The CMA must—

(a) arrange for the report to be laid before[—

(i) Parliament,

(ii) the Scottish Parliament,

(iii) Senedd Cymru, and

(iv) the Northern Ireland Assembly];

(b) publish the report in whatever way it considers appropriate.

15. The CMA may—

(a) prepare other reports about matters relating to any of its functions;

(b) publish a report prepared under this paragraph.

Concurrency report

16. (1) As soon as practicable after the end of each financial year, the CMA must prepare a report containing an assessment of how the concurrency arrangements have operated during the year.

(2) The concurrency arrangements are the arrangements for co-operation between the CMA and the sectoral regulators in respect of functions which are exercisable concurrently by the CMA and one or more of the regulators under Part 1 of the Competition Act 1998 (the "1998 Act") and Part 4 of the Enterprise Act 2002 (the "2002 Act").

(3) The report must, in particular, include information about—

(a) the exercise during the year by the CMA of its functions under Part 1 of the 1998 Act or Part 4 of the 2002 Act in cases in which the functions are or were exercisable concurrently by one or more sectoral regulators,

(b) the exercise during the year by each sectoral regulator of its functions under Part 1 of the 1998 Act or Part 4 of the 2002 Act, and

(c) any decision made during the year by a sectoral regulator, in respect of a case in relation to which the regulator considers that its functions under Part 1 of the 1998 Act were exercisable, that it was more appropriate for it to proceed by exercising functions other than those it has under that Part of that Act.

(4) The CMA is not required to include information in a report under this paragraph if it considers that doing so would, or would be likely to, prejudice the exercise of any of the functions of the CMA or a sectoral regulator.

(5) In preparing a report under this paragraph, the CMA must consult each sectoral regulator.

(6) The CMA must publish a report prepared under this paragraph in whatever way it considers appropriate.

(7) Each of the following is a sectoral regulator—

(a) the Office of Communications;

(b) the Gas and Electricity Markets Authority;

(c) the Water Services Regulation Authority;

(d) [the Office of Rail and Road]

(e) the Northern Ireland Authority for Utility Regulation;

(f) the Civil Aviation Authority;

(g) Monitor;

[(h) the Payment Systems Regulator established under section 40 of the Financial Services (Banking Reform) Act 2013];

[(i) the Financial Conduct Authority].

Documents

17. (1) The application of the CMA's seal must be authenticated by the signature of—

(a) a person who is a member of the CMA Board, or

(b) a person authorised (generally or specifically) for that purpose by the CMA.

(2) A document purporting to be duly executed under the CMA's seal or signed on its behalf—

(a) is to be received in evidence;

(b) is to be taken to be duly signed or sealed unless the contrary is shown.

(3) But this paragraph does not apply in relation to a document which is, or is to be, signed in accordance with the law of Scotland.

Membership of committees and sub-committees

18. (1) The members of a committee or sub-committee of the CMA may include persons who are not members of the CMA.

(2) A sub-committee may include persons who are not members of the committee that established it.

Additional powers

19. The CMA may—

(a) if so requested by the Secretary of State, represent the government of the United Kingdom in matters relating to international relations in any field connected to its functions, and

(b) promote good practice outside the United Kingdom in the carrying on of activities which may affect the economic interests of consumers in the United Kingdom.

20. (1) The CMA may do anything that is calculated to facilitate, or is conducive or incidental to, the performance of its functions.

(2) The power in sub-paragraph (1) is subject to any restrictions imposed by or under any enactment.

21–26. *(Amend the Public Records Act 1958, the Parliamentary Commissioner Act 1967, the House of Commons Disqualification Act 1975, the Northern Ireland Assembly Disqualification Act 1975, the Freedom of Information Act 2000, and Equality Act 2010.)*

NOTES

Paras 1, 3, 4, 6, 9, 10: all amendments to these paragraphs were made by the United Kingdom Internal Market Act 2020, s 32, Sch 3, paras 2–7, as from IP completion day (as defined in the European Union (Withdrawal Agreement) Act 2020, s 39).

Paras 12–14: words in square brackets substituted by the United Kingdom Internal Market Act 2020, s 40, as from 20 September 2021.

Para 16: words in square brackets in sub-para (7)(d) substituted by the Office of Rail Regulation (Change of Name) Regulations 2015, SI 2015/1682, reg 2(2), Schedule, Pt 1, para 4(v)(iii). Sub-paras (7)(h), (i) inserted by the Financial Services (Banking Reform) Act 2013, ss 67(5), 129, Sch 8, Pt 2, para 12.

Transitional provisions: the Enterprise and Regulatory Reform Act 2013 (Commencement No 3, Transitional Provisions and Savings) Order 2013, SI 2013/2227, art 3 provides as follows—

> "**3.**—(1) Any member of the Competition Commission whose term of office as such is not due to expire before the abolition of the Competition Commission under section 26 of the Act may be appointed to the Competition and Markets Authority ("CMA") panel under paragraph 1(1)(b) of Schedule 4 to the Act for the purpose in paragraph (2).
>
> (2) The purpose is to enable anything in the process of being done by that person immediately before the abolition of the Competition Commission, as a member of a group constituted under any enactment through which functions of the Competition Commission are being performed, to be completed on behalf of the CMA by that person after the abolition of the Competition Commission as a member of a group constituted (or treated as constituted) under Schedule 4 of the Act or any other enactment.
>
> (3) An appointment made by virtue of this article may be made only for the purpose in paragraph (2).".

See also, for various transitional provisions (including those relating to the abolition of the OFT and the Competition Commission, existing references to those bodies and provisions relating to continuity), the Enterprise and Regulatory Reform Act 2013 (Commencement No 6, Transitional Provisions and Savings) Order 2014, SI 2014/416, Schedule at **[2.13]**.

PART 2 THE CMA BOARD

Membership

[1.461]

27. The CMA Board is to consist of—

(a) the chair;

(b) the members appointed under paragraph 1(1)(b) to membership of the CMA Board.

Functions

28. Except where otherwise provided by or under any enactment, the functions of the CMA are exercisable by the CMA Board on behalf of the CMA.

Delegation

29. (1) Anything that the CMA Board is required or permitted to do (including conferring authorisation under this sub-paragraph) may be done by—

(a) a member of the CMA Board, or a member of staff of the CMA, who has been authorised for that purpose by the CMA Board, whether generally or specifically;

(b) a committee or sub-committee of the CMA Board that has been so authorised.

(2) Sub-paragraph (1) does not apply to the functions of deciding—

(a) whether the duty to publish a market study notice under section 130A of the Enterprise Act 2002 applies;

(b) whether to propose to make, or to make, a reference under section 131 of that Act;

(c) for the purposes of the requirement imposed by section 131A(2)(b) of that Act, whether the CMA is proposing to make a decision as to whether to make a reference under section 131 of that Act in a way that is likely to have a substantial impact on the interests of any person;

(d) whether section 140A of that Act applies in respect of a particular case;

(e) whether to accept an undertaking under section 154 of that Act, or to vary or supersede or release an undertaking under that section;

(f) for the purposes of the requirement imposed by section 169(2) of that Act, whether the CMA is proposing to make a decision to make a reference under section 131 of that Act in a way that is likely to have a substantial impact on the interests of any person.

(3) Sub-paragraph (1)(b) does not apply to a committee or sub-committee whose members include any person who is not a member of the CMA or of its staff.

30. Paragraph 29(1) is subject to provision in rules made under section 51 of the Competition Act 1998, by virtue of paragraph 1A of Schedule 9 to that Act, in respect of the exercise of a function of the CMA under Part 1 of that Act.

Proceedings

31. (1) The CMA Board may regulate its own proceedings.

(2) The CMA Board must consult the Secretary of State before making or revising rules and procedures, under sub-paragraph (1), for dealing with—

(a) conflicts of interest, or
(b) quorum.

Validity

32. The validity of anything done by the CMA Board is not affected by—

(a) a vacancy;
(b) a defective appointment.

Reference of matter to the chair

33. (1) This paragraph applies where the CMA Board is to consider whether a matter should be referred to the chair for the constitution of a group under this Schedule.

(2) Before the CMA Board considers whether to refer the matter to the chair, the chair must determine whether a person who is a member of the CMA Board might reasonably be expected to be a member of a group constituted in connection with the matter.

(3) If the chair determines that a person who is a member of the CMA Board might reasonably be expected to be a member of such a group, that person is not to participate in the CMA Board's consideration of whether to refer the matter to the chair.

NOTES

For various transitional provisions (including those relating to the abolition of the OFT and the Competition Commission, existing references to those bodies and provisions relating to continuity), see the Enterprise and Regulatory Reform Act 2013 (Commencement No 6, Transitional Provisions and Savings) Order 2014, SI 2014/416, Schedule at **[2.13]**.

PART 3 THE CMA PANEL

The CMA panel

[1.462]

34. The CMA panel is a panel of persons available for selection as members of a group constituted in accordance with this Part of this Schedule.

Membership of CMA panel

35. (1) The CMA panel is to consist of—

(a) at least one person (a "newspaper panel member") appointed to the CMA panel under paragraph 1(1)(b) for the purpose of being available for selection as a member of a group constituted to carry out functions on behalf of the CMA with respect to a newspaper merger reference (a "newspaper merger reference group");
(b) at least three persons ("specialist communications panel members") appointed to the CMA panel under paragraph 1(1)(b) for the purpose of being available for selection as members of a group constituted to carry out functions on behalf of the CMA with respect to a specialist communications reference (a "specialist communications reference group");
(c) at least six persons ("specialist utility panel members") appointed to the CMA panel under paragraph 1(1)(b) for the purpose of being available for selection as members of a group constituted to carry out specialist utility functions on behalf of the CMA (a "specialist utility group");
[(ca) at least one person (a "payment systems panel member") appointed to the CMA panel under paragraph 1(1)(b) for the purpose of being available for selection as a member of a group constituted to carry out functions on behalf of the CMA with respect to an appeal made in accordance with section 79 of the Financial Services (Banking Reform) Act 2013 (a "specialist payment systems group");]
(d) at least one person (a "reporting panel member") appointed to the CMA panel under paragraph 1(1)(b) for the purpose of being available for selection as a member of any group constituted to carry out functions on behalf of the CMA.
(e) . . .

(2) A person who is appointed to the CMA panel as a member of a kind mentioned in one of paragraphs (a) to [(d)] of sub-paragraph (1) may also be appointed as a member of one or more of the other kinds mentioned in those paragraphs.

(3) For the purposes of this paragraph and paragraph 38—

a "newspaper merger reference" is—

(a) a reference under section 45 of the Enterprise Act 2002 that specifies a newspaper public interest consideration (within the meaning of paragraph 20A of Schedule 8 to that Act);
(b) a reference under section 62 of that Act that specifies a consideration specified in section 58(2A) or (2B) of that Act;

a "specialist communications reference" is a reference under section 193 of the Communications Act 2003;

"specialist utility functions" are functions with respect to—

(a) an appeal under section 23B, or a reference under section 41E, of the Gas Act 1986;
(b) an appeal under section 11C, or a reference under section 56C, of the Electricity Act 1989;
(c) a reference under section 12, 14 or 17K of the Water Industry Act 1991;

[(ca) an appeal under section 12D of that Act;]
(d) the giving of a direction or the making of modifications under section 16A or 17P of that Act;
[(da) an appeal under article 14B of the Electricity (Northern Ireland) Order 1992 (SI 1992/231 (NI 1));
(db) an appeal under article 14B of the Gas (Northern Ireland) Order 1996 (SI 1996/275 (NI 2));]
(e) an appeal under section 173 of the Energy Act 2004;
[(ea) an appeal under regulation 4 of the Water Industry Designated Codes (Appeals to the Competition and Markets Authority) Regulations 2017 (SI 2017/447);]
(f) a reference under article 3 of the Water Services etc (Scotland) Act 2005 (Consequential Provisions and Modifications) Order 2005 (SI 2005/3172);
(g) the giving of a direction or the making of modifications under article 9 of that Order.

Constitution of CMA groups

36. Where the chair is, by or under any enactment, required to constitute a group under this Schedule (a "CMA group"), the chair must constitute the group in accordance with this Part of this Schedule.

Membership of CMA groups

37. (1) The members of a CMA group are to be selected by the chair.

(2) In selecting the members of a CMA group, the chair must comply with any requirements imposed by or under any enactment.

(3) Subject to that, paragraph 38 has effect for the purposes of the membership of a CMA group.

38. (1) Each CMA group is to consist of at least three members of the CMA panel.

(2) Subject to sub-paragraphs (3) to (6), those members are to be such persons as the chair may select.

(3) In the case of a newspaper merger reference group—
(a) the group must include at least one newspaper panel member;
(b) the members of the group (if any) who are not newspaper panel members must be reporting panel members.

(4) In the case of a specialist communications reference group, the group must include at least one, but not more than three, of the specialist communications panel members.

(5) In the case of a specialist utility group, the group must include at least one of the specialist utility panel members.

[(5A) In the case of a specialist payment systems group, the group must include at least one payment systems member.]

(6) A newspaper panel member is not to be selected as a member of a CMA group that is not a newspaper merger reference group.

(7) The chair may at any time appoint a reporting panel member to be an additional member of a CMA group.

(8) The chair must appoint one of the members of a CMA group to chair the group (the "group chair").

39. The validity of anything done by a CMA group is not affected by—
(a) a vacancy;
(b) a defective appointment.

Termination of person's membership of a CMA group

40. A member of the CMA panel may at any time resign from a CMA group by giving written notice to this effect to the chair.

41. (1) Sub-paragraph (2) applies if the chair considers that—
(a) a member of a CMA group will be unable, for a substantial period, to perform his or her duties as a member of the group, or
(b) because of a particular interest of a member of a CMA group, it is inappropriate for him or her to remain a member of the group.

(2) The chair may remove the person in question from membership of the group.

42. A person ceases to be a member of a CMA group on ceasing to be a member of the CMA panel.

Replacement of a member of a CMA group

43. (1) Sub-paragraph (2) applies if a person ceases to be a member of a CMA group, whether by being removed under paragraph 41, or otherwise.

(2) The chair may select a replacement member of the group from the CMA panel.

Continuity on removal or replacement

44. (1) A person's ceasing to be a member of a CMA group, whether by being removed under paragraph 41, or otherwise, does not prevent—
(a) the group from continuing with anything begun before the person ceased to be a member of it;
(b) any decision made or direction given by the person while a member of the group from having effect after he or she has ceased to be a member of the group.

(2) Sub-paragraph (1)—
(a) applies whether or not a replacement member of the group is selected under paragraph 43;
(b) does not affect any requirements imposed by or under any enactment with respect to the constitution of a CMA group.

Attendance of other members

45. (1) At the invitation of the group chair of a CMA group, any reporting panel member who is not a member of the group may attend its meetings or otherwise take part in its proceedings.

(2) But a person attending in response to such an invitation may not—

(a) vote in any proceedings of the group, or
(b) have a statement of his or her dissent from a conclusion of the group included in a report made by the group.

(3) Nothing in sub-paragraph (1) is to be taken to prevent a CMA group from consulting any member of the CMA panel with respect to any matter or question with which the group is concerned.

Powers of chair pending group's constitution and first meeting

46. (1) While a CMA group is being constituted, the chair may take such steps as he or she considers appropriate to facilitate the work of the group once it has been constituted.

(2) The steps taken must be steps that it would be within the power of the group to take, had it already been constituted.

47. (1) The chair may, on behalf of the CMA, exercise the power conferred by section 37(1), 48(1) or 64(1) of the Enterprise Act 2002 in respect of the reference of a matter—
(a) while a CMA group is being constituted in connection with the reference;
(b) after a CMA group has been so constituted, but before it has held its first meeting.

(2) Sections 34C, 46D and 62A of the Enterprise Act 2002 have effect subject to sub-paragraph (1).

Performance of functions of chair with respect to constitution etc of CMA group

48. (1) A function of the chair that is specified in sub-paragraph (4) may, with the consent of the CMA Board, be exercised on behalf of the chair by—
(a) a person who is a member of both the CMA panel and the CMA Board, or
(b) a member of the CMA panel designated by the Secretary of State (whether generally or specifically) for the purposes of this paragraph.

(2) The consent referred to in sub-paragraph (1) must specify the identity of the person by whom a function of the chair is to be exercised.

(3) It may be given—
(a) by reference generally to functions specified in sub-paragraph (4);
(b) by reference to specific functions, or functions of a particular description;
(c) by reference generally to CMA groups;
(d) by reference to specific matters or specific CMA groups, or by reference to matters or CMA groups of a particular description.

(4) The functions are—
(a) the chair's functions under paragraph 33 and under this Part of this Schedule;
(b) the chair's functions by or under any other enactment in respect of the constitution of a CMA group;
(c) the chair's functions under—
(i) Schedule 4A to the Gas Act 1986;
(ii) Schedule 5A to the Electricity Act 1989;
[(iia) Schedule 5A to the Electricity (Northern Ireland) Order 1992 (SI 1992/231 (NI 1));
(iib) Schedule 3A to the Gas (Northern Ireland) Order 1996 (SI 1996/275 (NI 2));]
[(iic) Schedule A1 to the Transport Act 2000;]
(iii) Schedule 22 to the Energy Act 2004;
(iv) Schedule 2 to the Civil Aviation Act 2012;
[(v) Schedule 5 to the Financial Services (Banking Reform) Act 2013];
[(vi) the Water Industry Designated Codes (Appeals to the Competition and Markets Authority) Regulations 2017 (SI 2017/447)].

Independence of groups

49. (1) In making decisions that they are required or permitted to make by virtue of any enactment, CMA groups must act independently of the CMA Board.

(2) Nothing in sub-paragraph (1) prevents—
(a) the CMA Board from giving information in its possession to a CMA group, or
(b) a CMA group giving information in its possession to the CMA Board.

Casting votes

50. If a CMA group's vote on any decision is tied, the group chair is to have a casting vote.

Requirement to make rules of procedure for certain groups

51. (1) The CMA Board must make rules of procedure for merger reference groups, market reference groups, and special reference groups.

(2) Those rules are subject to any provision made by or under any enactment in respect of the procedure of a CMA group.

(3) Before making rules under this paragraph, the CMA Board must consult such persons as it considers appropriate.

(4) The CMA Board must publish rules made under this paragraph in whatever manner it considers appropriate for bringing them to the attention of those likely to be affected by them.

(5) Subject to rules made under this paragraph, and to any provision made by or under any enactment, a CMA group of a type referred to in sub-paragraph (1) may determine its own procedure.

(6) In this paragraph and paragraph 53—
(a) "market reference group" means a CMA group constituted in connection with a reference under section 131, 132 or 140A of the Enterprise Act 2002;
(b) "merger reference group" means a CMA group constituted in connection with a reference under section 32 of the Water Industry Act 1991 or section 22, 33, 45, or 62 of the Enterprise Act 2002;

(c) "special reference group" means a CMA group constituted in connection with a reference under—
   (i) section 11 of the Competition Act 1980;
   (ii) section 41E of the Gas Act 1986;
   (iii) section 56C of the Electricity Act 1989;
   (iv) section 12, 14 or 17K of the Water Industry Act 1991;
   (v) . . .
   (vi) section 13 of, or Schedule 4A to, the Railways Act 1993;
   (vii) . . .
   (viii) section 12 of the Transport Act 2000;
   (ix) section 193 of the Communications Act 2003;
   (x) article 3 of the Water Services etc (Scotland) Act 2005 (Consequential Provisions and Modifications) Order 2005 (SI 2005/3172).

52. (1) In determining how to proceed in accordance with rules made for it by the CMA Board under paragraph 51(1), and in determining its own procedure under paragraph 51(5), a group must have regard to any guidance issued by the CMA Board.

(2) Before issuing guidance for the purposes of this paragraph, or amending or revoking it, the CMA Board must consult such persons as it considers appropriate.

53. (1) Rules made under paragraph 51 may—
(a) make different provision for different cases or different purposes;
(b) be varied or revoked by rules subsequently made under that paragraph.

(2) They may in particular make provision—
(a) for particular stages of a merger investigation, market investigation, or special investigation to be dealt with in accordance with a timetable and for revision of that timetable;
(b) as to the documents and information that must be given to a relevant group in connection with a merger investigation, market investigation or special investigation;
(c) as to the documents and information that a relevant group must give to other persons in connection with such an investigation.

(3) Rules making provision as described in sub-paragraph (2)(a) or (2)(b) may, in particular, permit or require a relevant group to disregard documents or information given after a particular date.

(4) Rules making provision as described in sub-paragraph (2)(c) may in particular make provision for the notification or publication of, and for consultation about, provisional findings of a relevant group.

(5) Rules made under paragraph 51 may make provision as to the quorum of relevant groups.

(6) They may make provision—
(a) as to the extent (if any) to which persons interested or claiming to be interested in a matter under consideration that is specified or described in the rules are allowed—
   (i) to be present before or heard by a relevant group, either by themselves or by their representatives;
   (ii) to cross-examine witnesses;
   (iii) otherwise to take part;
(b) as to the extent (if any) to which sittings of a relevant group are to be held in public;
(c) generally in connection with any matters permitted by rules making provision as described in paragraph (a) or (b) (including, in particular, provision for a record of any hearings).

(7) Rules made under paragraph 51 may make provision for—
(a) the notification or publication of information relating to merger investigations, market investigations or special investigations;
(b) consultation about such investigations.

(8) Rules made under paragraph 51 for market reference groups may make provision as to the involvement of any public interest expert in the market investigation in connection with the reference under section 140A of the Enterprise Act 2002 in relation to which the expert was appointed.

(9) For the purposes of this paragraph—

"market investigation" means an investigation carried out by a market reference group in connection with a reference under section 131, 132 or 140A of the Enterprise Act 2002;

"merger investigation" means an investigation carried out by a merger reference group in connection with a reference under section 32 of the Water Industry Act 1991 or section 22, 33, 45, or 62 of the Enterprise Act 2002;

"public interest expert" means a person appointed under section 141B of the Enterprise Act 2002 in relation to a reference under section 140A(6) of that Act;

"relevant group" means a market reference group, a merger reference group, or a special reference group;

"special investigation" means an investigation carried out by a special reference group in connection with a provision listed in paragraph 51(6)(c).

Procedure of other CMA groups

54. (1) Subject to any special or general directions given by the Secretary of State, and to any provision made by or under any enactment, a CMA group that is not a group of a type referred to in paragraph 51(1) may determine its own procedure.

(2) It may, in particular, determine its quorum, and determine—
(a) the extent (if any) to which persons interested or claiming to be interested in a matter under consideration are allowed—
   (i) to be present before or heard by it, either by themselves or by their representatives;
   (ii) to cross-examine witnesses;

(iii) otherwise to take part;

(b) the extent (if any) to which its sittings are to be held in public.

(3) In determining its procedure under sub-paragraph (1), a CMA group must have regard to any guidance issued by the CMA Board.

CMA group decision: requirement for two thirds majority

55. For the purposes of paragraphs 56 to 58, a "qualifying majority decision" is a decision made by a CMA group which is that of at least two-thirds of the members of the group.

56. (1) This paragraph applies for the purposes of Part 3 of the Enterprise Act 2002.

(2) Where a decision of a CMA group under section 35(1) or 36(1) of that Act that there is an anti-competitive outcome is not a qualifying majority decision, it is to be treated as a decision under that section that there is not an anti-competitive outcome.

(3) Where a decision of a CMA group under section 47 of that Act is not a qualifying majority decision—

(a) in the case of a decision that a relevant merger situation has been created, it is to be treated as a decision under section 47 that no such situation has been created;

(b) in the case of a decision that the creation of a relevant merger situation has resulted, or may be expected to result, in a substantial lessening of competition within any market or markets in the United Kingdom for goods and services, it is to be treated as a decision under section 47 that the creation of that situation has not resulted, or may be expected not to result, in such a substantial lessening of competition;

(c) in the case of a decision that arrangements are in progress or in contemplation which, if carried into effect, will result in the creation of a relevant merger situation, it is to be treated as a decision under section 47 that no such arrangements are in progress or in contemplation;

(d) in the case of a decision that the creation of such a situation as is mentioned in paragraph (c) may be expected to result in a substantial lessening of competition within any market or markets in the United Kingdom for goods and services, it is to be treated as a decision under section 47 that the creation of that situation may be expected not to result in such a substantial lessening of competition.

(4) Where a decision of a CMA group under section 63 of that Act is not a qualifying majority decision—

(a) in the case of a decision that a special merger situation has been created, it is to be treated as a decision under section 63 that no such situation has been created;

(b) in the case of a decision that arrangements are in progress or in contemplation which, if carried into effect, will result in the creation of a special merger situation, it is to be treated as a decision under section 63 that no such arrangements are in progress or in contemplation.

(5) Expressions used in this paragraph are to be construed in accordance with Part 3 of the Enterprise Act 2002.

57. (1) This paragraph applies for the purposes of Part 4 of the Enterprise Act 2002.

(2) Where a decision under section 134, 141 or 141A of that Act is not a qualifying majority decision—

(a) in the case of a decision on an ordinary reference that a feature or combination of features of a relevant market prevents, restricts or distorts competition in connection with the supply or acquisition of any goods or services in the United Kingdom or a part of the United Kingdom, it is to be treated as a decision that the feature or (as the case may be) combination of features of that relevant market does not prevent, restrict or distort such competition;

(b) in the case of a decision on a cross-market reference that a feature or a combination of the features specified in the reference, as that feature or combination of features relates to goods or services of one or more than one of the descriptions so specified, prevents, restricts or distorts competition in connection with the supply or acquisition of any goods or services in the United Kingdom or a part of the United Kingdom, it is to be treated as a decision that that feature or (as the case may be) combination of features as it relates to goods or services of those descriptions does not prevent, restrict or distort such competition.

(3) Accordingly, a CMA group is to be treated as having decided under section 134, 141 or 141A that there is no adverse effect on competition in relation to an ordinary reference or a cross-market reference if—

(a) one or more than one decision of the group, in relation to the reference, is to be treated as mentioned in sub-paragraph (2)(a) or (as the case may be) (b), and

(b) there is, in relation to the reference, no other relevant decision of the group.

(4) "Relevant decision", in sub-paragraph (3)(b), means—

(a) in relation to an ordinary reference, a decision that is not to be treated as mentioned in sub-paragraph (2)(a), and which is that a feature or combination of features of a relevant market prevents, restricts or distorts competition in connection with the supply or acquisition of any goods or services in the United Kingdom or a part of the United Kingdom;

(b) in relation to a cross-market reference, a decision that is not to be treated as mentioned in sub-paragraph (2)(b), and which is that a feature or a combination of the features specified in the reference, as that feature or combination of features relates to goods or services of one or more than one of the descriptions so specified, prevents, restricts or distorts competition in connection with the supply or acquisition of any goods or services in the United Kingdom or a part of the United Kingdom.

(5) Where a decision of a CMA group under section 141A of that Act is not a qualifying majority decision, in the case of a decision under section 141A(4) that the feature or combination of features in question operates or may be expected to operate against the public interest, it is to be treated as a decision under section 141A that the feature or combination of features in question does not operate nor may be expected to operate against the public interest.

(6) Expressions used in this paragraph are to be construed in accordance with Part 4 of the Enterprise Act 2002.

58. A decision made by a CMA group is also subject to any other provision made by or under any enactment about decisions that are not qualifying majority decisions.

NOTES

Para 35 is amended as follows:

Sub-para (1)(ca) inserted by the Financial Services (Banking Reform) Act 2013, s 79(8), Sch 5, para 2(1), (2).

Sub-para (1)(e) repealed, figure in square brackets in sub-para (2) substituted and paras (da), (db) of the definition "specialist communications reference" in sub-para (3) inserted, by the Enterprise and Regulatory Reform Act 2013 (Amendment) (Gas and Electricity Appeals) Regulations 2015, SI 2015/16, reg 2(1), (2), subject to transitional provisions in relation to on-going references to the CMA made by the Northern Ireland Authority for Utility Regulation under the Gas (Northern Ireland) Order 1996 and the Electricity (Northern Ireland) Order 1992.

Para (ca) of the definition "specialist communications reference" in sub-para (3) inserted by the Environment Act 2021, s 86(7), as from a day to be appointed.

Para (ea) of the definition "specialist communications reference" in sub-para (3) inserted by the Water Industry Designated Codes (Appeals to the Competition and Markets Authority) Regulations 2017, SI 2017/447, reg 20(a).

Para 38: sub-para (5A) inserted by the Financial Services (Banking Reform) Act 2013, s 79(8), Sch 5, para 2(1), (3).

Para 48: sub-para (4)(c)(iia), (iib) inserted by SI 2015/16, reg 2(1), (3), subject to transitional provisions as noted above. Sub-para (4)(c)(iic) inserted by the Air Traffic Management and Unmanned Aircraft Act 2021, s 11, Sch 7, para 11, as from 29 June 2021. Sub-para (4)(c)(v) inserted by the Financial Services (Banking Reform) Act 2013, s 79(8), Sch 5, para 2(1), (4). Sub-para (4)(c)(vi) inserted by SI 2017/447, reg 20(b).

Para 51: sub-para (6)(c)(v), (vii) repealed by SI 2015/16, reg 2(1), (4), subject to transitional provisions as noted above.

For various transitional provisions (including those relating to the abolition of the OFT and the Competition Commission, existing references to those bodies and provisions relating to continuity), see the Enterprise and Regulatory Reform Act 2013 (Commencement No 6, Transitional Provisions and Savings) Order 2014, SI 2014/416, Schedule at **[2.13]**.

Modifications: this Part of this Schedule is modified by the Enterprise Act 2002 (Protection of Legitimate Interests) Order 2003, SI 2003/1592, art 16, Sch 4, para 18 (as added by the Enterprise Act 2002 (Protection of Legitimate Interests) (Amendment) Order 2014, SI 2014/891, arts 2, 19(1), (5)), which provides as follows—

"**18.** In Schedule 4 to the Enterprise and Regulatory Reform Act 2013 (the Competition and Markets Authority)—

(a) in paragraph 35(3) the reference in the definition of a "newspaper merger reference" to section 45 of the Enterprise Act 2002 shall have effect as if it included a reference to article 5 of the Enterprise Act 2002 (Protection of Legitimate Interests) Order 2003;

(b) the reference in paragraph 47(1) to section 64(1) of the Enterprise Act 2002 shall have effect as if it included a reference to article 7(1) of the Enterprise Act 2002 (Protection of Legitimate Interests) Order 2003;

(c) the reference in paragraph 47(2) to section 62A of the Enterprise Act 2002 shall have effect as if it included a reference to article 5A of the Enterprise Act 2002 (Protection of Legitimate Interests) Order 2003;

(d) the reference in paragraph 51(6)(b) to section 62 of the Enterprise Act 2002 shall have effect as if it included a reference to article 5 of the Enterprise Act 2002 (Protection of Legitimate Interests) Order 2003;

(e) in paragraph 53(9) the reference in the definition of "merger investigation" to section 62 of the Enterprise Act 2002 shall have effect as if it included a reference to article 5 of the Enterprise Act 2002 (Protection of Legitimate Interests) Order 2003;

(f) paragraph 56(1) shall have effect as if it also provided that paragraph 56(4) also applies for the purposes of the Enterprise Act 2002 (Protection of Legitimate Interests) Order 2003; and

(g) in paragraph 56(4)—

(i) a reference to section 63 of the Enterprise Act 2002 shall have effect as if it included a reference to article 6 of the Enterprise Act 2002 (Protection of Legitimate Interests) Order 2003; and

(ii) a reference to a special merger situation shall have effect as if it included a reference to a European relevant merger situation.".

Note that s 68 of the Enterprise Act 2002 (under which the 2003 Order was made) was repealed by the Competition (Amendment etc) (EU Exit) Regulations 2019, SI 2019/93, regs 32, 47, as from IP completion day (as defined in the European Union (Withdrawal Agreement) Act 2020, s 39). See, however, Sch 4, Pt 7, paras 25–27 to the 2019 Regulations (at **[7.76]**) which provides for the continued application of the 2003 Order in the circumstances specified in those paragraphs.

[PART 3A THE OIM PANEL

The OIM panel

[1.463]

58A. (1) The OIM panel is a panel of persons available for selection as members of a group constituted in accordance with this Part of this Schedule.

(2) The OIM panel is to consist of—

(a) the OIM panel chair appointed under paragraph 1(1)(b)(iv), and

(b) the other members of the panel appointed under paragraph 1(1)(b)(v).

Constitution of OIM task groups

58B. (1) The OIM panel chair may at any time constitute a group in accordance with this Part of this Schedule for the purpose of carrying out on the CMA's behalf functions of the CMA under Part 4 of the United Kingdom Internal Market Act 2020.

(2) A group constituted as mentioned in sub-paragraph (1) is to be known as an Office for the Internal Market task group (or "OIM task group").

Membership of OIM task groups

58C. (1) The members of an OIM task group are to be selected by the OIM panel chair.

(2) Each OIM task group is to consist of at least three members of the OIM panel.

(3) The OIM panel chair must appoint one of the members of an OIM task group to chair the group ("the task group chair").

58D. The validity of anything done by an OIM task group is not affected by—

(a) a vacancy;

(b) a defective appointment.

Termination of person's membership of an OIM task group

58E. A member of the OIM panel may at any time resign from an OIM task group by giving written notice to this effect to the OIM panel chair.

58F. (1) Sub-paragraph (2) applies if the OIM panel chair considers that—

(a) a member of an OIM task group will be unable, for a substantial period, to perform their duties as a member of the group, or

(b) because of a particular interest of a member of an OIM task group, it is inappropriate for that person to remain a member of the group.

(2) The OIM panel chair may remove the person in question from membership of the task group.

58G. A person ceases to be a member of an OIM task group on ceasing to be a member of the OIM panel.

Replacement of a member of an OIM task group

58H. (1) Sub-paragraph (2) applies if a person ceases to be a member of an OIM task group, whether by being removed under paragraph 58F, or otherwise.

(2) The OIM panel chair may select a replacement member of the group from the OIM panel.

Continuity on removal or replacement

58I. (1) A person's ceasing to be a member of an OIM task group, whether by being removed under paragraph 58F, or otherwise, does not prevent—

(a) the group from continuing with anything begun before the person ceased to be a member of it;

(b) any decision made or direction given by the person while a member of the group from having effect after they have ceased to be a member of the group.

(2) Sub-paragraph (1) applies whether or not a replacement member of the group is selected under paragraph 58H.

Powers of chair pending group's constitution and first meeting

58J. (1) While an OIM task group is being constituted, the OIM panel chair may take such steps as the OIM panel chair considers appropriate to facilitate the work of the group once it has been constituted.

(2) The steps taken must be steps that it would be within the power of the group to take, had it already been constituted.

Independence of OIM task groups

58K. (1) In exercising functions which they are authorised to exercise by virtue of any enactment, OIM task groups must act independently of the CMA Board.

(2) Nothing in sub-paragraph (1) prevents—

(a) the CMA Board giving information in its possession to an OIM task group, or

(b) an OIM task group giving information in its possession to the CMA Board.

Casting votes

58L. If an OIM task group's vote on any decision is tied, the task group chair is to have a casting vote.

Procedure of OIM task groups

58M. (1) An OIM task group may determine its own procedure (including determining its quorum).

(2) In determining its procedure under sub-paragraph (1), an OIM task group must have regard to any guidance issued by the CMA Board.]

NOTES

Commencement: IP completion day (as defined in the European Union (Withdrawal Agreement) Act 2020, s 39).

Inserted by the United Kingdom Internal Market Act 2020, s 32, Sch 3, para 8, as from IP completion day (as defined in the European Union (Withdrawal Agreement) Act 2020, s 39).

PART 4 INTERPRETATION AND TRANSITIONAL AND TRANSITORY PROVISION

Interpretation

[1.464]

59. (1) In this Schedule, "enactment" means—

(a) an enactment contained in this or any other Act;

(b) an enactment comprised in subordinate legislation within the meaning of the Interpretation Act 1978;

(c) an enactment contained in, or in an instrument made under, an Act of the Scottish Parliament;

(d) a Measure or Act of the National Assembly for Wales;

(e) an enactment contained in, or in an instrument made under, Northern Ireland legislation (within the meaning of the Interpretation Act 1978).

(2) Any reference in this Schedule to an enactment includes a reference to an enactment whenever passed or made.

60. References in this Schedule to the commencement date are to the date on which section 25(3) comes into force.

Members of the Competition Commission

61. (1) This paragraph applies—

(a) in relation to any appointments under paragraph 1(1)(b) to the CMA panel that are made before the abolition of the Competition Commission under section 26, to any person who is a panel member of the Competition Commission and whose term of office as such is not due to expire before the abolition of the Competition Commission under that section;

(b) in relation to any other appointment under paragraph 1(1)(b) to the CMA panel, to a person who was a panel member of the Competition Commission immediately prior to its abolition under section 26.

(2) A person to whom this paragraph applies may be appointed under paragraph 1(1)(b) as a member of the CMA panel.

(3) But the terms of the person's appointment as a member of the CMA panel must not be such that the sum of the period of his or her office as a member of the CMA panel, and of the period of his or her office as a panel member of the Competition Commission (excluding any period when he or she also holds office as a member of the CMA panel), exceeds eight years.

(4) Paragraph 4(1) applies for the purposes of the person's re-appointment as a member of the CMA panel as it does for the purposes of the re-appointment of a CMA panel member to whom this paragraph does not apply.

(5) The power conferred by section 100 includes power to make provision for the appointment of panel members of the Competition Commission as members of the CMA panel, or for the re-appointment of persons who are appointed as members of the CMA panel by virtue of sub-paragraph (2), for the purpose of enabling anything in the process of being done by or on behalf of the Competition Commission immediately prior to its abolition to be completed by or on behalf of the CMA; and nothing in sub-paragraphs (1) to (4) restricts the provision that may be made for that purpose.

62. Except as provided for by paragraph 61, a person who holds or has held office as a panel member of the Competition Commission at any time prior to its abolition may not be appointed under paragraph 1(1)(b) as a member of the CMA panel.

63. References in paragraphs 61 and 62 to a panel member of the Competition Commission are to a person appointed as a member of the Competition Commission of a kind mentioned in paragraph 2(3) of Schedule 7 to the Competition Act 1998.

Financial years of the CMA

64. (1) If the duration of the period beginning with the commencement date and ending with the next 31 March is six months or more, the first financial year of the CMA is that period.

(2) But if the duration of that period is less than six months, the first financial year of the CMA is the period beginning with the commencement date, and ending with the 31 March in the year following the next 31 March after the commencement date.

(3) The subsequent financial years of the CMA are each successive period of 12 months.

First annual plan of the CMA

65. (1) The CMA is to publish its first annual plan within the period of three months beginning with the commencement date.

(2) The first annual plan is to relate to the period beginning with the date of publication of the plan, and ending with the date on which the CMA's first financial year ends.

NOTES

For various transitional provisions (including those relating to the abolition of the OFT and the Competition Commission, existing references to those bodies and provisions relating to continuity), see the Enterprise and Regulatory Reform Act 2013 (Commencement No 6, Transitional Provisions and Savings) Order 2014, SI 2014/416, Schedule at **[2.13]**.

National Assembly for Wales: see further, in relation to the renaming of the National Assembly for Wales as the Senedd Cymru or the Welsh Parliament, the Senedd and Elections (Wales) Act 2020. See also ss 3–9 of the 2020 Act in relation to the renaming of Acts of the National Assembly for Wales, Members of the National Assembly for Wales, etc.

Orders: the Enterprise and Regulatory Reform Act 2013 (Commencement No 3, Transitional Provisions and Savings) Order 2013, SI 2013/2227.

SCHEDULES 5–15

(Sch 5 (Proceedings under Part I of the 1998 Act), Sch 6 (Regulatory Appeals: Minor and Consequential Amendments), Sch 7 (Mergers: Interim Measures), Sch 8 (Mergers: Time Limits), Sch 9 (Markets: Cross-market References), Sch 10 (Markets: Public Interest Interventions), Sch 11 (Markets: Investigation Powers), Sch 12 (Markets: Time Limits), Sch 13 (Extension of Power to Issue Warrants Under the 1998 Act Extended to CAT), Sch 14 (Regulators: Use of Powers under the 1998 Act), and Sch 15 (Minor and Consequential Amendments: Part 4) contain amendments to the Competition Act 1980, the Competition Act 1998, and the Enterprise Act 2002 which have been incorporated in the appropriate place. They also contain amendments to various other enactments.)

FINANCIAL SERVICES (BANKING REFORM) ACT 2013

(2013 c 33)

ARRANGEMENT OF SECTIONS

PART 5
REGULATION OF PAYMENT SYSTEMS

The Payment Systems Regulator

An Act to make further provision about banking and other financial services, including provision about the Financial Services Compensation Scheme; to make provision for the amounts owed in respect of certain deposits to be treated as a preferential debt on insolvency; to make further provision about payment systems and securities settlement systems; to make provision about the accounts of the Bank of England and its wholly owned subsidiaries; to make provision in relation to persons providing claims management services; and for connected purposes

[18 December 2013]

NOTES

Only the provisions of this Act most relevant to competition law are reproduced; provisions omitted are not annotated.

PART 5 REGULATION OF PAYMENT SYSTEMS

The Payment Systems Regulator

[1.465]

40 The Payment Systems Regulator

(1) The FCA must establish a body corporate to exercise the functions conferred on the body by or under this Part.

(2) The body established under subsection (1) is referred to in this Part as the Payment Systems Regulator.

(3) The FCA must take such steps as are necessary to ensure that the Payment Systems Regulator is, at all times, capable of exercising the functions referred to in subsection (1).

(4) In complying with the duty imposed by subsection (3) the FCA may, in particular—

- (a) provide staff to the Payment Systems Regulator, and
- (b) provide services to the Payment Systems Regulator which the FCA considers would facilitate the exercise of any of those functions.

(5) Schedule 4 (which contains further provision about the Payment Systems Regulator) has effect.

"Payment system" etc

[1.466]

41 Meaning of "payment system"

(1) In this Part "payment system" means a system which is operated by one or more persons in the course of business for the purpose of enabling persons to make transfers of funds, and includes a system which is designed to facilitate the transfer of funds using another payment system.

(2) But "payment system" does not include—

- (a) any arrangements for the physical movement of cash;
- (b) a system which does not make any provision for the transfer of funds by payers, or to recipients, in the United Kingdom;
- (c) a securities settlement system operated by a [recognised CSD];
- (d) a system operated by a recognised clearing house [or a recognised CSD];
- (e) any other system whose primary purpose is not that of enabling persons to transfer funds.

(3) In this section—

["recognised CSD" has the meaning given by section 285(1) of FSMA 2000;]

"recognised clearing house" has the meaning given by section 285(1) of FSMA 2000;

"securities settlement system" means a computer-based system, and procedures, which enable title to units of a security to be evidenced and transferred without a written instrument, and which facilitate supplementary and incidental matters.

(4) The Treasury may by order amend this section so as to—

(a) add descriptions of systems or arrangements that are not to be regarded as payment systems, or

(b) vary or remove any such description.

NOTES

Sub-s (2): words in square brackets in para (c) substituted by the Central Securities Depositories Regulations 2017, SI 2017/1064, reg 10, Schedule, Pt 1, para 16(1), (2)(a). Words in square brackets in para (d) inserted by the Uncertificated Securities (Amendment and EU Exit) Regulations 2019, SI 2019/679, reg 3(1), (2).

Sub-s (3): definition "recognised CSD" inserted by SI 2017/1064, reg 10, Schedule, Pt 1, para 16(1), (2)(b).

[1.467]

42 Participants in payment systems etc

(1) This section applies for the purposes of this Part.

(2) The following persons are "participants" in a payment system—

(a) the operator of the payment system (see subsection (3));

(b) any infrastructure provider (see subsection (4));

(c) any payment service provider (see subsection (5)).

(But see also subsection (8).)

(3) "Operator", in relation to a payment system, means any person with responsibility under the system for managing or operating it; and any reference to the operation of a payment system includes a reference to its management.

(4) "Infrastructure provider", in relation to a payment system, means any person who provides or controls any part of the infrastructure used for the purposes of operating the payment system.

(5) "Payment service provider", in relation to a payment system, means any person who provides services to persons who are not participants in the system for the purposes of enabling the transfer of funds using the payment system.

(6) A payment service provider has "direct access" to a payment system if the payment service provider is able to provide services for the purposes of enabling the transfer of funds using the payment system as a result of arrangements made between the payment service provider and the operator of the payment system.

(7) Any reference to participation in a payment system is to be read in accordance with this section, and in particular—

(a) in the case of an operator of a payment system, includes a reference to developing the system, and

(b) in the case of a payment service provider with direct access to a payment system, includes a reference to entering into an agreement with a person to enable the person to become a payment service provider in relation to the system.

(8) The Bank of England is not to be regarded as a participant of any kind in any payment system.

General duties of Regulator

[1.468]

49 Regulator's general duties in relation to payment systems

(1) In discharging its general functions relating to payment systems the Payment Systems Regulator must, so far as is reasonably possible, act in a way which advances one or more of its payment systems objectives.

(2) The payment systems objectives of the Payment Systems Regulator are—

(a) the competition objective (see section 50),

(b) the innovation objective (see section 51), and

(c) the service-user objective (see section 52).

(3) In discharging its general functions relating to payment systems the Payment Systems Regulator must have regard to—

(a) the importance of maintaining the stability of, and confidence in, the UK financial system,

(b) the importance of payment systems in relation to the performance of functions by the Bank of England in its capacity as a monetary authority, and

(c) the regulatory principles in section 53.

(4) The general functions of the Payment Systems Regulator relating to payment systems are—

(a) its function of giving general directions under section 54 (considered as a whole),

(b) its functions in relation to the giving of general guidance under section 96 (considered as a whole), and

(c) its function of determining the general policy and principles by reference to which it performs particular functions.

[1.469]

50 The competition objective

(1) The competition objective is to promote effective competition in—

(a) the market for payment systems, and

(b) the markets for services provided by payment systems,

in the interests of those who use, or are likely to use, services provided by payment systems.

(2) The reference in subsection (1) to promoting effective competition includes, in particular, promoting effective competition—

(a) between different operators of payment systems,

(b) between different payment service providers, and

(c) between different infrastructure providers.

(3) The matters to which the Payment Systems Regulator may have regard in considering the effectiveness of competition in a market mentioned in subsection (1) include—

(a) the needs of different persons who use, or may use, services provided by payment systems;
(b) the ease with which persons who may wish to use those services can do so;
(c) the ease with which persons who obtain those services can change the person from whom they obtain them;
(d) the needs of different payment service providers or persons who wish to become payment service providers;
(e) the ease with which payment service providers, or persons who wish to become payment service providers, can provide services using payment systems;
(f) the ease with which payment service providers can change the payment system they use to provide their services;
(g) the needs of different infrastructure providers or persons who wish to become infrastructure providers;
(h) the ease with which infrastructure providers, or persons who wish to become infrastructure providers, can provide infrastructure for the purposes of operating payment systems;
(i) the needs of different operators of payment systems;
(j) the ease with which operators of payment systems can change the infrastructure used to operate the payment systems;
(k) the level and structure of fees, charges or other costs associated with participation in payment systems;
(l) the ease with which new entrants can enter the market;
(m) how far competition is contributing to the development of efficient and effective infrastructure for the purposes of operating payment systems;
(n) how far competition is encouraging innovation.

Regulatory and competition functions

[1.470]
54 Directions
(1) The Payment Systems Regulator may give directions in writing to participants in regulated payment systems.
(2) A direction given to a participant in a regulated payment system may—
(a) require or prohibit the taking of specified action in relation to the system;
(b) set standards to be met in relation to the system.
(3) A direction under this section may apply—
(a) generally,
(b) in relation to—
(i) all operators, or every operator of a regulated payment system of a specified description,
(ii) all infrastructure providers, or every person who is an infrastructure provider in relation to a regulated payment system of a specified description, or
(iii) all payment service providers, or every person who is a payment service provider in relation to a regulated payment system of a specified description, or
(c) in relation to specified persons or persons of a specified description.
(4) The Payment Systems Regulator must publish any direction given under this section that applies as mentioned in subsection (3)(a) or (b).
(5) A direction under this section that applies as mentioned in subsection (3)(a) or (b) is referred to in this Part as a "general direction".

[1.471]
55 System rules
(1) The Payment Systems Regulator may require the operator of a regulated payment system—
(a) to establish rules for the operation of the system;
(b) to change the rules in a specified way or so as to achieve a specified purpose;
(c) to notify the Payment Systems Regulator of any proposed change to the rules;
(d) not to change the rules without the approval of the Payment Systems Regulator.
(2) A requirement under subsection (1)(c) or (d) may be general or specific.
(3) A requirement under this section that is imposed on—
(a) all operators of regulated payment systems, or
(b) every operator of a regulated payment system of a specified description,
is referred to in this Part as a "generally-imposed requirement".

[1.472]
56 Power to require granting of access to payment systems
(1) This section applies where a person ("the applicant") applies for an order under this section.
(2) The Payment Systems Regulator may by order require the operator of a regulated payment system to enable the applicant to become a payment service provider in relation to the system.
(3) The Payment Systems Regulator may by order require any payment service provider with direct access to a regulated payment system to enter into an agreement with the applicant to enable the applicant to become a payment service provider in relation to the system.
(4) An order under this section may provide for the applicant to become a payment service provider in relation to a payment system—
(a) for a period specified in the order;
(b) on terms and conditions specified in the order.

[1.473]
57 Variation of agreements relating to payment systems
(1) This section applies to the following agreements—
(a) any agreement made between the operator of a regulated payment system and a payment service provider;

(b) any agreement made between a payment service provider with direct access to a regulated payment system and another person for the purpose of enabling that other person to become a payment service provider in relation to the system;
(c) any agreement concerning fees or charges payable in connection with—
(i) participation in a regulated payment system, or
(ii) the use of services provided by a regulated payment system.

(2) The Payment Systems Regulator may, on the application of a party to an agreement to which this section applies, vary the agreement by—
(a) varying any of the fees or charges payable under the agreement, or
(b) in the case of an agreement within subsection (1)(a) or (b), varying any other terms and conditions relating to the payment service provider's participation in the payment system.

(3) In the case of an agreement within subsection (1)(b), the reference in subsection (2)(b) to the payment service provider is to the payment service provider which does not have direct access to the payment system.

(4) The power under this section to vary any fee or charge includes power to specify a maximum fee or charge.

(5) If the Payment Systems Regulator varies an agreement under this section, the agreement has effect subject to the variation.

[1.474]

58 Power to require disposal of interest in payment system

(1) The Payment Systems Regulator may require a person who has an interest in[—
(a) the operator of a regulated payment system, or
(b) an infrastructure provider in relation to such a system,
to dispose of all or part of that interest].

(2) The power conferred by subsection (1) may be exercised only if the Payment Systems Regulator is satisfied that, if the power is not exercised, there is likely to be a restriction or distortion of competition in—
(a) the market for payment systems, or
(b) a market for services provided by payment systems.

[(2A) The reference in subsection (2) to a restriction or distortion of competition includes, in particular, a restriction or distortion of competition—
(a) between different operators of payment systems,
(b) between different payment services providers, or
(c) between different infrastructure providers.]

(3) The Payment Systems Regulator may not exercise the power conferred by subsection (1) without the consent of the Treasury.

(4) If the Payment Systems Regulator decides to exercise the power conferred by subsection (1) in relation to a person who has an interest in the operator of a regulated payment system—
(a) the Payment Systems Regulator must notify the relevant competition authorities (see subsection (5)), and
(b) the relevant competition authorities may not take any action in relation to the person that would require the person to dispose of all or part of that interest.

(5) The relevant competition authorities are—
(a) the Secretary of State,
(b) the Competition and Markets Authority, and
(c) the FCA.

NOTES

Sub-s (1): words in square brackets substituted by the Small Business, Enterprise and Employment Act 2015, s 14(1)–(3).
Sub-s (2A): inserted by the Small Business, Enterprise and Employment Act 2015, s 14(1), (2), (4).

[1.475]

59 The Regulator's functions under Part 4 of the Enterprise Act 2002

(1) The functions to which this subsection applies are to be concurrent functions of the Payment Systems Regulator and the Competition and Markets Authority ("the CMA").

(2) Subsection (1) applies to the functions of the CMA under Part 4 of the Enterprise Act 2002 (market investigations), so far as those functions—
(a) are exercisable by the CMA Board (within the meaning of Schedule 4 to the Enterprise and Regulatory Reform Act 2013), and
(b) relate to participation in payment systems.

(3) But subsection (1) does not apply to functions under the following sections of the Enterprise Act 2002—
section 166 (duty to maintain register of undertakings and orders);
section 171 (duty to publish guidance).

(4) So far as is necessary for the purposes of, or in connection with, subsections (1) and (2)—
(a) references in Part 4 of the Enterprise Act 2002 to the CMA (including references in provisions of that Act applied by that Part) are to be read as including references to the Payment Systems Regulator,
(b) references in that Part to section 5 of that Act are to be read as including references to section 64 of this Act, and
(c) references in that Part to consumers are to be read as including references to any person who uses, or is likely to use, services provided by payment systems in the course of a business carried on by the person.

(5) But subsection (4) does not apply—
(a) in relation to section 166 or 171 of that Act, or
(b) where the context otherwise requires.

(6) Section 130A of the Enterprise Act 2002 is to have effect in relation to the Payment Systems Regulator by virtue of subsections (1) and (2) as if—

(a) in subsection (2)(a) of that section, the reference to the acquisition or supply of goods or services of one or more than one description in the United Kingdom were a reference to the participation in payment systems used to provide services in the United Kingdom, and
(b) in subsection (2)(b) of that section, the reference to the extent to which steps can and should be taken were a reference to the extent to which steps that might include steps under Part 4 of that Act can and should be taken.

[1.476]
60 Restrictions on exercise of functions under Part 4 of the Enterprise Act 2002
(1) Before the CMA or the Payment Systems Regulator first exercises any of the concurrent functions in relation to any matter, it must consult the other.
(2) Neither the CMA nor the Payment Systems Regulator may exercise any of the concurrent functions in relation to any matter if any of those functions have been exercised in relation to that matter by the other.
(3) In subsections (1) and (2) "the concurrent functions" means the functions which by virtue of section 59 are concurrent functions of the Payment Systems Regulator and the CMA.
(4) Before the FCA or the Payment Systems Regulator first exercises any of the concurrent functions in relation to any matter, it must consult the other.
(5) Neither the FCA nor the Payment Systems Regulator may exercise any of the concurrent functions in relation to any matter if any of those functions have been exercised in relation to that matter by the other.
(6) In subsections (4) and (5) "the concurrent functions"—
(a) in relation to the Payment Systems Regulator, means the functions which by virtue of section 59 are concurrent functions of the Payment Systems Regulator and the CMA, and
(b) in relation to the FCA, means the functions which by virtue of section 234I of FSMA 2000 are concurrent functions of the FCA and the CMA.
(7) In this section "the CMA" means the Competition and Markets Authority.

[1.477]
61 The Regulator's functions under the Competition Act 1998
(1) The functions to which this subsection applies are to be concurrent functions of the Payment Systems Regulator and the Competition and Markets Authority ("the CMA").
(2) Subsection (1) applies to the functions of the CMA under the provisions of Part 1 of the Competition Act 1998, so far as relating to any of the following that relate to participation in payment systems—
(a) agreements, decisions or concerted practices of the kind mentioned in section 2(1) of that Act,
(b) conduct of the kind mentioned in section 18(1) of that Act, [and]
[(c) transferred EU anti-trust commitments or transferred EU anti-trust directions (as defined in section 40ZA of that Act)].
(3) But subsection (1) does not apply to functions under the following sections of that Act—
section 31D(1) to (6) (duty to publish guidance);
section 38(1) to (6) (duty to publish guidance about penalties);
section 40B(1) to (4) (duty to publish statement of policy on penalties);
section 51 (rules).
(4) So far as necessary for the purposes of, or in connection with, the provisions of subsections (1) and (2), references to the CMA in Part 1 of the Competition Act 1998 are to be read as including references to the Payment Systems Regulator.
(5) But subsection (4) does not apply—
(a) in relation to sections 31D(1) to (6), 38(1) to (6), 40B(1) to (4), 51, 52(6) and (8) and 54 of that Act, or
(b) where the context otherwise requires.

NOTES
Sub-s (2): word in square brackets in para (b) inserted, and para (c) substituted (for the original paras (c) and (d)), by the Competition (Amendment etc) (EU Exit) Regulations 2019, SI 2019/93, reg 60, Sch 1, para 15, as from IP completion day (as defined in the European Union (Withdrawal Agreement) Act 2020, s 39) (for transitional provisions and savings in relation to the operation of the 2019 Regulations, see Sch 4 to those Regulations at **[7.69]** et seq). Note that Sch 1, para 15 to the 2019 Regulations was amended by the Competition (Amendment etc) (EU Exit) Regulations 2020, SI 2020/1343, reg 27, with effect from immediately before IP completion day; and the effect of those amendments has been incorporated in the text set out above. Note also that the original paras (c) and (d) read as follows—

"(c) agreements, decisions or concerted practices of the kind mentioned in Article 101(1) of the Treaty on the Functioning of the European Union, and
(d) conduct which amounts to abuse of the kind mentioned in Article 102 of the Treaty on the Functioning of the European Union.".

[1.478]
62 Duty to consider exercise of powers under Competition Act 1998
(1) Before exercising any power within subsection (2), the Payment Systems Regulator must consider whether it would be more appropriate to proceed under the Competition Act 1998.
(2) The powers referred to in subsection (1) are—
(a) its power to give a direction under section 54 (apart from the power to give a general direction);
(b) its power to impose a requirement under section 55 (apart from the power to impose a generally-imposed requirement);
(c) its powers under sections 56, 57 and 58.
(3) The Payment Systems Regulator must not exercise the power if it considers that it would be more appropriate to proceed under the Competition Act 1998.

[1.479]
63 Provision of information and assistance to a CMA group

(1) For the purpose of assisting a CMA group in carrying out a relevant investigation, the Payment Systems Regulator must give the CMA group—

(a) any relevant information which it has in its possession, and

(b) any other assistance which the CMA group may reasonably require in relation to any matters falling within the scope of the investigation.

(2) A "relevant investigation" is an investigation carried out on a reference made by the Payment Systems Regulator under section 131 of the Enterprise Act 2002 by virtue of section 59.

(3) "Relevant information", in relation to a relevant investigation, is information—

(a) which relates to matters falling within the scope of the investigation, and

(b) which—

(i) is requested by the CMA group for the purpose of the investigation, or

(ii) in the opinion of the Payment Systems Regulator, it would be appropriate to give to the CMA group for that purpose.

(4) A CMA group, in carrying out a relevant investigation, must take into account any information given to it under this section.

(5) In this section "CMA group" has the same meaning as in Schedule 4 to the Enterprise and Regulatory Reform Act 2013.

[1.480]
64 Function of keeping markets under review

(1) For the purpose of the functions conferred on it by sections 58 to 63 the Payment Systems Regulator is to have the function of keeping under review—

(a) the market for payment systems, and

(b) the markets for services provided by payment systems.

(2) The function conferred by subsection (1) is to be carried out with a view to (among other things) ensuring that the Payment Systems Regulator has sufficient information to take informed decisions and to carry out its other functions effectively.

[1.481]
65 Exclusion of general duties

(1) Section 49 (the Payment Systems Regulator's general duties) does not apply in relation to anything done by the Payment Systems Regulator in the carrying out of its functions by virtue of sections 59 to 63.

(2) But in the carrying out of any functions by virtue of sections 59 to 63, the Payment Systems Regulator may have regard to any of the matters in respect of which a duty is imposed by section 49 if it is a matter to which the Competition and Markets Authority is entitled to have regard in the carrying out of those functions.

[1.482]
66 Concurrent competition powers: supplementary provision

(1) If any question arises as to whether, by virtue of section 59 or 61, any functions fall to be, or are capable of being, carried out by the Payment Systems Regulator in relation to any particular case, that question is to be referred to, and determined by, the Treasury.

(2) No objection is to be taken to anything done under the Competition Act 1998 or Part 4 of the Enterprise Act 2002 by or in relation to the Payment Systems Regulator on the ground that it should have been done by or in relation to the Competition and Markets Authority.

67 *(S 67 (Amendments relating to Regulator's competition powers) amends the Company Directors Disqualification Act 1986, s 9E, the Competition Act 1998, s 54, the Enterprise Act 2002, s 136, and the Enterprise and Regulatory Reform Act 2013, s 52, Sch 4.)*

Consultation, accountability and oversight

[1.483]
107 Competition scrutiny

(1) Chapter 4 of Part 9A of FSMA 2000 (competition scrutiny) applies to the Payment Systems Regulator's practices and regulating provisions in relation to payment systems as it applies to the FCA's practices and regulating provisions within the meaning of that Chapter.

(2) In subsection (1)—

(a) the reference to the Payment Systems Regulator's practices in relation to payment systems is a reference to practices adopted by it in the exercise of functions under this Part, and

(b) the reference to the Payment Systems Regulator's regulating provisions in relation to payment systems is a reference to the following—

(i) any general directions given under section 54;

(ii) any generally-imposed requirements under section 55;

(iii) any guidance given under section 96.

PART 8 FINAL PROVISIONS

[1.484]
147 Extent

(1) The provisions of this Act extend to England and Wales, Scotland and Northern Ireland.
This is subject to subsection (2).

(2) The amendments made by the following sections have the same extent as the enactments amended—

(a) section 13 (preferential debts: Great Britain),

(b), (c) . . .

NOTES

Sub-s (2): paras (b), (c) repealed by the Financial Services and Markets Act 2000 (Claims Management Activity) Order 2018, SI 2018/1253, art 98(1), (4).

[1.485]

148 Commencement and short title

(1) This Part comes into force on the day on which this Act is passed.

(2)–(4) (*Outside the scope of this work.*)

(5) The remaining provisions of this Act come into force on such day as the Treasury may by order appoint.

(6) Different days may be appointed for different purposes.

(7) This Act may be cited as the Financial Services (Banking Reform) Act 2013.

NOTES

Orders: the commencement orders relevant to the provisions of the Act reproduced here are the Financial Services (Banking Reform) Act 2013 (Commencement No 1) Order 2014, SI 2014/377, the Financial Services (Banking Reform) Act 2013 (Commencement No 4) Order 2014, SI 2014/823 and the Financial Services (Banking Reform) Act 2013 (Commencement No 6) Order 2014, SI 2014/2458.

NATIONAL SECURITY AND INVESTMENT ACT 2021

(2021 c 25)

An Act to make provision for the making of orders in connection with national security risks arising from the acquisition of control over certain types of entities and assets; and for connected purposes

[29 April 2021]

ARRANGEMENT OF SECTIONS

PART 2
REMEDIES

Assessment period

Interim and final orders

Financial assistance

CMA functions

PART 3
ENFORCEMENT AND APPEALS

Offences

Prosecution and penalties

Civil sanctions

Civil proceedings

Judicial review and appeals

Territorial application

PART 4
MISCELLANEOUS

Administrative requirements

Information gateways

CMA information

Data protection

Defamation

Annual report

PART 5
FINAL PROVISIONS

SCHEDULES

NOTES

Editorial note: the government has indicated that this Act will fully come into force on 4 January 2022. See www.gov.uk/government/news/new-and-improved-national-security-and-investment-act-set-to-be-up-and-running. But as of 24 November 2021, no commencement orders or regulations had been made to commence the remaining provisions of this Act.

PART 1 CALL-IN FOR NATIONAL SECURITY

CHAPTER 1 CALL-IN POWER

[1.486]

1 Call-in notice for national security purposes

(1) The Secretary of State may give a notice if the Secretary of State reasonably suspects that—

(a) a trigger event has taken place in relation to a qualifying entity or qualifying asset, and the event has given rise to or may give rise to a risk to national security, or

(b) arrangements are in progress or contemplation which, if carried into effect, will result in a trigger event taking place in relation to a qualifying entity or qualifying asset, and the event may give rise to a risk to national security.

(2) For the purposes of this Act, in considering whether a trigger event has taken place, or whether arrangements are in progress or contemplation which, if carried into effect, will result in a trigger event taking place, the effect of section 13(1) (notifiable acquisitions that are void) must be disregarded.

(3) A notice under subsection (1) is referred to in this Act as a call-in notice.

(4) If the Secretary of State decides to give a call-in notice, the notice must be given to—

(a) the acquirer,

(b) if the trigger event relates to a qualifying entity, the entity, and

(c) such other persons as the Secretary of State considers appropriate.

(5) The call-in notice must include a description of the trigger event to which it relates and state the names of the persons to whom the notice is given.

(6) The Secretary of State may not give a call-in notice unless a statement has been published (and not withdrawn) for the purposes of section 3.

(7) The Secretary of State must have regard to that statement before giving a call-in notice.

(8) But nothing in the statement limits the power to give a call-in notice.

NOTES

Commencement: to be appointed.

[1.487]

2 Further provision about call-in notices

(1) No more than one call-in notice may be given in relation to each trigger event.

(2) Subject to subsections (3) and (4), a call-in notice given on the grounds mentioned in section 1(1)(a)—

(a) may not be given after the end of the period of 6 months beginning with the day on which the Secretary of State became aware of the trigger event, and

(b) may not be given after the end of the period of 5 years beginning with the day on which the trigger event took place.

(3) Subsection (2)(b) does not apply where the trigger event is one in relation to which section 13(1) has effect.

(4) In relation to a trigger event taking place during the period beginning with 12 November 2020 and ending with the day before commencement day, a call-in notice given on the grounds mentioned in section 1(1)(a)—

(a) if the Secretary of State became aware of the trigger event before commencement day, may not be given after the end of the period of 6 months beginning with commencement day,

(b) if the Secretary of State became aware of the trigger event on or after commencement day—

(i) may not be given after the end of the period of 6 months beginning with the day on which the Secretary of State became aware of the trigger event, and

(ii) may not be given after the end of the period of 5 years beginning with commencement day.

(5) In this section "commencement day" means the day on which this section comes into force.

(6) This section is subject to section 22 (and see section 62).

NOTES

Commencement: to be appointed.

[1.488]

3 Statement about exercise of call-in power

(1) The Secretary of State may publish a statement for the purposes of this section if the requirements set out in section 4(1) are satisfied.

(2) The statement is a statement prepared by the Secretary of State that sets out how the Secretary of State expects to exercise the power to give a call-in notice.

(3) The statement may include, in particular—

(a) details of sectors of the economy in relation to which the Secretary of State considers that trigger events are more likely to give rise to a risk to national security,

(b) details of the trigger events, qualifying entities and qualifying assets in relation to which the Secretary of State expects to exercise the power to give a call-in notice, and

(c) details of factors that the Secretary of State expects to take into account when deciding whether or not to exercise the power.

(4) The Secretary of State must review a statement published under this section at least once every 5 years.

(5) A statement published under this section may be amended or replaced by a subsequent statement, and this section and section 4 apply in relation to any amended or replacement statement as in relation to the original statement.

(6) Nothing in a statement published under this section affects the power of the Secretary of State to make notifiable acquisition regulations (see section 6).

NOTES

Commencement: 1 July 2021.

[1.489]

4 Consultation and parliamentary procedure

(1) Before the Secretary of State may publish a statement for the purposes of section 3 the Secretary of State must—

(a) carry out such consultation as the Secretary of State thinks appropriate in relation to a draft of the statement,

(b) make any changes to the draft that appear to the Secretary of State to be necessary in view of the responses to the consultation, and

(c) lay the statement before Parliament.

(2) Either House of Parliament may at any time before the expiry of the 40-day period resolve not to approve the statement.

(3) If either House of Parliament resolves not to approve the statement under subsection (2), the Secretary of State must withdraw the statement.

(4) Any such resolution under subsection (2) does not affect the validity of a call-in notice given following the publication of the statement prior to its withdrawal, and does not affect the publication of a new statement.

(5) "The 40-day period" is the period of 40 days beginning with the day on which the statement is laid before Parliament (or, if it is not laid before each House of Parliament on the same day, the later of the days on which it is laid).

(6) When calculating the 40-day period, ignore any period during which Parliament is dissolved or prorogued or during which both Houses are adjourned for more than 4 days.

(7) The requirements in subsection (1)(a) and (b) may be met by consultation carried out before this section comes into force.

NOTES

Commencement: 1 July 2021.

CHAPTER 2 INTERPRETATION

[1.490]

5 Meaning of "trigger event" and "acquirer"

(1) For the purposes of this Act, a "trigger event" takes place when—

(a) a person gains control of a qualifying entity, as set out in section 8, or

(b) a person gains control of a qualifying asset, as set out in section 9.

(2) In this Act "acquirer" means the person who gains the control referred to in subsection (1) (or in relation to a trigger event that has not yet taken place, would gain that control).

NOTES

Commencement: to be appointed.

[1.491]

6 Notifiable acquisitions

(1) The Secretary of State may make regulations for the purposes of this section ("notifiable acquisition regulations").

(2) A notifiable acquisition takes place when a person gains control, by virtue of one or more of the cases described in subsection (2), (5) or (6) of section 8, of a qualifying entity of a specified description.

(3) But a notifiable acquisition does not take place if complying with the requirement to give a mandatory notice under section 14(1) would be impossible for the person within subsection (2).

(4) A description of qualifying entity that is specified must include provision that the entity carries on activities in the United Kingdom which are of a specified description (whether or not it also carries on other activities).

(5) Notifiable acquisition regulations may—

(a) amend this section in relation to the circumstances in which a notifiable acquisition takes place or does not take place,

(b) make provision for exemptions by reference to the characteristics of the person within subsection (2),

(c) make consequential amendments of other provisions of this Act.

(6) Notifiable acquisition regulations may by virtue of subsection (5)(a) include, in particular, provision about the circumstances in which the gaining of control of a qualifying asset of a specified description is a notifiable acquisition.

(7) A description specified under subsection (6) may only include qualifying assets within section 7(6) if it includes provision that any such asset is used in connection with activities carried on in the United Kingdom which are of a specified description (whether or not it is also used in connection with other activities).

(8) In this section "specified" means specified in notifiable acquisition regulations.

NOTES

Commencement: 29 April 2021 (sub-s (1)); 1 July 2021 (otherwise).

Regulations: the National Security and Investment Act 2021 (Notifiable Acquisition) (Specification of Qualifying Entities) Regulations 2021, SI 2021/1264 at **[2.205]**.

[1.492]

7 Qualifying entities and assets

(1) This section defines "qualifying entity" and "qualifying asset" for the purposes of this Act.

(2) A "qualifying entity" is (subject to subsection (3)) any entity, whether or not a legal person, that is not an individual, and includes a company, a limited liability partnership, any other body corporate, a partnership, an unincorporated association and a trust.

(3) An entity which is formed or recognised under the law of a country or territory outside the United Kingdom is a "qualifying entity" only if it—

(a) carries on activities in the United Kingdom, or

(b) supplies goods or services to persons in the United Kingdom.

(4) A "qualifying asset" is (subject to subsection (6)) an asset of any of the following types—

(a) land,

(b) tangible (or, in Scotland, corporeal) moveable property,

(c) ideas, information or techniques which have industrial, commercial or other economic value.

(5) Examples of assets within subsection (4)(c) include—

(a) trade secrets,

(b) databases,

(c) source code,

(d) algorithms,

(e) formulae,

(f) designs,

(g) plans, drawings and specifications,

(h) software.

(6) Land or moveable property situated outside the United Kingdom or the territorial sea, or any asset within subsection (4)(c), is a "qualifying asset" only if it is used in connection with—

(a) activities carried on in the United Kingdom, or

(b) the supply of goods or services to persons in the United Kingdom.

NOTES

Commencement: to be appointed.

[1.493]

8 Control of entities

(1) For the purposes of this Act, a person gains control of a qualifying entity if the person acquires a right or interest in, or in relation to, the entity and as a result one or more of the cases described in this section arises.

(2) The first case is where the percentage of the shares that the person holds in the entity increases—

(a) from 25% or less to more than 25%,

(b) from 50% or less to more than 50%, or

(c) from less than 75% to 75% or more.

(3) In subsection (2), the reference to holding a percentage of shares is—

(a) in the case of an entity that has a share capital, to holding shares comprised in the issued share capital of the entity of a nominal value (in aggregate) of that percentage of the share capital,

(b) in the case of an entity that does not have a share capital, to holding a right to a share of that percentage of the capital or profits of the entity,

(c) in the case of a limited liability partnership, to holding a right to a share of that percentage of any surplus assets of the partnership on a winding up.

(4) For the purposes of subsection (3)(c), to the extent that rights to share in any surplus assets of the limited liability partnership on a winding up are not expressly provided for, each member of the partnership is to be treated as holding the right to an equal share of such assets.

(5) The second case is where the percentage of the voting rights that the person holds in the entity increases—

(a) from 25% or less to more than 25%,

(b) from 50% or less to more than 50%, or

(c) from less than 75% to 75% or more.

(6) The third case is where the acquisition is of voting rights in the entity that (whether alone or together with other voting rights held by the person) enable the person to secure or prevent the passage of any class of resolution governing the affairs of the entity.

(7) In subsections (5) and (6), a reference to the voting rights in an entity is—
- (a) in the case of an entity that has a share capital, to the rights conferred on shareholders in respect of their shares to vote at general meetings of the entity on all or substantially all matters,
- (b) in the case of an entity that does not have a share capital, to the rights conferred on members to vote at general meetings of the entity on all or substantially all matters,

and, in the case of an entity that does not have general meetings at which matters are decided by such votes, includes any rights in relation to the entity that are of the equivalent effect.

(8) The fourth case is (subject to subsection (9)) where the acquisition, whether alone or together with other interests or rights held by the person, enables the person materially to influence the policy of the entity.

(9) Subsection (8) does not include a case where the person already holds any interest or right that enables the person materially to influence the policy of the entity.

NOTES

Commencement: to be appointed.

[1.494]

9 Control of assets

(1) For the purposes of this Act, a person gains control of a qualifying asset if the person acquires a right or interest in, or in relation to, the asset and as a result the person is able—
- (a) to use the asset, or use it to a greater extent than prior to the acquisition, or
- (b) to direct or control how the asset is used, or direct or control how it is used to a greater extent than prior to the acquisition.

This is subject to section 11.

(2) In this section, references to the use of an asset include references to its exploitation, alteration, manipulation, disposal or destruction.

NOTES

Commencement: to be appointed.

[1.495]

10 Holding and acquiring interests and rights: supplementary

(1) Schedule 1 provides for particular cases in which a person is to be treated for the purposes of this Act as holding an interest or right.

(2) A person is to be treated for the purposes of this Act as acquiring an interest or right (to the extent that the person would not otherwise be regarded as doing so) where—
- (a) the interest or right becomes treated as held by the person by virtue of Schedule 1, or
- (b) the person is already treated as holding the interest or right by virtue of that Schedule and something occurs in relation to the interest or right which would be regarded as its acquisition by the person (including by virtue of paragraph (a)) if the person was not already treated as holding it.

NOTES

Commencement: to be appointed.

[1.496]

11 Exceptions relating to control of assets

(1) For the purposes of this Act a person is not to be regarded as gaining control of a qualifying asset by reason of an acquisition made by an individual for purposes that are wholly or mainly outside the individual's trade, business or craft.

(2) Subsection (1) does not apply in relation to an asset that—
- (a) is land, or
- (b) falls within any of the following (as it has effect from time to time)—
  - (i) the Schedule to the Export of Radioactive Sources (Control) Order 2006 (SI 2006/1846),
  - (ii) article 4A of, or Schedule 2 or 3 to, the Export Control Order 2008 (SI 2008/3231),
  - (iii) Annex I or IV to Council Regulation (EC) No 428/2009 of 5 May 2009,
  - (iv) Annex I to Regulation (EU) No 258/2012 of the European Parliament and of the Council of 14 March 2012,
  - (v) Annex II or III to Regulation (EU) 2019/125 of the European Parliament and of the Council of 1 January 2019.

(3) The Secretary of State may by regulations—
- (a) amend subsection (2) so as to add, vary or remove any asset or description of asset,
- (b) prescribe other circumstances, or descriptions of circumstances, in which a person is not to be regarded for the purposes of this Act as gaining control of a qualifying asset.

NOTES

Commencement: 29 April 2021 (sub-s (3)); to be appointed (otherwise).

[1.497]

12 Trigger events: supplementary

(1) If a trigger event takes place over a period of more than one day, or if it is unclear when during a period of more than one day the event has taken place, it is treated for the purposes of this Act as taking place on the last day of the period.

(2) Subsections (3) and (4) apply if a person enters into an agreement or arrangement that enables the person (contingently or not) to do something in the future that would result in a trigger event taking place.

(3) For the purposes of this Act, entering into the agreement or arrangement does not necessarily establish that arrangements are in progress or contemplation which, if carried into effect, would result in a trigger event taking place.
(4) The question of whether such arrangements are in progress or contemplation (at the time of entry into the agreement or arrangement or subsequently) is to be determined by reference to all the circumstances, including how likely it is in practice that person will do the thing that would result in a trigger event taking place.

NOTES

Commencement: to be appointed.

CHAPTER 3 APPROVAL OF NOTIFIABLE ACQUISITION

[1.498]
13 Approval of notifiable acquisition

(1) A notifiable acquisition that is completed without the approval of the Secretary of State is void.
(2) The Secretary of State may approve a notifiable acquisition by—
- (a) giving a notification under section 14(8)(b)(ii),
- (b) making a final order under section 26, subject to subsection (3),
- (c) giving a final notification under section 26.

(3) A notifiable acquisition, in relation to which a final order has been made, that is completed otherwise than in accordance with the final order, is void.

NOTES

Commencement: to be appointed.

CHAPTER 4 PROCEDURE

Procedure in respect of notifiable acquisition

[1.499]
14 Mandatory notification procedure

(1) Subject to subsection (2), a person must give notice to the Secretary of State before the person, pursuant to a notifiable acquisition, gains control in circumstances falling within section 6(2).
(2) Subsection (1) does not apply if the Secretary of State has already given a call-in notice, which has not been revoked, in relation to the proposed notifiable acquisition.
(3) A notice under subsection (1) is referred to in this Act as a mandatory notice.
(4) The Secretary of State may by regulations prescribe the form and content of a mandatory notice.
(5) As soon as reasonably practicable after receiving a mandatory notice, the Secretary of State must decide whether to reject or accept the notice.
(6) The Secretary of State may reject the mandatory notice on one or more of the following grounds—
- (a) it does not meet the requirements of this section,
- (b) it does not meet the requirements prescribed by the regulations,
- (c) it does not contain sufficient information to allow the Secretary of State to decide whether to give a call-in notice in relation to the proposed notifiable acquisition.

(7) If the mandatory notice is rejected, the Secretary of State must, as soon as practicable, provide reasons in writing for that decision to the person who gave the notice.
(8) If the mandatory notice is accepted, the Secretary of State must—
- (a) as soon as practicable, notify each relevant person, and
- (b) before the end of the review period—
  - (i) give a call-in notice in relation to the proposed notifiable acquisition, or
  - (ii) notify each relevant person that no further action will be taken under this Act in relation to the proposed notifiable acquisition.

(9) The "review period" is the period of 30 working days beginning with the day on which the notification under subsection (8)(a) is given to the person who gave the mandatory notice.
(10) In this section "relevant person" means the person who gave the mandatory notice and such other persons as the Secretary of State considers appropriate.

NOTES

Commencement: 29 April 2021 (sub-s (4)); to be appointed (otherwise).
Regulations: the National Security and Investment Act 2021 (Prescribed Form and Content of Notices and Validation Applications) Regulations 2021, SI 2021/1272 at **[2.233]**.

[1.500]
15 Requirement to consider retrospective validation without application

(1) This section and section 16 apply to a notifiable acquisition that is completed without the approval of the Secretary of State and, accordingly, is void (see section 13(1)).
(2) The Secretary of State must, before the end of the period of 6 months beginning with the day on which the Secretary of State becomes aware of the notifiable acquisition—
- (a) give a call-in notice in relation to the acquisition, or
- (b) give a validation notice in relation to the acquisition to each relevant person and notify those persons that no further action will be taken under this Act in relation to the acquisition.

(3) The effect of a validation notice given under this section or section 16 or 17, is that the notifiable acquisition to which it relates is to be treated as having been completed with the approval of the Secretary of State (and, accordingly, is not void).
(4) In this section "relevant person" means—

(a) the person who was required to give a mandatory notice to the Secretary of State in relation to the acquisition (see section 14(1)), and

(b) such other persons as the Secretary of State considers appropriate.

NOTES

Commencement: to be appointed.

[1.501]

16 Application for retrospective validation of notifiable acquisition

(1) Any person materially affected by the fact that a notifiable acquisition to which this section applies (see section 15(1)) is void, may apply to the Secretary of State for a validation notice in relation to the acquisition.

(2) An application under subsection (1) is referred to in this Act as a validation application.

(3) The Secretary of State may by regulations prescribe the form and content of a validation application.

(4) Subject to subsection (8), as soon as reasonably practicable after receiving a validation application, the Secretary of State must decide whether to reject or accept the application.

(5) The Secretary of State may reject the application on one or more of the following grounds—

(a) it does not meet the requirements of this section,

(b) it does not meet the requirements prescribed by the regulations,

(c) it does not contain sufficient information to allow the Secretary of State to decide whether to give a call-in notice in relation to the acquisition.

(6) If the application is rejected, the Secretary of State must, as soon as practicable, provide reasons in writing for that decision to the person who made the application.

(7) If the application is accepted, the Secretary of State must—

(a) as soon as practicable, notify each relevant person, and

(b) before the end of the review period—

(i) give a call-in notice in relation to the acquisition, or

(ii) give a validation notice in relation to the acquisition to each relevant person and notify those persons that no further action will be taken under this Act in relation to the acquisition.

(8) The Secretary of State is not required to consider a validation application in relation to an acquisition if, in the opinion of the Secretary of State, there has been no material change in circumstances since a previous validation application in relation to the acquisition was made.

(9) In this section—

"relevant person" means the person who made the validation application and such other persons as the Secretary of State considers appropriate;

the "review period" is the period of 30 working days beginning with the day on which the notification under subsection (7)(a) is given to the person who made the validation application.

NOTES

Commencement: 29 April 2021 (sub-s (3)); to be appointed (otherwise).

Regulations: the National Security and Investment Act 2021 (Prescribed Form and Content of Notices and Validation Applications) Regulations 2021, SI 2021/1272 at **[2.233]**.

[1.502]

17 Retrospective validation of notifiable acquisition following call-in

(1) This section applies where the Secretary of State has given a call-in notice pursuant to—

(a) subsection (2)(a) of section 15, or

(b) subsection (7)(b)(i) of section 16,

(and, accordingly, the trigger event to which the call-in notice relates is, or includes, a notifiable acquisition to which those sections apply.)

(2) If the Secretary of State gives a final notification in relation to the call-in notice, the Secretary of State must also give a validation notice in relation to the acquisition.

(3) A validation notice under this section must be given to—

(a) each person to whom the final notification is given,

(b) the person (if any) who made an application in relation to the acquisition under section 16, and

(c) such other persons as the Secretary of State considers appropriate.

(4) Subsection (5) applies if the Secretary of State makes a final order in relation to the call-in notice.

(5) So much of the notifiable acquisition as would, had it been completed after the making of the final order, have been completed in accordance with the order is to be treated as having been completed with the approval of the Secretary of State (and, accordingly, is not void).

NOTES

Commencement: to be appointed.

Voluntary notification of trigger event

[1.503]

18 Voluntary notification procedure

(1) This section does not apply in relation to—

(a) arrangements which would result in a notifiable acquisition,

(b) a trigger event that is, or includes, a notifiable acquisition.

(2) A seller, acquirer or the qualifying entity concerned may give a notice to the Secretary of State stating that —

(a) a trigger event has taken place in relation to a qualifying entity or a qualifying asset, or

(b) arrangements are in progress or contemplation which, if carried into effect, will result in a trigger event taking place in relation to a qualifying entity or a qualifying asset.

(3) A notice under subsection (2) is referred to in this Act as a voluntary notice.

(4) The Secretary of State may by regulations prescribe the form and content of a voluntary notice.

(5) As soon as reasonably practicable after receiving the voluntary notice, the Secretary of State must decide whether to reject or accept the notice.

(6) The Secretary of State may reject the voluntary notice on one or more of the following grounds—

- (a) it does not meet the requirements of this section,
- (b) it does not meet the requirements prescribed by the regulations,
- (c) it does not contain sufficient information to allow the Secretary of State to decide whether to give a call-in notice,
- (d) there is no reasonable prospect of being able to give a call-in notice due to the operation of the time-limits in subsection (2) or (4) of section 2.

(7) If the voluntary notice is rejected, the Secretary of State must, as soon as practicable, provide reasons in writing for that decision to each relevant person.

(8) If the voluntary notice is accepted, the Secretary of State must—

- (a) as soon as practicable, notify each relevant person, and
- (b) before the end of the review period—
  - (i) give a call-in notice in relation to the trigger event, or
  - (ii) notify each relevant person that no further action will be taken under this Act in relation to the trigger event.

(9) The "review period" is the period of 30 working days beginning with the day on which the notification under subsection (8)(a) is given to the person who gave the voluntary notice; but this does not affect the operation of the time-limits in subsections (2) and (4) of section 2.

(10) In this section—

"relevant person" means the person who gave the voluntary notice and such other persons as the Secretary of State considers appropriate,

"seller", in relation to a trigger event, means a person who has ceded control of the qualifying entity or a qualifying asset (or in relation to a trigger event that has not yet taken place, would cede that control).

NOTES

Commencement: 29 April 2021 (sub-s (4)); to be appointed (otherwise).

Regulations: the National Security and Investment Act 2021 (Prescribed Form and Content of Notices and Validation Applications) Regulations 2021, SI 2021/1272 at **[2.233]**.

Information, etc

[1.504]

19 Power to require information

(1) The Secretary of State may give a notice to a person (subject to section 21) to require the person to provide any information in relation to the exercise of the Secretary of State's functions under this Act which—

- (a) is specified or described in the notice, or falls within a category of information specified or described in the notice, and
- (b) is within that person's possession or power.

(2) The Secretary of State is not to require the provision of information under this section except where the requirement to provide information is proportionate to the use to which the information is to be put in the carrying out of the Secretary of State's functions under this Act.

(3) A notice under subsection (1) is referred to in this Act as an information notice.

(4) An information notice may—

- (a) specify the manner in which the information is to be provided,
- (b) specify a time limit for—
  - (i) providing the information,
  - (ii) notifying the Secretary of State that the information is not in the person's possession or power, or
- (c) require the person to provide any information within their possession or power which would enable the Secretary of State to find the information required by the notice.

(5) An information notice must—

- (a) specify the purpose for which the notice is given, and
- (b) state the possible consequences of not complying with the notice.

(6) A person is not required under this section to provide any information which that person could not be compelled to provide in evidence in civil proceedings before the court.

(7) A reference in this section to the provision of information includes a reference to the provision of a legible and intelligible copy of information recorded otherwise than in legible form.

(8) A person to whom information is provided under this section may copy the information.

(9) In this section "the court" means—

- (a) in relation to England and Wales or Northern Ireland, the High Court,
- (b) in relation to Scotland, the Court of Session, and
- (c) in relation to a person outside the United Kingdom, the High Court of England and Wales.

NOTES

Commencement: to be appointed.

[1.505]

20 Attendance of witnesses

(1) The Secretary of State may give a notice to a person (subject to section 21) to require the person—

- (a) to attend at a time and place specified in the notice, and
- (b) to give evidence to the Secretary of State in relation to the exercise of the Secretary of State's functions under this Act.

(2) The Secretary of State is not to require the giving of evidence under this section except where the requirement to give evidence is proportionate to the use to which the evidence is to be put in the carrying out of the Secretary of State's functions under this Act.
(3) A notice under subsection (1) is referred to in this Act as an attendance notice.
(4) An attendance notice must—
  (a) specify the purpose for which the notice is given, and
  (b) state the possible consequences of not complying with the notice.
(5) A person is not required under this section to give any evidence which that person could not be compelled to give in civil proceedings before the court.
(6) A person is not required, in compliance with an attendance notice, to go more than 10 miles from their place of residence unless necessary travelling expenses are paid or offered to that person.
(7) In this section "the court" means—
  (a) in relation to evidence given in England and Wales or Northern Ireland, the High Court,
  (b) in relation to evidence given in Scotland, the Court of Session, and
  (c) in relation to evidence given outside the United Kingdom, the High Court of England and Wales.

NOTES

Commencement: to be appointed.

[1.506]

21 Information notices and attendance notices: persons outside the UK

(1) The Secretary of State may give an information notice or an attendance notice to a person outside the United Kingdom only if the person falls within subsection (2), (3) or (4) of this section.
(2) A person falls within this subsection if the person is—
  (a) a United Kingdom national,
  (b) an individual ordinarily resident in the United Kingdom,
  (c) a body incorporated or constituted under the law of any part of the United Kingdom, or
  (d) carrying on business in the United Kingdom.
(3) A person falls within this subsection if—
  (a) a trigger event has taken place in relation to a qualifying entity which is formed or recognised under the law of any part of the United Kingdom, or
  (b) arrangements are in progress or contemplation which, if carried into effect, will result in a trigger event taking place in relation to a qualifying entity of that description,

and the person is the acquirer.
(4) A person falls within this subsection if—
  (a) a trigger event has taken place in relation to a qualifying asset which —
    (i) is within section 7(4)(a) or (b) and is situated in the United Kingdom or the territorial sea, or
    (ii) is within section 7(4)(c) and is used in connection with activities carried on in the United Kingdom, or
  (b) arrangements are in progress or contemplation which, if carried into effect, will result in a trigger event taking place in relation to a qualifying asset within paragraph (a),

and the person is the acquirer.

NOTES

Commencement: to be appointed.

[1.507]

22 False or misleading information

(1) This section applies where false or misleading information is provided to the Secretary of State—
  (a) in a mandatory notice,
  (b) in a validation application,
  (c) in a voluntary notice,
  (d) in response to an information notice, or
  (e) in response to an attendance notice.
(2) Where a decision made by the Secretary of State under this Act is materially affected by the false or misleading information, the Secretary of State may reconsider the decision and may affirm, vary or revoke it.
(3) Where a decision is varied or revoked under this section, the Secretary of State must give notice to that effect to such persons as the Secretary of State considers appropriate.
(4) If a revoked decision was—
  (a) a decision to give a call-in notice,
  (b) a decision to make or revoke a final order, or
  (c) a decision to give a final notification,

the Secretary of State may give a further call-in notice and section 2(1) does not apply.
(5) Where a decision is revoked under this section, the time limits in section 2(2) and (4) do not apply to the case concerned, but a call-in notice (or a further call-in notice) may not be given after the end of the period of 6 months beginning with the day on which the information was discovered to be false or misleading.

NOTES

Commencement: to be appointed.

PART 2 REMEDIES

Assessment period

[1.508]

23 Meaning of "assessment period"

(1) This section defines "assessment period" in relation to a call-in notice.

(2) The assessment period begins with the day on which the call-in notice is given to the acquirer.

(3) In this section—

(a) "the initial period" is the period of 30 working days beginning with the day mentioned in subsection (2),

(b) "the additional period" is the period of 45 working days beginning with the first working day after the day on which the initial period ends,

(c) a "voluntary period" is such period of working days, beginning with the first working day after the day on which the additional period (or the previous voluntary period) ends, as may be agreed in writing between the Secretary of State and the acquirer.

(4) The assessment period ends at the end of the initial period unless, before the end of the initial period, the Secretary of State gives an additional period notice to each person to whom the call-in notice was given (see subsection (8)).

(5) If an additional period notice is given, the assessment period ends at the end of the additional period unless, before the end of the additional period, a voluntary period is agreed.

(6) If a voluntary period is agreed, the assessment period ends at the end of the voluntary period, or at the end of any further voluntary period which is agreed.

(7) The Secretary of State must give notice of any voluntary period, or further voluntary period to each person to whom the call-in notice was given.

(8) An "additional period notice" is a notice which the Secretary of State may give if the Secretary of State—

(a) reasonably believes that—

(i) a trigger event has taken place or that arrangements are in progress or contemplation which, if carried into effect, will result in a trigger event, and

(ii) a risk to national security has arisen from the trigger event or would arise from the trigger event if carried into effect, and

(b) reasonably considers that the additional period is required to assess the trigger event further.

(9) A voluntary period or further voluntary period may be agreed by the Secretary of State only if the Secretary of State—

(a) is satisfied, on the balance of probabilities, that—

(i) a trigger event has taken place or that arrangements are in progress or contemplation which, if carried into effect, will result in a trigger event, and

(ii) a risk to national security has arisen from the trigger event or would arise from the trigger event if carried into effect, and

(b) reasonably considers that the period is required to consider whether to make a final order or what provision a final order should contain.

NOTES

Commencement: to be appointed.

[1.509]

24 Effect of information notice and attendance notice

(1) This section applies if an information notice or an attendance notice is given at any time during the assessment period in relation to a call-in notice.

(2) As soon as practicable after giving the information notice or attendance notice, the Secretary of State must notify each relevant person of—

(a) the fact that an information notice or attendance notice has been given, and

(b) the time limit specified in the notice for complying with the requirements of the notice.

(3) As soon as practicable after—

(a) the Secretary of State is satisfied that the requirements of the information notice or the attendance notice have been complied with, or

(b) (if earlier) the time specified in the information notice or the attendance notice for complying with those requirements has passed,

the Secretary of State must notify each relevant person confirming that fact.

(4) Any day falling within the period beginning with the day on which the notice under subsection (2) is given and ending with the day on which a notice under subsection (3) is given does not count for the purposes of calculating the initial, additional or voluntary period under section 23.

(5) In this section "relevant person" means each person to whom the call-in notice was given.

NOTES

Commencement: to be appointed.

Interim and final orders

[1.510]

25 Interim orders

(1) The Secretary of State may, during the assessment period in relation to a call-in notice, make an order if the Secretary of State reasonably considers that the provisions of the order are necessary and proportionate for the purpose of preventing or reversing pre-emptive action, or mitigating its effects.

(2) In subsection (1), "pre-emptive action" means action which might prejudice the exercise of the Secretary of State's functions under this Act in relation to the call-in notice.

(3) An order under subsection (1) is referred to in this Act as an "interim order".

(4) An interim order may include—

(a) provision requiring a person, or description of person, to do, or not to do, particular things,

(b) provision for the appointment of a person to conduct or supervise the conduct of activities on such terms and with such powers as may be specified or described in the order,

(c) provision requiring a person, or description of person, not to disclose the contents of the order except to the extent permitted by the order,

(d) consequential, supplementary or incidental provision.

(5) Provision made by or under an interim order may extend to a person's conduct outside the United Kingdom or the territorial sea only if the person is—

(a) a United Kingdom national,

(b) an individual ordinarily resident in the United Kingdom,

(c) a body incorporated or constituted under the law of any part of the United Kingdom, or

(d) carrying on business in the United Kingdom.

(6) An interim order comes into force at such time as is determined by or under the order.

(7) An interim order ceases to have effect at the earliest of—

(a) the giving of a final notification or the coming into force of a final order in relation to the call-in notice,

(b) such time as is determined by or under the order,

(c) such time as it is revoked.

NOTES

Commencement: to be appointed.

[1.511]

26 Final orders and final notifications

(1) The Secretary of State must, before the end of the assessment period in relation to a call-in notice—

(a) make a final order, or

(b) give a final notification to each person to whom the call-in notice was given.

(2) In this section—

(a) a "final notification" is a notification that no further action in relation to the call-in notice is to be taken under this Act,

(b) a "final order" is an order under subsection (3).

(3) The Secretary of State may, during the assessment period, make a final order if the Secretary of State—

(a) is satisfied, on the balance of probabilities, that—

(i) a trigger event has taken place or that arrangements are in progress or contemplation which, if carried into effect, will result in a trigger event, and

(ii) a risk to national security has arisen from the trigger event or would arise from the trigger event if carried into effect, and

(b) reasonably considers that the provisions of the order are necessary and proportionate for the purpose of preventing, remedying or mitigating the risk.

(4) Before making a final order the Secretary of State must consider any representations made to the Secretary of State.

(5) A final order may include—

(a) provision requiring a person, or description of person, to do, or not to do, particular things,

(b) provision for the appointment of a person to conduct or supervise the conduct of activities on such terms and with such powers as may be specified or described in the order,

(c) provision requiring a person, or description of person, not to disclose the contents of the order except to the extent permitted by the order,

(d) consequential, supplementary or incidental provision.

(6) Provision made by or under a final order may extend to a person's conduct outside the United Kingdom or the territorial sea only if the person is—

(a) a United Kingdom national,

(b) an individual ordinarily resident in the United Kingdom,

(c) a body incorporated or constituted under the law of any part of the United Kingdom, or

(d) carrying on business in the United Kingdom.

(7) A final order comes into force at such time as is determined by or under the order.

(8) A final order ceases to have effect at such time as is determined by or under the order, unless it is revoked before that time.

NOTES

Commencement: to be appointed.

[1.512]

27 Review, variation and revocation of orders

(1) This section applies in relation to an interim order and a final order.

(2) The Secretary of State must keep each order under review and may vary or revoke it.

(3) If a person required to comply with an order requests that the Secretary of State vary or revoke it, the Secretary of State must consider the request as soon as practicable after receiving it.

(4) But the Secretary of State is not required to consider such a request in relation to a final order if, in the opinion of the Secretary of State, there has been no material change of circumstances—

(a) since the order was made or last varied, or

(b) in the case of a request from a person who has made a previous request in relation to the order, since the previous request was made.

NOTES

Commencement: to be appointed.

[1.513]

28 Orders: supplementary

(1) This section applies in relation to an interim order and a final order.

(2) As soon as practicable after making or varying an order, the Secretary of State must serve the order, or the order as varied, on—

(a) each person who is required to comply with the order,

(b) each person to whom the call-in notice was given, and

(c) such other persons as the Secretary of State considers appropriate.

(3) As soon as practicable after varying an order, the Secretary of State must give notice to any person who was previously required to comply with the order but is no longer required to comply with it.

(4) Subject to subsection (5), each order (including each order as varied) or explanatory material accompanying the order must—

(a) state the date on which the order or any variation comes into force or how that date is to be determined,

(b) state each person, or description of person, who is required to comply with the order,

(c) describe the trigger event and entity or asset concerned,

(d) state the reasons for making or varying the order,

(e) state the possible consequences of not complying with the order,

(f) provide information about—

(i) how to apply to the Secretary of State for an order to be varied or revoked, and

(ii) the procedure for judicial review or, in Scotland, an application to the supervisory jurisdiction of the Court of Session.

(5) The Secretary of State may exclude from the copy of an order served on any person within subsection (2), or from any explanatory material accompanying the order, anything the disclosure of which the Secretary of State considers—

(a) would be likely to prejudice the commercial interests of any person, or

(b) would be contrary to the interests of national security.

(6) As soon as practicable after revoking an order, the Secretary of State must give notice to the persons mentioned in subsection (2) that the order has been revoked.

NOTES

Commencement: to be appointed.

[1.514]

29 Publication of notice of final order

(1) Subject to subsection (3), the Secretary of State must publish, in such manner as the Secretary of State considers appropriate, notice of the fact that—

(a) a final order has been made,

(b) a final order has been varied or revoked.

(2) The notice under subsection (1) must be published as soon as practicable and must—

(a) state the date on which the order, variation or revocation comes into force, or how that date is to be determined,

(b) state each person, and each description of person, who is required to comply with the order,

(c) describe the trigger event and entity or asset concerned,

(d) include a summary of the order, variation or revocation, its effect and the reasons for it,

(e) include any other information that the Secretary of State considers it appropriate to include.

(3) The Secretary of State may exclude from the notice under subsection (1) anything the publication of which the Secretary of State considers—

(a) would be likely to prejudice the commercial interests of any person, or

(b) would be contrary to the interests of national security.

NOTES

Commencement: to be appointed.

Financial assistance

[1.515]

30 Financial assistance

(1) The Secretary of State may, with the consent of the Treasury, give financial assistance to or in respect of an entity in consequence of the making of a final order.

(2) "Financial assistance" means loans, guarantees or indemnities, or any other kind of financial assistance (actual or contingent).

(3) If during any relevant period the amount given under this section totals £100 million or more, the Secretary of State must as soon as practicable lay a report of the amount before the House of Commons.

(4) If during a relevant period in which a report has been laid under subsection (3) any further amount is given under this section, the Secretary of State must as soon as practicable lay a report of the amount before the House of Commons.

(5) "Relevant period" means—

(a) the period beginning with the day on which this section comes into force and ending with the following 31 March, and

(b) each subsequent period of 12 months.

NOTES

Commencement: to be appointed.

CMA functions

[1.516]

31 Interaction with CMA functions under Part 3 of Enterprise Act 2002

(1) This section applies at any time when a final order is in force, or a final notification has been given, in relation to a trigger event which involves, or would involve, two or more enterprises ceasing to be distinct enterprises for the purposes of Part 3 of the Enterprise Act 2002 ("the 2002 Act").

(2) The Secretary of State may direct the Competition and Markets Authority ("the CMA") to do, or not to do, anything under Part 3 of the 2002 Act in relation to the trigger event if the Secretary of State reasonably considers that the direction is necessary and proportionate for the purpose of preventing, remedying or mitigating a risk to national security.

(3) Before giving a direction under this section, the Secretary of State must consult the CMA and such other persons as the Secretary of State considers appropriate.

(4) The Secretary of State must publish a direction given under this section in such manner as the Secretary of State considers appropriate.

(5) The duty of the CMA to comply with a direction given under this section applies regardless of any other duty imposed on the CMA.

NOTES

Commencement: to be appointed.

PART 3 ENFORCEMENT AND APPEALS

Offences

[1.517]

32 Offence of completing notifiable acquisition without approval

(1) A person who, pursuant to a notifiable acquisition, gains control in circumstances falling within section 6(2) commits an offence if, without reasonable excuse, that person completes the notifiable acquisition without the approval of the Secretary of State in one of the ways mentioned in section 13(2).

(2) Subsection (1) applies even if a call-in notice or a validation notice has been given in relation to the notifiable acquisition.

(3) An offence is committed under this section notwithstanding the effect of section 13(1).

NOTES

Commencement: to be appointed.

[1.518]

33 Offence of failing to comply with order

(1) A person commits an offence if, without reasonable excuse, the person fails to comply with a requirement to which the person is subject under or by virtue of an interim order or a final order.

(2) Where a person is convicted of an offence under this section, the court may make an order requiring that person, within such period as may be specified by the order, to comply with a requirement to which the person is subject under or by virtue of an interim order or a final order.

NOTES

Commencement: to be appointed.

[1.519]

34 Offences: information and attendance of witnesses

(1) A person commits an offence if—

- (a) the person fails, without reasonable excuse, to comply with a requirement of an information notice or an attendance notice, or
- (b) the person intentionally or recklessly alters, suppresses or destroys or causes or permits the alteration, suppression or destruction of any information the person has been required by an information notice to provide.

(2) A person commits an offence if the person intentionally obstructs or delays the making of a copy of information provided in response to an information notice.

(3) A person commits an offence if—

- (a) the person supplies any information to the Secretary of State (including by way of giving evidence pursuant to an attendance notice) in connection with a function of the Secretary of State under this Act,
- (b) the information is false or misleading in a material respect, and
- (c) the person knows that, or is reckless as to whether, it is false or misleading in a material respect.

(4) A person commits an offence if—

- (a) the person supplies any information to another person (other than the Secretary of State),
- (b) the person supplying the information knows that the information is to be used for the purpose of supplying information to the Secretary of State in connection with a function of the Secretary of State under this Act,
- (c) the information is false or misleading in a material respect, and
- (d) the person supplying the information knows that, or is reckless as to whether, it is false or misleading in a material respect.

(5) Where a person is convicted of an offence under subsection (1) or (2), the court may make an order requiring that person, within such period as may be specified by the order—

(a) to comply with a requirement in an information notice,
(b) to comply with a requirement in an attendance notice, or
(c) to permit the making of a copy of information.

(6) Any reference in subsection (1) to destroying information includes a reference to destroying the means of reproducing information recorded otherwise than in legible form.

NOTES

Commencement: to be appointed.

[1.520]

35 Offences in relation to sharing information

(1) It is an offence for a person to use or disclose information in contravention of section 54 or 55(1).

(2) It is a defence for a person charged with an offence under this section to prove that the person reasonably believed that—

(a) the use or disclosure was lawful, or
(b) the information had already and lawfully been made available to the public.

NOTES

Commencement: to be appointed.

[1.521]

36 Offences by bodies corporate etc

(1) If an offence under this Act is committed by a body—

(a) with the consent or connivance of an officer of the body, or
(b) due to any neglect on the part of such an officer,

the officer, as well as the body, is guilty of the offence and liable to be proceeded against and punished accordingly.

(2) In this section—

"body" means a body corporate, a partnership or an unincorporated association other than a partnership,

"officer of a body"—

(a) in relation to a body corporate, means a director, member of the committee of management, chief executive, manager, secretary or other similar officer of the body, or a person purporting to act in any such capacity,
(b) in relation to a partnership, means a partner or person purporting to act as a partner,
(c) in relation to an unincorporated association other than a partnership, means a person who is concerned in the management or control of the body or purports to act in the capacity of a person so concerned.

(3) In subsection (2) "director" includes—

(a) a person occupying in relation to a body corporate the position of a director (by whatever name called),
(b) a person in accordance with whose directions or instructions (not being advice given in a professional capacity) the directors of that body are accustomed to act, and
(c) a person who has an interest or right in, or in relation to, the body corporate that (whether alone or together with other interests or rights held by the person) enables the person materially to influence the policy of the body corporate.

(4) If the affairs of a body corporate are managed by its members, subsection (1) applies in relation to the acts and defaults of a member in connection with the member's functions of management as if the member were a director of the body.

(5) The Secretary of State may by regulations provide for the modification of any provision of this section in its application to a body corporate or unincorporated association formed or recognised under the law of a country or territory outside the United Kingdom.

NOTES

Commencement: 29 April 2021 (sub-s (5)); to be appointed (otherwise).

Prosecution and penalties

[1.522]

37 Prosecution

Proceedings for an offence under this Act may be instituted—

(a) in England and Wales, only by the Director of Public Prosecutions, and
(b) in Northern Ireland, only by the Director of Public Prosecutions for Northern Ireland.

NOTES

Commencement: to be appointed.

[1.523]

38 Proceedings against partnerships etc

(1) Proceedings for an offence under this Act may be brought—

(a) where the offence is alleged to have been committed by a partnership, against the partnership in the firm name,
(b) where the offence is alleged to have been committed by an unincorporated association other than a partnership, against the association in its own name.

(2) Rules of court relating to the service of documents have effect in relation to such proceedings as if the partnership or unincorporated association were a body corporate.

(3) For the purposes of such proceedings the following provisions apply as they apply in relation to a body corporate—

(a) section 33 of the Criminal Justice Act 1925 and Schedule 3 to the Magistrates' Courts Act 1980,

(b) section 18 of the Criminal Justice Act (Northern Ireland) 1945 (c 15 (NI)) and Schedule 4 to the Magistrates' Court (Northern Ireland) Order 1981 (SI 1981/1675 (NI 26)).

(4) A fine imposed on a partnership on its conviction for an offence is to be paid out of the partnership assets.

(5) A fine imposed on an unincorporated association other than a partnership on its conviction for an offence is to be paid out of the funds of the association.

NOTES

Commencement: to be appointed.

[1.524]

39 Offences: penalties

(1) A person who commits an offence under section 32 (completing notifiable acquisition without approval) or 33 (failing to comply with interim or final order) is liable—

(a) on summary conviction in England and Wales, to imprisonment for a term not exceeding 12 months, or a fine (or both),

(b) on summary conviction in Scotland, to imprisonment for a term not exceeding 12 months, or a fine not exceeding the statutory maximum (or both),

(c) on summary conviction in Northern Ireland, to imprisonment for a term not exceeding 6 months, or a fine not exceeding the statutory maximum (or both),

(d) on conviction on indictment, to imprisonment for a term not exceeding 5 years, or a fine (or both).

(2) A person who commits an offence under section 34 (offences in relation to supplying information and attendance of witnesses) or 35 (offences in relation to sharing information) is liable—

(a) on summary conviction in England and Wales, to imprisonment for a term not exceeding 12 months, or a fine (or both),

(b) on summary conviction in Scotland, to imprisonment for a term not exceeding 12 months, or a fine not exceeding the statutory maximum (or both),

(c) on summary conviction in Northern Ireland, to imprisonment for a term not exceeding 6 months, or a fine not exceeding the statutory maximum (or both),

(d) on conviction on indictment, to imprisonment for a term not exceeding 2 years, or a fine (or both).

(3) In relation to an offence committed before paragraph 24(2) of Schedule 22 to the Sentencing Act 2020 comes into force, the references in subsections (1)(a) and (2)(a) to 12 months are to be read as references to 6 months.

NOTES

Commencement: to be appointed.

Civil sanctions

[1.525]

40 Power to impose monetary penalties

(1) Subject to section 43(1), the Secretary of State may give a notice imposing a monetary penalty on a person if the Secretary of State is satisfied, beyond reasonable doubt, that the person has committed an offence under—

(a) section 32 (completing notifiable acquisition without approval),

(b) section 33 (failing to comply with interim or final order), or

(c) section 34 (offences in relation to supplying information and attendance of witnesses),

(including where the person is liable to be proceeded against by virtue of section 36).

(2) A notice under this section is referred to in this Act as a penalty notice.

(3) In this Act "monetary penalty" means a requirement to pay to the Secretary of State a penalty of an amount determined by the Secretary of State.

(4) For an offence under section 33 or 34(1)(a), a monetary penalty may be—

(a) a fixed amount ("a fixed penalty"),

(b) an amount calculated by reference to a daily rate ("a daily rate penalty"), or

(c) a combination of a fixed penalty and a daily rate penalty.

(5) For an offence under section 32 or for any other offence under section 34, the monetary penalty may be a fixed penalty only.

(6) The amount of the monetary penalty is to be such amount as the Secretary of State considers appropriate but it may not exceed the permitted maximum, as set out in section 41.

(7) When determining a monetary penalty under this section, the Secretary of State must have regard, in particular, to—

(a) the seriousness of the offence,

(b) the desirability of deterring both the person on whom the penalty is imposed and others from committing the offence to which the penalty relates,

(c) the possibility, and desirability, of rectifying any failure to which the offence relates,

(d) any steps taken by the person on whom the penalty is imposed towards rectifying any failure to which the offence relates, and

(e) the ability of the person on whom the penalty is imposed to pay the penalty.

(8) A penalty notice must include information as to—

(a) the grounds for imposing the monetary penalty,

(b) whether the penalty is a fixed penalty, a daily rate penalty or a combination of both and how it is calculated,

(c) in the case of a fixed penalty, the amount of the penalty,

(d) in the case of a daily rate penalty, the amount of the daily rate, the day on which the amount first starts to accumulate and the day on which, or the circumstances in which, it ceases to accumulate,

(e) how the amount of the penalty was determined,

(f) how payment may be made,

(g) the period within which payment is to be made (which must be at least 28 days),

(h) rights of appeal,
(i) the consequences of non-payment.

(9) For the purposes of a daily rate penalty—
(a) the first day on which the amount may start to accumulate is the day after the day on which the penalty notice is given,
(b) unless the Secretary of State determines an earlier date, the daily rate ceases to accumulate at the beginning of the earliest of—
(i) the day on which the requirement to comply to which the offence relates is satisfied,
(ii) the day on which that requirement no longer applies.

(10) A monetary penalty imposed under this section is to be paid out of—
(a) the partnership assets where imposed on a partnership, and
(b) the funds of the association where imposed on an unincorporated association other than a partnership.

NOTES
Commencement: to be appointed.

[1.526]
41 Permitted maximum penalties

(1) The following are the permitted maximum fixed penalties for an offence under section 32 or 33—
(a) if the offence is committed by a business, the higher of 5% of the total value of the turnover of the business (both in and outside the United Kingdom and including any business owned or controlled by the business) and £10 million,
(b) if the offence is committed otherwise than by a business, £10 million.

(2) The following are the permitted maximum amounts per day for a daily rate penalty for an offence under section 33—
(a) if the offence is committed by a business, the higher of 0.1% of the total turnover of the business (both in and outside the United Kingdom and including any business owned or controlled by the business) and £200,000,
(b) if the offence is committed otherwise than by a business, £200,000.

(3) The permitted maximum fixed penalty for an offence under section 34(1)(a) is £30,000.
(4) The permitted maximum amount per day for a daily rate penalty for an offence under section 34(1)(a) is £15,000.
(5) The permitted maximum fixed penalty for an offence under section 34(1)(b) is £30,000.
(6) The permitted maximum fixed penalty for an offence under section 34(2) is £30,000.
(7) The permitted maximum fixed penalty for an offence under section 34(3) or (4) is £30,000.

(8) The Secretary of State may by regulations—
(a) provide that a person of a description specified in the regulations is or is not a business for the purposes of this section,
(b) make provision for determining when a business is to be treated as controlled by another business for the purposes of this section,
(c) make provision for determining the turnover (both in and outside the United Kingdom) of a business for the purposes of this section,
(d) amend subsection (1) or (2) so as to alter the percentage for the time being specified there,
(e) amend any of subsections (1) to (7) by substituting a different sum for any sum for the time being specified there.

(9) The regulations may in particular—
(a) include by virtue of subsection (8)(c) provision as to the amounts which are, or which are not, to be treated as comprising the turnover of a business, or provision as to the date or dates by reference to which the turnover of a business is to be determined,
(b) make provision for the Secretary of State to determine matters of a description specified in the regulations (including the matters mentioned in paragraph (a)).

NOTES
Commencement: 29 April 2021 (sub-s (8)); 1 July 2021 (sub-s (9)); to be appointed (otherwise).
Regulations: the National Security and Investment Act 2021 (Monetary Penalties) (Turnover of a Business) Regulations 2021, SI 2021/1262 at **[2.200]**.

[1.527]
42 Review, variation and revocation of monetary penalties

(1) The Secretary of State must keep a monetary penalty imposed by a penalty notice under review and may vary or revoke the penalty notice as the Secretary of State considers appropriate.
(2) If a penalty is revoked under this section, the Secretary of State must, as soon as practicable, give a notice to the person upon whom the penalty was imposed.
(3) If a penalty, or the period within which a penalty is to be paid, is varied under this section, the Secretary of State must, as soon as practicable, give a notice to the person on whom the penalty was imposed which—
(a) states the variation and the reasons for the variation,
(b) includes information about rights of appeal and consequences of non-payment.
(4) A notice under subsection (3) is referred to in this Act as a penalty variation notice.

NOTES
Commencement: to be appointed.

[1.528]
43 Monetary penalties: criminal proceedings and convictions

(1) A penalty notice may not be given to a person in respect of an offence if—
(a) criminal proceedings have been instituted but not concluded in respect of the offence, or

(b) the person has been convicted of the offence.

(2) Where a person has paid, or is required to pay, a monetary penalty under a penalty notice, no criminal proceedings may be instituted against the person in respect of the offence to which the notice relates.

NOTES

Commencement: to be appointed.

[1.529]

44 Recovering penalties

(1) Subsections (2) to (8) apply if all or part of a monetary penalty imposed by a penalty notice is unpaid by the time it is required to be paid.

(2) The unpaid balance carries interest from time to time at the rate for the time being specified in section 17 of the Judgments Act 1838.

(3) Where the Secretary of State considers it appropriate to do so, the Secretary of State may require so much of the penalty as has not already been paid to be paid immediately.

(4) The Secretary of State may recover any of the penalty and any interest that has not been paid if—

- (a) no appeal relating to the penalty has been brought under section 50 during the period within which such an appeal may be brought, or
- (b) an appeal has been determined or withdrawn.

(5) In England and Wales, and in Northern Ireland, the penalty is recoverable as if it were payable under an order of the High Court.

(6) In Scotland, the penalty may be enforced in the same manner as an extract registered decree arbitral bearing a warrant for execution issued by the sheriff court of any sheriffdom in Scotland.

(7) Where action is taken under this section for the recovery of a sum payable under a penalty notice, the penalty is—

- (a) in relation to England and Wales, to be treated for the purposes of section 98 of the Courts Act 2003 (register of judgments and orders etc) as if it were a judgment entered in the High Court, and
- (b) in relation to Northern Ireland, to be treated for the purposes of Article 116 of the Judgments Enforcement (Northern Ireland) Order 1981 (SI 1981/226 (NI 6)) (register of judgments) as if it were a judgment in respect of which an application has been accepted under Article 22 or 23(1) of that Order.

(8) Any sums received by the Secretary of State by way of a monetary penalty, or interest in respect of such a penalty, under this Act must be paid into the Consolidated Fund.

NOTES

Commencement: to be appointed.

[1.530]

45 Monetary penalties: cost recovery

(1) The Secretary of State may give a notice to a person requiring the person to pay to the Secretary of State the costs incurred by the Secretary of State in relation to the imposition of a monetary penalty on that person under section 40.

(2) A notice under subsection (1) is referred to in this Act as a cost recovery notice.

(3) The reference to "costs" in subsection (1) includes, in particular—

- (a) investigation costs,
- (b) administration costs,
- (c) costs of obtaining expert advice (including legal advice).

(4) A cost recovery notice must specify the amount to be paid and include information as to—

- (a) the grounds for giving the notice,
- (b) how payment may be made,
- (c) the period within which payment is to be made (which must be at least 28 days),
- (d) rights of appeal,
- (e) the consequences of non-payment.

(5) A person required to pay an amount to the Secretary of State under this section may require the Secretary of State to give a detailed breakdown of that amount.

(6) Costs imposed under this section are to be paid out of—

- (a) the partnership assets where imposed on a partnership, and
- (b) the funds of the association where imposed on an unincorporated association other than a partnership.

NOTES

Commencement: to be appointed.

[1.531]

46 Review, variation and revocation of cost recovery notice

(1) The Secretary of State must keep a cost recovery notice under review and may vary or revoke it as the Secretary of State considers appropriate.

(2) If a cost recovery notice is revoked under this section, the Secretary of State must, as soon as practicable, give a notice to the person to whom the cost recovery notice was given.

(3) If the costs, or the period within which the costs are to be paid, is varied under this section, the Secretary of State must, as soon as practicable, give a notice to the person to whom the cost recovery notice was given which—

- (a) states the variation and the reasons for the variation,
- (b) includes information about rights of appeal and consequences of non-payment.

(4) A notice under subsection (3) is referred to in this Act as a cost variation notice.

NOTES

Commencement: to be appointed.

[1.532]

47 Enforcement of cost recovery notice

(1) Subsections (2) to (8) apply if some or all of the costs payable under a cost recovery notice are unpaid by the time when they are required to be paid.

(2) The unpaid balance carries interest from time to time at the rate for the time being specified in section 17 of the Judgments Act 1838.

(3) Where the Secretary of State considers it appropriate to do so, the Secretary of State may require so much of the costs as have not already been paid to be paid immediately.

(4) The Secretary of State may recover from the person any of the costs and any interest as has not been paid if—

(a) no appeal relating to the costs has been brought under section 51 during the period within which such an appeal may be brought, or

(b) an appeal has been determined or withdrawn.

(5) In England and Wales, and in Northern Ireland, the costs are recoverable as if they were payable under an order of the High Court.

(6) In Scotland, the costs may be enforced in the same manner as an extract registered decree arbitral bearing a warrant for execution issued by the sheriff court of any sheriffdom in Scotland.

(7) Where action is taken under this section for the recovery of a sum payable under a cost recovery notice, the costs are—

(a) in relation to England and Wales, to be treated for the purposes of section 98 of the Courts Act 2003 (register of judgments and orders etc) as if they were a judgment entered in the High Court, and

(b) in relation to Northern Ireland, to be treated for the purposes of Article 116 of the Judgments Enforcement (Northern Ireland) Order 1981 (SI 1981/226 (NI 6)) (register of judgments) as if they were a judgment in respect of which an application has been accepted under Article 22 or 23(1) of that Order.

(8) Any sums received by the Secretary of State by way of costs, or interest in respect of such costs, under this Act must be paid into the Consolidated Fund.

NOTES

Commencement: to be appointed.

Civil proceedings

[1.533]

48 Enforcement through civil proceedings

(1) A person's duty to comply with a requirement to which the person is subject under or by virtue of an information notice, an attendance notice, an interim order or a final order is enforceable by civil proceedings by the Secretary of State for an injunction, or for specific performance of a statutory duty under section 45 of the Court of Session Act 1988, or for any other appropriate relief or remedy.

(2) Subsection (1) applies whether or not the person is in the United Kingdom.

NOTES

Commencement: to be appointed.

Judicial review and appeals

[1.534]

49 Procedure for judicial review of certain decisions

(1) This section applies to a claim for judicial review of a relevant decision.

(2) A "relevant decision" means—

(a) a decision or action under or by virtue of any of the following provisions, but not including any such decision or action that is directly related to a Part 3 function of the Secretary of State—

(i) section 19,

(ii) section 20,

(iii) section 21,

(iv) section 54(1) and (2)(a),

(v) section 54(6) to (8), insofar as the decision or action is related to the disclosure of information under section 54(2)(a),

(vi) section 55(1) and (3), insofar as the decision or action is related to the disclosure of information under section 54(2)(a),

(vii) section 56,

(viii) section 57, other than a decision or action related to the disclosure of information under section 54(2)(b) to (f) or (3),

(b) a decision or action under or by virtue of section 54(9), insofar as the decision or action is related to a decision or action falling within paragraph (a)(iv) or (v),

(c) a decision or action under or by virtue of—

(i) any provision of Part 1 of this Act not mentioned in paragraph (a),

(ii) Part 2 of this Act,

(iii) section 53, or

(iv) section 62,

and "action" includes a failure to act.

(3) A "Part 3 function" means a function under or by virtue of this Part of this Act.

(4) The court may entertain proceedings for a claim to which this section applies only if the claim form is filed before the end of the period of 28 days beginning with the day after the day on which the grounds to make the claim first arose, unless the court considers that exceptional circumstances apply.

(5) In the application of this section to Scotland—

(a) subsection (1) has effect with the substitution of "an application to the supervisory jurisdiction of the court in respect" for "a claim for judicial review",

(b) subsection (4) has effect with the substitution of—

(i) "an application" for "a claim",

(ii) "application is made" for "claim form is filed",

(iii) "the application" for "the claim".

(6) In the application of this section to Northern Ireland—

(a) subsection (1) has effect with the substitution of "an application" for "a claim",

(b) subsection (4) has effect with the substitution of—

(i) "an application" for "a claim",

(ii) "application for leave to apply for judicial review" for "claim form is filed",

(iii) "the application" for "the claim".

(7) In this section "the court" means—

(a) the High Court in England and Wales,

(b) the Court of Session in Scotland, and

(c) the High Court in Northern Ireland.

NOTES

Commencement: to be appointed.

[1.535]

50 Appeals against monetary penalties

(1) A person who is given a penalty notice or a variation notice may appeal to the court.

(2) A person may not appeal under this section after the end of the period of 28 days beginning with the day after the day on which the notice is given to the person.

(3) On an appeal against a penalty notice the court may—

(a) confirm or quash the decision to impose the monetary penalty,

(b) confirm or reduce the amount of the penalty,

(c) confirm or vary the period within which all or part of the penalty is to be paid.

(4) On an appeal against a variation notice the court may confirm, vary or quash the variation but may not increase the amount of the monetary penalty.

(5) In this section "the court" means—

(a) the High Court in England and Wales,

(b) the Court of Session in Scotland, and

(c) the High Court in Northern Ireland.

(6) Where an appeal is brought under this section, the monetary penalty is not payable until the appeal is determined or withdrawn, unless the court orders otherwise.

NOTES

Commencement: to be appointed.

[1.536]

51 Appeals against costs

(1) A person given a cost recovery notice or a cost variation notice may appeal to the court.

(2) A person may not appeal under this section after the end of the period of 28 days beginning with the day after the day on which the notice is given to the person.

(3) On an appeal against a cost recovery notice the court may—

(a) confirm or quash the decision to impose costs,

(b) confirm or reduce the amount payable,

(c) confirm or vary the period within which payment is to be made.

(4) On an appeal against a cost variation notice the court may confirm, vary or quash the variation but may not increase the amount payable.

(5) In this section "the court" means—

(a) the High Court in England and Wales,

(b) the Court of Session in Scotland, and

(c) the High Court in Northern Ireland.

(6) Where an appeal is brought under this section, the costs are not payable until the appeal is determined or withdrawn, unless the court orders otherwise.

NOTES

Commencement: to be appointed.

Territorial application

[1.537]

52 Extra-territorial application and jurisdiction to try offences

(1) Sections 32, 33, 34 and 35 apply—

(a) whether the offence is committed in the United Kingdom or elsewhere,

(b) if the offence is committed by an individual, whatever the nationality of the individual committing the offence,

(c) if the offence is committed otherwise than by an individual, regardless of whether the body corporate or unincorporated association is formed or recognised under the law of a country or territory outside the United Kingdom.

(2) Where an offence under this Part is committed outside the United Kingdom—

(a) proceedings for the offence may be taken at any place in the United Kingdom, and

(b) the offence may for all incidental purposes be treated as having been committed at any such place.

(3) In the application of subsection (2) to Scotland, any such proceedings against a person may be taken—

(a) in any sheriff court district in which the person is apprehended or is in custody, or

(b) in such sheriff court district as the Lord Advocate may determine.

(4) In subsection (3) "sheriff court district" is to be read in accordance with the Criminal Procedure (Scotland) Act 1995 (see section 307(1) of that Act).

NOTES

Commencement: to be appointed.

PART 4 MISCELLANEOUS

Administrative requirements

[1.538]

53 Procedure for service, etc

(1) The Secretary of State may by regulations make provision for the procedure which must be followed when a provision of or made under this Act requires or allows a notice, order, notification or document of any kind to be given or served.

(2) The regulations may, in particular, make provision—

(a) as to the manner in which a document must be given or served,

(b) as to the address to which a document must be sent,

(c) requiring, or allowing, a document to be sent electronically,

(d) for treating a document as having been given, received or served on a date or at a time determined in accordance with the regulations,

(e) as to what must, or may, be done if a sender or an intended recipient is not an individual,

(f) as to what must, or may, be done if a person is treated by virtue of Schedule 1 as holding an interest or right for the purposes of this Act,

(g) as to what must, or may, be done if a sender or an intended recipient is outside the United Kingdom.

(3) Section 7 of the Interpretation Act 1978 (service of notice by post) has effect in relation to provisions made under this Act subject to any provision made by regulations under this section.

NOTES

Commencement: 29 April 2021 (sub-s (1)); 1 July 2021 (otherwise).

Regulations: the National Security and Investment Act 2021 (Procedure for Service) Regulations 2021, SI 2021/1267 at **[2.226]**.

Information gateways

[1.539]

54 Disclosure of information

(1) A public authority may disclose information to the Secretary of State for the purpose of facilitating the exercise by the Secretary of State of functions under this Act.

(2) The Secretary of State may disclose information received under this Act to a public authority or an overseas public authority—

(a) for the purpose of facilitating the exercise by the Secretary of State of functions under this Act,

(b) for the prevention or detection of crime,

(c) for the purposes of a criminal investigation,

(d) for the purposes of criminal proceedings,

(e) for the purposes of civil proceedings under this Act, or

(f) for the purpose of protecting national security.

(3) The Secretary of State may also disclose such information to an overseas public authority for the purpose of the exercise of corresponding functions of overseas public authorities.

(4) A person who receives information under subsection (2) or (3) may not—

(a) use the information for a purpose other than the purpose for which it was disclosed, or

(b) further disclose the information,

except with the consent of the Secretary of State (which may be general or specific).

(5) Subsection (4) does not apply to information to which section 55 applies (information received from HMRC).

(6) In deciding whether to disclose information under this section, the Secretary of State must consider whether the disclosure would prejudice, to an unreasonable degree, the commercial interests of any person concerned.

(7) In deciding whether to disclose information to an overseas public authority under this section, the Secretary of State must have regard, in particular, to the following considerations—

(a) whether the law of the country or territory to whose authority the disclosure would be made provides protection against self-incrimination in criminal proceedings which corresponds to the protection provided in any part of the United Kingdom, and

(b) whether the matter in respect of which the disclosure is sought is sufficiently serious to justify making the disclosure.

(8) Except as provided by section 57, the disclosure of information under this section does not breach—

(a) any obligation of confidence owed by the person making the disclosure, or

(b) any other restriction on the disclosure of information (however imposed).

(9) In this section—

"overseas public authority" means a person in any country or territory outside the United Kingdom which appears to the Secretary of State to exercise functions of a public nature which—

(a) correspond to the functions of the Secretary of State under this Act, or

(b) relate to any of the purposes mentioned in paragraphs (b) to (f) of subsection (2),

"public authority" has the same meaning as in section 6 of the Human Rights Act 1998.

NOTES

Commencement: to be appointed.

[1.540]

55 Disclosure of information held by HMRC

(1) A person who receives information disclosed under section 54 by Her Majesty's Revenue and Customs (or anyone acting on their behalf) may not—

(a) use the information for a purpose other than the purpose mentioned in section 54(1), or

(b) further disclose the information,

except with the consent of the Commissioners for Her Majesty's Revenue and Customs (which may be general or specific).

(2) If a person discloses information in contravention of subsection (1)(b) which relates to a person whose identity—

(a) is specified in the disclosure, or

(b) can be deduced from it,

section 19 of the Commissioners for Revenue and Customs Act 2005 (offence of wrongful disclosure) applies in relation to that disclosure as it applies in relation to a disclosure of information in contravention of section 20(9) of that Act (and, accordingly, section 35 of this Act does not apply to that disclosure).

(3) Except as provided by section 57, the disclosure of information under this section does not breach—

(a) any obligation of confidence owed by the person disclosing the information, or

(b) any other restriction on the disclosure of information (however imposed).

NOTES

Commencement: to be appointed.

CMA information

[1.541]

56 Duty of CMA to provide information and assistance

The Competition and Markets Authority must give the Secretary of State—

(a) such information in its possession as the Secretary of State may by direction reasonably require to enable the Secretary of State to exercise functions under this Act,

(b) any other assistance which the Secretary of State may by direction reasonably require for the purpose of facilitating the exercise by the Secretary of State of functions under this Act and which it is within the power of the Authority to give.

NOTES

Commencement: to be appointed.

Data protection

[1.542]

57 Data protection

(1) This section applies to a duty or power to disclose or use information where the duty or power is imposed or conferred by or under any provision of Parts 1 to 4 of this Act.

(2) A duty or power to which this section applies does not operate to require or authorise the disclosure or use of information if the disclosure or use—

(a) would contravene the data protection legislation (but the duty or power is to be taken into account in determining whether the disclosure or use would contravene that legislation), or

(b) is prohibited by any of Parts 1 to 7 of, or Chapter 1 of Part 9 of, the Investigatory Powers Act 2016.

(3) In this section "data protection legislation" has the same meaning as in the Data Protection Act 2018 (see section 3 of that Act).

NOTES

Commencement: to be appointed.

58, 59 *(S 58 introduces Sch 2 to this Act (Minor and consequential amendments and revocations). S 59 amends the Enterprise Act 2002, s 243.)*

Defamation

[1.543]

60 Defamation

For the purposes of the law relating to defamation, absolute privilege attaches to any notice or direction given, or decision, report or order made, by the Secretary of State or the Competition and Markets Authority in the exercise of functions under or by virtue of this Act.

NOTES

Commencement: to be appointed.

Annual report

[1.544]

61 Annual report

(1) The Secretary of State must, in relation to each relevant period—

(a) prepare a report in accordance with this section, and

(b) lay a copy of it before each House of Parliament as soon as is practicable after the end of that period.

(2) Each report must provide details of—

(a) the expenditure incurred by the Secretary of State in giving, or in connection with giving, financial assistance falling within section 30,
(b) the amount of the actual or contingent liabilities of the Secretary of State at the end of the relevant period in respect of such financial assistance,
(c) the number of mandatory notices accepted,
(d) the number of mandatory notices rejected,
(e) the average number of working days—
 (i) from receipt of a mandatory notice to notification of a decision to accept that notice, and
 (ii) from receipt of a mandatory notice to giving written reasons for a decision to reject that notice,
(f) the sectors of the economy in relation to which mandatory notices were given,
(g) the number of voluntary notices accepted,
(h) the number of voluntary notices rejected,
(i) the average number of working days—
 (i) from receipt of a voluntary notice to notification of a decision to accept that notice, and
 (ii) from receipt of a voluntary notice to giving written reasons for a decision to reject that notice,
(j) the sectors of the economy in relation to which voluntary notices were given,
(k) the number of call-in notices given,
(l) the sectors of the economy in relation to which call-in notices were given,
(m) the number of final notifications given,
(n) the number of final orders made,
(o) the number of final orders varied,
(p) the number of final orders revoked.

(3) "Relevant period" means—
(a) the period beginning with the day on which this section comes into force and ending with the following 31 March, and
(b) each subsequent period of 12 months.

NOTES

Commencement: to be appointed.

PART 5 FINAL PROVISIONS

[1.545]

62 Transitional and saving provision in relation to the Enterprise Act 2002

(1) Nothing in this Act has effect in relation to anything that took place before 12 November 2020.

(2) Subsections (3) and (4) apply in relation to events which constitute a trigger event described in section 2(4), unless any action has been taken under this Act in relation to the events.

(3) If, disregarding the effect of any amendment made by this Act to the Enterprise Act 2002, the Secretary of State could, in relation to the events—
(a) give an intervention notice under section 42(2) of that Act,
(b) give a special intervention notice under section 59(2) of that Act, or
(c) give a European intervention notice under section 67(2) of that Act,

the Secretary of State may give the notice on or after the day on which this section comes into force.

(4) If any such notice is given in relation to events to which this section applies—
(a) before the day on which this section comes into force, or
(b) by virtue of subsection (3), on or after the day on which this section comes into force,

nothing in this Act has effect in relation to the events (and, accordingly, the Enterprise Act 2002 continues to have effect in relation to the events, disregarding the effect of any amendment made by this Act to that Act.)

(5) Regulations under section 66(4)(b) may make further provision for the purposes of this section.

NOTES

Commencement: 29 April 2021.

[1.546]

63 Regulations under this Act

(1) This section applies to regulations under this Act other than regulations under section 66 (commencement regulations).

(2) Regulations are to be made by statutory instrument.

(3) Regulations may contain consequential, transitional, transitory or saving provision.

(4) Subject to subsection (5), a statutory instrument containing regulations is subject to annulment in pursuance of a resolution of either House of Parliament.

(5) A statutory instrument containing (whether alone or with other provision) regulations under any of the following may not be made unless a draft of it has been laid before Parliament and approved by a resolution of each House—
(a) section 6(1),
(b) section 11(3),
(c) section 41(8).

NOTES

Commencement: 29 April 2021.

[1.547]

64 Financial provision

Any expenditure incurred by the Secretary of State under or by virtue of this Act is to be paid out of money provided by Parliament.

NOTES

Commencement: 29 April 2021.

[1.548]

65 Interpretation

In this Act—

"acquirer" has the meaning given by section 5(2),

"assessment period" has the meaning given in section 23,

"attendance notice" means a notice given under section 20(1),

"business" includes—

(a) a professional practice,

(b) an undertaking which is carried on for gain or reward,

(c) an undertaking in the course of which goods or services are supplied otherwise than free of charge, and

references to a person carrying on business include references to a person carrying on business in partnership with one or more other persons,

"call-in notice" means a notice given under section 1(1),

"cost recovery notice" means a notice given under section 45(1),

"cost variation notice" means a notice given under section 46(3),

"final notification" has the meaning given by section 26(2),

"final order" means an order made under section 26(3),

"information notice" means a notice given under section 19(1),

"interim order" means an order made under section 25(1),

"mandatory notice" means a notice given under section 14(1),

"monetary penalty" has the meaning given by section 40(3),

"notifiable acquisition" has the meaning given by section 6(2) (and see subsection (3) of that section),

"notifiable acquisition regulations" means regulations made under section 6(1),

"penalty notice" means a notice given under section 40(1),

"penalty variation notice" means a notice given under section 42(3),

"qualifying asset" has the meaning given by section 7(4),

"qualifying entity" has the meaning given by section 7(2),

"the territorial sea" means the territorial sea adjacent to the United Kingdom,

"trigger event" has the meaning given by section 5(1) and includes, where the context requires, a trigger event that has not yet taken place,

"United Kingdom national" means an individual who is—

(a) a British citizen, a British overseas territories citizen, a British National (Overseas) or a British Overseas citizen,

(b) a person who under the British Nationality Act 1981 is a British subject, or

(c) a British protected person within the meaning of that Act,

"validation application" has the meaning given by section 16(2),

"validation notice" means a notice given under section 15(2)(b), 16(7)(b)(ii) or 17(2) (and see section 15(3)),

"voluntary notice" means a notice given under section 18(2),

"working day", in relation to a part of the United Kingdom, means a day other than—

(a) a Saturday or Sunday, or

(b) a day which is a bank holiday under the Banking and Financial Dealings Act 1971 in that or any other part of the United Kingdom.

NOTES

Commencement: 29 April 2021.

[1.549]

66 Short title, commencement and extent

(1) This Act may be cited as the National Security and Investment Act 2021.

(2) This Part of this Act and the following provisions of this Act (which contain powers to make regulations) come into force on the day on which this Act is passed—

(a) section 6(1),
(b) section 11(3),
(c) section 14(4),
(d) section 16(3),
(e) section 18(4),
(f) section 36(5),
(g) section 41(8),
(h) section 53(1).

(3) The rest of this Act comes into force on such day as the Secretary of State may by regulations made by statutory instrument appoint.

(4) Regulations under subsection (3) may—

(a) appoint different days for different purposes;
(b) make transitional, transitory or saving provision.

(5) This Act extends to England and Wales, Scotland and Northern Ireland, except that the amendment or repeal of any enactment has the same extent as the enactment amended or repealed.

NOTES

Commencement: 29 April 2021.

Regulations: the National Security and Investment Act 2021 (Commencement No 1 and Transitional Provision) Regulations 2021, SI 2021/788.

Editorial note: the government has indicated that this Act will fully come into force on 4 January 2022. See www.gov.uk/government/news/new-and-improved-national-security-and-investment-act-set-to-be-up-and-running. But as of 24 November 2021, no commencement orders or regulations had been made to commence the remaining provisions of this Act.

SCHEDULES

SCHEDULE 1
TRIGGER EVENTS: HOLDING OF INTERESTS AND RIGHTS

Section 10

[1.550]

Joint interests

1. If two or more persons each hold an interest or right jointly, each of them is treated as holding that interest or right.

Joint arrangements

2. (1) If interests or rights held by a person and interests or rights held by another person are the subject of a joint arrangement between those persons, each of them is treated as holding the combined interests or rights of both of them.

(2) A "joint arrangement" is an arrangement between the holders of interests or rights that they will exercise all or substantially all the rights conferred by their respective interests, or their respective rights, jointly in a way that is pre-determined by the arrangement.

Indirect holdings

3. (1) An interest or right held indirectly by a person is to be treated as held by the person.

(2) A person holds an interest or right "indirectly" if the person has a majority stake in an entity and that entity—

- (a) holds the interest or right, or
- (b) is part of a chain of entities—
  - (i) each of which (other than the last) has a majority stake in the entity immediately below it in the chain, and
  - (ii) the last of which holds the interest or right.

(3) For these purposes, A has a "majority stake" in B if—

- (a) A holds a majority of voting rights in B,
- (b) A is a member of B and has the right to appoint or remove a majority of the board of directors of B,
- (c) A is a member of B and controls alone, pursuant to an agreement with other shareholders or members, a majority of the voting rights in B, or
- (d) A has the right to exercise, or actually exercises, dominant influence or control over B.

(4) In the application of this paragraph to the right to appoint or remove a majority of the board of directors, an entity is to be treated as having the right to appoint a director if—

- (a) a person's appointment as director follows necessarily from that person's appointment as director of the entity, or
- (b) the directorship is held by the entity itself.

(5) In this paragraph—

- (a) the reference to the right to appoint or remove a majority of the board of directors of an entity is to the right to appoint or remove directors holding a majority of the voting rights at meetings of the board on all or substantially all matters,
- (b) the reference to the board of directors, in the case of an entity that does not have such a board, is to be read as a reference to the equivalent management body of that entity,
- (c) references to "voting rights" are to be read in accordance with section 8(7).

Interests held by nominees

4. An interest held by a person as nominee for another is to be treated as held by the other (and not by the nominee).

Rights treated as held by person who controls their exercise

5. (1) Where a person controls a right, the right is to be treated as held by that person (and not by the person who in fact holds the right, unless that person also controls it).

(2) A person "controls" a right if, by virtue of any arrangement between that person and others, the right is exercisable only—

- (a) by that person,
- (b) in accordance with that person's directions or instructions, or
- (c) with that person's consent or concurrence.

Rights exercisable only in certain circumstances etc

6. (1) Rights that are exercisable by a person only in certain circumstances are to be treated as held by the person only—

- (a) when the circumstances have arisen, and for so long as they continue to obtain, or
- (b) when the circumstances are within the control of the person.

(2) But rights that are exercisable by an administrator or by creditors while an entity is in relevant insolvency proceedings are not to be regarded as held by the administrator or creditors even while the entity is in those proceedings.

(3) "Relevant insolvency proceedings" means—

(a) administration within the meaning of the Insolvency Act 1986,

(b) administration within the meaning of the Insolvency (Northern Ireland) Order 1989 (SI 1989/2405 (NI 19)), or

(c) proceedings under the insolvency law of another country or territory during which an entity's assets and affairs are subject to the control or supervision of a third party or creditor.

(4) Rights that are normally exercisable but are temporarily incapable of exercise are not for that reason to be treated as not being held.

Rights attached to shares held by way of security

7. Rights attached to shares held by way of security provided by a person are to be treated as held by that person—

(a) where apart from the right to exercise them for the purpose of preserving the value of the security, or of realising it, the rights are exercisable only in accordance with that person's instructions, and

(b) where the shares are held in connection with the granting of loans as part of normal business activities and apart from the right to exercise them for the purpose of preserving the value of the security, or of realising it, the rights are exercisable only in that person's interests.

Connected persons

8. Two or more persons who are connected with each other (within the meaning given by paragraph 9 or 10) are each to be treated as holding the combined interests or rights of both or all of them.

9. (1) Two or more undertakings are connected if they are group undertakings in respect of each other.

(2) In sub-paragraph (1), "undertaking" and "group undertaking" have the same meanings as in the Companies Act 2006 (see section 1161 of that Act).

10. (1) An individual, A, is connected with another individual, B, if—

(a) A is B's spouse, civil partner or cohabitee,

(b) A is a relative of B,

(c) A is the spouse, civil partner or cohabitee of a relative of B,

(d) A is a relative of B's spouse, civil partner or cohabitee, or

(e) A is the spouse, civil partner or cohabitee of a relative of B's spouse, civil partner or cohabitee.

(2) For the purposes of sub-paragraph (1)—

(a) two persons who are living together as if they were a married couple or civil partners are cohabitees,

(b) references to a spouse, civil partner or cohabitee include a former spouse, civil partner or cohabitee, and

(c) "relative" means a brother, sister, uncle, aunt, nephew, niece, lineal ancestor or descendant (the stepchild of any person, or anyone adopted by a person, whether legally or otherwise, as their child, being regarded as a relative or taken into account to trace a relationship in the same way as that person's child).

Common purpose

11. (1) Two or more persons who share a common purpose in relation to an asset or entity are each to be treated as holding the combined interests or rights of both or all of them.

(2) The cases in which persons share a common purpose in relation to an entity include (but are not limited to) cases in which the persons co-ordinate their influence on the activities, operations, governance or strategy of the entity.

(3) The cases in which persons share a common purpose in relation to an asset include (but are not limited to) cases in which the persons co-ordinate their influence on the way in which the asset is used, and section 9(2) applies for the purposes of this sub-paragraph.

Arrangements

12. (1) In this Schedule "arrangement" includes—

(a) any scheme, agreement or understanding, whether or not it is legally enforceable, and

(b) any convention, custom or practice of any kind.

(2) But something does not count as an arrangement unless there is at least some degree of stability about it (whether by its nature or terms, the time it has been in existence or otherwise).

NOTES

Commencement: to be appointed.

SCHEDULE 2

(Sch 2 amends the Enterprise Act 2002 (at **[1.184]** *et seq), and revokes the following: the Enterprise Act 2002 (Share of Supply Test) (Amendment) Order 2018 (SI 2018/578); the Enterprise Act 2002 (Turnover Test) (Amendment) Order 2018 (SI 2018/593); the Enterprise Act 2002 (Share of Supply) (Amendment) Order 2020 (SI 2020/748); and the Enterprise Act 2002 (Turnover Test) (Amendment) Order 2020 (SI 2020/763).)*

PART 2
STATUTORY INSTRUMENTS

A.
PROCEDURAL MATTERS

COMPETITION ACT 1998 (APPEALABLE DECISIONS AND REVOCATION OF NOTIFICATION OF EXCLUDED AGREEMENTS) REGULATIONS 2004

(SI 2004/1078)

NOTES

Made: 6 April 2004.

Authority: Competition Act 1998, ss 12(3) (repealed), 46(3), 47(1), 59(1), 71, Sch 13 para 19(3).

Commencement: 1 May 2004.

[2.1]

1 Citation and commencement

These Regulations may be cited as the Competition Act 1998 (Appealable Decisions and Revocation of Notification of Excluded Agreements) Regulations 2004 and shall come into force on 1st May 2004.

[2.2]

2 Appealable decisions

The following are prescribed as decisions for the purposes of sections 46 and 47 of the Competition Act 1998:

(a) a decision of the [CMA] imposing conditions or obligations subject to which a [retained exemption] is to have effect;

(b) a decision of the [CMA] imposing one or more additional conditions or obligations subject to which a [retained exemption] is to have effect; and

(c) a decision of the [CMA] varying or removing any such condition or obligation.

NOTES

References to the "CMA" substituted by the Enterprise and Regulatory Reform Act 2013 (Competition) (Consequential, Transitional and Saving Provisions) (No 2) Order 2014, SI 2014/549, art 2, Sch 1, Pt 1, para 12. For transitional provisions in relation to the abolition of the OFT and the Competition Commission and the continuity of functions, etc, see art 3 of the 2014 Order at **[2.21]**.

Words "retained exemption" in square brackets in paras (a) and (b) substituted (for the original words "parallel exemption") by the Competition (Amendment etc) (EU Exit) Regulations 2019, SI 2019/93, reg 61, Sch 2, Pt 1, para 3, as from IP completion day (as defined in the European Union (Withdrawal Agreement) Act 2020, s 39) (for transitional provisions and savings in relation to the operation of the 2019 Regulations, see Sch 4 to those Regulations at **[7.69]** et seq).

3 (*Revokes the Competition Act 1998 (Notification of Excluded Agreements and Appealable Decisions) Regulations 2000, SI 2000/263.*)

COMPETITION ACT 1998 AND OTHER ENACTMENTS (AMENDMENT) REGULATIONS 2004

(SI 2004/1261)

NOTES

Made: 30 April 2004.

Authority: European Communities Act 1972, s 2(2); Enterprise Act 2002, s 209. Note that the European Communities Act 1972 was repealed by the European Union (Withdrawal) Act 2018, s 1, as from exit day (as defined in s 20 of that Act), and the Enterprise Act 2002, s 209 was repealed by the Competition (Amendment etc) (EU Exit) Regulations 2019, SI 2019/93, regs 32, 58, as from IP completion day (as defined in the European Union (Withdrawal Agreement) Act 2020, s 39). For the status of "EU-derived domestic legislation" after IP completion day, see s 2 of the 2018 Act at **[7.4]**. See also Sch 4, Pt 7, para 35 to the 2019 Regulations (at **[7.76]**) which provides that the repeal of s 209 of the 2002 Act does not affect the validity of any provision made under that section before IP completion day.

Commencement: 1 May 2004 (certain purposes); 1 May 2007 (otherwise).

[2.3]

1 Citation and commencement

These Regulations may be cited as the Competition Act 1998 and other enactments (Amendment) Regulations 2004 and shall come into force—

(a) for the purposes of regulation 4 as it gives effect to paragraphs 50(a) and 54(8) of Schedule 1, on 1st May 2007; and

(b) for all other purposes, on 1st May 2004.

[2.4]

2 Interpretation

In these Regulations—

"the 1998 Act" means the Competition Act 1998;

"the appointed day" means the 1st May 2004;

"the EC Competition Regulation" means Council Regulation (EC) No 1/2003 of 16th December 2002 on the implementation of the rules on competition laid down in Articles 81 and 82 of the Treaty;

"the OFT" means the Office of Fair Trading; and

"the Treaty" means the [Treaty on the Functioning of the European Union].

NOTES

Definition "the EC Competition Regulation" revoked by the Competition (Amendment etc) (EU Exit) Regulations 2019, SI 2019/93, reg 61, Sch 2, Pt 3, para 11, as from IP completion day (as defined in the European Union (Withdrawal Agreement) Act 2020, s 39) (for transitional provisions and savings in relation to the operation of the 2019 Regulations, see Sch 4 to those Regulations at **[7.69]** et seq).

Definition "the Treaty" substituted by the Treaty of Lisbon (Changes in Terminology or Numbering) Order 2012, SI 2012/1809, art 3(1), Schedule, Pt 2.

[2.5]

3 Designation of national competition authorities

(1) Subject to [paragraph (3)] below, the following persons are hereby designated as national competition authorities pursuant to Article 35 of the EC Competition Regulation—

(a) . . .

(b) any regulator mentioned in section 54(1) of the 1998 Act.

(2) . . .

(3) Any person mentioned in paragraph (1)(b) above is designated as a national competition authority for the purposes of exercising all of the powers and functions of a competition authority of a Member State under Chapters I, II, IV, VIII and IX of the EC Competition Regulation.

NOTES

This regulation was revoked by the Competition (Amendment etc) (EU Exit) Regulations 2019, SI 2019/93, reg 61, Sch 2, Pt 3, para 11, as from IP completion day (as defined in the European Union (Withdrawal Agreement) Act 2020, s 39) (for transitional provisions and savings in relation to the operation of the 2019 Regulations, see Sch 4 to those Regulations at **[7.69]** et seq).

Para (1): words in square brackets substituted, and sub-para (a) revoked, by the Enterprise and Regulatory Reform Act 2013 (Competition) (Consequential, Transitional and Saving Provisions) (No 2) Order 2014, SI 2014/549, art 2, Sch 1, Pt 1, para 13(1), (2)(a). For transitional provisions in relation to the abolition of the OFT and the Competition Commission and the continuity of functions, etc, see art 3 of the 2014 Order at **[2.21]**.

Para (2): revoked by SI 2014/549, art 2, Sch 1, Pt 1, para 13(1), (2)(b) and subject to transitional provisions as noted to para (1) above.

4, 5 *(Reg 4 introduces Sch 1 (amendments to the Competition Act 1998); reg 5 introduces Sch 2 (amendments to other enactments).)*

[2.6]

6 Savings and consequential provision

(1) Paragraph (2) applies if an individual exemption from the prohibition imposed by section 2(1) of the 1998 Act has been granted before the appointed day and has not expired or been cancelled before that day.

(2) The repeals made by these Regulations do not affect that exemption (or a condition or an obligation relating to it); but this does not allow the OFT, on or after the appointed day, to extend that exemption under section 4(6) of the 1998 Act.

(3) Section 5 of the 1998 Act, despite its repeal by these Regulations, shall continue in effect while any individual exemption has effect.

(4) In this regulation "individual exemption" means an exemption granted under section 4 of the 1998 Act (including one granted by virtue of paragraph 3(2)(c) of Schedule 8 to that Act).

[2.7]

7

(1) Paragraph (2) applies if, before the appointed day, the European Commission adopted a decision pursuant to Article 81(3) of the Treaty in relation to an agreement and that decision has not expired or been revoked.

(2) Section 10 of the 1998 Act has effect in relation to the agreement without the amendment made by paragraph 7(2) of Schedule 1.

(3) Section 2(5) of the 1998 Act applies to this regulation as it applies to Part 1 of that Act.

[2.8]

8

(1) This regulation applies where, before the appointed day, the OFT has made a decision falling within paragraph (c), (d) or (e) of section 46(3), or has made a decision falling within paragraph (f) of section 46(3) in relation to an individual exemption.

(2) This regulation also applies where, on or after the appointed day, the [CMA] (by virtue of regulation 6) makes under section 5 of the 1998 Act a decision falling within paragraph (d)(i) or (ii) or (f) of section 46(3).

(3) Where this regulation applies—

(a) sections 46 and 47 of and Schedule 8 to the 1998 Act shall have effect in relation to the decision in question without the amendments made by these Regulations; and

(b) on an appeal in respect of that decision, the powers under paragraph 3(2) of Schedule 8 to that Act are not affected by the repeal by these Regulations of section 4 or 5 of this Act; but this does not allow the Competition Appeal Tribunal, on or after the appointed day, to extend the individual exemption.

(4) In this regulation—

(a) references to section 46(3) are to section 46(3) of the 1998 Act as that subsection had effect before the appointed day; and

(b) "individual exemption" has the same meaning as in regulation 6.

NOTES

Para (2): reference to the "CMA" substituted by the Enterprise and Regulatory Reform Act 2013 (Competition) (Consequential, Transitional and Saving Provisions) (No 2) Order 2014, SI 2014/549, art 2, Sch 1, Pt 1, para 13(1), (3). For transitional provisions in relation to the abolition of the OFT and the Competition Commission and the continuity of functions, etc, see art 3 of the 2014 Order at **[2.21]**.

Note that SI 2014/549 does not substitute the reference to the OFT in para (1) above.

[2.9]
9

(1) Paragraph (2) applies if—

(a) an agreement has been notified before the appointed day to the OFT under section 13 or 14 of the 1998 Act and, on the appointed day, the OFT has not determined the application made in respect of the agreement, or

(b) an agreement has been notified before the appointed day to the European Commission for a decision as to whether an exemption will be granted under Article 81(3) of the Treaty with respect to the agreement and, on the appointed day, the European Commission has not determined the matter.

(2) No penalty may be imposed under Part 1 of the 1998 Act in respect of any infringement of the Chapter I prohibition by the agreement which occurred during the period beginning with the date on which notification was given and ending with the appointed day.

[2.10]
10

Where section 5 of the 1998 Act continues to have effect by virtue of regulation 6, paragraph 6 of Schedule 9 to that Act shall continue to have effect despite its repeal by these Regulations.

(Sch 1 (Amendments to the Competition Act 1998) and Sch 2 (Amendments to other enactments): where relevant to this Handbook, these amendments have been incorporated at the appropriate place.)

ENTERPRISE AND REGULATORY REFORM ACT 2013 (COMMENCEMENT NO 6, TRANSITIONAL PROVISIONS AND SAVINGS) ORDER 2014

(SI 2014/416)

NOTES

Made: 3 March 2014.

Authority: Enterprise and Regulatory Reform Act 2013, ss 100, 103(3), (4).

[2.11]
1 Citation

This Order may be cited as the Enterprise and Regulatory Reform Act 2013 (Commencement No 6, Transitional Provisions and Savings) Order 2014.

[2.12]
2 Provisions coming into force on 1st April 2014

(1) *(Provides that ss 25(3), 26, 29–51, 54–58 of, and Schs 4–13, Sch 14, paras 1–19, 23–29, Sch 15 to, the Act come into force on 1 April 2014 (so far as not already in force).)*

(2) The Schedule contains transitional provisions and savings relating to the provisions brought into force by paragraph (1).

3 *(Provides for commencement on 6 April 2014 of provisions of the Act that are outside the scope of this work.)*

SCHEDULE
TRANSITIONAL PROVISIONS AND SAVINGS: THE COMPETITION AND MARKETS AUTHORITY AND COMPETITION REFORM

Article 2(2)

Introductory

[2.13]
1 Interpretation

(1) In this Schedule—

"the Act" means the Enterprise and Regulatory Reform Act 2013;

"amendments" includes repeals;

"the CMA" means the Competition and Markets Authority;
"the commencement date" means 1st April 2014;
"the Commission" means the Competition Commission;
"enactment" includes—

(a) an enactment comprised in subordinate legislation (within the meaning of the Interpretation Act 1978), and

(b) an enactment comprised in (or in an instrument made under) an Act of the Scottish Parliament, a Measure or Act of the National Assembly for Wales or Northern Ireland legislation;

"the OFT" means the Office of Fair Trading; and
"the 2002 Act" means the Enterprise Act 2002.

(2) For the purposes of this Schedule, the OFT has publicly launched a market study before the commencement date if it has publicly begun before that date activity which, if proposed to be undertaken by the CMA on or after that date, would require the publication of a market study notice under section 130A of the 2002 Act.

(3) References in this Schedule to amendments made by provisions of the Act include references to any other amendments made by virtue of the Act in consequence of, or for the purposes of, those amendments.

Abolition of OFT and Competition Commission

2 Abolition of OFT and Competition Commission

(1) Anything which, immediately before the commencement date, is in the process of being done by or in relation to the transferor may, so far as it relates to a relevant function, be continued by or in relation to the transferee.

(2) Anything done (or having effect as if done) by or in relation to the transferor for the purposes of or in connection with a relevant function is, if in force or effective immediately before the commencement date, to have effect as if done by or in relation to the transferee so far as that is required for continuing its effect on or after the commencement date.

(3) In the application of sub-paragraph (1) or (2)—

(a) any reference made before the commencement date under section 22, 33, 45, 62, 131 or 132 of the 2002 Act or section 59 of the Legal Services Act 2007 to the Commission is to be treated, so far as provided by those sub-paragraphs, as a reference under that section to the chair of the CMA for the constitution of a CMA group,

(b) where any functions exercisable immediately before the commencement date by a Commission group are to be exercisable on or after that date by a CMA group—

(i) any person who, immediately before the commencement date, is a member of the Commission group is to be treated, on or after that date, as a member of the CMA group concerned if the person is a member of the CMA panel,

(ii) any person who, immediately before the commencement date, is the chairman of the Commission group is to be treated, on or after that date, as the chair of the CMA group if the person is a member of the CMA panel, and

(iii) the persons treated as mentioned in sub-paragraph (i) or (ii) are to be treated, on or after the commencement date, as if they have been constituted in accordance with Part 3 of Schedule 4 to the Act as the chair and other members of the CMA group (and that Part applies accordingly in relation to the operation of the group), and

(c) an authorisation given (whether by warrant or otherwise) before the commencement date, so far as it authorises a named member, or member of staff, of the OFT or the Commission, continues to authorise that individual (but no other) on or after the commencement date if, and only if, the individual is a member, or (as the case may be) a member of staff, of the CMA.

(4) Any enactment, instrument or other document passed or made before the commencement date is to have effect, so far as necessary for the purposes of or in consequence of sub-paragraphs (1) to (3), as if any references (however expressed) to the transferor were references to the transferee.

(5) Sub-paragraphs (1) to (4)—

(a) do not apply in relation to any matter dealt with by a transfer scheme under section 27 of the Act or by any other transitional provision made by virtue of the Act; and

(b) do not apply so as to convert an appointment as a member of the OFT or the Commission into an appointment as a member of the CMA.

(6) Any enactment, instrument or other document passed or made before the commencement date is to have effect, so far as necessary for the purposes of or in consequence of its continued effect by virtue of sub-paragraph (8), (10) or (11) below or any of paragraphs 4 to 7, 9 to 12 and 16, as if any references (however expressed) to the transferor were references to the transferee.

(7) The repeals of section 45(4) of the Competition Act 1998 and section 2(3) of the 2002 Act (general conversion of references to the Monopolies and Mergers Commission and the Director General of Fair Trading) by paragraphs 220 and 229 of Schedule 5 to the Act do not apply so far as those sections create references to the transferor to which sub-paragraph (4) or (6) above are capable of applying.

(8) The repeal of paragraph 12(1) to (3) of Schedule 7 to the Competition Act 1998 (annual accounts) by paragraph 222 of Schedule 5 to the Act does not apply in relation to any accounts for the financial year ending with 31st March 2014; and those provisions of the Act of 1998 continue to apply as if the obligations of the Commission in relation to its accounts were obligations of the CMA in relation to the Commission's accounts.

(9) The CMA must prepare accounts (and send them to the Comptroller and Auditor General) under section 5 of the Government Resources and Accounts Act 2000 for the financial year ending with 31st March 2014 in respect of the OFT.

(10) The repeals of paragraph 12A of Schedule 7 to the Competition Act 1998 and section 4(1) to (3) of the 2002 Act (annual reports) by paragraphs 222 and 229 of Schedule 5 to the Act do not apply in relation to any report for the financial year ending with 31st March 2014; and those provisions of the Act of 1998 and the 2002 Act continue to apply as if the obligation to make (and, in the case of the OFT, lay) a report about the Commission or OFT were an obligation of the CMA to make (or lay) such a report.

(11) The repeal of Part 2 of Schedule 3 to the 2002 Act (transfers between the Commission and the Competition Service) by paragraph 226 of Schedule 5 to the Act does not apply in relation to any transfer effected by virtue of that Part before the commencement date so far as that Part is capable of continuing to apply on or after the commencement date in relation to the transfer.

(12) The abolition of the OFT or the Commission does not affect the validity of anything done (or having effect as if done) by or in relation to the transferor before the commencement date.

(13) In this paragraph—

"CMA Board" has the same meaning as in Schedule 4 to the Act (see Part 2 of that Schedule);

"CMA group" means a group constituted in accordance with Part 3 of Schedule 4 to the Act;

"CMA panel" has the same meaning as in Schedule 4 to the Act (see Part 3 of that Schedule);

"Commission group" means a group constituted under any enactment to perform functions of the Commission;

"the Council" means the Competition Commission Council;

"relevant function" means any function of the transferor which is transferred to the transferee by virtue of Part 3 or 4 of the Act or sub-paragraph (6) above;

"transferee" means the CMA, the CMA Board, a CMA group, the chair of the CMA, another member of the CMA or (as the case may be) a member of staff of the CMA;

"transferor" means the OFT, the Commission, the Council, a Commission group, the chairman of the OFT or Commission, another member of the OFT or Commission or a member of staff of the OFT or Commission;

and references in this paragraph to things done include references to things omitted to be done.

Mergers

3 General: existing matters

(1) The amendments made by Chapter 1 of Part 4 of the Act, section 49 or 50 of the Act and paragraphs 16 to 20, 21(3) to (5), (6)(a) and (8) to (10), 23, 24, 26, 28, 29 and 35 of Schedule 15 to the Act (mergers) apply in relation to—

(a) any reference under section 22, 33, 45 or 62 of the 2002 Act made before the commencement date, or

(b) any possible reference under section 22, 33, 45 or 62 of that Act which arose before that date,

as they apply in relation to any such reference made, or arising, on or after that date.

(2) In particular—

(a) the amendments mentioned in sub-paragraph (1) apply in relation to investigations begun, notices given, reports published, undertakings accepted or adopted and orders made or adopted before the commencement date as they apply in relation to investigations begun, notices given, reports published, undertakings accepted or adopted and orders made or adopted on or after that date, and

(b) the amendments made by section 29(2) to (9) of the Act (investigation powers) apply in relation to a matter which, before the commencement date, was the subject of a reference or possible reference under section 22, 33, 45 or 62 of the 2002 Act as they apply in relation to—

(i) a matter that is or has been the subject of a reference made on or after that date under section 22, 33, 45 or 62 of the 2002 Act, or

(ii) a matter that is or has been the subject, on or after that date, of a possible reference under section 22, 33, 45 or 62 of that Act.

(3) Sub-paragraph (2) is without prejudice to the generality of sub-paragraph (1).

(4) This paragraph is subject to paragraphs 4 to 7 and 16.

4 Investigation powers

(1) The amendments made by section 29 of the Act (investigation powers) do not apply in relation to any notice given before the commencement date under section 109 of the 2002 Act.

(2) The amendments made by paragraphs 16 to 20, 21(3) to (5), (6)(a) and (8) to (10), 23, 24, 26, 28, 29 and 35 of Schedule 15 to the Act (other amendments in relation to investigation powers) do not apply in relation to any notice given before the commencement date under section 31, 34B, 46C or (as the case may be) 99(2) of the 2002 Act.

5 Undertakings and orders

(1) The amendments made by section 30(1) of, and paragraphs 2(5) to (7) and 4(2) of Schedule 7 to, the Act (initial and interim undertakings) do not apply in relation to undertakings accepted under section 71 of, or paragraph 1 of Schedule 7 to, the 2002 Act before the commencement date.

(2) In their continued application by virtue of sub-paragraph (1)—

(a) section 71 of the 2002 Act has effect as if there were no power under that section for an undertaking under that section to be varied or superseded,

(b) section 80(4) of that Act continues to permit the varying or superseding of an undertaking under section 71 which has been adopted under section 80(3), and

(c) paragraph 1 of Schedule 7 to that Act has effect as if there were no power under that paragraph for an undertaking accepted or adopted under that paragraph to be varied or superseded.

(3) The amendments made by paragraphs 3(5) to (7) and 4(5) of Schedule 7 to the Act (interim orders) do not apply in relation to orders adopted before the commencement date.

(4) The amendments made by section 31 of the Act (financial penalties in relation to interim measures) do not apply in relation to a failure to comply which—

Part 2 Statutory Instruments

(a) occurs before the commencement date, and
(b) does not continue on or after it,

but otherwise do apply in relation to undertakings accepted, or orders made, before that date.

6 Time-limits: general

(1) The amendments made by paragraphs 2 to 4 and 7 to 12 of Schedule 8 to the Act (time-limits) do not apply in relation to any possible reference under section 22 or 33 of the 2002 Act which is active before the commencement date.

(2) For the purposes of this paragraph, a possible reference is active before the commencement date if (and only if) condition A, B, or C is met.

(3) Condition A is that, before the commencement date, the OFT—

(a) has not received a merger notice under section 96 of the 2002 Act in relation to the subject-matter of the reference,
(b) either—
 (i) has notified any relevant person that it has received a satisfactory submission for the purpose of considering whether to make the reference, or
 (ii) has received the case from the European Commission as mentioned in section 34A(1) of that Act, and
(c) has neither made the reference nor decided not to make it.

(4) Condition B is that, before the commencement date—

(a) the OFT has received a merger notice under section 96 of the 2002 Act in relation to the subject-matter of the reference,
(b) the period under section 97 of that Act for considering the notice has not expired,
(c) the notice has not been rejected under section 99(5) of that Act or withdrawn, and
(d) the OFT has neither made the reference nor decided not to make it.

(5) Condition C is that, before the commencement date—

(a) the OFT has received a merger notice under section 96 of the 2002 Act in relation to the subject-matter of the reference,
(b) the notice has been rejected under section 99(5) of that Act or withdrawn,
(c) the OFT has subsequently notified any relevant person that it has received a satisfactory submission for the purpose of considering whether to make the reference, and
(d) the OFT has neither made the reference nor decided not to make it.

(6) In its application, on or after the commencement date, to any possible reference under section 22 or 33 of the 2002 Act which is active before that date, section 97 of that Act has effect as if, for subsections (5) and (6), there were substituted—

"(5) The CMA may by notice to the person who gave the merger notice extend the period for considering a merger notice if it considers that the person has failed (with or without reasonable excuse) to comply with any requirement of a notice under section 109 or (before, on or after the commencement date) with a notice given before that date under section 99(2).

(6) An extension under subsection (5) shall end—

(a) when the person concerned provides the information or documents to the satisfaction of the CMA or (as the case may be) appears as a witness in accordance with the requirements of the CMA; or
(b) if earlier, when the CMA cancels the extension."

(7) In its application, on or after the commencement date, to any possible reference under section 22 or 33 of the 2002 Act which is active before that date, subsection (2) of section 98 of that Act has effect as if, for that subsection, there were substituted—

"(2) A notice under section 97(5)—

(a) shall also be given within 5 days of—
 (i) the end of the period within which the information is to be provided and which is stated in the notice under section 99(2); or
 (ii) the date for compliance with a notice served under section 109; and
(b) shall also inform the person who gave the merger notice of—
 (i) the CMA's opinion as mentioned in section 97(5) (in the case of a notice under section 99(2)) or the permitted purpose included in the notice in accordance with section 109(4) (in the case of a notice under section 109); and
 (ii) the CMA's intention to extend the period for considering the merger notice."

(8) In its application, on or after the commencement date, to any possible reference under section 22 or 33 of the 2002 Act which is active before that date, section 110B of that Act has effect as if—

(a) for subsection (1)(d) there were substituted—

 "(d) the making of the reference is prevented by section 96(3);",

(b) subsection (1)(f) and (2)(f) were omitted, and
(c) in subsection (2)(d), for the words "the expiry of the initial period" there were substituted "the time when the reference becomes prevented".

(9) The amendments made by paragraph 7 of Schedule 8 to the Act (time-limits for consideration of undertakings in lieu of references) do not apply in relation to any case received, on or after the commencement date, by the CMA from the European Commission as mentioned in section 34A(1) of the 2002 Act where the European Commission's decision or deemed decision (whenever made) relates to—

(a) a notification, under Article 4(1) of the EU Merger Regulation, which is made before the commencement date, or

(b) a request, under Article 4(4) of that Regulation, which is made before that date.

(10) In this paragraph—

"EU Merger Regulation" means Council Regulation (EC) No 139/2004 of 20th January 2004 on the control of concentrations between undertakings;

"relevant person" means any person carrying on an enterprise to which the possible reference relates and which has or might have ceased, or (as the case may be) would or might cease, to be distinct (within the meaning of section 26 of the 2002 Act).

7 Time-limits for duty to remedy adverse effects

The amendments made by paragraph 6 of Schedule 8 to the Act (time-limits for remedying adverse effects) do not apply in relation to a report of the Commission—

(a) of the kind mentioned in section 41(1) of the 2002 Act, and

(b) published before the commencement date.

Markets

8 General: existing matters

(1) The amendments made by Chapter 2 of Part 4 of the Act or section 49 or 50 of the Act (markets) apply in relation to—

(a) any reference made under section 131 or 132 of the 2002 Act before the commencement date, or

(b) any possible reference under section 131 or 132 of the 2002 Act which arose before that date,

as they apply in relation to any such reference made, or arising, on or after that date.

(2) In particular, the amendments mentioned in sub-paragraph (1) apply in relation to investigations begun, notices given, reports published, undertakings accepted and orders made before the commencement date as they apply in relation to investigations begun, notices given, reports published, undertakings accepted and orders made on or after that date.

(3) Sub-paragraph (2) is without prejudice to the generality of sub-paragraph (1).

(4) This paragraph is subject to paragraphs 9 to 12 and 16.

9 Public interest interventions

(1) The amendments made by section 35 of, and Schedule 10 to, the Act (public interest interventions in markets investigations) do not apply in relation to—

(a) any reference made under section 131 or 132 of the 2002 Act before the commencement date, or

(b) any case where the OFT has published a notice of a proposed undertaking in lieu under section 155(1) or (4) of the 2002 Act before the commencement date.

(2) In their application to cases where the OFT has publicly launched a market study before the commencement date but sub-paragraph (1) does not apply, sections 139 to 140A of the 2002 Act have effect as if—

(a) section 139(A1) provided for section 139 to apply where the OFT has publicly launched a market study in relation to a matter,

(b) the permitted period for the purposes of section 139(1) were the period beginning with the public launch of the market study and ending with—

(i) the acceptance by the CMA of an undertaking under section 154 instead of the making of a reference under section 131 in relation to the matter,

(ii) the publication of notice of the fact that the CMA has otherwise decided not to make such a reference in relation to the matter, or

(iii) the making of such a reference in relation to the matter,

(c) section 140(1)(a) and (b) required an intervention notice under section 139(1) to state—

(i) the matter to which the publicly launched market study relates, and

(ii) the date of the public launch,

(d) the references in section 140(4B)(b) and 140A(1) to preparing a market study report in relation to a matter within the period permitted by section 131B(4) were references to preparing a report on the market study concerned in relation to a matter,

(e) sections 140(4C) and (5)(zc) and 140A(2), (3)(c) and (11) were omitted,

(f) in section 140(6)(a) the word ""(zc)," were omitted,

(g) the reference in section 140A(1)(b) to the CMA being required to publish the report were a reference to the CMA publishing the report on the market study concerned,

(h) section 140A(3)(b) required the CMA not to publish the report but to give it to the Secretary of State, and

(i) the reference in section 140A(10) to the market study report were a reference to the report.

10 Investigation powers

(1) The amendments made by section 36 of, and Schedule 11 to, the Act (investigation powers) do not apply in relation to any notice given before the commencement date under section 174 of the 2002 Act or section 109 of that Act as applied by section 176 of that Act.

(2) In their continued application by virtue of sub-paragraph (1), sections 109 to 116 of the 2002 Act and any related provisions have effect without the amendments made by section 29 of the Act.

(3) In its application to cases where the OFT has publicly launched a market study before the commencement date—

(a) section 174(1)(a) of the 2002 Act has effect as if the reference to the publication of a market study notice were a reference to the public launch of a market study,
(b) section 174C(1) has effect as if for paragraphs (a) and (b) there were substituted "the CMA publishes the report on the market study concerned or (as the case may be) gives it to the Secretary of State under section 140A(3)(b)", and
(c) section 174C(2) has effect as if for paragraphs (a) and (b) there were substituted "the publication of the report or (as the case may be) the giving of it to the Secretary of State".

11 Time-limits for market studies and market references

(1) The amendments made by paragraphs 1, 2, and 10 of Schedule 12 to the Act (market studies and time-limits) do not apply in relation to any market study publicly launched by the OFT before the commencement date (or any reference made under section 131 or 132 of that Act before that date).

(2) The amendments made by paragraphs 3 and 6 of Schedule 12 to the Act (time-limits for market investigations and reports) do not apply in relation to any reference made under section 131 or 132 of the 2002 Act before the commencement date.

12 Time-limits for duty to remedy adverse effects

The amendments made by paragraphs 4 and 5 of Schedule 12 to the Act (time-limits for remedying adverse effects) do not apply in relation to a report of the Commission—
(a) of the kind mentioned in section 138(1) of the 2002 Act, and
(b) published before the commencement date.

Anti-trust

13 General: existing anti-trust investigations

Subject to paragraph 14, the amendments made by Chapter 3 of Part 4 of the Act (anti-trust) apply in relation to any investigation begun before, and continuing on, the commencement date as they apply in relation to any investigation begun on or after that date.

14 Penalties

The amendments made by section 40 of the Act (civil enforcement of investigation powers) do not apply in relation to any requirement imposed on a person under the Competition Act 1998 before the commencement date.

Price control references

15 Recovery of CMA's costs in respect of price control references

(1) The amendments made by section 54 of, and paragraphs 42 to 45 of Schedule 15 to, the Act (recovery of CMA's costs in respect of price control references) do not apply in relation to a determination on a price control reference if the notice of the appeal which gave rise to the price control reference was received by the Competition Appeal Tribunal before the commencement date.

(2) For the purposes of this paragraph, "price control reference" means a price control matter referred to the Commission before the commencement date or to the CMA on or after that date by virtue of section 193 of the Communications Act 2003 and "price control matter" has the same meaning as in that section.

General

16 Enactments applied by other enactments

(1) Subject as follows, this Schedule applies in relation to enactments as applied by other enactments as it applies in relation to the enactments themselves.

(2) In its application to provisions applied by Part 4 of the 2002 Act, paragraph 3(1) has effect as if the references to sections 22, 33, 45 or 62 of the 2002 Act were references to sections 131 or 132 of that Act.

(3) Paragraph 4(1) does not apply in relation to any notice given before the commencement date under section 109 of the 2002 Act as applied by section 176 of that Act (for which see paragraph 10).

(4) In its application to provisions applied by the Enterprise Act 2002 (Protection of Legitimate Interests) Order 2003, paragraph 3 has effect as if the references to sections 22, 33, 45 or 62 of the 2002 Act were references to article 5 of that Order.

(5) In its application to provisions applied by virtue of Schedule 4ZA to the Water Industry Act 1991, paragraph 3 has effect as if the references to sections 22, 33, 45 or 62 of the 2002 Act were references to section 32 of the Act of 1991.

(6) In their application to functions exercisable under the 2002 Act concurrently with a sectoral regulator, paragraphs 8 to 12 (other than paragraphs 9(2), 10(3) and 11(1)) have effect as if any reference to the OFT includes a reference to the sectoral regulator concerned.

(7) In their application to sectoral regulators (and without prejudice to paragraphs 8(1) and 9(1)), sections 139(A1)(b) and (1B) and 140A(2)(a) of the 2002 Act and any related provisions have effect as if the references to consultation under section 169 of that Act in respect of a decision of the kind mentioned in section 169(6)(a)(i) of that Act included references to consultation begun before the commencement date in respect of a decision of the kind mentioned in section 169(6)(a)(i) of that Act as it had effect before that date.

(8) In this paragraph "sectoral regulator" means—
(a) the Office of Communications,
(b) the Gas and Electricity Markets Authority,
(c) the Water Services Regulation Authority,
(d) the Office of Rail Regulation,
(e) the Northern Ireland Authority for Utility Regulation,
(f) the Civil Aviation Authority, or
(g) Monitor.

(9) This paragraph is subject to any provision made otherwise than by this Schedule and dealing specifically with the enactments as applied.

NOTES

National Assembly for Wales: see further, in relation to the renaming of the National Assembly for Wales as the Senedd Cymru or the Welsh Parliament, the Senedd and Elections (Wales) Act 2020, s 2 (with effect from 6 May 2020). See also ss 3–9 of the 2020 Act in relation to the renaming of Acts of the National Assembly for Wales, Members of the National Assembly for Wales, etc.

COMPETITION ACT 1998 (COMPETITION AND MARKETS AUTHORITY'S RULES) ORDER 2014

(SI 2014/458)

NOTES

Made: 23 February 2014.

Authority: Competition Act 1998, ss 51(5), (6), 71(3), 75A(3), (4). Note that s 75A of the 1998 Act was repealed by the Competition (Amendment etc) (EU Exit) Regulations 2019, SI 2019/93, regs 2, 27, as from IP completion day (as defined in the European Union (Withdrawal Agreement) Act 2020, s 39) (for transitional provisions and savings in relation to the operation of the 2019 Regulations, see Sch 4 to those Regulations at **[7.69]** et seq).

Commencement: 1 April 2014.

[2.14]

1 Citation and Commencement

This Order may be cited as the Competition Act 1998 (Competition and Markets Authority's Rules) Order 2014 and shall come into force on 1st April 2014.

[2.15]

2 Approval of the Competition and Market Authority's Rules

The Secretary of State approves the Rules made by the CMA set out in the Schedule.

3 *(Revokes the Competition Act 1998 (Office of Fair Trading's Rules) Order 2004, SI 2004/2751.)*

SCHEDULE
COMPETITION AND MARKET AUTHORITY'S COMPETITION ACT 1998 RULES

Article 2

[2.16]

1 Interpretation

(1) In these Rules—

"the Act" means the Competition Act 1998;

"CMA" means the Competition and Markets Authority;

"confidential information" means—

(a) commercial information whose disclosure the CMA or a regulator thinks might significantly harm the legitimate business interests of the undertaking to which it relates, or

(b) information relating to the private affairs of an individual whose disclosure the CMA or a regulator thinks might significantly harm the individual's interests, or

(c) information whose disclosure the CMA or a regulator thinks is contrary to the public interest;

["infringement decision" means a decision of the CMA that the Chapter I prohibition or the Chapter II prohibition has been infringed;]

"internal document" means—

(a) a document produced by, or exchanged between, the CMA, a regulator or another public authority and which has not been produced for the purpose of public disclosure by the CMA, a regulator or another public authority, or

(b) a document produced by, or exchanged between, any person from time to time retained under a contract for services by the CMA, a regulator or another public authority and the CMA, a regulator or another public authority and which has not been produced for the purpose of public disclosure;

"notice" means a notice that the CMA is required to give to a person under any of—

(a) rule 5,

(b) rule 11, [or]

(c) rule 15(3), *or*

(d) rule 16(1);

"oral hearing" means a hearing in which a relevant party may make oral representations on any matter referred to in a notice;

"Procedural Officer" means any relevant person who is required to exercise any function under rules 6(5) and 8(1);

"public authority" includes—

(a) in the United Kingdom, a court or tribunal and any person exercising functions of a public nature, and

(b) in any country or territory outside the United Kingdom, a court or tribunal and any person or body which appears to the CMA or a regulator to be exercising functions of a public nature;

"relevant party" means a person to whom a notice is required to be given, except where the CMA does not address a proposed infringement decision or infringement decision to that person in accordance with rules 5(3) or 10(2);

"relevant person" means any of the following categories of person who has been authorised by the CMA or a regulator's Board to exercise any function under these Rules—
(a) one or more members of the CMA Board or a regulator's Board,
(b) one or more members of the CMA panel or a regulator's Panel,
(c) one or more members of staff of the CMA or a regulator,
(d) jointly by one or more of the persons mentioned in paragraph (a), (b) or (c).

(2) Except where these Rules otherwise provide, expressions used in the Act which are also used in these Rules have the same meaning in these Rules as they have in section 59 of the Act.

(3) Any reference in these Rules to the CMA means the CMA or a regulator, except in—
(a) this rule,
(b) rule 20.

2 Application of the Rules

(1) *Subject to paragraphs (2) and (3),* these Rules apply when the CMA takes investigation or enforcement action under the Act in relation to [the Chapter I prohibition or the Chapter II prohibition].

(2) Rule 15 and rule 17 apply only when the CMA takes investigation or enforcement action in relation to the Chapter I prohibition or the Chapter II prohibition.

(3) Rule 16 applies only when the CMA takes investigation or enforcement action in relation to the prohibition in Article 101(1).

3 Delegation of functions

(1) There is to be a relevant person who oversees the investigation under the Act and who is to decide whether notice of a proposed infringement decision under rule 5 is given.

(2) Subject to rule 9(4) there is to be a different relevant person from the relevant person referred to in paragraph (1), who has not been involved in the investigation, who decides whether any supplementary notice of a proposed infringement decision under rule 5 is given, whether to make an infringement decision under rule 10 and whether to impose a penalty under rule 11.

(3) For the purposes of paragraph (2) the different relevant person must comprise at least two relevant persons.

4 Legal advice during investigations and inspections

(1) An officer entering a premises must, upon request, allow a reasonable time for the occupier's legal adviser to arrive at the premises before the investigation continues, if the officer—
(a) considers it reasonable in the circumstances to do so and
(b) is satisfied that such conditions as he considers it is appropriate to impose in granting the occupier's request are being, or will be, complied with.

(2) A person required by the CMA under section 26(6)(a)(ii) or (b) *or section 65E(6)(a)(ii) or (b)* of the Act to provide an oral explanation of a document or orally confirm the location of a document may be accompanied by a legal adviser.

(3) Where an individual is given notice under section 26A of the Act requiring them to answer questions immediately on receipt of the notice, an officer must upon request allow a reasonable time for the individual's legal adviser to arrive before starting the interview, if the officer—
(a) considers it reasonable in the circumstances to do so, and
(b) is satisfied that such conditions as he considers it appropriate to impose in granting the individual's request are being, or will be, complied with.

(4) For the purposes of paragraphs (1) and (3), a "reasonable time" means such period of time as the officer considers is reasonable in the circumstances.

(5) In this rule, "officer" means an investigating officer within the meaning of section 27(1) *or 65F(1)* of the Act or a named officer of the CMA authorised by a warrant issued under section 28, [or 28A] of the Act.

5 Statement of objections

(1) If the CMA proposes to make an infringement decision, subject to rules 18 and 19, the notice referred to in paragraph (2) must be given to each person who the CMA considers is a party to the agreement, or is engaged in conduct, which the CMA considers infringes [either or both] of the prohibitions mentioned in that paragraph.

(2) The CMA must give notice stating [whether it considers the Chapter I prohibition or the Chapter II prohibition or both] has been infringed and the provisions of rule 6 are to apply.

(3) Where the CMA considers that an agreement infringes the Chapter I prohibition *or the prohibition in Article 101(1)* the CMA may address that proposed infringement decision to fewer than all the persons who are or were party to that agreement or are or were engaged in that conduct.

6 Notices, access to file and representations

(1) A notice under rule 5 must state—
(a) the facts on which the CMA relies, the objections raised by the CMA, the action the CMA proposes and its reasons for the proposed action;
(b) the period within which a relevant party may make written representations to the CMA identifying the information contained in the notice which that relevant party considers the CMA should treat such information as confidential information; and
(c) the period within which a relevant party may make written representations to the CMA on the matters referred to in the notice.

(2) The CMA must give a relevant party a reasonable opportunity to inspect the documents in the CMA's file that relate to the matters referred to in a notice given to that relevant party, except that the CMA may withhold any document—

(a) to the extent that it contains confidential information; or
(b) which is an internal document.

(3) The CMA must offer a relevant party the opportunity to attend an oral hearing in order to make oral representations to the CMA on any matter referred to in a notice.

(4) Where the relevant party confirms that it wishes to attend an oral hearing, the CMA must give that relevant party a reasonable opportunity to attend an oral hearing to make such oral representations.

(5) The oral hearing must be chaired by a Procedural Officer who, other than in acting as the Procedural Officer under this rule or rule 8, has not been involved in the investigation in respect of which notice has been given.

(6) The Procedural Officer must prepare a report following the hearing and give that report to the persons set out in rule 3(2) who are to decide whether to make an infringement decision.

(7) The report must—

(a) contain an assessment of the fairness of the procedure followed in holding the oral hearing; and
(b) identify any other concerns about the fairness of the procedure followed in the investigation which have been brought to the attention of the person preparing the report in that person's role as the chairperson of the oral hearing.

(8) Where, upon the expiry of the period mentioned in paragraph (1)(c), no written representations on the matters referred to in a notice given to a relevant party have been made by that relevant party, the CMA may proceed with the case in the absence of such written representations.

(9) Where the CMA has given a relevant party a reasonable opportunity to make oral representations under paragraph (3) but no oral representations have been made, the CMA may proceed with the case in the absence of such representations.

(10) Paragraph (1)(b) does not restrict the application of rule 7(1) and (2).

7 Confidential information

(1) Where a person who has supplied information to the CMA has made representations to the CMA identifying such information as being information that the CMA should treat as confidential information and the CMA proposes to disclose such information under these Rules, the CMA must take all reasonable steps to—

(a) inform that person of the CMA's proposed action; and
(b) give that person a reasonable opportunity to make representations to the CMA on the CMA's proposed action.

(2) The CMA may at any time request a person who has supplied information to the CMA to make written representations to the CMA in respect of the information supplied—

(a) identifying the information which that person considers the CMA should treat as confidential information; or
(b) explaining why that person considers the CMA should treat the information as confidential information.

(3) If a person who has supplied information to the CMA makes written representations to the CMA in respect of the information supplied identifying the information which that person considers the CMA should treat as confidential information or explaining why the CMA should treat the information as confidential information, whether or not such representations are made under this rule, the CMA may seek from that person such further clarification as the CMA considers is needed.

(4) If the CMA requests any person to make representations or to give further clarification under this rule, the CMA may specify the period within which such representations or further clarification should be made.

(5) For the purposes of this rule, where, in the CMA's opinion, information supplied to the CMA by any person relates to or originates from another person, that other person may be treated as a person who has supplied the information to the CMA.

8 Procedural complaints

(1) Complaints about the procedures followed during the course of an investigation under the Act may be made to a Procedural Officer. The Procedural Officer, who, other than in acting as Procedural Officer under this rule or rule 6, must not have been involved in the investigation, is to consider a significant procedural complaint where that complaint has not been determined or settled by the relevant person overseeing the investigation to the satisfaction of a complainant.

(2) The Procedural Officer must give notice to the person who made the complaint of the decision in respect of the complaint within 20 working days.

(3) The Procedural Officer may extend the period to give notice of the decision in respect of the complaint by no more than 20 working days if the Procedural Officer considers that there are special reasons why the notice of the decision in respect of the complaint cannot be given within the period under paragraph (2).

9 Settlement

(1) The CMA may decide to follow a settlement procedure in respect of an investigation under the Act where a party to that investigation—

(a) admits that it has been a party to an agreement or has been engaged in conduct which infringes [the Chapter I prohibition or the Chapter II prohibition] in relation to that investigation, and
(b) agrees to an expedited administrative procedure for the remainder of the investigation.

(2) A single relevant person may only take the decision to follow a settlement procedure in respect of an investigation pursuant to paragraph (1) if a different relevant person approves that decision.

(3) For the purposes of paragraph (2) the different relevant person must comprise at least two relevant persons.

(4) Where a single relevant person takes the decision to follow a settlement procedure pursuant to paragraph (1) that relevant person may also propose to make an infringement decision under rule 5 and take the decision to make an infringement decision under rule 10 in respect of that investigation.

(5) Where the CMA decides to follow a settlement procedure pursuant to paragraph (1) the CMA must comply with rule 5 to the extent that it has not already been complied with and rule 10.

(6) Where the CMA decides to follow a settlement procedure pursuant to paragraph (1), the CMA may elect to impose a penalty on that party and the provisions of rule 12(2)(a) and 12(4) are to apply.

10 Notice of decision

(1) Where the CMA has made an infringement decision, it must without delay—

(a) subject to rules 18 and 19, give notice of the infringement decision to each person to whom the CMA considers is or was a party to the agreement, or is or was engaged in conduct, stating the facts on which the CMA bases the infringement decision and the CMA's reasons for making the infringement decision; and

(b) publish the infringement decision.

(2) Where the CMA considers that an agreement infringes the Chapter I prohibition *or the prohibition in Article 101(1)* the CMA may address an infringement decision to fewer than all the persons who are or were party to that agreement or are or were engaged in that conduct.

(3) The CMA may delay publication of the infringement decision under paragraph (1)(b) where the CMA considers that such publication may prejudice a criminal investigation or prosecution pursuant to section 192 of the Enterprise Act 2002 relating to the same or similar agreement or conduct.

(4) Where the CMA has made a decision that there are no grounds for action in respect of—

(a) an agreement either because the conditions of the Chapter I prohibition are not met or because the agreement is excluded from the Chapter I prohibition or satisfies the conditions in section 9(1) of the Act; or

(b) an agreement either because the conditions of the prohibition in Article 101(1) are not met or because the agreement satisfies the conditions of Article 101(3); or

(c) conduct because the conditions of the Chapter II prohibition *or the prohibition in Article 102* are not met;

the CMA must without delay, subject to rules 18 and 19, give notice of the decision, to any person whom it has undertaken to inform of the decision and to any person in respect of whom the CMA or an officer has issued any notice under rule 5, stating the facts on which the CMA bases the decision and the CMA's reasons for making the decision.

(5) Where the CMA is required to give notice of a decision under paragraph (4), it may publish the decision.

(6) In this rule, "officer" has the same meaning as in rule 4.

11 Notice of proposed penalty

If the CMA proposes to require an undertaking to pay a penalty under section 36 of the Act—

(a) the CMA must give notice of this to the undertaking stating [whether it considers the Chapter I prohibition or the Chapter II prohibition or both] has been infringed; and

(b) the provisions of rule 6 are to apply to the extent that they have not already been applied.

12 Directions and penalties

(1) Where the CMA gives a direction to a person under section 32 or 33 of the Act, it must at the same time inform that person in writing of the facts on which it bases the direction and its reasons for giving the direction.

(2) If the CMA requires an undertaking to pay a penalty under section 36 of the Act—

(a) the CMA must at the same time inform that undertaking in writing of the facts on which it bases the penalty and its reasons for requiring that undertaking to pay the penalty; and

(b) the provisions of rule 11 are to apply to the extent that they have not already been applied.

(3) The CMA must publish directions given under section 32 or 33 of the Act.

(4) The CMA must publish penalties imposed under section 36 of the Act.

13 Interim measures

(1) Subject to paragraph (2), if the CMA proposes to give a direction under section 35 of the Act, it must give each person to whom it proposes to give the direction a reasonable opportunity to inspect the documents in the CMA's file relating to the proposed direction.

(2) The CMA may withhold any document—

(a) to the extent that it contains confidential information; or

(b) which is an internal document.

(3) When giving a person an opportunity to make representations under section 35(3)(b) of the Act, the CMA must specify the period within which that person may make such representations.

(4) Where the CMA gives a direction to a person under section 35 of the Act, it must at the same time inform that person in writing of the facts on which it bases the direction and its reasons for giving the direction, and it must publish the direction.

14 Election to apply a relevant prohibition to a case

(1) The CMA may, at any time prior to making an infringement decision, elect to apply [the Chapter I prohibition or the Chapter II prohibition to a case] (whether or not any such election has previously been made by the CMA in that case).

(2) The CMA must make an election pursuant to paragraph (1) before it may make any decision under paragraph (3).

(3) If the CMA proposes—

(a) to make a decision that one or both of the prohibition in Article 101(1) and the prohibition in Article 102 has been infringed, but in any notice given under rule 5 the CMA has stated that it considers that only one or both of the Chapter I prohibition and the Chapter II prohibition has been infringed; or

(b) to make a decision that one or both of the Chapter I prohibition and the Chapter II prohibition has been infringed but in any notice given under rule 5 the CMA has stated that it considers that only one or both of the prohibition in Article 101(1) and the prohibition in Article 102 has been infringed,

the provisions of rules 5 and 6 are to apply to the extent that they have not already been applied.

(4) In paragraph (3), "any notice given under Rule 5" means any notice given under Rule 5 that has not been superseded by a supplemental notice given under Rule 5.

15 Cancellation, etc of a [retained exemption]

(1) The circumstances in which the CMA may exercise the powers in section 10(5)(a), 10(5)(c) and 10(5)(d) of the Act are where it finds that an agreement which benefits from a [retained exemption] nevertheless has effects in the United Kingdom, or a part of it, which are incompatible with the conditions laid down in section 9(1) of the Act.

(2) The circumstances in which the CMA may exercise the powers in section 10(5)(b) of the Act are where, having previously exercised the powers in section 10(5)(a) or 10(5)(c) of the Act in respect of an agreement, the CMA finds that—

(a) as a result of a material change in circumstances since the exercise of those powers, any condition or obligation it has imposed in exercise of those powers is no longer necessary to ensure that the effects of the agreement in the United Kingdom, or a part of it, are compatible with the conditions laid down in section 9(1) of the Act; or

(b) as a result of a material change in circumstances since the exercise of those powers, or as a result of information supplied in response to a notice given under paragraph (3) being incomplete, false or misleading in a material particular, the agreement has effects in the United Kingdom, or a part of it, which are incompatible with the conditions laid down in section 9(1) of the Act.

(3) Subject to rules 18 and 19, if (other than in the circumstances referred to in paragraph (2)(a)) the CMA proposes to exercise any of the powers in section 10(5) of the Act it must give notice to each person who it considers is a party to the agreement and the provisions of rule 6 are to apply.

(4) Subject to rules 18 and 19, if the CMA proposes to exercise any of the powers in section 10(5)(b) of the Act in the circumstances referred to in paragraph (2)(a) it must consult each person who it considers is a party to the agreement.

(5) If the CMA proposes to exercise any of the powers in section 10(5) of the Act it may consult the public.

(6) If the CMA has made a decision in exercise of any of its powers in section 10(5) of the Act it must—

(a) subject to rules 18 and 19, give notice of the decision to each person who the CMA considers is a party to the agreement, stating the facts on which it bases the decision and its reasons for the decision; and

(b) publish the decision.

16 Withdrawal of the benefit of a Commission Regulation pursuant to Article 29(2) of the EC Competition Regulation

(1) Subject to rules 18 and 19, if the CMA proposes, in any particular case, to withdraw in the whole or any part of the United Kingdom the benefit of a Commission Regulation pursuant to Article 29(2) of the EC Competition Regulation, it must give notice to each person who the CMA considers is a party to the agreement, and the provisions of rule 6 are to apply.

(2) If the CMA proposes to exercise its powers under Article 29(2) of the EC Competition Regulation it may consult the public.

(3) If the CMA has made a decision withdrawing in the whole or any part of the United Kingdom the benefit of a Commission Regulation pursuant to Article 29(2) of the EC Competition Regulation it must—

(a) subject to rules 18 and 19, give notice of the decision to each person who the CMA considers is a party to the agreement, stating the facts on which it bases the decision and its reasons for the decision; and

(b) publish the decision.

17 Withdrawal of an exclusion

(1) Subject to rules 18 and 19, if the CMA proposes to give a direction under paragraph 4 of Schedule 1 to the Act or paragraph 9 of Schedule 3 to the Act, or in accordance with an order made under section 50 of the Act, to the effect that an exclusion made by a provision specified in paragraph (2) does not apply to an agreement, it must consult each person who it considers is a party to the agreement.

(2) The provisions specified for the purposes of paragraph (1) are—

(a) paragraph 1 of Schedule 1 to the Act;

(b) paragraph 9(1) of Schedule 3 to the Act; and

(c) an order made under section 50 of the Act.

(3) The period specified for the purposes of paragraph 4(4) of Schedule 1 to the Act and paragraph 9(6) of Schedule 3 to the Act is ten working days starting with the date the notice is given.

(4) If the CMA has given a direction referred to in paragraph (1), it must publish the direction.

18 Associations of undertakings and government organisations

(1) Where the Rules require the CMA to give notice of any matter to an association of undertakings, the CMA is to give such notice to the director, secretary, manager or other similar officer of the association on its behalf.

(2) Where the Rules require the CMA to give notice of any matter to each of more than twenty members of an association of undertakings the CMA may, instead of giving such notice to any such member, give such notice to the director, secretary, manager or other similar officer of the association or government organisation on that member's behalf.

19 Time limits and giving notice

"(1) Where—

(a) the CMA has taken all reasonable steps to give notice to a person under rules 5, 10(1)(a), 10(4), 15(3), 15(4), 15(6)(a), *16(1) 16(3)(a)* or 17(1) but does not consider that the notice has been received; or

(b) in accordance with rules 5(3) and 10(2), an infringement decision or proposed infringement decision is not addressed to a person under rules 5, 10(1)(a), 10(4), 15(3), 15(4), 15(6)(a), *16(1), 16(3)(a)* or 17(1),

the CMA may publicise the matter in accordance with paragraph (2) in order to give notice to that person.".

(2) The CMA may publicise the matter by—

(a) publishing a summary of the notice by means of entry in the register maintained by the CMA under rule 20; and

(b) providing for a reference to the summary of the notice published in that register to be published in—

(i) the London Gazette, the Edinburgh Gazette and the Belfast Gazette;

(ii) at least one national daily newspaper; and

(iii) if there is in circulation an appropriate trade journal which is published at intervals not exceeding one month, in such trade journal.

(3) Except where paragraph (1) applies, where the Rules allow or require notice to be given to a person, such notice is to be treated as having been given on the date on which that person receives it.

(4) Where paragraph (1) applies, the notice is to be treated as having been given on the date of its publication in accordance with paragraph (2).

(5) Any notice given under the Rules must be in writing.

(6) Where the time prescribed by the Rules for performing an action expires on a non-working day, the action is in time if done at or before 5.30 pm on the following working day.

(7) Where an action required by the Rules is performed on a non-working day, or after 5.30 pm on a working day, the action is deemed to be completed on the following working day.

20 Public register

(1) The CMA must maintain a register in which there must be entered—

(a) all decisions required to be published under the Rules;

(b) all decisions published under rule 10(5);

(c) all directions required to be published under the Rules;

(d) all notices required to be published under rule 21(2); and

(e) all penalties required to be published under rule 12(4).

(2) The register is to be open to public inspection—

(a) at the CMA's head office between 10.00 am and 4.30 pm on every working day; and

(b) on the CMA's website.

21 Consultation

(1) Where the CMA, if it proposes to take action, is required to consult a person under the Rules, it must—

(a) subject to rules 18 and 19, give notice to that person; and

(b) state in that notice the action the CMA proposes to take, its reasons for proposing such action and the period within which that person may make written representations to the CMA on these matters.

(2) Where the CMA, if it proposes to take action—

(a) is required to consult the public under the Rules; or

(b) proposes to consult the public in exercise of its discretion to do so under the Rules,

it must publish a notice stating the action it proposes to take, its reasons for proposing such action and the period within which written representations may be made to the CMA on these matters.

NOTES

Rule 1 is amended as follows:

The definition "infringement decision" was substituted, the word "or" in square brackets in para (b) of the definition "notice" was inserted, and para (d) of that definition (and the preceding word "or" in italics) was revoked, by the Competition (Amendment etc) (EU Exit) Regulations 2019, SI 2019/93, reg 61, Sch 2, Pt 1, para 4(1), (2), as from IP completion day (as defined in the European Union (Withdrawal Agreement) Act 2020, s 39) (for transitional provisions and savings in relation to the operation of the 2019 Regulations, see Sch 4 to those Regulations at **[7.69]** et seq). The original definition "infringement decision" read as follows—

> ""infringement decision" means a decision that one or more of the Chapter I prohibition, the Chapter II prohibition, the prohibition in Article 101(1) and the prohibition in Article 102 has been infringed;".

Rule 2: the words in italics in para (1) were revoked, the words in square brackets in that paragraph were substituted (for the original words "any one or more of the Chapter I prohibition, the Chapter II prohibition, the prohibition in Article 101(1) and the prohibition in Article 102"), and paras (2) and (3) were revoked, by SI 2019/93, reg 61, Sch 2, Pt 1, para 4(1), (3), as from IP completion day (as defined in the European Union (Withdrawal Agreement) Act 2020, s 39) (for transitional provisions and savings in relation to the operation of the 2019 Regulations, see Sch 4 to those Regulations at **[7.69]** et seq).

Rule 4: the words in italics were revoked, and the words in square brackets in para (5) were substituted (for the original words ", 28A, 65G or 65H"), by SI 2019/93, reg 61, Sch 2, Pt 1, para 4(1), (4), as from IP completion day (as defined in the European Union (Withdrawal Agreement) Act 2020, s 39) (for transitional provisions and savings in relation to the operation of the 2019 Regulations, see Sch 4 to those Regulations at **[7.69]** et seq).

Rule 5: the words in the first pair of square brackets were substituted (for the original words "one or more"), the words in the second pair of square brackets were substituted (for the original words "which one or more of the Chapter I prohibition, the Chapter II prohibition, the prohibition in Article 101(1) and the prohibition in Article 102 the CMA considers"), and the words in italics in para (3) were revoked, by SI 2019/93, reg 61, Sch 2, Pt 1, para 4(1), (5), as from IP completion day (as defined in the European Union (Withdrawal Agreement) Act 2020, s 39) (for transitional provisions and savings in relation to the operation of the 2019 Regulations, see Sch 4 to those Regulations at **[7.69]** et seq).

Rule 9: in para (1)(a) the words in square brackets were substituted (for the original words "one or more of the Chapter I prohibition, the Chapter II prohibition, the prohibition in Article 101(1) and the prohibition in Article 102") by SI 2019/93, reg 61, Sch 2, Pt 1, para 4(1), (6), as from IP completion day (as defined in the European Union (Withdrawal Agreement) Act 2020, s 39) (for transitional provisions and savings in relation to the operation of the 2019 Regulations, see Sch 4 to those Regulations at **[7.69]** et seq).

Rule 10: the words in italics were revoked by SI 2019/93, reg 61, Sch 2, Pt 1, para 4(1), (7), as from IP completion day (as defined in the European Union (Withdrawal Agreement) Act 2020, s 39) (for transitional provisions and savings in relation to the operation of the 2019 Regulations, see Sch 4 to those Regulations at **[7.69]** et seq).

Rule 11: the words in square brackets were substituted (for the original words "which one or more of the Chapter I prohibition, the Chapter II prohibition, the prohibition in Article 101(1) and the prohibition in Article 102 the CMA considers") by SI 2019/93, reg 61, Sch 2, Pt 1, para 4(1), (8), as from IP completion day (as defined in the European Union (Withdrawal Agreement) Act 2020, s 39) (for transitional provisions and savings in relation to the operation of the 2019 Regulations, see Sch 4 to those Regulations at **[7.69]** et seq).

Rule 14: the words in square brackets in para (1) were substituted (for the original words "to a case one or more of the Chapter I prohibition, the Chapter II prohibition, the prohibition in Article 101(1) and the prohibition in Article 102"), and paras (2)–(4) were revoked, by SI 2019/93, reg 61, Sch 2, Pt 1, para 4(1), (9), as from IP completion day (as defined in the European Union (Withdrawal Agreement) Act 2020, s 39) (for transitional provisions and savings in relation to the operation of the 2019 Regulations, see Sch 4 to those Regulations at **[7.69]** et seq).

Rule 15: the words in square brackets were substituted (for the original words "parallel exemption") by SI 2019/93, reg 61, Sch 2, Pt 1, para 4(1), (10), as from IP completion day (as defined in the European Union (Withdrawal Agreement) Act 2020, s 39) (for transitional provisions and savings in relation to the operation of the 2019 Regulations, see Sch 4 to those Regulations at **[7.69]** et seq).

Rule 16: revoked by SI 2019/93, reg 61, Sch 2, Pt 1, para 4(1), (11), as from IP completion day (as defined in the European Union (Withdrawal Agreement) Act 2020, s 39) (for transitional provisions and savings in relation to the operation of the 2019 Regulations, see Sch 4 to those Regulations at **[7.69]** et seq).

Rule 19: the figures in italics in para (1) were revoked by SI 2019/93, reg 61, Sch 2, Pt 1, para 4(1), (12), as from IP completion day (as defined in the European Union (Withdrawal Agreement) Act 2020, s 39) (for transitional provisions and savings in relation to the operation of the 2019 Regulations, see Sch 4 to those Regulations at **[7.69]** et seq).

DESIGNATION OF THE COMPETITION AND MARKETS AUTHORITY AS A NATIONAL COMPETITION AUTHORITY REGULATIONS 2014

(SI 2014/537)

NOTES

Made: 6 March 2014.

Authority: European Communities Act 1972, s 2(2)(a).

Commencement: 1 April 2014.

Revocation: these Regulations were revoked by the Competition (Amendment etc) (EU Exit) Regulations 2019, SI 2019/93, reg 61, Sch 2, Pt 3, para 13, as from IP completion day (as defined in the European Union (Withdrawal Agreement) Act 2020, s 39) (for transitional provisions and savings in relation to the operation of the 2019 Regulations, see Sch 4 to those Regulations at **[7.69]** et seq).

[2.17]

1 Citation and commencement

These Regulations may be cited as the Designation of the Competition and Markets Authority as a National Competition Authority Regulations 2014 and shall come into force on 1st April 2014.

NOTES

These Regulations were revoked by the Competition (Amendment etc) (EU Exit) Regulations 2019, SI 2019/93, reg 61, Sch 2, Pt 3, para 13, (for transitional provisions and savings in relation to the operation of the 2019 Regulations, see Sch 4 to those Regulations at **[7.69]** et seq).

[2.18]

2 Designation as a national competition authority

(1) The Competition and Markets Authority is designated as a national competition authority pursuant to Article 35 of the EC Competition Regulation for the purposes of exercising all of the powers and functions of a competition authority of a Member State under Chapters I, II, IV, V, VIII and IX of the EC Competition Regulation.

(2) In this regulation, "EC Competition Regulation" means Council Regulation (EC) No 1/2003 of 16th December 2002 on the implementation of the rules on competition laid down in Articles 81 and 82 of the Treaty.

NOTES

These Regulations were revoked by the Competition (Amendment etc) (EU Exit) Regulations 2019, SI 2019/93, reg 61, Sch 2, Pt 3, para 13, (for transitional provisions and savings in relation to the operation of the 2019 Regulations, see Sch 4 to those Regulations at **[7.69]** et seq).

ENTERPRISE AND REGULATORY REFORM ACT 2013 (COMPETITION) (CONSEQUENTIAL, TRANSITIONAL AND SAVING PROVISIONS) (NO 2) ORDER 2014

(SI 2014/549)

NOTES

Made: 6 March 2014.
Authority: Enterprise and Regulatory Reform Act 2013, s 99(1)–(3).
Commencement: 1 April 2014.

[2.19]
1 Citation, commencement, interpretation and extent

(1) This Order may be cited as the Enterprise and Regulatory Reform Act 2013 (Competition) (Consequential, Transitional and Saving Provisions) (No 2) Order 2014 and comes into force on 1st April 2014.

(2) In this Order—
"the Act" means the Enterprise and Regulatory Reform Act 2013;
"CMA" means the Competition and Markets Authority;
"commencement date" means 1st April 2014;
"Commission" means the Competition Commission;
"OFT" means the Office of Fair Trading; and
"the 2002 Act" means the Enterprise Act 2002.

(3) An amendment or revocation made by this Order has the same extent as the provision to which it relates.

[2.20]
2 Consequential amendments to other legislation etc

Schedule 1 (which amends secondary legislation to make provision for the transfer of certain functions from the OFT and the Commission to the CMA and contains amendments consequential on Parts 3 and 4 of the Act) has effect.

[2.21]
3 Continuity of functions

(1) Anything which, immediately before the commencement date, is in the process of being done by or in relation to the transferor may, so far as it relates to a relevant function, be continued by or in relation to the transferee.

(2) Anything done (or having effect as if done) by or in relation to the transferor for the purposes of or in connection with a relevant function is, if in force or effective immediately before the commencement date, to have effect as if done by or in relation to the transferee so far as that is required for continuing its effect on or after the commencement date.

(3) In the application of paragraph (1) or (2)—

(a) any reference made before the commencement date under section 32 of the Water Industry Act 1991 to the Commission is to be treated, so far as provided by those paragraphs, as a reference under that section to the chair of the CMA for the constitution of a CMA group,

(b) where any functions exercisable immediately before the commencement date by a Commission group are to be exercisable on or after that date by a CMA group—

(i) any person who, immediately before the commencement date, is a member of the Commission group is to be treated, on or after that date, as a member of the CMA group concerned if the person is a member of the CMA panel,

(ii) any person who, immediately before the commencement date, is the chairman of the Commission group is to be treated, on or after that date, as the chair of the CMA group if the person is a member of the CMA panel, and

(iii) the persons treated as mentioned in paragraph (i) or (ii) are to be treated, on or after the commencement date, as if they have been constituted in accordance with Part 3 of Schedule 4 to the Act as the chair and other members of the CMA group (and that Part applies accordingly in relation to the operation of the group), and

(c) an authorisation given (whether by warrant or otherwise) before the commencement date, so far as it authorises a named member, or member of staff, of the OFT or the Commission, continues to authorise that individual (but no other) on or after the commencement date if, and only if, the individual is a member, or (as the case may be), a member of staff, of the CMA.

(4) Paragraphs (1) to (3)—

(a) do not apply in relation to any matter dealt with by a transfer scheme under section 27 of the Act or by any other transitional provision made by virtue of the Act; and

(b) do not apply so as to convert an appointment as a member of the OFT or the Commission into an appointment as a member of the CMA.

(5) Any enactment, instrument or other document passed or made before the commencement date is to have effect, so far as necessary for the purposes of or in consequence of its continued effect by virtue of Schedule 2, as if any references (however expressed) to the transferor were references to the transferee.

(6) Any enactment, instrument or other document passed or made before the commencement date is to have effect, so far as necessary for the purposes of or in consequence of anything transferred from the transferor to the transferee by virtue of this Order as if any references (however expressed) to the transferor were references to the transferee.

(7) The repeals of section 45(4) of the Competition Act 1998 and section 2(3) of the 2002 Act by Parts 3 and 4 of Schedule 5 to the Act do not apply so far as those sections create references to the transferor to which paragraph (5) or (6) above are capable of applying.

(8) The abolition of the OFT or the Commission does not affect the validity of anything done (or having effect as if done) by or in relation to the transferor before the commencement date.

(9) In this article—

"CMA Board" has the same meaning as in Schedule 4 to the Act (see Part 2 of that Schedule);

"CMA group" means a group constituted in accordance with Part 3 of Schedule 4 to the Act;

"CMA panel" has the same meaning as in Schedule 4 to the Act (see Part 3 of that Schedule);

"Commission group" means a group constituted under any enactment or instrument to perform functions of the Commission;

"relevant function" means any function of the transferor which is transferred to the transferee by this Order;

"transferee" means the CMA, the CMA Board, a CMA group, the chair of the CMA or another member of the CMA or (as the case may be) a member of staff of the CMA;

"transferor" means the OFT, the Commission, a Commission group, the chairman of the OFT or Commission, another member of the OFT or Commission, or a member of staff of the OFT or the Commission;

and references in this article to things done include references to things omitted to be done.

(10) Schedule 2 (which makes further transitional provision in relation to amendments in Schedule 1) has effect.

SCHEDULES

SCHEDULE 1

(Sch 1 contains amendments which, in so far as relevant to this work, have been incorporated at the appropriate place.)

SCHEDULE 2
TRANSITIONAL PROVISION AND SAVINGS

Article 3(10)

[2.22]

1. Merger Notices: The Enterprise Act 2002 (Merger Prenotification) Regulations 2003

The revocations made by paragraph 9(2), (5)(a) and (c) and (6) of Schedule 1 do not apply insofar as the continued application of the provisions so revoked is necessary for the purposes of or in consequence of paragraphs 4(2) or 6 of the Schedule to the Enterprise and Regulatory Reform Act 2013 (Commencement No 6, Transitional Provisions and Savings) Order 2014.

2. In their continued application by virtue of paragraph 1, regulations 8 to 11 of the Enterprise Act 2002 (Merger Prenotification) Regulations 2003 are to have effect as if any references to the OFT were references to the CMA.

3. Water mergers: investigation powers

The amendments made by paragraph 22(19) and (20) of Schedule 1 do not apply in relation to any notice given before the commencement date under section 109 of the 2002 Act as applied by virtue of Schedule 4ZA to the Water Industry Act 1991.

4. The amendments made by paragraph 22(5) and (6) of Schedule 1 do not apply in relation to any notice given before the commencement date under section 31 of the 2002 Act as applied by virtue of Schedule 4ZA to the Water Industry Act 1991.

5. Water mergers: undertakings

The amendment made by paragraph 22(13) of Schedule 1 does not apply in relation to undertakings accepted before the commencement date under section 71 of the 2002 Act as applied by virtue of Schedule 4ZA to the Water Industry Act 1991.

6. Postal services: investigation powers in connection with regulatory appeals

The amendments made by section 29 of the Act, to sections 109 to 111 of the 2002 Act, do not have effect in relation to those sections as applied by the Postal Services Act 2011 (Appeals to the Competition Commission) (Investigations and Extension of Time Limits) Order 2011 in relation to any notice given under section 109 of the 2002 Act before the commencement date.

7. The amendments made by paragraph 51(3) and (4) of Schedule 1 do not apply in relation to any notice given before the commencement date under section 109 of the 2002 Act as applied by the Postal Services Act 2011 (Appeals to the Competition Commission) (Investigations and Extension of Time Limits) Order 2011.

B. ENFORCEMENT AND PENALTIES

COMPETITION ACT 1998 (DEFINITION OF APPROPRIATE PERSON) REGULATIONS 1999

(SI 1999/2282)

NOTES

Made: 10 August 1999.
Authority: Competition Act 1998, ss 71, 73(5).
Commencement: 1 March 2000.

[2.23]
1 Citation and commencement

These Regulations may be cited as the Competition Act 1998 (Definition of Appropriate Person) Regulations 1999 and shall come into force on 1st March 2000.

[2.24]
2 Definition of appropriate person

For the purposes of section 73(4)(a) of the Competition Act 1998 "appropriate person" means—

(a) in relation to any land which is occupied by a government department that department; and
(b) in relation to any other land which is otherwise occupied for purposes of the Crown the person occupying the land for such purposes.

COMPETITION ACT 1998 (SMALL AGREEMENTS AND CONDUCT OF MINOR SIGNIFICANCE) REGULATIONS 2000

(SI 2000/262)

NOTES

Made: 7 February 2000.
Authority: Competition Act 1998, ss 39, 40, 59(1), 71.
Commencement: 1 March 2000.

[2.25]
1 Citation and commencement

These Regulations may be cited as the Competition Act 1998 (Small Agreements and Conduct of Minor Significance) Regulations 2000 and shall come into force on 1st March 2000.

[2.26]
2 Interpretation

In these Regulations—

"the Act" means the Competition Act 1998;

"applicable turnover" means the turnover of an undertaking for a business year determined in accordance with the Schedule to this Order; and where a business year does not equal twelve months the applicable turnover shall be the amount which bears the same proportion to the applicable turnover during that business year as twelve months does to that period;

"business year" means a period of more than six months in respect of which an undertaking publishes accounts or, if no such accounts have been published for the period, prepares accounts.

[2.27]
3 Small agreements

The category of agreements prescribed for the purposes of section 39(1) of the Act is all agreements between undertakings the combined applicable turnover of which for the business year ending in the calendar year preceding one during which the infringement occurred does not exceed £20 million.

[2.28]
4 Conduct of minor significance

The category of conduct prescribed for the purposes of section 40(1) of the Act is conduct by an undertaking the applicable turnover of which for the business year ending in the calendar year preceding one during which the infringement occurred does not exceed £50 million.

[2.29]
5

Where in the application of regulation 3 or 4 there is a calendar year in respect of which an undertaking has no business year ending in the preceding calendar year then the applicable turnover shall be the turnover for the preceding calendar year.

SCHEDULE
APPLICABLE TURNOVER

Article 2

Interpretation

[2.30]

1. In this Schedule:

["credit institution" means a credit institution for the purposes of Article 4(1)(1) of Regulation (EU) No 575/2013 of the European Parliament and of the Council of 26 June 2013 on prudential requirements for credit institutions and investment firms and amending Regulation (EU) No 648/2012;]

["financial institution" means a financial institution for the purposes of Article 4(1)(26) of Regulation (EU) No 575/2013 of the European Parliament and of the Council of 26 June 2013 on prudential requirements for credit institutions and investment firms and amending Regulation (EU) No 648/2012 or any undertaking located outside the [United Kingdom] which does not fall within the definition in that Article but which carries on equivalent activities;]

["insurance undertaking" means—

(a) an insurance undertaking carrying on the business of direct insurance of a class set out in Article 2 of, or Annex 1 to, Directive 2009/138/EC of the European Parliament and Council of 25 November 2009 on the taking-up and pursuit of the business of Insurance and Reinsurance (Solvency II);

(b) a reinsurance undertaking;

(c) a third-country reinsurance undertaking;]

["reinsurance undertaking" means an undertaking which—

(a) has its head office in the United Kingdom;

(b) has permission under Part 4A of the Financial Services and Markets Act 2000 to carry on one or more regulated activities;

(c) effects or carries out contracts of insurance that are limited to reinsurance contracts; and

(d) would require authorisation in accordance with Article 14 of Directive 2009/138/EC, if the United Kingdom were a Member State;

"third-country reinsurance undertaking" means an undertaking which, if its head office were in the United Kingdom—

(a) would require permission under Part 4A of the Financial Services and Markets Act 2000 to carry out regulated activities relating to reinsurance; and

(b) immediately before [IP completion day], would have required authorisation as a reinsurance undertaking in accordance with Article 14 of Directive 2009/138/EC; and]

terms used in this Schedule in respect of the determination of the applicable turnover of credit institutions, financial institutions and insurance undertakings shall (except where the contrary intention appears) have the same meaning as in the relevant Directive.

2. The provisions of this Schedule shall be interpreted in accordance with generally accepted accounting principles and practices.

General

3. The applicable turnover of an undertaking, other than a credit institution, financial institution, insurance undertaking, or an association of undertakings, shall be limited to the amounts derived by the undertaking from the sale of products and the provision of services falling within the undertaking's ordinary activities after deduction of sales rebates, value added tax and other taxes directly related to turnover.

4. Where an undertaking consists of two or more undertakings that each prepare accounts then the applicable turnover shall be calculated by adding together the respective applicable turnover of each, save that no account shall be taken of any turnover resulting from the sale of products or the provision of services between them.

Credit institutions and financial institutions

5. The applicable turnover of a credit institution or financial institution shall be limited to the sum of the following income items listed in Council Directive (EEC) 86/635 received by that institution after deductions of value added tax and other taxes directly related to those items:

(i) interest income and similar income;

(ii) income from securities:

— income from shares and other variable yield securities,

— income from participating interests,

— income from shares in affiliated undertakings,

(iii) commissions receivable;

(iv) net profit on financial operations; and

(v) other operating income.

Insurance undertakings

6. The applicable turnover of an insurance undertaking shall be limited to the value of gross premiums received which shall comprise all amounts received and receivable in respect of insurance contracts issued by or on behalf of the undertaking, including outgoing reinsurance premiums, and after deduction of taxes and parafiscal contributions or levies charged by reference to the amounts of individual premiums or the total volume of premiums.

Turnover of associations of undertakings

7. The turnover of an association of undertakings shall be the aggregate applicable turnover of the undertakings that are members of the association.

Aid granted to undertakings

8. Any aid granted by a public body to an undertaking which relates to one of the undertaking ordinary activities shall be included in the calculation of turnover if the undertaking is itself the recipient of the aid and if the aid is directly linked to the sale of products or the provision of services by the undertaking and is therefore reflected in the price.

NOTES

Para 1 is amended as follows:

Definitions "credit institution" and "financial institution" substituted by the Capital Requirements Regulations 2013, SI 2013/3115, reg 46(1), Sch 2, Pt 3, para 49.

The words in square brackets in the definition "financial institution" were substituted (for the original word "EEA"), the definition "insurance undertaking" was substituted, and the definitions "reinsurance undertaking" and "third-country reinsurance undertaking" were inserted, by the Competition (Amendment etc) (EU Exit) Regulations 2019, SI 2019/93, reg 61, Sch 2, Pt 1, para 1, as from IP completion day (as defined in the European Union (Withdrawal Agreement) Act 2020, s 39) (for transitional provisions and savings in relation to the operation of the 2019 Regulations, see Sch 4 to those Regulations at **[7.69]** et seq). Note that Sch 2, Pt 1, para 1 to the 2019 Regulations was amended by the Competition (Amendment etc) (EU Exit) Regulations 2020, SI 2020/1343, reg 29, with effect from immediately before IP completion day; and the effect of that amendment has been incorporated in the text set out above. Note also that the original definition "insurance undertaking" (as amended by the Solvency 2 Regulations 2015, SI 2015/575, reg 60, Sch 2, para 9) read as follows—

> ""insurance undertaking" means an insurance undertaking carrying on the business of direct insurance of a class set out in [Article 2 of or Annex 1 to, or a reinsurance undertaking carrying on the business of reinsurance under Directive 2009/138/EC of the European Parliament and Council of 25 November 2009 on the taking-up and pursuit of the business of Insurance and Reinsurance (Solvency II);]".

COMPETITION ACT 1998 (DETERMINATION OF TURNOVER FOR PENALTIES) ORDER 2000

(SI 2000/309)

NOTES

Made: 10 February 2000.

Authority: Competition Act 1998, ss 36(8), 71.

Commencement: 1 March 2000.

[2.31]

1 Citation and commencement

(1) This Order may be cited as the Competition Act 1998 (Determination of Turnover for Penalties) Order 2000 and shall come into force on 1st March 2000.

NOTES

Note: there is no para (2) in the Queen's Printer's copy of this Order.

[2.32]

2 Interpretation

(1) In this Order—

"the Act" means the Competition Act 1998;

"applicable turnover" means the turnover of an undertaking for a business year determined in accordance with the Schedule to this Order; and where a business year does not equal 12 months the applicable turnover shall be the amount which bears the same proportion to the applicable turnover during that business year as 12 months does to that period;

"business year" means a period of more than six months in respect of which an undertaking publishes accounts or, if no such accounts have been published for the period, prepares accounts;

. . .

NOTES

Para (1): definition "length of the infringement" (omitted) revoked the Competition Act 1998 (Determination of Turnover for Penalties) (Amendment) Order 2004, by SI 2004/1259, art 2(1), (2).

Note: there is no para (2) in the Queen's Printer's copy of this Order.

[2.33]

[3 Determination of turnover for the purposes of section 36(8)

The turnover of an undertaking for the purposes of section 36(8) is the applicable turnover for the business year preceding the date on which the decision of the [CMA] is taken or, if figures are not available for that business year, the one immediately preceding it.]

NOTES

Substituted by the Competition Act 1998 (Determination of Turnover for Penalties) (Amendment) Order 2004, SI 2004/1259, art 2(1), (3).

Reference to the "CMA" substituted by the Enterprise and Regulatory Reform Act 2013 (Competition) (Consequential, Transitional and Saving Provisions) (No 2) Order 2014, SI 2014/549, art 2, Sch 1, Pt 1, para 2. For transitional provisions in relation to the abolition of the OFT and the Competition Commission and the continuity of functions, etc, see art 3 of the 2014 Order at **[2.21]**.

[2.34]
4
Where in the application of article 3 there is any period in respect of which there is no preceding business year then the applicable turnover shall be the turnover for that period.

SCHEDULE
APPLICABLE TURNOVER

Article 2

Interpretation

[2.35]
1. (1) In this Schedule—

["credit institution" means a credit institution for the purposes of Article 4(1)(1) of Regulation (EU) No 575/2013 of the European Parliament and of the Council of 26 June 2013 on prudential requirements for credit institutions and investment firms and amending Regulation (EU) No 648/2012;]

["financial institution" means a financial institution for the purposes of Article 4(1)(26) of Regulation (EU) No 575/2013 of the European Parliament and of the Council of 26 June 2013 on prudential requirements for credit institutions and investment firms and amending Regulation (EU) No 648/2012 or any undertaking located outside the [United Kingdom] which does not fall within the definition in that Article but which carries on equivalent activities;]

"insurance undertaking" means—

(a) an insurance undertaking carrying on the business of direct insurance of a class set out in Article 2 of, or Annex 1 to, Directive 2009/138/EC of the European Parliament and Council of 25 November 2009 on the taking-up and pursuit of the business of Insurance and Reinsurance (Solvency II);
(b) a reinsurance undertaking; or
(c) a third-country reinsurance undertaking;]

["reinsurance undertaking" means an undertaking which—

(a) has its head office in the United Kingdom;
(b) has permission under Part 4A of the Financial Services and Markets Act 2000 to carry on one or more regulated activities;
(c) effects or carries out contracts of insurance that are limited to reinsurance contracts; and
(d) would require authorisation in accordance with Article 14 of Directive 2009/138/EC, if the United Kingdom were a Member State;

"third-country reinsurance undertaking" means an undertaking which, if its head office were in the United Kingdom—

(a) would require permission under Part 4A of the Financial Services and Markets Act 2000 to carry out regulated activities relating to reinsurance; and
(b) immediately before [IP completion day], would have required authorisation as a reinsurance undertaking in accordance with Article 14 of Directive 2009/138/EC; and]

terms used in this Schedule in respect of the determination of the applicable turnover of credit institutions, financial institutions and insurance undertakings shall (except where the contrary intention appears) have the same meaning as in the relevant Directive.

2. The provisions of this Schedule shall be interpreted in accordance with generally accepted accounting principles and practices.

General

3. The applicable turnover of an undertaking, other than a credit institution, financial institution, insurance undertaking, or an association of undertakings, shall be limited to the amounts derived by the undertaking from the sale of products and the provision of services falling within the undertaking's ordinary activities . . . after deduction of sales rebates, value added tax and other taxes directly related to turnover.

4. Where an undertaking consists of two or more undertakings that each prepare accounts then the applicable turnover shall be calculated by adding together the respective applicable turnover of each, save that no account shall be taken of any turnover resulting from the sale of products or the provision of services between them.

Credit institutions and financial institutions

5. The applicable turnover of a credit institution or financial institution shall be limited to the sum of the following income [items listed] in Council Directive (EEC) 86/635 received by . . . that institution . . . after deduction of value added tax and other taxes directly related to those items—

(i) interest income and similar income;
(ii) income from securities—
  — income from shares and other variable yield securities;
  — income from participating interests;
  — income from shares in affiliated undertakings;
(iii) commissions receivable;
(iv) net profit on financial operations;
(v) other operating income.

Insurance undertakings

6. The applicable turnover of an insurance undertaking shall be limited to the value of gross premiums received . . . which shall comprise all amounts received and receivable in respect of insurance contracts issued by or on behalf of the undertaking, including outgoing reinsurance premiums, and after deduction of taxes and parafiscal contributions or levies charged by reference to the amounts of individual premiums or the total volume of premiums.

Turnover of associations of undertakings

7. The turnover of an association of undertakings shall be the aggregate applicable turnover of the undertakings that are members of the association.

Aid granted to undertakings

8. Any aid granted by a public body to an undertaking which relates to one of the undertaking's ordinary activities shall be included in the calculation of turnover if the undertaking is itself the recipient of the aid and if the aid is directly linked to the sale of products or the provision of services by the undertaking and is therefore reflected in the price.

NOTES

Para 1 is amended as follows:

Definition "branch" (omitted) revoked by the Competition Act 1998 (Determination of Turnover for Penalties) (Amendment) Order 2004, SI 2004/1259, art 2(1), (4)(a).

Definitions "credit institution" and "financial institution" substituted by the Capital Requirements Regulations 2013, SI 2013/3115, reg 46(1), Sch 2, Pt 3, para 50.

The words in square brackets in the definition "financial institution" were substituted (for the original word "EEA"), the definition "insurance undertaking" was substituted, and the definitions "reinsurance undertaking" and "third-country reinsurance undertaking" were inserted, by the Competition (Amendment etc) (EU Exit) Regulations 2019, SI 2019/93, reg 61, Sch 2, Pt 1, para 2, as from IP completion day (as defined in the European Union (Withdrawal Agreement) Act 2020, s 39) (for transitional provisions and savings in relation to the operation of the 2019 Regulations, see Sch 4 to those Regulations at **[7.69]** et seq). Note that Sch 2, Pt 1, para 2 to the 2019 Regulations was amended by the Competition (Amendment etc) (EU Exit) Regulations 2020, SI 2020/1343, reg 30, with effect from immediately before IP completion day; and the effect of that amendment has been incorporated in the text set out above. Note also that the original definition "insurance undertaking" (as amended by the Solvency 2 Regulations 2015, SI 2015/575, reg 60, Sch 2, para 10) read as follows—

> ""insurance undertaking" means an insurance undertaking carrying on the business of direct insurance of a class set out in [Article 2 of or Annex 1 to, or a reinsurance undertaking carrying on the business of reinsurance under Directive 2009/138/EC of the European Parliament and Council of 25 November 2009 on the taking-up and pursuit of the business of Insurance and Reinsurance (Solvency II);]".

Paras 3, 6: words omitted revoked by SI 2004/1259, art 2(1), (4)(b), (d).

Para 5: words in square brackets substituted, and words omitted revoked, by SI 2004/1259, art 2(1), (4)(c).

ENTERPRISE ACT 2002 (SUPER-COMPLAINTS TO REGULATORS) ORDER 2003

(SI 2003/1368)

NOTES

Made: 23 May 2003.

Authority: Enterprise Act 2002, s 205.

Commencement: 20 June 2003.

[2.36]

1 Citation and commencement

This Order may be cited as the Enterprise Act 2002 (Super-complaints to regulators) Order 2003 and shall come into force on 20th June 2003.

[2.37]

2 Application of section 11 of the Enterprise Act 2002 to super-complaints to regulators other than the [CMA]

Section 11 of the Enterprise Act 2002 (Super-complaints to [CMA]), other than subsection (7)(a), shall apply to complaints made to a regulator specified in column (1) of the Schedule ("a specified regulator") as it applies to complaints made to the [CMA] under that section, if the complaint to a specified regulator concerns a market in relation to which that regulator has functions pursuant to the relevant enactment specified in column (2) of the Schedule.

NOTES

References to the "CMA" substituted by the Enterprise and Regulatory Reform Act 2013 (Competition) (Consequential, Transitional and Saving Provisions) (No 2) Order 2014, SI 2014/549, art 2, Sch 1, Pt 1, para 8. For transitional provisions in relation to the abolition of the OFT and the Competition Commission and the continuity of functions, etc, see art 3 of the 2014 Order at **[2.21]**.

SCHEDULE
REGULATORS AND RELEVANT ENACTMENTS CONFERRING FUNCTIONS

Article 2

[2.38]

(1) Regulator	*(2) Enactment*
[The Office of Communications	Communications Act 2003]
The Gas and Electricity Markets Authority	Gas Act 1986; Electricity Act 1989
The Director General of Electricity Supply for Northern Ireland	Electricity (Northern Ireland) Order 1992
The Director General of Gas for Northern Ireland	Gas (Northern Ireland) Order 1996
[The Water Services Regulation Authority]	Water Industry Act 1991
[The Office of Rail Regulation]	Railways Act 1993
The Civil Aviation Authority	Transport Act 2000[; Civil Aviation Act 2012]

NOTES

Entry "The Office of Communications" substituted by the Communications Act 2003 (Consequential Amendments No 2) Order 2003, SI 2003/3182, art 4. Words "The Water Services Regulation Authority" substituted by the Enterprise Act 2002 (Water Services Regulation Authority) Order 2006, SI 2006/522, art 2. Words "The Office of Rail Regulation" substituted by virtue of the Railways and Transport Safety Act 2003, s 16(4), (5), Sch 3, para 4. In the entry "The Civil Aviation Authority" words in square brackets in column 2 added by the Civil Aviation Act 2012 (Regulation of Operators of Dominant Airports) (Consequential Amendments) Regulations 2013, SI 2013/610, reg 2(1), Sch 1, para 3.

ENTERPRISE ACT 2002 (BODIES DESIGNATED TO MAKE SUPER-COMPLAINTS) ORDER 2004

(SI 2004/1517)

NOTES

Made: 16 June 2004.
Authority: Enterprise Act 2002, s 11.
Commencement: 14 July 2004.

[2.39]

1 Citation and commencement

This Order may be cited as the Enterprise Act 2002 (Bodies Designated to make Super-complaints) Order 2004 and shall come into force on 14th July 2004.

[2.40]

2 Designation of Bodies

Each body listed in the Schedule to this Order is hereby designated under section 11(5) and (6) of the Enterprise Act 2002 as a designated consumer body for the purpose of making super-complaints under section 11 of that Act.

SCHEDULE
DESIGNATED CONSUMER BODIES

Article 2

[2.41]

[The Campaign for Real Ale Limited.

The Consumer Council for Water.

The Consumers' Association.

The General Consumer Council for Northern Ireland.

The National Association of Citizens Advice Bureaux.

. . .

The Scottish Association of Citizens Advice Bureaux.]

NOTES

Substituted by the Enterprise Act 2002 (Bodies Designated to make Super-complaints) (Amendment) Order 2009, SI 2009/2079, art 2.

Entry "The National Consumer Council" (omitted) revoked by the Public Bodies (Abolition of the National Consumer Council and Transfer of the Office of Fair Trading's Functions in relation to Estate Agents etc) Order 2014, SI 2014/631, art 3, Sch 1, Pt 4, para 22.

ENTERPRISE ACT 2002 (DISCLOSURE OF INFORMATION FOR CIVIL PROCEEDINGS ETC) ORDER 2007

(SI 2007/2193)

NOTES

Made: 23 July 2007.
Authority: Enterprise Act 2002, s 241A.
Commencement: 1 October 2007.

[2.42]

1 Citation, commencement and interpretation

(1) This Order may be cited as the Enterprise Act 2002 (Disclosure of Information for Civil Proceedings etc) Order 2007 and shall come into force on 1st October 2007.

(2) In this Order a reference to a section, Part or Schedule is a reference to a section, Part or Schedule of the Enterprise Act 2002.

[2.43]

2 Prescribed information

All specified information to which section 237 applies (other than the categories of information set out in section 241A(2)) is prescribed for the purposes of section 241A(1) with the exception of—

(a) information which comes to the [CMA] in connection with the exercise of its functions under—

(i) subsection (1) of section 5 (acquisition of information etc) with a view to exercising its functions under—

(aa) section 6 (provision of information etc to the public),

(bb) section 7 (provision of information and advice to Ministers etc), or

(cc) section 8 (promoting good consumer practice);

(ii) section 11 (super-complaints to [CMA]);

(iii) section 92 (duty of [CMA] to monitor orders and undertakings relating to mergers);

(iv) section 162 (duty of [CMA] to monitor orders and undertakings relating to market investigations);

(v) Part 6 (cartel offence);

(vi) paragraphs 14 to 18 (monopoly references, enforcement undertakings and orders) of Schedule 24;

(b) information which comes to a regulator in connection with the exercise of its functions under section 11 (super-complaints to [CMA]) as applied by section 205 (super-complaints to regulators other than [CMA]); and

(c) information which comes to Her Majesty's Revenue and Customs in connection with the exercise of their functions under the Customs & Excise Management Act 1979 and the Value Added Tax Act 1994.

NOTES

References to the "CMA" substituted by the Enterprise and Regulatory Reform Act 2013 (Competition) (Consequential, Transitional and Saving Provisions) (No 2) Order 2014, SI 2014/549, art 2, Sch 1, Pt 1, para 21. For transitional provisions in relation to the abolition of the OFT and the Competition Commission and the continuity of functions, etc, see art 3 of the 2014 Order at **[2.21]**.

[2.44]

3 Prescribed proceedings

(1) The following civil proceedings are prescribed for the purposes of section 241A(1)—

(a) proceedings relating to or arising out of a legal right or obligation of a consumer;

(b) proceedings relating to or arising out of the infringement of an intellectual property right;

(c) proceedings relating to or arising out of passing off or the misuse of a trade secret.

(2) In paragraph (1)(a) a "consumer" is an individual who—

(a) is acting outside his trade, business or profession; or

(b) is acting with a view to carrying on a business but not in the course of a business carried on by him.

(3) In paragraph (1)(b) an "intellectual property right" includes a patent, copyright, and analogous or related right, database right, registered or unregistered design right, registered trade mark, topography right, supplementary protection certificate, plant variety right, protected designation of origin or a protected geographical indication.

ENTERPRISE ACT 2002 (PUBLISHING OF RELEVANT INFORMATION UNDER SECTION 188A) ORDER 2014

(SI 2014/535)

NOTES

Made: 6 March 2014.
Authority: Enterprise Act 2002, s 188A(1)(c).
Commencement: 1 April 2014.

[2.45]

1 Citation and commencement

This Order may be cited as the Enterprise Act 2002 (Publishing of Relevant Information under section 188A) Order 2014 and comes into force on 1st April 2014.

[2.46]

2 Publishing of Relevant Information

For the purposes of section 188A(1)(c) of the Enterprise Act 2002 relevant information about the arrangements is published if it is advertised once in either the London Gazette, the Edinburgh Gazette or the Belfast Gazette.

COMPETITION ACT 1998 (CONCURRENCY) REGULATIONS 2014

(SI 2014/536)

NOTES

Made: 6 March 2014.
Authority: Competition Act 1998, ss 54(4)–(6B), 71.
Commencement: 1 April 2014.

ARRANGEMENT OF REGULATIONS

[2.47]

1 Citation and commencement

These Regulations may be cited as the Competition Act 1998 (Concurrency) Regulations 2014 and come into force on 1st April 2014.

[2.48]

2 Interpretation

(1) In these Regulations—

"the Act" means the Competition Act 1998;

"the CMA's Rules" means the Competition and Markets Authority's Rules set out in the Schedule to the Competition Act 1998 (Competition and Market Authority's Rules) Order 2014;

"notify" means to notify in writing (including electronically) and "notice" shall be construed accordingly;

"Part 1 functions" means any functions under Part 1 of the Act which are, or (but for provision under these Regulations) would be, exercisable concurrently by two or more competent persons;

"prescribed functions" means—

(i) any of the functions of the CMA under section 25 of the Act;

[(ia) any of the functions of the CMA under section 40ZB, 40ZC or 40ZD of the Act;]

(ii) the function of making a decision, as defined in section 46(3) of the Act;

(iii) any of the functions of the CMA under paragraph 4 of Schedule 1 to the Act or under an order made under section 50 of the Act; and

"relevant competent persons" has the meaning given in regulation 4(2).

(2) References in these Regulations to "health care", "the NHS" and the provision of health care services for the purposes of the NHS each have the meaning given in section 64 of the Health and Social Care Act 2012.

NOTES

Para (1): sub-para (ia) of the definition "prescribed functions" was inserted by the Competition (Amendment etc) (EU Exit) Regulations 2019, SI 2019/93, reg 61, Sch 2, Pt 1, para 5(1), (1A), as from IP completion day (as defined in the European Union (Withdrawal Agreement) Act 2020, s 39) (for transitional provisions and savings in relation to the operation of the 2019 Regulations, see Sch 4 to those Regulations at **[7.69]** et seq). Note that Sch 2, Pt 1, para 5(1A) to the 2019 Regulations was inserted by the Competition (Amendment etc) (EU Exit) Regulations 2020, SI 2020/1343, reg 31, with effect from immediately before IP completion day.

[2.49]

3 Information regarding potential cases

For the purpose of determining which competent persons have jurisdiction to exercise Part 1 functions in respect of a case or for the purpose of facilitating the performance by another competent person of its Part 1 functions, a competent person may send to any other competent person details of any information in its possession that an infringement of—

(a) the Chapter I prohibition, [or]

(b) the Chapter II prohibition,

(c) the prohibition in Article 101(1), or

(d) the prohibition in Article 102,

may have taken place.

NOTES

The word in square brackets at the end of para (a) was inserted, and paras (c) and (d) were revoked, by the Competition (Amendment etc) (EU Exit) Regulations 2019, SI 2019/93, reg 61, Sch 2, Pt 1, para 5(1), (2), as from IP completion day (as defined in the European Union (Withdrawal Agreement) Act 2020, s 39) (for transitional provisions and savings in relation to the operation of the 2019 Regulations, see Sch 4 to those Regulations at **[7.69]** et seq).

[2.50]

4 Determination of the exercise of Part 1 functions

(1) If a competent person proposes to exercise any of the prescribed functions in respect of a case and it considers that another competent person has or may have concurrent jurisdiction to exercise Part 1 functions in respect of that case, it must inform that other competent person in writing of its intention to exercise prescribed functions in respect of that case.

(2) Where a competent person has informed another competent person of its intention to exercise prescribed functions in accordance with paragraph (1) in respect of a case, all such competent persons ("the relevant competent persons") must agree who is to exercise Part 1 functions in respect of that case.

(3) When agreement has been reached in accordance with paragraph (2), the CMA must as soon as practicable inform in writing the other relevant competent persons which competent person is to exercise Part 1 functions in respect of the case.

[2.51]

5 Dispute

(1) If the relevant competent persons are not able to reach agreement in accordance with regulation 4(2) within a reasonable time, the CMA must notify the other relevant competent persons that it intends to determine which relevant competent person is to exercise Part 1 functions in respect of the case.

(2) Any relevant competent person may make representations in writing to the CMA no later than 5 working days after the date upon which the CMA notifies its intention to make a determination in accordance with paragraph (1).

(3) The CMA must within 10 working days of notifying its intention in accordance with paragraph (1)—

(a) determine which competent person is to exercise Part 1 functions in respect of the case; and

(b) inform in writing all other relevant competent persons—

(i) which competent person is to exercise jurisdiction in respect of the case,

(ii) the date of the determination, and

(iii) the reasons for the determination.

(4) In making a determination in accordance with paragraph (3)(a) the CMA—

(a) must take into consideration any representations made in accordance with paragraph (2); and

(b) (subject to paragraph (5)) may decide that it is to exercise Part 1 functions in respect of the case rather than another relevant competent person, where the CMA is satisfied that its doing so would further the promotion of competition, within any market or markets in the United Kingdom, for the benefit of consumers.

(5) Where Monitor is one of the relevant competent persons, the CMA may not make a determination in accordance with paragraph (1) and (3)(a) that a competent person other than Monitor is to exercise Part 1 functions in relation to the case unless the CMA is satisfied that the case is not principally concerned with matters relating to the provision of health care services for the purposes of the NHS in England.

[2.52]

6 Avoidance of double jeopardy

(1) Where two or more competent persons may have concurrent jurisdiction to exercise Part 1 functions in respect of a case, no competent person shall exercise any prescribed functions in respect of that case before agreement has been reached in accordance with regulation 4(2) or a determination has been made in accordance with regulation 5(3)(a) as to which competent person is to exercise Part 1 functions in respect of that case.

(2) Subject to regulations 7 and 8, once agreement has been reached in accordance with regulation 4(2) or a determination has been made in accordance with regulation 5(3)(a) as to which competent person is to exercise Part 1 functions in respect of a case, no other competent person shall exercise any Part 1 functions in respect of that case.

[2.53]

7 Transfer

(1) A competent person who has exercised any Part 1 functions in respect of a case ("the transferor") may agree with another competent person who but for regulation 6 would have, concurrent jurisdiction to exercise Part 1 functions in respect of that case ("the transferee") to transfer the case to the transferee.

(2) If the transferor and the transferee propose to agree a transfer in accordance with paragraph (1), the transferor must first—

(a) notify the undertaking which is the subject of the exercise of Part 1 functions in that case (the undertaking concerned) and any other person likely to be materially affected by the transfer, of the proposed transfer, and

(b) give such recipients of the notice the opportunity to make written representations upon the proposal within no less than 10 working days of the date of that notice.

(3) The transferor and transferee must take into account any written representations made in accordance with paragraph (2)(b) before agreeing the transfer.

(4) Once the transferor and transferee have reached a decision about the proposed transfer, the transferor must—

(a) inform the recipients of the notice under paragraph (2) in writing of their decision and the reasons for it, and

(b) if the transfer has been agreed, that the transferee is to exercise jurisdiction in respect of the case from the date of the transfer.

(5) The transferor is not under any obligation to notify any person in accordance with paragraph (2) or to inform any person in accordance with paragraph (4) if the transferor has not informed the that person that it has exercised Part 1 functions in respect of the case.

[2.54]

8 Circumstances in which the CMA may decide that it is to exercise Part 1 functions

(1) The CMA may direct a regulator to transfer a case in respect of which the regulator is exercising Part 1 functions to the CMA where the CMA is satisfied that—

(a) it exercising the Part 1 functions rather than the regulator would further the promotion of competition, within any market or markets in the United Kingdom, for the benefit of consumers; and

(b) where the regulator is Monitor, the case is not principally concerned with matters relating to the provision of health care services for the purposes of the NHS in England.

(2) If the CMA proposes to exercise the power in paragraph (1) the CMA must first consult the regulator who is exercising Part 1 functions in respect of the case, explaining the reasons why the CMA considers it appropriate to exercise that power.

(3) If, following the consultation referred to in paragraph (2), the CMA still proposes to exercise the power in paragraph (1), the CMA must—

(a) notify—

(i) the regulator who is exercising Part 1 functions in respect of the case,

(ii) the undertaking which is the subject of the exercise of Part 1 functions in the case (the undertaking concerned), and

(iii) any other persons likely to be materially affected by the transfer,

of what it proposes,

(b) give such recipients of the notice the opportunity to make written representations upon the proposal within no less than 10 working days of the date of that notice, and

(c) take into account any representations made in accordance with paragraph (3)(b).

(4) Once the CMA has reached a decision whether to exercise the power in paragraph (1), the CMA must—

(a) inform the recipients of the notice under paragraph (3)(a) in writing of its decision and the reasons for it; and

(b) if the CMA has decided to exercise the power in paragraph (1), inform such recipients in writing that the CMA is to exercise jurisdiction in respect of the case from the date of the transfer.

(5) The CMA is not under any obligation to notify or inform any person referred to in paragraph (3)(a)(ii) or (iii) in accordance with this regulation if the regulator has not informed that person that it has exercised Part 1 functions in respect of the case.

(6) The CMA may not exercise the power in paragraph (1) in respect of a case where a regulator has given notice under section 31(1) of the Act that it proposes to make a decision (within the meaning given by section 31(2) of the Act) in that case.

[2.55]

9 Information sharing

(1) Each competent person must put in place arrangements for sharing with other competent persons the following information in connection with concurrent cases—

(a) details of any information in the possession of the competent person that an infringement of—

(i) the Chapter I prohibition, [or]

(ii) the Chapter II prohibition,

(iii) the prohibition in Article 101(1), or

(iv) the prohibition in Article 102,

may have taken place, whether or not the competent person proposes to exercise any of the prescribed functions in respect of the case;

(b) a draft of any notice which the competent person proposes to give under section 31 of the Act (decisions following an investigation) or rule 5 of the CMA's Rules (statement of objections), before the notice is given;

(c) a draft of any commitments which the competent person proposes to accept under section 31A of the Act (commitments) before those commitments are accepted;

(d) a draft of any notice which the competent person proposes to give under section 35(3) (notice of interim measures), before the notice is given;

(e) a draft of any notice which the competent person proposes to give under rule 10(1) of the CMA's Rules (notice of infringement decision), before the notice is given;

(f) a draft of any notice which the competent person proposes to give under rule 10(4) of the CMA's Rules (notice of no grounds for action decision), before the notice is given;

(g) a draft of any notice which the competent person proposes to give under rule 15(3) or (6) of the CMA's Rules (notice of proposed cancellation of [retained exemption] and notice of decision), before the notice is given;

Part 2 Statutory Instruments

(h) a draft of any notice of a decision by the competent person not to proceed with a case, before the notice is given;

(i) a draft of any notice which the competent person proposes to give under section 112 of the Enterprise Act 2002 as applied by section 40A(9) of the Act (notice of administrative penalty), before the notice is given;

(j) such other information in the possession of the competent person as any other competent person may reasonably require to facilitate the performance of its functions under the Act.

(2) This regulation does not affect any power or duty to disclose information which exists apart from this regulation.

NOTES

Para (1): the word in square brackets at the end of sub-para (a)(i) was inserted, sub-paras (a)(iii) and (iv) were revoked, and the words "retained exemption" in square brackets in sub-para (g) were substituted (for the original words "parallel exemption"), by the Competition (Amendment etc) (EU Exit) Regulations 2019, SI 2019/93, reg 61, Sch 2, Pt 1, para 5(1), (3), (4), as from IP completion day (as defined in the European Union (Withdrawal Agreement) Act 2020, s 39) (for transitional provisions and savings in relation to the operation of the 2019 Regulations, see Sch 4 to those Regulations at **[7.69]** et seq).

[2.56]

10 Use of staff

(1) A competent person who wishes to exercise Part 1 functions in respect of a case ("the appointor") may appoint an officer of another competent person ("the appointee") to act as his officer in relation to that case provided that the competent person of which the appointee is an officer gives his written consent to the appointment on or before the date upon which the appointment commences.

(2) An appointee—

(a) is an officer of the appointor for the purposes of sections 27 to 29 inclusive of the Act, and

(b) may exercise such other functions in relation to the case as may be agreed as if the appointee were an employee of the appointor.

(3) Any act or omission of the appointee within the terms of the appointment is to be deemed to be an act or omission of the appointor.

[2.57]

11 Service of Notices

(1) Any notice to be served on any person under regulations 7 and 8 may be served by post or by sending it by electronic means to an electronic address notified by the person for the purpose.

(2) A letter containing that notice is to be deemed to be properly addressed if it is addressed to that person at its registered office or last known residence or last known place of business in the United Kingdom.

[2.58]

12 Revocation and transitional provision

(1) (*Revokes the Competition Act 1998 (Concurrency) Regulations 2004, SI 2004/1077.*)

(2) Where a competent person (other than the CMA) is entitled to exercise prescribed functions within the meaning of and in accordance with the 2004 Regulations in respect of a case before the date these Regulations come into force, that competent person is to be treated as having jurisdiction to exercise Part 1 functions in respect of that case for the purposes of these Regulations as though an agreement to that effect had been reached in accordance with regulation 4(2) of these Regulations.

(3) Where the Office of Fair Trading is entitled to exercise prescribed functions within the meaning of and in accordance with the 2004 Regulations in respect of a case before the date these Regulations come into force, the CMA is to be treated as having jurisdiction to exercise Part 1 functions in respect of that case for the purposes of these Regulations as though an agreement to that effect had been reached in accordance with regulation 4(2) of these Regulations.

CMA REGISTERS OF UNDERTAKINGS AND ORDERS (AVAILABLE HOURS) ORDER 2014

(SI 2014/558)

NOTES

Made: 6 March 2014.
Authority: Enterprise Act 2002, ss 91(6), 166(6).
Commencement: 1 April 2014.

[2.59]

1 Citation, commencement and interpretation

(1) This Order may be cited as the CMA Registers of Undertakings and Orders (Available Hours) Order 2014 and comes into force on 1st April 2014.

(2) In this Order—

"the register" means a register maintained by the CMA under section 91 or 166 of the Enterprise Act 2002; and

"working day" means any day which is not Saturday, Sunday, Good Friday, Christmas Day, a bank holiday or public holiday in England and Wales or any other day on which the office of the CMA at which the register is available to the public is closed for business.

[2.60]
2 Available Hours

The CMA shall ensure that the contents of the register are available to the public (as a minimum) between the hours of 10.00 am and 4.00 pm on any working day.

3 *(Revokes the OFT Registers of Undertakings and Orders (Available Hours) Order 2003, SI 2003/1373.)*

COMPETITION AND MARKETS AUTHORITY (PENALTIES) ORDER 2014

(SI 2014/559)

NOTES

Made: 6 March 2014.
Authority: Competition Act 1998, s 40A(3); Enterprise Act 2002, ss 111(4), (6), 124(2)(b), 174D(4), (5).
Commencement: 1 April 2014.

[2.61]
1 Citation, commencement and interpretation

(1) This Order may be cited as the Competition and Markets Authority (Penalties) Order 2014 and is to come into force on 1st April 2014.

(2) In this Order—
(a) "the EA 2002" means the Enterprise Act 2002; and
(b) "the CA 1998" means the Competition Act 1998.

[2.62]
2 The Specified Amounts: Mergers

(1) For the purposes of section 111(4)(a) of the EA 2002 the fixed amount specified is £30,000.

(2) For the purposes of section 111(4)(b) of the EA 2002 the amount per day specified is £15,000.

(3) For the purposes of section 111(4)(c) of the EA 2002 the fixed amount specified is £30,000 and the amount per day specified is £15,000.

(4) For the purposes of section 111(6) of the EA 2002 the fixed amount specified is £30,000.

[2.63]
3 The Specified Amounts: Markets

(1) For the purposes of section 174D(4)(a) of the EA 2002 the fixed amount specified is £30,000.

(2) For the purposes of section 174D(4)(b) of the EA 2002 the amount per day specified is £15,000.

(3) For the purposes of section 174D(4)(c) of the EA 2002 the fixed amount specified is £30,000 and the amount per day specified is £15,000.

(4) For the purposes of section 174D(5) of the EA 2002 the amount specified is £30,000.

[2.64]
4 The Specified Amounts: Anti-trust

(1) For the purposes of section 40A(3)(a) of the CA 1998 the fixed amount specified is £30,000.

(2) For the purposes of section 40A(3)(b) of the CA 1998 the amount per day specified is £15,000.

(3) For the purposes of section 40A(3)(c) of the CA 1998 the fixed amount is £30,000 and the amount per specified is £15,000.

5 *(Revokes the Competition Commission (Penalties) Order 2003, SI 2003/1371 and the Competition Commission (Water Industry) Penalties Order 2007, SI 2007/461.)*

[2.65]
6 Transitional provision

(1) The amounts specified in Article 2 do not apply in relation to a notice given under section 109 of the EA 2002 (and section 109 as applied by any other enactment) before 1st April 2014.

(2) Despite the revocation of the Competition Commission (Penalties) Order 2003 by article 5, that Order (which specifies the maximum penalties that apply) shall continue to apply to a notice given under section 109 (and section 109 as applied by any other enactment) before 1st April 2014.

COMPETITION ACT 1998 (REDRESS SCHEME) REGULATIONS 2015

(SI 2015/1587)

NOTES

Made: 4 August 2015.
Authority: Competition Act 1998, ss 49C(8), 71(3)(b); Interpretation Act 1978, s 14A.
Commencement: 1 October 2015.

Part 2 Statutory Instruments

ARRANGEMENT OF REGULATIONS

[2.66]
1 Citation and commencement

(1) These Regulations may be cited as the Competition Act 1998 (Redress Scheme) Regulations 2015.

(2) These Regulations come into force on 1st October 2015.

[2.67]
2 Interpretation

(1) In these Regulations—

"the Act" means the Competition Act 1998; and

"applicant" means a person making an application to the CMA for approval of a redress scheme under section 49C of the Act.

(2) Any reference in these Regulations to the CMA means the CMA or a regulator.

[2.68]
3 Application for approval of a redress scheme

An application to the CMA for approval of a redress scheme under section 49C of the Act must be made in writing and must contain a summary of the scheme.

[2.69]
4 Approval of redress scheme

(1) Subject to paragraph (2), the CMA may approve a redress scheme under section 49C of the Act only if it—

(a) has been devised in accordance with the process specified in regulation 5;

(b) contains all of the information required by regulation 6; and

(c) contains all of the terms required by regulation 7.

(2) Paragraph (1) does not apply where the CMA approves a redress scheme at the same time as making the infringement decision to which the scheme relates; but the CMA may only approve a scheme in such cases if—

(a) the applicant has provided information to the CMA about the time when, and how, the scheme will comply with the requirements in paragraphs (1)(a), (b) and (c); and

(b) the CMA is satisfied that any conditions imposed under section 49C(4) or (5)(a) of the Act will ensure that the scheme will comply with those requirements within a period of time specified in those conditions.

[2.70]
5 Process for devising a redress scheme

(1) For the purposes of regulation 4, the process for devising a redress scheme is as follows.

(2) The scheme must be devised by—

(a) the person appointed by the applicant to be the chairperson of the scheme ("the chairperson"); and

(b) the persons appointed by the chairperson to constitute the board of the scheme ("the board").

(3) A person may only be appointed as the chairperson of the scheme if that person—

(a) satisfies the judicial-appointment eligibility condition on a five-year basis, or is an advocate or solicitor in Scotland of at least five years' standing, or is a member of the Bar of Northern Ireland or solicitor of the Court of Judicature of Northern Ireland of at least five years' standing; and

(b) does not have any interests which conflicts with the interests of the applicant or any person who may seek compensation under the scheme.

(4) A person may only be appointed to the board if that person does not have any interests which conflicts with the interests of the applicant or any person who may seek compensation under the scheme.

(5) The board appointed by the chairperson must comprise—

(a) an economist with appropriate experience and knowledge of competition economics to be able to consider the redress scheme;

(b) a person with experience of the industry of the applicant;

(c) a person who is able to represent the interests of those who may be entitled to compensation under the redress scheme; and

(d) any other person considered suitable by the chairperson.

(6) The scheme must be recommended by the chairperson to the CMA for approval, and the chairperson may only make such a recommendation if—

(a) the chairperson and the board have considered the relevant matters; and

(b) the majority of the persons comprising the chairperson and the board agree that it should be recommended for approval by the CMA.

(7) In this regulation, "the relevant matters" means—

(a) evidence of loss caused to persons entitled to compensation relating to the infringement decision;
(b) who is to be entitled to compensation under the redress scheme;
(c) the process for applying for compensation under the redress scheme, including any requirements to produce evidence in support of an application; and
(d) how those entitled to compensation under the scheme will be notified of their entitlement.

[2.71]
6 Required information

(1) The information required by this regulation is—
(a) the names of the redress scheme's chairperson and members of the redress scheme's board, and confirmation that none of them had a conflict of interest when they were appointed or when they considered whether to recommend approval of the scheme to the CMA;
(b) details of arrangements to ensure that the chairperson and the board had access to relevant information held by the applicant prior to deciding whether to recommend the redress scheme for approval to the CMA;
(c) details of the process for applying for compensation under the redress scheme, and estimates as to how long it will take to determine such applications for compensation; and
(d) details of an independent complaints process available for those applying for compensation under the redress scheme.

(2) In this regulation, "conflict of interest" has the meaning given by regulations 5(3)(b) and 5(4).

[2.72]
7 Required terms

The terms required by this regulation are—
(a) that a third party may not submit a claim on behalf of those entitled to compensation under the redress scheme;
(b) that the scheme will operate for a period of at least nine months.

[2.73]
8 Review

(1) The Secretary of State must from time to time—
(a) carry out a review of these Regulations,
(b) set out the conclusions of the review in a report, and
(c) publish the report.

(2) The report must in particular—
(a) set out the objectives intended to be achieved by the regulatory system established by these Regulations,
(b) assess the extent to which those objectives are achieved, and
(c) assess whether those objectives remain appropriate and, if so, the extent to which they could be achieved with a system that imposes less regulation.

(3) The first report under this regulation must be published before 1st October 2020.

(4) Reports under this regulation are afterwards to be published at intervals not exceeding five years.

C.
EXCLUSIONS AND EXEMPTIONS

COMPETITION ACT 1998 (SECTION 11 EXEMPTION) REGULATIONS 2001

(SI 2001/2993)

NOTES

Made: 28 August 2001.

Authority: Competition Act 1998, ss 11(2), 71. Note that s 11 of the 1998 Act was repealed by the Competition (Amendment etc) (EU Exit) Regulations 2019, SI 2019/93, regs 2, 5, as from IP completion day (as defined in the European Union (Withdrawal Agreement) Act 2020, s 39). Subject to any applicable transitional provisions and savings in relation to the operation of the 2019 Regulations (see Sch 4 to those Regulations at **[7.69]** et seq), these Regulations, therefore, lapsed on IP completion day.

Commencement: 30 September 2001.

References to the "European Community", "Community", etc: see the Treaty of Lisbon (Changes in Terminology) Order 2011, SI 2011/1043, which provides (with effect from 22 April 2011): (1) that for references to the "European Communities" or to the "European Community" (including references to "the Communities", "the Community", "the EC" or "the EEC") substitute references to the European Union; and (2) that "EU" should be substituted for the word "Community" (subject to certain exceptions) in references to "Community treaties", "Community customs duty", "Community institution", "Community instrument", "Community obligation", "enforceable Community right", "Community law", "Community legislation", and "Community provision". Also, where such a term is preceded by the word "a", for "a" substitute "an". For more details, see arts 3, 4, 6 of the 2011 Order as set out in the introductory notes to the Company Directors Disqualification Act 1986 preceding **[1.23]**.

[2.74]

1 Citation

These Regulations may be cited as the Competition Act 1998 (Section 11 Exemption) Regulations 2001 and shall come into force on 30th September 2001.

[2.75]

2 Interpretation

In these Regulations—

"the Act" means the Competition Act 1998;

"the Community prohibition" means the prohibition contained in—

(a) paragraph 1 of [Article 101] of the Treaty;

(b) any corresponding provision replacing, or otherwise derived from, that provision;

["the CMA's Rules" means the CMA's rules set out in the Schedule to the Competition Act 1998 (Competition and Market Authority's Rules) Order 2014;]

. . .

NOTES

Words in square brackets in the definition "the Community prohibition" substituted by the Treaty of Lisbon (Changes in Terminology or Numbering) Order 2012, SI 2012/1809, art 3(1), Schedule, Pt 2.

Definition "the CMA's rules" substituted by the Enterprise and Regulatory Reform Act 2013 (Competition) (Consequential, Transitional and Saving Provisions) (No 2) Order 2014, SI 2014/549, art 2, Sch 1, Pt 1, para 6(1), (2). For transitional provisions in relation to the abolition of the OFT and the Competition Commission and the continuity of functions, etc, see art 3 of the 2014 Order at **[2.21]**.

Definition "the enforcement regulations" (omitted) revoked by the EC Competition Law (Articles 84 and 85) Enforcement (Revocation) Regulations 2007, SI 2007/1846, reg 3(1), Schedule.

References to the European Community and related expressions: see the note "References to "the European Community", "Community", etc" in the introductory notes to these Regulations.

[2.76]

3 Exemption

(1) The prescribed circumstances in which agreements in relation to which a ruling may be given by virtue of [Article 104] of the Treaty are exempt from the Chapter I prohibition are—

(a) . . .

(b) that the [CMA] has not found that an agreement which would otherwise benefit from a section 11 exemption has effects in the United Kingdom, or a part of it, which are incompatible with the conditions laid down in section 9 of the Act.

(2) A section 11 exemption—

(a) subject to paragraph (3), takes effect on the date on which the relevant exemption from the Community prohibition takes effect, and

(b) ceases to have effect on the date on which—

(i) . . .

(ii) the relevant exemption from the Community prohibition otherwise ceases to have effect; or

(iii) a finding is made by the [CMA] that the agreement to which the relevant exemption relates has effects in the United Kingdom, or a part of it, which are incompatible with the conditions laid down in section 9 of the Act.

(3) A section 11 exemption may, if the [CMA] considers it appropriate and so determines, take effect from a date specified by the [CMA] which is earlier than the date on which the exemption from the Community prohibition takes effect.

(4) The [CMA] shall not make a finding that the agreement to which the relevant exemption relates has effects in the United Kingdom, or a part of it, which are incompatible with the conditions laid down in section 9 of the Act unless [it] does so in the manner specified in [rule 15 of the CMA's rules].

NOTES

Para (1): words in first pair of square brackets substituted by the Treaty of Lisbon (Changes in Terminology or Numbering) Order 2012, SI 2012/1809, art 3(1), Schedule, Pt 2. Sub-para (a) revoked by the EC Competition Law (Articles 84 and 85) Enforcement (Revocation) Regulations 2007, SI 2007/1846, SI 2007/1846, reg 3(1), Schedule. Reference to the "CMA" in sub-para (b) substituted by the Enterprise and Regulatory Reform Act 2013 (Competition) (Consequential, Transitional and Saving Provisions) (No 2) Order 2014, SI 2014/549, art 2, Sch 1, Pt 1, para 6(1), (3)(a) (for transitional provisions in relation to the abolition of the OFT and the Competition Commission and the continuity of functions, etc, see art 3 of the 2014 Order at **[2.21]**).

Para (2): sub-para (b)(i) revoked by SI 2007/1846, reg 3(1), Schedule. Reference to the "CMA" in sub-para (b)(iii) substituted by SI 2014/549, art 2, Sch 1, Pt 1, para 6(1), (3)(a) and subject to transitional provisions as noted to para (1) above.

Para (3): references to the "CMA" substituted by SI 2014/549, art 2, Sch 1, Pt 1, para 6(1), (3)(a) and subject to transitional provisions as noted to para (1) above.

Para (4): words in square brackets substituted by SI 2014/549, art 2, Sch 1, Pt 1, para 6(1), (3)(b) and subject to transitional provisions as noted to para (1) above.

References to the European Community and related expressions: see the note "References to "the European Community", "Community", etc" in the introductory notes to these Regulations.

COMPETITION ACT 1998 (LAND AGREEMENTS EXCLUSION REVOCATION) ORDER 2010

(SI 2010/1709)

NOTES

Made: 29 June 2010.
Authority: Competition Act 1998, s 50.
Commencement: 6 April 2011.

[2.77]

1 Citation and commencement

This Order may be cited as the Competition Act 1998 (Land Agreements Exclusion Revocation) Order 2010 and shall come into force on 6th April 2011.

[2.78]

2 Revocation

The Competition Act 1998 (Land Agreements Exclusion and Revocation) Order 2004 is hereby revoked.

D.
MERGER CONTROL

EEC MERGER CONTROL (DISTINCT MARKET INVESTIGATIONS) REGULATIONS 1990

(SI 1990/1715)

NOTES

Made: 20 August 1990.

Authority: European Communities Act 1972, s 2(2).

Commencement: 21 September 1990.

Revocation: these Regulations were revoked by the Competition (Amendment etc) (EU Exit) Regulations 2019, SI 2019/93, reg 61, Sch 2, Pt 3, para 9, as from IP completion day (as defined in the European Union (Withdrawal Agreement) Act 2020, s 39). For transitional provisions and savings in relation to the operation of the 2019 Regulations, see Sch 4 to those Regulations at **[7.69]** et seq. See, in particular, Sch 4, Pt 7, para 35B to the 2019 Regulations which provides that where, on or after IP completion day, the European Commission has requested information under the second sentence of Article 19(2) of the EC Merger Regulation in relation to a case for which it has continued competence in accordance with Article 92 of the EU withdrawal agreement, these Regulations continue to have effect on and after IP completion day in relation to the case despite their repeal by the 2019 Regulations.

References to the "European Community", "Community", etc: see the Treaty of Lisbon (Changes in Terminology) Order 2011, SI 2011/1043, which provides (with effect from 22 April 2011): (1) that for references to the "European Communities" or to the "European Community" (including references to "the Communities", "the Community", "the EC" or "the EEC") substitute references to the European Union; and (2) that "EU" should be substituted for the word "Community" (subject to certain exceptions) in references to "Community treaties", "Community customs duty", "Community institution", "Community instrument", "Community obligation", "enforceable Community right", "Community law", "Community legislation", and "Community provision". Also, where such a term is preceded by the word "a", for "a" substitute "an". For more details, see arts 3, 4, 6 of the 2011 Order as set out in the introductory notes to the Company Directors Disqualification Act 1986 preceding **[1.23]**.

[2.79]

1

(1) These Regulations may be cited as the EEC Merger Control (Distinct Market Investigations) Regulations 1990 and shall come into force on 21 September 1990.

(2) In these Regulations, "the Merger Control Regulation" means Council Regulation [(EC) No 139/2004] on the control of concentrations between undertakings, and expressions used in that Regulation shall bear the same meaning in these Regulations.

NOTES

These Regulations were revoked by the Competition (Amendment etc) (EU Exit) Regulations 2019, SI 2019/93, reg 61, Sch 2, Pt 3, para 9, as from IP completion day (as defined in the European Union (Withdrawal Agreement) Act 2020, s 39) (for transitional provisions and savings in relation to the operation of the 2019 Regulations, see Sch 4 to those Regulations at **[7.69]** et seq).

Para (2): words in square brackets substituted by the EC Merger Control (Consequential Amendments) Regulations 2004, SI 2004/1079, reg 2, Schedule, para 3.

[2.80]

2

At any time after the Commission has transmitted to the competent authorities of the United Kingdom a copy of the notification to the Commission of a concentration with a Community dimension, the [Competition and Markets Authority ("the CMA")] may, for the purpose of furnishing information to the Commission under the second sentence of Article 19(2) of the Merger Control Regulation, and by notice in writing signed [on behalf of the [CMA]]—

(a) require any person to produce, at a time and place specified in the notice, to the [CMA] or to any person appointed by [the [CMA]] for the purpose, any documents which are specified or described in the notice and which are documents in his custody or under his control and relating to any matter relevant to the furnishing of information as aforesaid, or

(b) require any person carrying on any business to furnish to the [CMA] such estimates, returns or other information as may be specified or described in the notice, and specify the time, the manner and the form in which such estimates, returns or information are to be furnished;

but no person shall be compelled by virtue of this regulation to produce any documents which he could not be compelled to produce in civil proceedings before the High Court or, in Scotland, the Court of Session or, in complying with any requirement for the furnishing of information, to give any information which he could not be compelled to give in evidence in such proceedings.

NOTES

These Regulations were revoked by the Competition (Amendment etc) (EU Exit) Regulations 2019, SI 2019/93, reg 61, Sch 2, Pt 3, para 9, as from IP completion day (as defined in the European Union (Withdrawal Agreement) Act 2020, s 39) (for transitional provisions and savings in relation to the operation of the 2019 Regulations, see Sch 4 to those Regulations at **[7.69]** et seq).

Words in first pair of square brackets substituted, and references to the "CMA" substituted, by the Enterprise and Regulatory Reform Act 2013 (Competition) (Consequential, Transitional and Saving Provisions) (No 2) Order 2014, SI 2014/549, art 2, Sch 1, Pt 1, para 1(1), (2) (for transitional provisions in relation to the abolition of the OFT and the Competition Commission and the continuity of functions, etc, see art 3 of the 2014 Order at **[2.21]**). Other words in square brackets substituted by the Enterprise Act 2002 (Consequential and Supplemental Provisions) Order 2003, SI 2003/1398, art 2, Schedule, para 17(1), (2).

References to the European Community and related expressions: see the note "References to "the European Community", "Community", etc" in the introductory notes to these Regulations.

[2.81]

[3

(1) The court may, on an application by the [CMA], enquire into whether any person ("the defaulter") has refused or otherwise failed, without reasonable excuse, to comply with a notice under regulation 2.

(2) An application under paragraph (1) shall include details of the possible failure which the [CMA] considers has occurred.

(3) In enquiring into a case under paragraph (1), the court shall hear any witness who may be produced against or on behalf of the defaulter and any statement which may be offered in defence.

(4) Paragraphs (5) and (6) apply where the court is satisfied, after hearing any witnesses and statements as mentioned in paragraph (3), that the defaulter has refused or otherwise failed, without reasonable excuse, to comply with a notice under regulation 2.

(5) The court may punish the defaulter as it would have been able to punish him had he been guilty of contempt of court but in punishing the defaulter the court shall not impose any penalty which could not be imposed on summary conviction for an offence created in exercise of the powers conferred by section 2(2) of the European Communities Act 1972.

(6) Where the defaulter is a body corporate or is a partnership constituted under the law of Scotland, the court may punish any director, officer or (as the case may be) partner of the defaulter as it would have been able to punish that director, officer or partner had he been guilty of contempt of court.

(7) In this regulation "the court"—

(a) in relation to England and Wales or Northern Ireland, means the High Court, and

(b) in relation to Scotland, means the Court of Session.]

NOTES

These Regulations were revoked by the Competition (Amendment etc) (EU Exit) Regulations 2019, SI 2019/93, reg 61, Sch 2, Pt 3, para 9, as from IP completion day (as defined in the European Union (Withdrawal Agreement) Act 2020, s 39) (for transitional provisions and savings in relation to the operation of the 2019 Regulations, see Sch 4 to those Regulations at **[7.69]** et seq).

Substituted by the Enterprise Act 2002 (Consequential and Supplemental Provisions) Order 2003, SI 2003/1398, art 2, Schedule, para 17(1), (3).

Paras (1), (2): references to the "CMA" substituted by the Enterprise and Regulatory Reform Act 2013 (Competition) (Consequential, Transitional and Saving Provisions) (No 2) Order 2014, SI 2014/549, art 2, Sch 1, Pt 1, para 1(1), (3). For transitional provisions in relation to the abolition of the OFT and the Competition Commission and the continuity of functions, etc, see art 3 of the 2014 Order at **[2.21]**.

References to the European Community and related expressions: see the note "References to "the European Community", "Community", etc" in the introductory notes to these Regulations.

[2.82]

[4

(1) A person commits an offence if he intentionally alters, suppresses or destroys a document which he has been required to produce by a notice under regulation 2.

(2) A person who commits an offence under paragraph (1) shall be liable—

(a) on summary conviction, to a fine not exceeding the statutory maximum;

(b) on conviction on indictment, to imprisonment for a term not exceeding two years or to a fine or to both.]

NOTES

These Regulations were revoked by the Competition (Amendment etc) (EU Exit) Regulations 2019, SI 2019/93, reg 61, Sch 2, Pt 3, para 9, as from IP completion day (as defined in the European Union (Withdrawal Agreement) Act 2020, s 39) (for transitional provisions and savings in relation to the operation of the 2019 Regulations, see Sch 4 to those Regulations at **[7.69]** et seq).

Substituted by the Enterprise Act 2002 (Consequential and Supplemental Provisions) Order 2003, SI 2003/1398, art 2, Schedule, para 17(1), (4).

[2.83]

[5

Section 117 (false or misleading information) and Part 9 (information) of the Enterprise Act 2002 shall apply as if these Regulations were contained in Part 3 of that Act.]

NOTES

These Regulations were revoked by the Competition (Amendment etc) (EU Exit) Regulations 2019, SI 2019/93, reg 61, Sch 2, Pt 3, para 9, as from IP completion day (as defined in the European Union (Withdrawal Agreement) Act 2020, s 39) (for transitional provisions and savings in relation to the operation of the 2019 Regulations, see Sch 4 to those Regulations at **[7.69]** et seq).

Added by the Enterprise Act 2002 (Consequential and Supplemental Provisions) Order 2003, SI 2003/1398, art 2, Schedule, para 17(1), (5).

ENTERPRISE ACT 2002 (MERGER PRENOTIFICATION) REGULATIONS 2003

(SI 2003/1369)

NOTES

Made: 23 May 2003.
Authority: Enterprise Act 2002, ss 101, 124(2).
Commencement: 20 June 2003.

ARRANGEMENT OF REGULATIONS

[2.84]
1 Citation and commencement

This Order may be cited as the Enterprise Act 2002 (Merger Prenotification) Regulations 2003 and shall come into force on 20th June 2003.

[2.85]
2 Interpretation

(1) In these Regulations
"the Act" means the Enterprise Act 2002; and
"working day" means any day which is not—
(a) Saturday, Sunday, Good Friday or Christmas Day; or
(b) a bank holiday in England and Wales.

(2) A reference in these Regulations to a person who does anything on behalf of a person who is authorised to give a merger notice or who has given such notice shall be construed as limited to a reference to a person who does so having been authorised so to act in accordance with regulation 14 of these Regulations.

[2.86]
3 Person authorised to give a merger notice

A merger notice may be given under section 96(1) of the Act by any person carrying on an enterprise to which the notified arrangements relate.

4 (*Revoked by the Enterprise and Regulatory Reform Act 2013 (Competition) (Consequential, Transitional and Saving Provisions) (No 2) Order 2014, SI 2014/549, art 2, Sch 1, Pt 1, para 9(1), (2). For transitional provisions in relation to the abolition of the OFT and the Competition Commission and the continuity of functions, etc, see art 3 of, and Sch 2, paras 1, 2 to, the 2014 Order at* **[2.21]**, **[2.22]**.)

[2.87]
5 Time at which a merger notice is to be treated as received

A merger notice given under section 96(1) of the Act shall be treated as having been received by the [CMA]—
(a) subject to paragraph (b), on the day on which it is in fact received by the [CMA];
(b) where it is received by the [CMA] on any day which is not a working day or after 5.00 pm on any working day, on the next working day,
and section 7 of the Interpretation Act 1978 shall not apply.

NOTES

References to the "CMA" substituted by the Enterprise and Regulatory Reform Act 2013 (Competition) (Consequential, Transitional and Saving Provisions) (No 2) Order 2014, SI 2014/549, art 2, Sch 1, Pt 1, para 9(1), (3). For transitional provisions in relation to the abolition of the OFT and the Competition Commission and the continuity of functions, etc, see art 3 of the 2014 Order at **[2.21]**.

[2.88]
6 Rejection of a merger notice

A rejection of a merger notice under section 99(5) of the Act shall be given in writing and such a notice shall be treated as having been rejected at the time when the rejection is sent to the person who gave the merger notice or a person acting on his behalf.

[2.89]

7 Withdrawal of a merger notice

A merger notice may be withdrawn by or on behalf of the person who gave the notice by a notice in writing sent to the [CMA].

NOTES

Reference to the "CMA" substituted by the Enterprise and Regulatory Reform Act 2013 (Competition) (Consequential, Transitional and Saving Provisions) (No 2) Order 2014, SI 2014/549, art 2, Sch 1, Pt 1, para 9(1), (4). For transitional provisions in relation to the abolition of the OFT and the Competition Commission and the continuity of functions, etc, see art 3 of the 2014 Order at **[2.21]**.

[2.90]

8 Provision of information to the [CMA]

(1) Any information which—

(a) is, or ought to be, known to the person who gave the merger notice or any connected person, and

(b) is material to the notified arrangements,

. . . shall be provided or disclosed in writing.

(2) Subject to paragraph (3), any information provided or disclosed to the [CMA] under this regulation shall be treated as having been so provided or disclosed on the day on which it is in fact received by the [CMA].

(3) Where information provided or disclosed to the [CMA] under this regulation is received by the [CMA] on any day which is not a working day or after 5.00 pm on any working day, it shall be treated as having been provided or disclosed to the [CMA] on the next working day.

(4) Section 7 of the Interpretation Act 1978 shall not apply to the provision or disclosure of any information under this regulation.

(5) . . .

NOTES

Provision heading, paras (2), (3): references to the "CMA" substituted by the Enterprise and Regulatory Reform Act 2013 (Competition) (Consequential, Transitional and Saving Provisions) (No 2) Order 2014, SI 2014/549, art 2, Sch 1, Pt 1, para 9(1), (5)(b). For transitional provisions in relation to the abolition of the OFT and the Competition Commission and the continuity of functions, etc, see art 3 of, and Sch 2, paras 1, 2 to, the 2014 Order at **[2.21]**, **[2.22]**.

Para (1): words omitted revoked by SI 2014/549, art 2, Sch 1, Pt 1, para 9(1), (5)(a) (subject to transitional provisions as noted above).

Para (5): revoked by SI 2014/549, art 2, Sch 1, Pt 1, para 9(1), (5)(c) (subject to transitional provisions as noted above).

9–13 (*Revoked by the Enterprise and Regulatory Reform Act 2013 (Competition) (Consequential, Transitional and Saving Provisions) (No 2) Order 2014, SI 2014/549, art 2, Sch 1, Pt 1, para 9(1), (6). For transitional provisions in relation to the abolition of the OFT and the Competition Commission and the continuity of functions, etc, see art 3 of, and Sch 2, paras 1, 2 to, the 2014 Order at* **[2.21]**, **[2.22]**.)

[2.91]

14 Circumstances in which a person is or is not to be treated as acting on behalf of the giver of a merger notice

(1) A person shall be treated as acting on behalf of a person who is authorised to give a merger notice or who has given such a notice only if the person on whose behalf he is to be treated as acting has authorised him so to act in accordance with paragraph (2).

(2) An authorisation to act on behalf of another person for the purposes of paragraph (1) shall be given to the [CMA] in writing and an authorisation to act on behalf of a company shall be signed by a director or other officer of that company.

(3) A person who has given an authorisation in accordance with paragraph (1) may revoke it by a notice in writing given to the [CMA] and, where that person is a company, the notice shall be signed by a director or other officer of that company.

NOTES

Paras (2), (3): references to the "CMA" substituted by the Enterprise and Regulatory Reform Act 2013 (Competition) (Consequential, Transitional and Saving Provisions) (No 2) Order 2014, SI 2014/549, art 2, Sch 1, Pt 1, para 9(1), (7). For transitional provisions in relation to the abolition of the OFT and the Competition Commission and the continuity of functions, etc, see art 3 of the 2014 Order at **[2.21]**.

ENTERPRISE ACT 2002 (MERGER FEES AND DETERMINATION OF TURNOVER) ORDER 2003

(SI 2003/1370)

NOTES

Made: 23 May 2003.

Authority: Enterprise Act 2002, ss 28, 121, 124(2).

Commencement: 20 June 2003.

ARRANGEMENT OF ARTICLES

PART 1 GENERAL

[2.92]
1 Citation and commencement

This Order may be cited as the Enterprise Act 2002 (Merger Fees and Determination of Turnover) Order 2003 and shall come into force on 20th June 2003.

[2.93]
2 Interpretation

In this Order—

(a) "the Act" means the Enterprise Act 2002;

(b) "applicable turnover" means the turnover of an enterprise in the preceding business year, or in a case to which article 11(4) applies, in the period referred to in that article, determined in accordance with the Schedule to this Order; and where a business year or a period under article 11(4) does not equal 12 months the applicable turnover shall be the amount which bears the same proportion to the applicable turnover during that business year as 12 months does to that period;

(c) "business year" means a period of more than six months in respect of which an enterprise or, if applicable, the business of which it forms part, prepares or is required to prepare accounts; . . .

[(d) "merger reference" means a reference by the CMA to its chair under section 22 or 33 of the Act or section 32 of the Water Industry Act 1991, or a reference by the Secretary of State to the chair of the CMA under section 45 of the Act; and]

[(e) "water enterprise" means an enterprise carried on by a water undertaker or sewerage undertaker.]

NOTES

Word omitted from para (c) revoked, and para (e) added, by the Enterprise Act 2002 (Merger Fees and Determination of Turnover) (Amendment) Order 2004, SI 2004/3204, art 2(1), (2)(a), (c).

Para (d) substituted by the Enterprise Act 2002 (Merger Fees and Determination of Turnover) (Amendment) Order 2014, SI 2014/534, arts 2, 3.

PART 2 MERGER FEES

[2.94]
3 Matters in respect of which fees are payable

A fee of the amount specified in Article 5 shall be payable in respect of—

(a) . . .

(b) subject to article 4(1) and (2), the decision by the [CMA] in relation to a possible reference under section 22 or 33 of the Act that it is or may be the case that a relevant merger situation has been created or (as the case may be) that arrangements are in progress or in contemplation which, if carried into effect, will result in the creation of a relevant merger situation;

(c) subject to article 4(1), the decision by the Secretary of State in relation to a possible reference under section 45 of the Act that it is or may be the case that a relevant merger situation has been created or (as the case may be) that arrangements are in progress or in contemplation which, if carried into effect, will result in the creation of a relevant merger situation;

[(d) subject to article 4(3) and (4), the decision by the CMA in relation to a possible merger reference under section 32(a) or (b) of the Water Industry Act 1991 that it is or may be the case—

(i) that arrangements are in progress which, if carried into effect, will result in a merger of any two or more water enterprises; or

(ii) that such a merger has taken place otherwise than as a result of the carrying into effect of arrangements that have been the subject of a reference by virtue of sub-paragraph (i) above].

NOTES

Para (a) revoked, and reference to the "CMA" in para (b) substituted, by the Enterprise Act 2002 (Merger Fees and Determination of Turnover) (Amendment) Order 2014, SI 2014/534, arts 2, 4.

Para (d) added by the Enterprise Act 2002 (Merger Fees and Determination of Turnover) (Amendment) Order 2004, SI 2004/3204, art 2(1), (3). Subsequently substituted by the Water Mergers (Miscellaneous Amendments) Regulations 2015, SI 2015/1936, regs 2(2), 23.

[2.95]

4 Circumstances in which certain fees are not payable

[(1) Except where the decision in respect of which a fee is payable under article 3(b) or (c) is made in relation to arrangements or proposed arrangements of which the CMA was given notice under section 96 of the Act, a fee shall not be payable under article 3(b) or (c) where the creation or possible creation of the relevant merger situation depends or would depend on the operation of section 26(3) or (4)(b) of the Act.]

(2) A fee shall not be payable under article 3(b) in relation to arrangements that are in progress or in contemplation which, if carried into effect, will result in the creation of a relevant merger situation, where [the CMA decides pursuant to section 33(2)(b) of the Act that the arrangements concerned are not sufficiently far advanced, or are not sufficiently likely to proceed, to justify the making of a merger reference].

[(3) A fee shall not be payable under article 3(d)—

(a) where the merger or prospective merger of two or more water enterprises depends or would depend on the operation of section 26(3) or (4)(b) of the Act; or

(b) in relation to arrangements of a kind specified in paragraph (4), where the CMA decides pursuant to section 33A(1)(a) of the Water Industry Act 1991 that they are not sufficiently far advanced, or are not sufficiently likely to proceed, to justify the making of a merger reference.

(4) The arrangements are those in progress or in contemplation which, if carried into effect, will result in a merger of any two or more water enterprises.]

NOTES

Para (1): substituted by the Enterprise Act 2002 (Merger Fees and Determination of Turnover) (Amendment) Order 2014, SI 2014/534, arts 2, 5(a).

Para (2): words in square brackets substituted by SI 2014/534, arts 2, 5(b).

Paras (3), (4): added by the Water Mergers (Miscellaneous Amendments) Regulations 2015, SI 2015/1936, regs 2(2), 24.

[2.96]

5 Amount of fees

(1) The amount of the fee payable under [article 3(b) or (c)] shall be—

(a) where the value of the turnover in the United Kingdom of the enterprise which has been taken over or (as the case may be) which it is proposed or contemplated should be taken over, does not exceed £20 million, [£40,000];

(b) where the value of such turnover exceeds £20 million but does not exceed £70 million, [£80,000];

(c) where the value of such turnover exceeds £70 million, [but does not exceed £120 million, £120,000;]

[(d) where the value of such turnover exceeds £120 million, £160,000].

(2) For the purposes of [paragraph (1)] the value of the turnover in the United Kingdom of the enterprise which has been taken over or (as the case may be) which it is proposed or contemplated should be taken over, shall be determined by taking the total value of the turnover in the United Kingdom of the enterprises which cease to be distinct enterprises and deducting—

(a) the turnover in the United Kingdom of any enterprise which continues to be carried on under the same ownership and control; or

(b) if no enterprise continues to be carried on under the same ownership and control, the turnover in the United Kingdom which, of all the turnovers concerned, is the turnover of the highest value.

(3) For the purposes of [paragraph (2)] the turnover in the United Kingdom of an enterprise shall be determined in accordance with article 11(2) to (4).

[(4) The amount of the fee payable under article 3(d) shall be—

(a) where the value of the turnover in England and Wales of the water enterprise which has been taken over or (as the case may be) which it is proposed should be taken over, does not exceed £20 million, [£40,000];

(b) where the value of such turnover exceeds £20 million but does not exceed £70 million, [£80,000];

(c) where the value of such turnover exceeds £70 million, [but does not exceed £120 million, £120,000;]

[(d) where the value of such turnover exceeds £120 million, £160,000].

(5) For the purposes of paragraph (4) the value of the turnover in England and Wales of the water enterprise which has been taken over or (as the case may be) which it is proposed should be taken over, shall be determined by taking the total value of the turnover of the water enterprises ceasing to be distinct enterprises and deducting—

(a) the turnover of any water enterprise continuing to be carried on under the same ownership and control; or

(b) if there is no water enterprise continuing to be carried on under the same ownership and control, the turnover which, of all the turnovers concerned, is the turnover of the highest value.

(6) For the purposes of paragraph (5) the turnover in England and Wales of a water enterprise shall be determined in accordance with the Regulations made pursuant to section 33(4) of the Water Industry Act 1991.]

NOTES

Para (1): words in first pair of square brackets substituted by the Enterprise Act 2002 (Merger Fees and Determination of Turnover) (Amendment) Order 2014, SI 2014/534, arts 2, 6. Sums and words in square brackets in sub-paras (a)–(c) substituted, and sub-para (d) inserted, by the Enterprise Act 2002 (Merger Fees) (Amendment and Revocation) Order 2012, SI 2012/1878, art 2(1)–(5).

Paras (2), (3): words in square brackets substituted by SI 2004/3204, art 2(1), (4)(b), (c).

Para (4): added, together with para (5), (6), by SI 2004/3204, art 2(1), (4)(d). Sums and words in square brackets in sub-paras (a)–(c) substituted, and sub-para (d) inserted, by SI 2012/1878, art 2(1), (6)–(9).

Paras (5), (6): added as noted above.

[2.97]

6 Person by whom fees are payable

[(1) Where the decision in respect of which a fee is payable under article 3(b) or (c) is made in relation to arrangements or proposed arrangements of which the CMA was given notice under section 96 of the Act and the person who gave the notice still exists at the time when the fee is payable under article 9, the fee is payable by the person who gave the notice.

(2) In any other case, the fee payable under article 3 is payable by the acquirer.]

(3) For the purposes of this article and article 7 "the acquirer" means the person, or group of persons, who has or have acquired or will, if those arrangements are carried into effect, acquire either—

(a) a controlling interest in one of the enterprises which was or is involved in the creation or possible creation of a relevant merger situation [or the merger or prospective merger of two or more water enterprises] which is the subject of the merger reference or, as the case may be, the [CMA's] or the Secretary of State's decision not to make such a merger reference, and in which he or they did not previously have such an interest; or

(b) in the case of such an enterprise carried on by a body corporate in which he or they did not previously have a controlling interest, a controlling interest in that body corporate.

(4) In a case where paragraph (3) applies to more than one person, whether by virtue of them being treated as associated persons, as defined in section 127 of the Act, or otherwise, the persons to whom it applies shall be jointly and severally liable for the fee in that case.

(5) . . .

NOTES

Paras (1), (2): substituted by the Enterprise Act 2002 (Merger Fees and Determination of Turnover) (Amendment) Order 2014, SI 2014/534, arts 2, 7(a).

Para (3): words in first pair of square brackets inserted by SI 2004/3204, art 2(1), (5)(b). Word in second pair of square brackets substituted by SI 2014/534, arts 2, 7(b).

Para (5): revoked by the Enterprise Act 2002 (Merger Fees) (Amendment) Order 2005, SI 2005/3558, art 2.

[2.98]

[7 Exemption for acquisitions by small and medium sized enterprises

(1) In a case in which, by virtue of article 6(1), the obligation to pay the fee under article 3(b) or (c) falls on a person who gave a merger notice under section 96 of the Act, no fee shall be payable if—

(a) that person is the acquirer;

(b) the notified arrangements relate to the enterprise that has been, or will be, taken over by the acquirer; and

(c) the acquirer qualifies as small or medium sized.

(2) In any other case, no fee is payable under article 3 where the acquirer qualifies as small or medium sized.

(3) But paragraphs (1) and (2) do not apply where the acquirer is an individual.

(4) For the purposes of paragraphs (1) and (2) an acquirer qualifies as small or medium sized if—

(a) the acquirer (whether or not it is a company) met, in its most recent financial year before the time when the fee would otherwise become payable, the qualifying conditions to be small specified in section 382(3) to (6) of the Companies Act 2006 or the qualifying conditions to be medium-sized specified in section 465(3) to (6) of that Act; and

(b) where the acquirer is a member of a group as defined in section 474 of the Companies Act 2006 (whether or not the acquirer is a company), that group met, in its most recent financial year before the time when the fee would otherwise become payable, the qualifying conditions to be small specified in section 383(4) to (7) of that Act or the qualifying conditions to be medium-sized specified in section 466(4) to (7) of that Act.]

NOTES

Substituted by the Enterprise Act 2002 (Merger Fees and Determination of Turnover) (Amendment) Order 2014, SI 2014/534, arts 2, 8.

[2.99]

8 Person to whom fees are payable

In a case falling within article 3 the fee shall be payable to the [CMA].

NOTES

Reference to the "CMA" substituted by the Enterprise Act 2002 (Merger Fees and Determination of Turnover) (Amendment) Order 2014, SI 2014/534, arts 2, 9.

[2.100]

[9 Time when fees are payable

(1) In a case falling within article 3(b) or (d), the fee shall be payable when the CMA publishes the merger reference or, as the case may be, publishes its decision that the duty to make such a merger reference does not apply.

(2) In a case falling within article 3(c), the fee shall be payable when the Secretary of State publishes the merger reference, or as the case may be, when the Secretary of State's decision not to make such a merger reference is published.]

NOTES

Substituted by the Enterprise Act 2002 (Merger Fees and Determination of Turnover) (Amendment) Order 2014, SI 2014/534, arts 2, 10.

10 (*Revoked by the Enterprise Act 2002 (Merger Fees and Determination of Turnover) (Amendment) Order 2014, SI 2014/534, arts 2, 11.*)

PART 3 DETERMINATION OF TURNOVER

[2.101]

11 Determination of turnover in the United Kingdom of an enterprise

(1) This article shall apply for the purposes referred to in section 28(2) of the Act and [article 5(3)].

(2) The turnover in the United Kingdom of an enterprise shall be, subject to paragraph (3), the applicable turnover for the business year preceding—

(a) where the question whether a relevant merger situation has been created is being determined, the date when the enterprises concerned ceased to be distinct enterprises or such earlier date as the decision-making authority considers appropriate;

(b) where the question whether it is or may be the case that arrangements are in progress or in contemplation which, if carried into effect, will result in the creation of a relevant merger situation is being determined, the date when the decision in relation to a possible reference has been or is to be made, or such earlier date as the decision-making authority considers appropriate.

(3) Where an acquisition or divestment or other transaction or event has occurred since the end of the preceding business year which the decision-making authority considers may have a significant impact on the turnover of the enterprise, that acquisition or divestment or other transaction or event may be taken into account if the decision-making authority considers it appropriate to do so.

(4) Where in the application of this article there is any period in respect of which there is no preceding business year then the applicable turnover shall be the turnover for that period.

NOTES

Para (1): words in square brackets substituted the Enterprise Act 2002 (Merger Fees and Determination of Turnover) (Amendment) Order 2004, SI 2004/3204, art 2(1), (8).

SCHEDULE
APPLICABLE TURNOVER

Article 2

Interpretation

[2.102]

1. In this Schedule:

["aid" means a measure which—

(a) fulfils the conditions set out in Article 1.1 of the Agreement on Subsidies and Countervailing Measures contained in Annex 1A to the WTO Agreement, and

(b) is specific within the meaning of Article 2 of that Agreement, irrespective of whether the recipient deals in goods or services;]

"branch" means a place of business in the United Kingdom which forms a legally dependent part of a credit institution or financial institution and which conducts directly all or some of the operations inherent in the business of the undertaking and any number of branches set up in the United Kingdom shall for the purposes of this Order be regarded as a single branch;

["credit institution" means a credit institution for the purposes of Article 4(1)(1) of Regulation (EU) No 575/2013 of the European Parliament and of the Council of 26 June 2013 on prudential requirements for credit institutions and investment firms and amending Regulation (EU) No 648/2012;]

["financial institution" means a financial institution for the purposes of Article 4(1)(26) of Regulation (EU) No 575/2013 of the European Parliament and of the Council of 26 June 2013 on prudential requirements for credit institutions and investment firms and amending Regulation (EU) No 648/2012;]

"insurance undertaking" means an insurance undertaking carrying on the business of direct insurance of a class set out in [Article 2(3) or Annex I of Directive 2009/138/EC of the European Parliament and of the Council of 25 November 2009 on the taking-up and pursuit of the business of Insurance and Reinsurance (Solvency II);]

and terms used in this Schedule in respect of the determination of the applicable turnover of credit institutions, financial institutions and insurance undertakings shall (except where the contrary intention appears) have the same meaning as in the relevant Directive.

2. Save in paragraphs 4 to 9, the provisions of this Schedule shall be interpreted in accordance with accounting principles and practices that are generally accepted in the United Kingdom.

General

3. The applicable turnover of an enterprise, other than an enterprise which is a credit institution, financial institution or insurance undertaking shall be limited to the amounts derived from the sale of products and the provision of services falling within the ordinary activities of the enterprise to businesses or consumers in the United Kingdom after deduction of sales rebates, value added tax and other taxes directly related to turnover.

4. Subject to paragraphs 8 and 9, where an enterprise consists of two or more enterprises which are under common ownership or control the applicable turnover shall be calculated by adding together the respective applicable turnover of each of the enterprises under common ownership or control.

5. For the purposes of paragraphs 4 and 7 to 9, enterprises shall in particular be treated as being under common control if they are—

(a) enterprises of interconnected bodies corporate;

(b) enterprises carried on by two or more bodies corporate of which one and the same person or group of persons has control; or

(c) an enterprise carried on by a body corporate and an enterprise carried on by a person or group of persons having control of that body corporate.

6. A person or group of persons able, directly or indirectly, to control or materially influence the policy of a body corporate, or the policy of any person in carrying on an enterprise but without having a controlling interest in that body corporate or in that enterprise, may, for the purposes of paragraph 4, be treated by the decision-making authority as having control of it.

7. Section 127 of the Act shall apply to the determination of whether enterprises are under common control for the purposes of paragraphs 5 and 6 as it applies, for the purposes specified in section 127, to section 26 of the Act.

8. Subject to paragraph 9, applicable turnover shall not include amounts derived from the sale of products or the provision of services between enterprises under common ownership or control.

9. Where, as a result of the merger situation, one or more enterprises ceases or will cease to be under common ownership or control with the enterprise being taken over, the decision-making authority may treat amounts derived from the sale of products or the provision of services between the enterprise being taken over and any enterprises ceasing to be under common ownership or control with that enterprise as applicable turnover and if such sale of products or provision of services has not resulted in any turnover or the decision-making authority considers that the turnover attributed to them does not reflect open market value, the decision-making authority may attribute such value to them as it considers appropriate and include them in the calculation of applicable turnover.

10. Where an enterprise has applicable turnover part of which is attributable to a credit institution, financial institution or insurance undertaking, that part or those parts of the applicable turnover shall be calculated in accordance with paragraphs 3, 11 and 12.

Credit institutions and financial institutions

11. The applicable turnover of an enterprise which is a credit institution or financial institution shall be limited to the sum of the following income as defined in Council Directive (EEC) 86/635 received by the branch or division of that institution established in the United Kingdom after deduction of value added tax and other taxes directly related to those items:

(a) interest income and similar income;

(b) income from securities:

— income from shares and other variable yield securities;

— income from participating interests;

— income from shares in affiliated undertakings;

(c) commissions receivable;

(d) net profit on financial operations;

(e) other operating income.

Insurance undertakings

12. The applicable turnover of an enterprise which is an insurance undertaking shall be limited to the value of gross premiums received from residents of the United Kingdom which shall comprise all amounts received and receivable in respect of insurance contracts issued by or on behalf of the undertaking, including outgoing reinsurance premiums, and after deduction of taxes and parafiscal contributions or levies charged by reference to the amounts of individual premiums or the total volume of premiums.

Aid granted to businesses

13. Any aid granted by a public body to a business which relates to one of the ordinary activities of the business shall be included in the calculation of turnover if the business is itself the recipient of the aid and if the aid is directly linked to the sale of products or the provision of services by the business and is therefore reflected in the price.

NOTES

Para 1 is amended as follows:

Definition "aid" substituted by the State Aid (Revocations and Amendments) (EU Exit) Regulations 2020, SI 2020/1470, reg 7(2), Sch 2, Pt 2, para 4, as from IP completion day (as defined in the European Union (Withdrawal Agreement) Act 2020, s 39).

Definitions "credit institution" and "financial institution" substituted by the Capital Requirements Regulations 2013, SI 2013/3115, reg 46(1), Sch 2, Pt 3, para 60.

Words in square brackets in definition "insurance undertaking" substituted by the Solvency 2 Regulations 2015, SI 2015/575, reg 60, Sch 2, para 16.

ENTERPRISE ACT 2002 (PROTECTION OF LEGITIMATE INTERESTS) ORDER 2003

(SI 2003/1592)

NOTES

Made: 17 June 2003.

Authority: Enterprise Act 2002, ss 68, 124(2), (4). Note that s 68 of the 2002 Act was repealed by the Competition (Amendment etc) (EU Exit) Regulations 2019, SI 2019/93, regs 32, 47, as from IP completion day (as defined in the European Union (Withdrawal Agreement) Act 2020, s 39). See, however, Sch 4, Pt 7, paras 25–27 to the 2019 Regulations (at **[7.76]**) which provides for the continued application of this Order in the circumstances specified in those paragraphs.

Note that this Order is reproduced as amended (inter alia) by the Enterprise Act 2002 (Protection of Legitimate Interests) (Amendment) Order 2014, SI 2014/891. The 2014 Order was also made under the powers conferred by the Enterprise Act 2002, s 68, and consequently lapsed on the repeal of that section as noted above. The 2014 Order contained various savings and transitional provisions and is reproduced at **[2.179]** *post* out of historical interest.

Commencement: 20 June 2003.

ARRANGEMENT OF ARTICLES

SCHEDULES

[2.103]

1 Citation, commencement and interpretation

(1) This Order may be cited as the Enterprise Act 2002 (Protection of Legitimate Interests) Order 2003 and shall come into force on 20th June 2003.

(2) In this Order—

"the Act" means the Enterprise Act 2002;

"a European intervention notice" means a notice given by the Secretary of State to the [CMA] pursuant to section 67 of the Act;

["media public interest consideration" means any consideration which, at the time of the giving of the European intervention notice concerned, is specified in section 58(2A) to (2C) of the Act, or in the opinion of the Secretary of State, is concerned with broadcasting or newspapers and ought to be specified in section 58 of the Act;]

"public interest consideration" means a consideration which, at the time of the giving of the European intervention notice concerned, is specified in section 58 of the Act, or is not so specified but, in the opinion of the Secretary of State, ought to be so specified.

NOTES

Para (2): in definition "a European intervention notice" reference to the "CMA" substituted by the Enterprise Act 2002 (Protection of Legitimate Interests) (Amendment) Order 2014, SI 2014/891, arts 2, 3. Definition "media public interest consideration" inserted by the Enterprise Act 2002 and Media Mergers (Consequential Amendments) Order 2003, SI 2003/3180, art 2, Schedule, para 10(1), (2).

[2.104]

2 Determination of a relevant merger situation

For the purposes of deciding whether a relevant merger situation has been created or whether arrangements are in progress or in contemplation which, if carried into effect, will result in the creation of a relevant merger situation, for the purposes of section 68(2)(a) of the Act and this Order, sections 23 to 32 of the Act (read together with section 34 of the Act and any Order made pursuant to that section) shall apply, but subject to the modifications mentioned in Schedule 1.

[2.105]

3 European intervention notices under section 67 of the Act

(1) A European intervention notice shall come into force when it is given and shall cease to be in force when the matter to which it relates is finally determined in accordance with paragraphs (2) and (3).

(2) A matter to which a European intervention notice relates is finally determined if—

- *(a) the time within which the [CMA] [or (if relevant) OFCOM] is to report to the Secretary of State under article 4 [or (as the case may be) 4A] has expired and no such report has been made;*
- *(b) the Secretary of State decides to accept an undertaking or group of undertakings under paragraph 3 of Schedule 2 instead of making a reference under article 5;*
- *(c) the Secretary of State otherwise decides not to make a reference under article 5;*
- *(d) the [CMA] cancels such a reference under article 7(1) or article 11(1);*
- *(e) the time within which the [CMA] is to prepare a report under article 8 and give it to the Secretary of State has expired and no such report has been prepared and given to the Secretary of State;*
- *(f) the time within which the Secretary of State is to make and publish a decision under article 12(2) has expired and no such decision has been made and published;*
- *(g) the Secretary of State decides under paragraph (2) of article 12 otherwise than as mentioned in paragraph (6) of that article;*
- *(h) the Secretary of State decides under paragraph (2) of article 12 as mentioned in paragraph (6) of that article but decides neither to accept an undertaking under paragraph 9 of Schedule 2 nor to make an order under paragraph 11 of that Schedule; or*
- *(i) the Secretary of State decides under paragraph (2) of article 12 as mentioned in paragraph (6) of that article and accepts an undertaking under paragraph 9 of Schedule 2 or makes an order under paragraph 11 of that Schedule.*

(3) The time when a matter to which a European intervention notice relates is finally determined is—

- *(a) in a case falling within paragraph (2)(a), (e) or (f), the expiry of the time concerned;*
- *(b) in a case falling within paragraph (2)(b), the acceptance of the undertaking or group of undertakings concerned;*
- *(c) in a case falling within paragraph (2)(c), (d) or (g), the making of the decision concerned;*
- *(d) in a case falling within paragraph (2)(h), the making of the decision neither to accept an undertaking under paragraph 9 of Schedule 2 nor to make an order under paragraph 11 of that Schedule; and*
- *(e) in a case falling within paragraph (2)(i), the acceptance of the undertakings concerned or (as the case may be) the making of the order concerned.*

NOTES

Para (2): reference to the "CMA" substituted by the Enterprise Act 2002 (Protection of Legitimate Interests) (Amendment) Order 2014, SI 2014/891, arts 2, 4. Words in second and third pairs of square brackets in sub-para (a) inserted by the Enterprise Act 2002 and Media Mergers (Consequential Amendments) Order 2003, SI 2003/3180, art 2, Schedule, para 10(1), (3).

[2.106]

4 Initial investigation and report by [CMA]

(1) Paragraph (2) applies where the Secretary of State has given a European intervention notice in relation to a relevant merger situation under section 67 of the Act.

(2) The [CMA] shall, within such period as the Secretary of State may require, give a report to the Secretary of State in relation to the case.

(3) The report shall contain—

- *(a) advice from the [CMA] on the considerations relevant to the making of a reference under section 22 or 33 of the Act which are also relevant to the Secretary of State's decision as to whether to make a reference under article 5; and*
- *(b) a summary of any representations about the case which have been received by the [CMA] and which relate to any public interest consideration mentioned in the European intervention notice concerned [(other than a media public interest consideration)] and which is or may be relevant to the Secretary of State's decision as to whether to make a reference under article 5.*

(4) The report shall include a decision as to whether the [CMA] believes that it is, or may be, the case that a European relevant merger situation has been created or (as the case may be) arrangements are in progress or in contemplation which, if carried into effect, will result in the creation of a European relevant merger situation.

[(4A) The report may, in particular, contain a summary of any representations about the case which have been received by the [CMA] and which relate to any media public interest consideration mentioned in the European intervention notice concerned and which is or may be relevant to the Secretary of State's decision as to whether to make a reference under article 5.]

(5) The report may, in particular, include advice and recommendations on any public interest consideration mentioned in the European intervention notice concerned and which is or may be relevant to the Secretary of State's decision as to whether to make a reference under article 5.

(6) The [CMA] shall carry out such investigations as it considers appropriate for the purpose of producing a report under this article.

NOTES

References to the "CMA" substituted by the Enterprise Act 2002 (Protection of Legitimate Interests) (Amendment) Order 2014, SI 2014/891, arts 2, 5.

Para (3): words in second pair of square brackets in sub-para (b) inserted by the Enterprise Act 2002 and Media Mergers (Consequential Amendments) Order 2003, SI 2003/3180, art 2, Schedule, para 10(1), (4)(a).
Para (4A): inserted by SI 2003/3180, art 2, Schedule, para 10(1), (4)(b).

[2.107]

[4A Additional investigation and report by OFCOM: media mergers

(1) Paragraph (2) applies where—

(a) the Secretary of State has given a European intervention notice in relation to a relevant merger situation under section 67 of the Act; and

(b) the European intervention notice mentions any media public interest consideration.

(2) OFCOM shall, within such period as the Secretary of State may require, give a report to the Secretary of State on the effect of the consideration or considerations concerned on the case.

(3) The report shall contain—

(a) advice and recommendations on any media public interest consideration mentioned in the European intervention notice concerned and which is or may be relevant to the Secretary of State's decision as to whether to make a reference under article 5; and

(b) a summary of any representations about the case which have been received by OFCOM and which relate to any such consideration.

(4) OFCOM shall carry out such investigations as they consider appropriate for the purposes of producing a report under this article.]

NOTES

Inserted by the Enterprise Act 2002 and Media Mergers (Consequential Amendments) Order 2003, SI 2003/3180, art 2, Schedule, para 10(1), (5).

[2.108]

5 Power of Secretary of State to refer the matter

(1) Paragraphs (2) and (3) apply where the Secretary of State—

(a) has given a European intervention notice in relation to a relevant merger situation; and

(b) has received a report of the [CMA] under article 4[, and any report of OFCOM which is required by virtue of article 4A,] in relation to the matter.

(2) The Secretary of State may make a reference to [the chair of the CMA for the constitution of a group under Schedule 4 to the Enterprise and Regulatory Reform Act 2013] if she believes that it is or may be the case that—

(a) a European relevant merger situation has been created;

(b) one or more than one public interest consideration mentioned in the European intervention notice is relevant to a consideration of the European relevant merger situation concerned; and

(c) taking account only of the relevant public interest consideration or considerations concerned, the creation of that situation operates or may be expected to operate against the public interest.

(3) The Secretary of State may make a reference to [the chair of the CMA for the constitution of a group under Schedule 4 to the Enterprise and Regulatory Reform Act 2013] if she believes that it is or may be the case that—

(a) arrangements are in progress or in contemplation which, if carried into effect, will result in the creation of a European relevant merger situation;

(b) one or more than one public interest consideration mentioned in the European intervention notice is relevant to a consideration of the European relevant merger situation concerned; and

(c) taking account only of the relevant public interest consideration or considerations concerned, the creation of that situation operates or may be expected to operate against the public interest.

(4) No reference shall be made under this article if the making of the reference is prevented by . . . paragraph 4 of Schedule 2.

(5) The Secretary of State, in deciding whether to make a reference under this article, shall accept the decision of the [CMA] included in its report under article 4 by virtue of paragraph (4) of that article.

(6) Where the decision to make a reference under article 5 is made at any time on or after the end of the period of 24 weeks beginning with the giving of the European intervention notice concerned, the Secretary of State shall, in deciding whether to make such a reference, disregard any public interest consideration which is mentioned in the European intervention notice but which has not been finalised before the end of that period.

(7) The Secretary of State may, if she believes that there is a realistic prospect of the public interest consideration mentioned in paragraph (6) being finalised within the period of 24 weeks beginning with the giving of the European intervention notice concerned, delay deciding whether to make the reference concerned until the public interest consideration is finalised or, if earlier, the period expires.

(8) A reference under this article shall, in particular, specify—

(a) the paragraph of this article under which it is made;

(b) the date on which it is made; and

(c) the public interest consideration or considerations mentioned in the European intervention notice concerned which the Secretary of State is not under a duty to disregard by virtue of paragraph (6) and which she believes are or may be relevant to a consideration of the relevant merger situation concerned.

NOTES

Para (1): reference to the "CMA" in sub-para (b) substituted by the Enterprise Act 2002 (Protection of Legitimate Interests) (Amendment) Order 2014, SI 2014/891, arts 2, 6(a). Words in second pair of square brackets in sub-para (b) inserted by the Enterprise Act 2002 and Media Mergers (Consequential Amendments) Order 2003, SI 2003/3180, art 2, Schedule, para 10(1), (6)(a).
Paras (2), (3): words in square brackets substituted by SI 2014/891, arts 2, 6(b).

Para (4): words omitted revoked by SI 2003/3180, art 2, Schedule, para 10(1), (6)(b).
Para (5): reference to the "CMA" substituted by SI 2014/891, arts 2, 6(c).

[2.109]

[5A Functions to be exercised by CMA groups

Where a reference is made to the chair of the CMA under article 5 for the constitution of a group under Schedule 4 to the Enterprise and Regulatory Reform Act 2013, the functions of the CMA under or by virtue of the following provisions in relation to the matter concerned are to be carried out on behalf of the CMA by the group so constituted—

- *(a) articles 6 to 11;*
- *(b) article 14, so far as relating to anything done on behalf of the CMA by the group;*
- *(c) where a reference is treated by virtue of article 7(4) as having been made under article 5(2), paragraph (ab) of section 23(9) of the Act as applied by article 2;*
- *(d) sections 104 and 104A of the Act as applied by article 15;*
- *(e) section 109 of the Act as applied by article 15, where the permitted purpose relates to a function that (by virtue of this article) is being or is to be carried out on behalf of the CMA by the group;*
- *(f) sections 110 to 115 of the Act as applied by article 15, so far as relating to a notice given under section 109 (as so applied) on behalf of the CMA by the group;*
- *(g) section 118(4) of the Act as applied by article 15;*
- *(h) section 120(5)(b) of the Act as applied by article 15, so far as relating to a decision of the group.]*

NOTES

Inserted by the Enterprise Act 2002 (Protection of Legitimate Interests) (Amendment) Order 2014, SI 2014/891, arts 2, 7.

[2.110]

6 Questions to be decided on references under article 5

(1) The [CMA] shall, on a reference under article 5(2), decide whether a European relevant merger situation has been created.

(2) The [CMA] shall, on a reference under article 5(3), decide whether arrangements are in progress or in contemplation which, if carried into effect, will result in the creation of a European relevant merger situation.

(3) If the [CMA] decides that a European relevant merger situation has been created, or that arrangements are in progress or in contemplation which, if carried into effect, will result in the creation of a European relevant merger situation, it shall, on a reference under article 5, decide whether, taking account only of the admissible public interest consideration or considerations concerned, the creation of that situation operates or may be expected to operate against the public interest.

(4) The [CMA] shall, if it has decided on a reference under article 5 that the creation of a European relevant merger situation operates or may be expected to operate against the public interest, decide the following additional questions—

- *(a) whether action should be taken by the Secretary of State under article 12 for the purpose of remedying, mitigating or preventing any of the effects adverse to the public interest which have resulted from, or may be expected to result from, the creation of the European relevant merger situation concerned;*
- *(b) whether the [CMA] should recommend the taking of other action by the Secretary of State or action by persons other than itself and the Secretary of State for the purpose of remedying, mitigating or preventing any of the effects adverse to the public interest which have resulted from, or may be expected to result from, the creation of the European relevant merger situation concerned; and*
- *(c) in either case, if action should be taken, what action should be taken and what is to be remedied, mitigated or prevented.*

(5) In this article "admissible public interest consideration" means any public interest consideration which is specified in the reference under article 5 and which the [CMA] is not under a duty to disregard.

NOTES

References to the "CMA" substituted by the Enterprise Act 2002 (Protection of Legitimate Interests) (Amendment) Order 2014, SI 2014/891, arts 2, 8.

[2.111]

7 Cancellation or variation of references under article 5

(1) The [CMA] shall cancel a reference under article 5(3) if it considers that the proposal to make arrangements of the kind mentioned in the reference has been abandoned.

(2) In relation to the question whether a European relevant merger situation has been created or the question whether a European relevant merger situation will be created, a reference under article 5 may be framed so as to require the [CMA] to exclude from consideration—

- *(a) subsection (1) of section 23 of the Act;*
- *(b) subsection (2) of that section; or*
- *(c) one of those subsections if the [CMA] finds that the other is satisfied.*

(3) In relation to the question whether [for the purpose of section 23(2)(b), the share of supply test is or will be met], a reference under article 5 may be framed so as to require the [CMA] to confine its investigation to the supply of goods or services in a part of the United Kingdom specified in the reference.

(4) The [CMA] may, if it considers that doing so is justified by the facts (including events occurring on or after the making of the reference concerned), treat a reference made under paragraph (2) or (3) of article 5 as if it had been made under paragraph (3) or (as the case may be) (2) of that article; and, in such cases, references in this Order to references under those enactments shall, so far as may be necessary, be construed accordingly.

(5) Where by virtue of paragraph (4), the [CMA] treats a reference made under paragraph (2) or (3) of article 5 as if it had been made under paragraph (3) or (as the case may be) (2) of that article, paragraphs . . . 2, 7 and 8 of Schedule 2, in particular, apply as if the reference had been made under paragraph (3) or (as the case may be) (2) of that article instead of under paragraph (2) or (3) of that article.

(6) Paragraph (7) applies in relation to [any order made under paragraph 2 of Schedule 2], which is in force immediately before the [CMA], by virtue of paragraph (4), treats a reference made under paragraph (2) or (3) of article 5 as if it had been made under paragraph (3) or (as the case may be) (2) of that article.

(7) The . . . order shall, so far as applicable, continue in force as if it were—

(a) in the case of an . . . order which relates to a reference under paragraph (2) of article 5, . . . made in relation to a reference made under paragraph (3) of that article; and

(b) in the case of an . . . order which relates to a reference made under paragraph (3) of that article, . . . made in relation to a reference made under paragraph (2) of that article;

and the . . . order concerned may be varied . . . or revoked accordingly.

(8) The Secretary of State may at any time vary a reference under article 5.

(9) The Secretary of State shall consult the [CMA] before varying any such reference.

(10) Paragraph (9) shall not apply if the [CMA] has requested the variation concerned.

(11) No variation by the Secretary of State under this article shall be capable of altering the public interest consideration or considerations specified in the reference or the period permitted by virtue of article 8 within which the report of the [CMA] under that article is to be prepared and given to the Secretary of State.

NOTES

References to the "CMA" substituted by the Enterprise Act 2002 (Protection of Legitimate Interests) (Amendment) Order 2014, SI 2014/891, arts 2, 9(a), (e). Other amendments to this article are as follows:

Para (3): words in first pair of square brackets substituted by the Enterprise Act 2002 (Turnover Test) (Amendment) Order 2020, SI 2020/763, art 3.

Para (5): figure omitted revoked, by SI 2014/891, arts 2, 9(b).

Para (6): words in square brackets substituted by SI 2014/891, arts 2, 9(c).

Para (7): words omitted revoked by SI 2014/891, arts 2, 9(d).

[2.112]

8 Investigations and reports on references under article 5

(1) The [CMA] shall prepare a report on a reference under article 5 and give it to the Secretary of State within the period permitted by article 9.

(2) The report shall, in particular, contain—

(a) the decisions of the [CMA] on the questions which it is required to answer by virtue of article 6;

(b) its reasons for its decisions; and

(c) such information as the [CMA] considers appropriate for facilitating a proper understanding of those questions and of its reasons for its decisions.

[(2A) Where the report relates to a reference under article 5 which has been made after a report of OFCOM under article 4A, the [CMA] shall give a copy of its report (whether or not published) to OFCOM.]

(3) The [CMA] shall carry out such investigations as it considers appropriate for the purpose of producing a report under this article.

NOTES

References to the "CMA" substituted by the Enterprise Act 2002 (Protection of Legitimate Interests) (Amendment) Order 2014, SI 2014/891, arts 2, 10.

Para (2A): inserted by the Enterprise Act 2002 and Media Mergers (Consequential Amendments) Order 2003, SI 2003/3180, art 2, Schedule, para 10(1), (7).

[2.113]

9 Time-limits and investigations and reports by [CMA]

(1) The [CMA] shall prepare its report under article 8 and give it to the Secretary of State under that article within the period of 24 weeks beginning with the date of the reference concerned.

(2) The [CMA] may extend, by no more than 8 weeks, the period within which a report under article 8 is to be prepared and given to the Secretary of State if it considers that there are special reasons why the report cannot be prepared and given to the Secretary of State within that period.

(3) The [CMA] may extend the period within which a report under article 8 is prepared and given to the Secretary of State if it considers that a relevant person has failed (whether with or without a reasonable excuse) to comply with any requirement of a notice under section 109 of the Act.

(4) In paragraph (3) "relevant person" means—

(a) any person carrying on any of the enterprises concerned;

(b) any person who (whether alone or as a member of a group) owns or has control of any such person; or

(c) any officer, employee or agent of any person mentioned in sub-paragraph (a) or (b).

(5) For the purposes of paragraph (4) a person or group of persons able, directly or indirectly, to control or materially to influence the policy of a body of persons corporate or unincorporate, but without having a controlling interest in that body of persons, may be treated as having control of it.

(6) An extension under paragraph (2) or (3) shall come into force when published in accordance with article 14.

(7) An extension under paragraph (3) shall continue in force until—

(a) the person concerned provides the information or documents to the satisfaction of the [CMA] or (as the case may be) appears as a witness in accordance with the requirements of the [CMA]; or

(b) the [CMA] publishes its decision to cancel the extension.

NOTES

References to the "CMA" substituted by the Enterprise Act 2002 (Protection of Legitimate Interests) (Amendment) Order 2014, SI 2014/891, arts 2, 11.

[2.114]

10 Article 9: supplementary

(1) A period extended under paragraph (2) of article 9 may also be extended under paragraph (3) of that article and a period extended under paragraph (3) of that article may also be extended under paragraph (2) of that article.

(2) No more than one extension is possible under article 9(2).

(3) Where a period within which a report under article 8 is prepared and given to the Secretary of State is extended or further extended under article 9(2) or (3), the period as extended or (as the case may be) further extended, shall, subject to paragraphs (4) and (5), be calculated by taking the period being extended and adding to it the period of the extension (whether or not those periods overlap in time).

(4) Paragraph (5) applies where—

(a) the period within which the report under article 8 is to be prepared and given to the Secretary of State is further extended;

(b) the further extension and at least one previous extension is made under article 9(3); and

(c) the same days or fractions of days are included in or comprise the further extension and are included in or comprise at least one such previous extension.

(5) In calculating the period of the further extension, any days or fractions of days of the kind mentioned in paragraph (4)(c) shall be disregarded.

(6) Any Regulations made pursuant to section 52(12) of the Act shall apply for the purposes of article 9(7).

[2.115]

11 Restrictions on action where public interest considerations not finalised

(1) The [CMA] shall cancel a reference under article 5 if—

(a) the European intervention notice concerned mentions a public interest consideration which was not finalised on the giving of that notice or public interest considerations which, at the time, were not finalised;

(b) no other public interest consideration is mentioned in the notice;

(c) at least 24 weeks has elapsed since the giving of the notice; and

(d) the public interest consideration mentioned in the notice has not been finalised within that period of 24 weeks or (as the case may be) none of the public interest considerations mentioned in the notice has been finalised within that period of 24 weeks.

(2) Where a reference to the [CMA] under article 5 specifies a public interest consideration which has not been finalised before the making of the reference, the [CMA] shall not give its report to the Secretary of State under article 8 in relation to that reference unless—

(a) the period of 24 weeks beginning with the giving of the European intervention notice has expired; or

(b) the public interest consideration has been finalised.

(3) The [CMA] shall, in reporting on any of the questions mentioned in article 6(3) and (4), disregard any public interest consideration which was not finalised on the giving of the European intervention notice and has not been finalised within the period of 24 weeks beginning with the giving of the notice concerned.

(4) Paragraphs (1) to (3) are without prejudice to the power of the [CMA] to carry out investigations in relation to any public interest consideration to which it might be able to have regard in its report.

NOTES

References to the "CMA" substituted by the Enterprise Act 2002 (Protection of Legitimate Interests) (Amendment) Order 2014, SI 2014/891, arts 2, 12.

[2.116]

12 Decision and enforcement by Secretary of State

(1) Paragraph (2) applies where the Secretary of State has received a report of the [CMA] under article 8 in relation to a European relevant merger situation.

(2) The Secretary of State shall, in connection with a reference under article 5(2) or (3), decide the questions which the [CMA] is required to decide by virtue of article 6(1) to (3).

(3) The Secretary of State shall publish her decision under paragraph (2) within a period of 30 days beginning with the receipt of the report of the [CMA] under article 8.

(4) In making her decisions under paragraph (2), the Secretary of State shall disregard any public interest consideration not specified in the reference under article 5 and any public interest consideration disregarded by the [CMA] for the purposes of its report.

(5) In making her decisions under paragraph (2), the Secretary of State shall accept the decisions of the report of the [CMA] under article 8 as to whether a European relevant merger situation has been created or whether arrangements are in progress or in contemplation which, if carried into effect, will result in the creation of a European relevant merger situation.

(6) Paragraph (7) applies where the Secretary of State has decided under paragraph (2) that—

(a) a European relevant merger situation has been created or arrangements are in progress or in contemplation which, if carried into effect, will result in the creation of a European relevant merger situation;

(b) at least one public interest consideration which is mentioned in the European intervention notice concerned is relevant to a consideration of the European relevant merger situation concerned; and

(c) *taking account only of the relevant public interest consideration or considerations concerned, the creation of that situation operates or may be expected to operate against the public interest;*

and has so decided, and published her decision, within the period required by paragraph (3).

(7) The Secretary of State may take such action under paragraph 9 or 11 of Schedule 2 as she considers reasonable and practicable to remedy, mitigate or prevent any of the effects adverse to the public interest which have resulted from, or may be expected to result from, the creation of the European relevant merger situation concerned.

(8) In making a decision under paragraph (7), the Secretary of State shall, in particular, have regard to the report of the [CMA] under article 8.

(9) In determining for the purpose of paragraph (3) the period of 30 days no account shall be taken of—

(a) *Saturday, Sunday, Good Friday and Christmas Day; and*
(b) *any day which is a bank holiday in England and Wales.*

NOTES

References to the "CMA" substituted by the Enterprise Act 2002 (Protection of Legitimate Interests) (Amendment) Order 2014, SI 2014/891, arts 2, 13.

[2.117]

13 Enforcement action in European intervention notice cases

(1) Schedule 2 (which provides for enforcement action in European intervention notice cases) shall have effect.

(2) The [CMA] may advise the Secretary of State in relation to the taking by her of enforcement action under Schedule 2.

NOTES

Para (2): reference to the "CMA" substituted by the Enterprise Act 2002 (Protection of Legitimate Interests) (Amendment) Order 2014, SI 2014/891, arts 2, 14.

[2.118]

14 Publicity requirements

(1) The [CMA] shall publish—

(a) *any cancellation made by it under article 7(1) of a reference under article 5;*
(b) *any extension by it under article 9 of the period within which a report under article 8 is to be prepared and published;*
(c) *any decision made by it under article 9(7)(b) to cancel such an extension; and*
(d) *any decision made by it under article 7(4) to treat a reference made under paragraph (2) or (3) of article 5 as if it had been made under paragraph (3) or (as the case may be) (2) of that article.*

(2) The Secretary of State shall publish—

(a) *any European intervention notice given by her;*
(b) *any report of the [CMA] under article 4 which has been received by her;*
[(ba) any report of OFCOM under article 4A which has been received by her;]
(c) *any reference made by her under article 5 or any decision made by her not to make a reference;*
(d) *any variation by her under article 7 of a reference under article 5;*
(e) *any report of the [CMA] under article 8 which has been received by her;*
(f) *any decision made by her neither to accept an undertaking under paragraph 9 of Schedule 2 nor to make an order under paragraph 11 of that Schedule;*
(g), (h) . . .
(i) *any decision made by her as mentioned in paragraph 6(6)(b) of Schedule 2; and*
(j) *any decision to dispense with the requirements of Schedule 10 of the Act.*

(3) Where any person is under a duty by virtue of paragraphs (1) or (2) to publish the result of any action taken by that person or any decision made by that person, the person concerned shall, subject to paragraph (4), also publish that person's reasons for the action concerned or (as the case may be) the decision concerned.

(4) Such reasons need not, if it is not reasonably practicable to do so, be published at the same time as the result of the action concerned or (as the case may be) as the decision concerned.

(5) The Secretary of State shall publish her reasons for any decision made by her under article 12(2).

(6) Such reasons may be published after the publication of the decision concerned if it is not reasonably practicable to publish them at the same time as the publication of the decision.

(7) The Secretary of State shall publish—

(a) *the report of the [CMA] under article 4[, and any report of OFCOM under article 4A,] in relation to a matter no later than publication of her decision as to whether to make a reference under article 5 in relation to that matter; and*
(b) *the report of the [CMA] under article 8 in relation to a matter no later than publication of her decision under article 12(2) in relation to that matter.*

(8) Where the Secretary of State has decided under article 12(7) to accept an undertaking under paragraph 9 of Schedule 2 or to make an order under paragraph 11 of that Schedule, she shall (after the acceptance of the undertaking or (as the case may be) the making of the order) lay details of her decision and her reasons for it, and the [CMA's] report under article 8, before each House of Parliament.

NOTES

Para (1): reference to the "CMA" substituted by the Enterprise Act 2002 (Protection of Legitimate Interests) (Amendment) Order 2014, SI 2014/891, arts 2, 15(a).

Para (2): sub-para (ba) inserted by the Enterprise Act 2002 and Media Mergers (Consequential Amendments) Order 2003, SI 2003/3180, art 2, Schedule, para 10(1), (8)(a). References to the "CMA" in sub-paras (b), (e) substituted, and paras (g), (h) revoked, by SI 2014/891, arts 2, 15(b).

Para (7): references to the "CMA" in sub-paras (a), (b) substituted by SI 2014/891, arts 2, 15(c). Words in second pair of square brackets in sub-para (a) inserted by SI 2003/3180, art 2, Schedule, para 10(1), (8)(b).

Para (8): word in square brackets substituted by SI 2014/891, arts 2, 15(d).

[2.119]

15 Other provisions of the Act applicable to this Order

The other provisions of the Act mentioned in Schedule 3 shall apply for the purposes of this Order with the modifications mentioned in that Schedule.

16 *(Introduces Sch 4 (consequential amendments).)*

SCHEDULES

SCHEDULE 1
MODIFICATIONS TO SECTIONS 23 TO 32 OF THE ACT

Article 2

[2.120]

Sections 23 to 32 of the Act shall apply as if—

- *(a) references in those sections to "the decision-making authority" were references to the [CMA] or (as the case may be) the Secretary of State;*
- *(b) in section 23(1) and (2) the words "For the purposes of this Part," were omitted;*
- *(c) in section 23(9) the words "For the purposes of this Chapter," were omitted;*
- *(d) for section 23(9)(a) there were substituted—*

  "(a) in relation to the giving of a European intervention notice, the time when the notice is given;

  (aa) in relation to the making of a report by the [CMA] under article 4 of the Enterprise Act 2002 (Protection of Legitimate Interests) Order 2003, the time of the making of the report;

  (ab) in the case of a reference which is treated as having been made under article 5(2) of the Enterprise Act 2002 (Protection of Legitimate Interests) Order 2003 by virtue of article 7(4) of that Order, such time as the [CMA] may determine; and";

- *(e) the references to the [CMA] in section 24(2)(a) and (b) included references to the Secretary of State;*
- *(f) the references to the [CMA] in [sections 25(1) to (3), (6) and (8)] included references to the Secretary of State;*
- *(g) the references to the [CMA] in section 25(4) and (5) were references to the Secretary of State;*
- *(h) the reference in section 25(4) to section 73 were a reference to paragraph 3 of Schedule 2 to this Order;*
- *(i) after section 25(5) of the Act there were inserted—*

  "(5A) The Secretary of State may by notice to the persons carrying on the enterprises which have or [may have ceased] to be distinct enterprises extend the four month period mentioned in section 24(1)(a) or (2)(b) if, by virtue of article 5(7) of the Enterprise Act 2002 (Protection of Legitimate Interests) Order 2003 or paragraph 3(5) of Schedule 2 to that Order, he decides to delay a decision as to whether to make a reference under article 5 of that Order.

  (5B) An extension under subsection (5A) shall be for the period of the delay.";

- *(j) in section 25(10)(b) after word "(4)" there were inserted ", (5A)";*
- *(k) the reference in section 25(12) to one extension were a reference to one extension by the [CMA] and one extension by the Secretary of State;*
- *(l) the powers to extend time-limits under section 25 . . . were not exercisable by the [CMA] or the Secretary of State before the giving of a European intervention notice;*
- *(m) in section 26(1) the words "For the purposes of this Part" were omitted;*
- *(n) in section 28(2) the words from "For the purposes" to "121(4)(c)(ii))" were omitted;*
- *(o) . . .*
- *(p) in the case of the giving of European intervention notices, the references in sections 23 to 29 to the making of a reference or a reference were, so far as necessary, references to the giving of a European intervention notice or a European intervention notice . . .*
- *(q) . . .*

NOTES

Words in square brackets substituted, and words omitted revoked, by the Enterprise Act 2002 (Protection of Legitimate Interests) (Amendment) Order 2014, SI 2014/891, arts 2, 16.

SCHEDULE 2
ENFORCEMENT ACTION IN EUROPEAN INTERVENTION NOTICE CASES

Article 13

Pre-emptive . . . orders

[2.121]

1. . . .

2. (1) Sub-paragraph (2) applies where a European intervention notice is in force.

(2) The Secretary of State may by order, for the purpose of preventing pre-emptive action—

(a) prohibit or restrict the doing of things which the Secretary of State considers would constitute pre-emptive action;

(b) impose on any person concerned obligations as to the carrying on of any activities or the safeguarding of any assets;

(c) provide for the carrying on of any activities or the safeguarding of any assets either by the appointment of a person to conduct or supervise the conduct of any activities (on such terms and with such powers as may be specified or described in the order) or in any other manner;

(d) do anything which may be done by virtue of paragraph 19 of Schedule 8 to the Act.

[(2A) Sub-paragraph (2B) applies where—

(a) a European intervention notice is in force; and

(b) the Secretary of State has reasonable grounds for suspecting that pre-emptive action has or may have been taken.

(2B) The Secretary of State may by order, for the purpose of restoring the position to what it would have been had the pre-emptive action not been taken or otherwise for the purpose of mitigating its effects—

(a) do anything mentioned in sub-paragraph (2)(b) to (d);

(b) impose such other obligations, prohibitions or restrictions as the Secretary of State considers appropriate for that purpose.

(2C) A person may, with the consent of the Secretary of State, take action or action of a particular description where the action would otherwise constitute a contravention of an order under this paragraph.]

(3) An order under this paragraph—

(a) shall come into force at such time as is determined by or under the order; and

(b) may be varied or revoked by another order.

(4) An order which is in force under this paragraph in relation to a reference or possible reference under article 5 shall cease to be in force if an undertaking under paragraph . . . 3 comes into force in relation to that reference.

(5) An order under this paragraph shall, if it has not previously ceased to be in force, cease to be in force when the European intervention notice concerned ceases to be in force.

(6) No order shall be made by the Secretary of State under this paragraph before the making of a reference under article 5 unless[—

(a) the Secretary of State has reasonable grounds for suspecting that it is or may be the case that two or more enterprises have ceased to be distinct or that arrangements are in progress or in contemplation which, if carried into effect, will result in two or more enterprises ceasing to be distinct; or

(b)] the order relates to a European relevant merger situation which has been, or may have been, created.

(7) The Secretary of State shall, as soon as reasonably practicable, consider any representations received by her in relation to varying or revoking an order under this paragraph.

[(8) In this paragraph "pre-emptive action" means action which might prejudice the reference or possible reference concerned under article 5 or impede the taking of any action under this Order which may be justified by the Secretary of State's decisions on the reference.]

Undertakings in lieu of reference under article 5

3. (1) Sub-paragraph (2) applies if the Secretary of State has power to make a reference to the [CMA] under article 5 and otherwise intends to make such a reference.

(2) The Secretary of State may, instead of making such a reference and for the purpose of remedying, mitigating or preventing any of the effects adverse to the public interest which have or may have resulted, or which may be expected to result, from the creation of the European relevant merger situation concerned accept from such of the parties concerned as she considers appropriate undertakings to take such action as she considers appropriate.

(3) In proceeding under sub-paragraph (2), the Secretary of State shall, in particular, accept the decisions of the [CMA] included in its report under article 4 so far as they relate to the matters mentioned in paragraphs (3)(a) and (4) of that article.

(4) No undertaking shall be accepted by the Secretary of State under this paragraph in connection with a possible reference under article 5 if a public interest consideration mentioned in the European intervention notice concerned has not been finalised and the period of 24 weeks beginning with the giving of that notice has not expired.

(5) The Secretary of State may delay making a decision as to whether to accept any such undertaking (and any related decision as to whether to make a reference under article 5) if she considers that there is a realistic prospect of the public interest consideration being finalised within the period of 24 weeks beginning with the giving of the European intervention notice concerned.

(6) A delay under sub-paragraph (5) shall not extend beyond—

(a) the time when the public interest consideration is finalised; or

(b) if earlier, the expiry of the period of 24 weeks mentioned in that sub-paragraph.

(7) An undertaking under this paragraph—

(a) shall come into force when accepted;

(b) may be varied or superseded by another undertaking; or

(c) may be released by the Secretary of State.

(8) An undertaking under this paragraph which is in force in relation to a European relevant merger situation shall cease to be in force if an order comes into force under paragraph 5 or 6 in relation to that undertaking.

(9) The Secretary of State shall, as soon as reasonably practicable, consider any representations received by her in relation to varying or releasing an undertaking under this paragraph.

4. (1) The Secretary of State shall not make a reference under article 5 in relation to the creation of a European relevant merger situation if—

(a) the Secretary of State has accepted an undertaking or group of undertakings under paragraph 3; and

(b) the European relevant merger situation is the situation by reference to which the undertaking or group of undertakings was accepted.

(2) Sub-paragraph (1) does not prevent the making of a reference if material facts about relevant arrangements or transactions, or relevant proposed arrangements or transactions, were not notified (whether in writing or otherwise) to the Secretary of State or the [CMA] or made public before any undertaking concerned was accepted.

(3) For the purposes of sub-paragraph (2) arrangements or transactions, or proposed arrangements or transactions, are relevant if they are the ones in consequence of which the enterprises concerned ceased or may have ceased, or may cease, to be distinct enterprises.

(4) In sub-paragraph (2) "made public" means so publicised as to be generally known or readily ascertainable.

5. (1) Sub-paragraph (2) applies where the Secretary of State considers that—

(a) an undertaking accepted by her under paragraph 3 has not been, is not being or will not be fulfilled; or

(b) in relation to an undertaking accepted by her under that paragraph, information which was false or misleading in a material respect was given to her or the [CMA] by the person giving the undertaking before she decided to accept the undertaking.

(2) The Secretary of State may, for any of the purposes mentioned in paragraph 3(2), make an order under this paragraph.

(3) Sub-paragraph (3) of paragraph 3 shall apply for the purposes of sub-paragraph (2) above as it applies for the purposes of sub-paragraph (2) of that paragraph.

(4) An order under this paragraph may contain—

(a) anything permitted by Schedule 8 to the Act; and

(b) such supplementary, consequential or incidental provision as the Secretary of State considers appropriate.

(5) An order under this paragraph—

(a) shall come into force at such time as is determined by or under the order; and

(b) may contain provision which is different from the provision contained in the undertaking concerned.

(6) No order shall be varied or revoked under this paragraph unless the [CMA] advises that such a variation or revocation is appropriate by reason of a change of circumstances.

6. (1) Sub-paragraph (2) applies where—

(a) the Secretary of State has the power to make an order under paragraph 5 in relation to a particular undertaking and intends to make such an order; or

(b) the Secretary of State has the power to make an order under paragraph 10 in relation to a particular undertaking and intends to make such an order.

(2) The Secretary of State may, for the purpose of preventing any action which might prejudice the making of that order, make an order under this paragraph.

(3) No order shall be made under sub-paragraph (2) unless the Secretary of State has reasonable grounds for suspecting that it is or may be the case that action which might prejudice the making of the order under paragraph 5 or (as the case may be) 10 is in progress or in contemplation.

(4) An order under sub-paragraph (2) may—

(a) prohibit or restrict the doing of things which the Secretary of State considers would prejudice the making of the order under paragraph 5 or 10;

(b) impose on any person concerned obligations as to the carrying on of any activities or the safeguarding of any assets;

(c) provide for the carrying on of any activities or the safeguarding of any assets either by the appointment of a person to conduct or supervise the conduct of any activities (on such terms and with such powers as may be specified or described in the order) or in any other manner;

(d) do anything which may be done by virtue of paragraph 19 of Schedule 8 to the Act.

(5) An order under this paragraph shall come into force at such time as is determined by or under the order.

(6) An order under this paragraph shall, if it has not previously ceased to be in force, cease to be in force on—

(a) the coming into force of an order under paragraph 5 or (as the case may be) 10 in relation to the undertaking concerned; or

(b) the making of the decision not to proceed with such an order.

(7) The Secretary of State shall, as soon as reasonably practicable, consider any representations received by her in relation to varying or revoking an order under this paragraph.

Statutory restrictions following reference under article 5

7. (1) Sub-paragraphs (2) and (3) apply where—

(a) a reference has been made under article 5 but not finally determined; and

[(b) no orders under paragraph 2 are in force in relation to the European relevant merger situation concerned.]

(2) No relevant person shall, without the consent of the Secretary of State—

(a) complete any outstanding matters in connection with any arrangements which have resulted in the enterprises concerned ceasing to be distinct enterprises;

(b) make any further arrangements in consequence of that result (other than arrangements which reverse that result); or

(c) transfer the ownership or control of any enterprises to which the reference relates.

(3) No relevant person shall, without the consent of the Secretary of State, assist in any of the activities mentioned in paragraphs (a) to (c) of sub-paragraph (2).

(4) The prohibitions in sub-paragraphs (2) and (3) do not apply in relation to anything which the person concerned is required to do by virtue of any enactment.

(5) The consent of the Secretary of State under sub-paragraph (2) or (3)—
- *(a) may be general or specific;*
- *(b) may be revoked by the Secretary of State; and*
- *(c) shall be published in such manner as the Secretary of State considers appropriate for bringing it to the attention of any person entitled to the benefit of it.*

(6) Paragraph (c) of sub-paragraph (5) shall not apply if the Secretary of State considers that publication is not necessary for the purposes mentioned in that paragraph.

(7) Sub-paragraphs (2) and (3) shall apply to a person's conduct outside the United Kingdom if (and only if) he is—
- *(a) a United Kingdom national;*
- *(b) a body incorporated under the law of the United Kingdom or of any part of the United Kingdom; or*
- *(c) a person carrying on business in the United Kingdom.*

(8) For the purpose of this paragraph a reference under article 5 is finally determined if—
- *(a) the time within which the [CMA] is to prepare a report under article 8 in relation to the reference and give it to the Secretary of State has expired and no such report has been so prepared and given;*
- *(b) the [CMA] decides to cancel the reference under article 11(1);*
- *(c) the time within which the Secretary of State is to make and publish a decision under article 12(2) has expired and no such decision has been made and published;*
- *(d) the Secretary of State decides under paragraph (2) of article 12 otherwise than as mentioned in paragraph (6) of that article;*
- *(e) the Secretary of State decides under paragraph (2) of article 12 as mentioned in paragraph (6) of that article but decides neither to accept an undertaking under paragraph 9 of this Schedule nor to make an order under paragraph 11 of this Schedule; or*
- *(f) the Secretary of State decides under paragraph (2) of article 12 as mentioned in paragraph (6) of that article and accepts an undertaking under paragraph 9 of this Schedule or makes an order under paragraph 11 of this Schedule.*

(9) For the purposes of this paragraph the time when a reference under article 5 is finally determined is—
- *(a) in a case falling within sub-paragraph (8)(a) or (c), the expiry of the time concerned;*
- *(b) in a case falling within sub-paragraph (8)(b) or (d), the making of the decision concerned;*
- *(c) in a case falling within sub-paragraph (8)(e), the making of the decision neither to accept an undertaking under paragraph 9 of this Schedule nor to make an order under paragraph 11 of this Schedule; and*
- *(d) in a case falling within sub-paragraph (8)(f), the acceptance of the undertaking concerned or (as the case may be) the making of the order concerned.*

(10) In this paragraph "relevant person" means—
- *(a) any person who carries on any enterprise to which the reference relates or who has control of any such enterprise;*
- *(b) any subsidiary of any person falling within paragraph (a); or*
- *(c) any person associated with any person falling within paragraph (a) or any subsidiary of any person so associated.*

***8.** (1) Sub-paragraph (2) applies where—*
- *(a) a reference has been made under article 5, and*
- *[(b) no orders under paragraph 2 are in force in relation to the European relevant merger situation concerned.]*

(2) No relevant person shall, without the consent of the Secretary of State, directly or indirectly acquire during the relevant period an interest in shares in a company if any enterprise to which the reference relates is carried on by or under the control of that company.

(3) The consent of the Secretary of State under sub-paragraph (2)—
- *(a) may be general or specific;*
- *(b) may be revoked by the Secretary of State; and*
- *(c) shall be published in such manner as the Secretary of State considers appropriate for bringing it to the attention of any person entitled to the benefit of it.*

(4) Paragraph (c) of sub-paragraph (3) shall not apply if the Secretary of State considers that publication is not necessary for the purpose mentioned in that paragraph.

(5) Sub-paragraph (2) shall apply to a person's conduct outside the United Kingdom if (and only if) he is—
- *(a) a United Kingdom national;*
- *(b) a body incorporated under the law of the United Kingdom or of any part of the United Kingdom; or*
- *(c) a person carrying on business in the United Kingdom.*

(6) In this paragraph—

"company" includes any body corporate;

"relevant period" means the period beginning with the publication of the decision of the Secretary of State to make the reference concerned and ending when the reference is finally determined;

"relevant person" means—
- *(a) any person who carries on any enterprise to which the reference relates or who has control of any such enterprise;*
- *(b) any subsidiary of any person falling within paragraph (a); or*
- *(c) any person associated with any person falling within paragraph (a) or any subsidiary of any person so associated; and*

"share" means share in the capital of a company, and includes stock.

(7) For the purposes of the definition of "relevant period" in sub-paragraph (6), a reference under article 5 is finally determined if—

(a) the [CMA] cancels the reference under article 7(1) or article 11(1);

(b) the time within which the [CMA] is to prepare a report under article 8 in relation to the reference and give it to the Secretary of State has expired and no such report has been so prepared and given;

(c) the time within which the Secretary of State is to make and publish a decision under article 12(2) has expired and no such decision has been made and published;

(d) the Secretary of State decides under paragraph (2) of article 12 otherwise than as mentioned in paragraph (6) of that article;

(e) the Secretary of State decides under paragraph (2) of article 12 as mentioned in paragraph (6) of that article but decides neither to accept an undertaking under paragraph 9 of this Schedule nor to make an order under paragraph 11 of this Schedule; or

(f) the Secretary of State decides under paragraph (2) of article 12 as mentioned in paragraph (6) of that article and accepts an undertaking under paragraph 9 of this Schedule or makes an order under paragraph 11 of this Schedule.

(8) For the purposes of the definition of "relevant period" in sub-paragraph (6) above, the time when a reference under article 5 is finally determined is—

(a) in a case falling within sub-paragraph (7)(a) or (d), the making of the decision concerned;

(b) in a case falling within sub-paragraph (7)(b) or (c), the expiry of the time concerned;

(c) in a case falling within sub-paragraph (7)(e), the making of the decision neither to accept an undertaking under paragraph 9 of this Schedule nor to make an order under paragraph 11 of this Schedule; and

(d) in a case falling within sub-paragraph (7)(f) the acceptance of the undertaking concerned or (as the case may be) the making of the order concerned.

(9) Section 79 of the Act shall apply for the purposes of paragraph 7 and this paragraph in relation to a reference under article 5 as it applies for the purposes of sections 77 and 78 in relation to a reference under section 22 or 33 of the Act.

(10) In its application by virtue of sub-paragraph (9) section 79 shall have effect as if—

(a) subsections (1) and (2) were omitted; and

(b) for the reference in subsection (4) to the [CMA] there were substituted a reference to the Secretary of State.

Final undertakings and orders

***9.** (1) The Secretary of State may, in accordance with article 12(6) to (8) accept, from such persons as she considers appropriate, undertakings to take action specified or described in the undertakings.*

(2) An undertaking under this paragraph—

(a) shall come into force when accepted;

(b) may be varied or superseded by another undertaking; and

(c) may be released by the Secretary of State.

(3) An undertaking which is in force under this paragraph in relation to a reference under article 5 shall cease to be in force if an order under paragraph 6(1)(b) or 10 comes into force in relation to the subject-matter of the undertaking.

(4) No undertaking shall be accepted under this paragraph in relation to a reference under article 5 if an order has been made under—

(a) paragraph 6(1)(b) or 10 in relation to the subject-matter of the undertaking; or

(b) paragraph 11 in relation to that reference.

(5) The Secretary of State shall, as soon as reasonably practicable, consider any representations received by her in relation to varying or releasing an undertaking under this paragraph.

***10.** (1) Sub-paragraph (2) applies where the Secretary of State considers that—*

(a) an undertaking accepted by her under paragraph 9 has not been, is not being or will not be fulfilled; or

(b) in relation to an undertaking accepted by her under that paragraph, information which was false or misleading in a material respect was given to her or the [CMA] by the person giving the undertaking before she decided to accept the undertaking.

(2) The Secretary of State may, for any purpose mentioned in article 12(7), make an order under this paragraph.

(3) Paragraph (8) of article 12 shall apply for the purpose of sub-paragraph (2) above as it applies for the purposes of article 12(7).

(4) An order under this paragraph may contain—

(a) anything permitted by Schedule 8 to the Act; and

(b) such supplementary, consequential or incidental provision as the Secretary of State considers appropriate.

(5) An order under this paragraph—

(a) shall come into force at such time as is determined by or under the order; and

(b) may contain provision which is different from the provision contained in the undertaking concerned.

(6) No order shall be varied or revoked under this paragraph unless the [CMA] advises that such a variation or revocation is appropriate by reason of a change of circumstances.

***11.** (1) The Secretary of State may, in accordance with article 12(7), make an order under this paragraph.*

(2) An order under this paragraph may contain—

(a) anything permitted by Schedule 8 to the Act; and

(b) such supplementary, consequential or incidental provision as the Secretary of State considers appropriate.

(3) An order under this paragraph shall come into force at such time as is determined by or under the order.

(4) No order shall be made under this paragraph in relation to a reference under article 5 if an undertaking has been accepted under paragraph 9 in relation to that reference.

(5) No order shall be varied or revoked under this paragraph unless the [CMA] advises that such a variation or revocation is appropriate by reason of a change of circumstances.

NOTES

Words omitted from the heading preceding para 1 revoked by the Enterprise Act 2002 (Protection of Legitimate Interests) (Amendment) Order 2014, SI 2014/891, arts 2, 17(1), (3).

Para 1: revoked by SI 2014/891, arts 2, 17(1), (2).

Para 2: sub-paras (2A)–(2C) inserted, words omitted from sub-para (4) revoked, words in square brackets in sub-para (6) inserted, and sub-para (8) added, by SI 2014/891, arts 2, 17(1), (4).

Paras 3–5, 10, 11: references to the "CMA" substituted by SI 2014/891, arts 2, 17(1), (5)–(7), (10), (11).

Para 7: sub-para (1)(b) substituted, and references to the "CMA" in sub-para (8) substituted, by SI 2014/891, arts 2, 17(1), (8).

Para 8: sub-para (1)(b) substituted, and references to the "CMA" in sub-paras (7), (10) substituted, by SI 2014/891, arts 2, 17(1), (9).

SCHEDULE 3
OTHER PROVISIONS OF THE ACT APPLICABLE TO THE ORDER

Article 15

[2.122]

1. *(1) The following sections of Part 3 of the Act shall apply, with the modifications mentioned in sub-paragraphs (2) to (27) below, for the purposes of this Order—*

(a) . . .
(b) section 86 (enforcement orders: general provisions);
(c) section 87 (delegated power of directions);
(d) section 88 (contents of certain enforcement orders);
(e) section 89 (subject-matter of undertakings);
(f) section 91 (register of undertakings and orders);
(g) section 92 (duty of [CMA] to monitor undertakings and orders);
(h) section 93 (further role of [CMA] in relation to undertakings and orders);
(i) section 94 (rights to enforce undertakings and orders);
[(ia) section 94A (interim undertakings and orders: penalties);]
(j) section 95 (rights to enforce statutory restrictions);
(k) section 103 (duty of expedition in relation to references);
(l) section 104 (certain duties of relevant authorities to consult);
[(la) section 104A (public consultation in relation to media mergers);]
(m) section 105 (general information duties of [CMA]);
[(ma) section 106B (general advisory functions of OFCOM);]
(n) section 108 (defamation);
(o) section 109 (attendance of witnesses and production of documents etc);
(p) section 110 (enforcement of powers under section 109: general);
[(pa) section 110A (restriction on powers to impose penalties under section 110);
(pb) section 110B (section 110A: supplemental provision);]
(q) section 111 (penalties);
(r) section 112 (penalties: main procedural requirements);
(s) section 113 (payments and interest by instalments);
(t) section 114 (appeals in relation to penalties);
(u) section 115 (recovery of penalties);
(v) section 116 (statement of policy);
(w) section 117 (false or misleading information);
(x) section 118 (excisions from reports);
(y) section 119 (minority reports of [CMA]);
[(ya) section 119A (other general functions of OFCOM);]
(z) section 120 (review of decisions under Part 3);
(aa) section 124 (orders and regulations under Part 3);
(bb) section 125 (offences by bodies corporate);
(cc) section 126 (service of documents);
(dd) section 127 (associated persons);
(ee) section 128 (supply of services and market for services etc); and
(ff) section 129 (other interpretation provisions).

(2) . . .

(3) Section 86 shall apply as if—
(a) subsection (5) were omitted; and
(b) in subsection (6)—
(i) the words from "section 72" to "under", where it appears for the second time, were omitted; and
(ii) for the words "Schedule 7" there were substituted "Schedule 2 to the Enterprise Act 2002 (Protection of Legitimate Interests) Order 2003".

(4) Section 88 shall apply as if in subsection (1)—
(a) the words from "section 75" to "under" were omitted; and

(b) for the words "Schedule 7" there were substituted "Schedule 2 to the Enterprise Act 2002 (Protection of Legitimate Interests) Order 2003".

(5) Section 89 shall apply as if in subsection (2)—

(a) the words from "[section 73]" to "under", where it appears for the second time, were omitted; and

(b) for the words "Schedule 7" there were substituted "Schedule 2 to the Enterprise Act 2002 (Protection of Legitimate Interests) Order 2003".

(6) Section 91 shall apply as if—

(a) in subsections (1), (3)(a) and (b) for the words "this Part" there were substituted "the Enterprise Act 2002 (Protection of Legitimate Interests) Order 2003";

(b) in subsection (3)(d)—

(i) the words from "by the [CMA]" to "78(2) or" were omitted; and

(ii) for the words "Schedule 7" there were substituted "Schedule 2 to the Enterprise Act 2002 (Protection of Legitimate Interests) Order 2003"; and

(c) . . .

(7) Section 92 shall apply as if—

(a) in subsections (1)(b), (3)(f) and (4)(f)—

(i) the words from "in sections 77(2)" to "78(2) and" were omitted; and

(ii) for the words "Schedule 7" there were substituted "Schedule 2 to the Enterprise Act 2002 (Protection of Legitimate Interests) Order 2003";

(b), (c). . .

(d) in subsection (3)(e) for the word "to" there were substituted "and";

(e) in subsection (3)(f) the words "(4) and" were omitted;

(f) subsections (4)(a) to (d) were omitted; and

(g) in subsection (5) for the words "this Part" in both places where they appear there were substituted "the Enterprise Act 2002 (Protection of Legitimate Interests) Order 2003".

(8) Section 93 shall apply as if—

(a) . . .

(b) in subsections (1)(b), (2) and (4) for the words "Schedule 7" there were substituted "Schedule 2 to the Enterprise Act 2002 (Protection of Legitimate Interests) Order 2003";

(c), (d) . . .

(9) Section 94 shall apply as if—

(a) . . .

(b) in subsection (8) for the words "Schedule 7" there were substituted "Schedule 2 to the Enterprise Act 2002 (Protection of Legitimate Interests) Order 2003";

(c) in subsection (9) for the words "to (8)" there were substituted "and (8)".

[(9A) Section 94A shall apply as if—

(a) in subsection (1)—

(i) for the words "the appropriate authority" there were substituted "the Secretary of State"; and

(ii) for the word "it" (in both places where it occurs) there were substituted "the Secretary of State";

(b) in subsection (5), for "the appropriate authority" there were substituted "the Secretary of State";

(c) in subsection (7), for the words "the person who imposed the penalty under this section" there were substituted "the Secretary of State"; and

(d) for subsection (8) there were substituted—

"(8) In this section, "interim measure" means an order under paragraph 2 of Schedule 2 to the Enterprise Act 2002 (Protection of Legitimate Interests) Order 2003.".]

(10) Section 95 shall apply as if—

(a) in subsections (1), (3) and (6)—

(i) the words from "section 77(2)" to "78(2) or" were omitted; and

(ii) for the words "Schedule 7" there were substituted "Schedule 2 to the Enterprise Act 2002 (Protection of Legitimate Interests) Order 2003";

(b) subsection (4) were omitted;

(c) in subsection (5) for the words "Schedule 7" there were substituted "Schedule 2 to the Enterprise Act 2002 (Protection of Legitimate Interests) Order 2003"; and

(d) in subsection (6) for the words "Subsections (4) and" there were substituted "Subsection".

(11) Section 103 shall apply as if—

(a) subsection (1) were omitted; and

(b) in subsection (2) for the words "section 45 or 62" there were substituted "article 5 of the Enterprise Act 2002 (Protection of Legitimate Interests) Order 2003".

(12) Section 104 shall apply as if—

(a) in subsection (5) for the words "this Part" there were substituted "the Enterprise Act 2002 (Protection of Legitimate Interests) Order 2003";

(b) . . .

[(c) for paragraph (a) in the definition of "relevant decision" there were substituted—

"(a) in the case of the CMA, any decision by the CMA on the questions mentioned in article 6 of the Enterprise Act 2002 (Protection of Legitimate Interests) Order 2003;"]

(d) . . .

(e) in paragraph (c)(i) in the definition of "relevant decision" in subsection (6), for the words "section 45 or 62" there were substituted "article 5 of the Enterprise Act 2002 (Protection of Legitimate Interests Order) 2003"; and

(f) in paragraph (c)(ii) in the definition of "relevant decision" in subsection (6), for the words "section 49 or (as the case may be) 64" there were substituted "article 7 of the Enterprise Act 2002 (Protection of Legitimate Interests) Order 2003".

[(12A) Section 104A shall apply as if—

(a) for the words in subsection (1) there were substituted—

"(1) Subsection (2) applies where the [CMA] is preparing a report under article 5 of the Enterprise Act 2002 (Protection of Legitimate Interests) Order 2003 which specifies a media public interest consideration."; and

(b) in subsection (2) the words "or special merger situation" were omitted.]

(13) Section 105 shall apply as if—

(a) in subsection (1)—

(i) for the words from "so as to enable" to "44 or 61" there were substituted "so as to make a report under article 4 of the Enterprise Act 2002 (Protection of Legitimate Interests) Order 2003"; and

(ii) for the words from "relevant merger situation" to the end of that subsection there were substituted "European relevant merger situation concerned";

[(ab) in subsection (1A) for the words "section 44A or 61A" there were substituted "article 4A of the Enterprise Act 2002 (Protection of Legitimate Interests) Order 2003";]

(b) subsection (2) were omitted; and

(c) in subsections (3)(a) and (3)(b), (4), (5)(a) and (5)(b) and (6) for the words "this Part" there were substituted "the Enterprise Act 2002 (Protection of Legitimate Interests) Order 2003".

[(13A) Section 106B shall apply as if—

(a) for the words in subsection (1) there were substituted—

"(1) OFCOM may, in connection with any case on which they are required to give a report by virtue of article 4A of the Enterprise Act 2002 (Protection of Legitimate Interests) Order 2003, give such advice as they consider appropriate to the Secretary of State in relation to—

(a) any report made by the [CMA] under article 8 of the Enterprise Act 2002 (Protection of Legitimate Interests) Order 2003; and

(b) the taking by the Secretary of State of enforcement action under Schedule 2 to the Enterprise Act 2002 (Protection of Legitimate Interests) Order 2003";

(b) in subsection (2) for the words "section 44A or 61A" there were substituted "article 4A of the Enterprise Act 2002 (Protection of Legitimate Interests) Order 2003"; and

(c) in subsection (3) for the words "section 50 or 65" there were substituted "article 8 of the Enterprise Act 2002 (Protection of Legitimate Interests) Order 2003".]

(14) Section 108 shall apply as if for the words "this Part" there were substituted "the Enterprise Act 2002 (Protection of Legitimate Interests) Order 2003".

[(15) Section 109 shall apply as if—

(a) for subsection (A1) there were substituted—

"(A1) For the purposes of this section, the permitted purposes are assisting the CMA or the Secretary of State in carrying out any functions, including enforcement functions, of the CMA or (as the case may be) the Secretary of State under or by virtue of the Enterprise Act 2002 (Protection of Legitimate Interests) Order 2003 in connection with a matter that is or has been the subject of a reference or possible reference under article 5 of that Order."; and

(b) in subsection (8A)—

(i) paragraph (a)(ii) were omitted;

(ii) in paragraph (a)(iii), the words "75, 76, 83 or" were omitted; and

(iii) in paragraph (b)(iii), for the words "Schedule 7" there were substituted "Schedule 2 to the Enterprise Act 2002 (Protection of Legitimate Interests) Order 2003".]

(16) Section 110 shall apply as if in subsections (2) and (9) for the words from "section 39(4)" to "65(3))" there were substituted "article 9(3) of the Enterprise Act 2002 (Protection of Legitimate Interests) Order 2003".

[(16A) Section 110A shall apply as if—

(a) subsections (5) and (6) were omitted;

(b) in subsections (7) and (8)—

(i) for the words "section 109(A1)(b)" (in both places where those words occur) there were substituted "section 109(A1)"; and

(ii) for the words "section 45 or 62" (in both places where those words occur) there were substituted "article 5 of the Enterprise Act 2002 (Protection of Legitimate Interests) Order 2003".

(16B) Section 110B shall apply as if—

(a) subsections (1) and (2) were omitted;

(b) in subsection (3), in the words before paragraph (a), for the words "section 45 or 62" there were substituted "article 5 of the Enterprise Act 2002 (Protection of Legitimate Interests) Order 2003";

(c) in subsection (3)(b), for the words "Schedule 7" there were substituted "Schedule 2 to the Enterprise Act 2002 (Protection of Legitimate Interests) Order 2003";

(d) in subsection (3)(c), for the words "Schedule 7" there were substituted "Schedule 2 to the Enterprise Act 2002 (Protection of Legitimate Interests) Order 2003";

(e) subsection (3)(d) were omitted;
(f) in subsection (4), in the words before paragraph (a), for the words "section 45 or 62" there were substituted "article 5 of the Enterprise Act 2002 (Protection of Legitimate Interests) Order 2003";
(g) subsection (4)(d) were omitted; and
(h) for subsections (5) and (6) there were substituted—

"(5) Paragraph 7(8) and (9) of Schedule 2 to the Enterprise Act 2002 (Protection of Legitimate Interests) Order 2003 applies for deciding if and when a reference under article 5(2) of that Order is finally determined for the purpose of section 110A(8) as it applies for deciding those questions for the purpose of paragraph 7 of that Schedule.

(6) Paragraph 8(7) and (8) of Schedule 2 to the Enterprise Act 2002 (Protection of Legitimate Interests) Order 2003 applies for deciding if and when a reference under article 5(3) of that Order is finally determined for the purpose of section 110A(8) as it applies for deciding those questions for the purpose of the definition of "relevant period" in paragraph 8(6) of that Schedule.".]

(17) . . .

(18) Section 117 shall apply as if in subsections (1)(a) and (2) for the words "this Part" there were substituted "the Enterprise Act 2002 (Protection of Legitimate Interests) Order 2003".

(19) Section 118 shall apply as if—
(a) in subsection (1)(a) for the words "section 44 or 61" there were substituted "article 4 of the Enterprise Act 2002 (Protection of Legitimate Interests) Order 2003";
[(aa) in subsection (1)(aa) for the words "section 44A or 61A" there were substituted "article 4A of the Enterprise Act 2002 (Protection of Legitimate Interests) Order 2003";]
(b) in subsection (1)(b) for the words "section 50 or 65" there were substituted "article 8 of the Enterprise Act 2002 (Protection of Legitimate Interests) Order 2003"; and
(c) in subsection (5) for the words "sections 38(4) and 107(11)" there were substituted "article 14(8) of the Enterprise Act 2002 (Protection of Legitimate Interests) Order 2003".

(20) Section 119 shall apply as if in subsection (1) for the words "this Part", in both places where they appear, there were substituted "the Enterprise Act 2002 (Protection of Legitimate Interests) Order 2003".

[(20A) Section 119A shall apply as if in subsections (1) and (4) for the words "this Part" there were substituted "the Enterprise Act 2002 (Protection of Legitimate Interests) Order 2003".]

(21) Section 120 shall apply as if—
(a) in subsections (1) and (2)(b) for the words "this Part" there were substituted "the Enterprise Act 2002 (Protection of Legitimate Interests) Order 2003"; and
(b) in subsection (1) for the words "relevant merger situation or a special merger situation" there were substituted "European relevant merger situation".

(22) Section 124 shall apply as if—
(a) in subsections (1) and (2) for the words "this Part" there were substituted "the Enterprise Act 2002 (Protection of Legitimate Interests) Order 2003";
(b) subsections (3) and (4) and (6) to (10) were omitted; and
(c) for subsection (5) there were substituted—

"(5) An order made by the Secretary of State under section 28, [94A(3) or (6),] 111(4) or (6) or 114(3)(b) or (4)(b) as applied by the Enterprise Act 2002 (Protection of Legitimate Interests) Order 2003, or under Schedule 2 to that Order shall be subject to annulment in pursuance of a resolution of either House of Parliament.".

(23) Section 125 shall apply as if in subsections (1) and (3) for the words "this Part" there were substituted "the Enterprise Act 2002 (Protection of Legitimate Interests) Order 2003".

(24) Section 126 shall apply as if in subsections (1), (4) and (6) for the words "this Part" there were substituted "the Enterprise Act 2002 (Protection of Legitimate Interests) Order 2003".

(25) Section 127 shall apply as if in subsection (3) for the words "section 22, 33, 45 or 62" there were substituted "article 5 of the Enterprise Act 2002 (Protection of Legitimate Interests) Order 2003".

(26) Section 128 shall apply as if in subsection (1) for the words "this Part" where they appear on both occasions there were substituted "the Enterprise Act 2002 (Protection of Legitimate Interests) Order 2003".

(27) Section 129 shall apply as if in subsections (1) to (4) for the words "this Part" where they appear on all occasions there were substituted "the Enterprise Act 2002 (Protection of Legitimate Interests) Order 2003".

2. (1) The following Schedules of the Act shall apply, with the modifications mentioned in sub-paragraphs (2) and (3) below, for the purposes of this Order—
(a) Schedule 8 (provision that may be contained in certain enforcement orders); and
(b) Schedule 10 (procedural requirements for certain enforcement undertakings and orders).

(2) Schedule 8 shall apply as if—
(a) in paragraph 1 for the words "this Part and Part 4" there were substituted "the Enterprise Act 2002 (Protection of Legitimate Interests) Order 2003";
(b) in paragraph 14—
  (i) the words "an order under section 75, 83, 84, 160 or 161, or" were omitted; and
  (ii) for the words "Schedule 7" there were substituted "Schedule 2 to the Enterprise Act 2002 (Protection of Legitimate Interests) Order 2003"; . . .
[(ba) in paragraph 20A(1)(a) for the words "intervention notice" there were substituted "European intervention notice" and in paragraph 20A(1)(a)(ii) for the words "relevant merger situation" there were substituted "European relevant merger situation"; . . .]

[(bb) in paragraph 20BA—

(i) in sub-paragraph (1) for the words "Schedule 7" there were substituted "Schedule 2 to the Enterprise Act 2002 (Protection of Legitimate Interests) Order 2003" and for the words "this Part or Part 4" there were substituted "the Enterprise Act 2002 (Protection of Legitimate Interests) Order 2003"; and

(ii) in sub-paragraph (5)(a) for the words "an intervention notice or special intervention notice" there were substituted "a European intervention notice"; and]

(c) in paragraph 24 for paragraphs (a) to (c) there were substituted "the Secretary of State".

(3) Schedule 10 shall apply as if—

(a) in paragraphs 1(a) and 6(a)—

(i) the words "section 73 or 82 or" were omitted; and

(ii) for the words "Schedule 7" there were substituted "Schedule 2 to the Enterprise Act 2002 (Protection of Legitimate Interests) Order 2003";

(b) in paragraphs 1(b) and 6(b)—

(i) the words "section 75, 83 or 84 or" were omitted; and

(ii) for the words "Schedule 7" there were substituted "Schedule 2 to the Enterprise Act 2002 (Protection of Legitimate Interests) Order 2003"; and

(c) in paragraph 2(1) the words "[the CMA or (as the case may be)]" were omitted.

***3.** Section 243(1) of the Act (overseas disclosures) shall not apply to information which comes to a public authority in connection with an investigation under this Order.*

NOTES

Para 1: sub-paras (1)(la), (ma), (ya), (12A), (13)(ab), (13A), (20A) inserted by the Enterprise Act 2002 and Media Mergers (Consequential Amendments) Order 2003, SI 2003/3180, art 2, Schedule, para 10(1), (9)–(15).

All other amendments to para 1 were made by the Enterprise Act 2002 (Protection of Legitimate Interests) (Amendment) Order 2014, SI 2014/891, arts 2, 18(1)–(17).

Para 2 is amended as follows:

Word omitted from sub-para (2)(b)(ii) revoked, and sub-para (2)(ba) inserted, by SI 2003/3180, art 2, Schedule, para 10(1), (16).

Word omitted from sub-para (2)(ba) revoked, and sub-para (2)(bb) inserted, by the Enterprise Act 2002 (Specification of Additional Section 58 Consideration) Order 2020, SI 2020/627, art 4.

Words in square brackets in sub-para (3)(c) substituted by SI 2014/891, arts 2, 18(1), (18).

(Sch 4 (consequential amendments) in so far as relevant to this work, these have been incorporated where appropriate.)

ENTERPRISE ACT 2002 (ANTICIPATED MERGERS) ORDER 2003

(SI 2003/1595)

NOTES

Made: 17 June 2003.

Authority: Enterprise Act 2002, ss 34, 124(2), (3).

Commencement: 20 June 2003.

As to the application of this Order in relation to water mergers, see the Water Mergers (Modification of Enactments) Regulations 2004, SI 2004/3202, reg 10, which provides as follows—

"10 Section 34: supplementary provision in relation to anticipated mergers

(1) Section 34 (supplementary provision in relation to anticipated mergers) has effect as if, in subsection (1)(a), for the words from "this Part" to "contemplation" there were substituted "section 32(a) of the 1991 Act".

(2) The Enterprise Act 2002 (Anticipated Mergers) Order 2003 shall have effect, for the purposes of references under section 32(a) of the 1991 Act, as if it had been made under section 34 of the 2002 Act as modified by paragraph (1) and as if—

(a) in article 2, for the definition of "reference" there were substituted—

""reference" means a reference under section 32(a) of the Water Industry Act 1991;"; and

(b) in article 4, for "36(2)(a) and (b)" there were substituted "36(4)(a) and (b)".".

Transitional provisions: see the Competition (Amendment etc) (EU Exit) Regulations 2019, SI 2019/93, Sch 4, Pt 7, paras 25–27 to the 2019 Regulations (at **[7.76]**).

[2.123]

1 Citation, commencement and interpretation

This Order may be cited as the Enterprise Act 2002 (Anticipated Mergers) Order 2003 and shall come into force on 20th June 2003.

[2.124]

2

In this Order—

"the Act" means the Enterprise Act 2002;

"reference" means a reference under Part 3 of the Act which relates to arrangements which are in progress or in contemplation; and

"notice" means a notice under section 42(2) [or 59(2)] of the Act which relates to such arrangements.

NOTES

The words in square brackets in the definition "notice" were substituted (for the original words ", 59(2) or 67(2)") by the Competition (Amendment etc) (EU Exit) Regulations 2019, SI 2019/93, reg 61, Sch 2, Pt 2, para 6, as from IP completion day (as defined in the European Union (Withdrawal Agreement) Act 2020, s 39. For transitional provisions and savings in relation to the operation of the 2019 Regulations, see Sch 4 to those Regulations at **[7.69]** et seq (see, in particular, Sch 4, Pt 7, paras 25–27 to the 2019 Regulations (at **[7.76]**)).

Application in relation to water mergers: see the introductory notes to this Order *ante*.

[2.125]

3 Supplementary provision in relation to anticipated mergers

Sections 27 and 29 of the Act shall apply in relation to references and notices with the following modifications:

(a) in section 27, for subsections (5) and (6) there shall be substituted the following subsections:

"(5) The decision-making authority may, for the purposes of a reference, treat successive events to which this subsection applies as if they will occur simultaneously on the date on which the latest of the events will occur.

(6) Subsection (5) applies to successive events—

(a) which consist of—

(i) one or more than one event which has occurred within the period of two years before the date of the reference; and

(ii) one or more than one event which will occur;

(b) which are events which have occurred or will occur under or in consequence of the same arrangements or transactions, or successive arrangements or transactions between the same parties or interests; and

(c) by virtue of each of which, under or in consequence of the arrangements or the transaction or transactions concerned, any enterprises cease as between themselves to be distinct enterprises."; and

(b) in section 29, for subsections (1) to (4) there shall be substituted;

"(1) Where an enterprise will be brought under the control of a person or group of persons in the course of two or more transactions (in this section a "series of transactions") to which subsection (2) applies, those transactions may, if the decision-making authority considers it appropriate, be treated for the purposes of a reference as if they will occur simultaneously on the date on which the latest of them will occur.

(2) This subsection applies to—

(a) any transaction which has occurred or which will occur and which—

(i) enables that person or group of persons directly or indirectly to control or materially to influence the policy of any person carrying on the enterprise;

(ii) enables that person or group of persons to do so to a greater degree; or

(iii) is a step (whether direct or indirect) towards enabling that person or group of persons to do so; and

(b) any transaction which has occurred or which will occur and by virtue of which that person or group of persons acquires a controlling interest in the enterprise or, where the enterprise is carried on by a body corporate, in that body corporate.

(3) Where a series of transactions includes a transaction falling within subsection (2)(b), any transaction occurring after the occurrence of that transaction is to be disregarded for the purposes of subsection (1).

(4) Where the period within which any relevant transactions have occurred exceeds two years before the date of the reference, the relevant transactions that may be treated as mentioned in subsection (1) are any of those transactions that have occurred within the period of two years.

(4A) In subsection (4) "relevant transactions" means transactions which have occurred and which are transactions in the series of transactions.".

[2.126]

4

In the case of any reference where the [CMA] exercises its discretion under section 27(5) or 29(1) of the Act (as substituted by this Order) section 36(2)(a) and (b) of the Act shall have effect as if the words "or has resulted" were inserted after "result".

NOTES

Reference to the "CMA" substituted by the Enterprise and Regulatory Reform Act 2013 (Competition) (Consequential, Transitional and Saving Provisions) (No 2) Order 2014, SI 2014/549, art 2, Sch 1, Pt 1, para 11. For transitional provisions in relation to the abolition of the Competition Commission and the continuity of functions, etc, see art 3 of the 2014 Order at **[2.21]**.

Application in relation to water mergers: see the introductory notes to this Order *ante*.

WATER MERGERS (MODIFICATION OF ENACTMENTS) REGULATIONS 2004

(SI 2004/3202)

NOTES

Made: 2 December 2004.

Authority: Water Industry Act 1991, s 213(2)(f), Sch 4ZA, paras 1, 2.

Commencement: 29 December 2004.

References to the "European Community", "Community", etc: see the Treaty of Lisbon (Changes in Terminology) Order 2011, SI 2011/1043, which provides (with effect from 22 April 2011): (1) that for references to the "European Communities" or to the "European Community" (including references to "the Communities", "the Community", "the EC" or "the EEC") substitute references to the European Union; and (2) that "EU" should be substituted for the word "Community" (subject to certain exceptions) in references to "Community treaties", "Community customs duty", "Community institution", "Community instrument", "Community obligation", "enforceable Community right", "Community law", "Community legislation", and "Community provision". Also, where such a term is preceded by the word "a", for "a" substitute "an". For more details, see arts 3, 4, 6 of the 2011 Order as set out in the introductory notes to the Company Directors Disqualification Act 1986 preceding **[1.23]**.

See further, in relation to the application of this Order to the Isles of Scilly as it applies to the rest of England, the Isles of Scilly (Application of Water Legislation) Order 2020, SI 2020/214, art 5(i)

ARRANGEMENT OF REGULATIONS

Part 2 Statutory Instruments

[2.127]

1 Citation, commencement and interpretation

(1) These Regulations may be cited as the Water Mergers (Modification of Enactments) Regulations 2004 and shall come into force on 29th December 2004.

(2) In these Regulations—

"the 1991 Act" means the Water Industry Act 1991; and

"the 2002 Act" means the Enterprise Act 2002.

[2.128]

2 Modification of Part 3 of the 2002 Act

In its application in relation to water mergers and merger references under section 32 of the 1991 Act, Part 3 of the 2002 Act has effect with the modifications prescribed in these Regulations.

[2.129]

3 Omitted provisions

(1) Part 3 of the 2002 Act has effect as if the following provisions were omitted—

(a) section 28 (turnover test);

(b) [section 34A] (cases referred by the European Commission);

[(ba) . . .]

(c) Chapter 2, section 85 and Schedule 7 (public interest cases);

(d) sections 59 [to 66] (other special cases);

[(e) section 73 (undertakings in lieu of references under section 22 or 33);]

(f) sections 96 to 102 (merger notices); . . . [and]

[(fa) . . .]

(g) section 123 (power to alter share of supply test).

(2) Accordingly, any reference in Part 3 of the 2002 Act to those provisions (and any provisions of that Part so far as applying to them) shall be disregarded.

NOTES

Para (1) is amended as follows:

Words in square brackets in sub-para (b) inserted, sub-paras (ba), (fa) originally inserted, and words omitted from sub-para (f) revoked, by the Enterprise and Regulatory Reform Act 2013 (Competition) (Consequential, Transitional and Saving Provisions) (No 2) Order 2014, SI 2014/549, art 2, Sch 1, Pt 1, para 22(1), (2).

Sub-para (b) was revoked, and the words in square brackets in sub-para (d) were substituted (for the original words "to 68"), by the Competition (Amendment etc) (EU Exit) Regulations 2019, SI 2019/93, reg 61, Sch 2, Pt 3, para 12(1), (2), as from IP completion day (as defined in the European Union (Withdrawal Agreement) Act 2020, s 39) (for transitional provisions and savings in relation to the operation of the 2019 Regulations, see Sch 4 to those Regulations at **[7.69]** et seq).

Sub-paras (ba), (fa) subsequently revoked, sub-para (e) substituted, and word in square brackets in sub-para (f) inserted, by the Water Mergers (Miscellaneous Amendments) Regulations 2015, SI 2015/1936, regs 2(1), 3.

[2.130]

4 Sections 22 to 24: References in relation to completed mergers

Part 3 of the 2002 Act has effect as if, for sections 22 to 24, there were substituted—

"22 References in relation to completed water mergers

(1) A reference under section 32(b) of the 1991 Act shall specify—

(a) the enactment under which it is made; and

(b) the date on which it is made.

(2) In this Part "the decision-making authority" means the [CMA].

[(3) No reference shall be made under section 32(b) of the 1991 Act if the period within which the CMA is required by section 34ZA of the 2002 Act to decide whether the duty to make a reference applies has expired without such a decision having been made.]

23 Water mergers

(1) For the purposes of this Chapter and Chapter 3 of Part 2 of the 1991 Act, the question whether a water merger has taken place shall be determined as at—

(a) in the case of a reference which is treated as having been made under section 32(b) of the 1991 Act by virtue of section 37(2), such time as the [CMA] may determine; and

(b) in any other case, immediately before the time when the reference has been, or is to be, made.

(2) In this Part—

(a) "water merger" means a merger of any two or more water enterprises;

(b) "water enterprise" means an enterprise carried on by a water undertaker or sewerage undertaker; and

(c) a reference to a merger of any two or more water enterprises is a reference to those enterprises ceasing to be distinct enterprises.

24 Time-limits for enforcement action

(1) No enforcement action shall be taken on a merger reference under section 32(b) of the 1991 Act in respect of an actual merger unless the reference was made within the period of four months beginning with whichever is the later of—

(a) the day on which the merger took place; and

(b) the day on which the material facts about the transactions which resulted in the merger first came to the attention of the [CMA] or were made public.

(2) In this section "made public" means so publicised as to be generally known or readily ascertainable."

NOTES

References to the "CMA" substituted by the Enterprise and Regulatory Reform Act 2013 (Competition) (Consequential, Transitional and Saving Provisions) (No 2) Order 2014, SI 2014/549, art 2, Sch 1, Pt 1, para 22(1), (3).

In the Enterprise Act 2002, s 22 (as set out above) para (3) was added by the Water Mergers (Miscellaneous Amendments) Regulations 2015, SI 2015/1936, regs 2(1), 4.

[2.131]

5 Section 25: Extension of time-limits

Section 25 (extension of time-limits) has effect as if—

(a) [in subsections (1), (2), (4), (9) and (10)], for "section 24(1)(a) or (2)(b)" there were substituted "section 24(1)";

[(aa) in subsection (4), for "section 73" there were substituted "section 33D of the 1991 Act"; [and]]

(b) [subsections (6) to (8)] were omitted; and

(c) in subsection (9), the words "Subject to subsections (10) and (11)," were omitted;

[(d) in subsection (10)(b), for "subsections (2), (4) and (6)" there were substituted "subsections (2) and (4)"].

NOTES

Words in square brackets in paras (a) and (b) substituted, and para (aa) inserted, by the Water Mergers (Miscellaneous Amendments) Regulations 2015, SI 2015/1936, regs 2(1), 5(a)–(c).

Note also that reg 5(d) of the 2015 Regulations provides that for the existing para (c) of this regulation there is substituted a new para (d). It is unclear whether the intention was actually to substitute a new para (d) for the existing para (c), or to insert a new para (d) after the existing para (c). Both paragraphs have been included in the text above.

The word in square brackets at the end of para (aa) was inserted, and paras (b) and (d) were revoked, by the Competition (Amendment etc) (EU Exit) Regulations 2019, SI 2019/93, reg 61, Sch 2, Pt 3, para 12(1), (3), as from IP completion day (as defined in the European Union (Withdrawal Agreement) Act 2020, s 39) (for transitional provisions and savings in relation to the operation of the 2019 Regulations, see Sch 4 to those Regulations at **[7.69]** et seq).

[2.132]

6 Section 30: Relevant customer benefits

Part 3 of the 2002 Act has effect as if, for section 30 (relevant customer benefits), there were substituted—

"30 Relevant customer benefits in relation to water mergers

(1) For the purposes of this Part a benefit is a relevant customer benefit if—

(a) it is a benefit to relevant customers in the form of—

(i) lower prices, higher quality or greater choice of goods or services in any market in the United Kingdom (whether or not the market or markets in relation to which the prejudice to the Authority has, or may have, occurred or (as the case may be) may occur); or

(ii) greater innovation in relation to such goods or services; and

(b) the [CMA] believes—

(i) in the case of a merger reference under section 32(a) of the 1991 Act, as mentioned in subsection (2); and

(ii) in the case of a merger reference under section 32(b) of the 1991 Act, as mentioned in subsection (3).

(2) The belief, in the case of a merger reference under section 32(a) of the 1991 Act, is that—

(a) the benefit may be expected to accrue within a reasonable period as a result of the merger concerned; and

(b) the benefit is unlikely to accrue without the merger concerned or a similar prejudice to the Authority.

(3) The belief, in the case of a merger reference under section 32(b) of the 1991 Act, is that—

(a) the benefit has accrued as a result of the merger concerned or may be expected to accrue within a reasonable period as a result of the merger concerned; and

(b) the benefit was, or is, unlikely to accrue without the merger concerned or a similar prejudice to the Authority.

(4) In subsection (1) "relevant customers" means—

(a) customers of any person carrying on an enterprise which, in the merger concerned, has ceased to be, or (as the case may be) will cease to be, a distinct enterprise;

(b) customers of such customers; and

(c) any other customers in a chain of customers beginning with the customers mentioned in paragraph (a);

and in this subsection "customers" includes future customers.

(5) For the purposes of subsection (1) "market in the United Kingdom" includes—

(a) so far as it operates in the United Kingdom or a part of the United Kingdom, any market which operates there and in another country or territory or in a part of another country or territory; and

(b) any market which operates only in a part of the United Kingdom;

and references to a market for goods or services include references to a market for goods and services.".

NOTES

Reference to the "CMA" substituted by the Enterprise and Regulatory Reform Act 2013 (Competition) (Consequential, Transitional and Saving Provisions) (No 2) Order 2014, SI 2014/549, art 2, Sch 1, Pt 1, para 22(1), (4).

7 *(Revoked by the Enterprise and Regulatory Reform Act 2013 (Competition) (Consequential, Transitional and Saving Provisions) (No 2) Order 2014, SI 2014/549, art 2, Sch 1, Pt 1, para 22(1), (5).)*

[2.133]

8 Section 32: Supplementary provision for purposes of [section 25]

Section 32 (supplementary provision for purposes of [section 25]) has effect as if—

(a) . . .

(b) in subsection (4), the words "or (5)(b)" were omitted.

NOTES

Words in square brackets substituted, and words omitted revoked, by the Enterprise and Regulatory Reform Act 2013 (Competition) (Consequential, Transitional and Saving Provisions) (No 2) Order 2014, SI 2014/549, art 2, Sch 1, Pt 1, para 22(1), (6).

[2.134]

9 Section 33: Duty to make references in relation to anticipated mergers

[(1)] Part 3 of the 2002 Act has effect as if, for section 33 (duty to make references in relation to anticipated mergers), there were substituted—

"33 References in relation to anticipated water mergers

A reference under section 32(a) of the 1991 Act shall specify—

(a) the enactment under which it is made; and

(b) the date on which it is made.".

[(2) No reference shall be made under section 32(a) of the 1991 Act if the period within which the CMA is required by section 34ZA of the 2002 Act to decide whether the duty to make a reference applies has expired without such a decision having been made.]

NOTES

Para (1) numbered as such, and para (2) added, by the Water Mergers (Miscellaneous Amendments) Regulations 2015, SI 2015/1936, regs 2(1), 6.

[2.135]

10 Section 34: Supplementary provision in relation to anticipated mergers

(1) Section 34 (supplementary provision in relation to anticipated mergers) has effect as if, in subsection (1)(a), for the words from "this Part" to "contemplation" there were substituted "section 32(a) of the 1991 Act".

(2) The Enterprise Act 2002 (Anticipated Mergers) Order 2003 shall have effect, for the purposes of references under section 32(a) of the 1991 Act, as if it had been made under section 34 of the 2002 Act as modified by paragraph (1) and as if—

(a) in article 2, for the definition of "reference" there were substituted—

""reference" means a reference under section 32(a) of the Water Industry Act 1991;"; and

(b) in article 4, for "36(2)(a) and (b)" there were substituted "36(4)(a) and (b)".

[2.136]

[10ZA Section 34ZA: Time-limits for decisions about references

Section 34ZA (time-limits for decisions about references) has effect as if—

(a) in subsection (1)—

(i) in the words before paragraph (a), for "section 22 or 33" there were substituted "section 32(a) or (b) of the 1991 Act"; and

(ii) in paragraph (a), for "(taking account of the power under section 22(2) or (as the case may be) 33(2) and the operation of section 22(3) or (as the case may be) 33(3))" there were substituted "(taking account of the operation of sections 33(1) and 33A(4) of the 1991 Act and the power under section 33A(1) or (as the case may be) (2) of the 1991 Act)";

(b) in subsection (2)—

(i) in the words before paragraph (a), for "section 22 or 33" there were substituted "section 32(a) or (b) of the 1991 Act"; and

(ii) in paragraph (a), for "section 73" there were substituted "section 33D of the 1991 Act";

(c) in subsection (3), in the definition of "the initial period"—

(i) paragraph (a) were omitted; and

(ii) in paragraph (b), "in any other case," were omitted and the remaining text ceased to be paragraph (b); and

(d) [subsection 4] were omitted.]

NOTES

Inserted by the Water Mergers (Miscellaneous Amendments) Regulations 2015, SI 2015/1936, regs 2(1), 7.

The words in square brackets in para (d) were substituted (for the original words "subsections (4) and (5)") by the Competition (Amendment etc) (EU Exit) Regulations 2019, SI 2019/93, reg 61, Sch 2, Pt 3, para 12(1), (4), as from IP completion day (as defined in the European Union (Withdrawal Agreement) Act 2020, s 39) (for transitional provisions and savings in relation to the operation of the 2019 Regulations, see Sch 4 to those Regulations at **[7.69]** et seq).

[2.137]

[10ZB Section 34ZB: Extension of time-limit

Section 34ZB (extension of time-limits) has effect as if subsections (5) and (8) were omitted.]

NOTES

Inserted by the Water Mergers (Miscellaneous Amendments) Regulations 2015, SI 2015/1936, regs 2(1), 7.

This regulation was revoked by the Competition (Amendment etc) (EU Exit) Regulations 2019, SI 2019/93, reg 61, Sch 2, Pt 3, para 12(1), (5), as from IP completion day (as defined in the European Union (Withdrawal Agreement) Act 2020, s 39) (for transitional provisions and savings in relation to the operation of the 2019 Regulations, see Sch 4 to those Regulations at **[7.69]** et seq).

[2.138]

[10ZC Section 34ZC: Sections 34ZA and 34ZB: supplementary

Section 34ZC (sections 34ZA and 34ZB: supplementary) has effect as if the references to subsection (5) of section 34ZB were omitted.]

NOTES

Inserted by the Water Mergers (Miscellaneous Amendments) Regulations 2015, SI 2015/1936, regs 2(1), 7.

This regulation was revoked by the Competition (Amendment etc) (EU Exit) Regulations 2019, SI 2019/93, reg 61, Sch 2, Pt 3, para 12(1), (5), as from IP completion day (as defined in the European Union (Withdrawal Agreement) Act 2020, s 39) (for transitional provisions and savings in relation to the operation of the 2019 Regulations, see Sch 4 to those Regulations at **[7.69]** et seq).

[2.139]

[10A Section 34C: functions to be exercised by CMA groups

Section 34C (functions to be exercised by CMA groups) has effect as if, in subsection (1)—

(a) in the words before paragraph (a), for "section 22 or 33" there were substituted "section 32(a) or (b) of the 1991 Act",

(b) in paragraph (a), for "sections 35(6) and (7), 36(5) and (6) and" there were substituted "section", and

(c) in paragraph (b), for "section 22, section 23(9)(a)" there were substituted "section 32(b) of the 1991 Act, section 23(1)(a)".]

NOTES

Inserted by the Enterprise and Regulatory Reform Act 2013 (Competition) (Consequential, Transitional and Saving Provisions) (No 2) Order 2014, SI 2014/549, art 2, Sch 1, Pt 1, para 22(1), (7).

[2.140]

11 Sections 35 to 36: Questions to be decided in relation to mergers

Part 3 of the 2002 Act has effect as if, for sections 35 and 36, there were substituted—

"35 Questions to be decided in relation to completed water mergers

(1) Subject to section 127(3), the first questions to be decided by the [CMA] on a merger reference under section 32(b) of the 1991 Act shall be—

(a) whether a water merger has taken place; and

(b) if so, whether that merger has prejudiced, or may be expected to prejudice, the ability of the Authority, in carrying out its functions by virtue of the 1991 Act, to make comparisons between different water enterprises.

(2) Any decision of the [CMA] on a merger reference under section 32(b) of the 1991 Act that a water merger has taken place shall be treated as a decision that no water merger has taken place if the decision is not that of at least two-thirds of the members of the group constituted in connection with the reference [under Schedule 4 to the Enterprise and Regulatory Reform Act 2013].

(3) Any decision of the [CMA] on a merger reference under section 32(b) of the 1991 Act that a water merger has prejudiced, or may be expected to prejudice, the ability of the Authority, in carrying out its functions by virtue of the 1991 Act, to make comparisons between different water enterprises shall be treated as a decision that the water merger has not prejudiced, or may be expected not to prejudice, that ability of the Authority if the decision is not that of at least two-thirds of the members of the group constituted in connection with the reference [under Schedule 4 to the Enterprise and Regulatory Reform Act 2013].

(4) For the purposes of this Part there is a prejudicial outcome if—

(a) a water merger has taken place and that merger has prejudiced, or may be expected to prejudice, the ability of the Authority, in carrying out its functions by virtue of the 1991 Act, to make comparisons between different water enterprises; or

(b) arrangements are in progress which, if carried into effect, will result in a water merger and that merger may be expected to prejudice the ability of the Authority, in carrying out its functions by virtue of the 1991 Act, to make comparisons between different water enterprises.

(5) The [CMA] shall, if it has decided on a reference under section 32(b) of the 1991 Act that there is a prejudicial outcome (within the meaning given by subsection (4)(a)), decide the following additional questions—

(a) whether action should be taken by it under section 41(2) for the purpose of remedying, mitigating or preventing the prejudice to the Authority or any adverse effect which has resulted from, or may be expected to result from, the prejudice to the Authority;

(b) whether it should recommend the taking of action by others for the purpose of remedying, mitigating or preventing the prejudice to the Authority or any adverse effect which has resulted from, or may be expected to result from, the prejudice to the Authority; and

(c) in either case, if action should be taken, what action should be taken and what is to be remedied, mitigated or prevented.

(6) In deciding the questions mentioned in subsection (5) the [CMA] shall, in particular, have regard to the need to achieve as comprehensive a solution as is reasonable and practicable to the prejudice to the Authority and any adverse effects resulting from it.

(7) In deciding, on a merger reference under section 32(b) of the 1991 Act, whether to take action for the purpose of remedying, mitigating or preventing the prejudice to the Authority or any adverse effect which has resulted from, or may be expected to result from, the prejudice to the Authority and, if so, what action should be taken, the [CMA] may, in particular, have regard to the effect of any such action on any relevant customer benefits in relation to the merger concerned provided that—

(a) a consideration of those benefits would not prevent a solution to the prejudice concerned; or

(b) the benefits which have accrued, or may be expected to accrue, are substantially more important than the prejudice concerned.

36 Questions to be decided in relation to anticipated water mergers

(1) Subject to section 127(3), the first questions to be decided by the [CMA] on a merger reference under section 32(a) of the 1991 Act shall be—

(a) whether arrangements are in progress which, if carried into effect, will result in a water merger; and

(b) if so, whether that merger may be expected to prejudice the ability of the Authority, in carrying out its functions by virtue of the 1991 Act, to make comparisons between different water enterprises.

(2) Any decision of the [CMA] on a merger reference under section 32(a) of the 1991 Act that arrangements are in progress which, if carried into effect, will result in a water merger shall be treated as a decision that no arrangements are in progress which, if carried into effect, will result in a water merger if the decision is not that of at least two-thirds of the members of the group constituted in connection with the reference [under Schedule 4 to the Enterprise and Regulatory Reform Act 2013].

(3) Any decision of the [CMA] on a merger reference under section 32(a) of the 1991 Act that a water merger may be expected to prejudice the ability of the Authority, in carrying out its functions by virtue of the 1991 Act, to make comparisons between different water enterprises shall be treated as a decision that the water merger may be expected not to prejudice that ability of the Authority if the decision is not that of at least two-thirds of the members of the group constituted in connection with the reference [under Schedule 4 to the Enterprise and Regulatory Reform Act 2013].

(4) The [CMA] shall, if it has decided on a reference under section 32(a) of the 1991 Act that there is a prejudicial outcome within the meaning given by section 35(4)(b), decide the following additional questions—

(a) whether action should be taken by it under section 41(2) for the purpose of remedying, mitigating or preventing the prejudice to the Authority or any adverse effect which may be expected to result from the prejudice to the Authority;

(b) whether it should recommend the taking of action by others for the purpose of remedying, mitigating or preventing the prejudice to the Authority or any adverse effect which may be expected to result from the prejudice to the Authority; and

(c) in either case, if action should be taken, what action should be taken and what is to be remedied, mitigated or prevented.

(5) In deciding the questions mentioned in subsection (4) the [CMA] shall, in particular, have regard to the need to achieve as comprehensive a solution as is reasonable and practicable to the prejudice to the Authority and any adverse effects resulting from it.

(6) In deciding, on a merger reference under section 32(a) of the 1991 Act, whether to take action for the purpose of remedying, mitigating or preventing the prejudice to the Authority or any adverse effect which may be expected to result from the prejudice to the Authority and, if so, what action should be taken, the [CMA] may, in particular, have regard to the effect of any such action on any relevant customer benefits in relation to the merger concerned provided that—

(a) a consideration of those benefits would not prevent a solution to the prejudice concerned; or

(b) the benefits which may be expected to accrue are substantially more important than the prejudice concerned.".

NOTES

All words in square brackets were substituted by the Enterprise and Regulatory Reform Act 2013 (Competition) (Consequential, Transitional and Saving Provisions) (No 2) Order 2014, SI 2014/549, art 2, Sch 1, Pt 1, para 22(1), (8).

[2.141]

12 Section 37: Cancellation and variation of references

Section 37 (cancellation and variation of references) has effect as if—

(a) in subsection (1), for "section 33" there were substituted "section 32(a) of the 1991 Act"; and

(b) for subsections (2) and (3) there were substituted—

"(2) The [CMA] may, if it considers that doing so is justified by the facts (including events occurring on or after the making of the reference concerned), treat a reference made under paragraph (a) or paragraph (b) of section 32 of the 1991 Act as if it had been made under paragraph (b) or (as the case may be) paragraph (a) of that section; and, in such cases, references in this Part to references under those paragraphs shall, so far as may be necessary, be construed accordingly.

(3) Where, by virtue of subsection (2), the [CMA] treats a reference made under paragraph (a) or paragraph (b) of section 32 of the 1991 Act as if it had been made under paragraph (b) or (as the case may be) paragraph (a) of that section, sections 77 to 81 shall, in particular, apply as if the reference had been made under paragraph (b) or (as the case may be) paragraph (a) of section 32 of that Act instead of under paragraph (a) or paragraph (b) of that section.";

(c) in subsection (4), for "section 22 or 33 as if it had been made under section 33 or (as the case may be) 22" there were substituted "paragraph (a) or paragraph (b) of section 32 of the 1991 Act as if it had been made under paragraph (b) or (as the case may be) paragraph (a) of that section";
(d) in subsection (5)(a)—
  (i) for "section 22" there were substituted "section 32(a) of the 1991 Act"; and
  (ii) for "section 33" there were substituted "section 32(b) of that Act";
(e) in subsection (5)(b)—
  (i) for "section 33" there were substituted "section 32(b) of the 1991 Act"; and
  (ii) for "section 22" there were substituted "section 32(a) of that Act"; and
(f) in subsection (6), for "section 22 or 33" there were substituted "section 32(a) or (b) of the 1991 Act".

NOTES

Reference to the "CMA" substituted by the Enterprise and Regulatory Reform Act 2013 (Competition) (Consequential, Transitional and Saving Provisions) (No 2) Order 2014, SI 2014/549, art 2, Sch 1, Pt 1, para 22(1), (9).

[2.142]
13 Section 38: Investigations and reports on references

Section 38 (investigations and reports on references) has effect as if—
(a) in subsection (1), for "section 22 or 33" there were substituted "section 32 of the 1991 Act"; and
(b) in subsection (2)—
  (i) in paragraph (b), the word "and" were omitted; and
  (ii) after paragraph (c), there were inserted—

"; and
(d) if the merger reference is under section 32(b) of the 1991 Act and the [CMA] is satisfied that the reference was not made within the period of four months mentioned in section 24, a statement of that fact.".

NOTES

Reference to the "CMA" substituted by the Enterprise and Regulatory Reform Act 2013 (Competition) (Consequential, Transitional and Saving Provisions) (No 2) Order 2014, SI 2014/549, art 2, Sch 1, Pt 1, para 22(1), (10).

[2.143]
[13A Section 39: Time-limits for investigations and report]

Section 39 (time-limits for investigations and reports) has effect as if, in subsection (8A), for "section 33" there were substituted "section 32(a) of the 1991 Act".]

NOTES

Inserted by the Enterprise and Regulatory Reform Act 2013 (Competition) (Consequential, Transitional and Saving Provisions) (No 2) Order 2014, SI 2014/549, art 2, Sch 1, Pt 1, para 22(1), (11).

[2.144]
14 Section 40: Section 39: supplementary

Section 40 (section 39: supplementary) has effect as if, in subsection (10), for "section 22 or 33" there were substituted "section 32 of the 1991 Act".

[2.145]
15 Section 41: Duty to remedy effects of completed or anticipated mergers

Section 41 (duty to remedy effects of completed or anticipated mergers) has effect as if—
(a) in subsection (1), for "an anti-competitive" there were substituted "a prejudicial";
(b) in paragraphs (a) and (b) of subsection (2), and in subsection (4), for "substantial lessening of competition" there were substituted "prejudice to the Authority ";
(c) in subsection (3)—
  (i) for "35(3)" there were substituted "35(5)"; and
  (ii) for "36(2)" there were substituted "36(4)"; and
(d) for subsection (5) there were substituted—

"(5) In making a decision under subsection (2), the [CMA] may, in particular, have regard to the effect of any action on any relevant customer benefits in relation to the merger concerned in accordance with section 35(7) or (as the case may be) section 36(6)".

NOTES

Reference to the "CMA" substituted by the Enterprise and Regulatory Reform Act 2013 (Competition) (Consequential, Transitional and Saving Provisions) (No 2) Order 2014, SI 2014/549, art 2, Sch 1, Pt 1, para 22(1), (12).

16 (*Revoked by the Enterprise and Regulatory Reform Act 2013 (Competition) (Consequential, Transitional and Saving Provisions) (No 2) Order 2014, SI 2014/549, art 2, Sch 1, Pt 1, para 22(1), (13).*)

[2.146]
17 Section 72: Initial enforcement orders: [completed or anticipated mergers]

Section 72 (initial enforcement orders: [completed or anticipated mergers]) has effect as if—
[(a) in subsection (1)—
  [(i) in paragraph (a), for "section 22 or 33" there were substituted "section 32(a) or (b) of the 1991 Act"; and]
  (ii) in paragraph (b), after "two or more" (in both places where it occurs), there were inserted "water";]

(b) . . .
(c) . . . and
(d) in subsection (6)—
[(i) in paragraph (a), for "section 22 or 33" there were substituted "section 32(a) or (b) of the 1991 Act";]
[(ia) in paragraph (b), for "section 73" there were substituted "section 33D of the 1991 Act"; and]
[(ii) in paragraph (d), for "section 22 or 33" there were substituted "section 32(a) or (b) of the 1991 Act"].

NOTES

The words in square brackets in the regulation heading, the words "completed or anticipated mergers" in square brackets, and para (a) were substituted, and paras (b), (c) were revoked, by the Enterprise and Regulatory Reform Act 2013 (Competition) (Consequential, Transitional and Saving Provisions) (No 2) Order 2014, SI 2014/549, art 2, Sch 1, Pt 1, para 22(1), (14).

The other words in square brackets were substituted or inserted by the Water Mergers (Miscellaneous Amendments) Regulations 2015, SI 2015/1936, regs 2(1), 8.

[2.147]

[17A Section 73A: Time-limits for consideration of undertakings

Section 73A (time-limits for consideration of undertakings) has effect as if—
(a) in subsection (1)—
(i) in the words before paragraph (a), for "section 73(2)" there were substituted "section 33D(1) of the 1991 Act"; and
(ii) paragraph (b) and the "or" preceding it were omitted; and
(b) in subsection (2), for "section 73(2)" there were substituted "section 33D(1) of the 1991 Act".]

NOTES

Inserted by the Water Mergers (Miscellaneous Amendments) Regulations 2015, SI 2015/1936, regs 2(1), 9.

Sub-para (a)(ii) was revoked by the Competition (Amendment etc) (EU Exit) Regulations 2019, SI 2019/93, reg 61, Sch 2, Pt 3, para 12(1), (6), as from IP completion day (as defined in the European Union (Withdrawal Agreement) Act 2020, s 39) (for transitional provisions and savings in relation to the operation of the 2019 Regulations, see Sch 4 to those Regulations at **[7.69]** et seq).

[2.148]

[17B Section 74: Effect of undertakings under section 73

Section 74 (effect of undertakings under section 73) has effect as if—
(a) in the heading, for "section 73" there were substituted "section 33D of the 1991 Act";
(b) in subsection (1)—
(i) in the words before paragraph (a), for "relevant authority shall not make a reference under section 22, 33 or 45" there were substituted "CMA shall not make a reference under section 32(a) or (b) of the 1991 Act"; and
(ii) in paragraph (a), for "section 73" there were substituted "section 33D of the 1991 Act"; and
(c) subsection (5) were omitted.]

NOTES

Inserted by the Water Mergers (Miscellaneous Amendments) Regulations 2015, SI 2015/1936, regs 2(1), 9.

[2.149]

[17C Section 75: Order making power where undertakings under section 73 not fulfilled etc

Section 75 (order making power where undertakings under section 73 not fulfilled etc) has effect as if—
(a) in the heading, for "section 73" there were substituted "section 33D of the 1991 Act";
(b) in subsection (1)(a), for "section 73" there were substituted "section 33D of the 1991 Act";
(c) in subsection (2), for "section 73(2)" there were substituted "section 33D(2) of the 1991 Act"; and
(d) for subsection (3) there were substituted—

"(3) Subsections (4) and (5) of section 33D of the 1991 Act shall apply for the purposes of subsection (2) above as they apply for the purposes of subsection (1) of that section.".]

NOTES

Inserted by the Water Mergers (Miscellaneous Amendments) Regulations 2015, SI 2015/1936, regs 2(1), 9.

[2.150]

18 Section 77: Restrictions on certain dealings: completed mergers

Section 77 (restrictions on certain dealings: completed mergers) has effect as if—
(a) in paragraph (a) of subsection (1), for "section 22" there were substituted "section 32(b) of the 1991 Act"; and
(b) in paragraph (b) of subsection (1)—
(i) for "relevant merger situation" there were substituted "water merger"; and
(ii) for "that situation" there were substituted "that merger".

[2.151]

19 Section 78: Restrictions on certain share dealings: anticipated mergers

Section 78 (restrictions on certain share dealings: anticipated mergers) has effect as if—
(a) in paragraph (a) of subsection (1), for "section 33" there were substituted "section 32(a) of the 1991 Act "; and
(b) in paragraph (b) of subsection (1)—
(i) for "relevant merger situation" there were substituted "proposed water merger"; and

(ii) for "that situation" there were substituted "that merger".

[2.152]

20 Section 79: Sections 77 and 78: further interpretation provisions

Section 79 (sections 77 and 78: further interpretation provisions) has effect as if—

(a) in subsections (1) and (2), for "section 22 or 33" there were substituted "section 32(a) or (b) of the 1991 Act"; and

(b) in paragraphs (c), (d) and (e) of subsection (1), for "an anti–competitive" there were substituted "a prejudicial".

[2.153]

21 Section 80: Interim undertakings

Section 80 (interim undertakings) has effect as if, in subsections (1), (7) and (8), for "section 22 or 33" there were substituted "section 32(a) or (b) of the 1991 Act".

[2.154]

22 Section 81: Interim orders

Section 81 (interim orders) has effect as if, in subsections (1), (7) and (8), for "section 22 or 33" there were substituted "section 32(a) or (b) of the 1991 Act".

[2.155]

23 Section 82: Final undertakings

Section 82 (final undertakings) has effect as if, in subsections (3) and (4), for "section 22 or 33" there were substituted "section 32(a) or (b) of the 1991 Act".

[2.156]

24 Section 84: Final orders

Section 84 (final orders) has effect as if, in subsection (5), for "section 22 or 33" there were substituted "section 32(a) or (b) of the 1991 Act".

[2.157]

[24A Section 89: Subject-matter of undertakings

Section 89 (subject-matter of undertakings) has effect as if for subsection (2) there were substituted—

"(2) In this Part "enforcement undertaking" means an undertaking under section 33D of the 1991 Act or an undertaking under section 80 or 82.".]

NOTES

Inserted by the Water Mergers (Miscellaneous Amendments) Regulations 2015, SI 2015/1936, regs 2(1), 10.

25 *(Revoked by the Enterprise and Regulatory Reform Act 2013 (Competition) (Consequential, Transitional and Saving Provisions) (No 2) Order 2014, SI 2014/549, art 2, Sch 1, Pt 1, para 22(1), (15).)*

[2.158]

[25A Section 103: Duty of expedition in relation to references

Section 103 (duty of expedition in relation to references) has effect as if in subsection (1), after "making and determining references under this Part" there were inserted "or under sections 32 to 35 of the 1991 Act".]

NOTES

Inserted by the Water Mergers (Miscellaneous Amendments) Regulations 2015, SI 2015/1936, regs 2(1), 11.

[2.159]

26 Section 104: Certain duties of relevant authorities to consult

Section 104 (certain duties of relevant authorities to consult) has effect as if, in subsection (6), in the definition of "relevant decision"—

[(a) in sub-paragraph (i) of paragraph (a), for "section 22 or 33 or accept undertakings under section 73" there were substituted "section 32(a) or (b) of the 1991 Act or accept undertakings under section 33D of that Act"; and]

(b) [in sub-paragraph (iii) of paragraph (a)], for " (3), 36(1) or (2)" there were substituted " (5), 36(1) or (4)".

NOTES

Para (a) substituted by the Water Mergers (Miscellaneous Amendments) Regulations 2015, SI 2015/1936, regs 2(1), 12.

Words in square brackets in para (b) substituted by the Enterprise and Regulatory Reform Act 2013 (Competition) (Consequential, Transitional and Saving Provisions) (No 2) Order 2014, SI 2014/549, art 2, Sch 1, Pt 1, para 22(1), (16).

[2.160]

27 Section 105: General information duties of OFT and Commission

Section 105 (general information duties of OFT and Commission) has effect as if, in subsection (1)—

[(a) for "section 22 or 33" there were substituted "section 32(a) or (b) of the 1991 Act"; and]

(b) for "creation of the relevant merger situation" there were substituted "water merger".

NOTES

Para (a) substituted by the Water Mergers (Miscellaneous Amendments) Regulations 2015, SI 2015/1936, regs 2(1), 13.

[2.161]

[28 Section 106: Advice and information about references under sections 22 and 33

Section 106 (advice and information about references under sections 22 and 33) has effect as if—

(a) in the heading, for "sections 22 and 33" there were substituted "section 32 of the 1991 Act";
(b) in subsection (1), for "section 22 or 33" there were substituted "section 32(a) or (b) of the 1991 Act"; and
(c) in subsection (6), after "a function conferred by this Part" there were inserted "or by sections 32 to 35 of the 1991 Act".]

NOTES

Substituted by the Water Mergers (Miscellaneous Amendments) Regulations 2015, SI 2015/1936, regs 2(1), 14.

[2.162]

29 Section 107: Further publicity requirements

Section 107 (further publicity requirements) has effect as if—

(a) in subsection (1)—
  (i) in paragraphs (a) and (b), for "section 22 or 33" there were substituted "section 32(a) or (b) of the 1991 Act"; and
  [(ii) in paragraph (aa), for "subsection (2)(b) of section 33" there were substituted "section 33A(1)(a) of the 1991 Act";
  (iii) in paragraph (ab), "paragraph (b) of" were omitted;
  (iv) paragraphs (ae) to (ah) were omitted;
  (v) paragraph (c) were omitted;
  (vi) in paragraph (eb), for "section 73" there were substituted "section 33D of the 1991 Act;" and
  (vii) paragraph (i) were omitted; and]
(b) in subsection (2)—
  (i) in paragraph (a), for "section 33" there were substituted "section 32(a) of the 1991 Act"; . . .
  (ii) in paragraph (b), for "section 22 or 33 as if it had been made under section 33 or (as the case may be) 22" there were substituted "paragraph (a) or paragraph (b) of section 32 of the 1991 Act as if it had been made under paragraph (b) or (as the case may be) paragraph (a) of that section"[; and
  (iii) paragraphs (g) to (m) were omitted;
(c) in subsection (3), paragraphs (b) to (j) were omitted; and
(d) subsections (6) to (11) were omitted].

NOTES

Sub-para (a)(ii)–(vii) substituted (for the original sub-para (a)(ii)), words omitted from sub-para (b)(i) revoked, and final words in square brackets added, by the Water Mergers (Miscellaneous Amendments) Regulations 2015, SI 2015/1936, regs 2(1), 15.

Sub-para (a)(iv) was revoked by the Competition (Amendment etc) (EU Exit) Regulations 2019, SI 2019/93, reg 61, Sch 2, Pt 3, para 12(1), (7), as from IP completion day (as defined in the European Union (Withdrawal Agreement) Act 2020, s 39) (for transitional provisions and savings in relation to the operation of the 2019 Regulations, see Sch 4 to those Regulations at **[7.69]** et seq).

[2.163]

[29A Section 108: Defamation

Section 108 (defamation) has effect as if after "under this Part" there were inserted "or sections 32 to 35 of the 1991 Act".]

NOTES

Inserted by the Water Mergers (Miscellaneous Amendments) Regulations 2015, SI 2015/1936, regs 2(1), 16.

[2.164]

30 Section 109: Attendance of witnesses and production of documents etc

Section 109 (attendance of witnesses and production of documents etc) has effect as if, [in subsection (A1)(a)—

(a) after "this Part" there were inserted "or section 32 of the 1991 Act", and
(b) for "section 22 or 33" there were substituted "section 32(a) or (b) of the 1991 Act]".

NOTES

Words in square brackets substituted by the Enterprise and Regulatory Reform Act 2013 (Competition) (Consequential, Transitional and Saving Provisions) (No 2) Order 2014, SI 2014/549, art 2, Sch 1, Pt 1, para 22(1), (19).

[2.165]

[30A Section 110A: Restriction on powers to impose penalties under section 110

Section 110A has effect as if—

(a) in subsections (5) and (6), for "section 22 or 33" there were substituted "section 32(a) or (b) of the 1991 Act . . .
(b) . . .]

NOTES

Inserted by the Enterprise and Regulatory Reform Act 2013 (Competition) (Consequential, Transitional and Saving Provisions) (No 2) Order 2014, SI 2014/549, art 2, Sch 1, Pt 1, para 22(1), (20).

Para (b) and the preceding word revoked by the Water Mergers (Miscellaneous Amendments) Regulations 2015, SI 2015/1936, regs 2(1), 17.

[2.166]

[30B Section 110B: Section 110A: supplementary provision

Section 110B (section 110A: supplementary provision) has effect as if—

(a) in subsection (1)—

(i) in the words before paragraph (a), for "section 22 or 33", there were substituted "section 32(a) or (b) of the 1991 Act"; [and]

(ii) in paragraphs (b) and (c), for "section 73", there were substituted "section 33D of the 1991 Act"; *and*

(iii) paragraph (e) were omitted;

(b) in subsection (2)—

(i) in the words before paragraph (a), for "section 22 or 33", there were substituted "section 32(a) or (b) of the 1991 Act"; and

(ii) paragraph (e) were omitted; and

(c) subsections (3) to (6) were omitted.]

NOTES

Inserted by the Water Mergers (Miscellaneous Amendments) Regulations 2015, SI 2015/1936, regs 2(1), 18.

The word in square brackets at the end of sub-para (a)(i) was inserted, and all words in italics were revoked, by the Competition (Amendment etc) (EU Exit) Regulations 2019, SI 2019/93, reg 61, Sch 2, Pt 3, para 12(1), (8), as from IP completion day (as defined in the European Union (Withdrawal Agreement) Act 2020, s 39) (for transitional provisions and savings in relation to the operation of the 2019 Regulations, see Sch 4 to those Regulations at **[7.69]** et seq).

[2.167]

31 Section 117: False or misleading information

Section 117 (false or misleading information) has effect as if, in subsections (1) and (2), after the word "Part" there were inserted "or section 32 of the 1991 Act".

[2.168]

[31A Section 119: Minority reports of CMA

Section 119 (minority reports of CMA) has effect as if, in subsection (1), for "this Part" there were substituted "section 32 of the 1991 Act".]

NOTES

Inserted by the Water Mergers (Miscellaneous Amendments) Regulations 2015, SI 2015/1936, regs 2(1), 19.

[2.169]

32 Section 120: Review of decisions under Part 3

Section 120 (review of decisions under Part 3) has effect as if—

[(za) in the heading, after "Part 3" there were inserted "or sections 32 to 35 of the 1991 Act";]

(a) for subsection (1), there were substituted—

"(1) Any person aggrieved by a decision of the [CMA] under this Part or [sections 32 to 35 of the 1991 Act] in connection with a reference or possible reference in relation to a water merger may apply to the Competition Appeal Tribunal for a review of that decision."; *and*

[(aa) subsection (1A) were omitted; and]

(b) in subsection (2)(b), after the words "this Part" there were inserted "[or sections 32 to 35 of the 1991 Act]".

NOTES

Reference to the "CMA" substituted by the Enterprise and Regulatory Reform Act 2013 (Competition) (Consequential, Transitional and Saving Provisions) (No 2) Order 2014, SI 2014/549, art 2, Sch 1, Pt 1, para 22(1), (21).

The word in italics in para (a) was revoked, and para (aa) was inserted, by the Competition (Amendment etc) (EU Exit) Regulations 2019, SI 2019/93, reg 61, Sch 2, Pt 3, para 12(1), (8A), as from IP completion day (as defined in the European Union (Withdrawal Agreement) Act 2020, s 39) (for transitional provisions and savings in relation to the operation of the 2019 Regulations, see Sch 4 to those Regulations at **[7.69]** et seq). Note that Sch 2, Pt 3, para 12(8A) to the 2019 Regulations was inserted by the Competition (Amendment etc) (EU Exit) Regulations 2020, SI 2020/1343, reg 33, with effect from immediately before IP completion day.

All other words in square brackets in this regulation were inserted or substituted by the Water Mergers (Miscellaneous Amendments) Regulations 2015, SI 2015/1936, regs 2(1), 20.

[2.170]

33 Section 122: Primacy of EC law

Section 122 (primacy of EC law) has effect as if—

(a) in subsection (1), after the word "Part" there were inserted "or sections 32 to 35 of the 1991 Act"; and

(b) subsections (2) to (5) were omitted.

NOTES

This regulation was revoked by the Competition (Amendment etc) (EU Exit) Regulations 2019, SI 2019/93, reg 61, Sch 2, Pt 3, para 12(1), (9), as from IP completion day (as defined in the European Union (Withdrawal Agreement) Act 2020, s 39) (for transitional provisions and savings in relation to the operation of the 2019 Regulations, see Sch 4 to those Regulations at **[7.69]** et seq).

References to the European Community and related expressions: see the note "References to "the European Community", "Community", etc" in the introductory notes to these Regulations.

[2.171]
34 Section 127: Associated persons

Section 127 (associated persons) has effect as if, in subsection (3), for "section 22, 33, 45 or 62" there were substituted "section 32(a) or (b) of the 1991 Act".

[2.172]
35 Section 129: Other interpretation provisions

Section 129 (other interpretation provisions) has effect as if, in subsection (1), the following definitions were inserted—

(a) before the definition of "action"—

""the 1991 Act" means the Water Industry Act 1991;";

(b) before the definition of "business"—

""the Authority" means the Water Services Regulation Authority or, until the coming into force of section 36 of the Water Act 2003, the Director General of Water Services;".

[2.173]
[36 Schedule 10: procedural requirements for certain enforcement undertakings and orders

Schedule 10 (procedural requirements for certain enforcement undertakings and orders) has effect as if, in paragraphs 1(a) and 6(a), for "section 73 or 82 or paragraph 3 or 9 of Schedule 7" there were substituted "section 33D of the 1991 Act or section 82 of, or paragraph 3 or 9 of Schedule 7 to, this Act".]

NOTES

Added by the Water Mergers (Miscellaneous Amendments) Regulations 2015, SI 2015/1936, regs 2(1), 21.

[2.174]
[37 Review

(1) The Secretary of State must—

(a) carry out reviews of these Regulations; and
(b) for each review, publish a report setting out the conclusions of the review.

(2) The reports must, in particular—

(a) set out the objectives intended to be achieved by these Regulations;
(b) assess the extent to which those objective are achieved; and
(c) assess whether those objectives remain appropriate, and if so, the extent to which they could be achieved with a system that imposes less regulation.

(3) The first report must be published by 17th December 2020.

(4) Subsequent reports must be published at intervals not exceeding five years.]

NOTES

Added by the Water Mergers (Miscellaneous Amendments) Regulations 2015, SI 2015/1936, regs 2(1), 22.

ENTERPRISE ACT 2002 (MERGERS) (INTERIM MEASURES: FINANCIAL PENALTIES) (DETERMINATION OF CONTROL AND TURNOVER) ORDER 2014

(SI 2014/533)

NOTES

Made: 6 March 2014.
Authority: Enterprise Act 2002, ss 94A(3)–(5), 124(2).
Commencement: 1 April 2014.

[2.175]
1 Citation and commencement

This Order may be cited as the Enterprise Act 2002 (Mergers) (Interim Measures: Financial Penalties) (Determination of Control and Turnover) Order 2014 and comes into force on 1st April 2014.

[2.176]
2 Control of an enterprise

(1) For the purposes of section 94A(2) of the Enterprise Act 2002 (penalty for breach of interim undertakings and orders), an enterprise is to be treated as controlled by a person (P) where—

(a) the enterprise is carried on by P otherwise than in partnership or as a member of an unincorporated association or group of persons;
(b) the enterprise is carried on by a body corporate in which P has a controlling interest;
(c) the enterprise is carried on by a body corporate, and P is able directly or indirectly to control or materially to influence the policy of that body corporate without having a controlling interest in that body corporate;
(d) the enterprise is carried on by a partnership or by an unincorporated association or group of persons, and P (whether or not P is a member of that partnership, association or group) is able directly or indirectly to control or materially to influence the policy of that partnership, association or group in carrying on the enterprise; or

(e) the enterprise is carried on by an individual, and P is able directly or indirectly to control or materially to influence the policy of that individual in carrying on the enterprise.

(2) For the purposes of paragraph (1)(b) and (c), P has a controlling interest in a body corporate if P—

(a) is a parent undertaking of that body corporate within the meaning of section 1162 of the Companies Act 2006; or

(b) would be a parent undertaking of that body corporate within the meaning of that section if P were an undertaking within the meaning of section 1161 of that Act.

(3) For the purposes of paragraph (2), subsections (2)(c) and (4)(a) of section 1162 of the Companies Act 2006 are to be disregarded.

(4) For the purposes of paragraph (1)(c), (d) and (e) the appropriate authority may, having regard to all the circumstances, determine whether any person is able directly or indirectly to control or materially to influence the policy of a body corporate or the policy of an individual or a partnership or an unincorporated association or group of persons in carrying on an enterprise.

(5) References in this article to a body corporate include a body incorporated outside the United Kingdom; and references to a partnership or an unincorporated association or group of persons include a partnership or unincorporated association or group of persons formed or established, or having any members incorporated, formed or established, outside the United Kingdom.

[2.177]

3 Turnover of an enterprise

(1) For the purposes of section 94A(2) of the Enterprise Act 2002 (penalty for breach of interim undertakings and orders), the turnover of an enterprise is the turnover of the enterprise in its relevant accounting period, determined in accordance with the Schedule.

(2) An enterprise's "relevant accounting period" is its accounting period immediately preceding the date on which the interim measure in question came into force.

(3) An "accounting period" of an enterprise is a period of more than six months in respect of which accounts are prepared or required to be prepared in relation to the enterprise.

(4) Where for the purposes of paragraph (1) the figures necessary for the appropriate authority to calculate the turnover of an enterprise in its relevant accounting period are not available to the appropriate authority when the appropriate authority decides to impose the penalty under section 94A(1) of the Enterprise Act 2002, the turnover of the enterprise is its turnover in its accounting period immediately preceding its relevant accounting period, determined in accordance with the Schedule.

(5) Where paragraph (4) applies but the figures necessary for the appropriate authority to calculate the turnover of an enterprise in its accounting period immediately preceding its relevant accounting period are not available to the appropriate authority when the appropriate authority decides to impose the penalty under section 94A(1) of the Enterprise Act 2002, the turnover of the enterprise for the purposes of section 94A(2) of that Act is its turnover, determined in accordance with the Schedule, in the period beginning with the day after the last day of its relevant accounting period and ending with the date on which the interim measure in question came into force.

(6) Where paragraph (4) applies but the enterprise has no accounting period immediately preceding its relevant accounting period, the turnover of the enterprise for the purposes of section 94A(2) of the Enterprise Act 2002 is its turnover, determined in accordance with the Schedule, in the period beginning with the date on which the activities constituting the enterprise began to be carried on and ending with the date on which the enterprise's relevant accounting period began.

(7) Where paragraph (6) applies but the figures necessary for the appropriate authority to calculate the turnover of the enterprise in the period beginning with the date on which the activities constituting the enterprise began to be carried on and ending with the date on which its relevant accounting period began are not available to the appropriate authority, the turnover of the enterprise for the purposes of section 94A(2) of the Enterprise Act 2002 is its turnover, determined in accordance with the Schedule, in the period beginning with the day after the last day of its relevant accounting period and ending with the date on which the interim measure in question came into force.

(8) Where for the purposes of paragraph (1) an enterprise has no relevant accounting period, the turnover of the enterprise for the purposes of section 94A(2) of the Enterprise Act 2002 is its turnover, determined in accordance with the Schedule, in the period beginning with the date on which the activities constituting the enterprise began to be carried on and ending with the date on which the interim measure in question came into force.

(9) Where an enterprise's relevant accounting period or other period in which its turnover is required to be determined by this article does not equal 12 months, the turnover of the enterprise in that period is the amount which bears the same proportion to the turnover of the enterprise in that period, determined in accordance with the Schedule, as 12 months does to that period.

SCHEDULE
TURNOVER OF AN ENTERPRISE

Article 3

[2.178]

1 Interpretation

(1) In this Schedule—

"credit institution" means a credit institution as defined in Article 4(1)(1) of Regulation (EU) No 575/2013 of the European Parliament and of the Council of 26th June 2013 on prudential requirements for credit institutions and investment firms and amending Regulation (EU) No 648/2012;

"financial institution" means a financial institution as defined in Article 4(1)(26) of Regulation (EU) No 575/2013 of the European Parliament and of the Council of 26th June 2013 on prudential requirements for credit institutions and investment firms and amending Regulation (EU) No 648/2012, or any undertaking located outside the [United Kingdom] which does not fall within that definition but which carries out equivalent activities; *and*

"insurance undertaking" means—

(a) an insurance undertaking (whether or not established in the [United Kingdom]) carrying on the business of direct non-life insurance of a class set out in [Annex I to Directive 2009/138/EC of the European Parliament and of the Council of 25 November 2009 on the taking-up and pursuit of the business of Insurance and Reinsurance (Solvency II)];

(b) an insurance undertaking (whether or not established in the [United Kingdom]) carrying on the business of . . . life insurance of a kind described in [Article 2(3) of Directive 2009/138/EC of the European Parliament and of the Council of 25 November 2009 on the taking-up and pursuit of the business of Insurance and Reinsurance (Solvency II)]; *or*

[(c) a reinsurance undertaking; or

(d) a third-country reinsurance undertaking];

["reinsurance undertaking" means an undertaking which—

(a) has its head office in the United Kingdom;

(b) has permission under Part 4A of the Financial Services and Markets Act 2000 to carry on one or more regulated activities;

(c) effects or carries out contracts of insurance that are limited to reinsurance contracts; and

(d) would require authorisation in accordance with Article 14 of Directive 2009/138/EC of the European Parliament and of the Council of 25 November 2009 on the taking-up and pursuit of the business of Insurance and Reinsurance (Solvency II), if the United Kingdom were a Member State; and

"third-country reinsurance undertaking" means an undertaking which, if its head office were in the United Kingdom—

(a) would require permission under Part 4A of the Financial Services and Markets Act 2000 to carry out regulated activities relating to reinsurance; and

(b) immediately before [IP completion day], would have required authorisation as a reinsurance undertaking in accordance with Article 14 of Directive 2009/138/EC].

(2) Except where the contrary intention appears, expressions used in this Schedule in relation to the determination of turnover in respect of the activities of a credit institution, a financial institution or an insurance undertaking have the same meaning as in the relevant Directive.

(3) The provisions of this Schedule are also to be interpreted in accordance with generally accepted accounting principles and practices.

2 Turnover of an enterprise

(1) The turnover of an enterprise is the sum of all amounts derived from the sale of products and the provision of services falling within the ordinary activities of the enterprise to businesses or consumers, after the deduction of sales rebates, value added tax and other taxes directly related to turnover.

(2) Paragraph 5 also applies to determine the turnover of an enterprise.

(3) But where all or any of the activities constituting an enterprise are the activities of a credit institution, a financial institution or an insurance undertaking, paragraph 3 or (as the case may be) paragraph 4 applies instead of this paragraph to determine the turnover of the enterprise in respect of those activities.

3 Turnover in respect of activities of a credit institution or financial institution

(1) The turnover of an enterprise in respect of the activities of a credit institution or financial institution is the sum of the following income items listed in Council Directive (EEC) 86/635 of 8th December 1986 on the annual accounts and consolidated accounts of banks and other financial institutions received by the institution, after deduction of value added tax and other taxes directly related to those items—

(a) interest income and similar income;

(b) the following income from securities—

(i) income from shares and other variable yield securities;

(ii) income from participating interests;

(iii) income from shares in affiliated undertakings;

(c) commissions receivable;

(d) net profit on financial operations;

(e) other operating income.

(2) Paragraph 5 also applies to determine the turnover of an enterprise in respect of the activities of a credit institution or financial institution.

4 Turnover in respect of activities of an insurance undertaking

(1) The turnover of an enterprise in respect of the activities of an insurance undertaking is the total value of gross premiums received, comprising all amounts received and receivable in respect of insurance contracts issued by or on behalf of the undertaking, including outgoing reinsurance premiums, and after deduction of taxes and parafiscal contributions or levies charged by reference to the amounts of individual premiums or the total volume of premiums.

(2) Paragraph 5 also applies to determine the turnover of an enterprise in respect of the activities of an insurance undertaking.

5 Further provisions about determining turnover

(1) The turnover of an enterprise is its turnover both in and outside the United Kingdom.

(2) The turnover of an enterprise also includes any aid granted in respect of the enterprise by a public body (in or outside the United Kingdom) to the business whose activities or part of whose activities constitute the enterprise, where—

(a) the aid relates to the ordinary activities of the business;

(b) the business is itself the recipient of the aid; and

(c) the aid is directly linked to the sale of products or the provision of services by the business and is therefore reflected in the price of those products or services.

(3) Where the person on whom a penalty under section 94A(1) of the Enterprise Act 2002 is imposed owns or controls more than one enterprise, the turnover of those enterprises does not include amounts derived from the sale of products or the provision of services between them.

(4) Where in the accounts or other information used by the appropriate authority to calculate the turnover (or any part of the turnover) of an enterprise any figure is expressed in a currency other than sterling, the appropriate authority may determine the equivalent in sterling, applying whatever rate or rates of exchange the authority considers appropriate and rounding the resulting figure up or down as it considers appropriate.

(5) Where an acquisition, divestment or other transaction or event has occurred since the end of the enterprise's relevant accounting period which the appropriate authority considers may have a significant impact on the turnover of the enterprise, the appropriate authority may take account of that transaction or event if it considers it appropriate to do so and accordingly increase or (as the case may be) reduce by such amount as it considers appropriate the amount which would otherwise constitute the enterprise's turnover for the purposes of section 94A(2) of the Enterprise Act 2002.

NOTES

Para 1 is amended as follows:

In the definition "financial institution" the words in square brackets were substituted (for the original "EU"), and the word "and" in italics at the end of that definition was revoked, by the Competition (Amendment etc) (EU Exit) Regulations 2019, SI 2019/93, reg 61, Sch 2, Pt 2, para 7(2), as from IP completion day (as defined in the European Union (Withdrawal Agreement) Act 2020, s 39) (for transitional provisions and savings in relation to the operation of the 2019 Regulations, see Sch 4 to those Regulations at **[7.69]** et seq).

In the definition "insurance undertaking" the words "United Kingdom" in square brackets in paras (a) and (b) were substituted (for the original words "European Economic Area"), the word "or" in italics at the end of para (b) was revoked, and paras (c) and (d) were substituted (for the original para (c)), by SI 2019/93, reg 61, Sch 2, Pt 2, para 7(3), as from IP completion day (as defined in the European Union (Withdrawal Agreement) Act 2020, s 39) (for transitional provisions and savings in relation to the operation of the 2019 Regulations, see Sch 4 to those Regulations at **[7.69]** et seq). The original para (c) (as amended by the Solvency 2 Regulations 2015, SI 2015/575, reg 60, Sch 2, para 36) read as follows—

> ""(c) a reinsurance undertaking carrying on the business of reinsurance under [Directive 2009/138/EC of the European Parliament and of the Council of 25 November 2009 on the taking-up and pursuit of the business of Insurance and Reinsurance (Solvency II)], or an equivalent undertaking having its head office outside the European Economic Area".

In the definition "insurance undertaking" the words in the second pair of square brackets in paras (a) and (b) were substituted, and the word omitted from para (b) was revoked, by the Solvency 2 Regulations 2015, SI 2015/575, reg 60, Sch 2, para 36.

The definitions "reinsurance undertaking" and "third-country reinsurance undertaking" were inserted by SI 2019/93, reg 61, Sch 2, Pt 2, para 7(4), as from IP completion day (as defined in the European Union (Withdrawal Agreement) Act 2020, s 39) (for transitional provisions and savings in relation to the operation of the 2019 Regulations, see Sch 4 to those Regulations at **[7.69]** et seq). Note that Sch 2, Pt 2, para 7(4) to the 2019 Regulations was amended by the Competition (Amendment etc) (EU Exit) Regulations 2020, SI 2020/1343, reg 32, with effect from immediately before IP completion day; and the effect of that amendment has been incorporated in the text set out above.

ENTERPRISE ACT 2002 (PROTECTION OF LEGITIMATE INTERESTS) (AMENDMENT) ORDER 2014

(SI 2014/891)

NOTES

Made: 31 March 2014.

Authority: Enterprise Act 2002, ss 68, 124(2), (4). Note that s 68 of the 2002 Act was repealed by the Competition (Amendment etc) (EU Exit) Regulations 2019, SI 2019/93, regs 32, 47, as from IP completion day (as defined in the European Union (Withdrawal Agreement) Act 2020, s 39). Subject to any applicable transitional provisions and savings in relation to the operation of the 2019 Regulations (see Sch 4 to those Regulations at **[7.69]** et seq), this Order, therefore, lapsed on IP completion day. See also the introductory notes to the Enterprise Act 2002 (Protection of Legitimate Interests) Order 2003, SI 2003/1592 at **[2.103]** *ante*.

Commencement: 1 April 2014.

[2.179]

1 Citation and commencement

This Order may be cited as the Enterprise Act 2002 (Protection of Legitimate Interests) (Amendment) Order 2014 and comes into force on 1st April 2014.

2–19 *(Arts 2–19 amend the Enterprise Act 2002 (Protection of Legitimate Interests) Order 2003, SI 2003/1592 at* **[2.103]** *et seq.)*

[2.180]

20 Transitional provision and savings: general

(1) Anything which was, immediately before 1st April 2014, in the process of being done by or in relation to the transferor may, so far as it relates to a transferred function, be continued by or in relation to the transferee.

(2) Anything done (or having effect as if done) by or in relation to the transferor for the purposes of or in connection with a transferred function, and which was in force or effective immediately before 1st April 2014, has effect as if done by or in relation to the transferee so far as that is required for continuing its effect on or after that date.

(3) In the application of paragraph (1) or (2)—

(a) any reference made before 1st April 2014 to the Competition Commission under article 5 of the Enterprise Act 2002 (Protection of Legitimate Interests) Order 2003 is to be treated, so far as provided by those paragraphs, as a reference under that article to the chair of the CMA for the constitution of a group under Schedule 4 to the Enterprise and Regulatory Reform Act 2013; and

(b) any authorisation given before 1st April 2014, so far as it authorises a named member or member of staff of the Office of Fair Trading or the Competition Commission, continues to authorise that individual (but no other) on or after that date if, and only if, the individual is a member or (as the case may be) a member of staff of the CMA.

(4) Where, in the application of paragraph (1) or (2), any functions exercisable immediately before 1st April 2014 by a Commission group are to be exercisable on or after that date by a CMA group—

(a) any person who, immediately before that date, was a member of the Commission group is to be treated, on or after that date, as a member of the CMA group concerned if the person is a member of the CMA panel;

(b) any person who, immediately before that date, was the chairman of the Commission group is to be treated, on or after that date, as the chair of the CMA group if the person is a member of the CMA panel; and

(c) the persons treated as mentioned in sub-paragraph (a) or (b) are to be treated, on or after that date, as if they have been constituted in accordance with Part 3 of Schedule 4 to the Enterprise and Regulatory Reform Act 2013 as the chair and other members of the CMA group (and that Part applies accordingly in relation to the operation of the group).

(5) So far as necessary for the purposes or in consequence of paragraphs (1) to (4), any notice, order, undertaking or other instrument or document given, accepted or made before 1st April 2014 has effect as if any references (however expressed) to the transferor were references to the transferee.

(6) The following are to have effect, so far as they continue to have effect by virtue of article 22 or 23, as if any references (however expressed) to the transferor were references to the transferee—

(a) any provision of the Enterprise Act 2002 (Protection of Legitimate Interests) Order 2003 as it was in force immediately before 1st April 2014;

(b) any notice, undertaking or other document given, accepted or made before that date.

(7) In this article—

"CMA Board" means the Board constituted under Part 2 of Schedule 4 to the Enterprise and Regulatory Reform Act 2013;

"CMA chair" means the person appointed to chair the CMA and the CMA Board under paragraph 1(1)(a) of Schedule 4 to that Act;

"CMA group" means a group constituted in accordance with Part 3 of Schedule 4 to that Act;

"CMA panel" means the panel constituted in accordance with Part 3 of Schedule 4 to that Act;

"Commission group" means a group constituted under paragraph 15 of Schedule 7 to the Competition Act 1998 to perform functions of the Competition Commission under the Enterprise Act 2002 (Protection of Legitimate Interests) Order 2003;

"transferee" means the CMA, the CMA Board, a CMA group, the CMA chair, another member of the CMA or (as the case may be) a member of staff of the CMA;

"transferor" means the Office of Fair Trading, the Competition Commission, a Commission group, the chair of the Office of Fair Trading or Competition Commission, another member of the Office of Fair Trading or Competition Commission or a member of staff of the Office of Fair Trading or the Competition Commission; and

"transferred function" means a function conferred by this Order on the transferee which was immediately before 1st April 2014 conferred by the Enterprise Act 2002 (Protection of Legitimate Interests) Order 2003 on the transferor.

(8) References in this article to things done include references to things omitted to be done.

[2.181]

21 Transitional provision and savings: general provision about effect of amendments in relation to existing matters

(1) The amendments made by articles 3 to 15, 17, 18(2)(c) and (e), (9), (14), (15) and (17) and 19 apply in relation to—

(a) any reference under article 5 of the Enterprise Act 2002 (Protection of Legitimate Interests) Order 2003 made before 1st April 2014, or

(b) any possible reference under article 5 of that Order which arose before that date,

as they apply in relation to any such reference made, or arising, on or after that date.

(2) In particular those amendments apply in relation to investigations begun, notices given, undertakings accepted and orders made before 1st April 2014 as they apply to investigations begun, notices given, undertakings accepted and orders made on or after that date.

(3) Paragraph (2) is without prejudice to the generality of paragraph (1).

(4) This article is subject to articles 22 and 23.

[2.182]

22 Transitional provision and savings: investigation powers

(1) The amendments made by article 16(5)(b), (9)(a) and (10) do not apply in relation to any notice given before 1st April 2014 under section 31 of the Enterprise Act 2002 as applied by the Enterprise Act 2002 (Protection of Legitimate Interests) Order 2003.

(2) The amendments made by article 18(2)(e) and (13) to (15) do not apply in relation to any notice given before 1st April 2014 under section 109 of that Act as applied by that Order.

[2.183]

23 Transitional provision and savings: interim undertakings and orders

(1) The amendments made by articles 9(b)(ii), (c)(i) and (d), 15(b)(iii) and 17(2), (3), (4)(b), (8)(a) and (9)(a) do not apply in relation to undertakings accepted under paragraph 1 of Schedule 2 to the Enterprise Act 2002 (Protection of Legitimate Interests) Order 2003 before 1st April 2014.

(2) In its continued application by virtue of paragraph (1), paragraph 1 of Schedule 2 to the Enterprise Act 2002 (Protection of Legitimate Interests) Order 2003 has effect as if it contained no power for an undertaking accepted under that paragraph to be varied or superseded.

(3) Any provision of the Enterprise Act 2002 applied by the Enterprise Act 2002 (Protection of Legitimate Interests) Order 2003 which—

(a) was applied by that Order immediately before 1st April 2014, and

(b) as so applied referred to an undertaking accepted under paragraph 1 of Schedule 2 to that Order, but

(c) as a result of an amendment made to the provision by the Enterprise and Regulatory Reform Act 2013, ceased to refer to such an undertaking

is, in relation to an undertaking accepted before that date, to be treated in its application by that Order as continuing to refer to such an undertaking despite that amendment.

(4) The amendments made by article 18(2)(c), (9) and (17) do not apply in relation to a failure to comply with an order under paragraph 2 of Schedule 2 to the Enterprise Act 2002 (Protection of Legitimate Interests) Order 2003 which—

(a) occurred before 1st April 2014, and

(b) did not continue on or after that date,

but otherwise do apply in relation to such orders made before that date.

E.
LITIGATION

COMPETITION APPEAL TRIBUNAL RULES 2003 (NOTE)

(SI 2003/1372)

[2.184]

NOTES

Part 6 of this Handbook (UK and EU Court Materials) contains all relevant material with regard to litigation etc. These Rules were set out in full in previous editions of this Handbook (in Section A of Part 6 (UK Courts)) but have been omitted this year due to pressure on space. These Rules were revoked by the Competition Appeal Tribunal Rules 2015, SI 2015/1648, as from 1 October 2015, and only apply to proceedings commenced before that date. See **[6.1]**.

SECTION 16 ENTERPRISE ACT 2002 REGULATIONS 2015

(SI 2015/1643)

NOTES

Made: 3 September 2015.
Authority: Enterprise Act 2002, s 16(1)(a).
Commencement: 1 October 2015.

[2.185]

1 Citation, commencement and interpretation

(1) These Regulations may be cited as the Section 16 Enterprise Act 2002 Regulations 2015 and come into force on 1st October 2015.

(2) In these Regulations "the court" means—

(a) in relation to England and Wales, the High Court of England and Wales;
(b) in relation to Scotland, the Court of Session or a sheriff court;
(c) in relation to Northern Ireland, the High Court or the county court in Northern Ireland;

[2.186]

2 Transfer of proceedings from the court to Competition Appeal Tribunal

Where in any proceedings before the court, there falls for determination an infringement issue the court—

(a) may by order transfer to the Tribunal for its determination so much of the proceedings as relates to the infringement issue;
(b) may give such directions or make such order as it thinks fit to give effect to the determination of that issue by the Tribunal.

COMPETITION APPEAL TRIBUNAL RULES 2015 (NOTE)

(SI 2015/1648)

[2.187]

NOTES

Part 6 of this Handbook (UK and EU Court Materials) contains all relevant material with regard to litigation etc. These Rules are set out in full in Section A of Part 6 (UK Courts) and apply to proceedings commenced after 1 October 2015. See **[6.8]**.

F.
STATE AID

FINANCIAL TRANSPARENCY (EC DIRECTIVE) REGULATIONS 2009

(SI 2009/2331)

NOTES

Made: 27 August 2009.

Authority: European Communities Act 1972, s 2(2). Note that the European Communities Act 1972 was repealed by the European Union (Withdrawal) Act 2018, s 1, as from exit day (as defined in s 20 of that Act). For the status of "EU-derived domestic legislation" after IP completion day, see s 2 of the 2018 Act at **[7.4]**.

Commencement: 22 September 2009.

Note that these Regulations are the domestic implementation of Commission Directive 2006/111/EC on the transparency of financial relations between Member States and public undertakings as well as on transparency within certain undertakings (at **[5.25]**).

PART 1 GENERAL

[2.188]

1 Citation and commencement

These Regulations may be cited as the Financial Transparency (EC Directive) Regulations 2009 and shall come into force on 22nd September 2009.

[2.189]

2 Interpretation

(1) In these Regulations—

"compensation" shall be construed as aid in any form whatsoever, including grant or support in accordance with [Article 107(1)] of the Treaty;

["contract" shall be construed as any agreement linking a public authority—

(a) to a public undertaking in respect of compensation; or

(b) to an undertaking which is either—

(i) granted a special or an exclusive right, or

(ii) entrusted with any service of general economic interest and receives public service compensation, in any form whatsoever, in relation to that service;]

"entrusted" shall be construed in accordance with [Article 106(2)] of the Treaty;

"exclusive right" means any right granted by a public authority to an undertaking through any legislative, regulatory or administrative means, reserving to it the right to provide a service or undertake an activity within a geographical area;

"Financial Transparency Directive" means Commission Directive 2006/111/EC of 16 November 2006 on the transparency of financial relations between Member States and public undertakings as well as on financial transparency within certain undertakings [(as that Directive applies to the United Kingdom under Article 10 of the Northern Ireland Protocol)];

["Northern Ireland Protocol" means the Protocol on Ireland/Northern Ireland in the EU withdrawal agreement;]

"public authority" includes the Crown and any regional, local or other territorial authority;

"public undertaking" means any undertaking over which a public authority may exercise, directly or indirectly, a dominant influence by virtue of its ownership of it, its financial participation in it, or the rules which govern it; a dominant influence is presumed when a public authority, directly or indirectly, in relation to an undertaking—

(a) holds the major part of the undertaking's subscribed capital;

(b) controls the majority of votes attaching to shares issued by the undertaking; or

(c) can appoint more than half the members of the undertaking's administrative, managerial or supervisory body;

"public undertaking operating in the manufacturing sector" means any public undertaking which has at least 50% of its total annual turnover arising from operations which are included in Section D of the Annex to Council Regulation (EEC) No 3037/90 of 9 October 1990 on the statistical classification of economic activities in the European Community [(as that Regulation had effect in EU law immediately before IP completion day)];

"services of general economic interest" shall be construed in accordance with [Article 106(2)] of the Treaty;

"share" shall be construed in accordance with section 540 of the Companies Act 2006;

"special right" means any right that is granted by a public authority through any legislative, regulatory or administrative means, which, within a geographical area and otherwise than in accordance with objective, proportional and non-discriminatory criteria—

(a) limits to two or more the number of undertakings authorised to provide a service or undertake an activity;

(b) designates several competing undertakings as being authorised to provide a service or undertake an activity; or

(c) confers on any undertaking any legal or regulatory advantages which substantially affect the ability of any other undertaking to operate the same activity in the same geographical area under substantially equivalent conditions;

"Treaty" means the Treaty [on the Functioning of the European Union]; and

"undertaking" means any entity engaged in an economic activity, regardless of the legal status of the entity or the way in which it is financed.

(2) These Regulations do not apply where [Article 346(1)] of the Treaty applies to a contract.

[(3) In these Regulations a reference to Article 106(2), Article 107(1) or Article 346(1) of the Treaty is a reference to that Article as it applies to the United Kingdom under Article 10 of the Northern Ireland Protocol.]

NOTES

Para (1) is amended as follows:

The words in square brackets in the definition "compensation" were substituted by the State Aid (Revocations and Amendments) (EU Exit) Regulations 2020, SI 2020/1470, reg 7(1), Sch 1, Pt 2, para 11(2)(a), as from IP completion day (as defined in the European Union (Withdrawal Agreement) Act 2020, s 39) (for transitional provisions and savings in relation to claims before a court or tribunal relating to State aid infringement before IP completion day, see Sch 3 to those Regulations at **[7.89]**. The original words were "Article 87".

Definition "contract" substituted by the Financial Transparency (EC Directive) (Amendment) Regulations 2011, SI 2011/1275, reg 2(2).

The words in square brackets in the definition "entrusted" were substituted by SI 2020/1470, reg 7(1), Sch 1, Pt 2, para 11(2)(b), as from IP completion day (as defined in the European Union (Withdrawal Agreement) Act 2020, s 39) (for transitional provisions see the first note relating to the 2020 Regulations above). The original words were "Article 86(2)".

The words in square brackets in the definition "Financial Transparency Directive" were inserted by SI 2020/1470, reg 7(1), Sch 1, Pt 2, para 11(2)(c), as from IP completion day (as defined in the European Union (Withdrawal Agreement) Act 2020, s 39) (for transitional provisions see the first note relating to the 2020 Regulations above).

Definition "Northern Ireland Protocol" inserted by SI 2020/1470, reg 7(1), Sch 1, Pt 2, para 11(2)(d), as from IP completion day (as defined in the European Union (Withdrawal Agreement) Act 2020, s 39) (for transitional provisions see the first note relating to the 2020 Regulations above).

The words in square brackets in the definition "public undertaking operating in the manufacturing sector" were inserted by SI 2020/1470, reg 7(1), Sch 1, Pt 2, para 11(2)(e), as from IP completion day (as defined in the European Union (Withdrawal Agreement) Act 2020, s 39) (for transitional provisions see the first note relating to the 2020 Regulations above).

The words in square brackets in the definition "services of general economic interest" were substituted by SI 2020/1470, reg 7(1), Sch 1, Pt 2, para 11(2)(f), as from IP completion day (as defined in the European Union (Withdrawal Agreement) Act 2020, s 39) (for transitional provisions see the first note relating to the 2020 Regulations above). The original words were "Article 86(2)".

The words in square brackets in the definition "Treaty" were substituted by SI 2020/1470, reg 7(1), Sch 1, Pt 2, para 11(2)(g), as from IP completion day (as defined in the European Union (Withdrawal Agreement) Act 2020, s 39) (for transitional provisions see the first note relating to the 2020 Regulations above). The original words were "establishing the European Community".

Para (2): words in square brackets substituted by SI 2020/1470, reg 7(1), Sch 1, Pt 2, para 11(3), as from IP completion day (as defined in the European Union (Withdrawal Agreement) Act 2020, s 39) (for transitional provisions see the first note relating to the 2020 Regulations above). The original words were "Article 296".

Para (3): added by SI 2020/1470, reg 7(1), Sch 1, Pt 2, para 11(4), as from IP completion day (as defined in the European Union (Withdrawal Agreement) Act 2020, s 39) (for transitional provisions see the first note relating to the 2020 Regulations above).

PART 2 PUBLIC UNDERTAKINGS

[2.190]

3 Maintenance of records

(1) A public undertaking shall maintain records of any public funds made available to it—

(a) directly by a public authority, or

(b) by a public authority through another public undertaking or financial institution.

(2) For the purposes of paragraph (1) the activities regarded as making public funds available to a public undertaking shall include—

(a) the setting-off of operating losses;

(b) the provision of capital;

(c) the provision of non-refundable grants or loans on privileged terms;

(d) the granting of financial advantages by forgoing profits or recovery of sums due;

(e) the forgoing of a normal return on public funds; or

(f) the provision of compensation for financial burdens imposed by a public authority.

(3) Nothing in paragraph (2) shall be construed as affecting the generality of paragraph (1).

(4) A public undertaking which receives public funds in relation to which it is required to maintain records under paragraph (1) shall maintain a record of the use to which those public funds are put.

(5) The obligations in paragraphs (1) and (4) shall not apply—

(a) where a public authority makes public funds available to another public authority;

[(b) in relation to any public funds which—

(i) were received by a public undertaking prior to IP completion day in relation to services supplied by a public undertaking which were not liable to affect trade between Member States (within the meaning of the Treaty as it applied to the United Kingdom prior to IP completion day) to an appreciable extent; or

(ii) are received by a public undertaking on or after IP completion day in relation to activities carried out by a public undertaking which are not liable to affect that trade between Northern Ireland and the

European Union which is subject to the Northern Ireland Protocol (within the meaning of Article 10 of the Northern Ireland Protocol) to an appreciable extent;]

(c) to the Bank of England;

(d) to deposits of public funds placed with a public credit institution by a public authority on normal commercial terms;

(e) to a public undertaking, other than a public credit institution, whose total annual net turnover—

(i) in each of the two financial years preceding any financial year in which the funds referred to in paragraph (1) are made available, in relation to the obligation in paragraph (1), or

(ii) in each of the two financial years preceding any financial year in which the funds referred to in paragraph (1) are used, in relation to the obligations in paragraph (4),

is less than 40 million euros; or

(f) to a public credit institution whose balance sheet total—

(i) in each of the two financial years preceding any financial year in which the funds referred to in paragraph (1) are made available, in relation to the obligation in paragraph (1), or

(ii) in each of the two financial years preceding any financial year in which the funds referred to in paragraph (1) are used, in relation to the obligation in paragraph (4),

is less than 800 million euros.

NOTES

Para (5): sub-para (b) substituted by the State Aid (Revocations and Amendments) (EU Exit) Regulations 2020, SI 2020/1470, reg 7(1), Sch 1, Pt 2, para 11(5), as from IP completion day (as defined in the European Union (Withdrawal Agreement) Act 2020, s 39) (for transitional provisions and savings in relation to claims before a court or tribunal relating to State aid infringement before IP completion day, see Sch 3 to those Regulations at **[7.89]**). The original paragraph read as follows—

"(b) in relation to any public funds received by a public undertaking in relation to services supplied by a public undertaking which are not liable to affect trade between Member States within the meaning of the Treaty to an appreciable extent;".

[2.191]

4 Retention of records by public undertakings

(1) A public undertaking shall retain the records which are required to be maintained under regulation 3(1) from the time that the public funds are provided until a period of five years has elapsed from the last day of the financial year in which the public funds were last used.

(2) A public undertaking shall retain the records which are required to be maintained under regulation 3(4) from the time that the public funds are used until a period of five years has elapsed from the last day of the financial year in which the public funds were last used.

[2.192]

5 Provision of information by public undertakings

Within 28 days of receipt of a written request by the Secretary of State, a public undertaking shall provide the Secretary of State with—

(a) such information, in such form, as is requested concerning the records (this may include copies of the records) which the undertaking is required to maintain under regulation 3(1) and 3(4); and

(b) such further information as is requested and considered necessary by the Secretary of State to fulfil the United Kingdom's obligations under the Financial Transparency Directive.

PART 3 UNDERTAKINGS REQUIRED TO MAINTAIN SEPARATE ACCOUNTS

[2.193]

6 Maintenance of separate accounts

(1) An undertaking which is—

(a) granted a special right or an exclusive right, or

(b) entrusted with any service of general economic interest and receives public service compensation, in any form whatsoever, in relation to that service,

and carries on an activity not covered by (a) or (b), shall maintain separate accounts in respect of its activities under paragraphs (a) and (b) and any other of its activities which fall outside of those paragraphs.

(2) The separate accounts referred to in paragraph (1) shall—

(a) show the costs and revenues associated with each of its activities;

(b) show the full details of the methods by which costs and revenues are assigned or allocated to each of its activities;

(c) show that the internal accounts corresponding to each of its activities are separate; and

(d) be based on clearly established, consistently applied and objectively justifiable cost accounting principles.

(3) This regulation shall not apply—

(a) to activities in respect of which other provisions in relation to financial transparency within undertakings have been laid down by [retained EU law];

[(b) in relation to—

(i) services which were supplied by an undertaking prior to IP completion day and which were not liable to affect trade between Member States (within the meaning of the Treaty as it applied to the United Kingdom prior to IP completion day) to an appreciable extent; or

(ii) activities carried out by an undertaking on or after IP completion day and which are not liable to affect that trade between Northern Ireland and the European Union which is subject to the Northern Ireland Protocol (within the meaning of Article 10 of the Northern Ireland Protocol) to an appreciable extent;]

(c) to an undertaking, other than a public credit institution, whose total annual net turnover in each of the two financial years preceding the financial year in which it enjoys a special right or an exclusive right, or in which it is entrusted with a service of general economic interest, is less than 40 million euros;

(d) to a public credit institution whose balance sheet total in each of the two financial years preceding the financial year in which it enjoys a special right or an exclusive right, or in which it is entrusted with a service of general economic interest, is less than 800 million euros; or

(e) to an undertaking which is entrusted with the operation of a service of general economic interest pursuant to [Article 106(2)] of the Treaty if the compensation it receives, in any form, was fixed for an appropriate period following an open, transparent and non-discriminatory procedure.

NOTES

Para (3) is amended as follows:

The words in square brackets in sub-para (a) were substituted by the State Aid (Revocations and Amendments) (EU Exit) Regulations 2020, SI 2020/1470, reg 7(1), Sch 1, Pt 2, para 11(6)(a), as from IP completion day (as defined in the European Union (Withdrawal Agreement) Act 2020, s 39) (for transitional provisions and savings in relation to claims before a court or tribunal relating to State aid infringement before IP completion day, see Sch 3 to those Regulations at **[7.89]**). The original words were "the European Union".

Sub-para (b) substituted by SI 2020/1470, reg 7(1), Sch 1, Pt 2, para 11(6)(b), as from IP completion day (as defined in the European Union (Withdrawal Agreement) Act 2020, s 39) (for transitional provisions see the first note relating to the 2020 Regulations above). The original paragraph read as follows—

"(b) in relation to services supplied by an undertaking which are not liable to affect trade between Member States within the meaning of the Treaty to an appreciable extent;".

The words in square brackets in sub-para (e) were substituted by SI 2020/1470, reg 7(1), Sch 1, Pt 2, para 11(6)(c), as from IP completion day (as defined in the European Union (Withdrawal Agreement) Act 2020, s 39) (for transitional provisions see the first note relating to the 2020 Regulations above). The original words were "Article 86(2)".

[2.194]

7 Retention of separate accounts

An undertaking required to maintain separate accounts under regulation 6(1) shall retain the separate accounts for a period of five years starting on the last day of the financial year to which those accounts relate.

[2.195]

8 Provision of information by undertakings required to maintain separate accounts

Within 28 days of receipt of a written request by the Secretary of State, an undertaking required to maintain separate accounts under regulation 6(1) shall provide the Secretary of State with—

(a) such information, in such form, as is requested concerning the separate accounts (this may include copies of the separate accounts) which the undertaking is required to maintain under regulation 6(1); and

(b) such further information as is requested and considered necessary by the Secretary of State to fulfil the United Kingdom's obligations under the Financial Transparency Directive.

PART 4 PUBLIC UNDERTAKINGS OPERATING IN THE MANUFACTURING SECTOR

[2.196]

9 Provision of information by public undertakings operating in the manufacturing sector

(1) A public undertaking operating in the manufacturing sector shall provide the following information to the Secretary of State relating to each financial year—

(a) a copy of its annual report and annual accounts (as each term is defined in section 471 of the Companies Act 2006), explanatory notes, accounting policies, statements by directors, segmental and activity reports and any other pertinent information;

(b) a copy of any notices of shareholder meetings relating to that financial year; and

(c) information concerning the occurrences described in paragraph (4), insofar as that information is not included in its annual report and annual accounts.

(2) The information required under paragraph (1) shall—

(a) where appropriate, specify the relationship between the provider of finance and the public undertaking operating in the manufacturing sector;

(b) where appropriate, include details of intra-group and inter-group transactions between different public undertakings; and

(c) where appropriate, include details of transactions conducted between public undertakings and public authorities.

(3) The information required under paragraph (1) shall be provided to the Secretary of State within—

(a) 10 working days of the date of the publication, if any, of the annual report of the public undertaking concerned, or

(b) eight months following the end of the undertaking's financial year, whichever is the earlier.

(4) The occurrences for the purposes of paragraph (1)(c) are—

(a) the provision of any share capital (including by a public authority, a public holding company or another public undertaking) or quasi-capital funds similar in nature to equity, specifying the terms of its or their provision (whether ordinary, preference, deferred or convertible shares, and interest rates and any dividend or conversion rights attaching thereto);

(b) the award to it of any non-refundable grants which are only refundable in certain circumstances;
(c) the award to it of any loans including overdrafts and advances on capital injections, specifying the interest rates and the terms of the loan and the security given, if any, to the lender by the undertaking receiving the loan;
(d) any guarantees given to it by a public authority in respect of loan finance (specifying the terms and charges, if any, paid by the public undertaking for the guarantee);
(e) any dividends paid out and profits retained; and
(f) any other financial advantage provided by a public authority, including the forgiving of sums due to a public authority by the public undertaking, such as the repayment of loans, grants, payment of corporate or social taxes or any similar charges.

(5) Within 28 days of receipt of a written request by the Secretary of State, a public undertaking operating in the manufacturing sector shall provide the Secretary of State with such further information as is requested and considered necessary to fulfil the United Kingdom's obligations under the Financial Transparency Directive.

(6) Paragraphs (1) and (5) shall not apply to public undertakings with a turnover in the previous financial year of 250 million euros or less.

[2.197]
10 Consolidated information by groups

Where two or more public undertakings subject to regulation 9 are members of a group of public undertakings and carry out activities in the same or closely related sectors, the information required by regulation 9(1) may be provided in relation to those undertakings in consolidated form rather than in relation to each undertaking separately.

PART 5 CONTRACT TERMS

[2.198]
11

Where a public authority is a party to a contract that public authority shall ensure that the contract contains the elements specified in—
(a) Regulations 3, 4 and 5, in respect of public undertakings;
(b) Regulations 6, 7 and 8, in respect of an undertaking required to maintain separate accounts; and
(c) Regulation 9 in respect of public undertakings operating in the manufacturing sector.

[2.199]
[12

(1) In the event that a contract does not expressly contain the elements required by Regulation 11, then it is an implied term of that contract that any undertaking that is a party to that contract shall comply with the provisions of—
(a) Regulations 3, 4 and 5, in respect of public undertakings;
(b) Regulations 6, 7 and 8, in respect of an undertaking required to maintain separate accounts; and
(c) Regulation 9 in respect of public undertakings operating in the manufacturing sector.

(2) Any term of a contract is void to the extent that it purports to exclude the application of paragraph (1).]

NOTES

Substituted by the Financial Transparency (EC Directive) (Amendment) Regulations 2011, SI 2011/1275, reg 2(1), (3).

Part 2 Statutory Instruments

G.
NATIONAL SECURITY AND INVESTMENT

NATIONAL SECURITY AND INVESTMENT ACT 2021 (MONETARY PENALTIES) (TURNOVER OF A BUSINESS) REGULATIONS 2021

(SI 2021/1262)

NOTES

Made: 10 November 2021.
Authority: National Security and Investment Act 2021, s 41(8), (9).
Commencement: 4 January 2022.

[2.200]
1 Citation, commencement, extent and interpretation

(1) These Regulations may be cited as the National Security and Investment Act 2021 (Monetary Penalties) (Turnover of a Business) Regulations 2021, and come into force on 4th January 2022.

(2) These Regulations extend to England and Wales, Scotland and Northern Ireland.

(3) In these Regulations, "the Act" means the National Security and Investment Act 2021.

NOTES

Commencement: 4 January 2022.

[2.201]
2 Meaning of "business"

For the purposes of section 41 of the Act (permitted maximum penalties), "business" includes a sole trader.

NOTES

Commencement: 4 January 2022.

[2.202]
3 Control of a business

(1) For the purposes of section 41 of the Act (permitted maximum penalties), a business is to be treated as controlled by another business ("A") where—

(a) the business is a body corporate in which A has a controlling interest;

(b) the business is a body corporate, and A is able to control directly or indirectly or materially to influence the policy of that body corporate without having a controlling interest in that body corporate;

(c) the business is a partnership or an unincorporated association or group of persons, and A (whether or not A is a member of that partnership, association or group) is able to control directly or indirectly or materially to influence the policy of that partnership, association or group; or

(d) the business is a sole trader, and A is able to control directly or indirectly or materially to influence the policy of that sole trader in carrying on the activities of the business.

(2) For the purposes of paragraph (1)(a) and (b), A has a controlling interest in a body corporate if A—

(a) is a parent undertaking of that body corporate within the meaning of section 1162 of the Companies Act 2006; or

(b) would be a parent undertaking of that body corporate within the meaning of that section if A were an undertaking within the meaning of section 1161 of that Act.

(3) For the purposes of paragraph (2), subsections (2)(c) and (4)(a) of section 1162 of the Companies Act 2006 are to be disregarded.

(4) For the purposes of paragraph (1)(b), (c) and (d), the Secretary of State may, having regard to all the circumstances, determine whether A is able to control directly or indirectly or materially to influence the policy of a body corporate or the policy of an individual or a partnership or an unincorporated association or group of persons in carrying on the activities of that business.

(5) References in this regulation—

(a) to a body corporate include a body incorporated outside the United Kingdom; and

(b) to a partnership or an unincorporated association or group of persons include a partnership or unincorporated association or group of persons formed or established, or having any members incorporated, formed or established, outside the United Kingdom.

NOTES

Commencement: 4 January 2022.

[2.203]
4 Turnover of a business

(1) This regulation applies to determine the turnover of a business ("A") and any business owned or controlled by A for the purposes of section 41 of the Act (permitted maximum penalties).

(2) The turnover of a business is its turnover in—

(a) the complete accounting period immediately preceding the decision date (the "relevant accounting period") (subject to paragraph (3)); or

(b) if the business has no relevant accounting period, the period beginning with the date on which the activities of the business began to be carried on and ending with the last day of the month preceding the month in which the decision date falls.

(3) If the figures necessary to calculate turnover of the business in the relevant accounting period are not available to the Secretary of State on the decision date, the turnover is (subject to paragraph (4)) its turnover in—

(a) the complete accounting period immediately preceding the relevant accounting period (the "preceding accounting period"); or

(b) if the business has no preceding accounting period, the period beginning with the date on which the activities of the business began to be carried on and ending with the day immediately preceding the date on which the relevant accounting period began.

(4) If the figures necessary to calculate the turnover of the business under paragraph (3)(a) or (b) are not available to the Secretary of State on the decision date, the turnover of the business is its turnover in the period beginning with the day after the last day of the relevant accounting period and ending with the last day of the month preceding the month in which the decision date falls.

(5) Where a period described in this regulation does not equal 12 months, the turnover of the business is the turnover in that period divided by the number of days in that period and multiplied by 365 or, if the period includes 29th February, 366.

(6) The amount of a business's turnover for the purposes of this regulation is, in the event of a disagreement between that business and the Secretary of State, the amount determined by the Secretary of State.

(7) For the purposes of this regulation—

(a) an "accounting period" of a business is a period of more than six months in respect of which accounts are prepared or required to be prepared in relation to the business;

(b) the "decision date" means the date on which the Secretary of State decides to impose a monetary penalty;

(c) the provisions of the Schedule apply in the determination of turnover.

NOTES

Commencement: 4 January 2022.

SCHEDULE
TURNOVER OF A BUSINESS

Regulation 4

[2.204]

1 Interpretation

(1) In this Schedule—

"credit institution" means a credit institution as defined in Article 4(1)(1) of Regulation (EU) No 575/2013 of the European Parliament and of the Council of 26 June 2013 on prudential requirements for credit institutions and investment firms and amending Regulation (EU) No 648/2012;

"financial institution" means a financial institution as defined in Article 4(1)(26) of Regulation (EU) No 575/2013 of the European Parliament and of the Council of 26 June 2013 on prudential requirements for credit institutions and investment firms and amending Regulation (EU) No 648/2012, or any undertaking located outside the United Kingdom which does not fall within the scope of that definition but which carries out equivalent activities;

"insurance undertaking" means—

(a) an undertaking which—

(i) has its head office in the United Kingdom;

(ii) has permission under Part 4A of the Financial Services and Markets Act 2000 to carry on one or more regulated activities; and

(iii) effects or carries out contracts of insurance or reinsurance; or

(b) a third-country insurance undertaking;

"third-country insurance undertaking" means an undertaking which, if its head office were in the United Kingdom, would require permission under Part 4A of the Financial Services and Markets Act 2000 to carry out regulated activities relating to insurance or reinsurance.

(2) The provisions of this Schedule are to be interpreted in accordance with generally accepted accounting principles and practices.

2 Turnover of a business

(1) The turnover of a business is the sum of all amounts derived from the sale of products and the provision of services falling within the ordinary activities of the business to businesses or consumers, after the deduction of sales rebates, value added tax and other taxes directly related to turnover.

(2) But where all or any of the activities of a business are the activities of a credit institution, a financial institution or an insurance undertaking, paragraph 3 or 4 (as the case may be) applies instead of sub-paragraph (1) to determine the turnover of the business in respect of those activities.

(3) Paragraph 5 also applies to determine the turnover of a business for the purposes of this Schedule.

3 Turnover in respect of activities of a credit institution or financial institution

(1) The turnover of a business in respect of the activities of a credit institution or financial institution is the sum of the following income items received by the institution, after deduction of value added tax and other taxes directly related to those items—

(a) interest income and similar income;
(b) the following income from securities—
(i) income from shares and other variable yield securities;
(ii) income from participating interests;
(iii) income from shares in affiliated undertakings;
(c) commissions receivable;
(d) net profit on financial operations;
(e) other operating income.

(2) Expressions used in sub-paragraph (1) have the meanings given by Council Directive (EEC) 86/635 of 8 December 1986 on the annual accounts and consolidated accounts of banks and other financial institutions.

4 Turnover in respect of activities of an insurance undertaking

The turnover of a business in respect of the activities of an insurance undertaking is the total value of gross premiums received, comprising all amounts received and receivable in respect of insurance contracts issued by or on behalf of the undertaking, including outgoing reinsurance premiums, and after deduction of taxes and parafiscal contributions or levies charged by reference to the amounts of individual premiums or the total volume of premiums.

5 Further provisions about determining turnover

(1) The turnover of a business is its turnover both in and outside the United Kingdom.

(2) The turnover of a business includes any subsidy given to the business, determined in accordance with paragraph 6.

(3) Where a business ("A") owns or controls one or more businesses, the turnover of the businesses owned or controlled by A does not include amounts derived from the sale of products or the provision of services between any of those businesses, or any of those businesses and A.

(4) Where in the accounts or other information used by the Secretary of State to calculate the turnover (or any part of the turnover) of a business any figure is expressed in a currency other than sterling, the Secretary of State may determine the equivalent in sterling, applying whatever rate or rates of exchange the Secretary of State considers appropriate and rounding the resulting figure up or down as the Secretary of State considers appropriate.

(5) Where an acquisition, divestment or other transaction or event has occurred since the end of the period in which the turnover of the business is determined in accordance with regulation 3 which the Secretary of State considers may have a significant impact on the turnover of the business, the Secretary of State may take account of that transaction or event if the Secretary of State considers it appropriate to do so and accordingly increase or (as the case may be) reduce by such amount as the Secretary of State considers appropriate the amount which would otherwise constitute the business's turnover.

6 Subsidies

(1) For the purposes of paragraph 5(2), "subsidy" means financial assistance which—
(a) is given, directly or indirectly, from public resources by a public authority;
(b) confers an economic advantage on one or more businesses; and
(c) is specific, that is, is such that it benefits one or more businesses over one or more other businesses with respect to the production of goods or the provision of services.

(2) For the purposes of sub-paragraph (1), the means by which financial assistance may be given include—
(a) a direct transfer of funds (such as grants or loans);
(b) a contingent transfer of funds (such as guarantees);
(c) the forgoing of revenue that is otherwise due;
(d) the provision of goods or services;
(e) the purchase of goods or services.

(3) For the purposes of sub-paragraph (1)(a), "public authority" means a person who exercises functions of a public nature.

(4) Financial assistance given from the person's resources by a person who is not a public authority is to be treated for the purposes of sub-paragraph (1)(a) as financial assistance given from public resources by a public authority if the involvement of a public authority in the decision to give financial assistance is such that the decision is, in substance, the decision of the public authority.

(5) For the purposes of sub-paragraph (4), the factors which may be taken into account when considering the involvement of a public authority in the decision of a person to give financial assistance include, in particular, factors relating to—
(a) the control exercised over that person by that public authority, or
(b) the relationship between that person and that public authority.

(6) For the purposes of this paragraph, financial assistance is to be treated as given to a business if the business has an enforceable right to the financial assistance.

NOTES

Commencement: 4 January 2022.

NATIONAL SECURITY AND INVESTMENT ACT 2021 (NOTIFIABLE ACQUISITION) (SPECIFICATION OF QUALIFYING ENTITIES) REGULATIONS 2021

(SI 2021/1264)

NOTES

Made: 10 November 2021.
Authority: National Security and Investment Act 2021, s 6(1), (2), (4), (8).
Commencement: 4 January 2022.

ARRANGEMENT OF REGULATIONS

SCHEDULES

[2.205]

1 Citation, commencement and extent

(1) These Regulations may be cited as the National Security and Investment Act 2021 (Notifiable Acquisition) (Specification of Qualifying Entities) Regulations 2021.

(2) These Regulations come into force on 4th January 2022.

(3) These Regulations extend to England and Wales, Scotland and Northern Ireland.

NOTES

Commencement: 4 January 2022.

[2.206]

2 Notifiable acquisitions

(1) Schedules 1 to 17 specify descriptions of qualifying entity for the purposes of section 6(2) of the National Security and Investment Act 2021 (notifiable acquisitions).

(2) A qualifying entity falls within a description in the Schedules by reason of the carrying on of an activity specified in the Schedules only if it carries on the activity in the United Kingdom.

NOTES

Commencement: 4 January 2022.

[2.207]

3 Interpretation

In these Regulations—

"the Act" means the National Security and Investment Act 2021;

"development" means all stages prior to production, including design, design research, design analyses, design concepts, assembly and testing of prototypes, pilot production schemes, design data, process of transforming design data into goods or software, configuration design, integration design, layouts;

"production" means all production stages, including product engineering, manufacture, integration, assembly (mounting), inspection, testing and quality assurance.

NOTES

Commencement: 4 January 2022.

Part 2 Statutory Instruments

[2.208]
4 Review

(1) The Secretary of State must from time to time—

(a) carry out a review of the regulatory provision contained in these Regulations; and

(b) publish a report setting out the conclusion of the review.

(2) The first report must be published before the end of the period of three years beginning with the day on which these Regulations come into force for any purpose.

(3) Subsequent reports must be published at intervals not exceeding three years.

(4) Section 30(4) of the Small Business, Enterprise and Employment Act 2015 requires that a report published under this regulation must, in particular—

(a) set out the objectives intended to be achieved by the regulatory provision referred to in paragraph (1)(a);

(b) assess the extent to which those objectives are achieved;

(c) assess whether those objectives remain appropriate; and

(d) if those objectives remain appropriate, assess the extent to which they could be achieved in another way which involves less onerous regulatory provision.

(5) In this regulation, "regulatory provision" has the same meaning as in sections 28 to 32 of the Small Business, Enterprise and Employment Act 2015 (see section 32 of that Act).

NOTES

Commencement: 4 January 2022.

SCHEDULES

SCHEDULE 1
ADVANCED MATERIALS

Regulation 2

[2.209]
1 Interpretation

In this Schedule—

"2D" means two-dimensional;

"3D" means three-dimensional;

"advanced composites" relates to structural composite materials with either metallic or ceramic matrices and includes 3D reinforcing architectures for any matrix (polymer, metal or ceramic);

"advanced materials" means completely new materials and materials that are developments on traditional materials, where such materials provide any of the following—

(a) targeted properties;

(b) advantageous properties;

(c) outstanding structural properties; or

(d) outstanding functional properties;

"enabler" means any material or process which is not a material described in paragraph 2(3) or 3 but is used in the manufacture or application of such materials;

"fabrication" in sector (7) (semiconductors) of the table set out in paragraph 3 means the process of producing a microelectronic circuit on a semiconductor substrate or using other advanced materials;

"graphene and related 2D" are those materials with attributes as defined within ISO/TS 80004-13:2017;

"metamaterial"—

(a) means a composite material in which the constituents are designed and spatially arranged through a rational design-led approach to change the manner in which electromagnetic, acoustic or vibrational energy interacts with the material, in order to achieve a property or performance that is not possible naturally and includes a metasurface and for this purpose "composite material" means a solid material formed from two or more constituents and "constituent" includes a region containing a vacuum, gas or liquid;

(b) does not include the types of composite materials the advanced composites described in paragraph 5 and composites or coatings containing pigments or fillers that are mixed in or blended into a binder material where both of these types of composite materials can be a constituent from which a metamaterial may be formed;

"metasurface" means a two-dimensional form of metamaterial which includes one or more layers of material that are intentionally patterned or textured (irrespective of whether they are periodic or not) through a rational design-led approach;

"nanotechnology" means the manipulation and control of matter predominantly in the nanoscale to make use of size-and-structure-dependent properties and phenomena distinct from those associated with individual atoms or molecules, or extrapolation from larger sizes of the same material (where "manipulation and control" includes material synthesis in relation to nanotechnology) with current or potential utility for defence, including nanomaterials, nanodevices, nanocomponents and nanosystems (including nanomachines) in accordance with ISO/TR 10993-22:2017;

"nanomaterials" means materials with any external dimension in the nanoscale or having internal structure or surface structure in the nanoscale and include nano-objects, dispersions or mixtures containing nano-objects, and nanostructured material (including structuring at an interface between materials, including air, and within a material) in accordance with ISO/TR 10993-22:2017;

"packaging" in sector (7) (semiconductors) of the table set out in paragraph 3 means the process of turning a microelectronic circuit on an appropriate substrate into a package suitable for use in an electronic circuit but does not include the assembly and packaging of chips and devices into circuit boards;

"photonic and optoelectronic materials and devices" in sector (8) of the table set out in paragraph 3 relate to high power lasers that are characterised by a combination of power at the output apertures (values of 1 kilowatt and above), beam quality (M^2 of less than 1.2), intended operating ranges (greater than 1 kilometre) and at wavelengths compatible with propagation over those distances (typically 1 micrometre to 2 micrometres wavelengths);

"semiconductor" means—

(a) semiconductors used to form radio frequency and microwave devices;

(b) semiconductors used to realise imaging sensor arrays;

(c) the accessibility of design and production for semiconductor devices and chips where "chips" include Field Programmable Gate Array devices, System on Chip, Application Specific Integrated Circuits and Readout Integrated Circuits and where "devices" includes radio and microwave frequency control circuitry, power amplifiers, low noise amplifiers and monolithic microwave integrated circuits and detectors;

"technical textiles" means textiles (and their processes and enablers) specifically developed for their functional performance including additional functionality (such as integrated computing, processing or data transmission), 3D architectures, protection against blast and ballistic events but does not include sportswear or clothing that is ordinarily available to consumers or household goods.

2 Activities

(1) A qualifying entity carrying on activities that consist of or include any of the activities set out in sub-paragraph (2) in relation to—

(a) any of the matters described in sub-paragraph (3); or

(b) any of the matters described in relation to the sectors set out in paragraph 3.

(2) The activities referred to in sub-paragraph (1) are—

(a) research;

(b) development or production;

(c) development or production of anything designed as an enabler;

(d) development or production of anything designed to be used for the purpose of production;

(e) the provision of qualified or certified designs, materials, parts or products;

(f) owning, creating, supplying or exploiting intellectual property;

(g) provision of know-how or services of enablers;

(h) recycling or re-using.

(3) The matters referred to in sub-paragraph (1)(a) are materials, the export or transfer of which is controlled by virtue of their being specified in—

(a) Schedule 2 to the Export Control Order 2008; or

(b) Annex I and Annex IV to Council Regulation (EC) No 2009/428 setting up a Community regime for the control of exports, transfer, brokering and transit of dual-use items.

3 Sectors and matters

The following Table sets out the sectors and matters referred to in paragraph 2(1)(b).

Table

Sector	*Matters*
(1) Advanced composites	1. The matters are, in relation to the sector of advanced composites, those set out in paragraphs 2 to 4.
	2. In relation to test, inspection and production equipment— (a) production technologies and capabilities for the manufacture of metal matrix composites; (b) production technologies and capabilities for the manufacture of ceramic matrix composites; (c) manufacture of 3D fibre architectures (that is with interlaminar reinforcement) for all composite types.
	3. In relation to materials— (a) metal matrix composites, powder-based metal matrix composites and continuous fibre reinforced metal matrix composites; (b) fibre reinforced ceramic matrix composites; (c) continuous silicon carbide fibres with diameters at and below 140 micrometres; (d) continuous oxide-based ceramic fibres with diameters at or below 20 micrometres; (e) coatings for the protection of ceramic matrix composites from degradation in the environment, for example ytterbium mono- and di-silicates;
	4. In relation to software and data— (a) capabilities for the design and design for manufacturing of metal matrix composites and fibre reinforced ceramic matrix composites; (b) software and computer-aided design for 3D fibre architectures and 3D preforms (with interlaminar reinforcement) for all composite types.
(2) Metals and alloys	1. The matters are, in relation to the sector of metal and alloys, those set out in paragraphs 2 to 5.
	2. In relation to systems, equipment and components, magnets utilising rare earth element-lean or element-free permanent magnetic materials with remanent magnetism, known as "B_r", greater than 1.0 Tesla and all rare-earth magnetic materials;

Sector	Matters
	3. In relation to testing, inspection and production equipment— (a) any processes that are involved in the reduction of either pure or mixed oxides in the solid state into either metals or alloys in or into crude or semi-fabricated forms, including powders, in batches of at least 1 kilogram; (b) hot isostatic pressing (also referred to as "HIP"); (c) spark plasma sintering (also referred to as "SPS") or field assisted sintering technology (also referred to as "FAST"); (d) diffusion and friction-based joining processes for steel for power transmission shafts described in paragraph 4(e) of this sector (metal and alloys), titanium alloys, nickel alloys or cobalt alloys; (e) friction-based processes to join metallic material layer by layer to create a structure; (f) superplastic forming of titanium and aluminium alloys; (g) electron beam, laser and weld arc-based metal additive manufacturing capabilities.
	4. In relation to materials— (a) any alloys that are formed by chemical or electrochemical reduction of feedstocks in the solid state directly from their oxides; (b) titanium alloys with continuous temperature-of-use capabilities above 350 Celsius; (c) powder metallurgy alloys; (d) nickel and cobalt based superalloys with continuous temperature-of-use capabilities above 700 Celsius; (e) steels for power transmission shafts with yield strengths of at least 1030 megapascals at 20 Celsius and 760 megapascals at 450 Celsius, ultimate tensile strengths of at least 1240 MPa at 20 Celsius and 950 megapascals at 450 Celsius and fracture toughnesses of at least 40 megapascals square root metres at 20 Celsius; (f) high strength high toughness weldable marine grade steels (toughness levels D, E and F); (g) armour grade steels; (h) armour grade aluminium alloys; (i) high entropy alloys and compositionally complex alloys (alloys that are formed by five or more elements where the composition is not dominated by one or two elements); (j) rare earth element-lean or element-free permanent magnetic materials with remanent magnetisation (also known as "B_r"), greater than 1.0 Tesla, and all rare-earth magnetic materials; (k) magnetic materials with high total saturation flux densities greater than 2.0 Tesla, which may include monolithic and laminate forms, and particulate and fibre reinforced composite materials.
	5.In relation to software and data— (a) computer models of complex metallic components, formed by powder-based additive manufacture, that embody a fluid and heat transfer function within their structure; (b) data on the performance of complex metallic components, formed by powder-based additive manufacture, that embody a fluid and heat transfer function within their structure.
(3) Engineering and technical polymers	1. The matters are, in relation to engineering and technical polymers, those set out in paragraphs 2 and 3.
	2. In relation to test, inspection and production equipment, machines for additively manufacturing the materials listed in paragraph 3 of this sector (Engineering and technical polymers), including loaded polymer filaments to enable electrically insulating and electrically conducting, thermally conducting and insulating, or magnetic and non-magnetic materials (or any further combination).
	3. In relation to materials— (a) engineering polymer materials and formulations with a glass transition temperature greater than 190 Celsius; (b) polymers responsive to external stimuli such as electromagnetic, load, chemical and biological stimuli (for example electroactive polymers, thermoactive polymers and self-healing systems) but not hydrogels in applications such as nappies; (c) high temperature, high pressure and chemically resistant elastomeric seals and systems; (d) polymer electrical insulation materials with high temperature (greater than 200 Celsius) and high voltage (above 1kilovolt)) capabilities for application in aviation electrical power management systems; (e) filaments and feedstocks for additive manufacturing or 3D printing with bespoke and elevated electrical, magnetic, or electromagnetic properties (typically formed from filled polymer compositions); (f) adhesives capable of retaining performance at high temperatures (above 190 Celsius); (g) adhesives with underwater curing capabilities; (h) void-filling viscoelastic polymers, created using at least a thermoplastic polyester and curing agent, intended for use to damp vibrations in metallic structures.
(4) Engineering and technical ceramics	1. The matters are, in relation to engineering and technical ceramics, those set out in paragraphs 2 and 3.
	2. In relation to test, inspection and production equipment, spark plasma sintering or field assisted sintering technology.

Sector	*Matters*
	3. In relation to materials— (a) boron carbide and silicon carbide ceramics for the manufacture of hard armour plates; (b) ultra-high temperature ceramics (with melting temperatures of at least 3000 Celsius) including transition metal diborides, either as monolithic or composite forms, including other ceramic monoliths or composites where ultra-high temperature ceramics have been added to their bulk or into surfaces; (c) magnetic materials, including fibres and particulates, for electromagnetic applications at frequencies above 500 megahertz; (d) functional ceramics (including ferroelectrics, magneto-dielectrics, or multi-ferroics) for acoustic applications, or electromagnetic applications above 100 megahertz; (e) dielectric and ferroelectric materials for use in the generation of, and manipulation of, high energy or high power radio frequency radiation, including functioning under high voltage conditions.
(5) Technical textiles	1. The matters are, in relation to technical textiles, those set out in paragraphs 2 to 6.
	2. In relation to systems, equipment and components, textile materials and products manufactured primarily for technical performance and functional properties rather than aesthetic or decorative characteristics but not sportswear or clothing ordinarily available to consumers or household goods;
	3. In relation to test, inspection and production equipment— (a) knitting, weaving, nonwoven or hybrid manufacturing processes related to the textile materials and products described in paragraph 2 of this sector; (b) fibre manufacturing processes related to the textile materials and products described in paragraph 2 of this sector (Technical textiles); (c) yarn manufacturing and texturing, dry fabric coating and laminating; (d) manufacture of 3D textiles; (e) closed loop recycling processes associated with the textile materials and products described in paragraph 2 of this sector.
	4. In relation to materials— (a) smart fabrics with fibres or yarns equipped with embedded sensors that respond to stimuli and perform a specific function; (b) fabrics made of smart polymers and textiles to protect and prevent injury or damage from blast and ballistic events; (c) energy harvesting fabrics; (d) textiles or fibres incorporating activated carbon; (e) fabrics with embedded devices for data storage and communication.
	5. In relation to software and data— (a) software and computer-aided design for 3D textiles and preforms; (b) machine learning software systems for smart textile manufacturing facilities, or for data-driven design and manufacturing of textile materials and systems.
	6. In relation to technology— (a) textile-based wearable electronics with potential to enable subtle integration of electronics with the human body for human-machine interfacing; (b) integration technologies to enable functionalities such as energy harvesting, data storage and communication, camouflage, structural and personnel health monitoring and protection.
(6) Metamaterials	1. The matters are, in relation to metamaterials, those set out in paragraphs 2 to 6.
	2. In relation to systems, equipment and components, metamaterials used in— (a) electromagnetic components including antennas, arrays, lens, devices; (b) electromagnetic applications including radio frequencies and microwave through to ultraviolet wavelengths; (c) nano-photonics or quantum technology as an enabler; (d) thermal control or protection; (e) airborne or underwater acoustics; or (f) structural applications.
	3. In relation to test, inspection and production equipment— (a) test, inspection and production equipment associated with the fabrication of 2D and 3D arrangements of one or more material and/or device constituents to form a metamaterial (including additive manufacturing, printed electronics methods, nano-fabrication, chemical self-assembly or engineering biology); (b) equipment associated with the non-destructive test and assurance of assembled or produced metamaterial, including composition, spatially varying composition and spatial arrangement parameters.
	4. In relation to materials— (a) a metamaterial; (b) tailored or bespoke feedstocks used in fabricating metamaterials including blended or formulated filaments referred to in paragraph 3(e) of sector (3) (engineering and technical polymers)), inks or dispersions used for additive manufacturing or printing but excluding inks or dispersions commercialised for forming electrically conducting pathways (known as "wires") in printed electronics.
	5. In relation to software and data, accumulations of metamaterial designs, or of elements comprising metamaterials, any of which that enable artificial intelligence, machine learning design or optimisation of metamaterials.

Sector	Matters
	6. In relation to technology, the inclusion with a metamaterial of technology in the form of systems or components, as well as material constituents, as part of the means and methods that enable metamaterials to alter their function and behaviour once installed or produced.
(7) Semiconductors	1. The matters are, in relation to semiconductors, those set out in paragraphs 2 to 5.
	2. In relation to systems, equipment and components— (a) high performance thermal imaging systems, equipment and components providing system sensitivity less than 30 milli-Kelvin for large format systems with more than 1 megapixels; (b) integrated systems having multiple operating wavebands on a single camera including mid-wavelength and long-wavelength infrared; (c) imaging systems with on-chip (smart) processing; (d) type II superlattice detectors; (e) single photon counting detector arrays operating at wavelengths longer than the visible band (wavelength greater than 750 nanometres), and with a size of at least 32x32 elements, or linear arrays with a size of at least 1x256 elements; (f) low noise CMOS (complementary metal-oxide-semiconductor) and EMCCD (electron multiplying charge coupled device) cameras where low noise would be less than 1 photoelectron/pixel/second; (g) technology and components for non-Von Neumann computing architectures, including but not limited to neuromorphic computing systems.
	3. In relation to test, inspection and production equipment— (a) the production of radio and microwave frequency systems, equipment and components incorporating compound semiconductors; example components include but are not limited to control circuitry, power amplifiers, low noise amplifiers and monolithic microwave integrated circuits, detectors and photonic devices; (b) facilities operating as a compound semiconductor foundry or providing compound semiconductor processing capability; (c) chip and device fabrication; (d) ceramic and polymeric packaging of processed semiconductor chips; (e) the production and integration capabilities for the high-performance imaging systems described in paragraph 2 of this sector (semiconductors).
	4. In relation to materials— (a) all compound semiconductors for radio frequency and microwave application including gallium nitride, gallium arsenide, gallium oxide, silicon germanium and indium phosphide; (b) imaging camera detector materials including cadmium mercury telluride, aluminium gallium arsenide, indium gallium arsenide and germanium silicon. 5. In relation to software and data, chip and device design
(8) Photonic and optoelectronic materials and devices	1. The matters are, in relation to photonic and optoelectronic materials and devices, those set out in paragraphs 2 to 6.
	2. In relation to systems, equipment and components— (a) polarisation control components including materials (solid and liquid) especially for high power applications (greater than 100 watts); (b) optical fibre designs mitigating nonlinear effects and enabling polarisation control of the output light for high power applications in both transverse single-mode and multimode optical fibre formats; (c) optical fibre based components such as light diodes, tap couplers and fibre Bragg gratings; (d) nonlinear components for nonlinear frequency conversion such as optical fibre geometries, crystal materials and optical patterning techniques; (e) low loss, high bandwidth optical fibre technologies (for laser sources and amplifier stages) and manufacturing techniques where the output power is capable of being scaled up for lasers that meet the characteristics set out in the description of "photonic and optoelectronic material and devices" in paragraph 1 of this Schedule (Interpretation); (f) phase modulators, where the spectral linewidth of fibre laser amplifiers is limited to no more than 16 gigahertz.
	3. In relation to test, inspection and production equipment— (a) optical fibre designs and production techniques, including coating techniques and test methodologies; (b) laser materials manufacturing techniques, host material doping techniques and characterisation techniques.
	4. In relation to materials— (a) materials that enable increased amplification, improved quality, improved robustness, improved increased electro-optical efficiency or reduced size or volume; (b) materials and or coatings or treatments that reduce optical losses of lenses or mirrors; (c) materials and or coatings or treatments that improve or increase the physical stability or robustness of lenses or mirrors; (d) materials enabling non-mechanical beam steering for detectors, sensors and imaging systems; (e) materials that reduce the size, weight and power requirements of optical detection, sensing and imaging systems; (f) materials suitable for aberration correction of high-power lasers (greater than 1 kilowatt) in the atmosphere.

Sector	*Matters*
	5. In relation to software and data— (a) algorithms, and their implementation in firmware, that compensate for the adverse atmospheric effects on laser beam propagation at distances greater than1 kilometre; (b) software, hardware and algorithm developments that improve phase control/coherent beam combination and efficiency.
	6. In relation to technology— (a) any approaches that enable high average optical power (greater than 3 kilowatts) combined with high quality (M2 <1.2) amplifiers; (b) any aspects that enable the propagation of light over significant distances (greater than 1 kilometre), including aberration correction devices.
(9) Graphene and related 2D materials	1. The matters are, in relation to graphene and related 2D materials, those set out in paragraphs 2 to 5.
	2. In relation to systems, equipment and components— (a) developing and operating equipment to synthesise single to few layer graphene and related 2D materials, including controlling the desired structure of the materials or their properties for application; (b) using processes including chemical exfoliation, electrochemical exfoliation, atom or molecule intercalation, surface growth, solution phase growth, vapour deposition and large area chemical vapour deposition.
	3. In relation to test, inspection and production equipment— (a) synthesis and manufacturing routes to either or both— (i) graphene and related 2D; or (ii) graphene and related 2D materials with bespoke or optimised functional properties, including but not limited to functioning as semi-conductors; (b) research, development and production of materials at scale for use as a filler or pigment including forming or using graphene and related two-dimensional materials in dispersions or mixed with other binders; (c) research, development and production to integrate the use of materials in devices and systems; (d) conversion of graphene and other 2D materials into intermediaries using processes including surface treatment and functionalisation, dispersion in matrices, mechanical and laser shaping, coating and ink printing processes.
	4. In relation to materials, all graphene and related 2D materials, including— (a) graphene, hexagonal boron nitride and transition metal dichalcogenides (such as MoS_2 and WS_2); (b) graphene and related 2D materials as thin films or coatings, powder form or mixtures with other materials; and (c) energetic materials (such as propellants or explosives).
	5. In relation to technology— (a) stacking of different 2D crystals resulting in either or both a charge redistribution between neighbouring crystals or causing structural changes; (b) components with finely tuned properties made by combining different 2D materials, including stacking different 2D materials.
(10) Nanotechnology	1. The matters are, in relation to nanotechnology, those set out in paragraphs 2 to 5.
	2. In relation to systems, equipment and components— (a) sensors or detectors including quantum dots with very high sensitivity to— (i) chemical, biological or nuclear materials (where the threshold is close to and including single molecule levels); or (ii) light or other forms of radiation (where the threshold is close to and including single photon levels); (b) autonomous remote or remotely activated sensing and reporting systems that are enabled by nanotechnology including Smart Dust; (c) nanomachines or nanoscale robots either with physically moving parts or capable of physical movement.
	3. In relation to test, inspection and production equipment— (a) test, inspection or production of nanotechnology or nanomaterials but not including services only offering test and inspection requiring the prior destruction of the produced nanotechnology or nanomaterials to form a test artefact (such as using Scanning Electron Microscopy or Atomic Force Microscopy); (b) methods to create or integrate nanotechnology for use in any of the following— (i) computer processing or memory devices (excluding commoditised silicon microelectronics technologies); (ii) communications or electronic warfare devices or components; (iii) precision navigation and timing systems; (iv) detectors, sensing or imaging systems; (v) counter-measure devices or systems; (vi) moving parts or soft robotics.
	4. In relation to materials, high-density nanoceramics and carbon nanotubes to reinforce ceramics for ballistic and blast protection.

Sector	Matters
	5. In relation to technology— (a) technology that exploits nanoscale phenomena or technology that is nano-enhanced or nano-science that further enhances nanoscale phenomena; (b) materials possessing exploitable magnetic, quantum or atomic spin states, or in combination for spinwave effects or technologies including defect centres in nanomaterials or utilising skyrmions; (c) electro-optic, magneto-optic, photonic or nanophotonic effects or devices (including vertical cavity emitting lasers) and circuits; (d) micromechanical, nanomechanical, electromechanical, optomechanical, or electro-opto-mechanical effects or systems; (e) metamaterials.
(11) Critical materials	1. The matters are, in relation to critical materials, the extraction, refinement, processing, production and end of life recovery (in single element, compound or product form) of any the following— (i) activated carbon; (ii) antimony (iii) arsenic; (iv) beryllium; (v) bismuth; (vi) boron; (vii) cadmium; (viii) cerium; (ix) chromium; (x) cobalt; (xi) dysprosium; (xii) erbium; (xiii) europium; (xiv) fluorspar; (xv) gadolinium; (xvi) gallium; (xvii) germanium; (xviii) graphite; (xix) holmium; (xx) indium; (xxi) iridium; (xxii) lead; (xxiii) lithium; (xxiv) lutetium; (xxv) mercury; (xxvi) molybdenum; (xxvii) neodymium; (xxviii) niobium; (xxix) osmium; (xxx) palladium; (xxxi) platinum; (xxxii) praseodymium; (xxxiii) rhenium; (xxxiv) ruthenium; (xxxv) samarium; (xxxvi) scandium; (xxxvii) selenium; (xxxviii) tantalum; (xxxix) tellurium; (xl) terbium; (xli) thulium; (xlii) tungsten; (xliii) vanadium; (xliv) ytterbium; (xlv) yttrium.
(12) Other materials	1. The matters are, in relation to other materials, those set out in paragraphs 2 to 6.
	2. In relation to systems, equipment and components— (a) capacitors based on tantalum; (b) components used in equipment or systems for the purpose of protecting optical systems and human vision from dazzle or damage by lasers.

Sector	*Matters*
	3. In relation to test, inspection and production equipment— (a) machines for additively manufacturing fully-assembled robotic, soft-robotic, sub-systems and systems or autonomous robotic sub-systems, systems and vehicles but not including machines for additively manufacturing individual components for such sub-systems systems and vehicles; (b) circuit board manufacturing of pitch, track or gap dimensions less than 30 micrometres; (c) new component placement technologies, including multi-axis component placement; (d) additive manufacturing or printing of moving parts, components and machines (known as "4D printing"); (e) battery pack assembly specifically for defence and security applications at the stage of integration, not isolated battery cell construction.
	4. In relation to materials— (a) materials (including paints or other forms of coating or surface) that are capable of modifying (including in real time) the appearance, detectability, traceability or identification of any object to a human or to sensors within the range of 15 terahertz up to and including ultraviolet; (b) foams with designed electrical, electromagnetic or thermal protection properties; (c) honeycombs with designed electrical or electromagnetic properties; (d) smart materials (including micro-fluidic systems) the properties of which can be repeatedly altered once installed at rates exceeding 1 megahertz; (e) materials enabling extreme size, weight and power reduction for energy, power and propulsion sources, or sensing or communications devices and systems for use in micro or smaller unmanned systems; (f) materials used in equipment or systems for the purpose of protecting optical systems and human vision from dazzle or damage from lasers.
	5. In relation to software and data— (a) creative artificial intelligence algorithms for material discovery and optimisation; (b) quantum simulation for material discovery and optimisation.
	6. In relation to technology, neuromorphic or quantum technologies enabling creative artificial intelligence or quantum simulation for materials discovery.

NOTES

Commencement: 4 January 2022.

SCHEDULE 2
ADVANCED ROBOTICS

Regulation 2

[2.210]

1 Interpretation

In this Schedule—

"cognitive" means having the abilities of reasoning, perception, communication, learning, planning, problem solving, abstract thinking, decision making or organisation;

"core components" means—

(a) sensors enabling advanced robotics to track and sense its environment;
(b) end effectors or other devices attached to advanced robotics allowing it to interact with its task or perform its operation;
(c) locomotion, where the advanced robotics is capable of moving in its environment;
(d) an energy source, including passive sources such as solar energy, providing power delivery enabling advanced robotics to move independently and to carry out its functions;
(e) hardware or software enabling sophisticated computational capabilities, including the use of artificial intelligence to process data and data sets received from the sensors and adapt the behaviour of the advanced robotics;
(f) communications capability, including the ability to communicate with a human operator or other advanced robotics.

2 Activities—advanced robotics

A qualifying entity carrying out any of the following activities—

(a) developing advanced robotics;
(b) producing advanced robotics;
(c) developing or producing core components specially designed or modified for use in advanced robotics.

3 Advanced robotics

Subject to paragraph 6, "advanced robotics" means a machine that meets either or both the descriptions set out in paragraph 4 and is capable of carrying out multifunctional physical actions, including positioning or orientating materials, parts, tools, special devices or itself through variable movements in three-dimensional space.

4 Description of advanced robotics

The descriptions referred to in paragraph 3 are—

(a) having the characteristic of autonomy set out in paragraph 5; and
(b) being capable of using its sensors to carry out sophisticated surveillance and data collection in respect of any aspects of its environment in order to collect, store or communicate to the operator, significant volumes of high-fidelity data.

5 Characteristic of autonomy

(1) Advanced robotics has the characteristic of autonomy where it is capable of performing actions—

(a) independent of human control; or

(b) independent of human control but complemented by—

(i) manual (including tele-operation) control;

(ii) pre-programmed operations or controls; or

(iii) control derived from other robotics or software control systems.

(2) The characteristics of autonomy may include either or both of the following—

(a) using physical, sensory and cognitive capabilities in combination, to decide on and implement a course of action that will vary depending on—

(i) the environment; or

(ii) the behaviour, dynamics, properties or arrangement of objects in the environment, which may include the ability to self-navigate or react to stimuli or changes in order to improve performance; or

(b) adapting or learning by carrying out actions to improve the performance of tasks from iteration and experience, which may include—

(i) the ability to self-heal;

(ii) the capability to identify and repair damaged robotics or components; or

(iii) having soft robotics capabilities (robotics made from compliant materials that mimic capabilities in living organisms that enable them to adapt or respond to their surroundings).

6 Exclusions

(1) Subject to sub-paragraph (2), "advanced robotics" does not include—

(a) machines containing robotic systems that are readily available for purchase by consumers, including robotic toys, domestic appliances described as "smart", vacuum cleaning robots and consumer-focussed drones, where "consumer" means an individual acting for purposes that are wholly or mainly outside of that individual's trade, business or craft;

(b) industrial automation systems that use mechanical tools performing repetitive functions with very basic or no sensors or cognitive ability, including—

(i) simple sensing or imaging devices that do not confer any ability to react or change their behaviour given a change in circumstances, without human intervention;

(ii) devices that carry out functions that require pre-set sequences of actions or require pre-set sensing of the environment;

(c) smart speakers or similar devices lacking end effectors or locomotion.

(2) The description of exceptions set out in sub-paragraph (1)(a) does not include self-driving vehicles.

NOTES

Commencement: 4 January 2022.

SCHEDULE 3
ARTIFICIAL INTELLIGENCE

Regulation 2

[2.211]

1 Interpretation

In this Schedule—

"artificial intelligence" means technology enabling the programming or training of a device or software to—

(i) perceive environments through the use of data;

(ii) interpret data using automated processing designed to approximate cognitive abilities; and

(iii) make recommendations, predictions or decisions;

with a view to achieving a specific objective;

"advanced robotics" has the same meaning as in Schedule 2;

"cognitive abilities" means reasoning, perception, communication, learning, planning, problem solving, abstract thinking, decision-making or organisation;

"cyber security" means the activities necessary to protect network and information systems, the users of such systems, and other persons affected by cyber threats;

"cyber threat" means any potential circumstance, event or action that could damage, disrupt or otherwise adversely affect network and information systems, the users of such systems and other persons;

"network and information system" has the same meaning as in regulation 1 of the Network and Information Systems Regulations 2018;

"technology" has the same meaning as in Schedule 2 to the Export Control Order 2008.

2 Activities—artificial intelligence

(1) A qualifying entity carrying on any of the following activities for one or more of the purposes set out in sub-paragraph 2—

(a) research into artificial intelligence; or

(b) developing or producing goods, software or technology that use artificial intelligence.

(2) The purposes are—

(a) the identification or tracking of objects, people or events;

(b) advanced robotics;

(c) cyber security.

NOTES

Commencement: 4 January 2022.

SCHEDULE 4
CIVIL NUCLEAR

Regulation 2

[2.212]

1 Activity—civil nuclear

A qualifying entity carrying on activities that consist of or include any of the following—

(a) subject to paragraph 2, holding a nuclear site licence granted in accordance with section 3 of the Nuclear Installations Act 1965 or applying for such a licence;

(b) subject to paragraph 2, being a tenant on a site in respect of which a nuclear site licence has been granted in accordance with section 3 of the Nuclear Installations Act 1965;

(c) holding either or both Category I/II or Category III nuclear material as defined in regulation 3(3) and (4) of the Nuclear Industries Security Regulations 2003;

(d) being a Class A carrier or a Class B carrier of nuclear material as approved under regulation 14 of the Nuclear Industries Security Regulations 2003;

(e) being in receipt of an order granting development consent under the Planning Act 2008 in relation to a nuclear reactor (as defined in section 26(1) of the Nuclear Installations Act 1965), or applying for such development consent;

(f) being, or having been, required to pay a fee to the Office for Nuclear Regulation under regulation 16(1) of the Health and Safety and Nuclear (Fees) Regulations 2021, where the outcome of the assessment for which that fee is to be, or has been, paid has not been determined;

(g) holding any equipment, software or information to which regulation 2(3) or (4), of the Uranium Enrichment Technology (Prohibition on Disclosure) Regulations 2004 applies;

(h) holding sensitive nuclear information as defined in section 77(7) of the Anti-Terrorism, Crime and Security Act 2001;

(i) being given financial support under section 5 of the Science and Technology Act 1965, or under section 93 of the Higher Education and Research Act 2017, for or in relation to nuclear reactors (as defined in section 26 of the Nuclear Installations Act 1965).

2 Exclusion

Paragraph 1(a) or (b) do not apply where the site to which the nuclear site licence relates is controlled or operated wholly or mainly for defence purposes as defined in section 70(3) of the Energy Act 2013.

NOTES

Commencement: 4 January 2022.

SCHEDULE 5
COMMUNICATIONS

Regulation 2

[2.213]

1 Interpretation

In this Schedule—

"cable landing station" means a cable landing station for a submarine cable system;

"electronic communications service" has the meaning given by section 32(2) of the Communications Act 2003

"public electronic communications network" means a public electronic communications network as defined by section 151(1) of the Communications Act 2003 and includes a submarine cable system that is provided for purposes which include the purpose of making electronic communications services available to the public;

"public electronic communications service" means a public electronic communications service as defined by section 151(1) of the Communications Act 2003, and includes an electronic communications service that is provided by means of a submarine cable system so as to be available for use by members of the public;

"submarine cable system" means a system of fibre optic cables which—

(a) are beneath the sea (whether on or in the seabed or in a tunnel); and

(b) are used for the conveyance of signals.

2 Public electronic communications providers

(1) A qualifying entity which—

(a) carries on activities which consist of or include either or both of the following—

(i) providing a public electronic communications network;

(ii) providing a public electronic communications service; and

(b) meets the turnover condition in sub-paragraph (2).

(2) The turnover condition is that the turnover of the entity's relevant business for the relevant period is at least £50,000,000.

(3) In sub-paragraph (2)—

(a) "relevant business" means so much of any business carried on in the United Kingdom by the entity in question or any of its associated entities as consists of either or both of the following—

(i) the provision of a public electronic communications network;

(ii) the provision of a public electronic communications service;

(b) "relevant period" means—

(i) the period of one year ending with the 31st March last before the time when a person gains control of the qualifying entity, by virtue of one or more of the cases described in subsection (2), (5) or (6) of section 8 of the Act; and

(ii) in the case of an entity which at that time has been carrying on that business for a period of less than a year, the period, ending with that time, during which it has been carrying it on.

(4) For the purposes of sub-paragraph (3)(a), another qualifying entity is an associated entity of the entity in question if—

(a) the entity in question owns, or has a controlling interest in, the other qualifying entity;

(b) the other qualifying entity owns, or has a controlling interest in, the entity in question; or

(c) a person or group of persons owns, or has a controlling interest in, both entities.

(5) For the purposes of sub-paragraph (4), a person has a controlling interest in a qualifying entity if the person holds more than 50% of the shares or voting rights in the entity; and subsections (3), (4), and (7) of section 8 of the Act apply for the interpretation of this sub-paragraph.

(6) For the purposes of this paragraph—

(a) turnover is to be calculated in conformity with accounting practices and principles which are generally accepted in the United Kingdom;

(b) turnover is to be limited to the amounts derived by an entity from the relevant business after deduction of sales rebates, value added tax and other taxes directly related to amounts so derived;

(c) where the relevant business of the entity in question is carried on by two or more entities that each prepare accounts the turnover shall be calculated by adding together the turnover of each, except that no account shall be taken of any turnover resulting from the supply of goods or the provision of services between them.

3 Associated facilities

(1) A qualifying entity carrying on activities which consist of or include the making available of anything that—

(a) is an associated facility by reference to a qualifying network or qualifying service; and

(b) is not excluded by sub-paragraph (2) or (3).

(2) An associated facility consisting of a building or an entry to a building is excluded by this sub-paragraph unless the main purpose of the building is to host a network element that is active.

(3) An associated facility other than a building or an entry to a building is excluded by this sub-paragraph if the associated facility is an element (such as a pipe, mast, duct, antenna installation, tower or pole) which—

(a) is not itself active; and

(b) is designed merely to host either or both of the following—

(i) other network elements that are not active;

(ii) cables (including strands of optical fibre).

(4) In this paragraph—

"associated facility" has the meaning given by section 32(3) of the Communications Act 2003 but as if the reference in that provision to a "facility, element or service" included a reference to a cable landing station;

"qualifying network" means a public electronic communications network provided by a qualifying entity falling within paragraph 2;

"qualifying service" means a public electronic communications service provided by a qualifying entity falling within paragraph 2.

4 Repair or maintenance of submarine cable systems or cable landing stations

(1) A qualifying entity carrying on activities which consist of or include the provision of services for the repair or maintenance of—

(a) a submarine cable system (in the United Kingdom or elsewhere) forming part of a public electronic communications network that—

(i) is provided in the United Kingdom by a qualifying entity falling within paragraph 2; or

(ii) interconnects with a public electronic communications network provided in the United Kingdom by a qualifying entity falling within paragraph 2; or

(b) a cable landing station in the United Kingdom that is used in connection with a public electronic communications network or public electronic communications service provided in the United Kingdom by a qualifying entity falling within paragraph 2.

(2) In this paragraph "interconnect" is to be read in accordance with section 151(2) of the Communications Act 2003.

5 Information systems

(1) A qualifying entity carrying on activities that consist of or include supplying to persons in the United Kingdom services which consist of or include one or more of the following—

(a) providing a top-level domain name registry which, in any relevant 168-hour period, serviced 14 billion or more queries from devices located in the United Kingdom for domains registered within the Internet Corporation for Assigned Names and Numbers;

(b) providing a domain name system resolver service which, in any relevant 168-hour period, serviced 500,000 or more different Internet Protocol addresses used by persons in the United Kingdom;

(c) providing a domain name system authoritative hosting service servicing 100,000 or more domains registered to persons with an address in the United Kingdom.

(2) A qualifying entity which—

(a) carries on activities which consist of or include supplying to persons in the United Kingdom services which consist of or include providing an internet exchange point; and

(b) has 30% or more of the market share among operators of internet exchange points in the United Kingdom in terms of interconnected autonomous systems.

(3) In this paragraph—

"domain name system" has the meaning given to "Domain Name System" in paragraph 10(5)(a) of Schedule 2 to the Network and Information Systems Regulations 2018;

"internet exchange point" has the meaning given in paragraph 10(5)(c) of Schedule 2 to the Network and Information Systems Regulations 2018;

"relevant 168-hour period" means any consecutive period of 168 hours falling within the 12 months ending with the time when a person gains control of the qualifying entity by virtue of one or more of the cases described in subsection (2), (5) or (6) of section 8 of the Act;

"top-level domain name registry" has the meaning given in paragraph 10(5)(d) of Schedule 2 to the Network and Information Systems Regulations 2018.

NOTES

Commencement: 4 January 2022.

SCHEDULE 6
COMPUTING HARDWARE

Regulation 2

[2.214]

1 Interpretation

In this Schedule—

"computer processing unit" means—

- (a) a central processing unit (also referred to as "CPU");
- (b) a field programmable gate array (also referred to as "FPGA");
- (c) a microcontroller;
- (d) a system on chip;
- (e) a graphics processor unit; or
- (f) a specialist processor for artificial intelligence applications;

"fabrication" means the process of producing a microelectronic circuit on a semiconductor substrate or using other advanced materials;

"packaging" means the process of turning a microelectronic circuit on an appropriate substrate into a package suitable for use in an electronic circuit but does not include the assembly and packaging of chips and devices into circuit boards;

"roots of trust" means hardware, firmware or software components that are inherently trusted to perform critical security functions.

2 Activity—computing hardware

A qualifying entity whose activities consist of one or more of the activities set out in paragraph 3.

3 The activities referred to in paragraph 2 are—

- (a) the ownership, creation, supply or exploitation of intellectual property relating to any of the following—
  - (i) computer processing units;
  - (ii) architectural, logical or physical designs for such units;
  - (iii) the instruction set architecture for such units;
  - (iv) code, written in a low-level language, that can control how such units operate;
  - (v) integrated circuits with the purpose of providing memory;
- (b) the design, maintenance or delivery of a service for the secure provisioning or management of either or both of the following—
  - (i) roots of trust of computer processing units;
  - (ii) code, written in a low level language, that can control how such units operate;
- (c) the fabrication or packaging of either or both of the following—
  - (i) computer processing units;
  - (ii) integrated circuits with the purpose of providing memory.

NOTES

Commencement: 4 January 2022.

SCHEDULE 7
CRITICAL SUPPLIERS TO GOVERNMENT

Regulation 2

[2.215]

1 Interpretation

In this Schedule—

"government" has the same meaning as "contracting authorities" in regulation 2 of the Public Contracts Regulations 2015;

"relevant public contract" means a contract for pecuniary interest between one or more persons and government, where the contract has as its object the execution of works, the supply of products or the provision of services.

2 Activity—critical suppliers to government

A qualifying entity being a party to a relevant public contract where the contract contains one or more of the features set out in paragraph 2.

3 The features referred to in paragraph 1 are—

(a) either or both the processing or storage of material to which a security classification of SECRET or TOP SECRET has been applied in accordance with the document titled "Government Security Classifications Version 1.1—May 2018" published by the Cabinet Office;
(b) a requirement to have List X accreditation as described in the document titled "Security Requirements for List X Contractors Version 10.0—April 2014" published by the Cabinet Office;
(c) a requirement for employees of the qualifying entity to be vetted at or above 'Security Check' level as described in guidance titled "National security: vetting clearance levels" published on 12 February 2020 by the United Kingdom Security Vetting.

NOTES
Commencement: 4 January 2022.

SCHEDULE 8
CRYPTOGRAPHIC AUTHENTICATION

Regulation 2

[2.216]
1 Interpretation

In this Schedule—

"consumer" means an individual acting for purposes that are wholly or mainly outside that individual's trade, business, craft or profession;

"authentication" means verifying—
(a) the identity of a user, process or device; or
(b) the origin or content of a message or other information;

"cryptography" means the discipline which embodies principles, means and methods for the transformation of data in order to hide its information content, prevent its undetected modification or prevent its unauthorised use and is limited to the transformation of information using one or more secret parameters or associated key management;

"secret parameter" means a variable, constant or key kept from the knowledge of others or shared only within a group.

2 Activity—cryptographic authentication

A qualifying entity carrying on activities consisting of or including research into, developing or producing, any product which—
(a) has authentication as a primary function;
(b) employs cryptography in performing that function; and
(c) is not ordinarily supplied to or made available for acquisition by consumers.

NOTES
Commencement: 4 January 2022.

SCHEDULE 9
DATA INFRASTRUCTURE

Regulation 2

[2.217]
1 Interpretation

In this Schedule—

"administrative access" refers to either or both authorisation or access granted via either or both logical or administrative access controls by virtue of which an entity may access relevant data infrastructure or control access to relevant data infrastructure where such access would otherwise be restricted or compartmented and where such access would permit the modification of the relevant data infrastructure in a way that was not authorised;

"electronic communications network" has the meaning given in section 32(1) of the Communications Act 2003;

"public electronic communications network" has the meaning given in section 151(1) of the Communications Act 2003;

"public electronic communications service" has the meaning given in section 151(1) of the Communications Act 2003;

"public sector authority" means an authority listed in paragraph 2;

"relevant activity" means storing, processing or transmitting data in digital form which are used in connection with the administration and operation of a public sector authority;

"relevant data infrastructure" is physical or virtualised infrastructure, which—
(a) is used for a relevant activity and the qualifying entity—
  (i) has a contract with a public sector authority to provide the relevant activity; or
  (ii) is a sub-contractor who has been notified that it is in a chain of sub-contractors which begins with the contractor that has a contract with the public sector authority for the purpose of providing the relevant activity, where the sub-contractor is providing a relevant activity that would fulfil or contribute towards the fulfilment of the main contract;
(b) is provided for peering, interconnection or exchange of digital data between providers of public electronic communications networks and/or providers of public electronic communications services but which is not owned by a provider of public electronic communications networks or a provider of a public electronic communications service; or

(c) enables the interconnection of one or more public electronic communications networks with an electronic communications network where part of that network is provided by means of a submarine cable system;

"specialist or technical services" means either or both—

(a) equipment installation services;

(b) equipment repair and maintenance services;

"submarine cable system" means a system of fibre optic cables which—

(i) are beneath the sea (whether on or in the seabed or in a tunnel); and

(ii) are intended for the conveyance of signals.

2 Interpretation—public sector authority

The authorities referred to in the definition of a "public sector authority" in paragraph 1 are set out in the following Table.

Table

Public sector authority
Prime Minister's Office
Attorney General's Office
Crown Prosecution Service
Government Legal Department
Serious Fraud Office
Cabinet Office
Crown Commercial Service
Government Property Agency
The Electoral Commission
UK Statistics Authority
Department for Business, Energy and Industrial Strategy
Competition and Markets Authority
HM Land Registry
Intellectual Property Office
Meteorological Office
Nuclear Decommissioning Authority
Office of Gas and Electricity Markets (Ofgem)
United Kingdom Space Agency
Department for Digital, Culture, Media and Sport
Information Commissioner
The National Archives
Office of Communications (Ofcom)
Department for Education
Education and Skills Funding Agency
Office of Qualifications and Examinations Regulation (Ofqual)
Office for Standards in Education, Children's Services and Skills (Ofsted)
Teaching Regulation Agency
Department for Environment, Food and Rural Affairs
Water Services Regulation Authority (Ofwat)
Department for International Trade
UK Export Finance (also known as the Exports Credit Guarantee Department)
Department for Transport
Civil Aviation Authority
Driver and Vehicle Licensing Agency

Public sector authority
Maritime and Coastguard Agency
Office of Rail and Road
Department for Work and Pensions
Health and Safety Executive
Office for Nuclear Regulation
Department of Health and Social Care
Health and Social Care Information Centre
Joint Committee on Vaccination and Immunisation
Medicines and Healthcare products Regulatory Agency
Public Health England
UK Health Security Agency
Foreign, Commonwealth and Development Office
Wilton Park
GCHQ
HM Treasury
Bank of England
Financial Conduct Authority
Government Actuary's Department
Government Internal Audit Agency
HM Revenues and Customs
National Audit Office
National Infrastructure Commission
National Savings and Investments
Office for Budget Responsibility
UK Debt Management Office
Valuation Office Agency
Home Office
National Crime Agency
Investigatory Powers Commissioner's Office
Ministry of Defence
Defence Electronics and Components Agency
Defence Equipment and Support
Defence Science and Technology Laboratory
Submarine Delivery Agency
United Kingdom Hydrographic Office
Ministry of Housing, Communities and Local Government
Queen Elizabeth II Centre
Ministry of Justice
Criminal Injuries Compensation Authority
HM Courts and Tribunals Service
HM Prison and Probation Service
Legal Aid Agency
Office of the Public Guardian

Public sector authority
Supreme Court of the United Kingdom
Northern Ireland Office
Office of the Advocate General for Scotland
Office of the Leader of the House of Commons
Office of the Leader of the House of Lords
Office of the Secretary of State for Scotland
Office of the Secretary of State for Wales
Secret Intelligence Service
Security Service
Northern Ireland Executive
The Executive Office
Department of Agriculture, Environment and Rural Affairs
Department for Communities
Department for the Economy
Department of Education
Department of Finance
Department of Health
Department for Infrastructure
Department of Justice
Invest Northern Ireland
The Scottish Government
Crown Office and Procurator Fiscal Service
Disclosure Scotland
Education Scotland
Office of the Accountant in Bankruptcy
Registers of Scotland
Revenue Scotland
Scottish Courts and Tribunals Service
Scottish Fiscal Commission
Scottish National Investment Bank
Scottish Public Pensions Agency
Social Security Scotland
Student Awards Agency for Scotland
The Scottish Ministers
Transport Scotland
The Welsh Government
Permanent Secretary's Group
Office of the First Minister Group
The Health and Social Services Group
The Economy, Skills and Natural Resources Group
The Education and Public Services Group

3 Activity—data infrastructure

A qualifying entity carrying on any of the activities set out in paragraph 4.

4 The activities referred to in paragraph 3 are—

(a) owning or operating relevant data infrastructure;
(b) managing relevant data infrastructure on behalf of other entities;
(c) managing facilities where relevant data infrastructure is located;
(d) providing specialist or technical services to entities carrying on activities described in sub-paragraphs (a), (b) or (c), which give the entity providing those specialist or technical services physical access to relevant data infrastructure;
(e) providing services where the provision of such services gives the entity providing those services administrative access to relevant data infrastructure;
(f) producing or developing software designed for use in the services in sub-paragraph (e) which configures or manages the provision of administrative access.

NOTES

Commencement: 4 January 2022.

SCHEDULE 10
DEFENCE

Regulation 2

[2.218]

1 Interpretation

In this Schedule—

"defence" has the meaning given to it by section 2(4) of the Official Secrets Act 1989; and
"government contractor" has the meaning given to it by section 12 of the Official Secrets Act 1989.

2 Activity—defence

A qualifying entity carrying on activities that comprise or include the research, development, production, creation or application of goods or services which are used or provided for defence or national security purposes where that entity meets a condition in paragraph 3.

3 The conditions referred to in paragraph 2 are that the entity—

(a) is a government contractor or any sub-contractor in a chain of sub-contractors which begins with the government contractor which provides goods or services within the scope of paragraph 2; or
(b) has been notified by or on behalf of the Secretary of State of information, documents or other articles of a classified nature which the entity or an employee of the entity may hold or receive relating to the activities within the scope of paragraph 2.

NOTES

Commencement: 4 January 2022.

SCHEDULE 11
ENERGY

Regulation 2

[2.219]

1 Interpretation

In this Schedule—

"aggregation" means combining multiple customer loads or generated electricity for sale, purchase or auction in the electricity market of Great Britain;
"downstream oil activity" means any of the following activities—
(a) the import of any of crude oil, intermediates, components and finished fuels;
(b) the storage of any of crude oil, intermediates, components and finished fuels;
(c) the production of intermediates, components and finished fuels through refining or blending processes;
(d) the distribution of petroleum-based fuels to storage sites by road, pipeline, rail or ship;
(e) the delivery of petroleum-based fuels to retail sites, airports or end users;
"existing upstream petroleum facility" means an upstream petroleum facility that began operating before the first day of the month that is 12 calendar months before the month in which a person gains control, by virtue of one or more of the cases described in subsection (2), (5) or (6) of section 8 of the Act, of the qualifying entity;
"gas" means any substance which is or (if it were in a gaseous state) would be gas within the meaning set out in section 48(1) of the Gas Act 1986;
"gas interconnector" has the meaning set out in section 5(8) of the Gas Act 1986;
"gas processing facility" has the meaning set out in section 90(1) of the Energy Act 2011;
"gas processing operation" has the meaning set out in section 90(2) of the Energy Act 2011;
"generate" in relation to electricity means carrying on an act within section 4(1)(a) of the Electricity Act 1989;
"generating asset" means an asset used to generate electricity;
"group undertaking" has the meaning set out in section 1161(5) of the Companies Act 2006;
"LNG import or export facility" has the meaning set out in section 12(6) of the Gas Act 1995 but does not include facilities in the territorial sea adjacent to Great Britain or the sea in any area designated under section 1(7) of the Continental Shelf Act 1964;

"new upstream petroleum facility" means an upstream petroleum facility that had not begun operating before the first day of the month that is 12 calendar months before the month in which a person gains control, by virtue of one or more of the cases described in subsection (2), (5) or (6) of section 8 of the Act, of the qualifying entity;

"oil equivalent" means petroleum and, for the purposes of assessments of throughput, where petroleum is in a gaseous state 1,100 cubic meters of this petroleum at a temperature of 15 degrees Celsius and pressure of one atmosphere is counted as equivalent to one tonne;

"petroleum" has the same meaning as in Part 1 of the Petroleum Act 1998, and includes petroleum that has undergone any processing;

"petroleum licence" means a licence granted under section 3 of the Petroleum Act 1998 or section 2 of the Petroleum (Production) Act 1934;

"petroleum production project" has the meaning set out in section 90(2) of the Energy Act 2011;

"terminal" has the meaning set out in section 90(2) of the Energy Act 2011, but does not include gas processing facilities in the United Kingdom or LNG import or export facilities;

"upstream petroleum facility" means a terminal, upstream petroleum pipeline or unit of infrastructure that is or will be necessary to a petroleum production project;

"upstream petroleum pipeline" has the meaning set out in section 90(2) of the Energy Act 2011, but does not include gas interconnectors.

2 Activity—energy

A qualifying entity carrying on any of the activities set out in paragraph 3.

3 The activities referred to in paragraph 2 are—

(a) in respect of any existing upstream petroleum facility that meets the conditions set out in paragraph 4(2)—
  (i) owning;
  (ii) operating;
  (iii) holding a petroleum licence in respect of; or
  (iv) where the qualifying entity meets the condition set out in paragraph 4(3), enabling the operation of;

(b) in respect of any new upstream petroleum facility that meets the conditions set out in paragraph 4(4)—
  (i) owning;
  (ii) operating;
  (iii) holding or applying for a petroleum licence in respect of; or
  (iv) where the qualifying entity meets the condition set out in paragraph 4(5)—
    (aa) developing;
    (bb) enabling the operation of; or
    (cc) enabling the development of;

(c) holding a transmission licence, distribution licence or interconnector licence under section 6 of the Electricity Act 1989 or carrying on any activity in pursuance of an exemption from section 4(1)(b), 4(1)(bb) or 4(1)(d) of the Electricity Act 1989 granted to the qualifying entity by order under section 5(1) of the Electricity Act 1989;

(d) where the qualifying entity meets the condition set out in paragraph 4(6)—
  (i) holding a generation licence under section 6 of the Electricity Act 1989 or carrying on any activity in pursuance of an exemption from section 4(1)(a) of the Electricity Act 1989 granted to the qualifying entity by order under section 5(1) of the Electricity Act 1989; or
  (ii) carrying on aggregation;

(e) holding a licence under section 7 or 7ZA of the Gas Act 1986 or carrying on any activity in pursuance of an exemption from sections 5(1)(a) or 5(1)(aa) of the Gas Act 1986 granted to the qualifying entity by order under section 6A(1) of the Gas Act 1986;

(f) owning or operating—
  (i) any gas processing facility in Great Britain that meets the condition set out in paragraph 4(8); or
  (ii) any LNG import or export facility that meets the condition set out in paragraph 4(9);

(g) where the qualifying entity meets the conditions set out in paragraph 4(10), supplying petroleum-based road, aviation or heating fuels (including liquefied petroleum gas) to persons in the United Kingdom.

4 Conditions

(1) This paragraph sets out the conditions referred to in paragraph 3.

(2) The conditions referred to in paragraph 3(a) are that the existing upstream petroleum facility—
  (a) has a throughput of greater than 3,000,000 tonnes of oil equivalent over the 12 calendar months preceding the month in which a person gains control, by virtue of one or more of the cases described in subsection (2), (5) or (6) of section 8 of the Act, of the qualifying entity; and
  (b) is—
    (i) situated in whole or in part in the United Kingdom; or
    (ii) used in connection with the supply of petroleum to persons in the United Kingdom.

(3) The condition referred to in paragraph (3)(a)(iv) is that the qualifying entity is an owner or operator of the existing upstream petroleum facility.

(4) The conditions referred to in paragraph 3(b) are that the new upstream petroleum facility—
  (a) has an expected throughput of greater than 3,000,000 tonnes of oil equivalent in its first 12 calendar months of operation; and
  (b) is or will be—
    (i) situated in whole or in part in the United Kingdom; or
    (ii) used in connection with the supply of petroleum to persons in the United Kingdom.

Part 2 Statutory Instruments

(5) The condition referred to in paragraph 3(b)(iv) is that the qualifying entity is or will be an owner or operator of the new upstream petroleum facility.

(6) The condition referred to in paragraph 3(d) is that—

(a) the qualifying entity is an owner or operator of any individual generating asset that has a total installed capacity equal to or greater than 100 megawatts; or

(b) the relevant capacity of the qualifying entity is equal to or greater than one gigawatt.

(7) For the purposes of sub-paragraph (6)(b), the "relevant capacity" of the qualifying entity is the total of—

(a) the total installed capacity of any generating assets owned or operated by the qualifying entity;

(b) the total installed capacity of any generating assets owned or operated by the acquirer or group undertakings of the acquirer;

(c) the amount of customer load and generated electricity available to the qualifying entity for aggregation; and

(d) the amount of customer load and generated electricity available to the acquirer or group undertakings of the acquirer for aggregation.

(8) The condition referred to in paragraph 3(f)(i) is that the gas processing facility has the technological capacity to carry on gas processing operations in relation to greater than 6 million cubic metres of gas per day.

(9) The condition referred in paragraph 3(f)(ii) is that the LNG import or export facility has the technological capacity to carry on the importation, regasification or liquefaction of greater than 6 million cubic metres of gas per day.

(10) The conditions referred to in paragraph 3(g) are that—

(a) the qualifying entity carries on any downstream oil activity; and

(b) the qualifying entity—

(i) has capacity of greater than 500,000 tonnes; or

(ii) owns a facility in the United Kingdom that has capacity of greater than 50,000 tonnes.

(11) For the purposes of sub-paragraph (10)—

(a) a qualifying entity "has capacity of greater than" a specified number of tonnes if any downstream oil activity was carried on in the United Kingdom by that qualifying entity in relation to greater than that number of tonnes of oil in at least one of the three calendar years preceding the year in which a person gains control, by virtue of one or more of the cases described in subsection (2), (5) or (6) of section 8 of the Act, of the qualifying entity; and

(b) a facility "has capacity of greater than" a specified number of tonnes if it was used for the purposes of any downstream oil activity in relation to greater than that number of tonnes of oil in at least one of the three calendar years preceding the year in which a person gains control, by virtue of one or more of the cases described in subsection (2), (5) or (6) of section 8 of the Act, of the qualifying entity.

NOTES

Commencement: 4 January 2022.

SCHEDULE 12
MILITARY AND DUAL-USE

Regulation 2

[2.220]

1 Interpretation

In this Schedule—

"restricted goods" and "restricted technology" are respectively goods and technology, including software or information (other than information in the public domain), the export or transfer of which is controlled by virtue of their being specified in the relevant export control legislation;

"relevant export control legislation" means—

(a) Schedules 2 and 3 to the Export Control Order 2008;

(b) the Schedule to the Export of Radioactive Sources (Control) Order 2006;

(c) Annex I to Council Regulation (EC) No 2009/428 setting up a Community regime for the control of exports, transfer, brokering and transit of dual-use items.

2 Activity—military and dual-use

A qualifying entity carrying on activities that consist of or include researching, developing or producing restricted goods or restricted technology.

NOTES

Commencement: 4 January 2022.

SCHEDULE 13
QUANTUM TECHNOLOGIES

Regulation 2

[2.221]

1 Interpretation

In this Schedule—

"quantum technology" means—

(a) quantum communications;

(b) quantum connectivity;

(c) quantum imaging, sensing, timing or navigation;

(d) quantum information processing, computing or simulation; or

(e) quantum resistant cryptography;

"quantum communications" means—

(a) the transmission of information, using the properties of quantum mechanics, specifically superposition, entanglement, single photon technology, the use of conjugate variable technologies or a combination of these;

(b) the use of a communication network (quantum or otherwise) to distribute quantum states or quantum state information; or

(c) the establishment of cryptographic keys or the generation of provably random numbers using a quantum physical process;

"quantum connectivity" means the ways in which quantum coherence, during processes such as transmission, propagation or amplification, is preserved;

"quantum imaging" means using the phase or amplitude properties of quantum mechanics, specifically superposition, entanglement, the use of sub-Poissonian sources or detectors of photons or a combination of these, to create images of objects;

"quantum information processing, computing or simulation" means—

(a) the simulation or realisation of systems that use certain properties of quantum mechanics, specifically superposition or entanglement, to acquire, encode, manipulate or process information, run algorithms or perform operations or measurements on data;

(b) algorithms, applications, software, error correction, noise reduction and operating systems that enable the functionality of the system;

(c) the capability of a classical computer to represent the internal state and operations of a quantum computer ("quantum emulation"); or

(d) the hosting or provision of third-party access of a quantum information processing, computing or simulation cloud-based service;

"quantum navigation" means using phase properties of quantum mechanics, specifically measurements of atoms or ions, or atom-ion interferometry, to establish the location or inertia of, and to guide, objects;

"quantum resistant cryptography" means methods of securing information or data being transmitted or stored, with a view to resisting attack by a quantum computing or simulation device;

"quantum sensing" means utilising the phase properties of quantum mechanics, specifically measurements of atoms or ions or atomic spin systems, to determine a property or rate of change in the property of an object, or the effect of an object on a measurable quantity;

"quantum timing" means using the phase properties of quantum mechanics, specifically measurements of atoms or ions or atomic gases, and the application of associated hardware including stable frequency mixers, optical or microwave sources, crystal oscillators and frequency combs, to provide a timing or synchronisation signal, or frequency reference.

2 Activity—quantum technology

A qualifying entity carrying on activities that consist of developing or producing quantum technology.

NOTES

Commencement: 4 January 2022.

SCHEDULE 14
SATELLITE AND SPACE TECHNOLOGY

Regulation 2

[2.222]

1 Interpretation

In this Schedule—

"defence" has the meaning given to it by section 2(4) of the Official Secrets Act 1989;

"infrastructure" includes any of the following—

(a) command and control stations;

(b) ground stations, ground sites and ground support equipment;

(c) software (including analysis software);

(d) information technology and telecommunications networks (including fibre cables);

(e) uplink and downlink terminals;

(f) data processing and storage facilities (including databases);

(g) satellites;

(h) technological systems and equipment deployed in outer space or on earth;

"outer space" has the meaning given to it by section 13(1) of the Outer Space Act 1986;

"space activity" and "sub-orbital activity" have the meaning given to them by section 1(4) of the Space Industry Act 2018;

"spacecraft" has the meaning given to it by section 2(6) of the Space Industry Act 2018;

"space derived data" means data obtained from space activity or from ground stations receiving data from outer space or from both space activity and ground stations receiving data from outer space, including data relating to—

(a) position, navigation and timing;

(b) earth observation;

(c) space situational awareness;

(d) telecommunications;

(e) signal intelligence;

(f) remote sensing; and

(g) research and development;

"space situational awareness" includes surveillance and tracking of satellites in outer space, monitoring and forecasting of weather in outer space, and mapping or detection of near earth objects or debris in outer space;

"testing" includes any service that provides quality assurance assessment of—

(a) equipment or systems for space activity or services derived from space activity, including engines, component parts, radio frequency, software and systems;
(b) facilities that manufacture, design or create any of the equipment set out in paragraph 3(e);
(c) launch site equipment or facilities; and
(d) equipment or facilities for transport of satellites, launch vehicles or their component parts between sites.

2 Activity—satellite and space technology

A qualifying entity carrying on activities that consist of or include operating, developing, producing, creating or using facilities for any of the activities set out in paragraph 3.

3 The activities referred to in paragraph 2 are—

(a) management of debris in outer space, including sending an object into outer space to remove debris;
(b) the provision of—
 (i) in-orbit servicing, maintenance or manoeuvring of satellites;
 (ii) in-orbit capabilities, including inspection services or life extension services, including refuelling, repair or relocation services; or
 (iii) any technology or system—
  (aa) that performs any of the activities set out in sub-paragraphs (a), (b)(i) and (b)(ii); or
  (bb) which is designed to, or may be used to, disrupt, modify or interfere with satellites;
(c) the provision of satellite communications links, including radio frequency or optical links—
 (i) between satellites in orbit;
 (ii) between spacecraft and satellites in orbit;
 (iii) between satellites in orbit and celestial bodies; or
 (iv) from earth to outer space, and from outer space to earth;
(d) operating or maintaining the capability of secure infrastructure related to—
 (i) space activity; or
 (ii) sub-orbital activity;
(e) the manufacture or testing of spacecraft, launch vehicles, satellites, planetary probes, orbital stations, ground support equipment, or component parts of, or materials used in, any equipment set out in this sub-paragraph;
(f) the use of space-derived data for a defence purpose;
(g) the operation or control of infrastructure;
(h) the provision or processing of space situational awareness data by activity on earth or by space activity or by means of infrastructure for any of the following—
 (i) sub-orbital activity;
 (ii) orbital activity;
 (iii) a defence purpose.

NOTES

Commencement: 4 January 2022.

SCHEDULE 15
SUPPLIERS TO THE EMERGENCY SERVICES

Regulation 2

[2.223]

1 Interpretation

In this Schedule—

"ambulance services provider" means—

(a) in England—
 (i) an NHS trust or NHS foundation trust established pursuant to Part 2 of the National Health Service Act 2006 (or their subsidiaries), which has a function of providing ambulance services;
 (ii) any private, public or voluntary sector entity which has been commissioned under any arrangement by or on behalf of the NHS Commissioning Board or a Clinical Commissioning Group pursuant to Parts 1 and 4 of the National Health Service Act 2006 to provide ambulance services;
 (iii) any private, public or voluntary sector entity which has been commissioned under any arrangement by or on behalf of the Secretary of State pursuant to Part 1 of the National Health Service Act 2006 to provide ambulance services;
(b) in Wales, an NHS Trust established by the Welsh Ambulance Services National Health Service Trust (Establishment) Order 1998;
(c) in Northern Ireland, the Northern Ireland Ambulance Service Trust as defined in the Northern Ireland Ambulance Service Health and Social Services Trust (Establishment) Order (Northern Ireland) 1995;
(d) in Scotland, the Special Health Board constituted by the Scottish Ambulance Service Board Order 1999 or any other private, public or voluntary sector entity providing ambulances and other means of transport under section 45 of the National Health Service (Scotland) Act 1978 (ambulances);

"associated facility" has the meaning given in section 32(3) of the Communications Act 2003;

"the British Transport Police Force" means the police force established by Part 3 of the Railways and Transport Safety Act 2003;

"the Civil Nuclear Constabulary" means the constabulary established under section 52(1) of the Energy Act 2004 (the Civil Nuclear Constabulary);

"emergency service" means—

(a) Border Force;
(b) the British Transport Police Force;
(c) the Civil Nuclear Constabulary;
(d) a fire and rescue authority;
(e) the Ministry of Defence Police;
(f) the National Crime Agency;
(g) a police body;

"a fire and rescue authority" is—

(a) in England—
  (i) an authority constituted by a scheme under section 2 of the Fire and Rescue Services Act 2004 (a combined fire and rescue authority);
  (ii) an authority constituted by a scheme to which section 4 of the Fire and Rescue Services Act 2004 applies (a combined fire and rescue authority constituted under the Fire Services Act 1947);
  (iii) an authority created by an order under section 4A of the Fire and Rescue Services Act 2004 (a police and crime commissioner as fire and rescue authority);
  (iv) a metropolitan county fire and rescue authority;
  (v) the London Fire Commissioner;
  (vi) a combined authority established under section 103 of the Local Democracy, Economic Development and Construction Act 2009 (combined authorities and their areas);
(b) in Wales—
  (i) for a county, a county council;
  (ii) for a county borough, a county borough council;
(c) in Northern Ireland, the Northern Ireland Fire and Rescue Service Board, as defined in article 3 of the Fire and Rescue Services (Northern Ireland) Order 2006 (the Northern Ireland Fire and Rescue Service Board);
(d) in Scotland, the Scottish Fire and Rescue Service, as defined in section 1A the Fire (Scotland) Act 2005 (the Scottish Fire and Rescue Service);

"electronic communications network" has the meaning given in section 32(1) of the Communications Act 2003;

"electronic communications service" has the meaning given in section 32 of the Communications Act 2003;

"fuel card" means a card, the production of which enables the person to whom it is issued to discharge his obligation to a supplier of fuel in respect of payment for that fuel, the supplier being reimbursed by a person other than the person producing the card;

"Ministry of Defence Police" means the police force established under the Ministry of Defence Police Act 1987;

"National Crime Agency" means the agency established under the Crime and Courts Act 2013;

"personal data" has the meaning given in section 3(2) of the Data Protection Act 2018;

"police body" means—

(a) in England and Wales—
  (i) a local policing body as defined in section 101 of the Police Act 1996 (interpretation); or
  (ii) the chief officer of police as defined in section 101 of the Police Act 1996;
(b) in Northern Ireland, the Police Service of Northern Ireland and Police Service of Northern Ireland Reserve;
(c) in Scotland—
  (i) the Scottish Police Authority, as defined in section 1 of the Police and Fire Reform (Scotland) Act 2012 (the Scottish Police Authority);
  (ii) the Chief Constable of the Police Service of Scotland, as appointed under section 7 of the Police and Fire Reform (Scotland) Act 2012 (senior officers);

"public electronic communications network" has the meaning given in section 151(1) of the Communications Act 2003;

"public electronic communications service" has the meaning given in section 151(1) of the Communications Act 2003;

"unmanned aircraft" means any aircraft operating or designed to operate autonomously or to be piloted remotely without a pilot on board.

2 Activity—suppliers to emergency services

A qualifying entity which supplies directly to—

(a) an emergency service of one or more of the goods and services set out in paragraph 3;
(b) an ambulance services provider of one or more of the goods and services set out in paragraph 4.

3 Good and services—emergency services

The goods and services referred to in paragraph 2(a) are the following—

(a) unmanned aircraft, any component, part or product of an unmanned aircraft, and any equipment, including an electronic device, relating to an unmanned aircraft;
(b) equipment designed to disrupt the operational system of an unmanned aircraft;
(c) equipment designed to detect, track or identify unmanned aircraft;
(d) firearms as defined in section 57(1) of the Firearms Act 1968 (interpretation: firearm);

(e) ammunition as defined in section 57(2) of the Firearms Act 1968 (interpretation: ammunition);
(f) certification, maintenance, support or repairs to vessels operated by Border Force for frontline operational purposes;
(g) maintenance or repairs of unmanned aircraft, any component, part or product of an unmanned aircraft, and any equipment, including an electronic device, relating to an unmanned aircraft;
(h) an electronic communications network, electronic communications service or associated facility, that—
 (i) is not a public electronic communications network or public electronic communications service; and
 (ii) is used by the emergency service for the purposes of—
  (aa) the prevention or detection of crime; or
  (bb) fulfilling the functions of a fire and rescue authority;
(i) hardware, systems or platforms to facilitate the storage of electronic data, used exclusively or primarily by the emergency service for the purposes of—
 (i) the prevention or detection of crime;
 (ii) fulfilling the functions of a fire and rescue authority; or
 (iii) the storage of personal data, including personnel data;
(j) the maintenance and repair of the goods and services referred to in sub-paragraphs (g) and (h);
(k) fuel cards;
(l) services to control systems relating to access and security of buildings;
(m) front line operational delivery of firefighting services in the event of strike action.

4 Goods and services—ambulance services provider

The goods and services referred to in paragraph 2(b) are an electronic communications network or electronic communications service that—
(a) is not a public electronic communications network or a public electronic communications service; and
(b) is used by the ambulance services provider for the purposes of fulfilling its functions.

NOTES

Commencement: 4 January 2022.

SCHEDULE 16
SYNTHETIC BIOLOGY

Regulation 2

[2.224]

1 Interpretation

In this Schedule—

"basic scientific research" means experimental or theoretical work undertaken principally to acquire new knowledge of the fundamental principles of phenomena or observable facts and not primarily directed towards a specific practicable aim or objective;

"medicine" means—
 (i) any substance or combination of substances presented as having properties of preventing or treating disease in human beings or animals;
 (ii) any substance or combination of substances that may be used by or administered to human beings or animals with a view to—
  (aa) restoring, correcting or modifying a physiological function by asserting a pharmacological, immunological or metabolic action;
  (bb) making a medical diagnosis;

"services" means routine synthetic biology processes that are outsourced to specialist providers for completion before being re-integrated into the original work stream to assemble into an experiment or goods, including making a specific strand of DNA or running a proprietary algorithm on a dataset.

2 Activities

Subject to the exceptions referred to in paragraphs 5 and 6, a qualifying entity carrying on activities that consist of or include any of the following—
(a) carrying on basic scientific research into synthetic biology;
(b) the development of synthetic biology;
(c) the production of goods using synthetic biology;
(d) the formulation of synthetic biology to enable the degradation of materials;
(e) the provision of services that enable the activities in paragraphs (a) to (d).

3 Meaning of synthetic biology

In this Schedule, "synthetic biology" means the process of applying engineering principles to biology to design, redesign or make biological components or systems that do not exist in the natural world.

4 Synthetic biology includes but is not limited to—
(a) the design and engineering of biological-based parts of—
 (i) enzymes;
 (ii) genetic circuits and cells;
 (iii) novel devices and systems;
(b) redesigning existing natural biological systems;
(c) using microbes to template materials;
(d) cell-free systems;
(e) gene editing and gene therapy;
(f) the use of DNA for data storage, encryption and bio-enabled computing.

5 Exceptions—general

Exceptions to the activities described in paragraph 2 are—

(a) general services or servicing not related to core synthetic biology, where "core" means those activities without which experiments cannot be conducted, such as DNA synthesis or cloning;

(b) the use of microorganisms to remove harmful contaminants, pollutants or toxins from the environment (known as bioremediation), including bio-based reagents that allow for testing for contaminants;

(c) any approach used to gather clinical information for the purpose of making a clinical decision or making a diagnosis (known as diagnostics) but not the storage or ownership of sensitive human genetic information that enables the identification of an individual;

(d) industrial biotechnology research, development or production using enzymes or organisms that have not been modified through the application of synthetic biology;

(e) the production of substances ordinarily consumed as food or used as feed, including any ingredient or component of such substances;

(f) gene therapy, where it is used solely for the purpose of replacing missing or defective genes to restore phenotypes to achieve a therapeutic effect;

(g) cell therapy, where cells are modified by genetic engineering and then introduced into a patient to treat disease.

6 Exceptions—human or veterinary medicines or immunomodulatory approaches

(1) Exceptions to the activities described in paragraph 2 are the ownership, ownership of intellectual property or development of the matters set out in sub-paragraph (2) that employ synthetic biology at any stage of the development or production, unless the circumstances set out in sub-paragraph (3) apply.

(2) The matters referred to in sub-paragraph (1) are—

(a) human or veterinary medicines;

(b) immunomodulatory approaches.

(3) The circumstances referred to in sub-paragraph (1) are where the matter described in sub-paragraph (2)—

(a) has a synthetic biology technology that could be employed or modified to produce, deliver or produce and deliver—

(i) toxic chemicals to achieve an incapacitating or lethal effect on humans or animals;

(ii) materials restricted under Schedule 5 to the Anti-terrorism, Crime and Security Act 2001; or

(b) uses substances or pathogens set out in Schedule 5 to the Anti-terrorism, Crime and Security Act 2001.

NOTES

Commencement: 4 January 2022.

SCHEDULE 17
TRANSPORT

Regulation 2

[2.225]

1 Interpretation—ports and harbours

In paragraph 2—

"harbour" is to be construed in accordance with section 313(1) of the Merchant Shipping Act 1995;

"infrastructure" means infrastructure, facilities and equipment within a port or harbour directly related to the movement of freight, passengers or seafarers;

"operating" means controlling the functioning of the port, harbour, terminal, wharf or other infrastructure;

"port" means an area of land and water made up of infrastructure which permits—

(a) the receiving and departing of ships;

(b) the loading and unloading of ships;

(c) the storage of cargo;

(d) the receipt and delivery of cargo; or

(e) the embarkation and disembarkation of passengers, crew and other persons;

"ship" is to be construed in accordance with section 313(1) of the Merchant Shipping Act 1995.

2 Activity—ports and harbours

A qualifying entity carrying on activities that consist of or include—

(a) owning or operating a port or harbour in the United Kingdom that handled 1 million tonnes or more of cargo as recorded in the Port Freight Annual Statistics published by the Department for Transport, in the year preceding the year in which the acquisition is due to be completed; or

(b) owning and operating terminals, wharves or other infrastructure situated in a port or harbour described in sub-paragraph (a).

3 Interpretation—airports and air traffic control

(1) In paragraph 4—

"airport" has the meaning set out in section 66(1) of the Civil Aviation Act 2012;

"en route air traffic control services" mean services provided pursuant to a licence under section 6 of the Transport Act 2000;

"operating an airport" means having overall responsibility for its management;

"parent undertaking" has the meaning set out in section 1162 of the Companies Act 2006;

(2) The entities that are to be regarded as owning an airport for the purposes of paragraph 4 are—

(a) a company which owns the airport ("C"); and

(b) any parent undertaking of C ;

(3) The entities that are to be regarded as owning a provider of en route air traffic control services for the purposes of paragraph 4 are—
- (a) a company which owns such a provider ("C"); and
- (b) any parent undertaking of C.

4 Activity—airports and air traffic control

A qualifying entity carrying on activities that consist of or include—
- (a) owning or operating an airport in the United Kingdom that handled at least six million passenger movements or 100,000 tonnes of freight in 2018, as recorded in the UK Airports Annual Statements of Movements, Passengers and Cargo published by the Civil Aviation Authority;
- (b) providing en route air traffic control services in the United Kingdom;
- (c) owning a provider of en route air traffic control services in the United Kingdom.

NOTES

Commencement: 4 January 2022.

NATIONAL SECURITY AND INVESTMENT ACT 2021 (PROCEDURE FOR SERVICE) REGULATIONS 2021

(SI 2021/1267)

NOTES

Made: 15 November 2021.
Authority: National Security and Investment Act 2021, s 53(1), (2).
Commencement: 4 January 2022.

ARRANGEMENT OF REGULATIONS

PART 1 INTRODUCTION

[2.226]

1 Citation, commencement, extent and application

(1) These Regulations may be cited as the National Security and Investment Act 2021 (Procedure for Service) Regulations 2021, and come into force on 4th January 2022.

(2) These Regulations extend to England and Wales, Scotland and Northern Ireland.

(3) These Regulations do not apply to a document if rules of court make provision about its service.

NOTES

Commencement: 4 January 2022.

[2.227]

2 Interpretation

(1) In these Regulations—

"the Act" means the National Security and Investment Act 2021;

"the NSI electronic portal" means an online facility provided by the Secretary of State for sending documents required or allowed to be given in connection with the Act;

"representative" means a person who has been appointed to act on behalf of another person in connection with the giving of documents under the Act.

(2) In these Regulations—
- (a) references to the giving of a document (however expressed) include references to the service of a document;
- (b) references to documents include references to orders, notices, notifications and applications required or allowed to be given under the Act.

NOTES

Commencement: 4 January 2022.

PART 2 SERVICE BY THE SECRETARY OF STATE

[2.228]

3 Service of documents by the Secretary of State

(1) A document required or allowed by the Act to be given to a person by the Secretary of State must be given—

(a) by sending it by email to that person's email address (or the email address of their representative), as provided for in regulation 4, or

(b) by posting it to that person's postal address (or the postal address of that person's representative), as provided for in regulation 5.

(2) For the purposes of paragraph (1)(b), "posting" a document means sending that document pre-paid by a postal service intended to ensure expeditious delivery.

(3) A document sent by email in accordance with paragraph (1)(a) is to be treated as having been given immediately after it is sent.

(4) A document posted in accordance with paragraph (1)(b)—

(a) to an address within the United Kingdom, is to be treated as having been given on the second working day after posting;

(b) to an address outside the United Kingdom, is to be treated as having been given on the fifth working day after posting.

(5) When giving a document under this regulation, the Secretary of State must mark it as being for the attention of the person to whom it is required or allowed to be given under the Act.

(6) Where the person referred to in paragraph (5) is a body corporate or unincorporate, the document being given to that person must additionally be marked as being for the attention of an officer or member of that body (as the case may be) whom the Secretary of State considers to be appropriate.

NOTES

Commencement: 4 January 2022.

[2.229]

4 Address for service by email under regulation 3(1)(a)

(1) For the purposes of regulation 3(1)(a), a person's email address (or the email address of their representative) is the email address provided by that person to the Secretary of State in connection with the giving of documents under the Act.

(2) Where an email address as referred to in paragraph (1) has not been provided, a person's email address is—

(a) in the case of an individual, an email address published for the time being by that person as an email address for contacting that person, or

(b) in the case of a body corporate or unincorporate, the general email address published for the time being by that body.

(3) Where an email address as referred to in paragraphs (1) and (2) has not been provided or published (as the case may be), or if the Secretary of State has reason to believe that such an address is unsuitable or inadequate, a person's email address is any email address by means of which the Secretary of State reasonably believes that the document will come to the attention of that person (or their representative).

NOTES

Commencement: 4 January 2022.

[2.230]

5 Address for service by post under regulation 3(1)(b)

(1) For the purposes of regulation 3(1)(b), a person's postal address (or the postal address of their representative) is the postal address provided by that person to the Secretary of State in connection with the giving of documents under the Act.

(2) Where a postal address as referred to in paragraph (1) has not been provided, a person's postal address is—

(a) where that person is a body corporate, the address of its registered office or principal office, or

(b) where that person is a partnership or an unincorporated association or body, the address of its principal office.

(3) In the case of—

(a) a body corporate registered outside the United Kingdom,

(b) a partnership carrying on business outside the United Kingdom, or

(c) an unincorporated association or body with offices outside the United Kingdom,

the references in paragraph (2) to its principal office include references to its principal office in the United Kingdom (if any).

(4) Where a postal address as referred to in paragraphs (1) and (2) has not been provided or is not known (as the case may be), or if the Secretary of State has reason to believe that such an address is unsuitable or inadequate, a person's postal address is any postal address by means of which the Secretary of State reasonably believes that the document will come to the attention of that person (or their representative).

NOTES

Commencement: 4 January 2022.

PART 3 SERVICE ON THE SECRETARY OF STATE

[2.231]

6 Service of documents on the Secretary of State

(1) The following documents required or allowed by the Act to be given by a person to the Secretary of State must be sent using the NSI electronic portal—

(a) a mandatory notice under section 14(1) of the Act;

(b) a validation application under section 16(1) of the Act;

(c) a voluntary notice under section 18(2) of the Act.

(2) Where a document is given to the Secretary of State in accordance with paragraph (1), the document is to be treated as having been given once it is registered on the NSI electronic portal.

(3) A document not covered by paragraph (1) which is required or allowed by the Act to be given by a person to the Secretary of State must be sent by email, to the email address specified for that purpose on the gov.uk website.

(4) Where a document is given to the Secretary of State in accordance with paragraph (3), the document is not to be treated as having been given until it is received by the Secretary of State in a form which is legible and capable of being used for subsequent reference.

(5) A document required or allowed by the Act to be given by a person to the Secretary of State may be given by that person's representative.

(6) This regulation is subject to regulation 7.

NOTES

Commencement: 4 January 2022.

[2.232]

7 Exceptions to regulation 6 requirements

(1) Paragraph (2) applies where a person who is required or allowed by the Act to give a document to the Secretary of State (or where that person's representative) considers that—

(a) they are unable to comply with the requirements in regulation 6, or

(b) there is a good reason not to comply with the requirements in regulation 6.

(2) The person (or their representative) must—

(a) establish contact with the Secretary of State by alternative means, within the time limit (if any) for giving the document to the Secretary of State, and

(b) propose to the Secretary of State an alternative means for giving the document to the Secretary of State (which may or may not be the same as the alternative means referred to in sub-paragraph (a)).

(3) Where the Secretary of State has been contacted in accordance with paragraph (2) and is satisfied that the person (or their representative) is unable or has good reason not to comply with the requirements in regulation 6, the Secretary of State must agree to be given the document by alternative means (which may or may not be the same as the alternative means referred to in paragraph (2)(a) or (b)).

(4) Where the Secretary of State agrees to be given a document by alternative means under this regulation—

(a) if there is a time limit for giving the document under the Act, that remains unchanged, and

(b) the document is not to be treated as having been given until it is received by the Secretary of State in a form which is legible and capable of being used for subsequent reference.

NOTES

Commencement: 4 January 2022.

NATIONAL SECURITY AND INVESTMENT ACT 2021 (PRESCRIBED FORM AND CONTENT OF NOTICES AND VALIDATION APPLICATIONS) REGULATIONS 2021

(SI 2021/1272)

NOTES

Made: 15 November 2021.

Authority: National Security and Investment Act 2021, ss 14(4), 16(3), 18(4).

Commencement: 4 January 2022.

ARRANGEMENT OF REGULATIONS

SCHEDULES

[2.233]
1 Citation, commencement and extent

(1) These Regulations may be cited as the National Security and Investment Act 2021 (Prescribed Form and Content of Notices and Validation Applications) Regulations 2021 and come into force on 4th January 2022.

(2) These Regulations extend to England and Wales, Scotland and Northern Ireland.

NOTES

Commencement: 4 January 2022.

[2.234]
2 Interpretation

In these Regulations—

"the Act" means the National Security and Investment Act 2021;

"body" means a body corporate, a partnership or an unincorporated association other than a partnership;

"dual-use items" means goods and technology, including software or information (other than information in the public domain), the export or transfer of which is controlled by virtue of their being specified in the relevant export control legislation;

"national infrastructure sector" means one of the following sectors listed by the Centre for the Protection of National Infrastructure as being sectors capable of containing critical national infrastructure—

(a) chemicals,
(b) civil nuclear,
(c) communications,
(d) defence,
(e) emergency services,
(f) energy,
(g) finance,
(h) food,
(i) government,
(j) health,
(k) space,
(l) transport, and
(m) water;

"notifying party" means the person who submits a mandatory notice, a validation application or a voluntary notice;

"relevant export control legislation" means—

(n) Annex 1 to Council Regulation (EC) No 428/2009 of 5 May 2009 setting up a Community regime for the control of exports, transfer, brokering and transit of dual-use items,
(o) the Schedule to the Export of Radioactive Sources (Control) Order 2006, and
(p) Schedules 2 and 3 to the Export Control Order 2008,

"representative" means a person who has been appointed to act on behalf of another person in connection with the giving of documents under the Act.

NOTES

Commencement: 4 January 2022.

[2.235]
3 Prescribed form and content of a mandatory notice

A mandatory notice must be in writing and contain—

(a) the information specified in Part 1 of Schedule 1,
(b) a declaration that the information provided in the notification is true and complete to the notifying party's knowledge, in the form set out in paragraph 39 of Part 2 of Schedule 1 and referred to as Declaration A, and
(c) where the notifying party has appointed a representative, a declaration that the notifying party confirms that the representative is authorised to submit the notice and to accept service, in the form set out in paragraph 40 of Part 2 of Schedule 1 and referred to as Declaration B.

NOTES

Commencement: 4 January 2022.

[2.236]
4 Prescribed form and content of a voluntary notice

A voluntary notice must be in writing and contain—

(a) the information specified in Part 1 of Schedule 2,
(b) a declaration that the information provided in the notification is true and complete to the notifying party's knowledge, in the form set out in paragraph 58 of Part 2 of Schedule 2 and referred to as Declaration A, and

(c) where the notifying party has appointed a representative, a declaration that the notifying party confirms that the representative is authorised to submit the notice and to accept service, in the form set out in paragraph 59 of Part 2 of Schedule 2 and referred to as Declaration B.

NOTES

Commencement: 4 January 2022.

[2.237]

5 Prescribed form and content of a validation application

A validation application must be in writing and—

(a) contain the information specified in Part 1 of Schedule 3,

(b) a declaration that the information provided in the application is true and complete to the notifying party's knowledge, in the form set out in paragraph 48 of Part 2 of Schedule 3 and referred to as Declaration A, and

(c) where the notifying party has appointed a representative, a declaration that the notifying party confirms that the representative is authorised to submit the application and to accept service, in the format set out in paragraph 49 of Part 2 of Schedule 3 and referred to as Declaration B.

NOTES

Commencement: 4 January 2022.

SCHEDULES

SCHEDULE 1

Regulation 3

PART 1 INFORMATION REQUIRED IN A MANDATORY NOTICE

Notifying party name and contact details

[2.238]

1. The acquirer's full name.

2. The acquirer's address.

3. Where the acquirer is an entity, the full name of an individual who holds or occupies a position in relation to the entity and who can be contacted in relation to the notice and the following information in relation to that individual—

(a) the position held in the entity,

(b) email address, and

(c) telephone number.

4. Where the acquirer has authorised a representative to submit the form and to accept service under the Act, the following information in relation to the representative—

(a) full name,

(b) business name,

(c) address,

(d) email address,

(e) telephone number, and

(f) details of the relationship between the representative and the acquirer.

Additional acquirers

5. (1) Where there is more than one acquirer involved in the acquisition, the information set out in subparagraphs (2) to (4), if known.

(2) The following information about each additional acquirer—

(a) name,

(b) address, and

(c) telephone number.

(3) Where an additional acquirer is an entity, the full name, of an individual who holds or occupies a position in relation to the entity and who can be contacted in relation to the notice, and the following information in relation to that individual—

(a) the position held in the entity,

(b) email address, and

(c) telephone number.

(4) The control thresholds set out in subsections (2), (5) and (6) of section 8 of the Act which are expected to be met by the additional acquirer and a description of the shares or voting rights expected to be acquired by the additional acquirer.

Related notifications

6. A statement of whether the acquirer (or in a case where there is more than one acquirer any of the acquirers) has submitted a notification to any overseas investment screening regimes within the last 12 months and specifying, if applicable, the following information about the notification—

(a) the name of the investment screening regime,

(b) the country, and

(c) any applicable case numbers or reference numbers.

Acquisition details

7. The areas of the economy as set out in the headings to the Schedules to the National Security and Investment Act 2021 (Notifiable Acquisition) (Specification of Qualifying Entities) Regulations 2021 in which the qualifying entity carries on activities and a description of those activities.

8. The control thresholds set out in subsections (2), (5) and (6) of section 8 of the Act which are expected to be met and provide a description of the shares or voting rights expected to be acquired by the acquirer.

9. The expected date of completion of the acquisition being notified.

Regulatory approvals

10. If applicable, the following information about any approvals given by a regulatory authority in the United Kingdom (including any approvals already given) required prior to completion of the acquisition—

(a) the name of the regulatory authority,
(b) details of the nature of the approval, and
(c) any key dates associated with those approvals.

Details of the qualifying entity

11. The qualifying entity's full name.

12. The qualifying entity's address.

13. If applicable, the qualifying entity's website address.

14. If known, the full name of an individual who holds or occupies a position in relation to the qualifying entity and who can be contacted in relation to the notice and the following information about that person—

(a) the position held in the qualifying entity,
(b) email address, and
(c) telephone number.

15. If the qualifying entity is registered in the United Kingdom, the following information—

(a) the Companies House registration number, and
(b) the Standard Industrial Classification code.

16. If the qualifying entity is formed or recognised under the law of a country or territory outside the United Kingdom, the following information in relation to the qualifying entity—

(a) the country of incorporation, and
(b) the full registration details within the country of incorporation.

17. A description of the activities which the qualifying entity carries out.

18. If known, a statement as to whether the qualifying entity is authorised to receive and/or store information which has been given a United Kingdom government security classification and, if it is, the following information—

(a) the classification level,
(b) the government department, agency or public body from which the information came, and
(c) a description of the information held by the qualifying entity under the authorisation.

19. A statement as to whether the qualifying entity requires any licences to operate within the areas of the economy as set out in the headings to the Schedules to the National Security and Investment Act 2021 (Notifiable Acquisition) (Specification of Qualifying Entities) Regulations 2021in the United Kingdom and, if it does, the following information in relation to each licence—

(a) the licence name,
(b) the name of the issuer of the licence, and
(c) the date when the licence was issued.

20. If known, a statement as to whether the qualifying entity owns or holds any dual-use items and, if it does, the name of each item and a description.

21. A statement as to whether the qualifying entity currently supplies, or in the past five years, has supplied, goods or services to a United Kingdom government department, agency or public body that relates to any one or more of the following areas—

(a) defence,
(b) national security responsibilities,
(c) law enforcement,
(d) national infrastructure.

22. If the qualifying entity supplies, or has supplied, goods or services for the purposes of paragraph 21, the following information—

(a) the name of the government department, agency or public body,
(b) a description of the supply relationship, and
(c) a statement of which of the areas referred to in paragraph 21 the supply relationship relates to.

23. A statement as to whether the qualifying entity currently, or in the past five years, has undertaken any research and development project that has been partly or wholly funded by any United Kingdom government department, agency or public body that relates to any one or more of the areas referred to in paragraph 21.

24. If the qualifying entity undertakes, or has undertaken, a research and development project as described in paragraph 23, the following information—

(a) the name of the research and development project,
(b) a description of the research and development undertaken,
(c) a statement of which area in paragraph 21 it relates to, and
(d) the name of the United Kingdom government department, agency or public body that provided the funding.

25. A statement as to whether, if known, the qualifying entity is party to any contracts which require personnel of the qualifying entity to hold national security vetting security clearance and, if so, the following information, if known—

(a) the level of clearances held, and

(b) the number of personnel holding that level of clearance.

Ownership and structure of the qualifying entity

26. The following information about the pre-acquisition structure of the qualifying entity which must be provided in a chart attached to the notice—

(a) the full names of shareholders with share ownership or voting rights of 5% or more specifying the percentage held by each, and

(b) the nationality (for individuals) or country of incorporation or constitution (for entities) of any shareholder listed in subparagraph (a).

27. The following details of the expected post-acquisition structure of the qualifying entity which must be provided in a chart attached to the notice—

(a) the full names of shareholders with share ownership or voting rights of 5% or more specifying the percentage held by each, and

(b) the nationality (for individuals) or country of incorporation or constitution (for entities) of any shareholders listed in subparagraph (a).

28. A statement as to whether any non-United Kingdom government has a direct or indirect role in the operation or decision making of the qualifying entity and, if it has, the following information in relation to each non-United Kingdom government—

(a) the name of the non-United Kingdom government or representative, and

(b) a description of the non-United Kingdom government's role and interests.

Details of the acquirer

29. A statement as to whether the acquirer is an individual or an entity.

30. The acquirer's nationality (for individuals) or country of incorporation or constitution (for entities).

31. Where the acquirer is an entity, the following information—

(a) if the acquirer is registered in the United Kingdom, the following information—

(i) the Companies House registration number, and

(ii) the Standard Industrial Classification code.

(b) if the acquirer is formed or recognised under the law of a country or territory outside the United Kingdom, the following information—

(i) the country of incorporation, and

(ii) the full registration details within the country of incorporation.

32. A description of the activities that the acquirer carries out.

33. A statement as to whether any non-United Kingdom government or any person acting on behalf of a non-United Kingdom government has any share ownership or voting rights in the acquirer and, if it has, the following information—

(a) the name of the non-United Kingdom government or the full name of the person acting on behalf of the non-United Kingdom government, and

(b) information on the amount of share ownership or voting rights held in the acquirer.

34. A statement of whether any non-United Kingdom government has a direct or indirect role in the operation or decision-making of the acquirer and, if it has, the following information in relation to each non-United Kingdom government—

(a) the name of the non-United Kingdom government or the full name of the person acting on behalf of the non-United Kingdom government, and

(b) a description of the government's role and interests.

35. A statement as to whether there will be any contractual arrangements in place regarding share ownership or voting rights between the acquirer and any other party in relation to the qualifying entity once the proposed acquisition has been completed and a description of any such contractual arrangements.

36. If applicable, the following information about the structure of the acquirer which must be provided in a chart attached to the notice—

(a) the full names of shareholders with share ownership or voting rights of 5% or more specifying the percentage held by each, and

(b) the country of nationality (for individuals) or country of incorporation or constitution (for entities) of any shareholders listed in subparagraph (a).

37. Where the acquirer will be acquiring indirect control over the qualifying entity, a statement—

(a) confirming that indirect control is to be acquired, and

(b) specifying the chain of entities which holds an interest or right in the acquirer, up to the last entity which holds the interest or right.

38. A statement of whether the acquirer has a board of directors and if applicable, the following information about each of the members of the board of directors or equivalent within the acquirer at the time of submitting the notification—

(a) the individual's full name,

(b) the individual's date of birth,

(c) the position held within the acquirer, and

(d) whether the person is classified as a politically exposed person (PEP) within the meaning given in regulation 35(12)(a) and (14) of the Money Laundering, Terrorist Financing and Transfer of Funds (Information on the Payer) Regulations 2017/692.

NOTES

Commencement: 4 January 2022.

PART 2 DECLARATIONS

Form of Declaration A

[2.239]

39. The form of Declaration A is—

"Declaration A

I declare that, to the best of my knowledge and belief, the information given in response to the questions in this Notice is true, correct, and complete in all material respects.

I understand that:

It is a criminal offence under section 34 of the National Security and Investment Act 2021 for a person recklessly or knowingly to supply to the Secretary of State information which is false or misleading in any material respect. This includes supplying such information to another person knowing that the information is to be used for the purpose of supplying information to the Secretary of State.

Signed:

Name: (block letters)

Position: (block letters)

Date:"

Form of Declaration B

40. The form of Declaration B is—

"Declaration B

I confirm that [full name of the representative] is authorised for the purpose of the acquisition described in this mandatory notice to submit this notice I hereby specify [the [email] address of the representative named in the notification] as an [email] address at which [name of the notifying party] will accept service of documents of any kind in connection with the National Security and Investment Act 2021 in relation to this Notice.

Signed:

Name: (block letters)

Position: (block letters)

Date:"

NOTES

Commencement: 4 January 2022.

SCHEDULE 2

Regulation 4

PART 1 INFORMATION REQUIRED IN A VOLUNTARY NOTICE

Notifying party name and contact details

[2.240]

1. A statement setting out whether the notifying party is the acquirer, seller or qualifying entity.

2. The notifying party's full name.

3. The notifying party's address.

4. Where the notifying party is an entity, the full name of an individual who holds or occupies a position in relation to the entity and who can be contacted in relation to the notice and the following information in relation to that individual—

(a) the position held in the notifying party,

(b) email address, and

(c) telephone number.

5. Where the notifying party has authorised a representative to submit the form and accept service, the following information in relation to the representative—

(a) full name,

(b) business name,

(c) address,

(d) email address,

(e) telephone number, and

(f) the relationship between the representative and the notifying party.

Acquirer's name and contact details

6. A statement as to whether there is more than one acquirer.

7. If the notifying party is not the acquirer, the following information in relation to the acquirer—

(a) full name, and

(b) address.

8. Where the acquirer is an entity, the full name, if known, of an individual who holds or occupies a position in relation to the entity and who can be contacted in relation to the notice, and the following information in relation to that individual—

(a) the position held in the entity,
(b) email address, and
(c) telephone number.

9. The control thresholds set out in subsections (2), (5) and (6) of section 8 or section 9 of the Act which are or are expected to be met by the acquirer and a description of the shares or voting rights being acquired by the acquirer.

10. Where the acquirer has authorised a representative to accept service under the Act on behalf of the acquirer, the following information in relation to the representative—
(a) full name,
(b) business name,
(c) address,
(d) email address,
(e) telephone number, and
(f) details of the relationship between the representative and the acquirer.

11. Where there is more than one acquirer involved in this acquisition, the information specified in paragraphs 7 to 10 must be provided in relation to each additional acquirer.

Related notifications

12. If known, a statement of whether the acquirer (or in a case where there is more than one acquirer, any of the acquirers) has submitted a notification to any overseas investment screening regimes within the last 12 months and specifying, if applicable, the following information about the notification—
(a) the name of the investment screening regime,
(b) the country, and
(c) any case numbers or reference numbers given.

Acquisition details

13. A statement specifying—
(a) whether the acquisition is in contemplation, in progress or has taken place,
(b) whether the notice is related to the acquisition of a qualifying asset or a qualifying entity, and
(c) if known, the date or the expected date of completion of the acquisition being notified.

14. If applicable, the following information about any approvals from a regulatory authority in the United Kingdom (including any approvals already given) required prior to completion of the acquisition—
(a) the name of the regulatory authority, and
(b) details of the nature of the approval, and
(c) any key dates associated with those approvals.

Details of the qualifying entity being acquired (to be provided in relation to an entity acquisition only)

15. The qualifying entity's full name.

16. The qualifying entity's address.

17. If applicable, the qualifying entity's website address.

18. If known, the full name of an individual who holds or occupies a position in relation to the qualifying entity and who can be contacted in relation to the notice and the following information about that person—
(a) the position held in the qualifying entity,
(b) email address, and
(c) telephone number.

19. If the qualifying entity is registered in the United Kingdom, the following information—
(a) the Companies House registration number, and
(b) the Standard Industrial Classification code.

20. If the qualifying entity is formed or recognised under the law of a country or territory outside the United Kingdom, the following information in relation to the qualifying entity—
(a) the country of incorporation, and
(b) the full registration details within the country of incorporation.

21. A description of the activities or services the qualifying entity provides or carries out.

22. If known, a statement as to whether the qualifying entity is authorised to receive and/or store information which has been given a United Kingdom government security classification and, if it is, the following information—
(a) the classification level,
(b) the government department, agency or public body from which the information came, and
(c) a description of the information held by the qualifying entity under the authorisation.

23. If known, a statement as to whether the qualifying entity holds any licences to operate in the United Kingdom and. if it does, the following information—
(a) the licence name,
(b) the name of the issuer of the licence, and
(c) the date when the licence was issued.

24. If known, a statement as to whether the qualifying entity owns or holds any dual-use items and, if it does, provide the name of each item and a description.

25. If known, a statement as to whether the qualifying entity currently supplies, or in the past five years, has supplied goods or services to a United Kingdom government department, agency or public body that relates to any one or more of the following areas—
(a) defence,

(b) national security responsibilities,
(c) law enforcement, or
(d) national infrastructure.

26. If the entity does supply, or has supplied, goods or services for the purposes of paragraph 25, the following information—
(a) the name of the department, agency or public body,
(b) a description of the supply relationship, and
(c) a statement of which of the areas referred to in paragraph 25 the supply relationship relates to.

27. If known, a statement as to whether the qualifying entity currently, or in the past five years, has undertaken any research and development project that has been partly or wholly funded by any United Kingdom government department, agency or public body that relates to any one or more of the areas referred to in paragraph 25.

28. If the qualifying entity undertakes, or has undertaken a research and development project for the purposes of paragraph 27, the following information—
(a) the name of the research and development project,
(b) a description of the research and development undertaken,
(c) a statement of which area in paragraph 25 it relates to, and
(d) the name of the United Kingdom government department, agency or public body that provided the funding.

29. If known, a statement as to whether, the qualifying entity is party to any contracts which require personnel of the qualifying entity to hold national security vetting security clearance and, if so, the following information—
(a) the level of clearances held; and
(b) the number of personnel holding that level of clearance.

Ownership and structure of the qualifying entity

30. The following information about the pre-acquisition structure of the qualifying entity which must be provided in a chart attached to the notice—
(a) the full names of shareholders with share ownership or voting rights of 5% or more specifying the percentage held by each, and
(b) the nationality (for individuals) or country of incorporation or constitution (for entities) of any shareholder listed in subparagraph (a).

31. The following details of the expected post-acquisition structure of the qualifying entity which must be provided in a chart attached to the notice—
(a) the full names of shareholders with share ownership or voting rights of 5% or more specifying the percentage held by each, and
(b) the nationality (for individuals) or country of incorporation or constitution (for entities) of any shareholders listed in subparagraph (a).

32. If known, a statement as to whether any non-United Kingdom government has a direct or indirect role in the operation or decision making of the qualifying entity and, if it has, the following information in relation to each non-United Kingdom government—
(a) the name of the non-United Kingdom government or representative, and
(b) a description of the non-United Kingdom government's role and interests.

Details of the qualifying asset being acquired (to be provided in relation to an asset acquisition only)

33. The category of a qualifying asset set out in subsection (4) of section 7 of the Act that the asset belongs to.

34. The location of the qualifying asset.

35. A description of the qualifying asset.

36. If known, a statement as to whether the qualifying asset has been given a United Kingdom government security classification and if it has, the following information—
(a) the classification level,
(b) the government department, agency or public body from which the classification came, and
(c) the reasons why the qualifying asset has a United Kingdom government security classification.

37. If a licence is required to operate the qualifying asset in the United Kingdom, details of—
(a) the licence name,
(b) the name of the issuer of the licence, and
(c) the date when the licence was issued.

38. If known, a statement as to whether the qualifying asset is considered a dual-use item and if it is, provide the name of the item and a description.

39. If known, a statement as to whether the qualifying asset is used to gather and/or hold data on United Kingdom citizens and, if it does, provide a description of the data gathered or held.

40. If known, a statement as to whether the qualifying asset holds any United Kingdom or internationally recognised standards, accreditations or certification.

41. If known, in case of a qualifying asset which is land or tangible (or, in Scotland, corporeal) moveable property, the full names of any person who has previously gained control over the qualifying asset before the acquisition takes place, which must be provided in a chart attached to the notice.

42. Specify the following information on the structure of the qualifying asset after the acquisition, in a chart attached to the notification—
(a) full names of those with rights or interests in the qualifying asset before the acquisition (if known), and
(b) specify the changes in rights or interests held in the qualifying asset as a result of the acquisition.

43. If known, a statement as to whether any non-United Kingdom government has a direct or indirect role in the control of the asset and, if it has, provide the name of the non-United Kingdom government and describe their role and interests.

44. If known, a statement as to whether there will be any contractual arrangements in place regarding share ownership or voting rights between the acquirer and any other party once the acquisition will have been completed.

Details of the acquirer

45. The acquirer's full name.

46. A statement as to whether the acquirer is an individual or an entity.

47. The country of incorporation or constitution (for entities) or the country of nationality (for individuals) of the acquirer.

48. If the acquirer is a qualifying entity registered in the United Kingdom, the following information—

(a) the Companies House registration number, and

(b) the Standard Industrial Classification code.

49. If the acquirer is formed or recognised under the law of a country or territory outside the United Kingdom, the following information—

(a) the country of incorporation, and

(b) the full registration details within the country of incorporation.

50. A description of the acquirer's main activities, products or services.

51. If known, a statement as to whether any non-United Kingdom government or any person acting on behalf of a non-United Kingdom government has any share ownership or voting rights in the acquirer and, if it has, the following information—

(a) the name of the non-United Kingdom government or the full name of the person acting on behalf of the non-United Kingdom government, and

(b) information on share ownership or voting rights held in the acquirer.

52. If known, a statement as to whether any non-United Kingdom government has a direct or indirect role in the operation or decision making of the acquirer and, if it has, the following information in relation to each non-United Kingdom government—

(a) the name of the non-United Kingdom government or the full name of the person acting on behalf of the non-United Kingdom government, and

(b) a description of the non-United Kingdom government's role and interests.

53. If known, a statement as to whether there will be any contractual arrangements in place regarding share ownership or voting rights between the acquirer and any other party in relation to the qualifying entity once the proposed acquisition has been completed and a description of any such contractual arrangements.

54. If applicable, the following information about the structure of the acquirer which must be provided in a chart attached to the notice—

(a) the full names of shareholders with share ownership or voting rights of 5% or more specifying the percentage held by each, and

(b) the country of nationality (for individuals) or country of incorporation or constitution (for entities) of any shareholders listed in subparagraph (a).

55. A statement as to whether any individual or entity is acquiring indirect control over the qualifying entity and if this is the case, provide details of the chain of individuals or entities that hold an interest or right.

56. A statement as to whether the acquirer has a board of directors and, if applicable, the following information about each of the members of the board of directors or equivalent within the acquirer at the time of submitting the notification—

(a) the individual's full name,

(b) the individual's date of birth,

(c) the position held within the acquirer, and

(d) whether the person is classified as a politically exposed person within the meaning given in regulation 35(12)(1)(a) and (14) of the Money Laundering, Terrorist Financing and Transfer of Funds (Information on the Payer) Regulations 2017/692.

Other

57. Any additional information the notifying party considers relevant to the notification.

NOTES

Commencement: 4 January 2022.

PART 2 DECLARATIONS

Form of Declaration A

[2.241]

58. The form of Declaration A is—

"Declaration A

I declare that, to the best of my knowledge and belief, the information given in response to the questions in this Notice is true, correct, and complete in all material respects.

I understand that:
It is a criminal offence under section 34 of the National Security and Investment Act 2021 for a person recklessly or knowingly to supply to the Secretary of State information which is false or misleading in any material respect. This includes supplying such information to another person knowing that the information is to be used for the purpose of supplying information to the Secretary of State.
Signed:
Name: (block letters)
Position: (block letters)
Date:"

Form of Declaration B

59. The form of Declaration B is—

"Declaration B
I confirm that [full name of the representative (if any)] is authorised for the purpose of the acquisition described in this form to act on behalf of the notifying party and to submit this form. I hereby specify [the [email] address of the representative named in the notification] as an [email] address at which [name of the notifying party] will accept correspondence and accept service of documents in accordance with the National Security and Investment Act 2021 (Procedure for Service) Regulations 2021.
Signed:
Name: (block letters)
Position: (block letters)
Date:"

NOTES

Commencement: 4 January 2022.

SCHEDULE 3

Regulation 5

PART 1 INFORMATION REQUIRED IN A VALIDATION APPLICATION

Notifying party name and contact details

[2.242]

1. A statement setting out whether the notifying party is the acquirer, seller, the qualifying entity or otherwise materially affected by the fact that the notifiable acquisition to which the application relates is void.

2. Details of how the notifying party has been materially affected by the fact that the notifiable acquisition to which the application relates is void.

3. A statement as to whether the information is provided by the notifying party or a representative.

4. The notifying party's full name.

5. The notifying party's address.

6. If applicable, where the notifying party is an entity, the full name of an individual who holds or occupies a position in relation to the entity and who can be contacted in relation to the notice and the following information in relation to that individual—

(a) the position held in the notifying party,
(b) email address, and
(c) telephone number.

7. Where the notifying party has authorised a representative to submit the application and to accept service under the Act, the following information in relation to the representative—

(a) full name,
(b) business name,
(c) address,
(d) email address,
(e) telephone number, and
(f) details of the relationship between the representative and the notifying party.

Acquirer's name and contact details

8. A statement as to whether there was more than one acquirer.

9. If the notifying party was not the acquirer, the following information in relation to the acquirer—

(a) name, and
(b) address,

10. Where the acquirer is an entity, the full name, if known, of an individual who holds or occupies a position in relation to the entity and who can be contacted in relation to the notice, and the following information in relation to that individual—

(a) the position held in the body,
(b) email address, and
(c) telephone number.

11. Details of which of the control thresholds set out in subsections (2), (5) and (6) of section 8 or section 9 of the Act that were met by the acquirer and a description of the shares or voting rights acquired by the acquirer.

12. If the notifying party was not the acquirer, and the acquirer has authorised a representative to accept service under the Act, the following information in relation to the acquirer's representative—

(a) full name,
(b) business name,
(c) registered address,
(d) email address,
(e) telephone number, and
(f) the relationship between the representative and the acquirer.

13. Where there was more than one acquirer involved in the acquisition, the information specified in paragraphs 9 to 12 in relation to each additional acquirer, if known.

Related notifications

14. A statement of whether the acquirer (or in a case where there is more than one acquirer any of the acquirers) has submitted a notification to any other overseas investment screening regimes within the last 12 months and specifying, if applicable the following information about the notification—
(a) the name of the investment screening regime,
(b) the country, and
(c) any case numbers or reference numbers given.

Acquisition details

15. If known, the reasons why the notifiable acquisition was not notified to the Secretary of State as required by section 14(1) of the Act.

16. The areas of the economy as set out in the headings to the Schedules in the National Security and Investment Act 2021 (Notifiable Acquisition) (Specification of Entities) Regulations 2021 in which the qualifying entity carries on activities and provide a description of those activities.

17. The control thresholds set out in subsections (2), (5) and (6) of section 8 of the Act 2021 that would have been met and provide a description of the shares or voting rights that would have been acquired by the acquirer had the notifiable acquisition not been void

18. The date that the notifiable acquisition completed.

Regulatory approvals

19. If applicable, the following information about any approvals given by a regulatory authority in the United Kingdom (including any approvals already given) that were required prior to completion of the acquisition—
(a) the name of the United Kingdom regulator,
(b) details of the nature of the approval, and
(c) any key dates associated with those approvals.

Details of the qualifying entity

20. The qualifying entity's full name.

21. The qualifying entity's address.

22. If known, the full name of an individual who holds or occupies a position in relation to the qualifying entity and the following information about that individual—
(a) the position held in the qualifying entity,
(b) email address, and
(c) telephone number.

23. If the qualifying entity is registered in the United Kingdom, the following information—
(a) the Companies House registration number, and
(b) the Standard Industrial Classification code.

24. If the qualifying entity is formed or recognised under the law of a country or territory outside the United Kingdom, the following information—
(a) the country of incorporation, and
(b) the full registration details within the country of incorporation.

25. A description of the activities which the qualifying entity carries out.

26. If known, a statement of whether the qualifying entity is authorised to receive and/or store information which has been given a United Kingdom government security classification and, if it is, the following information—
(a) the classification level,
(b) the government department, agency or public body from which the information came, and
(c) a description of the information held by the qualifying entity under the authorisation.

27. If known, a statement as to whether the qualifying entity requires any licences to operate within the areas of the economy as set out in the headings to the Schedules to the National Security and Investment Act 2021 (Notifiable Acquisition) (Specification of Qualifying Entities) Regulations 2021 in the United Kingdom and, if it does, the following information in relation to each licence—
(a) the licence name,
(b) the name of the issuer of the licence, and
(c) the date when the licence was issued.

28. If known, a statement as to whether the qualifying entity owns or holds any dual-use items and, if it does, the name of each item and a description.

29. If known, a statement as to whether the qualifying entity currently supplies, or in the past five years, has supplied, goods or services to a United Kingdom government department, agency or public body that relates to any one or more of the following areas—
(a) defence,

(b) national security responsibilities,
(c) law enforcement,
(d) critical national infrastructure.

30. If the entity does supply, or has supplied, goods or services for the purposes of paragraph 29, the following information—
(a) the name of the government department, agency or public body,
(b) a description of the supply relationship, and
(c) a statement of which of the areas referred to in paragraph 29 the supply relationship relates to.

31. If known, a statement as to whether the qualifying entity currently, or in the past five years, has undertaken any research and development project that has been partly or wholly funded by any United Kingdom government department, agency or public body that relates to any one or more of the areas referred to in paragraph 29.

32. If the qualifying entity undertakes, or has undertaken, a research and development project for the purposes of paragraph 31, the following information—
(a) the name of the research and development project,
(b) a description of the research and development undertaken,
(c) a statement of which area in paragraph 29 it relates to, and
(d) the name of the United Kingdom government department, agency or public body that provided the funding.

33. If known, a statement as to whether the qualifying entity is party to any contracts which require personnel of the qualifying entity to hold national security vetting security clearance and, if so, the following information, if known—
(a) the level of clearances held; and
(b) the number of personnel holding that level of clearance.

Ownership and structure of the qualifying entity

34. The following information about the pre-acquisition structure of the qualifying entity which must be provided in a chart attached to the notice—
(a) the full names of shareholders with share ownership or voting rights of 5% or more specifying the percentage held by each, and
(b) the nationality (for individuals) or country of incorporation or constitution (for entities) of any shareholder listed in subparagraph (a).

35. The following details of the post-acquisition structure of the qualifying entity which must be provided in a chart attached to the notice—
(a) the full names of shareholders with share ownership or voting rights of 5% or more specifying the percentage held by each, and
(b) the nationality (for individuals) or country of incorporation or constitution (for entities) of any shareholders listed in subparagraph (a).

36. If known, a statement as to whether any non-United Kingdom government has a direct or indirect role in the operation or decision making of the qualifying entity and, if it has, the following information in relation to each non-United Kingdom government—
(a) the name of the non-United Kingdom government or representative, and
(b) a description of the non-United Kingdom government's role and interests.

Details of the acquirer

37. A statement as to whether the acquirer is an individual or an entity.

38. The acquirer's nationality (for individuals) or country of incorporation or constitution (for entities).

39. Where the acquirer is an entity, the following information—
(a) if the acquirer is registered in the United Kingdom—
(i) the Companies House registration number, and
(ii) the Standard Industrial Classification code.
(b) if the acquirer is formed or recognised under the law of a country or territory outside the United Kingdom—
(i) the country of incorporation, and
(ii) the full registration details within the country of incorporation.

40. A description of the activities that the acquirer carries out.

41. If known, a statement as to whether any non-United Kingdom government or any person acting on behalf of a non-United Kingdom government has any share ownership or voting rights in the acquirer and, if it has, the following information—
(a) the name of the non-United Kingdom government or the full name of the person acting on behalf of the non-United Kingdom government, and
(b) information on the amount of share ownership or voting rights held in the acquirer.

42. If known, statement whether any non-United Kingdom government has a direct or indirect role in the operation or decision making of the acquirer and, if it has, the following information in relation to each non-United Kingdom government—
(a) the name of the non-United Kingdom government or the full name of the person acting on behalf of the non-United Kingdom government, and
(b) a description of the non-United Kingdom government's role and interests.

43. A statement as to whether there are any contractual arrangements in place regarding share ownership or voting rights between the acquirer and any other party in relation to the qualifying entity and a description of any such contractual arrangements.

44. The following information about the structure of the acquirer which must be provided in a chart attached to the application—

(a) the full names of shareholders with share ownership or voting rights of 5% or more specifying the percentage held by each, and
(b) the country of nationality (for individuals) or country of incorporation or constitution (for entities) of any shareholders listed in subparagraph (a).

45. Where the acquirer acquired indirect control over the qualifying entity, a statement—

(a) confirming that indirect control was acquired, and
(b) specifying the chain of entities which hold an interest or right in the acquirer, up to the last entity which holds the interest or right.

46. A statement as to whether the acquirer has a board of directors and, if applicable, the following information about each of the members of the board of directors or equivalent within the acquirer at the time of submitting this application—

(a) the individual's full name,
(b) the individual's date of birth,
(c) the position held within the acquirer, and
(d) whether the individual is classified as a politically exposed person within the meaning given in regulation 35(12)(a) and (14) of the Money Laundering, Terrorist Financing and Transfer of Funds (Information on the Payer) Regulations 2017.

Other

47. Any additional information the notifying party considers relevant to the application.

NOTES

Commencement: 4 January 2022.

PART 2 DECLARATIONS

Form of Declaration A

[2.243]

48. The content of Declaration A is—

"Declaration A

I declare that, to the best of my knowledge and belief, the information given in response to the questions in this Application is true, correct, and complete in all material respects.

I understand that:

It is a criminal offence under section 34 of the National Security and Investment Act 2021 for a person recklessly or knowingly to supply to the Secretary of State information which is false or misleading in any material respect. This includes supplying such information to another person knowing that the information is to be used for the purpose of supplying information to the Secretary of State.

Signed:
Name: (block letters)
Position: (block letters)
Date:"

Form of Declaration B

49. The content of Declaration B is—

"Declaration B

I confirm that [full name of the representative] is authorised for the purpose of the acquisition described in this form to act on behalf of the notifying party and to submit this form. I hereby specify [the [email] address of the representative named in the application] as an [email] address at which [name of the notifying party] will accept correspondence and accept service of documents in accordance with the National Security and Investment Act 2021 (Procedure for Service) Regulations 2021.

Signed:
Name: (block letters)
Position: (block letters)
Date:"

NOTES

Commencement: 4 January 2022.

PART 3
COMPETITION AND MARKETS AUTHORITY AND OTHER GUIDELINES

A. GENERAL

NOTES

The Director General of Fair Trading and sectoral regulators

The Director General of Fair Trading: the Enterprise Act 2002, s 2(1) provided that, as from the coming into force of that section (on 1 April 2003), the functions of the Director General of Fair Trading, his property, rights and liabilities were transferred to the Office of Fair Trading. Accordingly, (by virtue of s 2(2), (3) of the 2002 Act) the office of the Director was abolished, and any reference to the Director in any enactment, instrument or other document passed or made before the commencement of s 2(1) had, in so far as was necessary, effect as if it were a reference to the Office of Fair Trading. For transitional provisions in connection with the transfer, see Sch 24, para 6 to the 2002 Act at **[1.445]**. References in this Part to the Director General of Fair Trading should be construed accordingly. S 2 of the 2002 Act was repealed by the Enterprise and Regulatory Reform Act 2013, s 26(3), Sch 5, Pt 4, para 229, as from 1 April 2014 (see further the note relating to the Competition and Markets Authority below).

The Rail Regulator: the Railways and Transport Safety Act 2003, s 16 provided that, as from the coming into force of that section (on 5 July 2004), the functions, property, rights and liabilities, etc, of the Rail Regulator were transferred to the Office of Rail Regulation. Sch 3, para 4 to that Act further provided that references in any enactment, instrument or other document to the Rail Regulator shall, so far as necessary or appropriate in consequence of s 16, be treated after commencement as a reference to the Office of Rail Regulation (for transitional provisions in relation to, inter alia, the transfer of functions from the Rail Regulator to the Office of Rail Regulation, see Sch 3 to the 2003 Act). References in this Part to the Rail Regulator should be construed accordingly. The Office of Rail Regulation was subsequently renamed as the Office of Rail and Road on 16 October 2015 following ORR's appointment as Monitor for Highways England under the Infrastructure Act 2015.

Director General of Water Services: the functions, etc, of the Director General of Water Services were transferred to the Water Services Regulation Authority (Ofwat) on 1 April 2006 (see the Water Act 2003, s 36(1)). As to the transfer of the property, rights and liabilities of the Director General of Water Services to the Water Services Regulation Authority, see s 36(3) of, and Sch 3 to, the 2003 Act. References in this Part to the Director General of Water Services should be construed accordingly.

Director General of Telecommunications: as to the transfer of functions (etc) from the Director General of Telecommunications to OFCOM, see the Communications Act 2003, ss 30, 406, Schs 2, 17. For transitional provisions in connection with the transfer see s 31 of, and Sch 18 to, the 2003 Act. See also s 31(4) of the 2003 Act which provides that, on such day as the Secretary of State may by order appoint, the office of the Director General of Telecommunications shall be abolished. References in this Part to the Director General of Telecommunications should be construed accordingly.

The Competition and Markets Authority (references to the OFT and Competition Commission etc)

On 1 April 2014 the Competition and Markets Authority replaced the Office of Fair Trading and the Competition Commission as part of the wider reform to the UK competition regime. As a consequence, many of the OFT and Competition Commission guidance documents reproduced in previous editions of this Handbook have been replaced or rendered obsolete. Others have been adopted by the CMA Board, in some cases with amendments. See further the CMA's summary of responses to its consultation on the treatment of existing OFT and Competition Commission guidance CMA12resp (March 2014) which is available on the CMA's website at: www.gov.uk/government/uploads/system/uploads/attachment_data/file/288759/
CMA12resp_Proposed_approach_to_the_treatment_of_existing_OFTand_CC_guidance_FINAL.pdf, as well as the Publications section of the CMA's website.

With regard to the adoption of OFT and Competition Commission guidance documents by the CMA, the following should be noted:

— references to the OFT or CC (except where referring to specific past OFT or CC practice or case law) should be read as referring to the CMA

— references to 'referral to the CC' or 'a reference to the CC' should be read as the referral of a case by the CMA (or Secretary of State) either for a Phase 2 investigation involving an Inquiry Group of CMA panel members or for a market investigation by a market reference group of CMA panel members

— all references to issues of legal assessment and procedure in investigations under the Competition Act 1998 (CA98) must be read in the light of Competition Act 1998: Guidance on the CMA's investigation procedures in Competition Act 1998 cases (CMA8); in the case of conflict, CMA8 prevails.

— references to 'OFT Rules', 'Rules of Procedure' or equivalent should be read as referring to The Competition Act 1998 (Competition and Markets Authority's Rules) Order 2014 SI 2014/458 (the CA98 Rules) but note that in the case of any conflict between the Article numbers or content of the CA98 Rules and the previous OFT Rules, the CA98 Rules prevail.

— references to the substantive powers of investigation or assessment of the approach to applying legal powers (for example, the approach to publishing notices of investigation, interim measures or penalties for non-cooperation with an investigation under the CA98), should be read in light of CMA8.

— certain OFT or CC departments, teams or individual roles may not be replicated in the CMA, or may have been renamed; the CMA's structure is set out in their organisation chart (see **[3.74]**).

The Treaty of Lisbon, etc

The Treaty Establishing the European Community (the Treaty of Rome) was renamed and consolidated by the Treaty of Lisbon, which came into force on 1 December 2009 (ie, the Consolidated Version of the Treaty on the Functioning of the European Union). Articles 81 and 82 of the Treaty Establishing the European Community became Articles 101 and 102 of the TFEU. References to the former Treaty and to Articles 81 and 82 in this Part should be construed accordingly. References to the European Community (EC) should now also be read as references to the European Union (EU). The UK left the European Union at 11pm on 31 January 2020. The implementation period (as defined in the European Union (Withdrawal) Act 2018, s 1A(6) ended on 31 December 2020 (at 11pm).

COMPETITION COMMISSION SUGGESTED BEST PRACTICE FOR SUBMISSIONS OF TECHNICAL ECONOMIC ANALYSIS FROM PARTIES TO THE COMPETITION COMMISSION (CC2COM3 FEBRUARY 2009)

[3.1]

NOTES

As to the construction of this document (following the abolition of the OFT and Competition Commission), see further the note "The Competition and Markets Authority (references to the OFT and Competition Commission etc)" in the introductory notes to Part 3 *ante*.

Note also that all references to issues of jurisdiction or procedure in mergers cases, or to market studies or investigations, must be read in the light of Mergers: Guidance on the CMA's jurisdiction and procedure (CMA2) and Market studies and market investigations: Supplemental guidance on the CMA's approach (CMA3); in the case of conflict, CMA2 or CMA3 prevail.

CONTENTS

OBJECTIVES

[3.2]

1. Over the past few years, the Competition Commission (CC) has received an increasing number of submissions that involve formal economic modelling and sophisticated empirical work. These have come both from economic consulting firms and from academic experts working on behalf of parties to an inquiry, as well as from the parties directly. We expect the number of these submissions to increase further in the future and welcome this trend. We believe the use of empirical and quantitative methods can help us reach more informed decisions.

2. This document sets out some guiding principles for parties' submissions reporting the results of technical economic analysis in CC investigations.[1] These submissions, although undoubtedly of a technical nature, should as far as possible be comprehensible to non-economists – it is in parties' best interests to set out their analysis as clearly and completely as possible if they wish it to have the maximum impact.

3. As well as being of greater evidential value, presenting economic analysis in accordance with these guidelines will avoid disruption and delay to the CC's investigation—considerable time and resources can be wasted debating points that have not been properly explained. Submissions that follow the principles set out in this document are likely to be more persuasive.

NOTES

1 By technical economic analysis we mean any empirical analysis (statistical and econometric work), the results of simulation and profitability models, surveys and formal theoretical work that supports or counters a particular theory of harm or other line of inquiry. This may sometimes include analysis that is not purely economics-based, such as surveys of customers.

GENERAL PRINCIPLES

[3.3]

4. Before providing more detail, we set out below three general principles, which apply across a range of submissions.

CLARITY AND TRANSPARENCY

5. Submissions should not only present clearly the results and conclusions of the economic analysis undertaken, but they should also clearly state the methodology used, the assumptions made in reaching results, the justification for the methodology and the assumptions, and the robustness of the results to any assumptions made. Submissions should be understandable to non-economists, and CC economists should be able to determine how the analysis enables the parties' economic experts to reach the submitted conclusions.

COMPLETENESS

6. Submissions should contain a complete description of the analysis undertaken. All relevant assumptions should be discussed and choice of techniques explained. Relevant econometric output, diagnostic tests and checks for robustness should be included. Where references to academic literature have been made, these should also be cited.

7. The CC should be able to understand fully both the results and the economic theory and modelling that are generating those results, without having to seek more information from the submitting party.

REPLICATION OF RESULTS

8. In a number of cases, the CC will want to replicate the results of the analysis that has been submitted. This means that parties should be prepared to respond to a CC request, at very short notice, for all relevant computer code and data files necessary for the CC's economists to reproduce the results presented in the parties' submission. This will include the raw and the cleaned data and the programs for obtaining the latter from the former.

DETAILED GUIDANCE ON WRITTEN SUBMISSIONS

[3.4]
9. The following section contains more detailed advice on a range of issues that might be covered in a submission.

STRUCTURE OF SUBMISSIONS

10. When presenting technical analysis, any submission should contain:

(a) First, an executive summary of no more than five pages, which is accessible to non-economists and covers the purpose of the analysis, the nature of the data used, the methodology employed, the assumptions made, the results obtained and the robustness of the technical work.

(b) Secondly, an overview that might also include, for example, further reference to economic theory, literature, methodology and explanations of how common econometric problems have been solved (eg, endogeneity), how the model is identified and the choice of instrumental variables.

(c) Finally, a technical appendix presenting the methodology and results in much greater detail, including any algebraic manipulation of models, econometric output and diagnostic tests as appropriate.

11. The summaries and the technical appendix should always be totally consistent.

DATA ANALYSIS AND ECONOMETRIC ESTIMATION

12. When submitting the results of empirical analysis that relies on data, parties should take particular care to explain how any economic concerns have been addressed, and to ensure that relevant diagnostic robustness tests have been reported.

Econometric modelling

13. The submission should contain a clear explanation of any economic modelling that underpins the empirical analysis. Although formal economic modelling is not required in every case, econometric analysis is often based on important assumptions. The CC should be able to understand any assumptions that parties have made in setting up their analysis, so that it can assess the reasonableness of those assumptions and test them against all the evidence it has received in the case.

14. A list of references, including relevant articles that use a similar methodology, should also be included. These should include articles by academics and practitioners.

15. The submission should always contain a clear explanation of the rationale for the choice of methodology used to analyse the data. In doing this, any technical concerns should be addressed. By way of example, some particular concerns that might arise, and should be tackled, include:

(a) The economic concept of 'identification' – that is to explain if and how the model can identify the economic impacts that are being measured, separated from other factors and events. For example, an analysis of spending on a product before and after some event should be able to identify the impact of that event, separated from other factors that may have changed at the same time; or, when comparing levels of prices in different geographic areas, it should be able to identify whether this is due to the factor being considered, or some other factor that is often correlated with it.

(b) The choice of 'instrumental variables'. Sometimes, it may be preferable to use an alternative 'instrument' to substitute for the actual variable of interest, as a solution to certain econometric problems. However, in these cases, parties should explain why particular instruments have been chosen and consider the robustness of such choices.

(c) A common econometric method involves the estimation of reduced-form equations (eg reduced-form price equations), as opposed to structural equations that are directly derived from a formal economic model. However, the specifications of a reduced-form equation are best understood with an understanding of the underlying structural parameters. It will sometimes be difficult but, where possible, submissions relying on this type of modelling approach should provide the motivation for the econometric specification of a reduced-form equation.

(d) Omitted variables can be a common source of bias in econometric models. Where relevant and possible, submissions should include a consideration of what omitted variables there might be and the possible consequences their omission could have for the matter at hand.

16. This is by no means a comprehensive list and a similarly thorough approach should also be taken with any other econometric issues as they arise.

Presenting results

17. When presenting the results of statistical and econometric modelling in written submissions, parties should always include the appropriate diagnostic test results (t-statistics, R2, etc). Unless the CC is able to understand both the statistical and economic significance of the reported results it will not be able properly to evaluate the importance of modelling output and the results will be less influential. Accordingly, the economic significance of results should also be explained, especially when this is not clear from the econometric output.

Testing robustness

18. It is good practice to test the robustness of econometric analysis—in other words, to test whether the results are sensitive to plausible changes in the assumptions. The CC may want to carry out its own tests, but would expect evidence of the robustness of a piece of analysis to be provided by the parties.

Underlying data and files

19. As mentioned in the general principles above, parties should be prepared to submit data and files at very short notice, to enable the CC to replicate any analysis. The code should be clear, with a description provided such that it is easy to match it with the reported results.

Providing data

20. 'Raw' data should be provided wherever possible. For example, if a piece of analysis is based on daily transaction price data but only uses monthly average prices, the CC will require access to the daily data. Because the aggregation and cleaning of data may have a significant impact on the outcome of statistical or econometric analysis, it is important that the CC has access to the underlying data.

21. Parties should also make clear how raw data has been compiled and what steps have been taken to ensure its reliability. For instance, if the raw data is based on a sample of individual customer accounts, an explanation of how these accounts have been chosen and why they are representative of all customers should also be provided.

Providing program files

22. Parties should provide the program files that manipulate and clean the raw data in preparation for the analysis. Analysis often relies on data that has been 'cleaned' – for a variety of reasons one may want to discard some observations, either because they are considered as outliers, or because there is a reporting error. Although data cleaning is perfectly legitimate, the CC will want to see for itself how this process has been performed in any given case. Parties should provide a precise description of the data-cleaning process, preferably provided as annotated computer code, and specifying the nature and number of data records eliminated or changed at each step.

23. The files generating the econometric and statistical analyses should also be provided to the CC. Again, clear and complete comments should be included along with the code in the program files.

24. Using procedures in statistical packages tends to provide a better audit trail than using spreadsheets, so we encourage their use where possible. Although we do not mind receiving spreadsheet analysis, it can be more difficult to unpick the procedures from the data.

Survey evidence

25. Parties sometimes submit evidence which relies on surveys—for example, the percentages of customers who hold particular opinions. When the CC is to rely on survey evidence prepared or commissioned by the parties, as well as needing to see the precise questions that have been asked, it will also require additional supporting information and submissions should include the following:

Description of the research process

- A short statement of the purpose of the survey and the brief given to the research team, describing the members of the team that managed the research, including their roles in the team and their affiliations, and the timeline of the research project, including fieldwork.

Description of the sample and research process

- A short description of the sampling design and research methodology, which should cover:
  - (i) How respondents were selected and approached, including which quotas were used and how they were determined and implemented, the locations and timing of fieldwork and the rationale for such choices.
  - (ii) The methods used to collect data and the rationale, if any, for these methods.
  - (iii) A short description of the final sample that was achieved, including counts of the numbers not responding or excluded by category, and a comparison of the characteristics of the sample with those of the population from which the sample was drawn (eg age, social grade).
  - (iv) Research input materials, including the question script containing the questions with any pre-coded responses, code-frames used to categorize verbatim answers, and supplementary instructions or materials given to respondents, fieldworkers or interviewers where these are not obvious from the question script.

Description of output

- Research output materials, including any original presentation files or reports arising from the research; any tables of results used either to generate the presentation files or reports; and any tables of results otherwise being used by the party as evidence. Where tables or charts report weighed results, parties should provide counts of unweighted responses and detail of weights used.

26. In addition, where the CC believes that the survey may contain further evidence that would be of value to its inquiry, the CC may require the party to submit further information from the survey. In doing so, the CC will wish to respect the professional code of the Market Research Society regarding any assurances provided to respondents (such as assurances of confidentiality or anonymity at the time of interview).

Formal economic modelling

27. The submission of formal economic models is welcomed, as it can formalize the logic of economic arguments in a rigorous manner.

Identifying key assumptions

28. All economic models make assumptions for convenience and tractability. The sub-mission should present all assumptions clearly, and discuss the reasons for making each in turn. As for the empirical modelling discussed above, it is important that the CC is able to test any assumptions that parties have made against all the evidence it has received in the case.

Algebraic manipulations and proof

29. All key results should be clearly derived, setting out the relevant algebraic manipulations and proofs.

Sensitivity analysis

30. Because a formal economic model is based on a set of assumptions, a discussion of the robustness of the results is warranted. For example, the submission should make clear whether the results would hold generally when a specific functional form is adopted. Alternatively, assuming a particular market structure might have some impact on the final results.

31. It would also be helpful to provide a numerical simulation to see how the results vary with different parameter values.

Relevant economic literature

32. The submission should also contain references to the relevant economic literature.

Simulation models

33. Simulation models are based on formal, structural economic models. Therefore, the same requirements also apply for this type of submission.

34. The parties should provide all program files that generated the simulation results.

Models of economic profitability

35. Models of economic profitability are welcome because they can be useful in helping to understand the deficiencies in profit calculations based purely on accounting data. Parties should bear in mind that such models will normally be scrutinized within the CC by Chartered Accountants, rather than economists, however the general principles set out earlier in this document apply equally to these models as to other economic models.

36. The following specific points should be borne in mind when submitting material of this type:

(a) Explanatory notes should be provided, including a clear explanation of the approach taken to the modelling and why this is to be preferred over other approaches; a clear explanation of how the spreadsheet model has been constructed, including the use of any macros; and an explanation of the sources of data used as inputs to the model. All assumptions should be clearly listed and the derivation of these assumptions should be fully explained.

(b) An explanation of how input data can be traced back to, or reconciled to, audited financial data should be provided. Where this is not possible, it is important to explain the reasons for this. Consideration will also be given to whether the input data and assumptions are used by the business in reviewing its financial performance.

(c) The full spreadsheet model should be submitted, including integral formulae, to enable the model to be replicated by the CC.

Part 3 CMA and other Guidelines

CHAIRMAN'S GUIDANCE ON DISCLOSURE OF INFORMATION IN MERGER INQUIRIES, MARKET INVESTIGATIONS AND REVIEWS OF UNDERTAKINGS AND ORDERS ACCEPTED OR MADE UNDER THE ENTERPRISE ACT 2002 AND FAIR TRADING ACT 1973 (CC7 (REVISED) APRIL 2013)

[3.5]

NOTES

As to the construction of this document (following the abolition of the OFT and Competition Commission), see further the note "The Competition and Markets Authority (references to the OFT and Competition Commission etc)" in the introductory notes to Part 3 preceding **[3.1]**.

Note also that this guidance must be read in the light of Transparency and disclosure: Statement of the CMA's policy and approach (CMA6). In particular, paragraph 9.9 *post* has been amended by CMA6 to read as follows: "Groups are reminded of the opportunity provided to parties to make further representations to the Procedural Officer if they wish to dispute the proposal of a Group to disclose information. This is additional to the opportunity for parties to make known their concerns to the Group. Groups are required to have regard to the views of the Procedural Officer if the party has made representations to him. The decision to disclose will, however, remain that of the Group."

Note also that the CMA has published updated guidance on market investigation procedures, contained within CMA3. The following paragraphs are particularly affected by the changes: 6.5, 6.13, 7.1 to 7.3, 8.3, 8.4, 9.8 and the table in the Explanatory Note. In the case of conflict, CMA3 prevails.

The fines that could be imposed on summary conviction for certain criminal offences referred to in this document were, at that time, subject to specific caps of £5,000 or above. With effect from 12 March 2015, these caps have been removed and those specific offences are now punishable by a fine of any amount.

CONTENTS

1. INTRODUCTION

[3.6]

1.1 This is the Guidance of the Chairman of the Competition Commission (the CC Chairman) to the groups of the Competition Commission (the CC) appointed to consider merger inquiries and market investigations and to review undertakings and orders under the Enterprise Act 2002 (the Act) and the Fair Trading Act 1973 (FTA 1973) (referred to below as 'Groups') on the disclosure of information. The Guidance has been issued by the CC Chairman under paragraphs 19A (7) and (8) of Schedule 7 to the Competition Act 1998 following consultation with the members of the CC and other appropriate persons.

1.2 The Guidance explains the CC's transparency aims and the statutory framework relating to the CC's handling and disclosure of information. It provides guidance on disclosure during merger inquiries, market investigations and reviews of undertakings and orders. Finally, it provides guidance on various practical aspects of handling information received and requests for confidentiality.

1.3 The Guidance should be read in conjunction with the CC's *Rules of Procedure*,[1] which bind Groups.

NOTES

[1] *Competition Commission Rules of Procedure*, 2006 (CC1).

2. TRANSPARENCY AIMS

[3.7]

2.1 The CC aims to be open and transparent in its work while, as appropriate, maintaining the confidentiality of information that it obtains during its inquiries and reviews.[2]

2.2 Transparency facilitates inquiries for a number of reasons:

(a) First, it is a means of achieving due process and of ensuring that by having a better understanding of the CC's analysis affecting them, the main parties in inquiries are treated fairly.

(b) Secondly, it enables other interested persons, such as consumers and their representative bodies, suppliers and customers and other persons who may be affected by the CC's decision, to understand the issues that the CC is considering and then to form effectively their input to the process.

(c) Thirdly, transparency helps main parties and other interested persons when they are providing the CC with information, including identifying inaccuracies and incomplete or misleading information.

(d) Fourthly, as a result of the above, the effectiveness, efficiency and quality of CC inquiries and decisions are improved.

NOTES

[2] Unless stated to the contrary, reference to inquiries is to merger inquiries, and market investigations. References to reviews are to reviews of undertakings and orders under the Act or the FTA 1973.

3. SCOPE AND APPLICATION OF THIS GUIDANCE

[3.8]

3.1 The Guidance applies to all merger and market inquiries investigated by the CC and also to the review by the CC of undertakings accepted and orders made under the Act and the FTA 1973. It applies throughout these inquiries or reviews (for example, from the reference through to final determination, including the reconsideration of any decisions that are remitted back to it).

3.2 The Guidance provides guidance on the treatment of information as provided for in Part 9 of the Act.[3]

3.3 Although this Guidance sets out the general framework within which the CC considers disclosure issues, the circumstances of an individual case (including practical considerations) may call for a flexible approach to the means by which the CC achieves its transparency aims.[4] There can be many reasons for this including, for example:

(a) the nature of the inquiry or review—for example, market investigations typically involve several main parties, and there is often widespread interest in the investigation leading to extensive use of the CC's website as a means of disclosure;

(b) the nature of the information—the information may be confidential information or may be information to which the Data Protection Act 1998 applies so it may be appropriate for any disclosure to be on a limited and restricted basis;

(c) the relevance of the information to the case—the information may be confidential but nonetheless disclosure may be necessary because of its relevance; and

(d) practical and timing considerations—for example, in a merger inquiry information about the CC's developed thinking on remedies and submissions received may be included in a remedies working paper provided to the main party but not usually published.[5]

3.4 The Guidance reflects the current practices of the CC. However, the CC is continuously developing its procedures as it aims to develop best practice. If a Group encounters a situation not covered in this Guidance, or if it considers that it wishes to depart from the Guidance, the Chairman of the Group should normally consult the CC Chairman.

NOTES

3 Unless stated to the contrary, references in this guidance to sections are to sections of the Act.

4 The possible manner of disclosure is discussed in Part 9.

5 As described in *Merger Remedies: Competition Commission Guidelines*, November 2008 (CC8), a provisional decision on remedies may be set out in the form of a remedies working paper or provisional decision document published on the CC website or circulated to relevant parties.

4. STATUTORY CONSIDERATIONS RELEVANT TO DISCLOSURE

[3.9]

4.1 The Act imposes a general restriction on the disclosure by the CC of 'specified information'. Specified information includes information that the CC obtains in merger inquiries or market investigations,[6] but does not include information which is already lawfully in the public domain.[7] Where that information relates to the affairs of an individual or to the business of an undertaking disclosure is prohibited during the lifetime of the individual or while the undertaking continues in existence, save as permitted by the Act.

4.2 The Act permits the CC to disclose 'specified information':

(a) if the CC obtains the required consent or consents;[8]

(b) if the disclosure is required for the purpose of a Community obligation;[9]

(c) if the disclosure is made for the purpose of facilitating the exercise by the CC of any function it has under or by virtue of the Act or any other enactment;[10]

(d) if the information is disclosed to another person for the purpose of facilitating the exercise by that person of any function he has under or by virtue of the Act or another enactment specified in Schedule 15 to the Act or such subordinate legislation as the Secretary of State may specify in an order;[11] or

(e) if the information is disclosed:
  (i) in connection with the investigation of any criminal offence in any part of the UK;
  (ii) for the purposes of any criminal proceedings there; and
  (iii) for the purpose of any decision whether to start or bring to an end such an investigation or proceedings.[12]

4.3 The circumstances described in paragraph 4.2 are often referred to as 'information gateways'. Where the CC discloses information to a person there may be restrictions on the further disclosure or use of the information by that person.[13] In some instances the CC's consent is required before the disclosed information may be disclosed further.[14]

4.4 If any of these information gateways apply and before disclosing any specified information, the CC must have regard to three considerations:[15]

(a) the need to exclude from disclosure (so far as practicable) any information whose disclosure the CC thinks is contrary to the public interest;

(b) the need to exclude from disclosure (so far as practicable):
  (i) commercial information whose disclosure the CC thinks might significantly harm the legitimate business interests of the undertaking to which it relates; or
  (ii) information relating to the private affairs of an individual whose disclosure the CC thinks might significantly harm the individual's interests; and

(c) the extent to which the disclosure of the information mentioned in (b)(i) or (ii) is necessary for the purpose for which the CC is permitted to make disclosure.

4.5 These three considerations apply on each occasion that the CC is considering disclosure of specified information: for example, in correspondence, at hearings and in a disclosed or published document. The Act does not contain specific provision for excisions from reports, save in some cases concerning public interest considerations.[16]

4.6 The CC will give special consideration to the potential harms associated with disclosure where 'sensitive information' is concerned, sensitive information being information referred to in the first and second of the considerations (ie 4.4(a) and (b)). The CC's processes provide persons with the opportunity to state a view on the sensitivity of the information they have provided (see Part 9). It is the Group's responsibility to consider whether the disclosure of the information claimed by a party to be sensitive would in fact harm a person. If harm or potential harm is established, the Group will go on to consider whether the circumstances of the case merit disclosure of the information in any event.

NOTES

6 See sections 237 and 238 of the Act. This general restriction on disclosure also applies to any information obtained by the CC under Part 7 (Miscellaneous Competition Provisions), under any of the enactments listed in Schedule 14 to the Act, or under any secondary legislation specified by the Secretary of State in an order (section 238).

7 Section 237(3).

8 Section 239 specifies the consents that are required.

9 Section 240.

10 Section 241(1).

11 Section 241(3).

12 Section 242(1).

13 Sections 241(2)(4) and 242(2).

14 Section 241(2).

15 Section 244.

16 Sections 118 and 177.

5. APPROACH TO DISCLOSURE OF INFORMATION RECEIVED DURING INQUIRIES OR REVIEWS

[3.10]

5.1 When determining how best to achieve the transparency aims of the CC (see paragraph 2.2), Groups must have regard to the statutory framework (see Part 4) and the CC's Rules and guidance published by the CC or the CC Chairman relating to the CC's process and conduct of investigations.[17]

5.2 Additionally, Groups should have regard to:

(a) the desirability of Groups taking a consistent approach when applying the principles of disclosure;

(b) the desirability of avoiding unnecessary burdens on business, the need to conduct investigations effectively and efficiently, the need to reach properly reasoned decisions within statutory and administrative timescales;

(c) the need to disclose information supplied to the CC so that interested persons (main parties or other interested persons) are able to comment on matters affecting them and so that they can draw to the CC's attention any inaccuracies, incomplete or misleading information;

(d) the need to protect some information provided to it in the course of its inquiries or reviews and the importance of maintaining the CC's reputation for doing so;

(e) the CC's analysis as it affects them; and

(f) the desirability of making sufficient information available to the public so that the public may become aware of the main issues arising in inquiries and reviews and are in a more informed position to provide information to the Group.

These considerations may inform the Group as to whether particular information should be disclosed, to whom and the manner of disclosure.

5.3 For the most part these factors will not be in conflict with the CC's transparency aims and its statutory functions. However, when decisions are finely balanced, Groups should pay particular attention to the need to achieve due process.

5.4 In the following parts guidance is provided by reference to the various types of information the CC receives during an inquiry or review and to the format in which it is received. Guidance is also provided on the considerations relevant to the disclosure by the CC of its assessment, analysis and thinking. More information about the manner and timing of disclosure can be found in subsequent parts of this Guidance.

NOTES

17 For example, Groups contemplating the disclosure of information to a public body (during investigations) should have regard to the CC's guidance on the *Disclosure of information by the Competition Commission to other public authorities*, April 2006 (CC12). Groups should also have regard to the CC's *Merger Procedural Guidelines* (CC18) and *Guidelines for market investigations: Their role, procedures, assessment and remedies*, April 2013 (CC3), as appropriate.

6. INFORMATION RECEIVED BY THE CC

[3.11]

6.1 This part lists the main types of information received by the CC in the course of an inquiry or review by reference to the format in which information is received and provides guidance to Groups on their approach to disclosure for each type. In respect of each type this Guidance suggests the usual approach, timing and manner of disclosure. These may need to vary according to the circumstances.

(A) RESPONSES TO INFORMATION REQUESTS IN THE FIRST DAY LETTER, CC QUESTIONNAIRES, ETC

6.2 The information received through such responses from main and third parties is predominantly of a factual nature (often of confidential information relating to the firm's business) although there may be some content that expresses the party's views. The factual information in particular may be revised or supplemented in the course of the CC's inquiry or review. Particularly in inquiries, some of the information initially received may enable the development of the CC's understanding of the market and the parties concerned but may not be of relevance to the CC's analysis and ultimately, its findings.

6.3 In most inquiries and reviews it will not be appropriate to disclose these responses. However, as the inquiry or review develops, the Group may need to consider which of the factual information provided is relevant to its analysis and as such should be disclosed. The usual form of disclosure of such information will be through the incorporation of relevant material into the CC's documents (eg annotated issues statement, any disclosed working papers, provisional findings decision and report, and for reviews, the provisional decision and final decision or notice of intention to vary or terminate the remedy). Data will often be aggregated (see Part 9). See paragraphs 6.4 to 6.8 below in relation to the handling of any views included in such responses.

(B) OTHER WRITTEN SUBMISSIONS FROM MAIN PARTIES

6.4 During the course of an inquiry or review main parties are likely to make numerous submissions, either at the party's initiative or in response to a request from the CC. A distinction can generally be drawn in submissions between key arguments and detailed evidence, the latter often containing confidential information though the former may also contain some confidential information. The latter type of information should be treated in a similar way as responses to CC information requests (see paragraphs 6.2 and 6.3).

6.5 Groups should aim to disclose the main parties' key arguments on the issues raised in the inquiry or review, in particular from their responses to the First Day letter and the CC's key publications (eg issues statement, annotated issues statement in market investigations, notice of provisional findings and notice of possible remedies in inquiries and provisional decision on remedies (usually published in market investigations only) and responses to any views of other main or third parties or working papers disclosed to it.[18] However, it is unlikely to be necessary or practical for all such submissions to be disclosed. For example, the CC often receives the same key arguments repeatedly.

6.6 Generally, Groups should aim to disclose key arguments through publication because of the second, third and fourth of the aims mentioned in paragraph 2.2. An exception is when the response is to a communication (eg an annotated issues statement or a working paper) that was not published. In cases where there are several interested persons (eg market investigations involving several main parties or when there are interested third parties) publication may also be a practical means of ensuring due process. When publication is not practical or appropriate, Groups should consider whether disclosure to one or more parties is appropriate for the purpose of achieving due process.

(C) OTHER WRITTEN SUBMISSIONS OF THIRD PARTIES

6.7 Similarly, Groups should aim to disclose third parties' key arguments on the issues raised in the inquiry or review, in particular in third parties' responses to the CC's key publications and responses to the disclosed submissions of other parties and any disclosed working papers.

6.8 Generally, Groups should aim to disclose responses to publications through publication because of the second, third and fourth reasons mentioned in paragraph 2.2. However, when that is not practical or appropriate, Groups should consider whether disclosure to main and sometimes other third parties by some other means is appropriate for the purpose of achieving due process.

(D) SURVEYS COMMISSIONED BY MAIN AND THIRD PARTIES

6.9 Groups should aim to disclose reports of surveys commissioned by main and third parties. This is particularly the case if the survey was commissioned in contemplation of the inquiry or review by the party submitting the survey. A summary of the survey methodology should similarly be disclosed, when available. However, Groups should be sensitive to concerns about the commercial value of the survey, particularly if the survey was prepared for purposes unrelated to that party's involvement in the CC's inquiry or review.

6.10 Generally, Groups should aim to disclose such reports through publication for the reasons that apply to other aspects of key submissions. However, when that is not practical or appropriate, Groups should consider other means of disclosure to main and sometimes interested third parties.

6.11 Sometimes the CC will also receive underlying data or information relating to the survey. Because of the likely sensitivity of that data, particularly when it is personal data for the purposes of the Data Protection Act 1998, it is not presumed that the information will be disclosed. Generally, it will not be necessary to disclose the underlying data. Additional comment on the manner of any disclosure is found in Part 9.

(E) INFORMATION RECEIVED IN THE COURSE OF HEARINGS, MEETINGS AND TELEPHONE CONVERSATIONS

6.12 During inquiries or reviews there will be numerous oral communications between a party and the CC including hearings, meetings and telephone conversations. The purpose of such communications and the nature of the information exchanged will vary, and these factors will be relevant to the consideration of whether any disclosure is necessary. For example, communications concerned with the administration and conduct of the case will seldom, if ever, merit disclosure. In contrast, hearings are occasions on which submissions relevant to the CC's analysis are made by main or third parties, so that it is necessary for Groups to consider the appropriateness of disclosing the content of hearings and the manner of that disclosure.

6.13 For hearings with main or third parties[19] held by Groups or CC staff, Groups should consider whether any points arising should be disclosed to another main or third party.[20] Generally, when hearings are held in private (including joint hearings), transcripts or notes prepared of the hearings should not be disclosed except to the parties in attendance.[21] However, Groups should consider the need to disclose key arguments by providing a summary of the key points (such an approach would help ensure consistency with the approach to written submissions (see paragraphs 6.4 to 6.8)). In contrast, the transcripts of round-table hearings with experts should be disclosed and may often be suitable for publication.[22]

6.14 When preparing summaries of key points, Groups should have regard to the need to exclude confidential information. Generally, summaries should be disclosed through publication. However, there may be occasions when it is not appropriate to disclose the summaries due to the sensitivity of the information or the identity of the person providing evidence (or both). The information may, for example, refer to a party's future business strategy. In such circumstances, Groups will need to consider whether alternative means of disclosure of the key points raised is appropriate.

(F) INFORMATION FROM REFERRING BODY ON MAKING A REFERRAL OR ADVISING ON THE NEED FOR REVIEW OF REMEDIES

6.15 When making a reference, the Office of Fair Trading (OFT), or the Minister or regulator who has made the reference (the 'referring body'), is required by law to publish the reasons for making the reference. Similarly, when the OFT advises on the need for a review of an undertaking accepted or order made under the Act or the FTA 1973, the OFT usually publishes a non-confidential version of its advice on its website together with its reasons either at the time of submitting the advice or to coincide with the publication by the CC of its provisional decision.[23] Typically, the referring body will also provide the CC with additional information from its files which may be of use to the CC at the early stage of its inquiry (for example, to identify issues which enable the CC to explore and formulate its theories of harm). The information shared with the CC may include written submissions from main and third parties, analysis conducted by or reports commissioned by the referring body, and clarification of the approach taken by the referring body. Similarly, in reviews, the OFT will provide to the CC any application that originated the review and any further submissions received.

6.16 Discussions between the referring body and the CC (which may take place either shortly before or following the reference or request for review) are likely to be useful to the CC as it prepares for the inquiry or review, but these discussions are unlikely to involve the exchange of information that ought to be disclosed.

6.17 Groups should consider whether there is a need to disclose any information received in writing from the referring body to parties for reasons of due process but generally, this will not be necessary for a number of reasons.

6.18 For example, in inquiries *(a)* to the extent the issues raised are relevant to the CC's investigations, the issues will be explored in hearings, requests for information and various CC publications; and *(b)* submissions or analysis made or undertaken prior to the reference may be irrelevant to the direction the CC's inquiry takes. The submissions and analysis may be out of date or may be superseded by later submissions and responses to the CC during its inquiry or review. Examples of when the content of documents passed to the CC may need to be disclosed, however, are: *(a)* where the CC is making use of economic or profitability analysis undertaken by the referring body; and *(b)* where parties have indicated that submissions made to the referring body are to be treated as submissions to the CC (in this second example, the guidance provided in paragraphs 6.2 to 6.11 will be applicable).

6.19 A further example is when the CC is reviewing remedies and bases its assessment on the published advice of the OFT. There will generally be no need to disclose the submissions received by the OFT because the information will be contained in the OFT's decision disclosed to the relevant party. However, should that not be the case, the Group will need to consider whether disclosure by it is appropriate.

(G) OTHER INFORMATION FROM PUBLIC BODIES

6.20 During the course of an inquiry or review, the CC may have contact with a variety of public bodies, notably the OFT, sector regulators or other government departments. Often, these will be for the purpose of seeking clarification about an existing regulatory regime or their experience of a regulated industry. Such clarification provides assistance to the CC as it seeks to understand the industry that is the subject of the inquiry or review and may also be useful when considering candidate remedies. Public bodies (including the referring body) may also submit evidence to the CC's inquiry or review.

6.21 When considering the appropriateness of disclosure, a distinction can be made between assistance provided to aid the CC's understanding of the industry and submissions of views from the body concerned on the evidence submitted and the CC's thinking. Any materials provided to aid the CC's understanding will feed into the Group's thinking and will not usually be appropriate to disclose on a stand-alone basis. However, when the body is providing views, these should be treated in the same way as evidence received from any other third party and the guidance on disclosure of third party evidence will apply to it.

NOTES

18 Groups should also consider whether any additional key arguments were provided earlier in response to the CC's questionnaires etc that should be disclosed.

19 This includes hearings held via telephone conference calls and also meetings on the substance of the inquiry or review.

20 As explained in CC18, summaries of main party hearings in merger inquiries will not normally be published. For timing, resource and confidentiality reasons, summaries of hearings in response to notices of possible remedies are seldom prepared in merger decisions, though the key points are included in provisional remedies decisions.

21 The CC *Rules of Procedure* provide for hearings to be held in public or private at the Group's discretion (Rule 7).

22 For example, in the Groceries market investigation (reported in 2008) the CC published the transcripts of two economic round tables on local competition and buyer power.

23 See paragraph 22 of the Memorandum of Understanding between the OFT and the CC on variation and termination of merger, monopoly and market undertakings and orders under the FTA 1973 and the Act (10 March 2011).

7. VIEWS AND FINDINGS OF THE CC, CC ANALYSIS AND REPORTS OF SURVEYS COMMISSIONED BY THE CC AND ANALYSIS

(A) VIEWS AND FINDINGS OF THE CC INCLUDING KEY DECISION DOCUMENTS

[3.12]

7.1 The CC's Rules require the CC to publish a number of documents, notably the provisional findings and notice of possible remedies, during an investigation.[24] Additionally, the CC has developed a practice of consulting on its provisional decision on remedies (usually through disclosure to the merger parties in merger inquiries and publication in market investigations).[25] The disclosure of provisional findings and a provisional decision on remedies is the main means by which the CC ensures due process and fulfils its duty to consult on certain decisions under section 104 of the Act. When reviewing remedies, the CC similarly publishes a provisional decision either before or as part of publishing a notice of intention to vary or terminate undertakings or orders.[26]

7.2 The CC is not subject to a general obligation to disclose all its thinking in advance of consulting on its provisional decisions. However, the CC's practices have developed to provide insight prior to this. Earlier disclosure can improve the efficiency of the inquiry or a particularly complex review as it gives main parties (and interested third parties) the opportunity to comment before the publication or disclosure of the key documents mentioned in the paragraph above. At an early stage of either a merger or a market investigation the CC should publish an issues statement which will set out the theories of harm the CC proposes to explore. It should also disclose an annotated issues statement at a later stage (typically before the hearings with main parties).[27] The annotated issues statement provides an overview of the CC's current thinking with reference to the theories of harm and analysis conducted to date. In the case of mergers, the annotated issues statement is disclosed to the merger parties (but is not usually published)[28] and in the case of market investigations, it is disclosed to the main parties (usually by publication).

(B) INTERNAL PAPERS

7.3 In the course of conducting an inquiry or review, there will be many written communications among the Group or with the CC staff and CC advisers. These are internal papers and there is no general obligation to disclose all working papers.[29] However, Groups may disclose some working papers (or extracts from them) during the course of an inquiry or review, where they consider that to do so would assist parties to understand their developing thinking. Whether it is appropriate or practical to do so may depend upon timing considerations; for example, it would not be sensible to do so when the CC is soon to disclose that thinking in an annotated issues statement or provisional findings. However, parties will have the ability to comment following disclosure.

7.4 In merger inquiries it is generally more appropriate to disclose working papers (or extracts) to main parties (and occasionally interested third parties) by supplying the party concerned with the document. For market investigations, the purpose of the disclosure and the content of the paper will be relevant to the Group's consideration of the manner of disclosure. Sometimes in market investigations, exclusive disclosure to certain parties will be appropriate (for example, when the analysis is the assessment of a firm's profitability), but often disclosure through publication will be appropriate. If working papers are disclosed, Groups generally need not revise and disclose subsequent versions of these papers. This is because the more developed analysis and comment within the paper is usually included in the next key publication of the CC.

(C) SURVEYS COMMISSIONED BY THE CC OR CONDUCTED IN-HOUSE

7.5 Reports of surveys commissioned or prepared by the CC should generally be disclosed. Usually this will be through publication (accompanied with an explanation of the methodology) but there may be instances when it is inappropriate to publish the report.

7.6 Groups should also consider the need to provide other information relating to the survey. For example, it will often be appropriate to disclose cross-tabulations of the survey results to the merger parties and one or more main party in a market investigation.[30] On occasion, a Group may consider it appropriate to disclose other underlying information. If so, the Group would need to have regard to the particular considerations that arise in relation to that information (for further information see Part 9).

NOTES

24 CC1.

25 As described in CC8, in merger inquiries a provisional decision on remedies may be set out in the form of a remedies

working paper or provisional decision document published on the CC website or circulated to relevant parties.

26 See the Memorandum of Understanding, op cit, paragraphs 36, 38, 43 and 46–50.

27 To enable a party to respond to CC questions at a hearing, it may be necessary, for the purpose of due process, to make a disclosure of certain information held by the CC (Sports Direct International PLC v CC [2009] CAT 35. The disclosure of an annotated issues statement will generally be the means of providing the necessary information but Groups should consider whether this needs to be supplemented (see paragraph 7.4).

28 See CC18, paragraph 3.47.

29 The working papers provide a snapshot of the issues, analysis and views that are relevant at the time of disclosure and may change.

30 A cross-tabulation, or contingency table, is a grid that shows the numbers or percentages of answers to a survey question by a selection of subgroups within the total sample. Cross-tabulations may be used to study the correlation between two variables.

8. TIMING OF DISCLOSURE OF INFORMATION

[3.13]

8.1 Inevitably, information will be received throughout the course of an inquiry or review. As confidentiality claims can affect the timing of disclosure, it is not possible to be prescriptive in this Guidance, nor in the administrative timetable, about the timing of disclosure. In the following paragraphs, further guidance is provided as to some factors to be taken into account. Furthermore, this Guidance is supplemented by the additional detail provided in respect of particular types of documents listed in Parts 6 and 7.

8.2 When considering the timing of disclosure, Groups should have regard to the requirement to conduct inquiries and reviews fairly.[31] The purpose of the disclosure as well as its practical aspects will be relevant considerations. Timing may also be affected by the CC's developing practice when conducting inquiries and reviews, particularly as it aims to increase efficiency and meet its statutory deadlines.

8.3 There are, however, several key stages in inquiries: for example, the publication of the issues statement, disclosure of the annotated issues statement, main party hearings, the provisional findings, the notice of possible remedies and disclosure of the CC's provisional decision on remedies) and similarly in reviews (for example, provisional decision or notice of intention to vary or terminate the remedy). When a Group has identified that disclosure is appropriate, it should aim to make the disclosure by the time of the next key stage of the inquiry or as soon as possible afterwards. For example, by the time of publishing provisional findings, the Group should aim to have disclosed all key submissions received. If information is disclosed during a consultation period under section 104 of the Act (for example, the period for the consideration of provisional findings), a Group should consider whether the consultation period should be extended or additional time allowed to enable a party to respond specifically to the additional material that has been disclosed. Relevant considerations will include the nature, materiality and relevance of the information to a Group's findings, the administrative and statutory timetable and issues of practicality.

8.4 The appropriateness of disclosure is not limited to these key stages. As noted (see paragraphs 7.3 and 7.4) in merger and market inquiries it may be helpful for a Group to share its approach and developing thinking prior to the provisional findings by the disclosure of some working papers, in addition to the disclosure of the annotated issues statement.

NOTES

31 Sports Direct International PLC v CC [2009] CAT 35.

9. PRACTICAL ASPECTS OF HANDLING INFORMATION RECEIVED AND REQUESTS FOR CONFIDENTIALITY

(A) RECEIPT OF INFORMATION AND PREPARATION PRIOR TO DISCLOSURE

[3.14]

9.1 Groups are able to provide an assurance that before making a disclosure and when considering the manner of disclosure (see paragraph 9.14) they will take into account the representations made as to the sensitivity of the information supplied (see paragraph 4.4) but because of the need to ensure that the CC's processes are fair they should avoid providing a commitment that the information provided to it will not be disclosed.[32] Taking into account any explanation provided by the party submitting information (see paragraph 9.2) they will be able to assess whether disclosure is necessary and if so the manner of disclosure to provide necessary protection of the information. In the past, main and third parties have cooperated with the CC's information requests in the knowledge that the CC would be sensitive to such requests for confidentiality.

9.2 In respect of all information supplied (whether or not it appears likely that the Group will wish to disclose the information to others), parties should be required to make known to the Group which information they claim to be confidential, and provide sufficient information as to why by explaining, for example, the nature of the information, the harm that could be caused, the likelihood of harm and magnitude of that harm. For example, a party will have failed to give sufficient explanation about the sensitivity of information if a document is marked 'confidential' without further explanation. Where information supplied by a party is about another person or business, the party supplying the information should supply full details of its source and the circumstances in which it was obtained.

9.3 When providing key submissions, parties should also provide a second version of the same that excludes information that the party considers to be confidential (together with the explanation referred to above).[33] Groups may consider allowing a short interval (up to a week) between the receipt of the full version and the non-confidential version, though care should be taken to avoid the CC's administrative timetable being adversely affected.

9.4 All information excluded should be clear to the Group so that it may assess whether the non-confidential version is satisfactory, having regard to its intention to disclose information, the purpose of such disclosure, and this Guidance. A black-lined version of the original document is suitable for this purpose and Groups should ask for this.

9.5 On receipt of any non-confidential versions of submissions or summaries of documents, Groups should consider the need to make any modification to ensure adequate and appropriate disclosure for their purposes. In addition to considering the representations from the person that provided the information, Groups should also consider whether disclosure of the information will harm another person (for example, because it relates to another person or because the disclosure would enable information that is confidential to another person to become known).

9.6 The following are examples of information for which disclosure is unlikely to cause harm to the person to whom it relates so that any person claiming likely harm should ensure that it has supplied sufficient information to assist the Group when deciding whether disclosure is appropriate (see paragraph 9.2):

(a) financial information or data relating to a business that is more than two years old; and
(b) information which can readily be deduced from information in the public domain.

9.7 The following are examples of information the disclosure of which may be harmful or which may need to be protected. In such cases, if a Group considers that disclosure is necessary, it will need to consider the manner of disclosure:[34]

(a) financial information or data relating to a business that is less than two years old;
(b) responses to surveys (in aggregate or individually) the disclosure of which could be harmful to a firm or individual or where the identity of the person providing the information should be protected;
(c) information relating to the future strategy of a business or information relating to the past strategy of a business; and
(d) information which, if disclosed, may adversely affect the competitive process in the market.

9.8 It is the usual practice of the CC to be in contact with the party that is claiming that information should not be disclosed in the course of preparing material that is to be posted on the CC's website (including summaries of hearings, key submissions, provisional findings, provisional decisions on remedies (usually only on markets), any provisional decision of a review and final decision or notice of intention to vary or terminate the remedy). Often it is possible to use ranges, redactions etc to allay concerns about disclosure (see paragraph 9.14).

9.9 Groups are reminded of the opportunity provided to parties to make further representations to the Procedural Officer if they wish to dispute the proposal of a Group to disclose information. This is additional to the opportunity for parties to make known their concerns to the Group. Groups are required to have regard to the views of the Procedural Officer if the party has made representations to him. The decision to disclose will, however, remain that of the Group.

9.10 Before disclosing information that a party has claimed is confidential (including when it proposes to make limited or restricted disclosure), a Group should consider whether to inform the party to whom the information relates of its intention to make a disclosure. It might choose not to do so when the Group believes that the party has had sufficient opportunity to explain the nature of the sensitivity and likely harm, or when the Group has sought to protect the information to be disclosed or when to do so would jeopardize the proposed publication date of key CC publications or otherwise delay the progress of the inquiry or review (for example, delay would allow others insufficient time to comment on the document once disclosed).

(B) MANNER OF DISCLOSURE OF INFORMATION

9.11 A distinction can be made between the need to make a disclosure having taken the considerations in paragraph 4.4 into account and the form the disclosure will take to meet the purpose of the disclosure and may in some cases be subject to limits on onward disclosure by the recipient, so that any onward disclosure of the information would be an offence under section 245 of the Act. Disclosure can be achieved in various ways. With the exception of certain key CC documents (see paragraph 6.5) there is no presumption that disclosure is in a particular manner. In this section, further guidance is provided on the manner of disclosure of information.

9.12 The preceding paragraphs provide an indication only of when disclosure through publication may be appropriate based on the CC's experience. The CC's website can be an effective and practical way of making a disclosure. In particular, it can be an effective means of making disclosure to a large number of parties (and therefore may be useful in market investigations). However, the sensitivity and nature of the information concerned and practical issues arising may mean that publication of a particular document or piece of information is not appropriate.

9.13 As explained below, there may be a number of options open to Groups when considering the manner of disclosure. When determining which is appropriate, Groups should consider such factors as fairness, the nature of and sensitivity of the information, the materiality of the information to the inquiry or review and the CC's analysis, the phase of the inquiry or review, the impact upon the administrative or statutory timetable and the resources of the CC. When contemplating the method of disclosure, a balance will need to be struck between these factors, the starting point being consideration of section 244.

9.14 Groups will often have to consider how information contained in any disclosed documents should be presented or how access should be allowed to confidential information in order to provide protection. There are a number of possible ways in which confidential information may be protected including:

(a) provision of ranges as an alternative to providing exact figures (for example, when indicating market shares (see paragraph 9.16));
(b) provision of aggregated data as an alternative to individual responses or data (for example, by aggregating sales or purchase figures or by providing a summary of responses from customers);
(c) provision of aggregated summaries of submissions and responses to questionnaires;
(d) excision of the confidential information from documents (for example, of names, locations and data) when the information excised is not material to the CC's inquiries or its decision or where the excision does not affect the comprehension of the document for the reader concerned;
(e) anonymising the information;
(f) disclosure to one or more parties but without publication;
(g) disclosure subject to restrictions (for example, disclosure to parties' professional advisers subject to receipt of undertakings); and
(h) use of a data room (for example, when a Group considers that access to specific data should be provided but that the sensitivity of the information concerned necessitates additional safeguards to protect the information (see paragraphs 9.17 to 9.19)).

9.15 Of the forms identified in paragraph 9.14, the first four methods will be the usual approaches to take. The sixth, (f) is generally applicable when a Group considers it necessary to disclose a working paper (or part of a working paper) to a party for reasons of due process, and the information is pertinent to one party only. This may also be the method deployed when a Group is concerned that wider publication could be harmful to the functioning of the market.

Market share by range

9.16 Usually the ranges appropriate to use in respect of market shares in non-confidential versions of disclosed documents will be:

Between 0 and 4.99 per cent	[0–5] per cent
Between 5.0 and 9.99 per cent	[5–10] per cent
Between 10.0 and 19.99 per cent	[10–20] per cent
Between 20.0 and 29.99 per cent	[20–30] per cent
Between 30.0 and 39.99 per cent	[30–40] per cent
Between 40.0 and 49.99 per cent	[40–50] per cent
Between 50.0 and 59.99 per cent	[50–60] per cent
Between 60.0 and 69.99 per cent	[60–70] per cent
Between 70.0 and 79.99 per cent	[70–80] per cent
Between 80.0 and 89.99 per cent	[80–90] per cent
Between 90.0 and 100 per cent	[90–100] per cent

Data rooms

9.17 The use of a data room is an option that may be considered when a Group is satisfied of the need to disclose the information for reasons of due process but considers that, due to the nature of the information, additional safeguards are appropriate. Use of a data room has the advantage of limiting further use of the information (and, in the case of surveys, may be a way of ensuring that the identity of individual respondents remains anonymous). However, because of the resource implications associated with their operation they should be used sparingly.

9.18 As their name implies, data rooms may be used when a Group concludes that it is appropriate to provide access to data in order to enable the parties' economic advisers to gain further understanding of the CC's analysis and to examine the data in order to respond to the CC's findings. It will seldom be appropriate to allow access to the parties' other advisers or to use a data room to enable greater access to other information. Those having access to a data room are bound by the rules which the CC applies to the data room and also to undertakings which they provide. These make provision for the proper conduct of the data room and restrict the use and further disclosure of information to which the advisers have access.

9.19 The point at which access should be provided will depend upon the circumstances of the case. Generally, a Group should be resistant to requests made early in an investigation when the relevance of the information requested remains unclear. This is because of the sensitivity of the information and also the resource implications of setting up a data room. Groups may wish to consider both the need for and alternatives to a data room. In merger inquiries, because of the relative brevity of the investigatory period, it is likely that the need for a data room will not become clear until the inquiry has reached provisional findings. In this circumstance the CC will be mindful of the need to allow the parties adequate time to make representations after access has been provided, within the confines of the need for the CC to comply with its statutory and administrative deadlines.

Surveys

9.20 Particular issues arise in respect of the handling and disclosure of underlying data. Relevant considerations will include the application of the Data Protection Act 1998, which applies to personal data and the Code of Conduct of the Market Research Society (Groups should have regard to the version that is current when considering a particular disclosure issue), the latter requiring the anonymity of respondents to be preserved unless they have given informed consent. If a Group considers it necessary to disclose any of the underlying data, it must ensure that the identities of the persons who participated in the survey are protected. Anonymization is not always sufficient, and additional protection may be necessary to ensure that the identity of those who participated is not traceable.

NOTES

Paragraph 9.9 of this Guidance is reproduced as amended by CMA6, Annex A (at **[3.34]**).

32 In respect of CC surveys, the CC will seek to ensure that survey respondents are informed about how confidentiality will be protected at the time they agree to participate in the survey.

33 Parties are responsible for ensuring that the format of the non-confidential version prevents excised text from being read.

34 For guidance on manner of disclosure see paragraphs 9.11–9.20.

EXPLANATORY NOTE

[3.15]

This note does not form part of the Guidance. This note and the table below are intended to assist the reader in understanding whether a Group may decide to disclose or publish any of the information it receives during the course of a merger inquiry or market investigation. While the table below gives a general indication, it should be read in conjunction with the Guidance and in the event of conflict between the table and the *Chairman's Guidance on Disclosure of Information in Merger Inquiries, Market Investigations and Reviews of Undertakings and Orders accepted or made under the Enterprise Act 2002 and Fair Trading Act 1973*, the Guidance prevails.

Type of information	*Publication on CC website*	*Disclose to main or one or more third parties*	*Chairman's guidance*
Main party responses to CC questionnaires	No	May be disclosed	6(*a*)
Third party responses to CC questionnaires	No	May be disclosed	6(*a*)
Main party key arguments and views in submissions	√	Additional information may be disclosed	6(*b*)
Third party key arguments and views in submissions	√	N/A	6(*c*)
Surveys commissioned by main and third parties	√	√	6(*d*)
Oral communications—administration and conduct of case	No	No	6(*e*)
Summaries of hearings with main parties	No (mergers) √ (markets)	No (mergers) N/A (markets)	6(*e*)
Summaries of hearings with third parties	√ Unless (*a*) anonymity needs to be maintained or (*b*) response is to notice of possible remedies (mergers)	Additional information may be necessary	6 (e)
Information from referring body on making a reference or request for review	No	No	6(*f*)
Information from public bodies	No unless information submitted as evidence to investigation	No unless evidence submitted as evidence to investigation	6(*g*)
Issues statement, theories of harm, provisional findings, notices of possible remedies and final report	√	Additional information may be disclosed	CC Rules 7(*a*)
Annotated issues statement	√ (markets)	Disclosed to main parties (mergers)	7(*a*)
Provisional decision on remedies (markets only)	√ (markets)	√ Disclosed to main parties (mergers)	7(*a*)
Papers internal to the CC	No	No	7(*b*)
Working papers	Some	Some	7(*b*)

Type of information	*Publication on CC website*	*Disclose to main or one or more third parties*	*Chairman's guidance*
Surveys commissioned by the CC	√	√	7(*c*)

ADMINISTRATIVE PENALTIES: STATEMENT OF POLICY ON THE CMA'S APPROACH (CMA4, JANUARY 2014)

[3.16]

NOTES

The fines that could be imposed on summary conviction for certain criminal offences referred to in this document were, at that time, subject to specific caps of £5,000 or above. With effect from 12 March 2015, these caps have been removed and those specific offences are now punishable by a fine of any amount.

CONTENTS

1 INTRODUCTION

[3.17]

1.1 This document sets out the CMA's statement of policy regarding its powers under the Enterprise Act 2002 (EA02) and Competition Act 1998 (CA98), as amended by the Enterprise and Regulatory Reform Act 2013 (ERRA13),[1] to impose administrative penalties on a person who fails to comply with:

- notices requiring the attendance of witnesses, production of documents or supply of estimates, forecasts, returns or other information in Phase 1 and Phase 2 mergers and markets investigations[2] (EA02 Requirements)
- requirements to provide information or documents or certain other requirements in antitrust investigations[3] (CA98 Requirements), and
- interim measures[4] in mergers cases[5] (Merger IMs).

In this document EA02 Requirements and CA98 Requirements will be referred to collectively as Investigatory Requirements. A person that fails to comply with any Investigatory Requirements or Merger IMs is referred to as **P**. In this context, P refers to individuals and to both bodies corporate and unincorporated.

1.2 Where applicable, this document also sets out the considerations relevant to extending the period in which the CMA will carry out its investigations, consider undertakings in lieu of a reference (UILs) and prepare and publish its reports and/or decisions in mergers and markets cases.

REQUIREMENT FOR A STATEMENT OF POLICY AND SCOPE OF THIS DOCUMENT

1.3 The CMA is required to prepare and publish a statement of policy in relation to the use of its enforcement powers under sections 94, 94A, 110(1) and (3) and 174 of the EA02 and section 40A of the CA98; in respect of powers under sections 94 and 94A of the EA02 the statement may not be published until the Secretary of State has approved it.[6,7]

1.4 This statement of policy (Statement) – which was approved by the Secretary of State on 8 January 2014 – reflects the views of the CMA at the time of publication. The CMA may publish a revised statement of policy from time to time to reflect changes in best practice, legislation and the results of experience, legal judgments and research.[8] It may in due course be supplemented, revised or replaced. When preparing or revising its Statement the CMA must consult such persons as it considers appropriate (in respect of Merger IMs powers under sections 94 and 94A of the EA02 the Secretary of State must be consulted).[9] The CMA's webpages will always display the latest version of the Statement.

1.5 Although it covers many of the points likely to be of immediate concern to businesses and their advisers, this document makes no claim to be comprehensive. It cannot, therefore, be seen as a substitute for the EA02 and the regulations and orders made under the EA02, nor can it be cited as a definitive interpretation of the law. Anyone in any doubt about whether they may be affected by the legislation should consider seeking legal advice.

1.6 When reaching decisions regarding enforcement action for failure to comply with the investigatory powers described above, the CMA must have regard to this Statement.[10] The CMA will apply this Statement flexibly according to the circumstances of the case. However, different considerations may be relevant to the assessment of the appropriate administrative penalty, depending on which statutory power the CMA is using. For example, although daily penalties may be used for failure to comply with Investigatory Requirements in mergers, markets and CA98 cases, they may in practice be used to a greater extent in Phase I merger investigations which involve shorter deadlines, where statutory deadlines are approaching in mergers or markets cases or where the relevant information is needed for analysis at a pivotal point in the investigation, in order to incentivise swift compliance with Investigatory Requirements.

1.7 You may find it useful to read this document alongside other CMA, OFT and/or CC documents, including *Mergers: Guidance on the CMA's jurisdiction and procedure* (CMA2); *Market studies and market investigations: Supplemental guidance on the CMA's approach* (CMA3); *Competition Act 1998: Guidance on the CMA's investigation procedures in Competition Act 1998 cases* (CMA8); *Competition and Markets Authority Competition Act 1998 Rules* and the documents listed in Annexe C,[11] which were first published by the OFT and CC, and have been adopted by the CMA. This document supersedes the CC's *Statement of Policy on Penalties* (CC5).[12]

1.8 This Statement has effect from 1 April 2014. The powers made available to the CMA by the ERRA13 apply to all investigations, subject to the transitional arrangements provided for by the Secretary of State for mergers, markets and CA98 investigations that are ongoing as at 1 April 2014. For information on the transitional arrangements that apply to mergers, markets and CA98 investigations, please see *Transitional Arrangements: Guidance on the CMA's proposed approach to transitional arrangements – Part 1* (CMA 14).

NOTES

1 Sections 94A and 110 (mergers) and 174A and 174B (markets) of the EA02 and section 40A of the CA98. Further details on these powers are contained in the CMA publications *Mergers: Guidance on the CMA's jurisdiction and procedure* (CMA2) and *Market studies and market investigations: Supplemental guidance on the CMA's* approach (CMA3). As at 1 April 2014, markets powers under Part 4 of the EA02 and CA98 powers are applied and enforced, concurrently with the CMA, by the regulators for communications and postal matters, gas, electricity, water and sewerage, railway, airports and air traffic services and health services (the Regulators). Accordingly, where the Regulators have concurrent powers, references to the CMA in this statement of policy should be taken to include the Regulators in relation to their respective industries. It should be noted that the Regulators may have their own guidance on penalties in relation to the exercise of their regulatory, rather than concurrent, powers.

2 Sections 110 (mergers) and 174A (markets) of the EA02. The powers in section 110 also apply to some regulatory references. See, for example, references made under Section 12 of the Transport Act 2000 pursuant to section 12B(1) of that Act.

3 Section 40A of the CA98.

4 By virtue of section 94A(8) of the EA02, interim measures for these purposes are undertakings under section 80 or orders under section 72 or 81 or paragraph 2 of Schedule 7 of the EA02.

5 Section 94A of the EA02. As required by section 94B(1) of the EA02, this statement also covers the CMA's powers to bring civil proceedings to enforce mergers interim measures under section 94(6) of the EA02.

6 Sections 94B(1) and 94B(5), 116(1) and (2) and 174E(1) of the EA02 and section 40B(1) of the CA98.

7 In particular, it must include a statement about the considerations relevant to the determination of the amount and, in certain circumstances, the nature of any penalty imposed under the above mentioned sections of the CA98 and EA02 (sections 94B(2), 116(2) and 174E(2) of the EA02 and section 40B(2) of the CA98).

8 The CMA may revise its statement of policy at any time and must publish any revised statement of policy (in respect of mergers interim measures powers under section 94A of the EA02 the revised statement may not be published until the Secretary of State has approved it) (sections 94B(3) and (5), 116(3) and 174E(3) of the EA02 and section 40B(3) of the CA98).

9 Sections 94B(4), 116(4) and 174E(4) of the EA02 and section 40B(4) of the CA98.

10 Sections 110(9) and 174A(8) of the EA02 and section 40B(6) of the CA98 provide that the CMA must have regard to the statement of policy most recently published at the time of the relevant failure. A similar requirement applies to the Regulators by virtue of the legislation that conferred on them concurrent powers under the CA98 and EA02. However, it should be noted that while the Regulators must have regard to this statement of policy their approach may differ in some respects. It is therefore advisable to consider also any procedural guidance published by the Regulators in an investigation carried out by them.

11 These documents are available at www.gov.uk/cma/.

12 To the extent that it refers to powers the CC had to impose penalties for failure to comply with certain investigatory powers prior to the ERRA13, it also supersedes the CC document *General Advice and Information* (CC4).

2 LEGAL FRAMEWORK

PENALTIES FOR FAILURE TO COMPLY WITH INVESTIGATORY REQUIREMENTS[13]

[3.18]

2.1 Under the EA02 (in relation to markets or mergers investigations), the CMA may impose administrative penalties on persons who fail, either intentionally or without reasonable excuse, to comply with requirements imposed on them under sections 109 and 174 of the EA02.[14] These include failures to attend interviews or meetings with the CMA, failures to provide evidence, or failures to produce documents required by the CMA. Penalties may also be imposed on persons who intentionally obstruct or delay another person in copying documents produced to that other person.[15]

2.2 Similarly, under the CA98, the CMA may impose administrative penalties on persons who fail, either intentionally or without reasonable excuse, to comply with requirements imposed on them under sections 26, 26A, 27, 28 or 28A of the CA98.[16] These include failures to answer questions asked by the

CMA, failures to produce documents required by the CMA or to comply with the CMA's powers to enter premises (either with or without a warrant). They also include failure to provide adequate or accurate information in response to a request.

Criminal offences

2.3 Certain criminal offences in relation to interference with the CMA's investigatory powers operate alongside the enforcement powers detailed in this Statement. It is a criminal offence where a person:

- intentionally alters, suppresses or destroys any document which the person has been required to produce by the CMA under its EA02 powers in mergers and markets cases[17]
- knowingly or recklessly provides false or misleading information to the CMA or the Secretary of State in connection with any of their mergers functions under Part 3 of the EA02, or[18]
- in relation to CA98 investigations
  - obstructs the CMA in the exercise of its powers to carry out inspections under sections 27, 28 or 28A of the CA98
  - intentionally or recklessly destroys or otherwise disposes of, falsifies or conceals a document which they have been required to produce under the CMA's CA98 powers, or
  - knowingly or recklessly provides false or misleading information to the CMA or another person in connection with a CA98 investigation.[19]

In relation to obstructing the exercise of powers under section 27 of the CA98, a person is liable, on summary conviction, to a fine not exceeding the statutory maximum[20] and, on conviction on indictment, to a fine. For all the other EA02 and CA98 offences, a person is liable, on summary conviction, to a fine not exceeding the statutory maximum and, on conviction on indictment, to imprisonment for a term not exceeding two years or to a fine or to both.[21]

2.4 For mergers and markets investigatory powers, where an act is capable of constituting both (a) a failure warranting an administrative penalty **and** (b) a criminal offence, the CMA cannot impose an administrative penalty if P has been found guilty of the criminal offence.[22] Similarly, a criminal offence is not committed by P where the CMA has imposed an administrative penalty in respect of the same act.[23]

Amount of penalty

2.5 The CMA may impose such administrative penalty as it considers appropriate,[24] subject to the statutory maxima specified by order of the Secretary of State. The current maxima specified by the Competition and Markets Authority (Penalties) Order 2014 are as follows:

- £30,000 (fixed amount)
- £15,000 (daily rate), and
- £30,000 and £15,000 (fixed amount and daily rate together).

2.6 Where the penalty is being imposed because P has intentionally obstructed or delayed another person in copying documents produced to them (in the context of mergers and markets investigations), the penalty must be a fixed amount.[25] For other failures, committed without reasonable excuse, the penalty may be:

- a fixed amount
- an amount calculated by reference to a daily rate, or
- a combination of a fixed amount and an amount calculated by reference to a daily rate.[26]

Where the CMA is entitled to impose both a fixed and a daily penalty for a particular failure to comply, it may simultaneously impose fixed and daily penalties up to the maximum specified for each type of penalty.[27]

INTERACTION WITH POWER TO EXTEND MERGERS AND MARKETS INVESTIGATIONS

2.7 In certain circumstances, the CMA may extend the period within which certain duties to carry out mergers and markets investigations or to consider UILs or implement remedies must be discharged. This will apply if it considers that a relevant person has failed (with or without reasonable excuse) to comply with any EA02 Requirement issued by the CMA in relation to a merger reference or investigation or where any person has failed (with or without reasonable excuse) to comply with a EA02 requirement issued by the CMA during the remedies implementation phase of a market investigation.[28] In appropriate cases, the CMA has the power to both extend its statutory timetable and impose a fine on parties who fail to comply with EA02 Requirements.[29] This is discussed further in chapter 4 below.

PENALTIES FOR FAILURE TO COMPLY WITH MERGER IM POWERS[30]

2.8 The CMA may impose a fixed penalty (but not a daily penalty) for failure to comply with Merger IMs, for example an undertaking or order to suspend pre- or post-merger integration.[31] The penalty may not exceed 5% of the total value of the turnover (both in and outside the UK) of the enterprises owned or controlled by P.[32,33] The maximum amount of the penalty will therefore depend on the size of the enterprises owned or controlled by P.

2.9 This power to impose penalties sits alongside the ability of any person who may be affected by a breach of the Merger IM to bring an action where they have sustained loss or damage.[34] The CMA is also able to bring such civil proceedings to enforce interim measures. The interaction between these two powers is explained further in paragraph 4.21 below.

NOTES

13 See also Annexe B below, which contains a high-level summary table of the CMA powers and corresponding penalties for non-compliance covered by this Statement.

14 Sections 110(1) and 174A(1) of the EA02.
15 Sections 110(1) and (3) EA02 (mergers) and 174A(1) and (3) of the EA02 (markets).
16 Section 40A(1) of the CA98.
17 Section 110(5) of the EA02 (mergers) and section 174A(4) of the EA02 (markets).
18 Section 117 of the EA02. This provision also applies where such information is provided to OFCOM or Monitor under Part 3 of the EA02.
19 Sections 42 to 44 of the CA98.
20 It should be noted that section 85 of the Legal Aid, Sentencing and Punishment of Offenders Act 2012 (the LASPOA) provides for the statutory maximum fine on summary conviction to become an unlimited fine. If and when this section comes into force, references in the EA02, CA98 and this guidance to the statutory maximum fine on summary conviction should be read in light of the changes made by the LASPOA.
21 Sections 110(7) and 174A(6) of the EA02 and sections 42(6) and (7), 43(2) and 44(3) of the CA98.
22 Sections 110(8) and 174A(7) of the EA02.
23 Sections 110(6) and 174A(5) of the EA02.
24 Section 111(1) of the EA02 (mergers) and section 174D(1) of the EA02 (markets) and section 40A(1) of the CA98.
25 Sections 111(3) (mergers) and 174D(3) (markets) of the EA02.
26 Sections 111(2) and (3) (mergers) and 174D(2) and (3) (markets) of the EA02 and section 40A(2) of the CA98.
27 Section 111(7)(c) (mergers) and section 174D(6)(c) (markets) of the EA02 and section 40A(3)(c) of the CA98.
28 Sections 34ZB(1) and 39(3) (mergers) and section 138A(3) (markets) of the EA02. This power is in addition to the power to extend the timetable where there are special reasons to do so (see *Mergers: Guidance on the CMA's jurisdiction and procedure* (CMA2) and *Market studies and market investigations: Supplemental guidance on the CMA's approach* (CMA3).
29 Section 110(2) (mergers) and section 174A(2) (markets) of the EA02.
30 See also Annexe B below which contains a high-level summary table of the CMA powers and corresponding penalties for non-compliance covered by this statement of policy.
31 Section 94A(1) (mergers) of the EA02. Pursuant to section 94A(8) (mergers) of the EA02, 'interim measure' for these purposes means an undertaking under section 80 of the EA02 or an order under section 72 or 81 of the EA02.
32 Section 94A(2) (mergers) of the EA02.
33 The Enterprise Act 2002 (Mergers) (Interim Measures: Financial Penalties) (Determination of Control and Turnover) Order 2014 provides for the circumstances in which an enterprise is to be treated as 'controlled' by P and contains the rules for determining the turnover of an enterprise.
34 Section 94(4) (mergers) of the EA02. See also *Mergers: Guidance on the CMA's jurisdiction and procedure* (CMA2).

3 POLICY OBJECTIVES

[3.19]
3.1 Given the importance to businesses and consumers of substantive decisions in mergers, markets and CA98 investigations, and the need for such decisions to be taken in accordance with statutory or other timetables, it is vital for the CMA to be able to take such decisions based on information that is accurate and complete, and to gather that information as quickly as possible. Consistent with this, the legislative intention behind the enhanced investigatory powers available to the CMA is to provide appropriate investigatory powers during all phases of its investigations to be able to carry out its functions. Use of the CMA's investigatory and interim measures powers is therefore intended to:

- ensure that the CMA can expediently gather information to carry out its functions with the best available evidence in compliance with relevant investigation timetables (in particular but not limited to statutory timetables in mergers and markets cases)
- prevent action which might prejudice any reference, impede the taking of action following a reference, or cause detrimental and irreversible changes to market dynamics, and
- ensure that the threat of penalties will deter future non-compliance with relevant CMA powers, by those on whom penalties have been imposed and other persons who may be considering future non-compliance.

3.2 It follows that there are a number of possible adverse consequences for the CMA if a person fails to comply with Investigatory Requirements or Merger IMs:

- the costs of the investigation may increase
- the investigation may be delayed, which could have commercial and other adverse implications for the CMA, parties and consumers, and again increase costs for the CMA and parties
- the accuracy or quality of the CMA's decisions may be reduced
- any remedial action that may be required in Phase 2 of a merger investigation may be prejudiced, and/or
- in the most extreme circumstances the CMA could come to a different decision from the one it would have reached if the information had been available.

3.3 The CMA's penalty powers play an important role in incentivising compliance with Investigatory Requirements and Merger IMs and avoiding the adverse consequences described above. Therefore, the CMA will take failures to comply very seriously and will not hesitate to impose a penalty where appropriate.

4 STATEMENT OF POLICY ON WHETHER AND IN WHAT AMOUNT ADMINISTRATIVE PENALTIES WILL BE IMPOSED

[3.20]
4.1 The CMA considers that penalties imposed on P should, on the one hand, achieve the CMA's policy objectives of incentivising compliance with its investigatory and interim measures powers and deterring

future failures to comply, while not being disproportionate or excessive in all the circumstances of the case. When assessing whether and in what amount a penalty should be set, the CMA will have regard to the factors referred to in this chapter in the round, including the nature and gravity of the failure, any adverse effects on the CMA's investigation, P's reason for the failure and the size and administrative and financial resources available to P.

A. FACTORS INFLUENCING DECISION TO IMPOSE A PENALTY

General

4.2 The CMA will consider whether to impose an administrative penalty on a case-by-case basis, taking into account all relevant circumstances.[35] However, the CMA may be more likely to impose a penalty where it considers one or more of the following factors are present:

- the failure to comply is likely to have an adverse impact on the CMA's investigation, in particular the ability to obtain evidence relevant to the determination of issues being investigated and the ability to meet statutory or administrative timetables
- the failure to comply is significant and/or flagrant (whether committed intentionally or negligently)[36]
- P has previously failed to comply with an information request or CMA decision, whether in the current investigation or previously (that is, there is an element of 'recidivism')
- the imposition of a penalty is required to encourage (swift) compliance by P, and
- P sought to obtain an advantage or derive benefit from the failure.

4.3 The procedure used by the CMA when imposing Investigatory Requirements may also be relevant to the imposition of penalties. The CMA may be more likely to impose a penalty for failure to comply with Investigatory Requirements where the CMA has provided a draft request or set a deadline for compliance which takes P's comments into account.[37] Parties should raise any potential difficulties in responding as early as possible within the timeframe set out in an Investigatory Requirement – for example relating to administrative, resourcing, financial, logistical and practical issues – or any matters they do not understand with the case team as soon as possible after receiving a request, or as soon as they become aware that they may not meet the stipulated deadline.

Reasonable excuse

4.4 For the majority of the CMA's Investigatory Requirements and for Merger IMs, penalties can only be imposed if a failure to comply is 'without reasonable excuse'.[38] The EA02 and CA98 do not define the phrase. The circumstances that constitute a reasonable excuse are not fixed and the CMA will consider whether any reasons for failure to comply amount to a reasonable excuse on a case-by-case basis. However, the CMA will consider whether a significant and genuinely unforeseeable or unusual event and/or an event beyond P's control has caused the failure and the failure would not otherwise have taken place. For example, a significant and demonstrable IT failure (which could not reasonably have been foreseen or avoided) which prevented P from meeting a deadline might, depending on the circumstances, amount to a reasonable excuse.

4.5 The CMA will expect the person to whom the Investigatory Requirement or Merger IM applies to be responsible for ensuring Investigatory Requirements and Merger IMs are fully understood and that the CMA's powers are complied with, even when, for example, using external advisers to assist them with their response. As noted in paragraph 4.3 above, parties should make known any difficulties and raise any queries in relation to an information request as soon as possible. The CMA is unlikely (save in exceptional circumstances) to accept an excuse where P has not made a reasonable effort to meet the deadline in respect of an Investigatory Requirement, for example because it was forgotten.

Decision to extend timetables/deadlines

4.6 In certain circumstances, the CMA may extend the time limit within which certain duties to carry out merger and markets investigations and to consider UILs or impose remedies must be discharged if it considers that P has failed (with or without reasonable excuse) to comply with any EA02 Requirement which is given in relation to the reference or investigation.[39,40]

4.7 In reaching a decision on whether to extend the time limit, the CMA will consider all relevant factors on a case-by-case basis. These might, for example, include the CMA's assessment of whether the extension is necessary to enable the EA02 Requirements to be complied with and for the CMA to complete its functions, and whether any extension may jeopardise the effectiveness of any remedy the CMA might wish to impose (for example a divestment in the case of a completed merger). Any decision not to extend the relevant statutory deadline will be kept under review. The CMA would not usually expect to use isolated minor occurrences of non-compliance, or those with limited impact alone or in aggregate, to justify extensions to statutory timetables. In addition, the fact that a failure to comply is particularly serious (for example a deliberate failure by a recidivist designed to achieve an advantage) will not necessarily make an extension more likely.

4.8 In relevant circumstances, when considering whether to impose a penalty for non-compliance the CMA will have regard to the fact that it may also extend a timetable deadline for non-compliance. Where the CMA may both impose a penalty and extend the timetable in relation to the same failure,[41] there should be no expectation that the CMA will only use one of these powers. For example, where the failure has delayed the timetable the CMA may decide to extend the timetable **and** impose a penalty.

B. FACTORS AFFECTING THE TYPE OF PENALTY IMPOSED

4.9 Depending on the type of case and the powers concerned, the CMA may impose:

- **a fixed penalty only**: for failure, without reasonable excuse, to comply with Merger IMs[42] and for intentionally obstructing or delaying another person in copying documents produced to them,[43] or
- **a fixed penalty and/or a daily penalty**: for failure, without reasonable excuse, to comply with other investigatory powers under the EA02 (mergers and markets cases) or the CA98.[44]

4.10 Where the CMA has a choice as to the type of penalty that may be imposed, it will consider a number of factors, in the round, on a case-by-case basis. These may include the factors referred to in sections A and C of this chapter. The CMA may also consider the following non-exhaustive factors:

- **The factual circumstances in which a penalty is being considered.** The assessment of whether to impose a fixed or daily penalty, or a combination of the two, will involve consideration of the need to incentivise timely compliance with Investigatory Requirements. Daily penalties, for example, (either alone or in combination with a fixed penalty) may create greater incentives for parties to comply swiftly with Investigatory Requirements since the penalty imposed on P is directly related to the time P takes to comply with the request. It is also likely that daily penalties may result in a greater overall penalty than the maximum fixed penalty if P fails to comply promptly. They may be particularly appropriate in situations where timely compliance is likely to be of utmost importance, for example where statutory timetables are involved.
- **The deterrent effect of the penalty**. The CMA will consider the level of penalty that is likely to have the requisite deterrent effect, both on P and more generally on those who may be subject to Investigatory Requirements or Merger IMs in the present or in future investigations, having regard to the need for the penalty to be proportionate in all the circumstances. This assessment may affect the level of fixed, daily or combined penalty that is set. Further, where it is important to send a strong deterrent message, for example where there is an egregious or persistent failure to comply, it may be important to impose a penalty at a level that can only be reached by the combination of fixed and daily penalties.
- **Whether the failure to comply has been remedied**. In some cases where an initial failure has been remedied, it may still be appropriate to impose a penalty to reflect the nature and gravity of the failure and/or to achieve deterrence. In those circumstances, only a fixed penalty would be available as daily penalties can only be used for a continuing period of non-compliance after formal notice of the imposition of a penalty.[45] In cases of an extended and unremedied failure to comply with Investigatory Requirements, the CMA may be more likely to impose a daily penalty for the duration of the failure,[46] together with an additional fixed penalty to underline the seriousness of the failure and/or achieve deterrence, while still ensuring that the penalty is proportionate in all the circumstances.

C. FACTORS AFFECTING THE LEVEL OF PENALTY IMPOSED

4.11 The CMA will assess all the relevant circumstances of the case in the round in order to determine a penalty that is reasonable, appropriate and thus proportionate in the circumstances. The CMA is likely to set penalties towards the upper end of the relevant statutory maxima for the most serious failures to comply and/or where it is necessary to do so having regard to P's size and financial position. The assessment may include the factors referred to in sections A and B of this chapter. The CMA may also consider the following non-exhaustive factors on a case-by-case basis:

- the scale of any adverse effects on the case (including costs) that will be incurred by the CMA if the investigation has to be extended to take account of information provided late
- any prejudice failure to comply with Merger IMs might cause to the CMA's ability to take remedial action if that would be deemed necessary following the merger investigation
- the nature and gravity of the failure, including: whether the failure was intentional, the extent of any negligence involved in the failure, whether there was any attempt to conceal the failure from the CMA and the extent, if any, to which P complied with other aspects of the Investigatory Requirements or Merger IMs
- the reasons given by P for the failure to comply with the Investigatory Requirements or Merger IMs
- whether P derived any advantage from its failure or might reasonably be expected to do so
- any steps taken in mitigation by P to avoid the failure and/or ensure that failures do not occur in the future, or to discipline responsible individuals
- continuation or cessation of the failure after P became aware of the contravention or failure, or of the CMA's concern that there might have been a contravention or failure
- whether the involvement of senior management or officers contributed to any failure, including whether such individuals made arrangements for suitable resources to be made available to comply with the Investigatory Requirements or Merger IMs
- the size of, and administrative and financial resources available to, P,[47] and
- whether P has ever failed to comply with an Investigatory Requirement, Merger IM or CMA decision, either in the current investigation or previously (that is, whether there is an element of 'recidivism'). The seriousness of any past failure(s), the time that has elapsed since the failure(s) occurred, and any other relevant factors may be taken into account.

SPECIFIC FACTORS RELATING TO THE LEVEL OF PENALTY FOR FAILURE TO COMPLY WITH MERGER IMS

4.12 A penalty for failure to comply with Mergers IMs may not exceed 5% of the total value of the turnover (both in and outside the UK) of the enterprises owned or controlled by P. For these purposes the

Enterprise Act 2002 (Mergers) (Interim Measures: Financial Penalties) (Determination of Control and Turnover) Order 2014 (the Interim Measures Order) makes provision for determining:

- when an enterprise is to be treated as controlled by P, and
- the turnover (both in and outside of the UK) of an enterprise.[48]

Control

4.13 The Interim Measures Order provides that control is not limited to outright voting control of an enterprise, but includes situations falling short of outright voting control. These include:

- the ability materially to influence the policy of the entity carrying on the enterprise (known as 'material influence')
- the ability to directly or indirectly control the policy of the entity carrying on the enterprise (known as 'de facto' control), and
- having a 'controlling interest' in a body corporate carrying on the enterprise.[49]

4.14 The CMA considers that penalties should be applied fairly and proportionately in all scenarios and to all kinds of business structures to ensure they act as a meaningful deterrent. The CMA will consider the enterprises that P controls (that is, that it has de facto control over, a controlling interest in or – exceptionally – a material interest in, as detailed in the Interim Measures Order) on a case-by-case basis.

4.15 The CMA may, having regard to all the circumstances, determine whether P is able directly or indirectly to control or materially to influence the policy of a body corporate (without having a controlling interest in it) or the policy of an individual, a partnership or an unincorporated association or group of persons in carrying on an enterprise.[50] The CMA will generally rely on de facto control or controlling interest for determining turnover. It will only exceptionally rely also on material influence. This will be where relying only on de facto control and/or controlling interest would lead to a perverse or unfair outcome, for example because a party would receive a disproportionately low penalty because of their particular business structure.

4.16 Exceptional circumstances in which the CMA will include material influence turnover principally include, but are not limited to, the following:

- when reliance only on controlling interest and de facto control produces a very low figure for turnover in the relevant financial year for penalty-setting (and therefore a disproportionately low penalty), or
- where the business structure of the entity failing to comply has a number of interests that are not under its legal or de facto control, such that turnover assessed on a controlling interest or de facto control basis cannot accurately reflect that entity's true financial position and/or would lead to a penalty that would not achieve the CMA's objectives of incentivising compliance with its investigatory powers and deterring future failures to comply.

4.17 **Assessing material influence** – Where it assesses material influence, the CMA will do so on a case-by-case basis, focusing on the overall relationship between P and the entity carrying on the particular enterprise and on P's ability materially to influence policy relevant to the behaviour of a particular enterprise in the marketplace. 'Policy' in this context means the management of a business, and thus includes the strategic direction of an entity or group of entities and its ability to define and achieve its commercial objectives. In conducting its analysis, the CMA expects to follow the detailed factors and approach to assessing material influence contained in paragraphs 4.14 to 4.27 of the CMA document *Mergers: Guidance on the CMA's jurisdiction and procedure* (CMA2),[51] used when considering material influence for jurisdictional purposes.

4.18 **Assessing de facto control** – The CMA will consider whether, in all the circumstances, P has de facto control of an entity carrying on an enterprise, notwithstanding that it does not have a controlling interest). This is likely to include situations where in practice P has control over more than half of the votes actually cast at a shareholders' meeting. It might also involve situations where an investor's industry expertise leads to its advice being followed to a greater extent than its shareholding would seem to warrant (although this factor could equally be relevant to a finding of material influence). As with assessing material influence, the CMA expects to follow the approach in the CMA document *Mergers: Guidance on the CMA's jurisdiction and procedure* (CMA2).

4.19 **Assessing controlling interest** – Broadly speaking, under the Interim Measures Order P will have a controlling interest in an enterprise where it (a) holds a majority of the voting rights in a company, or (b) is a member of the company and either (i) has the right to appoint or remove a majority of its board of directors, or (ii) controls alone a majority of the voting rights in the company (pursuant to an agreement with other shareholders or members).[52] Only one shareholder can have a controlling interest, but it is not uncommon for a company to be subject to the control (in the wider sense described above) of two or more major shareholders at the same time – in a joint venture, for instance. Thus it is possible for a minority shareholder to have material influence over a company's policy even though someone else owns a controlling interest.

Turnover

4.20 The Interim Measures Order provides that turnover for present purposes is the turnover (both in and outside the UK) of the enterprises owned or controlled by P in the accounting period immediately preceding the date on which the relevant Merger IM came into force.[53] Generally, the CMA will take the turnover[54] figure from an enterprise's latest published accounts, where these are available. However, in exceptional circumstances, it may be appropriate to use different sources of information as better reflecting an enterprise's turnover for these purposes. In addition, the Interim Measures Order makes special provision for determining the turnover of credit institutions, financial institutions and insurance undertakings.

Interaction between penalty powers and power to bring civil proceedings

4.21 As noted at paragraph 2.9 above, the CMA may bring civil proceedings to enforce Merger IMs in addition to imposing administrative penalties in relation to a failure to comply with Merger IMs. The CMA does not generally expect to bring civil proceedings. However, it will consider whether to use the power on a case-by-case basis having regard to the nature of the failure, and in particular whether an administrative penalty will be sufficient to ensure that the failure will not prejudice possible remedial action if the CMA were to conclude that there was a substantial lessening of competition. In addition to enforcement by the CMA, any person affected by the contravention of Merger IMs who has sustained loss or damage as a result of such contravention may bring an action against the party bound by the Merger IMs.

NOTES

35 Persistent and repeated unreasonable behaviour that delays the OFT's enforcement action is an aggravating factor under the *OFT's Guidance as to the appropriate amount of penalty* for substantive infringements of competition law (OFT 423, September 2012), which has been adopted by the CMA. Where necessary and proportionate, the CMA will consider on a case-by-case basis whether any non-compliance with information gathering powers merits both an administrative penalty and the application of the aggravating factor in OFT423.

36 For the purposes of this guidance, a failure is 'intentional' if P must have been aware, or could not have been unaware, that its conduct was of such a nature as to lead to a failure to comply and a failure is 'negligent' if P ought to have known that its conduct would result in a failure to comply with an Investigatory Requirement or Merger IM.

37 Where practicable and appropriate, the CMA will discuss Investigatory Requirements with the intended recipient prior to giving the relevant notice so as to enable requests to be prepared that do not impose unnecessary burdens on recipients. The CMA will also seek to set reasonable deadlines for Investigatory Requirements and where draft Investigatory Requirements have been issued the final Investigatory Requirements will have considered any representations on proposed deadlines. For further details, see for example, *Transparency and disclosure: Statement of the CMA's policy and approach* (CMA6).

38 Sections 94A(1) and 110(1) (mergers) and 174A(1) (markets) of the EA02 and section 40A(1) of the CA98.

39 Sections 34ZB(1), 39(3) and 41A(3) (mergers) of the EA02, provided that P is a relevant person within the meaning of sections 34ZB(2), 39(5) and 41A(4) (mergers) and section 138A(3) (markets) of the EA02 (where the concept of relevant person does not apply). Such an extension comes into force when published by the CMA and continues in force until (a) the person concerned provides the information or documents to the satisfaction of the CMA, or (as the case may be) appears as a witness in accordance with the requirements of the CMA, or (b) the CMA publishes its decision to cancel the extension. See section 107 and sections 34ZB(7), 39(8) and 41A(7)(b) of the EA02 (mergers) and section 138A(5)(b) (markets) of the EA02.

40 See *Mergers: Guidance on the CMA's jurisdiction and procedure* (CMA2) and *Market studies and market investigations: Supplemental guidance on the CMA's approach* (CMA3).

41 Section 110(2) (mergers) of the EA02 provides that the CMA may impose a penalty for failure to comply with requirements imposed under section 109 of the EA02 and extend the timetable under section 39(4) of the EA02. Similarly, section 174A(2) (markets) of the EA02 provides that the CMA may both impose a penalty for failure to comply with requirements imposed under section 174 of the EA02 and extend the timetable under section 138A(3) of the EA02.

42 Section 94A(1) (mergers) of the EA02.

43 Sections 111(3) (mergers) and 174D(3) (markets) of the EA02.

44 Sections 111(2) and (3) (mergers) and 174D(2) and (3) (markets) of the EA02 and section 40A(2) of the CA98. See also Annexe B below, which contains a high-level summary table of the CMA powers and corresponding penalties for non-compliance covered by this statement of policy.

45 See sections 111(5)(b) (mergers) and 174D(9)(a) (markets) of the EA02 and section 40A(6)(b) of the CA98.

46 Unless the duration falls in a period after which the CMA cannot impose a fine. See sections 110A(1) (mergers) and 174B(1) (markets) of the EA02 and section 40A(7)(b) and (c) of the CA98.

47 As noted at paragraph 1.1 above, P refers to individuals and to both bodies corporate and unincorporated.

48 It should be noted that the Interim Measures Order and the CMA's approach to control set out in this Statement relate solely to determining the penalty for failure to comply with Merger IMs under sections 94A(2) and (3) (mergers) of the EA02.

49 See Article 2(1) of the Interim Measures Order.

50 See Article 2(4) of the Interim Measures Order.

51 See also paragraphs 3.2.8 to 3.2.12 of the publication *Merger Assessment Guidelines* (OFT1254/CC2).

52 See Article 2(2) of the Interim Measures Order.

53 See Article 3 of the Interim Measures Order.

54 The relevant turnover will be calculated after the deduction of sales rebates, value added tax and other taxes directly related to turnover.

5 PROCEDURE

GENERAL

[3.21]

5.1 In addition to the statutory procedural requirements noted at paragraphs 5.4 to 5.7 below, the CMA will follow the procedures set out in paragraphs 5.2 and 5.3 below. It should be noted that, notwithstanding the procedures below, time for the purposes of assessing duration relevant to a fine will start to run from when the failure takes place, other than in relation to daily penalties in relation to EA02 Requirements where no account is taken of any days before service of the notice imposing the penalty.

5.2 Where it appears that P has failed to comply with an Investigatory Requirement or Merger IM without reasonable excuse, before making a final decision to impose a penalty the CMA will issue a provisional decision setting out the reasons for its proposed action, the approach that it proposes to take in imposing a penalty and the proposed nature and level of penalty. P will be given a reasonable opportunity to make representations on the provisional decision to the CMA. The period within which representations must be received will be determined on a case-by-case basis having regard to the nature of the failure to comply and the constraints of the relevant statutory or administrative timetable, and in any event will not usually exceed one week. The CMA will consider any representations received and consult with the General Counsel's Office on its reasons for the proposed approach to and level of the penalty.

5.3 If the CMA decides to impose a penalty for non-compliance with an Investigatory Requirement or Merger IM, it will notify P of its decision as soon as practicable thereafter and will issue a notice (see paragraph 5.4 below).

STATUTORY PROCEDURAL POINTS

5.4 The following statutory procedural requirements apply to all administrative penalties the CMA may impose. Once the CMA has reached a decision to impose an administrative penalty, the CMA shall give notice of the penalty to P as soon as practicable.[55] This notice must specify:

- that the CMA has imposed a penalty on P
- whether the penalty is a fixed penalty, calculated by reference to a daily rate, or both
- the amount of the penalty, and where calculated by reference to a daily rate, the day on which the amount starts to accumulate and might cease to accumulate[56]
- the failure, obstruction or delay which the CMA considers gave it the power to impose a penalty
- any other facts which the CMA considers justify the imposition of a penalty and the amount of the penalty
- the manner in which, and the place at which, the penalty is required to be paid to the CMA
- the date or dates by which the penalty or (as the case may be) different portions of it are required to be paid
- that the penalty or different portions of it may be paid earlier than the date or dates by which it or they are required to be paid, and
- details of P's rights to apply to have the dates on which payments are due varied or to appeal the imposition or nature of the penalty, or the amount of the penalty or the specified date or dates of payment.[57]

APPEALS

5.5 Where P is aggrieved by the imposition or the nature of the penalty for failure to comply with EA02 Requirements or CA98 Requirements, its amount or the date by which the penalty is required to be paid, P may appeal to the Competition Appeal Tribunal.[58] Similarly, where P is aggrieved by the imposition or nature of a penalty for failure to comply with Merger IMs, the amount of the penalty or any date by which the penalty is required to be paid, P may appeal to the Competition Appeal Tribunal.[59]

5.6 If the whole or any portion of a penalty is not paid by the date by which it is required to be paid, interest will be payable on the unpaid balance at the rate specified in section 17 of the Judgments Act 1838.[60]

5.7 Where a penalty, or any portion of such penalty, has not been paid by the date on which it is required to be paid and there is no pending appeal against the decision, the CMA may recover the penalty and any interest which has not been paid; in England and Wales and Northern Ireland such penalty and interest may be recovered as a civil debt due to the CMA.[61]

DECISION-MAKING IN RELATION TO ADMINISTRATIVE PENALTIES

5.8 The way that the CMA makes decisions in its investigations depends on the statutory power in question. The CMA has issued procedural guidance in relation to mergers, markets and CA98 investigations, which sets out how key decisions in relation to investigations under those statutory powers will be made. See *Mergers: Guidance on the CMA's jurisdiction and procedure* (CMA2), *Market studies and market investigations: Supplemental guidance on the CMA's approach* (CMA3) and *Competition Act 1998: Guidance on the CMA's investigation procedures* (CMA8).

5.9 Decisions in relation to the imposition of the penalties covered in this Statement will be made by the person who makes substantive decisions in mergers, markets and CA98 investigations as described in the aforementioned guidance documents. As noted at paragraph 5.2 above, the decision-maker will consult the General Counsel's Office on its reasons for, and proposed approach to, imposing any penalty. Broadly speaking, administrative penalty decisions will be made as follows:

- **Mergers investigations** (in relation to penalties for failure to comply with mergers investigatory or interim measures powers):
  - Phase 1 (investigation before a decision to refer a merger has been made): the Phase 1 decision maker (either the Senior Director of Mergers or another senior member of CMA staff) and
  - Phase 2 (investigation after a decision to refer a merger has been made): the CMA inquiry group.
- **Market investigations**:
  - Phase 1 (investigation before a decision to make a market investigation reference has been made): generally the CMA Board, and
  - Phase 2 (investigation after a decision to make a market investigation reference has been made): the CMA market reference group appointed to conduct the investigation.

- **CA98 investigations**:
  - 'Phase 1' (up until the issue of a Statement of Objections): the Senior Responsible Officer, who has overall charge of the investigation, and
  - 'Phase 2' (after a Statement of Objections has been issued): the Case Decision Group.

NOTES

55 Sections 94A(7), 112(1) (mergers) and section 174D(10) (markets) of the EA02 and section 40A(9) of the CA98.

56 No account is taken of any days before service of the notice imposing the penalty.

57 Section 112(2) (mergers) and 174D(10) (markets) of the EA02.

58 Sections 114 (mergers) and 174D(10) (markets) of the EA02 and section 40A(9) of the CA98.

59 Section 94A(7) (mergers) of the EA02, which provides that the right to appeal against the imposition of a penalty in section 114 (mergers) of the EA02 applies to penalties imposed for failure to comply with interim measures.

60 Sections 113 (mergers) and 174D(10) (markets) of the EA02.

61 Sections 115 (mergers) and 174D(10) (markets) of the EA02.

ANNEXE(S)

A. PRACTICAL EXAMPLES

[3.22]

A.1 To assist relevant stakeholders, this annexe sets out some non-exhaustive illustrative examples of how the CMA powers described in the Statement might apply in selected potential scenarios. They do not form part of the Statement and are without prejudice to the CMA's ability to determine its approach to the imposition of a penalty on a case-by-case basis.

EXAMPLE 1

Scenario

A is a small enterprise. Two of A's competitors, B and C, have notified their proposed merger to the CMA. In the circumstances of the case, the CMA sends a formal information request under section 109 of the EA02 to A as part of its investigation into the effects of the merger of B and C. The information request is sent to A's Chief Executive, who accidentally misfiles the request and forgets about it. When contacted by the CMA the day after the deadline has passed, the Chief Executive is hugely apologetic and offers to provide the majority of the requested information later that day, with the remainder to follow the next day. A has provided several complete and timely responses to CMA information requests in the past.

Analysis

The CMA would be likely to consider this a minor/mitigated failure committed without reasonable excuse. It is based on an administrative error, which:

- A has taken immediate and satisfactory steps to rectify – A did not seek to benefit in any way from the failure to comply, and
- given the limited delay in providing the information (provided the outstanding information is indeed received promptly) is unlikely to have a material adverse impact on the CMA's investigation.

While the CMA does not consider that the circumstances of this failure to comply constitute a reasonable excuse, in some cases of this nature the CMA may decide not to impose an administrative penalty.

EXAMPLE 2

Scenario

D is a major operator in a market with three other key players. The CMA has received numerous complaints that prices in the market have increased exponentially in recent years, and believes there may be features of the market which are producing anti-competitive effects. It therefore decides to conduct a market study, sending information requests under section 174 of the EA02 to D and several of its competitors. D's response to the information request is incomplete and inadequate. Many questions are ignored completely or receive inadequate one-word responses that do not answer the question properly. When asked to estimate its market share and explain its reasoning for the estimate, D states 'around 20%' with no explanation of the basis for its estimate. The responses from D's competitors, however, indicate that D's share is close to 40%. Further investigation reveals a recent presentation to D's Board estimating its market share to be 42% at the relevant time and including data on which the estimate was based that was not provided to the CMA.

Analysis

The CMA would be likely to consider this a serious failure, committed without reasonable excuse, which would certainly warrant a penalty. Inadequate and indeed inaccurate information has been provided to the CMA, in all likelihood in order to prejudice the CMA's investigation to D's benefit. In order to reflect the seriousness of the failure to comply and deter future failures of this sort, the CMA would be likely to consider both a fixed penalty (which is likely to be at the upper end of the range) and a daily penalty (likely to be at the upper end of the range) until D provides complete, adequate and accurate responses to the information request.

EXAMPLE 3

Scenario

The CMA is investigating a major company, E, in relation to suspected breaches of a dominant position under the CA98. During a dawn raid of E's premises under section 28 of the CA98, a director refuses to provide the combination to unlock a filing cabinet, claiming that the contents are 'personal and confidential'. The director also attempts to prevent the CMA from taking copies of a number of documents, arguing that they are covered by legal professional privilege. It is later revealed that these documents and the contents of the filing cabinet were neither personal nor privileged, but were highly incriminating. The obstructive behaviour caused considerable delays to the CMA's investigation.

Analysis

The CMA would consider this a deliberate/aggravated failure, committed without reasonable excuse. The failure constitutes an unjustified obstruction of the CMA's investigation which may prevent the CMA from obtaining important evidence of possible further infringements. The director clearly acted intentionally and company E did not take sufficient and/or timely steps to investigate the director's claims in respect of the nature of the documents. In order to mark the seriousness of the failure to comply with its powers and to send a strong deterrent message about such behaviour, the CMA would likely impose the maximum fixed penalty as well as the maximum daily penalty on company E until the requests were complied with. The director's conduct might also be capable of constituting a criminal offence under section 42(7) of the CA98 and the CMA might consider whether it was appropriate to prosecute the director. Consideration of an administrative penalty as described is without prejudice to the CMA's ability to consider prosecution for the criminal offence.

EXAMPLE 4

Scenario

The CMA, through its market intelligence functions, has become aware of a recently completed acquisition by company F of its competitor, company G. The CMA has reasonable grounds for suspecting that the two enterprises have ceased to be distinct. In order to prevent the companies from starting integration of their respective businesses, the CMA makes an interim enforcement order under section 72 of the EA02 to prevent pre-emptive action by the companies, including that:

- the business of company F should be carried on separately and under a separate brand identity from the business of company G, and
- the assets of each of company F and company G are maintained and preserved.

F and G do not own or control any other enterprises. However, shortly thereafter company F begins to market the products produced by company G under the company F brand. The CMA also receives complaints from third parties that company F has been actively seeking to sell the site occupied by company G to a property developer.

In the business year preceding the date when the interim measures came into force, the turnover of company F and all of the enterprises it owned or controlled (including company G) was £10 million.

Analysis

The CMA would be likely to consider this an egregious failure committed without reasonable excuse. The steps taken to integrate the businesses could seriously prejudice the CMA's ability to impose an effective remedy if that was considered justified following its merger investigation. Company F has ignored an express order from the CMA and has not offered any explanation for its actions. Moreover, company F would be profiting from its failure to comply with the interim measures. Accordingly, the CMA is likely to impose a very significant penalty on company F to encourage swift compliance with the interim measures, potentially at or close to the maximum penalty of 5% of turnover (in and outside the UK) of the enterprises owned or controlled by company F (section 94A of the EA02), which would be £500,000 in this case. The interim measures are also enforceable by civil proceedings (section 94 of the EA02). In the particular circumstances of this case the CMA might also consider seeking an injunction from the High Court to ensure compliance for the duration of its investigation.

EXAMPLE 5

Scenario

The CMA is conducting a CA98 investigation into a suspected market-sharing agreement. Following inspections without notice under section 27 of the CA98, the CMA is seeking information from a hotel, part of a large chain, at which it suspects a cartel meeting took place. The CMA requests certain information by notice under section 26 of the CA98. In response to a draft information request proposing to give the hotel a week to respond, the hotel manager says the relevant data is stored on one of many external hard drives stored offsite. He also notes that he and staff are extremely busy preparing for their most important and lucrative conference of the year, to be held in three weeks' time. He therefore requests three weeks rather than one in which to respond. The CMA explains that it needs the information before it conducts a series of interviews that it has lined up for four weeks time, so although it is prepared to give the hotel the three weeks requested the hotel should take extra care to ensure it responds on time. The CMA sends the formal section 26 notice with the deadline requested by the hotel. The hotel fails to respond to the section 26 notice in the agreed timescale.

When contacted by the CMA following expiry of the agreed deadline, the hotel manager apologises but says that the IT expert he left to deal with the matter has been off sick for two weeks and is still off sick. The manager says that he does not know when the IT expert will be back and that he and his other staff are either too busy or do not have sufficient IT skills to obtain the information required. He says he will prioritise the CMA's request straight after the conference.

Analysis

The CMA would be likely to consider that there was no reasonable excuse for the failure to comply and that the failure merited a moderate to severe penalty. While the CMA understands that staffing difficulties may arise unexpectedly, in this case the IT expert had been sick for two weeks, during which time it would have become apparent to the manager that he would likely have problems meeting the CMA's deadline. The manager did not, however, discuss this with the CMA. Also, he was already aware of the work relating to the conference and was granted an additional week to respond taking that into account. The interviews that the CMA had scheduled will need to be postponed if the information is not received quickly, adding significant time to the investigation as the relevant individuals are on pre-booked overseas trips for six weeks after the scheduled interview dates. Finally, the manager has not made appropriate efforts to remedy the failure in a timely fashion, for example getting additional resources to help with the conference preparation and/or obtain the data required by the CMA. The CMA would likely impose a fixed penalty as well as a daily penalty to incentivise compliance with the investigatory requirement and to ensure that a deterrent (but proportionate) penalty was set.

B. SUMMARY TABLE OF CMA INVESTIGATORY AND MERGERS IM POWERS AND PENALTIES FOR FAILURE TO COMPLY

[3.23]

CMA power	Penalty for failure to comply	Further information
Mergers investigatory powers		
Section 109 EA02 – powers to require evidence, documents and/or attendance at interviews/meetings	Fixed penalty of up to £30,000 and/or daily penalty of up to £15,000	These powers are available to the CMA throughout the whole merger review process, from before Phase 1 up to any period of monitoring and enforcement after Phase 2 Penalties may be imposed where there is no reasonable excuse for the failure to comply
	Fixed penalty of up to £30,000 (but not a daily penalty) may be imposed on those who obstruct or delay copying of documents (section 110(3) EA02)	These powers are available to the CMA throughout the whole merger review process, from before Phase 1 up to any period of monitoring and enforcement after Phase 2 Obstruction or delay must be intentional
	Criminal offence to intentionally alter, suppress or destroy any document requested under section 109 EA02 (section 110(5) of the EA02)	For mergers investigatory powers under sections 109 and 110 EA02, where an act constitutes both (a) a failure warranting administrative penalty and (b) a criminal offence, the CMA cannot impose an administrative penalty if a person has been found guilty of the criminal offence. Equally, a criminal offence is not committed where the CMA has imposed an administrative penalty in relation to the same act.
	It is also a criminal offence knowingly or recklessly to provide false or misleading information to the CMA, the Secretary of State (and OFCOM and Monitor) in connection with any of their functions under Part 3 of the EA02 (mergers) (section 117 of the EA02) For both offences, a person is liable, on summary conviction, to a fine not exceeding the statutory maximum and, on conviction on indictment, to imprisonment for a term not exceeding two years or to a fine or to both	
Markets investigatory powers		

CMA power	Penalty for failure to comply	Further information
Section 174 EA02 – powers to require evidence, documents and/or attendance at interviews/meetings	Fixed penalty of up to £30,000 and/or daily penalty of up to £15,000 Fixed penalty of up to £30,000 (but not a daily penalty) may be imposed on those who obstruct or delay copying of documents (section 174A(3) EA02)	These powers are available to the CMA once it has published a market study notice and so may be used during market studies (Phase 1) as well as market investigations (Phase 2) Penalties may be imposed where there is no reasonable excuse for the failure to comply Obstruction or delay must be intentional.
	Criminal offence to alter, suppress or destroy any document requested under section 174 EA02. A person is liable, on conviction on indictment, to imprisonment for a term of up to two years and/or to a fine (section 174A(6) of the EA02) It is also a criminal offence knowingly or recklessly to provide false or misleading information to the CMA, the Secretary of State (and OFCOM and Monitor) in connection with any of their functions under Part 4 of the EA02 (markets) (section 180 of the EA02)	For markets investigatory powers under sections 174 and 174A EA02, where an act constitutes both (a) a failure warranting administrative penalty and (b) a criminal offence, the CMA cannot impose an administrative penalty if a person has been found guilty of the criminal offence. Equally, a criminal offence is not committed where the CMA has imposed an administrative penalty in respect of the same act.
CA98 investigatory powers		
Section 26 CA98 – power to require information and documents by notice	Fixed penalty of up to £30,000 and/or daily penalty of up to £15,000	Financial penalties may be imposed where there is no reasonable excuse for the failure to comply
Section 26A CA98 – power to require questions to be answered by notice	In addition to the CMA's administrative penalty powers, it is a criminal offence to obstruct the exercise of the CMA's powers under sections 27, 28 and 28A of the CA98 (section 42 CA98), to destroy or falsify documents (section 43 CA98) or to provide false or misleading information (section 44 CA98) In relation to obstructing the exercise of powers under section 27, a person is liable, on conviction on indictment, to a fine. For the other offences, a person is liable, on conviction on indictment, to imprisonment for a term of up to two years and/or to a fine	
Section 27 CA98 – power to enter business premises without a warrant		
Section 28 CA98 – power to enter business premises under a warrant		
Section 28A CA98 – power to enter domestic premises under a warrant		
Mergers interim measures powers		
Section 94A EA02 – power to impose penalty for failure to comply with an interim measure (without reasonable excuse)	Fixed penalty of up to 5% of the total value of the turnover (both in and outside the UK) of the enterprises owned or controlled by the person on whom the penalty is imposed	This power is available to the CMA at both Phase 1 and Phase 2 of a merger review process Penalties may be imposed where there is no reasonable excuse for the failure to comply

C. STATUS OF OFT AND CC PUBLICATIONS

[3.24]

C.1 The table below indicates the status of OFT and CC guidance documents and publications relevant to the administrative penalty powers covered in the Statement that had been published and were in effect prior to the transfer of the mergers, markets and CA98 functions to the CMA on 1 April 2014. Certain of those documents have been adopted by the CMA Board in order to facilitate transition to the new UK merger, markets and CA98 regime, and to minimise disruption to parties and the CMA.

OFT/CC Code	Title	Status of document	
		Replaced/ obsolete[1]	Adopted by the CMA Board[2]
CC4	General Advice and Information	√	-
CC5	Statement of Policy on Penalties	√	-

OFT/CC Code	Title	Status of document	
		Replaced/ obsolete[1]	Adopted by the CMA Board[2]
CC6	Competition Commission: guidance to merger reference groups, market reference groups and special reference groups	√	-
CC18	Merger procedural guidelines	√	-
OFT441	How will the Enterprise Act 2002 change the Competition Act 1998 regime?	√	-
OFT511	Market investigation references	-	√
OFT518	Overview of the Enterprise Act	√	-
OFT519	Market studies: guidance on the OFT approach	-	√
OFT527	Mergers jurisdictional and procedural guidance	√	-
OFT530	Practical information – everything you need to know about the Enterprise Act	√	-
OFT1254/CC2	Merger assessment guidelines	-	√
OFT1263rev	The OFT's CA98 procedures guide	√	-
SI 2004/2751	The Competition Act 1998 (Office of Fair Trading's Rules) Order 2004	√	-

NOTES

[1] The OFT and the CC publications listed in this column have, with effect from 1 April 2014, been replaced, or rendered obsolete, by the CMA guidance or publications.

[2] OFT and CC publications listed in this column have been adopted by the CMA Board (subject to any guidance prepared by the CMA in the future). They are available at www.gov.uk/cma/.

C.2 Parties should refer to those documents listed above as having been adopted by the CMA board (the adopted guidance) for further details on the substance and procedure around the substantive powers which the CMA may impose penalties for failure to comply with. This is subject, in particular, to the following general limitations:

- all references in the adopted guidance listed above to issues of jurisdiction or procedure in mergers and markets cases must be read in the light of the CMA mergers and markets guidance documents *Mergers: Guidance on the CMA's jurisdiction and procedure* (CMA2) and *Market studies and market investigations: Supplemental guidance on the CMA's approach* (CMA3)
- in the cases of conflict between those guidance documents and the adopted guidance, those guidance documents prevail
- the original text of the adopted guidance has been retained unamended: as such, that text does not reflect or take account of developments in case law, legislation or practice since its original publication, and
- all the adopted guidance should be read subject to the following cross-cutting amendments:
  - references to the 'OFT' or the 'CC' (except where referring to specific past OFT or CC practice or case law), should be read as referring to the CMA
  - references to 'referral to the CC' or 'a reference to the CC' should be read as referring to the referral of a case by the CMA (or Secretary of State) of a case for a Phase 2 investigation involving an Inquiry Group of the CMA panel members
  - references to articles of the EC Treaty should be read as referring to the equivalent articles of the Treaty on the Functioning of the European Union (TFEU)
  - certain OFT or CC departments, teams or individual roles may not be replicated in the CMA, or may have been renamed; a copy of the CMA's organisational chart is available on www.gov.uk/cma, and
  - parties should check any contact details against those listed on www.gov.uk/cma, which will be the most up to date.

TRANSPARENCY AND DISCLOSURE: STATEMENT OF THE CMA'S POLICY AND APPROACH (CMA6, JANUARY 2014)

[3.25]

NOTES

See also the CMA6 Clarification Note (Clarification on publishing market sensitive announcements (2016)) at **[3.70]**.

The fines that could be imposed on summary conviction for certain criminal offences referred to in this document were, at that time, subject to specific caps of £5,000 or above. With effect from 12 March 2015, these caps have been removed and those specific offences are now punishable by a fine of any amount.

CONTENTS

1. INTRODUCTION

[3.26]

1.1 The Enterprise and Regulatory Reform Act 2013 (ERRA13) established the Competition and Markets Authority (CMA) as the UK's economy-wide competition authority responsible for ensuring that competition and markets work well for consumers. On 1 April 2014, the functions of the Competition Commission (CC) and the Office of Fair Trading (OFT) were transferred to the CMA and those bodies abolished. The CMA's primary duty is to promote competition, both within and outside the UK, for the benefit of consumers.

1.2 This Statement constitutes an umbrella document guidance which aims to set out the CMA's policy and approach to transparency and disclosure at a high level. In brief, this Statement provides an overview of:

- the aims of the CMA in relation to transparency, information requests and handling of information
- the CMA's approach to transparency when involved in cases and projects[1]
- the CMA's approach to gathering information from and disclosing information to parties, and
- the CMA's approach when considering whether to disclose information to other UK or overseas public authorities.

It also notes the CMA's obligations regarding the protection and disclosure of information under the Enterprise Act 2002 (EA02), Competition Act 1998 (CA98), Freedom of Information Act 2000 (FOIA) and the Data Protection Act 1998 (DPA98).

1.3 This Statement applies to the CMA's cases, except where stated to the contrary, in particular such work under the CA98, EA02 and consumer enforcement actions.

1.4 More detailed guidance on transparency and disclosure as it relates to specific areas of the CMA's work, including the applicable legal provisions, is available in other CMA documents, including:[2]

- *Mergers: Guidance on the CMA's jurisdiction and procedure* (CMA2)
- *Market Studies and Market Investigations: Supplemental guidance on the CMA's approach* (CMA3)
- *Consumer Protection: Guidance on the CMA's approach to use of its consumer powers* (CMA7)
- *Competition Act 1998: Guidance on the CMA's investigation procedures in Competition Act 1998 cases* (CMA8)
- *Applications for leniency and no-action in cartel cases* (OFT1495), and
- *Chairman's Guidance on Disclosure of Information in Merger Inquiries, Market Investigations and Reviews of Undertakings and Orders accepted or made under the Enterprise Act 2002 and Fair Trading Act 1973* (CC7 (revised)).[3]

1.5 Amendments to the *Chairman's Guidance on Disclosure of Information in Merger Inquiries, Market Investigations and Reviews of Undertakings and Orders accepted or made under the Enterprise Act 2002 and Fair Trading Act 1973* (CC7 (revised)) as a result of the changes that are outlined in this Statement are listed in Annexe A to this document.

1.6 This Statement reflects the views of the CMA as at 1 April 2014 and may be revised from time to time to reflect changes in best practice, legislation and the results of experience, legal judgments and research. This Statement may in due course be supplemented, revised or replaced. The CMA's webpages will always display the latest version of the Statement.

1.7 Although it covers most of the points likely to be of immediate concern to businesses and their advisers, this Statement makes no claim to be comprehensive. It cannot, therefore, be seen as a substitute for the law itself, nor can it be cited as a definitive interpretation of the law. Anyone in any doubt about whether they may be affected by the points covered here should consider seeking legal advice.

1.8 The CMA will apply this Statement flexibly. This means that the CMA will have regard to the Statement when dealing with transparency and disclosure but that, when the facts of an individual case reasonably justify it, the CMA may adopt a different approach.

NOTES

1 For ease of reference, references to a case or cases in the remainder of this document also cover the CMA's projects.

2 In the event of apparent conflict between this guidance and the detailed guidance, the latter prevails.

3 These documents are available in full on www.gov.uk/cma. The webpages also contains a complete list of the CMA's guidance documents.

2. CMA AIMS IN RESPECT OF TRANSPARENCY, INFORMATION REQUESTS, AND HANDLING OF INFORMATION

OVERVIEW

[3.27]
2.1 The CMA is committed to its aims to be open and transparent about the work it does and how it engages with those directly involved in or affected by its work, while seeking to maintain (as appropriate) the confidentiality of information it obtains in the exercise of its functions. It also aims to be reasonable when requesting and handling information, and to protect confidential information in a manner that is appropriate in the circumstances of the case. Furthermore, the CMA aims to carry out its cases with appropriate efficiency and timeliness, including by having due regard to published timetables and statutory deadlines.

2.2 In regard to these aims, the CMA recognises the desirability of taking a consistent approach both when exercising the same functions and across functions. However, for some of the CMA's functions, the procedures and approach the CMA takes in an individual case are influenced or determined by legislation. Similarly the circumstances of a case may determine the CMA's approach in the particular instance.[4]

TRANSPARENCY

2.3 Transparency is important for a number of reasons. Transparency is a means of achieving due process and ensuring that parties directly involved in a case are treated fairly. It also enables other interested persons to engage effectively with the CMA and to contribute to its work. Ensuring due process for those directly involved in the CMA's work and effectively engaging with other interested persons in turn improves the effectiveness and efficiency of the CMA's work, and the quality and robustness of its decision-making.

2.4 Providing clear information about its cases also enhances the visibility of the CMA's work, thereby increasing its impact, predictability and accountability. Transparency further fosters closer cooperation with overseas competition and consumer authorities.

2.5 The CMA aims to achieve transparency in its work by:

- ensuring the parties directly involved and other interested persons (if appropriate) are informed during the course of a case of key developments, for example by notifying them of the formal commencement of a case (unless this may prejudice the investigation), sharing developing thinking with relevant parties at appropriate stages of a case, providing indicative timetables, and identifying contacts and decision makers
- engaging with the parties directly involved at an early stage of its cases (unless doing so may prejudice the case)
- ensuring that at appropriate times during the case parties directly involved and other interested persons have an opportunity to raise their concerns and provide their views regarding a particular case
- placing announcements on www.gov.uk/cma when a formal case has been opened (unless doing so may prejudice the case or would otherwise be inappropriate), and
- placing announcements on www.gov.uk/cma when a case, in relation to which a formal case opening announcement has been issued, reaches particular significant milestones and when it is completed.

INFORMATION REQUESTS

2.6 The CMA's cases require it to make evidence based decisions. The receipt of information is therefore important to the quality and effectiveness of the CMA's work. When formulating and determining the scope of information requests, determining to whom to address information requests, and determining the date by which the information should be provided, the CMA will aim to be fair and reasonable in its approach and will seek to avoid imposing unnecessary burdens across all of its work. In particular it will be receptive to parties' concerns about the burdens placed on them by the CMA's requests while seeking to balance those concerns with the efficient and effective operation of the CMA. Further information relating to information requests in respect of many of its functions is provided in chapter 4.

HANDLING INFORMATION

2.7 The CMA's commitment to transparency is provided in the context of the CMA's duty under the ERRA13 to promote competition for the benefit of consumers. The CMA is also under certain statutory obligations to protect confidential information. These obligations apply to the confidentiality of information relating to individuals and businesses that comes to the CMA in connection with the exercise of its statutory functions. Restrictions on the further disclosure of information apply to the CMA and to other persons to whom it makes disclosure. In particular a person making an unlawful disclosure commits a criminal offence.

2.8 Under the EA02 such specified information[5] may be disclosed in certain specific circumstances, generally referred to as 'information gateways'. When handling information and considering the appropriateness of making a disclosure, the CMA will be mindful of the need to protect confidential information from unlawful disclosure.

2.9 Further information about these statutory provisions of the EA02 and the DPA98, including the relevant considerations for the CMA before making a disclosure, is to be found in chapters 4, 6, 7 and 8.

Further information about the disclosure of information in the course of cases is available in chapter 4. Further information about the disclosure of information to other public bodies (UK and overseas) is provided in chapters 6 and 7 respectively.

NOTES

4 In particular, the CMA acknowledges that in criminal cartel and criminal consumer investigations, the public interest may weigh in favour of maintaining confidentiality of information rather than disclosure. Where there are parallel criminal and civil cartel investigations, the approach taken in relation to the CA98 investigation will be informed by the approach taken in the criminal case.

5 As defined under sections 237 and 238 of the EA02.

3. TRANSPARENCY DURING THE COURSE OF A CASE

PREPARATORY WORK

[3.28]

3.1 Before formally opening a case, the CMA typically carries out some preparatory work. For example, it may assess market intelligence and analyse trends in aggregated complaints data. The CMA may also engage with the parties directly involved,[6] for example through pre-notification discussions with merging parties in merger cases or informal preliminary inquiries in markets[7] and CA98 cases. The CMA may also engage with other interested persons, for example through discussions with complainants or other businesses in the market concerned, when it would be helpful to the CMA's case. This enables the CMA to gather information which will inform its early thinking and, where relevant, the decision as to whether to formally open a case. It also enables the parties directly involved to understand at an early stage the potential competition or consumer concerns under consideration.

3.2 The CMA will not engage with parties directly involved or other interested persons before the formal case opening decision where doing so may prejudice the investigation, for example in CA98 cases prior to unannounced site visits or witness interviews. This is particularly relevant, for example, in the case of suspected cartels, where the CMA is unlikely to contact the persons under investigation until after a formal investigation has been opened, unless they are already cooperating as leniency applicants or if the party directly involved is an informant.

ANNOUNCING A FORMAL CASE OPENING DECISION

3.3 For the purposes of this Statement, cases are formally opened when:

- in Phase 1 merger cases, the CMA confirms by notice to the merging parties that the merger notice is satisfactory[8] or (where the CMA is not dealing with a merger notice) that it otherwise has sufficient information to enable it to begin its investigation[9]
- in Phase 2 merger cases, the CMA makes a merger reference[10]
- in relation to market studies, the CMA serves notice of the launch of a market study[11]
- in relation to market investigations, the CMA makes a market investigation reference[12]
- in relation to super complaints, the CMA receives the super complaint[13]
- in CA98 investigations, the CMA decides that the legal test in the CA98[14] has been met (thus allowing the CMA to use its formal investigation powers) and that the case falls within its prioritisation principles
- in criminal cartel investigations, the CMA decides that there are reasonable grounds for suspecting that a criminal cartel offence has been committed[15] and that the case falls within its prioritisation principles
- in consumer enforcement actions, the CMA decides to launch an investigation of a case which falls within its prioritisation principles,[16] and
- in relation to the review of undertakings and orders,[17] the CMA launches a review of the undertakings or orders.[18]

3.4 In regulatory reference and appeal cases the CMA's involvement in the case will be on a formal footing when the reference or appeal is made. Similarly with market references, referred by a regulator or minister, the CMA's formal involvement commences when the reference is made. On other occasions the CMA may work with concurrent regulators on a pre-launch or market study prior to the market reference being made.

3.5 The CMA will, usually inform the parties directly involved of the decision to formally open a case (see paragraph 3.7). This may be done during the course of otherwise regular contact between the case team and the parties directly involved, through a notice to the notifying parties in Phase 1 mergers and market studies, through a Phase 2 opening letter[19] in Phase 2 merger inquiries and market investigations, or through a case initiation letter in CA98 investigations and civil consumer enforcement actions. However, it will not be appropriate to inform the parties directly involved (as soon as a case is opened) when doing so may prejudice an investigation. For example, in CA98 and cartel investigations such information may prejudice the investigation by undermining the CMA's ability to conduct unannounced site visits or execute search warrants. In such cases, the parties directly involved will be informed of the formal case opening decision, and an announcement will be made, as soon as it is possible to do so without prejudicing the investigation. In cartel cases suspects are usually made aware of the investigation when they are arrested and/or when search warrants are executed.

3.6 In relation to cases involving many parties, for example market studies, market investigations or certain consumer cases, undertakings in the relevant sector will not always be informed individually of the CMA's decision before the case opening announcement is placed on www.gov.uk/cma. Use of the webpages in such circumstances is an efficient means of communicating with the possibly large number of parties directly involved and may be the only means when not all such parties are identified by the CMA.

3.7 When the parties directly involved are informed of the formal case opening decision, the CMA will also provide them with the following information:

- a brief description of the case, the relevant legislation, the industry sector concerned and the CMA's reasons for starting a formal case. The level of information may vary according to the circumstances of the case. It may not be appropriate to name the parties directly involved at this early stage of a case
- an indicative timetable showing the anticipated dates of key milestones,[20] and
- the contact details for the main CMA contacts for the case including the first point of contact for general queries and submission of information.

3.8 At this early stage or shortly afterwards, the CMA may be able to provide the parties directly involved with other information about the case, such as potential timescales for state of play meetings (for example, in Phase 1 merger cases and CA98 investigations) and the identity of the person or persons within the CMA who will be responsible for key decisions.[21]

3.9 In all cases other than criminal cartel and criminal consumer investigations,[22] the CMA will place a case opening announcement on www.gov.uk/cma announcing its decision to formally begin a case except if to do so would prejudice the case or would otherwise be inappropriate. At the same time as or following the public announcement of a case opening, the CMA will also publish, if and as soon as reasonably practicable, the information referred to in paragraph 3.7.

3.10 The CMA will review the information provided on the status of the case and consider whether it is appropriate to update the information provided to the parties directly involved or the published information. For example, it will consider the need to do so in the light of changes to the indicative and any statutory timetable that may change as the case progresses.

ENGAGEMENT WITH RELEVANT PARTIES AND ANNOUNCEMENTS DURING A CASE

3.11 An important aspect of ensuring that the CMA is transparent in its work is the way it engages with relevant parties over the course of a case. The timing and manner of engagement will vary depending on the type of work involved.[23] When considering the manner and timing of engagement, the CMA will have regard to the need to ensure due process for both the parties directly involved and other interested persons. The CMA will also have regard to the need to conduct investigations effectively and efficiently, and the need to reach properly reasoned decisions.

3.12 The CMA must, in some cases, take certain steps to share its provisional thinking or proposed decisions. For example:

- in CA98 investigations, if it proposes to make a decision, the CMA must issue a Statement of Objections (SO) to any party suspected of a breach of the CA98[24]
- in relation to a provisional decision to make a market investigation reference, the CMA must consult in such a manner as it considers practicable any persons on whose interest the decision is likely to have substantial impact and publish a notice of the proposal[25]
- in mergers and markets cases the CMA must consult affected parties on undertakings in lieu,[26] proposed final orders and undertakings, and publish its provisional findings and possible remedies in Phase 2 merger inquiries and market investigations,[27] and
- in civil consumer enforcement actions it must generally (but not always), before making an application for an enforcement order, engage in appropriate consultation with the party against whom the enforcement order would be made.[28]

3.13 The CMA is not subject to a general obligation to disclose its thinking in advance of consulting on its provisional decisions. However, the CMA will take a flexible approach to sharing its developing thinking and/or evidence with parties directly involved and (if appropriate) other interested persons prior to this, having regard to the desirability of ensuring that such parties are kept informed of key developments in the progress of their case. The CMA may share its developing thinking or evidence when doing so would be helpful to the progression of the case at appropriate stages, to verify the information it has received or when it is otherwise appropriate to do so. For example, the CMA may provide to the parties directly involved and other interested persons the results of research or surveys relevant to a market study or investigation; or disclose publicly parties' key submissions in Phase 2 merger inquiries and market investigations.[29] The CMA may also share its developing thinking more widely through publishing the fact and/or details of such thinking, including on www.gov.uk/cma. This includes an announcement on the issuing of an SO in CA98 investigations, on making an application for an enforcement order in civil consumer enforcement actions and on a decision to prosecute in a criminal investigation in appropriate cases.

3.14 The CMA will seek to ensure that the parties directly involved are aware of the decision making procedures which apply to their case, and the identity of the person or persons within the CMA who will be responsible for key decisions during the course of the case. Other interested persons are also able to contact the CMA to share their views. The CMA may also itself contact other parties to request information or seek their views on the case, where doing so would assist the CMA in exercising its functions.

CASE CLOSURE ANNOUNCEMENTS AND DECISIONS

3.15 Publication of case closure announcements and decisions is a means of enhancing the visibility of the CMA's completed work, and of widening its impact, as well as enabling interested persons to hold the CMA to account.

3.16 On completing a case in relation to which a formal case opening announcement has been made, the CMA will publish the outcome on www.gov.uk/cma and usually issue a press notice with a link to the relevant pages on www.gov.uk/cma. The potential outcomes that will be announced include:

- in Phase 1 merger cases, a clearance decision, a Found Not to Qualify Notice or the CMA deciding to make a merger reference or accept undertakings in lieu of a reference[30]
- in Phase 2 merger case, a no Substantial Lessening of Competition (SLC) decision, an SLC with or without remedies (including a prohibition) or cancellation of reference decision[31]
- in Phase 1 markets cases (that is, market studies), the CMA deciding not to make a market reference, to make a market reference or to accept undertakings in lieu of a reference[32]
- in Phase 2 markets cases, a no Adverse Effects on Competition (AEC) finding, an AEC finding with or without remedies[33]
- in relation to super-complaints, a response stating what action, if any, it proposes to take in response[34]
- in CA98 investigations, where the CMA's investigation is resolved through closing an investigation on administrative priorities, issuing a non-infringement decision, a decision that there are no grounds for action by the CMA, by accepting commitments from a business about their future conduct, or a final decision that particular conduct amounts to an infringement of the CA98[35]
- in criminal investigations, the outcome of a prosecution or a decision to close an investigation[36]
- in consumer enforcement actions, the outcome of a court action (with a link to the decision where possible), the successful negotiation of undertakings, a conclusion that there is insufficient evidence to continue an investigation, or a case closure decision on prioritisation grounds[37]
- in reviews of undertakings and orders,[38] a decision to vary, release, revoke or continue to enforce an undertaking or order,[39] and
- in regulatory references and appeals, the final decision on the reference or appeal.[40]

3.17 The level of detail published will reflect the CMA's statutory requirements and depend on the nature of the outcome, while also having regard to the CMA's transparency aims and the need to protect confidential information. In cases where a detailed decision has been issued, the CMA will publish a non-confidential version of the decision on www.gov.uk/cma. For those cases in relation to which a formal case opening announcement has been made, if the CMA decides to close a case on the basis of prioritisation grounds, the CMA will explain why this is the case.

NOTICE OF ANNOUNCEMENTS

3.18 The CMA will in the majority of cases give the parties directly involved such advance notice as it considers fair and sufficient before making any public announcements, either during or at the end of the case. The CMA will aim to balance an open approach with the need to ensure the orderly announcement of full information.

3.19 It will in particular be mindful of the risk of leakage of information shared on a confidential basis with parties in advance of the CMA's public announcement. Such leakage may result in selective and/or misleading reporting in the press.

3.20 The points below are a general guide. It may be the case that the particular complexities of the issue the CMA is dealing with mean that it departs from its standard practice.

MARKET AND NON-MARKET SENSITIVE ANNOUNCEMENTS

3.21 Where there are no market or other sensitivities about the fact or date of the announcement, the CMA will be open about the date and will generally inform media organisations of this before the date. The CMA will inform the parties directly involved in advance of informing the media. As a general rule, in non-market-sensitive announcements, the CMA aims to give the parties directly involved advance sight of the content of the CMA's announcement, in confidence, unless there is a compelling reason not to do so. However, the CMA will not, as a matter of course, discuss the text of press releases with parties in advance of issue.

3.22 When making a market-sensitive announcement, the CMA will, when appropriate, apply the Financial Conduct Authority's (FCA) 'Guidelines for the control and release of price sensitive information by Industry Regulators' (originally published by the Financial Services Authority (FSA)).

3.23 Where the CMA considers an announcement to be market-sensitive, it will:

- aim to make the announcement before relevant financial markets open and generally at 7am on the date of issue, except in Phase 1 mergers cases and in other exceptional circumstances (for example because of information leaking to the media or where legal proceedings are concerned)
- when the announcement date is not already in the public domain, the CMA will advise those directly affected of the announcement the evening before issue once relevant financial markets have closed – this might be out of hours, in which event the CMA will have requested out of hours contact details in advance, and
- typically, including where there are multiple parties, the CMA will provide those directly involved with a confidential text of the press release and any document which is to be published alongside the press release at least one hour in advance of issue.

NOTES

See also the CMA6 Clarification Note (Clarification on publishing market sensitive announcements) at **[3.70]**.

DEALING WITH THE MEDIA WHEN MAKING AN ANNOUNCEMENT

3.24 For non-market-sensitive announcements, the CMA may sometimes brief the media in advance of the making a public announcement under an agreed 'embargo'. When this happens the parties and other relevant stakeholders such as trade bodies will be notified of the embargo. On occasion this may involve spokespeople giving interviews to both broadcast and print media in advance under an embargo.

3.25 When making a market-sensitive announcement, the CMA never discusses the content with the media beforehand. The CMA may confirm that an announcement will take place on a certain day, at a certain time, and in some cases the CMA will agree in advance to interview requests for broadcast media.

3.26 Where the CMA statement is not known about in advance by the media due to market sensitivity issues, and where giving broadcasting interviews is appropriate, it will be the CMA's practice to have spokespeople available in the expectation of receiving interview requests shortly after an announcement.

3.27 Once a market-sensitive announcement has been made, the CMA will respond to media enquiries and, where appropriate, make spokespeople available for broadcast and print interviews.

NOTES

6 For the purposes of this document, 'parties directly involved' does not include complainants. In CA98 investigations, the CMA may provide Formal Complainants with access to the same information as available to the parties directly involved at the outset of its formal investigation. Refer to the guidance on *Involving third parties in Competition Act investigations (OFT451) and Competition Act 1998: Guidance on the CMA's investigation procedures in Competition Act 1998 cases* (CMA8) for further guidance on the involvement of third parties in CA98 investigations, including guidance on when complainants may be given Formal Complainant status.

7 For example, using its general review functions the CMA might engage with market participants prior to any launch of a market study (see *Market Studies and Market Investigation: Supplemental guidance on the CMA's approach* (CMA3)).

8 A merger notice must meet the requirements under section 96(2) of the EA02. Where the CMA is satisfied that these requirements are met it must give notice to that effect to the person who submitted the merger notice (section 92(2A) of the EA02).

9 Under section 34ZA(3) of the EA02.

10 Under section 22(1) or 33(1) of the EA02.

11 Under section 5 and 130A of the EA02.

12 Under section 131(1) of the EA02.

13 The super-complaint must satisfy the criteria in section 11(1) of the EA02.

14 Under section 25 of the CA98, the CMA may use its formal investigation powers where it has reasonable grounds for suspecting that competition law has been breached.

15 Under section 192(1) of the EA02.

16 Under the relevant consumer protection legislation.

17 This does not apply to undertakings and orders under Part 8 of the EA02 or the Unfair Terms in Consumer Contracts Regulations 1999 (UTCCRs).

18 Sections 92(1) and (2)(b) and (c) and 162(2)(b) and (c) of the EA02.

19 Previously called 'First Day Letter'.

20 At this stage in a case, there may be few key milestones – for example, in merger cases, the only milestone at this stage will be the statutory deadline for a Phase 1 review.

21 Further information regarding the decision making procedures across the CMA can be found in the *Mergers: Guidance on the CMA's jurisdiction and procedure* (CMA2) (chapter 7), *Market Studies and Market Investigations: Supplemental guidance on the CMA's approach* (CMA3) (chapter 1), *Competition Act 1998: Guidance on the CMA's investigation procedures in Competition Act 1998 cases* (CMA8) (chapters 11 and 13) and *Consumer Protection: Guidance on the CMA's approach to use of its consumer powers* (CMA7) (for detail on CMA's approach to compliance and enforcement of consumer protection law, see chapter 5), referred to in paragraph 1.4.

22 As noted in footnote 4, where there are parallel civil cartel investigations, the approach taken in civil cartel investigations will be informed by the approach taken in the criminal case.

23 Refer to the CMA guidance relating to mergers, markets, CA98, and consumer protection referred to in paragraph 1.4 for further guidance.

24 Rule 4 of the Competition and Markets Authority Competition Act 1998 Rules 2014.

25 Section 131A(2) and 169(6)(a)(i) of the EA02.

26 Sections 90 and Schedule 10 in respect of mergers and 155(1) of the EA02 (the CMA must publish a notice of the proposed undertakings in relation to market studies).

27 Section 104(1) and (2) of the EA02.

28 Section 214(1) of the EA02.

29 Further detail on the CMA's approach to disclosure in such inquiries or investigations may be found in *Chairman's Guidance on Disclosure of Information in Merger Inquiries, Market Investigations and Reviews of Undertakings and Orders accepted or made under the Enterprise Act 2002 and Fair Trading Act 1973* (CC7 (revised)).

30 Made under sections 22(2), 33(2) and 73 of the EA02. Publicity requirements in respect of these decisions are in section 107(1) of the EA02.

31 Section 37(1) of the EA02.

32 Made under sections 131(1) and 154(2) of the EA02. Publicity requirements in respect of these decisions are in section 172(1) of the EA02.

33 Section 136(1) of the EA02.

34 Section 11 of the EA02.

35 Sections 31(2), 31A and 31B.

36 Sections 188, 188A, 188B and 192(1) of the EA02.

37 Sections 215(1), 219(2) and 220(2) and (3) of the EA02 and other relevant consumer protection legislation.

38 This does not apply to undertakings and orders under Part 8 of the EA02 or the UTCCRs.

39 Sections 82(2), 84(3)(b), 92(2), 159(4) and (5), 161(4)(b) and 162 of the EA02.

40 Under relevant sectoral legislation. See Schedule 6 of the ERRA13 for more detail as to the amended form of the relevant provisions of sectoral regulation concerning regulatory appeals and references.

4. OBTAINING AND USING INFORMATION

REQUESTS FOR INFORMATION

[3.29]

4.1 In respect of many of the CMA's functions the CMA has formal information gathering powers.[41] Such powers enable the CMA to request, for example, data, documents or forecasts, or require persons to attend as witnesses to give evidence. When it does not have, or does not use, formal powers, it relies upon the co-operation of parties and requests information on an informal, voluntary, basis. In practice, even where formal information gathering powers exist, the CMA will often request information on an informal basis. In either case, the CMA's approach as set out below is similar.[42]

4.2 The CMA will make evidence based decisions. Therefore the availability to it of evidence and accurate information is a key factor affecting the performance of the CMA, as is the ability to conduct cases in a timely manner. The CMA fully recognises that when making information requests, this will have an impact on others, whether they are businesses, consumers or organisations. While formulating information requests, the CMA will therefore strive to avoid imposing unnecessary burdens on such persons while considering also the need for the CMA to operate efficiently and effectively.

4.3 The CMA seeks to address these aims by:

- considering the information that is required for the CMA's purposes
- preparing clear and focused information requests
- addressing requests to those best placed to provide the information
- discussing, where practicable and appropriate, the request with the intended recipient prior to sending a request, including discussion of the information held by the recipient and the form in which it is held
- considering the likely timescale in which the intended recipient will be able to provide the information, and
- considering how soon the CMA requires the information, having regard to the administrative or statutory timetable of the case and the impact a delay in receiving the information may have on the CMA's efficiency or quality of the CMA's work.

4.4 These factors may be relevant to many of the CMA's information requests, whether at the outset of a case or while the case is ongoing. The extent of engagement prior to making an information request may vary. For example, at the outset of a Phase 2 merger inquiry or market investigation the CMA will generally discuss with key parties the information they hold and the form in which they hold it. This will help to influence the preparation of the information questionnaires that are typically used in the early stage of such inquiries or investigations.

4.5 Where it is practicable and appropriate, the CMA will discuss a draft of its information requests with the intended recipients so as to enable requests to be prepared that reduce the burden on the recipients (for example, by helping to shape requests, having regard to how information is held by the relevant parties). However, this approach may not always be possible, for example when the case involves multiple parties, each holding the information differently; or where the CMA is under time pressure to meet a statutory (or administrative) deadline. Examples of when the CMA may not provide any advance notice of a proposed information request prior to exercising its formal investigation powers include when it is concerned that there is a risk that the information could be destroyed, urgency or because the request is for a small amount of information, making it inefficient to do so. The CMA will consider representations about the scope of any information request and deadline for compliance.

4.6 The CMA will seek to set a reasonable deadline for all information requests and where draft formal requests have been issued the final request will have considered any representations on the proposed deadline.

4.7 It is likely that during the course of a case the CMA will seek additional information. When doing so, the same factors identified in paragraphs 4.3 to 4.6 are again likely to be relevant.

4.8 Parties should make known any difficulties and discuss any queries raised by any information request including any difficulties in responding within the timeframe set out in a request by contacting the case team as soon as possible after receiving a request, or as soon as they become aware that they may not meet the stipulated deadline.

4.9 The CMA may impose administrative financial penalties for non-compliance with some of the CMA's formal information gathering powers in relation to CA98 investigations, and its mergers and markets cases. Any decision to impose a penalty for failure to comply with a formal request for information may take into account (but will not depend on) whether the CMA had sent a draft request and set a deadline for compliance which took into account comments from that party.[43]

4.10 Prior to commissioning a survey as part of the information gathering process, the CMA will consult such of the parties directly involved as it considers appropriate on the draft survey design and content. The CMA may also require parties directly involved to provide information about their customers and suppliers.

IDENTIFYING CONFIDENTIAL INFORMATION

4.11 The CMA recognises that the confidentiality of parties' information is an important consideration for those who participate in a CMA case.

4.12 The CMA may therefore require that, in respect of all information supplied, parties should make known to the case team which information they consider to be confidential, and provide sufficient explanations for their claim, for example, regarding the nature of the information, the harm that could be caused, the likelihood of harm and the magnitude of that harm. The explanations provided will be taken into account when considering whether to disclose any of the information provided. The CMA's commitment to transparency means that confidentiality claims will be rigorously assessed. Such claims should be kept to the minimum extent necessary to protect confidentiality, and the CMA will not accept blanket or unsubstantiated claims for confidentiality. Having taken into account parties' confidentiality representations, the CMA will ultimately decide whether it is appropriate to disclose the information and, if so, the manner in which that disclosure should occur.

4.13 When providing key or substantial submissions, parties should also provide a second, non-confidential version. The CMA will permit a short interval for the provision of a non-confidential version, but the exact period permitted will differ depending on the type of work and will take into account the possibility that a delay in receiving confidentiality claims may adversely affect the CMA's statutory or administrative timetable.

4.14 Information may be viewed as 'confidential information' if it is:
- information whose disclosure the CMA thinks is contrary to the public interest
- commercial information whose disclosure the CMA thinks might significantly harm the legitimate business interests of the undertaking to which it relates, or
- information relating to the private affairs of an individual whose disclosure the CMA thinks might significantly harm the individual's interests.[44]

4.15 Whether in fact the CMA accepts that information is confidential will depend on the relevant circumstances and will therefore be assessed on a case-by-case basis. By way of indication only, the following are examples of information that the CMA will usually consider unlikely to cause harm to the person or business to whom it relates:
- information that is already in the public domain or can readily be deduced from information in the public domain, and
- financial information or other data[45] relating to a business which is more than two years old.

4.16 The following information will normally be considered to be confidential so that if the CMA is considering whether disclosure is appropriate, it will need to consider the manner of disclosure:
- financial information or other data[46] relating to a business which is less than two years old
- information which, if disclosed, may adversely affect the competitive process in the market
- information relating to the strategy (past or future) of a business, and
- responses to surveys (in aggregate or individually), the disclosure of which could be harmful to a firm or individual or where the identity of the person providing the information should be protected.

DISCLOSURE OF INFORMATION OBTAINED BY THE CMA

4.17 The CMA may use any information that it obtains during a case for the purposes of facilitating the exercise of any of its statutory functions. Part 9 of the EA02 imposes a general restriction on the disclosure of information which the CMA obtains during the exercise of any of its functions (referred to as 'specified information') to other persons.[47] The restriction applies during the lifetime of an individual or while the undertaking continues in existence. Only disclosure falling within one of the 'information gateways' (see below) is permitted.

4.18 The CMA may disclose specified information if:
- the CMA obtains the required consents (section 239 of the EA02)
- the disclosure is required for the purpose of a European obligation (section 240 of the EA02)
- the disclosure is made for the purpose of facilitating the exercise by the CMA of any of its statutory function (section 241(1) of the EA02)
- the information is disclosed to another public authority in the UK for the purpose of facilitating the exercise by that authority of its functions under the EA02 and/or the legislation set out in Schedule 15 of the EA02[48] (under section 241(3) of the EA02)
- the information is disclosed to any person (after the CMA satisfies itself that the disclosure is proportionate to what is sought to be achieved by it) (under section 242 of the EA02)
  - — in connection with the investigation of any criminal offence in any part of the UK
  - — for the purposes of any criminal proceedings there or
  - — for the purpose of any decision whether to start or bring to an end such an investigation or proceedings,
- the disclosure is to facilitate the performance of an overseas public authority's functions (under section 243 of the EA02).

4.19 The CMA may also disclose (under section 241A of the EA02) specified information which has been ordered by the Secretary of State to be 'prescribed'[49] information to any person for the purposes of:
- actual or prospective prescribed civil proceedings in the UK or elsewhere
- obtaining legal advice in relation to such proceedings, or
- establishing, enforcing or defending legal rights that are or may be the subject of such proceedings.

4.20 The information gateways of section 241A and 243 of the EA02 do not apply to all information received by the CMA (for example, in connection with a merger, market or CA98 investigation).[50]

4.21 Where the CMA discloses information to a person there are restrictions on the further disclosure or use of the information by that person. These restrictions vary between the information gateways. It is a criminal offence to disclose information in circumstances where such disclosure is not permitted under Part 9 of the EA02, where a person contravenes a direction under section 243(4) of the EA02 not to do so, or where a person uses the information disclosed to him for a purpose not permitted under the Part 9 of the EA02.[51]

4.22 Generally, if the CMA is considering making a disclosure for the purpose of its investigation, it will most commonly consider making the disclosure with the consent of the person to whom the information relates or by the information gateway under section 241(1) of the EA02.

4.23 Even when an information gateway applies, the CMA is required to have regard to certain considerations before making a disclosure. In particular, the CMA must have regard to the three considerations set out in section 244 of the EA02, namely:

- the need to exclude from disclosure (so far as it is practicable to do so) any information whose disclosure the CMA considers to be contrary to the public interest
- the need to exclude from disclosure (so far as practicable)
  - — commercial information the CMA considers might significantly harm the legitimate business interests of the undertakings or
  - — information relating to the private affairs of an individual which the authority thinks might significantly harm that individual's interests,
- the extent to which the disclosure of information relating to the private affairs of an individual or commercial information is necessary for the purpose for which the authority is permitted to make the disclosure.

4.24 These three considerations are applied by the CMA on a case-by-case basis when the CMA is considering disclosure of specified information. When decisions are finely balanced, the CMA will have particular regard to the need for disclosure to achieve due process.

CMA'S APPROACH TO DISCLOSURE IN CONNECTION WITH THE CONDUCT OF A CASE

4.25 The remainder of chapter 4 provides an overview of the CMA's approach to disclosure, both to parties directly involved and to others, in connection with the conduct of the CMA's case. Chapter 4 also applies when a public authority is a party in Phase 2 references and appeals. The CMA's approach to the disclosure of specified information to other public authorities, including sectoral regulators and overseas public authorities in other circumstances, is explained in chapters 6 and 7 of this Statement.

4.26 If an information gateway other than the consent gateway in section 239 of the EA02 applies, and the CMA considers, having taken into account the relevant statutory considerations, that it is appropriate to make the disclosure, it is not obliged to obtain the consent of the party to whom the information relates. However, the CMA will consider a party's representations regarding the confidential nature of any information they have provided.

4.27 The CMA will generally seek to inform the party claiming confidentiality or the party to whom the information relates of its intention to make a disclosure. When giving such advance notice, the CMA will provide details of the information it proposes to disclose relevant to the person concerned for example by way of a description, inventory or draft of the proposed disclosure. Other than when legally required to provide notice and besides the circumstances set out in chapter 6 and 7, the CMA might choose not do so if, for example, it considers that the party has already had sufficient opportunity to submit confidentiality claims, or if the CMA has sought to protect the information to be disclosed (for example, by anonymising or aggregating data).

4.28 When the CMA considers it appropriate to disclose information it will consider how best to protect confidential information. For example, the CMA may redact, anonymise or aggregate confidential information, such as by providing ranges in relation to market share data.[52]

4.29 Sometimes, the CMA may use confidentiality rings or data rooms as a means of making disclosure of confidential information while recognising the restrictive nature of the disclosure (see below). Their use will be restricted to when it is necessary to make the disclosure for the purpose of facilitating the CMA's functions by ensuring due process although in CA98 investigations, the CMA may also use confidentiality rings at access to file stage to handle the disclosure of confidential information where there appear to be identifiable benefits in doing so.[53]

4.30 Confidentiality rings enable disclosure of specific quantitative and/or qualitative data or documents to a defined group.[54] The group is determined on a case-by-case basis but, generally, disclosure is made to the relevant parties' external (legal and/or economic) advisers.

4.31 Data rooms enable access to a specific category of confidential data or documents to a defined group. As for confidentiality rings, the group is determined on a case-by-case basis. Data rooms are typically used to provide access to data to enable parties' advisers to gain further understanding of the CMA's analysis and to confirm or challenge the CMA's findings or conclusions. They may also be used to allow advisers to carry out an assessment of a specific set of qualitative documents. A data room provides access to the confidential data or documents on the CMA premises, and in so doing has the advantage of providing additional protection.

4.32 Access to documents in a confidentiality ring or data room will be subject to confidentiality undertakings provided by the persons with access (and for employees, their employer firm) which address, amongst other matters, how they may use the information disclosed to them and the restrictions that apply to onward disclosure. In the case of data rooms, the CMA will also require advisers to follow data room rules concerning the proper conduct of the data room, including making provision for bringing into and taking out of the data room such items as materials, notes and equipment.

4.33 It will be a condition of access to a confidentiality ring or data room that information reviewed by advisers is not shared with their client(s). It is for advisers to satisfy themselves of the steps they are required to take under any relevant professional conduct rules to ensure that they are able to operate on this basis.

4.34 Requests for the use of confidentiality rings and data rooms will be considered on a case-by-case basis. The CMA has discretion as to whether to agree to such requests, and is likely to do so only where it is proportionate, there are clear benefits in doing so, and potential legal and practical difficulties can be resolved swiftly in agreement with the parties concerned. The CMA will also take into account whether it is appropriate to provide access at the time the request is made, having regard to the progress of the case, the resource implications of operating confidentiality rings and data rooms, and of risks of human error and information leaks.

NOTES

41 For example, formal powers are available in mergers (see chapter 7 of *Mergers: Guidance on the CMA's jurisdiction and procedure* (CMA2)), market cases (see *Market Studies and Market Investigations: Supplemental guidance on the CMA's approach* (CMA3): chapter 2 for market studies, chapter 3 for market investigation references and chapter 4 for remedies), CA98 investigations (see chapter 6 of the *Competition Act 1998: Guidance on the CMA's investigation procedures in Competition Act 1998 cases* (CMA8)), criminal cartel investigations, regulatory reference and appeal cases and in respect of various consumer enforcement cases (see *Consumer Protection: Guidance on the CMA's approach to use of its consumer powers* (CMA7), chapters 6 and 7 on investigatory powers).

42 See relevant tool specific guidance for more details in specific areas of work.

43 Detailed guidance on the CMA's approach to penalties and other sanctions is available in *Administrative Penalties: Statement of policy on the CMA's approach* (CMA4).

44 See also Rule 1 of the Competition and Markets Authority Competition Act 1998 Rules 2014, which defines confidential information in the context of CA98 investigations.

45 This could include, for example, parties' turnover, sales, market share data, etc.

46 See footnote 45.

47 Section 237 of the EA02.

48 See chapter 6 for further detail on the application of Part 9 of the EA02 to disclosures to UK public authorities, and chapter 7 for detail on the application of Part 9 to disclosures to overseas public authorities.

49 For these purposes 'prescribed' means prescribed by order of the Secretary of State. As at the date of publication of this Statement, the Secretary of State has issued one order prescribing certain information and proceedings for the purposes of this section (the Enterprise Act 2002 (Disclosure of Information in Civil Proceedings etc) Order 2007, SI 2007/2193).

50 See section 241A(2) and section 243(3) of the EA02 respectively.

51 Section 245 of the EA02.

52 Particular procedures apply to the disclosure of information provided by would-be leniency applicants (see *Applications for leniency and no-action in cartel cases* (OFT1495), in particular chapter 7). For further guidance on disclosure in Phase 2 merger inquiries and market investigations, see *Chairman's Guidance on Disclosure of Information in Merger Inquiries, Market Investigations and Reviews of Undertakings and Orders accepted or made under the Enterprise Act 2002 and Fair Trading Act 1973* (CC7 (revised)), paragraphs 9.11-9.15.

53 See *Competition Act 1998: Guidance on the CMA's investigation procedures in Competition Act 1998 cases* (CMA8), chapter 11 for further guidance.

54 Subject to any restrictions in the DPA98 in relation to personal information.

5. COMPLAINTS AND ACCOUNTABILITY

DISPUTES REGARDING THE CONDUCT OF A CASE

[3.30]

5.1 Parties should raise any complaints about the conduct of an ongoing CMA case with the most senior CMA contact responsible for that case, who will review the case team's actions and aim to either put things right, or give an explanation for the course of action taken by the case team.

5.2 If a party is not satisfied with the senior CMA contact's response, they may request a review of the handling of their complaint by:

- the Procedural Officer (PO), where the complaint concerns certain procedural disputes in CA98 investigations,[55] and disputes relating to requests for confidentiality in merger cases[56] and market studies and investigations, or
- the General Counsel's Office (GCO) in relation to any disputes falling outside the PO's remit.

5.3 This does not alter the procedures in place for submitting general complaints about the CMA or about closed cases, which should be addressed in the first instance to the CMA Enquiries Unit, who will then escalate as and when appropriate.

5.4 The CMA's decisions in merger cases, market studies and market investigations are subject to appeal to the Competition Appeal Tribunal (Tribunal), which will apply the same principles as would be applied by a court on an application for judicial review in dealing with the review. The CMA's decisions in CA98 investigations are subject to a full merits review by the Tribunal. In addition, parties with sufficient interest have the right to seek judicial review of administrative decisions.

ACCOUNTABILITY

5.5 The CMA is accountable to the public through Parliamentary scrutiny in Westminster and the devolved administrations, for example through inquiries by select committees.

5.6 A member of the public may complain to the Parliamentary and Health Service Ombudsman (Ombudsman)[57] via a Member of Parliament about the CMA's administrative actions, after seeking to resolve the complaint with the CMA. The CMA will have regard to the Ombudsman's Principles of Good Administration, which are:

- getting it right
- being customer-focused
- being open and accountable
- acting fairly and proportionately
- putting things right, and
- seeking continuous improvement.

PUBLICATIONS

5.7 Each financial year, the CMA will produce an Annual Plan, setting out its objectives for the year, which is laid before Parliament. The CMA is accountable to Parliament for the delivery of these objectives via the presentation of its Performance Report.

5.8 The CMA will aim to provide consistent information in its Performance Report[58] for all closed consumer and competition enforcement cases, mergers casework, markets casework, reviews of undertakings and orders and regulatory appeals. This information will include:

- the date the case was opened
- a summary of the findings and/or recommendations, and
- the date the case was closed and the time taken to complete it.

5.9 The CMA will also provide information in its Performance Report on its ongoing work that is in the public domain.

5.10 The CMA will publish a Business Plan for each spending review period, setting out its vision, high-level priorities and planned expenditure over the spending review period. Information regarding the Business Plan will be available on www.gov.uk/cma.

5.11 The CMA is required to prepare resource accounts for each financial year, which are audited by the National Audit Office.

NOTES

55 Further information on the role of the Procedural Officer can be found in *Competition Act 1998: Guidance on the CMA's investigation procedures in Competition Act 1998 cases* (CMA8).

56 In Phase 1 merger cases, the procedure will only apply to disputes regarding the confidentiality of information that the CMA proposes including in published decisions.

57 Further information available on the Ombudsman's website at www.ombudsman.org.uk/.

58 The CMA is required, under paragraph 14 of Schedule 4 of the ERRA13, to provide certain information in an annual performance report.

6. DISCLOSURE TO UK PUBLIC AUTHORITIES[59]

[3.31]

6.1 As explained in chapter 4, Part 9 of the EA02 imposes a general restriction on the disclosure of information which the CMA obtain during the exercise of any of its functions (referred to as 'specified information') to other persons. The restriction applies during the lifetime of an individual or while the undertaking continues in existence. Only disclosure falling within one of the 'information gateways' is permitted. These restrictions apply to the exchange of information between public authorities.

6.2 The CMA may however disclose specified information where an information gateway exists.[60] The information gateways that most commonly apply when the CMA is considering disclosure to another UK public authority are:

- the CMA obtains consent (section 239 of the EA02)
- to facilitate the CMA's functions (section 241(1) of the EA02)
- to facilitate the exercise of other UK public authorities' functions under the EA02 and/or other legislation as set out in Schedule 15 of the EA02 (section 241(3) of the EA02)[61]
- for the purpose of civil proceedings (section 241A of the EA02),[62]
- for the purpose of criminal proceedings (section 242 of the EA02).[63]

6.3 As explained in chapter 4, there are restrictions that apply to the use and further disclosure of information disclosed under the information gateways. For further information see chapter 4. When information is disclosed by the CMA for the purpose of the CMA's functions, the receiving authority may not further disclose that information without the agreement of the CMA,[64] and the receiving authority may only use the information for the purpose for which the CMA disclosed it.[65] When information is disclosed by the CMA under other information gateways (apart from section 239 of the EA02) the information may only be used for the purpose of the disclosure.

6.4 As explained in chapter 4, it is a criminal offence to disclose information in circumstances where such disclosure is not permitted under Part 9 of the EA02, where a person contravenes a direction under section 243(4) of the EA02 not to do so, or where a person uses the information disclosed to him for a purpose not permitted under the Part 9 of the EA02.[66]

CMA'S APPROACH TO DISCLOSURE UNDER THE INFORMATION GATEWAYS

6.5 Even where an information gateway is relevant, the CMA must consider the statutory considerations in section 244 of the EA02 (see paragraph 4.23 for more details) before deciding whether or not to disclose the information. In assessing whether the disclosure is 'necessary for the purpose'[67] the CMA will have regard to the extent to which it believes the disclosure of the information may be relevant to the receiving authority's investigation or other statutory function.

6.6 The CMA will therefore assess the function or purpose for which the information is required and the scope of the information requested. In this context, the CMA will require the authority requesting the information (the requesting authority) to provide details of the function or purpose for which the information is required and/or, if it is an information request, to specify the scope of the information request. In cases where the CMA is considering whether to disclose information on its own initiative, it will form a preliminary view on whether there is a suitable statutory gateway, although it will normally liaise with the relevant public authority to clarify the point.

6.7 When considering whether to disclose information under the information gateways, the CMA will take into account the sensitivity of the information and any representations received from the person to whom the information relates. In some circumstances, the CMA may consider it appropriate to restrict the information disclosed for example through anonymisation, aggregation or provision of ranges.

6.8 The CMA will take into account the protection of the information afforded by any restrictions that apply on the use and further disclosure of the information. In the absence of information to the contrary, and provided the Part 9 of the EA02 restrictions on use and further disclosure (or equivalent legislative provisions affording the same or greater protection) apply, the CMA will consider that a recipient public authority will be mindful of the need to protect any specified information passed on to it so that the risks of inappropriate use or disclosure are limited. The CMA will not regard the disclosure of specified information to another public authority to enable that authority to carry out its statutory functions as being contrary to the public interest. As to the obligation to protect certain information exchanged within the UK Competition Network (UKCN), see paragraph 6.15.

6.9 Even when an information gateway is available, there may be circumstances when the CMA will decline to provide the information to the other public authority. For example, when overall it may be more efficient or speedier for the public authority to request the information. Another circumstance might be when the limitations on the use or further disclosure that will apply, were the CMA to make the disclosure, would not be suitable to the public authority's purpose for requesting the information.

ENHANCED INFORMATION SHARING WITH SECTORAL REGULATORS UNDER THE ERRA13

6.10 Under the ERRA13 the CMA and sectoral regulators having concurrent CA98 powers are required to put into place information sharing arrangements to disclose certain kinds of information to each other in connection with CA98 cases relevant to their regulated sectors in order to facilitate the exercise of their functions.[68] They are also permitted, but not required, to share information about a broader range of complaints than those where there are sufficient grounds for suspecting a CA98 infringement. For further information about these arrangements, see *Regulated Industries: Guidance on concurrent application of competition law to regulated industries* (CMA10).

6.11 To give effect to the statutory requirement and in order to strengthen the collaborative framework through which sectoral regulators and the CMA will work to further the interests of UK consumers, the CMA and the sectoral regulators have established the UKCN. The UKCN brings together the CMA with the Financial Conduct Authority (FCA), the Office of Communications (Ofcom), the Gas and Electricity Markets Authority (Ofgem), the Water Services Regulation Authority (Ofwat), the Northern Ireland Authority for Utility Regulation (URegNI), the Office of Rail Regulation (ORR), the Civil Aviation Authority (CAA), and Monitor (the latter having observer status). The mission of the UKCN[69] is to promote competition for the benefit of consumers and to prevent anticompetitive behaviour both through facilitating use of competition powers and the development of pro-competitive regulatory frameworks, as appropriate.

6.12 The exchange of information between the CMA and sectoral regulators within the UKCN is subject to Part 9 of the EA02.

CMA'S APPROACH TO GIVING NOTICE

6.13 The CMA will (subject to the circumstances described in this and the following paragraphs) usually give notice of its proposal to disclose specified information. However, in line with established case law,[70] it may decide that it is not appropriate to do so in some circumstances such as:

- where the giving of prior notice may hamper the CMA and/or requesting authority's investigation (for example, if the CMA or sectoral regulator are investigating a possible infringement of CA98, the subject of such an investigation may seek to destroy evidence if he becomes aware of the investigation)
- where information is being passed on to another UK public authority, or investigating or prosecuting authority
- the information is required as a matter of urgency, in which case the CMA will consider whether it is appropriate to inform the owner after the disclosure is made, or
- advance notice would be impracticable due to the number of persons to whom notice would otherwise need to be given in which case the CMA will consider whether it is appropriate to publish a notice on www.gov.uk/cma announcing that it intends to disclose a certain class or type of information to another authority and inviting representations from interested parties.

6.14 If the CMA considers it necessary or appropriate to pass information deriving from a leniency applicant to another UK agency, such as the Serious Fraud Office (SFO), the CMA would inform the applicant or its legal adviser first. However, applicants must accept that the CMA may refer cases to the SFO and the expectation should be that such referrals will be on the basis of a full disclosure of all material in the CMA's possession.[71]

6.15 Having regard to the enhanced partnership working, the responsibility of members (and observers) of the UKCN to protect any information disclosed to each other, including under Part 9 of the EA02 (or equivalent legislative provisions affording the same or greater protection apply), the CMA will generally not give the person to whom the information relates prior notice of its proposal to make a disclosure.

6.16 When giving advance notice, the CMA will provide details of the information it proposes to disclose relevant to the person concerned for example by way of a description, inventory or draft of the proposed disclosure.

NOTES

[59] The explanations in chapter 4 about making information requests and the handling of information may also be applicable to public authorities when they are treated as a party in Phase 2 merger and market references and appeals. This chapter applies when the CMA is considering disclosure of information to another UK public authority.

[60] The full list of information gateways is provided in paragraph 4.18 of chapter 4.

[61] For example, other governmental departments, Trading Standards Service and sectoral regulators

[62] This gateway is not applicable in relation to information received by the CMA while exercising its merger, market and CA98 functions. Further information about this information gateway is set out in paragraphs 4.19 and 4.20.

[63] See also footnote 4.

[64] Section 241(2) of the EA02.

[65] Section 241(2A) of the EA02.

[66] Section 245 of the EA02.

[67] Section 244(4) of the EA02.

[68] Regulation 4(1) of the Competition Act 1998 (Concurrency) Regulations 2004.

[69] See the UKCN Statement of Intent.

[70] R Kent Pharmaceuticals Ltd v Serious Fraud Office, [2004] EWCA Civ 1494, 11 November 2004

[71] See *Applications for leniency and no-action in cartel cases* (OFT1495) for further guidance.

7. COOPERATION WITH OVERSEAS PUBLIC AUTHORITIES

[3.32]

7.1 The CMA works with its international counterparts to promote convergence and a consistent approach to tackling anti-competitive practices, assessing multi-jurisdictional mergers and protecting consumers' interests. It may share information about its experiences and cases to assist in identifying issues of common interest and coordinating efforts, as well as comparing results and findings.

7.2 The CMA is a member of various international organisations, such as the Organisation for Economic Cooperation and Development (OECD), International Competition Network (ICN), European Competition Network (ECN) and the EU Consumer Protection and Co-ordination Network, and is also a party to a number of bilateral agreements entered into on an ad hoc basis with other agencies.

7.3 While the CMA may freely share general information about its work and experiences with overseas public authorities,[72] or through international fora, the disclosure of specified information is only permissible if an information gateway is available under Part 9 of the EA02. The information gateway permitting disclosure of specified information for the purposes of facilitating the exercise by the CMA of its own statutory functions applies in relation to disclosures to overseas public authorities, as it does to UK public authorities.[73]

7.4 The CMA may also seek the necessary consents to the disclosure of information to an overseas authority.[74] Consent is generally sought in the form of a waiver, permitting the CMA to disclose information to another (named) authority.[75]

7.5 Where a gateway for disclosure of specified information exists other than that contained in section 243(1) of the EA02 described below (for example if the CMA's disclosure is for the purpose of facilitating the exercise by the CMA of any of its statutory functions), the CMA will need to have regard to the considerations contained in section 244 of the EA02 (and to those in section 243(6) of the EA02).

DISCLOSURE OF SPECIFIED INFORMATION UNDER AN EU OBLIGATION

7.6 The CMA may disclose information to another person if the disclosure is required for the purpose of an EU obligation.

7.7 The CMA is obliged, under certain EU obligations, to disclose certain information it receives in the course of exercising its statutory functions to the Commission and/or other European competition and consumer protection authorities. The CMA will still nevertheless need to have regard to the three considerations in section 244 of the EA02 in deciding whether to disclose the specified information.

7.8 The EU obligations relevant to the CMA include Articles 11 and 12 of Regulation 1/2003[76] and paragraphs 2.2.3 and 2.3.3 of the Commission Notice on cooperation within the network of competition authorities,[77] which provide for the disclosure of information for the purpose of applying Articles 101 and 102 of the Treaty on the Functioning of the European Union, Articles 4, 9, 21 or 22 of the EU Merger Regulation,[78] and the Regulation on Consumer Protection Cooperation.[79]

DISCLOSURE OF SPECIFIED INFORMATION TO OVERSEAS PUBLIC AUTHORITIES UNDER SECTION 243 OF THE EA02

7.9 The CMA may also disclose specified information to overseas public authorities[80] in order to facilitate:

- the investigation and bringing of criminal proceedings[81]
- the investigation and bringing of civil proceedings in connection with the enforcement of specified legislation,[82] or
- a decision as to whether to start or bring to an end such investigations or proceedings.[83]

Disclosure to overseas authorities for these purposes is not permitted where the information is obtained by the CMA in connection with the CMA's mergers and markets functions under the EA02,[84] and under other specified legislation.[85]

7.10 Information disclosed to an overseas public authority may be disclosed subject to the condition that it must not be further disclosed without the agreement of the CMA.[86] The disclosed information may not be used by the overseas pubic authority for any purpose other than that for which it was first disclosed.[87]

7.11 The Secretary of State has the power to prevent a disclosure to an overseas authority which the CMA would be permitted to make under Part 9 of the EA02 where he or she thinks it would be more appropriate for any investigation or proceedings to be carried out in the UK or another country.[88]

7.12 In deciding whether to disclose information to an overseas public authority for the purposes listed in paragraph 7.9, the CMA must have regard to a number of other factors, including:

- whether the matter in respect of which disclosure is sought is sufficiently serious to justify making the disclosure
- whether the law of the overseas country to whose authority disclosure would be made provides appropriate protection against self-incrimination in criminal proceedings
- whether the law of that country provides appropriate protection for the storage and disclosure of personal data, and
- whether any mutual assistance arrangements apply.[89]

7.13 Before disclosing information under section 243 of the EA02, the CMA must have regard to the considerations in both section 243(6) of the EA02 and section 244 of the EA02.

7.14 The CMA will balance the considerations in section 243(6) of the EA02 on a case-by-case basis having regard to the particular circumstances of the disclosure in question. However, the CMA considers that the disclosure of information for the purpose of bringing civil and criminal proceedings on matters relating to competition law and consumer protection, or for conducting investigations leading to these proceedings, will generally be 'sufficiently serious' for the purpose of section 243(6) of the EA02. Criminal proceedings covered by mutual assistance agreements to which the UK is party will also normally be deemed sufficiently serious.

7.15 Section 243(7) of the EA02 states that protections are 'appropriate' if the relevant protection corresponds to that provided in any part of the UK. Therefore, protections which are directly analogous to those afforded in the UK will satisfy this consideration.

7.16 For example, in respect of the protection in relation to the storage and disclosure of personal data, the CMA is minded to consider that the protection afforded by the EU Directive 95/46 on the Protection of Individuals with the regard to the Processing of Personal Data (the Data Protection Directive) – which has been implemented in the UK through the DPA 98 – is appropriate for the purposes of section 243(6)(c) of the EA02. The laws of the countries which have implemented the Data Protection Directive would accordingly be considered to give appropriate protection under section 243(6)(c) of the EA02. Similarly, the European Commission – which affords protection in the area concerned equivalent to that contained in the Data Protection Directive[90] and whose officials are bound by the obligation of professional secrecy – is also considered to give appropriate protection under section 243(6)(c) of the EA02.

7.17 In addition to the considerations in section 243(6) of the EA02, the CMA may also take into account additional considerations although it is not legally required to do so. One such consideration is the past record of an overseas public authority as regards compliance with disclosure conditions in relation to previous requests. This may be particularly relevant when there are no mutual assistance arrangements in place between the country concerned and the UK; or where it was in doubt about the adequacy of protections for the storage and disclosure of personal data but the considerations in section 243(6) of the EA02 were otherwise met. Another consideration which may also be taken into account is reciprocity (that is, whether the overseas authority concerned has previously declined to disclose information although it had the power to do so).

7.18 When the CMA intends to make a disclosure to an overseas authority, the CMA will take into account parties' representations regarding the confidential nature of any information they have provided.[91] Also, if appropriate, the CMA will seek to protect the information to be disclosed (for example by anonymising or aggregating data or using ranges).

7.19 Although not required to do so, the CMA will generally seek to give notice of a possible disclosure. When giving such advance notice, the CMA will provide details of the information it proposes to disclose relevant to the person concerned for example by way of a description, inventory or draft of the proposed disclosure.

7.20 However, in line with established case law,[92] it may decide that it is not appropriate to give notice in some circumstances, such as:

- where the giving of prior notice may hamper an investigation
- where information is being passed on to another investigating or prosecuting authority
- the information is required as a matter of urgency,

- it would be impracticable to do so (for example, because of the number of persons to whom notice would otherwise need to be given).

7.21 In these circumstances, the CMA will take into account the protection of the information afforded by any restrictions that apply on the use and further disclosure of the information.

NOTES

72 Meaning a person or body outside the UK which appears to the CMA to exercise functions of a public nature in the enforcement of consumer or competition legislation (sections 243(11) and (12) of the EA02).

73 Section 241(1) of the EA02.

74 Section 239 of the EA02.

75 The CMA will consider the format of a waiver on a case by case basis, as the content will differ based on the circumstances of the case. For reference, the ICN model waiver form in relation to merger cases, and the model waiver forms used by a number of other competition agencies, can be viewed here: www.internationalcompetitionnetwork.org/.

76 Council Regulation 1/2003/EC on the implementation of the rules on competition laid down in Articles 81 and 82 of the Treaty.

77 Commission Notice 2004/C101/03.

78 Council Regulation (EC) No 137/2004 on the control of concentrations between undertakings.

79 Regulation (EC) No 2006/ 2004.

80 See footnote 72.

81 Section 243(2)(c) and (d) of the EA02.

82 Sections 243(2)(a) and (b) and 243(12) of the EA02.

83 Section 243(2)(e) of the EA02.

84 Section 243(3)(d) of the EA02.

85 Section 243(a), (b), (c) of the EA02.

86 Section 243(10)(a) of the EA02.

87 Section 243(10)(b) of the EA02.

88 Section 243(4) of the EA02.

89 Section 243(6) of the EA02.

90 Regulation (EC) 45/2001 of the European Parliament and of the Council of 18 December 2000 on the protection of individuals with regard to the processing of personal data by the European institutions and bodies and on the free movement of such data. See OJ L0008, 12/01/2001.

91 See *Applications for leniency and no-action in cartel cases* (OFT1495), paragraphs 7.31 and 7.32 which state that disclosure of information supplied as part of an application for leniency or immunity will never take place without consent except for in the two circumstances explained.

92 R Kent Pharmaceuticals Ltd v Serious Fraud Office, [2004] EWCA Civ 1494, 11 November 2004.

8. FREEDOM OF INFORMATION AND DATA PROTECTION

FOIA

[3.33]

8.1 The FOIA was introduced to improve the transparency and accountability of public bodies and gives anyone a general right of access to information held by the CMA.

8.2 When a person makes a request for recorded information, the FOIA requires the CMA to (i) inform the requester whether or not it holds the requested information; and (ii) if it does, it must disclose the information to the requester unless there is an applicable exemption. A request for information will be dealt with within 20 working days.[93]

8.3 There are a number of exemptions from disclosure under the FOIA of particular relevance to a request for information held by the CMA, including where disclosure would be prohibited under any statutory enactment, including the EA02.[94] Part 9 of the EA02 therefore continues to apply.

8.4 The CMA might also seek to rely on the law enforcement qualified exemption at section 31(1)(g) of the FOIA to withhold information if it considered its disclosure would, or would be likely to, prejudice the exercise by the CMA of its statutory functions for the purposes set out at section 31(2) of the FOIA. Section 31 of the FOIA is a qualified exemption requiring the carrying out of a public interest test to determine whether, in all the circumstances of the case, the public interest in maintaining the exemption outweighs that in disclosing the information.

8.5 The CMA might also seek to rely on section 32 of the FOIA which provides for an absolute exemption from disclosure where the requested information is held by a public authority in a document placed in the custody of a person conducting an inquiry, for the purpose of the inquiry. For the purposes of section 32 of the FOIA, an 'inquiry' includes any inquiry or hearing held under any provision contained in, or made under, an enactment. It includes, for example, the CMA when exercising its Phase 2 merger and market and regulatory appeal functions.

8.6 Requests for information under the FOIA should be submitted to the Information Access Team. Any person not satisfied with the CMA's refusal to provide information in response to an FOIA request has the right to an internal review of the CMA's decision, and a further right to complain to the Information Commissioner's Office (ICO) if that person is not satisfied with the internal review decision.

8.7 The CMA is required to have a publication scheme, approved by the ICO, and to publish information covered by the scheme. More information about the FOIA generally is available on the ICO website.[95]

DPA98

8.8 The DPA98 sets out rules for processing personal data relating to living individuals (the data protection principles). The principles include the need for those who process personal data (that is, do anything at all with it, such as collecting, recording, using or transferring it) to be open with those whose data they process about how that personal data is used.

8.9 The CMA is bound by the provisions of the DPA98 where it is processing personal data. No personal data will be disclosed by the CMA unless that disclosure is compliant with the DPA98.

8.10 Particular issues arise in respect of the handling and disclosure of underlying data from surveys conducted by the CMA, or by other parties. Both the DPA98, as mentioned, and the Code of Conduct of the Market Research Society apply to personal data, and the latter requires the anonymity of respondents to be preserved unless they have given informed consent. If the CMA considers it necessary to disclose any of the underlying data, it must ensure that the identities of the persons who participated in the survey are protected. The CMA will consider what protection may be necessary to ensure that the identity of survey respondents is not revealed. Anonymisation is not always sufficient to prevent someone being identifiable.

8.11 Any person may ask the CMA whether it is processing any personal data about them and if so, to be provided with a copy of it. If not satisfied with the CMA's response, that person may complain to the ICO.

NOTES

93 This deadline may be extended if the CMA reasonably requests further information or is considering the public interest test (sections 10(2) and (3) of the FOIA).

94 Section 44(1)(a) of the FOIA provides for an absolute exemption in this regard.

95 www.ico.org.uk.

ANNEXE(S)

A. KEY CHANGES TO EXISTING GUIDANCE

[3.34]

The following table lists those sections of the *Chairman's Guidance on Disclosure of Information in Merger Inquiries, Market Investigations and Reviews of Undertakings and Orders accepted or made under the Enterprise Act 2002 and Fair Trading Act 1973* (CC7 (revised)) that are significantly amended or superseded by the changes that are outlined in this Statement.

Existing guidance reference	Amendment
Chairman's Guidance on Disclosure of Information in Merger Inquiries, Market Investigations and Reviews of Undertakings and Orders accepted or made under the Enterprise Act 2002 and Fair Trading Act 1973 (CC7 (revised))	
Paragraph 9.9	Groups are reminded of the opportunity provided to parties to make further representations to the Procedural Officer if they wish to dispute the proposal of a Group to disclose information. This is additional to the opportunity for parties to make known their concerns to the Group. Groups are required to have regard to the views of the Procedural Officer if the party has made representations to him. The decision to disclose will, however, remain that of the Group.

B. STATUS OF OFT AND CC GUIDANCE DOCUMENTS

[3.35]

B.1 The table below indicates the status of OFT and CC guidance documents related to transparency and disclosure that had been published and were in effect prior to the transfer of their functions to the CMA on 1 April 2014. The *Chairman's Guidance on Disclosure of Information in Merger Inquiries, Market Investigations and Reviews of Undertakings and Orders accepted or made under the Enterprise Act 2002 and Fair Trading Act 1973* (CC7 (revised)) has been adopted by the CMA Board in order to facilitate the exercise by the CMA of its functions.

OFT/CC Code	Title	Status of document	
		Replaced/ obsolete[96]	Adopted by the CMA Board[97]
OFT1234	Transparency – a statement of the OFT's approach	√	–
CC7 (revised)	Chairman's Guidance on Disclosure of Information in Merger Inquiries, Market Investigations and Reviews of Undertakings and Orders accepted or made under the Enterprise Act 2002 and Fair Trading Act 1973	–	√

Part 3 CMA and other Guidelines

OFT/CC Code	Title	Status of document	
		Replaced/ obsolete[96]	Adopted by the CMA Board[97]
CC12	Disclosure of information by the Competition Commission to other public authorities	√	–
CC6	Competition Commission: guidance to merger reference groups, market reference groups and special reference groups	√	–
OFT518	Overview of the Enterprise Act	√	–

B.2 Parties should refer to the CC7 (revised) (the adopted guidance) for further guidance on the CMA's approach to transparency and disclosure, subject in particular to the following general limitations:

- in the case of conflict between this Statement and the adopted guidance, the adopted guidance prevails
- the original text of the adopted guidance has been retained unamended, except as indicated in Annexe A: as such, that text does not reflect or take account of developments in case law, legislation or practice, since its original publication, and
- the adopted guidance should be read subject to the following cross-cutting amendments:
  - — references to the 'OFT' and 'CC' (except where referring to specific past OFT or CC practice or case law), should be read as referring to the CMA
  - — certain OFT or CC departments, teams or individual roles may not be replicated in the CMA, or may be renamed. A copy of the CMA's organisational chart is available on www.gov.uk/cma, and
  - — parties should check any contact details against those listed on www.gov.uk/cma, which will be the most up to date.

NOTES

[96] OFT and CC publications listed in this column have, at the date of publication of this Statement, been replaced, or rendered obsolete, by CMA guidance or publications.

[97] OFT and CC publications listed in this column have been adopted by the CMA Board (subject to any guidance or publications prepared by the CMA in the future).

PRIORITISATION PRINCIPLES FOR THE CMA (CMA16, APRIL 2014)

[3.36]

NOTES

CONTENTS

1 INTRODUCTION

[3.37]

1.1 The CMA's mission is to make markets work well in the interests of consumers, businesses and the economy. Markets work well when businesses compete vigorously and fairly to win customers' business. In well-functioning markets consumers have confidence that market processes deliver excellent outcomes for them in terms of price, quality, variety, innovation and service. When markets work well, efficient businesses are rewarded and productivity growth is higher.

1.2 Markets usually work well for consumers and the economy without any need for intervention, in a virtuous circle. Competition provides firms with incentives to deliver what consumers want, to provide value for money, to produce efficiently and to innovate; whilst well-informed, active consumers can play a key role in driving competition between firms. The CMA only intervenes where necessary to protect competition or when it believes it can improve the way in which markets work. The CMA's interventions therefore seek to promote open competition, and to encourage greater availability of products and services and the provision of accurate, non-deceptive information between businesses and consumers.

1.3 We therefore focus our efforts and resources on deterring and influencing behaviour that poses the greatest threat to consumer welfare, and intervene in order to protect consumer welfare and, in the process, drive higher productivity growth. We also recognise the need to avoid imposing unnecessary burdens on business.

1.4 In order to make the best use of our resources in terms of real outcomes for UK consumers, we need to ensure that we make appropriate decisions about which projects and programmes of work we undertake across all areas of our responsibility. The CMA has agreed with the Treasury that we will deliver direct financial benefits to consumers of at least ten times our relevant costs to the taxpayer (measured over a rolling three-year period)

1.5 In seeking to target both our resources and enforcement strategy, the CMA needs to consider a range of factors including impact on consumers, strategic significance, risks and resources. We also need to take account of the activity, capacity and interests of our partners.

1.6 The principles for prioritisation set out in this document build on the principles introduced by the Office of Fair Trading in 2008.

1.7 In this document we set out how we use the principles, along with detail of the principles and explanatory notes. The discussion of the principles and how we use them is not intended to be exhaustive. As well as consideration of the principles, it may be necessary for the CMA to take other factors into account where appropriate. We will continue to keep the principles under review.

2 HOW WE USE THE PRINCIPLES

[3.38]

2.1 We generally prioritise according to the impact of work on consumers and according to the strategic significance of the work. We balance this against the risks and resources involved. Our vision, values and high-level strategy[1] guide our actions and our annual plans and other corporate documents[2] describe what we intend to do. We are also required to have regard to the Government's non-binding Ministerial statement of strategic priorities for the CMA.[3]

2.2 The list of factors to consider under different principles is illustrative and not exhaustive. We will not apply the principles in a mechanical way: judgement and a reasoned balancing exercise are required for each case which necessitates that we consider the principles in the round and on a case-by-case basis. Where appropriate, we may also consider other relevant factors. In other words, prioritisation will not take place in isolation but will always be a relative question which necessitates considerations of the CMA's overall portfolio and resources available at that time. It is therefore not possible to give guidance such as to allow an advance external assessment of whether a particular case would or would not be taken on by the CMA.

2.3 When deciding which new projects and programmes of work to take on, we will consider the timing and resource requirements of projects and other work going on across the CMA at that time. As part of this we will assess the resources required over the life of the projects under consideration as well as their potential impact. At particular points in the life cycle of a project we may consider whether it warrants the continued commitment of resources, especially when weighed against other potential work that we could take forward using those resources.

2.4 In some cases we have a legal duty to act once certain relevant circumstances have materialised. For instance:

- once we have received a 'super-complaint'[4] from a designated consumer body we must respond to this within 90 days
- we have a duty actively to assist the European Commission in carrying out its inspections if we receive a request for assistance from the Commission
- where we apply national competition law we are obliged to apply Articles 101 and 102 of the EC Treaty as appropriate and applicable
- we have a function to obtain and review information relating to merger situations, and a duty to refer for an in-depth 'Phase 2' investigation any relevant merger situation where we believe that it is or may be the case that the merger has resulted or may be expected to result in a substantial lessening of competition in a UK market
- we have a duty to conduct regulatory appeals and references in relation to price controls, terms of licences or other regulatory arrangements under sector specific legislation

NOTES

1 Published after consultation in January 2014.

2 www.gov.uk/cma.

3 Published after consultation at the time of the CMA's launch on 1 October 2013.

4 Receipt of a complaint from a designated consumer body that any feature or combination of features of a market in the UK for goods or services is or appears to be significantly harming the interests of consumers.

3 CMA PRIORITISATION PRINCIPLES

[3.39]

We generally prioritise our work according to the principles set out below. Where appropriate, we may also take account of other relevant factors. All relevant considerations will be balanced in the round.

Account will also be taken of whether we have a legal duty to act once certain circumstances have materialised. During prioritisation we will consider the timing and resource requirements of our work and ensure that our duties are appropriately met within the confines of the resources available to the CMA.

A. IMPACT

3.1 What would be the likely direct effect on consumer welfare in the market or sector where the intervention takes place? Consumer welfare includes better value for consumers in terms of price, quality, range or service, both static and dynamic, and may also include non-financial detriment such as the avoidance of physical harm or emotional distress. We may prioritise work because the direct effects would specifically benefit disadvantaged consumers.

3.2 What would be the likely indirect effect on consumer welfare? This principle captures further improvement to consumer welfare and consumer confidence that results from changes in consumer, business or government behaviour which is prompted by the CMA's action. It thus captures deterrence and improved awareness for consumers, business and government.

3.3 What would be the expected additional economic impact on efficiency, productivity and the wider economy? This captures whether, as a result of our actions, efficiency would be expected to increase or growth be encouraged in a particular sector or across the economy.

B. STRATEGIC SIGNIFICANCE

3.4 Does the work fit with the CMA's strategy and/or with other CMA objectives? This will include whether there are elements of strategic significance of the work that are additional to impact. The CMA will periodically review and publish its strategy in line with its overall ambition of being consistently one of the leading competition and consumer agencies in the world.[5]

3.5 Is the CMA best placed to act? Alternatives to CMA action could include:

- private enforcement
- action by CMA partners such as members of the Consumer Protection Partnership or the UK Competition Network, other UK regulators or law enforcement bodies, or the European Commission
- market developments, self-regulation, or new UK or EU regulatory or legislative developments.

3.6 What would be the impact of the new work on the balance of the CMA's current portfolio of work?

C. RISKS

3.7 What is the likelihood of a successful outcome?

D. RESOURCES

3.8 What are the resource implications of doing the work? This includes:

- whether the resource requirements of the work are proportionate to the benefits from doing the work
- the period over which the resources will be needed
- any savings created for the CMA by enabling us to meet our objectives more efficiently.

NOTES

5 The vision, values and strategy published at its shadow launch are on its website at: www.gov.uk/government/uploads/system/uploads/attachment_data/file/245454/CMA_vision_strategy_values_FINAL_ GOV_UK.pdf.

4 EXPLANATORY NOTES

DIRECT EFFECT ON CONSUMER WELFARE (IMPACT)

[3.40]

4.1 This is the benefit arising to consumers as a result of the change in behaviour of those that are the subject of CMA intervention. It will most likely arise from a CMA action that leads to preventing or terminating activity that would have negatively affected consumers for some time into the future. We will have regard to the potential effect if an action is taken, regardless of whether it is due to direct action by the CMA or by others (for example, the courts or the Government) pursuant to a CMA intervention.

4.2 Where the problem is in an upstream market and benefit arises in the first instance to businesses, we assume that benefits will be passed on to final consumers as a direct effect unless there is evidence to the contrary. Accordingly, for example, an increase in manufacturer competition that resulted in a reduction in wholesale prices that were passed on to final consumers in terms of lower retail prices would be treated as a direct effect. The effects of increased competition in a market serving businesses would therefore also be considered as a positive direct impact.

4.3 Disadvantaged consumers may be particularly vulnerable to exploitation within markets or may simply not share in the benefits of greater competition. Disadvantaged consumers may be served less well by markets because, for example, they may be more expensive to serve, they have less market access, they are in debt, or they cannot afford the higher risk that often accompanies better value. While the CMA has no legal or other mandate to redistribute wealth or power to intervene in individual disputes, we may sometimes favour projects that would benefit disadvantaged consumers, in order to build overall consumer confidence in markets.

4.4 Similarly, we recognise that some or all customers in certain markets may be subject to information asymmetries or may make decisions based on behavioural biases. We will take account of the observed behaviour of customers in our analysis of markets and in the design of any market interventions.

4.5 The CMA sets out examples of direct benefits to consumers in its evaluation work[6] and its Annual Reports.

INDIRECT EFFECT ON CONSUMER WELFARE (IMPACT)

4.6 Indirect effects arise from changes to the behaviour of those other than the direct subject of the CMA's intervention. While the deterrent effect of civil or criminal enforcement is the most obvious example, another example may be the increased consumer and business confidence in the correct functioning of the markets.

4.7 Whether a specific action will be likely to lead to wider behavioural changes can be difficult to gauge. Our work will be informed by the evidence available on deterrence and other indirect effects.[7]

4.8 Examples of where indirect effects might exist include:

- the deterrent effect of taking action in a market where similar issues exist in other markets (for example, we might expect a successful case relating to a particular drug to influence behaviour across the wider pharmaceutical sector)
- action that clarifies the law in a way that enables other businesses to engage in pro-competitive practices that were previously considered potentially illegal
- action that demonstrates to national or local government the benefits from removing disproportionate public restrictions on competition
- action that leads to consumers being more or better informed, empowered or active
- publication of guidance which affects policy and practice across all sectors

EFFECT ON EFFICIENCY/PRODUCTIVITY (IMPACT)

4.9 Competition is crucial in stimulating efficient and strong economies and encouraging growth; it drives productivity growth as more efficient firms win business from less efficient ones and all firms are motivated to become more efficient, often through innovation, in order to survive. We will look at whether there is the potential for additional economic impact on efficiency or productivity in the market in question or other markets. In markets where competition is weak or absent, substantial inefficiency may arise. This could take the form of poor cost control, weak internal managerial or strategic incentives, lack of innovation, or high levels of rent-seeking to prevent increased competition.

4.10 An initial action that increases competition in the market may deliver further consumer benefits over time resulting from the improved competitive process.

For example, liberalisation of the air passenger transport market had initial direct effects on consumer welfare, and also long-term productivity effects as new entrants drove cost reduction and innovation in areas ranging from online booking to airport competition.

4.11 Evidence of such inefficiency could take many forms, including lack of responsiveness to customer demand, high costs or low innovation relative to comparable industries, or high levels of anticompetitive lobbying.

FIT WITH THE CMA'S STRATEGY AND OBJECTIVES (STRATEGIC SIGNIFICANCE)

4.12 We will consider whether the proposed new project or piece of work would help further our key strategic objectives. Our five strategic goals, which support our mission, are:

- deliver effective enforcement
- extend competition frontiers
- refocus consumer protection
- achieve professional excellence
- develop integrated performance

4.13 In selecting and delivering our portfolio of work, we will seek to improve the skills and talent of our staff, the quality of our intelligence, our leadership ability and excellence on consumer and competition issues, our ability to work in partnership, or the capacity of our partners in areas where they work with us to achieve our objectives. Taking forward work that supports these aims will enhance the long-term ability of both the CMA and its partners in the UK consumer and competition policy framework to target intervention and deliver better outcomes.

4.14 Examples of the types of work that could enhance our capacity in this way include:

- innovation: establishing or testing new legal and economic approaches (for example, intervening in private actions involving alleged CA98 infringements)[8]
- work that clarifies the law in areas of practical commercial importance, therefore facilitating compliance and potentially promoting productivity
- policy work that leads to improvement in the consumer and competition policy framework (for example, new legislation)
- work that results in greater international quality or consistency in approach
- work that coordinates our activities with those of partners, for example sector regulators, in a way that promotes and reinforces consistency and increases impact
- work that enhances our ability to deal with complex cases where deterrence considerations play a role in our decision to pursue

IS THE CMA BEST PLACED? (STRATEGIC SIGNIFICANCE)

4.15 We always examine whether any work is best carried out by the CMA, having regard to whether there are alternative ways of achieving the desired or similar result. The CMA works in partnership with a number of bodies with which it shares competition and consumer powers, most notably through the UK Competition Network and the Consumer Protection Partnership, and it may be more appropriate for these partners to lead in some cases. Other bodies that might, in some cases, be better placed to take particular pieces of work forward include the Financial Ombudsman Service, the Serious Fraud Office and the Lord Advocate in Scotland. We also work in partnership with competition and consumer authorities in other countries, including the European Commission (DG Comp), and national competition authorities around the world.

POTENTIAL IMPACT ON THE CMA'S PORTFOLIO (STRATEGIC SIGNIFICANCE)

4.16 As well as considering individual projects, we will also consider the impact on the CMA's ongoing portfolio of work. The performance framework we have agreed with the Government[9] requires us, among other things, to demonstrate direct financial benefits to consumers of at least ten times our relevant costs to the taxpayer (measured over a rolling three-year period). We will therefore also consider work in terms of its contribution to our portfolio as well as its individual impact.

4.17 Important portfolio considerations will include an appropriate balance:

- between tackling both public and private restrictions on competition
- across the full range of legislative tools available to the CMA
- between established approaches and more innovative work
- between work which builds capacity (investment) and work that uses that capacity (output)
- across sectors of the economy
- of delivery over time
- between risk and return in terms of outcomes for consumers

LIKELIHOOD OF SUCCESSFUL OUTCOME (RISKS)

4.18 We take into account how likely the new project or programme of work is to achieve its desired impact. In some cases, recognition of there being only a relatively small likelihood of success could be a reason not to proceed with the project. In other cases, the likely scale of the detriment may be such that a project should be pursued despite there being a small likelihood of success because it will nevertheless provide clarity on the law. We also consider the overall balance of risk across the whole of the CMA's work portfolio.

4.19 In some cases the desired impact may be to establish consistent standards, create legal certainty and send clear long-term messages rather than 'win' a case. We will balance the risk of short-term failure with the chances of long-term success. We are obviously also subject to appeal to the Competition Appeal Tribunal and take account of this in our decisions.

4.20 Risk is inherent in everything that an organisation does. Consequently, good risk management at all levels is a critical success factor for any organisation. A core component of good corporate governance is risk management. The CMA will therefore carefully manage risk throughout the process of making decisions on its work programme.

RESOURCE IMPLICATIONS OF DOING THE WORK (RESOURCES)

4.21 When considering the resource implications of a proposed new project or programme of work, we will take into account all resources required to undertake the work. Over the course of a piece of work the resource allocated to it may change, depending on its requirements and the requirements of other projects, so that the CMA's resources are allocated in the most efficient way to cover all of our work.

4.22 We will take into account the resource availability of other parties, including our enforcement partners.

NOTES

6 This comprises annual reports on the positive impact of our work, and evaluation of the impact of individual cases or groups of cases.

7 The CMA will continue to assess the deterrent effect of its work, building on work done by the OFT which is available on the OFT website at www.oft.gov.uk/shared_oft/reports/Evaluating-OFTs-work/oft1391.pdf.

8 Article 15 of Council Regulation (EC) No 1/2003.

9 The performance framework is included in our Annual Plan.

PROCEDURAL OFFICER: RAISING PROCEDURAL ISSUES IN CMA CASES (CMA GUIDANCE, 31 MARCH 2014)

[3.41]

NOTES

This Guidance is available on the Competition and Markets Authority website at: www.gov.uk/guidance/procedural-officer-raising-procedural-issues-in-cma-cases.

Role, scope, process and how to apply for a review of a procedural decision

INTRODUCTION

If you are a party involved in one of the CMA's Competition Act, market or merger cases, the CMA's Procedural Officer provides a way in which you can raise procedural issues that you have not been able to resolve with the CMA Group or staff member responsible for the investigation.

The procedural issues that you can raise with the Procedural Officer vary depending on the type of case.

The Procedural Officer is independent from CMA investigations, case teams and decision makers. The role of the Procedural Officer is intended to ensure that procedural issues can be addressed quickly, efficiently and cost effectively.

The Procedural Officer also chairs oral hearings with parties in Competition Act investigations.

PROCEDURAL OFFICER ROLE, SCOPE AND PROCESS: COMPETITION ACT 1998 INVESTIGATIONS

SCOPE

The Procedural Officer determines procedural complaints in Competition Act investigations that relate to the following:

- deadlines for parties to respond to information requests, submit non-confidential versions of documents or to submit written representations on the Statement of Objections or Supplementary Statement of Objections
- requests for confidentiality redactions of information in documents on the CMA's case file, in a Statement of Objections or in a final decision
- requests for disclosure or non-disclosure of certain documents on the CMA's case file
- issues relating to oral hearings, including, for example, with regard to issues such as the date of the hearing
- other significant procedural issues that may arise during the course of an investigation.

The Procedural Officer is not able to review CMA decisions beyond those listed above, for example decisions on the scope of requests for information or decisions relating to the substance of a case.

APPLICATIONS TO THE PROCEDURAL OFFICER

The Procedural Officer becomes involved only at the request of a party to an investigation and only after the party has been unable to resolve the issue with the Senior Responsible Officer (SRO) of the investigation. A party wishing to refer an issue to the Procedural Officer needs to make an application as soon as possible after being notified of the SRO's decision on the issue in question and, in any event, within five working days of that notification.

The application should be no longer than five sides of A4 paper and should include:

- the name and contact details of the applicant
- the name and contact details of lawyers acting for the applicant (where appropriate)
- the CMA case name and reference number
- the date of the determination of the issue by the SRO responsible for the investigation
- a short summary of the issue in question, including a summary of the case team's original decision (where relevant), the decision of the SRO responsible for the investigation, the reason that the applicant is applying for a review of that decision and the outcome that the applicant is seeking

The applicant must also provide copies of relevant correspondence between the applicant and the CMA relating to the issue in question and copies of any relevant information or documents where these are in the applicant's possession. If the applicant has concerns about providing a copy of such information or documents to the Procedural Officer, they should raise these concerns with the Procedural Officer before submitting the application.

On receipt of an application, the Procedural Officer will provide an opportunity for each of the case team and the party to present their arguments orally on the telephone or at a meeting, before issuing a decision on the issue.

THE PROCEDURAL OFFICER'S DECISIONS IN COMPETITION ACT INVESTIGATIONS

The Procedural Officer will deal with the application as quickly as possible. There is an indicative administrative target that decisions will be taken in most cases within 10 working days from receipt of the application. The Procedural Officer will reach a decision within 20 working days from receipt of the application. This timeframe is extendable by no more than 20 working days if there are special reasons to do so.

The Procedural Officer's decision will be binding on the CMA case team. The Procedural Officer's decision, or a summary of it, will be published on the CMA's webpages, generally at the time the decision is made by the Procedural Officer or at the end of the CMA's investigation. Publication will be subject to redaction of confidential information.

PUBLISHED PROCEDURAL OFFICER DECISIONS IN COMPETITION ACT INVESTIGATIONS:

- Procedural Officer decision 2019/1 – Application by Amilco
- Procedural Officer decision 2019/3 – Application by Advanz Pharma
- Procedural Officer decision 2018/5
- Procedural Officer decision 2018/4
- Summary of Procedural Officer decision 2018/1
- Summary of Procedural Officer decision 2018/2
- Procedural Officer decision 2018/3

- Procedural Officer decision 2016/1 – Application by the AMA, Storm Model Management, Models One and Premier Model Management
- Procedural Officer decision 2015/1 – Application by Flynn
- Procedural Officer decision 2015/2 – Application by Pfizer.

MORE INFORMATION

You can find more information on the Procedural Officer's role and procedures in Competition Act investigations in:

Guidance on the CMA's investigation procedures in Competition Act 1998 cases

Competition Act 1998 (Competition and Markets Authority's Rules) Order 2014

Transparency and disclosure: Statement of the CMA's policy and approach

PROCEDURAL OFFICER ROLE, SCOPE AND PROCESS: MERGER AND MARKET CASES

SCOPE

The Procedural Officer provides a mechanism for handling disputes relating specifically to the confidentiality of information that the CMA proposes to publish in mergers and markets cases. This comprises information relating to a party which the CMA proposes to include:

- in its published Phase 1 merger decisions, or
- in its decisions, reports or other documents published in the course of market studies and Phase 2 merger or market investigations.

PROCESS

A party may make representations to the Procedural Officer if it has been unable to resolve the concern with:

- the CMA staff member with overall responsibility for the conduct of the investigation in Phase 1 merger investigations and market studies, or
- the Inquiry Group in Phase 2 merger investigations and market investigation references

The procedure followed by the Procedural Officer is flexible and will be tailored to the nature of the issue which has been raised. It will also reflect any specific timing constraints to which the CMA's investigation is subject.

The Procedural Officer's decision is binding on the case team in Phase 1 merger investigations and market studies.

The Procedural Officer advises the Inquiry Group acting on Phase 2 merger investigations or market investigation references, having considered the parties' representations. The Inquiry Group will have all due regard to that advice, but the final decision remains with the Inquiry Group.

MORE INFORMATION

You can find more information on the Procedural Officer's role and procedures in merger and market cases in:

Mergers: Guidance on the CMA's jurisdiction and procedure

Transparency and disclosure: Statement of the CMA's policy and approach.

HOW TO INVOLVE THE PROCEDURAL OFFICER

If you wish to apply to the Procedural Officer, you should make an application by email to Procedural.Officer@cma.gsi.gov.uk with a hard copy also sent by post to:

Frances Barr

Procedural Officer,

Competition and Markets Authority,

The Cabot

25 Cabot Square

London E14 4QZ

United Kingdom

The process to be followed in relation to each application will be indicated when the application is acknowledged.

If there is any reason why the Procedural Officer is unable personally to consider the application, the applicant will be informed of any alternative arrangements put in place when the application is acknowledged.

THE PROCEDURAL OFFICER

The CMA has appointed Frances Barr as Procedural Officer from 1 April 2014. Prior to joining the CMA, Frances was the General Counsel at the Office of Fair Trading. Previously she held a variety of legal, policy and project delivery roles at the OFT and worked on secondments at the Competition Commission and at the Department of Trade and Industry. Frances began her legal career in private practice at Slaughter and May, where she worked in London and Brussels.

RELATED INFORMATION

The Office of Fair Trading, one of the CMA's predecessors, trialled a Procedural Adjudicator role for procedural matters in Competition Act 1998 investigations. More information on the OFT's trial and copies of the decisions taken by its Procedural Adjudicator can be found at:

Procedural Adjudicator Trial.

(https://webarchive.nationalarchives.gov.uk/ukgwa/20140402154439/http://oft.gov.uk/about-the-oft/legal-powers/legal/competition-act-1998/procedural-adjudicator-trial)

REMEDIES: GUIDANCE ON THE CMA'S APPROACH TO THE VARIATION AND TERMINATION OF MERGER, MONOPOLY AND MARKET UNDERTAKINGS AND ORDERS (CMA11, JANUARY 2014 (REVISED AUGUST 2015))

[3.42]

NOTES

CONTENTS

1 INTRODUCTION

[3.43]

1.1 This guidance covers the Competition and Markets Authority's (CMA's) approach to the variation and termination of merger, monopoly and market final undertakings and orders.[1]

1.2 This guidance does not cover variation or termination of initial and interim undertakings or orders, such as undertakings under section 80 or orders under section 72 or 81 of the Enterprise Act 2002 (EA02).[2] Accordingly, unless otherwise specified, the term 'undertaking or order' in this guidance should be read as referring only to final undertakings and orders.

1.3 Further, in a small number of instances, the CMA retains a duty to advise the Secretary of State on orders and undertakings made under the Fair Trading Act 1973 (FTA) which have not been transferred from the Secretary of State to the CMA by statutory instrument. The Secretary of State is also responsible for varying or terminating undertakings or orders given following public interest cases.[3] This guidance does not relate to the process by which the CMA provides advice to the Secretary of State in these instances.[4]

1.4 This guidance supersedes the *Memorandum of Understanding between the Office of Fair Trading and the Competition Commission on the variation and termination of merger, monopoly and market undertakings and orders under the Fair Trading Act 1973 and the Enterprise Act 2002*, Version 2, published 10 March 2011 (the MoU).

1.5 The CMA will apply this guidance flexibly. This means that the CMA will have regard to the guidance when it deals with reviews of undertakings and orders but that, when the facts of an individual case reasonably justify it, the CMA may adopt a different approach.

1.6 This document is not a definitive statement of, or a substitute for, the law itself and should not be relied upon as an alternative to seeking appropriate legal advice.

1.7 This guidance sets out the CMA's practice as of 1 April 2014. Please see *Transitional Arrangements: Guidance on the CMA's approach – Part 1* (CMA14), chapter 6 for information on the applicable transitional arrangements. Please refer to www.gov.uk/cma to ensure you have the latest version of this guidance as it may be revised from time to time to reflect changes in best practice or the law and our developing experience.

1.8 You may find it useful to read this document alongside other documents published by the CMA or adopted by its Board, including *Merger Assessment Guidelines* (OFT1254/CC2), *Guidelines for market investigations* (CC3 (revised)), *Chairman's Guidance on Disclosure of Information in Merger Inquiries, Market Investigations and Reviews of Undertakings and Orders accepted or made under the Enterprise Act 2002 and Fair Trading Act 1973* (CC7 (revised)) and *Merger Remedies: Competition Commission Guidelines* (CC8). To the extent that any conflict arises between the content of such existing guidance documents and this guidance, the content of this guidance will prevail. Annexe A sets out the status of the Office of Fair Trading (OFT) and the Competition Commission (CC) guidance documents and publications that are relevant to the variation and termination of undertakings and orders and that had been published and were in effect prior to the transfer of the mergers and markets functions to the CMA on 1 April 2014.

NOTES

1 Variation and termination has been used as shorthand throughout this document. The statutory language in sections 92(2) and 162(2) of the EA02 refers to the release, variation or superseding of undertakings; and the variation or revocation of orders. See paragraph 2.2 below.

2 In the case of mergers, guidance for variation of initial and interim undertakings or orders is available in *Mergers: Guidance on the CMA's jurisdiction and procedure* (CMA2).

3 Sections 159 and 161 of the EA02.

4 Sections 92(3) and 162(3) of the EA02, as amended by the Enterprise and Regulatory Reform Act 2013 (ERRA13).

2 THE CMA'S STATUTORY ROLE

[3.44]

2.1 Undertakings and orders are the primary means by which remedies are implemented following the determination of merger and market investigation references under the EA02, as amended by the Enterprise and Regulatory Reform Act 2013 (ERRA13). Under the EA02,[5] undertakings are accepted or orders imposed by the CMA,[6] except in certain public interest cases where the Secretary of State is responsible for accepting undertakings or imposing orders.[7]

2.2 The CMA has a statutory duty[8] to keep under review undertakings and orders made under the FTA and under the EA02. From time to time, the CMA must consider whether, by reason of any change of circumstances:

- undertakings are no longer appropriate and need to be varied, superseded or released, and
- an order is no longer appropriate and needs to be varied or revoked.[9]

2.3 Responsibility for deciding on variation or termination of undertakings or orders lies with the CMA in respect of all but a very limited number of undertakings and orders (see paragraph 1.3).

NOTES

5 Prior to the EA02, under the FTA, the Secretary of State accepted undertakings or imposed orders to remedy the adverse effects identified during a merger and monopoly reference.

6 Under the EA02, the CMA may accept undertakings or impose orders (sections 82 and 84 of the EA02 (mergers) and sections 159 and 161 of the EA02 (markets)), and, where the conditions for a reference are met, the CMA may accept binding undertakings as an alternative to making a reference (section 73 of the EA02 (mergers) and section 154 of the EA02 (markets)).

7 Sections 55 and 66 and Schedule 7 of the EA02 (mergers) and sections 139, 147 and 159 of the EA02 (markets).

8 Under sections 92(1), (2) and (3) and 162 (1), (2) and (3) of the EA02; sections 88(4) and (5) of the FTA (as preserved in Schedule 24 of the EA02).

9 See footnote 1 above.

SUBSTANTIVE TEST IN CONSIDERING VARIATION AND TERMINATION OF UNDERTAKINGS AND ORDERS

2.4 In considering variation and termination of undertakings and orders, either upon request from a party or under the CMA's own initiative (see paragraphs 3.2 to 3.8), the CMA will consider whether there has been a change of circumstances. If there has, the CMA will then consider what action, if any, should be taken.

2.5 The precise nature of the CMA's consideration of any change of circumstances will depend entirely on the individual circumstances affecting a particular undertaking or order. However, the change of circumstances must be such that the undertaking or order is no longer appropriate in dealing with the competition problem and/or adverse effects which it was designed to remedy, if it is to lead to either variation or termination.

2.6 Types of circumstances that have led to variation or termination in the past include:

- undertakings or orders that have time-expired or clearly become obsolete (see for example, the review of Provident's trading checks undertakings (2012), where Provident was found no longer to provide trading checks and such products were not likely to re-emerge)
- undertakings or orders that are affected by new legislation (see, for example, the review of the Northern Ireland PCA Banking Market Investigation Order 2008 (2011), where the coming into force of two EU directives—the Payment Services Directive and the Consumer Credit Directive, both of which had been implemented into UK law—included articles that either were duplicated by the same subject matter or were different from requirements in the order), and
- undertakings or orders that are affected by changes in market conditions (see, for example, the review of Yellow Pages undertakings (2013), where increased internet access and usage by both consumers and advertisers had had a significant effect on the constraints faced, such that the owner of Yellow Pages was no longer able to operate as a price setter independent of the behaviour of competitors).

2.7 Experience of reviews of undertakings and orders suggests that the complexity of analysis required in a review varies significantly depending on the change of circumstances identified and the characteristics of the market. In some cases, detailed investigation may be required in order to evaluate whether there has been a change of circumstances and, if so, what, if any, changes to undertakings or an order may be justified.

3 PROCESS FOR REVIEWS OF UNDERTAKINGS AND ORDERS

[3.45]

3.1 This section sets out the process for reviews of undertakings and orders. It sets out:

- initial screening, including the ways in which a review may be initiated and deciding whether to conduct a review
- the process for a review, including: timescale, the CMA's assessment, the key stages of the CMA's decision-making process, and the conclusion of a review, and
- the procedure for dealing with undertakings or orders that are time-expired, lapsed or superseded by new CMA undertakings or orders.

INITIAL SCREENING

The ways in which a review may be initiated

3.2 There are two ways in which a review may be initiated – (i) at the request of parties who have given undertakings or who are subject to orders, or other interested parties; or (ii) by the CMA on its own initiative.

Requests from parties

3.3 Parties may request that undertakings or orders be varied or terminated by reason of a change of circumstances. Any submission making such a request should set out clearly and with supporting evidence:

- what the change of circumstances is
- how and why this makes it appropriate to vary or terminate the undertakings or order
- the possible consequences for consumers and businesses impacted by the remedy[10]
- why a review of the order and undertakings meets the CMA's published prioritisation principles, and 6 CMA11
- whether the request is being raised in order to avoid a breach of the undertakings or order.[11]

3.4 It is open to parties to approach the CMA prior to submitting a request in order to discuss what sort of evidence would be expected to be included in any request.

3.5 Parties should provide both a confidential and a non-confidential version of their submission.

3.6 The CMA will typically, upon receipt of a request for a review, issue an invitation to comment by publishing information about the request for review. The CMA will typically invite interested parties to comment on the request for review and to submit any relevant evidence.[12] The consultation period for the invitation to comment will typically be three weeks. The form of publication and extent of detail will depend on the circumstances of the case. This could range from publication of the non-confidential elements of the submission itself, to a statement confirming that the CMA is considering whether to conduct a review. In exceptional circumstances, publication of an invitation to comment may not occur if, for example, the CMA believes that the claimed change of circumstances, in and of itself, constitutes specified information which needs to be excluded from disclosure.[13]

NOTES

10 Where the request is made by other interested parties (that is, those not subject to the undertakings or order), they should explain their interest in the undertakings or order.

11 Where the possible change of circumstances is such that it would lead to a breach of the undertakings or order, the CMA will consider it as quickly as possible. However, parties can assist the CMA by giving it notice of such changes of circumstances in good time and thereby avoid being placed in potential breach.

12 Where the request for a review has been made by other interested parties (that is, those not subject to the undertakings or order) or the review is an own-initiative CMA review (see paragraphs 3.7 and 3.8 ANNEXE(S)3.8), and in order to ensure an effective public consultation and to establish whether such a public consultation can take place, the CMA will normally consult informally with those directly affected by the undertakings or order prior to the public consultation. This informal consultation is likely to be a short period of no more than two weeks.

13 See Part 9 of the EA02. See paragraph 3.23 ANNEXE(S)3.23 for further discussion of the CMA's approach to disclosure.

The CMA's own-initiative activity

3.7 The CMA is also able to begin a review on its own initiative, without any person having made a request. In practice, the CMA is likely to do so when, based on its own intelligence, it has identified possible changes of circumstances analogous to those referred to at paragraph 2.6 above, or where the Monopolies and Mergers Commission (MMC), the CC or the CMA has recommended a timeframe for review in the report in which the remedy was originally determined (see also paragraph 3.10).

3.8 If the CMA is intending to conduct a review on its own initiative it will typically issue an invitation to comment to all parties affected by the undertakings or order, asking for their view as to whether such a review should take place and to submit any relevant evidence. As noted at paragraph 3.6 above, the form of publication will depend on the circumstances of the case and the consultation period will typically be three weeks.

Deciding whether to conduct a review

3.9 The CMA will assess the request for a review and the responses to any consultation on the request, or the responses to a consultation on whether the CMA should conduct an own-initiative review. The

CMA will then decide whether a review should take place at a particular point in time. This decision will be taken by a senior member of CMA staff, supported and challenged by a further two individuals with the appropriate level of skill and expertise. The decision-maker may also consult the CMA's Case and Policy Committee to seek views on any policy issues arising out of the proposed decision on whether or not to conduct a review.

3.10 In deciding whether to conduct a review, the CMA will act in accordance with its published prioritisation principles. This may mean that the CMA will choose not to conduct a review within time frames recommended by a MMC, CC or CMA report in which the remedy was originally determined. Factors relevant in deciding whether to conduct a review will include whether there is a realistic prospect of finding a change of circumstances.

3.11 If the CMA decides not to proceed with a review, it will inform the relevant parties that a review will not take place. If particular parties made a request for a review, the CMA will typically set out briefly its reasons for not conducting a review. This decision will typically be published, although the CMA will have due regard to its obligation not to disclose certain specified information, as set out in Part 9 of the EA02.

3.12 If, on the other hand, the CMA decides to undertake a review, it will generally appoint a group of CMA panel members to conduct the review.[14] In cases dealing with undertakings given or an order made under EA02, where the original group has ceased to exist, a group will generally be formed as a Remedy Group (RG).[15] In cases dealing with undertakings given or orders made under the FTA, a group will be appointed by the Chair of the CMA.[16] Each group will be advised by a case team of CMA staff.

3.13 The CMA will inform relevant parties as soon as practicable of its intention to commence a review. At the same time, or as soon as practicable thereafter, the CMA will also provide them with the following information:

- a brief description of the case, the relevant legislation, the industry sector concerned and the CMA's reasons for commencing a review. The level of information may vary according to the circumstances of the case
- an indicative timetable showing the anticipated dates of key milestones (see paragraph 3.18 below), and
- the contact details for the main CMA contacts for the case including specifying the first point of contact for general queries and submission of information.

3.14 The CMA will place a review opening announcement on www.gov.uk/cma announcing its decision to commence a review (except if to do so would prejudice the case or would otherwise be inappropriate). At the same time as or following the public announcement, the CMA will also publish, as soon as reasonably practicable, the information referred to in paragraph 3.13.[17]

3.15 The CMA will review from time to time the information provided and consider whether it is appropriate to update the information provided to the parties directly involved or the published information.

3.16 Where undertakings or orders under review relate to a regulated sector, and especially where a sectoral regulator has a role in monitoring compliance with the undertakings or order,[18] the CMA will liaise with the relevant sectoral regulator as appropriate.[19] In other cases, for example, when reviewing merger undertakings or orders the relevant sectoral regulator may make a submission to the CMA setting out its views and any supporting evidence on the possible variation or termination.[20]

NOTES

Paragraphs 3.9 and 3.12 are reproduced as amended by the CMA11: minor amendments notice – August 2015, which is available on the CMA's website at www.gov.uk/government/publications/remedies-guidance-on-the-cmas-approach-to-the-variation-and-termination-of-merger-monopoly-and-market-undertakings-and-orders#history.

14 The appropriate approach may vary from case to case. For example, minor issues may be dealt with by CMA staff without the need to appoint a group of panel members. The appointment of panel members to form groups will be conducted in a manner consistent with the Rules of Procedure for CMA Groups.

15 The RG will be a sub-committee of the Case and Policy Committee, accountable to the CMA Board. The RG will follow broadly the same approach to its decision making as other groups of panel members.

16 Under the ERRA13, the Chair of the CMA is responsible for identifying and appointing the group of members that will conduct a particular inquiry and for selecting one of them to act as chair of the group. In practice, the Chair of the CMA will delegate these responsibilities to the CMA Panel Chair (or one of the CMA Inquiry Chairs). The CMA Panel Chair is a member of the CMA Board.

17 There may be a delay between the public announcement and the publication of the information in paragraph 3.13 if, for example, the group has not yet been appointed.

18 For example, the Office of Rail Regulation (ORR) in the Rolling Stock Leasing Market Investigation Order 2009.

19 The CMA's approach to the disclosure of specified information **to** other public authorities, including sectoral regulators, is explained in more detail in chapter 6 of *Transparency and disclosure: Statement of the CMA's policy and approach* (CMA6).

20 The CMA's approach to information received **from** sectoral regulators is set out at paragraphs 6.20 and 6.21 of the *Chairman's Guidance on Disclosure of Information in Merger Inquiries, Market Investigations and Reviews of Undertakings and Orders accepted or made under the Enterprise Act 2002 and Fair Trading Act 1973* (April 2013, CC7 (revised)).

THE PROCESS FOR A REVIEW

Timescale

3.17 Once the group has been appointed, it will decide upon an appropriate timetable for the review. The CMA will endeavour to conduct its review as efficiently as possible. However, the time taken to conduct a review will vary depending on the complexity of the issues involved, the available resources at the time and the extent to which parties engage in a timely manner.

3.18 The CMA will publish on www.gov.uk/cma an administrative timetable for the review that will assist in providing an indication of the expected time frame for the review. The administrative timetable will set out the key stages of the review, including what documents the CMA expects to publish and when. The administrative timetable may be revised during the course of the review.

The CMA's assessment

3.19 As part of the CMA's assessment it will first consider whether the initial submissions from all relevant parties are sufficient to allow it to reach a provisional decision:

- if the CMA considers that relevant parties have had sufficient opportunity to make their case and the initial submissions indicate a clear change of circumstances and clear cut grounds for variation or termination, it will provisionally decide whether the undertakings or order should be varied or terminated and, if so, how (see paragraphs 3.24 to 3.30 for the process thereafter). This approach is likely to be used in only the most straightforward of cases, such as where no material concerns have been expressed by third parties in response to the invitation to comment (see paragraph 3.6). Where variations are minor or urgent, the CMA will seek to deal with these as swiftly as possible,[21]
- if the CMA considers that further information and/or analysis is necessary before it can reach a provisional decision, it will consider what steps should be undertaken and how the further information and/or analysis required affects the timetable for the review. This approach is likely to be required in most reviews.

3.20 Where the CMA has identified the need for further information and/or analysis, it may invite or request submissions from those parties subject to the undertakings or order and/or interested third parties, including those that have not responded to any initial invitation to comment (see paragraph 3.6). In certain circumstances, particularly complex reviews,[22] the CMA may consider it necessary to hold a hearing with relevant parties.

3.21 The timing and manner of engagement with relevant parties will vary depending on the type of work involved in any given review. The CMA will have regard to the need to ensure due process for both parties directly involved and other interested persons. The CMA will also have regard to the need to conduct reviews effectively and efficiently, and the need to reach properly reasoned decisions.

3.22 Where the CMA wishes to test some of its initial thinking on the review, the CMA may decide to disclose working papers or sections of working papers to parties for comment. The CMA will take a flexible approach to sharing its developing thinking and/or evidence with parties directly involved and other interested persons, having regard to the desirability of ensuring that such parties are kept informed of key developments in the progress of the review. In most cases, however, the process of putting back materials to parties will be primarily to comment on factual accuracy and commercial sensitivity.

3.23 When considering what documents may be disclosed during the course of a review, the CMA will have regard to the *Chairman's Guidance on Disclosure of Information in Merger Inquiries, Market Investigations and Reviews of Undertakings and Orders accepted or made under the Enterprise Act 2002 and Fair Trading Act 1973* (CC7 (revised)). The Chairman's Guidance also provides information to parties on how information and submissions received by the CMA during its review will typically be disclosed, the usual form being the incorporation of relevant material into the CMA's published documents, including the initial invitation to comment, provisional decision, final decision and/or notice of intention to vary or terminate a remedy.[23]

NOTES

21 For example, the CC's review of FirstGroup's Scotrail undertakings in 2012 was completed in three months.

22 For example, where there are changes in market conditions which require detailed analysis or where the change of circumstances suggests a range of possible variations for the undertakings or order.

23 Part 9 of CC7 (revised) explains the practical aspects of handling information received and requests for confidentiality, including the presentation of data in aggregated form in the CMA's documents.

Key stages of the CMA's decision-making process

3.24 The CMA's decision-making process will typically comprise the following three key stages:

- a provisional decision (see paragraphs 3.25 to 3.30)
- a final decision (see paragraphs 3.31 to 3.32), and, as necessary,
- implementation notices and documents – a Notice of intention to vary or terminate and a Notice of variation or termination (see paragraphs 3.33 to 3.35).

Provisional decision

3.25 Before reaching a final decision, the group will make a provisional decision on which it will consult. The provisional decision will be published on www.gov.uk/cma. The consultation period will depend on the circumstances of the case but will typically be 21 days from the date of the provisional decision, and will be no less than 14 days.

3.26 The CMA's provisional decision will state what decision the CMA proposes to take and the reasons underpinning it. The provisional decision will address the question of whether there has been a change of circumstances. If the CMA is proposing a variation to the terms of the undertaking or order, at the time of publishing the provisional findings it will also seek views on the nature and scope of the proposed variation either as part of the provisional decision (see paragraphs 3.28 and 3.29) or in a separate notice of possible variation (see paragraph 3.30).

3.27 The CMA will consider variations proposed by parties (if any) as well as its own proposals. Parties will be expected to explain how their proposed variations will effectively address the competition problem and its adverse effects in light of the change of circumstances provisionally identified.[24] The CMA will normally set out a time limit within which any proposed variations must be submitted.

3.28 Usually the CMA will form a provisional decision on the substance of the necessary variation at the same time as the change of circumstances and will seek views on the proposed variation prior to consulting on the text of revised undertakings or a revised order. In these cases, the provisional decision will therefore also contain sufficient detail on the nature and scope of any proposed variations (if variation is appropriate) to provide a firm basis for subsequent implementation (see paragraphs 3.33 to 3.35).

3.29 In some reviews, the case for termination or the precise nature of the appropriate variation may be sufficiently clear at the time of making the provisional decision that the CMA may be in a position to draft the text of revised undertakings or a revised order at the same time as its provisional decision. The CMA may therefore decide to set out its provisional decision and reasoning as part of a notice of intention to vary or terminate the undertakings or order.[25] Such a notice will be given in accordance with the procedural requirements set out in Schedule 10 to the EA02 (see paragraphs 3.33 to 3.35).

3.30 At the time of consultation on the provisional decision, the precise nature of the variation may not always, however, have been decided upon. For example, there may be some circumstances in which the party or parties subject to the undertakings or order have not engaged in discussion of possible variations prior to the publication of the CMA's provisional decision.[26] In these circumstances, the CMA may consider it appropriate to consult on a range of possible variations. In order to do so, the CMA will publish a separate notice of possible variations at the same time as its provisional decision (which would focus on the change of circumstances only).[27] This separate notice of possible variations will set out the range of possible variations which the CMA is considering given the change of circumstances identified.

NOTES

24 The CMA will have regard to its guidance for assessing remedies when considering variations (see *Guidelines for Market Investigations* (CC3 (revised)) and *Merger Remedies: Competition Commission Guidelines* (CC8)).

25 This process was adopted, for example, in the reviews of the Store cards and Home credit market investigation orders (final decisions in both cases published in 2011).

26 This might be because the question of whether or not there is a change of circumstances is not clear cut and hence the CMA will need to reach a view on that first before engaging in discussions on possible variations.

27 This process was adopted, for example, in the review of ITV's Contracts Rights Renewal undertakings (2010).

Final decision

3.31 The CMA will consider all submissions received during the consultation period before reaching a final decision. The final decision and the reasons for it will be published.

3.32 If the final decision is that there has been no change of circumstances, or that the change of circumstances is not sufficient to warrant any variation or termination, the existing undertakings or order remain in force and continue to bind the parties.

Documents relating to implementation of any variation or termination

3.33 If the final decision is that there has been a change of circumstances and that variation or termination is appropriate, at the same time as the CMA's final decision or as soon as possible thereafter the CMA will give notice of its intention to vary or terminate the undertakings or order (unless the process has already been commenced, see paragraph 3.29). Such notice shall be given in accordance with the procedural requirements set out in Schedule 10 to the EA02. Changes to undertakings will be consulted upon for at least 15 days and changes to an order will be consulted upon for at least 30 days.[28]

3.34 The CMA will have regard to any representations made in response to the notice and may make modifications to the proposed revised undertakings or order as a result. If the CMA considers that any representation necessitates material change to the proposed revised undertakings or order, it will give notice of the proposed modifications with a further consultation period of no less than seven days.

3.35 In the absence of any representations, or in the event that the CMA decides on consideration of representations made not to amend materially the revised undertakings or order, it will proceed with accepting revised undertakings or making a revised order by issuing a Notice of variation. Similarly, in the absence of any representations to a Notice of intention to terminate the undertakings or order, the CMA will proceed with releasing parties from the undertakings or revoking the order by issuing a Notice of release or Notice of revocation.

NOTES

28 Schedule 10, paragraph 7(2) of the EA02.

Conclusion of a review

3.36 The CMA's review concludes either once a final decision has been made that there is no change of circumstances (see paragraph 3.32) or once the undertakings or order have been varied or terminated (see paragraph 3.35).[29]

3.37 The group appointed to undertake the review will normally be disbanded following the conclusion of the CMA's review.[30]

3.38 When the CMA gives notice of varying or terminating undertakings or an order, it will make any appropriate amendment to its published register of orders and undertakings. The CMA is responsible for monitoring and enforcing any undertakings and orders that remain in force, except where specifically indicated otherwise.

NOTES

29 A review may also be concluded if a new market investigation reference is made under section 131 of the EA02 by the CMA Board, or by the Secretary of State (sections 132 and 140A of the EA02), or by a sectoral regulator, which relates to the existing undertakings or order under review. In these exceptional circumstances, the CMA will notify relevant parties that this action is being taken and publish the fact the review is concluding on www.gov.uk/cma. The existing undertakings or order remain in force and continue to bind the parties unless or until such time as varied or terminated following the market investigation.

30 See paragraph 3.12.

PROCEDURE WHERE UNDERTAKINGS OR ORDERS ARE TIME-EXPIRED, LAPSED OR SUPERSEDED BY NEW CMA UNDERTAKINGS OR ORDERS

3.39 There may be cases in which undertakings or orders are time-expired or have lapsed as the result of a predetermined event, or where they have been superseded by new CMA undertakings or orders. For example:

- where undertakings or an order contain within them a time period for their application which has ended or where undertakings or orders contain an expiry date which has passed
- where undertakings or an order specify that they will expire upon a certain event happening, or
- where they are superseded by new undertakings or a new order resulting from a new CMA inquiry.[31]

3.40 In the case of such time-expired, lapsed or superseded undertakings or orders, there is no requirement for further investigation or consultation, as the undertakings or orders will already have time-expired, lapsed or been superseded. In such circumstances, the CMA will remove the undertakings or orders from its register of orders and undertakings, notify the parties subject to the undertakings or order, and publish a notice that the order or undertakings have been removed.

NOTES

31 For example, as was the case in the groceries market where the Groceries Supply Code of Practice superseded the Supermarkets Code of Practice.

A. STATUS OF THE OFT AND THE CC GUIDANCE DOCUMENTS AND PUBLICATIONS

[3.46]

A.1 The table below indicates the status of the OFT and the CC documents and publications that are relevant to the variation and termination of merger, monopoly and market undertakings and orders and that had been published and were in effect prior to the transfer of the mergers and markets functions to the CMA on 1 April 2014. Certain of those documents have been adopted by the CMA Board in order to facilitate transition to the new UK mergers and markets regime, and to minimise disruption to parties and the CMA.

OFT/CC Code	Title	Status of document	
		Replaced/ obsolete[1]	Adopted by the CMA Board[2]
OFT1060	Memorandum of understanding between the OFT and the CC on the variation and termination of merger, monopoly and market undertakings and orders under the Fair Trading Act 1973 and the Enterprise Act 2002	√	
CC1	Competition Commission: Rules of Procedure	√	-
OFT1254/CC2	Merger Assessment Guidelines	-	√
CC3 (revised)	Guidelines for Market Investigations	-	√
CC7 (revised)	Chairman's Guidance on Disclosure of Information in Merger Inquiries, Market Investigations and Reviews of Undertakings and Orders accepted or made under the Enterprise Act 2002 and Fair Trading Act 1973	-	√
CC8	Merger Remedies: Competition Commission Guidelines	-	√
OFT953	Prioritisation principles	√	-

NOTES

1 The OFT and the CC publications listed in this column have, with effect from 1 April 2014, been replaced, or rendered obsolete, by the CMA guidance or publications.

2 The OFT and the CC publications listed in this column have been adopted by the CMA Board (subject to any guidance

prepared by the CMA in the future).

A.2 Parties should refer to those documents listed above as having been adopted by the CMA Board (the adopted guidance) for further details on the substance and procedure around the variation and termination of merger, monopoly and market undertakings and orders. This is subject, in particular, to the following general limitations:

- all references in the adopted guidance listed above to issues regarding the variation and termination of undertakings and orders or jurisdiction or procedure in mergers and markets cases must be read in the light of this guidance and *Mergers: Guidance on the CMA's jurisdiction and procedure* (CMA2) and *Market Studies and Market Investigations: Supplemental guidance on the CMA's approach* (CMA3)
- in the cases of conflict between this guidance and the adopted guidance, this guidance prevails, and
- all the adopted guidance should be read subject to the following cross-cutting amendments:
  - references to the 'OFT' or the 'CC' (except where referring to specific past OFT or CC practice or case law), should be read as referring to the CMA
  - references to 'referral to the CC' or 'a reference to the CC' should be read as referring to the referral of a case by the CMA (or Secretary of State) of a case for a Phase 2 investigation involving an Inquiry Group of the CMA panel members
  - references to articles of the EC Treaty should be read as referring to the equivalent articles of the Treaty on the Functioning of the European Union
  - certain OFT or CC departments, teams or individual roles may not be replicated in the CMA, or may have been renamed; a copy of the CMA's organisational chart is available on www.gov.uk/cma, and
  - parties should check any contact details against those listed on www.gov.uk/cma, which will be the most up to date.

COMPETITION IMPACT ASSESSMENT (CMA50, PART 1: OVERVIEW (SEPTEMBER 2015))

[3.47]

NOTES

1. PURPOSE AND SCOPE OF THESE GUIDELINES

[3.48]

1.1 The Competition and Markets Authority (CMA) is a non-ministerial government department, established by the Enterprise and Regulatory Reform Act 2013, to carry out certain functions on behalf of the Crown. The CMA's stated mission is to make markets work well for consumers, businesses and the economy. In pursuit of this mission, the CMA can give information and advice to Ministers and their departments in respect of any proposed changes in law, regulation or policy.[1]

1.2 The CMA can provide advice and training, on request, to policymakers and other specialists (economists and lawyers) who are introducing a new measure and need to understand whether the changes are likely to have an impact on competition in existing or new markets.

1.3 Given that the CMA has limited resources, policymakers should in the first instance conduct their own assessment of whether or not their proposals will have an impact on competition. This publication aims to help policymakers conduct such an assessment. Where there is a complex competition or consumer issue, the CMA may be able to provide further assistance and support.

NOTES

1 Section 7(1), Enterprise Act 2002.

WHY CONSIDER THE IMPACT A POLICY OR REGULATORY PROPOSAL WILL HAVE ON COMPETITION?

1.4 Competition is a process of rivalry between firms and, where it is effective, encourages firms to deliver benefits to customers in terms of lower prices, higher quality and more choice.

1.5 Competing firms may focus on offering the lowest price, particularly where products are standardised. Most suppliers[2] will try to compete in a number of ways in addition to price, for example by developing new improved products, by offering products of differing quality or characteristics, by branding and advertising the differences in their products relative to their competitors', or by using different sales channels. This list is not exhaustive. Competing suppliers will seek to find a unique selling point that offers consumers advantages over rival goods or services.

1.6 The CMA's publication on Productivity and Competition: a summary of the evidence outlines the theoretical and empirical evidence on the relationship between competition and productivity. The evidence suggests that competition drives productivity in three main ways. First, within firms, competition acts as a disciplining device, placing pressure on the managers of firms to become more efficient. Secondly, competition ensures that more productive firms increase their market share at the expense of the less productive. These low productivity firms may then exit the market, to be replaced by higher productivity firms. Thirdly, and perhaps most importantly, competition drives firms to innovate, coming up with new products and production processes which can lead to step-changes in efficiency.

1.7 Laws, regulations and government interventions that bear on economic activity can restrict competition in a market. There is a significant body of literature demonstrating that removing regulatory restrictions on markets can have a positive impact on competition.[3] There is also strong evidence that low levels of product market regulation tend to be associated with greater productivity. Removing unnecessary restraints on competition, or preventing the introduction of unnecessarily restrictive regulations can ensure government supports competition, productivity and economic growth.

1.8 Policymakers in the UK Government who seek Reducing Regulation Committee clearance for their regulatory proposal may need to conduct an impact assessment. The Better Regulation Framework Manual states that, as part of the impact assessment process, policymakers should consider whether the proposal might have an impact on competition.[4] If the policy is likely to have an impact on competition, policymakers should carry out further analysis of the impact on competition. These guidelines provide policymakers and economists with assistance in identifying markets that might be affected by a new policy and in undertaking a competition impact assessment.

1.9 Whilst impact assessment processes in the Devolved Administrations differ, these guidelines should also provide a framework to help policymakers working in Devolved Administrations to consider the impact of their policies on competition.

1.10 Early consideration of the competition implications of a policy may also help to mitigate the risk that the CMA raises concerns about a policy once the proposal becomes draft legislation. The Small Business, Enterprise and Employment Act 2015 amended Section 7 of the Enterprise Act 2002 to give the CMA a new power, to use at its discretion, to make and publish written recommendations to ministers on the impact of proposals for legislation on competition within any UK market(s) for goods or services.[5] Considering competition early in the policy making process may mean that the CMA is less likely to publicly comment at a later date.

1.11 These guidelines replace an earlier version published by the Office of Fair Trading in 2007 and should be read in conjunction with the Better Regulation Executive's Better Regulation Framework Manual and the Treasury Green Book.

1.12 These guidelines are written for policymakers and do not assume technical knowledge or understanding of economics. However, the CMA recommends that at an early stage in the process policymakers advise their departmental specialists (economists and lawyers) that they are considering the effect of the proposed policy on competition.

1.13 Policymakers and economists who wish to speak to the CMA about undertaking a competition assessment with complex issues or who want to request further explanation of this document or training should email us at advocacy@cma.gsi.gov.uk.

NOTES

2 The term 'suppliers' includes any private entity, any public body acting in as an 'undertaking' engaging in economic activity, and any not-for-profit firm that is competing in the market.

3 For a fuller review of the literature please see CMA (2015), Productivity and Competition: a review of the evidence.

4 The Better Regulation Framework Manual was published under the last administration and provides further guidance on when Reducing Regulation Committee clearance is needed and when an impact assessment should accompany clearance requests

5 For more information about the power to comment, see: CMA (2015), CMA gains power to make written recommendations on proposals for legislation.

2. WHAT YOU NEED TO DO TO COMPLETE A COMPETITION IMPACT ASSESSMENT

[3.49]

2.1 In order to compete a competition impact assessment, policymakers need to conduct the steps shown in Figure 1 below.

Figure 1: Completing a competition impact assessment

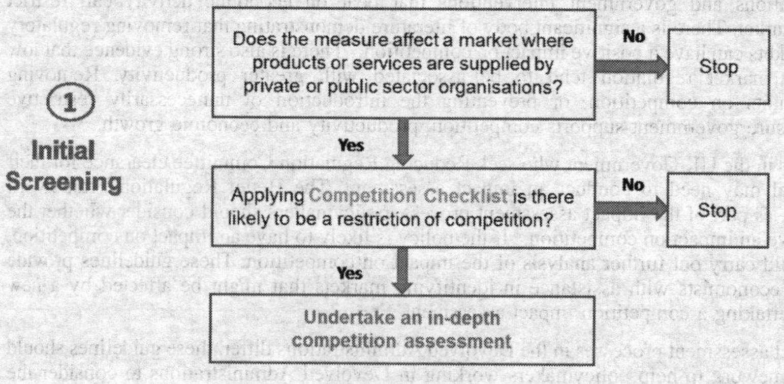

Competition checklist

1	**Will the measure directly or indirectly limit the number or range of suppliers?**
2	**Will the measure limit the ability of suppliers to compete?**
3	**Will the measure limit suppliers' incentives to compete vigorously?**
4	**Will the measure limit the choices and information available to consumers?**

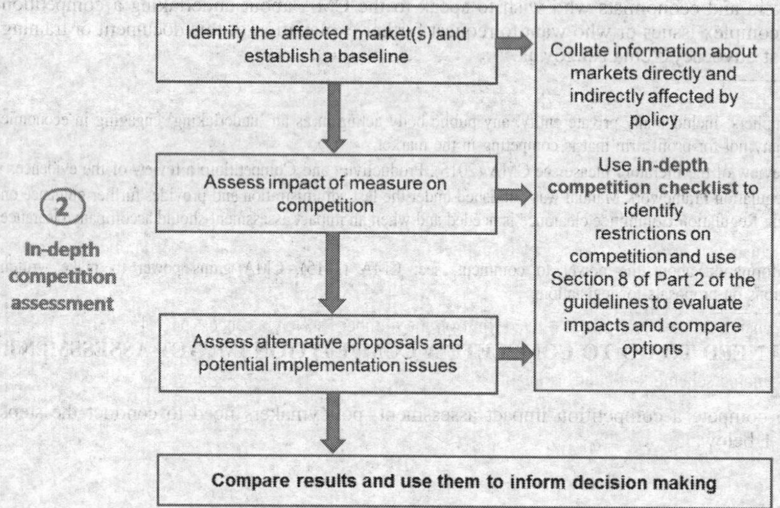

STAGE 1: INITIAL SCREENING

2.2 Before starting the impact assessment, policymakers should set out the purpose of their proposed measure.[6] This requires policymakers to think about why government intervention is necessary. Once the purpose of the new measure has been understood, it is important to undertake an initial screening to see whether an in-depth assessment of the impact on competition is warranted.

2.3 Step 1 of the initial screening asks whether the proposal affects a market where products or services are supplied by the private or public sector.[7] It could be that the measure clearly impacts on the supply of certain products or services. For example, a ban on apple advertising would directly impact on the market for apples and potentially the market for fruit. However, in certain cases the proposal may lead to changes in areas where no market exists and there is no possibility of an impact on competition arising from the change. For example, a proposal requiring government departments to be structured in a certain way is unlikely to have a significant impact on a market and, in turn, competition.

2.4 Should a market be affected by the proposal, policymakers should move to the next stage in the initial screening and apply the four questions which form the competition checklist, as set out below. In doing so, it should be possible to identify whether the proposal falls into one of the areas likely to raise concern. A competition concern may be identified if at least one of these conditions outlined in Table 1 below are met.

TABLE 1: COMPETITION CHECKLIST

1	Will the measure directly or indirectly limit the number or range of suppliers?
2	Will the measure limit the ability of suppliers to compete?
3	Will the measure limit suppliers' incentives to compete vigorously?
4	Will the measure limit the choices and information available to consumers?

2.5 If the answer to any of these question is 'yes', then policymakers should move to undertake an in-depth assessment of the likely impact.

NOTES

6 These guidelines are relevant to different types of government intervention, including regulation, changes in entitlement to services, buying or selling assets, and licencing, franchising and contracting. We use the terms proposal and measure to capture the wide range of interventions to which these guidelines are relevant.

7 These guidelines are relevant to proposals that affect existing markets and to proposals that will create new markets, for example, purchasing a new service which is not currently supplied by the private sector.

STAGE 2: IN-DEPTH COMPETITION ASSESSMENT

2.6 Should policymakers consider that an in-depth competition assessment is required then they will then need to identify the affected market(s), establish a baseline and conduct an assessment of the likely impact the policy will have on the market compared to the baseline. Part 2 of these guidelines provides further detail on how to conduct an in-depth assessment.

2.7 In doing so, policymakers should seek to provide an in-depth answer to the relevant competition checklist question(s). These questions are presented in the in-depth competition checklist at Table 2 below.

TABLE 2: IN-DEPTH COMPETITION CHECKLIST

Competition Checklist Question	Reference for further information in Part 2
Q1a: will the measure directly limit the number or range of suppliers by: • Awarding exclusive rights to supply? • Purchasing, franchising or licencing from a single supplier or a restricted group of suppliers? • Introducing a licensing scheme that places a fixed limit on the number of suppliers? • Introducing a licencing scheme that controls quality?	See Chapter 3. Examples to help you consider whether this issue applies to your proposal: • Commercial Use of Public Information (CUPI) market study, page 12, Part 2 • Taxi Licences, page 15, Part 2 • Licensing scheme for will writers, page 17, Part 2
Q1b: will the measure indirectly limit the number or range of suppliers by: • Significantly raising the costs of current suppliers, causing them to leave the market? • Significantly raising the costs of new suppliers relative to existing suppliers? • Significantly raising the costs of some current suppliers relative to other current suppliers?	See Chapter 3. Examples to help you consider whether this issue applies to your proposal: • Grandfathering taxi slots at a train station, page 19 • Competitive neutrality in the higher education sector, page 21
Q2: will the measure limit the ability of suppliers to compete by: • Controlling or substantially influencing the price a supplier may charge? • Controlling or substantially influencing the characteristics of the products supplied?	See Chapter 4. Examples to help you consider whether this issue applies to your proposal: • Price controls in Greece, page 23

Competition Checklist Question	Reference for further information in Part 2
• Limiting the sales channels a supplier can use, or the geographic area in which a supplier can operate? • Substantially restricting the ability of suppliers to advertise their products? • Introducing restrictions on production processes or how suppliers are governed?	• Price caps in the payday lending sector, page 24-25 • Regulating the quality of bottled water, page 26 • US motor vehicle manufacturers, page 28
Q3: will the measure limit suppliers' incentives to compete vigorously by:	See Chapter 5.
• Incentivising suppliers to coordinate activities over which they would ordinarily compete?	Examples to help you consider whether this issue applies to your proposal: • Risks created by policies that encourage information sharing, page 32
Q4: will the measure limit the choices and information available to consumers by: • Limiting the ability of consumers to decide from whom they purchase? • Changing the information available to consumers but not improving their ability to make informed decisions? • Increasing the cost of changing supplier?	See Chapter 6.

2.8 Conducting the in-depth impact assessment may require the policymaker to:

- consider whether the reasoning and issues outlined in the relevant chapters in Part 2 applies to their policy proposal;
- gather further information through engagement with suppliers and customers to get a better indication of what impact the proposal will have on supplier and consumer incentives in the affected markets; and/or
- employ more sophisticated empirical techniques to assess the likely impact of the proposal on price, quality, quantity and innovation in the affected markets.

2.9 Part 2 sets out in detail how impact can be assessed using both qualitative and quantitative techniques.

Considering alternative policy proposals

2.10 Where a proposal is likely to adversely affect competition in an affected market, policymakers should consider whether there are alternative proposals that will achieve the same policy objective but with less adverse effects. Part 2 provides an overview of some alternatives and the techniques that can be used to compare different options.

2.11 Ideally, alternative policy proposals should be identified that have a less adverse effect on competition but still enable policy objectives to be achieved. If this not possible, then, as a principle of good policy making, it is important that the issue is raised in discussions with decision makers and there is a clear justification as to whether and why other considerations are trumping the impact on markets.

Predicting implementation issues

2.12 Policymakers should also consider the means by which the measure is implemented. It may be the case that implementation creates competition issues that were not foreseen at the consultation or early stage of impact assessment.

2.13 For example, a consultation following the initial impact assessment might conclude that changes to product standards are required. So, for example, a consultation on the roll-out of solar panels might conclude that minimum efficiency standards are required in order for solar panel firms to be eligible for a subsidy. Such a requirement might distort the market for panels themselves as fewer models or manufacturers might be compliant than originally envisaged. The price for solar panels might subsequently be higher than was originally envisaged when a competitive market with a full range of suppliers was predicted.

2.14 When policymakers use the consultation process to check data and information about the market(s) affected by their proposals, they should remain aware that views expressed, or data or information supplied, may be selective and could well reflect vested interests. Policymakers should carefully consider stakeholders' interests when assessing the validity of their views and whether the evidence supports assertions made.

Plan to evaluate impact on competition

2.15 It is also advisable at an early stage of the policy making process to consider how to evaluate the impact of a regulatory proposal. HM Treasury's Green Book provides further guidance of evaluating policies against their stated objectives.

2.16 Table 3 below provides further insight into the types of indicator and data that could usefully be analysed to determine whether the policy has had a negative impact on competition. Most of these can either be directly observed, drawn from readily available public sources or developed using limited research and basic analysis.

TABLE 3: PLANNING TO EVALUATE IMPACT ON COMPETITION

Has the policy led to worsening market trends, demand and supply conditions . . .	. . . and have market outcomes got worse?
Market trends	• Reduction in product diversity or production of close substitutes
• Significant increase in market concentration levels	• Increase in prices
• Reduction in market entry, expansion and exit	• Decrease in consumption levels
Availability of information to consumers	• Reduction in efficiency
• Reduction in availability of useful information	• Decrease in quality of supply
• Increase in the complexity of information	
Entry and expansion conditions	
• Increase in the cost of entering and operating at the Minimum Efficient Scale needed to achieve reasonably competitive level of costs	
• Decrease in the likelihood of entry within a timescale that would affect incumbents' incentives	
• Firms becoming more capacity constrained	
• Increase in the cost of exiting the market	
Firms' behaviour	
• Closer correlation between firms' behaviour (eg investment decisions and pricing decisions)	
• Retrenchment into 'core' territories and a reduction in head-to-head competition	
• A reduction in production of close substitutes	
• Decline or absence of innovation in product characteristics or business models	
Consumer behaviour	
• More obstacles to switching between suppliers	
• Reduction in switching levels	
• Increase in firms exploiting behavioural biases	

POSITIVE IMPACT ON COMPETITION

2.17 These guidelines are designed to help policymakers analyse whether policy proposals will have a negative impact on competition. Nevertheless, the guidelines may also be useful for policymakers seeking to introduce pro-competitive policy changes. For example, the four competition impact assessment questions explored in the guidance can be reversed to identify potentially pro-competitive measures:

- Does the proposal directly or indirectly increase the number or range of suppliers?
- Does the proposal remove restrictions on the ability of suppliers to compete?
- Does the proposal increase suppliers' incentives to compete?
- Does the proposal allow consumers to make more informed choices?

2.18 Considering whether a policy may have a pro-competitive effect is important as measures that increase competition can reasonably be expected to drive economic growth and benefit society.

COMPETITION IMPACT ASSESSMENT (CMA50, PART 2: GUIDELINES (SEPTEMBER 2015))

[3.50]

NOTES

1. SUMMARY

[3.51]

1.1 Healthy competition between firms in a market can deliver benefits to consumers through lower prices, more choice and innovation and can help increase productivity and growth. This publication aims to help policymakers design proposals[1] that support competition. It does so by providing detail on how to conduct an in-depth assessment of the impact a proposal will have on competition.

Part 3 CMA and other Guidelines

1.2 Policymakers should conduct an in-depth competition assessment if their proposals:

1	Directly or indirectly limit the number or range of suppliers
2	Limit the ability of suppliers to compete
3	Limit suppliers' incentives to compete vigorously
4	Limit the choices and information available to consumers

1.3 This document provides policymakers and analysts with guidelines in how to conduct an in-depth competition assessment. The document should be read alongside Part 1 which provides an overview of the competition impact assessment process. Policymakers and analysts should refer to the appropriate chapter in this document depending on what competition issue is likely to affect their proposal. The document is structured as follows:[2]

- Chapter 2 addresses how to identify the affected markets and establish a baseline
- Chapter 3 outlines competition checklist question 1 – will the measure directly or indirectly limit the number or range of suppliers?
- Chapter 4 outlines competition checklist question 2 – will the measure limit the ability of suppliers to compete?
- Chapter 5 outlines competition checklist question 3 – will the measure limit suppliers' incentives to compete vigorously?
- Chapter 6 outlines competition checklist question 4 – will the measure limit the choices or information available to consumers?
- Chapter 7 considers alternatives
- Chapter 8 outlines methodologies that can be used to assess impact

NOTES

1 These guidelines are relevant to different types of government intervention, including regulation, changes in entitlement to services, buying or selling assets, and licencing, franchising and contracting. We use the terms proposal and measure to capture the wide range of interventions to which these guidelines may be relevant.

2 Chapters 1–7 of the guidelines have been written by the Competition and Markets Authority (CMA). Chapter 8 was written by Sean Ennis, a Senior Economist in the OECD's Competition Division. We are very grateful for Sean's support and to others who commented on earlier drafts.

2. IDENTIFYING AFFECTED MARKETS AND ESTABLISHING A BASELINE

[3.52]

2.1 The starting point for any in-depth assessment of the impact a proposal might have on competition should be to look at the product and geographic market affected by the measure. A product market for the purposes of this guidance comprises all those products and/or services which are regarded as interchangeable or substitutable by their consumers. A geographic market comprises the area in which the firms concerned compete in the supply of products or services. Depending upon the circumstances, it could be local, regional, national or international.[3] No formal market definition is needed for a competition impact assessment but it is useful to identify:

- products and geographical areas which are directly impacted by the measure;
- wider product markets which might be indirectly affected;
- wider geographic market which might be indirectly affected; and
- related upstream or downstream markets.

2.2 Developing an understanding of the affected markets can help to determine the likely impact of the proposal, will help to assess whether the proposed measure will have the desired effect (particularly if the aim is to reduce or change patterns of consumption) and will make it easier to identify what information needs to be collected and from whom in order to assess the impact of the proposal.

2.3 It might be the case, for example, that on closer analysis a regulatory proposal actually affects two or more economic markets. The impact of the proposal might be different in these different markets depending on the extent and nature of competition in these markets. If one market were more concentrated than the other, then the impact of a new regulation might potentially lead to a greater reduction in competition in the concentrated market.

2.4 Alternatively, it might be the case that the economic market is wider than those suppliers directly affected by the regulation. As outlined in the hypothetical example below, suppliers in the wider market might act as a source of competitive constraint on suppliers affected by a regulatory proposal. The extent to which affected suppliers could pass on the costs of regulation to consumers may be limited as a result of the competition they face from the wider geographic market.

2.5 Further it may be the case that customers will switch from buying the product or service affected by the measure to alternative products or services which are not affected. Such switching may also affect the extent to which the policy achieves its desired effect. The extent to which they will do so will depend on the willingness and ability of consumers to switch and the willingness and ability of suppliers to increase their production.

NOTES

3 See Market definition: OFT403, adopted by the CMA Board.

THE WIDER PRODUCT MARKET

2.6 Consideration should be given to whether or not the proposal will affect wider product markets, including those products or services that may be indirectly affected by the measure because consumers or suppliers would substitute to other products in response to the new measure.

New regulation requiring professional towel laundering imposed on hairdressers

Suppose a new regulation was proposed that required all towels used in a hair-dressing salon to be laundered professionally. The proposal would affect hair-dressing salons. The regulation would raise hairdressers' costs directly. Hairdressers would likely respond by raising their prices. Consumers, faced with higher prices in hairdressers' salons, may choose to have their hair cut elsewhere where the regulation did not apply and there was no increase in price. Hairdressers themselves may respond by offering to cut hair at customers' homes or in any other location than a salon.

THE WIDER GEOGRAPHIC MARKET

2.7 Policymakers should consider whether the wider geographic market will be affected by the proposal. Geographic markets may be local, regional, national or international. While policies may be limited in their jurisdiction they may have wider effects because of the ability of consumers and suppliers to purchase or supply in a broader geographic area.

New regulation imposed on hairdressers (continued)

Extending the hypothetical example above, the restriction on hairdressers requiring hairdressers to launder towels professionally may be introduced only in England. Customers living near the English borders could switch to having their hair cut in Scotland or Wales to circumvent the effect of the regulation (and higher prices in England). In effect the regulation will lead to a step change in costs and prices leading to a diversion along the borders away from English hairdressers. Policymakers might wish to quantify this effect to see if it makes a material difference to the effectiveness of the regulation they are seeking to introduce.

RELATED UPSTREAM OR DOWNSTREAM MARKETS

2.8 When identifying affected markets it is important to consider whether or not there will be knock-on effects in related upstream and downstream markets. In making this assessment, policymakers should identify the supply chain for the product or service affected by the proposed measure.

2.9 In doing so, policymakers will need to consider the effect of their proposals on suppliers of inputs required to produce the affected product and those who distribute, wholesale or retail the affected products. This requires a reasonable understanding of the production process – where policymakers do not have this information, they should use the consultation process to gather it. In general one would expect the supply chain to respond to regulations that increase demand for a product (such as microchips for dog tagging in the example below). The question that is relevant to policymakers is over what time and at what price.

Regulation requiring microchipping dogs

Suppose there were concern about stray dogs, and policymakers wanted to introduce a regulation that would require all dogs to be fitted with microchip identification tags. The aim of the policy is to reduce irresponsible dog ownership. Local authorities and charities can no longer bear the cost of having to treat and care for abandoned dogs. Policymakers have been advised that it would be sensible to allow pet shop owners who have received the relevant training to fit microchips in dogs.

What markets would be affected?

The proposed regulation would have a direct impact on the services provided to dog owners. Vets and pet shop owners would need to undertake training, acquire equipment and fit tags in dogs. The cost of this would likely be borne by dog owners who would need to pay more for dogs and dog ownership. The wider market for 'companion animals' might also be affected. The increased cost associated with dog ownership may lead some pet owners to switch to ownership of other pets. Related upstream markets would also be affected by this proposal including:

- UK trainers providing training to vets and pet shop owners
- UK or overseas manufacturers, wholesalers, and retailers of microchips
- UK or overseas manufacturers, wholesalers, and retailers of microchip scanners

What could be the potential competition issues?

The regulation could create a large fixed cost for all vets and pet shop owners who have to provide dog tagging. Fixed costs (those do not vary depending on the number of dogs tagged) could create a barrier to entry and result in dampening of competition in markets for veterinary services and pet supplies. Policymakers would need to assess the impact of these costs relative to likely overall firm revenues after the implementation of the regulatory reform to assess the likely effects.

Related upstream markets will need to expand their capacity in order to respond to the increased demand for microchipping. It would be useful to analyse over what time period existing or new suppliers would be able to respond to the increase in demand. If existing providers would remain capacity constrained and entry is costly, it may be that incumbent upstream suppliers would be able to charge higher amounts for the inputs needed to fit tags.

Policymakers could check with upstream suppliers whether or not they would be able to supply sufficient microchips, training and scanners to meet demand for these inputs. These parties may also be able to provide information on the cost of the inputs and the level of current demand, as well as their estimates of the impact of the regulation on prices, which would allow policymakers to estimate the cost of the proposed regulation.

ESTABLISH A BASELINE

2.10 Once the affected markets have been identified, policymakers will then need to identify the baseline option against which to assess the impact of the proposal. This is often the 'do nothing' option considered as the baseline in the wider Impact Assessment.

2.11 To identify this baseline, policymakers should collate information on:

- the characteristics of products and services in the markets affected by the proposed regulation;
- the nature of competition, including whether competition is between relatively standardised products focused on price, or whether competition is focused on product quality and differentiation; and
- basic indicators of the strength of competition/market power.

2.12 For the baseline it is also important to gauge the current state of competition in both directly and indirectly affected markets. The CMA's guidance on assessment of market power sets out how this can be done.[4] Relevant factors include the ease with which customers can switch between competing products and services and ease with which new suppliers can enter the market (and the history of recent entry).

2.13 Where new markets will be created by measure (such as markets for trading permits) there may be no baseline information and the impact of the proposal may need to be considered from scratch.

NOTES

4 CMA guidance (2014), Assessment of market power: OFT415.

3. COMPETITION QUESTION 1 – WILL THE MEASURE DIRECTLY OR INDIRECTLY LIMIT THE NUMBER OR RANGE OF SUPPLIERS?

[3.53]

3.1 Regulations might reduce competition directly (by placing limits on who can participate in a market) or indirectly (by raising costs and resulting in firms leaving the market or by reducing entry and subsequently enhancing the market power for the firms that remain), which may lead to price increases or a reduction in choice for consumers.[5] A reduction in the number of firms in the market might also increase the risk of collusive behaviour amongst suppliers leading to customers paying higher prices.[6]

3.2 Given the importance of maintaining competitive pressure on existing suppliers, the first question that policymakers should ask when conducting a competition impact assessment is:

NOTES

5 Market power of suppliers is the ability to profitably increase price, decrease quality, or decrease innovation relative to the levels that would prevail in a competitive market.

6 Whilst a separate consideration to the competition assessment, some regulations, such as requirements to invest in new production methods, will result in a direct cost-driven price increase. This will be particularly likely when the supplier is able to pass on increased costs via a price rise, rather than the costs decreasing the profitability of the firm. A report by the OFT commissioned from RBB Economics shows that the likelihood and extent of cost pass-through by a business differs depending on whether the cost change is firm-specific or industry-wide; the responsiveness of the demand and supply conditions it faces; and the degree of competition between businesses up and down the supply chain.6 For more information please see a report prepared for the OFT by RBB Economics (2014), *Cost pass-through: theory, measurement, and potential policy implications*.

WILL THE MEASURE DIRECTLY LIMIT THE NUMBER OR RANGE OF SUPPLIERS?

3.3 A proposal might directly limit the number or range of suppliers through:

- the award of exclusive rights to supply;
- procurement from a single supplier or a restricted group of suppliers;
- the creation of a licensing scheme that limits the number of suppliers; and
- the creation of a licensing scheme for quality standards.

Will the measure award exclusive rights to supply?

3.4 Exclusive rights to supply exist when an organisation is granted rights by the state to be the sole supplier of goods or services. Historically, suppliers of electricity, natural gas, telecommunications, water, postal services and railways, for example, were granted legal monopoly status – or exclusive rights – to provide the service.

3.5 Policymakers may consider there is a case for granting exclusive rights to supply goods or services where there are natural monopolies[7] and substantial investments in infrastructure are required that may not otherwise be supplied by the private sector. However, even when there is justification, policymakers should take into account that granting an exclusive right to supply amounts to the establishment of a private monopoly. As a result, the granting of exclusive rights may:

- give the firm market power, allowing it to raise prices of the products over which it has exclusive rights; and
- create an opportunity for the firm to leverage market power in related markets.

3.6 Given that the granting of exclusive rights may lead to monopoly pricing and market power, less restrictive ways to achieve the same objectives should be considered.

3.7 One such alternative is to consider distributing exclusive rights through a competitive bidding process known as 'competition *for* the market'.[8] To ensure competition for the market has the desired effect of introducing the threat of competition over time, policymakers should ensure that the length of licences, franchises or contracts is suitable for the market in question. Regular competition for exclusive rights is likely to be beneficial unless there is a requirement for long term investment. Care must also be taken to ensure that the current provider is not placed in an advantageous position relative to others because of its previous experience and other factors relevant to the bidding process.

Exclusive rights to manage the data and communications network to connect smart meters

The Department of Energy & Climate Change granted Smart Data Communications Company Ltd (DCC) a licence in September 2013 to establish and manage the data communications network connecting smart meters to the business systems of energy suppliers, network operators and other authorised service users of the network.

In order to mitigate the risk that DCC faces no competition it has been granted an exclusive licence, through a competitive tender process, for a fixed term.

DCC also operates under an ex-post price control regime whereby Ofgem closely scrutinises costs and revenues to ensure value for money.

3.8 Where exclusive rights are awarded, there may also be a need for further regulation to ensure the monopoly provider does not abuse its market power. In relation to the example above, Ofgem is able to ensure that DCC applies its charging methodology in line with its licence obligations as well as regulating the quality and service levels delivered by DCC.

3.9 Where awarding exclusive rights to supply confer advantages to a vertically integrated provider in downstream markets then policymakers will need to assess the likely impact. The upstream part of the company may, for example, be able to supply inputs to its downstream operations at a lower price than it supplies to its competitors. This would put the vertically integrated company at a competitive advantage with respect to other providers in the downstream market. In extreme cases a dominant position in a market may be conferred. Abuse of a dominant position is an infringement of competition law even where that dominant position is the result of Government action.

Commercial use of public information (CUPI) market study

The OFT's CUPI market study recommended that public sector information holders (PSIHs) should draw a distinction between the information solely gathered and supplied by the PSIH ('unrefined' information) and information that could be competitively supplied ('refined' information). The study recommended that refined information should be supplied in a way that would not limit or restrict competition. Issues the OFT identified that raised concern included:

- PSIHs were not defining unrefined and refined information so as to separate the monopoly products from those where there were or could be competition for supply.
- PSIHs were not providing businesses with complete knowledge about the information assets they held that could be considered for commercial use and reuse.
- Negotiations over licence terms and licences could be complex and could impose overly restrictive conditions on businesses that wished to use and reuse unrefined information.
- There could be quality of service issues where there were delays in provision by PSIHs or data provided that was not accurate.
- Some PSIHs did not separately account for costs related to unrefined and refined information and even where they did so some costs were not allocated appropriately. It was possible that prices for unrefined information charged to businesses were recovering some costs that should be attributed to refined information. If this was occurring it would have given the PSIH an undue advantage in the sale of refined information products.

As the diagram below shows, limited access to refined information can restrict the extent that downstream competitors can compete to provide refined products:

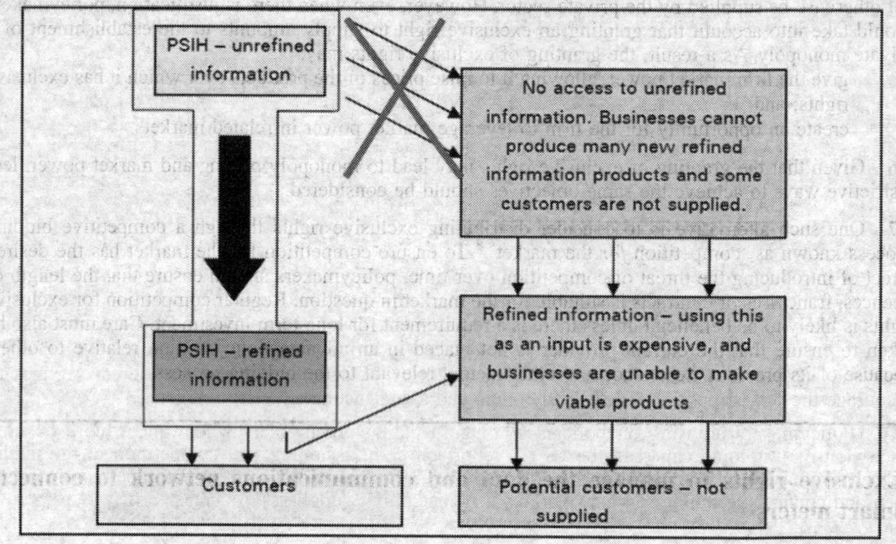

Best practice examples, identified at the time of the OFT study

The Environment Agency took a proactive approach to identifying information to be made available for reuse by developing a topic map and amending the terms on which raw data series were offered for reuse.

The Met Office allocated its indirect/common costs using an activity-based costing approach and separated the information for which it is sole supplier to that where it faces competition from businesses.

Source: *OFT, The commercial use of public information (CUPI) market study, December 2006*

3.10 Where the assessment points to potential distortions in related markets then policymakers might consider steps to mitigate the effect.[9] These include:

- Periodically reviewing special/exclusive rights.
- Separating regulatory powers (for example, granting access to the essential facility and issuing of technical standards) from the task of supplying the goods/services to different operators.[10]
- Considering whether there is a case for functional or structural separation that would prevent cross subsidy from the activity covered by the exclusive rights to downstream markets in which they compete with other providers.[11]
- If not, consider making the monopoly provider set up an activity-based accounting system that distinguishes between activities relating to the supply of goods or services in the sector for which exclusive or special rights are granted and other activities relating to the supply of goods and services.
- Where an essential input is being made available for reuse to all customers this should be on comparable terms to those that the vertically integrated company provide to their own internal operations.

NOTES

7 A natural monopoly is a monopoly in an industry in which it is most efficient (involving the lowest long-run average cost) for production to be permanently concentrated in a single firm rather than contested competitively.

8 Another mitigation is to seek to introduce at least some competition or contestability in part of the value chain. For example, competition introduced in the non-domestic water supply.

9 Autorité de la concurrence, *Guide for competition impact assessment of draft legislation*.

10 A UK example of split ownership in practice – Eurotunnel is operated entirely separately from train companies (such as Eurostar) who use the facility.

11 Structural unbundling as was seen in Ofcom's decision to split BT's wholesale and retail activity into two companies with the creation of BT Openreach.

Will the measure result in procurement from a single supplier or a restricted group of suppliers?

3.11 Large public sector organisations, such as prisons, may purchase all of their requirements from a single supplier. They may do so because they consider it is logistically easier to deal with a single supplier who understands their particular requirements and can supply across a number of regions. There may also be benefits resulting from efficiencies in the procurement administration and lower costs from awarding a single contract.

3.12 However, where a proposal would lead to a single supplier gaining a public sector contract, and that single supplier is the sole supplier or one of a few suppliers in the market, then procurement process is akin to the award of an exclusive right to supply and the same competition issues apply. The benefits of restricted procurement processes should be weighed against the loss of competition and choice.

3.13 As with the awarding of exclusive rights to supply, procurement from a single supplier or a restricted group of suppliers should involve a competitive bidding process. Bidding markets are often used in situations where it is known that there will be no competition in the market, and thus no competitive pressure, to ensure that potential suppliers face competitive pressures in bidding for the contracts.

3.14 In order to maximise competitive pressures in bidding for contracts, policymakers should consider whether the design and implementation of commissioning and procurement policies and processes can be designed to encourage bidding. Long and complex bidding processes can create barriers to entry by increasing the costs of entering public markets and by disproportionately favouring large suppliers and incumbents that will typically have more resource to devote to the bidding process.

3.15 The size of the contract on offer may also limit the number of firms able to bid, and this may itself restrict the number of potential suppliers frequently from managing large contracts, sub-contracts to smaller, and often more specialist, suppliers. In the absence of significant countervailing economies of scale and scope, consideration should be given to disaggregating contracts for different services to encourage the widest possible range of suppliers and avoid incumbency advantages.

3.16 Policymakers advising on policies relating to public procurement who want a more detailed discussion of this topic can read the OFT's report on commissioning and competition in the public sector.[12] An earlier OFT report also provides useful guidance on how to leverage competition to create open and contestable public services markets that incentivise suppliers to increase efficiency, improve quality of service provision and innovate.[13]

NOTES

[12] OFT (2011), *Commissioning and competition in the public sector* (OFT1314).

[13] OFT (2004), *Assessing the impact of public sector procurement on competition* (OFT742a).

Will the measure introduce a licensing scheme that controls market entry through a fixed limit on the number of suppliers?

3.17 In certain sectors such as dentistry, pharmacies and taxis, licensing schemes have been used to limit the number of firms that can operate in the market. The limit may relate to the absolute number of firms that can operate or can be based on population or demand estimates.

3.18 Policymakers may introduce a limit on the number of suppliers because they believe that there is an optimum level of provision in these sectors and too much entry will lead to oversupply, resulting in inefficiency and lack of profitability. As a result, policymakers may set a limit on the number of suppliers or, at the extreme, grant existing suppliers' rights to veto new entry. Such restrictions would protect incumbents from competitive pressure and are likely to result in less competition and consumers will be faced with less choice. Such restrictions may also be used to limit the supply of goods or services of questionable social value or the externalities they give rise to. In these circumstances policy interventions need to be wary of preserving the position of incumbents who may not be the best or most efficient suppliers.

Taxi licences

Imagine there was a concern about the number of taxis competing in a city. Local residents are concerned about congestion and the taxi trade body has written to your minister expressing concerns that their members are likely to be put out of business because of unfair competition from new taxi firms.

One option would be to introduce a licensing system which places a fixed limit on the number of taxis that are allowed to operate in the city.

The impact of such entry restrictions is likely to be an increase in the price of journeys (assuming there is price competition between taxis) and reduced availability. The regulation of taxi licence numbers creates a high probability that supply will reduce below free entry levels, leading to the development of very high licence values, reflecting the existence of large monopoly rents. Consumers will experience reduced service levels and, in most cases, increased prices.

In addition, evidence suggests that restrictive approaches to taxi licensing taken in many countries, together with resulting upward price pressures, leads consumers to substitute away from the taxi industry or to use unlicensed operators. The taxi drivers that the regulation was intended to protect might still ultimately lose out.

For more discussion about taxi licensing please see: Organisation for Economic Co-operation and Development (OECD) (2007) Taxi Services: Competition and Regulation.

3.19 Policymakers may at times seek to promote suppliers from certain regions or small suppliers by limiting the ability of other types of suppliers to participate in a business activity. The OECD, in its latest competition impact assessment guidance,[14] notes that such restrictions are typically excessive and encourages alternatives to be considered such as direct subsidies and/or tax benefits. However the use of direct subsidies must be done in a way that does not raise state aid concerns. Department for Business, Innovation and Skills (BIS) guidance provides an assessment of whether this poses a problem.[15]

NOTES

14 Competition Assessment Toolkit, Volume 3: Operational Manual, June 2015.

15 BIS (2015), State aid: the basics.

Will the measure introduce a licensing scheme that controls market entry through quality standards?

3.20 Licensing is frequently used as a means of ensuring suppliers have achieved a minimum level of competency or are fit to operate in a particular market. In some professions, such as the legal and accountancy professions, only persons holding certain qualifications are allowed to work in that profession. Restrictions such as this are a form of licensing. While benefits may arise in terms of ensuring a consistent standard of service, licensing schemes that control market entry through quality standards can harm competition.

3.21 Setting quality standards through licences may result in reduced numbers of suppliers or professionals in the market which may help to keep fee levels high. The higher standard of provision may also restrict choices and ultimately result in reduced supply for those consumers with low price and low quality preferences.

3.22 Many licensing schemes are self-funding and the cost of entry is directly linked to the licence fee. The cost of new entry should be considered against the revenues that a new entrant could expect to receive. Should licensing costs be high relative to expected revenues then the cost may create a barrier to entry. Further, depending on market conditions, licensing costs may be passed on to consumers in higher prices.

3.23 Given the potential for licensing systems to restrict choice and create barriers to entry, careful consideration should be given to the pros and cons of introducing a licensing scheme.

Introduction of licensing scheme for will writers

The Department for Constitutional Affairs (DCA), now part of the Ministry of Justice, in 2009 found problems in will writing services, notably:

- poorly drafted wills provided by will writers with little experience;
- misleading and high pressure (eg home visits) selling practices, especially to vulnerable consumers;
- no indemnity insurance or redress procedures; and
- potential difficulties of tracing wills when a will writing business ceased trading.

Will writing services are best categorised as 'experience goods', which means it is difficult for the consumer to evaluate the quality of service provided prior to the purchase.

The DCA considered the introduction of a licensing scheme for will writers. The OFT advised that there were pros and cons of introducing a licensing scheme that needed to be considered:

Pros:

- could ensure that suppliers have received a minimum level of competency improving the quality of will writing;
- could prescribe standards that must be followed by suppliers in the market to prevent pressure selling;
- could introduce a requirement to hold indemnity insurance or have a redress scheme; and
- could prescribe how wills are stored to ensure they can be traced when a will writing business ceases trading.

Cons:

- any regulation limiting the number of will writers would result in "rent creating" barriers to entry which reduce competition by giving licensed will writers market power to charge a price premium;
- limits consumer choice in the segment of the market written by will writers; and
- any licensing costs associated with licensing scheme would be expected to give rise to cost-creating barriers to entry and be passed on to consumers in higher prices.

The OFT advocated a less restrictive alternative comprising a consumer code, consumer education campaigns and reliance on existing consumer protection law which was followed by DCA.

For further discussion see the report prepared for the OFT by London Economics (2010), *Evaluation of OFT Competition Advocacy* (OFT866).

WILL THE MEASURE INDIRECTLY LIMIT THE NUMBER OR RANGE OF SUPPLIERS?

3.24 Policymakers undertaking a competition assessment should assess whether the proposals may indirectly limit the number or range of suppliers in a market. A proposal could have this effect if it:

- significantly raises the costs of incumbent firms, causing them to exit the market;
- significantly raises the costs of new suppliers (including small businesses) relative to existing suppliers; and
- significantly raises the costs of some existing suppliers relative to other existing suppliers.

Will the measure raise the costs of incumbent firms and cause them to exit the market?

3.25 A proposal may increase the cost of doing business to such a level that it is no longer profitable to compete in the market. Should sufficient numbers of firms leave the market, or should particular competitors leave the market that were an important source of competitive constraint, then the competitive dynamic may change. Gaining an understanding of which types of business (if any) might leave the market will provide insight into the likely changes in the structure of the market and whether there will be a subsequent reduction in competition.

3.26 In order to assess the impact measure will have on competition, policymakers can ask:
- What are the components of the costs that have to be incurred? Are these costs fixed or variable costs?[16]
- How large are the costs relative to businesses annual sales revenues?
- Will these costs lead businesses to exit the market?
- Which types of businesses are more likely to exit and will there be an ongoing source of competitive constraint in the event of exit?

NOTES

16 If regulations impose high levels of fixed costs these are more likely to represent a barrier to entry than variable costs which vary depending on the scale of production.

Will the measure significantly raise the costs of new suppliers relative to existing suppliers?

3.27 Policies raising the cost of entry may deter entry. Policymakers should consider the risk that policies raise the costs of all new suppliers relative to existing firms and whether the measure will have a disproportionate impact on entry from small and medium-sized enterprises.

3.28 Existing suppliers can persuade policymakers to exempt them from the impact of new policies, at least for a time. This exemption, even if temporary, may deter new entrants who face higher costs in complying with the measure. When faced with scarce inputs, such as airport landing slots and radio spectrum, existing suppliers may argue that they should be given preferential access ('grandfather rights') or preferential rates for these inputs in contrast to new entrants to the market. In both these cases, new suppliers may face higher costs than existing suppliers and may be deterred from entering the market as a result. It is important therefore that regulatory proposals that raise barriers to entry are proportionate and do not unduly serve to protect incumbents.

Accessing taxi customers at a railway station

Imagine your minister had asked you to design a system through which taxis could be given access to pick up consumers from a railway station. It is seen as desirable to have a system that regulates access to this group of consumers in order to prevent long tailbacks on the road leading up to the railway station.

One option would be to grant taxis time slots for picking up customers. Taxis would need a slot for a particular time of day in order to pick up customers at that time. The slots could be allocated using grandfather rights: taxis that used their slots in the previous year could have the right to continue using the slots in the following year (a 'use it or lose it' approach).

However, this approach to allocation would create an asymmetry between incumbent taxi drivers and new entrants. Inefficient, high-cost taxis that are already in the market would be protected from competition from new entrants, even though a new low-cost taxi could potentially use the slot more productively. An alternative option could be to limit the number of years for which grandfathering occurs.

Depending on the extent of the cost asymmetry, grandfathered regulations can: deter new entry, dampen new investment by incumbent businesses, allow continuation of inefficient production by older more inefficient firms and lead to higher prices.

3.29 Small businesses can be an important source of dynamic competition in a market. Government regulation and policies usually have a disproportionate impact on small businesses (up to 49 employees) – including micro businesses (up to ten employees) mainly because they have significantly less resources available to cope with regulatory change and ongoing compliance costs.[17] Regulations that are likely to have a disproportionate impact on small firms can potentially cut off an important route of entry and source of competitive constraint.[18]

3.30 Policies may raise the costs of firms wanting to exit the market and this may itself deter new entry. For example, if regulations require large investments in specialist equipment to meet quality standards which cannot be recouped on exit from the market then this may deter companies from entering at all.

3.31 In order to determine whether the measure will deter suppliers from entering a market, the costs should be compared with the likely revenues of firms to assess their deterrent effect.

Part 3 CMA and other Guidelines

NOTES

17 BIS (2015), *Better regulation framework manual, Practical Guidance for UK Government Officials*.

18 The previous administration required a regulatory scrutiny process requires a small and micro-business assessment (SAMBa) to be undertaken to ensure that major new regulatory proposals are designed and implemented so as to mitigate disproportionate burdens. The assumption was that there would be a legislative exemption for small and micro-businesses where a large part of the intended benefits of the measure could be achieved without including them. Where this was not possible the Framework Manual set out other ways the impact on small businesses could be mitigated such as by extending transition periods or temporary exemptions where immediate compliance would harm their business.

Will the measure significantly raise the costs of some existing suppliers relative to other existing suppliers?

3.32 Policies may, deliberately or inadvertently, favour some suppliers over others. For example, a regulation that imposes new technology on firms will favour those firms who have already adopted this technology. Such firms would then face lower costs than their rivals, for example, because they don't need to reconfigure their existing arrangements.

3.33 Similarly, a regulation that specifies a product standard may favour suppliers already meeting that standard over others that are not. This situation may be further exacerbated if one supplier holds intellectual property rights that enable it to achieve the specified product standard. Alternative suppliers may be inhibited from competing by the need to licence the technology from the right holder or innovate around the existing right.

3.34 Policies may also create competition distortions by favouring certain types of business models over others. Policymakers, particularly those overseeing mixed markets where private, voluntary and state owned undertakings compete alongside one another, can consider whether their proposals are 'competitively neutral'. This means that no firm should have a significant competitive advantage purely as a result of its ownership or control. Conferring advantages as a result of ownership or control may result in some inefficient firms remaining in the market and more efficient firms being unable to grow and innovate effectively. This inefficiency may lead to lower quality and higher prices for consumers and also to lower levels of innovation in the sector than would otherwise have been the case.[19]

3.35 Key barriers to competitive neutrality include:

- differences in regulation, pension, and tax treatment between public private and voluntary providers; and
- incumbency advantages enjoyed by existing firms, such as access to information, pre-qualification and bid criteria, and transition costs.

3.36 Ensuring policies are competitively neutral may also require policymakers to consider whether consumers are afforded the same level of protection regardless of the type of provider they choose.

Competitive neutrality in higher education

In a report on the higher education sector in England, the CMA raised concerns that some providers were operating outside the regulatory regime designed to protect students from poor quality. The nature of the higher education experience, namely that students cannot fully appreciate the quality on offer before they choose which university to attend, justifies a market intervention to assure quality.

The CMA was concerned that students would not appreciate that some institutions operated outside the quality assurance regime. Further concerns were raised that institutions operating outside the regulatory framework would not have sufficient incentives to focus on providing students with a quality learning experience.

Source: *An effective regulatory framework for higher education: a policy paper*

NOTES

19 Further information about competitive neutrality can be found in OFT (2010), *Competition in mixed markets: ensuring competitive neutrality* (OFT1242).

4. COMPETITION CHECKLIST QUESTION 2 – WILL THE MEASURE LIMIT THE ABILITY OF SUPPLIERS TO COMPETE?

[3.54]

4.1 Competition between suppliers may focus on price, quality, service or innovation. In some circumstances, policymakers may seek to place limits on these parameters. Policies that restrict the means by which suppliers compete with each other can inhibit competition between those suppliers to the detriment of consumers. Regulations may also prevent suppliers from developing new products, carrying out new advertising and marketing initiatives, or using alternative sales channels.

4.2 Policymakers should ask whether proposals limit the ability of suppliers to compete, for example where a measure:

- controls or substantially influences:
  — the price a supplier may charge; and/or

— the characteristics of the products supplied, for example by setting minimum quality standards;

- limits the sales channels a supplier can use, or the geographic area a supplier may supply in;
- substantially restricts the ability of suppliers to advertise their products; and
- limits the suppliers' freedom to organise their own production processes or their choice of organisational form.

WILL THE MEASURE CONTROL OR SUBSTANTIALLY INFLUENCE THE PRICE A SUPPLIER MAY CHARGE?

4.3 Concern about the price of goods and services may result in a regulation that sets minimum or maximum prices (price floors or ceilings) for particular products or services. The policy objective may be to protect consumers in some respects but there may be significant adverse effects on competition, meaning that in some cases consumers may pay more than they would absent the floor or ceiling.

4.4 Minimum prices (price floors) have sometimes been proposed to ensure that certain quality or safety standards are maintained, or to limit consumption for public health reasons. Whether or not they achieve their social goal, the unintended side effect may be to protect producers from the competitive process. The price increase may also generate windfall gains for producers/retailers, depending on whether and where there is market power in the supply chain. Unlike an increase in tax, additional consumer spending would go to retailers rather than government. The unintended consequence may be to give retailers an incentive to sell more, rather than less, of the product in question as retailers would gain additional profit for every extra unit they sold.

4.5 If the policy objective is to raise product quality, direct regulation of product quality might be a less restrictive means of delivery, although policymakers should note that some forms of quality regulation can themselves limit competition. If the policy objective is to limit harmful effects from excess consumption, imposing or increasing any duties or taxes payable on a product may help to ensure that suppliers will continue to compete and innovate over the portion of the final purchase price on which they can make a profit.

4.6 On the other side of the spectrum, maximum prices (price ceilings) which are aimed at protecting consumers or purchasers from high prices may act as a focal point for suppliers, with prices drawn to the ceiling, reducing the intensity of price competition between suppliers. The imposition of maximum prices may distort the choice of products supplied, may limit innovation, and may lead to the imposition of hidden charges to circumvent the price ceiling.

Price controls on fruit and vegetables in Greece

In June 2011 the Greek government removed mandated maximum mark-up prices on fresh fruit and vegetables. Research found that abolishing mark-ups led to a significant cut in wholesale prices of previously 'protected' products and as a result retail prices also went down. The researchers suggested that mandated mark-ups enabled wholesalers to set their prices very close to the maximum allowed margin. Once this restriction was removed, wholesalers were no longer constrained by the mark-up requirement and this encouraged further competition.

Source: OECD, Evaluation of competitive impacts of government interventions (Paper by C. Genakos, Pantelis Koutroumpis, and Mario Pagliero).

4.7 Price ceilings may be intended to protect consumers from producers with market power but there may be less restrictive means of delivering this objective. Educating consumers and providing sources of comparative information, establishing disclosure requirements and standards for presenting information, or mandating cooling-off periods can be less restrictive alternatives. If a price ceiling is still judged desirable, care should be taken that it is sufficiently flexible to accommodate different business models.

The CMA's view of price caps in the payday lending sector

In 2015 the CMA concluded its market investigation into the payday lending market. As part of the investigation, it considered the impact of the Financial Conduct Authority's (FCA) price cap on the features of the market that the CMA had identified as giving rise to competition concerns.

The CMA considered the price cap would lead to some advantages:

- The price cap may have led to some simplification of the products on offer in the market (for example, in relation to late fees and charges), which might have increased the comparability of different payday products, making it easier for customers to identify the best-value loan for their requirement;
- To the extent that the cap – together with the FCA's enhanced regulation of the payday lending sector more generally – improved the reputation of the sector and offered borrowers additional protection, it may have reduced the risk perceived by customers of switching lender; and
- The level of customer detriment arising from the Adverse Effect on Competition found by the CMA would be reduced as prices were reduced.

However, the CMA did not expect these effects of the cap to be sufficient to address the competition concerns it found. Further competition-enhancing measures were required because:

- Features of the market which limited customers' responsiveness to prices would be expected to continue to restrict competition between lenders even in the presence of the price cap. For example, the cap was highly unlikely to reduce the perceived urgency underpinning many borrowers' decisions to take out a payday loan, or remove the uncertainty that many customers face when deciding which lender to borrow from; and
- The cap was also unlikely to mitigate any of the characteristics of the payday lending market which limit the constraint that lenders face from the threat of entry and expansion.

The CMA also identified some potential negative impacts of the price cap on competition

- The cap may have weakened the competitive constraint in the market if, by reducing expected post-entry profitability, the cap reduced the incentive for new lenders to enter and increased the resources and time required by a new entrant to overcome its initial disadvantages and establish itself in the market. Similarly the cap might lead to less efficient lenders leaving the market;
- The cap may also have further dampened price competition between lenders by providing a 'focal point' or 'going rate' for payday loan pricing. It was possible that lenders priced up to the level of the cap, facilitated by the barriers to entry and expansion in the market; and
- The nature of the cap might affect the relative profitability of different types of product or make it more difficult to structure certain types of products in ways that complied with the structure of the cap which could reduce customer choice and competition.

However, while the CMA acknowledged the possibility that the price cap might become a 'focal point' for coordination, it also noted that the significant variation in market shares, efficiency, costs and products offered by different lenders would likely frustrate coordination efforts, particularly if the obstacles to competition the CMA had identified were addressed effectively.

Source: CMA (2015), Payday lending market investigation – Final report

WILL THE MEASURE CONTROL OR SUBSTANTIALLY INFLUENCE THE CHARACTERISTICS OF THE PRODUCTS SUPPLIED?

4.8 Policies may be introduced to safeguard consumers from products that are poor quality, or restrictions set on the nature of the product or service to be supplied. The justification may be that consumers are unable to monitor the quality of products and may suffer harm as a result, or that certain content standards are required by consumers (for example, the provision of information in multiple languages).

4.9 Such policies may restrict the ability of suppliers to compete with each other by differentiating their products, and may prevent informed consumers from purchasing a lower quality, low cost product. Where safety is not an issue and if standards are set above the level that a well-informed consumer would choose, minimum quality levels may have the effect of removing the offer of certain products/services for which there is demand from certain customers, and reducing the choices available to them. For example, a regulation requiring all airlines to provide all passengers with a hot meal on short-haul flights would require 'no-frills' airlines to offer customers hot meals when those customers may prefer a cheaper flight with no hot meal.

4.10 The specification of certain content or quality standards may also increase suppliers' costs. Higher costs incurred by businesses will typically translate into higher prices paid by consumers and reduction in the variety of products and services available.

Regulating the quality of bottled water

Imagine there was a concern about consumers being misled about the origins of bottled water. A group of consumers have written to your minister expressing their concerns that they purchased bottled water assuming it was mineral water captured straight from the source. But when they read the small print on the bottle they found that they had purchased filtered tap water.

One solution to protect consumers might be to improve the quality of bottled water by regulating so that all firms selling bottled water have to sell directly sourced mineral water. Consumers would not be misled into purchasing lower quality filtered water in the future.

However, the effect of such a regulation would be an eradication of other types of bottled water, including table water and filtered water. Consumers who prefer these lower quality, lower cost options would no longer be able to purchase, resulting in a reduction of consumer welfare. In addition, the market for bottled water might become more concentrated as a result of the regulatory change (with producers of table and filtered water having to leave the market), potentially resulting in remaining bottle water producers having sufficient market power to raise prices.

An alternative to regulating water quality would be to introduce an information remedy which requires producers to clearly indicate the origins of the bottled water.

4.11 In considering the impact on the market of a minimum standard, it is important to take the nature of competition in the market into account. For example, if aspects of the product or service that are decisive for the competitive positioning of operators are harmonised, negative impacts on competition are more likely than with harmonisation of parameters over which operators do not compete. Policymakers should also consider if the standard could inhibit entry, for example by setting minimum interoperability standards which carry high compliance costs for new entrants.

4.12 Hard restrictions on quality may not always be necessary to achieve the desired result. Seller reputation can safeguard quality, particularly where consumers can observe and understand quality and make repeat purchases. Ensuring the supply of information on product quality and safety may be sufficient to allow consumers to make informed decisions at the time of purchase, and requirements to include certain information on labels provide consumers with more information about the competing products on offer.

4.13 Quality standards need not always be set by the government. Industry participants may be able to develop standards themselves through self-regulation. As the standard setters are specialists and have an incentive to reach a solution which minimises regulatory burden on them, this may result in a standard which is more fit for purpose and has less impact on competition. Self-regulation can be a lighter touch way of achieving a solution but, in some instances, industry may use self-regulation to further their own interests. In these circumstances legislating might be a preferable approach to protect competition – for more detail on this see paragraph 7.11.

4.14 If it is desirable to impose a minimum standard, policymakers should consider carefully what form this should take. Ensuring quality through performance-based standards is preferable to prescriptive standards, and less likely to harm innovation, since suppliers are able to tailor their products to the standard, compete over efficient modes and methods of production, and ultimately provide more choice for consumers. For example, pollution controls on car emission limits are preferable to restrictions on engine capacity limits since they will introduce incentives on producers to develop new technology that minimises pollution.

WILL THE MEASURE LIMIT THE SALES CHANNELS A SUPPLIER CAN USE, OR THE GEOGRAPHIC AREA IN WHICH A SUPPLIER CAN OPERATE?

4.15 Some policies may limit how products or services can be supplied, or place restrictions on the area in which they can be supplied. Both of these types of restriction may limit innovation or act as a direct restriction on the number of suppliers in an area, weakening the competitive constraints that existing suppliers face. Such restrictions are likely to be particularly harmful where there is limited inter-brand competition (competition between different manufacturers or different suppliers is weak).[20]

US motor vehicle manufacturers

In 2015, staff of the US Federal Trade Commission (FTC) commented in support of proposed amendments to a Michigan law prohibiting motor vehicle manufacturers from selling new motor vehicles to consumers except through independent franchised dealers. The restriction on sales channels was having the effect of preventing a prospective manufacturer from choosing to sell its new product through a direct distribution method that it believed would reduce the costs of distribution and be more responsive to consumer preferences.

Although the amendments were drafted narrowly to cover only the prospective manufacturer's new product category, the FTC staff recommended more broadly that all restrictions on sales channels for motor vehicles should be removed. Absent public policy considerations, the law should permit manufacturers to choose whether to distribute their products directly, through third parties, or a mixture of both. Distribution methods resulting in higher prices or poorer service to consumers would be weeded out through the process of competition, without the need for government intervention.

Source: US Federal Trade Commission website.

4.16 It is rare that a restriction such as government limiting supply channels or areas will be needed to meet policy objectives. The primary justification for the restriction above was to protect independent dealers from the excessive exercise of market power by their suppliers. However, the FTC noted that a narrowly crafted provision to protect franchised dealers from abuse in their franchise relationships could achieve this goal without stifling competition.

NOTES

20 Government intervention to limit sales channels or areas should further be distinguished from circumstances where suppliers choose to limit sales or distribution channels of their own volition (eg through vertical integration), which is likely to bring efficiency benefits.

WILL THE MEASURE SUBSTANTIALLY RESTRICT THE ABILITY OF SUPPLIERS TO ADVERTISE THEIR PRODUCTS?

4.17 Advertising provides an important means by which suppliers promote their products and by which they differentiate their product from those of their rivals. Restrictions on advertising may limit competition, particularly if they deter new entrants because they would be unable to make consumers aware of their new products.

4.18 Advertising restrictions may be imposed as part of a mechanism to ensure quality or to moderate consumption of goods or services which may be harmful (such as problem gambling and irresponsible lending). Whilst these policy objectives may be worthwhile, consideration should be given to the effect on competition to ensure the restrictions are not overly prohibitive.

4.19 In some cases, industries or professional bodies may support restrictions on advertising as a way of softening competition. Historically, many professions have restricted advertising tightly. Although various arguments were advanced to support these restrictions, it was widely considered that they restricted competition disproportionately. Advertising of professional services is now generally permitted, subject to limitations in relation to advertising which is held to be misleading or harmful to the reputation of the profession.

4.20 Policymakers should note that restrictions on misleading advertising are generally pro-competitive in that they ensure suppliers compete on equal terms and that consumers are protected from false claims.

4.21 In order to determine what effect an advertising restriction might have on competition, it is useful to understand:

- To what extent are firms dependent on advertising in this 'window'? Are there other routes to attracting customers and competing to win market share, and what could be the cost implications of investing in alternative routes?
- Would the restriction affect new entrants in particular? Is there any evidence that building market share via advertising in this window is particularly important?

American opticians

A US study into opticians advertising restrictions compared cities with advertising restrictions for opticians with those without. The study found that, on average the price of an eye test was 33.6 per cent higher in the most restrictive cities than in the least restrictive cities with no appreciable difference in quality.

Original source: Bond, Ronald S, Kwoka, John E Jr, Phelan, John J, and Whitten, Ira Taylor (1980) 'Staff Report on Effects of Restrictions on advertising and commercial practice in the professions: the case of optometry.' Washington, DC: FTC, Bureau of Economics.

Summary, OECD (2004), *Enhancing Beneficial Competition in the Health Professions.*

WILL THE MEASURE IMPOSE RESTRICTIONS ON SUPPLIERS' PRODUCTION PROCESSES OR CHOICE OF ORGANISATIONAL FORM?

4.22 Policies that restrict the production process may have legitimate social objectives such as the protection of employees. Such policies, if they are excessive, may limit the freedom of producers to be inventive and innovative and may reduce the quantity of products that can be supplied. A reduction in quantity supplied may harm consumers as it is likely to lead to a price increase. This is because demand and supply can be expected to reach a new equilibrium at a higher price.

4.23 Policies may also limit organisational forms. For example, in 2001 the OFT examined competition in the professions and found that where certain professionals (such as accountants) are prevented from organising themselves as public limited companies, or were restricted from forming partnership with other qualified professionals, the regulations limited the freedom of professionals to develop their services in efficient and innovative ways, and inhibited competition between partnerships.[21]

NOTES

21 OFT (2001) Competition in the Professions

5. COMPETITION CHECKLIST QUESTION 3 – WILL THE MEASURE LIMIT SUPPLIERS' INCENTIVES TO COMPETE VIGOROUSLY?

[3.55]

5.1 The essence of competition is that suppliers compete against each other by offering lower prices, better service, or better quality products or services to win customers and market share.

5.2 Occasionally suppliers might decide, implicitly or explicitly, not to compete with each other. Suppliers might agree a common price (or range of prices) for goods or decide not to undercut each other. Alternatively, suppliers might agree not to compete in respect of certain customers or certain products, or agree terms that make it difficult for customers to switch to competing suppliers.

5.3 Government policies and regulations can make it more or less likely that suppliers will enter into and be able to sustain anti-competitive agreements. As a result, the competition assessment asks whether proposals may reduce suppliers' incentives to compete vigorously, for example where a measure:

- incentivises suppliers to coordinate their behaviour;
- exempts suppliers from competition law; or
- introduces or amends an intellectual property regime.

5.4 It may be that a proposal also reduces suppliers' incentives to compete by increasing the costs to customers of switching between suppliers. This is covered in the following chapter.

WILL THE MEASURE INCENTIVISE SUPPLIERS TO COORDINATE THEIR BEHAVIOUR AND THEREBY DAMPEN COMPETITION?

5.5 Policy or regulation can create a situation in which it is in suppliers' commercial interests to coordinate their activities in an anti-competitive manner. Such policies may be introduced with the aim of helping consumers. For example, in some markets, particularly where the product or service on offer is highly differentiated (such as mobile telephone contracts), customers may find it difficult or costly to compare prices. This difficulty may be resolved by a proposal requiring the publication of prices which aims to reduce search costs and making it easier for consumers to compare alternative offers. In most cases where this is being done to overcome barriers to searching, it should be positive for competition.

5.6 However, there are also possible anti-competitive effects associated with information sharing between competitors. Suppliers may use information on prices, costs, sales or outputs to coordinate behaviour amongst themselves to the detriment of consumers. The publication of prices may lead suppliers to raise their prices to those achieved by others.

5.7 Some seemingly harmless information may also dampen competition. Publication of market share information, or capacity utilisation information, may give suppliers an insight into the competitive constraints faced by their rivals. The table below sets out the broad level of risk presented by categories of commercial information.

5.8 The likelihood of information disclosure and exchange leading to collusion is more likely if there are few suppliers in the market, the product is relatively standardised, and entry barriers are high. It is less likely where the information is made available to consumers publicly and there is no asymmetry between firms and consumers.

5.9 It should be noted that in some circumstances a degree of information exchange (for example, to set a technical standard) may be preferable from a competition perspective than a centrally-mandated standard.

TABLE 1: RISKS OF COLLUSION PRESENTED BY INFORMATION SHARING[22]

Higher risk from information being shared	Lower risk from information being shared
Specific information	Aggregated information
Individualised information	Anonymised information
Non-public information	Genuinely public information
Future information/plans	Historic information
Information will need to be disclosed frequently	Disclosure of information is a one off
Information is sent directly by competitor	Information is sent by an independent source
Quantitative information	Qualitative information

Part 3 CMA and other Guidelines

NOTES

22 For further details refer to CMA guidelines on *Trade associations, professions and self-regulatory bodies*, OFT408 (2004).

5.10 Other types of measures can create incentives for suppliers to coordinate their activities in an anti-competitive manner. For example, policymakers may encourage the formation of trade associations, encourage the setting of best practice rules for members or encourage suppliers to coordinate on product design and compatibility. Whilst there may be legitimate reasons for encouraging these types of coordination, an unintended side-effect may be that competitors are better able to exchange commercially sensitive information and collude.

5.11 In addition to sharpening suppliers' incentives to coordinate their behaviour, policies and regulations may also affect market conditions, which in turn may make collusion more likely and sustainable. To collude effectively, firms must be able to reach an agreement, to detect breaches of the agreement, and to punish firms that breach it. A variety of market characteristics make collusion more likely, for example:

- there are relatively few firms in the market, they are relatively similar, and their cost base is broadly equivalent;
- products are standardised. Fewer variables in terms of design, quality or service make it easier to reach a common pricing scheme;
- there are low switching costs and customers move around in response to price changes;
- fewer products make it easier to coordinate;
- there are frequent, repetitive bids for specific goods; and
- competitors regularly socialise with each other, through personal connections or trade associations.

5.12 Policies which result in or increase the presence of these conditions may increase the likelihood of collusion.

5.13 Whilst not all policies that incentivise suppliers to coordinate their behaviour will result in suppliers breaching competition law,[23] policies that do so are particularly likely to harm competition and consumers. European and UK competition laws prohibit anti-competitive agreements between undertakings, and prohibit dominant undertakings from abusing their market power.[24] The fact that an agreement is sanctioned by government (national or local), or that discussion takes place in the presence of government officials, does not necessarily prevent it from falling foul of national or European competition law. The types of measures that raise greater risk of suppliers breaching competition rules are set out in the table below.

Are you encouraging suppliers to break competition law?

CA98 almost certainly infringed

- Government encourages or brokers an agreement between businesses to raise/fix prices or set minimum prices

Relatively high risk of CA98 being infringed

- Government acts as a mechanism to co-ordinate the otherwise independent commercial decision-making of businesses through non-mandatory means, effectively substituting individual/unilateral decision-making with a coordination of economic activity (including on price and non-price factors)
- Government encourages or facilitates the sharing of commercially sensitive information from one business to another (directly or indirectly) including information on individual retailer's future commercial policies or intentions

Relatively low risk of CA98 being infringed

- Government imposes legal requirements that businesses must comply with (although government should consider any potential adverse impact of legislation on competition and seek to mitigate that as far as possible)
- Government disseminates to a business a public policy message (for example, explaining potential social health and safety benefits of business activities) and invites business to make unilateral commitments to address the concern
- Government seeks the views of business, for example through a meeting at which businesses make high-level suggestions to inform government policy

NOTES

[23] In the UK, anti-competitive agreements and abuses of dominance are prohibited under the Competition Act 1998 (CA98) and (where the conduct may affect trade between EU member states) the Treaty on the Functioning of the European Union (TFEU).

[24] For further details refer to the CMA guidelines on *Agreements and concerted practices*, OFT401d (2004). CMA guidelines on *Assessment of market power*, OFT415 (2004) adopted by the CMA board, and CMA guidelines on *Abuse of a dominant position*, OFT402 (2004) adopted by the CMA board.

HOW DOES THE PROPOSAL INTERFACE WITH COMPETITION LAW?

5.14 Policymakers should ensure that their proposals would not require undertakings to act in a way that would infringe EU competition law.[25] Policies that do so may be incompatible with the TFEU, breach the UK's treaty obligations of sincere cooperation and result in the rules being unenforceable. This has been held to apply to situations where legislation gives regulatory effect to prohibited anti-competitive activity, as in the example below. Ensuring the proposal is compatible with TFEU will also help to ensure that competition is maintained. Policymakers concerned about this issue should consult their in-house legal team.

Italian match manufacturers

In 1923 Italian national legislation created a professional body for match manufacturers, who in turn established production quotas. As noted elsewhere, quotas may limit the incentives on suppliers to compete with each other. The European Court of Justice ruled that this legislation infringed the Treaty and that the national competition authority had a duty to disapply national legislation that requires or facilitates anti-competitive conduct that infringes what is now Article 101(1) of the TFEU.

Source: Consorzio Industrie Fiammiferi (CIF) v Autorità Garante della Concorrenza e del Mercato, C-198/01.

NOTES

[25] EU law would apply in addition to domestic legislation where an agreement may affect trade between EU member states.

6. COMPETITION CHECKLIST QUESTION 4 – WILL THE MEASURE LIMIT THE CHOICES OR INFORMATION AVAILABLE TO CONSUMERS?

[3.56]

6.1 Customers have an important part to play in stimulating rivalry between suppliers by making informed decisions which reward those firms that best meet their preferences. Markets work best when both the supply side (the firms) and the demand side (the customers) interact effectively. There is a virtuous circle between the actions of well-informed consumers in the market and competition.

Figure 1: The virtuous competitive circle

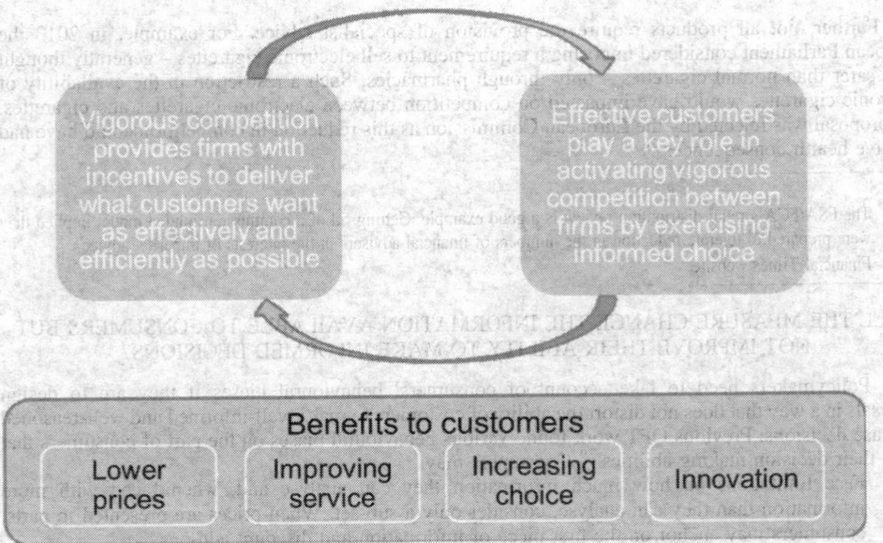

6.2 Evidence from numerous competition investigations shows that making markets work well not only requires the right supply side conditions, but also requires sufficiently engaged consumers who have the ability to assess, access, and act on information to select the goods or services that offer the best value to influence suppliers.[26] This highlights the crucial role that consumer policy, and other forms of demand side intervention, plays in driving effective markets.

6.3 There are a number of reasons why the demand side of a market might not work well. For example:

- The characteristics of some goods and services may make it difficult for consumers to make informed choices (such as when the product is an 'experience' good) such that the value of the product can only be fully appreciated after consumption;
- The characteristics of consumers may mean that they do not have the time or capability to make informed decisions; and
- Actions taken by providers (such as to obfuscate product information), can impede consumers' ability or willingness to access, assess and act on the available information.

6.4 For example, some financial services are inherently complex or require consumers to make difficult judgements about their future circumstances (for example, knowing what type of mortgage will best suit future circumstances). These complexities can make it difficult for consumers to make the best decisions and, in some cases, can deter consumers from trying altogether.

6.5 Such complexities might result in policymakers considering that a market intervention is needed to help consumers navigate complex products and make more informed decisions. In doing so, policymakers need to ensure that they do not make the functioning of the demand side of the market worse. Such effects may arise if the measure:

- limits ability of consumers to decide from whom they purchase;
- changes the information available to consumers but does not improve their ability to make informed decisions; and/or
- reduces the mobility of consumers by increasing the cost of changing suppliers.

6.6 These considerations are also relevant to policymakers who are introducing proposals with aims other than to improve the functioning of the demand side of a market, but where the proposal has the potential effect of making it more difficult for consumers to find a good deal.

NOTES

26 OFT (2010), *What does Behavioural Economics mean for Competition policy?*

WILL THE MEASURE LIMIT THE ABILITY OF CONSUMERS TO DECIDE FROM WHOM THEY PURCHASE?

6.7 Measures that limit the sales channels a supplier can use (as outlined in paragraphs 4.15 and 4.16) may also restrict the suppliers from whom a consumer can purchase. Restrictions of this nature may reflect a concern that it is important that consumers get specialist advice at the point of sale where, for example, certain health products or complex financial products are being supplied. However, the effect of the regulations may be to protect the traditional businesses from competition and may restrict choice at the point of sale, to the detriment of consumers and potentially public policy objectives.[27] Consumers may not receive the desired price or quality for a service as they are forced to purchase from higher cost suppliers or products that are not their preferred choice.

6.8 For example, regulations may impose rules on what pharmaceutical products can be supplied over the internet. This is to protect consumers so that they obtain advice from the pharmacist when they collect their prescriptions on how to take the medications. However, in certain countries, long-distance pharmacies have proven track records of safe and effective operations and so such restrictions may unduly restrict consumer choice.

6.9 Further, not all products require the provision of specialist advice. For example, in 2013 the European Parliament considered imposing a requirement to sell electronic cigarettes – generally thought to be safer than normal cigarettes – only through pharmacies. Such a restriction in the availability of electronic cigarettes would have impacted on competition between electronic cigarettes and cigarettes. The proposal was rejected by the European Commission as this reduction in competition could have had negative health consequences.[28]

NOTES

[27] The FSA/FCA's retail distribution review is a good example. Getting rid of a commission funded model implied they were prepared to tolerate reduction in the numbers of financial advisers in the interests of impartial advice.

[28] Financial Times website.

WILL THE MEASURE CHANGE THE INFORMATION AVAILABLE TO CONSUMERS BUT NOT IMPROVE THEIR ABILITY TO MAKE INFORMED DECISIONS?

6.10 Policymakers need to take account of consumers' behavioural biases if they are to design proposals in a way that does not distort the ability of customers to make well-informed and well-reasoned purchase decisions. Previous OFT work found various behavioural biases on the part of consumers that affect their decision making abilities.[29] Consumers may:

- Face limitations on how much information they can analyse and, when faced with more information than they can analyse, consider only a sub-set. When prices are presented in parts, consumers may anchor on the first piece of information and discount add-ons.
- Overweigh the present and be too optimistic. Consumers may over-estimate how much they will use a good or under-estimate how much it will cost them.
- Be overconfident about their ability to act in the future. For example they may overestimate their propensity to cancel automatically renewed contracts.

6.11 Similarly, research conducted by the Financial Conduct Authority has identified ten behavioural biases that affect consumers in retail financial markets.[30]

TABLE 2: APPLYING BEHAVIOURAL ECONOMICS TO FINANCIAL MARKETS

Our preferences are influenced by emotions and psychological experiences	**Rules of thumb can lead to incorrect beliefs**	**We use decision-making short cuts when assessing available information**
Present bias eg spending on a credit card for immediate gratification	***Overconfidence*** eg excessive belief in one's ability to pick winning stocks	***Framing, salience and limited attention*** eg overestimating the value of a packaged bank account because it is presented in a particularly attractive way
Reference dependence and loss aversion eg believing that insurance added on to a base product is cheaper because the base price is much higher	***Over-extrapolation*** eg extrapolating from just a few years of investment returns to the future	***Mental accounting and narrow framing*** eg investment decisions may be made asset-by-asset rather than considering the whole investment portfolio
Regret and other emotions eg buying insurance for peace of mind	***Projection bias*** eg taking out a payday loan without considering payment difficulties that might arise in the future	***Decision-making rules of thumb*** eg investment may be split equally across all the funds in a pension scheme, rather than making a careful allocation decision
		Persuasion and social influence eg following financial advice because an adviser is likeable

6.12 Consumers' tendency to frame their decisions with respect to certain reference points means that they often focus on a few headline rates and ignore the additional information about features or charges that is provided to them. As a result, the provision of extra information may lead customers to make poorer decisions by increasing the likelihood that they are made on the basis of incorrect beliefs using rules of thumb.

6.13 A 2007 Better Regulation Executive and National Consumer Council report provides a useful framework for considering whether regulations requiring information disclosure will have a positive impact on consumer behaviour and the demand side of the market.

Recommendations in the Better Regulation Executive and National Consumer Council 2007 report

Five policy design tests to assess information requirements:

(1) Have you defined the behavioural outcomes that you wish to achieve? (What do you want to achieve?)

(2) Will information provide a sufficient incentive for consumers to change their behaviour? (Is the information likely to be of value to consumers?)

(3) To what extent does the information fit with the wider system and simplify choices for consumers? (Will the information help consumers make choices?)

(4) Is the information aligned with business incentives, where this is possible (Will businesses support or oppose what you are trying to achieve?)

(5) Have you considered the fit with existing regulated information requirements?

Source: A final report by the Better Regulation Executive and National Consumer Council on maximising the positive impact of regulated information for consumers and markets (2007).

6.14 In addition, it is useful for policymakers to consider whether their proposal will exacerbate behavioural biases and lead to worse outcomes for consumers. For example, a report prepared for the Centre for Competition Policy notes that 'cooling-off' periods are often introduced by financial regulators to provide consumers with the opportunity to review and potentially reverse purchasing decisions made when they were in an emotionally 'hot' state and hence without adequate reflection.[31] However there is the potential for the cooling-off period to trigger even less reflection at the point of sale, leading to outcomes that are possibly worse compared to the situation in which there is no intervention at all.

NOTES

29 OFT (2010), Advertising of prices, Market study report (OFT1291).

30 FCA (2013), *Applying behavioural economics at the Financial Conduct Authority.*

31 Behavioural Remedies and Cost Benefit Analysis: A Cautionary Note, Michael Harker and Judith Mehta, Chapter 7 Behavioural Economics in Competition and Consumer Policy, 2013.

WILL THE MEASURE REDUCE THE MOBILITY OF CUSTOMERS BY INCREASING THE COST OF CHANGING SUPPLIERS?

6.15 Policymakers need to be aware that increasing switching costs might lead to a softening of competition.[32] Hence where a measure leads to an increase in switching costs, this might have a negative impact on competition. For example, the government may introduce a new regulation which requires consumers to provide more detailed information when applying for a mortgage. This may raise switching costs and may deter consumers from switching altogether leading to a lessening of competition.

6.16 In some cases switching costs can also arise from behavioural biases. For example, faced with increasingly complex products and increasing constraints on their time, behavioural economics has shown that consumers may choose to make decisions by limiting their search (and therefore not necessarily purchasing the best value package for them), deferring to an intermediary for advice, employing a heuristic technique ('rule of thumb'), or forgoing the purchase because of the time and effort required to fully research and evaluate the offer. It is important for policymakers in these circumstances to be aware of these difficulties and design policies accordingly.

6.17 Measures that help consumers to make more informed choices and overcome behavioural biases have included requirements to simplify tariff structures or to develop price comparison websites to aid transparency.

6.18 Policymakers should also be aware that while reducing switching costs generally leads to competition benefits there can be cases where interventions to reduce switching costs may not always be welfare enhancing. For example US research studied the impact of policies that nudge consumers towards better decision making by reducing inertia in the health insurance markets.[33] In these markets insurers have less information than consumers about their state of health and so are unable to price all risk characteristics. As a result it is those riskier consumers that take out the more comprehensive health plans, driving up the equilibrium price for these plans. In this situation giving consumers more information on which to make choices actually exacerbated the problem and resulted in still higher prices and a reduction in welfare.

NOTES

32 Paul Klemperer, Oxford University (1991), *Competition when Consumers have Switching Costs: An Overview with Applications to Industrial Organization, Macroeconomics and International Trade.*

33 Manuscript, UC Berkeley (2011), *Adverse Selection and Switching Costs in Health Insurance Markets: When Nudging Hurts.*

7. CONSIDERING ALTERNATIVES

[3.57]

7.1 Policymakers are advised to consider alternatives should they conclude that their proposal has the potential to significantly distort competition. Ways to mitigate the detrimental impact of specific interventions have been outlined in the previous chapters. This chapter draws these insights together and outlines a range of possible alternatives. The impact of such alternatives can be assessed and compared against the original proposal using some of the methodologies outlined in Chapter 8.

NO NEW INTERVENTION

7.2 In some circumstances policymakers may conclude it is not necessary to introduce new regulation. This does not necessarily mean accepting the status quo, and could also involve improving the use, clarity or enforcement of existing regulation. Unless existing regulations have significant impacts on competition and would benefit from replacement or revision, this approach would tend to be most competition-neutral.

7.3 Policymakers may also consider alternatives to the regulatory proposal. Alternatives can be conceptualised as rules based, incentives based, information based and self-regulatory, all existing in a framework of more and less distorting options.

TABLE 3: SPECTRUM OF INTERVENTIONS[34]

Policy objectives	**More distorting options**		**Less distorting options**
Deliver natural monopolies	Exclusive permanent rights to supply	Time limited exclusive rights to supply	Competition for the market (plus economic regulation) Ensure competition in downstream markets
Oversee access to scarce resources	Permanent access to incumbents (grandfather rights)	Time limited access	Auction to grant access
Reduce negative externalities (eg pollution and congestion)	Fixed quota on the number of suppliers		Tradable permits
Limiting consumer consumption	Minimum prices	Tax on the product	Information and education
Bringing prices down and/or enhancing international competitiveness	Maximum prices	Subsidy	Opening up the market to greater competition
Ensuring quality of goods/services or improve business practice	Prescriptive standards	Performance based standards Self-regulation (but see caveats below)	Consumer awareness (so poor practices are punished through reduced demand)

NOTES

[34] Adapted from the National Audit Office (2014), *Using alternatives to regulation to achieve policy objectives* (full report).

INCENTIVES BASED APPROACH

7.4 The government can use economic instruments, such as taxes, subsidies, quotas and permits, vouchers and auctions to incentivise business and citizens to change their behaviour. Often these sorts of systems need regulation to establish the framework. Some forms of economic instruments are more competition-neutral than others.

- **Taxes:** taxes on end-products may be a less distortionary option. For example, a significant element of the final purchase price for alcohol is duty, but suppliers still compete to supply, launch new products, and increase their market share. A rise in taxation may have a less distortionary impact on competition than, for example, a minimum price regulation, and be equally effective if it directly impacts on consumers' pattern of consumption. However, some taxes may affect small businesses disproportionately and therefore dampen competition by limiting new entry (such as tax exemptions, or differing rates of taxation which are easier for larger businesses to obtain).
- **Subsidies:** the government may choose to subsidise certain industries as a way of (for example) bringing prices down to maintain competitiveness or encourage the uptake of a certain technology. Subsidies may be competition-neutral nationally, if they apply across an industry, but may well be incompatible with EU rules on state aid if they confer an advantage on UK firms relative to those operating elsewhere in the EU.
- **Auctions:** in industries where resources (such as essential infrastructure) are scarce and must be shared by companies in order to provide a service, the government may choose to make control of them subject to auctions or tender processes. This 'competition for the market' can ensure that companies are incentivised to offer good terms to secure provision of the service over other suppliers, and can go some way to compensating for a loss of competition 'in the market' if the number of suppliers active is necessarily limited. However, it is usually preferable to preserve competition in the market where possible.

- **Ownership:** it may be possible to separate control of a given asset (for example, a natural monopoly wires business) from the operators who use it in the provision of a service (for example, generation and supply). This is may result in better outcomes as the upstream owner has an incentive to ensure efficient use of the asset without favouring a particular downstream firm.
- **Quotas:** quotas are likely to have a negative impact on competition. Maximum quotas will often limit competition as they constitute a capacity constraint; minimum quotas may raise barriers to entry for potential new entrants. Setting up a market for quotas may be one way of ensuring resources are used effectively.

7.5 These approaches can have advantages in principle over a rules based approach if they result in the right incentives being created to change behaviour. However, these approaches can also have disadvantages. It may, for example, be difficult to determine the size of the incentive required to change the behaviour needed among businesses and citizens. Predicting the effects of incentives may be difficult and there is often uncertainty when the effects will occur. As noted above, some types of economic incentive may harm competition as much as would a rule-based regime.

7.6 Particular care should be taken that these types of economic incentives do not contravene the EU rules on state aid that are enforced by the European Commission. BIS have published guidance on state aid and there is a unit at BIS that can provide specialist advice in this area.[35] State aid is considered as any advantage granted by public authorities through state resources on a selective basis to any undertakings that could potentially distort competition and trade in the EU.

7.7 Although the Treaty on the Functioning of the European Union does not include a precise definition of what constitutes state aid, the Commission has stated that it includes: grants, direct subsidies, tax exemptions, preferential interest rates, loans guarantees, provision of goods or services on preferential terms, indemnities against losses, and contracts not open to competitive tendering.

7.8 Policymakers should consult their in-house legal teams as a first step when considering this issue. BIS state aid guidance lists a number of suitable contacts for state aid issues in different areas. Further advice is available from sapt@bis.gsi.gov.uk.

NOTES

[35] Further government guidance on state aid can be found on GOV.UK.

INFORMATION AND EDUCATION

7.9 As set out in Chapter 6, ensuring customers have the information they need to make purchasing decisions helps competition to work well. In some cases, direct regulation may not be needed if consumers would be able to make better purchasing decisions through easier access to information. For example, the display of health and safety cleanliness standards at restaurants allows consumers to avoid poor quality, while having less impact on the natural process of competition than direct quality regulation. The advantage of this approach is that it offers relative freedom for the consumer and does not restrict the choices available. Instead it provides consumers with the information to help make a more informed decision.

SELF-REGULATION AND CO-REGULATION

7.10 An industry or a profession can self-regulate, for example through the use of codes of conduct, customer charters, standards or accreditation. In many cases rules and codes of conduct will be formulated by a trade association, or other industry representatives under their own initiative. In other cases, an industry or profession might self-regulate in response to delivering a stated government objective. Through self-regulation, the industry is solely responsible for monitoring and enforcing members' compliance. This enforcement can be achieved either first hand, or through other bodies set up by the industry. When a system of co-regulation is in place, there is an element of government monitoring.

7.11 Self-regulation often has benefits in terms of the lower costs it imposes on the industry. The approach may be more informed than government designed regulations if it is designed by industry specialists. However, care should be taken when considering self-regulation as an alternative that it would not be likely to facilitate anti-competitive agreements. Concerns about self-regulation include the greater likelihood of price coordination, coordination to prevent new entry, restrictions on the range of services produced (to the detriment of consumers) and agreements reduce to reduce product and process innovation. Further, unless the governance of self-regulation is very strong, there is a risk that arrangements will suit the interests of the subset of suppliers who design it.

8. METHODOLOGIES

[3.58]

8.1 Once it has been decided that an in-depth competition assessment is required then it is useful to consider how the impact of the proposal on competition will be assessed and measured. This assessment can be performed through a combination of qualitative and quantitative methods. In practice, most decisions about which options to prefer are qualitative, that is, not based on quantitative comparisons of options. Relevant data for a quantitative comparison is not always available and, even when available, may not be amenable to analysis. This chapter will lay out techniques of both qualitative and quantitative comparison.

8.2 Qualitative analysis combines facts and economic argumentation to arrive at reasoned judgments about which options to prefer. Quantitative analysis involves careful and rigorous use of numbers to estimates benefits of particular options compared to others. Table 4 shows the pros and cons of qualitative and quantitative methods.

TABLE 4: PROS AND CONS OF QUALITATIVE AND QUANTITATIVE METHODS

	Pros	Cons
Qualitative methods	Widely understood Requires little data Potentially quick	Does not identify the numerical impact of the measure (eg impact on price and quantity produced) Require more reliance on judgment
Quantitative methods	Requires less need for judgment Provides estimates of the numerical impact of the measure (eg likely price rises or change to quality)	Requires data to be available Requires more technical skills Requires more time

8.3 For particularly significant or controversial issues, quantitative analysis is preferred, when possible. However, the limit on data that is available or time to perform a comparison will often restrict the occasions on which quantitative analysis can be performed. It can also be difficult or impossible to quantify the consumer harm that will arise as a result of a new policy or regulation. So while quantitative analysis can help in selecting regulatory options that have the least restrictive effect on competition, it will often have to be buttressed by qualitative evidence.

8.4 A useful guide to assessing impacts of regulations on competition is the OECD's Manual for Competition Assessment (OECD (2015)), which has recently been updated to include more detailed guidance on methodologies that can be adopted to assess impact and contains many practical examples of how to perform the competition assessment of regulations.[36]

NOTES

36 OECD Competition Assessment Toolkit.

QUALITATIVE ANALYSIS

8.5 Policymakers will wish to be able to demonstrate that they have thought through in a structured way the likely impact of their policies on competition. For this reason argumentation based on economic principles is probably the most common form of qualitative analysis. In addition to the OECD's specific guidance on assessing impact of measures on competition, it is worth reviewing general guidance on impact assessment such as that contained in HM Treasury's Green Book.[37]

8.6 Qualitative analysis that uses "critical thinking" or "informal logic" to select among alternatives will:

- combine economic reasons, evidence and appropriate assumptions to reach conclusions;
- account for the credibility of sources, to ensure that no undue weight is placed on self-interested and biased argument;
- gather information to complete arguments and test plausible hypotheses;
- consider challenges that may be made to conclusions and have appropriate responses; and
- evaluate the quality of arguments about the strengths and weakness of alternative policies.

8.7 Examples of using arguments to compare options can be found in Annex B of the OECD's Competition Assessment Toolkit: Guidance.

8.8 The starting point of such analysis is to state the overall situation, including the reasons for developing the current proposals and establishing a baseline (as set out in Chapter 2). The analysis then states the objectives of the proposal and sets forth the alternatives, such as those considered in Chapter 7. Each option is analysed, considering its strengths and weaknesses, using any available evidence, including information about the rationale for a regulation, how each given option would achieve that goal and the likely impacts on consumers from each option based on economic principles. The analysis can identify assumptions, particularly where the assumptions may be questioned. Finally, a value judgment is made about which option is strongest, weighing the analyses of the options and considering the evidence and reasons, especially economic, to support each option.

8.9 Information that is particularly useful for such analysis can come from comparison of regulations across different jurisdictions. This allows different ways that a policy can be delivered to be identified and draws on research that has already been done to the likely impact on competition. The usefulness of comparisons depends on having common features between the jurisdictions, such as common consumer preferences and responses.[38]

8.10 Stakeholder consultation may also be a useful way to find out about the likely impact of a proposed measure. Stakeholders may have a good knowledge of the sector and of what alternatives can and cannot be implemented. Consulting with stakeholders can therefore provide a useful mechanism for ensuring that important facts have not been missed and that relevant options have not been ignored. However, companies that benefit or could benefit from a grant of market power via the proposal may be more likely to participate in stakeholder consultations and may also be more likely to argue in favour of an option that gives them market power, to the detriment of the public interest.

NOTES

37 HM Treasury, *The Green Book: Appraisal and Evaluation in Central Government*.

38 Common jurisdictions for comparison, depending on the focus of the regulatory framework, may include local authorities, England, Northern Ireland, Scotland, Wales, countries within the European Union, the OECD, and other

countries that may be relevant for a particular regulation.

QUANTITATIVE ANALYSIS

8.11 Quantitative assessment is particularly useful for providing a clear line of reasoning to examine whether regulations should be changed and how much public value comes from such changes. Quantitative analysis can be particularly useful as a counterweight to arguments in favour of a regulatory change, which may come from certain stakeholders who would enjoy market power as a result of the regulation.

8.12 Simple methods of providing quantitative estimates often provide results that are comprehensible, testable and transparent. One of the advantages of simple methods is that they are typically easy to explain and consequently more convincing for decision makers than complex methods.[39] If simple methods are not available, quantitative estimates will often not be made at all. Given the time constraints often present, this chapter focuses on simple methods for quantification.

8.13 Two particularly common sources of comparative quantitative information are quantification coming from predictive economic studies of a regulation's impact and quantification from before and after studies.

8.14 Economic studies that predict impacts of regulatory reform based on economic principles can show impact of regulations under consideration. Often such analyses have estimates of impacts on price, cost or other variables of interest. Such studies can provide useful insight should the study have looked at the impact of similar regulatory proposals to those under consideration.[40]

8.15 Before-and-after studies show the impact of a change in regulation, while adjusting or holding constant other factors. The intention of such studies is to identify the impact of a reform on variables of interest, such as price. The OECD in its Competition Impact Assessment Toolkit has produced a database identifying more than 300 research studies of the impact of pro-competitive regulatory reform, the vast majority of which are taken from developed countries that are members of the OECD. This database finds that the average price change from removing a restriction on competition is 19 per cent. This suggests that moving towards more competitive outcomes can reduce prices by up to 19 per cent on average.

8.16 Policymakers can use the OECD's assessment of average price impacts from different types of restriction (as outlined in the table below) as a 'rule of thumb' to estimate the price effect of introducing a regulatory restriction that impacts on competition. A rule of thumb is an alternative to a more detailed analysis in specific cases. Rules of thumb may be faster and use available data. These estimates can be used when there is a binding restriction from the regulation. So, for example, a rule that limits the number of taxis to 10,000 in a city is not binding if there are only 3,000 taxis operating in the area. The results, however, should be considered a benchmark, recognising that detailed studies may come up with different results, particularly if there are feasible ways to estimate elasticities and expected changes in variables like price.

8.17 The table can be used in the following way. Should a regulatory proposal to establish a licence as a requirement of operation be considered, for example, based on the average price effect from before-and-after empirical studies, a 23 per cent price rise could be anticipated (see the third row in the table below), assuming that the measure actually has a binding effect on the number of firms in the market.

TABLE 5: MEAN PRICE IMPACT FROM NOT IMPOSING A REGULATORY RESTRICTION THAT IMPACTS ON COMPETITION

Benchmark price change (ρ) (ratio of price change to less competitive price)	**Category and sub-category of regulatory restriction**
-0.20	(A) Limits the number or range of suppliers
-0.19	1 Grants exclusive rights for a supplier to provide goods or services
-0.23	2 Establishes a license, permit or authorization process as a requirement of operation
-0.15	3 Limits the ability of some types of suppliers to provide a good or service
-0.19	4 Significantly raises cost of entry or exit by a supplier
-0.12	5 Creates a geographical barrier to the ability of companies to supply goods services or labour, or invest capital
-0.18	(B) Limits the ability of suppliers to compete
-0.19	1 Limits sellers' ability to set the prices for goods or services
-0.14	2 Limits freedom of suppliers to advertise or market their goods or services
-0.16	3 Sets standards for product quality that provide an advantage to some suppliers over others or that are above the level that some well-informed customers would choose

Part 3 CMA and other Guidelines

Benchmark price change (ρ) (ratio of price change to less competitive price)	**Category and sub-category of regulatory restriction**
-0.39	4 Significantly raises costs of production for some suppliers relative to others (especially by treating incumbents differently from new entrants)
-0.20	(C) Reduces the incentive of suppliers to compete
-0.28	1 Creates a self-regulatory or co-regulatory regime
-0.10	2 Requires or encourages information on supplier outputs, prices, sales or costs to be published
-0.25	3 Exempts the activity of a particular industry or group of suppliers from the operation of general competition law
-0.20	(D) Limits the choices and information available to customers
-0.32	1 Limits the ability of consumers to decide from whom they purchase
-0.12	2 Reduces mobility of customers between suppliers of goods or services by increasing the explicit or implicit costs of changing suppliers
-0.16	3 Fundamentally changes information required by buyers to shop effectively

Source: OECD database of ex post studies of pro-competitive regulatory reform, 2015 version. This table will be updated as the database is updated, with new versions posted on the OECD website.

NOTES

39 Complex econometric methods which estimate the impact of a measure on cost and demand functions underlie more sophisticated analysis.

40 The variables that the study cover can depend on the product under consideration. For taxi services, for example, price is not the only variable of importance; quality matters to users, notably based on waiting time and quality of the vehicle. For retail sale of cars, price is again a variable of importance, but reliability of the vehicle may also be of particular importance for some users, with other characteristics of more importance to other users, due to the wide variety of users.

Measuring consumer harm

8.18 The competitive effects of proposals can often be examined by estimating the likely change from one point on the demand curve for a product to another. Where a proposal has the effect of limiting supply or raising price, an estimate of the likely consumer harm can be calculated relatively easily. The benefit of estimating the likely consumer harm is that a monetary value (in terms of consumer welfare lost as a result of the regulation) can be allocated to the regulatory proposal. While the estimate will not necessarily reflect consumer harm over time (the dynamic effect of the regulation), the studies summarised in Table 5 would often include results from entry and exit and potential innovations, as they are before and after studies of reforms affecting competition.

8.19 The logic of change in equilibrium approach is captured in Figure 2. Figure 2 shows the impact of moving from a competitive equilibrium (E*c*) to a restrictive equilibrium (E*r*). The movement makes price rise from P*c* to P*r* and quantity decrease from Q*e* to Q*r*. The consumer harm is represented by the joint area of the shaded rectangle and triangle. Even when detailed information is lacking, these areas can be estimated using relatively simple and standardised, default techniques.

Figure 2: Consumer harm from introduction of a restrictive measure

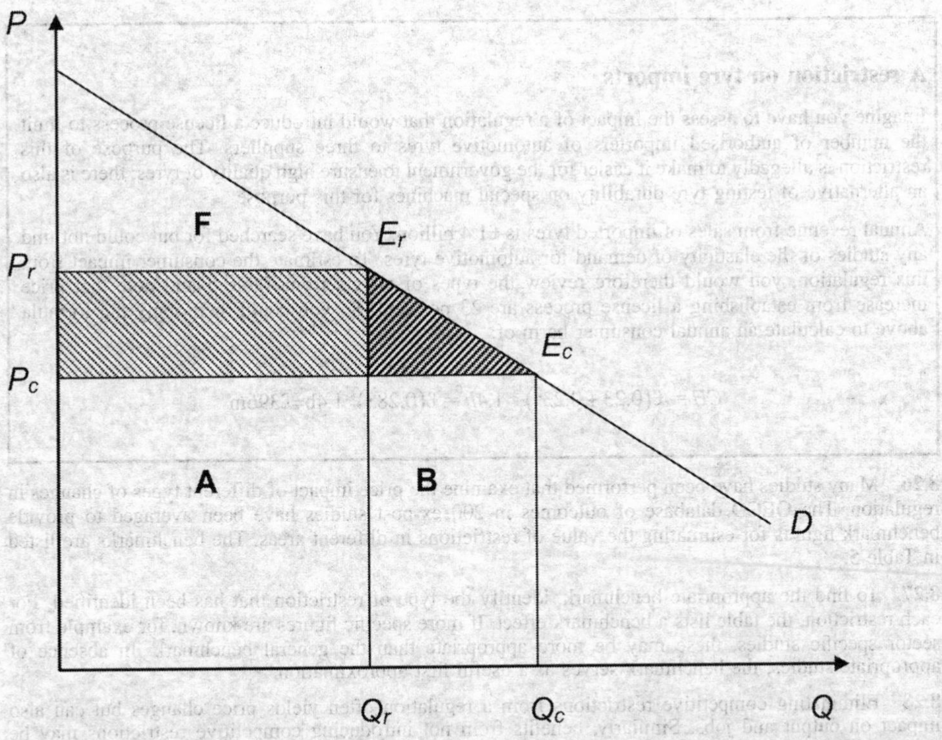

8.20 Policymakers can estimate impacts by measuring the consumer benefit that arises from not introducing a restrictive regulation (and thus conversely the consumer harm that will arise were such a restrictive regulation to be introduced). The OECD has set out a formula than can be utilised to perform this calculation. This requires the policymaker to know the total revenue, the expected price change following the introduction of the regulation (which can be taken from Table 5 above as explained in paragraph 8.27 below) and the elasticity of demand.

$$CB = \left(\rho + \frac{1}{2}|\varepsilon|\rho^2\right)R_r$$

Where:

CBs: standard measure of consumer benefit

ρ: percentage change in price related to restriction[41]

R: sector revenue

|ε|: absolute value of elasticity of demand

8.21 This formula can be divided into two parts, with the first part (ρRr) effectively representing the shaded box in Figure 2 and the second part (½ |ε|ρ2Rr) approximating the shaded triangle in Figure 2.

8.22 Where the elasticity for the sector is known, this should be used in the calculation. If the elasticity is unknown, the assumption of |ε|=2 can be assumed, for a reasonably typical market with competitors, some consumers willing to cease purchases in response to higher prices and no price regulation, to yield an estimated benefit from not introducing the restriction of:

$$CB = (\rho + \rho^2)R_r$$

8.23 Revenues are a valuable measure because they are often readily available and are less commercially sensitive than the two constituent elements of revenues, price and quantity sold.

8.24 The revenues should be those in the market directly affected by the regulation. More distant, but related markets would typically not have their revenue included in the revenue figure. Some judgment must be exercised in determining the bounds of the market for the purpose of the revenue estimate. Suppose revenues are known for a national market, but the measure has only a local effect. The local revenue can be estimated from national revenue, for example by making per capita revenue calculations, per outlet revenue calculations, or calculations per unit of geographic area.

8.25 Revenues are measured in currency units, allowing for the calculation of benefits that arise from not introducing a regulation that restricts competition measured in £s.

A restriction on tyre imports

Imagine you have to assess the impact of a regulation that would introduce a license process to limit the number of authorised importers of automotive tyres to three suppliers. The purpose of this restriction is allegedly to make it easier for the government to ensure high quality of tyres; there is also an alternative of testing tyre durability on special machines for this purpose.

Annual revenue from sales of imported tyres is £1.4 billion. You have searched for but could not find any studies of the elasticity of demand for automotive tyres. To estimate the consumer impact from this regulation, you would therefore review the types of effects from Table 5 and note that price increase from establishing a license process are 23 per cent. So you could then apply the formula above to calculate an annual consumer harm of:

$$CH = £(0.23 + 0.23^2) * 1.4b = £(0.283)*1.4b=£396m$$

8.26 Many studies have been performed that examine the price impact of different types of changes in regulation. The OECD database of outcomes in 200 ex-post studies have been averaged to provide benchmark figures for estimating the value of restrictions in different areas. The benchmarks are listed in Table 5.

8.27 To find the appropriate benchmark, identify the type of restriction that has been identified. For each restriction, the table lists a benchmark effect. If more specific figures are known, for example from sector specific studies, these may be more appropriate than the general benchmark. In absence of appropriate studies, the benchmark serves as a useful first approximation.

8.28 Eliminating competitive restrictions from a regulation often yields price changes but can also impact on output and jobs. Similarly, benefits from not introducing competitive restrictions may be measured in other ways than through price. For example, at times prices are regulated, but the quantity supplied is restricted. This restriction of quantities also harms consumers. A 1 per cent reduction in quantity supplied, even with prices fixed, may harm consumers more than a 1 per cent price increase.[42] This is because the 1 per cent price increase will result in those consumers with the lowest marginal benefit from the product stopping their purchases. In contrast, a decline of quantity will not necessarily be allocated to those consumers with the lowest marginal benefit, but could equally likely apply to all consumers, including those with very high personal benefit from consumption.

8.29 There are other variables that can be used in addition to price and quantity. The best variables to measure will depend on the product, the sector, what matters to consumers, and the available data.

8.30 More technical methods to estimate impacts can be used when very detailed information is available about pricing, firm sales and consumer preferences, allowing for an estimation of the demand curve.[43] Commonly, such detailed data is not immediately available.[44]

8.31 Once benefits and costs have been quantified a cost-benefit analysis can be undertaken. In many cases, benefits and costs provided by proposed measures will occur over years, and the timing of benefits and costs generated by different options may vary. In such cases, discounting is often required to correctly compare proposed options. Discounting can allow for costs and benefits that occur over time to be compared based on societal preferences for receiving benefits earlier, and other factors, such as the opportunity cost of funds and inflation. Where benefits and costs occur over time, selecting the appropriate discount rate can be critical to the selection of the best option. Guidance on how to undertake option appraisal and the choice of the underlying real discount rate to be used has been set out by HM Treasury in the Green Book. It is common in estimates of competitive benefits to truncate the benefits (by limiting the length of time considered, for example, to five years) to account for the imperfect foresight of regulators.[45]

NOTES

41 Note that expected price changes will often be given by ranges of percentage price changes.

42 This covers cases like price regulation combined with entry limits (taxis), where non-equilibrium outcomes may be enforced via regulation.

43 These sources could have helped to determine the supply curves that would apply in the baseline and under alternative proposals.

44 The standard measure assumes a market elasticity of -2 (or $|\varepsilon|=2$, in a constant elasticity demand function). It is intended to represent a typical product's elasticity with moderate competition and distant but feasible alternatives. The measure may be made more accurate if further information is available, or if there are reasons to believe the demand is either particularly inelastic, as with electricity or insulin, or particularly elastic, as may be the case with certain basic commodities.

45 For more detailed discussion see section 4.4.3.1 of Volume 3 of the OECD Competition Assessment Toolkit.

CMA RULES OF PROCEDURE FOR MERGER, MARKET AND SPECIAL REFERENCE GROUPS (CMA17, REVISED NOVEMBER 2015)

[3.59]

NOTES

An updated version of this guidance was published on 23 November 2015, correcting three small typographical errors. For more information see www.gov.uk/government/consultations/cmas-procedural-rules-for-groups-proposed-corrections.

CONTENTS

PART 1: GENERAL

1. INTRODUCTORY

[3.60]

1.1 These rules of procedure of the Competition and Markets Authority (CMA) are those referred to in, and required by, paragraph 51 of Schedule 4 to the Enterprise and Regulatory Reform Act 2013 (the ERR Act). These rules supersede the *Competition Commission Rules of Procedure* 2006.

1.2 Before making these rules the CMA Board consulted such persons as it considered appropriate.[1]

2. APPLICATION OF THE RULES

2.1 The rules shall apply from 1 April 2014.

2.2 The rules shall apply in relation to merger reference groups and market reference groups.[2]

2.3 Where a special reference group is appointed, its procedure is provided for in Part 7 of these rules.[3]

3. EFFECT OF THE RULES

3.1 The rules are supplementary to those statutory provisions which apply to the CMA under any enactment, or instrument made thereunder, and, in the event of any conflict between the rules and any statutory provision, the latter shall prevail.

3.2 The rules are binding on:

(a) the CMA Chair
(b) a CMA panel chair
(c) any group chair
(d) any CMA group
(e) any member of the CMA panel

3.3 If, at any time, a group encounters a situation which is not provided for in these Rules, then it shall determine its own procedure, but before doing so it shall consult the Chair and shall have regard to any guidance issued by the CMA Board.[4]

4. INTERPRETATION

4.1 In these rules:

- 'the Act' means the Enterprise Act 2002 as amended by the ERR Act
- 'Chair' means the Chair of the CMA appointed under paragraph 1(1)(a) of Schedule 4 to the ERR Act or any CMA panel chair, as appropriate
- 'CMA' means the Competition and Markets Authority
- 'CMA Board' means the Chair and members appointed under paragraph 27 of Schedule 4 to the ERR Act
- 'CMA panel chair' means a person who may, with the consent of the CMA Board, exercise a function of the Chair referred to in paragraph 48(4) of Schedule 4 to the ERR Act
- 'CMA panel' means the panel of persons available for selection as members of a group constituted in accordance with Part 3 of Schedule 4 to the ERR Act[5]
- 'ERR Act' means the Enterprise and Regulatory Reform Act 2013
- 'group' means a group constituted by the Chair under Schedule 4 to the ERR Act[6]
- 'group chair' means the member of a group appointed by the Chair to chair the group[7]
- 'main parties' means, in the case of a merger reference, those parties which, in the opinion of the group, are the main parties to the reference

- 'main parties' means, in the case of a market investigation reference, those parties which, in the opinion of the group, are the main parties to the inquiry
- 'market reference group', 'merger reference group' and 'special reference group' have the meanings given to them in paragraph 51(6) of Schedule 4 to the ERR Act[8]
- 'third parties' means those parties which are not main parties but which, in the opinion of the group, have a sufficient interest in the subject matter of the reference or the inquiry to be treated as such
- 'Ofcom price control reference' means a reference made under section 193 of the Communications Act 2003

5. TITLE

5.1 These rules may be referred to as the Competition and Markets Authority Rules of Procedure for Merger, Market and Special Reference Groups 2014.

NOTES

1. This is required by paragraph 51(3) of Schedule 4 to the ERR Act.
2. Defined in paragraph 51(6) of Schedule 4 to the ERR Act.
3. Defined in paragraph 51(6) of Schedule 4 to the ERR Act.
4. See paragraph 52(1) of Schedule 4 to the ERR Act.
5. Paragraph 34 of Schedule 4 to the ERR Act.
6. Paragraph 36 of Schedule 4 to the ERR Act.
7. Paragraph 38(8) of Schedule 4 to the ERR Act.
8. See Explanatory Note.

PART 2: APPOINTMENT AND CONDUCT OF GROUPS

6. APPOINTMENT AND CONDUCT

[3.61]

6.1 When a reference has been made to the Chair, the Chair shall promptly appoint members to form a group and a member of the group to be the group chair.[9]

6.2 In making appointments to a group, the Chair shall:

(a) have regard to any guidance published by the CMA on handling conflicts of interest and take into account any other factors which, in their opinion, might prejudice the independence and impartiality of the group

(b) not appoint a member of the CMA panel to the group if that member participated in the CMA Board's consideration of whether to refer the matter to the Chair for the constitution of a group

6.3 A group must consist of at least three members of the CMA panel.[10]

6.4 The group chair shall have a casting vote on any question to be decided by the group.[11]

6.5 In making decisions that a group is required or permitted to make by virtue of any enactment, it must act independently of the CMA Board.[12]

6.6 Rule 6.5 does not prevent:

(a) the CMA Board from giving information in its possession to a group

(b) a group giving information in its possession to the CMA Board[13]

6.7 Any reporting panel member[14] of the CMA panel who is not a member of the group may, at the invitation of the group chair, attend its meetings or otherwise take part in its proceedings for the purpose of offering the group advice about the exercise of its functions.[15]

6.8 It shall be the duty of a group to have regard to any advice given to it by the member of the CMA panel referred to in Rule 6.7 but that member may not vote or have any statement of their dissent from a conclusion of the group included in the group's report.[16]

6.9 A group may consult any member of the CMA panel with respect to any matter or question with which the group is concerned but, before doing so, the group shall consult the group chair, to avoid any conflict of interest arising.[17]

6.10 All members of the group shall have regard to any guidance issued by the CMA Board under paragraph 52 of Schedule 4 to the ERR Act, the advice and information requirements in sections 106, and 171 of the Act and to the CMA's *Administrative penalties: statement of policy on the CMA's approach (CMA4)*[18] made under sections 94B(1), 116(1) and 174E(1) of the Act.

6.11 If, during the proceedings of a group:

(a) a member of the group ceases to be a member of the CMA panel

(b) the Chair is satisfied that a member of the group will be unable for a substantial period to perform their duties as a member of the group, or

(c) it appears to the Chair that because of a particular interest of a member of the group it is inappropriate for that member to remain in the group

the Chair may appoint a replacement.[19]

NOTES

9. Where the CMA Board considers whether to make a reference to the Chair, before it does so, the Chair must determine whether a person who is a member of the CMA Board might reasonably be expected to be a member of a group

constituted in connection with the matter (paragraph 33(2) of Schedule 4 to the ERR Act). If the Chair determines that a person who is a member of the CMA Board might reasonably be expected to be a member of such a group, that person is not to participate in the CMA Board's consideration of whether to refer the matter to the Chair (paragraph 33(3) of Schedule 4 to the ERR Act).

10 Paragraph 38(1) of Schedule 4 to the ERR Act.

11 Paragraph 50 of Schedule 4 to the ERR Act.

12 Paragraph 49(1) of Schedule 4 to the ERR Act.

13 Paragraph 49(2) of Schedule 4 to the ERR Act.

14 See paragraph 35(2)(d) of Schedule 4 to the ERR Act.

15 See paragraph 45(1) of Schedule 4 to the ERR Act.

16 Paragraph 45(2) of Schedule 4 to the ERR Act.

17 See paragraph 45(1) and (3) of Schedule 4 to the ERR Act.

18 www.gov.uk/government/publications/administrative-penalties-statement-of-policy-on-the-cmas-approach.

19 Paragraphs 40–43 of Schedule 4 to the ERR Act.

PART 3: PROCEDURES FOR MARKET AND MERGER REFERENCE GROUPS

7. TIMETABLE

[3.62]

7.1 It shall be the duty of the group to comply with the relevant statutory timetable provided by the Act for the reference in question. After the group has been appointed, it shall, as soon as practicable, make arrangements for an administrative timetable to be drawn up which shall make provision for the major stages of the reference.

7.2 The major stages of the reference may include, in particular, the following:

(a) gathering information
(b) issuing questionnaires
(c) hearing of witnesses
(d) verifying information
(e) providing a statement of issues
(f) considering responses to a statement of issues
(g) notifying provisional findings
(h) notifying and considering possible remedies
(i) considering exclusions from disclosure
(j) publishing reports

provided that these stages need not necessarily take place within the administrative timetable in the order in which they are mentioned in this rule.

7.3 The group shall, when drawing up the administrative timetable, have regard to any views which the main parties to the reference have submitted to it.

7.4 Once the administrative timetable has been produced, the group shall make such arrangements as it thinks appropriate in order for it to be notified to all parties to the reference and to the public. The CMA may publish the timetable on its website.

7.5 The group may proceed on the basis that the main parties to the reference will comply with the administrative timetable.

7.6 If, at any point during the reference, the group has reason to believe that the administrative timetable will not be met for any reason, including any unforeseen circumstance, any difficulty concerning any stage of it, or any change to the statutory timetable, then the group shall prepare a revised timetable to which the notification and publication requirements contained in Rule 7.4 shall apply.

8. HEARINGS

8.1 It shall be the duty of the group to decide which, if any, of its hearings are to be held in public.

8.2 In taking that decision, the group shall have regard to:

(a) the views of the main and third parties
(b) the likelihood that a matter relating to the private affairs of an individual or body might be made known to the public and, being made known, might significantly harm the interests of that individual or body
(c) the extent to which an individual or body might be inhibited from providing information to the group if the hearing were to be held in public
(d) the extent to which an individual or body might be encouraged to provide information to the group if the hearing were to be held in public
(e) the efficient and proper conduct of the reference
(f) the administrative timetable
(g) the resource implications for the hearing
(h) the transport implications of the location of the hearing

8.3 If, during the course of any hearing in public, the group considers that it would be appropriate, having regard to the factors set out in Rule 8.2*(b)*, *(c)*, *(d)* and *(e)*, that the hearing should no longer continue to be held in public, it shall hold the hearing in private, after having given its reasons in public for doing so.

8.4 The group may, if it considers that it would assist a proper consideration of the reference, hold joint hearings with one or more of the parties.

8.5 If the group decides to hold joint hearings then it shall be the duty of the group to consider which, if any of those joint hearings are to be held in public, and in taking that decision the group shall have regard to the factors described in Rule 8.2.

9. APPEARANCES AT HEARINGS

9.1 The group shall decide the extent, if any, to which persons interested or claiming to be interested in the subject matter of the reference are allowed:

(a) to be present or to be heard, either by themselves or by their representatives
(b) to cross-examine witnesses
(c) otherwise to take part[20]

9.2 For the purpose of any investigation in connection with a reference, a group, or any person nominated by it, may take evidence on oath and for that purpose may administer oaths.[21]

9.3 Any person who objects to being sworn shall be permitted to make a solemn affirmation instead of taking an oath.

10. INVESTIGATION POWERS

10.1 A group may during the course of its proceedings exercise any of the investigation powers contained in sections 109 to 117 and sections 174 to 174D of the Act.

10.2 Where a group is minded to impose a penalty under section 94A or section 110(1) or (3) or section 174A(1) or (3) of the Act, it shall have regard to the CMA's Statement of Policy on Approach to Administrative Penalties made under sections 94B(1), 116(1) and 174E(1) of the Act.

10.3 Where, at any stage of a reference, any individual or body has been asked to provide information within a reasonable period of time and has failed to do so, without a reasonable explanation, the group shall not be obliged to have regard to any information received from that person or body after the date specified.[22]

NOTES

20 Paragraph 53(6) of Schedule 4 to the ERR Act.
21 Sections 109(5) and 174(6A) of the Act.
22 Section 53(3) of Schedule 4 to the ERR Act.

PART 4: FINDINGS ON THE TERMS OF REFERENCE

11. PROVISIONAL FINDINGS

[3.63]

11.1 A group shall make provisional findings on any reference it has been appointed to determine.

11.2 Provisional findings shall include the group's provisional decisions on the statutory questions it has to decide in relation to mergers and market investigation references.

11.3 When a group makes provisional findings on any reference it shall notify the main parties to the reference as soon as practicable after it has made them.

11.4 The notice shall describe the group's provisional findings and give an explanation of its reasons for coming to them.

11.5 Every notice:

(a) shall invite the main party affected, within such period being not less than 21 days as may be specified in the notice, to provide the group with its reasons in writing as to why such provisional findings should not become final (or, as the case may be, should be varied)
(b) shall, provided the group has formed a view, inform the main party affected of the procedure the group is minded to follow on receipt of such reasons
(c) shall not contain any information which the group considers should be excluded from the notice having regard to the three considerations set out in section 244 of the Act (specified information: considerations relevant to disclosure)

11.6 If any main party fails to provide reasons in writing by the date specified in the notice then the group shall not be obliged to take them into account.

11.7 A copy of any notice given under this rule shall be published on the CMA's website.

12. REMEDIES

12.1 A group shall have regard to the need to give as much notice as is practicable of the actions which it considers might be taken by the CMA for the purpose of remedying the effects of completed or anticipated mergers or for the purpose of remedying the adverse effects found in a market investigation.

12.2 Any notice of those actions may be contained in the provisional findings but, if it is not, the group shall notify the main parties as soon as practicable after it has notified them of its provisional findings.

12.3 A copy of any notice given under this rule shall be published on the CMA's website.

12.4 Any notice under this rule published on the CMA's website shall not contain any information which the group considers should be excluded from the notice having regard to the three considerations set out in section 244 of the Act (specified information: considerations relevant to disclosure).

12.5 The group shall consult the parties upon whom it has given notice under this rule and have regard to any representations received from them.

13. FINAL FINDINGS

13.1 Once the group has had regard to any reasons in writing or oral evidence submitted to or given to it following the notice of provisional findings then it shall take its final decisions on the statutory questions and actions, and proceed to make and publish the report as required by the Act.

PART 5: REPORTS

14. PREPARATION

[3.64]
14.1 A group may, for the purpose of preparing its report, send any material which it has produced back to any person or body so that its accuracy can be verified.

14.2 A group may, for the purposes of Rule 14.1, ask any person or body to identify any matter which that person or body might wish to have excluded from its report.

14.3 Where the final decision of a group is taken by a majority then the report may contain a statement or statements from the member or members in the minority of their dissent from that decision.

15. EXCLUSION OF MATTER

15.1 A group may exclude any matter from its report if it considers that publication of the matter would be inappropriate and in deciding what is inappropriate for this purpose the group shall have regard to the considerations mentioned in section 244 of the Act (specified information: considerations relevant to disclosure).

16. PUBLICATION

16.1 As soon as practicable after deciding which matter is to be excluded from the report, the group shall make arrangements for its publication in accordance with the provisions of sections 39, 137, 143, 143A and 144 of the Act.

16.2 A copy of the report shall be published on www.gov.uk/cma.

PART 6: UNDERTAKINGS AND ORDERS

17. CONSIDERATION OF ACTIONS

[3.65]
17.1 In any case where the report of a group contains a decision that, in the case of a merger reference, there is or may be a substantial lessening of competition, or, in the case of a market investigation, that there is one or more than one adverse effect on competition, and that remedial action should be taken, the group shall, in accordance with sections 41, 41A, 138 and 138A of the Act, consider what further reasonable and practicable actions it should take.[23]

17.2 As part of its considerations the group shall consult any individual or undertaking likely to be affected by those actions and shall have regard to any representations submitted to it by them.[24]

17.3 After the consultation has taken place, the group shall proceed to consider whether to accept an undertaking under sections 82 and 159 of the Act or to make an order under sections 84 and 161 of the Act, as the case may be.

NOTES

23 The order-making powers are set out in sections 84, 86, 87, 88, 161, 164, 165 of, and Schedule 8 to, the Act.

24 Paragraph 2(f) and paragraph 5(c) of Schedule 10 to the Act.

PART 7: RULES FOR SPECIAL REFERENCE GROUPS

18. SPECIAL REFERENCE GROUPS

[3.66]
18.1 The rules in Parts 1, 2, 3, 5 and 6 shall apply to the procedure of special reference groups.

18.2 Instead of complying with Part 4, special reference groups shall determine their own procedures for findings on the reference, but when doing so they shall have regard to any guidance issued by the CMA Board under paragraph 52(1) of Schedule 4 to the ERR Act.[25]

18.3 In their application to Ofcom price control references, these rules shall have effect subject to the rules made under section 15 of the Act (rules with respect to proceedings before the Competition Appeal Tribunal) and any directions given to the CMA by the Competition Appeal Tribunal in exercise of powers conferred by those rules.[26]

NOTES

25 Given effect to by section 25(4) of the ERR Act.

26 See section 193 of the Communications Act 2003.

EXPLANATORY NOTE

[3.67]
This note is not part of the rules.

1. These rules replace *CC1, Competition Commission Rules of Procedure* of 2006.

2. The rules apply to merger reference groups, market reference groups and special reference groups as defined in paragraph 51 of Schedule 4 to the ERR Act:

'market reference group' means a CMA group constituted in connection with a reference under section 131, 132 or 140A of the Act.

'merger reference group' means a CMA group constituted in connection with a reference under section 32 of the Water Industry Act 1991 or section 22, 33, 45 or 62 of the Act.[27]

'special reference group' means a CMA group constituted in connection with a reference under:
(a) section 11 of the Competition Act 1980
(b) 41E of the Gas Act 1986
(c) 56C of the Electricity Act 1989
(d) section 12, 14 or 17K of the Water Industry Act 1991
(e) Article 15 of the Electricity (Northern Ireland) Order 1992 (SI 1992/231 (NI 1))
(f) section 13 of, or Schedule 4A to, the Railways Act 1993
(g) Article 15 of the Gas (Northern Ireland) Order 1996 (SI 1996/275 (NI 2))
(h) section 12 of the Transport Act 2000
(i) section 193 of the Communications Act 2003
(j) Article 3 of the Water Services etc (Scotland) Act 2005 (Consequential Provisions and Modifications) Order 2005 (SI 2005/3172)

3. Subject to any special or general directions given by the Secretary of State, and to any provision by or under any enactment, a CMA group that is not a merger reference group, market reference group or special reference group may determine its own procedure.[28]

4. As at the date of making these rules the CMA has made as procedural rules for other CMA groups the following rules (previously made by the Competition Commission):

CC10: The Energy Code Modification Rules

CC14: Competition Commission Energy Licence Modification Rules

CC16: Postal Services Appeal Rules

CC19: Competition Commission Airport Licence Condition Appeal Rules

CC21: National Tariff Methodology Reference Rules

NOTES

27 The reference in this definition to section 62 of the Act has effect as if it included a reference to Article 5 of the Enterprise Act 2002 (Protection of Legitimate Interests) Order 2003 (SI 2003/1592), as amended by Enterprise Act 2002 (Protection of Legitimate Interests) (Amendment) Order 2014.

28 See paragraph 54 of Schedule 4 to the ERR Act.

CODE OF CONDUCT FOR CMA PANEL MEMBERS (MARCH 2016)

[3.68]

NOTES

This Code is available on the Competition and Markets Authority website at: www.gov.uk/government/publications/cma-panel-code-of-conduct.

OBJECTIVES OF THIS CODE

[3.69]
1. The Competition and Markets Authority's ('CMA') activities have important implications for society and can have considerable financial and reputational implications for particular parties. The purpose of this Code of Conduct ('the Code') is to enable CMA Panel Members to help the CMA to maintain its reputation for fairness, independence, integrity, rigorous analysis, careful handling of sensitive information, and efficient use of public money.

BACKGROUND

2. The CMA is a public body whose primary responsibility is to seek to promote competition, both within and outside the United Kingdom, for the benefit of consumers. The functions of the CMA include giving advice to government and other public bodies, studying and investigating competition issues in markets, investigating and enforcing civil and criminal prohibitions in competition and consumer law, and considering appeals and references from other public bodies under various economic regulatory statutes.

3. The CMA is a non-ministerial government department, funded by the taxpayer, reporting to parliament through its annual plan and report. Its staff are civil servants.

4. The CMA is a corporate body, established under the Enterprise and Regulatory Reform Act 2013 (ERRA 2013). It consists of a Chair, the CMA Board and the CMA panel, all appointed by the Secretary of State. The CMA Board comprises the Chair, the Chief Executive, executive and non-executive directors, and a number of members of the CMA panel. The Chief Executive acts as the CMA's accounting officer, responsible for the economy and efficiency of its handling of public monies.

5. Some functions of the CMA must be performed by members of the CMA panel (referred to in this Code as 'Members'), some by the CMA Board, and some by specifically authorised persons. Other functions are performed by or on behalf of the CMA Board, with many delegated to staff or committees or sub-committees. Members help perform a variety of these roles and often act as representatives of the CMA in dealing with third parties.

6. Members are appointed on the basis of their specialist skills and knowledge, such that they can be expected to be robust and weighty contributors able to take their own decisions on issues. The CMA will provide support and training to help them perform their functions at the CMA.

GENERAL

7. As holders of public office, Members' behaviour and actions must be governed by the principles set out in this Code. It is each Member's responsibility to ensure familiarity and compliance the Code. Compliance with the Code forms part of Members' terms of appointment. The Panel Chair is responsible for compliance of Members with this Code.

8. Members must, in carrying out their responsibilities, have regard to the principles of public life:[1] selflessness, integrity, objectivity, accountability, openness, honesty and leadership, and act at all times in the best interests of the CMA.

9. Members are expected to endorse and exemplify the CMA values of ambition, excellence, commitment, fairness and teamwork.[2]

10. Members must not occupy paid political posts or hold particularly sensitive or high profile unpaid roles in a political party. On matters directly affecting the CMA's work, Members should not make political speeches or engage in other political activities.

11. Members must not use information obtained in the course of their functions for personal gain, nor seek to use the opportunity presented by public service to promote their private interests.

12. Members must comply with the CMA's policy on acceptance of gifts and hospitality and rules in respect of claiming travel and subsistence expenses.

13. Members are expected to participate in the CMA's appraisal arrangements for review of the performance of members.

NOTES

[1] Committee on Standards in Public Life (May 1995), The 7 principles of public life.

[2] Competition and Markets Authority (January 2014), Vision, values and strategy for the CMA (CMA13).

RESPONSIBILITIES AS A MEMBER

14. Members may perform a variety of roles on behalf of the CMA including acting as a member of:

(a) the CMA Board;
(b) a merger reference group;
(c) a market reference group;
(d) a remedies review group;
(e) a special reference group (to decide a regulatory redetermination or appeal);
(f) a Case Decision Group (following the issue of a Statement of Objections in a Competition Act 1998 case);
(g) a Case Management Panel (in criminal cartel cases);
(h) the CMA's Case and Policy Committee; and

assisting with other internal governance roles.

15. In each case, Members must ensure that they:

(a) perform the duties imposed on the CMA by any relevant legislation;[3]
(b) exercise the powers of the CMA in accordance with the legislation and any CMA rules made to enable them to do so;[4] and
(c) have regard to any CMA guidance and policies relevant to the performance of the relevant functions of the CMA.

16. Members must have regard to the performance objectives of the CMA set out in its annual plan, and must help to ensure the CMA makes proper, economical, effective and efficient use of its resources. The plan takes account of the obligation of the CMA to perform many of its functions to tight statutory and administrative timetables. In this regard, Members should ensure that they are familiar with the CMA's project management guidance and prioritisation principles,[5] which are designed to help the CMA act in a timely way, and have regard to them where relevant during the performance of their functions.

17. The CMA is committed to being transparent about and enhancing the visibility of its work. Members should have regard to the CMA's Transparency Statement[6] and endeavour to conduct inquires and cases in an open fashion, providing information at appropriate stages and reasons for their decisions.

NOTES

3 The main statutes relevant to Members are likely to be the Competition Act 1998 and Parts 3 (mergers), 4 (market investigations), 7 (cartel offence) and 9 (restrictions on disclosure and use of information) of the Enterprise Act 2002. Regulatory references and appeals are made under specific regulatory statutes, including the Communications Act 2003. However in addition, other laws may be applicable in particular situations, including human rights law and EU law.

4 For example, members of mergers and markets reference groups must have regards to the Rules of procedure for merger, market and special reference groups (CMA17); members of Case Decisions Groups must have regard to the Guidance on the CMA's investigation procedures in Competition Act 1998 cases (CMA8).

5 Competition and Markets Authority (April 2014), Prioritisation principles for the CMA (CMA16).

6 Competition and Markets Authority (January 2014), Transparency and disclosure: Statement of the CMA's policy and approach (CMA6).

INDEPENDENCE OF PHASE 2 INQUIRIES

18. When establishing the CMA, parliament considered it important that Members should act independently of the CMA Board when taking decisions as members of CMA groups. The purpose of this requirement is to ensure that decision taking by groups is based on their own judgement reached after analysis of the evidence before them. This requirement does not prevent information passing between CMA groups and the CMA Board, or CMA groups seeking a variation of the terms of a merger or market investigation reference from the CMA Board.[7]

19. CMA Board Members involved in the decision to make a market investigation reference or a merger reference cannot be members of the resulting merger or markets group.[8]

NOTES

7 ERRA 2013, Schedule 4, paragraph 49.

8 ERRA 2013, Schedule 4, paragraph 33.

CONFLICTS OF INTEREST

20. The CMA must be, and be seen to be, impartial. This is essential in order to maintain public confidence in the decisions made by the CMA. The outside interests of Members and their close family relatives (including financial interests, those arising from their outside activities such as directorships or consultancies, previous roles and publishing activities) can threaten that impartiality because they create the possibility of bias, or the appearance of bias. (The latter risk may materialise if the fair-minded and informed observer would conclude that there was a real possibility of bias (even without any evidence of actual bias)).

21. Members must therefore comply with the CMA's policy for dealing with of interest set out in Annex D to the Board Rules of Procedure.[9] Members should note that this policy does not set out every circumstance in which a conflict of interest may arise. Details of any interests potentially relevant to particular appointments will be sought from Members before appointments are made. Members may also raise any concerns they have from time to time as cases develop or as personal circumstances change with the Compliance Officer or the Panel Chair. It is the responsibility of each Member, if in any doubt as to whether their external activities and other matters might pose a risk to the impartiality of the CMA, to seek advice from the Compliance Officer and/or Panel Chair. While Members may be in the best position to identify whether they have an outside interest of potential concern, they are not in the best position to judge any consequences for the CMA.

22. The Panel Chair is ultimately responsible for ensuring that Members appointed to inquiries and cases are not conflicted at any time and may remove a Member from a CMA group if, because of a particular interest of the Member, it is inappropriate for him or her to remain a member of the group.[10]

23. The Compliance Officer is responsible day to day for ensuring that the CMA's policy on conflicts of interest is applied and enforced. If a Member is in any doubt about the significance of an outside interest or activity, they should consult the Compliance Officer, who will advise on the appropriate action and make recommendations to the Panel Chair as appropriate.

24. Where a Member is a member of the CMA Board and/or a CMA committee or sub-committee (for example, the CMA's Case and Policy Committee, or a remedies review group) and receives the agenda for a meeting, that Member must ensure that they declare any potential and/or actual conflicts of interest in respect of specific matters which may be discussed at the meeting.

25. When taking on any outside appointments or acquiring financial interests, Members should be aware that those interests may restrict the scope of work the Member may be able to perform for the CMA.

26. A brief biography of Members with some details of their interests will be maintained on the CMA website. In addition, Members' interests of possible relevance to any role they may play for the CMA may be disclosed to particular parties or publicly on its website, either prior to the appointment of the Member to perform that role, or subsequently as a case progresses.

NOTES

9 Competition and Markets Authority (April 2014), Board Rules of Procedure.

10 Members may also be removed from a group if the Panel Chair considers that they will be unable, for a substantial period, to perform their duties as a member of the group. See ERRA 2013, Schedule 4, paragraph 41.

USE OF INFORMATION

27. Members are subject to a general duty of confidentiality in relation to the conduct of the affairs of the CMA and information they obtain in the course of their work. They must also comply with any relevant statutory restrictions in relation to the handling of such information, in particular those relating to commercial confidences and personal data under Part 9 of the Enterprise Act 2002 and the Data Protection Act 1998. These obligations are personal, and must be respected while complying with the transparency commitments of the CMA.

28. When handling information either provided or created in the course of the CMA's work, Members must comply with the CMA's information security policies, procedures and guidance and ensure that the confidentiality of the information is maintained and that it is protected from unauthorised disclosure or access. Specifically, Members must comply with the CMA's ICT Acceptable Usage Policy and whilst working away from the CMA's office they must access information securely, and communicate confidential information using specified systems for the secure transmission of information.

29. Members should take care not to discuss or comment on potential or ongoing inquiries or investigations in public, including via social media, without the prior agreement of the CMA, consulting CMA project teams or the central Communications team, as necessary.

30. Members must not misuse information gained in the course of their public service for personal gain or for political purposes.

INSIDER DEALING

31. Members who misuse information gained by virtue of their position may be committing a criminal offence of insider dealing under Part V of the Criminal Justice Act 1993.

CONTACT WITH THE MEDIA/GENERAL PUBLIC

32. All enquiries from the media should be directed to CMA's Press Office. Members should not engage directly with the media, other than via the CMA's press office.

33. All other enquiries should be directed to the CMA's general enquiries team.

RESPONSIBILITIES TOWARDS EMPLOYEES

34. Members must treat any staff or contractors employed by the CMA and other Members with courtesy and respect. Members should respect individual differences and act in accordance with the CMA's policies and procedures in respect of equality and diversity, bullying, harassment and discrimination.

35. Members should be willing to give feedback when sought on CMA employees and other Members whose performance they are well placed to assess.

RESPONSIBILITIES ON CEASING TO BE A MEMBER

36. After ceasing to be a Member, Members will remain bound by the statutory restrictions in relation to the handling of information mentioned in paragraph 27 above, and the restrictions that may be caused by conflicts of interests related to their activities when a Member; certain appointments and activities in relation to parties and advisers to parties they dealt with as Members require the consent of the Secretary of State for a period after they cease to be a Member.

CLARIFICATION ON PUBLISHING MARKET SENSITIVE ANNOUNCEMENTS (CMA6 CLARIFICATION NOTE) (2 DECEMBER 2016)

[3.70]

NOTES

This clarification note is available on the CMA's website at: www.gov.uk/government/publications/transparency-and-disclosure-statement-of-the-cmas-policy-and-approach.

Paragraph 3.23 of the CMA's transparency and disclosure statement (CMA 6) and paragraphs 12.19 and 13.14 of its guidance on jurisdiction and procedure in merger investigations (CMA 2), set out the CMA's approach to the publication of provisional and final decisions in markets and mergers investigations involving UK listed companies. To ensure the continued orderly announcement of such decisions, the CMA's practice will now be:

- In Phase 2 market investigations involving UK listed companies, parties will receive advance copies of the press release and other documents to be published at 6am, one hour before their publication at 7.00 am. This follows the process trialled earlier this year after confidential information entered the public domain having been shared the evening before.
- In Phase 2 merger investigations involving UK listed companies, parties will continue to receive advance copies of the press release, and any other documents to be published, after 4.30 pm on the preceding evening, ahead of their publication at 7.00 am (see paragraph 13.14 of CMA2).
- In Phase 1 merger decisions involving UK listed companies, parties will receive notification of the decision after 4.30 pm on the preceding evening, ahead of announcement at 7.00 am.

The CMA will keep these practices under review and may depart from this approach where there is an appropriate and reasonable justification for doing so.

PRO FORMA TEMPLATES FOR CMA CONFIDENTIALITY RINGS UNDERTAKINGS (JANUARY 2017)

NOTES

This template is available on the CMA's website at: www.gov.uk/government/publications/confidentiality-ring-and-disclosure-room-undertakings-templates.

[3.71]

This document contains pro forma templates and associated drafting notes for the undertakings to be given to the CMA regarding access to confidentiality rings in CMA investigations, by:

1. **External advisers retained by parties to advise in relation to CMA investigations (see *Confidentiality Ring Undertakings: Adviser*)**
2. **The firms to which those advisers belong (see *Confidentiality Ring Undertakings: Firm*)**

These templates are based on recent CMA practice and are intended to provide advisers and parties with an indication of the basic terms/provisions and conditions that may typically be included in CMA Confidentiality Rings undertakings.

If/as appropriate, these may be tailored for each particular case, taking into account, for example, the nature of the CMA's investigation and purpose of the disclosure exercise; the nature and sensitivity of the data/information to be disclosed; etc.

CONFIDENTIALITY RING UNDERTAKINGS: ADVISER

[When drafting the Undertakings using this template, your attention is drawn to the 'Confidentiality Ring Undertakings: Drafting Notes which will help clarifying certain concepts and tailoring this document to the specific needs of the particular Investigation.]

[NAME OF INVESTIGATION]

UNDERTAKINGS GIVEN BY [NAME OF ADVISER] TO THE COMPETITION AND MARKETS AUTHORITY REGARDING ACCESS TO THE [XXX] CONFIDENTIALITY RING [FOLLOWING/BEFORE XXX]

WHEREAS

(1) [Brief overview of the Investigation (including the empowering statutory provision(s)]
   (a) **See Drafting Note ('DN') 1 for example text for CA98, market investigations and merger inquiries**
   (b) **Incorporate definitions of:**
      - **the Competition and Markets Authority ('the CMA')**
      - **relevant legislation e.g. the Enterprise Act 2002 ('the EA02'), the Competition Act 1998 ('the CA98') and**
      - **'the Investigation'.**

(2) [Background information: i.e. description of stage of the Investigation; CMA/CAT actions so far]
   (a) **See DN2 for example text**

(3) [Background continued: e.g. request made by party/ies; rationale for the disclosure which is being facilitated by these undertakings etc.]

(4) The CMA has decided to disclose the following:
   (a) [Description of disclosed material]
   (b) [Description of disclosed material]
   (c) [etc.]

   (the 'Disclosed Material') by means of a confidentiality ring commencing on [insert date] ('the Confidentiality Ring'). A reference to the Disclosed Material in these undertakings includes a reference to any part of the Disclosed Material.

See DN 3 and DN4

OR

[*The CMA has decided to disclose the material set out in Schedule 1 [which may be amended from time to time by the CMA] ('the Disclosed Material') by means of a confidentiality ring commencing on [insert date] ('the Confidentiality Ring'). A reference to the Disclosed Material in these undertakings includes a reference to any part of the Disclosed Material*]

(5) The CMA considers that the 'Disclosed Material' [is/includes] specified information within the meaning of section 238 of the [EA02] [Enterprise Act 2002 ('the EA02')] to which the general restriction on disclosure in section 237 of the EA02 applies. The CMA may disclose specified information to any other person in circumstances permitted by the EA02.

(6) The CMA has decided to disclose the Disclosed Material [to certain parties the Investigation], [to Name of Party]] ([each a] [the] 'Relevant Party') by means of

the Confidentiality Ring pursuant to section [X] of the EA02. [**See DN5**]. Access to the Confidentiality Ring is restricted to the [external legal and/or economic [**See DN6**] advisers] of the Relevant Parties and is provided for the sole purpose of allowing the advisers of a Relevant Party, on behalf of the Relevant Party, [to review and understand [X]], to prepare submissions and representations to the CMA regarding [X], and (if relevant) to prepare and conduct an appeal against any decision of the CMA in connection with the Investigation, including an appeal in which the Relevant Party is, or is intending to apply to be, an intervener, in which case the arrangements established by these Undertakings may be extended to apply for the purposes of such appeal ('the Permitted Purpose'); [**See DN7**].

(7) Access to the Confidentiality Ring will be granted to, and only to, an adviser:

(a) who has been approved in writing by the CMA;

(b) who has given written undertakings acceptable to the CMA ('the Individual Undertakings'); and

(c) if relevant, in respect of whom the adviser's firm/employer has given written undertakings acceptable to the CMA ('the Firm Undertakings');

in accordance with [*the arrangements in recital (9)*][*arrangements specified by the CMA*] (each such adviser being an 'Authorised Adviser'); [**See DN8**]

(8) *[The number of Authorised Advisers is limited to [number – X] [for each Relevant Party]]* **[see DN9].**

(9) [The arrangements for obtaining CMA approval of an adviser and for giving undertakings in respect of an adviser are:

a. notice of not less than [insert time – e.g. 2 CMA working days[1]] must be given to the CMA of the date on which the adviser first wishes be granted access the Confidentiality Ring ('the Access Date');

b. by 4pm on the CMA Working Day before the Access Date the Individual Undertakings signed by the adviser and, if relevant, the Firm Undertakings signed on behalf of the adviser's firm/employer, must be provided to (and received by) the CMA;

c. before the adviser attempts to access the Confidentiality Ring confirmation in writing must be obtained from the CMA that it has approved the adviser and has accepted the signed Individual Undertakings and, if relevant, the signed Firm Undertakings.] **[see DN 10]**

(10) Subject to the Individual Undertakings and the Firm Undertakings, the CMA will make the Disclosed Material available to [the Authorised Advisers] [Name of Adviser] by encrypted Egress email [*unless otherwise specified in Schedule 1*]. [Each Authorised Adviser] [[Name of Adviser] will then be permitted:

(a) [*provided the Disclosed Material is password-protected,* to download the Disclosed Material via Egress onto a computer or into a secure folder on a server of the Authorised Adviser's firm/employer; and

(b) to print copies provided each Authorised Adviser only has one hard copy in existence at any one time (each a 'Permitted Copy')

[See DN11]

(11) Disclosure of the Disclosed Material other than in accordance with the Individual Undertakings is not permitted without the express and prior written consent of the CMA. Breach of the Individual Undertakings by an Authorised Adviser may result in:

(a) the CMA:

(i) terminating the Authorised Adviser's access to the Confidentiality Ring and refusing the Authorised Advisor access to any subsequent disclosure room or confidentiality ring run by the CMA, whether relating to the Investigation or any other investigation;

(ii) where relevant, referring the breach to the Authorised Adviser's regulatory body which may decide to take disciplinary action in relation to the breach.

(b) a breach by the Authorised Adviser of his or her obligations under Part 9 of the EA02 (as regards the disclosure and use of the Disclosed Material) which constitutes a criminal offence under section 245 of the EA02;

(12) [Name of Firm] has been instructed by [Name of Party], which is a Relevant Party, for the purpose of providing [legal/economic] advice to [Name of Party] in relation to the Investigation. [Name of Adviser] is [employed by [Name of Firm] as a [legal/economic adviser]] [a partner in [Name of Firm]].

NOW THEREFORE

I, [Name of Adviser], [Job title] at [Name of Firm], which has been engaged by [Name of Party] in connection with the Investigation, undertake to the CMA in my own name:

1. To access the Disclosed Material only through the Permitted Copies and in the secure electronic format provided by the CMA using only:

(a) a computer which is password-protected and accessible to only the Authorised Advisers of [Name of Party] [Name of Firm] ; or

(b) a secure folder on the server of the Authorised Adviser's firm/employer to which only the Authorised Advisers of [Name of Party] [Name of Firm] have access (such access to be controlled by appropriate information barriers and privacy settings of no less a standard than would be applied to personal data or price sensitive client information held by the Authorised Adviser's firm/employer, or the firm/employer's own commercially sensitive information, and any variation of these access permissions is to be made only with the express written consent of the CMA);

2. To use the Disclosed Material for, and only for, the Permitted Purpose;
3. [Save as provided in paragraphs 6 and 7], to hold the Disclosed Material in strict confidence and not to disclose or make available in any manner the Disclosed Material to any other person (including any other legal adviser, economic adviser, officer or employee of [Name of Firm] and [Name of Party]) except:
   (a) another Authorised Adviser of [Name of Party], or
   (b) a member of CMA staff or a CMA panel member working on the Investigation (or the court if in the course of an appeal),

   (such a person being a 'Non-Authorised Person');
4. Not to make any electronic or non-electronic copy in any format of the Disclosed Material other than the Permitted Copies, save that I may copy the Disclosed Material for, and only for, the purposes of preparing a [summary,] report or submission within the scope of the Permitted Purpose;
5. To ensure that, [save as provided in paragraphs 6 and 7], any document (including any [summary], report or submission) I prepare, or analysis I undertake, which contains or refers to the Disclosed Material or which derives wholly or partially from the Disclosed Material is not used, disclosed or made available in any way to:
   (a) disclose the Disclosed Material to any Non-Authorised Person; or
   (b) enable or assist any Non-Authorised Person to gain an understanding of [Name of Party]'s position or potential future position in any market relative to any other market operator (other than relative to a market wide benchmark) [any other description of information]; **[DN12]**

   [DN 13 – sharing with clients]
6. [For the avoidance of doubt] while I may share a non-confidential version of any report or submission with [Name of Party] to facilitate the Permitted Purpose, I will ensure, including by making any necessary redactions, that (i) the restrictions in paragraph [5] are complied with in relation to any such non-confidential report or submission; and that (ii) the non-confidential report or submission is only shared with [Name of Party] after the CMA has confirmed in writing to an Authorised Adviser of [Name of Party] that the non-confidential [summary]/report or submission does not include any of the Disclosed Material and meets the requirements in paragraph 5.
7. [*While I may share [a general summary of/the conclusion of my assessment of/key trends arising from] the Disclosed Material with [Name of Party], to facilitate the Permitted Purpose [only to the extent that . . .], I will ensure that, if so required by the CMA, [the non-confidential [summary] is only shared with [Name of Party] after the CMA has confirmed in writing to an Authorised Adviser of [Name of Party] that the non-confidential summary does not include any of the Disclosed Material and meets the requirements in paragraph 5.*]

   [*or*]

   [*such general summary/conclusion/key trends] is/are not used or made available in any way to:*

   a. disclose to any Non-Authorised Person, [specific] information regarding:
      i. the Disclosed Material relating to [X]; and
      ii. the Disclosed Material relating to [Y];

   b. enable or assist any Non-Authorised Person to gain an understanding of [Name of Party]'s position or potential future position in any market relative to any other market operator (other than relative to a market wide benchmark) and in particular does not reveal [description of information which should not be given to the party – if different from 7a(i) and (ii)];

   [*and, if so required by the CMA, that these are not shared with [Name of Party] until after the CMA has confirmed in writing to an Authorised Adviser of [Name of Party] that they comply with the requirements above*]
8. To ensure that any submission I prepare containing or referring to the Disclosed Material is submitted to the CMA separately from any other submission on behalf of [Name of Party], highlights any Disclosed Material [*and is accompanied by any working files (including 'stata-do-files') used to perform any analysis referred to in the submission*]; **DN 14**
9. To keep secure at all times:
   (a) the Disclosed Material and the Permitted Copies provided to me; and
   (b) any [summary] report, submission or other document prepared by or provided to me which contains or refers to the Disclosed Material

   (together the 'Relevant Material and Documents'), including in a manner which means the Relevant Material and Documents are not accessible to any Non-Authorised Person;
10. That, save as provided in paragraph 11, within 5 CMA working days of the relevant concluding event I will:

(a) return to the CMA or destroy the Relevant Material and Documents or, where the Relevant Material and Documents are in electronic form and their destruction is not possible, to return them to the CMA or render them inaccessible from any computer system, disk or device so that they are not readily available to any person; and

(b) where the Relevant Material and Documents are destroyed or rendered inaccessible, inform the CMA of the manner of the destruction or rendering inaccessible;

The relevant concluding event is:

(i) if there is an appeal against a decision of the CMA in connection with the Investigation in which [Name of Party] is a party or is intervening, the conclusion of the appeal;

(ii) if there is no such appeal, the expiry of the period for bringing such an appeal, or

(iii) if I cease to advise [Name of Party] in relation to the Investigation or appeal before the event specified by (i) or (ii), my ceasing to advise [Name of Party] in relation to the Investigation or appeal.

11. That, while the Authorised Advisers of [Name of Firm] may retain one copy (between them) of the Disclosed Material, Permitted Copies and any [summary] report, submission or other document which contains or refers to the Disclosed Material if it is required to comply with [Name of Firm]'s professional indemnity insurance policy or any applicable law, legislation or court order, I will ensure that:

(a) the copy is stored securely in accordance with the undertaking in paragraph 9;

(b) the CMA is notified of the retention within 5 CMA working days of the relevant concluding event specified by paragraph 10(i) or (ii); and

(c) the CMA is consulted as far as practicable prior to any disclosure of the copy under [Name of Firm]'s professional indemnity insurance policy or any applicable law, legislation or court order;

12. To notify the CMA immediately if I become aware of or suspect that there has been a breach of:

(a) these undertakings;

(b) the Individual Undertakings given by another Authorised Adviser of [Name of Party] [Name of Firm]]; or

(c) [the Firm Undertakings given in respect of any of the Authorised Advisers of Name of Party]].

PROVIDED THAT

These undertakings shall not apply to any part of the Disclosed Material that:

(i) belongs or relates solely to [Name of Party] or to [Name of Party]'s business and which does not include any confidential information belonging to, relating to or deriving solely or partially from any other party to the Investigation;

(ii) is information that has previously been disclosed by the CMA to [Name of Party in the Investigation;]

(iii) at the time of disclosure is in the public domain or subsequently comes into the public domain, except through breach of these undertakings, the Individual Undertakings given by other Authorised Advisers or the Firm Undertakings;

(iv) is required to be disclosed by law, legislation or court order, as long as, and unless prohibited by law, legislation or court order, I consult with the CMA as far as practicable prior to the proposed disclosure on the proposed forum, timing, nature and purpose of the proposed disclosure; or

(v) is covered by a confidentiality ring established by the Competition Appeal Tribunal in the course of an appeal against the decision of the CMA in connection with the Investigation in which [Name of Party] is a party or is intervening.

AND IN AGREEMENT THAT

These undertakings shall be governed by and construed in accordance with English law and I submit to the exclusive jurisdiction of the courts of England and Wales to hear and decide any action or proceedings which may arise out of, or in connection with these undertakings.

[Name of Party] has given full and informed consent to the terms of these undertakings, including the restrictions placed upon [Name of Adviser] on the disclosure of information by these undertakings.

[Name of Adviser] of [Name of Firm]

[*signature*]

[Date]

NOTES

[1] A 'CMA working day' is any day of the week, Monday to Friday, on which the CMA's offices are open (and excludes public or bank holidays).

1. CONFIDENTIALITY RING UNDERTAKINGS: FIRM

[When drafting the Undertakings using this template, your attention is drawn to the 'Confidentiality Ring Undertakings: Drafting Notes which will help clarifying some concepts and in tailoring this document to the specific needs of the particular Investigation.]

[NAME OF INVESTIGATION]

UNDERTAKINGS GIVEN BY [NAME OF FIRM] TO THE COMPETITION AND MARKETS AUTHORITY REGARDING ACCESS TO THE [XXX] CONFIDENTIALITY RING [FOLLOWING/BEFORE XXX]

WHEREAS

(1) [Brief overview of the Investigation (including the empowering statutory provision(s)]

a. See the Drafting Guide at Drafting Note ('DN') 1 for example text for CA98, market investigations and merger inquiries

b. Incorporate definitions of:

i. the Competition and Markets Authority ('the CMA')

ii. relevant legislation e.g. the Enterprise Act 2002 ('the EA02'), the Competition Act 1998 ('the CA98') and

iii. 'the Investigation'.

(2) [Background information: i.e. description of stage of the Investigation; CMA/CAT actions so far]

c. See DN2 for example text

(3) [Background continued: e.g. request made by party/ies; rationale for the disclosure which is being facilitated by these undertakings etc.]

(4) [The CMA has decided to disclose the following:

(a) [Description of disclosed material]

(b) [Description of disclosed material]

(c) [etc.]

(the 'Disclosed Material') by means of a confidentiality ring commencing on [insert date] ('the Confidentiality Ring').] A reference to the Disclosed Material in these undertakings includes a reference to any part of the Disclosed Material;

See DN3 and DN4

OR

[The CMA has decided to disclose the material set out in Schedule 1 [which may be amended from time to time by the CMA] ('the Disclosed Material') by means of a confidentiality ring commencing on [insert date] ('the Confidentiality Ring'). A reference to the Disclosed Material in these undertakings includes a reference to any part of the Disclosed Material;]

(5) The CMA considers that the 'Disclosed Material' [is/includes] specified information within the meaning of section 238 of the [EA02] [Enterprise Act 2002 ('the EA02') to which the general restriction on disclosure in section 237 of the Act applies. However, the CMA may disclose specified information to any other person in circumstances permitted by the EA02.

(6) The CMA has decided to disclose the Disclosed Material [to certain parties], [to Name of Party] ([each a] [the] 'Relevant Party' /] by means of the Confidentiality Ring pursuant to section [X] of the EA02. [**See DN5**]. Access to the Confidentiality Ring is restricted to the [external legal and/or economic **See DN6**] advisers] of the Relevant Parties and is provided for the sole purpose of [allowing the advisers of a Relevant Party, on behalf of the Relevant Party, to review and understand [X], to prepare submissions and representations to the CMA regarding [X], and (if relevant) to prepare and conduct an appeal against any decision of the CMA in connection with the Investigation, including an appeal in which the Relevant Party is, or is intending to apply to be, an intervener in which case the arrangements established by these Undertakings may be extended to apply for the purposes of such appeal ('the Permitted Purpose') [**See DN7**]

(7) Access to the Confidentiality Ring will be granted to, and only to, an adviser:

(a) who has been approved in writing by the CMA;

(b) who has given written undertakings acceptable to the CMA ('the Individual Undertakings'); and

(c) where relevant, in respect of whom the adviser's firm/employer has given written undertakings acceptable to the CMA ('the Firm Undertakings');

in accordance with [*the arrangements in recital (9)*] [*arrangements specified by the CMA*] (each such adviser being an 'Authorised Adviser'); [**See DN8**]

(8) [*The number of Authorised Advisers is limited to [number – X] [for each Relevant Party*]]; **[see DN9].**

(9) The arrangements for obtaining CMA approval of an adviser and for giving undertakings in respect of an adviser are:

a. notice of not less than [insert time – e.g. 2 CMA working days] must be given to the CMA of the date on which the adviser first wishes be granted access the Confidentiality Ring ('the Access Date');

b. by 4pm on the CMA Working Day before the Access Date the Individual Undertakings signed by the adviser and, if relevant, the Firm Undertakings signed on behalf of the adviser's firm/employer, must be provided to (and received by) the CMA;

c. before the adviser attempts to access the Confidentiality Ring, confirmation in writing must be obtained from the CMA that it has approved the adviser and has accepted the signed Individual Undertakings and, if relevant, the signed Firm Undertakings;

(10) Subject to the Individual Undertakings and the Firm Undertakings, the CMA will make the

Disclosed Material available to [the Authorised Advisers] [Name of Adviser] by encrypted Egress email [*unless otherwise specified in Schedule 1*]. [Each Authorised Adviser] [[Name of Adviser] will then be permitted:

(a) [*provided the Disclosed Material is password-protected,* to download the Disclosed Material via Egress onto a computer or into a secure folder on a server of the Authorised Adviser's firm/employer]; and

(b) to print copies provided each Authorised Adviser only has one hard copy in existence at any one time (each a 'Permitted Copy')

(11) Disclosure of the Disclosed Material other than in accordance with the Individual Undertakings, is not permitted without the express and prior written consent of the CMA. Breach of the Individual Undertakings by an Authorised Adviser or of the Firm Undertakings by an Authorised Adviser's firm/employer may result in:

(a) the CMA:

(i) in the case of a breach by an Authorised Adviser, terminating the Authorised Adviser's access to the Confidentiality Ring and refusing the Authorised Advisor access to any subsequent disclosure room or confidentiality ring run by the CMA, whether relating to the Investigation or any other investigation;

(ii) in the case of a breach by a firm/employer, terminating the firm/employer's participation in the Confidentiality Ring and refusing a request to participate in any subsequent disclosure room or confidentiality ring run by the CMA, whether relating to the Investigation or any other investigation;

(iii) where relevant, referring the breach to the regulatory body of the Authorised Adviser or firm/employer which may decide to take disciplinary action in relation to the breach;

(b) a breach of the obligations under Part 9 of the EA02 (as regards the disclosure and use of the Disclosed Material) which constitutes a criminal offence under section 245 of the EA02.

(12) [Name of Firm] has been instructed by [Name of Party], which is a Relevant Party, for the purpose of providing [legal/economic] advice to [Name of Party] in relation to the Investigation. [Name of Adviser[s]] [is/are] employed by [Name of Firm] as a [legal/economic advisers]] [is/are] [a] partner[s] in [Name of Firm]].

NOW THEREFORE

[Name of Firm] which has been engaged by [Name of Party] in connection with the Investigation undertakes to the CMA that:

1. It will give only Authorised Advisers of [Name of Party *or* Name of Firm] access to the Disclosed Material and only in accordance with the terms of the Individual Undertakings given by those Authorised Advisers; **DN 15**
2. It will notify the CMA immediately if it becomes aware of or suspects that there has been any breach of:
   a. these undertakings;
   b. the Individual Undertakings given by an Authorised Advisers of [Name of Party *or* [Name of Firm]; or
   c. [the other Firm Undertakings given in respect of any of the Authorised Advisers of [Name of Party]'. **DN 15**
3. It will notify the CMA immediately if any Authorised Adviser ceases to be at [Name of Firm] before:
   a. if there is an appeal against a decision of the CMA in connection with the Investigation in which [Name of Party] is a party or is intervening, the conclusion of the appeal;
   b. if there is no such appeal, the expiry of the period for bringing such an appeal.

Further, [Name of Firm] undertakes to the CMA to use its reasonable endeavours to ensure that the Authorised Advisers at [Name of Firm] comply with the Individual Undertakings which they have given.

PROVIDED THAT

These undertakings shall not apply to any part of the Disclosed Material that:

(i) belongs or relates solely to [Name of Party] or to [Name of Party]'s business and which does not include any confidential information belonging to, relating to or deriving solely or partially from any other party to the Investigation;

(ii) is information that has previously been disclosed by the CMA to [Name of Party] in the Investigation;

(iii) at the time of disclosure is in the public domain or subsequently comes into the public domain, except through breach of these undertakings, the Individual Undertakings or the other Firm Undertakings;

(iv) is required to be disclosed by law, legislation or court order, as long as, and unless prohibited by law, legislation or court order, [Name of Firm] consults with the CMA prior to the proposed disclosure on the proposed forum, timing, nature and purpose of the proposed disclosure; or

(v) is covered by a confidentiality ring established by the Competition Appeal Tribunal in the course of an appeal against the decision of the CMA in connection with the Investigation in which [Name of Party] is a party or is intervening.

AND IN AGREEMENT THAT

These undertakings shall be governed by and construed in accordance with English law and [Name of Firm] submits to the exclusive jurisdiction of the courts of England and Wales to hear and decide any action or proceedings which may arise out of, or in connection with these undertakings.

[Name of Party] has given full and informed consent to the terms of these undertakings and the Individual Undertakings given by the Authorised Advisers of [Name of Firm], including the restrictions placed upon those Authorised Advisers on the disclosure of information.

[Name of Firm]

[*signature*]

[Date]

2. CONFIDENTIALITY RING DRAFTING NOTES

CONFIDENTIALITY RING UNDERTAKINGS: DRAFTING NOTES

Drafting Note ('DN') 1: "Brief overview of the Investigation'

The following examples provide a reflection on the amount and nature of the information to be included in the recital:

CA98 example: 'In exercise of its powers under section 25 of the Competition Act 1998, the Competition and Markets Authority ('CMA') is investigating the conduct of [name of party] for suspected breaches of Chapter [I] / [II] of CA98 and/or the Treaty of the functioning of the European Union ('the Investigation').'

Markets example (Phase 2): 'On [Date], in exercise of its powers under sections 131 and 133 of the Enterprise Act 2002 ('the Act'), the Competition and Markets Authority (CMA) made a reference for a market investigation in to the supply or acquisition of [relevant market] ('the Investigation').'

Mergers example (Phase 2): 'On [Date], in exercise of its powers under [section 22] / [section 33] of the Enterprise Act 2002 ('the Act'), the Competition and Markets Authority (CMA) referred the [completed] [anticipated] acquisition by [name of acquiring party] of [name of acquired party] / [name of acquired party assets] for investigation and report ('the Investigation').'

DN2: 'Background Information'

CA98 example: 'On [Date] the CMA issued a Statement of Objections (the 'S.O') to [Name of Party] and [Name of Party] (together 'the Parties') alleging, on a provisional basis, a breach of the prohibition contained in Chapter [I] / [II] of CA98, and subsequently gave the Parties an opportunity to inspect the case file.'

Mergers and Markets example: 'On [Date] the CMA published its provisional findings in the Investigation ('the Provisional Findings'), in which it found a [summary of findings] and a consequent [substantial lessening of competition] / [adverse effect on competition] [in the [X] market].'

DN3: 'Description of the material to be disclosed'

This section of the template is the opportunity to describe what is being disclosed in the ring. The more descriptive and specific this section can be, the better.

If the description is lengthy it may be preferable to put it in a schedule. The second version of recital (4) provides for this. If required, this section reserves the ability to amend the description so that material can be added to the confidentiality ring. However, any amendment should be done formally, for example, by the advisers signing (or at least acknowledging receipt in writing of) a replacement schedule. The revised schedule (or other amendment) should be kept by the CMA with the original undertakings.

DN4: 'Disclosed Material'

The defined term which has been chosen is 'Disclosed Material', as this is a general term which can be used to cover data, information or documents.

DN5: Statutory Gateway

The CMA may disclose specified information under the Enterprise Act 2002 ('the EA02') if one or more statutory gateway applies. The gateway most likely to be relevant is that in section 241: disclosure is made for the purpose of facilitating the exercise by the CMA of any of its statutory functions, though the 'consent' gateway in section 239 may also be relevant.

DN6: Type of Adviser

The question of who is permitted to participate in a confidentiality ring or disclosure room is determined on a case by case basis, taking into account matters including the nature of the disclosed information and the reason for its disclosure. However, the CMA's usual approach is to limit access to the **parties' external legal and/or economic advisers**. Occasionally, however, it may be appropriate to allow participation by internal personnel such as employees of parties.

DN7: the 'Permitted Purpose'

In addition to the reference provided in the Undertakings regarding allowing the parties to be provided with the gist, the following are possibilities for the Permitted Purpose:

(1) To review the CMA's figures, economic analysis and/or modelling.

(2) To enable the parties' Advisers to further understand the CMA's analysis in order to allow such Advisers to prepare submissions and representations to the CMA.

The following text could be used for either, adapted as appropriate:

Example text:

'for the purpose of understanding and providing observations to the CMA on the latter's [Provisional Findings] / [Statement of Objections] / [[X] Working Paper] / [Insured Price Analysis] / [Price Concentration Analysis].'

For CA98 cases, consider also:

(3) To enable [Name of Party] to exercise fully its rights of defence.

To enable the same Undertakings to be used in the event of any appeal, Permitted Purpose is defined to include use for such an appeal.

DN8: Definition of Authorised Adviser

Note, this definition does not limit the definition of an Authorised Adviser to the Authorised Adviser of a particular party.

DN9: Limit on the number of Authorised Advisers

This recital is optional – it may be used if helpful to clarify the point.

DN10

This recital is optional as the arrangements for obtaining CMA approval of an adviser and giving undertakings could just as well be set out in other communications with advisers.

Receipt of scanned copies of signed undertakings is acceptable to the CMA.

DN11: Method of Disclosure

The usual way to make the Disclosed Material available is via encrypted Egress email. The email can be sent to each Authorised Adviser who can download and print his or her own copy or the email can be sent to a named Authorised Adviser who can then distribute hard copies to the other Authorised Advisers in his or her firm.

Where a stricter regime is wanted and a Confidentiality Ring with additional protections (also referred to as Confidentiality Ring+) is envisaged, the Disclosed Material is/may be provided on a hard drive.

There may be other ways of making information available, for example by encrypted CD Rom/ Memory stick being handed to the party's legal advisers who then have permission to provide copies to the other permitted advisers of that party. These possibilities should be discussed on a case by case basis.

DN12

Paragraph 5(b) is intended to cover confidential/market sensitive information that, while not falling within the definition of Disclosed Material, is created or derived from the Disclosed Material.

DN13

Paragraphs 6 and 7 may be mixed and matched depending on what, in the circumstances of the case, it is considered that advisers may be able to share with their clients. (For example, one could simply have paragraph 6 but not 7, or both paragraph 6 and 7 etc.)

Note the second option in paragraph 7 (by implication) permits advisers to share some Disclosed Material with their clients.

If a stricter regime is appropriate, **requirements for the CMA to check what is shared could be added here.** For example, paragraph 6 could be redrafted:

That [for the avoidance of doubt,] while I may share a non-confidential version of any [summary], report or submission with [Name of Party] to facilitate the Permitted Purpose, I will not share any such document until [written] confirmation has been obtained from the CMA that the restrictions in paragraph [5] have been complied with (including by making the necessary redactions) in relation to that document.

DN14

Provision for supplying working files to the CMA should be considered where it is expected that advisers will undertake quantitative work/analysis on the basis of the Disclosed Material. Such files will enable the CMA to understand and assess the merits of the arguments/challenges made by advisers.

DN15

The firm undertakings can relate to the Authorised Advisers of either the particular firm or (more broadly) the particular Party (this latter would include Authorised Advisers from different firms e.g. from a firm of solicitors and a firm of economists). The broader option [should be used if firm A is going to allow Authorised Advisers from firm B to work on the Disclosed Material in firm A's offices.

PRO FORMA TEMPLATES FOR CMA DISCLOSURE ROOM UNDERTAKINGS (JANUARY 2017)

NOTES

This template is available on the CMA's website at: www.gov.uk/government/publications/confidentiality-ring-and-disclosure-room-undertakings-templates.

[3.72]

This document contains pro forma templates and associated drafting notes for the undertakings to be given to the CMA regarding access to disclosure rooms in CMA investigations, by:

(1) **External advisers retained by parties to advise in relation to CMA investigations (see *Disclosure Room Undertakings: Adviser*)**

(2) **The firms to which those advisers belong (see *Disclosure Room Undertakings: Firm*)**

These templates are based on recent CMA practice and are intended to provide advisers and parties with an indication of the basic terms/provisions and conditions that may typically be included in CMA Disclosure Room undertakings.

If/as appropriate, these may be tailored for each particular case, taking into account, for example, the nature of the CMA's investigation and purpose of the disclosure exercise; the nature and sensitivity of the data/information to be disclosed; the types of document proposed to be prepared in a Disclosure Room, etc.

1. DISCLOSURE ROOM UNDERTAKINGS: ADVISER

When drafting the Undertakings using this template, your attention is drawn to the 'Disclosure Room Undertakings: Drafting Notes ('DN') which will help clarifying certain concepts and tailoring this document to the specific needs of the investigation at hand.

These undertakings and rules cover both the case where the Disclosure Room is used to prepare a Report to be taken out by advisers and the case where advisers prepare their submissions to the CMA in the disclosure room. Your attention is drawn to Drafting Note 14.

[NAME OF INVESTIGATION]

UNDERTAKINGS GIVEN BY [Name of Adviser] TO THE COMPETITION AND MARKETS AUTHORITY REGARDING ACCESS TO THE [X] DISCLOSURE ROOM [BEFORE/FOLLOWING X] [DN1]

WHEREAS

(1) [Brief overview of the Investigation (including the empowering statutory provision(s)]
   a. **See DN2 for example text for CA98, market investigations and merger inquiries**
   b. **Incorporate definitions of:**
      i. **the Competition and Markets Authority ('the CMA')**
      ii. **relevant legislation e.g. the Enterprise Act 2002 ('the EA02'), the Competition Act 1998 ('the CA98') and**
      iii. **'the Investigation'.**

(2) [Background information: i.e. description of stage of the Investigation; CMA/CAT actions so far]
   a. **See DN3 for example text**

(3) [Background continued: e.g. request made by party/ies; rationale for the disclosure which is being facilitated by these undertakings etc.]

(4) The CMA has decided to disclose the following:
   a. [Description of disclosed material]
   b. [Description of disclosed material]
   c. [etc.]

   ('the Disclosed Material') by means of a disclosure room commencing on [insert date] ('the Disclosure Room'). A reference to the Disclosed Material in these undertakings includes a reference to any part of the Disclosed Material;

   See DN4 and DN5

   OR

   [The CMA has decided to disclose the material set out in Schedule 1 [which may be amended from time to time by the CMA] ('the Disclosed Material') by means of a disclosure room commencing on [insert date] ('the Disclosure Room'). A reference to the Disclosed Material in these undertakings includes a reference to any part of the Disclosed Material;]

(5) The CMA considers that the 'Disclosed Material' [is/includes] specified information within the meaning of section 238 of the [EA02] [Enterprise Act 2002 ('EA02')] to which the general restriction on disclosure in section 237 of the EA02 applies. The CMA may disclose specified information to any other person in circumstances permitted by the EA02.

(6) The CMA has decided to disclose the Disclosed Material [to certain parties the Investigation], [to Name of Party]] ([each a] [the] 'Relevant Party') by means of the Disclosure Room pursuant to section [X] of the EA02. [**See DN6**]. Access to the Disclosure Room is restricted to the [external legal and/or economic [**See DN7**] advisers] of the Relevant Parties and is provided for the sole purpose of allowing the advisers of a Relevant Party, on behalf of the Relevant Party, [to review and understand [X], to prepare submissions and representations to the CMA regarding [X], and (if relevant) to prepare and conduct an appeal against any decision of the CMA in connection with the Investigation including an appeal in which the Relevant Party is, or is intending to apply to be, an intervener in which case the arrangements established by these Undertakings may be extended to apply for the purposes of such appeal ('the Permitted Purpose'); [**See DN8**].

(7) Access to the Disclosure Room will be granted to, and only to, an adviser:

a. who has been approved in writing by the CMA;

b. who has given written undertakings acceptable to the CMA ('the Individual Undertakings'); and

c. if relevant, in respect of whom the adviser's firm/employer has given written undertakings acceptable to the CMA ('the Firm Undertakings');

in accordance with [*the arrangements in recital (9)] OR [arrangements specified by the CMA*] (each such adviser being an 'Authorised Adviser'); [**See DN9**]

(8) [*The number of Authorised Advisers is limited to [number – X] [for each Relevant Party*] [**see DN10**].

(9) [*The arrangements for obtaining CMA approval of an adviser and for giving undertakings in respect of an adviser are:*

a. notice of not less than [insert time – e.g. 2 CMA working days[1]*] must be given to the CMA of the date on which the adviser first wishes be granted access to the Disclosure Room ('the Access Date');*

b. by 4pm on the CMA Working Day before the Access Date the Individual Undertakings signed by the adviser and, if relevant, the Firm Undertakings signed on behalf of the adviser's firm/employer, must be provided to (and received by) the CMA;

c. before the adviser attempts to access the Disclosure Room, confirmation in writing must be obtained from the CMA that it has approved the adviser and has accepted the signed Individual Undertakings and, if relevant, the signed Firm Undertakings.]

(10) The Disclosure Room is to operate in accordance with the Disclosure Room Rules which are annexed to these undertakings and subject to the Individual Undertakings and the Firm Undertakings.

(11) Disclosure, or removal from the Disclosure Room, of the Disclosed Material other than in accordance with the Individual Undertakings is not permitted without the express and prior written consent of the CMA. Breach of the Individual Undertakings by an Authorised Adviser may result in:

a. the CMA:

i. terminating the Authorised Adviser's access to the Disclosure Room and refusing the Authorised Advisor access to any subsequent disclosure room or confidentiality ring run by the CMA, whether relating to the Investigation or any other investigation;

ii. where relevant, referring the breach to the Authorised Adviser's regulatory body which may decide to take disciplinary action in relation to the breach.

b. a breach by the Authorised Adviser of his or her obligations under Part 9 of the EA02 (as regards the disclosure and use of the Disclosed Material) which constitutes a criminal offence under section 245 of the EA02;

(12) [Name of Firm] has been instructed by [Name of Party], which is a Relevant Party, for the purpose of providing [legal/economic] advice to [Name of Party] in relation to the Investigation. [Name of Adviser] is [employed by [Name of Firm] as a [legal/economic adviser]] [a partner in [Name of Firm]].

NOTES

1 A 'CMA working day' is any day of the week, Monday to Friday, on which the CMA's offices are open (and excludes public or bank holidays).

NOW THEREFORE

I, [Name of Adviser], [Job title] at [Name of Firm], who has been engaged by [Name of Party] in connection with the Investigation undertake to the CMA in my own name:

General

1. To abide by the Disclosure Room Rules which are annexed to these undertakings;

2. To use the Disclosed Material for, and only for, the Permitted Purpose;
3. Save as provided in paragraphs [*], to hold the Disclosed Material in strict confidence and not to disclose or make available in any manner the Disclosed Material to any other person (including any legal adviser, economic adviser, officer or employee of [Name of Firm] and [Name of Party]) except:
   a. another Authorised Adviser of [Name of Party]; or
   b. a member of CMA staff or a CMA panel member working on the Investigation (or the court if in the course of an appeal),

   (such a person being a 'Non-Authorised Person');
4. Save as provided in paragraph [8 or 9], not to make any electronic or non-electronic copy in any format of the Disclosed Material;
5. Save as provided in paragraph [8 or *], not to remove the Disclosed Material from the Disclosure Room;
6. [Save as provided in paragraph [*],] to ensure that any analysis I undertake, or any document I prepare, which contains or refers to the Disclosed Material or which derives wholly or partially from the Disclosed Material, or any knowledge I obtain in the Disclosure Room, is not used, disclosed or made available in any way to:
   a. disclose the Disclosed Material to any Non-Authorised Person;
   b. enable or assist any Non-Authorised Person to gain an understanding of [Name of Party]'s position or potential future position in any market relative to any other market operator (other than relative to a market wide benchmark) [any other description of information]; **[DN11]**
7. To notify the CMA immediately if I become aware of or suspect that there has been a breach of:
   a. these undertakings;
   b. the Individual Undertakings given by another Authorised Adviser of [Name of Party] [Name of Firm];
   c. the Disclosure Room Rules; or
   d. [the Firm Undertakings given in respect of any of the Authorised Advisers of Name of Party]';

Disclosure Room Report

8. That while I may, in order to facilitate the Permitted Purpose, prepare in the Disclosure Room, by myself or with one or more other Authorised Advisers of [Name of Party], [one report] on behalf of [Name of Party] which may contain the Disclosed Material (the 'Report) and which may be removed from the Disclosure Room, I will ensure:
   a. the Report does not include or refer to any Disclosed Material [that is/relating to] [description of information which the CMA considers confidential/highly sensitive, hence should not leave the building
      i.
      ii.
      iii.];
   b. the Report is no longer than is reasonably necessary for the Permitted Purpose;
   c. any working files (including 'stata-do-files') used to perform analysis referred to in the Report are saved in [X] of a laptop provided in the Disclosure Room;
   d. only one copy of the Report is removed from the Disclosure Room, subject to the procedure in sub-paragraph (e) except that:
      i. drafts of the Report may be taken into a breakout room used for internal discussion (as permitted in the Disclosure Room Rules);
      ii. [on [one/two] occasions during the period when the Disclosure Room is open and prior to removal of the Report, one copy of a draft of the Report may be removed from the Disclosure Room, subject to the procedure in sub-paragraph (e) **DN 12**];
   e. prior to removal of the Report [(*or a draft of the Report*)] from the Disclosure Room and no later than [time and date of last day of the Disclosure Room], the Report [(*or draft Report*)] is provided to a member of CMA staff for inspection and is removed from the Disclosure Room only after the member of CMA staff has confirmed to an Authorised Adviser of [Name of Party] that the Report [(or draft Report)] has been prepared in accordance with sub-paragraphs (a) to (d).
9. That once the Report [*or any draft Report*] has been removed from the Disclosure Room, I will ensure:
   a. the Report [or draft Report] is used for, and only for, the Permitted Purpose (which may include the preparation of one or more submissions to the CMA);
   b. any copies of the Report [or draft Report] or the Disclosed Material contained or referred to in the Report [or draft Report] I make are solely for my use or the use of any other Authorised Adviser of [Name of Party] for the Permitted Purpose and in accordance with these undertakings];
   c. I keep secure at all times:
      i. the Report [and any draft Report];
      ii. all copies of the Report [or draft Report] prepared by or provided to me; and

iii. any report, submission or other document prepared by or provided to me which contains or refers to the Disclosed Material

(together 'the Relevant Material and Documents') including in a manner which means the Relevant Material and Documents are not accessible to any Non-Authorised Person;

d. any submission I prepare containing or referring to the Disclosed Material is submitted to the CMA separately from any other submission on behalf of [Name of Party] and highlights any Disclosed Material.

10. That while I may, in order to facilitate the Permitted Purpose, share a non-confidential version of the Report or a non-confidential version of the submission with [Name of Party], I will not share any such document until [written] confirmation has been obtained from a member of CMA staff that the restrictions in paragraph [6] have been complied with (including by making the necessary redactions) in relation to that document.

11. **DN 13**[*That while I may share [a general, non-confidential, [summary] of the Report [including an explanation of the methodology used in the CMA's analysis]] the conclusion of my assessment of/key trends arising from] with [Name of Party], to facilitate the Permitted Purpose [only to the extent that . . . .], I will ensure that, if so required by the CMA, [the non-confidential [summary], is only shared with [Name of Party] after the CMA has confirmed in writing to an Authorised Adviser of [Name of Party] that the non-confidential summary does not include any of the Disclosed Material and meets the requirements in paragraph 6.]*

[or]

[such general summary/conclusion/key trends] is/are not used or made available in any way to:

a. disclose to any Non-Authorised Person, [specific] information regarding:

i. the Disclosed Material relating to [X]; and

ii. the Disclosed Material relating to [Y];

b. enable or assist any Non-Authorised Person to gain an understanding of [Name of Party]'s position or potential future position in any market relative to any other market operator (other than relative to a market wide benchmark) and in particular does not reveal [description of information which should not be given to the party – if different from 7a(i) and (ii)];

[and, if so required by the CMA, these are not shared with [Name of Party] until after the CMA has confirmed in writing to an Authorised Adviser of [Name of Party] that they comply with the requirements above]

12. That save as provided in sub-paragraph [13], within 5 CMA working days of the relevant concluding event I will:

a. return to the CMA or destroy the Relevant Material and Documents or, where the Relevant Material and Documents are in electronic form and their destruction is not possible, return them to the CMA or render them permanently inaccessible to any person from any computer system, disk or device so that they are not readily available to any person; and

b. where the Relevant Material and Documents are destroyed or rendered inaccessible, inform the CMA of the manner of the destruction or rendering inaccessible;

The relevant concluding event is:

i. if there is an appeal against a decision of the CMA in connection with the Investigation in which [Name of Party] is a party or is intervening, the conclusion of the appeal;

ii. if there is no such appeal, the expiry of the period for bringing such an appeal, or

iii. if I cease to advise [Name of Party] in relation to the Investigation or appeal before the event specified by (i) or (ii), my ceasing to advise [Name of Party] in relation to the Investigation or appeal.

13. That while the Authorised Advisers of [Name of Firm may retain one copy (between them) of the Report and any submission or other document containing the Disclosed Material if it is required to comply with [Name of Firm]'s professional indemnity insurance policy or any applicable law, legislation or court order, I will ensure that:

a. the copy is stored securely in accordance with the undertaking in paragraph [9];

b. the CMA is notified of the retention within 5 CMA working days of the relevant concluding event specified by paragraph [12](i) or (ii); and

c. the CMA is consulted as far as practicable prior to any disclosure of the copy under [Name of Firm]'s professional indemnity insurance policy or any applicable law, legislation or court order;

[Disclosure Room Submission See DN14

14. That while I may, in order to facilitate the Permitted Purpose, prepare in the Disclosure Room, by myself or with one or more of the other Authorised Advisers of [Name of Party], one or more submissions on behalf of [Name of Party] to the CMA in respect of [case team to complete] (each a 'Confidential Submission') which will constitute a 'response' to [[case team to complete], and may contain any of the Disclosed Material relating to [[case team to complete] (the 'Sensitive Information'), I will ensure:

a. any Confidential Submission is provided to the CMA by 5 pm [case team to insert date – usually the last day of the Disclosure Room];
b. any working files (including 'stata-do-files') used to perform analysis referred to in any Confidential Submission submitted to the CMA are saved in [X] of a laptop provided in the Disclosure Room;
c. any Confidential Submission is not removed from the Disclosure Room except that:
   i. drafts of any Confidential Submission may be taken into a breakout room used for internal discussion (as permitted in the Disclosure Room Rules);
   ii. during the period after any Confidential Submission has been submitted to the CMA up to the relevant concluding event [specified by paragraph 12(i) or (ii)], Authorised Advisers of [Name of Party] will be given access to that Confidential Submission at the CMA's offices on such terms as the CMA reasonably specifies;

15. That while I may, in order to facilitate the Permitted Purpose, prepare in the Disclosure Room, by myself or with one or more of the Authorised Advisers [Name of Party], a non-confidential version of any Confidential Submission (each a 'Non-Confidential Submission') which may be removed from the Disclosure Room and shared with [Name of Party, I will ensure that:
a. any Non-Confidential Submission must not include any of the Sensitive Information, [including/in particular case team to complete];
b. any Non-Confidential Submission must be no longer than is reasonably necessary for the Permitted Purpose;
c. only one copy of any Non-Confidential Submission is removed from the Disclosure Room subject to the procedure in sub-paragraph (d);
d. prior to the removal of any Non-Confidential Submission from the Disclosure Room and no later than [time and date of last day of the Disclosure Room], the Non-Confidential Submission is provided to a member of CMA staff for inspection and is removed from the Disclosure Room only after the member of CMA staff has confirmed to an Authorised Adviser of [Name of Party] that it has been prepared in accordance with sub-paragraphs (a) to (c).

PROVIDED THAT

These undertakings shall not apply to any part of the Disclosed Material that:
(i) belongs or relates solely to [Name of Party] or to [Name of Party]'s business and which does not include any confidential information belonging to, relating to or deriving solely or partially from any other party to the Investigation;
(ii) is information that has previously been disclosed by the CMA to [Name of Party in the Investigation;
(iii) at the time of disclosure is in the public domain or subsequently comes into the public domain, except through breach of these undertakings, the Individual Undertakings given by other Authorised Advisers or the Firm Undertakings;
(iv) is required to be disclosed by law, legislation or court order, as long as, and unless prohibited by law, legislation or court order, I consult with the CMA as far as practicable prior to the proposed disclosure on the proposed forum, timing, nature and purpose of the proposed disclosure; or
(v) is covered by a confidentiality ring established by the Competition Appeal Tribunal in the course of an appeal against the decision of the CMA in connection with the Investigation in which [Name of Party] is a party or is intervening.

AND IN AGREEMENT THAT

These undertakings and the Disclosure Room Rules shall be governed by and construed in accordance with English law and I submit to the exclusive jurisdiction of the courts of England and Wales to hear and decide any action or proceedings which may arise out of, or in connection with these undertakings and the Disclosure Room Rules.

[Name of Party] has given full and informed consent to the terms of these undertakings and the Disclosure Room Rules, including the restrictions placed upon [Name of Adviser] on the disclosure of information by these undertakings.

[Name of Adviser] of [Name of Firm]

[*signature*]

[Date]

2. DISCLOSURE ROOM UNDERTAKINGS: FIRM

When drafting the Undertakings using this template, your attention is drawn to the 'Disclosure Room Undertakings: Drafting Notes ('DN') which will help clarifying certain concepts and in tailoring this document to the specific needs of your particular investigation.

These undertakings and rules cover both the case where the Disclosure Room is used to prepare a Report to be taken out by advisers and the case where advisers prepare their submissions to the CMA in the disclosure room. Your attention is drawn to Drafting Note 13.

[NAME OF INVESTIGATION]

UNDERTAKINGS GIVEN BY [[Name of Firm] TO THE COMPETITION AND MARKETS AUTHORITY REGARDING ACCESS TO THE [X] DISCLOSURE ROOM [BEFORE/FOLLOWING X] [DN1]

WHEREAS

(1) [Brief overview of the Investigation (including the empowering statutory provision(s))]

a. **See DN2 for example text for CA98, market investigations and merger inquiries**

b. **Incorporate definitions of:**

i. **the Competition and Markets Authority ('the CMA')**

ii. **relevant legislation e.g. the Enterprise Act 2002 ('the EA02'), the Competition Act 1998 ('the CA98') and**

iii. **'the Investigation'.**

(2) [Background information: i.e. description of stage of the Investigation; CMA/CAT actions so far]

a. **See DN3 for example text**

(3) [Background continued: e.g. request made by party/ies; rationale for the disclosure which is being facilitated by these Undertakings etc.]

(4) The CMA has decided to disclose the following:

a. [Description of disclosed material]

b. [Description of disclosed material]

c. [etc.]

('the Disclosed Material') by means of a disclosure room commencing on [insert date] ('the Disclosure Room'). A reference to the Disclosed Material in these undertakings includes a reference to any part of the Disclosed Material;

See DN4 and DN5

OR

[The CMA has decided to disclose the material set out in Schedule 1 [which may be amended from time to time by the CMA] ('the Disclosed Material') by means of a disclosure room commencing on [insert date] ('the Disclosure Room'). A reference to the Disclosed Material in these undertakings includes a reference to any part of the Disclosed Material;]

(5) The CMA considers that the 'Disclosed Material' [is/includes] specified information within the meaning of section 238 of the [EA02] [Enterprise Act 2002 ('EA02')] to which the general restriction on disclosure in section 237 of the EA02 applies. The CMA may disclose specified information to any other person in circumstances permitted by the EA02.

(6) The CMA has decided to disclose the Disclosed Material [to certain parties the Investigation], [to Name of Party]] ([each a] [the] 'Relevant Party') by means of the Disclosure Room pursuant to section [X] of the EA02. [**See DN6**]. Access to the Disclosure Room is restricted to the [external legal and/or economic [**See DN7**] advisers] of the Relevant Parties and is provided for the sole purpose of allowing the advisers of a Relevant Party, on behalf of the Relevant Party, [to review and understand [X], to prepare submissions and representations to the CMA regarding [X], and (if relevant) to prepare and conduct an appeal against any decision of the CMA in connection with the Investigation including an appeal in which the Relevant Party is, or is intending to apply to be, an intervener in which case the arrangements established by these Undertakings may be extended to apply for the purposes of such appeal ('the Permitted Purpose'); [**See DN8**].

(7) Access to the Disclosure Room will be granted to, and only to, an adviser:

a. who has been approved in writing by the CMA;

b. who has given written undertakings acceptable to the CMA ('the Individual Undertakings'); and

c. if relevant, in respect of whom the adviser's firm/employer has given written undertakings acceptable to the CMA ('the Firm Undertakings');

in accordance with [*the arrangements in recital (9)] OR [arrangements specified by the CMA*] (each such adviser being an 'Authorised Adviser'); [**See DN9**]

(8) [*The number of Authorised Advisers is limited to [number – X] [for each Relevant Party]* **[see DN10]**.

(9) [*The arrangements for obtaining CMA approval of an adviser and for giving undertakings in respect of an adviser are:*

a. notice of not less than [insert time – e.g. 2 CMA working days[2]*] must be given to the CMA of the date on which the adviser first wishes be granted access the Disclosure Room ('the Access Date');*

b. by 4pm on the CMA Working Day before the Access Date the Individual Undertakings signed by the adviser and, if relevant, the Firm Undertakings signed on behalf of the adviser's firm/employer, must be provided to (and received by) the CMA;

c. before the adviser attempts to access the Disclosure Room, confirmation in writing must be obtained from the CMA that it has approved the adviser and has accepted the signed Individual Undertakings and, if relevant, the signed Firm Undertakings.]

(10) The Disclosure Room shall operate in accordance with the Disclosure Room Rules which are annexed to these undertakings and subject to the Individual Undertakings and the Firm Undertakings.

(11) Disclosure of the Disclosed Material other than in accordance with the Individual Undertakings, is not permitted without the express and prior written consent of the CMA. Breach of the Individual Undertakings by an Authorised Adviser or of the Firm Undertakings by an Authorised Adviser's firm/employer may result in:

a. the CMA:

i. in the case of a breach by an Authorised Adviser, terminating the Authorised Adviser's access to the Disclosure Room and refusing the Authorised Advisor access to any subsequent disclosure room or confidentiality ring run by the CMA, whether relating to the Investigation or any other investigation;

ii. in the case of a breach by a firm/employer, terminating the firm/employer's participation in the Disclosure Room and refusing a request to participate in any subsequent disclosure room or confidentiality ring run by the CMA, whether relating to the Investigation or any other investigation;

iii. where relevant, referring the breach to the regulatory body of the Authorised Adviser or firm/employer which may decide to take disciplinary action in relation to the breach;

b. a breach of the obligations under Part 9 of the EA02 (as regards the disclosure and use of the Disclosed Material) which constitutes a criminal offence under section 245 of the EA02.

(12) [Name of Firm] has been instructed by [Name of Party], which is a Relevant Party, for the purpose of providing [legal/economic] advice to [Name of Party] in relation to the Investigation. [Name(s) of Adviser[s]] [is/are employed by Name of Firm] as a [legal/economic adviser]] [is/are [a] partner[s] in Name of Firm]].

NOTES

[2] A 'CMA working day' is any day of the week, Monday to Friday, on which the CMA's offices are open (and excludes public or bank holidays).

NOW THEREFORE

[Name of Firm] which has been engaged by [Name of Party] in connection with the Investigation undertakes to the CMA that:

(1) It will give only Authorised Advisers of [Name of Party *or* Name of Firm] access to the Disclosed Material and only in accordance with the terms of the Individual Undertakings given by those Authorised Advisers; **DN 15**

(2) It will notify the CMA immediately if it becomes aware of or suspects that there has been any breach of:

(a) these undertakings;

(b) the Individual Undertakings given by an Authorised Advisers of [Name of Party *or* [Name of Firm];

(c) the Disclosure Room rules by an Authorised Adviser of [Name of Party] *or* [Name of Firm

(d) [the other Firm Undertakings given in respect of any of the Authorised Advisers of [Name of Party]']; **DN 15**

(3) It will notify the CMA immediately if any Authorised Adviser ceases to be at [Name of Firm] before:

(a) if there is an appeal against a decision of the CMA in connection with the Investigation in which [Name of Party] is a party or is intervening, the conclusion of the appeal;

(b) if there is no such appeal, the expiry of the period for bringing such an appeal.

Further, [Name of Firm] undertakes to the CMA to use its reasonable endeavours to ensure that the Authorised Advisers at [Name of Firm] comply with the Individual Undertakings which they have given.

PROVIDED THAT

These undertakings shall not apply to any part of the Disclosed Material that:

(i) belongs or relates solely to [Name of Party] or to [Name of Party]'s business and which does not include any confidential information belonging to, relating to or deriving solely or partially from any other party to the Investigation;

(ii) is information that has previously been disclosed by the CMA to [Name of Party in the Investigation;

(iii) at the time of disclosure is in the public domain or subsequently comes into the public domain, except through breach of these undertakings, the Individual Undertakings given by other Authorised Advisers or the Firm Undertakings;

(iv) is required to be disclosed by law, legislation or court order, as long as, and unless prohibited by law, legislation or court order, I consult with the CMA as far as practicable prior to the proposed disclosure on the proposed forum, timing, nature and purpose of the proposed disclosure; or

(v) is covered by a confidentiality ring established by the Competition Appeal Tribunal in the course of an appeal against the decision of the CMA in connection with the Investigation in which [Name of Party] is a party or is intervening.

AND IN AGREEMENT THAT

These undertakings shall be governed by and construed in accordance with English law and [Name of Firm] submits to the exclusive jurisdiction of the courts of England and Wales to hear and decide any action or proceedings which may arise out of, or in connection with these Undertakings.

[Name of Party] has given full and informed consent to the terms of these undertakings and the Individual Undertakings given by the Authorised Advisers of [Name of Firm], including the restrictions placed upon those Authorised Advisers on the disclosure of information.

[Name of Firm]

[*signature*]

[Date]

3. DISCLOSURE ROOM DRAFTING NOTES

DISCLOSURE ROOM UNDERTAKINGS: DRAFTING NOTES

These Drafting Notes have been prepared to assist in the preparation of Disclosure Room Undertakings. They should be read with the Disclosure Room Undertakings template, according to the instructions given in that template.

Drafting Note ('DN') 1: "the [X] Disclosure Room'

As multiple disclosure rooms may be held during the course of an investigation, it is advisable to define the disclosure room in each case by reference to the topic at issue or the material which is being disclosed. This will be helpful for case management purposes.

DN2: Brief overview of the Investigation

The following examples provide a reflection on the amount and nature of the information to be included in the recital:

CA98 example: 'In exercise of its powers under section 25 of the Competition Act 1998, the Competition and Markets Authority ('CMA') is investigating the conduct of [name of party] for suspected breaches of Chapter [I] / [II] of CA98 and/or the Treaty of the functioning of the European Union ('the Investigation').'

Markets example (Phase 2): 'On [Date], in exercise of its powers under sections 131 and 133 of the Enterprise Act 2002 ('the Act'), the Competition and Markets Authority (CMA) made a reference for a market investigation in to the supply or acquisition of [relevant market] ('the Investigation').'

Mergers example (Phase 2): 'On [Date], in exercise of its powers under [section 22] / [section 33] of the Enterprise Act 2002 ('the Act'), the Competition and Markets Authority (CMA) referred the [completed] [anticipated] acquisition by [name of acquiring party] of [name of acquired party] / [name of acquired party assets] for investigation and report ('the Investigation').'

DN3: Background Information

CA98 example: 'On [Date] the CMA issued a Statement of Objections (the 'S.O') to [Name of Party] and [Name of Party] (together 'the Parties') alleging, on a provisional basis, a breach of the prohibition contained in Chapter [I] / [II] of CA98, and subsequently gave the Parties an opportunity to inspect the case file.'

Mergers and Markets example: 'On [Date] the CMA published its provisional findings in the Investigation ('the Provisional Findings'), in which it found a [summary of findings] and a consequent [substantial lessening of competition] / [adverse effect on competition] [in the [X] market].'

DN4: Description of material being disclosed

This section of the template is the opportunity to describe what is being disclosed in the room. The more descriptive and specific this section can be, the better.

If the description is lengthy it may be preferable to put it in a schedule. The second version of recital (4) provides for this. If required, it reserves the ability to amend the description. However, any amendment should be done formally, for example, by the advisers signing a replacement schedule or amendment. The revised schedule or amendment should be kept by the CMA with the original undertakings.

DN5: Disclosed Material

The defined term which has been chosen is 'Disclosed Material', as this is a more general term which could be used in a disclosure room whether that room contains data or documents or both.

DN6: Statutory Gateway

The CMA may disclose specified information under the Enterprise Act 2002 ('the EA02') if one or more statutory gateway applies. The gateway most likely to be relevant is that in section 241: disclosure is made for the purpose of facilitating the exercise by the CMA of any of its statutory functions, though the 'consent' gateway in section 239 may also be relevant.

DN7: Advisers

The question of who is permitted to participate in a confidentiality ring or disclosure room is determined on a case by case basis, taking into account matters including the nature of the disclosed information and the reason for its disclosure. However, the CMA's usual approach is to limit access to the **parties' external legal and/or economic advisers**. Occasionally, however, it may be appropriate to allow participation by internal personnel such as employees of parties.

DN8: the 'Permitted Purpose'

In addition to the reference provided in the undertakings regarding allowing the parties to be provided with the gist, the following are possibilities for [X]:

(1) To review the CMA's figures, economic analysis and/or modelling.

(2) To enable the parties' Advisers to further understand the CMA's analysis in order to allow such Advisers to prepare submissions and representations to the CMA.

The following text could be used for either, adapted as appropriate:

Example text:

'for the purpose of understanding and providing observations to the CMA on the latter's [Provisional Findings] / [Statement of Objections] / [[X] Working Paper] / [Insured Price Analysis] / [Price Concentration Analysis].'

For CA98 cases, consider also:

(3) To enable [Name of Party] to exercise fully its rights of defence.

To enable the same Undertakings to be used in the event of any appeal, Permitted Purpose is defined to include use for such an appeal.

DN9: Definition of Authorised Adviser

Note, this definition does not limit the definition of an Authorised Adviser to the Authorised Adviser of a particular party.

DN10: Limit on the number of Authorised Advisers

This recital is optional – it may be used if helpful to clarify the point

DN11

Paragraph 6(b) is intended to cover confidential/market sensitive information that, while not falling within the definition of Disclosed Material, is created or derived from the Disclosed Material

DN12

These arrangements for taking out drafts may be formalised depending on the circumstances.

DN13

Paragraphs 10 and 11 may be mixed and matched depending on what, in the circumstances of the case, it is considered that advisers may be able to share with their clients. (For example, one could simply have paragraph 10 but not 11, or both etc.)

Note the second option in paragraph 11 (by implication) permits advisers to share some Disclosed Material with their clients.

If a stricter regime is envisaged, requirements for the CMA to check what is shared under paragraph 11 as well as under paragraph 10 could be added here.

DN14: Advisers Preparing Submissions in the Disclosure Room?

The usual position is that advisers should be permitted to prepare a Report in the Disclosure Room and then prepare a submission on the basis of the Report outside the Disclosure Room. However, there may be rare occasions where case teams consider that, *submissions* should be prepared in the Disclosure Room – generally where the information is too sensitive to be permitted to leave the CMA's offices. The template allows for case teams to provide for such an eventuality. A combination of both approaches may be used.

DN15

The firm undertakings can relate to the Authorised Advisers of either the particular firm or (more broadly) the particular Party (this latter would include Authorised Advisers from different firms e.g. from a firm of solicitors and a firm of economists). The broader option should be used if firm A is going to allow Authorised Advisers from firm B to work on the Disclosed Material in firm A's offices

DN16: Format

- CD-Rom
- USB
- Secure e-mail file transfer e.g. Egress

DN17: Breakout rooms

As far as practicable, more than one breakout room may be required depending on the number of Advisers involved in the disclosure.

We envisage two different uses for breakout rooms:

(1) Providing a space for Advisers of the same party to discuss the Disclosed Materials
- In this situation, Advisers are permitted to take into the breakout room handwritten and typed notes prepared in the Disclosure Room or their own materials that they have been permitted to bring into the Disclosure Room. This reflects the CAT's view, expressed in *BMI v. CC*, about the facilities which could be provided by the CMA in order to enable the Permitted Purpose to be fulfilled. However, Advisers are not permitted to take in phones, as we consider that there is too much of a risk in allowing Advisers to have materials from the Disclosure Room in a room where they also have a means of external communication, especially as no member of CMA staff will be present in the breakout room.

(2) Providing a space for Advisers to make external calls
- In this situation, phones are permitted. However, no notes of any kind prepared in the Disclosure Room (or pre-existing documents) are permitted to be taken into the breakout room (although blank paper is permitted so that advisers can take notes). Given that phones cannot be taken in to the Disclosure Room, the CMA may need to assist the Advisers by retrieving the necessary phones from where they have been deposited in advance of the Disclosure Room.

PRO FORMA TEMPLATE FOR CMA DISCLOSURE ROOM RULES (JANUARY 2017)

NOTES

This template is available on the CMA's website at: www.gov.uk/government/publications/confidentiality-ring-and-disclosure-room-undertakings-templates.

[3.73]

This document contains a pro forma template for the Disclosure Room Rules used by the CMA where Disclosure Rooms are utilised in CMA investigations. Individuals and firms must agree and adhere to these rules in order to be granted access to a CMA Disclosure Room.

The Disclosure Room Rules make provision for the practical operation of the disclosure room including the facilities that will be provided to participants and the conduct of participants whilst in the disclosure room and break out rooms.

The template has been produced based on recent CMA practice and is intended to provide advisers and parties with an indication of the basic terms/provisions and conditions that the CMA may typically include in Disclosure Room rules.

If/as appropriate, these may be tailored for each particular case, taking into account, for example, the nature of the CMA investigation and purpose of the disclosure exercise; the nature and sensitivity of the data/information to be disclosed; the types of document proposed to be prepared in a DR; etc.

Disclosure Room Rules are typically annexed to the Disclosure Room Undertakings.

('THE DISCLOSURE ROOM RULES')

1. The Disclosure Room Rules apply to the Disclosure Room referred to in the undertakings to which the Disclosure Room Rules are attached ('the Undertakings') [and any breakout room provided by the CMA under paragraph 15 of the Disclosure Room Rules].

2. Terms used in the Disclosure Room Rules have the meaning they are given in the Undertakings.

3. The CMA will make the Disclosure Room available at its offices at Victoria House, Southampton Row, London, WC1B 4AD to the Authorised Advisers (as described in recital (7) of the Undertakings).

4. Entry to the Disclosure Room, conduct within it and use of the Disclosed Material by an Authorised Adviser is conditional on:

(a) the Adviser complying with the Disclosure Room Rules;

(b) the Adviser complying with the Individual Undertakings which he or she has given; and

(c) where relevant, the Adviser's firm/employer complying with the Firm Undertakings which it has given in respect of the Adviser.

5. The number of Authorised Advisers is limited to [number – X] [per Relevant Party] (see recital (8) of the Undertakings). A maximum of [number ‹ X] Authorised Advisers per Relevant Party will be permitted to be present in the Disclosure Room at any one time.

6. The Disclosure Room will be open on each CMA Working Day[1] **from [insert dates X until Y] inclusive**. Its hours of operation will be from 9.30am until 5pm on each day. Should the CMA decide to open the Disclosure Room beyond that time or period, access will continue to be governed by the Individual Undertakings, Firm Undertakings, and the Disclosure Room Rules.

7. At all times that the Disclosure Room is open, a member of CMA staff will be present to oversee compliance with the Disclosure Room Rules and shall be the person any Authorised Adviser should contact in the event of a query or difficulty concerning the operation of the Disclosure Room (including IT matters).

8. In addition to the Disclosed Material, the following material will be made available in the Disclosure Room:

(a) [list of other materials that will be provided];
(b) and stationery.

9. The Disclosure Room will contain one laptop per Authorised Adviser with the following specification:

(a) Word, Excel and PowerPoint software;
(b) Stata software;
(c) access to a specific subfolder containing the Disclosed Material;
(d) access to [X] printers;
(e) no storage medium other than the hard disk will be available (ie the USB ports and the CD writer – if any – will be disabled);
(f) no internet or email capacity; and
(g) the computers available for use by the Authorised Advisers of each Relevant Party will be networked to each other.

10. Within reason, other software may be installed on one or more computer(s) in the Disclosure Room, provided that the following procedures are followed:

(a) an Authorised Adviser must notify the CMA at least two CMA working days before the opening of the Disclosure Room if the Authorised Adviser wishes to have alternative software installed;
(b) such software must be provided on [format] only, which must contain nothing other than the software to be installed **see Drafting Note (DN)16** (see drafting notes associated with the templates for Disclosure Room undertakings);
(c) CMA staff will check such [format] prior to installation;
(d) compliance with the licence arrangements for such software remains at all times the responsibility of the Authorised Adviser(s) wishing to install it.

11. All printing activity will be logged automatically.

12. Authorised Advisers will be provided with A4 sized envelope(s) in which they may store any printed materials and any handwritten notes. The envelope(s) will be sealed and placed in a secure location at the CMA's offices, which will be locked overnight. After the closure of the Disclosure Room any such materials will be destroyed by the CMA.

13. In accordance with paragraph [X] of the Individual Undertakings, one copy of the Report, per Relevant Party, produced by the Authorised Advisers on the computers provided in the Disclosure Room, may be removed from the Disclosure Room. Where necessary, CMA staff will redact from the Report any information which may, in their opinion, lead to a breach of the Individual Undertakings. For the avoidance of doubt, Authorised Advisers will not be considered to have been in breach of the Disclosure Room Individual Undertakings where the CMA has deemed it necessary to redact information from the Report or non-confidential Submission (hereby ensuring that such information is not removed from the Disclosure Room).

14. Authorised Advisers may talk to each other in the Disclosure Room but any conversations must be kept as brief and as quiet as possible to avoid disturbing other users of the Disclosure Room.

15. The CMA will, upon request and subject to availability, provide a breakout room during the opening hours of the Disclosure Room for reasonable use by the Authorised Advisers for:

(a) Discussions between Authorised Advisers who are present in the breakout room ('internal communications'); or
(b) External telephone conversations ('external communications');

but a breakout room may not be used for internal communications and external communications at the same time. **DN17** (see drafting notes associated with the templates for Disclosure Room undertakings)

16. A maximum of [number ‹ X] Authorised Advisers per Relevant Party will be permitted to be present in a breakout room at any one time.

17. Requests to use a breakout room must be made to the member of CMA staff present in the Disclosure Room on the day the Authorised Advisers wish to use the breakout room and when making the request an Authorised Adviser must indicate whether the breakout room is to be used for internal communications or external communications. In the event that the Authorised Advisers of more than one Relevant Party wish to use the breakout room, each party concerned shall be able to use the breakout room for a maximum of 2 hours at any one time and the priority given to parties will be determined by the order in which the Authorised Advisers made the request to the member of CMA staff. In the event of a dispute, the matter shall be resolved by the member of CMA staff the Disclosure Room.

18. An Authorised Adviser must not bring into the Disclosure Room or breakout room any device allowing external communication (for example, mobile phones, PDAs, laptop computers) or storage devices (eg memory sticks or dictaphones) except as permitted in Rule 21.

19. An Authorised Adviser must not bring into the Disclosure Room or breakout room his/her own material (for example, notes, copies of working papers or other documents or textbooks) except an Adviser may bring into the Disclosure Room his/her own material if:

(a) the material is in non-electronic format;
(b) the material is reasonably required to facilitate the Permitted Purpose;
(c) the material has not been supplied by the CMA;
(d) the Authorised Adviser has informed the CMA, by 4pm of the CMA Working Day[2] before, of the specific material that he/she intends to bring into the Disclosure Room;
(e) the Authorised Adviser presents, in advance of bringing into the Disclosure Room, the material for inspection by a member of CMA staff;
(f) the CMA has approved the material presented for inspection;
(g) the material is not removed from the Disclosure Room (except to be taken to a breakout room used for internal communications as permitted by Rule 20); and
(h) the material is given to the CMA for destruction by the end of the Disclosure Room.

20. Where a breakout room is to be used for internal communications:

(a) an Authorised Adviser may take into the breakout room copies of a draft Report and/or Confidential Submission(s) and handwritten and printed notes prepared in the Disclosure Room, as well as his/her own material brought into the Disclosure Room under Rule 19 but in doing so the Authorised Adviser must not breach the Individual Undertakings he/she has given; and
(b) an Authorised Adviser must not bring into the breakout room any device allowing communication with a person outside the breakout room (for example, mobile phones, PDAs, laptop computers, memory sticks).

21. Where the breakout room is to be used for external communications:

(a) an Authorised Advisers may, with the approval of a member of CMA staff, bring a mobile phone into the breakout room and use it for external communications; and
(b) an Authorised Adviser must not take into the breakout room copies of a draft Report, Confidential Submission(s), any other material prepared in the Disclosure Room or his/her own material whether brought into the Disclosure Room under Rule 19 or otherwise.

22. The usual rules for access to the CMA's offices will apply. In particular, visitor badges must be worn visibly at all times. The Authorised Advisers must not leave the Disclosure Room at any time without informing a member of the CMA staff and outside the Disclosure Room will be accompanied by a member of CMA staff where appropriate.

23. The CMA may without consultation vary the Disclosure Room Rules where it considers there is a good reason, which may include a reasonable suspicion that there has been a breach of the Disclosure Room Rules, the Individual Undertakings or the Firm Undertakings. The variations will have effect as regards an Authorised Adviser (and, if relevant, an Authorised Adviser's firm/employer) as soon as the variations are notified to the Authorised Adviser (and, if relevant, the Adviser's firm/employer).

NOTES

1 CMA 'Working Day' means any day of the week, Monday to Friday, on which the CMA office is open, excluding public or bank holidays.

2 CMA 'Working Day' means any day of the week, Monday to Friday, on which the CMA office is open, excluding public or bank holidays.

CMA STRUCTURE (18 FEBRUARY 2020)

[3.74]

NOTES

This document is available on the Competition and Markets Authority website at: www.gov.uk/government/publications/cma-structure. It lists the Senior Executives and key contacts for other areas. It is not a full list of the CMA's Senior Civil Service staff. More information is available on the CMA governance page at www.gov.uk/government/organisations/competition-and-markets-authority/about/our-governance.

Editorial note: the CMA website states that the document was last updated in February 2020, however, the current version of this document on the website is different from then one published in the 2020 edition of this Handbook. The version reproduced below is the current version on www.gov.uk/government/publications/cma-structure.

Chief Executive

Andrea Coscelli

Enforcement Directorate

Executive Director	Michael Grenfell
Senior Director, Cartels	Juliette Enser
Senior Director, Antitrust	Ann Pope
Senior Director, Consumer Protection	George Lusty

Markets & Mergers Directorate

Executive Director	New Executive Director starting in January 2022*

Part 3 CMA and other Guidelines

Senior Director, Markets	Daniel Gordon
Senior Directors, Mergers	Colin Raftery, Joel Bamford
Senior Director, Remedies, Business and Financial Analysis	Adam Land
Senior Director, Office for the Internal Market	Rachel Merelie
Digital Markets Unit	
Senior Director, Digital Markets Unit	Will Hayter
Legal Service / Policy and International	
General Counsel	Sarah Cardell
Senior Director, Policy and International and Digital Markets Unit	John McInnes
Senior Legal Director, Cartels and Consumer Protection	Stephen Blake
Senior Legal Director, Antitrust Enforcement	Ronan Flanagan
Senior Legal Director, Markets and Mergers	Jenny Coombes
Office of the Chief Economic Adviser	
Chief Economic Adviser	Mike Walker
Deputy Chief Economic Adviser	Julie Bon
Deputy Chief Economic Adviser	Jenny Haydock
Chief Data and Technology Insights Officer	Stefan Hunt
Corporate Services Directorate	
Chief Operating Officer	Erik Wilson
Senior Director, People, Capability and Culture	Lucy Robbins
Director, Executive Office, Security and Performance	Kate Bridge
Director Human Resources	Victoria Tricarico
Director, Commercial and Contract Management	David Moss
Director of Property Transformation	Nigel Bunclark
Director, Finance	Paul Ellis
Director, Technology and Business Services	Phil Urquhart
Strategy, Communications and Advocacy	
Senior Director, Strategy, Communications, Advocacy	Stuart Hudson
Director, Advocacy, UK Regions and Nations	Jennifer Halliday
Director, Communications	Anthony Wright
Director, Strategy	Susan Oxley

NOTES

* See www.gov.uk/government/news/cma-appoints-new-executive-director--2?=0 which announces the appointment of David Stewart to this role in January 2022.

MERGER AND MARKET REMEDIES – GUIDANCE ON REPORTING, INVESTIGATION AND ENFORCEMENT OF POTENTIAL BREACHES (CMA136, 29 JANUARY 2021)

[3.75]

NOTES

CONTENTS

1. INTRODUCTION

[3.76]

1.1 This guidance covers the Competition and Markets Authority's (CMA's) approach to actual or potential breaches of final undertakings and orders put in place to address concerns identified in merger, monopoly and market investigations, either under the Enterprise Act 2002 (EA02)[1] or under the previous legislation, the Fair Trading Act 1973.

1.2 This guidance does not cover initial and interim undertakings or orders in relation to mergers.[2] Accordingly, unless otherwise specified, the terms undertaking or order in this guidance should be read as referring to final undertakings and orders imposed at the end of CMA investigations as well as undertakings in lieu of reference.

1.3 Taking action to address breaches of undertakings and orders is important for the CMA to deliver the outcomes of its markets and mergers work. Breaches of undertakings and orders can mean that benefits for customers from the CMA's work are not being realised, rivalry is reduced and that markets are not working as well as they otherwise would.

1.4 The CMA will apply this guidance flexibly, which means that the CMA will have regard to the guidance when it deals with potential and actual breaches of final undertakings and orders, but that, when the facts of an individual case reasonably justify it, the CMA may take a different approach.

1.5 This document is not a definitive statement of, or a substitute for, the law itself and should not be relied upon as an alternative to seeking appropriate legal advice.

1.6 This guidance sets out the CMA's practice as at 29 January 2021. The CMA consulted on a draft version of this guidance during October 2020 and took account of all comments received in finalising this guidance. Please refer to www.gov.uk/cma to ensure you have the latest version of this guidance as it may be revised from time to time to reflect changes in practices or the law and the CMA's developing experience.

1.7 You may find it useful to read this guidance alongside other documents published by the CMA, including:

- *Remedies: Guidance on the CMA's approach to the variation and termination of merger, monopoly and market undertakings and orders, CMA11*;
- *Market studies and investigations - guidance on the CMA's approach, CMA3*; and
- several guidance documents relating to the assessment of merger cases by the CMA (www.gov.uk/government/collections/cma-mergers-guidance).

NOTES

1 As amended by the Enterprise and Regulatory Reform Act 2013 (ERRA13).

2 such as undertakings under section 80 (covering interim undertakings) or orders under section 72 (initial enforcement orders) or section 81 (interim orders).

2. THE CMA'S APPROACH TO BREACHES OF UNDERTAKINGS AND ORDERS

THE CMA'S STATUTORY ROLE

[3.77]
2.1 Undertakings and orders are the primary means by which remedies are implemented following the final determination of merger and market investigation references under the EA02, as amended by the Enterprise and Regulatory Reform Act 2013 (ERRA13). Under the EA02, undertakings are accepted, or orders imposed by the CMA,[3] except in certain public interest cases where the Secretary of State is responsible for accepting undertakings or imposing orders.[4, 5]

2.2 The CMA has a statutory duty to keep under review undertakings and orders made under the EA02.[6] Sections 92 and 162 of the EA02 provide that the CMA shall, in particular, from time to time, consider whether an enforcement undertaking or order has been or is being complied with.[7] In addition, and as part of the same statutory duty, the CMA considers whether undertakings and orders remain appropriate, and whether they should be varied or released/revoked. The CMA's reviews of its orders and undertakings are covered in separate guidance, *Variation of undertakings and orders: CMA11*.

2.3 The CMA allocates resources in this area by reference to its prioritisation principles.

COMPLIANCE WITH REMEDIES

2.4 The CMA's undertakings and orders are designed during the course of an investigation to remedy identified competition problems, by placing effective and proportionate obligations on specific firms, within an appropriate timeframe. They are subject to extensive consultation prior to introduction. As a consequence, the CMA expects all firms that have agreed undertakings or that are within the scope of its orders to be compliant with these at all times from their introduction and throughout the time they remain in force.

2.5 Where firms breach the CMA's undertakings and orders, this can be the result of, for example:

(a) conduct whereby a firm did not directly intend to breach undertakings or an order, but:
  (i) did not properly implement a remedy when it first came into force and so has never achieved compliance; or
  (ii) although it implemented the remedy initially, the existing practices of the firm are not sufficiently robust or it has failed to dedicate sufficient resource and expertise to ensure it can provide ongoing compliance with the undertakings or order (either in isolation or as part of its wider regulatory obligations);

(b) the firm being unaware of the legal obligations on it; or

(c) the firm deliberately choosing not to comply with its legal obligations.

2.6 As noted above, taking action to address breaches of undertakings and orders is an important way in which the CMA delivers the outcomes of its markets and mergers work. Breaches of undertakings and orders can mean that benefits for customers from the CMA's work are not being realised, rivalry is reduced and that markets are not working as well they otherwise would.

WHAT CONSTITUTES A BREACH?

2.7 The CMA considers a breach of an undertaking or an order to be any instance in which a firm fails to comply with any obligation which is required in an undertaking or order, regardless of any effect on competition or customers. The CMA considers such failures to represent breaches irrespective of how they occurred, including whether deliberate, accidental or through ignorance of the obligations. Section 4 of this guidance addresses the CMA's response to specific breaches, including how the CMA considers a range of factors in determining on a case by case basis whether, and if so, what enforcement action to take in response to a specific breach.

NOTES

3 Under the EA02, the CMA may accept undertakings or impose orders (sections 82 and 84 of the EA02 (mergers) and sections 159 and 161 of the EA02 (markets)), and, where the conditions for a reference are met, the CMA may accept binding undertakings (UIL) as an alternative to making a reference (section 73 of the EA02 (mergers) and section 154 of the EA02 (markets)).

4 See sections 55 and 66 and Schedule 7 of the EA02 (mergers) and sections 147, 147A, 159 and 161 of the EA02 (markets).

5 The CMA has obtained the option of seeking agreement with the European Commission for the CMA to monitor and enforce certain EU merger and anti-trust remedies in future within the UK. The CMA has issued separate guidance on this matter (CMA125: Guidance on the functions of the CMA after the end of the Transition Period).

6 The CMA has a corresponding duty under the previous legislation, the Fair Trading Act 1973.

7 Specifically sections 92(2)(a) and 162(2)(a) of the EA02. and Schedule 24 of the EA02

3. MONITORING, REPORTING, INVESTIGATION AND TRANSPARENCY OF BREACHES

MONITORING COMPLIANCE

[3.78]

3.1 The CMA has a team responsible for monitoring and enforcing compliance with its orders and undertakings. In some instances, the CMA also has monitoring trustees or other appointed bodies that have specific responsibilities in relation to specific orders and undertakings, while overall responsibility for compliance remains with the CMA. Such trustees and organisations are normally put in place for more complex behavioural orders and undertakings. Some orders and undertakings impose compliance reporting requirements on parties, while in other cases the CMA proactively seeks information and monitors compliance.

REPORTING BREACHES OF REMEDIES TO THE CMA

3.2 To date, the CMA has found out about breaches of its undertakings and orders through a variety of routes, including:

(a) its proactive monitoring of individual firms and markets;
(b) the investigations of firms carried out by the CMA under a variety of tools;[8]
(c) liaison with sector regulators and industry or other representative bodies;
(d) third parties, including individual consumers and firms or whistle-blowers, assessing and reporting on the compliance of others;
(e) compliance reports submitted to the CMA by firms; and
(f) self-assessments of compliance carried out at other times by firms.

3.3 It is important for the CMA to find out about all breaches of its undertakings and orders as soon as reasonably possible, irrespective of whether such breaches are considered material. This is because such early notification allows for the CMA to work with the firm concerned on actions to end the breach quickly and effectively and to understand whether specific enforcement action is necessary to end the breach. This facilitates the efficient use of investigative resource both in the CMA and the firm concerned.

3.4 The CMA is aware that its portfolio of market and merger undertakings and orders have varying types of legal obligation in relation to reporting breaches, with some imposing specific deadlines on firms for reporting breaches, while others require firms to report on an annual basis about breaches.

3.5 These legal obligations will remain in place and take precedence over this guidance document. However, in this guidance, the CMA encourages all firms to report to the CMA all breaches of its undertakings and orders as soon as these are discovered, even where a full account of the details is not yet available. As described above, this will allow the CMA and the firm concerned to work together, in a timely and efficient manner to assess the scale of the breach, and what action necessary in response, including potential enforcement action.

3.6 If a firm is aware of a breach and takes action to remedy the breach without informing the CMA at the time, there is a risk that the CMA may not be content with the action taken, leading to costly changes in approach and an increased likelihood of formal enforcement action to address the breach.

3.7 Where a firm becomes aware that it will breach a set of undertakings or an order in the near future, the CMA would also encourage the firm to contact the CMA as soon as it is aware of this possibility, to explain the circumstances surrounding this and to explore with the CMA what actions the firm can take to mitigate the duration and the effects of the breach.

3.8 All contact in relation to breaches of the CMA's orders and undertakings should be with the CMA's monitoring and enforcement team (*remediesmonitoringteam@cma.gov.uk*).

3.9 While the exact details the CMA will need to know about a breach will depend on the individual circumstances of a particular breach, the CMA would expect to receive the following information with all reports of breaches, while recognising that all aspects of this list may not be available at the point at which a breach is first identified and notified to the CMA:

(a) a description of the relevant provision(s) of the order or undertakings to which the breach relates;

(b) a full description of the breach itself, including whether, and if so how, it might have an impact on relevant third parties, and consumers;

(c) how the breach occurred and how and when it was discovered;

(d) the duration of the breach and whether it is ongoing;

(e) the size and significance of the breach and harm caused, both for the firm and for third parties and consumers;

(f) details of whether any third parties are involved, including suppliers, systems providers and other contracted parties; and

(g) whether any relevant regulators have been informed (for breaches in regulated sectors).

INVESTIGATIONS OF BREACHES

3.10 The CMA's approach to an investigation into breaches of its undertakings and orders will depend on the nature and severity of the breach. The CMA may use information-gathering powers contained in particular clauses of undertakings and orders, or broader information-gathering powers, such as section 109 EA02 notices for mergers, section 174 EA02 notices for markets, or use of the CMA's general function in section 5 EA02 to obtain, compile and keep under review information about matters relating to the carrying out of its functions.

3.11 Certain breaches of the CMA's undertakings and orders could also represent a breach of the CMA's broader jurisdictions, including competition and consumer protection legislation. Where the CMA considers this to be the case, the CMA will select the most appropriate legal tool or tools under which to conduct its investigation, based on the circumstances of the breach concerned, including, where appropriate, the enforcement mechanisms available to deliver redress to consumers.

3.12 The CMA notes that firms providing information to it have an obligation to provide truthful, complete and accurate information. It is an offence under section 117 of the Enterprise Act 2002 to knowingly or recklessly provide information to the CMA that is false or misleading in a material respect. The CMA also notes that failure to comply with a requirement of a notice issued under s109 or s174 EA02 without reasonable excuse can lead to the imposition of a penalty.[9]

PUBLIC REGISTER OF BREACHES OF UNDERTAKINGS AND ORDERS

3.13 The CMA has several public registers displayed on its website and generally seeks to promote transparency in relation to identified breaches of undertakings and orders, and the action the CMA is taking.

3.14 The CMA provides information on current markets and mergers orders and undertakings on its register of orders and undertakings (www.gov.uk/government/collections/markets-orders-and-undertakings-register). It has recently introduced a register of time-expired merger remedies (www.gov.uk/government/publications/mergers-orders-and-undertakings/expired-merger- remedies) (ie, those where the remedy itself included an automatic end-date for the obligations, or has otherwise expired).

3.15 On 1 April 2020, the CMA announced that it would begin publication of information about all material breaches of its undertakings and orders. The register of breaches will be updated quarterly. The objective in publishing this register is to provide transparency about the firms that breach the CMA's undertakings and orders and the frequency and nature of such breaches. It will also provide a description of any enforcement work carried out in respect of the breach.

3.16 Each potential breach the CMA becomes aware of will be investigated and the CMA will reach a decision on the basis of the information available to it on whether a particular issue represents a breach and, if so, whether it should appear on the register.

Material breaches

3.17 In considering whether a breach should appear on the register, the CMA will form a view as to whether the breach in question is material on a case by case basis. Breaches which are less likely to be found to be material are those which the CMA determines as having had no substantive effect on customers, consumers or competition (and which did not have the potential to have such an effect), and which were also of a very short duration with clear confirmation that they have ceased and will not recur. For example, some orders and undertakings impose information requirements on all customers, and while a failure to meet such obligations would generally be material, this might not be the case where a breach occurred for a very small group of customers (for example fewer than 50 customers of a mass market product or service), and specifically in a situation where the information had already been superseded (due to actions they had taken such as cancelling a policy etc). Another example could be the slightly late delivery of a reporting obligation to the CMA. Where only a few days late, such a delay may have limited impact on compliance and the work of the CMA. The intention of this definition is to ensure that those bound by orders and undertakings are not devoting resource unnecessarily to exploring very small breaches with no substantive impact on customers, and for the CMA to ensure it focuses its monitoring and enforcement resources on material breaches.

3.18 As noted in paragraph 3.3 above, all breaches and potential breaches should be reported to the CMA, and it is for the CMA to determine whether an issue represents a breach and whether it considers that to be material.

3.19 The CMA will record the following information about material breaches in its public register once a decision has been reached on whether an issue represents a material breach:

(a) the order or undertakings breached;
(b) the firm that breached the remedy;
(c) a short description of the breach including whether it is a breach of administrative, reporting or substantive obligations;
(d) the duration of the breach;
(e) when the breach was notified to the CMA;
(f) any action taken by the firm to address the breach and to put things right for consumers (such as through providing refunds to compensate for any loss or damage); and
(g) action taken by the CMA in response, whether formal or informal.

3.20 Prior to publishing details of a breach on the register of breaches, the CMA will notify the relevant firm of its decision to make an entry on the register and provide such of its reasoning as the CMA considers appropriate in the circumstances. Where the CMA has decided that enforcement action is appropriate in relation to such a breach, the CMA would normally expect the register of breaches to be updated when details of the enforcement action are published or, if sooner, when any enforcement action has been completed.

NOTES

[8] Including, Competition Act 1998 investigations, merger investigations, market studies, market investigations and investigations of previous breaches of orders and undertakings under the Enterprise Act 2002, and consumer protection investigations under Part 8 of the Enterprise Act 2002.

[9] As set out in Section 111 or Section 174D of the Enterprise Act 2002.

4. ENFORCEMENT AGAINST BREACHES OF REMEDIES

[3.79]

4.1 In relation to some identified breaches, the CMA may decide, as part of its statutory duty explained in paragraphs 2.1 to 2.3 above, that it is appropriate to take enforcement action. For example, this may occur where a breach is ongoing or where although a breach has been remedied, existing processes and procedures are inadequate to ensure ongoing compliance.

4.2 Before proposing any enforcement action in relation to a breach, the CMA will ensure that the firm involved is aware of the breach and has had an opportunity to liaise with the CMA over this.

4.3 In assessing the nature of a breach, and considering the possible enforcement action, the CMA will take a case-by-case approach, taking into account all relevant circumstances. This may include:

(a) **significance** – including the magnitude of the breach in terms of cost or value, the harm caused, and the number of suppliers, customers or consumers affected, as well as the duration of the breach;
(b) **the actions taken by the firm in reporting to the CMA and addressing the breach** – including whether the firm has reported the breach to the CMA in a timely and complete manner. Other relevant factors here include whether it has decided itself to take proactive steps to stop the breach (in advance of any indication that the CMA intends to take specific action), and the extent to which a firm has taken appropriate steps to remedy any detriment suffered by customers, and improve its procedures sufficiently to prevent further breaches;
(c) **recidivism and previous conduct** – including an assessment of the nature of any previous breaches, and whether a business is already subject to a heightened compliance regime resulting from previous breaches;
(d) **the need for the CMA to take action to address the breach** – including whether a breach is ongoing, and what, if any, action the CMA needs to take to bring the breach to an end, or to put in place improved and more substantial controls on a firm to seek to prevent further breaches; and
(e) **contextual factors, such as the status and age of the undertaking or order** – where an order or undertakings are new and in the process of being implemented and where firms have some legitimate uncertainty over their exact obligations, this might lead to different action being taken compared to when an order or undertakings have been in force continuously for a number of months or years and firms will be expected to be more familiar with the obligations. For older cases, we will give consideration to whether, and if so how, the relevant market has evolved since the undertakings or order were put in place, to ensure that our proposed enforcement remains proportionate.

4.4 The CMA's action typically falls into one of the two categories considered below.

INFORMAL ACTIONS

4.5 Informal action describes a response to a breach where the CMA is not engaging its formal enforcement powers (such as issuing directions – see paragraph 4.8 onwards). This can include the CMA agreeing actions with firms to end a breach and to improve practices and processes in the future. In these cases, the CMA may decide to publish a letter to businesses on its website which provides detail on the nature of the breach and acknowledges any action taken by a business to put things right. This is so that customers and any interested stakeholders are made aware of the action taken. Irrespective of whether or not the CMA decides to publish a letter, any material breaches will be recorded in the register of breaches as set out in paragraphs 3.13 to 3.20 above.

4.6 While the CMA will take a case-by-case approach, taking into account all relevant circumstances, informal action is more likely for breaches where the following are true:

(a) this is the first occasion that the firm has breached the remedy concerned;
(b) the breach is of limited scale and scope;
(c) the breach has limited practical impact on suppliers, customers and consumers;
(d) details of the breach were passed in full to the CMA as soon as was practical in the circumstances;
(e) the breach has been brought to an end by the firm concerned taking steps on a voluntary basis, considered as sufficient by the CMA, to resolve the root cause of the breach; and
(f) the firm has committed, on a voluntary basis, to take all steps, considered as sufficient and appropriate by the CMA, to prevent future breaches.

The process for informal enforcement

4.7 The process for issuing public letters involves the CMA engaging with the firm concerned as follows:

(a) Having understood the nature and extent of the breach, if the CMA reaches a provisional view that certain informal action would be appropriate, the CMA will write to the firm concerned to explain this provisional view and the reasons for it. The CMA shall explain the action it proposes to take and attach any draft public letter where appropriate. The firm will then have typically two weeks (and possibly more in complex cases) to provide any representations it wishes to provide to the CMA on both the principle and the substance of the action the CMA is proposing.
(b) The CMA will consider the representations received on both the principle and the substance before reaching a final view on the appropriate action. The CMA will then communicate this to the firm concerned, and will continue to liaise with the firm over the timing of any public announcements where relevant.

FORMAL ENFORCEMENT ACTION

4.8 To ensure compliance with its undertakings and orders, the CMA has formal enforcement tools available to ensure firms take all actions the CMA considers necessary for the firms to become compliant. These tools are used for more significant breaches, such as those:

(a) which may have a significant impact in terms of scale, harm caused, scope or the number of customers affected;
(b) which may have a significant impact on individual customers or consumers;
(c) which are ongoing, including those still being explored by the firm concerned, or where the necessary steps to remedy the breach and prevent future breaches were not identified, volunteered, agreed or taken by the firm responsible;
(d) which raise issues of recidivism and ongoing compliance problems; or
(e) where the CMA has concerns that a firm is not capable of, or willing to, take all the necessary steps voluntarily to prevent further breaches.

4.9 The use of the CMA's formal enforcement tools can result in the CMA seeking an order from the court requiring a firm to remedy a breach. A failure to comply with such an order may lead to contempt of court proceedings. Consequently , firms which persistently fail to comply with the relevant undertakings or order could face a fine, or imprisonment of individuals for up to two years (or both).

4.10 For breaches where formal enforcement powers are considered necessary (as described in paragraph 4.8), the CMA can either:

(a) Apply to a court to seek compliance with the original enforcement order or undertakings; or
(b) Issue directions to the firm concerned.

4.11 The CMA will determine which form of formal action to take based on the individual circumstances of the case, including the nature of the breach as further described in paragraph 4.3. Both seeking compliance directly through court or issuing directions can lead ultimately to contempt of court proceedings.

Issuing directions

4.12 In its directions, the CMA can require a firm to take specific steps to bring to an end a breach of an order or undertakings, as well as to improve its practices and procedures to prevent similar problems arising in the future. The CMA can also impose additional, generally more onerous, compliance and reporting obligations to allow for more detailed monitoring activities.[10]

Potential content of directions

4.13 The directions that the CMA issues to a firm will be specific to the firm and the particular breach. However, there are a number of types of directions which are commonly used, sometimes individually and at other times in combination with each other and with other relevant obligations. The list of types of directions below is not exhaustive and does not constrain the CMA from considering different directions where they are considered appropriate to a particular breach by a particular business. The main categories of directions include:

(a) **ending a breach** – where a breach is ongoing, the CMA may find it necessary to direct the firm concerned to take specific steps to end the breach within a certain timeframe;
(b) **changes to policies, processes and procedures to prevent further breaches** – depending on the cause of a breach, the CMA may consider it necessary to direct a firm to make specific changes to its policies, processes and procedures (including staff training where appropriate) to avoid further breaches in the future;

(c) **auditing internal processes and procedures** – where a number of policies, processes and procedures may have contributed to a breach, or for example where these are complex, the CMA may consider it necessary for the firm to procure a business independent of the firm to carry out either a one-off or a regular audit of all its processes and procedures relevant to achieving compliance with an order or undertaking;

(d) **enhanced compliance measures or new/additional reporting requirements** – in response to a firm breaching a remedy, the CMA may consider it appropriate to introduce compliance monitoring if this were not provided before the breach to understand the specific actions taken by firms to ensure and/or maintain compliance. Alternatively, where compliance monitoring was already required by the remedy concerned, the CMA may introduce new reporting obligations or increase the frequency of any existing compliance reporting. This can provide the CMA with valuable visibility of actions taken within the firm and the likelihood of further breaches; and

(e) **requiring a firm to inform affected customers about a breach** – where a breach affects a firm's customers, the CMA may direct that firm to provide certain information to its customers that were affected including informing them of their rights to refunds and / or redress from the firm.

CMA process for issuing directions

4.14 When the CMA believes it has all the information required to make a provisional decision, the CMA will generally expect to follow these steps:

(a) the CMA will write to the firm concerned, noting that it is minded to issue directions, on the basis of the information available from its investigation into the breach;

(b) the CMA will allow the firm concerned at least two weeks to provide any representations on whether the issuing of directions as an approach is appropriate and proportionate;

(c) the CMA will consider any representations provided and where it continues to consider it appropriate to issue directions, the CMA will provide the firm concerned with the draft directions that it intends to issue and seek an action plan detailing the timescales within which the tasks directed will be undertaken;

(d) the CMA will allow the firm concerned a reasonable period of time (a minimum of two weeks) to provide any representations on the specific requirements in the draft directions. The firm may also put forward any new information which is relevant to whether directions are appropriate or not;

(e) the CMA will consider any representations on the draft directions, and will reach a final decision on whether to issue directions and, where appropriate, will determine the exact directions to be issued; and

(f) the CMA will issue directions to the firm concerned, publishing the action plan and records this information on its public register of directions, the register of breaches, and relevant webpage for the order or undertakings concerned.

4.15 At the time the CMA issues directions to parties, it is normal practice for the CMA to take a number of steps to highlight the breach and any enforcement action publicly. This helps to inform affected customers and potential customers of a business of the breach and the action taken. While the CMA will inform parties of its intended actions in publicising breaches and enforcement action, the choice of materials, the approach, and their content is not part of the consultation described above.

Enforcing directions through the courts

4.16 If firms fail to comply with the CMA's directions, the CMA can enforce these directly through the courts. If a firm were to ignore a court order the CMA could pursue contempt of court proceedings. Contempt of court is an offence which includes disobeying or ignoring a court order, and can result in a fine, or imprisonment of up to two years (or both).

Duration of directions

4.17 The directions issued by the CMA will be considered on a case by case basis, and in some instances these directions may place an ongoing restriction on businesses for the duration of the order or undertakings to which they refer. This means that such directions will be expected to remain in place until such time as the parties are released from their commitments by the variation or revocation/release of the underlying undertakings or order.

4.18 In other cases, the directions given by the CMA may be to carry out a one-off, time-limited or event-limited activity and once this has been completed the directions may have no ongoing obligation or value.

4.19 For both ongoing and time/event limited directions, it is open to the parties bound by these to apply to the CMA for the directions to be varied or terminated (in whole or in part). Any submission making such a request should set out clearly and with supporting evidence matters such as:

(a) why it is appropriate to vary or terminate the directions in the way suggested. For time-limited and event-limited instances, this will normally involve demonstrating that the obligations have been completed;

(b) the possible consequences for consumers and businesses impacted by the remedy;

(c) why a review of the order and undertakings meets the CMA's published prioritisation; and

(d) whether the request is being raised in order to avoid a breach of the undertakings or order.

4.20 It is open to parties to approach the CMA prior to submitting a request in order to discuss what sort of evidence would be expected to be included in any request.

THE ROLE OF THIRD PARTIES IN BREACHES

4.21 In relation to some breaches, the firm responsible for compliance may rely, in part, on one or more third parties to deliver certain actions to ensure it remains compliant. The CMA's role in enforcing compliance with its undertakings and orders involves the CMA taking specific action against the firm that either gave undertakings or is within the scope of specific order. The CMA will expect the firm concerned to liaise with any third parties involved during the decision-making process for both informal and formal action, so that the views of these third parties can be understood by the CMA before a final decision is reached. The CMA will also expect the firm to ensure that such third parties take the necessary steps to ensure the relevant firm complies with either informal or formal enforcement action taken by the CMA.

CHALLENGING THE CMA'S APPROACH

4.22 While the CMA is able to determine the enforcement action it considers to be necessary and proportionate to end a breach and prevent similar problems arising in the future, firms that wish to challenge the CMA's approach can do so:

(a) by making representations during the opportunities provided for in the process described above for informal or formal enforcement. This is the most efficient way in which firms can ensure their representations are considered by the CMA;

(b) by seeking a judicial review of a relevant decision by the CMA; or

(c) in a case where the CMA is seeking to enforce an undertaking, order or directions in the courts, the relevant firm would be a party to those proceedings and able to make appropriate representations in court.

BREACHES OF OTHER LEGISLATION AND ALTERNATIVE ROUTES OF ENFORCEMENT

4.23 The CMA has a number of investigative and legislative tools and powers at its disposal, and in a limited number of cases, a breach of an undertaking or an order may also breach other legislation enforced by the CMA, and such powers could be applicable to addressing breaches of our orders or undertakings. For each breach, the CMA will determine which powers are most appropriate to be used to achieve the desired outcomes.

NOTES

10 See section 87 of the EA02.

CMA BOARD RULES OF PROCEDURE (REVISED APRIL 2021)

[3.80]

NOTES

These Rules and the associated Annexes are available on the Competition and Markets Authority website at: www.gov.uk/government/publications/cma-board-rules-of-procedure.

[3.81]

The Competition and Markets Authority (CMA) is a body corporate established under section 25 of the Enterprise and Regulatory Reform Act 2013. It performs its functions on behalf of the Crown and must seek to promote competition, both within and outside the United Kingdom, for the benefit of consumers.[1] The CMA will carry out its functions independently, impartially and fairly.

The CMA Rules of Procedure (the Rules), which are set out below, have been made by the Board.[2] These Rules shall, where applicable, be read and interpreted together with the CMA's statutory powers and functions. The meaning of certain words and phrases contained within these Rules are set out in the interpretation section below.

NOTES

1 Section 25 and paragraph 8, Schedule 4 of the Act.

2 These Rules of Procedure were made by the Board on 1 April 2021 under the power in paragraph 31(1), Schedule 4 of the Act .

INTERPRETATION

'the Act' means the Enterprise and Regulatory Reform Act 2013;

'the Board' means the Chair and Members appointed under paragraph 1, Schedule 4 of the Act;

'Board Member' means a member of the CMA appointed by the Secretary of State under paragraph 1(1)(b)(i) or (iii), Schedule 4 of the Act;

'Board Secretary' means the employee of the CMA who is appointed from time to time to act as secretary to the Board;

'Chair' means a person appointed to hold the office of Chair by the Secretary of State under paragraph 1(1)(a), Schedule 4 of the Act;

'Chief Executive' means the person appointed to hold the office of Chief Executive by the Secretary of State under paragraph 9(1), Schedule 4 of the Act;

'Chief Operating Officer' means the Executive Director appointed to hold the office of chief operating officer;

'clear days' in relation to a period of notice means a period excluding the day on which the notice is given and the day for which it is given or on which it is to take effect;

'the CMA' means the Competition and Markets Authority;

'Executive Director means a Board Member of the CMA who is also an employee of the CMA;

'Non-executive Director' means a Board Member of the CMA other than Executive Directors;

'ordinary resolution' means a resolution that is passed by a simple majority of such Board Members and the Chair in attendance as are entitled to vote on that resolution;

'Panel Member' means a member of the CMA appointed by the Secretary of State under paragraph 1(1)(b)(ii), Schedule 4 of the Act;

'the Principal Accounting Officer' means a person appointed by HM Treasury as accounting officer pursuant to s 5(6) of the Government Resources and Accounts Act 2000;[3]

'Replacement Chair' means the Non-executive Director who is appointed in accordance with paragraph 18 of these Rules to chair all or part of a Board meeting at which the Chair is absent or has declared a relevant conflict of interest in relation to any matter;

'Senior Independent Director' means the Non-executive Director who is appointed in accordance with paragraph 52 of these Rules.

NOTES

[3] For the avoidance of doubt, as the Principal Accounting Officer for the CMA, the Chief Executive is also charged with meeting the responsibilities of the Accounting Officer as described in Chapter 3 of Managing Public Money.

THE BOARD

The Board consists of the Chair and at least five Board Members, at least one of whom must also be a Panel Member. Of the Panel Members appointed to the Board, one shall be the designated chair of the Panel.[4]

The Board is responsible for:

- establishing the overall strategic direction of the CMA within the statutory framework laid down under the Act, setting organisational priorities and scrutinising the CMA's performance in meeting its goals
- ensuring that the CMA's independence is maintained and that the CMA's reputation for independence and impartiality is protected
- ensuring that the CMA fulfils its statutory duties and functions, and acts within the limits of its statutory authority
- overseeing the use of public funds (including considering the opinions and reports of the Principal Accounting Officer) and ensuring that public funds are used appropriately
- establishing a framework of prudent and effective controls, which enable risk to be assessed and managed
- ensuring that staff policies and practices are consistent with the CMA's values and, in particular, with promoting a working environment where harassment, bullying or other inappropriate or discriminatory behaviour is not tolerated
- demonstrating high standards of corporate governance, in line with the Corporate Governance in Central Government Departments Code of Good Practice, and by using an Audit and Risk Assurance Committee to help the Board address key financial and other risks.

In particular, the Board is responsible for:

- proposals for the annual plan and consultation on these proposals made under paragraph 13, Schedule 4 of the Act
- the annual plan made under paragraph 12, Schedule 4 of the Act
- the annual report made under paragraph 14, Schedule 4 of the Act
- the concurrency report made under paragraph 16, Schedule 4 of the Act
- making rules of procedure for merger reference groups, market reference groups, and special reference groups, as defined in paragraph 51, Schedule 4 of the Act.

The Chair, with the support of the Senior Independent Director (SID), will ensure a review of the effectiveness of the Board and its committees is carried out annually, with independent input at least once every three years.

The Board will review these Rules every two years.

MATTERS RESERVED FOR BOARD INVOLVEMENT

The matters listed in Annex A are reserved for the involvement of the Board.

The list of matters reserved for Board involvement does not preclude other matters or decisions being reserved by the Board or, in the case of matters that have been delegated by the Board, being referred to the Board.

NOTES

4 As constituted under Part 3, Schedule 4 of the Act.

BOARD MEETINGS

ARRANGING MEETINGS

The Board shall meet at least six times a year and at such other times as necessary.

A meeting may be called by the Chair; or by the SID and the Chief Executive; or by any two Non-executive Directors.

Subject to paragraph 13, not less than fourteen clear days' notice of a meeting will be provided to Board Members and the Chair.

A meeting may exceptionally be called on less than fourteen clear days' notice. Such shorter notice will be effective only if ratified either by the Chair or jointly by the Chief Executive and SID.[5]

Notice of a meeting shall be communicated in writing including by email. Such notice shall contain details of the meeting and of the business to be conducted at the meeting.

Failure of a Board Member or the Chair to receive notice of a meeting shall not invalidate that meeting or any business conducted at it.

Meetings may take place at the CMA's administrative offices or at any other convenient location, and may include virtual attendance (in accordance with paragraph 21 of these Rules). Any employee of the CMA or any other person may be invited to attend all or part of a Board meeting. Any confidential information (as referred to in paragraph 23) must not be shared with any person from outside of the CMA who attends a meeting.

PROCEDURE AT MEETINGS

The quorum for a meeting of the Board shall be: four Non-executive Directors (which may include a Board Member who is also a Panel Member); two Executive Directors; and must include either the Chair or the Chief Executive. Neither the Chair nor a Board Member will be counted towards quorum for an item in respect of which they have declared a relevant conflict of interest.

In the absence of the Chair at any meeting, the SID appointed under paragraph 52 below shall be the Replacement Chair for that meeting. In the absence of both the Chair and the SID at any meeting, those Non-executive Directors present will appoint a Non-executive Director as Replacement Chair for that meeting but such appointment cannot be of a Board Member who has also been appointed to the Panel.

Where decisions are made by the Board, they shall be made by ordinary resolution. In the case of equal votes the Chair, or the Replacement Chair, shall have a second or casting vote.

The Board will take collective responsibility for any decision made by it and will seek to achieve unanimity in decisions. Where Board Members have concerns that cannot be resolved in relation to a particular matter or a proposed action, they should ensure that these concerns are recorded.

Participation will usually be in person. However, unless the Chair has requested 'in person' attendance, Board Members may also participate by telephone, video or web conferencing facility and will be deemed to be present and constitute part of the Board for that meeting. Any Board Member who leaves a meeting prior to the conclusion of a meeting shall be taken to be a non-participating Board Member for the purpose of any decision taken by the Board during that person's absence. All attendances and absences by the Chair or by Board Members for all or part of a Board meeting will be recorded in the minutes of the meeting.

Any resolution capable of being passed by the Board at a meeting may instead be passed by written resolution. A response received by email will be effective. Any such written resolution shall be deemed passed when it has been authorised by the last of the Board Members approving the resolution, provided that a simple majority of Board Members entitled to vote on the resolution authorises it and provided that those Members entitled to vote on the resolution satisfy the quorum requirement in paragraph 17

MINUTES OF MEETINGS

Minutes of Board meetings shall be published on the CMA website and will not contain any confidential information. Examples of confidential information may include: information the disclosure of which is prohibited or restricted by a provision of any enactment; information that is otherwise subject to a duty of confidentiality; information which is subject to legal professional privilege; market-sensitive information; information the publication of which could hinder the performance of the functions of the CMA; and information about individuals such as employees of the CMA.

NOTES

5 As set out in the Board Emergency Procedure which sets out the process for convening the Board outside the usual schedule of meetings, including at short notice.

DELEGATION OF FUNCTIONS

CMA PANEL CHAIR

The Board may consent to the performance of those functions of the Chair listed in paragraph 48(4), Schedule 4 of the Act by a person who is appointed both to the Board and to the Panel[6] or by a Panel Member who is designated for this purpose by the Secretary of State.

CMA COMMITTEES AND SUB-COMMITTEES

Save in respect of functions of the CMA which are to be carried out on behalf of the CMA by a CMA group,[7] the Board may authorise any committee or sub-committee to perform anything authorised or required to be done by the CMA, subject to certain restrictions.[8] The Board shall receive regular reports from committees or sub-committees it has established as it shall direct.

The members of a committee or sub-committee of the CMA may include persons who are not Board Members provided that, if it is authorised to perform functions delegated to it by the Board, they are employees of the CMA or are Panel Members. A sub-committee may include persons who are not members of the committee which established it.

There shall be an Audit and Risk Assurance Committee (ARAC) established by the Board. Membership of ARAC and its terms of reference are set out in Annex B to these Rules.

There shall be a Remuneration Committee established by the Board. Membership of the Remuneration Committee and its terms of reference are set out in Annex C to these Rules.

There shall be a Nominations Committee established by the Board. Membership of the Nominations Committee and its terms of reference are set out in Annex D to these Rules.

AUTHORISATION OF INDIVIDUAL BOARD MEMBERS AND STAFF OF THE CMA

Save in respect of functions which the Board has reserved to itself or which it has authorised committees or sub-committees to exercise, the Board may authorise at any time any Board Member of the CMA or CMA staff member to perform anything authorised or required to be done by the CMA , subject to certain restrictions.[9]

Annex E sets out the Board authorisations of staff, Panel Chair and Inquiry Chairs, including in relation to the merger, market, competition, litigation and criminal enforcement functions of the CMA.

OBLIGATIONS OF BOARD AND COMMITTEE MEMBERS

The Chair, Board Members and members of committees and sub-committees must, in carrying out their respective responsibilities, comply with the Civil Service Code[10] and the Cabinet Office Code of Conduct for Board Members of Public Bodies[11]; have regard to the principles of public life[12]: selflessness, integrity, objectivity, accountability, openness, honesty and leadership; and act at all times in the best interests of the CMA.

The Chair, Board Members and members of the committees and sub-committees are also required to comply with the CMA's Respect agenda by ensuring that they:

- treat everyone with respect and ensure the workplace is free of bullying and harassment;
- encourage and enable colleagues to do their best; acknowledge and value diversity; and listen to different views with courtesy;
- give and receive honest, objective and supportive feedback in a mutually respectful way, with a genuine intention to assist each other's development; and
- take seriously concerns about inappropriate behaviour reported to them and ensure appropriate action is taken as a result of issues being raised.

Board Members and committee members shall have access to the CMA's governance, compliance and risk function which is responsible for providing advice to the Board and committee members to ensure compliance with, and adherence to: these Rules; the CMA framework agreement with BEIS; and other relevant guidance from government departments (including the Cabinet Office Code of Conduct and the Civil Service Code).

CONFLICTS OF INTEREST

The Chair and Board Members shall be subject to the procedures and guidelines for dealing with conflicts of interest set out in the CMA's Conflicts of Interest policy at Annex F to these Rules.

TRANSPARENCY

The CMA is publicly committed to openness and transparency in relation to the conduct of its affairs and is subject to the provisions of the Freedom of Information Act 2000 (FoIA) and data protection legislation. The Chair, Board Members and members of committees and sub-committees shall act in accordance with the guidelines and policies relating to these matters issued or adopted by the CMA from time to time.

CONFIDENTIALITY

The Chair and Board Members shall be subject to a general duty of confidentiality in relation to the conduct of the affairs of the CMA and information they obtain in the course of their work for it. This duty includes complying with relevant statutory restrictions on disclosure[13] and maintaining confidentiality of information where it is subject to legal professional privilege. This duty is personal and shall be without prejudice to the commitment of the Board and the CMA as a whole to transparency and compliance with the FoIA and data protection legislation.

CONCERNS ABOUT PROPRIETY

Board Members should raise any concerns that they have about the propriety of the Board, any Board Member or the Chief Executive confidentially with the Chair.

Board Members should raise any concerns that they have about the propriety of the Chair confidentially with the SID appointed under paragraph 52 below.

RESOLVING AND RECORDING CONCERNS OR DISPUTES BETWEEN BOARD MEMBERS

Where concerns about propriety or other significant issues or disputes arise between Board Members which affect the stability of the Board, the issue should be raised with the Chair (if the issue does not involve the Chair) or the SID (if the issue involves the Chair but does not involve the SID). If the issue involves both the Chair and the SID, the Chief Executive will nominate a Non-executive Director with whom to raise the issue.

That person with whom the issue is raised will investigate (with assistance, if required, from the Chief Operating Officer) and facilitate the resolution of the issue. This process will be carried out in consultation with other Board Members unless, exceptionally, it would be inappropriate to do so. A record of the nature of the issue and the steps taken to resolve it should be recorded by the Compliance Officer on a strictly confidential basis.

Where all reasonable channels have been exhausted and the resolution process is unsuccessful, the issue should be raised (by the person who has conducted the investigation) with the Director General of Market Frameworks at the Department for Business, Energy and Industrial Strategy (BEIS).

Where underlying allegations to an issue are considered by the person investigating to be particularly urgent or serious, that person may choose to escalate the issue directly with the Director General of Market Frameworks at BEIS.

Details of any dispute or issue, together the steps taken to resolve it, will be included in the report sent to BEIS as part of the annual appraisal process in respect of the Chair and Non-executive Directors (see paragraphs 55–57 below).

NOTES

6 Under paragraph 1(1)(b)(iii), Schedule 4 of the Act.

7 As constituted under paragraphs 36 and 37, Schedule 4 of the Act.

8 Paragraph 29 (1), Schedule 4 of the Act, subject to restrictions in paragraph 29(2)-(3) and paragraph 30 of Schedule 4 of the Act.

9 Paragraph 29 but subject to paragraph 30, Schedule 4 of the Act.

10 The Civil Service code - GOV.UK (www.gov.uk/government/publications/civil-service-code/the-civil-service-code).

11 Code of conduct for board members of public bodies, 2019 (The Cabinet Office Code of Conduct) (www.gov.uk/government/publications/code-of-conduct-for-board-members-of-public-bodies).

12 The Seven Principles of Public Life (www.gov.uk/government/publications/the-7-principles-of-public-life/the-7-principles-of-public-life--2).

13 For example, the EA02, the Data Protection Act 2018 and the Official Secrets Act 1989.

ROLES AND RESPONSIBILITIES OF THE CHAIR, CHIEF EXECUTIVE, NON-EXECUTIVE DIRECTORS

THE CHAIR

The Chair's role and responsibilities are set out in: the appointment letter; the legislation; the CMA Framework Agreement with BEIS; and these Rules. A summary of the Chair's role and responsibilities is set out in Annex G.

THE CHIEF EXECUTIVE

The Chief Executive's role and responsibilities are set out in: the appointment letter; the legislation; the CMA Framework Agreement with BEIS; and these Rules. A summary of the Chief Executive's role and responsibilities is set out in Annex G.

The roles of Chair and Chief Executive are distinct. The focus of the Chair's role is, in general terms, providing effective leadership at Board level, and determining the strategic direction for the CMA. By contrast, the focus of the Chief Executive's role is, in general terms, leading the CMA, as a whole organisation, in implementing the Board's strategy and discharging the function of the CMA's Principal Accounting Officer (as designated by HM Treasury).

The Chair and Chief Executive will discuss all major issues and emerging policies through frequent (and normally informal) meetings and will specifically discuss any contentious matters or those likely to set significant precedent.

NON-EXECUTIVE DIRECTORS

The responsibilities of Non-executive Directors are set out in their appointment letter and a summary of those is set out in Annex G.

In consultation with the Chair and the SID, Non-executive Directors may take the lead on some of the Board's activities, for example performing the role of chair of non-executive committees such as ARAC.

Non-executive Directors, other than the Chair, should meet by themselves at least once a year.

SENIOR INDEPENDENT DIRECTOR

In consultation with the Non-executive Directors, the Chair shall appoint a SID, who must be a Non-executive Director appointed to the Board under paragraph 1(1)(b)(i), Schedule 4 of the Act, and therefore cannot be a member of both the Board and the Panel.

The SID is, in general terms, responsible for providing a sounding board for the Chair and for serving as an intermediary between the Chair and the other Board Members, when necessary.

The SID's role and responsibilities are set out in the appointment letter and a summary of those is set out in Annex G.

CHAIR AND BOARD MEMBER EVALUATION PROCESS

The Chair's performance will be formally assessed on an annual basis by the Director General of Market Frameworks at BEIS, in consultation with the Board . The SID will lead on the consultation on behalf of other Board Members, ensuring all Board Members have an opportunity to feed into the process.

An appraisal of the performance of the Non-executive Directors will be conducted annually, led by the Chair, using an appropriate feedback process. Reports will be made to the Director General of Market Frameworks at BEIS.

Evaluations of the performance of individual Board Members should show whether each continues to contribute effectively and to demonstrate commitment to the role (including commitment of time for Board and committee meetings and other duties).

ANNEX A
MATTERS RESERVED FOR BOARD INVOLVEMENT

[3.82]

1. The functions of deciding:

(a) whether the duty to publish a market study notice under section 130A of the Enterprise Act 2002 applies;

(b) whether to propose to make, or to make, a reference under section 131 of that Act;

(c) for the purposes of the requirement imposed by section 131A(2)(b) of that Act, whether the CMA is proposing to make a decision as to whether to make a reference under section 131 of that Act in a way that is likely to have a substantial impact on the interests of any person;

(d) whether section 140A of that Act applies in respect of a particular case;

(e) whether to accept an undertaking under section 154 of that Act, or to vary or supersede or release an undertaking under that section;

(f) for the purposes of the requirement imposed by section 169(2) of that Act, whether the CMA is proposing to make a decision to make a reference under section 131 of that Act in a way that is likely to have a substantial impact on the interests of any person.

2. The approval of the CMA's conflicts of interest policy.

3. The Board will consider matters and provide an advisory steer in relation to large operational projects or programmes that, in the view of either the Principal Accounting Officer or ARAC, could have a significant long term impact on the CMA's costs or the space available for the CMA to carry out its work.

ANNEX B
AUDIT AND RISK ASSURANCE COMMITTEE TERMS OF REFERENCE

PURPOSE

[3.83]

1. The purpose of the Audit and Risk Assurance Committee is to advise the Principal Accounting Officer (the Chief Executive) and the Board on the adequacy of audit arrangements (internal and external) and on the implications of assurances provided in respect of risk and control, with a view to enabling the Board to assure itself of the effectiveness of the CMA's risk management system and procedures and its internal controls including business continuity and information technology.

STATUS

2. The Audit and Risk Assurance Committee acts only in an advisory capacity and has no executive powers.

3. The Audit and Risk Assurance Committee is authorised to investigate any activity within its terms of reference. It is authorised to seek any information it requires from any Board Member or employee of the CMA and all Board Members and employees of the CMA are directed to co-operate with any reasonable request made by the Committee.

4. The Audit and Risk Assurance Committee is authorised to obtain independent professional advice (including legal advice) and to arrange for the attendance of persons who are not CMA employees with relevant experience and expertise if it considers this necessary.

RESPONSIBILITIES

5. The Audit and Risk Assurance Committee's remit encompasses all aspects of corporate governance, risk management and internal control within the CMA. In particular, the Committee shall review, advise, and prepare a report, as appropriate, in relation to the following:

- the effectiveness of mechanisms employed for the identification, assessment and management of risk;
- the robustness of internal control systems, including the statements to be included in the annual report concerning internal controls and risk management;
- compliance with the Government's policies on Corporate Governance, together with such generally accepted principles of good corporate governance as it is reasonable to regard as applicable to the CMA;
- the suitability of the whistle-blowing arrangements, whereby employees can raise concerns in confidence about possible wrongdoing in financial reporting or other matters, including the proportionate and independent investigation of such matters and the appropriateness of any follow-up action;
- the effectiveness of the procedures for detecting fraud;
- the Annual Account and Trust Statement, focussing particularly on:
    - the quality of financial reporting and ensure that such reporting presents a balanced and understandable assessment of the position and performance of the CMA
    - critical accounting policies and practices, including the consistency of accounting policies on a year to year basis
    - major financial reporting issues and judgmental areas
    - the extent to which the financial statements are affected by any unusual transactions in the year and how they are disclosed
    - the propriety of major adjustments processed at year end
    - significant adjustments resulting from the audit;
- external audit reports, including:
    - meeting with external auditors at least twice a year, once at the planning stage, where the scope of the audit will be considered, and once at the reporting stage
    - discussing problems and reservations arising from the audit, and any matters the auditor may wish to discuss (where requested by the Committee, in the absence of Executive Members and any other person who is not a member of the Committee)
    - reviewing the external auditors' proposed audit opinion
    - reviewing the external auditors' management letter and management's response
    - facilitating the resolution of any difference between management and the auditor regarding financial reporting;
- the effectiveness of the internal audit function in the context of the overall risk management system, including:
    - the internal audit strategy and plan
    - its remit and resourcing
    - its standing and freedom from management and other restrictions
    - reviewing all internal audit reports promptly
    - the adequacy of management responses to audit reports
    - the performance of the internal auditor; and
    - the Principal Accounting Officer's CMA governance statement.

6. The Audit and Risk Assurance Committee shall recommend to the Board, Executive Committee and Principal Accounting Officer, as appropriate, such changes to existing practices and systems as is necessary.

MEMBERSHIP

7. The Audit and Risk Assurance Committee shall be comprised, as appropriate from time to time, of Non-executive Directors of the Board and one independent member. The Committee shall have the power to co-opt a person or persons with appropriate specialist qualifications and/or experience for a period not exceeding a year and subject to the approval of the appointment by the Board.

8. The CMA Board may not delegate anything that it is required or permitted to do to committees and sub-committees that include people who are not members of the CMA or its staff.

9. The Chair of the CMA Board, the Chief Executive (in his role as Principal Accounting Officer), the Chief Operating Officer, the Director of Finance, the Head of Risk, the Compliance Officer, the Head of Internal Audit and a representative from the External Audit team may also attend at the discretion of the Committee.

10. A Non-executive Director shall chair the Audit and Risk Assurance Committee.

11. The Chair of the Audit and Risk Assurance Committee shall be rotated on an appropriate cycle to provide for objectivity in the long term and to avoid over or under representation of particular aspects of the CMA's business and administrative interests.

12. A quorum shall be a minimum of two members.

MEETINGS

13. The Audit and Risk Assurance Committee shall meet as required, at least four times each year.

14. The Committee may ask any or all of those who normally attend but who are not members to withdraw to facilitate open and frank discussion of particular matters.

15. The Board or the Principal Accounting Officer may ask the Audit and Risk Assurance Committee to convene further meetings to discuss particular issues on which they want the Committee's advice

REPORTING

16. The Corporate Services Directorate and the Board Secretary support the work of the Audit and Risk Assurance Committee.

17. The Audit and Risk Assurance Committee is a sub-committee of the Board and its minutes shall be circulated to the Board.

18. The Chair of the Audit and Risk Assurance Committee shall report once a year to the Principal Accounting Officer, and inform the Board, on the findings and conclusions of the Committee for the past year.

ACCESS RIGHTS

19. The Head of Internal Audit and the representation of the External Audit team have the right of access to the Committee Chair and shall normally be present at meetings (as attendees rather than members).

CONFLICTS OF INTEREST

20. Members of the Audit and Risk Assurance Committee will:

- Have regard to the CMA's policy on conflicts of interest;
- Review before each meeting whether there are any interests which may conflict with their duties as members of the Committee and, if so, disclose them to the Board Secretary and, where appropriate, the CMA Compliance Officer;
- Be asked by the Chair of the Committee at each meeting to confirm they have carried out such a review and made such disclosure;
- Not participate in any activity of the Committee in relation to which they believe they have a conflict or possible conflict of interest without the consent of the Chair of the Committee.

REVIEW

21. These terms of reference will be reviewed by the Audit and Risk Assurance Committee every two years at least and any changes considered necessary will be recommended to the Board for approval.

VERSION CONTROL

22. These terms of reference were last updated in April 2021.

ANNEX C
REMUNERATION COMMITTEE
TERMS OF REFERENCE

PURPOSE

[3.84]

1. The purpose of the Remuneration Committee is to make final recommendations to the Board on all aspects of remuneration decisions for the CMA's senior civil servants in accordance with the guidance in the Pay Strategy and with particular regard to equal opportunities. It will also provide a strategic steer on pay issues relating to the CMA's non-senior civil servants.

STATUS

2. The Remuneration Committee is a sub-committee of the Board and acts on delegated authority from the Board.

RESPONSIBILITIES

3. The Remuneration Committee's responsibilities are:

- to ensure that the CMA's senior civil servants are rewarded fairly and differentially according to their contribution to the CMA, both in achieving their objectives and in developing their competencies, skills and knowledge
- to keep under review the criteria for allocating the CMA's senior civil servants to performance tranches and awarding bonuses
- to determine the performance tranche and, where applicable, bonus distribution for the CMA's senior civil servants, taking account of the CMA's overall performance and recommendations of line managers
- to monitor the operation of the system and provide a report of recommendations on pay decisions
- to provide a strategic steer on pay issues relating to the CMA's non-senior civil servants and to have oversight of the performance management ratings for non-senior civil servants, with a particular focus on equality and diversity.

MEMBERSHIP

4. The Remuneration Committee shall be Chaired by a Non-executive Director of the Board, and its members will include at least one other Non-executive Director of the Board and the Chair of the Board.

5. The CMA Board may not delegate anything that it is required or permitted to do to committees and sub-committees that include people who are not members of the CMA or its staff.

6. The Chief Executive and the Chief Operating Officer may also attend.

7. A quorum shall be a minimum of two members

MEETINGS

8. The Remuneration Committee shall meet as required, at least once a year.

REPORTING

9. Meetings of the Remuneration Committee will be minuted by Human Resources.

10. As soon as practicable after each meeting and at such other times as the Committee may consider appropriate, the Chair of the Committee shall report to the Board and, once approved by members of the Committee, the minutes of any Committee meeting shall be circulated to the Board unless, exceptionally, it would be inappropriate to do so.

11. The Chair of the Remuneration Committee will report once a year to the Board, on the findings, conclusions and recommendations of the Committee for the past year.

CONFLICTS OF INTEREST

12. Members of the Remuneration Committee will:

- Have regard to the CMA's policy on conflicts of interest;
- Review before each meeting whether there are any interests which may conflict with their duties as members of the Committee and, if so, disclose them to the Board Secretary and, where appropriate, the CMA Compliance Officer;
- Be asked by the Chair of the Committee at each meeting to confirm they have carried out such a review and made such disclosure;
- Not participate in any activity of the Committee in relation to which they believe they have a conflict or possible conflict of interest without the consent of the Chair of the Committee.

REVIEW

13. These terms of reference will be reviewed by the Committee every two years at least and any changes considered necessary will be recommended to the Board for approval.

VERSION CONTROL

14. These terms of reference were last updated in April 2021.

ANNEX D
NOMINATIONS COMMITTEE
TERMS OF REFERENCE

PURPOSE

[3.85]

1. The purpose of the Nominations Committee (the "Committee") is to advise the CMA Board on succession planning for executive and non-executive members of the Board. The Committee will provide advice to Government on future CMA Board appointments.

STATUS

2. The Committee is a sub-committee of the Board. It acts in an advisory capacity and has no executive powers.

3. The Committee is authorised to obtain independent professional advice (including legal advice) on any matters within its terms of reference and to arrange for the attendance of persons with relevant experience and expertise who are not CMA employees, if it considers this necessary.

RESPONSIBILITIES

4. The Committee shall advise the CMA Board on issues relating to:

(a) the structure, size and composition of the Board (including the skills, knowledge, experience and diversity), based on a regular review, and make recommendations to the Board with regard to any potential change;

(b) plans for the orderly succession to executive and non-executive Board positions, overseeing the development of a diverse pipeline for succession, taking into account the challenges and opportunities facing the CMA and the skills and expertise needed on the Board in the future; and

(c) CMA systems for identifying and developing SCS staff with high potential for Board roles in the future.

5. As appropriate, and in consultation with the Board, the Committee shall make recommendations to Government on appointments and re-appointments to the CMA Board based on an evaluation of the balance of skills, knowledge, experience and diversity required in respect of a particular vacancy.

MEMBERSHIP

6. The Committee shall comprise at least two non-executive Members of the Board (of whom one can be the Chair of the Board) and the CMA Chief Executive. An independent member (for example, a Panel Member) may also be asked to join the Committee.

7. Appointments to the Committee are made by the Board on the recommendation of the Committee.

8. The Chair of the Committee shall be a non-executive Member of the Board.

9. A quorum shall be two members, at least one of whom should be a non-executive Member of the CMA Board.

10. In the event that a member of the Committee is unable to attend a meeting s/he may, with the agreement of other Committee members, appoint a deputy to attend.

11. The Senior Director for People, Capability and Culture, the Director of the Executive Office & Performance and the HR Director may also attend at the invitation of the Committee.

12. .Representatives from the Department of Business, Energy and Industrial Strategy or other relevant government officials may attend at the invitation of the Committee.

MEETINGS

13. The Committee shall meet as required, but at least once a year

REPORTING

14. The Executive Office team shall support the work of the Committee, including by minuting the proceedings and decisions of all Committee meetings.

15. As soon as practicable after each meeting and at such other times as the Committee may consider appropriate, the Chair of the Committee shall report to the Board and, once approved by members of the Committee, the minutes of any Committee meeting shall be circulated to the Board unless, exceptionally, it would be inappropriate to do so.

CONFLICTS

16. Members of the Nominations Committee will:

- Have regard to the CMA's policy on conflicts of interest;
- Review before each meeting whether there are any interests which may conflict with their duties as members of the Committee and, if so, disclose them to the Board Secretary and, where appropriate, the CMA Compliance Officer;
- Be asked by the Chair of the Committee at each meeting to confirm they have carried out such a review and made such disclosure;
- Not participate in any activity of the Committee in relation to which they believe they have a conflict or possible conflict of interest without the consent of the Chair of the Committee.

REVIEW

17. These terms of reference will be reviewed by the Committee every two years at least and any changes considered necessary will be recommended to the Board for approval.

VERSION CONTROL

18. These terms of reference were last updated in April 2021.

ANNEX E
AUTHORISATION OF STAFF OF THE CMA AND NAMED CMA INQUIRY CHAIRS

(*This Annex has been omitted. The "Authorisation of staff of the CMA and named CMA Inquiry Chairs" document is reproduced as a separate document at* **[3.88]**. *Note also that the "Designation of officers of the CMA for the purpose of section 34 of the Regulation of Investigatory Powers Act 2000 and section 94 of the Police Act 1997") has been omitted as outside the scope of this work.*)

ANNEX F
CONFLICTS OF INTEREST POLICY (REVISED MARCH 2016)

[3.86]

NOTES

Editorial note: the Conflicts of Interest Policy (revised March 2016) was contained in Annex D of the 2016 version of this document reproduced in the previous edition.

INTRODUCTION

1. A conflict of interest may arise where a public official has a financial or other interest arising from their outside activities which influences, or might reasonably be perceived to influence, their impartiality or independence in performing their duties.

2. This document explains how the Competition and Markets Authority (CMA) handles actual or potential conflicts of interest arising from the outside interests of its Board, Panel members or staff members and external consultants.

3. This document sets out general guidance to Board, Panel members and staff members on how they can ensure that actual or potential conflicts of interest do not:

- enable decisions of the CMA to be impugned; or
- damage the reputation of the CMA for independence and impartiality.

4. However, the handling of particular conflict risks in relation to particular projects or inquiries will be considered by the CMA on a case-by-case basis, having regard to the approach the courts apply to assessing whether there is actual or apparent bias. This asks whether a fair minded observer, having considered the facts, would conclude that there was a real possibility that the decision maker was biased (see *Porter v Magill* (2002), 2 AC 357).

THE GENERAL APPROACH OF THE CMA TO HANDLING CONFLICTS OF INTEREST

5. The CMA expects its Board and Panel members to behave in accordance with the Principles of Public Life and its staff to follow the Civil Service Code,[1] both of which include the following values: integrity, honesty, objectivity and impartiality.

6. The CMA must be, and be seen to be, impartial. This is an essential ingredient of the public confidence enjoyed by the CMA. The outside interests of Board, Panel members or staff members and external consultants can threaten that impartiality because they create the possibility of bias, of apparent bias, or of insufficient independence in the CMA and its decisionmaking. The consequences for the CMA and its work could be extremely serious.

7. Some outside interests will create a clear conflict of interests. Others will not do so but may, nonetheless, prompt the CMA to take some action on a prudential basis.

8. Board, Panel members or staff members and consultants must be alert to the risk of conflicts arising at all times and review the position from time-to-time during all projects, cases or inquiries. Some potential conflicts can be identified in advance; others may only become apparent as the matter develops, or circumstances change (eg, because of the involvement of a new party, or a change in the personal circumstances of a Board, Panel member or staff member).

9. Board, Panel members or staff members should, therefore, always disclose any relevant facts to the CMA if they are in any doubt as to the compatibility of an outside interest with their work for the CMA. While they may be in the best position to identify whether they have an outside interest of potential concern, they are not in the best position to judge any consequences for the CMA.

The Compliance Officer

10. A Compliance Officer within the CMA is responsible for ensuring that the CMA's policies on conflicts of interest are applied and enforced on a day-today basis. If a Board, Panel member or staff member is in any doubt about the significance of an outside interest at any time, he or she may consult the Compliance Officer, who will advise on appropriate action.

Financial interests

11. Financial interests held by Board members, Panel members and staff which may be of potential concern include:

- shares, stocks, debentures or bonds (including options or rights in or over any such securities); and
- investment trusts, insurance policies, collective investment schemes (such as unit trusts) and dealing through intermediaries or with lending institutions (eg building society mortgages or bank loans), subject to paragraph 17 below.

12. They may also include:

- the financial interests of others to whom they give investment advice; and
- those of anyone with whom they may have a close family, domestic or other relationship and over whose decisions on investment matters they may reasonably be thought to exert an influence and where knowledge of such matters can reasonably be attributed to them. A close family member would include any co-habiting spouse/partners, any co-habiting children or any co-habiting dependant family members.

13. They may include not only financial interests relating to a company which is the subject of a project, case or inquiry but also those which relate to other companies which are likely to take a significant part in proceedings before the CMA, such as main competitors, customers or suppliers, or whose value is likely to be significantly affected by a CMA decision.

14. Where a financial interest belongs to a person with whom a Board, Panel member or staff member has a personal relationship, the CMA has regard to the nature of the personal association or relationship in deciding what, if any, action must be taken. Where the interest belongs to a close family member, it will normally treat the interest as if it was an interest of the Board, Panel member or staff member for the purpose of assessing conflicts.

15. Where assets are held by discretionary managers or in a trust, the CMA will adopt a prudent approach in deciding whether they raise concern. Relevant matters may include the duties to which a trustee or manager is subject and the degree of knowledge a person has or may acquire of the particular assets held by a trust or manager.

16. Where assets are held by a Board, Panel member or staff member as trustee for or otherwise on behalf of another person, the CMA will normally treat them for conflicts purposes as if they were assets of the Board, Panel member or staff member.

Financial interests which are unlikely to cause concern

17. The CMA will not usually consider financial interests of potential concern where:

- the value of assets is too low to be material; the CMA may from time-to-time set a general benchmark of value below which it will generally consider an interest of no concern – currently the *de minimis* level is set at £5000; and/or
- assets comprise goods and/or services bought on the open market on normal commercial terms available to other buyers (eg banking or insurance services, such as the mortgages and loans referred to in paragraph 11 above, telephone services, travel and tangible assets purchased on normal terms on the open market).

Other Interests

18. A conflict of interest may also arise out of connections which are non-financial.

Personal relationships

19. A conflict of interest may arise where the outcome of a project, case or inquiry could have real consequences for a person a Board, Panel member or staff member has a close personal association or relationship with. Such persons could include not only any co-habiting spouse or partners, any co-habiting children or any co-habiting dependent family members but also other associates, eg a close friend or close business associate who is working for or advising a company the CMA is investigating.

Outside activities

20. Conflicts of interest may also arise from past, current or future outside activities of Board, Panel members or staff members, eg:

- directorships (CMA staff, including Executive members, are usually prevented from being Directors under the terms of their employment by the Civil Service);
- equivalent positions with high-level responsibility for governance and performance;
- elected positions in government at local or national level;
- senior paid or unpaid roles with charities and not-for-profit organisations; and
- consultancy or advisory roles, whether remunerated or not, particularly where they involve the provision of advisory or other services on competition and/or economic regulation issues, potentially relevant to activities of the CMA.

Outside activities unlikely to cause concern

21. The CMA will not usually consider ordinary membership of charities or not-for-profit organisations where no role in governance or management is undertaken to be a matter of concern (although some activities by Board, Panel members or staff members, such as lobbying on matters of national interest or debate relevant to an project, case or inquiry, may raise concerns)

22. The significance of such organisational relationships generally diminishes over time. In particular, in the absence of complicating factors, Board, Panel members or staff members who were formerly partners in firms providing professional services to any party to a CMA case, project or inquiry are not normally considered to have a disqualifying interest in relation to that matter if two years have elapsed since they left the firm, provided that they have no continuing financial interest in or relationship with the firm.

Prejudgement

23. It is important that Board, Panel members and staff members approach decision-taking on behalf of the CMA with an open mind. Their ability to work on or consider a particular case, project or inquiry might appear to be compromised, for example, if they were involved in a private legal dispute with a company, or had written an article or made a speech expressing strong views about a particular matter.

24. The important question in such cases will be not whether a Board, Panel member or staff member may have an initial view on a particular issue, but whether they will bring a closed mind to bear in their work for the CMA. The fact that a Board, Panel member or staff member may have taken part in a previous case, project or inquiry in the same sector or involving the same party will not normally be regarded as giving rise to a risk of prejudgement.

PROCEDURES FOR HANDLING CONFLICTS OF INTEREST

Board and Panel members

Registration of interests

25. The CMA maintains registers of interests for Board members who must register the following interests of themselves and their families (ie any cohabiting spouse or partners, any co-habiting children or any co-habiting dependant family members).

26. Such interests may include:

(a) relevant Securities;
(b) remunerated employment, office or profession;
(c) other regular sources of income or remuneration from business, professional or public activities or interests;

(d) directorships, whether remunerated or not; and
(e) membership of public bodies (hospital trusts, governing bodies of universities, colleges and schools, and local authorities), trusteeships (of museums, galleries and similar bodies), and acting as an office holder or trustee for pressure groups, trade unions and voluntary or not-for-profit organisations.

Registration of (a) is only required for current interests. Registration of (b) to (e) must cover both current and recent (at least the last five years') interests.

27. 'Relevant Securities' means shares, stocks, debentures or bonds (including interests, options or rights in or over any such securities) held by the Board or Panel members or any co-habiting partner or co-habiting members of their family (including trust holdings) other than:

- units or interests in collective investment schemes or holdings in investment trusts or managed funds, bonds, policies or similar vehicles (including pension schemes, plans and policies) where investments are made and managed by professional managers in a significant number of enterprises without the Board or Panel member's involvement in investment decisions; and
- securities held under arrangements where the investment decisions are made by a professional investment manager, such as a stockbroker or bank, who has absolute discretion as to the purchase, sale and management of the investments and where the Board or Panel member has no involvement in such decisions.

28. Board members' interests will be disclosed in a public register which will be available on the CMA website for scrutiny by the public. Each Board member is responsible for keeping his or her entries in the register up-to-date. Panel members' interests will be disclosed as part of the appointment process for the inquiries in which they are involved and only those interests of relevance to the particular inquiry will be publicly disclosed.

Handling other interests of Board and Panel members

29. From time to time Board or Panel members may have or become aware of outside interests which do not require registration, but which in the context of a particular matter or issue before the CMA or the Board could nonetheless give rise, or be perceived as giving rise, to a conflict of interest.

30. A Board or Panel member must disclose to the Compliance Officer any such interest as soon as they become aware that it may cause a conflict, for example on receipt of an agenda for a meeting.

31. If in doubt as to whether or not there may be a conflict of interest, Board or Panel members are advised to inform the Compliance Officer in order to provide an opportunity for the CMA to determine an appropriate response.

32. In making decisions as to the possible conflicts of Board and Panel members the CMA will have regard to all the circumstances including the need to exercise an appropriate degree of caution to safeguard the CMA's independence and integrity.

33. The Compliance Officer will consider all potential conflicts that are brought to their attention on a case-by-case basis before making recommendations to the Panel Chair, in cases involving Panel members, and to the CMA Chair in the case of Board members, on what, if any, action should be taken.

34. During the conduct of an inquiry by a CMA Group, the Chair of the Inquiry Group is responsible for ensuring that the outside interests of Panel members are monitored and that any new issues that may arise during an inquiry (for example, from a change in their situation or a change in the interests affected by an inquiry) are brought to the attention of the Compliance Officer and the Panel Chair to advise as necessary on what, if any, action should be taken.

35. There are a number of actions that can be taken where a potential conflict of interest is identified in relation to a particular inquiry and the handling of particular cases will be a matter of judgement. In some cases the CMA may decide that an outside interest must be disposed of or be severed if the Panel member is to participate in a particular inquiry. Where the outside interest is less significant, the CMA may simply decide to address it by disclosure; if so, it will normally make a declaration that it is satisfied that the outside interest will not actually affect the impartiality of the CMA. In such cases, the CMA will nevertheless consider any representations that are made to it subsequently about the appointment in the particular circumstances of the case. In some cases, where the CMA considers that it may be particularly desirable that a Panel member act, or continue to act, in an inquiry, despite having a degree of concern, the CMA may seek to deal with the matter by disclosure and seeking to obtain acceptance of the appointment from parties to the inquiry.

36. In relation to any actual or potential conflict of interest, the CMA Chair, having consulted the Compliance Officer, and where they consider it necessary the General Counsel and other Board, Panel or staff members, will have the power to decide whether:

- the interest is one that is reasonably likely to influence the Board or Panel member's performance of his/her function; and
- in the opinion of a fair-minded and informed observer, the interest would suggest a real possibility of bias on the part of the Board or Panel member.

37. If having considered both questions the CMA Chair is satisfied that it is appropriate, the Board or Panel member may be permitted to participate fully or in a limited capacity in a decision or discussion. If the CMA Chair is not satisfied, the Board or Panel member shall withdraw from further participation in the decision or discussion in question and, in the case of a Panel member, if necessary the Chair may remove the person in question from membership of a relevant CMA Group.

38. In the event of the CMA Chair having an actual or potential conflict of interest, whether arising from a registrable or disclosable interest, the Compliance Officer and General Counsel, in conjunction with the Senior Independent Member, will have the same powers as the CMA Chair in deciding whether, or in what capacity the CMA Chair may participate in a decision or discussion.

INTERESTS OF STAFF

39. The staff who are substantively involved in making a decision may include not only the decision-taker but also others who contribute to decisions, for example, staff who contribute research and advice. The potential effect of outside interests of staff on their participation in a particular case, project or inquiry will be assessed on a case by case basis having regard to their potential involvement or influence over the decision-making of the CMA.

40. As with Board and Panel members, staff should always consider whether they hold any financial interests or other interests which could result in a perception of bias in any decision made by the CMA. When thinking about such interests, staff are reminded to read paragraphs 11–22 above which provide guidance as to those interests the CMA considers potentially problematic.

41. In particular, staff are reminded to consider the interests of any close family member or dependant, and be aware that any financial interest held by a staff member as a trustee will be considered as a personal holding when assessing potential conflict.

42. If a staff member holds any memberships of public bodies (hospital trusts, governing bodies of universities, colleges and schools, and local authorities), trusteeships (of museums, galleries and similar bodies), or acts as an office holder or trustee for pressure groups, trade unions and voluntary or not-for-profit organisations, these too should be disclosed to their staff manager.

43. Staff should also disclose to their staff manager any of the above interests which were held in the previous two years.

44. Staff should also consider whether any close family member holds an interest such as those held in paragraph 42, as these should also be disclosed to the staff manager. The Compliance Officer should also be consulted if there are any concerns.

Previous employment in the private sector

45. If during the first two years of CMA employment, staff members are involved in a case, project or inquiry relating to firms, consultancies or companies for which they previously worked, or competitors to those organisations, they should inform their staff manager and project director.

46. It is for the staff manager and project director to decide, with advice from the Compliance Officer and the General Counsel as necessary, on the appropriateness of the staff member continuing to work on the matter. Staff may be prohibited from working on a matter, depending on circumstances, for a period of twelve months or longer.

Other business and employment interests

47. The following general principles must be observed by staff in respect of business interest and outside occupations:

- No staff members may take a remunerated position within a concurrent or sectoral regulator without the express consent of the CMA.
- No staff may at any time engage in private activities which would require their attendance during CMA hours or in any way impair their usefulness as civil servants.
- No staff may engage in occupations or other activities, which might in any way conflict with the interests of the CMA or be inconsistent with their positions as civil servants.
- no staff may engage in outside activities involving the use of official experience, or experience acquired in the course of official duties, or payment from a Government Department, without first obtaining the consent of their senior manager (at SCS level). In cases of doubt managers should consult HR.
- The criteria of the Business Appointment Rules[2] also apply if staff wish to undertake outside employment whilst still employed by CMA.
- Staff must inform their senior staff manager if they have any private business interests which could possibly conflict with their position in the CMA. Staff must carry out any instructions from the CMA about the retention or disposal of those interests where it could be suggested that a conflict of interest may arise (see paragraph 1).

Directorships

48. Staff may not in general hold directorships in, or undertake work in, public or private companies, firms or other organisations. However, directorships may be allowed where staff members have been nominated by the CMA or have the express permission of the Compliance Officer. (The holding of nonexecutive directorships in small, private 'family type' companies may be permitted, if no conflict of interest is caused.) Staff should consult their senior staff manager before undertaking any such commitment. Appointments to outside bodies, eg as a non-executive director, for CMA purposes should be cleared with the Compliance Officer.

Consultancy work

49. Staff may not, without prior consent of the CMA, engage in consultancy work on behalf of any company:

- with which the CMA has a contractual relationship; or
- with which a staff member's group or area has some other close official relationship.

50. In any case of doubt regarding contractual relationships, staff should consult both their own senior management who can, if needs be, consult the Compliance Officer. In respect of other 'official' relationships, senior staff management should be consulted who should, in cases of doubt, then consult the Compliance Officer. Any consultancy work not of the prohibited type and undertaken by any staff member should be reported to their senior staff manager.

PROCEDURES FOR HANDLING INTERESTS FOR STAFF

51. Staff should first contact their staff manager, who should first make an assessment of the conflict in question, in conjunction with the work manager, where applicable. The staff manager may then feel able to come to a view on the point; if not, they should consult their own staff manager, the Compliance Officer and/or General Counsel. They will exercise their judgment, considering each case on its merits having regard to the particular circumstances.

ACCEPTANCE OF OUTSIDE APPOINTMENTS FOR CIVIL SERVANTS

52. The Business Appointment Rules[8] provide for the approval of appointments which certain former Civil Servants propose to take up in the first two years after they leave the service.

53. In summary, staff must obtain approval before accepting any new appointment or employment where an application under the Rules is required. For staff in SCS pay bands 2 and above, an application is required for any new appointment or employment that they wish to take up during the two year period after their last day of paid service. For staff in SCS pay band 1 and below, an application is only required if the individual's circumstances match one or more of the following criteria:

- They have been involved in developing policy affecting their prospective employer, or have had access to unannounced Government policy or other privileged information affecting their prospective employer, at any time in their last two years in the Civil Service.
- They have been responsible for regulatory or any other decisions affecting their prospective employer, at any time in their last two years in the Civil Service.
- They have had any official dealings with their prospective employer at any time in their last two years in the Civil Service.
- They have had official dealings of a continued or repeated nature with their prospective employer at any time during their Civil Service career.
- They have had access to commercially sensitive information of competitors of their prospective employer in the course of their official duties.
- The proposed appointment or employment would involve making representations to, or lobbying, the Government on behalf of a new employer.
- The proposed appointment or employment is consultancy work, either self-employed or as a member of a firm, and they have had official dealings with outside bodies or organisations in their last two years in the Civil Service that are involved in their proposed area of consultancy work.

54. Any staff member must report to their Staff Manager any offer of an appointment or employment which would need to be approved under the Rules if they plan to follow up the offer. Staff engaged on the letting or management of contracts must report all offers of an appointment or employment to their Staff Manager whether or not they intend to follow it up.

55. Staff must also have regard to the risk of conflicts of interest arising when conducting procurement exercises on behalf of the CMA and, when considering external employment, appointments or consultancy work. The need to consider the risk of conflicts arising is one of the reasons why the CMA requires staff to obtain its prior consent to external employment, appointments or consultancy work.

Interests of consultants

56. During the course of an inquiry or project, the CMA may instruct consultants to assist with aspects of its investigation. The roles played by consultants may vary considerably and the appropriate approach to their outside interests will be determined according to their role in the inquiry. However, where consultants act as the equivalent to members of staff, their outside interests will be assessed as if they were members of staff for conflicts purposes.

57. Where the CMA is considering whether to instruct a consulting firm to advise it on a particular matter, the CMA will take account of the outside interests of both the staff of the consulting firm and of the firm itself. In considering the interests of the firm, the CMA will take account of all relevant matters, which may include:

- the present and future clients of the firm (insofar as they can be ascertained), the nature of the work for those clients, and the extent to which the firm is independent of parties which may be affected by the inquiry;
- the degree to which the staff of the firm engaged on behalf of the CMA are protected from improper influence, for example, by being ring-fenced from other staff of the firm;
- any professional conduct rules which apply to the firm and its staff; and
- the record of the consulting firm in providing impartial advice to the CMA.

General

58. While this guidance addresses some actual or potential conflicts of interest that can be readily anticipated, it is not possible to provide a comprehensive list of all of the actual or potential conflicts of interest that might arise. Therefore:

- these guidelines must be interpreted and applied with regard to their spirit and purpose; and
- if a Board, Panel member or staff member has any doubt as to whether a conflict of interest may arise, the matter should be raised with the Compliance Officer.

Audit

59. The CMA carries out an annual audit of the conduct of the CMA's conflicts of interest policies and a report is published in its Annual Report.

NOTES

Editorial note: the paragraph numbered as paragraph 59 (immediately above) was numbered as a second paragraph 58 in the original document.

[1] See The 7 principles of public life (www.gov.uk/government/publications/the-7-principles-of-public-life/the-7-principles-of-public-life--2) and Civil Service: values and standards of behaviour (www.gov.uk/government/publications/civil-service-code).

[2] See Business Appointment Rules (assets.publishing.service.gov.uk/government/uploads/system/uploads/attachment_data/file/579758/ Business_Appointment_Rules_for_civil_servants.pdf).

ANNEX G
ROLES AND RESPONSIBILITIES OF BOARD MEMBERS

1. THE CHAIR'S RESPONSIBILITIES

[3.87]

1.1 The Chair of the CMA is to provide effective leadership and strategic direction for the CMA, forming a cohesive and focused Board. The Chair should enable the Board to take consistent, proportionate and fair decisions.

1.2 To achieve this, the Chair will:

- Facilitate Board meetings and maintain a high standard of discussion and debate
- Help steer the organisation by facilitating collective working
- Ensure systems are in place to provide Board Members accurate and timely information of good quality to allow the Board to consider properly all matters before it
- Ensure that a Board effectiveness review is performed annually, with independent input at least every three years, and that results are acted upon
- Collate feedback on the Chief Executive on their performance in leading the organisation and delivering its objectives
- Review the performance of Non-executive Directors annually and ensuring assessments are shared with the Director General of Market Frameworks in BEIS
- Liaise with BEIS and HMT as necessary, and as provided for in the CMA Framework Agreement
- Represent the CMA in discussions with Ministers and in forging strong relations with Parliament, Government and other relevant parties, and represent the views of the Board to the general public
- Ensure adherence to the comply or explain principle set out in the *Corporate governance in central government departments: code of good practice*.

1.3 Further details of the Chair's responsibilities can be found in:

- the Chair's appointment letter
- the CMA's Framework Agreement with BEIS
- the CMA Board's Rules of Procedure
- and other relevant legislative provisions.

2. INDIVIDUAL BOARD MEMBERS' RESPONSIBILITIES

2.1 Board Members should:

- Act objectively when discharging their responsibilities
- Act in the public interest, in keeping with the Nolan principles of public life and in accordance with the Code of Conduct for board members of public bodies
- Support actions to ensure that members of staff comply with the Civil Service Code.

3. RESPONSIBILITIES OF THE NON-EXECUTIVE DIRECTORS (NEDS)

3.1 In addition to the responsibilities outlined in paragraph 2 above, NEDs will exercise their role through influence and advice, supporting as well as challenging the executive, and covering issues such as:

- Support, guidance and challenge on the progress and implementation of the CMA's strategic plan
- Ensuring that the Board obtains and considers all appropriate information
- Advising on the operational and delivery implications of policy proposals
- Forming an audit and risk assurance committee and a nominations committee
- Involvement in the recruitment, appraisal and suitable succession planning of senior executives, as appropriate within the principles set out by the Civil Service Commission
- Involvement in the processes for the recruitment of public appointees.

4. RESPONSIBILITIES OF THE SENIOR INDEPENDENT DIRECTOR

4.1 One of the NEDs will be designated as the senior independent director (SID) who will:

- Support the Chair

- Meet other NEDs regularly, ensuring that their views are given due weight at the Board and that the Chair is made aware of any concerns
- Ensure that the NEDs meet the Chair alone, from time to time
- Ensure that NEDs meet the Chief Executive alone, from time to time
- Support the responsible BEIS Director General in the annual review of the performance of the Chair.

5. RESPONSIBILITIES OF THE CHIEF EXECUTIVE

5.1 The CMA's Chief Executive is the Principal Accounting Officer[1] for the CMA and is accountable to Parliament for the CMA's use of public money.

5.2 The Chief Executive is personally responsible for safeguarding the public funds for which he or she has charge, and for ensuring propriety, regularity, value for money and feasibility in the handling of those public funds for the day-to-day operations and management of the CMA. In addition, the Chief Executive ensures that the CMA is run on the basis of the standards (in terms of governance, decision-making and financial management) set out in Box 3.1 of HMT's "Managing Public Money".[2]

5.3 The Chief Executive may, at their discretion, designate an additional accounting officer.

5.4 In relation to the CMA Board, the Chief Executive's responsibilities include:

- Advising the CMA Board on the discharge of its responsibilities as set out in the legislation, the CMA's Framework Agreement with BEIS and in any other relevant instructions and guidance that may be issued from time to time
- Advising the Board on the CMA's performance compared with its aims and objectives
- Supporting the responsible BEIS Director General in the annual review of the performance of the Chair
- Discharging the role of Chief Executive and ensuring that financial considerations are taken fully into account by the Board at all stages in reaching and executing its decisions, and that financial appraisal techniques are followed
- Taking action as set out in paragraph 3.8.6 of Managing Public Money if the Board, or its Chair, is contemplating a course of action involving a transaction which the Chief Executive considers would infringe the requirements of propriety or regularity or does not represent prudent or economical administration, efficiency or effectiveness, is of questionable feasibility, or is unethical.

NOTES

1 For the avoidance of doubt, as the Principal Accounting Officer for the CMA, the Chief Executive is charged with meeting the responsibilities of the Accounting Officer as described in Chapter 3 of Managing Public Money.

2 https://assets.publishing.service.gov.uk/government/uploads/system/uploads/attachment_data/file/994901/MPM_Spring_21__without_annexes_180621.pdf.

AUTHORISATION OF STAFF OF THE CMA AND NAMED CMA INQUIRY CHAIRS (UPDATED 24 MAY 2021)

[3.88]

NOTES

This document is available on the Competition and Markets Authority website at: www.gov.uk/government/publications/cma-board-authorisation-of-staff-at-the-cma/authorisation-of-staff-of-the-cma-and-named-cma-inquiry-chairs--2.

Editorial note: See further, the CMA Board minutes of 10 February 2021 which states: "The Board agreed to extend the Covid-related Board authorisations put in place last year, by 12 months, until March 2022". See assets.publishing.service.gov.uk/government/uploads/system/uploads/attachment_data/file/972978/10_Feb_21_Public_Board_minutes.pdf.

Note also that this document is also included as Annex E in the CMA Board Rules of Procedure (Revised April 2021). Note also that the "Designation of officers of the CMA for the purpose of section 34 of the Regulation of Investigatory Powers Act 2000 and section 94 of the Police Act 1997") has been omitted as outside the scope of this work

I, Jonathan Scott , Chair of the Competition and Markets Authority (the CMA), being duly authorised to do so by the CMA Board on 13th October 2020,[1] hereby authorise the staff and committees of the CMA to exercise the functions of the CMA pursuant to paragraph 29 of Schedule 4 to the Enterprise and Regulatory Reform Act 2013 (the Act), subject to paragraph 30 of that Schedule, as follows.

NOTES

1 Under paragraph 29, Schedule 4 to the Enterprise and Regulatory Reform Act 2013, subject to the limitations set out in paragraphs 29(2) and 29(3).

PART 1: AUTHORISATIONS

FULLY AUTHORISED

1. The Chief Executive and Executive Directors are each authorised individually, and the Executive Committee of the CMA is authorised collectively, to do anything authorised or required to be done by the CMA by or under any enactment.

FULLY AUTHORISED SUBJECT TO EXCEPTIONS

2. The General Counsel is fully authorised, subject to Exception i of Part 2.

3. The Chief Economist and each Senior Director is fully authorised, subject to Exceptions i and ii of Part 2.

4. Each Director is fully authorised, subject to Exceptions i, ii and ix of Part 2.

5. Each Assistant Director allocated to a Phase 1 merger project, conducted under Part 3 of the Enterprise Act 2002, is authorised to the same extent as a Director as set out at paragraph 4 above, but subject also to Exceptions iii–viii and xi–xvi.

6. Each staff member of the CMA is authorised to the same extent as a Senior Director or Director as set out at paragraphs 3 and 4 above, save that Exceptions iii–xvi of Part 2 shall also apply.

7. Notwithstanding the exceptions set out at paragraphs 3 and 4 above, each Senior Director or Director who is legally qualified and is appointed to conduct a criminal prosecution under any legislation or law, is fully authorised in respect of the CMA's criminal enforcement functions under that legislation or law, subject to Exception i of Part 2.

8. Notwithstanding the exception set out at paragraph 6 above, each Assistant Director who is legally qualified and is appointed to conduct a criminal prosecution under any legislation or law, is fully authorised in respect of the CMA's criminal enforcement functions under that legislation or law, subject to Exceptions i and iii–xv of Part 2.

9. Notwithstanding the exceptions applicable to Senior Directors and Directors set out at paragraphs 3 and 4 above, Directors of Litigation and, for a period ending on 11.59 pm on 11th March 2021 (unless otherwise extended), Senior Legal Directors are fully authorised in respect of all of the CMA's powers to bring and conduct legal proceedings.

DELEGATION OF AUTHORISATION

10. Subject to any express restrictions contained in an authorisation and to any applicable professional requirements, any person or committee authorised to perform a function may, using any suitable means, authorise any member of staff or committee of the CMA, and any committee may authorise a sub-committee or decision group, to perform that function for such period and under such conditions as may be considered appropriate.

PART 2: EXCEPTIONS

11. The following exceptions apply to authorisations as specified in Part 1 above.

(i) Withholding information pursuant to an opinion of the qualified person under section 36 of the Freedom of Information Act 2000.

(ii) Bringing and conducting legal proceedings on behalf of the CMA.

(iii) Giving a direction or giving written notice of a proposed direction arising from a finding or suspicion that an infringement of competition law has occurred.

(iv) Making or publishing a decision, or giving written notice of a proposed decision that an infringement of competition law has occurred.

(v) Requiring payment of a penalty in respect of an infringement of competition law.

(vi) Accepting commitments (including variations and substitutions of commitments) or releasing commitments under section 31A of the Competition Act 1998.

(vii) Authorising the disclosure of information or production of documents under section 196(2)(b) of the Enterprise Act 2002.

(viii) Issuing or varying a written notice under section 190(4) of the Enterprise Act 2002.

(ix) Making a merger reference to the chair of the CMA under Part 3 of the Enterprise Act 2002.

(x) Making, releasing, revoking, varying or superseding an initial undertaking or enforcement order made or accepted, as appropriate, under Chapter 4 of Part 3 or Schedule 7 of the Enterprise Act 2002.

(xi) Accepting, releasing, varying or superseding undertakings in lieu of a merger reference.

(xii) Advising the Secretary of State in public interest merger cases (Chapter 2 of Part 3 of the Enterprise Act 2002).

(xiii) Authorising any person to do any of the following (whether or not under warrant or on notice): enter premises; inspect, seize or detain goods; break open or require the opening of a container or machine; or make a test purchase.

(xiv) Taking any decision as to whether, in a particular case, the CMA or another public authority should perform a function which is exercisable concurrently with that authority.

(xv) Giving a notice under section 174 of the Enterprise Act 2002 in relation to Phase 1 work conducted under Part 4 of that Act and imposing a penalty under section 174A of that Act in respect of such a notice.

(xvi) Carrying out a function of the CMA listed under section 133A(2) of the Enterprise Act 2002 where the group constituted under section 133A(1) of that Act has ceased to exist.

PART 3: AUTHORISATION OF THE PANEL CHAIR AND DESIGNATED PANEL MEMBERS

12. Martin Coleman, as a member of the CMA Panel appointed under Part 3 of Schedule 4 to the Act and a person appointed to membership of the CMA Board under paragraph 1(1)(b)(iii) of Schedule 4 to the Act and, for a period ending on 11.59 pm on 11th March 2021 (unless otherwise extended), Kirstin Baker and Kip Meek, each a member of the CMA Panel appointed under Part 3 of Schedule 4 to the Act who is designated by the Secretary of State for the purpose of paragraph 48 of Schedule 4 to the Act, are authorised to exercise on my behalf those functions listed in paragraph 48(4) of Schedule 4 to the Act.

PART 4: INTERPRETATION AND ENTRY INTO FORCE

13. The Interpretation Act 1978 applies to these authorisations as it applies to an Act of Parliament.

14. In these authorisations:

'legal proceedings' means proceedings before any Court or Tribunal established by law;

'legally qualified' refers to a person who is a barrister in England and Wales or Northern Ireland, a solicitor of the Senior Courts of England and Wales or a solicitor of the Court of Judicature of Northern Ireland;

'Phase 1' means work of the CMA up to and including the making of a reference to the Chair of the CMA for the constitution of a group under Schedule 4 to the Act;

'professional requirements' includes the requirement for an individual to be legally qualified to carry out certain CMA functions.

15. For the avoidance of doubt:

any reference to a position held by a staff member of the CMA is a reference to the staff member who holds that position from time to time, whether permanently or temporarily and includes persons working on secondment to the CMA

any person or committee authorised hereunder to perform any function of the CMA is, pursuant to paragraph 20 of Schedule 4 to the Act, authorised to do anything which is calculated to facilitate, or is conducive to or incidental to, the performance of that function. Any authorisation granted by a person or committee may be revoked by that person or committee.

16. These authorisations shall come into force on 13th October 2020.

Signed by: Jonathan Scott, Chair of the Competition and Markets Authority.

ADDRESSES OF THE REGULATORS

[3.89]

Competition and Markets Authority	**CMA** ***(Continued)***
The Cabot	Cartel Hotline: 020 3738 6888
25 Cabot Square	Email: cartelshotline@cma.gov.uk
London, E14 4QZ	Web: www.gov.uk/government/organisations/competition-and-markets-authority
Tel (general enquiries): 020 3738 6000	
Email: general.enquiries@cma.gov.uk	
Financial Conduct Authority	**Office of Rail and Road**
FCA Head Office	ORR Head Office
12 Endeavour Square	25 Cabot Square
London, E20 1JN	London, E14 4QZ
Tel (for firms): 0300 500 0597	Tel: 020 7282 2000
Email (for firms): firm.queries@fca.org.uk	Email: contact.cct@orr.gov.uk
Web: www.fca.org.uk	Web: www.orr.gov.uk
Office of Communications	**Office of Water Services**
Riverside House	Centre City Tower
2a Southwark Bridge Road	7 Hill Street
London, SE1 9HA	Birmingham, B5 4UA
Tel: 020 7981 3000 or 0300 123 3000	Tel: 0121 644 7500
Fax: 020 7981 3333	Email (General Enquiries): mailbox@ofwat.gsi.gov.uk
Web: www.ofcom.org.uk	Web: www.ofwat.gov.uk
Monitor (part of NHS Improvement)	**Payment Systems Regulator**
Wellington House	12 Endeavour Square
133–155 Waterloo Road	London, E20 1JN
London, SE1 8UG	Email: contactus@psr.org.uk
Tel (corporate enquiries): 0113 825 0000	Contact centre: 0300 456 3677
Email (corporate enquiries): enquiries@improvement.nhs.uk	Switchboard: 020 7066 1000
Web: www.england.nhs.uk/	Web: www.psr.org.uk
Utility Regulator (Northern Ireland)	**Office of Gas and Electricity Markets**
Queens House	10 South Colonnade, Canary Wharf
14 Queen Street	London, E14 4PU
Belfast, BT1 6ED, Northern Ireland	Tel (general enquiries) 020 7901 7295
Tel: 028 9031 1575	Fax: 020 7901 7066
Fax: 028 9031 1740	Email (general enquiries): consumeraffairs@ofgem.gov.uk
Email: info@uregni.gov.uk	Email (legal correspondence): OGC@ofgem.gov.uk
Web: www.uregni.gov.uk	Web: www.ofgem.gov.uk
Civil Aviation Authority	
11 Westferry Circus	
Canary Wharf, London, E14 4HE	
Tel: 0330 022 1500	
Web: www.caa.co.uk	

B. COMPETITION ACT 1998 INVESTIGATIONS AND CARTELS

1. GENERAL

AGREEMENTS AND CONCERTED PRACTICES (OFT 401, DECEMBER 2004)

[3.90]

NOTES

As to the construction of this document (following the abolition of the OFT and Competition Commission), see further the note "The Competition and Markets Authority (references to the OFT and Competition Commission etc)" in the introductory notes to Part 3 preceding **[3.1]**.

CONTENTS

1. INTRODUCTION

[3.91]

1.1 Article 81 of the EC Treaty[1] and the Chapter I prohibition contained in the Competition Act 1998 (the Act) both prohibit, in certain circumstances, agreements[2] which prevent, restrict or distort competition. Regulation 1/2003 (the Modernisation Regulation),[3] which took effect on 1 May 2004, substantially changed the framework for the enforcement of EC competition law.

1.2 This guideline sets out some of the circumstances in which the Office of Fair Trading (OFT) considers that agreements will or may be regarded as anti-competitive. It explains how the OFT will operate its powers under the Modernisation Regulation and under the Act when assessing agreements between undertakings. It is intended that this guideline should be of assistance not only to those undertakings which are parties to an agreement, but also to their customers and other businesses.

1.3 The provisions prohibiting agreements preventing, restricting or distorting competition are contained in Article 81(1) of the EC Treaty (Article 81(1)) and section 2(1) of the Act (the Chapter I prohibition). The terms used in relation to these provisions and the concepts relevant to their application are considered in Part 2 of this guideline.

1.4 Types of anti-competitive agreements to which Article 81 and/or the Chapter I prohibition may apply are considered in Part 3.

1.5 Part 4 of this guideline deals with the relationship between EC and national competition law. It considers the issue of consistency between Community and national competition law, and the approach the OFT will take to agreements which may fall within both Article 81 and the Chapter I prohibition.

1.6 Agreements which fall within Article 81 and/or the Chapter I prohibition but which satisfy certain specified conditions[4] are not prohibited, no prior decision to that effect being required. The conditions which need to be satisfied are set out in Part 5. Part 5 also discusses EC and domestic block exemptions and United Kingdom parallel exemptions.

1.7 Certain categories of agreement are excluded from the scope of Article 81 and/or the Chapter I prohibition. These categories of agreements are discussed in Part 6.

1.8 Breach of Article 81 or the Chapter I prohibition means that the agreement is void and each party is liable to a financial penalty of up to 10 per cent of its worldwide turnover. In addition, third parties who consider they have suffered loss as a result of any unlawful agreement may bring an action for damages in the Competition Appeal Tribunal (the CAT) or the courts. These consequences of infringement are considered in Part 7.

1.9 In certain circumstances where a case raises novel or unresolved questions about the application of Article 81 and/or the Chapter I prohibition and where the OFT considers there is an interest in issuing clarification for the benefit of a wider audience the OFT may publish written guidance in the form of an Opinion. The OFT also offers confidential informal advice. Further details can be found in Part 8.

NOTES

1 The Treaty establishing the European Community.

2 References in this guideline to agreement(s) should, unless otherwise stated or the context demands it, be taken to include

Part 3 CMA and other Guidelines

decisions by associations of undertakings and concerted practices.

3 Council Regulation (EC) No 1/2003 of 16 December 2002 on the implementation of the rules on competition laid down in Articles 81 and 82 of the Treaty (OJ L1, 4.1.03, p 1).

4 The conditions in Article 81(3) or section 9(1) of the Act.

2. ANTI-COMPETITIVE AGREEMENTS: THE PROVISIONS

SCOPE OF THE PROVISIONS

[3.92]

2.1 There are two substantive provisions which may be applied by the OFT to anti-competitive agreements: Article 81 and the Chapter I prohibition. The key difference between the two is their geographic scope. Both these provisions apply to agreements between undertakings which have as their object or effect the prevention, restriction or distortion of competition:

- within the common market and which may affect trade between Member States in the case of Article 81, and
- within the United Kingdom and which may affect trade within the United Kingdom in the case of the Chapter I prohibition.

2.2 Article 81(1) and section 2(2) of the Act provide an identical list of agreements to which the provisions apply, namely those which:

'(a) *directly or indirectly fix purchase or selling prices or any other trading conditions*

(b) *limit or control production, markets, technical development or investment*

(c) *share markets or sources of supply*

(d) *apply dissimilar conditions to equivalent transactions with other trading parties, thereby placing them at a competitive disadvantage*

(e) *make the conclusion of contracts subject to acceptance by the other parties of supplementary obligations which, by their nature or according to commercial usage, have no connection with the subject of such contracts.*'

2.3 This is a non-exhaustive, illustrative list and does not set a limit on the investigation and enforcement activities of the OFT under Article 81 or the Chapter I prohibition. Discussion of the OFT's approach to these types of agreement, and other potentially anti-competitive agreements can be found in Part 3 of this guideline. It should be noted, however, that any agreement that has an appreciable adverse effect on competition is likely to fall within Article 81(1) and/or the Chapter I prohibition irrespective of whether or not it is of a type described in the illustrative list in Article 81(1) and section 2(2) of the Act (or is considered in Part 3 of this guideline). Such an agreement may nevertheless be enforceable without prior approval if it meets the conditions set out in Article 81(3) and/or section 9(1) of the Act. This is considered in Part 5.

TERMS USED IN THE PROVISIONS

2.4 The terms used in Article 81 and the Chapter I prohibition and the concepts relevant to their application are dealt with in this section. These are terms and concepts used throughout this guideline.

Undertakings

2.5 The term undertaking is not defined in the EC Treaty or the Act but its meaning has been set out in Community law. It covers any natural or legal person engaged in economic activity, regardless of its legal status and the way in which it is financed.[5] It includes companies, firms, businesses, partnerships, individuals operating as sole traders, agricultural co-operatives, associations of undertakings (eg trade associations), non profit-making organisations and (in some circumstances) public entities that offer goods or services on a given market. The key consideration in assessing whether an entity is an undertaking for the application of Article 81 and/or the Chapter I prohibition is whether it is engaged in economic activity. An entity may engage in economic activity in relation to some of its functions but not others.

2.6 Article 81 and the Chapter I prohibition do not apply to agreements where there is only one undertaking: that is, between entities which form a single economic unit. In particular, an agreement between a parent and its subsidiary company, or between two companies which are under the control of a third, will not be agreements between undertakings if the subsidiary has no real freedom to determine its course of action on the market and, although having a separate legal personality, enjoys no economic independence.[6] Whether or not the entities form a single economic unit will depend on the facts of each case.

Agreement

2.7 Agreement has a wide meaning and covers agreements whether legally enforceable or not, written or oral; it includes so-called gentlemen's agreements. There does not have to be a physical meeting of the parties for an agreement to be reached: an exchange of letters or telephone calls may suffice.

2.8 The fact that a party may have played only a limited part in the setting up of the agreement, or may not be fully committed to its implementation, or may have participated only under pressure from other parties does not mean that it is not party to the agreement (although these facts may be taken into account in deciding the level of any financial penalty: for further details see the *OFT's guidance as to the appropriate amount of a penalty* (OFT 423)).

Decisions by associations of undertakings

2.9 Article 81 and the Chapter I prohibition also cover decisions by associations of undertakings. Trade associations are the most common form of associations of undertakings, but the provisions are not limited to any particular type of association. A decision by a trade association may include, for example, the constitution or rules of an association of undertakings or its recommendations or other activities.[7] In the day to day conduct of the business of an association, resolutions of the management committee or of the full membership in general meeting, binding decisions of the management or executive committee of the association, or rulings of its chief executive may all be 'decisions' of the association. The key consideration is whether the object or effect of the decision, whatever form it takes, is to influence the conduct or coordinate the activity of the members. A trade association's co-ordination of its members' conduct in accordance with its constitution may also be a decision even if its recommendations are not binding on its members, and may not have been fully complied with. It will be a question of fact in each case whether an association of undertakings is itself a party to an agreement.

2.10 The competition law guideline *Trade associations, professions and self-regulating bodies* (OFT 408) deals with the application and enforcement of Article 81 and the Chapter I prohibition in respect of both trade associations and the rules of self-regulating bodies.

Concerted practices

2.11 Article 81 and the Chapter I prohibition apply to concerted practices as well as to agreements. The boundary between the two concepts is imprecise. The key difference is that a concerted practice may exist where there is informal co-operation without any formal agreement or decision.

2.12 In considering if a concerted practice exists, the OFT will follow relevant Community precedents established under Article 81. The OFT will need to establish that the parties, even if they did not enter into an agreement, knowingly substituted cooperation between them for the risks of competition.

2.13 The following are examples of factors which the OFT may consider in establishing if a concerted practice exists:

- whether the parties knowingly entered into practical co-operation
- whether behaviour in the market is influenced as a result of direct or indirect contact between undertakings
- whether parallel behaviour is a result of contact between undertakings leading to conditions of competition which do not correspond to normal conditions of the market
- the structure of the relevant market and the nature of the product involved
- the number of undertakings in the market and, where there are only a few undertakings, whether they have similar cost structures and outputs.

THE PREVENTION, RESTRICTION OR DISTORTION OF COMPETITION

2.14 Article 81 and/or the Chapter I prohibition apply where the object or effect of the agreement is to prevent, restrict or distort competition within the common market (in the case of Article 81) or within the United Kingdom (in the case of the Chapter I prohibition). Any agreement between undertakings might be said to restrict the freedom of action of the parties. That does not, however, necessarily mean that the agreement is prohibited. The OFT does not adopt such a narrow approach. The OFT will assess an agreement in its economic context.

The appreciable effect on competition test

2.15 An agreement will fall within Article 81 and/or the Chapter I prohibition only if it has as its object or effect an appreciable prevention, restriction or distortion of competition within:

- the common market in the case of Article 81, or
- the United Kingdom in the case of the Chapter I prohibition.

2.16 The European Commission's *Notice on Agreements of Minor Importance*[8] (*the Notice on Agreements of Minor Importance*) sets out, using market share thresholds, what is **not** an appreciable restriction of competition under Article 81. The European Commission considers that agreements between undertakings which affect trade between Member States do not appreciably restrict competition within the meaning of Article 81 if:

- the aggregate market share of the parties to the agreement does not exceed 10 per cent on any of the relevant markets affected by the agreement where the agreement is made between competing undertakings (ie undertakings which are actual or potential competitors on any of the markets concerned), or
- the market share of each of the parties to the agreement does not exceed 15 per cent on any of the relevant markets affected by the agreement where the agreement is made between non-competing undertakings, (ie undertakings which are neither actual nor potential competitors on any of the markets concerned).

In both cases, these thresholds are reduced to five per cent where competition on the relevant market is restricted by the cumulative foreclosure effect of parallel networks of agreements[9] having similar effects on the market.

2.17 The above approach does **not** apply to an agreement containing any of the restrictions set out in paragraph 11 of the *Notice on Agreements of Minor Importance*. These include:

- in the case of an agreement between competing undertakings a provision which:
  - directly or indirectly fixes prices, shares markets or limits production, or

- in the case of an agreement between non-competing undertakings a provision which:
  - — limits a buyer's ability to determine its resale price,[10] or
  - — restricts a buyer operating at a retail level from selling to any end user in response to an unsolicited order (passive selling), or
  - — restricts active or passive selling by the authorised distributors to end-users or other authorised distributors in a selective distribution network, or
  - — restricts, by agreement between a supplier of components and a buyer who incorporates those components in its products, the supplier's ability to sell the components as spare parts to end-users or independent repairers not entrusted by the buyer with the repair or servicing of its products.

For the full list of restrictions please see paragraph 11 of the Notice. Agreements containing any of the restrictions set out in paragraph 11 of the *Notice on Agreements of Minor Importance* are regarded as being capable of having an appreciable effect even where the market shares fall below the thresholds explained in paragraph 2.16.

2.18 In determining whether an agreement has an appreciable effect on competition for the purposes of Article 81 and/or the Chapter I prohibition, the OFT will have regard to the European Commission's approach as set out in the *Notice on Agreements of Minor Importance*.

2.19 As a matter of practice the OFT is likely to consider that an agreement will not fall within either Article 81 or the Chapter I prohibition when it is covered by the *Notice on Agreements of Minor Importance*. Where the OFT considers that undertakings have in good faith relied on the terms of the *Notice on Agreements of Minor Importance*, the OFT will not impose financial penalties for an infringement of Article 81 and/or the Chapter I prohibition. A review of the types of agreements which would generally fall within Article 81 and/or the Chapter I prohibition are covered in Part 3 of this guideline.

2.20 The mere fact that the parties' market shares exceed the thresholds set out in paragraph 2.16, does **not** mean that the effect of an agreement on competition **is** appreciable. Other factors will be considered in determining whether the agreement has an appreciable effect.[11] Relevant factors may include for example, the content of the agreement and the structure of the market or markets affected by the agreement, such as entry conditions or the characteristics of buyers and the structure of the buyers' side of the market (see the competition law guideline *Assessment of market power* (OFT 415)).

2.21 When applying the market share thresholds discussed above, the relevant market share will be the combined market share not only of the parties to the agreement but also of other undertakings belonging to the same group of undertakings as the parties to the agreement. These will include, in the case of each party to the agreement: (i) undertakings over which it exercises control; and (ii) undertakings which exercise control over it as well as any other undertakings which are controlled by those undertakings. Further details on defining the relevant market are given in the competition law guideline *Market definition* (OFT 403).

Applicable law and territorial scope

2.22 In determining whether Article 81 and/or the Chapter I prohibition apply, the OFT will take into account the difference in the territorial scope of the two provisions.

Article 81

2.23 Article 81 only applies to agreements which may affect trade between Member States, ie it will only apply where there may be an appreciable effect on interstate trade. The case law of the European courts has interpreted this phrase broadly. Given the breadth of this interpretation, it is likely that in many cases agreements will fall within both Article 81 and the Chapter I prohibition. The European Commission has issued guidelines on the criteria it will apply to assess whether or not an agreement has an effect on trade between Member States in its Notice entitled *Guidelines on the Effect on Trade Concept contained in Articles 81 and 82 of the Treaty*.[12] The OFT will have regard to this Notice when considering whether agreements are likely to affect trade between Member States appreciably.

The Chapter I prohibition

2.24 The Chapter I prohibition only applies to agreements that may affect trade within the United Kingdom.

2.25 In practice it is very unlikely that an agreement which appreciably restricts competition within the United Kingdom does not also affect trade within the United Kingdom. So, in applying the Chapter I prohibition the OFT's focus will be on the effect that an agreement has on competition, discussed in paragraph 2.20 above.

2.26 The Chapter I prohibition applies only if an agreement is, or is intended to be, implemented in the United Kingdom.

2.27 The United Kingdom means Great Britain (England, Wales and Scotland and the subsidiary islands, excluding the Isle of Man and the Channel Islands) and Northern Ireland. For the purposes of the Chapter I prohibition, the United Kingdom includes any part of the United Kingdom where an agreement operates or is intended to operate.

Administrative priorities

2.28 It is the OFT's practice to consider, on a case by case basis, whether an agreement falls within its administrative priorities so as to merit investigation.

NOTES

[5] See Case C-41/90 *Höfner and Elser v Macrotron* [1991] ECR I-1979, [1993] 4 CMLR 306 and Case T–319/99 *Fenin v Commission*, [2003] ECR IT-357.

[6] See Case 22/71 *Beguelin Import v GL Import Export* [1971] ECR 949, [1972] CMLR 81.

[7] See *Re National Sulphuric Acid Association Ltd* OJ L260, 3.10.80, p 24, [1980] 3 CMLR 429.

[8] OJ C368, 22.12.01, p 13.

[9] Network effects are explained in Part 5 of the competition law guideline *Assessment of market power* (OFT 415).

[10] Except that a supplier may impose a maximum resale price or recommend a resale price, provided that pressure from the parties to the agreement does not result in that becoming a fixed or minimum price.

[11] See the Commission *Guidelines on the application of Article 81(3) of the Treaty*, OJ C101, 27.04.2004, p 97.

[12] OJ C101, 27.04.2004, p 81.

3. EXAMPLES OF ANTI-COMPETITIVE AGREEMENTS

[3.93]

3.1 This Part contains a discussion of various types of agreement which might appreciably restrict competition and fall within Article 81 and/or the Chapter I prohibition. The principles discussed are general and apply to agreements considered under both provisions.

3.2 Although an agreement may appreciably restrict competition within the meaning of Article 81 and/or the Chapter I prohibition, it will not be prohibited (and will still be valid and enforceable) where it satisfies the conditions in Article 81(3) and/or section 9(1) of the Act respectively. Further details on these conditions can be found in Part 5 and in the European Commission's Notice entitled *Guidelines on the Application of Article 81(3) of the Treaty*.[13]

EXAMPLES OF AGREEMENTS WHICH MIGHT APPRECIABLY RESTRICT COMPETITION

3.3 The types of agreements discussed in this part are agreements which have the object or effect of:

- directly or indirectly fixing prices
- fixing trading conditions
- sharing markets
- limiting or controlling production or investment
- collusive tendering (bid-rigging)
- joint purchasing or selling
- sharing information
- exchanging price information
- exchanging non-price information
- restricting advertising
- setting technical or design standards.

There is also a short discussion of other types of agreements which may be anti-competitive. The examples provided in this part are not exhaustive.

Directly or indirectly fixing prices

3.4 An agreement whose object is directly or indirectly to fix prices, or the resale prices of any product or service, almost invariably infringes Article 81 and/or the Chapter I prohibition. The OFT considers that such price-fixing agreements, by their very nature, restrict competition to an appreciable extent.

3.5 There are many ways in which prices can be fixed. Price fixing may involve fixing either the price itself or the components of a price, setting a minimum price below which prices are not to be reduced, establishing the amount or percentage by which prices are to be increased, or establishing a range outside which prices are not to move.

3.6 Price fixing may also take the form of an agreement to restrict price competition. This will include, for example, an agreement to adhere to published price lists or not to quote a price without consulting potential competitors, or not to charge less than any other price in the market. An agreement may restrict price competition even if it does not entirely eliminate it. Competition may, for example, remain in the ability to grant discounts or special deals on a published list price or ruling price. Recommendations of a trade association in relation to price are dealt with in the competition law guideline *Trade associations, professions and self-regulating bodies* (OFT 408).

3.7 An agreement may also have the object of fixing prices while only indirectly affecting the price to be charged. It may cover the discounts or allowances to be granted, transport charges, payments for additional services, credit terms or the terms of guarantees, for example. The agreement may relate to the charges or allowances quoted themselves, to the ranges within which they fall, or to the formulae by which ancillary terms are to be calculated.

3.8 Price fixing issues are not limited to agreements between competing undertakings. They can also arise between undertakings operating at different levels in the supply chain, where an agreement directly or indirectly (whether on its own or in combination with other factors under the control of the parties) has the object of restricting a buyer's ability to determine its resale price.[14]

Agreements to fix trading conditions

3.9 Undertakings may agree to regulate the terms and conditions on which goods or services are to be supplied, in addition to prices. Use of standard terms and conditions are dealt with in the competition law guideline *Trade associations, professions and self-regulating bodies* (OFT 408).

Agreements to share markets

3.10 Undertakings may agree to share markets, whether by territory, type or size of customer, or in some other way. This may be as well as or instead of agreeing on the prices to be charged, especially where the product is reasonably standardised. Where the object of the agreement is to share markets in this way, it will almost invariably infringe Article 81 and/or the Chapter I prohibition. The OFT considers that such market-sharing agreements, by their very nature, restrict competition to an appreciable extent.

3.11 There can be agreements, however, which have the effect (rather than the object) of sharing the market to some degree as a consequence of the main object of the agreement. Parties may agree, for example, each to specialise in the manufacture of certain products in a range, or of certain components of a product, in order to be able to produce in longer runs and therefore more efficiently. Such an agreement may fall within Article 81 and/or the Chapter I prohibition where there is, or is likely to be, an appreciable effect on competition. In assessing research and development (R&D) agreements[15] and joint production or specialisation agreements,[16] the OFT has regard to the European Commission's *Guidelines on the applicability of Article 81 of the EC Treaty to horizontal cooperation agreements*[17] (*Guidelines on Horizontal Cooperation Agreements*). R&D agreements may have the benefit of the European Commission block exemption for categories of research and development agreements.[18] Similarly, joint production or specialisation agreements may have the benefit of the European Commission block exemption for categories of specialisation agreements.[19]

Agreements to limit or control production or investment

3.12 An agreement whose object is to limit or control production will almost invariably infringe Article 81 and/or the Chapter I prohibition. Such an agreement may be the way in which prices are fixed, or it may relate to production levels or quotas, or it may be intended to deal with structural overcapacity. In some cases, it will be linked to other agreements which may affect competition.

3.13 Competitive pressures may be reduced if undertakings in an industry agree to limit investment or at least to coordinate future investment plans. The OFT considers that any agreement whose object is to limit or control investment will, by its very nature, restrict competition to an appreciable extent.

Collusive tendering ('bid-rigging')

3.14 Tendering procedures are designed to provide competition in areas where it might otherwise be absent. An essential feature of the system is that prospective suppliers prepare and submit tenders or bids independently. Any tender submitted as a result of collusion between prospective suppliers will almost invariably infringe Article 81 and/or the Chapter I prohibition. The OFT considers that bid-rigging agreements, by their very nature, restrict competition to an appreciable extent.

Joint purchasing/selling

3.15 An agreement between purchasers to fix (directly or indirectly) the price that they are prepared to pay, or to purchase only through agreed arrangements, limits competition between them. An example of one type of agreement which might be made between purchasers is an agreement as to those with whom they will deal. Such an arrangement may fall within Article 81 and/or the Chapter I prohibition if it has an appreciable effect on competition. In assessing joint purchasing/selling agreements, the OFT has regard to the European Commission's *Guidelines on Horizontal Cooperation Agreements*.

3.16 The same issues potentially arise in agreements between sellers, in particular where sellers agree to boycott certain customers. This type of agreement may have an appreciable effect on competition. In assessing agreements involving co-operation between competitors in the selling, distribution or promotion of their products, the OFT has regard to the European Commission's *Guidelines on Horizontal Cooperation Agreements*.[20]

Information sharing

3.17 As a general principle, the more informed customers are, the more effective competition is likely to be and so making information publicly available to customers does not usually harm competition.

3.18 In the normal course of business, undertakings exchange information on a variety of matters legitimately and with no risk to the competitive process. Indeed, competition may be enhanced by the sharing of information, for example, on new technologies or market opportunities. There are therefore circumstances where there is no objection to the exchange of information, even between competitors, and whether or not under the aegis of a trade association (see the competition law guideline *Trade associations, professions and self-regulating bodies* (OFT 408)).

3.19 The exchange of information may however have an adverse effect on competition where it serves to reduce or remove uncertainties inherent in the process of competition. The fact that the information could have been obtained from other sources is not necessarily relevant. Whether or not exchange of information has an appreciable effect on competition will depend on the circumstances of each individual case: the market characteristics, the type of information and the way in which it is exchanged. As a general principle, the OFT will consider that there is more likely to be an appreciable effect on competition the smaller the number of undertakings operating in the market, the more frequent the exchange and the more sensitive, detailed and confidential the nature of the information which is exchanged. There is also more likely to be an appreciable effect on competition where the exchange of information is limited to certain participating undertakings to the exclusion of their competitors and consumers.[21]

Exchange of price information

3.20 The exchange of information on prices may lead to price co-ordination and therefore diminish competition which would otherwise be present between the undertakings. This will be the case whether the information exchanged relates directly to the prices charged or to the elements of a pricing policy, for example discounts, costs, terms of trade and rates and dates of change.

3.21 The more recent or current the information exchanged, the more likely it is that exchange will have an appreciable effect on competition. Therefore, the circulation of purely historical information or the collation of price trends is unlikely to have an appreciable effect on competition, for example, where the exchange forms part of a scheme of inter-business comparison which is intended to spread best industrial practice. Exchange of information that is aggregated, and which cannot be disaggregated is also unlikely to have an appreciable effect on competition.

Exchange of non-price information

3.22 The exchange of information on matters other than price may have an appreciable effect on competition depending on the type of information exchanged and the structure of the market to which it relates. The exchange of aggregated statistical data, market research, and general industry studies for example are unlikely to have an appreciable effect on competition, since exchange of such information is unlikely to reduce individual undertakings' commercial and competitive independence.

3.23 In general, the exchange of information on output and sales should not affect competition provided that it is aggregated or, if it enables participants to identify individual undertakings' competitive behaviour, provided that it is sufficiently historic. In such circumstances, it is unlikely that an agreement to exchange such information would influence the participants' competitive market behaviour. There may however be an appreciable effect on competition if the information exchanged is current or recent or concerns future plans, and if it can be ascribed to particular undertakings, whether because it is broken down in this way or because it can be disaggregated.

Advertising

3.24 Restrictions on advertising, whether relating to the amount, nature or form of advertising, have the potential to restrict competition. Whether the effect is appreciable depends on the purpose and nature of the restriction, and on the market in which it is to apply. Decisions aimed at curbing misleading advertising, or at ensuring that advertising is legal, truthful and decent are unlikely to have an appreciable adverse effect on competition (see the competition law guideline *Trade associations, professions and self-regulating bodies* (OFT 408)).

Standardisation agreements

3.25 An agreement on technical or design standards may lead to an improvement in production by reducing costs or raising quality, or it may promote technical or economic progress by reducing waste and consumers' search costs. Some such agreements will, however, be likely to infringe Article 81 and/or the Chapter I prohibition if they are, in effect, a means of limiting competition from other sources, for example by raising entry barriers. Standardisation agreements which prevent the parties from developing alternative standards or products that do not comply with the agreed standard may also infringe Article 81 and/or the Chapter I prohibition. In assessing standardisation agreements, the OFT has regard to the European Commission's *Guidelines on Horizontal Cooperation Agreements.*

Other anti-competitive agreements

3.26 Competition in a market can be restricted in less direct ways than by fixing prices or sharing markets or the other examples set out above – for example, a scheme under which a customer obtains better terms the more business it places with the parties to the scheme could be regarded as anti-competitive. Each case will need to be considered in its own circumstances.

3.27 Other agreements where the parties agree to cooperate may fall within Article 81 and/or the Chapter I prohibition if they have an appreciable effect on competition. However, not all these, or other, agreements having appreciable effect on competition will necessarily be prohibited. As mentioned at paragraph 3.2, certain agreements which have an appreciable effect on competition within the meaning of Article 81 and/or the Chapter I prohibition will not be prohibited (and will still be valid and enforceable) where they satisfy the conditions in Article 81(3) and/or in section 9(1) of the Act respectively.

NOTES

13 OJ C101, 27.04.2004, p 97.

14 Except that a supplier may impose a maximum resale price or recommend a resale price, provided that pressure from the parties to the agreement does not result in that becoming a fixed or minimum price. For further detail, see the competition law guideline *Vertical agreements* (OFT 419).

15 An R&D agreement may range in scope from outsourcing certain research and development activities, to the joint improvement of existing products or to a co-operation concerning the research, development and marketing of completely new products.

16 A joint production agreement is an agreement between parties to produce certain products jointly, whereas a specialisation agreement is an agreement whereby the parties agree (unilaterally or reciprocally) to cease production of a product and to purchase it from the other party.

17 OJ C3, 6.1.01, p 2.

18 Commission Regulation (EC) No 2659/2000 on the application of Article 81(3) of the Treaty to categories of research and development agreements.

19 Commission Regulation (EC) No 2658/2000 on the application of Article 81(3) of the Treaty to categories of specialisation agreements.

20 Such agreements are termed **commercialisation agreements** in the European Commission's *Guidelines on Horizontal Cooperation Agreements*.

21 Case T-141/94 *Thyssen Stahl AG v Commission* [1999] ECR II-347, upheld on appeal in Case C-194/99 P, judgement of 2 October 2003.

4. RELATIONSHIP BETWEEN EC AND NATIONAL COMPETITION LAW

ARTICLE 3 OF THE MODERNISATION REGULATION

[3.94]

4.1 Article 3 of the Modernisation Regulation governs the relationship between Article 81 and national competition law. Article 3(1) provides that where national competition authorities or courts apply national competition law to agreements which may affect trade between Member States within the meaning of Article 81(1), they must also apply Article 81 to those agreements. Article 3(2) provides that national competition law cannot prohibit agreements which may affect trade between Member States:

- that do not restrict competition within the meaning of Article 81(1)
- that fulfil the conditions of Article 81(3), or
- that are covered by an EC block exemption regulation.

4.2 In all cases where the OFT examines an agreement between undertakings under the Chapter I prohibition it also considers whether Article 81 is applicable. The OFT's determination of whether Article 81 is applicable will consist of assessing whether the agreement may have an effect on trade between Member States. Where it is clear that the effect on trade between Member States test is met (see paragraph 2.23 above), the OFT will usually apply both Article 81 and the Chapter I prohibition. Equally, however, it is open to the OFT to apply Article 81 alone in such cases.

4.3 Under the OFT's Rules,[22] the OFT may, at any time prior to making an infringement decision, elect to apply to a case one or both of Article 81 and the Chapter I prohibition. This means that a case started under the Chapter I prohibition can be continued under Article 81 alone or (as is more likely) under both the Chapter I prohibition and Article 81 if it is subsequently concluded that there may be an effect on trade between Member States. Similarly a case started under the Chapter I prohibition and Article 81 can be continued under the Chapter I prohibition alone if it is subsequently concluded that there is no effect on trade between Member States.

4.4 In cases where an undertaking has committed an infringement of both an EC prohibition (ie Article 81 or Article 82) and the equivalent UK prohibition (ie the Chapter I or the Chapter II prohibition respectively), the undertaking will not be penalised again for the same anti-competitive effects. For further details see the OFT's *Guidance as to the appropriate amount of a penalty* (OFT 423).

4.5 As noted in paragraph 2.23 above, the OFT will have regard to the guidance set out in the European Commission's Notice entitled *Guidelines on the Effect on Trade Concept contained in Articles 81 and 82 of the Treaty*[23] when considering whether a particular agreement may have an effect on trade between Member States to determine whether Article 81 applies.

PRIMACY OF COMMUNITY LAW

4.6 In applying Article 81 the OFT is bound by the fundamental principle of the primacy of Community law and must follow the case law of the European Court in interpreting Community legislation. As a consequence, and in addition to the Article 3 obligations set out in paragraph 4.1 above, an agreement prohibited by Article 81 cannot be permitted under national law. The OFT cannot therefore permit an agreement which has been prohibited under Article 81.

4.7 The Modernisation Regulation also makes further provision to ensure consistency in the application of Article 81. Article 16(2) of the Modernisation Regulation provides that where the European Commission has taken a decision on an agreement, the OFT and other NCAs cannot take a decision under Article 81 in respect of the same agreement which would run counter to the decision adopted by the European Commission. Further detail on the Modernisation Regulation can be found in the competition law guideline *Modernisation* (OFT 442).

CONSISTENCY AND CASES BROUGHT UNDER THE CHAPTER I PROHIBITION

4.8 In addition to its obligations under Community law, under section 60 of the Act the OFT is under an obligation to deal with questions arising under Part I of the Act in relation to competition within the UK in such a way as to ensure consistency with the treatment of corresponding questions arising in Community law in so far as this is possible, having regard to any relevant differences between any of the provisions concerned.

NOTES

22 The Competition Act 1998 (Office of Fair Trading's Rules) Order 2004 (SI 2004/2752), rule 10.

23 OJ C101, 27.04.2004, p 81.

5. THE LEGAL EXCEPTION REGIME

[3.95]

5.1 The Modernisation Regulation introduces a legal exception regime. This means that an agreement that falls within Article 81(1) but which satisfies the conditions set out in Article 81(3) shall not be prohibited, no prior decision to that effect being required. Such an agreement is valid and enforceable from the moment that the conditions in Article 81(3) are satisfied and for as long as that remains the case. The Modernisation Regulation provides that the burden of proving that the conditions are satisfied rests on the undertaking(s) claiming the benefit of Article 81(3).

5.2 The Act has been amended to mirror this approach so that an agreement that falls within the Chapter I prohibition but which satisfies the conditions set out in section 9(1) of the Act is not prohibited, no prior decision to that effect being required. Such an agreement is valid and enforceable from the moment the conditions in section 9(1) are satisfied and for as long as that remains the case. The Act provides that the burden of proving that the conditions are satisfied rests on the undertaking(s) claiming the benefit of section 9(1) of the Act.

THE CONDITIONS IN ARTICLE 81(3) AND SECTION 9(1)

5.3 Article 81(3) and section 9(1) set out four conditions which must all be met for an agreement to have the benefit of either provision. Article 81(3) provides that Article 81(1) is inapplicable in respect of any agreement:

> *'which contributes to improving the production or distribution of goods or promoting technical or economic progress, while allowing consumers a fair share of the resulting benefit, and which does not:*
>
> (a) *impose on the undertakings concerned restrictions which are not indispensable to the attainment of these objectives;*
>
> (b) *afford such undertakings the possibility of eliminating competition in respect of a substantial part of the products in question.'*

5.4 The wording of section 9(1) is similar to that of Article 81(3) except that in the first condition in section 9(1) the phrase 'of goods' is not included. The omission of these words is intended to make clear (consistent with the practice of the European Commission in relation to Article 81(3)) that improvements in production or distribution in relation to services may also satisfy the first condition in section 9(1). The European Commission's practice has been either to apply Article 81(3) to services by analogy, or to invoke the promotion of technical and economic progress provision in Article 81(3) in relation to services agreements.

5.5 The European Commission has issued a Notice entitled *Guidelines on the Application of Article 81(3) of the Treaty*[24] to assist companies and their advisers in determining whether an agreement satisfies the conditions in Article 81(3). The OFT will have regard to this Notice in considering the application of Article 81(3) and section 9(1) of the Act.

BLOCK EXEMPTIONS

Article 81

5.6 The European Commission may adopt block exemption regulations so that particular categories of agreement which it considers satisfy the conditions in Article 81(3) are not prohibited under Article 81.[25] Where an agreement is covered by an EC block exemption regulation[26] the parties to the restrictive agreement are relieved of the burden of showing that their agreement satisfies the conditions in Article 81(3). They only have to prove that the restrictive agreement is block exempted.

Withdrawal of block exemptions

5.7 The European Commission may withdraw the benefit of any EC block exemption regulation if it finds that in a particular case the agreement in question has effects that are incompatible with Article 81(3).[27]

5.8 The OFT may also, under Article 29(2) of the Modernisation Regulation, withdraw the benefit of any EC block exemption regulation from any agreements if the following conditions are met:

- the agreements in question have effects that are incompatible with Article 81(3) in the territory of the United Kingdom, or a part of the United Kingdom, and
- the relevant territory has all the characteristics of a distinct geographic market.[28]

In the case of withdrawal of an EC block exemption regulation by the OFT, it will be for the OFT to demonstrate that the agreement infringes Article 81(1) and that it does not satisfy the conditions of Article 81(3) in the United Kingdom (or part of the United Kingdom) that is a distinct geographic market. The United Kingdom courts have no power to withdraw the benefit of an EC block exemption regulation.

5.9 In practice, the OFT is likely to exercise this power only rarely. An example of when the OFT might exercise its power to withdraw a block exemption is given in the competition law guideline *Vertical agreements* (OFT 419).

5.10 Where the OFT proposes to exercise its powers to withdraw the benefit of a block exemption from an agreement it must, following the procedures specified in the OFT's Rules,[29] give written notice to the parties to that agreement and give them an opportunity to make representations. It may also consult the public. If the OFT has decided to withdraw the benefit of a block exemption, it will notify the parties to that agreement of its decision and will publish the decision on a public register on the OFT's website.

Consequences of withdrawal

5.11 Where the OFT decides to withdraw the benefit of a block exemption from a particular agreement it at the same time establishes that the agreement infringes Article 81. Such an infringement finding can have effect only from the date of the withdrawal. The agreement will be void only from the date of withdrawal and any financial penalties imposed in respect of that agreement can relate only to the period after the withdrawal of the block exemption.

5.12 Withdrawal of the block exemption in a particular case will result in any parallel exemption also ceasing to have effect, by virtue of section 10(4)(b) of the Act.

The Chapter I prohibition

5.13 Under the Act the Secretary of State may, acting on the OFT's recommendation, make domestic block exemptions that specify particular categories of agreement which the OFT considers are likely to be exempt from the Chapter I prohibition as a result of section 9(1). An agreement which falls within a category specified in the block exemption will not be prohibited under the Chapter I prohibition.[30] Any such block exemption may impose conditions or obligations subject to which the block exemption will have effect.[31]

5.14 Breach of a condition imposed by the block exemption cancels the block exemption in respect of an agreement. The failure to comply with an obligation imposed by the block exemption enables the OFT to cancel the block exemption in respect of an agreement. Furthermore if the OFT thinks that an agreement is not exempt from the Chapter I prohibition as a result of section 9(1) of the Act, the OFT may cancel the block exemption in respect of that agreement.

Parallel exemption under the Act

5.15 An agreement is exempt from the Chapter I prohibition if it is covered by a finding of inapplicability by the European Commission[32] or an EC block exemption regulation, or would be covered by an EC block exemption regulation if the agreement had an effect on trade between Member States. These types of agreement are not prohibited under the Chapter I prohibition, no prior decision to that effect being required.

5.16 Where an agreement has no effect on trade between Member States but it would be covered by an EC block exemption regulation if the agreement had an effect on trade between Member States and therefore benefits from a parallel exemption, the OFT may nevertheless impose conditions on the parallel exemption or cancel the exemption following procedures specified in the OFT's Rules[33] if the agreement has effects in the United Kingdom, or a part of it, which are incompatible with the conditions in section 9(1).

Individual exemptions

5.17 Each individual exemption granted by the OFT prior to 1 May 2004 has been time limited. All such individual exemptions are valid until their expiry, although the OFT retains the power to cancel such exemptions. After expiry, individual exemptions will not be renewed.

5.18 An individual exemption decision made by the European Commission prior to 1 May 2004 is binding on the OFT until the expiry date of the individual exemption. In such cases the OFT will not apply Article 81 or the Chapter I prohibition for the duration of the individual exemption. The OFT will consider comfort letters issued by the European Commission, but these are not binding on the OFT.

NOTES

24 OJ C101. 27.04.2004, p 97.

25 The European Commission may only issue an EC block exemption regulation where it has been empowered to do so by an EC Council Regulation. For instance Council Regulation (EEC) 19/65 (JO, 06.03.1965, p 533, Spec. ed. (1965–1966) p 35)) (as amended, most recently, by Council Regulation (EC)1215/1999 and the Modernisation Regulation) allows the European Commission to adopt EC block exemption regulations in respect of vertical agreements and industrial property rights.

26 EC block exemption regulations in force include: Commission Regulation (EC) No 2658/2000 on the application of Article 81(3) of the Treaty to categories of specialisation agreements (OJ, L304, 5.12.2000, p 3); Commission Regulation (EC) No 2659/2000 on the application of Article 81(3) of the Treaty to categories of research and development agreements (OJ L304, 5.12.2000, p 7); Commission Regulation (EC) No 2790/1999 on the application of Article 81(3) of the Treaty to categories of vertical agreements and concerted practices (OJ L336, 29.12.1999, p 21); Commission Regulation (EC) No 1400/2002 on the application of Article 81(3) to categories of vertical agreement and concerted practices in the motor vehicle sector (OJ L203, 1.8.2002, p 30); and Commission Regulation (EC) No 772/2004 of 27 April 2004 on the application of Article 81(3) of the Treaty to categories of technology transfer agreements, OJ L123, 27.04.2004, p 11.

27 Article 29(1) of the Modernisation Regulation.

28 Article 29(2) of the Modernisation Regulation.

29 The Competition Act 1998 (Office of Fair Trading's Rules) Order 2004 (SI 2004/2751), rule 13.

30 A domestic block exemption does not exempt agreements affecting trade between Member States for the purposes of Article 81. An agreement falling within a domestic block exemption which affects trade between Member States and falls within Article 81, will be invalid and unenforceable if it does not benefit also from an EC block exemption or does not otherwise satisfy the conditions in Article 81(3).

31 The only United Kingdom block exemption that has been adopted to date is the Competition Act 1998 (Public Transport Ticketing Schemes Block Exemption) Order 2001 (SI 2001/319).

32 Under Article 10 of the Modernisation Regulation, the European Commission can find that Article 81 is inapplicable to an agreement either because the conditions of Article 81(1) are not fulfilled or because the conditions of Article 81(3) are satisfied.

33 The Competition Act 1998 (Office of Fair Trading's Rules) Order 2004 (SI 2004/2751), rule 12.

6. EXCLUSIONS

ARTICLE 81

[3.96]

6.1 Although the concept of an exclusion is not specifically recognised in relation to Article 81, under Community competition law certain categories of agreement are, in effect, excluded from the application of Article 81. These include:

- an agreement which would result in a concentration with a Community dimension and thereby be subject to the EC Merger Regulation[34]
- an agreement made by an undertaking entrusted with the operation of services of general economic interest or having the character of a revenue-producing monopoly, in so far as the application of Article 81 would obstruct the performance, in law or in fact, of the particular tasks assigned to the undertaking
- certain agreements which relate to production of, or trade in, the agricultural products listed in Annex I of the EC Treaty. Derogations in respect of these agreements are contained in Council Regulation (EEC) No 26/62 which provides that Article 81(1) does not apply where agreements:
  - — form an integral part of a national market organisation in agricultural products, or
  - — are necessary for the attainment of the objectives of the common agricultural policy.

This is not an exhaustive list.

THE CHAPTER I PROHIBITION

6.2 Schedules 1–3 of the Act specifically exclude from the Chapter I prohibition certain categories of agreement:

- an agreement to the extent to which it would result in a merger or joint venture within the merger provisions of the Enterprise Act 2002 (see the Enterprise Act publication *Mergers: substantive assessment guidance* (OFT 506) for further detail)
- an agreement which would result in a concentration with a Community dimension and thereby be subject to the EC Merger Regulation
- an agreement which is subject to competition scrutiny under the Financial Services and Markets Act 2000, the Broadcasting Act 1990 or the Communications Act 2003
- an agreement which is required in order to comply with, and to the extent that it is, a planning obligation
- (until 1 May 2005) an agreement to the extent that it is a land agreement, as defined in the Competition (Land and Vertical Agreements) Exclusion Order 2000 (see the competition law guideline *Land agreements* (OFT 420) for further detail)
- (from 1 May 2005) an agreement to the extent that it is a land agreement, as defined in the Competition Act 1998 (Land Agreements Exclusion and Revocation) Order 2004 (see the competition law guideline *Land agreements* (OFT 420) for further detail)
- (until 1 May 2005) an agreement to the extent that it is a vertical agreement, as defined in the Competition Act 1998 (Land and Vertical Agreements) Exclusion Order 2000, and does not have the object or effect of fixing resale prices (see the competition law guideline *Vertical agreements* (OFT 419) for further detail)
- (until 1 May 2007) an agreement which is the subject of a direction under section 21(2) of the Restrictive Trade Practices Act 1976[35]
- an agreement for the constitution of a European Economic Area regulated market, to the extent that it relates to the rules made or guidance issued by that market
- an agreement made by an undertaking entrusted with the operation of services of general economic interest or having the character of a revenue-producing monopoly, insofar as the prohibition would obstruct the performance of the particular tasks assigned to the undertaking (see the competition law guideline *Services of general economic interest* (OFT 421))
- an agreement to the extent to which it is made to comply with a legal requirement
- an agreement which is necessary to avoid conflict with international obligations and which is also the subject of an order by the Secretary of State
- an agreement which is necessary for compelling reasons of public policy and which is also the subject of an order by the Secretary of State
- an agreement where it relates to production of, or trade in, 'agricultural products' as defined in the EC Treaty and in Council Regulation (EEC) No 26/62, or to farmers' co-operatives.

The Secretary of State has the power to add, amend or remove exclusions in certain circumstances.

6.3 A domestic exclusion does not exclude agreements or conduct from applicable EC law: any agreements or conduct affecting trade between Member States that are excluded under the Act remain subject to Article 81. Accordingly, should conduct or agreements affecting trade between Member States infringe Article 81, all the usual consequences will follow, irrespective of any domestic exclusion.

NOTES

34 Council Regulation (EC) No 139/2004 on the control of concentrations between undertakings (OJ L24, 29.01.2004, p 1).

35 Paragraph 2 of Schedule 3 to the Act. This exclusion is repealed with effect from 1 May 2007.

Part 3 CMA and other Guidelines

7. CONSEQUENCES OF INFRINGEMENT

VOIDNESS

[3.97]

7.1 Any agreement which falls within Article 81(1) or the Chapter I prohibition and does not satisfy the conditions set out in Article 81(3) or section 9(1) of the Act, respectively, is void and unenforceable.[36]

FINANCIAL PENALTIES

7.2 Section 36 of the Act provides that the OFT may impose a financial penalty on an undertaking which has intentionally or negligently committed an infringement of Article 81 and/or the Chapter I prohibition. The amount of the penalty imposed may be up to 10 per cent of the worldwide turnover of the undertaking. See *OFT's Guidance as to the appropriate amount of a penalty* (OFT 423) for further details. Further information on penalties and other consequences of an infringement may be found in the competition law guideline *Enforcement* (OFT 407).

7.3 In order to avoid the prohibition regime being unduly burdensome on small businesses, the Act provides limited immunity from financial penalties for 'small agreements' in relation to infringements of the Chapter I prohibition.[37] This immunity does not apply to infringements of Article 81 or to price-fixing agreements. The term 'small agreements' relates to agreements between undertakings whose combined annual turnover does not exceed £20 million.[38] The immunity applies only to financial penalties: an anti-competitive agreement by such undertakings is still an infringement of the Chapter I prohibition, and consequently the OFT may take other enforcement action. The immunity does not prevent third parties from claiming damages for the loss caused by such an agreement.

7.4 Undertakings will benefit from immunity from financial penalties under the Act if the OFT is satisfied that they acted on the reasonable assumption that on the facts they qualified for the limited immunity for 'small agreements' in relation to infringements of the Chapter I prohibition.

7.5 The OFT may still investigate small agreements and can decide to withdraw the immunity from financial penalties if, having investigated the agreement, it considers that the agreement is likely to infringe the Chapter I prohibition. Withdrawal of the immunity in this way cannot have effect before the date of this decision.

THIRD PARTY ACTION

7.6 Third parties adversely affected by an agreement which they believe is prohibited by Article 81 and/or the Chapter I prohibition may take action in the courts to stop the behaviour and/or to seek damages.

7.7 Where a decision of the OFT or the CAT (on appeal from a decision of the OFT) has already found an infringement of Article 81 and/or the Chapter I prohibition, third parties who consider they have suffered loss as a result may bring an action for damages, against the undertaking or undertakings concerned, in the CAT or the courts. The CAT and the courts will be bound, in such proceedings, by the relevant infringement decision, provided that the decision is no longer capable of being overturned on appeal.[39]

NOTES

36 Article 81(2) and section 2(4) of the Act.

37 Section 39 of the Act.

38 Full details of how turnover is to be calculated can be found in the Competition Act 1998 (Small Agreements and Conduct of Minor Significance) Regulations 2000 (SI 2000/262).

39 Sections 47A(9) and 58A(2) of the Act.

8. OPINIONS AND INFORMAL ADVICE

[3.98]

8.1 Undertakings will generally be well placed to analyse the effect of their own conduct under Article 81 and under the Chapter I prohibition in the light of relevant Community case law and Community instruments including EC block exemption regulations and European Commission notices. Further, United Kingdom case law and OFT competition law guidelines, such as this one, are available to assist undertakings in considering the application of the law under the Act.

8.2 However, in specific cases that raise novel or unresolved questions of law, it may be possible to obtain guidance from the European Commission or from the OFT.

THE EUROPEAN COMMISSION'S APPROACH

8.3 The European Commission has published a Notice setting out its intention to issue Guidance Letters in certain circumstances, most particularly where a case gives rise to genuine uncertainty because it presents novel or unresolved questions for the application of the law. Further information about the European Commission's approach can be found in its *Notice on informal guidance relating to novel questions concerning Articles 81 and 82 of the EC Treaty that arise in individual cases (guidance letters)*.[40]

THE OFT'S APPROACH

8.4 Where a case raises novel or unresolved questions about the application of Article 81 and/or the Chapter I prohibition in the United Kingdom, and where the OFT considers there is an interest in issuing clarification for the benefit of a wider audience, it may publish written guidance in the form of an Opinion.

8.5 An Opinion published by the OFT cannot prejudge the assessment of the same question by the European Commission, the European Court or the CAT. An Opinion from the OFT does not bind any NCA or court having the power to apply Article 81 and/or the Chapter I prohibition. An Opinion also cannot bind the subsequent assessment of the same issues by the OFT, although the OFT will have regard to its Opinion when carrying out the assessment. See the competition law guideline *Modernisation* (OFT 423) for further details on Opinions.

INFORMAL ADVICE

8.6 The OFT also offers confidential informal advice to undertakings on the application of Article 81 and/or the Chapter I prohibition through contact with OFT officials on an ad hoc basis. Views given by way of informal advice are not binding. Requests for informal advice should be made in the first place by calling the OFT enquiries line at 08457 224499, or emailing enquiries@oft.gsi.gov.uk

NOTES

40 OJ C101, 27.04.2004, p 78.

ABUSE OF A DOMINANT POSITION (OFT 402, DECEMBER 2004)

[3.99]

NOTES

As to the construction of this document (following the abolition of the OFT and Competition Commission), see further the note "The Competition and Markets Authority (references to the OFT and Competition Commission etc)" in the introductory notes to Part 3 preceding **[3.1]**.

CONTENTS

1. INTRODUCTION

[3.100]

1.1 The EC Treaty[1] and the Competition Act 1998 (the Act) both prohibit, in certain circumstances, conduct by one or more undertakings which amounts to an abuse of a dominant position. The prohibitions are set out in Article 82 of the EC Treaty (Article 82) and section 18(1) of the Act (the Chapter II prohibition). EC Regulation 1/2003 (the Modernisation Regulation)[2] requires the designated national competition authorities of the Member States (NCAs) and the courts of the Member States to apply and enforce Article 82 as well as national competition law when national competition law is applied to an abuse prohibited by Article 82.

1.2 This guideline explains how the OFT will operate its powers under the Act and under the Modernisation Regulation in assessing the conduct of dominant undertakings. It indicates some of the factors which the OFT considers are relevant in determining whether an undertaking is dominant and whether its behaviour will or may be regarded as abusive.

1.3 It is intended that this guideline should be of assistance not only to those undertakings which are dominant in their market or markets, but also to their customers and other businesses. In addition to this guideline, the competition law guideline *Assessment of market power* (OFT 415) provides further guidance on how the OFT assesses dominance.

1.4 The scope and application of Article 82 and the Chapter II prohibition are explained in Part 2 of this guideline. Part 3 of the guideline deals with the relationship between EC and national competition law. Parts 4 and 5 consider the definitions of dominance and abuse respectively. The OFT offers confidential informal advice to undertakings, and may, in certain circumstances, publish written guidance in the form of an Opinion. Further details about this can be found in Part 5.

NOTES

1 The Treaty establishing the European Community.

2 Council Regulation (EC) No 1/2003 of 16 December 2002 on the implementation of the rules on competition laid down in Articles 81 and 82 of the Treaty (OJ L1, 4.1.2003, p 1).

2. ABUSE OF A DOMINANT POSITION: THE PROVISIONS

SCOPE OF THE PROVISIONS

[3.101]

2.1 The OFT is empowered to apply two substantive provisions which prohibit conduct by one or more dominant undertakings[3] which amounts to abusive behaviour: Article 82 and the Chapter II prohibition. The Chapter II prohibition is based on Article 82. Article 82 provides that:

> 'Any abuse by one or more undertakings of a dominant position within the common market or in a substantial part of it shall be prohibited as incompatible with the common market in so far as it may affect trade between Member States.'

The Chapter II prohibition provides that:

> '. . . any conduct on the part of one or more undertakings which amounts to the abuse of a dominant position in a market is prohibited if it may affect trade within the United Kingdom.'

2.2 The tests applied under Article 82 and the Chapter II prohibition have two common elements: whether an undertaking is dominant in a relevant market; and, if so, whether it is abusing that dominant position. The prohibition under both Article 82 and the Chapter II prohibition is on the **abuse** of the dominant position, not the **holding** of the position. The OFT would find an undertaking's behaviour an abuse only after detailed examination of the market concerned and the effects of the undertaking's conduct.

2.3 Article 82 applies to conduct which 'may affect trade between Member States'. The case law of the European Court has interpreted this phrase broadly. Given the breadth of this interpretation, it is likely that in many cases conduct will be caught by both Article 82 and the Chapter II prohibition (see paragraphs 3.1 to 3.7 for further details on the application of this test).

2.4 In determining whether Article 82 and/or the Chapter II prohibition apply, the dominant position must be held within the appropriate territory. In the case of Article 82, the dominant position must be held within the common market or in a substantial part of it. In the case of the Chapter II prohibition, the dominant position must be held within the United Kingdom or any part of it. It is possible that a dominant position held within the United Kingdom or any part of it may also constitute a dominant position held within the common market or a substantial part of it (see paragraphs 4.26 to 4.28 below).

2.5 Both Article 82 and the Chapter II prohibition provide, in similar terms, that conduct may constitute an abuse if it consists of:

(a) directly or indirectly imposing unfair purchase or selling prices or other unfair trading conditions
(b) limiting production, markets or technical development to the prejudice of consumers
(c) applying dissimilar conditions to equivalent transactions with other trading parties, thereby placing them at a competitive disadvantage
(d) making the conclusion of contracts subject to acceptance by the other parties of supplementary obligations which, by their nature or according to commercial usage, have no connection with the subject of the contracts.[4]

2.6 These are no more than examples, and are not exhaustive. The important issue is whether the dominant undertaking is using its dominant position in an abusive way. This may occur if it uses practices that have the effect of restricting the degree of competition which it faces, or of exploiting its market position unjustifiably.

EXCLUSIONS

2.7 Although the concept of an **exclusion** is not specifically recognised in relation to Article 82, under EC law certain types of conduct are, in effect, excluded from the application of Article 82. These include conduct:

- which would result in a concentration with a Community dimension and thereby be subject to the EC Merger Regulation,[5] or
- which is carried out by an undertaking entrusted with the operation of services of general economic interest or having the character of a revenue producing monopoly, insofar as the application of Article 82 would obstruct the performance, in law or fact, of the particular tasks assigned to the undertaking.

2.8 The Act sets out a number of specific exclusions from the Chapter II prohibition for certain categories of conduct:[6]

- to the extent that the conduct would result in enterprises ceasing to be distinct within the meaning of the merger provisions of the Enterprise Act 2002 (see the Enterprise Act guidance *Mergers: substantive assessment guidance* (OFT 506) for further detail)
- which would result in a concentration with a Community dimension and thereby be subject to the EC Merger Regulation
- which is carried out by an undertaking entrusted with the operation of services of general economic interest or having the character of a revenue-producing monopoly, insofar as the prohibition would obstruct the performance, in law or in fact, of the particular tasks assigned to the undertaking (see the competition law guideline *Services of general economic interest exclusion* (OFT 421))
- to the extent to which the conduct is engaged in in order to comply with a legal requirement
- which is necessary to avoid conflict with international obligations and the conduct is the subject of an order by the Secretary of State, or
- which is necessary for compelling reasons of public policy and the conduct is the subject of an order by the Secretary of State.

2.9 The Secretary of State has the power to add, amend or remove the exclusions from the Chapter II prohibition in certain circumstances.

EXEMPTIONS

2.10 Unlike Article 81 and the Chapter I prohibition, there are no block or parallel exemptions from Article 82 or the Chapter II prohibition.

2.11 If an undertaking's behaviour involves an agreement which is exempt from Article 81 or the Chapter I prohibition, the position under Article 82 and/or the Chapter II prohibition will depend on the type of exemption:

- the benefit of a United Kingdom or EC block exemption does not prevent the undertaking's behaviour from being an abuse under Article 82 or the Chapter II prohibition. This position also applies when the agreement benefits from a parallel exemption from the Chapter I prohibition because the agreement falls within a category of agreements which is covered by an EC block exemption regulation, but
- in cases where an agreement, prior to 1 May 2004, has been granted an individual exemption by the OFT under section 9 of the Act or benefits from a parallel exemption under section 10 of the Act because it has an individual exemption under Article 81(3), then it is unlikely to be examined again by the OFT under Article 82 and/or Chapter II, in the absence of a material change of circumstances.

CONSEQUENCES OF INFRINGEMENT

2.12 Conduct which amounts to the abuse of a dominant position is prohibited and the undertaking or undertakings involved may be subject to a financial penalty and/or to directions appropriate to bring the infringement to an end.

2.13 The OFT may impose a financial penalty of up to 10 per cent of the worldwide turnover of an undertaking for an infringement of Article 82 and/or the Chapter II prohibition. When setting the amount of any penalty, the OFT must have regard to its *Guidance as to the appropriate amount of a penalty* (OFT 423). Further details on penalties and directions (and other consequences of an infringement of Article 82 and/or the Chapter II prohibition) are available in the competition law guideline *Enforcement* (OFT 407).

CONDUCT OF MINOR SIGNIFICANCE

2.14 In order to avoid the prohibition regime being unduly burdensome on small businesses, the Act provides limited immunity from financial penalties for **conduct of minor significance** in relation to infringements of the Chapter II prohibition.[7] This immunity does not apply to infringements of Article 82. Conduct will be considered to be of minor significance if the annual turnover of the undertaking concerned does not exceed £50 million.[8] Undertakings will benefit from immunity from financial penalties for infringement of the Chapter II prohibition if the OFT is satisfied that they acted on the reasonable assumption that on the facts they qualified for the limited immunity for conduct of minor significance.

2.15 The OFT may still investigate conduct of minor significance and can decide to withdraw the immunity from financial penalties if, having investigated the conduct, it considers the conduct is likely to infringe the Chapter II prohibition. Withdrawal of the immunity in this way cannot have effect before the date of the decision.

THIRD PARTY ACTION

2.16 Third parties adversely affected by conduct which they believe infringes Article 82 and/or the Chapter II prohibition may, in addition to or instead of making a complaint to the OFT, take action in the courts to stop the behaviour and/or to seek damages.

2.17 Where a decision of the OFT or the Competition Appeal Tribunal (the CAT) on appeal from a decision of the OFT has already found an infringement of Article 82 and/or the Chapter II prohibition, third parties who consider they have suffered loss as a result of the infringement may bring an action for damages, against the undertaking or undertakings concerned, in the CAT or the courts. The CAT and the courts will be bound, in such proceedings, by the relevant infringement decision, provided that the decision is no longer capable of being overturned on appeal.

NOTES

3 The term undertaking is not defined in the EC Treaty or the Act, but its meaning has been set out in Community law. It covers any natural or legal person engaged in economic activity, regardless of its legal status and the way in which it is financed. It includes companies, partnerships, firms, businesses, individuals operating as sole traders, agricultural cooperatives, associations of undertakings (eg trade associations), non-profit making organisations and (in some circumstances) public entities that offer goods or services on a given market.

4 Section 18(2) of the Act.

5 Council Regulation (EC) No 139/2004 on the control of concentrations between undertakings. (OJ L24, 29.1.04, p 1).

6 A domestic exclusion does not, however, exclude conduct from applicable EC law. Any conduct affecting trade between Member States that is excluded under the Act remains subject to Article 82, unless there is an equivalent exclusion at EC level. Accordingly should conduct infringe Article 82, all the consequences of infringement described at paragraphs 2.12 and 2.13 below will follow, irrespective of any domestic exclusion.

7 Section 40 of the Act.

8 Full details of how turnover is to be calculated can be found in the Competition Act 1998 (Small Agreements and Conduct of Minor Significance) Regulations 2000 (SI 2000/262).

3. RELATIONSHIP BETWEEN EC AND NATIONAL COMPETITION LAW

ARTICLE 3 OF THE MODERNISATION REGULATION

[3.102]

3.1 The relationship between EC competition law and national competition law is governed by Article 3 of the Modernisation Regulation. Article 3(1) provides that where national competition authorities or courts apply national competition law to conduct which would be caught by Article 82, they must also apply Article 82.

3.2 In all cases where the OFT examines whether undertakings have abused a position of dominance under the Chapter II prohibition, it also considers whether Article 82 is applicable. The OFT's determination of whether Article 82 is applicable will consist of assessing whether the conduct 'may affect trade between Member States'.[9] In practice, where the OFT considers that conduct under investigation may have an effect on trade between Member States, it will, in addition to applying Article 82, usually also apply the Chapter II prohibition. Equally, however, it is open to the OFT to apply Article 82 alone in such cases.

3.3 Conduct may affect trade between Member States, and yet not be prohibited by Article 82 either because the undertaking is not dominant, or because the conduct is not an abuse. In such instances, Article 3 does not prevent the application of stricter national competition law (see the competition law guideline *Modernisation* (OFT 442) for further details on Article 3). In the United Kingdom the unilateral conduct of undertakings may, for example, be examined under the market investigation provisions of the Enterprise Act 2002 (the Enterprise Act) (see the Enterprise Act guidance on *Market investigation references* (OFT 511) for further details).

3.4 Under the OFT's Rules,[10] the OFT may, at any time prior to making an infringement decision, elect to apply to a case one or both of Article 82 and the Chapter II prohibition. This means that a case started under Chapter II can be continued under Article 82 or (as is more likely) can be continued under both Article 82 and Chapter II, and vice versa.

3.5 In cases where both Chapter II and Article 82 are applied, the decision and any remedies will be taken under both the Chapter II prohibition and Article 82. However, in such cases, when imposing penalties in respect of an infringement of both Article 82 and the Chapter II prohibition, the undertaking will not be penalised twice for the same anti-competitive effects. For further details see the OFT's *Guidance as to the appropriate amount of a penalty* (OFT 423).

3.6 The European Commission has issued a Notice entitled *Guidance on the effect on trade concept contained in Articles 81 and 82 of the Treaty*[11] (the Effect on Trade Notice) to assist with the assessment as to whether or not agreements or conduct have an effect on trade between Member States. The Effect on Trade Notice sets out the principles developed by the European Court in interpreting the effect on trade concept and spells out a rule which will be applied by the European Commission in deciding whether or not agreements or conduct are likely to appreciably affect trade between Member States. A brief summary of some of the key points of the Effect on Trade Notice is set out in the competition law guideline *Modernisation* (OFT 442).

3.7 The OFT will have regard to the guidance set out in the Effect on Trade Notice when considering whether particular conduct may have an effect on trade between Member States to determine whether Article 82 applies.

PRIMACY OF COMMUNITY LAW

3.8 In applying Article 82, the OFT is bound by the fundamental principle of the primacy of EC law and must follow the case law of the European Court in interpreting EC legislation. As a consequence, conduct prohibited by Article 82 cannot be permitted under national law. National law can, however, be stricter than Article 82 so that conduct permitted under Article 82 may be prohibited under national law. The Modernisation Regulation also makes further provision to ensure consistency in the application of EC law. Article 16(2) of the Modernisation Regulation provides that where the European Commission has taken a decision on the conduct of an undertaking, the OFT and other NCAs cannot take a decision in respect of the same conduct which would run counter to the decision adopted by the European Commission.

CONSISTENCY AND CASES BROUGHT UNDER THE CHAPTER I AND CHAPTER II PROHIBITIONS

3.9 In addition to its obligations under EC law, the OFT is under an obligation under section 60 of the Act to deal with cases brought under the Chapter II prohibition in such a way as to ensure consistency with EC law in so far as this is possible and having regard to any relevant differences between any of the provisions concerned. Further details about the operation of section 60 are set out in the competition law guideline *Modernisation* (OFT 442).

NOTES

9 Article 82.

10 The Competition Act 1998 (Office of Fair Trading's Rules) Order 2004 (SI 2004/2751), rule 10.

11 OJ C101, 27.4.04, p 81.

4. DOMINANCE

[3.103]

4.1 There are two tests common to assessing whether Article 82 or the Chapter II prohibition applies:

- whether an undertaking is dominant, and
- if it is, whether it is abusing that dominant position.

4.2 The first test raises two questions which are considered below: (i) the definition of the market in which the undertaking is alleged to be dominant (the relevant market); and (ii) whether it is dominant within that market.

4.3 In addition, in determining whether Article 82 and/or the Chapter II prohibition apply, it is necessary to consider in which territory the dominant position is held (see paragraphs 4.26 to 4.28 below).

MARKET DEFINITION

4.4 Before assessing whether an undertaking is dominant, the relevant market must be determined. This relevant market will have two dimensions:

- the relevant goods or services (the product market), and
- the geographic extent of the market (the geographic market).

4.5 The OFT's approach to market definition is provided in the competition law guideline *Market definition* (OFT 403), which follows a similar approach to that of the European Commission.[12] Market definition provides an appropriate frame of reference for competition analysis. In order to establish which products or geographic areas are included in the relevant market, a conceptual framework known as the hypothetical monopolist test is usually employed.

THE PRODUCT MARKET

4.6 The market is determined by taking the product (or service) relevant to the investigation — the **focal product** — and looking at the closest substitute products, usually those products to which consumers would switch, if the price of the focal product rose. These substitute products are included in the same market as the focal product if customers would switch to them in sufficient volumes in response to the hypothetical situation where the price of the focal product is sustained significantly above competitive levels.[13] The alternative products do not need to be perfect substitutes for the focal product, but alternatives which would fill a similar role to the focal product.

4.7 In addition to this substitution by customers (**demand-side substitution**), the price of the focal product can also be constrained by the potential behaviour of suppliers producing other products (**supply-side substitution**). This might occur where businesses which are not currently supplying the focal product could, at short notice, switch some of their existing facilities to supplying the focal product (or close substitutes) in response to prices of the focal product being sustained significantly above competitive levels. Where such switching would occur within one year and without substantial sunk costs,[14] supply-side substitutes may also be included in the relevant market.

THE GEOGRAPHIC MARKET

4.8 Similar methods are used to define the geographic market. Usually, the OFT would consider an area in which the focal product was sold as a candidate for the relevant geographic market. Then the OFT would consider whether, in response to the hypothetical situation where the price of the focal product in that area was being sustained significantly above competitive levels, customers would switch a sufficient volume of purchases to the same products sold in other areas. If so, these other areas will be included in the relevant geographic market. Supply side substitution might also occur whereby suppliers in other areas would quickly (for example, within one year), and without substantial investment, supply the candidate market in response to the higher prices there. The geographic market may be national (ie the United Kingdom), smaller than the United Kingdom (eg local or regional), wider than the United Kingdom (eg part of Europe, including the United Kingdom) or even worldwide.

PRECEDENT

4.9 In some cases a market may previously have been investigated and defined by the OFT or by another competition authority. While such precedents can provide useful insights, the market definition used in a previous case may not always be the correct one to use in subsequent cases.

ASSESSING DOMINANCE

4.10 The European Court has defined a dominant market position as: '. . . a position of economic strength enjoyed by an undertaking which enables it to prevent effective competition being maintained on the relevant market by affording it the power to behave to an appreciable extent independently of its competitors, customers and ultimately of its consumers.'[15]

4.11 An undertaking will not be dominant unless it has substantial market power.

4.12 Market power arises where an undertaking does not face sufficiently strong competitive pressure. Both suppliers and buyers can have market power. However, for clarity, market power will in this guideline refer to supplier market power. Where buyer market power is the issue, the term **buyer power** is employed to differentiate such market power from supplier market power. Market power and buyer power are not absolute but are matters of degree; the degree of power will depend on the circumstances of each case (see the competition law guideline *Assessment of market power* (OFT 415)).

4.13 Market power can be thought of as the ability profitably to sustain prices above competitive levels or to restrict output or quality below competitive levels. An undertaking with market power might also have the ability and incentive to harm the process of competition in other ways, for example by weakening existing competition, raising entry barriers or slowing innovation. However, although market power is not solely concerned with the ability of a supplier to raise prices, this guideline, for convenience, often refers to market power as the ability profitably to sustain prices above competitive levels.

4.14 In assessing whether an undertaking is dominant, the OFT considers whether that undertaking faces constraints on its ability to behave independently. The most important constraints are existing competition and potential competition. Other factors, such as the countervailing influence of powerful buyers, or regulation, are sometimes relevant as well.

4.15 These constraints, which are relevant when assessing dominance under both Article 82 and the Chapter II prohibition, are discussed briefly below and explained in detail in the competition law guideline *Assessment of market power* (OFT 415).

EXISTING COMPETITION

4.16 Existing competition refers to competition from undertakings already in the relevant market, to whom consumers might switch if the alleged dominant undertaking sustained prices above competitive levels. The market shares of competitors in the relevant market are one measure of the competitive constraint from existing competitors.

MARKET SHARES

4.17 There are no market share thresholds for defining dominance under Article 82 or the Chapter II prohibition. An undertaking's market share is an important factor in assessing dominance but does not, on its own, determine whether an undertaking is dominant. For example, it is also necessary to consider the position of other undertakings operating in the same market and how market shares have changed over time. An undertaking is more likely to be dominant if its competitors enjoy relatively weak positions or if it has enjoyed a high and stable market share.

4.18 The European Court has stated that dominance can be presumed in the absence of evidence to the contrary if an undertaking has a market share persistently above 50 per cent.[16] The OFT considers it unlikely that an undertaking will be individually dominant if its share of the relevant market is below 40 per cent, although dominance could be established below that figure if other relevant factors (such as the weak position of competitors in that market and high entry barriers) provided strong evidence of dominance.

POTENTIAL COMPETITION

4.19 Potential competition refers to the possibility that undertakings would enter the relevant market and gain market share at the expense of an alleged dominant undertaking that sustained prices above competitive levels. The strength of potential competition is affected by **barriers to entry**. For further details on barriers to entry see competition law guideline *Assessment of market power* (OFT 415).

OTHER FACTORS

4.20 The ability of an alleged dominant supplier to exercise market power may be diminished by the existence of powerful buyers. Nevertheless, the existence of powerful buyers in a relevant market would not, in itself, preclude the OFT from finding a supplier to be dominant in that market.[17]

4.21 Economic regulation is a further relevant factor when assessing market power in industry sectors where, for example, prices and/or service levels are subject to controls by the government or an industry sector regulator. In this situation an undertaking may still be considered to be dominant. Economic regulation may, however, limit the extent to which that dominant position may be abused, see the competition law guideline *Assessment of market power* (OFT 415).

INTELLECTUAL PROPERTY RIGHTS (IPRS)

4.22 The OFT considers that ownership of an IPR does not necessarily create a dominant position.[18] Whether or not dominance results from the ownership of an IPR depends upon the extent to which there are substitutes for the product, process or work to which the IPR relates.

COLLECTIVE DOMINANCE

4.23 Article 82 and the Chapter II prohibition prohibit conduct on the part of one **or more** undertakings which amounts to the abuse of a dominant position. A dominant position need not be held by a single undertaking. Separate undertakings may be found to hold a dominant position together where certain conditions are met. Their conduct may then be dealt with together under Article 82 and/or the Chapter II prohibition.

4.24 A dominant position may be held collectively when two or more legally independent undertakings are linked in such a way that they adopt a common policy on the market. The European Court confirmed the principle of collective dominance in the *Italian Flat Glass* case: 'There is nothing, in principle, to prevent two or more independent economic entities from being, on a specific market, united by such economic links that, by virtue of that fact, together they hold a dominant position vis à vis the other operators on the same market.'[19]

4.25 The links may be structural or they may be such that the undertakings adopt a common policy on the market.[20] For example, the nature of the market may be that undertakings might adopt the same pricing policy on the market without ever explicitly agreeing on price (see the competition law guideline *Assessment of market power*, OFT 415)).

TERRITORIAL SCOPE

4.26 In determining whether Article 82 and/or the Chapter II prohibition apply, it is necessary to consider the territory within which a dominant position is held. In the case of Article 82, the dominant position must be held in the whole or a substantial part of the common market. In respect of the Chapter II prohibition, the dominant position must be held within the United Kingdom or any part of it. A dominant position held within the UK or any part of it may also be a dominant position within a substantial part of the common market. In particular, where a dominant position is held within the UK as a whole, it will most likely also be a dominant position within a substantial part of the common market.

4.27 The analysis for determining whether a market constitutes a substantial part of the common market encompasses not just a determination of the geographic scope of the market but also an assessment of the economic importance of the product market relative to the total EC market.

4.28 Whether an area will constitute a substantial part of the common market for the purposes of Article 82 is dependent on the facts of each individual case. In the past the European Court has considered that the Belgium-Luxembourg sugar market was a substantial part of the common market even though it constituted just nine per cent of Community sugar production and five per cent of the sugar consumption in the Community[21]. In the same case the European Court also found that southern Germany was a substantial part of the common market, and in a further case the European Court found that the Port of Genoa was a substantial part of the common market[22] for the purposes of applying Article 82.

NOTES

12 See the European Commission's Notice on the definition of relevant market for the purposes of Community competition law, OJ C372, 9.12.97, p 5.

13 For further details, see competition law guideline Market definition (OFT 403).

14 Sunk costs are costs which cannot be recovered when an undertaking leaves a market.

15 Case 27/76 *United Brands v Commission* [1978] ECR 207, [1978] 1 CMLR 429. This definition has been used in other cases.

16 Case C62/86, *AKZO Chemie BV v Commission* [1993] 5 CMLR 215.

17 An undertaking with strong buyer power may itself be dominant.

18 See, for example, Cases C-241 & 242/91P *Radio Telefis Eireann v Commission (Magill)* [1995] ECR I-743 at paragraph 46.

19 Cases T-68/69 etc *Società Italiano Vetro SpA v Commission*, [1992] II ECR 1403, [1992] 5 CMLR 302.

20 Joined Cases C-395/96 P and C-396/96 P *Compagnie Maritime Belge SA* and others, [2000] ECR I-1365 paragraph 45.

21 Case 40/73 *Suiker Unie v Commission* [1975] ECR 1663.

22 Case C-179/90 *Merci convenzionale porto di Genova SpA* [1991] ECR I-5889.

5. ABUSE

[3.104]

5.1 The following paragraphs give some guidance on the second part of the test for assessing whether Article 82 or the Chapter II prohibition applies, that is, when an undertaking's behaviour might be regarded as an **abuse of a dominant position**.

CONCEPT OF ABUSE

5.2 The Act[23] and Article 82 list broad categories of business behaviour, within which particular examples of abusive conduct are most likely to be found. In general, the OFT considers that the likely **effect** of a dominant undertaking's conduct on customers and on the process of competition is more important to the determination of an abuse than the specific **form** of the conduct in question. Conduct may be abusive when, through the effects of conduct on the competitive process, it adversely affects consumers directly (for example, through the prices charged) or indirectly (for example, conduct which reduces the intensity of existing competition or potential competition). A dominant undertaking is under a special responsibility not to allow its conduct to impair undistorted competition.

5.3 Neither Article 82 nor the Act contains a provision under which an abuse can be exempted because it produces benefits, but conduct may not be regarded as an abuse, even if it restricts competition, where there is an objective justification for the conduct. For example, a refusal to supply might be justified by the poor creditworthiness of the customer. However, it will still be necessary for a dominant undertaking to show that its conduct is proportionate.

5.4 The OFT recognises the role of IPRs in encouraging creative and innovative activity. The legitimate exercise of an IPR by a dominant undertaking is not an abuse. It is, however, possible that the way in which an IPR is exercised may give rise to concern if it goes beyond the legitimate exploitation of the IPR; for example, if it is used to leverage market power from one market to another or to prevent the development of a new market.

CATEGORIES OF ABUSE

5.5 Abusive conduct generally falls into one or both of the following categories:

- conduct which exploits customers or suppliers (for example, excessively high prices), or
- conduct which amounts to exclusionary behaviour, because it removes or weakens competition from existing competitors, or establishes or strengthens entry barriers, thereby removing or weakening potential competition.

5.6 Exclusionary behaviour may include excessively low prices and certain discount schemes, where its (likely) effect is to foreclose a market, as well as vertical restraints or refusals to supply where these (are likely to) foreclose markets or dampen competition. However, whatever the form of the behaviour in question, its likely effect on competition will depend on the circumstances at hand and the OFT assesses alleged abuses on a case-by-case basis.

ABUSE IN RELATED MARKETS

5.7 As explained at paragraph 4.1 above, Article 82 and the Chapter II prohibition imply two tests: whether an undertaking is dominant, and whether it is abusing that dominant position. It is not necessary to show that the abuse was committed in the market which the undertaking dominates. In certain circumstances, Article 82 and the Chapter II prohibition may apply where an undertaking that is dominant in one market commits an abuse in a different but closely associated market. This principle was set out by the European Court in the case of *Tetra Pak II*.[24]

NOTES

[23] Section 18(2) of the Act.

[24] Case T-83/91 *Tetra Pak v European Commission* [1994] ECR II-755. In this case the European Court found that Tetra Pak's activities in relation to the markets in non-aseptic machines and cartons constituted an abuse of its dominant position in the distinct, but closely associated, markets for aseptic machines and cartons intended for the packaging of liquid foods.

6. INFORMAL ADVICE AND OPINIONS

[3.105]

6.1 Undertakings will generally be well placed to analyse the effect of their own conduct under Article 82 and under the Chapter II prohibition in the light of relevant EC case law and EC legislation, including European Commission Notices which clarify the application of the law.

6.2 In addition to OFT competition law guidelines (such as this one) which are available to assist undertakings in the application of the law under the Act, the OFT also offers confidential informal advice to undertakings on the application of Article 81, Article 82 and/or the prohibitions in the Act through contact with OFT officials on an ad hoc basis. Views given by way of informal advice cannot bind the OFT or the national courts. Requests for informal advice are best made by calling the OFT enquiries line at 08457 22 44 99, or emailing enquiries@oft.gsi.gov.uk.

6.3 Further, where a case raises novel or unresolved questions of law, it may be possible to obtain written guidance in the form of an Opinion from the European Commission or from the OFT. See the competition law guideline *Modernisation* (OFT 442) for further details on European Commission[25] and OFT Opinions.

NOTES

[25] Further information about the European Commission's approach can also be found in its *Notice on informal guidance relating to novel questions concerning Articles 81 and 82 of the EC Treaty that arise in individual cases (guidance letters)* (OJ C101, 24.4.04, p 78).

MARKET DEFINITION (OFT 403, DECEMBER 2004)

[3.106]

NOTES

As to the construction of this document (following the abolition of the OFT and Competition Commission), see further the note "The Competition and Markets Authority (references to the OFT and Competition Commission etc)" in the introductory notes to Part 3 preceding **[3.1]**.

CONTENTS

1. INTRODUCTION

[3.107]

1.1 Article 81 and Article 82 of the Treaty[1] (Article 81 and Article 82) and the Chapter I and Chapter II prohibitions contained in the Competition Act 1998 (the Act) prohibit agreements[2] which prevent, restrict or distort competition and conduct which constitutes abuse of a dominant position. EC Regulation 1/2003 (the Modernisation Regulation)[3] requires the designated national competition authorities of the Member States (NCAs) and the courts of the Member States to apply and enforce Articles 81 and 82 of the Treaty establishing the European Community (Article 81 and Article 82 respectively) as well as national competition law when national competition is applied to agreements which may affect trade between Member States or to abuse prohibited by Article 82.

1.2 This guideline follows a similar approach to the European Commission's *Notice on market definition*.[4] This guideline provides a conceptual framework within which evidence on market definition can be organised. It also discusses practical issues that may arise in market definition. The OFT will not follow mechanically every step described below in every case. Instead, the OFT will look at evidence that is reasonably attainable and relevant to the case in question.[5]

NOTES

1 The Treaty establishing the European Community.

2 References in this guideline to **agreements** should be taken to include decisions by associations of undertakings (see footnote 8 below) and concerted practices, unless otherwise stated or the context demands it.

3 Council Regulation (EC) No 1/2003 of 16 December 2002 on the implementation of the rules on competition laid down in Articles 81 and 82 of the Treaty (OJ L1, 4.1.03, p 1).

4 European Commission *Notice on the definition of the relevant market for the purposes of Community competition law* (OJ C372, 9.12.97, p 5). A similar approach is also used in the US Department of Justice and Federal Trade Commission *Horizontal Merger Guidelines*, revised 1992.

5 While this guideline is specific to Articles 81 and Article 82 and the Act, the OFT will generally use the same approach to market definition in other areas of casework, including mergers and market investigation references. In this regard, it should be noted that the appropriate market definition can differ according to the specific facts of each case. Part 5 of this guideline gives more details.

2. MARKET DEFINITION

THE PURPOSE OF MARKET DEFINITION

[3.108]

2.1 Market definition is not an end in itself but a key step in identifying the competitive constraints acting on a supplier of a given product or service. Market definition provides a framework for competition analysis. For example, market shares can be calculated only after the market has been defined and, when considering the potential for new entry, it is necessary to identify the market that might be entered. Market definition is usually the first step in the assessment of market power.

2.2 Therefore, market definition is important in the process of establishing whether or not particular agreements or conduct fall within the scope of the competition rules:

- Article 81 and section 2(1) of the Act (**the Chapter I prohibition**) apply only to agreements which have as their object or effect an 'appreciable' prevention, restriction or distortion of competition (see the competition law guideline *Agreements and concerted practices* (OFT 401)). The appreciability test usually requires definition of a relevant market and demonstration that the agreement would have an appreciable effect on competition within that market,[6] and
- Article 82 and section 18(1) of the Act (**the Chapter II prohibition**) apply only to dominant undertakings.[7] The OFT would not consider an undertaking to be dominant unless that undertaking had substantial market power. The definition of the relevant market(s) is a necessary first step in assessing whether an undertaking is dominant.

2.3 In addition to its value in providing a framework for competition analysis, an appropriately defined relevant market may provide information that allows an investigation to be closed at an early stage. For analysis under Article 81 and/or the Chapter I prohibition, where an agreement involves undertakings whose combined share of the relevant market is low, the agreement is unlikely to raise competition concerns unless it contains price fixing, market sharing or bid rigging restrictions.[8] Market definition is also important when assessing whether an undertaking's market share is below market share thresholds set out in certain block exemptions.

2.4 For analysis under Article 82 and/or the Chapter II prohibition, undertakings with low market shares will usually not possess market power individually. Therefore, an investigation of an individual undertaking whose market share is low can normally be closed at an early stage.[9]

THE HYPOTHETICAL MONOPOLIST TEST

2.5 The process of defining a market typically begins by establishing the closest substitutes to the product[10] (or group of products) that is the focus of the investigation. These substitute products are the most immediate competitive constraints on the behaviour of the undertaking supplying the product in question. In order to establish which products are 'close enough' substitutes to be in the **relevant market**, a conceptual framework known as the hypothetical monopolist test (the test) is usually employed.

2.6 Before describing the test in detail, it should be emphasised that defining a market in strict accordance with the test's assumptions is rarely possible. Even if the test described below could be conducted precisely, the relevant market is in practice no more than an appropriate frame of reference for analysis of the competitive effects. Nevertheless, the conceptual framework of the test is important as it provides a structure within which evidence on market definition can be gathered and analysed.

2.7 In essence the test seeks to establish the smallest product group (and geographical area) such that a hypothetical monopolist controlling that product group (in that area) could profitably sustain 'supra competitive' prices, ie prices that are at least a small but significant amount above competitive levels. That product group (and area) is usually the relevant market.

2.8 If, for example, a hypothetical monopolist over a candidate product group could not profitably sustain supra competitive prices, then the candidate product group would be too narrow to be a relevant market. If, on the other hand, a hypothetical monopolist over a subset of a candidate product group could profitably sustain supra competitive prices, then the relevant market would usually be narrower than the candidate product group.

2.9 The steps in applying this approach are as follows. We start by considering a hypothetical monopolist of the **focal product** (ie the product under investigation)[11] which operates in a **focal area** (ie an area under investigation in which the focal product is sold).

2.10 We then ask whether it would be profitable for the hypothetical monopolist to sustain the price of the focal product a small but significant amount (eg 5 to 10 per cent)[12] above competitive levels.[13] If the answer to this question is 'yes', the test is complete. The product and area under the hypothetical monopolist's control is (usually) the relevant market.

2.11 If the answer to this question is 'no', this is typically because a sufficiently large number of customers would switch some of their purchases to other substitute products (or areas).[14] In this case, we assume further that the hypothetical monopolist controls both the focal product **and** its closest substitute.[15] We then repeat the process, but this time in relation to the larger set of products (or areas) under the hypothetical monopolist's control.

2.12 As before, we ask whether it would be profitable to sustain prices 5 to 10 per cent above competitive levels. If so, the test is complete. The relevant market is (usually) the focal product and its closest substitute. If not, we assume that the hypothetical monopolist also controls the second closest substitute to the focal product and repeat the process once more. We continue expanding the product group in this way (ie by adding the next best substitute) until we have found a group of products (or areas) for which it is profitable for the hypothetical monopolist to sustain prices 5 to 10 per cent above competitive levels (by adding the next best substitute).[16]

2.13 When the test is complete for the first time, the relevant market has usually been defined. However, occasionally it will be appropriate to define the relevant market to be wider than the narrowest product group (or area) that passes the test (see, for example, the discussion of supply side substitution in Parts 3 and 4).

PRACTICAL ISSUES

2.14 In practice, defining a market requires balancing various types of evidence and the exercise of judgement. However, it is not an end in itself. Where there is strong evidence that the relevant market is one of a few plausible market definitions, and the competitive assessment is shown to be largely unaltered by which one of these market definitions is adopted, it may not be necessary to define the market uniquely.

2.15 A market definition should normally contain two dimensions: a **product** and **geographic area.**[17] It is often practical to define the relevant product market first and only then to define the relevant geographic market. Parts 3 and 4 below discuss some of the issues that may arise when defining product and geographic markets and applying the principles set out above.

2.16 Part 5 discusses further practical issues such as market definition when prices may already exceed competitive levels. It also describes how the relevant market should be defined according to the facts and competition issues of each case. Part 6 discusses market definition in the context of after markets.

NOTES

6 An exception is where agreements have as their object the prevention, restriction or distortion of competition. In these cases, market definition is not necessarily a prerequisite for finding an infringement: see Case T-62/98 *Volkswagen AG v Commission* [2000] ECR II-2707 at paragraphs 230 to 232. The relevant market would, however, need to be defined in order to determine the **relevant turnover** of an undertaking, one of the factors which the OFT takes into account for the purpose of determining the amount of any penalty (see the *OFT's Guidance as to the appropriate amount of a penalty* (OFT 423)).

7 The term **undertaking** is not defined in the Treaty establishing the European Community or the Act but its meaning has been set out in Community law. It covers any natural or legal person engaged in economic activity, regardless of its legal status and the way in which it is financed. It includes companies, firms, businesses, partnerships, individuals operating as sole traders, agricultural cooperatives, associations of undertakings (eg trade associations), charities, non profit making organisations and (in some circumstances) public entities that offer goods or services on a given market. For further details, see the competition law guideline *Agreements and concerted practices* (OFT 401).

8 See the competition law guideline *Agreements and concerted practices* (OFT 401).

9 See the competition law guidelines *Abuse of a dominant position* (OFT 402) and *Assessment of market power* (OFT 415).

10 The focus of the investigation may be a product or a service. The term **product** is used for convenience and should be interpreted throughout this guideline to mean good, service or property right.

11 Where there is more than one product under investigation, the test will usually be applied separately for each of the products.

12 The OFT will normally consider a price 5 to 10 per cent above competitive levels to be **small but significant**. However, this is only an indicative range. If a price sustained 5 to 10 per cent above competitive levels would not be profitable but a higher price would be, a hypothetical monopolist could profitably sustain prices significantly above competitive levels and so the test is complete.

13 When carrying out the test, we assume that the hypothetical monopolist is not subject to economic regulation that would affect its pricing behaviour and that the prices of products outside of the hypothetical monopolist's control are held constant at their competitive levels. However, while not considered as part of the test, the issues of regulation and the pricing strategies of competitors would be considered as part of the overall competitive assessment.

14 Sometimes the pricing strategy would not be profitable because of responses by other suppliers – this is known as supply side substitution and is discussed in Parts 3 and 4.

15 The best substitute to the focal product could be another product sold in the same area or the focal product sold in a different area.

16 Although the test discussed here refers to a hypothetical monopolist, it should be noted that an undertaking with less than 100 per cent of a relevant market may nevertheless have market power. For example, suppose the market has been defined such that a hypothetical monopolist would profitably sustain prices at, say, 10 per cent above competitive levels. First, since market power is a matter of degree, this leaves sufficient room for an undertaking with less than 100 per cent of the market to exercise market power by sustaining prices above competitive levels, even if that undertaking would not increase prices by as much as a hypothetical monopolist. Second, an undertaking with less than 100 per cent market share may have the ability to weaken any competition that it faces and thereby consolidate its market power even further. Third, undertakings in the market may dampen competition by co-ordinating their behaviour. In the extreme, if they colluded perfectly, a group of undertakings could behave as if they were a hypothetical monopolist. These issues should be considered as part of the assessment of market power. See the competition law guideline *Assessment of market power* (OFT 415).

17 Time is a further dimension that is sometimes relevant, see Part 5.

3. THE PRODUCT MARKET

THE DEMAND SIDE

[3.109]

3.1 This part discusses some of the practical issues that need to be addressed when defining the relevant product market.

3.2 As described above in Part 2, the market definition process usually starts by looking at a relatively narrow potential definition. This would normally be one (or more) of the products which two parties to an agreement both produce, or one (or more) of the products which are the subject of a complaint about conduct, ie the focal product (or focal group of products). Previous experience and common sense will normally indicate the narrowest potential market definition, which will be taken as the starting point for the analysis.

3.3 As set out in Part 2, the next question is whether a hypothetical monopolist of the focal product could profitably sustain prices a small but significant amount above competitive levels. The price increase must be large enough that a response from customers is reasonably likely, but not so large that the price rise would inevitably lead to a substantial shift in demand, and so lead to markets being defined so widely that market shares convey no meaningful information on market power. The OFT will normally consider a price 5 to 10 per cent above competitive levels to be **small but significant**.[18]

3.4 Following the price rise, customers may switch some of their purchases from the focal product to other substitute products (**demand side substitution**). It is not necessary for all customers, or even the majority, to switch. The important factor is whether the volume of purchases likely to be switched is large enough to prevent a hypothetical monopolist profitably sustaining prices 5 to 10 per cent above competitive levels.[19]

3.5 Substitute products do not have to be identical to be included in the same market. For example, in its report on *Matches and Disposable Lighters*,[20] the then Monopolies and Mergers Commission included matches and disposable lighters in the same market because customers viewed them as close substitutes. Similarly, the products' prices do not have to be identical. For example, if two products perform the same purpose, but one is of a higher price and quality, they might be included in the same market. The question is whether the price of one sufficiently constrains the price of the other. Although one is of a lower quality, customers might still switch to this product if the price of the more expensive product rose such that they no longer felt that the higher quality justified the price differential.

3.6 The important issue is whether the undertaking could **sustain** prices sufficiently above competitive levels. Customers may take time to respond to a sustained rise in the price of the focal product. As a rough rule of thumb, if substitution would take longer than one year, the products to which customers eventually switched would not be included in the same market as the focal product. Products to which customers would switch within a year without incurring significant switching costs[21] are more likely to be included in the relevant market. However, the relevant time period in which to assess switching behaviour may be significantly shorter than one year: for example, in industries where transactions are made very frequently. A case by case analysis of switching is therefore appropriate.

3.7 Evidence on substitution from a number of different sources may be considered. Although the information used will vary from case to case and will be considered in the round[22] the following evidence and issues are often likely to be important:

- Evidence from the undertakings active in the market and their commercial strategies may be useful. For example, company documents may indicate which products the undertakings under investigation believe to be the closest substitute to their own products. Company documents such as internal communications, public statements, studies on consumer preferences or business plans may provide other useful evidence.[23]
- Customers and competitors will often be interviewed. In particular, customers can sometimes be asked directly how they would react to a hypothetical price rise, although because of the hypothetical nature of the question, answers may need to be treated with a degree of caution. Survey evidence might also provide information on customer preferences that would help to assess substitutability: for example, evidence on how customers rank particular products, whether and to what extent brand loyalty exists, and which characteristics of products are the most important to their decision to purchase.

- A significant factor in determining whether substitution takes place is whether customers would incur costs in substituting products. High switching costs relative to the value of the product will make substitution less likely.
- Evidence on product characteristics may provide useful information where customer substitution patterns are likely to be influenced significantly by those characteristics. Where the objective characteristics of products are very similar and their intended uses the same this would be good evidence that the products are close substitutes. However, the following caveats should be noted. First, even where products apparently have very similar characteristics and intended use, switching costs and brand loyalty may affect how substitutable they are in practice. Second, just because products display similar physical characteristics, this does not necessarily mean that customers would view them to be close substitutes. For example, peak customers may not view rail travel during off peak times to be a close substitute for rail travel at peak times.[24] Third, products with very different physical characteristics may be close substitutes if, from a customer's point of view, they have a very similar use.[25]
- Patterns in price changes can be informative. For example, two products showing the same pattern of price changes, for reasons not connected to costs or general price inflation, would be consistent with (although not proof of) these two products being close substitutes. Customer reactions to price changes in the past may also be relevant. Evidence that a relatively large proportion of customers had switched to a rival product in response to a relatively small price rise in the focal product would provide evidence that these two goods are close substitutes.[26] Equally price divergence over time, without significant levels of substitution, would be consistent with the two products being in separate markets.
- Evidence on own or cross price elasticities of demand may also be examined if it is available. The own price elasticity of demand measures the rate at which demand for a product (eg the focal product) changes when its price goes up or down. The cross price elasticity of demand measures the rate at which demand for a product (eg a rival product) changes when the price of another product (eg the focal product) goes up or down.
- In some cases **critical loss** analysis may be relevant. One definition of critical loss is the minimum percentage loss in volume of sales required to make a 5 (or 10) per cent price increase on a product unprofitable. The critical percentage tends to be lower when an undertaking has a high mark up over unit costs (since each sale lost entails a relatively large loss in profit). However, the fact that an undertaking can set a high mark up might also demonstrate that its current customer base is not particularly price sensitive. These potentially opposing effects might need to be balanced and assessed in conjunction with other evidence (eg estimates of elasticities of demand); and
- Evidence on the price:concentration relationship may also be informative. Price:concentration studies examine how the price of a product in a distinct area varies according to the number (or share of supply) of other products sold in the same area. These studies are useful where data are available for several distinct areas with varying degrees of concentration. For example, if observations of prices in several geographic areas suggest that when two products are sold in the same area, prices are significantly lower than when they are not, this might suggest that the two products are close substitutes (provided that it is possible to distinguish this from the effect of other factors which might explain the price differences).

PRICE DISCRIMINATION

3.8 The test described in Part 2 assumes that the hypothetical monopolist charges all customers the same price for the focal product. However, in some cases the hypothetical monopolist may be able to charge some customers a higher price than others, where the price difference is not related to higher costs of serving those customers. This is called **price discrimination**. Price discrimination requires that customers cannot arbitrage.[27] The undertaking could be able to discriminate between customers due to a variety of reasons, for example:

- some customers may face such high switching costs that they might be **locked in** to purchasing a particular product (eg a customer might use a product as an input to its production process and switching to a rival product might entail costs of quality assuring that product, as well as adjusting its production process)
- customer demand may differ according to time, eg demand for transport services at peak times is much less price sensitive than off peak demand for the same service, and
- customer demand for an input may differ according to the purpose for which it is used (for example, if different manufacturers transform the same input into different end products, they may have different derived demands for that input).[28]

3.9 Where a hypothetical monopolist would (or would be likely to) price discriminate significantly between groups of customers, each of these groups may form a separate market. If so, a relevant market might be defined as sales of the relevant product in the relevant geographic area to a particular customer group. For example, a hypothetical monopolist of a train service might be able to price discriminate between peak and off peak customers. In this case, peak travel and off peak travel might be in separate markets.[29]

3.10 By contrast, where an undertaking is unable to price discriminate, this may lead to the relevant market being wider than the focal product or focal area. For example, suppliers may face price constraints[30] such that they must set a uniform price across products or across geographical areas. Although it might in theory be profitable for a hypothetical monopolist to raise price in the focal area, perhaps because substitutes are unavailable, the existence of a price constraint may make such a price rise unprofitable, because it would require that prices are also raised in other areas where substitutes are present. Price constraints may thus lead to the relevant market being widened beyond the focal area. In a given case, evidence on the extent to which prices are constrained and the effect of the constraint on substitution would need to be considered when assessing the appropriate relevant market.

CHAINS OF SUBSTITUTION

3.11 Sometimes a focal product will be part of a long and unbroken chain of substitutes. For example, consider five products labelled A to E, which are differentiated by their perceived quality.[31] The closer two products are in the alphabet, the more substitutable they are from the point of view of customers. Thus consumers whose favourite product is C consider B and D to be very good substitutes for C but consider A and E to be poorer substitutes for C. Even though all products in the chain are substitutes, this does not mean that the whole chain is the relevant market. For example, it may be that a hypothetical monopolist of three products next to each other in the chain could profitably sustain prices 5 to 10 per cent above competitive levels.[32] In short, the hypothetical monopolist test is a way of determining what range of products in the chain constitutes the relevant product market.

THE SUPPLY SIDE

3.12 This section addresses how the supply side of the market might be relevant to market definition.

3.13 If prices rise, undertakings that do not currently supply a product might be able to supply it at short notice and without incurring substantial sunk costs.[33] This may prevent a hypothetical monopolist profitably sustaining prices 5 to 10 per cent above competitive levels. This form of substitution is carried out by suppliers and hence is known as **supply side substitution**.

3.14 An example is the supply of paper for use in publishing.[34] Paper is produced in various different grades dependent on the coating used. From a customer's point of view, the different types of paper may not be viewed as substitutes, but because they are produced using the same plant and raw materials, it may be relatively easy for manufacturers to switch production between different grades. A hypothetical monopolist in one grade of paper might not profitably sustain supra competitive prices because manufacturers currently producing other grades would rapidly start supplying that grade.

3.15 Analysing supply side substitution raises similar issues to the analysis of barriers to entry (discussed further in the competition law guideline *Assessment of market power* (OFT 415)). Supply side substitution can be thought of as a special case of entry – entry that occurs quickly (eg less than one year), effectively (eg on a scale large enough to affect prices), and without the need for substantial sunk investments. Supply side substitution addresses the questions of whether, to what extent, and how quickly, undertakings would start supplying a market in response to a hypothetical monopolist attempting to sustain supra competitive prices.

3.16 When assessing the scope for supply side substitution, the evidence from some or all of the following sources may be relevant:

- potential suppliers might be asked whether substitution was technically possible, about the costs of switching production between products, and the time it would take to switch production. The key question is whether it would be profitable to switch production, given a small (eg 5 to 10 per cent) price increase above competitive levels
- potential suppliers might be asked whether they had spare capacity or were free or willing to switch production. Undertakings may be prevented from switching production because all their existing capacity was tied up, eg they may be committed to long term contracts. There might also be difficulties obtaining necessary inputs or finding distribution outlets. Undertakings may be unwilling to switch production from an existing product to a new one, if producing the former product is more profitable than the latter
- although potential suppliers may be able to supply the market, there may be reasons why customers would not use their products, so the views of customers might be sought, and
- more generally customers may also be able to supply wider information about potential suppliers. Customers that are businesses (not consumers) might take actions to encourage potential suppliers to enter.

3.17 In some cases, where there are high levels of supply-side substitutability, it may be appropriate to define a market with reference to the similarity of production methods. For example, in the paper example used above, it may be more appropriate to define the market as 'the supply of paper for use in publishing', rather than have numerous defined markets for individual grades of paper in which, given the high levels of supply-side substitutability, the competitive assessment would be qualitatively similar.

3.18 The OFT will not factor supply side substitution into market definition unless it is reasonably likely to take place, and already has an impact by constraining the supplier of the product or group of products in question. What matters ultimately is that all competitive constraints from the supply side are properly taken into account in the analysis of market power. Whether a potential competitive constraint is labelled **supply side substitution** (and so part of market definition) or **potential entry** (and so not within the market) should not matter for the overall competitive assessment.[35] If there is any serious doubt about whether or not to account for possible supply side substitution when defining the market and calculating market shares, the market will be defined only on the basis of demand side substitutability, and the supply side constraint in question will be considered when analysing potential entry.[36]

NOTES

18 See Part 5 for a discussion of whether the current price is a reasonable proxy for the competitive price.

19 The customers most likely to switch are sometimes called 'marginal' customers. Where a relatively high proportion of

marginal customers purchase a product, a sustained 5 to 10 per cent price rise above competitive levels is less likely to be profitable.

20 Cm 1854, 1992.

21 From a customer's point of view, switching costs can be defined as the real or perceived costs that are incurred when changing supplier but which are not incurred by remaining with the current supplier.

22 *Aberdeen Journals Limited v Office of Fair Trading (No. 2)* [2003] CAT 11 at paragraph 128.

23 *Ibid*, at paragraph 175 *et seq.*

24 See Part 5 for a discussion of how time may affect market definition.

25 See paragraph 3.5 for example.

26 Although switching behaviour may be distorted if current prices are significantly different from competitive prices. See Part 5 for a discussion of market definition when prices are not competitive.

27 For example, customers purchasing at low prices must not be able to sell on sufficient quantities to customers paying higher prices to undermine price discrimination.

28 Derived demand describes the situation where the input purchaser's demand for the input is derived from the demand for the final product that the input is used to make.

29 However, from a supply side perspective peak and off peak travel may be in the same market. Supply side substitution is discussed below.

30 This may be a legal or technical constraint on price setting or may be a commercial constraint on the supplier.

31 eg speed of spin cycle for washing machines, or sharpness of picture definition for digital cameras.

32 It is worth noting that market definition may differ according to the focal product. In the example given, products A, B and C may form the relevant market when product B is the focal product, while products B, C and D may form the relevant market when product C is the focal product.

33 In this context, a sunk cost is a cost incurred on entering a market that is not recoverable on exiting that market. These could, for example, include investments in product placement, distribution and production technology.

34 The European Commission, in the course of a merger investigation, defined the market for the supply of paper for use in publishing based on supply side substitution in Case IV/M166 *Torras/Sarrio OJ* [1992] C58/00, [1992] 4 CMLR 341.

35 Although this distinction may be relevant when determining whether market share thresholds have been met. It will also affect an undertaking's 'relevant turnover' for the purpose of calculating any penalty.

36 Some competition authorities prefer to define markets solely on the demand side, leaving supply side issues to the analysis of new entry. Both approaches are valid and should produce the same conclusions on the question of market power, provided that supply side issues are examined at some point.

4. THE GEOGRAPHIC MARKET

[3.110]

4.1 Geographic markets are defined using the same process as that used to define product markets. The geographic market may be national (ie the United Kingdom), smaller than the United Kingdom (eg local or regional), wider than the United Kingdom (eg part of Europe including the United Kingdom), or even worldwide. This part outlines some practical issues which are particularly relevant to geographic market definition:

- demand side issues
- supply side issues, and
- imports.

THE DEMAND SIDE

4.2 As with the product market, the objective is to identify substitutes which are sufficiently close that they would prevent a hypothetical monopolist of the focal product in one area from profitably sustaining prices 5 to 10 per cent above competitive levels. The process starts by looking at a relatively narrow area – the **focal area**. This might be the area supplied by the parties to an agreement or the subject of a complaint about conduct or, if that area were relatively wide, past experience might suggest a narrower area that is more appropriate. The hypothetical monopolist test is applied to this area, and repeated over wider geographic areas as appropriate until the hypothetical monopolist would find it profitable to sustain prices 5 to 10 per cent above competitive levels in the area(s) in question (see Part 2 for further details of the test).

4.3 The principles applied in defining the geographic market are the same as those for the product market. For example, the analysis of price discrimination and chains of substitution would proceed in the same way as set out in Part 3 above. The evidence used to define geographic markets on the demand side will usually be similar to the information used to define the product market (see paragraph 3.7). In addition to that evidence, the value of a product in relation to costs of search and transport is often an important factor in defining geographic markets. The higher the relative value, the more likely customers are to travel further in search of cheaper supplies. The mobility of customers may also be a relevant factor.

4.4 For consumer products, geographic markets may often be quite narrow, eg where sufficient numbers of consumers are unlikely to switch to products sold in neighbouring towns or regions, let alone countries. For wholesaling or manufacturing markets, customers may be in a better position to switch between suppliers in different regions, providing transport costs are not too high.

THE SUPPLY SIDE

4.5 This entails looking at the potential for undertakings in other (eg neighbouring) territories to supply the focal area. When defining the geographic market, supply side substitution is analysed using the same conceptual approach set out for the product market. Therefore, the main evidence will usually mirror the information gathered on product market definition (see paragraph 3.16). Where the price of a product is low relative to its transport costs, this might indicate a relatively narrow geographic market.

IMPORTS

4.6 When considering whether the geographic market should be defined more widely than a national market, data on imports may be informative. Significant imports of the product may indicate that the market is wider than a national market. However, the presence of imports in a territory will not always mean that the market is international, for a number of reasons. First, imports may come only from international operations of domestic suppliers, in which case they may not act as an independent constraint on domestic firms. Second, in order to import on a larger scale, international suppliers may require substantial investments in establishing distribution networks or branding their products in the destination country. Third, there may be quotas which limit the volume of imports into the destination country. These factors may mean that suppliers of the relevant product located outside the national market would not provide a sufficient constraint on domestic suppliers to be included in the same relevant geographic market.

4.7 Conversely a lack of imports does not necessarily mean that the market cannot be international. The potential for imports may still be an important source of substitution should prices rise. For example, when the European Commission looked at a merger between bus manufacturers in Germany, it found that although imports were low at the time, there were no significant barriers to imports from the rest of the EC should prices in Germany rise.[37]

NOTES

[37] Case IV/M477 *Mercedes- Benz/Kassbohrer* OJ [1995] L211/1, [1995] 4 CMLR 573.

5. OTHER ISSUES

TEMPORAL MARKETS

[3.111]

5.1 A third possible dimension to market definition is time. Examples of how the timing of production and purchasing can affect markets include:

- peak and off peak services. This can be a factor in transport services or utilities such as electricity supply
- seasonal variations, such as summer versus winter months, and
- innovation/inter-generational products. Customers may defer expenditure on present products because they believe innovation will soon produce better products or because they own an earlier version of the product, which they consider to be a close substitute for the current generation.

5.2 A time dimension might be appropriate where:

- it is not possible for customers to substitute between time periods. For example, peak customers might not view peak and off peak train tickets as substitutes, and
- suppliers cannot substitute between time periods. For example, capacity to produce fruit may vary between time periods and it may not be possible to store fruit from one period to another.

5.3 To some extent, the time dimension is simply an extension of the product dimension: ie the product can be defined as the supply of train services at a certain time of day.

THE COMPETITIVE PRICE VERSUS THE CURRENT PRICE

5.4 Throughout this guideline, the test has been couched in terms of a hypothetical monopolist profitably sustaining prices above **competitive levels**. However, where an undertaking has market power, it may operate in a market where the current price is substantially different from the competitive price.

5.5 For example, an undertaking with market power may well have already raised prices above competitive levels to its profit maximising level. If so, the undertaking would not profitably sustain prices above **current** levels. If it tried to sustain higher prices, consumers would switch to purchasing other products. However, it would be wrong to argue that these products prevented the undertaking from exercising market power and so it would usually be inappropriate to include them in the relevant market. This problem is sometimes known as the **cellophane fallacy** after a US case involving cellophane products.[38]

5.6 The possibility that market conditions are distorted by the presence of market power (or other factors) will be accounted for when all the evidence on market definition is weighed in the round. For example, where prices are likely to differ substantially from their competitive levels, caution must be exercised when dealing with the evidence on switching patterns as such evidence may not be a reliable guide to what would occur in normal competitive conditions.[39]

PREVIOUS CASES

5.7 In many cases a market may have already been investigated and defined by the OFT or by another competition authority. Sometimes earlier definitions can be informative when considering the appropriate product or area to use on commencing the hypothetical monopolist test. However, although previous cases can provide useful information, the market definition used may not always be the appropriate one for future cases. First, competitive conditions may change over time. In particular, innovation may make substitution between products easier or more difficult, and so change the market definition. Therefore, the relevant market concerned must be identified according to the particular facts of the case in hand.[40]

5.8 Second, a previous product market definition that concerned an area outside the United Kingdom would not necessarily apply to an area in the United Kingdom if the purchasing behaviour of customers differed significantly between those two areas.

5.9 Third, behaviour by an undertaking with market power can affect market definition. For example, suppose an earlier investigation had defined a market to be relatively wide because of the scope for both demand side and supply side substitution. A dominant undertaking in that market might raise customer switching costs or foreclose some possibilities for supply side substitution. If so, this might affect the appropriate definition of the relevant market.

DIFFERENTIATED PRODUCTS

5.10 When markets contain differentiated products (ie products that are differentiated by features such as brand, location or quality) there may not be a clear cut off point delineating the boundary of the market. This can mean that there is no clear distinction between products that are 'in' the market and those that lie outside it. Therefore, even if two products do not lie within the same market for the purposes of one investigation, this does not rule out the possibility that they will be in the same relevant market in another[41].

MARKETS WITH PORTFOLIOS OF PRODUCTS

5.11 In some cases the relevant product market may consist of 'bundles' of what are otherwise distinct products. For example, if a relevant product market was 'one stop grocery shopping', the market may include bundles of groceries that normally make up a weekly shop. Whether this is appropriate depends on the investigation. For example, if the investigation concerned the supply of a particular grocery item to a retailer, it would usually be appropriate to consider that item as a distinct product as opposed to bundled together with other products. The perspective of customers will be important in assessing the appropriate frame of reference.

WHOLESALE PRODUCTS

5.12 When considering the substitutes of a wholesale product, it may be necessary to consider substitution possibilities at the downstream level. For example, suppose a supplier produces a wholesale product A which is a necessary input for supply of a retail product B. Suppose also that a vertically integrated supplier that does not supply a substitute wholesale product supplies a product C which is a substitute for B at the retail level. The ability of customers to substitute to product C from product B at the retail level may constrain the ability to raise the price of the wholesale product A.

NOTES

38 *US v El Du Pont de Nemours & Co* [1956] 351 US 377.

39 Evidence on market definition may be distorted if prices are sustained below competitive levels, as, for example, may occur in an investigation of predatory pricing. See *Aberdeen Journals (No 2)* at paragraph 262.

40 *Aberdeen Journals Limited v Director General of Fair Trading (No 1)* [2002] CAT 4 at paragraph 139.

41 For example, recall the discussion of chains of substitution at paragraph 3.11 where products A to E were all substitutes for each other (to varying degrees) and where a hypothetical monopolist of three products next to each other in the chain could profitably sustain supra competitive prices. In this case, if the focal product is B alone, it is possible to define products A, B and C to be the relevant market. However, when investigating the conduct of an undertaking that supplies both products B and E, the appropriate frame of reference for the competitive assessment may include products A to E. (Of course, the analysis of competitive effects would account for the fact that customers do not view all products to be equally good substitutes.)

6. MARKET DEFINITION FOR AFTER MARKETS

[3.112]

6.1 An after market is a market for a **secondary product**, that is, a product which is purchased only as a result of buying a **primary product**. For example, a customer would purchase a printer cartridge (a secondary product) only for use with a printer (the primary product). Another example is replacement heads for razors (the secondary product) and razors (the primary product). The primary product and the secondary product are **complementary**.[42]

6.2 Three possible types of market definition are often put forward as regards after markets:

- a **system** market: a unified market for the primary product and the secondary product (eg a market for all razors **and** replacement heads)
- **multiple markets**: a market for primary products and separate markets for the secondary product(s) associated with each primary product (eg one market for all razors, individual markets for each type of replacement head), and
- **dual markets**: a market for the primary product and a separate market for the secondary product (eg one market for all razors, a separate market for all replacement heads).

6.3 The appropriate definition depends on the facts of the case. A system market may be appropriate either where customers engage in **whole life costing** (see paragraphs 6.5 to 6.6 below) or where reputation effects mean that setting a supra competitive price for the secondary product would significantly harm a supplier's profits on future sales of its primary product.

6.4 Where neither of the conditions set out in paragraph 6.3 applies, a multiple markets or a dual markets definition may be appropriate. The former is likely where, having purchased a primary product, customers are locked in to using only a restricted number of secondary products that are compatible with the primary product. A dual markets definition is appropriate where secondary products are compatible with all primary products (and perceived to be so by customers).

WHOLE LIFE COSTING

6.5 Whole life costing occurs where customers correctly anticipate the cost of future necessary purchases of the secondary market product when buying the primary product. For example, if a razor (with a 'life' of five replacement heads) costs £10, and each replacement head costs £2, the whole life cost of the razor would be £20. This depends on customers being able to form reasonable expectations on future prices of the secondary product when purchasing the primary product.

6.6 Whole life costing means that customers view the purchase of the primary and secondary product as a **system**, or a **unified deal**. Where whole life costing would make it unprofitable for a hypothetical monopolist to raise the price of the secondary market product above the competitive level it may be appropriate to adopt a system market definition. In this context it is appropriate to consider whether:

- it is relatively easy to obtain and comprehend information on the secondary market product, and relatively easy to predict how much of the secondary market product is likely to be required over the life time of the primary product, so that customers are **able** to whole life cost
- the price of (or likely expenditure on) the secondary product is a relatively high proportion of the primary product's price, so that customers are **likely** to whole life cost, and
- **sufficient** customers are able and likely to whole life cost so that it would be unprofitable for a supplier to set a supra competitive secondary market product price due to the number of customers that would adapt their purchasing behaviour in the primary market (within a reasonable period of time).[43]

REPUTATION

6.7 A supplier might not wish to increase prices of its secondary product for existing customers if that would earn it a reputation for exploitation and significantly reduce its ability to attract new or repeat customers to its primary product. Reputation is more likely to be important where suppliers have the prospect of relatively large numbers of new or repeat customers and where undertakings cannot price discriminate between new or repeat customers and other customers.

NOTES

42 Products A and B are complementary products if the demand for product B goes up when the price of product A goes down by a relatively small amount, other things being equal.

43 This requires that enough, but not necessarily all, customers whole life cost and that it is not possible to price discriminate between those who do and those who do not.

TRADE ASSOCIATIONS, PROFESSIONS AND SELF-REGULATING BODIES (OFT 408, DECEMBER 2004)

[3.113]

NOTES

As to the construction of this document (following the abolition of the OFT and Competition Commission), see further the note "The Competition and Markets Authority (references to the OFT and Competition Commission etc)" in the introductory notes to Part 3 preceding **[3.1]**.

CONTENTS

1. INTRODUCTION

[3.114]

1.1 Article 81 of the EC Treaty[1] (Article 81) and section 2 (the Chapter I prohibition) of the Competition Act 1998 (the Act) prohibit agreements[2] between undertakings, decisions by associations of undertakings or concerted practices which have as their object or effect the prevention, restriction or distortion of competition. Article 82 of the EC Treaty (Article 82) and section 18 of the Act (the Chapter II prohibition) prohibit conduct by one or more undertakings which amounts to the abuse of a dominant position. Such activities within the common market which may affect trade between Member States will fall within Article 81 and/or Article 82; activities which may affect trade in the United Kingdom (or part of it) will fall within the Chapter I prohibition and/or the Chapter II prohibition.

Part 3 CMA and other Guidelines

Further details of the prohibitions contained in the Act and the EC Treaty are available in the competition law guidelines *Agreements and concerted practices* (OFT 401) and *Abuse of dominant position* (OFT 402).

1.2 EC Regulation 1/2003 (the Modernisation Regulation)[3] requires designated national competition authorities of the Member States (NCAs) and the courts of the Member States to apply and enforce Articles 81 and 82 as well as national competition law when national competition law is applied to agreements which may affect trade between Member States or to abuse prohibited by Article 82.

1.3 This guideline explains how the OFT will apply Article 81 and the Chapter I prohibition when assessing the activities of trade associations, professions and self-regulating bodies. It should be read in conjunction with the competition law guideline *Agreements and concerted practices* (OFT 401).

1.4 This guideline refers to trade associations, professions and other self-regulating bodies but there are no definitions of these terms in Article 81 or the Act and, in practice, the boundaries between the three may be indistinct. The term used in both Article 81 and the Chapter I prohibition is an **association of undertakings**. Any body formed to represent the interests of its members in commercial matters may be an association of undertakings. An association of undertakings is deemed to represent the interests of those undertakings which have chosen to join, and it is therefore irrelevant how the association is organised. It is not necessary for it to have any formal constitution for its activities to fall within the scope of Article 81 and/or the Chapter I prohibition. An association of undertakings will fall within Article 81 and/or the Chapter I prohibition if its decisions, rules, recommendations or other activities lead to an appreciable restriction of competition, regardless of the exact form that the association takes.[4]

1.5 Part 2 of this guideline focuses on the application of Article 81 and the Chapter I prohibition to the decisions of associations of undertakings although, as explained above, the prohibition applies equally to agreements between undertakings. The definition of 'undertaking' is wide and may include an association of undertakings (see the competition law guideline *Agreement and concerted practices* (OFT 401)). The relationship of an association of undertakings with third parties is likely to be considered an agreement between undertakings for the purposes of Article 81 and the Chapter I prohibition. The internal relationship between the undertakings which form the association is likely to be considered as a decision of that association, although this will depend upon the facts of the case. Other activities of an association of undertakings may also fall within Article 81 and the Chapter I prohibition, either as a decision or because they constitute agreements (or both), and this too will depend upon the circumstances of the case. (See also paragraph 2.1 below.)

1.6 Examples of the decisions, rules, recommendations or other activities of associations of undertakings that may prevent, restrict or distort competition and therefore fall within the scope of Article 81 and/or the Chapter I prohibition are described in Part 3 of this guideline.

1.7 Decisions which fall within Article 81 and/or the Chapter I prohibition but which satisfy certain specified conditions are not prohibited, no prior decision to that effect being required. The conditions which need to be satisfied as part of the legal exception regime as well as the kinds of activities of associations of undertakings which might meet these conditions are explained in Part 4. The specific relevance of the application of Article 81 and/or the Chapter I prohibition to associations of undertakings and the possible exclusion from the application of the Chapter I prohibition that is available to certain self-regulating bodies are described in Parts 5, 6 and 7 of this guideline.

1.8 Article 82 and/or the Chapter II prohibition may also apply to the conduct of trade associations, professions and self-regulating bodies and/or their members. Article 82 and the Chapter II prohibition apply to 'conduct on the part of **one or more undertakings** which amounts to the abuse of a dominant position'; therefore such organisations themselves may constitute undertakings, or their members may comprise 'one or more undertakings' the conduct of which may fall within the scope of *Article 82 and the Chapter II prohibition*. These provisions are not covered in detail in this guideline and further reference should be made to the competition law guideline *Abuse of a dominant position* (OFT 402).

1.9 The involvement of an association of undertakings in an infringement of Article 81, Article 82 and/or the prohibitions contained in the Act may result in financial penalties being imposed on the association itself, its members, or both. Further details on the imposition on and enforcement of penalties against trade associations, professions and other self-regulating bodies are given in Part 8 of this guideline. More general information on penalties is available in the competition law guideline *Enforcement* (OFT 407) and in the *OFT's guidance as to the appropriate amount of a penalty* (OFT 423).

1.10 Section 60 of the Act sets out principles for ensuring that the United Kingdom authorities deal with questions arising in relation to the application of the Chapter I and Chapter II prohibitions in such a way as to ensure consistency with the treatment of corresponding questions arising in Community law in so far as this is possible, having regard to any relevant differences between any of the provisions concerned. This is considered in more detail in the competition law guideline *Modernisation* (OFT 442).

NOTES

1 The Treaty establishing the European Community.

2 References in this guideline to **agreement(s)** should, unless otherwise stated or the context demands it, be taken to include decisions by associations of undertakings and concerted practices.

3 Council Regulation (EC) No 1/2003 of 16 December 2002 on the implementation of the rules on competition laid down in Articles 81 and 82 of the EC Treaty (OJ L1, 4.1.03, p 1).

4 See Case 209/78 *Heintz van Landewyck* [1980] ECR 3125; Joined Cases 96/82 etc *NAVEWA v Commission* [1983] ECR 3369; Case 123/83 *BNIC v Clair* [1985] ECR 391.

2. APPLICATION OF ARTICLE 81 AND THE CHAPTER I PROHIBITION TO ASSOCIATIONS OF UNDERTAKINGS

DECISIONS BY ASSOCIATIONS OF UNDERTAKINGS AND AGREEMENTS BETWEEN UNDERTAKINGS

[3.115]
2.1 Article 81 and the Chapter I prohibition cover **decisions by associations of undertakings** in addition to **agreements between undertakings** and **concerted practices**. It will be a matter of fact in each case if an agreement between undertakings which is carried out within the structure of an association (for example, an agreement to abide by the rules of the association) is considered to be a 'decision' or an 'agreement' for the purposes of Article 81 or the Chapter I prohibition (see also paragraph 1.5 above). This part explains the nature of decisions for the purposes of Article 81 and the Chapter I prohibition; elsewhere the guideline deals with the application of Article 81 and the Chapter I prohibition to associations of undertakings by virtue of their activities more generally.

DECISIONS

2.2 Decision has a wide meaning. It may include, for example, the constitution or rules of an association of undertakings or its recommendations or other activities.[5] In the day to day conduct of the business of an association, resolutions of the management committee or of the full membership in general meeting, binding decisions of the management or executive committee of the association, or rulings of its chief executive, the effect of which are to limit the commercial freedom of action of the members in some respect, will all be **decisions** of the association. The key consideration is whether the effect of the decision, whatever form it takes, is to limit the freedom of action of the members in some commercial matter.

RULES

2.3 The rules of an association may constitute a decision of the association, as may any co-ordination of the members' conduct in accordance with its constitution. Any rule which has an appreciable effect on competition within the common market and which may affect trade between Member States will fall within Article 81. A rule which has an appreciable effect on competition within the United Kingdom and which may affect trade in the United Kingdom will fall within the Chapter I prohibition. It may be possible for a rule to fall within both Article 81 and the Chapter I prohibition.

RECOMMENDATIONS

2.4 A recommendation of an association of undertakings may also be a decision, as may an oral exhortation which it is intended that members should follow. This will be the case even if the recommendation is not binding on the members or has not been fully complied with.[6] Any recommendation which has an appreciable effect on competition within the common market and which may affect trade between Member States will fall within Article 81. A recommendation which has an appreciable effect on competition within the United Kingdom and which may affect trade in the United Kingdom will fall within the Chapter I prohibition. It may be possible for a recommendation to fall within both Article 81 and the Chapter I prohibition.

OTHER ACTIVITIES

2.5 Other activities which are organised by or through associations of undertakings may fall within Article 81 if they have an appreciable effect on competition within the common market and may affect trade between Member States and/or they may fall within the Chapter I prohibition if they have an appreciable effect on competition within the United Kingdom and may affect trade in the United Kingdom. As noted in paragraph 2.1 above, these other activities may take the form of decisions of associations of undertakings or agreements between the undertakings which form part of the association. For example, they would cover the exchange of specific price information as discussed in Part 3 below.

NOTES

5 See *National Sulphuric Acid Association Ltd, Re* OJ L260, 3.10.80, p 24; [1980] 3 CMLR 429.

6 See Case C-96/82 *IAZ International Belgium NV v Commission* [1983] ECR 3369, [1984] 3 CMLR 276.

3. SCOPE OF ARTICLE 81 AND THE CHAPTER I PROHIBITION

[3.116]
3.1 The fact that members of an association of undertakings are acting through the association does not affect the way in which Article 81 and/or the Chapter I prohibition apply to their decisions, rules, recommendations or other activities; their position is no better and no worse than if they were acting in the same manner outside the forum of such an association. In each case Article 81 and/or the Chapter I prohibition will only apply if the relevant activity has an appreciable effect on competition in the relevant market. Any such activity which appreciably restricts competition under Article 81(1) and/or the Chapter I prohibition may however still be valid and enforceable where it satisfies the conditions in Article 81(3) and section 9(1) of the Act respectively. A number of the examples below may satisfy these conditions and therefore will not be prohibited. (Further details on the legal exception regime are provided in Part 4 below.)

3.2 The remainder of this part sets out examples of the decisions, rules, recommendations or other activities of associations of undertakings that have the potential to appreciably prevent, restrict or distort competition for the purposes of Article 81(1) and/or the Chapter I prohibition. This is a non-exhaustive list; it includes types of activities which would generally fall within Article 81(1) and/or the Chapter I prohibition, although the particular circumstances of a case may mean that an activity of one of these types does not do so. Equally, there will clearly be instances of activities not listed in the types shown below which are prohibited. More general examples of anticompetitive behaviour which may fall within Article 81(1) and/or the Chapter I prohibition can be found in the competition law guideline *Agreements and concerted practices* (OFT 401). In assessing specific agreements, the OFT will also have regard to the European Commission's *Guidelines on the applicability of Article 81 of the EC Treaty to horizontal cooperation agreements.*[7]

PRICING

3.3 The OFT believes that any decision including any recommendation as to prices and charges, including discounts and allowances, is likely to have an appreciable effect on competition.

INFORMATION SHARING

General

3.4 As a general principle, the more informed customers are, the more effective competition is likely to be and so making information publicly available to customers does not usually harm competition.

3.5 In the normal course of business, undertakings exchange information on a variety of matters legitimately and with no risk to the competitive process. Indeed, competition may be enhanced by the sharing of information, for example, on new technologies or market opportunities. There are therefore circumstances where there is no objection to the exchange of information, even between competitors, and whether or not under the aegis of a trade association. For example, the collection and publication of statistics are legitimate functions of associations of undertakings.

3.6 The exchange of information may, however, have an adverse effect on competition where it serves to reduce or remove uncertainties inherent in the process of competition. The fact that the information could have been obtained from other sources is not necessarily relevant. Whether or not the information exchange has an appreciable effect on competition will depend on the circumstances of each individual case: the market characteristics, the type of information and the way in which it is exchanged. As a general principle, the OFT will consider that there is more likely to be an appreciable effect on competition the smaller the number of undertakings operating in the market, the more frequent the exchange and the more sensitive, detailed and confidential the nature of the information which is exchanged. There is also more likely to be an appreciable effect on competition where the exchange of information is limited to certain participating undertakings to the exclusion of their competitors and consumers.[8]

3.7 The general approach of the OFT to information exchange, based on the relevant principles established by the European Court[9] as appropriate, is set out below.

Exchange of price information

3.8 The exchange of information on prices may lead to price co-ordination and therefore diminish competition which would otherwise be present between the undertakings. This will be the case whether the information exchanged relates directly to the prices charged or to the elements of a pricing policy, for example discounts, costs, terms of trade and rates and dates of change.

3.9 The more recent or current the information exchanged, the more likely that exchange will have an appreciable effect on competition. Therefore, the circulation of purely historical information or the collation of price trends is unlikely to have an appreciable effect on competition, particularly if, for example, the exchange forms part of a scheme of inter-business comparison which is intended to spread best industrial practice, or if the information is collected, aggregated and disseminated by an independent body.

3.10 The regular and systematic exchange of specific information on prices between competitors is, however, likely to reduce the uncertainties inherent in the competitive process and to facilitate the coordination of market conduct, whether the exchange is organised by the members themselves or, as is often the case, by or through an association of undertakings. While the compilation of general information, for example general price trends for an industry, may not have an appreciable effect on competition, it must not cover (or enable undertakings to divine) confidential information relating to individual undertakings.[10]

Exchange of non-price information

3.11 The exchange of information on matters other than price may have an appreciable effect on competition depending on the type of information exchanged and the market to which it relates. The exchange of historical statistical data, market research, and general industry studies for example are unlikely to have an appreciable effect on competition, since exchange of such information is unlikely to inhibit individual undertakings' commercial and competitive independence.

3.12 In general, the exchange of information on output and sales should not affect competition provided that it is sufficiently historic and aggregated and cannot influence future competitive market behaviour. There may however be an appreciable effect on competition if it is possible to disaggregate the information and identify the participants. This may also be the case if the exchange relates to recent or current information, or information which relates to future plans.

3.13 As an example of this, in *United Kingdom Agricultural Tractor Registration Exchange*, the exchange of information by members of the trade association on sales and market shares, broken down by territory, product line and time period, was found to have infringed Article 81(1).[11] Significant to this decision was the detail of the information exchanged and the fact that the market was concentrated, with four undertakings accounting for 80 per cent of total sales. It was held that the information exchanged created a degree of transparency in such an oligopolistic market which could destroy any remaining competition and enhance entry barriers by identifying any newcomers to the market thus facilitating a strategic response by the established undertakings.

ADVERTISING

3.14 Restrictions on advertising, whether relating to the amount, nature or form of advertising, have the potential to restrict competition. Whether the effect is appreciable depends on the purpose and nature of the restriction, and on the market in which it is to apply. Rules or decisions of associations of undertakings aimed at curbing misleading advertising, or at ensuring that advertising is legal, truthful and decent are unlikely to have an appreciable effect on competition, but restrictions which more generally prevent members from using advertising are another matter. Rules or decisions of associations of undertakings prohibiting members from soliciting for business, from competing with other members, or from advertising prices, or prices below a minimum or recommended level, are all likely to have an appreciable effect on competition.

JOINT PURCHASING/SELLING

3.15 An agreement between purchasers to fix (directly or indirectly) the price that they are prepared to pay, or to purchase only through agreed arrangements, limits competition between them. An example of one type of agreement which might be made between purchasers is an agreement as to those with whom they will deal. Any joint activity, for example joint purchasing, joint selling or joint research, coordinated through an association of undertakings will be subject to Article 81 and/or the Chapter I prohibition to the same extent as if it were done outside the medium of an association of undertakings, for example, by the undertakings individually in an agreement.

CODES OF CONDUCT

3.16 A code of conduct may seek to introduce best practice into a particular sector and may include provisions, for example, for dealing with consumer complaints and a redress procedure. A code is unlikely to be successful in promoting consumer protection unless it is widely adopted and effectively enforced, but at the same time it may limit the way participants can compete. If, however, the structure of the market is competitive and the code does not deal with prices or involve any element of market sharing or customer sharing, the effects on competition are less likely to be appreciable. For further information on the OFT's consumer codes scheme, please visit the OFT's website or call the Codes Team on 020 7211 8815. It should be kept in mind that the process of approval of a code by the OFT's Codes Team and subsequent compliance with a code of conduct do not mean that an undertaking complies with the competition rules contained in Chapter I, Chapter II, Article 81 or Article 82.

TECHNICAL STANDARDS

3.17 Associations of undertakings may play a role in the negotiation and promulgation of technical standards in an industry. This will limit the members in the make-up of the products or services that they can offer and there is therefore a restriction of competition. If entry barriers were to be significantly raised as a result of adoption of the standard, the effects on competition could be appreciable.

STANDARD TERMS AND CONDITIONS

3.18 Associations of undertakings may be involved in the formulation of standard terms and conditions to be applied by members. This may be no more than a useful simplification of what otherwise might be complex and, to the customer, potentially confusing conditions. If an association of undertakings imposes on its members an obligation to use common terms and conditions of sale or purchase, this will inevitably restrict competition to some degree. Such standard conditions are less likely to have an appreciable effect on competition where members remain free to adopt different conditions if they so wish. Standard conditions may also have an appreciable effect on competition if a large proportion of members adopt those standard conditions leaving customers little choice in practice.

TERMS OF MEMBERSHIP

3.19 Rules of admission as a member of an association of undertakings should be transparent, proportionate, non-discriminatory and based on objective standards. Those that are not may appreciably restrict competition for the purposes of Article 81(1) and/or the Chapter I prohibition. Terms of membership will have an appreciable effect on competition where the effect of exclusion from membership is to put the undertaking(s) concerned at a competitive disadvantage. Similarly, procedures for expelling members of an association may have an appreciable effect on competition, particularly where they are not based on reasonable and objective standards or where there is no proper appeals procedure in the event of refusal of membership or expulsion.

CERTIFICATION

3.20 An association of undertakings may certify or award quality labels to its members to demonstrate that they have met minimum industry standards. While such a scheme has benefits for consumers in the form of quality assurances, it may lead to a restriction of competition. A scheme is less likely to have an appreciable effect on competition for the purposes of Article 81(1) and/or the Chapter I prohibition where certification is available to all manufacturers that meet objective and reasonable quality requirements. Where manufacturers must accept additional obligations governing the products which they can buy or sell, or restrictions as to pricing or marketing, the scheme is likely to have an appreciable effect on competition for the purposes of Article 81(1) and/or the Chapter I prohibition.

NOTES

7 OJ C3, 6.1.01, p 2.

8 Case T-141/94 *Thyssen Stahl AG v Commission* [1999] ECR II-347, upheld on appeal, Case C-194/99P.

9 See for example, *United Kingdom Agricultural Tractor Registration Exchange* OJ L68, 17.02.92, p 19, [1993] 4 CMLR 358, upheld on appeal, Case T34/92; Case C-8/95 *New Holland Ford Limited v Commission* [1998] 5 CMLR 311 and Case T-35/92 *John Deere v Commission* [1994] II ECR 957.

10 See *Bundesverband Deutscher Stahlhandel eV* OJ L62, 7.03.80, p 34; [1980] 3 CMLR 193.

11 *United Kingdom Agricultural Tractor Registration Exchange* OJ L68, 17.02.92, p 19, [1993] 4 CMLR 358, upheld on appeal, Case T34/92.

4. THE LEGAL EXCEPTION REGIME

GENERAL

[3.117]

4.1 The Modernisation Regulation introduces a legal exception regime. This means that an agreement that falls within Article 81(1) but which satisfies the conditions set out in Article 81(3) shall not be prohibited, no prior decision to that effect being required. Such an agreement is valid and enforceable from the moment that the conditions in Article 81(3) are satisfied and for as long as that remains the case. The Modernisation Regulation provides that the burden of proof rests on the undertaking(s) claiming the benefit of Article 81(3).

4.2 The Act has been amended to mirror this approach so that an agreement that falls within the Chapter I prohibition but which satisfies the conditions set out in section 9(1) of the Act shall not be prohibited, no prior decision to that effect being required. Such an agreement is valid and enforceable from the moment that the conditions in section 9(1) are satisfied and for as long as that remains the case. The Act provides that the burden of proof rests on the undertaking(s) claiming the benefit of section 9(1) of the Act.

The conditions in Article 81(3) and section 9(1)

4.3 *Article 81(3) and section 9(1) set out four conditions which must all be met. Article 81(3) provides that the prohibition in Article 81(1) is inapplicable in respect of any agreement:*

> *'which contributes to improving the production or distribution of goods or to promoting technical or economic progress, while allowing consumers a fair share of the resulting benefit, and which does not:*
>
> *(a) impose on the undertakings concerned restrictions which are not indispensable to the attainment of these objectives;*
>
> *(b) afford such undertakings the possibility of eliminating competition in respect of a substantial part of the products in question.'*

4.4 The wording of section 9(1) is similar to that of Article 81(3) except that in the first condition in section 9(1) the phrase **of goods** is not included. The omission of these words is intended to make clear (consistent with the practice of the European Commission in relation to Article 81(3)) that the conditions in section 9(1) apply also to agreements which contribute to improvements in relation to services.

4.5 The European Commission has issued a Notice entitled *Guidelines on the Application of Article 81(3) of the Treaty*[12] to assist companies and their advisers in determining whether an agreement satisfies the conditions in Article 81(3). The OFT will have regard to this Notice in considering the application of Article 81(3) and section 9(1) of the Act.

4.6 The following paragraphs provide examples of the kinds of activities of associations of undertakings which, where they have an appreciable effect, might meet the above conditions and so be legally enforceable without requiring any prior approval. Each activity will be judged on the facts of each case against the criteria set out in paragraph 4.3 above.

STANDARD TERMS AND CONDITIONS

4.7 Given the potential benefit to consumers from clearly expressed standard terms and conditions, such terms and conditions may fall within the conditions in Article 81(3) and/or in section 9(1) and result in the standard terms not being prohibited, notwithstanding that competition is inevitably restricted to some degree. The restrictions on competition are, however, likely to outweigh the benefits to consumers – and thus not meet the conditions in Article 81(3) and/or section 9(1) – if the standardisation covers terms that are likely to be relevant to a customer in choosing between competing suppliers, for example, if they indirectly affect the prices to be charged.

TECHNICAL STANDARDS

4.8 Technical standards can help to promote safety and protect consumers. The benefits would have to be assessed against any effects on competition in deciding whether the conditions in Article 81(3) and/or section 9(1) of the Act are satisfied.

NOTES

[12] OJ C101, 27.4.04, p 81.

5. TRADE ASSOCIATIONS

[3.118]

5.1 Trade associations are the most common form of association of undertakings. There are trade associations in almost every sector of the United Kingdom economy. Further, many United Kingdom companies are members of international trade associations. The functions of such associations in furthering the trade interests of their members are diverse but they can be broadly categorised as:

- representing to Government, the European Commission and other public bodies the interests of members on legislation, regulations, taxation and policy matters likely to affect them
- promoting and protecting the interests of members in the media
- collecting and disseminating statistics and market information, and information about legislation and Government policy
- promulgating standards, codes of practice or standard terms and conditions of sale
- providing a range of services of an advisory or consultancy nature on, for example, legal, accounting, training or environmental matters, and
- providing advice of a more commercial nature.

5.2 The functions of trade associations are clearly useful to members – especially, perhaps, to smaller firms – and they may also be beneficial in increasing the efficiency of the market system as a whole. Activities of trade associations which have no appreciable effect on competition will be of no concern. A trade association may, however, provide directly or indirectly the vehicle for anti-competitive, or even collusive, activity, and any decision, rule or recommendation of a trade association or agreement between its members which has an appreciable effect on competition may fall within Article 81 and/or the Chapter I prohibition. Where the activities of a trade association fall within Article 81 but satisfy the conditions in Article 81(3), or fall within the Chapter I prohibition but satisfy the conditions in section 9(1) of the Act, they will not be prohibited, no prior decision to that effect being required.

5.3 The nature of the membership of a trade association is likely to be relevant in assessing whether an activity has an appreciable effect. An association will usually seek to make its membership as comprehensive as possible to maximise its influence on behalf of its members. A wide membership will also increase the effectiveness of any code of practice on members' conduct, devised and implemented by a trade association in its self-regulatory role. However, the wider the membership among those engaged in a market within the United Kingdom, the greater the risk that any anti-competitive behaviour carried on by the association will have an appreciable effect. This will be of greater significance where members of a trade association are likely to be actual or potential competitors. The appreciable effect test is looked at in more detail in the competition law guideline *Agreements and concerted practices* (OFT 401).

6. PROFESSIONS

[3.119]

6.1 A professional body may lay down educational and experience qualifications for membership, keep a register of members, promulgate standards of conduct to be maintained by the members, and enforce the standards through a complaints and disciplinary procedure. A professional body represents its members' interests in dealing with Government and other public bodies and the media. Organisationally, the functions of representation and of registration and the establishment and enforcement of standards may be separated, as, for example, in the medical profession, between the British Medical Association and the General Medical Council. Increasingly, professional bodies have involved themselves in wider matters of professional practice such as professional indemnity insurance and relationships with other professions.

6.2 A professional body is capable of being an **association of undertakings** within the meaning of Article 81(1) and the Chapter I prohibition. As such, the rules and decisions of professional bodies are subject to the application of Article 81 and the Chapter I prohibition. The legal framework within which such decisions are taken, for example, whether or not the professional body is set up by and operates under statute or charter is irrelevant to the question of the applicability of Article 81 or the Chapter I prohibition to its decisions. However, in assessing their rules and decisions, professional bodies should be aware that not every agreement between undertakings or every decision of an association of undertakings which restricts competition necessarily infringes Article 81 or the Chapter I prohibition.[13]

6.3 The OFT has conducted a detailed study on competition within the professions. The report that resulted from this study was published in March 2001[14] and identified several restrictions on competition within the provision of professional services in England and Wales. The report focused on three professions — law, accountancy and architecture — and highlighted restrictions, whether arising from law, professional rules or other sources, which continued to constrain freedom to compete in those professions. The OFT noted in the report its intention that the lessons of the report would inform work across the whole range of professions and throughout the United Kingdom.

6.4 A number of restrictions were found to originate in professional rules. These include restrictions on advertising (including comparative advertising), restrictions on forms of service provision (such as rules against partnership), and the issuing by professional bodies of recommendations on fees. The professional bodies concerned were called upon to take prompt action to remove the unjustified restrictions. In April 2002 the OFT issued a progress statement indicating the progress that had been made in addressing the restrictions identified and indicating areas of continuing concern.[15]

6.5 The concerns identified in the OFT's report are not limited to the three professions that were reviewed. They may arise across the whole range of professions. The OFT encourages all professions to take account of the conclusions in the report in assessing whether their rules and practices may fall within Article 81 and/or the Chapter I prohibition.

6.6 The European Commission has also identified concerns with restrictions originating in certain professional rules in its *Report on Competition in Professional Services.*[16]

6.7 The Commission's report recommends[17] that in assessing whether any of their rules and decisions infringe Article 81, professional bodies should apply a proportionality test, ie. they should consider whether existing restrictions pursue a clearly articulated and legitimate public interest objective, whether they are necessary to achieve that objective and whether there are no less restrictive means to achieve this.

NOTES

13 In Case C-309/99 *Wouters* [2002] ECR I-1577, the European Court of Justice found that there was no infringement of Article 81 because the professional regulation in question, despite its inherent restrictive effects could be reasonably considered to be necessary for the proper practice of the legal profession as it was organised in the Member State concerned.

14 *Competition in professions* (OFT328).

15 *Competition in professions* (OFT328).

16 COM (2004) 83 final, 9 February 2004, paragraphs 37 to 47, available at: europa.eu.int/comm/competition/liberal_professions/final_communication_en.pdf. Note also the European Commission's decision in relation to the Belgian architects' fee system, see European Commission's press release at: europa.eu.int/rapid/pressReleasesAction.do?reference=IP/04/800&format=HTML&aged=0&language=EN&guiLanguage=en.

17 COM (2004) 83 Final at paragraphs 93 and 94.

7. SELF-REGULATING BODIES

[3.120]

7.1 There are self-regulating bodies that fall outside the field of the professions. An example is the Committee on Advertising Practice which devises and enforces the British Codes of Advertising and Sales Promotion and the members of which include organisations representing the advertising and sales promotion industries and most media businesses. Self-regulating bodies may have statutory backing, such as those concerned with investment business set up under the Financial Services and Markets Act 2000. The essence of any system of self-regulation is that the conduct of the members of a profession, trade or industry is subject to a degree of monitoring and control by its representative body, or an organisation set up by that body or its members, to ensure that users or consumers are protected from unethical or otherwise unacceptable behaviour.

7.2 Self-regulating bodies are associations of undertakings and Article 81 and the Chapter I prohibition apply to their rules and decisions in exactly the same way as to those of any other association of undertakings. The discussion as to the scope of Article 81(1) and the Chapter I prohibition above applies equally to self-regulating bodies. Article 81(1) and/or the Chapter I prohibition apply to self-regulating bodies only where their decisions or rules have an appreciable effect on competition and, where they have such an effect, they will not be prohibited if they meet the conditions contained in Article 81(3) and/or section 9(1) of the Act.

7.3 The agreements or conduct of some self-regulating bodies, notably those operating under the Financial Services and Markets Act 2000, are excluded from the Chapter I prohibition and Chapter II prohibition. In these cases, competition scrutiny of the self-regulating body's rules is already provided for under its own specific legislation.

8. CONSEQUENCES OF INFRINGEMENT

VOIDNESS

[3.121]

8.1 Any agreement which has an appreciable effect on competition for the purposes of Article 81 and/or the Chapter I prohibition is void unless it meets the conditions contained in (respectively) Article 81(3) and/or section 9(1) of the Act.

FINANCIAL PENALTIES

8.2 Section 36 of the Act provides that the OFT may impose a financial penalty on an undertaking which has intentionally or negligently committed an infringement of Article 81 and/or the Chapter I prohibition. The amount of the penalty imposed may be up to 10 per cent of the worldwide turnover of the undertaking. See *OFT's Guidance as to the appropriate amount of a penalty* (OFT 423) for further details.

8.3 The involvement of an association of undertakings in an infringement of Article 81 and/or the Chapter I prohibition may result in financial penalties being imposed on the association itself, its members or both.

8.4 Where the infringement of an association of undertakings relates to the activities of its members, the penalty shall not exceed 10 per cent of the sum of the worldwide turnover of each member active on the market affected by the infringement.

8.5 If the penalty is not paid within the date specified by the OFT, and an appeal against the imposition or amount of the penalty within the time allowed has not been brought or such an appeal has been made and the penalty upheld, the OFT may commence proceedings to recover the required amount as a civil debt.

THIRD PARTY CLAIMS

8.6 Third parties adversely affected by an agreement which they believe is prohibited by Article 81 and/or the Chapter I prohibition may take action in the courts to stop the behaviour and/or to seek damages.

8.7 Where a decision of the OFT or the Competition Appeal Tribunal (CAT), on appeal from a decision of the OFT, has already found an infringement of Article 81 and/or the Chapter I prohibition, third parties who consider they have suffered loss as a result of the infringement may bring an action for damages, against the undertaking or undertakings concerned, in the CAT or the courts. The CAT and the courts will be bound, in such proceedings, by the relevant infringement decision, provided that the decision is no longer capable of being overturned on appeal. For further details, see the competition law guideline *Enforcement* (OFT 407).

ASSESSMENT OF MARKET POWER (OFT 415, DECEMBER 2004)

[3.122]

NOTES

As to the construction of this document (following the abolition of the OFT and Competition Commission), see further the note "The Competition and Markets Authority (references to the OFT and Competition Commission etc)" in the introductory notes to Part 3 preceding **[3.1]**.

CONTENTS

1. INTRODUCTION

[3.123]

1.1 The EC Treaty[1] and the Competition Act 1998 (the Act) both prohibit agreements[2] which prevent, restrict or distort competition and conduct which constitutes abuse of a dominant position. EC Regulation 1/2003 (the Modernisation Regulation)[3] requires the designated national competition authorities of the Member States (NCAs) and the courts of the Member States to apply and enforce Articles 81 and 82 of the EC Treaty (Article 81 and Article 82 respectively) as well as national competition law when national competition law is applied to agreements which may affect trade between Member States or to abuse prohibited by Article 82. A more detailed explanation of the Modernisation Regulation is set out in the competition law guideline *Modernisation* (OFT 442).

1.2 The concept of market power is not part of the statutory framework of the EC Treaty or the Act, but it is a useful concept in assessing potentially anti-competitive agreements or conduct. This guideline explains how the OFT will assess whether undertakings[4] possess market power when investigating cases under Articles 81 and 82 and sections 2(1) and 18(1) of the Act (the 'Chapter I prohibition' and 'Chapter II prohibition' respectively).

1.3 Market power arises where an undertaking does not face effective competitive pressure. Both suppliers and buyers can have market power. However, for clarity, market power will usually be referred to here to describe supplier market power. Where buyer market power is the issue, the term **buyer power** is employed. Market power and buyer power are not absolute, but are matters of degree; the degree of power will depend on the circumstances of each case.

1.4 Market power can be thought of as the ability profitably to sustain prices above competitive levels or restrict output or quality below competitive levels. An undertaking with market power might also have the ability and incentive to harm the process of competition in other ways; for example, by weakening existing competition, raising entry barriers or slowing innovation. However, although market power is not solely concerned with the ability of a supplier to raise prices, this guideline often for convenience refers to market power as the ability profitably to sustain prices above competitive levels.

1.5 Market power can exist in a variety of contexts, some of which are discussed in this guideline. In some markets, a single undertaking may possess market power. In others where, for example, a number of undertakings have agreed explicitly or tacitly not to compete with each other, a group of undertakings may collectively possess market power.

1.6 The approach described in this guideline is not a mechanical test, but a conceptual framework within which evidence can be organised. It is not possible to give a prescriptive guide to market power since whether and the extent to which it exists will depend on the circumstances of each case.

Part 3 CMA and other Guidelines

1.7 An assessment of market power generally involves considering a wide range of relevant evidence on market definition,[5] market structure, entry conditions, the behaviour of undertakings and their financial performance before coming to a view of market power.

LAYOUT OF THIS GUIDELINE

1.8 Part 2 of this guideline describes why the assessment of market power can be useful under Article 81 and the Chapter I prohibition of the Act in considering the **appreciability** test (ie the appreciability of the effect on competition) and why it is central under Article 82 and the Chapter II prohibition in the identification of **dominance**. Although the concepts of appreciable effect and dominance are different, it is helpful in both cases to consider the competitive constraints that act on the undertaking (or undertakings). This guideline refers to these constraints as the factors which affect whether or not undertakings have market power.

1.9 Parts 3 to 6 of this guideline address theory and evidence relevant in the assessment of market power. Part 3 sets out a framework for assessing market power. Part 4 considers how to measure market shares, noting that they need to be considered in the context of other factors (such as entry barriers) before they are used as indicators of market power.

1.10 Part 5 considers various types of entry barrier and how they may be assessed in practice. Part 6 considers other factors that are important in the assessment of market power such as buyer power, evidence of excessive prices and profits and economic regulation.

NOTES

1 The Treaty establishing the European Community.

2 References in this guideline to **agreements** should be taken to include decisions by associations of undertakings (see footnote 5 below) and concerted practices, unless otherwise stated or the context demands it.

3 Council Regulation (EC) No 1/2003 of 16 December 2002 on the implementation of the rules on competition laid down in Articles 81 and 82 of the Treaty (OJ L1, 4.1.03, p 1).

4 The term **undertaking** is not defined in the EC Treaty or the Act, but its meaning has been set out in Community law. It covers any natural or legal person engaged in economic activity, regardless of its legal status and the way in which it is financed. It includes companies, partnerships, firms, businesses, individuals operating as sole traders, agricultural cooperatives, associations of undertakings (eg trade associations), non profit making organisations and (in some circumstances) public entities that offer goods or services on a given market,

5 See the competition law guideline *Market definition* (OFT 403).

2. APPRECIABLE EFFECT AND DOMINANCE

[3.124]

2.1 This part describes why the assessment of market power can be useful in considering the concepts of **appreciability** and **dominance** in competition law.

APPRECIABILITY UNDER ARTICLE 81 AND THE CHAPTER I PROHIBITION

2.2 An agreement will infringe Article 81 or the Chapter I prohibition only if it has as its object or effect an appreciable prevention, restriction or distortion of competition within:

- the common market in the case of Article 81, or
- the United Kingdom or a part of it in the case of the Chapter I prohibition.

Further details are provided in the competition law guideline *Agreements and concerted practices* (OFT 401).

Market power

2.3 If it is clear that none of the parties to an agreement possesses market power (either individually or collectively) and that market power would not arise as a result of the agreement, it is unlikely that the OFT will take further action unless it is considering a price fixing, market sharing or bid rigging agreement.[6]

2.4 Relevant factors in the assessment of market power include market shares, entry conditions, and the degree of buyer power from the undertaking's customers (which may include distributors, processors and commercial users). These factors are discussed in Parts 3 to 6 of this guideline.

Administrative priority

2.5 It is the OFT's practice to consider, on a case by case basis, whether an agreement falls within its administrative priorities so as to merit investigation.

Calculating market shares

2.6 When applying the market share thresholds, the relevant market share will be the combined market share not only of the parties to the agreement, but also of other undertakings belonging to the same group of undertakings as the parties to the agreement. These will include, in the case of each party to the agreement, undertakings over which they exercise control and undertakings that exercise control over them (and any other undertakings that are controlled by those undertakings).

DOMINANCE UNDER ARTICLE 82 AND THE CHAPTER II PROHIBITION

2.7 Article 82 and the Chapter II prohibition prohibit conduct by one or more undertakings which amounts to the abuse of a dominant position within:

- the common market in the case of Article 82, or
- the United Kingdom or a part of it in the case of the Chapter II prohibition.

2.8 The European Court has defined a dominant market position as:

'a position of economic strength enjoyed by an undertaking which enables it to prevent effective competition being maintained on the relevant market by affording it the power to behave to an appreciable extent independently of its competitors, customers and ultimately of consumers.'[7]

2.9 The OFT considers that an undertaking will not be dominant unless it has **substantial market power**.

2.10 Market power is not an absolute term but a matter of degree, and the degree of market power will depend on the circumstances of each case. In assessing whether an undertaking has substantial market power, it is helpful to consider whether and the extent to which an undertaking faces competitive constraints. Those constraints might be existing competitors, potential competitors and other factors such as strong buyer power from the undertaking's customers. These constraints are discussed further in Parts 3 to 6 of this guideline.

Market shares

2.11 There are no market share thresholds for defining dominance under Article 82 or the Chapter II prohibition. An undertaking's market share is an important factor in assessing dominance but does not determine on its own whether an undertaking is dominant. For example, it is also necessary to consider the position of other undertakings operating in the same market and how market shares have changed over time. An undertaking is more likely to be dominant if its competitors enjoy relatively weak positions or if it has enjoyed a high and stable market share.

2.12 The European Court has stated that dominance can be presumed in the absence of evidence to the contrary if an undertaking has a market share persistently above 50 per cent.[8] The OFT considers that it is unlikely that an undertaking will be individually dominant if its share of the relevant market is below 40 per cent, although dominance could be established below that figure if other relevant factors (such as the weak position of competitors in that market and high entry barriers) provided strong evidence of dominance.

COLLECTIVE DOMINANCE UNDER ARTICLE 82 AND THE CHAPTER II PROHIBITION

2.13 Article 82 and the Chapter II prohibition prohibit conduct on the part of 'one or more' undertakings that amounts to the abuse of a dominant position. Conduct by undertakings within the same corporate group which are not considered to operate as a single economic unit may be treated together under Article 82.[9] A dominant position may be held collectively (a **collective dominant position**) when two or more legally independent undertakings are linked in such a way that they adopt a common policy on the market.

2.14 The European Court confirmed the principle of collective dominance in the *'Italian Flat Glass' case*:

'There is nothing, in principle, to prevent two or more independent economic entities from being, on a specific market, united by such economic links that, by virtue of that fact, together they hold a dominant position vis-à-vis the other operators on the same market'.[10]

2.15 The links may be structural or they may be such that the undertakings adopt a common policy on the market. For example, the nature of the market may mean that undertakings might adopt the same pricing policy on the market without ever explicitly agreeing on price.[11] This is sometimes called **tacit coordination**.

2.16 Tacit coordination requires that undertakings are able to align their behaviour in the market. It also requires that:

- each undertaking is able to the compliance of the other undertakings with the common policy (ie transparency),
- the undertakings have incentives to maintain coordinated behaviour over time, so that coordination is sustainable (eg because deviations from the common policy are easy to detect and punish), and
- the foreseeable reactions of current and future competitors, as well as of customers, would not jeopardise the results expected from the common policy (eg new entrants, 'fringe' undertakings[12] or powerful buyers could not successfully challenge the common policy).[13]

NOTES

6 See the competition law guideline *Article 81 and the Chapter I prohibition* (OFT 401).

7 Case 27/76 *United Brands v Commission* [1978] ECR 207. This definition has been used in other cases.

8 Case C62/86 *AKZO Chemie BV v Commission* [1991] ECR I-3359.

9 The behaviour of undertakings that operate as a single economic unit within the same corporate group will however usually be treated as that of a single undertaking (see the competition law guideline *Agreements and concerted practices* (OFT 401).

10 Case T-68/89 etc *Società Italiano Vetro SpA v Commission* [1992] II ECR 1403.

11 Case C396/96 *Compagnie Maritime Belge Transports v Commission* [2000] ECR I-1365 at paragraph 45.

12 A 'fringe' undertaking is one not participating in the coordinated behaviour.

13 See the judgment in Case T-342/99 *Airtours plc v Commission* [2002] ECR II-2585.

3. A FRAMEWORK FOR ASSESSING MARKET POWER

[3.125]

3.1 Market power can be thought of as the ability profitably to sustain prices above competitive levels or restrict output or quality below competitive levels. An undertaking with market power might also have the ability and incentive to harm the process of competition in other ways; for example, by weakening existing competition, raising entry barriers or slowing innovation. However, although market power is not solely concerned with the ability of a supplier to raise prices, this guideline often refers to market power for convenience as the ability profitably to sustain prices above competitive levels.[14]

3.2 When assessing whether and to what extent market power exists, it is helpful to consider the strength of any **competitive constraints**, ie market factors that prevent an undertaking from profitably sustaining prices above competitive levels.

3.3 Competitive constraints include:

- **Existing competitors** – 'Existing competitors' are undertakings already in the relevant market.[15] If an undertaking (or group of undertakings) attempts to sustain prices above competitive levels, this might not be profitable because customers would switch their purchases to existing competitors. The market shares of competitors in the relevant market are one measure of the competitive constraint from existing competitors. It can also be important to consider how the market shares of undertakings in the market have moved over time. Market shares are discussed further in Part 4 of this guideline
- **Potential competition** – This refers to the scope for new entry. Where entry barriers are low, it might not be profitable for one or more undertakings in a market to sustain prices above competitive levels because this would attract new entry which would then drive the price down – if not immediately, then in the long term. Entry barriers are the subject of Part 5 of this guideline
- **Buyer power** – Buyer power exists where buyers have a strong negotiating position with their suppliers, which weakens the potential market power of a seller. This is discussed further in Part 6 of this guideline.

3.4 Economic regulation is a further relevant factor when assessing market power in industry sectors where, for example, prices and/or service levels are subject to controls by the government or an industry sector regulator. While economic regulation is not a competitive constraint in itself, it can limit the extent to which undertakings can exploit their market power.[16] This is also discussed further in Part 6 of this guideline.

3.5 Evidence about the behaviour and financial performance of undertakings is also relevant. Where there is direct evidence that, over the long term, prices substantially exceed relevant costs or profits substantially exceed competitive levels, this may point to market power. Behaviour and performance are dealt with further in Part 6.

3.6 For analytical clarity, this approach sets out the various indicators of market power as if they were separate. In practice, however, the factors are often related. Available evidence from all indicators will be considered in the round before coming to an assessment on market power.

NOTES

14 Where market power is exercised with the effect that quality, service or innovation is reduced, customers can be thought of as paying higher prices for a given level of quality, service or innovation, thus deriving poorer value for money than competition would deliver.

15 Where supply side substitution is likely, existing competitors include undertakings that would move very quickly into the market without incurring substantial sunk costs. See the competition law guideline *Market definition* (OFT 403).

16 Note, however, that the existence of regulation does not necessarily preclude a finding that, for example, the conduct of a dominant undertaking constitutes an abuse of a dominant position-see, for example, the judgment of the Competition Commission Appeal Tribunal in *Napp Pharmaceutical Holdings Limited and Subsidiaries v Director General of Fair Trading* [2002] CAT 1 at paragraph 411 *et seq.*

4. MARKET SHARES

[3.126]

4.1 As part of the framework for assessing market power, the OFT will usually define the market and assess how market shares have developed over time.[17] This part considers the extent to which market shares indicate whether an undertaking possesses market power, how market shares may be measured, the sort of evidence likely to be relevant, and some potential problems. These issues are important when considering the intensity of existing competition.

MARKET SHARES AND MARKET POWER

4.2 In general, market power is more likely to exist if an undertaking (or group of undertakings) has a persistently high market share.[18] Likewise, market power is less likely to exist if an undertaking has a persistently low market share. Relative market shares can also be important. For example, a high market share might be more indicative of market power when all other competitors have very low market shares.

4.3 The history of the market shares of all undertakings within the relevant market is often more informative than considering market shares at a single point in time, partly because such a snapshot might not reveal the dynamic nature of a market. For example, volatile market shares might indicate that undertakings constantly innovate to get ahead of each other, which is consistent with effective competition. Evidence that undertakings with low market shares have grown rapidly to attain relatively large market shares might suggest that barriers to expansion are low, particularly when such growth is observed for recent entrants.

4.4 Nevertheless, market shares alone might not be a reliable guide to market power, both as a result of potential shortcomings with the data (discussed in the next section) and for the following reasons:

- **Low entry barriers** – An undertaking with a persistently high market share may not necessarily have market power where there is a strong threat of potential competition. If entry into the market is easy, the incumbent undertaking might be constrained to act competitively so as to avoid attracting entry over time by potential competitors (see Part 5).
- **Bidding markets** – Sometimes buyers choose their suppliers through procurement auctions or tenders. In these circumstances, even if there are only a few suppliers, competition might be intense. This is more likely to be the case where tenders are large and infrequent (so that suppliers are more likely to bid), where suppliers are not subject to capacity constraints (so that all suppliers are likely to place competitive bids), and where suppliers are not differentiated (so that for any particular bid, all suppliers are equally placed to win the contract). In these types of markets, an undertaking might have a high market share at a single point in time. However, if competition at the bidding stage is effective, this currently high market share would not necessarily reflect market power.
- **Successful innovation** – In a market where undertakings compete to improve the quality of their products, a persistently high market share might indicate persistently successful innovation and so would not necessarily mean that competition is not effective.[19]
- **Product differentiation** – Sometimes the relevant market will contain products that are differentiated. In this case undertakings with relatively low market shares might have a degree of market power because other products in the market are not very close substitutes.
- **Responsiveness of customers** – Where undertakings have similar market shares, this does not necessarily mean that they have similar degrees of market power. This may be because their customers differ in their ability or willingness to switch to alternative suppliers (see also the discussion of buyer power in Part 6).
- **Price responsiveness of competitors** – Sometimes an undertaking's competitors will not be in a position to increase output in response to higher prices in the market. For example, suppose an undertaking operates in a market where all undertakings have limited capacity (eg are at, or close to, full capacity and so are unable to increase output substantially). In this case, the undertaking would be in a stronger position to increase prices above competitive levels than an otherwise identical undertaking with a similar market share operating in a market where its competitors were not close to full capacity.

4.5 Therefore, while consideration of market shares over time is important when assessing market power, an analysis of entry conditions and other factors is equally important. All relevant factors will be viewed in the round.

MEASURING MARKET SHARES

Evidence

4.6 Data on market shares may be collected from a number of sources including:

- information provided by undertakings themselves. Undertakings are usually asked for data on their own market shares, and to estimate the shares of their competitors,
- trade associations, customers or suppliers who may be able to provide estimates of market shares, and
- market research reports.

4.7 The appropriate method for calculating market shares depends on the case in hand. Usually sales data by value and by volume are both informative. Often value data will be more informative, for example, where goods are differentiated.

4.8 The following issues may arise when measuring market shares:

- **Production, sales and capacity** – Market share is usually determined by an undertaking's sales to customers in the relevant market. Market share is normally measured using sales to direct customers in the relevant market rather than an undertaking's total production (which can vary when stocks increase or decrease). Sometimes market shares will be measured by an undertaking's capacity to supply the relevant market: for example, where capacity is an important feature in an undertaking's ability to compete or in some instances where the market is defined taking into account supply side considerations.[20]
- **Sales values** – When considering market shares on a value basis, market share is valued at the price charged to an undertaking's direct customers. For example, when a manufacturer's direct customers are retailers, it is more informative to consider the value of its sales to retailers as opposed to the prices at which the retailers sell that manufacturer's product to final consumers.
- **Choice of exchange rates** – Where the relevant geographic market is international, this may complicate the calculation of market shares by value, as exchange rates vary over time. It may then be appropriate to consider a range of exchange rates over time, including an assessment of the sensitivity of the analysis to the use of different exchange rates.
- **Imports** – If the relevant geographic market is international, market shares will be calculated with respect to the whole geographic market. If the relevant geographic market is not international, it is possible that imports will account for a share of that market. If so, and if information is available, the sales of each importing undertaking are usually considered and market shares

calculated accordingly, rather than aggregating shares as if they were those of a single competitor. Where the relevant geographic market is domestic, the share of an undertaking that both supplies within and imports into that market[21] would usually include both its domestic sales and its imports.

- **Internal production** – In some cases, a supplier may be using some of its capacity or production to meet its own internal needs. In the event of a rise in price on the open market, the supplier may decide to divert some or all of its 'captive' capacity or production to the open market if it is profitable to do so, taking into account effects on its downstream business that is now deprived of the captive supply. The extent to which 'captive' capacity or production is likely to be released onto the open market (or might otherwise affect competition on the open market) will be taken into account in assessing competitive constraints.

NOTES

17 The OFT's approach to market definition is set out in the competition law guideline *Market definition* (OFT 403).

18 See, for example, *Aberdeen Journals Limited v Office of Fair Trading (No. 2)* [2003] CAT 11 at paragraphs 309 to 310.

19 For example, effective competition in innovation might mean that, in order to stay ahead of its rivals, the market leader must improve its products and processes on a regular basis. Innovation as a way to overcome entry barriers is discussed in Part 5.

20 See the competition law guideline *Market definition* (OFT 403).

21 This includes situations where the undertaking in question is part of the same group as an importer into that market.

5. ENTRY BARRIERS

[3.127]

5.1 This Part considers barriers to entry and expansion and how they may be assessed in practice.

5.2 Entry barriers are important in the assessment of potential competition. The lower are entry barriers, the more likely it is that potential competition will prevent undertakings already within a market from profitably sustaining prices above competitive levels.

5.3 Entry barriers are factors that allow an undertaking profitably to sustain supra-competitive prices in the long term, without being more efficient than its potential rivals. If it currently faced no existing competitors, an undertaking could not sustain supra-competitive prices in the long term in the absence of entry barriers.

5.4 An undertaking even with a large market share in a market with very low entry barriers would be unlikely to have market power. However, an undertaking with a large market share in a market protected by significant entry barriers is likely to have market power.

5.5 Entry barriers arise when an undertaking has an advantage (not solely based on superior efficiency) over potential entrants from having already entered the market and/or from special rights (eg to production or distribution) or privileged access to key inputs. Entry barriers may make new entry[22] less likely or less rapid by affecting the expected sunk costs of entry and/or the expected profits for new entrants once they are in the market, or by establishing physical, geographic or legal obstacles to entry.[23]

5.6 There are many ways in which different types of entry barrier can be classified, but it is useful to distinguish between the following factors which, depending on the circumstances, can contribute to barriers to entry:

- sunk costs
- poor access to key inputs and distribution outlets
- regulation
- economies of scale
- network effects, and
- exclusionary behaviour.[24]

5.7 Most of the following examples refer for simplicity to a situation where there is one incumbent already in the market[25] and one potential entrant or 'rival'. Although in reality the existence of several incumbents and several potential entrants may complicate the analysis, the principles outlined remain valid.

SUNK COSTS

5.8 Entry will occur only if the expected profit from being in the market exceeds any sunk costs of entry.[26]

5.9 Sunk costs of entry are those costs which must be incurred to compete in a market, but which are not recoverable on exiting the market.[27] When a new entrant incurs sunk costs when entering a market, it is as if that entrant has paid a non-refundable deposit to enable it to enter.[28]

5.10 Sunk costs might give an incumbent a strategic advantage over potential entrants. Suppose an incumbent has already made sunk investments necessary to produce in a market while an otherwise identical new entrant has not. In this case, even if the incumbent charges a price at which entry would be profitable (if the price remained the same following entry), entry may not occur. This would be the case if the entrant does not expect the post-entry price to be high enough to justify incurring the sunk costs of entry.[29]

5.11 It is useful to consider the extent to which sunk costs give an incumbent undertaking an advantage over potential new entrants and to what extent sunk costs might affect entry barriers.[30] The mere existence of sunk costs in any particular industry, however, does not necessarily mean that entry barriers are high or that competition within the market is not effective.

POOR ACCESS TO KEY INPUTS AND DISTRIBUTION OUTLETS

5.12 Entry barriers may arise where inputs or distribution outlets are scarce, and where an incumbent obtains an advantage over a potential entrant due to privileged access (or special rights) to those inputs or outlets.

Essential facilities

5.13 At one extreme, an incumbent might own or have privileged access to an essential facility, which its rival does not. Although the assessment of whether a particular facility is essential must be on a case-by-case basis, essential facilities are rare in practice. A facility will only be viewed as essential where it can be demonstrated that access to it is indispensable in order to compete in a related market and where duplication is impossible or extremely difficult owing to physical, geographic or legal constraints (or is highly undesirable for reasons of public policy). Generally if a rival does not have access to an essential facility, it cannot enter the market.

5.14 There will be circumstances in which difficulties accessing inputs or resources constitute an entry barrier without those assets or resources meeting the strict criteria required to be defined as 'essential facilities'.

Intellectual property rights

5.15 Intellectual property rights (IPRs) can be entry barriers, although this is not always the case. In particular, when an IPR does not prevent others from competing with the IPR holder in the relevant market, it would not normally be a barrier to entry. In those cases where IPRs do constitute a barrier to entry, it does not always imply that competition is reduced. Although an IPR may constitute an entry barrier in the short term, in the long term a rival undertaking may be able to overcome it by its own innovation. The short term profit which an IPR can provide acts an incentive to innovate and can thus stimulate competition in innovation.

REGULATION

5.16 Regulation may affect barriers to entry. For example, regulation may limit the number of undertakings which can operate in a market through the granting of licences. Also, licences may be restricted so that there is an absolute limit to the number of undertakings that can operate in the market. In this case a licence can be thought of as a necessary input before production can take place and so regulation will act as an entry barrier.[31]

5.17 Sometimes regulation sets objective standards. Where these apply equally to all undertakings, such as health and safety regulations, they might not affect the cost for new entrants any more than they affect the cost for incumbents. However, regulation can lead to entry barriers when it does not apply equally to all undertakings. For example, incumbents might lobby for standards that are relatively easy for them to meet, but harder for a new entrant to achieve.

ECONOMIES OF SCALE

5.18 Economies of scale exist where average costs fall as output rises.[32] In the presence of large economies of scale, a potential entrant may need to enter the market on a large scale (in relation to the size of the market) in order to compete effectively. Large scale entry might require relatively large sunk costs and might be more likely to attract an aggressive response from incumbents.[33] These factors may in some circumstances constitute barriers to entry.

5.19 Attaining a viable scale of production may take time and so require the new entrant to operate in the market for some time at a loss. For example, a new entrant at the manufacturing level might need to secure many distribution outlets to achieve a viable scale. If, perhaps due to long term contracts, many input suppliers or distributors are locked-in to dealing with the incumbent, the new entrant might not be able to achieve an efficient scale of production over the medium term. This could deter entry.

5.20 Even when entry is not completely deterred, entrants may take time to achieve efficient levels of production, obtain the relevant information, raise capital and build the necessary plant and machinery. In this case, even if entry occurs, the incumbent could nevertheless retain market power for a substantial period of time.

NETWORK EFFECTS

5.21 Network effects occur where users' valuations of the network increase as more users join the network. For example, as new customers enter a telephone network, this might add value to existing customers because they would be connected to more people on the same network. If customers benefit from being on the same network (eg due to incompatibility with other networks), an incumbent with a well established network might have an advantage over a potential entrant that is denied access to the established network and so has to establish its own rival network.

5.22 Network effects, just like economies of scale, may make new entry harder where the minimum viable scale (eg in terms of users of the network) is large in relation to the size of the market.

EXCLUSIONARY BEHAVIOUR

5.23 The term 'exclusionary behaviour' refers to anti-competitive behaviour which harms existing or potential competition: for example, by eliminating efficient competitors or raising barriers to entry and expansion. The following paragraphs set out some examples of how exclusionary behaviour can create barriers to entry.

Predatory response to entry

5.24 An undertaking contemplating entering a market weighs up its expected profit from being in the market with the expected sunk costs of entering. Expected profits from being in the market may depend on how the entrant expects the incumbent to react when it enters the market: the potential entrant might believe that the incumbent would, for example, reduce prices substantially if it entered and so reduce the prospective profits available.

5.25 While low prices are generally to be encouraged, if a new entrant expected an incumbent to respond to entry with predatory prices, this could deter entry. For example, if an incumbent has successfully predated in the past, it may have secured a reputation for its willingness to set predatory prices.[34] Any future potential entrants to this market (or to any other market where the incumbent operates) might then be deterred from entering due to the likelihood of facing an aggressive response.[35]

Vertical restraints

5.26 In general, vertical restraints are provisions made between undertakings operating at different levels of the supply chain which restrict the commercial freedom of one or more parties to the agreement. Many vertical restraints may be beneficial or benign, especially if there is effective competition at both the upstream and downstream levels. However, vertical restraints may also affect entry barriers.[36]

5.27 For example, a manufacturer might have a series of exclusive purchasing agreements with most retailers in a particular geographic market. This might limit the ability of a new manufacturer to operate on a viable scale in that market and therefore deter entry.

Other exclusionary practices

5.28 Discounts designed to foreclose markets, margin squeezes, and refusals to supply might also be used in a way that raises entry barriers.

ASSESSING ENTRY BARRIERS

5.29 Assessing the effects of entry barriers and the advantages they give to incumbents can be complex. A variety of steps may be involved. For example, incumbents and potential entrants might be asked for their views on: the sunk costs associated with a commitment to entry; the relative ease of obtaining the necessary inputs and distribution outlets; how regulation affects the prospect of entry; the cost of operating at the minimum viable scale; and any other factors that may impede entry or expansion in the market.

5.30 Claims that potential competition is waiting in the wings are more persuasive if there is fully documented evidence of plans to enter a market or where hard evidence of successful entry in the recent history of the market is provided. In the latter case, such evidence might include a historical record of entry into the market (or closely related markets), including evidence that new entrants had attained in a relatively short period of time a sufficient market share to become effective existing competitors.

5.31 It is important, but not necessarily straightforward, to assess the time that may elapse before successful entry would occur. Some producers, most likely those in neighbouring markets, may be able to enter speedily (eg in less than a year) and without substantial sunk costs by switching the use of existing facilities. Where this is possible, it will sometimes be taken into account in defining the market (as supply-side substitutability: see the competition law guideline *Market definition* (OFT 403)).[37] New entry from scratch tends to be slower than entry from a neighbouring market, for a variety of reasons which depend on the market concerned – obtaining planning permission, recruiting and training staff, ordering equipment, appointing distributors and so on. The nature of the market may also limit the times at which entry may occur. For example, where customers award long-term contracts, a potential entrant may have to wait until these contracts are renewed before it has an opportunity to enter the market. It may also be important to assess whether enough contracts would come up for renewal to allow the entrant to attain a viable scale.

5.32 Sometimes the relevant geographic market will be international. Where this is not the case, foreign suppliers may nevertheless exert a constraint on domestic undertakings, in the absence of entry barriers, as potential competitors. However, trade barriers – whether tariff or non-tariff – are an example of a barrier to entry that could impede international competition and shield market power.

5.33 Growth, or prospective growth, of a market will usually have a bearing on the likelihood of entry: entry will usually be more likely in a growing market than in a static or declining one because it will be easier for an entrant to achieve a viable scale, for example by selling to new customers.

5.34 In markets where products are differentiated, undertakings compete not only on price but also on features such as quality, service, convenience and innovation. Where there is scope for differentiation, this may facilitate entry, for example where a new entrant targets untapped demand by differentiating itself from incumbents (provided that incumbents have not already pre-empted all possible niches in the market).

5.35 In markets where brand image is important, a new entrant may have to invest heavily in advertising before it can attain a viable scale. However, even where advertising expenditure is a sunk cost, this does not necessarily mean that entry barriers are high. For example, incumbents may have had to establish their brands and may also have to advertise heavily to maintain them, and so will not necessarily have a cost advantage over potential entrants.

5.36 The rate of innovation is also important: in markets where high rates of innovation occur, or are expected, innovation may overcome product market barriers to entry relatively quickly (provided that there are no barriers to entry into innovative activity). Indeed, any profits that result from an advantage created by successful innovation (eg from intellectual property rights) may be an important incentive to innovate.

BARRIERS TO EXPANSION

5.37 New entry is not simply about introducing a new product to the market. To be an effective competitive constraint, a new entrant must be able to attain a large enough scale to have a competitive impact on undertakings already in the market. This may entail entry on a small scale, followed by growth. Barriers to entry are closely related to barriers to expansion and can be analysed in a similar way. Many of the factors discussed above that may make entry harder might also make it harder for undertakings that have recently entered the market to expand their market shares and hence their competitive impact.

NOTES

22 New entry into a market requires that both a new undertaking is established in the industry and that new productive capacity is set up in that industry.

23 For the purposes of this guideline, entry barriers include not only those factors that prevent new entry entirely but also those that impede (without necessarily preventing) new entry.

24 Exclusionary behaviour does not refer only to behaviour that raises entry barriers. Exclusionary behaviour also refers to practices that make it harder for existing competitors to become more forceful competitors, including practices which lead to the elimination of an existing competitor.

25 This gives the incumbent a '**first-mover advantage**': an advantage from being in the market before its rival.

26 Note that the expected profit from being in a market would also account for the possibility that exit occurs and that any associated 'exit costs' are incurred.

27 For example, suppose an entrant to a hypothetical market for long distance coach services in the North of England purchases a fleet of vehicles. On exiting that market it might be able to sell its coaches to another undertaking (eg one offering coach services in the South of England) and so some of the initial costs are recoverable and not sunk. However, not all of the expenditure will be recoverable. For example, any expenditure on the undertaking's livery is unlikely to be of use to another company. This latter expenditure is therefore sunk.

28 Where undertakings can determine their own sunk costs, these are sometimes called 'endogenous' sunk costs. For example, the non-recoverable components of spending on advertising and on research and development (R&D) are endogenous sunk costs. These might be used to differentiate products by brand image and/or by quality (see 5.35).

29 Provided entry would not drive prices below average avoidable cost, the incumbent would find it profitable to remain in the market following entry. Knowing this, the potential entrant decides to stay out of the market.

30 In the economics literature there are many models which describe how an incumbent might use sunk costs strategically to deter entry or, if entry is accommodated, reduce the share of the market available to the new entrant. Some examples are given below in the discussion of exclusionary behaviour.

31 If licences were tradeable in a competitive market, a potential entrant could purchase a licence and enter the market if a profitable opportunity arose. However, entry by one undertaking would require exit by another and so overall output might not rise. Therefore, the fact that the licences are limited might allow those undertakings in the market to sustain prices above competitive levels even though licences were tradeable.

32 Economies of **scope** mean that it costs less to produce two types of products together than to produce them separately. Economies of scope may have similar implications to economies of scale, as a potential entrant would prefer to enter the market with many as opposed to few products.

33 See paragraph 5.25.

34 In *Aberdeen Journals (No. 2)*, the Competition Appeal Tribunal accepted that Aberdeen Journals' predatory reaction to the launch of a rival newspaper would have been likely to deter others from seeking to enter the market.

35 Another example might be where an incumbent sinks costs in a way that sends a credible signal as to how it would behave if another undertaking decided to enter a market: it might 'over-invest' in sunk assets so that when it operated as the only undertaking in the market, it had significant spare capacity. From the potential entrant's point of view, the mere existence of that capacity might imply that the incumbent would 'flood' the market in response to entry. The entrant might then decide not to enter if it believed that the incumbent was likely to respond to entry by lowering the price to a low level where the entrant would earn insufficient revenue to cover its sunk costs.

36 For a further discussion see the competition law guideline *Vertical agreements* (OFT 419).

37 Some rivals will be able to enter the market more quickly and with a smaller sunk investment than others. Whether this is classified as supply side substitution or new entry should not make a difference to the assessment of market power. Ultimately what matters are the competitive constraints, not the way in which they are classified.

6. OTHER FACTORS IN THE ASSESSMENT OF MARKET POWER

BUYER POWER

[3.128]

6.1 The strength of buyers and the structure of the buyers' side of the market may constrain the market power of a seller. Size is not sufficient for buyer power. Buyer power requires the buyer to have choice.

6.2 The analysis of buyer power requires an understanding of the way that buyers interact with suppliers. Buyer power is most commonly found in industries where buyers and suppliers negotiate, in which case buyer power can be thought of as the degree of bargaining strength in negotiations.[38] A buyer's bargaining strength might be enhanced if the following conditions hold:

- the buyer is well informed about alternative sources of supply and could readily, and at little cost to itself, switch substantial purchases from one supplier to another while continuing to meet its needs[39]
- the buyer could commence production of the item itself or 'sponsor' new entry by another supplier (eg through a long-term contract) relatively quickly and without incurring substantial sunk costs
- the buyer is an important outlet for the seller (ie the seller would be willing to cede better terms to the buyer in order to retain the opportunity to sell to that buyer)
- the buyer can intensify competition among suppliers through establishing a procurement auction or purchasing through a competitive tender (see Part 4).

6.3 In general, buyer power is beneficial in two circumstances:

- when there are large efficiency gains that result from the factors (eg size) that give the buyer its power and these are passed on to the final consumer (eg through downstream competition), and
- when it exerts downward pressure on a supplier's prices and the lower prices are passed on to the final consumer.

6.4 However, buyer power does not always benefit the final consumer. First, where only some buyers are powerful, for example, a supplier with market power might harm downstream competition through actions which lead to weaker buyers facing higher input prices. Second, buyer power might be weakened as a result of the agreement or behaviour under investigation. Third, where the buyer also has market power as a seller in the downstream market, it may not pass on lower prices to the final consumer. Fourth, conduct by a dominant buyer may harm competition. A careful analysis of vertical relationships in the market, on a case-by-case basis, is therefore often required to assess buyer power.[40]

EVIDENCE ON BEHAVIOUR AND PERFORMANCE

6.5 An undertaking's conduct in a market or its financial performance may provide evidence that it possesses market power. Depending on other available evidence, it might, for example, be reasonable to infer that an undertaking possesses market power from evidence that it has:

- set prices consistently above an appropriate measure of costs, or
- persistently earned an excessive rate of profit.

6.6 High prices or profits alone are not sufficient proof that an undertaking has market power: high profits may represent a return on previous innovation, or result from changing demand conditions. As such, they may be consistent with a competitive market, where undertakings are able to take advantage of profitable opportunities when they exist. However, persistent significantly high returns, relative to those which would prevail in a competitive market of similar risk and rate of innovation, may suggest that market power does exist. This would be especially so if those high returns did not stimulate new entry or innovation.

ECONOMIC REGULATION

6.7 In some sectors the economic behaviour of undertakings (such as the prices they set or the level of services they provide) is regulated by the government or an industry sector regulator, and an assessment of market power may need to take that into account. Although an undertaking might not face effective constraints from existing competitors, potential competitors or the nature of buyers in the market, it may still be constrained from profitably sustaining prices above competitive levels by an industry sector regulator. However, that is not to say that market power cannot exist when there is economic regulation. It is feasible, for example, that regulation of the average price or profit level across several markets supplied by an undertaking may still allow for the undertaking profitably to sustain prices above competitive levels in one (or more) of these markets and/or to engage in exclusionary behaviour of various kinds.[41]

NOTES

[38] Another form of buyer power occurs where, under certain conditions, a dominant purchaser from a competitive industry would have an incentive to withhold purchases in order to buy at a lower price.

[39] This need not mean that the buyer stops buying the product entirely, just that it reduces purchases by a substantial amount. This may include ceasing to promote the product in question and promoting the products of rival suppliers instead. Reducing purchases of a must-have product might not be profitable for a buyer. However, where suppliers produce must-have products and other, less important, products the buyer might exercise power by threatening to de-list a weaker product unless it obtains better terms on the must-have product.

[40] Article 82 and the Chapter II prohibition prohibit abuses of buyer power by dominant undertakings. An agreement between customers to suppress prices would be likely to fall within Article 81 and/or the Chapter I prohibition.

[41] See, for example, *Napp* at paragraph 411 et seq.

VERTICAL AGREEMENTS (OFT 419, DECEMBER 2004)

[3.129]

NOTES

As to the construction of this document (following the abolition of the OFT and Competition Commission), see further the note "The Competition and Markets Authority (references to the OFT and Competition Commission etc)" in the introductory notes to Part 3 preceding **[3.1]**.

See also the list of consultations and draft documents in the Appendix at **[A1]**.

CONTENTS

1. INTRODUCTION

[3.130]
1.1 The prohibitions contained in Article 81 of the EC Treaty[1] (Article 81) and section 2 of the Competition Act 1998 (the Act) (the Chapter I prohibition) prohibit agreements[2] between undertakings which have as their object or effect the prevention, restriction or distortion of competition. Article 82 of the EC Treaty (Article 82) and section 18 of the Act (the Chapter II prohibition) prohibit conduct by one or more undertakings which amounts to an abuse of a dominant position. Such activities within the common market which may affect trade between Member States will fall within either Article 81 or Article 82; activities which may affect trade in the United Kingdom will fall within the Chapter I prohibition or the Chapter II prohibition.

1.2 EC Regulation 1/2003[3] (the Modernisation Regulation) requires the designated national competition authorities of the Member States (NCAs) and the courts of the Member States to apply and enforce Articles 81 and 82 of the EC Treaty as well as national competition law when national competition law is applied to agreements which may affect trade between Member States or to abuse prohibited by Article 82.

1.3 This guideline explains how the OFT applies Article 81 and the Chapter I prohibition to vertical agreements. In particular, it describes the application of the EC Block Exemption for Vertical Agreements[4] (the Block Exemption) to vertical agreements and explains how the OFT assesses vertical agreements. It also deals with other issues in relation to vertical agreements.

1.4 Vertical agreements do not generally give rise to competition concerns unless one or more of the parties to the agreement possesses market power on the relevant market or the agreement forms part of a network of similar agreements. The Block Exemption avoids placing on business the unnecessary burden of scrutinising a large number of essentially benign agreements and helps to ensure that the OFT is able to concentrate resources on matters giving rise to significant competition concern.

1.5 Part 2 of this guideline describes the OFT's application of Article 81 and the Chapter I prohibition to vertical agreements. Part 3 describes the scope and effects of the Block Exemption, as applied by the OFT in the context of Article 81 and the Chapter I prohibition. Categories of agreements likely to benefit from the exemption for vertical agreements in the Block Exemption include exclusive distribution agreements, exclusive purchasing agreements, selective distribution agreements and franchise agreements.

1.6 Part 4 discusses the possible application of Article 81(3) or section 9(1) of the Act to vertical agreements which may not benefit from the Block Exemption. Part 5 briefly explains the current operation of the Competition Act 1998 (Land and Vertical Agreements) Order 2000[5] (the UK Exclusion Order). The UK Exclusion Order largely covers vertical agreements that are also covered by the parallel application of the Block Exemption. The UK Exclusion Order is repealed with effect from 1 May 2005 upon entry into force of the Competition Act 1998 (Land Agreements Exclusion and Revocation) Order 2004.[6]

1.7 Other possible UK scrutiny of vertical agreements is set out in Part 6, including scrutiny under Article 82 and/or the Chapter II prohibition. There is no exemption or exclusion from Article 82 or the Chapter II prohibition for vertical agreements and restraints.

1.8 Part 7 of this guideline describes many of the factors that the OFT considers when assessing whether a vertical restraint in an agreement harms competition and/or whether it leads to any beneficial effects.

Part 3 CMA and other Guidelines

NOTES

1 The Treaty establishing the European Community.

2 References in this guideline to 'agreement(s)' should, unless otherwise stated or the context demands it, be taken to include decisions by associations of undertakings and concerted practices. The meaning of the terms 'undertakings', 'agreement', 'decisions by associations of undertakings' and 'concerted practices' in the context of the EC Treaty and the Act are described in the competition law guideline *Agreements and concerted practices* (OFT 401).

3 Council Regulation (EC) No 1/2003 of 16 December 2002 on the implementation of the rules on competition laid down in Articles 81 and 82 of the Treaty (OJ L1, 4.1.03, p 1).

4 Commission Regulation (EC) No 2790/1999 on the application of Article 81(3) of the Treaty to categories of vertical agreements and concerted practices (OJ L336, 29.12.99, p 21).

5 SI 2000/310.

6 SI 2004/1260. The competition law guideline *Land agreements* (OFT 420) explains how the Competition Act 1998 (Land

Agreements Exclusion and Revocation) Order 2004 operates in relation to land agreements, including vertical land agreements.

2. ARTICLE 81 AND THE CHAPTER 1 PROHIBITION

[3.131]

2.1 There are two substantive provisions which may be applied by the OFT to anti-competitive agreements: Article 81 and the Chapter I prohibition. The key difference between the two is their geographic scope. The Chapter I prohibition is based on Article 81. Both these provisions apply to agreements between undertakings which have as their object or effect the prevention, restriction or distortion of competition:

- within the common market and which may affect trade between Member States in the case of Article 81, and
- within the United Kingdom and which may affect trade within the United Kingdom in the case of the Chapter I prohibition.

Further guidance on the two provisions is given in the competition law guideline *Agreements and concerted practices* (OFT 401).

2.2 An agreement will fall within Article 81 and/or the Chapter I prohibition only if it has as its object or effect an **appreciable** prevention, restriction or distortion of competition within the geographic areas as set out above for each provision. In applying the Chapter I prohibition the OFT's focus will be on the effect on competition, as in practice it is very unlikely that an agreement which appreciably restricts competition within the United Kingdom does not also affect trade within the United Kingdom.

2.3 The European Commission's *Notice on Agreements of Minor Importance*[7] sets out, using market share thresholds, what is not an appreciable restriction of competition under Article 81. In determining whether an agreement has an appreciable effect on competition for the purposes of Article 81 and/or the Chapter I prohibition, the OFT will have regard to the European Commission's approach as set out in the *Notice on Agreements of Minor Importance* (see the competition law guideline *Agreements and concerted practices* (OFT 401)).

2.4 It is the OFT's practice to consider, on a case by case basis, whether an agreement falls within its administrative priorities so as to merit investigation.

NOTES

[7] OJ C368, 22.12.01, p 13.

3. THE BLOCK EXEMPTION

[3.132]

3.1 The Block Exemption creates a 'safe harbour' for large numbers of vertical agreements under Article 81(3), so that agreements falling within the terms of the Block Exemption are automatically exempt from the application of Article 81(1). The Block Exemption also has the parallel effect of creating a 'safe harbour' exempting agreements from the application of the Chapter I prohibition, by virtue of section 10 of the Act.[8] Thus agreements falling within the terms of the Block Exemption will be exempt from the application of both Article 81 and the Chapter I prohibition. The Block Exemption does not apply to agreements whose subject matter falls within the scope of any other EC block exemption regulation.[9]

3.2 The European Commission's Notice *Guidelines on Vertical Restraints*[10] sets out the principles for the assessment of vertical agreements under Article 81, including the application of the Block Exemption to vertical agreements. The OFT will have regard to this Notice in its assessment of vertical agreements, in relation to both Article 81 and the Chapter I prohibition. This guideline should be read together with the Block Exemption and the Notice.

3.3 The Block Exemption states that:

> 'Article 81(1) shall not apply to agreements or concerted practices entered into between two or more undertakings each of which operates, for the purposes of the agreement, at a different level of the production or distribution chain, and relating to the conditions under which the parties may purchase, sell or resell certain goods or services.'

3.4 There are two elements to consider:

- the economic relationship between the parties to the agreement, and
- the provisions of the agreement.

These two elements are considered below. Separate conditions applying to vertical agreements which include certain aspects relating to the assignment or use of intellectual property rights are also considered below.

ECONOMIC RELATIONSHIP BETWEEN THE PARTIES TO THE AGREEMENT

3.5 For an agreement to fall within the Block Exemption, the economic relationship between the parties must be such that each of the parties to the agreement operates **at a different level of the production or distribution chain** for the purposes of the agreement. Examples of activities at different levels of the production or distribution chain include supplying raw materials, manufacturing, wholesaling and retailing. An agreement between a food manufacturer and a supermarket for the supply of baked beans would be an example of a vertical agreement between undertakings operating at different levels of the production or distribution chain.

3.6 Different levels of the production or distribution chain may be found within each of the broad categories mentioned above. Within manufacturing, for example, one undertaking may manufacture a component part of a final product (such as a light bulb) and make an agreement to sell that part to a second undertaking which uses that part in its manufacture of the final product (such as a car). Although each of these undertakings is a manufacturer (one of light bulbs and one of cars), they would be regarded as operating at different levels of the production or distribution chain when they entered into an agreement for the supply of light bulbs to be incorporated into a car. Such an agreement may, therefore, benefit from the Block Exemption.

3.7 Each undertaking must operate at a different level of the production or distribution chain for an agreement to benefit from the Block Exemption. For example, an agreement between one manufacturer and a group of six competing wholesalers (where each of the six wholesalers operates at the same level of the production or distribution chain), while being an agreement between undertakings at different levels of the production or distribution chain (that is, manufacturing and wholesaling), would not benefit from the Block Exemption. The agreement would involve more than one undertaking at one particular level of the production or distribution chain (wholesaling). An agreement between a supplier of raw materials, a manufacturer, a distributor and a retailer could, however, benefit from the Block Exemption because each undertaking operates at a different level of the production or distribution chain.

3.8 Undertakings often operate at more than one level of the production or distribution chain. Whilst the Block Exemption in general does not apply to vertical agreements between competitors, an agreement between undertakings that operate at one or more of the same levels of the production or distribution chain may still benefit from the Block Exemption in certain limited circumstances. The agreement can benefit from the Block Exemption because the parties to the agreement each operate at different levels of the production or distribution chain **for the purposes of the agreement**.

3.9 Article 2(4) of the Block Exemption provides that the Block Exemption shall not apply to vertical agreements entered into between competing undertakings,[11] subject to certain limited exceptions. The Block Exemption sets out three exceptions to the general exclusion of vertical agreements between competitors, all of which relate to non-reciprocal agreements. Non-reciprocal means, for instance, that while one manufacturer becomes the distributor of the products of another manufacturer, the latter does not become a distributor of the products of the first manufacturer.

3.10 For example, non-reciprocal vertical agreements between competing undertakings are permitted where the supplier is a manufacturer and distributor of goods, whilst the buyer is a distributor that does not manufacture goods competing with the contract goods.

PROVISIONS OF THE AGREEMENT

Conditions of the agreement

3.11 The agreement must relate to the conditions under which the parties to the agreement may purchase, sell or resell certain goods or services to benefit from the Block Exemption. This covers final and intermediate goods and services. The goods or services may be resold by the buyer or may be used as an input by the buyer in producing its own goods or services. Conditions which relate to matters other than the conditions of purchase, sale and resale are not covered by the Block Exemption.

Intellectual property rights provisions

3.12 A vertical agreement that contains provisions relating to the assignment to, or use by, the buyer of intellectual property rights may benefit from the Block Exemption. Where such provisions are included, however, there are four elements with which provisions relating to intellectual property rights must comply in order for the agreement to benefit from the Block Exemption. They must:

- relate to the assignment to the buyer or use by the buyer of intellectual property rights
- not constitute the primary object of the agreement
- be directly related to the use, sale or resale of the goods or services by the buyer or its customers, and
- in relation to the contract goods or services, not contain restrictions that have the same object or effect as vertical restraints which are not exempted under the Block Exemption.

These elements are considered below.

3.13 In order to benefit from the Block Exemption, any provisions relating to intellectual property rights must relate to the assignment of the rights to the buyer or the use by the buyer of those rights. For example, an agreement under which a licence is given to a distributor to distribute and market the contract goods in a particular territory may benefit from the Block Exemption.

3.14 The assignment or use of the intellectual property rights must not be the primary object of the agreement. A simple patent licence, for example, would not benefit from the Block Exemption since the primary object of the agreement is to license the patent. It may, however, benefit from the EC technology transfer block exemption.[12]

3.15 The provisions must relate directly to the activity of the buyer or its customers in relation to the use, sale or resale of goods or services. The provisions will normally concern the marketing of goods or services, such as in a franchise agreement where the franchisor sells to the franchisee goods for resale and in addition licences the franchisee to use his trade mark and know-how to market the goods.

3.16 The intellectual property rights provisions must not have the same object or effect as restrictions which are not exempted under the Block Exemption. Vertical agreements containing intellectual property rights provisions having such object or effect fall outside the scope of the Block Exemption. The limits to the scope of the Block Exemption are discussed below, in paragraphs 3.17 to 3.29.

LIMITS TO THE SCOPE OF THE BLOCK EXEMPTION
(INCLUDING EXCLUDED OBLIGATIONS)

3.17 There are two key limits to the scope of the Block Exemption. The Block Exemption will **not** apply to a vertical agreement where:

- the market share of the supplier (or buyer, in the case of an agreement with an exclusive supply obligation)[13] exceeds 30 per cent of the relevant market (Article 3), or
- the agreement contains one or more of the 'hardcore' restrictions listed in the Block Exemption, including price-fixing (Article 4).

3.18 In addition, the Block Exemption does not apply to certain obligations, in particular non-compete obligations, unless specific conditions are fulfilled (Article 5).

Market share

3.19 Generally, the market share of the supplier on the market in which it sells the contract goods or services will determine whether the market share threshold is exceeded. The market share of the buyer on the relevant market in which it purchases the contract goods or services will only be relevant where the agreement includes an exclusive supply obligation.

3.20 In order to calculate market share, it is necessary to determine the relevant market. This means defining the relevant product and geographic markets. The analysis the OFT undertakes to determine the relevant market is described in the competition law guideline *Market definition* (OFT 403). The OFT's approach to assessment of market shares is described in the competition law guideline *Assessment of market power* (OFT 415).

3.21 Vertical agreements in which the market share threshold is exceeded will be subject to scrutiny under Article 81 and/or the Chapter I prohibition. However, it is possible for an agreement that falls within Article 81(1) but which satisfies the conditions set out in Article 81(3) not to be prohibited even where it does not fall under the Block Exemption. This is explained further in Part 4 below.

Hardcore restrictions

3.22 There are five 'hardcore' restrictions which, if included in a vertical agreement, have the effect of taking the entire agreement outside the scope of the Block Exemption. The most significant restriction is price-fixing. This is explained in paragraphs 3.23 to 3.25 below. The other four restrictions relate to specific types of sales restrictions and are described briefly in paragraphs 3.26 to 3.27 below.

3.23 The benefit of the Block Exemption does not apply to vertical agreements that fix prices. The Block Exemption provides that the exemption for vertical agreements does not apply to any vertical agreement which directly or indirectly (whether on its own or in combination with other factors under the control of the parties) has the object of restricting a buyer's ability to determine its sale price.

3.24 An agreement where the supplier imposes a maximum or recommended sale price may benefit from the Block Exemption unless such a maximum or recommended sale price results, in practice, in a fixed or minimum sale price because of pressure from, or any incentives offered by, any of the parties to the agreement. Where pressure and/or incentives in relation to recommended or maximum prices have such an effect the agreement will not benefit from the Block Exemption. Examples of the types of practices that may result in fixed or minimum sale prices include:

- an agreement fixing the maximum level of discount a distributor can grant from a prescribed price level, or
- intimidation, delay or suspension of deliveries and contract terminations in relation to the observance of a certain price level.

3.25 Price-fixing agreements that do not benefit from the Block Exemption are subject to scrutiny under Article 81 and/or the Chapter I prohibition and are capable of having an appreciable effect on competition even if the parties' combined share of the relevant market is less than the thresholds specified in the Commission's Notice on *Agreements of Minor Importance*. Details of how price-fixing agreements that fall within Article 81 and/or the Chapter I prohibition will be treated by the OFT can be found in the competition law guideline *Agreements and concerted practices* (OFT 401).

3.26 In addition to price-fixing, there are a further four 'hardcore' restrictions in the Block Exemption. Where an agreement directly or indirectly (whether on its own or in combination with other factors under the control of the parties) has as its object one of these restrictions, it will not benefit from the Block Exemption and will be subject to scrutiny under Article 81 and/or the Chapter I prohibition. These are:

- **Restrictions concerning the territory into which, or the customers to whom, the buyer may sell** – as a general principle a buyer must remain free to decide where and to whom he sells the contract goods or services and this cannot be restricted by the agreement. This general principle is subject to certain exceptions.[14]
- **Restrictions on sales to end-users by authorised retail distributors in a selective distribution system** – a producer applying a selective distribution system cannot restrict active or passive selling by the authorised distributors (operating at the retail level of trade) to end-users, except that the supplier can require the distributor to sell only from a given location.
- **Restrictions on authorised distributors in a selective distribution system selling or purchasing from other members of the network** – the appointed distributors in a selective distribution system cannot be restricted from buying or selling the contract goods to or from other appointed distributors within the network operating either at the same or at a different level of trade.

- **Restrictions on the sale of components as spare parts by the manufacturer of the component to end-users, independent repairers and service providers** – an agreement between a supplier of component parts and a buyer which incorporates these parts into its own products (the original equipment manufacturer) may not prevent or restrict sales by the supplier of these component parts as spare parts to end-users, independent repairers or service providers.

3.27 These restrictions are discussed in further detail in the European Commission's Notice *Guidelines on Vertical Restraints*.

Excluded obligations

3.28 Article 5 of the Block Exemption imposes specific conditions for certain types of obligations. If such obligations are contained in a vertical agreement and they do not comply with the conditions in Article 5, the Block Exemption will not apply to those obligations. This does not prevent the remainder of the agreement from benefiting from the Block Exemption, if the obligations are severable from the remainder of the agreement.

3.29 The Block Exemption does **not** apply to the following obligations:

- **Non-compete obligations[15] during the term of the contract which exceed five years** – any direct or indirect non-compete obligation which is indefinite (including those which are tacitly renewable beyond five years) or exceeds five years. The five year time limit does not apply if the contract goods or services are sold by the buyer from premises and land owned or leased by the supplier. In such cases, the time limit must not exceed the buyer's occupancy.
- **Non-compete obligations after the termination of the contract** – any direct or indirect non-compete obligation on the buyer not to manufacture, purchase, sell or resell goods or services after termination of the contract. However, such an obligation can be covered by the Block Exemption provided that the obligation is limited to a period of **one** year after termination of the agreement, relates to goods or services which compete with the contract goods or services, is limited to the premises and land from which the buyer has operated during the contract, and is indispensable to protect know-how[16] transferred from the supplier to the buyer.
- **Obligations not to sell particular competing brands in a selective distribution system** – any direct or indirect obligation causing the members of a selective distribution system not to sell the brands of particular competing suppliers.

WITHDRAWAL OF THE BLOCK EXEMPTION

3.30 As mentioned above, the Block Exemption exempts vertical agreements because they do not generally give rise to competition concerns. The OFT may, under Article 29(2) of the Modernisation Regulation, withdraw the benefit of the Block Exemption from any agreement if the following conditions are met:

- the agreement in question has effects that are incompatible with Article 81(3) in the territory of the United Kingdom, or a part of the United Kingdom, and
- the relevant territory has all the characteristics of a distinct geographical market.[17]

In the case of withdrawal of the Block Exemption by the OFT, it will be for the OFT to demonstrate that the agreement infringes Article 81(1) and that it does not satisfy the conditions of Article 81(3) of the United Kingdom (or part of the United Kingdom) that is a distinct geographic market. In practice the OFT is likely to exercise this power only rarely. The United Kingdom courts have no power to withdraw the benefit of the Block Exemption.

3.31 Where the OFT proposes to exercise its powers to withdraw the benefit of the Block Exemption from an agreement it must, following the procedures specified in the OFT's Rules,[18] give written notice to the parties to that agreement and give them the opportunity to make representations. It may also consult the public. If the OFT has decided to withdraw the benefit of the Block Exemption it will notify the parties to that agreement of its decision and will publish the decision on a public register on the OFT's website.

Consequences of withdrawal

3.32 Where the OFT decides to withdraw the benefit of the Block Exemption from a particular agreement it at the same time establishes that the agreement infringes Article 81. Such an infringement finding can have effect only from the date of the withdrawal. The agreement will be void only from the date of withdrawal and any financial penalties imposed in respect of that agreement can relate only to the period after the withdrawal of the Block Exemption.

3.33 Withdrawal of the Block Exemption in a particular case will result in any parallel exemption also ceasing to have effect, by virtue of section 10(4)(b) of the Act.

NOTES

8 Section 10(1) provides that an agreement is exempt from the Chapter I prohibition if it is exempt from the Community prohibition 'by virtue of a regulation', and section 10(2) provides that 'an agreement is exempt from the Chapter I prohibition if it does not affect trade between Member States but otherwise falls within a category of agreement which is exempt from the Community prohibition by virtue of a Regulation'.

9 EC block exemption regulations currently in force include: Commission Regulation (EC) No 2658/2000 on the application of Article 81(3) of the Treaty to categories of specialisation agreements; Commission Regulation (EC) No 2659/2000 on the application of Article 81(3) of the Treaty to categories of research and development agreements; Commission Regulation (EC) No 1400/2002 on the application of Article 81(3) of the Treaty to categories of vertical agreements and concerted practices in the motor vehicle sector; and Commission Regulation (EC) No 772/2004

on the application of Article 81(3) of the Treaty to categories of technology transfer agreements.

10 Commission Notice 2000/C 291/01 (OJ C291, 13.10.2000, p 1).

11 Competing undertakings for the purpose of the Block Exemption means actual or potential suppliers in the same product market; the product market includes goods or services which are regarded by the buyer as interchangeable with or substitutable for the contract goods or services, by reason of the product's characteristics, their prices and their intended use.

12 Commission Regulation (EC) No 772/2004 of 27 April 2004 on the application of Article 81(3) of the Treaty to categories of technology transfer agreements, OJ L123, 27.04.04, p 11.

13 Article 1(c) of the Block Exemption defines exclusive supply obligation as 'any direct or indirect obligation causing the supplier to sell the goods or services specified in the agreement only to one buyer inside the Community for the purposes of a specific use or for resale'.

14 The supplier can restrict a buyer from making 'active sales' into a territory allocated exclusively to another buyer or which the supplier has reserved exclusively to itself; the supplier can restrict sales by a wholesaler to end-users; the supplier can restrict distributors in a selective distribution system from selling to unauthorised distributors in markets where such a system is operated; and the supplier can restrict a buyer of components supplied for incorporation from re-selling them to competitors of the supplier (Article 4(b) of the Block Exemption).

15 Non-compete obligations for the purposes of the Block Exemption are obligations that directly or indirectly cause the buyer not to manufacture, purchase, sell or resell competing goods or services, or to purchase from the supplier, or another designated undertaking, more than 80 per cent of the buyer's total purchases of the contract goods or services and their substitutes on the relevant market, thereby preventing the buyer from purchasing competing goods and services or limiting such purchases to 20 per cent (Article 1(b) of the Block Exemption).

16 According to the definition in article 1(f) of the Block Exemption, the know-how needs to be 'substantial', meaning that the know-how includes information which is indispensable to the buyer for the use, sale or resale of the contract goods or services.

17 Article 29(2) of the Modernisation Regulation.

18 The Competition Act 1998 (Office of Fair Trading's Rules) Order 2004 (SI 2004/2751), rule 13.

4. ARTICLE 81(3) AND SECTION 9(1) OF THE ACT

[3.133]

4.1 A vertical agreement that does not benefit from the Block Exemption or from any other block exemption may still not be prohibited if it falls under the **legal exception regime**, introduced by the Modernisation Regulation. The phrase **legal exception regime** means that an agreement that falls within Article 81(1) but which satisfies the conditions set out in Article 81(3) shall not be prohibited, no prior decision to that effect being required. Such an agreement is valid and enforceable from the moment that the conditions in Article 81(3) are satisfied and for as long as that remains the case.

4.2 The Act has been amended similarly to mirror this approach so that an agreement that falls within the Chapter I prohibition but which satisfies the conditions set out in section 9(1) of the Act shall not be prohibited, no prior decision to that effect being required. Such an agreement is valid and enforceable from the moment that the conditions in section 9(1) are fulfilled and for as long as that remains the case.

4.3 Article 81(3) sets out four conditions which must all be met. It provides that the prohibition in Article 81(1) is inapplicable in respect of any agreement:

> 'which contributes to improving the production or distribution of goods or to promoting technical or economic progress, while allowing consumers a fair share of the resulting benefit, and which does not:
>
> (a) impose on the undertakings concerned restrictions which are not indispensable to the attainment of these objectives
>
> (b) afford such undertakings the possibility of eliminating competition in respect of a substantial part of the products in question.'

4.4 The wording of section 9(1) is similar to that of Article 81(3) except that in the first condition in section 9(1) the phrase 'of goods' is not included. The omission of these words is intended to make clear (consistent with the practice of the European Commission in relation to Article 81(3)) that improvements in production or distribution in relation to services may also satisfy the first condition in section 9(1).

4.5 Part 7 of this guideline describes some of the ways in which vertical agreements might contribute to improving production or distribution, or promoting technical or economic progress.[19]

4.6 The European Commission has issued a Notice entitled *Guidelines on the application of Article 81(3) of the Treaty*[20] to assist companies and their advisers in determining whether an agreement satisfies the conditions in Article 81(3). The OFT will have regard to this Notice in considering the application of Article 81(3) and section 9(1) of the Act. More detailed information on the legal exception regime can be found in the competition law guideline *Agreements and concerted practices* (OFT 401).

NOTES

19 This part of the guideline should be read together with the European Commission's Notice *Guidelines on Vertical Restraints*, in which the Commission has set out the principles and factors relevant for the assessment of individual agreements under Article 81(1) and Article 81(3). As mentioned in paragraph 3.2 above, the OFT will have regard to this Notice in its assessment of vertical agreements, in relation to both Article 18 and Chapter I prohibition.

20 OJ C101, 27.04.04, pp 97–118.

5. THE UK EXCLUSION ORDER

[3.134]

5.1 The UK Exclusion Order, made under section 50 of the Act, excludes vertical agreements (as defined in the UK Exclusion Order) from the application of the Chapter I prohibition. It is repealed with effect from 1 May 2005 upon entry into force of the Competition Act 1998 (Land Agreements Exclusion and Revocation) Order 2004[21] (Land Agreements Exclusion Order). During the transitional period the operation of the UK Exclusion Order remains unchanged. Following the repeal of the UK Exclusion Order vertical agreements that do not benefit from the Land Agreements Exclusion Order will need to be assessed for compatibility within the Chapter I prohibition. Such agreements may benefit from the parallel application of the Block Exemption, which is discussed in Part 3 above, or under the legal exception regime which is discussed in Part 4 above.

5.2 The UK Exclusion Order and, when it comes into force, the Land Agreements Exclusion Order, only offer protection from the Chapter I prohibition and do not preclude the application of Article 81 where there is an effect on trade between Member States.

5.3 The UK Exclusion Order largely applies to the same types of agreements as the Block Exemption, as it was intended to follow closely the treatment of vertical agreements in the European Community. The main differences between the operation of the UK Exclusion Order and the Block Exemption are:

- The UK Exclusion Order does not preclude the application of Article 81 where there is an effect on trade between Member States, whereas the Block Exemption has a parallel effect and thereby precludes the application of both Article 81 and the Chapter I prohibition
- The UK Exclusion Order is not subject to a market share threshold test (although, like the Block Exemption, the OFT may withdraw the benefit of the exclusion in certain cases, and where one party is dominant it does not preclude the application of Article 82 and/or the Chapter II prohibition)
- The UK Exclusion Order has only one 'hardcore' restriction, which relates to price-fixing. An agreement which includes a price-fixing restriction cannot benefit from the exclusion.

5.4 The UK Exclusion Order provides that the Chapter I prohibition does not apply to an agreement **to the extent that** it is a vertical agreement. The exclusion may therefore apply only to certain parts of an agreement rather than an agreement in its entirety. It is therefore possible for some provisions in an agreement to benefit from the exclusion while others do not.

5.5 Where an agreement is only partly covered by the exclusion, and the OFT has competition concerns about the object or effect of the agreement, it is able to have regard to the whole agreement (including those parts of the agreement that benefit from the exclusion for vertical agreements) to assess whether the Chapter I prohibition has been infringed. The OFT is not, however, able to take any action against the parts which benefit from the exclusion without first withdrawing the UK Exclusion Order. The process for, and consequences of, withdrawal of the UK Exclusion Order are discussed in the competition law guideline *Land agreements* (OFT 420).

NOTES

[21] SI 2004/1260. The competition law guideline *Land agreements* (OFT 420) explains how the Competition Act 1998 (Land Agreements Exclusion and Revocation) Order 2004 operates in relation to land agreements, including vertical land agreements.

6. OTHER POSSIBLE UNITED KINGDOM COMPETITION SCRUTINY OF VERTICAL AGREEMENTS

ARTICLE 82 AND THE CHAPTER II PROHIBITION

[3.135]

6.1 A vertical agreement entered into by an undertaking which holds a dominant position in a market may be subject to Article 82 and/or the Chapter II prohibition. There is no exemption or exclusion for vertical agreements from Article 82 or the Chapter II prohibition. The OFT's application of these prohibitions is described in the competition law guideline *Abuse of a dominant position* (OFT 402).

6.2 The economic analysis of vertical restraints is often similar whether a vertical restraint is assessed under Article 81 and/or the Chapter I prohibition or Article 82 and/or the Chapter II prohibition. The factors described in Part 7 of this guideline (below) therefore also apply to the analysis of a vertical restraint when it is assessed in the context of Article 82 or the Chapter II prohibition.

THE ENTERPRISE ACT 2002

6.3 The market investigation provisions in the Enterprise Act 2002 (see the Enterprise Act guidance *Market investigation references* (OFT 511)) may, in certain circumstances, be relevant for dealing with possible competition problems in relation to vertical agreements. A market investigation may, for example, be appropriate where vertical agreements are prevalent in a market and have the effect of preventing the entry of new competitors into the market, but there is no evidence of collusion between the firms involved which might have caused this situation to arise.

7. ASSESSMENT OF VERTICAL AGREEMENTS

[3.136]

7.1 This Part describes many of the factors that the OFT considers when assessing whether a vertical agreement restricts competition and/or whether it leads to any beneficial effects. These factors relate to the economic analysis of vertical agreements in the context of Article 81 and the Chapter I prohibition. Vertical agreements may also be assessed in the context of Article 82 and the Chapter II prohibition, where the economic analysis will often be similar. This Part does not describe the application of the Block Exemption: see Part 3 above for a discussion of its application.

7.2 In this Part, reference is usually made to agreements between a manufacturer and a retailer for convenience, but the same principles apply to agreements between any two parties which, for the purposes of the agreement, operate at different stages in the supply chain and in the supply of goods or services.

7.3 There are many contracts between manufacturers and retailers which place some restriction on the commercial freedom of one or both parties, but most will not raise competition concerns because they relate to undertakings which do not have market power, either individually or collectively.

7.4 Generally, for a vertical agreement to raise competition concerns, one or more parties to the agreement must have market power, or obtain market power as a result of the agreement.[22] Even where none of the undertakings party to a vertical agreement possesses market power individually, there may be a series of similar agreements which cover a group of undertakings that collectively possess market power. Such networks of agreements may raise competition concerns.

7.5 Vertical agreements may also produce benefits, even where they do not fall under the Block Exemption or the UK Exclusion Order. Therefore vertical agreements generally need to be assessed on a case by case basis.

TYPES OF VERTICAL RESTRAINT

7.6 The term **restraint** in this Part is used to describe a restriction occurring within a vertical agreement. However, a vertical restraint may also occur as a result of the unilateral conduct of an undertaking and a similar analysis would apply to those situations in the context of Article 82 and the Chapter II prohibition.

7.7 There is a wide range of restraints which might appear in vertical agreements and which might potentially restrict competition. The following list is not exhaustive but covers the main types.

- **resale price maintenance (RPM)**: where the supplier specifies the resale price of the product. Where fixed or minimum resale prices are specified these are hardcore restrictions which will almost invariably infringe Article 81 and/or the Chapter I prohibition.[23] Price-fixing agreements, by their very nature, restrict competition to an appreciable extent. Maximum prices and recommended resale prices will not usually infringe competition law, unless their effect is to fix prices and dampen price competition
- **selective distribution**: where a manufacturer supplies only a limited number of dealers that are then restricted in their ability to re-sell products
- **exclusive distribution**: a particular form of distribution where the manufacturer supplies only one retailer in a particular territory or allows only one retailer to supply a particular class of customer (eg businesses or consumers)
- **non-compete or exclusive dealing**: where the retailer agrees to purchase, or deal in, goods from only one manufacturer
- **tie-in sales and bundling**: where the manufacturer makes the purchase of one product (the tying product) conditional on the purchase of a second product (the tied product). A set of tied products is sometimes referred to as a bundle of products
- **full-line forcing**: an extreme form of tie-in sale where, in order to obtain one product in the retailer's range, the retailer must stock all the products in that range and
- **quantity forcing**: where the retailer is required to purchase a minimum quantity of a certain product.

7.8 The following paragraphs explain briefly possible anti-competitive effects of vertical restraints and some countervailing benefits they might produce.

COMPETITION EFFECTS

7.9 The important issue is generally not the form of the vertical restraint but its effect on competition. Usually, the first step in the analysis of a vertical restraint is to assess whether one or more parties to the agreement has market power.[24] Where this is the case, the restraint may have anti-competitive effects if its (likely) effect is to foreclose (a substantial part of) a market to competition or to dampen competition and/or in the context of Articles 81 and 82, to create obstacles to market integration. The following paragraphs provide some examples.

Example of foreclosure

7.10 A market is foreclosed either completely or partially when undertakings face barriers to entering that market, or barriers to expansion once in that market.

7.11 Selective distribution may foreclose a market to retail competition, where it is practised by a sufficient proportion of manufacturers. For example, if manufacturers of the most popular brands of a product have similar distribution agreements with their retailers (with the effect that relatively few retailers are authorised to stock the full range of popular brands), this may prevent unauthorised retailers from providing effective competition and thereby provide the authorised retailers with market power.

7.12 Selective distribution may be less likely to lead to foreclosure if, rather than imposing an absolute restriction on the number of retailers in the distribution network, any retailer may join the network provided it meets certain objective standards (where these standards are not clearly designed to favour existing retailers over new entrants).

Examples of competition dampening

7.13 Vertical restraints can also affect competition by reducing its intensity, or 'dampening' competition.

7.14 Competition dampening might occur in various ways. For instance, RPM will generally have direct negative effects on competition. Where prices are fixed absolutely, or minimum prices are specified, there will be no price competition between the retailers affected for the product concerned (ie no 'intra-brand' competition). RPM can also facilitate collusion, for example, by becoming a focal point for colluding undertakings, or by allowing undertakings to detect deviations from the collusive price more easily. Competition dampening of this sort could occur with other vertical restraints, for example exclusive distribution.

7.15 Another way is that vertical restraints can dampen not only intra-brand competition but also inter-brand competition ('inter-brand' competition refers to competition among manufacturers). For example, suppose manufacturers distribute exclusively to different retailers. Each retailer would then sell only one manufacturer's brand and so there would be no in-store inter-brand competition (ie competition among competing brands in the same retail outlet). Where the retailers in question are differentiated by location, this might make it harder for customers to compare each manufacturer's product. This could lead to demand for each manufacturer's brand becoming less price sensitive, thereby dampening competition at the manufacturing level.

Other effects

7.16 Vertical restraints might be used in combination, with a mutually reinforcing effect. For example, a selective distribution system when combined with full-line forcing might have the effect that retailers in a manufacturer's distribution system sell only that manufacturer's product.

7.17 Different forms of vertical restraints may, in some cases, have similar effects. For example, a manufacturer might require that its retailers purchase a minimum quantity of its product. If the minimum quantity is set just below each retailer's total input requirement, the effect is de facto exclusive dealing.

7.18 The parties to a vertical agreement might both benefit from a vertical restraint at the expense of consumers. For example, where a vertical restraint provides a retailer with market power, that retailer may generate excessive profits some of which are paid to the manufacturer (known as 'rent sharing').

BENEFITS OF VERTICAL RESTRAINTS

7.19 While vertical restraints, in the presence of market power, can lead to anti-competitive effects, they may also produce economic benefits. For example, vertical restraints can generate benefits through:

- promoting efficiencies
- promoting non-price competition, and
- promoting investment and innovation.

Efficiencies

7.20 Vertical restraints may generate efficiencies. For example, selective or exclusive distribution might reduce 'transaction costs' between undertakings, such as where, by limiting the number of retailers in a distribution network, a manufacturer significantly reduces its costs of distribution and of monitoring any promotional efforts required of its retailers.

7.21 In the above example, in order to reduce transaction costs the manufacturer may wish to limit the number of retailers in its network to such a degree that each retailer gains market power. If retailers exploited this market power, the manufacturer might suffer lower profits through reduced sales. Therefore, the manufacturer might set a maximum price to ensure that some of the savings in transaction costs are passed on to consumers.

Non-price competition

7.22 In some cases, a manufacturer may use vertical restraints to overcome 'free-rider' problems, for example, by dampening price competition in order to set stronger incentives for its retailers to promote non-price factors (eg pre-sales services). Overall, customers might gain, where their valuations of non-price features of the product are sufficiently high.

Example of free-riding among retailers

7.23 In some markets, 'full-service' retailers provide 'promotional effort' such as demonstrating new products, and providing pre-sales advice to potential purchasers. These services might bring benefits to the customer and help manufacturers increase sales of their products. However, strong promotional effort by full-service retailers might benefit other 'discount' retailers who sell but do not promote the product. The discount retailers could undercut the full-service retailers, since they would not incur its promotional cost. Customers might then opt to use the demonstration facilities at the full-service retailer but purchase the products from the lower-cost discount retailer. The discount retailer would then be free-riding on the demonstration services of the high-cost retailer who would lose sales and therefore be likely to cut back on its demonstration services. This might have a material adverse effect on consumers where they place a high value on pre-sales service.[25]

7.24 These problems might be more likely to arise where customers lack prior knowledge of the product and so need pre-sales information as might be the case with new or complex products or expensive, one-off purchases.

7.25 Manufacturers may use vertical restraints to overcome the problems resulting from free-riding by, for example, selective distribution conditions which would require all retailers selling their products to provide the necessary demonstration services. At the extreme, the manufacturer could use a system of exclusive distribution to ensure there was only one outlet in a particular area and therefore no prospect of free-riding. While dampening price competition between retailers, the latter may have a stronger incentive to provide promotional or other pre-sales services and overall customers might gain.

7.26 However, the free-rider problem might be capable of being solved more effectively and in a way less restrictive of competition. For example, rather than using a selective distribution network, another way to encourage promotional effort by retailers is for the manufacturer to contribute to its retailers' promotional costs.

Example of free-riding between manufacturers

7.27 Free-riding between manufacturers normally arises when a manufacturer provides support to a retailer. This might include providing information on potential customers, funding technical support for staff training and providing generic promotional equipment or material.[26] If the retailer sells the products of a number of the manufacturer's competitors, this support may generate sales for the competitors as well as the manufacturer. In this sense, the manufacturer's competitors might free-ride on the investments and support it provides the retailer.

7.28 The manufacturers might try to remedy this problem by requiring the retailer to commit to an exclusive purchasing obligation, or by using some form of quantity or line-forcing.

Investment and innovation

7.29 Vertical restraints might promote investment and innovation. For example, if a retailer contributed to the cost of a manufacturer developing a new product (eg financially or by transferring important know-how) then, once the product was developed, the retailer might be in a weak bargaining position since the manufacturer could sell its new product to rival retailers. Therefore, the retailer might require that prior to contributing finance or know-how, the manufacturer must agree that, once developed, the product will be sold exclusively to the retailer for a reasonable period.

NOTES

22 See the competition law guideline *Assessment of market power* (OFT 415).

23 See Part 3, above.

24 See the competition law guideline *Market definition* (OFT 403) for a discussion of the analysis the OFT undertakes to determine the relevant market, and the competition law guideline *Assessment of market power* (OFT 415) for a discussion of the OFT's approach to assessment of market shares.

25 Similar free-riding arguments might arise when retailers advertise on behalf of the manufacturer and thereby generate sales for competing retailers that also stock the manufacturer's product.

26 Where the manufacturer has a strong brand image, it might even provide the retailer with a mark of quality assurance, the idea being that the manufacturer would not allow its product to be stocked in a low quality retail outlet.

SERVICES OF GENERAL ECONOMIC INTEREST EXCLUSION (OFT 421, DECEMBER 2004)

[3.137]

NOTES

As to the construction of this document (following the abolition of the OFT and Competition Commission), see further the note "The Competition and Markets Authority (references to the OFT and Competition Commission etc)" in the introductory notes to Part 3 preceding **[3.1]**.

CONTENTS

1. INTRODUCTION

[3.138]

1.1 Article 81 of the EC Treaty[1] (Article 81) and section 2 (the Chapter I prohibition) of the Competition Act 1998 (the Act) prohibit agreements[2] between undertakings which have as their object or effect the prevention, restriction or distortion of competition. Article 82 of the EC Treaty (Article 82) and section 18 of the Act (the Chapter II prohibition) prohibit conduct by one or more undertakings which amounts to an abuse of a dominant position. Such activities within the common market which may affect trade between Member States fall within Article 81 and/or Article 82; activities which may affect trade in the United Kingdom (or part of it) will fall within the Chapter I and/or the Chapter II prohibition. Further details on the prohibitions contained in the Act and the EC Treaty are available in the competition law guideline *Modernisation* (OFT 442).

1.2 EC Regulation 1/2003 (the Modernisation Regulation)[3] requires the designated national competition authorities of the Member States (NCAs) and the courts of the Member States to apply and enforce

Articles 81 and 82 as well as national competition law, when national competition law is applied to agreements which may affect trade between Member States or to abuse prohibited by Article 82.

1.3 The OFT and the Regulators, within their particular sectors,[4] have concurrent powers to enforce the prohibitions of the Act and Article 81 and 82. Further details as to how the concurrent powers operate are given in the competition law guideline *Concurrent application to regulated industries* (OFT 405).

1.4 The Act and Article 86(2) of the EC Treaty exclude from the application of the prohibitions certain categories of agreements and types of conduct.

1.5 This guideline explains how the OFT interprets and applies the exclusion for 'services of general economic interest' and 'revenue-producing monopolies'.

1.6 Article 86(2) of the EC Treaty provides for an exclusion from the application of Articles 81 and 82 in respect of undertakings entrusted with the operation of services of general economic interest or monopolies producing revenue for the State. Article 86(2) states:

> 'Undertakings entrusted with the operation of services of general economic interest or having the character of a revenue-producing monopoly shall be subject to the rules contained in this Treaty, in particular to the rules on competition, insofar as the application of such rules does not obstruct the performance, in law or in fact, of the particular tasks assigned to them. The development of trade must not be affected to such an extent as would be contrary to the interests of the Community.'

1.7 The exclusion from the Chapter I prohibition and Chapter II prohibition (the Competition Act prohibitions) for 'services of general economic interest' and 'revenue-producing monopolies' is contained in paragraph 4 of Schedule 3 of the Act. Although not identical this is closely modelled on Article 86(2). The exclusion states that:

> 'Neither the Chapter I prohibition nor the Chapter II prohibition applies to an undertaking entrusted with the operation of services of general economic interest or having the character of a revenue-producing monopoly in so far as the prohibition would obstruct the performance, in law or in fact, of the particular tasks assigned to that undertaking.'

1.8 The exclusion contained in the Act was introduced in order to ensure that, as under EC law, undertakings entrusted with services of general economic interest, or having the character of a revenue producing monopoly, are protected from the full application of the UK domestic competition law prohibitions. For ease of reference, unless otherwise stated, the exclusions contained in the Act and Article 86(2) will be referred to as 'the exclusion' for the purposes of this guideline.

1.9 The OFT will interpret the exclusion strictly. Undertakings seeking to benefit from the exclusion will have to demonstrate that all the requirements of the exclusion are met. In considering whether the exclusion applies, the OFT will, in particular, need to be satisfied that the undertaking has been 'entrusted' with the operation of a service of general economic interest, and that the application of the Competition Act prohibitions or Articles 81 and 82 would obstruct the performance, in law or in fact, of the particular task entrusted to it.

1.10 Section 60 of the Act sets out principles for ensuring that the United Kingdom authorities deal with questions arising in relation to the application of the Competition Act prohibitions in such a way as to ensure consistency with the treatment of corresponding questions arising in Community law in so far as this is possible having regard to any relevant differences between any of the provisions concerned.

1.11 When applying the Competition Act prohibitions, the United Kingdom authorities are under a dual obligation. First, they must ensure that there is no inconsistency with either the principles laid down by the EC Treaty and the European Court or any relevant decision of the European Court. Second, the United Kingdom authorities must have regard to any relevant decision or statement of the European Commission. In the OFT's view, this is limited to decisions or statements which have the authority of the European Commission as a whole, such as, for example, decisions on individual cases under Articles 81 and 82. It would also include European Commission Notices and clear statements about its policy approach which the European Commission has published in its Annual Reports on Competition Policy. Section 60 of the Act is considered in more detail in the competition law guideline *Modernisation* (OFT 442).

1.12 The OFT considers that due to the extent of deregulation and liberalisation of the economy that has occurred in the United Kingdom compared to other parts of the EU, it is unlikely that there will be a significant number of cases in which previous European Commission decisions will be directly relevant when considering whether the exclusion applies in the United Kingdom. When considering the relevance of previous European Commission decisions, the OFT will consider the extent to which those decisions address questions which correspond to those raised in a particular case before the OFT.

STRUCTURE OF THE GUIDELINE

1.13 For an undertaking to benefit from the exclusion, it must satisfy the requirements of the exclusion as set out in paragraph 4 of Schedule 3 of the Act or Article 86(2), as applicable. This guideline considers each of the requirements of the exclusion in turn.

1.14 Part 2 considers the meaning of an undertaking under the Act and the EC Treaty, explains the requirements to be met for an undertaking to be considered to have been entrusted with a service of general economic interest and discusses the characteristics of 'services of general economic interest'.

1.15 Part 3 discusses how the OFT will assess whether the application of the Competition Act prohibitions or Article 81 and Article 82 would obstruct the performance, in law or in fact, of the particular tasks entrusted to an undertaking.

1.16 Part 4 discusses the factors relevant to determining whether tasks entrusted to an undertaking have the character of a revenue-producing monopoly.

NOTES

1 The Treaty establishing the European Community.

2 Reference in this guideline to **agreement(s)** should, unless otherwise stated or the context demands it, be taken to include decisions by associations of undertakings and concerted practices. The meaning of the term **undertakings** is set out in Part 2 of this guideline. The meaning of the terms **agreement**, **decisions by associations of undertakings** and **concerted practices** in the context of the EC Treaty and the Act are described in the competition law guideline *Agreements and concerted practices* (OFT 401).

3 Council Regulation (EC) 1/2003 of 16 December 2002 on the implementation of the rules on competition laid down in Articles 81 and 82 of the Treaty (OJ L1, 4.1.2003, p 1).

4 For a list of the Regulators please see inside cover.

2. SERVICES OF GENERAL ECONOMIC INTEREST

[3.139]

2.1. In order to benefit from the exclusion from the Competition Act prohibitions and Articles 81 and 82, an undertaking must be able to demonstrate that it has been **entrusted** with the operation of a 'service of general economic interest'. This part of the guideline explains what is meant by an **undertaking**, discusses how an undertaking might be entrusted with the operation of such a service and provides guidance on the interpretation of the terms **service** and **general economic interest**.

'UNDERTAKINGS' CAPABLE OF BENEFITING FROM THE EXCLUSION

2.2 The Competition Act prohibitions and Articles 81 and 82 only apply to undertakings. This section of the guideline explains when an organisation will be considered to be acting as an **undertaking** for the purpose of competition law and, in particular, for the application of the exclusion for services of general economic interest and revenue-producing monopolies. In addition, the guideline explains the circumstances in which public sector bodies or state-owned organisations will be considered to be undertakings.

COMMERCIAL/ECONOMIC ACTIVITY

2.3 The term **undertaking** is not defined in the EC Treaty or the Act, but its meaning has been set out in Community law. An undertaking includes any natural or legal person engaged in economic activity, regardless of its legal status or the way it is financed.[5] It includes companies, firms, businesses, partnerships, individuals operating as sole traders, agricultural co-operatives, associations of undertakings (for example, trade associations), non profit-making organisations and (in some circumstances) public entities that offer goods or services on a given market.[6] The key consideration in assessing whether an entity is an undertaking is whether it is engaged in economic activity. An entity may engage in economic activity in relation to some of its functions but not others. A parent company and its subsidiaries will usually be treated as a single undertaking if they operate as a single economic unit, depending on the facts of each case.

THE STATE

2.4 A public sector body will be considered to be an undertaking in so far as it carries out economic activities. The Competition Act prohibitions and Articles 81 and 82 will not apply to the public sector body in so far as it carries out non-economic administrative or social functions.

2.5 When assessing whether the provision of state services is economic in nature or relates to non-economic administrative or social functions, the OFT will, while taking into account the particular circumstances of each case, consider how the characteristics of the service provided by the state meet the general principles established by the relevant EC jurisprudence.

2.6 As stated, in considering whether state functions are economic or administrative, the legal status of a state organisation and the way in which it is financed are not relevant considerations. Whether the organisation is profit making will also not be determinative. An entity does not engage in economic activity simply through buying goods or services; the buying must be considered in conjunction with the end use of the goods or services bought. For example, an entity buying goods or services to advance a purely social activity is unlikely to be engaging in economic activity.[7] Equally, the supply of goods or services in the execution of an exclusively social function (such as the provision of health services on a non-profit making basis on the principle of solidarity, where the entitlement to services is not dependent on the amount of contributions) is unlikely to be an economic activity.[8] It is expected that the circumstances in which a public body operates as an undertaking for the purposes of the Competition Act prohibitions and Articles 81 and 82 will be clarified once the European Court of Justice has handed down its judgment in the appeal of the Court of First Instance's decision in *FENIN*.[9]

2.7 The policy of successive UK governments has been to expose the activity of parts of the public sector to competition or economic regulation, sometimes coupled with privatisation. It is therefore possible that, over time, functions that may once have been considered to be exclusively administrative or social will come to be regarded as economic.

2.8 It should be noted that these questions cannot be looked at in isolation, and that the OFT will in each case take into account all relevant factors.

ENTRUSTED

2.9 The Act and Article 86 require an undertaking seeking to benefit from the exclusion for services of general economic interest to demonstrate that it has been **entrusted** with the service in question by a public authority. This part of the guideline explains the circumstances in which a public authority might be considered to have **entrusted** an undertaking with the operation of a service of general economic interest.

2.10 A public authority capable of entrusting a task to an undertaking can be part of national, regional or local government. It can also include the Regulators.

2.11 The act of entrustment may be by way of legislative measures or regulation.[10] An undertaking may also be entrusted through the grant of a concession,[11] or licence governed by public law. In *Almelo*[12] the European Court held that the state-owned regional electricity distribution company Energiebedrijf IJsselmij, through being granted a non-exclusive licence governed by public law, had been entrusted with the operation of the provision of a service of general economic interest, as laid out in the licence.

2.12 Alternatively, the method of entrustment could be through an act of a public authority. In *IJsselcentrale*,[13] the European Commission concluded that an electricity distribution company was entrusted with a task, even though the grant was awarded by a ministerial order and not by statute. However, mere approval by a public authority of the activities carried out by the undertaking will be insufficient.[14]

2.13 The exclusion applies only to the particular tasks entrusted to the undertaking and not in respect of the undertaking or its activities generally.

2.14 For obligations imposed on an undertaking entrusted with the operation of a service of general economic interest to fall within the particular tasks entrusted to it, they must be linked to the subject matter of the service of general economic interest in question and contribute directly to that interest.[15] In a number of regulated sectors, organisations participating in these sectors are required to sign agreements that ensure the safe and secure operation of networks. If obligations under parts of these agreements were found to be services of general economic interest and therefore benefit from the exclusion, it should not be presumed that other parts of the agreement also benefit from the exclusion. This is discussed in more detail in Part 3 of this guideline.

2.15 While a public authority can entrust the operation of a service to an undertaking, it can only do so in its role as a public authority. The OFT will not consider a private contract entered into by a public authority, the purpose of which is for the authority itself to undertake an economic activity, to amount to an entrustment of the service. An example of this type of private agreement would be a local authority that 'self wins' a franchise awarded by the authority for the provision of refuse services.

SERVICES OF GENERAL ECONOMIC INTEREST

2.16 The definition of **services** in this context is broad and may include the distribution of goods[16] as well as the provision of services. The OFT will interpret 'services' in accordance with EC case law.

2.17 The European Commission has stated[17] that services of general economic interest are services that public authorities consider should be provided in all cases, whether or not there is an incentive for the private sector to do so. It has also stated that EU Member States are free to determine those services which they consider to be in the general interest.[18] Where public authorities consider that such services will not be satisfactorily provided by the market, the European Commission has stated that public authorities are free to set specific service obligations on undertakings that are entrusted to operate the services of general interest.[19]

2.18 Although the OFT recognises the need to ensure the provision of certain services which the market would not otherwise provide, it considers that, in the majority of cases, the free operation of the market will be best able to provide services of general economic interest to meet the needs of consumers.

DISTINCTION BETWEEN SERVICES OF GENERAL INTEREST AND SERVICES OF GENERAL ECONOMIC INTEREST

2.19 The European Commission has distinguished between services of general economic interest and services of general interest. Services of general interest include all services whether of an economic nature or not. In general, the internal market and competition rules under the Treaty have no impact on services of general interest to the extent that these services constitute non-economic activities.[20] Therefore, the exclusion is only services of a general economic interest.

2.20 The term **economic** has been interpreted as referring to the nature of the service itself, rather than the **interest**. The European Court has held that services of an economic nature may include activities in the cultural, social, public health and educational fields if their aim is to make an economic profit.[21]

2.21 To be a service of general economic interest, a service must not be one that is concerned with managing private interests. For example, the service of managing the copyrights of an association's members is not a service of general economic interest.[22]

2.22 To be a service of general economic interest the European Commission and the European Court have considered that the service must be widely available and not restricted to a class, or classes, of customers. However, a service directed at a particular group of customers may be able to benefit from the exclusion if the assessment of whether to offer the service was based on furthering the general economic interest. For example, a service of general economic interest may include the provision of services which aid regional development and are restricted to certain geographical areas.[23]

NOTES

5 Case C-41/90 *Höfner & Elser v Macrotron GmbH* [1991] ECR 1-1979, and Case T-319/99 *FENIN v Commission* [2003] ECR II-357, CFI; on appeal C-205/03P judgment pending.

6 See OFT's Policy Note 1/2004 available on its website at www.oft.gov.uk.

7 Case T-319/99 *FENIN v Commission* [2003] ECR II-357; on appeal C-205/03P judgment pending. C.f. the approach taken by the Competition Commission Appeal Tribunal in Case 1006/2/1/01 *Bettercare Group Limited v Director General of Fair Trading* [2002] CompAR 229 (*Bettercare II*).

8 Case C-264/01, C-306/01, C-354/01 and C-355/01 *AOK Bundesverband*, judgment of 16 March 2004 (unpublished). See also Cases C-159 and 160/91 *Poucet & Pistre* [1993] ECR 1-637 [Cf *Bettercare II*]. See also OFT Policy Note 1/2004 available on its website at www.oft.gov.uk/nr/rdonl yres/b63accdc-73bc-4af9-b452-a8b46535d069/0/oft443.pdf

9 Case T-319/99 *Fenin v Commission* [2003] ECR II-357; on appeal C-205/03P judgment pending.

10 *British Telecommunications* OJ 1983 L360/36.

11 C-159/94 and C-160/94 *EC Commission v the French Republic* [1997] ECR I-05815.

12 Case C-393/92 *Municipality of Almelo and Others v NV Energiebedrijf IJsselmij* [1994] ECR I-1477.

13 Commission Decision 91/50/EEC relating to a proceeding under Article 85 of the EEC Treaty (IV/32.732 – *IJselcentrale and others*) OJ 1991 L28/32.

14 See Commission Decision 85/77/EEC relating to a proceeding under Article 85 of the EEC Treaty (IV/30.717 – *Uniform Eurocheques*) OJ L 35 7.2.1985 p.43.

15 Case C-159/94 *Commission v. France (French Gas and Electricity Monopolies)* [1997] ECR I-5815.

16 Case C-172/82 *Fabricants Raffineurs D'huile de Graissage v Inter-Huiles* [1983] ECR 555.

17 Communication from the Commission, Services of general interest in Europe, European Commission, 19 January 2001 OJ 2001 C17/4.

18 Communication from the European Commission, Services of general interest in Europe, European Commission, 19 January 2001 OJ 2001 C17/4, paragraph 22.

19 Communication from the European Commission, Services of general interest in Europe, European Commission, 19 January 2001 OJ 2001 C17/4, paragraph 14.

20 Communication from the Commission, Services of general interest in Europe, European Commission, 19 January 2001 OJ 2001 C17/4.

21 Case C-109/92 *Wirth v Landeshauptstadt Hannover* [1993] ECR I – 6447. This case related to the provisions of the Treaty on the freedom to provide services and not to the interpretation of Article 86.

22 Case 127/73 *Belgische Radio en Televisie et Societe Belge des Auteurs, Compositeurs et Editeurs v. SV SABAM et NV Fonior* [1974] ECR 313.

23 Case 66/86 *Ahmed Saeed Flugreisen and Silver Line Reiseburo GmbH v Zentrale zur Bekampfung unlauteren Wettbewerbs e.V.* [1989] ECR 803.

3. EXTENT TO WHICH RESTRICTIONS ON COMPETITION BENEFIT FROM THE EXCLUSION

[3.140]

3.1 Restrictions on competition from other economic operators must be allowed in so far as they are necessary in order to enable the undertaking entrusted with the service of general economic interest to provide the service in question. In that regard, it is necessary to take into consideration the economic conditions in which the undertaking operates and the constraints placed on it, in particular the costs which it has to bear.[24] The European Court has held that the exclusion may apply where the restriction on competition is necessary for an undertaking to perform the service of general economic interest under economically acceptable conditions.[25] An undertaking seeking to benefit from the services of general economic interest exclusion must show that the application of the Competition Act prohibitions or Articles 81 and 82 would require it to perform the task entrusted to it under economically unacceptable conditions.

3.2 The OFT would need to be satisfied that the obligations on the undertaking could not be discharged in ways which would have a less restrictive or distorting effect on competition.

3.3 The European Court has held that it is sufficient that the performance, in law or fact, of the obligations on the undertaking would not be possible were the prohibitions to apply. It is not necessary that the survival of the undertaking itself is threatened for the exclusion to apply.[26]

3.4 In a number of cases[27] the exclusion was found to apply to exclusive rights to provide a service of general economic interest in order to protect a 'universal service' obligation, as otherwise the undertakings in question would not have been able to meet their service obligations. Without the benefit of the exclusion, competition would allow new entrants to target profitable customers (so called 'cherry picking' or 'cream skimming'), while leaving unprofitable customers to the incumbent (leading to higher prices being charged to those customers or a reliance on state subsidies).

3.5 Over the last two decades privatisation and liberalisation in the United Kingdom has significantly reduced the number of services for which exclusive rights are held. In addition, the introduction of EC Directives concerning common rules for the internal market in electricity[28] natural gas[29] and postal services[30] and the development of measures to promote competition in electronic communications and rail services since the above Article 86(2) cases were considered will also render these precedents less relevant in the EU as more of the markets are opened up to competition and the number of exclusive rights over aspects of services are reduced.

3.6 The OFT considers that, in general, effective competition will best serve the interests of consumers over time. Therefore, as stated, the OFT will interpret the exclusion strictly.

3.7 The OFT considers that it will in principle be for the undertaking seeking to benefit from the exclusion to show that the application of the Competition Act prohibitions or Article 81 or 82 would require it to perform the task entrusted to it under economically unacceptable conditions. The OFT will expect to see evidence that applying one or more prohibitions would necessarily result in economically unacceptable conditions.[31] The OFT considers that it is insufficient to show that there is a mere possibility that the application of one or more of the prohibitions would lead to a situation where the prevailing economic conditions were unacceptable.

3.8 The OFT will also need to be satisfied by the undertaking that the obligations on the undertaking could not be discharged in other ways, which would have a less restrictive or distorting effect on competition.

NOTES

24 Case C-393/92 *Municipality of Almelo and Others v NV Energiebedrijf Ijsselmij* [1994] ECR I-1477.

25 Case C-157/94 *Commission v Netherlands*, Case C-158/94 *Commission v Italy* [1997] and Case C-159/94 *Commission v France* [1997] ECR I-5815, ECR 1-5699, 5789, 5815.

26 Joined cases C-157/94 *Commission v Netherlands*, C-158/94 *Commission v Italy* and C-159/94 and C-160/94 *Commission v France* [1997] ECR I-5699, 5789, 5815.

27 Including Case C-320/91 *Criminal proceedings against Paul Corbeau* [1993] ECR I-2533, and Case C-266/96 *Corsica Ferries France SA v Gruppo Antichi Ormeggiatori del Porto di Genova Coop. and Others* [1998] ECR I-3949.

28 Directive 2003/54/EC of the European Parliament and of the Council of 26 June 2003 Concerning Common Rules for the Internal Market in Electricity and repealing Directive 96/92/EC, OJ 176 17.7.2003, p 37.

29 Directive 2003/55/EC of the European Parliament and of the Council of 26 June 2003 concerning the Common Rules for the Internal Market in Natural Gas and repealing Directive 98/30/EC, OJ 176 15.7.2003, p 57.

30 Directive 97/67/EC of the European Parliament and the Council of 15 December 1997 on common rules for the development of the internal market of Community postal services and the improvement of quality of service OJ 015, 21.1.1998, p 14, as amended by directive 2002/39/EC with regard to further opening to competition of Community postal services OJ L176, 5.7.2002, p 21.

31 See Case C-157/94 *Commission v Netherlands* at paragraph 51 and Case 159/94 *Commission v France* at paragraph 94 [1997] ECR I-5815, ECR I-5699, 5815.

4. UNDERTAKINGS HAVING THE CHARACTER OF A REVENUE-PRODUCING MONOPOLY

[3.141]

4.1 The exclusions contained in paragraph 4 of schedule 3 of the Act and Article 86(2) also allow for tasks entrusted to undertakings which have the character of a revenue-producing monopoly to be excluded from the prohibitions of the Act and of Articles 81 and 82. This part of the guideline discusses the criteria that need to be met in order to benefit from the exclusion as a revenue-producing monopoly and discusses why the OFT considers it extremely unlikely that any revenue-producing monopolies exist or will exist in the United Kingdom.

4.2 The OFT considers that in order to benefit from the exclusion as a revenue-producing monopoly, an undertaking must have as its principal objective the raising of revenue for the state through the provision of a particular service. Undertakings must have been granted an exclusive right to provide the service, and hence be the monopoly provider of that service. A revenue-producing monopoly must also show that the application of the prohibitions of the Act or Article 81 or Article 82 would obstruct the performance, in law or in fact, of the particular tasks assigned to it.[32]

4.3 There are very few cases in the jurisprudence of the EC courts or in the decisions of the European Commission in which the revenue-producing monopoly exclusion has been considered.[33] The main reason for this is that very few monopolies are established with the principal objective of raising revenue for the state.

4.4 The OFT considers that it is unlikely that there are any revenue-producing monopolies in the United Kingdom at this time. None of the privatised utilities would qualify nor would they have done so when under state ownership, as the raising of revenue was not their principal objective.

NOTES

32 See the wording of the exclusion.

33 The application of exclusion to the French and Italian match monopolies was considered and rejected in two Commission recommendations in 1962. (*Recommendation de la Commission a la République Française au sujet de l'amenagement du monopole des allumettes*; not available in English [1962] JO 48/1502; and *Recommendation de la Commission à la République Italienne au sujet de l'amenagement du monopole des allumettes*; not available in English [1962] JO 48/1505).

MODERNISATION (OFT 442, DECEMBER 2004)

[3.142]

NOTES

As to the construction of this document (following the abolition of the OFT and Competition Commission), see further the note "The Competition and Markets Authority (references to the OFT and Competition Commission etc)" in the introductory notes to Part 3 preceding **[3.1]**.

Note also that references to dishonesty in respect of the cartel offence are only relevant for cartels entered into prior to 1 April 2014. The Enterprise and Regulatory Reform Act 2013 (ERRA13) removes dishonesty as an element of the cartel offence for agreements entered into on or after 1 April 2014 or which relate to arrangements made or to be made on or after that date. The ERRA13 also introduces statutory exclusions and defences to the offence. For further information, see Cartel Offence Prosecution Guidance (CMA9).

CONTENTS

1. INTRODUCTION

[3.143]

1.1 On 1 May 2004, EC Regulation 1/2003 (the Modernisation Regulation)[1] came into force. The Modernisation Regulation substantially changes the framework for enforcement of European competition law. It requires the designated national competition authorities of the Member States[2] (NCAs) and the courts of the Member States to apply and enforce Articles 81 and 82 of the EC Treaty[3] (Article 81[4] and Article 82[5] respectively) when national competition law is applied to agreements which may affect trade between Member States or to abuse prohibited by Article 82. It also establishes a 'legal exception' regime. These changes are referred to in this guideline as 'modernisation'.

1.2 The Competition Act 1998 (the Act) has been amended both to take account of the Modernisation Regulation and in order to ensure that the United Kingdom system remains aligned with the EC system post-modernisation.

1.3 This guideline sets out how the Modernisation Regulation and related changes to the Act will be applied by the OFT.

1.4 An outline of the Modernisation Regulation is set out in Part 2 of this guideline. Part 3 describes the 'legal exception' regime introduced by the Modernisation Regulation. Part 4 considers the relationship between EC and national competition laws. Part 5 explains how the OFT will apply Articles 81 and 82. Part 6 deals with block exemption regulations under the EC and United Kingdom 'legal exception' regimes. Part 7 sets out the details of opinions that may be issued by the OFT on novel or unresolved questions relating to the application of Article 81, Article 82, the Chapter I prohibition, and the Chapter II prohibition and informal advice given by the OFT on an ad hoc basis.

1.5 The new framework established by the Modernisation Regulation makes co-operation between the OFT, the European Commission and other NCAs more important. Part 8 explains how cooperation will be achieved in practice. Part 9 addresses confidentiality and disclosure of information under the Modernisation Regulation and the Enterprise Act 2002 (the Enterprise Act). Part 10 sets out how the changes will affect the role of the courts and Part 11 explains the transitional arrangements that will apply to pending notifications, to individual exemptions granted by the OFT or the European Commission, and to ongoing cases.

NOTES

1 Council Regulation (EC) No 1/2003 of 16 December 2002 on the implementation of the rules on competition laid down in Articles 81 and 82 of the Treaty (OJ L1, 4.1.03, p 1).

2 As from 1 May 2004 the Member States are: Austria, Belgium, Cyprus, the Czech Republic, Denmark, Estonia, France, Finland, Germany, Greece, Hungary, Ireland, Italy, Latvia, Lithuania, Luxembourg, Malta, the Netherlands, Poland, Portugal, the Slovak Republic, Slovenia, Spain, Sweden, and the United Kingdom.

3 The Treaty establishing the European Community.

4 Article 81(1) prohibits agreements which may affect trade between Member States and which have as their object or effect the prevention, restriction or distortion of competition within the common market. Agreements which fall within Article 81(1) are prohibited unless the conditions in Article 81(3) are met. Further details on Article 81 are provided in the competition law guideline *Agreements and concerted practices* (OFT 401).

5 Article 82 prohibits conduct by one or more undertakings which amounts to an abuse of a dominant position within the common market or in a substantial part of it and which may affect trade between Member States. Further details on Article 82 are provided in the competition law guideline *Abuse of a dominant position* (OFT 402).

2. THE MODERNISATION REGULATION

[3.144]

2.1 The Modernisation Regulation has introduced a new framework for the application of Articles 81 and 82 with the aim of creating a more effective enforcement regime across the European Union. NCAs may now apply Articles 81 and 82 alongside the European Commission. This contrasts with the situation prior to modernisation under Council Regulation (EEC) 17/62, whereby the European Commission alone had the competence to apply Article 81(3) to agreements[6] that infringed Article 81(1). Article 81(1) and Article 82 were directly applicable, but there was no requirement for NCAs to have the power to apply Article 81(1) or Article 82 – and the OFT did not have this power in the United Kingdom.

2.2 The Modernisation Regulation:

- decentralised the application of Articles 81 and 82: the OFT, as an NCA, is competent to apply Articles 81 and 82 in the United Kingdom alongside the European Commission
- abolished the system of notifying agreements for exemption under Article 81(3) and the exclusive competence of the European Commission to apply Article 81(3)
- created a more level playing field for the treatment of agreements throughout the European Community: the application of national competition laws (and decisions of courts) cannot prohibit agreements, which may affect trade between Member States, which are permitted under Article 81, and
- established a network of competition authorities (European Competition Network or ECN), consisting of the European Commission and NCAs, to co-ordinate enforcement.

2.3 The Modernisation Regulation requires NCAs to apply Articles 81 and/or 82 respectively where they apply national competition law to an agreement within the meaning of Article 81(1) or an abuse prohibited by Article 82 which may affect trade between Member States. The Modernisation Regulation does not, however, lay down the procedures to be followed by NCAs in applying Articles 81 and 82.

2.4 In order to ensure the effective application of the new framework, the Modernisation Regulation requires each of the Member States to designate NCAs for the purpose of applying Articles 81 and 82. The OFT and the Regulators have been designated as NCAs for the United Kingdom.[7] The Regulators will fulfil their role as NCAs in relation to their respective sectors.

2.5 The Modernisation Regulation also addresses how the European Commission will apply Articles 81 and 82. These provisions of the Modernisation Regulation are not dealt with in this guideline, but the European Commission has issued a number of Notices explaining how it will operate under the Modernisation Regulation.[8]

NOTES

6 Reference in this guideline to 'agreement(s)' should, unless otherwise stated or the context demands it, be taken to include decisions by associations of undertakings and concerted practices.

7 Note that the Competition Commission is not designated as an NCA for the purpose of applying Articles 81 and 82. The Competition Commission is an independent public body established by the Act. The Competition Commission conducts in-depth inquiries into mergers, markets and the regulation of the major regulated industries, undertaken in response to a reference made to it by another authority.

8 The Notices are as follows: *Notice on cooperation within the Network of Competition Authorities* (OJ C101, 27.04.2004, p 43), *Notice on the co-operation between the Commission and the courts of the EU Member States in the application of Articles 81 and 82 EC* (OJ C101, 27.04.2004, p 54), *Notice on informal guidance relating to novel questions concerning Articles 81 and 82 of the EC Treaty that arise in individual cases (guidance letters)* (OJ C101, 27.04.2004, p 78), *Notice on the handling of complaints by the Commission under Articles 81 and 82 of the EC Treaty* (OJ C101, 27.04.2004, p 65), *Notice – Guidelines on the effect on trade concept contained in Articles 81 and 82 of the Treaty* (OJ C101, 27.04.2004, p 81), and *Notice – Guidelines on the Application of Article 81(3) of the Treaty* (OJ C101, 27.04.2004, p 97).

3. FRAMEWORK FOR THE APPLICATION OF ARTICLES 81 AND 82

[3.145]

3.1 The Modernisation Regulation sets out the framework for the application of Articles 81 and 82.

3.2 The Modernisation Regulation introduces a 'legal exception' regime. This means that an agreement that falls within the scope of Article 81(1) but which satisfies the conditions set out in Article 81(3) shall not be prohibited, no prior decision to that effect being required. Such an agreement is valid and enforceable from the moment that the conditions in Article 81(3) are satisfied and for as long as that remains the case.

3.3 In respect of Article 82, the Modernisation Regulation provides that abuse of a dominant position caught by Article 82 is prohibited without the need for a prior decision to that effect.

ABOLITION OF THE EC AND UNITED KINGDOM NOTIFICATION SYSTEMS

3.4 The legal exception regime, with its direct application of Article 81(3), means that undertakings are no longer required to notify agreements to the European Commission in order for those agreements to be exempt from the application of Article 81(1).

3.5 In order to ensure consistency with the EC regime, the system of notifications under the Act has been abolished. It has been amended so that an agreement that falls within the scope of section 2 of the Act (the Chapter I prohibition) but which satisfies the conditions set out in section 9(1) of the Act shall not be prohibited, no prior decision by the OFT to that effect being required. From 1 May 2004, it is not possible for the OFT to accept notifications for decision or guidance under the Act. However, the OFT will continue to offer informal advice and may (as set out in paragraphs 7.4 to 7.19 below) provide published guidance in the form of Opinions where a case presents novel or unresolved questions about the application of Article 81, Article 82 and/or the prohibitions in the Act. The OFT's treatment of individual exemptions granted before 1 May 2004 and pending United Kingdom notifications as at 1 May 2004 is set out in Part 11 below.

BURDEN AND STANDARD OF PROOF

3.6 Article 2 of the Modernisation Regulation sets out who will bear the burden of proving the facts relating to the conditions for applying Articles 81 and 82. The burden of proving an infringement of Article 81(1) or Article 82 is placed on the European Commission, the NCA or the party alleging the infringement. If an undertaking is seeking to rely on Article 81(3) then it bears the burden of proving that the conditions in Article 81(3) are met.

3.7 In order to ensure the consistent application of EC and United Kingdom law an identical approach to the burden of proof to that under Article 2 of the Modernisation Regulation applies under section 9(2) of the Act. This means that the OFT or party alleging an infringement of the Chapter I prohibition and/or the Chapter II prohibition will be required to prove the infringement. If an undertaking seeks to rely on section 9(1) of the Act in any proceedings, then it will bear the burden of proving that section 9(1) applies.

3.8 The standard of proof applied to infringement decisions under Articles 81 and 82 is that applied in the United Kingdom in relation to the Chapter I and Chapter II prohibitions.

4. RELATIONSHIP BETWEEN EC AND NATIONAL COMPETITION LAWS

ARTICLE 3 OF THE MODERNISATION REGULATION

[3.146]

4.1 The relationship between EC competition law and national law is governed by Article 3 of the Modernisation Regulation. Article 3(1) provides that where the OFT applies national competition law to agreements within the meaning of Article 81(1) which may affect trade between Member States, it must also apply Article 81 to such agreements. Where it applies national competition law to an abuse of a dominant position prohibited by Article 82, it must also apply Article 82.

4.2 What happens in the event that national competition law would lead to a stricter outcome than the position under EC competition law is also dealt with under Article 3. The position is different according to whether Article 81 or Article 82 applies.

4.3 In relation to agreements within the meaning of Article 81(1) which may affect trade between Member States, applying national competition law may not lead to the prohibition of an agreement if the agreement would be permitted under Article 81. This could be because the agreement in question does not restrict competition within the meaning of Article 81(1), the conditions in Article 81(3) are met or the agreement is covered by an EC block exemption regulation.

4.4 In relation to conduct which may affect trade between Member States, Article 3(2) permits the application of stricter national law than Article 82 to prohibit or sanction unilateral conduct. In the United Kingdom the unilateral conduct of undertakings may, for example, be examined under the market investigation provisions of the Enterprise Act.

EFFECT ON TRADE BETWEEN MEMBER STATES

4.5 As outlined above, the OFT is required to apply Articles 81 and/or 82 in addition to national competition law if an agreement or an abuse prohibited by Article 82 'may affect trade between Member States'.

4.6 The European Commission has issued a Notice entitled *Guidance on the effect on trade concept contained in Articles 81 and 82 of the Treaty*[9] (the *Effect on Trade Notice*) to assist with the assessment as to whether or not agreements or conduct have an effect on trade between Member States. The OFT will have regard to the *Effect on Trade Notice* in its application of competition law. Further information on the concept of effect on trade is available in the competition law guidelines *Agreements and concerted practices* (OFT 401) and *Abuse of a dominant position* (OFT 402).

PRIMACY OF COMMUNITY LAW

4.7 In applying Articles 81 and 82, the OFT and the national courts are bound by the fundamental principle of the primacy of Community law and must follow the case law of the European Court in interpreting Community legislation. As a consequence, an agreement prohibited by Article 81 or conduct prohibited by Article 82 cannot be permitted under national law.

4.8 The Modernisation Regulation also makes further provision to ensure consistency in the application of Community law by NCAs. Article 16(2) of the Modernisation Regulation provides that where the European Commission has taken a decision on an agreement or conduct under Article 81 or Article 82, NCAs cannot take a decision in respect of the same agreement or conduct which would run counter to the decision adopted by the European Commission.

INTERACTION WITH THE ACT

4.9 In addition to the obligations under Community law, section 60 of the Act aims to ensure that the United Kingdom authorities deal with cases under Part I of the Act consistently with Community law in so far as this is possible having regard to any relevant differences between the provisions concerned.

4.10 The provisions of section 60 of the Act apply to all United Kingdom authorities which are involved with the administration and enforcement of Part I of the Act: the OFT, the Regulators, the Competition Appeal Tribunal (the CAT) and the domestic courts.

4.11 When dealing with questions arising under Part I of the Act in relation to competition within the United Kingdom, the United Kingdom authorities are under a dual obligation. First, they must ensure that there is no inconsistency with either the principles laid down by the EC Treaty and the European Court, or any relevant decision of the European Court. Second, the United Kingdom authorities must have regard to any relevant decision or statement of the European Commission. In the OFT's view, this is limited to decisions or statements which have the authority of the European Commission as a whole, such as, for example, decisions on individual cases under Articles 81 and/or 82. It would also include European Commission Notices and clear statements about its policy approach which the European Commission has published in its Annual Reports on Competition Policy.

4.12 The obligation to ensure consistency applies only to the extent that this is possible, having regard to any relevant differences between the provisions concerned.

INTERACTION BETWEEN ARTICLES 81 AND 82 AND THE PROHIBITIONS IN THE ACT

Dual Application

4.13 In cases where an undertaking has committed an infringement of both an EC prohibition (ie Article 81 or Article 82) and the equivalent UK prohibition (ie the Chapter I prohibition or Chapter II prohibition respectively), the undertaking will not be penalised twice for the same anti-competitive effects.

4.14 Under the OFT's Rules[10] the OFT may, at any time prior to making an infringement decision, elect to apply to a case one or more of the Chapter I prohibition, the Chapter II prohibition, the prohibition in Article 81(1) and the prohibition in Article 82 (whether or not any such election has previously been made by the OFT in that case). This means that a case started under the Chapter I prohibition can be continued under Article 81 alone or (as is more likely) under both the Chapter I prohibition and Article 81 if it is subsequently concluded that there may be an effect on trade between Member States. It also means that a case started under Article 81 can be continued under the Chapter I prohibition alone if it is subsequently concluded that there is no effect on trade between Member States. The same principles apply in relation to cases commenced under the Chapter II prohibition and/or Article 82. The provisions of rules 4 (on statement of objections) and 5 (on notices, access to file and representations) of the OFT's rules shall apply to the extent that they have not already been applied.

Exclusions

4.15 Although the concept of an exclusion is not specifically recognised in relation to Article 81, under EC competition law certain categories of agreement are, in effect, excluded from the application of Article 81.

4.16 In certain limited circumstances agreements and/or conduct may benefit from an exclusion from the application of either the Chapter I and/or II prohibitions. Lists of potentially available exclusions may be found in the competition law guidelines *Agreements and concerted practices* (OFT 401) and *Abuse of a dominant position* (OFT 402). It should be noted that there are more potentially available exclusions under the Act than are available under EC law. Accordingly an agreement and/or conduct that benefits from an exclusion from the Chapter I and/or Chapter II prohibitions may still be subject to scrutiny under Article 81 and/or 82.

INTERACTION WITH OTHER NATIONAL LAW

General

4.17 As more fully explained in paragraphs 4.1–4.4 above, Articles 3(1) and (2) apply when national competition law is applied to agreements or conduct which may affect trade between Member States. However, Article 3(3) disapplies Articles 3(1) and (2) with respect to national merger control law. Furthermore, it states that Articles 3(1) and (2) do not preclude the application of national law that predominately pursues **objectives different from those pursued by Articles 81 and 82**.

4.18 The following paragraphs address key areas in which Articles 81 and 82 may interact with the application of national law. There may, however, be other areas in which such interactions occur.

Mergers

4.19 Article 3(3) of the Modernisation Regulation disapplies the requirement to apply Articles 81 and/or 82 as well as national competition law in cases where an NCA or the courts apply national merger control. As a consequence, where a merger, acquisition or joint venture is subject to investigation under the merger control provisions of the Enterprise Act there is no obligation to apply Articles 81 and/or 82 to the transaction whether or not it may have an effect on trade between Member States. This is so even if a merger, acquisition or joint venture has a Community dimension as defined in the EC Merger Regulation[11] but is subject to a reference back to the United Kingdom authorities by the European Commission. The OFT would not seek to apply Articles 81 and/or 82 in such circumstances. Market investigation references

4.20 Under the Enterprise Act, the OFT and, in certain circumstances, the Secretary of State have powers to make a reference to the Competition Commission for investigation where there are reasonable grounds for suspecting that any feature, or combination of features, of a market in the UK for goods or services prevents, restricts or distorts competition in connection with the supply or acquisition of any goods or services in the UK or part of it. The OFT's guidance on *Market investigation references* (OFT 511) explains how this power is exercised by the OFT.

The cartel offence

4.21 The cartel offence under the Enterprise Act and Article 81 and the Chapter I prohibition are aimed at different legal persons. The cartel offence is aimed at dishonest activity by **individuals** whereas Article 81 and the Chapter I prohibition are aimed at anti-competitive activity by **undertakings**. The Modernisation Regulation does not apply to national laws which impose criminal sanctions on natural persons, except to the extent that such sanctions are the means whereby competition rules applying to undertakings are enforced. The OFT considers that the cartel offence is not a means whereby competition rules applying to undertakings are enforced.

4.22 The OFT, therefore, considers that the investigation or prosecution of an individual under the cartel offence would **not** require the OFT to apply Article 81 as well.

4.23 However, the circumstances leading to an infringement of Article 81 or the Chapter I prohibition may also give rise to the prosecution of an individual under the cartel offence. This may lead to parallel investigations under the criminal provisions in the Enterprise Act and Article 81 and/or the Chapter I prohibition.

4.24 Where parallel investigations are underway, the investigating officers of the OFT will, where appropriate, act in accordance with criminal law and procedures in collecting evidence and gathering information. Where information has been exchanged between NCAs or between NCAs and the European Commission pursuant to the Modernisation Regulation, the information exchanged will not be used in evidence for the purposes of proving the cartel offence.

4.25 In certain cases, parallel investigations may be progressed where the Serious Fraud Office is leading the criminal investigation. Suitable procedures will be adopted to ensure that the two investigation teams maintain an on-going dialogue and to ensure that an investigation under Article 81 and/or the Chapter I prohibition does not prejudice a parallel criminal investigation.

4.26 In cases where the European Commission is investigating an infringement of Article 81 involving a potential criminal cartel offence in the United Kingdom, the OFT and the European Commission will co-operate to co-ordinate the investigations.

4.27 Further details on parallel investigations under the cartel offence and Article 81 and/or the Chapter I prohibition are provided in the OFT guidance on *Powers for investigating criminal cartels* (OFT 505).

Regulated industries

4.28 The Regulators are able to apply the Chapter I and Chapter II prohibitions in relation to their regulated industries by virtue of their concurrent powers under the Act. Additionally the Regulators are NCAs for the purposes of the Modernisation Regulation and are therefore able to apply Articles 81 and 82 in relation to their respective industries. Where the Regulators apply the Chapter I and/or Chapter II prohibitions, and there may be an effect on trade between Member States, they are also obliged, by Article 3 of the Modernisation Regulation, to apply Articles 81 and/or 82.

4.29 The Regulators also possess sectoral powers under national law in relation to their respective industries. Some of these powers may, in certain circumstances, be capable of being used to pursue the same or similar objectives to Articles 81 and 82, ie the protection of competition on the market, and may therefore be considered to be 'national competition law' within the meaning of Article 3 of the Modernisation Regulation. If so the application of such sectoral powers may give rise to an obligation to apply Articles 81 and/or 82 as well as the sectoral power if trade between Member States may be affected. Sectoral powers may, however, be used predominantly to pursue a different objective to that of Articles 81 and 82. In such cases these sectoral powers would not be considered to be 'national competition law' and so the obligation in Article 3(1) would not arise.

4.30 If an agreement or conduct could potentially fall within the scope of both Articles 81 and/or 82 and sector-specific powers which predominantly pursue a different objective to that of Articles 81 and 82, the Regulators will consider which regime is the most appropriate to address the agreement or conduct in question. In doing so, they will be required to bear in mind their obligations as NCAs under the Modernisation Regulation and their obligations as Regulators under national law.

NOTES

[9] OJ C101, 27.04.2004, p 81.

[10] The Competition Act 1998 (Office of Fair Trading's Rules) Order 2004 (SI 2004/2751) (the OFT's Rules), rule 10.

[11] Council Regulation (EC) No 139/2004 of 20 January 2004 on the control of concentrations between undertakings (the EC Merger Regulation) OJ L24, 29.01.2004, p 1.

5. APPLICATION AND ENFORCEMENT OF ARTICLES 81 AND 82 BY THE OFT

GENERAL

[3.147]

5.1 The OFT will generally examine anti-competitive agreements or conduct either by starting an investigation on its own initiative or as a result of a complaint received from a third party. Whilst the Modernisation Regulation gives NCAs the power to apply Article 81 and Article 82, it leaves the mechanisms for investigating infringements and enforcing decisions to procedures laid down in national law. In order to enable the application and enforcement of Articles 81 and 82 by the OFT the Act has been amended. The OFT therefore uses the powers of investigation and enforcement it has under the Act in Article 81 and Article 82 investigations. The level of financial penalties imposed will also be determined in accordance with national law.[12]

POWERS TO INVESTIGATE SUSPECTED INFRINGEMENTS OF ARTICLES 81 AND 82

5.2 The OFT's powers to investigate suspected infringements of United Kingdom competition law under the Act have been extended to cover Article 81 and Article 82. The OFT may investigate on its own behalf or at the request of other NCAs or the European Commission.[13] A detailed description of the powers of investigation available to the OFT is provided in the competition law guideline *Powers of investigation* (OFT 404).

THE OFT'S ENFORCEMENT POWERS UNDER THE MODERNISATION REGULATION

5.3 Article 5 of the Modernisation Regulation provides that NCAs may take certain decisions applying Articles 81 and 82. When applying Articles 81 and 82, the OFT may:

- require an infringement be brought to an end
- order interim measures
- accept binding commitments, and
- impose financial penalties.

5.4 These powers are broadly the same as those the OFT has under the Act to enforce the Chapter I and Chapter II prohibitions, including the power to accept binding commitments.

5.5 The Modernisation Regulation does not provide for the harmonisation of powers of enforcement or procedures between Member States. Accordingly, other NCAs may apply different powers of enforcement or procedures to those applied by the OFT. The European Commission's enforcement powers are often similar to those of the OFT, but the OFT is not required to follow the enforcement procedures of the European Commission. For instance, the OFT uses court orders to enforce interim measures and binding commitments under Articles 81 and 82. The European Commission, by contrast, uses periodic penalty payments.

5.6 A detailed description of the scope of the various powers of enforcement available to the OFT is provided in the competition law guideline *Enforcement* (OFT 407) and details of the imposition of financial penalties are provided in the *OFT's guidance as to the appropriate amount of a penalty* (OFT 423).

NOTES

[12] see OFT's *guidance as to the appropriate amount of a penalty* (OFT 423) for further details.

[13] Article 22 of the Modernisation Regulation.

6. BLOCK EXEMPTIONS

EC BLOCK EXEMPTION REGULATIONS

[3.148]

6.1 The Modernisation Regulation does not remove the existing EC block exemption regulations, nor does it affect the ability of the European Commission or the European Council to adopt further EC block exemption regulations.

6.2 Where the Commission has adopted a block exemption regulation, it may, in accordance with Article 29(1) of the Modernisation Regulation, withdraw the benefit of such an exemption when it finds that in any particular case an agreement, decision or concerted practice to which the exemption regulation applies has certain effects which are incompatible with Article 81(3) of the Treaty.

6.3 The OFT may also, in accordance with Article 29(2) of the Modernisation Regulation, withdraw the benefit of an EC block exemption regulation in a particular case from any agreement if the following conditions are met:

- the territory of the United Kingdom, or a part of it, has all the characteristics of a distinct geographic market, and
- the agreements in question have effects that are incompatible with Article 81(3) in the territory of the United Kingdom.

6.4 In cases where networks of vertical agreements fall within the terms of EC block exemption regulations and the OFT has a reasonable suspicion that the conditions set out in paragraph 6.3 apply to one or more markets in the United Kingdom, it may (as an alternative to taking action itself) decide to refer the relevant markets to the Competition Commission for investigation under the Enterprise Act. If the Competition Commission finds that the above conditions are met and that competition has been prevented, restricted or distorted by the network of similar vertical agreements, the Competition Commission may recommend to the OFT that it withdraws the benefit of the relevant block exemption regulation.

EFFECT ON THE UNITED KINGDOM BLOCK EXEMPTION REGIME

6.5 The Modernisation Regulation does not affect the Secretary of State's power under the Act to make national block exemption regulations on the recommendation of the OFT (although it may affect the circumstances in which such a recommendation would be made). Existing national block exemption regulations continue to apply.[14] In respect of EC block exemption regulations, the operation of the Act parallel exemption similarly remains unaffected. National block exemption regulations do not apply for the purpose of Article 81.

NOTES

14 Currently there is one United Kingdom block exemption: Competition Act 1998 (Public Transport Ticketing Schemes Block Exemption) Order 2001 (SI 2001/319).

7. OPINIONS AND INFORMAL ADVICE

GENERAL

[3.149]

7.1 Undertakings will generally be well placed to analyse the effect of their own conduct under Article 81 and Article 82 and under the Chapter I and Chapter II prohibitions in the light of relevant Community case law and Community instruments including EC block exemption regulations and European Commission notices. Further, United Kingdom case law and competition law guidelines such as this one are also available to assist undertakings in considering the application of the law under the Act.

7.2 Undertakings may request confidential informal advice on the application of Article 81, Article 82 and/or the prohibitions in the Act by contacting OFT officials on an ad hoc basis. However, in specific cases that raise novel or unresolved questions of law, it may be possible to obtain fuller written guidance from the European Commission in the form of a Guidance Letter or from the OFT in the form of an Opinion.

THE EUROPEAN COMMISSION'S APPROACH

7.3 The European Commission has published a notice setting out its intention to issue Guidance Letters in certain circumstances, most particularly where a case gives rise to genuine uncertainty because it presents novel or unresolved questions for the application of the law. Further information about the European Commission's approach can be found in its *Notice on informal guidance relating to novel questions concerning Articles 81 and 82 of the EC Treaty that arise in individual cases (guidance letters)*.[15]

THE OFT'S APPROACH

Opinions

7.4 Where a case raises novel or unresolved questions about the application of Article 81, Article 82 and/or the prohibitions in the Act in the United Kingdom, and where the OFT considers there is an interest in issuing clarification for the benefit of a wider audience it may publish written guidance in the form of an Opinion.

7.5 In order for the OFT to consider a request for an Opinion relating to the application of Article 81, Article 82 and/or the prohibitions in the Act all of the following conditions must be fulfilled:

- There is not sufficient precedent in Community or United Kingdom case law, or decisions, practice or previously published opinions given by the European Commission's competition services or the OFT to answer the question posed.
- The OFT considers that there is a need for a published Opinion. The OFT's view of the need for a published Opinion will be guided in particular by the following:
  - (a) the economic importance from the point of view of the consumer of the goods or services to which the agreement or conduct relates
  - (b) the extent to which a new type of agreement or conduct is likely to result in wide-spread usage in the market place, and
  - (c) the scope of the investments related to the agreement or conduct in relation to the size of the companies concerned.
- The Opinion can be prepared on the basis of the information provided, ie no further substantial fact finding is required. However, the OFT may make requests for further information to assist its assessment.

7.6 The OFT will not consider a request for an Opinion in any of the following circumstances:

- the question(s) raised in the request are identical or similar to issues raised in a case pending before the European Court or the European Commission
- the agreement or conduct to which the request refers is subject to proceedings pending before a Member State court or NCA, or
- the European Commission or another NCA is already considering a request for an Opinion in respect of the agreement or conduct which is the subject of the request before the OFT
- the request relates to hypothetical questions.

7.7 A request for an Opinion should only be made to the OFT in relation to an agreement or conduct that has or could potentially have substantial, direct, actual or foreseeable effects on competition in the United Kingdom or is implemented within or originates from the United Kingdom. It follows that the OFT will only give an Opinion where there exists a material link between the agreement or conduct and the United Kingdom.

7.8 Any request based on the above criteria is without prejudice to the power of the OFT to commence an investigation under Article 81, Article 82 and/or the prohibitions in the Act with regard to the facts presented in the request.

7.9 Whilst not obliged to do so under the Concurrency Regulations,[16] the OFT and the Regulators will always consult with each other when considering a request for an Opinion where it appears they may have concurrent jurisdiction.

7.10 Undertakings considering making a request should approach the OFT informally to establish the best way to proceed.

7.11 The OFT will, in principle, evaluate the request on the basis of the information provided but may use additional information available from public sources, former proceedings or any other source. The OFT can also undertake whatever informal fact finding measures it thinks necessary, but is under no obligation to do so.

7.12 Failure to provide either additional information requested by the OFT or conclusive reasoning why such information cannot be provided will be considered as a withdrawal of the request for an Opinion.

7.13 In relation to a request for an Opinion in relation to Article 81, Article 82 and/or the prohibitions in the Act, the OFT may share the information submitted to it with the Regulators, the European Commission and other members of the ECN, request comments from these other authorities and discuss the substance of the request with them in any appropriate forum. In relation to a request in relation to the Chapter I and Chapter II prohibitions, the OFT may share information submitted to it with the Regulators, seek input from these other authorities and discuss the substance of the request with them in any appropriate forum.

7.14 An undertaking can withdraw its request at any point although the information supplied with the request will remain with the OFT and can be used in subsequent proceedings under Articles 81 or 82 or the prohibitions in the Act.

7.15 The Opinion, together with the request (or a summary of it), will be published in the public register section on the OFT's website.

7.16 Parties requesting an Opinion should provide confidential information[17] in a separate annexe clearly marked as containing such material and provide a written explanation as to why they consider that the OFT should treat the information as confidential. If the OFT proposes to disclose any of the information which has been set out in such a separate annexe it will, to the extent that it is practicable to do so, consult the person who provided the information.

7.17 Opinions may be given by the OFT to help undertakings make their own informed assessment of their agreements. In these Opinions the OFT will set out its understanding of unresolved questions regarding the application of Articles 81 and 82 and/or the prohibitions in the Act.

7.18 An Opinion cannot prejudge the assessment of the same question by the European Commission, the European Court, or the CAT. An Opinion from the OFT does not bind other NCAs or courts having the power to apply Articles 81 and 82 or the prohibitions in the Act.

7.19 An Opinion also cannot bind the subsequent assessment of the same or similar issues by the OFT, although the OFT will have regard to its Opinion when carrying out any such assessment.

Informal Advice

7.20 The OFT offers confidential informal advice to undertakings on the application of Article 81, Article 82 and/or the prohibitions in the Act through contact with OFT officials on an ad hoc basis. Views given by way of informal advice are not binding. Requests for informal advice should be made in the first place by calling the OFT enquiries line at 08457 22 44 99, or emailing enquiries@oft.gsi.gov.uk.

NOTES

15 OJ C101, 27.04.2004, p 78.

16 Competition Act 1998 (Concurrency) Regulations 2004 (SI 2004/1077). Further details about the Concurrency Regulations are set out in the competition law guideline *Concurrent application to regulated industries* (OFT 405).

17 For these purposes, information is confidential if it is:

"(a) commercial information whose disclosure the OFT or a regulator thinks might significantly harm the legitimate business interests of the undertaking to which it relates, or

(b) information relating to the private affairs of an individual whose disclosure the OFT or a regulator thinks might significantly harm the individual's interests, or

(c) information whose disclosure the OFT or a regulator thinks is contrary to the public interest."

See the Competition Act 1998 (Office of Fair Trading's Rules) Order 2004 (SI 2004/2751) (the OFT's Rules), rule 1(1).

8. CO-OPERATION WITH THE EUROPEAN COMMISSION AND OTHER NCAS

[3.150]

8.1 NCAs and the European Commission will work closely together to ensure the effective and consistent enforcement of Articles 81 and 82. The ECN facilitates close co-operation between NCAs and the European Commission and provides support for the consistent application of EC competition rules.

8.2 The Modernisation Regulation and the Joint Statement of the Council and the European Commission on the Functioning of the Network of Competition Authorities[18] (the Joint Statement) set out the main principles governing the ECN. The details of co-operation within the ECN are set out in the European Commission's *Notice on Cooperation within the Network of Competition Authorities* (the *Network Notice*).[19] The OFT acknowledges the principles set out in the Commission's Notice and will

Part 3 CMA and other Guidelines

abide by those principles, which include principles relating to the protection of applicants claiming the benefit of a leniency programme, in any case in which it is acting or may act and those principles apply.

8.3 In the United Kingdom, the obligation to inform the European Commission under Article 11(3) of the Modernisation Regulation will arise before or without delay after using the powers of investigation set out in sections 26 to 28A of the Act.

8.4 Where the OFT has taken a first formal investigative measure when investigating under Article 81 or Article 82 and the case is allocated (in whole or in part) to the European Commission or to one or more other NCAs, or is to be shared with one or more other NCAs, the OFT will notify the parties it considers are concerned by the allocation of the case as soon as is reasonably practicable. Once such an allocation has occurred, the rights and obligations of the parties in relation to that case or parts of the case allocated to any other NCA will be determined in accordance with the law that is applicable to the NCA dealing with the case.

8.5 Article 13 of the Modernisation Regulation gives the OFT the power to suspend or terminate proceedings under Article 81 or Article 82 where the same agreement or practice that it is considering is being dealt with by the European Commission or another NCA, and to reject a complaint where the agreement or practice has already been dealt with by the European Commission or another NCA.[20] This is in addition to the OFT's existing ability to suspend or terminate proceedings or reject a complaint.

NOTES

18 Available from the European Council Register at register.consilium.eu.int (Document No 15435/02 ADD 1).

19 OJ C101, 27.04.04, p 43.

20 Article 13 of the Modernisation Regulation.

9. CONFIDENTIALITY AND DISCLOSURE OF INFORMATION

GENERAL

[3.151]

9.1 There are separate provisions under the Modernisation Regulation and under the Enterprise Act as regards confidentiality and the disclosure of information.

DISCLOSURE UNDER THE MODERNISATION REGULATION

9.2 As regards disclosure under the Modernisation Regulation, the OFT acknowledges the principles set out in the *Network Notice* and will abide by those principles, which include principles relating to the protection of applicants claiming the benefit of a leniency programme, in any case in which it is acting or may act and those principles apply.

CONFIDENTIALITY AND DISCLOSURE UNDER THE ENTERPRISE ACT

9.3 The Enterprise Act sets out the requirements for safeguarding certain information and lays down the requirements that have to be met before certain public authorities, including the OFT and the Regulators, may disclose such information. The provisions in Part 9 of the Enterprise Act apply to information which has been gathered for the purpose of the OFT's and the Regulator's Enterprise Act functions and for the purposes of the OFT's and the Regulators' competition and consumer functions under specified legislation (including the Act).

9.4 The provisions apply where the information obtained relates to the affairs of an individual or any business of an undertaking. There is a general restriction on the disclosure of information during the lifetime of the individual or during the existence of the undertaking, unless that disclosure is permitted by one of the gateways in Part 9 (as explained in paragraph 9.5 below), or the information has been lawfully made public previously or is disclosed by a public authority under powers or duties which exist apart from Part 9 of the Enterprise Act.

9.5 The gateways under Part 9 of the Enterprise Act allow the OFT to disclose information in the following circumstances:

- the disclosure is made with the consent of the individual or undertaking to which the information relates and, if different, the provider of the information (if the provider's identity is known by the OFT and the provider lawfully held the information)[21]
- the disclosure is required in order to fulfil an EC obligation[22]
- the disclosure is made by the public authority (in this case the OFT or a Regulator) for the purpose of facilitating the exercise of one of its functions under the Enterprise Act or any other enactment.[23] Information that is disclosed to another person in this way, but which is not made available to the public, must not be further disclosed by that person unless the public authority agrees, and the further disclosure is made for the same purpose[24]
- the disclosure is made to any other person to facilitate the exercise of certain statutory functions of the recipient. Information disclosed in this way may not be used for any purpose other than that for which it was disclosed[25]
- the disclosure is made in connection with the investigation of a criminal offence or bringing of criminal proceedings in any part of the United Kingdom. The disclosing authority must be satisfied that disclosure is proportionate in the circumstances. The recipient may only use the information for the specific purpose for which it was disclosed,[26] or
- disclosure is made to an overseas authority in accordance with section 243 of the Enterprise Act.[27]

9.6 Before making any disclosure of information covered by Part 9, the disclosing authority must consider whether there is a need to exclude any information whose disclosure would be contrary to the public interest and whether there is a need to exclude any information whose disclosure might cause significant harm to the legitimate business interests of an undertaking (for commercial information) or information whose disclosure might significantly harm the interests of an individual (for information relating to that individual's private affairs). If the authority considers that the disclosure might significantly harm legitimate business interests or the interests of an individual, the authority is required to consider the extent to which disclosure of that information is necessary for the purpose for which disclosure is permitted to be made.[28]

9.7 The disclosure gateways set out in Part 9 of the Enterprise Act do not apply to the power to exchange information with other members of the ECN under the Modernisation Regulation (as this is a power to disclose information which exists apart from Part 9 of the Enterprise Act, as explained in paragraph 9.4). However, the considerations set out in section 244 of the Enterprise Act apply to the exchange of information covered by Part 9 with other members of the ECN under the Modernisation Regulation.

NOTES

21 Section 239 of the Enterprise Act.

22 Section 240 of the Enterprise Act.

23 Section 241(1) of the Enterprise Act.

24 Section 241(2) of the Enterprise Act.

25 Section 241(3) and 241(4) of the Enterprise Act.

26 Section 242 of the Enterprise Act.

27 Details of this type of disclosure can be found in the Enterprise Act publication *The overseas disclosure of* information (OFT 507).

28 Section 244 of the Enterprise Act.

10. ROLE OF THE COURTS

APPLICATION OF COMPETITION LAW BY UNITED KINGDOM COURTS

[3.152]

10.1 By virtue of Articles 1 and 6 of the Modernisation Regulation, United Kingdom courts have the power to apply Articles 81 and 82, including Article 81(3). As a result of changes to the Act, the United Kingdom courts also have the power to apply the conditions in section 9(1) of the Act. Further details on Article 81(3) may be found in the Commission's *Notice – Guidelines on the Application of Article 81(3) of the Treaty*[29] and in the competition law guideline *Agreements and concerted practices* (OFT 401). The latter also gives further details on the application of section 9(1) of the Act. In the same way in which the OFT is obliged to apply Articles 81 and 82, as outlined in paragraphs 4.1 to 4.4 above, the United Kingdom courts are obliged under the terms of Article 3 of the Modernisation Regulation to apply Articles 81 and 82 as well as national competition law.

10.2 The Modernisation Regulation contains certain provisions in order to achieve consistency in the application of Articles 81 and 82 by the courts across the European Union.[30]

NATIONAL COURTS AND THE EUROPEAN COMMISSION

10.3 In any case concerning Article 81 and/or Article 82 before a court in the United Kingdom, and when the coherent application of Article 81 or Article 82 so requires, the European Commission has the right to submit written observations to the court. With the court's permission, the European Commission may also submit oral observations. Further details on the European Commission's interaction with the courts in the framework of the Modernisation Regulation are set out in the European Commission's *Notice on the co-operation between the Commission and the courts of the EU Member States in the application of Articles 81 and 82 EC*.[31]

NATIONAL COURTS AND THE OFT

10.4 The Modernisation Regulation also allows the OFT, acting on its own initiative, to submit written observations to United Kingdom courts on issues relating to the application of Articles 81 or 82.[32] With the court's permission, the OFT may also submit oral observations to the court. The OFT has similar powers in cases before the High Court and the Court of Appeal in England and Wales on issues relating to the application of the Chapter I or Chapter II prohibitions. Further details can be found in the competition law guideline *Enforcement* (OFT 407).

NOTES

29 OJ C101, 27.04.2004, p 97. [Note: this footnote was numbered as a second footnote 28 in the original text; it is believed that this was an error and the above text has been amended accordingly].

30 See, in particular, Articles 3, 15 and 16.

31 OJ C101 27/04/04, p 54.

32 Article 15(3) of the Modernisation Regulation.

11. TRANSITIONAL ARRANGEMENTS

TRANSITIONAL ARRANGEMENTS FOR MODERNISATION

[3.153]

11.1 The following paragraphs set out the transitional arrangements that apply to United Kingdom notifications pending as at 1 May 2004, to individual exemptions granted by the OFT and the European Commission, and to cases ongoing as at 1 May 2004.

Notifications

11.2 Prior to 1 May 2004, undertakings were able to notify agreements or conduct to the OFT for a decision or for guidance. The OFT would determine the notification by deciding that, or by giving guidance as to whether it would be likely that, the agreement or conduct was (i) outside the relevant prohibition, or (ii) prohibited, or (iii) in the case of agreements only, exempt. From 1 May 2004, it is no longer possible for the OFT to accept notifications for decision or guidance under the Act.

11.3 Notifications made to the OFT but which did not result in a final decision or guidance by the OFT before 1 May 2004 are treated from that date as requests for informal advice. Any fees paid by an undertaking in accordance with the notification process will be refunded in full.

Individual exemptions granted

11.4 Individual exemptions granted by the OFT prior to 1 May 2004 were time limited. Each individual exemption will be valid until expiry, although the OFT retains the power to cancel such exemptions. After expiry, individual exemptions will not be renewed.

11.5 An individual exemption decision made by the European Commission prior to 1 May 2004 is binding on the OFT in its application of Article 81 until the expiry date of the individual exemption. The operation of the parallel exemption provisions under the Act will continue to apply.

11.6 The OFT will consider comfort letters issued by the European Commission, but these are not binding on the OFT.

Existing cases

11.7 As more fully explained in paragraphs 4.1–4.4 above, as from 1 May 2004 the OFT is required to apply Articles 81 and 82 to agreements within the meaning of Article 81 and abuses prohibited by Article 82 where there may be an effect on trade between Member States[33] and where the OFT is applying national competition law.

TRANSITIONAL ARRANGEMENTS APPLYING SINCE ENTRY INTO FORCE OF THE ACT

11.8 Provisions for the transition from competition legislation pre-dating the Act are set out in Schedule 13 to the Act. Some of these transitional arrangements still apply to agreements made prior to the introduction of the Chapter I prohibition.

11.9 There are no transitional periods available in respect of the Chapter II prohibition.

11.10 The Chapter I and Chapter II prohibitions came into force on 1 March 2000 (the starting date). Most agreements made prior to the starting date which complied with pre-existing laws benefit or benefited from periods of transition during which the Chapter I prohibition does not or did not apply (transitional periods). Generally the transitional period was one year commencing on the starting date. However, in some cases, the transitional periods run from the starting date and last for five years.

11.11 The following agreements made before the starting date, benefit from a five year transitional period:

- agreements to the extent to which, immediately before the starting date, they have been found not to be contrary to the public interest by the Restrictive Practices Court[34]
- agreements relating to goods which, immediately before the starting date, were exempt under section 14 of the Resale Prices Act 1976 (the Resale Prices Act), to the extent to which they consist of exempt provisions[35]
- certain agreements which have been subject to scrutiny under the Financial Services Act 1986 or the Broadcasting Act 1990,[36] and
- certain agreements in the electricity, gas and railway industries.

11.12 In addition, agreements which, immediately before the starting date, benefited from a section 21(2) Restrictive Trade Practices Act direction were excluded from the Chapter I prohibition for their duration.[37] This exclusion has now been repealed, although the repeal will not take effect until 1 May 2007. The exclusion, its repeal and the circumstances where its benefit may be lost during the period prior to its repeal are explained further in paragraphs 11.18 to 11.22 below.

11.13 Agreements which benefit from the transitional arrangements in Schedule 13 of the Act or which benefit from the Schedule 3 exclusion relating to agreements benefiting from a section 21(2) Restrictive Trade Practices Act direction are not immune from the application of Articles 81 and 82. Where there is an effect on trade between Member States the OFT may apply Articles 81 and 82 to such agreements.

THE OPERATION OF THE TRANSITIONAL PERIODS

11.14 Generally, the transitional periods began on the starting date.[38] There is an exception to this rule for certain agreements relating to the utilities (see paragraph 11.16 below).

11.15 The Chapter I prohibition does not apply to the extent to which a transitional period is available.[39] Similarly, a number of the transitional periods set out in paragraph 11.11 above apply to the extent to which an agreement meets the relevant criteria. Therefore a particular transitional period may apply only to certain provisions of an agreement rather than its entirety. Where an agreement is only partly covered by a transitional period, the OFT is still able to have regard to the whole agreement in order to assess whether the Chapter I prohibition has been breached.[40]

Utilities agreements

11.16 Schedule 13 provides transitional periods for particular agreements in the electricity, gas and railway industries.[41] In summary, the pre-existing arrangements under the Restrictive Trade Practices Act were retained for five years from the starting date, in that agreements which were exempt from the application of the Restrictive Trade Practices Act benefit from transitional periods excluding them from the Chapter I prohibition during that period.

11.17 Further details on the transitional arrangements relating to these agreements are set out in the competition law guidelines *The application of the Competition Act in the energy sector* (OFT 428) and *Application to services relating to railways* (OFT 430).

Section 21(2) of the Restrictive Trade Practices Act

11.18 Section 3 and Schedule 3 of the Act provide for an exclusion for agreements which benefited from directions by the Secretary of State under section 21(2) of the Restrictive Trade Practices Act (ie directions that the restrictions or information provisions contained in the agreements were not of such significance as to call for investigation by the Restrictive Practices Court). The majority of agreements which were furnished to the OFT under the Restrictive Trade Practices Act received section 21(2) directions.

11.19 All agreements which, immediately before the starting date, benefited from a direction under section 21(2) were excluded from the Chapter I prohibition for their duration.[42]

11.20 This exclusion has been repealed, although the repeal will not come into effect until 1 May 2007.

11.21 Where particulars of subsequent variations, made prior to the starting date, to an agreement which benefited from section 21(2) directions were duly furnished under the terms of the Restrictive Trade Practices Act, and the Secretary of State did not withdraw the section 21(2) directions, the exclusion covers the agreement as varied.

11.22 The OFT has the power to withdraw the exclusion. In addition, the benefit of this exclusion from the Chapter I prohibition is lost if, after the starting date, there is a material variation to such an agreement.[43]

EXTENSION OF TRANSITIONAL PERIODS

11.23 The OFT is able to extend transitional periods either on application by one of the parties to the agreement or on its own initiative.[44] The OFT may grant a single extension of up to six months in respect of all current transitional periods apart from the period relating to the exclusion in relation to agreements benefiting from a section 21(2) direction.

11.24 Applicants for an extension should apply to the OFT (in the first instance) in writing not less than three months before the end of the transitional period, enclosing the agreement and other relevant information, as required by the OFT's Rules.

11.25 The OFT will not grant extensions as a matter of course. It is likely to grant them only where:

- it appears from the information provided that the agreement may infringe the Chapter I prohibition if it were not for the transitional period, but not seriously infringe it, and
- there are good reasons why an extension is required – for example, the agreement is being re-negotiated, or the agreement is due to expire shortly after the end of the unextended transitional period.

11.26 Agreements involving what would be serious infringements of the Chapter I prohibition (for example, price-fixing or market-sharing) which would be unlikely to satisfy the exemption conditions in section 9(1) of the Act will not be granted an extension.

Termination of transitional periods

11.27 The OFT may require parties to provide information about an agreement subject to a transitional period and may terminate transitional periods early (clawback).[45] The OFT's Rules set out the procedural requirements for the termination of transitional periods in addition to those in Schedule 13. Failure to provide the information required within the time limit specified in the OFT's Rules without reasonable excuse may in itself result in the OFT giving a direction to terminate the transitional period.

11.28 The OFT is likely to exercise its power of clawback where it is concerned that an agreement may be having an appreciable effect on competition, such that it is appropriate to review the agreement under the Chapter I prohibition immediately rather than waiting for the transitional period to run its course. It will consider carefully complaints from third parties in respect of agreements subject to transitional periods.

11.29 The OFT has equivalent information-gathering and clawback powers in respect of agreements benefiting from a direction under section 21(2) of the Restrictive Trade Practices Act and consequently excluded from the Chapter I prohibition.[46] The OFT's Rules set out the procedural requirements for the exercise of its powers to withdraw this and other exclusions.

NOTES

[33] Article 3 of the Modernisation Regulation.

[34] Schedule 13, paragraph 23(1) of the Act.

Part 3 CMA and other Guidelines

[35] Schedule 13, paragraph 24(1) of the Act.
[36] Schedule 13, paragraph 26 of the Act.
[37] Schedule 3, paragraph 2 of the Act.
[38] Schedule 13, paragraph 19(1) of the Act.
[39] Schedule 13, paragraph 19(2) of the Act.
[40] Schedule 13, paragraph 1(5) of the Act.
[41] Schedule 13, paragraphs 27–34 of the Act.
[42] Schedule 3, paragraph 2(1) of the Act.
[43] Schedule 3, paragraph 2(2) of the Act.
[44] Schedule 13, paragraph 36 of the Act.
[45] Schedule 13, paragraph 37–39 of the Act.
[46] Schedule 3, paragraph 2(3)–(9) of the Act.

APPLICATIONS FOR LENIENCY AND NO-ACTION IN CARTEL CASES (OFT 1495, JULY 2013)

OFT's detailed guidance on the principles and process

[3.154]

NOTES

See also: (i) the CMA's information note of 3 November 2017 "Arrangements for the handling of leniency applications in the regulated sectors" at **[3.244]**; (ii) the CMA's Addendum to OFT 1495 of September 2020 at **[3.171]**

As to the construction of this document (following the abolition of the OFT and Competition Commission), see further the note "The Competition and Markets Authority (references to the OFT and Competition Commission etc)" in the introductory notes to Part 3 preceding **[3.1]**.

Note also that references to dishonesty in respect of the cartel offence are only relevant for cartels entered into prior to 1 April 2014. The Enterprise and Regulatory Reform Act 2013 (ERRA13) removes dishonesty as an element of the cartel offence for agreements entered into on or after 1 April 2014 or which relate to arrangements made or to be made on or after that date. The ERRA13 also introduces statutory exclusions and defences to the offence. For further information, see Cartel Offence Prosecution Guidance (CMA9).

See also the list of consultations and draft documents in the Appendix at **[A1]**.

CONTENTS

FOREWORD

[3.155]

The OFT's leniency policy enhances and facilitates its enforcement actions against cartel conduct. Not only does the policy help to uncover cartels that would otherwise go undetected, it also encourages firms that have been involved in wrong-doing to provide first-hand, direct 'insider' evidence and to cooperate proactively in the bringing of successful enforcement action. In return, firms who fully and actively assist us in pursuing those purposes may benefit from immunity from, or a reduction in, financial penalties. Similarly, cooperating individuals receive protection from personal sanctions in the form of immunity from criminal prosecution and/or protection from director disqualification proceedings.

The benefits of offering leniency as a key part of anti-cartel enforcement action may be summarised as:

- Detection – promoting the discovery of cartels, which are difficult to detect by customers, competitors, enforcement agencies or other outsiders.
- Desistence – causing cartels to cease operation, as termination of the cartel activity is a condition for obtaining lenient treatment.
- Deterrence – making sanctioning of cartels more likely, and thereby making cartel membership less attractive and destabilising cartel arrangements.

- Redress – facilitating compensation for victims, through publicity of otherwise undetected cartels and a greater likelihood of infringement decisions that can be used as the basis for compensation claims.

Taking all of these together, the OFT's leniency policy serves to improve the level of compliance with competition law. Although an offer of immunity or other lenient treatment to those who have infringed the law is not undertaken lightly, it is justified by the greater benefits to the community and the economy. More effective compliance with competition law will increase competition, leading to lower prices, better service, higher quality, greater innovation and greater efficiency.

1. INTRODUCTION

[3.156]

1.1 This guidance sets out the detail of how the OFT will handle applications for civil leniency for undertakings (leniency agreements) and criminal immunity from prosecution for individuals (no-action letters). This document is primarily intended for legal practitioners, as it aims to provide the reader with a thorough understanding of the OFT's approach to leniency – the overarching principles, as well as the detail.[1]

1.2 The guidance is structured to follow the natural progress of a leniency application and subsequent investigation and enforcement action. The application process is summarised in two overview charts which appear at the end of this chapter: one for applications made before the OFT is investigating and the other for situations where the applicant is already aware of an OFT investigation into the relevant cartel activity.[2]

1.3 The guidance covers requirements and procedures applicable to both civil investigations into Competition Act 1998 (CA98) infringements by undertakings and criminal investigations into cartel offences by individuals under the Enterprise Act 2002 (EA02). Applicants should note from the outset that either or both types of investigation may arise, regardless of whether the application is made by an undertaking or an individual. Leniency applicants will be required to cooperate with all relevant enforcement action. Undertakings and their advisers will therefore need to be familiar with, and follow, guidance and requirements relating to criminal investigations and prosecutions in any case where the cartel activity is potentially criminal in nature.[3] Similarly, individual no-action letter applicants may be required to cooperate with civil investigations under the CA98.

1.4 The interaction between civil and criminal procedures, and the variety of different circumstances that can give rise to leniency applications, mean that this is a complex topic. We aim to strike an appropriate balance in this guidance between detailed guidance offering certainty and maintaining sufficient flexibility to adapt the policy as appropriate in individual cases, for example where novel points or circumstances arise. It should always be remembered that would-be applicants and their advisers who are unsure about particular aspects of the policies can seek further guidance – if necessary on a no-names basis. See further paragraph 3.3.

1.5 This guidance is not published pursuant to any statutory obligation and should not be read as if it were akin to a statutory enactment. The OFT's policy in relation to the handling of leniency applications is evolving and the OFT reserves the right to depart from this guidance, where it considers it appropriate to do so in all the circumstances of the particular case. Furthermore, this guidance note does not attempt to address in advance every conceivable situation which might arise. Where there are particular issues of the policy which are of crucial significance to an applicant or would-be applicant for leniency and these are not considered to have been directly and specifically addressed in this guidance, or it is important for the applicant to be certain that a particular aspect of the note accurately reflects the OFT's current thinking, it is incumbent on the applicant to raise the matter as early as possible with the OFT so that specific guidance can be given.

1.6 The reader should take particular note of the definitions used. A glossary of terms is included at the end of this guidance.

1.7 This guidance note and the other OFT leniency documents are all available on the OFT's website (www.oft.gov.uk).

KEY FEATURES OF THE UK LENIENCY SYSTEM

1.8 The key features of the UK leniency system are:

- the availability of confidential guidance on a no-names basis about 'hypothetical' cases on request
- the ability of legal advisers to determine whether immunity is available for their client prior to the client's identity being revealed
- the availability of 'markers' for leniency pending formal agreement on the scope of leniency protection
- guarantees of criminal immunity for all cooperating current and former employees and directors in cases where the applicant informs the OFT of cartel activity that it was not previously investigating
- the availability of immunity or a reduced penalty for undertakings and/or employees/directors where an applicant is the first to approach the OFT but there is already a pre-existing investigation
- the availability of a reduction of any penalty which might be imposed on applicants who are not the first to apply and the possibility that some cooperating current or former employees and directors in such circumstances will be granted individual immunity
- a commitment that the OFT will not apply for a Competition Disqualification Order against any current or former[4] director of a company which benefits from leniency in respect of the activities to which the grant of leniency relates[5]

- the possibility of oral applications, where appropriate
- the possibility of applications by undertakings or by individuals
- a high threshold, both as to the circumstances and standard of proof, for finding an undertaking or individual to be a coercer and therefore ineligible for corporate and/or criminal immunity.

1.9 In addition to the above, the OFT hopes that the following will also be considered to be key features of the UK leniency regime:

- a reputation for fair application of the guidance
- the availability of detailed guidance, with a view to enhancing clarity, transparency and certainty for applicants
- accessibility and approachability, and
- erring in favour of the applicant where it is genuinely a 'close call'.

OVERVIEW OF TYPES OF LENIENCY AND THE APPLICATION PROCESS

1.10 Table A below summarises the different types of leniency that are available, by reference to the stage at which the application is made, the level of information provided, the conditions of leniency and the level of protection available. This is a quick reference guide and not intended as a substitute for the fuller guidance in Chapter 2 of this guidance. Note that the table relates primarily to applications by undertakings, but individuals can also apply other than as part of a corporate application.

1.11 Overview Charts A and B below illustrate the processes to be followed when applying for leniency. They refer principally to applications by undertakings, although they would also be a good starting point for any individuals contemplating making an application separately from a corporate application.

1.12 Overview Chart A shows the processes for making applications where the applicant is not aware of the OFT having already commenced an investigation into the cartel activity or closely related activity. Overview Chart B relates to the situation where the applicant is already aware of an OFT investigation.

TABLE A — TYPES OF LENIENCY (SUMMARY)

Stage of application	**Minimum information**	**Conditions** (for undertaking and any individuals seeking to benefit)	**Level of protection**
'Type A' • First applicant • No pre-existing investigation	Information must give the OFT a sufficient basis for taking forward a credible investigation.	(a) Accept participation in a cartel activity (which by definition is a breach of the law). (b) Provide the OFT with all relevant information, documents and evidence. (c) Maintain continuous and complete cooperation throughout the investigation. (d) Refrain from further participation in the cartel activity. (e) Must not have coerced another to take part in the cartel.	• Guaranteed corporate immunity from financial penalties. • Guaranteed 'blanket' immunity from criminal prosecution for individual employees or officers. • Guaranteed director disqualification protection.
'Type B' • First applicant • Pre-existing investigation, but prior to statement of objections	Information must add significant value to the OFT's investigation.		• Discretionary corporate immunity from financial penalties, or reductions of up to 100%. • Discretionary immunity from criminal prosecution for individual employees or officers, which may be 'blanket' or for some but not all individuals. • Director disqualification protection, if corporate immunity or a leniency reduction is granted.
'Type C' • Second or later applicant (or coercer) • Prior to statement of objections	Information must add significant value to the OFT's investigation.	Conditions (a), (b), (c) and (d) as above.	• Discretionary corporate leniency reductions in financial penalties of up to 50%. • Discretionary immunity from criminal prosecution for specific individuals. • Director disqualification protection if a corporate leniency reduction is granted.

NOTES

1 The OFT's general policy as to leniency (immunity from, or reductions in, penalties in civil cases) is set out in the OFT Penalty Guidance *OFT's guidance as to the appropriate amount of a penalty* (OFT 423, September 2012). The availability of criminal immunity is established in section 190(4) of the EA02.

2 Cases where the OFT has commenced an investigation but then receives a related leniency application from an applicant who was not aware of that investigation are expected to be rare. In such cases, the OFT will be able to advise the applicant of the appropriate procedure.

3 It is important to realise that the criminal activity could have been undertaken by an individual in another cartel member.

4 The OFT may consider applying for a CDO against a former director who has been removed or otherwise ceases to act as a director because of a breach of competition law and/or opposing the relevant leniency application. For further guidance *Director disqualification orders in competition cases* (OFT510, June 2010) paragraph 4.14.

5 Provided that the director cooperates with the leniency process. For further guidance see *Director disqualification orders in competition cases* (OFT510, June 2010) paragraph 4.14.

Overview Chart A: Immunity applications under OFT's leniency policy (no pre-existing investigation)

Stage 1: Decision to approach OFT

Prospective applicant conducts internal enquiries leading to an internal decision to apply for immunity (if available)

- Follow guidance on internal investigations from the time that the possibility of a leniency application is in contemplation (including keeping records of all steps) and securing evidence
- Limit enquiries to those necessary to reach a decision whether to apply (due to risks of tip-off, prejudice to future proceedings, etc)
- Keep prospect of application confidential

If in doubt and needing additional guidance on eligibility, making internal enquiries or consequences of applying for leniency, speak to OFT on a confidential basis for guidance (can be no-names)

Stage 2: Obtaining a marker

Initial enquiry made to OFT as to availability of immunity (can be no names)

- Outline information and other essential commitments required

OFT confirms availability of immunity; applicant reveals identity to obtain a preliminary marker

- See checklist for:
  - Information required (on cartel, evidence, contacts, jurisdictions)
  - Other essential commitments

Provide application package
- written or oral statement
- readily available evidence
- description of enquires/ searches made so far

OFT response (one of):
- Confirm marker but not launch investigation (prioritisation decision)
- Confirm marker and discuss next steps
- Reject marker, or
- Ask for more before confirming or rejecting

Applicant commits to complete and continuous cooperation, including measures specified by OFT

Stage 3: OFT Investigation

Extensive cooperation required from applicant

- Provision of information identified as relevant by the applicant, in addition to meeting specific requests from the OFT
- Applicant to cooperate promptly in any investigative steps by the OFT, which will usually be similar to the investigative steps conducted in relation to non-applicant parties
- Applicant to keep (and provide if required) a record of any internal investigation steps

Regular dialogue throughout the investigation, regarding:
- Specific information and tasks required from the applicant
- General progress updates from OFT
- General updates from applicant (e.g. any change in circumstances of firm or individuals, new leads/enquiries pursued)

Comfort letter may be issued if no criminal investigation is pursued

Stage 4: Agreement / No action letters

Pre-agreement meeting/ correspondence
- OFT to propose refined scope of leniency protection, in line with results of investigation
- Opportunity for party to comment on scope, noting in particular the forthcoming admission of infringement

Formal agreement signed, prior to issue of SO
- Defines scope of protection
- Applicant confirms acceptance that the reported activity amounts to an infringement
- Standard form agreement

Individual no-action letters sent, where criminal prosecution is in contemplation

Comfort letters may be issued to specific individuals not at risk of criminal prosecution

Stage 5: SO to decision/ prosecution and appeal

Applicant's duty to cooperate continues, until determination of any decision, prosecution or appeal

- OFT may require further document disclosure and/or availability of witnesses
- Continued provision of information identified as relevant by the applicant, in addition to meeting specific requests made
- Continued liaison with OFT over steps taken by applicant that may have a bearing on the OFT's enforcement action, including any further investigative steps (e.g. when preparing responses to SO)

Continued acceptance of infringement (relevant to permissible extent of challenges to SO)

Continued dialogue between OFT and applicant

- OFT to discuss with applicant any changes to the scope of its case that are significant in light of the defined scope of leniency protection

Overview Chart B: Immunity/Leniency applications under OFT's leniency policy (after commencement of an investigation)

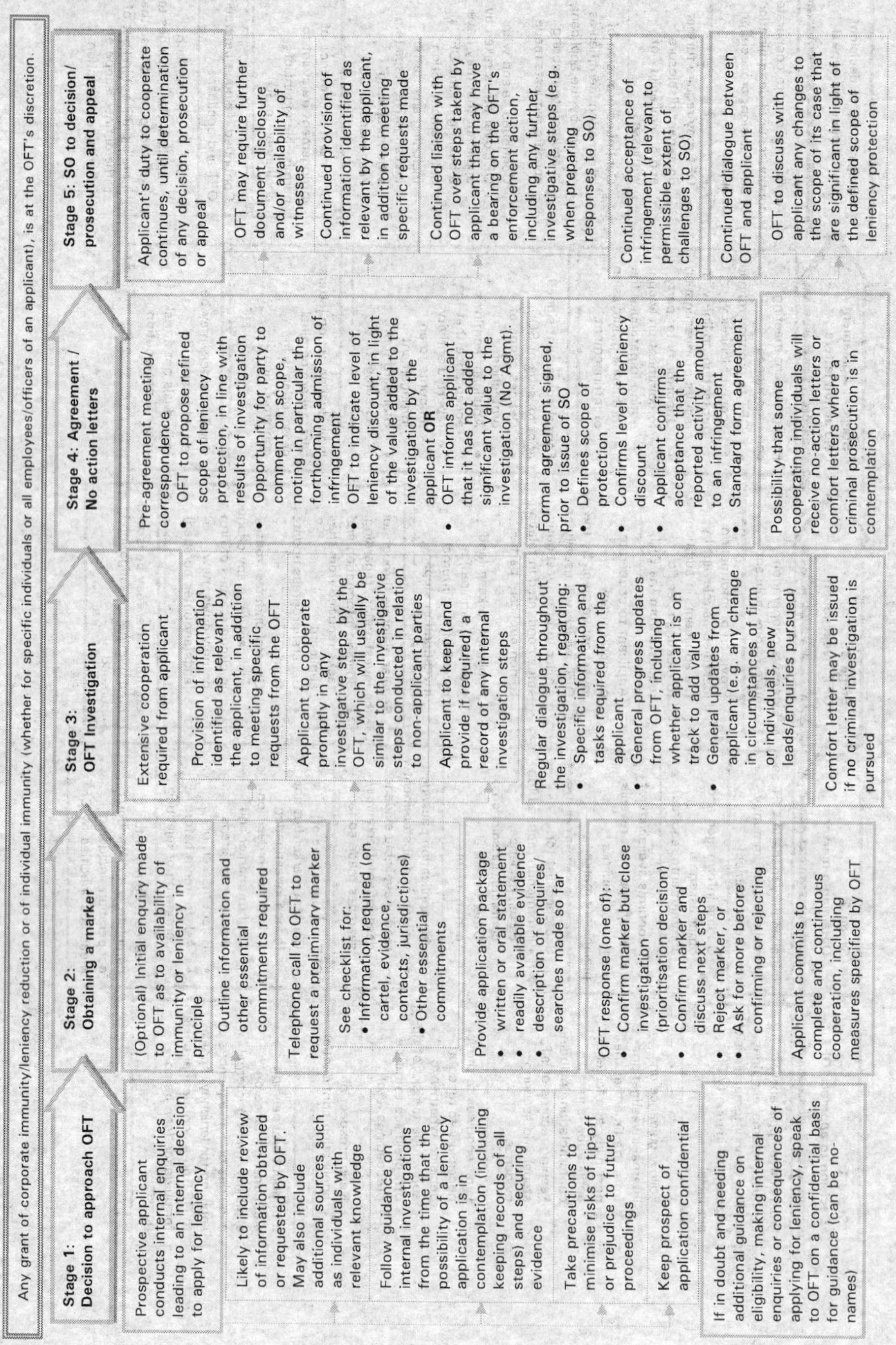

Any grant of corporate immunity/leniency reduction or of individual immunity (whether for specific individuals or all employees/officers of an applicant), is at the OFT's discretion.

Stage 1: Decision to approach OFT

Prospective applicant conducts internal enquiries leading to an internal decision to apply for leniency

- Likely to include review of information obtained or requested by OFT. May also include additional sources such as individuals with relevant knowledge
- Follow guidance on internal investigations from the time that the possibility of a leniency application is in contemplation (including keeping records of all steps) and securing evidence
- Take precautions to minimise risks of tip-off or prejudice to future proceedings
- Keep prospect of application confidential

If in doubt and needing additional guidance on eligibility, making internal enquiries or consequences of applying for leniency, speak to OFT on a confidential basis for guidance (can be no-names)

Stage 2: Obtaining a marker

(Optional) Initial enquiry made to OFT as to availability of immunity or leniency in principle

- Outline information and other essential commitments required

Telephone call to OFT to request a preliminary marker

- See checklist for:
  - Information required (on cartel, evidence, contacts, jurisdictions)
  - Other essential commitments

Provide application package

- written or oral statement
- readily available evidence
- description of enquires/ searches made so far

OFT response (one of):

- Confirm marker but close investigation (prioritisation decision)
- Confirm marker and discuss next steps
- Reject marker, or
- Ask for more before confirming or rejecting

Applicant commits to complete and continuous cooperation, including measures specified by OFT

Stage 3: OFT Investigation

Extensive cooperation required from applicant

- Provision of information identified as relevant by the applicant, in addition to meeting specific requests from the OFT
- Applicant to cooperate promptly in any investigative steps by the OFT, which will usually be similar to the investigative steps conducted in relation to non-applicant parties
- Applicant to keep (and provide if required) a record of any internal investigation steps

Regular dialogue throughout the investigation, regarding:

- Specific information and tasks required from the applicant
- General progress updates from OFT, including whether applicant is on track to add value
- General updates from applicant (e.g. any change in circumstances of firm or individuals, new leads/enquiries pursued)

Comfort letter may be issued if no criminal investigation is pursued

Stage 4: Agreement / No action letters

Pre-agreement meeting/ correspondence

- OFT to propose refined scope of leniency protection, in line with results of investigation
- Opportunity for party to comment on scope, noting in particular the forthcoming admission of infringement
- OFT to indicate level of leniency discount, in light of the value added to the investigation by the applicant **OR**
- OFT informs applicant that it has not added significant value to the investigation (No Agmt).

Formal agreement signed, prior to issue of SO

- Defines scope of protection
- Confirms level of leniency discount
- Applicant confirms acceptance that the reported activity amounts to an infringement
- Standard form agreement

Possibility that some cooperating individuals will receive no-action letters or comfort letters where a criminal prosecution is in contemplation

Stage 5: SO to decision/ prosecution and appeal

Applicant's duty to cooperate continues, until determination of any decision, prosecution or appeal

- OFT may require further document disclosure and/or availability of witnesses
- Continued provision of information identified as relevant by the applicant, in addition to meeting specific requests made
- Continued liaison with OFT over steps taken by applicant that may have a bearing on the OFT's enforcement action, including any further investigative steps (e.g. when preparing responses to SO)

Continued acceptance of infringement (relevant to permissible extent of challenges to SO)

Continued dialogue between OFT and applicant

- OFT to discuss with applicant any changes to the scope of its case that are significant in light of the defined scope of leniency protection

2. ELIGIBILITY FOR DIFFERENT TYPES OF LENIENCY

CARTEL ACTIVITY

[3.157]

2.1 Leniency is available to undertakings and individuals who have participated in cartel activity.

2.2 Cartel activity is defined for the purposes of the OFT's leniency policy for undertakings as agreements and/or concerted practices which infringe Article 101 of the TFEU and/or the Chapter I prohibition and involve price-fixing (including resale price maintenance), bid-rigging (collusive tendering), the establishment of output restrictions or quotas and/or market sharing or market-dividing.[6] The OFT notes that, by definition, cartel activities have as their **object** the prevention, restriction or distortion of competition and therefore neither the applicant nor the OFT will be required to assess the actual **effects** of the cartel activity before proceeding with an application.

2.3 Leniency in relation to vertical arrangements[7] is limited to price fixing (for example, resale price maintenance cases). The OFT's leniency policy does not cover other stand-alone vertical restrictions of competition as these tend to be (at least to an extent) visible on the market and therefore over time self-detecting. However, where vertical behaviour might be said to be facilitating horizontal cartel activity, leniency is available in principle to the parties involved in such behaviour (including the facilitator), as participation in such cartel activity can lead to exposure to significant sanctions.

2.4 For individuals, no-action letters can cover any type of activity that would amount to the criminal cartel offence under section 188 EA02.

2.5 The list below contains non-exhaustive examples of cartel activities for which leniency has in the past been granted:

(a) Agreements between competitors to coordinate the prices for the supply of goods or services, including coordination of the extent of price rises or elements of a price as well as agreeing absolute or total prices.

(b) Direct or indirect communication of specific, not publicly available, information regarding future pricing intentions between two or more competitors in a market. Indirect communication can include exchanges of information between direct competitors via one or more companies in a different level of the supply chain (for example a common supplier of goods or services).

(c) Various forms of bid-rigging (also known as collusive tendering), including (but not limited to) bid rotation, cover pricing (which occurs when a potential bidder submits a price obtained from a competitor in a tender process which is not designed to win the contract but to give the appearance of competition) and agreements to pay compensation to unsuccessful competing bidders in a tender process.

(d) Arrangements between suppliers and retailers of a good or services, which restrict the ability of the retailers to determine their retail prices by reference to the prices charged by different suppliers.

(e) Arrangements to restrict marketing or sales activities of competing undertakings to particular territories or groups of customers.

2.6 The OFT will have regard to the case law of the UK and EU courts on the interpretation of price-fixing, bid-rigging (collusive tendering), output restrictions or quotas and market sharing or market-dividing.

CONDITIONS FOR THE GRANT OF LENIENCY

2.7 In order to benefit from leniency from financial penalties or immunity from criminal prosecution, and subject to the limitations on availability described below, an applicant must meet the following conditions, each of which will apply throughout the application process and until final determination of any prosecution, infringement decision and resulting appeal proceedings.

Condition (a) – Admission

Applicants that are undertakings must accept that the undertaking participated in a cartel activity (which by definition includes an acceptance of an infringement of the law, see paragraph 2.2). Individual applicants must admit participation in the cartel offence under section 188 of the EA02.

Condition (b) – Information

The applicant must provide the OFT with all the non-legally privileged information, documents and evidence available to it regarding the cartel activity (see paragraphs 5.12 onwards).

Condition (c) – Cooperation

The applicant must maintain continuous and complete cooperation throughout the investigation and until the conclusion of any action (including criminal proceedings and defending civil or criminal appeals) by the OFT arising as a result of the investigation (see Chapter 5 of this guidance).

Condition (d) – Termination

The applicant must refrain from further participation in the cartel activity from the time of disclosure of the cartel activity to the OFT (except as may be directed by the OFT) (see paragraphs 4.44 onwards).

Condition (e) – Coercer test

In relation to a grant of immunity,[8] the applicant must not have taken steps to coerce another undertaking to take part in the cartel activity (see paragraphs 2.50 to 2.59).

AVAILABILITY OF DIFFERENT TYPES OF LENIENCY

2.8 In the OFT's experience, applications from undertakings (on behalf of the undertaking and also its employees and directors) are much more common than applications from individuals. Accordingly, this chapter approaches the availability of leniency/immunity by dealing primarily with applications from undertakings, but noting any points relating to applications from individuals where relevant.

TYPE A IMMUNITY

2.9 The first applicant to report and provide evidence of a cartel, when the OFT does not have a pre-existing investigation into the reported cartel activity and does not otherwise have sufficient information to establish the existence of the reported cartel activity, will be granted Type A immunity.

2.10 Type A immunity provides:

- guaranteed corporate immunity (that is, total immunity from financial penalties under CA98), together with
- guaranteed 'blanket' immunity from criminal prosecution for all cooperating current and former employees and directors of the undertaking (see paragraphs 2.38 to 2.40),[9] and
- protection from director disqualification proceedings for all directors of the undertaking.[10]

in relation to the reported cartel activity.

2.11 The grant of Type A immunity is subject to the applicant meeting the conditions of leniency (see paragraph 2.7), including not having coerced another undertaking to take part in cartel activity. Where an undertaking has been a coercer only Type C leniency will be available (Condition (e) of paragraph 2.7, see also paragraphs 2.50 to 2.59 below). The information provided in relation to condition (b) must, as a minimum, give the OFT a sufficient basis for taking forward a credible investigation.

2.12 If the Type A applicant is an individual, he/she alone will be guaranteed immunity from criminal prosecution, but his/her employer undertaking and colleagues may be eligible for immunity or leniency protection as a Type B applicant (see footnote 11).

2.13 A pre-existing investigation will exist from the point where the OFT considers it has reasonable grounds to suspect cartel activity, such that it may conduct an investigation under one or both of section 192 of the EA02 and section 25 of the CA98, and has taken active steps in relation to that investigation. Active steps may be overt or covert and may or may not involve the use of statutory information gathering powers. Examples would include (but are not limited to) voluntary interviews of witnesses, inspections of premises (under Section 28 of the CA98 or Section 194 of the EA02) or preparing applications for warrants.

2.14 Type A immunity therefore ceases to be available if:

- the OFT has a pre-existing investigation into the reported cartel activity
- the OFT has previously received a leniency application regarding the reported cartel activity, whether from an undertaking or an individual, or
- the OFT has sufficient information to establish the existence of the reported cartel activity.

TYPE B IMMUNITY/LENIENCY

2.15 The first applicant[11] to report and provide evidence of a cartel, when the OFT is conducting a pre-existing investigation into the reported cartel activity will be a Type B applicant.

2.16 Type B applicants will be eligible for:

- discretionary corporate immunity from penalties or reductions in penalty of anything up to 100 per cent, and/or
- discretionary criminal immunity for cooperating current and former employees and directors of the undertaking, which may be granted on a 'blanket' basis (see paragraphs 2.38 to 2.40), or for specific individuals, or for all employees other than named individuals, and
- protection from director disqualification proceedings[12] for all directors of the undertaking (which will be automatic if corporate leniency or immunity is granted),

in relation to the reported cartel activity.

2.17 The grant of any form of immunity or reduction in penalty to a Type B applicant is subject to the applicant meeting the conditions of leniency (see paragraph 2.7), including not having coerced another undertaking to take part in cartel activity. Where an undertaking has been a coercer only Type C leniency will be available (Condition (e) of paragraph 2.7, see also paragraphs 2.50 to 2.59 below). The information provided in relation to condition (b) must, as a minimum, add significant value to the OFT's investigation, that is, it must be information which genuinely advances the investigation.

2.18 The OFT's exercise of its discretion to grant immunity or a reduction in penalties will depend on its assessment of where the public interest lies in the particular case. In particular, the OFT will perform a balancing exercise, assessing the benefits of gaining additional evidence by reason of a grant of leniency against the disbenefit of granting immunity or a reduction in penalties after an investigation has already commenced, resources have been expended and after the OFT may already have further fruitful lines of enquiry to pursue and some probative evidence already in its possession.

2.19 The grant of corporate immunity/reduction in penalties will be assessed independently from the grant of any individual criminal immunity, noting in particular that there may be differences in the extent of information already available to us in relation to the civil infringement and the related criminal offence. The public interest in granting immunity from fines may not extend to immunity from criminal prosecution for some or all individuals.

2.20 Although Type B does not offer guaranteed immunity, Type B applications made at an early stage of the OFT's investigation are inherently more likely to result in the grant of corporate immunity and/or criminal immunity than late-stage Type B applications or Type C applications.

2.21 Moreover, where the OFT has a pre-existing investigation which relates to a suspected infringement of the CA98 but not a criminal cartel offence, the OFT would normally expect to grant 'blanket' criminal immunity (or issue a comfort letter confirming that the case is not being investigated criminally). Similarly, where the OFT has only a pre-existing criminal investigation, it would normally expect to grant corporate immunity.

2.22 In practice, approaches for Type B immunity are most likely to be triggered by inspections.[13] The OFT will, where possible, give prospective applicants an indication of whether corporate immunity and/or blanket criminal immunity are in principle available before the undertaking's identity is revealed. Would-be applicants therefore have nothing to lose by enquiring about the availability of Type B immunity after the commencement of an investigation. Applicants should however note that there may be some delay between the initial inspections and the OFT being in a position to assess properly whether there is a public interest in granting immunity. It is therefore for applicants to decide whether to wait for a firm indication from the OFT as to whether immunity is available, or to avoid the risk of others applying first by making an early application for Type B immunity or leniency.

2.23 The grant of any form of immunity or reductions in penalties to Type B applicants is discretionary in all circumstances. However, Type B protections will definitely cease to be available where:

- the OFT has previously received a leniency application regarding the reported cartel activity from an undertaking, or
- the OFT has sufficient information to establish the existence of the reported cartel activity.

TYPE C LENIENCY

2.24 In circumstances where another undertaking has already reported the cartel activity, or where the applicant has coerced another undertaking to participate in the cartel activity, only Type C leniency is available. The grant of Type C leniency is always discretionary.

2.25 In the Type C position, the applicant will be eligible for:

- discretionary reductions in corporate penalties of up to 50 per cent, and/or
- discretionary criminal immunity to specific individuals, and
- protection from director disqualification proceedings[14] for all directors of the undertaking (if a reduction in corporate penalty is granted).

2.26 The grant of Type C leniency is subject to the applicant meeting the conditions of leniency (see paragraph 2.7), save for Condition (e) (coercer test). The information provided in relation to condition (b) must, as a minimum, add significant value to the OFT's investigation, that is, it must be information which genuinely advances the investigation.

2.27 The OFT's exercise of its discretion to grant leniency will depend on its assessment of where the public interest lies in the particular case. In particular, the OFT must perform a balancing exercise, assessing the benefits of gaining additional evidence by reason of a further grant of leniency against the disbenefit of granting leniency to multiple parties in a single investigation, when the OFT may already have some probative evidence and further fruitful lines of enquiry to pursue and already has the cooperation of at least one applicant.

2.28 The grant of a reduction in corporate penalty will be assessed independently from the grant of any individual criminal immunity, noting that there may be differences in the extent of information already available to the OFT in relation to the civil infringement and the related criminal offence. The public interest in granting a reduction in fines may not extend to immunity from criminal prosecution for any individuals.

2.29 'Blanket' criminal immunity, that is, immunity for all cooperating current and former employees and directors at risk of prosecution for the cartel offence, will not be granted in Type C leniency cases, but comfort letters may be available in cases not investigated criminally.

2.30 However, the OFT will consider, on an individual-by-individual basis, whether one or more current or former employees or directors of an undertaking qualifying for Type C leniency should be granted individual immunity. Whether the OFT will grant individual immunity will depend on an assessment of the overall public interest.

2.31 In circumstances where the OFT has sufficient information to establish the existence of the reported cartel activity in relation to an applicant, such that it could prove the involvement of that applicant in cartel activity, the OFT is highly unlikely to exercise its discretion to grant leniency, but may do so where it considers that the public interest is best served by using information and cooperation from the applicant to prove the participation by others in the cartel.

2.32 The OFT will, where possible, give prospective applicants an indication of whether Type C leniency reductions and/or individual immunity are in principle available at the time of the application. However, depending on the stage at which the application is made and the extent of information already in the OFT's possession, it is possible that the OFT will only be able to assess whether the applicant could potentially add significant value to the investigation once it has fully assessed both the information already gathered from other sources and that put forward by the applicant, and hence it may not be able to confirm in principle whether or not leniency is available until a late stage.[15]

WHEN CAN INDIVIDUAL IMMUNITY BE GRANTED?

2.33 Individual immunity in this guidance refers to a situation where one or more individuals are granted criminal immunity but not as part of a 'blanket' grant of criminal immunity to all current and former employees and directors of an undertaking in a Type A or Type B case.[16]

2.34 Individual immunity is most likely to be granted when an individual makes an approach for criminal immunity on their own account, but it may also be granted to one or more individuals where their employer or former employer undertaking qualifies for Type B or C leniency.

2.35 Individuals in Type A circumstances will be guaranteed a no-action letter if they need it, or comfort letter, subject to meeting the conditions for leniency (see paragraph 2.7).

2.36 If there is already a pre-existing investigation, but the individual self-reports to the OFT about the cartel activity before any other individual or undertaking, the individual may still be granted individual immunity provided they add significant value to the OFT's investigation, subject to meeting the conditions for leniency (see paragraph 2.7). However, it is important to understand that the OFT always retains a residual discretion in such cases and will conduct a public interest assessment, weighing up the benefits of gaining additional evidence by reason of a grant of immunity against the disbenefit of making an immunity grant after an investigation has already commenced, resources have been expended and after the OFT may already have further fruitful lines of enquiry to pursue and some probative evidence already in its possession.

2.37 The ability of an individual to apply for individual immunity independently of an undertaking, and before the undertaking has itself applied for immunity, is one of the key reasons why undertakings who discover potential wrongdoing should promptly make a Type A immunity application and not postpone it in the hope of being able to make a successful Type B immunity application once an investigation has started. Furthermore, undertakings should be aware that individuals may now also seek to take advantage of the OFT's informant reward programme to report cartel conduct which their employer has failed to report.[17]

'BLANKET' CRIMINAL IMMUNITY

2.38 It is **not** a pre-condition for gaining a marker for Type A immunity that the applicant produces an up-front list of names of its current and former employees and directors who may be implicated in the cartel. Rather, where an undertaking benefits from Type A immunity, it can be assumed with certainty that any current or former employee or director of the undertaking, wherever they are in the world and whatever their precise role in the cartel activity, will receive a no-action letter if they would otherwise be at risk of prosecution for the cartel offence or an individual comfort letter if appropriate.[18] Furthermore, the same principle applies to blanket immunity that the OFT has granted in Type B cases.

2.39 Where an individual benefitting from blanket immunity would otherwise be at risk of prosecution for the cartel offence and is therefore eligible for a no-action letter, the individual must meet the conditions for leniency set out at paragraph 2.7 above, including cooperation with the OFT's investigation, or they will lose the benefit of the 'blanket' immunity.

2.40 References to employees and directors throughout this guidance should also be read as including other officers of the company, even where they are not technically directors or employees, such as company secretaries.

CESSATION OF AVAILABILITY OF LENIENCY GENERALLY

2.41 The OFT will not accept leniency applications from undertakings after the OFT has issued a statement of objections in relation to the reported cartel activity. The OFT will not accept immunity applications from an individual after that individual has been charged with a cartel offence in relation to the reported cartel activity.

2.42 In exercising its discretion in relation to the grant of immunity or leniency in cases where it has a pre-existing investigation into cartel activity, the OFT may in some cases conclude that it will no longer accept any further leniency applications.

2.43 This may be because the OFT considers that it already has sufficient information to establish the infringement or offence in relation to all relevant parties, or that any additional information is unlikely to add significant added value such as to justify the resources necessary to handle the application, or that it would not be a priority for the OFT to extend the investigation beyond its existing scope.

GUIDANCE ON THE LIKELIHOOD OF CRIMINAL ENFORCEMENT

2.44 Not all cases of cartel activity will involve the commission of any offence, and even where an offence has been committed the OFT may determine that, in all the circumstances, it is not appropriate to commence a criminal investigation. We recognise that the possibility of a criminal investigation is a relevant factor for applicants in deciding whether to proceed with an application for leniency.

2.45 The OFT's thinking on which cartel cases it will be appropriate to investigate criminally will continue to evolve as the EA02 regime becomes more established. For example, in recent years, it has become common for the early stages of cartel investigations to be carried out with a view to using both criminal and civil enforcement powers.

2.46 The prime consideration will be the extent to which there is likely to be evidence that one or more individuals behaved dishonestly. It is important to note that the individuals who acted dishonestly may be employees of a cartel member other than the applicant.[19]

2.47 Additionally, the factors set out in the OFT's published prioritisation principles such as the extent of consumer detriment will also be taken into account.[20] In cartel cases which have had an impact on a number of EU member states, it may be that unless there is a significant relative impact on the UK and/or the evidence for, or organisation of, the cartel is relatively 'concentrated' in the UK, that the OFT will conclude that action by the Commission under Article 101 of the TFEU alone would be more appropriate. However, each case will obviously turn on its own facts.

2.48 A potential applicant who is concerned about the likelihood of a criminal investigation can provide details of the relevant conduct to the OFT on a 'no names' basis (see further paragraphs 4.1 onwards), and the OFT may be able to give an assurance that criminal enforcement would not be in contemplation in the scenario given.

2.49 In cases where the OFT decides only to undertake an investigation under the CA98 or chooses not to investigate at all, it will not generally issue no-action letters to any individuals. Instead, if requested, a comfort letter will be sent to the undertaking qualifying for immunity and expressed to apply to all current and former employees of the undertaking.[21] The letter will state that the OFT has decided not to commence a criminal investigation, having regard to the nature of the cartel behaviour reported, the role of the individuals and the overall public interest. The OFT is satisfied in the light of experience that a comfort letter in these circumstances will be effective in achieving its objectives.

THE APPLICATION OF THE COERCER TEST

2.50 Undertakings who have taken steps to coerce another undertaking to take part in the cartel activity are not eligible for corporate immunity (whether Type A or Type B) but can receive a maximum reduction in penalty of 50 per cent for Type C leniency.

2.51 It is always possible to contact the OFT for no-names confidential guidance about whether the bar on granting a coercer immunity may be an issue in a prospective application. The OFT has already given such guidance in past cases and then received successful immunity applications. The OFT believes the coercer bar will not lead to a significant number of refusals to grant immunity. The OFT has, at the time of the publication of this guidance never refused corporate immunity on coercer grounds.

2.52 The OFT does not believe that it would be fruitful to develop a detailed definition of 'coercer', but there must be evidence of clear, positive and ultimately successful steps from a participant (that is, the coercer) to pressurise an unwilling participant to take part in the cartel. The bar is high in relation to both the type of behaviour which will be regarded as coercive and the evidence necessary to prove that behaviour.

2.53 For example, conduct may amount to coercion in the following situations:

- actual physical violence or proven threats of violence which have a realistic prospect of being carried out, or blackmail (these would apply equally to cases of horizontal as well as vertical collusion),[22] or
- such strong economic pressure as to make market exit a real risk, where, for example, a large player organises a collective boycott of a small player or refuses to supply key inputs to such a small player – these scenarios are more likely to apply in cases where there is at least a significant vertical element and are less likely to be relevant where an arrangement is purely horizontal and there are no significant cross-supplies between competitors.

2.54 The OFT takes the view that there will not be a coercer issue in the following situations:

- harmful market pressure which falls short of risking market exit but may reduce profit margins
- mere agreed enforcement or punishment mechanisms to enforce the operation of a cartel, and
- standard term contracts in a resale price maintenance case, even where there is a significant inequality of bargaining power.

2.55 Even if an undertaking were to lose eligibility for corporate immunity as a result of finding out subsequent to its initial application that it had been a coercer:

- it would still be eligible for up to a 50 per cent reduction in any financial penalty (Type C leniency), and
- the undertaking's current and former employees or directors (except for the 'rogue' coercing employee(s) or officer(s)) would remain eligible for criminal immunity.[23]

THE COERCER TEST AS IT APPLIES TO INDIVIDUALS

2.56 The coercer test for an individual under the no-action policy is fully aligned with that for an undertaking seeking corporate immunity.

2.57 In other words the question is whether another **undertaking** has been coerced, not specifically whether one individual has coerced another or others within the undertaking. Therefore, if the undertaking is not deemed a coercer, no employee or director within it will be refused criminal immunity on the coercer ground, save in the exceptional circumstance of an employee/director somehow enjoying a position of power independent of his/her position within the undertaking, who used that power to coerce another undertaking.

2.58 If an undertaking is found to be a coercer, individuals within the undertaking who did not themselves play a coercing role will not be denied criminal immunity on coercer grounds.

2.59 The OFT has, at the time of the publication of this guidance never had cause to refuse criminal immunity on the basis of the coercer test.

NOTES

6 See paragraph 3.1 of the OFT's the revised Penalty Guidance *OFT's guidance as to the appropriate amount of a penalty* (OFT 423), September 2012.

7 Vertical agreements are agreements between undertakings, each of which operates, for the purposes of the agreement, at a different level of the production or distribution chain (for example, between a supplier and a distributor). They are capable of infringing Article 101 of the TFEU and/or the Chapter I prohibition but do not fall within the scope of the criminal cartel offence.

8 This condition does not apply to Type C leniency for undertakings.

9 Though please see paragraphs 8.21 to 8.22 below with respect to criminal prosecutions in Scotland.

10 The OFT will not apply for a Competition Disqualification Order against any current or former director of a company which benefits from leniency in respect of the activities to which the grant of leniency relates. This applies provided that the director in question maintains complete and continuous cooperation with the OFT investigation and, in the case of a former director, the director has not been removed from office or otherwise ceased to act as a director as a result of his/her involvement in the breach of competition law. Note that this does not preclude a criminal court from making a Director Disqualification Order following a conviction for a cartel offence. Orders can be made in such cases without an application by the OFT.

11 Where the first applicant (Type A or B) is an individual, that individual's employer undertaking will be eligible to apply for Type B provided it remains the first **undertaking** to apply.

12 See above footnote 10.

13 On-site inspections under sections 27 or 28 of the CA98 or sections 193 or 194 of the EA02.

14 See footnote 10.

15 Paragraphs 7.14 to 7.18 provide guidance on the use of information provided by an applicant who, despite having acted in good faith, has failed to qualify for leniency.

16 Blanket immunity may be granted in some Type B cases. In others individual immunity may be granted to specific individuals, or for all employees other than named individuals.

17 See '*Rewards for Information about cartels*' on the OFT's website at www.oft.gov.uk.

18 See paragraphs 8.14 to 8.16 below that set out the way in which the OFT will decide whether individuals receive no-action letters or, alternatively, comfort letters.

19 Section 47 of the Enterprise and Regulatory Reform Act 2013 (ERRA) amends section 188(1) of the Enterprise Act 2002 by omitting 'dishonestly' from the cartel offence. This amended offence will come into force on 1 April 2014. Until this amended offence comes into force, the OFT will continue to consider whether to investigate a cartel under its criminal powers with regard to whether it is likely that there will be evidence of dishonesty.

20 See *OFT Prioritisation Principles* (OFT 953, October 2008).

21 This only applies in Type A and Type B immunity situations.

22 See paragraphs 2.2 and 2.3 above.

23 See also paragraph 2.57.

3. BEFORE APPLYING FOR LENIENCY

[3.158]

3.1 The OFT recognises that firms and individuals will want and need to consider carefully the decision whether to apply for leniency and that for firms, such a decision will ordinarily be made at a very senior level. The OFT appreciates that potential leniency applicants require sufficient information on which to base such a decision. This chapter sets out certain important considerations and guidance which firms, individuals and their advisers should have regard to before applying for leniency. Many of these matters will affect the OFT's ability to take effective enforcement action as a result of the leniency application. Disregarding these issues so that the OFT's own investigation might risk being prejudiced may therefore result in the applicant putting itself in a position where it cannot meet the requirement of continuous and complete cooperation which is a condition of immunity or leniency.

3.2 Firms and individuals considering applying for leniency should therefore ensure that they are familiar with the conditions of leniency (see paragraph 2.7) and in particular the requirements for the provision of information and for complete and continuous cooperation with the OFT's investigation, that will follow any application (see Annexe D and Chapter 5).

SEEKING CONFIDENTIAL GUIDANCE

3.3 Undertakings or individuals thinking about applying for leniency may, before doing so, approach the OFT for confidential guidance. For the avoidance of doubt, such guidance may be sought on any aspect of the OFT's leniency and no-action programmes – not just in those situations referred to in this guidance note where specific reference is made to the option of seeking such guidance. Confidential guidance discussions would usually involve a discussion on a no-names basis about a given factual matrix (perhaps expressed 'hypothetically') with a view to the undertaking or individual obtaining comfort on an issue before deciding whether to make an application.

3.4 The OFT handles many such requests on a wide range of topics, covering, for example:

(a) whether certain evidence amounts to a concrete basis for suspicion of cartel activity, sufficient to secure a marker

(b) whether particular investigative steps by the applicant prior to making an application are appropriate or necessary to secure a marker (see also paragraph 3.8 to 3.13)

(c) the OFT's preferred approach to briefing/interviewing employees in the company's own pre-application investigation

(d) the OFT's preferred approach to ceasing participation in a particular cartel activity
(e) whether particular arrangements fall within the definition of cartel activities, where there is genuine and reasonable doubt as to the characterisation of conduct, for example where there is an absence of legal precedent,[24] or
(f) the OFT's proposed handling of particular factual scenarios that are not covered by this guidance.

3.5 Any person seeking confidential guidance on leniency from the OFT should ring the Leniency Enquiry Line on 0207 211 8833. Once the purpose of your call has been assessed, you will be transferred to an appropriate senior officer experienced in leniency cases.

3.6 The OFT will give its views, by which it will consider itself bound, provided the discussion is followed-up by an application within a reasonable time and provided the information given when the advice was sought was not false or misleading and there has been no material change of circumstance.

3.7 The OFT will not use information given in consequence of seeking confidential guidance for any other purpose. In the event that leniency is not applied for, or not subsequently granted to the undertaking or individual on whose behalf the guidance was sought, the OFT will not attempt to establish the undertaking's identity by a process of 'reverse engineering'.

CONDUCTING INTERNAL INVESTIGATIONS

3.8 The establishment in the UK of a criminal cartel regime has made it particularly important for internal investigations prior to an approach for leniency to be conducted with care and precision and to be limited to that which is necessary. The OFT only requires that undertakings act reasonably, reducing the risks as best they can having regard to all relevant considerations. The OFT accepts that what is reasonable for these purposes may depend upon the circumstances of the case. Undertakings can be guided by the established rules of evidence, particularly as they apply to criminal proceedings, and may wish to take advice from a criminal lawyer for this purpose.

3.9 Even where it appears that a criminal investigation is unlikely to result, potential applicants for leniency are asked to have regard to the importance of internal investigations being carried out with appropriate care.

3.10 Annexe C provides important guidance on the conduct of internal investigations. This sets out the steps and precautions the OFT expects applicants to take, with respect to:

- minimising the risk of 'tipping off' other parties to cartel activity
- preserving and securing electronic evidence
- preserving and securing physical evidence
- interviewing witnesses, and
- keeping a record of the investigative steps taken.[25]

3.11 When conducting an internal investigation before making a leniency application, applicants should also bear in mind that the OFT sets a relatively low evidential threshold for the gaining of a marker. All that is necessary is to establish a concrete basis for a suspicion of cartel activity and a demonstration of a genuine intention to confess. Leniency applicants are encouraged to approach the OFT as early as possible. However, the OFT does accept that some other agencies set a higher threshold and that a more significant investigation may be necessary in order to make leniency applications in multiple jurisdictions. Potential applicants who are concerned about the interaction between the OFT's leniency application threshold and those in other jurisdictions can approach the OFT for confidential guidance.[26]

3.12 Experience has shown that the way in which a (prospective) applicant and its advisers conduct their internal investigations both prior to and following[27] an approach to the OFT for leniency is capable of having a substantial bearing on the success of the OFT's own subsequent investigations and enforcement action, especially where these include a criminal investigation with a view to a possible prosecution. For this reason, the way in which internal investigations are conducted by an applicant cannot be considered exclusively a matter for the applicant concerned. It is crucial to ensure that such internal investigations are conducted in a manner that minimises the risk of tipping-off persons involved in the cartel as well as to ensure that such investigations are not conducted in such a way as would risk diminishing the probative value of the evidence obtained in that investigation or any subsequent investigation by the OFT.

3.13 Except in the case of an oral application,[28] all leniency applicants will be expected to take a careful note of all the actions they have taken as part of an internal investigation, including the identities of any witnesses who were interviewed in the investigation process, the nature of the questions asked and the replies obtained. The note will need to be retained until the conclusion of any proceedings. A refusal or inability to do so may mean that the applicant is not meeting the conditions for leniency.

3.14 In addition to enabling the OFT to focus its own investigative steps or to direct the applicant in making further enquiries following the application, there may be circumstances where the OFT will need to rebut arguments that an internal investigation has compromised the integrity of the OFT's own case, and the provision of a clear note explaining the steps taken in such an investigation will be invaluable for this purpose.

APPLICATION OF LEGAL PRIVILEGE

3.15 The OFT will not as a condition of leniency **require** waivers of legal professional privilege (LPP) over any relevant information[29] in either civil or criminal investigations.[30]

3.16 However, save where the position is uncontroversial and clear to the OFT's satisfaction, the OFT will ordinarily require a review of any relevant information in respect of which LPP is claimed, by an independent counsel (IC) selected, instructed and funded on a case by case basis by the OFT.[31] An IC in such a situation will be instructed by the OFT to provide an independent opinion to the OFT on whether the relevant information in question is protected by LPP.[32] Failure or refusal in such a situation to provide the relevant information in question to an IC could result in the withdrawal of the leniency marker or revocation of the leniency agreement (as the case may be), on the grounds of non-compliance with the duty of complete and continuous cooperation.[33]

3.17 During the course of such a review by an IC, the relevant information in respect of which LPP is claimed will not be provided to the OFT. A copy of an IC's opinion to the OFT on the matter will be provided to the leniency applicant after it has been received by the OFT.

3.18 When the leniency applicant provides the relevant information to an IC, it may make observations to that IC on why it considers that the relevant information in question benefits from LPP. While the OFT will not be provided with the relevant information in question at this time, the OFT reserves the right to make its own observations to that IC, which will be provided to the leniency applicant. Such observations might set out the OFT's understanding of the relevant law of LPP, for example. An IC may, if requested by the OFT, provide the OFT with a copy of the leniency applicant's observations (or parts or a summary thereof), insofar as in that IC's view this would not undermine the claim to LPP or disclose the substance of the information in respect of which LPP is claimed. An IC will be instructed by the OFT to take both sets of observations into consideration when formulating their opinion.

3.19 Where an IC advises the OFT that the relevant information is not protected by LPP, then the OFT will expect that relevant information to be provided to it by the leniency applicant as a condition of leniency. On the other hand, where an IC advises the OFT that the relevant information benefits from LPP, then the OFT will not require it to be provided by the leniency applicant as a condition of leniency.

3.20 Where an IC advises the OFT that only parts of the relevant information are protected by LPP, then the leniency applicant will be required to provide the non-privileged relevant information to the OFT. To assist the leniency applicant in doing so, an IC will identify to the leniency applicant the precise parts which can be redacted. An IC may be asked by the OFT to confirm that only these redactions have been made.

3.21 If the leniency applicant refuses or fails in any such situation to provide to the OFT relevant information that in the opinion of the instructed IC does not benefit from LPP, the OFT may decide to withdraw the leniency marker or to revoke the leniency agreement on the grounds of non-compliance with the obligation to provide all relevant information.[34]

3.22 The IC process does not absolve the leniency applicant from their duty of complete and continuous cooperation.[35] When considering whether the leniency applicant has discharged this duty in relation to the IC process, the OFT will consider case-specific factors, for example whether the leniency applicant had made what, on any objective view, were manifestly baseless claims to LPP; whether a blanket claim was made in respect of a large volume of documents without sufficient specificity in relation to individual documents or categories of documents; and whether the leniency applicant appeared to be motivated by a desire to delay or otherwise prejudice the OFT investigation.[36]

3.23 The conclusions of the IC will ordinarily be regarded as determinative as between the leniency applicant and the OFT. However, the OFT will expect the leniency applicant to make available for review by the court, if required, any material over which LPP is claimed but where the claim is disputed, in order that the court can conclusively determine whether LPP is properly claimed.

MAINTAINING CONFIDENTIALITY AND SECURING EVIDENCE

3.24 In order to avoid 'tipping off' other parties to the reported cartel activity of the likelihood of an OFT investigation,[37] it is essential that applicants maintain complete confidentiality of the fact that they have applied for leniency, or even that a leniency application is in contemplation.

3.25 Disclosures to lawyers with a view to obtaining legal advice about an intended or actual leniency application are acceptable. In addition, where parallel leniency applications have been made in other jurisdictions, there is no prohibition on those jurisdictions' appropriate competition authorities being informed that an application to the OFT is either pending or has been made as the case may be.

3.26 The OFT sometimes receives requests from leniency applicants to make disclosures to banks and/or auditors after an application for leniency has been made. In general this is acceptable provided the OFT is consulted in advance as to whether and when such disclosures can be made and how much information can be given. The OFT may insist that a list be maintained of all individuals who have knowledge of the leniency approach and that such individuals be required to enter into confidentiality undertakings. See also paragraph 10.3 below.

3.27 Clearly the need for the utmost confidentiality in the circumstance described above arises from the OFT's desire to maintain the element of surprise should it wish to use its statutory powers such as those relating to inspections and searches. Once the OFT's investigation has reached the 'overt' stage, disclosures by leniency applicants of their status – including public disclosures – are less of an issue, but even at this stage the OFT must be consulted in advance about any proposed disclosure.

3.28 To this end, the OFT recommends that undertakings maintain lists of all current (and indeed former) employees or directors of an undertaking who are aware of the potential or actual[38] leniency application and have access to potentially relevant material and that each such individual be required to sign a declaration that they will observe strict confidentiality and that they will not remove, destroy, tamper with, or otherwise interfere with potentially relevant material. The OFT also recommends that potentially relevant material be secured, as far as possible, to avoid such destruction or tampering. For example, if mobile devices such as laptops or phones may contain relevant evidence, it may be sensible for the undertaking's lawyers or security department to take those promptly into secure custody so that they cannot be interfered with.

NOTES

24 As a general matter, it is for businesses and their advisers to self-assess their compliance with competition law. The OFT may decline to give guidance in circumstances when it considers that the caller is seeking general comfort on the OFT's assessment of conduct rather than genuinely with a view to making a leniency application.

25 Except in the case of an oral application, see paragraph 4.31.

26 See paragraph 3.3 and following, above.

27 There may be some cases (usually civil investigations under CA98) where the OFT may agree with the applicant, after grant of the marker, that the applicant and its advisers should conduct relatively extensive further enquiries including some of the interviews

28 Oral applications are discussed in paragraph 4.31. This includes discussion of the circumstances in which the OFT may accept an oral application as well as the cooperation expected from the oral applicant.

29 See paragraph 5.12 below for a definition of 'relevant information'.

30 The OFT does not rule out **inquiring** as to whether a leniency applicant may be prepared to waiver LPP over certain material during the course of a possible criminal cartel prosecution. In such circumstances, it will be made clear that any refusal to waive LPP **will not** have any adverse consequences for the leniency application and furthermore, that granting such a waiver **will not** yield any additional leniency discount or any other advantage to the leniency applicant. Any such inquiry would be made for the purposes of clarity in a possible criminal cartel prosecution, so that the defence and the court can know as early as possible the leniency applicant's position with respect to LPP material.

31 An IC will be instructed on a case by case basis. Any IC instructed for the purposes of a case will be a lawyer who is not an OFT official and who is regarded by the OFT as having suitable expertise in LPP and disclosure issues. An IC will not be instructed by the OFT to advise on any aspect of the case in question other the claims to LPP made by a leniency applicant.

32 The instructions will be disclosed to the leniency applicant after they have been sent to the IC.

33 See paragraph 10.6 and following for a discussion of the process of withdrawal or revocation.

34 See paragraph 10.6 and following for a discussion of the process of withdrawal or revocation.

35 See, for example, paragraphs 5.4 and following for a discussion of the duty of continuous and complete cooperation. See also paragraphs 10.1 and following for a discussion of the concept of bad faith.

36 See paragraph 10.6 and following for a discussion of the process of withdrawal or revocation.

37 Where an applicant 'tips off' other parties to the cartel activity, this may amount to 'bad faith' on the part of the applicant. See paragraph 10.1.

38 Up until the time when the OFT's investigation becomes overt.

4. CHECKING AVAILABILITY AND INITIAL APPLICATION

[3.159]

4.1 All initial contacts with the OFT with a view to making leniency applications or ascertaining the availability of leniency should be made by telephoning the Leniency Enquiry Line on 0207 211 8833. Once the purpose of your call has been assessed, you will be transferred to an appropriate senior officer experienced in leniency cases. Leniency enquiries should be made during office hours.

ASCERTAINING THE AVAILABILITY OF TYPE A IMMUNITY

4.2 Before making a leniency application, and if the undertaking is not aware of a pre-existing investigation, undertakings may wish to ascertain whether guaranteed immunity (Type A) is available. This can be done by either a representative from the undertaking or its legal adviser telephoning the OFT's Leniency Enquiry Line.[39] You will be asked for the following information and essential commitments:

- Confirmation from the legal adviser that he/she has instructions to apply for Type A immunity if it is available[40] (conditional instructions)[41] and that the undertaking understands that such an application will entail a commitment to cooperate with the OFT in any subsequent investigation.
- Confirmation that there is a 'concrete basis' for the suspicion of cartel activity, see paragraph 4.23
- Confirmation that the undertaking has a 'genuine intention to confess'. This means that there must be an acceptance by the undertaking that, as a matter of fact and law, the available information suggests that it has been engaged in cartel conduct in breach of the Chapter I prohibition and/or Article 101 of the TFEU, see paragraph 4.22.
- Specify the relevant sector, dates and broad nature of the cartel activity, or otherwise provide sufficient information to allow the OFT to determine whether there is a pre-existing civil and/or criminal investigation and/or a pre-existing leniency applicant. The level of detail required will depend on whether there have been previous investigations or applications in the sector.
- The name and telephone number of the person making the enquiry. The name of the undertaking or individual that they represent does not need to be disclosed at this point ('no-names enquiry').

4.3 The OFT officer will then make internal enquiries, and will revert to the named contact to confirm whether or not Type A immunity is in principle available. In the great majority of approaches, the OFT will be able to confirm within a short time (around one to two working days) whether Type A is available. However, this will not always be the case. For example, on some complex investigations, applicants may approach the OFT hoping to gain Type A immunity notwithstanding that an investigation is already underway. Applicants may claim to have discovered a 'new' related infringement. However, it will not always be possible for the OFT to determine quickly whether the 'new' matter is one which may properly be described as being outside the scope of its investigation and/or outside the scope of any earlier leniency application from another undertaking.[42]

4.4 If Type A immunity is not available, the applicant is free to consider all the available options, including whether to submit an application for Type B or C leniency or whether to withdraw without its identity having been made known to the OFT. The OFT will not use for any other purpose information that a would-be leniency applicant has provided to enable the OFT to establish whether any type of leniency is available. Where, for example, an undertaking has had to disclose the precise sector concerned in order to determine the availability of Type A (or B) immunity only for it to be informed by the OFT that immunity is no longer available, the OFT will not attempt to establish the undertaking's identity by a process of 'reverse engineering'. In most cases this would in any event be impossible.[43]

4.5 If Type A immunity is available, the legal adviser/representative must disclose the identity of the applicant, unless paragraph 4.36 applies due to a parallel application to the Commission. During the same telephone call, the OFT will request the information required in order to grant a preliminary marker, as set out in the checklist at Annexe D. If the applicant has also applied to other competition authorities in respect of the same cartel activity, it must also give the OFT limited waivers of confidentiality[44] sufficient to enable the OFT to discuss jurisdiction and handling of the application with those other authorities.

4.6 The preliminary marker will then be given (that is, a marker pending consideration of the full application package). This will be operational from the moment the applicant's identity has been disclosed to the OFT, and from that time on, no other Type A or B marker will be granted for the same cartel activity, unless the preliminary marker is subsequently rejected.

OBTAINING A MARKER WHEN AN INVESTIGATION HAS STARTED

4.7 In the event that the prospective applicant is already aware of an investigation into the cartel activity, it may wish to contact the OFT to ascertain whether any form of immunity or leniency is in principle available. Calls in relation to these issues should be made to the OFT's Leniency Enquiry Line.[45]

4.8 The OFT will, where possible, give prospective applicants an indication of whether the applicant is in the Type B position and if so, whether corporate immunity and/or blanket criminal immunity are in principle available, before the undertaking's identity is revealed.

4.9 If the OFT states that Type B corporate immunity and/or blanket criminal immunity is indeed available in principle, the would-be applicant can then seek to establish whether the information it can provide would be sufficient to warrant a marker for Type B immunity in its particular case by specifying the form and substance of the information it expects to be in a position to provide to the OFT.[46] The OFT will then advise whether, if such evidence were to be provided, it would be minded to grant immunity (corporate and/or criminal) or only a reduction in penalties. In principle, there is no reason why this cannot be done on a no-names basis. However, there would be no marker protection until disclosure of the applicant's identity.

4.10 If an approach is made to the OFT during or immediately after on-site inspections or other information requests, the OFT may have to defer a definite answer on whether corporate and/or criminal immunity is available, in order to assess the likelihood of information provided by the applicant adding significant value to the investigation in light of information gathered.[47] Similarly, for some time after the inspections or information requests, the OFT may not be in a position to assess whether a grant of corporate and/or criminal immunity is in the public interest (see paragraph 2.18). In those circumstances, it is up to the applicant whether to disclose its identity to mark the undertaking's position in the queue, in which case a Type B marker will be granted, with the extent of leniency protection to be assessed once the OFT has a better understanding of the evidence it has, including that which has been obtained during the inspection. Alternatively, if the applicant is not prepared to disclose its identity without a definite answer that immunity is available, no marker will be granted.

4.11 If the OFT already has one or more previous leniency applications in relation to the cartel activity, only Type C markers will be available. In some circumstances, the OFT will have determined that it is not prepared to accept any further leniency applications, and will respond to enquiries accordingly. (See paragraphs 2.41 to 2.43.)

4.12 If leniency, of whatever type, is in principle available, the legal adviser/representative must disclose the identity of the applicant to obtain a preliminary marker (that is, a marker pending consideration of the full application package). This will be operational from the moment the applicant's identity has been disclosed to the OFT.[48] As in the case of an application for Type A immunity, the applicant will need to satisfy the OFT that:

- the evidential threshold for the grant of a marker has been reached, that is, that there is a 'concrete basis' for a suspicion of participation in cartel activity, and
- the undertaking must have a 'genuine intention to confess'.[49]

4.13 During the same telephone call, the OFT will request the information required in order to grant a preliminary marker, as set out in the checklist at Annexe D, which should be followed by the application package (see below).

4.14 Note that the grant of a Type B or Type C preliminary marker will always be subject to applicants continuing to meet the conditions of leniency, and the information provided by the applicant adding significant value to the OFT's investigation, see paragraphs 2.7 above and 5.21 and 5.22 below.

APPLICATION PACKAGE AND NEXT STEPS

4.15 During or immediately following the telephone call to grant the preliminary marker, the OFT and the applicant will discuss the timing and process for the prompt provision by the applicant of the application package. The minimum contents of the package are set out in the checklist at Annexe D. In complex or particularly urgent cases, the OFT may ask for certain information or material to be provided promptly, followed by the full package at a later date.

4.16 If the cartel activity is ongoing, the OFT and the applicant will also discuss cessation of the cartel activity without tipping off others and/or any requirement by the OFT for the applicant to continue to participate in the cartel (see paragraphs 4.44 to 4.48).

4.17 Once the OFT has had an opportunity to consider the information provided it will revert to the applicant as soon as is reasonably practicable, having regard to all the circumstances of the case. The possible outcomes are:

(a) Confirm marker but not launch investigation
Most likely in relation to Type A applications, the OFT may decide to accept the marker but not to proceed with an investigation. This may be because it has higher priorities for its resources at that point in time or because the Commission is investigating the undertakings and the OFT has decided not to proceed with a criminal investigation into individuals. In that situation, the OFT will tell the applicant what precautions it needs to take in order to preserve its marker for leniency protection.[50] Provided the applicant cooperates as instructed, in the (unlikely) event that the OFT were to change its assessment of its priorities and commence an investigation, the applicant would be able to proceed with its application with the same level of marker protection.

(b) Confirm marker and discuss next steps
If the OFT intends to proceed with an investigation (whether criminal and/or civil) it will confirm the marker and promptly start discussions with the applicant on what cooperation is expected. See Chapter 5.

(c) Reject preliminary marker
There are a number of reasons why, following consideration of the application package, OFT may reject the marker. For example: the activity described may not amount to cartel activity within the scope of the leniency policy; the information provided may not give reasonable grounds to suspect cartel activity (Type A) or add significant value (Type B or C) or; the information provided may disclose that the applicant does not have a genuine intention to confess to cartel activity.

(d) Ask for more before confirming or rejecting
In some instances, the OFT may require more information before it can assess whether the application should be accepted or whether the case will be a priority for investigation. In those instances, the OFT will make clear to the applicant what more it is asking for, and why.

4.18 In some applications covering complex activities, the OFT's response may be a mixture of the above, for example because it is focusing its investigation on only part of the reported activity.

4.19 If the OFT confirms the marker, it will normally write to the applicant with this confirmation, unless the applicant has requested to receive such confirmation orally in which case this would typically be done in a telephone call.

4.20 A senior representative of the applicant undertaking, which the OFT considers should be a company director where the undertaking is a company ('the applicant's representative') — or in the case of an individual application, the applicant — will be asked to sign a letter indicating that the applicant understands the conditions for the grant of leniency and in particular that it is committed to complete and continuous cooperation throughout the OFT's investigation and subsequent enforcement action. Where the confirmation of a marker has been given orally, such a document may be signed at the OFT's premises and retained in OFT's records, rather than forming a written communication between the OFT and the applicant.[51] The OFT does not intend the applicant's representative to incur any personal liability to the OFT for the actions of the undertaking simply as result of signing such a letter. The original applicant's representative may be replaced in that role by another senior representative of the applicant undertaking,[52] but the undertaking must promptly notify the OFT of the replacement and the new applicant's representative will be expected to sign a letter in the same terms as their predecessor. The undertaking must ensure that the position of applicant's representative is never vacant.

4.21 The OFT may be able to indicate to the applicant some of the particular actions or information that will be required from the applicant, but at this early stage of the investigation, will not be able to present an exhaustive list of requirements.

MEANING OF KEY TERMS IN THE APPLICATION PROCESS

Genuine intention to confess

4.22 There must be an acceptance by the undertaking that, as a matter of fact and law, the available information suggests that it has been engaged in cartel conduct in breach of the Chapter I prohibition and/or Article 101 of the TFEU. It is recognised that in certain circumstances a party applying for a marker may be genuinely uncertain, at that stage, as to whether it has engaged in cartel conduct. In one case, for example, the applicant for a marker had received, via its compliance officer, an anonymous tip-off that its staff had been engaging in price-fixing. The tip-off had some credibility having regard to the information given, but at the stage at which a marker was sought the tip-off remained untested. The applicant accepted that if the tip-off was accurate, it would have been guilty of cartel conduct but the OFT considered that it was reasonable in the circumstances for the applicant to place a qualification on its possible involvement. However, there have been other cases where the OFT has been faced with requests for markers from applicants who believe that they are in possession of much of the basic facts but seek to deny that those facts constitute cartel conduct. They ask for a marker 'in case' the OFT were minded to take a different view. This will not satisfy the requirement of a genuine intention to confess.[53]

'Concrete basis' to suspect cartel activity

4.23 A 'concrete basis' for suspecting cartel activity may take many forms but might include, for example, documentary evidence which plainly indicates the existence of a cartel, or information from a potential witness alleging cartel activity, or a combination of evidence from documentary and/or witness sources which together point to cartel activity. Alternative plausible non-cartel explanations for documents do not preclude those documents giving rise to a suspicion of cartel activity, provided the applicant can explain why a cartel is a likely explanation.[54]

EMERGING DETAILS AND EXPANDING THE SCOPE OF APPLICATIONS FOR LENIENCY AND/OR NO-ACTION

4.24 The OFT will discuss the scope of the application during the applicant's initial approach, based on the emerging details of the cartel activity as known to the applicant at that time. For these purposes, scope might include the extent of products or services affected, the geographic scope, the duration of the activity, the characterisation of the cartel activity and the number of undertakings or individuals involved.

4.25 The scope of the application should cover the suspected cartel activity. The OFT will be realistic about what can sensibly be identified at the initial application stage and the scope can be further specified/refined as progress is made with the OFT's investigation. Ultimately, the scope of leniency protection should be limited to the minimum necessary to protect the applicant, both to ensure that the OFT does not preclude future applications into similar but distinct cartels and so that the applicant does not confess to more than the evidence would support.

4.26 The OFT recognises that at the time of the initial approach to the OFT, and potentially at the time of submission of the application package, the full details of the cartel activity will not be known to those preparing and submitting the application (and, in relation to certain types of cartel activity, relevant details will only be apparent from information in the possession of other parties). The OFT will therefore be understanding where there is genuine uncertainty on the part of the applicant as to the extent or particulars of the activity, provided always that there remains a 'concrete basis' to suspect cartel activity. In complex cases, it may be appropriate to grant the preliminary marker on a wide basis that goes beyond the direct evidence available at the time of the initial application, provided the applicant can explain why such an approach is reasonable in the circumstances.

4.27 The scope of the marker or preliminary marker may be adjusted in light of further emerging details and evidence as the investigation progresses, and will inform the scope of the leniency agreement or no-action letter, which are signed at a later stage of the investigation.

4.28 It is important for applicants to alert the OFT to any areas of doubt, for example by differentiating between known facts supported by evidence already uncovered, statements based on the belief or best recollection of witnesses and suspicions or assumptions. The applicant should inform the OFT of further enquiries it proposes to make to resolve any such doubts, noting that the OFT may wish to take such investigative steps directly, particularly where they relate to uncertainty on the part of potential witnesses.

4.29 Where an undertaking discovers any innocent omissions up to and after the signing of the leniency agreement it should inform the OFT immediately and satisfy the OFT that:

- the omission was indeed innocent, and
- the information subsequently discovered has been provided to the OFT without undue delay.

4.30 If the OFT is satisfied that the above is the case, and such information affects the scope of the suspected infringement, it will normally be prepared to draft (or modify) the scope of the leniency agreement and/or no-action letters accordingly.

OTHER MATERIAL PROCEDURAL POINTS RELATING TO MARKERS AND APPLICATIONS

Oral applications and written confirmation

4.31 The entire application process can be oral if requested and provided there is good reason for it.[55] However:

- all pre-existing written evidence of the cartel will need to be provided to the OFT
- witnesses will need to be made available for interview and to sign statements, setting out their evidence
- the leniency agreement and any no-action letters (usually entered into shortly prior to issue of a statement of objections) will be in writing, and
- If the case proceeds to a prosecution or statement of objections, reference to the leniency application(s) and identity of the applicant(s) will be made in formal documents disclosed to other parties and/or made public at that stage.[56]

4.32 The grant of a preliminary marker or confirmation of a marker can be confirmed in writing if desired, for all types of leniency.

Joint approaches for leniency not accepted

4.33 The OFT will generally not accept joint approaches made simultaneously by or on behalf of two or more undertakings participating in the same cartel activity. If the OFT were to receive such approaches, the would-be applicants would not be able to 'share' Type A immunity and the OFT would not be able to confirm that a particular undertaking was the 'first' to apply and so grant it a marker for Type A (or Type B) immunity. Moreover, undertakings who discuss a possible leniency application with other participants in the cartel activity are at risk of being found to have acted in bad faith by having tipped off others of their intended approach to the OFT.[57]

Applications during inspections

4.34 Where an approach is made during an inspection,[58] the inspection will continue in the normal way. To the extent that an undertaking merely complies with its obligations pursuant to the OFT's mandatory powers of investigation it will not be treated as having provided information under the OFT's civil leniency or no-action policies.

4.35 Markers can only be granted by certain senior OFT officials who will generally need to make checks within the OFT before they do so, so approaches during an inspection should be made by telephone in the normal way (see paragraph 4.7), not to the OFT officials present at the inspection.

OFT no-names markers in 'Commission immunity application' cases

4.36 As an exception to the usual rule, the OFT will be willing to allow no-names markers[59] for Type A applicants where the undertaking's legal adviser confirms that he/she also has instructions to make an application for immunity to the Commission under section II of the Commission Leniency Notice. The adviser will need to provide his/her own name and firm and sufficient details of the affected sector to enable the OFT to exclude the existence of a pre-existing UK civil and/or criminal investigation and/or applicant. The legal adviser would also need to confirm the applicant's genuine intention to confess. Once the marker has been given on this basis, the OFT will expect the adviser to revert to it within a specified (and generally short) time frame – to be agreed case-by-case – to confirm:

- that an application has been made to the Commission
- the identity of the applicant undertaking, and
- the nature and emerging details of the suspected infringement and the underlying evidence.

4.37 Where Commission immunity is no longer available, the applicant is free to withdraw its no-names marker without having to reveal its identity. Alternatively, the applicant may nevertheless decide to keep its OFT marker. In such a case the marker would be required to become a named marker and the applicant would need to submit an application package in the usual way (see paragraph 4.15 to 4.21, above).

4.38 It is the OFT's intention that allowing no-names markers in Type A immunity cases, in advance of an approach to the Commission, will provide certainty to undertakings on the issue of whether there is possible exposure to a risk of prosecution in the UK for the cartel offence of any of its current and former employees and directors. It is intended that this will give further encouragement to the Commission's leniency programme.

4.39 Apart from 'Commission immunity application' cases, strong justification will be needed for obtaining no-names markers, as the OFT will ordinarily expect the legal adviser to have obtained conditional instructions to apply for immunity if the availability of Type A immunity is confirmed.

Requests for waivers

4.40 In cases where leniency has been applied for in other jurisdiction(s), the OFT would expect to be given 'waivers' of confidentiality so as to be able to discuss appropriate matters with those other jurisdiction(s). Generally any transfer of information in these circumstances is limited to that which is necessary to coordinate planned concerted action such as on-site investigations. Where there are particular sensitivities for a leniency applicant about such waivers, these should be raised promptly with the OFT. Ideally, therefore, applicants' advisers should take instructions on the issue of waivers in advance of making the application because the OFT may need to discuss matters with other jurisdictions with some urgency once the application has been made.

OFT SUMMARY APPLICATIONS IN 'COMMISSION IMMUNITY APPLICATION' CASES

4.41 The OFT accepts short form 'summary applications' as contemplated in the European Competition Network (ECN) Model Leniency Programme[60] in cartel cases where:

- the Commission is 'particularly well-placed' to deal with a case in accordance with paragraph 14 of the Network Notice
- the OFT is in its opinion also 'well-placed' to act in accordance with paragraph 8 of the Network Notice
- the applicant has made or is in the process of filing an application for immunity with the Commission, and
- the applicant is in a Type A position in the UK.

4.42 Where the 'summary application' route is available to an applicant, the OFT will apply the procedures set out in paragraphs 22 to 25 of the ECN Model Leniency Programme. In addition to the information required in accordance with paragraph 22 of the ECN Model Leniency Programme, the OFT may also need to be provided with relevant UK-specific information relating to the reported cartel, such as the details of any UK-based individuals and conduct and an estimate of the size of the UK market and market shares of the parties. Where this is the case, the applicant should ensure that it is in a position to provide such additional UK-specific information promptly.

4.43 In the event that the OFT commences a criminal investigation in relation to the reported cartel, the OFT will require complete and continuous cooperation from the applicant, as further described in this guidance, even where it is not conducting a civil investigation into the undertaking (for example because the Commission is conducting such an investigation under Article 101 of the TFEU). Failure to cooperate with the OFT in this way will lead to rejection of the applicant's marker, with potential consequences for individual directors and employees of the applicant who will no longer benefit from the protection of the Type A immunity.

DIRECTIONS TO CONTINUE CARTEL ACTIVITY

4.44 Ordinarily the applicant (whether an undertaking or an individual) will be required to refrain from further participation in the cartel activity unless the OFT directs otherwise. Such a direction will be rare. The objective in most such cases will be to protect the element of surprise of any forthcoming inspections.

4.45 The OFT will never expect individuals within an undertaking or an individual immunity applicant to take inappropriate risks. They will usually only be asked to carry on their basic activities in the same way as if they had never approached the OFT. The OFT will provide clear guidance as to what is expected in such cases.

4.46 In exceptional cases, the objective may also be to allow the coming into existence of further evidence of the cartel activity and this may involve the use by the OFT of its powers under the Regulation of Investigatory Powers Act 2000 (RIPA).

4.47 The general expectation is that, where necessary, individuals benefitting from criminal immunity will be expected to give evidence, including where the individual has been directed to continue his or her participation in ongoing cartel activity.

4.48 In cases where a person has had and/or continues to have an involvement in cartel activity and applies for immunity on his/her own account and is able to continue to make use of a relationship to obtain further information about a cartel for the OFT and under the OFT's close direction, the individual may be granted individual immunity but remain a secret source. The OFT will not disclose the identity or role of a secret source in any subsequent investigation or proceedings. An individual immunity applicant will generally only be treated as a secret source where the safety of the individual would be in jeopardy or other serious adverse consequences would follow if the person's approach to the OFT were to become known.

NOTES

39 See paragraph 4.1.

40 If the application is made by a representative of the undertaking rather than a legal adviser, they would be asked to confirm their intention to apply for Type A immunity if it is available.

41 The OFT will not require a professional undertaking from the legal adviser as to his/her conditional instructions to make a Type A immunity application.

42 In such circumstances, if the applicant elects to continue the application and reveal its identity, it may be possible for a marker for Type C leniency to be given immediately, with the possibility that such a marker might in future 'convert' to Type A once the circumstances are clearer.

43 The same applies in the case of a would-be applicant for individual immunity who is seeking to establish whether they will be entitled to automatic criminal immunity by reason of being the first to confess absent a pre-existing investigation.

44 Please see paragraph 4.40 for a discussion of such waivers.

45 See paragraph 4.1.

46 The OFT will be sensible about comparing this indication with the information actually given subsequently (that is, in the application package and beyond). Some variation is acceptable provided that, overall, the initial information does not turn out to have been misleading in a material way and the information actually provided has, in fact, added significant value and genuinely advanced the OFT's investigation.

47 An application for leniency after commencement of an inspection or receipt of a formal information request will not interrupt or avoid the need for the applicant to comply with the formal investigative measures. Nor will information compulsorily obtained by the OFT under such measures be considered as information provided as part of the leniency application when assessing whether the application has added significant value to the OFT's investigation.

48 If a Type B marker is granted no other Type B marker will be granted for the same cartel activity, unless the preliminary marker is subsequently rejected. For Type C markers, note that queue position does not determine the level of discount (see paragraph 6.10), so the timing of the marker is less critical than for Types A or B.

49 As elaborated upon at paragraph 4.22 below.

50 For example, securing physical and electronic evidence, keeping track of relevant witnesses who leave the applicant's employment and continuing to keep the application confidential.

51 See, for example, paragraphs 5.7 and 5.20 below.

52 For example, if the original applicant's representative leaves the undertaking.

53 Parties with concerns or questions about how the genuine intention to confess might relate their specific situation can avail themselves of confidential guidance from the OFT. See paragraphs 3.3 and following, above.

54 Parties with questions about whether there is a concrete basis to suspect cartel activity can avail themselves of confidential guidance from the OFT. See paragraphs 3.3 and following, above.

55 When considering an oral application, the OFT will, among other things, have regard to paragraph 51 of the European Competition Network Model Leniency Programme Explanatory note (ec.europa.eu/competition/ecn/mlp_revised_2012_en.pdf). See paragraphs 4.41 and following of this guidance for further discussion of the Model Leniency Programme.

56 Information provided by the applicant will also generally be disclosed as part of 'access to the file' for other recipients of the statement of objections or disclosure to criminal defendants. See further Chapter 7.

57 See paragraphs 10.1 to 10.4 below

58 On-site inspections under Sections 27 or 28 of the CA98 or Sections 193 and 194 of the EA02.

59 This is a marker which is granted without the applicant having immediately to reveal its identity to the OFT.

[60] For a copy of the ECN Model Leniency Programme and the Explanatory Notes see the ECN website at ec.europa.eu/comm/competition/ecn/model_leniency_en.pdf. The ECN Model Leniency Programme was launched on 29 September 2006 and was revised in November 2012. It sets out the principal elements which the ECN members believe should be common in all programmes. This includes the type of information an applicant should be prepared to provide in order to get immunity, a coherent set of termination and cooperation duties and a streamlined procedure for processing applications.

5. EXPECTED COOPERATION THROUGHOUT THE INVESTIGATION

[3.160]
5.1 Once the OFT has launched an investigation into any cartel activity, whether using its criminal or civil powers, it must take full control of all investigative steps to ensure that the investigation is carried out fairly, thoroughly and carefully. The case team will therefore engage in regular dialogue with the applicant regarding any steps that the OFT wishes the applicant to take and also to communicate steps that the OFT intends to undertake directly concerning the applicant, its premises or current or former employees/officers.[61]

5.2 Although this dialogue will provide applicants with an opportunity to suggest further or alternative steps, or ways to achieve the results required whilst reducing disruption to business, ultimately it will be for the OFT to determine what steps are necessary and appropriate. In general, the types of investigative steps that will be required will be similar to those required for non-leniency parties, albeit that they will be carried out with the cooperation of the applicant rather than through use of compulsory investigative powers.

5.3 In some cases, the need for the OFT to ensure that the investigation has been carried out to the requisite standard may involve the OFT repeating or conducting 'spot-checks' of searches or other steps already carried out by the applicant, for example to ensure that all relevant material has been correctly identified.

THE REQUIREMENT TO MAINTAIN 'CONTINUOUS AND COMPLETE' COOPERATION

5.4 The requirement to maintain continuous and complete cooperation throughout the OFT's investigation and any subsequent proceedings is at the heart of the leniency process and is a condition for the grant of any immunity or type of leniency, whether for an undertaking or individual. Clearly the requirement necessitates compliance with the rules and principles set out in this guidance note. However, continuous and complete cooperation also implies that the overall approach to the leniency process by an applicant must be a constructive one, designed genuinely to assist the OFT in efficiently and effectively detecting, investigating and taking enforcement action against cartel conduct, so that the public policy objectives of the OFT's leniency policy are achieved.

5.5 This constructive approach would, for example, extend to positively and proactively engaging in discussions regarding efficient handling of procedural matters, for example where the OFT is considering streamlined access to file or alternative processes for providing confidentiality representations.

5.6 Cooperation must also be timely, with information being provided promptly and individuals being made available for interviews or preparation of witness statements in accordance with the reasonable requests of OFT investigators. If the applicant foresees or encounters difficulties meeting OFT deadlines or requests, these should be raised with the OFT as early as possible, but applicants should not expect that extensions to deadlines will be common.

5.7 If at any time, the OFT has concerns that the applicant is not adopting such a constructive approach,[62] or that there are unreasonable delays in providing information or otherwise cooperating with OFT requirements, the matter will be raised with the applicant's representative and the applicant's legal advisers by the case team, and if necessary the applicant's representative will be invited to meet with the Senior Responsible Officer (SRO),[63] that is, the senior official responsible for the investigation to discuss those concerns.

5.8 If, following the meeting with the SRO, those concerns have not been adequately addressed to the satisfaction of the OFT, then the applicant may lose all protection under the leniency programme.

CONTINUING ACCEPTANCE OF CARTEL INFRINGEMENT

5.9 Leniency is given in exchange for admissions of participation in cartel conduct.[64] After the marker has been granted, the conditions of leniency necessitate that there should be a continuing acceptance of having engaged in cartel activity, including an acceptance that such activity infringed the Chapter I prohibition or Article 101 of the TFEU or, in the case of individual applicants, amounted to the cartel offence (see paragraph 2.7, condition (a)). Ultimately, this will be reflected in the leniency agreement (see paragraphs A.4(a) and B.3(a) of the pro forma leniency and no-action letters respectively).

5.10 One issue which has arisen is the extent to which a leniency applicant is entitled to dispute the OFT's analysis of the evidence or law. If, at any stage, the applicant's representations to the OFT, for example during the written and oral representations stage following the issue of a statement of objections, amount expressly or implicitly to a denial of cartel participation, the OFT will consider such representations to be inconsistent with any actual or proposed grant of leniency.

5.11 What if the applicant continues to accept that it has been a party to cartel behaviour but disputes specific elements of the OFT's analysis, for example, as to the precise duration of the infringement? The OFT does not exclude that the making of certain limited representations, such as identifying material factual inaccuracies, provided they are made in a spirit of cooperation, is consistent with the grant of leniency. However, the OFT does not consider that it would be possible or desirable to seek in the abstract to draw a clear dividing line between such representations and the sorts of representations that would transgress an applicant's duty to provide constructive and genuine assistance in proving admitted cartel conduct. The OFT will nevertheless take a common sense approach in each case and hear what the applicant has to say before making any decision as to how the applicant's leniency position may be affected. See also paragraph 6.2.

INFORMATION TO BE PROVIDED BY LENIENCY APPLICANTS

5.12 Leniency applicants must provide all non-legally privileged information, documents and evidence available to them regarding the existence and activities of the reported cartel activity (hereafter referred to as the 'relevant information').

5.13 A checklist of specific information that will be required in every case is included at Annexe D, but this should not be interpreted as a limitation on the previous paragraph.

5.14 This requirement to provide all relevant information should be interpreted widely so as to include any information, in whatever form, which is capable of having some reasonable bearing on the OFT's investigation of the cartel. As well as pre-existing documents, this will include the provision of evidence from current and former employees and directors, including the provision of witness statements by them as may be required by the OFT.

5.15 Information which has a bearing on the OFT's investigation will include information that supports a finding of cartel activity, information which suggests an absence of cartel activity (generally, or on the part of specific undertakings or individuals) – 'exculpatory' material[65] – and information on possible leads or sources of information that the OFT may wish to pursue.

5.16 Relevant information will typically be available to the applicant from a number of different sources. Applicants should note paragraphs A.4(b) and A.4(c) of the pro forma leniency agreement at Annexe A in relation to securing and making available documents, IT systems and evidence from current and former directors, officers, employees and agents. Such measures may be required from applicants at any time in the investigation, whether before or after the signing of the leniency agreement.

5.17 After receipt of the application package, the OFT will give advice to the applicant, as best it can, as to the broad categories of information the OFT considers are likely to be relevant in the context of the particular case and the form in which any further information should be provided. The OFT will also advise the applicant on steps which the OFT will take directly and steps which it expects the applicant to undertake as part of its ongoing cooperation. This guidance will be regularly updated and/or refined through ongoing dialogue between the OFT and the applicant as the OFT's investigation progresses.

5.18 Furthermore, the applicant should, as part of this dialogue, inform the OFT of any developments that may affect the OFT's ability to gather or analyse relevant information. This might include, for example, changes to IT systems, change of employment/location of individual witnesses, or commencement of related investigations by other regulatory authorities.

5.19 When providing information to the OFT via e-mail, leniency applicants and their advisers should ensure that they use the CJSM (Criminal Justice Secure e-Mail) system, access to which is available free of charge.[66]

INFORMATION INSUFFICIENT FOR A CREDIBLE INVESTIGATION (TYPE A)

5.20 Information provided by applicants for Type A immunity must, as a minimum give the OFT a sufficient basis for taking forward a credible investigation.[67] If, after a reasonable opportunity following the initial application package (the duration of which will be assessed on a case-by-case basis), the relevant information provided by the applicant does not meet this minimum threshold the OFT will withdraw the applicant's marker. Before withdrawing the marker, the OFT will discuss with the applicant's representative its assessment that it does not have a basis for taking forward a credible investigation and consider with the applicant's representative any options or possibilities for producing sufficient evidence to reach that threshold.

INFORMATION DOES NOT ADD SIGNIFICANT VALUE (TYPES B AND C)

5.21 Information provided by Type B and Type C applicants must, as a minimum, be such that it adds 'significant value' to the OFT's investigation, that is, it must genuinely advance the investigation.

5.22 If, after examining the information provided by the applicant and the material obtained from other sources prior to the application, the OFT considers that the relevant information provided by the applicant does not meet this minimum threshold, the OFT will withdraw the applicant's marker. Before withdrawing the marker, the OFT will discuss with the applicant's representative its assessment that the information provided does not add significant value and consider with the applicant's representative any options or possibilities for producing sufficient evidence to reach that threshold. Paragraphs 7.14 to 7.18 below include discussion of how the information provided by the applicant will be treated by the OFT, where the marker is withdrawn.

DISCOVERY OF GENUINELY UNRELATED MATERIAL

5.23 There is no obligation to submit material which is clearly outside the scope of the leniency application to the OFT – the OFT will not be asking US-style 'omnibus questions'.

5.24 To the extent the information relates to an entirely separate infringement, it is treated in the normal way. Undertakings are, therefore, encouraged also to apply for leniency for that (entirely separate) infringement. To the extent that the undertaking is not benefiting from immunity in relation to the original leniency application, the OFT's leniency plus policy should be taken advantage of. (See paragraph 9.1 below.)

INVESTIGATIVE MEASURES BY OFT

5.25 It is the OFT's responsibility to ensure that investigations, whether criminal or civil, are carried out to the necessary standard. It is therefore normal practice for the OFT to carry out various investigative steps directly in relation to leniency applicants, in the same way that it does in relation to non-leniency parties under investigation.

5.26 Leniency applicants will be expected to comply with requests to cooperate in such steps, including anything that could be required from a non-applicant by the use of OFT's formal powers, without the OFT having to resort to formal powers in relation to the applicant.

5.27 Bearing in mind that there may be strong financial and personal incentives for undertakings and individual witnesses to present the conduct as falling within the scope of the leniency policy, the OFT's investigation must robustly assess the probative value of information provided by the leniency applicant, including witness evidence from employees and directors. The OFT will need to probe any changes in story or inconsistencies, look for independent corroborative material where possible, and pursue any lines of enquiry which call into question evidence from the leniency applicant. Where there is a clear dispute over the facts of the case between the leniency applicant and another alleged party to the cartel, the OFT will consider carefully both parties' accounts before deciding which it regards to be the most credible.

5.28 Cartel investigations vary, and so the following guidance is indicative rather than intended to list measures that will apply in every case. For example, the types of investigative steps required in criminal investigations may be more extensive and potentially more intrusive than those undertaken in purely civil investigations. Also, the OFT may need to undertake more steps directly where the applicant is genuinely unable to meet the cost of undertaking such steps to the standards required for a proper investigation.

5.29 Typical investigative steps that the OFT will or may wish to carry out directly include:

- Interviewing witnesses.
- Assisting to prepare witness statements.
- Retaining a secure, forensically sound image of relevant electronic material. As well as being important to enable verification of the authenticity of electronic evidence, the OFT may also wish to conduct searches of such material directly (with or without the assistance of specialist IT consultants), instead of/as well as receiving the results of electronic searches conducted by the applicant.[68]
- Reviewing original hard copy documents (essential in criminal cases, where originals will be retained as evidence).
- Physical searches of relevant premises.
- Assessing the relevance of specific documents within categories identified by the applicant as potentially relevant (noting that the OFT's assessment of relevance will be informed by information from other sources not available to the applicant).
- Spot checks of searches undertaken by the applicant or its advisers.

INTERVIEWS WITH LENIENCY APPLICANT WITNESSES WHERE THERE IS A CRIMINAL INVESTIGATION

5.30 If an individual has applied for individual immunity and the OFT is, in principle, prepared to issue a no-action letter, the individual applying for immunity from prosecution will be interviewed. Any information they provide in such interviews will not be used against them in criminal proceedings except in the following circumstances:

- where a no-action letter is not issued, if the individual applying for immunity from prosecution has knowingly or recklessly provided information that is false or misleading in a material particular, or
- where a no-action letter is issued, if it is subsequently revoked (see further paragraphs 7.20 to 7.24 below).

5.31 In Type A cases, or Type B cases where the OFT has confirmed that it is minded to grant blanket criminal immunity, the individual knows, before being interviewed, that they will be granted criminal immunity provided they satisfy all the usual conditions. The purpose of the interview is therefore to obtain all relevant information from the individual with a view to advancing the OFT's investigation – not to decide whether the individual will be granted criminal immunity in principle. However, in cases where the grant of individual immunity is discretionary, including other Type B and Type C cases, interviews of individuals may be conducted for two reasons:

- to elicit sufficient information to enable the OFT to decide whether it is in the public interest to exercise its discretion to grant a no-action letter in principle, and
- to obtain information from the individual with a view to advancing the OFT's investigation.

5.32 In Type A and B immunity cases the OFT will interview the individual under the protections laid out in paragraph 5.30. In Type B and C leniency cases the interview may also be under the protections laid out in paragraph 5.30. However, in Type B and C leniency cases where the individual is a suspect and the OFT does not believe that it is in the public interest to offer an interview under the protections laid out in paragraph 5.30, interviews will be conducted under caution.[69] Where a voluntary interview has been conducted under caution in a Type B or C leniency case, the OFT may nonetheless decide later that the individual will be offered criminal immunity depending on the OFT's assessment as to what is in the public interest.

5.33 Where individuals have been granted interviews under the protections laid out in paragraph 5.30, the principle of protection of incriminating information given in the interview will also extend to the giving of information in documentary form, whether directly or through the applicant's legal adviser.

5.34 If desired, a Type B or C leniency applicant's adviser could seek confidential guidance from the OFT about whether interviews are likely to be offered under the protections laid out in paragraph 5.30. If the OFT is not conducting a criminal investigation into the cartel activity the issue of whether or not an interview will need to be conducted under caution will not arise.

COOPERATION FROM CURRENT OR FORMER EMPLOYEES OR DIRECTORS

5.35 It is important to note that in the case of the standard form leniency agreement for corporate immunity/leniency, cooperation extends to an undertaking using its best endeavours to procure the ongoing cooperation of its current and former employees and directors in relation to any subsequent appeal proceedings before the Competition Appeal Tribunal.[70] Where the matter is being investigated criminally, the OFT will require such cooperation to extend also to any criminal investigation and subsequent proceedings.[71] This is because it will not necessarily be the case that all current and former directors and employees will already be the subject of cooperation obligations under no-action or comfort letters. There may be a number of employees or directors who are not recipients of such letters but who may still be called upon to assist in the criminal matter, including by being available as witnesses in criminal proceedings. The mechanism to help secure their cooperation will be the leniency agreement with the undertaking which employs or employed the individuals concerned.[72] In the case of the standard form no-action letter, the cooperation requirement continues until the conclusion of any criminal proceedings – so that where required, the individual may have to give oral evidence in criminal proceedings.

5.36 In principle, leniency protection from individual sanctions can extend to former employees and directors even where those individuals now work for another company that is under investigation for the same cartel activity, provided that they fulfil the requirement to cooperate with the OFT's investigation. However, the OFT strongly recommends that applicant undertakings do not contact such individuals prior to discussing the approach with the OFT, given the issues of confidentiality and the risks of tip-off that may arise, and the potential consequences for the applicant if tip-off results.

Consequences for an undertaking applying for leniency of failure to cooperate by a current or former employee or director

5.37 A failure, at any stage, to cooperate with the OFT on the part of a current or former employee or director of an applicant undertaking will not necessarily mean that the undertaking's leniency application will fail or that leniency, once given, will be revoked. The leniency application will not fail or be revoked in cases where:

- the applicant can show that it used its best endeavours to secure the cooperation of that individual[73] (albeit unsuccessfully), and
- overall the applicant provided the OFT with sufficient evidence of the reported cartel activity to pass the applicable evidential threshold.[74]

5.38 In this context, it should be noted that the applicant's general cooperation obligation includes a positive duty to inform the OFT without delay about any concerns the applicant may have as to the level of cooperation provided by any of its current or former employees or directors. In particular, the applicant must inform the OFT without delay about any concerns the applicant may have regarding the completeness and/or accuracy of any statements made by any of its current and former employees and directors during the course of the OFT's investigation.

5.39 It follows from the above that where an undertaking's application for Type A or B immunity does not fail, or is not revoked, despite an individual failing to cooperate, all other implicated current or former employees or directors of the undertaking who are maintaining cooperation will continue to qualify for immunity. By contrast, the non-cooperating individual will of course lose all protection under the leniency programme.

5.40 In the event of the undertaking's application failing, or being revoked, those current or former employees or directors of the undertaking who had cooperated throughout the investigation will no longer be eligible for 'blanket' criminal immunity but they will have been interviewed under the terms of paragraph 5.30 above and, as such, no information given by them whether orally or in writing as part of the leniency process will be used in evidence against them and they may still be able to apply for individual immunity.

NOTES

61 This does not preclude the OFT from engaging directly with former employees/officers without informing the applicant. Direct engagement with current employees, without involving the applicant or its advisers, may also be appropriate in criminal investigations.

62 This will include where the leniency applicant has been careless in its approach to the leniency application.

63 See '*A guide to the OFT's investigation procedures in competition cases*' (OFT1263, March 2011), in particular, Chapter 5 for a description of the role of the SRO.

64 See also the points made at paragraph 4.22 above on the need for a genuine intention to confess.

65 'Exculpatory material' for these purposes will include information known to the leniency applicant which could reasonably be seen as calling into question the credibility, as a witness, of anyone who provides relevant information.

66 For more information on the CJSM, including how to create an account, please see www.cjsm.net

67 The OFT may, for example, be of the view that there is no basis for taking forward a credible investigation in a case where

the applicant has provided the OFT with documentary evidence which is prima facie probative of the reported cartel conduct (and was thereby sufficient for the initial grant of a marker) but the strength of which is then materially undermined by statements given by implicated current or former employees or directors of the applicant.

68 The OFT may also require information on the type of electronic software and hardware used by the applicant or its individual employees. The OFT may also require a record of the 'continuity of evidence' stating where electronic documents were initially produced or obtained. Please see footnote 124 for a definition of continuity of evidence.

69 If there are grounds to suspect that a person has committed an offence, the person must be cautioned before any questions about an offence, or further questions if the answers provide the grounds for suspicion, are put to him/her in circumstances where the suspect's answers or refusal to answer may be given in evidence to a court in a prosecution. See Code C of the Codes of Practice issued to accompany the Police and Criminal Evidence Act 1984 (PACE). A caution in these circumstances does not indicate that the OFT is minded to charge the individual concerned, but will be used where the possibility of charge cannot be ruled out.

70 Paragraph A.4(c) (x) of the pro forma leniency agreement in Annexe A.

71 Paragraph A.4(c) (xi) of the pro forma leniency agreement in Annexe A.

72 The OFT recognises the limitations for the undertaking in relation to procuring the ongoing cooperation of former employees and directors who have no independent cooperation obligations under a no-action or comfort letter.

73 Where the applicant proposes disciplinary action against an individual, including dismissal, arising from that individual's role in the cartel, the OFT will expect the undertaking to discuss this matter with the OFT. The OFT will be keen to ensure that any action proposed by the undertaking against an individual does not have the perverse effect of reducing incentives to cooperate with the OFT. So far as is reasonable, the incentives placed on the individual by the undertaking and the OFT should be aligned, that is, there should be the maximum possible incentive on the individual's part to tell the full truth about his or her involvement in the cartel. The OFT will expect to see cooperation in this respect from the undertaking.

74 In this context, please also see footnote 67 above (which refers to the possible difficulty in achieving the relevant evidential threshold if an individual's account of events materially undermines documentary evidence provided by the undertaking that would otherwise have been probative of the existence of the cartel).

6. THE LENIENCY AGREEMENT OR NO-ACTION LETTER AND RELATED ISSUES

TIMING OF LENIENCY AGREEMENTS

[3.161]

6.1 Leniency agreements will be signed in the later stages of the OFT's investigation, shortly prior to the issue of the statement of objections in a CA98 investigation, or shortly before any individuals are charged with the cartel offence. At this point in time, the OFT will have received and assessed substantially all of the information that is relevant to its case, and will accordingly be in a position to ascertain the necessary scope/characterisation of the cartel activity to be covered in the leniency agreement and also the scope of the 'undertaking', that is, the relevant legal entities that need to benefit from leniency protection.

6.2 The OFT will share its proposals as to scope/characterisation with the applicant. Applicants will have an opportunity to comment and discuss the proposed scope/characterisation before signing the agreement,[75] which will include an acceptance that the reported cartel activity infringed the Chapter I prohibition and/or Article 101 of the TFEU.

6.3 In relation to Type B and C leniency, the OFT will also by this point be in a position to ascertain the appropriate level of reduction in penalty based on the value added by the leniency applicant (see paragraphs 6.8 to 6.10 below).

6.4 Before signing the leniency agreement, the OFT will need to be and remain[76] satisfied that the conditions for the grant of leniency have been and continue to be met, namely the continued acceptance of participation in cartel activity, the information requirements set out above,[77] the requirement of continuous and complete cooperation, that the applicant has refrained from any further participation in the cartel and, in relation to immunity agreements, that the applicant was not a coercer.

TIMING OF ISSUE OF NO-ACTION AND COMFORT LETTERS

6.5 A proper determination of whether a person should receive a no-action or comfort letter cannot generally be made until at or near the conclusion of the OFT's criminal investigation. It may not be necessary for all lines of enquiry to have been completed. However, as a minimum, the OFT will expect to have received and duly analysed the substantial and most probative elements of the relevant information in the possession or control of the immunity applicant and that of its current and former employees and directors before it issues any no-action or comfort letters.[78] This is likely to mean that relevant individuals will have been interviewed at least once about their role in the cartel activity and possibly more than once before a no-action or comfort letter is issued.[79] Where a person applies and qualifies in principle for criminal immunity on his or her own account, the position on timing is broadly analogous to that which applies as part of a corporate approach.

6.6 Where requested and where there is good reason to do so,[80] the OFT will be willing to issue interim comfort letters to certain individuals to the effect that, as at that time, the OFT is content that the individual(s) concerned appear to be cooperating fully and consequently that no-action or final comfort letters, where needed, will be issued in due course provided that cooperation and compliance with all the usual requirements continues.

FORM OF LENIENCY AND NO-ACTION AGREEMENTS

6.7 Leniency and no-action agreements are in standard form. They are attached at Annexe A and Annexe B of this guidance. It should be noted that the OFT will not generally expect to negotiate amendments to the terms of these agreements – however reasonable suggestions for minor variations addressing specific concerns will be considered.

DISCOUNTS GRANTED IN TYPE B AND C LENIENCY CASES

6.8 The key criterion for determining the discount available will be the overall added value of the material provided by the leniency applicant. This will generally be a function of the stage at which the undertaking comes forward, the evidence already in the OFT's possession and the probative value of the evidence provided by the undertaking. The OFT will also take into account the overall level of cooperation provided.[81]

6.9 In Type B cases, it is possible that the value added by the application will be high, as it will be the OFT's first application in the case and, as such, even where the application does not result in a grant of corporate immunity, awards of up to 100 per cent are possible. However, the OFT has insufficient experience of Type B reductions in penalty to give any more guidance about the percentage reductions that are likely to be on offer in the majority of cases. That said, it should be noted that in general, awards are unlikely to be close to 100 per cent as the OFT would otherwise probably have granted corporate immunity to the Type B applicant. In Type C cases, however, experience suggests that applicants can generally expect to achieve discounts in the range of 25 per cent to 50 per cent. However, it is possible that low value and/or late applications may gain awards of less than 25 per cent.[82]

6.10 Queue position in Type C cases is not decisive. It is possible that an applicant who is third in the queue may get a discount greater than an applicant who was second to apply. That said, it is the usual experience of the OFT that the further ahead in the queue an applicant is, the greater the value added by its application. Therefore, would-be applicants are encouraged to apply at the earliest possible stage.

NOTES

75 This is not, however, an opportunity for the applicant to negotiate changes to the OFT's ultimate findings.

76 These requirements, in particular that of continuous and complete cooperation, also remain conditions of leniency after the signing of the leniency agreement.

77 Although the OFT expects that signing of leniency agreements will take place towards the end of the OFT's investigation after the most substantial and most evidentially probative elements of the relevant information have been received, following signing, the applicant's duty to provide all relevant information will nonetheless be ongoing after that point. For example, the applicant may need to cooperate in the finalisation of witness statements, or to produce relevant information which comes to the attention of the applicant only at a late stage.

78 This accords with the position in regard to the timing of the issue of any leniency agreement. See paragraph 6.1 above.

79 For the procedure under which such interviews will be conducted, see paragraphs 5.31 to 5.34 above.

80 For example, where an investigation has been running on for an unusually long period or where the individuals are overseas nationals and there are particular anxieties given the unfamiliarity with the UK legal system.

81 In this respect the points in paragraphs 5.4 to 5.11 above should be noted.

82 While the OFT will consider any limited representations as to the amount of the award proposed, it will not negotiate over the matter. See also footnote 94 below to the effect that dissatisfaction with an award is not an 'exceptional circumstance' justifying withdrawal from leniency.

7. DISCLOSURE AND USE OF INFORMATION

DISCLOSURE OF LENIENCY INFORMATION DURING A CIVIL OR CRIMINAL INVESTIGATION

[3.162]

7.1 The OFT recognises the importance of confidentiality for leniency applicants. Accordingly, the fact that an undertaking has applied for leniency will not normally be revealed to other undertakings until the statement of objections has been issued. However, in the course of the OFT's civil investigation it may be necessary, directly or indirectly, to disclose information provided by a leniency applicant to third party witnesses or to those suspected of direct involvement in the cartel. Consequently, there is a risk that parties will conclude that the information has been supplied by a leniency applicant, which may in turn reveal the identity of the applicant. The OFT will not formally confirm whether there is a leniency applicant, however.

7.2 Where there are particular sensitivities about the possibility of a leniency applicant's identity being revealed in the course of the investigation, these should be discussed with the OFT at the start of the application process.

7.3 Similar circumstances arise when the OFT is conducting a criminal investigation. Prior to interviewing suspects, the OFT is required to provide disclosure of any material to which the OFT wishes to refer or allude during the interview.

DISCLOSURE OF LENIENCY MATERIAL TO SUPPORT A STATEMENT OF OBJECTIONS, INFRINGEMENT DECISION AND AS PART OF THE ACCESS TO FILE PROCESS

7.4 Where the OFT is conducting a civil investigation, the fact that a party has applied for leniency, together with the information it has submitted and on which the OFT intends to rely, will be set out in the statement of objections issued to the other parties to the proceedings.[83]

7.5 Similarly, subject to the OFT's rules on the protection of confidential information,[84] material submitted as part of the leniency application will be disclosed to the parties during the course of access to the file.

7.6 Before making any disclosure either in the statement of objections or as part of access to the file, however, the OFT will give the leniency applicant a reasonable opportunity to make representations as to whether the OFT should treat any or all of the information as confidential within the meaning of the OFT's rules.

7.7 Disclosure of application statements may be of particular concern to applicants because application statements sometimes disclose certain aspects of the application that the OFT has chosen not to pursue or the applicant's own analysis of the emerging details of the cartel at the time of the application, and there is therefore a potential risk that any unnecessary disclosures may put leniency applicants at a disadvantage relative to non-leniency parties. Accordingly, whilst application statements, including transcripts of oral statements, will be placed on the OFT's file, when assessing the need for disclosure, the OFT will give weight to the strong public interest in encouraging full and frank applications, and notes that non-disclosure of such material may be in the public interest in order to protect the efficacy of the leniency regime. In practice, this means that the OFT will not ordinarily grant access to the application statement to other recipients of a statement of objections. However, in the event that the application statement contains relevant evidential material that has not been presented in other forms that can be made available as part of access to the file,[85] it may be necessary to grant access to the application statement, for rights of defence purposes.[86] In such cases, we will keep confidential any parts of the statement that are not relevant to the case in question. We will also discuss with the applicant whether any additional protective measures in relation to how information is disclosed, for example to third parties is appropriate. This protection will not extend to other documents provided by the applicant, such as witness statements, which refer to or include information from the application statement, which will ordinarily need to be disclosed.

7.8 Even in the case of an unsuccessful leniency applicant or in the case of a leniency applicant which is not proceeded against or where the leniency application was subsequently withdrawn, it cannot be excluded that disclosure of some or all of the material provided as part of the leniency application, including the identity of the applicant, may have to be disclosed to other parties in the course of access to the file.

7.9 Any person to whom information is disclosed in a statement of objections or as part of access to the file will be bound by the restrictions on further disclosure as set out in Part 9 of the EA02.[87]

7.10 Where the OFT's investigation results in an infringement decision, the fact that a party to the proceedings has been granted leniency, together with the leniency information relied on by the OFT, will be apparent from the infringement decision. This will be notified to the parties and a non-confidential version published under the OFT's rules.[88] Undertakings applying for leniency should therefore be aware that at that stage, the fact that a party has been granted leniency, together with the nature of at least some of the evidence provided will become public.

DISCLOSURE OF LENIENCY MATERIAL TO SUPPORT A CRIMINAL PROSECUTION

7.11 If a prosecution is commenced, full disclosure of 'used' and relevant 'unused' material must be made to defendants, to comply with requirements under the Criminal Procedure and Investigations Act 1996 as amended by the Criminal Justice Act 2003, and the associated Code of Practice. This will inevitably include material provided by the leniency applicant, and would typically include application statements (whether written or transcripts of oral statements), where such statements are capable of having an impact on issues arising in the criminal case. Where individuals who have been issued with no-action letters provide witness statements, the fact of those letters having been issued will ordinarily have to be disclosed, although protection of the identities of individuals who are secret sources will be sought by applications for public interest immunity where necessary.

7.12 Given that one of the objectives of the leniency policy is to facilitate effective enforcement action, applicants will be expected to respond promptly and constructively to requests for information which the OFT is under a duty to disclose in order to proceed to a prosecution. In this regard, applicants should note that the grounds for withholding relevant material from defendants in a criminal prosecution are more limited than the scope to withhold information from disclosure in a civil investigation.

7.13 Material disclosed for the purpose of criminal proceedings remains subject to the prohibition on further disclosure imposed by Part 9 of the EA02 save to the extent that it has been disclosed to the public.[89] In the OFT's view disclosure to defendants in criminal proceedings would not of itself amount to disclosure to the public.

DISCLOSURE OF INFORMATION TO SUPPORT PRIVATE CIVIL PROCEEDINGS ETC.

7.14 As a matter of general policy, the OFT would firmly resist, on public interest grounds, requests for disclosure of leniency material, or the fact that leniency has been sought, where such requests are made, for example, in connection with private civil proceedings whether in the UK or overseas.[90] In any event the OFT must observe the general prohibitions on disclosure in Part 9 of the EA02. It follows, however, from paragraphs 7.10 and 7.11 above, that the identity of leniency applicants and certain information they have provided, will enter the public domain through any published infringement decision or through any criminal proceedings held in open court.

USE OF INFORMATION SUBMITTED BY A FAILED OR WITHDRAWN LENIENCY APPLICANT

7.15 Information which is self-incriminatory and which was submitted after a marker approach by an undertaking applying for leniency will not subsequently be relied on as evidence by the OFT against that undertaking (hereafter referred to as a 'failed bona fide applicant') or any of its cooperating current and former employees and directors which, despite having acted in good faith throughout, has failed to qualify for leniency.[91] However, this does not preclude the OFT from pursuing a case against a failed bona fide applicant in such circumstances. The OFT may make use of such information against third parties. Where it proposes to do so, it will consider any representations from the failed bona fide applicant and whether, in using information in this way, it would be fair and reasonable to award a reduction of any fine which might be imposed on the failed bona fide applicant at the mitigation stage of the penalty-setting process.[92]

7.16 If the OFT proposes to use information provided by the failed bona fide applicant which could have been obtained through public sources, such as material available on the internet, it will consider itself free to use that information whether it be to support a case against the failed bona fide applicant or against third parties and whether or not it can be regarded as self-incriminatory.[93]

7.17 Where the OFT proposes to use any information provided by a failed bona fide applicant which was not available from public sources and is of a purely factual nature (as distinct from being self-incriminatory) the OFT may make use of such information whether it be to support a case against the failed applicant or against third parties. Where it proposes to do so, it will consider any representations from the failed bona fide applicant (including as to whether the material should properly be regarded as 'factual' or 'self-incriminatory') and whether it would be fair and reasonable to award a reduction of any fine which might be imposed on that applicant at the mitigation stage of the penalty-setting process.

7.18 Where an undertaking, having made an application for leniency and received confirmation of a marker, has chosen to withdraw its application of its own volition, the OFT may use any information provided by the applicant either against the applicant or any third party.[94] However, in so doing the OFT will consider whether it is fair and reasonable to award a reduction of any fine which might be imposed on the withdrawn applicant at the mitigation stage of the penalty-setting process.

7.19 Some practitioners have expressed concern over the use of information in failed and withdrawn leniency application cases, but the OFT's experience is that disputes over the use of information in such circumstances arise rarely in practice. Where a bona fide application has failed, it will generally be because there was an insufficient basis to take forward a credible investigation or because the value added to an existing investigation was small. It is therefore relatively unlikely that the OFT will have any desire to use the information for any purpose. Instances of withdrawal of applications have proven to be rare and the OFT sees no reason why the frequency of such instances would increase in the future.

USE OF INFORMATION IN CASES OF BAD FAITH AND NON-COOPERATION

7.20 Where a leniency applicant, at any stage, acts in bad faith and/or fails to cooperate fully, the OFT reserves the right to use information derived from an approach or application against that failed applicant (and any third parties). Nonetheless, in such circumstances, the OFT will still consider whether the use of information makes it fair and reasonable to award a reduction of any fine which might be imposed on the failed applicant at the mitigation stage of the penalty-setting process.

USE OF INFORMATION IN THE CASE OF FAILED NO-ACTION APPLICANTS

7.21 The principles governing the use of information in the case of failed no-action applications largely parallel the principles in relation to failed leniency approaches by undertakings.

7.22 As set out above at paragraph 5.30, if an individual has applied for individual immunity and been interviewed, any information they provide in such interviews will not be used against them in criminal proceedings except in the following circumstances:

- where a no-action letter is not issued, if the individual applying for immunity from prosecution has knowingly or recklessly provided information that is false or misleading in a material particular, or
- where a no-action letter is issued, if it is subsequently revoked.

7.23 The effect of this, in conjunction with paragraph 10.11 below (concerning revocation), is that where an applicant has intentionally or recklessly misled the OFT or is in breach of the conditions in paragraph 2.7 above, in particular as a result of a failure to cooperate, the OFT will revoke the no-action letter, and consequently all information given under the no-action process may be used against the individual in evidence. In addition, the OFT would also consider itself free to use the information against any third party including any undertaking.[95]

7.24 Similarly, where a no-action letter is not issued following an interview under paragraph 5.30, information provided could only be used against the interviewed individual applicant in criminal proceedings if he/she knowingly or recklessly provided information that is false or misleading in a material particular. The OFT would also consider itself free to use the information against third parties and other undertakings in those circumstances.

7.25 The OFT has not had experience of voluntary withdrawals of applications for no-action letters, but would be likely to take a similar approach to that taken in relation to voluntary withdrawals by undertakings from leniency. See paragraph 7.17.

USE OF INFORMATION IN THE CASE OF OFT DECIDING NOT TO PROCEED

7.26 If the OFT decides, at any stage, that it does not wish to proceed with its investigation into the infringement on administrative priority grounds, the OFT will generally have no desire to use the information provided against the applicant or for any other purpose.

7.27 One exception to this position is where the OFT has decided to proceed against certain parties to a group of related infringements, but has not pursued all possible parties for administrative priority reasons. In those circumstances, the OFT may need to rely on evidence provided by a leniency applicant which is no longer under investigation, against third parties. Where it proposes to do so, it will consider any representations from the leniency applicant, for example as to whether the information can be provided in another form or disclosed in a way which does not reveal that it was received as part of a leniency application.

7.28 There may also be cases where, in criminal proceedings against an individual, material provided by a leniency applicant in relation to a separate case would be 'relevant' and may need to be disclosed, despite the fact that that case was not proceeded with. In such cases, the material will be treated as sensitive and only be disclosed to the defence if it meets the statutory test for disclosure.

7.29 Where the OFT decides not to open an investigation at all or a case is closed on administrative priority grounds, the applicant's marker will remain on the OFT's file and, provided the conditions for leniency continue to be met,[96] the applicant's position would be preserved in the unlikely event that the OFT decided to open or re-open the investigation, for example if new information came to light. To the extent that the case closure is publicised, the OFT would seek to avoid disclosing the fact of any leniency application.

TRANSFER OF INFORMATION TO OTHER UK AGENCIES

7.30 If the OFT considers it necessary or appropriate to pass information deriving from a leniency applicant to another UK agency, such as the Serious Fraud Office (SFO), the OFT would inform the applicant or its legal adviser first. However, applicants must accept that the OFT may refer cases to the SFO and the expectation should be that such referrals will be on the basis of a full disclosure of all material in the OFT's possession.

TRANSFER OF INFORMATION TO OVERSEAS AUTHORITIES, THE COMMISSION AND OTHER MEMBERS OF THE ECN

7.31 Information supplied by an undertaking as part of an application for leniency will never be passed to an overseas agency without the consent of the provider save for one exception. Such information may be disclosed to the Commission and/or another EU national competition authority but only in accordance with the provisions and safeguards set out in paragraphs 40 and 41 of the Network Notice. Also, where such a disclosure was being contemplated by the OFT, the OFT would always consult the provider.

7.32 Information supplied as part of an application for individual immunity will also never be passed to an overseas agency without the consent of the provider save again for one exception. The OFT may wish to provide the information to the Commission or to another EU national competition authority for the purpose of applying Article 101 of the TFEU. In the case of the Commission and the vast majority of EU national competition authorities, the enforcement of Article 101 is by way of proceedings against the undertakings concerned and will not therefore expose any individual to the risk of personal sanctions. Even where this is not the case, however, the OFT would, in any event, only transmit such information in accordance with the provisions and safeguards set out in paragraphs 40 and 41 of the Network Notice. The Commission or national authority would also be required to guarantee to the OFT that the information would not be provided to any other agency. There should therefore be no risk of any personal exposure of sanction to the applicant. Again, and for the reasons set out above where the OFT was considering such a disclosure to the Commission or to another EU national competition authority and the disclosure might lead to the identity of the provider being revealed, the OFT would always consult the provider.

NOTES

83 Once a formal investigation is opened, generally a case initiation letter will be sent to the parties under investigation containing basic details of the investigation. However for some cases, such as in cartel investigations, it may not be appropriate to do so as this may prejudice the investigation such as prior to unannounced inspections or witness interviews. If the OFT does consider it appropriate to send a case initiation letter to the parties it may limit any information provided in the letter to protect the identity of a leniency applicant. Generally once the parties have been informed of the investigation the OFT will generally publish on the OFT's website, a case opening notice containing basic details of the case including the administrative timetable for the case. In the case of cartel investigations the OFT will limit the details in the notice to ensure the ongoing investigation is not prejudiced and would not mention publicly that any undertaking had applied for leniency. It is OFT normal practice publicly to announce the issue of the Statement of Objections on our website and to make an announcement on the Regulatory News Service, however the OFT would not mention publicly that any undertaking whose identity had been revealed as party to a statement of objections had applied. If, of its own volition, an undertaking wanted to disclose that it was a leniency applicant in these circumstances, then the applicant would be free to do so. See OFT's Competition Act Procedures Guidance, A guide to the *OFT's investigation procedures in competition cases* (OFT 1263rev, October 2012). www.oft.gov.uk/news-and-updates/press/2012/91-12.

84 Competition Act 1998 (OFT's Rules) Order 2004 (SI 2004/2751), Rules 1(1), 4(3) and 6. See also Section 244 of the EA02.

85 The OFT expects applicants to provide all primary source material that led to the generation of the application statement that the OFT considers is relevant to its case, so this situation is expected to be exceptional, rather than the norm.

Part 3 CMA and other Guidelines

86 Depending on the relevance of such information, it cannot be excluded that it may also need to be set out in the statement of objections and any subsequent infringement decision.

87 See in particular Section 241(2) of the EA02.

88 The Competition Act 1998 (Office of Fair Trading's Rules) Order 2004 (SI 2004/2751), Rule 7.

89 See, for example, section 241(2) EA02.

90 Obviously where a court has made an order with which the OFT was bound to comply, the OFT would discharge its duty to the court. Additionally, if disclosure of leniency material, or at least the fact that a leniency applicant existed, was genuinely necessary for the OFT to defend general civil proceedings, for example a judicial review on the correctness of the OFT's decision to open an investigation, some limited disclosure may have to be made. However, the OFT would always give utmost consideration to the public interest in maintaining an effective leniency policy.

91 This may, for example, occur because (a) the information supplied was insufficient, in the absence of other information, to provide the OFT with a basis for taking forward a credible investigation, (b) the information failed to add significant value to an existing investigation (c) the applicant provided evidence of an infringement which had only a minimal impact on trade in the UK but was instead focused on other jurisdictions or (d) because at the time of the marker approach the parties and the OFT had a reasonable expectation that the reported conduct amounted to cartel activity but subsequent investigation revealed that the nature of the infringement was not such as to amount to cartel activity.

92 In particular, as to whether a reduction should be granted under paragraph 2.16 of the revised OFT's Penalty Guidance, *OFT's guidance as to the appropriate amount of a penalty* (OFT 423, September 2012).

93 Assuming the material did not become publicly available only because of the leniency application.

94 However, there may be exceptional circumstances which, in the OFT's view, justify the withdrawal of the leniency application. If so, the OFT would apply the same principles as those relating to the use of information against a failed bona fide leniency applicant. Given the OFT's very limited experience of voluntary withdrawals, it does not intend to draw up a list of possible exceptional circumstances. However, the OFT will not regard as an exceptional circumstance justifying a withdrawal from leniency, that an applicant is dissatisfied with the level of award made in a Type B or C leniency case.

95 It will be recalled from paragraph 540 of this guidance note that the position is different where an individual has cooperated fully under the no-action process but his/her application is under the umbrella of an immunity approach by an undertaking whose corporate application has failed. In those circumstances no information provided by any cooperating individual will be used against him/her because the protections laid out in paragraph 5.30 continue to apply.

96 For example, leniency applicants should consider preserving relevant documents so that they are in a position to offer full cooperation, and should preserve the confidentiality of their leniency applications.

8. OTHER ISSUES RELATING TO CRIMINAL INVESTIGATIONS/PROSECUTIONS

INTERACTION BETWEEN THE CARTEL OFFENCE IN THE UK AND THE COMMISSION LENIENCY NOTICE

[3.163]

8.1 The OFT is aware that some practitioners might have a concern that undertakings approaching the Commission under the Commission Leniency Notice might inadvertently increase exposure for the undertaking's current and former employees and directors to the risk of prosecution in the UK for the cartel offence, in those cases where the infringement had some effect on the UK. The OFT believes that the points set out in this section should be sufficient to allay any concerns which might exist.

8.2 Based on past experience, the OFT expects that most undertakings that qualify for immunity under the Commission Leniency Notice will also be able to gain 'blanket' criminal immunity in the UK for current and former employees and directors, by virtue of that undertaking applying separately to the UK and gaining Type A immunity. Thus any fears of exposure to prosecution for the cartel offence would be allayed. Indeed, using the procedure referred to in paragraph 4.36 above, applicants, if they so wish, are able to request a no-names marker in the UK before they even approach the Commission.

8.3 What happens if the result of such an approach under paragraph 4.36 is that the OFT tells the applicant that Type A immunity is not available (and that 'blanket' criminal immunity for a Type B applicant is not available either) and that relevant current and former employees and directors are not therefore guaranteed criminal immunity in the UK? In that situation, the OFT might still be able to reassure the undertaking's adviser, on the basis of the provision of a 'hypothetical' set of facts provided by him/her, that the case would not be of a type where the OFT would contemplate bringing a criminal prosecution.

8.4 What if individual immunity was not available and in addition, the OFT was not prepared to give any assurances that it would not contemplate bringing a criminal prosecution in a case of that kind? It is at least possible that in such cases an undertaking might nonetheless qualify for immunity under the Commission Leniency Notice. If so, the OFT will normally be prepared to grant no-action letters[97] to any implicated current or former employee or director of such an undertaking. This would be so even if another undertaking had already qualified for UK Type A immunity and consequent criminal immunity for all of its current and former employees and directors.

8.5 In theory therefore, a possible outcome is that the current and former employees and directors of two undertakings could be granted criminal immunity – in the one case because the undertaking obtains Type A immunity in the UK and in the other case because the undertaking obtains immunity under the Commission Leniency Notice and then obtains criminal immunity for all of its current and former employees and directors on the back of its grant of Commission immunity. The OFT expects this to be very rare, however, as the great majority of undertakings that qualify for immunity under the Commission Leniency Notice will also have put down a prompt marker to secure Type A immunity in the UK. Indeed, attempting to secure criminal immunity by reason of the undertaking applying for Type A immunity is the safer option of the two because it is guaranteed and not subject to the qualification that it would **normally** be granted.

8.6 Why does the OFT say it would only **normally** grant criminal immunity on the back of immunity granted under the Commission Leniency Notice? First, where there is already a pre-existing criminal investigation in the UK (the chances of which will obviously be increased if there is already a Type A applicant in the UK), there should be no guarantee of no-action letters to current and former employees and directors of an undertaking even if it qualifies for immunity under the Commission Leniency Notice.[98] Second, the OFT will be mindful of any attempts to 'game the system'. For example, if an undertaking is too late for Type A immunity in the UK and the OFT suspects that an application has subsequently been made to the Commission largely as a device for trying to procure no-action letters, the OFT might decline to offer criminal immunity. The OFT is more likely to decline to grant criminal immunity in such instances where the cartel is not one which the Commission would be 'particularly well placed' to investigate within the terms of the Network Notice.[99] Third, the OFT might refuse to grant criminal immunity when there is unreasonable delay between the approach to the Commission and the subsequent approach to the UK.

8.7 Therefore, the best option when applying for immunity under the Commission Leniency Notice is also to make a prompt approach to the OFT to try to secure UK Type A immunity – through the no-names marker procedure or otherwise.

8.8 The final set of circumstances to be considered here are those where an undertaking:

- is not in a Type A position and is unable to secure discretionary Type B immunity in the UK
- is not given an assurance that a prosecution for the cartel offence would not be contemplated in a case of that type, and
- does not qualify for immunity, but only a reduction of fine, under the Commission Leniency Notice.

The OFT believes that even in such cases, potential Commission applicants need have no concern that an approach to the Commission will **increase** the probability of prosecution for the cartel offence of any of its current and former employees and directors. This is because of the various information restriction safeguards set out in Regulation 1/2003 as supplemented by the Network Notice, together with the OFT's commitment to use internal 'information barriers'.

8.9 The principal route for disclosure of information from the Commission to the OFT is Article 12 of Regulation 1/2003. However, any information disclosed by the Commission to the OFT under Article 12 can only be used for the purpose of applying Articles 101 or 102 of the TFEU and cannot be used as evidence to impose sanctions against natural persons. Notwithstanding this, there may still be a residual concern that any information disclosed by the Commission to the OFT for the purpose of applying Article 101, might still be used by the OFT as **intelligence** to start or further a criminal investigation, even though it could not be used as **evidence** in such a criminal case. So far as information deriving from a Commission leniency applicant is concerned, there should be no such concerns, however, owing to the safeguards in paragraphs 37 to 42 of the Network Notice.[100] These safeguards generally act to prevent any leniency-derived material from being submitted to the OFT under Article 12. The same safeguards also apply to information that has been obtained by the Commission during, by means of, or following any fact-finding measure which could not have been carried out except as a result of leniency.

8.10 The OFT also receives information from the Commission:

- sent under the 'close cooperation' principle (Article 11(1) and (2))
- sent with a view to the OFT assisting the Commission during its investigations (Articles 19 to 22), and
- sent to the OFT as a member of the Advisory Committee (Article 14).

Such material (whether from a leniency source or otherwise) could not be used in evidence in a criminal cartel prosecution because of the limitation in Article 28 of the Regulation and the case law of the European Court.[101]

8.11 Furthermore, in leniency cases, the effect of paragraph 39 of the Network Notice is that if a Commission case started as a result of leniency, the OFT will not be able to rely on information received from the Commission in that case under any of the Articles mentioned above, as a basis for starting[102] its own criminal investigation.[103]

8.12 In summary, the OFT could not use, either as intelligence or evidence, any leniency-derived information obtained from the Commission to further its criminal cartel enforcement functions. Nevertheless, as a further measure designed to provide reassurance to potential Commission leniency applicants, the OFT will use an internal information barrier between staff having access to information derived from the Commission under the above-mentioned provisions on a given case and staff on a team investigating the same cartel activity under section 188 of the EA02.[104] The former group of staff would therefore not be permitted to pass on information directly or indirectly derived from the Commission to the latter group.

8.13 For the above reasons, the OFT believes that the existence of the cartel offence in the UK should not deter applications for immunity or leniency under the Commission Leniency Notice.

WHEN WILL AN INDIVIDUAL HAVE TO ADMIT TO THE CARTEL OFFENCE, IN PARTICULAR DISHONESTY, AND WHEN WILL 'COMFORT LETTERS' INSTEAD OF NO-ACTION LETTERS BE ISSUED?

8.14 Concern has been expressed in the past that the OFT may require certain individuals who qualify in principle for criminal immunity to admit to participation in the cartel offence, including dishonesty, where such an admission is neither necessary nor appropriate. In particular, it has been said that if the

OFT were to reach a view about the role of a particular individual in the cartel arrangements at an early stage of the OFT's investigation, the OFT may require an admission of participation which might later turn out to be inappropriate once the investigation has been completed and all the evidence has been thoroughly scrutinised. It is for this reason that the OFT will not reach a final decision on whether an individual will be required to admit participation in the offence, including dishonesty, until the investigation is at or near its conclusion and after specialist criminal counsel has had the opportunity to review sufficient evidence gathered in the case to be able to advise the OFT on the issue.[105] If the adviser to the would-be no-action letter recipient wishes to put forward any material relevant to the dishonesty point, this will be considered before a final decision is made.

8.15 If the OFT duly decides that it is appropriate that an individual in the cartel who qualifies for criminal immunity in principle should make an admission of participation in the cartel offence, including dishonesty, then that individual will only be offered a no-action letter on condition that such an admission is made. Alternatively, if such an admission is deemed not to be appropriate, then the individual will be offered a 'comfort letter'. The comfort letter will state that after analysis of the evidence it has been concluded that there is insufficient evidence to implicate the individual in the cartel offence and that the OFT does not, therefore, consider that there is any risk of prosecution for the cartel offence by either the OFT or any other agency. For those other individuals who qualify in principle for criminal immunity, but who are judged not to have had any, or any significant, role in the cartel at all, the OFT would generally not consider it necessary to issue them with either a no-action or comfort letter as they do not even face a hypothetical risk. Concern has previously been expressed that a comfort letter in the terms described does not give the would-be applicant sufficient certainty as to their position. However, given that the cartel offence has now been in force since June 2003 and a number of comfort letters have been issued in a number of cases, the OFT considers that the comfort letter procedure has proven to be effective in achieving its objectives.

8.16 In the majority of cases therefore only a small proportion of those who qualify for criminal immunity will ultimately receive a no-action letter. If at any stage an individual who qualifies for criminal immunity but has not received a no-action letter subsequently appears to be at risk of prosecution for the cartel offence, whether by the OFT or any other agency, a no-action letter will be issued.

CARTEL CASES REFERRED TO THE SERIOUS FRAUD OFFICE

8.17 Where an undertaking or individual approaches the OFT for immunity in respect of cartel activity that has already been referred to the SFO or in respect of which such a referral is in contemplation, the SFO will in such cases be consulted about the possible grant of criminal immunity. This is appropriate given that the SFO will be leading the investigation. The final decision on whether to grant a no-action letter rests with the OFT.

8.18 Where a case has already been referred to the SFO, the circumstances may be such that the granting of immunity is no longer in the public interest (see paragraph 2.36).

8.19 However, the ability of an applicant to obtain certainty is not reduced. The legal adviser may still ask the OFT if criminal immunity is available and there is simply a greater prospect that the answer will be no where a referral to the SFO has already been made.

OTHER CRIMINAL OFFENCES

8.20 The grant of a no-action letter cannot prevent prosecution for conduct which, though it may be related to the cartel activity, amounts to a separate and distinct offence, such as bribery. However, to the extent that the cartel conduct particularised in a no-action letter would also be capable of being prosecuted as another offence (for example under the Fraud Act 2006), the OFT would only refer the case to another UK agency, such as the SFO, on the understanding that that agency would not circumvent the effect of the no-action letter by using that other offence to prosecute the recipient for the conduct particularised in the letter. This is subject, of course, to the proviso that the applicant complies with the usual conditions as set out in this guidance.

CRIMINAL IMMUNITY IN SCOTLAND

8.21 Guarantees of immunity from prosecution cannot be given by the OFT in relation to alleged criminality wholly or partly in Scotland/that falls to be prosecuted in Scotland, as the Lord Advocate has the final say on such matters. However, the OFT would bring to the Lord Advocate's attention the cooperation being offered by individuals, or which has been provided. Where a would-be applicant is concerned to know the likely approach of the Scottish prosecution authorities, the OFT will, if desired, contact those authorities in order to seek a view from them about whether individuals might be exposed to prosecution.

8.22 The OFT is, as at the date of publication, in discussion with the Serious and Organised Crime Division of the Crown Office (SOCD), Scotland regarding the renewal of their Memorandum of Understanding (MoU) in relation to the cooperation in the investigation and prosecution of cartel offences that have been committed within the jurisdiction of the Scottish Courts (including the handling of leniency applications).[106] The OFT recommends that applicants who consider their application may potentially require consideration under the Memorandum of Understanding should inform the OFT of this at the earliest opportunity.

NOTES

[97] Or where appropriate, comfort letters as per paragraph 8.15 of this guidance.

[98] This would not preclude an undertaking from applying to the OFT for Type C leniency (or Type B if it is available), in

which case the OFT may be willing to grant discretionary individual immunity to some of the undertaking's current and former employees and directors

99 See paragraph 14 of the Commission Notice on Co-operation Within the Network of Competition Authorities (OJ 2004 C101/3 for a description of the circumstances in which the European Commission will be 'particularly well placed'.

100 The Commission would only be permitted to transmit leniency information to the OFT with the consent of the applicant or where the applicant had also made a leniency application to the OFT relating to the same case or where the OFT had made a written commitment not to use the information to impose sanctions on the leniency applicant or any current or former employee or director of the leniency applicant.

101 Case C-67/91 *Dirección General de Defensa de la Competencia v Asociación Española de Banca Privada a.o.* [1992] ECR I-4785 (Spanish Banks).

102 It might be argued that there is a 'lacuna' here in as much as there is apparently no prohibition on using such information for an existing criminal investigation. However, the OFT would consider that to interpret the provision in this way would be contrary to the spirit of the Network Notice and in any event the information barriers referred to in paragraph 8.12 would apply as a 'long-stop' assurance.

103 Although the Network Notice only refers expressly to information exchanged under Articles 11 and 20 to 22 of Regulation 1/2003, the OFT would also not rely on such information to start an EA02 investigation where it was received under Articles 14 (Advisory Committee) or 19 (Power to take statements).

104 It may sometimes be the case that both the staff at the OFT assisting the Commission and the staff working on an EA02 case may all be based in the OFT's Cartels and Criminal Enforcement Group. In this situation, the information barrier is maintained through clear guidance and training to all staff. A clear breach of the information barrier will be viewed internally as a serious performance management issue for the staff member(s) concerned. In particular cases, the Commission will also expect the OFT to explain to it the measures the OFT will be taking to ensure that the information barrier is maintained.

105 In most cases, the OFT will seek counsel's advice on the matter to assist the OFT in making its determination. However, the OFT is not bound to seek advice. For example, it is not likely to seek advice where the decision as to whether or not a dishonesty admission should be made is considered to be a relatively straightforward one.

106 (OFT546, June 2009). The MoU has been renewed annually from 2009. The SOCD is the successor to the NCD within the Crown Office.

---

9. OTHER PROCEDURAL ISSUES: LENIENCY PLUS/PENALTIES

LENIENCY PLUS

[3.164]

9.1 An undertaking co-operating with an investigation by the OFT under CA98 in relation to cartel activity in one market (the first market) may also be involved in a completely separate cartel activity in another market (the second market). If the undertaking obtains total immunity from financial penalties or a reduction of up to 100 per cent in the amount of the financial penalty because it is the Type A or Type B applicant in relation to its activities in the second market, it will also receive a reduction in the financial penalties imposed on it which is additional to the reduction which it would have received for its cooperation in the first market alone.[107] The additional reduction granted in the first market, because of the successful application in the second market, is known as 'leniency plus'.

9.2 For example, as a result of an investigation by the OFT of producers, including ABC Limited, in the widgets market, ABC Limited carries out an internal investigation and discovers that, as well as having participated in cartel activity in the widgets market, one of its divisions has participated in separate cartel activity in the sprockets market. ABC Limited has been co-operating with the OFT's widgets investigation and is interested in seeking lenient treatment by disclosing its participation in the sprockets cartel activity. Assuming ABC Limited qualifies for total immunity or a reduction of up to 100 per cent in the amount of the financial penalty because it is the Type A or Type B applicant in relation to its activities in relation to the sprockets market, it can also obtain a reduction in financial penalty in relation to the widgets market in addition to the reduction it would have received for co-operation in the widgets investigation alone, that is, the leniency plus reduction will apply in respect of the widgets market (the first market) as a result of its successful leniency application in the investigation into the sprockets market (the second market).

9.3 The key question here is whether the novel evidence relates to a 'completely separate cartel activity'. In determining what would be an appropriate additional reduction by way of leniency plus, the OFT will have regard to all the relevant circumstances. As a general rule, however, the OFT considers that the primary benefit for an immunity applicant is immunity from financial penalties and, where the applicant qualifies for Type A or Type B immunity, criminal immunity for all its cooperating current and former directors and employees as well as protection from director disqualification proceedings for all directors of the undertaking. Leniency plus in respect of any existing OFT investigation should be regarded as a secondary benefit only.[108] Consistent with that principle, reductions for leniency plus are not likely to be high. The level of any discounts would depend on such factors as the scale of the consumer detriment involved in the additional reported cartel, including the number and size of the affected markets, the amount of effort gone to by the immunity applicant to investigate the additional cartel and the likelihood that the OFT would have uncovered the additional cartel in any event.[109]

9.4 As a general rule, where an undertaking is already cooperating with the OFT in respect of more than one cartel investigation and it applies for immunity in respect of a further completely separate cartel, the OFT will only award the undertaking leniency plus in respect of one of those prior investigations. However, the OFT will consider all the relevant circumstances before reaching a decision.

PENALTY CALCULATIONS

9.5 In the past, the OFT has calculated financial penalties for successful corporate immunity applicants in the same way as for other parties and then reduced the figure to zero. However, where total immunity from financial penalties is being granted the OFT will no longer calculate penalties as a matter of course. This applies whether the immunity applicant is in the Type A or Type B position. In the event that the OFT considers that there are significant reasons why in a particular case it would be appropriate to calculate the level of penalty that an immunity applicant would have received, the OFT will discuss those reasons with the applicant.

'BUT FOR' TEST

9.6 Where a Type B or Type C applicant that is granted a reduction in financial penalties, has provided evidence of previously unknown facts relevant to the gravity or duration of the infringement, the OFT will not take account of such information to the detriment of the applicant when assessing the appropriate amount of penalties. In other words, if the finding of duration would have been shorter, or the infringement less serious, 'but for' the evidence provided by the applicant, the penalty for that applicant will be assessed against the short duration or lesser gravity that the OFT would otherwise have found.

9.7 The same principle applies where an OFT investigation covers multiple related infringements, and the OFT would not have investigated a particular infringement involving the applicant 'but for' evidence provided by that applicant. In that situation, the applicant would not be penalised for the particular infringement in question, even though it is granted a reduction in penalties, rather than corporate immunity, for the wider investigation.

NOTES

107 For the avoidance of doubt, the undertaking does not need to be in receipt of leniency in respect of the first market to receive this reduction. It is sufficient for the undertaking to be receiving a reduction, by way of mitigation, for cooperation.

108 Similarly, where a Type B applicant is not granted immunity but is granted a reduction in financial penalties, any leniency plus awarded in respect of an existing cartel investigation should be regarded as a secondary benefit.

109 The considerations cited here are not to be considered exhaustive.

10. BAD FAITH/WITHDRAWAL OF LENIENCY/REVOCATION OF NO-ACTION LETTERS

'BAD FAITH': UNAUTHORISED DISCLOSURE OR DESTRUCTION ETC OF MATERIAL

[3.165]

10.1 The OFT uses the term 'bad faith' in this context to describe situations which go beyond non-cooperation and which instead involve positive steps to hinder an OFT investigation and any consequent enforcement action. For example, the OFT will consider bad faith[110] to have been shown by a leniency applicant where the applicant:

- tips off another person or undertaking about an intended or actual approach for leniency to the OFT, or
- destroys or tampers with evidence either prior to or at any time after an approach to the OFT for leniency.[111]

CONSEQUENCES FOR INDIVIDUALS AND COMPANIES WHERE BAD FAITH IS SHOWN

10.2 If bad faith has been shown, the potential consequences will depend on the stage at which it has been discovered. The consequences are likely to be:

- a refusal to grant a leniency marker or the withdrawal of a leniency marker as the case may be, or
- the revocation of a leniency agreement and any no-action or comfort letters granted pursuant to the undertaking's approach or, as the case may be, the withdrawal of a no-action letter arising out of an individual immunity approach, and
- possible prosecution of one or more individuals under sections 43 and 44 of the CA98 and section 201 of the EA02, depending on the precise circumstances.

10.3 In relation to the likely consequences referred to at paragraph 10.2, the OFT recognises that even where an undertaking took all reasonable steps to ensure that there was no 'tipping off' or document destruction or tampering by a current or former employee or director, a dishonest or negligent person may nonetheless act contrary to the undertaking's clear instructions and in spite of its precautions. In such cases, the OFT would be understanding[112] of the undertaking's position[113] but it will be incumbent on the undertaking to demonstrate the reasonable steps it took to avoid the breach occurring. (See paragraphs 3.24 to 3.28 with respect to maintaining confidentiality and securing evidence.)

10.4 Where instances of bad faith on the part of individuals have been discovered by the undertaking they should be reported to the OFT promptly.

THE RELATIONSHIP BETWEEN NON-COOPERATION AND BAD FAITH

10.5 There are similarities between non-cooperation as described in paragraphs 5.37 to 5.40 above and bad faith as described in paragraphs 10.1 to 10.4 above. In both cases, where an undertaking has acted reasonably as a whole, the consequences may be confined only to the individuals who failed to cooperate or showed bad faith as the case may be. In general though, bad faith is viewed more seriously than 'simple' failure to cooperate – in particular the OFT may consider that prosecution of relevant individuals is appropriate where the elements of the offences described in paragraph 10.2 above are met. As to the use by the OFT of information arising from leniency applications which have failed, or been revoked, due to non cooperation or bad faith, see paragraph 7.19 above.

WITHDRAWAL OF LENIENCY MARKER/REVOCATION OF LENIENCY AGREEMENT

10.6 Withdrawal of leniency is expected to be rare, but the OFT takes the conditions of leniency very seriously and will not permit applicants to benefit from reductions in fines or immunity from prosecution in circumstances where that applicant has failed to cooperate or otherwise failed to meet the conditions.

10.7 If at any time after the grant of a leniency marker, the OFT has concerns that an applicant has acted or is acting in a way that puts its leniency status at risk, it will raise those concerns with the applicant's representative and give the applicant an opportunity to respond, and if possible to address the concerns, prior to withdrawing the leniency marker.

10.8 If the OFT is minded to revoke a leniency agreement because it considers that the applicant has breached the terms of the agreement, the applicant will be notified in writing and given a reasonable opportunity to make representations.

10.9 The decision on withdrawal of a leniency marker or revocation of a leniency agreement will be taken by the OFT's Senior Responsible Officer (SRO) in the investigation. For cases where the SRO is not the Senior Director of Cartels and Criminal Enforcement, the SRO will consult the Senior Director prior to taking any decision on withdrawal of leniency.

REVOCATION OF NO-ACTION LETTERS

10.10 A no-action letter may be revoked if:

- the recipient of a letter ceases to satisfy in whole or in part any of the relevant conditions (set out at paragraph 2.7 above), or
- the recipient of a letter has knowingly or recklessly provided information that is false or misleading in a material particular.

10.11 On revocation any immunity granted by the no-action letter will cease to exist as if it had never been granted and the OFT may rely on any information given by the applicant in a prosecution against them for the cartel offence.

10.12 If the OFT is minded to revoke a no-action letter the recipient of the letter will be notified in writing and given a reasonable opportunity to make representations.

10.13 The decision on revocation of a no-action letter will be taken by the Senior Director of Cartels and Criminal Enforcement.

NOTES

110 The list of bad faith examples here is not to be considered exhaustive.

111 If the destruction or tampering occurred prior to the approach, these provisions only operate where the undertaking is contemplating applying for leniency. See also ECN Model Leniency Programme, Section V, paragraph 13(3).

112 This does not mean that the OFT will guarantee that the undertaking's application will always be safe in bad faith cases where the company took the various precautions described. There may be cases where the breach is so fundamental, for example a tip-off by a senior director or employee, that the public interest demands that the entire leniency application should fail. It is to be imagined that such cases will be extremely rare. Of course, in the hopefully equally rare instance of the bad faith having been corporately rather than individually sanctioned, the undertaking's leniency application is bound to fail.

113 The individual concerned is nevertheless likely to face some kind of sanction by the OFT, for example, the revocation of any actual or intended no-action letter protection.

GLOSSARY OF TERMS

[3.166]

In this guidance note, the following terms have the following meanings:

- applicant – an applicant for any form of leniency, including after the applicant's marker has been confirmed and/or the leniency agreement and/or any no-action letters or comfort letters have been signed.
- CA98 – the Competition Act 1998.
- cartel offence – the offence contained in section 188 EA02.
- Chapter I prohibition – the prohibition contained in section 2 CA98.
- Commission – the European Commission.
- Commission Leniency Notice – Commission Notice on Immunity from fines and reduction of fines in cartel cases (OJ C298, 8.12.2006, p 17).
- EA02 – the Enterprise Act 2002.
- TFEU – the Treaty on the Functioning of the European Union.
- leniency – a 'catch all' term used throughout this document to refer collectively to all of (or, where it is clear from the context, some of) corporate immunity, corporate reductions in penalties or individual immunity. Where reference is made within this document to an **undertaking** having applied for 'leniency' that includes all the sub-types below but obviously excludes individual immunity.
  - criminal immunity – refers to immunity granted to an individual from prosecution for the cartel offence

  - 'blanket' criminal immunity – refers to a situation where all of the current and former employees and directors of an undertaking are granted criminal immunity.
  - corporate immunity – refers to a situation where an undertaking is granted immunity from any financial penalty under the CA98[114] and
  - individual immunity – refers to a situation where one or more individuals are granted criminal immunity but not as part of a 'blanket' grant of criminal immunity.
- Leniency Enquiry Line – Telephone number 0207 211 8833, for all initial contacts with the OFT with a view to making leniency applications, ascertaining the availability of leniency or seeking confidential guidance. Once the purpose of your call has been assessed, you will be transferred to an appropriate senior officer experienced in leniency cases.
- marker – a formal acknowledgement of a leniency application which records the timing of the application and priority relative to other applicants. The grant of a marker must be followed by the provision of a full application package and continued compliance with the conditions of leniency, in which case the marker will be retained pending signing of the formal leniency agreement or no-action letter later in the investigation.
- Network Notice – Commission Notice on cooperation within the Network of Competition Authorities (OJ C101, 27.4.2004, p 43–53).
- no-action letter – letter issued by the OFT pursuant to section 190(4) EA02 guaranteeing immunity from prosecution for the cartel offence in England and Wales.
- OFT's Penalties Guidance – *OFT's Guidance as to the appropriate amount of a penalty* (OFT 423, September 2012).pre-existing investigation – refers to a situation where the OFT considers it has reasonable grounds to suspect cartel activity, such that it may conduct an investigation under one or both of s192 of EA02 and s25 CA98, and has taken active steps in relation to that investigation. Active steps may be overt or covert and may or may not involve the use of statutory information gathering powers.
- Regulation 1/2003 – Council Regulation (EC) No 1/2003 of 16 December 2002 on the implementation of the rules of competition laid down in Articles 81 and 82 of the Treaty (Now Articles 101 and 102 of the TFEU) (OJ L1, 4.1.03, p 1).
- SRO – Senior Responsible Officer. See *'A guide to the OFT's investigation procedures in competition cases'* (OFT1263rev, October 2012), in particular, Chapter 5 for a description of the role of the SRO.
- Type A, Type B, Type C – summary terms used to indicate the different levels of leniency protection available according to the stage at which a leniency application is received, as set out in Table A above.

NOTES

114 The OFT may impose financial penalties under the CA98 for infringements of the Chapter I prohibition and/or of Article 101 of the TFEU. Article 101 prohibits agreements between undertakings, decisions by associations of undertakings and concerted practices which may affect trade between Member States and which have as their object or effect the prevention, restriction or distortion of competition within the common market. The Chapter I prohibition is based on Article 101 of the TFEU but applies to anti-competitive practices which affect trade within the United Kingdom. For further details see the competition law guidance *Agreements and Concerted Practices* (OFT 401, December 2004).

ANNEXES

ANNEXE A. PRO FORMA CORPORATE LENIENCY AGREEMENT COMPETITION ACT 1998 (THE ACT) AND ARTICLE 101 OF THE TFEU:

[3.167]

A.1 This letter sets out an agreement between [**Applicant**] (the Applicant) and the Office of Fair Trading (the OFT).

Grant of immunity

A.2 The OFT grants the Applicant [immunity from **OR** a reduction of [*X*] per cent in the amount of] any financial penalty which may otherwise be imposed by the OFT under section 36 of the Act (leniency) in respect of the reported cartel activity as defined in paragraph A.3 below. Leniency is granted on the terms and conditions set out below and in accordance with paragraph [3.9 **OR** 3.11 **OR** 3.13] of the *OFT's guidance as to the appropriate amount of a penalty*[115] issued under section 38 of the Act (a copy of which is attached to the original signed version of this letter).

A.3 Leniency is granted on the application of the Applicant in connection with the following cartel activity in the United Kingdom [and, if appropriate relevant Member States], namely [description of the reported cartel activity] ('the reported cartel activity'). Subject to the provisions of paragraphs A.4 and A.7 below, this means that [immunity from **OR** a reduction **of** [*X*] per cent in the amount of] financial penalty will be imposed by the OFT on the Applicant in relation to any finding by the OFT that the reported cartel activity or any part of it constitutes an infringement of section 2 of the Act [and/or Article 101 of the TFEU].

Conditions

A.4 This grant of leniency is made and remains conditional on the Applicant throughout its dealings with the OFT in relation to the reported cartel activity having satisfied and continuing to satisfy each of the conditions set out below.

(a) The Applicant accepts that the reported cartel activity infringed section 2 of the Act [and/or Article 101 of the TFEU].

(b) The Applicant has provided the OFT with all the non-legally privileged information, documents and evidence[116] available to it as at the date of this agreement regarding the existence and activities of the reported cartel activity.

(c) The Applicant maintains continuous and complete cooperation throughout the OFT's civil and any criminal investigations and until the conclusion of any action by the OFT arising as a result of the investigations, and reference to such action includes (a) any action taken by the OFT in any proceedings before the Competition Appeal Tribunal (CAT) arising from a decision of the OFT in connection with the reported cartel activity and (b) any action taken by the OFT, or any other prosecuting agency, to charge and prosecute any individuals in connection with the reported cartel activity. Save as otherwise agreed with the OFT, this includes but is not limited to:

   (i) not disclosing (either directly or indirectly) to any third party without the OFT's express prior consent the fact that the Applicant has approached the OFT and is cooperating with the OFT under the provisions of the OFT's leniency programme

   (ii) in addition to the non-legally privileged information, documents and evidence already provided, voluntarily and without prompting providing the OFT with all the facts that become known to the Applicant, together with all the non-legally privileged information, documents and evidence, wherever located, that come into the possession, custody or control of the Applicant, or otherwise become available to it, relating to the reported cartel activity

   (iii) to the extent that they have not already been provided, voluntarily and without the OFT using its powers under any of sections 26 to 28A of the Act or any of sections 193 to 194 of the Enterprise Act 2002 [or any national competition authority exercising at the request of the OFT its powers under Article 22 of Council Regulation 1/2003/EC], promptly providing the OFT with all the non-legally privileged information, documents, evidence or other items in its possession, custody or control, or otherwise available to it, wherever located, requested by the OFT in the furtherance of its investigation into the reported cartel activity

   (iv) making the IT systems and equipment[117] under its control and/or accessible from its premises available for analysis by such means and in such manner as determined by the OFT to be most appropriate for the purposes of its investigation. In making this determination the OFT will have regard to the legitimate interests of the undertaking in protecting confidentiality of its information, and maintaining the protections of legal professional privilege

   (v) ensuring that any potentially relevant IT systems are not removed, destroyed, tampered with or modified, and that relevant data are not removed, destroyed, tampered with or modified prior to, during or following any analysis by the OFT in accordance with paragraph (iv) above

   (vi) using its best endeavours to secure the complete and truthful cooperation of its current and former directors, officers, employees and agents and encouraging such persons voluntarily to provide the OFT with any information (directly or indirectly) relevant to the reported cartel activity

   (vii) facilitating the ability of current and former directors, officers, employees and agents to appear for such interviews as the OFT may reasonably require at the times and places reasonably designated by the OFT

   (viii) using its best endeavours to ensure that current and former directors, officers, employees and agents who provide information to the OFT respond completely and truthfully to all questions asked in interviews with the OFT

   (ix) using its best endeavours to ensure that current and former directors, officers, employees and agents who provide information to the OFT make no attempt either falsely to protect or falsely to implicate any undertaking in any infringement of the Act [and/or of Article 101 of the TFEU] or any individual in relation to the cartel offence under section 188 of the Enterprise Act 2002

   (x) in relation to CAT proceedings arising from a decision by the OFT in connection with the reported cartel activity, using its best endeavours to facilitate, and secure the complete and truthful cooperation, of its current and former directors, officers, employees and agents, even if the Applicant is not a party to the CAT proceedings, in:

      (a) assisting the OFT or its counsel in the preparation for any CAT proceedings

      (b) if requested by the OFT or its counsel attending any CAT proceedings, and

      (c) speaking to their witness statements and being cross-examined on such witness statements in any CAT proceedings,

   (xi) in relation to any criminal proceedings in connection with the reported cartel activity, providing equivalent cooperation to the OFT or any other UK prosecuting agency (in a manner compatible with the rules and principles of criminal law and procedure) as that referred to at paragraph (x) above in relation to any CAT proceedings, and

   (xii) recording and retaining on a continuing basis any material which might have any bearing on the reported cartel activity and which remains in the possession of the Applicant or under its control until the conclusion of any civil or criminal proceedings in connection with the reported cartel activity.

(d) The Applicant has refrained from further participation in the reported cartel activity from and including [**X**], that is, the date of application for leniency, and shall continue to do so.

(e) [The Applicant has not taken steps to coerce another undertaking to take part in the reported cartel activity [Only relevant for an Applicant seeking immunity].]

In addition to the above-mentioned conditions, the Applicant understands that it is bound by all the other relevant conditions, provisos and qualifications referred to in the OFT's published guidance documents on leniency.

Use of information provided by the Applicant

A.5 All information, documents and other evidence provided by the Applicant to the OFT under this agreement shall, notwithstanding the termination of the agreement (whether by revocation, the conclusion of the case, including any proceedings before the CAT, in relation to the reported cartel activity, or otherwise), remain the property of the OFT and may be used by the OFT to facilitate the performance of its functions by or under any enactment.

Revocation

A.6 If, at any time before the conclusion of the case (whether by the adoption of a decision or otherwise) including any proceedings before the CAT or other appeal proceedings, the OFT determines that any of the conditions in paragraph A.4 above have not been complied with, the OFT may, subject to the provisions of paragraph A.7 below, revoke the grant of leniency to the Applicant and impose any penalty in accordance with section 36 of the Act in relation to any finding by the OFT that the reported cartel activity or any part of it constitutes an infringement of section 2 of the Act and/or Article 101 of the TFEU.

A.7 Before revoking the grant of leniency, the OFT will give written notice to the Applicant of the nature of the alleged non-compliance and that the OFT is considering revoking the grant to the Applicant of leniency. The Applicant will be given an opportunity to respond to the notice and, if the OFT considers it possible and appropriate, to remedy any breach within a reasonable period of time from the service of the notice.

Entire agreement

A.8 This letter constitutes the entire agreement between the OFT and the Applicant and, save as may be expressly referred to, supersedes all prior representations, writings, negotiations or understandings, if any, whether oral or written, relating to the grant by the OFT of leniency to the Applicant in connection with the reported cartel activity.[118]

Jurisdiction

A.9 This agreement is subject to English law and the jurisdiction of English Courts.

Execution

A.10 The signatories to this letter on behalf of each party have all the authority and capacity necessary to sign this letter and to bind the respective parties hereto. The signatories below acknowledge acceptance of the terms and conditions set out above which shall only take effect when both parties have signed this letter in duplicate, one original to be retained by each party.

Signed: Date:

Name:

Position: Senior Director of Cartels and Criminal Enforcement

For and on behalf of the Office of Fair Trading

Signed: Date:

Name:

Position:

For and on behalf of the Applicant

NOTES

115 OFT 423, December 2004. Though please see footnote 1 above.

116 References to 'evidence' in this agreement include evidence in any form, and could include, for example, mobile telephones which may contain relevant material such as call logs and (deleted or undeleted) text messages.

117 This would include, but not be limited to, servers, personal computers, laptops, mobile telephones, blackberries, palmtops, electronic organisers, digital media and all other similar networking or personal devices.

118 However, for the avoidance of doubt, this clause does not oust the application of the OFT's published leniency guidance.

ANNEXE B. PRO FORMA INDIVIDUAL NO-ACTION LETTER ENTERPRISE ACT 2002 (THE ACT) – NOTICE UNDER SECTION 190(4)

[3.168]

B.1 This letter gives written notice to [**Applicant**] (the Applicant) that he/she will not be prosecuted in England and Wales or Northern Ireland for an offence under section 188 of the Act that falls within the description specified in paragraph B.2 of this letter (except in the circumstances specified in paragraph B.6).

Grant of immunity

B.2 The offence for which immunity from prosecution is granted (the Reported Offence) is that [**describe**, for example, 'the Applicant dishonestly agreed with one or more other persons to make or implement, or to cause to be made or implemented, arrangements relating to [Undertaking A] and [Undertaking B] to fix a price for the supply by [Undertaking A] in the United Kingdom (otherwise than to Undertaking B) of [a product or service]] (the Cartel Agreement).

Conditions

B.3 This grant of immunity from prosecution is made and remains conditional on the Applicant having satisfied and continuing to satisfy each of the conditions set out below.

(a) The Applicant must admit participation in the Reported Offence described in paragraph B.2 of this letter.

(b) The Applicant must provide the Office of Fair Trading (the OFT) with all non-legally privileged facts, statements, documents, evidence or any other items (Information) available to him/her relating to the Reported Offence and the existence and activities of the Cartel Agreement.

(c) The Applicant must maintain continuous and complete cooperation throughout the investigation of the Reported Offence and the Cartel Agreement and until the conclusion of any criminal proceedings arising as a result of the investigation. Save as otherwise agreed with the OFT, such cooperation includes but is not limited to the Applicant:

- (i) not disclosing (either directly or indirectly) to any third party without the OFT's express prior consent the fact that the Applicant is cooperating with the OFT under the provisions of the OFT's no-action policy
- (ii) voluntarily and without prompting, providing the OFT with all Information that becomes known to him/her or available to him/her relating to the Reported Offence or the Cartel Agreement, in addition to any such Information already provided
- (iii) making the IT systems and equipment [119] under his/her control and/or accessible to him/her available for analysis by such means and in such manner as determined by the OFT to be most appropriate for the purposes of its investigation. In making this determination the OFT will have regard to the legitimate interests of the Applicant in protecting confidentiality of the information made available, and maintaining the protections of legal professional privilege.
- (iv) to the extent that it has not already been provided, providing voluntarily and promptly, and without the OFT using its powers under any section of the Act, all Information available to him/her wherever located, requested by the OFT in relation to the Reported Offence or the Cartel Agreement
- (v) where required providing evidence upon oath in any criminal proceedings arising out of the Reported Offence or the Cartel Agreement
- (vi) recording and retaining on a continuing basis any material which might have any bearing on the Reported Offence or the Cartel Agreement and which remains in the possession of the Applicant or under his/her control until the conclusion of any criminal proceedings arising out of the Reported Offence or the Cartel Agreement.

(d) The Applicant must have refrained from participation in the Cartel Agreement (except as may have been directed by the investigating authority) from and including [date of disclosure to the OFT].

(e) The Applicant must refrain from any further participation in the Cartel Agreement (except as may be directed by the investigating authority).

(f) The Applicant must not have taken steps to coerce another undertaking to take part in the Cartel Agreement.

In addition to the above-mentioned conditions, the Applicant understands that it is bound by all the other relevant conditions, provisos and qualifications referred to in the OFT's published guidance documents on leniency.

B.4 The Applicant hereby (i) admits having committed the Reported Offence, (ii) confirms that he/she has complied with conditions (b), (c), (d) and (e) above, and (iii) undertakes to continue to comply with condition (c) above and to comply with condition (f) above.

Revocation

B.5 If, in the view of the OFT, at any time before the conclusion of any criminal proceedings arising as a result of the investigation into the Reported Offence, the conditions which are set out in this letter have not been complied with in full by the Applicant or the Applicant has knowingly or recklessly provided Information that is false or misleading in a material particular, the OFT shall give immediate written notice to the Applicant of the nature of the alleged non-compliance and that the OFT is considering revoking the grant of immunity. The Applicant will be given a reasonable opportunity to explain the alleged non-compliance and, if the OFT considers it possible and appropriate, to remedy the breach within a reasonable period of time from the service of the notice.

B.6 If the OFT then determines that the conditions set out in this letter have not been fully complied with, or that the Applicant knowingly or recklessly provided Information that is false or misleading in a material particular to the OFT, the OFT may revoke the grant of immunity from prosecution. On revocation, the grant of immunity will cease to exist as if it had never been granted and any Information provided by the Applicant may be used against him/her in criminal proceedings.

B.7 Irrespective of whether the OFT has revoked the grant of immunity, all Information provided to the OFT by the Applicant shall remain the property of the OFT.

Entire agreement

B.8 This letter sets out all of the terms and conditions on which the OFT grants immunity from prosecution to the Applicant for the Reported Offence. It supersedes all prior representations, writings, negotiations or understandings, if any, whether oral or written, relating to the Reported Offence.[120]

Execution

B.9 The signatories below acknowledge acceptance of the terms and conditions set out above which shall only take effect when both parties have signed this letter in duplicate, one original to be retained by each party.

Signed: Date:

Name:

Position: Senior Director of Cartels and Criminal Enforcement

For and on behalf of the Office of Fair Trading

Signed: Date:

Name:

NOTES

[119] This would include, but not be limited to, servers, personal computers, laptops, mobile telephones, blackberries, palmtops, electronic organisers, digital media and all other similar networking or personal devices.

[120] However, for the avoidance of doubt, this clause does not oust the application of the OFT's published leniency guidance.

ANNEXE C. CONDUCTING INTERNAL INVESTIGATIONS BEFORE A LENIENCY APPLICATION

[3.169]

C.1 In addition to the detection of cartels, the purpose and function of the OFT's leniency policy is also to facilitate the bringing of successful enforcement action by the OFT, in part through the provision of direct 'insider' evidence of the cartel activity.

C.2 In order to fulfil this objective, it is essential that applicants take precautions to ensure that they do not, either before or after making their applications, conduct their own investigations into the suspected cartel activity in ways that diminish the probative value of the evidence obtained in that investigation or any subsequent investigation by the OFT.

C.3 This part of the guidance therefore highlights some of the potential risks that arise and some key points for those investigating to follow. Persons conducting such investigations should have regard to all relevant legal requirements (such, for example, those arising in relation to employment, data protection and privacy law) to ensure that their investigation is conducted lawfully and may wish to seek specialist legal advice for this purpose.

Limit enquiries to the necessary

C.4 The OFT recognises that undertakings and their advisers will need to make sufficient enquiries to reach a decision as to whether to apply for leniency. However, due to the various possible risks described below, in conjunction with the OFT's responsibilities to ensure the standard of the investigation, it is important that the OFT is able to conduct its own investigation from the earliest possible opportunity. It is of prime importance that would-be applicants **conduct an enquiry that is as limited to what is necessary at the pre-leniency stage in order to make a decision as to whether to apply for leniency**. The OFT accepts that what is necessary for these purposes will depend upon the circumstances of the case and that a business will need to have a suitable information base in order to make such a decision.

Tip-off

C.5 On more than one occasion, the OFT has conducted 'surprise' inspections of premises only to find evidence to suggest that the undertaking being visited had prior knowledge of the OFT's investigation. This could have occurred as a result of a tip-off emanating from the leniency applicant. Tip-off is obviously a real risk when individuals within a leniency applicant have close links with individuals working in a 'target' undertaking likely to be the subject of a surprise visit. The risk may be particularly high where individuals in the applicant undertaking previously worked for the target undertaking. It is also likely to be very risky to approach former employees or directors of the leniency undertaking and making such an approach during the pre-marker period (or indeed any time up to the OFT's own investigations becoming overt) should be an exceptional course. The OFT will expect an undertaking to take a sensible risk-based approach and to conduct its internal investigations in such a way as to minimise as far as possible the risk of tip-off.

C.6 It should also be noted that, given the possibility of a subsequent criminal investigation, an individual may be prosecuted for any unauthorised disclosures[121] and that such disclosures may, if discovered, also result in the undertaking and the individual losing the immunity which they would otherwise have qualified for.

Minimising risk of 'tip-off'

- Knowledge of any leniency application, already made or in contemplation, should be restricted to those who need to know.

- Consider carefully which individuals need to be approached and, as far as possible, avoid questioning 'high-risk' individuals about the cartel activity at all or in such a way as to increase the chance of tip-off.
- Consideration should also be given, to the extent that the relevant legal framework permits, to which covert investigations can be conducted to establish sufficient material to make the approach for leniency, for example, covert examination of relevant individuals' email accounts or other electronic material.
- Take care when explaining the reasons why individuals are being questioned. For example, compare, bearing in mind any relevant legal requirements, the relative merits of telling an individual that the interview is with a view to a possible approach to the OFT and the full consequences of tipping off with the alternative approach of questioning the individual in a more low-key way such as to establish the facts, which may in some instances be a better way of reducing the chance of him or her tipping others off.
- The approach to be taken in a given case will depend on a risk assessment of the individual(s) concerned.

Tampering and 'corruption' avoidance

C.7 It is a sensible precaution to secure any items of evidence, so far as possible, to prevent tampering or corruption of material such as would undermine its evidential value in any future legal proceedings, especially criminal proceedings. 'Corruption' in this context can mean any physical amendment to evidential sources that may affect their probative value, and could be inadvertent rather than deliberate. What precautions are possible and reasonable will naturally depend on the circumstances of the case and the OFT only expects undertakings to take sensible and prudent measures. The taking of such measures could have an impact upon the success of any future OFT investigation, as sophisticated cartels can often only be evidenced through fragmentary material, such as emails or text messages.

C.8 When securing evidence (whether physical or electronic), the evidence should be physically located in such a way that access to it is limited to as few people as possible, who are aware of the importance of its preservation. Ideally, original materials should be kept in secure, locked storage. There should be clear records of how evidence has been secured and of who has had access to it and for what purposes (for example to review, to copy, to show to others).

C.9 Ultimately, the applicant needs to be able to inform the OFT of where any evidential material originated from and be in a position to confirm that evidential material has not been altered between being removed from that location and being handed to the OFT.

C.10 Records of where evidence came from should indicate which person or persons had possession or control of the material and its location, including any description of the file(s) that particular papers were taken from and where the file or other document was kept. Any records, schedules or lists of evidence gathered as part of an internal investigation must give a sufficiently detailed description of the material to ensure there can be no confusion at a later stage in identifying the material referred to.

Preserving and securing electronic evidence

- When preserving and securing electronic evidence, relevant legal requirements should always be borne in mind and legal advice sought where necessary.
- If certain individuals have used laptop computers, mobile telephones or other electronic devices which might contain relevant evidence, consideration should be given to removing those items from further use, at the earliest possible opportunity, so as to prevent evidence loss or to allow a forensically sound image to be created.
- When examining any electronic media, take care to ensure that it is examined in such a way that the evidential integrity of the material in question is not adversely affected.
- Wherever practicable, forensic experts should be used, who are familiar with universally accepted standards for the recovery of electronic data.[122]
- Back-up tapes of electronic media should be located and secured.

Preserving and securing physical evidence

- Original hard copy documents which provide evidence of a cartel should be safely secured, including diaries and workbooks of relevant individuals.
- Working copies should be made if the documents are to be used at all for the purposes of the investigation and/or for any continued business use.
- No amendments or annotations should be made to original documents at any time during the investigation.
- A note should be kept of the source location, and where known, the author(s) of relevant documents that are removed in the course of the investigation.

Witness interviews

C.11 The secret nature of cartels means that the evidence of witnesses can be of paramount importance to successful enforcement action. Any individual who has information relevant to establishing the existence of the cartel can be a witness for these purposes.

C.12 Interviewing witnesses to obtain the maximum possible information but without distorting their evidence can be difficult. Because of these difficulties, it is preferable for applicants to limit the number and scope of interviews to the minimum necessary to decide whether to make a leniency application.

C.13 The following precautions must be taken in any internal investigation, notwithstanding that the OFT will conduct its own interviews and prepare statements for witnesses to sign.

Interviewing witnesses

- Any interviews must be conducted in a balanced way with a view to establishing the facts, and without any pressure being placed on any witness to give or confirm a particular version of events.
- Witness evidence must not be 'contaminated' by exposure to the evidence of other witnesses. Do not tell any individual what another individual has said about the alleged cartel activity.
- Witness evidence must not be 'contaminated' by exposure to documents or records that the witness did not create or have access to at the relevant time. Witnesses must be interviewed separately and asked not to discuss their evidence with any other witness.
- The importance of being able to provide an account of interviews with witnesses is particularly acute (see below).
- Careful consideration should be given to the conduct of the investigation where senior managers who are witnesses would normally expect to see the results of the investigation and be involved in decisions whether or not to apply for leniency.

Explanation of steps taken in the internal investigation

C.14 Except in the case of an oral application,[123] all leniency applicants will be expected to take a careful note of all the actions they have taken as part of an internal investigation, including the identities of any witnesses who were interviewed in the investigation process, the nature of the questions asked and the replies obtained. The note will need to be retained until the conclusion of any proceedings. A refusal or inability to do so may mean that the applicant is not meeting the conditions for leniency.

C.15 In addition to enabling the OFT to focus its own investigative steps or to direct the applicant in making further enquiries following the application, there may be circumstances where the OFT will need to rebut arguments that an internal investigation has compromised the integrity of the OFT's own case, and the provision of a clear note explaining the steps taken in such an investigation will be invaluable for this purpose.

C.16 The OFT recommends that, from the moment a leniency application is in contemplation, all notes, including manuscript/rough notes, should be kept in a separate notebook from notes relating to unrelated matters. In the event of a criminal case, the pre-trial disclosure requirements may extend to such material, and so this precaution will facilitate the protection of completely unrelated material from disclosure.

C.17 Ultimately, and depending on whether the case results in a criminal prosecution, the OFT, and hence the applicant, may need to demonstrate a full audit trail of the enquiries that have been carried out and this may, in some cases, necessitate witness statements from those involved in conducting the investigation. An inability or refusal on the part of a leniency applicant to assist the OFT in doing so in an effective manner may mean that the leniency applicant cannot fulfil the conditions of leniency.

C.18 Therefore, at a minimum, save to the extent that LPP applies, applicants should be able to provide an account of the following:

Interviews/meetings with potential witnesses

- Names of interviewees, with time and date of interview(s)
- Names of interviewers, any other persons present and the capacity in which they act (for example, legal representative (and who they represent), company representative)
- Nature of pre-interview briefing, that is, what the interviewee was told about the purpose of the interview, what they knew about the company's position (whether they were aware of the potential leniency application), what they had been told about their own position or possible personal consequences arising from the investigation.
- Whether the interview was recorded
- If no tape recording or detailed transcript was made, details of questions asked and answers given

Physical Searches

- Locations searched (address, types of rooms searched, occupiers of particular offices/desks searched)
- Search and sift criteria, for example the briefing given to persons conducting the search
- Specific locations of relevant material, including any file names and information on who had possession or control of the material
- Where and how relevant material has been secured
- Who found relevant material, and the continuity of evidence[124]

Electronic Searches

- Locations searched (servers, personal computers, laptops, mobile telephones, palmtops, electronic personal organisers, digital media, other similar networking or personal devices)
- Means of searching, in particular whether searches were conducted on a forensically secure image or on the original data
- Search and sift criteria, for example the briefing given to persons conducting the search, the list of search terms used
- Number of hits generated through electronic searches, and details of any 'manual' sifts to assess relevance of those hits.
- Where and how relevant material has been secured, and the continuity of evidence[125]
- Who found/identified relevant material

NOTES

121 See, in particular, section 201(4) of the EA02 which provides that any individual who knows or suspects that an investigation by the SFO or OFT into an offence under section 188 (the cartel offence) is being carried out **or is likely to be carried out** and falsifies, conceals, destroys or otherwise disposes of **or causes or permits the falsification etc** of information which he knows or suspects to be relevant to such an investigation is guilty of an offence carrying a prison term of up to five years and an unlimited fine.

122 In determining whether electronic evidence is forensically sound, the OFT will in particular have regard to the *ACPO Good Practice Guide for Computer-Based Electronic Evidence*. If a small undertaking is concerned that cost is a barrier to precautions such as this, it is advised to seek confidential guidance from the OFT as to the best course of action (see paragraph 3.3 onwards).

123 Oral applications are discussed in paragraph 4.31. This includes discussion of the circumstances in which the OFT may accept an oral application as well as the cooperation expected from the oral applicant.

124 Continuity of evidence means being able to establish how a particular document or item has been handled from the time when it was first acquired or created to the point at which it is used in evidence (such as when it is cited in a statement of objections or produced in court). This is achieved by ensuring that items are stored securely, and by keeping full and accurate records of who has been in possession of the material, where and when.

125 Please see footnote 124.

ANNEXE D. CHECKLIST OF INFORMATION REQUIREMENTS DURING A LENIENCY APPLICATION

[3.170]

Leniency applicants must provide all non-legally privileged information, documents and evidence available to them regarding the existence and activities of the reported cartel activity (hereafter referred to as the 'relevant information').

This checklist identifies specific information that will be required in every case, but this should not be interpreted as a limitation on the requirement to provide all relevant information (see further paragraph 5.12 onwards).

	Information regarding cartel	**Other information/confirmations**
Confidential guidance (optional)	• Sufficient details to enable the OFT to give the guidance required. The identity of the undertaking does not need to be disclosed at this point ('no-names enquiry')	• Name and contact telephone number of enquirer (legal adviser or representative of the undertaking)
Immunity availability enquiry (only relevant before investigation has started)	• Specify the relevant sector, dates and broad nature of the activity or otherwise provide sufficient information to allow the OFT to determine whether there is a pre-existing investigation and/or a pre-existing leniency applicant. – The level of detail required will depend on whether there have been previous investigations or applications in the sector. – The identity of the undertaking does not need to be disclosed at this point ('no-names enquiry')	• Name and telephone number of the person making the enquiry. • Confirm that the legal adviser has instructions to apply for Type A immunity if it is available • Confirm that the undertaking understands that such an application will entail a commitment to cooperate with the OFT in any subsequent investigation; • Confirm that there is a 'concrete basis' for the suspicion of cartel activity; • Confirm that the undertaking has a 'genuine intention to confess'.
Application for marker (all types of leniency)	• The identity of the applicant • Emerging details of the cartel: – Type of arrangement – Affected product market(s) – Dates (is it ongoing?) – Evidence uncovered so far (sufficient to give a 'concrete basis' for suspicion of cartel activity, describe form and substance) – Names and locations of employees involved – To the extent known, names and locations of other involved undertakings and individuals – Geographic scope	• Contact names and details for the undertaking and its legal representative(s) • Information on whether those or any other legal advisers represent any individual employees/directors of the applicant undertaking. • Details of other competition authorities from whom markers have been obtained or will be requested – Waivers to share information with other competition authorities sufficient to coordinate investigations
Application package	• All of the above, in a written or oral statement	• All of the above, in a written or oral statement

	Information regarding cartel	Other information/confirmations
	– Clarity on which aspects are facts supported by evidence, assumptions, likely explanations, gaps in knowledge • All relevant documentary evidence uncovered so far (hard or electronic copies) and its provenance • Names of employees/directors who may give evidence, with an outline of matters of which they have personal knowledge	• Description of enquiries and searches conducted so far by the applicant or its legal advisers
On confirmation of the marker	• OFT will direct further searches/inquiries to be made at this stage	• Signed commitment from the applicant (direct) to complete and continuous cooperation
Ongoing throughout investigation and enforcement proceedings (before and after signing of the leniency agreement/no-action letters)	• Applicant must continue to provide any emerging relevant evidence/information, whether inculpatory or exculpatory – Applicant must draw OFT's attention to any information which alters the applicant's understanding as set out in the application statement • OFT will direct further searches/inquiries to be made – Retention of forensically sound image of relevant IT material likely to be required, as well as information on the steps taken in obtaining the forensically sound image. • Individual witnesses must be made available (promptly on request) for interviews by OFT, and subsequently to sign witness statements	• Description of ongoing enquiries and searches conducted by the applicant or its legal advisers • Any changes to contact details for the applicant, its advisers and individuals' advisers • Any changes to the employment status (and where possible, contact details) for key individuals (including any employees/directors interviewed by OFT) • Details of any significant developments regarding investigations by other competition authorities, such as formal findings, or interviews/other investigative steps that may uncover evidence or create documents relevant to the OFT's investigation

ADDENDUM TO OFT1495 (SEPTEMBER 2020)

[3.171]

NOTES

This Addendum was published by the CMA on 24 September 2020.

1. This Addendum to the Leniency Guidance[1] sets out the way in which the CMA will exercise its discretion in relation to the grant of Type B leniency in Resale Price Maintenance (RPM) cases.

2. The CMA may grant successful Type B applicants immunity or up to a 100% discount on any financial penalty.[2]

3. However, the CMA **would not generally expect to grant immunity or discounts on any financial penalty of more than 50% to Type B applicants in RPM cases, and the detailed provisions of the Leniency Guidance should be read accordingly**.

4. This Addendum applies to new leniency applications made on or after 24 September 2020.

NOTES

[1] OFT 1495, *Applications for leniency and no-action in cartel cases, OFT's detailed guidance on the principles and process*, July 2013.

[2] CMA73, *Guidance as to appropriate amount of a penalty*, 18 April 2018, paragraph 3.1; and OFT1495, paragraph 2.2.

CARTEL OFFENCE PROSECUTION GUIDANCE (CMA9, MARCH 2014)

[3.172]

NOTES

See the Memorandum of understanding between the CMA and Crown Office, Scotland (at **[3.179]**) in relation to co-operation between the CMA and the Crown Office to investigate/prosecute cartel offences committed in Scotland.

Note that the fines that could be imposed on summary conviction for certain criminal offences referred to in this document were, at that time, subject to specific caps of £5,000 or above. With effect from 12 March 2015, these caps have been removed and those specific offences are now punishable by a fine of any amount.

CONTENTS

1 INTRODUCTION

[3.173]

1.1 Section 47 of the Enterprise and Regulatory Reform Act 2013 (ERRA13) comes into force on 1 April 2014. This section makes important changes to the criminal cartel offence which was created by the Enterprise Act 2002 (EA02).

1.2 In this guidance references to 'the Act' mean references to the EA02 as amended by the ERRA13 and references to 'the offence' mean the criminal cartel offence under section 188(1) of the Act. All section references are to the Act unless otherwise stated.

1.3 In summary, a person commits the offence if he or she agrees with one or more other persons that two or more undertakings will engage in certain prohibited cartel arrangements, namely price fixing, market sharing, bid-rigging, and limiting output. The offence is subject to certain exclusions and defences. The maximum penalty on conviction on indictment is five years imprisonment and/or an unlimited fine.

1.4 In England and Wales, and in Northern Ireland, prosecutions may only be brought by the Competition and Markets Authority (CMA) or the Serious Fraud Office (SFO), or with the consent of the CMA. Prosecutions will generally be undertaken by the CMA.

1.5 In Scotland, prosecutions will be brought by the Crown Office and Procurator Fiscal Service (COPFS), the sole prosecution authority in Scotland which is headed by the Lord Advocate. The question of the publication of prosecution guidance in relation to offences committed in Scotland is a matter for the Lord Advocate alone.

1.6 Where cross-jurisdictional issues arise within England, Wales, Northern Ireland and Scotland, the jurisdiction in which a case will be brought will depend on the outcome of discussions between the CMA, the SFO and the COPFS, and will follow the normal principles that govern prosecutions for other offences.

1.7 This guidance is issued under section 190A of the Act, which stipulates that the CMA must prepare and publish guidance on the principles to be applied in determining, in any case, whether proceedings for an offence under the Act should be instituted. This guidance has been prepared for that purpose and does not seek to set out a list of cases which the CMA will or will not prosecute. The CMA may at any time issue revised or new guidance; please refer to the CMA webpages on www.gov.uk/cma for the latest version.

1.8 The CMA has consulted with the SFO and the COPFS and other interested parties in the preparation of this guidance.

1.9 The guidance is not intended to be exhaustive and the CMA will be mindful of the wide range of circumstances and culpability which may arise in any particular case.

1.10 This guidance relates to agreements made on or after 1 April 2014 and which relate to arrangements made or to be made on or after that date. It sets out how the Code for Crown Prosecutors ('the Code') will be applied in such cases. The unamended criminal cartel offence under EA02 will still apply to agreements made before 1 April 2014 or which relate to arrangements made or to be made before that date. The Code will continue to be applied in the usual way in respect of such agreements and arrangements.

1.11 The Code does not apply to offences committed in Scotland. These are subject to considerations in the COPFS Prosecution Code.

2 THE LEGISLATIVE BACKGROUND

[3.174]

2.1 The criminal cartel offence was created by the EA02 with the intention of criminalising and deterring behaviour by individuals leading to the most serious and damaging forms of anti-competitive agreements, namely 'hardcore cartels'.[1]

2.2 In essence, a hardcore cartel is an agreement between competitors to fix prices, share markets, rig bids or limit output at the expense of the interests of customers and without any countervailing customer benefits. Typically, hardcore cartels are secret arrangements under which competitor businesses agree to coordinate their activity, usually in order to preserve or drive up prices.

2.3 There is an inherent public interest in individuals involved in such hardcore cartels being prosecuted, giving practical effect to Parliament's intentions in criminalising such behaviour.

Part 3 CMA and other Guidelines

2.4 The cartel offence originally required the individual to have acted dishonestly.[2] Dishonesty as an element of the offence has been removed, and statutory exclusions and defences have been added.

2.5 The offence was amended following publication of draft legislation and a full consultation process.[3]

2.6 A full copy of the Act and its Explanatory Notes can be accessed at www.legislation.gov.uk/ukpga/2013/24/pdfs/ukpga_20130024_en.pdf.

2.7 In summary, the Act:

- provides a revised framework for combating behaviour by individuals leading to hardcore criminal cartels, removing the need to prove dishonesty
- creates two new exclusions from the offence: (i) the notification exclusion;[4] and (ii) the publication exclusion[5]
- retains the exclusion relating to the notification of bid-rigging arrangements[6]
- provides that an individual will not commit an offence if the agreement is made in order to comply with a legal requirement[7]
- creates three new defences to the cartel offence:[8] (i) where, at the time of the making of the agreement, there is no intention to conceal the nature of the arrangements from customers; (ii) where, at the time of the making of the agreement, there is no intention to conceal the nature of the arrangements from the CMA; and (iii) where the defendant, before the making of the agreement, took reasonable steps to ensure that the nature of the arrangements would be disclosed to professional legal advisers for the purposes of obtaining advice about them before their making or (as the case may be) their implementation.

NOTES

1 Department of Trade and Industry (DTI), A World Class Competition Regime. Cm 5233. (2001)

2 See subsection 188(1) of the EA02.

3 BIS: A Competition Regime for Growth – a consultation on options for reform (March 2011) and BIS: Growth, Competition and the Competition Regime, Government Response to Consultation (March 2012).

4 See subsection 188A(1)(a) of the Act.

5 See subsection 188A(1)(c) of the Act.

6 See subsection 188A(1)(b) of the Act.

7 See subsection 188A(3) of the Act.

8 See section 188B of the Act.

3 THE DECISION-MAKING PROCESS

[3.175]

3.1 The CMA's decision to prosecute the offence will be made by application of the Full Code Test as set out in the Code www.cps.gov.uk/publication/code-crown-prosecutors. The Full Code Test has two stages: (i) the evidential stage; and (ii) the public interest stage. In most cases the evidential stage must be considered before the public interest stage. A case which does not pass the evidential stage must not proceed. Further guidance on this is set out in paragraphs 4.1–4.24 below.

3.2 If the evidential stage is passed, meaning the CMA considers that there is sufficient evidence against a suspect to provide a realistic prospect of conviction of that suspect, then the CMA will go on to consider whether a prosecution is in the public interest. Further guidance on this is set out in paragraphs 4.26–4.41 below.

3.3 There may be cases where it is clear, prior to the collection and consideration of all likely evidence, that the public interest does not require a prosecution. In these instances the CMA may decide that the case should not proceed further.

3.4 A decision by the CMA that a prosecution should not proceed on either evidential or public interest grounds does not preclude the CMA from considering whether the collusive arrangements between undertakings should be subject to civil enforcement for infringements of EU or national competition law under Article 101 of the Treaty on the Functioning of the European Union (TFEU)[9] or section 2 of the Competition Act 1998 (CA98) respectively, nor whether a Competition Disqualification Order should be sought against any individual.[10]

SCOTLAND

3.5 In Scotland, the Procurator Fiscal (a prosecutor acting under the authority of the Lord Advocate) considers the evidence and decides whether to prosecute in the public interest.

3.6 Where there is sufficient evidence in the case, the Procurator Fiscal will consider a number of additional factors when deciding whether to prosecute. These are set out in full in the COPFS Prosecution Code www.crownoffice.gov.uk/images/Documents/Prosecution_Policy_Guidance/Prosecution20Code20_Final20180412__1.pdf but include the following:

- seriousness of the offence
- length of time since the offence took place
- interests of the victim and other witnesses
- age of the offender, any previous convictions and other relevant factors
- local community interests or general public concern, and
- any other factors at his discretion, according to the facts and circumstances of the case.

NOTES

9 Article 101, – OJ2008/C115/88–89

10 Provision for Competition Disqualification Orders are made in section 9A to 9E to the Company Directors

Disqualification Act 1986 as amended by the EA02

4 THE OFFENCE AND THE APPLICATION OF THE CODE FOR CROWN PROSECUTORS

THE EVIDENTIAL STAGE

[3.176]

4.1 At the evidential stage, the CMA must be satisfied that there is sufficient evidence to provide a realistic prospect of conviction against each suspect. It must be satisfied that the evidence is admissible, reliable and credible. The Act contains statutory exclusions which the CMA must consider. If they apply then no offence will have been committed – see paragraphs 4.11–4.16 below.

4.2 At the evidential stage, the CMA must also consider what the defence case may be and how it is likely to affect the prospects of conviction. It must consider the credibility and impact of any defence and any other information that the suspect has put forward or on which he or she might rely. In particular, the Act contains three statutory defences which may be raised – see paragraphs 4.18–4.24 below.

4.3 The offence is contained in subsection 188(1) of the Act. The necessary conduct element is that an individual agrees with one or more other persons that undertakings will engage in one or more of the prohibited cartel activities. These are price fixing, limitation of supply or production, market sharing and bid-rigging.[11,12]

4.4 The offence applies in respect of agreements both to make or implement such arrangements and also to cause such arrangements to be made or implemented. The offence will be committed irrespective of whether the agreement reached is actually implemented by the undertakings.

4.5 If the agreement between the individuals is made outside the United Kingdom, proceedings may only be brought where the agreement has been implemented in whole or in part in the United Kingdom.

4.6 The cartel offence applies only to individuals who 'agree' arrangements between them. The cartel offence does not cover conduct that falls short of an agreement. For example, the mere fact of an individual passing on confidential future pricing information to an individual at a competitor would not in and of itself be caught by the offence, although it may be evidence of a cartel agreement by which the offence is committed.

4.7 In respect of arrangements restricting pricing, supply or production, the offence also requires that the restriction is reciprocal,[13] and that the arrangement relates to undertakings operating at the same level of the supply chain.[14]

4.8 The offence will not therefore be committed in the case of arrangements that: (i) contain unilateral restrictions (that is, restrictions on only one party); (ii) contain restrictions on more than one party but that do not relate to the same level of the production or supply chain; or (iii) do not contain restrictions that relate to the pricing, supply or production of a product or service, or to bid-rigging arrangements.

4.9 The following is a non-exhaustive list of examples of arrangements between undertakings which would not constitute evidence of the commission of the offence on the part of the individuals who reach agreement about them (though the undertakings may be subject to enforcement under EU or national competition law):

Unilateral restrictions

- cooperation agreements that contain restrictions on only one party to limit production or supply of the contract product
- non-reciprocal non-compete restrictions in a joint venture; for example, investment vehicles whereby an undertaking invests in a new production joint venture with a manufacturer and, in return, the manufacturer agrees not to compete with the joint venture, and
- a non-compete restriction on a seller in the context of the sale of an undertaking.

Operate at different levels of the supply chain

- co-operation agreements that impose restrictions on supply or production on more than one party but at different levels of the supply or production chain.

4.10 The criminal cartel offence is therefore reserved for agreements between individuals to make reciprocal arrangements that relate to at least two undertakings and whose purpose is to fix prices, restrict output, allocate markets or rig bids.

EXCLUSIONS

4.11 Section 188A of the Act makes further provision for circumstances where the offence will not be committed. Parties to arrangements that would otherwise fall within the offence may bring the arrangements outside the scope of the offence by ensuring that the arrangements satisfy the requirements of the notification exclusion,[15] the bid-rigging notification exclusion,[16] or the publication exclusion,[17] each of which involves the provision of 'relevant information'.

4.12 '**Relevant information**' for the purpose of the exclusions means (a) the names of the undertakings to which the arrangements relate; (b) a description of the nature of the arrangements which is sufficient to show why they are or might be arrangements which fall within the scope of the offence; (c) the products or services to which they relate; and (d) any other information as may be specified in an order made by the Secretary of State.[18]

Part 3 CMA and other Guidelines

4.13 The notification exclusion provides that an individual will not commit an offence if under the terms of the arrangement customers would be given relevant information about the arrangements before they enter into agreements for the supply to them of the product or service so affected. The exclusion will not be satisfied if the arrangement merely provides that customers would be provided with a broad general disclaimer that its agreements may contain price fixing/market sharing provisions.

4.14 The bid-rigging notification exclusion provides that an individual will not commit an offence if, in the case of bid-rigging arrangements, the person requesting bids would be given relevant information about them at or before the time when a bid is made.

4.15 The publication exclusion provides that an individual will not commit an offence if, under the arrangement, relevant information about the arrangement would be published, before the arrangements are implemented, in the manner specified at the time of the making of the agreement in an order made by the Secretary of State. The manner in which the arrangements are to be published is by advertising them once in any of the London Gazette, the Edinburgh Gazette or the Belfast Gazette.

4.16 The exclusions are framed in terms of how it was intended that the arrangements would operate at the time the individual agreed to make or to implement them. Evidence of genuine steps being taken in relation to one of the statutory exclusions will be relevant to whether or not there was such an intention even if they failed to meet the requirements of section 188A, for example:

- customers were notified of the agreement as required by subsections 188A(1)(a) or (b), but there is evidence of an inadvertent failure to notify a minority of all relevant customers, or
- a limited number of products or services covered by the agreement were inadvertently sold shortly before the relevant disclosures were made to customers under subsection 188A(1)(a) or (b), or published in the appropriate format under subsection 188A(1)(c).

4.17 In addition to the exclusions identified above, an individual will not commit an offence if the agreement is made in order to comply with a legal requirement.[19] **'Legal requirement'**[20] means a requirement:

(a) imposed by or under any enactment in force in the United Kingdom
(b) imposed by or under TFEU or the European Economic Area Agreement and having legal effect in the United Kingdom without further enactment, or
(c) imposed by or under the law in force in another European Union Member State and having legal effect in the United Kingdom.

DEFENCES

4.18 The insertion of section 188B into the Act creates three statutory defences to the offence. It will be sufficient for the defendant to prove that any one of the defences applies. The standard of proof the defendant will need to discharge in order to prove one of the defences is the balance of probabilities.

4.19 It is a defence (under subsection 188B(1)), where the arrangements would (operating as the parties intend) affect the supply in the United Kingdom of a product or service, for an individual to show that at the time of the making of the agreement, he or she did not intend that the nature of the arrangements would be concealed from customers at all times before they enter into agreements for the supply to them of the product or service.[21]

4.20 It is a defence (under subsection 188B(2)) for an individual to show that, at the time of the making of the agreement, he or she did not intend that the nature of the arrangements would be concealed from the CMA.[22]

4.21 It is a defence (under subsection 188B(3)) for an individual to show that, before making the agreement, he or she took reasonable steps to ensure that the nature of the arrangements would be disclosed to professional legal advisers for the purpose of obtaining advice about them before they were made or implemented.[23]

4.22 The CMA will need to consider whether there is evidence that any of the defences may apply. It will need to assess the credibility and strength of that evidence. In relation to the defences under subsection 188B(1) and 188B(2) it will need to consider whether the evidence shows that it is likely there was an absence of intention to conceal the arrangements.

4.23 The defence under subsection 188B(2) does not place an obligation on the individual to notify the CMA about the agreement and there is no duty on the CMA to respond to any such notifications that are made. Any evidence of attempts by an individual to bring the arrangements to the attention of the CMA will be considered. If an arrangement is notified to the CMA, this will not preclude the CMA from taking civil enforcement action in relation to it under EU or national competition law, either at the time or at any later date.

4.24 The CMA takes the view that the term 'professional legal advisers' under subsection 188B(3) is intended to cover both external and in-house legal advisers qualified in the UK and that it could also apply to legal advisers qualified in foreign jurisdictions with an equivalent legal qualification. For the defence under section 188B(3) to succeed, an individual must show that the purpose for which he or she took steps to disclose the arrangements to a professional legal adviser was to obtain advice about them. The steps must also have been 'reasonable'. The CMA takes the view that this must genuinely be an attempt to seek legal advice about the arrangement.

NO ACTION LETTERS

4.25 The CMA will not prosecute any individual who has received a written notice under subsection 190(4) of the EA02 except in the circumstances specified in that notice.

THE PUBLIC INTEREST STAGE

4.26 It has never been the rule that a prosecution will automatically take place once the evidential stage is met. A prosecution will usually take place unless the CMA is satisfied that there are public interest factors tending against prosecution which outweigh those tending in favour. In making an assessment of the public interest in order to decide whether to bring a prosecution, the CMA will focus on those cases where the harmful nature of the individual's behaviour is obvious without the need for any detailed assessment. As a result, the potential for any conflict between the application of, on the one hand, the criminal offence and, on the other, the civil competition law regime is negligible.

4.27 When deciding the public interest, the CMA will consider each of the questions set out in paragraph 4.12 of the Code, and in particular those set out and expanded upon below, so as to identify and determine the relevant general public interest factors tending for and against prosecution. These general factors, together with the explanatory text for them in the Code and the more offence specific factors set out in this guidance, will enable the CMA to form an overall assessment of the public interest.

4.28 Assessing the public interest is not simply a matter of adding up the number of factors on each side and seeing which side has the greater number. The questions identified are not exhaustive, and not all the questions may be relevant in every case. The weight to be attached to each of the questions, and the factors identified, will also vary according to the facts and merits of each case. It is possible that one factor alone may outweigh a number of other factors which tend in the opposite direction. There may be an overlap between factors.

4.29 Although there may be public interest factors tending against prosecution in a particular case, the CMA should consider whether, nonetheless, a prosecution should go ahead and those factors put before the court for consideration before sentencing.

4.30 These public interest factors relate to matters which are not elements of the offence that need to be proved before a jury.

4.31 The CMA will consider each of the following questions.

How serious is the offence committed?

4.32 The more serious the offence the more likely it is that a prosecution is required. Hardcore cartels are generally serious and individuals involved in them are likely to have caused serious harm requiring prosecution.

4.33 The more serious and potentially harmful the cartel conduct the more likely it is that a prosecution is required. Factors that are likely to be relevant to assessing the degree of harm involved will include the CMA's assessment as to the impact of the cartel on any particular market or the risk of that impact, the degree of limitation on consumer choice created by the arrangements, and the potential for the cartel to raise prices or restrict the supply of goods or services, as well as issues such as the vulnerability of the customers affected or potentially affected by the cartel.

4.34 Cartels that have been carried on for a prolonged period are more likely to require prosecution.

What is the level of culpability of the suspect?

4.35 This is likely to be determined by the individual's level of involvement in the making or enforcing of the arrangements concerned. The CMA will consider the extent to which the individual was the instigator or ringleader in the cartel. It will also consider whether the individual is or was in a position of authority or trust within the undertaking. If an individual had a very limited role in the arrangements, for a short period of time, and/or was in a vulnerable position acting under the direct instructions of others, that will be a factor in deciding whether a prosecution of that individual will be required.

4.36 The CMA will look at the extent to which the individual's purpose was to preserve or increase the profits of their organisation or to profit personally, by overcharging customers or by depriving them of choices between products or services, and so harming their interests.

4.37 Whether an individual was acting openly or not is an important factor to be considered by the CMA. The greater the degree of evidence of clandestine conduct and of conscious participation in a hardcore cartel, the more likely it is that a prosecution will be required. Conduct such as deliberate concealment, covert behaviour or misrepresentation are likely to be relevant.

4.38 Whether an individual's conduct was contrary to guidelines laid down in an undertaking's compliance policy will be a relevant factor, as will evidence of attempts by individuals to report arrangements to senior management within the undertaking.

4.39 If an individual has previously been found by a competition authority or a court to have participated in, or has admitted to previous participation in, cartel conduct, either criminal or civil, it is more likely that a prosecution will be required.

What is the impact on the community?

4.40 Criminal cartels can have a wider impact on the community and markets than will be apparent to individual customers and, where present, this will be a factor that the CMA will need to consider. Such wider effects can include a diminution of public funds, an effect on public safety or the stifling of innovation.

Is prosecution a proportionate response?

4.41 The CMA should also consider whether prosecution is proportionate to the likely outcome.

NOTES

[11] See subsection 188(2) of the Act.

[12] 'Bid-rigging arrangements' are arrangements under which, in response to a request for bids for the supply of a product or service in the United Kingdom, or for the production of a product in the United Kingdom: (a) A but not B may make a bid, or (b) A and B may each make a bid but, in one case or both, only a bid arrived at in accordance with the arrangements.

[13] See subsection 188(3) of the Act.

[14] See section 189 of the Act.

[15] See subsection 188A(1)(a) of the Act.

[16] See subsection 188A(1)(b) of the Act.

[17] See subsection 188A(1)(c) of the Act.

[18] As at the date of publication, no order under subsection 188A(2)(d) has been made.

[19] See subsection 188A(3) of the Act.

[20] See paragraph 5 of Schedule 3 to the CA98.

[21] See subsection 188B(1) of the Act.

[22] See subsection 188B(2) of the Act.

[23] See subsection 188B(3) of the Act.

5 TRANSITIONAL ARRANGEMENTS

[3.177]

5.1 The Act applies to agreements falling within section 188(1) which are made after the commencement of the Act and which relate to arrangements made or to be made after that commencement.[24]

NOTES

[24] Section 47(8) ERRA13

COMPETITION AND MARKETS AUTHORITY: REWARDS FOR INFORMATION ABOUT CARTELS

(March 2014)

[3.178]

NOTES

This document is available on the Competition and Markets Authority website at: www.gov.uk/government/publications/cartels-informant-rewards-policy.

The CMA offers financial rewards of up to £100,000 (in exceptional circumstances) for information about cartel activity. If you have information, or have access to information, about cartels and you are considering approaching us to offer that information in exchange for a possible reward, you will find it useful to read the guidance set out here.

WHY DOES THE CMA OFFER FINANCIAL REWARDS FOR INFORMATION ABOUT CARTEL BEHAVIOUR?

Cartels, particularly illegal agreements between businesses to fix prices and share markets, cause serious damage to businesses and the economy and cost consumers money.

Cartels are illegal under both the civil and criminal law.

Under the civil law (the Competition Act 1998), the CMA is able to fine companies up to 10 per cent of their turnover if they are found guilty of cartel activity.

Individuals who engage in cartel activity may commit a criminal offence and may be imprisoned for up to five years and may be given an unlimited fine.

Any company directors implicated in cartel activities could also be disqualified from acting as a director in the future for up to 15 years.

Cartels are generally conducted in secret and they can be hard to detect and prove. For this reason the CMA believes it should offer financial rewards for information which helps in the detection and investigation of cartels and which, in appropriate cases, leads to the fining of the companies or the criminal prosecution of the individuals involved.

WHAT IS A CARTEL?

The term 'cartel' is a catch-all that covers any of the following collusive arrangements between businesses:

- Directly or indirectly fixing prices between businesses – where two or more businesses agree to raise the price of their product or service instead of setting their prices independently of each other and competing in the market place. This is known as price fixing.

- Limiting or preventing supply or production between businesses – where two or more businesses agree to limit or prevent the supply or production of a product.
- Dividing up customers or prospective customers between businesses – where two or more businesses agree that they will not poach each other's customers and/or that business 1 will not compete with business 2 in area A if business 2 agrees to a similar arrangement for the benefit of business 1 in area B. This is known as market sharing.
- In response to a request by a third party to tender for a contract, a secret agreement between businesses that one or more of them will agree not to bid for the contract or one or more of them will put in an artificially high price for the contract to allow another business to win the contract – perhaps for a return of favour on another occasion when another contract is tendered. This is known as bid rigging.

IF I HAVE ANY INFORMATION ABOUT CARTELS, WHO SHOULD I CALL?

To contact us you can call our cartels hotline on 0800 085 1664 or 020 3738 6888. You will immediately be put through to a voice mailbox. Please leave a message with your contact details and an investigator will try to respond to your call within two business days. Alternatively email: cartelshotline@cma.gsi.gov.uk.

AT WHAT STAGE SHOULD I APPROACH THE CMA?

We prefer you to approach us before you have obtained all of the information about the cartel. This is so we can discuss with you in advance what risks there might be in obtaining that information and how those risks could be reduced – or whether they should be taken at all.

In addition, an early approach allows us to discuss with you what information will be of most value to us.

Of course, some people will already have the information that they wish to impart and there is no prospect they will be able to get anymore. Again, the earlier the approach the better. Old information relating to a cartel that was in operation some while ago is generally going to be of less importance to us than information about a cartel that is still ongoing or ended only recently. Having said that, if you have information about a really significant cartel which ended some while ago, it is still worth approaching us as we may still wish to investigate.

HOW WILL I KNOW THAT IF I GIVE INFORMATION IT WILL BE TREATED IN STRICTEST CONFIDENCE?

We recognise that many people who want to give us information about cartel activity will only be prepared to do so if there is a guarantee that their identity as a 'whistle-blower' will not become known to third parties.

For this reason only specially trained officers, mostly with a law enforcement background, will deal with you. They will very carefully safeguard any information you give to protect your identity from disclosure.

HOW WILL THE PROCESS OF GIVING INFORMATION ACTUALLY WORK?

Our officer will want to talk to you to obtain as much detail as possible. Initially the conversation could be conducted on a no-names basis if necessary, though we will always prefer to know your identity from the very start.

If the officer's initial assessment is that you have information and/or can gain information that is likely to be of value to us and might well give us a basis for further investigation, we will want to meet you to discuss the information in more detail. At that meeting we will need to know your identity as an essential part of assessing your credibility and the likely reliability of the information you may be able to give us.

People may be tempted to give information for all sorts of reasons and it is important that we can explore all of your motivations for approaching us. This is for our protection as well as that of any persons or businesses which might otherwise be susceptible to unfounded allegations.

WHEN WILL I KNOW IF I WILL GET A FINANCIAL REWARD AND HOW DOES THE CMA CALCULATE ANY AMOUNT?

It is essential to understand that rewards are granted at the discretion of the CMA. The CMA is entirely free to reject offers of information and it does not have to give reasons for doing so. Furthermore, where the CMA has agreed to accept some information from a person and the information provides a credible basis for further investigation, the CMA is still free to decide, on the basis of other more pressing priorities, that it will not use the information given and will not therefore give a financial reward. This is another reason why it is best to discuss with us in advance what information you may be able to gain for us and how useful that would be to us.

Where a reward is available, its amount will depend on a number of factors:

- the value of the information in terms of what we have been able to achieve from it
- the amount of harm to the economy and consumers which we believe the information given has helped to put a stop to and/or has helped to disclose
- the effort you have had to invest in order to give us the information
- the risk you have had to take in order to give us the information.

It is important to understand that we won't bargain over how much will be paid – but we do aim to pay a fair price.

The CMA cannot calculate 'up-front' what amount of reward you will get – in particular because it depends on the ultimate value of the information given which will only become fully apparent at the end of an investigation. It follows from this that we can only pay rewards at the end of the investigation. However, we will reimburse expenses as they are incurred. Although we will not calculate amounts up-front, we will try to give you some idea early on in our dealings with you as to the broad range within which a possible financial reward amount might fall. It should be understood though, that this very broad estimate will not bind us to give a reward falling within the estimate given – or indeed any reward.

SHOULD I TAKE LEGAL ADVICE BEFORE DECIDING WHETHER TO OFFER INFORMATION TO THE CMA?

Obviously the CMA will operate entirely within the law in the way in which it uses informants. In particular, if circumstances require it, a special form of authorisation will be obtained by the CMA under a piece of legislation known as the Regulation of Investigatory Powers Act 2000. If obtained, this protects the actions of an informant in providing the CMA with information, provided those actions are in accordance with the authorisation. So, provided you only act in the way we have directed you, your actions in providing us with information cannot be subject to any civil or criminal liability.

Even so, you may still be concerned about other legal aspects such as your employment law position if, for example, you were planning to give information about your employer. It is entirely a matter for you whether to take legal advice in such circumstances. However, if you do want to take legal advice, you may wish to contact us first and see whether the information you have, or may have access to, will be of possible use to us and what the risks to you would be in obtaining the information. If you then feel it would be good to take legal advice before proceeding further, you will have every opportunity to do so, but the CMA will not pay for you to take that advice. The CMA will not be able to offer you legal advice – though we will do our best to ensure that you have a reasonable appreciation of any risks involved which you can consider carefully.

The important additional thing to remember is that except in those rare cases where you agree to be a witness, we will only be using your information as intelligence so as to protect your identity from disclosure. As such, your employer should never know that you have assisted us. Nonetheless, it is worth noting that an employer cannot dismiss or otherwise victimise an employee for whistle-blowing on illegal activity. See the Public Interest Disclosure Act 1998 on the Public Concern at Work website.

The organisation Public Concern at Work also has useful information on its website about whistle-blowing in a workplace context and operates an advice line. Visit the Public Concern at Work website for more information.

I HAVE BEEN DIRECTLY INVOLVED IN THE CARTEL ACTIVITY I WISH TO REPORT. WILL I STILL BE ELIGIBLE FOR A FINANCIAL REWARD?

Under the CMA's leniency policy any company or individual who has been directly involved in a cartel can gain complete civil and criminal immunity from sanction provided that:

- they are the first to report and confess involvement in the cartel
- they cooperate fully with the CMA throughout the investigation
- the CMA did not have any pre-existing investigation into the cartel.

The CMA does not consider that an individual in such circumstances should ordinarily also gain a financial reward.

However, there may be circumstances where the CMA will consider a reward in addition to immunity from sanction under the leniency policy. This is most likely to be considered where the role of the person in the cartel was relatively peripheral – for example that of an employee who was occasionally directed by his superiors to attend a cartel meeting and who was not asked to take an active part in decision-making about the cartel.

IF I AM RUNNING A BUSINESS AND BELIEVE THAT I HAVE BEEN THE VICTIM OF A CARTEL, WILL I GAIN A REWARD FOR REPORTING MY CONCERNS?

The financial reward programme is really intended for those who have what might be called 'inside' information about the existence of a cartel. The CMA often receives complaints from businesses that their competitors or suppliers have been involved in anti-competitive activities and generally such complaints are not, for obvious reasons, able to be supported by significant 'inside' information about the cartel. As such, a reward is highly unlikely to be available in cases where complainants simply report their general concerns about possible cartel activity by competitors – even if those concerns are backed up by at least some evidence.

MEMORANDUM OF UNDERSTANDING BETWEEN THE COMPETITION AND MARKETS AUTHORITY AND THE CROWN OFFICE AND PROCURATOR FISCAL SERVICE

(July 2014)

[3.179]

NOTES

INTRODUCTION

[3.180]

1. This Memorandum of Understanding (MOU) records the basis on which the Competition and Markets Authority (CMA) and Crown Office and Procurator Fiscal Service (COPFS) (the Parties) will cooperate to investigate and/or prosecute individuals in respect of the cartel offence established by the Enterprise Act 2002 (EA02)[1] where such an offence may have been committed within the jurisdiction of the Scottish Courts.

2. The Parties recognise that this MOU may require amendment in the light of future experience.

NOTES

[1] The Enterprise and Regulatory Reform Act 2013 (ERRA13) amended the EA02 and created the CMA. The powers of the Office of Fair Trading (OFT) under the EA02 in respect of competition and criminal cartel enforcement were transferred to the CMA on 1 April 2014. In this MOU references to EA02 mean references to the EA02 as amended by the ERRA13.

INITIAL ENQUIRIES AND REFERENCES TO COPFS

3. Where the CMA receives information, through use of Competition Act 1998 (CA98) powers or otherwise, that criminal cartel activity may have occurred, the Cartels and Criminal Group (CCG) of the CMA will undertake any necessary initial criminal enquiries. Therefore, if COPFS receives information suggestive of criminal cartel activity, prior to any related referral from the CMA, COPFS, via its Serious and Organised Crime Division (SOCD) will, in the first instance, refer that information to CCG.

4. If, after any necessary initial enquiries (and informal discussions with COPFS), the CMA identifies a cartel case as one that might involve criminality wholly or partly within the Scottish jurisdiction, the case will be referred formally to the Procurator Fiscal, Organised Crime and Counter Terrorism at SOCD or their representative. The referral will provide such background information as is necessary to enable COPFS to make an informed decision as to whether or not the matter should be accepted for investigation or alternatively, whether the CMA should undertake further enquiries.

5. If COPFS considers that the CMA should make further enquiries, the parties will discuss and agree the nature and scope of such enquiries (which are likely to be conducted by CCG under EA02 powers). Once the further enquiries have been completed, COPFS will reconsider its decision in the light of any additional evidence so obtained.

6. Where the CMA identifies a criminal cartel case as potentially falling within the remit of the Serious Fraud Office (SFO) or COPFS, it will ensure that there is suitable liaison among the three organisations with a view to determining the most appropriate way to deal with the case.

THE COPFS CRIMINAL INVESTIGATION

7. If COPFS accepts a CMA referral, the way in which the investigation will proceed, including whether it would be appropriate to second any CMA staff to the SOCD for the purpose and duration of the investigation, will be agreed with CCG.

USE OF POWERS DURING A COPFS CRIMINAL INVESTIGATION

8. The presumption will operate that once COPFS has accepted a criminal cartel investigation, powers under the Criminal Law (Consolidation) (Scotland) Act 1995 will be used rather than those under the EA02 where the two sets of powers would achieve essentially the same objectives. However, depending upon the precise circumstances it may be decided that EA02 powers could and should be used to pursue particular objectives.

CMA INVESTIGATION COSTS

9. Where CMA staff are working on a case which has been accepted by COPFS for investigation, the CMA will bear its own staff costs, including all case-related travel and subsistence.

TRAINING OF CCG STAFF

10. COPFS will provide the CMA with appropriate training in Scottish law and procedure, as needed, so as to enable CCG staff to conduct criminal investigations in Scotland.

CA98 INVESTIGATIONS AND EC CASES

11. In certain cases, the CCG will progress an investigation using CA98 powers (which may or may not have commenced prior to any COPFS referral), while the SOCD will progress a related criminal investigation. Suitable procedures will be adopted to ensure that the two investigation teams maintain an ongoing dialogue. Both case teams will thereby seek to ensure that the CA98 investigation does not prejudice the parallel criminal investigation or any resulting prosecution.

12. Subject to any applicable restrictions under EC law, where the CMA becomes aware of an investigation by the Directorate General for Competition of the European Commission (DG Comp) which might involve a potential cartel offence in Scotland, it will draw the investigation to the attention of COPFS and, if COPFS accepts such a case for investigation, the CMA will seek to facilitate coordination of the progress of both investigations.

LENIENCY AND IMMUNITY FROM PROSECUTION

13. Decisions about whether to grant leniency to undertakings rest with the CMA. However, if any such decision could have an impact on the outcome of an existing COPFS cartel investigation or prosecution, the CMA will consult COPFS.

14. Where the CMA has received an application for immunity from prosecution in respect of a cartel that falls to be prosecuted in Scotland, the Senior Director of CCG will report the level of cooperation of relevant individual(s) to the Lord Advocate, via the Procurator Fiscal, Organised Crime and Counter Terrorism and where the CMA recommends that conditional criminal immunity should be granted, the Lord Advocate will accord such a recommendation serious weight in exercising his discretion in the grant of criminal immunity in Scotland.

15. In determining whether to grant conditional criminal immunity, the Lord Advocate will take cognisance of the CMA's own rules on leniency as set out in the CMA's detailed guidance on the principles and process of applications for leniency and no-action in cartel cases (OFT1495) and in particular whether the applicant has fully cooperated with the relevant authorities. The Lord Advocate will also require the applicant to disclose and self-certify the completeness and accuracy of any criminal convictions or associations.

16. Where possible, the Lord Advocate will give an early indication at the commencement of a leniency application and before the applicant's identity (or that of any related economic undertaking) has been revealed to the authorities by their advisers of whether criminal immunity is likely to be granted, assuming full ongoing cooperation with the authorities were to be maintained and on the basis that there are no criminal convictions or associations to be disclosed.

DECISION IN RELATION TO CRIMINAL INVESTIGATION

17. Where the CMA considers in respect of a cartel case falling within Scottish jurisdiction that it should be dealt with solely by the CMA using CA98 powers, the CMA will report to the Lord Advocate, via the Procurator Fiscal, Organised Crime and Counter Terrorism, the circumstances in relation to the operation of the particular cartel and seek an indication from the Lord Advocate at the commencement of a leniency application and before the applicant's identity (and that of any related economic undertaking) is revealed to the authorities by their advisers of whether a criminal investigation is likely to be initiated at all.

USE OF INFORMATION

18. Where the Lord Advocate declines to grant or to give a favourable early indication of immunity, or declines to give an early indication that a criminal investigation will not be initiated, any information from an applicant which was provided to enable the Lord Advocate to reach his decision will not be used in evidence (or as intelligence for that or any other investigation) against the applicant, provided the information was not false or misleading in a material particular or materially incomplete.

19. In the event that disclosed and self-certified details of any criminal convictions or criminal associations are false or misleading in a material particular, or materially incomplete, any grant of or favourable early indication of immunity will be withdrawn and any information from the applicant may be used in evidence (or as intelligence) in any investigation against the applicant.

SIGNATORIES

For and on behalf of the Competition and Markets Authority

Alex Chisholm Chief Executive Officer 8th July 2014

For and on behalf of the Crown Office and Procurator Fiscal Service

Catherine Dyer Crown Agent 3rd July 2014

BACKGROUND NOTE TO THE MOU BETWEEN THE CMA AND COPFS

[3.181]

The EA02 makes it a criminal offence, including in Scotland, for an individual to agree with one or more other persons that two or more undertakings will engage in certain prohibited cartel agreements, including price-fixing, limitation of production or supply, market-sharing and bid-rigging. This is subject to a number of exclusions and defences introduced by the ERRA13 with effect from 1 April 2014.[1] Any individual convicted of the offence may receive a maximum of five years' imprisonment and/or an unlimited fine. The criminal cartel offence will operate alongside the existing CA98 regime under which anti-competitive agreements between undertakings are prohibited.

In order to investigate the criminal cartel offence, the EA02 provides the CMA with a number of powers, including the power to compel persons to answer questions or otherwise provide information or documents relevant to the investigation; the power to enter premises under warrant and to take possession of relevant documents and certain powers of surveillance exercised in accordance with the Regulation of Investigatory Powers Act 2000 and the Police Act 1997.

In addition to conducting criminal investigations, members of the CCG exercise the CMA's powers of investigation under the CA98, including in Scotland to determine whether undertakings have engaged in cartel agreements. If the CMA decides that a cartel has been formed in breach of the CA98, the CMA can impose a financial penalty against the undertakings involved of up to 10% of their worldwide turnover.

In Scotland, the Lord Advocate is solely responsible for the investigation and prosecution of crime. His local representatives are Procurators Fiscal. The National Casework Division (NCD) operates under his direction and control and is responsible inter alia for the investigation and prosecution of serious or complex fraud.

The Criminal Law (Consolidation) (Scotland) Act 1995 provides that the Lord Advocate may nominate a person to exercise his powers to require persons to answer questions, provide information or produce documents for the purposes of an investigation into serious or complex fraud. The Act also makes provision for the obtaining of search warrants, with the assistance of police officers.

The CMA operates a leniency programme for those involved in cartels who come forward with information. In the context of the CA98, an undertaking may receive total or partial immunity from financial penalties if it comes forward with information about its role in a cartel. In the context of the cartel offence, whilst guarantees of immunity from prosecution cannot be given by the CMA in relation to Scotland (unlike in England, Wales and Northern Ireland), the Crown Office and CMA have put in place arrangements aimed at achieving a high degree of consistency of outcome with respect to criminal cartel immunity as between Scotland and the rest of the UK, while recognising the particular features of the Scottish criminal justice system and the constitutional position of the Lord Advocate.

For further information on DG Comp, which investigates cartels that may affect interstate trade between the members of the EU, visit its website ec.europa.eu/competition/index_en.html.

NOTES

1 For agreements made before 1 April 2014 or which relate to arrangements made before that date the offence will only have been committed where the individual making the agreement did so dishonestly.

GUIDANCE ON THE APPROVAL OF VOLUNTARY REDRESS SCHEMES FOR INFRINGEMENTS OF COMPETITION LAW (CMA40, AUGUST 2015)

[3.182]

NOTES

See also the *Approval application form - where there is no existing infringement decision* and the *Approval application form - where there is an existing infringement decision* at www.gov.uk/government/publications/approval-of-redress-schemes-for-competition-law-infringements. The Competition Act 1998 (Redress Scheme) Regulations 2015 (SI 2015/1587) govern the approval process and operation of voluntary redress schemes (see **[2.66]**).

CONTENTS

1. INTRODUCTION AND OVERVIEW

POWER TO APPROVE VOLUNTARY REDRESS SCHEMES

The legal background

[3.183]

1.1 This guidance outlines the provisions in the Competition Act 1998 (CA98), introduced by the Consumer Rights Act 2015 (CRA15),[1] which permit a person (the applicant) to submit a voluntary redress scheme to the Competition and Markets Authority (CMA)[2] or a concurrent regulator (Regulator)[3] for approval.

1.2 Under the CA98 as amended and the Competition Act 1998 (Redress Scheme) Regulations 2015, the CMA and Regulators are empowered to approve certain voluntary redress schemes. The remainder of this guidance uses the term 'the Authority' (which means the CMA or a Regulator as appropriate),[4] in order to reflect that both the CMA and Regulators may approve schemes. Where an application for scheme approval is made to the CMA or a Regulator, where appropriate it may be referred to the CMA or another Regulator to assess instead.[5]

1.3 Where a business offers a redress scheme, those affected by the infringement are able to claim compensation through such a scheme without the need to pursue litigation in the courts.

1.4 The CMA and Regulators are required to publish guidance on applications for approval of redress schemes, the approval of such schemes, and the power to enforce approved schemes.[6] This is the CMA's guidance and was approved by the Secretary of State as required under section 49C(10) of the CA98 on 6 August 2015. It was published and came into effect on 14 August 2015. The CMA will take this guidance into account when carrying out its approval role under the CA98.[7]

1.5 The guidance is aimed principally at businesses seeking to provide compensation under a redress scheme and chairpersons and members of independent boards[8] appointed to determine compensation in relation to such a scheme. Businesses, Chairpersons and Board members appointed to devise redress schemes are expected to have regard to this guidance as appropriate when applying for approval of schemes or carrying out their roles and obligations under the legislative framework for scheme approval.

1.6 The guidance will be kept under review and may be revised from time to time to reflect the Authority's developing experience of its approval role and any relevant developments in the wider competition redress landscape.

NOTES

1 Section 49C of the CA98, as amended by the CRA15.

2 The CMA was established under the Enterprise and Regulatory Reform Act 2013 as the UK's economy-wide competition and consumer authority. It is responsible for ensuring that competition and markets work well for consumers, businesses and the economy as a whole. Further information on the CMA can be found on the CMA's webpages. The CMA's primary duty is to promote competition, both within and outside the UK, for the benefit of consumers. To enable it to carry out its functions, the CMA has a range of statutory powers.

3 As at 13 August 2015, the concurrent regulators, and the scope of their competition concurrency, are:

- Civil Aviation Authority (CAA) (air traffic services and airport operation services) (www.caa.co.uk)
- Financial Conduct Authority (FCA) (the provision of financial services) (www.fca.org.uk)
- Monitor (the provision of health-care services in England) (www.gov.uk/government/organisations/monitor)
- Ofcom (electronic communications and post) (www.ofcom.org.uk)
- Ofgem (gas and electricity markets in Great Britain) (www.ofgem.gov.uk)
- Ofwat (water and sewerage markets in England and Wales) (www.ofwat.gov.uk)
- Office of Rail and Road (ORR) (railway services in Great Britain) (www.orr.gov.uk)
- Payment Systems Regulator (participation in payment systems) (www.psr.org.uk)
- Utility Regulator, Northern Ireland (NIAUR) (gas, electricity, water and sewerage services in Northern Ireland) (www.uregni.gov.uk)

4 See definition of 'the Authority' in Annex A.

5 The CMA and Regulators together form the UK Competition Network (UKCN), save that Monitor is an observer only of the UKCN. Any decision to transfer an application to another UKCN member or to Monitor will be taken having regard to the Competition Act Concurrency Regulations 2014 and the published guidance on the *Concurrent application of competition law to regulated industries* (CMA10).

6 Section 49C(9) of the CA98, as amended by the CRA15.

7 The CMA expects that regulators will take this CMA guidance into account when producing their own guidance on the approval power.

8 The roles of the Board and the Chairperson are explained in paragraphs 2.42–2.78 below.

Overview of the process for the Authority's approval of voluntary redress schemes

General

1.7 Approved voluntary redress schemes are a form of alternative dispute resolution (ADR). A flowchart of the process for the Authority's approval of redress schemes is set out in Figure 1 on page 9 below.

1.8 A person (which may include more than one undertaking applying jointly) who has infringed competition law[9] may apply to the Authority for approval of a voluntary redress scheme. An application can be submitted to the Authority either during the course of an ongoing investigation or where an infringement decision has already been made by the Authority or the European Commission. Although the Authority may consider an application before it adopts an infringement decision, it may only approve the scheme at the time it makes an infringement decision (if the scheme relates to that decision) or after the infringement decision has been made (if the scheme relates to a decision of the European Commission).[10]

1.9 The Secretary of State has made regulations relating to the Authority's approval of redress schemes under section 49C(8) of the CA98 – the Competition Act 1998 (Redress Scheme) Regulations 2015 (the Regulations) – which govern how the Authority considers redress schemes.[11]

NOTES

9 See paragraphs 1.22–1.26 below.

10 Redress schemes for these purposes arise where there is a decision by a relevant authority and not in the context of a private action (see Annex C for the distinction between follow-on and stand-alone actions).

[11] SI 2015/1587. The Regulations will come into force on 1 October 2015.

Unconditional approval of full schemes

1.10 The Regulations provide that the Authority may approve a redress scheme only if it:

- has been devised in accordance with the process specified in the Regulations (Required Process);
- contains all of the information required by the Regulations (Required Information); and
- contains all of the terms required by the Regulations (Required Terms).[12]

1.11 As regards the **Required Process**, a person wishing to offer a voluntary redress scheme will need to appoint a Chairperson who will in turn appoint the members of the Board in accordance with paragraphs 2.42 to 2.59 below. The Chairperson and the Board will then devise the terms of the redress scheme, including the level of compensation, taking into consideration the relevant matters.[13] According to the Regulations, the relevant matters include:

- evidence of loss caused to persons entitled to compensation relating to the infringement decision;
- who is entitled to compensation under the redress scheme;
- the process for applying for compensation under the redress scheme, including any requirements to produce evidence in support of an application; and
- how those entitled to compensation under the scheme will be notified of their entitlement.[14]

1.12 Although under the Regulations it is the responsibility of the Chairperson and Board to devise a scheme, applicants will need to decide on the key parameters within which a scheme will be devised, and ensure that they are communicated clearly to the Chairperson and Board. Also, an applicant may have an idea as to how it would like specific aspects of a redress scheme to operate. For example, it may have explored internally various options for a redress scheme, including what evidence may be required from potential beneficiaries, or arrangements to advertise a scheme. An applicant can share its ideas with the Chairperson and the Board, so as to assist them in devising the scheme, and the Chairperson and the Board may take into account any initial suggestions made by the applicant, should it consider them to be appropriate.

1.13 The **Required Information** includes:

- the names of the Chairperson and Board members and confirmation that none of them had a conflict of interest, neither when they were appointed nor when they considered whether to recommend approval of the scheme to the Authority;
- details of the arrangements to ensure that the Chairperson and Board members had access to relevant information held by the applicant prior to deciding whether to recommend the redress scheme for approval to the Authority;
- details of the process for applying for compensation under the redress scheme, and estimates as to how long it will take to determine such applications for compensation; and
- details of an independent complaints process available for those applying for compensation under the redress scheme.[15]

1.14 The **Required Terms** that the redress scheme must include are:

- that a third party may not submit a claim under the scheme on behalf of those entitled to compensation under the scheme; and
- that the scheme will operate for at least nine months.[16]

1.15 For ease of reference, the remainder of this guidance refers to the Required Process, the Required Information, and the Required Terms collectively as the **Regulation Requirements**.

NOTES

[12] Article 4(1) of the Regulations.
[13] See paragraphs 2.60–2.78 below.
[14] Article 5(7) of the Regulations.
[15] Article 6(1) of the Regulations.
[16] Article 7 of the Regulations.

Conditional approval of outline schemes

1.16 Even if all the Regulation Requirements have not been met yet (for example a Chairperson or Board have not been appointed), if the applicant has provided the Authority with information about the time when, and how, the scheme will comply with the Regulation Requirements, the Authority may approve an outline scheme subject to conditions which must include conditions to ensure such compliance by a particular date.[17] An applicant will also need to provide the Authority with sufficient information for it to consider that it is appropriate to approve a scheme in principle (see further paragraph 1.20 below). The deadline the Authority sets for satisfying the Regulation Requirements will depend, among other things, on how quickly the Chairperson and the Board members can be appointed and the complexity of the case. However, the Authority will expect businesses to act as quickly as reasonably possible.

1.17 As well as imposing conditions relating to the Regulation Requirements, the Authority may also impose further conditions requiring the provision of information about the operation of the scheme more generally,[18] including for example about the amount or value of compensation to be offered under the scheme and how this will be determined. Moreover, where such information conditions relating to the Regulation Requirements or other matters are imposed, the Authority may also impose other conditions,[19] such as, for example:

- that other information required is provided by a particular date;
- that the Authority, the Board and the Chairperson must be provided with complete and accurate information in all material respects; and
- that the Authority must be satisfied with the Chairperson and Board members' final determination of, and the level of compensation ultimately offered under, the scheme.[20]

1.18 The Authority may revoke conditional approval of an outline redress scheme if any of the conditions (information and/or non-information related) are not met.[21] The Authority may take into account any representations made by the compensating party and/or any discussions with the Chairperson and Board before reaching its decision. Alternatively, where appropriate, the Authority's concerns about a breach of one or more conditions may be addressed by the offer of a suitable full replacement scheme from the applicant, which must satisfy the Regulation Requirements and be capable of unconditional approval, since no further conditions can be imposed in relation to a replacement scheme.

1.19 The Authority is not able to grant conditional approval of schemes that relate to existing infringement decisions of the Authority or the European Commission. In respect of such infringement decisions, the Authority is able to consider only full schemes rather than outline schemes and, if granting approval, will do so without conditions.

1.20 A business wishing to submit an outline scheme for conditional approval will in practice need to provide the Authority with sufficient information for it to assess whether it considers the outline scheme being offered is – in principle, and subject to the Chairperson and Board devising the detailed scheme in due course – appropriate for approval. The information required for that assessment may to some extent vary case by case, but the Authority would expect an outline scheme submitted for conditional approval to include sufficient information on the key parameters of the scheme set out at paragraph 2.9 below. In particular, applicants should provide available details about:

- the agreement or conduct, and the aspects of the relevant investigation in relation to which, the scheme is being offered;
- the persons who will be entitled to claim compensation under the redress scheme;
- the scope of the compensation to be offered under the scheme, as initially proposed by the applicant;
- the proposed Chairperson and Board members, and proposed arrangements to ensure they will have access to relevant information held by the applicant;
- the process for applying for compensation under the redress scheme;
- the possible types of evidence that potential beneficiaries may submit in support of an application under the proposed scheme;
- the independent complaints process available for those applying for compensation under the redress scheme;
- how the redress scheme will be advertised and those entitled to compensation under the scheme will be notified of their entitlement; and
- evidence or information about the expected cost to the applicant of administering the scheme, including details as to how the scheme will be resourced.

1.21 Further details about applications for redress scheme approval and the assessment and approval process can be found in chapters 2 and 3 of this guidance.

Figure 1: The redress scheme approval process

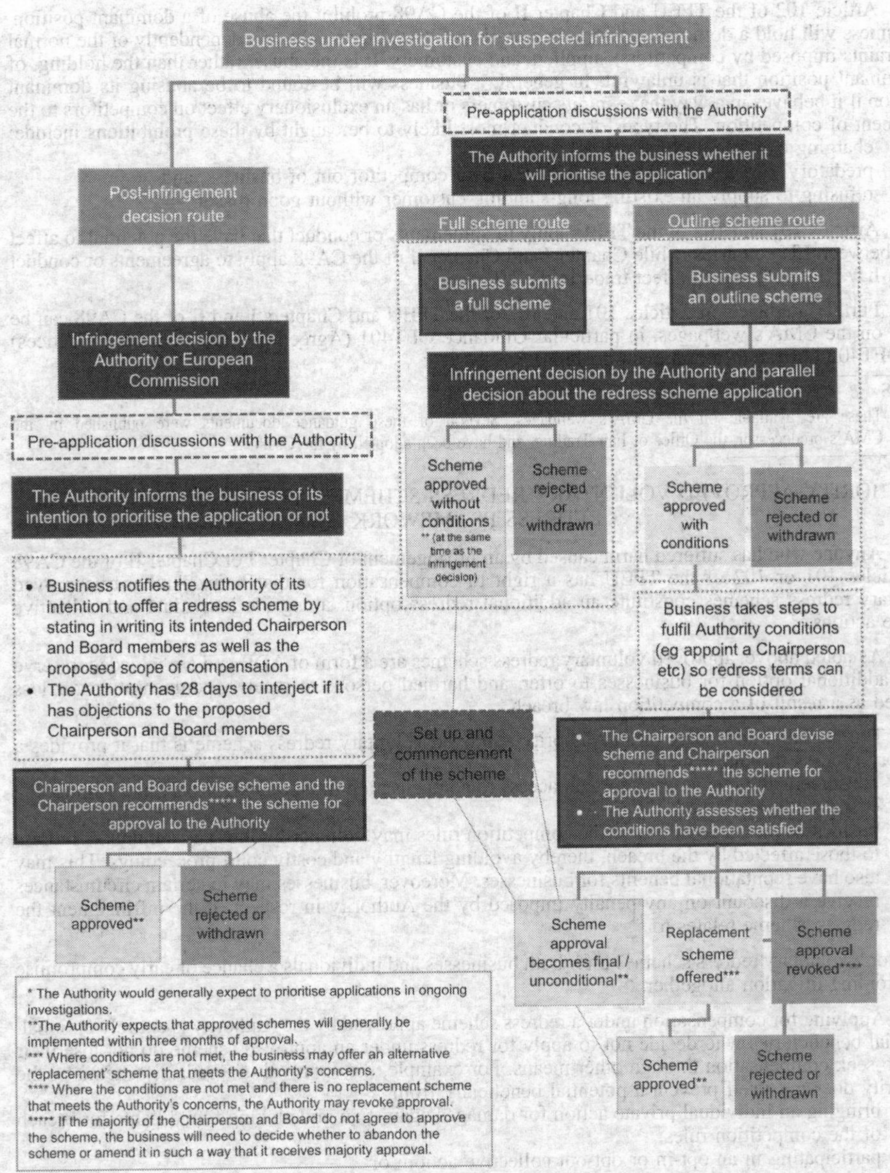

NOTES

17 Sections 49C(4) and (5)(a) of the CA98 and Article 4(2) of the Regulations.

18 That is, information not falling within the Regulation Requirements. See section 49C(4) of the CA98.

19 Section 49C(5)(a) of the CA98.

20 For further details on the conditions that the CMA may impose, see paragraph 3.14 below.

21 Section 49C(5)(b) of the CA98.

BREACHES OF COMPETITION LAW THAT MAY BE COVERED BY AN AUTHORITY-APPROVED REDRESS SCHEME

1.22 Redress schemes eligible for Authority approval may relate to decisions made by the Authority or the European Commission. These decisions may find that the UK and/or EU prohibitions against anti-competitive agreements or abuse of a dominant position have been breached. These prohibitions are contained, respectively, in the Chapter I and Chapter II prohibitions of the CA98 and Articles 101 and 102 of the Treaty on the Functioning of the European Union (TFEU).

1.23 Article 101 of the TFEU and Chapter I of the CA98 prohibit any agreements or concerted practices between businesses which prevent, restrict or distort competition, unless an exemption applies. The types of agreement most likely to be caught by these prohibitions include those that:

- fix the prices to be charged for goods or services;

- limit production; or
- allocate customers or share markets.

1.24 Article 102 of the TFEU and Chapter II of the CA98 prohibit the abuse of a dominant position. A business will hold a dominant position in a market if it is able to behave independently of the normal constraints imposed by competitors, suppliers and customers. It is the abuse, rather than the holding, of a dominant position that is unlawful. In general, a business will be found to be abusing its dominant position if it behaves in a way that exploits customers or has an exclusionary effect on competitors to the detriment of competition. The types of conduct most likely to be caught by these prohibitions include:

- charging excessively high prices;
- predatory low pricing aimed at driving a rival competitor out of business; and
- refusing to supply an existing long-standing customer without good reason.

1.25 Articles 101 and 102 of the TFEU apply to agreements or conduct that have the potential to affect trade between EU countries, while Chapter I and Chapter II of the CA98 apply to agreements or conduct which have the potential to affect trade in the UK.

1.26 Further guidance on Articles 101 and 102 of the TFEU and Chapters I and II of the CA98 can be found on the CMA's webpages, in particular Guidance OFT401 (Agreements and concerted practices) and OFT402 (Abuse of a dominant position).[22]

NOTES

[22] These are available on the CMA's webpages. Several of these guidance documents were published by the CMA's predecessor, the Office of Fair Trading, and have been adopted by the CMA.

AUTHORITY-APPROVED VOLUNTARY REDRESS SCHEMES AS PART OF THE OVERALL REDRESS FRAMEWORK

1.27 Anyone who has suffered harm caused by an infringement of Chapter I or Chapter II of the CA98 or Articles 101 or 102 of the TFEU has a right to compensation for that harm. Authority-approved voluntary redress schemes constitute an additional redress option, alongside individual and collective private actions.[23]

1.28 As noted above, approved voluntary redress schemes are a form of ADR and are intended to serve as an additional option for businesses to offer, and harmed persons to receive, compensation for loss suffered as a result of a competition law breach.

1.29 The potential advantage of an Authority-approved voluntary redress scheme is that it provides a statutory process through which:

- consumers and businesses can gain access to compensation more quickly, easily and without the costs of litigation; and
- businesses that have infringed the competition rules may voluntarily offer and administer redress to those affected by the breach, thereby avoiding lengthy and costly court proceedings. This may also have reputational benefits for businesses. Moreover, businesses may in certain circumstances receive a discount on any penalty imposed by the Authority in respect of the infringement the redress scheme relates to.[24]

Therefore, voluntary redress schemes offer both businesses and individuals a chance of early compromise and avoiding litigation altogether.

1.30 Applying for compensation under a redress scheme approved by the Authority is entirely optional. Potential beneficiaries who decide not to apply for redress under an approved scheme do not lose their right to seek compensation through other means. For example, the approval of a redress scheme by the Authority does not itself prevent a potential beneficiary from:

- bringing an individual private action for damages against an undertaking found liable for breach of the competition rules;
- participating in an opt-in or opt-out collective action; or
- otherwise seeking to obtain compensation.

1.31 The Competition Appeal Tribunal (CAT) may, however, as part of its active case management powers, consider whether ADR has been undertaken for these purposes.[25] This may include use of an Authority-approved redress scheme. In particular, the CAT Rules of Procedure provide that:

- a collective proceedings claim form must state whether the parties have used an ADR procedure;[26]
- in the first case management conference, the CAT may consider staying proceedings while the parties attempt to reach a compromise to avoid proceedings, by ADR or other means;[27]
- as part of the CAT's certification of whether claims are eligible for inclusion in collective proceedings, one of the factors the CAT will take into account includes the availability of ADR and any other means of resolving the dispute;[28] and
- the CAT will also take into account the availability of ADR in determining whether collective proceedings should be opt-in or opt-out.[29]

1.32 In relation to the costs of bringing litigation, both the ordinary courts and the CAT have a wide discretion as to the costs and expenses which are recoverable. In making an order in relation to the payment of costs, the ordinary courts and the CAT will take into account a number of factors. In relation to the CAT, the factors are set out in the CAT Rules of Procedure[30] and include any admissible offer to settle made by a party which is drawn to the CAT's attention. Moreover, in certain circumstances the CAT may take into account in its assessment as to costs any 'without prejudice save as to costs' offers to settle that the business formally makes in litigation.[31] Such an offer might be based on the amount of compensation that the compensating party had proposed earlier in the context of a voluntary redress scheme.

NOTES

23 See Annex C for further details on the private actions framework for competition law.

24 See chapter 3 below.

25 As set out in the Governing principles of the CAT Rules of Procedure (the CAT Rules).

26 See the CAT Rules on collective proceedings.

27 See the CAT Rules on the response to a collective proceedings claim form.

28 See the CAT Rules on the certification of claims as eligible for inclusion in collective proceedings.

29 See the CAT Rules on the certification of claims as eligible for inclusion in collective proceedings.

30 See the CAT Rules on costs.

31 So-called Calderbank offers. Offers made pursuant to the Part 36 regime of the Civil Procedure Rules in the ordinary courts are not discussed in further detail here; such offers attract cost consequences for refusing offers to settle in certain circumstances in order to encourage parties to settle their disputes.

2. APPLYING FOR AUTHORITY APPROVAL AND DEVISING A VOLUNTARY REDRESS SCHEME

[3.184]

2.1 This chapter provides information on: (a) how to apply for Authority approval of a voluntary redress scheme; and (b) how to devise a redress scheme. In particular, the chapter presents the requirements that according to the CA98 and/or the Regulations a redress scheme must satisfy in order to be approved as well as the additional specifications that the Authority would expect a voluntary redress scheme to contain.

APPLICATIONS FOR AUTHORITY APPROVAL OF VOLUNTARY REDRESS SCHEMES

When to apply

2.2 A business wishing to obtain the Authority's approval for a voluntary redress scheme may apply after an infringement decision has been issued by the Authority or the European Commission by submitting a full scheme. The Authority may consider a redress scheme even where a business has challenged the infringement decision, though normally this would be where it contests only the fine (if a fine has been imposed) and not its liability or the existence of a competition law infringement.[32]

2.3 Equally, if there is no infringement decision yet but the Authority is investigating conduct that may constitute a breach of the competition rules, the undertakings under investigation may still apply for approval of a voluntary redress scheme by submitting either a full or an outline scheme. Applications for scheme approval during the course of an ongoing Authority competition investigation are in practice expected to be submitted after the Authority has issued its Statement of Objections to parties under investigation, since that is the point at which businesses will have seen the infringements alleged against them in detail. Nevertheless, it is possible for an undertaking under investigation to apply for redress scheme approval at any time before an infringement decision is adopted. The Authority will not consider it inconsistent for a party to seek approval of a scheme while exercising its rights of defence during the course of an investigation. In multi-party infringements or investigations, parties may choose to seek approval for schemes jointly with one or more other parties to the infringement or the investigation.

NOTES

32 The Authority does not rule out that it might consider applications for redress scheme approval in other circumstances of appeal. In practice, however, it will do so only exceptionally in view of the tension between challenging the existence of the infringement and providing compensation for harm caused by that same infringement.

Pre-application discussions

2.4 Where a potential applicant is considering offering a redress scheme it wishes the Authority to approve, it should approach the Authority at the earliest opportunity for an initial discussion in order to avoid wasting resources. At the end of the pre-application discussions the Authority will inform the potential applicant whether it is minded to prioritise assessing an application for scheme approval or not (see paragraph 3.2 below).

2.5 Where a potential scheme relates to an ongoing Authority competition investigation, the Authority will not consider any expression of interest in setting up a redress scheme as an admission of the suspected infringement being considered by it.

How to apply

2.6 The application must be made in writing[33] using the relevant template application form available on the Authority's webpages.[34] There are two application forms available – one where an infringement decision has already been issued at the time of application, and the other (to be used in relation to an Authority investigation only) where no infringement decision has been issued yet.

2.7 The relevant form must be signed by an appropriate senior representative of the business who is authorised to act on behalf of the business, such as a director or a delegated proxy with power of attorney. Forms may be submitted electronically.

Part 3 CMA and other Guidelines

NOTES

33 Article 3 of the Regulations.

34 The application form contains CMA contact details, and different details will apply if an application is being submitted to a Regulator. See note 3 above for details of Regulators' websites.

Application content

2.8 The application form must comply with the Regulation Requirements and must contain the information set out in paragraph 2.9 below, which includes some information that would ultimately form part of the final terms of a redress scheme under which potential beneficiaries would seek compensation.[35] Where an applicant is seeking unconditional approval of a full scheme, all the information should be supplied with the application for approval. However, as explained above,[36] while an application for conditional approval of an outline scheme must contain sufficient information to enable the Authority to decide whether it is appropriate to grant conditional approval, it will not need to contain all of the information in the first instance.

2.9 The information is as follows:

- Details about the agreement or conduct and the aspects of the relevant infringement decision or investigation in relation to which the scheme is being offered.
- Details about the proposed starting date of the redress scheme. Generally, this should be no more than three months after the date of approval by the Authority or, in the case of conditional approval, no more than three months after the Authority has confirmed that the conditions of the scheme have been met. However, where the compensating parties provide convincing reasons, for example because of complexities around the business' internal governance required to execute the scheme, a later commencement date may be considered appropriate.
- Details about the terms and duration of the redress scheme, and confirmation that it will operate for a period of at least nine months.[37]
- Details about the persons who will be entitled to compensation under the redress scheme,[38] and confirmation that a third party may not submit a claim on behalf of those entitled to compensation under the redress scheme.[39]
- Details about the **scope** of the compensation to be offered under the scheme as determined by the Board and the Chairperson (within any parameters previously suggested by the business).
- Details about the **level** of compensation to be offered under the scheme as determined by the Board and the Chairperson.
- Details about the appointed Chairperson and Board members, including their names and qualifications, as well as confirmation that none of them had a conflict of interest, neither at the time they were appointed nor when they considered whether to recommend approval of the scheme to the Authority.[40]
- The arrangements the applicant made to ensure the Chairperson and Board members had access to relevant information held by the applicant prior to deciding whether to recommend the scheme for approval to the Authority (in the case of a full scheme).[41]
- Confirmation that the Chairperson and Board members considered the relevant matters as defined in the Regulations[42] and anything else deemed relevant, and that they agreed by majority vote that it should be recommended to the Authority for approval.[43]
- Details about the process for applying for compensation under the redress scheme, including estimates as to how long it will take to determine applications for compensation.[44]
- Details about the possible types of evidence that persons entitled to compensation under the redress scheme may submit in support of their application.[45]
- Details about the independent complaints process available for those applying for compensation under the redress scheme.[46]
- Details about the consequences of accepting redress under the scheme.
- Details about how the redress scheme will be advertised and those entitled to compensation under the scheme notified of their entitlement.[47]
- Details about how the applicant will monitor whether the scheme is operating successfully.
- Information about the expected cost to the applicant of administering the scheme, including details as to how the scheme will be resourced.
- Details about any other matter considered to be relevant.
- Contact details for those who can deal with queries about schemes when the Authority announces that it has approved a scheme.

2.10 The application form must also contain:

- a summary of the redress scheme;[48]
- the Chairperson and Board members' recommendation that the Authority approves the redress scheme, along with a report of any minority views; and
- any other relevant document.

NOTES

35 The accompanying footnotes indicate where the information specified a Regulation Requirement. In the absence of a reference to the Regulations, the information is required by the Authority in the exercise of its discretion.

36 See paragraphs 1.16–1.20.

37 Article 7(b) of the Regulations.

38 Article 5(7)(b) of the Regulations.

39 Article 7(a) of the Regulations.

40 Article 6(1)(a) of the Regulations.
41 Article 6(1)(b) of the Regulations.
42 Articles 5(6)(a) and (7) of the Regulations.
43 Article 5(6)(b) of the Regulations.
44 Article 6(1)(c) of the Regulations.
45 Article 5(7)(c) of the Regulations.
46 Article 6(1)(d) of the Regulations.
47 Article 5(7)(d) of the Regulations.
48 Article 3 of the Regulations.

TERMS OF VOLUNTARY REDRESS SCHEMES

2.11 The terms of a voluntary redress scheme must provide potential beneficiaries with sufficient information to make an informed decision as to whether they should seek compensation under the scheme. While under the Regulations it is for the Chairperson and Board to devise a scheme, applicants may wish to decide on the key parameters within which the scheme will be devised and ensure that it is communicated clearly to the Chairperson and Board. For example, an applicant may wish to specify that a scheme should compensate direct purchasers only, or that it should compensate so-called umbrella[49] claims.

2.12 The terms should specify the following:
(a) the requirements to produce evidence in support of an application for redress under the scheme;
(b) who is to be entitled to compensation under the scheme;
(c) the process for applying for compensation under the redress scheme;
(d) how the redress scheme will be advertised and how those entitled to compensation under the scheme will be notified of their entitlement;
(e) the independent complaints process available for those applying for compensation under the scheme;
(f) the scope of compensation to be offered by the scheme; and
(g) the consequences of accepting redress under the scheme.[50]

NOTES

49 See paragraph 2.14 below.
50 Article 5(6)(a) of the Regulations – read in conjunction with Article 5(7) – requires the Chairperson and Board members to consider the matters at points *(a)* to *(e)*.

Entitlement to compensation under the redress scheme

2.13 The terms of the scheme must define the category of persons that the scheme is intended to compensate, ie those who are entitled to apply for compensation under the scheme. In this regard, the applicant will need to decide, for example, whether a scheme will cover indirect as well as direct purchasers. If a scheme covers both direct and indirect purchasers, the applicant may wish to consider taking appropriate steps to minimise the risk of double recovery.[51] This risk may arise where, for instance, a direct and indirect purchaser both seek to recover the same overcharge under the scheme, or where a direct purchaser seeks redress under the scheme and an indirect purchaser claims compensation for the same loss through the courts.

NOTES

51 According to article 2(23) and (24) of the Damages Actions Directive (Directive 2014/104/EU of 26 November 2014), 'direct purchaser' means a natural or legal person who acquired, directly from an infringer, products or services that were the object of an infringement of competition law, whereas 'indirect purchaser' means a natural or legal person who acquired, not directly from an infringer, but from a direct purchaser or a subsequent purchaser, products or services that were the object of an infringement of competition law, or products or services containing them or derived therefrom.

Scope of compensation offered under the scheme

2.14 The applicant must determine the scope of compensation to be offered under the scheme. For example, the applicant may need to decide whether compensation will cover only direct loss (such as the overcharge resulting from the infringement), or also other losses such as any reduced sales resulting from a potential beneficiary charging higher prices to customers because of the infringement overcharge.[52] Similarly, the applicant may need to determine whether redress under the scheme will compensate loss in respect of purchases made from infringing parties only, or also those from vendors not party to an infringement but who adapted to a price increase resulting from a cartel by increasing their own prices (so-called 'umbrella claims'). Furthermore, the applicant may need to determine whether the scheme will cover harm inflicted within the UK only, or also harm outside the UK. This may be appropriate, for example, where the redress scheme is offered in connection with a European Commission infringement decision.

2.15 Depending on the circumstances, the applicant may also need to make decisions about variable compensation, where victims may have suffered differing levels of harm depending on how much of the good or service affected by the competition infringement they purchased. For example, if the harm resulted from overcharges on airline tickets, a victim's harm would depend on the number of tickets they purchased during the relevant period. It might also depend on the precise ticket purchased. For example, there may be a greater overcharge on a ticket costing £1,000 than on one costing £100, although it would depend on the type of ticket purchased.

2.16 The applicant should also specify whether redress under the scheme will be provided in monetary or non-monetary form.[53] For example, in some limited circumstances it may be appropriate for compensation under the scheme to be provided in the form of non-monetary solutions, such as vouchers or coupons. However, potential beneficiaries should generally be given the option of choosing between monetary and non-monetary solutions.

2.17 Redress schemes should include a clear statement of the ambit of the redress scheme and in particular of the entitlement criteria and the type and extent of compensation that is being offered. This should enable potential beneficiaries to evaluate appropriately whether they are entitled to compensation and to decide whether to accept redress under a scheme or pursue redress through another route.

NOTES

52 Applicants should bear in mind that individuals who have suffered harm from their competition law infringement may still seek compensation in court for heads of loss which are not covered by the redress scheme. See also paragraph 2.40 below.

53 See section 49C(12)(a) of the CA98 as amended by the CRA15.

The process for applying for compensation under the redress scheme

2.18 The scheme must set out the process by which potential beneficiaries should apply for compensation and the procedures for handling applications. This may vary on a case by case basis, but as a minimum it should include an identification number per application and a reasonable timetable for notifying potential beneficiaries whether their application has been accepted and when compensation will be paid.

2.19 It is expected that a scheme will specify a scheme administrator (which may be an employee of the business or a third party) to whom applications for redress will be submitted, along with evidence of harm suffered that is capable of satisfying the evidential requirements of the scheme.

2.20 A scheme must also state specifically the closing date by which applications for redress must be submitted. According to the Regulations, schemes must be open for a period of at least nine months,[54] and applicants are expected to consider carefully whether in all the circumstances a particular scheme should be open for longer.

NOTES

54 Article 7(b) of the Regulations.

Evidence requirements

2.21 The terms of the scheme must stipulate what evidence a potential scheme beneficiary[55] needs to provide in support of an application for compensation under the redress scheme. Such evidence requirements must be fair and reasonable.

2.22 For example:

- in an infringement relating to air travel, the names of the passengers and the dates and place of departure and destination may be appropriate evidence;
- in an infringement relating to items of significant value, such as, for instance, televisions, laptops or manufacturing equipment, the receipt of purchase or the warranty for the product may be appropriate evidence. Other evidence such as entries on bank or credit card statements may also be acceptable;
- in an infringement relating to the sale of small-value items or everyday goods (such as milk or toothpaste) by a retailer, presentation of a loyalty card for the relevant retailer may constitute appropriate evidence. The Authority would expect businesses offering a redress scheme to use information at their disposal to facilitate applications for compensation by potential scheme beneficiaries, for example, by providing customer records; and
- in an infringement relating to items that potential scheme beneficiaries may have bought a long time ago, such as clothing or tools, a photograph of the item in question may be appropriate evidence.

2.23 The methods by which evidence would have to be submitted would need to be fair and reasonable. For example, a range of different methods such as post and electronic methods should be accepted.

2.24 Where compensating parties have in their possession data allowing them to identify all the individuals that have suffered harm as a result of the competition infringement, it may not be appropriate to require potential scheme beneficiaries to produce evidence of their harm. This approach would also reduce the cost to the compensating party of having to check and verify the evidence of harm submitted by potential scheme beneficiaries.

NOTES

55 In this guidance, references to 'scheme beneficiary' or 'potential scheme beneficiary' include consumers and/or businesses as appropriate.

The independent complaints process

2.25 The terms of the redress scheme must set out an independent complaints process that can be followed if a complaint arises in the course of an application for compensation under the scheme and must explain in detail how it will operate. As set out below, the complaints process covers both complaints about rejection of an application for compensation on non-entitlement grounds and failure to deliver compensation.

2.26 Recourse to the complaints process shall be free of charge for potential beneficiaries, and there should be no fee, whether refundable or not, for using it. The complaints process should be carried out by a person independent of the compensating party (the 'independent reviewer'), which might be a third party, the Chairperson or the Board. In the latter case, it may not be necessary to reconvene the whole Board; depending on the issue in question, a single Board member may be sufficient to perform this function.

2.27 The outcome of the complaints process will not affect the complainant's right to otherwise seek compensation for their loss. The Authority will not take part in considering complaints or any other forms of appeal against the scheme, its terms or its administration.

Complaints about the rejection of a potential beneficiary's application for compensation under the redress scheme on grounds of non-entitlement

2.28 There may be various reasons why an application for compensation under the redress scheme may be rejected on grounds of non-entitlement. For example:

- the potential beneficiary may mistakenly believe that they fall within the scope of the scheme as a result of having misunderstood its terms;
- the potential beneficiary may not have produced sufficient evidence of their entitlement to compensation under the scheme; or
- the compensating party may be applying the terms of the scheme too strictly.

2.29 While the former two reasons might be legitimate grounds for rejecting an application, the latter would not be.

2.30 A potential beneficiary whose initial application for compensation under the scheme has been rejected must be informed by the scheme administrator of the reasons for the rejection. They must also be informed of their right:

- to complain to an independent reviewer,[56] as specified in the scheme, through the independent complaints process; or
- if appropriate, to resubmit their original application for compensation under the scheme. For instance, if a potential beneficiary falls within the scope of the scheme but did not supply all the relevant evidence they have, they should have the chance to supply the missing evidence as an addition to their original application without having to go through the complaints process.

NOTES

56 Where the submitted complaints suggest the existence of a systemic problem with the decision-making or the administration of the scheme, it may be appropriate for the independent reviewer to bring this to the attention of the Chairperson and the Board.

Complaints about the compensating party's failure to deliver compensation to those found entitled to compensation under the scheme

2.31 It is possible that the compensating party or parties may fail to deliver compensation to those found entitled to compensation under the scheme.

2.32 When potential beneficiaries are informed that their application for compensation under the scheme has been accepted, they must also be notified by the scheme administrator about the complaints process in the event of a potential failure of the compensating party to deliver compensation. If compensation is not delivered, a potential beneficiary may wish, through the complaints process, to make a final request for the compensating party or parties to award redress in accordance with the terms of the scheme, before taking formal enforcement action (see chapter 4 for further details) and/or bringing the matter to the Authority's attention.

Advertising requirements

2.33 The terms of the scheme must also set out how it will be advertised[57] and those entitled to compensation under the scheme will be notified of their entitlement.

2.34 Compensating parties will be expected to consider what level of advertising is appropriate in their case, for example:

- targeting the advertising of their scheme through appropriate channels taking into account the nature of the product or service the compensation relates to and the geographical scope of the infringement, as appropriate, such as specialist press, internet advertising and social media campaigns;
- advertising the scheme on their own website (if they have one); and/or
- contacting potential beneficiaries they have contact details for (eg from the operation of a loyalty scheme).

2.35 Compensating parties should also consider advertising at point of sale if this is appropriate to the nature of the infringement, for example where the infringement relates to repeat purchase goods, such as milk or toothpaste.

2.36 Moreover, it may also be appropriate for compensating parties to notify consumer bodies and/or small business representatives (for example, Which?, Citizens Advice, or the Federation of Small Businesses). This may be the case, for example, where the infringement affects a large number of consumers and/or small businesses, or where consumers and/or small businesses are likely to contact such bodies and organisations to enquire about their redress options.

2.37 In addition to any specific forms of advertising provided for in a scheme, existing approved redress schemes will be publicised on the webpages of:

- the government;
- the Department for Business, Innovation & Skills; and
- the CMA and/or the relevant Regulator.[58]

NOTES

[57] Advertising would need to comply with applicable consumer protection laws, including the Consumer Protection from Unfair Trading Regulations 2008 and the Business Protection from Misleading Marketing Regulations 2008. Relevant sectoral legislation and rules may also be relevant to communications with customers.

[58] The Regulator webpages are provided in footnote 3 above.

The consequences of accepting redress under a scheme

2.38 The terms of the scheme must specify what the consequences of accepting redress under it are for potential beneficiaries.

2.39 A redress scheme may typically state that a scheme beneficiary who has accepted redress offered under the scheme does so on the basis of a full and final settlement and therefore cannot bring an individual private action for damages or participate in a collective action with respect to that loss. This may be necessary in order to ensure that the compensating party will not pay twice for the same harm.

2.40 Nevertheless, a redress scheme may not prevent a scheme beneficiary from bringing an individual private action or from participating in a collective action against:

- the compensating party for losses not falling within the scope of the scheme. For example, if the scheme covers only direct losses, beneficiaries will still be able to seek redress for their indirect losses through other means, including litigation;
- other parties to the competition infringement which have not set up a voluntary redress scheme for the harm inflicted by their conduct; or
- the compensating party where the beneficiary's claim under the scheme was rejected.

2.41 As set out at paragraph 1.31 above, in considering individual or collective actions for damages the CAT may take into account the existence of an alternative dispute resolution procedure, including an Authority-approved redress scheme. The time limits for a person to bring a claim outside of an Authority-approved scheme are not affected by the process of applying for compensation under the redress scheme.

APPOINTMENT AND ROLE OF THE CHAIRPERSON AND THE BOARD

2.42 As already noted above, a Chairperson and Board will need to be appointed to devise a scheme according to the Required Process. The Chairperson and all members of the Board must possess appropriate qualifications and experience to carry out their functions effectively.

Appointment of the Chairperson and the Board members

2.43 The applicant will appoint a Chairperson who must be a senior lawyer or judge. Specifically, the Chairperson must:

- satisfy the judicial appointment eligibility condition for England and Wales on a five-year basis;[59]
- be an advocate or solicitor in Scotland of at least five years' standing; or
- be a member of the Bar of Northern Ireland or solicitor of the Court of Judicature of Northern Ireland of at least five years' standing.

2.44 The Authority would also expect the Chairperson to demonstrate appropriate experience and knowledge of competition law and practice, or any other relevant law and practice.

2.45 The Chairperson, rather than the applicant, will be responsible for appointing the members of the Board. The Board must comprise:

- an economist with appropriate experience and knowledge of competition economics to be able to consider the redress scheme. The Authority would expect the economist Board member to demonstrate the requisite technical or specialist knowledge and expertise. This would be through a number of years' experience working as an economist and through having obtained the appropriate academic qualifications;
- a person with experience of the industry of the applicant;
- a person who is able to represent the interests of those who may be entitled to compensation under the redress scheme. If potential beneficiaries include consumers, the representative should be from a recognised consumer body (for example, Which? or Citizens Advice), a group specific to a particular industry (such as a passenger group), or an independent academic institution.[60] If the potential beneficiaries also include businesses, it may be appropriate for there to be an additional representative, such as from a trade association. Chairpersons should also consider carefully whether it may be appropriate for there to be more than one Board member representing the interests of potential beneficiaries. For example, where both direct and indirect purchasers have suffered harm from the infringement in question, it may be appropriate for the Chairperson to appoint a Board member for each of these categories of potential beneficiaries in order to ensure that their interests are adequately represented; and
- any other person considered suitable by the Chairperson, for example an accountant or a market expert where specialist knowledge of a particular sector, industry or consumer demographic is required (beyond the expertise provided by the industry representative).

2.46 In appointing the members of the Board, the Chairperson must take the requirements above into account.

2.47 The Chairperson and the Board are to be remunerated by the applicant. Before appointing the members of the Board, the Chairperson will consult with the applicant to ensure that it will undertake to pay the cost of their appointment. The Authority would expect the parties to agree a suitable and adequate remuneration structure and would expect the Chairperson and Board members to be remunerated in a way that does not impede their independence and objectivity. In particular, the Chairperson's and the Board members' remuneration must not be dependent on the outcome of any aspects of their assessment of the scheme as this would be a conflict of interest.

2.48 Depending on the circumstances, administrative or other support may be required to assist the Chairperson and the Board members in performing their functions. For example, depending on the case, the economist Board member may require support to consider questions relating to the amount of overcharge caused by an infringement. However, the Chairperson and the Board shall retain oversight at all times and cannot delegate its functions and responsibilities to other persons.

NOTES

59 The eligibility condition is to be a solicitor or barrister, or hold any other relevant legal qualification in England and Wales and have experience in law, for at least five years – for example, exercising judicial functions in a court or tribunal, giving legal advice, arbitration, teaching or researching law.

60 Such as a university.

Duties of the Chairperson and the Board members

2.49 The Chairperson and the Board members must act with:

- independence;
- impartiality;
- objectivity;
- integrity; and
- honesty.

2.50 The Chairperson and the Board members must act on the basis of the evidence, which may – where appropriate – include drawing reasonable inferences from that evidence or an absence of evidence.

2.51 The Chairperson and the Board members must act in accordance with their respective capacities and roles.

2.52 The Chairperson and the Board members must perform their functions:

- with reasonable skill and care;
- in accordance with the law; and
- where appropriate, in accordance with the rules governing their professional conduct.

2.53 Whether there is an actual or potential conflict of interest should be determined case by case. A conflict may be likely to arise where a Chairperson and Board members have interests that might reasonably be perceived to, or might actually, influence their independence and/or impartiality in performing their functions. In relation to the Chairperson or the economist Board member, where that person has a history of acting predominantly for claimants or defendants, the Authority does not consider that necessarily risks impeding their ability to perform Chairperson and Board functions impartially in the absence of specific evidence or concerns in a particular case.

2.54 Actual or potential conflicts of interests may arise out of, but are not limited to:

- acting or having acted in a professional capacity in relation to the competition infringement in question or a related infringement of the CA98 or the TFEU;
- any form of past or current employment with, or engagement by, the applicant within the previous two years, with the exception of their employment as members of a Board under an Authority-approved scheme;
- any financial interest in the applicant;
- publication of views or comments relating to the applicant and/or the specific competition infringement at hand;[61]
- a close personal association or relationship with a person who is working for or advising the applicant, such as close family or personal ties (for example spouse, partner, child, sibling, parent or close friend).

2.55 While the above examples illustrate potential conflicts of interest that could favour the applicant, the Chairperson and Board members must equally be free of conflicts of interest that may be expected to favour potential scheme beneficiaries.

2.56 Even without an actual or potential conflict, the Chairperson and Board members must refrain from any activities that might interfere with or in any way compromise the performance of their functions.

2.57 The Board members must disclose to the Chairperson any circumstances likely to give rise to any doubts about their impartiality and independence as soon as they become aware of their existence. In the case of the Chairperson, such disclosure should be made to the compensating party and the Authority.

2.58 The Chairperson and the members of the Board must sign a formal undertaking declaring that they will act in accordance with the principles and duties set out in this section of the guidance. A template undertaking can be found in Annex B.

2.59 If after appointment it becomes clear that the Chairperson or a Board member does not meet the impartiality criteria (for example, because they have an undisclosed conflict of interest), they should be removed and replaced with a new person who meets the relevant criteria described above. The applicant should make the Authority aware of such an eventuality at the earliest opportunity.

NOTES

[61] Having published views or comments in relation to the type of the competition infringement in question will generally be insufficient to trigger a conflict of interest.

Function of the Chairperson and the Board

2.60 The primary function of the Chairperson and the Board will be to devise the redress scheme, whether prior to the Authority's full unconditional approval or pursuant to a condition of outline approval. In particular, the Chairperson and the Board will consider the following matters:

- The scope of compensation to be offered under the scheme (within any parameters set by the applicant); for example, where a scheme covers both direct and indirect purchasers, the Chairperson and the Board will need to consider carefully where in the supply chain the loss has been suffered as well as any initial proposals made by the applicant for addressing the risk of double recovery.[62]
- The evidence that the applicant has provided about the loss caused to potential scheme beneficiaries, and how this has been aggregated. In certain cases it may also be necessary for the Chairperson and the Board to obtain further evidence of harm.[63]
- The appropriate level of redress for each potential category of scheme beneficiary (although in some cases it may be more appropriate for the Chairperson and the Board to determine the aggregate level of redress owed to potential scheme beneficiaries) and/or the methodology to be applied in determining that level of redress.
- Who is entitled to compensation under the redress scheme, the application process, including any evidence requirements, the independent complaints process available for those applying for compensation under the redress scheme and how the scheme will be advertised and those entitled to compensation will be notified of their entitlement.

2.61 In devising a redress scheme within any parameters suggested by the applicant, the Chairperson and the Board may take into account any initial suggestions made by the applicant as to how the redress scheme might operate, and its terms.

2.62 It is for the Chairperson and the Board to determine the amount of compensation they consider appropriate, based on relevant factual and economic evidence provided by the applicant, and using an appropriate framework/methodology. The Chairperson and the Board are expected to produce a report determining the exact level of redress to be provided under the scheme and/or the methodology to be applied by the applicant in determining the amount of redress for each beneficiary.

2.63 In this regard, the principles contained in the European Commission's practical guide to quantifying harm in private actions for damages for national courts may be of assistance to the Chairperson and the Board.[64] The Authority notes that the government created the possibility for the Authority to approve schemes in order to provide a swift and relatively low cost way of providing redress, while ensuring the interests of those harmed are properly considered and safeguarded. In those circumstances, it is expected that the use of independent economic evidence and experts (beyond the economist on the Board) in setting up and assessing the terms of the scheme should be significantly less than in, for example, a contested judicial process. As a result, such use should be kept to the minimum reasonably necessary to assess compensation. That said, it should be recognised that expert evidence may be necessary in certain situations. For example, in order to facilitate indirect/consumer purchaser redress, it may be needed to determine the level of, or any passing on of, any overcharge caused by the infringement. The need for such evidence may vary case by case. For instance, there might be a greater need for it where a full scheme is submitted for approval prior to a CMA infringement decision.

2.64 In addition to their primary function, the Chairperson and Board may, at the request of the compensating party, reconvene at a later date in order to provide any guidance it considers necessary. The guidance may be in relation to the implementation, interpretation or application of any determination the Chairperson and the Board have made, or regarding the administration of the scheme in respect of individual customers or customer classes. Whether such an approach is taken may vary case by case.

2.65 The Chairperson and the Board are expected to comply with the approach set out in this guidance when performing their roles in relation to the scheme, unless it can be demonstrated to the Authority's satisfaction that there are good reasons for taking a different approach.

NOTES

[62] See also paragraph 2.13 above.

[63] See also paragraphs 2.75 and 2.78 below.

[64] See the guide published in the Official Journal of the European Union.

Recommendation of the Chairperson and the Board

2.66 Once the Chairperson and Board have devised a redress scheme, they must then vote on whether to recommend it to the Authority for approval. The scheme can only be recommended to the Authority if a majority vote in favour of it. If the number of votes is equal, the majority requirement is not met.

2.67 If at least a majority of the Chairperson and the Board agree that a scheme should be recommended to the Authority, the Chairperson should make that recommendation to the Authority as soon as possible.[65]

2.68 If a majority of the Chairperson and Board members do not agree that the scheme should be recommended for approval (for example because of a difference of opinion over the level or scope of compensation), it cannot be put to the Authority. In those circumstances, the applicant will need to decide whether it is prepared to amend the scheme in a way that satisfies the concerns raised by those who voted against the scheme. If it was, the scheme would then need to be returned to the Chairperson and Board to reconsider recommending it for approval. If the applicant is unwilling or unable to amend the scheme in a way that garners majority approval, the applicant will need to abandon the scheme.

2.69 The Chairperson's and Board members' recommendation on the scheme must identify the information on the basis of which they reached their decision on the level of redress, alongside the methodology they applied. Moreover, where the recommendation for Authority approval is not unanimous, the report on the scheme should make it clear that there are dissenting opinions, and should include details of the material points of dissent and the reasoning behind them.

2.70 Whether a recommendation is unanimous or not, the Chairperson and the Board members will take collective responsibility for any decision made by them. However, the Authority would expect each member to take lead responsibility for the assessment of their particular area of expertise. For example, the economist member of the Board is likely to take the lead in assessing the economic evidence in determining the appropriate level of redress.

2.71 While the Chairperson and Board are normally expected to devise schemes with regard to the parameters suggested by the applicant (and, in the case of conditional outline approval, conditionally approved by the Authority), they may consider that a scheme should go beyond those parameters. In those circumstances, the Chairperson and Board might vote not to recommend a scheme for approval by the Authority on the grounds that the parameters suggested by the applicant were inappropriate. Equally, they might vote to recommend a scheme to the Authority that was wider than that specified by the applicant. The Authority would expect the applicant and the Chairperson and Board to explore whether an appropriate solution could be found. If ultimately the Chairperson and Board chose not to recommend a scheme for approval by the Authority, the scheme could not proceed. If instead the Chairperson and Board chose to recommend a scheme for approval, the Authority would consider whether it was appropriate to explore whether the application should be withdrawn and a new application made (in the case of a full scheme), or whether a replacement scheme could be approved (in the case of an outline scheme – see paragraphs 3.16 to 3.19 below).

NOTES

65 The Chairperson's role in making the recommendation is to convey the views of those who have considered the scheme.

Confidentiality and privilege

2.72 The Chairperson and the Board members are required to treat as confidential any information supplied to them in confidence (and appropriately identified as confidential) by the applicant and any other persons from whom they may obtain relevant information, unless otherwise agreed with the provider of that information. This includes any information that would be covered by privilege.[66] While it should not often be necessary, disputes over confidentiality should be settled by an independent person with appropriate experience and expertise.[67]

2.73 The Chairperson and the Board members must not disclose confidential (and, where relevant, privileged) information other than as permitted or required by law, or with the consent of the party to which the information relates. They may only use such information for the purposes of performing their functions in devising and recommending the scheme at hand. All communications with the Chairperson and the Board members must be made on a confidential and where relevant on a privileged/without prejudice basis. Any privilege over those communications is to be retained unless and until it is expressly waived by the person entitled to assert it. As a matter of practicality, parties may wish to consider marking all documents appropriately and entering into suitable confidentiality agreements to expressly provide for the terms on which information is provided to the Chairperson and the Board members, and how documents, electronic or otherwise, should be treated.

2.74 However, as an exception, the Chairperson and the Board may share with the Authority where necessary – and the Authority may use – details of communications in the performance of their roles in the redress scheme approval process. The Authority does not consider it is incompatible with any claims to privilege for documents associated with the redress scheme process to be shared by the Chairperson and the Board with the Authority for the limited purposes of the Authority carrying out its assessment. Documents that may be protected by privilege (whether in whole or in part) may be disclosed to the Authority in confidence and on a limited waiver basis. The Authority would continue to treat such documents in confidence[68] and would expect to resist any claim for onward disclosure in favour of any third parties to the extent possible under law. In the Authority's view, it would not be a waiver (implied or express) of any privilege for it to be provided with material in confidence for this specific and limited purpose. Insofar as it is consistent with applicable legal duties, the Authority would only use such documents for the sole purpose of carrying out any assessments required under the redress scheme approval process. In certain circumstances, it may be sufficient for the Authority to be provided with only a summary of the underlying information provided to the Chairperson and the Board members. However, the underlying information could be provided subsequently on request if the Authority considered it was required in order to carry out its assessment.

NOTES

66 Including legal advice privilege, litigation privilege, without prejudice privilege. Joint or common interest privilege may be relevant in certain circumstances.

[67] This may, for example, be independent legal counsel.

[68] The Authority has a common interest in maintaining the confidentiality of all such communications for the proper functioning of the redress scheme approval process. The Authority considers that the restrictions on disclosure in Part 9 of the Enterprise Act 2002 would also apply.

Fact-finding by the Chairperson and the Board members and cooperation by the applicant

2.75 The applicant is expected to cooperate fully with the Chairperson and the Board members within the timescales agreed with them. In particular, it is expected to provide the Chairperson and the Board with all the assistance and information they may reasonably and proportionately require in order to discharge their functions. This may include, but is not limited to:

- providing evidence of harm (by way of, for example, an expert report and the information/data used to prepare that report);
- providing full and complete access to all the applicant's personnel, books, records, documents and information that the Chairperson and the Board may require, in addition to the evidence referred to above;
- providing information that is not related to the applicant but is reasonably available to, or accessible by, them. What is considered reasonable may vary case by case, but it is not expected that the Chairperson and the Board members will need to request that an applicant obtains information that will require it to incur significant costs relative to the likely level of compensation; and
- providing any office and supporting facilities that the Chairperson and the Board members may require.

2.76 The applicant must not obstruct the Chairperson and the Board members from performing their functions, and the information and evidence it provides to the Authority as well as the Chairperson and the Board, must be complete and accurate in all material respects.[69] Provision of false or misleading information may in certain circumstances also amount to a criminal offence.[70]

2.77 The extent to which the Chairperson and the Board will take into account any evidence of harm submitted by the applicant will depend on its scope and quality. In any event, the Chairperson and the Board members are expected to take reasonable steps to obtain appropriate information from the applicant and/or third parties in order to satisfy themselves that the terms of the redress scheme and the amount of redress to be offered under it are appropriate, having regard to the principles in paragraph 2.75 above.

2.78 The applicant may ask the Chairperson and the Board to provide it with an estimate of the anticipated costs of the Chairperson and the Board early in the process so as to enable it to calculate the overall cost of running the redress scheme. If the estimated amount exceeds what the applicant had expected, the applicant will have to decide whether it is willing and able to cover the additional cost or whether it prefers to abandon the redress scheme altogether. If a business took the latter course of action where an outline scheme had already been approved, the Authority considers that would amount to a breach of conditions imposed. For example, the requirement in the Regulations that the Chairperson and the Board members have considered the relevant matters and have by majority vote recommended the scheme to the Authority for approval (which the Authority would have made a condition of outline approval) would not be met. Consequently, the Authority would expect to revoke scheme approval. In such circumstances the Authority would consider whether to seek recovery of any penalty reduction granted in recognition of conditional scheme approval.

NOTES

[69] The Authority may reject an application for approval of a redress scheme, or revoke conditional approval of such an application, if it is suspected that a compensating party has supplied to the Board, the Chairperson or the Authority information that is false or misleading in a material respect. Additionally, as noted in footnote 70 below, in certain circumstances provision of false or misleading information may amount to a criminal offence

[70] It is a criminal offence for a person to knowingly or recklessly supply information to the Authority in connection with a CA98 investigation which that person knows to be false or misleading in a material particular (section 44 of the CA98).

3. THE AUTHORITY'S ASSESSMENT OF APPLICATIONS FOR REDRESS SCHEME APPROVAL

[3.185]

3.1 This chapter sets out guidance on the process the Authority expects to follow when assessing applications for approval of a voluntary redress scheme.

PRIORITISATION AND TIMEFRAME

3.2 The Authority has discretion whether or not to consider schemes for approval. At the end of the pre-application discussions the Authority will tell the potential applicant whether it intends to prioritise an application for redress scheme approval or not. The Authority would generally expect to prioritise applications for redress scheme approval in relation to an ongoing investigation. In the case of an application for approval after an infringement decision has been made, the Authority will decide whether to consider it or not on a case by case basis according to its published prioritisation principles,[71] as appropriate.

3.3 If the Authority decides to consider an application for redress scheme approval (whether in respect of a full scheme or an outline scheme), it will in the majority of cases aim to assess it and notify applicants of the outcome within a three month timescale from the day when a complete formal application[72] is received.

3.4 In the case of applications submitted during the course of a competition investigation, formal scheme approval cannot take place until the point at which the Authority makes its infringement decision. However, if the Authority planned to approve a scheme, it would in the majority of cases expect to give compensating parties a preliminary indication of that fact within approximately three months of receiving a complete formal application[73] for approval, even if any approval is not formalised until later. Any preliminary indication that the Authority planned to approve a scheme would not prevent the Authority from making a later final decision to reject a scheme. Where the Authority has conditionally approved an outline scheme, it will in the majority of cases aim to assess whether the conditions have been satisfied and whether to confirm or revoke approval or seek a replacement scheme within a two to three month timescale after the Board and the Chairperson have produced their report on the scheme.

NOTES

71 See Prioritisation Principles for the CMA (CMA16).

72 A complete formal application is one that provides the Authority with sufficient information to assess whether conditional or full approval should be granted or whether the application should be rejected.

73 See note 72 above for definition of a complete formal application.

SCOPE OF THE AUTHORITY'S ASSESSMENT

3.5 In assessing whether it is appropriate to approve a scheme (including whether the scheme has been set up according to the Regulation Requirements), the Authority will not consider in detail the underlying elements of the scheme, particularly where such a detailed assessment would duplicate or undermine in practice the work of a Chairperson and a properly-constituted Board.

3.6 Nevertheless, the Authority may, although it is not obliged to, take into account:

- the terms of the redress scheme, and in particular:
  - — the duration of the scheme;
  - — the adequacy of the advertising plans;
  - — the fairness and reasonableness of the evidence requirements;
  - — the Chairperson's and the Board members' terms of engagement, which must be clear and ensure their independence and objectivity in carrying out theirs functions;
  - — the consequences of accepting redress under the scheme; and
  - — whether the scheme ensures vulnerable consumers' access to redress.
- whether the Chairperson and the Board members took into account all the relevant matters and complied with this guidance (or any explanation of why it was necessary to take a different approach to the guidance);
- the scope and level of compensation offered under the scheme[74] and the Chairperson's and the Board's relevant determination. For example, where on the face of the case indirect purchasers are likely to have suffered harm from the competition infringement, the Authority would normally expect schemes to cover damage that has been caused to both direct and indirect purchasers, unless a good reason for taking a different approach is provided;
- any dissenting views from Board members or the Chairperson; and
- the views of the applicant where the recommendation of the Chairperson and the Board includes elements of compensation that go beyond the scope of the scheme initially proposed by the applicant in the context of an outline scheme conditionally approved by the Authority.[75]

NOTES

74 Section 49C(3) of the CA98 as amended by the CRA15.

75 Consistent with paragraph 2.8 above, an applicant seeking conditional approval of an outline scheme will not need to have provided full details of the scheme. Consequently, when considering whether to conditionally approve an outline scheme the Authority assessment described at paragraph 3.6 above will be based on the available information provided by the applicant.

APPROVAL PROCESS AND OUTCOMES

General

3.7 Having assessed an application for approval of a redress scheme, the investigating Authority may:

- in the case of a full scheme, approve or reject it; and
- in the case of an outline scheme, approve it with conditions (see paragraphs 3.13 to 3.19 below) or reject it.[76, 77]

3.8 Given that the expert independent Board members and the Chairperson will have determined, or will subsequently have to determine, both the compensation under the scheme, and that they consider the terms of the scheme are appropriate, the Authority expects that in practice it will revoke conditional approval of an outline scheme or unconditional approval of a full scheme in exceptional circumstances only (see further paragraph 3.16 below). If during its assessment the Authority has concerns regarding any of the matters it may take into account when deciding whether to approve a scheme (whether outline or full) and is considering rejecting a scheme, it would expect to provide the applicant and the Chairperson and Board (as appropriate) with the opportunity to respond (including providing more information) before finally approving or rejecting the scheme. If the Chairperson and the Board provide any such information to the Authority, it should be with notice to the party that provided them with the information. Provision to the Authority by the Chairperson and the Board or by the applicant will be on a confidential and limited waiver basis, and will continue to attract 'without prejudice privilege' (save where this is expressly waived by the person entitled to assert that privilege).

3.9 If any changes to the terms of the scheme initially submitted to the Authority result from this exercise, or otherwise, the applicant will be given an opportunity to confirm the new terms of the scheme by which they would be bound if the Authority approved the scheme. A sufficiently senior representative of the compensating party, such as a director, will be expected to sign the final version of the scheme they are content to be bound by before any Authority approval of the scheme.

NOTES

76 Sections 49C(3) and (4) of the CA98 as amended by the CRA15.

77 As with other decisions of public bodies, the Authority's decision to approve or reject an application for scheme approval could potentially be challenged via judicial review.

Approval process where there is already an infringement decision at the time of the application for approval

3.10 Where an infringement decision has already been made, the Authority can only consider a full redress scheme. There will be no repayment of any penalty amount imposed and the Authority cannot consider an outline redress scheme. Because the Authority is unable to impose conditions where scheme approval relates to an infringement decision that has already been made, prior to submitting a formal application for approval of a full scheme, the applicant must:

- notify the Authority of its intention to offer a redress scheme by stating in writing the proposed Chairperson it has chosen and the Board members that the proposed Chairperson has chosen; and
- inform the Authority of the intended scope of compensation.

3.11 If the Authority considers that the Chairperson and the Board do not meet the relevant criteria, it has 28 days in which to object. If the Authority does not object, the applicant can proceed with formally appointing the Chairperson of the Board who will, in turn, formally appoint the members of the Board that he or she had proposed. The Chairperson and the Board members then determine the precise levels of compensation and decide, by majority vote, whether or not the scheme will be recommended to the Authority for approval.

3.12 If the application is submitted formally to the Authority for scheme approval, the Authority will then determine whether to reject the application or approve the scheme unconditionally, taking into account the relevant matters set out in paragraphs 3.5 and 3.6 above. If an application is rejected by the Authority, or withdrawn by the applicant, the Authority will return to the applicant all scheme-related documentation received from it.

Approval process where there is no pre-existing infringement decision at the time of the application for approval

3.13 Where a scheme is submitted for approval before an infringement decision has been made in an investigation, an outline scheme or a full scheme may be submitted to the Authority. Approval of the redress scheme will come into force only if the investigating Authority makes an infringement decision against the applicant.[78] The Authority does not expect to publicise that an application for approval of a scheme has been submitted during the course of an ongoing investigation. Similarly, applicants are expected not to disclose that they have applied, or taken steps to apply, to the Authority for approval of a scheme without first consulting the Authority.

3.14 Where an applicant submits an outline scheme, the Authority will consider whether or not to approve it. In accordance with section 49C of the CA98, the Authority's approval of an outline redress scheme will be subject to conditions requiring the applicant to comply with the Regulation Requirements by a specified time (likely to be after the Chairperson's and the Board's assessment).[79] The Authority may also set other conditions for approval:

- Most other conditions will require the applicant to provide further information to the Authority. Such information conditions will include (but are not limited to) applicants providing the Authority with information about how the redress scheme ultimately will satisfy the unfulfilled Regulation Requirements.[80] For example, the applicant may be requested to provide:
  - details of the Chairperson and Board members actually appointed; and
  - a copy of the Chairperson's and the Board's determination, specifying the exact level of redress to be offered under the scheme, and explaining the methodology that the Chairperson and the Board members applied to arrive at that level (and including details of any minority views where their determination was not unanimous).
- The Authority will consider whether, and if so, what, further conditions should be imposed alongside information conditions case by case. However, it would generally expect to impose at least the following conditions that:
  - any further information required under conditions must be provided by a particular date;
  - the Authority does not have significant concerns with the Chairperson's and the Board's subsequent determination of the precise level and details of compensation, or the compensation that businesses ultimately offer under the scheme;[81]
  - the applicant cooperates fully with the Chairperson and the Board members (including, for example, in relation to reasonable and proportionate information requests and providing all assistance the Chairperson and the Board may reasonably require in order to discharge its functions) and that the information it provides to the Chairperson and the Board, as well as the Authority, is accurate and complete in all material respects;
  - the Authority is satisfied that the specific Chairperson and individuals subsequently appointed to the Board meet the strict eligibility criteria regarding the terms of their appointment; and

— the Chairperson, the Board members and the applicant comply with the terms of this guidance document (unless they demonstrated to the Authority's satisfaction that there were good reasons for taking a different approach).

3.15 The Authority will discuss any conditions it plans to impose with the applicant before they are imposed. If agreement on the conditions cannot be reached, the applicant will be given the opportunity to withdraw its application before conditional approval is given, and therefore before a scheme binds them. This will ensure that participation in the scheme by the applicant remains entirely voluntary. If an application is rejected by the Authority, or withdrawn by the applicant, the Authority will return to the applicant all scheme-related documentation received from it. The Authority would also expect to return documents if the Authority closes its investigation without reaching an infringement decision.

3.16 Once conditions have been agreed and the applicant states that it has taken all necessary steps to fulfil them, the Authority may undertake the following actions:

- Approve the scheme unconditionally and finally, where it is satisfied that all conditions imposed have been met. Any Required Information or other information provided pursuant to a condition of approval will form part of the terms of the scheme.[82]
- Revoke approval of the scheme if any conditions imposed by the Authority are not met. Save in respect of a failure to meet the Regulation Requirements, the Authority expects only in exceptional circumstances to find that the conditions it has imposed have in its view not been satisfied. For example, the Authority may find that the imposed conditions have not been fulfilled if:
  - — it considers that there are material/manifest errors in the methodology followed by the Chairperson and the Board in calculating the precise level of compensation. In those circumstances the Authority may choose to request that the Chairperson and the Board reconsider and re-make their determination, or the relevant parts of it, with approval revoked only if the same or similar issues persist;
  - — it becomes apparent to the Authority that significant information and evidence was withheld from the Chairperson and the Board members when they were making their determination; or
  - — there are strong indications that there has been an attempt to deceive the Authority about the appropriate level of compensation to be offered under the scheme.
- Approve an alternative redress scheme voluntarily offered by the applicant as a replacement for the original scheme, where it considered that was necessary to ensure that the scheme operated as intended, or otherwise to ensure an appropriate outcome for potential beneficiaries. The replacement scheme must be capable of being approved without conditions:[83]
  - — The Authority might consider a replacement scheme offered by an applicant where it considered that the scheme devised by the Chairperson and Board should be revised. This might for example be the case where, exceptionally, the Authority had identified concerns about the methodology followed by the Chairperson and the Board, or there had been a material change of circumstances necessitating a change.[84] In those circumstances, in order to meet the Regulatory Requirements the applicant would need to go back to the Chairperson and Board and ask them to consider and recommend the replacement scheme to the Authority.
  - — The Authority might also consider a replacement scheme offered by the applicant where the scheme devised and recommended for approval by the Chairperson and Board went beyond the parameters of the outline scheme that the Authority had approved preliminarily, and the Authority agreed fully with that recommendation. This might for example be the case where the applicant had initially specified explicitly that it wished to offer compensation to only direct purchasers of a cartelised product but the Chairperson and Board recommended a scheme that covered indirect purchasers also.[85]
  - — The Authority is unlikely to approve a replacement redress scheme where the need for such a scheme results from the applicant having acted in bad faith.

3.17 If the Authority considers that a replacement scheme is necessary, the applicant will need to consider whether it is willing to proceed with the expanded scheme the Authority considers is appropriate, or whether instead it is willing to proceed only with the scheme originally approved by the Authority (or a variant of that scheme that did not go as far as the Authority considered was appropriate).

3.18 If the applicant is willing to proceed with the expanded replacement scheme the Authority considers is appropriate, the Authority will consider approving it. If the applicant does not choose to do that, the Authority will provide it with an opportunity to present its views before determining whether it is appropriate to revoke or finally approve the original or modified replacement scheme (as appropriate).

3.19 If the Authority revokes the conditional approval, the business would not be forced nonetheless to proceed with an (unapproved) scheme with which it did not agree. In those circumstances, the Authority would consider whether to seek recovery of any penalty reduction granted previously in recognition of conditional scheme approval.

NOTES

78 Section 49C(2) of the CA98 as amended by the CRA15.

79 Article 4(2)(b) of the Regulations and section 49C(3) of the CA98 as amended by the CRA15.

80 Article 4(2)(b) of the Regulations and section 49C(4) of the CA98 as amended by the CRA15.

81 This scenario might arise where, for example, the Board and the Chairperson determined compensation that went further than the scope of the outline scheme approved by the Authority (and the Authority agreed that was appropriate) but the business was not prepared to offer that level of compensation through a replacement scheme. See further paragraph 3.16 below.

82 Section 49C(7) of the CA98 as amended by the CRA15.
83 Section 49C(5)(c) of the CA98 as amended by the CRA15.
84 As noted above, in order to allow for the fact that the Authority might exceptionally have concerns with the Chairperson and Board's recommendation, the Authority will, when approving an outline scheme, generally impose a condition that its ultimate approval is subject to it not having significant concerns with the actual compensation ultimately offered for approval by the business.
85 The Authority considers that if the Chairperson and Board recommended a scheme that covered both direct and indirect purchasers where the outline scheme did not restrict the categories of purchaser to be compensated, a replacement scheme would not be required.

NOTIFICATION OF THE AUTHORITY'S DECISION

3.20 The Authority does not expect to publicise any preliminary intention to approve or reject an application for approval of a redress scheme.

3.21 After it has finalised its assessment of an application, the Authority will provide applicants with a short reasoned document that sets out:

- whether it has approved or rejected a scheme;
- on what grounds it has approved or rejected a scheme; and
- if an application for conditional approval of an outline scheme was made during the course of an Authority investigation, a brief description of any conditions to which its approval is subject (including any associated deadlines by which such conditions must be met).

3.22 Issue of this document will constitute the Authority's formal approval or rejection of a scheme.[86] If a scheme is approved, the decision document will include the agreed terms of the scheme that the Authority has approved and by which the business will be bound if the scheme ultimately proceeds, as well as any conditions that the Authority may have imposed.

3.23 The Authority will publish a brief summary of its decision to approve a scheme, whether subject to conditions or not, on its webpages, drawing attention to the compensating party's commitment to compensate individuals and businesses for the harm caused by its infringement.

3.24 Where the Authority issues an infringement decision at the same time as it approves a redress scheme, the infringement decision would generally note the existence of an Authority-approved voluntary redress scheme as well as any penalty reduction granted in connection with it. The Authority will also include on its webpages a link to the details of the scheme held on the compensating party's website or other contact details for the compensating party as appropriate.

NOTES

86 If the Authority has completed its assessment of an application in advance of having made an infringement decision, the Authority will typically provide the compensating party with a draft of this document. When the Authority makes its infringement decision, it will issue the document formally.

POSSIBILITY OF PENALTY REDUCTIONS IN CERTAIN CASES

3.25 If it is considering approving a scheme in relation to a potential Authority infringement decision,[87] the Authority will consider whether – were it to approve the scheme – it would be appropriate to make a penalty reduction in light of the infringing party's voluntary provision of redress. Where possible, the intention to grant a penalty discount in light of a redress scheme will be noted in the draft penalty statement that the Authority issues in accordance with its procedures in CA98 cases. It should be noted that, since draft penalty statements are put on the investigation file for inspection in multi-party cases, other parties to the investigation will become aware of the fact that an application has been submitted for approval in such a case.[88]

3.26 However, it is noted that, to the extent possible having regard to legal obligations, the Authority would in this context not expect to disclose the application for approval itself, nor any supporting documents, to other parties to the investigation. In particular, as noted at paragraph 2.74 above, documents that may be protected by privilege and that are disclosed to the Authority in confidence and on a limited waiver basis will be treated in confidence by the Authority, and it would expect to resist any claim for onward disclosure in favour of any third parties to the extent possible under law. In assessing whether exceptionally it might be necessary to disclose material relating to an approved application, the CMA would expect to apply the principles it uses for assessing potential disclosure of certain documents in relation to the use of its leniency and settlement tools.[89]

3.27 The Authority retains discretion to decide whether a scheme merits a penalty reduction – there is no absolute right to a penalty reduction.

3.28 However, if an applicant disagrees with the amount of any penalty reduction proposed by the Authority, it will be provided with an opportunity to withdraw its application before the Authority formally gives conditional approval to the outline scheme. This will ensure that participation in the scheme by the business remains entirely voluntary.

3.29 While there is no right to a penalty reduction, the Authority expects that in the majority of cases where it approves a scheme at the time of issuing an infringement decision it will reduce the penalty it would otherwise have imposed to recognise the provision of redress through the offer of the scheme.

3.30 Any penalty discount is likely to be up to a maximum of 20% of the penalty the Authority would otherwise have imposed.

3.31 When deciding the precise level of any penalty discount, the Authority may take into account, among other factors:

- the terms of the redress scheme;
- the size of the penalty imposed by the Authority;
- any appropriate evidence of the likely administrative costs of implementing the scheme; and
- any other discounts awarded to the compensating parties in the particular case, such as for leniency or settlement.

By contrast, the Authority expects that other factors it would generally consider when imposing a penalty – for example, the gravity of the infringement – are unlikely to be relevant in this respect.

3.32 The discount will be taken into account at step 6 of the Authority's framework for calculating financial penalties.[90]

3.33 The Authority would generally expect to seek recovery of any penalty reduction where:

- a business seeks to withdraw from a scheme after it has been approved;
- a business did not comply with conditions imposed on approval of an outline scheme and such approval was revoked by the Authority; or
- the scheme has been established but not used.[91] In this case, in deciding whether to recover some or all of the penalty discount that it has granted, the Authority will take into account whether the compensating party has acted in good faith as well as the administrative costs that it has already expended in running the scheme. If the penalty discount did not exceed the costs of scheme administration, the Authority may not be minded to recover its costs (as to which, see below).

NOTES

87 The Authority will only be able to consider making penalty reductions in its own investigations.

88 Once any written and oral representations made on the Statement of Objections have been considered, if the Authority is considering reaching an infringement decision and imposing a financial penalty on a party, it will provide that party with a draft penalty statement. This will set out the key aspects relevant to the calculation of the penalty that the Authority proposes to impose on that party, based on the information available to the Authority at the time. See the CMA's guidance on investigation procedures in CA98 cases (CMA8).

89 See the CMA's leniency guidance (OFT1495, adopted by the CMA Board) and its guidance on investigation procedures in CA98 cases (CMA8).

90 Penalty reductions for leniency and settlement are also applied at this step. See OFT's guidance as to the appropriate amount of a penalty (OFT423, adopted by the CMA Board).

91 See also paragraph 4.14 below.

RECOVERY OF THE AUTHORITY'S COSTS

3.34 Section 49D of the CA98 provides that the Authority may recover its reasonable costs relating to an application for approval of a redress scheme.

3.35 The Authority may impose such a requirement by giving the relevant person written notice that specifies:

- the amount to be paid;
- how that amount has been calculated; and
- the deadline by which that amount must be paid.[92]

3.36 Generally, the Authority expects to calculate its costs on the basis of the total number of hours that Authority staff have devoted to assessing the application for approval of a redress scheme multiplied by an average hourly rate. Where appropriate, the calculated amount may be revised downwards if proportionality so requires.

3.37 If the costs that need to be paid under this section relate to an approved scheme, the Authority may revoke scheme approval if the costs have not been paid by the date specified in the written notice.[93]

3.38 Costs that need to be paid under this section are recoverable by the Authority as a debt.[94]

3.39 The Authority will seek to recover its reasonable costs in the vast majority of cases but, in exceptional circumstances, it may seek to recover only a portion of its costs. In determining the amount of costs to be recovered, the Authority may also consider the size and financial position of the relevant parties applying for approval, as well as the compensating party's cooperation with the Authority.

3.40 If a party withdraws an application before the Authority has decided whether to approve or reject the scheme, the Authority has no power to enforce the scheme. However, in such a case the Authority would nevertheless generally expect to recover from the party in question the full amount of its reasonable costs of assessing the application.

3.41 A person required to pay costs under this section may appeal to the CAT against the amount.[95]

NOTES

92 Section 49D(2) of the CA98, as amended by the CRA15.

93 Section 49D(4) of the CA98, as amended by the CRA15.

94 Section 49D(5) of the CA98, as amended by the CRA15.

95 Section 49D(3) of the CA98, as amended by the CRA15. It should also be noted that authority decisions relating to voluntary redress schemes would be subject to judicial review under usual principles.

4. ENFORCEMENT OF AND RELEASE FROM AN AUTHORITY-APPROVED VOLUNTARY REDRESS SCHEME

[3.186]

4.1 This chapter considers how a voluntary redress scheme may be enforced, either by a scheme beneficiary or the Authority. It also considers the circumstances under which the Authority may release the compensating party from complying with the redress scheme.

ENFORCEMENT OF AUTHORITY-APPROVED VOLUNTARY REDRESS SCHEMES

Duty of a compensating party to comply with a redress scheme

4.2 The compensating party is under a statutory duty to comply with the terms of an approved redress scheme, which also include any information conditions attached to an outline scheme.[96]

4.3 This statutory duty is owed to any natural or legal person entitled to compensation under the terms of the scheme,[97] whether or not they have made a formal application under the scheme.

NOTES

[96] Section 49E(1) of the CA98, as amended by the CRA15.

[97] Section 49E(2) of the CA98, as amended by the CRA15.

Enforcement of a redress scheme by a scheme beneficiary

4.4 If a compensating party breaches its duty to comply with the terms of an approved redress scheme, legislation states that a scheme beneficiary who suffers loss or damage as a result of the breach may bring civil proceedings before the court[98] for damages, an injunction or interdict or any other appropriate relief or remedy.[99] In practice, the loss that such a beneficiary suffers is likely to be the compensation they have not received. The beneficiary does not need to have used the complaints process described at paragraphs 2.25 to 2.32 above before they exercise their right to bring civil proceedings, but in practice they may wish to consider doing so.

4.5 In any civil proceedings to enforce a scheme, it is a defence for the compensating party to show that it took all reasonable steps to comply with the duty to adhere to the terms of the approved redress scheme.[100]

NOTES

[98] In England and Wales/Northern Ireland, the High Court or county court; in Scotland, the Court of Session or the sheriff.

[99] Section 49E(3) of the CA98, as amended by the CRA15.

[100] Section 49E(6) of the CA98, as amended by the CRA15.

Enforcement of a redress scheme by the Authority

4.6 In addition to enforcement by a scheme beneficiary who has suffered loss or damage, if the Authority considers that the compensating party is in breach of the duty to comply with the terms of a redress scheme, it also has the power to bring civil proceedings before the court for an injunction or interdict, or any other appropriate relief or remedy.[101, 102]

4.7 This power is discretionary. The Authority will consider whether to use the power on a case by case basis, considering factors such as (but not limited to):

- the nature and gravity of the suspected breach;
- whether the independent appeals process under the redress scheme is potentially capable of resolving issues relating to the suspected breach; and
- the feasibility of the scheme beneficiary bringing civil proceedings in respect of the suspected breach.

4.8 The Authority would also expect generally to apply its prioritisation criteria[103] when it is considering whether to enforce a redress scheme.

NOTES

[101] Section 49E(4) of the CA98, as amended by the CRA15. Again, it is a defence for the compensating party to show it took all reasonable steps to comply with the duty to adhere to the terms of the approved redress scheme (section 49E(6) of the CA98, as amended by the CRA15).

[102] It should be noted that the fact a scheme is no longer open for new applications does not mean a compensating party is released from its duty to comply with its terms. For example, if an application for compensation had been accepted under the scheme but the compensation had not been paid, a beneficiary or the Authority would still be able to enforce that obligation.

[103] See paragraph 3.2 above.

RELEASE FROM A REDRESS SCHEME

The Authority's approach to considering release from a redress scheme

4.9 If the Authority considers that it is no longer appropriate for the compensating party to remain under a duty to comply with the terms of a redress scheme, it may release the compensating party from that duty.[104] In this context, the Authority would take into account the desirability of giving appropriate notification to beneficiaries under the scheme. The Authority would also consider the desirability of ensuring that any person who had relied reasonably on the scheme as their means of achieving compensation, and as a result was unable to claim separately through judicial means because the statutory limitation period for doing so had expired, was not prejudiced by releasing the compensating party from the duty.

4.10 Where a person has entered into a settlement agreement with the compensating party, that agreement remains enforceable as a matter of contract law, regardless of any subsequent release of the compensating party from the statutory duty to comply with the terms of the redress scheme.[105]

4.11 In considering the release of a compensating party from the duty to comply with the terms of a redress scheme, the Authority will consider whether there has been a material change of circumstances since the scheme commenced. The precise nature of the Authority's consideration will depend on the individual circumstances affecting a particular redress scheme. However, the change of circumstances must be such that it is no longer appropriate in the Authority's view for the compensating party to be bound to comply with the terms of the redress scheme.

4.12 The types of circumstances which may lead to the release of a compensating party may include (but are not limited to):

- a situation in which the redress scheme is superseded by a new (non-statutory) redress scheme; and
- a situation in which the redress scheme is obsolete, for example where the redress scheme has fulfilled its purpose. This may be the case, for example, where claims from all those entitled to claim under the scheme have been satisfied, but the period for which the scheme is open for applications is still to expire.

4.13 By contrast, the Authority is unlikely to release the compensating party from its duty to comply with the terms of the redress scheme where there remain outstanding obligations arising under it, regardless of whether the scheme has closed or not. Where obligations under a scheme have been satisfied and the scheme has closed, there will be no need for the Authority to release a compensating party.

4.14 The complexity of analysis the Authority will need to undertake in deciding whether to release a compensating party from its duty to comply with the terms of a redress scheme is likely to vary significantly depending on the change of circumstances identified and the nature and severity of the competition infringement. In some cases, a detailed investigation may be required in order to evaluate whether there has been a change of circumstances and, if so, whether the compensating party should be released. In some exceptional cases where a party is released from its obligations – for example where no compensation has been paid under a scheme – the Authority does not rule out reconsidering whether it would be appropriate for the party to retain its reduction in fine.

4.15 Where a scheme is approved and established but a compensating party has successfully appealed the relevant infringement decision, the Authority would consider on a case-by-case basis whether it would be appropriate to release that compensating party from its obligations under the scheme, or for those obligations to continue.

NOTES

[104] Section 49E(7) of the CA98, as amended by the CRA15.

[105] Section 49E(8) of the CA98, as amended by the CRA15.

The ways in which a release from the redress scheme may be initiated

4.16 A release from the terms of the redress scheme may be on the basis of:

- a review undertaken on the Authority's own initiative; or
- a request to the Authority by the compensating party.

4.17 A request from the compensating party must be set out clearly in writing and be accompanied by appropriate supporting evidence setting out:

- what the material change of circumstances is;
- how and why this makes it appropriate to release the compensating party from the redress scheme;
- the possible consequences for scheme beneficiaries; and
- whether the request is being made in order to avoid a breach of the redress scheme.

4.18 The Authority will consider whether and in what detail to carry out its review on a case-by-case basis. Parties can approach the Authority prior to submitting a request in order to discuss what sort of evidence would be expected to be included in any request.

4.19 If the Authority has decided to undertake a review, and plans to release a compensating party from its duty to comply with the terms of a redress scheme, it will consult with the people it considers appropriate on its proposed decision.

ANNEX A: GLOSSARY

[3.187]

In this guidance:

(1) '**the approved scheme**' means a redress scheme approved by the Authority;

(2) '**the applicant**' means a person making an application to the Authority for approval of a redress scheme under section 49C of the CA98;

(3) to the extent this guidance is applied or taken account of by the CMA or a Regulator, '**the Authority**' means either the CMA or a Regulator as appropriate;

(4) **'the Board'** means a group of people appointed by the Chairperson who do not have a conflict of interest, comprising: an economist with appropriate experience and knowledge of competition economics to be able to consider the redress scheme; a person with experience of the industry of the applicant; a person who is able to represent the interests of those who may be entitled to compensation under the redress scheme; and any other person deemed suitable by the Chairperson;

(5) the '**Chairperson**' means a person appointed by the applicant who does not have a conflict of interest and satisfies the judicial-appointment eligibility condition on a five-year basis, or is an advocate or solicitor in Scotland of at least five years' standing, or is a member of the Bar of Northern Ireland or solicitor of the Court of Judicature of Northern Ireland of at least five years' standing;

(6) **'the compensating party'** means a person offering compensation under an Authority-approved scheme;

(7) **'the conditions of redress scheme'** means the conditions that the Authority may impose on the applicant under section 49C of the CA98 when approving an outline scheme;

(8) **'full scheme'** means a scheme submitted to the Authority for approval under section 49C of the CA98 which complies with all the Regulation Requirements;

(9) **'the independent reviewer'** means any person who has been designated under the scheme as responsible for assessing complaints by potential scheme beneficiaries whose applications for compensation under the redress scheme have been rejected or have not been fulfilled by the compensating party;

(10) **'outline scheme'** means a scheme submitted to the Authority for approval under section 49C of the CA98 which does not yet comply with all the Regulation Requirements;

(11) **'redress scheme'** means a scheme under which a person offers compensation as a consequence of an infringement decision made in respect of that person;

(12) **'the Regulations'** means The Competition Act 1998 (Redress Scheme) Regulations 2015 (SI 2015/1587);

(13) **'the relevant matters'** means the matters specified in Article 5(7) of the Regulations;

(14) **'the Regulation Requirements'** means the requirements that according to Article 4(1) of the Regulations any redress scheme submitted to the Authority for approval must (either at the date of submission or at a specified later date) satisfy for the Authority to approve it;

(15) **'the scheme administrator'** means any person who is responsible for examining applications for compensation under the redress scheme and verifying whether the entitlement and evidence requirements are satisfied;

(16) **'scheme beneficiary'** or **'potential scheme beneficiary'** means any person whose application for compensation under the redress scheme has been approved or who is *prima facie* entitled to compensation under an Authority-approved redress scheme;

(17) **'the terms of the redress scheme'** means the provisions that specify the scope, operation and consequences of a redress scheme.

ANNEX B: TEMPLATE UNDERTAKING

DECLARATION OF INDEPENDENCE, COMMITMENT AND ABSENCE OF CONFLICT OF INTEREST

[3.188]

NOTE: *The sample text below provides an example of how Chairpersons and Board members might provide the required confirmations in respect of their roles in the context of an application for redress scheme approval.*[106] *However, Chairpersons and Board members must amend the sample text below, or use alternative text, as appropriate in view of their individual circumstances.*

I, [Chairperson / Board member's name], hereby declare that:

- I do not have, nor have I become exposed to, a conflict of interest that impairs my objectivity and independence in discharging my duties as a Chairperson/Board member.
- If a conflict of interest or circumstances likely to give rise to any doubts about my impartiality and independence arise or may arise during the execution of my tasks, I shall immediately notify the Chairman/the Authority[107] in writing without delay. In the event of such conflicts of interest, I undertake to immediately take all necessary steps to resolve it.
- I hereby undertake not to be bound by any instructions from the compensating party restricting my ability to determine whether compensation is appropriate, and shall be completely independent in the performance of my duties.
- I hereby undertake to take all necessary measures to prevent any situation that could compromise the impartial and objective performance of my tasks.
- I hereby undertake to perform my functions as a Chairperson/Board member with reasonable skill and care and in accordance with the law as well as any applicable rules governing my professional conduct.
- I undertake to abstain from any contact or conduct that could compromise, or appear to compromise, my independence as a Chairperson/Board member.
- Save for the remuneration agreed with the compensating party for the performance of my role in devising a scheme, I declare that:
    - — I will not derive any kind of advantage from the execution of my tasks as a Board member.

— I have not granted and will not grant, have not sought and will not seek, have not attempted and will not attempt to obtain, and have not accepted and will not accept, any advantage, financial or in kind, from any party whatsoever, where such advantage constitutes an illegal practice or involves corruption, either directly or indirectly, inasmuch as it is an incentive or reward relating to performance of my functions as a Chairperson/Board member.

Done at [. . .] on [. . .]

Signature [. . .]

NOTES

106 See paragraphs 2.43–2.59 above.

107 As appropriate.

ANNEX C: SUMMARY OF PRIVATE ACTIONS FRAMEWORK FOR COMPETITION LAW BREACHES

[3.189]

(1) Anyone who has suffered harm caused by an infringement of Chapter I or Chapter II of the CA98 or Articles 101 or 102 of the TFEU has a right to compensation for that harm.

(2) A natural or legal person who has suffered loss as a result of a relevant infringement of competition law may seek redress through the courts by bringing a private action.[108] Two forms of private action should be distinguished:

- **Follow-on actions** – if a relevant competition authority, such as the CMA, a Regulator or the European Commission, has made a decision that competition law has been infringed, a claimant may rely on the decision as proof of the breach.
- **Stand-alone actions** – if there is no previous decision by a competition authority finding an infringement of the competition rules, the claimant will have to obtain and submit evidence to the court to prove the breach of competition law.

(3) As well as showing that the defendant breached competition law, the claimant (in both follow-on and stand-alone actions) will also have to prove that the breach actually caused the claimant loss. In practice, a claimant will need to prove that its loss would not have occurred 'but for' the competition law breach.

(4) A private action may be brought on a collective basis by a representative[109] on behalf of a class of potential claimants who can be consumers or businesses, or a combination of the two. Under the CA98 (as amended by CRA15), it is possible for a class representative to bring collective proceedings before the CAT.[110] Such collective proceedings[111] must be brought by a person who proposes to be the representative in the proceedings. The CAT is required to authorise the class representative and certify whether the claims in question are eligible for inclusion in collective proceedings. The CAT will also determine whether collective proceedings should be on an 'opt-in' or an 'opt-out' basis:[112]

- **Opt-in collective proceedings** are brought on behalf of each class member who joins or 'opts-in' by notifying[113] the class representative that the claim should be included in the proceedings. This means that a person will be included in the action only if they expressly join the proceedings.
- **Opt-out collective proceedings** are brought on behalf of members of a class. To be included, a person must fall within the class described in the collective proceedings: they will be included in the proceedings unless they 'opt-out' by a certain date and in the manner prescribed by the CAT.[114]

(5) Collective proceedings are possible for both follow-on and stand-alone cases. The CAT Rules of Procedure[115] provide for a range of safeguards within the collective actions regime to protect against frivolous or unmeritorious cases being brought.[116]

(6) In addition to individual and collective private actions for damages, the CRA15 also introduces a new collective settlement regime for competition law cases in the CAT to allow victims of competition law infringements and businesses which have breached the competition rules to quickly and easily settle cases on a voluntary basis.[117] Further details on the operation of collective actions and the CAT's approval of collective settlements are set out in the CAT Rules of Procedure.

(7) Certain regulators have other redress powers that may be used related to their sector specific powers. For example, the FCA has separate redress powers under the Financial Services and Markets Act 2000 which the FCA can exercise using its own initiative.[118]

NOTES

108 Other forms of private action in competition law, for example an application to a court for an injunction or a declaration, are beyond the scope of this guidance. The UK courts that have jurisdiction to hear competition law cases are the following:

- the Chancery Division of the High Court of England and Wales (and in some circumstances, the Commercial Court) may hear cases. See the Practice Direction on competition law and Rule 58.1(2) of the Civil Procedure Rules);
- the Court of Session and Sheriff Court in Scotland;
- the High Court of Northern Ireland; and
- the Competition Appeal Tribunal (CAT).

For the remainder of this guidance, the term 'ordinary courts' is used to refer to the High Court of England and Wales, the Court of Session and Sheriff Court in Scotland, and the High Court of Northern Ireland.

109 Government policy is that only those who would fairly and adequately act in the interests of the class members will be authorised to act as the class representative in accordance with Rule 77 (Authorisation of the class representative).

110 Section 47B of the CA98 allows proceedings before the CAT combining two or more claims to which section 47A applies ('collective proceedings'). Collective proceedings are subject to the provisions of the CA98 and the CAT Rules of Procedure. The CAT also has general powers of case management including, where there are multiple claims, its power to consolidate proceedings, hear two or more claims together or transfer proceedings.

111 Collective proceedings are possible in the ordinary courts but under separate legal provisions. These are beyond the scope of this guidance, which refers to CAT collective proceedings only.

112 Section 47B of the CA98.

113 Notification must be made in the manner and by the time specified by the CAT.

114 However, any class member who is not domiciled in the UK at a time specified will need to opt-in by notifying the class representative that the claim should be included in the collective proceedings.

115 The CAT Rules of Procedure are available on the CAT webpages.

116 For example, the CAT may only authorise a person to act as the class representative in the collective proceedings if it considers that it is just and reasonable for that person to do so and will take into account a number of factors in its discretion, including whether that person would fairly and adequately act in the interests of the class members, according to the relevant provisions of the CAT Rules of Procedure. The CAT will also certify that the claims in question are eligible for inclusion in collective proceedings according to the relevant CAT Rules of Procedure.

117 Sections 49(A) and 49(B) of the CA98, as amended by the CRA15. The collective settlements regime is set out in the CAT Rules of Procedure.

118 The Financial Ombudsman Service (FOS) is also an option for customers in certain circumstances if the customer is unhappy with the response received (further information is available at the FOS website).

CMA'S GUIDANCE AS TO THE APPROPRIATE AMOUNT OF A PENALTY (CMA73, 18 APRIL 2018)

[3.190]

NOTES

With regard to this guidance, note that:

— all references to issues of legal assessment and procedure in investigations under the Competition Act 1998 must be read in the light of Competition Act 1998: Guidance on the CMA's investigation procedures in Competition Act 1998 cases (CMA8); in the case of conflict, CMA8 prevails;

— references to the substantive powers of investigation or assessment of the approach to applying legal powers (for example, the approach to publishing notices of investigation, interim measures or penalties for non-cooperation with an investigation under the CA98), should be read in light of CMA8.

See also the list of consultations and draft documents in the Appendix at **[A1]**.

CONTENTS

PREFACE

[3.191]

The Competition and Markets Authority (CMA) has the power to apply and enforce the Competition Act 1998 (CA98). The CMA also has the power[1] to apply and enforce Articles 101 and 102 of the Treaty on the Functioning of the European Union (TFEU) in the United Kingdom.[2] In relation to the regulated sectors these provisions are applied and enforced, concurrently with the CMA, by the regulators listed below (under section 54 and schedule 10 of the CA98) (the Regulators). Throughout this guidance, references to the CMA should be taken to include the Regulators in relation to their respective sectors, unless otherwise specified.

The following are the Regulators, as at 1 April 2018:

- the Office of Communications (Ofcom) (communications);
- Ofgem (gas and electricity markets in Great Britain);
- the Northern Ireland Authority for Utility Regulation (gas, electricity, water and sewerage services in Northern Ireland);
- the Water Services Regulation Authority (Ofwat) (water and sewerage markets in England and Wales);
- the Office of Rail and Road (ORR) (railway services in Great Britain);
- the Civil Aviation Authority (CAA) (air traffic services and airport operation services);
- NHS Improvement (healthcare services in England);
- the Financial Conduct Authority (FCA) (financial services); and
- the Payment Systems Regulator (PSR) (participation in payment systems).[3]

This guidance is issued in performance of the statutory obligation on the CMA, contained in sections 38(1) and 38(1A) of the CA98 (and pursuant to section 38(3) of the CA98), to publish guidance as to the appropriate amount of a penalty, including guidance as to the circumstances in which, in determining a penalty, the CMA may take into account the effects of an infringement in another member state. The CMA is required to have regard to the guidance for the time being in force when setting the amount of any penalty to be imposed. Although there is no equivalent statutory obligation on the Regulators to publish guidance as to the appropriate amount of a penalty, the Regulators are required to have regard to the CMA's published guidance for the time being in force when setting the amount of any penalty to be imposed under the CA98. The Competition Appeal Tribunal (CAT) also must have regard to the CMA's published guidance.[4]

NOTES

1 Under Council Regulation (EC) No 1/2003 of 16 December 2002 (the Modernisation Regulation).

2 Paragraph 1.2 provides describes the circumstances in which the CMA is required to apply Article 101 and 102.

3 The list is correct as at 1 April 2018. The list may change from time to time if further sector regulators are given concurrent powers or existing sectoral regulators are given concurrent powers over a wider range of markets. Some of these Regulators have or may issue guidance on other specific issues, such as competition law compliance, which may interact with this guidance. These documents are not referred to in this guidance.

4 Section 38(8) of the CA98.

1. INTRODUCTION

[3.192]

1.1 This guidance[5] sets out the basis on which the CMA will calculate penalties for infringements of the CA98 or of the TFEU where it decides to exercise its discretion to impose a penalty under section 36(1) and 36(2) of the CA98. The guidance also sets out the basic requirements for the grant of lenient treatment by the CMA under the CMA's leniency programme.[6] The CMA is issuing this guidance in performance of its statutory obligation to publish guidance as to the appropriate amount of a penalty, including guidance as to the circumstances in which, in determining a penalty, the CMA may take into account the effects of an infringement in another Member State.[7]

1.2 The Modernisation Regulation requires national competition authorities of the Member States (NCAs) and the courts of the member states to apply Articles 101 and 102 of the TFEU as well as national competition law when national competition law is applied to agreements or conduct which may affect trade between member states. The CA98 gives the CMA powers to enforce both the Chapter I and Chapter II prohibitions of the CA98 and Articles 101 and 102 of the TFEU.[8]

POLICY OBJECTIVES

1.3 Consistent with section 36(7A) of the CA98, the twin objectives of the CMA's policy on financial penalties are:

- to impose penalties on infringing undertakings[9] which reflect the **seriousness of the infringement**; and
- to ensure that the threat of penalties will **deter** both the infringing undertakings and other undertakings that may be considering anti-competitive activities from engaging in them.

The CMA has a discretion to impose financial penalties and intends, where appropriate, to impose financial penalties which are severe, in particular in respect of agreements[10] between undertakings which fix prices or share markets, other cartel activities[11] and serious abuses of a dominant position. The CMA considers that these are among the most serious infringements of competition law.

1.4 There are two aspects to the deterrence objective. First, there is a need to deter the undertakings which are subject to the decision from engaging in future anti-competitive activity (often referred to as 'specific deterrence'). Second, there is a need to deter undertakings at large which might be considering activities contrary to any of Article 101, Article 102, the Chapter I or Chapter II prohibitions from breaching the law (often referred to as 'general deterrence').

1.5 The CMA recognises that it is important to ensure that penalties imposed on individual undertakings are proportionate and not excessive.

1.6 The CMA also wishes to encourage undertakings to come forward with information relating to any cartel activity in which they are involved. The CMA therefore sets out in part 3 of this guidance when lenient treatment will be given to such undertakings.

STATUTORY BACKGROUND

1.7 Section 36 of the CA98 provides that the CMA may impose a financial penalty on an undertaking which has intentionally or negligently committed an infringement of Article 101, Article 102, the Chapter I and/or Chapter II prohibitions.[12] It is therefore for the CMA to determine in a given case whether or not a financial penalty should be imposed.

1.8 Sections 38(1) and 38(1A) of the CA98 require the CMA to prepare and publish guidance as to the appropriate amount of a penalty, including guidance as to the circumstances in which, in determining a penalty, the CMA may take into account the effects of an infringement in another member state. Section 38(2) of the CA98 provides that the CMA may alter the guidance on penalties at any time. Section 38(3) of the CA98 provides that, if altered, the CMA must publish the amended guidance. Under section 38(4) the Secretary of State must approve any guidance on penalties before it can be published. When preparing or altering guidance on penalties, sections 38(6) and (7) require the CMA to consult such persons as it considers appropriate, including the Regulators. These particular provisions apply to the CMA alone and not also to the Regulators.

1.9 This guidance was approved by the Secretary of State as required under section 38(4) of the CA98 on 16 April 2018. It was published and came into effect on 18 April 2018. Before finalising this revised guidance, the CMA conducted a consultation in accordance with sections 38(6) and (7) of the CA98.

1.10 By virtue of section 38(8) of the CA98, the CMA must have regard to the guidance for the time being in force when setting the amount of any financial penalty to be imposed. A similar requirement applies to the Regulators by virtue of the legislation that conferred on them concurrent powers under the CA98. The CAT also must have regard to the CMA's published guidance.[13] This guidance applies from the date of publication to ongoing and new CA98 cases. The CMA notes that the amendments made to the previous guidance (OFT423) are intended to be clarificatory and reflect recent CMA decisional practice. They do not substantively alter the CMA's penalty calculation mechanism.

1.11 The financial penalty may not in any event exceed the maximum penalty of 10% of the worldwide turnover of the undertaking.[14]

1.12 This guidance on penalties will continue to be kept under review in the light of experience in its application.

EXCEPTIONS

1.13 Sections 39 and 40 of the CA98 provide limited immunity from financial penalties for **small agreements** in relation to infringements of the Chapter I prohibition and for **conduct of minor significance** in relation to infringements of the Chapter II prohibition.[15] This immunity does not apply to any infringements of Articles 101 or 102 or to infringements of the Chapter I prohibition which are price-fixing agreements. It may be withdrawn by the CMA in certain circumstances. Further details are set out in the competition law guideline *Enforcement* (OFT407, adopted by the CMA Board).[16]

CRIMINAL CARTEL OFFENCE

1.14 Section 188 of the Enterprise Act 2002 introduced a criminal offence for individuals who engage in cartel arrangements that fix prices, limit supply or production, share markets or rig bids in the UK. The criminal cartel offence only applies to relevant agreements in respect of arrangements between undertakings operating at the same level of the supply chain, known as horizontal agreements. Vertical agreements which are intended to operate between undertakings at different levels in the supply chain, for example between a manufacturer and a distributor, or between a distributor and a retailer, are not covered by the offence.

1.15 The cartel offence operates alongside the provisions of the CA98, and further information can be found in the *Cartel Offence Prosecution Guidance* (CMA9, March 2014). The guidance document *Applications for leniency and no action in cartel cases* (OFT1495, adopted by the CMA Board) sets out how the CMA will handle applications for immunity from prosecution for the criminal cartel offence under section 190(4) of the Enterprise Act 2002. The prosecution or conviction of individuals under section 188 of the Enterprise Act 2002 in connection with an infringement is not relevant for the purpose of setting the amount of financial penalties payable by undertakings under section 36 of the CA98.

PARALLEL APPLICATION OF ARTICLES 101 AND 102 AND THE CHAPTER I AND CHAPTER II PROHIBITIONS

1.16 In cases where an undertaking has committed an infringement both of an EU prohibition (that is, Article 101 or Article 102) and the equivalent UK prohibition (that is, the Chapter I prohibition or Chapter II prohibition respectively), the undertaking will not be penalised twice for the same anti-competitive effects.

1.17 In most cases the penalty imposed in respect of an infringement of an EU prohibition will be the same as the penalty imposed in respect of an infringement of a UK prohibition, because the CMA will calculate the penalty for each infringement according to the same steps as set out in part 2 of this guidance. However, in some cases the penalties for infringement of an EU prohibition and its equivalent UK prohibition will differ, such as where the infringing agreement or conduct commenced before 1 March 2000 when the CA98 entered into force.

NOTES

5 This revised guidance replaces the CMA's *Guidance as to the appropriate amount of a penalty* (OFT423, issued December 2004, adopted by the CMA Board).

6 *Applications for leniency and no action in cartel cases* (OFT1495, adopted by the CMA Board).

7 See Statutory background section below for further details.

8 Article 101 prohibits agreements between undertakings (see notes 7 and 9 below) which may affect trade between Member States and which have as their object or effect the prevention, restriction or distortion of competition within the common market. Article 102 prohibits conduct by one or more undertakings which amounts to an abuse of a dominant position within the common market or a substantial part of it in so far as it may affect trade between Member States. The Chapter I prohibition and the Chapter II prohibition of the CA98 correspond to Article 101 and Article 102 respectively but apply to anti-competitive practices and conduct which affect trade within the United Kingdom. For further details see the competition law guidelines *Agreements and concerted practices* (OFT401, adopted by the CMA Board) and *Abuse of a dominant position* (OFT402, adopted by the CMA Board).

9 The term 'undertaking' is not defined in the TFEU or the CA98, but its meaning has been set out in EU law. It covers any natural or legal person engaged in economic activity, regardless of its legal status and the way in which it is financed. It includes companies, firms, businesses, partnerships, individuals operating as sole traders, agricultural cooperatives, associations of undertakings (for example, trade associations) non profit-making organisations and (in some circumstances) public entities that offer goods or services on a given market. A parent company and its subsidiaries will

usually be treated as a single undertaking if they operate as a single economic unit, depending on the facts of each case.

10 References in this guidance to 'agreements' should, unless otherwise stated or the context demands it, be taken to include decisions by associations of undertakings and concerted practices.

11 See below paragraph 3.1, containing a definition of 'cartel activities' for the purposes of this guidance.

12 Section 36(3) of the CA98 provides that the CMA may impose a penalty on an undertaking only if it is satisfied that the infringement has been committed intentionally or negligently. It does not, for the purposes of crossing that threshold, have to determine specifically which it was. See *Napp Pharmaceutical Holdings Limited and Subsidiaries v Director General of Fair Trading* [2002] CAT 1 at [455]-[457], [2002] CompAR 13 (*Napp*) and *Aberdeen Journals Limited v Office of Fair Trading* [2003] CAT 11 at [484] and [485] (*Aberdeen Journals (No.2)*). See also Case C-137/95 P, *SPO and Others v Commission* [1996] ECR I-1611 at paragraphs 53-57.

13 Section 38(8) of the CA98.

14 Calculated in accordance with The Competition Act 1998 (Determination of Turnover for Penalties) Order 2000 (SI 2000/309) (as amended by The Competition Act 1998 (Determination of Turnover for Penalties) (Amendment) Order 2004 (SI 2004/1259)).

15 See further The Competition Act 1998 (Small Agreements and Conduct of Minor Significance) Regulations 2000 (SI 2000/262).

16 *Enforcement: Incorporating the Office of Fair Trading's guidance as to the circumstance in which it may be appropriate to accept commitments* (OFT407, adopted by the CMA Board).

2. STEPS FOR DETERMINING THE LEVEL OF PENALTY

METHOD OF CALCULATION

[3.193]

2.1 A financial penalty imposed by the CMA under section 36 of the CA98 will be calculated following a six-step approach:[17]

- Calculation of the starting point having regard to the seriousness of the infringement and the relevant turnover of the undertaking.
- Adjustment for duration.
- Adjustment for aggravating or mitigating factors.
- Adjustment for specific deterrence and proportionality.
- Adjustment if the maximum penalty of 10% of the worldwide turnover of the undertaking[18] is exceeded and to avoid double jeopardy.
- Adjustment for leniency, settlement discounts and/or approval of a voluntary redress scheme.[19]

Details on each of these steps are set out in paragraphs 2.3 to 2.10 below.

2.2 An undertaking participating in cartel activity[20] may benefit from total immunity from, or a significant reduction in the level of, a financial penalty, if the requirements for lenient treatment set out in part 3 of this guidance are satisfied.

Step 1 – starting point

2.3 The starting point for determining the level of financial penalty which will be imposed on an undertaking is calculated having regard to:

- the seriousness of the infringement and the need for general deterrence;[21] and
- the relevant turnover of the undertaking.

The starting point will be calculated as described below.

Assessment of seriousness – application of percentage starting point to relevant turnover

2.4 The CMA will apply a starting point of up to 30% to an undertaking's relevant turnover in order to reflect adequately the seriousness of the particular infringement (and ultimately the extent and likelihood of actual or potential harm to competition and consumers). In applying the starting point, the CMA will also reflect the need to deter the infringing undertaking and other undertakings generally from engaging in that type of infringement in the future.

2.5 This is a case specific assessment of:

- first, how likely it is for the type of infringement at issue to, by its nature, harm competition;
- second, the extent and/or likelihood of harm to competition in the specific relevant circumstances of the individual case (as discussed in paragraph 2.8 below); and
- finally, whether the starting point is sufficient for the purpose of general deterrence.

2.6 At the first stage, the CMA will consider the likelihood that the type of infringement at issue will, by its nature, cause harm to competition. There is no pre-set 'tariff' of starting points for different types of infringement given the range of conduct that will be encountered in different cases and to which the CMA must have regard in setting an appropriate penalty for the case in question. However, in making its assessment, the CMA will have reference to the following principles:

- The CMA will generally use a starting point between 21 and 30% of relevant turnover for the most serious types of infringement, that is, those which the CMA considers are most likely by their very nature to harm competition. In relation to infringements of the Chapter I prohibition and/or Article 101, this includes cartel activities, such as price fixing and market sharing, and other, non-cartel object infringements which are inherently likely to cause significant harm to competition. In relation to infringements of the Chapter II prohibition and/or Article 102, this will typically include conduct which is inherently likely to have a particularly serious exploitative or exclusionary effect, such as excessive and predatory pricing.

- In relation to infringements of the Chapter I prohibition and/or Article 101, a starting point between 10 and 20% is more likely to be appropriate for certain, less serious object infringements, and for infringements by effect.[22] A 10 to 20% starting point is also more likely to be appropriate in relation to infringements of the Chapter II prohibition and/or Article 102 involving conduct which is less likely to be inherently harmful.

2.7 The above principles do not prevent the CMA from applying a starting point of below 10%. However the CMA considers that this is likely to occur as a result of the CMA having made a downwards adjustment to reflect the particular circumstances of the case, as described below.

2.8 At the second stage, the CMA will consider whether it is appropriate to adjust the starting point upwards or downwards to take account of specific circumstances of the case that might be relevant to the extent and likelihood of harm to competition and ultimately to consumers. When making its case-specific assessment, the CMA will consider the relevant circumstances of the case. These may include, for example:

- the nature of the product including the nature and extent of demand for that product;
- the structure of the market including the market share(s) of the undertaking(s) involved in the infringement, market concentration and barriers to entry;
- the market coverage of the infringement;
- the actual or potential effect of the infringement on competitors and third parties; and
- the actual or potential harm caused to consumers whether directly or indirectly.

2.9 Finally, the CMA will consider whether the starting point for a particular infringement is sufficient for the purpose of general deterrence. In particular the CMA will consider the need to deter other undertakings, whether in the same market or more broadly, from engaging in the same or similar conduct.

2.10 In the case of infringements involving more than one undertaking, the assessment outlined above will be consistent for each undertaking. The starting point is intended to reflect the seriousness of the infringement at issue, rather than the particular circumstances of each undertaking's unlawful conduct (which are taken into account at other steps). As a result, for infringements involving more than one undertaking, the CMA expects to adopt the same percentage starting point for each undertaking to the infringement.[23]

Determination of relevant turnover

2.11 The relevant turnover is the turnover of the undertaking in the relevant product market and relevant geographic market[24] affected by the infringement in the undertaking's last business year.[25] In this context, an undertaking's last business year is the financial year preceding the date when the infringement ended.

2.12 Generally, the CMA will base relevant turnover on figures from an undertaking's audited accounts. However, in exceptional circumstances it may be appropriate to use a different figure as reflecting the true scale of an undertaking's activities in the relevant market.[26]

2.13 The CMA recognises that such an exceptional approach may be appropriate where, in particular, the remuneration for services supplied is based on commission fees. When deciding whether it is appropriate to depart from its general rule of using turnover from audited accounts in this way, the CMA will consider a number of factors, in particular: (i) whether the remuneration for the services in question is decided by the seller of the services or the client, and (ii) whether the undertaking is purchasing inputs in order to supply a fresh product incorporating those inputs to its client.[27] Other factors such as whether a person is taking ownership of goods or services and whether the person bears risks resulting from the operation of the business in question may also be relevant. In addition, the CMA notes that specific situations for the calculation of 'turnover' may arise in the areas of credit, financial services and insurance, as is recognised in the statutory instrument which relates to the determination of the maximum penalty that the CMA may impose.[28]

2.14 In cases concerning infringements of Article 101 and/or Article 102, the CMA may, in determining the starting point, take into account effects in another member state of the agreement or conduct concerned. Where it does so, the CMA will take into account effects in another member state through its assessment of relevant turnover. The CMA may consider turnover generated in another member state if the relevant geographic market is wider than the UK and the express consent of the relevant member state or NCA, as appropriate, is given in each particular case.

2.15 As stated at paragraph 2.4 above, the starting point may not in any event exceed 30% of the relevant turnover of the undertaking.

Step 2 – adjustment for duration

2.16 The starting point may be increased or, in particular circumstances, decreased to take into account the duration of the infringement. Penalties for infringements which last for more than one year may be multiplied by not more than the number of years of the infringement. Part years may be treated as full years for the purpose of calculating the number of years of the infringement. Where the total duration of an infringement is less than one year, the CMA will treat that duration as a full year for the purpose of calculating the number of years of the infringement. In exceptional circumstances, the starting point may be decreased where the duration of the infringement is less than one year. Where the total duration of an infringement is more than one year, the CMA will round up part years to the nearest quarter year, although the CMA may in exceptional cases decide to round up the part year to a full year.

Step 3 – adjustment for aggravating and mitigating factors

2.17 The basic amount of the financial penalty, adjusted as appropriate at step 2, may be increased where there are aggravating factors, or decreased where there are mitigating factors. The CMA will consider whether any adjustments are appropriate in all cases for each undertaking based on the specific circumstances of the infringement. A list of non-exhaustive factors is provided in the following paragraphs.

2.18 Aggravating factors include:

- persistent and repeated unreasonable behaviour that delays the CMA's enforcement action;[29]
- role of the undertaking as a leader in, or an instigator of, the infringement;
- involvement of directors or senior management (notwithstanding paragraph 1.15 above);
- retaliatory or other coercive measures taken against other undertakings aimed at ensuring the continuation of the infringement;
- continuing the infringement after the start of the investigation;
- repeated infringements by the same undertaking or other undertakings in the same group (recidivism);[30]
- infringements which are committed intentionally rather than negligently;[31]
- retaliatory measures taken or commercial reprisal sought by the undertaking against a leniency applicant;
- failure to comply with competition law following receipt of a warning or advisory letter in respect of the same or similar conduct.[32]

2.19 Mitigating factors include:

- role of the undertaking, for example, where the undertaking is acting under severe duress or pressure;
- genuine uncertainty on the part of the undertaking as to whether the agreement or conduct constituted an infringement;
- adequate steps having been taken with a view to ensuring compliance with Articles 101 and 102 and the Chapter I and Chapter II prohibitions;[33]
- termination of the infringement as soon as the CMA intervenes;[34]
- cooperation which enables the enforcement process to be concluded more effectively and/or speedily.[35]

Step 4 – adjustment for specific deterrence and proportionality

2.20 In considering whether any adjustments should be made at this step for specific deterrence or proportionality, the CMA will consider appropriate indicators of the undertaking's size and financial position at the time the penalty is being imposed. The CMA may have regard to indicators – including, where they are available, total turnover, profitability (including profits after tax), net assets and dividends, liquidity and industry margins – as well as any other relevant circumstances of the case. The CMA will generally consider three year averages for profits and turnover. The CMA may also consider indicators of size and financial position from the time of the infringement.

2.21 The penalty figure reached after steps 1 to 3 may be increased to ensure that the penalty to be imposed on the undertaking will deter it from breaching competition law in the future, given its specific size and financial position and any other relevant circumstances of the case. Such an increase will generally be limited to situations in which an undertaking has a significant proportion of its turnover outside the relevant market or where the CMA has evidence that the infringing undertaking has made or is likely to make an economic or financial benefit from the infringement that is above the level of penalty reached at the end of step 3. Where relevant, the CMA's estimate would account for any gain which might accrue to the undertaking in other product or geographic markets as well as the 'relevant' market under consideration.[36] The assessment of the need to adjust the penalty will be made on a case-by-case basis for each individual infringing undertaking.

2.22 In addition, there might be exceptional cases where an undertaking's relevant turnover is very low or zero with the result that the figure at the end of step 3 would be very low or zero. In such cases, the CMA would expect to make more significant adjustments, both for general and specific deterrence, at this step. Such an approach may also be appropriate where the relevant turnover did not accurately reflect the scale of an undertaking's involvement in the infringement or the likely harm to competition. This might be the case, for example, in relation to bid-rigging cases or where an undertaking's turnover in the last business year before the infringement ended was unusually low.

2.23 In considering the appropriate level of uplift for specific deterrence, the CMA will ensure that the uplift does not result in a penalty that is disproportionate or excessive having regard to the undertaking's size and financial position and the nature of the infringement.

2.24 At this step, the CMA will assess whether, in its view, the overall penalty proposed is appropriate in the round. Where necessary, the penalty reached at the end of steps 1 to 3 may be decreased to ensure that the level of penalty is not disproportionate or excessive. In carrying out this assessment of whether a penalty is proportionate, the CMA will have regard to the undertaking's size and financial position, the nature of the infringement, the role of the undertaking in the infringement and the impact of the undertaking's infringing activity on competition.

Step 5 – adjustment to prevent maximum penalty being exceeded and to avoid double jeopardy

2.25 The final amount of the penalty calculated according to the method set out above may not in any event exceed 10% of the worldwide turnover of the undertaking in its last business year.[37] The business year on the basis of which worldwide turnover is determined will be the one preceding the date on which the decision of the CMA is taken or, if figures are not available for that business year, the one immediately preceding it. The penalty will be adjusted if necessary to ensure that it does not exceed this maximum.

2.26 In addition, where an infringement ended prior to 1 May 2004, any penalty imposed in respect of an infringement of the Chapter I prohibition or the Chapter II prohibition (but not any penalty imposed in respect of an infringement of Article 101 or Article 102) will, if necessary, be adjusted further to ensure that it does not exceed the maximum penalty applicable in respect of an infringement of the Chapter I prohibition or the Chapter II prohibition prior to 1 May 2004, that is, 10% of turnover in the UK of the undertaking in the financial year preceding the date when the infringement ended (multiplied pro rata by the length of the infringement where the length of the infringement was in excess of one year, up to a maximum of three years).[38] The adjustments referred to in paragraphs 2.25 and 2.26 will be made after all the relevant adjustments have been made in steps 2 to 4 above and also before adjustments are made in respect of leniency, settlement or approval of a voluntary redress scheme discounts under step 6.

2.27 Where any infringement by an association of undertakings (for example, a trade association) relates to the activities of its members, the penalty shall not exceed 10% of the sum of the worldwide turnover of each member of the association of undertakings active on the market affected by the infringement. See the competition law guideline *Trade associations, professions and self-regulating bodies* (OFT408, adopted by the CMA Board) for further details on the imposition and enforcement of penalties on associations of undertakings.[39]

2.28 If a penalty or fine has been imposed by the European Commission, or by a court or other body in another member state in respect of an agreement or conduct, the CMA must take that penalty or fine into account when setting the amount of a penalty in relation to that agreement or conduct.[40] This is to ensure that where an anti-competitive agreement or conduct is subject to proceedings resulting in a penalty or fine in another member state, an undertaking will not be penalised again in the UK for the same anti-competitive effects.

Step 6 – application of reductions under the CMA's leniency programme, settlement and approval of voluntary redress schemes

2.29 The CMA will reduce an undertaking's penalty where the undertaking has a leniency agreement with the CMA, entered into as a result of an application pursuant to part 3 of this guidance below and in accordance with the CMA's published guidance on leniency, provided always that the undertaking meets the conditions of the leniency agreement.[41]

2.30 The CMA will also apply a penalty reduction where an undertaking settles with the CMA, which will involve, among other things, the undertaking admitting its participation in the infringement.[42]

2.31 The CMA may also apply a penalty reduction where an undertaking obtains approval for a voluntary redress scheme.[43] The procedure for applying for approval is set out in the CMA's *Guidance on the approval of voluntary redress schemes for infringements of competition law* (CMA40).

2.32 Where the CMA applies discounts at this step, these discounts will be applied consecutively.[44]

FINANCIAL HARDSHIP

2.33 In exceptional circumstances, the CMA may reduce a penalty where the undertaking is unable to pay the penalty proposed due to its financial position. The CMA emphasises that such financial hardship adjustments will be exceptional and there can be no expectation that a penalty will be adjusted on this basis.[45]

NOTES

17 In applying the steps to individual undertakings in multi-party cases, the CMA will observe the principle of equal treatment, which is articulated by the Court of First Instance (now the General Court) in the *Tokai Carbon* case as follows: 'The fact none the less remains that . . . [the Commission] must comply with the principle of equal treatment, according to which it is prohibited to treat similar situations differently and different situations in the same way, unless such treatment is objectively justified (FETTCSA, paragraph 406).' (See Case T-236/01 *Tokai Carbon Co. Ltd and Others v Commission* [2004] ECR II-1181, at paragraph 219). In doing so, the CMA will take account of the judgment of the Competition Appeal Tribunal (the CAT) in the *Kier* Construction judgment that, ' . . . it is perfectly rational for a bigger undertaking to receive a more severe penalty than a smaller company . . . However, this does not mean that penalties should be precisely proportionate to the relative sizes of the undertakings on which they are imposed . . . it will not necessarily be fair or proportionate to impose on a bigger company a penalty which reflects the same proportion of its total worldwide turnover as a penalty imposed on a smaller company represents in relation to the latter's turnover.' (See *Kier Group plc and others v Office of Fair Trading* [2011] CAT 3, at [177]).

18 See note 14 above.

19 A voluntary redress scheme is a method of alternative dispute resolution, via which a business may apply to the CMA for approval of a scheme where it is seeking to offer compensation to victims of competition law breaches.

20 For the purposes of this guidance, 'cartel activities' are agreements and/or concerted practices which infringe Article 101 of the TFEU and/or the Chapter I prohibition and involve price-fixing (including resale price maintenance), bid-rigging (collusive tendering), the establishment of output restrictions or quotas and/or market-sharing or market-dividing.

21 This is distinct from the need to deter the specific infringing undertaking from further breaches of the Chapter I or Chapter II prohibitions and/or Article 101 or 102 ('specific deterrence'), which is assessed at Step 4 (see paragraphs 2.20 to 2.24).

22 For further information on object and effect infringements see, *Agreements and concerted practices* (OFT401, adopted by the CMA Board).

23 See *Eden Brown v Office of Fair Trading* [2011] CAT 8, paragraph 80.

24 See the competition law guideline *Market Definition* (OFT403, adopted by the CMA Board) for further background information on the relevant product market and relevant geographic market. The CMA notes also that the Court of Appeal in its judgment in the *Toys and Kits* appeals stated that: ' . . . neither at the stage of the OFT investigation, nor on appeal to the Tribunal, is a formal analysis of the relevant product market necessary in order that regard can properly be had to step 1 of the Guidance in determining the appropriate penalty' and that it was sufficient for the OFT to 'be satisfied, on a reasonable and properly reasoned basis, of what is the relevant product market affected by the infringement.' See Argos *Limited and Littlewoods Limited v Office of Fair Trading and JJB Sports plc v Office of Fair Trading* [2006] EWCA Civ 1318, at paragraphs 169 and 170 to 173 respectively.

25 Relevant turnover will be calculated after the deduction of sales rebates, value added tax and other taxes directly related to turnover.

26 See *Eden Brown Ltd and others v Office of Fair Trading* [2011] CAT 8 (the *Construction Recruitment Forum* judgment), at [44]-[59].

27 Ibid.

28 See The Competition Act 1998 (Determination of Turnover for Penalties) Order 2000 (SI 2000/309) as amended by The Competition Act 1998 (Determination of Turnover for Penalties) (Amendment) Order 2004 (SI 2004/1259).

29 This will include situations where an undertaking persistently and repeatedly disrespects CMA time limits specified (for example for providing representations on confidentiality) or otherwise persistently delays the CMA's investigation. The CMA will not treat the full exercise of the party's rights of defence as unreasonable behaviour.

30 Where an undertaking **continues or repeats** the same or a similar infringement after the CMA, one of the Regulators or the European Commission has made a decision that the undertaking infringed Article 101 and/or the Chapter I prohibition, or Article 102 and/or the Chapter II prohibition, the amount resulting from the application of steps 1 and 2 may be increased by up to 100% for each such infringement established. The CMA would expect to apply such an increase only where the prior decision found that the infringement or infringements had a UK impact. The actual amount of any such increase for recidivism will be determined on a case-by-case basis having regard to all relevant circumstances. The CMA would not expect to apply an uplift for recidivism in respect of prior infringement decisions made more than 15 years before the start of the infringement for which the current penalty is being set. The CMA considers that infringements are the 'same or similar' where they fall under the same provision of the CA98 or equivalent provision of the TFEU. For instance, an infringement decision under the Chapter I prohibition or Article 101 could be counted as a 'same or similar' infringement when assessing the penalty for another infringement of Chapter I or Article 101.

31 In *Napp* at [456] and [457] the Competition Commission Appeal Tribunal (now the CAT) stated that, in its judgment, an infringement is committed 'intentionally' if the undertaking must have been aware that its conduct was of such a nature as to encourage a restriction or distortion of competition and an infringement is committed 'negligently' if the undertaking ought to have known that its conduct would result in a restriction or distortion of competition. This approach was followed by the CAT in *Aberdeen Journals* (No.2) at [484] and [485].

32 When considering whether to uplift, the CMA will take into account the individual circumstances of the failure and will impose an uplift in these circumstances only where the *warning letter or advisory letter* related to conduct the CMA considers to be the same or similar to the conduct under investigation. See CMA guidance on warning and advisory letters. The Regulators may use different terminology for their equivalents of warning and advisory letters.

33 The CMA will consider carefully whether evidence presented of an undertaking's compliance activities in a particular case merits a discount from the penalty of up to 10%. The mere existence of compliance activities will not be treated as a mitigating factor. Compliance activities are likely to be treated as a mitigating factor where an undertaking demonstrates that adequate steps, appropriate to the size of the business concerned, have been taken to achieve a clear and unambiguous commitment to competition law compliance throughout the undertaking (from the top down). This will be expected to include appropriate steps relating to competition law risk identification, risk assessment, risk mitigation and review activities, including making a public statement regarding a commitment to compliance on the undertaking's relevant website(s) and conducting periodic review of its compliance activities, and reporting that to the CMA. The undertaking will also need to present evidence on the steps it took to review its compliance activities, and change them as appropriate, in light of the events that led to the investigation at hand. The CMA will expect compliance activities and the steps taken to be appropriate to the size of the undertaking. Save for exceptional cases, the CMA will not treat the existence of compliance activities as an aggravating factor justifying an increase in the financial penalty. Such exceptional circumstances could include situations where, for example, compliance activities are used to conceal or facilitate an infringement, or to mislead the CMA during its investigation. It should be noted that the CMA has published *guidance to assist businesses to achieve competition law compliance*.

34 Intervention by the CMA would be by the exercise of its powers under sections 26 to 28A of the CA98.

35 Respecting CMA time limits specified or otherwise agreed will be a necessary but not sufficient criterion to merit a reduction at this step, that is to say, cooperation over and above this will be expected. An example of such cooperation may be the provision of staff for voluntary interviews and/or arranging for staff to provide witness statements. Note that in cases of cartel activity an undertaking which cooperates fully with the investigation may benefit from total immunity from, or a significant reduction in the level of, a financial penalty, if it satisfies the requirements for lenient treatment set out in part 3 of this guidance. Undertakings benefiting from the leniency programme will not receive an additional reduction in financial penalties under this head (since continuous and complete cooperation is a condition of leniency).

36 For example, in a predation case the relevant market may be very small. However, the act of predation might provide an undertaking with a reputation for aggressive behaviour which it could use to its advantage in many other markets. In cases concerning infringements of Articles 101 and/or 102 of the TFEU, the gain in another member state may be taken into account, provided the express consent of the relevant member state or NCA, as appropriate, is given in each particular case.

37 See note 14 above.

38 Calculated in accordance with The Competition Act 1998 (Determination of Turnover for Penalties) Order 2000 (SI 2000/309) immediately prior to its amendment by The Competition Act 1998 (Determination of Turnover for Penalties) (Amendment) Order 2004 (SI 2004/1259).

39 *Trade associations, professions and self-regulating bodies* (OFT408, adopted by the CMA Board).

40 See section 38(9) of the CA98.

41 See the CMA's guidance *Applications for leniency and no-action in cartel cases* (OFT1495, adopted by the CMA Board).

42 See Chapter 14, *Guidance on the CMA's investigation procedures in Competition Act 1998 cases* (CMA8).

43 See paragraph 3.32, *Guidance on the approval of voluntary redress schemes for infringements of competition law* (CMA40).

44 For example, any leniency discount will be applied to penalty after Step 5, then any settlement discount will be applied to the figure reached after application of the leniency discount, with finally any discount in respect of an approved voluntary redress scheme being applied to the figure reached after the application of the settlement discount.

45 See *Sepia Logistics Limited (formerly known as Double Quick Supplyline Limited) v Precision Concepts Ltd* [2007] CAT 13, at [94]. See also *GF Tomlinson Group Limited and Others v Office of Fair Trading* [2011] CAT 7, at [262].

3. LENIENT TREATMENT FOR UNDERTAKINGS COMING FORWARD WITH INFORMATION IN CARTEL ACTIVITY CASES

IMMUNITY FROM OR REDUCTION IN FINANCIAL PENALTY FOR UNDERTAKINGS COMING FORWARD WITH INFORMATION IN CARTEL ACTIVITY CASES

[3.194]

3.1 For the purposes of this guidance, 'cartel activities' are agreements and/or concerted practices which infringe Article 101 of the TFEU and/or the Chapter I prohibition and involve price-fixing (including resale price maintenance), bid-rigging (collusive tendering), the establishment of output restrictions or quotas and/or market-sharing or market-dividing.

3.2 Undertakings participating in cartel activities might wish to terminate their involvement and inform the CMA of the existence of the cartel activity, but be deterred from doing so by the risk of incurring large financial penalties.

3.3 The CMA considers that it is in the interest of the economy of the UK, and the European Union more generally, to have a policy of granting lenient treatment to undertakings which inform it of cartel activities and which then cooperate with it in the circumstances set out below. It is the often secret nature of cartel activities which justifies such a policy. The interests of customers and consumers in ensuring that such activities are detected and prohibited outweigh the policy objectives of imposing financial penalties on those undertakings which participate in cartel activities but which cooperate to a significant degree with the CMA as set out below.

3.4 In order to encourage undertakings participating in cartel activities to come forward, the CMA **will** grant total immunity from financial penalties for an infringement of Article 101 and/or the Chapter I prohibition to a participant in cartel activity who is the first to come forward before the CMA has commenced an investigation and who satisfies the requirements set out in paragraphs 3.13 and 3.14. Alternatively, the CMA **may** offer total immunity or a reduction of up to 100% from financial penalties to a participant who is the first to come forward and who satisfies the requirements set out in paragraphs 3.16 and 3.17. An undertaking which is not the first to come forward, or does not satisfy these requirements may benefit from a reduction of up to 50% in the amount of the financial penalty imposed if it satisfies the requirements set out in paragraphs 3.18 to 3.20.

PROCEDURE FOR REQUESTING IMMUNITY OR A REDUCTION IN THE LEVEL OF PENALTIES

3.5 An undertaking which wishes to take advantage of the lenient treatment set out in this part must contact the CMA following the procedures set out in the CMA's guidance on Applications for leniency and no-action in cartel cases (OFT1495) or any equivalent guidance issued by the Regulators.[46] This step has to be taken by a person who has the power to represent the undertaking for that purpose.

3.6 Initial contact can be made by telephone.[47] Prospective applications may be discussed with the CMA without disclosing the identity of the undertaking if preferred, perhaps with the prospective applicant's legal adviser.[48] However, before an application can then be taken forward, the applicant's name must be given to the CMA.

3.7 The CMA document, *Applications for leniency and no-action in cartel cases* (OFT1495) provides detailed guidance on the interaction between the CMA's approach to lenient treatment for undertakings as described in this guidance and the CMA's approach to granting no-action letters confirming immunity from prosecution from the criminal cartel offence under section 190(4) of the Enterprise Act 2002.

LENIENCY APPLICATIONS AND THE EUROPEAN COMPETITION NETWORK

3.8 The European Commission and a number of NCAs also have leniency programmes that facilitate the detection of infringements.[49]

3.9 As set out at paragraph 1.2 above, the Modernisation Regulation creates a system in which NCAs and the European Commission will apply Articles 101 and 102. The European Competition Network ('the ECN') facilitates close cooperation between NCAs and the European Commission and ensures an effective and consistent application of EU competition rules. An NCA will be considered well placed to deal with a case where the cumulative case allocation criteria are met. Details of these criteria are provided in the *Commission Notice on Cooperation within the Network of Competition Authorities* (the Network Notice).[50]

3.10 In most instances, where the CMA receives a leniency application (and it is well placed to deal with the case), it will remain in charge of the case. An application for leniency to the CMA will not be considered as an application for leniency to another authority within the ECN, even where that other authority deals with the case in parallel with or in place of the CMA. It is therefore in the interest of the applicant to apply for leniency to all the competition authorities which have the power to apply Article 101 in the territory affected by the infringement and which may be considered well placed to deal with the infringement in question. In view of the importance of timing in most existing leniency programmes, applicants will also need to consider whether it would be appropriate to make leniency applications to the relevant authorities simultaneously. A list of competition authorities in member states which offer a leniency programme can be found on the European Commission's website.[51] Individual applications may be discussed with the CMA.[52]

3.11 The CMA accepts short form 'summary applications' as contemplated in the ECN Model Leniency Programme[53] in appropriate cartel cases[54], where:

- the Commission is 'particularly well-placed' to deal with a case in accordance with paragraph 14 of the Network Notice;
- the CMA is in its opinion also 'well-placed' to act in accordance with paragraph 8 of the Network Notice;
- the applicant has made or is in the process of filing an application for immunity with the Commission; and
- the applicant is in a position where it could have benefited from immunity under paragraph 3.13 below.

3.12 Details on how information may be exchanged within the ECN, and the safeguards in place to protect the position of a leniency applicant with regard to such information exchange, can be found in the Network Notice (see paragraphs 39 to 42).

TOTAL IMMUNITY FOR THE FIRST TO COME FORWARD BEFORE AN INVESTIGATION HAS COMMENCED IN CARTEL ACTIVITY CASES

3.13 An undertaking **will** benefit from total immunity from financial penalties if the undertaking is the first[55] to provide the CMA with evidence of cartel activity in a market before the CMA has commenced an investigation[56] of the cartel activity; provided that the CMA does not already have sufficient information to establish the existence of the alleged cartel activity, and conditions (a) to (e) below are satisfied. The undertaking must:[57]

(a) accept that the undertaking participated in cartel activity;
(b) provide the CMA with all the information, documents and evidence available to it regarding the cartel activity;
(c) maintain continuous and complete cooperation throughout the investigation and until the conclusion of any action (including criminal proceedings and defending civil or criminal appeals) by the CMA arising as a result of the investigation;
(d) refrain from further participation in the cartel activity from the time of disclosure of the cartel activity to the CMA (except as may be directed by the CMA); and
(e) not have taken steps to coerce another undertaking to take part in the cartel activity.

3.14 The information, documents and evidence provided by the undertaking must, as a minimum, give the CMA a sufficient basis for taking forward a credible investigation.

3.15 If an undertaking does not qualify for total immunity under paragraphs 3.13 and 3.14 above, it may still benefit from a reduction of financial penalties of up to 100% under paragraphs 3.16 and 3.17 below or a reduction of up to 50% under paragraphs 3.18 to 3.20 below.

IMMUNITY OR REDUCTION IN THE LEVEL OF FINANCIAL PENALTIES OF UP TO 100% FOR THE FIRST TO COME FORWARD AFTER AN INVESTIGATION HAS COMMENCED IN CARTEL ACTIVITY CASES

3.16 An undertaking **may** benefit from immunity or a reduction in the level of the financial penalty of up to 100% if the following conditions are satisfied:

- the undertaking seeking immunity or a reduction in the level of financial penalty under this paragraph is the first[58] to provide the CMA with evidence of cartel activity in a market before the CMA has issued a statement of objections;[59]
- conditions (a) to (e) in paragraph 3.13 above are satisfied; and
- the information, documents and evidence provided by the undertaking, as a minimum, add significant value to the CMA's investigation, that is they must constitute or contain information which genuinely advances the investigation.

3.17 Immunity or a reduction in the level of the financial penalty of up to 100% by the CMA in these circumstances is discretionary. In order for the CMA to exercise this discretion it must be satisfied that the undertaking should benefit from a reduction in the level of the financial penalty, taking into account the overall added value provided by the leniency applicant. This will generally depend on the stage at which the undertaking comes forward, the information, documents and other evidence already in the CMA's possession and the probative value of the information, documents and other evidence provided by the undertaking. The CMA will also take into account the overall level of cooperation provided.

REDUCTION IN THE LEVEL OF FINANCIAL PENALTIES OF UP TO 50% IN CARTEL ACTIVITY CASES

3.18 Undertakings which provide evidence of cartel activity before a statement of objections is issued, but are not the first to come forward, or do not qualify for total immunity or a reduction in the level of financial penalty under paragraphs 3.13 and 3.14 or 3.16 and 3.17 above (as the case may be), may be granted a reduction of up to 50% in the amount of a financial penalty which would otherwise be imposed, if conditions (a) to (d) in paragraph 3.13 above are met. The information, documents and evidence provided by the undertaking must, as a minimum, add significant value to the CMA's investigation, that is, they must genuinely advance the investigation.

3.19 The key criterion for determining the discount available will be the overall added value of the information, documents and evidence provided by the leniency applicant. This will generally depend on the stage at which the undertaking comes forward, the information, documents and evidence already in the CMA's possession and the probative value of the information, documents and evidence provided by the undertaking. The CMA will also take into account the overall level of cooperation provided.

3.20 The grant of a reduction by the CMA in these circumstances is discretionary. In order for the CMA to exercise this discretion it must be satisfied that the undertaking should benefit from a reduction, taking into account the factors described in paragraphs 3.18 and 3.19 above.

ADDITIONAL REDUCTION IN FINANCIAL PENALTIES ('LENIENCY PLUS')

3.21 An undertaking cooperating with an investigation by the CMA under the CA98 in relation to cartel activities in one market (the first market) may also be involved in completely separate cartel activity in another market (the second market) which also infringes Article 101 and/or the Chapter I prohibition.

3.22 If the undertaking obtains total immunity from financial penalties under paragraph 3.13 and 3.14 or a reduction of up to 100% in the amount of the financial penalty under paragraphs 3.16 and 3.17 above in relation to its activities in the second market, it will also receive a reduction in the financial penalties imposed on it which is additional to the reduction which it would have received for its cooperation in the first market alone.[60]

3.23 For example, as a result of an investigation by the CMA of producers, including ABC Limited, in the widgets market, ABC Limited carries out an internal investigation and discovers that, as well as having participated in cartel activities in the widgets market, one of its divisions has participated in separate cartel activities in the sprockets market. ABC Limited has been cooperating with the CMA's widgets investigation and is interested in seeking lenient treatment by disclosing its participation in the sprockets cartel activity. Assuming ABC Limited qualifies for total immunity or a reduction of up to 100% of the financial penalty in relation to the sprockets market, it can also obtain a reduction in financial penalty in relation to the widgets market in addition to the reduction it would have received for cooperation in the widgets investigation alone, that is, an additional reduction in respect of the widgets market (the first market) as a result of its cooperation in the investigation into the sprockets market (the second market).

CONFIDENTIALITY

3.24 An undertaking coming forward with evidence of cartel activity may be concerned about the disclosure of its identity as an undertaking which has volunteered information. The CMA will therefore endeavour, to the extent possible and allowing for the exchange of information as required within the ECN, to keep the identity of such undertakings confidential throughout the course of its investigation until the issue of a statement of objections. Further detailed guidance is provided in the CMA's guidance on *Applications for leniency and no-action in cartel cases*[61] on the circumstances in which it will or may be necessary to disclose the identity of, or information, documents and evidence provided by, undertakings that have applied for lenient treatment.

NOTES

46 See the CMA's guidance *Applications for leniency and no-action in cartel cases* (OFT1495).

47 Prospective applicants may call the following number: 020 3738 6833.

48 See paragraph 3.24 as regards confidentiality.

49 The European Commission document, *Commission Notice on immunity from fines and reduction of fines in cartel cases* (published in the Official Journal of the European Communities: Official Journal C298, 08.12.06, page 17) concerns 'secret cartels'. Cartels are defined in this Notice as 'agreements and/or concerted practices between two or more competitors aimed at coordinating their competitive behaviour on the market and/or influencing the relevant parameters of competition through practices such as the fixing of purchase or selling prices or other trading conditions, the allocation of production quotas, the sharing of markets including bid-rigging, restrictions of imports or exports and/or anti-competitive actions against other competitors'. Therefore, the European Commission's Notice applies to horizontal agreements only. The CMA's civil leniency policy applies to cartel activities (as defined in paragraph 3.1 above), namely horizontal agreements and any form of price-fixing including resale price maintenance.

50 *Commission Notice on Cooperation within the Network of Competition Authorities*, Official Journal C101, 27.04.04, page 43.

51 See the document on the European Commission's website: List of National Competition Authorities which operate a leniency programme.

52 See paragraph 3.24 as regards confidentiality.

53 ECN Model Leniency Programme.

54 Further details on the circumstances in which summary applications are accepted can be found in the CMA's guidance *Applications for leniency and no-action in cartel case* (OFT1495, adopted by the CMA Board).

55 Guaranteed immunity under this paragraph will not be available if the CMA has been informed of the cartel activity by either an undertaking applying for immunity from financial penalties or an individual seeking immunity from criminal prosecution under section 190(4) of the Enterprise Act 2002.

56 For these purposes, the CMA will have commenced an investigation from the point where the CMA (a) considers there are reasonable grounds for suspecting cartel activity, such that it may conduct an investigation under one or both of

section 192 of the Enterprise Act 2002 and section 25 of the CA98, and (b) has taken active steps in relation to that investigation. Active steps may be overt or covert and may or may not involve the use of statutory information gathering powers.

57 Further details on the interpretation of these conditions is provided in the CMA's guidance *Applications for leniency and no-action in cartel cases* (OFT1495, adopted by the CMA Board).

58 Immunity or reductions in financial penalty under this paragraph will not be available if the CMA has previously been informed of the same cartel activity by either an undertaking applying for immunity under paragraph 3.13 or under this paragraph, or by an individual seeking immunity from criminal prosecution under section 190(4) of the Enterprise Act 2002, except where the only prior applicant is an individual employee or officer of the applicant **undertaking** and it remains the first undertaking to come forward.

59 Under Rule 5 of The Competition Act 1998 (Competition and Markets Authority's Rules) Order 2014 (SI 2014/458).

60 For the avoidance of doubt, the undertaking does not need to be in receipt of leniency in respect of the first market to receive this reduction. It is sufficient for the undertaking to be receiving a reduction, by way of mitigation, for cooperation.

61 The CMA's guidance on *Applications for leniency and no-action in cartel cases* (OFT1495, adopted by the CMA Board).

GUIDANCE ON COMPETITION DISQUALIFICATION ORDERS (CMA 102, FEBRUARY 2019)

[3.195]

NOTES

CONTENTS

1. INTRODUCTION

[3.196]

1.1 This guidance relates to the exercise of powers of the Competition and Markets Authority ('CMA') under the Company Directors Disqualification Act 1986 ('CDDA').[1] The CDDA applies to England, Wales and Scotland. The CMA's powers relating to the disqualification of persons for being directors of companies in Northern Ireland are contained in the Company Directors Disqualification (Northern Ireland) Order 2002 which are the same in all material respects as those under the CDDA.[2] Save for the description of the provisions in the CDDA, this guidance also applies to the exercise of the CMA's powers under the Company Directors Disqualification (Northern Ireland) Order 2002.

1.2 This guidance does not offer any commentary on the court's procedure relating to competition disqualification orders ('CDOs').[3]

1.3 This guidance provides an overview of the legal framework for the CMA's powers to seek CDOs or accept Competition Disqualification Undertakings ('CDUs') and the CMA's approach to the exercise of its powers.

1.4 Chapter 2 of this guidance provides an overview of the CMA's statutory powers to apply for CDOs. Chapter 3 outlines the statutory basis for CDUs. Chapter 4 sets out an indication of the factors which the CMA will consider when deciding whether to apply for a CDO. Chapter 5 outlines the procedure which the CMA will follow before applying to the court for a CDO. Chapter 6 explains the CMA's approach to transparency and disclosure in CDO cases.

1.5 This guidance was published and came into effect on 6 February 2019. It replaces the CMA's previous guidance – OFT510 *Director disqualification orders in competition cases.*

NOTES

1 Sections 9A to 9E CDDA. The following 'specified regulators' can also exercise these powers: the Office of Communications; the Gas and Electrical Markets Authority; the Water Services Regulation Authority; the Office of Rail and Road; the Civil Aviation Authority; NHS Improvement; the Payment Systems Regulator; and the Financial Conduct Authority. See section 9E(2) CDDA.

2 SI 2002/3150. Articles 13A-13E.

3 In England and Wales 'court' means the High Court and in Scotland 'court' means the Court of Session (section 9E(3) CDDA).

2. COMPETITION DISQUALIFICATION ORDERS

[3.197]

2.1 Under the CDDA, the court **must** make a CDO against a person if the court considers that the following two conditions are satisfied in relation to that person:

- an undertaking which is a company of which that person is a director commits a breach of competition law; **and**
- the court considers that person's conduct as a director makes him or her unfit to be concerned in the management of a company.[4]

CONDITION 1 – BREACH OF COMPETITION LAW

2.2 An 'undertaking' for the purposes of section 9A of the CDDA has the same meaning as it does for the purposes of the Competition Act 1998 ('CA98') and Articles 101 and 102 of the Treaty on the Functioning of the European Union ('TFEU').[5] An undertaking includes any natural or legal person carrying on commercial or economic activities relating to goods or services, irrespective of legal status. It follows that a sole trader, partnership, company or a group of companies can each be an undertaking.

2.3 A CDO can only be made against a **director** or a **former director of a company**. A 'director' for these purposes includes a de facto director and a shadow director.[6]

2.4 A company means a registered company but also includes any unregistered company that is capable of being wound up under Part 5 of the Insolvency Act 1986.[7] Further the term 'company' also encompasses building societies,[8] incorporated friendly societies,[9] NHS foundation trusts[10] and limited liability partnerships.[11]

2.5 A breach of competition law for the purposes of section of the 9A CDDA means an infringement of **any** of:

- the Chapter 1 prohibition of the CA98;
- the Chapter 2 prohibition of the CA98;
- Article 101 of the TFEU; or
- Article 102 of the TFEU.

2.6 The Chapter 1 prohibition is established by section 2(1) of CA98 and provides that:

> '. . . agreements between undertakings, decisions by associations of undertakings or concerted practices which:
>
> (a) may affect trade within the United Kingdom, and
>
> (b) have as their object or effect the prevention, restriction or distortion of competition within the United Kingdom,
>
> are prohibited . . .'.

2.7 The Chapter 2 prohibition is established by section 18 of CA98 and provides that:

> '. . . any conduct on the part of one or more undertakings which amounts to the abuse of a dominant position in a market is prohibited if it may affect trade within the United Kingdom'.

2.8 Article 101 of the TFEU provides that:

> '(1) The following shall be prohibited as incompatible with the internal market: all agreements between undertakings, decisions by associations of undertakings and concerted practices which may affect trade between Member States and which have as their object or effect the prevention, restriction or distortion of competition within the internal market . . .'

2.9 Article 102 of the TFEU provides that:

> 'Any abuse by one or more undertakings of a dominant position within the internal market or in a substantial part of it shall be prohibited as incompatible with the internal market in so far as it may affect trade between Member States'.

CONDITION 2 – A PERSON'S CONDUCT AS A DIRECTOR MAKES HIM OR HER UNFIT TO BE CONCERNED IN THE MANAGEMENT OF A COMPANY

2.10 When deciding whether the second condition is satisfied, the court:

- **must** have regard to whether:
  - — the director's conduct contributed to the breach of competition law;[12]
  - — the director's conduct did not contribute to the breach but he or she had reasonable grounds to suspect that the conduct of the undertaking constituted the breach and he took no steps to prevent it; or
  - — the director did not know but ought to have known that the conduct of the undertaking constituted the breach.
- **may** have regard to his conduct as a director of a company in connection with any other breach of competition law.
- **must not** have regard to any of the matters specified in Schedule 1 of the CDDA.[13]

EFFECT OF A CDO

2.11 Unless the person has the permission of the court, during the period in which a person is subject to a CDO, it is a criminal offence for him or her to:

- be a director of a company;
- act as a receiver of a company's property; and
- in any way, whether directly or indirectly, be concerned in or take part in the promotion, formation or management of a company.[14]

2.12 That person can also not act as an insolvency practitioner.[15]

2.13 The maximum period of disqualification is 15 years.[16]

2.14 In addition, any person involved in the management of a company in contravention of a CDO is personally liable for all of the relevant debts of the company.[17]

NOTES

4 Sections 9A(1) to (3) CDDA.

5 Section 9A(11) CDDA.

6 Section 22(4) CDDA which provides that a '*director . . . includes any person occupying the position of director, by whatever name called*'. Further section 9E(5) which provides that '*director includes shadow director*'. A shadow director is any person in accordance with whose directions or instructions the directors of a company are accustomed to act (section 22(5) CDDA). A person shall not be deemed to be a shadow director by reason only that the directors act on the advice given by that person in a professional capacity (section 22(5) CDDA). Director also includes a shadow director or officer of a building society, a member of the committee of management or officer of an incorporated friendly society, a director or officer of an NHS foundation trust and a member or shadow member of a limited liability partnership.

7 Section 22(2) CDDA.

8 Section 22A CDDA.

9 Section 22B CDDA.

10 Section 22C CDDA.

11 Limited Liability Partnerships Regulations 2001 (SI 2001/1090 reg.4(2)).

12 See paragraph 2.5 above for 'breach of competition law'.

13 Sections 9A(5) and (6) CDDA. Schedule 1 CDDA specifies matters to be considered when determining unfitness of directors in non-CDO cases including the director's responsibility for the causes of any material contravention by a company of any applicable legislative or other requirement; the director's responsibility for the causes of the company's insolvency; and any misfeasance or breach of any fiduciary duty by the director in relation to the company.

14 Sections 1(1)(a) and 13 CDDA.

15 Section 1(1) CDDA.

16 Section 9A(9) CDDA.

17 Section 15(1)(a) CDDA. Similarly, a person involved in the management of a company who acts or is willing to act on instructions given without leave of the court by a person whom he or she knows at that time to be the subject of a CDO will also be personally liable for all of the relevant debts of the company (section 15(1)(b) CDDA).

3. COMPETITION DISQUALIFICATION UNDERTAKINGS

[3.198]

3.1 The CMA may accept a competition disqualification undertaking ('CDU') from a director either **instead** of applying for a CDO or, where a CDO has been applied for, **instead** of continuing with the application for a CDO.[18]

3.2 A CDU has the same effect as a CDO. For the period specified in the undertaking the person will not:

- be a director of a company;
- act as a receiver of a company's property;
- in any way, whether directly or indirectly, be concerned or take part in the promotion, formation or management of a company; or
- act as an insolvency practitioner.[19]

3.3 The maximum period which may be specified in a CDU is 15 years.[20] Breach of a CDU has the same consequences as a breach of a CDO.[21]

3.4 A director can offer to give a CDU at any time during an investigation or during court proceedings.

3.5 If the CMA accepts a CDU offered by a director before court proceedings are commenced the CMA will not seek to recover any costs of its investigation from that director.

3.6 Once court proceedings have been commenced, a director may still offer to give a CDU. If the CMA accepts the CDU, the court proceedings will stop. However, the court may order that the director pay the legal costs that the CMA has incurred up to the date of the CDU.

3.7 The CMA will normally consider a reduction in the disqualification period where a director offers a CDU in terms acceptable to the CMA. The stage in the proceedings at which the CDU is offered will be a relevant consideration when the CMA is considering whether to accept a reduction in the disqualification period and, if so, the extent of any such reduction.

NOTES

18 Section 9B(2) CDDA.

19 Section 9B(3) CDDA. However, a CDU may provide that a prohibition covering the categories in the first three bullet points does not apply if the person first obtains the permission of the court.

20 Section 9B(5) CDDA.

21 Sections 13 and 15 CDDA. See also paragraphs 2.11 to 2.14 above.

4. APPLICATIONS FOR COMPETITION DISQUALIFICATION ORDERS

[3.199]

4.1 The CMA has the power to apply to the court for a CDO.[22]

INVESTIGATIVE POWERS

4.2 In addition to relying on information obtained for the purpose of an investigation under section 25 of the CA98 or otherwise, the CMA may also use any or all the information-gathering powers in sections 26 to 28 of the CA98 specifically for the purposes of deciding whether to apply for a CDO.[23]

GENERAL PRINCIPLES

4.3 The CMA will decide whether to investigate the conduct of a director and whether to apply for a CDO by reference to the facts and circumstances of each individual case, the evidence available and the public interest in the disqualification of the director. In making this assessment, the CMA will consider the factors described at paragraphs 4.4 – 4.8 amongst others.

4.4 The CMA will consider whether a company of which the person is a director (and which is an undertaking) has committed a breach of competition law.[24] Other factors relating to the breach of competition law that the CMA may take into account include:

- the nature and seriousness of the infringement;[25]
- the duration of the infringement;
- the impact or potential impact of the infringement on consumers;
- the conduct of the undertaking during the CMA's investigation; and
- any previous breaches of competition law committed by the undertaking.

4.5 The nature and extent of the director's responsibility for, or involvement in, the breach, whether by act or omission will be considered by the CMA in order to assess whether the director is unfit to be concerned in the management of a company. In all cases the CMA must, as directed by section 9A of the CDDA, consider whether:

- the director's conduct contributed to the breach of competition law;
- the director's conduct did not contribute to the breach of competition law but he or she had reasonable grounds to suspect that the undertaking's conduct constituted a breach and took no steps to prevent it; or
- the director did not know but ought to have known that the undertaking's conduct constituted a breach.

4.6 The CMA will consider whether the director has been involved directly or indirectly in previous breaches of competition law.

4.7 The CMA will also consider other matters such as the conduct of the director during the CMA's investigation into the breach of competition law and whether the director co-operated with the CMA during the investigation.

4.8 The deterrent effect of a CDO in the relevant market, and more widely, will also be taken into account by the CMA recognising the importance of the public interest in deterring breaches of competition law.

4.9 The above principles and factors are not exhaustive. The CMA retains full discretion when deciding whether to investigate the conduct of a director, to apply for a CDO, or to accept a CDU.

DIRECTORS OF PARENT AND SUBSIDIARY COMPANIES

4.10 An undertaking may in some cases constitute a group of companies (treated for the purposes of competition law as a 'single economic entity') and more than one company in the same group may be liable for a breach of competition law by the undertaking. When considering whether to apply for a CDO against the director of a company or companies which constitute the undertaking, the CMA will carefully consider the director's conduct in relation to the breach of competition law in accordance with the principles outlined at paragraphs 4.4 – 4.9 above.

IMMUNITY AND LENIENCY

4.11 Subject to paragraph 4.13 below, the CMA will not apply for a CDO against any current or former director of a company that has benefitted from leniency in respect of the activities to which the grant of leniency relates.[26]

4.12 'Leniency' for these purposes means immunity from, or any reduction in, financial penalty as described in the *CMA's Guidance as to the Appropriate Amount of a Penalty* (the 'Penalties Guidance')[27] or as described in the European Commission's *Notice on Immunity from Fines and Reduction of Fines in Cartel Cases*[28]. 'Reduction' for these purposes does not mean a reduction in the amount of financial penalty imposed for a breach owing to the application of any mitigating factors or circumstances discussed in the Penalties Guidance or the European Commission's *Guidelines on the Method of Setting Fines*[29] or to the application of a settlement or early resolution discount.

4.13 Irrespective of whether the relevant company has been granted immunity or leniency by the CMA or the European Commission, the CMA may, however, consider applying for a CDO against:

- a director who has at any time been removed or has otherwise ceased to act as a director of a company owing to his or her role in the breach of competition law in question or for opposing the relevant application for leniency; or
- a director who fails to co-operate with the leniency process – that is, a director who fails to maintain continuous and complete co-operation throughout the CMA's investigation (including any criminal investigation by the CMA) and until the conclusion of any action taken by the CMA as a result of its investigation.[30]

4.14 To minimise the risk of a CDO application being made against them, company directors whose companies have been involved in cartel activities should therefore seek to ensure that their companies approach the CMA and, if appropriate, the European Commission for leniency.

COOPERATION

4.15 In cases where a director does not qualify for leniency, the CMA may take into account the extent to which the director has provided material assistance and co-operation to the CMA in its investigations, both when considering whether to apply for a CDO against him or her and, if so, whether such co-operation merits a reduction in the period of disqualification either in the form of a CDU or a recommendation to the court when it is making a CDO.

CARTEL OFFENCE: CONVICTION/NO-ACTION LETTERS

4.16 Any court[31] by or before which an individual is convicted of an indictable offence (whether tried on indictment or summarily) committed in connection with the management of a company may make a disqualification order against that individual.

4.17 Where a director has been convicted of the cartel offence under section 188 of the Enterprise Act 2002 and that offence has been committed in connection with the management of a company, the convicting court has the power to make a disqualification order against that director.[32] The CMA takes the view that where the court by or before which the director is convicted has considered whether to make a disqualification order, that will be the most appropriate venue for consideration of the matter, so the CMA would not ordinarily expect to exercise its powers under section 9A of the CDDA in these circumstances.

4.18 Provided the applicable conditions have been met, the CMA will **not** apply for a CDO against **any** beneficiary of a no-action letter in respect of the cartel activities specified in that letter.[33] The CMA will provide recipients of no-action letters with confirmation of this policy.

NOTES

22 Section 9A(10) CDDA.

23 Section 9C(2) CDDA.

24 This is the first condition for making a CDO (see paragraph 2.1).

25 As explained in paragraph 2.5, the CMA may pursue a CDO application in respect of any infringement of Chapter 1 CA98; Chapter 2 CA98; Article 101 TFEU; or Article 102 TFEU (section 9A(2) and (4) CDDA).

26 The CMA's policy on leniency is set out in OFT1495 *Applications for leniency and no action in cartel cases, OFT's detailed guidance on the principle and process*, July 2013 or any publication replacing it ('Leniency Guidance').

27 CMA73 *CMA's guidance as to the appropriate amount of a penalty.*

28 OJ 2006 C298/11.

29 OJ 2006 C210/02.

30 See the Leniency Guidance.

31 Sections 2(1) and 2(2)(b) CDDA.

32 This is because the cartel offence is an indictable offence (section 190 Enterprise Act 2002).

33 A no-action letter is a letter sent by the CMA to an individual stating that they will not be prosecuted for the criminal cartel offence in respect of the cartel activities specified in the letter.

5. PROCEDURE

[3.200]

5.1 Before making an application for a CDO against a person, the CMA will give notice to the person likely to be affected by the application (a 'section 9C notice').[34]

5.2 The section 9C notice will include the following information:

- that the CMA proposes to apply for a CDO against that person;
- the consequences for that person of a CDO being made against him or her;
- the grounds for the proposed application;
- a summary of the evidence that the CMA will rely on in support of its proposed application, together with an index of relevant documents;
- that the person may request a copy of any of the documents listed in the index of relevant documents that are not already in his or her possession, and a deadline by which any such request should be made;[35]
- that the person has an opportunity to make written representations prior to the CMA making the proposed application, and a deadline by which that person should submit written representations;
- that the person's representations may be made by a legal advisor on the person's behalf;
- that the person may wish to offer the CMA a CDU, which, if accepted by the CMA, would mean that the CMA would not make the application for a CDO;
- an assurance that, if a CDU offered by that person is accepted by the CMA before proceedings are issued, the CMA will not seek to recover any costs from that person; and
- a statement that once a CDO application has been made to the court, the award of costs will be at the discretion of the court and that the general principle is that costs will be awarded against the unsuccessful party.

NOTES

34 Sections 9C and 16(1), CDDA.

35 Any documents which are provided may be subject to excisions for reasons of confidentiality and data protection.

6. PUBLICATION

[3.201]
The CMA will register CDOs and CDUs at Companies House, which is required to maintain a register of all disqualified directors. The Companies House register of disqualified directors can be accessed through its website: www.gov.uk/search-the-register-of-disqualified-company-directors.

The CMA will publish CDOs and CDUs on the relevant pages of its website and will make announcements, including informing media organisations, at key stages during a case such as the issue of court proceedings, the acceptance of a CDU and the making of a CDO. Further detail on the CMA's policy and approach to transparency and disclosure can be found in *Transparency and disclosure: Statement of the CMA's policy and approach.*[36]

NOTES

[36] CMA6 *Transparency and disclosure: Statement of the CMA's policy and approach.*

MEMORANDUM OF UNDERSTANDING BETWEEN THE COMPETITION AND MARKETS AUTHORITY AND THE SERIOUS FRAUD OFFICE

(October 2020)

[3.202]

NOTES

CONTENTS

1. INTRODUCTION

[3.203]
1.1 This Memorandum of Understanding (MoU) records the basis on which the Competition and Markets Authority (CMA) and the Serious Fraud Office (SFO) (referred to jointly as 'the Parties' or 'a Party' in the singular) will co-operate to investigate and/or prosecute individuals in respect of the criminal cartel offence, established by section 188 of the Enterprise Act 2002 (EA02).

1.2 The criminal cartel offence may be investigated by the CMA, by the SFO, or by way of a joint investigation between the Parties.

1.3 In accordance with section 190(2) EA02, proceedings for the criminal cartel offence may only be instituted:

- by the Director of the Serious Fraud Office (the Director), or
- by or with the consent of the CMA

1.4 The Parties envisage collaborating in this area to ensure effective and efficient investigation or prosecution of the criminal cartel offence in appropriate cases.

1.5 The Parties recognise that this MoU may require amendment in the light of future experience.

2. THE ROLE OF THE CMA

[3.204]
2.1 The CMA is the UK's economy wide competition authority established by the Enterprise and Regulatory Reform Act 2013 (ERRA13). Its statutory duty is to promote competition for the benefit of consumers both within and outside the UK. The CMA is a non-ministerial government department.

2.2 The CMA has a range of statutory powers to address problems in markets including the ability to investigate individual undertakings or groups of undertakings to determine whether they may be in breach of the prohibitions against anti-competitive agreements and the abuse of a dominant position under the Competition Act 1998 ('CA98'). As outlined above, the CMA is also able to investigate and institute criminal proceedings against individuals in respect of the criminal cartel offence.

3. THE ROLE OF THE SFO

[3.205]
3.1 The SFO was created in 1988 by the Criminal Justice Act 1987 (CJA87) following recommendations in the Fraud Trials Committee Report (known as the Roskill Report). It is a non-ministerial government department with power to investigate and prosecute serious or complex fraud, bribery and corruption. In cases of sufficient seriousness or complexity this remit encompasses the criminal cartel offence.

3.2 Section 1(1) CJA87 provides that the Director may investigate any suspected offence which appears to her on reasonable grounds to involve serious or complex fraud. Under section 1(4) of the same Act it is also open to her to conduct a joint investigation in conjunction with any other person who is in her opinion a proper person to be concerned in it and this can include other agencies such as the CMA.

3.3 In considering whether to accept a case for investigation the Director applies the SFO Statement of Principle and will take into account the actual or intended harm that may be caused to:

- the public, or
- the reputation and integrity of the UK as an international financial centre; or
- the economy and prosperity of the UK

and whether the complexity and nature of the suspected offence warrants the application of the SFO's specialist skills, powers and capabilities to investigate and prosecute.

3.4 The principal investigative tools of the SFO are contained in section 2 CJA87 and include powers to require persons to answer questions, furnish information and produce documents.

4. COOPERATION

[3.206]
4.1 The Parties will cooperate and support each other in cases of mutual interest to enhance sharing of know-how and wider cooperation including, but not limited to:

- their respective technical expertise;
- relevant know-how and training;
- targeted secondments between the Parties; and
- regular update meetings and information sharing.

5. INTELLIGENCE AND EXCHANGE OF INFORMATION

[3.207]
5.1 Each of the Parties is subject to restrictions on the disclosure of confidential information, but these are qualified by statutory 'gateways' by which they may share information with each other. The CMA's gateway is contained in Part 9 of the EA02 and the SFO's in section 3(5) CJA87. In addition, both Parties must comply with the law relating to data protection including the provisions of the Data Protection Act 2018, the General Data Protection Regulation (Regulation (EU) 2016/679) and any successor legislation.

Part 9 of the EA02

5.2 Part 9 of the EA02 prohibits the disclosure of 'specified information' except in certain circumstances. Specified information is defined in section 237 EA02 as information which relates to the affairs of an individual or the business of an undertaking which has come to the public authority in connection with listed functions or by virtue of listed enactments and specified subordinate legislation. Information which falls within this definition must not be disclosed unless disclosure is permitted under Part 9.

5.3 The CMA is empowered by section 242 EA02 to disclose specified information to the SFO in the following three circumstances:

(I) in connection with the investigation of any criminal offence in any part of the United Kingdom;
(II) for the purposes of any criminal proceedings there;
(III) for the purpose of any decision whether to start or bring to an end such an investigation or proceedings.

5.4 The CMA also needs to ensure that the considerations relevant to disclosure of specified information (section 244 EA02) have been considered and that the making of the disclosure is proportionate to what is sought to be achieved by it (section 242(3) EA02).

Section 3(5) CJA87

5.5 Section 3(5) CJA87 allows for information obtained by any person in their capacity as a member of the SFO to be disclosed to the CMA on the basis that it is a government department; on the basis that it is a competent authority having regulatory functions in relation to commercial activity; or for the purposes of a criminal investigation or criminal proceedings (see section 3(5)(a) to (c) and (6)(l)). This is subject to the caveat that there must be no statutory prohibition on disclosure.

Single Points of Contact (SPOCs)

5.6 The CMA has an Intelligence Unit and the SFO has an Intelligence Division whose staff have specific responsibility for developing channels of communication with a wide range of external organisations including financial institutions, enforcement authorities, regulators and other bodies charged with detecting and preventing fraud, criminal cartels and other criminal offences.

5.7 In order to facilitate the flow of information with both confidence and confidentiality, the Parties will appoint a nominated senior officer and deputy as SPOCs to liaise with each other. This officer or deputy will act as a filter and with authority in order to ensure that information and intelligence passing between the Parties is screened and processed with an appropriate degree of uniformity and speed and in compliance with the provisions of Part 9 of the EA02. Some information will be of a sensitive nature and source protection may therefore be essential. Care will need to be taken that the Parties are not burdened with trivial or speculative matters.

5.8 Contact between the Parties will normally be through the respective SPOCs. However, contact on investigations and/or prosecutions may be directly with nominated investigative officers and/or prosecutors subject to oversight by senior managers.

5.9 When the SFO receives evidence of an allegation of fraud or other criminal activity which could involve criminal cartel activity, an authorised person will in appropriate cases communicate with CMA's nominated SPOC as soon as practicable, and where appropriate, before any overt action is taken. The Parties can then consider the proper course of action having regard to their respective priorities and any requirement for confidentiality.

5.10 In order to ensure effective working relationships, the nominated SPOCs will meet periodically in order to discuss cases of mutual interest and to discuss the progress of cases. The Parties agree that such meetings will take place at least once every six months.

6. INITIAL ENQUIRIES AND REFERENCES TO THE SFO

[3.208]

6.1 Where the CMA receives information, through use of CA98 powers or otherwise, that criminal cartel activity may have occurred, it will undertake any necessary initial criminal enquiries, if appropriate. If the SFO receives information suggestive of criminal cartel activity, prior to any related referral from the CMA, the SFO will, in the first instance, refer that information to the CMA.

6.2 If, after any necessary initial enquiries (and informal discussions with the SFO), the CMA identifies a criminal cartel case as being likely to fall within the SFO acceptance criteria, the case may be referred to the Director if the CMA considers that the investigation of the case would be more appropriately dealt with by the SFO. The referral will provide such background information as is necessary to enable the Director to make an informed decision as to whether or not the matter should be accepted for investigation or, alternatively, whether the CMA should undertake further enquiries.

6.3 If the Director considers that the CMA should make further enquiries, the Parties will discuss and seek to agree the nature and scope of such enquiries. If the CMA agrees to undertake further enquiries, once they have been completed, the Director will reconsider the decision in the light of any additional evidence so obtained.

7. THE CRIMINAL CASE TEAM

[3.209]

7.1 Criminal cartel investigations may be led by either of the Parties. Where one Party leads an investigation it may request assistance by the provision of staff and support from the other Party

7.2 Any staff working on a criminal cartel investigation, regardless of which Party they are employed by, will work for the purpose of that investigation under the leadership and direction of the Party taking the lead (e.g. if the SFO takes the lead, the SFO may request that CMA staff assist the investigation – in such a case, the CMA staff would be working under the supervision of the relevant SFO case controller).

7.3 The provision of cross-Party staff to assist the relevant investigation will depend on the circumstances of the case and the availability of appropriate resource at the relevant time. A case conference will be convened as soon as reasonably practicable to discuss preliminary matters including the need for additional resource or collaboration from a police force or other agency.

7.4 Throughout the case, the presumption will operate that the relevant team members and management from both Parties will have access to all case-related documentation including records of decisions, advices and submission papers. It may be necessary to use the statutory gateways contained in Part 9 of the EA02 and section 3(5) CJA87 in order to share information with team members and management from the other Party.

7.5 It is also open to the Parties to conduct a joint investigation where the Director exercises her discretion under section 1(4) CJA87 to investigate in conjunction with the CMA. This would obviate the need for the SFO to rely on section 3(5) CJA87 in order to share confidential information concerning the case with the CMA as such sharing would constitute an internal transfer rather than a disclosure to an external third party.

7.6 Whether one Party leads an investigation or the Parties agree to a joint investigation it is best practice for their respective roles and responsibilities to be set out in an operational Memorandum of Understanding (MoU).

8. USE OF POWERS DURING A CRIMINAL INVESTIGATION

[3.210]

8.1 The presumption will operate that once the SFO has accepted a criminal cartel investigation;

powers under the CJA87 will be used rather than those under the EA02 where the two sets of powers would achieve essentially the same objective. However, depending upon the precise circumstances of the case, a criminal case team may determine that EA02 powers could and should be used to pursue particular objectives.

8.2 In a joint investigation consideration will need to be given as to whether to use powers under the CJA87, the EA02 or both.

9. COSTS OF THE INVESTIGATION

[3.211]
9.1 Where one Party leads the investigation, it will be responsible for setting the budget for the case (even if the case came about through a referral from the other Party). Subject to [9.2] below, the Party taking the lead will be responsible for all the costs of the investigation.

9.2 Where a Party has agreed to support the Party taking the lead by making any of its staff available, it will bear the costs of those staff (including all case-related travel and subsistence).

9.3 In a joint investigation the distribution of costs between the Parties will be agreed in writing or set out in the operational MoU.

10. CA98 INVESTIGATIONS

[3.212]
10.1 In certain cases, the CMA will progress a civil investigation using CA98 powers, while an SFO-led case team will progress an overlapping criminal investigation. Suitable procedures will be adopted to ensure that the two investigation teams maintain an ongoing dialogue and consideration should be given to entering an operational MoU. Both case teams will thereby seek to ensure that the CA98 investigation does not prejudice the parallel criminal investigation. Where there are issues in dispute between the two case teams which they cannot resolve, the Parties will attempt to resolve matters at a more senior level.

11. LENIENCY AND NO-ACTION LETTERS

[3.213]
11.1 The power of the CMA to grant criminal immunity from prosecution to individuals (no-action letters) is established by section 190(4) EA02 and use of this power is governed by the detailed guidance in its leniency policy entitled 'Applications for leniency and no-action in cartel cases'. As a matter of law the SFO is bound by any no action letter issued by the CMA.

11.2 Decisions in respect of leniency or the issue or withdrawal of no-action letters rest with the CMA. However, if any such decision could have an impact on the outcome of an existing SFO-led cartel investigation or prosecution, the CMA will consult the SFO.

11.3 Where the issue or withdrawal of a no-action letter concerning a suspect or defendant in an SFO-led case is under consideration the CMA will be reliant on the SFO's assessment as to the degree to which that individual has cooperated with the criminal case. The Parties will liaise closely in such scenarios to ensure consistency of approach in the operation of the leniency policy.

11.4 In circumstances where the SFO decides (in a SFO-led cartel investigation or prosecution) that an individual fails or has failed to cooperate with an investigation/prosecution, the SFO will consult with the CMA before any SOCPA agreement that the SFO have granted is revoked.

11.5 The grant of a no-action letter by the CMA cannot prevent prosecution for conduct, which, though related to the cartel activity, amounts to a separate and distinct offence such as a Bribery or Fraud Act offence.

11.6 The SFO agrees that if a person has been given a no-action letter in relation to particular cartel activity – and provided that letter is not subsequently revoked for any reasons set out in the CMA's no-action guidance – the SFO will not attempt to prosecute that individual for the cartel behaviour with another offence (such as conspiracy to defraud) as a device for circumventing the effects of the no-action letter.[1]

NOTES

1 See paragraph 8.20 of the CMA's leniency guidance

12. DECISIONS TO CEASE INVESTIGATION AND WHETHER TO PROSECUTE

[3.214]
12.1 Decisions about whether to cease an SFO-led criminal cartel investigation, or whether to charge or prosecute in such a case, rest with the SFO. However, in all cases, the SFO will consult the CMA.

13. CONCLUSION

[3.215]
13.1 The Parties recognise and respect their differing statutory remits, operational priorities and constraints, and confidentiality requirements. However, in the public interest they commit themselves to improve professional co-operation and to the systematic exchange of information in preventing dishonesty, corruption or serious fraud.

SIGNATORIES

For and on behalf of the Competition and Markets Authority

Andrea Coscelli **Chief Executive Officer**

Signature

Date 21 October 2020

For and on behalf of Serious Fraud Office

Lisa Osofsky **Director**

Signature

Date 21 October 2020

GUIDANCE ON THE CMA'S INVESTIGATION PROCEDURES IN COMPETITION ACT 1998 CASES (CMA8, UPDATED 4 NOVEMBER 2020)

[3.216]

NOTES

See also the list of consultations and draft documents in the Appendix at **[A1]**.

CONTENTS

1. PREFACE

[3.217]

1.1 The Competition and Markets Authority (CMA) has set out, in this guidance document, general information for the business and legal communities and other interested parties on the processes that the CMA uses when using its powers under the Competition Act 1998 (CA98) to investigate suspected infringements of competition law.

1.2 This guidance updates and supersedes the previous version issued in January 2019.

1.3 This guidance should be read alongside the CMA publications Administrative Penalties: Statement of policy on the CMA's approach (CMA4), Transparency and Disclosure: Statement of the CMA's policy and approach (CMA6) and Prioritisation principles for the CMA (CMA16), which outline the basis on which the CMA decides which cases to investigate.

1.4 This guidance sets out the CMA's procedures and explains how the CMA generally conducts investigations into suspected competition law infringements. This represents the CMA's practice as at the date of publication of this document. It may be revised from time to time to reflect changes in best practice or the law and the CMA's developing experience in assessing and investigating cases.

1.5 The CMA will apply this guidance flexibly. This means that the CMA will have regard to the guidance when dealing with suspected competition law infringements but that, when the facts of an individual case reasonably justify it, the CMA may adopt a different approach.

1.6 This guidance is concerned exclusively with the CMA's investigations under the CA98. It does not cover CMA investigations into individuals suspected of having committed the criminal cartel offence nor does it cover investigations under the Company Directors Disqualification Act 1986 (CDDA) for the purpose of deciding whether to make an application for a competition disqualification order (CDO).[1]

1.7 This guidance does not cover the procedures used by sectoral regulators[2] in their competition law investigations. Further guidance on the enforcement of competition law by the sectoral regulators is available in the CMA guideline Regulated Industries: Guidance on concurrent application of competition law to regulated industries (CMA10) or from the relevant organisation's website.

1.8 This document incorporates the commitments made in the CMA's published guideline Transparency and Disclosure: Statement of the CMA's policy and approach (CMA6) insofar as they apply to investigations under the CA98.

1.9 This guidance document also incorporates the CMA's guidance as to the circumstance in which it may be appropriate to accept commitments under section 31A of the CA98, see paragraphs 10.17 to 10.20 which constitute this guidance.

STATUTORY BACKGROUND

1.10 Section 31D(1) of the CA98 requires the CMA to prepare and publish guidance as to the circumstances in which it may be appropriate to accept commitments. Section 31D(2) of the CA98 provides that the CMA may alter this guidance at any time. Section 31D(3) of the CA98 provides that, if the guidance is altered, the CMA must publish the guidance as altered. Under section 31D(4) of the CA98 the Secretary of State must approve any guidance on commitments before it can be published. When preparing or altering guidance on commitments, sections 31D(6) and (7) of the CA98 require the CMA to consult such persons as it considers appropriate, including the Regulators. These particular provisions apply to the CMA alone and not to the Regulators.

1.11 Paragraphs 10.17 to 10.20 (the Commitments Guidance) were approved by the Secretary of State as required under section 31D(4) of the CA98 on 14 January 2019, following a consultation conducted by the CMA in accordance with section 31D(6) and (7) of the CA98. The Commitments Guidance was published and came into effect on 18 January 2019. The Commitments Guidance was re-issued unaltered in this guidance on 4 November 2020, and has been in effect since 18 January 2019.

1.12 By virtue of section 31D(8) of the CA98, the CMA must have regard to the guidance for the time being in force when exercising its discretion to accept commitments under section 31A. A similar requirement applies to the Regulators by virtue of legislation that conferred on them concurrent powers under the CA98.

1.13 This guidance (other than the Commitments Guidance included in it) takes effect from 4 November 2020. The changes in it will apply to all ongoing and future cases from 4 November 2020. See paragraph 1.11 above for the date that the re-issued Commitments Guidance entered into force.

1.14 The decision-making procedures set out in this guidance will apply to ongoing and future civil cases under the CA98. The CMA has published guidance on the principles to be applied in determining, in any case, whether criminal proceedings should be brought under section 188 of the Enterprise Act 2002 (the EA02). More information is available in the CMA guideline Cartel Offence: Prosecution Guidance (CMA9).

1.15 This document is not a definitive statement of, or a substitute for, the law itself and the legal tests which the CMA applies in assessing breaches of competition law are not addressed in this guidance. A range of publications on how the CMA carries out this substantive assessment is available on the CMA's webpages. The CMA recommends that any person who considers that they or their business may be affected by an investigation into suspected anti-competitive practices should seek independent legal advice.

1.16 This guidance sets out the procedures the CMA follows within the legal framework outlined in Chapter 2. It addresses each stage of a typical investigation in turn. The key stages of an investigation into a suspected infringement and a summary of the CMA's action at these stages are set out at Figure 1.1.

Figure 1.1 – Key stages in an investigation

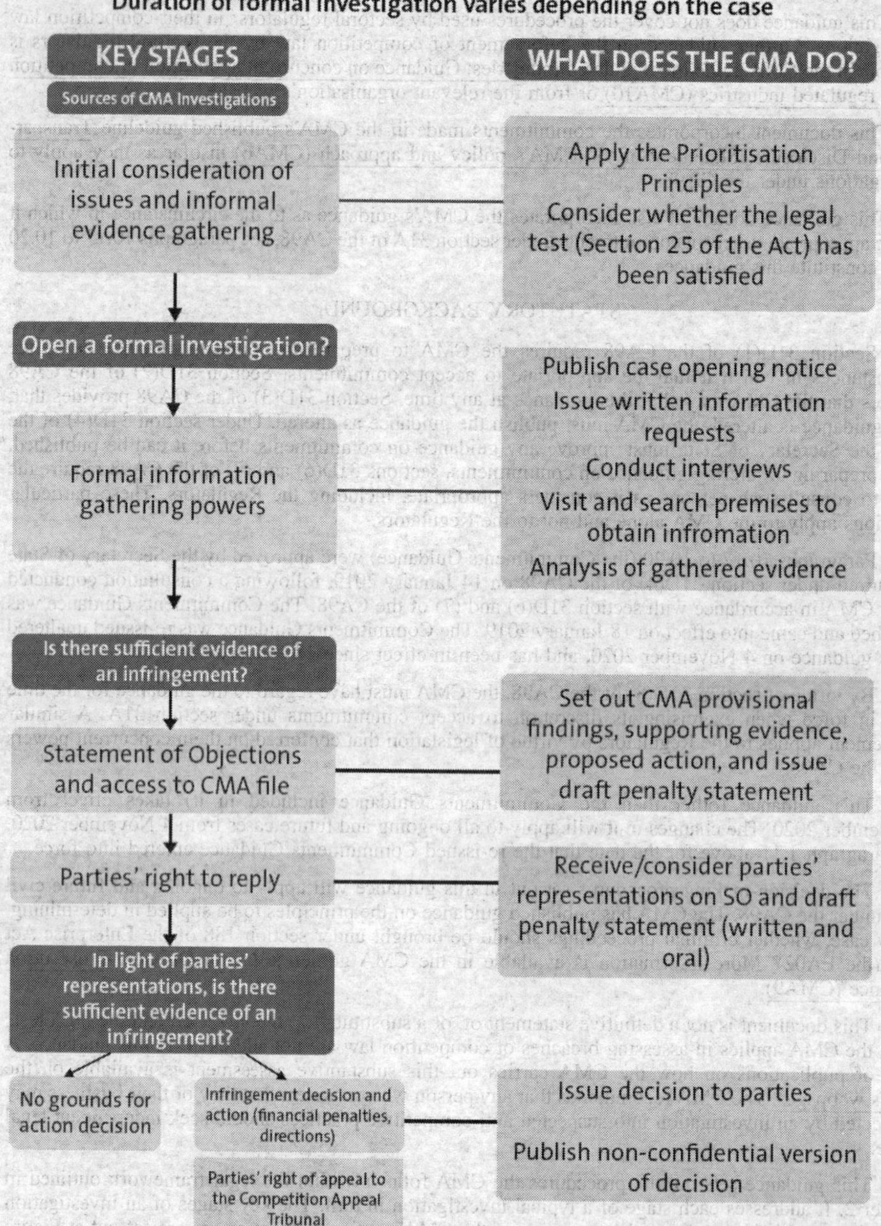

For a description of what this chart shows, see the chart descriptions section, below.

NOTES

[1] See CMA's Guidance on Competition Disqualification Orders (CMA102).

[2] The Office of Communications, the Gas and Electricity Markets Authority, the Northern Ireland Authority for Utility Regulation, the Water Services Regulation Authority, the Office of Rail and Road, NHS Improvement, the Civil Aviation Authority, the Financial Conduct Authority and the Payment Systems Regulator. This list is correct as at 4 November 2020. The list may change from time to time if further sectoral regulators are given concurrent powers.

2. THE LEGAL FRAMEWORK

[3.218]

2.1 The legal framework that applies to the investigation and enforcement of suspected civil breaches of competition law is described below.

2.2 The CA98 prohibits, in certain circumstances, agreements and conduct which prevent, restrict or distort competition, and conduct which constitutes an abuse of a dominant position.

2.3 More information on the laws on anti-competitive behaviour is available in the quick guide Competing Fairly (OFT447) and in the more detailed guidance on Agreements and Concerted Practices (OFT401) and Abuse of a dominant position (OFT402).

2.4 In the UK, competition law is applied and enforced principally by the CMA[3]. The CA98 gives the CMA powers to apply, investigate and enforce the Chapter I and Chapter II prohibitions in the CA98.[4]

2.5 There are procedural rules that apply when the CMA takes investigative or enforcement action.[5] In addition, the CMA is required to carry out its investigations and make decisions in a procedurally fair manner according to the standards of administrative law.[6]

2.6 In exercising its functions, as a public body, the CMA must also ensure that it acts in a manner that is compatible with the Human Rights Act 1998.

NOTES

3 However, certain sectoral regulators (see paragraph 1.7 above) have concurrent powers with the CMA to apply and enforce the Chapter I and Chapter II prohibitions in the CA98 within their respective regulated sectors. These sectoral regulators also have concurrent competition law powers in respect of market studies and investigations under Part 4 of the EA02.

4 See Chapter III (Investigation and Enforcement) of the CA98. At present, the CMA and sectoral regulators with concurrent powers are also required by EU law to apply the EU competition prohibitions (Articles 101 and/or 102 of the Treaty on the Functioning of the EU) alongside the domestic UK prohibitions in certain cases. This will continue to be the case until the end of the Transition Period envisaged by the UK/EU Withdrawal Agreement. During the Transition Period, existing arrangements for the discharge of the functions of the CMA will be largely unaffected. For further information on how EU Exit affects the CMA's powers and processes for competition law enforcement ('antitrust', including cartels), during the Transition Period, towards the end of that period, and after it ends, as well as the treatment of 'live' cases, which are those cases that are being reviewed by the European Commission or the CMA during and at the end of the Transition Period, see the CMA's Guidance on the functions of the CMA under the Withdrawal Agreement.

5 The Competition Act 1998 (Competition and Markets Authority's Rules) Order 2014 SI 2014/458 (the CA98 Rules).

6 See in particular *Pernod Ricard SA and Campbell Distillers Limited v Office of Fair Trading* [2004] CAT 10.

3. THE SOURCES OF THE CMA'S INVESTIGATIONS

[3.219]

3.1 There are a variety of ways in which information can come to the CMA's attention, leading the CMA to investigate whether competition law may have been breached.

3.2 The CMA's own research and market intelligence may prompt the CMA to make initial enquiries into suspected anti-competitive conduct. Alternatively, evidence gathered through other CMA workstreams, such as the CMA's merger or markets functions, or use of the CMA's powers under the Regulation of Investigatory Powers Act 2000, or information received from international partners may reveal potentially anti-competitive behaviour. In these circumstances, the CMA gathers publicly available information and may write to businesses or individuals seeking further information that the CMA considers could be relevant.

3.3 The CMA also relies on information from external sources to bring to its attention potentially anti-competitive conduct. This could be from individuals with so called 'inside' information about a cartel[7] or from a complainant.

CARTELS AND LENIENCY

3.4 A business which is or has been involved in a cartel[8] may wish to take advantage of the benefits of the CMA's leniency programme prompting them to approach the CMA with information about its operation.

3.5 By confessing to the CMA, a business could gain total immunity from, or a significant reduction in, any financial penalties the CMA can impose if it decides that the arrangement breaches the Chapter I prohibition.[9]

3.6 It is also a criminal offence for an individual to agree with one or more other persons to make or implement, or cause to be made or implemented, any cartel arrangements in the United Kingdom.[10] Cooperating current and former employees and directors of companies which obtain immunity from financial penalties will normally receive immunity from prosecution. Also, an individual who comes forward with information about a cartel may receive immunity from criminal prosecution.[11]

3.7 In addition, the CMA will not apply for a competition disqualification order against any current director of a company whose company has benefited from leniency.[12] However, the CMA may apply for an order against a director who has been removed or has otherwise ceased to act as a director of a company owing to his role in the breach of competition law and/or for opposing the application for leniency, or against a director who fails to co-operate with the leniency process.

3.8 The CMA encourages business representatives who suspect that their business has been involved in cartel activity to blow the whistle on the cartel.

3.9 For more information on what constitutes a cartel, see the CMA's quick guide Cartels and the Competition Act (OFT435) and the guideline Agreements and Concerted Practices (OFT401).

HOW TO APPLY FOR LENIENCY

3.10 The CMA handles leniency applications in strict confidence. Applications for lenient treatment under the CMA's leniency programme should be made to the Senior Director or Director of Cartels in the first instance. More detailed information on the CMA's leniency programme is available in Applications for leniency and no-action in cartel cases (OFT1495).

COMPLAINTS ABOUT POSSIBLE BREACHES OF COMPETITION LAW

3.11 Another way in which the CMA receives information from external sources is where an individual or a business complains to the CMA about the behaviour of another business. Complaints can be a useful and important source of information relating to potentially anti-competitive behaviour.

HOW TO MAKE A COMPETITION COMPLAINT

3.12 If an individual or a business suspects that another business is infringing competition law, they should contact the CMA.

3.13 Complaints about suspected cartels should be made by calling the CMA's Cartel Hotline on 0800 085 1664 or 020 3738 6888 or by emailing the CMA at cartelshotline@cma.gov.uk. These complaints are handled in confidence by the CMA. Guidance on reporting a suspected cartel to the CMA is available in the quick guide Cartels and the Competition Act (OFT435).

3.14 For all other competition related complaints, the CMA should be informed via its webpages in the first instance,[13] which will set out the format and method for making the CMA aware of competition concerns. It is also possible to make a complaint to the CMA anonymously using a non-name-based email account, a private masked phone number, by post or via a representative (such as a trade association). The CMA webpages provide information on how to do so.

3.15 Complaints made via the CMA's webpages which appear to relate to a suspected cartel will be redirected to the Cartel Hotline.[14]

PRE-COMPLAINT DISCUSSIONS

3.16 Where a complainant is considering investing significant resource into a complaint, it can approach the CMA with an outline in the first instance and ask for the possibility of having a pre-complaint discussion. This may be helpful to businesses in deciding whether to commit the necessary time and effort in preparing a reasoned complaint.

3.17 In such cases, the CMA may give an initial view as to whether the CMA would be likely to investigate the matter further if an in-depth complaint were to be made. This view would be based both on the likelihood of the complaint raising competition concerns and on the assessment of the complaint against the CMA's Prioritisation Principles to see if it falls within the CMA's casework priorities at the time (see Chapter 4 for more information on how the CMA prioritises cases). However, any view given at this stage will not commit the CMA to opening an investigation.

3.18 To be able to engage in pre-complaint discussions, the CMA would expect to receive a basic level of information submitted via its webpages from the complainant covering the key aspects of their concerns. This should include:

- the identity of the complainant and the party/ies to the suspected infringement, and their relationship to one another (for example, whether they are competitors, customers or suppliers), and
- the reasons for making the complaint, including a brief description of:
- the product(s)/service(s) concerned;
- the agreement or conduct the complainant believes to be anti-competitive;
- the type of business operated by the complainant and the party/ies to the suspected infringement (for example, manufacturer, wholesaler, retailer) and an indication of their geographic scale (for example, local, national, or international); and
- if known, the size of the market and of the parties involved (for example, market shares).

3.19 Whether the CMA engages in pre-complaint discussions will depend on the availability of CMA resources and whether the issue(s) outlined in the basic information suggest to the CMA that the case is one that would merit a prioritisation assessment by the CMA.

CONFIDENTIALITY OF COMPLAINTS

3.20 The CMA understands that individuals and businesses may want to ensure that details of their complaints are not made public. If a complainant has specific concerns about disclosure of its identity or its commercially sensitive information, it should let the CMA know at the same time as submitting its complaint. The CMA is prohibited[15] from disclosing certain confidential information and while the CMA is considering whether to pursue a complaint it aims to keep the identity of the complainant confidential. Furthermore, as noted at paragraph 3.14 above, complainants who have particular concerns in this regard can make a complaint anonymously.

3.21 If the CMA decides to open a formal investigation, it may, at some point during the course of that investigation, need to reveal a complainant's identity and/or the information[16] supplied by it, so as to allow the business under investigation to respond properly to the information provided. The CMA will aim not to – and generally will in practice not need to – reveal a complainant's identity without their consent until a Statement of Objections is issued. Before disclosing a complainant's identity or any of their information, the CMA will contact the complainant (or its representative, as appropriate) to give it an opportunity to comment. Further information is available on the CMA's contact webpages.

INVOLVEMENT OF COMPLAINANTS WHERE THE CMA PRIORITISES AN INVESTIGATION

3.22 The CMA may provide a complainant with information during an investigation. For example, a complainant may be provided with a non-confidential version of a Statement of Objections or an opportunity to comment on a draft case closure letter, where certain circumstances are met.[17]

NOTES

[7] The CMA operates a financial reward programme in exchange for information about the operation of a cartel, see Cartels: policy for witnessing and reports.

[8] A cartel is an agreement between businesses not to compete with each other. The agreement can often be verbal. Typically, illegal cartels involve cartel members agreeing on price fixing, bid rigging, output quotas or restrictions, and/or market sharing arrangements. In some cartels, more than one of these elements may be present. For the purposes of the CMA's leniency programme, price-fixing includes resale price maintenance.

[9] More information on how the CMA sets penalties is available: CMA's guidance as to the appropriate amount of a penalty (CMA73).

[10] Section 188 of the EA02. Section 188A of the EA02 sets out circumstances in which the cartel offence has not been committed. Section 188B of the EA02 provides statutory defences to the cartel offence. See further CMA guideline Cartel Offence: Prosecution Guidance (CMA9).

[11] See further the CMA's guidance on Applications for leniency and no action in cartel cases (OFT1495).

[12] In respect of the activities to which the grant of leniency relates. For further detail, see CMA's Guidance on Competition Disqualification Orders (CMA102).

[13] Complaints can also be made by calling the CMA on 020 3738 6000.

[14] The CMA offers financial rewards of up to £100,000 (in exceptional circumstances) for information about cartel activity. See the CMA's Informant reward policy for further details.

[15] Part 9 of the EA02. However, Part 9 does permit the CMA to disclose confidential information in certain specified circumstances.

[16] Complaints made anonymously should therefore avoid including information that could allow the complainant's identity to be deduced.

[17] See, for example, paragraphs 10.3—10.6 and 12.7–12.11 below.

4. WHAT THE CMA DOES WHEN IT RECEIVES A COMPLAINT

[3.220]

4.1 The CMA welcomes submissions from businesses and consumers regarding competition concerns. Due to resource constraints the CMA may not be able to respond to all complaints it receives. The CMA may engage in informal dialogue with the complainant if the CMA needs to clarify any information provided to it at this stage or the CMA requires additional information. Although the CMA considers all complaints it receives, the CMA cannot formally investigate all suspected infringements of competition law. The CMA decides which cases to investigate on the basis of its Prioritisation principles. These take into account the likely impact of the investigation in the form of direct or indirect benefits to consumers, the strategic significance of the case, the risks involved in taking on the case, and the resources required to carry out the investigation.

4.2 However, the CMA's ability to follow up on a complaint and to determine whether to open a formal investigation depends to a great extent on the timely cooperation of the complainant and the amount and quality of information they provide to the CMA. The CMA will be better able to consider a complaint that includes the information set out in paragraph 3.18 above. As noted above at paragraph 3.14, the CMA should be informed of complaints via its webpages in the first instance

4.3 If the CMA decides not to prioritise a complaint at this stage, in appropriate cases it may send an advisory letter or a warning letter to the company or companies whose conduct is the subject of the complaint.[18] This would inform them that the CMA has been made aware of a possible breach of competition law by them and that, although the CMA is currently not minded to pursue an investigation, it may do so in future if the CMA receives further evidence of a suspected infringement or the CMA's prioritisation assessment changes.

4.4 Where the CMA prioritises a complaint, the case will be allocated to the appropriate area of the Enforcement Directorate for further investigation.[19]

OVERVIEW OF PROCESS

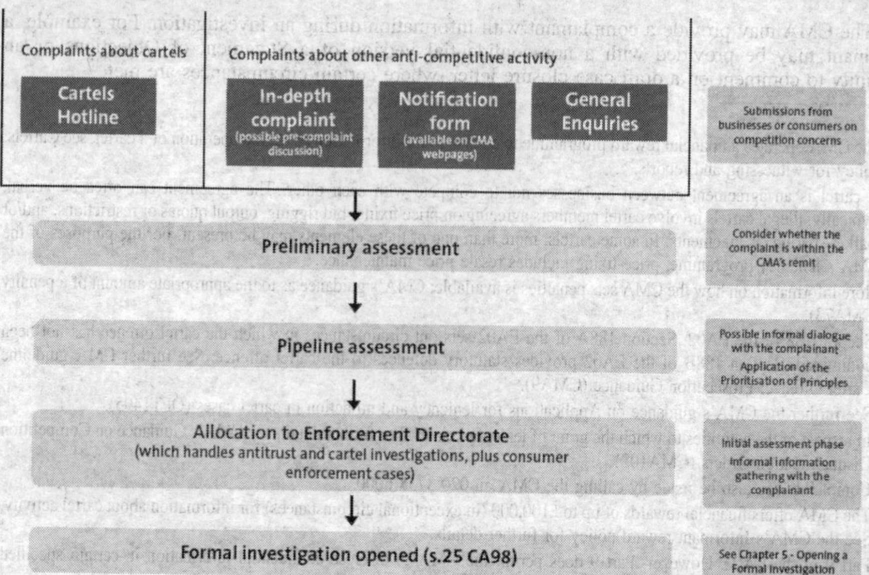

For a description of what this chart shows, see the chart descriptions section, below.

INITIAL ASSESSMENT PHASE

4.5 Once the CMA has decided to take forward a case within the Enforcement Directorate, the CMA may gather more information from the complainant, the company/ies under investigation, and/or third parties. This may involve sending an informal request for information, a request for clarification of information already provided in the complaint, or an invitation to meet with the CMA. Information will be requested at this stage on an informal basis, i.e. the CMA will rely on voluntary cooperation rather than using its formal powers to gather information.

4.6 However, it is unlikely that the CMA would gather information informally, where it considers that contacting the businesses under investigation informally at this stage may prejudice the investigation, for example in the case of suspected cartels.

NOTES

[18] See the CMA's Essential information for businesses: warning and advisory letters.

[19] In some cases, members of the Enforcement Directorate may be involved in considering the complaint.

5. OPENING A FORMAL INVESTIGATION

[3.221]

5.1 If a complaint is likely to progress to a formal investigation, the case is allocated:

- a designated case team, responsible for day-to-day running of the case, and
- a Senior Responsible Officer (SRO), who is responsible for authorising the opening of a formal investigation and taking certain other decisions, including, where the SRO considers there is sufficient evidence, authorising the issue of a Statement of Objections and any Draft Penalty Statement(s).[20]

5.2 After the decision has been taken to open a formal investigation, the CMA will send the businesses under investigation a case initiation letter setting out brief details of the conduct that the CMA is looking into, the relevant legislation, the case-specific timetable, and key contact details for the case team such as the Assistant Project Director, Project Director and SRO.[21]

5.3 The receipt of a case initiation letter will often coincide with the CMA's use of its formal powers, for example, with the business also receiving a formal notice or information request. See Chapter 6 for more information on the CMA's formal powers of investigation.

5.4 In some cases, it will not be appropriate to issue a case initiation letter at the start of a case, as to do so may prejudice the investigation, such as prior to unannounced inspections or witness interviews. In these cases, the CMA will send out the letter as soon as possible.

5.5 Once a formal investigation is opened and the parties have been informed of this, the CMA will generally publish a notice of investigation on its webpages[22] as soon as practicable after the formal investigation has been opened and updated thereafter, as appropriate. However, the CMA will generally not publish or update any notice where doing so may prejudice the investigation – or any criminal investigation or any investigation under the CDDA for the purpose of deciding whether to make an application for a CDO –.[23]

5.6 Section 25A(1) of the CA98 sets out the type of information that a notice of investigation may contain. The notice will generally include basic details of the case, such as whether the case is being investigated under the Chapter I and/or II prohibitions, a brief summary of the suspected infringement, the industry sector involved, and the identity of the businesses being investigated and may include on the case webpage an explanation of the reasons for prioritising the case. The CMA will also outline the administrative timetable for the case.[24] If the timetable changes during the investigation, the timetable will be updated in the notice of investigation including, where possible, reasons for the changes that have been made.

5.7 The CMA will normally publish the names of the parties under investigation in the notice, other than in exceptional circumstances, such as where doing so could in the CMA's view prejudice a CMA investigation or an investigation of one of the CMA's enforcement partners.[25] If it has not already done so when opening the investigation, the CMA will usually include parties' names in the notice of investigation at a later stage of an investigation, and if a Statement of Objections is issued.

5.8 In some cases, such as cartel investigations, it may not be possible to include many details of the investigation at the stage of publishing the notice of investigation, as to do so might prejudice the CMA's ongoing investigation. Save where a party has done so itself with the consent of the CMA, the CMA also will not mention publicly at the opening of an investigation whether any party to the suspected infringement had applied for leniency.[26]

NOTES

[20] The categories of decision for which the SRO is responsible are listed in more detail at paragraph 9.6 below.

[21] See Transparency and Disclosure Statement of the CMA's policy and approach (CMA6).

[22] Section 25A of the CA98 permits the CMA to publish a notice of investigation.

[23] Further information on the CMA's approach to treatment and disclosure of information is available in the guideline Transparency and Disclosure: Statement of the CMA's policy and approach (CMA6). For information regarding investigations under the CDDA for the purpose of deciding whether to make an application for a CDO, see the CMA's Guidance on Competition Disqualification Orders (CMA102).

[24] Initially, the timetable will cover the investigative stages up to the CMA's decision on whether to issue a Statement of Objections. If the CMA issues a Statement of Objections, the timetable will be updated with indicative timing of the steps to the end of the investigation.

[25] Where the CMA has published a notice identifying a party under investigation and subsequently decides to terminate the investigation of that party without making an infringement decision against it, the CMA will publish a notice stating that the party's activities are no longer being investigated (see section 25A(4) of the CA98).

[26] See further the CMA's guidance on Applications for leniency and no-action in cartel cases (OFT1495).

6. THE CMA'S FORMAL POWERS OF INVESTIGATION

INFORMATION GATHERING POWERS

[3.222]

6.1 The CMA has a range of powers to obtain information to help it establish whether an infringement has been committed.[27] The CMA can require the production of specified documents or information, ask individuals oral questions and/or carry out interviews with individuals, enter premises without a warrant, and enter and search premises with a warrant. The entering of premises can be with or without notice.[28]

WRITTEN INFORMATION REQUESTS

6.2 The CMA will send out formal information requests (also referred to as section 26 notices)[29] in writing to obtain information that it considers relates to any matter relevant to the investigation from a range of sources such as the business/es under investigation, their competitors and customers, complainants, and suppliers.

6.3 The information request will tell the recipient what the investigation is about, specify or describe the documents and/or information that the CMA requires, and set out the offences and/or sanctions that may apply if the recipient does not comply. The request may also give details of where and when the documents and/or information must be produced.

6.4 Examples of the types of documents[30] and information the CMA may ask for include internal business reports, copies of emails and other internal data. Under this power, the CMA can ask for information that is not already written down, for example market share estimates based on knowledge or experience. The CMA can also require past or present employees of the business providing the document to explain any document that is produced. If a document cannot be produced, the CMA can require the recipient to state, to the best of their knowledge, where the document can be found.

6.5 The CMA may send out more than one request to the same person or company during the investigation. For example, the CMA may ask for additional information after considering material submitted in response to an earlier request.

6.6 The CMA will ask for documents or information which, in its opinion, are relevant to the investigation at the time the request is sent out. Any queries about the scope of an information request or the time given to respond should be raised with the case team as soon as possible.

GIVING ADVANCE NOTICE AND USING DRAFT INFORMATION REQUESTS

6.7 In appropriate cases, the CMA will seek to give recipients of large information requests advance notice so that they can manage their resources accordingly.

6.8 In certain circumstances, where it is practical and appropriate to do so, the CMA may send the information request in draft. The CMA can then take into account comments on the scope of the request, the actions that will be needed to respond, and the deadline by which the information must be received. The time frame for comment on the draft will depend on the nature and scope of the request.

RESPONDING TO A WRITTEN INFORMATION REQUEST

6.9 The written information request will also set a deadline by which the response must be received.

6.10 The deadline specified in the information request will depend on the nature and the amount of information that the CMA has requested. If a request has been provided in draft and the timescale for response to the final request already discussed, the CMA will only agree to an extension in exceptional circumstances, so as to minimise any delay to the investigation. In all circumstances, recipients must provide reasons for requesting an extension to the deadline set for response.

6.11 Where a recipient has a complaint about the deadline set for a response to a written information request, the recipient should raise this as soon as possible with the SRO. If it is not possible to resolve the dispute with the SRO, the recipient may refer the matter to the Procedural Officer.[31]

6.12 The CMA expects recipients to comply fully with any information request within the given deadline. This is especially the case where the CMA has engaged with them on the scope and purpose of the request and the proposed deadline for its completion, in order to help them comply. The CMA can fine any person who fails, without reasonable excuse, to comply with a formal information request.[32] This may be either a fixed or daily penalty, or a combination of the two, depending on what is appropriate in the circumstances.[33] It is also a criminal offence punishable by fine and/or imprisonment to provide false or misleading information,[34] or to destroy, falsify or conceal documents[35] (subject in each case to certain defences or conditions set out in the CA98).

6.13 Unless otherwise indicated, the response should be sent to the case team in electronic format. The process for providing representations where a response contains commercially sensitive information or details of an individual's private affairs and the sender considers that disclosure might significantly harm their interests or the interests of the individual, is detailed in Chapter 7.

POWER TO REQUIRE INDIVIDUALS TO ANSWER QUESTIONS

6.14 The CMA can require any individual who has a 'connection with'[36] a business which is a party to the investigation to answer questions on any matter relevant to the investigation after giving formal written notice.[37] This may be a current connection or a former connection, for example where the individual used to work for the undertaking under investigation. The CMA will determine whether an individual has a 'connection with' the relevant undertaking on a case-by-case basis, taking account of the circumstances of the case.[38]

6.15 The CMA will give a formal notice to the person it wishes to interview, informing them that it intends to ask questions under formal powers. The notice will explain what the CMA's investigation is about, give details of when and where the questions will be asked or the interview will take place (which could be immediately after receipt of the notice – see paragraphs 6.18 to 6.20 below), and may indicate that the interviewee is to answer the questions via a videolink or similar technology. It also sets out both the penalties that the CMA may impose if the recipient fails, without reasonable excuse, to comply with the formal notice to answer the CMA's questions[39] and the statutory limitations on the use against them of statements made in the interview.[40]

6.16 Where the individual the CMA wishes to interview has a current connection with the relevant undertaking at the time the formal notice is given,[41] the CMA must also give a copy of the notice to that undertaking.[42] The CMA will take such steps as are reasonable in all the circumstances to provide the notice before the interview takes place. In general, the CMA will provide a copy of a notice to a relevant undertaking at the same time as, or as soon as reasonably practicable after, giving the notice to the individual.[43]

6.17 Any queries about the details of an interview notice should be raised with the case team as soon as possible.

CONDUCT OF INTERVIEWS

6.18 As indicated above, in certain circumstances the CMA may interview an individual under formal powers immediately after giving a formal notice to that person.[44]

6.19 This may include, for example, where the CMA considers that an individual may have information that would enable the CMA to take steps to prevent damage to a business or consumers, or where the effective conduct of the investigation means that the CMA considers it necessary to ask an individual questions about facts or documents immediately after having given a notice (which will generally be during the course of an inspection pursuant to the CMA's power to enter premises).

6.20 Ordinarily interviews will be recorded, but in circumstances where this is unnecessary or impracticable a contemporaneous note will be taken of the questions and the interviewee's response. The interviewee will be asked to read through and check any transcript of the recording or the questions and answers in the note and to confirm, in writing, that they are an accurate account of the interview.[45] Further information on the CMA's approach to handling confidential information can be found in Chapter 7. The CMA will not seek comments on accuracy and representations on confidentiality of the transcript (or note) of the interview until it is satisfied that it can do so without risk to the investigation.

CAN A LEGAL ADVISER BE PRESENT?

6.21 Any person being formally questioned or interviewed by the CMA may request to have a legal adviser present to represent their interests. In some cases, an individual may choose to be represented by a legal adviser who is also acting for the undertaking under investigation. While the CMA recognises that the interview power may be used in a range of circumstances, the starting point for the CMA is that it will be generally inappropriate for a legal adviser only acting for the undertaking to be present at the interview. The CMA also considers that in certain circumstances there may be a risk that the presence at the interview of a legal adviser only acting for the business will prejudice the investigation, for example if their presence reduces the incentives on the individual being questioned to be open and honest in their account. In cases where the CMA wishes to question a person having entered into premises as described at paragraph 6.38 below, the questioning may be delayed for a reasonable time to allow the individual's legal adviser to attend.[46] During this time, the CMA may make this subject to certain conditions for the purpose of reducing the risk of contamination of witness evidence. Such conditions could include requesting that a CMA officer accompanies the individual in the period before the interview takes place and/or suspending the individual's use of electronic devices, including telephones.

POWER TO ENTER PREMISES

6.22 In some cases, the CMA will visit premises to obtain information. The power the CMA uses to gain entry will depend on whether the CMA intends to inspect business premises[47] (such as an office or a warehouse) or domestic premises[48] (such as the home of an employee).

6.23 Under certain circumstances the CMA can enter business premises, but not domestic premises, without a warrant. Where the CMA has obtained a warrant[49] in advance of entry, the CMA can enter and search both business and domestic premises. These two powers (to enter premises without a warrant and to enter premises with a warrant) are explained below.

6.24 The occupier of the premises does not have to be suspected of having breached competition law.[50]

ENTERING PREMISES WITHOUT A WARRANT

See footnote 51[51]

6.25 A CMA officer who is authorised by the CMA in writing to enter premises but does not have a warrant may enter business premises in connection with an investigation if they have given the premises' occupier at least two working days' written notice.[52]

6.26 In certain circumstances, the CMA does not have to give advance notice of entry.[53] For example, the CMA does not have to give advance notice if it has reasonable suspicion that the premises are, or have been, occupied by a party to an agreement that the CMA is investigating or a business whose conduct the CMA is investigating, or if a CMA authorised officer has been unable to give notice to the occupier, despite taking all reasonably practicable steps to give notice.

WHAT POWERS DOES THE CMA HAVE WHEN ENTERING BUSINESS PREMISES WITHOUT A WARRANT?

6.27 When an inspection without a warrant is taking place, CMA officers may require any person to:

- produce any document that may be relevant to the CMA's investigation – CMA officers can take copies of, or extracts from, any document produced
- provide an explanation of any document produced, and/or
- tell the CMA where a document can be found if CMA officers consider it to be relevant to the investigation.

6.28 CMA officers may also require any relevant information electronically stored to be produced in a form that can be read and taken away, and they may also take steps necessary to preserve documents, including electronic material, or prevent interference with them.[54]

ENTERING AND SEARCHING PREMISES WITH A WARRANT

See footnote 55[55]

6.29 The CMA can apply to the court[56] for a warrant to enter and search business or domestic premises.

6.30 The CMA would usually seek a warrant to search premises where the CMA suspects that the information relevant to the investigation may be destroyed or otherwise interfered with if the CMA requested the material via a written request. Therefore, the CMA mostly uses this power to gather information from businesses or individuals suspected of participating in a cartel.

WHAT POWERS DOES THE CMA HAVE WHEN ENTERING PREMISES WITH A WARRANT?

6.31 Where an inspection is carried out under a warrant, CMA officers are authorised to enter premises using such force as is reasonably necessary, but only if they are prevented from entering the premises. CMA officers cannot use force against any person.

6.32 In addition to the CMA's powers described above, the warrant also authorises CMA officers[57] to search the premises for documents that appear to be of the kind covered by the warrant and take copies of or extracts from them.[58]

6.33 The search may cover offices, desks, filing cabinets, electronic devices such as computers, mobile phones and tablets, as well as any documents, on the premises. The CMA can also take away from the premises[59]:

- original documents that appear to be covered by the warrant if the CMA thinks it is necessary to preserve the documents or prevent interference with them or where it is not reasonably practicable to take copies of them on the premises

- any document, or copies of it, to determine whether it is relevant to the investigation, when it is not practicable to do so at the premises. If the CMA considers later on that the information is outside the scope of the investigation, the CMA will return it[60]
- any relevant document, or copies of it, contained in something else where it is not practicable to separate out the relevant document at the premises. As above, the CMA will return information if the CMA considers later on that it is outside the scope of the investigation, and/or
- copies of computer hard drives, mobile phones, mobile email devices and other electronic devices.

6.34 At the end of the inspection, the CMA officer will provide, where practicable, a list of documents and/or extracts that have been taken.

WHAT WILL HAPPEN UPON ARRIVAL?

6.35 The CMA's authorised officers will normally arrive at the premises during office hours. On entry, they will provide evidence of their identity, written authorisation by the CMA, and a document setting out what the investigation is about and describing what criminal offences may be committed if a person fails to co-operate. A separate document will also be provided that sets out the powers of the authorised officers and the right of the occupier to request that a legal adviser is present.

6.36 Where the CMA has obtained a warrant, the CMA officer will produce it on entry. The warrant will list the names of the CMA officers authorised to exercise the powers under the warrant and will state what the investigation is about and describe the criminal offences that may be committed if a person fails to co-operate.

6.37 Where possible, the person in charge at the premises should designate an appropriate person to be a point of contact for CMA authorised officers during the inspection.

CAN A LEGAL ADVISER BE PRESENT?

6.38 The occupier may ask legal advisers to be present during an inspection, whether conducted with or without a warrant. If the occupier has not been given notice of the visit, and there is no in-house lawyer on the premises, CMA officers may wait a reasonable time for legal advisers to arrive.[61]

6.39 During this time, the CMA may take necessary measures to prevent tampering with evidence or warning other businesses about the investigation.[62]

WHAT IF THERE IS NOBODY AT THE PREMISES?

6.40 If there is no one at the premises when CMA officers arrive, the officers must take reasonable steps to inform the occupier that the CMA intends to enter the premises. Once the CMA has informed them, or taken such steps as it is able to inform them, the CMA must allow the occupier or their legal or other representative a reasonable opportunity to be present when the CMA carries out a search under the warrant.[63]

6.41 If CMA officers have not been able to give prior notice, the CMA must leave a copy of the warrant in a prominent place on the premises. If, having taken the necessary steps, the CMA has entered premises that are unoccupied, upon leaving those premises the CMA must leave them secured as effectively as they were found.[64]

VOLUNTARY PROVISION OF INFORMATION

6.42 There may be circumstances under which a business may seek to provide information and documents voluntarily to the CMA. The business should discuss any voluntary provision with the case team prior to sending any material.

RETURN OF INFORMATION

6.43 Where it considers it appropriate, the CMA may return information it has gathered during the course of an investigation (irrespective of how that information has been obtained).[65] The CMA may return information where, after careful review, the CMA considers it is duplicate information or information that is outside the nature and scope of the investigation, including where information falls outside the scope of the investigation as a result of that scope having changed. Any such information that is returned will no longer form part of the CMA's investigation file.[66]

NOTES

27 Information gathered under the CMA's powers can also be used in any director disqualification proceedings the CMA brings. For further information, see the CMA's Guidance on Competition Disqualification Orders (CMA102).

28 At present, the CMA also has powers to gather information to assist other authorities in relation to their investigations into suspected competition infringements in other parts of the European Union. For example, the CMA may assist the Commission in obtaining information in relation to its investigations into suspected infringements of Articles 101 and 102 of the TFEU. This will remain the case until at least the end of the Transition Period. For further information see Chapter 16 below.

29 Section 26 of the CA98 gives the CMA the power to require the production of information and documents. when conducting a formal investigation.

30 The term 'document' includes 'information recorded in any form', section 59 of CA98.

31 See Chapter 15 and Rule 8 of the CA98 Rules. See Procedural Officer: raising procedural issues in CMA cases, for further details.

32 Any decision to impose a penalty for failure to comply with a formal information request may take into account whether

the CMA had issued a draft information request and set a deadline for compliance with the final information request that reflected comments received on the draft request from that party. For more information on potential financial penalties for failing to comply with the CMA's powers of investigation see Administrative Penalties: Statement of policy on the CMA's approach (CMA4).

33 Section 40A of the CA98. Failure to comply includes failures to answer questions asked by the CMA, failures to produce documents required by the CMA, or failures to provide adequate or accurate information in response to any requirement imposed on a person under section 26, 26A, 27, 28 or 28A of the CA98. See CMA guideline Administrative Penalties: Statement of policy on the CMA's approach (CMA4).

34 Section 44 of the CA98.

35 Section 43 of the CA98.

36 Section 26A(6) of the CA98 describes the meaning of 'connection with' an undertaking, being an individual who 'is or was (i) concerned in the management or control of the undertaking, or (ii) employed by, or otherwise working for, the undertaking'.

37 Section 26A of the CA98.

38 An individual who has a 'connection with' a business could include current or former directors, partners or equivalent officers; any person exercising management functions of any sort; temporary or permanent employees, consultants, volunteers or contract staff; professional advisers or any other person who has advised the business; and/or officers or controllers of shareholders that exercise or have exercised any degree of 'control' of the relevant business. A person does not need to have received a salary, fee, allowance, equity share, capital gain, or any other form of remuneration or payment from a business in order to have a 'connection with' a relevant business. For these purposes, a 'director' includes any person occupying the position of director, by whatever name called. This includes a person formally appointed to a company board, as well as any person who assumes to act as a director (a de facto director). It also includes a 'shadow director', defined as any person in accordance with whose directions or instructions the directors of a company are accustomed to act (other than advice given purely in a professional capacity).

39 Section 40A of the CA98. For more information on potential financial penalties for failing to comply with the CMA's powers of investigation see Administrative Penalties: Statement of policy on the CMA's approach (CMA4).

40 Section 30A(2) and (3) of the CA98 provide that a statement obtained from an individual through the use of the CMA's formal interview powers may only be used as evidence against that individual on a prosecution for an offence in providing false or misleading information, or on a prosecution for some other offence where in giving evidence in the proceedings the individual makes a statement that is inconsistent with the statement obtained by the CMA and evidence relating to the latter statement is adduced, or a question relating to it is asked, by or on behalf of the individual.

41 See footnote 36 above.

42 Section 26A(2) of the CA98.

43 Section 26A(3) of the CA98 requires the CMA to 'take such steps as are reasonable in all the circumstances to comply with the requirement [to provide a copy of the interview notice at the time it is given to the individual] . . . before the time at which the individual is required to answer questions.' The CMA may consider that, in all the circumstances, it is not in a position to provide a copy of the formal interview notice to the relevant undertaking before conducting an interview, for example where a delay in conducting an interview may compromise the investigation or otherwise undermine the CMA's ability to exercise its functions under the CA98.

44 Section 26A(1) of the CA98.

45 The CMA will also send a copy of the transcript or note to any undertaking with which the individual has a 'current connection', and to which the CMA has given a copy of the formal interview notice pursuant to section 26A(2) of the CA98, to allow such undertaking(s) to make confidentiality representations to the CMA. Additionally, if appropriate, the CMA will send a copy of the transcript or note to any undertaking with which the individual has a 'former connection', to allow such undertaking to make confidentiality representations to the CMA.

46 Rule 4 of the CA98 Rules.

47 Business premises are defined as meaning any premises (or part of any premises) not used as a dwelling, section 27(6) of the CA98.

48 Domestic premises are defined as premises (or any part of premises) used as a dwelling, and also used in connection with the affairs of an undertaking or association of undertakings, or where documents relating to the affairs of an undertaking or association of undertakings are kept, section 28A(9) of the CA98.

49 From the High Court of England and Wales or Northern Ireland, the Court of Session in Scotland, or the Competition Appeal Tribunal.

50 For example, the CMA could enter the premises of a supplier or a customer of the business suspected of breaching the law, so long as the CMA has taken all reasonably practicable steps to notify them in advance of the CMA's intended entry.

51 Section 27 of the CA98.

52 The written notice will set out what the investigation is about and the criminal offences that may be committed if a person fails to comply.

53 Section 27(3) of the CA98.

54 Section 27(5) of the CA98.

55 Section 28 of the CA98 in relation to business premises. Section 28A of the CA98 in relation to domestic premises.

56 The High Court in England and Wales or Northern Ireland, the Court of Session in Scotland, or the Competition Appeal Tribunal.

57 Other persons, such as IT specialists or industry experts, may also be authorised to carry out specific tasks under the supervision of authorised CMA officers.

58 For business premises, section 28(2)(b) of the CA98. For domestic premises, section 28A(2)(b) of the CA98.

59 For business premises, section 28(2)(c) of the CA98. For domestic premises, section 28A(2)(c) of the CA98. The CMA can only retain these documents for a maximum period of three months (for business premises, section 28(7) of the CA98. For domestic premises, section 28A(8) of the CA98).

60 However, the CMA may retain all of the material if it is not reasonably practicable to separate the relevant information from the irrelevant information without prejudicing its lawful use, for example as evidence.

61 Rule 4 of the CA98 Rules.

62 This could include sealing filing cabinets, keeping business records in the same state and place as when CMA officers arrived, suspending external email or the making and receiving of calls, and/or allowing CMA officers to enter and remain in offices of their choosing. It may be a criminal offence to tamper with evidence protected in this way.

63 Rule 4 of the CA98 Rules.

64 For business premises, section 28(5). For domestic premises, section 28A(6) of the CA98.

65 As noted, however, the CMA may retain all of the information or materials it has gathered in the course of its investigation if it is not reasonably practicable to separate the relevant information from the irrelevant information.

66 The CMA file will include all information which remains relevant to the investigation.

7. LIMITS ON THE CMA'S POWERS OF INVESTIGATION

PRIVILEGED COMMUNICATIONS

[3.223]

7.1 Under the CA98, the CMA is not allowed to use its powers of investigation to require anyone to produce or disclose[67] privileged communications.

7.2 Privileged communications are defined in the CA98.[68] They include communications, or parts of such communications, between a professional legal adviser and their client for the purposes of giving or receiving legal advice, or those which are made in connection with, or in contemplation of, legal proceedings, and for the purposes of those proceedings. For example, this would cover a letter from a company's lawyer to the company advising on whether a particular agreement infringed the law.

7.3 If there is a dispute during an inspection as to whether communications, or parts of communications, are privileged, a CMA officer may request that the communications are placed in a sealed envelope or package. The officer will then discuss the arrangements for the safe-keeping of these items by the CMA pending resolution of the dispute.

PRIVILEGE AGAINST SELF-INCRIMINATION

7.4 When the CMA requests information or explanations, the CMA cannot force a business to provide answers that would require an admission that it has infringed the law.[69] The CMA can, however, ask questions about or ask for the production of any documents already in existence, or information relating to facts, such as whether a given employee attended a particular meeting.

7.5 The law on privilege is complicated. As investigators of a possible infringement, the CMA is not able to advise on the circumstances in which a person can claim privilege. Anyone in any doubt about how it applies in practice should seek independent legal advice.

HANDLING CONFIDENTIAL INFORMATION

7.6 During the course of an investigation the CMA acquires a large volume of confidential information relating to both businesses and individuals.

7.7 There are strict rules governing the extent to which the CMA is permitted to disclose such information, as set out in Part 9 of the EA02. In many instances the CMA may have to redact documents the CMA proposes to disclose to remove any confidential information, for example, by blanking out parts of documents or by aggregating figures.

7.8 During the course of an investigation, the CMA may request confidentiality representations on the documents held on its file. Any such requests will generally provide an explanation as to the types of material the CMA considers are likely to be confidential under Part 9 of the EA02. It may also include a suggested framework according to which the information provider should detail any confidentiality representations. A deadline will be set for provision of confidentiality representations reflecting the extent of the material provided. Any request for an extension to the deadline, along with reasons for such a request, should be discussed well in advance of the deadline with the case team.

7.9 Representations should be provided where a person or business considers that any information they are giving the CMA, or that the CMA has acquired, is commercially sensitive or contains details of an individual's private affairs and that disclosing it might significantly harm the interests of the business or person. The CMA will not accept blanket or unsubstantiated confidentiality claims.

7.10 In the event that the CMA does not receive any confidentiality representations (and has not been notified that none will be provided) within the deadline stated the CMA will assume that no confidentiality is being claimed in respect of the information when deciding whether it should be disclosed.

7.11 The CMA may not agree with the person or business who provided it that the information in question is confidential,[70] or the CMA may agree that the information is confidential but consider that it is necessary to disclose the information to the parties in the investigation in order to enable them to exercise their rights of defence. In such circumstances, the CMA will give the person or business that provided the information prior notice of the proposed action and will give them a reasonable opportunity to make representations. The CMA will then inform the party whether or not the CMA still intends to disclose the information, after considering all the relevant facts.

7.12 In some cases, the CMA may consider the use of practices such as confidentiality rings or data rooms[71] at access to file stage to handle the disclosure of confidential information to a limited group of persons.

7.13 The CMA will only use these procedures where there are identifiable benefits in doing so and where any potential legal and practical difficulties can be resolved swiftly in agreement with the parties concerned.[72] In such cases, the person or business that provided the information will be informed of the CMA's proposed course of action and provided with a reasonable opportunity to comment. The CMA will then inform the person or business whether or not it still intends to use the proposed confidentiality ring and/or data room arrangement, after considering all the relevant facts.

7.14 Where a person or business is unhappy about the extent and/or method of disclosure, they should raise this as soon as possible with the SRO. If it is not possible to resolve the dispute with the SRO, the person or business may refer the matter to the Procedural Officer.[73]

7.15 Further information on the CMA's approach to the treatment and disclosure of information, including to identifying confidential information, is available in the guideline Transparency and Disclosure: Statement of the CMA's policy and approach (CMA6).

NOTES

67 Production of privileged communications may be through providing written documents or orally (for example, during an interview).

68 Section 30 of the CA98.

69 Privilege against self-incrimination is an aspect of the right to a fair trial guaranteed by Article 6 of the European Convention on Human Rights. This is given effect in the United Kingdom by the Human Rights Act 1998.

70 Particular types of information that the CMA is unlikely to consider to be 'confidential' includes financial information or certain other data relating to a business that is more than two years old and information that is already in the public domain or can be readily deduced from information in the public domain.

71 In practice, the CMA is only likely to use data rooms in exceptional circumstances.

72 See further detail at Chapter 11.

73 See Chapter 15 and Rule 8 of the CA98 Rules. See the CMA's webpage, raising procedural issues in CMA cases, for further details.

8. TAKING URGENT ACTION TO PREVENT SIGNIFICANT DAMAGE OR TO PROTECT THE PUBLIC INTEREST

[3.224]

8.1 The CMA has the power[74] to give temporary directions (referred to as 'interim measures') if:

(a) the CMA has begun, but not completed, an investigation under section 25 of the CA98; and

(b) the CMA considers that it is necessary for it to act as a matter of urgency for the purpose of:

 (i) preventing significant damage to a particular person or category of person; or

 (ii) protecting the public interest.

8.2 The CMA can give interim measures directions on its own initiative or in response to an application for interim measures if it considers that the conditions set out in paragraph 8.1 are met.

APPLICATION FOR INTERIM MEASURES

8.3 Any person who considers that the alleged anti-competitive behaviour of another business is causing them significant damage may apply to the CMA to take interim measures.

8.4 Potential applicants should contact the case team in the first instance[75] to discuss the information requirements and explain the procedure. Where a person is considering applying for interim measures but the CMA has not opened an investigation in relation to a relevant alleged infringement, that person may request a pre-complaint discussion (see paragraph 3.16). When doing so, that person should indicate their potential interest in making an interim measures application and the reasons for considering such an application.

8.5 Applicants should provide as much information and evidence as possible to demonstrate their case for interim measures and should also indicate as precisely as possible the nature of the interim measure being sought. The application should include a declaration of truth[76] by the applicant, or a person authorised to act on behalf the applicant, that:

- to the best of their knowledge and belief, the information and evidence provided to the CMA in support of the application is true, correct, and complete in all material particulars; and
- they understand that it is a criminal offence under section 44 of the CA98 for a person, recklessly or knowingly, to supply to the CMA information which is false or misleading in a material particular. This includes providing such information to another person knowing that the information is to be used for the purpose of providing information to the CMA.

8.6 The applicant should at the same time submit a separate, non-confidential version of the information and evidence they have provided in support of their application and, in an annex clearly marked as confidential, set out clearly why the redacted information should be regarded as confidential. The CMA may provide this non-confidential version to the party/ies in relation to which the application for interim measures has been made to enable the application to be considered expeditiously, where necessary. More information about how the CMA handles confidential information is available at paragraphs 7.6—7.15 above.

8.7 Moreover, the CMA may (such as in particular, to be able to consider the interim measures application expeditiously) decide that it is appropriate for any unredacted information that the applicant considers confidential to be placed into a confidentiality ring or data room (see paragraph 8.10 below).[77]

DECISION TO IMPOSE INTERIM MEASURES

8.8 The CMA has the discretion whether to make an interim measures direction. The SRO may provisionally decide to give an interim measures direction (a provisional decision which may follow a complaint or be on the CMA's own initiative). In this case, the CMA will write to the business to which the directions are addressed setting out the terms of the proposed directions and the reasons for giving them. The CMA will also allow them a reasonable opportunity to make representations on that provisional decision. Given the time-critical nature of the interim measures process, the time allowed may necessarily be short.

8.9 The business to which the directions are addressed will also be allowed a reasonable opportunity to inspect documents on the CMA's file that relate to the proposed directions. 'Reasonable opportunity' for these purposes will depend upon the circumstances of the case, taking into account factors such as the urgency of the situation and the likely impact of the proposed interim measures directions on the business to which they are addressed. Given the need to act as a matter of urgency in interim measures cases, the CMA will provide only those documents relied on in the provisional decision that relate to the proposed directions the CMA considers are necessary to prevent significant damage or protect the public interest. At the interim measures stage, the CMA will not normally provide access to documents on the CMA's file that relate to the suspected infringement of the Chapter I or Chapter II prohibitions. The business to which the directions are addressed will have the opportunity to inspect such documents should the CMA issue a Statement of Objections.[78] However, a schedule of additional documents on the CMA's file will also be provided, with an opportunity for the business to request the disclosure of additional documents where it can satisfy the CMA that this is necessary for it to respond to the CMA's provisional decision.

8.10 The CMA may withhold any documents to the extent to which they contain any confidential information (or are internal documents).[79] The CMA considers that it may be appropriate in some circumstances to provide access to certain documents by using a confidentiality ring or data room, having regard to the considerations set out in Chapter 11 below.[80]

8.11 After taking into account any representations, and having satisfied itself as to the adequacy of the evidence it is relying upon and taking into account all the circumstances of the case, the CMA will make its final decision and inform the applicant and the business against which the order is being sought. The SRO is responsible for deciding whether to give an interim measures direction. Before taking this decision, the SRO will consult other senior CMA officials as appropriate.

8.12 In deciding whether the imposition of interim measures is appropriate in the relevant circumstances, the CMA will seek to ensure that:

- it imposes interim measures only where it has identified specific behaviour or conduct that it considers is causing or is likely to cause significant damage to a particular person or category of person, or is or is likely to be contrary to the public interest; and
- the particular interim measures sought prevent, limit or remedy the significant damage that the CMA has identified, and are proportionate for the purpose of preventing, limiting or remedying that significant damage.

8.13 The CMA will assess whether conduct is causing or is likely to cause significant damage with regard to the facts of the case. In particular, the CMA will assess the nature of the market(s) in question and the dynamics of competition within the market(s), the effect the conduct is having or is likely to have on a particular business or categories of businesses in the market(s), or the effect that the conduct is having or is likely to have on the public interest. The CMA will also consider the impact of making such an interim measures direction on the potential addressee of such a decision and on other parties, and the extent to which the applicant has taken reasonable action to seek to avoid or mitigate the significant damage that may arise.

8.14 Damage will be significant where a particular person or category of persons is or is likely to be restricted in their ability to compete effectively in the market(s), such that this is causing or is likely to cause significant damage to their commercial position. Damage can include actual or potential:

- financial loss to a person or class of persons (to be assessed with reference to that person's size or financial resources as well as the proportion of the loss in relation to the person's total revenue);
- restriction on a person's or class of persons' ability to obtain supplies and/or access to customers; and
- damage to the goodwill or reputation of a person or class of persons.

8.15 Significant damage may be temporary or permanent – it does not require that the damage is irreparable, and/or that any business will or may exit the market(s) in question. The CMA will take into account the facts of the case, the nature of competition in the relevant market(s) and the potential duration of the interim measures in determining the period over which the relevant damage is to be assessed.

8.16 The CMA may also consider that it is necessary to act urgently to protect the public interest, for example, to prevent damage being caused to a particular industry, to consumers, or to competition more generally as a result of the suspected infringement. In determining whether interim measures may be appropriate in order to protect the public interest, the CMA will have particular regard to the effect or potential effect that the relevant conduct is having, or is likely to have, on consumers or categories of consumers.

8.17 Possible content of interim measures could include requiring a party to:

- continue the supply of goods, services or other inputs (for example, access to essential infrastructure) where that supply is required to prevent significant damage to a person or persons in the market(s) or any associated market(s) in question, or to enable customers to obtain access to goods or services; and
- reverse a price increase or decrease for any goods or services where that price increase or decrease has or is likely to cause significant damage to any person's or category of persons' ability to compete effectively or is likely to cause a detriment to the public.

8.18 Where the investigation concerns an agreement, the CMA will not seek interim measures where the CMA is satisfied that, on the balance of probabilities, the agreement meets the conditions for an individual exemption from the prohibition against anti-competitive arrangements.[81]

8.19 The SRO will assess each situation on a case-by-case basis to make a provisional decision as to whether interim measures may be appropriate in any particular scenario.

8.20 In most cases, interim measures will have immediate effect. However, if a person fails to comply with them without reasonable excuse, the CMA may apply to court for an order to require compliance within a specified time limit.

8.21 The court can require the person in default or any officer of a business responsible for the default to pay the costs of obtaining the order.

8.22 If the measures relate to the management or administration of a business, the court order can compel the business or any of its officers to comply with them. Failure to comply with a court order will be in contempt of court.

REJECTING AN APPLICATION FOR INTERIM MEASURES

8.23 If the SRO provisionally decides to reject an application for interim measures, the CMA will consult the applicant before doing so by sending a provisional dismissal letter setting out the principal reasons for rejecting the application. The CMA will give them an opportunity to submit comments and/or additional information within a certain time, the length of which will depend on the case.

8.24 If the comments from the applicant contain confidential information, a separate non-confidential version must be submitted at the same time (see 7 Limits on the CMA's powers of investigation on handling confidential information). The CMA may provide this non-confidential version to the business under investigation if, in the CMA's view, it would be appropriate to do so, such as where it may be relevant for the rights of defence.

8.25 The CMA will consider any comments and further evidence submitted within the specified time limit. After considering the additional information provided, if the SRO still decides to reject the application, the CMA will send a letter to the applicant and normally the business against which the directions are sought to inform them and give the CMA's reasons.

8.26 However, if the comments and/or additional information from any of these parties leads the SRO to change his/her provisional view and to decide that the CMA should make an interim measures direction, the CMA will inform the applicant and the business against which the directions are sought, and the investigation will continue in the normal way.

PUBLICATION

8.27 The CMA's interim measures directions are included in the public CA98 register and will be published on the CMA webpage. The CMA may also publish them in an appropriate trade journal.

NOTES

74 Section 35 of the CA98.

75 In circumstances, where no investigation has been opened, the Senior Director, Antitrust should be contacted.

76 A template declaration of truth is provided at Annex A.

77 See paragraphs 11.21 to 11.34 below for further discussion of confidentiality rings and data rooms.

78 See paragraph 10.30 and Chapter 11.

79 See Rule 13(2) of the CA98 Rules.

80 See, for example, paragraphs 11.22 to 11.34 below for further discussion of confidentiality rings and data rooms.

81 Section 9(1) of the CA98.

9. ANALYSIS AND REVIEW

[3.225]

9.1 The evidence that the CMA gathers using the powers described in 6 The CMA's formal powers of investigation is fundamental to the outcome of an investigation. Throughout an investigation, the CMA routinely reviews and analyses the information in the CMA's possession to test the factual, legal and economic arguments and to establish whether it supports or contradicts the theory/ies of competition harm.

9.2 In some cases, an investigation may start out by probing a particular set of circumstances that points to conduct of one type, but information may later surface which indicates the existence of another type of potentially anti-competitive behaviour or a different theory of competition harm from that advanced earlier in the investigation. Alternatively, the CMA's early analysis may suggest that a large number of businesses have been acting unlawfully but later on it emerges that the CMA only has enough evidence to warrant further investigation of some of those businesses. The CMA may also exercise its administrative discretion to focus resources on investigating a limited set of activities or businesses.

INTERNAL SCRUTINY

9.3 The CMA regularly scrutinises the way it handles the investigation and routinely assesses the evidence before it, to ensure that its actions and decisions are well-founded, fair and robust. This involves seeking internal advice from specialist advisers on the legal, policy and economic issues that arise throughout the investigation. In some instances, the CMA may also seek advice from external sources, such as external counsel.

9.4 The General Counsel and the Chief Economic Adviser are responsible for ensuring that there has been a thorough review of the robustness of the legal and the economic analysis (and of the evidence being used to support this), respectively, before a Statement of Objections and any Draft Penalty Statement are issued or a final decision on infringement is taken. This includes ensuring the decision maker(s) is/are aware of any significant risks before the decision to issue a Statement of Objections, a Draft Penalty Statement or a final infringement decision is taken.

9.5 The General Counsel and the Chief Economic Adviser (or their representative(s)) will attend the oral hearing on liability and penalty and may ask questions of the parties.

9.6 The SRO decides whether:

- there are sufficient grounds to open a formal investigation;
- there is sufficient evidence to issue a Statement of Objections;
- to close a case prior to issue of a Statement of Objections;
- to issue a Draft Penalty Statement;[82]
- to make an interim measures direction;[83]
- to accept commitments offered by a party under investigation;[84] and
- a case is appropriate for settlement.[85]

In addition to taking advice from specialist advisers as detailed above, the SRO will consult two other senior officials as appropriate at key stages of the investigation prior to issuing a Statement of Objections and any Draft Penalty Statement. The SRO will consult and where appropriate seek approval from the Case and Policy Committee[86] in relation to decisions on commitments and settlement.

9.7 Where a Statement of Objections is issued, a Case Decision Group[87] is appointed by the Case and Policy Committee to act as the decision-maker on whether, based on the facts and evidence before it, the legal test for establishing an infringement has been met and, where a Draft Penalty Statement has been issued to a party, whether a financial penalty should be imposed on that party in respect of any infringement found and the appropriate amount of that penalty. Before taking this decision, the Case Decision Group will be made aware of any significant legal risks or risks on the economic analysis (as described in paragraph 9.4), and may consult the Case and Policy Committee.

SHARING THE CMA'S EARLY THINKING AND GIVING REGULAR UPDATES

9.8 The time taken to establish the facts and whether they point to an infringement of competition law will vary from case to case depending on a range of factors such as the number of parties under investigation, the extent to which they cooperate with the CMA, and the complexity of the conduct under consideration.

9.9 The CMA generally provides case updates to businesses under investigation either by telephone or in writing. The CMA will also offer each party under investigation separate opportunities to speak with representatives of the case team (which may include the SRO) to ensure that they are aware of the stage the investigation has reached.[88] At 'state of play' meetings, which may be held by telephone or video conference, parties will be provided with further information on the nature and scope of the investigation. In particular, the CMA will inform parties of the next stages of the investigation and the likely timing of these, subject to any restrictions the CMA may have if the timing is market sensitive.[89] The CMA may also share the case team's provisional thinking on a case, where the investigation is sufficiently advanced (see paragraph 9.10 below).

9.10 The CMA will usually hold a state of play meeting once it has undertaken some investigatory steps and invite parties to a further state of play meeting before a decision is taken on whether to issue a Statement of Objections. At this further state of play meeting the CMA will be able to update parties on its provisional thinking on the case, including the key potential competition concerns identified.

9.11 In all cases where a Statement of Objections is issued, the CMA will provide an update, usually by telephone, to each party after it has received all parties' written and (where applicable) oral representations on the Statement of Objections and, where the CMA proposes to require a party to pay a financial penalty, on the Draft Penalty Statement. At least one member of the Case Decision Group and the case team will be on the call. The CMA will update parties on its preliminary views on how the CMA intends to proceed with the case in light of the written and oral representations that have been received.

9.12 In appropriate circumstances, the CMA may also have discussions with parties on other occasions. This may be where they have new information that can materially assist the CMA in taking forward the case. Parties who believe that an oral update of this kind would be useful should contact the case team in the first instance to discuss the matter.

9.13 As a matter of routine, the CMA will keep parties to the investigation informed of the anticipated case timetable and any changes to this, as well as publishing and updating this information on the relevant case page.[90]

9.14 If a party has a concern or complaint about the CMA's procedures or the handling of a case, it should contact the SRO in the first instance. If the party is unable to resolve the dispute with the SRO, certain procedural complaints may be referred to the Procedural Officer.[91] If a dispute falls outside the scope of the Procedural Officer's role, the CMA publication Transparency and Disclosure: Statement of the CMA's policy and approach (CMA6) sets out the options available to pursue the complaint.

NOTES

82 See paragraphs 11.15 to 11.19.
83 See paragraphs 8.8 to 8.26.
84 See paragraphs 10.15 to 10.16.

85 See paragraph 11.4. See 14 Settlement for more information on settlement.

86 The Case and Policy Committee operates under delegated authority from the CMA Board. The purpose of the Case and Policy Committee includes overseeing and scrutinising the development of CMA casework, projects, decisions and policy relating to the CA98.

87 See paragraph 11.35.

88 On occasion, the CMA may, if the CMA considers it useful or appropriate, invite the parties under investigation to a multi-party meeting. For example, the CMA may consider offering a multi-party meeting where there are differing views on a key issue such as market definition or differing interpretations offered in respect of a key piece of evidence.

89 As to market sensitivity considerations, see Transparency and Disclosure: Statement of the CMA's policy and approach (CMA6).

90 See 5 Opening formal investigation.

91 See 15 Complaints about the CMA's investigation handling, right of appeal and reviewing the CMA's processes and Rule 8 of the CA98 Rules. See Procedural Officer: raising procedural issues in CMA cases, for further details.

10. INVESTIGATION OUTCOMES

[3.226]

10.1 CMA investigations can be resolved in a number of ways. The CMA:

- can decide to close an investigation on grounds of administrative priorities (see paragraphs 10.2 – 10.12);
- can issue a decision that there are no grounds for action if the CMA has not found sufficient evidence of an infringement of competition law (see paragraphs 10.13 – 10.14);
- can accept commitments from a business relating to its future conduct where the CMA is satisfied that these commitments address the competition concerns (see paragraphs 10.15 – 10.29); and
- will issue a Statement of Objections where the CMA's provisional view is that the conduct under investigation amounts to an infringement of competition law and, where the CMA provisionally considers a financial penalty should be imposed on a party in respect of the alleged infringement, it will also issue a Draft Penalty Statement to that party (see 11 Issuing the CMA's provisional findings – the Statement of Objections and Draft Penalty Statement below). After allowing the business/es under investigation an opportunity to make representations on the Statement of Objections and any Draft Penalty Statement(s) issued (see 12 Right to apply below), if the CMA still considers that they have committed an infringement, the CMA can issue an infringement decision against them and impose penalties and/or such directions as the CMA considers appropriate to bring the infringement to an end.

CLOSING INVESTIGATIONS ON THE GROUNDS OF ADMINISTRATIVE PRIORITIES

10.2 Not all of the CMA's investigations result in a finding that there has been a breach of competition law. The CMA may decide that a formal investigation no longer merits the continued allocation of resources because it no longer fits within the CMA's casework priorities and/or because the CMA does not have sufficient evidence in its possession to determine whether a breach has been committed and the CMA considers that further investigation is not warranted. The CMA may take this decision at any stage of the investigation.[92]

10.3 If the CMA is considering closing an investigation on the grounds of administrative priorities, the CMA may, where it considers it appropriate, inform in writing any complainants whose complaint led to the investigation and whose interests are, in the CMA's view, directly and materially affected by the outcome of the CMA's investigation, setting out the principal reasons for not taking forward the investigation. The amount of detail given will vary according to the circumstances of each case. In more advanced investigations, the CMA is likely to give more details than in the case of complaints which have not been the subject of extensive investigation.

10.4 The CMA will assess whether a complainant[93] is directly and materially affected by the outcome of the CMA's investigation on the basis of the information it has provided to the CMA. This may include complainants who are:

- actual or potential competitors of the business or businesses under investigation who allege that the agreement or conduct under investigation restricts their ability to compete effectively;
- customers of the business or businesses under investigation who allege that they have been harmed by the activity; and
- a trade or consumer association that alleges that some or all of its members have been harmed by the agreement or conduct under investigation.

10.5 The CMA will give such complainants an opportunity to submit their comments or any additional information within a specified time frame. The time frame provided will depend on the circumstances of the case, but will generally be no longer than four weeks.

10.6 If that complainant's response contains confidential information, it will be asked to submit a separate non-confidential version at the same time (see 7 Limits on the CMA's powers of investigation on handling confidential information). The CMA may provide this to the business/es the CMA is investigating if the CMA thinks it appropriate, such as if it is likely to change the CMA's preliminary view.

10.7 The CMA will also give a copy of the provisional closure letter to the business/es under investigation, giving them an opportunity to comment within the same time frame.

10.8 The CMA will consider any comments and further evidence submitted within the specified time limit before reaching a final view on whether to close an investigation.

10.9 If the CMA decides to close the case, the CMA will write to any complainants whose comments it has sought in accordance with paragraphs 10.4 and 10.5 above, as well as the business under investigation, explaining why any additional information sent to the CMA has not led the CMA to change its view. The level of detail given will depend on the case and the nature of the additional information provided.

10.10 In these circumstances, the CMA may also issue a warning or advisory letter to the business under investigation to inform it that the CMA has been made aware of a possible breach of competition law by that business and that, although the CMA is currently not minded to pursue an investigation, it may do so in the future if its priorities change (for example, in response to further evidence received).[94]

10.11 The CMA will also issue a public statement linking to the case page on www.gov.uk/cma and explain why the CMA has closed the case on administrative priority grounds. Where the CMA has published a notice that identifies a party whose activities are being investigated, the CMA will publish a further notice stating that the activities of the party in question are no longer being investigated.

10.12 If the response to the CMA's provisional closure letter leads the CMA to change its preliminary view and decide that an investigation should be continued, the CMA will inform the company under investigation and the complainant in question and continue the investigation in the normal way.

ISSUING A NO GROUNDS FOR ACTION DECISION

10.13 If the CMA does not find sufficient evidence of a competition law infringement, the CMA may publish a reasoned no grounds for action decision when closing the case.[95]

10.14 In such cases, the CMA may, where it considers it appropriate, provide a non-confidential version of its proposed decision to any complainant whose complaint led to the investigation and whose interests are, in the CMA's view, directly and materially affected by the outcome of the CMA's investigation.[96] The consultation process on the proposed decision will be the same as for closure on the ground of administrative priorities.

ACCEPTING COMMITMENTS ON FUTURE CONDUCT

10.15 If the CMA considers that the case gives rise to competition concerns, instead of continuing its investigation (which may result in the CMA issuing an infringement decision), the CMA may be prepared to accept binding promises, called 'commitments', from a business, relating to its future conduct.[97] The CMA must be satisfied that the commitments offered address its competition concerns.

10.16 Commitments may be structural or behavioural in nature, or a combination of both. For example, they may involve a business agreeing to cease or modify its conduct, terminating an arrangement, removing a particular clause from an agreement, withdrawing from a particular activity, licensing specific assets, or even divesting itself of part of its business.

CIRCUMSTANCES IN WHICH IT MAY BE APPROPRIATE TO ACCEPT COMMITMENTS

10.17 The decision to accept commitments is at the CMA's discretion.

10.18 The CMA is likely to consider it appropriate to accept commitments only in cases where the competition concerns are readily identifiable, will be addressed by the commitments offered, and the proposed commitments can be implemented effectively and, if necessary, within a short period of time.

10.19 The CMA is very unlikely to accept commitments in cases involving secret cartels between competitors[98] or a serious abuse of a dominant position.[99]

10.20 The CMA will not accept commitments in circumstances:

- where compliance with and the effectiveness of any commitments would be difficult to discern; and/or
- where it considers that not to complete its investigation and make a decision would undermine deterrence.

PROCEDURE

10.21 A business under investigation can offer commitments at any time during the investigation, until a decision on infringement is made. However, the CMA is unlikely to consider it appropriate to accept commitments at a very late stage in an investigation, such as after the CMA has considered representations on the Statement of Objections. The CMA has a broad discretion in determining which cases are suitable for commitments.

10.22 If a business would like to discuss offering commitments, it should contact the case team in the first instance. The CMA may ask, for example, at a State of Play meeting, whether the business wishes to offer commitments.[100] If, following that contact, the CMA thinks that commitments may be appropriate, the CMA will send a summary of its competition concerns to the business[101] (where the case is still at pre-Statement of Objections stage). Once commitments have been offered, the CMA may discuss these with the business to see if they would be acceptable to the CMA.

10.23 If the CMA proposes to accept the commitments offered, the CMA will consult those who are likely to be affected by them and give them an opportunity to give their views within a time limit of at least 11 working days.[102] After receipt of the responses to this consultation, the CMA will hold a meeting with each business that offered commitments to inform them of the general nature of responses received and to indicate whether the CMA considers that changes are required to the commitments before the CMA would consider accepting them.

10.24 If the business/es offer revised commitments including significant changes, the CMA will allow another opportunity for complainants and any other third parties to express their views within a time limit of at least six working days.

10.25 The SRO is responsible for deciding whether to accept the commitments offered, having consulted with the Case and Policy Committee and other senior CMA officials as appropriate. The SRO's decision will require the approval of the Case and Policy Committee before the commitments can be formally accepted by the CMA. Once accepted, the CMA will publish the commitments on its webpages.

DECISION TO ACCEPT COMMITMENTS

10.26 Once commitments have been accepted in respect of an agreement or conduct, the CMA may not continue its investigation, make an infringement decision or give interim measures directions in relation to the aspects of the alleged infringement addressed by the commitments, except under limited circumstances.[103]

10.27 However, the CMA is not prevented from taking any action in relation to competition concerns that are not addressed by the commitments it has accepted.

10.28 Where the CMA has accepted commitments it may, for the purposes of addressing its current competition concerns, accept a variation of the commitments or commitments in substitution for them.[104] If the CMA's current competition concerns are different from the competition concerns it identified when the commitments were accepted, when considering the appropriateness of accepting varied or substitute commitments, the CMA will take into account the considerations in paragraphs 10.17 to 10.20, above.

10.29 The CMA may consider it appropriate to release commitments where:[105]

- It is requested to do so by the person(s) who gave the commitments. In such cases, the CMA will generally consider it appropriate to release commitments only where it has reasonable grounds for believing that the competition concerns identified by it at the time, or their acceptance or variation, no longer arise; or
- The competition concerns identified at the time of their acceptance or variation no longer arise.

ISSUING A STATEMENT OF OBJECTIONS

10.30 The CMA will issue a Statement of Objections where its provisional view is that the conduct under investigation amounts to an infringement. Where the CMA provisionally considers a financial penalty should be imposed on a party in respect of the alleged infringement, it will also issue a Draft Penalty Statement to that party at the same time as the Statement of Objections. See Chapter 11 for more detail on this.

NOTES

92 The SRO is responsible for deciding whether to close a case on administrative priorities grounds prior to issue of a Statement of Objections (see paragraph 9.6 for further information on the decision making process). After any Statement of Objections has been issued, case closure decisions are the responsibility of the Case Decision Group.

93 Or a third party when considering requests for disclosure of a Statement of Objections.

94 See paragraph 4.3 above.

95 Rule 10 of the CA98 Rules.

96 See paragraph 10.4 for examples of when a complainant is likely to be regarded as being "directly and materially affected by the outcome of the CMA's investigation".

97 Section 31A of the CA98.

98 These include cartels relating to price-fixing, bid-rigging (collusive tendering), establishing output restrictions or quotas, market sharing.

99 That is, those which the CMA considers are most likely by their very nature to harm competition. In relation to infringements of the Chapter II prohibition and/or Article 102, this will typically include conduct which is inherently likely to have a particularly serious exploitative or exclusionary effect, such as excessive and predatory pricing.

100 The business is under no obligation to do so and this is without prejudice to the outcome of the investigation.

101 Such a summary is not a replacement for a Statement of Objections. It will set out the CMA's competition concerns and a summary of the main facts on which those concerns are based. However, it will not generally include detail of the source of the facts on which the CMA relies.

102 Procedural requirements for the acceptance or variation of commitments are set out in Part 1 of Schedule 6A to the CA98.

103 These are listed in section 31B(4) of the CA98.

104 See section 31(A)(3) of the CA98. The procedure in paragraphs 10.21 to 10.25 will also apply to any variation of commitments. Also, the procedural requirements for the acceptance or variation of commitments are set out in part 1 of Schedule 6A to the CA98.

105 Pursuant to Section 31A(4)(b) of the CA98. Procedural requirements for the release of commitments are set out in part 2 of Schedule 6A to the CA98.

11. ISSUING THE CMA'S PROVISIONAL FINDINGS – THE STATEMENT OF OBJECTIONS AND DRAFT PENALTY STATEMENT

[3.227]

11.1 Following the analysis of the evidence on the files, if the CMA's provisional view is that the conduct under investigation amounts to an infringement, the CMA will issue a Statement of Objections to each business it considers to be responsible for the infringement and give them an opportunity to inspect the CMA's file.[106] Where the CMA provisionally considers that the infringement alleged in

Part 3 CMA and other Guidelines

the Statement of Objections warrants the imposition of a financial penalty, it will at the same time issue a Draft Penalty Statement to each business on which it proposes to impose such a penalty.[107] Each of these documents is discussed below.

STATEMENT OF OBJECTIONS

11.2 If the case involves more than one party, each party will receive a copy of the Statement of Objections. Information that is confidential will be disclosed through the Statement of Objections to other parties only if disclosure is strictly necessary in order for them to exercise their rights of defence. Before disclosing any confidential information, the CMA will consider whether there is a need to exclude any information whose disclosure would be contrary to the public interest or whose disclosure might significantly harm the interests of the company or individual it relates to. If the CMA considers that disclosure might significantly harm legitimate business interests or the interests of an individual, the CMA will consider the extent to which disclosure of that information is nevertheless necessary for the purpose for which the CMA is allowed to make the disclosure.[108]

11.3 Where the CMA considers that an agreement or conduct infringes the Chapter I prohibition the CMA may use its discretion to address the Statement of Objections to fewer than all the persons who are, or were, a party to that agreement or conduct.[109] The CMA will notify any party who is not an addressee under Rule 5(3) that a Statement of Objections has been issued and will provide a non-confidential version of the Statement of Objections, following a request by such a party, where it is deemed that it is necessary for them to review it to protect their rights of defence. The CMA will only provide access to documents on its file where it is established that access is required in order for such a party to make representations on the Statement of Objections.

11.4 At this stage, the CMA may also invite addressees of a Statement of Objections to contact the CMA if they would like to enter into discussions on the possible settlement of the case. This settlement procedure applies where a business under investigation is prepared to admit that it has breached competition law and confirms that it accepts that a streamlined administrative procedure will govern the remainder of the investigation of that business's conduct. If so, the CMA will impose a reduced penalty on the business.

11.5 Businesses may wish to approach the CMA earlier on in the investigation to discuss the possibility of exploring settlement. If so, they should contact the case team in the first instance. See 14 Settlement for more information on settlement.

11.6 The Statement of Objections represents the CMA's provisional view and proposed next steps. It allows the businesses being accused of breaching competition law an opportunity to know the full case against them and, if they choose to do so, to respond formally in writing and orally.

11.7 The Statement of Objections will set out the facts and the CMA's legal and economic assessment of them which led to the provisional view that an infringement has occurred. The CMA will also set out any action it proposes to take, such as imposing financial penalties[110] and/or issuing directions to stop the infringement if the CMA believes it is ongoing, as well as the CMA's reasons for taking that action. Where the CMA provisionally considers that the infringement alleged in the Statement of Objections warrants the imposition of a financial penalty, it will at the same time issue a Draft Penalty Statement to each business on which it proposes to impose such a penalty.[111]

11.8 The CMA will generally send the Statement of Objections (together with any Draft Penalty Statement) and covering letter to recipients by secure email in PDF format.

11.9 It is the CMA's normal practice to publicly announce the issue of the Statement of Objections on its webpages and to make an announcement to the media, and on the Regulatory News Service where the matter is judged market sensitive.[112] The CMA will also update the administrative timetable on the case page. The CMA will not include reference to the amount of any proposed penalty in its public announcement about the issue of a Statement of Objections, other than in respect of Statements of Objections issued to parties that have settled with the CMA.[113]

11.10 The timing of the announcement and any advance notice will depend on whether there is any market sensitivity in respect of the announcement. The CMA has to balance its responsibilities concerning the control and release of market sensitive information against the objective of, as far as possible, giving directly affected parties fair and sufficient notice.

11.11 In both market-sensitive and non-market sensitive situations, the CMA will aim to balance an open approach with the need to ensure the orderly disclosure of information. Generally, in non-market sensitive announcements, the CMA aims to give parties advance notice of its announcement, in confidence, unless there is a compelling reason not to do so. In such situations, it may also give advance indication on its website about the expected date, but not contents, of the announcement.

11.12 In the case of market sensitive announcements, where appropriate, the CMA will apply the Guideline for the control and release of price sensitive information by Industry Regulators (originally published by the Financial Services Authority, the predecessor of the Financial Conduct Authority).[114]

11.13 If the date and content of the announcement is market-sensitive (for example, where nothing about the investigation has previously been announced), the CMA will not publicise the expected date on its webpages. It will notify directly affected parties in strict confidence the evening before the announcement is to be made, once relevant financial markets have closed (including, where appropriate, financial markets in other countries).

11.14 More details about the way in which the CMA publicly announces the issue of a Statement of Objections is available in the CMA's guideline Transparency and Disclosure: Statement of the CMA's policy and approach (CMA6).

DRAFT PENALTY STATEMENT

11.15 Where the CMA issues a Statement of Objections to a party and the CMA provisionally considers that the alleged infringement warrants the imposition of a financial penalty, the CMA will at the same time provide each party on which it proposes to impose a penalty with a Draft Penalty Statement addressed to that party.[115]

11.16 The Draft Penalty Statement will set out the key aspects[116] relevant to the calculation of the penalty that the CMA proposes to impose on that party, based on the information available to the CMA at the time.[117] It will also include a brief explanation of the CMA's reasoning for its provisional findings on each aspect of the penalty calculation.

11.17 Where a Draft Penalty Statement is issued to more than one party under investigation, the CMA will – in order to provide parties with transparency as to the CMA's application of the principle of equal treatment in the CMA's draft calculations[118] – place a non-confidential version of each party's Draft Penalty Statement on the file. Each non-confidential version will generally be disclosed to the other parties under investigation.[119]

11.18 The CMA will normally send a party's Draft Penalty Statement in PDF format, in the same secure e-mail in which the Statement of Objections is sent to that party.

11.19 As noted above at paragraph 11.9, the CMA will not include reference to the amount of any proposed penalty in its public announcement about the issue of a Statement of Objections, other than in respect of Statements of Objections issued to parties that have settled with the CMA.[120]

WHO DECIDES WHETHER TO ISSUE A STATEMENT OF OBJECTIONS AND ANY DRAFT PENALTY STATEMENT?

11.20 The SRO decides whether to issue a Statement of Objections as well as any Draft Penalty Statement. Before doing so, the SRO will consult the General Counsel and the Chief Economic Adviser (or their representatives) to ensure that the SRO is aware of any significant legal and economic risks that have been identified.[121] The SRO will also consult other senior CMA officials as appropriate.

INSPECTION OF THE FILE AND TREATMENT OF CONFIDENTIAL INFORMATION

11.21 At generally the same time as issuing the Statement of Objections and any Draft Penalty Statement, the CMA will also give the addressees of the Statement of Objections and any Draft Penalty Statement the opportunity to inspect the file. This is to ensure that they can properly defend themselves against the allegation of having breached competition law and have an opportunity to make representations in respect of any proposed penalty.

11.22 The CMA's file contains documents that relate to matters contained in the Statement of Objections and any Draft Penalty Statement, excluding certain confidential information[122] and CMA internal documents.[123]

11.23 The CMA allows addressees of the Statement of Objections and any Draft Penalty Statement a reasonable opportunity to inspect the CMA's file. The time given for addressees will take into consideration a number of factors including the size of the file, the nature of the documents and the access to file process being used. The CMA considers that, in general, the period of time for inspecting the file will generally be the same as that given for the provision of written representations.[124]

11.24 Prior to issuing the Statement of Objections and any accompanying Draft Penalty Statement, the CMA will discuss with the businesses under investigation the process envisaged for giving access to the CMA's file. This may be discussed as part of a State of Play meeting[125] and/or in writing. In all cases, the CMA will seek to ensure that the access to file process is as efficient as practicable, both for addressees of the Statement of Objections (and any Draft Penalty Statement) as well as the CMA. The CMA will consider the most appropriate process for allowing parties to have access to its case file in each case, while ensuring that parties are able to exercise their rights of defence.

11.25 In some cases, the CMA may provide each party with:

(a) copies of the documents that are directly referred to in the Statement of Objections and any Draft Penalty Statement sent to that party; and
(b) a schedule containing a detailed list of all the documents on the CMA's file.

These will usually be given in electronic form by secure email.[126]

11.26 Under this process, businesses will have a reasonable opportunity to inspect additional documents listed in the schedule upon request. The CMA will set a reasonable deadline within which the business will be able to make any such requests, on a case-by-case basis. Where a business requests additional documents from the schedule, the CMA may consider whether it is appropriate to use a confidentiality ring to facilitate further disclosure of documents on the CMA's file.[127]

11.27 In some cases, the CMA may discuss with a business under investigation, in advance of the Statement of Objections, the use of a confidentiality ring to facilitate the disclosure of documents not referred to in the Statement of Objections or any Draft Penalty Statement sent to that business. The use of a confidentiality ring in these circumstances would allow parties' external advisers to carry out an assessment of documents that are not directly referred to in a Statement of Objections or any Draft Penalty Statement, in order to enable those advisers to make targeted requests for the disclosure of other documents on the CMA's file to the parties. Given the large volume of documents that are often on the CMA's file, the CMA considers that the use of confidentiality rings in this way to facilitate access to file is likely to give rise to identifiable benefits in terms of efficiencies, both for addressees of the Statement of Objections (and any Draft Penalty Statement) as well as the CMA.

11.28 The CMA would envisage that a confidentiality ring may also be appropriate where the disclosure of a specific category of confidential information or data would enable a defined group to further their understanding or prepare confidential submissions on behalf of their client regarding the CMA's analysis – for example, in relation to certain (confidential) quantitative data.[128]

11.29 The use of confidentiality rings or data rooms by the CMA in this way, as means of making disclosure of confidential information only to a party's external advisers, will be restricted to when it is necessary to make the disclosure for the purpose of facilitating the CMA's functions by ensuring due process.

11.30 The CMA has discretion as to whether to use confidentiality rings or data rooms in investigations under the CA98, either (i) as a means of facilitating access to file or (ii) to disclose a specific category of confidential information or data to allow a party's external advisers to further their understanding or prepare confidential submissions. The CMA will do so only where it is proportionate, there are clearly identifiable benefits, and where any potential legal and practical difficulties can be resolved swiftly in agreement with the parties concerned. In such cases, the person or business that provided the information will be informed of the CMA's proposed course of action and provided with a reasonable opportunity to comment. The CMA will then inform the person or business whether or not it still intends to use the proposed confidentiality ring and/or data room arrangement, after considering all the relevant facts.[129]

11.31 Requests from addressees for access to file using confidentiality rings or data rooms will be considered on a case-by-case basis. The CMA will also take into account whether it is appropriate to provide access at the time the request is made, having regard to the progress of the case, the resource implications of operating confidentiality rings and data rooms, and the risks of inadvertent disclosure through human error and information leaks.

11.32 Where the CMA decides on (or a party requests) the use of a confidentiality ring or data room process, the CMA will provide the relevant parties with details of how the CMA proposes this will work in practice. For example, providing copies of the proposed data room rules and the confidentiality undertakings[130] that will be required from those who are given access to the data room or confidentiality ring.[131] It will be a condition of access to a confidentiality ring or data room that information reviewed by advisers is not shared with their client(s).

11.33 If any party has a concern about the potential use of a confidentiality ring or data room procedure, they should raise their concerns first with the SRO and, if it is not possible to resolve the issue, with the Procedural Officer.[132]

11.34 It is a criminal offence, punishable by fine and/or imprisonment, for any person to whom information is disclosed by way of a confidentiality ring or data room to disclose or otherwise use the information other than for the purpose of facilitating the exercise of any of the CMA's functions under the CA98 or any other enactment.[133] In practical terms, this means that a person to whom information is disclosed which has not been made publicly available must not make any onward disclosure of that information.

APPOINTMENT OF A CASE DECISION GROUP

11.35 Once the CMA has issued a Statement of Objections, a three-member Case Decision Group is appointed by the Case and Policy Committee to be the decision-makers in the case.[134] The Case Decision Group is responsible for taking decisions on (a) whether to issue an infringement decision (with or without directions) or a 'no grounds for action' decision; and (b) on the appropriate amount of any penalty.[135] The CMA will inform the parties of the identity of the Case Decision Group members. At least one member of the Case Decision Group will be legally qualified.

11.36 The SRO will not be a member of the Case Decision Group, to ensure that the final decision is taken by officials who were not involved in the decision to issue the Statement of Objections and any Draft Penalty Statement(s).

11.37 The case team, including the SRO, will remain in place to progress the investigation under the direction of the Case Decision Group as appropriate. The case team will remain the primary point of contact for the parties.[136]

NOTES

106 Rule 6 of the CA98 Rules. Rules 18 and 19 set out the process for notification by the CMA of a Statement of Objections to each business it considers to be responsible for the infringement.

107 Rule 11 of the CA98 Rules.

108 Section 244 of the EA02.

109 Rule 5(3) of the CA98 Rules.

110 More information on how the CMA sets penalties is available in the CMA's Guidance as to the appropriate amount of a penalty (CMA73).

111 Rule 11 of the CA98 Rules. See paragraphs 11.15 to 11.19 below.

112 See London Stock Exchange.

113 And see paragraph Annexe(s)14.37 below.

114 See the FCA website.

115 Rule 11 of the CA98 Rules.

116 Including, for example, the starting point percentage, the relevant turnover figure to be used, the duration of the infringement, any uplift for specific deterrence, any aggravating/mitigating factors (and the proposed increase/decrease

in the penalty for these), and any adjustment proposed for proportionality.

117 Rule 11 of the CA98 Rules. For further information on how the CMA calculates a penalty, see CMA's Guidance as to the appropriate amount of a penalty (CMA73).

118 See CMA's Guidance as to the appropriate amount of a penalty (CMA73), at footnote 17.

119 The case team will prepare non-confidential versions of each party's draft penalty statement, based on any confidentiality representations previously made by that party in relation to the information included in the draft penalty statement. Where the draft penalty statement contains information regarding a party, which that party has not had a previous opportunity to assess for confidentiality, the CMA will allow it a reasonable opportunity to make such an assessment and to make any confidentiality claims to the CMA before the non-confidential version of the draft penalty statement is placed on the file.

120 And see paragraph Annexe(s)14.37 below.

121 As described further in paragraph 9.4 above.

122 Under Rule 1(1) of the CA98 Rules, confidential information means commercial information whose disclosure the CMA thinks might significantly harm the legitimate business interests of the undertaking to which it relates, or information relating to the private affairs of an individual whose disclosure the CMA thinks might significantly harm the individual's interests, or information whose disclosure the CMA thinks is contrary to the public interest.

123 Rule 6(2) of the CA98 Rules.

124 See paragraph 12.3 below.

125 See paragraphs 9.9 to 9.11 above.

126 Where a business does not have the relevant electronic means to view the documents in this way the CMA will send hard copies.

127 Confidentiality rings enable disclosure of specific quantitative and/or qualitative data or documents to a defined group. The group is determined on a case-by-case basis but, generally, disclosure is made to the relevant parties' external (legal and/or economic) advisers. The use of a confidentiality ring is subject to any restrictions in the Regulation (EU) 2016/679 (General Data Protection Regulation) (GDPR) and the DPA 2018 in relation to personal information. While the CMA will normally use a confidentiality ring in CA98 investigations it may, in exceptional circumstances, use a data room. This may, for example, be the case where additional enhanced security measures are appropriate because the information is considered by the CMA to be particularly sensitive. Like confidentiality rings, data rooms enable access to a specific category of confidential data or documents to a defined group and the group is also determined on a case-by-case basis. However, a data room provides access to the confidential data or documents on the CMA premises, and in so doing has the advantage of providing additional protection.

128 As noted above at footnote 135, the CMA will normally use a confidentiality ring in CA98 investigations, but may, in exceptional circumstances, use a data room.

129 If the CMA considers, having taken into account the relevant statutory provisions, that it is necessary to make the disclosure for the purpose of facilitating the CMA's functions, it is not obliged to obtain the consent of the party to which the information relates. However, the CMA will consider a party's representations regarding the confidential nature of any information that the party has provided.

130 See Confidentiality ring and disclosure room undertaking templates.

131 See Chapter 4 of the CMA's guideline Transparency and Disclosure: Statement of the CMA's policy and approach (CMA6) for further information on the CMA's general approach to the protection of confidential information disclosed through a confidentiality ring or data room.

132 See Chapter 15 and Rule 8 of the CA98 Rules. See Procedural Officer: raising procedural issues in CMA cases, for further details.

133 Section 241(2A) and section 245 of the EA02.

134 The Case Decision Group, generally comprising of members of the CMA's senior staff and, where appropriate the CMA panel, will operate under the delegated authority of the Case and Policy Committee.

135 The Case Decision Group may also decide to close a case on the grounds of administrative priorities. See further paragraphs 10.2 – 10.12 above.

136 Contact details for the case team will be included in the notice of investigation published on the CMA's webpages: www.gov.uk/cma.

12. RIGHT TO REPLY

WRITTEN REPRESENTATIONS THE RESPONSE TO THE STATEMENT OF OBJECTIONS AND ANY DRAFT PENALTY STATEMENT

[3.228]

12.1 When the CMA issues a Statement of Objections, the CMA will invite each addressee of the Statement of Objections (Addressee) to respond in writing, commenting on the matters referred to in the Statement of Objections.[137] Any Addressee to which the CMA has also issued a Draft Penalty Statement will have the opportunity to make written representations to the CMA on the proposed penalty.[138] However, there is no obligation to submit a response on either the Statement of Objections or any Draft Penalty Statement.

12.2 Where the CMA has provided a non-confidential version of the Statement of Objections to a person who is party to an agreement or conduct that the CMA considers infringes the Chapter I prohibition but who is not an Addressee,[139] the CMA will allow that person to make representations on the matters referred to in the non-confidential version of the Statement of Objections.

12.3 The deadline for submitting written representations will be specified in the Statement of Objections and any Draft Penalty Statement. The deadline will be set on a case-by-case basis having regard to the circumstances of each particular case. Such circumstances may include the volume of documentary evidence relied upon in the Statement of Objections, the particular situation of the Addressee themselves, and also whether any Draft Penalty Statement has been issued to the Addressee along with the Statement of Objections. The deadline for an Addressee to submit written representations will be no more than 12 weeks from the issue of the Statement of Objections and any Draft Penalty Statement. Any requests for an extension to the deadline should be communicated to the CMA as soon as possible, and in any event within five working days, following the receipt of the Statement of Objections and any Draft Penalty Statement, and must specify the reasons why an extension is required. In order not to delay investigations, extensions to the time for submitting written representations on the Statement of Objections and Draft Penalty Statement will be given only where there are particularly compelling reasons for doing so, and should not be regarded as normal practice.

12.4 Where an Addressee has a complaint about the deadline set for submitting written representations, the Addressee should raise this as soon as possible with the SRO. If it is not possible to resolve the dispute with the SRO, the Addressee may refer the matter to the Procedural Officer.[140]

12.5 When an Addressee submits written representations it should also provide a non-confidential version of its representations, along with an explanation which justifies why information should be treated as confidential. The CMA will not accept blanket or unsubstantiated confidentiality claims. The non-confidential version should be provided within two weeks of the date of submitting the original response. Any extension to this deadline should be agreed in advance of the deadline with the case team.

12.6 Where there is more than one Addressee the CMA will not cross disclose the written (or oral) representations made by an Addressee to each of the other Addressees, other than in exceptional circumstances.[141]

12.7 The CMA may on a case by case basis also provide an opportunity to submit written representations on a non-confidential version of the Statement of Objections to third parties who are:

- a complainant whose complaint has led to the relevant investigation and whose interests are, in the CMA's view, directly and materially affected by the outcome of the CMA's investigation;[142]
- third parties or complainants who in the CMA's view:
- are directly and materially affected by the outcome of the CMA's investigation but have not made a complaint to the CMA about the agreement or conduct under investigation;
- are likely materially to assist the CMA in its investigation; and
- have requested the opportunity to comment on the Statement of Objections; and
- current or former directors of an Addressee of the Statement of Objections, in respect of whom the CMA is carrying out an investigation under the CDDA for the purpose of deciding whether to make an application for a CDO.

12.8 The CMA is only likely to regard a third party as being able materially to assist it in its investigation where it considers that third party's comments are likely to be material over and above, and that are not otherwise duplicative of, views and information that the CMA has already taken into consideration in preparing the Statement of Objections.

12.9 The CMA will not provide complainants or third parties with an opportunity to comment, or may only consult them to a more limited extent, in this way where doing so risks prejudicing the CMA's investigation or another case.[143]

12.10 In most cases, disclosure of a non-confidential version of the Statement of Objections will be sufficient to enable third parties to provide the CMA with informed comments and this will not generally include any annexed documents or any Draft Penalty Statements. The non-confidential version of the Statement of Objections is for the relevant complainant or third party's use only in making representations to the CMA and must not be disclosed to others. The deadline for a complainant or third party to submit written representations (along with a non-confidential version of any written representations) will be set on a case-by-case basis.

12.11 The non-confidential version of the written representations that have been submitted by a relevant complainant or third party will generally be disclosed to Addressee(s) to allow them an opportunity to comment. However, in the case of representations made by a current or former director of an Addressee who is the subject of an investigation under the CDDA, for confidentiality reasons[144] these will not be disclosed to the Addressees, other than in exceptional circumstances.[145]

12.12 The CMA will not generally allow complainants and other third parties an opportunity to comment on the Addressees' written representations, although this may be appropriate in certain circumstances.[146]

ORAL REPRESENTATIONS THE ORAL HEARING

12.13 The CMA will offer all Addressees of a Statement of Objections the opportunity to attend a single oral hearing to discuss the matters set out in that Statement of Objections and any Draft Penalty Statement.[147]

12.14 The CMA encourages Addressees to take up the opportunity to attend an oral hearing and Addressees should make clear before or when submitting their written representations that they would like to do so. The Addressee can bring legal or other advisers to the oral hearing to assist in presenting its oral representations at the hearing, subject to any reasonable limits that the CMA may set in terms of the number of persons that may attend on behalf of the Addressee. While an Addressee may be accompanied by its legal or other advisers, the CMA would expect staff or directors of the Addressee's business to attend the oral hearing and the Case Decision Group would also expect to hear from them when presenting the Addressee's oral representations. Complainants and third parties will generally not be permitted to attend the Addressee's oral hearing.[148]

12.15 The oral hearing will be held after the deadline for the submission of the written representations on the Statement of Objections and any Draft Penalty Statement, allowing time for the Case Decision

Group to consider the representations. The hearing will be attended by the Case Decision Group, members of the case team, the Chief Economic Adviser and the General Counsel (or their representatives). Where necessary the CMA may arrange for attendees, from the Addressee and/or the CMA, to join the oral hearing via video conferencing. The hearing will be chaired by the Procedural Officer.

12.16 To promote a focussed and productive meeting, the case team will ask the Addressee to give an indication, in advance, of the matters it proposes to focus on in its oral representations at the hearing. The Addressee and the case team will agree an agenda in advance of the hearing, taking into account any matters which the Case Decision Group has indicated to the case team that it wishes to cover at the oral hearing. The agenda for the hearing will include reasonable periods of time for the Addressee to make oral representations on the Statement of Objections and, if the Addressee has indicated it would like to do so, any Draft Penalty Statement. The agenda will also include a reasonable period of time for the CMA staff present to ask the Addressee questions on its representations.[149]

12.17 In the event that an agenda and associated timings are not agreed between the Addressee and the case team at least three working days prior to the hearing, the agenda will be determined by the Procedural Officer.

12.18 The oral hearing provides the Addressee with an opportunity to highlight directly to the Case Decision Group issues of particular importance to its case, and which have been set out in its written representations. The oral hearing may also provide a useful opportunity for the Addressee to clarify the detail set out in its written representations. As a general rule, any points raised orally by the Addressee at this stage should be limited to those already submitted to the CMA in writing.

12.19 During the oral hearing, the Case Decision Group and other members of CMA staff present may ask questions on the Addressees' written representations or questions of clarification. It will be helpful for the CMA, and is likely to assist the progress of the investigation, if Addressees provide full responses to these questions. However, there is no obligation to answer. It is possible to respond to questions in writing after the hearing.

12.20 Where an Addressee indicates that it will respond to questions in writing post-hearing, the case team will set out these questions in writing and provide a deadline for response which is appropriate in the circumstances of the case.

12.21 A transcript of the oral hearing will be taken and the Addressee will be asked to confirm the accuracy of the transcript and, if necessary, to identify any confidential information. The CMA will not accept blanket or unsubstantiated confidentiality claims.

12.22 Following the oral hearing, the Procedural Officer will report to the Case Decision Group on the fairness of the procedure followed in the investigation.[150]

12.23 If a Case Decision Group member changes after the oral hearing(s) but before the CMA issues a final decision, the new member will, as well as considering parties' written representations, review the transcript of the oral hearing(s).

12.24 The CMA will consider multi-party oral hearings on specific issues in appropriate cases, such as where there are differing views on a key issue like market definition, or differing interpretations offered in respect of a key piece of evidence.

CONSIDERING REPRESENTATIONS

12.25 The case team, the Case Decision Group, and other CMA officials including legal and economic advisers, will carefully and objectively consider all written and oral representations to appraise the case as set out in the Statement of Objections and any Draft Penalty Statements, and to assess whether the provisional findings in the Statement of Objections and any Draft Penalty Statements are supported by the evidence and the facts.

12.26 An original set of all written representations and the transcript(s) from the oral hearing(s) will be placed on the case file.

LETTER OF FACTS

12.27 Where the CMA acquires new evidence at this stage which supports the objection(s) contained in the Statement of Objections or the draft penalty calculation set out in any Draft Penalty Statement and the Case Decision Group is considering relying upon it to establish that an infringement has been committed or for the purposes of determining the appropriate level of any penalty to be imposed, the CMA will put that evidence to the Addressee[151] in writing and give it an opportunity to respond to the new evidence.[152] The time frame for responding will be set according to the volume and complexity of the new evidence.

SUPPLEMENTARY STATEMENT OF OBJECTIONS

12.28 If new information received by the CMA in response to the Statement of Objections indicates that there is evidence of a different suspected infringement or there is a material change in the nature of the infringement described in the Statement of Objections,[153] the CMA will issue a Supplementary Statement of Objections. This will set out the new facts or changes in the nature of the infringement on which the CMA proposes to rely to establish an infringement. The Case Decision Group will be responsible for deciding whether to issue a Supplementary Statement of Objections, having consulted the case team and other CMA officials as appropriate. If the CMA proposes to impose a financial penalty in respect of the infringement alleged in the Supplementary Statement of Objections, it will, at the same time as the Supplementary Statement of Objections, issue a Draft Penalty Statement to each party on which it proposes to impose such a penalty. Whether to issue any such Draft Penalty Statement(s) in these circumstances will be a decision for the Case Decision Group.

12.29 The CMA will give the Addressee an opportunity to make representations on the Supplementary Statement of Objections and any Draft Penalty Statement. The CMA will set the time frame for responding after taking into account the extent of the difference in the objections raised in the first Statement of Objections compared with the Supplementary Statement of Objections and allow the Addressees an opportunity to inspect new documents on the file[154] The process will be the same as that set out in Chapter 11.

12.30 If it appears unlikely, when issuing a Supplementary Statement of Objections, that engaging with complainants or third parties who had previously been provided with an opportunity to comment on the Statement of Objections will materially assist the investigation, the CMA may decide to consult them on a more limited basis, or not at all. This may be the case, for example, where the Supplementary Statement of Objections is very narrow in scope.

NOTES

137 Rule 6 of the CA98 Rules.

138 Rule 11 of the CA98 Rules.

139 See Rule 5(3) of the CA98 Rules and paragraph 11.3 above.

140 See Chapter 15 and Rule 8 of the CA98 Rules. See Procedural Officer: raising procedural issues in CMA cases, for further details.

141 For instance, where the CMA considers it necessary for rights of defence of the other Addressees to cross disclose genuinely new relevant evidence (as opposed to arguments of fact or law) included in the representations of a party, or where it assists the CMA in clarifying a substantive factual or legal or economic issue.

142 See paragraph 10.4 for examples of when a complainant is likely to be regarded as being "directly and materially affected by the outcome of the CMA's investigation".

143 For example, a related criminal investigation or an investigation by another agency.

144 The fact that the CMA is carrying out an investigation under the CDDA in respect of a particular director will not normally be public at that stage of the CMA's investigation.

145 For example, where the CMA considers it necessary for the rights of defence of an Addressee to disclose genuinely new relevant evidence (as opposed to arguments of fact or law) included in the representations of the director, or where it assists the CMA in clarifying a substantive factual or legal or economic issue and, in the particular circumstances, considers that this outweighs the confidentiality concerns arising from such disclosure.

146 For example, when the Addressee and a third party put forward different versions or interpretations of the same facts and it is necessary to decide which version or interpretation is more credible.

147 Rule 6 and Rule 11 of the CA98 Rules.

148 In some cases, the CMA may decide that it is appropriate to hold a multi-party hearing, including complainants and/or other third parties. See paragraph 12.24 below.

149 See paragraph 12.19.

150 Rule 6(6) and (7) of the CA98 Rules.

151 Rule 5(3) parties will be notified that a letter of facts has been issued and may be provided with a non-confidential copy where they have established that it is necessary for their rights of defence.

152 The CMA may issue multiple letters of facts.

153 A Supplementary Statement of Objections will not be issued where, for example, the scope of a suspected infringement has reduced or the amount of the proposed penalty is reduced.

154 Rule 5(3) parties will be notified that a Supplementary Statement of Objections has been issued and may be provided with a non-confidential copy where they have established that it is necessary for their rights of defence.

13. THE FINAL DECISION

[3.229]

13.1 The Case Decision Group decides whether there is sufficient evidence to meet the legal test for establishing an infringement and, if so, the level of any financial penalty to be imposed. Prior to proceeding to issue a final decision, the Case Decision Group may consult the Case and Policy Committee on any legal, economic or policy issues arising out of the proposed decision.[155]

13.2 As noted in Chapter 10, if, having completed its consideration of the case, the Case Decision Group does not find sufficient evidence of a competition law infringement, it will close the case.[156] In those circumstances, the Case Decision Group may decide to publish a reasoned no grounds for action decision.

ISSUE OF AN INFRINGEMENT DECISION

13.3 The CMA will issue an infringement decision to each business the CMA has found to have infringed the law.[157] The CMA will also provide a non-confidential version of the decision to any person who is party to an agreement or conduct that the CMA considers infringes the Chapter I prohibition but who was not an addressee of the Statement of Objections.[158]

13.4 The infringement decision will set out fully the facts on which the CMA relies to prove the infringement and the action that it is taking, and will address any material representations that have been made during the course of the investigation.

IMPOSITION OF FINANCIAL PENALTIES

13.5 If a financial penalty is being imposed, the infringement decision will explain how the Case Decision Group decided upon the appropriate level of penalty, having taken into account the CMA's statutory obligations[159] and the parties' written and oral representations on the Draft Penalty Statement. More information on how the CMA sets penalties is available in the CMA's Guidance as to the appropriate amount of a penalty (CMA73).

13.6 The infringement decision will also specify the date before which the penalty must be paid. It is likely that payment will be required within a period of three months from the date of the infringement decision. If the business fails to pay within the date specified (and has not brought an appeal against the imposition or amount of the penalty within the time allowed or an appeal has been heard and the penalty upheld), the CMA may commence proceedings to recover the required amount as a civil debt.

ISSUING OF DIRECTIONS

13.7 The infringement decision may also give directions to bring the infringement to an end.[160] Directions may require the individual or business to modify or cease the conduct or agreement. This may include positive action, such as informing third parties that an infringement has been brought to an end. In some circumstances, the directions appropriate to bring an infringement to an end may be (or include) structural changes to its business.

13.8 Any directions will set out the facts on which the direction is based and the reasons for it.[161] In most cases directions will have immediate effect, although in some cases the CMA may allow a period of time for compliance.[162] The directions will be published on the public register maintained by the CMA.

ANNOUNCEMENT OF THE INFRINGEMENT DECISION

13.9 When an infringement decision is issued, the CMA will normally issue a press announcement, make an announcement on the Regulatory News Service and publish a page on the CMA's webpages which describes the case.

13.10 As a general rule, as described in Chapter 11, in non-market-sensitive announcements, the CMA aims to give parties advance notice of the announcement, in confidence, unless there is a compelling reason not to do so. In both market-sensitive and non-market sensitive situations, the CMA will aim to balance an open approach with the need to ensure the orderly announcement of full information.[163]

13.11 After the infringement decision and press announcement have been issued, the CMA may notify complainants whose complaint led to the investigation and other third parties (for example, third parties who have submitted written representations during the investigation) of the CMA's decision.

CONFIDENTIALITY

13.12 Information that is confidential will be disclosed through the infringement decision to other parties only if disclosure is strictly necessary. Before disclosing any confidential information, the CMA will consider whether there is a need to exclude any information whose disclosure would be contrary to the public interest or whose disclosure might significantly harm the interests of the company or individual it relates to. If the CMA considers that disclosure might significantly harm legitimate business interests or the interests of an individual, the CMA will consider the extent to which disclosure of that information is nevertheless necessary for the purpose for which the CMA is allowed to make the disclosure.[164]

13.13 The Addressee of the decision will have already had the opportunity to make confidentiality representations. Either shortly before or after the infringement decision has been issued, prior to publication of a non-confidential version, the CMA will usually allow the Addressee a final opportunity to make representations on information which the Addressee deems to be confidential and is contained in the decision. Any representations must be limited to confidentiality issues only and, as at the other stages in the process, the CMA will not accept blanket or unsubstantiated confidentiality claims.

FINAL PUBLICATION

13.14 The CMA will publish, as quickly as possible, a non-confidential version of the infringement decision on the case page on the CMA's webpages. The CMA also maintains a register of decisions in investigations under the CA98 and the details of the case will be placed on the register.

13.15 The CMA may delay publication of the final decision to avoid prejudicing any criminal investigation under section 192 of the EA02 that relates to the same or similar arrangements or conduct.

NOTES

155 As described in paragraph 9.7 above.

156 The Case Decision Group may consult the Case and Policy Committee as necessary.

157 Section 31 of the CA98 and Rule 10(1) of the CA98 Rules.

158 Rule 10(2) and Rule 19 of the CA98 Rules.

159 Section 36(7A) of the CA98.

160 Section 32 and 33 of the CA98.

161 Rule 12 of the CA98 Rules.

162 The CMA may apply to the court for an order requiring compliance with a direction within a specified time limit if a person fails to comply with it without reasonable excuse, section 34 of the CA98.

163 For a general guide to the CMA's approach when it makes a public announcement, see Transparency and

Disclosure: Statement of the CMA's policy and approach (CMA6).

164 Section 244 of the EA02.

14. SETTLEMENT

[3.230]

14.1 In the context of enforcement cases under the CA98, 'settlement' is the process whereby a business under investigation is prepared to admit that it has breached competition law and confirms that it accepts that a streamlined administrative procedure will govern the remainder of the CMA's investigation. If so, the CMA will impose a reduced penalty on the business.[165]

14.2 Settlement, in appropriate cases, allows the CMA to achieve efficiencies through a streamlined administrative procedure, resulting in earlier adoption of any infringement decision, and/or resource savings.

14.3 It is distinct from the CMA's leniency policy and the CMA's power to accept commitments under section 31A of the CA98.[166] The leniency policy and the use of settlements are not mutually exclusive – it is possible for a leniency applicant to settle a case under the CA98 and benefit from both leniency and settlement discounts.

DISCRETIONARY NATURE OF SETTLEMENT

14.4 The CMA will consider settlement for any case falling under the Chapter I or Chapter II prohibitions under the CA98 as long as the CMA considers that the evidential standard for giving notice of its proposed infringement decision is met.

14.5 Whether to settle any case is at the CMA's discretion. Moreover, there is no right or obligation to settle or enter into any settlement discussions where these are offered by the CMA.

14.6 In determining whether a case is suitable for settlement the CMA will have regard to a number of factors. The primary factor is whether the CMA considers that the evidential standard for giving notice of its proposed infringement decision is met. The CMA will not proceed with settlement discussions unless it considers that this standard is met. The CMA will also consider other factors such as the likely procedural efficiencies and resource savings that can be achieved. A further factor that may be relevant is the prospect of reaching settlement in a reasonable time frame. The CMA will continue to consider throughout the settlement discussions whether procedural efficiencies and resource savings can still be achieved from settlement, for example, taking into account the number of businesses who are interested in settlement out of the total number involved in the investigation.

REQUIREMENTS FOR SETTLEMENT

14.7 At a minimum, the CMA will require the settling business/es to:

- make a clear and unequivocal admission of liability in relation to the nature, scope and duration of the infringement. The scope of the infringement will include, as a minimum, the material facts of the infringement as well as its legal characterisation. An admission of the facts alone is not sufficient to constitute an admission of liability sufficient to form the basis of a settlement. Where appropriate the admission will also include the facts of any actual implementation of the infringement;
- cease the infringing behaviour immediately from the date that it enters into settlement discussions with the CMA, where it has not already done so. It must also refrain from engaging again in the same or similar infringing behaviour; and
- confirm it will pay a penalty set at a maximum amount.[167] As set out in paragraph 14.29 below, this maximum penalty – which will apply provided the business continues to follow the requirements of settlement – will reflect the application of the settlement discount to the penalty that would otherwise have been imposed. The level of settlement discount applied will reflect the particular circumstances of the case, in particular whether the case is being settled pre- or post- Statement of Objections (see paragraph 14.31 below).

14.8 In addition, in order to achieve the CMA's objective of resolving the case efficiently, settling businesses must confirm that they accept that:

- there will be a streamlined administrative process for the remainder of the investigation. This would normally include streamlined access to file arrangements, no Draft Penalty Statement, no written representations on
- the Statement of Objections or any Supplementary Statement of Objections (except in relation to manifest factual inaccuracies), no oral hearings after settlement has been reached and no Case Decision Group being appointed;[168]
- there will be an infringement decision against the settling business (except in the circumstances set out in paragraph 14.27);
- unless the settling party itself successfully appeals the infringement decision, the decision will remain final and binding as against it, even if another addressee of the infringement decision successfully appeals it;
- if the settling business appeals the decision, it will no longer benefit from the settlement discount (see further paragraph 14.30 below). The CMA will remain free to use the admissions made by the settling business and any documents, information or witness evidence provided by the settling business; and
- there are likely to be specific requirements that relate to the circumstances of the case and the stage which it has reached. For example, the settling business may be required to make some of its employees or officers available for interview and to provide additional witness statements

where the circumstances of a case demand it. The settling business is likely also to be required to confirm that it will use its best endeavours to ensure that employees or officers (who may have provided witness statements during the investigation) appear as witnesses on behalf of the CMA's case, should another addressee of the eventual infringement decision appeal any infringement decision to the Competition Appeal Tribunal.

BUSINESSES SETTLE VOLUNTARILY

14.9 A settling business may withdraw from settlement discussions at any time before confirming in writing[169] its acceptance of the requirements for settlement (including its admission). The settling business' decision to settle should be based on its full awareness of the requirements of settlement and the consequences of settling. The settling business should satisfy itself, and will be taken to have satisfied itself, as to the following:

- that, having seen the key evidence on which the CMA is relying, it is prepared to admit to the infringement by reference to the Summary Statement of Facts[170] or draft Statement of Objections or Statement of Objections (where the settlement occurs after issue of the Statement of Objections), including the nature, scope and duration of the infringement;
- the maximum level of penalty to be imposed; and
- the implications of settling, including the minimum requirements of settlement listed in paragraphs 14.7 and 14.8 above and that (except in the circumstances set out in paragraph 14.27) an infringement decision will be issued which may be relied on by third parties to bring follow-on damages actions.

SETTLEMENT PROCESS

14.10 Settlement discussions can be initiated either before or after the Statement of Objections is issued. Businesses may wish to approach the CMA during an investigation to discuss the possibility of exploring settlement by contacting the case team. The CMA will not make any assumptions about a business' liability from the fact that it is interested in engaging in or engages in settlement discussions.

14.11 Before the CMA case team can commence settlement discussions, the SRO will be required to obtain a mandate from the CMA's Case and Policy Committee to engage in settlement discussions. If settlement may be appropriate in a specific case, all businesses involved in an investigation (except, normally, any immunity applicant[171]) will be invited to explore the possibility of settlement.

14.12 Settlement discussions will be subject to a set timetable. However, the timetable will be appropriate to the circumstances of the case (for example to take account of the number of businesses entering into settlement discussions) rather than fixed at a set period. The appropriate procedure will also be partly determined by the stage in the administrative process at which settlement discussions take place. Settlement discussions will generally be overseen by the SRO.

14.13 In cases where one or more of the businesses does not wish to settle, the CMA may settle with the remaining businesses.[172] For non-settling businesses, the CMA will revert to the usual administrative procedure.[173]

SUMMARY STATEMENT OF FACTS

14.14 If the settlement discussions take place pre-Statement of Objections, each business that enters into settlement discussions will be presented with a Summary Statement of Facts[174] and will be provided with access to the key documents on which the CMA is relying as well as a list of the documents on the CMA's file. Access to specific documents can be requested, although the provision of such access will influence the CMA's ongoing assessment of the procedural efficiencies and resources savings that can be achieved from settlement.[175] The CMA will give the business the opportunity to provide limited representations, including identifying manifest factual inaccuracies on the Summary Statement of Facts as part of the settlement discussions. If the settling business' representations amount to a wholesale rejection of the facts of the alleged infringement as set out in the Summary Statement of Facts, the CMA will reassess whether the case remains suitable for settlement. This will be determined by the CMA on a case-by-case basis.

DRAFT PENALTY CALCULATION

14.15 Where settlement is being considered prior to the issue of a Statement of Objections, each business considering settlement will be presented with a draft penalty calculation which is likely to contain some aspects which will be the same for each business considering settlement, and some which will vary to reflect the relevant business' particular circumstances. The CMA will also give each business the opportunity to make limited representations on the draft penalty calculation within a specified time frame as part of settlement discussions, provided that these are not inconsistent with its admission of liability.

14.16 Where a party is considering settlement after receipt of the Statement of Objections and any Draft Penalty Statement, it will have the opportunity to submit limited representations on the Draft Penalty Statement within a specified time frame as part of settlement discussions, provided that these are not inconsistent with its admission of liability.

14.17 The CMA will not enter into negotiation or plea-bargaining during settlement discussions, for example by accepting an admission in relation to a lesser infringement in return for dropping a more serious infringement. Nor will the CMA be prepared to negotiate variations to the minimum standard requirements of the settlement procedure which will apply to all settling businesses in that investigation.

APPROVAL OF SETTLEMENT

14.18 The SRO must receive approval from the Case and Policy Committee to settle.[176]

14.19 While settlement discussions will be conducted orally, the business' acceptance of the settlement requirements, including its admission, must be confirmed in writing (with its company letterhead). However, the CMA may consider a reasoned request from the settling business to provide the confirmation that it accepts the settlement requirements (including its admission) orally. This will be recorded and transcribed.

14.20 If a business is settling pre-Statement of Objections, its admission will be made by reference to the infringement(s) as set out in the Summary Statement of Facts (incorporating any amendments necessitated by the representations referred to in paragraph 14.14). The business will also be given the opportunity to indicate in a concise memorandum any manifest factual inaccuracies in the Statement of Objections once it is issued to the business.[177]

14.21 Where a business is settling post-Statement of Objections the admission will be made by reference to the infringement as set out in the Statement of Objections and the business will be given the opportunity to indicate any manifest factual inaccuracies in the Statement of Objections as part of its admission. If the settling business has made representations on the Statement of Objections before settling, the CMA will require the business, in its confirmation that it has accepted the requirements of settlement (see paragraph 14.19 above), formally to withdraw those representations other than to the extent that they deal with manifest factual inaccuracies, as otherwise such representations may tend to undermine the clear and unequivocal admission of liability which is an essential feature of settlement.[178]

14.22 The letter containing the confirmation from the party that it has accepted the requirements of the settlement procedure and its admission to the infringement will be placed on the CMA's file.

14.23 Notes of the discussions will also be put on the CMA's file but will not be disclosed to other businesses involved in the investigation[179] or, if the discussions break down and no settlement is reached, the Case Decision Group.[180] Parties must not disclose the content of settlement discussions, the fact that discussions have taken place, or any documents they have had access to during the settlement procedure to any third parties (including any other parties engaging in settlement discussions) without the prior written authorisation of the CMA.

14.24 If, during settlement discussions, a business provides the CMA with new documentary evidence or information relevant to the infringement, those new documents or information will be placed on the file and may be disclosed to other parties to the investigation in the usual way. The CMA may also take further investigatory steps in relation to any such new documents or information provided to it. For example, the CMA may issue formal information requests or interview individuals in relation to the new documents or information where it is appropriate to do so. The CMA will make this clear to businesses when commencing settlement discussions.

14.25 If settlement discussions are not successful, the case will revert to the usual administrative procedure. Any decision to issue an infringement decision and any resulting penalty will be for a Case Decision Group. This means that any penalty imposed may be different from any penalty calculation provided during settlement discussions. Subject to paragraph 14.27 below, the case will then proceed to either an infringement decision (if the case has already passed Statement of Objections stage) or to a Statement of Objections followed by an infringement decision (if the Statement of Objections has not yet been issued).

ISSUE OF AN INFRINGEMENT DECISION

14.26 If settlement discussions are successful the SRO will generally issue an infringement decision and will consult the Case and Policy Committee on his/her proposed decision.[181]

14.27 An infringement decision will be issued in every settlement case unless the CMA decides not to make an infringement finding against the settling business, for example where new exculpatory evidence comes to light after settlement but before the CMA has adopted an infringement decision. Equally, the decision (and where relevant any Statement of Objections) will substantially reflect the admission made by the settling business unless the CMA considers it necessary to include amendments or issue a Supplementary Statement of Objections, for example where new evidence comes to light (see further paragraph 14.33). The decision will also include findings of fact and law, the amount, and an explanation of, the penalty imposed on the settling business as well as a description of the key requirements of the settlement procedure. The decision may include findings of effect if appropriate to the case.

SETTLEMENT DISCOUNT

14.28 As part of the minimum requirements for settlement, a business must accept that it will pay a maximum penalty. This is the maximum amount of penalty that the settling business will pay if the CMA issues an infringement decision.[182]

14.29 In the infringement decision, the CMA will set out the total penalty (£X) less the specified settlement discount of (Y%), provided the settling business follows any continuing requirements of settlement, which results in the reduced penalty after settlement of (£Z) (the maximum penalty).

14.30 The settlement discount set out in the infringement decision will no longer apply if a settling business appeals the infringement decision to the Competition Appeal Tribunal. The Competition Appeal Tribunal has full jurisdiction to review the appropriate level of penalty.

14.31 Settlement discounts will be capped at a level of 20%. The actual discount awarded will take account of the resource savings achieved in settling that particular case at that particular stage in the investigation. The discount available for settlement pre-Statement of Objections will be up to 20% and for settlement post-Statement of Objections will be up to 10%.

WITHDRAWAL FROM THE SETTLEMENT PROCEDURE FOLLOWING SETTLEMENT

14.32 Following the completion of successful settlement discussions the CMA will retain the right to withdraw from the settlement procedure if the settling business does not follow the requirements for settlement. Prior to withdrawing, the CMA will notify the settling business that it considers that it is not following the requirements of settlement and will give the business the opportunity to respond.

14.33 If the CMA does not intend to substantially reflect a settling business' admission in either the Statement of Objections or infringement decision (for example where new evidence comes to light, as referred to in paragraph 14.27), the settling business will be given the opportunity to withdraw from the settlement procedure and the case will revert to the usual administrative procedure. In these circumstances, the settling business' admission will not be disclosed to other businesses involved in the investigation or to the Case Decision Group, where this has not already occurred (for example, to other businesses as part of access to file, see paragraph 14.19). Nor will that admission be used in evidence against any of the parties to the investigation.

COMPETITION DISQUALIFICATION

14.34 The CMA has the discretion to decide that it will not pursue a competition disqualification order or undertakings against the directors of a business that is under investigation for a breach of competition law, including where it is a settling business. However, this will not be a part of the settlement procedure under the CA98. Where the CMA has decided not to prioritise a CDDA investigation against one or more directors of a company or not to seek their disqualification, it may make this known to the director and settling business at the time of the CA98 settlement. In some cases it may also be possible for the CMA to settle a CDDA investigation against one or more directors of a settling business by accepting competition disqualification undertakings from the director or directors concerned at the same time as the settlement of the CA98 case, but where this is the case the decision to accept a disqualification undertaking will nevertheless be separate from the decision to settle the CA98 case.

EXTERNAL COMMUNICATIONS DURING OR POST SETTLEMENT

14.35 The CMA's standard practice is not to make a public announcement that settlement discussions are taking place, or, where discussions break down, that they have broken down. As set out in paragraph 14.23 above, parties must not disclose the content of settlement discussions or the fact that those discussions have taken place to any third parties (including any other parties engaging in settlement discussions) without the prior written authorisation of the CMA.

14.36 In a case involving more than one business, the CMA is likely to inform other businesses involved in the investigation that one or more businesses are exploring the possibility of settlement. This is a necessary part of the process since the CMA is committed to ensuring transparency of case timetables, and entering into discussions on possible settlement will typically pause the case timetable whilst such discussions take place. At settlement discussion stage, the CMA will not name the business or businesses that have decided to explore the possibility of settlement, although in a case involving a small number of businesses, the CMA recognises that it may be possible for the business or businesses to infer which business is considering the possibility of settlement. The CMA will make it clear to other businesses involved in the investigation that the relevant business or businesses are only exploring the possibility of settlement at this stage.

14.37 The CMA may announce that a business has settled with a press release, in which case the CMA's webpages will be updated. Where possible the CMA will give the settling business or businesses at least one hour's advance notice of the press release's contents before it is published.[183]

NOTES

165 See Rule 9 of the CA98 Rules. See also paragraph 2.1 and 2.30 of the CMA's Guidance as to the appropriate amount of a penalty (CMA73), which provides that the CMA will reduce penalties where a business settles.

166 See, respectively, the CMA guidance Applications for leniency and no action in cartel cases (OFT1495) and paragraphs 10.15 to 10.29 above.

167 There may be rare cases where the CMA may settle where a penalty is not being imposed on a party, for example an immunity applicant. However, the CMA would not normally invite an immunity applicant to explore the possibility of settlement (see paragraph 14.11 below).

168 Following settlement the SRO would generally remain the decision-maker on the case. The SRO would consult the Case and Policy Committee on his/her proposed decision.

169 Although, as set out in paragraph Annexe(s)14.19, it may be possible for a business to confirm its acceptance orally.

170 For the purposes of settlement discussions initiated before a Statement of Objections is issued, a Summary Statement of Facts sets out the key evidence and facts upon which the CMA relies to support its provisional view that there has been an infringement of competition law. The Summary Statement of Facts together with the key documents relied upon in the Summary Statement of Facts are presented to a business interested in settling, to enable it to consider its position regarding a possible settlement.

171 As for the parties who settle, an immunity applicant involved in an investigation which is settled will be asked to confirm as part of the leniency process that they accept that there will be no involvement of a Case Decision Group.

172 The settlements with those business will need to be approved by the CMA's Case and Policy Committee: see paragraph Annexe(s)14.18 below.

173 Referred to as 'hybrid' cases.

174 Alternatively, a draft Statement of Objections may be presented. This will depend on a number of factors, such as, the

timing of the approach to settle and whether the issue of a draft Statement of Objections would provide additional procedural efficiencies and resource savings. Further references to Summary Statement of Facts should be read to include such a draft Statement of Objections, where issued for settlement purposes.

175 These may be subject to confidentiality redactions where appropriate.

176 Rule 9 of the CA98 Rules.

177 Where a business has received a draft Statement of Objections the CMA will normally not provide a further opportunity to indicate any manifest factual inaccuracies.

178 See paragraph Annexe(s)14.7 above.

179 See the disclosure provisions in Part 9 of the EA02.

180 If settlement discussions take place post-Statement of Objections, the Case Decision Group will be informed that one or more businesses are exploring the possibility of settlement. This is inevitable because settlement discussions will pause the case timetable. There may also be exceptional cases where the CMA considers it appropriate for the Case Decision Group to oversee the settlement discussions and remain decision makers on the case, in which case they would already be aware of the settlement discussions.

181 Rule 9 of the CA98 Rules.

182 The maximum penalty figure may include a reduction for cooperation that has been provided prior to settlement as a mitigating factor under step 3 of the penalty calculation (see CMA's Guidance as to the appropriate amount of a penalty (CMA73).

183 Further details of the way in which the CMA gives notice of announcements is available in the CMA's Guideline Transparency and Disclosure: Statement of the CMA's policy and approach (CMA6).

15. COMPLAINTS ABOUT THE CMA'S INVESTIGATION HANDLING, RIGHT OF APPEAL AND REVIEWING THE CMA'S PROCESSES

PROCEDURAL COMPLAINTS PROCESS FOR INVESTIGATIONS UNDER THE CA98

See footnote 184[184]

[3.231]

15.1 Parties to an investigation under the CA98 have recourse to a procedural complaints process in the event that they are unhappy with certain aspects of the investigation procedure after a formal investigation under section 25 of the CA98 has been opened.[185]

15.2 The CMA has also published a guideline Transparency and Disclosure: Statement of the CMA's policy and approach (CMA6) setting out the steps it takes to ensure the CMA's work is open and accessible. Individuals, businesses and their advisers are entitled to be treated with courtesy, respect and in a non-discriminatory manner when dealing with the CMA. If a party's dispute falls outside the scope of the CMA's procedural complaints process for CA98 investigations, this guideline sets out the options available to pursue the complaint.

15.3 Once a formal investigation has been opened, any concerns or complaints about the CMA's procedures or how investigations are handled should be made in writing to the SRO in the first instance. If a party wishes to complain to the SRO, it should set out details of its complaint and provide copies of any relevant supporting documents or correspondence.

15.4 If, during the course of an investigation under the CA98, a party is unable to resolve the dispute with the SRO, complaints about the procedures followed during the course of the investigation may be referred to the Procedural Officer. The Procedural Officer considers significant procedural complaints. Significant procedural complaints considered by the Procedural Office are in particular, those relating to:

- deadlines for parties to respond to information requests, submit non-confidential versions of documents or submit written representations on the Statement of Objections, Supplementary Statement of Objections or any Draft Penalty Statement;
- requests for confidentiality redactions of information in documents on the CMA's case file, in the Statement of Objections, in a Draft Penalty Statement or in the final decision;
- requests for disclosure or non-disclosure of certain documents on the CMA's case file; and
- issues relating to oral hearings, including, for example, with regard to issues such as the date of the hearing.

15.5 The Procedural Officer is independent of the investigation, the case team and the Case Decision Group.

15.6 The Procedural Officer does not have jurisdiction to review decisions on the scope of requests for information or other decisions relating to the substance of a case.[186] Decisions made by the Procedural Officer about complaints referred during the course of CA98 investigations, including those complaints found to fall outside the scope of the Procedural Officer's role, are published on the Procedural Officer's webpage.[187]

PROCESS FOR REFERRING A COMPLAINT TO THE PROCEDURAL OFFICER

See footnote 188[188]

15.7 If a party wishes to refer a dispute to the Procedural Officer for review, that party will need to make an application within five working days of being notified of the SRO's decision on the issue in question. A party must provide a short written summary of the issue in question and provide copies of relevant correspondence with the case team and SRO.

15.8 On receipt of a complaint reference, the Procedural Officer will provide an opportunity for the case team and the party to present their arguments to the Procedural Officer orally on the telephone or at a meeting, before issuing a short, reasoned decision either confirming the SRO's decision, or reaching a different decision in whole or in part. The Procedural Officer's decision will be binding on the case team.

15.9 The Procedural Officer will endeavour to deal with the complaint as quickly as possible, with an indicative administrative target of taking decisions in most cases within ten working days from receipt of the application. The Procedural Officer will reach a decision within 20 working days from receipt of the application, extendable by no more than 20 working days if there are special reasons[189] to do so.[190]

15.10 The Procedural Officer will carefully assess how long any extension will be and will endeavour to make only one extension where it is required. The party's cooperation will assist the Procedural Officer to make a robust and timely decision, in particular by attending meetings and/or providing information on short notice.

15.11 The CMA will publish the Procedural Officer's decision, or a summary of that decision, generally at the time of the decision or at the end of the case, subject to confidentiality redactions as appropriate.

RIGHT OF APPEAL TO THE COMPETITION APPEAL TRIBUNAL OR COURT

15.12 The role of the Procedural Officer does not prejudice the party's rights in respect of judicial review and/or any appeal before the Competition Appeal Tribunal.

15.13 Addressees of the CMA's appealable decisions and third parties with a sufficient interest in appealable decisions have a right to appeal them to the Competition Appeal Tribunal. Appealable decisions include decisions as to whether there has been a competition law infringement, interim measures decisions and decisions on the imposition of, or the amount of, a penalty.[191]

15.14 Where the law does not provide for an appeal, an application for judicial review may be brought in certain circumstances.[192] Parties should seek independent legal advice on their rights in this regard.

NOTES

184 The Procedural Officer can also deal with certain disputes in relation to merger investigations and market studies and investigations (see further Chapter 5 of the CMA guideline Transparency and Disclosure: Statement of the CMA's policy and approach (CMA6)).

185 Rule 8 of the CA98 Rules.

186 Section 26 of the CA98 provides the CMA with the power to require documents or information.

187 Procedural Officer: raising procedural issues in CMA cases.

188 See further Rule 8 of the CA98 Rules.

189 For example, where complaints require the Procedural Officer to deal with large volumes of data or materials, or where the Procedural Officer receives a number of complaints within a short period of time and is unable to deal with one or more complaints within the original 20 working day period.

190 See Rule 8 of the CA98 Rules.

191 Section 46 and section 47 of the CA98.

192 A judicial review application may be brought before the Administrative Court of the Queen's Bench Division under Part 54 of the Civil Procedure Rules.

16. APPLICATION AND ENFORCEMENT OF ARTICLES 101 AND 102

[3.232]

16.1 For the remainder of the Transition Period, the CMA can continue to use its powers of investigation and enforcement under the CA98 for Article 101 and Article 102 TFEU investigations. During this period, the CMA may also investigate at the request of the European Commission or National Competition Authorities of EU Member States (NCAs). Whether, and if so to what extent, the CMA will be able to continue to use its powers in this way following the end of the Transition Period may change. As such, the remainder of this section should be read as being of application only during the remainder of the Transition Period.[193]

POWERS TO ASSIST WITH EUROPEAN COMMISSION INVESTIGATIONS

16.2 Part 2 of CA98 and the EC Regulation 1/2003 (the Modernisation Regulation)[194] together provide the CMA[195] with powers to assist the European Commission to undertake investigations relating to Article 101 and Article 102.

16.3 The CMA may actively participate in European Commission investigations relating to Article 101 or Article 102 in three ways:

- the European Commission may request that the CMA carry out an inspection of business premises on its behalf;
- the CMA may be required to assist the European Commission when it carries out an inspection of business premises in the United Kingdom; and
- the CMA may be required to assist the European Commission when it carries out an inspection of non-business premises in the United Kingdom.

INSPECTIONS ON BEHALF OF THE EUROPEAN COMMISSION

16.4 When the CMA is carrying out an inspection of business premises on behalf of the European Commission, the CMA officers will have been given an authorisation[196] under CA98 which has the effect of providing them with the powers of an official authorised by the European Commission.[197]

16.5 This means that the CMA officers will possess further powers that are not available when the CMA investigates suspected infringements of Article 101 or Article 102 on itself. Primarily, in addition to

Part 3 CMA and other Guidelines

asking employees for explanations of documents, CMA officers can ask for an explanation of the facts or documents relating to the subject matter and purpose of the inspection.[198]

16.6 The CMA may obtain a warrant where an inspection of business premises which it is carrying out on behalf of the European Commission is being, or is likely to be, obstructed.[199] The warrant obtained must indicate the subject matter and purpose of the investigation and the nature of the offence for obstruction.[200]

ASSISTING WITH EUROPEAN COMMISSION INSPECTIONS

16.7 When assisting the European Commission with an inspection of business premises, CMA officers have the same powers as an official authorised by the European Commission.[201]

16.8 When assisting the European Commission with an inspection of non-business premises, the CMA must obtain a warrant before any inspection can be carried out. The CMA officers, in addition to being able to do anything which the warrant authorises them to do, will have the same powers as an official authorised by the European Commission.[202]

PRIVILEGED INFORMATION

16.9 Where an inspection is being conducted by the CMA on behalf of the European Commission (under sections 62B and/or 63 of CA98), the United Kingdom rules on legal professional privilege will apply.[203]

16.10 When assisting the European Commission with an inspection, the range of documents that can benefit from legal professional privilege is in some respects narrower than when the CMA is investigating suspected infringements of Article 101 or Article 102 on its own behalf or on behalf of another NCA.

16.11 The European Court of Justice has recognised that correspondence between a client and an external legal adviser, entitled to practice in one of the Member States, is subject to legal professional privilege where: (i) the correspondence follows the initiation of proceedings by the European Commission and concerns the defence of the client; or (ii) the correspondence existed before the initiation of proceedings but is closely linked with the subject matter of the proceedings.

16.12 Correspondence between a client and an external legal adviser who is not entitled to practise in one of the Member States or between a client and an in-house legal adviser (unless the in-house legal adviser is simply reporting the legal advice of an external legal adviser) is not recognised by the European Courts as being protected by legal professional privilege under European Union law.[204]

16.13 Where an inspection is being conducted to assist the European Commission, legal professional privilege can be claimed only for documents that fall within the category of correspondence that the European Court of Justice has recognised as being subject to legal professional privilege. In order to claim legal professional privilege for certain documents during an inspection the occupier must make a case to the European Commission demonstrating why the documents are covered by legal professional privilege.

POWER TO ASSIST NATIONAL COMPETITION AUTHORITIES OF EU MEMBER STATES

16.14 Under Part 2A of CA98, the CMA may carry out an inspection or other fact-finding measure[205] in the United Kingdom on behalf of an NCA in order to assist it in establishing whether there has been an infringement of Article 101 or 102.[206]

16.15 Part 2A provides the CMA with similar powers of investigation to those it uses to investigate suspected infringements of Article 101 and 102 under Part I of the Act. This means that, where there are reasonable grounds to suspect an infringement, the CMA will have the power to:

- require the production of specified documents and information;[207]
- enter business premises without a warrant;[208] and
- enter and search business or domestic premises with a warrant.[209]

16.16 Although NCAs of other Member States do not have any formal powers of investigation within the United Kingdom, NCAs officers may be authorised to accompany, and participate under the supervision of, authorised CMA officers on an inspection where the CMA uses its power to enter premises under a warrant.[210]

16.17 These powers of investigation are subject to the same restrictions concerning legal professional privilege and self-incrimination in relation to investigations under Part I of the CA98.

NOTES

193 For further information on how EU Exit affects the CMA's powers and processes for competition law enforcement after the end of the Transition Period, see the CMA's Guidance on the functions of the CMA after the end of the Transition Period.

194 Council Regulation (EC) No 1/2003 of 16 December 2002, OJ L 1, 4.1.2003, p. 1-25.

195 These powers are not available to the Regulators. They may, however, participate in inspections carried out by the CMA on behalf of the European Commission if the industry being investigated falls within their area of expertise.

196 The authorisation will identify the officers, the subject matter and purpose of the investigation and draw attention to the penalties which an undertaking may incur in connection with the inspection under the relevant provision of Community law. Article 23(1)(c) (fines) and Article 24(1)(e) (periodic penalty payments) of the Modernisation Regulation.

197 Section 62B(1) of CA98.

198 Article 20(2)(e) of the Modernisation Regulation.

199 Section 63 of the CA98.

200 A person will be guilty of an offence if they intentionally obstruct any person in the exercise of their powers under a warrant issued in relation to a European Commission investigation relating to Article 101 or 102. The sanction is a fine of up to the statutory maximum on summary conviction or an unlimited fine and/or a maximum of two years' imprisonment on conviction on indictment.

201 Article 20(5) of the Modernisation Regulation.

202 Article 21(4) of the Modernisation Regulation.

203 Section 65A of CA98.

204 Case 155/79 *AM & S Europe v Commission* [1982] ECR 1575, 1982 [CMLR] 264.

205 These powers are not available to the Regulators. They may, however, participate in inspections carried out by the CMA on behalf of other NCAs if the industry being investigated falls within their area of expertise.

206 Section 65D of CA98.

207 Section 65E of CA98.

208 Section 65F of CA98.

209 Sections 65G and 65H of CA98.

210 Section 65G(4) and 65H(4) of CA98.

ANNEXE A – TEMPLATE DECLARATION OF TRUTH

[3.233]
This Declaration should be included with the interim measures application and be signed by an individual or individuals with authority to bind the person applying for interim measures (the Applicant):

I declare that, to the best of my knowledge and belief, the information and evidence provided to the CMA in support of the application for interim measures made by [name of the Applicant] is true, correct, and complete in all material respects.

I understand that it is a criminal offence under section 44 of the Competition Act 1998 (CA98) for a person recklessly or knowingly to supply to the CMA information which is false or misleading in any material particular. This includes supplying such information to another person knowing that the information is to be used for the purpose of supplying information to the CMA.

Signed: Name: (block letters) Position: (block letters) Date:

CHART DESCRIPTIONS

FIGURE 1.1 KEY STAGES OF AN INVESTIGATION

Source of CMA investigations

Initial consideration of issues and informal evidence gathering. Apply the Prioritisation Principals and consider whether the legal test (section 25 of the Act) has been satisfied.

Open a formal investigation

Formal information gathering powers. Publish case opening notice and issue written information requests. Conduct interviews. Visit search premises to obtain information and analysis of gathered evidence.

Consider if there is sufficient evidence of an infringement and Parties' right to reply

Statement of Objections and access to CMA file. Set out CMA provisional findings, supporting evidence, proposed action, and issue draft penalty statement. Receive/consider parties' representations on SO and draft penalty statement (written and oral).

Consider if there is sufficient evidence of an infringement in light of parties' representations

At this point there will either be no grounds for action decision or an infringement decision will be issued and action will be taken (financial penalties, directions). We will publish the non-confidential version of the decision.

The parties have a right of appeal to the Competition Appeal Tribunal after we have made the decision.

Duration of formal investigation varies depending on the case.

OVERVIEW OF COMPLAINT PROCESS

Complaints

First, we receive submissions from businesses or consumers on competition concerns. We have a specific hotline where we receive complaints about cartels. Complaints about other anti-competitive activity can be made via General Enquiries, notification form (available on CMA webpages), an in-depth complaint with possible pre-complaint discussion.

Preliminary assessment

Consider whether the complaint is within the CMA's remit.

Pipeline assessment

Possible informal dialogue with the complainant and application of the Prioritisation Principals.

Allocation to Enforcement Directorate

This is the initial assessment phase which handles antitrust and cartel investigations, plus consumer enforcement cases. Informal information gathering with the complainant begins.

Formal investigation opened (s 25 CA98)

COMPETITION AND MARKETS AUTHORITY: GUIDANCE ON WHISTLEBLOWING

(Published 16 July 2021)

[3.234]

NOTES

INTRODUCTION

If you are an employee or ex-employee and wish to provide the CMA with information and/or raise a concern about your employer's possible involvement in anti-competitive or unfair trading practices, please contact us here:

— call: 020 3738 6556

— email: whistleblower@cma.gov.uk

If you are unsure whether the practices you are concerned about amount to anti-competitive or unfair trading practices, we still want to hear from you if you suspect a business is behaving unfairly.

Contact: general.enquiries@cma.gov.uk.

WHAT WILL HAPPEN IF I MAKE A REPORT?

We understand that it may be a significant decision to come forward and report potential wrongdoing or malpractice by your employer. If you contact us, we handle your details and the information you provide sensitively and in confidence. In particular, we would seek to protect your identity from the organisation you are reporting against. If you prefer, you can provide information anonymously. This would mean that we are unable to discuss your complaint with you. It may also make it more difficult for us to take action in respect of your concerns, but we will still do our best to investigate if as a result of the information you have reported to us we think there has been an infringement of competition or consumer law.

If you wish to provide your information anonymously you can use the following methods:

— phone – set your mobile phone to withhold your number

— email – set up a new account ensuring the address does not contain your name or other identifying information

— online – the CMA online form gives you the option not to provide your name

If you have provided us with contact details, a member of the CMA will contact you in confidence to discuss the information that you have provided and the next steps.

All information provided by you will be stored securely, assessed by a member of our intelligence team and, where appropriate, research conducted into the businesses and sector of the economy involved. We are not required to investigate every disclosure received. Nor are we required to assess and conclude whether a disclosure made by you qualifies for protection under the Public Interest Disclosure Act 1998.

Once we have assessed your information, a decision will be made on the appropriate action that we should take.

As a result of your information we may:

— contact businesses to remind them about the importance of complying with competition and consumer protection law

— investigate and take enforcement action against businesses we suspect are breaking competition or consumer protection law

— conduct studies or investigations into markets where there may be competition and consumer problems

— prosecute people involved if we think a criminal offence has been committed

— decide not to take any further action

— suggest that you contact other enforcement agencies directly or share intelligence with other enforcement agencies.

THINGS YOU NEED TO KNOW

The CMA has a prescribed role under the Public Interest Disclosure Act 1998 (which amends the Employment Rights Act 1996) for matters relating to the sale of goods or the supply of services, which adversely affect the interests of consumers; or about competition affecting markets in the UK. This means that you can report malpractice directly to the CMA as a 'Prescribed Person'. [see https://www.gov.uk/

government/publications/blowing-the-whistle-list-of-prescribed-people-and-bodies--2/whistleblowing-list-of-prescribed-people-and-bodies.]

This is known as making a protected disclosure.

You are a whistleblower if you want to disclose information and/or raise a concern about the activities of businesses or individuals, which you are aware of through work, about possible wrongdoing relating to the matters that fall within the CMA's remit.

Under the Act, you can make a disclosure to the CMA which, in your reasonable belief, is in the public interest and substantially true tending to show one or more of six matters listed in the Act has occurred, is occurring or is likely to occur, including:

— a criminal offence

— a breach of any legal obligation

— the covering up of any wrongdoing relating to the above

Under the Act, whistleblowers who make a report to the CMA as a 'Prescribed Person' will potentially qualify for the same employment rights as if they had made a report direct to their employer. Whistleblowers are protected by the Act and employees should not be treated unfairly by their employer or lose their job because they have spoken out.

You may have questions about the legal protection available to you and how the law applies. We are unable to advise you on your personal situation but there are organisations that may be able to help including:

— Protect (https://protect-advice.org.uk/)

— Whistleblowers UK (https://www.wbuk.org/)

— Acas (https://www.acas.org.uk/)

— Citizens Advice (https://www.citizensadvice.org.uk/)

We always recommend that you seek independent advice.

We cannot deal with personal employment/workplace issues such as raising a grievance about a personal employment situation (for example, bullying). You will need to use your employer's internal 'speak out' or complaints process or seek independent legal advice.

2. SECTOR SPECIFIC

(I) GENERAL

UNITED KINGDOM COMPETITION NETWORK (UKCN) STATEMENT OF INTENT

(December 2013)

[3.235]

NOTES

1. THE STATUTORY BASIS FOR THE UKCN

[3.236]

The Enterprise and Regulatory Reform Act 2013 (ERRA13) was enacted in April 2013. The Act creates the Competition & Markets Authority (CMA) as Non-Ministerial Government Department to replace the Office of Fair Trading and the Competition Commission,[1] with the main duty to:

"*promote competition, both within and outside the United Kingdom, for the benefit of consumers*"[2]

The Act makes provision for the strengthening of the primacy of general competition law, so that the sector regulators are expressly required, where they are not already required to do so, to consider whether the use of their competition law powers is more appropriate before taking enforcement action under their sector-specific, regulatory powers.[3]

Certain sector regulators[4] have concurrent competition powers alongside the CMA to enforce Articles 101 and Article 102 of the Treaty on the Functioning of the European Union (TFEU), the Competition Act, 1998 (CA98), to make Market Investigation References (MIRs) to the CMA with respect to activities in their sectors, and concurrency in respect of super-complaints under the Enterprise Act, 2002 (EA02).[5] ERRA13 amends the enabling power for the competition concurrency regulations, so as to:[6]

- require enhanced information sharing arrangements between the CMA and the sector regulators;
- allow the CMA to decide who will act in a case in a concurrent sector, following consultation; and
- allow the CMA, in certain circumstances, to take over a case from a concurrent regulator

The intent of these statutory reforms is to ensure that competition cases, business and the economy should benefit from greater consistency in approach through the use of general competition law and to ensure that the sector regulators consider whether a more appropriate way of proceeding would be under the competition law before using their sector-specific powers.

As soon as practicable after the end of each financial year, the CMA must prepare a report containing an assessment of how the concurrency arrangements have operated during the year.[7]

Under ERRA13, the Secretary of State may make an order to remove the competition functions from the sector regulator if the SoS considers that it is appropriate to do so for the purpose of promoting competition, within any market or markets in the UK, for the benefit of consumers. This clause applies to all sectoral regulators with concurrent competition powers, with the exception of Monitor.[8]

NOTES

1 Part 3, s. 26, ERRA13.

2 Part 3, s. 25, ERRA13.

3 Schedule 14, ERRA 14. The primacy provision will not be commenced for Monitor until a later date on Government agreement.

4 The present concurrent regulators, and the scope of their competition concurrency, are:
Civil Aviation Authority (CAA) (air traffic control services and airport operation services)
Monitor (the provision of health-care services in England)
Ofcom (electronic communications and post)
Ofgem (gas and electricity markets in Great Britain)
Ofwat (water and sewerage markets in England and Wales)
Office of Rail Regulation (ORR) (railway services in Great Britain)
Utility Regulator, Northern Ireland (NIAUR) (gas, electricity, water and sewerage services in Northern Ireland)

5 The various regulators are given their concurrent powers to deal with super-complaints by virtue of section 205 EA02 and the 2003 Regulations. Monitor does not have powers to deal with super-complaints.

6 Chapter 5, s.51, ERRA 13.

7 Part 1, s.16, *Concurrency report*, ERRA 13.

8 Chapter 5, s.52, ERRA13.

2. PURPOSE OF THE UK COMPETITION NETWORK AS AGREED BY REGULATORY HEADS

To give effect to the statutory requirements of ERRA13 and in order to strengthen the collaborative framework through which the sector regulators and CMA will work to further the interests of the consumer, the heads have agreed to establish a United Kingdom Competition Network (UKCN) and to develop a programme of work for the UKCN.

The UKCN brings together the CMA with the CAA, FCA, Ofcom, Ofgem, Ofwat, ORR and the Utility Regulator of Northern Ireland. These sector regulators all have a duty to promote competition in the interests of consumers. The health-care regulator, Monitor, which has a statutory duty to prevent anti-competitive behaviour, will attend the Network with observer status.

The mission of the UKCN will be to promote competition for the benefit of consumers and to prevent anti-competitive behaviour both through facilitating use of competition powers and development of pro-competitive regulatory frameworks, as appropriate.

The heads agreed to pursue this mission on the basis of six priority areas that are summarised in section 3, below.

3. PROPOSED AREAS OF FOCUS FOR UKCN MEMBERS

Within the overall mission of the UKCN, the UKCN will work individually and collectively in the following areas:

3.1 STRATEGIC DIALOGUE

The CMA and Sector Regulatory Heads should engage together within the UKCN in a broad strategic dialogue, identifying opportunities to use competition or regulatory powers to promote market mechanisms to further the interests of consumers[9] with a view to:

- mutual understanding of market developments, opportunities to shape regulatory frameworks to further competition/prevent anti-competitive behaviour and otherwise use competition tools to benefit consumers/users and the wider economy
- understanding developments in the EU and international regimes
- identifying common challenges in relation to litigation
- taking into account other *ex ante* regulatory objectives such as ensuring safety of networks and services

3.2 ENFORCEMENT COOPERATION UNDER COMPETITION LAW

To ensure consistent application of competition law in the United Kingdom in the areas of sector regulation, members of the UKCN will cooperate closely with respect to:

- cases, including the identification of potential CA98 and MIR cases in regulated sectors
- market studies (including, collaborative market studies where applicable)
- CMA proposals to allocate ongoing Competition Act cases to itself
- the role of the CMA taking cases in regulated sectors
- peer review of competition-related work products

3.3 ENHANCING CAPABILITIES

To ensure that UKCN members each have the capabilities needed to enforce competition powers correctly and effectively, members will contribute to:

- staff development and training
- establishing an effective information sharing and casework process structure (with suitable disclosure barriers)
- enhancing process handling, including considering the option of using a procedural adjudicator
- the sharing of staff through secondment programmes between the CMA and the sector regulators and between the sector regulators

3.4 SHARING BEST PRACTICE

Aligned to effective enforcement coordination, UKCN members will adopt means by which to share best practice which may include:

- the development of model procedures
- sharing of research findings
- participation in international benchmarking of best practice
- joint workshops

3.5 ADVOCACY

To ensure that the most significant competition and consumer issues are identified and expedited, UKCN members will:

- exchange ideas and expertise for competition advocacy.
- support mutually, as appropriate, each others' competition advocacy work
- support mutually, as appropriate, each others' work on best regulatory practice including the fundamental principle of day-to-day operational independence from Government
- input into the Annual Concurrency Report

Part 3 CMA and other Guidelines

3.6 ANNUAL CONCURRENCY REPORT

To ensure the timely publication of the annual Competition Concurrency Report under ERRA13, members of the UKCN will provide information with regard to:

- cases in progress as well as closed cases
- cases examined by sector regulators but where no infringement was found
- their contributions to developing a track record of competition cases and market investigations by UKCN members
- the operation of the concurrency arrangements
- the outcomes achieved alongside the delivery of the process
- the development of competition within their sectors in addition to specific cases in order to provide overall strategic context

NOTES

[9] Monitor does not have a duty to promote competition but will act to prevent anti-competitive behaviour where this is against patients' interests.

ANNEXE 1 – BACKGROUND TO THE ESTABLISHMENT OF THE UK COMPETITION NETWORK FOLLOWING THE REFORM OF THE UK COMPETITION LANDSCAPE.

A1. GOVERNMENT COMPETITION LANDSCAPE REVIEW

[3.237]

Competitive markets are a key driver of productivity, innovation and economic growth, providing greater choice and other benefits for consumers. In March 2011, the Government launched its consultation on reforming the UK competition regime[10] with the overarching objective to maximise the ability of the competition authorities to secure vibrant, competitive markets that work in the interests of consumers and to promote productivity, innovation and economic growth.

One of the key proposals was the creation of a new Competition and Markets Authority (CMA) to replace the Competition Commission and the Office of Fair Trading (OFT). The Government considered that creating a single competition authority and modernising its competition toolkit would improve markets and help consumers and businesses by providing greater coherence in competition practice and a more streamlined approach to decision-making. It would also facilitate faster and less burdensome processes for businesses and a single strong centre of competition expertise that could help business understand their competition law obligations and provide national and international leadership.

The package of proposals included options to enhance the competition concurrency regime affecting the sector regulators following the National Audit Office 2010 Review of the UK Competition Landscape that recommended the introduction of appropriate incentives for the sector regulators to use their competition powers.

The consultation also considered that competition cases, business and the economy could benefit from more consistency in approach through the use of general competition law. One of the conclusions of the consultation was that the Government wanted to encourage sector regulators to work more closely with the CMA and to use their competition powers where they considered them to be appropriate.

Following the consultation, the Government set out its specific reforms before Parliament in May 2012, in the Enterprise and Regulatory Reform Bill.

A2. ENTERPRISE AND REGULATORY REFORM ACT, 2013

New Primary Legislation

The Enterprise and Regulatory Reform Act 2013 (ERRA13) was enacted in April 2013. The Act creates the CMA as a Non-Ministerial Government Department with the main duty to:

"*promote competition, both within and outside the United Kingdom, for the benefit of consumers*"

This duty reflects the CMA's position as the UK's principal competition authority and its leadership role in tackling anti-competitive behaviour as part of ensuring markets work well for consumers, as well as its domestic and international advocacy role.

ERRA13 gives the CMA an important role to play in working with and through partner agencies to deliver positive competition outcomes by ensuring greater coherence in competition policy and practice, increased case flow and flexibility in resource allocation, and to advocate the benefits of competition and markets across the economy. ERRA13 also maintains the regulatory appeal function currently exercised by the Competition Commission and in future to be exercised by the CMA. This is subject to a wider review of the appeals system for competition cases and regulatory decisions.[11]

The Primacy of general competition law

The Act makes provision for the strengthening of the primacy of general competition law, so that the sector regulators are expressly required, where they are not already required to do so, to consider whether the use of their competition law powers is more appropriate before taking enforcement action under their sector-specific, regulatory powers.[12]

Changes to the Competition Concurrency Regime

The Act is designed to ensure that the CMA and the sector regulators work more closely together and for there to be greater sharing of information between them in respect of potential and ongoing competition cases.

The Secretary of State also has powers to prescribe circumstances in which the CMA may decide that it, rather than a sector regulator, should bring a Competition Act case. This will ensure the CMA can take action in cases where it is better placed to do so, and it is intended to further improve the robustness of decisions and to strengthen the regime.

It is envisaged that this power for the CMA to take over a case from a concurrent regulator will be used rarely in practice as the closer working and information sharing arrangements between the competition authorities will in any case ensure better and more consistent case management and competition enforcement outcomes for the benefit of consumers. Where the power is used, the CMA would have to consult the regulator before exercising this power and there will have to be a formal agreement with each regulator on how this will work in practice.[13]

The Power to remove competition functions from concurrent sector specific regulators

The Act also allows the Secretary of State to make an order to remove the competition functions from a sector regulator if it is considered that it is appropriate to do so for the purpose of promoting competition, within any market or markets in the UK, for the benefit of consumers.[14]

The Annual Competition Concurrency Report

Alongside this and in order to ensure transparency, accountability and greater certainty for business, the CMA will be required to report annually on the operation of the concurrency arrangements and on decisions on the use of concurrent competition powers by the CMA and sector regulators.

A3. GOVERNMENT'S STRATEGIC STEER

To increase transparency, the Government has committed to issuing a non-statutory statement of strategic priorities for the CMA (the Steer)[15] setting out how Government envisages the competition regime will fit into wider government economic policy.

The Steer is part of an overall accountability framework which also comprises the legal and performance management frameworks, e.g. the CMA's duty to 'promote competition, both within and outside the UK, for the benefit of consumers'. It provides an open and transparent statement which the CMA will be expected to have regard to, but the CMA retains full independence in how it approaches its work, and in its selection of cases, and the tools it uses to tackle them. Alongside this Steer will sit the Performance Management Framework established by BIS and HM Treasury.

As part of the Steer the CMA will be expected to identify markets where competition is not working well and tackle the constraints on competition in these cases.

The draft Steer also proposes that the CMA should assess specific sectors where enhanced competition could contribute to faster growth (for example, knowledge intensive sectors, financial services and infrastructure sectors including energy) – working with the responsible regulator where appropriate.

Alongside the Consultation on some of the CMA's new draft guidance, the Government invited comments on the Steer and certain key pieces of secondary legislation on 15 July.[16]

A.4 THE COMPETITION POWERS OF THE SECTOR REGULATORS

The CMA will need to work with other sector regulators, to build up and continue to share competition expertise, including through joint enforcement work, training and research. This will include engagement with those sector regulators with concurrent competition powers listed in the table below and with regulators such as the Financial Conduct Authority that have a duty to promote competition in the interests of consumers but that do not have concurrent competition powers.

Sector Regulators with Concurrent Competition Powers

Regulator	Scope of Concurrent Competition Powers
Civil Aviation Authority (CAA)	Air traffic services, and now under the Civil Aviation Act 2012, airport operation services in the United Kingdom.
Monitor	Health care services in England.[17]
Northern Ireland Authority for Utility Regulation (NIAUR)	Gas, electricity, water and sewerage services in Northern Ireland.
Office of Rail Regulation (ORR)	Railway services in Great Britain.
The Office of Communications (Ofcom)	Electronic communications, broadcasting and postal services in the United Kingdom.
The Office of Gas and Electricity Markets (Ofgem)	Gas and electricity in Great Britain.
Water Services Regulation Authority (Ofwat)	Water and sewerage in England and Wales.

The Financial Conduct Authority (FCA)

At present, the FCA is not specified as a sector regulator in ERRA13 because it does not have concurrent Competition Act 1998 (CA98) nor Market Investigation Reference (MIR) powers with the CMA.

The Government believes that the FCA should have a far stronger role in competition than the Financial Services Authority had. This commitment is reflected in the FCA having a statutory mandate to promote effective competition in the interests of consumers. The FCA may use any of its regulatory powers to promote competition. The FCA also has the power of referral to the CMA. The FCA will take the lead in addressing competition issues where it is better placed to do so. In addition, The Financial Services (Banking Reform) Bill, 2013 envisages FCA receiving concurrent competition powers from April 2015.[18]

Monitor

Monitor has no duty to promote competition in the interest of consumers, unlike other sector regulators. Monitor's main duty is to protect and promote the interests of patients by promoting provision of health care services which is economic, efficient and effective, and maintains or improves the quality of the services. Monitor must exercise its functions with a view to preventing anti-competitive behaviour in the provision of NHS-funded health care services which is against patients' interests. The Health and Social Care Act gives Monitor the power to take enforcement action under the provider licence and the National Health Service (Procurement, Patient Choice and Competition) (No.2) Regulations 2013. Monitor also has concurrent powers which enable it to enforce the Competition Act, 1998 and to make market investigation references under the EA02.

A.5 PROGRESS REPORT OF THE JOINT REGULATORS GROUP WORK-GROUP ON CONCURRENCY TO THE MAY 2013JRG MEETING

The regulators, under the aegis of the Joint Regulators Group (JRG), have worked with the CMA transition team and colleagues from the Department for Business (BIS) and the Office of Fair Trading (OFT) to consider in more detail how operational relationships can be optimised.

In May 2013, the JRG published a report[19] on progress so far on this work, as well as setting out directions for future consideration, in particular how a vision for enhanced cooperation might be realised and the key areas that needed to be addressed, in particular:

- transparency: in order to demonstrate to stakeholders that effective action is being taken on emerging issues;
- flexibility: recognising the need to reflect differing regulatory and market conditions in each sector; and
- pragmatism and practicalities: for example in relation to the different levels of resources available to different regulators

A.6 MEETINGS OF THE REGULATORY HEADS

Subsequent to the working level cooperation between JRG and the CMA transition team, the first meeting of the regulatory heads was held on Thursday 11 July and the UKCN Statement of Intent was approved by the Chief Executives at a workshop held on 18 September 2013.

The initial meeting was convened to discuss how best to respond to the various reforms to the competition legislation, including the creation of the CMA, revision of the concurrency regime and additional competition responsibilities for some of the sector regulators as indicated above.

The CMA and sector regulator heads agreed that:

(i) a 'step-up' in the role of competition concurrency in the areas covered by sector regulators would be sought, following the introduction of ERRA13; and

(ii) each head should support the establishment of the UK Competition Network and should involve themselves personally in the establishment and supervision of an appropriate programme of work and to manage the delivery of agreed actions.

At the workshop, the heads considered the draft UKCN Statement of Intent (UKCN SoI), developed following the July meeting. It was agreed that the UKCN SoI should be a living document, which should be updated to reflect new regulators/powers and reviewed at least annually. Following adoption by the heads, it was then submitted to each agency's Board for agreement.

Following agreement by each Board, the UKCN Heads agreed the publication of the latest version of the UKCN Statement of Intent and associated press release on 2 December, 2013.

NOTES

10 A Competition Regime for Growth: A Consultation on options for reform, BIS, March 2011.

11 Streamlining regulatory and competition appeals: consultation on options for reform, BIS, June 2013.

12 The primacy provision will not be commenced for Monitor until a later date.

13 Where there is dispute, the CMA may not however decide that it or another Regulator other than Monitor is to exercise Part 1 functions which are primarily concerned with matters relating to the provision of health care services for the purposes of the NHS in England. The CMA and Monitor may nevertheless agree that the CMA is to act in such a case as will be reflected in the Concurrency Regulations.

14 This power applies to all sectoral regulators with concurrent competition powers except Monitor. Monitor does not have

a duty to promote competition but will act to prevent anti-competitive behaviour where this is against patients' interests.

15 Competition Regime: Consultation on CMA Priorities and Draft Secondary Legislation, BIS, July 2013.

16 A second tranche of consultations was launched on 17 September covering the new concurrency regulation, CMA Rules on Competition Act enforcement and CMA guidance on concurrency and Competition Act procedures. These consultations were closed on 11 November 2013 and responses are currently being reviewed.

17 There is a power for the Secretary of State to extend these powers to the area of social care in England.

18 Financial Services (Banking Reform) Bill Government Amendments: FCA Concurrent Powers, Briefing to Peers: www.gov.uk/government/uploads/system/uploads/attachment_data/file/245760/HoL_Policy_Brief_-_FCA_Concurrent_Powers.pdf

19 Building Confidence that Consumers in Regulated Sectors are Effectively Protected from Competition Failures: Concurrent enforcement with the Competition and Markets Authority, *Progress report of the Joint Regulators Group Work-Group on Concurrency to the May JRG meeting*, June 2013.

REGULATED INDUSTRIES: GUIDANCE ON CONCURRENT APPLICATION OF COMPETITION LAW TO REGULATED INDUSTRIES (CMA10, MARCH 2014)

[3.238]

NOTES

Since this Guidance was published, the Financial Conduct Authority (FCA) and the Payment Systems Regulator (PSR) have acquired concurrent competition powers under the Financial Services (Banking Reform) Act 2013. The FCA acquired concurrent competition powers to enforce against breaches of the UK and EU prohibitions on anti-competitive agreements and abuses of a dominant position under the Competition Act 1998 and to conduct market studies and make market investigation references under the Enterprise Act 2002 from 1 April 2015. The PSR acquired concurrent powers to conduct market studies and market investigation references under the Enterprise Act 2002 on 1 April 2014; it acquired powers to enforce against breaches of the UK and EU prohibitions on anti-competitive agreements and abuses of a dominant position on 1 April 2015. References in the document to the Regulators should be read as including the FCA and PSR (unless the context indicates otherwise). References (in the above) to the enforcement of EU prohibitions should now be read in light of the UK's exit from the European Union.

Since 1 April 2016, Monitor has been operating with the NHS Trust Development Authority as part of a single integrated organisation known as NHS Improvement.

CONTENTS

1 INTRODUCTION

[3.239]

1.1 For a number of industries the application and enforcement of Article 101 of the Treaty on the Functioning of the European Union (the TFEU) and Article 102 of the TFEU in the United Kingdom and of Chapter I and Chapter II of the Competition Act 1998 (CA98) (as amended by the Enterprise and Regulatory Reform Act 2013 (the ERRA13)) is carried out by the sectoral regulators listed in paragraph 2.1 (Regulator or Regulators (where referred to collectively)) concurrently with the Competition and Markets Authority (the CMA).[1] EC Regulation 1/2003 (Modernisation Regulation)[2] requires the designated national competition authorities of the Member States (NCAs) and the courts of the Member States to apply and enforce Article 101 and Article 102 of the TFEU as well as national competition law when national competition law is applied to agreements which may affect trade between Member States or to abuse prohibited by Article 102 of the TFEU. The CMA and the Regulators with concurrent competition powers under the CA98 are designated as NCAs with the power to apply Articles 101 and 102 of the TFEU. Throughout this guidance, references to the CMA should be taken to include the Regulators in relation to their respective industries, unless otherwise specified.

1.2 The CMA has set out in this guidance document general information for the business and legal communities and other interested parties on the application and enforcement of Articles 101 and 102 of the TFEU and Chapters I and II of the CA98 in the United Kingdom by the CMA and the Regulators.

1.3 In particular, this guidance sets out information about which regulated sectors are affected by the concurrency provisions and the scope of the concurrent powers and explains the way in which the concurrent application and enforcement of competition law works in practice.

1.4 Chapter 2 of this guidance sets out the concurrent powers of the Regulators.

1.5 Chapter 3 describes the operation of the concurrency regime. In particular, it outlines:

- the procedures for making complaints and the way in which they are dealt with under concurrent powers

- the coordination and leadership role of the CMA in relation to concurrent competition law application and enforcement, for the purpose of enhancing the efficient application and enforcement of Articles 101 and 102 of the TFEU and Chapters I and II of the CA98 in the regulated sectors.[3] This includes the forms of support that may be available to the Regulators and the availability of the CMA's collective case decision making model and procedural complaints procedure to the Regulators[4]
- the circumstances in which the CMA or a Regulator may decide to investigate a suspected infringement of competition law and the procedure for agreeing case allocation between the CMA and the Regulators
- the procedures for sharing information in respect of the application of Articles 101 and 102 of the TFEU and Chapters I and II of the CA98 between the CMA and the Regulators, including the categories of information that will be shared and when, and how that information will be dealt with by the CMA and the Regulators
- the process for and possible content of the annual report on the operation of the concurrency regime that the CMA is required to prepare[5]
- the operation and role of the United Kingdom Competition Network (UKCN). The UKCN is a forum which enables the Regulators and the CMA to share expertise, ideas and experience for the purpose of ensuring a consistent and high-quality approach to competition policy and enforcement in the regulated sectors, and to coordinate matters relating to concurrency[6]
- how the Regulators work with the CMA and with each other, using the powers in the CA98, including under the Competition Act 1998 (Concurrency) Regulations 2014 (the Concurrency Regulations) (SI 2014/536),[7] and
- how the CMA and the Regulators will work in the European Union (EU) with other NCAs who have been given the responsibility of applying Article 101 and Article 102 of the TFEU in their territories.

1.6 Chapter 4 explains how the use of these powers interacts with the Regulators' sectoral powers and duties and the powers under the Enterprise Act 2002 (EA02).

1.7 Chapter 5 describes the restrictions on the disclosure of information which are set out in the Modernisation Regulation and within the EA02.

1.8 Annexe A contains the Concurrency Regulations.

1.9 The UKCN Statement of Intent document, which provides further information about the UKCN, is included in Annexe B.

1.10 This guidance document supersedes the OFT's previous guide on concurrent competition law enforcement entitled *Concurrent Application to Regulated Industries*.[8] You may find it useful to read this document alongside other CMA, OFT and/or CC documents, including the CMA guideline *Competition Act 1998: Guidance on the CMA's investigation procedures in Competition Act 1998 cases* (CMA8) (*CMA CA98 Procedures Guidance*),[9] *The Application of the Competition Act in the Telecommunications Sector* (OFT417), *The Application of the Competition Act in the Water and Sewerage Sectors* (OFT422), *Application in the Energy Sector* (OFT428), *Application in Services Relating to Railways* (OFT430), and *Application to the Northern Ireland Energy Sectors* (OFT437), (Regulated Sector Publications).[10]

1.11 This is the CMA's current practice as at the date of publication of this document. It may be revised from time to time to reflect changes in best practice or the law and the CMA's developing experience. Please refer to www.gov.uk/cma to ensure you have the latest version of this guidance.

1.12 This guidance is intended to explain these provisions to those who are likely to be affected by them and to indicate how the CMA expects them to operate. Further information on how the CMA has applied and enforced competition law in particular cases may be found in the CMA's decisions, as available on the CMA's webpages.[11]

1.13 The CMA will apply this guidance flexibly. This means that the CMA will have regard to the guidance when dealing with suspected competition law infringements in the regulated sectors but that, when the facts of an individual case reasonably justify it, the CMA may adopt a different approach.

1.14 This guidance will take effect from 1 April 2014. The new approach established by the ERRA13 and outlined in this guidance will apply to all ongoing and future cases.

1.15 This document is not a definitive statement of, or a substitute for, the law itself. A range of publications on how the CMA carries out this substantive assessment is available on the CMA's webpages. In particular, this guidance is not a substitute for the TFEU, nor for regulations made under it. Neither is it a substitute for European Commission (Commission) notices and guidance. Furthermore, this guidance is not a substitute for the CA98 or the EA02 and the regulations and orders made under those Acts. It should be read in conjunction with these legal instruments, EU case law and United Kingdom case law. Anyone in doubt about how they may be affected by the TFEU, the CA98 or the EA02 should seek independent legal advice.

NOTES

1 Section 54 of the CA98 (combined with sector-specific legislation) provides that, in relation to the regulated sectors described in paragraph 2.1, the same provisions are applied and enforced, concurrently with the CMA, by the Regulators for communications matters, gas, electricity, water and sewerage, railway, air traffic, airport and healthcare (in respect of England only) services.

2 Council Regulation (EC) No 1/2003 of 16 December 2002 on the implementation of the rules on competition laid down in Articles 81 and 82 of the EC Treaty (OJ L1, 4.1.2003, p 1).

3 See section 54 of the CA98 (as amended by the ERRA13) and the Concurrency Regulations.

4 For further information on the CMA's approach to investigating and enforcing suspected infringements of Chapter I and Chapter II of the CA98 see *CMA guideline Competition Act 1998: Guidance on the CMA's investigation procedures in Competition Act 1998 cases* (CMA8), available at: www.gov.uk/cma.

5 See paragraph 16 of Schedule 4 of the ERRA13.

6 The UKCN Statement of Intent document is enclosed as Annexe B.

7 See Annexe A. The Concurrency Regulations are also available to download at www.legislation.gov.uk/id/uksi/2014/536.

8 Concurrent Application to Regulated Industries (OFT 405).

9 Competition Act 1998: Guidance on the CMA's investigation procedures in Competition Act 1998 cases (CMA8) available at: www.gov.uk/cma.

10 Regulated Sector Publications are available at: www.gov.uk/cma. Their content is not substantively affected by the ERRA13.

11 The CMA maintains a register of CA98 decisions, available at: www.gov.uk/cma.

2 THE CONCURRENT POWERS

[3.240]

2.1 The industry sectors where the Regulators have concurrent powers with the CMA as at 1 April 2014[12] are:[13]

Agreements[14] or conduct relating to:	Statute	Regulatory Body
The provision of airport operation services	The Civil Aviation Act 2012	CAA[15]
The supply of air traffic services	The Transport Act 2000	CAA
The provision of health care services in England	The Health and Social Care Act 2012	Monitor
Commercial activities connected with the generation, transmission or supply of electricity in Northern Ireland	The Electricity (Northern Ireland) Order 1992	NIAUR
Commercial activities connected with the supply of water or securing a supply of water or with the provision or securing of sewerage services in Northern Ireland	Water and Sewerage Services (Northern Ireland) Order 2006	NIAUR
The conveyance, storage or supply of gas in Northern Ireland	The Gas (Northern Ireland) Order 1996	NIAUR
Activities connected to electronic communications, broadcasting and postal services matters	The Communications Act 2003	Ofcom
The shipping, conveyance or supply of gas and activities ancillary thereto	The Gas Act 1986	Ofgem
Commercial activities connected with the generation, transmission or supply of electricity	The Electricity Act 1989	Ofgem
Commercial activities connected with the supply of water or securing a supply of water or with the provision or securing of sewerage services	The Water Industry Act 1991	Ofwat
The supply of services relating to railways	Railways Act 1993 (as amended by the Transport Act 2000)	ORR

2.2 The Regulators have all the powers of the CMA to apply and enforce Article 101 and Article 102 TFEU and the CA98 in order to deal with anti-competitive agreements or abuses of a dominant position which relate to activities in relation to their respective sectors, with the exceptions noted in paragraph 2.4 below. In many cases, the undertakings whose agreement or conduct is relevant will be licensees, franchisees or similar right holders under one of the statutes listed above, although it is the subject matter to which the agreement or conduct relates rather than the identity of the undertakings involved which will determine whether there is concurrent jurisdiction.

2.3 A Regulator may:

- consider complaints about possible infringements of any of Article 101 of the TFEU, Article 102 of the TFEU, the Chapter I prohibition and/or the Chapter II prohibition
- impose interim measures to prevent significant damage
- carry out investigations both on the Regulator's own initiative and in response to complaints. The Regulators have the same powers as the CMA to require the production of documents and information, to interview individuals that have a connection with a business under investigation and to search premises. Further details about these powers are given in the CMA CA98 Procedures Guidance (CMA8)[16]

- impose financial penalties, taking account of the statutory guidance on penalties issued by the CMA[17]
- give and enforce directions to bring an infringement to an end
- accept commitments that are binding on an undertaking
- adopt confidential informal advice and publish an opinion
- agree to settle a case where the business under investigation is prepared to admit that it has breached Article 101 and/or Article 102 of the TFEU, and/or the Chapter I prohibition and/or the Chapter II prohibition in the United Kingdom and to agree to a streamlined administrative procedure to govern the remainder of the investigation, in return for which the Regulator may agree to impose a reduced penalty on the business.[18]

2.4 The CMA alone, however, has powers to issue guidance on penalties, to issue guidance on commitments and to make procedural rules (the CA98 Rules).[19] The CA98 Rules set out the procedures to be followed in carrying into effect the provisions of the CA98.[20] In issuing guidance on penalties, in issuing guidance on commitments and in making and amending the CA98 Rules, the CMA is required to consult publicly and with the Regulators.[21]

2.5 Once it has been decided which United Kingdom authority will exercise **Part 1 functions** in relation to a case,[22] no other authority can exercise any of the **prescribed functions** in relation to that case. 'Part 1 functions' are any functions under Part 1 of the CA98 which are or would be exercisable concurrently (see definition in Regulation 2 of the Concurrency Regulations). 'Prescribed functions' arise from the CA98 and are defined in Regulation 2 of the Concurrency Regulations. They are

- the opening of a formal investigation pursuant to section of the CA98
- the withdrawal of an exclusion from the Chapter I prohibition in relation to an individual agreement, and
- the making of certain formal decisions, including requiring that an infringement be brought to an end, ordering interim measures, accepting commitments by decision and imposing fines.

2.6 Once jurisdiction in relation to a case has been allocated to a particular authority, Regulation 6 of the Concurrency Regulations prevents another authority from exercising Part 1 functions in relation to that case unless the case is formally transferred to that authority (Regulation 7 of the Concurrency Regulations) or the CMA decides to take over a case from a Regulator under Regulation 8 of the Concurrency Regulations.[23]

2.7 While not the subject of this guidance, the Regulators also have the power to carry out market studies and make market investigation references in their respective sectors under Part 4 of the EA02 (see *Markets Studies and Market Investigations: Supplemental guidance on the CMA's approach* (CMA3)).[24]

2.8 In addition, the Regulators may make regulatory references to the CMA or be appealed to the CMA in relation to certain price controls, access charges and other licence modifications (Regulatory Cases).[25] The CMA is also required to review qualifying mergers in certain regulated sectors (Regulatory Mergers). This guidance does not consider Regulatory Cases or Regulatory Mergers further. Should you wish to find out more about the procedure for Regulatory Cases or Regulatory Mergers, please refer to the CMA's webpages and, where it exists, to the relevant sector-specific guidance document.

NOTES

12 The identity of the concurrent regulators and scope of their concurrent powers may be subject to change. Please refer to the CMA's webpages for an up-to-date summary of all concurrent regulators and their concurrent powers on www.gov.uk/cma. On 18 December 2013, the Financial Services (Banking Reform) Act received Royal Assent, awarding the Financial Conduct Authority concurrent powers from 1 April 2015 to make Market Investigation References under EA02 and to enforce CA98 in respect of financial service activities.

13 The table is organised alphabetically by reference to each Regulator's acronym.

14 References in this guidance to 'agreement' should, unless otherwise stated or the context demands it, be taken to include decisions by associations of undertakings and concerted practices.

15 See CAA publication *The CAA's concurrent competition powers for airport operation services and air traffic services* (CAP 1016) for more information on the meaning of 'airport operation services' and 'air traffic services', as well as on the CAA's concurrent competition powers.

16 Available at: www.gov.uk/cma.

17 See *Guidance as to the appropriate amount of a penalty* (OFT 423) and *Administrative Penalties: Statement of policy on the CMA's approach* (CMA4), available at: www.gov.uk/cma.

18 See CMA CA98 Procedures Guidance (CMA8) for more details on settlement, available at: www.gov.uk/cma.

19 See *The Competition Act 1998 (Competition and Markets Authority's Rules) Order 2014* (SI 2014/458), available at: www.legislation.gov.uk/id/uksi/2014/458.

20 See further paragraph 3.12 below. Subject to the minimum procedural requirements that Regulators must follow in CA98 investigations as set out in the CA98 Rules, each Regulator may conduct investigations in accordance with its own procedures.

21 In addition, only the CMA and the Serious Fraud Office may prosecute suspected infringements of the criminal cartel prohibitions under section 190 of the EA02.

22 See paragraphs 3.23 to 3.36 for further information on case allocation.

23 See further paragraphs 3.26 to 3.29 for information on the CMA's power to take a case under Regulation 8 of the Concurrency Regulations.

24 *Markets Studies and Market Investigations: Supplemental guidance on the CMA's approach* (CMA3), available at: www.gov.uk/cma

25 As at 1 April 2014 the CMA has responsibility for Regulatory Cases in the aviation, communications, energy, railways, health and water sectors. Please refer to the CMA's webpages for the latest guidance in respect of these duties:

www.gov.uk/cma

3 CONCURRENCY IN PRACTICE

[3.241]

3.1 The ERRA 2013 introduced a number of measures to improve the use of general competition powers in the regulated sectors and to improve coordination between the authorities which have those powers.[26] In line with this, the Government issued a 'strategic steer' to the CMA in October 2013 which stated that 'the CMA should engage in a broad strategic dialogue with the Regulators and look for opportunities to promote effective competition'.[27] It is one of the strategic goals of the CMA, announced on its establishment on 1 October 2013, to extend the frontiers of competition into new areas, including by working with Regulators to ensure fuller use of competition law and policy in sectoral markets.[28] Moreover, the Regulators and the CMA, working together in the new UKCN established in 2013 (with Monitor having observer status), have declared that their mission in the UKCN 'will be to promote competition for the benefit of consumers and to prevent anti-competitive behaviour both through facilitating use of competition powers and development of pro-competitive regulatory frameworks, as appropriate.'[29]

3.2 The CMA will play a leading role to promote and coordinate the effective application of competition law in the regulated sectors. Cooperation between the CMA and the Regulators is central to the effective operation of the concurrency regime. The CMA's leadership role will facilitate the efficient allocation of resources, the appropriate sharing of information between the Regulators and the CMA, and the development of high standards of excellence in the application and enforcement of Article 101 and Article 102 of the TFEU, Chapter I and/or Chapter II of the CA98 within the regulated sectors.

3.3 The Concurrency Regulations contain provisions for the co-ordination of the performance by the CMA and the Regulators of their concurrent functions under the CA98. These provisions include:

- allowing for the exchange of information between the CMA and the Regulators, both for the purpose of determining who has jurisdiction to exercise Part 1 functions[30] in relation to a case under the CA98 and/or EU law (Regulation 3) and, generally, for the purpose of facilitating the performance by the CMA and the Regulators of their Part 1 functions
- determining who should exercise Part 1 functions in relation to a case (Regulation 4)
- resolving disputes as to who should exercise Part 1 functions in relation to a case, including specifying the circumstances in which the CMA must decide which competent person is to exercise Part 1 functions in relation to a case (Regulation 5)
- preventing the simultaneous exercise by more than one authority of Part 1 functions in relation to a case (Regulation 6)
- transfer of a case from one authority to another (Regulation 7)
- providing the CMA with the power in certain circumstances to take over a case that has been allocated to a Regulator (Regulation 8)[31]
- requiring the putting in place of information sharing arrangements between the CMA and the Regulators for the purpose of enhancing transparency and coordination in relation to the concurrent application of Article 101 and Article 102 of the TFEU and Chapter I and Chapter II of the CA98 generally and in relation to any particular case (Regulation 9)
- use of staff of the CMA or a Regulator by the CMA or another Regulator allowing for staff to be shared between the CMA and Regulators, or between Regulators (not involving the CMA). This includes the secondment of any officer[32] of the CMA or a Regulator by the Regulator or the CMA or another Regulator for any duration agreed between the relevant authorities (Regulation 10).

3.4 The Concurrency Regulations set out the process for determining which of the United Kingdom authorities will act in any particular case. Where Article 101 and/or Article 102 of the TFEU may apply, the case will also be subject to the case allocation principles for determining whether the United Kingdom NCA or an NCA from another Member State is well placed to act. The case allocation principles for determining which NCA in the European Competition Network is well placed to act are set out in the Commission's Notice on *Cooperation within the Network of Competition Authorities*.[33] Further details on case allocation within the European Competition Network are provided in the competition law guidance *Modernisation* (OFT442).[34]

3.5 The Concurrency Regulations are not intended to deal comprehensively with all aspects of the relationship between the CMA and the Regulators. Matters which are not addressed specifically in the Concurrency Regulations will be dealt with by means of Memoranda of Understanding between the CMA and the individual Regulators.

3.6 This document does not provide guidance on the Memoranda of Understanding between the CMA and the Regulators. However, the CMA expects that Memoranda of Understanding between itself and the Regulators under the new concurrency arrangements will outline in detail a framework for cooperation and coordination between the CMA and each Regulator within the relevant regulated sector in relation to various issues that are likely to include the:

- concurrent application and enforcement of competition law by the Regulator and the CMA
- prevention of anti-competitive behaviour and/or promotion of competition within the relevant regulated sector
- exchange of information between a Regulator and the CMA for the purpose of facilitating effective cooperation and coordination of activities and enforcement within the relevant regulated sector
- exchange of staff between the CMA and a Regulator for the purpose of enhancing the effective application and enforcement of competition law and other legal powers as appropriate

- procedure for sharing experience and expertise between the CMA and a Regulator, including through the use of meetings, joint training and the exchange of research, analysis, guidance and similar documents.

3.7 The Memoranda of Understanding may be reviewed from time to time by the CMA and a Regulator to ensure that they remain effective and appropriate. The Memoranda of Understanding will be available on the CMA's webpages[35] and the website of each relevant Regulator.

ENSURING CONSISTENCY OF DECISION-MAKING

Primacy of EU Law

3.8 In applying Articles 101 and 102 of the TFEU the CMA, the Regulators and the national courts are bound by the fundamental principle of the primacy of EU law and must follow the case law of the European Court interpreting EU legislation, and must have regard to any relevant decision or statement of the Commission. As a consequence, and in addition to the Article 3 obligations set out in chapter 4 below, an agreement or conduct prohibited by Article 101 or Article 102 cannot be permitted under national law. The CMA and the Regulators cannot therefore permit an agreement or conduct which is otherwise prohibited under Article 101 or Article 102.[36]

3.9 The Modernisation Regulation contains further provisions to ensure consistency in the application of EU law by NCAs. Article 16(2) of the Modernisation Regulation provides that where the Commission has taken a decision on an agreement or conduct under Article 101 or Article 102 of the TFEU, NCAs (including the CMA and the Regulators) cannot take a decision under Article 101 or Article 102 of the TFEU in respect of the same agreement or conduct which would run counter to the decision adopted by the Commission.

3.10 Chapter 4 provides further details on Article 3 of the Modernisation Regulation.

Consistency provisions under United Kingdom Law

3.11 In addition, section 60 of the CA98 sets out principles for ensuring that the United Kingdom authorities deal with questions arising in relation to the application of the Chapter I and Chapter II prohibitions of the CA98 in such a way as to ensure consistency with the treatment of corresponding questions arising in EU law in so far as this is possible, having regard to any relevant differences between any of the provisions concerned. This is considered in more detail in the competition law guidance *Modernisation* (OFT442).[37]

Decision-making procedure

3.12 Where the CMA exercises Part 1 functions in relation to a case within a regulated sector, it will apply its procedures for making any decisions in relation to that case in accordance with the CA98 and the CA98 Rules.[38]

3.13 Where a Regulator exercises Part 1 functions in relation to a case, that Regulator must make any decisions in relation to that case in accordance with the relevant requirements of the CA98, the CA98 Rules and any relevant sector-specific legislation applicable to the Regulators' exercise of Part 1 functions,[39] will do so based upon their own procedures. These procedures may, under the CA98 Rules applicable to the Regulators, include provisions for a decision-making role for CMA staff, CMA board members or CMA panel members.[40] In imposing any penalties under the CA98, the Regulators must have regard to the CMA's penalties guidance for the time being in force (see *OFT's guidance as to the appropriate amount of a penalty* (OFT423)).[41]

Appeals

3.14 Most final decisions taken by the CMA or a Regulator under Article 101, Article 102 of the TFEU and/or under the CA98 are subject to appeal to the Competition Appeal Tribunal (the CAT) on both the substance of the decision and on any penalties imposed.[42]

UKCN PRACTICE AND PROCEDURE

3.15 The UKCN brings together the CMA with the CAA, the FCA, Ofcom, Ofgem, Ofwat, the ORR and the Utility Regulator of Northern Ireland. All these Regulators are subject to new duties imposed on them by the concurrency provisions of the ERRA 13 and, with the exception of the health care regulator Monitor, have statutory duties in relation to the promotion of competition. The health care regulator, Monitor, which has a statutory duty to prevent anti-competitive behaviour, will attend the UKCN with observer status.

3.16 The UKCN is a new forum to promote competition and assist in deterring anti-competitive behaviour in regulated sectors[43] by:

- facilitating a consistent approach by the Regulators and the CMA in the exercise of their functions and powers under the CA98 and Part 4 of the EA02
- developing the practical working arrangements between the Regulators and the CMA
- providing a forum for discussion of matters of common interest and the sharing of information where appropriate and where legally permitted and required
- coordinating the provision of advice and information on the application of the Chapter I prohibition and the Chapter II prohibition and Article 101 and Article 102 of the TFEU to the public.

3.17 A UKCN Statement of Intent document is set out in Annexe B of this guidance.

3.18 The UKCN deals with issues such as:

- **the development and application of competition policy in the regulated sectors** – the UKCN provides a forum for the Regulators and the CMA to share expertise, ideas and experience for the purpose of preventing anti-competitive behaviour and/or promoting competition in the regulated sectors for the benefit of consumers and users of regulated services, by ensuring a consistent and high-quality approach to competition policy and enforcement in those sectors
- **general principles of information sharing** – subject to the obligations under the Modernisation Regulation and/or Part 9 of the EA02, information about cases in progress is shared. This includes matters of general policy and the way in which Articles 101 and 102 of the TFEU and the prohibitions in the CA98 are interpreted, applied and enforced. In each instance, this is with a view to ensuring consistency of decision-making. Information about the CA98 complaints received and investigations in progress or contemplated is also shared to facilitate the performance by the CMA and the Regulators of their functions under Part 1 of the CA98, for example to ascertain whether there is concurrent jurisdiction.

3.19 The UKCN may form working groups as appropriate in order to consider specific issues of the application of competition law, and/or the promotion of competition and tacking anti-competitive practices in one or more regulated sector.

3.20 At all times, the members of the UKCN are mindful of the confidentiality provisions of the EA02 and their obligations to safeguard information provided by other NCAs which are contained in the Modernisation Regulation (see chapter 5 below).

CASE HANDLING

General principles of case allocation

3.21 The CMA and the Regulators will always consult with each other before acting on a case where it appears that they may have concurrent jurisdiction. They must consult with each other under the Concurrency Regulations before exercising any of the prescribed functions in relation to a case. The CMA expects that such consultation will include the circulation of details of complaints.

3.22 Under the concurrency arrangements, the general principle is that the CMA or the relevant Regulator will be responsible for a case depending on which of them is better or best placed to do so.[44] The factors considered in determining which of the CMA or Regulators deals with the matter will be assessed by the CMA and relevant Regulator as appropriate and include:

- the sectoral knowledge of a Regulator and the CMA
- whether the case affects more than one regulated sector and/or non-regulated sectors not subject to concurrent competition law[45]
- previous contacts between the parties or complainants and a Regulator or the CMA
- experience in dealing with any of the undertakings which may be involved in the proceedings
- experience in dealing with any similar issues which may be involved in the proceedings
- whether the CMA considers it necessary to exercise Part 1 functions in relation to a case in order to develop United Kingdom competition policy or to provide greater deterrent and precedent effect for the benefit of competition and consumers, either within the relevant regulated sector, or more widely
- whether the case being allocated to the CMA and supported by the relevant Regulator (or vice versa) will provide the best combination of competition and sector-specific expertise.

Procedure for agreeing which authority will deal with a complaint or investigation

3.23 When a complaint has been made to the CMA or a Regulator and it gives rise to concurrent jurisdiction between two or more United Kingdom authorities, the complainant will be informed, as a matter of policy, which authority is handling the complaint. In line with the information sharing arrangements between the CMA and the Regulators, the CMA and the relevant Regulator may engage in discussions as they consider appropriate in relation to any particular complaint or matter.[46]

3.24 It is expected that agreement will ordinarily be reached promptly as to which United Kingdom authority is better or best placed to deal with a particular complaint and in any event, in no more than two months after receipt of the complaint by the first authority to receive it. In circumstances where Regulation 4 of the Concurrency Regulations applies and agreement cannot be reached between the relevant authorities within a reasonable time (which may differ from the two-month period above), the CMA will decide which United Kingdom authority should deal with a case (Regulation 5) and it will have regard to the principles set out in paragraph 3.22 in doing so. The CMA may decide in some circumstances that it is to exercise Part 1 functions in relation to that case during the initial case allocation process. Where there is dispute, the CMA may not however decide that it or another Regulator other than Monitor is to exercise Part 1 functions in any case which is principally concerned with matters relating to the provision of health care services for the purposes of the NHS in England.3.26 to 3.29 below in making such a decision.[47] The CMA will follow the process outlined in paragraphs

3.25 Where either the CMA or a Regulator proposes to commence a competition investigation on its own initiative into a regulated sector, the CMA or the relevant Regulator will inform the other of that investigation and engage in discussions as they consider appropriate in respect of the investigation. As a general principle, the authority which is best placed to deal with the case will have jurisdiction over that case in accordance with the case allocation principles under Regulation 4 of the Concurrency Regulations.

Circumstances in which the CMA may exercise jurisdiction where a case has already been allocated to a Regulator

3.26 Pursuant to Regulation 8 of the Concurrency Regulations, where a Regulator has been allocated a case under Regulation 4, the CMA may nonetheless take over that case where it is satisfied that doing so would further the promotion of competition within any market or markets in the United Kingdom for the benefit of consumers. For example, the power might be exercised where (consistent with the EU Commission's powers to take cases from NCAs) the CMA considers itself best placed to make a decision that sets an appropriate precedent, in particular when similar issues arise across different sectors or parts of the United Kingdom or in order to enforce the CA98 prohibitions more effectively. For example, because the Regulator lacks the necessary resources. However, the CMA may not take over a case from Monitor under Regulation 8 where the case is principally concerned with matters relating to the provision of health care services for the purposes of the NHS in England.

3.27 The CMA may make such a decision after consultation with the Regulator, the undertaking concerned and any other persons likely to be materially affected by the transfer at any stage before a Regulator has issued a Statement of Objections.[48] After a Statement of Objections has been issued, the CMA cannot exercise Part 1 functions in relation to that case, unless the Regulator wishes to transfer the case to the CMA.[49]

3.28 The CMA will consult with the relevant Regulator(s) in respect of its proposed decision to take over a case as soon as it reasonably can after reaching such a view and will give reasons for that proposed decision (Regulation 8 of the Concurrency Regulations). The CMA and the Regulator(s) will also discuss potential arrangements for further cooperation in relation to the case in the event that the CMA does take over that case. If, following such consultation, the CMA still proposes to take over the case, it is required under Regulation 8 to notify each of the following interested parties that it is taking over a case: the relevant Regulator(s), the undertaking(s) being investigated, and any other person likely to be materially affected by the transfer (which may include the complainant(s)). The CMA will work closely with the relevant Regulator(s) and interested parties in reaching a decision on whether it is to exercise Part 1 functions in relation to a case. In practice, the CMA expects that the circumstances in which it would take over a case under Regulation 8 are likely to be rare.

3.29 Any decision by the CMA to exercise Part 1 functions pursuant to Regulation 5 or Regulation 8 of the Concurrency Regulations is not irreversible. While the CMA expects that this may happen only in exceptional circumstances, the CMA and a Regulator may agree to transfer that case back from the CMA to the relevant Regulator. The CMA will follow the procedures laid down in Regulation 7 where it decides to transfer a case back to any relevant Regulator.

Consequences of allocation of a case to the CMA or a Regulator

3.30 Neither the CMA nor the Regulators may exercise any of the prescribed functions in relation to a case where it appears that they may have concurrent jurisdiction until the question of which authority is to exercise Part 1 functions in relation to the case has been determined under Regulations 4 or 5 of the Concurrency Regulations (Regulation 6). Once the matter has been determined under Regulations 4 or 5, Regulation 6 also prohibits any other United Kingdom authority from exercising Part 1 functions in relation to that case unless it is formally transferred to that authority under the procedures laid down in Regulation 7 or the CMA decides that it is likely to be the best placed authority to act under the procedures set out in Regulation 8.

3.31 As a matter of policy, once jurisdiction of a case has been allocated to the CMA or a Regulator, the relevant authority will be responsible for the investigation, decision making and enforcement for that case, unless the case is subsequently transferred from that authority to another (for example, pursuant to Regulation 8). Notwithstanding the exercise of Part 1 functions by one of the CMA or a Regulator, the CMA and the other relevant Regulators will consult each other and may cooperate further as appropriate in respect of a case. This cooperation may occur, for example, through joint attendance at meetings, regular discussions throughout the investigation, cooperation in the collection and/or review of evidence, and the use of secondments.

Procedure for transferring cases between authorities

3.32 The Concurrency Regulations set out the procedure which must be followed in the cases of transfers under Regulation 7. When the CMA and a Regulator intend to transfer a case, the undertaking which is the subject of the investigation and any other person likely to be materially affected by the transfer (which may include any complainant) will be given an opportunity to make representations on the proposed transfer, and will be notified of the outcome. This will not be the case where the undertaking has not yet been informed that it is the subject of the investigation (Regulation 7). Those making such representations should assume that such representations will be seen by both or all of the authorities concerned. Any other person likely to be materially affected by the transfer (which may include any complainant) will also be notified of any transfer.

Cooperative working between the CMA and the Regulators

3.33 The CMA and each Regulator may agree arrangements for the use of staff or members of the CMA or a Regulator by the CMA or another Regulator, allowing for staff to be shared between the CMA and Regulators, or between Regulators (not involving the CMA). This includes through the secondment of any officer of the CMA or a Regulator by the Regulator or the CMA or another Regulator for any duration agreed between the relevant authorities.

3.34 Such secondments may be agreed on a case by case basis for any duration and for the purposes agreed between the CMA and the Regulator and/or between Regulators. Under Regulation 10, secondments may be for the purpose of exercising any function under Part 1 of the CA98. For example, the CMA and a Regulator may agree to share staff in this way to provide case support, investigatory expertise, specialist guidance (such as may be provided by economically or legally qualified staff of either the CMA or a Regulator) or to make any decision in relation to a case. The CMA may also agree to the use by a Regulator of the CMA's procedural complaints process, including providing a Regulator with access to the Procedural Officer to determine any dispute or complaint that falls within the competence of the Procedural Officer under Rule 8 of the CA98 Rules.[50]

3.35 In addition to the use of staff by a Regulator or the CMA, the CMA and each Regulator may agree arrangements for the provision of training, guidance, advice or any other form of support on a case by case basis, or more generally.

3.36 The full provisions for the use of staff and provision of support by the CMA and/or a Regulator are outlined in Memoranda of Understanding between the CMA and each Regulator.

COMPLAINTS

3.37 Complaints about breaches of competition law may be made either to the CMA and copied to the relevant Regulator, or directly to the relevant Regulator and copied to the CMA.[51] Complainants should only make one complaint in relation to any particular agreement or conduct, unless the complainant has access to substantial new factual evidence which it did not possess at the time of the original complaint. The principles relating to case handling will apply as outlined above. Complainants will be told as soon as is practicable which authority is dealing with the case. They will also be notified of any subsequent change.

3.38 The principles of case allocation set out in the Commission's *Notice on Cooperation within the Network of Competition Authorities*[52] will also be taken into account where Article 101 and/or Article 102 of the TFEU may apply. Pursuant to those case allocation principles, a United Kingdom NCA can be considered well-placed to act in relation to a complaint where the following three cumulative criteria are met:

- the agreement or conduct has substantial, direct, actual or foreseeable effects on competition and is implemented within or originates from within the United Kingdom
- the United Kingdom NCA is capable of bringing effectively to an end the entire infringement
- the United Kingdom NCA can gather, possibly with the assistance of other authorities, the evidence required to prove the infringement.

3.39 It follows that the CMA or a Regulator will only deal with a complaint where there exists a material link between the infringement and the United Kingdom.[53] For further details on case allocation within the European Competition Network see the competition law guideline *Modernisation* (OFT442).[54]

3.40 Submissions that urgent interim measures are needed to prevent 'significant damage' as a result of a breach of Article 101 and/or Article 102 of the TFEU, the Chapter I prohibition and/or the Chapter II prohibition of the CA98 will be treated in the same way as complaints. That is, the CMA or a Regulator with jurisdiction over the case will require there to be a material link between the infringement and the United Kingdom in order to consider the use of interim measures. The CMA or a Regulator will apply the legal framework to the facts of the case in determining whether the legal test for interim measures is met.[55] Further guidance on interim measures and the CMA and Regulators' approach to seeking interim measures is given in the CMA CA98 Procedures Guidance (CMA8).[56]

INFORMATION SHARING

Purpose of sharing information

3.41 The timely and appropriate exchange of information between the Regulators and between each Regulator and the CMA for the purpose of exercising concurrent functions is essential for the efficient and effective functioning of the United Kingdom concurrency regime, for example to:

- establish transparent, cooperative and effective working practices between the CMA and the Regulators, or between the Regulators
- facilitate the effective allocation or reallocation of complaints or investigations pursuant to the Concurrency Regulations
- enable the CMA or a Regulator to provide effective support and guidance in the context of a case or more generally
- facilitate the effective sharing or secondment of any officer of the CMA or a Regulator by the Regulator or the CMA or another Regulator, including for the purpose of making decisions in relation to the exercise by that Regulator of Part 1 functions
- facilitate the efficient use by a Regulator of the CMA's Procedural Officer, where a Regulator wishes to make use of the CMA's procedural complaints process.[57]

Information sharing in practice

3.42 Regulation 9 requires that each competent person must put in place arrangements for sharing with other competent persons certain kinds of information in connection with concurrent cases under the CA98. A 'competent person' means each of the CMA or any of the Regulators.[58]

3.43 The full arrangements for the sharing of information will be outlined in individual Memoranda of Understanding between the CMA and each of the Regulators. However, the CMA envisages that each

Memorandum of Understanding will provide for regular, timely and appropriate exchange of information between Regulators and the CMA connected with the exercise of concurrent competition functions, and that there will be adequate safeguards in place in relation to the information exchanged.[59] Regulators and the CMA will maintain open lines of communication through the UKCN and by way of strong bilateral partnerships.

3.44 In particular, the CMA envisages that the Memoranda of Understanding will specify that each competent person will provide the details of any information in their possession giving them reasonable grounds to suspect that Article 101 and/or Article 102 of the TFEU, and/or the Chapter I prohibition and/or the Chapter II prohibition of the CA98 may have been infringed to any other competent person who has or may have concurrent jurisdiction in respect of the possible infringement. The CMA envisages that this information will be shared even if the competent person in possession of the information does not propose to exercise any prescribed functions in respect of the case.

3.45 Such notification should take place in a timely manner and, in all cases, within 15 working days of the competent person reaching the view that there are reasonable grounds to suspect that such a competition law infringement may have taken place.[60] In addition, each competent person may share information in respect of any complaint or case prior to undertaking an assessment as to whether that competent person has reasonable grounds to suspect that a competition law infringement may have taken place.

3.46 Following any such notification, the competent person(s) in receipt of such information may request further information in relation to the case from the other competent person. In practice, most such information exchanges are likely to occur between the Regulators and the CMA and vice versa, since the CMA shares concurrent jurisdiction with each Regulator. Nevertheless, there may also be exchanges between Regulators in appropriate circumstances, for example if a case raises issues in more than one regulated sector.

3.47 Neither the competent person providing the information, nor any competent person in receipt of that information will be required to take any further action in respect of the possible infringement and the exchange of information between the CMA and a Regulator does not imply that a case or complaint will be prioritised or investigated. Furthermore, these information sharing arrangements will be without prejudice to the procedure for determining which competent person will exercise prescribed functions in relation to a case discussed in paragraphs 3.23 to 3.29 above.

3.48 In addition to information on potential infringements, the CMA and Regulators will share certain information connected with the exercise of concurrent competition functions at appropriate stages in a case, in accordance with Regulation 9 of the Concurrency Regulations. The CMA expects that details of these arrangements will be contained in each Memorandum of Understanding.

3.49 However, in summary, where the CMA or a Regulator has opened an investigation into a suspected infringement pursuant to section 25 of the CA98[61] and proposes to take any of the following steps in relation to that investigation, the CMA and the Regulator will each share information with the other competent person who would, but for the allocation of the case under the Concurrency Regulation to another competent person, have concurrent jurisdiction in the case[62] and the CMA expects that the Memoranda of Understanding will include the following provisions:

- **Statement of Objections** – where the CMA or a Regulator proposes to issue a Statement of Objections to a party in relation to a suspected infringement of Article 101 and/or Article 102 of the TFEU, and/or the Chapter I prohibition or the Chapter II prohibition of the CA98, it will share a draft of its proposed Statement of Objections with each other competent person who had concurrent jurisdiction in the case, prior to the case being allocated under the Regulations. Such information will be shared no later than 15 working days prior to the date on which the investigating competent person proposes to issue the Statement of Objections to a party. The CMA and any other competent person in receipt of such information may, but is not required to, provide comments or guidance to the investigating competent person in response to the information shared with it. Any such comments will be made no later than 10 working days following receipt of the proposed Statement of Objections.[63] The investigating competent person will not issue any Statement of Objections for a period of 10 working days after sharing information with each other competent person in relation to that draft Statement of Objections. Irrespective of the level of engagement between the CMA and a Regulator in any case, the decision to issue a Statement of Objections will be taken by the competent person with jurisdiction over the case.[64]
- **Notice or decision** – similarly, where the CMA or a Regulator proposes to issue any preliminary or final commitment decision or notice, infringement decision or notice, no grounds for action decision or notice, or decision or notice not to proceed with a case (including in relation to any case closure decision or notice based on administrative priority grounds) (Proposed Decision or Notice),[65] it will share a draft of its proposed decision or notice with each other competent person who would, but for the allocation of the case under the Concurrency Regulation to another competent person, have concurrent jurisdiction in the case.[66] Such information will be shared no later than 10 working days prior to the date on which the investigating competent person proposes to issue any Proposed Decision or Notice. The CMA and any other competent person in receipt of such information may, but is not required to, provide comments or guidance to the investigating competent person in response to the information shared with it. Any such comments will be made no later than 10 working days following receipt of the Proposed Decision or Notice.[67] The investigating competent person will not issue the proposed decision or notice for a period of 10 working days after sharing information with each other competent person in relation to that draft Proposed Decision or Notice.

3.50 In addition, the CMA and the Regulators may share additional information at any appropriate stage during an investigation and in a timely manner agreed between them as required. Such information may include:

- information in relation to any CA98 complaint received by the CMA or a Regulator and any investigation undertaken at the CMA or a Regulator's own initiative, or in response to a complaint
- details of any notices issued pursuant to sections 26, 26A and 27 of the CA98, and the use of powers to enter premises pursuant to sections 28 and 28A of the CA98
- before commencing an investigation into any suspected infringement of Article 101, Article 102, the Chapter I prohibition or the Chapter II prohibition, notification of a proposed decision to commence an investigation, including the information on which the proposed decision to open an investigation was made
- before issuing a case opening notice pursuant to section 25A of the CA98
- any application or request received by the CMA or a Regulator to seek interim measures to prevent 'significant damage' in relation to any case
- a regular summary of the progress and substance of any investigation into any suspected infringement of Article 101 and/or Article 102 of the TFEU, the Chapter I prohibition or the Chapter II prohibition of the CA98 conducted by the CMA or a Regulator. Subject to confidentiality considerations, this may include providing information of the CMA's or the Regulator's working assumptions and general approach to the investigation.

3.51 The CMA or a Regulator may request information that they may reasonably require from any other competent person relating to an individual investigation at any stage during the investigation to facilitate the performance of its functions under the CA98. The competent person to whom the request is made will respond appropriately to such a request for further information.

3.52 The exchange of information between the CMA and the Regulators does not imply that any infringement of Article 101 and/or Article 102 of the TFEU, the Chapter I prohibition and/or the Chapter II prohibition of the CA98 has taken place. Similarly, such information sharing does not impose an obligation on each competent person to consider a matter in more detail than it would otherwise have done.

3.53 The exchange of information between the CMA and the Regulators connected with the exercise of concurrent competition functions is governed by Part 9 of the EA02, which ensures that adequate safeguards are in place to prevent the unlawful disclosure of information by the CMA or a Regulator. Further details on Part 9 of the EA02 are set out in paragraphs 5.5 to 5.7 below.[68]

3.54 In addition to these obligations, the exchange of information between the CMA and the Regulators is subject to procedural safeguards, including the use of confidentiality obligations that restrict the distribution and use of the information received. Moreover, any information contained in a leniency application made to the CMA will be treated in accordance with the principles and protections set out in OFT1495, *Applications for Leniency and No-Action in Cartel Cases.*[69]

ANNUAL CONCURRENCY REPORT

3.55 The CMA is required to prepare an annual report containing an assessment of how the concurrency arrangements have operated during the prior year.[70] This report must include information about the activities of the CMA and the Regulators in relation to the exercise of all concurrent functions (that is, under both Part 1 of the CA98 and Part 4 of the EA02).[71]

3.56 The report evaluates the operation of competition concurrency and key competition issues in concurrent sectors in the United Kingdom. It is intended to facilitate continuing improvement to the concurrency regime, the promotion of competition in the regulated sectors (or the preventing of anti-competitive behaviour in health-care services in England, in the case of Monitor), and to strengthen transparency and accountability within the Regulators and the CMA.

3.57 In each report, the CMA will outline the landscape of the CMA's and the Regulators' duties, powers and general market conditions in each concurrent sector. The report will outline the actions taken by the Regulators and the CMA during the reporting period to promote competition in the concurrent sectors (or, again, the preventing of anti-competitive behaviour in health-care services in England, in the case of Monitor).[72] The report will set out and assess the relevant outcomes in relation to promotion of competition and/or the preventing of anti-competitive behaviour and application of competition law to the concurrent sectors achieved during the reporting period.

3.58 The CMA may include the following type of information in the report in respect of the operation of concurrency under the CA98. This information will be aggregated and presented, as appropriate, in relation to each Regulator and the CMA:

- the number (and description) of decisions in which the use of competition powers under Part 1 of the CA98 was considered by a Regulator to be more appropriate than regulatory powers
- the number (and description) of decisions in which the use of regulatory powers was considered to be more appropriate than competition powers under Part 1 of the CA98 (in cases where competition powers could have been exercised)
- the number of formal investigations under the CA98 commenced in each concurrent sector
- whether the CMA and/or a Regulator issued any notices pursuant to sections 26, 26A and 27 of the CA98, or used powers to enter premises pursuant to sections 28 and 28A of the CA98 in those sectors
- whether the CMA and/or a Regulator accepted any commitments in relation to a case pursuant to section 31A of the CA98

Part 3 CMA and other Guidelines

- the number of notifications between the Regulators and the CMA (and vice versa) that an infringement of any or all of the Chapter I and/or Chapter II prohibitions or Article 101 and Article 102 of the TFEU may have taken place
- the number of statements of objection/statements of competition concerns issued in concurrent sectors by the CMA and the Regulators
- the number (and description) of final decisions notified by the CMA and the Regulators
- summaries of infringement decisions pursuant to Part 1 of the CA98 made in concurrent sectors, including a description of any financial penalty and/or other remedies imposed
- whether there have been secondments and/or joint projects between the CMA and the concurrent Regulators (or between the Regulators) and if so, how many people were involved, for what purpose and for how long
- whether any appeals have been brought to the CAT in respect of decisions under Part 1 of the CA98 in any of the concurrent sectors and the outcomes of any such appeals.

3.59 The annual report will also comment on the general operation of the co-operation arrangements discussed in this guidance. The CMA may offer its view on the nature and quality of such co-operation during the reporting year. It will also provide a high-level summary of the work of the UKCN during the relevant reporting year. The annual report will not, however, include any information that could jeopardise ongoing cases under Part 1 of the CA98, or the effectiveness of actual or proposed regulatory activity in any of the concurrent sectors.

3.60 The CMA will also report on the operation of concurrency in the regulated sectors under Part 4 of the EA02 (that is, market studies and market investigation references). In particular, the annual report may contain the following type of information:

- whether the CMA and/or any Regulator has exercised any powers to issue a market study notice pursuant to section 130A of the EA02 in any of the concurrent sectors
- whether the CMA and/or any Regulator has exercised any powers to make a market investigation reference pursuant to section 131 of the EA02 in any of the concurrent sectors
- whether the CMA and/or any Regulator has accepted undertakings in lieu of a market investigation reference pursuant to section 154 of the EA02 in any of the concurrent sectors
- whether the CMA and/or any Regulator has, following an issue of a market study notice pursuant to section 130A of the EA02 in any of the concurrent sectors, decided not to make a market investigation reference in any of the concurrent sectors at the conclusion of that market study.

3.61 The annual report will generally not refer to any Regulatory Case or Regulatory Merger made to, or determined by, the CMA during the relevant reporting period.

3.62 The CMA will cooperate and consult with the Regulators in preparing the annual report. The CMA will prepare a draft report that it will send to the Regulators asking them to provide any comments or suggestions on the content or conclusions of the annual report. The CMA will consider any comments or suggestions it receives from a Regulator and may seek further clarification on those comments or suggestions as appropriate. The CMA will prepare a final version of the annual report for publication that takes account of its consultation with the Regulators as appropriate. The annual report will be made available on www.gov.uk/cma.

NOTES

26 Department for Business Innovation and Skills, *Growth, competition and the competition regime – Government response to consultation*, March 2012, paragraph 8.4.

27 Department for Business, Innovation and Skills, *Strategic steer for the Competition and Markets Authority 2014–17*, in Annex 1 to *its Response to consultation on statement of specific priorities for the CMA*, 1 October 2013, paragraphs 6 and 9.

28 Statement by Alex Chisholm, Chief Executive of the CMA, *CMA mission and strategy*, 1 October 2013.

29 UK Competition Network, *Statement of Intent*, 2 December 2013. See Annexe B of this Guidance.

30 See paragraph 2.5 above for an explanation of this term.

31 The exercise of this power would prevent the Regulator from investigating (or continuing to investigate) the case unless and until the CMA transferred the case back to the Regulator.

32 'Officer' is used in this guidance to mean any member of staff of the CMA or a Regulator, any board member of the CMA or a Regulator, or any Panel member of the CMA.

33 OJ C101, 27.04.2004, p 43.

34 OFT guideline *Modernisation* (OFT442), available at: www.gov.uk/cma.

35 www.gov.uk/cma

36 The CMA and the Regulators may exercise their discretion either not to investigate, or to close an investigation into, conduct that is otherwise prohibited under Article 101 or Article 102 of the TFEU on administrative priority grounds.

37 OFT guideline *Modernisation* (OFT442), available at: www.gov.uk/cma

38 See the CMA CA98 Procedures Guidance (CMA8) (available at: www.gov.uk/cma) for more details on settlement and on the CMA's investigation and decision-making procedures under Chapter I and/or Chapter II of the CA98. For CA98 Rules, see *The Competition Act 1998 (Competition and Markets Authority's Rules) Order 2014, SI N. 458.*

39 Relevant sector-specific legislation may include, for example, legislation under which a Regulator is granted concurrent powers (see further the table at paragraph 2.1 above), and which outline a Regulator's duties in relation to the prevention of anticompetitive behaviour and/or promotion of competition (or similar duty) within their sector.

40 Similarly, where the CMA may use Regulators' staff, board or panel members (or equivalent) when making decisions in relation to a concurrent case.

41 OFT guideline *OFT's guidance as to the appropriate amount of a penalty*, available at: www.gov.uk/cma

42 See sections 46 and 47 of the CA98.

43 Note however that Monitor has a duty to exercise its functions with a view to preventing anti-competitive behaviour which is against the interests of people who use health care services in England, but not to promote competition.

44 In contrast to the other concurrent sectors (where either the CMA or the relevant Regulator may take responsibility for a case depending on which one is better or best placed to do so), under the Concurrency Regulations Monitor will normally be responsible for any case that is principally concerned with matters relating to the provision of health care services for the purposes of the NHS in England, though Monitor may nevertheless agree with the CMA that the CMA shall act in a case.

45 This may include, for example, a case affecting a regulated sector across the United Kingdom, including any nations which benefit from devolved powers.

46 See further paragraphs 3.41 to 3.54 below for further information.

47 Though the CMA and Monitor may nevertheless agree that the CMA is to act in such a case: see Regulation 4(2) of the Concurrency Regulations.

48 A Statement of Objections outlines the CMA's or Regulator's provisional conclusions in relation to the suspected infringement of competition law. The Statement of Objections is a formal procedural step in a case pursuant to Rule 5 of the CA98 Rules.

49 Regulation 8 of the Concurrency Regulations.

50 Rule 8 of the CA98 Rules sets out the CMA's procedural complaints process. Further guidance on the procedural complaints process and the role of the Procedural Officer is set out in Chapter 15 of the CMA CA98 Procedures Guidance (CMA8) for more details on settlement and CA98 Rules, both available at: www.gov.uk/cma

51 Complaints about breaches of sector legislation alone should be sent directly to the relevant Regulator.

52 OJ C101, 27.04.2004, p 43.

53 The CMA or a Regulator will determine whether there is a material link between the suspected infringement and the United Kingdom on a case-by-case basis, and will assess whether the suspected infringement may affect trade within the United Kingdom, and/or prevent, restrict or distort competition within the United Kingdom.

54 OFT guideline *Modernisation* (OFT442), available at: www.gov.uk/cma

55 Section 35 of the CA98.

56 Available at: www.gov.uk/cma

57 Rule 8 of the CA98 Rules sets out the CMA's procedural complaints process. Further guidance on the procedural complaints process and the role of the Procedural Officer is set out in Chapter 15 of the CMA CA98 Procedures Guidance (CMA8) for more details on settlement and CA98 Rules, both available at: www.gov.uk/cma

58 See Regulation 2 of the Concurrency Regulations and section 54(7) of the CA98.

59 Further detail on confidentiality and disclosure of information is set out in chapter 5 of this guidance.

60 The notification requirements will apply where the threshold for a CA98 investigation is met. Section 25 of the CA98 sets out the legal test for the CMA or a Regulator to commence an investigation of a suspected infringement of the prohibitions under Chapter I or Chapter II of the CA98, or Article 101 or Article 102 of the TFEU.

61 Section 25 of the CA98 sets out the legal test for the CMA or a Regulator to commence an investigation of a suspected infringement of the prohibitions under Chapter I or Chapter II of the CA98, or Article 101 or Article 102 of the TFEU. The information sharing arrangements do not apply to any complaint or preliminary investigation in which the investigating competent person concluded that there were no reasonable grounds for suspecting that there has been an infringement of the prohibitions under Chapter I or Chapter II of the CA98, or Article 101 or Article 102 of the TFEU in accordance with section 25 of the CA98.

62 See paragraphs 3.23 to 3.29 for a discussion of the case allocation process under the Regulations.

63 The CMA considers that the documents containing such comments will be 'internal documents' for the purposes of the CMA Rules and therefore may be withheld from access to the file following a Statement of Objections: see Rule 1(1) and Rule 6(2) of the CMA Rules (SI 2014/458).

64 Subject to the CMA exercising its discretion to take over a case under Regulation 8 of the Concurrency Regulations. For more information see paragraphs 3.26 to 3.29 above.

65 See Regulations 9(1)(b) to 9(1)(j) of the Concurrency Regulations for a description of the range of notices and decisions to which the information sharing requirements relate.

66 See paragraphs 3.23 to 3.29 for a discussion of the case allocation process under the Regulations.

67 See footnote 61 above.

68 See also *Transparency and disclosure: Statement of the CMA's policy and approach* (CMA6), and in particular Chapter 6 on disclosure to UK public authorities.

69 OFT1495 has been adopted by the CMA: see *Proposed Treatment of existing Office of Fair Trading and Competition Commission guidance, Summary of responses to the consultation* (CMA12) available at www.gov.uk/cma

70 See paragraph 16 of Schedule 4 of the ERRA13.

71 Paragraph 16(3) of Schedule 4 of the ERRA13 prescribes the information that must be included in the annual report.

72 Monitor has a duty to exercise its functions with a view to preventing anti-competitive behaviour which is against the interests of people who use health care services in England, but not to promote competition.

4 REGULATORS' OTHER POWERS AND DUTIES

STATUTORY SECTORAL DUTIES

[3.242]

4.1 The duties of the Regulators under the individual statutes listed in the table in chapter 2 above are set out in those statutes. In general, the Regulators must ensure that there is sufficient provision of the regulated service throughout the United Kingdom, they must promote or facilitate competition,[73] and they must protect the interests of customers, consumers or users. The Regulators are not generally required to have regard to those sectoral duties when exercising Part 1 functions[74] under the CA98. However, they may have regard to matters covered by their sectoral duties if they are matters to which the CMA could have regard in exercising its powers under the CA98. Consistent with the intention of the legislation to strengthen the primacy of general competition law, the Regulators[75] are required to consider

Part 3 CMA and other Guidelines

whether the use of their CA98 powers is more appropriate before using their sectoral powers to promote competition. The duty is tailored to the individual regimes, which have differently formulated duties on and powers for the regulators, and is discussed below.

RELATIONSHIP BETWEEN THE REGULATORS' POWERS UNDER THE CA98 AND THEIR OTHER FUNCTIONS AND POWERS CONTAINED IN SECTOR SPECIFIC LEGISLATION

4.2 In some circumstances, a particular agreement or practice may fall within the scope of a Regulator's sector specific legislation as well as within the Chapter I prohibition, the Chapter II prohibition, Article 101 and/or Article 102 of the TFEU. Regulated companies may, for example, have licences which prevent them from showing undue preference to, or undue discrimination against, any class of persons. Some types of price discrimination, for example, may also infringe the Chapter II prohibition and/or Article 102 of the TFEU. Further details are given in the competition law guidance *Abuse of a dominant position* (OFT402).[76]

4.3 In some circumstances, sector-specific legislation requires a Regulator to enforce a licence condition or a statutory provision; sometimes, however, it may be more effective or provide greater deterrent and precedent effect for the benefit of competition and consumers to use the powers available under the CA98. Before making any final or provisional enforcement order, a Regulator must consider whether, in a particular case, it is more appropriate to proceed under the CA98 (and take action in relation to an infringement of the Chapter I prohibition, the Chapter II prohibition, Article 101 and/or Article 102). Where a Regulator considers that it would be more appropriate to proceed under the CA98, they cannot then proceed with licence enforcement under sector-specific regulation; they must instead use their legal powers under the CA98.[77]

4.4 Each Regulator will determine whether it may be more appropriate to proceed under the CA98 on a case-by-case basis. In order to ensure the efficient and effective allocation of resources, a Regulator will consider which potential investigation and enforcement route would be most appropriate in a particular case when it commences an investigation in its sector. A Regulator will also keep under review the question of which route of investigation and enforcement is the most appropriate during the course of any investigation.

4.5 Where a Regulator has commenced an investigation or enforcement action pursuant to sector-specific powers but concludes during the course of that investigation or enforcement action that it would be more appropriate to proceed under the CA98 in respect of the relevant facts and evidence, they may begin proceedings under the CA98. In these circumstances the Regulators and the CMA will follow the case handling procedures for determining jurisdiction in a concurrent case as described in paragraphs 3.21 to 3.40 above. As a general principle, the authority which is best placed to deal with the case will have jurisdiction over that case in accordance with the case allocation principles under Regulation 4 of the Concurrency Regulations.

4.6 Where a Regulator proceeds under the CA98, they will be required to bear in mind their obligations as NCAs under the Modernisation Regulation, in particular under Article 3(1) in cases where trade between Member States may be affected (see paragraph 4.8 below) and those as Regulators under national law. The Regulators' approach to this process will be set out in their sector-specific guidance on the application of competition law to their particular sectors. If it appears during an investigation by a Regulator using its sector-specific powers that action under the CA98 is more appropriate (or, in the reverse case, under its sector-specific powers), the parties will be informed.

4.7 A decision by a Regulator to make any enforcement or penalty order under that Regulator's relevant sector powers does not prohibit the CMA from undertaking an investigation under the CA98 in relation to the same or similar facts.[78]

RELATIONSHIP BETWEEN EU COMPETITION LAW AND SECTOR SPECIFIC LEGISLATION

4.8 The relationship between EU competition law and national law is governed by Article 3 of the Modernisation Regulation. Article 3(1) provides that where the CMA and the Regulators apply national competition law to agreements which may affect trade between Member States, they must also apply Article 101 of the TFEU. Where they apply national competition law to conduct prohibited by Article 102 of the TFEU they must also apply Article 102. In applying their sectoral powers the Regulators will need to consider the extent to which, if any, the use of these powers may be considered to be the application of national competition law for the purposes of Article 3.

4.9 It is important to consider what happens in the event that the application of national competition law would lead to a stricter outcome than the position under EU law. The position is different according to whether Article 101 or Article 102 of the TFEU applies.

4.10 When applying Article 101 of the TFEU and national competition law in parallel, the CMA and the Regulators may not prohibit an agreement if the agreement would be permitted under Article 101 of the TFEU. An agreement could be permitted under Article 101 of the TFEU because the agreement in question does not restrict competition within the meaning of Article 101(1) of the TFEU, the conditions in Article 101(3) of the TFEU are met or the agreement is covered by an EU block exemption regulation.

4.11 However, the CMA and the Regulators are permitted under Article 3(2) to apply national law which is stricter than Article 102 of the TFEU to unilateral conduct. In the United Kingdom the unilateral conduct of undertakings may, for example, be examined under the market investigation provisions of the EA02 (see paragraphs 4.17 to 4.21 below).

4.12 Article 3 does not, however, preclude the application of national law that predominantly pursues objectives different from those pursued by Articles 101 and 102 of the TFEU. This means that the

Regulators may still apply powers set out in their sector-specific legislation to agreements which are compatible with EU competition law provided they do so predominantly in pursuit of objectives different from that pursued by Article 101 and Article 102 of the TFEU (the protection of competition on the market). The interaction of Article 3 and national competition law is dealt with in more detail in the competition law guideline *Modernisation* (OFT442).[79]

EXCEPTIONS IN THE CA98 FOR SERVICES OF 'GENERAL ECONOMIC INTEREST'

4.13 In line with Article 106(2) of the TFEU, the CA98 provides, in Schedule 3, an exclusion from the Chapter I and Chapter II prohibitions:

- where an undertaking has either been entrusted with a service of general economic interest, or has the character of a revenue-producing monopoly (that is, an undertaking that has been granted monopoly powers by the State to raise money for the State)[80]
- insofar as the application of the prohibitions in the CA98 would obstruct the performance of the particular task assigned to the undertaking.

4.14 The CMA and the Regulators are required to apply these principles when applying the exclusion in Schedule 3.

4.15 The fact that the CA98 may not apply to certain activities of a regulated business in these circumstances does not, however, mean that the Regulators cannot apply their sectoral powers to those activities. Indeed, it is precisely in these situations that the Regulators' ability to ensure services are available to consumers throughout the United Kingdom on reasonable terms through use of their sectoral powers is particularly relevant. Further information on the exclusions under the CA98 and Article 106(2) of the TFEU can be found in the competition law guideline *Services of general economic interest exclusion* (OFT421).[81]

REGULATORS AND THE EUROPEAN COMPETITION NETWORK

4.16 The CMA and the Regulators are designated as NCAs with the responsibility to apply Articles 101 and 102 of the TFEU in accordance with the provisions in the Modernisation Regulation in relation to their respective sectors. They are obliged to apply EU competition rules in close cooperation with the Commission and other NCAs. To this end, the Commission and designated competition authorities of the Member States have formed the European Competition Network (the ECN) which facilitates close cooperation in the enforcement of Articles 101 and 102 of the TFEU in the EU. Further details on the ways in which the Regulators can participate in the work of the ECN can be found in the Commission's *Notice on Cooperation within the Network of Competition Authorities*[82] and the competition law guidance *Modernisation* (OFT442).[83]

MARKET STUDIES AND MARKET INVESTIGATION REFERENCES

4.17 The EA02 makes provision for a system of market investigations by the CMA. Under the EA02 (and the provisions of the sector-specific legislation which give the Regulators concurrent powers under the EA02), the CMA and the Regulators may undertake market studies, and may make market investigation references to the Chair of the CMA for the constitution of a CMA group to conduct an in-depth market investigation into single or multiple markets for goods or services in the United Kingdom. In the case of the Regulators, market investigation references may only be made in relation to their respective sectors. Regulators may make single market or cross-market references within their respective sectors where the test for such a reference is met.[84] The purpose of these investigations is to examine the market(s) and (where required) implement appropriate remedies where the CMA determines that the structure of the market(s) or the conduct of the suppliers or customers is harming competition.

4.18 When making a reference, the CMA or the Regulator concerned must have reasonable grounds for suspecting that any feature or combination of features of a market or markets in the United Kingdom prevents, restricts or distorts competition in relation to the supply or acquisition of any goods or services in the United Kingdom (or a part of the United Kingdom).

4.19 Before initiating a market study or making a market investigation reference to the Chair of the CMA for the constitution of a CMA group, the CMA or the Regulator concerned will first consider whether a matter warrants investigation as an infringement of Article 101, and/or Article 102 of the TFEU, the Chapter I prohibition or the Chapter II prohibition. Regulators may, in addition, wish to exercise their discretion to consider whether it would be more appropriate to deal with an issue under any sector specific legislation or rules (subject to concluding that it would be more appropriate to deal within an issue under the CA98, in which case the Regulator must proceed under the CA98).[85]

4.20 Where the CMA or a Regulator identifies any conduct and/or receives information that an infringement of the CA98 or Article 101 or Article 102 of the TFEU may have taken place and believes it has sufficient grounds to conduct an investigation under the CA98, the CMA or the Regulator will proceed under the CA98 in the first instance. Any decision to conduct an investigation under the CA98 will not prevent the CMA or the Regulator from reviewing the same or similar market(s), conduct or arrangements pursuant to its market studies and market investigations powers under Part 4 of the EA02 if such a review is appropriate and reasonable. Any such action is only likely to occur in unusual circumstances, for example where:

- proceeding under the CA98 is not likely to address adequately the competition concerns identified
- the CMA or the relevant Regulator considers that the legal threshold for such an investigation is met
- such an investigation would be proportionate and appropriate in the circumstances.[86]

4.21 Further details concerning these powers under the EA02 can be found in *Markets Studies and Market Investigations: Supplemental guidance on the CMA's approach* (CMA3)[87] and in the competition law guideline *Modernisation* (OFT442).[88]

CONCURRENT SUPER-COMPLAINTS

4.22 The EA02 provides for a super-complaint to be made by a designated consumer body if any feature, or combination of features, of a market in the United Kingdom for goods or services is or appears to be significantly harming the interests of consumers.[89]

4.23 The Regulators with concurrent competition powers have a duty to respond to super-complaints made to them under the EA02 if the complaint concerns a regulated sector in relation to which that Regulator has functions (as set out in the table in chapter 2).[90] The coordination of super-complaint duties will be based on policies agreed and applied through the UKCN. Information on the super-complaint process can be found in *Super-complaints: guidance for designated consumer bodies* (OFT514).[91]

NOTES

73 Note however that Monitor has a duty to exercise its functions with a view to preventing anti competitive behaviour which is against the interests of people who use health care services in England, but not to promote competition.

74 See paragraph 2.5 above for an explanation of this term.

75 With the exception of Monitor at this time.

76 OFT guideline *Abuse of a dominant position* (OFT402), available at: www.gov.uk/cma

77 This duty will not be applied to Monitor at this time. However, the Secretary of State may commence this duty at a future date upon Government agreement.

78 In the event that any such CMA investigation resulted in directions, interim measures and/or financial penalties being imposed on the relevant undertaking, any such enforcement action would be subject to the statutory requirements under Chapter III of Part 1 of the CA98.

79 OFT guideline *Modernisation* (OFT442), available at: www.gov.uk/cma.

80 For further details see competition law guidance *Services of general economic interest exclusion* (OFT 421), available at: www.gov.uk/cma.

81 OFT guideline *Services of general economic interest exclusion* (OFT 421), available at: www.gov.uk/cma

82 OJ C101, 27.04.2004, p 43.

83 OFT guideline *Modernisation* (OFT442), available at: www.gov.uk/cma

84 For further information on single market and cross-market references, including the threshold for making a market investigation reference under the EA02, see further CMA guideline *Markets Studies and Market Investigations: Supplemental guidance on the CMA's approach* (CMA3), available at: www.gov.uk/cma

85 This duty will not be applied to Monitor at this time, however the Secretary of State may commence this duty at a future date upon Government agreement.

86 Please see footnote 81 above.

87 *Markets Studies and Market Investigations: Supplemental guidance on the CMA's approach* (CMA3), available at: www.gov.uk/cma

88 OFT guideline *Modernisation* (OFT442), available at: www.gov.uk/cma

89 Section 11 of the EA02.

90 The Enterprise Act 2002 (Super-complaints to Regulators) Order 2003 (SI 2003/1368).

91 OFT guideline *Super-complaints: guidance for designated consumer bodies* (OFT514), available at: www.gov.uk/cma

5 CONFIDENTIALITY AND DISCLOSURE OF INFORMATION

[3.243]

5.1 In the course of any investigation under the CA98, the CMA or the Regulator will indicate the purpose for which any requested document or information is required, and under which powers they are sought. Further detail on the information seeking powers is given in the competition law guideline *Powers of investigation* (OFT404)[92] and in the CMA CA98 Procedures Guidance (CMA8).

DISCLOSURE UNDER THE MODERNISATION REGULATION

5.2 The power of all members of the ECN to exchange and use information which has been collected for the purpose of applying Article 101 or 102 of the TFEU is important to the functioning of the ECN. Regulators will fulfil their role as NCAs in relation to their sectors, as described in paragraph 4.16 above.

5.3 Information on the exchange and use of confidential information within the Network can be found in the Commission's *Notice on Cooperation within the Network of Competition Authorities.*[93] Information on confidentiality and the disclosure of information can be found in the competition law guideline *Modernisation* (OFT442).[94]

5.4 The exchange between the CMA and the Regulators of information obtained by them under Part I of the CA98 is governed by Part 9 of the EA02 rather than the Modernisation Regulation. Further details on Part 9 of the EA02 are set out in paragraphs 5.5 to 5.7 below.

CONFIDENTIALITY AND DISCLOSURE UNDER NATIONAL LAW

5.5 The Concurrency Regulations provide for broad information sharing between the CMA and a Regulator in respect of investigations under the CA98.[95] In all cases, the CMA and the Regulators will treat any information so disclosed in accordance with their legal duties.

5.6 The EA02 sets out the requirements for safeguarding certain information and lays down the requirements that have to be met before public authorities, including the CMA and the Regulators, may disclose such information. These are set out in Part 9 of the EA02 which applies to information which has been gathered for the purpose of the CMA's and the Regulators' EA02 functions, and for the purposes of the CMA's and the Regulators' competition and consumer functions under specified legislation (including the CA98). Further information on confidentiality and the disclosure of information can be found in *Transparency and disclosure: Statement of the CMA's policy and approach* (CMA6),[96] as well as in the CMA CA98 Procedures Guidance (CMA8).[97]

5.7 Where information has been obtained under Part I of the CA98 or under the EA02, its disclosure by a Regulator for sector-specific purposes is subject to the restrictions set out in Part 9 of the EA02 rather than the provisions of any sector-specific legislation. In particular, this means that a Regulator may only disclose such information where it is permitted to do so pursuant to sections 239 to 243 of the EA02 and must have regard to the considerations relevant to disclosure set out in section 244 of the EA02.

NOTES

92 OFT guideline *Powers of investigation* (OFT404), available at: www.gov.uk/cma

93 OJ C101, 27.04.04, p 43.

94 OFT guideline *Modernisation* (OFT442), available at: www.gov.uk/cma

95 For further information on the information sharing provisions, see paragraphs 3.41 to 3.54 above.

96 *Transparency and disclosure: Statement of the CMA's policy and approach* (CMA6), available at: www.gov.uk/cma.

97 CMA CA98 Procedures Guidance (CMA8), available at: www.gov.uk/cma.

ANNEXE(S)

(Annexe A sets out the text of the Competition Act 1998 (Concurrency) Regulations 2014, SI 2014/536 which are reproduced in Part 2 of this Handbook at **[2.47]**. *Annexe B sets out the text of the United Kingdom Competition Network (UKCN) Statement of Intent, which is reproduced at* **[3.235]** *above.)*

CMA INFORMATION NOTE ARRANGEMENTS FOR THE HANDLING OF LENIENCY APPLICATIONS IN THE REGULATED SECTORS (3 NOVEMBER 2017)

[3.244]

NOTES

SUMMARY

1. This note provides businesses with information on the arrangements for the handling of leniency applications within the regulated sectors amongst the full members of the UK Competition Network (UKCN), so that there is clarity as to the process that should be followed, and to ensure the operation of a single queue system.

2. This note is published by the Competition and Markets Authority (CMA) and has been endorsed by the sectoral regulators that are the other full members of the UKCN.[1]

3. For the avoidance of doubt, the arrangements described in this information note apply **only** in respect of leniency applications in the UK, and do not reduce the need for applicants to apply for leniency to non-UK authorities (such as the European Commission and other National Competition Authorities) in order to obtain protection under the applicable leniency regimes of those authorities.

4. Case allocation is not covered by this information note. Case allocation is covered instead by the Concurrency Regulations,[2] the concurrency guidance[3] and the memorandums of understanding (MoUs) between the CMA and each of the sectoral regulators.

5. Any disclosure of leniency information under the leniency concurrency arrangements set out in this information note is subject to the provisions of Part 9 of the Enterprise Act 2002. Information sharing arrangements are set out in the relevant paragraphs of the MoUs between the CMA and each of the sectoral regulators.[4]

6. All businesses should in the first instance approach the CMA by calling the CMA's leniency number in order to secure their place in the leniency queue. The CMA's leniency number is 020 3738 6833.

7. The CMA's leniency number can be used for prospective leniency applications. That is, businesses may approach the CMA on a 'no names' basis in order to explore whether there is an existing investigation or an existing applicant for leniency.[5]

8. In the event that any initial leniency enquiries or leniency applications are made to a sectoral regulator, the sectoral regulator will immediately direct the person making the leniency enquiry or leniency application to the CMA. The applicant's place in the leniency queue is always determined by the order in which any business applied **to the CMA** for leniency.

9. From the earliest stage of any application, the CMA and sectoral regulators will work together closely so that leniency applications within the regulated sectors are dealt with swiftly and efficiently, and in accordance with the principles outlined below.

10. In all cases, decisions about the ultimate grant of leniency will be made by the authority to which the case has been allocated in accordance with the Concurrency Regulations.[6]

11. The approach of the CMA and the sectoral regulators is designed to ensure that:

— the process for granting leniency is fair, transparent, certain and consistent;

— no more than one business is granted Type A and Type B leniency in any one case;

— the incentives for applying for leniency are not undermined; and

— the CMA can properly retain control over the grant of criminal immunity and the management of investigations in relation to the cartel offence.

NOTES

1 The UK Competition Network (UKCN) is an alliance of the Competition and Markets Authority (CMA) with all the UK regulators that have a specific role to support and enable competition within their sectors. The network aims to encourage stronger competition across the economy for the benefit of consumers and to prevent anti-competitive behaviour in the regulated industries. The sectoral regulators with concurrent competition powers that are full members of the UKCN are the Office of Communications (Ofcom), the Gas and Electricity Markets Authority (Ofgem), the Utility Regulator (Northern Ireland), Water Services Regulation Authority (Ofwat), the Office of Rail and Road (ORR), the Civil Aviation Authority (CAA), the Financial Conduct Authority (FCA) and the Payment Systems Regulator (PSR).

2 The Competition Act 1998 (Concurrency) Regulations 2014 (SI 2014/536).

3 CMA10 (*Regulated Industries: Guidance on concurrent application of competition law to regulated industries*).

4 The relevant paragraphs provide: ' . . . if the CMA or [the sectoral regulator] consider it necessary or appropriate to pass leniency information to each other (or to another UK authority with concurrent powers), the transmitting authority will inform the applicant or its legal adviser first.' 'In addition . . . , where [the sectoral regulator] or the CMA receives leniency information from the other (or from another UK authority with concurrent powers) for the purpose of applying the Competition Prohibitions or, in the case of the CMA, the cartel offence under section 188 of the Enterprise Act 2002, that information will not be used for any other purpose. This restriction on use also applies to any information obtained by the receiving authority as a result of investigative measures relating to the Competition Prohibitions or the cartel offence following the receipt of leniency information from the other authority. This does not affect the use that may be made by the CMA or [the sectoral regulator] of information received from other sources, or if the leniency applicant's consent is obtained. . . . ' The MoU with the FCA further provides that when leniency information is shared with the FCA, the FCA may also contact the applicant to let it know it is aware of the leniency application and remind the applicant of any obligations it may have to notify relevant conduct, under Principle 11 of the FCA's Principles for Business or Principle 4 of the FCA's Statement of Principle for Approved Persons. The MoU with the PSR further provides that when leniency information is shared with the PSR, the PSR may also contact the applicant to remind it of its obligations under General Direction 1.

5 For further detail, see *Leniency and no-action applications in cartel cases*: OFT1495, Chapter 3.

6 Competition Act 1998 (Concurrency) Regulations 2014, SI 2014/536.

BACKGROUND

12. The sectoral regulators have concurrent powers with the CMA to enforce the competition prohibitions[7] in their respective sectors and, where they find that an infringement has taken place, to impose penalties on the businesses concerned.

13. When setting the level of a penalty, the CMA and the sectoral regulators are required to have regard to the *Guidance as to the appropriate amount of a penalty* (OFT423).[8]

14. In order to help detect and take action against cartels, OFT423 includes provision for the grant of immunity from, or a reduction in, financial penalties for businesses that report their participation in cartel activity and satisfy certain conditions.

15. The approach taken by the CMA in handling applications for leniency for businesses is set out in more detail in the *Applications for leniency and no-action in cartel cases* (OFT1495).

16. Three different types of leniency are available, subject to specified conditions being met:

— **Type A (first-in and no pre-existing investigation)** – guaranteed corporate immunity from financial penalties, automatic blanket immunity from criminal prosecution for individual employees and officers, and guaranteed protection from competition disqualification orders (CDOs).

— **Type B (first-in where there is a pre-existing investigation but a Statement of Objections has not yet been issued)** – discretionary corporate immunity from financial penalties or reductions of up to 100%, discretionary immunity from criminal prosecution for employees or officers, and CDO protection if immunity/leniency reduction is granted.

— **Type C (second or later applicant or coercer, and a Statement of Objections has not yet been issued)** – discretionary reduction in financial penalty of up to 50%, discretionary immunity from criminal prosecution for specific individuals, and CDO protection if a leniency reduction is granted.

NOTES

7 As set out in Chapter I and Chapter II of the Competition Act 1998 (CA98) and Articles 101 and 102 of the Treaty on the Functioning of the European Union (TFEU).

8 Section 38(8) CA98.

THE SINGLE QUEUE SYSTEM

17. The CMA and sectoral regulators operate a 'single queue system' for the handling of leniency applications within the regulated sectors.

18. Under this system, applicants need only make an application to the CMA and, provided the conditions for leniency are met, that application will secure the applicant's place in the leniency queue with all authorities.

19. This approach ensures that the applicant's place in the leniency queue is determined by the order in which any business applied for leniency. This, in turn:

— makes it clear that the granting of more than one type A or type B marker is precluded, as both require an applicant to be 'first-in';

— maximises the incentives to come in for leniency early: since it is clear that there can only be one type A or type B marker in respect of the same conduct, there is **no 'second chance'** for businesses which have waited to see how their fellow cartelists will act. This promotes fairness more generally: there is no reason why, as a point of principle, an applicant in a regulated sector should have an additional opportunity to obtain a type A or type B marker as compared with those in unregulated sectors;

— allows for certainty around an applicant's place in the queue and the type of marker granted. In particular, there is no risk that an applicant will become (significantly) worse off because the case has been transferred to another authority (with which the applicant may not have secured first place in the queue). This, in turn, deters any 'gaming' of the system, for example, by parties:

- waiting to see how their fellow cartelists will act; or
- lobbying for their case to be taken forward by a particular authority;

— reduces the burden on businesses, which only have to make one leniency application;

— provides certainty for businesses, which need not concern themselves with whether they have submitted applications to all the relevant authorities;

— avoids a duplication of work by the authorities, and within the competition regime as a whole.

THE SINGLE QUEUE SYSTEM IN PRACTICE

20. It may not be clear at the time a leniency application is made whether any particular conduct is under investigation (ie whether there is a pre-existing investigation) and by which authority. Therefore, in order to provide certainty for businesses, all initial leniency enquiries and applications, whether for types A, B or C leniency, should *begin* with the CMA.

21. Put simply, this means that **all businesses should approach the CMA for leniency in the first instance in order to secure their place in the leniency queue**. From that point onwards, the CMA and any relevant sectoral regulators will work together closely.

22. In the event that any initial leniency enquiries or leniency applications are made to a sectoral regulator, the sectoral regulator will immediately direct the person making the leniency enquiry or leniency application to the CMA. This approach ensures that the applicant's place in the leniency queue is determined by the order in which any business applied **to the CMA** for leniency.

23. However, given that CA98 cases may be investigated by either the CMA or the sectoral regulators, it would be neither sensible nor workable for the CMA to assess whether the conditions for leniency are met going forward, in a case for which it is no longer responsible.

24. Therefore, prior to case allocation under the Concurrency Regulations, the CMA will be responsible for the following, in consultation with all other relevant sectoral regulators:

— checking the availability of leniency and the grant of any provisional marker;

— the confirmation of any provisional marker (ie the grant of a confirmed marker);

— determining the scope of any confirmed marker; and

— where appropriate, the withdrawal of any marker.

25. Once a case has been allocated under the Concurrency Regulations:

— all initial leniency enquiries should still be made to the CMA.[9] In the event that any initial leniency enquiries or leniency applications are made to a sectoral regulator, the sectoral regulator will immediately direct the person making the leniency enquiry or leniency application to the CMA. This approach ensures that the applicant's place in the leniency queue is determined by the order in which any business applied **to the CMA** for leniency;

— the CMA will be responsible for the grant of any provisional marker, before handing the matter over to the authority to which the case has been allocated (if that is an authority other than the CMA);

— the authority to which the case has been allocated will be responsible for:

- the confirmation of any provisional marker (ie, the grant of a confirmed marker);
- determining the scope of any confirmed marker;
- where appropriate, the withdrawal of any marker; and
- the final grant or withdrawal of leniency.

NOTES

9 Where an existing leniency applicant is providing supplementary evidence after a case has been allocated, it should consider whether this might amount to a new leniency application (eg because it relates to a new product, party or time

period). If so, the applicant will need to apply to the CMA to secure its place in the queue.

CRIMINAL IMMUNITY

26. For the avoidance of doubt, the CMA will at all times remain responsible for the grant of criminal immunity, including where that criminal immunity arises 'automatically' in connection with a grant of type A immunity or is discretionary and arises in connection with a type B or type C leniency application, as described in OFT1495.

27. This means that all enquiries regarding criminal immunity and any application for criminal immunity should be **made to the CMA**.

28. In the event that such an enquiry or application is made to a sectoral regulator, the sectoral regulator will immediately direct the person making the leniency application or leniency enquiry to the CMA.

(II) COMMUNICATIONS

MEMORANDUM OF UNDERSTANDING BETWEEN THE COMPETITION AND MARKETS AUTHORITY AND THE OFFICE OF COMMUNICATIONS – CONCURRENT COMPETITION POWERS

2 February 2016

[3.245]

NOTES

FOREWORD

[3.246]

The changes to the United Kingdom's (UK) competition law system, introduced under the Enterprise and Regulatory Reform Act 2013 and in force since April 2014, are designed to improve the effectiveness of competition law enforcement in this country.

The Competition and Markets Authority (CMA) has competition law powers which apply across the whole economy. Sectoral regulators such as the Office of Communications (Ofcom) may exercise the competition law powers to enforce the prohibitions on anti-competitive agreements and on abuse of a dominant position, and to make market investigation references, concurrently with the CMA in those sectors for which they have responsibility.

The Enterprise and Regulatory Reform Act 2013 introduced a number of changes to enhance the working of concurrency and enable closer working between the CMA and sectoral regulators.

The CMA and the sectoral regulators have demonstrated their commitment to making the concurrency framework more effective through the establishment of the UK Competition Network (UKCN). This represents an enhanced forum for cooperation which will enable closer working with the objective of more consistent and effective use of competition powers across all sectors. In their statement of intent in December 2013, the members of the UKCN affirmed: 'The mission of the UKCN will be to promote competition for the benefit of consumers and to prevent anti-competitive behaviour both through facilitating use of competition powers and development of pro-competitive regulatory frameworks, as appropriate.'[1]

This memorandum of understanding (MoU) represents a further stage in the process of cooperation between the CMA and the regulators, setting out more practical detail on how the CMA and Ofcom will work together within the framework of competition law.[2]

The main purpose of this MoU is to establish an understanding between the CMA and Ofcom as to how this closer working will work in practice. It draws on the legislation which sets out the formal framework for how concurrency will operate and also, importantly, sets out our bilateral commitment to look for opportunities to work together, including within the framework of the UKCN, to promote competition for the benefit of consumers. We shall do this by the sharing of expertise, information, ideas and experience and each of us will commit to doing this efficiently and with a mutual regard for each other's statutory position and strategic objectives.

We believe that this MoU offers a valuable basis for that cooperation, in the interests of the CMA, Ofcom, the electronic communications, broadcasting and postal sectors and, most importantly of all, consumers.

Alex Chisholm	**Sharon White**
CEO, CMA	**Chief Executive, Ofcom**

NOTES

1 UKCN, Statement of Intent, 2 December 2013.

2 This MoU does not relate to 'regulatory appeals' – that is, the separate role that the CMA has in considering appeals against, or references relating to, proposed direct regulatory action by Ofcom under the sectoral statutes. This is a separate role, to be undertaken by the CMA panel, and the CMA is committed to ensuring that its cooperation with Ofcom – whether under this MoU (and under comparable MoUs agreed with other sectoral regulators), through the UKCN, or otherwise in connection with their concurrent powers – will not impair the impartiality and fairness of the CMA's conduct of such regulatory appeals (or indeed of market or merger investigations undertaken by the CMA panel).

MEMORANDUM OF UNDERSTANDING BETWEEN THE COMPETITION AND MARKETS AUTHORITY AND THE OFFICE OF COMMUNICATIONS

PURPOSE OF THIS MEMORANDUM OF UNDERSTANDING

[3.247]

1. This MoU sets out working arrangements between the CMA and Ofcom in relation to:

Part 3 CMA and other Guidelines

(a) their concurrent powers to apply the prohibitions on agreements that prevent, restrict or distort competition and on the abuse of a dominant position, under the Chapter I prohibition and the Chapter II prohibition of the Competition Act 1998 and under Article 101 and Article 102 of the Treaty on the Functioning of the European Union – referred to in this MoU as the 'competition prohibitions'; and

(b) their concurrent powers to undertake market studies, and to make references to the CMA for the constitution of a CMA group to conduct an in-depth market investigation into single or multiple markets for goods or services in the United Kingdom (UK) under the Enterprise Act 2002 – referred to in this MoU as the 'market provisions';

in the electronic communications, broadcasting and postal sectors.

2. This MoU is not intended to have legal effect.

3. This MoU is to be read alongside other material concerning the relations between the CMA and Ofcom, including: the Communications Act 2003; the Postal Services Act 2011; the Competition Act 1998; the Enterprise Act 2002; the Enterprise and Regulatory Reform Act 2013; the Competition Act 1998 and Other Enactments (Amendment) Regulations 2004; the Competition Act 1998 (Concurrency) Regulations 2014, referred to in this MoU as the concurrency regulations; the CMA's guidance on concurrent application of competition law to regulated industries, referred to in this MoU as the concurrency guidance,[3] and Ofcom's guidelines for the handling of competition complaints and complaints concerning regulatory rules.[4] This MoU supplements and does not supplant that material.

4. The arrangements covered by this MoU are, wherever possible, set out in terms providing sufficient flexibility for the relationship between Ofcom and the CMA to develop in the light of experience. The CMA and Ofcom commit to review these arrangements from time to time to evaluate their continuing fitness for purpose. Such review can be initiated at the request of the CMA, Ofcom or a member of the UKCN. This MoU may only be revised by agreement between the CMA and Ofcom.

5. Nothing in this MoU applies in relation to the functions of the CMA in its separate role of considering appeals against, or references related, to proposed action by Ofcom under the sectoral statutes. The CMA and Ofcom acknowledge the importance of maintaining the CMA's impartiality and fairness in carrying out those functions, and indeed of market or merger investigations undertaken by the CMA panel.

6. The arrangements between the CMA and Ofcom in relation to their concurrent consumer enforcement powers are set out in a separate MoU, and the CMA's guidance on merger jurisdiction and procedure sets out how the CMA and Ofcom will work together on mergers in the communications sectors.

NOTES

3 CMA (2014), *Regulated industries: Guidance on concurrent application of competition law to regulated industries* (CMA10).

4 Ofcom (25 July 2012), *Enforcement Guidelines*.

CONTEXT

7. This MoU operates within the framework of the legislative provisions referred to in paragraph 1 and any other applicable sector-specific legislation from time to time.

Role of the CMA

8. The CMA is a non-ministerial department, established under the Enterprise and Regulatory Reform Act 2013.

9. The CMA works to promote competition for the benefit of consumers, both within and outside the UK, to make markets work well for consumers, businesses and the economy.

10. The CMA's statutory responsibilities, in so far as relevant to the matters that are the subject of this MoU, include:

(a) investigating where there may be breaches of the competition prohibitions; and

(b) conducting market studies and market investigations where there may be competition and consumer problems.

11. In connection with its statutory responsibilities, the CMA will cooperate with sectoral regulators and encourage sectoral regulators to use their powers, including their power to apply the competition prohibitions, in the interests of competition for the benefit of consumers.

Role of Ofcom

12. Ofcom is the independent national regulatory authority for the UK's communications industries, with responsibilities across broadcasting (television and radio), telecommunications, spectrum and postal services. Ofcom is also a national competition authority with concurrent powers with the CMA to enforce competition law in the sectors which it regulates.

13. Ofcom's principal duties, set out in the Communications Act 2003, are to further the interests of citizens in relation to communications matters and to further the interests of consumers in relevant markets, where appropriate by promoting competition.

14. In relation to postal services, Ofcom's primary duty is to carry out its functions in a way that it considers will secure the provision of a universal postal service. Where it appears to Ofcom that, in relation to the carrying out of any of its functions in relation to postal service, that any of the general duties (including the principal duties set out above) conflict with its duty under section 29(1) of the Postal Services Act 2011 to secure the provision of a universal postal service, Ofcom must give priority to that latter duty.

15. Ofcom's role includes securing:

- the optimal use for wireless telegraphy of the electro-magnetic spectrum;
- that a wide range of electronic communications services is available throughout the UK;
- that a wide range of TV and radio services of high quality and wide appeal are available in the UK;
- that sufficient plurality in the providers of different television and radio services is maintained;
- adequate protection for members of the public and others against offensive or harmful material;
- that a universal postal service is provided in the UK; and
- adequate protection for members of the public and others against unfair treatment in programmes or unwarranted infringement of privacy.

16. Pursuant to section 371(10) of the Communications Act 2003, the duties set out above do not apply when Ofcom is carrying out its concurrent functions under the Competition Act 1998 or Article 101 and 102 of the Treaty on the Functioning of the European Union.[5]

NOTES

5 Save that Ofcom is permitted to have regard to any of the matters in respect of which a duty is imposed by section 3(1) to (4) of the Communications Act 2003 or section 29 of the Postal Services Act 2011 if it is a matter to which the CMA is entitled to have regard in the carrying out of its competition law functions – see section 371(11) of the Communications Act 2003.

AIMS

17. The Enterprise and Regulatory Reform Act 2013, as well as establishing the CMA, made provision for the better working of the CMA's and the sectoral regulators' concurrent powers in the regulated sectors; specifically, the Act: 'strengthens the role of the CMA and enhances the emphasis on early and proper consideration of the use of anti-trust powers (under Part 1 of the CA 1998 (i.e. the competition prohibitions) by the sector regulators.'[6]

18. It is one of the strategic goals of the CMA, announced on its establishment on 1 October 2013, to extend the frontiers of competition into new areas, including by working with sectoral regulators to ensure fuller use of competition law and policy in sectoral markets.[7]

19. The government's strategic steer to the CMA, issued on 1 December 2015, says that the CMA should build 'a strong dialogue with sectoral regulators using the UKCN to ensure that the overall competition regime is coordinated and regulatory practices complement each other.'[8]

20. The sectoral regulators and the CMA, working together in the UKCN established in 2013 (with Monitor having observer status), declared that: 'The mission of the UKCN will be to promote competition for the benefit of consumers and to prevent anti-competitive behaviour both through facilitating use of competition powers and development of procompetitive regulatory frameworks, as appropriate.'[9]

21. The CMA and Ofcom seek to use their respective powers to achieve more competitive outcomes in the electronic communications, broadcasting and postal sectors for the benefit of consumers so as to make markets in those sectors work well for consumers, businesses in the sector and businesses that use those services and the economy in which those services play an important part. It is the view of the CMA and Ofcom that such competitive outcomes can be achieved by various tools, including: their concurrent competition law powers under the competition prohibitions, the market provisions and merger control, but also through other tools such as direct regulatory action by Ofcom including through enforcement of regulatory obligations (for example, in providing for third party access to networks) and liberalisation measures introduced under national and European Union legislation.

22. This MoU aims to further the attainment of these objectives, and to make the changes introduced by the Enterprise and Regulatory Reform Act 2013 work effectively, maximising the complementary skills of the CMA and Ofcom, including through:

(a) promoting cooperation and coordination between the CMA and Ofcom when dealing with cases of suspected anti-competitive behaviour for which they have concurrent powers;
(b) promoting cooperation and coordination between the CMA and Ofcom when dealing with market studies and market investigation references for which they have concurrent powers;
(c) facilitating the efficient and effective handling of cases of suspected anti-competitive behaviour within the electronic communications, broadcasting and postal services markets;
(d) avoiding duplication of activity, wherever possible; and
(e) ensuring transparency as to the respective roles of the CMA and Ofcom for individuals and consumers affected.

NOTES

6 Enterprise and Regulatory Reform Act 2013 Explanatory Notes, paragraph 370.

7 Statement by Alex Chisholm, Chief Executive of the CMA, CMA mission and strategy, 1 October 2013.

8 Department for Business, Innovation and Skills, Strategic Steer for the Competition and Markets Authority, in Annex A to the *Government's response to the Consultation on the Strategic Steer to the CMA*, 1 December 2015, page 11

9 UKCN, Statement of Intent, 2 December 2013.

GENERAL COOPERATION

23. In addition to the provisions for cooperation between the CMA and Ofcom specific to particular powers of the CMA and Ofcom, as set out in this MoU, the CMA and Ofcom are committed to the following general principles and practices for cooperation between themselves in respect of the sectors for which Ofcom has responsibility.

24. Officials of the CMA and Ofcom will meet and communicate, at appropriate levels of seniority, to discuss matters of mutual interest, both through the UKCN and bilaterally. A framework for such meetings will, as far as possible, be determined in advance so as to ensure attendance at the appropriate level and expertise.

25. The CMA and Ofcom will, in respect of the electronic communications, broadcasting and postal sectors, always consult each other:

(a) before the initial exercise of concurrent competition law powers in all cases where it appears that they have concurrent jurisdiction and where there are reasonable grounds for suspecting an infringement of the competition prohibitions; and

(b) before launching a market study under the Enterprise Act 2002.[10]

26. Where either the CMA or Ofcom exercises its concurrent powers, the CMA and Ofcom will, to the extent permitted by law, engage with each other in open dialogue and by sharing relevant information as appropriate. This engagement may include attendance at internal meetings held by the investigating authority (ie the authority to which a case is allocated) by the supporting authority (ie the other authority which would be competent to exercise concurrent powers in relation to the case), in order to discuss the case as envisaged at paragraph 3.31 of the concurrency guidance. The supporting authority will not generally attend the investigating authority's constitutional decision-making meetings, meetings of governance bodies or meetings with external parties such as those under investigation or complainants. Attendance by the supporting authority at any meeting is at the discretion of the investigating authority.

27. The CMA and Ofcom will consult each other at an early stage on any issues that might have significant implications for the other. For example, where the CMA undertakes a market study which relates to a sector other than the electronic communications, broadcasting and postal sectors but which may have a significant impact on any of those sectors, the CMA will inform Ofcom and share appropriate information relating to that market study with Ofcom to the extent permitted by law.

28. Within the spirit of broader collaboration for the purposes of the promotion of competitive outcomes, the CMA and Ofcom will commit to discuss and share other relevant information, where legally permissible to do so, but subject to the need not to impair the impartiality and fairness of the CMA in carrying out the functions referred to in paragraph 5 of this MoU.

NOTES

[10] Instigation of a market study occurs on the publication of a market study notice, as defined in section 130A of the Enterprise Act 2002.

PART A – COOPERATION IN RELATION TO THE COMPETITION PROHIBITIONS (COMPETITION ACT 1998 AND ARTICLES 101 AND 102 OF THE TREATY ON THE FUNCTIONING OF THE EUROPEAN UNION)

CASE ALLOCATION

Basis of allocation

[3.248]

29. The CMA and Ofcom will endeavour to reach agreement on which authority will exercise its concurrent competition powers in respect of any particular case, under regulation 4(2) of the concurrency regulations. They will do so in a spirit of constructiveness and cooperation, while acknowledging the CMA's ultimate powers under regulations 5 and 8 of the concurrency regulations.

30. Their determination of which authority will exercise its powers will be based on assessing which authority is better placed to exercise those powers, having regard to the factors set out in paragraph 3.22 of the concurrency guidance. Specifically, the factors include:

- the sectoral knowledge of a regulator and the CMA;
- whether the case affects more than one regulated sector and/or non-regulated sectors not subject to competition law;
- previous contacts between the parties or complainants and a regulator or the CMA;
- experience with dealing with any of the undertakings which may be involved in the proceedings;
- experience with dealing with any similar issues which may be involved in the proceedings;
- whether the CMA considers it necessary to exercise Part 1 functions in relation to a case in order to develop UK competition policy or to provide a greater deterrent and precedent effect for the benefit of competition and consumers, either within the relevant regulated sector, or more widely;
- whether the case being allocated to the CMA and supported by the relevant regulator (or vice versa) will provide the best combination of competition and sector-specific expertise.

31. The CMA and Ofcom envisage that other factors may appear relevant in the light of practical experience and that, if so, such factors may be chosen to supplement or supplant the factors set out above and in paragraph 3.22 of the concurrency guidance.

Procedure for allocation

32. Where either the CMA or Ofcom has decided, on the basis of information in its possession, that there are reasonable grounds for suspecting that one of the competition prohibitions has been infringed (the reasonable suspicion test),[11] in relation to the electronic communications, broadcasting and postal services sectors, it will disclose to the other (ie receiving authority) sufficient information:

(a) to enable the receiving authority to understand the basis on which the disclosing authority has decided that the reasonable suspicion test is met; and

(b) for there to be an informed discussion on which authority (if either) is best placed to proceed in respect of the case.

33. The disclosing authority will provide this information within ten working days after it has decided that the reasonable suspicion test is met, whether or not it proposes to exercise concurrent powers.[12] Nothing in this paragraph prevents the CMA and Ofcom discussing the case prior to such a decision, subject to paragraph 46 below.

34. Within seven working days from receipt of the information described under paragraph 32, the receiving authority will respond in writing, settling out its initial view on the case and how it should be allocated and identifying any further information which it requires.

35. The CMA and Ofcom will endeavour to agree which authority will exercise its concurrent competition powers in relation to the case, as provided for in regulation 4(2) of the concurrency regulations, as soon as possible and in any event no later than one month from disclosure of the information described under paragraph 32. Other than in exceptional circumstances (which shall be set out in writing), the CMA will initiate the procedure set out in regulation 5 of the concurrency regulations if agreement is not reached within two months of the disclosing authority first receiving sufficient information in connection with a complaint to enable it to decide that the reasonable suspicion test is met.

36. The procedure for agreeing the transfer of a case that is already in progress from the CMA to Ofcom, or from Ofcom to the CMA, is as set out in regulation 7 of the concurrency regulations and in paragraph 3.32 of the concurrency guidance.

37. The procedure for the CMA to direct the transfer to itself from Ofcom, of a case that is already in progress, is as set out in regulation 8 of the concurrency regulations.

NOTES

[11] As provided in section 25 of the Competition Act 1998.

[12] As provided in regulation 9 of the Concurrency Regulations.

Implications of allocation

38. Any agreement or determination as to case allocation, under regulations 4, 5, 7 or 8 of the concurrency regulations, shall be notified to the person who has provided the information resulting in the case (for example, the person making a complaint), and so far as appropriate and lawful to any other affected person, by the authority which is exercising its concurrent competition powers in relation to the case, as soon as reasonably practicable.

39. Case allocation determines which of the CMA and Ofcom is to exercise concurrent functions and make any decisions under the competition prohibitions. The CMA or Ofcom will be publicly identified as having such responsibility if and when any such investigation is announced. The CMA and Ofcom envisage that, whichever authority has responsibility for a particular case, they and their officials will work cooperatively with each other on the case, pooling their expertise including as described in paragraphs 54 to 60 of this MoU and in paragraph 3.33 to 3.35 of the concurrency guidance.

SHARING INFORMATION

Principles of information sharing

40. The effective sharing of information between the CMA and Ofcom is fundamental to the successful exercise of their concurrent competition powers. It is needed both for the appropriate allocation of cases, as described in paragraphs 32 to 37 of this MoU, and for the successful handling of cases once allocated to make optimal use of the complementary experience and expertise of the two authorities.

41. The CMA and Ofcom are committed, in addition to their legal obligations to share information (set out in regulation 9 of the concurrency regulations), to open dialogue and continuing liaison, both bilaterally and through the UKCN, with a view not only to handling specific cases but to promoting competition, for the benefit of consumers in the electronic communications, broadcasting and postal sectors.

Information sharing mechanism – general liaison

42. The CMA and Ofcom recognise the importance of meeting regularly to share information on matters relevant to competition in the electronic communications, broadcasting and postal sectors, and to keep each other abreast of relevant work which they are considering or currently undertaking.

43. The CMA and Ofcom will meet regularly at multiple levels, bilaterally and through the UKCN.

44. The CMA and Ofcom will each designate in its organisation a relationship manager at official level to take responsibility for relations between the two authorities. In each authority, the relationship manager's responsibilities will include (but not be limited to):

(a) maintaining an overview of joint projects between the two authorities and matters of mutual interest;

(b) maintaining an overview of the authority's contacts from all areas of joint working and mutual interest; and

(c) holding meetings with the relationship manager in the other authority from time to time (whether bilaterally or in the context of the UKCN) to identify potential new issues with a view to circulating information to appropriate individuals within each organisation.

45. The existence of relationship managers does not in any way preclude direct communication between other staff at the CMA and Ofcom.

46. For the purposes of sharing information pursuant to paragraph 32, ie in circumstances where the reasonable suspicion test is met, such information will be shared by the disclosing authority to the extent permitted by law and whether or not it proposes to exercise concurrent powers.[13] Where disclosure would be appropriate and permitted by law, the CMA and Ofcom may also share information regarding potential infringements of the competition prohibitions in advance of having reached a view as to whether the reasonable suspicion test is met. In circumstances where either the CMA or Ofcom has taken the view that a matter is not an administrative priority, irrespective of whether a view has been reached on whether the reasonable suspicion test is met, each may share the details of the matter with the other, or with any other authority which would be able to exercise concurrent competition powers in relation to that matter, to the extent permitted by law. Where leniency information is being shared under this paragraph, special considerations apply, as set out in paragraphs 52 and 53.

NOTES

[13] For the avoidance of doubt, this does not entail an obligation to inform the other party if the regulator is carrying out general monitoring activity, where there is no active consideration of exercising its concurrent powers.

Information sharing mechanism – handling specific cases

47. The procedures for information sharing for the purpose of case allocation shall be as set out in paragraphs 32 to 34 and 40 to 53 of this MoU.

48. When either the CMA or Ofcom is exercising its powers in respect of the competition prohibitions in a particular case in the electronic communications, broadcasting and postal sectors, each of them will share with the other any of the following information in its possession (to the extent permitted by law and subject to the confidentiality obligations in paragraphs 51 to 53 of this MoU):

(a) as a minimum, the matters referred to in regulation 9(1)(b) – (j) of the concurrency regulations, and in paragraph 3.49 of the concurrency guidance, complying with the time limits specified in paragraph 3.49;

(b) all other information which it reasonably believes to be relevant for the other to carry out its functions in the conduct of the case; and

(c) in the case of the authority which is exercising the powers, reports to the other on the progress of the case of sufficient frequency and detail to enable the other to be appropriately informed; the means and frequency of such reporting will be decided on a case-by-case basis and in the light of experience as this enhanced framework of collaboration and its supporting arrangements develop over time.

Information sharing mechanism – for know-how purposes

49. The CMA will maintain on its webpages a central database of decisions taken in cases under the competition prohibitions with a view to having an accessible body of know-how that will help ensure the effective and consistent application of competition law. The CMA and Ofcom will, to the extent permitted by law, contribute information to that in the way best calculated to achieve that objective.

50. In any event, the CMA will report on cases in the regulated sectors under the competition prohibitions in the annual concurrency report which it is required under statute to issue. Further provisions on the annual concurrency report are in paragraphs 61 to 63 of this MoU.

Information sharing – confidentiality constraints

51. Any disclosure of information under paragraphs 32 to 34 and 40 to 50 of this MoU, and any use by the recipient of such information, shall only be to the extent permitted by law, including by reference to the provisions of Part 9 of the Enterprise Act 2002, relevant sector-specific legislative provisions and any other provisions relating to the disclosure, handling and use of information (such as the Data Protection Act 1998 and section 118 of the Financial Services and Markets Act 2000, to the extent relevant).

52. Prior to disclosing information to each other, the CMA and Ofcom will not generally give the person to whom the information relates prior notice of its intention to make the disclosure. However, if the CMA or Ofcom consider it necessary or appropriate to pass leniency information to each other (or to another UK authority with concurrent powers), the transmitting authority will inform the applicant or its legal adviser first. Leniency information for the purposes of this MoU is any information which came into the possession of any of the CMA, its predecessors, Ofcom or any other public authority as a direct or indirect result of having been provided in the context of an application for leniency. It includes information obtained by the transferring authority as a result of investigative measures resulting directly or indirectly from an application for leniency.

53. In addition to the general provisions referred to in paragraph 51, where Ofcom or the CMA receives leniency information from the other (or from another UK authority with concurrent powers) for the purpose of applying the competition prohibitions or, in the case of the CMA, the cartel offence under section 188 of the Enterprise Act 2002, that information will not be used for any other purpose. This restriction on use also applies to any information obtained by the receiving authority as a result of investigative measures relating to the competition prohibitions or the cartel offence following the receipt of leniency information from the other authority. This does not affect the use that may be made by the CMA or Ofcom of information received from other sources or if the leniency applicant's consent is obtained.[14] Where the provision of leniency information to either the CMA or Ofcom affords or might, under certain conditions, afford the leniency applicant, its subsidiaries or its employees protection from sanctions (including a reduction in penalties) under the leniency programme operated by that authority and that information has been passed to another authority, the receiving authority shall afford the leniency applicant, its subsidiaries or its employees no lesser protection.

NOTES

[14] The use restriction in this paragraph is intended to govern the use of leniency information in the context of the concurrency arrangements. It is not intended to prevent the disclosure of such leniency information by either one of the CMA or Ofcom to the other (to the extent permitted by Part 9 of the Enterprise Act 2002 and in accordance with Leniency and no-action applications in cartel cases: OFT1495) for purposes other than the application of the competition prohibitions or the cartel offence. However, any such disclosure of leniency information would only be likely to be justified in exceptional circumstances, given the strong public interest in maintaining the incentives for undertakings and, in the case of the cartel offence, individuals to apply for leniency.

POOLING RESOURCES

54. Paragraph 26, above, and the concurrency guidance, provide for support to be provided by the supporting authority to the investigating authority when it is exercising its concurrent powers in a case. The CMA and Ofcom will endeavour, so far as is reasonably practicable and permitted by law, and in the light of their respective ongoing priorities and resource availability at the time, to share their resources with each other in the interests of the effective enforcement of competition law in the electronic communications, broadcasting and postal sectors, and more generally the promotion of competition for the benefit of consumers in those sectors, and to ensure that their resources and expertise are used most efficiently for that purpose. This is subject to the proviso that, as stated in paragraph 5, this does not apply in relation to the function of the CMA in its role of considering appeals against, or references related to, proposed action by Ofcom under the sectoral statutes.

55. As a consequence, where it has been agreed or determined that one of the authorities is to exercise its concurrent competition powers in relation to a case, that authority will, to the extent that there are reasonable resources available, receive appropriate practical assistance and support from the other in the handling of the case, as agreed on a case by case basis.

Secondments of staff

56. One means of the practical assistance and support that might be given, as referred to in paragraph 54 and 55 of this MoU, is the secondment of staff, in accordance with regulation 10 of the concurrency regulations and paragraphs 3.33 and 3.34 of the concurrency guidance.

57. The CMA and Ofcom agree that secondments may, on a case-by-case basis, be appropriate for this purpose, and will endeavour to meet each other's requests for secondments to the extent that they are reasonable and resources permit; this may include making provision for any secondee to be available to work for part of his or her time at his or her existing employer during the course of the secondment, for example on such cases that are in progress.

58. Requests for secondments should be made by the relationship manager of one authority to the relationship manager of the other, setting out the following information:

(a) The number of secondees requested.
(b) The period for which each one is requested.
(c) The level of seniority of each one.
(d) The nature of the expertise or experience of each one.
(e) The proposed payment arrangements.
(f) A brief explanation of why the resource requested cannot adequately be met by deployment of staff from within the requesting authority.

OTHER MUTUAL SUPPORT

59. In addition to the sharing of information, expertise, experience and the secondment of staff, the CMA and Ofcom will provide each other with more informal forms of support to enable them to carry out their competition law functions in relation to the electronic communications, broadcasting and postal sectors – in each case to the extent that it is appropriate and permitted by law, and that resources permit – including (but not limited to):

(a) answering specific queries from time to time;
(b) providing information or views on a specific sector or market, or an area of competition law or policy; and
(c) providing training on a specific sector or market, or an area of competition law or policy.

60. Such support may be requested and provided in connection with a specific case or with the promotion of competition more generally.

ANNUAL CONCURRENCY REPORT

61. The CMA is required by statute to publish a report every year, starting after its first year of operation in 2014/15,[15] containing an assessment of how the concurrency arrangements between the CMA and the sectoral regulators, as regards both the competition prohibitions and the market provisions, have operated during the year. This MoU refers to that report as the annual concurrency report. There is further provision on the annual concurrency report in paragraphs 3.55 to 3.62 of the concurrency guidance.

62. The CMA will consult, and cooperate with, Ofcom and with other sectoral regulators in preparing the annual concurrency report. In connection with this, the CMA will:

(a) prepare a draft of the annual concurrency report that it will send to Ofcom and other sectoral regulators seeking comments or suggestions on the content or conclusions of the annual concurrency report and giving them adequate time to comment or make suggestions;

(b) take account of any comments or suggestions it receives from Ofcom and other sectoral regulators and the CMA may seek further clarification on those comments or suggestions as appropriate;

(c) prepare a final version of the annual concurrency report for publication that takes account of its consultation of Ofcom and other sectoral regulators as appropriate; and

(d) make the annual concurrency report available on the CMA webpages.

63. Ofcom will cooperate with the CMA in the preparation of the annual concurrency report including (but not limited to) by way of:

(a) providing information and data on general market conditions and on the application of the competition prohibitions and the market provisions in the electronic communications, broadcasting and postal sectors;

(b) responding to reasonable requests for information and data; and

(c) providing to the CMA any comments and suggestions it may have in connection with the process described in paragraph 62 of this MoU;

in each case promptly so as to facilitate the timely production and publication of the annual concurrency report.

NOTES

[15] Enterprise and Regulatory Reform Act 2013 Schedule 4 paragraph 16.

VOLUNTARY REDRESS SCHEMES

64. In cases relating to investigations under the competition prohibitions in the electronic communications, broadcasting and postal sectors, both the CMA and Ofcom have the power to approve voluntary redress schemes. When either authority proposes to exercise these powers, it shall liaise with the other authority as appropriate and will have regard to its own guidance.[16]

NOTES

[16] The CMA's guidance on the approval of voluntary redress schemes (CMA40) states at footnote 7: 'The CMA expects that regulators will take this CMA guidance into account when producing their own guidance on the approval power.'

SHORT FORM OPINIONS

65. The CMA shall inform Ofcom following an initial enquiry for a short form opinion relating to the electronic communications, broadcasting and postal sectors. Where the CMA is considering providing such an opinion, it will discuss with Ofcom before deciding to do so. If the CMA then decides to produce an opinion, it will engage with Ofcom, the nature and degree of that engagement to be considered on a case-by-case basis. In all cases, the CMA will give Ofcom the opportunity to provide comments on a draft opinion.

PART B – COOPERATION IN RELATION TO THE MARKET PROVISIONS: MARKET STUDIES AND MARKET INVESTIGATIONS (ENTERPRISE ACT 2002)

HOW CONCURRENCY WORKS UNDER THE MARKET PROVISIONS

[3.249]

66. Ofcom has the power, concurrently with the CMA, to carry out market studies, to make market investigation references, agree undertakings in lieu of a reference and make recommendations to the government in relation to the electronic communications, broadcasting and postal sectors under Part 4 of the Enterprise Act 2002 (as do other sectoral regulators in relation to the sectors for which they are responsible).

67. Under the Enterprise Act 2002, the CMA and Ofcom may, in relation to the electronic communications, broadcasting and postal sectors, undertake market studies, and may make market investigation references to the Chair of the CMA for the constitution of a CMA group to conduct an in-depth market investigation into single or multiple markets for goods or services in the UK. The purpose of these investigations is to examine the market(s) and (where required) implement appropriate remedies where the CMA determines that the structure of the market(s) or the conduct of the suppliers or customers is harming competition.

68. When making a reference, the CMA or Ofcom, as applicable, must have reasonable grounds for suspecting that any feature or combination of features of a market or markets in the UK prevents, restricts or distorts competition in relation to the supply or acquisition of any goods or services in the UK (or in a part of the UK).

69. The cooperation between the CMA and Ofcom provided for in this Part B shall not extend to conduct that could reasonably be expected to impair the impartiality or the fairness of the CMA panel in conducting market investigations.

SUPER-COMPLAINTS

70. Section 11 of the Enterprise Act 2002 provides for a super-complaint to be made by a designated consumer body that any feature, or combination of features, of a market in the UK for goods or services is or appears to be significantly harming the interests of consumers.

71. Ofcom has a duty to respond to super-complaints made to it under the Enterprise Act 2002 if the complaint concerns the electronic communications, broadcasting and postal services sector.

72. The coordination of the CMA's and the sectoral regulators' super-complaint duties will be consistent with that for the market provisions generally to the extent appropriate and otherwise will be based on policies agreed and applied through the UKCN.

MUTUAL CONSULTATION

73. Ofcom and the CMA have a duty to consult each other before exercising concurrent functions under the market provisions.[17]

NOTES

[17] Section 370 of the Communications Act 2003.

SHARING INFORMATION

74. The provisions of paragraphs 42 to 46, 48 (excluding 4848(a)) and 50 of this MoU apply to information sharing under the market provisions as they do under the competition prohibitions.

POOLING RESOURCES

75. The provisions of paragraph 54 to 60 of this MoU apply to pooling resources under the market provisions as they do under the competition prohibitions.

76. Where the CMA and Ofcom intend to pool resources in order to exercise powers under the market provisions of the Enterprise Act 2002, they shall, at the outset of any such project discuss the arrangements for how they will pool resources and work jointly.

ANNUAL CONCURRENCY REPORT

77. The provisions of paragraphs 61 to 63 of this MoU apply under the market provisions as they do under the competition prohibitions.

OFCOM ENFORCEMENT GUIDELINES FOR COMPETITION ACT INVESTIGATIONS

(28 June 2017)

[3.250]

NOTES

See also: Ofcom's approach to enforcement (June 2017); Procedures for investigating breaches of competition-related conditions in Broadcasting Act licences (June 2017); Advice for complainants: guidance on submitting a compliant to Ofcom (June 2017). All three documents are available on the Ofcom website at: www.ofcom.org.uk/consultations-and-statements/category-2/ofcoms-approach-to-enforcement.

CONTENTS

SECTION 1: INTRODUCTION

[3.251]

1.1 Ofcom is the independent regulator and competition authority for the UK communications industries. It has concurrent powers with the Competition and Markets Authority (the "**CMA**") to investigate suspected infringements of competition law.

WHAT DO THESE GUIDELINES COVER?

1.2 These Guidelines set out the procedures Ofcom will normally follow in Competition Act investigations. Competition Act investigations are investigations into anti-competitive conduct and/or agreements under Chapter I and/or Chapter II of the Competition Act 1998 (the "**Competition Act**" or the "**Act**") and/or Article 101 and/or Article 102 of the Treaty on the Functioning of the European Union (the "**TFEU**").

OUR OBJECTIVES

1.3 We take enforcement action in respect of non-compliance with competition law to prevent harm to competition and consumers, and to remedy this where we can. We may also impose a penalty to deter non-compliance.

1.4 We seek to ensure that Competition Act investigations are conducted in a fair, transparent, efficient and timely way.

STATUS OF THESE GUIDELINES

1.5 These Guidelines take effect from 28 June 2017. They set out Ofcom's general approach to enforcement in Competition Act investigations and they are designed to be flexible. Where we depart from the approach set out in these Guidelines, we will explain our reasons for doing so.

1.6 These Guidelines are not a substitute for any regulation or law, and are not legal advice.

1.7 They will be kept under review and amended as appropriate in light of further experience and developing law and practice and any change to Ofcom's powers and responsibilities.

SECTION 2: WHY AND HOW OFCOM OPENS CASES

[3.252]

2.1 This section sets out why and how Ofcom decides whether to open a Competition Act investigation.

HOW OFCOM DECIDES WHETHER TO INVESTIGATE

2.2 We cannot necessarily pursue every possible issue that comes to our attention and must make decisions about whether to open investigations by weighing up the likely benefits of conducting an investigation against the resources that would be required, and the comparative benefits of using those resources in other ways. We make decisions about whether to open investigations on a case-by-case basis, having considered all the matters that appear to us to be relevant to whether or not we should do so.

2.3 The matters we will generally consider include the following, so far as they are relevant to the case concerned:

(a) The risk of harm arising from/seriousness of the alleged conduct. For example:
- the risk to the interests of citizens or consumers resulting from the alleged contravention (including whether that risk is immediate or not and whether it is direct or indirect), and conversely the direct and indirect benefit to consumers of our taking action (e.g. to deter similar conduct by others);
- whether the conduct is on-going;
- whether the allegation concerns conduct that is, or that appears to be, a repeated, intentional or particularly flagrant contravention or infringement;
- whether the business which is under investigation has a history of similar contraventions or infringements, or a demonstrated record of poor compliance;

(b) The strategic significance of addressing the alleged conduct and whether alternative proceedings are likely to achieve the same ends. For example:
- whether an investigation would help clarify the regulatory or legal framework for stakeholders;
- whether the issue that has been identified directly relates to Ofcom's broader strategic goals or priorities (including those within Ofcom's Annual Plan);
- whether there are other alternative proceedings that are likely to achieve the same ends, or deal with the same issues, as the potential investigation. This could include, for example, whether other agencies may be better placed to investigate the complaint or whether planned market reviews may address the potential harm;
- in the case of complaints in relation to the Chapter II prohibition and/or Article 102 of the TFEU, whether Ofcom has recently found (for example in a market review) that no communications provider (including the subject of the investigation) occupies a position of significant market power in the market which appears relevant to the complaint; and

(c) The resource implications of our conducting an investigation, for example, what resources (in particular what specialist resources) are required to conduct an investigation, given the need to do justice to the interests of all parties likely to be affected.

2.4 Where appropriate we will also consider other factors as well.

2.5 In addition, before opening an investigation, under section 25 of the Competition Act, Ofcom must be satisfied that there are reasonable grounds for suspecting that a competition law infringement has occurred.

2.6 Ofcom will also consider whether it is the best placed competition authority to handle the case under the concurrency rules.

2.7 Ofcom exercises its powers as the UK competition authority for the communications industries in accordance with the Concurrency Regulations[1] and the European Commission's Network Notice[2]. When considering whether to open a Competition Act investigation, we will consider whether Ofcom or the

CMA is best placed to act on a case.[3] In certain circumstances, Ofcom may pass details on to the CMA (or vice versa) where the two regulators agree to the transfer and subject to notifying the subject of the investigation under Rule 7 of the Concurrency Regulations.[4]

2.8 Where a case raises issues under Article 101 and/or Article 102 of the TFEU, Ofcom will apply the case allocation principles set out in the Network Notice to decide whether we, the CMA, a national competition authority from another Member State or the European Commission is well placed to act.

SOURCES OF INFORMATION

2.9 Information which could trigger a Competition Act investigation can come to Ofcom's attention from a number of different sources. For example, Ofcom may consider opening an investigation:

- where a business comes to us to let us know that they believe they have or may have breached competition law (a "self-referral");
- in response to a complaint by an industry stakeholder or whistleblower;
- in response to information provided to us by other bodies (for example, where other regulatory bodies, MPs, consumer organisations or the press draw our attention to complaints they have received about a particular issue);
- where routine monitoring by us gives rise to a concern about compliance; and/or
- where we identify a particular concern through other areas of our work.

Complaints and whistleblowing

2.10 As noted above, some of our investigations begin because we have received a complaint about a potential infringement of competition law by a business, from another business or a trade association. Guidance for stakeholders who wish to make a complaint is set out in the document *Advice for complainants: Submitting a complaint to Ofcom*, available here: www.ofcom.org.uk/__data/assets/pdf_file/0013/102514/Advice-for-complainants.pdf.

2.11 In addition, Ofcom has published guidance on how individuals working in the communications sector may contact us if they have concerns about possible wrongdoings at their own organisation (or their former organisation) and where they have been unable to raise or resolve those concerns internally.[5] Such disclosures can be made in confidence to Ofcom's Corporation Secretary. Further guidance for whistleblowers is set out in *Advice for complainants* document.

Self-referrals

2.12 An undertaking that considers it has or may have breached competition law may contact Ofcom with details.

2.13 In the context of suspected involvement in a cartel, this is known as an application for "leniency". By confessing, an undertaking could gain total immunity from, or a significant reduction in, any financial penalties Ofcom can impose if it decides that the arrangement breaches the Chapter I prohibition and/or Article 101. Confessing may also protect staff and senior individuals from criminal prosecution and/or competition disqualification orders against directors.

2.14 All initial applications for leniency should be made to the CMA in accordance with its published leniency process and procedure.[6]

2.15 The CMA's process for applying for leniency is not repeated here. Further information on the types of leniency which may be available, and the conditions which must be met to secure those benefits, is contained in the CMA's guidance on leniency applications and penalty guidelines.[7]

INITIAL ASSESSMENT

2.16 Prior to opening an investigation, Ofcom will first carry out an initial assessment of the issue(s) to ascertain whether there is sufficient concern to warrant committing our resources to an investigation of the relevant matters, having considered all relevant factors as explained in paragraph 2.3 above. We do not make a substantive decision on whether or not there has been a breach of competition law during this initial assessment phase.

2.17 As part of our initial assessment, we will normally give the business whose conduct we are considering the opportunity to comment on the relevant issue(s) and to provide information to assist us in deciding whether to open an investigation. Where we are carrying out an initial assessment following receipt of a complaint, we will also generally tell the subject of the possible investigation that we are doing so on the basis of a complaint, and will generally share a non-confidential version of the complaint submission with the subject for comment.

2.18 However, we may decide not to provide the subject with the opportunity to comment and provide information if we consider that we already have sufficient information to conduct our initial assessment and decide whether to open an investigation. This could be based on previous engagement with the subject about the relevant issues, for example, through informal engagement, which might in some cases explore issues similar to those we would explore during our initial assessment. We may also decide not to provide an initial opportunity for comment and to provide information where there are reasons to proceed to an investigation more quickly. This could be, for example, due to the risk of particular consumer harm or where we consider this may prejudice the conduct of any subsequent investigation, such as in cases where we may need to use our information gathering powers to obtain and preserve evidence prior to alerting the subject of the investigation.

2.19 Where we are assessing a complaint, there may also be cases in which we consider that it is not appropriate to provide the subject of the complaint with the opportunity to comment on the complaint submission. This could be, for example, for one or more of the reasons explained in paragraph 2.18 above. There may also be cases where it is important to safeguard the anonymity of the complainant such that it is not appropriate to share a copy of the complaint at this stage.[8] In such cases, where we decide to open an investigation, we would (subject to anonymity concerns) share a non-confidential version of the complaint submission with the subject once we have opened the investigation (or at an appropriate point of time after we have done so, i.e. after we have exercised our information gathering powers).

2.20 Where we have sufficient information to decide that we should not open an investigation without obtaining comments from the subject of the complaint (for example, because the scale of any possible consumer harm appears too low to merit the resource required to investigate), we will normally only inform the complainant of our decision not to open an investigation and would not invite any further comment.

2.21 We aim to complete our initial assessment as quickly as reasonably possible, but the length of time that this will take is likely to vary on a case-by-case basis based on the issues under consideration.

2.22 In cases where we decide that it is appropriate to give the subject of the possible investigation an initial opportunity to comment and to provide information on the issues under consideration (including in response to a complaint), we will write to the subject setting out how long it will have to comment, and how soon after considering any comments or information received we aim to take our decision on whether to open an investigation. We will also provide contact details for the case leader who will act as the main point of contact while we are making our initial assessment. We will provide the same information to a complainant where we are completing our initial assessment of a complaint we have received. In those cases, we expect to keep the subject and any complainant updated should our initial assessment take longer than expected.

2.23 We are not able to exercise our information gathering powers under the Competition Act prior to opening an investigation, although we expect businesses we are considering investigating to ensure that the information they provide to Ofcom during our initial assessment is accurate. We may also ask complainants to provide further information, and also expect complainants to ensure that the information they provide to Ofcom during our initial assessment is accurate. In some cases, we may meet the subject of the possible investigation and/or a complainant where we consider this will assist us in reaching a decision on whether to open an investigation.

2.24 We do not publish details of, or comment publicly on, the matters we are considering during our initial assessment phase.

RESOLUTION THROUGH MEANS OTHER THAN FORMAL ENFORCEMENT ACTION

2.25 In some cases, Ofcom may be able to resolve an issue without the need for formal enforcement action. For example, we may be satisfied that the business has taken, or has offered assurances that it will take, appropriate steps to address any concerns we have identified such that there is no need for further action (although there may be a period of compliance monitoring).

2.26 In such cases, we will normally write to the business whose conduct we have been considering and any complainant to explain the basis on which we have decided not to proceed to formal enforcement action, and the circumstances in which we might reconsider the need to take formal enforcement action in future if relevant (for example, in the event that the organisation did not take the steps which it had said that it would or we received further evidence of a potential breach of competition law).

2.27 Such informal action will generally not involve Ofcom taking any decision about whether or not competition law has been breached.

2.28 Where Ofcom has decided not to pursue formal enforcement action in relation to an issue as a result of informal resolution, but we later become aware of further issues relating to the same or a similar issue, we may take formal enforcement action at that stage. If we did so, we would generally take into account any failure on the part of the relevant business to abide by assurances previously given to us relating to this conduct.

2.29 We may publish details of assurances that have been given about the steps the relevant business has taken and/or will take to address the issue, for example where we consider this would be in the interests of potentially affected customers or consumers more generally. We will usually inform the business concerned shortly before (and no more than one working day before) publication on Ofcom's website that we will be doing so, and provide them with a copy of the intended text for information only at that stage.

NEXT STEPS FOLLOWING OFCOM'S DECISION ON WHETHER TO OPEN AN INVESTIGATION

2.30 A senior member of Ofcom's executive with appropriate Board-delegated authority will decide whether to open an investigation. Typically, this will be the person who will be responsible for overseeing the investigation.

2.31 Where we decide not to open an investigation following our initial assessment, we will normally inform the business whose conduct we have been considering and any complainant, but will not usually give them the opportunity to comment before we take our decision.

2.32 Ofcom will not usually publicise a decision not to open an investigation unless the fact that a complaint has been made has been made public by either the complainant or the business that we were considering investigating, or a potential investigation is the subject of press speculation, and we consider we should clarify the position. In such cases, we would usually inform the subject of the investigation shortly before (and no more than one working day before) publication on Ofcom's website that we will be doing so, and provide them with a copy of the intended text for information only at that stage.

2.33 In most cases, when Ofcom decides to open an investigation, we will inform the subject and any complainant by sending them each a case opening letter explaining the scope of Ofcom's investigation, who the case leader and case supervisor are (as discussed further at paragraph 3.5 below) and next steps. However, there may be some cases where we delay doing so if we consider it may prejudice our ability to carry out an investigation, for example in cases where we may need to use our information gathering powers to obtain and preserve evidence prior to alerting the subject.

2.34 Shortly after sending the case opening letter(s), we will generally also announce that we have opened an investigation on the Competition and Consumer Enforcement Bulletin (**CCEB**) section of our website[9] (although we may delay doing so if we consider it may prejudice our ability to carry out an investigation). The case opening announcement will typically include the following details:

(a) the identity of the subject of the investigation;
(b) the identity of any complainant[10];
(c) whether the case is being investigated under Chapter I and/or Chapter II of the Act (and/or Article 101 and/or 102 of the TFEU);
(d) the scope of the investigation; and
(e) the case leader's contact details.[11]

2.35 Announcing the beginning of an investigation does not imply that Ofcom has formed any view about whether competition law has been breached.

2.36 If the investigation raises issues under Article 101 and/or Article 102 of the TFEU, Ofcom will notify the European Commission before (or without delay after) using its powers of investigation. In such investigations, Ofcom will co-operate with the European Commission and other national competition authorities in the European Competition Network (**ECN**) following the Network Notice. This may include the exchange of information by Ofcom within the ECN subject to the confidentiality and disclosure provisions of the Modernisation Regulation[12] and Part 9 of the Enterprise Act 2002 (the "**Enterprise Act**").

NOTES

1 The Competition Act 1998 (Concurrency) Regulations 2014 (SI 2014/536). These are available on www.legislation.gov.uk.

2 Commission Notice on cooperation within the Network of Competition Authorities (2004/C101/03) eur-lex.europa.eu/legal-content/EN/TXT/PDF/?uri=CELEX:52004XC0427(02)&from=EN

3 See further *Guidance on concurrent application of competition law to regulated industries* (CMA10), published March 2014 www.gov.uk/government/uploads/system/uploads/attachment_data/file/288958/CMA10_Guidance_on_concurrent_application_of_competition_law_to_regulated_industries.pdf and Modernisation (OFT442) www.gov.uk/government/uploads/system/uploads/attachment_data/file/284432/oft442.pdf

4 Ofcom has entered into a Memorandum of Understanding with the CMA in relation to our exercise of concurrent powers. See *Memorandum of understanding between the Competition and Markets authority and the Office of Communications – concurrent competition powers* (2 February 2016) www.ofcom.org.uk/__data/assets/pdf_file/0021/83523/cma_and_ofcom_mou_on_use_of_concurrent_consumer_powers_webversion.pdf

5 www.ofcom.org.uk/about-ofcom/policies-and-guidelines/procedure-for-making-a-disclosure

6 *Applications for leniency and no action in cartel cases* (OFT1495), www.gov.uk/government/uploads/system/uploads/attachment_data/file/284417/OFT1495.pdf

7 *Applications for leniency and no action in cartel cases* (OFT1495); and *OFT's guidance as to the appropriate amount of penalty* (OFT432) www.gov.uk/government/uploads/system/uploads/attachment_data/file/284393/oft423.pdf

8 Ofcom will consider requests from complainants to remain anonymous. However, it may not be feasible to carry out our initial assessment or open or conduct an investigation without revealing the identity of the complainant to the subject. This does not apply to whistleblowers.

9 www.ofcom.org.uk/about-ofcom/latest/bulletins/competition-bulletins

10 If a complainant has concerns about being publicly identified on Ofcom's website, the complainant should raise this concern with us, ideally at the time of making its complaint submission. For the avoidance of doubt, Ofcom will not publish a copy of the complaint submission itself.

11 Competition Act, section 25A(1)

12 Council Regulation (EC) No 1/2003 of 16 December 2002 on the implementation of the rules on competition laid down in Articles 81 and 82 of the Treaty eur-lex.europa.eu/legal-content/en/ALL/?uri=CELEX:32003R0001

SECTION 3: INVESTIGATING

[3.253]

3.1 This section sets out how Ofcom is likely to conduct an investigation. This includes guidance on Ofcom's likely engagement and contact with the subject of the investigation, complainants and third parties, and how we will gather information, publish information and deal with confidential information.

ENGAGEMENT WITH OFCOM DURING THE INVESTIGATION

3.2 We seek to ensure that Competition Act investigations are conducted in a fair, transparent, efficient and timely way. As set out in the relevant sections of this document, Ofcom may request representations from, and engage with, complainants and other relevant third parties.

3.3 We will endeavour to keep the subjects of our investigations up-to-date on the progress of the investigation. If we receive a request to meet to discuss the case, we will consider it. We will be prepared to meet with the subject of an investigation and complainants or other third parties, and/or provide written or verbal updates, where we consider it to be appropriate for reasons of fairness and transparency. We will decide whether and when it is appropriate to do so on a case-by-case basis, depending on the nature of the investigation and the stage that we have reached in our analysis.

3.4 We explain in the following sections of these Guidelines the type of engagement that businesses we are investigating, complainants and third parties can generally expect to have with Ofcom at key points during the investigation.

CASE TEAM

3.5 At the outset of the investigation, Ofcom will usually[13] inform the subject of the investigation, and any complainant, of:

- the case leader – this is the person who will be their main contact at Ofcom for the case during the course of the investigation; and
- the case supervisor – this is the person who will be overseeing the investigation.[14]

3.6 We will also explain how the Procedural Officer can be contacted (see paragraph 3.50 and Section 7 of this document).

3.7 At the same time Ofcom may ask the subject and any complainant to each nominate a principal point of contact for communications about the investigation.

3.8 If the case leader or the case supervisor changes during the course of the investigation, we will update the subject and any complainant.

3.9 Details of the case leader for an investigation will also be set out on the CCEB section of our website.

TIMESCALES

3.10 Ofcom recognises that it is important for all stakeholders that if we open an investigation we progress it in a timely manner and conclude it as soon as reasonably possible. We will give the subject and any complainant an indication of the likely timescale involved in completing an investigation – this will normally be at the point when we open the investigation.[15]

3.11 We will provide updates to the subject and any complainant on the progress of investigations, including when we expect to reach a specific milestone, and will provide updates where this changes.

3.12 We will also aim to publish on the CCEB section of our website details of how long we expect to take to reach key milestones in an investigation.

CHANGING THE SCOPE OF AN INVESTIGATION

3.13 We may widen the scope of an investigation if we become aware of new issues that warrant investigation, or reduce the scope if we decide that it is no longer appropriate to pursue particular aspects of the case. When we change the scope of an investigation, we will inform the subject of the investigation and any complainant, and will update the CCEB entry on our website. Where we consider it necessary for reasons of fairness we will give the subject and/or the complainant the opportunity to comment prior to deciding to change the scope of the investigation.

INFORMATION GATHERING

3.14 Ofcom relies on accurate information, provided in a timely manner, to carry out efficient investigations. Ofcom has powers to gather information under the Competition Act, and we can use these information gathering powers once we have opened a Competition Act investigation.

3.15 We will usually use these powers, once we have opened an investigation, to obtain relevant information to help us establish whether a competition law infringement has been committed. However, we cannot require the production or disclosure of privileged communications[16] or require a party to provide responses that would require an admission that it has infringed the law.

Written information requests

3.16 Ofcom has the power, under section 26 of the Competition Act, to issue written information requests requiring a person to produce specified documents or information which we consider relate to any matter relevant to the investigation. This is the power we would expect to use most often to gather information during Competition Act investigations.

3.17 Ofcom will set a deadline by which the response to a written information request must be received. This will depend on the demands of the investigation timetable, and the nature and amount of the information we have requested.

Other information gathering powers

3.18 Ofcom also has powers under sections 26A to 28A of the Act to:

- require an individual connected with the subject of the investigation to answer oral questions on any matter relevant to the investigation;[17] and
- enter, and in some instances to search, business and domestic premises.

3.19 We would expect to use these powers less frequently, and we would expect to have regard to the CMA's guidance in this regard when exercising these powers.[18]

Power to require an individual to answer oral questions

3.20 Where we wish to question a connected individual, we will provide the individual with a formal written notice requiring them to answer questions at a specified place and time or immediately on receipt of the notice. The notice will explain what the investigation is about and give details of when and where the questions will be asked.[19]

3.21 Where the individual has a current connection with the subject of the investigation at the time the notice is given, Ofcom will also give a copy of the notice to the subject. We will take reasonable steps in the circumstances to provide the notice before the interview takes place, and in general Ofcom will provide a copy of the notice to the subject at the same time as, or as soon as reasonably practicable after, giving the notice to the individual.[20]

3.22 The individual may request to have their legal adviser present. Where an interview is to take place immediately on receipt of the notice, we may delay it for a reasonable time to allow the individual's legal adviser to attend.[21]

3.23 Ordinarily interviews will be recorded, but in circumstances where this is unnecessary or impracticable a contemporaneous note will be taken of the interview. The individual will be asked to read through and check any transcript or note of the interview and to confirm, in writing, that it is an accurate account of the interview. Ofcom will also normally ask the individual to identify any confidential information in the transcript.[22]

Powers to enter and search premises

3.24 Ofcom has powers under the Act to enter a business premises (without a warrant),[23] and to enter and search a business or domestic premises (with a warrant).[24]

3.25 If Ofcom is entering and/or searching premises, Ofcom's authorised officers will normally arrive at the premises during office hours. If Ofcom intends to use its powers to enter business premises without a warrant we will give the premises' occupier at least two days' written notice of such arrival.[25] On entry, Ofcom's authorised officers will provide evidence of their identity, written authorisation by Ofcom, and a document setting out what the investigation is about and describing what criminal offences may be committed if a person fails to co-operate. Where Ofcom has obtained a warrant, Ofcom's authorised officers will also produce it on entry.

3.26 The occupier may ask legal advisers to be present during an inspection. If the occupier has not been given notice of the visit, and there is no in-house lawyer on the premises, Ofcom officers may wait a reasonable time for legal advisers to arrive.[26] During this time, Ofcom's officers may take necessary measures to prevent tampering with evidence or warning other businesses about the investigation.

3.27 Where possible, the person in charge at the premises should designate an appropriate person to be a point of contact for Ofcom authorised officers during the inspection.

3.28 When entering business premises without a warrant, Ofcom's officers may require any person to:

- produce any document which might be relevant to Ofcom's investigation, and Ofcom's officers may take copies of or extracts from any document produced;[27]
- provide any explanation of any document produced; and
- tell them where a document can be found if Ofcom's officers consider it to be relevant to the investigation.[28]

3.29 When entering a business or domestic premises with a warrant, in addition to the powers set out in paragraph 3.28 above, Ofcom's officers may also search the premises for documents which appear to be of the kind covered by the warrant. Ofcom may take away from the premises:

- copies or original versions[29] of documents which appear to be of the kind covered by the warrant;
- copies or original versions of documents to determine whether a document is relevant to the investigation, when it is not practicable to do so at the premises;
- any relevant documents, or copies, contained in something else where it is not practicable to separate out the relevant document at the premises; and
- copies of computer hard drives, mobile phones and other electronic devices.[30]

Non-compliance with Ofcom's information gathering powers

3.30 Ofcom's information gathering powers under the Competition Act are a critical tool in obtaining information necessary to carry out a Competition Act investigation. We expect recipients to provide correct and complete information in response to written information requests by the given deadline, and to comply with Ofcom's other information gathering powers. Ofcom may take enforcement action against failures to respond properly to information requests, and to comply with its other information gathering powers.

3.31 Ofcom may impose a penalty on any person who fails, without reasonable excuse, to comply with a requirement imposed by our information gathering powers under the Competition Act. This may be either a fixed or daily penalty, or a combination of the two, depending on what is appropriate in the circumstances.[31] It is also a criminal offence punishable by fine and/or imprisonment to knowingly or recklessly provide false or misleading information, or to intentionally or recklessly destroy, dispose of, falsify or conceal documents, or to intentionally obstruct an officer exercising their information gathering powers to enter or search a premises.[32]

3.32 If we decide to impose a penalty for failure to comply with our information gathering powers, we will have regard to the procedure set out in the CMA's Statement of Policy on administrative penalties.[33]

CONFIDENTIALITY

3.33 Information provided to Ofcom during the course of a Competition Act investigation is often confidential. Ofcom will always consider whether disclosure of information about a particular business is necessary for the purpose of facilitating the exercise by Ofcom of our functions.[34] In particular, Ofcom may judge that it is necessary to disclose information gathered from complainants or other third parties to the subject of the investigation in order to allow the subject to respond to Ofcom's case. Similarly, Ofcom may judge that disclosure of information gathered from the subject of the investigation to a complainant and other third parties is justified in order to facilitate the carrying out by us of our functions.

3.34 When Ofcom is considering disclosing confidential information, we must consider the extent to which the disclosure of the information is necessary for the purpose for which we are permitted to make the disclosure. We must also consider the need to exclude from disclosure (as far as practicable):

- information whose disclosure we consider is contrary to the public interest;
- commercial information whose disclosure we consider might significantly harm the legitimate business interests of the undertaking to which it relates; or
- information relating to the private affairs of an individual whose disclosure Ofcom considers might significantly harm the individual's interest.[35]

3.35 If the subject of the investigation, any complainant or a third party provides us with information that they consider to be confidential, they should clearly identify this information and explain why they consider it to be confidential, in accordance with the relevant statutory definition.[36]

3.36 It is for Ofcom to determine what it is, and is not, appropriate to disclose in accordance with the statutory framework, and Ofcom may consider it appropriate to disclose information notwithstanding that a party has asserted confidentiality over it. We will decide on the best means of dealing with confidential information on a case by-case basis, in accordance with the relevant statutory framework, having regard to the respective interests of the party that has provided the confidential information, and of the subject of the investigation.

3.37 If Ofcom is proposing to disclose information which a party considers to be confidential, we will take reasonable steps to inform that party and will give it a reasonable opportunity to make representations on our proposal,[37] before making a final decision on whether to disclose the information. This decision will be made by the case team and/or the case supervisor, and will be communicated to the party concerned in advance of the disclosure being made. Where the decision is to disclose the information despite the party whose information it is continuing to object to such disclosure, we would give that party the opportunity to escalate its concerns to the Procedural Officer (in accordance with Section 7). We would expect to delay disclosing the information until the Procedural Officer has reached his/her decision. If we intended to proceed to disclose the information after taking these steps, we would inform the party concerned in advance.

3.38 We may request that we are provided with a non-confidential version of a submission if needed for the purposes of publication and/or disclosure. Such a non-confidential version should normally include suggested non-confidential summaries of information (for example "confidential details of contracts") or ranges of numbers, rather than simply removing the confidential information.

PUBLICISING CASES

3.39 Ofcom ensures that its regulatory activities are transparent and accountable. Publicising the action we take can also usefully draw it to the attention of parties who have relevant information, can help deter non-compliance in future and educate others about what can go wrong.

3.40 As explained at paragraph 2.344 above, when we open an investigation, we will typically publicise it on the CCEB section of our website.[38]

3.41 We will also publish updates regarding the progress of an investigation on the CCEB when we reach key milestones (such as when we issue a statement of objections, when we change the scope of an investigation, when we issue a final infringement decision or when we close a case). This is explained in more detail in the relevant sections of these Guidelines.

3.42 We may also issue media releases regarding the outcome of our investigations, for example where we consider this would be in the interests of potentially affected customers or consumers more generally.

3.43 We do not agree the text of CCEB updates or media releases with the subject of the investigation or any complainant.

3.44 We will ordinarily inform the subject of the investigation shortly, and no more than one working day, before publication on the CCEB that we will be doing so, and provide it with a copy of the intended text of the CCEB update for information only at that stage.

3.45 Where we consider an announcement to be potentially market sensitive, we will generally inform the subject after markets have closed, with publication at 7.00am on Ofcom's website and via the Regulatory News Service, just before markets open. Where the subject is a listed company in other jurisdictions, we will, where possible, seek to avoid publication during stock exchange hours in those jurisdictions.

3.46 There may be certain cases which we consider it would be inappropriate to publicise, for example because they are particularly sensitive and/or publicity could have a detrimental impact on third parties. We would inform the subject and any complainant if we intend to take this approach to an investigation. We expect these cases to be exceptional.

INVOLVEMENT OF THIRD PARTIES

3.47 Ofcom recognises that in some cases third parties may be directly affected by the outcome of an investigation and can play a valuable role by drawing issues to our attention and by providing us with relevant information during the course of an investigation.

3.48 Ofcom may seek input from relevant third parties – for example, from trade associations, competitors or customers of the subject of the investigation, in order to assist us in reaching a decision on the case. Ofcom will involve third parties in an investigation to the extent we consider appropriate in order to carry out our functions fairly, transparently and effectively.

HOW TO RAISE CONCERNS WITH OFCOM

3.49 If a subject of an investigation, a complainant or third party (where relevant) is dissatisfied with the way in which Ofcom is proceeding, they should usually raise their concerns in writing with the case leader or case supervisor in the first instance.

3.50 Where engagement with the case leader/case supervisor does not resolve a party's concerns about a significant procedural issue, it may contact the Procedural Officer. The process for doing so is set out in Section 7.

NOTES

[13] As noted above, there may be circumstances in which we decide not to do this until a later point in the investigation, for example where we consider this could prejudice the conduct of the investigation, such as in cases where we may need to use our information gathering powers to obtain and preserve evidence prior to alerting the subject about our investigation.

[14] As explained at paragraph 4.4 below, the case supervisor is the person responsible for overseeing the investigation and for deciding whether to issue a statement of objections.

[15] Although we may delay doing so where we consider this may prejudice the conduct of the investigation, such as in cases where we may need to use our information gathering powers to obtain and preserve evidence prior to alerting the subject of the investigation about our investigation.

[16] Competition Act, section 30

[17] An individual has a connection with the subject of the investigation if they are or were concerned in the management or control of the subject or employed by, or otherwise working for the subject. An individual has a current connection with the subject if, at the time in question, they are so concerned, so employed or otherwise so working (Competition Act, section 26A(6)).

[18] CMA8, March 2014, *Competition Act 1998: Guidance on the CMA's investigation procedures in Competition Act 1998 cases* (paragraphs 6.18 – 6.46) www.gov.uk/government/organisations/competition-and-markets-authority

[19] Competition Act, section 26A(1), section 26A(5)

[20] Competition Act, section 26A(2), section 26A(3), section 26A(4)

[21] Competition Act 1998 (Competition and Markets Authority's Rules) Order 2014 (SI 2014/458) (the "**CMA Rules**"), Rule 4(3), available at: www.legislation.gov.uk/id/uksi/2014/458

[22] If the individual has a current connection with the subject of the investigation, we will also send a copy of the transcript or note to the subject, giving it the opportunity to make confidentiality representations. In addition, if appropriate, we may send a copy of the transcript to the subject if the individual has a former connection to it.

[23] Competition Act, section 27

[24] Competition Act, section 28, section 28A. See also Competition Act, section 29. For the procedure for making an application to the High Court for a warrant see *Civil Procedure Rules, Practice Direction – Application for a warrant under the Competition Act 1998* (May 2004) and the Alternative Procedure for Claims in Rule 8 CPR, as modified by the Practice Direction.

[25] Competition Act, section 27(2). Ofcom may enter business premises without giving notice if it reasonably suspects that the premises are or have been occupied by the subject of the investigation and we have taken all reasonably practicable steps to give written notice but have not been able to do so (Competition Act, section 27(3)).

[26] CMA Rules, Rule 4(1)

[27] Ofcom's officers may also require any relevant information electronically stored to be produced in a form that can be read and taken away, and they may also take steps necessary to preserve documents or prevent interference with them.

[28] Competition Act, section 27(5)

[29] If we consider it is necessary to preserve the documents or prevent interference with them, or where it is not reasonably practicable to take copies on the premises.

[30] Competition Act, section 28(2), section 28A(2)

[31] Competition Act, section 40A. In setting the penalty we will have regard to *Administrative penalties: Statement of Policy on the CMA's approach (CMA4)* www.gov.uk/government/uploads/system/uploads/attachment_data/file/270245/CMA4_-_Admin_Penalties_Statement_of_Policy.pdf

[32] Competition Act, sections 42 to 44

[33] *Administrative penalties: Statement of Policy on the CMA's approach (CMA4)*

[34] Under Part 9 of the Enterprise Act, we must not disclose information relating the affairs of an individual, or any business of an undertaking, unless it is permitted by one of the prescribed "gateways" under that Part. The gateway under section 241 of the Enterprise Act provides that a public authority may disclose such information for the purpose of facilitating the exercise of its functions. This gateway also provides that the recipient of information that is disclosed by Ofcom for these purposes may not disclose the information further without Ofcom's consent.

[35] Enterprise Act, section 244

[36] Confidential information is defined by Rule 1 of the CMA Rules as: (a) commercial information whose disclosure Ofcom considers might significantly harm the legitimate business interests of the undertaking to which it relates; (b) information relating to the private affairs of an individual whose disclosure Ofcom considers might significantly harm the individual's interests; or (c) information whose disclosure Ofcom considers is contrary to the public interest.

37 CMA Rules, Rule 7

38 www.ofcom.org.uk/about-ofcom/latest/bulletins/competition-bulletins. Stakeholders who are interested in following the progress of our investigations can also subscribe to receive email notifications of changes to the CCEB.

SECTION 4: OUTCOMES OF INVESTIGATIONS AND THE DECISION-MAKING PROCESS

[3.254]

4.1 This section sets out the possible ways in which Ofcom may conclude a Competition Act investigation. This includes reaching a decision that there has been an infringement of competition law, a decision that there is insufficient evidence to find an infringement, a decision to close the case without taking a decision on the merits, and accepting binding commitments from the subject of the investigation to address our competition concerns.

4.2 In some cases, we may be able to reach a settlement with the subject of an investigation as a way of resolving a case, in circumstances where we think we have grounds to find an infringement of competition law. The process for settlement is set out in Section 5 of these Guidelines.

4.3 This section also sets out who will make key decisions during an investigation.

DECISION MAKERS

4.4 Ofcom will nominate a person to oversee the investigation and to decide whether to issue a statement of objections (the case supervisor), who will be a senior member of Ofcom's executive with appropriate Board-delegated authority.[39]

4.5 Following the statement of objections, Ofcom will nominate three different relevant persons to collectively make the following subsequent decisions:

- whether to issue a supplementary statement of objections;
- whether to issue a draft penalty statement; and
- whether to issue an infringement decision (including any penalty and/or directions).

These decision makers will comprise three senior members of Ofcom's executive with appropriate Board-delegated authority. They will not have been involved in the investigation nor be the person who is responsible for overseeing the investigation and making the decision to the issue the statement of objections.[40]

INVESTIGATION OUTCOMES

Statement of objections

4.6 Where Ofcom reaches the provisional view that the conduct under investigation amounts to an infringement of competition law, we will issue a statement of objections to the subject of the investigation.[41]

4.7 The statement of objections represents Ofcom's provisional view, which may change in light of subsequent representations made, or material provided by, the subject of the investigation (or complainants or other third parties where relevant) or any further evidence which comes to light. It allows the subject of the investigation to know the full case against it, and if it chooses to do so, to formally respond in writing and orally.

4.8 The statement of objections will state:

- which of the competition law prohibitions Ofcom considers has been infringed;
- Ofcom's reasons for considering that the conduct under investigation amounts to an infringement of competition law;
- the facts on which Ofcom has relied;
- the action Ofcom proposes to take, such as imposing a financial penalty (although Ofcom will not include a provisional determination of the amount of the penalty) and/or issuing directions, and our reasons for the proposed action; and'
- the period in which the subject of the investigation may make written representations to Ofcom on the matters referred to in the statement of objections and on the confidentiality of the information contained in the statement of objections.[42]

4.9 If the subject of the investigation is a company, Ofcom will send the statement of objections in hard copy to the Company Secretary, copied by email to our main contact, unless it has agreed otherwise with us.

4.10 Ofcom will not publish the statement of objections, but we will generally publish an update on the CCEB section of our website. Our update will normally explain that we have issued a statement of objections and include a summary of the infringement which Ofcom is minded to find. The CCEB update will also state that the subject of the investigation will have the opportunity to make representations on the statement of objections before we make our final decision.

Access to file

4.11 Ofcom will give the subject of the investigation a reasonable opportunity to inspect copies of disclosable documents on Ofcom's investigation file ("**access to file**").[43] We will usually give access to file at the same time as we issue the statement of objections. Access to file will usually be given by supplying the file by electronic means.

4.12 Disclosable documents are documents on Ofcom's file which relate to the matters contained in the statement of objections.[44] Ofcom may withhold a document:

(a) to the extent that it contains confidential information;[45] or

(b) if it is an Ofcom internal document.[46]

4.13 Ofcom may also exclude routine administrative documents[47] from the file and list these in a schedule which will be placed on the file. Ofcom will provide the subject with a schedule of external documents on its file which have not been disclosed as part of the access to file process.

Written representations

4.14 The subject of the investigation will have the opportunity to make written representations to Ofcom on the proposed findings in the statement of objections.[48]

4.15 The deadline for submitting written representations will be set by Ofcom having regard to the circumstances of the case, and Ofcom will give a longer period in more complex cases. Usually the deadline for the subject to submit written representations will be at least 40 days from the issue of the statement of objections. If Ofcom is unable to give access to file at the same time as we issue the statement of objections, the time for submission of written representations will not start to run until access to file has been given.

4.16 Where we consider it to be appropriate for reasons of fairness, we may provide complainants or relevant third parties with the opportunity to comment on a non-confidential copy of the statement of objections. This will typically be where they may have further information relevant to the proposed decision and therefore could provide informed comments on the statement of objections. Another example may be where Ofcom's provisional findings may have a direct impact on the economic interests of a third party, such as where we comment in the statement of objections on the conduct of an agent of the subject of our investigation which we consider has given rise to the potential breach.

4.17 In such cases, Ofcom would expect the complainant or the third party to enter into appropriate agreements with us limiting its use of and onward disclosure of the document. We will set deadlines for representations depending on the circumstances of the case.

4.18 We will not usually provide a complainant or third parties with copies of, or access to, the underlying evidence relied on, but may do so where appropriate for reasons of fairness.

4.19 We will provide any written representations on the statement of objections received from the complainant or a third party to the subject of the investigation, providing it with an opportunity for comment.

Oral hearings

4.20 Ofcom will offer the subject of the investigation the opportunity to attend an oral hearing to make oral representations on matters referred to in the statement of objections.[49] The oral hearing provides the subject with an opportunity to highlight directly to the final decision makers issues of particular importance to its case and/or to clarify the detail set out in its written representations.

4.21 Ofcom will normally ask the subject to confirm by a given date if it wishes to make oral representations, and will then set a date for the oral hearing, which will normally be held 10 to 20 working days after the deadline for written representations has elapsed.

4.22 The oral hearing will be chaired by the Procedural Officer[50] and will usually be held at the Ofcom offices in which the investigating case team is based.

4.23 The case supervisor, case leader and other members of the case team may also be present and may comment during the course of the hearing. The final decision makers will also attend the oral hearing. Other personnel from Ofcom may attend as appropriate, for example, legal advisers, economic advisers and/or technical experts, depending on the circumstances of the case.

4.24 The subject may bring legal advisers or other relevant expert advisers to the oral hearing to assist in presenting its oral representations, although Ofcom may ask that the subject limits the number of persons attending the oral hearing on its behalf to a reasonable number.

4.25 Complainants and other third parties will not usually be invited to attend the oral hearing.

4.26 Ofcom will agree an agenda with the subject in advance of the oral hearing which will include reasonable periods of time for the subject to make oral representations and for the Ofcom personnel present to ask the subject questions on its representations.

4.27 The hearing will be transcribed and the transcript will be provided to the subject of the investigation, giving an opportunity for comment on its factual accuracy.[51]

4.28 The Procedural Officer will prepare a report following the oral hearing assessing the fairness of the procedure followed in the hearing and on any procedural issues that have been brought to his/her attention.[52]

Disclosure of additional evidence

4.29 Where Ofcom acquires new evidence at this stage which supports the case contained in the statement of objections, and Ofcom proposes to rely on it to establish that an infringement has been committed, as part of its on-going obligation to provide access to file, Ofcom will put this evidence to the subject of the investigation and give it the opportunity to respond. The timeframe for responding will depend on the volume and complexity of the new evidence.

Supplementary statement of objections

4.30 In some cases, new information or evidence may come to Ofcom's attention after we have issued the statement of objections, which leads us to consider making a material change to the nature of the proposed infringement (such as evidence of a different or more serious infringement, or a material change in our reasoning for proposing to find a breach of competition law). In such circumstances, we would issue a supplementary statement of objections.

4.31 If we issue a supplementary statement of objections, we will provide the subject of the investigation with any new documents on the file in accordance with paragraphs 4.11 to 4.13, above. We would also provide the subject, and may provide the complainant and any interested third parties, with the opportunity to respond in accordance with paragraphs 4.14 to 4.28, above. The period of time for making written representations on any supplementary statement of objections would typically be shorter than the time given to respond to the statement of objections. We would also generally expect to publish a CCEB update as per paragraph 4.10, above.

Draft penalty statement

4.32 If, following investigation, Ofcom finds that there has been an infringement of competition law, it may impose a financial penalty on the subject of the investigation of up to 10% of its turnover in a relevant market.[53] In determining penalties, Ofcom is required to have regard to the CMA's guidance on how it calculates the appropriate amount of a penalty,[54] including consideration of any grounds for leniency.[55] We must also have regard to the seriousness of the infringement and the desirability of deterring the subject and other stakeholders from infringing competition law.[56]

4.33 Where Ofcom has said it is minded to impose a penalty in the statement of objections or any supplementary statement of objections, it will issue a draft penalty statement to the subject on the level of that penalty after considering any written and oral representations on the statement of objections and any supplemental statement of objections.[57] The draft penalty statement will set out the level of the penalty Ofcom is minded to impose and its reasons.

4.34 The subject will be offered the opportunity to make written representations on the draft penalty statement. The deadline for submitting written representations on the draft penalty statement will be set on a case-by-case basis and will allow the subject the opportunity to inspect any new relevant documents on the file.[58] However, the deadline for submitting written representations will typically be shorter than the time given to respond to the statement of objections. The subject will also be given the opportunity to attend an oral hearing, chaired by the Procedural Officer and conducted in accordance with paragraphs 4.20 to 4.28 above.[59]

4.35 Ofcom will not publish the draft penalty statement and will not comment publicly about issuing a draft penalty statement.

The infringement decision

4.36 After considering any written or oral representations on the statement of objections, any supplementary statement of objections and any draft penalty notice, if the final decision makers determine there is sufficient evidence to establish an infringement of competition law, Ofcom will issue a final infringement decision to the subject of the investigation.[60] If the subject is a company, we will deliver the infringement decision in hard copy to the Company Secretary, copied by email to our main contact, unless it has agreed otherwise with us.

4.37 Ofcom will also normally inform any complainant that we have reached a final decision on the investigation.

4.38 The infringement decision will state the facts on which Ofcom bases the decision and the reasons for our decision. It will also set out the reasons for any decision to impose a financial penalty on the subject and the level of penalty.[61] The infringement decision may also include directions setting out actions the subject must take to bring the infringement to an end, and the reasons for imposing these directions.[62]

4.39 Once the infringement decision has been issued, Ofcom will close the case and update the details on the CCEB section of our website. This will generally include a summary of the contraventions Ofcom has found and details of any penalty and/or directions imposed.[63]

4.40 Ofcom will also publish a non-confidential version of the infringement decision on the CCEB section of our website[64] once we have finalised the relevant redactions of any confidential information. We will generally inform the subject and any complainant in advance of the intended date of publication of the final decision.

Investigations that do not lead to an infringement finding

4.41 Not all of Ofcom's Competition Act investigations result in a finding that the business under investigation has infringed competition law. Ofcom may decide that we do not have sufficient evidence to find a competition law infringement or that it is appropriate to close an investigation without making a finding on whether the subject of the investigation has infringed competition law. Alternatively, we may accept binding commitments as to future conduct from the subject of the investigation which address our competition concerns.

No grounds for action decision

4.42 Ofcom may decide, either before or after we issue a statement of objections, that we do not have sufficient evidence to find a competition law infringement.[65] In these circumstances Ofcom will issue a provisional "no grounds for action decision" to the subject of the investigation stating the facts on which we base our provisional decision and the reasons for this proposed decision. We will invite written representations from the subject of the investigation on the matters set out in our provisional decision.

4.43 We will usually provide the complainant with a non-confidential version of the provisional decision and invite written representations on it. We may also provide other relevant third parties with a non-confidential copy and the opportunity to make written representations, for example where we consider the relevant stakeholder(s) may have information which would assist us in reaching a decision on the outcome of the investigation. The deadline for written representations will depend on the circumstances of the case. We will not usually provide access to the underlying evidence.

4.44 Ofcom will consider any written representations and if our view is that we still do not have sufficient evidence to find a competition law infringement, we will issue a final no grounds for action decision to the subject.[66] Ofcom will also normally inform any complainant that we have reached a final decision on the investigation. If the representations change our view, we will continue the investigation.

4.45 If Ofcom decides to issue a no grounds for action decision, we will close the case and publish details of this on the CCEB section of our website.[67] Ofcom will also generally publish a non-confidential version of the decision[68] once we have finalised the relevant redactions of any confidential information, and we will generally inform the subject and any complainant in advance of the intended date of publication.

Case closure without a decision on the merits

4.46 Ofcom may close an investigation without taking a decision on the merits of the case and without making a finding on whether there has been a breach of competition law.[69]

4.47 If we decide to close an investigation on this basis, we will usually write to the subject of the investigation and the complainant in advance setting out the reasons why we are minded to make a decision to close the investigation, and invite comments from them. The timeframe for comment may be short, particularly where we consider there is limited scope for comment on the reasons underpinning our proposed decision to close the investigation. We will also pass details onto the CMA for them to decide whether they wish to pursue the case further.

4.48 Ofcom will inform the subject that we have decided to close the case and will also normally inform the complainant that we have reached a final decision on the investigation.

4.49 In the majority of cases, a case closure decision of this type is likely to be a brief statement indicating case closure and the basis on which we have decided to close the case. We will publish details of our decision to close the case on the CCEB section of our website.[70]

Commitments

4.50 Ofcom may accept binding commitments which fully address our competition concerns from the subject of an investigation in relation to its future conduct.[71]

4.51 The subject may offer binding commitments to Ofcom at any time during an investigation up until a final infringement decision is made. However, Ofcom is unlikely to consider it appropriate to accept commitments offered at a very late stage in an investigation, such as after considering representations on a statement of objections.

4.52 Ofcom is likely to consider it appropriate to accept commitments only in cases where the competition concerns are readily identifiable, will be fully addressed by the commitments offered, and the proposed commitments can be implemented effectively and, if necessary, within a short period of time. Ofcom is very unlikely to accept commitments in cases involving secret cartels between competitors or a serious abuse of a dominant position.

4.53 The fact that the subject of an investigation has approached us to discuss commitments, and the substance of commitments, is not relevant to our consideration of whether an infringement has occurred. We will therefore not use any offer of commitments as evidence in any subsequent decision about the agreement or conduct under investigation.

4.54 If a subject would like to discuss offering commitments, it should contact the case leader in the first instance. If, following that, Ofcom considers that commitments may be appropriate, then (if a statement of objections has not been issued) Ofcom will send a summary of its competition concerns to the subject. Ofcom may discuss with the subject the form and content of any commitments offered in order to reach an agreement as to what might be acceptable to Ofcom.

4.55 If Ofcom proposes to accept the commitments offered, we will consult those likely to be affected by them, including any complainant. We will give those persons an opportunity to make representations within a time limit of at least 11 working days.[72] Ofcom will then discuss these representations with the subject of the investigation and indicate whether Ofcom considers that changes are required to the commitments before we would consider accepting them.

4.56 If the subject offers revised commitments with significant changes, we will consult affected persons and give them another opportunity to make representations, within a time limit of at least 6 working days.[73] We will discuss these representations with the subject.

4.57 The decision on whether to accept commitments will be taken by a senior member of Ofcom's executive with appropriate Board-delegated authority. Depending on the stage at which this decision is reached, this will generally be the person responsible for deciding whether there are grounds for action (who, as noted above, will typically be the person responsible for overseeing the investigation, i.e. the case supervisor), or the final decision makers referred to at paragraph 4.5 above.

4.58 If Ofcom decides to accept commitments, we will notify the subject of the investigation and publish the commitments on the CCEB section of our website.[74]

COMPLIANCE MONITORING

4.59 Where Ofcom has made an infringement decision or closed a case having accepted commitments or informal assurances, we may decide to put "it into compliance". The purpose of the compliance phase is to ensure that the subject of the investigation does not repeat behaviour that Ofcom has deemed to breach competition law, that it complies with any commitments or assurances given, and/or that it implements any directions imposed by Ofcom.

4.60 The process that we follow during the compliance phases will differ from case to case. The length of the compliance phase will depend on the circumstances of the case and the measures that are to be monitored. Generally, Ofcom will not grant extensions to any deadline set for compliance with a direction, unless we receive an application prior to the expiry of the deadline together with an explanation of why the deadline should be extended, including supporting evidence.

4.61 The CCEB section of Ofcom's website includes a section for cases in compliance, where we will publish details of significant developments.[75]

4.62 Once we consider that compliance has been established, we will close the case and update the CCEB section of our website accordingly.

NOTES

39 CMA Rules, Rule 3(1)

40 CMA Rules, Rule 3(2)

41 CMA Rules, Rule 5(1)

42 CMA Rules, Rule 5(2), Rule 6(1)

43 CMA Rules, Rule 6(2)

44 CMA Rules, Rule 6(2)

45 CMA Rules, Rule 6(1); see also Rule 1(1) for the definition of "confidential information"

46 CMA Rules, Rule 6(1)

47 Routine administrative documents will generally include correspondence setting up meetings and documents which do not relate to the substance of the matters set out in the statement of objections.

48 CMA Rules, Rule 6(1)

49 CMA Rules, Rule 6(3), Rule 6(4)

50 CMA Rules, Rule 6(5)

51 To the extent multiple parties are given access to file, we will ask the subject of the investigation for representations on the confidentiality of the transcript.

52 CMA Rules, Rule 6(6), Rule 6(7).

53 Competition Act, section 36(8), calculated in accordance with the Competition Act 1998 (Determination of turnover for penalties order) (SI 2000/309) (as amended by SI 2004/1259)

54 *OFT's guidance as to the appropriate amount of penalty (OFT423)*, www.gov.uk/government/uploads/system/uploads/attachment_data/file/284393/oft423.pdf

55 Competition Act, section 38(8)

56 Competition Act, section 36(7A)

57 CMA Rules, Rule 11(a)

58 CMA Rules, Rule 6(2), Rule 11(b)

59 CMA Rules, Rule 6, Rule 11(b)

60 CMA Rules, Rule 10(1)(a)

61 CMA Rules, Rule 12(2); Competition Act, section 36

62 CMA Rules, Rule 12(1); Competition Act, section 32, section 33

63 Competition Act, section 25A(4); CMA Rules, Rules 12(3), Rule 12(4)

64 CMA Rules, Rule 10(1)(b)

65 Depending on the stage at which this decision is reached, the decision maker may be the person responsible for deciding whether to issue a statement of objections (who, as noted above, will typically be the person responsible for overseeing the investigation), or it may be the final decision makers referred to at paragraph 4.5 above.

66 CMA Rules, Rule 10(4)

67 Competition Act, section 25A(4)

68 CMA Rules, Rule 10(5)

69 Depending on the stage at which this decision is reached, the decision maker may be the person responsible for deciding whether to issue a statement of objections (who, as noted above, will typically be the person responsible for overseeing the investigation), or it may be the final decision makers referred to at paragraph 4.5 above.

70 Competition Act, section 25A(4)

71 Competition Act, section 31A

72 Competition Act 1998, Schedule 6A, paragraph 2

73 Competition Act 1998, Schedule 6A, paragraph 3

74 Competition Act 1998, Schedule 6A, paragraph 7

75 www.ofcom.org.uk/about-ofcom/latest/bulletins/competition-bulletins/cases-in-compliance

SECTION 5: SETTLEMENT PROCEDURE

INTRODUCTION

[3.255]

5.1 In some cases, Ofcom may consider that it is appropriate to settle a Competition Act investigation. Settlement is a voluntary process for resolving a Competition Act investigation which leads to a formal, legally binding infringement decision.[76] It involves the subject of the investigation admitting it has breached competition law and accepting that the remainder of the investigation will follow a streamlined administrative procedure.[77] In such cases, Ofcom will apply a discount to the level of the penalty imposed on the subject[78] in light of the resource savings involved in following a streamlined administrative procedure.

5.2 Those who we are investigating are not under any obligation to enter into a settlement process or to settle, and Ofcom has broad discretion to decide whether a case is appropriate for settlement or to agree to settlement.

5.3 Settlement is distinct from leniency (as discussed at paragraph 2.13 above) and Ofcom's power to accept commitments under section 31A of the Competition Act (as discussed at paragraphs 4.50 to 4.58 above). Leniency and the use of settlements are not mutually exclusive – it is possible for a leniency applicant to settle a case under the Competition Act and benefit from both leniency and settlement discounts.

5.4 Where the settlement process is successful, the legally binding enforcement decision will refer to the fact that settlement has been agreed and will reflect the substance of any admissions made by the subject of the investigation for the purposes of the settlement.

5.5 In the event that the settlement process is unsuccessful, the case will revert to the usual process and the content of any settlement discussions will not be revealed to the final decision makers. However, any additional documentary evidence provided during the settlement process would go onto the case file and could be taken into account by Ofcom for the purposes of our final infringement decision. In addition, Ofcom may follow up any new competition law issues which come to light during the settlement process.

5.6 For the avoidance of doubt, settlement is not a negotiation with Ofcom about what infringements Ofcom might be prepared to find or not to find. Nor is it a negotiation about the level of the penalty which Ofcom would impose, nor is it equivalent to the type of discussions which take place between parties to litigation or potential litigation on a "without prejudice" basis for the purposes of seeking to resolve or avoid litigation.

REQUIREMENTS FOR SETTLEMENT

5.7 As a minimum, Ofcom will require the subject of the investigation to:

- make a clear and unequivocal admission of liability in relation to the nature, scope and duration of the infringement.[79] This would need to reflect Ofcom's position on the nature of the infringement(s) we are minded to find and the appropriate level of penalty (as explained further below);
- cease the infringing behaviour immediately from the date it enters into a settlement process with Ofcom and refrain from engaging again in the same or similar infringing behaviour;
- confirm that it accepts that there will be a formal and published finding of infringement against it, will pay a penalty and will comply with any directions imposed;
- confirm that it will accept a streamlined administrative process.[80] This will be decided on a case-by-case basis depending on the stage at which the settlement process is commenced, but would include streamlined access to file arrangements (for example we would expect to provide the subject with access to key documents we are relying on as appropriate for reasons of fairness and transparency), limiting written representations to manifest factual inaccuracies only, no oral hearing and no separate draft penalty statement after settlement has been reached. The person responsible for deciding whether to issue a statement of objections will also be the final decision maker in a settlement case;[81] and
- confirm that it accepts that it will no longer benefit from the settlement discount if it appeals the decision.[82]

HOW DOES OFCOM DECIDE WHETHER A CASE IS SUITABLE FOR SETTLEMENT?

5.8 Ofcom may consider settlement for any investigation in which we have reached a stage where we believe that we have a sufficient basis for giving notice of our proposed infringement decision and come to a preliminary view on an appropriate level of penalty.

5.9 In determining whether a case is suitable for settlement, Ofcom will have regard to a number of factors such as the likely procedural efficiencies and resource savings that can be achieved through settlement.[83] We may decide that a case is not suitable for settlement due to public policy reasons (for example due to the nature of the harm caused by the infringement), or due to previous conduct of the subject during the course of the investigation (for example, where the subject has been obstructive or failed to co-operate).

SETTLEMENT DISCOUNTS

5.10 Where the settlement process results in a final infringement decision being issued, that decision will contain the penalty amount, which will include a settlement discount. Our aim will be to conclude the settlement process as swiftly as possible. In line with this aim, the earlier the settlement process is commenced, the greater the discount available, as the resource savings that Ofcom could achieve would be greater.

5.11 Settlement discounts will be capped at the level of 20%. The discount will be considered on a case-by-case basis. We would normally expect this discount to be:

- up to 20% where a successful settlement process is commenced before the statement of objections is issued; and
- up to 10% where a successful settlement process is commenced after the statement of objections is issued.

5.12 Where we are concerned that the process is not progressing as swiftly as possible due to delays or inefficiencies caused by the subject of the investigation or that it is not showing its full co-operation with the settlement process, Ofcom is likely to bring the settlement process to an end or reduce the available discount on account of the time taken and resources used. We would give the subject notice that we are minded to do so at that point.

DECISION MAKING IN A SETTLEMENT CASE

5.13 Typically, the decision maker in a settlement case will be the person responsible for overseeing the investigation and deciding whether to issue a statement of objections (the case supervisor). Before the settlement process can start in a particular case, the decision maker must obtain approval to engage in the settlement process from at least two senior members of Ofcom's executive with appropriate Board-delegated authority.[84] The relevant decision maker will then typically oversee the settlement process and, as noted above, in contrast to our usual process, we would expect this decision maker also to be responsible for taking the final infringement decision on the case in the event that the settlement process is successful.[85]

PROCESS

5.14 If the subject of an investigation wishes to discuss the possibility of exploring settlement, it should approach the case leader and/or the case supervisor in the first instance.

5.15 While we will engage positively with a subject that indicates an early willingness to settle, we will need to have reached a stage in our analysis where we are able to come to a provisional view on the nature of the infringement(s) and appropriate level of penalty.

5.16 The settlement process will be conducted by the case supervisor and members of the case team.

5.17 As noted at paragraph 5.11 above, the level of discount on the level of penalty as a result of settlement will depend on the stage at which a successful settlement process is commenced. There are two main stages at which a settlement process may be commenced:

- prior to a statement of objections being issued; or
- following a statement of objections being issued.

5.18 If the settlement process is unsuccessful and the subject wishes to enter into a further settlement process at a later stage of the investigation, it remains open for it to do so. However, as noted above, it is at Ofcom's discretion whether and on what bases to enter into a settlement process at any stage.

Settlement process prior to the issue of a statement of objections

5.19 If the subject of the investigation approaches Ofcom about settlement prior to the issue of a statement of objections, and Ofcom considers this to be an appropriate case in which to consider settlement, we will normally provide details of our initial thinking on the case in general terms to the subject where we consider this will be of assistance in order for the subject and Ofcom to decide whether to engage in a settlement process.

5.20 Following this, if Ofcom and the subject wish to continue with the settlement process, we will send to the subject a statement of facts setting out Ofcom's provisional findings and the evidence on which we are relying. We will also provide an indication of the provisional level of penalty that Ofcom would be minded to impose, including the settlement discount.[86] We will also provide access to key documents we are relying on, if appropriate for reasons of fairness and transparency.

5.21 The subject will be asked if it would be prepared in principle to agree to make admissions on the basis of the statement of facts. The timeframe for doing so will be set on a case-by-case basis having regard to possible resource savings through the settlement process. If the subject wishes to pursue settlement on the basis set out in the statement of facts, it will be asked to make written representations on manifest factual inaccuracies in the statement of facts. If its representations appear to go beyond this (for example into the merits of Ofcom's provisional findings or on the level of the penalty), we would reassess whether the case remained appropriate for settlement at this stage.

5.22 If the subject is not prepared to agree to a settlement on the basis of the position set out in the statement of facts, it is unlikely to be appropriate to pursue settlement at this stage and Ofcom would normally expect to proceed to issue a statement of objections in accordance with its usual process. If the subject wishes to enter into a further settlement process at a later stage of the investigation, it remains open for it to do so (subject to Ofcom also considering this to be appropriate), although a lower settlement discount would then apply.

5.23 If the subject indicates that it does wish to pursue settlement on the basis set out in the statement of facts, we would proceed to issue a statement of objections which would take account of any representations made on manifest factual inaccuracies in the statement of facts, and would contain the proposed penalty amount.[87] We would also provide a streamlined access to file process. We would expect to provide the subject with access to key documents we are relying on as appropriate for reasons of fairness and transparency, to the extent that access to such documents has not been provided following the statement of facts (as set out in paragraph 5.20 above).

5.24 As noted above, one of the settlement requirements would be that the subject agrees not to make written representations on the statement of objections, except in relation to manifest factual inaccuracies in the statement of objections. As the statement of objections will take account of representations made on manifest factual inaccuracies in the statement of facts, we would not expect to receive any further representations at this stage and we would expect the subject to provide written confirmation of admissions and its acceptance of the settlement requirements, as discussed further below.

Settlement process following the issue of a statement of objections

5.25 If the subject of the investigation is in principle prepared to agree to the settlement requirements and admit to the contraventions as set out in the statement of objections, it may inform Ofcom that it wishes to enter into a settlement on that basis. In such a case, one of the settlement requirements would be that the subject agrees not to make written representations on the statement of objections except in relation to manifest factual inaccuracies.

5.26 We will provide the subject with an indication of the penalty and level of the discount on the penalty which we would be minded to apply if a successful settlement process is commenced at this stage. If access to file has not yet been given, we would expect to provide a streamlined access to file process, in accordance with paragraph 5.23 above.

5.27 We expect to set a deadline for the subject to indicate its willingness to settle the case and will provide a short period of time for representations on manifest factual inaccuracies in the statement of objections. The timeframe for doing so will be set on a case-by-case basis having regard to possible resource savings through the settlement process.

5.28 We then expect the subject to provide written confirmation of admissions and its acceptance of the settlement requirements as discussed further below.

5.29 If the subject wishes to make written representations on the statement of objections (which are more extensive than identifying manifest factual inaccuracies), it may nonetheless indicate to Ofcom that it wishes to enter into a settlement process after doing so. Ofcom would consider any written representations made to it in line with our usual process before deciding whether to or not to engage in a settlement process.

5.30 As noted above, settlement is not a negotiation. Therefore, in the event that we consider it appropriate to engage in a settlement process, after considering the subject's written representations, we would expect to provide it with a written statement of our revised position. This would set out:

- the infringement we are minded to find; and
- an indication of the level of penalty we would be minded to impose, taking into account our revised assessment of the nature of the infringement and after having applied the settlement discount on the penalty at that stage of the process.[88]

5.31 We would expect to set a deadline for the subject to indicate to Ofcom its willingness to settle the case on the basis of the written statement. The timeframe for doing so will be set on a case-by-case basis having regard to possible resource savings through the settlement process.

5.32 Ofcom would not expect to receive any further representations at this stage, and will expect the subject to provide written confirmation of admissions and its acceptance of the settlement requirements as discussed further below. As set out above, one of the requirements for settlement would be that the broadcaster agrees that there would not be an oral hearing.

Successful conclusion of the settlement process

5.33 If the settlement process is successful and the subject of the investigation has indicated to Ofcom that it is prepared to agree to the settlement requirements and to make admissions on a basis which reflects Ofcom's position, it must provide written confirmation of its admissions and acceptance of the settlement requirements. That letter should be sent by its Chief Executive Officer or another senior member of its executive.

5.34 Before the subject provides its written confirmation letter, we will provide the subject with a draft of the terms of the infringement decision we would expect to take, reflecting the subject's admissions and having taken into account any representations from the subject on manifest factual inaccuracies:

- Where settlement is agreed prior to the subject making substantive written representations on the statement of objections, this will normally be in the form of the statement of objections. We normally expect in such cases that the final infringement decision would be in the same terms as the statement of objections (subject to any corrections of factual inaccuracies). We therefore expect the subject to provide its written confirmation of its admissions and acceptance of the settlement requirements following receipt of the statement of objections.
- Where settlement is agreed after the subject has made written representations on the statement of objections, this will normally be in the form of a draft of the final infringement decision. In practice, this is likely to be the written statement setting out Ofcom's position following consideration of the subject's written representations (as set out in paragraph 5.30 above), as we would normally expect in such cases the final infringement decision would be in the same terms

as that written statement (subject to any corrections of factual inaccuracies). We would therefore expect the subject to provide its written confirmation of its admissions and acceptance of the settlement requirements following receipt of Ofcom's written statement of position.

5.35 Once we have received the subject's written confirmation of its admissions and acceptance of the settlement requirements, the relevant decision maker will then formally make Ofcom's final decision, reflecting the position agreed during the settlement process and the subject's admissions.

What happens if the settlement process is unsuccessful?

5.36 The subject of the investigation may withdraw from the settlement process at any time before confirming that it has accepted the requirements for settlement and confirming its admission in writing (in accordance with paragraph 5.33 above). Ofcom may also withdraw from the settlement process at any stage, though prior to doing so, we would notify the subject and give it the opportunity to respond.

5.37 If settlement is unsuccessful then the case will revert to the usual procedure.

5.38 The subject of the investigation would not have entered into the settlement agreement and therefore would not have made any formal admissions.

5.39 The final decision makers may be aware of the fact that the possibility of settlement has been discussed between Ofcom and the subject. However, neither the substance of any oral discussions between the subject and Ofcom, nor any correspondence relating to, or written records of such discussions would be disclosed to the final decision makers, so that the decision could be taken impartially on the basis of the relevant evidence.

5.40 As noted above, settlement is not akin to "without prejudice" negotiations for the purposes of seeking to resolve litigation. Any additional documentary evidence provided during the settlement process would be placed on the case file and could be taken into account by Ofcom for the purposes of its final infringement decision even if the settlement process is unsuccessful. In addition, Ofcom may follow up any new competition law issues which come to light during the settlement process.

Publicity in settlement cases

5.41 Ofcom's standard practice is not to comment publicly on the fact that settlement discussions are taking place, or that the settlement process has been unsuccessful.

5.42 Following the conclusion of a successful settlement process, Ofcom will close the case and update the details on the CCEB section of Ofcom's website. This will generally refer to the fact that a settlement has been agreed and include a summary of the infringement(s) Ofcom has found and details of the penalty (including the level of the settlement discount) and any other directions imposed. Ofcom may also publicise the outcome of the case in a media release relating to the case. Ofcom will normally share in advance a copy of the CCEB update with the subject for information only shortly (and no more than one working day) before publication.

5.43 Ofcom will also publish a non-confidential version of the infringement decision, in accordance with our standard practice.[89]

NOTES

76 CMA Rules, Rule 9

77 CMA Rules, Rule 9(1)

78 See the CMA's *Guidance as to the appropriate amount of penalty* (OFT423), paragraph 2.26

79 CMA Rules, Rule 9(1)(a)

80 CMA Rules, Rule 9(1)(b)

81 CMA Rules, Rule 9(4)

82 The Competition Appeal Tribunal has full jurisdiction to review the appropriate level of penalty

83 Taking into account, among other things the stage at which settlement is initiated, whether settlement would result in shortening the case timetable and a reduction in resources, and whether settlement is likely to be reached in a reasonable timeframe.

84 Under the CMA Rules (Rules 9(2) – (3)), where a single individual, such as the case supervisor, is the decision maker in a settlement process, then they will need a mandate from at least two other individuals before taking a decision to follow a settlement procedure.

85 CMA Rules, Rule 9(4)

86 That discount would reflect the discount that Ofcom would be minded to apply to the penalty were the settlement process successful and concluded swiftly. Were Ofcom minded to reduce the available discount at any point on account of the time taken and the resources used during the settlement process, we would give the subject of the investigation notice of our intention to do so.

87 This would not typically include the settlement discount because, as discussed further below, we would not typically expect settlement to be formally agreed until after we have issued the statement of objections. We would, however, expect to confirm the level of the available settlement discount at this stage which would, for example, be the same amount as previously proposed to the subject were the settlement process successful and concluded swiftly. The discount may be reduced in the event the settlement process takes longer, as set out above.

88 That discount would reflect the discount that Ofcom would be minded to apply to the penalty were the settlement process successful and concluded swiftly. Were Ofcom minded to reduce the available discount at any point on account of the time taken and the resources used during the settlement process, we would give the subject notice of this at that point.

89 See paragraph 4.40 above.

SECTION 6: TAKING URGENT ACTION

[3.256]

6.1 Once Ofcom has formally opened a Competition Act investigation, we have the power to require a person to comply with temporary directions (known as "interim measures") while we complete our investigation.[90]

6.2 Where we consider that it is necessary to act as a matter of urgency for the purpose of:

(a) preventing significant damage to a particular person or category of person; or

(b) protecting the public interest,

we may impose such interim measures as we consider appropriate for that purpose.[91]

6.3 Ofcom may exercise these powers following a request to do so by an application or on its own-initiative. For guidance on making an application for Ofcom to take urgent action, see *Advice for complainants: Submitting a complaint to Ofcom*.[92]

PROCESS FOR CONSIDERING A REQUEST FOR INTERIM MEASURES

6.4 We will assess requests for interim measures against the relevant statutory criteria (as set out above). If we consider the test is met then we may impose interim measures at our discretion. In exercising this discretion, we will have regard to other relevant considerations including the impact on the person who would be subject to the interim measures direction and any relevant third party interests.

6.5 The decision on whether to impose interim measures will be taken by a senior member of Ofcom's executive with appropriate Board-delegated authority.

6.6 In most cases, where we are considering whether to grant interim measures in response to a third party request, where time allows, Ofcom will inform the undertaking about whom the request for interim measures has been made (the "subject") that we have received such a request, and will give it the opportunity to make representations to Ofcom on a non-confidential version of the request.

6.7 In some cases, we may receive a request for interim measures before we have decided whether to open a Competition Act investigation (for example, we might receive a request with a complaint submission). As stated above, Ofcom does not have powers to impose interim measures until we have formally opened a Competition Act investigation. Therefore, in such cases, before we can make a decision on whether to impose interim measures, we will need to decide whether the statutory test[93] for opening a Competition Act investigation has been met.

6.8 We will seek to do this expeditiously, but we may require information from the subject of the application in order to assess whether the statutory criteria to open a Competition Act investigation are met, and whether it is appropriate to take urgent action. In such cases, Ofcom may request information informally as we cannot use our statutory information gathering powers under the Competition Act until we have opened an investigation. Ofcom would expect timely co-operation from the subject in responding to such informal information requests. Assuming we decide that the statutory threshold for opening a Competition Act investigation has been met and we open an investigation, we would expect to follow up with information requests, using our statutory powers under the Act, as appropriate.

6.9 Before reaching a decision on whether to impose interim measures, the decision maker will first reach a provisional view based on the evidence set out in the applicant's request, any representations received from the subject of the application and any further information gathered during the course of the investigation up until that point.

6.10 Where we are minded to give a direction imposing interim measures, we will provide a provisional decision to the subject of the application[94] and the applicant, which will set out the proposed measures and Ofcom's reasons.[95] We will also allow the subject to inspect documents on the file which relate to the proposed measures, but may withhold confidential information and internal documents.[96] Ofcom will allow the subject the opportunity to make representations,[97] which may include written and/or oral representations as appropriate in the circumstances, having regard to the urgency of the case, and we may allow the applicant to do so if we consider it appropriate. Given the urgent nature of the interim measures process, we will normally set a short timeframe for representations.

6.11 Where our provisional decision is to reject an application for interim measures, we will normally inform the applicant and the subject and provide them with an opportunity to comment and submit any further information or evidence before reaching our final decision.

6.12 Ofcom will not publish the provisional decision, or any details of it.

6.13 As soon as reasonably practicable after the period for representations had ended, and after taking into account any representations, Ofcom will determine whether to impose interim measures. We will inform the subject of the application[98] and any applicant. Ofcom will publish details of our decision and a non-confidential version of it on the CCEB section of our website.[99]

NOTES

[90] Competition Act, section 35(1)

[91] Competition Act, section 35(2)

[92] www.ofcom.org.uk/__data/assets/pdf_file/0013/102514/Advice-for-complainants.pdf

[93] In accordance with section 25 of the Competition Act, before opening a Competition Act investigation, we must be satisfied there are reasonable grounds for suspecting that a competition law infringement has occurred

[94] Competition Act, section 35(3)(a)

[95] Competition Act, section 35(4)

96 CMA Rules, Rule 13(1), Rule 13(2)
97 Competition Act, section 35(3)(b)
98 CMA Rules, Rule 13(4)
99 CMA Rules, Rule 13(4)

SECTION 7: PROCEDURAL COMPLAINTS ABOUT INVESTIGATIONS

[3.257]

7.1 If the subject of an investigation, any complainant or a third party (where relevant) is dissatisfied about any aspect of the investigation procedure, it should usually raise its concerns in writing with the case leader in the first instance, and then with the person overseeing the investigation (i.e. the case supervisor).

7.2 If a party does not consider that its concerns have been satisfactorily resolved by the case leader and/or the case supervisor then, if an investigation has been formally opened, it may refer certain procedural complaints to Ofcom's Procedural Officer.[100]

THE PROCEDURAL OFFICER

7.3 A number of appropriately experienced Ofcom staff have Board-delegated authority to act as the Procedural Officer for the purposes of a Competition Act investigation. The relevant Procedural Officer will be appointed on a case-by-case basis, if a relevant procedural complaint is made, and in any event when the oral hearing takes place.

7.4 The Procedural Officer will be independent from the Competition Act investigation, case team and decision makers, and will not have been involved in the investigation (other than as the Procedural Officer).[101] The role of the Procedural Officer is intended to ensure that procedural issues can be addressed quickly, efficiently and cost effectively, and independently of the case team.

7.5 The Procedural Officer will also chair any oral hearings in Competition Act investigations.[102]

TYPES OF COMPLAINT WHICH CAN BE MADE TO THE PROCEDURAL OFFICER

7.6 Complaints about the procedure followed by Ofcom when conducting a Competition Act investigation can be made to the Procedural Officer by the subject of the investigation, complainant or a third party (where relevant) once the investigation has been formally opened.

7.7 The Procedural Officer will deal with complaints which relate to the following:

(a) deadlines for parties to respond to information requests, submit documents or provide representations;
(b) requests for redaction of confidential information in documents on Ofcom's case file, and in documents that Ofcom proposes to publish or disclose;
(c) requests for disclosure or non-disclosure of certain documents or information on Ofcom's case file;
(d) issues relating to the process for oral hearings; or
(e) other significant procedural issues that may arise during the course of an investigation.

7.8 The Procedural Officer is not able to deal with complaints which relate to decisions taken by Ofcom relating to substantive issues, for example decisions on the scope of information requests or decisions relating to the scope and substance of an investigation.

MAKING A COMPLAINT TO THE PROCEDURAL OFFICER

7.9 If a party is not satisfied with the decision of the case supervisor regarding the procedural issue it has raised, then it may refer its concerns to the Procedural Officer. If it wishes to do so, it should make an application to the Procedural Officer as soon as possible after receiving the decision from the case supervisor, and in any event within five working days.

7.10 The application should be no longer than five sides of A4 paper and should include:

(a) the name and contact details of the applicant;
(b) the name and contact details of the lawyers acting for the applicant (where relevant);
(c) the Ofcom case name and reference number;
(d) the date of decision made by the case supervisor; and
(e) a short summary of the issues including a summary of the case team's original decision, the decision of the case supervisor, the reason the applicant wants a review of that decision and the outcome the applicant is seeking.

7.11 The applicant should also provide copies of relevant correspondence between it and Ofcom relating to the issue in question and copies of any relevant information or documents which the applicant holds.

7.12 The application should be submitted by email to Procedural.Officer@ofcom.org.uk.

7.13 The Procedural Officer will provide members of the case team and the case supervisor, and the applicant, the opportunity to present their arguments orally on the telephone or at a meeting.

THE PROCEDURAL OFFICER'S DECISION

7.14 The Procedural Officer will deal with the application as quickly as possible, and will aim to take a decision in most cases within 10 working days from receipt of the application. In any event the

Procedural Officer will reach a decision within 20 working days from receipt of the application.[103] The Procedural Officer may extend this timeframe by no more than 20 working days if there are special reasons to do so.[104]

7.15 The Procedural Officer's decision will be submitted in writing to the applicant, and it will be binding on the case team and decision makers. A non-confidential version of the Procedural Officer's decision, or a summary of it, will be published on Ofcom's website, generally at the time the decision is made or at the end of Ofcom's investigation.

NOTES

100 CMA Rules, Rule 8(1)

101 CMA Rules, Rule 8(1)

102 CMA Rules, Rule 6(5)

103 CMA Rules, Rule 8(2)

104 CMA Rules, Rule 8(3)

ANNEX 1: OVERVIEW OF A COMPETITION ACT CASE

[3.258]

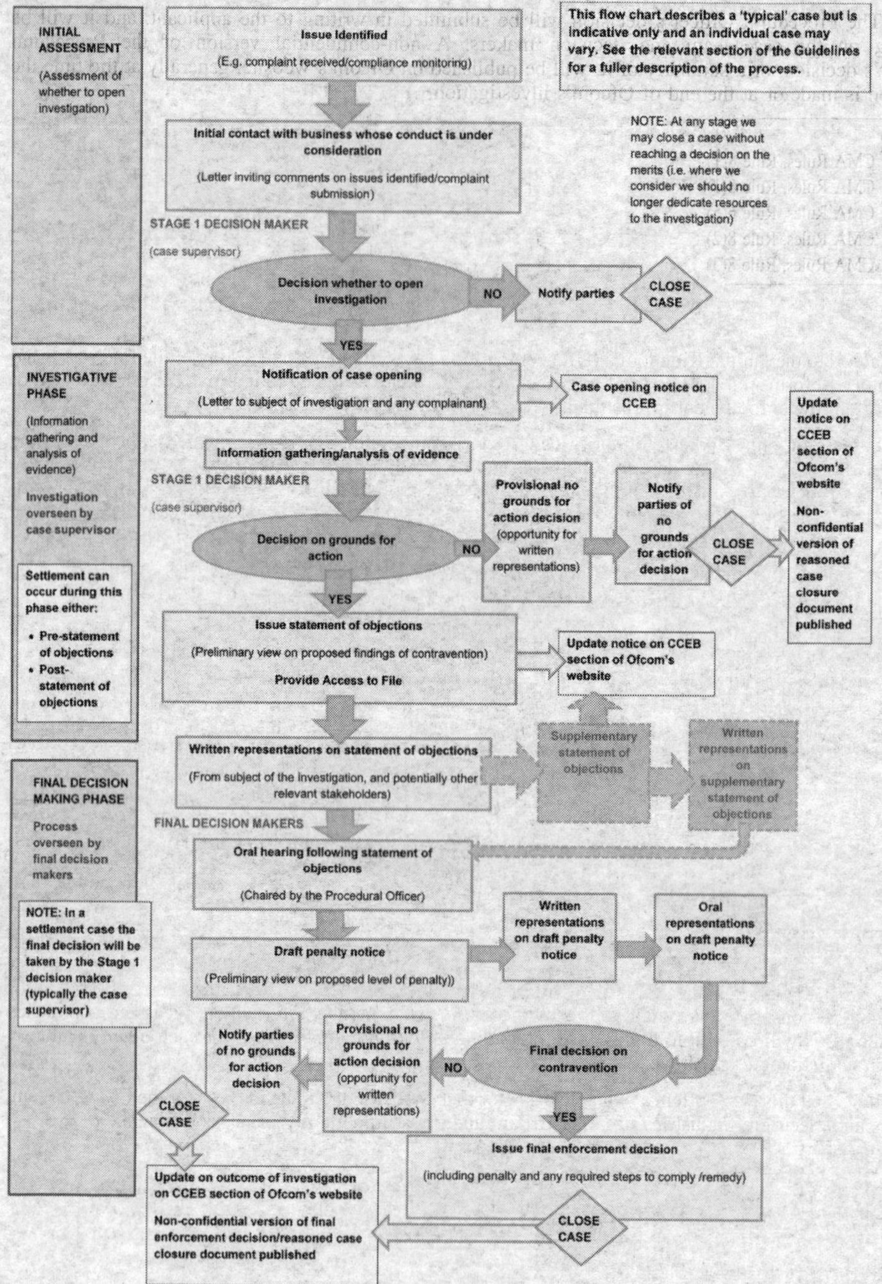

(III) ENERGY

MEMORANDUM OF UNDERSTANDING BETWEEN THE COMPETITION AND MARKETS AUTHORITY AND THE GAS AND ELECTRICITY MARKETS AUTHORITY[1] – CONCURRENT COMPETITION POWERS

18 January 2016

[3.259]

NOTES

FOREWORD

[3.260]
The changes to the United Kingdom's (UK) competition law system, introduced under the Enterprise and Regulatory Reform Act 2013 and in force since April 2014, are designed to improve the effectiveness of competition law enforcement in this country.

The Competition and Markets Authority (CMA) has competition law powers which apply across the whole economy. Sectoral regulators such as Gas and Electricity Markets Authority (Ofgem) may exercise the competition law powers to enforce the prohibitions on anti-competitive agreements and on abuse of a dominant position, and to make market investigation references, concurrently with the CMA in those sectors for which they have responsibility.

The Enterprise and Regulatory Reform Act 2013 introduced a number of changes to improve the working of concurrency and enable closer working between the CMA and sectoral regulators.

The CMA and the sectoral regulators have demonstrated their commitment to making the concurrency framework more effective through the establishment of the UK Competition Network (UKCN). This represents an enhanced forum for cooperation which will enable closer working with the objective of more consistent and effective use of competition powers across all sectors. In their statement of intent in December 2013, the members of the UKCN affirmed: 'The mission of the UKCN will be to promote competition for the benefit of consumers and to prevent anti-competitive behaviour both through facilitating use of competition powers and development of pro-competitive regulatory frameworks, as appropriate'.[2]

This Memorandum of Understanding (MoU) represents a further stage in the process of cooperation between the CMA and the regulators, setting out more practical detail on how the CMA and Ofgem will work together within the framework of competition law.[3]

The main purpose of this MoU is to establish an understanding between the CMA and Ofgem as to how this closer working will work in practice. It draws on the legislation which sets out the formal framework for how concurrency will operate and also, importantly, sets out our bilateral commitment to look for opportunities to work together, including within the framework of the UKCN, to promote competition for the benefit of consumers. We shall do this by the sharing of expertise, information, ideas and experience and each of us will commit to doing this efficiently and with a mutual regard for each other's statutory position and strategic objectives.

We believe that this MoU offers a valuable basis for that cooperation, in the interests of the CMA, Ofgem, the gas and electricity industries in Great Britain and, most importantly of all, consumers.

Alex Chisholm	**Dermot Nolan**
CEO, CMA	**CEO, Ofgem**

NOTES

1 Referred to throughout as Ofgem.

2 UKCN (2013), *Statement of Intent*.

3 This MoU does not relate to "regulatory appeals" – that is, the separate role that the CMA has in considering appeals against, or references relating to, proposed direct regulatory action by Ofgem under the sectoral statutes. This is a separate role, to be undertaken by the CMA panel, and the CMA is committed to ensuring that its cooperation with Ofgem – whether under this MoU (and under comparable MoU agreed with other sectoral regulators), through the UKCN or otherwise in connection with their concurrent powers – will not impair the impartiality and fairness of the CMA's conduct of such regulatory appeals (or indeed of market or merger investigations undertaken by the CMA panel).

MEMORANDUM OF UNDERSTANDING BETWEEN THE COMPETITION AND MARKETS AUTHORITY AND THE GAS AND ELECTRICITY MARKETS AUTHORITY

PURPOSE OF THIS MEMORANDUM OF UNDERSTANDING

[3.261]
1. This MoU sets out working arrangements between the CMA and Ofgem in relation to:

(a) their concurrent powers to apply the prohibitions on agreements that prevent, restrict or distort competition and on the abuse of a dominant position, under the Chapter I prohibition and the Chapter II prohibition of the Competition Act 1998 and under Article 101 and Article 102 of the treaty on the Functioning of the European Union – referred to in this MoU as the 'competition prohibitions'; and
(b) their concurrent powers to undertake market studies, and to make references to the CMA for the constitution of a CMA group to conduct an in-depth market investigation into single or multiple markets for goods or services in the UK under the Enterprise Act 2002 – referred to in this MoU as the 'market provisions',

in the gas and electricity sectors in Great Britain.

2. This MoU is not intended to have legal effect.

3. This MoU is to be read alongside other material concerning the relations between the CMA and Ofgem, including: the Gas Act 1986; the Electricity Act 1989; the Competition Act 1998; the Enterprise Act 2002; the Enterprise and Regulatory Reform Act 2013; the Competition Act 1998 and Other Enactments (Amendment) Regulations 2004; the Competition Act 1998 (Concurrency) Regulations 2014, referred to in this MoU as the concurrency regulations, and the CMA's guidance on concurrent application of competition law to regulated industries, referred to in this MoU as the concurrency guidance.[4] This MoU supplements and does not supplant that material.

4. The arrangements covered by this MoU are, wherever possible, set out in terms providing sufficient flexibility for the relationship between Ofgem and the CMA to develop in the light of experience. The CMA and Ofgem commit to review these arrangements from time to time to evaluate their continuing fitness for purpose. Such review can be initiated at the request of the CMA, Ofgem or a member of the UKCN. This MoU may only be revised by agreement between the CMA and Ofgem.

5. Nothing in this MoU applies in relation to the functions of the CMA in its separate role of considering appeals against, or references related, to proposed action by Ofgem under the sectoral statutes. The CMA and Ofgem acknowledge the importance of maintaining the CMA's impartiality and fairness in carrying out those functions, and indeed of market or merger investigations undertaken by the CMA panel.

6. Nothing in this MoU applies in relation to the functions of Ofgem in respect of its role as the designated regulatory authority for Great Britain in accordance with Article 35 of the Electricity Directive and Article 39 of the Gas Directive ('relevant functions'). The CMA and Ofgem acknowledge the importance of acting independently in respect of relevant functions and the need to ensure that Ofgem's members and staff do not seek or take any instructions that might compromise, or might reasonably be seen to compromise, Ofgem's independence in respect of relevant functions.

NOTES

4 CMA10.

CONTEXT

7. This MoU operates within the framework of the legislative provisions referred to in paragraph 1, the Gas Act 1986, the Electricity Act 1989 and any other applicable sector specific legislation from time to time.

Role of the CMA

8. The CMA is a non-ministerial department, established under the Enterprise and Regulatory Reform Act 2013.

9. The CMA works to promote competition for the benefit of consumers, both within and outside the UK, to make markets work well for consumers, businesses and the economy.

10. The CMA's statutory responsibilities, in so far as relevant to the matters that are the subject of this MoU, include:
(a) investigating where there may be breaches of the competition prohibitions; and
(b) conducting market studies and market investigations where there may be competition and consumer problems.

11. In connection with its statutory responsibilities, the CMA will cooperate with sectoral regulators and encourage sector regulators to use their powers, including their powers to apply the competition prohibitions, in the interests of competition for the benefit of consumers.

Role of Ofgem

12. Ofgem is the regulator of Great Britain's gas and electricity markets. Its powers, duties and objectives come from GB statutes and relevant EU legislation. Ofgem's principal objective is to protect the interests of existing and future energy consumers. These interests are taken as a whole and include the reduction of greenhouse gases, the security of the supply of gas and electricity to consumers, and Ofgem's fulfilment of the objectives in the EU Gas and Electricity Directives (such as the promotion of competition, helping to ensure consumer protection and contributing to the protection of vulnerable consumers).

13. When exercising regulatory functions, Ofgem is generally required to act in the manner it considers will best further the principal objective, by promoting effective competition in the activities it regulates wherever appropriate. However, before performing regulatory functions with a view to promoting competition, Ofgem must always first consider the extent to which the interests of consumers would be protected by the promotion of competition and whether there are other ways which would better protect those interests.

14. When performing regulatory functions, Ofgem is also subject to a wide range of other general duties which include (but are not limited to):

(a) a duty to act in the manner it considers is best calculated to secure a diverse and viable long-term energy supply;

(b) duties to have regard to a wide range of matters including:

- (i) better regulation principles;
- (ii) the need to secure that all reasonable demands for electricity are met;
- (iii) the need to secure that, so far as it is economical to meet them, all reasonable demands in Great Britain for gas conveyed through pipes are met;
- (iv) the need to secure that licence holders are able to finance their activities;
- (v) the need to contribute to the achievement of sustainable development; and
- (vi) the interests of individuals who are chronically sick, of pensionable age, with low incomes or live in rural areas, as well as to those of other consumers.

15. Ofgem conducts investigations into the conduct of companies that it believes may be breaching licence conditions and has concurrent powers with the CMA under the Competition Act 1998 or consumer protection laws. It also has powers under the Enterprise Act 2002 to conduct market studies or to make a market investigation reference to the CMA where it has reasonable grounds for suspecting that any feature or combination of features prevents, restricts or distorts competition in the gas and electricity markets.

AIMS

16. The Enterprise and Regulatory Reform Act 2013, as well as establishing the CMA, made provision for the better working of the CMA's and the sectoral regulators' concurrent powers in the regulated sectors; specifically, the act: 'strengthens the role of the CMA and enhances the emphasis on early and proper consideration of the use of anti-trust powers (under Part 1 of the CA 1998 [ie the competition prohibitions]) by the sector regulators'.[5]

17. It is one of the strategic goals of the CMA, announced on its establishment on 1 October 2013, to extend the frontiers of competition into new areas, including by working with sectoral regulators to ensure fuller use of competition law and policy in sectoral markets.[6]

18. The government's strategic steer to the CMA, issued on 1 December 2015, says that the CMA should build 'a strong dialogue with sectoral regulators using the UKCN to ensure that the overall competition regime is coordinated and regulatory practices complement each other'.[7]

19. The sectoral regulators and the CMA, working together in the UKCN established in 2013 (with Monitor having observer status), declared that: 'The mission of the UKCN will be to promote competition for the benefit of consumers and to prevent anti-competitive behaviour both through facilitating use of competition powers and development of pro-competitive regulatory frameworks, as appropriate'.[8]

20. The CMA and Ofgem seek to use their powers to achieve competitive outcomes in the gas and electricity industries in Great Britain for the benefit of consumers so as to make markets in the gas and electricity sectors in Great Britain work well for consumers of gas and electricity services, businesses in those sectors and businesses that use those services and the economy in which those services play an essential part. It is the view of the CMA and Ofgem that such competitive outcomes can be achieved by various tools, including their competition law powers under the competition prohibitions, the market provisions and merger control, but also through other tools such as direct regulatory action including through powers to make regulatory rules, licence modification, enforcement of licence provisions (for example, in providing for third party access to networks) and liberalisation measures introduced under national and European Union legislation.

21. This MoU aims to further the attainment of these objectives, and to make the changes introduced by the Enterprise and Regulatory Reform Act 2013 work effectively, maximising the complementary skills of the CMA and Ofgem, including through:

(a) promoting cooperation and coordination between the CMA and Ofgem when dealing with cases of suspected anti-competitive behaviour for which they have concurrent powers;

(b) promoting cooperation and coordination between the CMA and Ofgem when dealing with market studies and market investigation references for which they have concurrent powers;

(c) facilitating the efficient and effective handling of cases of suspected anti-competitive behaviour within the gas and electricity services markets in Great Britain;

(d) avoiding duplication of activity, wherever possible; and

(e) ensuring transparency as to the respective roles of the CMA and Ofgem for individuals and consumers affected.

NOTES

5 Enterprise and Regulatory Reform Act 2013 Explanatory Notes, paragraph 370.

6 Statement by Alex Chisholm, Chief Executive of the CMA, CMA mission and strategy, 1 October 2013.

7 Department for Business, Innovation and Skills (1 December 2015), *Strategic steer for the Competition and Markets Authority*, in Annex A to the Government's response to the Consultation on the Strategic Steer to the CMA, p11.

8 UKCN (2013), Statement of Intent.

GENERAL COOPERATION

22. In addition to the provisions for cooperation between the CMA and Ofgem specific to particular powers of the CMA and Ofgem, as set out in this MoU and elsewhere, the CMA and Ofgem are committed to the following general principles and practices for cooperation between themselves in respect of the sectors for which Ofgem has responsibility.

23. Officials of the CMA and Ofgem will meet and communicate, at appropriate levels of seniority, to discuss matters of mutual interest, both through the UKCN and bilaterally. A framework for such meetings will, as far as possible, be determined in advance so as to ensure attendance at the appropriate level and expertise.

24. The CMA and Ofgem will, in respect of Great Britain's gas and electricity markets, always consult each other:

(a) before the initial exercise of concurrent competition law powers in all cases where it appears that they have concurrent jurisdiction and where there are reasonable grounds for suspecting an infringement of the competition prohibitions; and

(b) before launching a market study under the Enterprise Act 2002.[9]

25. Where either the CMA or Ofgem exercises its concurrent powers, the CMA and Ofgem will, to the extent permitted by law, engage with each other in open dialogue and by sharing relevant information as appropriate. This engagement may include attendance at internal meetings held by the investigating authority (ie the authority to which a case is allocated) by the supporting authority (ie the other authority which would be competent to exercise concurrent powers in relation to the case), in order to discuss the case as envisaged at paragraph 3.31 of the concurrency guidance. The supporting authority will not generally attend the investigating authority's constitutional decision-making meetings, meetings of governance bodies or meetings with external parties such as those under investigation or complainants. Attendance by the supporting authority at any meeting is at the discretion of the investigating authority, but requests to attend should be considered by the investigating authority in the spirit of cooperation underpinning the new concurrency regime.

26. The CMA and Ofgem will consult each other at an early stage on any issues that might have significant implications for the other. For example, where the CMA undertakes a market study which relates to a sector other than Great Britain's gas or electricity sectors but which may have a significant impact on either of those sectors, the CMA will inform Ofgem and share appropriate information relating to that market study with Ofgem to the extent permitted by law.

27. Within the spirit of broader collaboration for the purposes of the promotion of competitive outcomes, the CMA and Ofgem will commit to discuss and share other information about a broader range of competition complaints and concerns, where legally permissible to do so, but subject to the particular need not to impair the impartiality and fairness of the CMA in carrying out the functions referred to in paragraph 5 of this MoU.

NOTES

[9] Instigation of a market study occurs on the publication of a market study notice, as defined in section 130A of the Enterprise Act 2002.

PART A – COOPERATION IN RELATION TO THE COMPETITION PROHIBITIONS (COMPETITION ACT 1998 AND ARTICLES 101 AND 102 OF THE TREATY ON THE FUNCTIONING OF THE EUROPEAN UNION)

CASE ALLOCATION

Basis of allocation

[3.262]

28. The CMA and Ofgem will endeavour to reach agreement on which authority will exercise its concurrent competition powers in respect of any particular case, under regulation 4(2) of the concurrency regulations. They will do so in a spirit of constructiveness and cooperation, while acknowledging the CMA's ultimate powers under regulations 5 and 8 of the concurrency regulations.

29. Their determination of which authority will exercise its powers will be based on assessing which of them is better placed to exercise those powers, having regard to the factors set out in paragraph 3.22 of the concurrency guidance. The CMA and Ofgem envisage that other factors may appear relevant in the light of practical experience and that, if so, such factors may be chosen to supplement or supplant the factors set out in paragraph 3.22 of the concurrency guidance.

Procedure for allocation

30. Where either the CMA or Ofgem has decided, on the basis of information in its possession, that there are reasonable grounds for suspecting that one of the competition prohibitions has been infringed (the reasonable suspicion test)[10] in relation to the gas and electricity markets in Great Britain, it will disclose to the other (ie the receiving authority) sufficient information:

(a) to enable the receiving authority to understand the basis on which the disclosing authority has decided that the reasonable suspicion test is met; and

(b) for there to be an informed discussion on which authority (if either) is best placed to proceed in respect of the case.

31. In practice, it may be helpful for the CMA and Ofgem to have discussed the case prior to such a decision having been reached, subject to paragraph 44 below. The disclosing authority will provide the information described under paragraph 30 within ten working days after it has decided that the reasonable suspicion test is met, whether or not it proposes to exercise concurrent powers.[11]

32. Within seven working days from receipt of this information, the receiving authority will respond in writing, setting out its initial view on the case and how it should be allocated and identifying any further information which it requires.

33. The CMA and Ofgem will endeavour to agree which authority will exercise its concurrent competition powers in relation to the case, as provided for in regulation 4(2) of the concurrency regulations, as soon as possible and in any event no later than one month from disclosure of the information described under paragraph 30. Other than in exceptional circumstances (which shall be set out in writing), the CMA will initiate the procedure set out in regulation 5 of the concurrency regulations if agreement is not reached within two months of the disclosing authority first receiving sufficient information in connection with a complaint to enable it to decide that the reasonable suspicion test is met.

34. The procedure for agreeing the transfer of a case that is already in progress from the CMA to Ofgem, or from Ofgem to the CMA, is as set out in regulation 7 of the concurrency regulations and in paragraph 3.32 of the concurrency guidance.

35. The procedure for the CMA to direct the transfer to itself from Ofgem of a case that is already in progress is as set out in regulation 8 of the concurrency regulations.

NOTES

[10] As provided in section 25 of the Competition Act 1998.

[11] As provided in regulation 9 of the concurrency regulations.

Implications of allocation

36. Any agreement or determination as to case allocation, under regulations 4, 5, 7 or 8 of the concurrency regulations, shall be notified to the person who has provided the information resulting in the case (for example, the person making a complaint), and so far as appropriate and lawful to any other affected person, by the authority which is exercising its concurrent competition powers in relation to the case, as soon as reasonably practicable.

37. Case allocation determines which of the CMA and Ofgem is to exercise concurrent functions and make any decisions under the competition prohibitions. The CMA or Ofgem will be publicly identified as having such responsibility if and when any such investigation is announced. The CMA and Ofgem envisage that, whichever authority has responsibility for a particular case, they and their officials will work cooperatively with each other on the case as appropriate, pooling their expertise including in the ways described in paragraphs 52 to 60 of this MoU and in paragraph 3.33 to 3.35 of the concurrency guidance.

SHARING INFORMATION

Principles of information sharing

38. The effective sharing of information between the CMA and Ofgem is fundamental to the successful exercise of their concurrent competition powers. It is needed both for the appropriate allocation of cases, as described in paragraphs 30 to 35 of this MoU, and for the successful handling of cases once allocated to make optimal use of the complementary experience and expertise of the two authorities.

39. The CMA and Ofgem are committed, in addition to their legal obligations to share information (set out in regulation 9 of the concurrency regulations), to open dialogue and continuing liaison, both bilaterally and through the UKCN, with a view not only to handling specific cases but to promoting competition for the benefit of consumers in the gas and electricity markets in Great Britain.

Information sharing mechanism – general liaison

40. The CMA and Ofgem recognise the importance of meeting regularly to share information on matters relevant to competition in the gas and electricity markets in Great Britain, and to keep each other abreast of relevant work which they are considering or currently undertaking.

41. The CMA and Ofgem will meet regularly at multiple levels, bilaterally and through the UKCN.

42. The CMA and Ofgem will each designate in its organisation a relationship manager at official level to take responsibility for relations between the two authorities. In each authority, the relationship manager's responsibilities will include (but not be limited to):

(a) maintaining an overview of joint projects between the two authorities and matters of mutual interest;

(b) maintaining an overview of the authority's contacts from all areas of joint working and mutual interest; and

(c) holding meetings with the relationship manager in the other authority from time to time (whether bilaterally or in the context of the UKCN) to identify potential new issues, with a view to circulating information to appropriate individuals within each organisation.

43. The existence of relationship managers does not in any way preclude direct communication between other staff at the CMA and Ofgem.

44. For the purposes of sharing information pursuant to paragraph 30, ie in circumstances where the reasonable suspicion test is met, such information will be shared by the disclosing authority to the extent permitted by law and whether or not it proposes to exercise concurrent powers.[12] Where disclosure would be appropriate and permitted by law, the CMA and Ofgem may also share information regarding potential infringements of the competition prohibitions in advance of having reached a view as to whether the reasonable suspicion test is met. In circumstances where either the CMA or Ofgem has taken the view that a matter is not an administrative priority, irrespective of whether a view has been reached on whether the reasonable suspicion test is met, each may share the details of the matter with the other, or with any other authority which would be able to exercise concurrent competition powers in relation to that matter, to the extent permitted by law. Where leniency information is being shared under this paragraph, special considerations apply, as set out in paragraphs 50 and 51.

NOTES

[12] For the avoidance of doubt, this does not entail an obligation to inform the other party if the regulator is carrying out general monitoring activity, where there is no consideration of exercising its concurrent powers.

Information sharing mechanism – handling specific cases

45. The procedures for information sharing for the purpose of case allocation shall be as set out in paragraphs 30 to 32 and 38 to 51 of this MoU.

46. When either the CMA or Ofgem is exercising its powers in respect of the competition prohibitions in a particular case in the gas and electricity markets in Great Britain, each of them will share with the other any of the following information in its possession (to the extent permitted by law and subject to the confidentiality obligations in paragraphs 49 to 51 of this MoU):

(a) as a minimum, the matters referred to in regulation 9(1)(b) – (j) of the concurrency regulations, and in paragraph 3.49 of the concurrency guidance, complying with the time limits specified in paragraph 3.49;

(b) other information which it reasonably believes to be relevant or helpful to the other in the conduct of the case; and

(c) in the case of the authority which is exercising the powers, reports to the other on the progress of the case, of sufficient frequency and detail to enable the other to be appropriately informed; the means and frequency of such reporting will be decided on a case-by-case basis and in the light of experience as this enhanced framework of collaboration and its supporting arrangements develop over time.

Information sharing mechanism – for know-how purposes

47. The CMA will maintain on its webpages a central database of decisions taken in cases under the competition prohibitions, with a view to having an accessible body of know-how that will help ensure the effective and consistent application of competition law. The CMA and Ofgem will, to the extent permitted by law, contribute information to that in the way best calculated to achieve that objective.

48. In any event, the CMA will report on cases in the regulated sectors under the competition prohibitions in the annual concurrency report which it is required under statute to issue. Further provisions on the annual concurrency report are in paragraphs 61 to 63 of this MoU.

Information sharing – confidentiality constraints

49. Any disclosure of information under paragraphs 30 to 32 and 38 to 48 of this MoU, and any use by the recipient of such information, shall only be to the extent permitted by law, including by reference to the provisions of Part 9 of the Enterprise Act 2002, relevant sector-specific legislative provisions and any other provisions relating to the disclosure, handling and use of information (such as the Data Protection Act 1998 and section 118 of the Financial Services and Markets Act 2000, to the extent relevant).

50. Prior to disclosing information to each other, the CMA and Ofgem will not generally give the person to whom the information relates prior notice of its intention to make the disclosure. However, if the CMA or Ofgem consider it necessary or appropriate to pass leniency information to each other (or to another UK authority with concurrent powers), the transmitting authority will inform the applicant or its legal adviser first. Leniency information for the purposes of this MoU is any information which came into the possession of any of the CMA, its predecessors, Ofgem or any other public authority as a direct or indirect result of having been provided in the context of an application for leniency. It includes information obtained by the transferring authority as a result of investigative measures resulting directly or indirectly from an application for leniency.

51. In addition to the general provisions referred to in paragraph 49, where Ofgem or the CMA receives leniency information from the other (or from another UK authority with concurrent powers) for the purpose of applying the competition prohibitions or, in the case of the CMA, the cartel offence under section 188 of the Enterprise Act 2002, that information will not be used for any other purpose. This restriction on use also applies to any information obtained by the receiving authority as a result of investigative measures relating to the competition prohibitions or the cartel offence following the receipt of leniency information from the other authority. This does not affect the use that may be made by the CMA or Ofgem of information received from other sources, or if the leniency applicant's consent is obtained.[13] Where the provision of leniency information to either the CMA or Ofgem affords or might, under certain conditions, afford the leniency applicant, its subsidiaries or its employees protection from sanctions (including a reduction in penalties) under the leniency programme operated by that authority and that information has been passed to another authority, the receiving authority shall afford the leniency applicant, its subsidiaries or its employees no lesser protection.

NOTES

[13] The use restriction in this paragraph is intended to govern the use of leniency information in the context of the concurrency arrangements. It is not intended to prevent the disclosure of such leniency information by either one of the CMA or Ofgem to the other (to the extent permitted by Part 9 of the Enterprise Act 2002 and in accordance with Leniency and no-action applications in cartel cases: OFT1495) for purposes other than the application of the competition prohibitions or the cartel offence. However, any such disclosure of leniency information would only be likely to be justified in exceptional circumstances, given the strong public interest in maintaining the incentives for undertakings and, in the case of the cartel offence, individuals to apply for leniency.

POOLING RESOURCES

52. Paragraph 25 above and the concurrency guidance provide for support to be provided by the supporting authority to the investigating authority when it is exercising its concurrent powers in a case. The CMA and Ofgem will endeavour, so far as is reasonably practicable and permitted by law, and in light of their respective ongoing priorities and resource availability at the time, to share their resources with each other in the interests of the effective enforcement of competition law in the gas and electricity markets in Great Britain, and more generally the promotion of competition for the benefit of consumers in that sector, and to ensure that their resources and expertise are used most efficiently for that purpose. This is subject to the proviso that, as stated in paragraph 5, this does not apply in relation to the functions of the CMA in its role of considering appeals against, or references related to, proposed action by Ofgem under the sectoral statutes.

53. As a consequence, where it has been agreed or determined that one of the authorities is to exercise its concurrent competition powers in relation to a case, that authority will, to the extent that there are resources available, receive appropriate practical assistance and support from the other in the handling of the case, as agreed on a case-by-case basis.

Secondments of staff

54. One means of the practical assistance and support that might be given, as referred to in paragraphs 52 and 53 of this MoU, is the secondment of staff, in accordance with regulation 10 of the concurrency regulations and paragraphs 3.33 and 3.34 of the concurrency guidance.[14]

55. The CMA and Ofgem are fully committed to the idea of secondments for this purpose, and will endeavour to meet each other's requests for secondments to the extent that they are appropriate and resources permit; this may include making provision for any secondee to be available to work for part of his or her time at his or her existing employer during the course of the secondment, for example on such cases that are in progress.

56. Requests for secondments should be made by the relationship manager of one authority to the relationship manager of the other, setting out the following information:
(a) The number of secondees required.
(b) The period for which each one is required.
(c) The level of seniority of each one.
(d) The nature of the expertise or experience of each one.
(e) The proposed payment arrangements.
(f) A brief explanation of why the requirement or requirements cannot adequately be met by deployment of staff from within the requesting authority.

57. To the extent that the recipient of a request for a secondment made under paragraph 56 of this MoU refuses that request or accedes to it on terms that are materially different from those requested, the recipient shall give reasons.

58. The CMA and Ofgem will develop appropriate arrangements for the pooling and secondment of staff. Such arrangements will have regard to the resource constraints of both parties and such calls for staff, therefore, will be made in reasonable time and with sufficient warning to enable appropriate resource planning, management of other work commitments and appropriate sign-off procedures within each authority.

NOTES

[14] Nothing in this section affects arrangements for the secondment of staff outside of the provisions of regulation 10 of the concurrency regulations and paragraphs 3.33 and 3.34 of the concurrency guidance.

OTHER MUTUAL SUPPORT

59. In addition to the sharing of information, expertise, experience and the secondment of staff, the CMA and Ofgem are fully committed to providing each other with more informal forms of support to enable them to carry out their competition law functions in relation to the gas and electricity markets in Great Britain – in each case to the extent that it is appropriate and permitted by law, and that resources permit – including (but not limited to):
(a) answering specific queries from time to time;
(b) providing information or views on a specific sector or market, or an area of competition law or policy; and
(c) providing training on a specific sector or market, or an area of competition law or policy.

60. Such support may be requested and provided in connection with a specific case or with the promotion of competition more generally. In this regard, both the CMA and Ofgem will act reasonably, including by providing sufficient time and information for requests for support to be responded to fully and effectively and for the relevant staff to be engaged.

ANNUAL CONCURRENCY REPORT

61. The CMA is required by statute to publish a report every year, starting after its first year of operation in 2014/15,[15] containing an assessment of how the concurrency arrangements between the CMA and the sectoral regulators, as regards both the competition prohibitions and the market provisions, have operated during the year. This MoU refers to that report as the annual concurrency report. There is further provision on the annual concurrency report in paragraphs 3.55 to 3.62 of the concurrency guidance.

62. The CMA will consult, and cooperate with, Ofgem and with other sectoral regulators in preparing the annual concurrency report. In connection with this, the CMA will:

(a) prepare a draft of the annual concurrency report that it will send to Ofgem and other sectoral regulators seeking comments or suggestions on the content or conclusions of the annual concurrency report and giving them adequate time to comment or make suggestions;

(b) take account of any comments or suggestions it receives from Ofgem and other sectoral regulators and the CMA may seek further clarification on those comments or suggestions as appropriate;

(c) prepare a final version of the annual concurrency report for publication that takes account of its consultation of Ofgem and other sectoral regulators as appropriate; and

(d) make the annual concurrency report available on the CMA webpages.

63. Ofgem will cooperate with the CMA in the preparation of the annual concurrency report including (but not limited to) by way of:

(a) providing information and data on general market conditions and on the application of the competition prohibitions and the market provisions in the gas and electricity markets in Great Britain;

(b) responding to reasonable requests for information and data; and

(c) providing to the CMA any comments and suggestions it may have in connection with the process described in paragraph 62 of this MoU;

in each case promptly so as to facilitate the timely production and publication of the annual concurrency report.

NOTES

15 Enterprise and Regulatory Reform Act 2013, Schedule 4, paragraph 16.

VOLUNTARY REDRESS SCHEMES

64. In cases relating to investigations under the competition prohibitions in the gas and electricity sectors in Great Britain, both the CMA and Ofgem have the power to approve voluntary redress schemes. When either authority proposes to exercise these powers, it shall liaise with the other authority as appropriate and will have regard to its own guidance.[16]

NOTES

16 The CMA's guidance on the approval of voluntary redress schemes (CMA40) states at footnote 7: 'The CMA expects that regulators will take this CMA guidance into account when producing their own guidance on the approval power.'

SHORT FORM OPINIONS

65. The CMA shall inform Ofgem following an initial enquiry for a short form opinion relating to the gas or electricity markets in Great Britain. Where the CMA is considering providing such an opinion, it will discuss with Ofgem before deciding to do so. If the CMA then decides to produce an opinion, it will engage with Ofgem, the nature and degree of that engagement to be considered on a case-by-case basis, having regard, in particular, to the extent to which the opinion has a multi-sector rather than single-sector dimension. In all cases, the CMA will give Ofgem the opportunity to provide comments on a draft opinion.

CHOICE OF INSTRUMENT – COMPETITION PROHIBITION OR DIRECT REGULATION BY LICENCE ENFORCEMENT

66. As a result of legislative changes introduced by Schedule 14 to the Enterprise and Regulatory Reform Act 2013,[17] Ofgem is required by sections 28(4A) and 30A(2) of the Gas Act 1986 and sections 25(4A) and 27A(2) of the Electricity Act 1989, to 'consider whether it would be more appropriate to proceed under the Competition Act 1998' before exercising its direct regulatory powers of licence enforcement.

67. The Explanatory Notes to the legislation explain that this provision 'enhances the emphasis on early and proper consideration of the use of anti-trust powers (under Part 1 of the CA98)[18] by the sector regulators'.[19]

68. The Government had previously indicated that the policy intention is to: 'strengthen the primacy of general competition law, so that the Sector Regulators are required to consider whether the use of their CA98 powers is more appropriate before using their sectoral powers to promote competition'.[20]

69. Under this provision, it is for Ofgem to determine, in any particular case, whether using its powers under the competition prohibitions would be more appropriate than exercising its licence enforcement powers.

70. Paragraph 4.4 of the concurrency guidance says that this determination will be made by the sectoral regulators 'on a case-by-case basis.' It may be that, in the light of experience accumulated over the coming months or years in applying this provision, it will be possible to develop more general principles that could serve as useful guidance in future cases, perhaps through the forum of the UKCN, while respecting the right of the sectoral regulator to make the determination.

NOTES

17 Having effect from April 2014.

18 That is, the competition prohibitions.

19 Enterprise and Regulatory Reform Act 2013 – Explanatory Notes, paragraph 370.

20 BIS (March 2012), *Growth, competition and the competition regime – Government response to consultation*, paragraph 8.16.

PART B – COOPERATION IN RELATION TO THE MARKET PROVISIONS: MARKET STUDIES AND MARKET INVESTIGATIONS (ENTERPRISE ACT 2002)

HOW CONCURRENCY WORKS UNDER THE MARKET PROVISIONS

[3.263]

71. Ofgem has the power, concurrently with the CMA, to carry out market studies, to make market investigation references, agree undertakings in lieu of a reference and make recommendations to the government in relation to the gas and electricity markets in Great Britain under Part 4 of the Enterprise Act 2002 (as do other sectoral regulators in relation to the sectors for which they are responsible).

72. Under the Enterprise Act 2002, the CMA and Ofgem may, in relation to the gas and electricity markets in Great Britain, undertake market studies, and may make market investigation references to the Chair of the CMA for the constitution of a CMA group to conduct an in-depth market investigation into single or multiple markets for goods or services in the UK. The purpose of these investigations is to examine the market(s) and (where required) implement appropriate remedies where the CMA determines that the structure of the market(s) or the conduct of the suppliers or customers is harming competition.

73. When making a reference, the CMA or Ofgem, as applicable, must have reasonable grounds for suspecting that any feature or combination of features of a market or markets in the UK prevents, restricts or distorts competition in relation to the supply or acquisition of any goods or services in the UK (or in a part of the UK).

74. As provided for by section 36A(5A) of the Gas Act 1986 and section 43(4A) of the Electricity Act 1989, neither the CMA nor Ofgem shall exercise functions under Part 4 of the Enterprise Act 2002 in relation to any matter if such functions have been exercised in relation to that matter by the other.

75. As provided for in section 36A(6) of the Gas Act 1986 and section 43(5) of the Electricity Act 1989, where a market investigation reference is made, Ofgem can be required to provide advice and assistance to the CMA, or can itself decide to provide information, and the CMA is then under an obligation to take the information into account.

76. The cooperation between the CMA and Ofgem provided for in this Part B shall not extend to conduct that could reasonably be expected to impair the impartiality or the fairness of the CMA panel in conducting market investigations.

SUPER-COMPLAINTS

77. Section 11 of the Enterprise Act 2002 provides for a super-complaint to be made by a designated consumer body that any feature, or combination of features, of a market in the UK for goods or services is or appears to be significantly harming the interests of consumers.

78. Ofgem has a duty to respond to super-complaints made to it under the Enterprise Act 2002 if the complaint concerns a market in relation to which Ofgem has functions under the Gas Act 1986 and/or the Electricity Act 1989.

79. The coordination of the CMA's and the sectoral regulators' super-complaint duties will be based on policies agreed and applied through the UKCN.

MUTUAL CONSULTATION

80. Ofgem and the CMA have a duty to consult each other before exercising concurrent functions under the market provisions.

SHARING INFORMATION

81. The provisions of paragraphs 40 to 44, 46 (excluding 46(a)) and 48 of this MoU apply to information sharing under the market provisions as they do under the competition prohibitions.

POOLING RESOURCES

82. The provisions of paragraph 52 to 60 of this MoU apply to pooling resources under the market provisions as they do under the competition prohibitions.

83. Where the CMA and Ofgem intend to pool resources in order to exercise powers under the market provisions of the Enterprise Act 2002, they shall, at the outset of any such project, discuss the arrangements for how they will pool resources and work jointly.

ANNUAL CONCURRENCY REPORT

84. The provisions of paragraph 61 to 63 of this MoU apply under the market provisions as they do under the competition prohibitions.

MEMORANDUM OF UNDERSTANDING BETWEEN THE COMPETITION AND MARKETS AUTHORITY AND THE NORTHERN IRELAND AUTHORITY FOR UTILITY REGULATION – CONCURRENT COMPETITION POWERS

18 January 2016

[3.264]

NOTES

FOREWORD

[3.265]

The changes to the United Kingdom's (UK) competition law system, introduced under the Enterprise and Regulatory Reform Act 2013 and in force since April 2014, are designed to improve the effectiveness of competition law enforcement in this country.

The Competition and Markets Authority (CMA) has competition law powers which apply across the whole economy. Sectoral regulators such as the Northern Ireland Authority for Utility Regulation (NIAUR) may exercise the competition law powers to enforce the prohibitions on anti-competitive agreements and on abuse of a dominant position, and to make market investigation references, concurrently with the CMA in those sectors for which they have responsibility.

The Enterprise and Regulatory Reform Act 2013 introduced a number of changes to improve the working of concurrency and enable closer working between the CMA and sectoral regulators.

The CMA and the sectoral regulators have demonstrated their commitment to making the concurrency framework more effective through the establishment of the UK Competition Network (UKCN). This represents an enhanced forum for cooperation which will enable closer working with the objective of more consistent and effective use of competition powers across all sectors. In their statement of intent in December 2013, the members of the UKCN affirmed: 'The mission of the UKCN will be to promote competition for the benefit of consumers and to prevent anti-competitive behaviour both through facilitating use of competition powers and development of pro-competitive regulatory frameworks, as appropriate.'[1]

This memorandum of understanding (MoU) represents a further stage in the process of cooperation between the CMA and the regulators, setting out more practical detail on how the CMA and the NIAUR will work together within the framework of competition law.[2]

The main purpose of this MoU is to establish an understanding between the CMA and the NIAUR as to how this closer working will work in practice. It draws on the legislation which sets out the formal framework for how concurrency will operate and also, importantly, sets out our bilateral commitment to look for opportunities to work together, including within the framework of the UKCN, to promote competition for the benefit of consumers. We shall do this by the sharing of expertise, information, ideas and experience, and each of us will commit to doing this efficiently and with a mutual regard for each other's statutory position and strategic objectives.

NIAUR is responsible for regulating the electricity, gas and water and sewerage industries in Northern Ireland. Its principal objectives can be summarised as follows:

- To protect the interests of electricity consumers (with regard to price and quality of service), wherever appropriate by promoting competition in the generation, transmission and supply of electricity.
- To promote the development and maintenance of an economic and coordinated gas industry and to protect the interests of gas consumers (with regard to price and quality of service).
- To protect the interests of water and sewerage consumers in relation to the supply of water and provision of sewerage services, wherever appropriate by facilitating effective competition.

We believe that this MoU offers a valuable basis for that cooperation, in the interests of the CMA, the NIAUR, the gas, electricity, water and sewerage industries in Northern Ireland and, most importantly of all, the consumers.

Alex Chisholm	**Jenny Pyper**
CEO, CMA	**CEO, NIAUR**

NOTES

1 UKCN, *Statement of Intent*, 2 December 2013.

2 This MoU does not relate to 'regulatory appeals' – that is, the separate role that the CMA has in considering appeals against, or references relating to, proposed direct regulatory action by the NIAUR under the sectoral statutes. This is a separate role, to be undertaken by the CMA panel, and the CMA is committed to ensuring that its cooperation with the

NIAUR – whether under this MoU (and under comparable MoU agreed with other sectoral regulators), through the UKCN, or otherwise in connection with their concurrent powers – will not impair the impartiality and fairness of the CMA's conduct of such regulatory appeals (or indeed of market or merger investigations undertaken by the CMA panel).

MEMORANDUM OF UNDERSTANDING BETWEEN THE COMPETITION AND MARKETS AUTHORITY AND THE NORTHERN IRELAND AUTHORITY FOR UTILITY REGULATION

PURPOSE OF THIS MEMORANDUM OF UNDERSTANDING

[3.266]

1. This MoU sets out working arrangements between the CMA and the NIAUR in relation to:

(a) their concurrent powers to apply the prohibitions on agreements that prevent, restrict or distort competition and on the abuse of a dominant position, under the Chapter I prohibition and the Chapter II prohibition of the Competition Act 1998 and under Article 101 and Article 102 of the Treaty on the Functioning of the European Union – referred to in this MoU as the 'competition prohibitions'; and

(b) their concurrent powers to undertake market studies, and to make references to the CMA for the constitution of a CMA group to conduct an in-depth market investigation into single or multiple markets for goods or services in the UK under the Enterprise Act 2002 – referred to in this MoU as the 'market provisions,'

in the gas, electricity, water and sewerage services in Northern Ireland.

2. This MoU is not intended to have legal effect.

3. This MoU is to be read alongside other material concerning the relations between the CMA and the NIAUR including: the Energy (Northern Ireland) Order 2003; the Gas (Northern Ireland) Order 1996; the Electricity (Northern Ireland) Order 1992; the Water and Sewerage Services (Northern Ireland) Order 2006; the Competition Act 1998; the Enterprise Act 2002; the Enterprise and Regulatory Reform Act 2013; the Competition Act 1998 and Other Enactments (Amendment) Regulations 2004; the Competition Act 1998 (Concurrency) Regulations 2014, referred to in this MoU as the 'concurrency regulations' and the CMA's guidance on concurrent application of competition law to regulated industries, referred to in this MoU as the 'concurrency guidance'.[3] This MoU supplements and does not supplant that material.

4. The arrangements covered by this MoU are, wherever possible, set out in terms providing sufficient flexibility for the relationship between the NIAUR and the CMA to develop in the light of experience. The CMA and the NIAUR commit to review these arrangements from time to time to evaluate their continuing fitness for purpose. Such review can be initiated at the request of the CMA, the NIAUR or a member of the UKCN. This MoU may only be revised by agreement between the CMA and the NIAUR.

5. Nothing in this MoU applies in relation to the functions of the CMA in its separate role of considering appeals against, or references related, to proposed action by the NIAUR under the sectoral statutes. The CMA and the NIAUR acknowledge the importance of maintaining the CMA's impartiality and fairness in carrying out those functions, and indeed of market or merger investigations undertaken by the CMA panel.

NOTES

[3] CMA10.

CONTEXT

6. This MoU operates within the framework of the legislative provisions referred to in paragraph 1 and any other applicable sector specific legislation from time to time.

Role of the CMA

7. The CMA is a non-ministerial department, established under the Enterprise and Regulatory Reform Act 2013.

8. The CMA works to promote competition for the benefit of consumers, both within and outside the UK, to make markets work well for consumers, businesses and the economy.

9. The CMA's statutory responsibilities, in so far as relevant to the matters that are the subject of this MoU, include:

(a) investigating where there may be breaches of the competition prohibitions; and

(b) conducting market studies and market investigations where there may be competition and consumer problems.

10. In connection with its statutory responsibilities, the CMA will cooperate with sectoral regulators and encourage sectoral regulators to use their powers, including their powers to apply the competition prohibitions, in the interests of competition for the benefit of consumers.

Role of the NIAUR

11. The NIAUR is a non-ministerial government department responsible for regulating the gas, electricity, water and sewerage industries in Northern Ireland and promoting the short and long term interests of consumers of services supplied by these industries.

12. The NIAUR's statutory duties in relation to gas and electricity are set out in the Energy (Northern Ireland) Order 2003. Its duties in relation to water and sewerage are set out in the Water and Sewerage Services (Northern Ireland) Order 2006. In so far as relevant to the matters that are the subject of this MoU, these statutory duties include:

(a) investigating where there may be breaches of the competition prohibitions in relation to the gas, electricity, water and sewerage industries in Northern Ireland;

(b) conducting market studies and market investigations where there may be competition and consumer problems in relation to the gas, electricity, water and sewerage industries in Northern Ireland;

(c) carrying out its functions in relation to electricity, water and sewerage industries in Northern Ireland in the matter best calculated to protect the interests of consumers of the services provided by those industries, wherever appropriate by promoting effective competition between persons engaged in, or in commercial activities connected with, the provision of those services;

(d) facilitating competition between persons whose activities consist of or include storing, supplying or participating in the conveyance of gas in Northern Ireland; and

(e) carrying out its functions in relation to the supply of water and sewerage services, having regard to the desirability of facilitating effective competition within the industries which supply those services.

AIMS

13. The Enterprise and Regulatory Reform Act 2013, as well as establishing the CMA, made provision for the better working of the CMA's and the sectoral regulators' concurrent powers in the regulated sectors; specifically, the Act: 'strengthens the role of the CMA and enhances the emphasis on early and proper consideration of the use of anti-trust powers (under Part 1 of the CA98 [ie the competition prohibitions]) by the sector regulators.'[4]

14. It is one of the strategic goals of the CMA, announced on its establishment on 1 October 2013, to extend the frontiers of competition into new areas, including by working with sectoral regulators to ensure fuller use of competition law and policy in sectoral markets.[5]

15. The government's strategic steer to the CMA, issued on 1 December 2015, says that the CMA should build 'a strong dialogue with sectoral regulators using the UKCN to ensure that the overall competition regime is coordinated and regulatory practices complement each other'.

16. The sectoral regulators and the CMA, working together in the UKCN established in 2013 (with Monitor having observer status), declared that: 'The mission of the UKCN will be to promote competition for the benefit of consumers and to prevent anti-competitive behaviour both through facilitating use of competition powers and development of procompetitive regulatory frameworks, as appropriate.'[5a]

17. The CMA and the NIAUR seek to use their powers to achieve more competitive outcomes in the gas, electricity, water and sewerage industries in Northern Ireland for the benefit of consumers so as to make markets in the gas, electricity, water and sewerage sectors in Northern Ireland work well for consumers of gas, electricity, water and sewerage services, businesses in those sectors and businesses that use those services and the economy in which those services play an essential part. It is the view of the CMA and the NIAUR that such competitive outcomes can be achieved by various tools, including their competition law powers under the competition prohibitions, the market provisions and merger control, but also through other tools such as direct regulatory action including through enforcement of licence provisions (for example, in providing for third party access to networks) and liberalisation measures introduced under national and European Union legislation.

18. This MoU aims to further the attainment of these objectives, and to make the changes introduced by the Enterprise and Regulatory Reform Act 2013 work effectively, maximising the complementary skills of the CMA and the NIAUR, including through:

(a) promoting cooperation and coordination between the CMA and the NIAUR when dealing with cases of suspected anti-competitive behaviour for which they have concurrent powers;

(b) promoting cooperation and coordination between the CMA and the NIAUR when dealing with market studies and market investigation references for which they have concurrent powers;

(c) facilitating the efficient and effective handling of cases of suspected anticompetitive behaviour within the gas, electricity, water and sewerage services markets in Northern Ireland;

(d) avoiding duplication of activity, wherever possible; and

(e) ensuring transparency as to the respective roles of the CMA and the NIAUR for individuals and consumers affected.

NOTES

4 Enterprise and Regulatory Reform Act 2013 Explanatory Notes, paragraph 370.

5 Department for Business, Innovation and Skills (1 December 2015), *Strategic steer for the Competition and Markets Authority*, in Annex A to the *Government's response to the Consultation on the Strategic Steer to the CMA*, p11.

5a UKCN (2013), Statement of Intent.

GENERAL COOPERATION

19. In addition to the provisions for cooperation between the CMA and the NIAUR specific to particular powers of the CMA and the NIAUR, as set out in this MoU and elsewhere, the CMA and the NIAUR are committed to the following general principles and practices for cooperation between themselves in respect of the sectors for which the NIAUR has responsibility.

20. Officials of the CMA and the NIAUR will meet and communicate, at appropriate levels of seniority, to discuss matters of mutual interest, both through the UKCN and bilaterally. A framework for such meetings will, as far as possible, be determined in advance so as to ensure attendance at the appropriate level and expertise.

21. The CMA and the NAIUR will, in respect of the gas, electricity, water and sewerage industries in Northern Ireland, always consult each other:

(a) before the initial exercise of concurrent competition law powers in all cases where it appears that they have concurrent jurisdiction and where there are reasonable grounds for suspecting an infringement of the competition prohibitions; and

(b) before launching a market study under the Enterprise Act 2002.[6]

22. Where either the CMA or the NIAUR exercises its concurrent powers, the CMA and the NIAUR will, to the extent permitted by law, engage with each other in open dialogue and by sharing relevant information as appropriate. This engagement may include attendance at internal meetings held by the investigating authority (ie the authority to which a case is allocated) by the supporting authority (ie the other authority which would be competent to exercise concurrent powers in relation to the case), in order to discuss the case as envisaged at paragraph 3.31 of the concurrency guidance. The supporting authority will not generally attend the investigating authority's constitutional decision-making meetings, meetings of governance bodies or meetings with external parties such as those under investigation or complainants. Attendance by the supporting authority at any meeting is at the discretion of the investigating authority, but requests to attend should be considered by the investigating authority in the spirit of cooperation underpinning the new concurrency regime.

23. The CMA and the NIAUR will consult each other at an early stage on any issues that might have significant implications for the other. For example, where the CMA undertakes a market study which relates to a sector other than gas, electricity, water or sewerage services in Northern Ireland but which may have a significant impact on any of those sectors, the CMA will inform the NIAUR and share appropriate information relating to that market study with the NIAUR to the extent permitted by law.

24. Within the spirit of broader collaboration for the purposes of the promotion of competitive outcomes, the CMA and the NIAUR will commit to discuss and share other relevant information, where legally permissible to do so, but subject to the need not to impair the impartiality and fairness of the CMA in carrying out the functions referred to in paragraph 5 of this MoU.

NOTES

6 Instigation of a market study occurs on the publication of a market study notice, as defined in section 130A of the Enterprise Act 2002.

PART A – COOPERATION IN RELATION TO THE COMPETITION PROHIBITIONS (COMPETITION ACT 1998 AND ARTICLES 101 AND 102 OF THE TREATY ON THE FUNCTIONING OF THE EUROPEAN UNION)

CASE ALLOCATION

Basis of allocation

[3.267]

25. The CMA and the NIAUR will endeavour to reach agreement on which authority will exercise its concurrent competition powers in respect of any particular case, under regulation 4(2) of the concurrency regulations. They will do so in a spirit of constructiveness and cooperation, while acknowledging the CMA's ultimate powers under regulations 5 and 8 of the concurrency regulations.

26. Their determination of which authority will exercise its powers will be based on assessing which of them is better placed to exercise those powers, having regard to the factors set out in paragraph 3.22 of the concurrency guidance.

The CMA and the NIAUR envisage that other factors may appear relevant in the light of practical experience and that, if so, such factors may be chosen to supplement or supplant the factors set out in paragraph 3.22 of the concurrency guidance.

Procedure for allocation

27. Where either the CMA or the NIAUR has decided, on the basis of information in its possession, that there are reasonable grounds for suspecting that one of the competition prohibitions has been infringed (the 'reasonable suspicion test')[7] in relation to the gas, electricity, water and sewerage sectors in Northern Ireland, it will disclose to the other (ie the receiving authority) sufficient information:

(a) to enable the receiving authority to understand the basis on which the disclosing authority has decided that the reasonable suspicion test is met; and

(b) for there to be an informed discussion on which authority (if either) is best placed to proceed in respect of the case.

28. In practice, it may be helpful for the CMA and the NIAUR to have discussed the case prior to such a decision having been reached, subject to paragraph 41 below. The disclosing authority will provide the information described under paragraph 27 within ten working days after it has decided that the reasonable suspicion test is met, whether or not it proposes to exercise concurrent powers.[8]

29. Within seven working days from receipt of this information, the receiving authority will respond in writing, setting out its initial view on the case and how it should be allocated and identifying any further information which it requires.

30. The CMA and the NIAUR will endeavour to agree which authority will exercise its concurrent competition powers in relation to the case, as provided for in regulation 4(2) of the concurrency regulations, as soon as possible and in any event no later than one month from disclosure of the information described under paragraph 27. Other than in exceptional circumstances (which shall be set out in writing), the CMA will initiate the procedure set out in regulation 5 of the concurrency regulations if agreement is not reached within two months of the disclosing authority first receiving sufficient information in connection with a complaint to enable it to decide that the reasonable suspicion test is met.

31. The procedure for agreeing the transfer of a case that is already in progress from the CMA to the NIAUR, or from the NIAUR to the CMA, is as set out in regulation 7 of the concurrency regulations and in paragraph 3.32 of the concurrency guidance.

32. The procedure for the CMA to direct the transfer to itself from the NIAUR of a case that is already in progress is as set out in regulation 8 of the concurrency regulations.

NOTES

[7] As provided in section 25 of the Competition Act 1998.

[8] As provided in regulation 9 of the concurrency regulations.

Implications of allocation

33. Any agreement or determination as to case allocation, under regulations 4, 5, 7 or 8 of the concurrency regulations, shall be notified to the person who has provided the information resulting in the case (for example, the person making a complaint), and so far as appropriate and lawful to any other affected person, by the authority which is exercising its concurrent competition powers in relation to the case, as soon as reasonably practicable.

34. Case allocation determines which of the CMA and the NIAUR is to exercise concurrent functions and make any decisions under the competition prohibitions. The CMA or NIAUR will be publicly identified as having such responsibility if and when any such investigation is announced. The CMA and the NIAUR envisage that, whichever authority has responsibility for a particular case, they and their officials will work cooperatively with each other on the case as appropriate, pooling their expertise including in the ways described in paragraphs 49 to 57 of this MoU and in paragraphs 3.33 to 3.35 of the concurrency guidance.

SHARING INFORMATION

Principles of information sharing

35. The effective sharing of information between the CMA and the NIAUR is fundamental to the successful exercise of their concurrent competition powers. It is needed both for the appropriate allocation of cases, as described in paragraphs 27 to 32 of this MoU, and for the successful handling of cases once allocated to make optimal use of the complementary experience and expertise of the two authorities.

36. The CMA and the NIAUR are committed, in addition to their legal obligations to share information (set out in regulation 9 of the concurrency regulations), to open dialogue and continuing liaison, both bilaterally and through the UKCN, with a view not only to handling specific cases but to promoting competition, for the benefit of consumers in the gas, electricity, water and sewerage sectors in Northern Ireland.

Information sharing mechanism – general liaison

37. The CMA and the NIAUR recognise the importance of meeting regularly to share information on matters relevant to competition in the gas, electricity, water and sewerage sectors in Northern Ireland and to keep each other abreast of relevant work which they are considering or currently undertaking.

38. The CMA and the NIAUR will meet regularly at multiple levels, bilaterally and through the UKCN.

39. The CMA and the NIAUR will each designate in its organisation a relationship manager at official level to take responsibility for relations between the two authorities. In each authority, the relationship manager's responsibilities will include (but not be limited to):

(a) maintaining an overview of joint projects between the two authorities and matters of mutual interest;

(b) maintaining an overview of the authority's contacts from all areas of joint working and mutual interest; and

(c) holding meetings with the relationship manager in the other authority from time to time (whether bilaterally or in the context of the UKCN) to identify potential new issues with a view to circulating information to appropriate individuals within each organisation.

40. The existence of relationship managers does not in any way preclude direct communication between other staff at the CMA and the NIAUR.

41. For the purposes of sharing information pursuant to paragraph 27, ie in circumstances where the reasonable suspicion test is met, such information will be shared by the disclosing authority to the extent permitted by law and whether or not it proposes to exercise concurrent powers.[9] Where disclosure would be appropriate and permitted by law, the CMA and the NIAUR may also share information regarding potential infringements of the competition prohibitions in advance of having reached a view as to whether the reasonable suspicion test is met. In circumstances where either the CMA or the NIAUR has taken the view that a matter is not an administrative priority, irrespective of whether a view has been reached on whether the reasonable suspicion test is met, each may share the details of the matter with the other, or with any other authority which would be able to exercise concurrent competition powers in relation to that matter, to the extent permitted by law. Where leniency information is being shared under this paragraph, special considerations apply, as set out in paragraphs 47 and 48.

NOTES

[9] For the avoidance of doubt, this does not entail an obligation to inform the other party if the regulator is carrying out general monitoring activity, where there is no consideration of exercising its concurrent powers.

Information sharing mechanism – handling specific cases

42. The procedures for information sharing for the purpose of case allocation shall be as set out in paragraphs 27 to 29 and 35 to 48 of this MoU.

43. When either the CMA or the NIAUR is exercising its powers in respect of the competition prohibitions in a particular case in the gas, electricity, water and sewerage sectors in Northern Ireland, each of them will share with the other any of the following information in its possession (to the extent permitted by law and subject to the confidentiality obligations in paragraphs 46 to 48 of this MoU):

(a) as a minimum, the matters referred to in regulation 9(1)(b) – (j) of the concurrency regulations, and in paragraph 3.49 of the concurrency guidance, complying with the time limits specified in paragraph 3.49;

(b) other information which it reasonably believes to be relevant or helpful to the other in the conduct of the case; and

(c) in the case of the authority which is exercising the powers, reports to the other on the progress of the case, of sufficient frequency and detail to enable the other to be appropriately informed; the means and frequency of such reporting will be decided on a case by case basis and in the light of experience as this enhanced framework of collaboration and its supporting arrangements develop over time.

Information sharing mechanism – for know-how purposes

44. The CMA will maintain on its webpages a central database of decisions taken in cases under the competition prohibitions, with a view to having an accessible body of know-how that will help ensure the effective and consistent application of competition law. The CMA and the NIAUR will, to the extent permitted by law, contribute information to that in the way best calculated to achieve that objective.

45. In any event, the CMA will report on cases in the regulated sectors under the competition prohibitions in the annual concurrency report which it is required under statute to issue. Further provisions on the annual concurrency report are in paragraphs 58 to 60 of this MoU.

Information sharing – confidentiality constraints

46. Any disclosure of information under paragraphs 27 to 29 and 37 to 45 of this MoU, and any use by the recipient of such information, shall only be to the extent permitted by law, including by reference to the provisions of Part 9 of the Enterprise Act 2002, relevant sector-specific legislative provisions and any other provisions relating to the disclosure, handling and use of information (such as the Data Protection Act 1998 and section 118 of the Financial Services and Markets Act 2000, to the extent relevant).

47. Prior to disclosing information to each other, the CMA and the NIAUR will not generally give the person to whom the information relates prior notice of its intention to make the disclosure. However, if the CMA or the NIAUR consider it necessary or appropriate to pass leniency information to each other (or to another UK authority with concurrent powers), the transmitting authority will inform the applicant or its legal adviser first. Leniency information for the purposes of this MoU is any information which came into the possession of any of the CMA, its predecessors, the NIAUR or any other public authority as a direct or indirect result of having been provided in the context of an application for leniency. It includes information obtained by the transferring authority as a result of investigative measures resulting directly or indirectly from an application for leniency.

48. In addition to the general provisions referred to in paragraph 46, where the NIAUR or the CMA receives leniency information from the other (or from another UK authority with concurrent powers) for the purpose of applying the competition prohibitions or, in the case of the CMA, the cartel offence under section 188 of the Enterprise Act 2002, that information will not be used for any other purpose. This restriction on use also applies to any information obtained by the receiving authority as a result of investigative measures relating to the competition prohibitions or the cartel offence following the receipt of leniency information from the other authority. This does not affect the use that may be made by the CMA or the NIAUR of information received from other sources, or if the leniency applicant's consent is obtained.[10] Where the provision of leniency information to either the CMA or the NIAUR affords or might, under certain conditions, afford the leniency applicant, its subsidiaries or its employees protection from sanctions (including a reduction in penalties) under the leniency programme operated by that authority and that information has been passed to another authority, the receiving authority shall afford the leniency applicant, its subsidiaries or its employees no lesser protection.

NOTES

[10] The use restriction in this paragraph is intended to govern the use of leniency information in the context of the concurrency arrangements. It is not intended to prevent the disclosure of such leniency information by either one of the

CMA or the NIAUR to the other (to the extent permitted by Part 9 of the Enterprise Act 2002 and in accordance with OFT1495) for purposes other than the application of the competition prohibitions or the cartel offence. However, any such disclosure of leniency information would only be likely to be justified in exceptional circumstances, given the strong public interest in maintaining the incentives for undertakings and, in the case of the cartel offence, individuals to apply for leniency.

POOLING RESOURCES

49. Paragraph 22 above and the concurrency guidance provide for support to be provided by the supporting authority to the investigating authority when it is exercising its concurrent powers in a case. The CMA and the NIAUR will endeavour, so far as is reasonably practicable and permitted by law, and in light of their respective ongoing priorities and resource availability at the time, to share their resources with each other in the interests of the effective enforcement of competition law in the gas, electricity, water and sewerage sectors in Northern Ireland, and more generally the promotion of competition for the benefit of consumers in those sectors, and to ensure that their resources and expertise are used most efficiently for that purpose. This is subject to the proviso that, as stated in paragraph 5, this does not apply in relation to the functions of the CMA in its role of considering appeals against, or references related to, proposed action by the NIAUR under the sectoral statutes.

50. As a consequence, where it has been agreed or determined that one of the authorities is to exercise its concurrent competition powers in relation to a case, that authority will, to the extent that there are resources available, receive appropriate practical assistance and support from the other in the handling of the case, as agreed on a case by case basis.

Secondments of staff

51. One means of the practical assistance and support that might be given, as referred to in paragraphs 49 and 50 of this MoU, is the secondment of staff, in accordance with regulation 10 of the concurrency regulations and paragraphs 3.33 and 3.34 of the concurrency guidance.

52. The CMA and the NIAUR are fully committed to the idea of secondments for this purpose, and will endeavour to meet each other's requests for secondments to the extent that they are appropriate and resources permit; this may include making provision for any secondee to be available to work for part of his or her time at his or her existing employer during the course of the secondment, for example on such cases that are in progress.

53. Requests for secondments should be made by the relationship manager of one authority to the relationship manager of the other, setting out the following information:

(a) the number of secondees required;
(b) the period for which each one is required;
(c) the level of seniority of each one;
(d) the nature of the expertise or experience of each one;
(e) the proposed payment arrangements; and
(f) a brief explanation of why the requirement or requirements cannot adequately be met by deployment of staff from within the requesting authority.

54. To the extent that the recipient of a request for a secondment made under paragraph 53 of this MoU refuses that request or accedes to it on terms that are materially different from those requested, the recipient shall give reasons.

55. The CMA and the NIAUR will develop appropriate arrangements for the pooling and secondment of staff. Such arrangements will have regard to the resource constraints of both parties and such calls for staff, therefore, will be made in reasonable time and with sufficient warning to enable appropriate resource planning, management of other work commitments and appropriate sign-off procedures within each authority.

OTHER MUTUAL SUPPORT

56. In addition to the sharing of information, expertise, experience and the secondment of staff, the CMA and the NIAUR are fully committed to providing each other with more informal forms of support to enable them to carry out their competition law functions in relation to the gas, electricity, water and sewerage sectors in Northern Ireland – in each case to the extent that it is appropriate and permitted by law, and that resources permit – including (but not limited to):

(a) answering specific queries from time to time;
(b) providing information or views on a specific sector or market, or an area of competition law or policy; and
(c) providing training on a specific sector or market, or an area of competition law or policy.

57. Such support may be requested and provided in connection with a specific case or with the promotion of competition more generally. In this regard, both the CMA and the NIAUR will act reasonably, including by providing sufficient time and information for requests for support to be responded to fully and effectively and for the relevant staff to be engaged.

ANNUAL CONCURRENCY REPORT

58. The CMA is required by statute to publish a report every year, starting after its first year of operation in 2014/15,[11] containing an assessment of how the concurrency arrangements between the CMA and the sectoral regulators, as regards both the competition prohibitions and the market provisions, have operated during the year. This MoU refers to that report as the 'annual concurrency report'. There is further provision on the annual concurrency report in paragraphs 3.55 to 3.62 of the concurrency guidance.

59. The CMA will consult, and cooperate with, the NIAUR and with other sectoral regulators in preparing the annual concurrency report. In connection with this, the CMA will:

(a) prepare a draft of the annual concurrency report that it will send to the NIAUR and other sectoral regulators seeking comments or suggestions on the content or conclusions of the annual concurrency report and giving them adequate time to comment or make suggestions;

(b) take account of any comments or suggestions it receives from the NIAUR and other sectoral regulators and the CMA may seek further clarification on those comments or suggestions as appropriate;

(c) prepare a final version of the annual concurrency report for publication that takes account of its consultation of the NIAUR and other sectoral regulators as appropriate; and

(d) make the annual concurrency report available on the CMA webpages.

60. The NIAUR will cooperate with the CMA in the preparation of the annual concurrency report including (but not limited to) by way of:

(a) providing information and data on general market conditions and on the application of the competition prohibitions and the market provisions in the gas, electricity, water and sewerage sectors in Northern Ireland;

(b) responding to reasonable requests for information and data; and

(c) providing to the CMA any comments and suggestions it may have in connection with the process described in paragraph 59 of this MoU,

in each case promptly so as to facilitate the timely production and publication of the annual concurrency report.

NOTES

[11] Enterprise and Regulatory Reform Act 2013 Schedule 4 paragraph 16.

CHOICE OF INSTRUMENT – COMPETITION PROHIBITION OR DIRECT REGULATION BY LICENCE ENFORCEMENT

61. As a result of legislative changes introduced by Schedule 14 to the Enterprise and Regulatory Reform Act 2013,[12] the NIAUR is required by Articles 42(5A) and 45(3) of the Energy (Northern Ireland) Order 2003 and Articles 31(1A) and 35(11) of the Water and Sewerage Services (Northern Ireland) Order 2006, to 'consider whether it would be more appropriate to proceed under the Competition Act 1998' before exercising its direct regulatory powers of licence enforcement.

62. The Explanatory Notes to the legislation explain that this provision: 'enhances the emphasis on early and proper consideration of the use of anti-trust powers (under Part 1 of the CA98)[13] by the sector regulators.'[14]

63. The government had previously indicated that the policy intention is to: 'strengthen the primacy of general competition law, so that the Sector Regulators are required to consider whether the use of their CA98 powers is more appropriate before using their sectoral powers to promote competition.'[15]

64. Under this provision, it is for the NIAUR to determine, in any particular case, whether using its powers under the competition prohibitions would be more appropriate than exercising its licence enforcement powers.

65. The guidance says that this determination will be made by the sectoral regulators 'on a case-by-case basis'.[16] It may be that, in the light of experience accumulated over the coming months or years in applying this provision, it will be possible to develop more general principles that could serve as useful guidance in future cases, perhaps through the forum of the UKCN, while respecting the right of the sector regulator to make the determination.

NOTES

[12] Having effect from April 2014.

[13] That is, the competition prohibitions.

[14] Enterprise and Regulatory Reform Act 2013 – Explanatory Notes, paragraph 370.

[15] BIS (March 2012), Growth, competition and the competition regime – Government response to consultation, paragraph 8.16.

[16] BIS (March 2012), Growth, competition and the competition regime – Government response to consultation, paragraph 4.3.

VOLUNTARY REDRESS SCHEMES

66. In cases relating to investigations under the competition prohibitions in the gas, electricity, water and sewerage sectors in Northern Ireland, both the CMA and the NIAUR have the power to approve voluntary redress schemes. When either authority proposes to exercise these powers, it shall liaise with the other authority as appropriate and will have regard to its own guidance.[17]

NOTES

[17] The CMA's guidance on the approval of voluntary redress schemes (CMA40) states at footnote 7: 'The CMA expects that regulators will take this CMA guidance into account when producing their own guidance on the approval power.'

SHORT FORM OPINIONS

The CMA shall inform the NIAUR following an initial enquiry for a short form opinion relating to the markets for gas, electricity, water or sewerage services in Northern Ireland. Where the CMA is considering providing such an opinion, it will discuss with the NIAUR before deciding to do so. If the CMA then decides to produce an opinion, it will engage with the NIAUR, the nature and degree of that engagement to be considered on a case by case basis, having regard, in particular, to the extent to which the opinion has a multi-sector rather than single-sector dimension. In all cases, the CMA will give the NIAUR the opportunity to provide comments on a draft opinion.

PART B – COOPERATION IN RELATION TO THE MARKET PROVISIONS: MARKET STUDIES AND MARKET INVESTIGATIONS (ENTERPRISE ACT 2002)

HOW CONCURRENCY WORKS UNDER THE MARKET PROVISIONS

[3.268]

68. The NIAUR has the power, concurrently with the CMA, to carry out market studies, make market investigation references, agree undertakings in lieu of a reference and make recommendations to the government in relation to the gas, electricity, water and sewerage sectors in Northern Ireland under Part 4 of the Enterprise Act 2002 (as do other sectoral regulators in relation to the sectors for which they are responsible).

69. Under the Enterprise Act 2002, the CMA and the NIAUR may, in relation to the gas, electricity, water and sewerage sectors in Northern Ireland, undertake market studies, and may make market investigation references to the Chair of the CMA for the constitution of a CMA group to conduct an in-depth market investigation into single or multiple markets for goods or services in the UK. The purpose of these investigations is to examine the market(s) and (where required) implement appropriate remedies where the CMA determines that the structure of the market(s) or the conduct of the suppliers or customers is harming competition.

70. When making a reference, the CMA or the NIAUR, as applicable, must have reasonable grounds for suspecting that any feature or combination of features of a market or markets in the UK prevents, restricts or distorts competition in relation to the supply or acquisition of any goods or services in the UK (or in a part of the UK).

71. The cooperation between the CMA and the NIAUR provided for in this Part B shall not extend to conduct that could reasonably be expected to impair the impartiality or the fairness of the CMA panel in conducting market investigations.

SUPER-COMPLAINTS

72. Section 11 of the Enterprise Act 2002 provides for a super-complaint to be made by a designated consumer body that any feature or combination of features, of a market in the UK for goods or services is or appears to be significantly harming the interests of consumers.

73. The NIAUR has a duty to respond to super-complaints made to it under the Enterprise Act 2002 if the complaint concerns the electricity or gas sectors in Northern Ireland.

74. The coordination of the CMA's and the sectoral regulators' super-complaint duties will be based on policies agreed and applied through the UKCN.

MUTUAL CONSULTATION

75. The NIAUR and the CMA have a duty to consult each other before exercising concurrent functions under the market provisions by virtue of Article 29(6) of the Water and Sewerage Services (NI) Order 2006, Article 23(4) of the Gas (NI) Order 1996 and Article 46(4) of the Electricity (NI) Order 1992.

SHARING INFORMATION

76. The provisions of paragraphs 37 to 41, 43 (excluding 43(a) and 45 of this MoU apply to information sharing under the market provisions as they do under the competition prohibitions.

POOLING RESOURCES

77. The provisions of paragraph 49 to 57 of this MoU apply to pooling resources under the market provisions as they do under the competition prohibitions.

78. Where the CMA and the NIAUR intend to pool resources in order to exercise powers under the market provisions of the Enterprise Act 2002, they shall, at the outset of any such project discuss the arrangements for how they will pool resources and work jointly.

ANNUAL CONCURRENCY REPORT

79. The provisions of paragraphs 58 to 60 of this MoU apply under the market provisions as they do under the competition prohibitions.

OFGEM ENFORCEMENT GUIDELINES

(October 2017)

[3.269]

NOTES

Publication date: 10 October 2017	**Contact:** Bruno Sheldon, Senior Enforcement Manager **Team:** Enforcement **Tel:** 020 7901 7000 **Email:** enforcement@ofgem.gov.uk

[3.270]

Overview:

As part of our duty to regulate the way in which energy businesses behave, it is important that we can act decisively to put things right if businesses breach their obligations.

This document describes how we will use our enforcement powers in such situations, how we will provide redress and remedies for consumers, and how breaches or infringements will be punished or deterred. It also sets out a number of actions we may take as an alternative to exercising our statutory enforcement powers.

The aim of these guidelines is to bring greater clarity, consistency and transparency to our enforcement policies and processes, and to highlight the processes we have in place to maximise the impact and efficiency of our work. This document is for anybody who is seeking more information on how we will use our enforcement powers. Consumers who wish to make a complaint about their gas or electricity supplier (or network operator) should contact their supplier (or network operator) in the first instance and then, if they are unhappy with the response, the Energy Ombudsman (see paragraph 1.5). Ofgem does not generally enter into individual correspondence with complainants.

CONTENTS

Changes to these guidelines:

Change number	**Date**	**Summary of change**
1	14-09-2016	Document updated to reflect a number of statutory, technical and other changes including in relation to: - the composition of Settlement Committees; - our consumer powers in light of changes brought into effect by the Consumer Rights Act 2015; and - our powers under competition law.
2	10-10-2017	Document updated to reflect a number of changes including: - streamlining of the criteria to decide when to open an investigation and use our enforcement powers; - clarification of our expectations regarding companies self-reporting potential non-compliance with licences; - ancillary changes to reflect the fact that enforcing the Standards of Conduct is no longer a new practice and to reflect our updated practices in relation to competition law investigations.

EXECUTIVE SUMMARY

[3.271]

The Gas and Electricity Markets Authority (the Authority) regulates the gas and electricity markets in Great Britain.[1] The Office of Gas and Electricity Markets (Ofgem) carries out the Authority's day-to-day work and investigates matters on its behalf.

Ofgem may open an investigation into a potential breach of a relevant legal requirement. Investigations may result in the Authority deciding to close the case because there is insufficient evidence of a breach, or it may decide to take enforcement action. Enforcement action includes issuing directions or orders to bring an end to a breach or remedy the harm that was caused, imposing financial penalties and accepting commitments or undertakings relating to future conduct or arrangements. The relevant legal requirements that the Authority can enforce, which are covered by these guidelines, include:

- imposing financial penalties, making consumer redress orders and issuing provisional/final orders, where appropriate, for breaches of relevant conditions and requirements under the Gas Act 1986 and the Electricity Act 1989
- imposing directions and penalties for breaches of the prohibitions on anti-competitive agreements and abusing positions of dominance in the Competition Act 1998 and in articles 101 and 102 of the of the Treaty on the Functioning of the European Union
- applying to the court for an order to stop breaches of certain consumer legislation, including under the Enterprise Act 2002, the Consumer Rights Act 2015 and the Business Protection from Misleading Marketing Regulations 2008.

Our vision is to achieve a culture where businesses put energy consumers first and act in line with their obligations. Enforcement action is a core part of our role and is essential to the delivery of our mission to make a positive difference for consumers. It ensures we can put right harm that is caused and there are meaningful consequences for companies that fail to comply and, as such, companies are deterred from breaching legal requirements.

However, enforcement action is not the only tool available to us for achieving a culture where businesses put energy consumers first. Through our monitoring and engagement with energy companies, we can prevent harm occurring in the first place or put it right quickly and satisfactorily through alternative action. Alternative action may include non-statutory undertakings or assurances to ensure future compliance, independent audits of conduct and/or voluntary action to remedy any concerns, which could include payments to affected parties and charitable organisations.

These guidelines set out our general approach to enforcing the legislation set out above, which includes explaining our powers to investigate and enforce, the criteria that we use to decide whether to open an investigation, the key investigative stages that we will usually follow and our decision making processes.

These guidelines cover the following:

- Section 1 explains what these guidelines cover and our objectives and regulatory principles in exercising our enforcement functions
- Section 2 describes the legislation and legal requirements covered by these guidelines
- Section 3 sets out the criteria for prioritising whether to investigate a potential breach of a legal requirement; it includes how we will take into account self-reporting
- Section 4 explains our general procedures for conducting investigations under the different types of legislation
- Section 5 covers our processes for settling or contesting cases
- Section 6 explains our decision-making bodies and our framework for delegating our decision-making powers
- Section 7 sets out our processes for closing cases including the publicity that may result, when follow-up compliance might be appropriate and how we evaluate cases and share lessons learned.

NOTES

1 The enforcement powers under the Electricity Act 1989 extend to the renewable energy zone. The Northern Ireland Authority for Energy Regulation is responsible for the regulation of the gas and electricity industries in Northern Ireland.

SECTION 1: INTRODUCTION

WHAT DO THESE GUIDELINES COVER?

[3.272]

1.1 As the sector regulator, we have a number of roles identifying and responding to conduct in the gas and electricity markets which may be unlawful, anti-competitive, or otherwise harm consumer interests.

1.2 We handle the following types of investigations which are covered by these guidelines:

- compliance with relevant conditions and requirements as defined in the Gas Act 1986 and the Electricity Act 1989[2]
- alleged anti-competitive agreements and abuses of dominant positions in the gas and electricity sectors under chapters I and II of the Competition Act 1998 for matters affecting trade within the United Kingdom, and Articles 101 and 102 of the Treaty on the Functioning of the European Union for matters affecting trade between EU member states
- compliance with consumer protection provisions under Part 8 of the Enterprise Act 2002, including the Consumer Protection from Unfair Trading Regulations 2008
- potentially unfair terms in consumer contracts and potentially unfair consumer notices under the Consumer Rights Act 2015[3]
- compliance with misleading marketing provisions in the Business Protection from Misleading Marketing Regulations 2008.

1.3 We have published separate guidance on:

- the Authority's policy on imposing financial penalties and making consumer redress orders under the Gas Act and the Electricity Act ("penalty and redress policy statement[4]")
- the Authority's policy on imposing financial penalties and seeking restitution for affected parties under REMIT[5]
- the procedures that we will normally follow when investigating potential REMIT breaches
- our prioritisation criteria and approach to dealing with applications for the approval of voluntary redress schemes for infringements of competition law.[6]

1.4 In certain cases conduct may amount to an offence which we have the power to prosecute (subject to any requirements for consent).[7] Our separate prosecution policy statement explains the process we will follow for criminal investigations[8]. We will launch any criminal investigations in accordance with statutory requirements and relevant codes of practice, notably the Criminal Procedure and Investigations Act 1996 and the Police and Criminal Evidence Act 1984 (PACE).

1.5 We do not generally intervene in individual disputes between consumers and energy companies. If consumers are worried about an issue concerning their energy supplier (or network operator), or have a complaint they wish to make, they should contact their supplier (or network operator) in the first instance. If they are not happy with the outcome they can contact the Energy Ombudsman. More information on how to make a complaint can be found on our website,[9] which also provides details about the Energy Ombudsman and the Citizens Advice consumer service.

OUR OBJECTIVES AND REGULATORY PRINCIPLES

1.6 The Authority's principal objective in carrying out its functions is to protect the interests of existing and future gas and electricity consumers. The interests of consumers include their interests in the reduction of gas and electricity supply emissions of greenhouse gases and the security of their supply of gas and electricity.[10] The Authority must carry out its functions in the manner best calculated to further that objective, wherever appropriate by promoting effective competition.[11] Before exercising its functions to promote competition, it must consider whether the interests of consumers would be better protected by exercising its functions in other ways.[12]

1.7 Our vision for our enforcement work is to **achieve a culture where businesses put energy consumers first and act in line with their obligations**.

1.8 Our strategic objectives are to:

- deliver credible deterrence across the range of our functions
- ensure visible and meaningful consequences for businesses who fail consumers and who do not comply
- achieve the greatest positive impact by targeting enforcement resources and powers.

1.9 We aim to achieve these objectives by:

- using a range of enforcement tools
- identifying poor behaviour early and taking action in a timely manner
- being transparent and fair in the enforcement process and visible in the actions that we take
- learning from everything we do.

1.10 We will have regard to better regulation principles of transparency, accountability, proportionality, consistency and targeting regulatory activities only at cases in which action is needed, and to other principles that we consider represent best regulatory practice.[13]

1.11 In relation to our enforcement activities this will include:

Transparency – We aim to be transparent in our enforcement work, having due regard to the need to maintain confidentiality in certain circumstances. We will aim to inform companies as soon as possible of our concerns and keep them appropriately informed through the key stages of our decision-making processes. Where appropriate, we will publish information when we open and close cases in line with these guidelines. In appropriate cases, we may also share information with other enforcement authorities to facilitate the exercise of our functions or those of other authorities involved.

Accountability – Our enforcement processes seek to ensure parties under investigation are treated fairly and appropriately; we are accountable for the decisions we take and make public. We also seek feedback following case closure and share lessons learnt in accordance with these guidelines (see paragraph 7.11).

Proportionality – We will prioritise our enforcement investigation and action in cases where the potential breach, if confirmed, is serious (our assessment will include harm to consumers, competition and our ability to regulate) and/or where there is a need to address poor conduct in the energy market. We will not normally prioritise enforcement action for isolated issues affecting small numbers of consumers unless any harm they have suffered is significant. We will generally focus on systemic weaknesses, including where those weaknesses adversely affect particular groups of consumers such as those in vulnerable situations.

Consistency – We will aim to ensure consistency in our enforcement decision making. Our Enforcement Oversight Board (see paragraphs 6.4-6.6) makes our case opening and related decisions and helps to achieve this by providing strategic oversight of our enforcement work.

Targeting – We will target our resources where they are most needed to tackle the most serious harm or poor conduct while delivering maximum impact. We have a range of enforcement tools which enable us to target action appropriately in line with these guidelines. Where appropriate, we will also work with other enforcement authorities to achieve these aims.

1.12 We will also have regard to the timeliness of our decision-making. One of our objectives is to respond more quickly to events and speed up our decision-making to promote consumer protection. We aim to reach a view on the appropriate way to handle issues which come to our attention, including case opening decisions, in a timely manner.

STATUS OF THESE GUIDELINES

1.13 These guidelines apply to all current and future investigations. We amend the guidelines from time to time and will use the version published on Ofgem's website. If the circumstances of a particular case justify it, we may depart from the general approach to enforcement set out in these guidelines. If we do, we will explain why.

1.14 These guidelines are not a substitute for any regulation or law and should not be taken as legal advice. Companies concerned about a complaint that has been made against them should consider seeking independent legal advice. These guidelines will be kept under review and amended in the light of further experience and developing law and practice.

NOTES

2 This includes requirements treated as such under other legislation.

3 The Unfair Terms in Consumer Contracts Regulations 1999 may also be relevant in certain circumstances. Please see paragraph 2.78 onwards for further details.

4 www.ofgem.gov.uk/publications-and-updates/statement-policy-respect-financial-penalties-and-consumer-redress

5 REMIT is the European Regulation (1227/2011) on wholesale energy market integrity and transparency. We have powers to enforce the prohibitions on a range of matters set out in REMIT, including energy market insider trading and market manipulation. These powers are set out in the Electricity and Gas (Market Integrity and Transparency)(Enforcement Etc.) Regulations 2013 (as amended).

6 www.ofgem.gov.uk/system/files/docs/2016/04/ofgem_guidance_on_voluntary_redress_schemes_for_infringements_of_competition_act_1998_open_letter_dated_14_april_2016.pdf.

7 Conduct may amount to an offence under the Gas Act, Electricity Act or Competition Act. Examples include carrying on licensable activities without a licence or without the benefit of an exemption, failing to provide information required under a notice or making false statements. By virtue of section 45 of the Gas Act, section 108 of the Electricity Act and section 72 of the Competition Act, an officer of a company may be personally liable to prosecution.

8 www.ofgem.gov.uk/publications-and-updates/ofgems-criminal-prosecution-policy-statement.

9 www.ofgem.gov.uk/consumers/business-gas-and-electricity-guide/complain-about-your-gas-or-electricity-bill-or-supplier

10 Section 4AA of the Gas Act and section 3A of the Electricity Act.

11 The Authority's principal objective does not apply when it is exercising functions under the Competition Act, consumer protection legislation or REMIT.

12 These provisions relate only to our functions under Part 1 of the Gas Act and Part 1 of the Electricity Act. Section 4AA(1C) of the Gas Act and section 3A(1C) of the Electricity Act.

13 These provisions relate only to our functions under Part 1 of the Gas Act and Part 1 of the Electricity Act. Section 4AA(5A) of the Gas Act and section 3A(5A) of the Electricity Act.

SECTION 2: OUR ENFORCEMENT POWERS

[3.273]

2.1 This section explains the legal basis for the main types of investigation that we conduct under the legislation covered by these guidelines.

2.2 It also describes our enforcement options under the different pieces of legislation. In appropriate cases, instead of or before using our enforcement powers, we may take alternative action to try to resolve issues that arise (see paragraphs 3.29-3.35).

2.3 Our powers in relation to the matters covered by these guidelines are principally derived from the following legislation:

- the Gas Act 1986 (the Gas Act)
- the Electricity Act 1989 (the Electricity Act)
- the Utilities Act 2000[14]
- the Competition Act 1998 (the Competition Act)
- the Enterprise Act 2002 (the Enterprise Act)
- the Consumer Rights Act 2015 (the Consumer Rights Act)
- the Business Protection from Misleading Marketing Regulations 2008 (the BPMMRs).

GAS ACT AND ELECTRICITY ACT

Compliance with relevant conditions and requirements

2.4 Under the Gas Act and the Electricity Act, the Authority has powers to ensure that regulated persons comply with relevant conditions and requirements.[15]

2.5 Relevant conditions are those contained in any licence held by a regulated person. Some licences contain conditions which require the regulated person to comply with industry codes and agreements.[16] Breaches of obligations under these codes and agreements may amount to breaches of licence conditions. We can take enforcement action in respect of these breaches under the relevant legislation.

2.6 Where we see opportunities to improve consumer protection as the markets we regulate evolve, we can amend or insert conditions into existing licences or new licences.

2.7 The Gas Act and the Electricity Act prohibit certain activities unless the person carrying on that activity is licensed, exempt from the requirement for a licence, or eligible (under the Gas Act only) for an exception to the prohibition on unlicensed activities.

2.8 Licensable activities include the transporting, shipping and supply of gas and the transmission, distribution, generation and supply of electricity. There are also interconnector licences for both gas and electricity, which concern the co-ordination and conveyance of gas and directing the flow of electricity via interconnectors. SMART meter communication licences for gas and electricity allow licensees to provide communication services to link smart meters in homes and small businesses with the systems of energy suppliers, network operators and energy service companies.

2.9 Licensees must comply with the conditions set out in their licence, including conditions in relation to becoming a party to, and complying with, industry codes and standards. Industry codes and standards establish rules that govern market operation and the terms for connection and access to energy networks.

2.10 Licence conditions can be prescriptive or principles-based and licences may contain both. Prescriptive conditions tend to be detailed and specific, identifying how licensees must achieve a certain outcome. Principles-based conditions have more general requirements, such as 'to treat customers fairly', which generally places the onus on licensees to determine how compliance should be achieved while also providing more space for innovation. Ofgem has committed over time to rely more on principles within the gas and electricity supply licences rather on prescriptive conditions.

2.11 The provisions that impose obligations on regulated persons, enforceable as relevant requirements for the purposes of Part 1 of the Gas Act and Part 1 of the Electricity Act, are specified in schedules to the Gas Act and Electricity Act.[17] We also have powers to enforce obligations or requirements treated as relevant requirements under other legislation.[18]

2.12 In these guidelines, "sectoral cases" refers to cases where obligations or requirements are enforced as breaches of relevant conditions or requirements. This is distinct from competition cases, for example, which we enforce using our competition powers.

2.13 If we believe that a regulated person may be in breach of any of their obligations, we may decide to investigate. We take a proportionate approach to enforcement and compliance and will consider alternatives to exercising our statutory enforcement powers, as described in paragraphs 3.29-3.37.

Provisional orders

2.14 A provisional order may be used, if considered necessary, to require a regulated person to do or not do something to prevent loss or damage that might arise before a final order can be made.[19]

2.15 This may include where a company is not taking steps to secure compliance, where behaviour needs to be stopped urgently, or where consumers are suffering continuing harm. For example, provisional orders have been used to:

- prevent serious harm to customers of one energy company who were at risk of having their supplies cut off during cold weather[20]
- require an energy company not to disconnect customers and to provide the option of prepayment meters for customers in payment difficulties
- require an energy company to lodge sufficient credit, pay any outstanding debts, and send us a business plan, updated monthly, on the measures it has taken to comply with industry code payment and credit requirements.

2.16 In deciding whether the imposition of a provisional order is appropriate in any case, we will seek to ensure that:

- we make a provisional order only where we suspect or have identified specific behaviour, conduct or outcomes for consumers, that we consider are causing or likely to cause loss or damage to a particular person or category of person
- the terms of the order sought prevent, limit or remedy the loss or damage that we have identified, and are proportionate for the purpose of preventing, limiting or remedying that loss or damage.

2.17 A provisional order will lapse after a maximum of three months if not subsequently confirmed.[21]

Final decisions

2.18 If the Authority is satisfied that a regulated person is contravening or is likely to contravene any relevant condition or requirement, it may impose a final order or confirm a provisional order to bring the breach to an end, after complying with certain procedural requirements.[22]

2.19 If satisfied that a contravention has occurred or is ongoing, or that a regulated person has failed or is failing to achieve any relevant standard of performance,[23] the Authority may impose a financial penalty, after complying with certain procedural requirements.[24] It may also, or instead, make a consumer redress order where one or more consumers have suffered loss, damage or inconvenience as a result of a contravention of a relevant condition or requirement, after complying with certain procedural requirements.[25] Section 6 describes how decisions are made and issued. Further information about penalties and redress can be found in paragraphs 6.43–6.50.

2.20 If the Authority concludes that the regulated person has not committed any breach, the case will be closed.

2.21 The Authority need not make a final order or confirm a provisional order if the regulated person has agreed to take, and is taking, appropriate steps to comply, or where it considers that the breach is trivial.[26]

2.22 The Authority's sectoral enforcement powers to impose a final order, confirm a provisional order, impose a penalty or make a consumer redress order, cannot be exercised if the Authority is satisfied it would be more appropriate[27] to proceed under the Competition Act.[28]

2.23 If a regulated person fails to comply with a final order, confirmed provisional order or does not pay any financial penalty, we may decide to revoke a licence.[29] The Authority can enforce a final order, provisional order or consumer redress order by civil proceedings.[30] Any outstanding financial penalty (and interest) may be recovered by the Authority as a civil debt.[31]

2.24 An outline of the process that we will usually follow in sectoral cases is set out in a flowchart in the appendix.

COMPETITION ACT AND TREATY ON THE FUNCTIONING OF THE EUROPEAN UNION

Prohibited agreements or conduct

2.25 Under the Competition Act and the Treaty on the Functioning of the European Union (TFEU)[32], the following are prohibited:

- agreements that may affect trade in the UK that have, or had, as their object or effect, the prevention, restriction or distortion of competition within the UK (the Chapter I prohibition of the Competition Act) unless they are exempt in accordance with the provisions of the Competition Act
- agreements that may affect trade between Member States that have, or had, as their object or effect, the prevention, restriction or distortion of competition within the European Union (Article 101(1) TFEU) unless they are exempt in accordance with the provisions of Article 101(3) TFEU)
- conduct that amounts to an abuse of a dominant position which may affect trade in the UK (the Chapter II prohibitions of the Competition Act)
- conduct that amounts to an abuse of a dominant position which may affect trade within the European Union (Article 102 TFEU).

2.26 We have concurrent powers[33] with the Competition and Markets Authority (CMA) to enforce these prohibitions, in relation to commercial activities in the gas and electricity sectors. Specifically, those activities are the following:

- commercial activities connected with the generation, transmission or supply of electricity or the use of electricity interconnectors
- licensable activities, or other activities that are ancillary to those subject to licences, for the transportation, shipping or supply of gas or for gas interconnectors or smart meter communication services (including, in particular, the storage of gas, the provision and reading of meters and the provision of pre-payment facilities).[34]

2.27 The relationship between the CMA and Ofgem in relation to their concurrent competition powers is set out in the Memorandum of Understanding (MoU) between the two bodies.[35]

2.28 The relevant competition law provisions apply to agreements between, and conduct by, 'undertakings'. Where these guidelines deal with competition law cases, the word 'company' should be understood to include all forms of undertaking (such as a sole trader, partnership, company or a group of companies).

2.29 An investigation may be conducted under the Competition Act where there are reasonable grounds for suspecting that the prohibitions in the Competition Act and/or TFEU have been infringed.[36]

2.30 Before exercising investigatory powers, we are required to consult with the CMA and any other concurrent regulator to decide which authority having concurrent powers will investigate the case. This means that although we may initially identify a competition concern, or receive a complaint that raises the issue of concern, the investigation might ultimately be carried out by another authority. Transfers between regulators may also occur at any stage.[37]

2.31 The process in the Competition Act (Concurrency) Regulations 2014 (the Concurrency Regulations) and associated CMA guidance on the concurrent application of competition law to regulated industries[38] (the Concurrency Guidance) will be followed to decide who will investigate the case.

2.32 Where a case raises issues under Article 101 and/or Article 102, we apply the case allocation principles set out in the European Commission's 'Notice on Cooperation within the Network of Competition Authorities' (the Network Notice)[39] to determine whether Ofgem, the CMA, a national competition authority (NCA) from another Member State, or the European Commission will investigate. We will notify the European Commission before, or without delay after, using our powers of investigation[40] in a competition case raising Article 101/102 issues.[41] In the context of an Ofgem investigation raising such issues, we will cooperate with the European Commission and other NCAs in the European Competition Network (ECN) following the Network Notice. This may include the exchange of information by us within the ECN.

2.33 As noted above (at paragraph 2.22) the Authority must also, before taking certain enforcement action using its sectoral powers, consider whether the use of its competition law powers is more appropriate. We will consider this at an early stage in the process.

2.34 When dealing with Competition Act cases we will follow the applicable parts of the Competition Act 1998 (Competition and Markets Authority's Rules) Order 2014 (the CA98 Rules).

2.35 Further information on the concurrency arrangements and the application of competition law in the energy sector can be found in applicable CMA guidance, including the Concurrency Guidance.[42]

2.36 If appropriate, we may consider alternatives to exercising our statutory enforcement powers as described in paragraphs 3.29–3.35.

2.37 We also have concurrent powers with the CMA to make a market investigation reference.[43] This is to determine whether the process of competition is working effectively in markets as a whole and to seek to remedy industry or market-wide competition problems.[44]

Commitments

2.38 We may accept binding commitments from a company that it will take appropriate action to address the competition concerns which we have identified.[45] In such cases, we will not take an infringement decision in relation to that company. We are required to have regard to the CMA's adopted guidance, 'Enforcement', when considering whether to accept commitments.[46]

2.39 In line with the above guidance, we are only likely to accept commitments once the competition concerns are readily identifiable,[47] where the concerns are fully addressed by the commitments offered and the commitments are capable of being implemented effectively, and if necessary, within a short space of time. We will not, other than in very exceptional circumstances, accept commitments in cases involving secret cartels between competitors which include price-fixing, bid-rigging, establishing output restrictions or quotas, sharing and/or dividing markets, or cases involving the serious abuse of a dominant position.[48]

2.40 It is for a company under investigation to offer commitments to us. Commitments can be accepted at any time up until an infringement decision is made. We are less likely to consider it appropriate to accept them at a very late stage in our investigation (for instance, after we have considered representations in response to the Statement of Objections). We may accept commitments in respect of some competition concerns and continue our investigation in respect of others arising from the same agreement or conduct.

2.41 Where we propose to accept commitments, we will comply with the procedural requirements[49] for notification and consultation. This is so that interested third parties and those likely to be affected by the commitments have an opportunity to make representations. Once accepted, commitments will usually be published on our website (after taking account of the appropriate confidentiality considerations under Part 9 of the Enterprise Act).

2.42 If a person fails, without a reasonable excuse, to adhere to commitments, the Authority can seek a court order for compliance (and costs).[50]

Final decisions

2.43 If the Authority finds that a prohibition has been infringed, it may issue written directions requiring the appropriate person to bring the infringement to an end.[51] If the Authority does not find sufficient evidence of an infringement, it may publish a reasoned no grounds for action decision when closing the case.[52] Paragraphs 7.4–7.6 describe other ways in which a Competition Act case may be closed.

2.44 In addition to issuing directions, or instead of doing so, if satisfied that the infringement was committed intentionally or negligently, the Authority may impose a financial penalty on the infringing party (subject to certain exceptions[53]). Section 6 describes how decisions are made and issued. Further information about penalties is set out in paragraphs 6.53–6.56.

2.45 If a person fails, without a reasonable excuse, to comply with written directions (or interim measures directions), the Authority can seek a court order to obtain compliance (and costs).[54] Any outstanding penalty sum may be recovered as a civil debt.[55]

Interim measures directions

2.46 Where a case under the Competition Act has been opened, the Authority may impose interim measures in order to prevent significant damage to a particular person or category of person, or to protect the public interest.[56]

2.47 In deciding whether the imposition of interim measures is appropriate in any case, we will seek to ensure that:

(1) we impose interim measures only where we suspect or have identified specific behaviour or conduct that we consider is causing, or is likely to cause, significant damage to a particular person or category of person, or is or is likely to be contrary to the public interest

(2) the particular interim measures sought will prevent, limit or remedy the significant damage that we have identified, and will be proportionate for the purpose of preventing, limiting or remedying that significant damage.

2.48 There is more information about the factors that we may take into account when deciding whether to impose interim measures in Chapter 8 of the CMA's guidance on investigation procedures in Competition Act 1998 cases.[57]

2.49 Equally, the Competition Appeal Tribunal (the CAT) may give such directions as it considers appropriate to prevent significant damage to a particular person or category of person, or protecting the public interest.[58]

2.50 An outline of the process that we will usually follow in Competition Act cases is set out in a flowchart in the Appendix.

ENTERPRISE ACT

2.51 We are a "designated enforcer" under Part 8 of the Enterprise Act.[59] This means that we are empowered to take action to enforce certain consumer protection legislation[60] such as the provisions on unfair terms in consumer contracts and unfair consumer notices of the Consumer Rights Act, the Consumer Contracts (Information, Cancellation and Additional Charges) Regulations 2013 and the Consumer Protection from Unfair Trading Regulations 2008.

2.52 We have powers to obtain an enforcement order (similar to an injunction) from the County Court or High Court (or before the Sheriff or Court of Sessions in Scotland) to prohibit a respondent (a company) from carrying on a particular course of conduct.[61]

2.53 Part 8 of the Enterprise Act only applies to an infringement which harms or has the potential to harm the collective interest of consumers. It is not a means of pursuing individual redress. It follows that the breach must affect, or have the potential to affect, consumers generally or a group of consumers.

2.54 This must be established by the evidence that we gather, which demonstrates how a particular infringement has, or may in the future have, an adverse effect on consumers. Further information on matters we may take into account when investigating under Part 8 can be found in the CMA's guidance on enforcement of consumer protection legislation.[62]

2.55 We may investigate if we believe that the evidence demonstrates a business practice that infringes the legislation, which we consider may be harming the collective interests of consumers.

2.56 As Ofgem is a concurrent designated enforcer of certain consumer protection legislation along with the CMA, the relationship between the CMA and Ofgem in relation to the exercise of these powers is set out in a Memorandum of Understanding.

2.57 The following general principles also underpin our enforcement of this legislation:

- action is necessary and proportionate
- companies will normally be given a reasonable opportunity to put matters right
- wherever possible, court action will only be taken after undertakings have been sought
- proceedings will be brought by the most appropriate body
- action is co-ordinated (so that the company is not subjected to unnecessary multiple approaches)
- publicity will be accurate, balanced and fair.

2.58 Before opening a case, we are required to notify the CMA (as the central co-ordinator for enforcement) of our intention to open a case.[63] A decision will be made by the CMA about who is best placed to take the investigation forward.[64]

2.59 Except where urgent action is necessary, companies will be contacted and provided with details of the alleged infringement(s). They will be given a reasonable opportunity to respond to the allegations and stop the infringement(s) before we seek a court order.

Interim enforcement orders

2.60 We may seek an interim enforcement order from the court only if it is expedient that the infringing conduct is prohibited or prevented.[65] This is a temporary order made to continue until the court finally determines whether or not to make an enforcement order.

2.61 We must give notice to the CMA of our intention to apply for an order. A minimum of seven days' consultation with the business is required unless the CMA thinks that the application should be made without delay.[66] A case is likely to be regarded as urgent when immediate action is vital to safeguard consumers' interests.

Undertakings

2.62 Instead of (or before) seeking an enforcement order we may secure undertakings under the Enterprise Act to address the relevant conduct. An undertaking will seek to ensure that a company does not continue, repeat or engage in the conduct that constitutes an infringement, or consent or connive with another company in the carrying out of the particular conduct.[67]

2.63 We may also include such further undertakings for the benefit of consumers as Ofgem considers just, reasonable and proportionate in the circumstances. The measures which may be included in such undertakings are often referred to as 'enhanced consumer measures'. They may include:

- measures offering compensation or other redress to consumers who have suffered loss as a result of the conduct
- measures offering consumers the option to terminate (but not vary) their contract
- where the consumers who have suffered loss as a result of the conduct cannot be identified (or cannot be identified without disproportionate cost), measures intended to be in the collective interests of consumers (eg a payment to an appropriate consumer charity)
- measures intended to prevent or reduce the risk of the infringing conduct re-occurring, including where this may improve compliance with consumer law more generally
- measures intended to enable consumers to choose more effectively between parties supplying or seeking to supply goods or services.

2.64 The terms of the undertaking will be agreed in discussion with the company. We may also require information or documents to be provided to determine if the enhanced consumer measures have been taken.

2.65 We will notify the CMA of any undertakings given.[68] We will usually publish undertakings on our website (after taking account of the appropriate confidentiality considerations under Part 9 of the Enterprise Act).

2.66 In appropriate cases, we may consider other alternatives such as those set out in paragraph 3.30.

Enforcement orders

2.67 Where suitable undertakings are not obtained, or are given but subsequently breached or found to be inadequate, an enforcement order may be sought to put a stop to the harmful conduct.

2.68 In assessing whether to seek an enforcement order the relevant factors are likely to include the:

- intent of the company and whether the breach was deliberate

- history of breaches by the company
- damage being done to consumers.

2.69 If seeking an enforcement order, we must give notice to the CMA and a minimum of 14 days'[69] consultation with the business is required, unless the CMA thinks that the order should be made without delay.[70] We will draw the court's attention to any breach of the undertaking and the court will have regard to this when deciding whether to make an enforcement order.

2.70 We will set the length of any consultation period with the company based on the complexity of the issues.

2.71 If we bring proceedings against a company, it will be notified and have an opportunity to dispute the Authority's case and to make representations to the court. We will comply with our duties of disclosure under the Civil Procedure Rules (CPR).[71]

2.72 If satisfied that the person named in the application has engaged or is engaging in conduct which amounts to a Community or Domestic Infringement, or in the case of a Community Infringement, is likely to engage in such conduct, the court may make an order.[72]

2.73 The order will indicate the nature of the infringing conduct, and direct the person not to continue, repeat or engage in the conduct, or consent or connive with another body corporate in the carrying out of the particular behaviour. If appropriate, the order may require the person to publish the order and a corrective statement. The court can alternatively accept undertakings from the person, which may also include a requirement to publish the undertaking and a corrective statement.[73]

2.74 An enforcement order may also require the company to take enhanced consumer measures. A summary of the enhanced consumer measures can be found in paragraph 2.63 of these guidelines. Any undertaking given to the court may also include enhanced consumer measures. There is no power to impose a penalty.

2.75 We will notify the CMA of any undertakings given or court order made, which it may publish.[74]

2.76 Breaching an enforcement order or undertaking to the court is a contempt of court and can lead to a fine or imprisonment.

2.77 An outline of the process that we will usually follow in cases under Part 8 of the Enterprise Act is set out in a flowchart in the appendix.

UNFAIR TERMS IN CONSUMER CONTRACTS AND UNFAIR CONSUMER NOTICES – CONSUMER RIGHTS ACT

2.78 We also have the power to enforce the provisions in the Consumer Rights Act relating to unfair terms in consumer contracts and unfair consumer notices directly, rather than under the provisions of Part 8 of the Enterprise Act.[75]

2.79 These provisions enable us to consider complaints about unfair terms in consumer contacts or unfair consumer notices[76], as well as to take action on our own initiative.

2.80 If we intend to consider a complaint about a potentially unfair contract term or consumer notice, we must notify the CMA of our intention to do so, and must then consider the complaint.[77]

2.81 We will generally consider potentially unfair contract terms in standard consumer contracts (between a consumer and a seller or supplier) or consumer notices under our powers in the Consumer Rights Act. We will usually use our powers under Part 8 of the Enterprise Act to enforce in relation to unfair terms provisions only where there is evidence that the collective interests of consumers in the UK are being harmed or the supplier's conduct raises issues under other consumer protection legislation as well.

2.82 Under both the Consumer Rights Act and Part 8 of the Enterprise Act, we may seek undertakings from a party that it will comply with conditions agreed with us about the use of the relevant terms or notices. We are required to notify the CMA of the conditions on which any undertaking is accepted and the party which gave it. The CMA is required to publish details of any such undertaking. If the party fails to comply with those undertakings, we may apply to the court for an injunction.[78] Proceedings may be issued in the same courts as they are for cases under Part 8 of the Enterprise Act and our disclosure duties are the same.

2.83 If seeking an injunction (or interim injunction), we must give the CMA at least 14 days' notice before the date of the application, unless the CMA consents to a shorter period.[79] The injunction granted by the court may relate to the particular term or notice or to any term or notice of a similar kind or with a similar effect.[80] The court may grant an injunction on such conditions, and against such parties, as it thinks appropriate. There is no power to impose a penalty. We will notify the CMA of the outcome of any application and, if an injunction is granted, the conditions on which (and the parties against whom) it is made. The CMA is required to publish those details.[81] If we have agreed to consider a relevant complaint but decide not apply for an injunction, then we are required to give reasons for our decision to the party who made the complaint.[82] In doing so, we may have regard to any undertakings given by the company.

2.84 Failure to comply with any injunction or undertaking made to the court is a contempt of court and can lead to a fine or imprisonment.

2.85 An outline of the process that we will usually follow in an unfair terms case is set out in a flowchart in the appendix.

2.86 The provisions set out above on unfair contract terms and consumer notices do not apply to:
- any contract entered into before 1st October 2015
- any consumer notice provided or communicated before 1st October 2015.

2.87 These matters are covered by the Unfair Terms in Consumer Contracts Regulations 1999 (UTCCRs). The UTCCRs have now been revoked other than for those purposes.[83] We have power to enforce the UTCCRs on a similar basis to the process set out above, although certain procedural differences may apply.

BUSINESS PROTECTION FROM MISLEADING MARKETING REGULATIONS 2008 (BPMMRS)

2.88 Under the BPMMRs, the following are prohibited:
- advertising which misleads traders (regulation 3)
- misleading comparative advertising (regulation 4)
- promotion by a code owner of misleading advertising and comparative advertising which is not permitted (regulation 5).

2.89 We have concurrent powers with the CMA and other regulators to enforce the BPMMRs to protect business customers from misleading marketing.[84] Our powers to enforce the above regulations are set out in regulation 13. If more than one regulator is contemplating bringing proceedings to enforce the BPMMRs, the CMA may decide that it is best placed to proceed or may direct that another regulator proceeds.[85]

2.90 If we consider that there may have been breaches of the regulations, we will follow similar initial procedures to those in cases under Part 8 of the Enterprise Act. If this does not secure compliance we may:
- seek undertakings from brokers or other organisations to put a stop to misleading marketing activity[86]
- apply to the court for an injunction (or interim injunction) to secure compliance with the regulations.[87]

2.91 We must give the CMA at least 14 days' notice before the date of the application of our intention to apply for an injunction (or interim injunction), unless the CMA consents to a shorter period. Our disclosure duties are as described in paragraph 2.71.

2.92 We can apply for an injunction if there has been or is likely to be a relevant breach and we think it is appropriate to do so. The court can grant an injunction even without proof of actual loss or damage, or intention or negligence by the advertiser. The injunction may relate to particular advertising and any in similar terms or likely to convey a similar impression.[88] When granting the injunction, the court may require the person against whom the order is made to publish the injunction and a corrective statement.[89] The court can alternatively accept undertakings. There is no power to impose a penalty. We will notify the CMA of any undertakings given or court order made, which it may publish.[90]

2.93 Breach of the injunction or undertaking given to the court is a contempt of court and can lead to a fine or imprisonment.

2.94 An outline of the process that we will usually follow in cases under the BPMMRs is set out in a flowchart in the appendix.

NOTES

14 The Utilities Act established the Gas and Electricity Markets Authority and amended the Gas Act and Electricity Act. Its provisions are therefore covered under paragraphs 2.4–2.13 which relate to those Acts.

15 'Regulated person', 'relevant condition' and 'relevant requirement' are defined in section 28(8) of the Gas Act and section 25(8) of the Electricity Act. 'Regulated person' includes licence holders, distribution exemption holders and supply exemption holders.

16 Examples include the Balancing and Settlement Code, the Connection and Use of System Code, the Uniform Network Code, and the System Operator – Transmission Owner Code.

17 Schedule 4B to the Gas Act and Schedule 6A to the Electricity Act.

18 For example, breaches under the rules and regulations implementing the Electricity Market Reform, such as under the Electricity Capacity Regulations 2014. Where appropriate, the Authority may also use other prescribed sanctions available in the relevant statutory instruments.

19 Section 28(2) of the Gas Act and section 25(2) of the Electricity Act.

20 The order required the company not to wrongfully block customers from switching suppliers, required improvements to its customer handling services, and prevented it from taking on new customers until it had satisfied us that it was able to handle its existing customer complaints.

21 Section 28(8) of the Gas Act and section 25(8) of the Electricity Act. It can be confirmed (with or without changes) for example if the company is continuing to commit breaches or it is suspected that further breaches are likely.

22 Sections 28(1) and 29 of the Gas Act and sections 25(1) and 26 of the Electricity Act.

23 Those prescribed in regulations made under sections 33A or 33AA of the Gas Act (standards of performance for gas suppliers and transporters) and sections 39 or 39A of the Electricity Act (standards of performance for electricity suppliers and distributors).

24 Section 30A of the Gas Act or 27A of the Electricity Act. It may not impose a financial penalty for a contravention that is likely to occur.

25 Section 30G and 30I of the Gas Act and section 27G and 27I of the Electricity Act.

26 Section 28(5A) of the Gas Act and section 25(5A) of the Electricity Act.

27 In relation to consumer redress orders the language 'most appropriate' is used. Section 30N(2) of the Gas Act and Section 27N(2) of the Electricity Act.

28 Sections 28(4A) and (4B), 30A(2) and (2A), and 30N(2) of the Gas Act and sections 25(4A) and (4B), 27A(2) and (2A) and 27N(2) of the Electricity Act require the Authority to consider this before exercising its powers. In practice this is likely to be considered much earlier. See paragraph 2.24.

29 See the list of revocation conditions at www.ofgem.gov.uk/licences-codes-and-standards/licences/revoking-licence.

30 Sections 30(8) and 30L of the Gas Act and sections 27(7) and 27L of the Electricity Act.

31 Section 30F of the Gas Act and section 27F of the Electricity Act.

32 We will review these guidelines in relation to powers under EU Treaties post BREXIT.

33 This means that more than one competition authority has the jurisdiction to investigate and take enforcement action.

34 Section 36A of the Gas Act and section 43 of the Electricity Act set out the Authority's precise jurisdiction under the Competition Act. These activities are broader than activities that require a licence under the Electricity Act or the Gas Act. We do not have powers to deal with criminal cartel offences under section 188 of the Enterprise Act.

35 The latest version of the MoU was published on 24 February 2016: www.ofgem.gov.uk/publications-and-updates/memorandum-understanding-between-competition-and-markets-authority-and-gas-and-electricity-markets-authority-concurrent-competition-powers.

36 The full test is set out in section 25 of the Competition Act.

37 Regulation 7 of the Concurrency Regulations.

38 www.gov.uk/government/publications/guidance-on-concurrent-application-of-competition-law-to-regulated-industries.

39 Commission Notice on cooperation within the Network of Competition Authorities, 2004/C 101/03 at: eur-lex.europa.eu/LexUriServ/LexUriServ.do?uri=CELEX:52004XC0427(02):EN:NOT.

40 Sections 26 to 28A of the Competition Act.

41 Article 11(3) of the Modernisation Regulation (EU Regulation 1/2003).

42 www.gov.uk/government/publications/guidance-on-concurrent-application-of-competition-law-to-regulated-industries.

43 Under Part 4 of the Enterprise Act.

44 For example, in 2014 we made a market investigation reference in respect of the supply and acquisition of energy in Great Britain: www.ofgem.gov.uk/publications-and-updates/decision-make-market-investigation-reference-respect-supply-and-acquisition-energy-great-britain

45 Section 31A of the Competition Act.

46 Chapter 4 of OFT407 www.gov.uk/government/publications/competition-law-application-and-enforcement. Further information is also in Chapter 8 and Chapter 10 of the CMA's guidance CMA8: www.gov.uk/government/publications/guidance-on-the-cmas-investigation-procedures-in-competition-act-1998-cases.

47 This means that if, for example, the full extent of the competition concerns are not yet identifiable because further investigation is needed, we are unlikely to accept commitments at this stage.

48 See footnote 16 in OFT407 at: www.gov.uk/government/publications/competition-law-application-and-enforcement.

49 These are described in Chapter 4 of OFT407 at: www.gov.uk/government/publications/competition-law-application-and-enforcement.

50 Section 31E of the Competition Act.

51 See sections 32 (modification or termination of a prohibited agreement), 33 (modification or ceasing of prohibited conduct) and 54 (functions exercisable by concurrent regulators) of the Competition Act.

52 Rule 10 of the CA98 Rules sets out the notice requirements should the Authority make such a finding.

53 Sections 36(4) and (5), 39 and 40 (reasonable assumption of immunity).

54 Section 34 of the Competition Act.

55 Section 37 of the Competition Act.

56 Section 35 of the Competition Act and rule 13 of the CA98 Rules. Further information on interim measures is in Chapter 3 of the CMA's adopted guidance, 'Enforcement' (OFT407) at: www.gov.uk/government/publications/competition-law-application-and-enforcement. The section on procedures is at paragraph 3.12. This OFT guideline, like any others referred to hereafter, has been adopted by the CMA Board but must be read in the light of changes to the legislation and the applicable CMA guidance and may be replaced or superseded. Check the CMA's website for the most recent and applicable document.

57 www.gov.uk/government/publications/guidance-on-the-cmas-investigation-procedures-in-competition-act-1998-cases.

58 See paragraph 24(2) of the Competition Appeal Tribunal Rules 2015.

59 Schedule to the Enterprise Act (Part 8 Designated Enforcers: Criteria for Designation, Designation of Public Bodies as Designated Enforcers and Transitional Provisions) Order 2003.

60 These are specified under section 211 of the Enterprise Act (Domestic infringements relate to breaches of a wide range of UK laws in statutory instruments made under Part 8) and section 212 (Community infringements harm the collective interest of consumers and breach the UK's and other European Economic Area states legislation and other provisions implementing the European Directives listed in Schedule 13 to the Act).

61 Section 215 of the Enterprise Act. Proceedings are issued in the High Court for more complex cases (Civil Procedure Rules (CPR) Practice Direction 7A) and otherwise in the County Court. CPR Part 8 is used for claims where there is unlikely to be a substantial dispute of fact (e.g. where the only issue is one of law). The CPR Part 7 procedure is used in all other cases. In certain cases, conduct may amount to an offence which could be prosecuted by Trading Standards or the CMA.

62 Consumer Protection: Enforcement Guidance dated 17 August 2016 (CMA58) available at: www.gov.uk/government/publications/consumer-protection-enforcement-guidance-cma58.

63 This is done via the National Anti-Fraud Network website.

64 See chapter 4 of the CMA's guidance on the use of its consumer powers www.gov.uk/government/publications/consumer-protection-guidance-on-the-cmas-approach-to-use-of-its-consumer-powers.

65 Section 218 of the Enterprise Act.

66 Section 214 of the Enterprise Act.

67 Section 219 of the Enterprise Act. Undertakings may be obtained in respect of a Domestic Infringement if the conduct

has occurred or is occurring, and in respect of a Community Infringement also if the conduct is likely to occur (ie, even before the conduct has occurred).

68 Section 219(6) of the Enterprise Act.

69 An extended consultation period of 28 days will apply in certain circumstances where the company against whom the enforcement order would be made is a member of, or is represented by, a trade association or other business representative body that operates an approved consumer code of practice. Section 214(4) to (4B) of the Enterprise Act.

70 Section 214 of the Enterprise Act. Any representations made to us by a company about why it failed to comply with any undertaking will be shared with the CMA when consulting on whether to seek an enforcement order.

71 CPR Part 31.

72 Section 217 of the Enterprise Act.

73 Section 217(9) and (10) of the Enterprise Act.

74 Section 215(9) of the Enterprise Act.

75 Part 2 and Schedule 3 to the Consumer Rights Act.

76 A consumer notice is defined broadly in the Consumer Rights Act as a notice to the extent that it: a) relates to rights or obligations as between a trader and a consumer; or b) purports to exclude or restrict a trader's liability to a consumer. It does not matter whether the notice is expressed to apply to a consumer, as long as it is reasonable to assume it is intended to be seen or heard by a consumer. A notice includes an announcement, whether or not in writing, and any other communication or purported communication.

77 Paragraph 2 of Schedule 3 to the Consumer Rights Act.

78 Paragraph 3 of Schedule 3 to the Consumer Rights Act.

79 Paragraph 4 of Schedule 3 to the Consumer Rights Act.

80 Paragraph 5 of Schedule 3 to the Consumer Rights Act.

81 Paragraph 7(1) of Schedule 3 to the Consumer Rights Act.

82 Paragraph 2(3) of Schedule 3 to the Consumer Rights Act.

83 The Consumer Rights Act 2015 (Commencement No. 3, Transitional Provisions, Savings and Consequential Amendments) Order 2015.

84 A trader may also be guilty of an offence under regulation 6 if they engage in advertising which is misleading which could be prosecuted by Trading Standards or the CMA.

85 Regulation 17 of the BPMMRs.

86 Regulation 16 of the BPMMRs.

87 Regulation 15 of the BPMMRs.

88 Regulation 18 of the BPMMRs.

89 Regulation 18 of the BPMMRs.

90 Regulations 19 and 20 of the BPMMRs.

SECTION 3: OPENING A CASE

[3.274]

3.1 This section describes how we identify and decide whether to investigate a potential breach and the sources of information that we most frequently use. It provides information about how we handle information (including confidential information).

3.2 It also explains how we prioritise cases and decide whether to open (or continue) a case. We provide an overview of how we assess whether there is a case to answer and, if there is, whether it would be consistent with our criteria to open an enforcement case.

3.3 Concerns may be resolved satisfactorily without opening an enforcement case; we have a range of alternative action tools that we will consider, as described in paragraph 3.30.

SOURCES OF INFORMATION

Self-reporting

3.4 A case may start because of self-reporting by a company[91] which has, for example, realised when carrying out internal checks that it may have breached a licence condition, code or relevant legislation.

3.5 We strongly encourage companies to promptly self-report potential breaches that may give rise to material harm to consumers, the market or to Ofgem's ability to regulate; our expectation is that they will do so. Companies should promptly open a dialogue with Ofgem[92] and provide as much detail as possible about the potential breach (or breaches), what caused it, the harm that may have resulted, including to customers, and the steps that have been or will be taken (including proposed timings) to remedy the situation. We recognise that the need to self-report promptly might mean companies have not necessarily established the full extent of problems but that should not prevent prompt and accurate self-reporting of the facts as they stand and taking steps, in a timely manner, to determine the full extent of problems and put things right.

3.6 For Competition Act cartel cases, companies should consider whether they may be eligible to receive total or partial immunity from fines and contact the CMA, in the first instance, if so.[93]

3.7 The fact that the breaches came to light as a result of prompt, accurate and comprehensive self-reporting, particularly when those breaches were unlikely to come to light via other information sources, will, in most cases, count in a company's favour; it will either be taken into account in our decision to prioritise enforcement action or will be reflected in any penalty.

3.8 Prompt, accurate and comprehensive self-reporting, combined with swift action to put things right (ensuring no repeat breach), is more likely to result in Ofgem seeking to resolve the matter via alternative action for sectoral cases. However, for serious breaches or breaches that indicate repeated poor compliance, opening an enforcement case is likely to be the most appropriate course of action. Given that potential breaches of competition law are by their nature serious, alternative action is unlikely to be appropriate.

3.9 Companies should also be aware that prompt, accurate and comprehensive self-reporting is one of the factors that tend to decrease the amount of any financial penalty that the Authority may decide to impose[94] in circumstances when an investigation is carried out and a breach (or breaches) is found. When setting the amount of a penalty, the Authority recognises the value of companies promptly reporting to Ofgem and putting right any non-compliance that they have identified.

3.10 Conversely, factors that tend to increase the amount of any financial penalty in sectoral cases include withholding relevant evidence and/or submitting it in a manner that hinders the investigation and any attempt to conceal all or part of a contravention or failure.[95] Similarly, persistent and repeated unreasonable behaviour that delays enforcement action is an aggravating factor to be taken into account in setting penalties in competition law cases.

Whistleblowers

3.11 Whistleblowing is when a person raises a concern about a wrongdoing, risk or malpractice that they are aware of through their work (for instance, licence breaches such as disconnecting vulnerable consumers in winter, or misselling of energy contracts identified by a customer services operative or a sales agent of the company). It is also sometimes described as making a disclosure in the public interest. We invite contact from all parties who may have such information relating to the gas and electricity markets. Disclosures made to "blow the whistle" about concerns regarding potential breaches of relevant regulations or legislation may lead to a case being opened.

3.12 To facilitate such disclosures, government has issued whistleblowing guidance[96] applicable to people considering disclosing information, which:

- sets out the circumstances in which disclosure would entitle a person to benefit from the legal protections (against victimisation or unfair dismissal by their employer) offered to whistleblowers
- details the process that should be followed in dealing with whistleblowers.

3.13 We have also produced our own whistleblowing guidance[97] document, which should be consulted before making a disclosure to us.

Own-initiative investigations

3.14 We have a general duty to monitor the gas and electricity markets for the purposes of considering whether any of our functions are exercisable.[98]

3.15 We also conduct own-initiative investigations to address issues concerning gas and electricity companies and across the industry on a particular regulatory requirement or industry risk (in other words, our regular compliance monitoring may identify an issue that needs to be investigated). We use monitoring programmes to ensure compliance with a new regulation when it is introduced (for example to help industry understand new requirements) or where we are assessing compliance with an existing regulation/obligation across industry.

3.16 Some licence conditions and regulations require companies to send us regular reports on their activities. Breaches may be identified when we analyse the information provided or may arise from a failure to comply with the reporting requirements.

3.17 Where our monitoring work reveals information that suggests it may be appropriate for us to investigate a particular company or multiple companies, we will use our prioritisation criteria (see paragraphs 3.36–3.49) to decide whether to open a case. If we do not open a case we may, as an alternative, resolve any problems via alternative action (see paragraphs 3.29–3.35). We will generally inform companies when we become aware of a potential breach (or breaches) that warrants referral to the Enforcement team for further consideration.

Other sources of information

3.18 We collect information and data from a range of sources as part of our market monitoring activity. Along with information we are given by industry participants and any individual complaints (usually received through our consumer affairs team), this information helps us to identify potential issues that may lead to an investigation. In addition, we may receive:

- information from organisations such as the Citizens Advice consumer service and the Energy Ombudsman about complaints that have been made to them
- super-complaints from designated consumer bodies about a feature or combination of features that is, or appears to be, significantly harming the interests of consumers[99]
- information from the CMA or other regulators such as evidence suggesting potential breaches of competition law that may fall within our jurisdiction.

3.19 If we receive an individual complaint, we will add the information to our database of intelligence. We analyse this material and keep it under review to help us decide if we need to take action. For this purpose, it is helpful if a complaint to us is specific, well-reasoned, clear and supported by evidence.[100] Due to resource constraints we will not generally be able to enter into individual correspondence with complainants, although we will confirm receipt of a complaint in writing. In general, individual consumer complaints should be directed toward the supplier (or network operator) in the first instance and then, if they are not satisfied with the outcome, to the Energy Ombudsman.[101]

3.20 If we need any further information, we will contact a complainant and tell them what we require. If we decide to take a case forward, the opening of the case will usually be published on our website (see paragraphs 4.7–4.14) and we will notify complainants of this.

HANDLING INFORMATION

3.21 Those who submit complaints (or otherwise provide us with information) should be aware that to take a case forward we may need to disclose the information provided, either to the company in question and/or to others connected to the subject matter of the complaint.

3.22 Where information is confidential or where complainants do not wish it to be disclosed, this should be made clear, including the reasons why, in writing.

3.23 If a person or company thinks that any information they are giving us or that we have acquired is commercially sensitive or contains details of an individual's private affairs, and that disclosing it might significantly harm the interests of the business or person, they should submit a separate non-confidential version of the information in which any confidential parts are removed. They should also, in an annex clearly marked as confidential, set out why the information that has been removed should be considered confidential. Non-confidential versions of documents should be provided at the same time as the original document or at an alternative time as required by us. If such a version is not provided within the timescale set by us we will presume that the provider of that information does not wish to continue to claim confidentiality.

3.24 We will make our own assessment of whether material should be treated as confidential. We may not agree that the information in question is confidential. This will depend on the circumstances and will be assessed on a case-by-case basis. Any request that information is treated as confidential will be considered in accordance with the appropriate legislation.[102]

3.25 In all cases, even if a person does not wish for certain information to be disclosed, there may still be circumstances in which its disclosure is required. Information provided, including personal information, may be published or disclosed in accordance with the access to information regimes (primarily the Data Protection Act 1998, the Freedom of Information Act 2000 and the Environmental Information Regulations 2004) or to facilitate the exercise of our functions.

INITIAL ENQUIRY PHASE

3.26 Before a decision is taken to open a case, we may seek further information from a complainant or from third parties, such as other stakeholders or competitors, and consumer bodies, so that we can assess whether a case should be opened.

3.27 We may also contact the company in question to seek clarification or information to help us assess whether there is a case to answer. Prompt responses may speed up the resolution of the issue and might avoid the need to take enforcement action.

3.28 In relevant cases, we will consider whether the use of our competition law powers is more appropriate.

ALTERNATIVE ACTION THAT WE WILL CONSIDER

3.29 When deciding how best to deal with a concern, we may engage in alternative action to bring a company into compliance. Alternative action can be used in lieu of opening an investigation into a potential breach, as part of closing an investigation or during an investigation to address any ongoing concerns. As explained in paragraph 3.8 above, we do not normally consider alternative action to be appropriate when addressing potential breaches of competition law. It is also unlikely to be sufficient in sectoral cases when potential breaches are serious or when we have significant concerns about a company's conduct (see paragraphs 3.36–3.49 on our case opening criteria).

3.30 We may undertake one or more of the following alternative actions with the company in question:

- enter into dialogue or correspondence and discuss potentially harmful or unlawful conduct, including what they have done or plan to do to put things right
- agree a period of reporting, either to ensure that behaviour is not repeated or to show that they have taken certain action to address the issue
- request that they engage independent auditors or other appropriately skilled persons to conduct a review focused on a particular area of concern
- accept non-statutory undertakings or assurances to ensure future compliance with a particular obligation
- agree other voluntary action, such as the implementation of specified remedial or improvement actions and/or making voluntary payments to affected consumers, other appropriate parties or to charitable organisations.[103]

3.31 We would expect a company to engage fully and proactively in helping to ensure a successful resolution of the alternative action. Steps might include, for example, providing us with comprehensive plans (independently audited where necessary) to ensure future compliance, developing proposals for our consideration and input to fully compensate customers for any financial losses or other detriment caused, or ensuring other appropriate forms of redress.

3.32 When deciding whether an issue can properly be resolved without the need to investigate or use our statutory enforcement powers, we will have regard to our prioritisation criteria for opening an investigation (see paragraphs 3.36–3.49 below).

3.33 If we decide that alternative action is sufficient to deal with the conduct, we will need to be satisfied that the action will fully address our concerns. In considering alternative action we will have regard to whether:

- where issues have been self-reported, we are satisfied the full extent of the potential breach has been self-reported promptly, accurately and comprehensively by the company
- where issues have come to light via other means, we are satisfied that the full extent of the potential breach has been established
- we are confident that the company will act promptly to put things right, including taking account of its willingness and ability to address the matter as well as its previous record in complying with its legal obligations
- we consider that the company has provided robust assurances (including supporting evidence where necessary) that the potential breach will not recur
- the relevant concerns can be appropriately addressed by the alternative action being considered and be implemented effectively
- not pursuing an investigation and potential enforcement action is a proportionate and targeted response given the nature of the concern and meets our vision and Strategic Objectives for enforcement action (see paragraphs 1.7 and 1.8).

3.34 If we seek and obtain a non-statutory undertaking or other agreed action from a company, this may result in the case being closed, although the company may be the subject of a period of compliance monitoring after the case is closed (see paragraphs 7.7–7.10). Failure to comply with non-statutory undertakings or assurances or any other agreed action could lead to enforcement action, and we may take a more serious view of any breach found to have occurred following such undertakings or assurances (see paragraph 3.47).

3.35 If we consider that a case cannot be resolved without the use of our statutory enforcement powers, the case may still be settled by agreement. This is dealt with in Section 5.

PRIORITISATION CRITERIA FOR DECIDING WHETHER TO OPEN (OR CONTINUE) A CASE

3.36 This section includes non-exhaustive details of the factors that we will normally take into account in deciding whether to open (or continue) a case.

3.37 We will make decisions on a case-by-case basis, considering the specific facts of the matter, the legal context and our available resources.

Case opening decisions

3.38 In determining whether an enforcement case is appropriate, we will consider how to meet our vision and Strategic Objectives for enforcement action (see paragraphs 1.7 and 1.8). When making our assessment we will consider in each case the following criteria:

(1) Do we have the power to take action and are we best placed to act?
(2) Is it a priority matter for us, due to the apparent seriousness of the potential breach?
(3) Is it a priority matter for us, due to the apparent conduct of the company in question?

3.39 We will consider whether we have the power to take action and are best placed to act as set out below. The decision to open a new case can then be taken by applying either criteria (2) or (3) above (both need not apply). For example, we may open a case to address apparent poor conduct even when our assessment suggests that any resulting harm or likely harm is limited. Similarly, we may open a case when we judge the harm or likely harm to be serious even if the company in question has a good compliance history and has put things right.

Do we have the power to take action and are we best placed to act?

3.40 This means asking whether the case falls within the scope of the relevant provisions of the legislation, so that we have the power to take enforcement action, and whether the tests set out in the relevant legislation can be fulfilled.[104] This means:

- in cases under the Gas Act and the Electricity Act, assessing if it appears likely that the behaviour in question could constitute a breach of any relevant condition or requirement
- in Competition Act and TFEU cases, considering whether there are reasonable grounds for suspecting that there has been an infringement of the applicable prohibitions
- in cases under Part 8 of the Enterprise Act, assessing whether it appears likely that there has been a breach of any of the consumer protection legislation which we have the power to enforce and, if so, whether that breach harms or has the potential to harm the collective interests of consumers
- for cases concerning unfair contract terms or consumer notices under the Consumer Rights Act, assessing whether it appears likely that there is a potentially unfair contract term or consumer notice
- for the Business Protection from Misleading Marketing Regulations 2008, assessing whether it appears likely that there has been any prohibited advertising which is misleading to traders.

3.41 Where there is a concurrent power to take enforcement action with another regulator, a decision will be made about who is best placed to act.[105] This may result in the case being referred to another regulator for investigation. Equally, sometimes other regulators will refer cases to us.

3.42 Where two or more concurrent regulators such as the CMA and Ofgem have the power to investigate a particular breach or infringement, the concurrency arrangements, which provide for co-ordination with other regulators, prevent a company from facing two separate investigations (and sanctions) by different regulators for the same behaviour.[106]

3.43 Action may be taken by us where another body is already investigating or taking action, where the power to act does not derive from concurrent powers (as distinct from the action envisaged in paragraph 3.42). For example, a code owner or panel[107] may be dealing with a breach of a code where the same conduct may also amount to a breach of a licence condition.

3.44 Whether an additional investigation may be justified will depend on the circumstances of the case. We will take into account the impact of any action already taken, or to be taken by another body, before deciding whether to launch a case into any breach of a licence condition also occasioned by the activity.

3.45 Provided the issue warrants an investigation under our prioritisation criteria (see paragraphs 3.29–3.35), we are more likely to launch a separate investigation if, for example:

- the action being taken by the other body appears not to deal with our concerns fully or does not cover all of the matters about which we have concerns
- a financial penalty or consumer redress order may be merited (which the other body does not have the power to impose)
- separate action should be taken as a deterrent to the company or others.

Is it a priority matter for us due to the apparent seriousness of the potential breach?

3.46 This means assessing a range of factors including the degree to which the suspected breach has caused, is causing or is likely to cause harm to consumers (financial or non-financial), to competition or to our ability to regulate effectively. The latter is important for breaches that, if confirmed, would harm our ability to regulate or could lead to a loss of confidence in the regulator if companies do not face meaningful consequences. We will also take account of the extent to which the company may have benefitted (financially or otherwise) from the suspected breach and the need to deter future poor practice, both by the company in question and others across the market.

Is it a priority matter for us, due to the apparent conduct of the company in question?

3.47 This means assessing a range of factors to determine whether the company is willing and able to comply with its obligations or whether it is a company with recurring non-compliance. Our assessment will include whether the alleged breach appears to be intentional, reckless, a sign of negligence or constitutes a failure to comply with previous undertakings. For principles-based rules, it will include considering whether a company intent on complying might have acted in the way it did. We will consider the compliance record of the company[108] and any history of similar breaches, including any that in isolation may not have been considered serious enough at the time to justify opening a new case. We will consider also whether the company self-reported promptly, accurately and comprehensively, is taking timely action (or has already taken action) to put matters right, and is willing and able to avoid repeat breaches. We are more likely to open an investigation if the breach is ongoing but may also take action if the company is no longer in breach.

Other case opening considerations

3.48 The criteria set out above are not exhaustive; we may consider other factors where relevant such as the resources we have available at the time. We may not have anticipated every scenario that could arise in a case. We also do not know what further changes there may be to the enforcement landscape.

3.49 On occasion, particularly when addressing a concern across the market, we may not open a case and instead focus our resources on a relevant policy project (we also have powers under the Enterprise Act to conduct market studies and make market investigation references) which we consider may better address the identified non-compliant conduct and any resulting harm.

NOTES

91 The Gas Act and Electricity Act impose obligations on 'regulated persons'. The Competition Act refers to 'undertakings' and consumer protection legislation refers to 'traders' or 'sellers or suppliers'. For simplicity we refer to the 'company' from this section onwards, except when describing specific decisions or appeals in section 6.

92 By writing to their usual contacts or the Enforcement Team, Ofgem, 9 Millbank, London, SW1P 3GE, emailing enforcement@ofgem.gov.uk or by telephoning via the main switchboard on 020 7901 7000.

93 See www.gov.uk/guidance/cartels-confess-and-apply-for-leniency.

94 Details of the other factors that may affect the penalty level in cases under the Gas Act and Electricity Act are in the Authority's financial penalties and consumer redress policy statement.

95 In relation to Competition Act investigations, persistent and repeated unreasonable behaviour that delays the Authority's enforcement action will be considered to be an aggravating factor in determining the level of any penalty imposed for breaching the relevant prohibitions contained in the Competition Act or the TFEU.

96 www.gov.uk/whistleblowing/dismissals-and-whistleblowing. The documents include a list of prescribed people and bodies to whom you can blow the whistle. Ofgem is the Gas and Electricity Markets Authority for these purposes.

97 www.ofgem.gov.uk/ofgem-publications/83570/whistleblowingguidance.pdf.

98 Section 34 of the Gas Act and section 47 of the Electricity Act.

99 Under section 11 of the Enterprise Act.

100 Where the complaint concerns an alleged breach of the Competition Act, complainants should have regard to the CMA's guidance CMA8.

101 www.ombudsman-services.org/energy.html.

102 We will comply with section 105 of the Utilities Act 2000 and Part 9 of the Enterprise Act when deciding whether information is confidential and/or whether it should be disclosed. We will also have regard to section 35 of the Gas Act and section 48 of the Electricity Act, as appropriate, in relation to the publication of information and advice.

103 We have appointed an expert independent third party to manage the allocation of voluntary redress payments from licensees to charitable organisations.

104 REMIT cases are covered in separate guidelines. However, when assessing the resource requirements of a potential case, consideration is given to other current and potential cases under all of our enforcement powers, including REMIT.

105 See further at paragraph 3.43 onwards.

106 The position is different in cases concerning European competition issues where the competition effects are felt in different territories. Parallel investigations may be carried out by two or more Member States' competition authorities for their respective territories.

107 Code owners are network operators required by licence to provide codes or agreements. Panels are comprised of consumer and industry representatives and are responsible for administering the code.

108 For supply licensees this could include an assessment of complaints registered with them, Citizen's Advice or the Energy Ombudsman

SECTION 4: CONDUCTING INVESTIGATIONS

[3.275]

4.1 This section sets out the general procedures we will follow once we have decided to open a case. It explains how we will deal with making public cases that we open and close. It also outlines the investigation powers that we may use in a case.

4.2 Where there are differences to the procedure, for example in competition cases or cases where orders are sought from a court, these have been set out below. The section also deals with how to raise procedural issues.

NOTIFICATION THAT WE ARE OPENING A CASE

4.3 If we decide to open a case we will normally inform the company under investigation. We may not, for example, where we consider that alerting the company before making an information request or conducting a dawn raid might prejudice the investigation. In these cases, we will notify as soon as it is appropriate to do so.

4.4 When notifying the company of the case, we will provide an outline of the allegations and the scope of the investigation. We will give a provisional timeline for the key steps of the investigation and when we expect to give updates. Companies under investigation can expect regular updates, often by telephone or email. The timeline may change as the case progresses. If it does we will notify the company. The scope of the inquiry may widen if we become aware of other matters requiring investigation.

4.5 We may invite the company for an initial meeting, to discuss the nature of the allegations, the timeline and how we intend to proceed. The company may comment on the allegations at this stage (for example, to say that it admits or denies breaches, or cannot say yet). It may wish to raise other matters, such as inviting Ofgem to visit a company site.

OFGEM'S TIMESCALES FOR CARRYING OUT AN INVESTIGATION

4.6 We aim to carry out investigations as quickly as possible. The cases that we investigate vary enormously in type, complexity and size. The provisional timeline provided to the company at the outset of every investigation will be set on a case-by-case basis. It will be updated as the case progresses.

MAKING CASES PUBLIC AND PUBLICITY

4.7 We believe that making cases public is important to ensure transparency of our work. It also serves to inform consumers about the work that we are doing, helps identify possible witnesses and maximises the deterrent effect of enforcement action by encouraging industry compliance.

4.8 In line with our commitment to transparency, we will publish on our website every case that we open[109] unless this would adversely affect the investigation (for example, where it may prejudice our ability to collect information), harm consumers' interests or is subject to confidentiality or other considerations.[110] We will consider on a case-by-case basis how best to publicise the opening of a case bearing in mind our Enforcement Vision and Strategic Objectives.[111] In some cases, we may also decide to make an announcement to the media. We will normally inform a company before we publish the opening of a case on our website or make an announcement to the media.

4.9 When we publish the opening of a case on our website we will make clear that this does not imply that we have made any finding(s) about non-compliance.

4.10 We will exclude information from publication only if we consider that failure to do so would harm consumers' interests or might seriously harm the interests of the company under investigation. We will consider these factors when deciding whether to offer anonymity to any company under investigation.[112]

4.11 In Competition Act cases, any notice that we have opened a case may include any of the information set out in section 25A of the Competition Act (our decision to open a case, the section that the investigation falls under, the matter being investigated, the identity of any company being investigated and the market affected). If publishing details of any company being investigated (or any other information set out in section 25A of the Competition Act) could adversely affect the investigation (as per paragraph 4.8) we may decide to exclude that information. In line with the CMA's approach, we will normally publicly announce the issue of the Statement of Objection.[113]

4.12 We will also usually publish case closures on our website. Findings of breach or infringement, penalties and/or consumer redress orders in settled and contested cases (subject to any confidentiality and other legal issues) will also be published. When a case has been made public on opening, then if we close it with no finding of breach or infringement (for example, due to lack of evidence, on the grounds of administrative priorities or because we are taking alternative action) we will also make this fact public.[114] We will normally inform a company before we publish the closing of a case on our website or make an announcement to the media.

4.13 In order to ensure the transparency of our work, to explain our expectations or to share lessons learned, details of cases resolved via alternative action will normally be made public. Where the issue was resolved quickly with limited intervention from Ofgem, some details may be included in reports that we publish from time-to-time on our compliance and enforcement activity.

4.14 Where alternative action involves more substantial activity or voluntary payments to put things right, we will normally publish information on the action taken. We will consult the company in advance of publishing any statements.

CONTACT WITH THE CASE TEAM

4.15 When we decide to open a case we will provide the company under investigation and any relevant third parties with contact details of the person who will be the main point of contact at Ofgem during the investigation. The name of the Senior Responsible Officer (SRO) in the case will also be provided to the company.

4.16 Any specific queries should be addressed to the Ofgem contact.

4.17 We will comply with our duties in respect of confidential information when providing updates.

INTERIM ORDERS

4.18 Where there is a need for immediate action, for example where consumers are suffering detriment that needs to be stopped, we may take steps to make a provisional order or interim measures direction, or obtain an interim enforcement order or interim injunction as appropriate. These orders are described in Section 2.

4.19 We will usually engage with companies under investigation before making an order, and where appropriate, we may invite written representations from them. However, there may be circumstances (such as where an ongoing or likely contravention requires immediate intervention to prevent detriment to consumers or competition) in which it may be necessary to make an order without representations from the company affected.

4.20 This does not apply to Competition Act cases, where we are required to give written notice to the proposed recipients of the interim measures direction before the direction is made, and offer them an opportunity to make representations and inspect documents on file.[115]

4.21 In cases under Part 8 of the Enterprise Act, consultation with the company before seeking an order is usually required.

INFORMATION GATHERING

4.22 We have wide-ranging powers to require the provision of information. These include powers under the following legislation:

- the Gas Act and Electricity Act[116]
- the Competition Act[117]
- the Consumer Rights Act.[118]

4.23 We will use these powers to collect the information and evidence which we need to progress an investigation. It will usually be necessary to issue several information requests in the course of an investigation, although we will aim to avoid requesting information more than once without good reason. We may ask for additional information after considering material submitted in response to an earlier request. The request will set out how the information should be submitted and the deadline.

4.24 We will set the length of any deadline based on the complexity of the issues raised and the breadth, type and amount of information required. We will give what we consider, in the circumstances, to be a reasonable amount of time for responses.

4.25 We may share drafts of the request with the company to give the company an opportunity to comment on the scope or form of the request (for instance, whether the data or documentation is available in the form requested), and on whether there is any practical issue with the deadline. After considering any comments and making any amendments we consider necessary, we will issue the actual information request.

4.26 Any problems understanding an information request or queries about the scope of it should be raised promptly with the Ofgem contact. Representations about the deadline should be made to the contact in writing as soon as possible. Companies should not wait until just before the deadline to request more time. We may allow further time if there are good reasons for needing an extension. These reasons should be set out in the request for an extension. We will aim to deal with all requests promptly and reasonably.

4.27 Delays in the provision of information can have an impact on overall timescales for the investigation. We expect stakeholders to respond within deadlines to the notices served upon them. Failure to cooperate fully with reasonable requests from the investigation team will be taken very seriously, in line with the appropriate policy on penalties/redress.

4.28 We may gather information by making a site visit. A visit may be made, either at the request of the company or Ofgem, if we think that this might help to clarify matters or is appropriate for some other reason. Any site visit should be arranged through the Ofgem contact.

4.29 In Competition Act cases, we may also ask questions of an individual connected with a company under investigation,[119] and enter, and in some instances search, business and domestic premises.[120]

4.30 In sectoral cases and those under the Enterprise Act and Consumer Rights Act, the Authority may apply to the court for an order requiring any default in complying with a notice to be made good (and costs).[121]

4.31 In Competition Act cases, the Authority may impose a civil sanction by way of a financial penalty on a person who fails to comply with a requirement imposed under section 26, 26A, 27, 28 or 28A.[122]

4.32 Failure to fully comply with notices to produce documents or information may amount to a criminal offence[123] and will be taken seriously.

MEETINGS

4.33 Meetings with a company under investigation may be held as part of an information or evidence-gathering exercise or be used for updates on the progress of the investigation. The company and Ofgem may deal with procedural or substantive issues, raise concerns or issues, for example in advance of the settlement phase (case direction meeting), or to discuss settlement terms (see Section 5).

4.34 If we think a meeting is necessary or would be helpful, we will contact the company to request a meeting. We will make the arrangements and confirm them. We will say who (from Ofgem) will attend. We may request that particular people attend from the company, such as those with knowledge of particular matters or with the authority to speak for the company).

OTHER SOURCES OF INFORMATION

4.35 We may seek information and evidence from third parties such as consumer bodies, industry competitors, whistleblowers or other witnesses, other stakeholders or from publicly available records.

4.36 Sometimes we instruct experts, for example to provide economic analysis or carry out a survey to help us assess detriment.

4.37 We may consider (where available):

- complaint statistics and any qualitative data
- market data
- market monitoring and surveillance material
- statistical reports
- economic or technical analysis
- information relating to how other parties have secured compliance
- any other relevant evidence.

RAISING PROCEDURAL ISSUES

4.38 If a company wishes to raise any procedural issues these should be taken up with the SRO.

4.39 In competition cases we will comply with requirements under the Competition Act Rules for there to be a Procedural Officer to whom complaints about the investigation procedures can be made, if not adequately resolved by the SRO[124] in the case.

NOTES

109 We will consider a case as open for publishing purposes once the Enforcement Oversight Board has decided to invest enforcement team resources investigating a case in accordance with our prioritisation criteria.

110 Section 35 of the Gas Act and section 48 of the Electricity Act. We will comply with any duties under section 105 of the Utilities Act 2000 and Part 9 of the Enterprise Act in respect of confidential information.

111 See paragraphs 1.11 and 1.12.

112 When deciding on anonymity, we will have regard to the applicable legislation.

113 In the case of market sensitive announcements, we will have regard to relevant guidance from the FCA.

114 We are required to do this under section 25A of the Competition Act and we are committing to do it for all other types of cases covered by these guidelines.

115 Section 35 of the Competition Act and Rule 13 of the CA98 Rules.

116 Section 38 of the Gas Act and section 28 of the Electricity Act. There are other powers to require information: for monitoring purposes under section 34A of the Gas Act and section 47A of the Electricity Act, in the standard licence conditions and in the statutory instruments relating to the environmental schemes.

117 Sections 26 of the Competition Act.

118 The investigatory powers of consumer law enforcement bodies have been consolidated so that they appear in a single piece of legislation (the Consumer Rights Act). Our powers to request information in consumer law cases can now therefore mainly be found in that Act. Guidance for businesses on these changes is available at: www.businesscompanion.info/sites/default/files/Investigatory-powers-of-consumer-law-enforcers-guidance-for-businesses-on-the-Consumer-Rights-Act-2015-Oct-2015.pdf.

119 Section 26A of the Competition Act.

120 Sections 27, 28 or 28A of the Competition Act.

121 Section 38(4) of the Gas Act, section 28(6) of the Electricity Act and Paragraph 16 of Part 3 of Schedule 5 to the Consumer Rights Act.

122 Section 40A of the Competition Act and the CMA's guidance entitled "*Administrative penalties: Statement of Policy on the CMA's approach*" (CMA4), to which Ofgem is required to have regard when proceeding under section 40A.

123 If a person fails to produce required documents or information; or alters, suppresses or destroys such documents, they may be guilty of a criminal offence and liable on conviction to a fine (section 38(2) and (3) of the Gas Act and section 28(4)

and (5) of the Electricity Act). If a person intentionally or recklessly destroys, falsifies or conceals a required document, or if a person provides false or misleading information, they may be guilty of a criminal offence and liable to a fine and in some cases to imprisonment for up to two years (sections 43 and 44 of the Competition Act).

124 Rule 8 of the CA98 Rules. Further information on the Procedural Officer's role and the sorts of complaints that may be referred for resolution can be found in Chapter 15 of the CMA's Guidance CMA8 at: www.gov.uk/government/publications/guidance-on-the-cmas-investigation-procedures-in-competition-act-1998-cases.

SECTION 5: SETTLING OR CONTESTING A CASE

[3.276]

5.1 This section describes our procedures for settling or contesting sectoral and Competition Act cases. Sectoral cases are covered in paragraphs 5.4–5.47.

5.2 Many of the processes described are the same for Competition Act cases. However, certain obligations in the Competition Act and associated legislation require us to adopt some differences of approach when dealing with competition cases. Paragraphs 5.48–5.76 explain how we deal with settling or contesting Competition Act cases.

5.3 This section and Section 6 do not apply to cases under the Enterprise Act 2002, the Consumer Rights Act 2015 or the Business Protection from Misleading Marketing Regulations 2008. Different procedures apply in these cases as orders are sought from a court and are not decisions of the Authority. We have set out these procedures in Section 2.

SECTORAL CASES

Settling a sectoral case

5.4 To settle a case, a company under investigation must be prepared to admit to the breaches that have occurred. The settlement will lead to a finding of breach. The company will be expected to agree with this finding and to any penalty and/or consumer redress order.

5.5 The company will also be expected to agree not to challenge or appeal any finding of breach, penalty or consumer redress order that is agreed to as part of the settlement. We will not enter into partial settlements with companies.

5.6 This settlement process is distinct from the resolution of a case by, for example, the acceptance of undertakings or other agreed action.

5.7 Due to the statutory time restrictions in cases where a provisional order has been made, the process described in this section will not apply. In cases where no penalty or consumer redress order is proposed, the process described in this section will not apply. In such cases, the case team will write to the company concerned setting out the process that will be followed.

5.8 It is important to appreciate that settlement in the regulatory context is not the same as the settlement of a commercial dispute. An Ofgem settlement is a regulatory decision taken by us, the terms of which are accepted by the company under investigation. In sectoral cases, we must have regard to our statutory objective when agreeing the terms. We must also have regard to our statutory obligations to consult on proposed penalties and consumer redress orders.[125]

5.9 It is also important to note that settling does not reduce the seriousness of any breach. It will, however, result in a lower penalty than would likely be imposed if the matters were contested, and the case will be dealt with more quickly.

5.10 Settlement is a voluntary process. There is no obligation on companies to enter into settlement discussions or to settle. Any decision to settle should be based on a full awareness of the requirements of settlement (described above) and the consequences of settling, including that a finding on breach will be made.

5.11 Companies should consider whether to obtain legal or other advice before settling a case. The fact that we have settled a case with a company does not prevent us from taking future action if further breaches occur, or if actions agreed by the company to reach settlement are not carried out.

5.12 Although there may be exceptional cases[126] where settlement is not appropriate, generally we will consider settlement in all sectoral cases.

5.13 Companies may ask to enter into settlement discussions. Whilst we will engage positively with a company that indicates a willingness to enter into early settlement discussions, in many cases it may not be possible to start such discussions until we have sufficient information to assess the nature and extent of the breaches and the harm caused. To speed up our investigations, we may ask the company to cooperate with us by providing information in the meantime.

5.14 We will expect companies to take appropriate steps to secure compliance irrespective of the stage at which the case is at. Similarly, in suitable cases we will also expect satisfactory arrangements for consumer redress to be put in place. The fact that a company has not completed such steps will not be a bar to settlement discussions taking place, so long as the company has shown a real commitment to resolve the outstanding issues. If actions are agreed and not carried out, enforcement action may be undertaken.

Settlement discounts

5.15 Early settlement results in cases being resolved more quickly, and saves resources for both the company and Ofgem. It may also result in consumers obtaining compensation earlier than would otherwise be the case. In recognition of the benefits of early settlement, we have a discount scheme.

5.16 The discount is applied to a penalty amount that has been agreed in the settlement. It is available on a sliding scale, depending on when the settlement agreement is signed by the company (the earlier the settlement, the greater the percentage discount).[127] The Authority has provided for three settlement windows, as follows:

Early settlement window

- greatest discount
- opens when the draft penalty notice and/or redress order and press notice are served on the company
- closes on expiry of the reasonable period (normally 28 days[128]) notified to the company when the above documents are served

Middle settlement window

- medium discount
- opens after the early settlement window has closed
- closes on expiry of the period for making written representations on the Statement of Case notified to the company when the Statement of Case is served

Late settlement window

- smallest discount
- opens after the middle settlement window has closed
- closes on a date notified to the company by the EDP Secretariat.[129]

5.17 The percentage discounts are set out in the Authority's penalties and redress policy statement.[130]

The settlement framework

5.18 In most cases, after we have carried out our enquiries to assess the breaches and any harm caused, we will serve the company with a Summary Statement of Initial Findings (the Summary Statement).

5.19 This document will cover the breaches that we consider have been committed and/or that may be ongoing, our thinking about the detriment and/or gain, and such other matters as may be appropriate.

5.20 We will allow a reasonable period (normally 21 days) for written representations in response to the Summary Statement. We will also offer the company an opportunity to make oral representations on the Summary Statement at an optional case direction meeting (or other contact).

5.21 The purpose of these steps is not to negotiate but for us to understand the company's position on the Summary Statement so that we can take account of it in making recommendations to the Settlement Committee. Late submission of written representations may affect our ability to reach a settlement agreement during the early settlement window.

5.22 After this, we will obtain a settlement mandate from a Settlement Committee.[131] The company will then be provided with a draft penalty notice and/or consumer redress order, and/or a draft final order and press notice. If there is a proposed penalty and/or redress order it will be notified at this point that the early settlement window has opened. At the same time, it will be told the date that this window closes.

5.23 If a company wishes to take advantage of the greatest settlement discount, it will have the duration of the window to sign a settlement. This agreement is subject to the processes set out in paragraphs 6.20–6.25 which need not happen before expiry of the deadline. There will be no extension to the deadline that we set, apart from in very exceptional circumstances.

5.24 We will contact the company to make the necessary arrangements for discussions to take place. Settlement discussions may take place over a number of meetings, telephone calls and/or emails.

5.25 Settlement discussions will take place on a "without prejudice" basis. This means that if discussions break down, neither party can rely on admissions or statements made during the settlement discussions in any subsequent contested case.[132]

5.26 The aim of discussions will be to agree the terms of a penalty notice and/or consumer redress order and get comments on press notices.[133] We may also agree other terms with the company as part of a settlement.[134]

5.27 If a settlement agreement is not signed by the close of the early settlement window, the company may still receive a lesser discount for an agreement subsequently reached, according to the sliding scale already described (further information about the windows is set out in paragraphs 5.30, 5.41 and 5.47).

5.28 If a settlement is agreed, the company will be expected to sign a settlement agreement. The settlement decision will be made and issued as described in paragraphs 6.20–6.25. If a settlement cannot be reached, the case will move to the contested route.

Contesting sectoral cases – the Statement of Case

5.29 If a case is not settled within the early settlement window we will draft and serve a Statement of Case on the company which sets out our findings and the case alleged against the company. The company's written representations will be invited. We will also disclose any relevant documents (see paragraphs 5.32–5.34).

5.30 We will usually write to the company to advise that the Statement of Case is being drafted and serve an updated timeline for the case. We may invite the company to attend a case direction meeting for discussions to take place. When the Statement of Case is ready we will serve it on the company, and notify them of the deadline for any written representations and the closure of the middle settlement window (which will be the same date).

5.31 If the case is to be contested, we will inform the Enforcement Decision Panel Secretariat so that a Panel can be selected to deal with the case.[135]

Disclosure

5.32 We will disclose a list of all of the documents that we will rely on. Many of them are likely to be documents that the company already has and may have provided to us in the course of the investigation. However, we will produce copies of any other documents on which we rely that are reasonably requested by the company, subject to any legal restrictions on disclosure including questions of confidentiality and privilege.

5.33 In some cases, we may rely on information contained in confidential documents. In these cases our disclosure list will note the documents where full disclosure is not possible. It may be necessary to limit the description of the documents themselves. We will explain the alternative arrangements, which will allow the recipient to review the evidence on which we rely. Typically this will mean that confidential material will be removed so that confidence is maintained. Other arrangements may sometimes be required.

5.34 We will also disclose, by list, documents in the knowledge or possession of the case team or the relevant policy team, which might undermine the case advanced in the Statement of Case. Again, we will note those documents where full disclosure is not possible and the alternative arrangements that will be made. Privileged documents may be listed by class and will not be disclosed.

Written representations

5.35 Making written representations in response to the Statement of Case is the company's opportunity to examine and seek to rebut some or all of the allegations against it. The company should submit the evidence it wishes to put forward to support its representations. There is no obligation to submit a response but note that there are restrictions on introducing new material in any subsequent oral hearing (as described in paragraph 6.35).

5.36 The length of time that we give for a company to respond will depend on:

- the number and complexity of the issues raised by us in the Statement of Case and on
- the amount of any material in the Statement of Case that has not previously seen by the company.

5.37 We will usually allow 28 days for a company to respond to a Statement of Case. However, we may decide to extend the period for written representations if it appears reasonable to do so in a particular case.

5.38 Once we have received any written representations and supporting evidence from the company, we will review the material and our case. This may lead to us deciding that issues raised may no longer be of concern and we may close the case or withdraw from parts of it. It may lead to us making a further information request to the company or replying to the company's representations.

5.39 If there is a material change in the nature of the breaches in the light of the written representations, we may prepare a Supplementary or Revised Statement of Case. The company will be given an opportunity to respond in writing to the new document. We will usually allow a further 28 days for this, and may shorten or extend the time subject to the complexity of the issues.

5.40 If there are difficulties in meeting any deadline, a request for an extension should be made in writing to the Ofgem contact (or in urgent cases by telephone). We will deal with such requests as described in paragraph 4.26.

5.41 If a company has not requested the opportunity to make oral representations to the decision-making body (the Panel) and the case is to be decided by consideration of the written representations only, the EDP Secretariat will issue a notice to the company informing it of the date that the late settlement window closes and any other relevant deadlines.

Oral representations

5.42 A company may, if it wishes, make oral representations to the Panel. There is no obligation to do so. A decision not to request to make oral representations will not be held against a company. A company may decide not to for reasons of convenience or to save costs. A company may choose to have legal representation when oral representations are made, although this is not required.

5.43 If the company does wish to make oral representations, this should be clearly stated in the response to the Statement of Case. The EDP Secretariat will then arrange a date for oral representations to be heard.

5.44 Even where a company has not requested the opportunity to make oral representations, we may do so. The Panel may also invite further representations, in any case, if it needs further clarification on the papers. It may request that these clarifications are made orally. It cannot compel attendance, so it will always be possible to submit clarifications in writing. Whether oral representations for clarification are necessary is a matter for the discretion of the Panel.

5.45 The form, length and procedures of any hearing will be decided by the Panel, taking account of all the circumstances of the case. The EDP Secretariat will fix the date taking into account the parties' availability. The EDP Secretariat will aim to find a date convenient to all parties where possible.

5.46 The EDP Secretariat will notify the parties in writing of the date that the late settlement window closes. At least 28 days prior to the date fixed for the hearing, the Panel will issue directions in writing to the parties (via the EDP Secretariat) indicating how it intends to conduct the hearing.

5.47 The parties may make written representations on the directions about the hearing within the time period set out in the directions (at least seven days). If the parties raise any issues, these will be resolved on the papers and the decision notified to the parties in writing.

COMPETITION ACT CASES

Settling in Competition Act cases

5.48 Settling in Competition Act cases follows a similar process to the one above for sectoral cases. However, there are a number of differences of approach that exist because of requirements imposed by relevant legislation, including the CA98 Rules. Where different terminology is used in Competition Act cases to describe a similar or the same process, that terminology is also set out below.

5.49 Due to the different legal framework for Competition Act cases, the nature of the allegations and the number of parties that may be involved, we will retain a broad discretion in determining which cases to settle. There should be no expectation that we will offer settlement in Competition Act cases. The assessment of whether a case is suitable for settlement will be made on a case-by-case basis. We will consider factors such as whether the evidential standard for giving notice of a proposed infringement decision is met (we will only enter into discussions where we consider that that standard is met) and the likely procedural efficiencies and resource savings that can be achieved.

5.50 For enforcement cases under the Competition Act, settlement is the process whereby a company under investigation is prepared to admit the infringement, stop the infringing behaviour, agree to a streamlined administrative process for the remainder of the investigation[136] and confirm that it will pay a maximum penalty amount.[137] These are minimum requirements in order to settle. If a company meets them, a reduced penalty will be imposed in accordance with the CMA's adopted guidance as to the appropriate amount of a penalty.[138]

5.51 The company must agree that the settlement discount set out in the infringement decision will no longer apply if it appeals the infringement decision to the CAT,[139] and that we will remain free to use the admissions made by it and any documents, information or witness evidence provided by it.

5.52 Settlement is a voluntary process. In Competition Act cases, the company should satisfy itself that, having seen the key evidence on which the Authority is relying, it is prepared to admit to the infringement, including the nature, scope and duration of the infringement.

5.53 If the company does not follow the requirements for settlement we may withdraw from the settlement procedure. Before doing so, we will notify the company and will give it an opportunity to respond.

5.54 When deciding how to deal with settling or contesting a Competition Act case, we will have regard to the CMA's guidance on investigation procedures in Competition Act 1998 cases (the CMA's Guidance).[140]

Early settlement discounts

5.55 We will apply the CMA's settlement discounts as described in the above guidance.[141] There are two settlement windows as follows:

Early settlement window
- greater discount up to a maximum
- opens when the parties are informed that the investigation has been opened
- closes just before the date for service of the Statement of Objections

Late settlement window
- lesser discount up to a maximum
- opens on service of the Statement of Objections
- closes on a date notified to the company by the EDP Secretariat.

5.56 The percentage discounts are set out in the CMA's guidance. The amount of any settlement discount to be applied (up to a maximum) will depend on how early in the settlement window an agreement is reached, the procedural efficiencies and resource savings resulting from the settlement, and the extent to which the company follows the requirements of settlement.

The settlement framework

5.57 Before service of the Statement of Objections, each company that enters into settlement discussions will be provided with a Summary Statement of Initial Findings (the Summary Statement). The Summary Statement will be used as the basis of the company's admission.

5.58 We will also provide the company with access to key documents as part of the streamlined administrative process. There may be an optional case direction meeting (or other contact).

5.59 The SRO will generally oversee the settlement discussions. All decisions to follow the settlement procedure must be approved by the Settlement Committee.

5.60 The company will be provided with a draft penalty statement and it will be notified that the early settlement window has opened. At the same time, it will be told that the window will close just before

Part 3 CMA and other Guidelines

the date for service of the Statement of Objections. We will write to the company subsequently to say when we expect to serve the Statement of Objections and set the date for closure of this window.

5.61 If a company wishes to take advantage of the greater settlement discount, it will have up until the early settlement window closes to agree a settlement. We will not extend the early settlement window for the purposes of reaching an agreement, apart from in very exceptional circumstances.

5.62 During discussions, the company will be given the opportunity to provide limited representations, including identifying manifest factual inaccuracies, on the Summary Statement (or Statement of Objections if already served) within a specified time frame. If the representations amount to a wholesale rejection of the alleged facts or rejection of any important part of the case, we will reassess, on a case-by-case basis, whether the case remains suitable for settlement.

5.63 The company will also be given the opportunity to make limited representations on the draft penalty calculation within a specified time frame, provided that they are not inconsistent with the company's admission of liability. We will not enter into negotiations or plea-bargaining during settlement discussions (for example, by accepting an admission in relation to a lesser infringement in return for dropping a more serious infringement).[142] We may also agree other terms with the company as part of a settlement.

5.64 If a settlement is not agreed by the close of the early settlement window, the company may still receive a lesser discount for an agreement subsequently reached before the late settlement window closes.

5.65 If the company is willing to settle on the basis of the requirements of the procedure covered in settlement discussions with us, it will confirm in a letter (with its company letterhead) its acceptance of those requirements which includes its admission. Even if a settlement is reached, we are still required to serve the Statement of Objections upon which the infringement decision will be based.[143] If a settlement is agreed, the infringement decision will be made and issued.

Contesting Competition Act cases – the Statement of Objections

5.66 Contested Competition Act cases follow similar procedures to those in sectoral cases whilst ensuring appropriate consistency with the CMA procedures for such matters including consistency with the CA98 Rules. The main differences, which are set out below, relate to documents served on the company, disclosure (which is called 'access to file' in competition cases) and the time usually allowed for responses to the Statement of Objections.

5.67 The case team will produce a Statement of Objections.[144] This is a notice to the company under investigation that the Authority proposes to make an infringement decision.

5.68 The document must set out the prohibition that we consider has been infringed, the facts we rely on, our reasons for considering that the conduct breaches competition law, the action we intend to take and our reasons, the period for written representations on the confidentiality of information in the document, and the period for written representations on the content of the document.[145] It will set out any proposed action, such as imposing a financial penalty and/or issuing directions and the reasons for taking the action. It will also provide the deadlines for any written representations.

5.69 If the case involves more than one party, each party will receive a copy of the Statement of Objections. We will also notify the company that the late settlement window has opened. Information that is confidential will be disclosed through the Statement of Objections to other parties only if disclosure is strictly necessary in order for them to exercise their rights of defence.

5.70 We may also offer third parties with a sufficient interest the opportunity to consider and make representations[146] on a non-confidential version of the Statement of Objections. We may, in the event of a request, consider granting access to documents on the file where that is permissible under Part 9 of the Enterprise Act.

5.71 Before disclosing any confidential information, we will consider whether there is a need to exclude any information where disclosure would be contrary to the public interest or might significantly harm the interests of the company or individual it relates to. If this is the case, we will consider the extent to which disclosure of that information is nevertheless necessary for the purpose for which we are allowed to make the disclosure.

Access to file

5.72 At the same time as we serve the Statement of Objections we will give the company access to certain documents on the case file as required by the legislation.[147] We may withhold any document to the extent that it contains confidential information or which is an internal document. In many instances we may have to remove any confidential information before disclosing documents.[148] We will adopt a similar procedure to handling confidential information as is described in paragraph 5.33.

Written representations

5.73 We will usually allow at least 40 working days and no more than 12 weeks for a company to respond in writing to the Statement of Objections. If there is a material change in the nature of the breaches in the light of the written representations, we may prepare a Supplementary Statement of Objections. The company will be given an opportunity to respond in writing to the new document. We will usually allow a further 28 days for this, and we may shorten or extend the time subject to the complexity of the issues.

5.74 If the case is to be contested, we will inform the EDP Secretariat so that a Panel can be selected from the EDP to deal with the case.[149]

5.75 If a company has not requested the opportunity to make oral representations to the Panel and the case is to be decided 'on the papers', the EDP Secretariat will issue a notice to the company informing it of the date that the late settlement window closes.

Oral representations

5.76 If oral representations are to be heard, the parties will be notified in writing of the date that the late settlement window closes and how the hearing is intended to be conducted.

NOTES

125 Sections 30A and 30I of the Gas Act and sections 27A and 27I of the Electricity Act.

126 Certain cases may not be suitable for settlement (for example, where a point of legal interpretation is at issue such as the interpretation of a relevant provision on which we would wish the EDP's guidance).

127 The discount does not apply to any monies to be recovered from the company. Any final penalty amount and/or consumer redress order is subject to consultation in accordance with statutory requirements (see paragraph 6.23).

128 For example, where an early settlement window coincides with a holiday period we may allow a longer period for agreement

129 The body that supports the Enforcement Decision Panel (EDP). The decision-making structure is described in section 6.

130 This can be found at: www.ofgem.gov.uk/sites/default/files/docs/2014/11/financial_penalties_and_consumer_redress_policy_statement_6_november_2014__0.pdf

131 The bodies with delegated powers to issue a settlement mandate prior to settlement discussions are described in section 6.

132 If for any reason a company that has entered into settlement discussions chooses to reveal to the Panel any of the detail of the settlement discussions, we reserve the right, similarly, to reveal information (including any admissions) that were made during those discussions.

133 This means that (unlike in contested cases) we will seek to reach agreement with the company on the wording that will appear in the penalty notice/consumer redress order. There will be an exchange of press notices and an opportunity for the parties to comment on the content before they are published. The final decision as to what we publish will be made by us.

134 For example, other terms of settlement may include the possibility of paying a sum of money in lieu of (or in addition to) a financial penalty, to appropriate charities, trusts or organisations for specific activities. We have published guidance which provides information on the current process and the set of principles involved in allocating voluntary redress payments in this respect, in the context of enforcement investigations conducted under the Gas Act and the Electricity Act. This guidance is available at www.ofgem.gov.uk/publications-and-updates/open-letter-guidance- allocation-voluntary-redress-payments for further information.

135 The decision making structure is described in Section 6.

136 The streamlined procedure is intended to achieve efficiencies and resource saving. It would include, for example, streamlined access to file by access to key documents only, no written representations (except limited representations identifying manifest factual inaccuracies) or oral representations.

137 This will be reduced by a settlement discount, provided that the company proposing to settle follows any continuing requirements of settlement.

138 www.gov.uk/government/publications/appropriate-ca98-penalty-calculation.

139 The CAT has full jurisdiction to review the appropriate level of penalty.

140 www.gov.uk/government/publications/guidance-on-the-cmas-investigation-procedures-in-competition-act-1998-cases.

141 Chapter 14 of the CMA's guidance CMA8 at: www.gov.uk/government/publications/guidance-on-the-cmas-investigation-procedures-in-competition-act-1998-cases.

142 Although we will seek to reach agreement with the company on the wording that will appear in the penalty notice. There will also be an exchange of press notices before they are published.

143 Rule 9(5) of the CA98 Rules.

144 Ofgem will ensure compliance with rule 3 of the CA98 Rules that the person responsible for overseeing the investigation and for deciding to issue a Statement of Objections must be a different person from the person responsible for deciding whether to issue a Supplementary Statement of Objections, an infringement decision or penalty decision.

145 The procedure we must follow is set out in Rules 5 and 6 of the CA98 Rules.

146 Non-confidential versions of these representations will be disclosed to the company or companies for comment.

147 Rule 6(2) of the CA98 Rules.

148 See also paragraphs 3.17–3.21 on the handling of confidential information.

149 The decision making structure is set out in Section 6.

SECTION 6: DECISION MAKING AND APPEALS

[3.277]

6.1 Decisions on breaches or infringements, the use of its enforcement powers, and the imposition of penalties or consumer redress payments may be delegated by the Authority. The Authority's decision-making bodies include the Enforcement Oversight Board, Settlement Committees, the Enforcement Decision Panel and, in certain circumstances, senior partners.

6.2 This section explains the Authority's power to delegate its decision-making powers and describes the Authority's decision-making bodies. It sets out how settlement decisions and final decisions in contested cases are made and issued. It also deals with appeals.

THE DECISION MAKERS

The power to delegate

6.3 The Authority is authorised to delegate its decision-making powers to any member or employee of the Authority, or any committee of the Authority which consists entirely of members or employees of the Authority.[150] Day-to-day decisions are made by the SRO (as discussed in paragraph 4.15).

The Enforcement Oversight Board (EOB)

6.4 The EOB provides strategic oversight and governance to our enforcement work and oversees the portfolio of cases, including monitoring their progress. Changes in the regulatory landscape and market environment mean that the priority of a case may change over time.

6.5 The EOB takes the decision[151] on whether to open (or not) an investigation into a potential breach, taking account of the prioritisation criteria (see paragraphs 3.36–3.49). The EOB also decides whether to accept alternative action that addresses harm via voluntary payments (other than those repaying consumers who have been directly impacted). It may also decide whether we should seek to exercise our Competition Act powers in a particular case.[152] It is usually consulted on whether interim orders should be made or commitments accepted.

6.6 The members of the EOB are usually senior civil servants from across Ofgem. It is chaired by a senior civil servant with responsibility for enforcement.

The Settlement Committee

6.7 A Settlement Committee may be constituted for any sectoral or Competition Act[153] case which is considered suitable for settling. Settlement Committees consider whether to authorise settlement agreements in respect of alleged contraventions and they reach decisions in accordance with Ofgem's powers under the applicable Acts. Our Settlement Committee Terms of Reference have been published on the Ofgem website[154].

6.8 In sectoral cases where the penalty amount is below £100,000[155] or the issues raised are unlikely to attract significant industry or media interest or are otherwise uncontentious, the case may be handled by a senior Ofgem employee, as described in paragraph 6.11.

6.9 A Settlement Committee generally consists of two members of the EDP and one Ofgem Partner or Senior Partner[156] and is constituted as and when required to deal with a case. The membership of the Committee in a particular case will be provided to the company in writing by the EDP Secretariat.

6.10 If settlement discussions break down, an EDP member will not hear the contested case if they have been on an earlier Settlement Committee that has considered the same case.

Senior Ofgem employees

6.11 A Senior Partner may, in sectoral cases, decide:

(a) the settlement mandate and, if required, approve any final settlement decision
(b) to make a final order or confirm a provisional order
(c) to make a final order or confirm a provisional order with modifications

where the level of penalty recommended by the case team is below £100,000 or the issues raised are unlikely to attract significant industry or media interest or are otherwise uncontentious. The Senior Partner will take advice, where necessary, from other senior Ofgem officials.

6.12 The identity of the Senior Partner will be provided to the company in writing.

6.13 The process in relation to Competition Act cases is set out in paragraphs 5.48–5.65.

The Enforcement Decision Panel (EDP)

6.14 The EDP consists of a pool of members who are employees of the Authority, one of whom is appointed as the EDP Chair.

6.15 EDP members are employed specifically for EDP duties and are independent from the case team.

6.15 Contested cases are decided by a decision-making Panel of usually three members appointed from the EDP by the EDP Chair. A Panel is constituted as and when required to deal with a particular case. There will be a Panel Chair who will chair the decision making discussions, and who has the casting vote in the event of a deadlock.

6.16 In contested Competition Act cases where it must exercise its decision-making powers, the EDP Chair appoints at least one legally qualified member to the Panel. In Competition Act cases, a Procedural Officer is also required to chair the oral hearing and report to the Panel on procedural fairness.[157]

6.17 The EDP Terms of Reference have been published on the Ofgem website.[158]

6.18 The identity of the Panel members (and the Procedural Officer in Competition Act cases) will be notified to the parties in writing by the EDP Secretariat.

6.19 The EDP Secretariat provides administrative and procedural support to the EDP members. This includes the management of correspondence, case papers and evidence. The EDP Secretariat is independent of the case team. It liaises with the parties on behalf of the Panel. The Panel, or its individual members, should not be contacted directly by any party or their representatives outside of any oral representations.

SETTLEMENT DECISIONS

Settlement decisions in sectoral cases

6.20 At the case team's request, a Settlement Committee will be constituted to provide a settlement mandate to the case team before discussions commence. The mandate will not be disclosed to the party under investigation. When setting the mandate (or subsequently approving an agreement where necessary), the Settlement Committee will have regard to the Authority's penalties and redress policy statement.

6.21 Details of the procedural steps involved in settling a case are set out in paragraphs 5.4–5.28.

6.22 In sectoral cases, if after settlement discussions an agreement cannot be reached between the company and the case team within the settlement mandate (for example, because new material has come to light during the discussions), the case team may, in exceptional circumstances, go back to the Settlement Committee to seek a revised mandate.

6.23 If an agreement is reached within the terms of the mandate given by the Settlement Committee, the decision and penalty notice and/or consumer redress order will be published in accordance with the statutory requirements,[159] for the purposes of consultation. Following the close of the consultation, any representations will be considered.

6.24 If, having received representations or objections, the Settlement Committee proposes to vary the level of a penalty or the amount of consumer redress ordered from that originally proposed, the consultation process must be repeated.

6.25 The company will then have the opportunity to make further representations. The company's agreement to waive its right to challenge or appeal against breach, penalty or a consumer redress order (see paragraph 5.5) will fall away if the proposed variation to the penalty and/or the consumer redress order is outside the scope of their original settlement agreement.

Settlement decisions in Competition Act cases

6.26 Details of the procedural steps involved in settling a Competition Act case are set out in paragraphs 5.48–5.65.

6.27 All decisions to follow the settlement procedure in Competition Act cases will be approved by the Settlement Committee. The Committee will have regard to the CMA's adopted guidance on the appropriate amount of a penalty[160] and applicable parts of the CMA's procedural guidance in Competition Act 1998 cases.[161]

6.28 If the Settlement Committee approves the SRO's decision to follow a settlement procedure, the procedure will continue as follows:

- **if the Statement of Objections has not been issued**,[162] the SRO will issue that document and the case will follow a streamlined administrative process (as set out in paragraph 5.50). If it is still appropriate to proceed with an infringement decision, the SRO will issue that decision together with a notice of penalty, if appropriate, and potentially, a notice of directions to bring the infringement to an end
- **if the Statement of Objections has already been issued,** the SRO will proceed to issue the infringement decision together with a notice of penalty, if appropriate, and potentially, a notice of directions to bring the infringement to an end
- **once the settlement is agreed in terms that have been approved**, an infringement decision and notice of penalty will be published.[163]

CONTESTED DECISIONS

What decisions can the appointed Panel make?

6.29 EDP members have delegated powers to make decisions in contested cases concerning the Gas and Electricity Acts and the Competition Act.

6.30 The appointed Panel will decide in sectoral cases whether

- there is or has been a contravention of any relevant condition or requirement, or a failure to achieve a standard of performance
- to make a final order or confirm a provisional order (see paragraph 6.11 on the potential delegation of these powers)
- to impose a financial penalty and/or consumer redress order and, if so, the amount of any penalty or compensation and time for payment/compliance.

6.31 The appointed Panel will decide in Competition Act cases whether

- there has been an infringement of competition law
- to issue written directions to the parties to bring an infringement to an end
- to impose a financial penalty and, if so, the amount and time for payment.

How will the appointed Panel make decisions?

6.32 The appointed Panel will act within the Authority's statutory powers. It will take account of any relevant guidance (including these guidelines).

6.33 If the Panel has not been asked to hear oral representations, whether representations are necessary or whether the case can be dealt with on the papers is a matter for the discretion of the Panel. The Panel may request further assistance from the parties.

6.34 The Panel will decide on a case-by-case basis whether it will exercise its decision-making powers on liability and penalty at the same time or separately. This will be decided at an early stage and communicated to the parties with details of how the Panel intends to proceed (issued via the EDP Secretariat). In Competition Act cases we would usually expect these to be dealt with separately.

6.35 Where oral representations are made, neither Ofgem nor the company will be permitted to introduce new material in oral representations save in exceptional circumstances or where the Panel requests additional material. If a party wishes to introduce new material, notice must be given to any other party and the permission of the Panel should be sought before it is introduced. No evidence can be introduced after the hearing other than at the request of the Panel.

6.36 Details of the procedural steps involved in contesting a sectoral case are set out in paragraphs 5.29–5.47. Details of the procedural steps involved in contesting a Competition Act case are set out in paragraphs 5.66–5.76.

6.37 When making decisions, the Panel will consider all of the relevant available information presented to it including, and not limited to:

- the Statement of Case or Statement of Objections and any Supplementary or Revised Statements
- any relevant evidence submitted to support the findings of the Statement of Case or Statement of Objections
- the affected parties' written representations and any other relevant evidence
- any oral representations of the case team and the affected parties and their respective legal representatives
- any information or evidence received in answer to a request from the Panel.

Outcome of the decision making process – sectoral cases

6.38 If the Panel concludes that the regulated person has not committed any breach, the company will be informed of the case closure and a statement will normally be published on our website (see paragraph 4.12).

6.39 If the Panel is satisfied that a regulated person is or is likely to be in contravention of a licence condition or relevant requirement, a notice will be published on our website setting out the decision that:

- a breach is ongoing, or likely to occur, and that the Panel proposes to make a final order[164] and/or
- a breach has occurred (or is ongoing) and that the Panel proposes to impose a financial penalty and/or consumer redress and/or
- a breach has occurred, and the Panel does not intend to propose a financial penalty and/or consumer redress.

A notice will also be served on the regulated person along with a copy of any order.

6.40 Where the Panel proposes to make a final order or confirm a provisional order the notice will set out:

- that the Panel proposes to make the order
- the relevant condition or requirement with which it seeks compliance
- the acts or omissions which constitute contraventions of it
- any other facts to justify the order
- the time (not less than 21 days) for representations or objections to be made.[165]

6.41 Following the close of the consultation, the Panel will consider any representations and decide whether to exercise the Authority's powers to confirm or make an order.

6.42 As soon as is practicable after making an order, a copy of the order will be served on the regulated person and it will be published.[166]

Imposing a financial penalty or consumer redress order

6.43 The Panel may exercise the Authority's power to impose a financial penalty and/or make a consumer redress order. In deciding whether to do so, the Panel will have regard to the Authority's penalties and redress policy statement.

6.44 In setting the amount of any financial penalty and/or payment under a consumer redress order, the Panel will have regard to the Authority's penalties and redress policy statement. The amount in each case (combined if both are imposed) in respect of a contravention must not exceed 10 per cent of the regulated person's turnover.[167]

6.45 Under a consumer redress order, the Panel may require a regulated person to take necessary action to remedy the consequences of the contravention or prevent a contravention of the same or similar kind being repeated. The Panel might order:[168]

- the payment of compensation to affected consumers (i.e. those consumers that have suffered loss or damage, or been caused inconvenience, as a result of the contravention)
- the preparation and/or distribution of a written statement setting out the contravention and its consequences
- the variation or termination of contracts with affected consumers
- some other remedial action as considered necessary.

6.46 If proposing a penalty or a consumer redress order, a notice[169] setting out relevant details will be served on the regulated person (and in the case of a consumer redress order, on each affected consumer, or published in such a manner to bring it to their attention[170]) and published in line with statutory requirements.[171] The notice will include the time (not less than 21 days) for representations or objections to the penalty amount or consumer redress order.

6.47 If both a penalty and consumer redress order are proposed, the Panel may serve a joint notice.

6.48 Following the close of the consultation period, the Panel will consider any representations or objections, which are duly made and not withdrawn, and decide whether to exercise the Authority's powers to impose, vary or withdraw the proposed penalty and/or consumer redress order.

6.49 Before varying any proposal, a further notice to this effect must be given[172] for consultation, and any further representations or objections must be considered.

6.50 Notice of the final decision and the period for compliance (minimum 42 days for payment of a penalty, minimum seven days for compliance with the requirements of a consumer redress order) will be published and served on the regulated person.[173]

Outcome of the decision making process – Competition Act cases

6.51 If the Panel finds an infringement of the Competition Act, it will make an infringement decision. Notice of the decision will be given to each person who is or was a party to the agreement and/or is or was engaged in conduct.[174] A final opportunity will be given to the addressee of the decision to make confidentiality representations. The non-confidential version of the decision and any summary will be published on our website.

6.52 If an infringement decision is made, the Panel will also decide whether to give written directions and, if so, decide the content of the directions.[175] When giving directions to a person, they must be informed in writing at the same time of the facts on which the direction is based and reasons for it.[176]

Imposing a financial penalty

6.53 Where the Panel intends to make an infringement decision, the Panel may also decide to impose a financial penalty if satisfied that the infringement was committed intentionally or negligently.[177] The Panel may impose a financial penalty on the infringing party of up to 10 per cent of the company's applicable turnover.[178]

6.54 When deciding on the appropriate amount of a penalty the Panel will have regard to the CMA's adopted guidance, 'The OFT's guidance as to the appropriate amount of a penalty'.[179]

6.55 Before making the final decision on infringement and the appropriate penalty, the Panel must give the company an opportunity to comment in writing and orally, within a time specified in the draft, on the draft penalty notice which sets out the calculation of the penalty amount.

6.56 Having taken account of any representations, final notice of the penalty will be given in writing and specify the period for payment.[180] The company must be informed of the facts on which the Panel bases the penalty and its reasons for requiring it.[181]

AUTHORITY STRATEGIC OVERSIGHT

6.57 The Authority will not seek to influence the outcome of particular matters or change any decision of a Panel or Settlement Committee. The Authority will retain oversight through its annual review of the decisions taken by Panel members in settled and contested cases. It may, if appropriate, issue further guidance to the EDP to inform future decisions.

APPEALS

Appeals to the court in sectoral cases

6.58 A regulated person may appeal against the making of a provisional or final order[182] on the grounds that it was not within the powers conferred on the Authority by, or the procedural requirements of, the Gas or Electricity Acts. They may make an application to the court[183] within 42 days from the date of the order being served on them.[184]

6.59 The court has the power to quash the order or any provision of it if it is satisfied that the order was not within those powers or that the interests of the regulated person have been substantially prejudiced by a failure to comply with those requirements.[185]

6.60 Where a regulated person is aggrieved by the imposition of a penalty, the amount or the date for payment and/or by the making of a consumer redress order, or any requirement imposed by the order, the regulated person may make an application to the court.[186] The application must be made within 42 days of receipt of notice of the decision.[187]

6.61 The court may quash the penalty, substitute a penalty of a lesser amount or substitute the date or dates for payment, as appropriate, if satisfied that one or more of the grounds of appeal are met, namely:

- the imposition of the penalty was not within the Authority's power
- relevant procedural requirements were not complied with and the regulated person has been substantially prejudiced by the non-compliance
- it was unreasonable of the Authority to require the penalty imposed, or any portion of it, to be paid by the date or dates by which it was required to be paid.

6.62 In the case of a consumer redress order, the court may quash the order or any provision in it, or vary any such provision, as appropriate, if satisfied that one or more of the grounds of appeal are met, namely:

- the making of the order was not within the Authority's powers

- relevant procedural requirements were not complied with and the interests of the regulated person were substantially prejudiced by that non-compliance
- it was unreasonable of the Authority to require something to be done under the order.

Appeals to the Competition Appeal Tribunal

6.63 Competition Act decisions[188] may be appealed to a specialist tribunal, the Competition Appeal Tribunal (the CAT), established under the Enterprise Act. Appealable decisions include, among others, infringement decisions, no grounds for action decisions, directions and the imposition of financial penalties.[189] Note that there is no appeal against the decision not to accept commitments.

6.64 Any party in respect of which the Authority has made a decision may appeal against that decision.[190] A third party who the CAT considers has sufficient interest may also appeal certain decisions to the CAT.[191]

6.65 If a party appeals an infringement decision that was made following a settlement agreement, the settlement discount set out in the decision will no longer apply[192] and the CAT will have full jurisdiction to review the appropriate amount of any penalty.

6.66 Any appeal to the CAT must be made so that it is received by the CAT within two months of the date of notification or publication of the decision (whichever is the earliest).[193]

6.67 The CAT's powers include the power to confirm or set aside the decision, to substitute its own decision for that of the Authority, to remit the matter to the Authority and to impose, revoke or vary the amount of penalty.[194]

Appeals against decisions made by the courts

6.68 Orders made under Part 8 of the Enterprise Act, the Consumer Rights Act 2015 and the Business Protection from Misleading Marketing Regulations 2008 are dealt with on appeal in the same way as other civil appeals. An appeal lies to the next level of judge in the court hierarchy against the order made by the lower court.[195]

6.69 Notice of appeal must be filed at the appeal court within the time directed by the lower court, or (where the court makes no such direction) within 21 days of the date of the lower court's decision that is to be appealed.[196]

NOTES

150 Paragraph 9(1) and (3) of Schedule 1 to the Utilities Act 2000.

151 Technically the senior civil servant who chairs the EOB takes the decision but does so after an EOB discussion in practice.

152 Decisions about whether to seek a court order under the Enterprise Act and related decisions under general consumer law are generally reserved to the Authority.

153 See paragraphs 6.26–6.29.

154 www.ofgem.gov.uk/system/files/docs/2017/07/committee_tors_approved_by_gema_july_2016.pdf.

155 For these purposes the amount of any consumer redress payment is not taken into account.

156 This includes Ofgem staff at equivalent or higher grades than Partner.

157 Rules 6(5) and (6) of the Competition Act 1998 (Competition and Markets Authority's Rules) 2014 (CA98 Rules). Note that the Procedural Officer will not have been involved in the investigation and is not a decision-maker in the case.

158 www.ofgem.gov.uk/system/files/docs/2017/07/committee_tors_approved_by_gema_july_2016.pdf.

159 Section 30A of the Gas Act and section 27A of the Electricity Act.

160 OFT423 at: www.gov.uk/government/publications/appropriate-ca98-penalty-calculation.

161 See Chapter 14 of the CMA's guidance at: www.gov.uk/government/publications/guidance-on-the-cmas-investigation-procedures-in-competition-act-1998-cases.

162 We are still required to serve the Statement of Objections in settled Competition Act cases. See Rule 9(5) of the CA98 Rules.

163 Rule 12 of the CA98 Rules.

164 The Panel decides whether or not to confirm a Provisional Order in accordance with statutory deadlines.

165 The procedural requirements are set out in section 29 of the Gas Act and section 26 of the Electricity Act. Representations may be made by anyone, including consumers.

166 See section 29(7) of the Gas Act or section 26(5) of the Electricity Act.

167 Section 30O of the Gas Act and section 27O of the Electricity Act. Turnover is determined in accordance with the Electricity and Gas (Determination of Turnover for Penalties) Order 2002.

168 Section 30H of the Gas Act and section 27H of the Electricity Act. Note that in the event that it is impractical to identify all affected consumers, payment could, for example, be ordered to a proxy group or to a suitable fund to recognise wider detriment to the market.

169 Under section 30A(3) of the Gas Act and section 27A(3) of the Electricity Act (penalties) and under section 30I of the Gas Act and section 27I of the Electricity Act (consumer redress orders). There are certain time limits on the imposition of penalties (section 30C of the Gas Act and section 27C of the Electricity Act) and time limits for making consumer redress orders (section 30K of the Gas Act and section 27K of the Electricity Act).

170 Section 30I(5) of the Gas Act and section 27I(5) of the Electricity Act.

171 Sections 30A(7) and 30I(5) of the Gas Act and sections 27A(7) and 27I(5) of the Electricity Act.

172 Section 30A(4) of the Gas Act and section 27A(4) of the Electricity Act.

173 Sections 30A(5) and 30G(5) of the Gas Act and sections 27A(5) and 27G(5) of the Electricity Act.

174 Rule 10 of the CA98 Rules.

175 Sections 32 and 33 of the Competition Act.

176 Rule 12 of the CA98 Rules.

177 Section 36 of the Competition Act.

178 See section 36(8) of the Competition Act. Turnover is determined in accordance with the Competition Act 1998 (Determination of Turnover for Penalties) Order 2000, as amended by the Competition Act 1998 (Determination of Turnover for Penalties) (Amendment) Order 2004.

179 www.gov.uk/government/publications/appropriate-ca98-penalty-calculation.

180 Section 36 of the Competition Act. The date before which the payment is due must not be earlier than the end of the period within which an appeal against the notice may be brought under section 46.

181 Rule 12 of the CA98 Rules.

182 Except when they have agreed not to as part of a settlement agreement.

183 In relation to England and Wales, the High Court and in relation to Scotland, the Court of Session, section 30(9) of the Gas Act and section 27(8) of the Electricity Act.

184 Section 30(1) Gas Act and section 27(1) Electricity Act.

185 Section 30(2) Gas Act and section 27(2) Electricity Act.

186 Section 30E(1) and 30M of the Gas Act and section 27E(1)and 27M of the Electricity Act.

187 Section 30E(2) and 30M(2) of the Gas Act and section 27E(2) and 27M(2) of the Electricity Act.

188 Appeals relating to enforcement decisions in respect of breaches of the Transmission Constraint Licence Condition predating 16 July 2017 may also be heard by the CAT. Further information can be found at: www.ofgem.gov.uk/publications-and-updates/final-decision-guidance-transmission-constraint-licence-condition.

189 Except in the case of an appeal against the imposition, or the amount, of a penalty, the making of an appeal does not suspend the effect of the decision to which the appeal relates: Section 46(4) of the Competition Act.

190 Section 46 of the Competition Act.

191 Section 47 of the Competition Act.

192 In accordance with the settlement agreement made with us.

193 Rule 9 of the Competition Appeal Tribunal Rules 2015. The CAT's Rules and Guidance are available on its website at: www.catribunal.org.uk/240/Rules-and-Guidance.html.

194 Paragraph 3 of Schedule 8 to the Competition Act.

195 The Access to Justice Act 1999 (Destination of Appeals) Order 2000 provides a summary of the destinations for different types of civil appeals.

196 Rule 52.4(2) of the Civil Procedure Rules and see Part 52 of the Civil Procedure Rules generally for further information about appeals.

SECTION 7: CLOSING CASES

[3.278]

7.1 A decision may be made very early on not to pursue a case where the issue raised does not satisfy the criteria for opening a case (see paragraphs 3.36–3.49).

7.2 If a case has been opened, it may be closed at any stage. Cases will be kept under review. A case may be closed where:

- it is concluded that there is no relevant breach or infringement (for example, after investigating the matter or following receipt of the response to the Statement of Case or Statement of Objections)
- the company under investigation has made commitments, or given assurances, undertakings, or has taken other action (including in the context of alternative action) to ensure that behaviour is stopped and relevant matters have been appropriately addressed and we do not consider further action to be appropriate
- we have obtained a court order to secure compliance (such as an enforcement order under Part 8 of the Enterprise Act or injunction under the Business Protection from Misleading Marketing Regulations 2008)
- a case has been contested or settled and a decision made or approved by the decision maker and published
- we have reviewed it against our prioritisation criteria and concluded that the case should be closed on the grounds of administrative priorities[197] (see also the specific comments below about competition cases).

7.3 Competition Act cases are complex and resource intensive. When we review a case to decide whether to continue, we may close it on the grounds of administrative priorities without reaching a decision as to whether or not there has been an infringement.[198] For example, this may be because:

- the evidence or our analysis suggests that the likelihood of consumer detriment from the conduct or agreement in question is less significant than anticipated at the outset or
- the resources needed to progress the investigation in a timely fashion are greater than planned and cannot be justified in the light of our overall portfolio of work and resource demands.

7.4 In Competition Act cases, we may decide to consult with a complainant or other third parties on a proposed decision to close the case on any grounds. In considering whether to consult with such persons, we will normally have regard to the CMA's guidance on involving third parties in Competition Act investigations.[199]

7.5 Where we close a Competition Act case on the grounds of administrative priorities, this will mean that we are taking no decision on the merits of the case.

PUBLICITY

7.6 We will usually make case closures public on our website (as set out in paragraph 4.8).

COMPLIANCE MONITORING

7.7 Where we have taken enforcement action, or secured undertakings or other agreements that adequately resolve the issues, we will close the case.

7.8 In some cases we may decide to put the company under investigation into a 'compliance phase'. This means we will monitor its behaviour to ensure that:

- there are no further behaviours of concern
- it complies with any undertakings or commitments and/or that
- it implements any agreements made with us (for example by paying compensation to affected consumers or ceasing the infringing behaviour).

7.9 The length of the compliance phase will depend on the particular circumstances of the case and the monitoring required.

7.10 Similar compliance monitoring steps may be agreed with the company in question following alternative action.

FEEDBACK

7.11 After closing a case, our case teams routinely evaluate the investigation process to assess what went well and how things could be improved. We will usually share the "lessons learned" with our colleagues at Ofgem so that we can learn from everything we do. In most cases we will also request feedback from others involved in the case (for example, companies under investigation) and use it to inform our future enforcement work.

NOTES

197 This means that we have weighed up the likely benefits of conducting the case against the resources that it requires, and the comparative benefits of using those resources in other ways, before deciding that the case should be closed.

198 Further information on the way in which we may deal with such decisions can be found in Chapter 10 of the CMA's guidance CMA8, '*Competition Act 1998: Guidance on the CMA's investigation procedures in Competition Act 1988 cases*', at: www.gov.uk/government/publications/guidance-on-the-cmas-investigation-procedures-in-competition-act-1998-cases.

199 www.gov.uk/government/publications/involving-third-parties-in-competition-act-investigations.

APPENDIX: PROCESS FLOWCHARTS

[3.279]

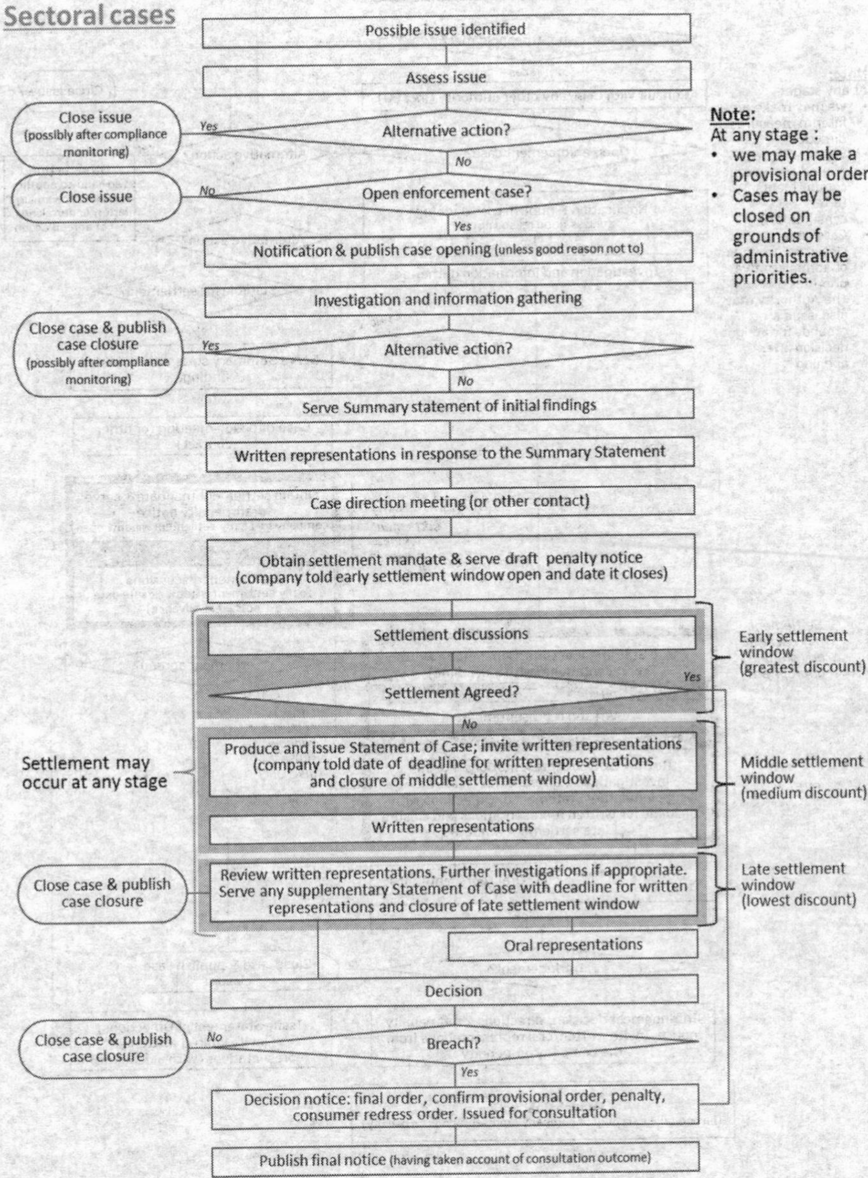

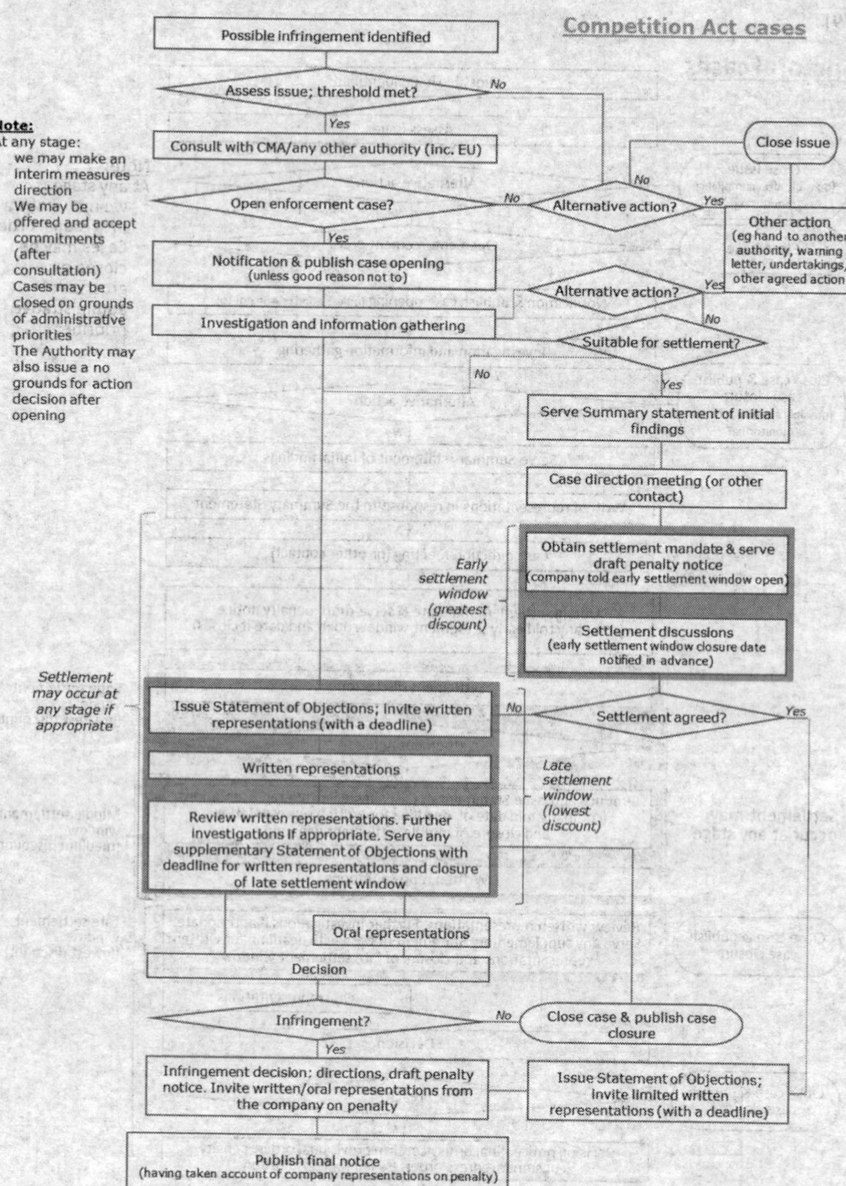
Competition Act cases
Note:
At any stage:
• we may make an interim measures direction
• We may be offered and accept commitments (after consultation)
• Cases may be closed on grounds of administrative priorities
• The Authority may also issue a no grounds for action decision after opening
Possible infringement identified
Assess issue; threshold met?
No
Yes
Consult with CMA/any other authority (inc. EU)
Close issue
Open enforcement case?
No
Alternative action?
No
Yes
Other action (eg hand to another authority, warning letter, undertakings, other agreed action
Yes
Notification & publish case opening (unless good reason not to)
Alternative action?
Yes
No
Investigation and information gathering
Suitable for settlement?
No
Yes
Serve Summary statement of initial findings
Case direction meeting (or other contact)
Obtain settlement mandate & serve draft penalty notice (company told early settlement window open)
Early settlement window (greatest discount)
Settlement discussions (early settlement window closure date notified in advance)
Settlement may occur at any stage if appropriate
Issue Statement of Objections; invite written representations (with a deadline)
No
Settlement agreed?
Yes
Written representations
Late settlement window (lowest discount)
Review written representations. Further investigations if appropriate. Serve any supplementary Statement of Objections with deadline for written representations and closure of late settlement window
Oral representations
Decision
Infringement?
No
Close case & publish case closure
Yes
Infringement decision: directions, draft penalty notice. Invite written/oral representations from the company on penalty
Issue Statement of Objections; invite limited written representations (with a deadline)
Publish final notice (having taken account of company representations on penalty)

Cases under Part 8 of the Enterprise Act, Consumer Rights Act, UTCCRs and BPMMRs

Note:
At any time:
- an interim order/interim injunction may be sought
- Cases may be closed on grounds of administrative priorities

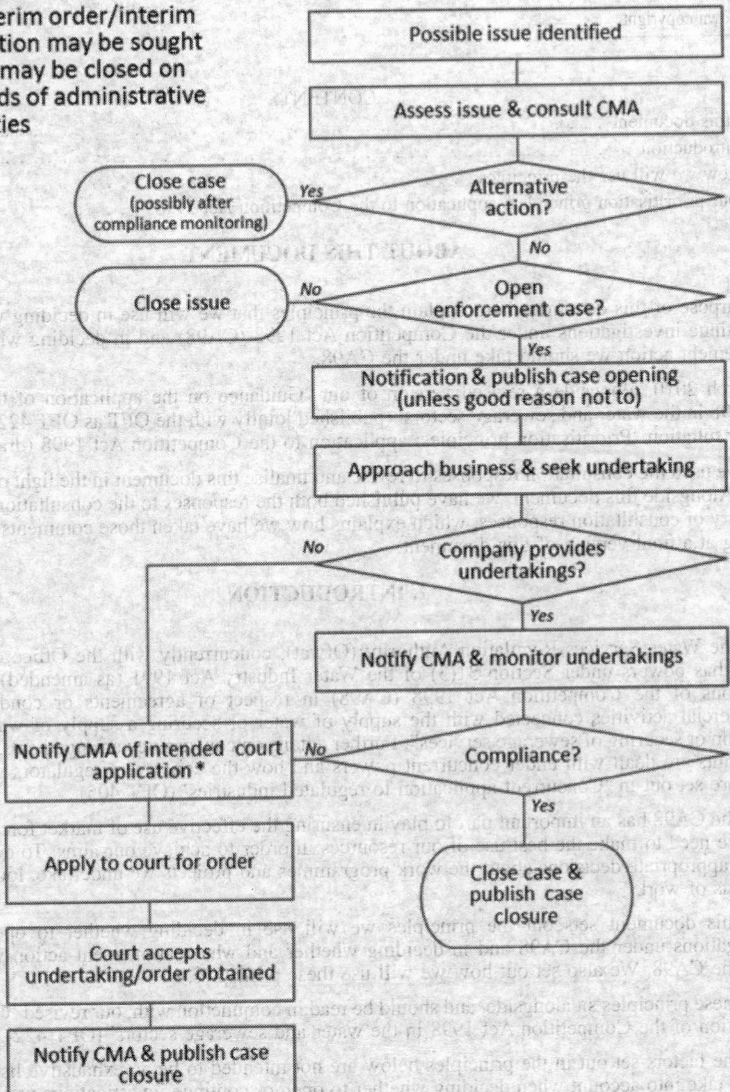

Possible issue identified

Assess issue & consult CMA

Alternative action? — Yes: Close case (possibly after compliance monitoring); No: continue

Open enforcement case? — No: Close issue; Yes: continue

Notification & publish case opening (unless good reason not to)

Approach business & seek undertaking

Company provides undertakings? — Yes: continue; No: Notify CMA of intended court application *

Notify CMA & monitor undertakings

Compliance? — Yes: Close case & publish case closure; No: Notify CMA of intended court application *

Notify CMA of intended court application *

Apply to court for order

Court accepts undertaking/order obtained

Notify CMA & publish case closure

*In cases under Part 8 of the Enterprise Act, consultation requirements also apply.

(IV) WATER

OFWAT: PRIORITISATION PRINCIPLES: APPLICATION TO THE COMPETITION ACT 1998 (SEPTEMBER 2010)

[3.280]

NOTES

CONTENTS

ABOUT THIS DOCUMENT

[3.281]
The purpose of this document is to explain the principles that we will use in deciding whether to open or continue investigations under the Competition Act 1998 (CA98) and in deciding whether and what enforcement action we should take under the CA98.

In March 2010, alongside a revised version of our 'Guidance on the application of the Competition Act 1998 in the water and sewerage sectors' (published jointly with the OFT as OFT 422), we published our consultation 'Prioritisation principles: application to the Competition Act 1998 (draft)'.

We have used the consultation responses to revise and finalise this document in the light of the comments made. Alongside this document, we have published both the responses to the consultation and a separate summary of consultation responses, which explains how we have taken those comments into account in arriving at a final version of this document.

1. INTRODUCTION

[3.282]
1.1 The Water Services Regulation Authority (Ofwat), concurrently with the Office of Fair Trading (OFT), has powers under Section 31(3) of the Water Industry Act 1991 (as amended) to enforce the provisions of the Competition Act 1998 (CA98) in respect of agreements or conduct relating to "commercial activities connected with the supply of water or securing a supply of water or with the provision or securing of sewerage services". Further details on concurrency arrangements, including how complaints are dealt with under concurrent powers and how the concurrent regulators work with each other, are set out in 'Concurrent application to regulated industries' (OFT 405).

1.2 The CA98 has an important part to play in ensuring the effective use of market forces. At the same time, we need to make the best use of our resources in order to achieve our aims. To do this, we need to take appropriate decisions about the work programmes and projects we undertake, looking across all our areas of work.

1.3 This document sets out the principles we will use in deciding whether to open or continue investigations under the CA98 and in deciding whether and what enforcement action we should take under the CA98. We also set out how we will use these principles.

1.4 These principles sit alongside, and should be read in conjunction with, our revised 'Guidance on the application of the Competition Act 1998 in the water and sewerage sectors' (OFT 422).

1.5 The factors set out in the principles below are not intended to be an exhaustive list of everything we will take into account when deciding whether to open or continue investigations under the CA98 or whether and what enforcement action we should take under the CA98. We may consider other factors as necessary or appropriate.

1.6 We will keep these principles under review and may revise them from time to time as appropriate.

2. HOW WE WILL USE THE PRINCIPLES

[3.283]
2.1 Under section 25 of the CA98, we may open an investigation into a possible breach of Article 101, Article 102, the Chapter I and/or Chapter II prohibitions if we have reasonable grounds for suspecting a breach.

2.2 We take exploitative or exclusionary behaviour very seriously, and we will use our CA98 powers if it is appropriate for us to do so. We decide whether we will open or continue a CA98 investigation, or whether or what enforcement action we should take, by balancing the impact the investigation is having or is expected to have on our strategic goals with the risks and resources it will involve. We will also compare the opening or continuation of a CA98 investigation or the taking of particular CA98 enforcement action with other courses of action open to us. Other powers available to us may provide the most appropriate way of addressing a particular issue.

2.3 We will exercise our judgement on a case-by-case basis, considering the principles and the facts of the case. We will also consider other relevant factors. A decision whether to open or continue a CA98 investigation or whether or what enforcement action we should take will always involve an assessment of the best use of our resources, taking into account their alternative uses. Thus, we will not take such decisions in isolation, but will always consider our portfolio of work and the resources available.

2.4 The question of whether to open or continue a CA98 investigation or whether or what enforcement action we should take will in part depend on the priority we attach to the possible investigation or action relative to other uses for our resources. It is therefore not possible to give guidance in advance on whether we would open or continue an investigation in a given set of circumstances.

2.5 In line with our commitment to delivering better regulation set out in our strategy 'Delivering sustainable water', we will seek to apply these prioritisation principles in line with the principles of better regulation. These are that our actions should be transparent, accountable, proportionate, consistent and targeted.

3. OUR PRIORITISATION PRINCIPLES: APPLICATION TO THE COMPETITION ACT 1998

[3.284]
3.1 We enforce the CA98 concurrently with the OFT, and have therefore adopted the broad prioritisation principles[1] used by the OFT. They are:

- impact;
- strategic significance;
- risks; and
- resources.

3.2 As a sectoral regulator, we are different in nature to the OFT – we have different tools available to us and a different portfolio of work. We may therefore use our principles in a different way to that in which the OFT uses its principles.

3.3 The OFT applies its prioritisation principles across its portfolio of work and across its tool-kit. In contrast, this guidance deals only with our decisions on whether to open or continue investigations under the CA98 and on whether or what enforcement action we should take under the CA98. We have therefore adopted an additional principle:

- interaction with our other powers.

3.4 In this section, we set out the way we will use each of these principles in deciding whether to open or continue a CA98 investigation or whether or what enforcement action we should take under the CA98. We discuss interaction with our other powers first, because in general we consider that this is likely to be a significant consideration in many cases. However, the order of the principles has no legal significance.

3.5 As noted, the principles and factors set out below are not exhaustive. We take decisions on a case-by-case basis and we will exercise our judgement, considering the principles and the facts of the case. Where other factors are relevant, we will also consider them.

A. INTERACTION WITH OUR OTHER POWERS

3.6 When considering whether to open or continue with an investigation or take enforcement action under the CA98, we will consider whether our other powers are a more appropriate means of addressing an issue.

3.7 It will not always be possible for us to address an issue using our other powers. If it is possible to do so, we will assess the impact, strategic significance, risk and resources that would be involved in using our other powers. We will then compare that with the impact, strategic significance, risk and resources involved in using our CA98 powers.

3.8 We will take account of possible different outcomes that might arise when using different powers, including the possibility of differing impacts on affected parties.

3.9 Balancing all these factors, we will choose the most appropriate route to address the particular issue.

B. IMPACT

3.10 The greater the positive impact on consumers from the decision, the more likely we are to open or continue an investigation or to take a particular course of enforcement action. Consumers may be positively affected if an investigation results in lower prices, better quality products or services, more choice and/or more innovation. Such impacts may be felt in the short term or over time.

3.11 When assessing the impact on consumers, we will consider direct and indirect effects. Consumers benefit directly from changes in the behaviour of those subject to the investigation or enforcement action. Consumers may benefit directly, for example, if we prevent or terminate activity that negatively affects them. Where an investigation concerns a related market or intermediate market (where customers may be suppliers in other markets), we will assume that benefits will be passed on to final consumers.

3.12 Consumers benefit indirectly through changes in the behaviour of others than those who were subject to the investigation or enforcement action. Such indirect effects may occur, for example, through deterrence and awareness effects. Consumers will benefit if our investigation or enforcement action results in changed behaviour and improved awareness by consumers, other customers, companies and the government. Indirect effects include effects in markets other than those under investigation or subject to enforcement action.

3.13 In considering the impact of an investigation or enforcement action, we will also consider any positive effects it may have on efficiency. We may consider effects on:

- productive efficiency (whether goods and services are provided at lowest cost);
- allocative efficiency (whether resources are used to produce goods and services that customers value sufficiently to pay their costs of production); and
- dynamic efficiency (the development of more efficient production methods over time by means of innovation and technological progress).

Improvements in efficiency may benefit consumers directly, if they occur in the market that is the subject of the investigation, or indirectly, if they occur in other markets.

3.14 Consumers may also benefit indirectly where an investigation has the effect of safeguarding or facilitating the competitive process, as the proper functioning of competitive process may help secure the efficiencies, lower prices, better quality products or services, more choice and/or more innovation.

3.15 In assessing the likely impact on consumers, we will consider these factors in the round (and as appropriate) to arrive at a reasonable overall assessment of the likely impact of an investigation in the particular case under consideration.

3.16 It is also possible that an investigation may have differential impacts on different groups of consumers. Where this is the case, we will consider those differential impacts as part of our overall assessment.

C. STRATEGIC SIGNIFICANCE

3.17 In our strategy, we set out a number of goals. They are:

- ensuring a fair deal for customers;
- keeping companies accountable;
- making monopolies improve;
- harnessing market forces;
- contributing to sustainable developments; and
- delivering better regulation.

3.18 We will not open or continue with CA98 investigations that, overall, are not consistent with our strategic goals. The more an investigation or enforcement action will contribute to one or more of our strategic goals, the more likely we are to open or continue it.

3.19 In some cases, it may be more appropriate for a body other than us to investigate or take action. We enforce the CA98 concurrently with the OFT (and other sectoral regulators). In line with the Competition Act 1998 (Concurrency) Regulations 2004 (SI 2004, No. 1077) and the OFT guidance 'Concurrent application to regulated industries' (OFT 405), we will consider whether the OFT or another regulator might be best placed to deal with a particular case.

D. RISKS

3.20 The higher the likelihood of a successful outcome, the more likely we are to open or continue an investigation or to take a particular enforcement action. A successful outcome is one that helps us to achieve one or more of our strategic goals.

3.21 In relation to CA98 investigations, we note that an infringement decision is not the only successful outcome. It is possible for an investigation to have a significant impact and generate significant strategic benefits, without resulting in an infringement decision (for example if it resolves an issue by means of undertakings, or clarifies an important issue).

E. RESOURCES

3.22 We will only decide to open or continue an investigation or to take particular enforcement action if we are satisfied that the resources required are proportionate to the expected benefits (taking into account any risk that they may not be achieved). We may decide to open or continue an investigation or to take enforcement action that is resource-intensive because we consider that, having regard to its impact, strategic significance and risk, it is a good use of our resources. Conversely, we may decide to terminate or not to open an investigation or not to take enforcement action that is relatively resource-light because it is still a poor use of our resources.

3.23 In considering our resources, we will have regard to:

- the level of resource that will be required;
- the period over which the resource will be required; and
- the alternative uses to which that resource could be put.

We will consider not only our internal resource requirement, but also what external resource we may need (such as counsel or consultancy advice).

NOTES

1 'OFT Prioritisation Principles' (OFT 953) – see www.oft.gov.uk/shared_oft/about_oft/oft953.pdf

MEMORANDUM OF UNDERSTANDING BETWEEN THE COMPETITION AND MARKETS AUTHORITY AND THE WATER SERVICES REGULATION AUTHORITY – CONCURRENT COMPETITION POWERS

23 February 2016

[3.285]

NOTES

FOREWORD

[3.286]

The changes to the United Kingdom's (UK) competition law system, introduced under the Enterprise and Regulatory Reform Act 2013 and in force since April 2014, are designed to improve the effectiveness of competition law enforcement in this country.

The Competition and Markets Authority (CMA) has competition law powers which apply across the whole economy. Sectoral regulators such as the Water Services Regulation Authority (Ofwat) may exercise the competition law powers to enforce the prohibitions on anti-competitive agreements and on abuse of a dominant position, and to make market investigation references, concurrently with the CMA in those sectors for which they have responsibility.

The Enterprise and Regulatory Reform Act 2013 introduced a number of changes to improve the working of concurrency and enable closer working between the CMA and sectoral regulators.

The CMA and the sectoral regulators have demonstrated their commitment to making the concurrency framework more effective through the establishment of the UK Competition Network (UKCN). This represents an enhanced forum for cooperation which will enable closer working with the objective of more consistent and effective use of competition powers across all sectors. In their statement of intent in December 2013, the members of the UKCN affirmed: 'The mission of the UKCN will be to promote competition for the benefit of consumers and to prevent anti-competitive behaviour both through facilitating use of competition powers and development of pro-competitive regulatory frameworks, as appropriate.'[1]

This memorandum of understanding (MoU) represents a further stage in the process of cooperation between the CMA and the regulators, setting out more practical detail on how the CMA and Ofwat will work together within the framework of competition law.[2]

The main purpose of this MoU is to establish an understanding between the CMA and Ofwat as to how this closer working will work in practice. It draws on the legislation which sets out the formal framework for how concurrency will operate and also, importantly, sets out our bilateral commitment to look for opportunities to work together, including within the framework of the UKCN, to promote competition for the benefit of consumers. We shall do this by the sharing of expertise, information, ideas and experience and each of us will commit to doing this efficiently and with a mutual regard for each other's statutory position and strategic objectives.

Water and sewerage markets are in the process of liberalisation, with the aim of fostering more competitive markets for the benefit of current and future customers. As markets evolve, competition enforcement under the Competition Act 1998 and review of markets under the Enterprise Act 2002 will be increasingly important tools to enable the development of effective competition in the sector.

We believe that this MoU offers a valuable basis for that cooperation, in the interests of the CMA, Ofwat, the water and sewerage industry in England and Wales and, most importantly of all, the consumers.

Alex Chisholm	**Richard Khaldi**
CEO, CMA	**Senior Director, Customers and Casework, Ofwat**

NOTES

1 UKCN (2013), Statement of Intent.

2 This MoU does not relate to 'regulatory appeals' – that is, the separate role that the CMA has in considering appeals against, or references relating to, proposed direct regulatory action by Ofwat under the sectoral statutes. This is a separate role, to be undertaken by the CMA panel, and the CMA is committed to ensuring that its cooperation with Ofwat – whether under this MoU (and under comparable MoU agreed with other sectoral regulators), through the UKCN, or otherwise in connection with their concurrent powers – will not impair the impartiality and fairness of the CMA's conduct of such regulatory appeals (or indeed of market or merger investigations undertaken by the CMA panel).

MEMORANDUM OF UNDERSTANDING BETWEEN THE COMPETITION AND MARKETS AUTHORITY AND THE WATER SERVICES REGULATION AUTHORITY

PURPOSE OF THIS MEMORANDUM OF UNDERSTANDING

[3.287]

1. This MoU sets out working arrangements between the CMA and Ofwat in relation to:

(a) their concurrent powers to apply the prohibitions on agreements that prevent, restrict or distort competition, and on the abuse of a dominant position, under the Chapter I prohibition and the Chapter II prohibition of the Competition Act 1998 and under Article 101 and Article 102 of the Treaty on the Functioning of the European Union – referred to in this MoU as the 'competition prohibitions'; and

(b) their concurrent powers to undertake market studies, and to make references to the CMA for the constitution of a CMA group to conduct an in-depth market investigation into single or multiple markets for goods or services in the UK under the Enterprise Act 2002 – referred to in this MoU as the 'market provisions';

in the water and sewerage sector.

2. This MoU is not intended to have legal effect.

3. This MoU is to be read alongside other material concerning the relations between the CMA and Ofwat, including: the Water Industry Act 1991; the Competition Act 1998; the Enterprise Act 2002; the Enterprise and Regulatory Reform Act 2013; the Competition Act 1998 and Other Enactments (Amendment) Regulations 2004; the Competition Act 1998 (Concurrency) Regulations 2014, referred to in this MoU as the concurrency regulations, and the CMA's guidance on concurrent application of competition law to regulated industries, referred to in this MoU as the concurrency guidance.[3] This MoU supplements and does not supplant that material.

4. The arrangements covered by this MoU are, wherever possible, set out in terms providing sufficient flexibility for the relationship between Ofwat and the CMA to develop in the light of experience. The CMA and Ofwat commit to review these arrangements from time to time to evaluate their continuing fitness for purpose. Such review can be initiated at the request of the CMA, Ofwat or a member of the UKCN. This MoU may only be revised by agreement between the CMA and Ofwat.

5. Nothing in this MoU applies in relation to the functions of the CMA in its separate role of considering appeals against, or references related, to proposed action by Ofwat under the sectoral statutes. The CMA and Ofwat acknowledge the importance of maintaining the CMA's impartiality and fairness in carrying out those functions, and indeed of market or merger investigations undertaken by the CMA panel.

NOTES

3 CMA (2014), Regulated industries: Guidance on concurrent application of competition law to regulated industries (CMA10).

CONTEXT

6. This MoU operates within the framework of the legislative provisions referred to in paragraph 1, the concurrent powers of Ofwat under section 31 of the Water Industry Act 1991 and any other applicable sector-specific legislation from time to time.

Role of the CMA

7. The CMA is a non-ministerial department, established under the Enterprise and Regulatory Reform Act 2013.

8. The CMA works to promote competition for the benefit of consumers, both within and outside the UK, to make markets work well for consumers, businesses and the economy.

9. The CMA's statutory responsibilities, in so far as relevant to the matters that are the subject of this MoU, include:

(a) investigating where there may be breaches of the competition prohibitions; and

(b) conducting market studies and market investigations where there may be competition and consumer problems.

10. In connection with its statutory responsibilities, the CMA will cooperate with sectoral regulators to promote effective competition and support the use of their powers, including their powers to apply the competition prohibitions, in the interests of competition for the benefit of consumers.

Role of Ofwat

11. Ofwat is a non-ministerial department established under the Water Industry Act 1991. Ofwat is the independent economic regulator of the water and sewerage industry in England and Wales. Ofwat is responsible for regulating the sectors, acting independently of the industry, government and other stakeholders, while working within the government policy framework. Ofwat's duties include protecting the interests of consumers, wherever appropriate by promoting effective competition. Ofwat is designated as a national competition authority under Article 35 of EU Regulation 1/2003 and has powers to enforce the competition prohibitions in the Competition Act 1998 and Articles 101 and 102 of the Treaty on the Functioning of the European Union, in relation to commercial activities connected with the supply of water or securing a supply of water or with the provision or securing of sewerage services.

AIMS

12. The Enterprise and Regulatory Reform Act 2013, as well as establishing the CMA, made provision for the better working of the CMA's and the sectoral regulators' concurrent powers in the regulated sectors; specifically, the act: 'strengthens the role of the CMA and enhances the emphasis on early and proper consideration of the use of anti-trust powers (under Part 1 of the CA 1998 [ie the competition prohibitions]) by the sector regulators.'[4]

13. It is one of the strategic goals of the CMA, announced on its establishment on 1 October 2013, to extend the frontiers of competition into new areas, including by working with sectoral regulators to ensure fuller use of competition law and policy in sectoral markets.[5]

14. The government's strategic steer to the CMA, issued on 1 December 2015, says that the CMA should build 'a strong dialogue with sectoral regulators using the UKCN to ensure that the overall competition regime is coordinated and regulatory practices complement each other.'[6]

15. The sector regulators and the CMA, working together in the UKCN established in 2013 (with Monitor having observer status), declared that: 'The mission of the UKCN will be to promote competition for the benefit of consumers and to prevent anti-competitive behaviour both through facilitating use of competition powers and development of pro-competitive regulatory frameworks, as appropriate.'[7]

16. The CMA and Ofwat seek to use their powers to achieve more competitive outcomes in the water and sewerage industry in England and Wales for the benefit of consumers so as to make markets in the water and sewerage sectors in England and Wales work well for consumers of water and sewerage services, businesses in those sectors and businesses that use those services and the economy in which those services play an essential part. It is the view of the CMA and Ofwat that such competitive outcomes can be achieved by various tools, including their competition law powers under the competition prohibitions, the market provisions and merger control, but also through other tools such as direct regulatory action including through enforcement of licence provisions (for example, in providing for third party access to networks) and liberalisation measures introduced under national and European Union legislation.

17. This MoU aims to further the attainment of these objectives, and to make the changes introduced by the Enterprise and Regulatory Reform Act 2013 work effectively, maximising the complementary skills of the CMA and Ofwat, including through:

(a) promoting cooperation and coordination between the CMA and Ofwat when dealing with cases of suspected anti-competitive behaviour for which they have concurrent powers;

(b) promoting cooperation and coordination between the CMA and Ofwat when dealing with market studies and market investigation references for which they have concurrent powers;

(c) facilitating the efficient and effective handling of cases of suspected anti-competitive behaviour within the water and sewerage services markets in England and Wales;

(d) avoiding duplication of activity, wherever possible; and

(e) ensuring transparency as to the respective roles of the CMA and Ofwat for individuals and consumers affected.

NOTES

4 Enterprise and Regulatory Reform Act 2013 Explanatory Notes, paragraph 370.

5 Statement by Alex Chisholm, chief executive of the CMA, CMA mission and strategy, 1 October 2013.

6 Department for Business, Innovation and Skills, Strategic steer for the Competition and Markets Authority, in Annex A to the *Government's response to the Consultation on the Strategic Steer to the CMA*, 1 December 2015, page 11.

7 UKCN (2013), Statement of Intent.

GENERAL COOPERATION

18. In addition to the provisions for cooperation between the CMA and Ofwat specific to particular powers of the CMA and Ofwat, as set out in this MoU and elsewhere, the CMA and Ofwat are committed to the following general principles and practices for cooperation between themselves in respect of the sectors for which Ofwat has responsibility.

19. Officials of the CMA and Ofwat will meet and communicate, at appropriate levels of seniority, to discuss matters of mutual interest, both through the UKCN and bilaterally. A framework for such meetings will, as far as possible, be determined in advance so as to ensure attendance at the appropriate level and expertise.

20. The CMA and Ofwat will, in respect of the water and sewerage sector, always consult each other:

(a) before the initial exercise of concurrent competition law powers in all cases where it appears that they have concurrent jurisdiction and where there are reasonable grounds for suspecting an infringement of the competition prohibitions; and

(b) before launching a market study under the Enterprise Act 2002.[8]

21. Where either the CMA or Ofwat exercises its concurrent powers, the CMA and Ofwat will, to the extent permitted by law, engage with each other in open dialogue and by sharing relevant information as appropriate. This engagement may include attendance at internal meetings held by the investigating authority (ie the authority to which a case is allocated) by the supporting authority (ie the other authority which would be competent to exercise concurrent powers in relation to the case), in order to discuss the case as envisaged at paragraph 3.31 of the concurrency guidance. The supporting authority will not generally attend the investigating authority's constitutional decision-making meetings, meetings of governance bodies or meetings with external parties such as those under investigation or complainants. Attendance by the supporting authority at any meeting is at the discretion of the investigating authority, but requests to attend should be considered by the investigating authority in the spirit of cooperation underpinning the new concurrency regime.

22. The CMA and Ofwat will consult each other at an early stage on any issues that might have significant implications for the other. For example, where the CMA undertakes a market study which relates to a sector other than water and sewerage but which may have a significant impact on water and sewerage, the CMA will inform Ofwat and share appropriate information relating to that market study with Ofwat to the extent permitted by law.

23. Within the spirit of broader collaboration for the purposes of the promotion of competitive outcomes, the CMA and Ofwat will commit to discuss and share other relevant information, where legally permissible to do so, but subject to the need not to impair the impartiality and fairness of the CMA in carrying out the functions referred to in paragraph 5 of this MoU.

NOTES

[8] Instigation of a market study occurs on the publication of a market study notice, as defined in section 130A of the Enterprise Act 2002.

PART A – COOPERATION IN RELATION TO THE COMPETITION PROHIBITIONS (COMPETITION ACT 1998 AND ARTICLES 101 AND 102 OF THE TREATY ON THE FUNCTIONING OF THE EUROPEAN UNION)

CASE ALLOCATION

Basis of allocation

[3.288]

24. The CMA and Ofwat will endeavour to reach agreement on which authority will exercise its concurrent competition powers in respect of any particular case, under regulation 4(2) of the concurrency regulations. They will do so in a spirit of constructiveness and cooperation, while acknowledging the CMA's ultimate powers under regulations 5 and 8 of the concurrency regulations.

25. Their determination of which authority will exercise its powers will be based on assessing which of them is better placed to exercise those powers, having regard to the factors set out in paragraph 3.22 of the concurrency guidance. The CMA and Ofwat envisage that other factors may appear relevant in the light of practical experience and that, if so, such factors may be chosen to supplement or supplant the factors set out in paragraph 3.22 of the concurrency guidance.

Procedure for allocation

26. Where either the CMA or Ofwat has decided, on the basis of information in its possession, that there are reasonable grounds for suspecting that one of the competition prohibitions has been infringed (the reasonable suspicion test)[9] in relation to the water and sewerage sector, it will disclose to the other (ie the receiving authority) sufficient information:

(a) to enable the receiving authority to understand the basis on which the disclosing authority has decided that the reasonable suspicion test is met; and
(b) for there to be an informed discussion on which authority (if either) is best placed to proceed in respect of the case.

27. In practice, it may be helpful for the CMA and Ofwat to have discussed the case prior to such a decision having been reached, subject to paragraph 40 below. The disclosing authority will provide the information described under paragraph 26 within ten working days after it has decided that the reasonable suspicion test is met, whether or not it proposes to exercise concurrent powers.[10]

28. Within seven working days from receipt of this information, the receiving authority will respond in writing, setting out its initial view on the case and how it should be allocated and identifying any further information which it requires.

29. The CMA and Ofwat will endeavour to agree which authority will exercise its concurrent competition powers in relation to the case, as provided for in regulation 4(2) of the concurrency regulations, as soon as possible and in any event no later than one month from disclosure of the information described under paragraph 26. Other than in exceptional circumstances (which shall be set out in writing), the CMA will initiate the procedure set out in regulation 5 of the concurrency regulations if agreement is not reached within two months of the disclosing authority first receiving sufficient information in connection with a complaint to enable it to decide that the reasonable suspicion test is met.

30. The procedure for agreeing the transfer of a case that is already in progress from the CMA to Ofwat, or from Ofwat to the CMA, is as set out in regulation 7 of the concurrency regulations and in paragraph 3.32 of the concurrency guidance.

31. The procedure for the CMA to direct the transfer to itself from Ofwat of a case that is already in progress is as set out in regulation 8 of the concurrency regulations.

NOTES

[9] As provided in section 25 of the Competition Act 1998.

[10] As provided in regulation 9 of the concurrency regulations.

Implications of allocation

32. Any agreement or determination as to case allocation, under regulations 4, 5, 7 or 8 of the concurrency regulations, shall be notified to the person who has provided the information resulting in the case (for example, the person making a complaint), and so far as appropriate and lawful to any other affected person, by the authority which is exercising its concurrent competition powers in relation to the case, as soon as reasonably practicable.

33. Case allocation determines which of the CMA and Ofwat is to exercise concurrent functions and make any decisions under the competition prohibitions. The CMA or Ofwat will be publicly identified as having such responsibility if and when any such investigation is announced. The CMA and Ofwat envisage that, whichever authority has responsible for a particular case, they and their officials will work cooperatively with each other on the case as appropriate, pooling their expertise including in the ways described in paragraphs 48 to 57 of this MoU and in paragraphs 3.33 to 3.35 of the concurrency guidance.

SHARING INFORMATION

Principles of information sharing

34. The effective sharing of information between the CMA and Ofwat is fundamental to the successful exercise of their concurrent competition powers. It is needed both for the appropriate allocation of cases, as described in paragraphs 26 to 31 of this MoU, and for the successful handling of cases once allocated to make optimal use of the complementary experience and expertise of the two authorities.

35. The CMA and Ofwat are committed, in addition to their legal obligations to share information (set out in regulation 9 of the concurrency regulations), to open dialogue and continuing liaison, both bilaterally and through the UKCN, with a view not only to handling specific cases but to promoting competition for the benefit of consumers in the water and sewerage sectors in England and Wales.

Information sharing mechanism – general liaison

36. The CMA and Ofwat recognise the importance of meeting regularly to share information on matters relevant to competition in the water and sewerage sectors in England and Wales, and to keep each other abreast of relevant work which they are considering or currently undertaking.

37. The CMA and Ofwat will meet regularly at multiple levels, bilaterally and through the UKCN.

38. The CMA and Ofwat will each designate in its organisation a relationship manager at official level to take responsibility for relations between the two authorities. In each authority, the relationship manager's responsibilities will include (but not be limited to):

(a) maintaining an overview of joint projects between the two authorities and matters of mutual interest;

(b) maintaining an overview of the authority's contacts from all areas of joint working and mutual interest; and

(c) holding meetings with the relationship manager in the other authority from time to time (whether bilaterally or in the context of the UKCN) to identify potential new issues, with a view to circulating information to appropriate individuals within each organisation.

39. The existence of relationship managers does not in any way preclude direct communication between other staff at the CMA and Ofwat.

40. For the purposes of sharing information pursuant to paragraph 26, ie in circumstances where the reasonable suspicion test is met, such information will be shared by the disclosing authority to the extent permitted by law and whether or not it proposes to exercise concurrent powers.[11] Where disclosure would be appropriate and permitted by law, the CMA and Ofwat may also share information regarding potential infringements of the competition prohibitions in advance of having reached a view as to whether the reasonable suspicion test is met. In circumstances where either the CMA or Ofwat has taken the view that a matter is not an administrative priority, irrespective of whether a view has been reached on whether the reasonable suspicion test is met, each may share the details of the matter with the other, or with any other authority which would be able to exercise concurrent competition powers in relation to that matter, to the extent permitted by law. Where leniency information is being shared under this paragraph, special considerations apply, as set out in paragraphs 46 and 47.

NOTES

[11] For the avoidance of doubt, this does not entail an obligation to inform the other party if the regulator is carrying out general monitoring activity, where there is no active consideration of exercising its concurrent powers.

Information sharing mechanism – handling specific cases

41. The procedures for information sharing for the purpose of case allocation shall be as set out in paragraphs 26 to 28 and 34 to 47 of this MoU.

42. When either the CMA or Ofwat is exercising its powers in respect of the competition prohibitions in a particular case in the water and sewerage sectors in England and Wales, each of them will share with the other any of the following information in its possession (to the extent permitted by law and subject to the confidentiality obligations in paragraphs 45 to 47 of this MoU):

(a) as a minimum, the matters referred to in regulation 9(1)(b) – (j) of the concurrency regulations, and in paragraph 3.49 of the concurrency guidance, complying with the time limits specified in paragraph 3.49;

(b) other information which it reasonably believes to be relevant or helpful to the other in the conduct of the case; and

(c) in the case of the authority which is exercising the powers, reports to the other on the progress of the case, of sufficient frequency and detail to enable the other to be appropriately informed; the means and frequency of such reporting will be decided on a case-by-case basis and in the light of experience as this enhanced framework of collaboration and its supporting arrangements develop over time.

Information sharing mechanism – for know-how purposes

43. The CMA will maintain on its webpages a central database of decisions taken in cases under the competition prohibitions, with a view to having an accessible body of know-how that will help ensure the effective and consistent application of competition law. The CMA and Ofwat will, to the extent permitted by law, contribute information to that in the way best calculated to achieve that objective.

44. In any event, the CMA will report on cases in the regulated sectors under the competition prohibitions in the annual concurrency report which it is required under statute to issue. Further provisions on the annual concurrency report are in paragraphs 58 to 60 of this MoU.

Information sharing – confidentiality constraints

45. Any disclosure of information under paragraphs 26 to 28 and 34 to 44 of this MoU, and any use by the recipient of such information, shall only be to the extent permitted by law, including by reference to the provisions of Part 9 of the Enterprise Act 2002, relevant sector-specific legislative provisions and any other provisions relating to the disclosure, handling and use of information (such as the Data Protection Act 1998 and section 118 of the Financial Services and Markets Act 2000, to the extent relevant).

46. Prior to disclosing information to each other, the CMA and Ofwat will not generally give the person to whom the information relates prior notice of its intention to make the disclosure. However, if the CMA or Ofwat consider it necessary or appropriate to pass leniency information to each other (or to another UK authority with concurrent powers), the transmitting authority will inform the applicant or its legal adviser first. Leniency information for the purposes of this MoU is any information which came into the possession of any of the CMA, its predecessors, Ofwat or any other public authority as a direct or indirect result of having been provided in the context of an application for leniency. It includes information obtained by the transferring authority as a result of investigative measures resulting directly or indirectly from an application for leniency.

47. In addition to the general provisions referred to in paragraph 45, where Ofwat or the CMA receives leniency information from the other (or from another UK authority with concurrent powers) for the purpose of applying the competition prohibitions or, in the case of the CMA, the cartel offence under section 188 of the Enterprise Act 2002, that information will not be used for any other purpose. This restriction on use also applies to any information obtained by the receiving authority as a result of investigative measures relating to the competition prohibitions or the cartel offence following the receipt of leniency information from the other authority. This does not affect the use that may be made by the CMA or Ofwat of information received from other sources, or if the leniency applicant's consent is obtained.[12] Where the provision of leniency information to either the CMA or Ofwat affords or might, under certain conditions, afford the leniency applicant, its subsidiaries or its employees protection from sanctions (including a reduction in penalties) under the leniency programme operated by that authority and that information has been passed to another authority, the receiving authority shall afford the leniency applicant, its subsidiaries or its employees no lesser protection.

NOTES

[12] The use restriction in this paragraph is intended to govern the use of leniency information in the context of the concurrency arrangements. It is not intended to prevent the disclosure of such leniency information by either one of the CMA or Ofwat to the other (to the extent permitted by Part 9 of the Enterprise Act 2002 and in accordance with Leniency and no-action applications in cartel cases: OFT1495) for purposes other than the application of the competition prohibitions or the cartel offence. However, any such disclosure of leniency information would only be likely to be justified in exceptional circumstances, given the strong public interest in maintaining the incentives for undertakings and, in the case of the cartel offence, individuals to apply for leniency.

POOLING RESOURCES

48. Paragraph 21 above, and the concurrency guidance provide for support to be provided by the supporting authority to the investigating authority when it is exercising its concurrent powers in a case. The CMA and Ofwat will endeavour, so far as is reasonably practicable and permitted by law, and in the light of their respective ongoing priorities and resource availability at the time, to share their resources with each other in the interests of the effective enforcement of competition law in the water and sewerage sectors in England and Wales, and more generally the promotion of competition for the benefit of consumers in those sectors, and to ensure that their resources and expertise are used most efficiently for that purpose. This is subject to the proviso that, as stated in paragraph 5, this does not apply in relation to the functions of the CMA in its role of considering appeals against, or references related to, proposed action by Ofwat under the sectoral statutes.

49. As a consequence, where it has been agreed or determined that one of the authorities is to exercise its concurrent competition powers in relation to a case, that authority will, to the extent that there are resources available, receive appropriate practical assistance and support from the other in the handling of the case, as agreed on a case-by-case basis.

50. Such support and assistance may include the provision of training or practical know-how and expertise by one authority to the other where appropriate to enable the authority exercising its concurrent competition powers in the case to carry out its statutory functions effectively (for example in relation to conduct of site visits).

Secondments of staff

51. One means of the practical assistance and support that might be given, as referred to in paragraphs 48 and 49 of this MoU, is the secondment of staff, in accordance with regulation 10 of the concurrency regulations and paragraphs 3.33 and 3.34 of the concurrency guidance.

52. The CMA and Ofwat are fully committed to the idea of secondments for this purpose, and will endeavour to meet each other's requests for secondments to the extent that they are appropriate and resources permit; this may include making provision for any secondee to be available to work for part of his or her time at his or her existing employer during the course of the secondment, for example on such cases that are in progress.

53. Requests for secondments should be made by the relationship manager of one authority to the relationship manager of the other, setting out the following information:

(a) The number of secondees required.
(b) The period for which each one is required.
(c) The level of seniority of each one.
(d) The nature of the expertise or experience of each one.
(e) The proposed payment arrangements.
(f) A brief explanation of why the requirement or requirements cannot adequately be met by deployment of staff from within the requesting authority.

54. To the extent that the recipient of a request for a secondment made under paragraph 53 of this MoU refuses that request or accedes to it on terms that are materially different from those requested, the recipient shall give reasons.

55. The CMA and Ofwat will develop appropriate arrangements for the pooling and secondment of staff. Such arrangements will have regard to the resource constraints of both parties and such calls for staff, therefore, will be made in reasonable time and with sufficient warning to enable appropriate resource planning, management of other work commitments and appropriate sign-off procedures within each authority.

OTHER MUTUAL SUPPORT

56. In addition to the sharing of information, expertise, experience and the secondment of staff, the CMA and Ofwat are fully committed to providing each other with more informal forms of support to enable them to carry out their competition law functions in relation to the water and sewerage sectors in England and Wales – in each case to the extent that it is appropriate and permitted by law, and that resources permit – including (but not limited to):

(a) answering specific queries from time to time;
(b) providing information or views on a specific sector or market, or an area of competition law or policy; and
(c) providing training on a specific sector or market, or an area of competition law or policy.

57. Such support may be requested and provided in connection with a specific case or with the promotion of competition more generally. In this regard, both the CMA and Ofwat will act reasonably, including by providing sufficient time and information for requests for support to be responded to fully and effectively and for the relevant staff to be engaged.

ANNUAL CONCURRENCY REPORT

58. The CMA is required by statute to publish a report every year, starting after its first year of operation in 2014/15,[13] containing an assessment of how the concurrency arrangements between the CMA and the sectoral regulators, as regards both the competition prohibitions and the market provisions, have operated during the year. This MoU refers to that report as the annual concurrency report. There is further provision on the annual concurrency report in paragraphs 3.55 to 3.62 of the concurrency guidance.

59. The CMA will consult, and cooperate with, Ofwat and with other sectoral regulators in preparing the annual concurrency report. In connection with this, the CMA will:

(a) prepare a draft of the annual concurrency report that it will send to Ofwat and other sectoral regulators seeking comments or suggestions on the content or conclusions of the annual concurrency report and giving them adequate time to comment or make suggestions;
(b) take account of any comments or suggestions it receives from Ofwat and other sectoral regulators and the CMA may seek further clarification on those comments or suggestions as appropriate;
(c) prepare a final version of the annual concurrency report for publication that takes account of its consultation of Ofwat and other sectoral regulators as appropriate; and
(d) make the annual concurrency report available on the CMA webpages.

60. Ofwat will cooperate with the CMA in the preparation of the annual concurrency report including (but not limited to) by way of:

(a) providing information and data on general market conditions and on the application of the competition prohibitions and the market provisions in the water and sewerage sectors in England and Wales;
(b) responding to reasonable requests for information and data; and
(c) providing to the CMA any comments and suggestions it may have in connection with the process described in paragraph 59 of this MoU;

in each case promptly so as to facilitate the timely production and publication of the annual concurrency report.

NOTES

[13] Enterprise and Regulatory Reform Act 2013 Schedule 4 paragraph 16.

VOLUNTARY REDRESS SCHEMES

61. In cases relating to investigations under the competition prohibitions in the water and sewerage sectors in England and Wales, both the CMA and Ofwat have the power to approve voluntary redress schemes. When either authority proposes to exercise these powers, it shall liaise with the other authority as appropriate and will have regard to its own guidance.[14]

NOTES

[14] The CMA's guidance on the approval of voluntary redress schemes (CMA40) states at footnote 7: 'The CMA expects that regulators will take this CMA guidance into account when producing their own guidance on the approval power.'

SHORT FORM OPINIONS

62. The CMA shall inform Ofwat following an initial enquiry for a short form opinion relating to the water and sewerage sector. Where the CMA is considering providing such an opinion, it will discuss with Ofwat before deciding to do so. If the CMA then decides to produce an opinion, it will engage with Ofwat, the nature and degree of that engagement to be considered on a case-by-case basis, having regard, in particular, to the extent to which the opinion has a multi-sector rather than single-sector dimension. In all cases, the CMA will give Ofwat the opportunity to provide comments on a draft opinion.

CHOICE OF INSTRUMENT – COMPETITION PROHIBITION OR DIRECT REGULATION BY LICENCE ENFORCEMENT

63. As a result of legislative changes introduced by Schedule 14 to the Enterprise and Regulatory Reform Act 2013,[15] Ofwat is required by sections 19(1A) and 22A(13) of the Water Industry Act 1991, to 'consider whether it would be more appropriate to proceed under the Competition Act 1998' before exercising its direct regulatory powers of enforcement in relation to statutory or other requirements which are enforceable by Ofwat under section 18 of the Water Industry Act 1991 or licence contravention by relevant companies.

64. The Explanatory Notes to the legislation explain that this provision 'enhances the emphasis on early and proper consideration of the use of anti-trust powers (under Part 1 of the CA98)[16] by the sector regulators'.[17]

65. The government had previously indicated that the policy intention is to: 'strengthen the primacy of general competition law, so that the Sector Regulators are required to consider whether the use of their CA98 powers is more appropriate before using their sectoral powers to promote competition'.[18]

66. Under this provision, it is for Ofwat to determine, in any particular case, whether using its powers under the competition prohibitions would be more appropriate than exercising its licence enforcement powers.

67. Paragraph 4.4 of the concurrency guidance says that this determination will be made by the sectoral regulators 'on a case-by-case basis'. It may be that, in the light of experience accumulated over the coming months or years in applying this provision, it will be possible to develop more general principles that could serve as useful guidance in future cases, perhaps through the forum of the UKCN, while respecting the right of the sectoral regulator to make the determination.

NOTES

[15] Having effect from April 2014.

[16] That is, the competition prohibitions.

[17] Enterprise and Regulatory Reform Act 2013 Explanatory Notes, paragraph 370.

[18] BIS (March 2012), *Growth, competition and the competition regime: government response to consultation*, paragraph 8.16.

PART B – COOPERATION IN RELATION TO THE MARKET PROVISIONS: MARKET STUDIES AND MARKET INVESTIGATIONS (ENTERPRISE ACT 2002)

HOW CONCURRENCY WORKS UNDER THE MARKET PROVISIONS

[3.289]

68. Ofwat has the power, concurrently with the CMA, to carry out market studies, to make market investigation references, agree undertakings in lieu of a reference and make recommendations to the government in relation to the water and sewerage sectors in England and Wales under Part 4 of the Enterprise Act 2002 (as do other sectoral regulators in relation to the sectors for which they are responsible).

69. Under the Enterprise Act 2002, the CMA and Ofwat may, in relation to the water and sewerage sectors in England and Wales, undertake market studies, and may make market investigation references to the Chair of the CMA for the constitution of a CMA group to conduct an in-depth market investigation into single or multiple markets for goods or services in the UK. The purpose of these investigations is to examine the market(s) and (where required) implement appropriate remedies where the CMA determines that the structure of the market(s) or the conduct of the suppliers or customers is harming competition.

70. When making a reference, the CMA or Ofwat, as applicable, must have reasonable grounds for suspecting that any feature or combination of features of a market or markets in the UK prevents, restricts or distorts competition in relation to the supply or acquisition of any goods or services in the UK (or in a part of the UK).

71. The cooperation between the CMA and Ofwat provided for in this Part B shall not extend to conduct that could reasonably be expected to impair the impartiality or the fairness of the CMA panel in conducting market investigations.

SUPER-COMPLAINTS

72. Section 11 of the Enterprise Act 2002 provides for a super-complaint to be made by a designated consumer body that any feature, or combination of features, of a market in the UK for goods or services is or appears to be significantly harming the interests of consumers.

73. Ofwat has a duty to respond to super-complaints made to it under the Enterprise Act 2002 if the complaint concerns the water and sewerage sectors in England and Wales.

74. The coordination of the CMA's and the sectoral regulators' super-complaint duties will be based on policies agreed and applied through the UKCN.

MUTUAL CONSULTATION

75. Ofwat and the CMA have a duty to consult each other before exercising concurrent functions under the market provisions.

SHARING INFORMATION

76. The provisions of paragraphs 36 to 40, 42 (excluding 42(a) and 44 of this MoU apply to information sharing under the market provisions as they do under the competition prohibitions.

POOLING RESOURCES

77. The provisions of paragraphs 48 to 57 of this MoU apply to pooling resources under the market provisions as they do under the competition prohibitions.

78. Where the CMA and Ofwat intend to pool resources in order to exercise powers under the market provisions of the Enterprise Act 2002, they shall, at the outset of any such project, discuss the arrangements for how they will pool resources and work jointly.

ANNUAL CONCURRENCY REPORT

79. The provisions of paragraphs 58 to 60 of this MoU apply under the market provisions as they do under the competition prohibitions.

GUIDANCE ON OFWAT'S APPROACH TO THE APPLICATION OF THE COMPETITION ACT 1998 IN THE WATER AND WASTEWATER SECTOR IN ENGLAND AND WALES

March 2017

[3.290]

NOTES

CONTENTS

ABOUT THIS DOCUMENT

[3.291]
This document sets out our guidance on Ofwat's approach to the application of the Competition Act 1998 (CA98) and the equivalent provisions under Articles 101 and 102 of the Treaty on the Functioning of the European Union (TFEU) to the water and wastewater sector in England and Wales. Our aim is to provide more clarity on how the competition law prohibitions may apply in the sector.

This guidance replaces our previous guidance on these issues. We have reflected developments in legislation and case law that have taken place since the publication of earlier guidance,[1] as well as our experience of applying CA98 to date.

When applying our concurrent competition powers, we will also take account of any changes to competition law guidance issued by the Competition and Markets Authority (CMA) and the European Commission.[2]

In line with best practice, we are issuing this guidance on competition law to provide a backdrop on how we may approach competition law issues that arise in the future. While the guidance is intended to assist companies in understanding potential competition law issues in the water and sewerage sector in England and Wales, all companies operating in the sector must be clear that it is their responsibility to assure themselves that they have taken the necessary steps to ensure compliance with competition law, whether that is enforced by:

- Ofwat;
- the Competition and Markets Authority; or
- the European Commission.

NOTES

[1] Notably the guidance reflects changes introduced by the Enterprise and Regulatory Reform Act 2013 to strengthen the primacy of competition law and to improve the operation of the competition concurrency regime. We have also updated our procedures to reflect improvements in best practice.

[2] It should be noted that this guidance does not take into account the result of the referendum in June 2016 in favour of the UK leaving the European Union (EU) or the consequences of the UK ceasing to be an EU Member State (or member of the European Economic Area). The guidance reflects current UK and EU law which Ofwat must follow. We would expect to update the guidance in light of developments in this respect.

1. INTRODUCTION

1.1 BACKGROUND

[3.292]

As the economic regulator of the water and sewerage sector, Ofwat's role is to help build customers' and wider society's trust and confidence in the vital public services the water sector provides. We do this in a number of ways including:

- overseeing how the sector is performing;
- being ready to step in if service providers fall short;
- using the right tools from our available toolkit to achieve the best results; and
- acting clearly and predictably.

As part of our responsibilities, we have concurrent powers to apply competition law with respect to water and sewerage activities in England and Wales. In particular we have concurrent jurisdiction to apply the prohibitions on restrictive agreements and concerted practices, and the abuse of a dominant position under the Competition Act 1998 (CA98) and the equivalent provisions under Articles 101 and 102 of the Treaty on the Functioning of the European Union (TFEU).

We exercise our competition law powers concurrently with the Competition and Markets Authority (CMA).

1.2 OUR APPROACH TO REGULATION

In January 2015, we launched our strategy, 'Trust in water',[3] which sets out our journey to become a regulator that is more:

- **outcomes focused** – focusing on the things that really matter to water and sewerage customers, the environment and society now and in the future;
- **relationships focused** – encouraging the water and sewerage sector to step up, take responsibility for its relationships, be open, honest, fair and transparent;
- **proportionate and targeted** – focusing our regulatory intervention where it is needed most, stepping in where necessary (and only where necessary) to protect customers; and
- **willing and able to use all the tools in our regulatory tool kit** – using both our traditional tools, as well as broader tools to shine a light on issues and provoke debate.

Our shared vision[4] for the water and sewerage sector in England and Wales is that customers and wider society have trust and confidence in vital public water and sewerage services. The need for effective competition in appropriate elements of the sector, where the contestability of services can promote further efficiencies and innovation, is reflected in part of our statutory duties[5] and is central to that vision.

Given our focus on realising the benefits of effective competition for water and sewerage customers, our concurrent powers under competition law are a critical part of our toolkit for intervening when markets are not performing or delivering as they should. Having competition law powers for the water and sewerage sector (alongside those held by the CMA ensures that we can protect the 'level playing field' and the dynamics of contestable markets in the sector from agreements, conduct or practices that distort competition and impact adversely on customers. In addition, we are now required to consider whether the use of our competition powers would be more appropriate instead of taking relevant enforcement action under our sector-specific, regulatory powers.[6]

In line with best practice, we are issuing this guidance on competition law to provide a backdrop on how we may approach competition law issues that arise in the future. However, while the guidance is intended to assist companies in understanding potential competition law issues in the water and sewerage sector in England and Wales, all companies operating in the sector must be clear that it is their responsibility to assure themselves that they have taken the necessary steps to ensure compliance with competition law, whether that is enforced by:

- Ofwat;
- the CMA; or
- the European Commission.

1.3 CHANGING TIMES

To date, although large parts of the water and wastewater sector have been characterised by monopoly, there are competitive markets in operation. These include:

- the appointment of new incumbent companies (known as 'NAVs')[7] to sites within the areas of existing incumbent companies;
- competition for the provision of new connections to incumbent companies' existing infrastructure (including where the new infrastructure is provided through 'self-lay' before being connected to the incumbent's existing infrastructure); and
- competition in the supply chain to the incumbent companies.

Despite these existing markets, this guidance comes at an important time. Water and sewerage markets are evolving further from being largely monopolistic and regulated to being more contestable and, in some parts of the value chain, subject to head to head competition. So, there are new challenges ahead for companies within the sector as they start to operate in, and interact with, those markets.

In particular, from April 2017 amendments to the Water Industry Act 1991 (WIA91) will allow approximately 1.2 million eligible business customers in England[8] to choose their supplier of water and sewerage retail services. For customers who use the system of an incumbent company whose area is wholly or mainly in England, the market will be extended to include all such business customers. There are already similar arrangements in the water and sewerage sector in Scotland and eligible business customers will be able to take advantage of both markets.

Where the incumbent's area is wholly or mainly in Wales, only business customers with premises that each use more than 50 megalitres of water per year will be able to choose their water supplier, reflecting the policy position of the Welsh Government (this position will not change in April 2017). In September 2016, we also published our report to Government on the costs and benefits of extending retail competition to residential customers in England. Should Government pursue this option, this will of course have implications for competition enforcement.

There is flexibility in the new markets that will be opened. For example, the Government issued supplier of first resort and exit regulations,[9] which enable new retailers in the relevant water and sewerage markets to exit the market efficiently, without disadvantaging customers. The existing incumbent monopoly companies in England can also choose to exit the relevant retail markets.[10] In addition, an in-area trading ban which prevented a new entrant owned by an existing incumbent monopoly company from competing in that company's own area has been removed – this will in particular stimulate competition for customers who want to be served more efficiently on a multi-site basis.

Looking ahead, amendments made by the Water Act 2014 will also enable the development of new markets for the upstream (non-retail) water and sewerage services provided by English water and sewerage companies. When the changes are brought into force (which currently will not happen before 2019), new entrants will have new opportunities to provide new sources of water or sewerage treatment services with obligations upon incumbents to provide access to their networks and treatment and storage systems. The Water Act 2014 will make it easier for the existing water and sewerage companies to buy and sell water and sewerage services to and from each other. There will also be a legal framework for owners of small-scale water storage to sell excess water into the public supply. In addition, there will be reforms to the existing framework for adopting water and sewerage infrastructure 'self-laid' by developers.

Separately, our Water2020 programme is promoting the use of markets to inform, enable and incentivise better use of resources and innovation through water resource trading and the contestable provision of bio-resources transportation, treatment and recycling/disposal. These markets will also be supported by direct procurement for customers on projects with a whole life cost of more than £100 million. These changes have the potential to:

- unlock substantial benefits for customers, companies, the environment and investors;
- help meet future challenges; and
- ensure that water and sewerage services are resilient, efficient and service providers are taking a long-term approach.

In Wales the Welsh Government has retained the existing scope for markets in relation to services provided by water and sewerage companies operating within Wales. The water supply licensing regime introduced by the Water Act 2014 therefore provides for the continuation of the pre-existing regime in relation to such companies. However, the Water Act 2014 does give the Welsh Government the power to extend the full new water supply and sewerage licensing regime if it considers it appropriate to do so.

The effective application of competition law will be a key tool for us in protecting the development of these new markets, ensuring their market dynamic and realising their benefits for customers and the environment. Without properly addressing competition concerns, markets will not work effectively for customers and society, which could erode trust and confidence in those markets and the sector as a whole.

We have already put in place regulatory structures to enable the new business retail market in England opening in April 2017 to work effectively. There will be a number of new codes, including a Wholesale Retail Code[11] and a Market Arrangements Code,[12] and a number of new charging rules. In particular, there will be charging rules issued by us that will cover charges from the existing incumbent companies to:

- end users;[13]
- new retailers (where the rules are referred to as wholesale charging rules);[14]
- relevant parties for new connections;[15] and
- other incumbent companies for bulk supply agreements.[16]

There will also be various codes and rules in relation to the additional new upstream markets in England enabled by the Water Act 2014 (which will not come into force before 2019).

Part 3 CMA and other Guidelines

Ofwat will monitor these existing and new competitive markets closely and will not hesitate to intervene in a proportionate way using the right tools, including enforcement under competition law, to ensure that competition works well for the benefit of consumers.

1.4 RESPONSIBILITIES

Although we have put in place regulatory structures to enable markets within the water and sewerage sector to work effectively, ultimately all companies operating in the sector, whether an incumbent water and sewerage company, a new retailer or any other business, are responsible for managing their own compliance with competition law. It is vital that companies view their approach to these new markets (and the other existing markets in the sector) through both a regulatory lens and a competition law lens.

For example, in relation to the specific markets operating, or planned, within the sector, although all of the companies operating within those markets must comply with any codes or rules that govern them, these obligations are broadly principles based (particularly our charging rules). It is therefore likely that companies will find more than one way of complying with their obligations under any of the codes and/or rules, particularly given their differing sizes and organisational structures.

It is important to note that, even if a company is compliant with a relevant obligation within the codes and/or rules for a market, it may still be in breach of competition law. Therefore, given the different likely approaches, this can lead to the possibility of one compliant approach to a particular obligation being a breach of competition law, while another may not. Accordingly, companies should ensure that they take into account competition law when deciding on their approach to such obligations. Further, the codes and/or rules for any of the markets within the water and sewerage sector will not cover every scenario faced by companies, nor are they designed to. In particular, incumbent companies will need to be conscious of their special responsibility under Chapter II of the CA98[17] where they are in a dominant position (or a "super-dominant" position).

In relation to existing markets, we have previously carried out investigations under the Competition Act 1998 into incumbent company behaviour in both the NAV market and the market for new water and sewerage connections. Importantly, as well as ensuring new markets are designed and run effectively, we will continue to monitor and, where appropriate, use our competition law powers in relation to existing markets within the sector to ensure they are working for the benefit of all customers.

We expect all companies (whether an existing incumbent, a new retailer or any other business) to respond to any competition law concerns that arise in a manner that reflects the best interests of water and sewerage customers. That will include engaging with and responding to us (or the CMA) quickly, openly and, where appropriate, proactively considering commitments, settlements, and/or voluntary redress. This approach to competition law issues is in line with our general regulatory approach as evidenced by our strategy and our company monitoring framework.

This guidance

Where companies and businesses operating in the water and sewerage sector do not meet their competition law obligations, Ofwat is committed to using its concurrent competition law powers to ensure that customers can realise the benefits of effective competition. This guidance provides companies and businesses with an important resource in understanding and meeting their obligations and in understanding how Ofwat will apply its powers. Our prioritisation principles[18] are unchanged.

NOTES

3 www.ofwat.gov.uk/about-us/

4 www.ofwat.gov.uk/about-us/vision/

5 Under sections 2(2A)(a) and 2(2B) of the Water Industry Act 1991 (as amended), Ofwat must further the consumer objective by protecting the interests of consumers, wherever appropriate by promoting effective competition.

6 Schedule 14, Enterprise and Regulatory Reform Act 2013 (and see section 2.2 below)

7 The reference to "NAVs" – New Appointments and Variations - is based on the appointment of a new undertaker and the variation of the existing undertaker's area – see sections 8 and 9 Water Industry Act 1991 in particular.

8 The market will be for all eligible business, charity and public sector customers who use the system of an incumbent company whose area is wholly or mainly in England.

9 The Water and Sewerage Undertakers (Exit from the Non-household Retail Market) Regulations 2016 (the 'Exit Regulations')

10 Regulation 4 of the Exit Regulations limits the ability to exit to companies whose supply area is wholly or mainly in England.

11 The WRC is a statutory code which includes the requirements placed on wholesalers and retailers for the operation of the market requirements for wholesalers and retailers to follow in maintaining the central register at the Market Operator and also contains the processes which inform the design and construction of the market's central operating system (CMOS).

12 The MAC is a non-statutory code, which sets out how the market will operate as well as the role and function of the market operator and systems and processes to support this.

13 Charges scheme rules have since 17 November 2015 set out the principles and specific requirements that apply to water undertakers and sewerage undertakers when making their charges schemes for end users.

14 These charging rules applicable to incumbents wholly or mainly in England will also replace the previous "costs principle" in section 66D WIA91 (prior to its amendment by the Water Act 214) which previously regulated the access prices paid by new entrants to existing incumbent companies for use of the incumbents' systems to supply their own customers. The UK Government will retain the "costs principle" in relation to introductions of water until the upstream market changes in the Water Act 2014 are brought into force.

15 See further www.ofwat.gov.uk/regulated-companies/markets/connections-market/new-connections/

16 See section 94(3) WA14. This does not cover the charges from undertakers to large user customers under section 56 WIA91.

17 The Chapter II prohibition and the concepts of 'dominance' and 'super-dominance' are explained in section 3.3

18 www.ofwat.gov.uk/publication/prioritisation-principles-application-competition-act-1998/

2. OUR COMPETITION LAW POWERS

[3.293]

Key messages

The Competition Act 1998 is a central component of our legal powers. Ofwat can enforce the prohibitions under UK and EU competition law in relation to water and sewerage services in England and Wales.

Our competition law functions are 'concurrent' with the CMA, which can also exercise its competition powers in the sector.

Ofwat and the CMA must agree which authority is best placed to conduct an investigation in relation to the water and sewerage sectors.

2.1 UK AND EU COMPETITION LAW

Our competition law powers derive primarily from the CA98 and Articles 101 and 102 TFEU.[19] Details about how the CA98 provisions are applied are set out in secondary legislation, including the 'CA98 Rules'[20] and the 'Concurrency Regulations'.[21] The latter deals specifically with the concurrent application of competition law by the CMA and sectoral regulators.[22] We are also required to have regard to CMA guidance in relation to the imposition of penalties and the acceptance of commitments[23] (both of which are discussed further in Chapter 4).

Where relevant, we refer in this guidance to guidelines published by the CMA and its predecessor body, the OFT, that have been adopted by the CMA. It should be noted that these documents state the law as it was at the time of their publication. In considering potential competition law infringements, we will take into account any relevant legislative and case law developments since publication.

2.2 THE COMPETITION ACT 1998 (CA98)

Both Ofwat and the CMA have the power to apply and enforce the Chapter I and Chapter II prohibitions under the CA98 and Articles 101 and 102 TFEU in relation to all commercial activities connected with the supply of water or securing a supply of water, or with the provision or securing of sewerage services in England and Wales (for simplicity referred to in this Guidance as water and sewerage services).[24] These are the main UK and EU competition law provisions, which prohibit anti-competitive agreements and abusive conduct by dominant undertakings respectively. The substance of these provisions is explained in Chapter 3.

Importantly, the activities of businesses that are not appointed under the WIA91 may fall within the scope of Ofwat's competition law jurisdiction. As a result, a company that is not subject to any form of other regulation by us could potentially find itself the subject of a competition law investigation by us.

2.3 TREATY ON THE FUNCTIONING OF THE EUROPEAN UNION (TFEU)

Where national competition authorities in EU Member States, including Ofwat, apply national competition law to agreements or conduct which may affect trade between EU Member States, they are required as a matter of EU law also to apply Articles 101 or 102 of the TFEU.[25]

Under section 60 CA98, so far as possible we must deal with competition law issues under Part I CA98 in a way that is consistent with the treatment of equivalent issues under EU law. As a result, the position under Chapter I and Chapter II of the CA98 will generally be the same as under Articles 101 and 102 TFEU, subject to the fact that the latter only apply where there is an effect on inter-state trade.

This guidance will therefore focus on the Chapter I and Chapter II prohibitions, but parties should be aware that the EU provisions may be applied in parallel in appropriate circumstances. Further information on the framework for applying Articles 101 and 102 TFEU, and how those EU provisions interact with the domestic competition law provisions, is available in the guidance 'Modernisation' (OFT442).[26]

2.4 CONCURRENCY

We cooperate with the CMA when exercising our competition law functions. We are part of the UK Competition Network which is a forum for co-operation between the CMA and UK sectoral regulators with concurrent competition powers.[27] We are also a designated National Competition Authority (NCA) within the European Competition Network for the purposes of the application of EU competition law.[28]

As with other UK sectoral regulators with concurrent competition powers, we have agreed a Memorandum of Understanding with the CMA setting out how we will work together for the purposes of applying and enforcing the CA98.[29] In addition, the CMA has published both rules[30] and detailed guidance[31] relating to the concurrent application and enforcement of competition law provisions by the CMA and sectoral regulators. This guidance should be read in conjunction with those documents.

Chapter 4 of this guidance outlines the procedure adopted by Ofwat and the CMA for the purpose of allocating competition law cases between them.

2.5 THE 'PRIMACY' OF THE COMPETITION ACT

We are required to consider whether the use of our CA98 powers is more appropriate before taking enforcement action or imposing penalties under the WIA91.[32] If we consider that the use of our CA98 powers would be more appropriate, we must exercise our CA98 powers rather than those WIA91 powers.

These 'primacy' obligations, introduced by the Enterprise and Regulatory Reform Act 2013, do not extend to our dispute resolution functions.

We routinely consider the CA98 at an early stage when considering whether to use any of our relevant regulatory powers for the purpose of assessing how we can best facilitate effective competition in the sector.

We will keep parties informed of what powers we are using in relation to ongoing investigations. Where we conclude that it is appropriate to use a different tool during the course of an investigation, we will inform the parties and provide reasons.

2.6 SUMMARY OF OUR CONCURRENT COMPETITION LAW POWERS

We have various powers we may exercise in respect of CA98 enforcement. In particular, we may:

- consider complaints about possible infringements of the Chapter I prohibition and the Chapter II prohibition;
- impose interim measures to prevent significant damage to a person or category of persons, or to protect the public interest;[33]
- carry out investigations, both on our own initiative and in response to complaints, including requiring the production of documents and the provision of information, and searching premises;[34]
- impose financial penalties on companies, taking account of the relevant statutory guidance on penalties;[35]
- give and enforce directions to bring an infringement to an end;
- accept binding commitments as to future conduct;
- reach settlements whereby a company admits an infringement in return for a reduction in penalty and a more expedited procedure;
- apply to court for a company director 'disqualification order' against directors of an infringing company (known as a 'Competition Disqualification Order');[36]
- decide there are 'no grounds for action';
- approve voluntary redress schemes; and
- publish written guidance in the form of an Opinion where:
  - a case raises novel or unresolved questions about the application of the Chapter I and/or the Chapter II prohibition; and
  - we consider there is an interest in issuing clarification for the benefit of a wider audience.

NOTES

19 Other pieces of domestic primary legislation containing relevant competition law provisions are the Enterprise Act 2002, the Enterprise and Regulatory Reform Act 2013 and the Consumer Rights Act 2015. However, Ofwat does not have jurisdiction to enforce the criminal cartel offence under the Enterprise Act 2002 and this Guidance does not apply to the market investigation or merger control provisions under that Act.

20 Competition Act 1998 (Competition and Markets Authority's Rules) Order 2014

21 Competition Act 1998 (Concurrency) Regulations 2014.

22 Further provision as to the application of Articles 101 and 102 TFEU can be found in Council Regulation (1/2003/EC) of 16 December 2002, OJ L1, 4.1.2003, p 1 ('the Modernisation Regulation').

23 Pursuant to sections 31D and 38 CA98: the CMA's guidance on the appropriate level of a penalty imposed under section 36 CA98 and the CMA's guidance as to the circumstances in which it may be appropriate to accept commitments under section 31A CA98

24 Section 54 of the CA98 and section 31 of the WIA91. Ofwat's competition law jurisdiction does not extend to the supply of water and sewerage services in Scotland and Northern Ireland. In these parts of the UK the CMA has the sole power to enforce CA98 and Articles 101 and 102 TFEU with respect to these services and activities.

25 Article 3 of the Modernisation Regulation. This obligation does not apply if the national law being applied pursues an objective which is predominantly different from those pursued by Article 101 and Article 102. We may also apply national law in a way which is stricter than Article 102 in relation to unilateral conduct.

26 www.gov.uk/government/uploads/system/uploads/attachment_data/file/284432/oft442.pdf

27 NHS Improvement has observer status.

28 ec.europa.eu/competition/ecn/index_en.html

29 Updated MoU Ofwat and CMA 2016, www.gov.uk/government/uploads/system/uploads/attachment_data/file/502668/Ofwat_MoU.pdf

30 The Competition Act 1998 (Concurrency) Regulations 2014 SI 2014 No.536 (the Concurrency Regulations)

31 CMA. www.gov.uk/government/publications/guidance-on-concurrent-application-of-competition-law-to- regulated-industries

32 The Enterprise and Regulatory Reform Act 2013, Schedule 14.

33 Section 35 CA98

34 For further details see the CMA's 'Guidance on the CMA's investigation procedures in Competition Act 1998 (CMA8) and the guidance (OFT404) 'Powers of Investigation'.

35 OFT423, 'Guidance as to appropriate amount of penalty'.
36 Sections 9C and 9E, Company Directors Disqualification Act 1986. Further guidance on Competition Disqualification Orders is available on the CMA website (OFT510) at www.gov.uk/government/publications/competition-disqualification-orders.

3. THE REQUIREMENTS OF COMPETITION LAW

[3.294]

Key messages

The Competition Act 1998 (CA98) imposes two key prohibitions on anti-competitive conduct.

- Chapter I CA98 prohibits agreements between undertakings and concerted practices that have as their object or effect the prevention, restriction or distortion of competition within the UK (the Chapter I prohibition).
- Chapter II CA98 prohibits the abuse of a dominant market position (the Chapter II prohibition) within the UK.

Articles 101 and 102 of the Treaty on the Functioning of the European Union (TFEU) contain equivalent prohibitions where the anti-competitive conduct may affect trade between EU Member States.

This chapter summarises the main aspects of the analysis in CA98 cases. We highlight issues that may be particularly likely to arise in the water and sewerage sector. However, this guidance does not cover all points that may arise in CA98 cases.

3.1 THE CHAPTER I AND CHAPTER II PROHIBITIONS: OVERVIEW

The Chapter I prohibition, contained in section 2(1) of the CA98, prohibits agreements between undertakings, decisions by associations of undertakings and concerted practices that have the object or effect of preventing, restricting or distorting competition. The Chapter I prohibition applies to agreements implemented or intended to be implemented in the whole or part of the United Kingdom, which may affect trade within the United Kingdom. An agreement is exempt from the Chapter I prohibition if it satisfies the criteria for exemption set out in section 9 of the CA98.

The Chapter II prohibition, contained in section 18(1) of the CA98, prohibits conduct by one or more undertakings which amounts to an abuse of a dominant position in a market. The Chapter II prohibition applies if the dominant position is held within the whole or part of the United Kingdom and the conduct in question may affect trade within the United Kingdom.

3.2 THE CHAPTER I: ANTI-COMPETITIVE AGREEMENTS AND CONCERTED PRACTICES

We set out below high level guidance on some of the key elements of the Chapter I prohibition on restrictive agreements. Some elements of this, in particular the discussion of the term 'undertaking' and discussion of market definition, are common to Chapter I and Chapter II CA98.

CA98 provides a non-exhaustive, indicative list of agreements to which the prohibition applies, namely those which:

- directly or indirectly fix purchase or selling prices or any other trading conditions;
- limit or control production, markets, technical development or investment;
- share markets or sources of supply;
- apply dissimilar conditions to equivalent transactions with other trading parties, thereby placing them at a competitive disadvantage; or
- make the conclusion of contracts subject to acceptance by the other parties of supplementary obligations which, by their nature or according to commercial usage, have no connection with the subject of such contracts.[37]

Undertakings

The competition law provisions apply to 'undertakings'. The term 'undertaking' is used in competition law to refer to any natural or legal person engaged in economic activity, regardless of its legal status and the way in which it is financed. It includes companies, firms, businesses, partnerships, individuals operating as sole traders, agricultural cooperatives, associations of firms, non-profit making organisations and (in some circumstances) public entities that offer goods or services on a given market.[38]

It should not be confused with the term 'undertaker', which is often used to describe a company holding an appointment under the WIA91 as a supplier of water and/or sewerage services.

3.3 MARKET DEFINITION

Market definition provides a framework for competition analysis. It is not an end in itself, but a starting point for cases under both the Chapter I and Chapter II prohibitions.

In Chapter I cases, market definition is considered when assessing the actual or potential competitive effects of agreements and concerted practices. The Chapter I prohibition applies only to agreements which have as their object or effect an 'appreciable' prevention, restriction or distortion of competition. Consideration of appreciability (and the application of certain **de minimis** rules) usually requires consideration of the relevant economic market. Agreements between undertakings are more likely to have an appreciable effect on competition where the undertakings concerned collectively have some degree of market power within the relevant market.

Market definition is also an important step in cases under the Chapter II prohibition. In order to determine whether an undertaking is dominant, it is generally necessary to define the relevant market in order to assess the extent of the undertaking's market power within the relevant market. This identifies the competitive constraints faced by an undertaking. Dominance is addressed in section 3.7 of this guidance, below.

We will assess the relevant market based on the facts of each individual case. In doing so, we will follow the framework set out in the CMA's guidance on market definition (OFT 403 'Market definition'). This will typically involve considering product and geographic dimensions, and may involve temporal dimensions. The appropriate market definitions may also change over time as more areas are opened up to competition.

The 'hypothetical monopolist' test

Defining the relevant market usually involves application of the 'hypothetical monopolist' test, which entails considering how customers (the 'demand side') and other suppliers (the 'supply side') would react to an attempt by a hypothetical monopolist to raise prices significantly above the competitive level. A significant price rise in this context is generally (and indicatively) taken to be in the region of 5 to 10 per cent of the price. This test is also sometimes referred to as the 'SSNIP' test (standing for 'small but significant non-transitory increase in price').

The application of the 'hypothetical monopolist' test will generally include consideration of the extent to which, following a hypothetical price increase:

- customers would switch to other products or services;
- suppliers not currently supplying that product or service would be able to switch their production within a short period of time;
- customers would be prepared to travel further than they currently do; and
- suppliers currently not supplying a given geographic area would be prepared to supply it.

The relevant market is defined as the narrowest set of products and geographic areas where a hypothetical monopolist could profitably raise prices.

The hypothetical monopolist test is primarily an intellectual framework for identifying a set of products, services, suppliers and geographic areas that can be usefully thought of as a market for the purposes of competition assessment. It needs to be applied flexibly and fit the industry in question. For instance, in some markets, price may not be the most relevant metric to use to assess competitive rivalry. Capacity or service changes may be more appropriate.

Product market

Goods and services will fall within the same product market where they are sufficiently inter-changeable. This issue can be considered both in terms of demand and supply substitutability.

- On the demand side, products will be substitutable if customers consider them to be close enough substitutes for each other that they would be willing to switch between them in response to small, significant changes in product or service characteristics.
- On the supply side, the issue is how easily and quickly suppliers would be able and willing to switch their production to produce the product or service under consideration following a small but significant change in conditions within the relevant market. In both cases, so far as possible where data is available (bearing in mind that some markets will only be opened to competition from April 2017 or later), we would consider changes in customer and supplier behaviour following relatively small changes in market conditions, such as a modest price increase of the product or service under investigation.
- Defining the product market requires analysis of the specific nature of the product or service in question. For example, in a context where some retail markets are open to competition and others are not, and differences exist on the basis of geography, it may be appropriate to draw a distinction between customer groups.

Notably after business retail market opening in England, a distinction between services for household and non-household customers may be appropriate. Further, it may be appropriate to define distinct markets for different products or services in the value chain, that are inputs into, or components of, the provision of water or sewerage services.

In general, in order to be included in the relevant market, substitution to or from a product or service must be a genuine possibility and capable of ready implementation.

For example, where a supplier could only expand its production after it had constructed new infrastructure, factors affecting that construction, including the time and cost required, would need be taken into account. Certainty of delivery may also be a relevant factor, for example, if new infrastructure requires a lengthy process of approvals and planning permission where the outcome is necessarily uncertain.

In these cases, we are unlikely to consider such supply expansion as sufficiently timely to include these suppliers within our definition of the relevant market.

However, we would consider them at a later stage in the assessment of competition when assessing the constraint that entry and expansion may impose on the competitors within the relevant market.

Market definition in the Fairfield CA98 investigation[39]

On 24 April 2014, we issued a Supplementary Statement of Objections (SSO) to Anglian Water which set out our provisional view that there had been an infringement of the CA98 in relation to a margin squeeze for the provision of sewerage services at the Fairfield development in Milton Keynes.

We provisionally concluded in the SSO that there were separate and distinct product markets for water and sewerage services at both the upstream and downstream levels, and that the relevant geographic market was limited to the Fairfield site.

Ofwat's decision following its investigation noted that market definition was not critical in the Fairfield case, as Anglian Water was undoubtedly dominant at the upstream level regardless of the precise market definition used. It was not therefore necessary for us to reach a final decision on issues of market definition and dominance. The final 'no grounds for action' decision issued in December 2015 stated that our indicative reasoning on the issues around market definition remained as set out in the SSO.

Geographic market

When defining the relevant geographic market, the issue is whether the supply of a product or service in one geographic area places a competitive constraint on the supply of the same product or service in a different geographic area. Like product market definition, this will need to be determined on the facts of each case.

While company boundaries, water resource zones or catchment areas may be relevant to geographic market definition, the appropriate geographic market may not necessarily be coterminous with these. For instance, if a large customer is located near a boundary with another water company, it might be reasonably served by both. In such a case, we might include both companies in the relevant geographic market.

Product and geographic markets in the water and sewerage sector

There are a number of separate **product markets** that might be defined, including providing retail water and sewerage services, providing connections to relevant water and waste water infrastructure, or the production of materials connected to anaerobic digestion or sludge. In determining the scope of the relevant markets for the purposes of an investigation, we will also take into account the statutory framework. This suggests that water and waste water services may be separate product markets, as they are subject to different regimes, and indeed they are not directly substitutable services. However, in any case we will take account of any bundling of services and integration along the value chain, and analyse both the demand and supply sides of the market as we did in the Fairfield investigation.

In determining the relevant **geographic market**, generally we will take into account the scope of an undertaker's area of appointment, as this is likely to confer a level of market power that is relevant to the assessment of dominance under the Chapter II prohibition. Within the current and proposed industry framework, actual and potential new appointments (where the appointed company is, or becomes, an undertaker), actual and potential water supply or sewerage licensees, customer self-supply, private supplies and on-site services might be important influences on geographic market definitions, generating different, or narrower relevant geographic markets.

For instance, considering a regional market for water services may be appropriate where the substitution of products or services can only usefully be considered within that geographic area. Similarly, the market can, but need not necessarily, widen beyond what appears to be substitutable products if that is how consumers purchase the product.

3.4 AGREEMENTS, DECISIONS AND CONCERTED PRACTICES

The Chapter I prohibition may apply to all forms of agreements and arrangements between undertakings, including in particular the so-called 'hard core' forms of collusion for which there may also be criminal sanctions.[40] An agreement does not need to be in writing to fall within the scope of the CA98, which also covers tacit understandings as well as express agreements. Concerted practices include forms of co-ordination that fall short of a full agreement but nonetheless allow the parties to substitute practical co-operation for the risks of competition.

The concept of a 'decision' by an association of undertakings includes the rules and recommendations of trade associations.

3.5 OBJECT OR EFFECT

The Chapter I prohibition applies to an agreement only if it has as its object or effect the prevention, restriction or distortion of competition.

The 'object' of an agreement does not refer to the subjective intention of the parties, but rather to the objective meaning and purpose of the agreement considered in its legal and economic context. The question is whether the coordination of conduct in itself reveals a sufficient degree of harm to competition, such that it is not necessary to examine its effects.

In practice, 'object' agreements tend to be those that obviously harm the competitive process or which have been established as object agreements in previous case law.[41]

Where it is not possible to say that an agreement has as its object the restriction of competition, it is necessary to consider its effects.

Any agreement between undertakings might be said to restrict the freedom of action of the parties in some sense. This is because the parties are then obliged to fulfil their side of the bargain. That does not, however, necessarily mean that the agreement is prohibited. An agreement will only be prohibited if it appreciably prevents, restricts or distorts competition. However, that includes potential as well as actual competition, such as where an agreement might have prevented a new entrant from entering the market.

In such effects cases, the assessment will typically require us to establish a 'counterfactual'. This is an idea of how competition would have developed if the agreement or arrangement had not existed. Once that has been done, the level of competition in the counterfactual can be compared with the level of competition arising or likely to arise under the agreement.

In assessing whether an agreement or concerted practice has an appreciable effect on competition, we will have regard to the European Commission's Notice on Agreements of Minor Importance.[42] This provides that, so long as they do not have the object of restricting competition, agreements will not appreciably restrict competition if:

- the aggregate market share of the parties does not exceed 10%, where the agreement is between actual or potential competitors; or
- the market share of each of the parties does not exceed 15%, where the agreement is between undertakings that are not actual or potential competitors.

Horizontal and vertical agreements

'Horizontal agreements' are those between undertakings operating at the same level of the market. Agreements between direct competitors to limit competition are regarded particularly seriously. Several types of horizontal agreement are considered to have the object of restricting competition. Of these, agreements or concerted practices between competitors to fix prices, share customers or markets, limit output or rig bids are treated as particularly serious infringements, and are referred to as cartels.[43] The sharing of commercially sensitive information which reduces uncertainty about future behaviour has also, in certain circumstances, been considered as a restriction of competition by object.

'Vertical agreements' are agreements between undertakings active at different levels of the market. For example, in the water and sewerage sector, vertical agreements may arise between appointed water and sewerage companies and downstream retailers.

The exemption conditions

An agreement may not be unlawful under CA98 even if it restricts competition. Section 9 CA98 provides that an agreement is exempt from the Chapter I prohibition if it:

(a) contributes to –
  (i) improving production or distribution, or
  (ii) promoting technical or economic progress, while allowing consumers a fair share of the resulting benefit, but
(b) does not –
  (i) impose on the undertakings concerned restrictions which are not indispensable to the attainment of those objectives; or
  (ii) afford the undertakings concerned the possibility of eliminating competition in respect of a substantial part of the products in question.

Unlike under section 2 CA98, where the entity alleging a restriction bears the burden of proof, the burden of proving that the exemption criteria are satisfied rests on the party claiming the benefit of the exemption.

However, if the conditions are satisfied, the agreement is not prohibited, and it is not necessary to have any prior decision to that effect. The agreement is valid and enforceable from the moment the conditions are satisfied and for so long as that remains the case.

Detailed guidance on the application of the exemption criteria can be found in European Commission guidance which details the position in respect of the exemption conditions under EU competition law,[44] but (as we explained above) the position under the Chapter I prohibition is likely to be the same.

An agreement will also be exempt from the Chapter I prohibition if it falls within a UK or EU 'block exemption'.[45] There are various block exemptions which may be of relevance and interest in the water and sewerage sectors, notably the block exemptions for:

- vertical agreements;[46] and
- research and development agreements.[47]

3.6 THE CHAPTER I PROHIBITION AND CHANGES IN THE WATER AND SEWERAGE SECTORS

Given the important changes taking place in the water and sewerage sector in the coming years, we expect to monitor closely whether any agreements or conduct may impede or interfere with the development of an effectively competitive market, for example by restricting the potential emergence of new competitors or forms of competition.

Collective agreements and the new retail market

A number of the structures set up to facilitate the operation of the business retail market from April 2017 may from time to time involve some forms of collaboration within industry. These interactions may take place in the context of trade association meetings, or within separate organisations or fora. It will nevertheless be the responsibility of companies involved in such arrangements, and any trade associations themselves, to ensure that they conduct their interactions in a manner that is consistent with competition law.

For example, the coordination or establishment of technical barriers to entry, collective or tacit agreements to inhibit the market from expanding or taking on larger scale self-supply, before and after opening of the retail market, could potentially result in enforcement action by us under the Chapter I prohibition.

3.7 THE CHAPTER II PROHIBITION/ARTICLE 102 TFEU

The Chapter II prohibition prohibits conduct by one or more companies which amounts to an abuse of a dominant position which may affect trade within the UK.

A central step in Chapter II cases is to determine whether a company is dominant on the relevant market. If an undertaking is dominant, then it is necessary to consider whether it has engaged in abusive conduct. Market definition is addressed in more detail above.

Dominance

In the context of an assessment of the relevant market, an assessment can be made of whether an undertaking has a dominant position.

The European Courts have defined a dominant position as

> 'a position of economic strength enjoyed by an undertaking which enables it to prevent effective competition being maintained on the relevant market by affording it the power to behave to an appreciable extent independently of its competitors, customers and ultimately of consumers'.[48]

In other words, dominant companies are those with significant market power, which can be thought of as the ability to sustain prices significantly above competitive levels or restrict output or quality significantly below competitive levels.

Further, as well as acting in ways that are harmful to customers, a dominant undertaking may have both the ability and incentive to harm the process of competition in order to maintain its position of strength on the market. For example, a dominant undertaking could use its market power to make it harder for actual or potential competitors to compete by raising their costs or barriers to entry.

Dominance may involve more than one undertaking. Undertakings may be jointly or collectively dominant[49] where they are linked in such a way as to adopt a common policy on the market.

Assessment of market power and dominance

Market share can be a useful indicator of market power, although it does not, on its own, determine whether an undertaking is dominant. In developing the case law on dominance, the courts have stated that dominance can be presumed, in the absence of evidence to the contrary, where an undertaking has a market share persistently above 50%.[50] Dominance has rarely been established in case law where an undertaking has a market share of below 40%, but this does not mean dominance in such cases may not be possible depending on features of a particular market.[51]

In assessing whether an undertaking enjoys a dominant position, we will have regard to the CMA's guidance: 'Assessment of Market Power' (OFT 415). We will look at a range of factors, including:

- the extent to which an undertaking faces competitive constraints (from, for example, existing competitors, potential competitors or because of strong buyer power on the part of its customers);
- customers' behaviour and options (for example, awareness of competition, the extent to which alternative providers are chosen, the extent to which substitutes are available, the time and costs involved in switching);
- competitors' behaviour and capacities (for example, their range of offers, their ability to increase available supplies within the relevant time period, the time and costs involved in acquiring customers);
- market operation (for example the extent of barriers to entry and exit, such as the regulation of water abstractions and discharges to the environment);
- an undertaking's conduct in a market with regard to price and output setting as well as its financial performance (such as persistently earning a rate of profit above competitive levels);
- market share and movements in market share over time; and
- the effect of regulation of prices, quality and other product characteristics.

Assessing market shares

We will generally assess market shares by volume and by value, and data may be collected from a number of sources. Assessments by value can often be more sensitive indicators of market power, because undertakings that are able to secure prices above the competitive level are more likely to have relatively high shares by value.

Assessing market shares

When assessing market share we will generally consider shares and movement in share over a period of time.

Special responsibility and 'super-dominance'

Dominant undertakings have a special responsibility not to allow their conduct to impair or distort competition. A dominant company is not absolved of this special responsibility as a result of the existence of sectoral regulation.

Undertakings are said to be 'super-dominant' where they enjoy very significant market power, where they operate as a monopoly or quasi-monopoly. Generally, such circumstances are relevant to the assessment of the lawfulness of an undertaking's conduct under the Chapter II/Article 102 prohibition.[52] In other words, 'super-dominant' undertakings have an even greater responsibility not to distort competition where such competition exists or not to prevent such competition from developing.

Abusive conduct

Dominance itself is not prohibited by the CA98. It is only the abuse of a dominant position that is unlawful. In Chapter II cases, once dominance has been established it is therefore necessary to determine whether there has been any abusive conduct.

Section 18 CA98 states:

'Conduct may, in particular, constitute such an abuse if it consists in –

(a) directly or indirectly imposing unfair purchase or selling prices or other unfair trading conditions;
(b) limiting production, markets or technical development to the prejudice of consumers;
(c) applying dissimilar conditions to equivalent transactions with other trading parties, thereby placing them at a competitive disadvantage;
(d) making the conclusion of contracts subject to acceptance by the other parties of supplementary obligations which, by their nature or according to commercial usage, have no connection with the subject of the contracts.'

This list is not exhaustive. Other types of conduct may also be abusive, if it amounts to the dominant undertaking having recourse to methods different from those which characterise 'normal' competition.

Dominant undertakings can engage in 'exploitative' conduct that seeks to take advantage of customers (for example by restricting output or raising prices) or to exploit certain groups of customers (such as those who are less able to switch to alternative products). In addition, dominant undertakings may also engage in anti-competitive conduct that harms the process of competition. This includes exclusionary conduct, which has the object or effect of eliminating competitors from a market or hindering market participation by current competitors or potential new entrants. However, conduct is not abusive simply because it harms competitors. The CA98 does not protect competitors in themselves, but rather seeks to protect the process of competition and ultimately the interests of customers and consumers.

Examples of anti-competitive exclusionary abuse include margin squeeze, predation, undue discrimination or selective discounting, refusal to supply (and constructive refusal to supply), and the use of long term and/or exclusive contracts. In some circumstances, bundling and tying can also be considered abusive.

The OFT guidance 'Abuse of a Dominant Position' (OFT 402) provides further details on the type of conduct which might be considered an abuse of a dominant position.

Dominance and abuse in related markets

It is not necessary for dominance and abuse to be on the same market. The Chapter II prohibition applies where an undertaking that is dominant in one market commits an abuse in a different but closely associated market.

This might occur, in particular, when a vertically integrated undertaking[53] that is dominant on one market commits an abuse on an upstream or downstream market on which it is not dominant, or on the market on which it is dominant in order to gain a competitive advantage in a related market.

When investigating this type of infringement Ofwat will take into account, among other things, the need for access to inputs from an upstream market in order to operate in the downstream market, and the setting of upstream and downstream prices by the dominant undertaking.

Predation, margin squeeze and refusal to supply

Types of abusive conduct that may be of particular concern where dominant undertakings are vertically integrated include predation, refusal to supply and margin squeeze (although the first two abuses are not limited to that context).

In the examples below, we refer to high level points of guidance only. All of these issues raise complex questions of fact, which will be case-specific, and complex questions of law and economics which continue to be refined. For example, competition authorities and courts have considered a number of different costing methodologies and benchmarks when assessing abusive conduct, and the approach taken is case specific, having regard to the relevant precedents. The assessment is particularly complex in multi-product markets where common infrastructure is used to deliver multiple products and in the context of vertically integrated undertakings operating in a sector such as water and waste water with high infrastructure costs which are either sunk, or only recoverable in the long run.

Cost-benchmark analysis is based on the premise that in order to break even (on a given market) companies that do not engage in abusive behaviour need to cover their incremental costs in the short run and their total costs (including incremental and fixed costs) in the long run.

The following paragraphs should be read with the above in mind and companies are strongly advised to seek legal advice in appropriate circumstances.

Predatory pricing occurs where a dominant undertaking sets prices below cost (deliberately incurring a loss) which is likely to eliminate or substantially weaken a competitor and thus enable the dominant undertaking to maintain or strengthen its market power. It is based on a comparison of the prices charged by a dominant undertaking and the costs incurred by it, taking into account its strategy. The key to assessment of predatory pricing (and indeed margin squeeze discussed below and many other forms of potentially abusive conduct) is to choose the correct cost benchmark by which to assess the dominant undertaking's conduct. This may vary by industry, and assessment of alleged predation will therefore need to be based on a careful, evidence-based analysis of the relevant circumstances.

Margin squeeze involves pricing behaviour on the part of the dominant undertaking which reduces the margin of the undertaking operating on the downstream market, preventing or limiting competition from efficient competitors in that market. Margin squeeze ordinarily requires consideration of the spread of prices and costs in the upstream and downstream markets. The aim of this enforcement is not to protect new entrants per se, but is rather concerned with ensuring that customers benefit as a result of healthy competition (in particular where such entrants would improve customer outcomes through better service or product quality, lower prices and innovative products and services).

A **refusal to supply** may take place in conjunction with abusive pricing conduct, or as a distinct abuse without a pricing element. It may occur where access to an upstream product (such as access to a monopoly network) is made impossible, more difficult or more costly for a downstream undertaking, particularly where the input is not replicable by the access seeker. We would be concerned in circumstances where such refusal or constructive refusal to supply could not be objectively justified (see below) and had as a consequence a reduction of competition in the downstream market.

Other abuses of dominance

In addition to the abuses of dominance discussed above, other types of conduct by dominant undertakings can have the object and/or effect of restricting competition and may amount to an abuse. We have set out the examples of price discrimination and tying and bundling below, but other conduct, such as exclusive dealing or the use of loyalty inducing rebates could also, potentially, amount to an abuse.

Tying and bundling refer to situations in which two or more products are supplied together. They are capable of raising competition law concerns as in certain circumstances they may allow a company which is dominant on one market to leverage its market power onto another market (on which it was not previously dominant) by foreclosing competitors from that latter market.

Price discrimination occurs where a dominant undertaking offers differential pricing to different customers (or the same pricing to customers in different circumstances). This may occur as part of vertical supply chain abuses such as margin squeeze (as discussed above), or at a single level of a market such as in retail markets. Price discrimination may be harmful where it is used to exclude competitors

Both types of conduct are more likely to occur in retail markets, and may be objectively justified as being of benefit to customers. Ofwat will assess any such behaviour and its likely competitive impacts on a case by case basis.

Objective justification

While the Chapter II prohibition does not, unlike the Chapter I prohibition, provide criteria for exemption, a dominant undertaking can defend itself against an allegation of abuse by demonstrating that it has an objective justification for its conduct.

A dominant undertaking must, however, put forward arguments and evidence to show that its conduct was objectively justified. Conduct must be proportionate in order to satisfy this test.

3.8 COMPETITION LAW AND REGULATION

The water and sewerage sector is subject to significant sectoral regulation. However, companies operating in the sector need to comply with both sectoral regulation and competition law.

The application of the CA98 will take into account the existence of regulation in the sector in a number of ways. For example, whether an agreement generates anti-competitive effects will be assessed in light of the economic context, which will include any regulatory framework. In addition, under the Chapter II prohibition, assessments of market definition and dominance may be influenced by aspects of the regulatory regime, for example where a company has a virtual monopoly over the supply of services in a region as a result of being an appointed undertaker.

Even where the scope for competition is limited, the CA98 provisions will continue to apply where there remains some residual scope for competition or potential competition. Similarly, even though the regulatory framework may, for example, encourage certain behaviour, the CA98 prohibitions continue to apply to the extent that an undertaking retains a degree of discretion in the way in which it implements sector specific rules or codes.[54]

For example, if there is more than one way to comply with a regulatory requirement, at least one of which is not anti-competitive, an undertaking is unlikely to be able to justify an agreement or conduct which is anti-competitive on the basis that it was undertaken for the purposes of regulatory compliance. Further, the fact that a company has complied with its regulatory obligations may not be sufficient to demonstrate that it has also complied with CA98.[55]

The exception is that Schedule 3 CA98 provides that the Chapter I and Chapter II prohibitions do not apply to an agreement or conduct to the extent that it is entered into or undertaken in order to comply with a legal requirement. For example, where anti-competitive conduct is required by national legislation or the national legal framework, and these provisions eliminate entirely any possibility of complying with them in a way which is not anti-competitive, the Chapter I and Chapter II prohibitions will not apply to the extent necessary to meet such requirements.[56]

Schedule 3 CA98 also excludes certain other categories of agreement and conduct from the Chapter I and Chapter II prohibitions, including in particular the activities of an undertaking entrusted by a public authority with the operation of services of general economic interest (SGEI). The SGEI exclusion applies to a firm entrusted with the provision of services of general economic interest, or having the character of a revenue-producing monopoly, only so far as the Chapter I or Chapter II prohibitions would obstruct the performance, in law or in fact, of the particular tasks assigned. The exclusion will be interpreted strictly, and Ofwat will have regard to the CMA's guidance on the SGEI exclusion.[57]

It is for undertakings to assess themselves whether any relevant exclusions may apply to their agreements, arrangements or conduct. We will have regard to guidance issued by the CMA when assessing any arguments to this effect.

In certain limited cases, the WIA91 prohibits the use by us of our powers under CA98.[58] In such cases, we will use the regulatory tools available to us under the WIA91 where we consider it appropriate.

3.9 CONSEQUENCES OF A COMPETITION LAW INFRINGEMENT

As discussed above, where we investigate an infringement of the CA98, we may:

- impose a financial penalty on the infringing undertaking;
- generally make directions as to future conduct; or
- agree to accept commitments.

We explain these powers further in Chapter 4.

In addition, infringements of the CA98 may give rise to claims from third parties. Claims for redress for breaches of the CA98 can be brought in the UK courts which have jurisdiction to hear competition cases, including the Competition Appeal Tribunal (CAT) and the High Court. The three main types of relief available to a successful claimant are:

- damages;
- an injunction; and
- a declaration.

Claims for damages resulting from a CA98 infringement may be brought as either 'stand-alone' or 'follow-on' actions. A standalone action is a claim brought where the claimant itself seeks to prove that the CA98 has been infringed, without relying on an infringement decision of a competition authority.

Where Ofwat, the CMA, the European Commission or another sector regulator has made a final decision that the CA98 has been infringed, that decision will be binding on both the ordinary courts and the CAT (unless that decision is being appealed). A claimant can therefore use the decision as proof of a CA98 breach and may rely on certain findings of fact in it, so that in most cases they will need to prove only that they have suffered loss as a result of the infringement (a 'follow-on' action).

Where an anti-competitive agreement has been found to be unlawful under the CA98, the relevant restrictive provisions in that agreement and, in some circumstances, the entire agreement will be void and unenforceable. We may also apply to the court for a Competition Disqualification Order against a company director in appropriate cases.[59]

NOTES

37 Section 2(2) CA98

38 See case C-41/90 *Höfner and Elser v Macrotron GmbH* [1991] ECR I-1979, [1993] 4 CMLR 306 and case T-319/99 *Fenin v Commission* [2003], ECR II-357, 4 March 2003 [2003] CMLR 1

39 www.ofwat.gov.uk/publication/fairfield-competition-act-1998-investigation-decision-summary/

40 See Section 4.10 below.

41 For more information see European Commission 'Guidance on restrictions of competition "by object" for the purpose of defining which agreements may benefit from the De Minimis Notice'

42 'Notice on agreements of minor importance which do not appreciably restrict competition under Article 101(1) of the Treaty on the Functioning of the European Union', OJ 2014 C291/1

43 See Part 6 of the Enterprise Act, 2002.

44 European Commission Guidelines on the application of Article 81(3) of the Treaty (2004/C101/08). The TFEU re-

numbered Article 81 as Article 101 and Article 82 as Article 102.

45 Section 6 CA98

46 Commission Regulation (EU) No 330/2010 of 20 April 2010 on the application of Article 101(3) of the Treaty on the Functioning of the European Union to categories of vertical agreements and concerted practices, OJ 2010 L102/1

47 Commission Regulation (EU) No 1217/2010 of 14 December 2010 on the application of Article 101(3) of the Treaty on the Functioning of the European Union to certain categories of research and development agreements, OJ 2010 L335/36

48 Case 27/76 *United Brands v Commission* [1978] ECR 207. This definition has been used in other cases.

49 The concept of joint dominance was first defined in cases T-66, 77 and 78/89 *Società Italiana Vetro v Commission (Italian Flat Glass)* [1992] ECR II-1403, [1992] 5 CMLR 302. See further case T-102/96 *Gencor v Commission* [1999] ECR II-753, [1999] 4 CMLR 971

50 Case C62/86, *AKZO Chemie BV v Commission* [1993] 5 CMLR 215

51 See for example case T-219/99 *British Airways v Commission* [2003] ECR II-5917, where British Airways was found to have a dominant position with a market share between 39 and 46 per cent.

52 *Konkurrensverketk v Teliasonera Sverige* AB Case C-52/09 [2011] 4 CMLR 18

53 This is where an undertaking acts on both the supply and retail markets, either as a single entity or through parent and subsidiary companies

54 Case C-280/08 *P Deutsche Telekom AG v Commission* [2010] ECR I-09552

55 Or indeed vice versa, as regulatory obligations may go further than competition law compliance requires.

56 Cases C-359 & 379/95P *Commission and France v Ladbroke Racing* [1997] ECR I-6265, [1998] 4 [CMLR] 27

57 OFT421, 'Services of general economic interest exclusion'

58 WIA91 ss.66D, 110A, 110B.

59 Sections 9C and 9E, Company Directors Disqualification Act 1986.

4. OUR PROCEDURAL APPROACH: INVESTIGATIONS AND ENFORCEMENT

[3.295]

Key messages

Only one regulator can exercise prescribed CA98 functions in any one case at any one time. There are procedures in place to ensure the best-placed competition authority takes a case forward.

Our 'primacy' obligations mean that before exercising our formal enforcement powers set out in the WIA91 we have a duty to consider whether it would be more appropriate to proceed under the CA98.

We will apply our prioritisation principles to all potential CA98 investigations in deciding whether to begin an investigation and will continue to keep this under review.

We will seek to exercise our functions under the CA98 transparently and fairly.

OPENING CASES

Potential cases involving a possible breach of the CA98 can come to our attention in a number of ways. This includes:

- complaints by the public and businesses;
- referrals from other authorities;
- proactive intelligence gathering;
- market studies and enquiries;
- applications for leniency; and
- other regulatory monitoring.

A CA98 investigation may also be opened following receipt of a super-complaint brought by a designated consumer body.[60]

Figure 1 below shows the stages that an investigation may include, from us becoming aware of an issue to a final decision. The column on the right indicates the body, team or individual (usually, the Senior Responsible Officer (SRO), Market Outcomes and Enforcement), within Ofwat that will generally be involved at each stage. The stages are described in further detail in this chapter. Further details on the procedure we follow is found in the CMA's Rules of Procedure[61] and the Concurrency Regulations.[62]

Figure 1 Stages that an Ofwat CA98 investigation may include

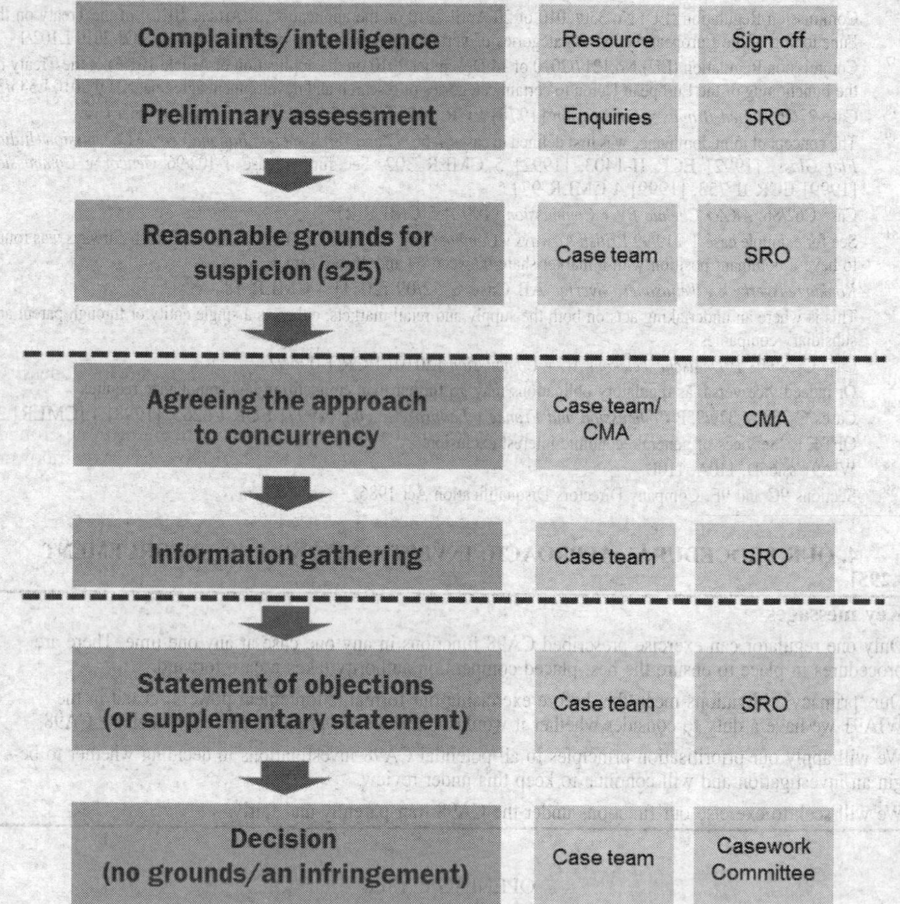

4.1 PRELIMINARY ASSESSMENT

When considering whether to open or continue with an investigation under the CA98, we are generally required to consider whether our other powers are a more appropriate means of addressing an issue. As explained above, before exercising our powers with regards to formal enforcement or financial penalties set out in WIA91, we must consider whether it would be more appropriate to proceed under the CA98.

It will be important for any complainant to present the best possible case to enable us to decide whether it is appropriate to open an investigation. Appendix 1 sets out the information that we would generally expect to see in any formal complaint if we are to take forward a CA98 investigation.

Complaints received by us will be assessed in the light of, for example:

- our jurisdiction;
- the nature of the alleged conduct;
- our applicable powers;
- the evidence;
- available resources; and
- our prioritisation principles.[63]

4.2 PRIORITISATION

As set out in our published prioritisation principles, our CA98 powers have an important part to play in ensuring the effective use of market forces. At the same time, we need to make the best use of our resources in order to achieve our aims. To do this, we need to take appropriate decisions about the work programmes and the projects we undertake, looking across all our areas of work. Our prioritisation principles are summarised below.

Our prioritisation principles

Impact – The greater the positive impact on consumers from the decision, the more likely we are to open or continue an investigation.

Strategic significance – The intervention must be compatible with Ofwat's strategy.

Our prioritisation principles

Risks – The higher the likelihood of a successful outcome, the more likely we are to open or continue an investigation given our finite resources.

Resources – Ofwat must be satisfied that the resources required are proportionate to the expected benefits.

Once a case is opened and a case team assembled, the team will regularly review a CA98 investigation as it develops, taking a view as to whether the investigation continues to be justified in light of our prioritisation principles. If it is not, the investigation may be closed on the grounds of administrative priority.

While part of the assessment may take into account the strength and quality of the available evidence, an administrative decision not to open or to close an investigation on the basis of our prioritisation principles is not a decision on the merits of the case or whether there has been a breach of competition law. Our choice of whether to take enforcement action is a question of how we use our resources effectively and efficiently. In some cases it may be appropriate to deal with suspected infringements of competition law without formal enforcement action. For example, we may alert parties to possible concerns without formally opening an investigation.

If we decide not to open a formal investigation under the CA98, or close an investigation on the grounds of administrative priority, it is open to the CMA (or another concurrent regulator) to exercise their powers under the CA98, following consultation with us.[64]

4.3 REASONABLE GROUNDS FOR SUSPECTING AN INFRINGEMENT

Once our case team has reviewed the available evidence and made a preliminary assessment of the agreement or conduct in question, they will consider whether there are 'reasonable grounds for suspecting'[65] an infringement of the CA98.

Once we have established that we have evidence suggesting there are reasonable grounds for suspecting that there is a breach of CA98, we must engage with the CMA within a set timeframe in order to agree the approach to concurrency (see section 4.5).

4.4 AGREEING THE APPROACH TO CONCURRENCY

Before launching any CA98 investigation, Ofwat and the CMA (and any other relevant regulator) will consult one another to agree which authority will exercise its concurrent competition powers in relation to the case,[66] as soon as possible and in any event no later than one month from disclosure of the relevant information.[67]

In determining case allocation the guiding principle is that a case will be allocated to the competition authority best placed to exercise the concurrent competition enforcement powers.[68] We will endeavour to:

- reach agreement on which competition authority will exercise its powers in each case as soon as reasonably practical; and
- engage constructively with the CMA and any other relevant sectoral regulators.

If agreement cannot be reached, the CMA may determine which competition authority should act (see the Concurrency Regulations and Ofwat's MoU with the CMA).[69]

The CMA may direct that a case in progress is transferred from Ofwat to the CMA, if it is satisfied that to do so would further the promotion of competition within any market or markets in the United Kingdom for the benefit of consumers. The CMA can only issue such a direction before Ofwat has issued a Statement of Objections.

The European Commission has the power to take over cases involving an alleged breach of Article 101 and/or Article 102 TFEU from NCAs by initiating proceedings.[70]

4.5 CONDUCTING A FORMAL INVESTIGATION

We seek to exercise our functions transparently and fairly. We carry out our CA98 investigations and make CA98 decisions in accordance with the principles of administrative law, ensuring our procedure is fair. We are required to follow the CMA's procedural rules[71] when undertaking an investigation or taking enforcement action under the CA98 or Articles 101 and 102 TFEU and we will also have regard to the CMA's procedural guidance.[72]

When we decide to open a formal investigation under the CA98 we will generally send the party or parties under investigation a case initiation letter. This letter will set out brief details of the agreement or conduct under investigation, the relevant legislation, our indicative proposed timetable for the initial stages of the investigation and contact details. Where relevant, we will also generally inform the person who has provided relevant information to us giving rise to the investigation (for example, the person making a complaint). However, we will not communicate with the party or parties under investigation or with third parties at the start of an investigation if this may be prejudicial (for example, where we intend to conduct unannounced inspections). We may need to limit the amount of information provided in some cases (for example, to protect the identity of a whistle-blower or a complainant).

We may in some circumstances publish basic information about the investigation in accordance with our powers under section 25A CA98 (for example, if we consider that it may assist us in our investigation or is necessary for market stability). If we publish information identifying a party whose activities (including being a party to a particular agreement) are being investigated, and subsequently decide to terminate the investigation, we will publish a notice stating that the activities of that party are no longer being investigated, in compliance with our statutory obligations.[73]

4.6 REQUESTING AND OBTAINING INFORMATION

In order to reach decisions on the basis of robust evidence, we will require detailed information and data. Information may be needed from the subjects of our investigations and from third parties. We appreciate that providing such information may be onerous in some cases, and we seek to make the process as efficient as possible without prejudicing the investigation. This may entail sharing draft information requests before they are formally issued, or discussing with parties how they hold data in order to tailor our requests.

In summary, our powers in conducting an investigation include the power to:

- issue requests for information and documents (commonly referred to as section 26 notices) in writing;
- conduct compulsory interviews with any individual connected to a party under investigation;[74]
- enter into business and/or domestic premises and require the production of documents and take copies of documents. Such entry may be either with, or (for business premises) without, a warrant. If we have obtained a warrant, we may search for and seize documents;
- impose a penalty on any business or individual which (without reasonable excuse) does not comply with our information gathering powers,[75] having regard to the CMA's Statement of Policy on Administrative penalties (CMA4).

We cannot:

- require the production or disclosure of privileged communications;[76]
- force a party to provide answers that would require an admission that it has infringed the law;
- disclose confidential and sensitive information other than in accordance with our statutory powers.[77]

When we have requested information, we expect:

- to be provided with relevant information in a clear and concise format and within the time period set. We will work with parties to ensure information is provided in a way that suits both Ofwat and the parties, where possible;
- to receive separate non-confidential versions of any document or materials provided which contain sensitive or otherwise confidential information;
- a clear explanation as to why any redacted information should be considered confidential.

We may return information where, after careful review, we consider it is outside the scope of the request. However, we will retain this information for as long as necessary to satisfy ourselves that this is the case.

Where the volume of information involved is large, we will typically discuss with the companies concerned how the information may best be provided. This may involve, for example, the use of an information portal.

In principle, where information on one matter has been gathered using powers under the CA98, we may use it to investigate other matters under the CA98, and we may use information gained under the CA98 for investigations under EU competition law or other relevant legislation.[78] However, this is subject to certain constraints and limitations, in particular with respect to the use of leniency information shared with us by other concurrent regulators.

Any information received from the European Commission or another NCA will only be used in accordance with Article 12 of the Modernisation Regulation.[79] This provides for information sharing (which can include confidential information) amongst NCAs and/or the European Commission. In general, information exchanged on this basis will only be used in evidence for the purpose of applying Articles 101 and 102 TFEU in respect of the subject-matter for which it was collected. However, where national competition law is applied in the same case and in parallel to EU competition law, and does not lead to a different outcome, information so exchanged may also be used for the application of national competition law.

4.7 INTERIM MEASURES

We have the power to impose interim measures either on our own initiative or in response to a request to do so, where we consider it necessary to:

- act urgently either to prevent significant damage to a person or category of persons, or
- in order to protect the public interest.[80]

Interim measures generally require a party to comply with temporary directions, for example, to continue supplying a particular product or service, in circumstances where an investigation has been started but not yet concluded.

Applications for interim measures should be made to the SRO of the Market Outcomes and Enforcement Programme, with sufficient information and evidence to demonstrate the need for interim measures.

In considering an application for interim measures we will follow the procedure outlined in the CMA's guidance[81] which outlines the right for representations to be made by applicants and the party against whom interim measures are sought. Applications are likely to be determined by the SRO of the Market Outcomes and Enforcement Programme.

Casework Committee

We established a Board Committee for Casework ('the Casework Committee') to make final decisions in strategic cases (as defined in Annex J of the Board's Rules of Procedure). In practice, a CA98 case will generally be classified as a strategic case and final decisions are likely to include key decisions after a Statement of Objections has been issued (including settlement decisions).

The terms of reference of the Casework Committee are interpreted in accordance with the CMA's Procedural Rules. The role played by the Casework Committee is similar to that played by the Case Decision Group in CMA investigations.[82]

The Casework Committee may voluntarily refer decisions back to Ofwat's Board, where it deems it appropriate to do so.

4.8 INVESTIGATION FINDINGS

There are several ways in which an investigation under the CA98 can be resolved. These are as follows.

- We may proceed to a formal infringement decision. Prior to doing so, we will issue a Statement of Objections setting out our provisional view as to why the agreement or conduct under investigation amounts to an infringement. If appropriate, having taken account of representations received and any new evidence, we may issue a final infringement decision, and impose a penalty and/or directions on the party or parties concerned.
- We may agree a settlement with the parties concerned which will permit an expedited process for reaching an infringement decision.
- We may issue a decision that there are no grounds for action (either before or after issuing a Statement of Objections) if we have not found sufficient evidence of an infringement.
- We may close our investigation on the grounds of administrative priorities at any time (before or after issuing a Statement of Objections), consulting formal complainants before taking a decision to do so.
- We may accept commitments from a party as to its future conduct which would not involve a finding of infringement.

If the Casework Committee decides to adopt an infringement decision, it will set out the key facts relied upon to prove the infringement and the nature of the sanction it will impose. It will also consider the material representations made during the course of the investigation. The infringement decision may impose a financial penalty and may contain directions to bring the infringement to an end. We will normally publish a summary of the investigation and a non-confidential version of the infringement decision.

Alternatively, the Casework Committee may adopt a 'No grounds for action decision' and close the investigation. In the same way as when issuing an infringement decision, we will set out the key facts relied upon to issue the decision - publishing either a case closure summary or a non-confidential version of the decision.

Statement of objections

Where we reach the provisional view that the agreement or conduct under investigation amounts to a CA98 infringement and at that stage consider it appropriate to proceed to a formal decision, our current approach is that the SRO of the Market Outcomes and Enforcement Programme will decide to issue a Statement of Objections to each business considered to be responsible for the infringement.

The Statement of Objections represents Ofwat's provisional view based on our legal and economic assessment of the case. It allows the business that is accused of breaching the CA98 to know the full case against it and, if it chooses to do so, to respond in writing and orally. We give each addressee of a Statement of Objections an opportunity to inspect our investigation file.

Further information on the Statement of Objections procedure is contained in the CMA's guidance. We will generally follow the CMA's approach. We will normally announce the issue of a Statement of Objections but may not do so in certain cases, or may publish limited information, in light of for example, particular market sensitivities that may arise in any given case.

Settlement

Settlement is a voluntary process in which a business must admit that it has breached the CA98 and accept that a streamlined administrative process will apply for the remainder of the investigation in return for a reduction in any financial penalty. The settlement process can be initiated at any time during the formal investigation, including after the issue of a Statement of Objections.

Ofwat will have regard to the CMA's guidance[83] when agreeing settlements in CA98 investigations and it should be noted that this process is substantially different from the settlement process in relation to other types of enforcement cases dealt with by Ofwat.

If settlement has been agreed before the issue of an SO, we will produce a statement setting out our findings so far and noting that the party concerned has accepted that it has infringed the CA98 and asked for settlement. Settlement decisions are likely be taken by the Casework Committee.

In order for us to consider settlement, the undertaking in question must:[84]

Part 3 CMA and other Guidelines

- make a clear and unequivocal admission of liability in relation to the nature, scope, and duration of the infringement;
- cease the infringing behaviour immediately; and
- confirm they accept a streamlined administrative process for the remainder of the investigation.

An infringement decision will be issued in every settlement case (unless exceptionally we decide not to make an infringement finding). We may impose a financial penalty on any settling business, including a settlement discount. This will be capped at:

- 20% for settlement pre-Statement of Objections; and
- 10% for settlement post-Statement of Objections.

Financial penalties

If we decide that there has been an infringement of the CA98, we may impose a penalty on the infringing undertaking(s). In practice, such a decision is likely to be taken by the Casework Committee which will have regard to the CMA's penalty guidance when setting the amount of a penalty.[85]

Where the Casework Committee is considering reaching an infringement decision under the CA98 and imposing a financial penalty on a party, it will provide that party with a draft penalty statement, setting out the key considerations relevant to the calculation of the proposed penalty, based on the information available to it at the time. Parties will be given an opportunity to comment on the draft penalty statement in writing and to attend an oral hearing.

The infringement decision will explain how the appropriate level of penalty was decided upon, having taken into account our statutory obligations in fixing a financial penalty and the parties' written and oral representations on the draft penalty calculation.

4.9 EARLY RESOLUTION: COMMITMENTS AND INFORMAL RESOLUTION

We may bring our investigation to an end without proceeding to an infringement or 'no grounds for action' decision in a number of ways.

Warning or advisory letters

We may from time to time issue warning or advisory letters where we are concerned that an undertaking might be infringing the CA98 in connection with the supply of water and sewerage services in England and Wales. Generally, we will follow the process outlined by the CMA.[86]

Our approach will be based on various factors, including:

- the seriousness of any potential anti-competitive practices;
- the strength of the evidence Ofwat has; and
- the potential for the practices to harm competition in the relevant market sector.

Our warning letter will:

- explain our concerns about the relevant business practices;
- recommend that the addressee carry out a self-assessment of its business practices to ensure it is complying with competition law;
- ask the addressee to write to us with details of what it has done, or is planning to do, to ensure that it complies with competition law.

Our advisory letter will:

- explain our concerns about the relevant business practices;
- recommend that the addressee carry out a self-assessment of its practices to ensure it is complying with competition law; and
- request that the addressee let the CMA know it has received the letter.

A warning or advisory letter does not necessarily mean the recipient has breached the CA98. However, it is important that the party takes the matter seriously and responds when requested to do so. Failure to do so may result in us opening a full CA98 investigation.

Commitments

Under section 31A CA98, we may accept commitments from one or more parties for the purpose of addressing the competition concerns at issue in a particular case. Commitments are binding promises from a party in relation to its future conduct. Ofwat may apply to the court if a party from whom we have accepted commitments fails (without reasonable excuse) to adhere to them.

We will have regard to the CMA's guidance on the circumstances in which it may be appropriate to accept commitments[87] and the process that the CMA adopts when considering commitments.[88] If we choose to accept commitments we will close our investigation and not make an infringement decision in relation to the issues covered by the commitments.

Undertakings under investigation can offer commitments at any time until an infringement decision is made. Commitments can be offered before we have issued a Statement of Objections even though we have not yet fully carried out our investigation but on the basis that we may have notified parties that we have reasonable suspicion of an infringement. To date, we have accepted such commitments in two cases.[89]

Commitments can also be offered after we have issued a Statement of Objections and generally after the parties have had an opportunity to make representations. However, we are unlikely to accept commitments at a very late stage.

Where we are offered commitments, we will consult those businesses affected by the agreement and/or conduct in question. We will seek views on, for example, whether the commitments address the potential harm arising from the agreement or conduct in question. If we propose to accept the final commitments offered, we may submit these to the Casework Committee for approval.

Bristol Water CA98 investigation

In March 2013, we launched a formal investigation into the price and non-price terms Bristol Water applied when providing services to self-lay organisations. We did this in response to two separate complaints. These related to the services provided by Bristol Water to enable the provision of new water connections for new development sites, either by itself or by self-lay organisations (SLOs).

The complainants alleged that Bristol Water had used its dominant position to harm competition in the contestable market for providing new water connections.

During the early stages of its investigation, we identified four competition concerns related to Bristol Water's conduct (including pricing and non-pricing behaviours) that could potentially restrict entry and expansion of competitors in the new water connections market in Bristol Water's area.

In March 2015, we gave notice of our intention to accept a comprehensive set of binding commitments to address our concerns.

4.10 LENIENCY, VOLUNTARY REDRESS, FINES AND PENALTIES

Leniency

Under both EU and UK competition law, competition authorities may grant leniency to undertakings who inform them of cartel activities and commit to ongoing cooperation during an investigation. This is a powerful tool to enable competition authorities to uncover cartel activities, which are often difficult to identify. The benefits of increasing detection of these most serious competition infringements generally outweigh the loss of the deterrent effect that would come from imposing financial penalties on all the undertakings that participated in the infringing agreement(s).

Leniency may take the form of total immunity from fines for the first undertaking to successfully apply, or a reduction in penalties.

It is vital that undertakings who are considering applying for leniency do not delay in seeking to obtain a leniency 'marker' (that is, a marker recognising their place in the 'queue' for leniency). We do not have concurrent jurisdiction to prosecute the 'cartel offence' (defined in the Enterprise Act 2002).[90] If we are made aware of conduct relating to a suspected cartel offence we will immediately refer the matter to the CMA. The CMA is the only authority empowered to grant criminal immunity and issue a no-action letter with respect to prosecutions under the criminal cartel offence and, for that reason, the CMA generally administers the grant of leniency markers (in collaboration with sectoral regulators where relevant).

All initial applications for leniency markers in cases involving water and waste water activities in England and Wales should be **made directly to the CMA** in accordance with its published leniency process and procedure.[91]

The CMA's process for applying for leniency is not repeated here. For further information on the types of leniency treatment which may be available to businesses, and the conditions which must be met to secure those benefits, see the CMA's 'Guidance as to the appropriate amount of a penalty' and guidance on leniency applications.[92]

Voluntary redress

Voluntary redress schemes are a form of alternative dispute resolution. Under changes introduced by the Consumer Rights Act 2015, we have powers concurrently with the CMA to approve a redress scheme in relation to a CA98 infringement.[93],[94] The CMA and relevant regulators are required to publish guidance on applications for approval of redress schemes, the approval of such schemes, and the power to enforce approved schemes.[95] We will follow the CMA guidance[96] on the approval and enforcement of such redress schemes, but will exercise our discretion to use our powers in accordance with our prioritisation principles.

Where an undertaking offers a redress scheme, those affected by the infringement are able to claim compensation through the scheme without the need to pursue litigation in the courts.

In cases relating to the supply of water and waste water services in England and Wales, undertakings which have infringed the CA98 may apply to Ofwat or the CMA for approval of a voluntary redress scheme. When either authority proposes to exercise relevant powers, it will liaise with the other authority as appropriate.

4.11 COMPETITION DISQUALIFICATION ORDERS

We have concurrent jurisdiction with the CMA to apply to a court for a competition disqualification order to be made against any director of a company which we have found to be in breach of competition law.[97] Such an order will be made if the court finds that the conduct of the director in relation to the breach of competition law makes him/her unfit to be concerned in the management of a company.

Before making such an application, we will give notice to the director concerned and give that person an opportunity to make representations to us.

Part 3 CMA and other Guidelines

4.12 APPEALS

A decision taken by us as to whether the Chapter I and/or the Chapter II prohibition under the CA98 or Articles 101 and/or 102 TFEU have been infringed may be appealed to the Competition Appeal Tribunal (CAT).[98] The CAT may:

- confirm or set aside our decision;
- impose, revoke or vary the amount of any penalty imposed by us;
- remit the matter to us; or
- make any other decision, including give any such directions or take such other steps that we ourselves could have made or taken.

The procedure applicable to appeals to the CAT is set out in the Competition Appeal Tribunal Rules 2015.[99]

Where the CA98 does not provide for an appeal, an application for judicial review may be brought in certain circumstances. Parties should seek independent legal advice on their rights in this regard.

NOTES

60 See section 11 Enterprise Act 2002. A super-complaint is a complaint submitted by a designated consumer body that any feature, or combination of features, of a market in the UK for goods or services is or appears to be significantly harming the interests of consumers.

61 Competition Act 1998 (Competition and Markets Authority's Rules) Order 2014/458

62 Competition Act 1998 (Concurrency) Regulations 2014

63 www.ofwat.gov.uk/wp-content/uploads/2016/03/prs_inf_100920ca98priority.pdf

64 Reg. 8, Competition Act 1998 (Concurrency) Regulations 2014

65 Section 25 CA98

66 Regulation 4(2) of the Concurrency Regulations (www.legislation.gov.uk/id/uksi/2014/536).

67 See above, footnote 33. See paragraph 26 of the MOU.

68 CMA10 contains a list of factors relevant to determining which regulator is 'better or best placed

69 Regulation 5 of the Concurrency Regulations

70 Further details on case allocation as between NCAs from different Member States are provided in guidance adopted by the CMA. www.gov.uk/government/publications/guidance-on-concurrent-application-of-competition-law-to- regulated-industries

71 The Competition Act 1998 (Competition and Markets Authority's Rules) Order 2014 SI 2014/458

72 'Competition Act 1998: Guidance on the CMA's investigation procedures in Competition Act 1998 cases', www.gov.uk/government/uploads/system/uploads/attachment_data/file/537006/CMA8_CA98_Guidance_on_the_CMA_investigation_procedures.pdf

73 See paragraph 10 of The Competition Act 1998 (Competition and Markets Authority's Rules) Order 2014 SI 2014/458

74 S26A CA98

75 S40A CA98

76 S30 CA98

77 Part 9 EA02 imposes a general restriction on the disclosure of information. The Concurrency Regulations require arrangements to be made for the sharing with concurrent authorities of specific information during an investigation.

78 There are restrictions on disclosure of such information under Part 9 Enterprise Act 2002.

79 EC Regulation 1/2003

80 See 'Competition Act 1998: Guidance on the CMA's investigation procedures in Competition Act 1998 cases'

81 'Competition Act 1998: Guidance on the CMA's investigation procedures in Competition Act 1998 cases' (CMA8)

82 Op. cit, page 64: Appointment of a Case Decision Group.

83 CMA8

84 See paras 14.7–14.8 CMA8

85 OFT 423, OFT's guidance as to the appropriate amount of a penalty, (September 2012) www.gov.uk/government/publications/appropriate-ca98-penalty-calculation

86 CMA8

87 See OFT407 'Enforcement' and CMA8 'Guidance on the CMA's investigation procedures in Competition Act 1998 cases'

88 See paragraph 10.20 of CMA8 'Guidance on the CMA's investigation procedures in Competition Act 1998 cases' (CMA8)

89 See www.ofwat.gov.uk/ib0415-ofwat-accepts-commitments-from-bristol-water/ and www.ofwat.gov.uk/wpcontent/uploads/2015/11/pap_pos20130117alcontrol1.pdf

90 EA2002, s.188: An individual is guilty of an offence if he agrees with one or more other persons to make or implement, or to cause to be made or implemented, arrangements of the kind specified in s.188(2). These include agreements to fix prices, limit supply or production, market-sharing agreements, and bid-rigging agreements. As to concurrent jurisdiction in respect of the cartel offence, see the CMA's guidance CMA9, www.gov.uk/government/publications/cartel-offence-prosecution-guidance

91 OFT1495

92 See OFT 423, OFT's guidance as to the appropriate amount of a penalty, (September 2012) www.gov.uk/government/publications/appropriate-ca98-penalty-calculation, and OFT1495, Applications for leniency and no-action in cartel cases, (July 2013). www.gov.uk/government/publications/leniency-and-no-action-applications-in-cartel-cases. In the event that we are initially approached by a leniency applicant, we will direct the applicant, in the first instance, to the CMA.

93 Voluntary redress schemes in respect of a CA98 infringement are not to be confused with redress schemes for the resolution of customer complaints, which retailers must have in pace in accordance with Ofwat's Customer Protection Code of Practice.

94 Competition Act 1998 (Redress Scheme) Regulations 2015, (S.I. 2015, No.1587

95 Section 49C(9) of the CA98, as amended by the CRA15.

96 www.gov.uk/government/uploads/system/uploads/attachment_data/file/453925/Voluntary_redress_schemes_guidance.pdf

97 Sections 9C and 9E, Company Directors Disqualification Act 1986. See also OFT510: www.gov.uk/government/publications/competition-disqualification-orders

98 See CA98 sections 46 and 47, and Schedule 8

99 www.catribunal.org.uk/240/Rules-and-Guidance.html

APPENDIX 1: HOW TO SUBMIT A COMPLAINT

WHERE TO SEND COMPLAINTS

[3.296]
Complaints should be submitted to:

Case Management Office
Ofwat
Centre City Tower
7 Hill Street
Birmingham
B5 4UA
E-mail: CaseManagementOffice@ofwat.gsi.gov.uk
Telephone: 0121 644 7500

CONTENTS OF A SUBMISSION

A submission should contain the following information to help us make a preliminary assessment of a relevant complaint.

A SUMMARY OF THE COMPLAINT

This should set out the CA98 or EU competition law prohibition(s) you believe have been infringed and why. It should also include details of:

- the alleged infringement, the parties involved and your relationship with the target of the complaint,
- the products or services connected to the supply of water and waste water services or activities in England and Wales,
- key dates of the alleged infringement,
- the detriment to the complainant,
- the detriment to customers and consumers in the market or related markets.

Please note that Ofwat is willing to receive anonymous complaints.

BACKGROUND MATERIAL

You should include the following information as a minimum.

- Business name, address, telephone number, e-mail address and the contact details of a person who can discuss the detail of the complaint.
- A brief explanation of the nature of your business and its scale (local, national, international, approximate turnover).
- Details of any closely related markets which are relevant to your complaint.
- Approximate market shares of key participants active in the market and any related markets which are relevant to your complaint,
- The nature of supply and/or demand for products/services in the market, and any related products/services in the market or related markets, which are relevant to your complaint.

SUPPORTING DOCUMENTATION

You should include:

- any relevant letters, emails, reports or other documents which detail the events which are the cause of your complaint,
- any other material that will assist us with understanding and substantiating your complaint.

If you cannot provide any of the above information, please explain why in your submission.

DECLARATION

If you are complaining on behalf of a regulated entity, whether a water undertaker or licensee, you should include a declaration that the information in your submission is correct and complete to the best of your knowledge. Your declaration should include:

- your name and signature;
- your position in the company; and
- the date.

PROCESS

Our case management office will acknowledge receipt of a complaint within ten working days, including an initial view as to whether the complaint meets the requirements set out above. If a submission does not meet these requirements, we will advise you what else may be needed before we will consider the complaint.

Should we decide to open a case in response to your complaint, Ofwat may send a non-confidential version of your submission to the parties named in your complaint. Ofwat may wish to do so prior to formally opening any investigation. If your submission contains confidential information, you should provide a separate non-confidential version that we can send to the target(s) of the complaint, as well as explaining why you believe the information to be confidential. We will consult you before revealing your identity and before revealing any confidential information that you have provided.

If Ofwat decides to investigate your complaint, we might request permission from you to publish details of the complaint, including your identity, on Ofwat's website.

If we issue a Statement of Objections, it is likely that we will need to reveal your identify to the addressee of the Statement of Objections. You should let us know if you are concerned about your identity being revealed.

If you need any further guidance on how to submit a complaint to Ofwat please contact our case management office.

(V) FINANCIAL SERVICES

FCA 2015/38
COMPETITION LAW INFRINGEMENT (DISCLOSURE) INSTRUMENT 2015

[3.297]

NOTES

The FCA Handbook is available on the FCA website at www.handbook.fca.org.uk/.

POWERS EXERCISED

[3.298]

(A) The Financial Conduct Authority makes this instrument in the exercise of the following powers and related provisions in the Financial Services and Markets Act 2000 ("the Act"):

(1) section 137A (The FCA's general rules);

(2) section 137T (General supplementary powers); and

(3) section 139A (Power of the FCA to give guidance).

(B) The rule-making powers listed above are specified for the purpose of section 138G (Rule-making instruments) of the Act.

COMMENCEMENT

(C) This instrument comes into force on 1 August 2015.

AMENDMENTS TO THE FCA HANDBOOK

(D) The Supervision manual (SUP) is amended in accordance with the Annex to this instrument.

CITATION

(E) This instrument may be cited as the Competition Law Infringement (Disclosure) Instrument 2015.

By order of the Board of the Financial Conduct Authority
2 July 2015

ANNEX
AMENDMENTS TO THE SUPERVISION MANUAL (SUP)

In this Annex, underlining indicates new text.

15.3 General notification requirements

. . .

Civil, criminal or disciplinary proceedings against a firm

15.3.15 R A *firm* must notify the *appropriate regulator* immediately if:

. . .

(3) disciplinary measures or sanctions have been imposed on the *firm* by any statutory or regulatory authority, competition authority, professional organisation or trade body (other than the *appropriate regulator*) or the *firm* becomes aware that one of those bodies has started an investigation into its affairs; or

. . .

. . .

Competition law infringements

15.3.32 R (1) *firm* must notify the *FCA* if it has or may have committed a significant infringement of any applicable competition law.

(2) A *firm* must make the notification as soon as it becomes aware, or has information which reasonably suggests, that a significant infringement has, or may have, occurred.

(3) (a) A *firm* must make the notification in writing unless (3)(b) applies.

(b) A *firm* may make the notification orally where it has made or will make an oral application for leniency or immunity covering the same subject matter to any competition authority.

15.3.33 G A notification under *SUP* 15.3.32R should include:

(1) information about any circumstances relevant to the infringement or possible infringement;

(2) identification of the relevant law; and

(3) information about any steps which the *firm* or other *person* has taken or intends to take to rectify or remedy the infringement or prevent any future potential occurrence.

15.3.34 G In determining whether a matter is significant, a *firm* should have regard to the actual or potential effect on competition, any customer detriment, and the duration of any infringement and implications for the *firm's* systems and controls.

15.3.35 G (1) Where a *firm* notifies the *FCA* under *SUP* 15.3.32R, the *firm* should not infer or assume that any lack of (or delay in) a response, objection or enforcement activity by the *FCA* or any other competition authority means that the agreement or conduct:

(a) does not infringe competition law; or

(b) is, or will be, immune from enforcement.

(2) Notification under *SUP* 15.3.32R is not sufficient to constitute an application for leniency or immunity from penalty in any subsequent investigation under Chapter 1 of the Competition Act 1998 or article 101 of the *Treaty.*

. . .

15 Annex 1 R Application of SUP 15 to incoming EEA firms and incoming Treaty firms

. . .

Applicable Sections		Application
SUP 15.3.2G	Insolvency, bankruptcy and winding up	Apply in so far as responsibility for the matter in question is not reserved by an *EU* instrument to the *firm's Home State regulator*
SUP 15.3.32R to SUP 15.3.35G	Competition law infringements	Apply in so far as responsibility for the matter in question is not reserved by an *EU* instrument to the *firm's Home State regulator*
. . .		

ENFORCEMENT OF THE COMPETITION ACT 1998 (PSR PS15/2.1)
A guide to the PSR's powers and procedures (CA98 Guidance)(August 2015)

[3.299]

NOTES

CONTENTS

1 OVERVIEW

[3.300]

- We have powers to enforce the prohibitions under UK and EU competition law on anticompetitive agreements and conduct in relation to participation in payment systems.
- Our competition law functions are 'concurrent' – the CMA and possibly other regulators such as the FCA may also exercise them in this sector.

INTRODUCTION

1.1 Part 1 of the Competition Act 1998 (CA98) and Article 101 and Article 102 of the Treaty on the Functioning of the European Union (TFEU) prohibit anti-competitive agreements and abuses of a dominant position.[1]

1.2 As from 1 April 2015, under the concurrency provisions in the Financial Services (Banking Reform) Act 2013 (FSBRA),[2] we have had powers under CA98 in relation to agreements and conduct relating to participation in payment systems.[3] The concept of 'participation' in payment systems is defined in section 42 FSBRA and includes the operation of the payment system and the provision of infrastructure and payment services.[4] The powers relate to all payment systems falling within the definition in section 41 FSBRA, and not only to those systems that have been designated by HM Treasury under section 43 FSBRA.

1.3 We also have powers to carry out market studies as provided by the Enterprise Act 2002 (EA02) and to refer markets to the Competition and Markets Authority (CMA) for detailed investigation. These powers are covered separately in the PSR's Markets Guidance.

1.4 These competition powers may also be exercised by the CMA with regard to all sectors of the economy so, in respect of payment systems, the CMA and the PSR have concurrent competition law functions ('concurrent functions') and the PSR is a 'concurrent regulator'.

1.5 This guidance explains how we will exercise our concurrent functions in respect of the prohibitions in Chapter I and Chapter II CA98 and/or Article 101 and Article 102 TFEU[5] in relation to participation in payment systems within the UK, in particular the enforcement processes we will follow, and how these relate to our other powers and duties.[6]

1.6 This document focuses on the procedural aspects of the PSR's powers of enforcement under CA98. For guidance on the application of the CA98 prohibitions, please refer to the CMA's guidance documents, including *Agreements and concerted practices* (OFT401) and *Abuse of a dominant position* (OFT402), both adopted by the CMA Board, which apply to all areas of economic activity, including the payments industry.[7] We have not sought to duplicate all the guidance that the CMA has issued, with its greater experience. However, where CMA guidance is more detailed than ours in a material respect, we shall consider such guidance in deciding how to proceed.

NOTES

1 We do not have powers to prosecute the criminal cartel offence in section 188 EA02.

2 Sections 59 to 66 FSBRA

3 As from 1 April 2015 the FCA, under the concurrency provisions in sections 234I to 234O of the Financial Services and Markets Act 2000 (FSMA), has had competition law powers, including powers under CA98 in relation to agreements and conduct relating to the provision of financial services. The FCA has published its own guidance on its concurrent competition powers which can be found at www.fca.org.uk/publication/policy/ps15-18.pdf

4 The Bank of England is not to be regarded as a participant of any kind in any payment system (see section 42(8) FSBRA).

5 Article 35 of Regulation 1/2003 requires Member States to designate National Competition Authorities (NCAs) to apply Articles 101 and Article 102 TFEU. The PSR is designated as a NCA by Regulation 3 of the Competition Act 1998 and Other Enactments (Amendment) Regulations 2004.

6 This document constitutes advice and information issued pursuant to section 52 CA98, referred to in this document as guidance for the sake of convenience.

7 These guidance documents are available on the CMA's website at www.gov.uk/cma, along with all other CMA guidance, or OFT guidance adopted by the CMA Board, referred to in this document.

LEGISLATIVE CONTEXT AND OTHER GUIDANCE DOCUMENTS

1.7 The legal framework for the PSR's CA98 concurrent enforcement powers in relation to participation in payment systems in the UK includes (but is not limited to):

- Articles 101 and 102 TFEU and Regulation 1/2003[8]
- Competition Act 1998
- Competition Act 1998 (Competition and Markets Authority's Rules) Order 2014 (CA98 Rules)
- Competition Act 1998 (Concurrency) Regulations 2014 (Concurrency Regulations)
- Financial Services (Banking Reform) Act 2013
- Enterprise Act 2002
- Enterprise and Regulatory Reform Act 2013

1.8 Additionally, we must have regard to:

- the CMA's guidance on the appropriate level of a penalty imposed under section 36 CA98[9]
- the CMA's statement of policy in relation to the imposition of penalties under section 40A CA98[10]
- the CMA's guidance as to the circumstances in which it may be appropriate to accept commitments under section 31A CA98[11]

1.9 The CMA's Guidance on concurrent application of competition law to regulated industries (Concurrency Guidance)[12] explains how the concurrency regime operates in relation to CA98.

1.10 This guidance sets out how we will carry out enforcement action under our powers under CA98.[13] Our approach will be informed by the statutory rules that apply to CA98 enforcement. We refer where relevant in this guidance to the CMA's Procedural Guidance[14] and other guidance documents.

1.11 This guidance represents the PSR's procedures as at the date of publication. We may revise this guidance from time to time – for example, to reflect changes to our practice and procedures in the light of our developing experience or because of changes in the law. Our website will always contain the most up-to-date version.

NOTES

8 Council Regulation (EC) No 1/2003 of 16 December 2002 on the implementation of the rules on competition laid down in Articles 101 and 102 of the Treaty, OJ L1, 4.1.2003, p 1.

9 The guidance in force as at the date of this document is OFT423 *OFT's guidance as to the appropriate amount of a penalty* (which has been adopted by the CMA Board). We are required to have regard to this guidance by virtue of section 38(8) CA98.

10 CMA4 *Administrative Penalties: Statement of Policy on the CMA's Approach.* We are required to have regard to this guidance by virtue of section 40B(6) CA98.

11 OFT407 *Enforcement* (which has been adopted by the CMA Board). We are required to have regard to this guidance by virtue of section 31D(8) CA98.

12 CMA10, available at

Part 3 CMA and other Guidelines

www.gov.uk/government/publications/guidance-on-concurrent-application-of-competition-law-to-regulated-industries

13 For guidance on the processes and procedures that the we will apply in relation to our regulatory functions under FSBRA, see our *Powers and Procedures Guidance*: www.psr.org.uk/powers-and-procedures-guidance

14 *Guidance on the CMA's Investigation Procedures in Competition Act 1998 cases* (CMA8)

2 OUR APPROACH TO USING OUR CA98 POWERS

[3.301]

- We seek to exercise our functions transparently and fairly, and parties are able to challenge our procedural and substantive decisions.
- We are a national competition authority under Regulation 1/2003, which places certain obligations on us in the application of EU competition law.
- Only one regulator can exercise prescribed CA98 functions in any one case at any one time, and there are procedures in place to ensure the best-placed authority takes a case forward.
- There may be instances in which we take enforcement action under our other powers as well as CA98.
- Our 'primacy' obligations mean that before exercising certain of our powers set out in FSBRA we have a duty to consider whether it would be more appropriate to proceed under CA98.

FAIR AND TRANSPARENT PROCESS

2.1 We aim to exercise our functions as transparently as possible, recognising the importance of ensuring that appropriate information is provided on our decision-making process and also that we should be open and accessible both to affected stakeholders and the general public. The legal framework for the disclosure of information gathered under CA98 is different from that for information gathered under our regulatory functions. This guidance sets out our approach to transparency in relation to CA98 investigations and how we will liaise with parties under investigation and third parties.

2.2 We are also committed to ensuring fair treatment in the exercise of our powers: this protects the rights of those we are investigating and of third parties, and assists us in our decision-making. We must carry out our investigations and make decisions in a procedurally fair, transparent and proportionate manner, according to the standards of administrative law. In addition, we must comply with the Human Rights Act 1998.

2.3 Conducting an investigation involves taking many administrative decisions, e.g. setting deadlines, determining the scope of information requests, and deciding on the disclosure of information. Anyone who wishes to query such a decision should raise it with the case team (see section 4).

2.4 If it is not possible to resolve the dispute in this way, procedural complaints can be made to the PSR's Procedural Officer,[15] whose details can be found on our website. They may consider complaints that relate to:

- deadlines for parties to respond to information requests, to submit non-confidential versions of documents or to submit written representations on the Statement of Objections or Supplementary Statement of Objections (see section 5 below)
- requests for treatment of confidential information in documents on the PSR's case file, in a Statement of Objections or in a final decision
- requests for disclosure or non-disclosure of certain documents on the PSR's case file
- issues relating to oral hearings, e.g. the date of the hearing
- other significant procedural issues that may arise during the course of an investigation

2.5 The Procedural Officer is not able to review PSR decisions beyond those listed above, e.g. decisions on the scope of requests for information or decisions relating to the substance of a case.

2.6 The Procedural Officer will also chair any oral hearing and prepare a report assessing its fairness (see section 5 below). They will not otherwise be involved in the investigation.

2.7 The PSR has a process for the investigation of complaints made against us. Anyone who is directly affected by the PSR's actions or inactions – or anyone acting on such a person's behalf – can file a complaint against the PSR. Details of the complaints scheme and guidance on how to make a complaint are available on our website.[16] However, we note that we expect complaints in relation to CA98 procedural matters to be within the scope of the Procedural Officer's jurisdiction and that they will be dealt with by the Procedural Officer, who is established for that purpose. Ultimately, a party with sufficient interest can seek judicial review in the High Court of an administrative decision taken by the PSR.

2.8 Parties whose agreements or conduct are the subject of a decision specified in section 46 CA98 have a right of appeal on its merits to the Competition Appeal Tribunal (CAT). These decisions are:

- whether the Chapter I or Chapter II prohibition, or the prohibition in Article 101 or 102 TFEU has been infringed
- the imposition of a penalty for an infringement of Chapter I or Chapter II CA98 or Article 101 or Article 102 TFEU or the amount of such a penalty
- the cancellation of a block or parallel exemption
- withdrawing the benefit of a regulation of the European Commission pursuant to Article 29(2) of Regulation 1/2003
- not releasing commitments pursuant to a request made under section 31A(4)(b)(i) CA98
- releasing commitments under section 31A(4)(b)(ii)
- directions and interim measures in relation to agreements or conduct

2.9 A party can also appeal the imposition of an administrative penalty imposed on it under section 40A CA98[17] to the CAT.

2.10 Third parties with a sufficient interest in a decision of the type set out in section 47 CA98 also have a right of appeal to the CAT. Such decisions include:

- a decision as to whether the Chapter I or Chapter II prohibition, or the prohibition in Article 101 or 102 TFEU has been infringed
- a decision to accept or release commitments, or to accept a variation of commitments (unless that variation is not material in any respect)
- a decision to make directions, or a decision not to make directions, under section 35 CA98

NOTES

15 Their role is similar to that carried out by the CMA's Procedural Officer in relation to procedural complaints. See www.gov.uk/proceduralofficer-raising-procedural-issues-in-cma-cases#procedural-officer-role-scope-and-process-competition-act-1998-investigations

16 See: www.psr.org.uk/complaints-against-psr

17 See footnote 33 in relation to administrative penalties.

REGULATION 1/2003

2.11 We are a national competition authority (NCA) for the purposes of Regulation 1/2003 and as such are a member of the European Competition Network (ECN). We have certain obligations under Article 3 of Regulation 1/2003, including that we must apply Article 101 and/or Article 102 TFEU in any case where we are applying the Chapter I or Chapter II prohibition respectively if trade between EU Member States may be affected. We must notify the European Commission if we open an investigation involving the application of Article 101 and/or Article 102 TFEU. This assists in the efficient allocation of cases between NCAs and as between NCAs and the European Commission.

2.12 The European Commission has the power to take over cases involving an alleged breach of Article 101 and/or Article 102 TFEU from NCAs such as the PSR, by initiating proceedings. If we have already opened an investigation, then the European Commission would consult with us before initiating its own proceedings.[18]

2.13 We may not prohibit an agreement or concerted practice under national competition law if it would not be prohibited under Article 101 TFEU. This does not prevent the application of stricter national law to an agreement if it predominantly pursues different objectives from those pursued by Article 101. We may apply national law which is stricter than Article 102 TFEU in respect of unilateral conduct.[19]

NOTES

18 Article 11(6), Regulation 1/2003

19 Article 3, Regulation 1/2003

CASE ALLOCATION UNDER CONCURRENCY ARRANGEMENTS AND THE UKCN

2.14 Our functions under CA98 in respect of participation in payment systems are concurrent with those of the CMA and, in certain instances, other regulators that have concurrent functions over some payment systems participants (for example, the FCA).

2.15 While cases may be transferred between concurrent authorities, only one authority can exercise prescribed functions in respect of a case at any moment.[20] The Concurrency Regulations and Concurrency Guidance set out how information will be shared between relevant competent authorities and how cases will be allocated. The general principle is that the authority that will be responsible for a case depends on which one is better or best placed to do so.[21] We will cooperate with the CMA and other concurrent regulators to ensure the effective and efficient handling of cases in relation to participation in payment systems. If agreement cannot be reached, the CMA may determine which relevant competent authority should exercise their power. The PSR's Memorandum of Understanding (MoU) with the CMA sets out the framework for our cooperation.[22]

2.16 We are part of the UK Competition Network (UKCN), which is an alliance of the CMA and UK sector regulators that have a duty to promote competition in the interests of consumers. The UKCN's Statement of Intent can be found as an annex to the Concurrency Guidance.

2.17 The PSR will participate in, and support the CMA in its lead participation in, the activities of the European Competition Network and the International Competition Network, and other international forums as appropriate.

NOTES

20 The prescribed functions include the opening of a formal investigation and the taking of a decision within the meaning of section 46(3) CA98, including a decision as to whether the Chapter I or Chapter II prohibition has been infringed.

21 See Concurrency Guidance paragraph 3.22, which contains a list of factors relevant to which authority will be best placed.

22 See: www.psr.org.uk/how-psr-regulates/memorandums-understanding. [*Note: Our wesbite will be updated with the MoU agreed and adopted by the CMA and the PSR.*]

RELATIONSHIP WITH FSBRA

2.18 The PSR has a broad range of legal tools to address competition concerns, and when considering a competition issue, we will assess the appropriateness of the available tools when deciding what action, if any, to take. These tools include market reviews under FSBRA and market studies under EA02 or enforcement action under CA98 or FSBRA. While we have a specific primacy obligation in section 62 FSBRA, this applies only to the five powers listed (see paragraphs 2.23 to 2.24).

2.19 Our guiding principle will be to choose the tool that will allow us most efficiently and effectively to investigate and if necessary remedy the possible harm that we have identified. To a large extent, this will be influenced by the facts in front of us (see paragraph 2.26 for examples). Procedural factors may be relevant: for instance, as noted (paragraph 1.2), our concurrent powers extend beyond the participants in the payment systems that we regulate.

2.20 Anti-competitive agreements or abusive conduct by participants in payment systems may breach regulatory obligations under FSBRA or other legislation, as well as competition law. Accordingly, there may be instances in which we take enforcement action under our other powers as well as CA98, in parallel or sequentially. We will act reasonably and proportionately when considering taking other enforcement action (such as imposing a penalty or publishing details of a compliance failure) and, for example, the level of any penalty to be imposed.[23] We will also take into account penalties levied by authorities in connected cases.

2.21 We will make clear when using our formal information gathering powers which powers we are using and the nature of the suspected infringement(s) that we are investigating. Where more than one of our enforcement powers is considered to be potentially appropriate, we may make separate information requests under different information gathering powers. However, we will seek to decide as early as possible what is likely to be the most appropriate power(s) to deal with the specific agreement or conduct in question, and we aim to be proportionate in respect of the use of our formal information gathering powers.

2.22 In some circumstances we may begin an investigation under CA98 and subsequently decide that action under our other powers is more appropriate, or vice versa. In such cases we will inform the party or parties involved.

NOTES

[23] The PSR's guidance on the imposition of penalties under FSBRA is set out in our *Penalties Guidance*, available at www.psr.org.uk/psrpenalties-guidance.

'Primacy'

2.23 We are bound by statutory provisions giving 'primacy' to CA98 enforcement in certain situations.[24] This means that, before exercising certain of our powers set out in FSBRA (listed in paragraph 2.24 below), we have a duty to consider whether it would be more appropriate to proceed under CA98. If we consider that it would be more appropriate to proceed under CA98, we must do so rather than exercise that other power.

2.24 The specified powers are the powers under:

- section 54 FSBRA to give a direction (apart from the power to give a general direction)
- section 55 FSBRA to impose a requirement (apart from the power to impose a generally-imposed requirement)
- section 56 FSBRA to require the operator a regulated payment system or a payment service provider (PSP) with direct access to grant access to that payment system
- section 57 FSBRA to change the fees, charges, terms and conditions of an agreement relating to a regulated payment system
- section 58 FSBRA to require the disposal of an interest in the operator of a regulated payment system

2.25 We will determine on a case-by-case basis whether it may be more appropriate to proceed under CA98. We will look at the potential harm to competition raised by the conduct or agreement in question, the resource and timing implications of the actions available to us, and the potential outcomes (including their suitability for addressing the issues identified) and deterrent effect of those actions. Other factors may also be relevant to our considerations.[25]

2.26 As noted above at paragraph 2.18, we have a broad range of legal tools to address competition concerns. Some cases would appear to fall more naturally for investigation under CA98 (such as collusion amongst rivals to fix prices or allocate customers or markets; unilateral strategic conduct by a participant to exclude rivals). In others it will be clear that CA98 is not the appropriate legal instrument, for example, if the proposed action relates to behaviour of a single undertaking that is not dominant, or if the behaviour does not appear likely to be capable of affecting competition.

NOTES

[24] Section 62 FSBRA

[25] See the CMA's *'Baseline' annual report on concurrency*, April 2014, CMA24, paragraph 47, which states that: the use of competition law may encourage companies to think in terms of the effects of their activities rather than compliance with specific rules; there may be greater flexibility with competition law, compared to ex ante regulation which may be reviewed only periodically; and the application of competition law in regulated sectors may set a precedent across the regulated sector and more widely in the economy.

3 CASE INITIATION

[3.302]

- We may be alerted to possible CA98 infringements from a variety of sources, including other work we are undertaking, or information shared with us by others.

- We cannot investigate every possible CA98 infringement of which we become aware, and must prioritise which cases to take forward.
- When we open an investigation, we will generally provide the parties we are investigating with basic information about the case, though we will delay doing so if it could prejudice our investigation.

SOURCES OF POTENTIAL CA98 INVESTIGATIONS

3.1 We may be alerted to possible CA98 infringements from a variety of sources:

- Complaints from the public or businesses. Such complainants may be granted 'Formal Complainant' status by the PSR.[26]
- Super-complaints from bodies designated under section 68 FSBRA.[27]
- Referrals from other authorities. This could include information shared by the CMA under the concurrency arrangements or information received from the European Commission or NCAs.
- Applications for leniency.
- Applications made under sections 56 and 57 FSBRA.
- Our own enquiries and activities in relation to payment systems.
- Market studies or other own-initiative work or intelligence-gathering.

3.2 Participants in regulated payment systems should bring actual and possible contraventions to the PSR's attention, as they are obliged to do under General Direction 1, thus: *'A participant must deal with the PSR in an open and cooperative way, and must disclose to the PSR appropriately anything relating to the participant which could materially adversely impact advancement of the PSR's statutory objectives and duties'*. See also paragraphs 6.5 to 6.9.

3.3 Complaints from the public or businesses about possible CA98 infringements can be made by contacting:

Payment Systems Regulator
25 The North Colonnade
Canary Wharf
London
E14 5HS
Email: PSRcomplaints@psr.org.uk

3.4 We also participate in the FCA's Whistleblowing programme, details of which can be found on the FCA's website (including contact details).[28] Whistleblowers are individuals who want to provide information about wrongdoing in the regulated sector and want their information and identity to be treated confidentially. Such whistleblowers can be employees/contractors of firms who meet the criteria in the Public Interest Disclosure Act 1998 or other individuals (for example, consultants, associates or employees of other regulated or non-regulated firms).

3.5 The PSR does not offer immunity from criminal offences. However, individuals who have been involved in the behaviour in question may wish to familiarise themselves with the CMA's leniency policy in relation to cartel activity (see section 6) to see if it may be relevant to them. They may be eligible to apply to the CMA for immunity from criminal prosecution for the cartel offence under section188 EA02.

NOTES

26 We will follow the CMA's Procedural Guidance (*Guidance on the CMA's investigation procedures in Competition Act 1998 cases*, March 2014 (CMA8)) and the OFT guideline *Involving third parties in Competition Act investigations* (OFT451), adopted by the CMA Board, with regard to the granting of Formal Complainant status to any person who meets the criteria set by the CMA.

27 We have produced guidance on how designated bodies can bring a super-complaint (*Super-Complaints Guidance*). See: www.psr.org.uk/how-psr-regulates/complaints-and-disputes/super-complaints

28 www.fca.org.uk/site-info/contact/whistleblowing

DECIDING WHETHER TO OPEN AN INVESTIGATION – PRIORITISATION ASSESSMENT

3.6 We cannot investigate every complaint or possible infringement of competition law of which we are made aware and must therefore prioritise which work to undertake.

3.7 We will decide on a case-by-case basis whether to open an investigation. In deciding whether to investigate a possible infringement of competition law, we will have regard to several factors, including:

- the likely impact of the investigation in terms of the direct and indirect consumer benefit that investigation may bring
- the significance of the case (including the possible deterrent effect of an investigation or decision)
- the risks involved in taking on a case (including the likelihood of determining whether or not there has been an infringement)
- whether other tools are available that would be more appropriate to achieve the same or a better outcome (see paragraphs 2.18 and 2.19)
- the resources required to carry out the investigation

3.8 These criteria are illustrative, rather than exhaustive. We also draw attention to the PSR's Administrative Priority Framework, which applies to the exercise of all our statutory objectives, functions and duties.[29] We will keep our prioritisation assessment of any particular case under review and it may be that we need to close an investigation once it has been opened, if our assessment of its priority changes. The CMA has the power to take over an investigation we have opened.

3.9 Before launching any CA98 investigation we will consult the CMA, and discuss whether it (or possibly another concurrent regulator) should lead the investigation. Ultimately, the CMA may decide this (see paragraphs 2.14 and 2.15).

3.10 While we may assess the strength and quality of the available evidence, an administrative decision not to conduct an investigation, or to close an investigation after it has been opened, is not a decision on the merits of the case. It does not imply any view about the merits of a complaint or whether there has been a breach of competition law. Our choice of whether to take enforcement action is a question of how we use our resources effectively and efficiently. In some cases it may be appropriate to deal with suspected infringements of competition law without formal enforcement action. For example, we may alert parties to possible concerns without formally opening an investigation. Our prioritisation assessment underlies our decision as to whether or not to investigate a matter. However, if the PSR decides not to open a formal investigation into a matter under CA98, it is open to the CMA (or any other regulator with concurrent jurisdiction over the agreement or conduct in question) to take action under CA98, following consultation with the PSR (see paragraphs 2.14 and 2.15 and the Concurrency Guidance with regard to case allocation).

NOTES

29 See: www.psr.org.uk/administrative-priority-framework

OPENING A FORMAL INVESTIGATION

3.11 If we decide to open a formal investigation under CA98, we will generally send the party or parties under investigation a case initiation letter setting out brief details of the conduct which we are investigating, the relevant legislation, our indicative proposed timetable and contact details. We will generally also inform the person who has provided the information resulting in the case (for example, the person making a complaint). However, we will not communicate with the party or parties under investigation nor with third parties at the start of an investigation if this may prejudice the investigation (for example, where we intend to conduct unannounced inspections), and we may need to limit the amount of information provided if there are good grounds for doing so (for example, to protect the identity of a whistleblower or a complainant).

3.12 We may in some circumstances publish basic information about the investigation, in accordance with our powers under section 25A CA98 (for example, if we consider that it may assist us in our investigation or is necessary for market stability). If we publish information identifying a party whose activities are being investigated, and subsequently decide to terminate the investigation into that party, we will (in compliance with our statutory obligations) publish a notice stating that the activities of that party are no longer being investigated.

4 CONDUCT OF THE INVESTIGATION

[3.303]

- We will assemble a case team to conduct the investigation, headed by a Case Sponsor who will take certain key decisions up to and including any decision to issue a Statement of Objections.
- We will keep parties informed on the progress of our investigation, including holding 'state of play' meetings.
- We have formal information gathering powers to investigate suspected CA98 infringements.
- We can order interim directions in order to prevent significant damage or protect the public interest.
- There are several potential outcomes of an investigation, including case closure, finding no grounds for action, accepting commitments or finding an infringement.

THE CASE TEAM AND DECISION-MAKERS

4.1 The PSR will assemble a case team to conduct the investigation. This may consist of case officers, investigators, lawyers, economists, financial analysts and others with the necessary expertise from across the PSR and the FCA, as appropriate. Each investigation will have a Case Sponsor, who will take the following decisions, as appropriate:

- To decide whether there is sufficient evidence to issue a Statement of Objections (see paragraphs 5.1 to 5.6).
- To close a case on grounds of administrative priorities (before or after the issue of a Statement of Objections (see paragraph 4.16).
- To make an interim measures direction (see paragraphs 4.12 to 4.15).
- To accept commitments offered by a party under investigation (see paragraphs 4.19 to 4.22).
- Whether a case is appropriate for settlement (see paragraphs 6.10 to 6.19).

4.2 These decisions are described in more detail in the relevant paragraphs, including in relation to the additional approvals needed for certain decisions.

KEEPING PARTIES INFORMED

4.3 The PSR expects to provide case updates to parties under investigation and Formal Complainants either by telephone or in writing. We will also offer 'state of play' meetings to parties under investigation. We use these meetings to ensure that the parties are aware of the stage the investigation has reached, and inform it of the next steps and the likely timing of these, subject to any restrictions due to confidentiality or market sensitivity.

4.4 We are likely to hold state of play meetings after a case has been formally opened (unless this could prejudice the ongoing investigation), before the decision is taken to issue a Statement of Objections (see section 5) and after we have received the oral and written representations on the statement of objections.

4.5 The PSR will keep parties under investigation and Formal Complainants to the investigation informed of the anticipated case timetable and any changes to this.

INFORMATION GATHERING

4.6 In order to reach well-evidenced decisions, we may need detailed information and data. We expect to require this both from the subjects of our investigations and from third parties. We appreciate that providing such information may be onerous, and we will seek to make the process as efficient as possible (without prejudicing the ongoing investigation). This may entail sharing draft information requests before they are formally issued, or discussing with parties how they hold data in order to tailor our requests to their systems.

4.7 Once we have 'reasonable grounds for suspecting'[30] an infringement of the prohibitions contained in Part 1 of the CA98 and/or Article 101 or Article 102 of the TFEU, we may use the information gathering powers provided by the CA98. These are described in the CMA's Procedural Guidance.[31] In summary, we:

- Can issue requests for information and documents (commonly referred to as section 26 notices) in writing.
- Can conduct compulsory interviews with any individual connected to a party under investigation.[32]
- Have the power to enter business and domestic premises, require the production of documents and take copies of documents. Such entry may be either with or (for business premises) without a warrant. If we have obtained a warrant, we may search for and seize documents.
- May impose a penalty on any business or individual who (without reasonable excuse) does not comply with our information gathering powers.[33]

4.8 We also have extensive powers to obtain information from those subject to our regulation under FSBRA (as set out in the PSR's *Powers & Procedures Guidance*),[34] and other than where prohibited by law, we may use information we obtain in other ways during an investigation under CA98. However, once we have decided to launch an investigation under CA98, we would use the tools provided by CA98 in order to conduct that investigation.

4.9 The CMA's Procedural Guidance describes the limits on its powers of investigation under CA98.[35] Those limits apply equally to the PSR so that we:

- cannot require the production or disclosure of privileged communications[36]
- cannot force a party to provide answers that would require an admission that it has infringed the law
- are subject to strict rules governing the extent to which we are permitted to disclose confidential and sensitive information (see section 7)

4.10 We expect to receive a separate non-confidential version of any document or materials containing sensitive or otherwise confidential information, along with a clear explanation as to why the redacted information should be considered confidential.[37]

4.11 Where information has been gathered using powers under CA98, we may use it to investigate other matters under CA98 or other legislation such as FSBRA, subject to and in accordance with the relevant legislation, case law and restrictions relating to the use of leniency information shared with us by other competition authorities set out in paragraph 6.7 (see also section 7).

NOTES

30 This is the legal test under section 25 CA98.

31 *Competition Act 1998: Guidance on the CMA's investigation procedures in Competition Act 1998 cases*, March 2014 (CMA8), Chapter 6

32 Under section 26A CA98

33 Under section 40A CA98, we may impose penalties for parties failing to comply with our investigation gathering powers without reasonable excuse. In determining whether, and if so how, to proceed under section 40A CA98, we will have regard to the CMA's Policy Statement on Administrative Penalties (*Administrative penalties: Statement of Policy on the CMA's approach* (CMA4)). In addition, it is a criminal offence to provide false or misleading information, or to destroy, falsify or conceal documents (subject to certain statutory defences and conditions).

34 See: www.psr.org.uk/powers-and-procedures-guidance

35 See its Chapter 7

36 See section 30 CA98

37 However, the PSR may nonetheless need to disclose such Information. Part 9 EA02 applies to the disclosure of information gathered under CA98.

TAKING URGENT ACTION TO PREVENT SIGNIFICANT DAMAGE OR TO PROTECT THE PUBLIC INTEREST

4.12 Under section 35 CA98, we have the power to require a party to comply with temporary directions (referred to as 'interim measures') while we complete the investigation. In summary, we can require a party to comply with temporary directions where:

- the investigation has been started but not yet concluded, and
- we consider it necessary to act urgently either to prevent significant damage to a person or category of persons, or to protect the public interest

Part 3 CMA and other Guidelines

4.13 We can impose interim measures on our own initiative or in response to a request to do so. Any person who considers that the alleged anti-competitive behaviour of another party is causing them significant damage may apply to us to take interim measures. If a person fails to comply with the interim measures without reasonable excuse, we will apply to court for an order to require compliance within a specified time limit. When we consider whether to impose interim measures, we will have regard to the factors set out in CMA8 paragraphs 8.12 to 8.16.

4.14 In terms of the procedure we will follow:

- Any application should be made to the case team in writing, providing as much detail as possible as to why the grounds set out in section 35 CA98 are met.
- The Case Sponsor may provisionally decide to give an interim measures direction (a provisional decision which may follow a complaint or be on our own initiative). We will write to the party to which the directions are addressed setting out the terms of the proposed directions and the reasons for giving them.
- We will also allow that party a reasonable opportunity to make representations. Given the nature of the interim measures process, the time allowed may be short.
- We will allow the party to inspect documents on our file, other than those parts that are confidential (see section 7).
- After taking into account any representations, and having satisfied ourselves as to the adequacy of the evidence we are relying upon, taking into account all the circumstances of case, we will make our final decision and inform the applicant and any Formal Complainants and the party against which the order is being sought. The Case Sponsor is responsible for deciding whether to give an interim measures direction, subject to obtaining the approval of PSR senior management.
- We will publish any interim measures direction we issue.

4.15 If the Case Sponsor provisionally decides to reject an application for interim measures:

- We will consult the applicant and any other Formal Complainants before doing so by sending a provisional dismissal letter setting out the principal reasons for rejecting the application.
- We will give them an opportunity to submit comments and/or additional information within a certain time, the length of which will depend on the case.
- If the comments from the applicant or Formal Complainant contain confidential information, a separate non-confidential version must be submitted at the same time (see section 7 on handling confidential information). We may provide this non-confidential version to the party under investigation if we think it would be appropriate to do so, such as where it may be relevant for the rights of defence.
- We will consider any comments and further evidence submitted within the specified time limit. After considering the additional information provided, if the Case Sponsor still decides to reject the application, we will send a letter to the applicant and any other Formal Complainants and normally the party against which the directions are sought to inform them and give our reasons.
- However, if the comments and/or additional information from any of these parties leads the Case Sponsor to change his or her provisional view and to decide that we should make an interim measures direction, we will inform the applicant, any other Formal Complainants, and the party against which the directions are sought, and the interim measures application will continue as set out in paragraph 4.14.

POSSIBLE OUTCOMES OF INVESTIGATION

4.16 There are several ways in which an investigation under CA98 can be resolved.[38] In summary:

- We will issue a Statement of Objections where our provisional view is that the conduct under investigation amounts to an infringement. After doing this and receiving the parties' representations, we can issue a final decision that the conduct amounts to an infringement, and can impose a penalty and/or directions on the party or parties concerned (see sections 5 and 6).
- We can issue a decision that there are no grounds for action (either before or after issuing a Statement of Objections) if we have not found sufficient evidence of an infringement (see section 5).
- We can close our investigation on the grounds of administrative priorities at any time (before or after issuing a Statement of Objections). In these circumstances, we may also write to parties explaining that, although we are not currently pursuing a formal investigation, we have concerns about their conduct. We will consult Formal Complainants before taking a decision to close an investigation on grounds of administrative priorities.
- We can accept commitments from a party about its future conduct (see paragraphs 4.19 to 4.22).

4.17 Infringement decisions,[39] penalty decisions and decisions that there are no grounds for action will be taken by the Competition Decisions Committee (see sections 5 and 6). All other decisions are the responsibility of the Case Sponsor, subject to obtaining the approval of PSR senior management for any decision to accept commitments.

4.18 As noted (paragraph 2.22), it is possible that information obtained during an investigation under CA98 may lead to and/or be used in enforcement action under FSBRA.

Commitments

4.19 Under section 31A CA98, we may accept commitments from one or more parties for the purposes of addressing the competition concerns that we are investigating in a particular case. Commitments are binding promises from a party in relation to its future conduct.

4.20 We will have regard to the CMA's guidance on the circumstances in which it may be appropriate to accept commitments[40] and the CMA's process when considering commitments (e.g. paragraph 10.20 of CMA8).[41] If we choose to accept commitments we will close our investigation and not take an infringement decision.

4.21 We will give notice of any proposal to accept commitments and allow at least eleven working days for interested third parties to give their views on the proposed commitments. After receiving responses to this consultation on the proposed commitments, we will have a meeting with each party that has offered commitments to inform them of the general nature of responses received and to indicate whether we consider that changes are necessary to the commitments before we would consider accepting them. If the parties offer material modifications to the proposed commitments, we will allow interested third parties a further period of at least six working days in which to comment on the modified commitments. We may repeat the process, although we do not wish the process of considering commitments to become unduly protracted.

4.22 If we accept commitments, then we cannot continue the investigation, make a final decision, or order interim measures.[42] However, we can take such action if we have reasonable grounds to suspect that there has been a material change in circumstances, a party has not adhered to the commitments we accepted, or if the information that led us to accept the commitments was incomplete, false, or misleading in a material particular.[43]

NOTES

[38] See paragraph 7.11 below in relation to taking action using the PSR's powers under other statutes, which could be in addition to one of the outcomes listed below.

[39] Other than in settlement cases, for which, see paragraphs 6.10 to 6.19 below.

[40] Annexe A in *Enforcement* (OFT407), which has been adopted by the CMA Board.

[41] *Competition Act 1998: Guidance on the CMA's investigation procedures in Competition Act 1998 cases* (CMA8), March 2014

[42] Section 31B(1) CA98

[43] Section 31B(2) CA98

5 THE STATEMENT OF OBJECTIONS AND FOLLOWING STEPS

[3.304]

- We will issue a Statement of Objections setting out our provisional findings if we consider that the conduct under investigation amounts to an infringement.
- We will provide the addressees of a Statement of Objections with access to the file of documents relating to the matters set out within it. We may provide third parties with access to the non-confidential version of the Statement of Objections, if they could materially assist our investigation.
- Addressees have the opportunity to make written and oral representations, which will be considered by a Competition Decisions Committee who will be appointed after the issuing of the Statement of Objections.
- If necessary, we may issue a Supplementary Statement of Objections or a Letter of Facts.
- If we propose to issue an infringement decision and impose a penalty, we will issue the addressee with a draft penalty statement setting out how the penalty will be calculated.
- The Competition Decisions Committee will be responsible for a final infringement decision or a decision that there are no grounds for action.

DECISION TO ISSUE A STATEMENT OF OBJECTIONS AND APPOINTMENT OF A COMPETITION DECISIONS COMMITTEE

5.1 Where our provisional view is that the conduct under investigation amounts to an infringement, we will issue a Statement of Objections to each party we consider to be responsible for the infringement (the addressee(s)). The Case Sponsor is responsible for the decision to issue a Statement of Objections, after consultation with other senior officials within the PSR.

5.2 A Competition Decisions Committee comprising at least three people will be appointed to be the final decision-maker on whether or not the party or parties under investigation have infringed the prohibitions contained in Chapter I or Chapter II of CA98/ Article 101(1) or 102 TFEU, once the Statement of Objections has been issued. It will be drawn from a panel appointed by the PSR Board to act as decision-makers in CA98 cases.

5.3 We will inform those parties of the identity of the Competition Decisions Committee members. However, the case team will remain the primary contact for parties, which will remain in place, and parties should not contact the Competition Decisions Committee directly.

THE STATEMENT OF OBJECTIONS

5.4 The Statement of Objections sets out our provisional view and proposed next steps. It gives the party accused of a breach of competition law an opportunity to know the full case against it and, if it chooses to do so, to respond formally.

5.5 The Statement of Objections will set out the facts and our legal and economic assessment of them which led to the provisional view that an infringement has occurred. It will also set out any action we propose to take, such as imposing financial penalties[44] and/or issuing directions to stop the infringement if we believe it is ongoing, as well as our reasons for taking that action.

5.6 We will keep parties under investigation and Formal Complainants informed of the anticipated case timetable and any changes to this as far as is possible and practicable while complying with our legal obligations, and to the extent that doing so would not prejudice ongoing investigations. We will normally announce the issue of a Statement of Objections on our website and make an announcement on a regulatory information service. However, we may decide not to announce the issue of a Statement of Objections, or may vary the extent of any publication, depending on the circumstances of the case and in particular the market sensitivity of any information we would otherwise publish. However, in any situation and at any time, listed companies may need to consider their own market disclosure obligations.

NOTES

44 See paragraphs 5.27 and 5.28 below in relation to the issuing of a draft penalty statement.

ACCESS TO THE FILE

5.7 At the same time as issuing the Statement of Objections, we will also give the addressee(s) of the Statement of Objections the opportunity to inspect the file. This is to ensure that they can properly defend themselves against the allegation of having breached competition law.

5.8 We will allow addressee(s) of the Statement of Objections a reasonable opportunity (typically six to eight weeks), to inspect copies of disclosable documents on the file. These are documents that relate to matters contained in the Statement of Objections, excluding certain confidential information and PSR internal documents.[45] Section 7 sets out the statutory framework for the disclosure of information. A person to whom we disclose information which is not made publicly available must not make any onward disclosure of that information without our consent.

5.9 We may, if appropriate, exclude routine administrative documents from the file and list them in a schedule, allowing parties to access specific documents upon request. Routine administrative documents would be those which do not relate to the substance of matters set out in a Statement of Objections, and could include, for example, correspondence setting up meetings.

5.10 In appropriate circumstances, we may consider establishing a confidentiality ring (within which confidential information may be disclosed to a defined group) or a data room at a specified location (within which access to confidential information may be given to a defined group).

NOTES

45 Confidential information and internal information are defined in Rule 1(1) of the CA98 Rules.

INVOLVING THIRD PARTIES

5.11 We may provide Formal Complainants (see paragraph 3.1 above) and third parties who may be able to assist materially our assessment of a case with an opportunity to submit written representations. We expect that disclosure of a non-confidential version of the Statement of Objections will be sufficient to enable third parties to provide us with informed comments: this will not generally include any annexed documents. Any such document is to be used only for making representations to us and must not be disclosed to others.

RESPONDING TO THE STATEMENT OF OBJECTIONS

5.12 We will give the recipients of the Statement of Objections the opportunity to make written and oral submissions to the Competition Decisions Committee.

5.13 We will set a reasonable time limit for parties to make written submissions. While this will depend on the circumstances, in particular the complexity of the case, we anticipate that we will give addressees between eight and twelve weeks to respond. We anticipate giving Formal Complainants and other third parties between four and six weeks to respond with any representations on the Statement of Objections.

5.14 Parties should submit non-confidential versions of their written submissions at the same time or shortly after submission of those submissions to us.

5.15 We will disclose non-confidential Formal Complainant and third party submissions to the addressees of the Statement of Objections. In some circumstances, it may be appropriate to share a party's representations with Formal Complainants and other third parties for their comment, e.g. where different versions of the facts have been put forward. We will seek submissions from the party regarding confidentiality before disclosing such representations to the Formal Complainant.

5.16 We will invite the addressee(s) of the Statement of Objections to make oral submissions to the Competition Decisions Committee. Any oral hearing will be chaired by the Procedural Officer.[46]

5.17 The oral hearing provides the addressee with an opportunity to highlight to the Competition Decisions Committee issues of particular importance to its case, and which have been set out in its written representations.

5.18 During the oral hearing, the Competition Decisions Committee and others present may ask questions about the addressee's written representations or questions of clarification. There is no obligation to answer, and addressees may respond to questions in writing after the hearing.

5.19 We will take a transcript of the oral hearing and the addressee will be asked to confirm the accuracy of the transcript and to identify any confidential information.

5.20 Following the oral hearing, the Procedural Officer will report to the Competition Decisions Committee, indicating any procedural issues that have been brought to the attention of the

Procedural Officer during the investigation and confirming whether the parties' right to be heard has been respected, including an assessment of the fairness of the procedure followed in the oral hearing.[47]

5.21 We will consider holding multi-party oral hearings in appropriate cases, such as where there are differing views on key issues. We will also consider on a case-by-case basis whether it is appropriate for interested third parties to be present at oral hearings.

NOTES

46 See paragraph 2.4 above.

47 Rule 6(7) and (8) of the CA98 Rules

STEPS FOLLOWING REPRESENTATIONS

Consideration

5.22 The Competition Decisions Committee will consider the Statement of Objections and representations from the addressee(s), Formal Complainants and third parties. It may draw on advice from PSR/FCA staff, including economists, lawyers and those with sectoral expertise.

Letter of facts

5.23 It may be that we acquire new evidence at this stage which supports the objection(s) contained in the Statement of Objections. If the Competition Decisions Committee proposes to rely on it to establish that an infringement has been committed, it will put that evidence to the addressee in a letter and give it an opportunity to respond to the new evidence. The time allowed for responding will depend on the volume and complexity of the new evidence. However, it will be shorter than the time given to respond to the Statement of Objections.

Supplementary Statement of Objections

5.24 If new information received by the Competition Decisions Committee in response to the Statement of Objections indicates that there is evidence of a different suspected infringement or there is a material change in the nature of the infringement described in the Statement of Objections, the Competition Decisions Committee will issue a Supplementary Statement of Objections setting out the new set of facts on which the Competition Decisions Committee proposes to rely to establish an infringement.

5.25 The Competition Decisions Committee will give the addressee a further opportunity to respond in writing and orally, and to inspect new documents on the file.

5.26 If it appears unlikely that engaging with Formal Complainants or other interested third parties at this stage will materially assist the investigation, the Competition Decisions Committee may decide to consult them on a more limited basis, or not at all.

Draft penalty statement

5.27 Where, once any written and oral representations made on the Statement of Objections have been considered, the Competition Decisions Committee is considering reaching an infringement decision and imposing a financial penalty on a party, we will provide that party with a draft penalty statement.[48] This will set out the key aspects[49] relevant to the calculation of the penalty that we propose to impose on that party, based on the information available to us at the time.[50] It will also include a brief explanation of the Competition Decisions Committee's reasoning for its provisional findings on each aspect. We will provide access to any new relevant documents on the file, which will include non-confidential versions of the draft penalty statements issued to other addressees of the Statement of Objections, if applicable.

5.28 Parties will be offered the opportunity to comment on the draft penalty statement in writing and to attend an oral hearing (in person or by telephone) with the Competition Decisions Committee.[51]

NOTES

48 Rule 11 of the CA98 Rules

49 Including, for example, the starting point percentage, the relevant turnover figure to be used, the duration of the infringement, any uplift for specific deterrence, any aggravating/mitigating factors (and the proposed increase/decrease in the penalty for these), and any adjustment proposed for proportionality.

50 Rule 11 of the CA98 Rules. For further information on how the CMA calculates the appropriate amount of a penalty, see *Guidance as to the appropriate amount of a penalty* (OFT423), which has been adopted by the CMA Board. We must have regard to the CMA's Guidance on penalties for the time being in force.

51 Rule 6 of the CA98 Rules

POSSIBLE DECISIONS

5.29 Following consideration of the Statement of Objections and representations from the addressees, Formal Complainants and third parties, including the possible additional steps described above (paragraphs 5.22 to 5.28), the Competition Decisions Committee will decide:

- that an infringement decision should be issued, or
- that a decision that there are no grounds for action[52] should be issued

5.30 As noted in paragraphs 2.18 to 2.20, we may consider that information discovered during a CA98 investigation may justify taking action under our powers under other legislation, such as FSBRA.

NOTES

52 There are alternative options for the closure of a case following the issuing of a Statement of Objections, which would not be taken by the Competition Decisions Committee. As noted (see paragraph 4.16), we may close a case on grounds

of administrative priorities at any time; however, we expect that we will rarely do so once it has reached the stage of issuing a Statement of Objections. The PSR may also accept commitments from parties to address its competition concerns at any stage, but we anticipate that we would be unlikely to do so at a very late stage, such as following receipt of the representations from the addressee(s) of the Statement of Objections.

Infringement decision

5.31 If the Competition Decisions Committee is satisfied that the legal test for establishing an infringement is met, we will issue an infringement decision to each party that has found to have infringed the law.[53] The infringement decision will set out the facts on which we rely to prove the infringement and the action that we are taking, and will address material representations made during the course of the investigation. In cases that involve more than one party, information that is confidential will be disclosed to other parties only if necessary. The infringement decision may impose a financial penalty (see section 6) and may also give directions to bring the infringement to an end.[54] If a party fails to comply with our directions, we may seek a court order to enforce them.[55]

5.32 We expect to issue a press announcement regarding any infringement decision, and to make an announcement on a regulatory information service. If so, we will inform the addressee(s) before the issue of the infringement decision and its announcement.

5.33 We will publish a summary, and a non-confidential version of the infringement decision, after seeking representations on confidentiality from the addressee(s) and third parties if relevant.

NOTES

[53] Section 31 CA98 and Rule 10(1) of the CA98 Rules

[54] Sections 32 and 33 CA98

[55] Section 34 CA98

Decision that there are no grounds for action

5.34 If, having completed its consideration of the case, the Competition Decisions Committee does not find sufficient evidence of a competition law infringement, it will decide to close the case.

5.35 Before a decision is taken that there are no grounds for action, we will consult any Formal Complainant in the case.

5.36 We will generally follow the same procedure as for issuing an infringement decision, including making an announcement and publishing a non-confidential version of the decision, although we may decide not to publish a no grounds for action decision, e.g. if it may affect an ongoing investigation under our other powers.

6 PENALTIES, LENIENCY AND SETTLEMENT

[3.305]

- If we find a competition law infringement, we may impose a penalty.
- We will have regard to the CMA's leniency policy when imposing penalties under CA98, meaning that we will grant immunity from, or a reduction in the penalty imposed on, a party meeting the criteria in the CMA's leniency policy.
- We may, at our discretion, agree a settlement with parties who admit that they have committed a CA98 infringement and agree to a streamlined procedure for the remainder of the investigation.

PENALTIES

6.1 If the Competition Decisions Committee finds an infringement of the prohibitions in Chapter I or Chapter II of CA98/ Article 101(1) or 102 TFEU, it may decide to impose a penalty on the infringing party or parties. The infringement decision will explain how the Competition Decisions Committee decided upon the appropriate level of penalty, having taken into account our statutory obligations in fixing a financial penalty[56] and the parties' written and oral representations on the draft penalty calculation.

NOTES

[56] Section 36(7A) CA98. We will have regard to the CMA's penalty guidance for the time being in force when setting the amount of a penalty (available at www.gov.uk/cma). The penalty guidance in force at the date of publication of this document is OFT423 *OFT's guidance as to the appropriate amount of a* penalty, which has been adopted by the CMA Board. See: www.gov.uk/government/uploads/system/uploads/attachment_data/file/284393/oft423.pdf

LENIENCY AND THE GENERAL DIRECTION 1 REGULATORY DUTY OF COOPERATION AND DISCLOSURE

6.2 Under leniency arrangements, parties who have participated in cartel activity such as price-fixing or market sharing can choose to give detailed confessions of their infringements. If that information provides a sufficient basis for a credible CA98 investigation to be taken forward, provided certain other conditions[57] are complied with, they will receive complete immunity from penalties for those infringements in return. Even where there is a pre-existing CA98 investigation, leniency and corresponding penalty reductions may also be available (in differing degrees) to parties that confess their infringements and provide information that adds significant value to that pre-existing CA98 investigation.

6.3 We will have regard to the CMA's penalties guidance and will apply the CMA's leniency policy when pursuing enforcement under CA98.[58] This means that we will grant immunity from a penalty, or give a reduction in the penalty, for the infringements of competition law, to an undertaking satisfying the criteria set out in the CMA's leniency policy.

6.4 We expect leniency applications to be made directly to the CMA (in particular, since we do not have concurrent powers under EA02 in relation to the prosecution of the cartel offence, and cannot grant immunity from prosecution in relation to this offence).

6.5 A participant in a regulated payment system must comply with its obligation under General Direction 1.[59] It must deal with the PSR in an open and cooperative way, and must disclose to the PSR appropriately anything relating to the participant which could materially adversely impact advancement of our statutory objectives and duties. This obligation is independent of the voluntary decision to apply for leniency: a step that a participant in a regulated payment system may choose not to take.[60]

6.6 Under the provisions for concurrent enforcement of the competition prohibitions by the CMA and sector regulators such as the PSR, we and the CMA will share between ourselves information on actual and possible cases relating to participation in payment systems (which may include leniency information),[61] subject to the restrictions in applicable legislation (including Part 9 EA02 and section 91 FSBRA).

6.7 We will use leniency information that we receive from the CMA only for the purpose of enforcement of the competition prohibitions unless the leniency applicant agrees otherwise. This restriction on use also applies to any information a resulting PSR CA98 investigation obtains. However, the fact that an applicant has applied for leniency will not prevent us from using information obtained by us from other sources or that applicant (e.g. pursuant to its General Direction 1 disclosure obligation), to take enforcement action under FSBRA or any other legislation.

6.8 When we receive leniency information from the CMA, we may also contact the leniency applicant to remind it of any obligation it might have to notify relevant matters to us under General Direction 1.

6.9 We expect prompt notification under General Direction 1 regardless of whether a participant in a regulated payment system is considering applying for leniency. While disclosures under General Direction 1 will depend on the event in question, the PSR expects to discuss matters with participants in regulated payment systems at an early stage. We do not think that the General Direction 1 regime and the CMA leniency regime conflict: participants in regulated payment systems can meet the requirements of both regimes if they act promptly.[62] However, participants who are concerned about the interaction of disclosures under General Direction 1 and the CMA's leniency regime should contact us and the CMA and we will work together and discuss how to proceed based on the individual circumstances of the case.

NOTES

57 The requirements for the grant of immunity and leniency can be found in full in OFT1495 *Applications for leniency and no-action in cartel cases – OFT's detailed guidance on the principles and process*, which has been adopted by the CMA Board. See: www.gov.uk/government/organisations/competition-and-markets-authority

58 See OFT423 and OFT1495, both of which have been adopted by the CMA Board.

59 See: www.psr.org.uk/psr-general-directions

60 This obligation is different from the conditions under which an applicant may receive leniency. A notification under General Direction 1 is not sufficient to constitute an application for leniency.

61 Leniency information for these purposes includes information which came into the possession of any of the CMA, its predecessor bodies, or any other public authority as a direct or indirect result of having been provided in the context of an application for leniency under the Chapter I prohibition CA98 or Article 101 TFEU. It includes any information that investigative measures resulting from the leniency application obtain.

62 Participants considering applying for leniency should have regard to the CMA's guidance. See OFT1495, adopted by the CMA Board, and in particular paragraphs 3.8 to 3.14 on conducting internal investigations and paragraphs 3.24 to 3.28 on maintaining confidentiality and securing evidence. Participants considering whether the criminal cartel offence is relevant should consult the CMA as necessary in order to ensure that, in complying with their General Direction 1 obligations, they do not prejudice the ability of their employees to benefit from immunity or leniency.

SETTLEMENT

6.10 Settlement is a voluntary process in which:

- a party admits that it has been party to an agreement or has been engaged in conduct which infringes one or more of the prohibitions in Chapter I or Chapter II of CA98/ Article 101(1) TFEU or 102 TFEU
- the party agrees to a streamlined administrative procedure for the remainder of the investigation (see paragraph 6.14) and
- we issue an infringement decision but impose a reduced penalty on the settling party (see paragraph 6.13)

6.11 The decision to engage in settlement discussions and to settle is at our discretion. The circumstances in which we are likely to consider it appropriate to settle a case will depend on several factors:

- Whether we consider that we have a sufficient understanding of the nature and gravity of the suspected infringement to make a reasonable assessment of the appropriate outcome.
- The likely procedural efficiencies and resource savings that can be achieved.
- The number of parties in a case.
- In multi-party cases, the number of parties interested in pursuing settlement discussions.

- The prospect of reaching a settlement in a reasonable time. We will not allow parties to use settlement discussions in order to delay an investigation. We will set clear and challenging timetables for settlement discussions to ensure that they result in a prompt outcome and do not divert resources unnecessarily from the formal process.

6.12 The settlement procedure is separate from leniency or the commitments procedure, though it is possible for a leniency applicant to benefit from both leniency and settlement discounts.

Requirements for settlement

6.13 We will require a settling party to take a number of actions:

- Admit liability in relation to the nature, scope and duration of the infringement. The scope of the infringement will include, as a minimum, the material facts of the infringement as well as the legal characterisation of the infringement.
- Cease the infringing behaviour immediately from the date that it enters into settlement discussions with us, where it has not already done so. It must also refrain from engaging again in the same or similar infringing behaviour.
- Confirm it will pay a penalty set at a maximum amount. This maximum penalty (which will apply provided the party continues to follow the requirements of settlement) will reflect the application of a settlement discount to the penalty that would otherwise have been imposed. This discount will reflect the circumstances of the case, in particular whether the case is being settled before or after issue of a Statement of Objections. Settlement discounts are capped at a level of 20% for settlement pre-Statement of Objections and at 10% for settlement post- Statement of Objections. The actual discount awarded will take account of the resource savings achieved in settling that particular case at that particular stage in the investigation.

6.14 In addition, in order to achieve our objective of resolving the case efficiently, settling parties must confirm that they accept that:

- There will be a streamlined administrative process for the remainder of the investigation. This may include streamlined access to file arrangements (e.g. through access to key documents only and/or through the use of a confidentiality ring), no written representations on the Statement of Objections (except in relation to manifest factual inaccuracies), no oral hearings, no separate draft penalty statement after settlement has been reached and no Competition Decisions Committee being appointed (see paragraph 5.2).
- There will be an infringement decision against the settling party.
- Unless the settling party itself successfully appeals the infringement decision, the decision will remain final and binding as against it, even if another addressee of the infringement decision successfully appeals it.
- If the settling party appeals the decision it will no longer benefit from the settlement discount.
- The settling party may be required to undertake to assist us in any continued investigation or in a defence should another party appeal a decision in the case.

6.15 Parties must not disclose without the consent of the PSR the fact or content of settlement discussions to other persons unless required by law or regulatory requirements, apart from information about the matter to which the infringement decision relates once made public.[63]

NOTES

[63] See also paragraph 14.20 of CMA8 on the same point.

Settlement decision procedure

6.16 A decision to initiate a settlement procedure will be taken by the Case Sponsor subject to obtaining the approval of at least two members of the PSR's senior management (the Settlement Decision Makers).

6.17 The Settlement Decision Makers will not have been directly involved in establishing the evidence on which the decision is based. They may, but need not, be involved in the discussions exploring possible settlement. If they approve the decision of the Case Sponsor to settle the case, they will formally issue the infringement and penalty decision.

6.18 We would expect to hold any settlement discussions on the basis that neither we nor the party concerned would seek to rely against each other on any admissions or statements made in the course of the settlement discussions if settlement discussions fail and the matter becomes contested (in an infringement decision or a subsequent appeal from a contested decision)[64] or in other proceedings. The Competition Decisions Committee (if it has been appointed) will be informed that one or more parties are exploring the possibility of settlement (because this will extend the case timetable) but would not be involved in the settlement discussions other than in exceptional circumstances.

6.19 The terms of any proposed settlement will be put in writing[65] and be agreed by us and the party concerned. The admission will be by reference either to the alleged infringement as set out in the Statement of Objections or, if the case settles before a Statement of Objections is issued, will be made by reference to the infringements as set out in a summary statement of facts that we will present to the party.

NOTES

[64] Where a party settles with the PSR and that party appeals the settlement decision against it, the PSR may use admissions made during the course of the settlement negotiations.

[65] The PSR may consider a reasoned request from the settling party to provide the confirmation that it accepts the settlement

requirements orally, however such oral statements must be transcribed at the PSR's premises.

7 DISCLOSURE AND USE OF INFORMATION BY THE PSR IN CA98 INVESTIGATIONS

[3.306]

- We must handle confidential information carefully and may not disclose it other than in accordance with either FSBRA or EA02 (as applicable).
- The framework for disclosure of information by us is governed by the context in which we have obtained it.
- Where specified information is received by us in connection with our CA98 functions, it will be dealt with under EA02 and is excluded from the FSBRA regime governing disclosure of information.
- Where appropriate, we may use information obtained during the course of a CA98 investigation to take action under other legislation.

DISCLOSURE OF INFORMATION BY THE PSR

7.1 The applicable legal framework for our use and disclosure of information is determined according to the statutory context in which the information was received by the PSR. We may use information that we have received from many lawful sources in conducting investigations under CA98. However, we may only disclose such information under the applicable legal regime. Accordingly, when we wish to disclose information that we have gathered under our FSBRA powers in a CA98 investigation, we must apply the relevant FSBRA disclosure provisions.[66]

NOTES

[66] The converse would also apply for disclosure of information gathered under a CA98 investigation in a FSBRA regulatory action (including compliance failure proceedings).

Disclosure under FSBRA

7.2 When we receive information for the purposes of, or in discharge of, our statutory functions under FSBRA which is not in the public domain and relates to a person's business or other affairs, the information will be 'confidential information' under section 91 FSBRA. Information which is already publicly available, or which is aggregated in a format so that it is not possible to ascertain from it information that can be attributed to a particular person, is not considered confidential information under FSBRA.

7.3 However, when we receive information for the purposes of, or in discharge of, our concurrent functions, this information is expressly excluded from the FSBRA regime and will instead be dealt with under the regime set out in EA02 (in other words, information we receive for the purposes of or in discharge of our concurrent competition law functions can only be disclosed by us under Part 9 EA02, i.e. not under FSBRA). (See paragraphs 7.6 to 7.10).[67]

7.4 Where we have obtained information under FSBRA rather than in connection with our concurrent functions (see paragraph 7.6), FSBRA provisions on disclosure will apply. Section 91 FSBRA restricts the disclosure of confidential information unless we have the consent of the person who provided the information (and the person about whom the information relates, if a different person) or a 'gateway' applies. A gateway is an exception to the restriction on disclosure, allowing the disclosure of confidential information to third parties in certain prescribed circumstances. If a gateway is not applicable, we may not release confidential information without the requisite consent(s).

7.5 The full set of gateways is set out in Regulations made under FSBRA.[68] They include disclosure to assist the PSR in the discharge of its functions, and disclosure to the FCA, the Prudential Regulation Authority and the CMA to assist them in the discharge of their functions. When we disclose information pursuant to a gateway, we may restrict the use to which it may be put.

NOTES

[67] Section 91(6) FSBRA

[68] The Financial Services (Banking Reform) Act 2013 (Disclosure of Confidential Information) Regulations 2014 (SI 2014/882)

Disclosure under EA02

7.6 When we receive information in connection with the exercise of our concurrent functions, Part 9 EA02 will apply to any disclosure of such information.[69] Part 9 EA02 imposes a general restriction on the disclosure of information relating to the affairs of an individual or any business of an undertaking which we obtain during the exercise of our CA98 functions (referred to as 'specified information') to other persons.[70] The restriction applies during the lifetime of an individual or while the undertaking continues in existence (for the individual or business to which the specified information relates, respectively).

7.7 Disclosure is permitted if it falls within one of the 'information gateways' as set out in sections 239 to 243 EA02. These gateways include where we obtain the required consents[71] or where the disclosure is made for the purpose of facilitating the exercise by us of any of our statutory functions.[72]

7.8 Even when Part 9 EA02 and one of its information gateways apply, we must have regard to certain considerations before making a disclosure. In particular, we must have regard to the three considerations set out in section 244 EA02, namely:

Part 3 CMA and other Guidelines

- the need to exclude from disclosure (so far as it is practicable to do so) any information whose disclosure we consider to be contrary to the public interest
- the need to exclude from disclosure (so far as practicable) commercial information we consider might significantly harm the legitimate business interests of the undertaking to which it relates; or information relating to the private affairs of an individual which we think might significantly harm that individual's interests, and
- the extent to which the disclosure of information relating to the private affairs of an individual or of commercial information is necessary for the purpose for which we are permitted to make the disclosure

7.9 We will apply these three considerations on a case-by-case basis when we are considering disclosure of specified information. When decisions are finely balanced, we will have particular regard to the need for disclosure to achieve fairness in our processes, for example to safeguard the rights of defence of an addressee of a Statement of Objections.

7.10 Where we disclose information to another person, there are restrictions on the further disclosure or use of the information by that person.

NOTES

[69] Section 91(6) FSBRA
[70] Section 237 EA02
[71] Section 239 EA02
[72] Section 241 EA02

TAKING ACTION UNDER OTHER POWERS

7.11 Given our other objectives and powers, in certain circumstances, it may be appropriate for us to use information that we receive during the course of a CA98 investigation to take action under different statutes, where applicable. Any restrictions that may apply to the use of information transferred to the PSR from a member of the European Competition Network (ECN) or the CMA do not apply to information received by the PSR directly from businesses or individuals.

MEMORANDUM OF UNDERSTANDING BETWEEN THE COMPETITION AND MARKETS AUTHORITY AND THE PAYMENT SYSTEMS REGULATOR – CONCURRENT COMPETITION POWERS

December 2015

[3.307]

NOTES

FOREWORD

[3.308]
The changes to the United Kingdom's (UK) competition law system, introduced under the Enterprise and Regulatory Reform Act 2013 and in force since April 2014, are designed to improve the effectiveness of competition law enforcement in this country.

The Competition and Markets Authority (CMA) has competition law powers that apply across the whole economy. Sectoral regulators such as the Payment Systems Regulator (PSR) may exercise the competition law powers to enforce the prohibitions on anti-competitive agreements and on abuse of a dominant position, and to make market investigation references, concurrently with the CMA in those sectors for which they have responsibility.

The Enterprise and Regulatory Reform Act 2013 introduced a number of changes to improve the working of concurrency and enable closer working between the CMA and sectoral regulators. When the PSR acquired its concurrent competition powers, these reflected the enhanced concurrency provisions introduced by the Enterprise and Regulatory Reform Act 2013.

The CMA and the sectoral regulators have demonstrated their commitment to making the concurrency framework more effective through the establishment of the UK Competition Network (UKCN). This represents an enhanced forum for cooperation that will enable closer working with the objective of more consistent and effective use of competition powers across all sectors. In their statement of intent in December 2013, the members of the UKCN affirmed: 'The mission of the UKCN will be to promote competition for the benefit of consumers and to prevent anti-competitive behaviour both through facilitating use of competition powers and development of pro-competitive regulatory frameworks, as appropriate.'[1]

This memorandum of understanding (MoU) represents a further stage in the process of cooperation between the CMA and the regulators, setting out more practical detail on how the CMA and the PSR will work together within the framework of competition law.[2]

The main purpose of this MoU is to establish an understanding between the CMA and the PSR as to how this closer working will work in practice. It draws on the legislation that sets out the formal framework for how concurrency will operate and also, importantly, sets out our bilateral commitment to look for opportunities to work together, including within the framework of the UKCN, to promote competition for the benefit of consumers. We shall do this by the sharing of expertise, information, ideas and experience and each of us will commit to doing this efficiently and with a mutual regard for each other's statutory position and strategic objectives.

We believe that this MoU offers a valuable basis for that cooperation, in the interests of the CMA, the PSR, the payment systems industry in the UK, and, most importantly of all, consumers.

Alex Chisholm	**Hannah Nixon**
CEO, CMA	**Managing Director, PSR**

NOTES

1 UKCN (2013), Statement of intent.

2 This MoU does not relate to 'regulatory appeals' – that is, the separate role that the CMA has in considering appeals against regulatory action by the PSR under the Financial Services (Banking Reform) Act 2013. This is a separate role, to be undertaken by the CMA panel, and the CMA is committed to ensuring that its cooperation with the PSR – whether under this MoU, through the UKCN, or otherwise in connection with the PSR's concurrent powers – will not impair the impartiality and fairness of the CMA's conduct of such regulatory appeals (or indeed of market or merger investigations undertaken by the CMA panel).

MEMORANDUM OF UNDERSTANDING BETWEEN THE COMPETITION AND MARKETS AUTHORITY AND THE PAYMENT SYSTEMS REGULATOR

PURPOSE OF THIS MEMORANDUM OF UNDERSTANDING

[3.309]

1. This MoU sets out working arrangements between the CMA and the PSR in relation to:

(a) their concurrent powers to apply the prohibitions on agreements that prevent, restrict or distort competition, and on the abuse of a dominant position, under the Chapter I prohibition and the Chapter II prohibition of the Competition Act 1998 and under Article 101 and Article 102 of the Treaty on the Functioning of the European Union – referred to in this MoU as the 'competition prohibitions';

(b) their concurrent powers to undertake Enterprise Act 2002 market studies, and to make references to the CMA for the constitution of a CMA group to conduct an in-depth market investigation into single or multiple markets for goods or services in the UK under the Enterprise Act 2002 – referred to in this MoU as the 'market provisions'; and

(c) cooperation in respect of competition scrutiny under the Financial Services and Markets Act 2000 (FSMA) as it applies to the PSR by virtue of the Financial Services (Banking Reform) Act 2013 (FSBRA);

in relation to participation in payment systems.

2. This MoU is not intended to have legal effect.

3. This MoU is to be read alongside other material concerning the relations between the CMA and the PSR, including: FSBRA; the Competition Act 1998; the Enterprise Act 2002; the Enterprise and Regulatory Reform Act 2013; the Competition Act 1998 and Other Enactments (Amendment) Regulations 2004; the Competition Act 1998 (Concurrency) Regulations 2014, referred to in this MoU as the concurrency regulations; the CMA's guidance on concurrent application of competition law to regulated industries,[3] referred to in this MoU as the concurrency guidance and the PSR's guidance on the application of its competition powers.[4] This MoU supplements and does not supplant that material.

4. The arrangements covered by this MoU are, wherever possible, set out in terms providing sufficient flexibility for the relationship between the PSR and the CMA to develop in the light of experience. The CMA and the PSR commit to review these arrangements from time to time to evaluate their continuing fitness for purpose. Such review can be initiated at the request of the CMA, the PSR or a member of the UKCN. This MoU may only be revised by agreement between the CMA and the PSR.

5. Nothing in this MoU applies in relation to the functions of the CMA in its separate role of considering appeals against regulatory action by the PSR under FSBRA. The CMA and the PSR acknowledge the importance of maintaining the CMA's impartiality and fairness in carrying out those functions, and indeed of market or merger investigations undertaken by the CMA panel.

NOTES

3 CMA (2014), *Regulated industries: Guidance on concurrent application of competition law to regulated industries* (CMA10).

4 PSR's *Enforcement of the Competition Act 1998 – a guide to the PSR's powers and procedures.*

CONTEXT

6. This MoU operates within the framework of the legislative provisions referred to in paragraph 1, the concurrent powers of the PSR under sections 59 to 66 of FSBRA and any other applicable sector specific legislation from time to time.

Role of the CMA

7. The CMA is a non-ministerial department, established under the Enterprise and Regulatory Reform Act 2013.

8. The CMA works to promote competition for the benefit of consumers, both within and outside the UK, to make markets work well for consumers, businesses and the economy.

9. The CMA's statutory responsibilities, in so far as relevant to the matters that are the subject of this MoU, include:
(a) investigating where there may be breaches of the competition prohibitions; and
(b) conducting market studies and market investigations where there may be competition and consumer problems.

10. In connection with its statutory responsibilities, the CMA will cooperate with sectoral regulators to promote effective competition and support the use of their powers, including their powers to apply the competition prohibitions, in the interests of competition for the benefit of consumers.

Role of the PSR

11. The PSR is established under FSBRA to exercise functions in relation to payment systems. It has regulatory functions that apply to payment systems designated for regulation by HM Treasury under section 43 of FSBRA, and under other applicable legislation (eg Part 8 of the Payment Services Regulations 2009).

12. The PSR has three statutory objectives under FSBRA:
(a) to promote effective competition in the market for payment systems and the markets for services provided by payment systems in the interests of service users;
(b) to promote the development of, and innovation in, payment systems in the interests of service users; and
(c) to ensure that payment systems are operated and developed in a way that takes account of, and promotes, the interests of service users.

AIMS

13. The PSR acquired competition powers in relation to participation in payment systems under the Enterprise Act 2002 in April 2014 and under the Competition Act 1998 in April 2015. These powers are exercisable concurrently with the CMA thereby bringing the PSR in line with the other sectoral regulators, which already had powers exercisable concurrently with the CMA in those sectors for which they have responsibility.

14. The Enterprise and Regulatory Reform Act 2013, as well as establishing the CMA, made provision for the better working of the CMA's and the sectoral regulators' concurrent powers in the regulated sectors; specifically, the act: 'strengthens the role of the CMA and enhances the emphasis on early and proper consideration of the use of anti-trust powers (under Part 1 of the CA 1998 [ie the competition prohibitions]) by the sector regulators.'[5]

15. It is one of the strategic goals of the CMA, announced on its establishment on 1 October 2013, to extend the frontiers of competition into new areas, including by working with sectoral regulators to ensure fuller use of competition law and policy in sectoral markets.[6]

16. The government's strategic steer to the CMA, issued on 1 December 2015, says that the CMA should build 'a strong dialogue with sectoral regulators using the UKCN to ensure that the overall competition regime is coordinated and regulatory practices complement each other'.[7]

17. The sectoral regulators[8] and the CMA, working together in the UKCN established in 2013 (with Monitor having observer status), declared that: 'The mission of the UKCN will be to promote competition for the benefit of consumers and to prevent anti-competitive behaviour both through facilitating use of competition powers and development of pro-competitive regulatory frameworks, as appropriate.'[9]

18. The CMA and the PSR seek to use their powers to achieve more competitive outcomes in the payment systems industry in the UK for the benefit of consumers so as to make the markets for payment systems and the services they provide in the UK work well for the individuals and businesses who use them and for the economy in which payment systems play an essential part. It is the view of the CMA and the PSR that such competitive outcomes can be achieved by various tools including: their concurrent competition law powers under the competition prohibitions and market provisions; the CMA's powers under specific consumer protection legislation and the CMA's merger control functions. However, the CMA and the PSR recognise that some of these outcomes can also be achieved through the PSR's sector-specific regulatory powers such as the power to give directions or impose requirements or to require the granting of access to a regulated payment system.

19. This MoU aims to further the attainment of these objectives, and to make the changes introduced by the Enterprise and Regulatory Reform Act 2013 and FSBRA work effectively, maximising the complementary skills of the CMA and the PSR, including through:
(a) promoting cooperation and coordination between the CMA and the PSR when dealing with cases of suspected anti-competitive behaviour for which they have concurrent powers;
(b) promoting cooperation and coordination between the CMA and the PSR when dealing with market studies and market investigation references for which they have concurrent powers;
(c) facilitating the efficient and effective handling of cases of suspected anti-competitive behaviour within the markets for payment systems and the services they provide in the UK;
(d) avoiding duplication of activity, wherever possible; and
(e) ensuring transparency as to the respective roles of the CMA and the PSR for businesses, individuals and consumers affected.

NOTES

5 Enterprise and Regulatory Reform Act 2013 Explanatory Notes, paragraph 370.

6 Statement by Alex Chisholm, Chief Executive of the CMA, *CMA mission and strategy*, 1 October 2013.

7 Department for Business, Innovation and Skills, *Strategic steer for the Competition and Markets Authority*, in Annex A to the *Government's response to the Consultation on the Strategic Steer to the CMA*, 1 December 2015, page 11.

8 The PSR has been a full member of the UKCN since its establishment in April 2014 even though it did not have full concurrent powers at that time. It was included as it had a statutory duty to promote effective competition in the interests of service users and concurrent powers under the Enterprise Act 2002 and it was due to acquire concurrent Competition Act 1998 powers in April 2015.

9 UKCN (2013), Statement of intent.

GENERAL COOPERATION

20. In addition to the provisions for cooperation between the CMA and the PSR specific to particular powers of the CMA and the PSR, as set out in this MoU and elsewhere, the CMA and the PSR are committed to the following general principles and practices for cooperation between themselves in respect of the sectors for which the PSR has responsibility.

21. Officials of the CMA and the PSR will meet and communicate, at appropriate levels of seniority, to discuss matters of mutual interest, both through the UKCN and bilaterally. A framework for such meetings will, as far as possible, be determined in advance so as to ensure attendance at the appropriate level and expertise.

22. The CMA and the PSR will, in respect of matters in relation to participation in payment systems, always consult each other:

(a) before the initial exercise of concurrent competition law powers in all cases where it appears that they have concurrent jurisdiction and where there are reasonable grounds for suspecting an infringement of the competition prohibitions; and

(b) before launching a market study under the Enterprise Act 2002,[10] or, in the PSR's case, a market review under FSBRA.

23. Where either the CMA or the PSR exercises its concurrent powers, the CMA and the PSR will, to the extent permitted by law, engage with each other in open dialogue and by sharing relevant information as appropriate. This engagement may include attendance at internal meetings held by the investigating authority (ie the authority to which a case is allocated) by the supporting authority (ie the other authority that would be competent to exercise concurrent powers in relation to the case), in order to discuss the case as envisaged at paragraph 3.31 of the concurrency guidance. The supporting authority will not generally attend the investigating authority's constitutional decision-making meetings, meetings of governance bodies or meetings with external parties such as those under investigation or complainants. Attendance by the supporting authority at any meeting is at the discretion of the investigating authority but requests to attend should be considered by the investigating authority in the spirit of cooperation underpinning the new concurrency regime.

24. The CMA and the PSR will consult each other at an early stage on any issues that might have significant implications for the other. For example, where the CMA undertakes a market study which relates to a sector other than payment systems and the services they provide but which may have a significant impact on that sector, the CMA will inform the PSR and share appropriate information relating to that market study with the PSR to the extent permitted by law.

25. Within the spirit of broader collaboration for the purposes of the promotion of competitive outcomes, the CMA and the PSR will commit to discuss and share other relevant information, where legally permissible to do so, but subject to the need not to impair the impartiality and fairness of the CMA in carrying out its functions referred to in paragraph 5 of this MoU.

NOTES

10 Instigation of a market study occurs on the publication of a market study notice, as defined in section 130A of the Enterprise Act 2002.

PART A – COOPERATION IN RELATION TO THE COMPETITION PROHIBITIONS (COMPETITION ACT 1998 AND ARTICLES 101 AND 102 OF THE TREATY ON THE FUNCTIONING OF THE EUROPEAN UNION)

CASE ALLOCATION

Basis of allocation

[3.310]

26. The CMA and the PSR will endeavour to reach agreement on which authority will exercise its concurrent competition powers in respect of any particular case, under regulation 4(2) of the concurrency regulations. They will do so in a spirit of constructiveness and cooperation, while acknowledging the CMA's ultimate powers under regulations 5 and 8 of the concurrency regulations.

27 Their determination of which authority will exercise its powers will be based on assessing which of them is better placed to exercise those powers, having regard to the factors set out in paragraph 3.22 of the concurrency guidance. The CMA and the PSR envisage that other factors may appear relevant in the light of practical experience and that, if so, such factors may be chosen to supplement or supplant the factors set out in paragraph 3.22 of the concurrency guidance.

Procedure for allocation

28. Where either the CMA or the PSR has decided, on the basis of information in its possession, that there are reasonable grounds for suspecting that one of the competition prohibitions has been infringed (the 'reasonable suspicion test')[11] in relation to participation in payment systems, it will disclose to the other (ie the receiving authority) sufficient information:

(a) to enable the receiving authority to understand the basis on which the disclosing authority has decided that the reasonable suspicion test is met; and

(b) for there to be an informed discussion on which authority (if either) is best placed to proceed in respect of the case.

29. In practice, it may be helpful for the CMA and the PSR to have discussed the case prior to such a decision having been reached, subject to paragraph 42 below. The disclosing authority will provide the information described under paragraph 28 within ten working days after it has decided that the reasonable suspicion test is met, whether or not it proposes to exercise concurrent powers.[12]

30. Within seven working days from receipt of this information, the receiving authority will respond in writing, setting out its initial view on the case and how it should be allocated and identifying any further information that it requires.

31. The CMA and the PSR will endeavour to agree which authority will exercise its concurrent competition powers in relation to the case, as provided for in regulation 4(2) of the concurrency regulations, as soon as possible and in any event no later than one month from disclosure of the information described under paragraph 28. Other than in exceptional circumstances (which shall be set out in writing), the CMA will initiate the procedure set out in regulation 5 of the concurrency regulations if agreement is not reached within two months of the disclosing authority first receiving sufficient information in connection with a complaint to enable it to decide that the reasonable suspicion test is met.

32. The procedure for agreeing the transfer of a case that is already in progress from the CMA to the PSR, or from the PSR to the CMA, is as set out in regulation 7 of the concurrency regulations and in paragraph 3.32 of the concurrency guidance.

33. The procedure for the CMA to direct the transfer to itself from the PSR of a case that is already in progress is as set out in regulation 8 of the concurrency regulations.

NOTES

11 As provided in section 25 of the Competition Act 1998.

12 As provided in regulation 9 of the concurrency regulations.

Implications of allocation

34. Any agreement or determination as to case allocation, under regulations 4, 5, 7 or 8 of the concurrency regulations, shall be notified to the person who has provided the information resulting in the case (for example, the person making a complaint), and so far as appropriate and lawful to any other affected person, by the authority that is exercising its concurrent competition powers in relation to the case, as soon as reasonably practicable.

35. Case allocation determines which of the CMA and the PSR is to exercise concurrent functions and make any decisions under the competition prohibitions. The CMA or the PSR will be publicly identified as having such responsibility if and when any such investigation is announced. The CMA and the PSR envisage that, whichever authority has responsibility for a particular case, they and their officials will work cooperatively with each other on the case as appropriate, pooling their expertise including in the ways described in paragraphs 51 to 58 of this MoU and in paragraphs 3.33 to 3.35 of the concurrency guidance.

SHARING INFORMATION

Principles of information sharing

36. The effective sharing of information between the CMA and the PSR is fundamental to the successful exercise of their concurrent competition powers. It is needed both for the appropriate allocation of cases, as described in paragraphs 28 to 33 of this MoU, and for the successful handling of cases once allocated to make optimal use of the complementary experience and expertise of the two authorities.

37. The CMA and the PSR are committed, in addition to their legal obligations to share information (set out in regulation 9 of the concurrency regulations), to open dialogue and continuing liaison, both bilaterally and through the UKCN, with a view not only to handling specific cases but to promoting competition, in the interests of service users in the markets for payment systems and the services they provide in the UK.

Information sharing mechanism – general liaison

38. The CMA and the PSR recognise the importance of meeting regularly to share information on matters relevant to competition in the markets for payment systems and the services they provide in the UK, and to keep each other abreast of relevant work that they are considering or currently undertaking.

39. The CMA and the PSR will meet regularly at multiple levels, bilaterally and through the UKCN.

40. The CMA and the PSR will each designate in its organisation a relationship manager at official level to take responsibility for relations between the two authorities. In each authority, the relationship manager's responsibilities will include (but will not be limited to):

(a) maintaining an overview of joint projects between the two authorities and matters of mutual interest;
(b) maintaining an overview of the authority's contacts from all areas of joint working and mutual interest; and
(c) holding meetings with the relationship manager in the other authority from time to time (whether bilaterally or in the context of the UKCN) to identify potential new issues, with a view to circulating information to appropriate individuals within each organisation.

41. The existence of relationship managers does not in any way preclude direct communication between other staff at the CMA and the PSR.

42. For the purposes of sharing information pursuant to paragraph 28, ie in circumstances where the reasonable suspicion test is met, such information will be shared by the disclosing authority to the extent permitted by law and whether or not it proposes to exercise concurrent powers.[13] Where disclosure would be appropriate and permitted by law, the CMA and the PSR may also share information regarding potential infringements of the competition prohibitions in advance of having reached a view as to whether the reasonable suspicion test is met. In circumstances where either the CMA or the PSR has taken the view that a matter is not an administrative priority, irrespective of whether a view has been reached on whether the reasonable suspicion test is met, each may share the details of the matter with the other, or with any other authority that would be able to exercise concurrent competition powers in relation to that matter, to the extent permitted by law. Where leniency information is being shared under this paragraph, special considerations apply, as set out in paragraphs 48 and 49.

NOTES

13 For the avoidance of doubt, this does not entail an obligation to inform the other party if the regulator is carrying out general monitoring activity, where there is no consideration of exercising its concurrent powers.

Information sharing mechanism – handling specific cases

43. The procedures for information sharing for the purpose of case allocation shall be as set out in paragraphs 28 to 30 and 36 to 50 of this MoU.

44. When either the CMA or the PSR is exercising its powers in respect of the competition prohibitions in a particular case in relation to participation in payment systems in the UK, each of them will share with the other any of the following information in its possession (to the extent permitted by law and subject to the confidentiality obligations in paragraphs 48 to 50 of this MoU):
(a) as a minimum, the matters referred to in regulation 9(1)(b) – (j) of the concurrency regulations, and in paragraph 3.49 of the concurrency guidance, complying with the time limits specified in paragraph 3.49;
(b) other information that it reasonably believes to be relevant or helpful to the other in the conduct of the case; and
(c) in the case of the authority that is exercising the powers, reports to the other on the progress of the case, of sufficient frequency and detail to enable the other to be appropriately informed; the means and frequency of such reporting will be decided on a case-by-case basis and in the light of experience as this enhanced framework of collaboration and its supporting arrangements develop over time.

Information sharing mechanism – for know-how purposes

45. The CMA will maintain on its webpages a central database of decisions taken in cases under the competition prohibitions in the regulated sectors, with a view to having a body of know-how that will help ensure the effective and consistent application of competition law. The CMA and the PSR will, to the extent permitted by law, contribute information to that in the way best calculated to achieve that objective.

46. In any event, the CMA will report on cases in the regulated sectors under the competition prohibitions in the annual concurrency report that it is required under statute to issue. Further provisions on the annual concurrency report are in paragraphs 61 to 63 of this MoU.

Information sharing – confidentiality constraints

47. Any disclosure of information under paragraphs 28 to 30 and 36 to 46 of this MoU, and any use by the recipient of such information, shall only be to the extent permitted by law, including by reference to the provisions of Part 9 of the Enterprise Act 2002, relevant sector-specific legislative provisions and any other provisions relating to the disclosure, handling and use of information (such as the Data Protection Act 1998 and section 118 of FSMA, to the extent relevant).

48. Prior to disclosing information to each other, the CMA and the PSR will not generally give the person to whom the information relates prior notice of its intention to make the disclosure. However, if the CMA or the PSR consider it necessary or appropriate to pass leniency information to each other (or to another UK authority with concurrent powers), the transmitting authority will inform the applicant or its legal adviser first. Leniency information for the purposes of this MoU is any information that came into the possession of any of the CMA, its predecessors, the PSR or any other public authority as a direct or indirect result of having been provided in the context of an application for leniency. It includes information obtained by the transferring authority as a result of investigative measures resulting directly or indirectly from an application for leniency.

49. In addition to the general provisions referred to in paragraph 47, where the PSR or the CMA receives leniency information from the other (or from another UK authority with concurrent powers) for the purpose of applying the competition prohibitions or, in the case of the CMA, the cartel offence under section 188 of the Enterprise Act 2002, that information will not be used for any other purpose. This restriction on use also applies to any information obtained by the receiving authority as a result of investigative measures relating to the competition prohibitions or the cartel offence following the receipt of leniency information from the other authority. This does not affect the use that may be made by the CMA or the PSR of information received from other sources, including but not limited to disclosures to the PSR under its General Direction 1[14], or if the leniency applicant's consent is obtained.[15] Where the provision of leniency information to either the CMA or the PSR affords or might, under certain conditions, afford the leniency applicant, its subsidiaries or its employees protection from sanctions (including a reduction in penalties) under the leniency programme operated by that authority and that information has been passed to another authority, the receiving authority shall afford the leniency applicant, its subsidiaries or its employees no lesser protection.

50. Where an application for leniency is made to the CMA by a participant in a payment system regulated by the PSR under FSBRA, the CMA will remind the applicant that it is obliged, under the PSR's General Direction 1, to disclose to the PSR appropriately anything relating to the applicant which could materially adversely impact advancement of the PSR's statutory objectives and duties. When leniency information is shared with the PSR, the PSR may also contact the applicant to remind it of its General Direction 1 obligations.[16]

NOTES

14 See the PSR's General directions.

15 The use restriction in this paragraph is intended to govern the use of leniency information in the context of the concurrency arrangements. It is not intended to prevent the disclosure of such leniency information by either one of the CMA or the PSR to the other (to the extent permitted by Part 9 of the Enterprise Act 2002 and in accordance with Leniency and no-action applications in cartel cases: OFT1495) for purposes other than the application of the competition prohibitions or the cartel offence. However, any such disclosure of leniency information would only be likely to be justified in exceptional circumstances, given the strong public interest in maintaining the incentives for undertakings and, in the case of the cartel offence, individuals to apply for leniency.

16 The PSR and CMA acknowledge that OFT1495 applies, in particular paragraphs 3.24–3.28, with respect to maintaining confidentiality.

POOLING RESOURCES

51. Paragraph 23 above, and the concurrency guidance provide for support to be provided by the supporting authority to the investigating authority when it is exercising its concurrent powers in a case. The CMA and the PSR will endeavour, so far as is reasonably practicable and permitted by law, and in the light of their respective ongoing priorities and resource availability at the time, to share their resources with each other in the interests of the effective enforcement of competition law in the markets for payment systems and the services they provide in the UK, and more generally the promotion of competition in the interests of service users in that sector, and to ensure that their resources and expertise are used most efficiently for that purpose. This is subject to the proviso that, as stated in paragraph 5, this does not apply in relation to the functions of the CMA in its role of considering appeals against regulatory action by the PSR under FSBRA.

52. As a consequence, where it has been agreed or determined that one of the authorities is to exercise its concurrent competition powers in relation to a case, that authority will, to the extent that there are resources available, receive appropriate practical assistance and support from the other in the handling of the case, as agreed on a case-by-case basis.

53. Such support and assistance may include the provision of training or practical know-how and expertise by one authority to the other where appropriate to enable the authority exercising its concurrent competition powers in the case to carry out its statutory functions effectively (for example in relation to conduct of site visits).

Secondments of staff

54. One means of the practical assistance and support that might be given, as referred to in paragraphs 51 and 52 of this MoU, is the secondment of staff, in accordance with regulation 10 of the concurrency regulations and paragraphs 3.33 and 3.34 of the concurrency guidance.

55. The CMA and the PSR are fully committed to the idea of secondments for this purpose, and will endeavour to meet each other's requests for secondments to the extent that they are appropriate and resources permit; this may include making provision for any secondee to be available to work for part of his or her time at his or her existing employer during the course of the secondment, for example on such cases that are in progress.

56. Requests for secondments should be made by the relationship manager of one authority to the relationship manager of the other, setting out the following information:

(a) The number of secondees required.
(b) The period for which each one is required.
(c) The level of seniority of each one.
(d) The nature of the expertise or experience of each one.
(e) The proposed payment arrangements.
(f) A brief explanation of why the requirement or requirements cannot adequately be met by deployment of staff from within the requesting authority.

57. To the extent that the recipient of a request for a secondment made under paragraph 56 of this MoU refuses that request or accedes to it on terms that are materially different from those requested, the recipient shall give reasons.

58. The CMA and the PSR will develop appropriate arrangements for the pooling and secondment of staff. Such arrangements will have regard to the resource constraints of both parties and such calls for staff, therefore, will be made in reasonable time and with sufficient warning to enable appropriate resource planning, management of other work commitments and appropriate sign-off procedures within each authority.

Other mutual support

59. In addition to the sharing of information, expertise, experience and the secondment of staff, the CMA and the PSR are fully committed to providing each other with more informal forms of support to enable them to carry out their competition law functions in relation to participation in payment systems in the UK – in each case to the extent that it is appropriate and permitted by law, and that resources permit – including (but not limited to):

(a) answering specific queries from time to time;
(b) providing information or views on a specific sector or market, or an area of competition law or policy; and
(c) providing training on a specific sector or market, or an area of competition law or policy.

60. Such support may be requested and provided in connection with a specific case or with the promotion of competition more generally. In this regard, both the CMA and the PSR will act reasonably, including by providing sufficient time and information for requests for support to be responded to fully and effectively and for the relevant staff to be engaged.

ANNUAL CONCURRENCY REPORT

61. The CMA is required by statute to publish a report every year, starting after its first year of operation in 2014/15,[17] containing an assessment of how the concurrency arrangements between the CMA and the sectoral regulators, as regards both the competition prohibitions and the market provisions, have operated during the year. This MoU refers to that report as the annual concurrency report. There is further provision on the annual concurrency report in paragraphs 3.55 to 3.62 of the concurrency guidance.

62. The CMA will consult, and cooperate with, the PSR and with other sectoral regulators in preparing the annual concurrency report. In connection with this, the CMA will:

(a) prepare a draft of the annual concurrency report that it will send to the PSR and other sectoral regulators seeking comments or suggestions on the content or conclusions of the annual concurrency report and giving them adequate time to comment or make suggestions;
(b) take account of any comments or suggestions it receives from the PSR and other sectoral regulators, and the CMA may seek further clarification on those comments or suggestions as appropriate;
(c) prepare a final version of the annual concurrency report for publication that takes account of its consultation of the PSR and other sectoral regulators as appropriate; and
(d) make the annual concurrency report available on the CMA webpages.

63. The PSR will cooperate with the CMA in the preparation of the annual concurrency report including (but not limited to) by way of:

(a) providing information and data on general market conditions and on the application of the competition prohibitions and the market provisions in relation to participation in payment systems in the UK;
(b) responding to reasonable requests for information and data; and
(c) providing to the CMA any comments and suggestions it may have in connection with the process described in paragraph 62 of this MoU;

in each case promptly so as to facilitate the timely production and publication of the annual concurrency report.

NOTES

[17] Enterprise and Regulatory Reform Act 2013 Schedule 4 paragraph 16.

VOLUNTARY REDRESS SCHEMES

64. In cases relating to investigations under the competition prohibitions in relation to participation in payment systems in the UK, both the CMA and the PSR have the power to approve voluntary redress schemes. When either authority proposes to exercise these powers, it shall liaise with the other authority as appropriate and will have regard to its own guidance.[18]

NOTES

[18] The CMA's guidance on the approval of voluntary redress schemes (CMA40) states at footnote 7: 'The CMA expects that regulators will take this CMA guidance into account when producing their own guidance on the approval power.'

SHORT FORM OPINIONS

65. The CMA shall inform the PSR following an initial enquiry for a short form opinion relating to the sector for payment systems and the services they provide. Where the CMA is considering providing such an opinion, it will discuss with the PSR before deciding to do so. If the CMA then decides to produce an opinion, it will engage with the PSR, the nature and degree of that engagement to be considered on a case-by-case basis, having regard, in particular, to the extent to which the opinion has a multi-sector rather than single-sector dimension. In all cases, the CMA will give the PSR the opportunity to provide comments on such a draft opinion.

PART B – COOPERATION IN RELATION TO THE MARKET PROVISIONS: MARKET STUDIES AND MARKET INVESTIGATIONS (ENTERPRISE ACT 2002)

HOW CONCURRENCY WORKS UNDER THE MARKET PROVISIONS

[3.311]

66. The PSR has the power, concurrently with the CMA, to carry out market studies, to make market investigation references, agree undertakings in lieu of a reference and make recommendations to the government in relation to participation in payment systems in the UK under Part 4 of the Enterprise Act 2002 (as do other sectoral regulators in relation to the sectors for which they are responsible).

67. Under the Enterprise Act 2002, the CMA and the PSR may, in relation to participation in payment systems in the UK, undertake market studies, and may make market investigation references to the Chair of the CMA for the constitution of a CMA group to conduct an in-depth market investigation into single or multiple markets for goods or services in the UK. The purpose of these investigations is to examine the market(s) and (where required) implement appropriate remedies where the CMA determines that the structure of the market(s) or the conduct of the suppliers or customers is harming competition.

68. When making a reference, the CMA or the PSR, as applicable, must have reasonable grounds for suspecting that any feature or combination of features of a market or markets in the UK prevents, restricts or distorts competition in relation to the supply or acquisition of any goods or services in the UK (or in a part of the UK).

69. The cooperation between the CMA and the PSR provided for in this Part B shall not extend to conduct that could reasonably be expected to impair the impartiality or the fairness of the CMA panel in conducting market investigations

SUPER-COMPLAINTS

70. The CMA[19] has an obligation to respond to super-complaints about any feature, or combination of features, of a market in the UK for goods or services which is or appears to be significantly harming the interests of consumers. The PSR[20] has a similar obligation for super-complaints relating to a market in the UK for services provided by payment systems.

71. The coordination of the CMA's and the sectoral regulators' super-complaint duties will be based on policies agreed and applied through the UKCN.

72. Subject to paragraph 71 above, the PSR intends, where permitted by law, to:

(a) inform the CMA of super-complaints received under section 68 of FSBRA;

(b) discuss with the CMA those super-complaints where the PSR considers that action by the CMA under any of the CMA's powers is more appropriate than regulatory action under FSBRA, bearing in mind the PSR's statutory objective in relation to promoting effective competition in the interests of service users set out in FSBRA;

(c) refer to the CMA super-complaints identifying competition issues that the PSR cannot address under its powers; and

(d) inform the CMA of super-complaints that identify issues in a market for services provided by payment systems which the PSR believes may have consequences for related non-payment systems/services markets.

73. Subject to paragraph 71 above, the CMA intends to:

(a) inform the PSR of super-complaints received under section 11 of the Enterprise Act 2002 where they relate to one or more markets for payment systems and the services they provide in the UK (or part thereof);

(b) discuss those super-complaints with the PSR where the CMA considers that regulatory action under FSBRA may be more appropriate than action under any of the CMA's powers, bearing in mind the CMA's mission to make markets work well in the interests of consumers, businesses and the economy;

(c) refer to the PSR super-complaints concerning the markets for payment systems and the services they provide in the UK to which the CMA cannot respond under its powers; and

(d) inform the PSR of super-complaints that identify competition issues in non-payment systems/services markets which the CMA believes may have consequences for the markets for payment systems and the services they provide.

NOTES

[19] Section 11 of the Enterprise Act 2002.

[20] Sections 68 and 69 of FSBRA.

MUTUAL CONSULTATION

74. The PSR and the CMA have a duty to consult each other before exercising concurrent functions under the market provisions.[21]

NOTES

[21] Section 60(1) of FSBRA.

SHARING INFORMATION

75. The provisions of paragraphs 38 to 42, 44 (excluding 44(a)) and 46 of this MoU apply to information sharing under the market provisions as they do under the competition prohibitions.

POOLING RESOURCES

76. The provisions of paragraphs 51 to 58 of this MoU apply to pooling resources under the market provisions as they do under the competition prohibitions.

77. Where the CMA and the PSR intend to pool resources in order to exercise powers under the market provisions of the Enterprise Act 2002, they shall, at the outset of any such project, discuss the arrangements for how they will pool resources and work jointly.

ANNUAL CONCURRENCY REPORT

78. The provisions of paragraphs 61 to 63 of this MoU apply under the market provisions as they do under the competition prohibitions.

PART C – COOPERATION IN RELATION TO COMPETITION SCRUTINY (THE FINANCIAL SERVICES AND MARKETS ACT 2000 AND THE FINANCIAL SERVICES (BANKING REFORM) ACT 2013)

INTERACTION BETWEEN THE PSR AND THE CMA UNDER FSMA AND FSBRA

[3.312]

79. For the purposes of this Part C and pursuant to section 140B of FSMA, the CMA gives 'section 140B advice' if:

(a) it gives advice, under section 7 of the Enterprise Act 2002, to the PSR and that advice states that one or more of the things listed in paragraph 80 below may cause or contribute to the prevention, restriction or distortion of competition in connection with the supply or acquisition of any goods or services in the UK or a part of the UK, or might be expected to do so in the future; or

(b) it publishes a report, under section 136 of the Enterprise Act 2002, which contains a decision that one or more of the things listed in paragraph 80 below may cause or contribute to the prevention, restriction or distortion of competition in connection with the supply or acquisition of any goods or services in the UK or a part of the UK, or might be expected to do so in the future, and the CMA recommends that any action be taken by the PSR.

80. The things mentioned in paragraph 79 are:

(a) a regulating provision or practice of the PSR, as defined under section 107(2) of FSBRA;

(b) two or more regulating provisions or practices;

(c) a particular combination of regulating provisions or practices; or

(d) a feature or combination of features of one or more markets in the UK that could be dealt with by regulating provisions or practices of the PSR.

81. Sections 140A to 140H of FSMA on competition scrutiny apply to the PSR's practices and regulating provisions in relation to payment systems.[22]

82. The CMA will consult with the PSR before officially publishing section 140B advice, and will provide the PSR with guidance as to how it intends to use this power.

83. Under section 140G of FSMA, the PSR must, within 90 days after the day on which it receives section 140B advice from the CMA, publish a response stating how it proposes to deal with the advice and in particular:

(a) whether it has decided to take any action, or to take no action, in response to the advice;

(b) if it has decided to take action, what action it proposes to take; and

(c) its reasons for its proposals.

NOTES

[22] By virtue of section 107 of FSBRA.

FINANCIAL CONDUCT AUTHORITY FINALISED GUIDANCE FG16/3: VOLUNTARY REDRESS SCHEMES UNDER THE COMPETITION ACT 1998 (NOTE)

(March 2016)

[3.313]

NOTES

This finalised guidance is issued pursuant to section 49C of the Competition Act 1998 and covers:

— applications for approval of redress schemes,

— the approval of redress schemes, and

— the enforcement of approved schemes, in particular the criteria we intend to adopt in deciding whether to enforce approved redress schemes.

This guidance was approved by the Secretary of State on 23.3.2016, and is available on the FCA's website at: www.fca.org.uk/publications/finalised-guidance/fg16-3-guidance-voluntary-redress-schemes-under-competition-act-1998.

FINALISED GUIDANCE FG15/8: THE FCA'S CONCURRENT COMPETITION ENFORCEMENT POWERS FOR THE PROVISION OF FINANCIAL SERVICES (NOTE)

A guide to the FCA's powers and procedures under the Competition Act 1998

(As updated in April 2018)

[3.314]

NOTES

This guidance explains how the Financial Conduct Authority will use its concurrent functions for the prohibitions in Chapter 1 and Chapter 2 the Competition Act 1998 and/or Article 101 and Article 102 TFEU for the provision of financial services within the UK, in particular the enforcement processes it will follow, and how these relate to its other powers and duties. This document constitutes advice and information issued pursuant to section 52 of the 1998 Act.

This is available on the Financial Conduct Authority's website at:
www.fca.org.uk/publications/finalised-guidance/fg15-8-fcas-powers-and-procedures-under-competition-act-1998.

FCA MISSION: APPROACH TO COMPETITION (NOTE)

October 2018

[3.315]

NOTES

In October 2018, the FCA published a Mission Document detailing its approach to competition law. It emphasises that the objective of the FCA is to promote competition in the interests of consumers, not for its own sake.

In chapter 1 (Our Role) the FCA states that it does three things to advance its competition objective. (1) It looks at market structure and dynamics through its market studies, adjusting the 'rules of the game' where necessary to improve consumer outcomes. (2) It investigates anti-competitive behaviour under the Competition Act 1998 and EU law. (3) It implements regulation with the aim of supporting, rather than inhibiting, competition in consumers' interests.

In chapter 2 (Our decision-making framework) the FCA covers its four-step decision-making framework. Ie, (i) identifying potential harm; (ii) diagnosing the cause of harm; (iii) remedying the features of a market that do not work well for consumers; and (iv) evaluating the success of those remedies to inform future decisions.

The guidance also contains two Annexes: Annex 1 (Market studies, calls for input and other competition reviews launched by the FCA), and Annex 2 (Feedback Statement for Approach to Competition consultation).

The full guidance is available on the FCA website at
www.fca.org.uk/publication/corporate/our-approach-competition-final-report-feedback-statement.pdf.

MEMORANDUM OF UNDERSTANDING BETWEEN THE COMPETITION AND MARKETS AUTHORITY AND THE FINANCIAL CONDUCT AUTHORITY – CONCURRENT COMPETITION POWERS

(July 2019)

[3.316]

NOTES

In April 2018, paragraphs 48 and 49 of this Memorandum of Understanding were amended to reflect changes introduced by the Senior Manager and Certification Regime.

It was further updated in July 2019 to reflect the FCA's new concurrent competition jurisdiction in relation to the provision of claims management services in Great Britain.

FOREWORD

[3.317]

The changes to the United Kingdom's (UK) competition law system, introduced under the Enterprise and Regulatory Reform Act 2013 and in force since April 2014, are designed to improve the effectiveness of competition law enforcement in this country.

The Competition and Markets Authority (CMA) has competition law powers which apply across the whole economy. Sectoral regulators such as the Financial Conduct Authority (FCA) may exercise the competition law powers to enforce the prohibitions on anti-competitive agreements and on abuse of a dominant position, and to make market investigation references, concurrently with the CMA in those sectors for which they have responsibility.

The Enterprise and Regulatory Reform Act 2013 introduced a number of changes to improve the working of concurrency and to enable closer working between the CMA and sectoral regulators. When the FCA acquired its concurrent competition powers, these reflected the enhanced concurrency provisions introduced by the Enterprise and Regulatory Reform Act 2013.

The CMA and the sectoral regulators have demonstrated their commitment to making the concurrency framework more effective through the establishment of the UK Competition Network (UKCN). This represents an enhanced forum for cooperation which will enable closer working with the objective of more consistent and effective use of competition powers across all sectors. In their statement of intent in December 2013, the members of the UKCN affirmed: 'The mission of the UKCN will be to promote competition for the benefit of consumers and to prevent anti-competitive behaviour both through facilitating use of competition powers and development of pro-competitive regulatory frameworks, as appropriate.'[1]

This memorandum of understanding (MoU) represents a further stage in the process of cooperation between the CMA and the regulators, setting out more practical detail on how the CMA and the FCA will work together within the framework of competition law.

The main purpose of this MoU is to establish an understanding between the CMA and the FCA as to how this closer working will work in practice. It draws on the legislation which sets out the formal framework for how concurrency will operate and also, importantly, sets out our bilateral commitment to look for opportunities to work together, including within the framework of the UKCN, to promote competition for the benefit of consumers. We shall do this by the sharing of expertise, information, ideas and experience and each of us will commit to doing this efficiently and with a mutual regard for each other's statutory position and strategic objectives.

We believe that this MoU offers a valuable basis for that cooperation, in the interests of the CMA, the FCA, the financial services industry in the UK and, most importantly of all, consumers.

Andrea Coscelli	**Andrew Bailey**
CEO, CMA	**CEO, FCA**

NOTES

1 UKCN (2013), Statement of intent.

MEMORANDUM OF UNDERSTANDING BETWEEN THE COMPETITION AND MARKETS AUTHORITY AND THE FINANCIAL CONDUCT AUTHORITY

PURPOSE OF THIS MEMORANDUM OF UNDERSTANDING

[3.318]

1. This MoU sets out working arrangements between the CMA and the FCA in relation to:

(a) their concurrent powers to apply the prohibitions on agreements that prevent, restrict or distort competition, and on the abuse of a dominant position, under the Chapter I prohibition and the Chapter II prohibition of the Competition Act 1998 and under Article 101 and Article 102 of the Treaty on the Functioning of the European Union – referred to in this MoU as the 'competition prohibitions';

(b) their concurrent powers to undertake Enterprise Act 2002 market studies, and to make references to the CMA for the constitution of a CMA group to conduct an in-depth market investigation into single or multiple markets for goods or services in the UK under the Enterprise Act 2002 – referred to in this MoU as the 'market provisions'; and

(c) cooperation in respect of competition scrutiny under the Financial Services and Markets Act 2000 (FSMA);

in the provision of financial services in the UK and the provision of claims management services in Great Britain (together, 'the FCA's concurrent jurisdiction'). The FCA and CMA have entered into a separate MoU in relation to consumer protection.

2. This MoU is not intended to have legal effect.

3. This MoU is to be read alongside other material concerning the relations between the CMA and the FCA, including: FSMA; the Competition Act 1998; the Enterprise Act 2002; the Enterprise and Regulatory Reform Act 2013; the Competition Act 1998 and Other Enactments (Amendment) Regulations 2004; the Competition Act 1998 (Concurrency) Regulations 2014, referred to in this MoU as the concurrency regulations; the CMA's guidance on concurrent application of competition law to regulated industries, referred to in this MoU as the concurrency guidance;[2] and the FCA's guidance on its powers and procedures under the Competition Act 1998.[3] This MoU supplements and does not supplant that material.

4. The arrangements covered by this MoU are, wherever possible, set out in terms providing sufficient flexibility for the relationship between the FCA and the CMA to develop in the light of experience. The CMA and the FCA commit to review these arrangements from time to time to evaluate their continuing fitness for purpose. Such review can be initiated at the request of the CMA, the FCA or a member of the UKCN. This MoU may only be revised by agreement between the CMA and the FCA.

NOTES

2 CMA (2014), Regulated industries: Guidance on concurrent application of competition law to regulated industries (CMA10).

3 FCA (2018), The FCA's concurrent competition enforcement powers for the provision of financial services (FG15/8).

CONTEXT

5. This MoU operates within the framework of the legislative provisions referred to in paragraph 1, the concurrent powers of the FCA under sections 234I to 234O of FSMA and any other applicable sector specific legislation from time to time.

Role of the CMA

6. The CMA is a non-ministerial department, established under the Enterprise and Regulatory Reform Act 2013.

7. The CMA works to promote competition for the benefit of consumers, both within and outside the UK, to make markets work well for consumers, businesses and the economy.

8. The CMA's statutory responsibilities, in so far as relevant to the matters that are the subject of this MoU, include:

(a) investigating where there may be breaches of the competition prohibitions; and

(b) conducting market studies and market investigations where there may be competition and consumer problems.

9. In connection with its statutory responsibilities, the CMA will cooperate with sectoral regulators to promote effective competition and support the use of their powers, including their powers to apply the competition prohibitions, in the interests of competition for the benefit of consumers.

Role of the FCA

10. The FCA is established under FSMA as the market conduct regulator in the financial services sector. It is also responsible for the prudential supervision of firms that are not regulated by the Prudential Regulation Authority (PRA). In addition, it is responsible for the regulation of claims management services in Great Britain.

11. The FCA has a single strategic objective which is to ensure that the relevant markets function well. It also has three operational objectives:

(a) to secure an appropriate degree of protection for consumers;

(b) to protect and enhance the integrity of the UK financial system; and

(c) to promote effective competition in the interests of consumers.

AIMS

12. The FCA acquired competition powers in relation to the provision of financial services, which are exercisable concurrently with the CMA, in April 2015 thereby bringing the FCA in line with the other sectoral regulators, which already had powers exercisable concurrently with the CMA in those sectors for which they have responsibility. In April 2019, it also obtained concurrent competition powers in relation to the provision of claims management services in Great Britain.[4]

13. The Enterprise and Regulatory Reform Act 2013, as well as establishing the CMA, made provision for the better working of the CMA's and the sectoral regulators' concurrent powers in the regulated sectors; specifically, the act: 'strengthens the role of the CMA and enhances the emphasis on early and proper consideration of the use of anti-trust powers (under Part 1 of the CA 1998 [ie the competition prohibitions]) by the sector regulators.'[5]

14. It is one of the strategic goals of the CMA, announced on its establishment on 1 October 2013, to extend the frontiers of competition into new areas, including by working with sectoral regulators to ensure fuller use of competition law and policy in sectoral markets.[6]

15. The government's strategic steer to the CMA, issued on 1 December 2015, says that the CMA should build 'a strong dialogue with sectoral regulators using the UKCN to ensure that the overall competition regime is coordinated and regulatory practices complement each other.'[7]

16. The sectoral regulators[8] and the CMA, working together in the UKCN established in 2013 (with Monitor having observer status), declared that: 'The mission of the UKCN will be to promote competition for the benefit of consumers and to prevent anti-competitive behaviour both through facilitating use of competition powers and development of pro-competitive regulatory frameworks, as appropriate.'[9]

17. The CMA and the FCA seek to use their powers to achieve more competitive outcomes in the financial services industry in the UK for the benefit of consumers so as to make the financial services markets in the UK work well for consumers of financial services, businesses in the sector and businesses that use those services and the economy in which those services play an essential part. The CMA and FCA are similarly working towards these outcomes in relation to the provision of claims management services in Great Britain. It is the view of the CMA and the FCA that such competitive outcomes can be achieved by various tools including: their concurrent competition law powers under the competition prohibitions and market provisions; their concurrent powers under specific consumer protection legislation; and the CMA's merger control functions. However, the CMA and the FCA recognise that some of these outcomes can also be achieved through the FCA's sector specific tools such as conduct regulation, supervision and enforcement.

18. This MoU aims to further the attainment of these objectives, and to make the changes introduced by the Enterprise and Regulatory Reform Act 2013, the Financial Services (Banking Reform) Act 2013 and Financial Guidance and Claims Act 2018 work effectively, maximising the complementary skills of the CMA and the FCA, including through:

(a) promoting cooperation and coordination between the CMA and the FCA when dealing with cases of suspected anti-competitive behaviour for which they have concurrent powers;
(b) promoting cooperation and coordination between the CMA and the FCA when dealing with market studies and market investigation references for which they have concurrent powers;
(c) facilitating the efficient and effective handling of cases of suspected anticompetitive behaviour within the FCA's concurrent jurisdiction;
(d) avoiding duplication of activity, wherever possible; and
(e) ensuring transparency as to the respective roles of the CMA and the FCA for individuals and consumers affected.

NOTES

4 These changes were introduced by the Financial Guidance and Claims Act 2018.

5 Enterprise and Regulatory Reform Act 2013 Explanatory Notes, paragraph 370.

6 Statement by Alex Chisholm, Chief Executive of the CMA, *CMA mission and strategy*, 1 October 2013.

7 Department for Business, Innovation and Skills, *Strategic steer for the Competition and Markets Authority*, in Annex A to the *Government's response to the Consultation on the Strategic Steer to the CMA*, 1 December 2015, page 11.

8 The FCA has been a full member of the UKCN since the UKCN's formation even though it did not have concurrent powers. It was included as it has had a statutory duty to promote effective competition in the interests of consumers since its formation in April 2013 and it was due to acquire concurrent powers in April 2015.

9 UKCN (2013), Statement of intent.

GENERAL COOPERATION

19. In addition to the provisions for cooperation between the CMA and the FCA specific to particular powers of the CMA and the FCA, as set out in this MoU and elsewhere, the CMA and the FCA are committed to the following general principles and practices for cooperation between themselves in respect of the sectors for which the FCA has responsibility.

20. Officials of the CMA and the FCA will meet and communicate, at appropriate levels of seniority, to discuss matters of mutual interest, both through the UKCN and bilaterally. A framework for such meetings will, as far as possible, be determined in advance so as to ensure attendance at the appropriate level and expertise.

21. The CMA and the FCA will, in respect of the FCA's concurrent jurisdiction, always consult each other:
(a) before the initial exercise of concurrent competition law powers in all cases where it appears that they have concurrent jurisdiction and where there are reasonable grounds for suspecting an infringement of the competition prohibitions; and
(b) before launching a market study (in the FCA's case, whether under the Enterprise Act 2002 or FSMA).

22. Where either the CMA or the FCA exercises its concurrent powers, the CMA and the FCA will, to the extent permitted by law, engage with each other in open dialogue and by sharing relevant information as appropriate. This engagement may include attendance at internal meetings held by the investigating authority (ie the authority to which a case is allocated) by the supporting authority (ie the other authority which would be competent to exercise concurrent powers in relation to the case), in order to discuss the case as envisaged at paragraph 3.31 of the concurrency guidance. The supporting authority will not generally attend the investigating authority's constitutional decision-making meetings, meetings of governance bodies or meetings with external parties such as those under investigation or complainants. Attendance by the supporting authority at any meeting is at the discretion of the investigating authority, but requests to attend should be considered by the investigating authority in the spirit of cooperation underpinning the concurrency regime.

23. The CMA and the FCA will consult each other at an early stage on any issues that might have significant implications for the other. For example, where the CMA undertakes a market study which relates to a sector other than one in the FCA's concurrent jurisdiction but which may have a significant impact on any sector in the FCA's concurrent jurisdiction, the CMA will inform the FCA and share appropriate information relating to that market study with the FCA to the extent permitted by law.

24. Within the spirit of broader collaboration for the purposes of the promotion of competitive outcomes, the CMA and the FCA will commit to discuss and share other relevant information, where legally permissible to do so.

PART A – COOPERATION IN RELATION TO THE COMPETITION PROHIBITIONS (COMPETITION ACT 1998 AND ARTICLES 101 AND 102 OF THE TREATY ON THE FUNCTIONING OF THE EUROPEAN UNION)

CASE ALLOCATION

Basis of allocation

[3.319]
25. The CMA and the FCA will endeavour to reach agreement on which authority will exercise its concurrent competition powers in respect of any particular case, under regulation 4(2) of the concurrency regulations. They will do so in a spirit of constructiveness and cooperation, while acknowledging the CMA's ultimate powers under regulations 5 and 8 of the concurrency regulations.

26. Their determination of which authority will exercise its powers will be based on assessing which of them is better placed to exercise those powers, having regard to the factors set out in paragraph 3.22 of the concurrency guidance. The CMA and the FCA envisage that other factors may appear relevant in the light of practical experience and that, if so, such factors may be chosen to supplement or supplant the factors set out in paragraph 3.22 of the concurrency guidance.

Procedure for allocation

27. Where either the CMA or the FCA has decided, on the basis of information in its possession, that there are reasonable grounds for suspecting that one of the competition prohibitions has been infringed (the reasonable suspicion test)[10] in relation to the FCA's concurrent jurisdiction it will disclose to the other (ie the receiving authority) sufficient information:

(a) to enable the receiving authority to understand the basis on which the disclosing authority has decided that the reasonable suspicion test is met; and

(b) for there to be an informed discussion on which authority (if either) is best placed to proceed in respect of the case.

28. In practice, it may be helpful for the CMA and the FCA to have discussed the case prior to such a decision having been reached, subject to paragraph 41 below. The disclosing authority will provide the information described under paragraph 27 within ten working days after it has decided that the reasonable suspicion test is met, whether or not it proposes to exercise concurrent powers.[11]

29. Within seven working days from receipt of this information, the receiving authority will respond in writing, setting out its initial view on the case and how it should be allocated and identifying any further information which it requires.

30. The CMA and the FCA will endeavour to agree which authority will exercise its concurrent competition powers in relation to the case, as provided for in regulation 4(2) of the concurrency regulations, as soon as possible and in any event no later than one month from disclosure of the information described under paragraph 27. Other than in exceptional circumstances (which shall be set out in writing), the CMA will initiate the procedure set out in regulation 5 of the concurrency regulations if agreement is not reached within two months of the disclosing authority first receiving sufficient information in connection with a complaint to enable it to decide that the reasonable suspicion test is met.

31. The procedure for agreeing the transfer of a case that is already in progress from the CMA to the FCA, or from the FCA to the CMA, is as set out in regulation 7 of the concurrency regulations and in paragraph 3.32 of the concurrency guidance.

32. The procedure for the CMA to direct the transfer to itself from the FCA of a case that is already in progress is as set out in regulation 8 of the concurrency regulations.

NOTES

10 As provided in section 25 of the Competition Act 1998.

11 As provided in regulation 9 of the concurrency regulations.

Implications of allocation

33. Any agreement or determination as to case allocation, under regulations 4, 5, 7 or 8 of the concurrency regulations, shall be notified to the person who has provided the information resulting in the case (for example, the person making a complaint), and so far as appropriate and lawful to any other affected person, by the authority which is exercising its concurrent competition powers in relation to the case, as soon as reasonably practicable.

34. Case allocation determines which of the CMA and the FCA is to exercise concurrent functions and make any decisions under the competition prohibitions. The CMA or FCA will be publicly identified as having such responsibility if and when any such investigation is announced. The CMA and the FCA envisage that, whichever authority has responsibility for a particular case, they and their officials will work cooperatively with each other on the case, pooling their expertise including as described in paragraphs 50 to 59 of this MoU and in paragraphs 3.33 to 3.35 of the concurrency guidance.

SHARING INFORMATION

Principles of information sharing

35. The effective sharing of information between the CMA and the FCA is fundamental to the successful exercise of their concurrent competition powers. It is needed both for the appropriate allocation of cases, as described in paragraphs 27 to 32 of this MoU, and for the successful handling of cases once allocated to make optimal use of the complementary experience and expertise of the two authorities.

36. The CMA and the FCA are committed, in addition to their legal obligations to share information (set out in regulation 9 of the concurrency regulations), to open dialogue and continuing liaison, both bilaterally and through the UKCN, with a view not only to handling specific cases but to promoting competition for the benefit of consumers in the sectors within the FCA's concurrent jurisdiction.

Information sharing mechanism – general liaison

37. The CMA and the FCA recognise the importance of meeting regularly to share information on matters relevant to competition in the FCA's concurrent jurisdiction, and to keep each other abreast of relevant work which they are considering or currently undertaking.

38. The CMA and the FCA will meet regularly at multiple levels, bilaterally and through the UKCN.

39. The CMA and the FCA will each designate in its organisation a relationship manager at official level to take responsibility for relations between the two authorities. In each authority, the relationship manager's responsibilities will include (but will not be limited to):

(a) maintaining an overview of joint projects between the two authorities and matters of mutual interest;

(b) maintaining an overview of the authority's contacts from all areas of joint working and mutual interest; and

(c) holding meetings with the relationship manager in the other authority from time to time (whether bilaterally or in the context of the UKCN) to identify potential new issues, with a view to circulating information to appropriate individuals within each organisation.

40. The existence of relationship managers does not in any way preclude direct communication between other staff at the CMA and the FCA.

41. For the purposes of sharing information pursuant to paragraph 27, ie in circumstances where the reasonable suspicion test is met, such information will be shared by the disclosing authority to the extent permitted by law and whether or not it proposes to exercise concurrent powers.[12] Where disclosure would be appropriate and permitted by law, the CMA and FCA may also share information regarding potential infringements of the competition prohibitions in advance of having reached a view as to whether the reasonable suspicion test is met. In circumstances where either the CMA or FCA has taken the view that a matter is not an administrative priority, irrespective of whether a view has been reached on whether the reasonable suspicion test is met, each may share the details of the matter with the other, or with any other authority which would be able to exercise concurrent competition powers in relation to that matter, to the extent permitted by law. Where leniency information is being shared under this paragraph, special considerations apply, as set out in paragraphs 47 and 48.

NOTES

12 For the avoidance of doubt, this does not entail an obligation to inform the other party if the regulator is carrying out general monitoring activity, where there is no consideration of exercising its concurrent powers.

Information sharing mechanism – handling specific cases

42. The procedures for information sharing for the purpose of case allocation shall be as set out in paragraphs 27 to 29 and 35 to 49 of this MoU.

43. When either the CMA or the FCA is exercising its powers in respect of the competition prohibitions in a particular case in the FCA's concurrent jurisdiction, each of them will share with the other any of the following information in its possession (to the extent permitted by law and subject to the confidentiality obligations in paragraphs 46 to 48 of this MoU):

(a) as a minimum, the matters referred to in regulation 9(1)(b) – (j) of the concurrency regulations, and in paragraph 3.49 of the concurrency guidance, complying with the time limits specified in paragraph 3.49;

(b) other information which it reasonably believes to be relevant or helpful to the other in the conduct of the case; and

(c) in the case of the authority which is exercising the powers, reports to the other on the progress of the case, of sufficient frequency and detail to enable the other to be appropriately informed; the means and frequency of such reporting will be decided on a case-by-case basis and in the light of experience as this enhanced framework of collaboration and its supporting arrangements develop over time.

Information sharing mechanism – for know-how purposes

44. The CMA will maintain on its webpages a central database of decisions taken in cases under the competition prohibitions, with a view to having an accessible body of know-how that will help ensure the effective and consistent application of competition law. The CMA and the FCA will, to the extent permitted by law, contribute information to that in the way best calculated to achieve that objective.

45. In any event, the CMA will report on cases in the regulated sectors under the competition prohibitions in the annual concurrency report which it is required under statute to issue. Further provisions on the annual concurrency report are in paragraphs 60 to 62 of this MoU.

Information sharing – confidentiality constraints

46. Any disclosure of information under paragraphs 27 to 29 and 35 to 45 of this MoU, and any use by the recipient of such information, shall only be to the extent permitted by law, including by reference to the provisions of Part 9 of the Enterprise Act 2002, relevant sector-specific legislative provisions and any other provisions relating to the disclosure, handling and use of information (such as the Data Protection Act 1998 and section 118 of FSMA, to the extent relevant).

47. Prior to disclosing information to each other, the CMA and the FCA will not generally give the person to whom the information relates prior notice of its intention to make the disclosure. However, if the CMA or the FCA consider it necessary or appropriate to pass leniency information to each other (or to another UK authority with concurrent powers), the transmitting authority will inform the applicant or its legal adviser first. Leniency information for the purposes of this MoU is any information which came into the possession of any of the CMA, its predecessors, the FCA or any other public authority as a direct or indirect result of having been provided in the context of an application for leniency. It includes information obtained by the transferring authority as a result of investigative measures resulting directly or indirectly from an application for leniency.

48. In addition to the general provisions referred to in paragraph 46, where the FCA or the CMA receives leniency information from the other (or from another UK authority with concurrent powers) for the purpose of applying the competition prohibitions or, in the case of the CMA, the cartel offence under section 188 of the Enterprise Act 2002, that information will not be used for any other purpose. This restriction on use also applies to any information obtained by the receiving authority as a result of investigative measures relating to the competition prohibitions or the cartel offence following the receipt of leniency information from the other authority. This does not affect the use that may be made by the CMA or the FCA of information received from other sources, including but not limited to disclosures to the FCA under Principle 11 of the FCA's Principles for Business, Principle 4 of the FCA's Statements of Principle for Approved Persons, Rule 4 of the FCA's Senior Manager Conduct Rules,[13] or if the leniency applicant's consent is obtained.[14] Where the provision of leniency information to either the CMA or the FCA affords or might, under certain conditions, afford the leniency applicant, its subsidiaries or its employees protection from sanctions (including a reduction in penalties) under the leniency programme operated by that authority and that information has been passed to another authority, the receiving authority shall afford the leniency applicant, its subsidiaries or its employees no lesser protection.

49. Where an application for leniency is made to the CMA by a firm active in the FCA's concurrent jurisdiction, the CMA will remind the applicant that it may have obligations to notify the FCA of its conduct under Principle 11 of the FCA's Principles for Business, Principle 4 of the FCA's Statements of Principle for Approved Persons, or Rule 4 of the FCA's Senior Manager Conduct Rules. When leniency information is shared with the FCA, the FCA may also contact the applicant to let it know it is aware of the leniency application and remind the applicant of any obligations it may have to notify relevant conduct, under the principles or rule mentioned above.[15] The FCA will have due regard for the need for appropriate handling of such contacts to minimise prejudice to the conduct of any ongoing or subsequent investigation.

NOTES

13 As set out in the FCA Handbook

14 The use restriction in this paragraph is intended to govern the use of leniency information in the context of the concurrency arrangements. It is not intended to prevent the disclosure of such leniency information by either one of the CMA or the FCA to the other (to the extent permitted by Part 9 of the Enterprise Act 2002 and in accordance with Leniency and no-action applications in cartel cases: OFT1495) for purposes other than the application of the competition prohibitions or the cartel offence. However, any such disclosure of leniency information would only be likely to be justified in exceptional circumstances, given the strong public interest in maintaining the incentives for undertakings and, in the case of the cartel offence, individuals to apply for leniency.

15 The FCA and CMA acknowledge that OFT1495 applies, in particular paragraphs 3.24–3.28, with respect to maintaining confidentiality.

POOLING RESOURCES

50. Paragraph 22 above, and the concurrency guidance provide for support to be provided by the supporting authority to the investigating authority when it is exercising its concurrent powers in a case. The CMA and the FCA will endeavour, so far as is reasonably practicable and permitted by law, and in the light of their respective ongoing priorities and resource availability at the time, to share their resources with each other in the interests of the effective enforcement of competition law in the FCA's concurrent jurisdiction, and more generally the promotion of competition for the benefit of consumers in those sectors, and to ensure that their resources and expertise are used most efficiently for that purpose.

51. As a consequence, where it has been agreed or determined that one of the authorities is to exercise its concurrent competition powers in relation to a case, that authority will, to the extent that there are resources available, receive appropriate practical assistance and support from the other in the handling of the case, as agreed on a case-by-case basis.

52. Such support and assistance may include the provision of training or practical know-how and expertise by one authority to the other where appropriate to enable the authority exercising its concurrent competition powers in the case to carry out its statutory functions effectively (for example in relation to conduct of site visits).

Secondments of staff

53. One means of the practical assistance and support that might be given, as referred to in paragraphs 50 and 51 of this MoU, is the secondment of staff, in accordance with regulation 10 of the concurrency regulations and paragraphs 3.33 and 3.34 of the concurrency guidance.

54. The CMA and the FCA are fully committed to the idea of secondments for this purpose, and will endeavour to meet each other's requests for secondments to the extent that they are appropriate and resources permit; this may include making provision for any secondee to be available to work for part of his or her time at his or her existing employer during the course of the secondment, for example on such cases that are in progress.

55. Requests for secondments should be made by the relationship manager of one authority to the relationship manager of the other, setting out the following information:

(a) The number of secondees required.

(b) The period for which each one is required.
(c) The level of seniority of each one.
(d) The nature of the expertise or experience of each one.
(e) The proposed payment arrangements.
(f) A brief explanation of why the requirement or requirements cannot adequately be met by deployment of staff from within the requesting authority.

56. To the extent that the recipient of a request for a secondment made under paragraph 55 of this MoU refuses that request or accedes to it on terms that are materially different from those requested, the recipient shall give reasons.

57. The CMA and the FCA will develop appropriate arrangements for the pooling and secondment of staff. Such arrangements will have regard to the resource constraints of both parties and such calls for staff, therefore, will be made in reasonable time and with sufficient warning to enable appropriate resource planning, management of other work commitments and appropriate sign-off procedures within each authority.

OTHER MUTUAL SUPPORT

58. In addition to the sharing of information, expertise, experience and the secondment of staff, the CMA and the FCA are fully committed to providing each other with more informal forms of support to enable them to carry out their competition law functions in relation to the FCA's concurrent jurisdiction – in each case to the extent that it is appropriate and permitted by law, and that resources permit – including (but not limited to):
(a) answering specific queries from time to time;
(b) providing information or views on a specific sector or market, or an area of competition law or policy; and
(c) providing training on a specific sector or market, or an area of competition law or policy.

59. Such support may be requested and provided in connection with a specific case or with the promotion of competition more generally. In this regard, both the CMA and the FCA will act reasonably, including by providing sufficient time and information for requests for support to be responded to fully and effectively and for the relevant staff to be engaged.

ANNUAL CONCURRENCY REPORT

60. The CMA is required by statute to publish a report every year, starting after its first year of operation in 2014/15,[16] containing an assessment of how the concurrency arrangements between the CMA and the sectoral regulators, as regards both the competition prohibitions and the market provisions, have operated during the year. This MoU refers to that report as the annual concurrency report. There is further provision on the annual concurrency report in paragraphs 3.55 to 3.62 of the concurrency guidance.

61. The CMA will consult, and cooperate with, the FCA and with other sectoral regulators in preparing the annual concurrency report. In connection with this, the CMA will:
(a) prepare a draft of the annual concurrency report that it will send to the FCA and other sectoral regulators seeking comments or suggestions on the content or conclusions of the annual concurrency report and giving them adequate time to comment or make suggestions;
(b) take account of any comments or suggestions it receives from the FCA and other sectoral regulators and the CMA may seek further clarification on those comments or suggestions as appropriate;
(c) prepare a final version of the annual concurrency report for publication that takes account of its consultation of the FCA and other sectoral regulators as appropriate; and
(d) make the annual concurrency report available on the CMA webpages.

62. The FCA will cooperate with the CMA in the preparation of the annual concurrency report including (but not limited to) by way of:
(a) providing information and data on general market conditions and on the application of the competition prohibitions and the market provisions to the sectors within the FCA's concurrent jurisdiction;
(b) responding to reasonable requests for information and data; and
(c) providing to the CMA any comments and suggestions it may have in connection with the process described in paragraph 61 of this MoU;

in each case promptly so as to facilitate the timely production and publication of the annual concurrency report.

NOTES

16 Enterprise and Regulatory Reform Act 2013 Schedule 4 paragraph 16.

VOLUNTARY REDRESS SCHEMES

63. In cases relating to investigations under the competition prohibitions in the FCA's concurrent jurisdiction, both the CMA and the FCA have the power to approve voluntary redress schemes. When either authority proposes to exercise these powers, it shall liaise with the other authority as appropriate and will have regard to its own guidance.[17]

NOTES

17 The CMA's guidance on the approval of voluntary redress schemes (CMA40) states in footnote 7: 'The CMA expects that regulators will take this CMA guidance into account when producing their own guidance on the approval power.'

SHORT FORM OPINIONS

64. The CMA shall inform the FCA following an initial enquiry for a short form opinion relating to the FCA's concurrent jurisdiction. Where the CMA is considering providing such an opinion, it will discuss with the FCA before deciding to do so. If the CMA then decides to produce an opinion, it will engage with the FCA, the nature and degree of that engagement to be considered on a case-by-case basis, having regard, in particular, to the extent to which the opinion has a multi-sector rather than single-sector dimension. In all cases, the CMA will give the opportunity to provide comments on a draft opinion.

PART B – COOPERATION IN RELATION TO THE MARKET PROVISIONS: MARKET STUDIES AND MARKET INVESTIGATIONS (ENTERPRISE ACT 2002)

HOW CONCURRENCY WORKS UNDER THE MARKET PROVISIONS

[3.320]

65. The FCA has the power, concurrently with the CMA, to carry out market studies, to make market investigation references, agree undertakings in lieu of a reference and make recommendations to the government in relation to the FCA's concurrent jurisdiction under Part 4 of the Enterprise Act 2002 (as do other sectoral regulators in relation to the sectors for which they are responsible).

66. Under the Enterprise Act 2002, the CMA and the FCA may, in relation to the FCA's concurrent jurisdiction, undertake market studies, and may make market investigation references to the Chair of the CMA for the constitution of a CMA group to conduct an in-depth market investigation into single or multiple markets for goods or services in the UK. The purpose of these investigations is to examine the market(s) and (where required) implement appropriate remedies where the CMA determines that the structure of the market(s) or the conduct of the suppliers or customers is harming competition.

67. When making a reference, the CMA or the FCA, as applicable, must have reasonable grounds for suspecting that any feature or combination of features of a market or markets in the UK prevents, restricts or distorts competition in relation to the supply or acquisition of any goods or services in the UK (or in a part of the UK).

68. The cooperation between the CMA and the FCA provided for in this Part B shall not extend to conduct that could reasonably be expected to impair the impartiality or the fairness of the CMA panel in conducting market investigations.

SUPER-COMPLAINTS

69. The CMA[18] has an obligation to respond to super-complaints about any feature, or combination of features, of a market in the UK for goods or services which is or appears to be significantly harming the interests of consumers. The FCA[19] has a similar obligation for super-complaints relating to the FCA's concurrent jurisdiction.

70. The coordination of the CMA's and the sectoral regulators' super-complaint duties will be based on policies agreed and applied through the UKCN.

71. Subject to paragraph 70 above, the FCA intends where permitted by law to:

(a) inform the CMA of super-complaints received under section 234C of FSMA;

(b) inform the CMA of formal references received under section 234D of FSMA which could raise matters that could be considered by the CMA by way of a market study and/or under section 131 of the Enterprise Act 2002;

(c) discuss with the CMA those super-complaints where the FCA considers that action by the CMA under any of the CMA's powers is more appropriate than regulatory action under FSMA, bearing in mind the FCA's operational objective in relation to promoting effective competition in the interests of consumers set out in FSMA;

(d) refer to the CMA super-complaints identifying competition issues which the FCA cannot address under its powers; and

(e) inform the CMA of super-complaints which identify issues in the FCA's concurrent jurisdiction which the FCA believes may have consequences for related non-financial services and non-claims management services markets.

72. Subject to paragraph 70 above, the CMA intends to:

(a) inform the FCA of super-complaints received under section 11 of the Enterprise Act 2002 where they relate to the FCA's concurrent jurisdiction;

(b) discuss those super-complaints with the FCA where the CMA considers that regulatory action under FSMA may be more appropriate than action under any of the CMA's powers, bearing in mind the CMA's mission to make markets work well in the interests of consumers, businesses and the economy;

(c) refer to the FCA super-complaints concerning the FCA's concurrent jurisdiction to which the CMA cannot respond under its powers; and

(d) inform the FCA of super-complaints which identify competition issues in markets not within the FCA's concurrent jurisdiction, which the CMA believes may have consequences for the FCA's concurrent jurisdiction.

NOTES

18 Section 11 of the Enterprise Act 2002.

19 Sections 234C and 234E of FSMA.

MUTUAL CONSULTATION

73. The FCA and the CMA have a duty to consult each other before exercising concurrent functions under the market provisions.[20] The FCA will also consult the CMA before launching a market study under FSMA.

NOTES

[20] Section 234I(7) of FSMA.

SHARING INFORMATION

74. The provisions of paragraphs 37 to 41, 43 (excluding 43(a)) and 45 of this MoU apply to information sharing under the market provisions as they do under the competition prohibitions.

POOLING RESOURCES

75. The provisions of paragraph 50 to 59 of this MoU apply to pooling resources under the market provisions as they do under the competition prohibitions.

76. Where the CMA and the FCA intend to pool resources in order to exercise powers under the market provisions of the Enterprise Act 2002, they shall, at the outset of any such project, discuss the arrangements for how they will pool resources and work jointly.

ANNUAL CONCURRENCY REPORT

77. The provisions of paragraphs 60 to 62 of this MoU apply under the market provisions as they do under the competition prohibitions.

PART C – COOPERATION IN RELATION TO COMPETITION SCRUTINY (FINANCIAL SERVICES AND MARKETS ACT 2000)

INTERACTION BETWEEN THE FCA AND THE CMA UNDER FSMA

[3.321]

78. For the purposes of this Part C and pursuant to section 140B of FSMA, the CMA gives 'section 140B advice"' if:

(a) it gives advice, under section 7 of the Enterprise Act 2002, to the FCA and that advice states that one or more of the things listed in paragraph 79 below may cause or contribute to the prevention, restriction or distortion of competition in connection with the supply or acquisition of any goods or services in the UK or a part of the UK, or might be expected to do so in the future; or

(b) it publishes a report, under section 136 of the Enterprise Act 2002, which contains a decision that one or more of the things listed in paragraph 79 below may cause or contribute to the prevention, restriction or distortion of competition in connection with the supply or acquisition of any goods or services in the UK or a part of the UK, or might be expected to do so in the future, and the CMA recommends that any action be taken by the FCA.

79. The things mentioned in paragraph 78 are:

(a) a regulating provision or practice of the FCA;

(b) two or more regulating provisions or practices (of the FCA or of both the FCA and PRA);

(c) a particular combination of regulating provisions or practices (of the FCA or of both the FCA and PRA); or

(d) a feature or combination of features of one or more markets in the UK that could be dealt with by regulating provisions or practices (of the FCA or of both the FCA and PRA).

80. The CMA will consult with the FCA before officially publishing section 140B advice, and will provide the FCA with guidance as to how it intends to use this power.

81. Under section of 140G of FSMA, the FCA must, within 90 days after the day on which it receives section 140B advice from the CMA, publish a response stating how it proposes to deal with the advice and in particular:

(a) whether it has decided to take any action, or to take no action, in response to the advice;

(b) if it has decided to take action, what action it proposes to take; and

(c) its reasons for its proposals.

(VI) TRANSPORT

CIVIL AVIATION AUTHORITY: GUIDANCE ON THE APPLICATION OF THE CAA'S COMPETITION POWERS (NOTE)

CAP 1235 (May 2015)

[3.322]

NOTES

This guidance sets out the application of the CAA's competition powers that covers the whole breadth of its powers in relation to airport operation services and air traffic services – to undertake sector reviews, carry out market studies, make market investigation references to the CMA, and investigate competition infringements and super complaints. The guidance has been prepared to inform stakeholders – businesses and their advisers, consumers, consumer groups, and other interested parties on how the CAA will apply its competition powers and duties. It sets out how the CAA will apply its concurrent competition powers and seeks to explain the interface between generally applicable competition law and aviation specific legislation.

This document is available on the Civil Aviation Authority website at: www.caa.co.uk/Commercial-industry/Airports/Economic-regulation/Competition-policy/Competition-powers/.

See also "Prioritisation Principles for the CAA's Consumer Protection, Competition Law and Economic Regulation Work" (May 2015) (same website as above). It explains the CAA's approach in deciding which pieces of work to take forward in the areas of consumer protection, competition law and economic regulation.

See also "CAP1343 – Guidance on the application of the CAA's powers under the Airport Charges Regulations 2011" (October 2015) on the CAA website at: www.caa.co.uk/Commercial-industry/Airports/Economic-regulation/Competition-policy/Airport-charges-regulations/.

MEMORANDUM OF UNDERSTANDING BETWEEN THE COMPETITION AND MARKETS AUTHORITY AND THE CIVIL AVIATION AUTHORITY – CONCURRENT COMPETITION POWERS

9 February 2016

[3.323]

NOTES

FOREWORD

[3.324]

The changes to the United Kingdom's (UK) competition law system, introduced under the Enterprise and Regulatory Reform Act 2013 and in force since April 2014, are designed to improve the effectiveness of competition law enforcement.

The Competition and Markets Authority (CMA) has competition law powers which apply across the whole economy. Sectoral regulators such as the Civil Aviation Authority (CAA) may exercise the competition law powers to enforce competition law concurrently with the CMA in those sectors for which they have responsibility, namely the prohibitions on anti-competitive agreements and on abuse of a dominant position, and the ability to make market investigation references.

The Enterprise and Regulatory Reform Act 2013 introduced a number of changes to improve the working of concurrency and to enable closer working between the CMA and sectoral regulators.

The CMA and the sectoral regulators have demonstrated their commitment to making the concurrency framework more effective through the establishment of the UK Competition Network (UKCN). This represents an enhanced forum for cooperation which enables closer working, with the objective of more consistent and effective use of concurrent competition powers across all sectors. In their statement of intent in December 2013, the members of the UKCN affirmed: 'The mission of the UKCN will be to promote competition for the benefit of consumers and to prevent anti-competitive behaviour both through facilitating use of competition powers and development of pro-competitive regulatory frameworks, as appropriate.'[1]

This memorandum of understanding (MoU) represents a further stage in the process of cooperation, setting out more detail on how the CMA and the CAA will, in practice, work together within the framework of competition law.[2]

It draws on the formal framework in the legislation and sets out our bilateral commitment to look for opportunities to work together, including within the framework of the UKCN, to promote competition for the benefit of consumers. We shall do this by the sharing of expertise, information, ideas and experience. Each of us will commit to doing this efficiently and with a mutual regard for each other's statutory duties and strategic objectives.

In particular, in working together with the CMA, the CAA will continue to discharge its primary statutory duties to maintain a high standard of safety in the provision of air traffic services, and to further the interests of users of air transport services regarding the range, availability, continuity, cost and quality of airport operation services. Wherever possible the interests of users will be best promoted through effective competition. In situations where effective competition is absent, or may not be achievable, regulation by licence may be more effective.

We believe that this MoU offers a valuable basis for that cooperation, in the interests of the CMA, the CAA, the aviation sector and most importantly of all, consumers.

Alex Chisholm	**Andrew Haines**
CEO, CMA	**CEO, CAA**

NOTES

[1] UKCN (2013), Statement of intent.

[2] This MoU does not relate to 'regulatory appeals' – that is, the separate role that the CMA has in considering appeals against, or references relating to, proposed direct regulatory action by the CAA under the sectoral statutes. This is a separate role, to be undertaken by the CMA panel, and the CMA is committed to ensuring that its cooperation with the CAA – whether under this MoU (and under comparable MoU agreed with other sectoral regulators), through the UKCN, or otherwise in connection with their concurrent powers – will not impair the impartiality and fairness of the CMA's conduct of such regulatory appeals (or indeed of market or merger investigations undertaken by the CMA panel).

MEMORANDUM OF UNDERSTANDING BETWEEN THE COMPETITION AND MARKETS AUTHORITY AND THE CIVIL AVIATION AUTHORITY

PURPOSE OF THIS MEMORANDUM OF UNDERSTANDING

[3.325]

1. This MoU sets out working arrangements between the CMA and the CAA in relation to their concurrent powers in the air traffic and airport operation services sectors:

(a) to apply the prohibitions on agreements that prevent, restrict or distort competition; and on the abuse of a dominant position, under the Chapter I prohibition and the Chapter II prohibition of the Competition Act 1998 and under Article 101 and Article 102 of the Treaty on the Functioning of the European Union – referred to in this MoU as the 'competition prohibitions'; and

(b) to undertake market studies, and to make references to the CMA for the constitution of a CMA group to conduct an in-depth market investigation into single or multiple markets for goods or services in the UK under the Enterprise Act 2002 – referred to in this MoU as the 'market provisions'.

2. This MoU is not intended to have legal effect.

3. This MoU is to be read alongside other material concerning the relations between the CMA and the CAA, including: the Civil Aviation Act 2012; the Transport Act 2000; the Competition Act 1998; the Enterprise Act 2002; the Enterprise and Regulatory Reform Act 2013; the Competition Act 1998 and Other Enactments (Amendment) Regulations 2004; the Competition Act 1998 (Concurrency) Regulations 2014, referred to in this MoU as the concurrency regulations, and the CMA's guidance on concurrent application of competition law to regulated industries, referred to in this MoU as the concurrency guidance[3] and the CAA's guidance on the application of its competition powers.[4] This MoU supplements and does not supplant that material.

4. The arrangements covered by this MoU are, wherever possible, set out in terms providing sufficient flexibility for the relationship between the CAA and the CMA to develop in the light of experience. The CMA and the CAA commit to review these arrangements from time to time to evaluate their continuing fitness for purpose. Such review can be initiated at the request of the CMA, the CAA or a member of the UKCN. This MoU may only be revised by agreement between the CMA and the CAA.

5. Nothing in this MoU applies in relation to the functions of the CMA in its separate role of considering appeals against, or references related to, proposed action by the CAA under the sectoral statutes. The CMA and the CAA acknowledge the importance of maintaining the CMA's impartiality and fairness in carrying out those functions, and indeed of market or merger investigations undertaken by the CMA panel.

NOTES

[3] CMA (2014), *Regulated industries: Guidance on concurrent application of competition law to regulated industries* (CMA10).

[4] CAA (2015), *CAP 1235 Guidance on the Application of the CAA's Competition Powers.*

CONTEXT

6. This MoU operates within the framework of the legislative provisions referred to in paragraph 1, the Transport Act 2000, the Civil Aviation Act 2012 and any other applicable sector specific legislation from time to time.

Role of the CMA

7. The CMA is a non-ministerial department, established under the Enterprise and Regulatory Reform Act 2013.

8. The CMA works to promote competition for the benefit of consumers, both within and outside the UK, to make markets work well for consumers, businesses and the economy.

9. The CMA's statutory responsibilities, in so far as relevant to the matters that are the subject of this MoU, include:
(a) investigating where there may be breaches of the competition prohibitions; and
(b) conducting market studies and market investigations where there may be competition and consumer problems.

10. In connection with its statutory responsibilities, the CMA will cooperate with sectoral regulators and encourage sectoral regulators to use their powers, including their powers to apply the competition prohibitions, in the interests of competition for the benefit of consumers.

Role of the CAA

11. The CAA is a public corporation established by Parliament in 1972 as an independent specialist aviation regulator. Its current functions and duties are found principally in the Civil Aviation Act 1982, the Transport Act 2000 and the Civil Aviation Act 2012 and in instruments made under them.

12. The CAA works to enhance aviation safety performance, improve choice and value for aviation consumers and to improve aviation's environmental performance. Its primary statutory duties in relation to activities within the scope of this MoU are:
(a) for airspace, to maintain a high standard of safety in the provision of air traffic services; and
(b) with regards to airports, the CAA must carry out its functions in a manner which it considers will further the interests of users of air transport services regarding the range, availability, continuity, cost and quality of airport operation services. It must do so, where appropriate, in a way which it considers will promote competition in the provision of airport operation services.

13. In both of these areas the CAA has a number of secondary duties.[5] Where appropriate, the CAA fulfils its duties primarily through the economic licensing of operators of dominant airports as defined by the Civil Aviation Act 2012 and of certain providers of air traffic services under the Transport Act 2000.

14. In so far as relevant to the matters that are directly the subject of this MoU, the relevant CAA functions are:
(a) those under the Competition Act 1998 of investigating where there may be breaches of the competition prohibitions within the supply of air traffic services or airport operation services; and
(b) those under the Enterprise Act 2002 of conducting market studies and market investigations within these sectors where there may be competition and consumer problems.

Under both the Transport Act 2000 and Civil Aviation Act 2012, the CAA has a duty to consider whether enforcement through the Competition Act 1998 is more appropriate than using its sectoral enforcement tools.

NOTES

[5] Section 2(2) to (7) of the Transport Act 2000 and section 1(3) to (7) of the Civil Aviation Act 2012.

AIMS

15. The Enterprise and Regulatory Reform Act 2013, as well as establishing the CMA, made provision for the better working of the CMA's and the sectoral regulators' concurrent powers in the regulated sectors; specifically, the act: 'strengthens the role of the CMA and enhances the emphasis on early and proper consideration of the use of anti-trust powers (under Part 1 of the CA 1998 [ie the competition prohibitions]) by the sector regulators.'[6]

16. It is one of the strategic goals of the CMA, announced on its establishment on 1 October 2013, to extend the frontiers of competition into new areas, including by working with sectoral regulators to ensure fuller use of competition law and policy in sectoral markets.[7]

17. The government's strategic steer to the CMA, issued on 1 December 2015, says that the CMA should build 'a strong dialogue with sectoral regulators using the UKCN to ensure that the overall competition regime is coordinated and regulatory practices complement each other.'[8]

18. The sectoral regulators and the CMA, working together in the UKCN established in 2013 (with Monitor having observer status), declared that: 'The mission of the UKCN will be to promote competition for the benefit of consumers and to prevent anti-competitive behaviour both through facilitating use of competition powers and development of pro-competitive regulatory frameworks, as appropriate.'[9]

19. The CMA and the CAA seek to use their respective powers to achieve more competitive outcomes in the air traffic and airport operation sectors for the benefit of consumers so as to make markets in those sectors work well for consumers, businesses in those sectors and businesses that use those services and the economy in which those services play an important part. It is the view of the CMA and the CAA that such competitive outcomes can be achieved by various tools, including their concurrent competition law powers under the competition prohibitions, the market provisions and merger control, but also through other tools such as direct regulatory action by the CAA including through enforcement of regulatory obligations (for example, in providing for non-discrimination by licence holders) and liberalisation measures introduced under national and European Union legislation.

20. This MoU aims to further the attainment of these objectives, and to make the changes introduced by the Enterprise and Regulatory Reform Act 2013 work effectively, maximising the complementary skills of the CMA and the CAA, including through:
(a) promoting cooperation and coordination between the CMA and the CAA when dealing with cases of suspected anti-competitive behaviour for which they have concurrent powers;

(b) promoting cooperation and coordination between the CMA and the CAA when dealing with market studies and market investigation references for which they have concurrent powers;

(c) facilitating the efficient and effective handling of cases of suspected anti-competitive behaviour within air traffic and airport operation services markets;

(d) avoiding duplication of activity, wherever possible; and

(e) ensuring transparency as to the respective roles of the CMA and the CAA for individuals and consumers affected.

NOTES

6 Enterprise and Regulatory Reform Act 2013 Explanatory Notes, paragraph 370.

7 Statement by Alex Chisholm, Chief Executive of the CMA, CMA mission and strategy, 1 October 2013.

8 Department for Business, Innovation and Skills, *Strategic steer for the Competition and Markets Authority*, in Annex A to the *Government's response to the Consultation on the Strategic Steer to the CMA*, 1 December 2015, page 11.

9 UKCN (2013), Statement of intent.

GENERAL COOPERATION

21. In addition to the provisions for cooperation between the CMA and the CAA specific to particular powers of the CMA and the CAA as set out in this MoU, the CMA and the CAA are committed to the following general principles and practices for cooperation between themselves in respect of the sectors for which the CAA has responsibility.

22. Officials of the CMA and the CAA will meet and communicate, at appropriate levels of seniority, to discuss matters of mutual interest, both through the UKCN and bilaterally. A framework for such meetings will, as far as possible, be determined in advance so as to ensure attendance at the appropriate level and expertise.

23. The CMA and the CAA will, in respect of the air traffic and airport operation services sectors, always consult each other:

(a) before the initial exercise of concurrent competition law powers in all cases where it appears that they have concurrent jurisdiction and where there are reasonable grounds for suspecting an infringement of the competition prohibitions; and

(b) before launching a market study under the Enterprise Act 2002.[10]

24. Where either the CMA or the CAA exercises its concurrent powers, the CMA and the CAA will, to the extent permitted by law, engage with each other in open dialogue and by sharing relevant information as appropriate. This engagement may include attendance at internal meetings held by the investigating authority (ie the authority to which a case is allocated) by the supporting authority (ie the other authority which would be competent to exercise concurrent powers in relation to the case), in order to discuss the case as envisaged in paragraph 3.31 of the concurrency guidance. The supporting authority will not generally attend the investigating authority's constitutional decision-making meetings, meetings of governance bodies or meetings with external parties such as those under investigation or complainants. Attendance by the supporting authority at any meeting is at the discretion of the investigating authority, but requests to attend should be considered by the investigating authority in the spirit of cooperation underpinning the new concurrency regime.

25. The CMA and the CAA will consult each other at an early stage on any issues that might have significant implications for the other. For example, where the CMA undertakes a market study which relates to a sector other than air traffic or airport operation services but which may have a significant impact on either of those sectors, the CMA will inform the CAA and share appropriate information relating to that market study with the CAA to the extent permitted by law.

26. Within the spirit of broader collaboration for the purposes of the promotion of competitive outcomes, the CMA and the CAA will commit to discuss and share other information about a broader range of competition complaints and concerns, where legally permissible to do so, but subject to the particular need not to impair the impartiality and fairness of the CMA in carrying out the functions referred to in paragraph 5 of this MoU.

NOTES

10 Instigation of a market study occurs on the publication of a market study notice, as defined in section 130A of the Enterprise Act 2002.

PART A – COOPERATION IN RELATION TO THE COMPETITION PROHIBITIONS (COMPETITION ACT 1998 AND ARTICLES 101 AND 102 OF THE TREATY ON THE FUNCTIONING OF THE EUROPEAN UNION)

CASE ALLOCATION

Basis of allocation

[3.326]

27. The CMA and the CAA will endeavour to reach agreement on which authority will exercise its concurrent competition powers in respect of any particular case, under regulation 4(2) of the concurrency regulations. They will do so in a spirit of constructiveness and cooperation, while acknowledging the CMA's ultimate powers under regulations 5 and 8 of the concurrency regulations.

28. Their determination of which authority will exercise its powers will be based on assessing which of them is better placed to exercise those powers, having regard to the factors set out in paragraph 3.22

of the concurrency guidance. The CMA and the CAA envisage that other factors may appear relevant in the light of practical experience and that, if so, such factors may be chosen to supplement or supplant the factors set out in paragraph 3.22 of the concurrency guidance.

Procedure for allocation

29. Where either the CMA or the CAA has decided, on the basis of information in its possession, that there are reasonable grounds for suspecting that one of the competition prohibitions has been infringed (the reasonable suspicion test)[11] in relation to the air traffic or airport operation services sectors, it will disclose to the other (ie the receiving authority) sufficient information:

(a) to enable the receiving authority to understand the basis on which the disclosing authority has decided that the reasonable suspicion test is met; and

(b) for there to be an informed discussion on which authority (if either) is best placed to proceed in respect of the case.

30. In practice, it may be helpful for the CMA and the CAA to have discussed the case prior to such a decision having been reached, subject to paragraph 43 below. The disclosing authority will provide the information described under paragraph 29 within ten working days after it has decided that the reasonable suspicion test is met, whether or not it proposes to exercise concurrent powers.[12]

31. Within seven working days from receipt of this information, the receiving authority will respond in writing, setting out its initial view on the case and how it should be allocated and identifying any further information which it requires.

32. The CMA and the CAA will endeavour to agree which authority will exercise its concurrent competition powers in relation to the case, as provided for in regulation 4(2) of the concurrency regulations, as soon as possible and in any event no later than one month from disclosure of the information described under paragraph 29. Other than in exceptional circumstances (which shall be set out in writing), the CMA will initiate the procedure set out in regulation 5 of the concurrency regulations if agreement is not reached within two months of the disclosing authority first receiving sufficient information in connection with a complaint to enable it to decide that the reasonable suspicion test is met.

33. The procedure for agreeing the transfer of a case that is already in progress from the CMA to the CAA, or from the CAA to the CMA, is as set out in regulation 7 of the concurrency regulations and in paragraph 3.32 of the concurrency guidance.

34. The procedure for the CMA to direct the transfer to itself from the CAA of a case that is already in progress is as set out in regulation 8 of the concurrency regulations.

NOTES

11 As provided in section 25 of the Competition Act 1998.

12 As provided in regulation 9 of the concurrency regulations.

Implications of case allocation

35. Any agreement or determination as to case allocation, under regulations 4, 5, 7 or 8 of the concurrency regulations, shall be notified to the person who has provided the information resulting in the case (for example, the person making a complaint), and so far as appropriate and lawful to any other affected person, by the authority which is exercising its concurrent competition powers in relation to the case, as soon as reasonably practicable.

36. Case allocation determines which of the CMA and the CAA is to exercise concurrent functions and make any decisions under the competition prohibitions. The CMA or CAA will be publicly identified as having such responsibility if and when any such investigation is announced. The CMA and the CAA envisage that, whichever authority has responsibility for a particular case, they and their officials will work cooperatively with each other on the case as appropriate, pooling their expertise including in the ways described in paragraphs 51 to 59 of this MoU and in paragraphs 3.33 to 3.35 of the concurrency guidance.

SHARING INFORMATION

Principles of information sharing

37. The effective sharing of information between the CMA and the CAA is fundamental to the successful exercise of their concurrent competition powers. It is needed both for the appropriate allocation of cases, as described in paragraphs 29 to 34 of this MoU, and for the successful handling of cases once allocated to make optimal use of the complementary experience and expertise of the two authorities.

38. The CMA and the CAA are committed, in addition to their legal obligations to share information (set out in regulation 9 of the concurrency regulations), to open dialogue and continuing liaison, both bilaterally and through the UKCN, with a view not only to handling specific cases but to promoting competition for the benefit of consumers in the air traffic and airport operation services sectors.

Information sharing mechanism – general liaison

39. The CMA and the CAA recognise the importance of meeting regularly to share information on matters relevant to competition in the air traffic and airport operation services markets, and to keep each other abreast of relevant work which they are considering or currently undertaking.

40. The CMA and the CAA will meet regularly at multiple levels, bilaterally and through the UKCN.

41. The CMA and the CAA will each designate in its organisation a relationship manager at official level to take responsibility for relations between the two authorities. In each authority, the relationship manager's responsibilities will include (but will not be limited to):

(a) maintaining an overview of joint projects between the two authorities and matters of mutual interest;

(b) maintaining an overview of the authority's contacts from all areas of joint working and mutual interest; and

(c) holding meetings with the relationship manager in the other authority from time to time (whether bilaterally or in the context of the UKCN) to identify potential new issues, with a view to circulating information to appropriate individuals within each organisation.

42. The existence of relationship managers does not in any way preclude direct communication between other staff at the CMA and the CAA.

43. For the purposes of sharing information pursuant to paragraph 29, ie in circumstances where the reasonable suspicion test is met, such information will be shared by the disclosing authority to the extent permitted by law and whether or not it proposes to exercise concurrent powers.[13] Where disclosure would be appropriate and permitted by law, the CMA and CAA may also share information regarding potential infringements of the competition prohibitions in advance of having reached a view as to whether the reasonable suspicion test is met. In circumstances where either the CMA or the CAA has taken the view that a matter is not an administrative priority, irrespective of whether a view has been reached on whether the reasonable suspicion test is met, each may share the details of the matter with the other, or with any other authority which would be able to exercise concurrent competition powers in relation to that matter, to the extent permitted by law. Where leniency information is being shared under this paragraph, special considerations apply, as set out in paragraphs 49 and 50.

NOTES

[13] For the avoidance of doubt, this does not entail an obligation to inform the other party if the regulator is carrying out general monitoring activity, where there is no consideration of exercising its concurrent powers.

Information sharing mechanism – handling specific cases

44. The procedures for information sharing for the purpose of case allocation shall be as set out in paragraphs 29 to 31 and 37 to 50 of this MoU.

45. When either the CMA or the CAA is exercising its powers in respect of the competition prohibitions in a particular case in the air traffic or airport operation services sectors, each of them will share with the other any of the following information in its possession (to the extent permitted by law and subject to the confidentiality obligations in paragraphs 48 to 50 of this MoU):

(a) as a minimum, the matters referred to in regulation 9(1)(b) – (j) of the concurrency regulations, and in paragraph 3.49 of the concurrency guidance, complying with the time limits specified in paragraph 3.49;

(b) other information which it reasonably believes to be relevant or helpful to the other in the conduct of the case; and

(c) in the case of the authority which is exercising the powers, reports to the other on the progress of the case, of sufficient frequency and detail to enable the other to be appropriately informed; the means and frequency of such reporting will be decided on a case-by-case basis and in the light of experience as this enhanced framework of collaboration and its supporting arrangements develop over time.

Information sharing mechanism – for know-how purposes

46. The CMA will maintain on its webpages a central database of decisions taken in cases under the competition prohibitions, with a view to having an accessible body of know-how that will help ensure the effective and consistent application of competition law. The CMA and the CAA will, to the extent permitted by law, contribute information to that in the way best calculated to achieve that objective.

47. In any event, the CMA will report on cases in the regulated sectors under the competition prohibitions in the annual concurrency report which it is required under statute to issue. Further provisions on the annual concurrency report are in paragraphs 60 to 62 of this MoU.

Information sharing – confidentiality constraints

48. Any disclosure of information under paragraphs 29 to 31 and 37 to 47 of this MoU, and any use by the recipient of such information, shall only be to the extent permitted by law, including by reference to the provisions of Part 9 of the Enterprise Act 2002, relevant sector-specific legislative provisions and any other provisions relating to the disclosure, handling and use of information (such as the Data Protection Act 1998 and section 118 of the Financial Services and Markets Act 2000, to the extent relevant).

49. Prior to disclosing information to each other, the CMA and the CAA will not generally give the person to whom the information relates prior notice of its intention to make the disclosure. However, if the CMA or the CAA consider it necessary or appropriate to pass leniency information to each other (or to another UK authority with concurrent powers), the transmitting authority will inform the applicant or its legal adviser first. Leniency information for the purposes of this MoU is any information which came into the possession of any of the CMA, its predecessors, the CAA or any other public authority as a direct or indirect result of having been provided in the context of an application for leniency. It includes information obtained by the transferring authority as a result of investigative measures resulting directly or indirectly from an application for leniency.

50. In addition to the general provisions referred to in paragraph 48, where the CAA or the CMA receives leniency information from the other (or from another UK authority with concurrent powers) for the purpose of applying the competition prohibitions or, in the case of the CMA, the cartel offence under section 188 of the Enterprise Act 2002, that information will not be used for any other purpose. This restriction on use also applies to any information obtained by the receiving authority as a result of investigative measures relating to the competition prohibitions or the cartel offence following the receipt of leniency information from the other authority. This does not affect the use that may be made by the CMA or the CAA of information received from other sources, or if the leniency applicant's consent is obtained.[14] Where the provision of leniency information to either the CMA or the CAA affords or might, under certain conditions, afford the leniency applicant, its subsidiaries or its employees protection from sanctions (including a reduction in penalties) under the leniency programme operated by that authority and that information has been passed to another authority, the receiving authority shall afford the leniency applicant, its subsidiaries or its employees no lesser protection.

NOTES

[14] The use restriction in this paragraph is intended to govern the use of leniency information in the context of the concurrency arrangements. It is not intended to prevent the disclosure of such leniency information by either one of the CMA or the CAA to the other (to the extent permitted by Part 9 of the Enterprise Act 2002 and in accordance with Leniency and no-action applications in cartel cases: OFT1495) for purposes other than the application of the competition prohibitions or the cartel offence. However, any such disclosure of leniency information would only be likely to be justified in exceptional circumstances, given the strong public interest in maintaining the incentives for undertakings and, in the case of the cartel offence, individuals to apply for leniency.

POOLING RESOURCES

51. Paragraph 24, above, and the concurrency guidance provide for support to be provided by the supporting authority to the investigating authority when it is exercising its concurrent powers in a case. The CMA and the CAA will endeavour, so far as is reasonably practicable and permitted by law, and in light of their respective ongoing priorities and resource availability at the time, to share their resources with each other in the interests of the effective enforcement of competition law in the air traffic and airport operation services sectors, and more generally the promotion of competition for the benefit of consumers in those sectors, and to ensure that their resources and expertise are used most efficiently for that purpose. This is subject to the proviso that, as stated in paragraph 5, this does not apply in relation to the functions of the CMA in its role of considering appeals against, or references related to, proposed action by the sectoral regulators under the sectoral statutes.

52. As a consequence, where it has been agreed or determined that one of the authorities is to exercise its concurrent competition powers in relation to a case, that authority will, to the extent that there are resources available, receive appropriate practical assistance and support from the other in the handling of the case, as agreed on a case-by-case basis.

Secondments of staff

53. One means of the practical assistance and support that might be given, as referred to in paragraphs 51 and 52 of this MoU, is the secondment of staff, in accordance with regulation 10 of the concurrency regulations and paragraphs 3.33 and 3.34 of the concurrency guidance.

54. The CMA and the CAA are fully committed to the idea of secondments for this purpose, and will endeavour to meet each other's requests for secondments to the extent that they are appropriate and resources permit; this may include making provision for any secondee to be available to work for part of his or her time at his or her existing employer during the course of the secondment, for example on such cases that are in progress.

55. Requests for secondments should be made by the relationship manager of one authority to the relationship manager of the other, setting out the following information:

(a) The number of secondees required.
(b) The period for which each one is required.
(c) The level of seniority of each one.
(d) The nature of the expertise or experience of each one.
(e) The proposed payment arrangements.
(f) A brief explanation of why the requirement or requirements cannot adequately be met by deployment of staff from within the requesting authority.

56. To the extent that the recipient of a request for a secondment made under paragraph 55 of this MoU refuses that request or accedes to it on terms that are materially different from those requested, the recipient shall give reasons.

57. The CMA and the CAA will develop appropriate arrangements for the pooling and secondment of staff. Such arrangements will have regard to the resource constraints of both parties and such calls for staff, therefore, will be made in reasonable time and with sufficient warning to enable appropriate resource planning, management of other work commitments and appropriate sign-off procedures within each authority.

OTHER MUTUAL SUPPORT

58. In addition to the sharing of information, expertise, and experience and the secondment of staff, the CMA and the CAA are fully committed to providing each other with more informal forms of support to enable them to carry out their competition law functions in relation to the air traffic and airport operation services sectors – in each case to the extent that it is appropriate and permitted by law, and that resources permit – including (but not limited to):

(a) answering specific queries from time to time;
(b) providing information or views on a specific sector or market, or an area of competition law or policy; and
(c) providing training on a specific sector or market, or an area of competition law or policy.

59. Such support may be requested and provided in connection with a specific case or with the promotion of competition more generally. In this regard, both the CMA and the CAA will act reasonably, including by providing sufficient time and information for requests for support to be responded to fully and effectively and for the relevant staff to be engaged.

ANNUAL CONCURRENCY REPORT

60. The CMA is required by statute to publish a report every year, starting after its first year of operation in 2014/15,[15] containing an assessment of how the concurrency arrangements between the CMA and the sectoral regulators, as regards both the competition prohibitions and the market provisions, have operated during the year. This MoU refers to that report as the annual concurrency report. There is further provision on the annual concurrency report in paragraphs 3.55 to 3.62 of the concurrency guidance.

61. The CMA will consult, and cooperate with, the CAA and with other sectoral regulators in preparing the annual concurrency report. In connection with this, the CMA will:

(a) prepare a draft of the annual concurrency report that it will send to the CAA and other sectoral regulators seeking comments or suggestions on the content or conclusions of the annual concurrency report and giving them adequate time to comment or make suggestions;
(b) take account of any comments or suggestions it receives from the CAA and other sectoral regulators and the CMA may seek further clarification on those comments or suggestions as appropriate;
(c) prepare a final version of the annual concurrency report for publication that takes account of its consultation of the CAA and other sectoral regulators as appropriate; and
(d) make the annual concurrency report available on the CMA webpages.

62. The CAA will cooperate with the CMA in the preparation of the annual concurrency report including (but not limited to) by way of:

(a) providing information and data on general market conditions and on the application of the competition prohibitions and the market provisions in the air traffic and airport operation services sectors;
(b) responding to reasonable requests for information and data; and
(c) providing to the CMA any comments and suggestions it may have in connection with the process described in paragraph 61 of this MoU;

in each case promptly so as to facilitate the timely production and publication of the annual concurrency report.

NOTES

15 Enterprise and Regulatory Reform Act 2013 Schedule 4 paragraph 16.

VOLUNTARY REDRESS SCHEMES

63. In cases relating to investigations under the competition prohibitions in the air traffic and air operation services sectors in the UK, both the CMA and the CAA have the power to approve voluntary redress schemes. When either authority proposes to exercise these powers, it shall liaise with the other authority as appropriate and will have regard to its own guidance.[16]

NOTES

16 The CMA's guidance on the approval of voluntary redress schemes (CMA40) states in footnote 7: 'The CMA expects that regulators will take this CMA guidance into account when producing their own guidance on the approval power.' The CAA has adopted the CMA's guidance.

SHORT FORM OPINIONS

64. The CMA shall inform the CAA following an initial enquiry for a short form opinion relating to the air traffic or airport operation services sectors. Where the CMA is considering providing such an opinion, it will discuss with the CAA before deciding to do so. If the CMA then decides to produce an opinion, it will engage with the CAA, the nature and degree of that engagement to be considered on a case-by-case basis. In all cases, the CMA will give the CAA the opportunity to provide comments on a draft opinion.

PART B – COOPERATION IN RELATION TO THE MARKET PROVISIONS: MARKET STUDIES AND MARKET INVESTIGATIONS (ENTERPRISE ACT 2002)

HOW CONCURRENCY WORKS UNDER THE MARKET PROVISIONS

[3.327]

65. The CAA has the power, concurrently with the CMA, to carry out market studies, to make market investigation references, agree undertakings in lieu of a reference and make recommendations to the government in relation to the air traffic and airport operation services sectors in the UK under Part 4 of the Enterprise Act 2002 (as do other sectoral regulators in relation to the sectors for which they are responsible).

66. Under the Enterprise Act 2002, the CMA and the CAA may, in relation to the air traffic and airport operation services sectors in the UK, undertake market studies, and may make market investigation references to the Chair of the CMA for the constitution of a CMA group to conduct an in-depth market investigation into single or multiple markets for goods or services in the UK. The purpose of these investigations is to examine the market(s) and (where required) implement appropriate remedies where the CMA determines that the structure of the market(s) or the conduct of the suppliers or customers is harming competition.

67. When making a reference, the CMA or the CAA, as applicable, must have reasonable grounds for suspecting that any feature or combination of features of a market or markets in the UK prevents, restricts or distorts competition in relation to the supply or acquisition of any goods or services in the UK (or in a part of the UK).

68. The cooperation between the CMA and the CAA provided for in this Part B shall not extend to conduct that could reasonably be expected to impair the impartiality or the fairness of the CMA panel in conducting market investigations.

SUPER-COMPLAINTS

69. Section 11 of the Enterprise Act 2002 provides for a super-complaint to be made by a designated consumer body that any feature, or combination of features, of a market in the UK for goods or services is or appears to be significantly harming the interests of consumers.

70. The CAA has a duty to respond to super-complaints made to it under the Enterprise Act 2002 if the complaint concerns the air traffic or airport operation services markets.

71. The coordination of the CMA's and the sectoral regulators' super-complaint duties will be based on policies agreed and applied through the UKCN.

MUTUAL CONSULTATION

72. The CAA and the CMA have a duty to consult each other before exercising concurrent functions under the market provisions.

SHARING INFORMATION

73. The provisions of paragraphs 39 to 43, 45 (excluding 45(a)) and 47 of this MoU apply to information sharing under the market provisions as they do under the competition prohibitions.

POOLING RESOURCES

74. The provisions of paragraph 51 to 59 of this MoU apply to pooling resources under the market provisions as they do under the competition prohibitions.

75. Where the CMA and the CAA intend to pool resources in order to exercise powers under the market provisions of the Enterprise Act 2002, they shall, at the outset of any such project, discuss the arrangements for how they will pool resources and work jointly.

ANNUAL CONCURRENCY REPORT

76. The provisions of paragraphs 60 to 62 of this MoU apply under the market provisions as they do under the competition prohibitions.

MEMORANDUM OF UNDERSTANDING BETWEEN THE COMPETITION AND MARKETS AUTHORITY AND THE OFFICE OF RAIL AND ROAD – CONCURRENT COMPETITION POWERS

9 February 2016

[3.328]

NOTES

FOREWORD

[3.329]

The changes to the United Kingdom's (UK) competition law system, introduced under the Enterprise and Regulatory Reform Act 2013 and in force since April 2014, are designed to improve the effectiveness of competition law enforcement in this country.

The Competition and Markets Authority (CMA) has competition law powers which apply across the whole economy. Sectoral regulators such as the Office of Rail and Road (ORR) may exercise the competition law powers to enforce the prohibitions on anti-competitive agreements and on abuse of a dominant position, and to make market investigation references, concurrently with the CMA in those sectors for which they have responsibility.

The Enterprise and Regulatory Reform Act 2013 introduced a number of changes to improve the working of concurrency and to enable closer working between the CMA and sectoral regulators.

The CMA and the sectoral regulators have demonstrated their commitment to making the concurrency framework more effective through the establishment of the UK Competition Network (UKCN). This represents an enhanced forum for cooperation which will enable closer working with the objective of more consistent and effective use of competition powers across all sectors. In their statement of intent in December 2013, the members of the UKCN affirmed: 'The mission of the UKCN will be to promote competition for the benefit of consumers and to prevent anti-competitive behaviour both through facilitating use of competition powers and development of pro-competitive regulatory frameworks, as appropriate.'[1]

This memorandum of understanding (MoU) represents a further stage in the process of cooperation between the CMA and the regulators, setting out more practical detail on how the CMA and the ORR will work together within the framework of competition law.[2]

The main purpose of this MoU is to establish an understanding between the CMA and the ORR as to how this closer working will work in practice. It draws on the legislation which sets out the formal framework for how concurrency will operate and also, importantly, sets out our bilateral commitment to look for opportunities to work together, including within the framework of the UKCN, to promote competition for the benefit of consumers. We shall do this by the sharing of expertise, information, ideas and experience and each of us will commit to doing this efficiently and with a mutual regard for each other's statutory position and strategic objectives.

We believe that this MoU offers a valuable basis for that cooperation, in the interests of the CMA, the ORR, the railways services industry in Great Britain and, most importantly of all, the consumers.

Alex Chisholm	**Joanna Whittington**
CEO, CMA	**CEO, ORR**

NOTES

1 UKCN (2013), Statement of Intent.

2 This MoU does not relate to 'regulatory appeals' – that is, the separate role that the CMA has in considering references relating to proposed direct regulatory action by the ORR under the sectoral statutes. This is a separate role, to be undertaken by the CMA panel, and the CMA is committed to ensuring that its cooperation with the ORR - whether under this MoU (and under comparable MoUs agreed with other sectoral regulators), through the UKCN, or otherwise in connection with their concurrent powers - will not impair the impartiality and fairness of the CMA's conduct of such regulatory appeals (or indeed of market or merger investigations undertaken by the CMA panel).

MEMORANDUM OF UNDERSTANDING BETWEEN THE COMPETITION AND MARKETS AUTHORITY AND THE OFFICE OF RAIL AND ROAD

PURPOSE OF THIS MEMORANDUM OF UNDERSTANDING

[3.330]

1. This MoU sets out working arrangements between the CMA and the ORR in relation to:

(a) their concurrent powers to apply the prohibitions on agreements that prevent, restrict or distort competition, and on the abuse of a dominant position, under the Chapter I prohibition and the Chapter II prohibition of the Competition Act 1998 and under Article 101 and Article 102 of the Treaty on the Functioning of the European Union – referred to in this MoU as the 'competition prohibitions'; and

(b) their concurrent powers to undertake market studies, and to make references to the CMA for the constitution of a CMA group to conduct an in-depth market investigation into single or multiple markets for goods or services in the UK under the Enterprise Act 2002 – referred to in this MoU as the 'market provisions';

in the rail sector.[3]

2. This MoU is not intended to have legal effect.

3. This MoU is to be read alongside other material concerning the relations between the CMA and the ORR, including: the Railways Act 1993; the Competition Act 1998; the Enterprise Act 2002; the Enterprise and Regulatory Reform Act 2013; the Competition Act 1998 and Other Enactments (Amendment) Regulations 2004; the Competition Act 1998 (Concurrency) Regulations 2014, referred to in this MoU as the concurrency regulations; and the CMA's guidance on concurrent application of competition law to regulated industries, referred to in this MoU as the concurrency guidance.[4] This MoU supplements and does not supplant that material.

4. The arrangements covered by this MoU are, wherever possible, set out in terms providing sufficient flexibility for the relationship between the ORR and the CMA to develop in the light of experience. The CMA and the ORR commit to review these arrangements from time to time to evaluate their continuing fitness for purpose. Such review can be initiated at the request of the CMA, the ORR or a member of the UKCN. This MoU may only be revised by agreement between the CMA and the ORR.

5. Nothing in this MoU applies in relation to the functions of the CMA in its separate role of considering references related to proposed action by the ORR under the sectoral statutes. The CMA and the ORR acknowledge the importance of maintaining the CMA's impartiality and fairness in carrying out those functions, and indeed of market or merger investigations undertaken by the CMA panel.

NOTES

[3] For the purpose of this MoU, the term 'rail sector' encompasses services relating to railways in Great Britain. These are defined in section 67(3ZA) of the Railways Act 1993 as: *(a)* railway services (meaning the carriage of passengers and goods by railway and light maintenance, station and network services); *(b)* the provision and maintenance of rolling stock; *(c)* the development, maintenance or renewal of a network, station or light maintenance depot; and *(d)* the development, provision or maintenance of information systems designed wholly or mainly for facilitating the provision of railway services.

[4] CMA (2014), *Regulated industries: Guidance on concurrent application of competition law to regulated industries* (CMA10).

CONTEXT

6. This MoU operates within the framework of the legislative provisions referred to in paragraph 1 and any applicable sector-specific legislation from time to time.

Role of the CMA

7. The CMA is a non-ministerial department, established under the Enterprise and Regulatory Reform Act 2013.

8. The CMA works to promote competition for the benefit of consumers, both within and outside the UK, to make markets work well for consumers, businesses and the economy.

9. The CMA's statutory responsibilities, in so far as relevant to the matters that are the subject of this MoU, include:

(a) investigating where there may be breaches of the competition prohibitions; and
(b) conducting market studies and market investigations where there may be competition and consumer problems.

10. In connection with its statutory responsibilities, the CMA will cooperate with sectoral regulators and encourage sectoral regulators to use their powers, including their powers to apply the competition prohibitions, in the interests of competition for the benefit of consumers.

Role of the ORR

11. The ORR is a body corporate established under the Railways and Transport Act 2003. It is a non-ministerial government department. The ORR is the safety and economic regulator of railways in Great Britain.

12. The ORR's principal economic direct regulatory functions are set out in the Railways Act 1993 and in various regulations implementing European rail liberalisation legislation. In summary, they are to:

(a) regulate Network Rail's stewardship of the national rail network;
(b) license operators of railway assets (the network, stations, light maintenance depots and trains);
(c) approve access by parties to track, stations and light maintenance depots; and
(d) keep under review the provision of railway services.

13. The ORR also has powers concurrently with the CMA to investigate where there may be breaches of the competition prohibitions and to conduct market studies and to refer markets where there may be competition and consumer problems in the rail sector.

14. The ORR has 24 duties (which it balances in the exercise of its sector-specific regulatory and Enterprise Act 2002 market study functions). These duties contain a number of objectives, for example, they require the ORR:

(a) to promote the use of the railway network in Great Britain for the carriage of passenger and goods, and the development of that railway network, to the greatest extent that it considers economically practicable;
(b) to promote competition in the provision of railway services for the benefit of users of railway services;
(c) to protect the interest of users of railway services;
(d) to have regard to the funds available to the Secretary of State for the purposes of his functions in relation to railways or railway services; and
(e) to contribute to the achievement of sustainable development.

15. The ORR will cooperate with the CMA and other sectoral regulators, in the exercise of its concurrent functions, for the purpose of strengthening the competition framework and to ensure consistency of approach. The ORR will also engage with the CMA broadly in the promotion of competition for the benefit of users of services relating to railways.

AIMS

16. The Enterprise and Regulatory Reform Act 2013, as well as establishing the CMA, made provision for the better working of the CMA's and the sectoral regulators' concurrent powers in the regulated sectors; specifically, the act: 'strengthens the role of the CMA and enhances the emphasis on early and proper consideration of the use of anti-trust powers (under Part 1 of the CA 1998 [ie the competition prohibitions]) by the sector regulators.'[5]

17. It is one of the strategic goals of the CMA, announced on its establishment on 1 October 2013, to extend the frontiers of competition into new areas, including by working with sectoral regulators to ensure fuller use of competition law and policy in sectoral markets.[6]

18. The government's strategic steer to the CMA, issued on 1 December 2015, says that the CMA should build 'a strong dialogue with sectoral regulators using the UKCN to ensure that the overall competition regime is coordinated and regulatory practices complement each other.'[7]

19. The sectoral regulators and the CMA, working together in the UKCN established in 2013 (with Monitor having observer status), declared that: 'The mission of the UKCN will be to promote competition for the benefit of consumers and to prevent anti-competitive behaviour both through facilitating use of competition powers and development of pro-competitive regulatory frameworks, as appropriate.'[8]

20. The CMA and the ORR seek to use their powers to achieve more competitive outcomes in the rail sector for the benefit of users and the economy in which those services play an essential part. It is the view of the CMA and the ORR that such competitive outcomes can be achieved by various tools, including: their concurrent competition law powers under the competition prohibitions and market provisions; their concurrent powers under specific consumer protection legislation; and the CMA's merger control functions. However, the CMA and ORR recognise that some of these outcomes can also be achieved through other tools such as those that are available to regulators through national and European Union legislation.

21. This MoU aims to further the attainment of these objectives, and to make the changes introduced by the Enterprise and Regulatory Reform Act 2013 work effectively, maximising the complementary skills of the CMA and the ORR, including through:

(a) promoting cooperation and coordination between the CMA and the ORR when dealing with cases of suspected anti-competitive behaviour for which they have concurrent powers;
(b) promoting cooperation and coordination between the CMA and the ORR when dealing with market studies and market investigation references for which they have concurrent powers;
(c) facilitating the efficient and effective handling of cases of suspected anti-competitive behaviour within the rail sector;
(d) avoiding duplication of activity, wherever possible; and
(e) ensuring transparency as to the respective roles of the CMA and the ORR for individuals and consumers affected.

NOTES

5 Enterprise and Regulatory Reform Act 2013 Explanatory Notes, paragraph 370.
6 Statement by Alex Chisholm, Chief Executive of the CMA, CMA mission and strategy, 1 Oct 2013.
7 Department for Business, Innovation and Skills, Strategic steer for the Competition and Markets Authority, in Annex A to the *Government's response to the Consultation on the Strategic Steer to the CMA*, 1 December 2015, page 11.
8 UKCN (2013), Statement of Intent.

GENERAL COOPERATION

22. In addition to the provisions for cooperation between the CMA and the ORR specific to particular powers of the CMA and the ORR, as set out in this MoU and elsewhere, the CMA and the ORR are committed to the following general principles and practices for cooperation between themselves in respect of the sectors for which the ORR has responsibility.

23. Officials of the CMA and the ORR will meet and communicate, at appropriate levels of seniority, to discuss matters of mutual interest, both through the UKCN and bilaterally. A framework for such meetings will, as far as possible, be determined in advance so as to ensure attendance at the appropriate level and expertise.

24. The CMA and the ORR will, in respect of the rail sector, always consult each other:

(a) before the initial exercise of concurrent competition law powers in all cases where it appears that they have concurrent jurisdiction and where there are reasonable grounds for suspecting an infringement of the competition prohibitions; and
(b) before launching a market study under the Enterprise Act 2002.[9]

25. Where either the CMA or the ORR exercises its concurrent powers, the CMA and the ORR will, to the extent permitted by law, engage with each other in open dialogue and by sharing relevant information as appropriate. This engagement may include attendance at internal meetings held by the investigating authority (ie the authority to which a case is allocated) by the supporting authority (ie the other authority which would be competent to exercise concurrent powers in relation to the case), in order to discuss the case as envisaged at paragraph 3.31 of the concurrency guidance. The supporting authority will not generally attend the investigating authority's constitutional decision-making meetings, meetings of governance bodies or meetings with external parties such as those under investigation or complainants. Attendance by the supporting authority at any meeting is at the discretion of the investigating authority, but requests to attend should be considered by the investigating authority in the spirit of cooperation underpinning the new concurrency regime.

26. The CMA and the ORR will consult each other at an early stage on any issues that might have significant implications for the other. For example, where the CMA undertakes a market study which relates to a sector other than the rail sector but which may have a significant impact on that sector, the CMA will inform the ORR and share appropriate information relating to that market study with the ORR to the extent permitted by law.

27. Within the spirit of broader collaboration for the purposes of the promotion of competitive outcomes, the CMA and the ORR will commit to discuss and share other information about a broader range of competition complaints and concerns, where legally permissible to do so, but subject to the need not to impair the impartiality and fairness of the CMA in carrying out the functions referred to in paragraph 5 of this MoU.

NOTES

9 Instigation of a market study occurs on the publication of a market study notice, as defined in section 130A of the Enterprise Act 2002.

PART A – COOPERATION IN RELATION TO THE COMPETITION PROHIBITIONS (COMPETITION ACT 1998 AND ARTICLES 101 AND 102 OF THE TREATY ON THE FUNCTIONING OF THE EUROPEAN UNION)

CASE ALLOCATION

Basis of allocation

[3.331]

28. The CMA and the ORR will endeavour to reach agreement on which authority will exercise its concurrent competition powers in respect of any particular case, under regulation 4(2) of the concurrency regulations. They will do so in a spirit of constructiveness and cooperation, while acknowledging the CMA's ultimate powers under regulations 5 and 8 of the concurrency regulations.

29. Their determination of which authority will exercise its powers will be based on assessing which of them is better placed to exercise those powers, having regard to the factors set out in paragraph 3.22 of the concurrency guidance. The CMA and the ORR envisage that other factors may appear relevant in the light of practical experience and that, if so, such factors may be chosen to supplement or supplant the factors set out in paragraph 3.22 of the concurrency guidance.

Procedure for allocation

30. Where either the CMA or the ORR has decided, on the basis of information in its possession, that there are reasonable grounds for suspecting that one of the competition prohibitions has been infringed (the reasonable suspicion test)[10] in relation to the rail sector, it will disclose to the other (ie the receiving authority) sufficient information:

(a) to enable the receiving authority to understand the basis on which the disclosing authority has decided that the reasonable suspicion test is met; and

(b) for there to be an informed discussion on which authority (if either) is best placed to proceed in respect of the case.

31. In practice, it may be helpful for the CMA and the ORR to have discussed the case prior to such a decision having been reached, subject to paragraph 44 below. The disclosing authority will provide the information described under paragraph 30 within ten working days after it has decided that the reasonable suspicion test is met, whether or not it proposes to exercise concurrent powers.[11]

32. With seven working days from receipt of this information, the receiving authority will respond in writing, setting out its initial view on the case and how it should be allocated and identifying any further information which it requires.

33. The CMA and the ORR will endeavour to agree which authority will exercise its concurrent competition powers in relation to the case, as provided for in regulation 4(2) of the concurrency regulations, as soon as possible and in any event no later than one month from disclosure of the information described under paragraph 30. Other than in exceptional circumstances (which shall be set out in writing), the CMA will initiate the procedure set out in regulation 5 of the concurrency regulations if agreement is not reached within two months of the disclosing authority first receiving sufficient information in connection with a complaint to enable it to decide that the reasonable suspicion test is met.

34. The procedure for agreeing the transfer of a case that is already in progress from the CMA to the ORR, or from the ORR to the CMA, is as set out in regulation 7 of the concurrency regulations and in paragraph 3.32 of the concurrency guidance.

35. The procedure for the CMA to direct the transfer to itself from the ORR of a case that is already in progress is as set out in regulation 8 of the concurrency regulations.

NOTES

10 As provided in section 25 of the Competition Act 1998.

11 As provided in regulation 9 of the concurrency regulations.

Implications of allocation

36. Any agreement or determination as to case allocation, under regulations 4, 5, 7 or 8 of the concurrency regulations, shall be notified to the person who has provided the information resulting in the case (for example, the person making a complaint), and so far as appropriate and lawful to any other affected person, by the authority which is exercising its concurrent competition powers in relation to the case, as soon as reasonably practicable.

37. Case allocation determines which of the CMA and the ORR is to exercise concurrent functions and make any decisions under the competition prohibitions. The CMA or ORR will be publicly identified as having such responsibility if and when any such investigation is announced. The CMA and the ORR envisage that, whichever authority has responsibility for a particular case, they and their officials will work cooperatively with each other on the case as appropriate, pooling their expertise including in the ways described in paragraphs 52 to 60 of this MoU and in paragraphs 3.33 to 3.35 of the concurrency guidance.

SHARING INFORMATION

Principles of information sharing

38. The effective sharing of information between the CMA and the ORR is fundamental to the successful exercise of their concurrent competition powers. It is needed both for the appropriate allocation of cases, as described in paragraphs 30 to 35 of this MoU, and for the successful handling of cases once allocated to make optimal use of the complementary experience and expertise of the two authorities.

39. The CMA and the ORR are committed, in addition to their legal obligations to share information (set out in regulation 9 of the concurrency regulations), to open dialogue and continuing liaison, both bilaterally and through the UKCN, with a view not only to handling specific cases but to promoting competition, for the benefit of users of railway services.

Information sharing mechanism – general liaison

40. The CMA and the ORR recognise the importance of meeting regularly to share information on matters relevant to competition in the rail sector in Great Britain, and to keep each other abreast of relevant work which they are considering or currently undertaking.

41. The CMA and the ORR will meet regularly at multiple levels, bilaterally and through the UKCN.

42. The CMA and the ORR will each designate in its organisation a relationship manager at official level to take responsibility for relations between the two authorities. In each authority, the relationship manager's responsibilities will include (but will not be limited to):

(a) maintaining an overview of joint projects between the two authorities and matters of mutual interest;

(b) maintaining an overview of the authority's contacts from all areas of joint working and mutual interest; and

(c) holding meetings with the relationship manager in the other authority from time to time (whether bilaterally or in the context of the UKCN) to identify potential new issues, with a view to circulating information to appropriate individuals within each organisation.

43. The existence of relationship managers does not in any way preclude direct communication between other staff at the CMA and the ORR.

44. For the purposes of sharing information pursuant to paragraph 30, ie in circumstances where the reasonable suspicion test is met, such information will be shared by the disclosing authority to the extent permitted by law and whether or not it proposes to exercise its concurrent powers in the case.[12] Where disclosure would be appropriate and permitted by law, the CMA and ORR may also share information regarding potential infringements of the competition prohibitions in advance of having reached a view as to whether the reasonable suspicion test is met. In circumstances where either the CMA or FCA has taken the view that a matter is not an administrative priority, irrespective of whether a view has been reached on whether the reasonable suspicion test is reached, each may share the details of the matter with the other, or with any other authority which would be able to exercise concurrent competition powers in relation to that matter, to the extent permitted by law. Where leniency information is being shared under this paragraph, special considerations apply, as set out in paragraphs 50 and 51.

NOTES

[12] For the avoidance of doubt, this does not entail an obligation to inform the other party if the regulator is carrying out general monitoring activity, where there is no active consideration of exercising its concurrent powers.

Information sharing mechanism – handling specific cases

45. The procedures for information sharing for the purpose of case allocation shall be as set out in paragraphs 30 to 32 and 38 to 51 of this MoU.

46. When either the CMA or the ORR is exercising its powers in respect of the competition prohibitions in a particular case in the rail sector, each of them will share with the other any of the following information in its possession (to the extent permitted by law and subject to the confidentiality obligations in paragraphs 49 to 51 of this MoU):

(a) as a minimum, the matters referred to in regulation 9(1)(b) – (j) of the concurrency regulations, and in paragraph 3.49 of the concurrency guidance, complying with the time limits specified in paragraph 3.49;

(b) other information which it reasonably believes to be relevant or helpful to the other in the conduct of the case; and

(c) in the case of the authority which is exercising the powers, reports to the other on the progress of the case, of sufficient frequency and detail to enable the other to be appropriately informed; the means and frequency of such reporting will be decided on a case-by-case basis and in the light of experience as this enhanced framework of collaboration and its supporting arrangements develop over time.

Information sharing mechanism – for know-how purposes

47. The CMA will maintain on its webpages a central database of decisions taken in cases under the competition prohibitions, with a view to having an accessible body of know-how that will help ensure the effective and consistent application of competition law. The CMA and the ORR will, to the extent permitted by law, contribute information to that in the way best calculated to achieve that objective.

48. In any event, the CMA will report on cases in the regulated sectors under the competition prohibitions in the annual concurrency report which it is required under statute to issue. Further provisions on the annual concurrency report are in paragraphs 61 to 63 of this MoU.

Information sharing – confidentiality constraints

49. Any disclosure of information under paragraphs 30 to 32 and 38 to 48 of this MoU, and any use by the recipient of such information, shall only be to the extent permitted by law, including by reference to the provisions of Part 9 of the Enterprise Act 2002, relevant sector-specific legislative provisions and any other provisions relating to the disclosure, handling and use of information (such as the Data Protection Act 1998 and section 118 of the Financial Services and Markets Act 2000, to the extent relevant).

50. Prior to disclosing information to each other, the CMA and the ORR will not generally give the person to whom the information relates prior notice of its intention to make the disclosure. However, if the CMA or the ORR consider it necessary or appropriate to pass leniency information to each other (or to another UK authority with concurrent powers), the transmitting authority will inform the applicant or its legal adviser first. Leniency information for the purposes of this MoU is any information which came into the possession of any of the CMA, its predecessors, the ORR or any other public authority as a direct or indirect result of having been provided in the context of an application for leniency. It includes information obtained by the transferring authority as a result of investigative measures resulting directly or indirectly from an application for leniency.

51. In addition to the general provisions referred to in paragraph 49, where the ORR or the CMA receives leniency information from the other (or from another UK authority with concurrent powers) for the purpose of applying the competition prohibitions or, in the case of the CMA, the cartel offence under section 188 of the Enterprise Act 2002, that information will not be used for any other purpose. This restriction on use also applies to any information obtained by the receiving authority as a result of investigative measures relating to the competition prohibitions or the cartel offence following the receipt of leniency information from the other authority. This does not affect the use that may be made by the CMA or the ORR of information received from other sources, or if the leniency applicant's consent is obtained.[13] Where the provision of leniency information to either the CMA or the ORR affords or might, under certain conditions, afford the leniency applicant, its subsidiaries or its employees protection from sanctions (including a reduction in penalties) under the leniency programme operated by that authority and that information has been passed to another authority, the receiving authority shall afford the leniency applicant, its subsidiaries or its employees no lesser protection.

NOTES

[13] The use restriction in this paragraph is intended to govern the use of leniency information in the context of the concurrency arrangements. It is not intended to prevent the disclosure of such leniency information by either one of the CMA or the ORR to the other (to the extent permitted by Part 9 of the Enterprise Act 2002 and in accordance with Leniency and no-action applications in cartel cases: OFT1495) for purposes other than the application of the competition prohibitions or the cartel offence. However, any such disclosure of leniency information would only be likely to be justified in exceptional circumstances, given the strong public interest in maintaining the incentives for undertakings and, in the case of the cartel offence, individuals to apply for leniency.

POOLING RESOURCES

52. Paragraph 25, above, and the concurrency guidance provide for support to be provided by the supporting authority to the investigating authority when it is exercising its concurrent powers in a case. The CMA and the ORR will endeavour, so far as is reasonably practicable and permitted by law, and in the light of their respective ongoing priorities and resource availability at the time, to share their resources with each other in the interests of the effective enforcement of competition law in the rail sector in Great Britain, and more generally the promotion of competition for the benefit of consumers in that sector, and to ensure that their resources and expertise are used most efficiently for that purpose. This is subject to the proviso that, as stated in paragraph 5, this does not apply in relation to the functions of the CMA in its role of considering references related to proposed action by the ORR under the sectoral statutes.

53. As a consequence, where it has been agreed or determined that one of the authorities is to exercise its concurrent competition powers in relation to a case, that authority will, to the extent that there are resources available, receive appropriate practical assistance and support from the other in the handling of the case, as agreed on a case-by-case basis.

Secondments of staff

54. One means of the practical assistance and support that might be given, as referred to in paragraphs 52 and 53 of this MoU, is the secondment of staff, in accordance with regulation 10 of the concurrency regulations and paragraphs 3.33 and 3.34 of the concurrency guidance.

55. The CMA and the ORR are fully committed to the idea of secondments for this purpose, and will endeavour to meet each other's requests for secondments to the extent that they are appropriate and resources permit; this may include making provision for any secondee to be available to work for part of his or her time at his or her existing employer during the course of the secondment, for example on such cases that are in progress.

56. Requests for secondments should be made by the relationship manager of one authority to the relationship manager of the other, setting out the following information:

(a) The number of secondees required.
(b) The period for which each one is required.
(c) The level of seniority of each one.
(d) The nature of the expertise or experience of each one.
(e) The proposed payment arrangements.
(f) A brief explanation of why the requirement or requirements cannot adequately be met by deployment of staff from within the requesting authority.

57. To the extent that the recipient of a request for a secondment made under paragraph 56 of this MoU refuses that request or accedes to it on terms that are materially different from those requested, the recipient shall give reasons.

58. The CMA and the ORR will develop appropriate arrangements for the pooling and secondment of staff. Such arrangements will have regard to the resource constraints of both parties and such calls for staff, therefore, will be made in reasonable time and with sufficient warning to enable appropriate resource planning, management of other work commitments and appropriate sign-off procedures within each authority.

Other mutual support

59. In addition to the sharing of information, expertise, experience and the secondment of staff, the CMA and the ORR are fully committed to providing each other with more informal forms of support to enable them to carry out their competition law functions in relation to the rail sector – in each case to the extent that it is appropriate and permitted by law, and that resources permit – including (but not limited to):
(a) answering specific queries from time to time;
(b) providing information or views on a specific sector or market, or an area of competition law or policy; and
(c) providing training on a specific sector or market, or an area of competition law or policy.

60. Such support may be requested and provided in connection with a specific case or with the promotion of competition more generally. In this regard, both the CMA and the ORR will act reasonably, including by providing sufficient time and information for requests for support to be responded to fully and effectively and for the relevant staff to be engaged.

ANNUAL CONCURRENCY REPORT

61. The CMA is required by statute to publish a report every year, starting after its first year of operation in 2014/15,[14] containing an assessment of how the concurrency arrangements between the CMA and the sectoral regulators, as regards both the competition prohibitions and the market provisions, have operated during the year. This MoU refers to that report as the annual concurrency report. There is further provision on the annual concurrency report in paragraphs 3.55 to 3.62 of the concurrency guidance.

62. The CMA will consult, and cooperate with, the ORR and with other sectoral regulators in preparing the annual concurrency report. In connection with this, the CMA will:
(a) prepare a draft of the annual concurrency report that it will send to the ORR and other sectoral regulators seeking comments or suggestions on the content or conclusions of the annual concurrency report and giving them adequate time to comment or make suggestions;
(b) take account of any comments or suggestions it receives from the ORR and other sectoral regulators, and the CMA may seek further clarification on those comments or suggestions as appropriate;
(c) prepare a final version of the annual concurrency report for publication that takes account of its consultation of the ORR and other sectoral regulators as appropriate; and
(d) make the annual concurrency report available on the CMA webpages.

63. The ORR will cooperate with the CMA in the preparation of the annual concurrency report including (but not limited to) by way of:
(a) providing information and data on general market conditions and on the application of the competition prohibitions and the market provisions in the railways services sector in Great Britain;
(b) responding to reasonable requests for information and data; and
(c) providing to the CMA any comments and suggestions it may have in connection with the process described in paragraph 62 of this MoU;

in each case promptly so as to facilitate the timely production and publication of the annual concurrency report.

NOTES

14 Enterprise and Regulatory Reform Act 2013 Schedule 4 paragraph 16.

VOLUNTARY REDRESS SCHEMES

64. In cases relating to investigations under the competition prohibitions in the rail sector, both the CMA and the ORR have the power to approve voluntary redress schemes. When either authority proposes to exercise these powers, it shall liaise with the other authority as appropriate and will have regard to its own guidance.[15]

NOTES

15 The CMA's guidance on the approval of voluntary redress schemes (CMA40) states at footnote 7: 'The CMA expects that regulators will take this CMA guidance into account when producing their own guidance on the approval power.'

SHORT FORM OPINIONS

65. The CMA shall inform the ORR following an initial enquiry for a short form opinion relating to the rail sector. Where the CMA is considering providing such an opinion, it will discuss with the ORR before deciding to do so. If the CMA then decides to produce an opinion, it will engage with the ORR, the nature and degree of that engagement to be considered on a case-by-case basis, having regard, in particular, to the extent to which the opinion has a multi-sector rather than a single-sector dimension. In all cases, the CMA will give the ORR the opportunity to provide comments on such a draft opinion.

CHOICE OF INSTRUMENT – COMPETITION PROHIBITION OR DIRECT REGULATION BY LICENCE ENFORCEMENT

66. As a result of legislative changes introduced by Schedule 14 to the Enterprise and Regulatory Reform Act 2013,[16] the ORR is required by sections 55(5A) and 57A(6) of the Railways Act 1993, to 'consider whether it would be more appropriate to proceed under the Competition Act 1998' before exercising its direct regulatory powers of licence enforcement.

67. The Explanatory Notes to the legislation explain that this provision 'enhances the emphasis on early and proper consideration of the use of anti-trust powers (under Part 1 of the CA98)[17] by the sector regulators'.[18]

68. The government had previously indicated that the policy intention is to: 'strengthen the primacy of general competition law, so that the Sector Regulators are required to consider whether the use of their CA98 powers is more appropriate before using their sectoral powers to promote competition'.[19]

69. Under this provision, it is for the ORR to determine, in any particular case, whether using its powers under the competition prohibitions would be more appropriate than exercising its licence enforcement powers.

70. Paragraph 4.4 of the concurrency guidance says that this determination will be made by the sectoral regulators 'on a case-by-case basis.' It may be that, in the light of experience accumulated over the coming months or years in applying this provision, it will be possible to develop more general principles that could serve as useful guidance in future cases, perhaps through the forum of the UKCN, while respecting the right of the sector regulator to make the determination.

NOTES

16 Having effect from April 2014.

17 That is, the competition prohibitions.

18 Enterprise and Regulatory Reform Act 2013 Explanatory Notes, paragraph 370.

19 BIS, *Growth, competition and the competition regime – Government response to consultation*, March 2012, paragraph 8.16.

PART B – COOPERATION IN RELATION TO THE MARKET PROVISIONS: MARKET STUDIES AND MARKET INVESTIGATIONS (ENTERPRISE ACT 2002)

HOW CONCURRENCY WORKS UNDER THE MARKET PROVISIONS

[3.332]

71. The ORR has the power, concurrently with the CMA, to carry out market studies, to make market investigation references, agree undertakings in lieu of a reference and make recommendations to the government in relation to the rail sector under Part 4 of the Enterprise Act 2002 (as do other sectoral regulators in relation to the sectors for which they are responsible).

72. Under the Enterprise Act 2002, the CMA and the ORR may, in relation to the rail sector, undertake market studies, and may make market investigation references to the Chair of the CMA for the constitution of a CMA group to conduct an in-depth market investigation into single or multiple markets for goods or services in the UK. The purpose of these investigations is to examine the market(s) and (where required) implement appropriate remedies where the CMA determines that the structure of the market(s) or the conduct of the suppliers or customers is harming competition.

73. When making a reference, the CMA or the ORR, as applicable, must have reasonable grounds for suspecting that any feature or combination of features of a market or markets in the UK prevents, restricts or distorts competition in relation to the supply or acquisition of any goods or services in the UK (or in a part of the UK).

74. The cooperation between the CMA and the ORR provided for in this Part B shall not extend to conduct that could reasonably be expected to impair the impartiality or the fairness of the CMA panel in conducting market investigations.

SUPER-COMPLAINTS

75. Section 11 of the Enterprise Act 2002 provides for a super-complaint to be made by a designated consumer body that any feature, or combination of features, of a market in the UK for goods or services is or appears to be significantly harming the interests of consumers.

76. The ORR has a duty to respond to super-complaints made to it under the Enterprise Act 2002 if the complaint concerns the rail sector in Great Britain.

77. The coordination of the CMA's and the sectoral regulators' super-complaint duties will be based on policies agreed and applied through the UKCN.

MUTUAL CONSULTATION

78. The ORR and the CMA have a duty to consult each other before exercising concurrent functions under the market provisions.

SHARING INFORMATION

79. The provisions of paragraphs 40 to 44, 46 (excluding 4646(a)) and 48 of this MoU apply to information sharing under the market provisions as they do under the competition prohibitions.

POOLING RESOURCES

80. The provisions of paragraphs 52 to 60 of this MoU apply to pooling resources under the market provisions as they do under the competition prohibitions.

81. Where the CMA and the ORR intend to pool resources in order to exercise powers under the market provisions of the Enterprise Act 2002, they shall, at the outset of any such project, discuss the arrangements for how they will pool resources and work jointly.

ANNUAL CONCURRENCY REPORT

82. The provisions of paragraphs 61 to 63 of this MoU apply under the market provisions as they do under the competition prohibitions.

COMPETITION ACT 1998 GUIDANCE

GUIDANCE ON ORR'S APPROACH TO THE ENFORCEMENT OF THE COMPETITION ACT 1998 IN RELATION TO THE SUPPLY OF SERVICES RELATING TO RAILWAYS

31 March 2016

[3.333]

NOTES

CONTENTS

INTRODUCTION

[3.334]

The Office of Rail and Road (**ORR**) is the independent safety and economic regulator of railways in Great Britain and monitor of Highways England. We are here to ensure the network operates safely, reliably and provides value for taxpayers and customers. We safeguard the public and the workforce by regulating the rail industry's health and safety performance. We hold Network Rail to account – and we require it to provide passengers with a punctual and reliable service. We make sure that train and freight operating companies have fair access to the rail network, and that the market is competitive and fair.

As part of this mandate we have powers, in relation to the supply of services relating to railways, to enforce the prohibitions on agreements[1] that prevent, restrict or distort competition and on the abuse of a dominant position, contained in Chapters I and II of the Competition Act 1998 (the **Act**) and in Articles 101 and 102 of the Treaty on the Functioning of the European Union (**TFEU**). ORR exercises these powers concurrently with the Competition and Markets Authority (**CMA**).[2]

We are part of the UK Competition Network (**UKCN**), a forum bringing together the CMA and UK sectoral regulators[3] to promote competition and assist in deterring anti-competitive behaviour in regulated sectors. We are also a designated National Competition Authority (**NCA**) within the European Competition Network (**ECN**)[4] for the purposes of exercising all of the powers and functions of a competition authority of a Member State of the European Union (**EU**).[5]

PURPOSE OF THIS GUIDANCE

The purpose of this guidance is to provide advice and information about how we expect to exercise our concurrent power to enforce the competition prohibitions under the Act and the TFEU and to give practical guidance on how the competition prohibitions may apply in the railways sector. In particular this guidance will provide information on:

- the scope of our jurisdiction to apply the competition prohibitions and how our relationship with the CMA will work in practice (Chapter 1);
- how we consider the competition prohibitions may apply in the railways sector and a number of particular considerations which businesses and individuals with an interest in this sector may wish to have regard to (Chapter 2);
- factors we will take into account when: prioritising our resources; determining whether to use our powers under the Act or alternative sector-specific tools which may be available to us to resolve issues in railways markets; and the inter-relationship of our sector-specific powers with competition law (Chapter 3);
- how we expect to conduct investigations under the Act, notably the procedures we will adopt and how we will engage with complainants and parties under investigation (Chapter 4); and
- the procedures we will follow in cases where we have issued a Statement of Objections and our approach to determining appropriate outcomes (Chapter 5).

This guidance supersedes and replaces the guidelines 'Application to services relating to railways'.[6] It reflects changes in: EU competition law; sector-specific legislation and policy; case law; and our approach to competition enforcement in light of our evolving experience. It is intended to constitute general advice and information about the application of the competition prohibitions in the railways sector and explain our approach to enforcing the competition prohibitions.[7] We are currently producing separate related guidance on our approach to monitoring and reviewing markets which will include information on how we will undertake our market investigation reference functions under Part 4 of the Enterprise Act 2002 (the **Enterprise Act**).

This guidance is not intended to be an exhaustive guide to the legal and economic framework for the application of the competition prohibitions to agreements and conduct. It is a complement, rather than a substitute, for relevant domestic or EU legislation, case law and guidance. The CMA alone has powers to make procedural rules, which we must follow when enforcing the competition prohibitions.[8] Only the CMA has powers to issue guidance on the specific areas of penalties and commitments; we must have regard to the CMA's policy and guidance in these reserved areas. As a general principle, where the CMA's guidance is more detailed than our own in a material respect, we will consider its guidance in deciding how to proceed.

It is the responsibility of each business to self-assess its compliance with competition law. We recommend that businesses involved in the provision of services relating to railways have regard to this guidance (and, where appropriate, other more detailed guidance published by the CMA) in the course of reviewing their compliance with competition law. We will not endorse or approve any particular compliance programme or give pre-approval to specific agreements or practices.

NOTES

1 For the purposes of this guidance, reference to 'agreements' should be taken to include decisions taken in trade or other associations of undertakings, and/or concerted practices. See paragraphs 2.14 to 2.18, below

2 Section 67(3) of the Railways Act 1993 (the **Railways Act**)

3 The other sectoral regulators are CAA (Civil Aviation Authority), Ofcom (Office of Communications), Ofgem (the Gas and Electricity Markets Authority), Ofwat (the Water Services Regulation Authority), FCA (the Financial Conduct Authority), PSR (Payment Systems Regulator), and the Northern Ireland Authority for Utility Regulation. Monitor (the regulator of healthcare services in England), has concurrent competition powers but not a statutory duty to promote competition; Monitor is not a member of the UKCN but attends its meetings with an observer status

4 Council Regulation 1/2003 on the implementation of the rules on competition laid down in Articles [101] and [102] of the Treaty, OJ L1, 4.1.2003, p 1. (**Regulation 1/2003**) and the Commission Notice on cooperation within the Network of Competition Authorities, (OJ C101, 27.4.2004, p 43–53), set out the main principles of how the network functions

5 The Competition Act 1998 and other Enactments (Amendment) Regulations 2004 (S.I. 2004 No. 1261), paragraph 3(1)(b)

6 ORR Competition Act Guidelines: Application to Services Relating to Railways (August 2005) and OFT Guidelines, OFT430, Application to Services Relating to Railways, (October 2005)

7 Published under ORR's concurrent powers under section 52 of the Act

8 Namely the Competition Act 1998 (Competition and Markets Authority's Rules) Order 2014 (S.I. 2014 No. 458) (the **CMA Rules**)

CHAPTER 1 – ORR'S POWERS AND CONCURRENCY

SUMMARY

[3.335]
This Chapter explains the scope of ORR's powers and how we expect concurrency with the CMA to work in practice.

A. ORR'S CONCURRENT JURISDICTION

1.1. ORR has all the powers of the CMA[9] to apply and enforce Articles 101 and 102 TFEU and the Act to deal with anti-competitive agreements or abuses of a dominant position where the relevant activities relate to the supply of services relating to railways in Great Britain.[10]

1.2. We will assess on a case by case basis whether a matter falls within our concurrent jurisdiction according to the subject matter to which the agreement or conduct relates rather than the identity of the undertakings involved.[11] Our jurisdiction is not limited to cases involving railway undertakings or directly related to railways infrastructure or rolling stock; for example, we have previously undertaken investigations in relation to the supply of grease for use in electric trackside lubricants[12] and in relation to the provision of real time train information.

1.3. The meaning of railway includes tramways and also any transport system which uses another mode of guided transport but which is not a trolley vehicle system.[13] This means that matters relating to or affecting infrastructure such as the London Underground network, or heritage railways, would be likely to fall within our concurrent jurisdiction.

CASE STUDY – SERVICES RELATING TO RAILWAYS

In November 2009 we concluded an investigation into the provision of Real Time Train Information (RTTI).[14] RTTI is a key input into many end applications including railway station departure boards and websites about travel by rail. In 2009, strong growth in the use of RTTI was being driven by the then relatively new range of travel 'apps' developed for mobile devices. We opened an investigation into this market following a complaint from a software developer arguing that it had been denied access to key RTTI inputs. RTTI is a '*service relating to railways*' because it involves the development of information systems that are designed for the provision of railway services.

i. ORR's powers

1.4. Where a matter relates to *services relating to railways* we may:

- consider complaints about possible infringements of Articles 101 and/or 102 TFEU, and/or the Chapter I and/or Chapter II prohibitions in the Act;
- impose interim measures to prevent significant damage;[15]
- carry out investigations both in response to complaints and on our own initiative, including requiring the production of documents and information and searching premises;[16]
- impose financial penalties on undertakings, taking into account the statutory guidance on penalties issued by the CMA;[17]
- give and enforce directions to bring an infringement to an end;[18]
- accept commitments that are binding on an undertaking;[19] and
- agree to settle a case where the business under investigation is prepared to admit that it has breached Article 101 and/or Article 102 of the TFEU, and/or the Chapter I prohibition and/or the Chapter II prohibition in the United Kingdom and to agree to a streamlined administrative procedure to govern the remainder of the investigation, in return for which ORR may agree to impose a reduced penalty on the business.

ii. Conforming with European competition law

1.5. As a designated NCA, when enforcing national competition law in relation to agreements and/or conduct which may affect trade between Member States, we are required to also apply Articles 101 and 102.[20]

1.6. We may not prohibit an agreement or concerted practice under national competition law if it would not be prohibited under Article 101. This does not however prevent the application of stricter national law to an agreement if the national law being applied pursues an objective which is predominantly different from those pursued by Article 101.

1.7. National competition law is not limited to the application of the domestic competition prohibitions in the Act. We will, where necessary, assess on a case by case basis whether a particular matter has as its objective the enforcement of national competition law or whether the objective pursued is predominantly different from those pursued by Article 101. We note that when exercising our functions and powers under the Railways Act we have a number of different duties to promote a variety of objectives in the UK rail industry. Only one of those duties is the promotion of competition in the provision of railway services for the benefit of users of railway services. Other objectives include consumer protection, the environment, safety, financing and efficiency. We must, on any particular issue or case, make a judgment on the priority and balance to be achieved among these different objectives. Therefore, as a general principle, "the protection of competition in the market" may not be the predominant objective for us when exercising our powers and functions under the Railways Act.

1.8. We may apply national law in a way which is stricter than Article 102 in respect of unilateral conduct.

1.9. When applying and enforcing the prohibitions in Articles 101 and 102 we are bound by the fundamental principle of the primacy of EU law. We must therefore follow the case law of the European Courts[21] in interpreting the scope of the prohibitions in the TFEU. We must also ensure, in so far as it is possible, that any questions arising in relation to the application and enforcement of the prohibitions in the Act, are dealt with in a manner which is consistent with the treatment of corresponding questions arising in EU law.[22]

NOTES

9 With the exception of powers to enforce the criminal cartel offence in the Enterprise Act (see paragraphs 1.17 to 1.18, below)

10 The term 'services relating to railways' is defined by section 67(3ZA) of the Railways Act as including:
- railway services (meaning the carriage of passengers and goods by railway and light maintenance, station and network services);
- the provision and maintenance of rolling stock;
- the development, maintenance or renewal of a network, station or light maintenance depot; and
- the development, provision or maintenance of information systems designed wholly or mainly for facilitating the provision of railway services

11 CMA10, Regulated Industries: Guidance on concurrent application of competition law to regulated industries, (March 2014), www.gov.uk/government/publications/guidance-on-concurrent-application-of-competition-law-to-regulated-industries

12 orr.gov.uk/what-and-how-we-regulate/competition/competition-issues/competition-complaints-investigated/ntm-sales

13 Sections 81 and 82 of the Railways Act

14 orr.gov.uk/what-and-how-we-regulate/competition/competition-issues/competition-complaints-investigated/real-time-train-information

15 Section 35 of the Act

16 Sections 26 to 29 of the Act

17 CMA4, Administrative Penalties: Statement of Policy on the CMA's Approach, (January 2014) www.gov.uk/government/uploads/system/uploads/attachment_data/file/270245/CMA4_-_Admin_Penalties_Statement_of_Policy.pdf

18 Sections 32 to 34 of the Act

19 Section 31A of the Act

20 Article 3(1) of Regulation 1/2003

21 Namely, the General Court and the European Court of Justice

22 For more information on the operation of Regulation 1/2003 see OFT442, Modernisation, (December 2004), www.gov.uk/government/uploads/system/uploads/attachment_data/file/284432/oft442.pdf

B. HOW CONCURRENCY WORKS IN PRACTICE

[3.336]

1.10. Our functions under the Act are exercised concurrently with the CMA and with other sectoral regulators where their respective concurrent jurisdiction overlaps with our own. We will cooperate with the CMA and other sectoral regulators in the exercise of our concurrent functions, for the purpose of strengthening the competition framework and to ensure consistency of approach. There are rules on concurrency to which we and other sectoral regulators must adhere.[23] The CMA has published detailed guidance on how the concurrent application and enforcement of competition law works in practice.[24] The CMA and ORR have agreed a Memorandum of Understanding which sets out working arrangements between the two organisations in relation to the application and enforcement of the competition prohibitions in circumstances where there is concurrent jurisdiction.[25] These documents contain greater detail on the concurrent enforcement of the competition prohibitions and should be read in conjunction with this guidance.

i. Case allocation

1.11. In all circumstances there will be an overlap between ORR and the CMA in terms of which authority should take forward a case. There may also be instances where there are overlaps between ORR and other sectoral regulators. As only one authority can exercise prescribed functions[26] in respect of a case at any moment in time, cases must be allocated to one authority, and, where appropriate, transferred between concurrent authorities.

1.12. In determining case allocation the guiding principle to be applied is that a case will be allocated to the regulator that is better or best placed to exercise the concurrent competition enforcement powers.[27] We will endeavour to reach agreement on which authority will have jurisdiction to exercise its powers to enforce the competition prohibitions in respect of each particular case and will engage with the CMA and any other sectoral regulators in a spirit of constructiveness and cooperation. If agreement cannot be reached, the CMA may determine which relevant competition authority should exercise its concurrent power.[28]

1.13. The CMA may direct that a case in progress be transferred from ORR to the CMA, if it is satisfied that to do so would further the promotion of competition within any market or markets in the United Kingdom, for the benefit of consumers.[29]

1.14. Where Article 101 and/or Article 102 may apply, a case will also be subject to the case allocation principles for determining whether a UK NCA or a NCA from another Member State is best placed to act. The European Commission has the power to take over cases involving an alleged breach of Article 101 and/or Article 102 TFEU from NCAs by initiating proceedings. Further details on case allocation as between NCAs from different Member States are provided in guidance adopted by the CMA.[30]

ii. Information sharing

1.15. We will share information with the CMA and other sectoral regulators for the purposes of general liaison and, in relation to specific cases where it is appropriate to do so, in order to facilitate the discharge of our functions under the Act. The procedures for sharing information with the CMA are set out in the Memorandum of Understanding.[31]

1.16. Prior to sharing any information with the CMA and other sectoral regulators we will have regard to the provisions in Part 9 of the Enterprise Act .[32]

iii. Criminal cartels

1.17. The criminal cartel offence was created with the intention of criminalising and deterring behaviour by individuals leading to the most serious and damaging forms of anti-competitive agreements, namely 'hard-core cartels'. In essence, a hard-core cartel is an agreement between competitors to fix prices, share markets, rig bids or limit output at the expense of the interests of customers and without any countervailing customer benefits. Typically, hard-core cartels are secret arrangements under which competitor businesses agree to coordinate their activity, usually in order to preserve or drive up prices.[33]

1.18. We do not have concurrent jurisdiction to prosecute the cartel offence. In the event that we uncover a suspected criminal cartel, we will refer the matter to the CMA.

iv. Leniency

1.19. It is in the interest of the economy of the UK, and the EU more generally, to have a policy of granting lenient treatment to undertakings which inform competition law enforcement authorities of cartel activities and which then cooperate with those authorities. It is the often secret nature of cartel activities which justifies such a policy. The interests of customers and consumers in ensuring that such activities are detected and prohibited outweigh the policy objectives of imposing financial penalties on those undertakings which participate in cartel activities but which cooperate to a significant degree with competition authorities.

1.20. Further information on the types of lenient treatment which may be available to businesses and the conditions which must be met to secure those benefits, is set out in guidance published by the OFT and adopted by the CMA.[34]

1.21. We would suggest that initial applications for leniency markers in cases involving the railways sector be made to the CMA in accordance with its published leniency process and procedure.[35] The CMA is the only authority empowered to grant a no-action letter with respect to prosecutions under the criminal cartel offence and, for that reason, generally administers the grant of markers (in collaboration with sectoral regulators where relevant). We will consider ourselves bound by the type of any marker granted by the CMA, subject to the conditions of leniency continuing to be met. However, the ORR will be responsible for deciding the amount of any leniency discount ultimately granted in cases which have been allocated to it for enforcement under the Act.

1.22. In leniency cases in the railways sector, leniency information given to the CMA may be passed to us if the case is allocated to ORR for enforcement under the Act. We will use leniency information passed to us only for the purposes of enforcing the Act unless the leniency applicant agrees otherwise.

1.23. In considering immunity from, or applying any reduction in, financial penalties under the Act, we will follow the CMA's guidance and policy,[36] though as noted at paragraph 1.21 above, we cannot grant a no-action letter with respect to prosecutions under the criminal cartel offence.

NOTES

23 The Competition Act 1998 (Concurrency) Regulations 2014 SI 2014 No. 536 (the **Concurrency Regulations**)

24 CMA10

25 Memorandum of Understanding between the Competition and Markets Authority and the Office of Rail Regulation: Concurrent competition powers, (May 2014), (the **Memorandum of Understanding**) www.gov.uk/government/uploads/system/uploads/attachment_data/file/318909/MoU_-_CMA_and_the_ORR.pdf

26 Prescribed functions are those functions in Part 1 of the Act which are, or would be, exercisable concurrently under Regulation 2 of the Concurrency Regulations. These include: the opening of a formal investigation pursuant to the Act, the withdrawal of an exclusion from the Chapter I prohibition in relation to an individual agreement, and the making of certain formal decisions including requiring that an infringement be brought to an end, ordering interim measures, accepting commitments by decision and imposing fines

27 CMA10 contains a list of factors relevant to determining which regulator is 'better or best placed' at paragraph 3.22

28 Regulation 5 of the Concurrency Regulations

29 Regulation 8 of the Concurrency Regulations; the CMA may only issue such a direction prior to a statement of objections being issued

30 OFT442

31 Paragraphs 37 to 48 of the Memorandum of Understanding

32 Notably the considerations in section 244 of the Enterprise Act

[33] See CMA9, Cartel Offence Prosecution Guidance, (March 2014)

[34] See OFT 423, OFT's guidance as to the appropriate amount of a penalty, (September 2012) www.gov.uk/government/publications/appropriate-ca98-penalty-calculation, and OFT1495, Applications for leniency and no-action in cartel cases, (July 2013)
www.gov.uk/government/publications/leniency-and-no-action-applications-in-cartel-cases. In the event that we are initially approached by a leniency applicant, we will direct the applicant, in the first instance, to the CMA

[35] OFT1495

[36] OFT423

CHAPTER 2 – APPLICATION IN A RAILWAY CONTEXT

SUMMARY

[3.337]
This Chapter describes how the competition prohibitions may apply in the context of the railways sector and how this is likely to affect our approach to enforcing the competition prohibitions.

A. THE COMPETITION ACT 1998 AND ARTICLES 101 AND 102 OF THE TREATY ON THE FUNCTIONING OF THE EUROPEAN UNION

2.1. For the purposes of this guidance, a competition infringement is a breach of any of the competition prohibitions contained in the Act or the TFEU. The UK prohibition in Chapter I of the Act is equivalent to the EU prohibition in Article 101 TFEU. The UK prohibition in Chapter II of the Act is equivalent to the EU prohibition in Article 102 TFEU.

2.2. This chapter first sets out principles applicable across all of the prohibitions, before providing guidance on how each of the prohibitions may apply in the railways sector.

i. Undertakings

2.3. The competition prohibitions apply only to agreements between *undertakings*, and, abuses committed by dominant *undertakings* respectively.

2.4. The term 'undertaking' is a broad concept which may, in the particular circumstances of each case, refer to any entity engaged in an economic activity, regardless of its legal status and the way in which it is financed. The term may therefore include: companies; firms; businesses; partnerships; individuals operating as sole traders; associations of undertakings (including trade associations); non-profit making organisations; and (in some circumstances) public entities that offer goods or services in a given market.[37] Key participants within the rail industry including train operating companies and fully or partly publicly owned players such as Network Rail, TfL, and others, are likely to be viewed as undertakings for most of their activities.

2.5. Organisations with separate legal personalities (for instance distinct limited companies) may be considered to be part of one and the same undertaking if they are found to form a 'single economic unit'. A parent company may be part of the same undertaking as a subsidiary if the parent exercises a decisive influence over the subsidiary.[38] Companies in the same corporate group will often be considered to constitute a single undertaking.

2.6. In the railways context, holding companies which exercise decisive influence over subsidiary companies that (for example) have been specifically incorporated to undertake defined activities, such as a rail franchise, should be aware that they may be held liable for the actions of the subsidiary.

2.7. It is for businesses to self-assess the extent to which they form part of the same undertaking with other legal entities.

ii. Market definition

2.8. To assess the application of the competition prohibitions, it will generally be necessary for us to define a relevant market or markets. Defining a relevant market is not an end in itself; rather, it provides a framework for competition analysis. Defining the market is generally a key step in identifying the competitive constraints acting on a supplier of a given product or service and analysing the effects of agreements or conduct. Markets are defined in terms of the products or services involved, geographical scope and, in some cases, the time period in which those products or services are sold.

2.9. In broad terms, defining markets involves an analysis of the extent to which identified products or services are substitutable, for example by reason of their characteristics, prices or intended use. 'Demand-side substitution' takes place when consumers switch from one product to another in response to a change in the relative prices of goods. Supply side substitution refers to suppliers switching production facilities in order to expand the range of goods that they sell. Where an identified product or service is readily interchangeable with another, it is likely to be considered to be within the same market. On the other hand where a product or service is not interchangeable or interchangeable only to a limited extent, it is likely to constitute a separate market. For example in relation to rail passenger transport, customers utilising railway services at peak times may not view rail travel during off peak times as a viable substitute for rail travel at peak times (because using off peak services would mean passengers would not get to work on time). Rail travel at peak times will constitute a separate market to rail travel at off peak times if customers with fixed preferences regarding time of travel are sufficiently numerous.

2.10. In cases involving transport markets, the definition of geographic and product markets are typically closely related as the geography in which a service is being delivered typically represents a key intrinsic element of the service's value.

2.11. There are a range of economic tools which may be used for the purposes of determining the substitutability of products and services. We will define the relevant market(s) for each individual case based on the particular facts of that case; in doing so we will follow the framework set out in guidance adopted by the CMA.[39] Typically in defining markets we will utilise the 'hypothetical monopolist' test, which involves assessing how customers (the demand side) and other suppliers (the supply side) would react to an attempt by a hypothetical monopolist to introduce a small but significant non-transitory increase in price (**SSNIP**) (usually 5% to 10%) to the product or service in question. Analysis of the hypothetical monopolist test will typically involve consideration of:

- the extent to which customers would switch to other products or services in response to a SSNIP, and how long this would take;
- the extent to which alternative suppliers would start supplying the product or service in question in response to a SSNIP and how long this would take; and
- the extent to which customers would switch to other suppliers in other areas in response to a SSNIP and the extent to which suppliers from other areas would start supplying the relevant product or service in the relevant geographic area.

2.12. We will also consider product characteristics in our definition of markets. For example, in a railway transport context, we may typically consider factors such as, for passenger services, journey purpose, and, for freight services, the relative merits of different modes of transport from a customer perspective.

CASE STUDY

In November 2006 we concluded an investigation into the market for coal haulage by rail.[40] In this investigation we had to carry out a market definition exercise. We concluded that, in Great Britain at the time, there was a national market for coal haulage by rail, distinct from other transport modes and from the haulage of other goods by rail. In order to reach this conclusion we examined factors such as: the relative costs and service quality levels that it was possible to achieve using rail as opposed to road transport; and from a supply side perspective the speed and ease with which rail freight operators could procure network capacity and rolling stock. Our conclusions rested on analysis that we carried out using evidence gathered from the companies involved using our powers of investigation.

NOTES

37 For further guidance on the application of competition law to the activities of public bodies see OFT 1389, *Public Bodies and Competition Law: A guide to the application of the Competition Act 1998*, (December 2011) www.gov.uk/government/publications/public-bodies-and-competition-law

38 This can apply, for example, to joint ventures and where the parent company has less than a 100% shareholding but still exercises decisive influence over the subsidiary

39 OFT403, Market Definition, (December 2004) www.gov.uk/government/publications/market-definition. We will also have regard to the Commission Notice on the definition of the relevant market for the purposes of Community competition law (OJ C372, 9.12.97, p 5)

40 orr.gov.uk/__data/assets/pdf_file/0017/3527/ca98_decision_ews-dec06.pdf

B. AGREEMENTS BETWEEN UNDERTAKINGS – CHAPTER I AND ARTICLE 101

[3.338]

2.13. ORR may investigate where it has reasonable grounds to suspect there are agreements between undertakings[41] which have as their object or effect the appreciable prevention, restriction or distortion of competition. Article 101 applies to agreements that may affect trade between Member States of the EU.[42] The Chapter I prohibition applies to agreements which may affect trade within the United Kingdom.

i. Anti-competitive agreements

2.14. Reference to 'agreements' includes informal co-operation falling short of a formal agreement,[43] concerted practices and decisions taken by associations of undertakings (often taking the form of trade associations).

2.15. In particular, these prohibitions apply to agreements which:

- directly or indirectly fix purchase or selling prices or any other trading conditions;
- limit or control production, markets, technical development or investment;
- share markets or sources of supply;
- apply dissimilar trading conditions to equivalent transactions with other trading parties, thereby placing them at a competitive disadvantage; or
- make the conclusion of contracts subject to acceptance by the other parties of supplementary obligations which, by their nature or according to commercial usage, have no connection with the subject of such contracts.

2.16. Examples of potentially anti-competitive agreements which may constitute infringements of the Chapter I prohibition and/or Article 101 that may arise in the railways sector include:

- **Agreements or conscious cooperation between companies not to compete for certain business, for example contracts, such as: passenger rail franchises; freight contracts; contracts to supply rolling stock; and contracts to supply Network Rail.**
- Agreements regarding the setting of technical standards for the supply of products and services to Network Rail or train operators. Such agreements may lead to efficiencies by reducing costs, and/or raising quality or compatibility, but could be harmful overall where their principal overall effect is to limit competition, for example by raising entry barriers.

- Agreements between competing train operators or other industry participants about prices to be charged for certain products or services. Recognising the benefits of a national network, the rail industry currently encourages a degree of co-operation between train operating companies,[44] but the lawfulness of such agreements must still be considered on a case by case basis.

2.17. Such agreements may also fall within the scope of the prohibitions if they are carried out in the context of discussions between members of a trade association or the agreement manifests itself in the form of a decision by a trade association to be recognised by its members.

2.18. This list is non-exhaustive and is only illustrative. We may apply the Chapter I prohibition and the Article 101 prohibition to other types of agreements which may restrict, distort or prevent competition to determine whether they constitute an infringement of competition law.

ii. Exemptions to Chapter I and Article 101

2.19. An agreement may be exempt from the Chapter I and Article 101 prohibitions if it meets certain criteria, which are set out at section 9(1) of the Act and Article 101(3) TFEU respectively.

2.20. The criteria are that the agreement in question:
- contributes to improving production or distribution or promoting technical or economic progress;
- allows consumers a fair share of the resulting benefit;
- does not impose on the undertakings concerned restrictions which are not indispensible to the attainment of these objectives; and
- does not afford the undertakings the possibility of eliminating competition in respect of a substantial part of the products or services in question.

2.21. We will not give pre-approval for a particular practice or agreement. It is for businesses to self-assess whether the agreement or arrangement in question is covered by this exemption; the European Commission has published guidance to assist businesses and their advisers for this purpose.[45]

iii. Block exemptions

2.22. The Secretary of State may, by order, on a recommendation from us or the CMA, exempt categories of agreement from the Chapter I prohibition[46] where they fall within the criteria set out in section 9 of the Act (**UK Block Exemptions**). The European Council and the European Commission may make block exemption regulations which have the effect of exempting particular categories of agreements which are considered to satisfy the criteria set out in Article 101(3) (**EU Block Exemptions**).

2.23. It is for businesses to self-assess whether their conduct falls within either a UK or a EU Block Exemption.

EU Block Exemptions – Council Regulation 169/2009

2.24. Where an agreement falls within a EU Block Exemption it is not prohibited under Article 101 and it will also be exempt from the Chapter I prohibition.[47]

2.25. Of particular relevance to the railways sector[48] is Council Regulation 169/2009.[49] By the terms of this Regulation the prohibition in Article 101(1) does not apply to agreements in rail, road and inland waterways, the object or effect of which is to apply technical improvements or to achieve technical cooperation by means of:
- the standardisation of equipment, transport supplies, vehicles or fixed installations;
- the exchange or pooling, for the purpose of operating transport services, of staff, equipment, vehicles or fixed installations;
- the organisation and execution of successive, complementary, substitute or combined transport operations and the fixing and application of inclusive rates and conditions for such operations, including special competitive rates;
- the use, for journeys by a single mode of transport, of the routes which are most rational from the operational point of view;
- the coordination of transport timetables for connecting routes;
- the grouping of single consignments; and
- the establishment of uniform rules as to the structure of tariffs and their conditions of application provided such rules do not lay down transport rates and conditions.

UK Block Exemptions– public transport ticketing schemes

2.26. An agreement which falls within the category of agreements specified in a UK Block Exemption order will be automatically exempt from the Chapter I prohibition.

2.27. The Competition Act 1998 (Public Transport Ticketing Schemes Block Exemption) Order (SI 2001 No 319) came into force on 1 March 2001 and was subsequently amended, by the Competition Act 1998 (Public Transport Ticketing Schemes Block Exemption) (Amendment) Order 2011 (SI 2011 No. 227 and the Competition Act 1998 (Public Transport Ticketing Schemes Block Exemption) (Amendment) Order 2016.[50] This domestic block exemption covers ticketing schemes that provide multi-operator travel cards, multi-operator individual tickets, through tickets and short and long distance add-on tickets for local travel on buses, trains, trams and domestic ferry services. The block exemption sets out a number of conditions which a ticketing scheme must satisfy in order to benefit from it.

2.28. The public transport ticketing schemes block exemption automatically exempts the agreements within its scope from Chapter I of the Act insofar as they meet certain specified conditions. It allows for public transport operators to enter into agreements to offer passengers tickets that they can use on the services of two or more operators. This normally increases the mobility of passengers and makes travel more flexible.

2.29. The CMA is proposing to issue revised guidance, to reflect amendments made to the block exemption, to clarify some areas which are thought to be unclear, and to update certain aspects of the guidance to take account of new formats and products that have emerged (such as the introduction of smart tickets).[51]

Withdrawal of block exemptions

2.30. We may withdraw the benefit of a EU Block Exemption in cases where the following conditions are met:

- the territory of the UK or part of it, in the relevant case, has all the characteristics of a distinct geographic market; and
- the agreements in question have effects that are incompatible with Article 101(3) TFEU in the territory of the UK.

2.31. No later than 30 days prior to adopting a decision withdrawing the benefit of a EU Block Exemption we will inform the European Commission.[52]

2.32. We may also, in certain circumstances, withdraw the benefits of a UK Block Exemption. For example, we may withdraw the benefit of the Public Transport Ticketing Services block exemption in relation to a particular agreement if we are satisfied it does not meet the statutory exemption criteria,[53] notwithstanding the fact that it would otherwise meet the conditions of the block exemption itself. Before taking this step, we must give notice in writing of our proposal and consider any representations made.

iv. Appreciable effect on trade between Member States, or, competition

2.33. In order for Article 101(1) to be applicable the agreement in question must affect trade between Member States, or, competition to an appreciable extent. In assessing whether or not an agreement has an appreciable effect on competition or trade between Member States we will have regard to the European Commission's *Notice on agreements of minor importance*[54] which sets out, using specified market share thresholds, the Commission's views as to what is and is not an appreciable restriction of competition under Article 101.

2.34. If an agreement has as its object[55] the prevention, restriction or distortion of competition it will, by its nature, have an appreciable effect on competition.[56]

NOTES

41 As noted above at paragraph 2.5, the Chapter I and Article 101 prohibitions do not apply to agreements between group companies which are part of a single undertaking

42 In assessing whether or not an agreement may affect trade between Member States, we will have regard to the European Commission's Notice – *Guidelines on the effect on trade concept contained in Articles 81[101] and 82[102] of the Treaty* (2004), OJ C101, 27.4.2004, p 81. This Notice states that the concept of trade is not limited to traditional exchanges of goods and services across borders, rather it is a wider concept, covering all cross-border economic activity, including establishment

43 General guidance on assessing whether agreements and concerted practices are anti-competitive is described in the OFT401, *Agreements and Concerted Practices* (December 2004) www.gov.uk/government/publications/agreements-and-concerted-practices-understanding-competition-law . General guidance on the application of competition law to the activities of trade associations, professions and self-regulating bodies is set out in the OFT408, *Trade Associations, Professions and Self-Regulating Bodies* (December 2004) www.gov.uk/government/publications/trade-associations-and-professionalself-regulating-bodies-and-competition-law

44 A notable example of this is the UK's system of interoperable fares, whereby customers are able to buy a single ticket to complete a journey which includes services provided by more than one operator

45 *Guidelines on the Application of Article 101(3) of the Treaty* (OJ C101 27.04.2004, p 97)

46 Under section 6 of the Act

47 Sections 10(1) and (2) of the Act provide that any agreement which benefits from a EU Block Exemption, or that would do so if it were to affect trade between Member States, will also be exempted from the domestic Chapter I prohibition

48 Other EU Block Exemptions which may be applicable in the railways sector include: Commission Regulation (EC) No 2658/2000 on the application of Article 101(3) of the Treaty to categories of specialisation agreements (OJ, L304, 5.12.2000 p 3); Commission Regulation (EC) No 2659/2000 on the application of Article 101(3) of the Treaty to categories of research and development agreements (OJ L304, 5.12.2000, p 7); Commission Regulation (EC) No 2790/1999 on the application of Article 101(3) of the Treaty to categories of vertical agreements and concerted practices (OJ L336, 29.12. 1999, p 21); and Commission Regulation (EU) 316/2014 on the application of Article 101(3) of the TFEU to categories of technology transfer agreements (OJ L93, 28.3.2014, p 17-23)

49 Council Regulation 169/2009 applying rules of competition to transport by rail, road and inland waterways (OJ L61, 5. 3.2009, p 1)

50 This order was published on 8 February 2016 (SI 2016/126). The order, which came into force on 29 February 2016, makes certain amendments to the block exemption and extends the duration for 10 years.

51 OFT439, Public transport ticketing schemes block exemption, (November 2006) www.gov.uk/government/publications/public-transport-ticketing-schemes-block-exemption

52 Article 11(4) of Regulation 1/2003

53 Namely those in Article 101(3) and the equivalent provisions in the Act

54 OJ C291, 30.8.2014, p 1–4 (commonly referred to as the *De Minimis* Notice)

55 In assessing whether an agreement has as its object the prevention, restriction or distortion of competition, we will look

at the objective meaning and purpose of the agreement in its economic context. If the object of an agreement is the prevention, restriction or distortion of competition, it is not necessary to show that it also has an anti-competitive effect in order to establish an infringement

56 Case C-226/11 *Expedia* [2012] ECR I-000, in particular paragraphs 35, 36 and 37

C. ABUSE OF A DOMINANT POSITION – CHAPTER II AND ARTICLE 102

[3.339]

2.35. Chapter II of the Act and Article 102 TFEU prohibit conduct by one or more undertakings which amounts to an abuse of a dominant position in a market. Article 102 applies to conduct within the EU or in a substantial part of it in so far as it may affect trade between Member States of the EU.[57] The Chapter II prohibition applies if the dominant position is held within the whole or part of the UK and the conduct in question may affect trade within the whole or part of the UK.

i. Dominance

2.36. In order to contravene the prohibitions in Chapter II and Article 102 an undertaking or undertakings must first be found to be dominant or collectively dominant[58] in a market.

2.37. A dominant market position is defined as a position of economic strength enjoyed by an undertaking which enables it to prevent effective competition from being maintained in the relevant market by affording it the power to behave to an appreciable extent independently of its competitors, customers and ultimately its consumers.[59] Central to the determination of whether an undertaking is in a dominant position in a market is an assessment of its market power. In assessing whether an undertaking enjoys a dominant position we will have regard to guidance adopted by the CMA[60] and guidance issued by the European Commission.[61]

2.38. A non-exhaustive list of factors that we will take into account when assessing dominance under Chapter II or Article 102 includes:

- the presence of existing competitors;
- the likelihood of potential competitors entering the market;
- whether countervailing buyer power exists;
- barriers to entry; and
- the market share of the undertaking(s) over a period of time. There are no specified market share thresholds for dominance under Chapter II or Article 102, although the European Court has stated that dominance can be presumed, in the absence of evidence to the contrary, if an undertaking has a market share persistently above 50%.[62]

ii. Abuse

2.39. In general terms, conduct may be abusive when it is directly exploitative of customers (for example through the charging of excessive prices) or where it has an adverse effect on the competitive process (for example conduct which raises barriers to entry or increases competitors' costs).

2.40. Examples of conduct within the railways sector which could potentially constitute an abuse of a dominant position include:

- **Owners of facilities that are essential to operating a downstream rail transport service, denying downstream competitors access to their facilities without justification, or charging excessive or discriminatory prices for those competitors to use those facilities. Similar issues may exist where firms have access to essential non-physical inputs, such as data or information.**
- **A dominant firm that is vertically integrated and controls an essential upstream input may be able to eliminate downstream competition by creating a 'margin squeeze' between downstream retail prices and costs, where the latter includes the cost of procuring the essential upstream input.**
- **Railway undertakings in a dominant position boycotting certain suppliers, as a result of, for instance, ancillary matters unrelated to the service being tendered for.**
- **Pricing practices by rail freight operators that limit rivals' ability to compete. Competition on prices (alongside quality, choice, etc.) is generally a sign of a market working well and of consumer benefits, but in certain circumstances low pricing and discounting, when exercised by firms with substantial market power, may be anti-competitive. One key example of anti-competitive pricing is 'predatory pricing', whereby a dominant firm sets very low prices with the aim of driving its competitors out of the market. Other examples include certain types of rebate schemes.**

2.41. An undertaking can also contravene Chapter II or Article 102 where it is dominant in one market but the abuse takes place in a separate related market. An example of this in a railway context could be a dominant supplier of specialist railway equipment tying in a purchaser (perhaps by means of warranty conditions which are not objectively justifiable) to long-term maintenance services or products, thereby preventing other suppliers of those services or products from competing effectively in the market.

iii. Exemptions from Chapter II/Article 102

2.42. There is no legal exemption regime specific to Chapter II or Article 102. Conduct which is otherwise anti-competitive may however be subject to the general exclusions from the competition prohibitions (see below). It is also a defence for the dominant undertaking to show that its conduct is objectively justified. A dominant undertaking may achieve this by demonstrating that its conduct is objectively necessary or by demonstrating that its conduct produces substantial efficiencies which outweigh any anti-competitive effects on consumers.[63]

2.43. Of particular interest in the railway context is that anti-competitive conduct may, in certain circumstances, be considered objectively necessary for health and safety reasons related to the nature of the product or service in question. We will draw upon our significant knowledge of health and safety in the railways sector in determining the merits of such arguments.

NOTES

57 In assessing whether conduct has an appreciable effect on trade between Member States we will take the same approach as outlined for Chapter I/Article 101(1), see footnote 42, above

58 The concept of collective or 'joint' dominance was first defined in cases T-66,77 and 78/89 *Società Italiana Vetro v Commission* (Italian Flat Glass) [1992] ECR II-1403, [1992] 5 CMLR 302. Further guidance on the concept of collective dominance is set out in OFT415 *Assessment of Market Power* (December 2004) www.gov.uk/government/publications/assessment-of-market-power paragraphs 2.13 to 2.16

59 Case 27/76 *United Brands v Commission* [1978] ECR 207, [1978] 1 CMLR 429

60 OFT415

61 Commission Communication: Guidance on the Commission's enforcement priorities in applying Article [102] of the EC Treaty to abusive exclusionary conduct by dominant undertakings (2009/C45/02) (OJ C45, 24.2.2009 p 7) (the **Commission's Article 102 Enforcement Priorities Guidance**), paragraphs 9 to 18

62 Case C62/86 *AKZO Chemie BV v Commission* [1991], ECR I-3359.

63 See the Commission's Article 102 Enforcement Priorities Guidance, paragraphs 28 to 31

D. GENERAL EXCLUSIONS TO THE COMPETITION PROHIBITIONS

[3.340]

2.44. In addition to the exemptions noted above there are a number of general exclusions from the competition prohibitions which apply regardless of the category of conduct. It is for businesses to self-assess whether conduct is excluded from the application of the competition prohibitions or whether conduct which may otherwise infringe the competition prohibitions may nonetheless benefit from the application of an exclusion.

i. Services of general economic interest

2.45. Conduct which is carried out by undertakings entrusted (by a public authority)[64] with the operation of services of general economic interest (**SGEI**) or which have the character of monopolies producing revenue for the State are excluded from the application of the competition prohibitions insofar as the application of those prohibitions[65] would obstruct the performance, in law or fact, of the particular tasks assigned to the undertaking.[66]

2.46. It is ultimately for businesses to self-assess whether their conduct, which may otherwise be prohibited, benefits from the SGEI exclusion.

2.47. We consider that the legal threshold for establishing that the SGEI exclusion should apply is a high one. In considering any argument that the SGEI exclusion should apply, we will have regard to the guidelines adopted by the CMA.[67]

2.48. We note that this exclusion may be relevant in the franchised passenger rail transport sector, to the extent that transport services provided pursuant to a public service contract (i.e. franchise agreement) may, in certain circumstances, be classified as a SGEI.[68] When considering the application of the exclusion in this context, we will take into account the extent to which the relevant service is a specified part of the franchise agreement, the nature of the obligation placed on the franchisee by virtue of that agreement, the degree and nature of competition, and the wider market structure. We will also consider on a case by case basis the extent to which a franchisee has the character of a revenue producing monopoly and whether the application of the competition prohibitions would obstruct the tasks assigned to it.

ii. Agreements and conduct which are subject to legal direction

2.49. In situations where national legislation or the legal framework created by such legislation requires undertakings to engage in certain conduct, and operates to entirely eliminate the possibility of competitive activity or autonomy on the part of the undertaking, the undertaking itself will not be in violation of the competition rules for carrying out the conduct required of it.[69] However, to the extent that an undertaking has any autonomy within a legal regime, or in situations where there is some scope for residual competition, the competition prohibitions will apply to the undertaking's conduct.

2.50. Therefore undertakings remain responsible for ensuring that their conduct does not infringe the competition prohibitions, even in cases where there has been an approval of conduct under sector specific legislation by a regulator (for instance in relation to pricing practices). We will consider, when applying the competition prohibitions, the extent that the undertaking has a degree of discretion within the limits set by the regulator and/or has the ability to revert to the regulator for further authorisation.[70]

2.51. In the railways sector there are agreements entered into by railway undertakings to meet licence obligations or by virtue of directions pursuant to sections 16A, 17, 18, 19, 19A (and Schedule 4A), 22A and 22C of the Railways Act.[71] We consider that conduct carried out as a result of these agreements will only be excluded from the application of the competition prohibitions to the extent that such conduct engaged in by undertakings relates specifically to meeting legal requirements placed on them by such licence obligations or directions which can be met in no other way.

NOTES

64 In order for a matter to be 'entrusted' with the operation of services of a general economic interest, there must have been an act of a public authority

65 The exclusion also disapplies other rules contained in the European Treaties

66 Article 106(2) TFEU

67 OFT421, Services of a general economic interest exclusion, (December 2004) www.gov.uk/government/publications/services-of-general-economic-interest-exclusion

68 We will carefully consider the criteria set out in Case C-280/00 *Altmark* [2003] ECR I-7747, [2003] 3 CMLR 339 which considered that there was no 'advantage' by way of a state aid if compensation is paid to an undertaking to discharge public service obligations in the following circumstances: (i) the recipient of compensation must actually have clearly defined public service obligations to discharge; (ii) the basis of compensation must be established in advance in an objective and transparent manner; (iii) the compensation cannot exceed the costs incurred in discharging the public service obligation (and taking into account the relevant receipts and also a reasonable profit margin); and (iv) where there is no public procurement procedure, the level of compensation must be determined by comparison with what a typical undertaking might incur

69 *Commission and France v Ladbroke Racing* [1997] ECR I-6265, 4 [CMLR] 27

70 *Deutsche Telekom v Commission* [2010] ECR I-09555

71 Namely: section 16A (directions to provide, improve or develop railway facilities); sections 17,18 and 19 (directions to enter into access agreements or installation access contracts); section 19A and Schedule 4A (directions to amend access agreements following a review by ORR of access charges); and sections 22A and 22C (directions to amend an access agreement following an application by the beneficiary, or to give effect to conditions of a licence)

E. FRANCHISING

[3.341]

2.52. The franchise process is one where potential competitors compete to offer a range of services over a group of routes.[72] This process means that there is 'competition for the market' as opposed to significant levels of competition in the market. Potential franchisees need to assess their expectation of overall costs and revenues which they will be able to achieve. The Department will regulate certain fares by price caps or tariff baskets whilst leaving other fares unregulated, and will also specify service levels, for example frequency of trains on any given route.

2.53. When considering competition complaints about services which fall within a franchise package (for example passenger rail fares), we will have regard to the fact that there has been competition for the market; however we will also consider the length of time that has passed since such competition took place, the number of participants in the franchising competition and the extent to which the franchisee has exercised its discretion within the parameters set by the franchise agreement.

NOTES

72 The most common form of passenger rail franchises in Great Britain are contracts which the franchisee (rail transport operator) enters into with the Department for Transport (the **Department**) following a competitive tender process conducted by the Department. There are other forms of contracts entered into by way of competition 'for the market'. We will assess the application of competition law to each form of franchise process on a case by case basis

CHAPTER 3 – PRIORITISATION, CHOICE OF TOOL, AND RELATIONSHIP WITH SECTOR SPECIFIC REGULATION

SUMMARY

[3.342]

This Chapter sets out how we will prioritise competition enforcement cases and how we will determine whether to use powers under the Act or use sector specific legislation.

A. INTRODUCTION

3.1. Our competition enforcement powers operate in parallel to a number of other regulatory tools which we may utilise in discharging our duties as an economic regulator. These regulatory tools include:

- consumer law enforcement powers;
- licensing powers (both in terms of modifications to licences and the enforcement of licence breaches);
- regulation of access to services and facilities on the rail network, including track access and access to stations and light maintenance depots, through the approval of access agreements; and
- setting the efficient price for delivery of performance and investment in the railways and monitoring and enforcing delivery of regulated outputs.

3.2. We have published separate guidance in relation to our licence enforcement functions[73] and will publish separately our approach to regulating access to services and facilities on the rail network.

NOTES

73 Available at orr.gov.uk/news-and-media/news-and-announcements/2015/rail-and-road-users-at-heart-of-orrs-approach-to-enforcement

B. PRIORITISATION CRITERIA

[3.343]

3.3. We apply prioritisation principles to help us focus our resource in a way that will deliver most value from our interventions. When applying the prioritisation principles in the context of discharging our concurrent functions under the Act, we will afford particular weight to prioritising the protection of consumers and other users of railway services. The weight attached to each of the criteria will also be influenced by our strategic objectives. Otherwise, the criteria below are not ordered by priority or significance.

3.4. Our prioritisation criteria are:

- **Strategic significance** – We will consider how our intervention will deliver outcomes which are in line with our strategic objectives; for example to secure value for money from the railway, for users and funders.
- **Is ORR better/best placed to act** – We will examine whether an investigation is best carried out by ORR. We work in partnership with a number of concurrent competition authorities, most notably through the UKCN. Consideration of this criterion will typically involve determining which regulator is better or best placed to investigate according to the factors set out in CMA10 (the concurrency guidance).[74]
- **Impact** – An important consideration for us will be the likely impact of our intervention. Factors which we will take into consideration in measuring that impact include:
  - the actual or potential level of harm (which, depending on the circumstances, could be harm to passengers, taxpayers or other users of the railways);
  - evidence to suggest a systemic issue, rather than an isolated incident;
  - circumstances that suggest conduct that is recurrent and/or on-going;
  - whether the conduct in question is leading or could lead to inefficiencies in the market, either in terms of costs or end prices to consumers; and
  - the likely deterrent effect or any other beneficial effects, such as raised awareness amongst consumers. This impact can be in the market in question or in related markets.
- **Costs** – We will estimate the internal and external costs attached to our intervention. The internal costs will include any opportunity costs (for example, knock-on effects on ORR's current and future portfolio of strategic work). It is important that the costs of our intervention are proportionate to the impact that we are seeking.
- **Risks** – We will adopt a risk-based approach when assessing whether or not a matter constitutes a priority. The risks that we will consider include:
  - the probability of a successful outcome particularly in terms of better outcomes for taxpayers, passengers or other users of the railways; the legal risks, notably the strength of the evidence available or likely to become available during the investigation; and
  - the impact of our decisions on our reputation, since credibility plays an important role in the overall effectiveness of the regime.

3.5. The list of criteria set out above is not exhaustive and we may consider other factors where appropriate. We will keep our prioritisation assessment of any particular case under review.

3.6. If we decide not to open an investigation into a matter under the Act on prioritisation grounds, it would nonetheless remain open to the CMA, or any other regulator with concurrent jurisdiction in relation to the matter in question, to take action under the Act, following consultation with us.

NOTES

[74] Under the current domestic concurrency arrangements a case will be allocated to the regulator that is better/best placed to exercise the concurrent competition enforcement powers. CMA10 contains a list of factors relevant to determining which regulator is 'better/best placed' at paragraph 3.22. Where Article 101 and/or Article 102 may apply, a case will also be subject to the case allocation principles for determining whether the United Kingdom NCA or a NCA from another Member State is best placed to act

C. CHOICE OF TOOL

[3.344]

3.7. Anti-competitive agreements or abusive conduct in the railways sector may breach conditions or requirements in licence agreements, or may give rise to grounds for us to take action under one, or a range, of our sector specific regulatory powers. There are therefore many conceivable circumstances in which we could proceed to address problems or issues that have come to our attention either by way of our powers under the Act or by using our sector specific tools.

3.8. In certain circumstances we are required to give 'primacy' to pursuing enforcement action under the Act. This 'primacy' duty stipulates that we must, before making a final order or confirming a provisional order for the purpose of securing compliance with a licence condition or requirement, consider whether it would be more appropriate to proceed under the Act. We must not make a final order or make or confirm a provisional order if we consider it would be more appropriate to proceed under the Act.[75]

3.9. In practice we will, at an early stage, both in relation to licensing and other matters, determine on a case by case basis which tool is most appropriate to deal with the particular issues being raised. The appropriateness of the tool being utilised to address a particular issue will be kept under review at regular stages in enforcement cases.

3.10. The overriding principle is that we will seek to use the most effective, efficient and expeditious solution where an issue is found to exist. In order to make this assessment we will have regard to our prioritisation criteria with particular consideration of:

- the resource and timing implications of the tool being used;
- the potential outcomes which may be achieved; and

- any other advantages or disadvantages between using particular tools, for example potential deterrent effect and establishing case precedent.

i. Procedure

3.11. We will endeavour to keep interested parties informed of what powers we are using in relation to on-going investigations. If we decide midway through an investigation to investigate under different powers, we will write to all parties involved and explain our reasons for switching between powers.

3.12. We will inform the CMA of all cases which we could have taken under the Act, even if ultimately we decide to deal with the case under sector specific legislation.

NOTES

[75] Sections 55(5A) and (5AA) of the Railways Act

D. INTER-RELATIONSHIP WITH SECTOR SPECIFIC REGULATION

i. Safety

[3.345]

3.13. Alongside our economic functions we also regulate health and safety for the entire mainline rail network in Great Britain, as well as the London Underground, light rail, trams and the heritage sector. As well as giving advice to the industry, we also have a range of formal enforcement powers given to us under the Health and Safety at Work etc. Act 1974.[76]

3.14. In cases raising issues relating to safety, for instance where compliance with health and safety law is raised as a possible justification for otherwise anti-competitive conduct, we will draw upon our expertise of enforcing health and safety law in a railway context.

3.15. In considering arguments that otherwise anti-competitive conduct is justified on health and safety grounds, we will take into account that it is usually for public authorities to set and enforce public health and safety standards. It is not the task of undertakings to take steps on their own initiative to exclude products or services which they regard, rightly or wrongly, as dangerous or inferior to their own or alternatives.[77]

ii. EU Railway Packages

3.16. The European Commission has recognised that differing frameworks and technical and operational standards across Member States can create barriers to competitive entry, which can frustrate the policy of liberalisation of rail markets in the EU. It has therefore enacted a number of railways packages which have been transposed into UK law to establish sector specific tools aimed at liberalising railway markets and harmonising standards across Member States.[78]

3.17. An example of a measure adopted under the railways packages is Directive 2012/34/EU (the **Directive**)[79] which has the objective of strengthening further the governance of railway infrastructure, thereby enhancing the competitiveness of the railways sector vis-à-vis other modes of transport. When implemented into UK law[80] the Directive will give us powers (exercisable on our own initiative) to monitor the competitive situation in rail services markets and control arrangements for access to rail infrastructure and services. Guidance on our approach to monitoring and reviewing markets is being produced separately; we are also preparing guidance in relation to how we will discharge our functions in relation to access to infrastructure.[81]

NOTES

[76] orr.gov.uk/what-and-how-we-regulate/health-and-safety/health-and-safety-enforcement

[77] The Commission's Article 102 Enforcement Priorities Guidance paragraph 29; *Hilti v Commission* [1991] ECR II-1439 paragraphs 118 to 119

[78] For more information, see ec.europa.eu/transport/modes/rail/market/index_en.htm

[79] Directive 2012/34/EU of the European Parliament and of the Council of 21 November 2012 establishing a single European railway area (recast) (OJ L343, 14.12.2012, p 32)

[80] The Department is currently consulting on the transposition of the Directive into UK law www.gov.uk/government/consultations/recast-first-railway-package

[81] We expect to consult on separate guidance shortly after the transposition of the Directive

CHAPTER 4 – CONDUCT OF AN INVESTIGATION

SUMMARY

[3.346]

This Chapter sets out how we expect to conduct investigations under the Act, and explains the possible outcomes of investigations.

A. INTRODUCTION

4.1. In conducting investigations under the Act we are required to follow the procedural rules set out in the CMA Rules. We will also have regard to the CMA's guidance on investigation procedures.[82] This guidance is intended to be a supplement to those documents and explain our particular approach to conducting investigations under the Act.

i. Transparency and proportionate use of powers

4.2. We aim to exercise our functions in a transparent manner. As such we aim to ensure that appropriate information is provided on our decision making process and that we are open and accessible to affected stakeholders. This applies throughout the course of any investigation which we undertake. Interested parties are encouraged to make representations to us at appropriate times during the course of investigations and otherwise engage with us so as to assist our decision making in cases.

4.3. We are committed to carrying out our investigations and making decisions in a procedurally fair, transparent and proportionate manner.

ii. The Procedural Officer

4.4. Parties who are aggrieved by any procedural step we take during our investigations have recourse to a procedural complaints process. Such complaints are determined by a Procedural Officer.[83]

NOTES

82 CMA8, Competition Act 1998 Guidance on the CMA's investigation procedures in Competition Act 1998 cases, (March 2014) www.gov.uk/government/publications/guidance-on-the-cmas-investigation-procedures-in-competition-act-1998-cases

83 To be appointed as and when necessary. The identity of the Procedural Officer will be communicated to relevant parties as soon as possible after an appointment is made. CMA Rules, Rule 8; see also CMA8, Chapter 15

B. OPENING AN INVESTIGATION

[3.347]

4.5. In order to open an investigation we must have reasonable grounds for suspecting that at least one of the competition prohibitions is being infringed, or has been infringed at some time in the past[84] (the '**Reasonable Suspicion**' test).

4.6. We may launch an investigation under the Act in response to a complaint made or information supplied by a customer, a competitor, a party to a possible infringement (for example a leniency applicant), or another third party (for example, a whistle-blower). Details of how to make a complaint about a possible infringement of the competition prohibitions are set out on our website.[85]

4.7. We may also decide to investigate a possible breach on our own initiative, for example following a market review or other research undertaken by us.

4.8. Designated consumer bodies[86] may make 'super-complaints' to sectoral regulators, where there are or appear to be market features that may be significantly harming consumers. A super-complaint may be made to us in relation to the rail industry. We will have 90 calendar days to respond to a super-complainant stating whether we will take action and what that action is likely to be. Only designated consumer bodies can make a super-complaint.[87]

i. Formal complainant status

4.9. We will grant formal complainant status to any person who has submitted a written, reasoned, complaint to us and whose interests are likely to be materially affected by the subject matter of the complaint. Formal complainants will have the opportunity to be involved in key stages of the case and, where appropriate, will be kept updated in writing and orally about the status of the investigation.

4.10. Individuals who make complaints but do not wish to have formal complainant status should inform us of this in writing. We will typically withdraw formal complainant status in response to such requests.

ii. Initial enquiry phase

4.11. In appropriate cases we may undertake an 'initial enquiry phase' in order to determine whether the threshold for opening an investigation is met. Any resources dedicated to an initial enquiry phase will be proportionate and commensurate with our continued assessment of the merits of the case and its likelihood of ultimately constituting an administrative priority for ORR.[88]

4.12. The initial enquiry phase may include engaging further with complainants, and, where there is minimal risk of any future investigation being jeopardised, may involve engaging with third parties and the party(ies) who may have committed an infringement. We may make informal requests for information at this stage; however, as our formal information powers under the Act are not engaged prior to the opening of an investigation, parties are not required by law to respond to our requests.

4.13. Where there is more than a minimal risk of any prospective investigation being jeopardised, for example where we would expect to utilise our powers to conduct a site inspection in order to obtain evidence which otherwise might be destroyed or difficult to obtain, we will not engage in any initial enquiries with third parties or the party(ies) who may have committed an infringement.

iii. Informing the CMA and the European Commission

4.14. If we determine, in relation to any matter, that the Reasonable Suspicion test is met, we will inform the CMA within 7 workings days in order to commence the case allocation procedure. We will inform the CMA of each case which we consider meets the threshold for opening an investigation.

4.15. We will inform the European Commission if we open an investigation involving the application of Article 101 and/or Article 102 TFEU.[89] If we have already opened an investigation, the European Commission will consult us before exercising its power to take over the investigation.[90]

Part 3 CMA and other Guidelines

vi. Communication with parties

4.16. If we decide to open an investigation under the Act, we will generally send the businesses under investigation a case initiation letter setting out brief details of the conduct which we are investigating, the relevant legislation, our indicative proposed timescale, and our relevant contact details.

v. Warning letters

4.17. In some cases we may consider it appropriate to deal with suspected infringements of competition law which do not constitute an administrative priority for ORR by issuing a warning letter. A warning letter will set out, amongst other things, that we have been made aware of a possible breach of competition law and although we are not currently minded to pursue an investigation at that stage, we may do so in future if we receive further evidence of a suspected infringement or if our prioritisation assessment changes.

NOTES

84 Section 25 of the Act

85 orr.gov.uk/what-and-how-we-regulate/competition/competition-issues/how-to-complain-under-competition-law

86 Entities designated as consumer bodies include: the Consumer Association; National Consumer Council; Citizens Advice; Energywatch; Consumer Council for Water; Postwatch; CAMRA and General Consumer Council for Northern Ireland

87 Further guidance on super-complaints is available in OFT514, Super-complaints, (July 2003) www.gov.uk/government/publications/how-consumer-bodies-can-make-super-complaints

88 See 'Prioritisation Criteria' above

89 Article 11(3) of Regulation 1/2003

90 Article 11(6) of Regulation 1/2003

C. THE CASE TEAM AND DECISION MAKING

[3.348]

4.18. We will assemble a case team to conduct the investigation, which is likely to consist of a case officer, lawyers, economists and others with the necessary expertise from across ORR, depending on the issues raised by the matter being investigated. For example, in cases involving access issues or those raising issues about safety we may include specialists from those areas of ORR within the case team, or ensure that the case team draws upon their experience as appropriate.

4.19. Each case team will always include a Senior Responsible Officer (**SRO**), the identity of whom will be notified to the parties as soon as practicable. During the course of the investigation, the SRO will have the responsibility of taking decisions in relation to whether:

- there is sufficient evidence to issue a Statement of Objections;
- to close the case on the grounds of administrative priorities;
- to make an interim measures direction;
- to accept commitments offered by a party under investigation; and
- the case is appropriate for settlement.

D. KEEPING PARTIES INFORMED

i. Publishing a timetable

[3.349]

4.20. We will publish indicative timetables for on-going investigations on our website. We will update case timetables where changes occur during the course of investigations. We will also, where possible and subject to the confidential nature of cases, provide broad details of the nature of the case under investigation.

ii. Communication with parties

4.21. The amount and frequency of communications with the party under investigation will vary depending on a number of factors, including the number of parties under investigation, the extent to which they co-operate with us and the complexity of the conduct under investigation.

4.22. Typically we will, as a minimum, hold 'state of play' meetings at appropriate points with each party under investigation. The proposed estimated dates of state of play meetings will be included on our published timetables. The first state of play meeting will usually take place soon after an investigation is opened.

4.23. State of play meetings are an opportunity for those being investigated to meet with the case team and the SRO. In state of play meetings we will keep each party informed of the stage the investigation has reached and provide information on the next steps in the investigation and proposed timings. We will provide as much information as possible to parties under investigation as is appropriate, bearing in mind any restrictions due to confidentiality and market sensitivity. We will endeavour, where it is appropriate to do so, to appraise parties of our preliminary thinking in relation to key aspects of the matter being investigated.

4.24. In addition to state of play meetings, we will provide, as appropriate, additional updates to parties under investigation either by telephone or in writing.

iii. Communication with complainants

4.25. Complainants will not, as a matter of course, be offered formal state of play meetings. We would expect however to provide regular updates to complainants either by telephone or in writing where it is appropriate to do so.

E. INFORMATION GATHERING AND SHARING

i. Information gathering powers under the Act

[3.350]
4.26. Once we have opened an investigation under the Act[91] we have a number of formal information gathering powers. Further detail on our information gathering powers is set out in the CMA's guidance.[92] In summary, under the Act our information gathering powers include that we:

- can issue requests for information and documents (commonly referred to as section 26 notices);
- can conduct compulsory interviews with any individual connected to a business under investigation; and
- have the power to enter business and domestic premises, require the production of documents and take copies of documents. Such entry may be either with or (for business premises) without a warrant. If we have received a warrant, we may search for and seize documents.

4.27. The CMA's guidance describes the limits on its information gathering powers under the Act.[93] These limits also apply to us. As such we:

- cannot require the production or disclosure of privileged communications; and
- cannot force a business to provide answers that would require an admission that it has infringed the law.

ii. Use of information gathered under the sector specific powers

4.28. There may be circumstances in which information gathered using our sector specific powers may be utilised for the purposes of enforcing the competition prohibitions; though once we have launched an investigation under the Act (or transferred a case for enforcement under the Act), we would expect to use our powers under the Act.

4.29. Our information gathering powers under sector specific legislation are primarily contained in the Railways Act, or are otherwise governed by its provisions. There are restrictions on the disclosure by ORR of information it has obtained under or by virtue of the Railways Act and which relates to the affairs of a business or an individual unless consent for such disclosure has been obtained from that business or individual. However, the Railways Act[94] does permit disclosure for the purpose of facilitating the carrying out by ORR of any of its functions under the Railways Act and the Transport Act 2000, including our concurrent competition powers. Therefore we can use or disclose information gathered under the Railways Act to facilitate our functions under the Act.

4.30. Similarly, Part 9 of the Enterprise Act restricts disclosure of information which has been obtained under the Act[95] if such information relates to the affairs of any individual or to any business of an undertaking, unless a relevant statutory gateway is available – for example, the individual or business concerned gives its consent[96] or the disclosure is made for the purpose of facilitating the performance of any function ORR has by virtue of any enactment.[97] It is possible for information obtained by us in the course of an investigation under the Act to be disclosed by us to facilitate our regulatory functions under the Railways Act.[98]

4.31. Before making any such disclosure, we must have regard to three considerations:[99]

- the need to exclude from disclosure (so far as practicable) any information whose disclosure we think is contrary to the public interest;
- the need to exclude from disclosure (so far as practicable):
  - commercial information the disclosure of which we think might significantly harm the legitimate business interests of the undertaking to which it relates; or
  - information relating to the private affairs of an individual the disclosure of which we think might significantly harm the individual's interests; and
- the extent to which the disclosure of the information is necessary for the purpose for which we are permitted to make the disclosure.

iii. Freedom of Information Act

4.32. The Freedom of Information Act 2000 (**FOIA**) gives any person the right to request non-published information from us, as a public authority. We, as an organisation, are committed to openness and transparency; however, we recognise that we will obtain information in the context of competition investigations that should not be widely disclosed, or in some circumstances not disclosed at all.

4.33. Where information obtained by us in the course of investigations made under the Act falls within the prohibition on disclosure contained in Part 9 of the Enterprise Act, such information would be exempt from disclosure under section 44 of the FOIA. This provides that where the disclosure of information is "*prohibited by another enactment*" it is considered exempt information for the purposes of the FOIA.[100]

4.34. We might also seek to rely on other absolute or qualified exemptions contained within the FOIA, including:

Part 3 CMA and other Guidelines

- section 31(1)(g) of the FOIA, which allows us to withhold information if we consider that its disclosure would, or would be likely to, prejudice our ability to exercise our statutory functions for the purposes set out at section 31(2) of the FOIA. This is a qualified exemption and is subject to a test of whether, in all the circumstances, the public interest in maintaining the exemption outweighs the public interest in disclosing the information; and
- section 32 of the FOIA, which provides an absolute exemption where the requested information is held by a public authority in a document placed in the custody of a person conducting an inquiry, for the purposes of that inquiry.

iv. Exchange of information and restrictions on use of information

4.35. As a designated NCA we are required to carry out our EU competition law functions in close cooperation with our European competition partners.[101] We may, for instance, share confidential information with the European Commission and NCAs of other Member States.[102] Prior to sharing any information in accordance with this obligation we will have regard to the provisions in Part 9 of the Enterprise Act.[103]

4.36. NCAs of Member States, when applying Articles 101 and 102, are permitted to provide each other with, and use in evidence, any matter of fact or law (including confidential information).[104] The information may only be used as evidence in the application of Articles 101 or 102 TFEU[105] and in respect of the specific investigation for which it was collected by the original NCA. Information gathered from another member of the ECN during the course of an investigation under the Act enjoys a similar degree of protection and therefore should not be used for any other purpose.

4.37. The exchange of information between ORR and the CMA is permitted both for the purpose of determining who has jurisdiction to exercise functions under the Act[106] in relation to a case under the Act and/or EU law, and generally for the purpose of facilitating the performance by us of our concurrent competition functions.[107]

v. Penalties for non-compliance

4.38. We may impose penalties if parties fail to comply with our information gathering powers without reasonable excuse.[108] In determining whether to proceed, we will follow the CMA's policy on administrative penalties.[109] In addition, it is a criminal offence to provide false or misleading information, or to destroy, falsify or conceal documents (subject to certain statutory conditions).[110]

NOTES

91 Under section 25 of the Act

92 See CMA 8, Chapters 6 and 7 and OFT404, Powers of investigation, (December 2004) www.gov.uk/government/publications/cma-powers-of-investigation-of-anti-competitive-behaviour

93 See CMA 8, Chapter 7

94 Section 145(2) of the Railways Act

95 Sections 237 and 238 of the Enterprise Act

96 Sections 239(3) and (4) of the Enterprise Act

97 Section 241(1) of Enterprise Act

98 Under Schedule 15 of the Enterprise Act, which lists both the Act and the Railways Act as enactments conferring functions

99 Section 244 of the Enterprise Act

100 To benefit from the section 44 exemption in FOIA, information must fall within the general prohibition on disclosure in section 237 of the Enterprise Act. To fall within the prohibition information must be specified information, namely it came to a public authority pursuant to a number of prescribed functions (including enforcement of the Act). Such specified information must also relate to the affairs of a living individual or the business of an undertaking which remains in existence

101 Article 11(1) of Regulation 1/2003

102 Article 12(1) and (2) of Regulation 1/2003. Information shared under this provision may only be used by the recipient NCA for the purposes of applying the EU competition prohibitions. However if national competition law is applied in parallel to the EU prohibitions, and does not lead to a different outcome, the information may also be used for the purposes of applying national competition laws. Further guidance on the operation of information sharing within the ECN is set out in the Commission Notice on cooperation within the Network of Competition Authorities (OJ 2004 C101 p 3)

103 Notably the considerations in section 244 of the Enterprise Act

104 Article 12 of Regulation 1/2003

105 Or national competition law, subject to the criteria at footnote 104 above

106 Namely, Part 1 functions which are any functions under the Act which are or would be exercisable concurrently (see the definition in regulation 2 of the Concurrency Regulations).

107 Regulation 3 and 9 of the Concurrency Regulations; CMA10 paragraphs 3.41 to 3.62; and, the Memorandum of Understanding paragraphs 37 to 48

108 Section 40A of the Act

109 CMA4, Administrative Penalties: Statement of Policy on the CMA's approach, (January 2014) www.gov.uk/government/publications/administrative-penalties-statement-of-policy-on-the-cmas-approach

110 Sections 43 and 44 of the Act

F. INTERIM MEASURES

[3.351]
4.39. We have the power to require a party to comply with temporary directions, called 'interim

measures', where an investigation has been started but not yet concluded and we consider it necessary to act urgently either to prevent significant damage to a person or category of persons, or in order to protect the public interest.[111]

4.40. We can impose interim measures on our own initiative or in response to a request to do so. If a person wishes to make an interim measures application, they should contact the case team leader and provide sufficient information to demonstrate the need for interim measures.

4.41. In considering an application for interim measures we will follow the procedure outlined in the CMA's guidance[112] which outlines rights for representations to be made by applicants and the party against whom an interim measure is sought. Each application will be assessed on a case by case basis, with determinations made by the SRO. In determining whether or not to impose interim measures in any particular case we will seek to ensure that:

- any interim measures are imposed only where specific conduct or behaviour is identified which we consider is causing or is likely to cause significant damage[113] to a particular person or category of person, or is likely to be contrary to the public interest; and
- any interim measures prevent, limit or remedy the significant damage identified by ORR and are proportionate to address any significant damage which is being caused or is likely to be caused.

NOTES

111 Section 35 of the Act

112 CMA8, Chapter 8

113 We consider damage may include actual or potential: financial loss; restrictions on obtaining supplies; or, loss of goodwill. Damage will be significant where a particular person or category of persons is or is likely to be restricted in their ability to compete effectively in the market(s) such that this is causing or is likely to cause significant damage to their commercial position

G. POSSIBLE OUTCOMES FOLLOWING INVESTIGATIONS

[3.352]

4.42. There are a number of possible outcomes which may arise following an investigation. Each of these possible outcomes is addressed below.

i. Issue a statement of objections

4.43. If the SRO reaches the provisional view that the conduct under investigation amounts to an infringement of competition law, the SRO can decide to issue a Statement of Objections to each business under investigation.

4.44. We will generally follow the CMA's approach in relation to the issue of a Statement of Objections.[114] We will normally announce the issue of a Statement of Objections on our website and on the Regulatory News Service. However depending on the circumstances of the case and any market sensitivities, we may vary the extent of publication or decide not to announce the issue of the Statement of Objections.

4.45. The Statement of Objections sets out our provisional view based on our legal and economic assessment of the case. It also sets out our proposed next steps, and gives the business under investigation an opportunity to know the full case against it and to respond formally in writing and orally. The processes to be followed and possible outcomes following a Statement of Objections are set out in Chapter 5, below.

ii. Closing a case on the grounds of administrative priorities

4.46. At any time before or after issuing a Statement of Objections, the SRO may decide that a formal investigation no longer merits the continued allocation of resources. At regular intervals throughout an investigation the merits of continuing the case will be assessed against our prioritisation principles.

4.47. If the SRO decides that a case no longer constitutes an administrative priority, we will inform the business under investigation as well as any formal complainants in writing and set out our reasons for not taking forward the investigation. We will give formal complainants an opportunity, usually within two to four weeks, to submit representations and any additional information. Businesses under investigation will also be allowed the same time frame to submit representations.

4.48. After considering any representations and further evidence received, the SRO will reach a view on whether to close the case. If the SRO decides to close the case on the grounds of administrative priorities, we will inform the business under investigation. In appropriate cases we may issue a warning letter stating that although we are not minded to pursue the investigation further at the current time, we may pursue an investigation in the future. We will always reserve the right to keep our prioritisation decisions under review.

4.49. A decision to de-prioritise a case by us is not binding on other competition authorities (e.g. the CMA and the European Commission). Other competition authorities with the requisite jurisdiction may wish to undertake an investigation in relation to a matter otherwise deprioritised by us.

iii. Issuing a no grounds for action decision

4.50. If the SRO considers that there is insufficient evidence of a competition law infringement the SRO may issue a decision that there are no grounds for action. In such a case, we will provide a non-confidential provisional version of our proposed 'non-infringement' decision to any formal complainant(s). We will invite representations from any formal complainants within a time frame of two to four weeks. We will consider any representations made before proceeding to make a non-infringement decision or not.

iv. Accepting commitments on future conduct

4.51. The SRO may accept commitments from one or more businesses for the purposes of addressing the competition concerns that we are investigating in a particular case.[115] Commitments may be offered at any time during a case;[116] however, the SRO is less likely to exercise their discretion to accept commitments the further a case has progressed.

4.52. Commitments constitute binding promises from a business in relation to its future conduct. We will follow the CMA's guidance on the circumstances in which it is appropriate to accept commitments.[117]

4.53. If the SRO accepts commitments we will discontinue our investigation and we cannot make a final decision or give a direction.[118] However, we can continue the investigation, make a decision or give a direction if we have reasonable grounds:

- to believe that there has been a material change of circumstances since the commitments were accepted;
- to suspect that a business has not adhered to the commitments it has accepted; or
- to suspect that the information that led us to accept the commitments was incomplete, false, or misleading in a material particular.

4.54. We will give notice of any proposal to accept commitments and allow at least eleven working days for interested parties to give their views on the proposed commitments. Where appropriate, we will have a meeting with each business that offered commitments to inform them of the general nature of responses received. If necessary we will indicate whether we consider that changes are required to the commitments before we would consider accepting them. If the parties offering commitments offer material modifications to the proposed commitments, we will allow interested third parties a further period of at least six working days in which to comment on the modified commitments.

4.55. The SRO will make the decision as to whether to accept commitments. Once accepted we will publish the commitments, and a decision explaining our reasons for accepting commitments, on our website.

v. Informing the CMA and the European Commission

4.56. We will share a draft notice, decision or copy of commitments with the CMA and any other competition authority with concurrent jurisdiction prior to:

- issuing a Statement of Objections;
- making a decision or publishing a notice of intention to accept commitments;
- issuing an infringement decision;
- issuing a non-infringement decision; or
- making any decision not to proceed with an investigation (including on administrative priority grounds.[119]

4.57. We will allow concurrent regulators ten working days to provide comments on the relevant documents shared with them. We will take into account any comments provided before reaching any final determination.

4.58. We will also, no less than 30 days before the adoption of a decision accepting commitments, inform the European Commission and provide sufficient information for the European Commission to assess the case.[120] We will take into account any comments provided by the European Commission before making any final determination.

NOTES

[114] CMA8, Chapter 11

[115] Section 31A of the Act

[116] Once a case has formally begun, but before any infringement decision has been made

[117] See OFT407 paragraphs 4.1 to 4:28; and, CMA8 paragraphs 10.15 to 10.23

[118] Section 31B(2) of the Act (giving a direction would include ordering interim measures)

[119] The full list of scenarios in which we would share a draft with concurrent competition authorities is set out at Regulation 9 of the Concurrency Regulations

[120] Article 11(4) of Regulation 1/2003

CHAPTER 5 – AFTER A STATEMENT OF OBJECTIONS

SUMMARY

[3.353]

This Chapter sets out the procedure we will follow in cases where we have issued a Statement of Objections and our approach to determining appropriate outcomes.

A. RIGHT TO REPLY

5.1. Businesses who receive a Statement of Objections have the opportunity to exercise their rights of defence (otherwise known as the 'right to reply'). The stages in this process and the approach we will take to allow parties to exercise this right are set out below.

i. Appointment of a case decision group

5.2. The right to reply involves the opportunity to make oral and written representations to a case decision group (**CDG**). This group consists of at least two expert individuals who were not part of the original case team, to be appointed by ORR's Board on a case by case basis.[121] The role of the CDG is to scrutinise the case as set out in the Statement of Objections and to carefully consider and take into account any representations made by businesses alleged to have infringed/be infringing the competition prohibitions. Parties will be informed of the identities of CDG members when they are appointed.

5.3. The CDG may receive advice and assistance from the original case team but will make its determination independently.

ii. Access to the file

5.4. After issuing a Statement of Objections to a business we will give it a reasonable opportunity (typically six to eight weeks) to inspect the disclosable documents which we have on our case file and which relate to the matters referred to within the Statement of Objections. We will follow the CMA's guidance in relation to access to the file.[122] We will exclude from disclosure certain confidential information and internal documents. We may also exclude routine administrative documents from the file, for example correspondence setting up meetings.

5.5. We will comply with the provisions in Part 9 of the Enterprise Act 2002 when considering what information is confidential and/or whether it is appropriate for such information to be disclosed for the purposes of facilitating our functions under the Act. We consider[123] that confidential information is:

- commercial information, disclosure of which might significantly harm the legitimate business interests of the undertaking to which it relates;
- information relating to the private affairs of an individual, disclosure of which might significantly harm the individual's interests; or
- information, disclosure of which would be contrary to the public interest.

5.6. In order for us to determine what information is confidential, it is our policy to request that third parties who provide information to us indicate which parts of that information they consider to be confidential, in line with the above criteria. We have discretion, even where third parties have claimed confidentiality, to disclose such information if we consider that it is necessary to do so in the exercise of our powers under the Act. Requests to restrict disclosure of confidential information should therefore be supported by reasoned arguments as to what harm would ensue from its disclosure and why.

5.7. We will consider representations on confidentiality from affected parties and assess the merits of each case put before us, following the procedure in the CMA Rules.[124] If we propose to disclose confidential information provided by a person, we will inform that person of the proposed disclosure and give them a reasonable opportunity to make representations on the proposed action. We will typically not accept blanket requests for confidentiality (i.e. confidentiality over an entire document, or part of it) and may request that parties specifically redact parts of documents which they consider to be confidential.

5.8. Depending on the nature of the information to be disclosed, we may make use of electronic disclosure techniques, or, where appropriate, utilise data rooms to effect access to file. The arrangements for disclosure of information will be assessed on a case by case basis.

iii. Written representations

5.9. Recipients of a Statement of Objections will have an opportunity to make written representations. We would expect to give parties between eight to twelve weeks to respond to the Statement of Objections, depending upon the complexity of the case. We will ask for a confidential and a non-confidential version of their representations.[125]

5.10. We may give formal complainants and third parties, who may be able to assist with the CDG's assessment of the case, an opportunity to submit written representations. In order to facilitate that process we will provide them with a non-confidential version of the Statement of Objections or the particular part on which we are seeking their representations, not usually including annexed documents. Any documents disclosed in this regard should be used solely for the purpose of providing representations to us and should not be disclosed to other third parties.

iv. Oral hearings

5.11. The CDG will invite the parties under investigation to attend an oral hearing to discuss the matters set out in the Statement of Objections. If appropriate, formal complainants may also be invited to attend and make representations at oral hearings. Hearings will be attended by members of the case team as well as the CDG.

5.12. The hearing will be conducted by a duly appointed Procedural Officer.

5.13. We will agree with the party under investigation an agenda for any oral hearing in which it is involved in advance of the hearing. The party under investigation will have an opportunity to highlight to the CDG directly any issues of importance to its case, and to clarify the detail set out in its written representations. Although it is helpful to us if the party under investigation answers the questions raised in the oral hearing, there is no obligation to do so and it is possible to respond to questions in writing following the hearing. A transcript of the hearing will be taken.

5.14. Following the oral hearing, the Procedural Officer will report to the CDG indicating any procedural issues that have been brought to the attention of the Procedural Officer during the investigation and an assessment of the fairness of the procedure followed during the oral hearing.[126]

NOTES

121 CMA Rules, Rules 3(2) and (3)

122 CMA8, Chapter 11

123 See Enterprise Act 2002 section 244

124 CMA Rules, Rule 7

125 See paragraph 5.6, above, for the principles we will apply

126 CMA Rules, Rules 6(6) and (7)

C. STEPS FOLLOWING ORAL HEARINGS

NOTES

Editorial note: the original document does not contain a Chapter B.

[3.354]

5.15. Following an oral hearing, the CDG will consider the Statement of Objections and the representations which have been submitted in writing and orally. It may then take any or all of the steps set out below.

i. Letter of Facts

5.16. If the CDG receives new evidence supporting the objections contained in the Statement of Objections, and the CDG intends to rely on it to establish an infringement, it will put the new evidence to the addressee of the Statement of Objections in a 'Letter of Facts' and allow time for it to respond.

ii. Supplementary Statement of Objections

If the CDG receives new information in response to the Statement of Objections which indicates that there is evidence of a different suspected infringement from that set out in the Statement of Objections, or that there is a material change in the alleged infringement, the CDG will issue a 'Supplementary Statement of Objections' setting out the new facts on which is proposes to rely, and giving the addressee an opportunity to respond in writing and orally, and to inspect the new documents.[127]

iii. Draft penalty statement

5.18. If the CDG is considering reaching an infringement decision and imposing a financial penalty on a party, it will provide that party with a draft penalty statement,[128] which will set out the key aspects relevant to the calculation of the proposed penalty, based on the information available to it at the time. Parties will be given an opportunity to comment on the draft penalty statement in writing and to attend a further oral hearing with the CDG.

NOTES

127 Subject to the considerations listed above in relation to access to the file

128 CMA Rules, Rule 11

D. POSSIBLE DECISIONS

[3.355]

5.19. Following consideration of the Statement of Objections and the representations received, the CDG will decide to either issue an infringement decision or a decision that there are no grounds for action.

i. Infringement decision

5.20. If the CDG issues an infringement decision, it will set out the facts on which it relies to prove the infringement and the action which it will take. It will also address the material representations made to us during the course of the investigation. The infringement decision may impose a financial penalty[129] and may issue directions to bring the infringement to an end.[130] If a party then fails to comply with our directions, we may seek a court order to enforce the directions.[131]

5.21. We would normally issue a press announcement regarding an infringement decision and make an announcement on the Regulatory News Service. We will also publish a summary and a non-confidential version of the infringement decision.

ii. No grounds for action

5.22. If the CDG does not find sufficient evidence of a breach of competition law, it will consult any formal complainant. Following any such consultation, the CDG may decide to close the case.

5.23. We would expect to follow the same procedure as for issuing an infringement decision, in terms of publication and announcements.

NOTES

129 Section 36 of the Act

130 Sections 32-33 of the Act

131 Section 34 of the Act

E. SANCTIONS FOR INFRINGEMENT

i. Penalties

[3.356]

5.24. If we find an infringement of competition law we may impose a penalty on the infringing undertaking(s). The infringement decision will explain how the CDG decided on the appropriate level of penalty, having taken into account our statutory obligations in fixing a financial penalty[132] and the parties' written and oral representations on the draft penalty calculation.

5.25. We will follow the CMA's penalty guidance when setting the amount of a penalty.[133]

ii. Settlements

5.26. In the context of enforcement cases under the Act, settlement is the process whereby a business under investigation is prepared to admit that it has infringed competition law and confirms that it accepts that a streamlined 'right to reply' procedure will govern the remainder of the investigation of that business's conduct in return for a reduction in its financial penalty.

5.27. We will retain a broad discretion in determining which cases are appropriate for settlement. Businesses do not have a right to settle in any given case. We will follow the CMA's guidance in relation to: determining which cases are appropriate for settlement; the procedure to be followed in settlement cases; and calculating discounts from financial penalties/granting immunity from sanctions such as competition disqualification orders.[134]

5.28. A party wishing to settle will have to admit liability in relation to the nature, scope and duration of its infringement, immediately cease the infringing behaviour and refrain from engaging in the same or similar infringing behaviour. A party wishing to settle will also have to accept that there will be a streamlined administrative process for the remainder of the investigation, including streamlined access to file arrangements and a streamlined process for making representations. A settling party will have to accept that there will be an infringement decision against it, and that such a decision will remain final and binding.[135]

iii. Voluntary redress schemes

5.29. Both we and the CMA are empowered to approve certain voluntary redress schemes.[136]

5.30. Approved voluntary redress schemes are a form of alternative dispute resolution. Where a business offers a redress scheme, those affected by the infringement are able to claim compensation through such a scheme without the need to pursue litigation in the courts.

5.31. In cases relating to the provision of services relating to railways, where there is no pre-existing investigation, a person (which may include more than one undertaking applying jointly) who has infringed competition law may apply to ORR or the CMA for approval of a voluntary redress scheme. When either authority proposes to exercise these powers, pursuant to the Concurrency Regulations, it shall liaise with the other authority as appropriate.

5.32. Where potential applications for approval of a scheme relate to a pre-existing decision of ORR or to an on-going ORR investigation, applications for approval should be made to ORR. Similarly, where proposed schemes relate to a pre-existing decision or to an on-going investigation of another UK competition authority, applications should be made to that authority.

5.33. If a potential scheme relates to a pre-existing decision of the European Commission:

- where the product or service concerns the supply of services relating to railways, applicants should apply for approval to ORR in the first instance.
- where the product or service does not concern the supply of services relating to railways and does not relate to an industry over which another regulator has concurrent powers only the CMA will have jurisdiction to consider scheme approval and applications should be made to the CMA.

5.34. ORR has discretion whether or not to consider applications for scheme approval. In exercising its discretion ORR will have regard to its prioritisation criteria.

5.35. Applications received by the CMA may be transferred to ORR and applications received by ORR may be transferred to either the CMA or another regulator, where appropriate. Any such transfer shall have regard to the Concurrency Regulations and other relevant rules.

5.36. Where ORR is deemed to be best placed to deal with an application for approval of a voluntary redress scheme (under the Concurrency Regulations and the Concurrency Guidance) it will follow the CMA's guidance on the approval of such schemes.[137]

iv. Directions

5.37. If we have made a decision that one of the competition prohibitions has been infringed, we may impose directions on the infringing parties which we consider are appropriate to bring the infringement to an end. If a party subject to directions fails to comply with them, we may apply to the court for an order requiring the relevant party to make good their default.

v. Competition disqualification orders

5.38. We can make an application to the court for a competition disqualification order to be made against any director of a company which we have found to be in breach of competition law.[138] Such an order will be made by the court if it finds that the conduct of the director in connection with that breach against whom the order is sought makes him unfit to be concerned in the management of a company.

5.39. Before making such an application, we will give notice to the director concerned and give that person an opportunity to make representations.[139]

vi. Informing the CMA and the European Commission

5.40. We will share a draft copy of any proposed infringement decision with any other competition authority with concurrent jurisdiction prior to finalising the decision. We will allow concurrent regulators 10 working days to provide comments on the draft infringement decision shared with them. We will take into account any comments provided before reaching any final determination.

5.41. We will also, no less than 30 days before the adoption of a decision requiring that an infringement be brought to an end, inform the European Commission and provide sufficient information for the European Commission to assess the case.[140] We will take into account any comments provided by the European Commission before making any final determination.

NOTES

132 Section 36(7A) of the Act

133 OFT 423, OFT's guidance as to the appropriate amount of a penalty, (September 2012) www.gov.uk/government/publications/appropriate-ca98-penalty-calculation

134 CMA8, Chapter 14

135 Unless the party concerned successfully appeals the decision

136 Competition Act 1998 (Redress Scheme) Regulations 2015, (S.I. 2015, No. 1587)

137 CMA40, Guidance on the approval of voluntary redress schemes for infringements of competition law, (14 August 2015) www.gov.uk/government/publications/approval-of-redress-schemes-for-competition-law-infringements

138 Section 9A(10) of the Company Directors Disqualification Act 1986 (CDDA 1986), see OFT510, Director disqualification orders in competition cases (June 2010) www.gov.uk/government/publications/competition-disqualification-orders

139 Section 9C of CDDA 1986

140 Article 11(4) of Regulation 1/2003

(VII) HEALTHCARE

MONITOR ENFORCEMENT GUIDANCE

28 March 2013

[3.357]

NOTES

Note that Monitor became part of NHS Improvement in April 2016.

CONTENTS

FOREWORD

[3.358]
The Health and Social Care Act 2012 (the Act) makes changes to the way health care is regulated, including expanding Monitor's role by giving us a number of additional responsibilities. As part of these changes we are given a new main duty to protect and promote the interests of people who use health care services by promoting the provision of services which is economic, efficient and effective, and maintains or improves the quality of the services.

As the foundation of our new role, the Act requires that Monitor issue licences for providers of NHS services and also gives Monitor powers to enforce this licence. These powers enable Monitor to investigate potential breaches of the licence and then to either impose requirements on NHS service providers where we find actual breaches, or accept undertakings from the provider, to make sure they return to compliance. The requirements we can impose range from obliging providers to take steps to restore compliance, requiring providers to restore the position before the breach or obliging them to pay a financial penalty. In exceptional circumstances, we can also consider revoking a licence.

Some of the enforcement powers of the Act can also be exercised against those who are not licence holders – such as those operating without a licence when required to hold one, and those in breach of a requirement to provide Monitor with information. The Act separately gives Monitor concurrent powers with the Office of Fair Trading to apply competition law in the health care sector in England.

This document sets out guidance on how we will exercise our enforcement powers. As examples, this guidance will apply to:

- complaints from a commissioner that a provider has acted unreasonably in refusing to supply a service as a Commissioner Requested Service, in breach of its licence;
- complaints that a provider is not charging in line with the national tariff as required by its licence;
- complaints that a provider has acted anti-competitively in breach of its licence and/or competition law;
- investigations into whether an NHS foundation trust may be in breach of its licence conditions about governance; and
- failures, by those obliged to do so, to provide information to Monitor.

In this document we explain when we may formally investigate potential breaches, the processes we are likely to follow, and the factors that we may consider when deciding what requirements to impose should Monitor find a breach of the provider licence.

We are very grateful for the support and engagement of stakeholders in helping develop this guidance through the recent consultation. This is a new enforcement framework which we will develop and refine over time as we learn through practice. But we are keen to start with an effective regime building on regulatory experience to date.

Adrian Masters

Managing Director of Sector Development

1. INTRODUCTION

[3.359]
The Health and Social Care Act 2012 (the Act) makes changes to the way providers of NHS health care services will be regulated and gives Monitor new duties and powers. Further information on our role can be found on our website: www.monitor.gov.uk

This guidance covers the general approach that Monitor will take to using our provider licence enforcement and competition law powers over health care providers. Parts of it apply to others who may be required to supply Monitor with information. This document explains:

- when Monitor may decide to take action, and what action we might take;
- how Monitor is likely to decide what kind of sanctions to impose using our powers under the Act; and
- the high-level processes Monitor intends to follow when taking enforcement action.

This guidance is designed to provide information about how Monitor generally expects to go about our enforcement work. The circumstances in some cases may make it appropriate for us to depart from the guidance.

We have written this guidance to be as clear as possible, and have tried to use straightforward language and avoided quoting sections of the Act where possible; this means that, sometimes, we do not use the exact wording used in the Act which would, of course, override this guidance.

All of this guidance is relevant to providers of NHS health care services in England. The sections that cover competition law are relevant to all providers of health care services in England. The sections covering enforcement action under sections 105 and 106 of the Act apply also to others where they may be in breach of a requirement to provide Monitor with information; this applies to the NHS Commissioning Board and clinical commissioning groups. This guidance does not cover Monitor's approach to using our enforcement powers under the *National Health Service (Procurement, Patient Choice and Competition) (No. 2) Regulations 2013*.

As we move from the current framework of regulating NHS foundation trusts through their terms of Authorisation to regulating them through the licence, we are following a similar approach to that set out in this guidance in 'translating' breaches of terms of the Authorisation into appropriate regulatory action under the licence, to take effect as the licence comes into force. We are working closely with the NHS foundation trusts affected by this to achieve a smooth transition.

1.1 SCOPE OF THE GUIDANCE

The Act requires Monitor to introduce a licence for providers of NHS health care services, the standard conditions for which are available here. The Act gives Monitor associated enforcement powers under sections 105 and 106. Monitor may use these specific enforcement powers to ensure that any provider that should hold a licence does in fact hold one, all licensed providers comply with their licence conditions and all providers and others who may be obliged to comply with requests from Monitor to provide information.

Section 89 of the Act gives Monitor the power to revoke a provider's licence if we are satisfied that the provider has failed to comply with a licence condition. Some of this guidance also applies to investigations which may result in revocation of a licence under section 89 of the Act.

Section 111 of the Act gives Monitor additional specific powers to take action where the governance of an NHS foundation trust is such that it is failing, or will fail, to comply with one or more of the conditions in its licence. These powers are in addition to those described above. Some of this guidance also applies to investigations which may result in an intervention under section 111 of the Act.

When carrying out the above functions, Monitor will seek to ensure that the enforcement actions we take enable us to best achieve our main duty to protect and promote the interests of people that use health care services (health care service users) by promoting the provision of health care services which is economic, efficient and effective, and maintains or improves the quality of the services.

The Act gives Monitor concurrent powers with the Office of Fair Trading (OFT) to apply competition law in relation to the provision of health care services in England meaning that either Monitor or the OFT may act in relation to a particular case. Some of this guidance also has relevance to investigations that Monitor may carry out under the Competition Act 1998 (the Competition Act) and the Treaty on the Functioning of the European Union (the TFEU). It gives an overview of the investigation process we intend to follow and contains links to information published by the OFT. Monitor and the OFT will decide on a case-by-case basis which organisation is best placed to investigate an issue. We may, in the future, publish more detailed guidance on Monitor's procedures around applying competition law.

This guidance also describes how we will prioritise our enforcement work in order to make the best use of resources. We intend to apply the same principles for prioritising all of our decisions that potentially involve a significant amount of resource to a case or project.

Table 1.1 Monitor's enforcement powers

How this guidance applies to Monitor's different enforcement powers:

Regulatory action / Section of guidance	Informal action	Enforcement undertakings (section 106)	Discretionary requirements (section 105)	Section 111 new licence condition	Section 111 remove, suspend or disqualify directors/governors	Revoking a provider's licence (section 89)	Competition law (section 72)
2.2 Prioritisation	√	√	√	√	√	√	√
2.3 Informal or formal action	√	√	√	√	√	√	√
3.2 to 3.4 Imposing discretionary requirements			√	√	√	√	
3.5 Accepting enforcement undertakings		√					
4.2.1 Case initiation	√	√	√	√	√	√	√
4.2.2 Investigations	√	√	√	√	√	√	√
4.2.3 Case updates	√	√	√	√	√	√	√
4.2.4 Entering into enforcement undertakings		√					
4.2.5 Discretionary requirements			√				
4.3 Procedures for licence revocation						√	
4.4 Actions under section 111 of the Act (applies to NHS foundation trusts)				√	√		
4.5 Investigations under competition law							√
5 Decision making	√	√	√	√	√	√	√
6.2 Rights of appeal		√*	√			√	√

*** Right of appeal for enforcement undertakings is only in relation to a refusal by Monitor to issue a certificate of compliance with undertakings.**

1.2 MONITOR'S ENFORCEMENT POWERS

In this section we explain the different enforcement powers that the Act gives Monitor. More details of Monitor's enforcement powers are in the Annex. This section outlines:

Licence enforcement

- what discretionary requirements are and when Monitor may impose them – section 105 of the Act;
- what enforcement undertakings are and when Monitor may accept them – section 106 of the Act;
- Monitor's power to revoke a provider's licence – section 89 of the Act;
- Monitor's powers to impose additional licence conditions on an NHS foundation trust, and to require a foundation trust to remove, suspend or disqualify one or more of its directors and/or governors – section 111 of the Act; and

Competition law enforcement

- Monitor's powers to apply competition law.

Licence enforcement

Discretionary requirements under the Act

Where Monitor finds that a provider is breaching, or has breached, one or more of its licence conditions, or has not met a requirement to hold a licence, or has failed to provide Monitor with information we require, Monitor may impose one or more of the 'discretionary requirements' specified in section 105 of the Act. Monitor may also impose such requirements on others in breach of a requirement to provide us with information.

The discretionary requirements that Monitor may impose are:

- **compliance requirements** which require a provider to take such steps as we may specify to ensure that the breach in question does not continue or recur;
- **restoration requirements** which require a provider to take such actions as we may specify to restore the situation to what it would have been, absent the breach; and
- **variable monetary penalties** which require a provider to pay a penalty.

The Act requires us to explain in guidance how we intend to exercise our powers to impose discretionary requirements including:

- when we are likely to impose a discretionary requirement – see Chapter 3;
- when we may not impose a discretionary requirement – see Chapter 3;
- the matters we are likely to take into account in determining a variable monetary penalty, including any discounts for voluntary reporting – see Chapter 3; and
- a provider's rights to make representations and rights of appeal – see Chapter 6.

Enforcement undertakings under the Act

If Monitor has reasonable grounds to suspect that a provider is breaching, or has breached, one or more of its licence conditions, or has not met a requirement to hold a licence, or has failed to provide Monitor with information we required, we may also accept 'enforcement undertakings', as described in section 106 of the Act. Monitor may also accept such undertakings from others in breach of a requirement to provide us with information.

Enforcement undertakings are actions that providers commit themselves to taking and which Monitor may decide to accept. They would usually be used as an alternative to investigating further with the attendant possibility of imposing discretionary requirements.

An enforcement undertaking may include one or more of the following commitments:

- action to ensure that the breach does not continue or recur;
- action to ensure that the position is, so far as possible, restored to what it would have been, absent the breach;
- action, including the payment of a sum of money, to benefit any other licensee affected by the breach, any provider of NHS health care services affected by the breach, or any commissioner of NHS health care services affected by the breach; or
- action of such a description as may be prescribed.

The Act requires us to include in our guidance information about how we intend to exercise our powers to accept enforcement undertakings – see Chapters 3 and 4.

Revoking a provider's licence

Monitor may also revoke a provider's licence if we are satisfied that the provider has failed to comply with a licence condition, as set out in section 89 of the Act.

Powers to impose additional licence conditions on NHS foundation trusts

Monitor has additional specific powers to take action where the governance of an NHS foundation trust is such that it is failing, or will fail, to comply with one or more of the conditions in its licence.

There are two parts to these powers:

(I) where Monitor is satisfied that an NHS foundation trust's directors and/or governors are failing to (a) secure compliance with conditions in the foundation trust's licence, or (b) take steps to reduce the risk of a breach of a condition in the foundation trust's licence under section 111 of the Act, Monitor may include in the licence such conditions relating to governance as Monitor considers appropriate; and

(II) where Monitor is satisfied that the NHS foundation trust has breached, or is breaching, an additional licence condition that was included under section 111 of the Act, we may use our powers to require the foundation trust to remove, suspend or disqualify one or more of the foundation trust's directors and/or governors or, if the foundation trust does not do so, Monitor may make such changes.

Competition law

Monitor has concurrent powers with the OFT to apply UK and European competition law to providers in the health care sector in England. Where Monitor establishes an infringement of the Competition Act and/or Articles 101/102 of the TFEU, our enforcement powers include:

- giving directions to bring an infringement to an end; and
- imposing financial penalties.

Before any finding of infringement, Monitor may accept binding commitments offered to us by an undertaking.

Monitor's powers to apply competition law are not limited to the NHS but apply to all undertakings involved in the provision of health care services in England. Further information on what constitutes an 'undertaking' can be found at www.oft.gov.uk/shared_oft/ca-and-cartels/OFT1389.pdf.

Overview of Monitor's formal provider enforcement powers (simplified)

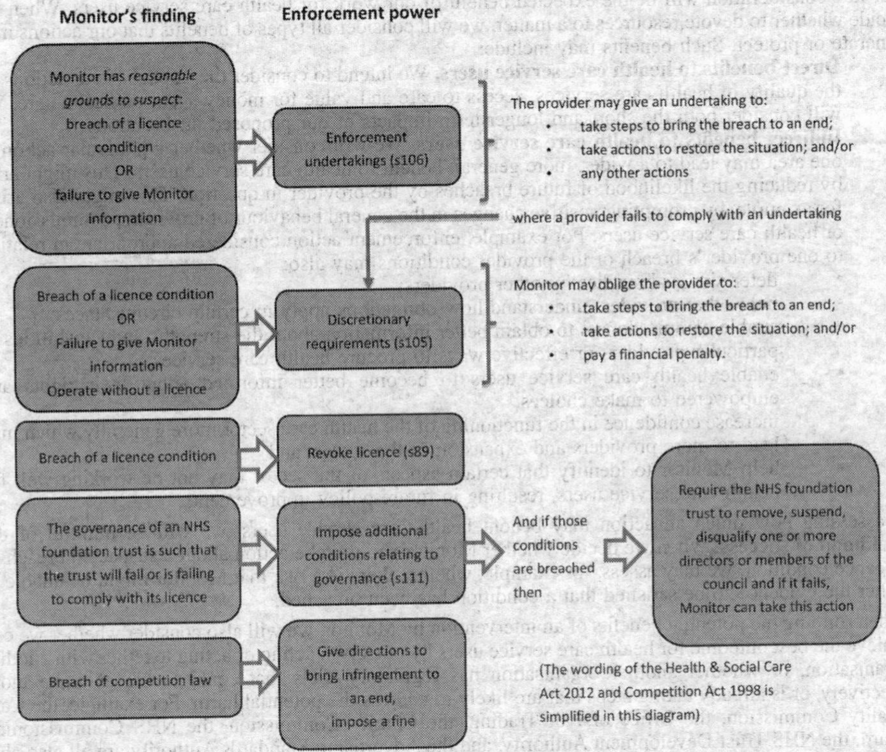

1.3 ABOUT THIS DOCUMENT

Chapter 2 explains how Monitor is likely to decide whether to take action, and what kind of action we might decide to take.

Chapter 3 is about enforcement actions and explains the factors Monitor will take into account when deciding which, if any, discretionary requirements to impose or what, if any, enforcement undertakings we will accept. This chapter also covers the matters Monitor may take into account when imposing a variable monetary penalty.

Chapter 4 describes the processes that Monitor will follow if we decide to investigate formally a potential breach. This includes the procedures for gathering information, the information that parties may receive about the investigation process, and the opportunity for the affected party to make representations.

Chapter 5 outlines the decision-making procedures that Monitor will follow.

Chapter 6 explains what rights of appeal exist if the affected party wishes to contest a Monitor enforcement decision or a competition law decision.

2. PRIORITISATION

[3.360]

This chapter sets out the prioritisation framework that we intend to follow to make sure Monitor focuses on the issues that best enable us to meet our duties and to make use of our resources.

2.1 PRIORITISATION FRAMEWORK

Monitor intends to apply this prioritisation framework to decisions about whether to pursue enforcement action and to all other significant cases where Monitor has discretion over whether to act. We will use this framework to inform our decisions on whether or not to begin cases, and to continue with them once under way. In developing this framework, Monitor has considered the approaches taken by other regulators, many of which also use prioritisation frameworks.

When assessing priorities for enforcement action, we would expect to draw on a range of information, including but not limited to: intelligence and information that Monitor may collect directly; information from patient representative bodies and commissioners; any complaints and representations made to Monitor; and information from providers themselves, including, for example, monitoring information supplied to us.

In weighing up the benefits and costs of taking action, we will consider, amongst any other relevant factors:

The likely benefits to health care service users

Our key consideration will be the expected benefit of our work for health care service users. When we decide whether to devote resources to a matter, we will consider all types of benefits that our actions may generate or protect. Such benefits may include:

- **Direct benefits to health care service users.** We intend to consider the impact of our actions on the quality of health care services, access to care and value for money spent on health care. We will consider both the short and longer term impacts of our proposed interventions.
- **Indirect benefits to health care service users.** We will consider whether a particular action in one area may lead to a wider, more general, benefit to health care service users. This might arise by reducing the likelihood of future breaches by the provider in question. This might also arise, for example, by prompting positive changes in the general behaviour of providers, commissioners or health care service users. For example, enforcement action considered appropriate in relation to one provider's breach of the provider conditions may also:
  - deter similar breaches by other providers;
  - help other providers understand how obligations apply in certain circumstances;
  - enable commissioners to obtain better information about the strengths and capabilities of particular providers or effective ways to procure health care services;
  - enable health care service users to become better informed about their rights and empowered to make choices;
  - increase confidence in the functioning of the health care sector more generally which may lead to more providers and expansion of the sector; and
  - help Monitor to identify that certain aspects of the sector may not be working well for health care service users, resulting in future policy improvements.

In assessing how much an action may benefit health care service users, we will be mindful of the **likelihood of success**. When we decide whether Monitor should take action about a suspected breach of a licence condition, we may assess, for example, whether there is a risk that Monitor might be unable to gather the evidence to be satisfied that a condition has been breached.

In determining the potential benefits of an intervention by Monitor, we will also consider whether we can achieve the best outcome for health care service users by ourselves acting or acting together with another organisation, or whether another organisation has regulatory tools that could tackle an issue more effectively, or is already taking steps that are likely to address the potential harm. For example, the Care Quality Commission, the Office of Fair Trading, the Charity Commission, the NHS Commissioning Board, the NHS Trust Development Authority, and the Advertising Standards Authority are all also able to take action within the health care sector.

If the breach relates to enabling integrated care, we will also consider the potential for action to reduce inequalities, in line with our duty under the Act.

The likely costs of taking action

To ensure that we make the best possible use of our resources, we will also consider the cost of any action. We will think about the resources needed to take a particular course of action and compare them to the potential benefits. We propose to consider staff and non-staff costs, and the likely duration of the work.

We also recognise that the actions we take may be costly for other organisations in the health care sector. So we intend to consider the impact of our possible actions on providers, and other parties, and will pay close attention to whether the burden they would impose is in proportion to the scale of the problem they aim to correct.

Deciding whether to take formal or informal action

When called on to act, Monitor may need to choose between taking informal action, formal action, or no action at all. We may also consider responding to a problem in ways that do not involve the use of our enforcement powers. For example, we may decide to review the situation, review our own policy approach, or consider addressing the matter by using other powers such as the power to set prices for some NHS services.

Even when a matter could appropriately be addressed by using Monitor's formal enforcement powers, it may still be appropriate to deal with it informally and give providers an opportunity to address any issues without a formal investigation. Monitor's decision on whether to take formal or informal action will take into account the individual circumstances of the matter in hand. We will make our decisions based on what is in the interests of health care service users in line with our main duty. Relevant considerations may include:

- the impact of the breach or potential breach on health care service users;
- whether the provider has already taken steps that suggest the breach is unlikely to recur, for example by:
  - notifying the breach to Monitor as soon as it was identified; or
  - voluntarily taking action to end the breach and limit the risk of similar future breaches;
- the context in which the breach has occurred. For example, we might consider: whether the conduct involves repeated breaches of the same condition; a provider that is repeatedly breaching different conditions; whether other regulators or relevant stakeholders have relevant concerns about the provider; a provider's history of responding to breaches; the likelihood that the action being considered resulting in compliance and the speed at which it will result in compliance; whether the type of breach is thought to be widespread in the health care sector; and/ or
- whether any third parties (eg, other regulators or litigants) are taking relevant action in relation to the same breach.

If Monitor considers that informal action is preferred over formal action, or as a first attempt to resolve a matter before moving to formal action, such informal action may involve one or more of the following:

- providing guidance, or working with providers to support them in maintaining or restoring compliance. For example, this may include the use of agreed action plans containing specific milestones and deadlines;
- issuing an advisory letter to explain a provider's obligations and what action may be advisable to maintain compliance; and
- issuing a warning letter which sets out Monitor's concerns, and notifying the provider that if it does not take action Monitor may commence a formal investigation.

In choosing the most effective response to a potential issue, we will consider which option is likely to create the most potential benefit to health care service users, with proportionate potential costs to Monitor and the sector, in line with the principles outlined above.

3. IMPOSING DISCRETIONARY REQUIREMENTS AND ACCEPTING ENFORCEMENT UNDERTAKINGS

3.1 INTRODUCTION

[3.361]
Monitor may impose discretionary requirements where we are satisfied that a provider is, or was, in breach of a licence condition, or the requirement to hold a licence, or a requirement to supply Monitor with information. A provider subject to a formal investigation may offer Monitor an enforcement undertaking which Monitor may accept instead of investigating further and, potentially, imposing discretionary requirements. Monitor may also accept enforcement undertakings from, others in breach of a requirement to provide us with information.

This chapter outlines:

- the nature of the discretionary requirements that Monitor may impose;
- the factors that Monitor may consider in determining what requirements are needed;
- issues relevant to each requirement and how they may be implemented, including the factors that Monitor may take into account when setting a variable monetary penalty; and
- when Monitor may accept enforcement undertakings.

3.2 DISCRETIONARY REQUIREMENTS

Discretionary requirements are formally specified in the Act and may be a:

- **Compliance requirement:** A compliance requirement is an instruction from Monitor to the provider to take specified steps within a set period to secure that the breach not continue or recur. The principal focus of a compliance requirement is to secure compliance;
- **Restoration requirement:** A restoration requirement obliges the provider to take such steps within such period as Monitor may specify to secure that the position is, so far as possible, restored to what it would have been, absent the breach. Restoration requirements may also be used to compensate any affected party, including health care service users and other providers. Such a requirement could require, for example, that the provider gives up any gains it has made from the breach and restores the position of those who have suffered harm as a result; and
- **Variable monetary penalty**: Variable monetary penalties require a provider to pay a financial penalty of such amount as Monitor may specify. The variable monetary penalty must not exceed 10% of the provider's turnover in England.

Discretionary requirements may be used in combination in relation to the same breach, where appropriate. However, Monitor must not impose discretionary requirements on more than one occasion in relation to the same breach.

3.3 DECIDING WHAT KIND OF DISCRETIONARY REQUIREMENTS TO IMPOSE

In considering what, if any, discretionary requirements to impose, Monitor's aim is to ensure that any action we take promotes compliance and fulfils Monitor's main duty to protect and promote the interests of people who use health care services, by promoting the provision of health care services which is economic, efficient and effective, and maintains or improves the quality of the services. We will ensure also that we take into account all our other duties as appropriate in exercising our enforcement functions.

In deciding what action is most appropriate in the circumstances of the individual case and which requirements, if any, to impose, we intend to consider, amongst other relevant considerations:

- the seriousness of the breach;
- ensuring provider compliance;
- deterring similar breaches;
- restoring the position to what it would have been without the breach; and
- the proportionality of the remedy to the nature of the breach.

Monitor may decide not to impose a discretionary requirement if we conclude that:

- the breach caused (or was capable of causing) no harm or harm that is not material;
- a discretionary requirement is not required to ensure provider compliance;
- a discretionary requirement is not required to restore the position to what it would have been without the breach; and
- a discretionary requirement is not required to deter similar breaches.

Monitor may also decide not to impose a discretionary requirement if we conclude that the only suitable discretionary requirement would be disproportionate to the nature of the breach.

Seriousness

Monitor will take into account a range of relevant factors in assessing seriousness, including:

- the nature and the scale of the harm that a breach or potential breach has caused or is capable of causing to health care service users. Monitor intends to assess:
  - who has been or is likely to be affected;
  - the extent to which any harm could be reversed or remedied;
  - the number of health care service users affected, or potentially affected, whether directly or indirectly;
  - the actual or potential impact on those health care users;
  - the duration of any harmful effects of potential effects;
- whether the provider knew or should have known that its actions would risk non-compliance; and/or
- whether the provider has committed a breach before.

The more serious the breach, the more likely Monitor will be to impose discretionary requirements.

Ensuring provider compliance

Monitor will consider what action may be needed to ensure: that a breach not continue; and/or that the provider end the breach and not repeat it. Monitor will also consider what forms of intervention may be needed to deter similar breaches from recurring.

In considering whether requirements are needed to ensure that a breach not continue, Monitor proposes to assess, amongst other relevant factors:

- whether the breach has been brought to an end;
- if the breach is continuing, what steps the provider has taken and/or proposes to take voluntarily in order to bring the breach to an end;
- whether, if the provider has proposed voluntary steps, it would still be beneficial to ensure that the breach does not continue by imposing requirements relating to those proposed steps;
- whether there are other steps which Monitor considers should be taken in order to ensure that the breach not continue; and
- whether any third parties (eg, other regulators or litigants) are taking relevant action in relation to the same breach.

If Monitor considers that discretionary requirements are needed to ensure a breach not continue, it is likely that Monitor will impose a compliance requirement.

In considering whether requirements are needed to deter further breaches by the provider, Monitor proposes to assess, amongst other relevant factors:

- Whether the provider knew, or should have known, that its actions would risk non-compliance; this may include evidence that the breach was genuinely accidental and that the provider has already taken steps to avoid non-compliance;
- How much the provider has gained, or is expected to gain, from the breach – relevant benefits may include financial and other benefits such as reputational benefits;
- Whether the provider has taken steps that suggest the breach in question will not recur – this could be, for example, by:
  - notifying the breach to Monitor as soon as it was identified;
  - voluntarily taking effective steps to ensure that the breach is remedied and to limit the risk of further breaches taking place in future;
  - cooperating generally with Monitor's enquiries and requirements; or

- taking action to compensate those affected.
- Whether the breach could represent part of a pattern of non-compliance, emerging or otherwise, such that Monitor considers that imposing requirements is necessary to incentivise compliance in the future; and
- Whether any third parties (eg, other regulators or litigants) are taking relevant action in relation to the same breach.

Monitor is likely to impose a discretionary requirement if we are satisfied that it is needed to deter future breaches. A compliance requirement is likely to be appropriate if there are practical steps which Monitor could require of the provider in order to ensure that the breach not recur. The greater the risk of future breach, the greater the likelihood that Monitor will impose a variable monetary penalty (whether instead of or in addition to other discretionary requirements) in order to deter a recurrence.

Deterring similar breaches by other providers

In order to deter similar breaches by other providers, Monitor will consider how the action we take in one case might also affect the incentives on other providers to comply. For example, Monitor may find it appropriate to adjust the severity of the requirements we impose according to:

- the extent to which the type of breach under consideration is thought to be widespread in the health care sector;
- the extent of harm the type of breach has caused (or is capable of causing) to health care service users; or
- whether previous sanctions have been effective or ineffective in deterring others from taking similar action.

If Monitor considers that it is necessary to adjust the proposed discretionary requirements in order to deter similar breaches by other providers, it is likely that Monitor would impose (or increase) a variable monetary penalty. However, in appropriate cases the objective of deterring similar breaches by other providers may be met through the imposition of, or modifications to, a compliance requirement or a restoration requirement.

Restoring the position to what it would have been without the breach

Monitor will consider whether it would be desirable and feasible to take steps to restore the position to what it would have been without the breach. If so, Monitor may impose a restoration requirement.

Restoration could require a provider to give up any gains it has made from a breach and restore the position of those who have suffered harm as a result. Restoration requirements may be financial or non-financial.

Where a breach of a regulatory requirement causes harm to another party, Monitor considers that a restoration requirement may have a number of advantages. It might be used to ensure that parties do not profit from a breach, and it may deter others from similar conduct in future. It may also compensate any affected parties.

However, there may be some practical limits to Monitor's ability to impose restoration requirements. For example, it may be difficult to establish which parties (whether individuals or categories of parties) have been harmed by a breach, or the extent of any such harm.

Proportionality

Monitor will ensure the action we take is proportionate and reasonable in the circumstances at hand, and that we balance the need to deter harmful conduct with the need to ensure the continued provision of health care services to health care service users.

Before imposing a requirement, Monitor therefore proposes to consider:

- the specific circumstances of the relevant provider;
- how any requirement is likely to affect the provider's delivery of health care services; and

In particular, Monitor will consider the impact of a particular requirement on the provider's future financial viability. We propose to consider factors such as:

- the cost of the requirement to the provider;
- the provider's current financial position;
- how much the provider has gained from the relevant breach;
- whether a requirement is likely to cause the provider financial hardship or distress that could:
    - threaten service continuity; or
    - cause further harm to health care service users by reducing competition and choice in the market; or
    - any wider harm to health care service users that might arise from reducing the resources available to the provider in line with our main duty.

3.4 VARIABLE MONETARY PENALTIES

This section sets out the factors which Monitor will consider when deciding on the appropriate amount of a variable monetary penalty.

Variable monetary penalties may require a provider to pay a monetary penalty to Monitor which Monitor must pay into the Government Consolidated Fund. The variable monetary penalty must not exceed 10%

of the provider's turnover in England. The Department of Health has published its intended definition of 'turnover' for these purposes, which is available at www.gov.uk/government/uploads/system/uploads/attachment_data/file/217119/130227-Licensing-consultation-response.pdf.

An important objective of imposing a penalty is deterring similar conduct in future. The amount of any penalty must be sufficient to ensure that it will act as an effective incentive to compliance, having regard to the seriousness of the breach. The factors Monitor will take into account, therefore, include amongst other relevant considerations:

- the seriousness of the breach;
- ensuring provider compliance;
- deterring similar breaches by other providers; and
- the proportionality of a variable monetary penalty to the nature of the breach.

The factors relevant to each of these considerations are described in section 3.3 above.

As well as these matters, Monitor will consider any relevant aggravating and mitigating factors. Penalties are likely to be higher when we identify one or more aggravating factors. Aggravating factors could be, but are not limited to, where:

- Monitor has previously imposed a discretionary requirement on, or accepted an enforcement undertaking from, the relevant provider concerning similar or related matters;
- there is a positive intent to contravene, in that the provider must have been aware, or could not reasonably have been unaware, that its conduct would lead to a breach; or
- a provider has not cooperated with Monitor's investigation.

Penalties are likely to be lower when we identify relevant mitigating factors. Mitigating factors could be, but are not limited to, where:

- a provider takes timely and effective action to remedy the effects of a breach, including action to restore any actual or potential harm caused;
- a provider self-reports a breach; or
- a provider has cooperated fully with Monitor's investigation and requirements.

3.5 ENFORCEMENT UNDERTAKINGS

A provider may offer an enforcement undertaking during the course of a formal investigation. Monitor may accept the undertaking if we have reasonable grounds to suspect that the provider is, or was, in breach of a licence condition, the requirement to hold a licence, or a requirement to supply Monitor with information. An enforcement undertaking may include a commitment to take steps to secure that the breach in question does not continue or recur. A provider may also undertake to restore the position to what it would have been had the breach in question not occurred, or action (including the payment of a sum of money) to benefit any other licence holder or commissioner affected by the breach.

The decision whether to accept an enforcement undertaking, rather than to continue an investigation and potentially impose discretionary requirements, is at Monitor's discretion and will depend on the circumstances. In considering an enforcement undertaking offered by a provider, Monitor intends to take into account the factors outlined in section 3.3 above.

Agreed enforcement undertakings may be less burdensome on the provider than the discretionary requirements which Monitor would otherwise have imposed. This is in recognition of:

- the cooperation demonstrated by that provider; and
- the fact that Monitor is then able to devote resources to other matters on the basis that Monitor can stop pursuing an investigation or parts of an investigation.

We intend to maintain a register of enforcement undertakings. We are likely to require providers that have given undertakings report on compliance. Any reporting commitments will be agreed as part of the agreement of the enforcement undertaking as a whole.

If the relevant provider complies with the enforcement undertaking, Monitor cannot take further action in relation to the relevant breach or suspected breach. For example, having accepted undertakings which are then complied with, Monitor cannot seek to impose additional discretionary requirements or to revoke the provider's licence in relation to the same breach.

Failing, or partially failing, to comply with an enforcement undertaking accepted by Monitor may result in the imposition of a discretionary requirement.

4. ENFORCEMENT – CASE PROCEDURES

4.1 INTRODUCTION

[3.362]
This chapter outlines the general procedures that Monitor intends, in general, to follow when conducting an investigation that may result in us taking formal enforcement action.

This chapter focuses first on the procedures relevant to licence enforcement and to imposing discretionary requirements or accepting enforcement undertakings. Under schedule 11 of the Act, Monitor is bound to follow certain processes when taking such enforcement action.

This chapter also outlines:

- the processes relevant to licence revocation;

- the processes Monitor intends to follow when using our additional powers where the governance of an NHS foundation trust is such that it is failing, or will fail, to comply with one or more of its licence conditions; and
- an introduction to the processes relevant to enforcement under competition law.

As we explained earlier, we are following a similar approach to that set out in this guidance in 'translating' breaches of NHS foundation trusts' terms of Authorisation into appropriate regulatory action under the licence, to take effect as the licence comes into force. The processes we follow, however, are likely to be more bespoke than the case procedures set out in this section. For example, we do not intend to publish case initiations or consult on draft findings for this transition activity. We are currently working closely with the relevant foundation trusts.

4.2 ENFORCEMENT PROCEDURES

4.2.1 Case initiation

When we become aware of a potential breach, we will consider how to proceed in accordance with our prioritisation principles – see chapter 2. Where we decide to begin an investigation of a potential breach, we will notify the relevant party or parties and set out what Monitor is investigating, the key contacts at Monitor, and the expected timetable for the investigation.

Information about the investigation will, where appropriate, be published on Monitor's website. Monitor considers that publication of case details will generally be beneficial, as it will help to highlight issues that are of concern to Monitor and deter inappropriate conduct, and help ensure that all interested parties are aware of an issue and can provide relevant information.

4.2.2 Investigation

Once Monitor has decided to start a formal investigation, we may use our powers under the Act to gather information – see section 104 of the Act. These powers allow us to ask parties specified in the Act (licence holders, provider licence applicants, providers who are exempt from requiring a licence, providers who should hold a provider licence, the NHS Commissioning Board and clinical commissioning groups) for any information, documents or other items Monitor considers are necessary or expedient to have in order to perform our regulatory functions.

Information includes information, documents or records kept by means of a computer. Monitor also has the power to require the provision of the information, documents or records in legible form. The Monitor provider licence will also require licence holders to provide Monitor with such information as we consider necessary to fulfil our licensing functions, which can be used in addition to or instead of the powers specified in section 104 of the Act.

During the course of an investigation, Monitor may need to issue several information requests to determine whether a provider has breached its obligations or for any other appropriate reason. Monitor will try to limit the burdens placed on parties to an investigation, as much as possible, and ensure that our information gathering is focused and proportionate – in line with our obligations under section 68 of the Act.

At any point during an investigation, Monitor may close a case without further action if, for example, we consider that there is insufficient evidence of a breach or that a formal investigation should no longer be prioritised. Where we consider it appropriate, we will also publish our reasons for making such decisions on our website.

There is no specific time period within which Monitor must complete an investigation, and how long an investigation lasts will vary depending on the complexity of the issue and how much relevant information is available. But when an investigation is opened, we will provide parties with our expected timescales and provide updates to the timescale as appropriate.

4.2.3 Case updates

In longer running cases, we intend to give the relevant parties regular updates about how the investigation is progressing, and when key decisions are likely to be taken.

We intend to:

- keep the parties to the investigation informed about the expected timetable and any changes; and
- provide regular case updates to parties, for example, each month, by telephone or in writing.

We will also offer providers under investigation the opportunity to meet representatives of the case team at appropriate intervals, for example every four to six months to ensure that parties have the opportunity to raise points directly with us and to discuss the progress of an investigation.

4.2.4 Entering into enforcement undertakings

This section sets out our proposed procedure for entering into enforcement undertakings, which we are required to publish in accordance with schedule 11 of the Act.

Where Monitor considers it appropriate we may discuss with the provider the possibility of accepting an enforcement undertaking. A provider may offer an enforcement undertaking at any point during the course of an investigation, up until a final decision is made as to whether the provider has acted in breach and as to any discretionary requirement, although the closer an investigation is to its conclusion, the smaller the resource saving to be made by accepting undertakings – see section 3.5.

Offering an enforcement undertaking Where a provider wishes to offer an enforcement undertaking, it should first discuss this with the case team. If after this it wishes to do so, it should write to the case team setting out the commitments it is offering, any timescales for implementing the commitments and their anticipated impact. If Monitor thinks that an enforcement undertaking may be an appropriate way to resolve a matter, we may invite a provider to consider making an offer of an enforcement undertaking. When a provider makes such an offer, Monitor expects that we will normally respond by telling the provider that we either:

- do not consider it appropriate to enter into discussions about undertakings at that time and intend to continue the formal investigation; or
- consider it appropriate to enter into discussions about undertakings.

In some circumstances, Monitor is likely to wish to continue with an investigation until we can be satisfied that an enforcement undertaking may or may not be an appropriate way forward. In most circumstances, Monitor will tell the provider when we expect to be in a position to respond to an offer of an enforcement undertaking.

When undertakings have been offered and Monitor considers they may be an appropriate way to resolve the matter; we are likely to discuss the form and content of the undertaking offered with the provider, and invite the parties to make any changes that we consider necessary. In deciding whether to accept enforcement undertakings, Monitor will assess the proposed undertaking by referring to the factors outlined in section 3.3 above.

Accepting an enforcement undertaking Where Monitor has received a proposed enforcement undertaking that we think may represent an appropriate resolution of the matter we may seek views on whether it is appropriate. When we choose to seek views, we will also give reasons why we propose to accept the draft enforcement undertaking, referring to the factors outlined in section 3.3.

Seeking views may range from formal and extensive public engagement to more informal, brief engagement with third parties. The decision on whether to seek views will be made on a case-by-case basis. In deciding whether to seek views we will consider all relevant matters including whether it is in the interests of health care service users to take action quickly, for example where there is a concern about patient safety, as well as any benefits of wider engagement. We will also consider the factors outlined in section 3.3.

After seeking views, Monitor would then need to decide whether the proposed undertakings should be modified, accepted, or rejected.

After an enforcement undertaking has been accepted Where Monitor accepts an enforcement undertaking, we are under a legal obligation to publish it. That means Monitor cannot accept an enforcement undertaking on the basis that any of the terms of the undertaking will be kept confidential. We can only withhold from publication any part of an enforcement undertaking which contains information which is:

- commercial, information whose disclosure would or might significantly harm the legitimate business interests of the affected party; or
- information about the private affairs of an individual, where disclosure would or might significantly harm that person's interests.

The terms of an enforcement undertaking – including, in particular, the action it specifies and the period within which the action must be taken – may be varied if both Monitor and the provider agree.

Where Monitor is satisfied that a provider has complied with an enforcement undertaking, we must issue a certificate to that effect – this is called a compliance certificate. A provider who has given an enforcement undertaking can apply to Monitor at any time for a compliance certificate, including in the application evidence to demonstrate that the provider has satisfactorily met the compliance requirement, and other relevant information to be required and specified by Monitor. Monitor must decide whether or not to issue a compliance certificate, and give notice to the applicant of the decision within 14 days after the day on which we receive the application. There is a right of appeal from a decision to refuse this application.

If at any point Monitor considers that a provider who has given an enforcement undertaking has supplied inaccurate, misleading or incomplete information in relation to the undertaking then we may treat the provider as having failed to comply with the undertaking. In that case, after giving notice, Monitor may revoke any compliance certificate given to that provider.

Table 4.1 summarises the process for entering into enforcement undertakings

1	Monitor informs the provider in writing that we have launched formal enforcement action in relation to a suspected breach.
2	If it wishes, the provider contacts the case team to discuss the possibility of undertakings and following this it writes to Monitor with an outline of a proposed enforcement undertaking. The provider may also write to Monitor with an outline of a proposed undertaking after an invitation from Monitor to do so.
3	Monitor responds to the provider indicating, if necessary, whether the matter is suitable for an enforcement undertaking and the terms and timescales on which discussions might proceed.
4	Discussions on an enforcement undertaking may proceed based on the provider's offer at 2 above and/or alternative suggestions made by Monitor.

5	If provisional agreement is reached, Monitor may seek views as set out above if it considers this appropriate.
6	Following consideration of views if sought Monitor either:
	• accepts the enforcement undertaking – with any necessary and agreed modifications – and closes our investigation; or
	• rejects the proposed undertakings and continues our investigation.
7	Monitor will publish the agreed enforcement undertaking.

4.2.5 Discretionary requirements

Notice of Intent

Under schedule 11 of the Act, if Monitor intends to impose a discretionary requirement on a provider we must issue the provider with a 'Notice of Intent' containing the following information:

- the proposal to impose a discretionary requirement;
- the effect of the discretionary requirement;
- the grounds for making the proposal – a statement of the evidence and reasoning behind the proposal as well as our preliminary conclusion;
- an explanation of the effect of section 106 of the Act (enforcement undertakings), including whether we have considered an enforcement undertaking, or may be considering them;
- the circumstances (if any) in which Monitor may not impose the requirement; and
- the period for making representations ('notice period').

Where Monitor is considering imposing discretionary requirements, we may seek views on whether they are appropriate. When we choose to seek views, we will also give reasons for our proposals, referring to the factors outlined in section 3.3.

Seeking views may range from formal and extensive public engagement to more informal, brief engagement with third parties. The decision on whether to seek views will be made on a case-by-case basis. In deciding whether to seek views we will consider all relevant matters including whether it is in the interests of health care service users to take action quickly, for example where there is a concern about patient safety, as well as any benefits of wider engagement. We will also consider the factors outlined in section 3.3.

After seeking views, Monitor would then need to decide whether the proposed requirements should be imposed and in the original or modified form.

Making representations to Monitor

Under schedule 11 of the Act, on receiving a Notice of Intent, the relevant parties will be invited to submit representations to Monitor in writing and in person within a specified period, known as the 'notice period' of at least 28 days from the day after the Notice of Intent was received.

On request, providers may also make oral representations to the relevant decision-makers within Monitor. In certain circumstances, Monitor may reduce the notice period to a minimum of five days. This may be the case, as specified in schedule 11, where:

- Monitor is proposing a compliance requirement or restoration requirement; and
- Monitor considers that a shorter notice period is necessary to prevent or minimise further breaches.

Final notice

Under schedule 11 of the Act, after the end of the notice period, Monitor must decide whether to impose the discretionary requirement, with or without modification, or impose any other discretionary requirement.

If, after issuing the Notice of Intent, Monitor has become aware of new information which the provider should in fairness be given an opportunity to comment on before Monitor decides whether to impose a discretionary requirement, Monitor will make arrangements for the provider to be given that opportunity.

If the decision-makers – see chapter 5 – decide to impose a discretionary requirement Monitor will issue a further notice, known as a 'final notice'. The final notice will contain the following information:

- the discretionary requirement which Monitor has decided to impose;
- the effect of the discretionary requirement;
- the reasons for imposing the requirement;
- the consequences of failing to comply with the requirement; and
- the right of appeal.

Although we are not required by the Act to do so, we expect that Monitor will always publish final notices unless the circumstances of the case make this inappropriate. Where appropriate, we will consider the need to obtain confirmation of factual accuracy prior to publication.

If Monitor imposes a variable monetary penalty, the final notice, as specified in schedule 11 of the Act, will also contain the following information:

- how to make the payment;
- the period within which payment must be made;
- any discount for early payment; and
- the rate of interest payable for late payment.

The provider will have a minimum period of 28 days, as specified in schedule 11 of the Act, from the day after the final notice was received to pay a monetary penalty. A monetary penalty may not be imposed unless the Notice of Intent was issued within five years of the last day of the period in which the licensee was in breach.

Any financial penalty paid to Monitor will be transferred to the Government Consolidated Fund. Under schedule 11 of the Act, if the provider does not pay a monetary penalty imposed by Monitor within the specified time, interest may be payable and, in addition to any other action to recover these amounts due, Monitor may take action to collect the money, and any interest owed, through the civil courts as a civil debt.

After the decision

Under schedule 11 of the Act, Monitor has some freedom to change a discretionary requirement after we have given a final notice. At that stage, Monitor may still:

- withdraw the requirement;
- reduce the amount of any variable monetary penalty;
- extend the time allowed for paying the penalty; or
- extend the time for taking steps specified in a compliance or restoration requirement.

Although we are not required to do so, we expect that where Monitor has decided to take any of the above steps, we will always publish notices setting out the steps decided on and our reasons for taking any of these steps, unless the circumstances of the case would make this inappropriate.

The provider may appeal a decision to impose a discretionary requirement. This is explained in chapter 6.

Non-compliance penalties

Under schedule 11 of the Act, if the provider fails to comply with a compliance or restoration requirement that Monitor has imposed, we may take further action against the provider.

Monitor may impose a financial penalty known as a 'non-compliance penalty' on the provider.

If we decide to take this action, we will first issue a 'non-compliance notice', as specified in schedule 11 of the Act, setting out:

- the amount of the non-compliance penalty;
- the reasons for imposing the non-compliance penalty;
- how to pay the non-compliance penalty;
- the period within which a provider must pay;
- any discount for early payment;
- the consequences of late payment; and
- the right of appeal.

Although we are not required to do so, we expect that Monitor will always publish non-compliance notices unless the circumstances of the case would make this inappropriate. Where appropriate, we will consider the need to obtain confirmation of factual accuracy prior to publication.

If any part of the original payment demanded is not paid by the deadline, Monitor may under schedule 11 of the Act increase the amount payable by up to 50% of the amount of the original penalty.

As with discretionary requirements, under schedule 11 of the Act Monitor has discretion to reduce the amount of the penalty or extend the payment period of a non-compliance penalty. We may make such changes at any time in the process after we have imposed a non-compliance penalty.

Payments from non-compliance penalties are recoverable as civil debts and we will pay them into the Government Consolidated Fund.

The provider can appeal against Monitor's decision to impose a non-compliance penalty. The process for appealing is explained in chapter 6.

4.3 PROCEDURES FOR LICENCE REVOCATION

As outlined in section 1.2, Monitor may revoke a provider's licence if we are satisfied that the provider has failed to comply with a licence condition – see section 89 of the Act. In making the decision that a provider has failed to comply with its licence condition, we intend the following parts of this proposed guidance to apply:

- Chapter 2 – deciding whether a matter is a priority;
- Chapter 4, section 4.2 – case initiation, investigation and case updates;
- Chapter 5 – decision making; and
- Chapter 6 – appeals.

Monitor expects that we would consider revoking a provider's licence only rarely, as to do so would prevent a provider from continuing to provide NHS health care services where it is obliged to hold a licence. If Monitor considers it appropriate to do so, we will consider revoking a provider's licence.

In considering whether to revoke a licence, Monitor's aim will be to fulfil Monitor's main duty to protect and promote the interests of people who use health care services by promoting the provision of health care services which is economic, efficient and effective, and maintains or improves the quality of the services. We intend to consider, amongst any other relevant factors, the following factors as set out in section 3.3 above, that is:

- the seriousness of the breach;
- ensuring provider compliance;
- deterring similar breaches; and
- the proportionality of the remedy to the nature of the breach.

Monitor considers that it would normally only be appropriate to revoke a licence if we are satisfied that the objectives could not be met through the imposition of discretionary requirements (or the acceptance of enforcement undertakings).

Case initiation, investigation, case update

We propose that the processes relevant to licence revocation will be as we set out in sections 4.2.1, 4.2.2, and 4.2.3.

Notice of Intent (section 90)

Where Monitor proposes to revoke a licence, we must give notice to the provider setting out our reasons for proposing to revoke the licence and the time that the licensee has to make representations – see section 90 of the Act. Monitor may take such action only where we are satisfied that a licence holder has failed to comply with a condition of its licence.

Monitor must provide the licence holder with no less than 28 days from date of receipt, within which representations may be made. Providers may, on request, also make oral representations to relevant decision-makers (see chapter 5 below) within Monitor.

Where Monitor is proposing this action, we may seek views on whether it is appropriate. When we choose to seek views, we will also give reasons for our proposal, referring to the factors outlined in section 3.3.

Seeking views may range from formal and extensive public engagement to more informal, brief engagement with third parties. The decision on whether to seek views will be made on a case-by-case basis. In deciding whether to seek views we will consider all relevant matters including whether it is in the interests of health care service users to take action quickly, for example where there is a concern about patient safety, as well as any benefits of wider engagement. We will also consider the factors outlined in section 3.3.

After seeking views, Monitor would then need to decide whether to take the proposed action or other action.

Notice of Decision (section 91)

Having considered the licence holder's representations Monitor will issue a Notice of Decision confirming whether or not the provider's licence has been revoked. Under section 91 of the Act, the Notice of Decision must explain the provider's right of appeal (see chapter 6 below).

A licence revocation can only have effect once the licensee's right to appeal has ended or once an appeal has been confirmed by the First-Tier Tribunal or the appeal has been abandoned – see sections 91 and 92 of the Act (see chapter 6 below).

Although we are not required by the Act, we expect that Monitor will always publish final notices unless the circumstances of the case mean that this would be inappropriate.

The licensee can appeal against Monitor's decision to revoke its licence. The process for appealing is explained in chapter 6.

4.4 PROCEDURES FOR IMPOSING ADDITIONAL LICENCE CONDITIONS ON NHS FOUNDATION TRUSTS AND REMOVING, SUSPENDING OR DISQUALIFYING DIRECTORS OR GOVERNORS OF NHS FOUNDATION TRUSTS

We intend that the following parts of this proposed guidance apply to Monitor's actions under section 111 of the Act:

- Chapter 2 – deciding whether a matter is a priority;
- Chapter 4, section 4.2 – case initiation, investigation and case updates; and
- Chapter 5 – decision making.

As outlined in section 1.2, there are two parts to Monitor's powers under section 111:

(I) where Monitor is satisfied that an NHS foundation trust's directors and/or governors are failing to (a) secure compliance with conditions in the foundation trust's licence, or (b) take steps to reduce the risk of a breach of a condition in the foundation trust's licence under section 111 of the Act, Monitor may include in the licence such conditions relating to governance as Monitor considers appropriate; and

(II) where Monitor is satisfied that the NHS foundation trust has breached or is breaching an additional licence condition that was included under section 111 of the Act, we may use our powers to require the foundation trust to remove, suspend or disqualify one or more of the foundation trust's directors and/or governors or, if the foundation trust does not do so, Monitor may make such changes.

A separate process must be followed to exercise the second power. The process that Monitor proposes to follow is set out below.

Case initiation, investigation, case update

We propose that the processes relevant to section 111 actions will be as we set out in sections 4.2.1, 4.2.2, and 4.2.3.

Notice of Intent (section 111)

If Monitor is minded to impose an additional licence condition on a foundation trust, Monitor will issue a notice to the foundation trust informing it of:

- the proposal to impose additional licence conditions;
- the anticipated effect of the additional licence conditions;
- any incidental or consequential modifications which may be necessary or expedient to other licence conditions in consequence of the additional licence conditions;
- the grounds for making the proposal; and
- the period for making representations ('notice period').

Monitor would follow the same procedure in the event that we were minded to vary any such licence condition.

Where Monitor is proposing such action, we may seek views on whether it is appropriate. When we choose to seek views, we will also give reasons for our proposals, referring to the factors outlined in section 3.3.

Seeking views may range from formal and extensive public engagement to more informal, brief engagement with third parties. The decision on whether to seek views will be made on a case-by-case basis. In deciding whether to seek views we will consider all relevant matters including whether it is in the interests of health care service users to take action quickly, for example where there is a concern about patient safety, as well as any benefits of wider engagement. We will also consider the factors outlined in section 3.3.

After seeking views, Monitor would then need to decide whether the proposed condition should be modified, retained or not included.

If Monitor is satisfied that a foundation trust has not complied with additional licence conditions and Monitor is minded to require a foundation trust to remove, suspend or disqualify one or more of its directors and/or governors, we will issue a notice to the foundation trust informing it of:

- the proposal to require the foundation trust to remove, suspend or disqualify one or more of its directors and/or governors;
- the grounds for making the proposal; and
- the period for making representations ('notice period').

Final notice (section 111)

At the end of the notice period, if Monitor has not changed its view following the foundation trust's representations, Monitor would issue a final notice.

If the decision-makers – see chapter 5 – decide to impose an additional licence condition, Monitor will issue a further notice, known as a 'final notice of additional licence conditions'. This notice will contain the following information:

- the licence conditions which Monitor has decided to impose; any incidental or consequential modifications which must be made to other licence conditions;
- the anticipated effect of the additional licence conditions;
- the reasons for imposing the additional licence conditions; and
- the consequences of failing to comply with them.

Monitor would follow the same procedure in the event that we decided to vary any such licence condition.

If the decision-makers – see chapter 5 – decide to impose governance changes, Monitor will issue a further notice, known as a 'final notice of governance changes'. It will contain the following information:

- the requirements of the foundation trust to remove, suspend or disqualify one or more of its directors and/or governors and appoint interim governors or directors;
- the reasons for imposing them; and
- the consequences of failing to comply with them.

Although we are not required to do so, we expect that Monitor will always publish final notices unless the circumstances of the case mean that this would be inappropriate.

Should the foundation trust not comply with this notice, Monitor will, if it considers appropriate, itself implement one or more of the requirements set out in the notice.

4.5 PROCEDURES FOR INVESTIGATIONS UNDER COMPETITION LAW

Where Monitor suspects anti-competitive behaviour in the health care sector in England, we may decide to use our powers under the provider licence, or apply the prohibitions on anti-competitive agreements and abuse of a dominant position set out in the Competition Act and Articles 101 and 102 of the Treaty on the functioning of the European Union.

Monitor will have concurrent powers to apply competition law, meaning that either Monitor or the OFT could act in relation to a particular case. Monitor and the OFT will decide which organisation is best placed to investigate an issue on a case-by-case basis.

As far as possible, we intend that the procedures Monitor follows are consistent whether taking action under the Act or the Competition Act or the TFEU. But when Monitor takes action under the Competition Act, we must adhere to the same statutory rules that the OFT would if it were taking the case (see Competition Act 1998 (Office of Fair Trading's Rules) Order 2004 Statutory Instrument 2751 of 2004 www.legislation.gov.uk/uksi/2004/2751/contents/made). Similarly, when enforcing Articles 101 and 102 of the TFEU, Monitor must comply with the requirements in European Union Regulation 1/2003.

In any enforcement proceedings under the Competition Act, Monitor will also be required to have regard to:

- the OFT's guidance on the circumstances in which it may be appropriate to accept binding commitments. This is contained in an annex to the OFT's Enforcement Guidelines, see www.oft.gov.uk/shared_oft/business_leaflets/ca98_guidelines/oft407.pdf.
- the OFT's guidance as to the appropriate amount of a penalty, see www.oft.gov.uk/shared_oft/business_leaflets/ca98_guidelines/oft423.pdf.

The following sections of this proposed guidance are also relevant to investigations under the Competition Act or TFEU:

- Chapter 2 – deciding whether a matter is a priority;
- Chapter 4, section 4.2 – case initiation and case updates;
- Chapter 5 – decision making; and
- Chapter 6 – appeals.

We may, in the future, publish more detailed guidance on Monitor's procedures in applying competition law.

5. DECISION-MAKING FOR ENFORCEMENT CASES

5.1 INTRODUCTION

[3.363]
This chapter sets out Monitor's proposed approach to taking three key decisions relevant to formal enforcement:

(I) the decision to formally investigate a potential breach or infringement;
(II) the decision to provisionally find a breach and to issue, for example, a 'Notice of Intent'; and
(III) the decision to find a breach and to issue, for example, a 'final notice'.

5.2 THE DECISIONS TO LAUNCH A FORMAL INVESTIGATION AND TO MAKE A PROVISIONAL FINDING

The first two decisions relevant to a formal investigation are: whether to formally investigate a matter; and whether to make a provisional finding that there has been a breach or infringement.

In both cases, Monitor proposes the decisions are taken by a senior staff member in the Monitor group, advised by technical experts as appropriate, responsible for the enforcement action. This person will oversee the investigation up to and including any provisional finding, and take decisions about whether or not enforcement undertakings should be accepted in relation to breaches of obligations by providers, or commitments in competition law cases.

5.3 THE DECISION TO FIND A BREACH OR INFRINGEMENT

For final decisions concerning a breach or an infringement, Monitor proposes that a decision-making committee comprising a number of Monitor's senior staff would take the decision as to whether there has been a breach/infringement, and what sanctions, if any, should be imposed.

The membership of the decision-making committee will be decided on a case-by-case basis, to suit the matter in hand and reflect the risk and complexity involved. It may involve staff from any discipline throughout Monitor. Monitor's Board may decide that it forms the decision-making committee in relation to enforcement matters that are of particular significance to health care service users. In other cases, Monitor's Executive team may form the decision-making committee, or it may be made up of other members of Monitor's senior staff.

However the final decision-making committee is composed, the majority of the decision makers on the committee would not have had any significant prior involvement in the investigation – that is, they would bring a 'fresh pair of eyes' to the matter. The senior staff member responsible for the first two decision-making points (decision to investigate and provisional finding) and other members of the investigating team may participate in the discussions around making the final decision, but will not be members of the decision-making committee for the purpose of making the decision. It is noted in this context that Monitor has processes in place for decision-makers to declare where necessary any conflicts of interest.

If a party offers an enforcement undertaking after a provisional finding, the decision-making committee would take the decision as to whether that undertaking should be accepted.

To ensure that parties have the opportunity to make representations directly to decision-makers, members of the decision-making committee would hear any oral representations made in response to a provisional finding.

6. RIGHTS OF APPEAL

6.1 INTRODUCTION

[3.364]
This chapter outlines the decisions that are appealable and the appeal processes as specified by law.

6.2 PROVIDER ENFORCEMENT

A provider may appeal a decision to impose a discretionary requirement, the imposition of a non-compliance penalty or the refusal by Monitor to issue a certificate of compliance in relation to an enforcement undertaking to the First-tier Tribunal.

The First-tier Tribunal is a specialist judicial body established under the Courts and Enforcement Act 2007. The main function of the First-tier Tribunal is to hear and decide appeals in specified areas of law (see www.justice.gov.uk/tribunals).

Discretionary requirements

A provider has a right of appeal to the First-tier Tribunal against a decision to impose a discretionary requirement. An appeal may be brought on one or more of the following grounds:

- that the decision was based on an error of fact;
- that the decision was wrong in law;
- that the amount of a variable monetary penalty is unreasonable;
- that the nature of a compliance requirement or restoration requirement is unreasonable; or
- that the decision was unreasonable for any other reason.

Once the provider has lodged an appeal, the discretionary requirement will be suspended until the appeal is determined.

When the Tribunal reaches a decision on the appeal, it may take any of the following actions:

- confirm, vary or withdraw the discretionary requirement;
- take such steps as Monitor could take in relation to the breach; or
- remit the decision whether to confirm the requirement, or any matter relating to the decision, to Monitor.

Non-compliance penalties

A provider may appeal to the First-tier Tribunal against one of Monitor's decisions to impose a non-compliance penalty on any of the following grounds:

- that the decision was based on an error of fact;
- that the decision was wrong in law; or
- that the decision was, or the amount of the penalty is, unfair or unreasonable.

If the provider lodges an appeal, the non-compliance penalty will be suspended until the appeal is determined.

When making a decision on the appeal, the Tribunal may take the following action:

- confirm, vary or withdraw the non-compliance penalty; or
- remit the decision whether to confirm the penalty, or any matter relating to that decision, to Monitor.

Enforcement undertakings

A provider may appeal, to the First-tier Tribunal, a refusal from Monitor to meet a request for a certificate of compliance on the following grounds:

- the decision was based on an error of fact;
- the decision was wrong in law; or
- the decision was unfair or unreasonable.

In making a decision on the appeal, the Tribunal may either confirm Monitor's decision or direct that it is not to have effect.

6.3 LICENCE REVOCATION

A licensee has a right of appeal to the First-tier Tribunal against a decision to revoke a licence under section 89(b). An appeal may be brought on one or more of the following grounds:

- that the decision was based on an error of fact;
- that the decision was wrong in law; or
- that the decision was unreasonable.

Once the provider has lodged an appeal, the licence revocation does not take effect until the appeal is confirmed or abandoned.

When making a decision on the appeal, the Tribunal may take any of the following actions:

- confirm Monitor's revocation decision;
- direct that Monitor's revocation decision is not to have effect; or
- remit the revocation decision to Monitor.

6.4 COMPETITION LAW ENFORCEMENT

Monitor's Competition Act and TFEU decisions may be appealed to the Competition Appeal Tribunal. Appeals can be brought by addressees of Monitor's decisions and by third parties with a sufficient interest. Appealable decisions include decisions as to whether there has been a competition law infringement; interim measures' decisions; and decisions on the imposition of, or the amount of, a penalty (see www.catribunal.org.uk/).

The Competition Appeal Tribunal was created by section 12 and Schedule 2 to the Enterprise Act 2002 which came into force on 1 April 2003. The Competition Appeal Tribunal is a specialist judicial body with cross-disciplinary expertise in law, economics, business and accountancy whose function is to hear and decide cases involving competition or economic regulatory issues.

The Competition Appeal Tribunal has wide powers to determine most appeals under competition law on their merits and may:

- confirm or set aside all or part of the decision;
- remit the matter to Monitor;
- impose, revoke or vary the amount of any penalty;
- give such directions, or take such other steps as Monitor could have given or taken; or
- make any other decision which Monitor could have made.

ANNEX
MONITOR'S POWERS OF ENFORCEMENT UNDER THE HEALTH AND SOCIAL CARE ACT 2012

1. COMPETITION

Functions under the Competition Act (section 72)

[3.365]
Monitor and the Office of Fair Trading have concurrent functions under Part 1 of the Competition Act, relating to the provision of health care services in England where:

(a) agreements, decisions or concerted practices are anti-competitive (anti-competitive practices); or
(b) there are abuses of a dominant position in a market (abuse of dominant position).

These powers relate to the Competition Act and the TFEU.

Functions under Part 4 of the Enterprise Act 2002 (section 73)

Monitor and the Office of Fair Trading have concurrent functions under Part 4 of the Enterprise Act 2002 (market investigations), relating to activities which concern the provision of health care services in England.

2. LICENSING PROCEDURE

Licence revocation (section 89)

Monitor may revoke a provider's licence on the application of the licensee, or if Monitor is satisfied that the licensee has failed to comply with a condition of its licence.

Monitor must give notice to the licensee if we propose to revoke its licence. The notice must set out Monitor's reasons for its proposal; and specify the period (not less than 28 days from the date of receipt) within which representations about it may be made to Monitor.

Right to make representations (section 90)

Monitor must give notice to the licensee if we propose to revoke its licence. That notice must:

(a) set out Monitor's reasons for our proposal; and
(b) specify the period (not less than 28 days beginning with the day after that on which the notice is received), for representations to be made on it to Monitor.

Notice of decisions (section 91)

If Monitor decides to revoke a licence, we must give notice of our decision to the licensee. The notice must explain the right of appeal against that decision.

The decision will take effect when we specify, subject to not being a day earlier than:

(a) the day on which a decision on appeal (if made) is confirmed or the appeal is abandoned;
(b) the day on which Monitor receives notification that the licensee does not intend to appeal (before the end of the period for bringing an appeal); or
(c) the day after the period for bringing an appeal.

Appeals to the Tribunal (section 92)

An appeal may be made to the First-tier Tribunal against Monitor's decision to revoke a licence. The grounds for an appeal are that the decision was:

(a) based on an error of fact;
(b) wrong in law; or

(c) unreasonable.

On hearing the appeal, the First-tier Tribunal may:
(a) confirm Monitor's decision;
(b) direct that the decision is not to have effect; or
(c) remit the decision to Monitor.

3. ENFORCEMENT

Information provision (section 104)

Monitor may require a person (any provider of NHS health care services in England whether licensed or not, the NHS Commissioning Board and a Clinical Commissioning Group) to provide us with any information, documents, records or other items which we consider is necessary or expedient for our functions. This includes information, documents or records kept by means of a computer and Monitor has the power to require the provision of the information, documents or records in legible form.

Discretionary requirements (section 105)

Monitor may impose one or more discretionary requirements on a person if Monitor is satisfied that the person:
(a) has provided, or is providing, an NHS health care service without either a licence or an exemption to hold a licence;
(b) is a provider licensee who is in breach of a licence condition; or
(c) is in breach of a requirement to provide information.

Discretionary requirement means:
(a) a requirement to pay a monetary penalty to Monitor (a "variable monetary penalty"). The variable monetary penalty must not exceed 10% of the person's turnover in England, such amount to be calculated in the manner set out in regulations by the Department of Health. If all or part of a variable monetary penalty is not paid by the time required, the unpaid balance carries interest at the rate specified in section 17 of the Judgments Act 1838; subject to the total interest not exceeding the amount of the penalty;
(b) a requirement to take such steps, within such period, to secure that the breach in question does not continue or recur (a "compliance requirement"); or
(c) a requirement to take such steps, within such period, to secure that the position is, so far as possible, restored to what it would have been if the breach in question was not occurring or had not occurred (a "restoration requirement").

Monitor must not impose discretionary requirements on a person on more than one occasion in relation to the same breach.

Enforcement undertaking requirements (section 106)

Monitor may accept an enforcement undertaking from a person if Monitor has reasonable grounds to suspect that the person:
(a) has or is providing, an NHS health care service without either a licence or an exemption to hold a licence:
(b) is a licensee who has or is providing, an NHS health care service in breach of a licence condition; or
(c) is in breach of a requirement to provide information.

An enforcement undertaking is that a specified action will be taken within a specified period. The action must be:
(a) to secure that the breach does not continue or recur;
(b) to secure that the position is, so far as possible, restored to what it would have been if the breach was not occurring or had not occurred;
(c) action (including the payment of a sum of money) to benefit:
  (i) any other licence holder affected by the breach;
  (ii) any commissioner of NHS health care services which is affected by the breach; or
(d) action of such a description as may be allowed in regulations to be made by the Department of Health.

Where Monitor accepts an enforcement undertaking, unless the person has failed to comply with the undertaking or any part of it:
(a) Monitor may not impose any discretionary requirement which we would otherwise have power to impose in respect of the breach; and
(b) Monitor may not revoke that person's licence if the breach is a breach of a licence condition.

Where the person has complied with only part of an enforcement undertaking, Monitor must take the partial compliance into account in deciding whether:
(a) to impose a discretionary requirement on the person; or
(b) to revoke the person's licence, if the breach is a breach of a licence condition.

Further provision about enforcement powers (section 107)

Monitor must follow schedule 11 provisions about procedures for discretionary requirements and enforcement undertakings.

Guidance on use of enforcement powers (section 108)

Monitor must publish guidance about how we intend to impose discretionary requirements, accept enforcement undertakings and the procedures we will follow to do so. Monitor may revise the guidance. Monitor must consult persons we consider appropriate before publishing or revising the guidance.

The guidance, in regard to discretionary requirements, must include information about:

(a) the circumstances in which Monitor is likely to impose a discretionary requirement;
(b) the circumstances in which Monitor may not impose a discretionary requirement;
(c) the matters likely to be taken into account by Monitor in determining the amount of any variable monetary penalty to be imposed (including, where relevant, any discounts for voluntary reporting); and
(d) rights to make representations and rights of appeal.

Monitor must have regard to the guidance or revised guidance in imposing discretionary requirements and accepting enforcement undertakings.

Publication of enforcement action (section 109)

Monitor must include, in our annual report, information about:

(a) cases in which a discretionary requirement has been imposed during the financial year of the report (except if it was overturned on appeal); and
(b) cases in which an enforcement undertaking has been accepted during that financial year.

But Monitor must not include information which we are satisfied is:

(a) commercial information where its disclosure might significantly harm the legitimate business interests of the relevant provider; or
(b) information relating to the private affairs of an individual where its disclosure might significantly harm that person's interests.

Notification of enforcement action (section 110)

As soon as is practicable after imposing a discretionary requirement or accepting an enforcement undertaking, Monitor must notify:

(a) the NHS Commissioning Board;
(b) Clinical Commissioning Groups who are likely to be affected by the requirement or undertaking; and
(c) any person exercising regulatory functions in relation to the relevant provider.

4. IMPOSITION OF LICENCE CONDITIONS ON NHS FOUNDATION TRUSTS AND REMOVING, SUSPENDING OR DISQUALIFYING DIRECTORS OR GOVERNORS OF NHS FOUNDATION TRUSTS (SECTION 111)

Where Monitor is satisfied that the governance of an NHS foundation trust is such that the foundation trust will fail to comply with the conditions of its licence, Monitor may include a governance condition(s) in its licence that we consider is appropriate to reduce that risk.

This includes where Monitor is satisfied that the council of governors, the board of directors or the council of governors and board of directors together are failing:

(a) to secure compliance with conditions in the foundation trust's licence; or
(b) to take steps to reduce the risk of a breach of a condition in the foundation trust's licence.

Monitor may modify such a condition once it has been included.

Such a condition will have effect until the Secretary of State for Health orders that section 111 of the Act ceases to have effect.

Where Monitor is satisfied that the trust has breached or is breaching this new condition Monitor may by notice require the foundation trust to:

(a) remove one or more of the directors or members of the council of governors and appoint interim directors or members of the council;
(b) suspend one or more of the directors or members of the council of governors from office as a director or member for a set period; or
(c) disqualify one or more of the directors or members of the council of governors from holding office as a director or member for a set period.

Where Monitor is satisfied that a foundation trust has failed or is failing to comply with such a notice, Monitor may do one or more of the things which we required the foundation trust to do.

Where Monitor includes a condition, we may also make such incidental or consequential modifications as we consider necessary or expedient to any other condition of the licence concerned which is affected.

Monitor can also, in relation to such a condition, use the enforcement powers under sections 105 and 106 of the Act.

Where Monitor includes a condition by modifying a standard condition of the licence concerned, the modification does not prevent any other part of the condition from continuing to be regarded as a standard condition.

MONITOR: APPLICATION OF THE COMPETITION ACT 1998 IN THE HEALTHCARE SECTOR: GUIDANCE FOR PROVIDERS (September 2014)

[3.366]

NOTES

Note that Monitor became part of NHS Improvement in April 2016.

See also: "Choice and competition licence conditions: guidance for providers of NHS funded services" (September 2014) at www.gov.uk/government/publications/nhs-healthcare-providers-working-with-choice-and-competition. This guidance explains the choice and competition conditions of the NHS provider licence and explains how Monitor applies these licence conditions in individual cases.

See also "Monitor's approach to market investigation references: guidance for providers" (same website as above).

CONTENTS

FOREWORD

[3.367]

Monitor's job as regulator is to protect and promote the interests of patients by ensuring that the whole healthcare sector works for their benefit. We recognise that providers and commissioners have challenging roles on the front line of healthcare: our philosophy is to help people do the right thing rather than punishing them for doing the wrong thing.

This guidance has been written to help you, as healthcare providers, make the best decisions for patients. It is one of a set of documents explaining how we apply competition rules, first published in March 2013 for a 12-week public consultation. We are grateful for all the support and engagement we received to help us develop our guidance, and we have acted on feedback.[1]

The full set of finalised guidance comprises this document, alongside:

- how we approach market investigation references (under Part 4 of the Enterprise Act 2002)
- how we apply the choice and competition conditions of the licence for providers of NHS healthcare services.

As an extra aid, we have published (and will continue to publish) hypothetical scenarios which help illustrate how the choice and competition conditions of the provider licence and competition law work in practice.

We have also previously published related guidance both to support NHS providers considering transactions[2] and to assist commissioners using the Procurement, Patient Choice and Competition Regulations.[3]

To help you use this guidance most fully and identify when it might be necessary to work with us, we briefly explain what we mean by choice and competition and set out how and why we are working in this area.

NOTES

1 Please see the consultation response document at www.gov.uk/government/publications/nhs-healthcare-providers-working-with-choice-and-competition

2 www.gov.uk/government/publications/supporting-nhs-providers-considering-transactions-and-mergers

3 www.gov.uk/government/publications/procurement-patient-choice-and-competition-regulations-guidance

OUR ROLE IN CHOICE AND COMPETITION

Choice and competition have existed in the NHS in England for many years and are powerful tools for improving the quality of care provided to patients. They enable patients and commissioners to select the providers which offer quality services that best meet the needs of patients.

Choice and competition are governed by specific rules which seek to make sure that:

- they operate in the best interests of patients
- procurement decisions by commissioners achieve the best results
- all providers are treated fairly
- no one behaves anti-competitively to the disadvantage of patients.

Our role is to make sure that this all works the way it is meant to: that the rules are applied taking into account the specific circumstances of the health sector, and above all that they are applied in the best interest of patients.

We take this responsibility seriously. We will enforce the competition rules affecting healthcare services to ensure that they operate fairly in the interests of patients, and to help both NHS providers and NHS commissioners meet the needs of patients.

To achieve this, we will explain in documents like this one how any breach of these rules might have negative effects on patients, and how we expect our intervention to maintain or improve service quality or innovation, or deliver better value for money.

INTRODUCTION TO THIS GUIDANCE

[3.368]

The Health and Social Care Act 2012 (the Health and Social Care Act) gives us concurrent (shared) powers with the Competition and Markets Authority (CMA)[4] to enforce provisions of the Competition Act 1998 (CA98) and the Treaty on the Functioning of the European Union (TFEU) in relation to the provision of healthcare services in England. We refer to these laws as competition law in this document and this guidance explains how we will use these powers.[5]

By investigating anti-competitive behaviour, we will seek to ensure that patients have access to high quality healthcare services. Preventing anti-competitive behaviour also means that providers can compete in a fair environment. This helps to ensure that providers are rewarded based on the quality and value of services they provide, which may incentivise them to make long-term investments and to improve services further for patients.

In applying our concurrent powers, we will draw on the approach of the CMA as set out in guidance (see 'Competition Act 1998: CMA Guidance and Rules of Procedure for investigation procedures under the Competition Act 1998'). The CMA has adopted certain guidance documents on CA98 that were previously published by the Office of Fair Trading (OFT) (see Annexe A to the guidance cited above). Unless stated, the OFT guidance we refer to in this document has been adopted by the CMA.

As we gain more experience in dealing with potential breaches of competition law we will update our guidance.

The rest of this guidance is structured as follows:

- our concurrent powers
- our investigation procedures in competition cases
- our enforcement powers in competition cases
- our approach to publishing decisions
- appeals against our decisions
- assessing anti-competitive practices in the health sector
- assessing abuse of dominance in the health sector
- glossary.

NOTES

4 The CMA replaced the Office of Fair Trading and Competition Commission on 1 April 2014. It is the UK's economy-wide competition authority responsible for ensuring that competition and markets work well for consumers.

5 This guidance is not a substitute for the TFEU nor for regulations made under it. Neither is it a substitute for European Commission notices and guidelines or a substitute for CA98 and the regulations and orders made under that Act. It should be read in conjunction with these legal instruments, Community case law and United Kingdom case law. Anyone in doubt about how they may be affected by the TFEU or CA98 should seek legal advice. This guidance reflects the views of Monitor at the time of publication and may be revised from time to time to reflect changes in best practice, legislation and the results of experience, legal judgments and research. It may in due course be supplemented, revised or replaced. Our website will always display the latest version of the guidance.

OUR CONCURRENT POWERS

[3.369]

Competition law prohibits:

- **Anti-competitive practices**: that is, agreements[6] between undertakings, decisions by associations of undertakings and concerted practices that have the object or effect of preventing, restricting or distorting competition. The term undertaking is described in guidance: 'Agreements and concerted practices' (OFT 401) and 'Assessment of market power' (OFT 415), and also in the glossary in this document.

  On the specific question of whether public bodies can be undertakings and subject to UK and European competition law, see 'Public bodies and competition law: A guide to the application of the Competition Act 1998' (OFT 1389). Not-for-profit organisations such as charities may be undertakings for the purposes of CA98 if they are carrying on some form of commercial or economic activity.[7]
- **Abuse of dominance**: that is, conduct[8] by one or more undertakings which amounts to the abuse of a dominant position in a market.

For more detail later in this guidance, see Anti-competitive practices and Abuse of dominant position.

Using our competition law powers, we can:

- impose interim measures to prevent significant damage[9] or protect the public interest

- carry out investigations, both on our own initiative and in response to complaints, including requiring the production of documents and the provision of information, and searching premises
- impose financial penalties, taking account of the statutory guidance on penalties adopted by the CMA
- give and enforce directions to bring an infringement to an end
- accept commitments that are binding on an undertaking
- offer information and confidential informal advice on how the competition law prohibitions apply in relation to the provision of healthcare services in England
- publish written guidance in the form of an opinion where a case raises novel or unresolved questions about the application of Article 101, Article 102, the Chapter I prohibition and/or the Chapter II prohibition in the United Kingdom, and where we consider there is an interest in issuing clarification for the benefit of a wider audience.

Our concurrent powers to apply competition law are not limited to NHS-funded services but apply to all healthcare[10] services in England.

NOTES

[6] See the Chapter I prohibition contained in section 2(1) of CA98 which applies where trade within the UK may be affected and Article 101 of the TFEU which applies where trade between Member States may be affected.

[7] For a practical example of the application of CA98 to charities see the OFT's decision CA98/05/2006 'Exchange of information on future fees by certain independent fee-paying schools' (20 November 2006).

[8] See the Chapter II prohibition in section 18(1) of CA98 which applies if the dominant position is held within the UK and the conduct in question may affect trade within the UK; and Article 102 of the TFEU which applies to conduct within the internal market or a substantial part of it in so far as it may affect trade between member states.

[9] Section 43 of the Enterprise and Regulatory Reform Act 2013 amended section 35(2)(a) of CA98 by replacing the current test for the imposition of interim measures of 'preventing serious, irreparable damage' with 'preventing significant damage'.

[10] Section 64(3) of the Health and Social Care Act defines 'health care' as all forms of health care provided for individuals, whether relating to physical or mental health.

OUR INVESTIGATION PROCEDURES IN COMPETITION CASES

ALLOCATION OF CASES

[3.370]
Both Monitor and the CMA can deal with cases relating to suspected anti-competitive conduct in relation to the provision of healthcare services in England.

Where it appears that we may have concurrent jurisdiction, the CMA and Monitor will always consult with each other before acting and cases will be investigated by the authority best placed to undertake the investigation. The Competition Act 1998 (Concurrency) Regulations 2014 set out the approach to allocating cases between Monitor and the CMA.

We will normally be responsible for any CA98 case that is principally concerned with matters relating to the provision of healthcare services for the purposes of the NHS in England.[11] However, we may nevertheless agree with the CMA that the CMA shall act in a case.

The types of cases that might be investigated by the CMA rather than Monitor are cases involving the provision of goods rather than healthcare services, or cases not principally concerned with healthcare services. In each case that falls within our concurrent jurisdiction, we will consider whether we are the best placed authority to conduct the investigation. The factors to be considered in determining which authority deals with the matter will include securing the maximum benefit for healthcare service users, the sectoral knowledge of the authorities, whether the case affects other sectors and the authority's experience of dealing with the parties or similar issues which may be involved in the proceedings.

NOTES

[11] The CMA will not be able to allocate or transfer a case to a regulator other than Monitor unless it is satisfied that the case is not principally concerned with matters relating to the provision of healthcare services for the purposes of the NHS in England.

PRIORITISATION PRINCIPLES

We expect to become aware of potential breaches in a number of ways: for example, through complaints from third parties, intelligence from another regulator or authority, facts that emerge from our current or completed cases and reviews, or through other information we receive in our role as sector regulator.

When we become aware of a possible breach, we will consider how to proceed in accordance with our prioritisation principles set out in our 'Enforcement guidance'.

As part of this process, we will consider whether the case meets the thresholds set in CA98 for us to have the power to investigate. We can investigate when there are reasonable grounds for suspecting that Article 101, Article 102, the Chapter I prohibition and/or the Chapter II prohibition of CA98 have been infringed.

The prioritisation principles set out in our 'Enforcement guidance' explain how we decide which course of action is appropriate in each case. We expect to have regard to factors such as the likely direct and indirect benefits to patients, the likelihood of success, and the likely cost of resources needed to take that particular action. We intend to apply the principles to decisions not only about whether to begin a case, but also whether to continue with a case once it is under way. We will also apply them to decisions about which course of enforcement action to take. We apply the principles to ensure we make the best use of the resources available to us.

RELATIONSHIP BETWEEN COMPETITION LAW AND THE CHOICE AND COMPETITION LICENCE CONDITIONS

Some types of behaviour may fall within the scope of the provider licence conditions[12] on choice and competition as well as competition law. We will decide at an early stage which powers we think are most appropriate and will advise interested parties accordingly. Our general approach is that we will use the most effective, efficient and expeditious solution where we find a problem. We have set out separate guidance on how we intend to take action under the provider licence.

NOTES

[12] The provider licence is Monitor's main tool for regulating providers of NHS services. It sets out conditions that healthcare providers must meet to help ensure that the health sector works for the benefit of patients.

MAKING A COMPLAINT

We may begin an investigation into a possible breach of competition law on our own initiative or in response to a complaint. A complaint should be supported by as much factual information as possible so that we can make an accurate and prompt assessment as to whether there are reasonable grounds for suspecting a breach of competition law. All complaints should also contain (as a minimum) the information set out below. General allegations that a complainant considers conduct to be inconsistent with competition law will not typically be sufficient for us to begin an investigation. We have published further guidance on making complaints to us about issues relating to patient choice and competition.

A complaint should include the following details:

- name, address, telephone number and email address of the complainant
- name and job title of the person(s) authorised to represent the organisation or person raising the complaint
- contact details for the party that is the subject of the complaint (the respondent)
- a description of the services involved
- an outline of the relationship between the complainant and the respondent
- a chronology outlining relevant events
- a statement of why, in the opinion of the complainant, the conduct in question is inconsistent with one or more of the rules governing choice and competition in the healthcare sector and any supporting evidence, where available
- an explanation of how the complainant's business has been affected by the alleged activity and/or how people who use healthcare services have been adversely affected by the alleged activity.

Complaints should be submitted to cooperationandcompetition@monitor.gov.uk or posted to:

Co-operation and Competition Directorate
Monitor
Wellington House
133-135 Waterloo Road
London SE1 8UG

Before disclosing a complainant's identity we will discuss the matter with them and give them an opportunity to make representations.

INFORMAL ADVICE

Anyone can approach us informally to seek advice about how we apply our concurrent powers or talk to us before making a complaint about a possible breach of competition law. Resources permitting, we will try to give an initial view as to whether we would be likely to investigate the matter further if a formal complaint were made. If you wish to seek informal advice please contact Monitor's Co-operation and Competition Directorate at: cooperationandcompetition@monitor.gov.uk

INVESTIGATION PROCEDURES

The investigation procedures described below will apply to investigations we begin on our own initiative or in response to a complaint.

We will conduct investigations into suspected breaches of CA98 in accordance with the procedural rules set out in relevant parts of our 'Enforcement guidance'[13] and the CMA's CA98 rules.[14]

We have a range of information-gathering powers under competition law. These include the power to require any person to produce specified document(s) and/or information which relates to any matter relevant to the investigation, and the power to enter premises in connection with an investigation in certain circumstances.

A person is guilty of an offence if he/she fails to comply with a requirement imposed on him/her under our information-gathering powers.

Where we decide to begin an investigation of a potential breach, we will notify the relevant party or parties and explain what we are investigating, the key contacts at Monitor, and the expected timetable for the investigation. Where appropriate, we will publish information about the investigation on our website.

There is no specific time period within which we must complete an investigation, but we will provide parties with our expected timescales and provide updates to the timescales as appropriate. In longer running cases we intend to give the relevant parties regular updates about how the investigation is progressing and when key decisions are likely to be taken.

Before making a decision that there has been a breach of competition law, we will give written notice to the person(s) likely to be affected by the proposed decision and give that person(s) an opportunity to make representations, including the opportunity to attend an oral hearing.

Complaints about the procedures followed during the course of an investigation under CA98 may be made to a procedural officer.[15]

NOTES

[13] The following sections of Monitor's 'Enforcement guidance' apply to the exercise of our competition law powers: 2.2, 2.3, 4.2.1, 4.2.2, 4.2.3, 4.5, 5 and 6.2.

[14] These rules replace the previous procedural rules that applied to OFT investigations under CA98 (See CA98 (OFT's Rules) Order 2004 SI 2004/2751.)

[15] The procedural officer is a person appointed to adjudicate procedural complaints that arise in CA98 investigations. They are independent of the investigation.

OUR ENFORCEMENT POWERS IN COMPETITION CASES

[3.371]

We have a number of enforcement powers in cases involving a breach of competition law.[16]

We have discretion as to what enforcement action is appropriate in each case. In exercising this discretion, we will ensure the action we take is proportionate and reasonable in the circumstances.

Where there are issues around the financial or clinical sustainability of a provider these may be relevant to our decision about whether to pursue enforcement action and what type of enforcement action is appropriate. For example, we are likely to consider the impact of our possible enforcement actions on providers and the local health economy, and whether this is proportionate to the scale of the problem we aim to correct.

NOTES

[16] For further guidance on the application of these principles see 'Enforcement' (OFT 407).

DIRECTIONS

Where we have decided there has been a breach of competition law, we may give such directions (legally binding instructions) as we consider appropriate to bring the infringement to an end. These may include requiring organisations to modify or terminate an agreement, or to modify or cease the conduct in question. We are able to give directions to such persons as we consider appropriate, and not just to the parties breaching competition law.[17] Directions may also require positive action, such as reporting to us or structural changes. The directions must be in writing.

If a person or organisation fails, without reasonable excuse, to comply with a direction given by us, we may apply to court for an order requiring compliance with the direction.

NOTES

[17] For example, directions may be addressed to the parent company which, though not the actual instigator of the infringement, has a subsidiary which is the immediate party to the infringement.

INTERIM MEASURES

During an investigation into a potential breach of competition law, we may give interim measures directions pending our final decision. These are temporary directions that require certain steps to be taken while an investigation is carried out. They will not affect the final decision.

We can give interim measures directions if we consider that it is necessary as a matter of urgency to:

- prevent significant damage to a particular person or category of person, or
- protect the public interest.

In deciding whether the imposition of interim measures is appropriate, we will draw on the approach of the CMA[18] and ensure that:

- we impose interim measures only where we have identified specific behaviour or conduct that we consider is causing or will cause significant damage to a person or category of persons, or is or will be contrary to the public interest
- the particular interim measures imposed will prevent, limit or remedy the significant damage identified and are proportionate for the purpose of preventing, limiting or remedying that significant damage.

NOTES

[18] See the CMA's guidance on their investigation procedures in CA98 cases.

COMMITMENTS

We may accept binding commitments from organisations suspected of infringing competition law. We are required to have regard to the CMA's guidance when considering whether to accept commitments offered.[19] Commitments may be structural or behavioural, or a combination of both.

In accordance with the CMA's guidance, we are likely to consider it appropriate to accept binding commitments only where:

- the competition concerns are readily identifiable
- the competition concerns are fully addressed by the commitments offered and
- the proposed commitments can be implemented effectively and, if necessary, within a short period of time.

Once we have accepted binding commitments, we will end our investigation into the aspects of the alleged infringement addressed by the commitments. This does not prevent us from taking action in relation to competition concerns that are not addressed by the commitments we have accepted.

We enforce binding commitments in the same way as directions.

NOTES

[19] See the Annexe to 'Enforcement' (OFT 407): www.gov.uk/government/uploads/system/uploads/attachment_data/file/284436/oft407.pdf

PENALTIES

We have the power to impose a financial penalty in relation to a breach of competition law if we are satisfied that the infringement has been committed intentionally or negligently.[20] We must have regard to the CMA's guidance[21] when determining the appropriate level of a penalty. The CMA or concurrent regulators, including Monitor, may impose a financial penalty on an undertaking of up to 10% of the undertaking's worldwide turnover.

In accordance with the CMA's guidance we will use the following six-step approach to calculate the amount of a penalty:

- calculation of the starting point having regard to the seriousness of the infringement and the relevant turnover of the undertaking
- adjustment for duration
- adjustment for aggravating or mitigating factors
- adjustment for specific deterrence and proportionality
- adjustment if the maximum penalty of 10% of the worldwide turnover of the undertaking is exceeded and to avoid double jeopardy[22]
- adjustment for leniency and/or settlement discounts.

NOTES

[20] Section 36(3), CA98

[21] OFT's 'Guidance as to the appropriate amount of a penalty' (OFT 423): www.gov.uk/government/uploads/system/uploads/attachment_data/file/284393/oft423.pdf

[22] If a penalty or fine has been imposed by the European Commission, or by a court or other body in another Member State in respect of an agreement or conduct, we must take that penalty or fine into account when setting the amount of a penalty in relation to that agreement or conduct. This is to ensure that where an anti-competitive agreement or conduct is subject to proceedings resulting in a penalty or fine in another Member State, an undertaking will not be penalised again in the UK for the same anti-competitive effects.

LENIENCY

The CMA's guidance on 'Applications for leniency and no-action in cartel cases' also sets out its policy and practice on leniency in cartel cases (including, subject to certain conditions, granting total immunity from financial penalties to a participant in cartel activity who is the first to come forward).[23] Where cartel cases are allocated to us under the concurrency arrangements, we will adopt the CMA's approach to leniency.

NOTES

[23] For the purposes of the CMA's leniency policy for undertakings, cartel activity is defined as agreements and/or concerted practices which infringe Article 101 of the TFEU and/or the Chapter I prohibition and involve price-fixing (including resale price maintenance), bid-rigging (collusive tendering), the establishment of output restrictions or quotas and/or market sharing or market dividing.

OUR APPROACH TO PUBLISHING DECISIONS

[3.372]
The non-confidential version of an infringement decision and a summary of the decision will be published on our website.

APPEALS AGAINST OUR DECISIONS

[3.373]
Our decisions under CA98 and the TFEU may be appealed to the Competition Appeal Tribunal.

The parties we investigate and third parties with a sufficient interest can appeal our decisions. Appealable decisions include decisions about whether there has been a competition law infringement; interim measures decisions; and decisions on the imposition of, or the amount of, a penalty.[24]

The Competition Appeal Tribunal is a specialist judicial body with cross-disciplinary expertise in law, economics, business and accountancy whose function is to hear and decide cases involving competition or economic regulatory issues.

The tribunal has wide powers to determine most appeals under competition law on their merits and may:

- confirm or set aside all or part of the decision
- remit the matter to us
- impose, revoke or vary the amount of any penalty
- give such directions, or take such other steps as we could have given or taken or
- make any other decision we could have made.

NOTES

24 See guidance from the Competition Appeal Tribunal on appeals under the 1998 Competition Act: www.catribunal.org.uk/240/Rules-and-Guidance.html

ASSESSING ANTI-COMPETITIVE PRACTICES IN THE HEALTH SECTOR

[3.374]

We have published examples of anti-competitive practices in relation to the provision of healthcare services that may breach the Chapter I prohibition and/or Article 101.

In assessing whether agreements infringe competition law, we will follow the approach set out by the CMA in the guidance 'Agreements and concerted practices' (OFT 401).

BENEFITS

If we find that an agreement prevents, restricts or distorts competition, we will consider whether it gives rise to benefits and assess whether these benefits outweigh the anti-competitive effects. We will apply the framework set out in the European Commission's notice 'Guidelines on the application of Article 101(3) TFEU'.[25]

The party or parties submitting that the agreement gives rise to benefits must demonstrate how the benefits will be passed on to healthcare users, for example, through lower prices to commissioners or increased financial surpluses that will be reinvested in services for patients.

Any restriction on competition must as a matter of law be necessary to achieve the benefits in order for the anti-competitive agreement to be permissible. We will therefore consider the extent to which efficiency gains could be realised without the restrictions on competition.

NOTES

25 Guidelines on the application of Article 101(3) TFEU (formerly Article 81(3) TEC) [Official Journal No C 101 of 27.4.2004]. To satisfy Article 101(3) an agreement must satisfy four conditions: it must contribute to improving the production or distribution of goods or to promoting technical or economic progress; allow consumers a fair share of the resulting benefit; it must not impose unnecessary restrictions on the undertakings concerned; nor offer the undertakings the possibility of eliminating competition in a substantial part of the products in question.

REPRESENTATIVE AND PROFESSIONAL BODIES

The healthcare sector features a wide range of representative and professional bodies. These organisations play an important role in the sector in representing the interests of members on a range of matters, and can help providers improve their effectiveness in the marketplace, for instance by disseminating clinical knowledge and sharing best practices.

Decisions by these organisations are also subject to competition law, and the organisations themselves can infringe competition law and be subject to enforcement action. Similarly, agreements entered into by an association or professional group might be construed as an agreement on the part of its members, which means the members could be held accountable for infringements.

Decisions by such organisations are most likely to raise concerns where they lead to the co-ordination of members' behaviour instead of the members competing with each other. In particular, representative and professional bodies should be careful that they do not facilitate or provide a forum for anti-competitive behaviour by their members.

COMMISSIONER INVOLVEMENT

It is important to keep in mind that the fact that a commissioner initiates or participates in an agreement does not protect participating providers or trade associations from the possibility of breaching competition law. Nor can providers justify infringing competition rules simply by claiming that a commissioner encouraged them to adopt particular arrangements.

ASSESSING ABUSE OF DOMINANCE IN THE HEALTH SECTOR

[3.375]

In assessing whether the conduct of an individual organisation infringes competition law, we will follow the approach set out by the CMA in the guidance 'Abuse of a dominant position' (OFT 402). We have also published examples of conduct in relation to the provision of healthcare services that may breach the Chapter II prohibition and/or Article 102.

Conduct by providers may frequently be motivated by good intention. Behaviour that might look like attempts to prevent rival organisations from competing effectively, for example, could be motivated by a desire to promote the interests of patients or protect the local health economy. However, providers should be mindful that such motivation does not necessarily imply that conduct will always be in the interests of patients and/or taxpayers.

GLOSSARY

[3.376]

Abuse of dominance: Conduct may constitute an abuse of dominance if, for example, it:

- directly or indirectly imposes unfair purchase or selling prices or other unfair trading conditions
- limits production, markets or technical development to the prejudice of consumers
- applies dissimilar conditions to equivalent transactions with other trading parties, thereby placing them at a competitive disadvantage
- makes the conclusion of contracts subject to the other parties accepting supplementary obligations which have no connection with the subject of the contracts.

Anti-competitive practices: The prohibition in Chapter I of CA98 and Article 101 of the TFEU applies to agreements, decisions or practices which have as their object or effect the prevention, restriction or distortion of competition within the United Kingdom. This includes agreements, decisions or practices which:

- directly or indirectly fix purchase or selling prices or any other trading conditions
- limit or control production, markets, technical development or investment
- share markets or sources of supply
- apply dissimilar conditions to equivalent transactions with other trading parties, thereby placing them at a competitive disadvantage
- make the conclusion of contracts subject to acceptance by the other parties of supplementary obligations which, have no connection with the subject of such contracts.
- **CA98:** Competition Act 1998
- **CMA:** Competition and Markets Authority
- **Competition law**: For the purposes of this guidance, competition law means Chapter I and Chapter II of the Competition Act 1998 and Articles 101 and 102 of the TFEU.
- **Concurrent powers:** Powers to enforce competition law that may be exercised by both the CMA and sector regulators.
- **OFT:** Office of Fair Trading
- **Sector regulator:** A regulator responsible for regulating matters (including competition) in a particular sector. Other sector regulators are the Office of Communications (Ofcom), the Water Services Regulation Authority (Ofwat), the Office of the Gas and Electricity Markets (Ofgem), the Northern Ireland Utility Regulator, the Office of Rail Regulation (ORR) and the Civil Aviation Authority (CAA).
- **TFEU:** Treaty on the Functioning of the European Union

Undertaking: The term undertaking is described in guidance adopted by the CMA. It is not defined in CA98 or the TFEU, but UK and EU case law has defined 'undertaking' as covering any natural or legal person engaged in 'economic activity', regardless of its legal form or the way in which it is financed. Assessment of whether a body is an undertaking therefore focuses on the nature of the activity undertaken, not the nature of the body that undertakes it.

MEMORANDUM OF UNDERSTANDING BETWEEN THE COMPETITION AND MARKETS AUTHORITY AND NHS IMPROVEMENT

1 April 2016

[3.377]

NOTES

FOREWORD

[3.378]

The Competition and Markets Authority (CMA) and NHS Improvement are committed to working together in the healthcare sector for the benefit of patients and service users. The CMA is the UK's economy-wide competition authority responsible for ensuring that competition and markets work well for consumers. NHS Improvement is the operational name for the organisation that brings together Monitor, NHS Trust Development Authority, Patient Safety, the National Reporting and Learning System, the Advancing Change Team and the Intensive Support Teams. NHS Improvement is a combination of the continuing statutory functions and legal powers vested in these bodies, including Monitor's functions in relation to competition.

This memorandum of understanding (MoU) describes how the CMA and NHS Improvement will work together. It draws on the legislation that sets out our functions, and sets out our commitment to look for opportunities to work together in the area of health. We shall do this by sharing expertise, information, ideas and experience. Each of us commits to doing this efficiently and with a mutual regard for each other's statutory position and strategic objectives.

Competition in the healthcare sector can be a powerful tool for improving quality of care. In exercising our functions, we will have regard to the distinctive characteristics of the sector and seek to ensure that our two organisations make the best use of our powers, skills and experience to make the sector work for patients and service users.

The CMA and NHS Improvement can both enforce provisions of the Competition Act 1998 and the Treaty on the Functioning of the European Union in the healthcare services sector in England. We can exercise our competition law powers to take action in relation to anti-competitive agreements and conduct.

The CMA and a sectoral regulator sharing powers in this way is referred to as concurrency. The CMA's competition law powers apply across the whole UK economy. Sectoral regulators such as NHS Improvement exercise their competition law powers in their own sector.

NHS Improvement also has concurrent powers with the CMA to refer features of markets in the healthcare services sector in England for investigation by the CMA's market reference group where we have concerns about competition in a market.

In addition to working together in relation to concurrency, the CMA and NHS Improvement will also work together in relation to mergers. NHS Improvement provides advice to the CMA on the effect of the merger on benefits for people who use NHS healthcare services and on such other matters relating to the merger as NHS Improvement considers appropriate.

We believe that this MoU offers a valuable framework for our cooperative working.

SUMMARY POINTS OF THE MOU

- The CMA and NHS Improvement will engage in open dialogue and continuing liaison with a view not only to handling specific cases but to making the healthcare sector work for patients. This cooperation will include regular meetings (both bilaterally and through the UK Competition Network (UKCN) (in which NHS Improvement has observer status)).
- The CMA and NHS Improvement will endeavour to share their resources with each other so far as is reasonably practicable, meet each other's requests for appropriate secondments, and provide other mutual support so that they can effectively carry out their functions in the healthcare services sector in England.
- The CMA and NHS Improvement will always consult each other before acting on a case (including instigating a market study) where it appears they have concurrent powers, and will apply the case allocation principles and procedures set out in this MoU.
- The CMA and NHS Improvement will share information relevant to their concurrent powers and relevant to their functions in relation to mergers.
- Improvement will cooperate with the CMA in relation to the CMA's preparation of an annual concurrency report, which will assess the operation of concurrency in all concurrent sectors. NHS

Alex Chisholm	**Jim Mackey**
CEO, CMA	**CEO, NHS Improvement**

MEMORANDUM OF UNDERSTANDING BETWEEN THE COMPETITION AND MARKETS AUTHORITY AND NHS IMPROVEMENT

PURPOSE

[3.379]

1. NHS Improvement is the organisation which brings together Monitor and the NHS Trust Development Authority, Patient Safety, the National Reporting and Learning System, the Advancing Change Team and the Intensive Support Teams. This MoU applies in relation to the exercise of the functions conferred on Monitor under or by virtue of the provisions of Chapter 2 of Part 3 of the Health and Social Care Act 2012 (competition). References to NHS Improvement must be read accordingly.

2. This MoU sets out working arrangements between the CMA and NHS Improvement in relation to their concurrent powers in the healthcare services sector in England:

(a) to apply the prohibitions on agreements that prevent, restrict or distort competition and on the abuse of a dominant position, under Chapter I and Chapter II of the Competition Act 1998 and under Article 101 and Article 102 of the treaty on the Functioning of the European Union – referred to in this MoU as the 'competition prohibitions'; and

(b) to undertake market studies, and to make references to the CMA to conduct an in-depth market investigation under the Enterprise Act 2002 – referred to in this MoU as the 'market provisions'.

3. It also sets out working arrangements between the CMA and NHS Improvement in relation to the review of mergers involving NHS foundation trusts under the Enterprise Act 2002.

4. This MoU is not intended to have legal effect.

5. This MoU is to be read alongside the legislation that sets out the powers and duties of the CMA and NHS Improvement[1] and guidance related to these laws.[2] This MoU supplements and does not supplant that material.

6. The arrangements covered by this MoU are, wherever possible, set out in terms providing sufficient flexibility for the relationship between NHS Improvement and the CMA to develop in the light of experience. The CMA and NHS Improvement commit to review these arrangements from time to time to evaluate their continuing fitness for purpose. This MoU may only be revised by agreement between the CMA and NHS Improvement.

7. Nothing in this MoU applies in relation to the functions of the CMA in its separate role of considering references related to proposed action by NHS Improvement under healthcare sector legislation, for example in relation to setting the national tariff for healthcare services. The CMA and NHS Improvement acknowledge the importance of maintaining the CMA's impartiality and fairness in carrying out those functions, and indeed of market or merger investigations undertaken by the CMA panel.

NOTES

[1] Including the Health and Social Care Act 2012, the Competition Act 1998, the Enterprise Act 2002, the Enterprise and Regulatory Reform Act 2013, the Competition Act 1998 and Other Enactments (Amendment) Regulations 2004, the Competition Act 1998 (Concurrency) Regulations 2014 (referred to in this MoU as 'concurrency regulations').

[2] Including CMA (2014), *Regulated industries: Guidance on concurrent application of competition law to regulated industries* (CMA10), NHS Improvement's guidance on the application of the Competition Act 1998 in the health care sector, NHS Improvement's guidance on its approach to market investigation references, NHS Improvement's guidance on merger benefits, NHS Improvement's and the CMA's short guide to the competition review of NHS mergers for managers of NHS providers and CMA (2014), *CMA guidance on the review of NHS mergers.*

CONTEXT

8. This MoU operates within the framework of the legislative provisions referred to in paragraphs 2 and 3 and any other applicable sector-specific legislation from time to time.

Role of the CMA

9. The CMA is a non-ministerial department, established under the Enterprise and Regulatory Reform Act 2013.

10. The CMA works to promote competition for the benefit of consumers, both within and outside the United Kingdom (UK), to make markets work well for consumers, businesses and the economy.

11. The CMA's statutory responsibilities, in so far as relevant to the matters that are the subject of this MoU, include:

(a) investigating where there may be breaches of the competition prohibitions;

(b) conducting market studies and market investigations where there may be competition and consumer problems; and

(c) review of mergers under Part 3 of the Enterprise Act 2002.

12. In connection with its statutory responsibilities, the CMA will cooperate with sectoral regulators, including NHS Improvement, and encourage the sectoral regulators to use their powers, including their powers to apply the competition prohibitions, in the interests of competition and for the benefit of consumers. The CMA acknowledges that NHS Improvement's role is limited to preventing anti-competitive behaviour that is detrimental to patients' interests.

Role of NHS Improvement

13. The Health and Social Care Act 2012 conferred functions on Monitor in respect of competition and mergers in the healthcare sector. The Health and Social Care Act 2012 also provides that in exercising those functions, Monitor's main duty is to protect and promote the interests of people who use healthcare services by promoting the provision of healthcare services which is economic, efficient and effective, and maintains or improves the quality of the services. NHS Improvement brings together Monitor and the NHS Trust Development Authority, Patient Safety, the National Reporting and Learning System, the Advancing Change Team and the Intensive Support Teams.

14. NHS Improvement's statutory responsibilities, relevant to the subject of this MoU, include:

(a) investigating where there may be breaches of the competition prohibitions that concern the provision of healthcare services in England;

(b) conducting market studies and making market investigation references to the CMA in relation to activities that concern the provision of healthcare services in England; and

(c) providing advice to the CMA on benefits and other matters relating to mergers involving NHS foundation trusts.

15. In addition to these powers and functions, NHS Improvement is responsible for overseeing foundation trusts, NHS trusts and independent providers, in particular through a licensing regime. It also oversees commissioners' responsibilities in relation to procurement, patient choice and competition, and regulates prices for NHS healthcare services.

GENERAL COOPERATION

16. In addition to the provisions for cooperation between the CMA and NHS Improvement specific to their powers, as set out in this MoU and elsewhere, the CMA and NHS Improvement are committed to the following general principles and practices for cooperation between themselves in relation to the sector for which NHS Improvement has responsibility.

17. The CMA and NHS Improvement will consult each other at an early stage on any issues that might have significant implications for the other. For example, where the CMA undertakes a market study which relates to a sector other than healthcare services in England but which may have a significant impact on healthcare services in England, the CMA will inform NHS Improvement and share appropriate information relating to that market study with NHS Improvement to the extent permitted by law.

18. Officials of the CMA and NHS Improvement will meet and communicate, at appropriate levels of seniority, to discuss matters of mutual interest, both through the UKCN (in which NHS Improvement has

Part 3 CMA and other Guidelines

observer status) and bilaterally. A framework for such meetings will, as far as possible, be determined in advance so as to ensure attendance at the appropriate level and expertise.

19. The CMA and NHS Improvement will engage in open dialogue and continuing liaison with a view not only to handling specific cases but to making the healthcare sector work for patients. The CMA and NHS Improvement recognise the importance of meeting regularly to share information relating to competition in the provision of healthcare services, and to keep each other abreast of relevant current or future work. The CMA and NHS Improvement will consult each other at an early stage on any issues that might have significant implications for the other.

CONCURRENCY

20. The Enterprise and Regulatory Reform Act 2013, which established the CMA, made provision for the better working of concurrent powers in the regulated sectors.

21. The government's strategic steer to the CMA, issued on 1 December 2015, says that the CMA should build 'a strong dialogue with sectoral regulators using the UKCN to ensure that the overall competition regime is coordinated and regulatory practices complement each other'.[3]

22. NHS Improvement does not have a duty to promote competition. NHS Improvement will use its powers to prevent anti-competitive behaviour when it is against patients' interests.

23. This MoU sets out how the CMA and NHS Improvement can make the changes introduced by the Enterprise and Regulatory Reform Act 2013 work effectively, including through:

(a) cooperating and coordinating when dealing with cases of suspected anti-competitive behaviour and with market studies and market investigation references, for which they have concurrent powers;

(b) facilitating the efficient and effective handling of cases of suspected anti-competitive behaviour concerning the provision of healthcare services in England;

(c) avoiding duplicating activity, wherever possible; and

(d) ensuring transparency as to the respective roles of the CMA and NHS Improvement.

24. The CMA and NHS Improvement will, in respect of the healthcare services sector in England, always consult each other:

(a) before the initial exercise of concurrent competition law powers in all cases where it appears that they have concurrent jurisdiction and where there are reasonable grounds for suspecting an infringement of the competition prohibitions; and

(b) before launching a market study under the Enterprise Act 2002.[4]

25. Within the spirit of broader collaboration, the CMA and NHS Improvement will commit to discuss and share other relevant information relating to competition concurrency, where legally permissible to do so, but subject to the particular need not to impair the impartiality and fairness of the CMA in carrying out the functions referred to in paragraph 7 of this MoU.

NOTES

[3] Department for Business, Innovation and Skills, *Strategic steer for the Competition and Markets Authority*, in Annex A to the *Government's response to the Consultation on the Strategic Steer to the CMA*, 1 December 2015, page 11.

[4] Instigation of a market study occurs on the publication of a market study notice, as defined in section 130A of the Enterprise Act 2002.

MERGER CONTROL

26. The CMA and NHS Improvement will cooperate with each other as appropriate in relation to UK merger control under the Enterprise Act 2002, including on the benefits of mergers for patients and commissioners, as set out in Part C below.

POOLING RESOURCES

27. The CMA and NHS Improvement will endeavour, so far as is reasonably practicable and permitted by law, and in the light of their respective ongoing priorities and resource availability at the time, to share their resources with each other in the interests of the effective enforcement of competition law and effective review of mergers in the healthcare sector. More generally, the two authorities will work together to ensure that anti-competitive behaviour in that sector is prevented in the interests of patients and, for that purpose, they will ensure that their resources and expertise are used efficiently. This is subject to the proviso that, as stated in paragraph 7, this does not apply in relation to the functions of the CMA in its role of considering references related to proposed action by the sectoral regulators under the sectoral statutes.

28. As a consequence, where it has been agreed or determined that one of the authorities is to exercise its concurrent competition powers in relation to a case, that authority will, to the extent that there are resources available, receive appropriate practical assistance and support from the other in the handling of the case, as agreed on a case-by-case basis.

Secondments of staff

29. One means of the practical assistance and support that might be given, as referred to in paragraphs 27 and 28 of this MoU, is the secondment of staff, in accordance with regulation 10 of the concurrency regulations and paragraphs 3.33 and 3.34 of the CMA's guidance on concurrent application of competition law to regulated industries (CMA10), referred to in this MoU as the concurrency guidance.

30. The CMA and NHS Improvement are fully committed to the idea of secondments for this purpose, and will endeavour to meet each other's requests for secondments to the extent that they are appropriate and resources permit; this may include making provision for any secondee to be available to work for part of his or her time at his or her existing employer during the course of the secondment, for example on such cases that are in progress.

31. The CMA and NHS Improvement will develop appropriate arrangements for the pooling and secondment of staff. Such arrangements will have regard to the resource constraints of both parties and such calls for staff, therefore, will be made in reasonable time and with sufficient warning to enable appropriate resource planning and management of other work commitments and appropriate sign-off procedures within each authority.

Other mutual support

32. In addition to the sharing of information, expertise and experience and the secondment of staff, the CMA and NHS Improvement are fully committed to providing each other with more informal forms of support to enable them to carry out their competition law enforcement and merger review functions in relation to the healthcare services sector in England. In each case, this will be to the extent that is appropriate and permitted by law, and that resources permit – including (but not limited to):

(a) answering specific queries from time to time;
(b) providing information or views on a specific sector or market, or an area of competition law or policy; and
(c) providing training on a specific sector or market, or an area of competition law or policy.

33. Such support may be requested and provided in connection with a specific case or in relation to the general exercise of the CMA's and NHS Improvement's functions. In this regard, both the CMA and NHS Improvement will act reasonably, including by providing sufficient time and information for requests for support to be responded to fully and effectively, and for the relevant staff to be engaged.

PART A – COOPERATION IN RELATION TO THE COMPETITION PROHIBITIONS (COMPETITION ACT 1998 AND ARTICLES 101 AND 102 OF THE TREATY ON THE FUNCTIONING OF THE EUROPEAN UNION)

BACKGROUND

[3.380]
34. The CMA and NHS Improvement are committed to ensuring that competition rules as they apply to the healthcare services sector in England operate in the interests of patients. The CMA and NHS Improvement share a mutual interest in ensuring competition law enforcement takes into account the specific circumstances of the healthcare sector. This will involve as frequent contact between the CMA and NHS Improvement as the circumstances require. The CMA understands that NHS Improvement has a duty to support providers and commissioners in their efforts to improve healthcare services in the interests of patients.

35. The Health and Social Care Act 2012 gives NHS Improvement concurrent powers with the CMA to enforce provisions of the Competition Act 1998 and the Treaty on the Functioning of the European Union in relation to the provision of healthcare services in England. Where it appears that the CMA and NHS Improvement may have concurrent jurisdiction, the CMA and NHS Improvement will always consult with each other before acting and cases will be investigated by the authority best placed to undertake the investigation, as set out below. The CMA and NHS Improvement will work closely together to ensure the competition rules are well understood.

CASE ALLOCATION

Basis of allocation

36. The CMA and NHS Improvement will endeavour to reach agreement on which authority will exercise its concurrent competition powers in respect of any particular case, under regulation 4(2) of the concurrency regulations. They will do so in a spirit of constructiveness and cooperation, while acknowledging the CMA's powers under regulations 5 and 8 of the concurrency regulations, noting regulation 5(5) and regulation 8(1)(b) as regards NHS Improvement.

37. Their determination of which authority will exercise its powers will be based on assessing which of them is better placed to exercise those powers, having regard to the following factors:

(a) Securing the maximum benefit for healthcare service users.
(b) The sectoral knowledge of NHS Improvement and the CMA.
(c) Whether the case affects more than one regulated sector and/or non-regulated sectors not subject to concurrent competition law.
(d) Previous contacts between the parties or complainants and NHS Improvement or the CMA.
(e) Experience in dealing with any of the undertakings that may be involved in the proceedings.
(f) Experience in dealing with any similar issues that may be involved in the proceedings.
(g) Whether the CMA considers it necessary to exercise concurrent competition powers in relation to a case in order to develop UK competition policy or to provide greater deterrent and precedent effect for the benefit of competition and consumers either within the relevant regulated sector, or more widely.
(h) Whether the case being allocated to the CMA and supported by NHS Improvement (or vice versa) will provide the best combination of competition and sector-specific expertise.

38. The CMA and NHS Improvement envisage that other factors may appear relevant in the light of practical experience and, if so, such factors may be chosen to supplement or supplant the above factors.

Procedure for allocation

39. Where either the CMA or NHS Improvement has decided, on the basis of information in its possession, that there are reasonable grounds for suspecting that one of the competition prohibitions has been infringed (the reasonable suspicion test)[5] in relation to the healthcare sector, it will disclose to the other (ie the receiving authority) sufficient information:

(a) to enable the receiving authority to understand the basis on which the disclosing authority has decided that the reasonable suspicion test is met; and

(b) for there to be an informed discussion on which authority (if either) is best placed to proceed in respect of the case.

40. In practice, it may be helpful for the CMA and NHS Improvement to have discussed the case prior to such a decision having been reached, subject to paragraph 53 below. The disclosing authority will provide the information described in paragraph 39 within ten working days after it has decided that the reasonable suspicion test is met, whether or not it proposes to exercise concurrent powers.[6]

41. Within seven working days from receipt of this information, the receiving authority will respond in writing, setting out its initial view on the case and how it should be allocated and identifying any further information that it requires.

42. The CMA and NHS Improvement will endeavour to agree which authority will exercise its concurrent competition powers in relation to the case, as provided for in regulation 4(2) of the concurrency regulations, as soon as possible and in any event no later than one month from disclosure of the information as described under paragraph 39. Other than in exceptional circumstances (which shall be set out in writing) and subject to regulation 5(5) of the concurrency regulations, the CMA will initiate the procedure set out in regulation 5 of the concurrency regulations if agreement is not reached within two months of the disclosing authority first receiving sufficient information in connection with a complaint to enable it to decide that the reasonable suspicion test is met.

43. The procedure for agreeing the transfer of a case that is already in progress from the CMA to NHS Improvement, or from NHS Improvement to the CMA is as set out in regulation 7 of the concurrency regulations and in paragraph 3.32 of the concurrency guidance.

44. The procedure for the CMA to direct the transfer to itself from NHS Improvement of a case already in progress is as set out in regulation 8 of the concurrency regulations.

NOTES

[5] As provided in section 25 of the Competition Act 1998.

[6] As provided in regulation 9 of the concurrency regulations.

Implications of allocation

45. Any agreement or determination as to case allocation, under regulations 4, 5, 7 or 8 of the concurrency regulations, shall be notified to the person who has provided the information resulting in the case (for example, the person making a complaint), and so far as appropriate and lawful to any other affected person, by the authority that is exercising its concurrent competition powers in relation to the case, as soon as reasonably practicable.

46. Case allocation determines which of the CMA and NHS Improvement is to exercise concurrent functions and make any decisions under the competition prohibitions. The CMA or NHS Improvement will be publicly identified as having such responsibility if and when any such investigation is announced. The CMA and NHS Improvement envisage that, whichever authority has responsibility for a particular case, they and their officials will work cooperatively with each other on the case, pooling their expertise including as described in paragraphs 27 to 33 of this MoU and in paragraphs 3.33 to 3.35 of the concurrency guidance.

SHARING INFORMATION

Principles of information sharing

47. The effective sharing of information between the CMA and NHS Improvement is fundamental to the successful exercise of their concurrent competition powers. It is needed both for the appropriate allocation of cases, as described in paragraphs 39 to 44 of this MoU, and for the successful handling of cases once allocated to make optimal use of the complementary experience and expertise of the two authorities.

48. The CMA and NHS Improvement are committed, in addition to their legal obligations to share information (set out in regulation 9 of the concurrency regulations), to open dialogue and continuing liaison, both bilaterally and through the UKCN (in which NHS Improvement has observer status), with a view not only to handling specific cases but to preventing anti-competitive behaviour, for the benefit of patients in the healthcare services sector.

Information sharing – general liaison

49. The CMA and NHS Improvement recognise the importance of meeting regularly to share information on matters relevant to competition in the healthcare sector, and to keep each other abreast of relevant work that they are considering or currently undertaking.

50. The CMA and NHS Improvement will meet regularly at multiple levels, bilaterally and through the UKCN (in which NHS Improvement has observer status).

51 The CMA and NHS Improvement will each designate in its organisation a relationship manager or key contacts to support effective collaboration between the two authorities, including by (but not limited to) assisting with:

(a) maintaining an overview of joint projects between the two authorities and matters of mutual interest;

(b) maintaining an overview of the authority's contacts from all areas of joint working and mutual interest; and

(c) holding meetings with the key contacts in the other authority from time to time (whether bilaterally or in the context of the UKCN (in which NHS Improvement has observer status)) to identify potential new issues with a view to circulating information to appropriate individuals within each organisation.

52. The existence of relationship managers or points of contact does not in any way preclude direct communication between other staff at the CMA and NHS Improvement.

53. For the purposes of sharing information pursuant to paragraph 39, ie in circumstances where the reasonable suspicion test is met, such information will be disclosed by the disclosing authority to the extent permitted by law and whether or not it proposes to exercise concurrent powers.[7] Where disclosure would be appropriate and permitted by law, the CMA and NHS Improvement may also share information regarding potential infringements of the competition prohibitions in advance of having reached a view as to whether the reasonable suspicion test is met. In circumstances where either the CMA or NHS Improvement has taken the view that a matter is not an administrative priority, irrespective of whether a view has been reached on whether the reasonable suspicion test is met, each may share the details of the matter with the other, or with any other authority which would be able to exercise concurrent competition powers in relation to that matter, to the extent permitted by law. Where leniency information is being shared under this paragraph, special considerations apply, as set out in paragraphs 61 and 63.

NOTES

[7] For the avoidance of doubt, this does not entail an obligation to inform the other party if the regulator is carrying out general monitoring activity, where there is no consideration of exercising its concurrent powers.

Information sharing mechanism – handling specific cases

54. Where either the CMA or NHS Improvement exercises its concurrent powers, the CMA and NHS Improvement will, to the extent permitted by law, engage with each other in open dialogue and by sharing relevant information as appropriate. This engagement may include attendance at internal meetings held by the investigating authority (ie the authority to which a case is allocated) by the supporting authority (ie the other authority which would be competent to exercise concurrent powers in relation to the case), in order to discuss the case as envisaged at paragraph 3.31 of the concurrency guidance.

55. The supporting authority will not generally attend the investigating authority's constitutional decision-making meetings, meetings of governance bodies or meetings with external parties such as those under investigation or complainants. Attendance by the supporting authority at any meeting is at the discretion of the investigating authority, but requests to attend should be considered by the investigating authority in the spirit of cooperation underpinning the concurrency regime.

56. The procedures for information sharing for the purpose of case allocation shall be as set out in paragraphs 39 to 41 and 47 to 63 of this MoU.

57. When either the CMA or NHS Improvement is exercising its powers in respect of the competition prohibitions in a particular case in the healthcare services sector in England, each of them will share with the other any of the following information in its possession (to the extent permitted by law and subject to the confidentiality obligations set out in paragraphs 60 to 63 of this MoU):

(a) as a minimum, the matters referred to in regulation 9(1)(b) – (i) of the concurrency regulations, and in paragraph 3.49 of the concurrency guidance, complying with the time limits specified in paragraph 3.49;

(b) all other information that it reasonably believes to be relevant or helpful to the other in the conduct of the case; and

(c) in the case of the authority that is exercising its powers, reports to the other on the progress of the case with sufficient frequency and detail to enable the other to be appropriately informed; the means and frequency of such reporting will be decided on a case-by-case basis and in the light of experience as this enhanced framework of collaboration and its supporting arrangements develop over time.

Information sharing mechanism – for know-how purposes

58. The CMA will maintain on its webpages a central database of decisions taken in cases under the competition prohibitions in the regulated sectors, with a view to having an accessible body of know-how that will help ensure the effective and consistent application of competition law. The CMA and NHS Improvement will, to the extent permitted by law, contribute information to that in the way best calculated to achieve that objective.

59. In any event, the CMA will report on cases in the regulated sectors under the competition prohibitions in the annual concurrency report which it is required under statute to issue.[8] Further provisions on the annual concurrency report are in paragraphs 64 to 66 of this MoU.

NOTES

8 Enterprise and Regulatory Reform Act 2013 Schedule 4 paragraph 16.

Information sharing – confidentiality constraints

60. Any disclosure of information under paragraphs 39 to 41 and 47 to 59 of this MoU, and any use by the recipient of such information, shall only be to the extent permitted by law, including by reference to the provisions of Part 9 of the Enterprise Act 2002, relevant sector-specific legislative provisions and any other provisions relating to the disclosure, handling and use of information (such as the Data Protection Act 1998 and section 118 of the Financial Services and Markets Act 2000, to the extent relevant).

61. Prior to disclosing information to each other, the CMA and NHS Improvement will not generally give the person to whom the information relates prior notice of its intention to make the disclosure. However, if the CMA or NHS Improvement consider it necessary or appropriate to pass leniency information to each other (or to another UK authority with concurrent powers), the transmitting authority will inform the applicant or its legal adviser first. Leniency information for the purposes of this MoU is any information which came into the possession of any of the CMA, its predecessors, NHS Improvement or any other public authority as a direct or indirect result of having been provided in the context of an application for leniency. It also includes any information obtained (whether by the transferring or receiving authority) as a result of investigative measures resulting directly or indirectly from an application for leniency.

62. Where the provision of leniency information to either the CMA or NHS Improvement affords or might, under certain conditions, afford the leniency applicant, its subsidiaries or its employees protection from sanctions (including a reduction in penalties) under the leniency programme operated by that authority and that information has been passed to the other authority, the receiving authority shall afford the leniency applicant, its subsidiaries or its employees no lesser protection.

63. Any disclosure of leniency information between the CMA and NHS Improvement will be subject to agreement on appropriate protections regarding the use of that information for other purposes.

ANNUAL CONCURRENCY REPORT

64. The CMA is required by statute to publish a report every year, starting after its first year of operation in 2014/15,[9] containing an assessment of how the concurrency arrangements between the CMA and the sectoral regulators, as regards both the competition prohibitions and the market provisions, have operated during the year. This MoU refers to that report as the annual concurrency report. There is further provision on the annual concurrency report in paragraphs 3.55 to 3.62 of the concurrency guidance.

65. The CMA will consult, and cooperate with, NHS Improvement and other sectoral regulators in preparing the annual concurrency report. In connection with this, the CMA will:

(a) prepare a draft annual concurrency report that it will send to NHS Improvement and other sectoral regulators seeking comments or suggestions on the content or conclusions of the annual concurrency report, giving them adequate time to comment or make suggestions;

(b) take into account any comments or suggestions it receives from NHS Improvement and other sectoral regulators and the CMA may seek further clarification on those comments and suggestions as appropriate;

(c) prepare a final version of the annual concurrency report for publication that takes account of its consultation with NHS Improvement and other sectoral regulators as appropriate; and

(d) make the annual concurrency report available on the CMA webpages.

66. NHS Improvement will cooperate with the CMA in preparing the annual concurrency report. This includes (but is not limited to):

(a) providing information and data on general market conditions and on the application of the competition prohibitions and the market provisions in the healthcare services sector in England;

(b) responding to requests for information and data; and

(c) providing to the CMA any comments and suggestions it may have in connection with the process described in paragraph 65 of this MoU; in each case promptly so as to facilitate the timely production and publication of the annual concurrency report.

NOTES

9 Enterprise and Regulatory Reform Act 2013 Schedule 4 paragraph 16.

VOLUNTARY REDRESS SCHEMES

67. In cases relating to investigations under the competition prohibitions in the healthcare services sector in England, both the CMA and NHS Improvement have the power to approve voluntary redress schemes. When either authority proposes to exercise these powers, it shall liaise with the other authority as appropriate and will have regard to its own guidance.[10]

NOTES

10 The CMA's guidance on the approval of voluntary redress schemes (CMA40) states at footnote 7: 'The CMA expects that regulators will take this CMA guidance into account when producing their own guidance on the approval power.'

SHORT FORM OPINIONS

68. The CMA shall inform NHS Improvement following an initial enquiry for a short form opinion relating to the provision of healthcare services in England. Where the CMA is considering providing such an opinion, it will discuss with NHS Improvement before deciding to do so. If the CMA then decides to produce an opinion, it will engage with NHS Improvement, the nature and degree of that engagement to be considered on a case-by-case basis, having regard, in particular, to the extent to which the opinion has a multi-sector rather than single sector dimension. In all cases, the CMA will give NHS Improvement the opportunity to provide comments on a draft opinion.

PART B – COOPERATION IN RELATION TO THE MARKET PROVISIONS: MARKET STUDIES AND MARKET INVESTIGATIONS (ENTERPRISE ACT 2002)

BACKGROUND

[3.381]
69. NHS Improvement also has the power, concurrently with the CMA, to carry out market studies and to make market investigation references, agree undertakings in lieu of a reference and make recommendations to the government in relation to activities concerning the provision of healthcare services in England under Part 4 of the Enterprise Act 2002 (as do other sectoral regulators in relation to the sectors for which they are responsible).

70. Under the Enterprise Act 2002, the CMA and NHS Improvement may, in relation to activities concerning the provision of healthcare services in England, undertake market studies, and make market investigation references to the Chair of the CMA for the constitution of a CMA group to conduct an in-depth market investigation into single or multiple markets for goods or services in the UK. The purpose of these investigations is to examine the market(s) and (where required) implement appropriate remedies where the CMA determines that the structure of the market(s) or the conduct of the suppliers or customers is harming competition.

71. When making a reference, the CMA or NHS Improvement, as applicable, must have reasonable grounds for suspecting that any feature or combination of features of a market or markets in the UK prevents, restricts or distorts competition in relation to the supply or acquisition of any goods or services in the UK (or in a part of the UK).

72. The cooperation between the CMA and NHS Improvement provided for in this Part B shall not extend to conduct that could reasonably be expected to impair the impartiality or the fairness of the CMA panel in conducting market investigations.

MUTUAL CONSULTATION

73. NHS Improvement and the CMA have a duty to consult each other before exercising concurrent functions under the market provisions.

SHARING INFORMATION

74. The provisions of paragraphs 49 to 53, 57 (excluding 57(a)) and 59 of this MoU apply to information sharing under the market provisions as they do under the competition prohibitions.

POOLING RESOURCES

75. The provisions of paragraphs 27 to 33 of this MoU apply to pooling resources under the market provisions as they do under the competition prohibitions.

76. Where the CMA and NHS Improvement intend to pool resources in order to exercise powers under the market provisions of the Enterprise Act 2002, they shall, at the outset of any such project, discuss the arrangements for how they will pool resources and work jointly.

ANNUAL CONCURRENCY REPORT

77. The provisions of paragraphs 64 to 66 of this MoU apply under the market provisions as they do under the competition prohibitions.

PART C – COOPERATION IN RELATION TO UK MERGER CONTROL (ENTERPRISE ACT 2002)

BACKGROUND

[3.382]
78. The CMA and NHS Improvement are committed to ensuring that mergers in the NHS are well planned and work well for patients. To this end, the CMA and NHS Improvement will work closely with each other to ensure the merger review process is well understood, and operates as quickly and predictably as possible. This will involve as frequent contact between the CMA and NHS Improvement as the circumstances require. During pre-notification discussions and throughout the formal merger review process, the CMA and NHS Improvement will provide each other with timely and reasoned explanations of their views and/or requirements.

79. NHS Improvement supports merger parties to develop a sound rationale for their anticipated transaction, ensuring the strategy is well considered and helps them determine whether a notification should be filed to the CMA, identifying potential competition issues and patient benefits. NHS Improvement will help merger parties understand the merger control process, to make informed decisions and to engage effectively with the CMA if the parties choose to notify the merger. Merger parties may also approach the CMA for informal advice on jurisdictional, procedural and substantive questions on

UK merger review and how it might affect the transaction. The CMA and NHS Improvement will each update the other on a regular basis on forthcoming mergers relevant to the healthcare sector.

80. Section 79(5) of the Health and Social Care Act 2012 requires NHS Improvement to provide advice to the CMA on relevant customer benefits[11] and on any other matter which it considers appropriate in relation to merger cases that are reviewed by the CMA under Part 3 of the Enterprise Act 2002:

(a) The first case is where the activities of two or more NHS foundation trusts cease to be distinct activities.

(b) The second case is where the activities of one or more NHS foundation trusts and the activities of one or more businesses cease to be distinct activities.

NHS Improvement will provide this advice to the CMA in phase 1 of the CMA's review.

81. Merger parties may submit further evidence on relevant customer benefits at phase 2 to the CMA or, in the event that they did not submit any relevant customer benefits during phase 1 of the CMA's review, they may make such submissions for the first time in phase 2. The CMA will seek NHS Improvement's views regarding the phase 2 relevant customer benefits proposal recognising its expertise as a sectoral regulator.

NOTES

11 Section 30 of the Enterprise Act 2002.

GENERAL PRINCIPLES

82. The CMA and NHS Improvement will observe the following general principles in relation to NHS Improvement's advice to the CMA pursuant to section 79(5) of the Health and Social Care Act 2012:

(a) the CMA and NHS Improvement will cooperate with each other in the exercise of their respective functions under Part 3 of the Enterprise Act 2002 and section 79(5) of the Health and Social Care Act 2012;

(b) the final conclusion on all aspects of the competitive analysis of the merger case under Part 3 of the Enterprise Act 2002 is for the CMA;

(c) NHS Improvement's analysis and advice in relation to such merger cases will draw on its expertise across the healthcare sector;

(d) the views that NHS Improvement presents in its advice will be its own, independent of the CMA;

(e) NHS Improvement's advice is not binding on the CMA; however, in phase 1 of its review, the CMA will place significant weight on NHS Improvement's expert advice on the relevant customer benefits of a merger;

(f) where NHS Improvement has provided advice to the CMA in phase 1, the CMA will attach such weight to that advice in phase 2 as it considers appropriate in the light of any changes to the proposed customer benefits and/or relevant evidence gathered and analysis undertaken during the course of its investigation; and

(g) the cooperation between the CMA and NHS Improvement provided for in this Part C shall not extend to conduct that could reasonably be expected to impair the impartiality and fairness of the CMA decision-maker and/or CMA group, as the case may be, in conducting merger reviews.

PROCESS FOR THE PROVISION OF ADVICE IN PHASE 1 OF THE CMA'S REVIEW

83. Under section 79(5) of the Health and Social Care Act 2012, NHS Improvement must provide its advice, including on relevant customer benefits, as soon as reasonably practicable after receiving notice that the CMA has decided to review a merger. NHS Improvement recognises the importance of its advice being provided in good time.[12]

NOTES

12 NHS Improvement notes that, in all cases, the CMA commits that, generally in the period between working days 15 and 20 of phase 1 of its review, it will have a 'state of play' discussion with the merger parties, typically by conference call. The purpose of this discussion is to give the merger parties information on any competition concerns, including feedback from the CMA's market test, whether or not the CMA is to send the merger parties an issues letter, and the theories of harm that the CMA proposes to include in the issues letter. The case team will also provide an update on the likely timetable for the case going forward.

Pre-notification period

84. The CMA will not commence a merger review until it considers that the merger parties have provided sufficient information on relevant customer benefits or indicated in the Merger Notice that they will not be making a submission in relation to relevant customer benefits in phase 1.

85. The CMA will liaise closely with NHS Improvement as to whether the information received with respect to relevant customer benefits will allow NHS Improvement to start its assessment of relevant customer benefits and provide advice to the CMA within the CMA's timetable.

86. If the merger parties decide not to make reasoned submissions in relation to relevant customer benefits and indicate their decision in writing to NHS Improvement, NHS Improvement will inform the CMA of the merger parties' decision as soon as reasonably practicable.

Phase 1 assessment period

87. As described above, the CMA and NHS Improvement will maintain close contact and dialogue throughout the pre-notification and formal merger review process. As part of this ongoing dialogue, NHS

Improvement will share its developing thinking (written or oral) including in relation to relevant customer benefits with the CMA as early as reasonably practicable and will supplement any initial advice on an ongoing basis as may be appropriate in the circumstances. Wherever possible, NHS Improvement will act with a view to the CMA being able to refer to NHS Improvement's advice on the 'state of play' call with the merger parties as well as reflect it in the issues letter.[13]

88. In any case where the CMA intends to proceed to a case review meeting,[14] and consequently sends an issues letter to the merger parties, the CMA will give NHS Improvement as much advance notice as is possible. NHS Improvement will share its developing thinking throughout and will communicate its advice to the CMA as soon as practicable following the start of the statutory timetable for the merger review. When providing its advice, NHS Improvement will be mindful of the CMA's timetable and the importance to the CMA of:

(a) being able to reflect NHS Improvement's views in the CMA's issues letter and at the case review meeting; and

(b) being able to reflect NHS Improvement's final advice at the CMA's decision meeting.[15]

89. NHS Improvement and the CMA will discuss NHS Improvement's views in relation to relevant customer benefits on an ongoing basis and in any event prior to the CMA's issues meeting and case review meeting.

90. Before providing its final advice to the CMA, NHS Improvement expects to provide the merger parties and the CMA with its provisional view on the relevant customer benefits arising from the merger. The CMA will be given the opportunity to seek clarifications on this provisional view within an appropriate period of time depending on the nature of the advice.

91. NHS Improvement staff involved in producing its advice, including on relevant customer benefits, will be available to meet the CMA case team to explain the reasoning and analysis underlying the advice provided. The CMA may ask NHS Improvement to provide further advice in relation to arguments raised in NHS Improvement's advice or in relation to additional evidence provided by the merger parties in response to the issues letter.

NOTES

13 Following the 'state of play' call and in the event that the case raises complex or material competition issues, an issues letter is sent to the merger parties, which they are given the opportunity to respond to at an issues meeting. Issues letters are normally sent approximately 20 working days from the start of the CMA's phase 1 review and followed a few days later by an issues meeting.

14 The case review meeting is an internal meeting held by the CMA following the issues meeting with the merger parties.

15 NHS Improvement notes that the CMA's decision meeting is normally held approximately 30 working days from the start of the CMA's phase 1 review and involves the decision-maker on the case, who is usually a senior member of CMA staff, deciding whether to clear the transaction or to refer it to phase 2 for further investigation.

Meetings with the merger parties

92. Meetings with the merger parties will generally be held separately by NHS Improvement and the CMA. Where appropriate, however, joint meetings may be held between the merger parties, the CMA and NHS Improvement in order to facilitate the review and ensure administrative efficiency.

PROCESS FOR THE PROVISION OF ADVICE IN PHASE 2 OF THE CMA'S REVIEW

93. As described in paragraph 81, merger parties may submit further evidence on relevant customer benefits at phase 2 to the CMA or, where they did not make submissions relating to relevant customer benefits during phase 1 of the CMA's review, they may make such submissions for the first time at phase 2. In the event that the CMA seeks NHS Improvement's views regarding the phase 2 relevant customer benefits, NHS Improvement will provide this advice after receiving notice from the CMA that the merger parties have made submissions relating to relevant customer benefits by the deadline specified in such notice.

REQUESTING AND SHARING INFORMATION

94. Paragraphs 49 to 53, 57 (excluding 57(a)) and 59 of this MoU apply to information sharing under the merger provisions as they do under the competition prohibitions.

95. To minimise the burden on merger parties, where appropriate, NHS Improvement and the CMA will coordinate information requests.

96. Sharing of information (including data) between the CMA and NHS Improvement is crucial for the effective fulfilment of their respective merger duties and should reduce the burden on merger parties which could otherwise arise, for example from duplicative information requests. The CMA and NHS Improvement may, where appropriate, discuss with each other anticipated or completed mergers that are brought to their attention; informal advice they will be providing or have provided; pre-notification drafts; and information obtained throughout the review.

97. The information and data sharing from the CMA to NHS Improvement will include any confidential information which the CMA considers will facilitate the effective fulfilment of its merger control statutory functions. In certain circumstances, whilst having regard to the confidentiality requests of the merger parties, the CMA may decide to disclose information to NHS Improvement without the consent of the merger parties. This may occur, for example, where it considers that disclosure is necessary to enable the CMA to exercise its statutory functions, including the need to have regard to NHS Improvement's advice on relevant customer benefits.

98. NHS Improvement's advice may contain information that is confidential (either as regards the merger parties or other confidential information known to NHS Improvement). NHS Improvement may share such information with the CMA.

99. NHS Improvement will provide the CMA with a confidential version of its advice for the purpose of the CMA's decision on the merger. For publication purposes, NHS Improvement will also provide the CMA with a non-confidential version of its advice.

POOLING RESOURCES

100. The provisions of paragraphs 27 to 33 of this MoU apply to pooling resources under the merger provisions as they do under the competition prohibitions and market provisions.

101. Where the CMA and NHS Improvement intend to pool resources in order to exercise powers under the merger provisions of the Enterprise Act 2002, they shall, at the outset of any such project, discuss the arrangements for how they will pool resources and work jointly. NHS Improvement will provide as much support as is practicable throughout the course of a merger control review, including meeting requests for additional expert resource as the need may arise.

(VIII) OTHER

NOTES

There are also a number of short "60 second summary" and "Case study" materials on the CMA's website aimed at participants in specific industries or professions, such as accountants and auditors, commercial vehicles, online sales, private medical practitioners, estate agents, and company secretaries. See www.gov.uk/government/collections/competition-and-consumer-law-compliance-guidance-for-businesses.

LAND AGREEMENTS (OFT 1280A, MARCH 2011)

The application of competition law following the revocation of the Land Agreements Exclusion Order

[3.383]

NOTES

As to the construction of this document (following the abolition of the OFT and Competition Commission), see further the note "The Competition and Markets Authority (references to the OFT and Competition Commission etc)" in the introductory notes to Part 3 preceding **[3.1]**.

CONTENTS

1 INTRODUCTION

PURPOSE OF THIS GUIDELINE

[3.384]

1.1 This guideline is aimed at businesses that are party to land agreements and their legal advisors. For the purposes of this guideline, land agreements are defined as agreements which create, alter, transfer or terminate an interest in land. Land agreements therefore include transfers of freehold interests, leases and assignments of leasehold interests. They also include agreements relating to easements, licences and, in Scotland, interests under a lease and other heritable rights in or over land, such as heritable securities.

1.2 Article 101 of the Treaty on the Functioning of the European Union (the TFEU) and the Chapter I prohibition contained in the Competition Act 1998 (the Act) both prohibit, in certain circumstances, agreements which prevent, restrict or distort competition. The UK law prohibiting anti-competitive agreements is referred to either as 'the Chapter I prohibition' or 'the prohibition' in this guideline.

1.3 Prior to 6 April 2011, many land agreements have been excluded[1] from the prohibition of anti-competitive agreements contained in Chapter I of the Act. From 6 April 2011 onwards, the Chapter I prohibition applies to land agreements that have been entered into prior to and continue to exist after 6 April 2011 and also to land agreements that are entered into on or after that date.[2,3]

1.4 This guideline aims to assist firms in understanding how the general principles of competition law apply to land agreements in the UK. In particular, it focuses on restrictions in land agreements which restrict the way in which land may be used, or how a right over land may be exercised (referred to in this guideline as 'restrictions').[4]

WHEN WILL A LAND AGREEMENT INFRINGE COMPETITION LAW?

1.5 There are many legitimate reasons why a person or business may impose or agree to restrictions which affect or limit the way in which land may be used or how a right over land may be exercised in a land agreement. Such restrictions do not necessarily infringe competition law and the OFT expects that only a minority of restrictions will do so.

1.6 In some cases, land will be an important 'input' to a related market where goods or services are being provided. Land agreements have the potential to restrict competition in such related markets. An agreement will not fall within the scope of the Chapter I prohibition unless its impact on competition in a related market is 'appreciable'.

1.7 Two main categories of restrictions in land agreements are more likely to restrict competition.

1.8 First, if the parties to a land agreement are competitors in a relevant market and a restriction regarding the use of land is aimed at sharing or carving-up markets between those parties, the agreement is very likely to constitute a serious infringement of the Chapter I prohibition.

1.9 Second, other types of restriction may fall within the Chapter I prohibition if they have the effect of restricting competition by raising barriers to entry (or expansion) in a particular market where a party to the agreement is carrying out an economic activity and a restriction makes access to that market by other competitors more difficult.[5] These types of restriction are unlikely to appreciably restrict competition unless one or more of the parties to the agreement possess 'market power' in a related market. Market power is the ability to maintain prices above competitive levels or to maintain output in terms of product quantities, product quality, and variety or innovation below competitive levels for a not insignificant period of time.[6]

1.10 Market power is unlikely to arise where there is sufficient competition from existing competitors in the related market, or other suitable land is available for use in the related market by other competitors. Chapter 4 provides further detail on how to assess such factors.

1.11 Agreements which appreciably restrict competition may nevertheless be exempt from the Chapter I prohibition, if certain criteria are satisfied (as explained further in chapter 5 of this guideline).

1.12 The compatibility of a land agreement with the prohibition needs to be assessed taking into account present and also possible future circumstances. An agreement which does not infringe the Chapter I prohibition at the time when it is entered into may, subsequently and as a result of change in its economic context, infringe the Chapter I prohibition.

WHAT HAPPENS IF AN AGREEMENT INFRINGES COMPETITION LAW?

1.13 Parties to a prohibited agreement (that is, an agreement which falls within the scope of the prohibition and does not benefit from exemption), or a party abusing a dominant position may face enforcement action by the OFT, a sectoral regulator,[7] or, where there may be an effect on trade between Member States, the European Commission. These authorities have the power to investigate suspected infringements, to impose financial penalties of up to 10 per cent of a firm's worldwide turnover and to give directions to take steps to bring an infringement to an end.[8]

1.14 A restriction which infringes the Chapter I prohibition is void and unenforceable. The effect of this on the remainder of an agreement is a matter for the law which governs the particular agreement. In some cases a court may consider it possible to 'sever' the provisions of an agreement which infringe the Chapter I prohibition and in such cases, the other terms of the agreement would remain valid and enforceable.[9]

1.15 Parties to a prohibited agreement may also be susceptible to private action before the UK courts for damages or injunctive relief for breaches of competition law, by any person who has suffered loss as a result of an infringement.

STRUCTURE OF THE REMAINDER OF THIS GUIDELINE

1.16 Chapter 2 explains the main elements of the law prohibiting agreements and certain other arrangements which prevent, restrict or distort competition.

1.17 Chapter 3 summarises the OFT's approach to defining markets.[10] Defining the relevant market is an important step in assessing agreements or conduct under the competition rules.

1.18 Chapter 4 sets out the types of restrictions that are more likely to restrict competition and the main factors relevant to assessing whether a land agreement prevents, restricts or distorts competition to an appreciable extent. Chapter 4 also notes certain other restrictions of competition which could potentially arise in the context of land agreements, but which are outside the scope of this guideline.

1.19 Chapter 5 explains the circumstances in which land agreements that appreciably restrict competition may nevertheless be exempt from the Chapter I prohibition.

1.20 Chapter 6 summarises the circumstances in which a firm which has a dominant market position may infringe competition law by abusing this position, in way that excludes its competitors from the relevant market, or exploits its customers.

1.21 Chapter 7 sets out the consequences of infringing competition law in further detail.

1.22 Chapter 8 explains the circumstances in which the OFT would be unlikely to take further action in cases involving land agreements. This chapter sets out that the OFT is generally unlikely to take further action in respect of a land agreement where none of the parties to the agreement has a market share exceeding 30 per cent on the relevant market.[11]

1.23 Chapter 9 sets out some worked examples of how land agreements may be assessed in relation to the Chapter I prohibition.[12]

1.24 Annexe A contains a flow-chart showing how businesses and their legal advisers can use the guideline to assess land agreements in practice. Annexe B is a glossary of terms referred to in this guideline.

NOTES

1 By virtue of the Competition Act 1998 (Land Agreements Exclusion and Revocation) Order 2004 (SI 2004/1260) and, prior to that, the Competition Act 1998 (Land and Vertical Agreements Exclusion) Order 2000 (SI 2000/310).

2 By virtue of the Competition Act 1998 (Land Agreements Exclusion Revocation) Order 2010 (SI 2010/1709). Planning obligations continue to benefit from exclusion from the Chapter I prohibition by virtue of paragraph 1, Schedule 3 of the Act.

3 From 6 April 2011, this guideline replaces the OFT's previous guideline on *Land Agreements* (OFT420), which explained the application of the Competition Act 1998 (Land Agreements Exclusion and Revocation) Order 2004.

4 The scope of this guideline is limited to explaining the application of competition law to the types of agreement that were previously excluded from the Chapter I prohibition. Given its specific purpose, the guideline focuses on the law of anti-competitive agreements. A succinct reference to the prohibitions on the abuse of a dominant position is made in chapter 6 of this guideline. The guideline does not cover merger control. Certain land agreements in connection with grocery retailing activities are subject to additional control under the Groceries Market Investigation (Controlled Land) Order 2010 (the Groceries Controlled Land Order). The provisions of the Groceries Controlled Land Order apply separately from general competition law. Land restrictions in the grocery sector which are not caught by the provisions of this Order may however be prohibited under general competition law.

5 This may be the case, for example, in relation to the following types of restrictions: (i) arrangements where a landlord agrees not to allow access to a site or sites owned by the landlord to competitors of the lessee; (ii) lease provisions which restrict the commercial activity that a lessee is permitted to undertake on leased premises; and (iii) restrictive covenants in the context of a sale of land where a restriction is imposed on the future use of that land.

6 The degree of market power that is normally required for a finding of an infringement of the Chapter I prohibition/Article 101 TFEU is less than the degree of market power required for a finding of dominance under Chapter II of the Act/Article 102 TFEU. See chapters 4 and 6.

7 The following sectoral regulators have concurrent powers to enforce competition law in the UK: the Office of Communications; the Gas and Electricity Markets Authority; the Water Services Regulation Authority; the Office of Rail Regulation; the Civil Aviation Authority; and the Northern Ireland Authority for Utility Regulation.

8 See the OFT guideline *Enforcement* (OFT407).

9 This has been stated, amongst others, by the High Court in *Inntrepreneur Estates Ltd v Mason*, [1994] 68 P&CR 53, [1993] 2 CMLR 293, QBD, and by the Court of Appeal in *Inntrepreneur Estates (GL) Ltd v Boyes*, [1995] ECC 16, [1993] 2 EGLR 112, CA.

10 Market definition is a tool used in all areas of competition law. Given the scope of this guideline, market definition is explained primarily in relation to the application of the Chapter I prohibition to land agreements.

11 This should not be regarded as a statement of how the Chapter I prohibition will apply to land agreements. Paragraphs 8.3 to 8.9 below apply to agreements which transfer an interest in land and relate to obligations or restrictions regarding the use of land. These paragraphs do not apply to other types of agreement which are outside the scope of this guideline, as explained in chapter 4).

12 This guideline cannot cover every possible scenario and other types of restrictions should be assessed in accordance with the legal framework explained in this guideline. Businesses should consider seeking legal advice on any specific agreements which they believe may raise competition law concerns.

2 ANTI-COMPETITIVE AGREEMENTS: THE PROVISIONS

SCOPE OF THE PROVISIONS

[3.385]

2.1 Both UK and EU competition law prohibit agreements and certain other arrangements which have as their object or effect the prevention, restriction or distortion of competition.[13] These prohibitions are set out, respectively, in Chapter I of the Act and Article 101 of the TFEU.[14]

2.2 Article 101 of the TFEU applies to agreements which have the potential to appreciably affect trade between EU Member States.[15] In most cases, individual land agreements will not have an effect on trade between EU Member States, and therefore, in practice, Articles 101 (and 102) TFEU are less likely to apply. However, for most practical purposes it is not necessary to distinguish between the EU and UK rules. For the remainder of this guideline, references to the Chapter I prohibition should also be understood to include the prohibition in Article 101 TFEU.[16]

2.3 The exclusion previously in place for land agreements did not apply to the equivalent prohibition in Article 101 TFEU, or the prohibitions on the abuse of a dominant position in Chapter II of the Act and Article 102 TFEU.

2.4 Any agreement which falls within the scope of the Chapter I prohibition or Article 101 TFEU will be void and unenforceable[17] unless it benefits from exemption.[18] When considering whether a land agreement is prohibited, it is therefore necessary to assess:

- whether the agreement prevents, restricts or distorts competition and, if it does
- whether it benefits from exemption.

2.5 In order to qualify for exemption four cumulative criteria must be satisfied. These are set out in chapter 5. In this guideline the term 'exemption' includes both the exemption regime of section 9 of the Act and the equivalent provisions in Article 101(3) TFEU.[19]

TERMS USED IN THE PROVISIONS

Undertakings

2.6 Competition law applies to agreements between, and conduct by, 'undertakings'. An undertaking means any natural or legal person carrying out commercial or economic activities relating to goods or services, irrespective of that person's legal status or the way that it is financed. This includes companies, firms, businesses, partnerships, individuals operating as sole traders, agricultural co-operatives, associations of undertakings (for example trade associations), non profitmaking organisations and (in some circumstances) public bodies that offer goods or services on a given market.

2.7 In this guideline the words 'firm', 'business' and 'company' should be understood to include all forms of undertaking.

2.8 The key consideration in assessing whether an entity is an undertaking for the purposes of the application of the Chapter I prohibition is whether it is engaged in economic activity. An entity may engage in an economic activity in relation to some of its functions but not others. For example, a public body such as a local authority may act as an undertaking if it leases land for commercial uses and acts as a landlord in that context, but would not be acting as an undertaking when carrying out activities that are connected with the exercise of the powers of a public authority (for example, granting planning permission).

2.9 The prohibition does not apply to individuals who are not acting as a business. Therefore agreements regarding the use of residential property, or transfers of leasehold or freehold interests in residential property, agreed with a private individual or between such individuals,[20] will not be caught by the prohibition.

Agreement

2.10 For the purposes of competition law, an 'agreement' does not need to be a formal written agreement. The prohibition extends also to informal arrangements, concerted practices and decisions of associations of undertakings.[21]

THE PREVENTION, RESTRICTION OR DISTORTION OF COMPETITION

The appreciable effect on competition test

2.11 An agreement will not fall within the scope of competition law unless its impact on competition is 'appreciable'. It should be noted that when assessing the impact on competition of an agreement, it is always necessary to consider the specific facts of the case. Any agreement between undertakings might be said to restrict the freedom of action of the parties. That does not, however, necessarily mean that the agreement appreciably restricts competition.

2.12 When determining whether the impact of an agreement is appreciable the OFT will have regard to the approach set out in the European Commission's *Notice on Agreements of Minor Importance*.[22]

2.13 This means that unless the agreement contains a restriction of competition listed as hardcore in the Commission's Notice (such as an agreement to fix prices or allocate customers), the OFT considers that agreements between firms do not appreciably restrict competition if:

- the aggregate market share of the parties to the agreement does not exceed 10 per cent on any of the relevant markets affected by the agreement where the agreement is between competing undertakings (often called 'horizontal agreements'), or
- the market share of each of the parties to the agreement does not exceed 15 per cent on any of the relevant markets affected by the agreement where the agreement is made between non-competing undertakings (that is, firms which are neither actual nor potential competitors on any of the markets concerned, which usually means firms operating at different levels of the supply chain).[23]

2.14 In both cases, the thresholds are reduced to five per cent where competition on the relevant market is restricted by the cumulative foreclosure effect of parallel networks of agreements having similar effects on the markets.[24]

2.15 The OFT does not consider that the impact of an agreement on competition is appreciable below these market share thresholds.

2.16 The mere fact that the parties' market shares exceed the thresholds set out in paragraph 2.13 above, does **not** mean that the effect of an agreement on competition **is** appreciable. Other factors will be considered in determining whether the agreement may have an appreciable effect on competition. Key factors that are relevant to this assessment are set out in chapter 4 and must be considered on a case by case basis.

2.17 Where the OFT considers that undertakings have in good faith relied on the terms of the *Notice on Agreements of Minor Importance*, the OFT will not impose financial penalties for an infringement of the Chapter I prohibition.[25]

Present and future circumstances

2.18 Finally, the compatibility of a land agreement with the prohibition needs to be assessed taking into account present and also possible future circumstances. An agreement which does not infringe the Chapter I prohibition at the time when it is entered into may, subsequently and as a result of change in its economic context, infringe the prohibition and become void and unenforceable.[26] Assessing the possibility of an agreement infringing competition law in the future is important when an agreement can make it more difficult for other businesses to compete effectively in a market – for example, the assessment may be affected by the entry and exit of competitors on that market or the availability of suitable sites for use in that market.

NOTES

13 Restrictions of competition by object are those that by their very nature have the potential to restrict competition. Once it has been established that an agreement has as its object the restriction of competition, there is no need to take account of its actual effect in order to conclude that the prohibition has been infringed. See, for example, the judgment of the European Court of Justice in Joined cases C-501/06 P, C-513/06 P, C-515/06 P and C-519/06 P *GlaxoSmithKline* [2009] ECR I-9291, [2010] 4 CMLR 2.

14 See the OFT guideline *Agreements and concerted practices* (OFT401).

15 This criterion is explained in the Commission *Guidelines on the effect of trade concept contained in Articles 81 and 82* [now 101 and 102] *of the Treaty* (OJ C101, 27.4.2004, p. 81). In exceptional cases, land agreements may appreciably

affect trade between Member States. This may be for example the case where a competitor from another Member State is foreclosed as a result of a restriction contained in a land agreement or land agreements.

16 UK competition law mirrors the substantive provisions of EU competition law. Under section 60 of the Act the courts and UK competition authorities are required to interpret UK competition law consistently with the equivalent EU provisions and have regard to relevant decisions of the European Commission.

17 In some cases a court may consider it possible to sever certain provisions which infringe the Chapter I prohibition in a land agreement, and let other terms of the agreement be valid and enforceable (as set out further in chapter 7).

18 Agreements benefiting from an exclusion from competition law are outside the scope of the prohibition. Planning obligations benefit from exclusion from the Chapter I prohibition by virtue of paragraph 1, Schedule 3 of the Act.

19 Certain categories of agreement benefit automatically from exemption by virtue of a block exemption. The only UK block exemption currently in force is the Public Transport Ticketing Schemes Block Exemption (SI 2001 No 319, as amended). EU block exemptions also apply under UK law by virtue of the parallel exemption regime under section 10 of the Act. There is no block exemption that relates specifically to land agreements.

20 If only one party to a lease agreement is acting as an undertaking and the other is not, the agreement would not be caught by the Chapter I prohibition.

21 For the purposes of the Chapter I prohibition, the OFT considers that the parties to an agreement will generally be the contracting parties executing the creation, alteration, transfer or termination of the interest in land. The position may be more complex where a restrictive covenant affecting freehold land 'runs with the land' (that is to say, it may be enforceable by not only the original contracting parties, but also between the successors in title of the land both burdened by and benefiting from the restriction). The OFT will consider on a case-by-case basis whether there is an 'agreement' between the successors in title of land with the benefit or burden of a restrictive covenant. It may be relevant to take into account, for example, whether a party is aware of a restriction and whether a party has sought or is seeking to enforce a restriction.

22 OJ C368, 22.12.2001, p. 13. See also the OFT guideline *Agreements and concerted practices* (OFT401), para 2.14 ff.

23 The relevant market share will be the combined market share not only of the parties to the agreement but also of other undertakings belonging to the same group of undertakings as the parties to the agreement. These will include, in the case of each party to the agreement: (i) undertakings over which it exercises control; and (ii) undertakings which exercise control over it as well as any other undertakings which are controlled by those undertakings.

24 The cumulative effect of parallel networks of agreements is explained in paragraph 8 of the European Commission's *Notice on Agreements of Minor Importance*.

25 See OFT guideline *Agreements and concerted practices* (OFT401), paragraph 2.19.

26 Similarly, an agreement which infringes the prohibition at the time when it is entered into may cease to be void and become enforceable at a later stage because of a change in circumstances. This is sometimes referred to as 'transient voidness' of an agreement. See the judgment of the Court of Appeal in *Passmore v Morland plc*, [1999] 1 CMLR 1129, CA. Paragraph 8.6 explains how the OFT may consider recent changes in parties' market shares as part of its overall assessment of whether further action by the OFT would be warranted in particular cases relating to land agreements.

3 MARKET DEFINITION

THE PURPOSE OF MARKET DEFINITION

[3.386]

3.1 Market definition is important in assessing agreements or conduct under the competition rules. For example, the Chapter I prohibition applies to agreements which have as their object or effect an appreciable prevention, restriction or distortion of competition. The appreciability test usually requires definition of a relevant market and demonstration that the agreement would have an appreciable effect on competition within that market.[27]

3.2 This chapter summarises the principles of market definition and how they apply in the context of land agreements. A fuller explanation of market definition is set out in the OFT guideline *Market Definition* (OFT403).[28]

3.3 Assessing the impact of a land agreement will generally involve the consideration of two relevant markets.

3.4 The first relevant market is the downstream or **related market**. This is the market involving the economic activity where the land affected by the agreement is used. For example, when considering a covenant in a lease that prevents the tenant from opening a coffee shop on leased premises, it will be necessary to consider the impact of that covenant on the market in which a coffee shop would compete. This will depend on both the product and geographic scope of the market.

3.5 The product scope of the related market will be defined by the economic activity for which the land is being used. The relevant product market comprises all the products[29] or services that customers consider substitutable. Using the coffee shop example referred to in paragraph 3.4 above, the product scope is defined by looking at all other types of shops that compete with and constrain coffee shops. These could include coffee shops and also other similar premises selling food and beverages such as sandwich bars and cafes, depending on the degree of competitive constraint that they provide on coffee shops.

3.6 The geographic scope of the related market will be defined by the relevant geographic area over which the product in question competes. The geographic scope of the relevant market may be global, international, national, regional or local. Continuing the above example, suppose that the product scope had been defined as the relevant market for coffee shops and competing premises also selling beverages, such as cafes. In this case the geographic market would be defined by looking at the geographic area over which the coffee shop competes with other coffee shops or similar premises selling beverages.

3.7 The second relevant market is the upstream **market for land** that is suitable for use in the related market. This second market can be important when assessing the impact of a restriction over a particular piece of land, because the land is an input into the related market.

3.8 Determining what land is suitable (and over what geographic area) will depend on the product and geographic scope of the related market. The scope of the market for land is defined as all land that is suitable for use in the related market where the land is being used. In the example of the coffee shop, the product scope for the land will include all the land that is suitable for use by a coffee shop and similar premises selling beverages, within the relevant geographic scope of that market.

3.9 A restriction on the use of land is more likely to impact on competition where the related market has a narrow geographic scope. In some retail markets, for example, the ability of customers to switch between retailers will be limited to a local level. In other markets, the related market may have a wider geographic scope and it is less likely that a restriction on the use of a particular piece of land will impact on competition in that market.

3.10 Market definition is not an end in itself but a key step in identifying the competitive constraints acting on a supplier of a given product or service. Market definition is usually the first step in the assessment of market power, which is explained further in chapter 4 of this guideline.

HOW TO DEFINE MARKETS

3.11 In identifying the product scope of the relevant market, particular regard is paid to demand-side factors (the behaviour of customers and its effects). However, it may also be relevant to consider supply-side factors (the capabilities and reactions of suppliers in the short term) and other market characteristics.

3.12 The relevant product market is identified primarily by considering the response of customers of the 'focal product' to an increase in the price of the product (demand-side substitution). In order to establish which products are substitutable and therefore form part of the relevant market, a conceptual framework known as the 'hypothetical monopolist test' is usually employed.

3.13 Applying this framework begins by determining the narrowest product in question, called the focal product. A set of substitutable products will satisfy the hypothetical monopolist test if a hypothetical firm that was the only present and future seller of the products in the candidate market would find it profitable to raise prices for these products.

3.14 A set of substitute products will fail the hypothetical monopolist test (that is to say, it will be too narrow to comprise the relevant market), if customers would respond to a small but significant and non-transitory increase in price (a SSNIP) by switching to products outside the set to such an extent that the price increase by the hypothetical monopolist would not be profitable. If customers switch to substitutable products, those alternative products will form part of the same market. This process is repeated on the wider group of products until a point is reached where a SSNIP would be profitable.

3.15 When applying the hypothetical monopolist test, the OFT will normally use a SSNIP of five per cent, although it may sometimes be appropriate to use a higher or lower number. In most cases, a hypothetical monopolist test would be conducted relative to prevailing prices. In cases where it is thought that prevailing prices might be the outcome of anti-competitive behaviour, the OFT may consider conducting the test using prices that are lower than prevailing prices as a starting point.

3.16 The OFT will consider a range of evidence when evaluating whether a SSNIP by the hypothetical monopolist would be profitable. Relevant evidence may include closeness of substitution, product characteristics, relative price levels, information on prices and sales volumes across time or areas, responses from customers or third parties, relevant documents and profit margins. This list is not definitive and information gathered on these factors may be supplemented by other information and by calculations which can help the OFT judge how likely it is that a SSNIP would be profitable.[30]

3.17 The boundaries of the relevant product market are generally determined by reference to demand-side substitution alone. However, there are circumstances where the OFT may consider the response of suppliers to changes in prices – known as supply side substitution. Supply-side substitution can be thought of as a special case of entry – entry that occurs quickly (for example less than one year), effectively (for example on a scale large enough to affect prices), and without the need for substantial sunk investments. Supply-side substitution addresses the questions of whether, to what extent, and how quickly, undertakings would start supplying a market in response to a hypothetical monopolist attempting to sustain supra-competitive prices.[31]

3.18 The same demand techniques are used to determine the geographic scope of a market. Correspondingly where available, similar information to that used to identify demand-side substitution between products can be used to assess the geographic boundaries of the relevant market. Useful evidence may include: product characteristics such as perishability; differences in pricing, advertising or sales by area; customer switching data; and responses from customers or third parties.[32]

3.19 In several previous merger cases in a retail context, the OFT has used a catchment area as a pragmatic approximation to geographic market definition. This has been done for example in some retail mergers involving physical (or 'bricks and mortar') stores. From the customer's perspective, most retail markets are inherently local if they require a visit to a physical store or outlet.

3.20 A catchment area can be usefully defined as the area from which a store derives a large percentage of its business. Catchment areas have sometimes been determined by relying on proxies or rules of thumb. Notably, the OFT has in the past considered the area from within which about 80 per cent of a stores' customers (or sales) are drawn as a useful starting point when considering catchment areas.[33] This is without prejudice to other rules being used in appropriate circumstances.

3.21 To delineate catchment areas, it is common to use a measure around the store which is being considered. The measure could be a distance or a drive time from the store.[34]

3.22 In the absence of sufficient information enabling the geographical market to be defined on the basis of catchment areas, or where these would not be a realistic representation of market definition of using the hypothetical monopolist test, other proxies may be relevant to determine the geographic market. For example, postal areas and Local Authority Licensing Areas have been used as a proxy for geographic markets by the OFT in the past.[35]

3.23 As noted above, in some retail markets, the ability of customers to switch between retailers will be limited to a local level. In other commercial and industrial markets, the related market may have a wider geographic scope, for example, where the scope is regional or national.[36]

OTHER CONSIDERATIONS

3.24 In some cases suppliers may be able to offer different customers different terms (for example, when suppliers are able to discriminate between customers by charging different prices for the same product depending on how much they are willing to pay). In these cases it is also necessary to consider whether the relevant market should be divided into different customer groups.[37]

3.25 In certain circumstances, it may be argued that a market is not 'local' if suppliers in that market (for example national retail chains) have a national pricing policy. However, the existence of national pricing policies is not in itself sufficient to conclude that a certain store competes in a national market. In such situations, it is relevant to consider whether other key aspects of the retail offer (such as product range, store aspect and layout, amount of pre- and post-sales service, targeted customer discounts or competitor price matching) are decided on the basis of local factors or are adaptable to those. Where there is evidence that companies compete locally in any of those factors, it is possible that the relevant geographic market is mostly local.[38]

3.26 Finally competition is not always symmetric. For example, a small grocery store may not impose a competitive constraint on a large supermarket in a given area, but at the same time that supermarket may constrain the pricing of the smaller store, as well as other supermarkets and other smaller stores over a wider area.

NOTES

27 An exception is where an agreement has as its object the prevention, restriction or distortion of competition. In these cases, market definition is not necessarily a pre-requisite for a finding of infringement but the relevant market would need to be defined for the purpose of determining the relevant turnover of an undertaking, which is taken into account when determining the appropriate amount of any penalty (see the *OFT's Guidance as to the appropriate amount of a penalty* (OFT 423)).

28 More specific guidance on how market definition is assessed for retail markets, in the context of the UK merger control regime, is set out in the OFT and CC joint *Merger Assessment Guidelines* (OFT1254/CC2 (Revised)) and a joint 'Commentary on retail mergers' by the Competition Commission and OFT published in March 2011. Such guidance is also illustrative for cases considered under the Act.

29 The term 'product' is used for convenience and should be interpreted throughout this guideline to include goods and services.

30 Further detail is set out in the OFT guideline *Market Definition* (OFT403).

31 More detail on supply side substitution is given in the OFT Guideline *Market Definition* (OFT403).

32 More details on evidence are provided in the OFT Guideline *Market Definition* (OFT403).

33 See, for example, *Travis Perkins plc/BSS Group plc* (OFT ME/4609/10, October 2010), *Completed acquisition by Lodge Brothers Funerals Ltd of two funeral homes in the London borough of Hillingdon* (OFT ME/4245/09, December 2009), *Home Retail Group plc / Focus (DIY) Ltd* (OFT ME/3427/07, April 2007) and *Nationwide Building Society/Derbyshire Building Society* (OFT ME/3872/08, November 2008).

34 For example, a 15-minute drive-time catchment area would encompass the area from which customers could reach a store by driving for 15 minutes or less. By way of illustration, drive times have been used by the OFT and the Competition Commission to define catchment areas in the following sectors: (i) cinemas – a 20-minute drive-time catchment area was used in *Terra Firma Investments (GP) 2 Ltd/United Cinemas International (UK) Limited and Cinema International Corporation (UK) Limited* (OFT ME/1322/04, January 2005) and *Vue Entertainment Holdings (UK) Ltd/A3 Cinema Ltd* (CC, February 2006); (ii) supermarkets – a 10- or 15-minute drive-time catchment area for supermarkets of 1400 square metres and over and a five- or 10-minute drive-time catchment area for supermarkets of under 1400 square metres were used in *Safeway PLC Safeway plc and Asda Group Limited (owned by Wal-Mart Stores Inc); Wm Morrison Supermarkets PLC; J Sainsbury plc; and Tesco plc: A report on the mergers in contemplation* (CC, August 2003); (iii) sports equipment stores – a 15-minute drive-time catchment areas was used in *Sports Direct/JJB Sports* (CC, March 2010). In relation to other businesses, such as licensed betting offices, a distance measure has been used to define the catchment area – a 400m and 880m distances from the betting office were used in *William Hill plc/Stanley plc* (OFT ME/1716/05, August 2005).

35 The OFT has used these proxies in past merger cases in the absence of a detailed study into local market conditions, but it has also noted that they may not accurately capture the geographic scope of competitive constraints on individual businesses.

36 An illustrative example of a 'regional' market is the OFT's merger decision in *Aggregate Industries Limited/Atlantic Aggregates Limited and Stone Haul Limited* (OFT ME/3978/08, March 2009), where the OFT examined the market for 'secondary' aggregates on the basis of 30-mile radii, whilst having regard to a 40–50 mile radius in relation to certain locations. See also OFT Decision No. CA98/01/2008 *Abuse of a dominance position by Cardiff Bus*. Other markets may be wider in scope (for example, national markets).

37 In other cases there may also be temporal characteristics of demand, which may lead to defining temporal or seasonal markets.

38 For example, merger analysis in the cinema sector has shown that firms that operate on a national basis may nevertheless set ticket prices and other aspects of their retail offer according to local competition (see, for example, *Vue Entertainment Holdings (UK) Ltd/A3 Cinema Ltd* (CC, February 2006)).

4 ASSESSING WHETHER A LAND AGREEMENT APPRECIABLY RESTRICTS COMPETITION

[3.387]

4.1 This chapter sets out the main factors relevant to assessing whether a land agreement prevents, restricts or distorts competition, and whether it does so to an appreciable extent. This guideline is designed to provide a framework to assist parties in assessing land agreements for compatibility with the Chapter I prohibition.

4.2 Restrictions in land agreements regarding the way in which land may be used, or how a right over land may be exercised, do not necessarily infringe competition law. Parties that own or have an interest in land are generally free to determine how that land should be used or whether the land is suitable for use for a particular purpose. The OFT expects that only a minority of land agreements will be caught by the Chapter I prohibition.

4.3 The nature of the restriction, the relationship between the parties to the agreement and the factual context of the restriction are particularly important in assessing whether a restriction will have negative effects on competition. This chapter sets out types of restriction that are more likely to appreciably restrict competition and types of restriction that generally are unlikely to do so.

4.4 When assessing whether a restriction may restrict competition, it is necessary to compare the actual or future situation on the relevant market with the land agreement and the restrictions that it contains in place, with the situation that would prevail in the absence of the agreement (the 'counterfactual'). A restriction will fall within the scope of the prohibition only if it has a negative impact on actual or potential competition when compared with the counterfactual.[39]

4.5 Chapter 9 of this guideline provides worked examples which illustrate the general framework set out in this chapter.

KEY FACTORS RELEVANT TO THE ASSESSMENT OF WHETHER AN AGREEMENT APPRECIABLY RESTRICTS COMPETITION

Type of restriction and relationship between the parties to the agreement

4.6 Where the parties to a land agreement are competitors and the object of a restriction regarding the use of land is for the parties to share markets by territory, type or size of customer, the agreement will almost invariably infringe the Chapter I prohibition. The OFT considers that such market-sharing agreements have as their object the restriction of competition and, by their very nature, restrict competition to an appreciable extent.

4.7 Other types of restrictions may have the effect of restricting competition, if they foreclose[40] (a substantial part of) a related market to the competitors of a party to the agreement, by raising barriers to entry or expansion, or dampen competition in that market.

4.8 The examples of restrictions described in paragraphs 4.9 to 4.14 below may appreciably restrict competition if one or more of the parties to the agreement has or obtains some degree of market power on a related market and the agreement contributes to the creation, maintenance or strengthening of that market power. Paragraphs 4.15 to 4.25 below describe the key factors in assessing whether parties to such an agreement possess market power.

Exclusivity arrangements

4.9 Where a land-owner leases land to a party and agrees not to allow a competitor of that party to operate on the land or other land that is owned by the land-owner, this may protect the lessee from competition and has the potential to foreclose competitors of the lessee in a related market.

4.10 For example, a landlord of a shopping centre might guarantee one tenant the exclusive right to operate a certain type of shop in that centre. By definition, such an agreement would protect that tenant from competition from other relevant competitors within that shopping centre and this has the potential to restrict competition on the related market.

Leasehold use restrictions

4.11 In many leases, a landlord will specify permitted uses for the land that is leased (often referred to as 'permitted user' clauses) or conversely, uses that are not permitted (often referred to 'restricted user' clauses). In most cases, permitted user and restricted user clauses are unlikely to restrict competition. However, where a land-owner is also active in a related market and seeks to limit the availability of its land to its downstream competitors by restricting the use of its land for a particular purpose, this has the potential to restrict competition.

4.12 For example, a land-owner who operates a number of convenience stores in a particular area may limit how a lessee of a particular site may use the property, by stipulating that the lessee may not use the site as a convenience store, or conversely by stipulating that it must be used for a particular purpose other than as a convenience store. This has the potential to restrict competition in the related market for convenience stores.

Freehold restrictive covenants

4.13 A restrictive covenant regarding the transfer of a freehold interest in land may restrict the use of a party's land in some way for the benefit of another party's land. In most cases, such restrictions will not restrict competition. However, where a land-owner stipulates how a property should be used in order to limit the availability of land to its competitors in a related market, this has the potential to restrict competition on the related market.

4.14 An example would be where the vendor of a property, who owns a betting shop or betting shops in a particular area, seeks to control how the property is used after it is sold by specifying that it cannot be used as a betting shop. A further example would be a restriction accepted by the purchaser of a property not to sell the property to a competitor of the vendor.

MARKET POWER ON THE RELATED MARKET

4.15 Market power arises where an undertaking does not face effective competitive pressure.[41]

4.16 In the context of land agreements, the stronger a party's competitors are on the related market and the greater their number, the less risk there is that parties to the agreement will possess market power in that market and that the types of restrictions outlined in paragraphs 4.9 to 4.14 above will foreclose access to the related market or dampen competition on this market. Further, an undertaking may not possess market power on the related market where there is a strong threat of potential competition (for example where there is other suitable land available for use in the related market).[42] These points are considered further below.

Existing competitors

4.17 Market shares and measures of concentration, assessed on the relevant market, may inform the degree of market power a party possesses on a related market. The market shares of competing firms in the relevant market, both in absolute terms and relative to each other, can give an indication of the potential extent of a firm's market power. Market shares may be calculated in a number of ways, including on the basis of turnover, sales, or the number of competitors in a particular area. A straightforward count of the number of firms in a market is a basic measure of concentration or market shares. When assessing local retail markets, a count of the number of independent fascias in a local area also conveys information about concentration or market share.[43]

4.18 Where the parties to an agreement have high market shares,[44] this is usually a good indicator of market power but this may not always be the case. For example, an undertaking may not have market power on the related market where entry barriers are low and there is a strong threat of potential competition.

Barriers to entry or expansion on the related market and availability of suitable land

4.19 The existence of barriers to entry or expansion – in particular, the availability of suitable land for use in the related market is also relevant to the assessment of market power on the related market.[45]

4.20 As outlined in chapter 3, the scope of the available land relevant to this assessment is defined by reference to the economic activity in the related market, including the geographic scope of that market.

4.21 Barriers to entry or expansion in a related market may be significant where a single land owner owns all (or substantially all) of the available land suitable for use in that market. Even if the suitable land is owned by many parties, it might not be available to the market if most of it is tied up in long term lease contracts.

4.22 It is also necessary to consider whether sites suitable for use in the related market have unique or special qualities. For example, a restriction which prevents land from being used for a superstore is more likely to have an impact on competition than a restriction which prevents an individual high street unit from being used as a particular type of retail business. This is because there are likely to be fewer sites suitable for a superstore development, and more sites suitable for a high street store (that are not subject to such a restriction).

4.23 Furthermore, barriers to entry or expansion may be more significant where the number of other sites suitable for use in the related market is limited as a result of planning restrictions.

4.24 Similarly, there may be circumstances where the ability to compete in a market requires access to land in a particular location, such as land in the proximity of a port or transport network. A restriction preventing potential competitors from using land in such a location is more likely to appreciably restrict competition.

4.25 Where effective entry which prevents or erodes market power in the related market is likely to occur within one to two years (for example as a result of land being sold, developed or converted from other uses), entry barriers can in general be regarded as low.[46]

Other considerations

4.26 It is not only the position of the parties to the agreement on the related market, or the availability of other suitable land in the affected market which is important, but also the extent of the relevant restriction. The longer the duration of the restriction the more significant the impact on competition is likely to be.

CUMULATIVE IMPACT OF MULTIPLE AGREEMENTS

4.27 Where an agreement forms part of a series or group of similar agreements on a given market, and access to the relevant market or competition on that market is significantly restricted by the cumulative effect of parallel networks of similar agreements practised by competitors on that market, an individual agreement may fall within the Chapter I prohibition if the agreement makes an appreciable contribution to the cumulative effect.[47]

TYPES OF RESTRICTIONS THAT ARE UNLIKELY TO APPRECIABLY RESTRICT COMPETITION

4.28 Obligations or restrictions in land agreements are unlikely to give rise to negative effects on competition where the agreement does not foreclose access to or dampen competition on a related market where the land is being used to carry out an economic activity.

4.29 Provisions in commercial property agreements that are unlikely to give rise to competition concerns include for example: (i) covenants relating to the payment of service charges and meeting of certain financial criteria, and (ii) restrictions imposed on a lessee regarding alterations, repairs, obstructions to the premises, applications for planning permission, advertisements, or hours of use.[48]

4.30 Provisions in commercial property agreements which relate to the use of premises are also generally unlikely to raise competition concerns.[49] This would include, for example, where the owner of a site such as a shopping centre or retail park restricts the specific line or lines of business that may be carried out by a lessee, in order to achieve its desired 'retail mix' and to ensure the attractiveness of a shopping centre to consumers.[50] However, where a restriction is reciprocal (for example, a lease in a shopping centre which restricts the lessee to selling a particular type of product and this is accepted by the lessee on the basis that no other lessee in the shopping centre will be permitted to sell that type of product), it will be necessary to consider whether the agreement may appreciably restrict competition (see paragraph 4.9 above).

4.31 Further, where an owner of one property benefits from a restrictive covenant that restricts activities that may be carried out on an adjacent property which could block access to or interfere with the enjoyment of their site, this would generally be unlikely to appreciably restrict competition (subject to the considerations in paragraph 4.28 above).

4.32 The Chapter I prohibition does not apply to an agreement to the extent it is a planning obligation, by virtue of paragraph 1, Schedule 3 of the Act. This includes planning obligations made, for example, under section 106 of the Town and Country Planning Act 1990.

OTHER TYPES OF RESTRICTIONS ON COMPETITION (OUTSIDE THE SCOPE OF THIS GUIDELINE)

4.33 This guideline covers restrictions in land agreements that affect or limit the way in which the land may be used, or how a right over land may be exercised. To the extent that an anti-competitive agreement is not a land agreement because it does not create, alter, transfer, or terminate an interest in land, or a land agreement includes other restrictions on competition (restrictions not relating to the way the land may be used or how a right over the land may be exercised), it may restrict competition within the meaning of the Chapter I prohibition and Article 101.

4.34 For example, if a retail firm leases land to a competitor on terms which require the competitor not to undercut the landlord's retail prices, this could constitute price-fixing behaviour. An agreement between tenants as to the nature of goods they will each sell in a particular area would not be a land agreement, but could constitute a form of market-sharing. Price-fixing, market-sharing and other forms of cartel behaviour are generally considered capable of having an appreciable impact on competition regardless of the parties' market shares. The OFT guideline *Agreements and concerted practices*[51] provides guidance on the prohibition on anti-competitive agreements more generally.

4.35 A land agreement may also be entered into in the context of a trading relationship between parties and/or may contain restrictions which relate to the conditions under which a trade or activity may be carried out or under which a party may purchase, sell or resell goods or services from the premises.

4.36 For example, a supplier of a certain product leases land to a retailer of that product on terms may require the retailer to source all of its requirements for a particular type of product from the supplier. This type of restraint may restrict competition where, for example, this significantly forecloses the relevant market to competing suppliers.

4.37 The European Commission's *Guidelines on Vertical Restraints*[52] sets out principles for the assessment of vertical agreements under Article 101 TFEU, including the application of the EU Block Exemption Regulation for vertical agreements.[53]

NOTES

[39] For example, it may be relevant to consider whether a particular agreement is necessary for an undertaking to enter a new market successfully. In such cases, it is necessary to appraise how likely it is that a party would be able to enter the relevant market in the absence of the agreement. It must be clear that such an agreement would be objectively necessary for undertakings to enter the market in a similar setting. See paragraph 18 of the European Commission's *Guidelines on the application of Article 81(3)* [now 101(3)], (OJ C101, 27.4.2004, p.97) and Case T-328/03 *O2 (Germany) v Commission* [2006] 5 CMLR 258. In the *O2* case, the European Court stated that the examination of competition in the absence of an agreement may be particularly necessary in markets undergoing liberalisation or emerging markets, where effective competition may be problematic owing to the presence of a dominant operator, the concentrated nature of the market structure or the existence of significant barriers to entry. See also Case 56/65 *Société Technique Minière v. Maschinenbau ULM GmbH*, [1966] ECR 235, [1966] CMLR 357, Case 258/78 *Nungesser (LC) KG and Kurt Eisele v Commission* [1982] ECR 2015, [1983] 1 CMLR 278, Case *Métropole Télévision SA v Commission* OJ C354, 23.11.1996, p.18, ECJ, Case T-65/98*Van den Bergh Foods vs. Commission* [1998] ECR II-2641, [1998] 5 CMLR 475, [2003] ECR II-4653, [2004] 4 CMLR 14, CFI). On the other hand, considerations

regarding the indispensability of a restriction to the profitability of a project or business on a particular market, in light of the competitive situation on that market, should be assessed under the exemption framework. If the assessment involves weighing up the precompetitive benefits of an agreement against its restrictive impact, this balancing should be carried out within the exemption framework. The application of the exemption criteria to land agreements is explained in chapter 6 of this guideline.

40 A market is foreclosed either completely or partially when undertakings face barriers to entering that market, or barriers to expansion once in that market.

41 See footnote 6 above.

42 The OFT guideline *Assessment of Market Power* (OFT 415) explains in further detail how the OFT will assess whether undertakings possess market power.

43 Whilst counting firms or fascias in a particular area may provide a good first proxy for market shares, counting firms or fascias does not take into account differences in shares of sales and the size distribution of firms. This may not be suitable when there are large differences in the sizes of firms or their sales. For the purposes of the assessment of independent fascias stores under common ownership should be treated as a single fascia (even if branded differently).

44 The relevant market share will be the combined market share not only of the parties to the agreement but also of other undertakings belonging to the same group of undertakings as the parties to the agreement. These will include, in the case of each party to the agreement: (i) undertakings over which it exercises control; and (ii) undertakings which exercise control over it as well as any other undertakings which are controlled by those undertakings.

45 The OFT will consider not only the scale of any barriers to entry and/or expansion that may impact on the likelihood of entry or expansion on a related market, but also whether firms have the ability and incentive to enter that market (or the intent to do so).

46 Paragraph 117 of the European Commission's *Guidelines on Vertical Restraints* OJ C130, 19.5.2010, p.1, is illustrative to note in this respect.

47 Case C-234/89 *Stergios Delimitis v Henniger Bräu AG* [1991] ECR I-935.

48 Such restrictions could in some cases be regarded as 'ancillary' to the transfer of an interest in land and may fall outside the scope of the Chapter I prohibition. Cases such as Case 161-84 [1986] ECR 353, *Pronuptia de Paris v Schillgalis* and Case 42/82 [1985] ECR 2545, *Remia BV and Verenidge Bedrijven and Nutricia v Commission* are illustrative in this respect. A restriction is directly related to a main transaction if it is subordinate to the implementation of that transaction and is inseparably linked to it. The test of necessity implies that the restriction must be objectively necessary for the implementation of the main transaction and be proportionate to it (see paragraphs 28 to 31 of the European Commission's *Guidelines on the application of Article 81(3)* [now 101(3)], (OJ C101, 27.4.2004, p.97)). If the assessment involves weighing up the pro-competitive benefits of an agreement against its restrictive impact, this balancing should be carried out within the exemption framework. The concept of 'ancillary' restraints must therefore be distinguished from the application of the exemption criteria, which concerns the economic benefits that may be produced by a restrictive agreement and which are balanced against the restrictive effects of an agreement.

49 Restrictions on the use of premise can be expressed positively (a permitted user clause) or negatively (a restricted user clause).

50 The owner of the site may also request certain types of retailers to be located within a particular 'zone' of the centre in order to ensure a logical layout.

51 *Agreements and concerted practices* (OFT401).

52 OJ C130, 19.5.2010, p.1.

53 Commission Regulation on the application of Article 101(3) TFEU to categories of vertical agreements and concerted practices OJ L102, 23.4.2010, p.1. As explained in footnote 19 above, the EU Block Exemption for vertical agreements also applies under UK law by virtue of the parallel exemption regime under section 10 of the Act. Certain restrictions will remove the benefit of the block exemption from an agreement, such as restrictions which impose fixed or minimum resale prices at which goods may be sold.

5 APPLYING THE EXEMPTION CRITERIA

[3.388]

5.1 Agreements which fall within the scope of the Chapter I prohibition or Article 101 may nevertheless be exempt from the prohibition if the criteria set out below are satisfied, with no prior decision to that effect being required.[54] Such an agreement is valid and enforceable from the moment that the conditions in section 9(1) are satisfied and will continue to benefit from exemption for so long as those criteria remain satisfied.

5.2 It is for the party wishing to rely on exemption to prove that the criteria are satisfied. Parties therefore need to assess whether the criteria apply on a case by case basis.[55]

5.3 The four cumulative criteria which must be satisfied to qualify for exemption are as follows.

- The agreement must contribute to improving production or distribution, or to promoting technical or economic progress.
- It must allow consumers a fair share of the resulting benefits.
- It must not impose restrictions beyond those indispensable to achieving those objectives.
- It must not afford the parties the possibility of eliminating competition in respect of a substantial part of the products in question.

5.4 The remainder of this chapter provides guidance on how to apply the criteria to land agreements. The European Commission has issued Guidelines on the application of Article 101(3) of the TFEU.[56] As set out in chapters 1 and 3, the provisions of Chapter I prohibition and Article 101 TFEU are in most respects identical in substance. The OFT will therefore have regard to the Commission's Guidelines when considering the exemption provisions in section 9(1) of the Act. Parties should also consider the Commission's Guidelines when assessing their own agreements.

CONDITION (I) – EFFICIENCY GAINS

5.5 For exemption to apply, the benefits of the agreement must outweigh (or at least match) its negative impact on competition. Parties must therefore show that a restrictive agreement contributes to improving production or distribution, or to promoting technical or economic progress. These benefits are sometimes referred to as the efficiency gains or benefits of the agreement.

5.6 There is no exhaustive list of the types of efficiency gain which might satisfy this criterion. Examples might include:

- the creation of one or more new retail outlets
- more efficient distribution of products, or
- a greater range of products being available to consumers.

5.7 By way of illustration, one retailer (a department store) might be granted the exclusive right to operate in a shopping centre. This agreement may give rise to efficiency gains because the owner of the centre considers that the department store will attract considerable footfall to the centre. Other retailers may benefit from the footfall generated by the department store, which also contributes to the profitability of the shopping centre overall.

CONDITION (III) – INDISPENSABILITY OF THE RESTRICTIONS

5.8 The third criterion is that the agreement must not contain restrictions that go beyond those which are indispensable to achieving the benefits identified. For practical purposes, it is usually simplest to apply criterion (iii) before criterion (ii).

5.9 The question is not whether in the absence of the restriction the agreement would not have been concluded, but whether the benefits could have been achieved by means of a less restrictive agreement. Put another way, a restriction will be considered indispensable if its absence would eliminate or significantly reduce the efficiencies that follow from the agreement, or make it significantly less likely that they will materialise **and** there is no less restrictive means of achieving the benefits.

5.10 When considering whether there are other less restrictive means of achieving the benefits, parties are not required to consider purely theoretical alternatives, only those which are economically practicable. This requires an assessment of the market conditions and business realities facing the parties to the agreement.

5.11 Using the shopping centre example referred to in paragraph 5.7 above, the department store may need to invest considerable amounts in order to set up its store within the shopping centre and may only be prepared to make this investment if it has a guarantee that it will be the only department store in the shopping centre for a certain period.[57]

5.12 Conversely, the indispensability criterion may not be met where a shopping centre owner is granting an exclusive right to a retailer to operate as a particular type of retailer in an area in order to ensure a particular mix of different types of retailer. Although customers may benefit from the shopping centre containing a mix of retailers (or from a more efficient use of space), this objective could potentially be achieved through covenants in lease agreements which restrict how different retail units may be used. Restrictions granting exclusivity to each retailer within the centre may therefore (while ensuring a mix of retailers) go further than is necessary to achieve this type of benefit.

5.13 In many cases, the question of indispensability will also relate to the duration of a restriction. It is necessary to consider the duration of the restriction and whether it is longer than necessary to achieve the benefits identified. Generally, restrictions of a longer duration are less likely to be considered indispensable.

5.14 Such a restriction would be justified only for so long as is necessary to give the parties sufficient certainty that they will be able to recoup their investment in a development. The appropriate duration of the exclusivity will depend on the specific facts of each case. In a retail context, for example, it may be relevant to take into account the time necessary for a store to reach mature sales (at a point when its sales are projected to grow at a rate at or around inflation) that is, a stable revenue and customer base to provide the required return on investment.

CONDITION (II) – FAIR SHARE FOR CONSUMERS

5.15 The restrictive agreement must allow consumers a fair share of the benefits identified under the first criterion. This means that it is not sufficient for benefits to accrue to the parties to the agreement – consumers must also benefit.

5.16 The concept of 'fair share' implies that the benefits passed on to consumers must compensate for the negative impact from the restriction of competition. The net effect of the agreement must at least be neutral from the point of view of those consumers that are likely to be affected by the agreement.

5.17 In the illustrative shopping centre example described in paragraph 5.7 above, the agreement restricts competition between retailers within the shopping centre. This restriction impacts on consumers who might otherwise benefit from greater competition between retailers. For example, if the shopping centre contained two department stores instead of one with exclusive rights, the competition between them could improve price, quality, range or service standards for the benefit of consumers.

5.18 In this scenario, other retailers may benefit from the footfall generated by the department store, which may lead to economies of scale which pass through to consumers. Further, there may be evidence that consumers value having this particular retailer in the centre and consumers may benefit from the shopping centre having a greater variety of different types of retailer as a result of the restriction.

5.19 The greater the restriction on competition, the greater must be the efficiencies and the pass-on to consumers to justify that restriction. This implies that if the restrictive effects of an agreement are relatively limited and the efficiencies substantial, it is more likely that consumers will receive a 'fair share' of the resulting benefits. If, on the other hand, the restrictive effects of the agreement are substantial and the efficiencies relatively limited, it is unlikely that this criterion will be fulfilled.

CONDITION (IV) – NO ELIMINATION OF COMPETITION

5.20 Finally, in order to benefit from exemption, a restrictive agreement must not allow the parties the possibility of eliminating competition in respect of a substantial part of the products in question.

5.21 Whether competition is being eliminated for these purposes will depend on the degree of competition existing prior to the agreement and on the impact of the restrictive agreement – that is, the extent of the reduction of competition brought about by the agreement.

5.22 Where competition within a market is already weak, a relatively small reduction may result in competition being 'eliminated' for the purposes of this criterion. Similarly, the greater the reduction of competition caused by the agreement, the greater the likelihood that competition in respect of a substantial part of the products concerned will be eliminated.

5.23 Both actual and potential competition must be considered. While sources of actual competition are usually the more important and easier to verify, sources of potential competition must also be taken into account. The assessment of potential competition requires an analysis of barriers to entry facing firms that are not already competing within the relevant market. The OFT would expect any party to a restrictive land agreement seeking to rely on potential competition and the absence of barriers to entry to be able to identify the sources of potential competition and provide evidence that these sources constitute a real competitive constraint.

NOTES

54 Section 9(1) of the Act and Article 101(3) TFEU.

55 Regulation 1/2003 (Council Regulation (EC) No 1/2003 of 16 December 2002, often referred to as the Modernisation Regulation) abolished the system of notifying agreements for exemption under Article 81(3) of the EC Treaty [now 101(3) TFEU]. The same system was adopted in the UK through the amendment of the Act.

56 *Guidelines on the application of Article 81(3)* [now 101(3)] (OJ C101, 27.4.2004, p. 97).

57 The profitability of a development such as a shopping centre may depend on certain conditions being offered by the developers such as exclusivity in order to secure the commitment of a particular lessee. This is different from a situation where market entry would not have occurred **at all** but for the existence of an equivalent agreement and the commitment of a particular lessee (such as an anchor tenant) is key to the commercial viability of a development. If market entry would not have occurred at all, absent the agreement in question, the agreement may not be restrictive of competition. This will require an objective assessment of the possibility of a party to penetrate the relevant market without the benefit of the restriction in question.

6 ABUSE OF DOMINANCE

[3.389]

6.1 Chapter II of the Act and Article 102 of the TFEU prohibit conduct by one or more undertakings which amounts to an **abuse of a dominant position** in a market and which:

- may affect trade within the United Kingdom or any part of it (in the case of the Chapter II prohibition), or which
- may affect trade in the internal market or a substantial part of it, in so far as it may affect trade between Member States (in the case of Article 102).

6.2 These provisions apply equally to conduct relating to land as they do to any other conduct. The exclusion previously in place for land agreements did not apply to the prohibitions on the abuse of a dominant position in Chapter II of the Act and Article 102 TFEU.

6.3 Firms are generally free to decide to whom they sell or lease land, and the price at which they do so. Conduct regarding land will only be prohibited by Chapter II of the Act and/or Article 102 in limited circumstances.

6.4 The tests applied under the Chapter II prohibition and Article 102 TFEU have two common elements:

- whether a firm is dominant, and
- if it is, whether it is abusing that dominant position.

6.5 The prohibition under both Article 102 TFEU and the Chapter II prohibition relates to the **abuse** of a dominant position, not the **holding** of the position.

DOMINANT POSITION

6.6 Whether a firm is dominant depends on two questions: the definition of the relevant market and whether the firm holds a dominant position within that market.[58]

6.7 A business holds a dominant position on a market if it is able to behave independently of the normal constraints imposed by competitors, suppliers and customers. A dominant position may be held by one firm on its own or by one or more legally independent firms where they are linked in such a way that they adopt a common policy in the market (joint or collective dominance).

6.8 A firm will not be dominant unless it possesses substantial market power. The OFT will assess the market power of a firm by looking at the competitive constraints it faces in the relevant market. Those constraints may include, but may not be limited to, the bargaining power of customers (including tenants) and the possibility of new entry onto the market by, for instance, converting other premises or building new premises.

6.9 The market share of a firm is an important factor in assessing market power but it does not, on its own, determine whether a firm is dominant. For example, it is also necessary to consider the position of other undertakings operating in the same market and how market shares have changed over time. An undertaking is more likely to be dominant if its competitors have relatively weak positions in the relevant market, or if it has enjoyed a high and stable market share.

6.10 Generally speaking, a market share above 50 per cent gives rise to a presumption of dominance, in the absence of evidence to the contrary.[59] The OFT considers that a position of dominance is unlikely where a firm's market share is below 40 per cent.

6.11 For further guidance on this topic see the OFT guideline *Abuse of a dominant position* (OFT402) and the European Commission's *Guidance on the Commission's enforcement priorities in applying Article 82 of the EC Treaty* [now Article 102 TFEU] *to abusive exclusionary conduct by dominant undertakings*.[60]

ABUSE

6.12 The prohibitions under Chapter II of the Act and Article 102 of the TFEU relate to the abuse of the dominant position. Holding a dominant position is not unlawful, but it is unlawful to abuse that position. The Act and Article 102 TFEU set out examples of conduct which may amount to abuse of a dominant position, but these lists are not exhaustive and are for illustration only. The important question is whether the conduct of a dominant firm can be regarded as an abuse of a dominant position. This may occur if a dominant firm pursues conduct which is different from conduct that is normally adopted in the course of competition in the market, in a way that exploits customers or has an exclusionary effect on competitors.

6.13 In certain circumstances, the prohibitions under Chapter II of the Act and Article 102 TFEU may apply where an undertaking that is dominant in one market commits an abuse in a different but closely associated market.[61]

6.14 Examples of conduct which may be considered to be an abuse of a dominant position are given in the OFT's guideline *Abuse of a dominant position*. In relation to land, this may include conduct which excludes competitors in a relevant market, for example by limiting access to a so-called 'essential facility' or where a dominant firm seeks to use restrictions in land agreements as part of a strategic campaign to exclude competitors from a market, particularly where regulatory constraints such as planning or licensing limit the supply of suitable land for the competing activity.[62] It is also possible for a firm to abuse a dominant position through 'exploitative' conduct such as the charging of excessive prices for land (that is, prices which are significantly above the competitive level) or unjustified discrimination between tenants.

6.15 Unlike the Chapter I prohibition and Article 101 TFEU, there are no exemptions (or a regime equivalent to that of Article 101(3) TFEU) from the Chapter II prohibition or Article 102 of the TFEU.[63]

NOTES

58 See chapter 3 regarding market definition.

59 The European Court has stated that dominance can be presumed in the absence of evidence to the contrary if an undertaking has a market share persistently above 50 per cent, see Case C62/86, *AKZO Chemie BV v Commission* [1993] 5 CMLR 215.

60 OJ C45, 24.2.2009, p. 7.

61 This principle was established by the European Court in Case T-83/91 *Tetra Pak v European Commission* [1994] ECR II-755.

62 Generally, a dominant firm will not be obliged to sell or lease land to any potential acquirer or lessee if there are objective reasons not to do so.

63 The Act sets out a number of specific exclusions from the Chapter II prohibition. Although the concept of exclusion is not specifically recognised in relation to Article 102 TFEU, under EU law certain types of conduct are in effect, excluded from the application of Article 102 TFEU. For further details on these exclusions, see OFT guideline *Abuse of a dominant position* (OFT402).

7 CONSEQUENCES OF BREACH

[3.390]

7.1 A breach of the Act has a number of potential consequences, as set out below. These include: (i) financial penalties, (ii) director disqualification orders, (iii) the unenforceability of an agreement which infringes the Chapter I prohibition, and (iv) private actions.

FINANCIAL PENALTIES

7.2 Parties to a prohibited agreement (that is, an agreement which falls within the scope of the prohibition and does not benefit from exemption), or a party abusing a dominant position are susceptible to enforcement action by the OFT, European Commission or a sectoral regulator.[64] These authorities have the power to investigate suspected infringements, to impose financial penalties and to give directions to take steps to bring an infringement to an end.[65] By statute,[66] the maximum penalty that can be imposed for an infringement is 10 per cent of a party's worldwide turnover.

7.3 The OFT and sectoral regulators cannot make a finding of infringement of the Chapter I prohibition or impose penalties for land agreements in respect of the period prior to 6 April 2011.[67]

7.4 The OFT has published guidance on the way in which it calculates financial penalties under the Act,[68] and the OFT's decisional practice and the case law of the UK courts gives further guidance on how this is applied in practice. The OFT calculates the appropriate amount of a penalty on a case-by-case basis according to the principles set out in the guidance.[69]

7.5 Small businesses may be immune from financial penalties under the Act in certain circumstances.[70]

7.6 Where a party has used best endeavours[71] to amend or remove a clause in breach of the Chapter I prohibition from an agreement (and where relevant, to remove this restriction from the relevant land register), and has not sought to enforce it, the OFT may, depending on the relevant facts of each case, consider this to be a mitigating factor when determining the appropriate amount of any financial penalty (if the OFT considers that it is in fact appropriate to impose a financial penalty).[72]

OTHER CONSEQUENCES

7.7 In addition to financial penalties, the OFT and certain sectoral regulators have the power to apply for disqualification orders against directors in certain circumstances following a competition law infringement.[73]

7.8 An agreement which contains a prohibited restriction is void and unenforceable.[74]

7.9 The effect of this on the remainder of an agreement is a matter for the law which governs the particular agreement. A court may consider it possible, as a matter of contract law, to sever provisions which infringe the Chapter I prohibition from the remainder of an agreement. If this is the case, the unenforceability will affect only the offending provisions in question and the remaining terms of the agreement will remain valid and enforceable.[75] This guideline does not cover the practical consequences of a land agreement being void and unenforceable.

7.10 In addition, the parties to a prohibited agreement, or a party abusing a dominant position, may also be susceptible to private actions before the UK courts for damages or injunctive relief for breaches of competition law by any person who has suffered a loss as a result of the infringement.[76]

NOTES

64 The following sectoral regulators have concurrent powers to enforce competition law in the UK: the Office of Communications; the Gas and Electricity Markets Authority; the Water Services Regulation Authority; the Office of Rail Regulation; the Civil Aviation Authority; and the Northern Ireland Authority for Utility Regulation.

65 See the OFT guideline *Enforcement* (OFT407).

66 Section 36(8) of the Act and Competition Act 1998 (Determination of Turnover for Penalties) (Amendment) Order 2000 (SI 2000/309), as amended.

67 By virtue of the Competition Act 1998 (Land Agreements Exclusion and Revocation) Order 2004 (SI 2004/1260) in place prior to 6 April 2011 and, prior to that, the Competition Act 1998 (Land and Vertical Agreements Exclusion) Order 2000 (SI 2000/310). Land agreements entered into before 6 April 2011 will continue to benefit from exclusion until that date, but will cease to benefit from exclusion from that date.

68 *OFT's Guidance as to the appropriate amount of a penalty* (OFT 423).

69 The OFT will generally impose penalties on all parties to an infringing agreement. However, depending on the precise circumstances of the case, the OFT may consider it appropriate to distinguish between a party with the benefit of a restriction and a party with the burden in assessing either the appropriate amount of a penalty, or whether it is appropriate to impose a penalty at all.

70 Sections 39 and 40 of the Act provide limited immunity from financial penalties for small agreements in relation to infringements of the Chapter I prohibition and for conduct of minor significance in relation to infringements of the Chapter II prohibition (see further Competition Act 1998 (Small Agreements and Conduct of Minor Significance) Regulations 2000 (SI 2000/262)). This immunity does not apply to any infringements of Article 101 or 102 TFEU or to infringements of the Chapter I prohibition which are price-fixing agreements. This immunity may be withdrawn by the OFT in certain circumstances. Further details are set out in the OFT guideline *Enforcement* (OFT407).

71 Best endeavours do not necessarily include an obligation to make any payment to procure that a party consents to the release of the restrictive covenant.

72 For an illustrative example of the steps that might be taken to remove a restriction from the relevant land register, where appropriate, see Article 4 of the Groceries Controlled Land Order.

73 See OFT guidance *Director disqualification orders in competition cases* (OFT510).

74 Section 2(4) of the Act.

75 This has been stated, amongst others, by the High Court in *Inntrepreneur Estates Ltd v Mason*, [1994] 68 P&CR 53, [1993] 2 CMLR 293, QBD, and by the Court of Appeal in *Inntrepreneur Estates (GL) Ltd v Boyes*, [1995] ECC 16, [1993] 2 EGLR 112, CA. See also *Byrne v Inntrepreneur Beer Supply Co Ltd* [1999] EuLR 634. Whether a provision that infringes the Act is in fact severable from the remainder of an agreement will depend on the relevant facts. For example, the courts have previously taken into account considerations such as whether the severing of the restriction materially changes the nature of the agreement between the parties and whether the restriction formed the whole or a substantial part of the consideration for the contract.

76 See the OFT's *Quick guide to private litigation in competition cases.*

8 THE OFT'S ADMINISTRATIVE PRIORITIES

[3.391]

8.1 The OFT is not obliged to investigate every suspected infringement. When deciding whether to take action in relation to a suspected infringement of competition law, the OFT will have regard to its prioritisation principles, which include expected impact of its work on consumers, the strategic significance of OFT action, and the risks and resources involved in possible work.[77]

8.2 Given that many types of agreements concerning the use of land have previously been excluded from the application of UK competition law and therefore parties in the property sector are adjusting to a change in the law, the OFT has set out a category of land agreements in relation to which the OFT is unlikely to consider taking further action, on the basis that it would be less likely that significant negative effects on competition and consumers would arise and/or the exemption criteria could be met in respect of such agreements.[78]

8.3 The OFT considers that only a minority of restrictions in land agreements will infringe the Chapter I prohibition. Chapter 4 of this guideline sets out examples of restrictions that generally do not give rise to competition concerns in the OFT's view and in respect of which the OFT is unlikely to take further action.

8.4 Chapter 4 of this guideline also sets out that there are two main categories of agreement that are more likely to restrict competition.

8.5 First, the OFT considers that if the parties to a land agreement are competitors in a relevant market and a restriction in a land agreement is aimed at sharing markets, the agreement is very likely to constitute a serious infringement of the Chapter I prohibition. The market share threshold set out in the paragraph below will not be applied in such cases.

8.6 Second, the OFT may be concerned where the parties to the agreement seek to use a land restriction to foreclose existing or potential competitors in a relevant market or dampen competition in this market. However, whether such an agreement will give rise to significant negative effects on competition will depend on the scope of the relevant market where the land is being used and whether one or more of the parties to the agreement possesses market power in this market. The OFT is unlikely to take further action if none of the parties to the agreement has (or, as a result of the agreement, obtains) a share of the relevant market which exceeds 30 per cent. The 'relevant market' for this purpose refers to the (downstream) related market where the land that is the subject of the agreement is being used to carry out an economic activity. Parties will need to consider the product and geographic scope of the related market in applying this threshold.

8.7 Chapter 4 of this guideline sets out relevant methods of assessing market shares. In most cases, the OFT considers that the most appropriate method of calculating market shares is according to value of sales in the relevant market. However in retail markets, it may be pragmatic to calculate market shares by counting the number of independent fascias in the relevant market. In retail markets, if there are four or more independent fascias in the relevant market (including the party to the agreement that is benefiting from the restriction in question), the OFT is likely to take the view that the market share threshold set out in paragraph 8.6 above is not exceeded.

8.8 It may also be relevant to consider how market shares have changed over time. In cases where a party's market share at the time of entering into an agreement is initially not more than 30 per cent but subsequently increases, the OFT will generally take the view that where a party's market share was initially not more than 30 per cent, but has subsequently increased to not more than 35 per cent, within a two-year period, the threshold is not met.

8.9 In exceptional cases, the OFT may decide to investigate an agreement or agreements where parties have market shares which do not exceed the 30 per cent threshold but where there appear to be significant negative effects on competition: for example, where a long-term exclusivity arrangement appears to be significantly restricting access to a particular market, or where there are cumulative effects arising from a number of similar agreements affecting a relevant market.

8.10 The approach set out in this chapter should not be regarded as a statement of how the Chapter I prohibition applies to land agreements (in particular, it is possible that appreciable effects on competition could arise below the market share threshold outlined in paragraph 8.6 above).

8.11 The OFT will keep this approach under review on the basis of further experience regarding land agreements.

NOTES

77 See *Prioritisation Principles* (OFT 953).

78 Paragraphs 8.3 to 8.9 apply to land agreements which contain restrictions or obligations regarding the use of land or the way that a right in land may be exercised. These paragraphs do not replace the OFT's prioritisation principles, which will apply in all cases relating to land agreements. Restrictions which are outside the scope of this guideline are referred to in chapter 4.

9 WORKED EXAMPLES

EXAMPLE 1 (RESTRICTIVE COVENANT FOR THE BENEFIT OF ADJACENT LAND)

[3.392]

9.1 A restrictive covenant prevents the owner of land adjacent to a theatre from being used for certain industrial purposes (regardless of permitted planning uses), for so long as the theatre remains in place. The restriction has been put in place to prevent noisy activities being carried out on land adjacent to the theatre, which may interfere with performances at the theatre.

Summary analysis:

9.2 The restriction is unlikely to infringe the Chapter I prohibition, since it is unlikely to have the object or effect of restricting competition on a related market. In particular, the restriction does not appear to foreclose competitors of the party which owns the theatre or reinforce its position on this related market.

9.3 The scope of the restriction (affecting industrial uses, rather than all uses and lasting only for so long as the theatre remains in place) does not appear to be wider than is necessary to achieve the objective of the restriction, which is to avoid interferences with the use of the theatre).[79]

EXAMPLE 2 (TERMS OF SALE – PLANNING PERMISSION ALLOCATION BETWEEN COMPETITORS)

9.4 Company A owns a large development site and is planning to build houses on it. Having considered alternative options, as well as its capacity and access to funding, Company A chooses to develop only a part of the site and sell the rest to other home builders. Company A divides the site into three plots, keeping one for itself and inviting offers for the other two plots from other house builders.

9.5 The planning permission for the whole site originally owned by Company A limits the number of houses that can be built to 300. Company A imposes a restriction on each of the two plots that are sold which specifies that a maximum of 100 houses can be built on each plot.

Summary analysis:

9.6 The restriction on the number of houses that can be built on each plot is unlikely to infringe the Chapter I prohibition. This is unlikely to constitute a restriction of competition, given that the restrictions are necessary for company A and the buyers of the two segregated parcels to know with a sufficient degree of certainty how the terms of the planning permission would apply to each of the plots, and neither of the parties would have been able to enter into the agreement without such knowledge.[80]

EXAMPLE 3 (PERMITTED USE RESTRICTION)

9.7 Buildco is a property developer. Buildco has developed an office complex and rents space in this complex to business lessees. All of Buildco's leases contain covenants preventing the lessee from using the space for any purpose other than as offices. They also contain covenants preventing Buildco from leasing any of the office space for any other purposes. The complex is in an area with plenty of other offices and retail outlets. The property market in the area is largely competitive and premises of both types are usually available to let.

9.8 One of the office lessees (Shopco) wants to open a shop in the office space that it is currently using, but is prevented to do so by the existing use restriction.

Summary analysis

9.9 As noted above, many leases contain permitted user restrictions and the vast majority of these restrictions are unlikely to give rise to competition concerns. In this example, the restrictions are designed to ensure the continuing use of the premises as offices, given that this is the land-owner's intended purpose for the site, as well as guaranteeing a certain type of environment for other lessees using the premises as offices. These restrictions do not appear to confer exclusive use of land to any lessee or otherwise protect lessees within the complex from competition on the related market where they carry out an economic activity.

9.10 In this example, the permitted use restrictions are unlikely to infringe the Chapter I prohibition.

9.11 There is no obligation on Buildco to allow Shopco to convert office space into shop space.

EXAMPLE 4 (DEVELOPMENT AGREEMENT INCLUDING A RESTRICTION ON THE USE OF LAND)

9.12 The University of Scholartown owns a large area of land on the fringes of Scholartown and wants to develop university accommodation for students on its land.

9.13 The University lacks the necessary capital to develop the land itself, so grants a long lease of part of that area to a developer. The developer agrees to build and provide accommodation at affordable prices for students (which are defined in the lease as a function of average student accommodation prices in the UK).

9.14 The University undertakes not to allow the construction of student accommodation on land that it owns unless a demand test for further accommodation is satisfied. The restriction ensures that, for the term of the lease, there is adequate demand for the accommodation constructed by the developer, hence ensuring sufficient profitability of the contract for the developer.

9.15 There are five existing student halls of residence in Scholartown. Three of these are owned by the University and the two others are owned by two different parties. Students look for accommodation both in student halls and the private accommodation market. There is also some undeveloped land near the University campus, owned by a third party, which would be suitable for the development of other halls of residence buildings.

Summary analysis

9.16 The restriction on the construction of student accommodation on other land owned by the University has the potential to restrict competition in the market for the provision of accommodation to students around the University.[81]

9.17 In this example, the restriction may not have an appreciable effect on competition in the market, as there is likely to be lots of private accommodation available in Scholartown and there are also a number of other alternative student accommodation sites in Scholartown (as well as the possibility of further sites being built on land not owned by the University).

9.18 If other alternative accommodation for students were more limited, this agreement could appreciably restrict competition. If this were the case, it is possible that this agreement could meet the criteria for exemption. First, the agreement facilitates the development of new accommodation for students and increases the accommodation available in Scholartown overall. Secondly, these benefits are passed on to consumers, in the form of new, affordable accommodation for students.

9.19 In this example, it may be the case that the developer would not commit its investment in the site without the exclusivity provision regarding the use of land that is owned by the University. Notably, the demand test should ensure that the restriction will be no greater than necessary to ensure profitability for the developer. The restrictive agreement is unlikely to substantially eliminate competition in any market.

EXAMPLE 5 (SHOPPING CENTRE — 'ANCHOR TENANT')

9.20 Landco is a property developer that builds shopping centres and leases retail units in those centres. Landco plans to build a large, state of the art shopping centre (the Shop Here Centre), located in the fringes of Townbridge. Landco is seeking to attract a high-profile anchor tenant in the shopping centre and plans to do so by offering favourable terms.

9.21 Buy&Buy operates large department stores across the country. Landco has offered Buy&Buy a 25-year lease agreement for a big store in Shop Here. The financial commitment of Buy&Buy to the project is key for Landco to obtain access to finance in this project. The presence of Buy&Buy in the shopping centre will also be crucial to attract customers and other businesses to the centre.

9.22 The lease with Buy&Buy will contain an exclusivity clause whereby Landco will not lease other retail plots at Shop Here to a department store competing with Buy&Buy. There will be about 20 more small and medium size retail units in the Shop Here Centre, which will compete with Buy&Buy to a certain extent on some products that are sold in its store.

9.23 The vast majority of Shop Here's customers come from within a drive time of 25 minutes. The Shop Here Centre will be located about a 10-minute drive from the centre of Townbridge. There is also a shopping centre of a similar size, called the Shop There Centre at the other end of Townbridge, located about a 15-minute drive from Shop Here. There is one large department store in the Shop There Centre owned by a rival retailer (Buy More). There are various retail businesses in the centre of Townbridge.

Summary analysis:

9.24 The exclusivity clause protects Buy&Buy from competition from other department stores within the Shop Here Centre. It is possible that the restriction may not fall within the Chapter I prohibition if it could be demonstrated that the agreement enables market entry (that is, as a result of the building of the shopping centre) which would not have occurred **at all** without the existence of an equivalent agreement.[82]

9.25 Otherwise, the restriction may appreciably restrict actual or potential competition in the related market in which Buy&Buy competes for customers.

9.26 The market where Buy&Buy competes is likely to include all stores of a similar size within the area where Buy&Buy draws its customers from. This may include other retailers within the shopping centre. On the assumption that this is a 25-minute drive-time area around Buy&Buy, it would also include the other shopping centres and retailers in the vicinity of the centre (including Buy More) and other retailers in Townbridge. On the basis that Buy&Buy competes in a sufficiently wide and competitive market, it may be that the exclusivity clause does not have an appreciable effect on competition in the related market. There may also be other land available for other potential department stores.

9.27 If the exclusivity clause were found to appreciably restrict competition, it would be necessary to consider whether the restrictive agreement would benefit from exemption.

9.28 First, the agreement gives rise to efficiencies as it facilitates the development of the new shopping centre which increases overall choice and competition in Townbridge. The presence of Buy&Buy within the centre increases footfall within the centre and contributes to the overall profitability of the centre.

9.29 The evidence in this case suggests that investment in the shopping centre could not have taken place without a period of guaranteed exclusivity and therefore the exclusivity provision is 'indispensable' to the benefits produced by the agreement.

9.30 However, an exclusivity provision of unlimited duration is unlikely to be necessary to protect the investment of Buy&Buy in the centre or to ensure the overall profitability of the centre.

9.31 A period of exclusivity of limited duration could benefit from exemption. The appropriate duration of the exclusivity provision for the agreement to benefit from exemption needs to be determined taking into account the economic and commercial conditions in which the agreement will be implemented. In this regard, it may be relevant to take into account the time necessary for a store to reach mature sales (at a point when its sales are projected to grow at a rate at or around inflation) that is, a stable revenue and customer base to provide the required return on investment.

9.32 The benefits described above are likely to be passed on to consumers, since consumers benefit from the competition created by the existence of the new shopping centre, the potential economies of scale created by greater footfall within the centre as a result of the investment of Buy&Buy in the centre and also from the variety of retailers within the centre.

9.33 Finally the agreement does not substantially eliminate competition in any market, since Buy&Buy continues to face competition from other retailers from within and outside the shopping centre.

EXAMPLE 6 (SHOPPING CENTRE – USE RESTRICTIONS)

9.34 The situation is the same as in Example 5. Landco is currently negotiating the leases of the small and medium size retail units in the Shop Here Centre with various retailers in different sectors, including fashion shops, electronics retailers, sports equipment retailers, bookstores, music stores and a pharmacy, as well as coffee shops and restaurants. The leases for small and medium size units will be of different durations, all between five and 10 years.

9.35 All lease agreements for units in the shopping centre contain a clause which restricts the use of the premise to a specific use. This enables Landco to achieve its desired 'retail mix' and to ensure the attractiveness of a shopping centre to consumers. Landco also requests certain types of retailers to be located within a particular 'zone' of the centre in order to ensure a logical layout.

Summary analysis:

9.36 Landco is generally free to decide which retailers take on leases within the shopping centre. As set out in paragraphs 4.28 and 4.30 above, restricted user provisions do not generally restrict competition, although it may be necessary to assess whether a restriction gives rise to appreciable effects on competition if it guarantees an exclusive right to the lessee to operate as a particular type of retailer within the Shop Here Centre or otherwise forecloses access to or dampens competition on a related market.

EXAMPLE 7 (SHOPPING CENTRE – EXCLUSIVITY ARRANGEMENTS)

9.37 The situation is the same as in Example 6. Landco has entered into a lease agreement with a coffee shop company (Nice Coffee), which guarantees that Nice Coffee will be the only coffee shop in the Shop Here Centre. Demand estimates suggest that multiple coffee shops would be viable in the Shop Here Centre.

9.38 The only other retailer selling hot beverages within the shopping centre is a fast food outlet. The nature of the restriction means that there are no other units available to other coffee shops within the shopping centre.

Summary analysis:

9.39 This restriction means that competing coffee shops are unable to establish a unit in the centre and therefore prevents Nice Coffee from facing competition within the shopping centre. This type of restriction could appreciably restrict competition, depending on the product and geographic scope of the related market where Nice Coffee is a competitor and the extent of competition that Nice Coffee faces within that market.

9.40 The product market in which Nice Coffee competes would be determined, in broad terms, by the products that customers see as substitutes of those offered by Nice Coffee. Nice Coffee is likely to face competitive constraints from a fairly limited geographic area, because most customers of the shopping centre are not prepared to go very far to buy alternative beverages.[83] The market that is affected by the exclusivity clause is therefore likely to be the market for coffee and other beverages in Shop Here.

9.41 The exclusivity in this context is likely to appreciably restrict competition, in particular if it effectively confers Nice Coffee a considerably large share of the relevant market, as there are no other coffee shops in the shopping centre and there may be very limited pressure from other lessees, such as restaurants, which offer similar beverages.

9.42 Although customers may benefit from the shopping centre containing a mix of retailers, it might be difficult to argue that the exclusivity clause is 'indispensable' to facilitate investment in the coffee shop (since there is demand to support multiple coffee shops in Shop Here and the specific investment necessary to open a coffee shop is likely to be low), or to argue that the exclusivity clause is necessary for Landco to ensure the presence of at least one coffee shop in Shop Here (which could equally be achieved through leasing a retail unit to a coffee shop with a user restriction in it).

9.43 In these circumstances the exclusivity clause is unlikely to satisfy the exemption criteria.

EXAMPLE 8 (RESTRICTIVE COVENANT REGARDING FUTURE USE OF PREMISES AFTER SALE)

9.44 There are two petrol stations in Townville. They are both owned and operated by an oil company, Phill-up. The petrol stations are located within a 10-minute drive of each other. There are no other petrol stations located within a 10-minute drive from either of Phill-up's petrol stations in Townville.

9.45 Phill-up decides to close one of these petrol stations and sell the land to a company without any interest in the petrol business. Phill-up also wants to prevent anyone else from purchasing the land and selling it in the future to potential rival petrol stations. It therefore includes a restrictive covenant in the sale of the land preventing any future owner of the land from using it as a petrol station.

Summary analysis:

9.46 The restrictive covenant prevents the land from being used as a petrol station and, more specifically, is aimed at preventing others from competing with Phill-up's retained petrol station. This restriction could appreciably restrict competition in the related market for the sale of petrol, depending on the scope of the related market for the sale of petrol and the extent of competition in the related market for the sale of petrol.

9.47 The geographic scope of the market for the sale of petrol can be determined by the distance that the majority of Phill-up customers are prepared to travel to fill their tanks at Phill-up's retained petrol station. For the purposes of this example, it is assumed that this is a 10-minute drive time isochrone.

9.48 Phill-up does not currently face any competition from other petrol stations within this related market.

9.49 It is unlikely that the covenant would have a negative impact on competition if there are many other suitable sites for use as petrol stations, as this would mean that new entrants could establish a petrol station in future. The availability of other suitable sites may vary over time, and so would vary the assessment of the agreement.

9.50 Given that there are no other petrol stations located within a 10-minute drive from either of Phill-up's petrol stations in Townville, the restrictive covenant is likely to appreciably restrict competition in the local petrol station market.

9.51 There is no evidence of any countervailing benefits which may outweigh any restriction on competition (assuming the agreement is found to appreciably restrict competition), and so the agreement would not benefit from exemption.

EXAMPLE 9 (RESTRICTIVE COVENANT REGARDING FUTURE USE OF PREMISES AFTER SALE)

9.52 Littleville is a small town in a rural area. The nearest town is 10 miles away.

9.53 There are five licensed betting offices (LBOs) in Littleville, each with a 20 per cent share of sales in this town. They are all within walking distance of one another on or within a close proximity to the High Street. There are a number of other retailers on or near the High Street.

9.54 About a year ago, one of the LBOs (Bet With Us) acquired the freehold to a vacant retail unit next door to its existing unit, with a view to extending into the vacant unit. However Bet With Us eventually decided to abandon the plan to expand its office. Instead, it has decided to sell the vacant unit to Fix It, a hardware store.

9.55 Bet With Us wants to ensure that if the outlet becomes available again, no other company will be able to open an LBO next door. It therefore includes a restrictive covenant in the sale, which prevents the unit being used as an LBO by future owners.

Summary analysis:

9.56 The restrictive covenant is aimed at preventing another business from competing with Bet With Us next door to it and preventing access to the site by competitors of Bet With Us. This type of restriction could appreciably restrict competition, depending on the geographic scope of the related LBO market and the extent of competition in this market.

9.57 The geographic dimension of the related market is broadly determined by the distance that users of an LBO in Littleville would go to find an alternative LBO in response to a small but significant sustained increase in prices. Given the absence of LBOs in a radius of 10 miles, the market is likely to include only the five LBOs in Littleville.

9.58 Based on Bet With Us's market share, the fact that it faces relatively strong competition from other betting shops in the area that there appear to be many other suitable retail outlets available to competitors (subject to planning permission and obtaining relevant licensing consents), the covenant may not appreciably restrict competition.

9.59 Although the covenant may not appreciably restrict competition at the time it is entered into, it may subsequently infringe the Chapter I prohibition as a result of changes in market circumstances. If Bet With Us's market share increases (for example, if three of the other LBOs in the area close) and if in the future, there is a shortage of other suitable sites available to potential competitors in Littleville over a short-term (one to two year) period, the analysis may differ. Therefore, the competitive assessment of the restrictive covenant may vary over time.

9.60 Assuming the restrictive covenant does appreciably restrict competition, there is no evidence of any countervailing benefits which may outweigh the restriction on competition at any present or future time, and so the agreement would be unlikely to benefit from exemption.

NOTES

79 See footnote 48 above.

80 See footnote 48 above.

81 The geographic scope of this market is likely to be determined by the distance that students are prepared to travel between their student homes and the University campus. This will be wider than the campus and will include the other halls of residence and some private accommodation in town.

82 This will require an objective assessment of the possibility of a party to penetrate the relevant market without the benefit of the restriction in question. See chapters 4 and 5 for further detail.

83 To the extent that Nice Coffee owns a number of coffee chains in the UK, it is also relevant to consider whether its retail offer is set according to conditions of local competition. The geographic dimension of the market where other retailers in Shop Here compete may vary in relation to each of them. Given the short distance from other high street shops, a majority of the businesses in Shop Here are likely to be constrained by these shops, together with the shops in Shop There and possibly businesses in a wider market (for example, where customers would consider shopping online for the same products that are sold in Shop Here).

ANNEXES

ANNEXE A: SELF-ASSESMENT FLOW-CHART

[3.393]

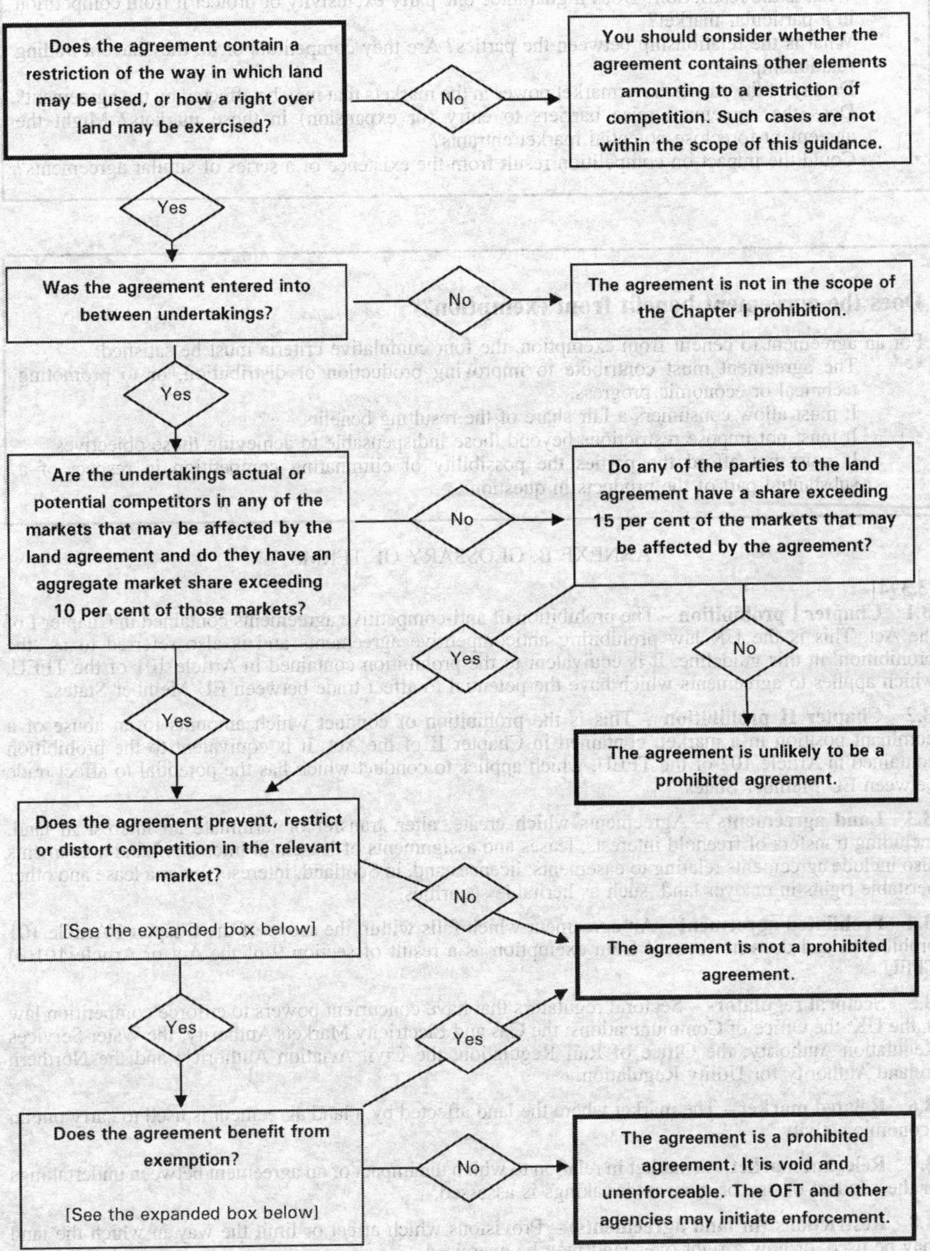

Does the agreement prevent, restrict or distort competition in the relevant market?

To answer this question, you should consider, amongst others, the following questions:

- What is the restriction? Does it guarantee one party exclusivity or protect it from competition in a particular market?
- What is the relationship between the parties? Are they competitors or do they have a trading relationship?
- Do any of the parties have market power in the markets that may be affected by the agreement?
- Does the agreement raise barriers to entry (or expansion) in those markets? Might the agreement foreclose potential market entrants?
- Could the impact on competition result from the existence of a series of similar agreements?

Does the agreement benefit from exemption?

For an agreement to benefit from exemption, the four cumulative criteria must be satisfied:

- The agreement must contribute to improving production or distribution, or to promoting technical or economic progress.
- It must allow consumers a fair share of the resulting benefits.
- It must not impose restrictions beyond those indispensable to achieving those objectives.
- It must not afford the parties the possibility of eliminating competition in respect of a substantial part of the products in question.

ANNEXE B: GLOSSARY OF TERMS

[3.394]

B.1 Chapter I prohibition – The prohibition of anti-competitive agreements contained in Chapter I of the Act. This is the UK law prohibiting anticompetitive agreements and is also referred to as 'the prohibition' in this guideline. It is equivalent to the prohibition contained in Article 101 of the TFEU, which applies to agreements which have the potential to affect trade between EU Member States.

B.2 Chapter II prohibition – This is the prohibition of conduct which amounts to an abuse of a dominant position in a market, contained in Chapter II of the Act. It is equivalent to the prohibition contained in Article 102 of the TFEU, which applies to conduct which has the potential to affect trade between EU Member States.

B.3 Land agreements – Agreements which create, alter, transfer or terminate an interest in land, including transfers of freehold interests, leases and assignments of leasehold interests. Land agreements also include agreements relating to easements, licences and, in Scotland, interests under a lease and other heritable rights in or over land, such as heritable securities.

B.4 Prohibited agreement – An agreement which falls within the scope of the Chapter I/Article 101 prohibition and does not benefit from exemption as a result of section 9 of the Act or Article 101(3) TFEU.

B.5 Sectoral regulators – Sectoral regulators that have concurrent powers to enforce competition law in the UK: the Office of Communications; the Gas and Electricity Markets Authority; the Water Services Regulation Authority; the Office of Rail Regulation; the Civil Aviation Authority; and the Northern Ireland Authority for Utility Regulation.

B.6 Related market – The market where the land affected by a land agreement is used to carry out an economic activity.

B.7 Relevant market – A market in relation to which the impact of an agreement between undertakings or the conduct of one or more undertakings is assessed.

B.8 Restrictions (in land agreements) – Provisions which affect or limit the way in which the land may be used, or how a right over land may be exercised.

HOW COMPETITION LAW APPLIES TO CO-OPERATION BETWEEN FARMING BUSINESSES: FREQUENTLY ASKED QUESTIONS (OFT 740REV, NOVEMBER 2011)

[3.395]

NOTES

As to the construction of this document (following the abolition of the OFT and Competition Commission), see further the note "The Competition and Markets Authority (references to the OFT and Competition Commission etc)" in the introductory notes to Part 3 preceding **[3.1]**.

Note also that references to dishonesty in respect of the cartel offence are only relevant for cartels entered into prior to 1 April 2014. The Enterprise and Regulatory Reform Act 2013 (ERRA13) removes dishonesty as an element of the cartel offence for agreements entered into on or after 1 April 2014 or which relate to arrangements made or to be made on or after that date. The ERRA13 also introduces statutory exclusions and defences to the offence. Please refer to Cartel Offence Prosecution Guidance (CMA9) for further information.

CONTENTS

1 INTRODUCTION

[3.396]

Farmers may want to enter into commercial agreements with other farmers for a variety of reasons ranging from simple agreements to share machinery and equipment to more complex arrangements involving common selling practices. The OFT recognises that many such forms of collaboration will be beneficial, increasing efficiency and benefiting consumers. We are also aware, however, that it is not always clear to farmers or their advisers whether a particular agreement will infringe competition law and this uncertainty may mean that some forms of beneficial co-operation do not happen.

The aim of these FAQs is to provide farm businesses with a brief outline of how competition law applies to the farming sector. In particular, the information provided aims to provide clarity about which sorts of behaviour and agreements are unlikely to breach competition law and which are more likely to do so.

This document should not be viewed as legal advice or relied upon as a complete statement of the law. The views and information provided in these FAQs do not bind the OFT nor are they intended as advice or a decision in specific cases. More detailed guidance on the application of competition law in the UK can be found in a number of guidance publications available from the OFT website. Links to the key ones can be found in the Annexe to this document.

SHORT FORM OPINIONS

In addition to consulting OFT guidance or obtaining independent legal advice, businesses seeking clarity on how competition law applies to **prospective** collaboration agreements between competitors which raise novel or unresolved competition issues may be able to seek **a short-form opinion** from the OFT.

The short-form opinion process was introduced by the OFT in April 2010 as a straightforward and quick way of providing clear advice on competition law to businesses planning innovative forms of collaboration and others in similar situations in the future.

We hope this process will help ensure companies are not prevented or discouraged from embarking on legitimate and beneficial co-operation for fear of infringing competition law. Further information on the short-form opinion process, as well as on the OFT's first short-form opinion, is available on the OFT's website.[1]

KEY MESSAGES

The aim of competition law is to prevent harmful anti-competitive agreements and behaviour. Many forms of collaboration are beneficial, both to farmers and their customers. The key question to ask when considering whether a potential agreement is likely to infringe competition law is what effect it will have on competition in the relevant market and on customers.

The practices set out below would **almost certainly** infringe competition law. These might be considered the 'black list' of things to be avoided if you want to stay on the right side of the law:

- Anti-competitive agreements between companies where competitors **fix prices or divide markets.**[2] These are viewed as serious, 'hard core' infringements. Because fixing prices is very unlikely to lead to more efficient production, or better outcomes for consumers, these agreements nearly always infringe the law.[3]
- The prohibition on anti-competitive agreements also extends to **concerted practices**. A concerted practice may exist where there is informal cooperation between competitors, for example where sensitive commercial information may be exchanged or conveyed. **This includes, in particular, any information that may reveal a business's future commercial behaviour – in particular, pricing or marketing strategy.** In effect, exchanging information which reduces uncertainty about a business's or a competitor's behaviour is likely to be problematic. While this problem may arise with current information, it is more likely to do so with information about future activity. Through these actions the businesses in question would knowingly substitute co-operation between them for the risks of competition, thus reducing the normal commercial uncertainty that should exist between competitors. On the contrary, businesses should determine their commercial conduct, including pricing, completely independently of one another.
- Abuse of a dominant position in a relevant market by a business, particularly if this leads to the exclusion of actual and/or potential entrants.

Outside the above, there are many other forms of co-operation and collaboration between businesses which farmers could undertake and which, in the absence of market power, would be less likely to, or would almost certainly not, infringe competition law (depending on the circumstances of the situation and the size of the market affected). In this context, the FAQs set out below are intended to provide some guidance to farmers who may be considering entering into some form of co-operative arrangement, but fear — and/or are not clear whether -the arrangement may be in breach of current competition law.

STRUCTURE OF THE FAQS

The FAQs are organised into the following sections:

- General questions on competition law in the farming sector and how the OFT applies the law.
- More detailed questions on collaboration and agreements between farming businesses.
- Mergers.

QUESTIONS AND ANSWERS

Navigate to the answer by holding down ctrl and clicking on the question:

NOTES

[1] www.oft.gov.uk/OFTwork/competition-act-and-cartels/short-form-opinions. See also OFT's first short-form opinion **P&H/Makro joint purchasing agreement.**

[2] Market sharing occurs where undertakings agree that they will not compete on some territories, type of customer or some other criterion.

[3] See A20 for the very limited circumstances under which a price-fixing agreement might be exempt from competition law.

2 COMPETITION LAW AND POLICY IN THE FARMING SECTOR

[3.397]

Q1 How can competition law and policy help farm businesses?

A1 Competition law helps farm businesses:

(i) by establishing the conditions under which farmers can develop sustainable forms of co-operation with a view to improving their farms' efficiency and strengthening their bargaining power, without undermining their incentives to become more efficient and to innovate.
(ii) by protecting them from anti-competitive practices which may limit access to potential customers or markets, and/or adversely affect the level of competition existing in the market or farmers' ability to compete effectively in that market.

If you believe your business is suffering because of the anti-competitive practices of others in the market, you may wish to make a complaint to the OFT. More information about how to make a complaint can be found at: www.oft.gov.uk/about-the-oft/legal-powers/legal/competition-act-1998/complaints

Q2 Why is the preservation of competition considered to be so important?

A2 Competition is at the heart of any successful market economy. As noted above, it provides a stimulus for businesses to improve their performance and to reduce their prices in order to gain an advantage over rivals and win more business. It encourages the development of new or improved products or processes and increases economic growth and living standards. Without competition in food production there would be less incentive for farmers to offer better produce to their customers and, ultimately, to final consumers.

Anti-competitive agreements and abuses of dominant market positions increase prices and harm consumer choice. They make the supply chain less efficient and undermine the performance of the economy as a whole. Stopping businesses from colluding to fix prices should ensure more choice for consumers and prices that reflect as much as possible the costs of production (including a reasonable profit).

An effective market economy means competing to produce in the most efficient manner. Producers cut costs to become more efficient so that they can meet or beat competitors' prices. New businesses coming into a market are more likely to flourish if existing businesses do not exploit their market power in an anti-competitive way. Existing businesses should innovate to respond to new rivals.

Q3 How are competition law and policy carried out in the UK?

A3 In the UK, competition law is applied and enforced principally by the OFT. The Competition Act 1998 ('the Act') gives the OFT powers to apply, investigate and enforce the following main prohibitions (referred to as Chapter I and Chapter II prohibitions respectively) and — since 2004 — the equivalent prohibitions under EU competition law if an agreement or conduct has an appreciable effect on trade between EU member states:[4]

- a prohibition on anti-competitive agreements between companies (Chapter I prohibition)
- a prohibition on the abuse of market power or of a dominant position (Chapter II prohibition), that focuses primarily on not excluding entrants to a particular market.

Companies which are found to have infringed the Act can face significant financial penalties of up to 10 per cent of world wide turnover. The most serious sanctions apply to cartels where competitors fix prices or divide markets.[5]

Q4 Is there any other key legislation farmers should be aware of?

A4 Yes. Under the Enterprise Act 2002, the OFT and the Competition Commission (CC) have respectively a duty to refer and, if appropriate, assess and remedy the adverse effects of mergers that would otherwise substantially lessen competition.

Also, the Enterprise Act 2002 makes provision for the OFT to carry out market studies. We may as a result of such studies refer markets to the CC to conduct more in-depth market investigations. Both the OFT and the CC may propose remedies in markets in which competition does not work well for consumers.

The OFT's decisions in competition investigations are subject to statutory rules, precedents and guidance derived from both UK and EC case law. Our decision-making is required to be transparent.[6] We publish versions of our infringement decisions, which are also subject to appeal to the Competition Appeal Tribunal (CAT). If we do not find evidence of a competition law infringement, we sometimes publish a document explaining our reasons for not taking action. Details of OFT decisions can be found on our website.[7]

Q5 How does the OFT assess whether there is a competition problem?

A5 The OFT takes the following steps when assessing allegations of anticompetitive agreements or behaviour.

Defining the relevant market

In most cases we begin by defining a 'relevant market', so as to determine the competitive constraints acting on a supplier or purchaser of a given product or service. These include actual or potential competitors or firms that are capable of constraining those firms' behaviour and of preventing them from behaving independently of effective competitive pressure (for example, by raising prices above the competitive level). This exercise also helps us to assess whether there is market power that may be being misused to restrict or prevent competition.[7]

Product markets

In brief, the relevant product market will consist of the products affected by the agreement or conduct in question, including substitute products, which are sufficiently close to the product concerned that customers or final consumers may switch to them should the price of the product concerned increase. If there are no such constraints, then that product group forms a separate market. For example, the OFT has concluded in previous merger decisions that raw milk forms a separate product market because processors cannot substitute other products for raw milk to produce dairy products.

Geographic markets

We also consider the geographic limits of these constraints. For example, the market for some agricultural products in the UK would not be considered a separate national market because, if prices were too high in the UK, produce could and would be imported from abroad. But this may not happen for all farm products. For example, the markets for perishable products, such as raw milk, which cannot be transported very far, are likely to be considered national or even regional markets.

Assessing competition in a relevant market

Once we have established a relevant market, we consider whether the restrictions in a particular collaborative arrangement or agreement are likely to have a significant adverse effect on competition. This will usually mean considering the impact on consumers in terms of prices, choice and quality.

As noted, under the law we consider certain collaborative practices such as price fixing and market sharing, and activities which may facilitate those practices, such as the sharing of future pricing and/or market strategy information as nearly always having an adverse effect on a market. We may also consider the effect on competition of conduct by single businesses that may have market power or a 'dominant position' in a particular market, to ascertain whether that business may be abusing that dominant position.

Q6 How might 'market power' and 'dominant position' be assessed in the farming sector?

A6 The prohibition on abuse of a dominant position applies if a farmer, an association of farmers or a co-operative is dominant in a relevant market. A business is said to hold a dominant position if it has substantial market power. As an indication, an undertaking[9] might be said to have substantial market power if it has a high (say 40 per cent or over) share of the relevant market and there are few restraints on its behaviour (for example, in setting prices) from competitors, customers and/or consumers. In other words, the OFT considers it unlikely that a business will be individually dominant if its share of the relevant market is under 40 per cent, and even market shares above this level may not indicate dominance if, for example, there is strong buyer power or barriers to entry to the market are low.[10]

It is highly unlikely that any individual farmer or local co-operative will hold a dominant position but a national co-operative may do so if the relevant geographic market is national or sub-national.

It should be noted that even where a firm does hold a dominant position, this does not automatically cause concern under competition law. It is only when that dominant position is abused that the law is broken. Accordingly, in the context of co-operation agreements in the agricultural sector, this prohibition is likely to be less relevant than the prohibition on anti-competitive agreements.

Q7 What sorts of behaviour may be an abuse of a dominant position?

A7 Abusive conduct may be conduct which exploits consumers or suppliers, for example, through excessively high prices. It may also be anticompetitive conduct against actual or potential rivals which amounts to 'exclusionary' behaviour, because it excludes, removes or weakens competition from existing competitors or establishes or strengthens barriers to entry to the market. Examples of exclusionary behaviour are:

- Predatory behaviour (excessively low prices to try to drive competitors out of the market, with a view to raising prices once the competitors have exited the market).
- Activities which unduly limit or foreclose competitors' access to the market.
- In some circumstances, refusing to supply existing or potential customers without justification.

Q8 In what circumstances would European competition law apply?

A8 As noted earlier, since 2004 the OFT can apply both national competition law (Chapter I and Chapter II prohibitions) and EU competition law (Articles 101 and 102 TFEU) to agreements and/or conduct which may affect trade between member states. Therefore, EU competition law will only directly apply to co-operation among UK farmers if those arrangements have the capability to appreciably affect trade between member states.

The EU has noted that in practice this means that if a group of farmers with a combined market share of less than five per cent and an EU aggregate turnover of less than 40 million euros were to decide to enter into any types of co-operation agreements, EU competition rules would simply not apply to them. However, UK legislation would still apply if the agreement affected trade in a relevant market in the UK.

Q9 In summary, what sorts of activity are most likely to infringe competition law in the farming sector?

A9 As noted in the introduction section, all agreements or collaborative arrangements between direct competitors in the farming sector which seek to fix prices or share markets and/or customers are considered highly likely to breach competition law. Hence they are generally prohibited. Similarly, agreements to limit supply of production to keep prices high or where the co-operation allows the parties to maintain, gain or increase market power and thereby to cause negative market effects with respect to prices, output, innovation, or the variety or quality of products would be likely to infringe competition law.

NOTES

[4] Article 101 of the Treaty on the Functioning of the EU ('TFEU') and Article 102 TFEU respectively.

[5] The Enterprise Act 2002 makes it a criminal offence for an individual to dishonestly agree with one or more other persons that two or more undertakings will engage in certain prohibited cartel arrangements, including those that involve price fixing, market sharing, limitation of production or supply and bid rigging.

[6] See the OFT publication *A guide to the OFT's investigation procedures in competition cases* (OFT1263 — March 2011). This is available from the OFT's website.

[7] www.oft.gov.uk/OFTwork/competition-act-and-cartels/ca98/decisions.

[8] See the OFT publication *Market Definition* (OFT 403 — December 2004). This is available on the OFT's website.

[9] In this document, the terms 'business' and 'undertaking' (the term used in competition legislation) are used interchangeably.

[10] See also the OFT publication *Abuse of a dominant position* (OFT 402 — December 2004). This is available on the OFT's website.

3 COLLABORATION IN THE FARMING SECTOR

[3.398]

Most forms of collaboration between farmers or between businesses in the farming sector will not raise any competition problems. It is only where cooperation could significantly affect the competitive process (for example, collaborating to fix prices, share markets or limit production) that the OFT is likely to have concerns. As noted, consumers are generally harmed by such collaboration.

As set out below, generally beneficial forms of collaboration (such as cooperatives, grouping together to purchase common inputs, to share expensive equipment or to engage in joint marketing or research and development and similar activities) do not cause problems under competition law, particularly when the businesses involved do not have market power.

Q10 Aren't all forms of agricultural collaboration excluded automatically from EU law and the Competition Act?

A10 No, but some are. The Treaty for the Functioning of the European Union (TFEU) and the Competition Act do exclude from consideration under EU and UK competition law many agreements between farmers or farmers' associations (or associations of such associations) which:

- concern the production or sale of agricultural products (including livestock, dairy, meat and fish products as well as fruit and vegetables and other crops), or the use of joint facilities for the storage, treatment and processing of agricultural products.

However, the exclusion only applies if the agreements meet certain conditions. The main ones are:

- The agreements are **only** between farmers or associations of farmers. For example, an agreement between a group of dairy farmers and milk processors would not come within the exclusion, nor would an agreement between livestock farmers and slaughterhouses.
- Crucially, the agreement must not involve an obligation on the farmers to charge identical prices for their products. Arrangements whereby farmers agree to sell through a co-operative and take whatever price the co-operative realises in the market should, however, be acceptable.

Q11 Presumably an association of farmers or an agreement between associations of farmers that only covers a small share of the relevant market will not raise competition concerns?

A11 Generally that is the case. Some agreements are considered not to restrict competition because they cover a small proportion of the relevant market (see A5 for a brief summary of the meaning of 'relevant market').

As a rule, if the parties to an agreement are competitors that together have less than a **10 per cent market share**, there will be no significant restriction of competition. Undertakings in a 'vertical' (supplier/buyer) relationship may in addition benefit from an exemption from competition law provided both parties have less than a **30 per cent** share of the relevant market.

Even where agreements or collaborative arrangements cover a higher proportion of the market, there is no presumption that they will infringe the law. Whether or not they infringe will depend upon the overall effects of the agreement, the nature and structure of the market(s) in question, the extent of the parties' market power and the precise terms of the agreement.

It should be emphasised that agreements that involve **price fixing** or **market sharing** will be regarded as being likely to restrict competition significantly no matter how small the proportion of the market they cover.

Q12 Does competition law apply to agreements between farm businesses and businesses in other parts of the supply chain (for example, those which purchase the farmers' products)?

A12 Yes, EU and UK competition law apply in principle to all agreements or concerted practices between producers and other market participants such as processors and retailers.

As noted, an agreement between farmers or a farmers' association and a business in another part of the supply chain, for example, between a buyer and a seller is sometimes called a 'vertical agreement'. It is recognised that many such agreements are harmless and even beneficial. Consequently, many such agreements are generally exempted from consideration under competition law. This is provided that they do not contain certain hard-core restrictions such as price fixing, restrictions concerning the territory into which, or the customers to whom, the buyer may sell etc.

Businesses need to satisfy themselves that they are able to benefit from the EU rules on this exemption, which will also apply in UK law. As noted in A11, to benefit from the exemption, the agreement must not involve serious anti-competitive practices, and both parties must have market shares of **30 per cent** or less. The protection given by these rules can be withdrawn in circumstances where particular competition concerns arise.[11] There is no presumption that agreements where parties have higher market shares than 30 per cent are in breach of the law, but they may be subject to closer scrutiny, depending on the circumstances.

Q13 Are there examples of agreements in the farming sector that have infringed competition law?

A13 There is no recent UK case law on the application of competition law to the farming sector as there have been no cases since the Competition Act was introduced that have directly involved farmers. In practice, competition law is applied in the same way to agricultural markets as any other market. For example, there are a number of European cases in which agreements between businesses in the farming sector were found to include an element of agreeing or fixing prices. These agreements were considered to have infringed the law. The 'French beef' example [in the shaded box] describes an actual case of anti-competitive behaviour by French associations in the beef sector which was not covered by the exceptions to the EU competition rules for agricultural undertakings.

French beef

On 24 October 2001 six French agricultural associations entered into an agreement in the beef sector. Four of the associations represented farmers, including the association representing the co-operative movement and the FNSEA, the main French farmers union. The two others represented slaughter-houses. Under the agreement the associations jointly set a minimum price for beef. They also undertook to suspend or at least limit imports of all types of beef. The organisations knew that their action was unlawful. During the inspections carried out by the EU Commission in December 2001 documents were found which noted that the agreements were 'a bit against the law but that can't be helped' and asked 'can we close ranks, without being caught by the DGCCRF (the French Competition Authority)?'

On 3 May 2003 the EU Commission imposed fines totalling euro 16.7 million on the six participants to the agreement, of which euro 12 million was on the FNSEA.

The 'French beef' agreement was found not to benefit from the agricultural exclusion to Article 101 (**and** to have broken the law), because it involved an obligation to charge identical prices. The Commission and courts noted the difficulties that the industry was experiencing at the time, which were reflected in a reduction of the penalty, but this did not prevent the agreement from being judged to have infringed the law. It is likely that a similar agreement in the UK would not benefit from the UK agricultural exclusion and would infringe the Competition Act prohibition on anti-competitive agreements.

Q14 I want to share farm overheads with other small farmers, for example to share the use of equipment to reduce my costs. Would this cause competition concerns?

A14 Generally no. For example, farm businesses may get together to share

equipment, to purchase or deliver training courses, recruit jointly or share support services such as accountancy, payroll services or website design.

These types of activity can bring about more efficient production and distribution and are very unlikely to harm competition especially if the businesses involved do not have market power. Set out below are some examples of co-operation that, in the absence of market power, could be considered to be 'efficiency-enhancing' and would therefore be highly unlikely to breach competition law:

- Sharing facilities of any kind; for example, storage, transport, processing facilities, other common equipment.
- Sharing of skills and knowledge including staff.
- Common marketing or branding of a product to add value which is of some benefit to consumers (but not simply increasing the sale price of a product without such justification).
- Common marketing or branding of a product to ensure availability of that product on the relevant market.
- Reducing waste through better management and potential use of all by-products to their highest value rather than for disposal or for commodities.

Q15 How would competition legislation apply to an agreement to set up a cooperative, a joint production agreement or farmers' buying group in order to negotiate better prices by joint production/bulk buying?

A15 Farmers' co-operatives (within which, for example, farmers co-operate in the area of production, collection or processing their products), joint production agreements and joint agreements for bulk buying of inputs have generally been recognised under EU and UK law as pro-competitive structures, which allow farmers to compete more effectively against other suppliers.

Competition concerns are unlikely to arise unless the businesses involved have market power. For these agreements, parties with a combined market share of **20 per cent** are unlikely to be judged to have market power.[12]

Q16 How would competition legislation apply to an agreement to set up a farmers' marketing or sales group?

A16 Most agreements of this type, often referred to as commercialisation agreements, will not raise competition concerns provided they do not involve price fixing. The agricultural exclusion might apply to a marketing or sales agreement but marketing or sales groups can cover a variety of arrangements and the competition assessment will depend on the details. For example, marketing might be generic advertising or producers selling under a common brand. Alternatively, joint marketing may be needed to have the scale and professional management to meet the specifications of large customers. None of these is likely to raise competition concerns.

It is crucial that the parties to a joint selling agreement are free to set their own prices but they can sell through a common organisation such as a co-operative or commercial agent, taking whatever price the agent can get for their produce. The co-operative or agent should not otherwise restrict competition, for example by limiting quantities sold by its members, which might amount to market sharing.

Competition concerns are unlikely to arise unless the businesses involved have market power. For these agreements, parties with a combined market share of **15 per cent** are unlikely to be considered to have market power.[13]

Q17 These collaborative arrangements, particularly joint commercialisation, are likely to require a reasonable amount of exchange of information. To what extent is this permissible?

A17 Competition authorities recognise that many such collaborative arrangements involve a degree of information exchange. Much of this is harmless, particularly if it concerns historical information. However, parties should not exchange sensitive commercial information, particularly on future (and possibly current) marketing strategy, volumes and prices. Such information may reveal a business's or competitor's future commercial behaviour. Exchanging information which reduces uncertainty about a business's behaviour is likely to be problematic. Through these actions the businesses in question would knowingly substitute cooperation between them for the risks of competition, thus reducing the normal commercial uncertainty that should exist between competitors. On the contrary, businesses should determine their commercial conduct, including pricing, completely independently of one another.

Even when sharing what would otherwise be considered 'harmless' information, parties should also guard against such discussions leading to, or facilitating, an opportunity for exchanges of the above type of more commercially sensitive information. Discussions that strayed into and/or facilitated direct and/or indirect exchanges of current and future commercially sensitive information are likely to fall foul of competition law. Commercialisation agreements where a certain degree of information exchange takes place should not be a mere cover for colluding on pricing and marketing strategies, otherwise the OFT would have scope to intervene and stop them.

Q18 There seem to be a number of different market share thresholds that are used as benchmarks to assess market power for different arrangements. How do I know which one applies?

A18 This table summarises the market share thresholds for types of agreements in the UK that, generally, will be unlikely to raise competition concerns because they would affect only a small part of the market.

Type of agreement	Applicable market share threshold	Likely competition assessment if parties to agreement are at or below market share threshold	Likely competition assessment if parties to agreement are above market share threshold
The parties form a **horizontal agreement** (that is, the parties are at the same level of the supply chain).	The parties' joint share of the relevant market is **10 per cent** or lower.	There will be no appreciable restriction of competition unless the agreement contains a provision which directly or indirectly fixes prices, shares markets or limits production.	See below.
The parties form a **joint commercialisation** agreement.	The parties' joint share of the relevant market is **15 per cent** or lower.	There will be no appreciable restriction of competition unless the agreement contains a provision which directly or indirectly fixes prices, shares markets or limits production.	Above a **15 per cent** market share there is no presumption of illegality under competition law, and the potential restrictive and efficiency-enhancing effects of the agreement will be assessed on a case by case basis.
The parties form a **production, bulk-buying, collection or processing cooperative** agreement.	The parties' joint share of the relevant market is **20 per cent** or lower.	There will be no appreciable restriction of competition unless the agreement contains a provision which directly or indirectly fixes prices, shares markets or limits production.	Above a **20 per cent** market share there is no presumption of illegality under competition law, and the potential restrictive and efficiency-enhancing effects of the agreement will be assessed on a case by case basis.

Type of agreement	Applicable market share threshold	Likely competition assessment if parties to agreement are at or below market share threshold	Likely competition assessment if parties to agreement are above market share threshold
A party, or parties, enter/s into a **'vertical' agreement** with another party at a different level of the supply chain (either higher or lower in the chain).	Both parties' share of the relevant market is lower than 30 **per** cent.	The parties would benefit from an exemption from competition law. Agreements which involve price fixing or market sharing will be regarded as likely to restrict competition no matter how small the proportion of the market they cover.	Above a 30 **per cent** market share there is no presumption of illegality under competition law, and the potential restrictive and efficiency-enhancing effects of the agreement will be assessed on a case by case basis.

Q19 If an agreement is likely to be caught by the TFEU or the Competition Act but the parties feel there are justifiable grounds for its retention, are there any criteria they can use to make an assessment against?

Yes, an agreement could be exempted (hence will not be prohibited) under the TFEU (if it affects other Member States) or the Competition Act if it satisfies the exemption criteria set out below.[14] The restrictions must:

(a) contribute to:
  (i) improving production or distribution, or
  (ii) promoting technical or economic progress,

while allowing consumers a fair share of the resulting benefit and

(b) not:
  (iii) impose on the undertakings concerned restrictions which are not indispensable to the attainment of those objectives, or
  (iv) afford the undertakings concerned the possibility of eliminating competition in respect of a substantial part of the products in question.

Since 2004, it has been the responsibility of the parties to an agreement themselves to assess that agreement under competition law. If parties consider that an agreement they have arranged or are contemplating might meet the above exemption criteria, and this is brought to the OFT's attention, we would take into account whether or not these criteria have been met when deciding whether the prohibition against anti-competitive agreements has been infringed.

Parties may be expected to provide evidence to support their view that their agreement meets the criteria. It should be noted that it is only in exceptional circumstances that hard core restrictions of competition would meet the criteria, but it is, in principle, possible.

Q20 Are there any circumstances in which price fixing would be allowed under competition law, such as where farmers may want to jointly sell, distribute, or promote their products?

A20 Only in very exceptional circumstances would price fixing be allowed under current competition law, as price fixing is considered a hard core restriction. Such arrangements would have to meet the criteria set out in A19 above — in particular the fixing of prices would have to be indispensable to the implementation of the agreement.

In this context, it may also be worth noting that the EU has suggested two specific circumstances where price fixing could be exempted as it might be considered as indispensible for a commercialisation agreement to be implemented, these are:

- if a large buyer does not want to deal with a number of prices and requests a single supply price, or
- if farmers agree on jointly launching new products, such as a common brand, which can only be credibly achieved if all aspects of marketing, including price, are standardised.

A favourable assessment would, however, depend on the collective bargaining group not holding appreciable market power.

NOTES

11 Further information is available at: eur-lex.europa.eu/LexUriServ/LexUriServ.do?uri=CELEX:52010SC0411:EN:NOT.

12 See European Commission publications: *How EU competition policy helps dairy farmers in Europe*, published February 2010: ec.europa.eu/competition/sectors/agriculture/summary_dairy.pdf,

13 See European Commission publications: *How EU competition policy helps dairy farmers in Europe*, published February 2010: ec.europa.eu/competition/sectors/agriculture/summary_dairy.pdf,

14 Part 9 of the Competition Act or Article 101 (3) of the TFEU.

4 MERGERS

[3.399]

Q21 How does merger control operate?

A21 Some forms of co-operation may amount to a merger if a party transfers some or all parts of its business to another party in the collaboration. The OFT can consider mergers, acquisitions and joint ventures under the mergers provisions of the Enterprise Act if they involve (a) two enterprises (businesses or parts of businesses) that cease to be distinct and (b) either (i) the merging businesses both supply or acquire particular goods or services in (a substantial part of) the UK with a combined share of at least 25 per cent, or (ii) the UK turnover of the acquired business exceeds £70m.

If the OFT finds a realistic prospect that the merger results in a substantial lessening of competition, it will in principle refer the merger to the Competition Commission (CC) for further investigation. The OFT and the CC have issued several guidelines with more information about its assessment of mergers.[15]

Q22 Is it true that the OFT/Competition Commission will seek to ban any mergers which will result in an enterprise having a market share of over 25 per cent?

A22 No. There is no presumption that a merger leading to a market share greater than 25 per cent raises competition concerns. Rather the competition authorities assess a merger to see if it may be expected to result in a substantial lessening of competition. As noted in A21, OFT and CC merger guidance describes how we go about this. Each case is considered on its own merits. For example, the proposed merger between First Milk and Milk Link, two dairy farmers' co-operatives, which was abandoned in 2008, would have resulted in significant combined shares in the procurement of raw milk and the supply of cheddar to retailers, but the OFT concluded that the merger would not have raised competition concerns because the merged firm would have faced sufficient competitive constraints.[16] Another example is the merger between Grainfarmers Group and Centaur Grain Group, two grain marketing farmers' co-operatives, which was cleared by the OFT despite shares exceeding 30 per cent in the procurement of grain in certain regions.[17]

NOTES

15 A brief overview is given in *A Quick Guide to UK Merger Assessment* (March 2011, OFT1313 and CC2 (summary)), with more detailed guidance in *Mergers jurisdictional and procedural guidance* (June 2009, OFT527) and *Merger Assessment Guidelines* (September 2010, OFT1254 and CC2). These can be found on the OFT's website.

16 See OFT decision of 12 December 2007.

17 See OFT decision of 23 September 2008.

ANNEXE

[3.400]

OFT has produced various guidelines on competition law and these should be used if further guidance in addition to the FAQs is needed.

The main booklets relating to these FAQs are:

- the major provisions
- Market definition
- Assessment of market power
- Abuse of a dominant position
- Agreements and concerted practices
- Vertical agreements
- Competing fairly

which can be found at: www.oft.gov.uk/about-the-oft/legal-powers/legal/competition-act-1998/publications

and:

- Overview of the Enterprise Act
- Mergers – substantive assessment guidance

which can be found at: www.oft.gov.uk/about-the-oft/legal-powers/legal/enterprise-act/publications2

Guidance booklets can also be ordered in hard copy from 0870 60 60 321.

Businesses considering making a request for a Short Form Opinion should approach the OFT informally to establish the best way to proceed. For further information, contact:

Jackie Holland; Director, Competition Policy and Procedural Adjudicator

jackie.holland@oft.gsi.gov.uk

or

Ann Pope; Director, Goods and Consumer Group

ann.pope@oft.gsi.gov.uk

The OFT is happy to receive any feedback on the views expressed in these FAQs.

Comments can be sent to:

Enquiries Unit: Farming collaboration FAQs
Office of Fair Trading
2–6 Salisbury Square
London, EC4Y 8JX
Tel 020 721 1 8000

PUBLIC BODIES AND COMPETITION LAW (OFT 1389, DECEMBER 2011)

A guide to the application of the Competition Act 1998

[3.401]

NOTES

As to the construction of this document (following the abolition of the OFT and Competition Commission), see further the note "The Competition and Markets Authority (references to the OFT and Competition Commission etc)" in the introductory notes to Part 3 preceding **[3.1]**.

Note also that references to dishonesty in respect of the cartel offence are only relevant for cartels entered into prior to 1 April 2014. The Enterprise and Regulatory Reform Act 2013 (ERRA13) removes dishonesty as an element of the cartel offence for agreements entered into on or after 1 April 2014 or which relate to arrangements made or to be made on or after that date. The ERRA13 also introduces statutory exclusions and defences to the offence. Please refer to Cartel Offence Prosecution Guidance (CMA9) for further information.

The fines that could be imposed on summary conviction for certain criminal offences referred to in this document were, at that time, subject to specific caps of £5,000 or above. With effect from 12 March 2015, these caps have been removed and those specific offences are now punishable by a fine of any amount.

CONTENTS

1 INTRODUCTION

[3.402]

1.1 Markets for public services continue to be opened up to the private and voluntary sectors. Effective competition in those markets can benefit the wider economy by encouraging greater productivity and innovation and preserving long term growth, while continuing to provide greater value for money for users and taxpayers. Public bodies are also increasingly seeking to generate revenues by utilising assets or spare capacity in markets beyond their core public functions. Such developments reinforce the need for public bodies to be aware of their existing and ongoing obligations under UK and EU competition law when carrying out their functions.

1.2 To that end, this guide[1] seeks to assist public bodies by providing a high level outline of the circumstances in which their activities will be subject to the UK and EU competition law prohibitions on:

- anti-competitive agreements, including price-fixing, market-sharing or bid-rigging arrangements and potentially, depending on their effect, agreements involving exclusivity, restrictions of long duration or certain collaborative arrangements with competitors such as joint selling or purchasing, and
- abuses of a dominant position, such as the setting of unfair prices or trading conditions or the refusal to supply an existing customer without objective justification.[2]

1.3 Those prohibitions, set out in the Competition Act 1998 (CA98)[3] and the Treaty on the Functioning of the European Union (TFEU)[4] apply to the conduct of all '**undertakings**'.

1.4 Public bodies will fall within the definition of an undertaking when they carry out an '**economic activity**'. It is for public bodies themselves to assess on a case-by-case basis whether, in carrying out any of their functions, they are acting as undertakings.

1.5 In making this assessment, it is the **nature of the particular activity being conducted** that is key, not the legal form, or public or private sector status, of the body that carries it out. Thus, a body – including a public body – may be an undertaking (and therefore subject to competition law) in respect of some of its activities, but not others. **Section 2** below discusses further the concept of 'economic activity'.

1.6 Where UK or EU competition law does apply to the activity of a public body, it is not necessarily the case that that body's existing conduct infringes such competition law or that it will have to amend its conduct. Indeed, compliance with competition law should not materially impede public bodies' efficient exercise of their functions.

1.7 However, non-compliance with competition law can have serious consequences. These include the unenforceability of the relevant agreement or decision and an adverse reputational impact, as well as the possibility of financial penalties and/or claims for damages. Breaches of competition law may also have consequences for the individuals involved in some cases. **Section 4** below discusses further the consequences of non-compliance with UK and EU competition law.

1.8 This guide sets out factors to which public bodies should have regard in determining whether they act as undertakings in any of their activities. It is not intended to be a comprehensive guide to the legal and economic frameworks for applying competition law to agreements and conduct.[5] Public bodies seeking a more definitive indication as to whether any of their specific activities are subject to UK or EU competition law should seek legal advice in the first instance.

1.9 In cases involving genuine uncertainty, the OFT should be approached, as it may – in appropriate circumstances – provide a public body with a non-binding 'Short-form Opinion' on the application of the CA98 to a specific collaborative activity.[6] To enquire as to the possibility of a Short-form Opinion, or for other queries about this guide that cannot be addressed through legal advice, please contact the OFT's Enquiries and Reporting Centre on 0845 7 22 44 99, who will be able to direct you to an appropriate person.

NOTES

1 This guide replaces the Office of Fair Trading's (OFT) policy note OFT443 *The Competition Act and public bodies* (August 2004).

2 Public bodies should be aware that their conduct may also (or alternatively) be subject to other laws within the field of competition law, including public procurement, merger control and/or State aid laws. Those laws are outside the scope of this guide. OFT guidance on the UK merger control rules is available on its website www.oft.gov.uk/OFTwork/mergers/publications Guidance on the application of the EU State aid laws in the UK can be found on the BIS website www.bis.gov.uk/policies/europe/state-aid

3 Anti-competitive agreements between undertakings are prohibited under Chapter I of the CA98 (the Chapter I prohibition). Chapter II of the CA98 prohibits undertakings with a dominant position in a market from abusing that dominant position (the Chapter II prohibition).

4 The Chapter I and Chapter II prohibitions are the UK law equivalents of, respectively, Articles 101 and 102 TFEU, which apply where the anti-competitive agreement or conduct may affect trade between EU Member States. European case law on these provisions of the TFEU is directly relevant to the interpretation of the equivalent CA98 provisions due to section 60 CA98.

5 The OFT has previously published guidelines on the general application of competition law. These are available from the OFT website (www.oft.gov.uk) See, in particular, OFT401 *Agreements and concerted practices* (December 2004); OFT402 *Abuse of a dominant position* (December 2004); and OFT1341 *How your business can achieve compliance with competition law* (June 2011).

6 See Section 4, paragraphs 4.12 and 4.13 below.

2 THE APPLICATION OF COMPETITION LAW TO PUBLIC BODIES

[3.403]

2.1 Below is a high-level overview of the key principles to which a public body should have regard when assessing whether its activities will be subject to UK or EU competition law.[7]

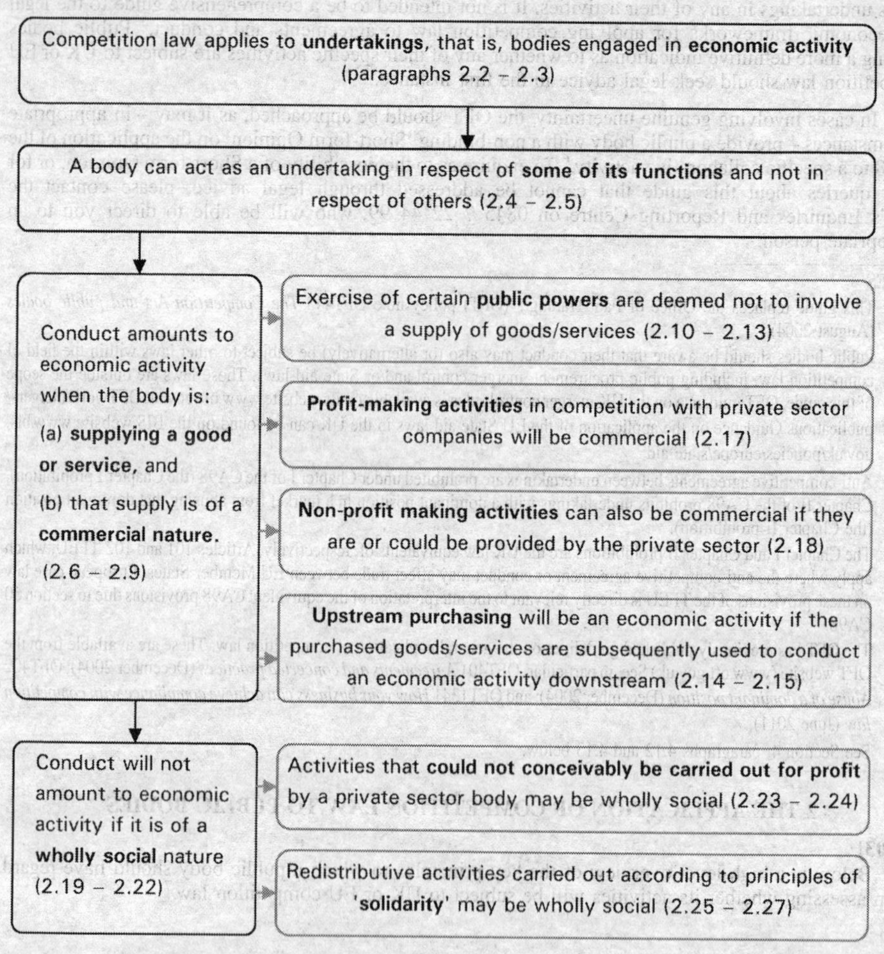

PUBLIC BODIES AS 'UNDERTAKINGS'

2.2 A public body will be subject to the UK and EU competition law prohibitions discussed in this guide if and when it acts as an 'undertaking'. The term 'undertaking' is not defined in the CA98 or the TFEU, but its meaning has been considered in UK and EU case law.

2.3 That case law has defined 'undertaking' as covering any natural or legal person engaged in 'economic activity', regardless of its legal form or the way in which it is financed.[8] The focus of the assessment of whether a body is an undertaking is therefore on the nature of the **particular activity** undertaken, not the nature of the body that undertakes it. As such:

- The term 'undertaking' can apply equally to public sector bodies and not-for-profit bodies, as well as to private sector bodies. Public authorities, State-controlled enterprises, charities,[9] etc. all fall within the definition of an undertaking, if they are carrying on an economic activity.
- The legal form of the body in question is also irrelevant to the question of whether it acts as an undertaking. A body need not, for example, be an incorporated company in order to be an undertaking.
- The fact that a body is intended to be non-profit making will not, of itself, be sufficient to deprive it of its status as an undertaking.[10]

2.4 It is also important to note that this 'functional' approach means that a public body may act as an undertaking – and therefore be subject to competition law – in respect of some of its activities, but not in respect of others.

- For example, a body vested with public powers to grant applications to organise motorcycling events was found not to be acting as an undertaking when making such authorisation decisions, but was considered to act as an undertaking when carrying out economic advertising and sponsorship activities relating to such events.[11]

2.5 As a result, each activity carried out by a public body must be considered separately to assess whether or not it is 'economic'.[12]

IDENTIFYING 'ECONOMIC ACTIVITY'

2.6 Whether a particular activity carried on by a public body is treated as an economic activity necessarily depends on the specific facts at hand. For this reason, past cases may provide only limited wider guidance to public bodies seeking to apply legal precedent to their own specific circumstances. Nevertheless, the case law has set out certain broad principles that public bodies should take into account when assessing whether their own conduct amounts to economic activity.

2.7 In broad terms, a public body should ask itself the following questions for each of its activities separately:

- Am I offering or supplying a good or service, as opposed to, for example, exercising a public power?
- If so, is that offer or supply of a 'commercial' – rather than an exclusively 'social' – nature?

2.8 If the answer to both these questions is yes, then – **for the purposes of that activity (and any related upstream purchasing)** – the public body is likely to be regarded as an undertaking subject to UK and EU competition law. Further detail on each of these elements of the assessment is set out below.

DOES THE PUBLIC BODY OFFER OR SUPPLY GOODS OR SERVICES?

2.9 It is the activity of **offering or supplying** goods or services on a given market[13] that is the characteristic feature of an economic activity.[14] Where – by contrast – an activity does not itself involve such offer or supply and is not related to a subsequent downstream offer or supply of goods and services by the body in question, that activity will generally not be considered economic activity.

Exercise of 'public powers'

2.10 The exercise by a body of powers which are 'typically those of a public authority' (that is, where it carries out State prerogatives or essential functions of the State) are deemed not to involve the offer or supply of goods or services on a market.[15]

2.11 Certain 'core' State activities, such as the provision of a national military or the administration of justice would typically be considered to involve the exercise of essential functions of the State, and thus not to involve the offer or supply of goods or services.

2.12 In past cases, certain functions relating to air traffic control,[16] environmental protection[17] and tax collection on behalf of the State[18] have, similarly, each been deemed to involve such an exercise of 'public powers'.

2.13 Ultimately, the distinction between such public functions and economic activities involving the provision of a good or service on a market will depend on the facts of each case. As noted above, the exercise by a body of certain 'public powers' would not prevent other 'non-core' activities carried out by the same body being subject to competition law.

- For example, where a body acts in a purely administrative capacity and merely regulates the provision of goods and services on a market, it has been considered not to be offering or supplying such goods or services.[19] That such administrative activity is undertaken in exchange for a fee will not necessarily render the activity 'economic'.[20] However, to the extent that the body also participates in the market, such participation may constitute an economic activity.[21]

Purchase of goods or services

2.14 Competition law may apply to agreements and conduct relating to a public body's **purchasing** activities (whether individually or jointly with others). However, in determining whether a public body is acting as an undertaking in relation to such purchase of goods or services in a market, the economic or non-economic nature of that purchasing activity depends on **the end use to which the public body puts the goods or services bought**:[22]

- If the purchased goods are related to a subsequent offer or supply of goods or services on a market by the public body in question (for example, the purchased goods form an input to such supply of goods or services), then, if the downstream supply is considered to be an economic activity, the purchasing activity is also likely to be deemed to be 'economic'.
- By contrast, where a public body purchases goods or services in a given market, but does **not** directly offer or supply any goods or services in that (or a related) market,[23] that body will not typically be acting as an undertaking for the purposes of UK or EU competition law when it makes such purchases.

2.15 Public bodies should note that, even where they are carrying out essential functions of the State, or merely purchasing goods, their conduct may — even if not subject to the UK and EU competition law prohibitions discussed in this guide —still be subject to other legal controls. These may include public and administrative law or public procurement law.[24] Discussion of such laws, including, for example, the extent to which public bodies are required to undertake an open competitive procurement when making purchases, is beyond the scope of this guide.

WHERE GOODS OR SERVICES ARE OFFERED OR SUPPLIED BY THE PUBLIC BODY, IS THAT OFFER OR SUPPLY OF A 'COMMERCIAL' NATURE, AS OPPOSED TO AN EXCLUSIVELY 'SOCIAL' NATURE?

2.16 Where public bodies do offer or supply goods or services, it is necessary to consider whether that downstream supply is of a commercial or, instead, an exclusively social nature.[25]

Commercial activity

2.17 The provision of goods or services on a 'commercial' basis will constitute economic activity. The clearest example of this is an activity undertaken for profit in direct competition with private sector companies:

- For example, Companies House has been found to act as an undertaking when competing with private sector information providers in the supply of online company data search tools.[26]
- Similarly, a public body will also generally be regarded as engaging in economic activity when it carries out 'wider markets activities' (being 'non-core', discretionary activities using capacity not needed for the body's statutory duties, which are provided in a competitive market with a view to generating revenues).

2.18 However, the concept of 'commercial' activity should not be considered limited to such examples: importantly, an activity need not in fact generate a profit[27] – or even have a profit-making motive[28] – in order to be deemed to be commercial in nature (and thus to be an 'economic' activity). Thus, the fact that a public body provided employment recruitment services free of charge did not prevent the EU courts finding that those services were an economic activity, as they could be (and had previously been) provided by private sector companies.[29]

'Social' activity

2.19 By contrast, where public bodies carry out an activity of an exclusively social nature, neither that activity, nor the bodies' purchase of goods or services for the purpose of that activity, will generally be treated as an economic activity.

2.20 Again, any assessment of whether an activity is of an exclusively social nature will necessarily be highly fact specific, and must take account of all aspects of the activity in question. While certain individual features of an activity – such as, for example, a lack of connection between the cost of providing a good or service and the price (if any) paid by end users[30] – may suggest that an activity is inherently 'uncommercial', all aspects of the activity must be considered as a package, rather than feature by feature.

2.21 Past case law on this issue does not provide a clear definition of when an activity will be considered to be 'social'. Those cases do establish certain principles, however, that public bodies can seek to apply when determining in a given case whether they are undertaking a social activity:

- The activity must be **exclusively** social – an activity that is fundamentally 'commercial' but also pursues some public service objectives will still be an economic activity.
- Activities which by their very nature could not – even in principle – be carried out for profit without State support have previously been characterised as being 'exclusively social'.
- In the context of social security and insurance schemes, the operation of a scheme according to certain wholly 'uncommercial', redistributive principles (known as '**solidarity**') has been considered to be an exclusively social activity.

Each of these is discussed further below.

Exclusively social

2.22 The activity must be of an **exclusively** social nature. An activity that would otherwise be deemed to be commercial in nature (and therefore 'economic') will not necessarily be sheltered from competition law simply because it also pursues some additional public service objectives.

- For example, a public body's operation of a pension fund was found by the EU court to be an economic activity as the fund operated on the principle of 'capitalisation' (the level of benefit it paid out was based on the financial results of its investment of contributions) and in competition with insurance companies.[31] That the fund also pursued some social objectives,[32] was governed to an extent by certain principles of solidarity and was non-profit making, was not, in the court's view, sufficient to render such activity 'non-economic'.

Impossibility of profit

2.23 Exclusively 'social' activities have previously been characterised as those which **by their very nature could not – even in principle – be carried out for profit without State support.**[33] Where the nature of the activity is such that profitable private sector involvement is impossible, no 'market' for the activity exists. Market forces do not (and could not) therefore play any part in the activity and, as such, that activity would not be capable of having anti-competitive effects.[34]

2.24 Importantly, however, the fact that private sector companies **currently** do not carry out activities in the market does not preclude the possibility of the activity being found to be 'economic'.[35]

- For example, where private sector companies have in fact carried out the activity in question in the past, this may indicate that it is not an activity that must necessarily be carried out by a public authority, and therefore that the activity is 'economic'.[36]
- Similarly, the fact that a government or public body decides not to allow private sector companies to provide a certain good or service (and, for example, instead provides it wholly in-house) does not necessarily mean that that activity is not 'economic'.[37]

'Solidarity'

2.25 Past cases in which public bodies' activities have been found to be 'exclusively social' have focused on the fields of compulsory social security and insurance. In that context, the EU courts have found the operation of certain compulsory healthcare and insurance schemes subject to State control to be 'exclusively social' where those schemes:

- provided members with the relevant service (for example, insurance cover) regardless of their financial status and state of health
- did not take a member's level of contributions into account when paying benefits, and
- were non-profit-making.[38]

Given those features, the schemes were said by the court to be governed by the principle of '**solidarity**' and not to constitute economic activity.

2.26 By contrast, an insurance scheme which was optional and operated according to the principle of 'capitalisation' (that is, the scheme paid benefits solely based on the amount of the beneficiary's contributions and the financial results of the investments made by the managing organisation) was deemed to be engaging in economic activity.[39]

2.27 To date, it appears that 'solidarity' has been found to exist where public bodies' activities led to the redistribution of income between those who are 'better off' (be that in terms of their finances, health, age, etc.) and those who, given their resources, would otherwise be deprived.[40] As set out above, however, an activity must be considered on its own specific facts in order to determine whether, as a whole, it could be considered to be governed entirely by principles of 'solidarity'.

NOTES

7 This overview is intended as a framework and to facilitate ease of reference to the remainder of this section. It is not a substitute for the more detailed paragraphs that follow, which explain how the various terms have been used and interpreted by the UK and EU courts in past cases.

8 Case C-41/90 *Höfner & Elser v Macrotron* [1991] ECR I-1979 ('*Höfner & Elser*'), paragraph 21.

9 See, for example, OFT decision of 20 November 2006, *Exchange of information on future fees by certain independent fee-paying schools* (Case CA98/05/2006).

10 Case C-67/96, *Albany International BV v Stichting Bedrijfspensioenfonds Textielindustrie* [1999] ECR I-5751 ('*Albany*'), paragraph 79.

11 Case C-49/07, *MOTOE v Elliniko Dimosio* [2008] ECR I-4863 ('*MOTOE*'), paragraph 25 onwards.

12 Joined cases C-264/01, C306/01, C-354/01, C-355/01 *AOK Bundesverband* [2004] ECR I-2493, paragraph 58.

13 The question of whether a good or service is offered or supplied 'on a market' is considered further below.

14 Case C-205/03 P *Federación Española de Empresas de Tecnología Sanitaria (FENIN) v Commission* [2006] ECR I-6295 ('*FENIN*'), paragraphs 25 to 26.

15 Case C-343/95 *Diego Cali & Figli SrL v Servizi Ecologici Porto di Genova Spa* [1997] ECR I-1547 ('*Diego Cali*'), paragraphs 22 to 23.

16 Case C-113/07 P, *SELEX Sistemi Integrati SpA v Commission* [2009] ECR I-2207 ('*SELEX*').

17 See *Diego Cali*.

18 Case C-207/01, *Altair Chimica SpA v ENEL Distribuzione* SpA [2003] ECR I-8875.

19 See, for example, case C-30/87, *Corinne Bodson v SA Pompes funebres des regions liberes*, [1988] ECR 2479 ('*Bodson*'), in which the grant by a public body of a concession to provide funeral services in a particular locality was found not to be an economic activity.

20 See, for example, *Bodson*, paragraph 18.

21 See *MOTOE*, paragraphs 24–26.

22 *FENIN*, paragraph 26. The Court of Justice (CJ), in examining whether organisations in charge of the Spanish health system were engaging in economic activity, confirmed that a public body's purchasing activity should not be dissociated from the downstream use (in that case, the management of the health system) to which those purchases are put. See also *SELEX*, paragraph 102 (cf. the approach taken in *BetterCare Group Limited v Director General of Fair Trading* [2002] CAT 7 ('*BetterCare II*'), referred to at n.34 below).

23 For example, where the good or service is purchased entirely for the public body's own use (that is, as an end consumer). See, by contrast, joined cases C-180/98–C184/98 *Pavel Pavlov and Others v Stichting Pensioenfonds Medische Specialisten* [2000] ECR I-6451, paragraphs 78–82, in which payments made by self-employed doctors into a single occupational pension fund were found not to have been made as end customers, but rather were held to relate to the doctors' downstream activity of providing private medical services to patients. As that downstream supply of medical services was an economic activity, the making of pension contributions (in effect, the activity of 'purchasing' pensions) was itself also an economic activity.

24 Furthermore, the OFT has used its broader markets-focused powers to investigate the impact of procurement activities on competition in markets. See, for example, OFT1314 *Commissioning and competition in the public sector* (March 2011) and OFT1214 *Choice and competition in public service markets* (March 2010).

25 As noted at paragraph 2.14, the commercial or social nature of the downstream supply is relevant not only to whether **that downstream supply** is an economic activity, but also to whether the public body's **upstream purchase** of goods or services required for such supply is itself also an economic activity.

26 See the OFT decision of 25 October 2002, *Companies House, the Registrar of Companies for England and Wales* (Case CP/1139-01).

27 Case C-244/94, *Fédération Française des Sociétés d'Assurance and Others v Ministère de l'Agriculture et de la Pêche* [1995] ECR I-4013 ('*FFSA*'), paragraph 21.

28 *MOTOE*, paragraph 27.

29 See *Höfner & Elser*.

30 See the opinion of Advocate General Maduro in *FENIN*, paragraph 31.

31 *Albany*, paragraph 86. See also *FFSA*, paragraph 18.

32 In that case, supplementing the low-level state pension for all workers within a particular sector.

33 See the opinion of AG Jacobs in *AOK Bundesverband*, paragraph 27, citing *Albany* and *Höfner & Elser*.

34 The fact that a public body's conduct **was** capable of having anti-competitive effects in the market has been taken by the UK Competition Appeal Tribunal as evidence that that conduct was economic (see *BetterCare II*). To the extent that that judgment focused on purchasing conduct, it must now be considered in the light of the principles subsequently endorsed by the CJ in *FENIN* and *SELEX* (n.22 above).

35 See Case C-475/99 *Firma Ambulanz Glöckner v Landkreis Südwestpfal* [2001] ECR I-8089 ('*Ambulanz Glöckner*'), paragraph 20 and *Höfner & Elser*, paragraph 22.

36 See *Ambulanz Glöckner*, paragraph 20: the ambulance transport services that the bodies in question had the exclusive right to provide had previously been carried out by private sector companies. As such, they were found to constitute an economic activity.

37 See *Höfner & Elser*, paragraph 22: German law prohibited any parties other than public bodies from providing the 'employment procurement' services under consideration. Such services were nonetheless held to be an economic activity, as they had not always been, and were not necessarily, carried out by public bodies.

38 Joined cases C-159/91 and C-160/91 *Poucet and Pistre* [1993] ECR I-637 ('*Poucet and Pistre*'), paragraph 10 (concerning management of the public social security system). See also cases C-350/07 *Kattner Stahlbau GmbH v Maschinenbau- und Metall- Berufsgenossenschaft* (insurance against accidents at work and occupational diseases) [2009] ECR I-1513, *AOK Bundesverband* (operation of sickness funds), and C-218/00 *Cisal di Battistello Venanzio v INAIL* [2002] ECR I-691 (compulsory insurance against accidents at work).

39 *FFSA*, paragraph 17.

40 *Poucet and Pistre*, paragraph 10.

3 SPECIFIC EXCLUSIONS FROM COMPETITION LAW

[3.404]

3.1 Where public bodies **do** act as undertakings, there may be certain limited circumstances in which their conduct may fall within the scope of a specific exclusion from competition law provided for in the relevant UK and/or EU legislation.

3.2 Schedule 3 paragraph 4 of the CA98 and its EU law equivalent, Article 106(2) TFEU, exclude from the application of the UK and EU prohibitions respectively undertakings that are entrusted with providing 'services of general economic interest' or that are 'revenue-producing monopolies', insofar as those prohibitions would obstruct, in law or in fact, the performance by those undertakings of the particular tasks assigned to them.[41] These exclusions therefore seek to ensure that the application of competition law does not prevent the effective provision of important public services or the proper operation of fiscal monopolies.[42]

3.3 The OFT will interpret these exclusions strictly, and the exclusions will generally be applicable in only a limited number of circumstances. In the past, the European courts have applied the 'services of general economic interest' exclusion in certain sectors in which a universal service obligation exists, such as core postal services or emergency ambulance transport services.[43]

3.4 The CA98[44] also excludes from the scope of its prohibitions any agreements that an undertaking must enter into, or conduct that it must engage in, in order for it to comply with a '**legal requirement**' (for example, a requirement imposed by primary or secondary UK legislation or directly-effective EU legislation). Again, the OFT expects that this exclusion will be applicable in only a very limited number of circumstances. These might include, for example:

- agreements that are entered into as a result of formal directions issued by a sector regulator,[45] or
- where a party is specifically required by legislation to disclose publicly certain information that would otherwise be considered competitively sensitive. Thus, the Chapter I prohibition has previously been found not to apply to a regulated undertaking's publication of its prices, insofar as such publication was mandated by the terms of its statutory licence.[46]

The legislation or other legal instrument must **require** (explicitly or in practice) undertakings to engage in the agreement or conduct in question. If that agreement or conduct is only encouraged or facilitated by the relevant legal instrument and the undertaking therefore retains some freedom of action, competition law will still apply.[47]

3.5 The CA98 also confers on the Secretary of State power to issue orders excluding certain categories of agreement between undertakings from the scope of the CA98,[48] if such exclusion is necessary either to avoid conflict with international obligations or for compelling reasons of public policy. To date, only three such orders have been made, each excluding on public policy grounds narrow categories of agreement in the defence sector from the application of the CA98. Furthermore, such orders do not serve to disapply EU competition law where the agreement affects trade between EU Member States.

NOTES

41 Note that where entrustment of a service of general economic interest to an undertaking involves the grant of State aid, it will be necessary to comply with applicable EU State aid rules. Those rules are beyond the scope of this guide.

42 For guidance on how the OFT interprets and applies these exclusions, see OFT421 *Services of general economic interest exclusion* (December 2004). Broadly, services of general economic interest are services that the State considers should be provided in all cases, whether or not there is an incentive for the private sector to do so. Revenue-producing monopolies are bodies granted a legal monopoly over the production or distribution of a particular good or service in order to raise revenue for the State.

43 See, respectively, case C-320/91 *Corbeau* [1993] ECR I-2533 and *Ambulanz Glöckner*. In the UK, such sectors are typically governed by sector specific regulation. It should be noted that the significant privatisation and liberalisation in the UK has significantly reduced the number of services where a single body has been entrusted with the exclusive right to provide the relevant service.

44 Schedule 3, paragraph 5 CA98.

45 For example, the Office of Rail Regulation considers that, where it directs undertakings to enter into access agreements under section 17 of the Railways Act 1993, those agreements are excluded from the scope of both the Chapter I and Chapter II prohibitions.

46 Decision of the Director General of Fair Trading of April 2002, *Vodafone: distribution agreements for pre-pay mobile phone vouchers* (Case 5/04/2002).

47 See Case C-280/08 P, *Deutsche Telekom v. Commission*, [2010] ECR I-0000, paragraphs 80–81: the fact that the undertaking's abusive pricing conduct was encouraged by pricing rules laid down by a national regulatory authority did not absolve the undertaking of competition law liability, as it retained some freedom to determine its prices. See also joined cases C-359/95 P and C-379/95 P *Commission and France v Ladbroke Racing* [1997] ECR I-6265, paragraphs 33–34.

48 Schedule 3, paragraph 7 CA98.

4 THE CONSEQUENCES FOR PUBLIC BODIES OF ENGAGING IN ECONOMIC ACTIVITY

[3.405]

4.1 The fact that a public body acts as an undertaking and is subject to UK and EU competition law does not necessarily mean that it will have to amend its practices. Indeed, compliance with competition law should not materially impede public bodies' efficient exercise of their functions. Instead, public bodies need to self-assess whether their conduct is compliant with competition law to determine whether any amendments are required.

4.2 However, the OFT is keen to ensure that, where public bodies do engage in economic activities, a level playing field and a similar commitment to compliance exists for all operators in those markets, particularly in mixed markets in which public bodies, private firms and third sector organisations (for example, charities) compete alongside one another. Effective competition in those markets can benefit the wider economy by encouraging greater productivity and innovation and preserving long term growth, while continuing to provide greater value for money to the taxpayer.

4.3 If a public body is acting as an undertaking, the types of agreement and conduct that are prohibited by competition law will be the same for that public body as for any other undertaking.

4.4 Thus, for example, types of agreement (whether formal or informal) that are likely to be prohibited under the Chapter I prohibition and/or Article 101 include those which fix the price charged for goods or services, limit production, allocate markets or customers (whether geographically or by some other division), or involve collusive tendering (also known as bid-rigging).

4.5 Other agreements between undertakings, such as those involving the joint purchase or sale of goods or services or those which have a long exclusivity period, may also breach competition law where they have anti-competitive effects. Anti-competitive effects include enabling the undertakings concerned to raise prices or to reduce quality or service standards, and/or making it difficult for other undertakings to compete. For these types of agreements, any competition law concerns will be assessed alongside any economic benefits arising from the arrangements.[49]

4.6 Under the Chapter II prohibition and/or Article 102, a public body acting as an undertaking must refrain from certain conduct where it holds a dominant position, which is only likely if that undertaking is able to behave independently of the normal constraints imposed by competitors, suppliers and consumers. Examples of the kind of conduct that might amount to an abuse of that dominant position include: charging prices so low that they do not cover the costs of the product or service sold in order to exclude competitors, offering different prices or terms to similar customers without objective justification, or refusing to supply an existing or long standing customer without objective justification.

4.7 The OFT has published separate guidance on how undertakings can achieve compliance with competition law.[50] The information above is therefore intended as a brief overview of the principal categories of potentially unlawful conduct, and not as a substitute either for that more detailed guidance or for bodies seeking legal advice, where appropriate.

SANCTIONS FOR BREACH OF COMPETITION LAW

4.8 Failure by a public body to comply with competition law in carrying out an economic activity can have serious consequences:

- An agreement entered into, or decision made, which breaches UK or EU competition law will be automatically void and unenforceable.
- Third parties (including injured competitors, customers and consumer groups) that have suffered loss as a result of an undertaking's infringement of competition law can bring a civil damages claim against that undertaking in the UK courts.

4.9 Furthermore, the OFT also has a wide range of powers to investigate undertakings (and in some cases individuals within those undertakings) that are suspected of breaching competition law[51] and, where appropriate, may impose substantial penalties:

- Undertakings that are found to have breached competition law can be fined up to 10 per cent of their annual worldwide turnover and directed to change their behaviour.
- Individuals who dishonestly engage in cartel activity can be prosecuted under the criminal cartel offence[52] and sentenced to up to five years in prison and/or a fine.
- To the extent that the undertaking in breach is formed as a company – whether in public or private ownership – directors of that company can be disqualified from managing a company for up to 15 years.[53]

4.10 The OFT uses its tools flexibly and applies a range of measures.[54] It will pursue the course of action that it deems to be the most suitable, effective and efficient, taking into account the specific circumstances of the case and the markets at issue, and the OFT's prioritisation principles.[55]

4.11 For example, in response to a competition concern in a public services market, the OFT will consider the range of options available to it, and will balance the beneficial deterrent effect of a formal decision and possible fine against the impact that payment of a fine might have on the public body and ultimately, the taxpayer.

Part 3 CMA and other Guidelines

FURTHER GUIDANCE

4.12 Notwithstanding the principle that bodies must self-assess whether they are compliant with competition law, the OFT may – where genuine uncertainty exists – provide public bodies that are proposing to enter into some form of collaboration agreement with existing or potential competitors with its non-binding views under the OFT's Short-form Opinion process.

4.13 The OFT will consider giving a Short-form Opinion where the proposed agreement raises novel or unresolved questions regarding the application of the CA98, the clarification of which would benefit a wider audience. The OFT will consider requests for such Short-form Opinions under its usual prioritisation principles.[56]

OFT publications

4.14 The OFT has published further guidance on the application of the CA98, including:

- OFT401 *Agreements and concerted practices* (December 2004)
- OFT402 *Abuse of a dominant position* (December 2004)
- OFT407 *Enforcement* (December 2004)
- OFT421 *Services of general economic interest exclusion* (December 2004)
- OFT953 *OFT Prioritisation Principles* (October 2008)
- OFT1330 *Quick Guide to competition law compliance* (June 2011)
- OFT1341 *How your business can achieve compliance with competition law* (June 2011)

4.15 These guidance documents are available to download from the OFT's website www.oft.gov.uk

European Commission publications

4.16 For information on the application of EU competition law to:

- agreements between competitors, see *European Commission Guidelines on the applicability of Article 101 of the Treaty on the Functioning of the European Union to horizontal co-operation agreements* (OJ 2011 C11/1)
- agreements between businesses at different levels of the distribution chain (such as suppliers and retailers), see *European Commission Guidelines on Vertical Restraints* (OJ 2010 C130/1).

4.17 These Guidelines are available to download from the European Commission website ec.europa.eu/competition

NOTES

49 For example, the agreement may be permitted under section 9 CA98 or Article 101(3) TFEU on the basis of the efficiencies and consumer benefits generated by that agreement, either in general terms or pursuant to a specific UK or EU block exemption.

50 See OFT1341 *How your business can achieve compliance with competition law* (June 2011) and OFT1330 *Quick Guide to competition law compliance* (June 2011).

51 See further OFT 404 *Powers of* investigation (December 2004), OFT407 *Enforcement* (December 2004), and OFT515 *Powers for investigating criminal cartels* (January 2004).

52 Section 188, Enterprise Act 2002. While the 'cartel offence' in section 188 is committed by individuals, the scope of the offence is determined by reference to arrangements between 'undertakings'. Section 188(7) makes clear that 'undertaking' for this purpose has the same meaning as under the CA98.

53 See further OFT510 *Competition Disqualification Orders* (June 2010) and OFT1340 *Company directors and competition law* (June 2011).

54 For example, if the OFT is made aware of a potential breach of competition law, but decides not to prioritise a full CA98 investigation, it may, in appropriate cases, send that body a warning letter (see further OFT1263 *A guide to the OFT's investigation procedures in competition cases* (March 2011), paragraph 4.8).

55 These describe the principles that the OFT uses in prioritising its enforcement and other work, based on the impact, strategic significance, risks and resources associated with such action. See OFT953 *OFT Prioritisation Principles* (October 2008).

56 Further detail on the circumstances in which the OFT may issue Short-form Opinions is provided in *OFT's Approach to Short-form Opinions* (April 2010).

C. MERGERS

1. GENERAL

COMPETITION AND MARKETS AUTHORITY REMEDIES FORM FOR OFFERS OF UNDERTAKINGS IN LIEU OF REFERENCE

(January 2014)

[3.406]

NOTES

This form is available on the Competition and Markets Authority website at: www.gov.uk/government/publications/undertakings-in-lieu-of-reference-form.

This form (the Remedies Form) specifies the information and documents to be submitted by the merger parties for the purpose of offering undertakings in lieu of reference (UILs) pursuant to section 73 of the Enterprise Act 2002 (as amended) (the Act).

The information requested allows the Competition and Markets Authority (CMA) to examine whether the proposed UILs offered by the merger parties (or a modified version of them) might be acceptable to remedy, mitigate or prevent in a clear cut manner the substantial lessening of competition (SLC) identified by the CMA in its decision pursuant to section 22 or 33 of the Act.

Guidance on the process for assessing UILs and on how the CMA assesses remedies is set out in chapter 8 of *Mergers: Guidance on the CMA's jurisdiction and procedure* (CMA2) and in *Mergers: Exceptions to the duty to refer and undertakings in lieu of reference guidance* (OFT1122), both of which are available on the CMA's webpages.[1]

The level of information required by the CMA will vary according to the type and structure of remedy proposed. This Remedies Form refers to a 'business' to be divested. This is because the CMA generally prefers divestiture of an existing business that can compete effectively on a stand-alone basis independently of the merger parties over divestiture of part of a business or a collection of assets. Nevertheless, the Remedies Form can be used when the proposed divestiture comprises part of a business. Similarly, the Remedies Form can be used where the UILs offered involve divestment of multiple businesses: a single Remedies Form should be submitted for the full UIL offer, but distinctions between the individual divestment packages making up that offer should be highlighted where relevant. In such circumstances, parties are encouraged to discuss with the CMA case team the likely information requirements of the CMA.

Parties are not obliged to complete all aspects of this Remedies Form but doing so as far as possible and relevant will enhance the CMA's ability to assess effectively the UILs offered. Failure to complete all aspects of this Remedies Form by the end of the five working day period for offering UILs will not automatically invalidate the UIL offer. If parties consider that any particular information requested by this Remedies Form may not be necessary or relevant for the CMA's assessment, they are asked to provide adequate reasons for this. Again, parties are encouraged to discuss such omissions with the case team in advance of making their submission.

The CMA does not automatically refuse behavioural remedies as UILs. However, in general, it is highly unlikely that behavioural remedies will be sufficiently clear cut to address identified competition concerns and therefore to be suitable for the purposes of UILs. This form therefore focuses on structural remedies. Nevertheless, if the merger parties wish to offer a behavioural remedy as a UIL they should provide answers to questions 1 to 3 of the Remedies Form as well as an indication of the timetable for implementation of the proposed remedy and any potential barriers to such implementation.

NOTES

[1] www.gov.uk/cma

DESCRIPTION OF THE UIL AND HOW IT WILL ADDRESS THE SLC

1. Provide:
(i) a general description of the UILs offered
(ii) any conditions for their implementation, and
(iii) the proposed text of the UILs offered (as a separate document), noting where relevant how this differs from the template UILs available on the CMA's webpages.

2. Describe how the UILs offered will remedy, mitigate or prevent in a clear cut manner the SLC identified by the CMA or any adverse effect which has or may have resulted from it or may be expected to result from it.

3. Provide a **non-confidential summary** of the nature and scope of the UILs offered and how, in your view, they will remedy, mitigate or prevent in a clear cut manner the SLC identified by the CMA or any adverse effect which has or may have resulted from it or may be expected to result from it. The CMA may use this summary in order to test the UILs offered with third parties (including potential purchasers).

INFORMATION ON THE BUSINESS TO BE DIVESTED

This section sets out information that should be provided in relation to the current operation of the business to be divested. For divestments that are currently divisions but not separate entities, the information provided should be at the divisional level, but parties are encouraged to discuss with the CMA how best to do this in order to ensure the right balance of information between questions 4 to 8 and questions 9 to 15.

4. Describe the business to be divested generally, including:
(i) the entity(ies) belonging to it (and which form a part of the divestment)
(ii) its registered place of business and head office
(iii) its other locations for production or provisions of services
(iv) how, in broad terms, it operates and is managed
(v) an overview of its organisational structure, and
(vi) whether a disposal of shares or assets is proposed.

5. List and describe the products or services supplied by the business to be divested and any new products or services planned.

6. Provide details[2] of the key assets and liabilities of the business to be divested including:
(i) staff, including those employees at managerial level who are critical for the operation of the business to be divested, describing their functions
(ii) production facilities
(iii) key intellectual property rights and licences
(iv) key intangible assets, including brands
(v) leases and freehold property
(vi) working capital and other such assets or liabilities
(vii) cash
(viii) debt and other financial liabilities
(ix) any debt or leasing obligations that will pass with the business to be divested, and
(x) other liabilities not covered above (for example, pensions).

Highlight if any of the above assets come from more than one party to the merger (that is, whether a 'mix and match' divestiture is proposed).

7. Provide a customer list for the business to be divested with revenue (in GBP) generated in the most recent financial year and list and describe key supplier contracts, including setting out when any key customer or supplier contracts are due for renewal.

8. Provide summary financial statements for the business to be divested at profit and loss level for each of the two most recent financial years, the current financial year and a forecast period of two financial years. The table below provides a guide to how you may wish to present the information. For the current financial year, you should, as necessary, split the information between actual and forecast information. Where the SLC relates to more than one product type or market, you should also provide a breakdown by product type/market.

Business to be divested	**Historical FY-2**	**Historical FY-1**	**Current FY**	**Forecast FY-1**	**Forecast FY-2**
Revenue (GBP)					
Cost of sales (GBP)					
Gross profit (GBP)					
EBITDA (GBP)					
Depreciation (GBP)					
EBIT(GBP)					
Source of data:					

NOTES

2 In some instances the information in this question can be submitted via an annual report or management report provided that the current position has not materially changed from that stated in the report. If so, please provide cross-references indicating where in the report(s) the information responsive to this question can be found.

ASSETS EXCLUDED FROM THE BUSINESS TO BE DIVESTED AND CONTINUING LINKS TO THE MERGER PARTIES

This section sets out information that should be provided in relation to the existing parts of the business to be divested that will not form part of the proposed divestiture package.

9. Where relevant, describe any of the operational or management functions which will not form a part of the business to be divested but which are currently necessary for the functioning of the business. This description should include such functions as:
(i) research and development
(ii) production
(iii) marketing and sales
(iv) logistics
(v) relations with customers
(vi) relations with suppliers, and
(vii) the maintenance and provision of IT systems and various support functions (for example, payroll, general finance, accounting and regulatory compliance).

Please note any material changes in such arrangements in the last two years.

10. Set out what transitional service arrangements you would include as part of the divestment with regard to the functions referred to in Question 9 in the event they are required by the purchaser. Please specify your proposed key terms and duration of any such arrangements.

11. Where relevant, describe in detail (including terms and duration) any continuing links between the business to be divested and other businesses controlled by the merger parties, such as:
(i) supply, production, distribution, service or other contracts
(ii) shared tangible or intangible assets
(iii) shared or seconded personnel
(iv) shared IT systems or other systems
(v) shared customers, and
(vi) administrative and other support functions.

12. For each of the links referred to in Question 11 describe any changes envisaged and the expected timing of these changes.

13. Describe the customers or groups of customers which will not form a part of the proposed business to be divested but which are currently customers of the business to be divested. Provide the total turnover generated by these customers (in GBP and as a percentage of the total turnover of the business to be divested).

14. Describe any other areas where the business to be divested differs from the nature and scope of the business as currently operated.

15. Where carve-out arrangements are likely to impact on the operation of the business to be divested, describe any arrangements envisaged for carving out or reconfiguring the business to be divested from its existing form.

REMEDY IMPLEMENTATION PROCESS

The purpose of this section is to allow you to explain to the CMA how the business will be divested to a suitable purchaser in an acceptable timeframe. The more information that you are able to provide when completing this part of the Remedies Form, the more the CMA is likely to be able to have confidence that a suitable purchaser will be found.

16. Provide a proposed timetable for divestment setting out key milestones including preparation of documentation and filtering of potential purchasers. Please note that the CMA has 50 working days beginning on the day after the CMA gives the notice required pursuant to section 34ZA(1)(b) or section 34A(2)(b) of the Act to accept UILs.[3]

17. State whether there are likely to be significant due diligence, statutory or regulatory issues that may delay the divestment process. These may include any third party rights, obligations, consents (including the transfer of leases), licences and regulatory approvals. Set out the expected timeframes for resolving each of these.

18. Suitable purchasers. Please answer either part (i) or (ii):
(i) If you have already identified a potential purchaser, explain why you consider this buyer would meet the CMA's purchaser suitability criteria.[4]
(ii) If you have not yet identified a potential purchaser, explain the reasons why, in your view, the business will be acquired by a suitable purchaser in the timeframe proposed in Question 16. List likely purchasers for the business to be divested highlighting those potential purchasers whom you have already approached with a view to a sale and summarising the strength of their interest and their capability to complete a transaction within the timescale proposed. Where you have already approached potential purchasers, submit any expressions of interest, informal or formal offers or any draft heads of terms.

19. If you do not consider that divestment to an upfront buyer is required in this case, please provide reasons for this.[5]

20. In instances of multiple businesses to be divested, state whether and why these are intended to be sold to several buyers or to one. If to several, explain whether you intend to 'package' some of the businesses to be divested together in order to achieve a sale.

21. Set out whether you consider the appointment of a monitoring trustee would be appropriate in this case. If you do not consider that a monitoring trustee is required in this case, please provide reasons for this.

NOTES

[3] Subject to a possible extension of up to 40 working days if the CMA considers that there are special reasons for doing so: see paragraphs 8.23 to 8.24 of *Mergers: Guidance on the CMA's jurisdiction and procedure* (CMA2).

[4] See *Mergers: Exceptions to the duty to refer and undertakings in lieu of reference guidance* (OFT1122).

[5] An 'upfront buyer' means having a buyer in place with a signed sale and purchase agreement (generally conditional from the buyer's perspective only on CMA acceptance of the UILs and completion of the main transaction if it remains anticipated) **before** the CMA accepts the UILs (see paragraphs 8.33 to 8.34 of *Mergers: Guidance on the CMA's jurisdiction and procedure* (CMA2)). The upfront buyer would need to meet the CMA's purchaser suitability criteria set out in *Mergers: Exceptions to the duty to refer and undertakings in lieu of reference guidance* (OFT1122).

COMPETITION AND MARKETS AUTHORITY TEMPLATE UNDERTAKINGS IN LIEU OF A REFERENCE

Version 28 October 2015

[3.407]

NOTES

This form is available on the Competition and Markets Authority website at: www.gov.uk/government/publications/undertakings-in-lieu-of-reference-form.

[3.408]

Note 1: If merger parties wish to offer an undertaking under section 73A(1) of the Enterprise Act 2002, they should provide the CMA with a version of this template showing the proposed changes.

Note 2: These template undertakings are for completed mergers. For anticipated mergers, please make the necessary (minor) amendments.

Note 3: These template undertakings have two alternative versions of paragraph 2, depending on whether an upfront buyer is offered.

Note 4: In this template X is the direct acquirer, Y is the target business. For upfront buyer cases, Z is the proposed purchaser.

ACQUISITION BY X OF Y
UNDERTAKINGS GIVEN BY X TO THE COMPETITION AND MARKETS AUTHORITY PURSUANT TO SECTION 73 OF THE ENTERPRISE ACT 2002

Whereas:

(a) X (**[define X]**) completed the acquisition of Y (**[define Y]**) on [date] by way of [details of transaction] (the **Transaction**) such that X and Y ceased to be distinct for the purposes of the Enterprise Act 2002 (the **Act**);

(b) Under section 22(1) of the Act the Competition and Markets Authority (**CMA**) has a duty to refer a relevant merger situation for a Phase 2 investigation where it believes that it is or may be the case that the creation of that merger situation has resulted or may be expected to result in a substantial lessening of competition within any market or markets in the UK for goods or services;

(c) Under section 73 of the Act the CMA may, instead of making such a reference and for the purpose of remedying, mitigating or preventing the substantial lessening of competition concerned or any adverse effect which has or may have resulted from it or may be expected to result from it, accept undertakings to take such action as it considers appropriate, from such of the parties concerned as it considers appropriate. In particular, the CMA shall have regard to the need to achieve as comprehensive a solution as is reasonable and practicable to the substantial lessening of competition and any adverse effects resulting from it;

(d) As set out in the CMA's decision of [date] (the **Decision**), the CMA believes that, in the absence of appropriate undertakings, it would be under a duty to refer the Transaction for a Phase 2 investigation;

(e) The CMA considers that the undertakings given below by X are appropriate to remedy, mitigate or prevent the substantial lessening of competition, or any adverse effect which has or may have resulted from the Transaction, or may be expected to result from it, as specified in the Decision;

(f) [in upfront buyer cases: Prior to the acceptance of these undertakings by the CMA, X entered into a legally binding agreement of [date] to divest the Divestment Business as a going concern to a Proposed Purchaser on terms approved by the CMA. This agreement was conditional only on formal CMA approval of the Proposed Purchaser and acceptance by the CMA of these undertakings. This agreement includes a warranty that the Proposed Purchaser has the financial resources, expertise (including the managerial, operational and technical capability), incentive and intention to maintain and operate the Divestment Business as part of a viable and active business in competition with X and other competitors in the [description of relevant market];] and

(g) [The CMA made an Initial Enforcement Order applying to [list addressees of Order] on [date] in respect of the Transaction pursuant to section 72 of the Act for the purposes of preventing pre-emptive action. Pursuant to section 72(6)(b) of the Act, this Initial Enforcement Order ceases to be in force on the acceptance by the CMA of the undertakings given below by X].

NOW THEREFORE X hereby gives to the CMA the following undertakings for the purpose of remedying, mitigating or preventing the substantial lessening of competition, or any adverse effect which has or may have resulted from it or may be expected to result from it.

1 EFFECTIVE DATE OF THE UNDERTAKINGS

1.1 These undertakings shall take effect from the date that, having been signed by X, they are accepted by the CMA.

[Paragraph 2 if an upfront buyer is offered:]

2 DIVESTMENT OF THE DIVESTMENT BUSINESS

2.1 X shall ensure that the completion of the divestment of the Divestment Business to the Proposed Purchaser contemplated by the agreement referred to in recital [f] of these undertakings takes place within a period not exceeding [one month] from the date these undertakings take effect.

2.2 X shall use all reasonable endeavours to ensure the transfer of Key Staff with the divestment of the Divestment Business.

2.3 [If applicable:] Where X divests a Divestment Business over which it holds[, or Y held,] a freehold interest by way of the grant of a long lease on normal commercial terms of not less than 25 years duration to the Proposed Purchaser, it shall in addition sell the freehold interest in the Divestment Business to a person independent of and unconnected to X and the Group of Interconnected Bodies Corporate to which X belongs and any Associated Person or Affiliate of X or such Group of Interconnected Bodies Corporate, within a period not exceeding three months from the date of the commencement of the lease.

2.4 In the event that X fails to complete the divestment of the Divestment Business in accordance with paragraphs 2.1 [and] 2.2 [and 2.3] above, the CMA may, whether or not initiating the Trustee Functions as set out in paragraph 4 below, require X to divest the Divestment Business as a going concern at no minimum price to a purchaser or purchasers approved by the CMA.

[Paragraph 2 if no upfront buyer is offered:]

2 DIVESTMENT OF THE DIVESTMENT BUSINESS

2.1 X shall, using its best endeavours and acting in good faith, as soon as reasonably practicable, effect to the satisfaction of the CMA the divestment of the Divestment Business as a going concern by the end of the Divestment Period to a purchaser approved by the CMA in accordance with the provisions of these undertakings.

2.2 Without prejudice to the generality of paragraph 2.1 above, X shall use all reasonable endeavours to ensure the transfer of Key Staff with the divestment of the Divestment Business.

2.3 X shall be deemed to have complied with its obligations at paragraph 2.1 above if, as soon as reasonably practicable and in any event by the end of the Divestment Period, it has entered into a legally binding agreement (or agreements) with a purchaser (or purchasers) approved in advance by the CMA in writing pursuant to these undertakings (or a legally binding agreement (or agreements) conditional on such approval), provided that the completion of the divestment of the Divestment Business contemplated by such agreement (or agreements), if later than the end of the Divestment Period, takes place:

(a) within a period not exceeding [one month] after the approval of the purchaser by the CMA (or within [one month] of the effective date of these undertakings, as set out in paragraph 1 above, whichever is later); or

(b) within a period not exceeding 10 Working Days after all the necessary approvals and consents from third parties have been obtained,

whichever is later.

2.4 Without prejudice to the generality of paragraph 2.1 above, X shall take the following measures to the extent they may be necessary in the opinion of the CMA to effect the sale of the Divestment Business in accordance with the provisions of these undertakings:

(a) the transfer or vesting of property, assets, rights, personnel, liabilities or obligations (including without prejudice any contracts, licences, authorisations, permits or consents);

(b) [any other transfer of interests that will take effect with the sale]

(c) the adjustment of contracts, whether by discharge or reduction or assignment of any liability or obligation or otherwise;

(d) the creation, allotment, transfer, surrender or cancellation of any shares, stock or securities; and

(e) the formation or winding up of a company.

2.5 [If applicable:] Where X divests a Divestment Business over which it holds[, or Y held,] a freehold interest by way of the grant of a long lease on normal commercial terms of not less than 25 years duration to the purchaser, it shall in addition sell the freehold interest in the Divestment Business to a person independent of and unconnected to X and the Group of Interconnected Bodies Corporate to which X belongs and any Associated Person or Affiliate of X or such Group of Interconnected Bodies Corporate, within a period not exceeding three months from the date of the commencement of the lease.

2.6 X shall ensure that the sale and purchase agreement entered into for the purposes of paragraph 2.1 and 2.3 above includes a warranty that the purchaser has the financial resources, expertise (including the managerial, operational and technical capability), incentive and intention to maintain and operate the Divestment Business as part of a viable and active business in competition with X and other competitors in the [description of relevant market].

2.7 In the event that X fails to divest the Divestment Business in accordance with paragraphs 2.1, 2.2, 2.3 [and 2.5] above, the CMA may, whether or not initiating the Trustee Functions as set out in paragraph 4 below, require X to divest the Divestment Business as a going concern at no minimum price to a purchaser approved by the CMA.

2.8 X shall notify the CMA in writing of the identity of each proposed purchaser that makes an offer for the Divestment Business together with the value and terms of such offers as soon as reasonably practicable following the receipt of such offers and in any event within 5 Working Days of receipt of such offers.

3 APPROVAL OF PURCHASER AND TERMS OF DIVESTMENT

3.1 For the purposes of the CMA approving a Proposed Purchaser [if an upfront buyer is offered: and the terms of the divestment] of the Divestment Business in accordance with these undertakings, X shall, save as required or permitted by the CMA, satisfy the CMA that:

(a) the acquisition by the Proposed Purchaser of the Divestment Business, on the terms set out above, remedies, mitigates or prevents the substantial lessening of competition concerned or any adverse effect which has or may have resulted from it, or may be expected to result from it, in particular having regard to the need to achieve as comprehensive a solution as is reasonable and practicable to the substantial lessening of competition and any adverse effects resulting from it;

(b) the Proposed Purchaser is independent of and unconnected to X and the Group of Interconnected Bodies Corporate to which X belongs and any Associated Person or Affiliate of X or such Group of Interconnected Bodies Corporate;

(c) the Proposed Purchaser has the financial resources, expertise (including the managerial, operational and technical capability), incentive and intention to maintain and operate the Divestment Business as a viable and active business in competition with X and other competitors in the [description of market] from the date of completion of the divestment of the Divestment Business;

(d) the Proposed Purchaser is reasonably to be expected to obtain all necessary approvals, licences and consents from any regulatory or other authority, including (where applicable) landlord's consent to the transfer of any leasehold interest; and

(e) the acquisition by the Proposed Purchaser of the Divestment Business does not create a realistic prospect of a substantial lessening of competition within any market or markets in the UK.

3.2 The CMA may require X to provide it with such information and documentation as it may reasonably require to satisfy the CMA that the Proposed Purchaser will fulfil the requirements in paragraph 3.1 above.

4 APPOINTMENT OF A TRUSTEE

4.1 The provisions of paragraph 4.2 to paragraph 4.7 below shall apply only as long as X has not satisfied, or where the CMA has reasonable grounds for believing that X will not satisfy, all or any part of the obligation to divest the Divestment Business in accordance with paragraph 2 above.

4.2 Within 5 Working Days of the CMA notifying X in writing that it must do so, X shall propose to the CMA for approval:

(a) the names of at least two individuals to exercise the Trustee Functions; and

(b) the full terms of a mandate in accordance with which the Trustee shall carry out the Trustee Functions.

4.3 X and/or any individuals nominated pursuant to paragraph 4.2 shall satisfy the CMA that, save as required or permitted by the CMA:

(a) such nominated individuals have the necessary qualifications to carry out their mandates, and are employees or partners of an investment bank, retail bank, commercial property agent, building society or law firm or accountancy firm with an established reputation either nationwide or in a substantial part of the UK or in another EU member state;

(b) such nominated individuals are each independent of X and of the Group of Interconnected Bodies Corporate to which X belongs and of any Associated Person or Affiliate of X or of such Group of Interconnected Bodies Corporate and of any Proposed Purchaser of the Divestment Business to be sold pursuant to these undertakings, and, in the reasonable opinion of X, are appropriate to be appointed as Trustee; and

(c) such nominated individuals neither are, nor are likely to become, exposed, either directly or indirectly, to a conflict of interest that impairs or may be likely to impair their objectivity or independence in discharging the Trustee Functions.

4.4 Within 2 Working Days of the CMA approving, at its discretion, one or more of the persons nominated by X and their proposed mandates pursuant to paragraph 4.2 above, and subject to any modifications the CMA deems necessary for the Trustee to carry out the Trustee Functions, X shall use its best endeavours to appoint from the persons so approved one person to carry out the Trustee Functions in accordance with the mandate approved by the CMA pursuant to paragraph 4.2 above.

4.5 In the event that:

(a) X fails to propose any person or persons in accordance with paragraph 4.2 above; or

(b) none of the persons proposed by X pursuant to paragraph 4.2 is approved by the CMA; or

(c) X is unable for any reason to appoint within the time limit stipulated in paragraph 4.4 above any such person following approval by the CMA,

X shall use its best endeavours to appoint from persons nominated by the CMA one person to carry out the Trustee Functions on the terms of a mandate approved by the CMA. X shall use its best endeavours to make such appointment within 5 Working Days of receiving the nominations from the CMA.

4.6 The appointment of the Trustee pursuant to paragraph 4.4 or paragraph 4.5 above shall be irrevocable unless:

(a) a conflict of interest that impairs or may be likely to impair the objectivity or independence of the Trustee in discharging the Trustee Functions arises;

(b) the Trustee ceases to perform the Trustee Functions; or

(c) the CMA is otherwise satisfied that there is good cause for the appointment to be terminated in advance of the satisfactory fulfilment of the Trustee Functions.

4.7 In the event that the appointment of the Trustee is terminated in accordance with paragraph 4.6 above, X shall, if requested to do so in writing by the CMA, use its best endeavours to appoint from persons nominated by the CMA one person to carry out the Trustee Functions in accordance with such mandate as is approved by the CMA. X shall use its best endeavours to make such appointment within seven Working Days of receiving the nominations from the CMA. Where required by the CMA, the outgoing Trustee shall continue as Trustee until a new Trustee is in place and a full handover of all relevant information has taken place.

5 THE MANDATE

5.1 The terms of the mandate proposed by X pursuant to paragraph 4.2 above shall, as a minimum, contain all provisions necessary to enable the Trustee to carry out the Trustee Functions including, without limitation to the generality of this paragraph:

(a) an exclusive, irrevocable mandate to sell the Divestment Business as required by paragraph 6.1 below to a purchaser as directed or approved in writing in advance by the CMA at no minimum price and on such reasonable terms and conditions as the Trustee considers appropriate to effect an expedient sale;

(b) a mandate to take any other steps necessary for, or incidental to, the Trustee's mandate under sub-paragraph (a) above;

(c) a comprehensive power of attorney to the Trustee (including the authority to grant sub-powers of attorney to the Trustee's officers, employees and agents) to enable it to take all steps necessary or appropriate to effect the sale of the Divestment Business;

(d) a mandate to comply with any orders and/or directions given by the CMA; and

(e) a mandate to appoint at X's expense such advisers as the CMA and/or the Trustee reasonably considers necessary or appropriate in connection with the performance of the Trustee Functions.

6 FUNCTIONS OF TRUSTEE

6.1 The Trustee shall seek to procure, within such period as may be specified in writing by the CMA, the completion of the sale of the Divestment Business at no minimum price, to a purchaser or purchasers approved by the CMA in accordance with paragraph 6.3 below.

6.2 Without prejudice to the generality of paragraph 6.1 above, the Trustee shall take the following measures in relation to the Divestment Business to the extent to which such measures may be necessary to effect the divestment of the Divestment Business in accordance with the provisions of these undertakings:

(a) the transfer or vesting of property, assets, rights, personnel, liabilities or obligations (including without prejudice any contracts, licences, authorisations, permits or consents);

(b) any other transfer of interests that will take effect with the sale;

(c) the adjustment of contracts, whether by discharge or reduction or assignment of any liability or obligation or otherwise;

(d) the creation, allotment, transfer, surrender or cancellation of any shares, stock or securities; and

(e) the formation or winding up of a company.

6.3 The Trustee shall not sell or permit the divestment of the Divestment Business to a Proposed Purchaser unless it has been directed to do so by the CMA or has obtained the CMA's prior written approval in respect of the identity of that Proposed Purchaser. The Trustee shall notify the CMA of the identity of a Proposed Purchaser as soon as reasonably practicable prior to the signing of a legally enforceable agreement and in any event at least 20 Working Days in advance of the proposed completion of the proposed sale and purchase agreement in question.

6.4 Pending the divestment of the Divestment Business pursuant to paragraph 6.1 above, the Trustee shall monitor X's compliance with its obligations under paragraph 7.1 and paragraph 7.2 below and shall promptly take such measures as it considers necessary to ensure such compliance, as well as reporting in writing to the CMA, if the Trustee concludes on reasonable grounds that X is failing or will fail to comply with such obligations.

6.5 The Trustee may give written directions to X to take such steps as may be specified or described in the directions for the purpose of securing X's compliance with its obligations under these undertakings or enabling the Trustee to carry out the Trustee Functions. The Trustee may not require X to:

(a) offer any reverse premium or similar inducement to a purchaser; or

(b) accept any actual or contingent liability towards a purchaser or otherwise in connection with the divestment of the Divestment Business which would be unusual in scope, duration or financially, having regard to the price and usual market practice in relation to similar disposals.

6.6 The Trustee shall, as soon as reasonably practicable, comply at all times with any reasonable instructions or written directions made by the CMA for the purposes of carrying out or securing compliance with the undertakings (or any matter incidental thereto) and shall provide to the CMA such information and reports in relation to the carrying out of the Trustee Functions as the CMA may require. The Trustee shall promptly report in writing to the CMA if the Trustee concludes on reasonable grounds that X is failing or will fail to comply with any of its obligations under these undertakings.

6.7 For the purpose of fulfilling the Trustee Functions, the Trustee shall not be bound by instructions of X nor shall the Trustee Functions be extended or varied in any way by X save with the prior express written consent of the CMA.

7 OBLIGATIONS OF X FOLLOWING APPOINTMENT OF TRUSTEE

7.1 X shall not give any instruction or request to the Trustee which conflicts with the Trustee Functions.

7.2 X shall take all such steps as are reasonably necessary to enable the Trustee to carry out the Trustee Functions, including but not limited to:

(a) complying with such written directions as the Trustee may from time to time give pursuant to paragraph 6.6 above; and

(b) providing the Trustee with all such assistance and information as it may reasonably require in carrying out the Trustee Functions.

8 REMUNERATION OF TRUSTEE

8.1 X shall pay the Trustee a reasonable remuneration for the services it provides in carrying out the Trustee Functions, and shall pay the Trustee in a way that does not impede the independent and effective fulfilment of the Trustee Functions, which shall be set out in the Trustee's mandate referred to in paragraph 5 above.

9 INTERIM ACTION

9.1 Pending the completion of the divestment of the Divestment Business to the satisfaction of the CMA in accordance with the provisions of these undertakings, save as otherwise agreed in advance in writing by the CMA, X shall minimise as far as possible any risk of loss of competitive potential of the Divestment Business and in particular ensure that: [**note**: if an Initial Enforcement Order is in force, it may be appropriate for the CMA to grant derogations similar to those granted for that Order]

(a) the Divestment Business is carried on separately from the X Business and the Divestment Business's separate sales or brand identity is maintained;

(b) the Divestment Business and the X Business are maintained as a going concern and sufficient resources are made available for the development of the Divestment Business and the X Business, on the basis of their respective pre-Transaction business plans;

(c) except in the ordinary course of business, no substantive changes are made to the organisational structure of, or the management responsibilities within, the Divestment Business or the X Business;

(d) the nature, description, range and quality of [goods and/or services] supplied in the UK by each of the Divestment Business and the X Business are maintained and preserved;

(e) except in the ordinary course of business for the separate operation of the Divestment Business and the X Business:

   (i) all of the assets of the Divestment Business and the X Business are maintained and preserved, including facilities and goodwill;

   (ii) none of the assets of the Divestment Business or the X Business are disposed of; and

   (iii) no interest in the assets of the Divestment Business or the X Business is created or disposed of;

(f) there is no integration of the information technology of the Divestment Business or X Businesses, and the software and hardware platforms of the Divestment Business shall remain essentially unchanged, except for routine changes and maintenance;

(g) the [customer and supplier] lists of the Divestment Business and the X Business shall be operated and updated separately and any negotiations with any existing or potential [customers and suppliers] in relation to the Divestment Business will be carried out by the Divestment Business alone and for the avoidance of doubt the X Business will not negotiate on behalf of the Divestment Business (and vice versa) or enter into any joint agreements with the Divestment Business (and vice versa);

(h) all existing contracts of the Divestment Business and the X Business continue to be serviced by the business to which they were awarded;

(i) no changes are made to Key Staff of the Divestment Business or X Business;

(j) no Key Staff are transferred between the Divestment Business and the X Business;
(k) all reasonable steps are taken to encourage all Key Staff to remain with the Divestment Business and the X Business; and
(l) no business secrets, know-how, commercially-sensitive information, intellectual property or any other information of a confidential or proprietary nature (**Confidential Information**) relating to either of the Divestment Business or the X Business shall pass, directly or indirectly, from the Divestment Business (or any of its employees, directors, agents or affiliates) to the X Business (or any of its employees, directors, agents or affiliates), or vice versa, except where strictly necessary in the ordinary course of business (for example, where required for compliance with external regulatory and/or accounting obligations) or any steps necessary in order for X to comply with these undertakings, including the transfer of information necessary for the divestment process, provided that, upon divestment of the Divestment Business, any records or copies (electronic or otherwise) of Confidential Information held by X in relation to the Divestment Business (or vice versa) shall be returned to the relevant business and any copies destroyed (except as may be necessary for the purposes of compliance with the obligations above).

9.2 At all times, X will actively keep the CMA informed of any material developments relating to the Divestment Business, which includes, but is not limited to:
(a) details of Key Staff who leave the X Business or the Divestment Business;
(b) any interruption of the X Business or the Divestment Business (including without limitation its procurement, production, logistics, sales and employee relations arrangements) that has prevented it from operating in the ordinary course of business for more than 24 hours;
(c) all substantial customer volumes lost by the Divestment Business; and
(d) substantial changes in the X Business's or the Divestment Business's contractual arrangements or relationships with key suppliers.

10 CONTINUED SEPARATION

10.1 Except with the prior written consent of the CMA, for a period of 10 years following the divestment of the Divestment Business pursuant to these undertakings, X, or any member of the Group of Interconnected bodies Corporate to which X belongs:
(a) shall not, directly or indirectly, hold, acquire, re-acquire or use:
    (i) an Interest in the Divestment Business [other than (a) any freehold interest in the property associated with the Divestment Business pending divestment of that freehold proprietary interest pursuant to paragraph [2.3/2.5] above]; or
    (ii) any Interest in any company carrying on or having Control of the Divestment Business (other than any investments made in the ordinary course of the operation of any of the employee benefit and pension schemes of X or of any members of the Group of Interconnected Bodies Corporate to which X belongs of not more than three per cent in aggregate of the issued equity share capital in any such company, whose shares are listed or dealt with on any recognised investment exchange, which carries no more than three per cent of the voting rights exercisable at meetings of such company); or
    (iii) other than in the normal course of business, any of the assets of the Divestment Business;
(b) shall procure that no employee or director of X or any member of the Group of Interconnected Bodies Corporate to which X belongs for as long as they are an employee or director of X or any member of the Group of Interconnected Bodies Corporate to which X belongs holds or is nominated to any directorship or managerial position in the Divestment Business or directorship or managerial position in any company or other undertaking carrying on or having control of the Divestment Business without the CMA's prior written consent;
(c) shall not participate in the formulation of, or (other than in the ordinary course of business) influence or attempt to influence, the policy of the Divestment Business or any company or other undertaking carrying on or having control of that Divestment Business; and
(d) shall not enter into or carry out any agreement or arrangement with any person, if the carrying out of the agreement or arrangement is intended to result or will result in any Associated Person or Affiliate of X or of any member of the Group of Interconnected Bodies Corporate to which X belongs directly or indirectly acquiring the Divestment Business or doing any of the things listed in sub-paragraphs 10.1(a), 10.1(b) and 10.1(c) above.

10.2 If applicable: Where X (or any member of the Group of Interconnected Bodies Corporate to which X belongs) divests a Divestment Business by way of granting a sub-lease and remains the landlord of the purchaser of the Divestment Business, then for the duration of the sub-lease, X shall within 10 Working Days of being requested to do so (unless agreed otherwise by the CMA):
(a) consent to any matter requiring landlord's approval under the terms of the lease between X and the purchaser of the Divestment Business (except where X is required to obtain such consent from another person); and/or
(b) pass on any request for consent to the freehold owner of the property or relevant third party, as appropriate.

11 IF APPLICABLE: NEW DIVESTMENT IF X OBTAINS POSSESSION OF A DIVESTMENT BUSINESS PROPERTY

11.1 In the event that, following divestment of a Divestment Business in a manner that has involved X assigning an existing lease or granting a sub-lease to the purchaser of the Divestment Business, X benefits from or becomes subject to an Occupation Interest (so long as X so benefits or becomes so subject during the term of the lease assigned or sub-lease granted by X as part of such divestment), X shall:

(a) within 10 Working Days of becoming aware that it is so benefitting or is so subject inform the CMA in writing of that fact; and

(b) using its best endeavours and acting in good faith comply with such written directions as the CMA may give to X to effect a new divestment of the Occupation Interest to a new purchaser approved by the CMA in accordance with the provisions of these undertakings, provided always that such written directions must be of a similar nature to those contained in these undertakings with regard to the original divestment of the Divestment Business.

11.2 In determining, for the purposes of sub-paragraph 11.1(b) above, whether to require X to effect a new divestment of the Occupation Interest to a new purchaser approved by the CMA in accordance with the provisions of these undertakings, the CMA may have regard to any change of circumstances since the Decision.

11.3 In the event that X fails to divest the Occupation Interest in accordance with paragraph 11.1 above, the CMA may, whether or not initiating the Trustee Functions set out in these undertakings, require X to divest the Occupation Interest at no minimum price to a purchaser approved by the CMA.

11.4 X shall notify the CMA in writing of the identity of each proposed purchaser that makes an offer for the Occupation Interest together with the value and terms of such offers as soon as reasonably practicable following the receipt of such offers and in any event within 10 Working Days of receipt of such offers.

11.5 In the event that the CMA gives written directions under paragraph 11.1 above for X to effect a new divestment of the Occupation Interest, paragraphs 3, 4, 5, 6, 7, 8 and 9 shall apply to the new divestment in the same way that they applied to the original divestment obligation save that references to 'Divestment Business' in those paragraphs shall be construed as references to 'Occupation Interest'.

12 COMPLIANCE

12.1 X shall comply promptly with such written directions as the CMA may from time to time give:

(a) to take such steps as may be specified or described in the directions for the purpose of carrying out or securing compliance with these undertakings; or

(b) to do or refrain from doing anything so specified or described which it might be required by these undertakings to do or to refrain from doing.

12.2 X shall co-operate fully with the CMA when the CMA is:

(a) monitoring compliance with the provisions of these undertakings; and

(b) investigating potential breaches of the provisions of these undertakings.

12.3 X shall procure that any member of the same Group of Interconnected Bodies Corporate as X complies with these undertakings as if it had given them and actions and omissions of the members of the same Group of Interconnected Bodies Corporate as X shall be attributed to X for the purposes of these undertakings.

12.4 Where any Affiliate of X is not a member of the same Group of Interconnected Bodies Corporate as X, X shall use its best endeavours to procure that any such Affiliate shall comply with these undertakings as if it had given them.

13 PROVISION OF INFORMATION

13.1 X shall furnish promptly to the CMA such information as the CMA considers necessary in relation to or in connection with the implementation and/or enforcement of and/or the compliance with these undertakings, including for the avoidance of doubt, any Confidential Information.

14 EXTENSION OF TIME LIMITS

14.1 The CMA may, in response to a written request from X, or otherwise at its own discretion, grant an extension to any time period referred to in these undertakings.

15 SERVICE

15.1 X hereby authorises [Organisation], whose address for service is [address], to accept service on its behalf of all documents connected with these undertakings (including any document of any kind which falls to be served on or sent to X, or any of its Subsidiaries in connection with any proceedings in Courts in the UK, orders, requests, notifications or other communications connected with these undertakings).

15.2 Unless X inform the CMA in writing that [Organisation] has ceased to have authority to accept and acknowledge service on its or any of its Subsidiaries' behalf, any document, order, request, notification or other communication shall be validly served on X if it is served on [Organisation]; and service shall be deemed to have been acknowledged by X if it is acknowledged by [Organisation] or such other nominee.

15.3 Paragraph 15.2 above has effect irrespective of whether, as between X and [Organisation] or other nominees, [Organisation] or other nominees has or continues to have any authority to accept and acknowledge service on X's or any of its respective Subsidiaries' behalf.

15.4 No failure or mistake by [Organisation] or other nominees (including a failure to notify X of the service of any document, order, request, notification or other communication) shall invalidate any action taken in respect of these undertakings including any proceedings or judgment.

15.5 Any communication from X to the CMA under these undertakings shall be addressed to Manager, Market and Mergers Remedies Monitoring, Competition and Markets Authority, Victoria House, Southampton Row, London WC1B 4AD or such other person or address as the CMA may direct in writing.

16 EFFECT OF INVALIDITY

16.1 Should any provision of these undertakings be contrary to law or invalid for any reason, X undertake to continue to observe the remaining provisions.

17 GOVERNING LAW

17.1 X recognises and acknowledges that these undertakings shall be governed and construed in all respects in accordance with English law.

17.2 In the event that a dispute arises concerning these undertakings, X undertakes to submit to the courts of England and Wales.

18 TERMINATION

18.1 X recognises and acknowledges that these undertakings shall be in force until such time as they are varied, released or superseded under the Act.

18.2 X recognises and acknowledges that the variation, release or supersession of these undertakings shall not affect the validity and enforceability of any rights or obligations that arose prior to such variation, release or supersession.

19 INTERPRETATION

19.1 The Interpretation Act 1978 shall apply to these undertakings as it does to Acts of Parliament.

19.2 References in these undertakings to any English law term for any legal status, interest, concept or thing shall in respect of any jurisdiction other than England and Wales be deemed to include what most nearly approximates in that jurisdiction to the English law term.

19.3 In these undertakings the word "including" shall mean including without limitation or prejudice to the generality of any description, definition, term or phrase preceding that word and the word "include" and its derivatives shall be construed accordingly.

19.4 For the purposes of these undertakings:

"**the Act**" means the Enterprise Act 2002;

"**Affiliate**" a person is an affiliate of another person if they or their respective enterprises would be regarded as being under common control for the purposes of section 26 of the Act;

"**Associated Person**" means a person or persons associated with X within the meaning of section 127(4) of the Act and includes any Subsidiary of such a person or persons;

"**business**" has the meaning given by section 129(1) and (3) of the Act;

"**CMA**" means the Competition and Markets Authority or any successor body;

"**Confidential Information**" means any business secrets, know-how, commercially sensitive information, intellectual property or any other information of a confidential or proprietary nature;

"**Control**" shall be construed in accordance with section 26 of the Act, and in the case of a body corporate, a person shall be deemed to Control it if he holds, or has an interest in, shares of that body corporate amounting to 10 per cent or more of its issued share capital or carrying an entitlement to vote at meetings of that body corporate of 10 per cent or more of the total number of votes which may be cast at such meetings;

"**Decision**" means the CMA's decision under section 22 of the Act dated [date] in connection with the Transaction;

"**Divestment Business**" means [details of the divestment business];

[if applicable – see paragraph 11 and the definition of "Occupational Interest" below:] "**Divestment Business Property**" means the relevant property associated with the Divestment Business as at the date of these undertakings;

[if no upfront buyer is offered:] "**Divestment Period**" means the period of time determined by the CMA and notified in writing to X by the CMA;

"**enterprise**" has the meaning given in section 129(1) of the Act;

"**Group of Interconnected Bodies Corporate**" has the meaning given in section 129(2) of the Act; references to a Group of Interconnected Bodies Corporate shall be to the Group of Interconnected Bodies Corporate as constituted from time to time;

"**Interest**" includes shares, an interest in shares and any other interest carrying an entitlement to vote at shareholders' meetings but does not include a contract to acquire shares in the future; and for this purpose "an interest in shares" includes an entitlement by a person other than the registered holder, to exercise any right conferred by the holding of these shares or an entitlement to Control the exercise of such right;

"**Key Staff**" means staff in positions of executive or managerial responsibility and/or whose performance affects the viability of the Divestment Business or the X Business, as the case may be;

[if applicable – see paragraph 11:] "**Occupation Interest**" means an interest in the Divestment Business Property by virtue of which X enjoys an unconditional right or is under an unconditional obligation to occupy the Divestment Business Property provided always that: (i) the original purchaser (or its successor) is not in occupation of the Divestment Business Property; and/or (ii) before such interest in the Divestment Business Property arose, the most recent use to which the Divestment Business Property had been put was that of carrying on [nature of the business];

"**Proposed Purchaser**" means [if an upfront buyer is offered: Z or such other proposed purchaser] [if no upfront buyer is offered: any proposed purchaser] for the Divestment Business;

"**Subsidiary**" shall be construed in accordance with section 1159 of the Companies Act 2006 (as amended), unless otherwise stated;

"**the Transaction**" means the [details of the transaction];

"**Trustee**" means the person appointed pursuant to paragraph 4.4, paragraph 4.5 or paragraph 4.7 to carry out the Trustee Functions;

"**Trustee Functions**" means the functions set out in paragraph 6;

"**UK**" means the United Kingdom of Great Britain and Northern Ireland;

"**Working Day**" means any day of the week other than a Saturday or a Sunday or any day that is a public holiday in [England and Wales] [Scotland];

"**X**" means [full registered name and company number of acquirer];

"**X Business**" means the business of X and its Group of Interconnected Bodies Corporate carried on as at [date of Transaction or date of Initial Enforcement Order if later];

"**Y**" means [full registered name and company number (or, in asset transaction, description of business) of target of Transaction];

[if an upfront buyer is offered:] "**Z**" means [full registered name of the proposed purchaser]; and

unless the context requires otherwise, the singular shall include the plural and vice versa.

FOR AND ON BEHALF OF X

Signature

Name

Title

Date

DATE ACCEPTED BY THE CMA:

COMPETITION AND MARKETS AUTHORITY MERGER ENQUIRY LETTER TEMPLATE (APRIL 2016)

[3.409]

NOTES

This document is available on the Competition and Markets Authority website at: www.gov.uk/government/publications/merger-enquiry-letter-template.

This document is the template for the enquiry letter that is used by the CMA when initiating an investigation into a merger that has not been formally notified to the CMA by the parties to the merger. Further information about the enquiry letter is available in *Mergers: Guidance on the CMA's jurisdiction and procedure*, paragraphs 6.15 to 6.18.

This template will be adjusted for the merger in question. The CMA may request additional or more specific information than listed in this template.

[Acquirer]

From:

Direct line: 020 3738 [xxxx]

Our ref: [xx]

[Date]

By email to [ ]@[ ]

Dear [name addressee]

[COMPLETED/ANTICIPATED] ACQUISITION BY [ACQUIRER] OF [TARGET]: SECTION 109 NOTICE

The Competition and Markets Authority (**CMA**) understands that [in [month and year],] [legal name of acquirer] ([**Acquirer**]), either itself or through an affiliated entity, [acquired/will acquire] [target] (this acquisition referred to as the **Transaction**).

Under section 5 of the Enterprise Act 2002 (**the Act**), the CMA has a function to obtain and keep under review information about matters relating to the carrying out of its other functions, including the competition assessment of mergers and acquisitions. This is done with a view to (among other things) ensuring that the CMA has sufficient information to take informed decisions and to carry out its other functions effectively. If a merger or acquisition qualifies for review by the CMA, [section 22 / section 33] of the Act imposes a duty on the CMA to refer this merger or acquisition to an in-depth Phase 2 assessment where it believes that it is or may be the case that the merger or acquisition [has resulted, or] may be expected to result, in a substantial lessening of competition in one or more markets in the UK.

The CMA is now assessing whether the Transaction gives rise to a relevant merger situation for the purposes of Part 3 of the Act and, if so, whether its statutory duty to refer the Transaction to a Phase 2 assessment set out in [section 22 / section 33] of the Act is triggered.

For the purposes of this assessment, I am now serving [Acquirer] with the attached notice (**the Notice**) made by the CMA in exercise of its powers under section 109 of the Act.

The Notice requires [Acquirer] to produce the documents specified and supply the information described in **questions 1 to 8** of Annex 1 to the Notice **by 4:30 pm on [deadline one]** and provide the response to **all remaining questions** in Annex 1 to the Notice **by 4:30 pm on [deadline two]**. In both cases, the documents and information should be provided to the CMA by email to me at [email] and to my colleague [name] at [email]. You may also send the documents and information by post to the CMA at Victoria House, Southampton Row, London WC1B 4AD, marked for the attention of me and [name].

[If [Acquirer] does not provide the documents specified and information described in Annex 1 to the Notice by the above deadlines (with or without reasonable excuse), the CMA may, in accordance with section 25(2) of the Act, extend its four month statutory deadline for reviewing the Transaction by the additional number of days that it takes [Acquirer] to provide the documents/ information and for the CMA to assess whether the documents/ information form a satisfactory response.]

[In addition,] if [Acquirer] fails to comply with the requirements of the Notice without reasonable excuse, the CMA may impose a financial penalty on [Acquirer] under the CMA's powers in section 110 of the Act. The financial penalty may be a fixed amount, an amount calculated by reference to a daily rate, or a combination of the two. Further information can be found in the CMA's *Administrative penalties: Statement of policy on the CMA's approach* (CMA4), which can be found at www.gov.uk/government/publications/ administrative-penalties-statement-of-policy-on-the-cmas-approach.

If you believe that [Acquirer] is not in a position to provide the documents specified and information described in Annex 1 to the Notice, please let me know as soon as possible. In that case, please also let me know which entity (if any) you believe would be better placed.

In addition to the specific documents and information requested in Annex 1 to the Notice, I encourage [Acquirer] to provide any additional data and documentary evidence that it considers may be useful for the CMA's assessment of the Transaction's impact on competition.

You may also find it useful to read the CMA publication *Quick Guide to UK Merger Assessment* (CMA18). You can find more detailed information about the CMA's processes in *Mergers: Guidance on the CMA's jurisdiction and procedure* (CMA2 – for example, the purpose of this 'enquiry letter' is set out from paragraph 6.15) and about the CMA's assessment of the impact of a merger on competition in *Merger Assessment Guidelines* (OFT1254/CC2). It may also be useful to review the guidance notes to the Merger Notice under section 96 of the Act that the CMA has published to assist notifying merger parties to understand the nature and extent of information that notifying parties should provide to the CMA to enable it to assess a notified merger. These documents are available at www.gov.uk/ mergers-how-to-notify-the-cma-of-a-merger.

If you have any questions, please contact me on the above number or my colleague [name] on [phone number]. We would be very happy to discuss this request for documents and information, as well as the CMA's processes more generally.

[I am copying this letter to [name of main contact at company/organisation].]

Yours sincerely

[add electronic signature]

[Name]

[Email]

[COMPLETED/ANTICIPATED] ACQUISITION BY [ACQUIRER] OF [TARGET] NOTICE UNDER SECTION 109 OF THE ENTERPRISE ACT 2002

NOTICE

1. Acting under section 109 of the Enterprise Act 2002 (the **Act**) and for the purpose of an investigation into the above acquisition (the **Transaction**), a permitted purpose under section 109(A1) of the Act, the Competition and Markets Authority (**CMA**) hereby gives notice to [legal name of acquirer] ([**define Acquirer**]) at [acquirer registered address] that it is required to produce the documents specified and supply the information described in the attached Annex 1.

2. [Acquirer] is required to produce the documents specified and supply the information described in **questions 1 to 8** of the attached Annex 1 **by 4:30 pm on [deadline one]** and provide the response to **all remaining questions** in the attached Annex 1 **by 4:30 pm on [deadline two]**.

3. It should be produced to the CMA by email to [name] at [email] and [name] at [email]. It may also be produced by post to the CMA at Victoria House, Southampton Row, London WCIB 4AD, marked for the attention of [name] and [name].

4. [Acquirer] is not required to produce any documents or supply any information which it would not be compelled to produce and/or supply in civil proceedings before the High Court in England and Wales or Northern Ireland or before the Court of Session in Scotland.

5. Any reference in this Notice to the production of a document includes a reference to the production of a legible and intelligible copy of information recorded otherwise than in legible form.

CONSEQUENCES OF NOT COMPLYING WITH THIS NOTICE

Non-compliance with this Notice

6. Under section 110 of the Act where the CMA considers that a person has, without reasonable excuse, failed to comply with any requirement of this Notice it may impose a penalty of such amount as it considers appropriate. The amount of such penalty may be a fixed amount or an amount calculated by reference to a daily rate or a combination of a fixed amount and an amount calculated by reference to a daily rate.

7. Such a penalty is subject to the following limits:

(a) In the case of a fixed amount, such amount shall not exceed £30,000.

(b) In the case of an amount calculated by reference to a daily rate, such amount per day shall not exceed £15,000.

(c) In the case of a fixed amount and an amount calculated by reference to a daily rate, the fixed amount shall not exceed £30,000 and the amount calculated by reference to a daily rate shall not exceed £15,000 per day.

8. Any penalty imposed by reference to a daily rate shall not take account of any days prior to the service of the notice of the penalty and the amount of the penalty payable shall cease to accumulate at the beginning of:

(a) the day on which the requirement of this Notice is satisfied

(b) if earlier, the relevant day as defined in section 110A of the Act, namely the day when the CMA finally decides on whether the Transaction is referred to Phase 2 for an in-depth investigation under [section 22 / section 33] of the Act.

Intentional obstruction or delay

Under section 110(3) of the Act, where the CMA considers that a person has intentionally obstructed or delayed another person in the exercise of his powers under section 109(6) of the Act, it may impose a fixed amount penalty. Such penalty shall not exceed £30,000.

10. No penalty shall be imposed by virtue of sections 110(1) and 110(3) of the Act where more than four weeks have passed since the relevant day as defined in section 110A of the Act (see paragraph 8(b) above). This provision does not apply in relation to any variation or substitution of a penalty which is permitted by the Act.

Suppression or destruction of documents

11. Under section 110(5) of the Act, an offence is committed where documents required to be produced in accordance with this Notice are intentionally altered, suppressed or destroyed. A person who commits an offence under this section shall be liable:

(a) on summary conviction, to a fine;

(b) on conviction on indictment, to imprisonment for a term not exceeding two years or to a fine or both.

STATEMENT OF POLICY ON PENALTIES

12. The CMA shall have regard to its *Administrative penalties: Statement of policy on the CMA's approach* (CMA4), which can be found at www.gov.uk/government/publications/administrative-penalties-statement-of-policy-on-the-cmas-approach.

[add electronic signature]

[AD]

Assistant Director, Mergers

[Date]

ANNEX 1 TO SECTION 109 NOTICE

The Competition and Markets Authority (**CMA**) understands that [in [month and year],] [legal name of acquirer], either itself or through an affiliated entity, [acquired/will acquire] [target entity/ assets amounting to an enterprise] (**[Target]**) (this acquisition referred to as the **Transaction**).

In this Annex we refer to [acquirer full legal name] when we refer to that specific legal entity. [Acquirer full legal name] together with all entities under common ownership or common control, or over which it exerts material influence, or which exert material influence over it within the meaning of section 26 of the Enterprise Act 2002, [but excluding [Target],] are collectively referred to as [**Acquirer**].

Please provide the documents specified and supply the information described in **questions 1 to 8** of this Annex 1 **by 4:30 pm on [deadline one]** and provide the response to **all remaining questions** in this Annex 1 **by 4:30 pm on [deadline two]**.

Further information on the CMA's merger process can be found on the CMA's website: www.gov.uk/mergers-how-to-notify-the-cma-of-a-merger. This includes links to further guidance listed under the heading "Detailed information" on this web page, as set out in the cover letter to the section 109 Notice.

REPRESENTATIVES

1. Provide the contact details of the person with whom the CMA should communicate in relation to the Transaction. This can be a person within [acquirer full legal name] or, for example, a solicitor acting for it. Those contact details should include:

1.1. Name
1.2. Position
1.3. Direct telephone line
1.4. Direct email address
1.5. Full postal address
1.6. Please confirm that such appointed representative is duly authorised as provided for in section 126(4) of the Enterprise Act 2002 to receive communications and service of documents from the CMA on behalf of [acquirer full legal name] and provide a copy of the document granting the authorisation.

2. Provide contact details (including the name and position of a contact person, his/her direct email address and direct telephone number) for [Target].

TRANSACTION DETAILS

3. Provide a copy of the contractual agreements or other documents forming and implementing the Transaction.

4. State whether the Transaction has completed and, if so state on which date this completion took place. If the Transaction has not completed, please state on which date completion is expected to take place.

5. Provide a diagram showing the pre- and post-Transaction ownership structure of [Acquirer], including the Target, showing all subsidiaries [Acquirer] controls which are active in the same economic sector as [Target].

6. Provide a copy of any press release and public report (such as a newspaper article) evidencing when and how [Acquirer]'s intention to engage in the Transaction and the completion of the Transaction were made public for the first time.

7. List all other jurisdictions in which the Transaction has been notified to the competition authorities.

8. List all other mergers, acquisitions, disposals and/or joint ventures undertaken by [Acquirer] in the last two years.

JURISDICTION

9. What was the turnover in the UK of [Target] in the last financial year?

10. To determine whether the 'share of supply test' is met for jurisdictional purposes:[1]

10.1. Provide your best estimate of the share of supply for any product or service of any description in relation to which [Acquirer] and [Target] have a combined share of supply in the UK, or in a substantial part of the UK, of 25% or more and where the merger causes an increment in such share. In addition to any other relevant product or service, please consider in any case [specific area of overlap CMA is aware of].

10.2. Please state the methodology and data sources you have used to produce your estimates.

NOTES

[1] Information about the share of supply test can be found in *Mergers: Guidance on the CMA's jurisdiction and procedure*, paragraphs 4.53-4.62.

BUSINESS ACTIVITIES

11. Describe the pre-Transaction business activities of [Acquirer] and [Target] in the UK, including a description of the products and services

11.1. where the businesses of [Acquirer] and [Target] overlapped before the Transaction, ie where there was a horizontal relationship between these businesses (the **Overlap Products**),[2] and

11.2. where before the Transaction the businesses of [Acquirer] or [Target] operate at different levels of the supply chain, ie where there was a vertical relationship between these businesses (the **Vertically Related Products**).[3]

12. Provide a list of all entities that form part of [Acquirer] (as defined in the second paragraph of this Annex above) and are active in the supply or purchase of the Overlap Products or the Vertically Related Products in the UK.

Part 3 CMA and other Guidelines

13. Provide a copy of the annual accounts and reports for the two most recent accounting periods for:
13.1. [acquirer full legal name]; and
13.2. [Acquirer] in consolidated form.

14. Provide a copy of the management accounts of [acquirer full legal name] for the twelve months prior to the Transaction.

15. If [Acquirer] has management accounts relating specifically to the business activities in which [Acquirer] and [Target] overlapped prior to the Transaction, please provide also those management accounts for the twelve months prior to the Transaction.

16. If [Acquirer] is in possession of the management accounts of [Target], provide a copy of those for the twelve months prior to the Transaction.

NOTES

2 Horizontal relationships relate to business activities in the same economic sector and at the same level of the supply chain, ie between competing (or potentially competing) businesses.

3 Vertical relationships relate to business activities at different levels of the supply chain. These can be, for example, the link between an upstream supplier (or potential supplier) and a downstream customer (or potential customer), either as an input into its own production or for resale.

GEOGRAPHIC AREA(S) OF ACTIVITIES

17. State the extent of the geographic area (or areas, if local or regional markets are relevant) in the UK in which, before the Transaction, (a) [Acquirer] and (b) [Target] supplied the Overlap Products and the Vertically Related Products. Explain how you have arrived at your response, including how you have assessed where most customers are located.[4]

NOTES

4 Further information about the geographic market is at *Merger Assessment Guidelines*, from paragraph 5.2.21.

COUNTERFACTUAL[5]

18. State your forecast for the short-term future of [Target] if the Transaction had not taken place. If your forecast is that [Target]'s position in this short-term future would have been materially different from its position before the Transaction, give your reasons for this forecast.

NOTES

5 The 'counterfactual' is the situation that would exist without the Transaction. See *Merger Assessment Guidelines*, from paragraph 4.3.1.

DOCUMENTS

Business plans and financial forecasts

19. Provide copies of the most recent business plan and financial forecasts of [Acquirer].

20. If available, provide copies of the most recent business plan and financial forecasts of [Acquirer] related specifically to one or more of the Overlap Products [and the Vertically Related Products].

The Transaction, its business rationale and investment case

21. Provide copies of all documents (including but not limited to minutes of meetings, studies, reports, presentations, surveys, analyses or recommendations) in the possession of [Acquirer] which:
(a) in the two years prior to the Transaction have been prepared by or for, or received by, any member of the board of directors (or equivalent body) or senior management or shareholders of any [Acquirer] entity (whether prepared internally or by external consultants) and
(b) set out the reasons for undertaking the Transaction, such as its investment case and/or the benefits for [Acquirer] of undertaking the Transaction.

22. To the extent accessible to [Acquirer], provide any Information Memorandum or Sale Information Brochure or similar document circulated by the seller of [Target] or its representatives when seeking expressions of interest for [Target] or during any 'due diligence' undertaken by or on behalf of [Acquirer].

Market studies and analysis

23. Provide copies of all documents (including but not necessarily limited to reports, presentations, studies, analysis, or industry market reports such as customer research and pricing studies) in the possession of [Acquirer] and either prepared by or for [Acquirer] or published in the last two years prior to the Transaction, which set out the competitive conditions, market conditions, estimated market shares and/or competitors in the industry or business areas in relation to which [Acquirer] and [Target] overlapped prior to the Transaction [or were in a (potential) vertical relationship], as identified in your response to Question 11 above.

Advertising and marketing

24. Provide copies of all internally or externally produced marketing and advertising strategy documents generated by, or on behalf of, [Acquirer] in the twelve months prior to the Transaction and which relate to the Overlap Products [or the Vertically Related Products].

Prices

25. As regards price lists of [Acquirer] for each of the Overlap Products:

25.1. Provide copies of these price lists, if available.

25.2. If [Acquirer] applies different price lists and/or discounts and/or rebates depending on the identity of the customer, the geographic area or any other factors, then provide each such list.

25.3. If there is more than one price list for the same Overlap Product, then please list any factors contributing to any differences in the price lists so that the CMA can identify the reasons for any differences.

25.4. If [Acquirer] does not have price lists for each Overlap Product, describe how [Acquirer] determines the prices it charges for those Overlap Products for which it does not have price lists.

Documents prepared by or for [Target]

26. To the extent accessible to [Acquirer], provide copies of the documents requested in questions 19 to 25 that were prepared by or on behalf of [Target].

Contractual arrangements with customers

27. Please list in an Excel spreadsheet the following details for the five largest customers of each of (a) [Acquirer] and (b) [Target] for each of the Overlap Products in each geographic area where [Acquirer] and [Target] overlap (as set out in your response to question 17 above):

27.1. Customer name;

27.2. Nature of the arrangement (for example, whether the contract was awarded by open tender, tender by invitation or bilateral negotiations);

27.3. Length of the arrangement;

27.4. Whether the arrangement has been rolled over or automatically renewed without further tender or negotiations, and, if so, how often;

27.5. Previous supplier (if known);

27.6. Total value of contract (annual);

27.7. Product or service supplied;

27.8. Value per unit of product or service (if known);

27.9. Competitors for the provision of this contract (if known);

27.10. Proportion of the revenues generated from this customer relative to [Acquirer]'s total revenue from each of the relevant product or service.

HORIZONTAL ISSUES

28. In relation to each Overlap Product:

28.1. State how each of (a) [Acquirer] and (b) [Target] market these products and services, for example whether the focus is on the price or quality of these products or services and whether they have specific characteristics that make them suitable for only specific customer groups.

28.2. [State whether each of (a) [Acquirer] and (b) [Target] sets the key competitive variables for these products and services at a local, regional or national level.]

29. State the revenues earned in the most recent financial year by each of [Acquirer] and, if known, [Target] for each of the products and services referred to in question 28.

30. Provide best estimates of the shares of supply held by each of [Acquirer], [Target] and their competitors based on volumes and revenues in each of the Overlap Products in each geographic area in which they are supplied by both [Acquirer] and [Target], as indicated in your response to question 17. State the methodology and data sources for your estimates.

[VERTICAL ISSUES

31. For each Vertically Related Product, provide your best estimates of the shares of supply held by [Acquirer] and [Target] based on volumes and revenues in each geographic area indicated in your response to question 17 above.]

ENTRY OR EXPANSION

32. List the main factors affecting entry or expansion for each of the Overlap Products.

33. Provide details of all entry, exit or significant expansion over the past five years of which [Acquirer] is aware in relation to the Overlap Products, stating in each case (a) the product or service for which such entry/exit/expansion took place, (b) the relevant firm(s), and (c) if known, the scope and size of such entry/exit/expansion (in volume or revenues terms).

EFFICIENCIES AND CUSTOMER BENEFITS

34. List the main efficiencies and customer benefits that the Transaction will give rise to, if any.

CONTACT DETAILS

35. All contact details requested in this question should include, where available: (i) the name of a contact person, (ii) his/her direct telephone number and (iii) his/her direct email address. If [Acquirer] does not hold the relevant data, please provide the contact details of the Company Secretary or CEO of the relevant company. Please provide the contact details of:

35.1. **ten customers** of each of [Acquirer] and [Target] for each of the Overlap Products in each geographic area where [Acquirer] and [Target] overlapped prior to the Transaction, as indicated in your response to question 17, which should constitute a representative selection of their customers (for example, a sample of large, medium-sized and small customers); please also explain the basis on which these customers have been selected. If there are fewer than ten customers in any category, then provide details in relation to all customers in that category;

35.2. **ten main competitors** that [Acquirer] considers to be credible alternatives to [Acquirer] and [Target] for each of the Overlap Products in each geographic area where [Acquirer] and [Target] overlapped prior to the Transaction, as indicated in your response to question 17;

35.3. [**five main competitors** [Acquirer] considers to be credible alternatives to [Acquirer] or [Target] for each product or service in each geographic area where there was a vertical relationship between [Acquirer] and [Target] prior to the Transaction, as indicated in your response to questions 11.2 and **Error! Reference source not found.**;]

35.4. **five main suppliers** of each of [Acquirer] and [Target] for each product or service in each geographic area where [Acquirer] and [Target] overlap, as indicated in your response to questions 11.1 and 17;

35.5. any sectoral **trade associations** of which [Acquirer] is aware in respect of the Overlap Products;

35.6. any **government departments or regulatory authority** holding relevant information on this economic sector or from which the CMA could seek information or data on competition in any of the markets identified in this response.

RETAIL MERGERS COMMENTARY (CMA62, APRIL 2017)

[3.410]

NOTES

CONTENTS

INTRODUCTION

[3.411]

Retail mergers account for a significant number of cases that come before the CMA. Moreover, some of the questions that such mergers raise are largely specific to the sector.

This paper provides a commentary on some of the most frequently asked questions from retailers and their advisers. It builds on the previous commentary (OFT1305/CC2) and has been updated to reflect recent Competition and Markets Authority (CMA)[1] experience of mergers in retail sectors.

As a commentary based on the analysis of past merger cases in the retail sector, this paper does not constitute guidance under section 106(1) of the Enterprise Act 2002. The OFT and CC published joint *Merger Assessment Guidelines*[2] in 2010, to which the CMA will have regard when investigating merger cases.

This commentary focuses on situations where a merger involves firms supplying competing products (so-called 'horizontal mergers') and as such, may remove the rivalry between them, allowing the merged firm to profitably increase prices or worsen other elements of its offering (so-called 'unilateral effects'). The paper relates solely to the analysis of retail merger cases and not to other types of investigations.

In recent years the CMA has considered mergers involving many different retail sectors, including grocery stores, mobile phone shops, pubs, betting shops, pharmacies and DIY retailers.

Retail businesses and markets have a number of common features which affect the CMA's analysis:

- Retail businesses typically have fixed physical outlets (sometimes called bricks-and-mortar), which consumers usually visit in order to acquire or consume goods or services. These businesses may also have an internet presence. In other cases retailers may operate exclusively on the internet. In many cases, retail businesses will have multiple outlets across a region or country.
- Retail businesses often supply a range of goods sourced from numerous (unrelated) suppliers, although other retailers may supply services or a mixture of goods and services.
- The decision to purchase from a retail business is made by the individual consumer.

The relevance of this commentary to a particular retail merger will therefore vary according to the characteristics of the businesses and market concerned. For example, the commentary on catchment areas will not be relevant to a business that is internet-based and does not have fixed retail outlets. Some of the techniques discussed in the commentary are also useful for analysing mergers in non-retail sectors. For example, the CMA has applied some aspects of the methodology in investigations of mergers in the wholesale and leisure sectors.

Retail markets are continually evolving and we note that online retailing is increasingly important. The competitive interaction between different retail channels depends on the characteristics of the market concerned. This update of the commentary includes a section on how the CMA has assessed the interaction between bricks-and-mortar and online retail.

The commentary explains the principles that the CMA has followed in past retail mergers. It also describes the information and evidence that we have relied upon. We have included technical boxes to provide more detailed information for advisers. However, merger analysis cannot be done mechanistically and the CMA will consider each merger with due regard to the particular circumstances of the case and will apply methodology flexibly. This commentary is not intended to provide a comprehensive overview of all analytical issues in a retail merger.

We have used examples from past phase 1 and phase 2 merger investigations to illustrate our approach. Under the two-phase merger control regime in the UK, the CMA is required to apply different thresholds when answering the statutory questions in phase 1 and in phase 2. In phase 1, the CMA applies a 'realistic prospect' threshold, whereas in phase 2 the CMA applies a 'balance of probabilities' threshold. This will inform the approach taken by the CMA to the analysis in the two stages. The difference in the evidential threshold and the reduced time available for review at phase 1 will sometimes require a difference in the emphasis attached to certain aspects of the analysis – the extent of analysis on particular aspects and the evidence considered is likely to vary according to whether the merger is being considered in a phase 1 or phase 2 investigation.

We have selected the following topics as being of greatest interest to merging parties (Parties) and their advisers:

- Local and national competition, including how the CMA examines the effects of mergers on local competition when prices are set centrally and uniformly at all stores and how the CMA analyses the effect of a retail merger on dynamic competition.
- Catchment areas, including how the CMA chooses the appropriate distance measure.
- Filtering, including how the CMA identifies the effective competitor set and how the CMA chooses the appropriate measure of concentration.
- Bricks-and-mortar and online retail, including how the CMA assesses the strength of the constraint on bricks-and-mortar retailers from retailers active online. This constraint may be assessed either when considering the effective competitor set or assessing the closeness of competition between the Parties and third parties.
- Diversion ratios and price pressure indices, including how the CMA calculates diversion ratios and how the CMA uses these techniques.
- Econometric evidence, including key techniques that are widely used in retail merger investigations.

Surveys are frequently used in the assessment of retail mergers and throughout the commentary we explain how they have been used in past cases. Information on the design and implementation of surveys can be found in *Good practice in the design and presentation of consumer survey evidence in merger inquiries*.[3]

The analysis carried out by the CMA of the issues covered in this commentary will feed into the CMA's assessment of whether or not a particular retail merger gives rise to a substantial lessening of competition (SLC) and the scope of any SLC finding. This in turn will help determine what, if any, remedies would be effective in dealing with the competitive harm arising from the merger.

In line with its general practice, the CMA has tended to use structural remedies, such as prohibition or divestiture, in problematic retail mergers. The CMA's analysis of local and national competition plays a key role in determining what scale and scope of divestiture package would be sufficient to remedy any SLC. Similarly, the CMA's consideration of the effective competitor set can play a role, alongside other factors in assessing the suitability of potential purchasers for any divested business. As such, we hope that this commentary will help retailers and their advisers to anticipate some of the factors leading to the potential remedial outcomes that might be required, as well as the issues that will be considered in analysing the competitive impact of retail mergers. Remedies are not covered further in this commentary, please see *CC8: Merger Remedies: Competition Commission Guidelines*. It is not possible to comment in detail on every aspect of the retail cases that the CMA has examined in recent years. We hope nevertheless that the commentary will be useful and bring out some of the key themes from our experience.

NOTES

[1] Note that any references to the CMA include its predecessor organisations the Office of Fair Trading (OFT) and the Competition Commission (CC).

[2] *Merger Assessment Guidelines*: CC2/OFT1254.

[3] *Good practice in the design and presentation of consumer survey evidence in merger inquiries*: CC2com1/OFT1230.

1. LOCAL AND NATIONAL COMPETITION

[3.412]

1.1 The CMA draws up theories of harm to provide a framework for assessing the effects of a merger.

These theories of harm are informed by an understanding of the nature of competition in the market, including the main dimensions over which firms compete in both the short run and the longer run.

1.2 Bricks-and-mortar retailers compete to attract customers to their stores. The CMA's starting point is therefore that retailers compete with other stores in the local area.

1.3 In this section we set out how the CMA analyses the effect of a retail merger involving bricks-and-mortar stores on local and national competition.

LOCAL COMPETITION

1.4 Some retail chains set elements of their retail offer centrally and uniformly across stores.[4] In this context, Parties have sometimes argued that:

(a) the merger would not have an impact on prices and the service to customers at a local level because many of the important aspects of their offer to customers are determined centrally and they would not change their policy to a local one as a result of the merger; and

(b) where the merger involves a firm with a central policy acquiring a small number of stores, there would be no increases in national prices or deterioration of other aspects of their retail offer.

1.5 When considering these arguments the CMA's assessment of local competition has examined whether:

(a) the Parties currently set some aspects of their retail offer with regard to local competitive conditions; and

(b) if the Parties do not currently set their retail offer with regard to local competitive conditions, whether they would have an incentive to do so post-merger.

Does the retail offer vary between stores?

1.6 The CMA's starting point has been to recognise that customers shop in local retail stores within a given travel time of their home or work. Against this background the CMA's strong starting assumption at phase 1 has been that there will be material local competition on one or more aspects of the retail offer. The CMA has previously found evidence of local competition across a wide variety of sectors, including: supermarkets,[5] cinemas,[6] pharmacies,[7] opticians,[8] and bookmakers.[9]

1.7 In some phase 2 investigations the CMA has conducted a more detailed assessment of whether firms vary some aspects of their retail offer locally according to the strength of local competition. It has considered a range of evidence of local competitive responses, including:

(a) internal documents describing how the Parties set their retail offer, including documents that set out the responsibilities of local management, or show responses to local entry;

(b) evidence on how retailers have responded to under-performance at one or more local stores; and

(c) business plans for refurbishments, store openings and closures.

1.8 The CMA has also conducted empirical analysis to test how the performance of a store (for instance its price or quality) is affected by the level of, and any changes in, competition in the local area (for more information on performance concentration analysis see paragraphs 6.5 and 6.9):

(a) In Ladbrokes/Coral (2016), the Parties flexed some elements of the retail offer locally, affecting both price (eg promotions) and quality (eg store refurbishments), and the CMA assessed the effect of the merger on local competition. The Parties set other aspects of the retail offer (eg odds) centrally and uniformly across all of their stores, so the CMA also assessed the effect of the merger on their incentive to degrade the retail offer at all stores (see paragraphs 1.13 to 1.17).

(b) In Celesio/Sainsbury's (2016) evidence showed that pharmacies are able to (and do in practice) vary a number of aspects of the retail offer at a local level in response to competition. These included location, quality and speed of service, opening hours, stocking levels and waiting times. As a result the CMA assessed the effect of the merger on local competition.

Does the retail offer vary between stores?

1.9 Where the evidence shows that the retail offer at a store does not reflect competitive conditions in local markets, the CMA has assessed whether the merger may create an incentive to flex some aspects of the retail offer locally. To assess this the CMA has analysed the costs and benefits of changing the policy.

1.10 The costs of local flexing might include the cost of carrying different ranges in different stores, the fragmenting of sales volumes with suppliers and the additional complexity associated with such a change in policy, which may require different systems.

1.11 The benefits of local flexing come from the ability to degrade the retail offer where a store faces less competition and to improve it where it faces more competition. The benefits are greater when local demand and the intensity of local competition differ between the areas where the retailer operates.[10]

1.12 The CMA has assessed the incentive to flex some aspects of the retail offer in past phase 2 investigations:

(a) In Holland & Barrett/Julian Graves (2009) the CC found that the Parties would incur costs if they changed to local pricing and that these costs would deter a change in policy. These costs included a loss of national brand identity resulting in reduced revenue, increased spending on local in-store advertising, new staff to manage local promotions and local stock management.

(b) In Sports Direct/JJB Sports (2010), the CC found that differences in Sports Direct's retail offer were not related to local competitive conditions and that this suggested that the benefits of flexing were outweighed by the costs. There were relatively few areas where the Parties' stores overlapped and the CC did not think it likely that the merger would significantly increase Sports Direct's incentives to flex its retail offer in response to local competition.

(c) In Poundland/99p Stores (2015), the CMA found that the Parties would be able to flex the retail offer at the local level and that the cost of doing so would not be prohibitive. The CMA analysed the incentive to flex the retail offer by assessing the effect of the merger on the proportion of areas in which Poundland faced few competitors. The merger did not change this proportion significantly, so the CMA found that it would not be likely to change Poundland's incentives.

LOCAL MARKETS AND CENTRALLY SET, UNIFORM COMPONENTS OF THE RETAIL OFFER

1.13 In some cases the CMA has found that Parties do not flex aspects of the retail offer locally and would not have the incentive to do so after the merger. The CMA has then assessed whether the loss of rivalry in the areas where they overlap would be sufficient for the Parties to deteriorate their centrally set retail offer. This would involve increasing prices, or deteriorating other aspects of the retail offer, at all stores.

1.14 A retailer will take account of the extent of local competition faced by its stores when making decisions regarding prices and other competitive variables, even if these are set uniformly across all stores.

1.15 The total effect of any change in the retail offer is determined by the aggregate change in competitive conditions across all individual stores operated by that retailer. This, in turn, depends on the local competitive conditions faced by each store. Where competitive conditions facing individual stores are weak, fewer customers will be lost if the retailer degrades the retail offer. A retailer that has a collection of stores facing weak local competition will, as a result, face less of a constraint from its competitors than a retailer that has stores facing stronger local competition.

1.16 For example, two retailers might each have 50% of national sales. In one case, this might reflect an equal market share in each local market. In this case, each retailer will be influenced by the actions of its competitor. However, in another case, a 50% share of national sales might reflect a monopoly position for each of the two retailers in half of the local markets across the country. In these circumstances, each retailer would not face any direct constraint from the other (except in the border region where their stores face each other).

1.17 To assess the effect of a merger on the centrally set, uniform retail offer the CMA has looked at evidence on closeness of competition between the Parties and other retailers at a local level and the extent of geographic overlap:

(a) In Holland & Barrett/Julian Graves (2009), the CC found that the local markets where competition might be lessened as a result of the merger represented a small proportion of the Parties' stores. The CC found that this would not be sufficient for the retailer to increase its prices substantially, or to adjust any other feature of its centrally set uniform retail offer.

(b) In Sports Direct/JJB Sports (2010), the CC found that less than 10% of Sports Direct stores were within 5 miles of an acquired JJB Sports store.[11] The CMA used quantitative techniques to assess post-merger upward price pressure (see Section 5 for more details on these techniques) and estimated potential price effects of less than 1%. The CC considered this alongside other evidence and concluded that the effect of this merger was likely to be too small to be significant.

(c) In Poundland/99p (2015) the CMA's quantitative analysis suggested that the merger would not significantly change the proportion of areas where Poundland would face limited competition. The CMA concluded that the merger would not create an incentive for Poundland to worsen any aspects of its centrally set, uniform retail offer.

(d) In Ladbrokes/Coral (2016), the CMA used quantitative techniques to estimate the aggregate diversion ratio reflecting the extent of local overlap between individual stores. This indicated that there was likely to be a material incentive for the Parties to worsen aspects of their centrally set, uniform retail offer at all stores. The CMA concluded that this SLC would be remedied by the sale of stores designed to address SLCs in local markets.

NATIONAL COMPETITION

1.18 There may be aspects of competition that are not related to the extent of local competition. The CMA has assessed two theories of harm associated with a reduction in national competition:

(a) A loss of national competition not related to the standard aggregation of local areas.

(b) A loss of dynamic competition, such as the expansion of the Parties into new locations.

Assessing national competition

1.19 The CMA has assessed the loss of national competition where there are elements of the competitive offering that are determined nationally and not in response to the aggregation of local competitive interactions. For example, in Ladbrokes/Coral (2016), the CMA investigated whether bookmakers competed against each other on a national basis to offer the best odds for a certain event, in a national newspaper. Even though consumers 'purchased' their bets locally, the CMA concluded that the Parties did not have regard to local levels of competition when bidding to offer the best price.

Dynamic competition

1.20 If retailers have plans to open new stores, an analysis based on the locations of their current stores may not fully capture the effect of merger. The CMA has investigated whether a merger will lessen dynamic competition where at least one of the Parties has extensive expansion plans, but has not yet decided on the location of new stores.[12]

1.21 The CMA has tested whether the following cumulative conditions are met:[13]
(a) One or both of the Parties would be likely to enter into a number of overlaps in local markets absent the merger.
(b) One or both of the Parties would be substantially more likely to enter into these overlap areas than other competitors.
(c) In the absence of the merger, the entry of one or both of Parties in overlap areas would have led to substantially greater competition.

1.22 The CMA investigated this theory of harm in a number of recent cases:
(a) In Pure Gym/The Gym (2014), the CMA at phase 1 found that the Parties were the two leading budget gym players and were each significantly larger than the third and fourth largest players. Their expansion plans were also materially more significant than those of other budget gym players, and meant that they would open a large number of new gyms in the near future. However, the CMA did not find it necessary to conclude on its concerns on potential competition beyond areas where the Parties had specific plans to enter to pass the test for reference, given it had other concerns about the merger.
(b) In Poundland/99p Stores (2015), there was evidence from Poundland's internal documents and public statements that it had plans to expand substantially. Analysis showed that the expansion would only create a small number of additional overlaps because most 99p stores already overlapped with a Poundland store. The CMA also found that the Parties were not better placed to expand than their competitors, who also had plans to expand significantly.
(c) In Ladbrokes/Coral (2016) the CMA had historical information on shop openings and closures in the industry. The CMA noted that the Parties had frequently opened stores in competition with each other over the five years preceding the merger. However, the CMA also noted that the Parties' expansion activity had considerably slowed down in the two most recent years, and that their forward-looking expansion plans were constrained by regulation and the changing economics of the betting industry. For these reasons, the CMA found that the merger would not cause a substantial lessening of dynamic competition post-merger.

NOTES

4 The retail offer includes elements such as price, quality, range and service (PQRS).

5 In Somerfield/Morrison, the CC found that although prices were set nationally, Somerfield had tiered pricing, leading to variation in local prices.

6 In various investigations in the cinema sector, the OFT found that cinemas set ticket prices and other aspects of the retail offer locally to account for local competition.

7 Boots/Alliance UniChem, Celesio/Sainsbury's.

8 Alliance Boots/Dolland & Aitchison.

9 Ladbrokes/Coral (although the CMA also found that there was national competition to offer the best odds for particular events).

10 Demand may differ between stores because of differences in demographics, for example, or differences in the size of the local market.

11 This transaction involved the sales of 31 out of 251 JJB stores. The remainder of the stores were kept by JJB Sports, which continued to operate them.

12 Where the CMA has information about where the Parties are planning to open stores, it uses the potential competition framework to assess their plans to enter specific local areas. *Merger Assessment Guidelines*, paragraphs 5.4.13–5.4.18.

13 These conditions are consistent with a theory of harm based on actual potential competition, but where the areas in which overlaps will occur are not yet known. 'Actual potential competition' occurs due to the removal of a potential constraint on a party present in an area. This constraint only occurs if and when entry occurs. *Merger Assessment Guidelines*, paragraph 5.4.14.

2. CATCHMENT AREAS

[3.413]

2.1 A store's catchment area is the area from which most of its customers are drawn. Catchment areas provide useful information on how far customers are willing to travel to visit a store.

2.2 The CMA has used analysis of catchment areas to identify areas where the Parties' stores overlap. Stores are likely to be alternatives for some customers, and therefore competitors, if their catchment areas overlap. If the Parties' catchment areas overlap then further analysis will be required to determine whether an SLC may arise.

2.3 The CMA has estimated catchment areas using distance or drive-times and using the range of sources set out in paragraph 2.5. The CMA usually centres catchment areas on the stores of the target and the acquirer. This approach has been used both in phase 1 and phase 2 assessments of retail mergers.

2.4 The section looks at the techniques and evidence used to estimate catchment areas. We consider the following issues:
(a) Data sources.
(b) Methodological issues:
  (i) Shopping mission.
  (ii) Choosing the distance measure.
  (iii) 80% catchment areas.
  (iv) Individual or average catchment areas.
  (v) Asymmetric catchment areas.
  (vi) Urban and rural catchment areas.

DATA SOURCES

2.5 The CMA has used a variety of evidence to identify the location of a store's customers. Sources include:

(a) data from loyalty cards – for example, Greene King/Spirit (2015);
(b) home/site delivery records – for example, Travis Perkins/BSS Group (2010), Saint-Gobain/Build Centre (2012), Edmundson Electrical/Western Electrical (2014);
(c) customer contact details – for example, Nationwide Building Society/Derbyshire Building Society (2008), Saint-Gobain/Build Centre (2012);
(d) customer surveys can be used to estimate customers' willingness to travel, which can be used to estimate catchment areas – for example, Saint-Gobain/Build Centre (2012), Poundland/99p Stores (2015), Ladbrokes/Coral (2016), Celesio/Sainsbury's (2016);
(e) company documents, such as business plans or internal company research – for example, Pure Gym/The Gym (2014), Martin McColl/Cooperative (2016), Ladbrokes/Coral (2016).

METHODOLOGICAL ISSUES

Shopping mission

2.6 The CMA has usually estimated catchment areas using data on the home address of the Parties' customers, where this data is available.

2.7 However, the CMA has adjusted this approach where there is evidence that customers do not visit the store from their home, or where the visit is part of a bigger shopping trip. In Saint-Gobain/Build Center (2012) the Parties' customers were tradesmen who may buy goods near to the site they are working on rather than near their home address. The OFT used evidence from competitors and from a consumer survey, which suggested that the appropriate catchment area was 10 miles.

Choosing the distance measure

2.8 The catchment area can be measured using the straight-line distance, the drive-time, or using postcode areas.

2.9 The choice of measure depends on what data is available as well as the number of overlaps and the characteristics of the market. Where relevant and appropriate, the CMA will also draw on experience from previous cases in the sector.

2.10 In some cases the CMA has tested the sensitivity of the results to different measures in order to ensure that all potentially problematic overlap stores are identified.

• Straight-line distance

2.11 Straight-line distance is measured 'as the crow flies' from the store.[14] It is easier to measure than drive-time.

2.12 The CMA has used straight-line distance where the results are unlikely to be sensitive to the measure used or for pragmatic reasons where the Parties have a large number of stores.

2.13 The CMA used straight-line distances to estimate catchment areas in a number of merger cases including Poundland/99p Stores (2015), Ladbrokes/Coral (2016) and Celesio/Sainsbury's (2016).

• Drive-time or walk-time

2.14 Drive-time (or walk-time) measures how far a customer can drive (or walk) in a given time. The area delineated by a drive-time is referred to as an isochrone.[15] For example, a 10-minute drive-time isochrone is the area covered by driving from a store for 10 minutes in all directions.

2.15 Isochrones follow the local road network and the CMA has used them when there are important topographic features in the local area that make straight-line distances inaccurate. For example, an isochrone will take account of the time taken to reach the crossing points of a river whereas a straight-line distance is based on the assumption that the river can be crossed at any place.

2.16 Assumptions about driving speeds must be clearly stated in any submission because they affect the size of a drive-time isochrone.

2.17 The CMA has used isochrones in many merger investigations, including Rontec/Total (2011), One Stop/Alfred Jones (2013), Asda/Co-operative Group (five stores) (2014), and Pure Gym/The Gym (2014).

• Postcode areas

2.18 The CMA has sometimes used postcode areas to measure catchment areas.[16] These are constructed by centring on the postcode area in which one of the Parties' stores is located and then adding neighbouring postcode areas until the catchment area captures 80% of customers. Using postcode areas can have advantages over straight-line distance and drive-time measures where it allows the CMA to use information on the local area to estimate shares of sales in a catchment area. For example, in mergers in the funeral home sector the CMA has used data on the number of deaths in each postcode area to estimate the total number of deaths in a catchment area and the share accounted for by a funeral home.

2.19 The CMA has used this approach in a number of mergers in the funeral sector, including Co-operative Group (CWS) Limited/United Co-operatives Limited (2007), Co-operative Group Limited/George Burgess & Son Ltd (2009) and Lodge Brothers Funerals Ltd/two funeral homes in the London Borough of Hillingdon (2009).

80% catchment areas

2.20 The CMA has usually used catchment areas that capture 80% of a store's sales or customers. However, the CMA may adjust its starting point where there is evidence that this is appropriate:

(a) In Pure Gym/The Gym (2014), the CMA found that the Parties assessed competition over a narrower area than the 80% catchment and analysed each overlap area in detail instead of relying on a catchment area-based filter (see Section 3 for more details on filters).

(b) In Greene King/Spirit Pub (2015), the CMA used 60% catchment areas because customers who lived nearer the pub were more likely to visit regularly and therefore account for a larger share of revenue.

Individual or average catchment areas

2.21 The CMA usually calculates an average catchment area for a sample of stores. However, in some cases the CMA has calculated the catchment area for individual stores as a sensitivity, or as the basis of the analysis.

2.22 Individual store catchment areas can be informative where people living in different places are willing to travel very different distances to visit a store, and where differences in travel patterns are not related to observable factors such as whether the area is in an urban or rural area. However, catchment areas for individual stores depend on the number of stores in the local area – customers do not need to travel far if there are lots of stores in the local area. Therefore, store catchment areas may not be related to customers' willingness to travel and it may be preferable to use average catchment areas to identify overlaps.

Asymmetric catchment areas

2.23 In some cases the CMA has used different catchment areas for different types of store. For example, a large one-stop shop grocery store typically has a 10- to 15-minute catchment area, whereas a small convenience store has a much smaller catchment area.[17]

2.24 Asymmetric catchment areas have been used in most mergers in the grocery sector, as well as in a number of other sectors:

(a) In Carpetright/Allied Carpets (2010) the OFT found that some independent stores had narrower catchment areas than the larger, often out-of-town, stores that were often located out of town.

(b) In Celesio/Sainsbury's (2016) the CMA found that Sainsbury's pharmacies drew customers from a wider area than Lloyds, partly because they were located in a supermarket. As a result, the CMA used different catchment areas for supermarket and non-supermarket pharmacies.

Rural or urban

2.25 In some cases the CMA has used different catchment areas for stores in rural and urban areas. For example:

(a) in Rontec/Total (2011) the OFT used 10-minute drive-time isochrones for urban areas and 20-minute drive-time isochrones in rural areas;

(b) in Asda/Co-operative Group (five stores) (2014) the CMA used 10-minute drive-time isochrones in urban areas and 15-minute drive-time isochrones in rural areas for one-stop shop grocery stores and 5-minute drive-time isochrones in urban areas and 10-minute drive-time isochrones in rural areas for mid-sized grocery stores; and

(c) in Greene King/Spirit Pub (2015) and Celesio/Sainsbury's (2016) the CMA distinguished between rural and urban areas using information from the Office of National Statistics.

NOTES

14 This gives a radial catchment area, which is referred to as an isoradial. An isoradial is a line that connects points that are an equal straight-line distance from a focal point.

15 An isochrone is a line that connects points that are an equal travel time away from a focal point.

16 A postcode area is typically defined as the first two to four digits of the postcode, depending on area (for instance N1 or SW19) plus the next digit.

17 See CC, Groceries market investigation.

3. FILTERING

[3.414]

3.1 A filter is a simple rule based, for example, on the number of competitors in the catchment area. A store passes the filter if there will be sufficient competitors in the catchment area after the merger.

3.2 The CMA mainly uses filters as a screen. When there are many overlaps between the Parties' stores the CMA uses filters to screen out overlap areas where there are unlikely to be competition concerns. This allows the CMA to focus on the remaining overlap areas, which are each analysed in more detail in an assessment that is informed by an understanding of the nature of competition and reflects the factors discussed in this and later sections.

3.3 In this section we focus on these screening filters that are used to rule out non-problematic overlap areas. In some phase 2 merger investigations the CMA has used more sophisticated rules to conduct a competitive assessment and to identify the local areas where the merger may be expected to result in an SLC. The CMA has taken this approach when there were a very large number of potentially problematic overlap areas (see, for example, Ladbrokes/Coral (2016)).

3.4 The screening filter is usually implemented early in a case, often in pre-notification. This allows the CMA to conduct further analysis of any areas that may give rise to competition concerns. In some cases, the CMA has refined the filter during the course of an investigation when it has received additional information.

3.5 Screening filters must be applied systematically and need to be based on a readily observable concentration measure, such as the fascia count (see paragraph 3.22).

3.6 The CMA has sometimes done additional filtering to check that stores have not been incorrectly screened out. This is done by flexing the catchment area or using a different filter.

3.7 Phase 2 merger investigations often involve more complex filters and may use the results of surveys or empirical evidence.

3.8 In this section, we discuss:
(a) identifying which competitors should be included in the filter (the effective competitor set);
(b) choosing a concentration measure;
(c) weighting the concentration measure; and
(d) setting a threshold.

THE EFFECTIVE COMPETITOR SET

3.9 The CMA uses information on the nature of the products or services offered by the Parties and customer preferences to identify the Parties' main competitors (the effective competitor set).

3.10 As discussed above, screening filters are conducted early in a case and for pragmatic reasons in most cases the CMA has identified the effective competitor set across local areas rather than identifying every competitor in every local area.

3.11 In past cases the CMA has drawn on a range of readily available information to assess whether a firm should be included as a competitor in the filter. This has included:
(a) internal documents;
(b) evidence on store characteristics;
(c) evidence from competitors and customers; and
(d) surveys.

3.12 In some more complex cases, the CMA has refined the effective competitor set using data and econometric analysis (see Section 6).

Internal documents

3.13 Internal documents can provide useful information on the competitors that the Parties benchmark their retail offer against. For example, in the casino merger Rank/Gala (2013) group-level internal documents provided useful information that suggested that other types of leisure venue such as cinemas should not be included in the competitor set.

3.14 Documents that have been prepared by the local store manager or the regional manager, or centrally prepared documents that have a local focus, may identify individual competitors in a local area:
(a) In Rank/Gala (2013) internal documents only identified nearby casinos as competitive threats and suggested that bingo venues did not constrain casinos.
(b) In Ladbrokes/Coral (2016) internal capital expenditure requests submitted by local store managers identified the rival store(s) with which they competed.

3.15 Competitors may provide useful information on the effective competitor set and they may have internal documents or research that provides useful insights.

Evidence on store characteristics

3.16 Information on store characteristics can indicate whether there are similarities between different stores and this can provide evidence to assess whether customers view them as close substitutes.

3.17 The relevant stores characteristics may include qualitative and quantitative measures such as range, store size, branding and opening hours. For example, in Poundland/99p Stores (2015) the CMA compared the ranges and prices for a selection of products of Poundland with those of a number of other retailers.

Survey evidence

3.18 A survey can provide useful information on the factors that matter to customers when they choose a store.

3.19 In some cases, customers are able to identify the set of alternative stores that they use, or would consider using. Diversion ratios (see Section 5) may also be used to provide a ranking of competitors and can be used to identify whether different types of competitors should be included in the effective competitor set. For example, in Ladbrokes/Coral (2016), the CMA's survey, along with other pieces of evidence, indicated that the Parties' customers considered independent LBOs to be a slightly less attractive alternative than LBOs managed by other national chains. The evidence also suggested that the Parties' customers did not perceive any significant differences between the LBOs of the different national chains.

WHAT CONCENTRATION MEASURES?

3.20 As noted in paragraph 3.1 the filter needs to be based on a readily observable measure, as filtering is usually carried out at an early stage in the investigation.

3.21 The CMA usually uses either a fascia count or a store count to measure concentration. The choice of measure depends on the characteristics of the market and the factors that drive customers' choice of store.

Fascia count

3.22 The CMA often uses a count of the number of independent fascias in a local market to measure concentration. Fascia counts have been used in mergers in a wide range of sectors, including; groceries, sports retailers, and cinemas, as well as builders' merchants.

3.23 Fascia count is likely to be the appropriate measure if brand is important to customers and customers choose between the fascias in their local area, irrespective of the number of stores that they have. Fascia count takes account of the fact that customers may perceive that stores of the same brand have similar retail offers. As such, the entry of a new fascia is likely to have a greater effect on competition than the entry of another store in a chain already present in the area:

(a) In Cineworld/City Screen Limited (2013) the CC used a count of the number of cinema fascias because consumers choose between brands.

(b) In Martin McColl/Co-operative (2016) the CMA used a count of the number of grocery fascias because consumers choose between brands.

Store count

3.24 Store count is a good measure of concentration if the brand is not very important or visible to the customer. Store count can also be a useful measure in cases where factors such as distance are an important driver of competition:

(a) In Greene King/Spirit (2015) the CMA used a count of the number of pubs in the local area because customers may not have been aware of the chain to which a pub belonged.

(b) In Ladbrokes/Coral (2016) the CMA used a count of the number of betting shops in the area because location was very important to consumers.

(c) In Celesio/Sainsbury's (2016) the CMA used a count of the number of pharmacies in the area because location was very important to consumers.

Market shares

3.25 The CMA has sometimes used market share estimates to measure concentration. This is only possible where there is data on the size of the local market and on the sales of each competitor. For example, the CMA was able to calculate local shares in Co-operative Group Limited/Funeral Business of George Burgess & Son Ltd (2009). The CMA used data on the number of deaths in each postcode district in the UK to estimate the size of the overall market for funeral services at a local level and determine the volume share of each market participant in the local area. However, in many retail sector cases involving local markets, local market share data may not be available.

WEIGHTING THE CONCENTRATION MEASURE

3.26 In some cases, the CMA has weighted the concentration measure. This additional complexity is more frequently used in phase 2 merger investigations. The CMA has used this approach in the design of screening filters as well as in the design of rules that identify the local areas where the merger may be expected to result in an SLC (for an example of the latter see Ladbrokes/Coral (2016)).

3.27 In using fascia count or store count we assume that each individual fascia or store in the effective competitor set in an area is equally close, and also that all competitors within a given distance impose the same competitive constraint. Depending on the facts of the case these may or may not be reasonable assumptions. Simple counts of fascias or stores may under or overstate the extent of competition in an area because they do not reflect important differences between fascia or stores.

3.28 Where there is evidence of systematic variations based on observable characteristics, the CMA has incorporated these into its analysis. This has either been done by adjusting the weight of stores or fascias used in the filter, or by excluding firms from the filter and taking account of the constraint they impose in the competitive assessment.

3.29 The adjustments have fallen into two categories: adjusting the weight that is assigned to a specific competitor; or weighting all stores based on distance.

Adjusting the weight that is assigned to a specific competitor

3.30 By adjusting the weight given to a specific competitor, the CMA is able to account for differences between different fascias, or between different types of competitors. The CMA has typically determined the weight using qualitative evidence, such as; internal competitor monitoring reports, and/or quantitative evidence such as; surveys, performance concentration analysis, or entry exit analysis:

(a) In Greene King/Spirit (2015), the CMA found that wet-led pubs (ie pubs that have a drink-focused offering) exerted some constraint on the Parties' dry-led pubs, though not as much as other dry-led pubs. The CMA included wet-led pubs in the effective competitor set, but applied a discount factor related to the diversion ratio (see Section 5) to reflect the reduced competitive constraint they imposed.[18]

(b) In Poundland/99p Stores (2015) the CMA found that although supermarkets and value general merchandise (VGM)[19] retailers competed with the Parties, they did not compete as closely as other single price point retailers. As a result, the CMA applied a 0.5 weight to both supermarkets and VGM retailers, based on the empirical analysis and the results of the consumer survey.

(c) In Ladbrokes/Coral (2016) the CMA found that independent LBO operators exerted less of a competitive constraint on the Parties than national LBO operators. As a result, the CMA applied a 0.9 weight to independent LBOs, before then applying a distance weighting (see paragraph 3.32(b)).

Weighting all stores based on distance

3.31 Where there is evidence that distance is an important driver of store choice for customers, stores located close together are likely to be closer competitors to each other than stores located further apart.

3.32 There are a number of different ways to control for the impact of distance on closeness of competition, all of which attach some form of decreasing weight to each store based on how far it is away from the focal store:

(a) In Celesio/Sainsbury's (2016) the CMA found that distance was an important factor for consumers when they choose which pharmacy to visit. The CMA used a weight based on straight-line distance from the focal store to each store in the catchment area. It then used this weighted store count to calculate the Parties' combined share of stores in the area and the increment due to the merger.[20]

(b) In Ladbrokes/Coral (2016) the CMA found that that distance was an important factor for consumers when they choose which bookmakers to visit. The CMA used a weight based on straight-line distance from the focal store. The CMA calculated a 'weighted share of shop' around each focal shop as its primary measure of competition.[21]

WHAT IS THE THRESHOLD FOR CONCERN?

3.33 The appropriate threshold for screening out non-problematic overlaps depends on the characteristics of the market and the definition of the effective competitor set. For example, the appropriate threshold for identifying overlaps that require a detailed competition assessment is likely to be higher if the effective competitor set is narrowly defined and excludes firms that are likely to exert some competitive constraint. The CMA designs the filters to minimise the risk of screening out overlaps that could be problematic.

3.34 Internal documents that provide insights into the nature and intensity of competition in the market are likely to be helpful in deciding the appropriate threshold. Empirical evidence can also provide useful information on the relationship between outcomes for customers and the number of firms in the market (see performance concentration analysis and entry/exit analysis (Section 6)).

Fascia count threshold

3.35 The CMA has used a 'four to three' fascia count threshold in mergers in the grocery sector. That is, the CMA has identified overlaps as potentially problematic where the merger reduces the number of fascia in the market from four to three. In other sectors, the CMA has often used a 'five to four' fascia count threshold:

(a) A four to three fascia count threshold was first used in Safeway (2003) and has been used in subsequent supermarket investigations. This has been consistent with evidence found during the course of merger enquiries and the Groceries market investigation.

(b) In Saint-Gobain/Build Center (2012) the OFT used a five to four fascia count threshold to screen out non-problematic areas. This was consistent with the approach taken in comparable cases.

(c) In Rank/Gala (2013), the CC used a five to four fascia count threshold to screen out non-problematic areas. It adopted this threshold to ensure that no potentially problematic areas were missed. This threshold was based on an assessment of the Parties' internal documents, the evidence from surveys and the econometric analysis.

(d) In Cineworld/City Screen Limited (2013), the CC used a four to three fascia count threshold which excluded independent cinemas. Given the evidence available, which included internal documents, econometrics and surveys, the CC considered that this was appropriately cautious.

Store count threshold

3.36 In past cases the CMA has calculated the share of stores from the store count. Previous CMA decisions in mergers in markets where products are undifferentiated suggest that combined market shares of less than 40% will not often give the CMA cause for concern over unilateral effects.[22] The CMA has taken this as a starting point when assessing the appropriate share of store threshold.

3.37 The share of store threshold usually has two elements: the combined share of stores and the increment due to the merger. If the combined share of stores is high, but the increment is low, this is likely to indicate that one of the Parties is not an important competitive constraint in the local area:

(a) In Greene King/Spirit (2015) the CMA used a 35% share of stores (pubs) with a 5% increment. This threshold was higher than in previous cases in the pub sector because evidence from a consumer survey and internal documents suggested that some customers would switch to alternatives outside the effective competitor set.

(b) In Celesio/Sainsbury's (2016) a 40% weighted share of stores, with an increment of 15% was used. This threshold was consistent with a diversion ratio from the consumer survey of around 30%.

(c) In Ladbrokes/Coral (2016) the CMA used the weighted store counts to calculate a proxy for the diversion ratio, this was referred to as a weighted share of stores. The CMA used a 35% weighted share of stores. This threshold was determined by analysing the results of a consumer survey and econometric analysis.

NOTES

18 The discount factor was determined by looking at both the survey results and the number of pubs in that category (in the isochrone) and setting the discount factor so that expected diversion to that category of pubs is equal to actual diversion.

19 This was defined as meaning any of the following retailers: B&M, Home Bargains, Poundstretcher, Wilko, Poundworld's Bargain Buys fascia and 99p's Family Bargains fascia.

20 This was calculated as the sum of the Parties' weighted store count, divided by the total weighted store count.

21 This was defined as the sum of the weights associated with the shops of the merging party divided by the sum of the weights associated with all shops present in the area.

22 *Merger Assessment Guidelines*, paragraph 5.3.5.

4. BRICKS-AND-MORTAR AND ONLINE RETAIL

[3.415]

4.1 One question that often arises in retail mergers is how the CMA assesses the competitive interaction between different distribution channels. In this section we focus on how the CMA has assessed whether bricks-and-mortar retailers are constrained by online retailers;[23] specifically, whether the online constraint is sufficient to prevent bricks-and-mortar retailers worsening their retail offer as a result of a merger. In general, this will occur if a significant share of those customers who shop at a bricks-and-mortar store would switch to online retailers in response to a small, but significant change in the relative PQRS.[24]

4.2 To assess the strength of the online constraint, the CMA has typically used the same sources of evidence as it uses for other aspects of its competitive assessment. These include customer surveys, internal documents, econometric analysis, and third party views.

4.3 In some retail sectors the CMA has found that the competitive interaction between the online and bricks-and-mortar channels is evolving rapidly and this needs to be taken into account in the analysis.

4.4 In the following section we set out some of the issues encountered:

(a) The use of customer surveys to test out-of-market constraints.
(b) The use of internal documents.
(c) Interpretation of price differences in different channels.
(d) The role of price discrimination.
(e) Interpretation of trends and migration versus diversion.
(f) Customer search.
(g) Multi-channel offers.
(h) Online retailer mergers.

CUSTOMER SURVEYS

4.5 In some cases the CMA has used a customer survey to obtain information on customer preferences with regard to different distribution channels. This has included information about current customer behaviour, search behaviour and an estimate of the proportion of bricks-and-mortar customers who would divert to online providers.

4.6 When looking at different distribution channels it is important to design the survey carefully, and to consider the appropriate survey mode. For example, a survey conducted online is likely to over-represent the views of customers who are more familiar with the digital environment and online shopping tools:

(a) In Poundland/99p Stores (2015) the Parties conducted an online survey of customers, who were recruited by encouraging customers to go to a website shown on the till receipt. The CMA was concerned that those customers willing to go online to complete a survey may not be representative of the population of customers, which was supported by the CMA's survey in phase 2.

(b) In Ladbrokes/Coral (2016) the CMA found that the results of a survey of an online panel were not representative across channel use and were likely to be heavily biased in favour of those who gamble online and who would divert online.

4.7 For more information on best practice in surveys, please see *Good practice in the design and presentation of consumer survey evidence in merger inquiries*.

INTERNAL DOCUMENTS

4.8 The CMA has used internal documents to help understand how retailers perceive the interaction between different channels and how it affects business decisions. For example, if bricks-and-mortar retailers regularly monitor online competitors alongside other bricks-and-mortar competitors and if this analysis is used to inform business decisions on pricing and quality, this could point to a relatively strong interaction between the two channels.

4.9 If internal documents point to online retailers as a 'strategic threat' but day-to-day business decisions are still primarily informed by the monitoring of bricks-and-mortar competitors, then the CMA may be less confident that the online channel constrains the bricks-and-mortar channel. For example, in Ladbrokes/Coral (2016), although the Parties argued that online suppliers constrained their business, their internal documents indicated that they tended to focus on their bricks-and-mortar competitors when tracking the performance of their retail estates. These internal documents did not indicate that the Parties responded to a change in the constraint imposed by the online channel.

DIFFERENCES BETWEEN THE PRICES CHARGED BY RETAILERS IN DIFFERENT CHANNELS

4.10 The CMA has found that, in and of itself, the existence of price differentials between the bricks-and-mortar and online channels does not necessarily imply that there is no competitive interaction between them. For example, bricks-and-mortar stores may be able to charge a higher price as they offer additional services – such as the ability to try the product – and no delivery times.

4.11 The magnitude of any price differential may be an indicator of the strength of customers' preferences for shopping in stores. More importantly, changes in such price differentials over time might shed some light on how competitive dynamics are evolving in the industry:

(a) In Waterstone's/Ottakar's (2006) the CC found that the Parties had increased their discounts from the recommended retail price (RRP) in response to increasing discounts by other retailers, including online retailers. The CC concluded that there were important competitors active in other distribution channels.

(b) In Ladbrokes/Coral (2016), the CMA looked at the extent to which retailers charged different prices and earned different margins for their products depending on whether they are sold online or in stores. The CMA found that there had been limited variation in the gross win margin differential in the last five years, which indicated that the competitive constraint exercised by online providers on bricks-and-mortar operators was changing only very slowly, and not for all products.

PRICE DISCRIMINATION

4.12 In past cases the CMA has found that the constraint from online retailers requires that bricks-and-mortar retailers cannot segment their customers and charge different prices to those who are likely to divert online and those that are unlikely to do so.

4.13 In most retail sectors, customers are anonymous and retailers have little information on their shopping habits. However, in some sectors, retailers that operate across both channels might be able to identify those bricks-and-mortar customers who also shop online and offer them cheaper prices in store without extending these offers to other customers.

MIGRATION VERSUS DIVERSION

4.14 Bricks-and-mortar retailers have often pointed to the growth of the online channel, and/or to specific evidence that some of their customers are migrating online. However, this type of evidence may not necessarily be informative of the strength of the online constraint.

4.15 In Ladbrokes/Coral (2016) the CMA assessed whether a sufficient share of bricks-and-mortar customers would respond to a small, but significant change in relative prices by switching to online providers. It concluded that the fact that a number of bricks-and-mortar customers regularly migrate online irrespective of changes in quality, or price, did not allow any strong inferences about how substitutable the two channels were for the remaining retail customers.

SEARCH

4.16 In some cases, the CMA has found that the online channel exerts pressure on the bricks-and-mortar channel by allowing easier search for customers, even if most customers end up purchasing the products in store. For example, in Thomas Cook/Co-operative Group Ltd/Midlands Co-operative Society Ltd (2011), the CC found that around half of customers searched online before booking a holiday in store, and a quarter of those who asked for a discount did so because they had seen lower prices online.

4.17 However, for this type of behaviour to be an effective constraint on bricks-and-mortar retailers, there must be some evidence that it impacts their business decisions (for example, in the form of internal documents, correlation in prices over time).

ONLINE RETAIL MERGERS

4.18 The CMA has also investigated mergers of online retailers and assessed the constraint from bricks-and-mortar retailers:

(a) In Amazon/The Book Depository (2011), the OFT found that the online retailers were not constrained by offline retailers, based primarily on the results of a survey conducted by the Parties.

(b) In Yoox/Net-a-Porter (2015), the CMA found that online fashion retailers and bricks-and-mortar retailers operated in separate markets, based primarily on the Parties' internal documents and third party views.

(c) In Mapil Bidco/Chain Reaction Cycles (2016), the CMA found that online retailers of bike components and accessories were not constrained by bricks-and-mortar retailers, based primarily on an analysis of the Parties' internal documents, third party views, and a qualitative analysis of the product ranges and prices available in the two channels. The Parties argued that many customers would need to visit a bricks-and-mortar store for fitting and technical assistance. The CMA noted that detailed online product information attempted to replicate this assistance.

NOTES

23 This can be pure play online retailers or bricks-and-mortar retailer with an online presence.

24 The CMA has also investigated mergers of online retailers and examined whether online stores are constrained by bricks-and-mortar stores has also arisen. For example: Amazon/The Book Depository (2011), Yoox/Net-a-Porter (2015), Mapil Bidco/Chain Reaction Cycles (2016).

5. DIVERSION RATIOS AND PRICE PRESSURE INDICES

[3.416]

5.1 In some retail mergers the CMA has used diversion ratios and simple quantitative indicators such as pricing pressure indices (PPIs) to evaluate the potential for the merger to create incentives for the merging firms to raise their price.

5.2 These measures can be used as part of a simple screen to rule out overlap areas that are not likely to be problematic, or as part of the more detailed competitive assessment of areas that have failed a filter. These measures are generally used as one input into the decision and are unlikely, on their own, to determine the outcome of a particular case.

5.3 In this section, we set out:

(a) how the CMA uses diversion ratios and PPIs;
(b) calculating diversion ratios;
(c) calculating profit margins;
(d) calculating pricing pressure indices; and
(e) deriving empirical estimates of pass-through

HOW THE CMA USES DIVERSION RATIOS AND PPIS

5.4 In many retail markets, retailers compete on a number of aspects of the retail offer. When altering aspects of the retail offer, there are both costs and benefits to the retailers concerned. For example, if a retailer raised its prices, a cost of doing so would be the profit lost through customers switching to its competitors. However, the retailer may also benefit from increased profit from those customers who do not switch but who pay the higher prices.

5.5 When reviewing a merger, the CMA considers whether some of the profits lost by one of the Parties (resulting from a hypothetical change in the retail offer) would be recaptured by the other Party. If so, the merger may create an incentive to change the retail offer (for example, raise prices). The strength of this incentive will depend, among other things, on the profits from sales that the Parties would recapture from the change to the retail offer.[25]

CALCULATING DIVERSION RATIOS

5.6 The diversion ratio provides an indicator of the closeness of competition between firms or products.

5.7 Diversion ratios can be calculated in a number of different ways, depending on the information available in a particular case. In retail mergers, the CMA has most often used the results of consumer surveys to calculate diversion ratios.

5.8 The diversion ratio attempts to capture what customers would do in response to an increase in prices. However, it can be difficult to survey a sufficiently large number of customers who would switch in response to a price rise to estimate a robust diversion ratio. Therefore, the CMA asks customers what they would do in response to the closure of a store (or stores).

5.9 The diversion ratio from firm A to B is then calculated by dividing the number of customers who switch from A to B by the total number of customers who gave eligible responses to the diversion question. (See Technical Box 4 for a discussion of how the CMA calculates diversion ratios and PPIs when one or both of the Parties has more than one store in any area and *Good practice in the design and presentation of consumer survey evidence in merger inquiries* for more detail on the precise calculation.)

5.10 Diversion ratios can either be combined with margins to give a measure of the pricing pressure or used on their own as a measure of closeness of competition:

(a) In Rank/Gala (2013) the CC focused on diversion ratios as a general measure of closeness of competition.
(b) In Ladbrokes/Coral (2016) the CMA carried out a survey in a sample of 15 local overlap areas. The survey results were used to inform the decision on the strength of the constraint from online, whether there were aggregated local effects and as an input to determining the local areas in which the merger would be likely to lead to an SLC.
(c) In Celesio/Sainsbury's (2016) the CMA carried out a survey in a sample of 16 local overlap areas. The survey was used to calculate the diversion ratio between the Parties, and between the Parties and third parties. This was used as in input into the initial filter as well as in the detailed assessment of areas failing the filter.

5.11 The CMA has adjusted the diversion ratio calculation when the merger involves the sale of just part of a retail chain. For example, in Asda/Cooperative Group (five stores) (2014) CGL was only selling a small proportion of stores to Asda and was keeping stores in a number of the overlap areas. The CMA considered that the diversion ratio to Asda gave a measure of the strength of the competitive constraint that would be lost as a result of the merger, and the diversion ratio to other retained CGL stores, gave a measure of the competitive constraint that would be gained by the merger. The combination of these two diversion ratios was used to calculate the PPI.

CALCULATING PRICING PRESSURE INDICES

5.12 Price pressure indices (PPIs) combine diversion ratios with information on product margins and prices to give an approximate measure of the incentives for the Parties to raise their price. PPIs are simple quantitative indicators. They do not attempt to predict the exact extent of post-merger price rises. They measure the extent of the upward price pressure or, if an assumption is made about the degree to which this pressure is passed through to customers, a measure of upward price movement.

Technical Box 1: Calculating variable profit margins

Variable margins are made up of the sales of the relevant products which both Parties supply less their variable costs. In past cases the CMA has considered that cost variability depends on the period over which the Parties could change their retail offer. The decisions on how to derive variable margins have therefore been made on a case-by-case basis and have required an element of judgement. In general, if margins are high, unilateral effects are more likely to arise as a result of a merger:[26]

(a) In Somerfield/Morrison (2005), the CC considered margins based on 'direct costs' including cost of sales, staff costs and distribution costs.

(b) In Asda/Netto (2010), the OFT used one month as a reasonable period over which to assess variable margins. The OFT considered that over a month, a supermarket can change a number of variables including its staffing levels for particular shifts, levels of stock and pricing decisions.

(c) In Cineworld/City Screen Limited (2013) the CC sought to calculate the margins and revenue that the Parties could expect to obtain from an additional film admission. This included both the margin and revenue associated with films and ancillary services such as food and drink. The CC analysis considered what percentage of each cost and revenue item was variable with admissions.

5.13 The choice of which PPI is most appropriate (and which form of the PPI)[27] depends on the circumstances of the case and on the information available, including that on the rate of cost pass-through (see Technical Box 3). Each PPI is based on strong assumptions about the nature of competition, costs and the way in which demand changes with price. In past cases the CMA has looked at how likely these assumptions are to hold and which best fits the facts of the case, whilst making the limitations of PPIs clear in its assessment.

Technical Box 2: Three main types of PPIs

The CMA and its predecessor bodies have used three main types of PPIs:

1. The Upward Pricing Pressure (UPP) metric compares an estimate of the value of lost sales (based on estimated diversion ratios and margins) with an estimate of efficiencies resulting from the merger. If the value of lost sales is higher than the value of efficiencies, the merger is likely to lead to a price increase.
2. The Gross Upward Pricing Pressure Index (GUPPI) is similar to UPP, but does not allow for any efficiencies. The GUPPI can be interpreted as equivalent to a notional cost increase for the Parties. If we make an assumption about the rate of cost pass-through, it can be interpreted as an upward price movement.
3. The Illustrative Price Rise (IPR) combines an estimate of the value of lost sales with an assumption about the form of demand, or an empirical estimate of cost pass-through, to provide an estimate of the upward price movement. It takes account of accommodating price reactions. IPR has historically considered that the relationship between prices and quantity is either linear or isoelastic.[28]

5.14 In general:

(a) GUPPI is the most commonly used measure. It requires the least information, but has no straightforward interpretation in terms of a price increase unless we make some additional assumptions about pass-through. The CMA has used GUPPI in a number of retail mergers including Shell/Rontec (2011), Saint-Gobain/Build Center (2012), Edmundson/Electric Center (2012), Rexel/Wilts (2012), Cineworld/City Screen (2013) and Original Bowling/Bowlplex (2015). For example:

(i) In Saint-Gobain/Build Centre (2012) the Parties conducted surveys in 49 local areas[29] that failed the initial filter. The OFT combined diversion ratios, margins and a measure of the pass-through to calculate the GUPPI in each area. The OFT considered that this was an indicator (among others) of the presence of horizontal unilateral effects, and that a value of this measure greater than 5% gave rise to concern.

(ii) In Cineworld/City Screen Limited (2013) the CC carried out a survey of Cineworld and Picturehouse members. The CC used this along with a measure of the local margin to calculate the GUPPI in each local area. This was used as part of the competitive assessment.

(b) The IPR is expressed as a percentage price increase, which makes interpretation easier. However, it requires additional information on the form of demand and/or the extent of cost pass-through. One disadvantage of the IPR approach is that its results are sensitive to assumptions about the way demand changes with price. The CMA has used IPR in most grocery mergers[30] as well as in other mergers including Carpetright/Allied Carpet (2010), Sports Direct/JJB (2010), and Edmundson Electrical/Western Electrical (2014).

(c) The UPP can be useful where the CMA has information on efficiencies.

Technical Box 3: Deriving empirical estimates of pass-through

In some mergers, Parties have submitted empirical evidence on cost pass-through. This attempts to show how prices have reacted to changes in costs in the past. These can be useful in understanding which PPI should be used in a particular case (or in calibrating GUPPI as a measure of the upward price movement). This is because each PPI makes different assumptions about how incentives to increase prices are passed through to consumers, which can then be compare to empirical evidence on pass-through.

Technical Box 3: Deriving empirical estimates of pass-through

For example, in Saint-Gobain/Build Centre (2012), the OFT analysed data on a revenue-weighted basket of goods, to estimate pass-through for the branch network as a whole. This suggested pass-through was around 100%. This evidence led the OFT to conclude that it was not appropriate to use isoelastic IPR, as this assumed a pass-through rate of greater than 100% at all times.

5.15 Where no reliable information is available on demand or efficiencies, the CMA has found it preferable to use GUPPI and consider other factors qualitatively rather than make simplifying assumptions to calculate more sophisticated indicators.

5.16 PPIs do not take account of other factors that are relevant to the competitive assessment, including merger efficiencies (with the exception of UPP – see Technical Box 2), product repositioning and entry. The CMA has taken these factors into account separately as part of its wider competitive assessment.

Technical Box 4: Calculating diversion ratios and PPIs in multi-store areas

• In some retail mergers there might be some areas where one or both Parties own more than one store. Where this is the case, the CMA must decide how to capture the interactions between the different stores owned by the same party in the calculation of diversion ratios and PPIs. This has implications for the formulation of the diversion question(s) in consumer surveys, and for the formulas used to calculate the PPIs.

• It is possible to formulate the 'diversion question' in a customer survey in two different ways:

○ the survey can ask respondents where they would go if the particular store they visited on that occasion was closed for a period of time; or

○ the survey can ask respondents where they would go if all stores of the same brand were closed.

• The first formulation leaves open the possibility that a proportion of customers might respond to a closure of a given store by going to another store of the same brand (ie there might be some 'own-brand diversion'); whereas the second question 'forces' customers to go to a store of another brand. As a result, diversion ratios based on the first approach will indicate a lower level of diversion between the Parties than diversion ratios based on the second approach.

• Which question to ask and how to treat own-brand diversion depends in the first instance on the theory of harm that is investigated:

○ If the CMA is investigating a theory of harm based on the aggregation of local concerns – as the Parties apply the same parameters of competition uniformly across their estates – the right approach is to use the second formulation of the diversion question and disallow own-brand diversion. In this context, a customer who decides to leave a shop of one party in response to a price increase is very unlikely to go a different shop of the same party as this will also experience the same price increase.

○ If the CMA is investigating a local theory of harm – where the firms flex the parameters of competition in individual shops – the interactions between the stores are more complex, and different approaches may be appropriate depending on the circumstances of the case.

• Consider the situation depicted in Figure 1, where one of the merging party owns two stores (1.a and 1.b), and the other merging party owns one store (2).
Suppose we observe significant own-brand diversion from store 1.a to store 1.b.

Figure 1

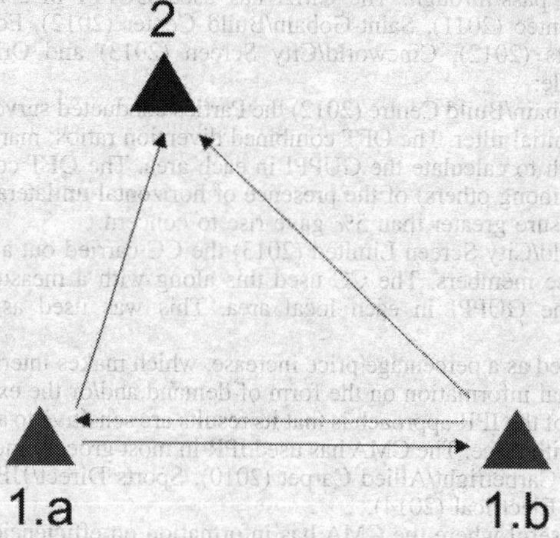

Technical Box 4: Calculating diversion ratios and PPIs in multi-store areas

• One possible argument is that the effect of own-brand diversion is already present pre-merger, and therefore to identify the effect of the merger we should use the first formulation of the diversion question and allow own-brand diversion to reduce diversion between the merging parties. The argument is that the owner of shop 1.a will already offer a high price-merger to reflect the fact they retain a share of the value of diverted sales. In other words, that aspect of market power is already 'priced in' pre-merger. Because we are interested in identifying the incremental effect of the merger, the diversion ration from store 1.a to store 2 should be reduced by allowing for the amount of own-brand diversion that exists pre-merger.

• The problem with this argument is that it considers the change in pricing incentives at store 1.a in isolation, and ignores the other effects of the merger on pricing incentives at other stores. If shop 1.b also has some positive diversion to store 2, it will also have an incentive to increase price. This will increase the value of diverted sales from store 1 .a to store 1.b, which will, in turn, prove a further incentive to increase price at shop 1.a. Moreover, if shop 1.b has some positive diversion to shop 1.a it will have a further incentive to increase its price to reflect the higher value of diverted sales at shop 1.a, and this will then further feedback on the pricing incentives at shop 1.a. So even though own-brand diversion is present pre-merger, its effects on pricing incentives change post-merger.

• If we know the diversion ratios between all shops in the area, then in principle it is possible to calculate an IPR to provide an approximation of the 'equilibrium price' in the market. The IPR methodology relies on diversion ratios that allow own-brand diversion, but it captures the interactions between different shops under common ownership by solving their equilibrium pricing conditions 'as a system'.

If we do not know the diversion ratios for all shops then we can potentially use GUPPIs to provide bounds for the effects of the merger. A GUPPI with a diversion ratio that allows for own-brand diversion is likely to underestimate the effects of the merger because it takes no account of these various feedback effects (it only considers the 'first order effects' of the merger on the pricing incentives of each shop considered in isolation). A GUPPI with a diversion ratio that disallows own-brand diversion might overestimate the effects of the merger because it does not truly reflect its incremental effect on pricing incentive. This approach is likely to be more appropriate in the context of a phase 1 inquiry.

NOTES

25 The CMA has often considered this by reference to the incentive to raise prices, such reference serving as a proxy for other aspects of the retail offer. However, the CMA has also considered separately and in more detail how other aspects of the retail offer may be altered by the merger.

26 See paragraph 5.4.9(b) of the *Merger Assessment Guidelines*.

27 For instance in cases where there are asymmetries in the cost structure between two firms it may be appropriate to use an asymmetrical form of the PPI. See Asda/Netto (2010).

28 Isoelastic demand is concave and assumes that consumers have a constant elasticity, ie that the ratio of a change in price to a change in quantity is the same at all points of the demand curve.

29 Surveys were not conducted in three local areas which failed the initial filter.

30 See for example, GCL/Somerfield (2008) and Asda/Co-operative Group (5 stores) (2014).

6. ECONOMETRIC EVIDENCE

INTRODUCTION

[3.417]

6.1 Econometric techniques are widely used in retail merger investigations to provide quantitative evidence on the nature and extent of competition, particularly at phase 2, but also occasionally at phase 1. Such evidence often relates to how closely the Parties compete, over which dimensions they compete, and who their main competitors are. These questions are fundamental to merger investigations, meaning that rigorous econometric and quantitative analysis are important tools to help us make more informed decisions.

6.2 A variety of empirical methods are used in retail merger investigations. In some instances, simple descriptive analysis can provide useful evidence. We may analyse price changes over time for example, or test whether prices are correlated with costs. Econometric analysis goes beyond simple correlations, by aiming to establish robust causal relationships between variables.

6.3 Econometric analysis can form an important piece of the evidence base in a merger investigation. The relative weight that is attached to this evidence depends crucially on the robustness of the results – whether, for example, reasonable changes to the model or data produce similar outcomes – and the extent to which the analysis is able to isolate causal effects rather than correlations. This will depend in large part on the availability and reliability of the data we have.

6.4 This section provides details on the most common econometric models used in retail mergers. For information on the submission of original econometric work, and the process for interacting with the CMA on its econometric evidence see *Suggested best practice for submissions of technical economic analysis from parties to the Competition Commission* (CC, 2009).

PERFORMANCE CONCENTRATION ANALYSIS

6.5 Performance concentration analysis (PCA) is the most common econometric model used in retail merger cases. A PCA tests how the performance of a retail store is affected by the level of competition in its local area. Performance may be measured by margin, revenue, prices or quality – such as the number of staff or opening hours. In areas where the Parties' stores face only one competitor for example, the Parties may offer a poorer service than areas where their stores face many competitors.

6.6 We measure the extent of local competition by the number of stores – or fascias – within a given distance of the store of interest. As a first approximation, this distance is often the catchment area. We can then extend this basic framework to allow for different distances and/or different types of competing stores. Doing so, we generate quantitative evidence along two important dimensions of local competition:

(a) What is the relevant geographic market – over what distances do retail stores compete with each other?

(b) What is the relevant competitor set – with which fascia or type of store do retail stores compete most closely?

6.7 A primary concern with such analysis is that unobserved local factors, such as the level of demand or rental costs, might influence both the level of competition and a store's performance or prices. This would bias the results, as we would wrongly be conflating the impact of such factors on performance with that of local competition. Stores based in areas of high demand, for example, can charge higher prices, and there are likely to be many competing stores to serve the high demand. The model could therefore, incorrectly, suggest that greater competition causes higher prices.

6.8 Furthermore, the absence of any correlation in performance concentration analysis cannot be interpreted as strong evidence of a lack of a relationship between performance and competition, only that the model has been unable to show that there is a linkage.

6.9 PCA's have been used by the CMA in a number of cases:

(a) In Rank/Gala (2013), the PCA analysis found that the number of competitors within a 30-minute drive-time reduced a casino's admissions and turnover, but there was no evidence of any effect beyond this distance. There was also some evidence that increases in local competition, caused by new entry, reduced a casino's margins.

(b) In Celesio/Sainsbury's (2016), the CMA found that entry of single-owner independents and large-chain high street pharmacies exerted a competitive constraint on Lloyds, with opening hours increasing in response to new entry. Similarly, the analysis showed that the entry of supermarket pharmacies exerted a competitive constraint on Sainsbury's.

ENTRY AND EXIT ANALYSIS

6.10 A (partial) solution to this problem is to consider how the store's performance varies over time in response to changes in the extent of local competition, while controlling for unobservable factors using fixed effects. This partially alleviates the problem above, because factors such as local demand are, to a large extent, constant over time. Changes in the extent of local competition are driven by the entry and exit of new stores; hence this methodology is also sometimes known as 'entry-exit analysis'.

6.11 Entry-exit analysis can still suffer from the concerns above though, because new entrants may target locations where demand is expected to increase. Again, this would cause the model to wrongly assign the impact of demand on performance to that of competition. For specific applications, we can assess the extent to which this is likely to be true and the expected impact on the results. In general, such issues cause the model to under-estimate the impact of competition on performance, so that the results can be interpreted as 'lower bound' estimates.

6.12 Entry-exit analysis has been used by the CMA in a number of cases:

(a) In Poundland/99p Stores (2015), the CMA found that local entry by the Parties had a larger impact on each other's sales than local entry by supermarkets or small single price point (SPP) retailers. Further, the CMA found that entry within 0.5 miles generally had a larger impact on sales than entry between 0.5 miles and 1 mile.

(b) In Ladbrokes/Coral (2016) the CMA found that betting and gaming stakes at the Parties' stores declined when rival stores entered the local area. This effect was larger when entrants located very nearby, and when the existing level of competition was weak.

7. REFERENCES

[3.418]

Alliance Boots/Dolland & Aitchison (2009): *Proposed joint venture between Alliance Boots Limited and Dolland & Aitchison Limited in relation to their respective optical businesses*, 19 May 2009 www.gov.uk/cma-cases/alliance-boots-limited-dollond-aitchison-limited

Amazon/The Book Depository (2011): *Anticipated acquisition by Amazon.com Inc of the Book Depository International Limited*, 14 December 2011 www.gov.uk/cma-cases/amazon-com-inc-the-book-depository-international-ltd

Asda/Co-operative Group (five stores) (2014): *Anticipated acquisition by Asda Stores Limited of five grocery stores and three petrol filling stations from Co-operative Group Limited*, 22 December 2014 www.gov.uk/cma-cases/asda-stores-limited-co-operative-group-limited-5-stores

Asda/Netto (2010): *Anticipated acquisition by Asda Stores Limited of Netto Foodstores Limited*, 20 October 2010 www.gov.uk/cma-cases/asda-netto

Boots/Alliance UniChem (2006): *Anticipated acquisition by Boots plc of Alliance UniChem plc*, 22 February 2006 www.gov.uk/cma-cases/boots-plc-alliance-unichem-plc

Carpetright/Allied Carpets (2010): *Completed acquisition by Carpetright plc of four Allied Carpet stores*, 29 September 2010 www.gov.uk/cma-cases/carpetright-allied-carpet

Celesio/Sainsbury's (2016): Celesio AG and Sainsbury's Supermarkets Limited, *A report on the anticipated acquisition by Celesio AG of Sainsbury's Pharmacy Business*, 29 July 2016 www.gov.uk/cma-cases/celesio-sainsbury-s-pharmacy-business-merger-inquiry

Cineworld/City Screen Limited (2013): *A report on the completed acquisition by Cineworld Group plc of City Screen Limited*, 8 October 2013 www.gov.uk/cma-cases/cineworld-city-screen-merger-inquiry

Co-operative Group Limited/George Burgess & Son Ltd (2009): *Anticipated acquisition by Co-operative Group Limited (formerly Cooperative Wholesale Society Limited) of the Funeral Business of George Burgess & Son Ltd*, 27 January 2009 www.gov.uk/cma-cases/co-operative-group -ltd-george-burgess-son-ltd

Co-operative Group Limited/Somerfield (2008): *Completed acquisition by Co-operative Group Limited of Somerfield Limited*, 17 November 2008 www.gov.uk/cma-cases/co-operative-group-ltd-somerfield-ltd

Co-operative Group (CWS) Limited/United Co-operatives Limited (2007): *Anticipated merger between Co-operative Group (CWS) Limited and United Co-operatives Limited*, 3 August 2007 www.gov.uk/cma-cases/co-operative-group-cws-ltd-united-co-operatives-ltd

Edmundson/Electric Centre (2012): *Completed acquisition by Edmundson Electrical Limited of Electric Center*, 23 July 2012 www.gov.uk/cma-cases/edmundson-electrical-electric-center

Edmundson Electrical/Western Electrical (2014): *Completed acquisition by Marlowe Holdings Investments LTD of Western Electrical Holding LTD*, 13 June 2014 www.gov.uk/cma-cases/edmundson-electrical-western-electrical

Greene/King Spirit (2015): *Anticipated acquisition by Greene King plc of Spirit Pub Company plc*, 29 May 2015. www.gov.uk/cma-cases/greene-king-spirit-pub-company-merger-inquiry

Holland & Barrett/Julian Graves (2009): *A report on the completed acquisition by NBTY Europe Limited of Julian Graves Limited*, 20 August 2009 www.gov.uk/cma-cases/nbty-europe -ltd-julian-graves-ltd-merger-inquiry-cc

Ladbrokes/Coral (2016): *A report on the anticipated merger between Ladbrokes plc and certain businesses of Gala Coral Group Limited*, 26 July 2016. www.gov.uk/cma-cases/ladbrokes -coral-group-merger-inquiry

Lodge Brothers Funerals Ltd/two funeral homes in the London Borough of Hillingdon (2009): *Completed acquisition by Lodge Brothers Funerals Ltd of two funeral homes in the London Borough of Hillingdon*, 17 December 2009 www.gov.uk/cma-cases/lodge-brothers-hillingdon

Mapil Bidco/Chain Reaction Cycles (2016): *Anticipated acquisition by Mapil Bidco Ltd of Chain Reaction Cycles Ltd, Hotlines Europe Ltd and Decade Europe Ltd*, 3 August 2016 www.gov.uk/cma-cases/mapil-bidco-chain-reaction-cycles-merger-inquiry

Martin McColl/Co-operative (2016): *Anticipated acquisition by Martin McColl Ltd of 298 groceries stores from Co-operative Group Ltd*, 26 January 2017 www.gov.uk/cma-cases/martin- mccoll-s-co-operative-merger-inquiry

Nationwide Building Society/Derbyshire Building Society (2008): *Anticipated acquisition by Nationwide Building Society of the Derbyshire Building Society*, 25 November 2008 www.gov.uk/cma-cases/nationwide-building-society-derbyshire-building-society

Original Bowling/Bowlplex (2015): *Anticipated acquisition by The Original Bowling Company Ltd of Bowlplex Ltd*, 17 August 2015 www.gov.uk/cma-cases/the-original-bowling -company-bowlplex-merger-inquiry

One Stop/Alfred Jones (2013): *Anticipated acquisition by One Stop Stores Limited of 33 stores from Alfred Jones (Warrington) Limited, trading as Spar*, 22 November 2013 www.gov.uk/cma-cases/one-stop-ltd-alfred-jones-warrington-ltd

Poundland/99p Stores (2015): *A report on the anticipated acquisition by Poundland Group plc of 99p Stores Limited*, 18 September 2015 www.gov.uk/cma-cases/poundland-99p-stores-merger-inquiry

Pure Gym/The Gym (2014): *Anticipated combination of Pure Gym Limited and The Gym Limited, 11 September 2014* www.gov.uk/cma-cases/pure-gym-the-gym

Rank/Gala (2013): *A report on the anticipated acquisition by The Rank Group Plc of Gala Casinos Limited*, 19 February 2013 www.gov.uk/cma-cases/rank-gala-merger-inquiry-cc

Rexel/Wilts (2012): *Completed acquisition by Rexel UK Limited of certain assets of Wilts Wholesale Electrical Company Limited*, 13 November 2012 www.gov.uk/cma-cases/rexel-uk-wilts- wholesale-electrical-company

Rontec/Total (2011): *Proposed acquisition by Rontec Investments LLP of petrol forecourts, stores and other assets from Total Downstream UK plc, Total UK Limited and their affiliates*, 9 November 2011 www.gov.uk/cma-cases/rontec-total-downstream-uk-total-uk-ltd

Safeway (2003): *Safeway plc and Asda Group Limited (owned by Wal-Mart Stores Inc); Wm Morrison Supermarkets PLC; J Sainsbury plc; and Tesco plc: A report on the mergers in contemplation*, 18 August 2003 http://webarchive.nationalarchives.gov.uk/+/http:/www.competition-commission.org.uk/rep_pub/reports/2003/481safeway.htm

Saint-Gobain/Build Centre (2012): *Completed acquisition by Saint-Gobain of Build Center*, 8 February 2012 www.gov.uk/cma-cases/jewson-build-center

Shell/Rontec (2011): *Anticipated acquisition by Shell UK Limited of 253 petrol stations from Consortium Rontec Investments LLP*, 13 February 2012 www.gov.uk/cma-cases/shell-uk-ltd-consortium -rontec-investments-llp

Somerfield/Morrison (2005): *A report on the acquisition by Somerfield plc of 115 stores from Wm Morrison Supermarkets plc*, September 2005 www.gov.uk/cma-cases/somerfield-plc- wm-morrison-supermarkets-plc-merger-inquiry-cc

Sports Direct/JJB Sports (2010): *A report on the acquisition by Sports Direct International plc of 31 stores from JJB Sports plc*, 16 March 2010 www.gov.uk/cma-cases/sports-direct- international-plc-jjb-sports-plc-merger-inquiry-cc

Thomas Cook/Co-operative Group Ltd/Midlands Co-operative Society Ltd (2011): *A report on the anticipated travel business joint venture between Thomas Cook Group plc, the Co-operative Group Limited and the Midlands Co-operative Society Limited*, 16 August 2011 www.gov.uk/cma-cases/ thomas-cook-group-plc-co-operative-group-ltd-midlands-co-operative-society-ltd-merger-inquiry-cc

Travis Perkins/BSS Group (2010): *Anticipated acquisition by Travis Perkins plc of the BSS Group plc*, 11 November 2010. www.gov.uk/cma-cases/travis-perkins-bss-group

Vodafone Limited/140 stores formerly controlled by Phones4U Limited (2015): *Completed acquisition by Vodafone Limited of 140 stores formerly controlled by Phones4U Limited*, 4 February 2015 www.gov.uk/cma-cases/ completed-acquisition-by-vodafone-limited-of-some-assets-formerly-controlled-by-phones4u-limited

Waterstone's/Ottakar's (2006): *Proposed acquisition of Ottakar's plc by HMV Group plc through Waterstone's Booksellers Ltd*, 12 May 2006 http://webarchive.nationalarchives.gov.uk/20140402141250/ http://www.competition-commission.org.uk/our-work/directory-of-all-inquiries/ hmv-group-plc-waterstones-plc-ottakars-plc/final-report-and-appendices-glossary

Yoox/Net-a-Porter (2015): *Anticipated acquisition relating to Compagnie Financière Richemont S.A., YOOX S.p.A and The Net-A-Porter Group Limited*, 2 September 2015 www.gov.uk/cma-cases/ richemont-yoox-net-a-porter-merger-inquiry

COMPETITION AND MARKETS AUTHORITY MERGER NOTICE UNDER SECTION 96 OF THE ENTERPRISE ACT 2002: TEMPLATE FOR COMPLETION

June 2017

[3.419]

NOTES

Note: paragraph 20 of this Notice was amended in November 2017 to include reference to a new template for recording documents submitted to the CMA and added information on how documents should be submitted. Annex 1 to merger notice template follows this document, and Annex 2 is at **[3.428]**.

This document is available on the Competition and Markets Authority website at: www.gov.uk/government/publications/ mergers-forms-and-fee-information.

PREAMBLE

PURPOSE OF THE NOTICE

[3.420]

1. This merger notice (Notice) is for the purpose of notifying an anticipated or completed merger to the Competition and Markets Authority (CMA) pursuant to section 96 of the Enterprise Act 2002 (as amended) (the Act).

Parties giving the Notice

2. A Notice may be submitted by any person carrying on an enterprise to which the notified arrangements relate.[1] Merger parties may submit a Notice jointly. This may in particular be appropriate in anticipated mergers where the acquirer may not have access to the target's internal information or documents, and will not therefore be able to verify the accuracy or completeness of the information provided, or – for similar reasons – in joint ventures.

3. The person(s) submitting the Notice (referred to below as notifying parties) take(s) responsibility for the accuracy and completeness of the information. Where merger parties are submitting a Notice jointly, each notifying party must sign the declaration below and each party is responsible for the accuracy and completeness of the information it has submitted in, or with, the Notice.

The UK merger control regime

4. The UK merger control regime is set out in the Act. Guidance on the procedures followed by the CMA in reviewing mergers is provided in *Mergers: Guidance on the CMA's jurisdiction and procedure*

(CMA2) (the Guidance). The text of the Act together with the Guidance and other relevant documents can be found on the CMA's webpages (www.gov.uk/cma).

5. The Act sets statutory time limits for the merger review process. The CMA has an initial period of 40 working days, subject to an extension in certain circumstances (the Phase 1 investigation) to decide whether its duty to make a reference for an in-depth Phase 2 investigation applies.[2] Where notifying parties voluntarily notify a merger to the CMA by submitting a Notice, the period of 40 working days begins on the first working day after the day on which the CMA gives notice to notifying parties that it is satisfied that the Notice is in the prescribed form, contains the prescribed information and states that the existence of a proposed merger has been made public (a Satisfactory Notification).[3]

Information required by the Notice

6. This Notice sets out the categories of information to be provided by merger parties when notifying a merger to the CMA to enable it to assess the notified merger.[4]

7. The 'prescribed information' necessary for the purposes of a Satisfactory Notification is information responsive to the questions in this Notice, insofar as it is relevant to the notified merger. The specific nature and extent of information required in response to each of these questions will vary from case to case, and will depend, for example, on the activities of the merger parties or the extent of overlap in their activities.

8. In order to advance pre-notification discussions, notifying parties are requested to submit a draft Notice with the information they consider necessary for the CMA's Phase 1 investigation (along with brief explanations setting out why any information requested in the Notice that has not been provided is not relevant in the circumstances of the case).

9. The Guidance provides further information for notifying parties on pre-notification contacts and the preparation of the draft Notice. Merger parties that are unsure about the extent of information required are encouraged to discuss this with the CMA's case team as early in the process as possible in order to avoid any unnecessary delay to the assessment of the notified merger.

The Guidance Notes

10. The CMA has published Guidance Notes to assist notifying parties in assessing the nature and extent of information that, in their individual case, they should provide in response to a particular question for the purposes of a Satisfactory Notification. To that end, the Guidance Notes provide examples of the type of information that may ordinarily be responsive. The questions in this Notice should therefore be read in the light of those Guidance Notes, and notifying parties should review the Guidance Notes in full before answering the questions.

11. However, the Guidance Notes cannot and do not list exhaustively all information that the CMA may, in a given case, consider should be provided in response to a particular question for the purposes of a Satisfactory Notification. The CMA may request additional information responsive to a question, beyond that indicated in the Guidance Notes, where it considers that, in the specific circumstances of the case, such additional information is required for the purposes of its Phase 1 investigation.[5] Where notifying parties have engaged in pre-notification discussions with the CMA and/or submitted draft(s) of the notification to the CMA (as to which, please see below and Chapter 6 of the Guidance), the CMA will make clear to notifying parties as part of such engagement what information it expects to be necessary for a Satisfactory Notification in the case at hand.

Other published sources of guidance or information

12. In addition to the Guidance and Guidance Notes, notifying parties are encouraged to refer to other sources of guidance on the information and evidence that the CMA will likely require parties to provide in support of their notification in a particular case, including:

- *Merger Assessment Guidelines* (OFT1254/CC2)
- *Mergers: Exceptions to the duty to refer and undertakings in lieu of reference guidance* (OFT1122)
- *Retail mergers commentary* (CMA62), and
- *Good practice in the design and presentation of consumer survey evidence in merger inquiries* (OFT1230/CC2com1).[6]

These documents also explain certain terminology used in this Notice and in the Guidance Notes,[7] and/or how the CMA is likely to approach its substantive assessment of notified mergers.

13. In addition, notifying parties may wish to refer to previous merger decisions published by the CMA (and its predecessors, the Office of Fair Trading (OFT) and the Competition Commission (CC) if relevant) on mergers in the relevant sector (available on or through the CMA's webpages), which may provide useful guidance on the issues that the CMA is likely to consider as part of its assessment of mergers in that sector and thus the nature of the information that notifying parties are likely to have to provide.

Pre-notification

14. The CMA strongly encourages notifying parties to engage in early pre-notification discussions with the CMA, in particular where they require further clarification as to the specific nature or extent of information that should be provided in the case at hand. These pre-notification contacts are extremely valuable both to notifying parties and to the CMA to determine precisely the information that will be required for a Satisfactory Notification, and provide the most efficient means of resolving any uncertainties notifying parties may have in this regard. Such early engagement is therefore likely to generate efficiencies in terms of timing and information gathering and may result in a reduction in the information notifying parties are required to provide.

15. If, during pre-notification and having reviewed the notifying parties' draft Notice, the CMA considers that additional information responsive to the questions in the Notice is required for the purposes of a Satisfactory Notification, beyond that already provided by notifying parties in their draft notification, the CMA will indicate this to notifying parties.

16. Merger parties should also note that, during the course of a Phase 1 investigation (that is, following the submission of a Satisfactory Notification and the commencement of the 40 working day period), the CMA may subsequently require further information from the merger parties for the purposes of its investigation, including information that the CMA did not require prior to giving notice to notifying parties that the Notice was satisfactory.

17. Merger parties are also advised to discuss with the CMA any additional information that they may wish to provide with their notification to aid the CMA's investigation. It is particularly important to discuss with the CMA any evidence supporting their notification (for example, econometric analysis or customer surveys) that merger parties intend to produce specifically for the purposes of the CMA's merger control investigation. Such discussions should occur in advance of notification and prior to commencing production of that evidence (see further paragraph 6.41 of the Guidance). This will help to minimise risks of the parties undertaking wasted or unnecessary work.

Completing the Notice

18. The CMA wishes to obtain the information necessary to carry out its responsibilities under the Act without placing undue burdens on the parties. Notifying parties can choose to supply the requisite information either in the format of this Notice template or in a written format of their choosing (that is signed and indicates clearly where the information responsive to each question in the Notice can be found in the submission). Irrespective of the format chosen, all of the information requested in the Notice should be provided (unless that information is not necessary in the circumstances of the case, for the reasons explained elsewhere in this Notice) and the notifying parties should provide the signed declaration set out in Part VI of this Notice.[8]

19. When completing this Notice, evidence (including contemporaneous documents) cited in support of statements made by notifying parties should be provided to the CMA, where reasonably practicable. The CMA is likely to attach more weight to supported statements and therefore encourages notifying parties to provide evidence in support of their statements wherever reasonably practicable.

20. In order to help the CMA's investigation proceed efficiently, any data or documents requested in the Notice should be submitted in a readable and searchable format and classified and indexed using the template in Annex 2. Annex 2 should be updated if additional data or documents are submitted in response to follow-up questions from the CMA. The contact details of the merger parties' customers, competitors and suppliers should be provided using the template in Annex 1.

21. Notifying parties may consider that it is not necessary to provide certain information requested in the Notice. This may be the case, for example, where:

- The question is not applicable as a factual matter (eg where there are no vertical relationships between the merging parties, it is not necessary to provide a response to Question 18 in relation to the potential vertical effects of the merger);
- The information requested is not relevant for the CMA's assessment (eg in cases in which there is little or no overlap between the merging parties, it may not be necessary to provide responses to Question 23 on Countervailing buyer power or Question 24 on Efficiencies and customer benefits); and
- The information requested is not available to the notifying party (eg where the merger is a 'hostile' transaction).[9]

22. In this circumstance, notifying parties should respond to the question by providing a brief explanation setting out why the information requested in the Notice has not been provided. The CMA will consider, at its discretion, whether the information provided by the notifying parties is sufficient for a Satisfactory Notification. While no formal process exists through which the CMA will grant "waivers" from the requirement to provide certain information, notifying parties are encouraged to discuss any information that they consider should not be necessary in pre-notification discussions.

23. In assessing if the information provided by the notifying parties is sufficient for a Satisfactory Notification, the CMA will consider whether it would be necessary and proportionate to request additional information in view of the complexity of the merger and the potential competition concerns on which the CMA is likely to focus its investigation.

24. For the avoidance of doubt, where the CMA has accepted that certain information requested in the Notice is not necessary for a Satisfactory Notification, this does not preclude the CMA from subsequently requesting this information at any other time during the merger review process (whether by way of a voluntary request for information or pursuant to section 109 of the Act).

25. As stated above, the initial period of 40 working days will not begin until the first working day after the CMA has confirmed to the notifying parties that it has received a Satisfactory Notification. As noted above, the nature and extent of information required for these purposes may vary from case to case and further information may be requested from the merger parties at a later stage, following commencement of that 40 working day period.

26. The CMA will endeavour to inform notifying parties in writing whether or not a submitted Notice amounts to a Satisfactory Notification as promptly as is practicable in the circumstances.[10] This will typically be within five (and no more than ten) working days of receipt of that Notice, and is likely to depend on, for example, the volume and length of submissions, the extent to which the CMA has previously considered earlier drafts of the same submissions, and the available CMA resource. In general, the CMA is likely to be able to provide such confirmation more promptly in those cases in which parties have engaged in pre-notification.

27. If any information contained in the Notice is found to be, in any material respect, false or misleading, the CMA may reject the Notice (including in instances where the CMA has previously confirmed that it considers the Notice to be a Satisfactory Notification).[11]

28. It is an offence punishable by a fine and/or imprisonment to intentionally or recklessly give the CMA information that is false or misleading in a material respect.[12]

Submission of the Notice

29. If, after submitting the Notice and during the course of the investigation, there are any changes in the circumstances of the merger or the merger parties which are relevant to the information provided in the Notice or other information the merger parties have provided to the CMA, they must inform the CMA immediately.

30. Information on how to submit a Notice to the CMA is available on the CMA's webpages.

NOTES

1 See the Enterprise Act 2002 (Merger Prenotification) Regulations 2003 (SI 2003/1369) (as amended) and Guidance Note to the Declaration in Part III.

2 See section 34ZA of the Act.

3 See sections 34ZA(3) and 96(2A) of the Act.

4 See section 96(2) of the Act.

5 That is, its investigation under sections 22 or 33 of the Act as to whether it has a duty to refer that merger to Phase 2.

6 The documents listed here were originally published by the CMA's predecessors, the OFT and/or CC, and have been adopted by the CMA. They are available on the CMA's webpages.

7 Merger parties are referred in particular to *Merger Assessment Guidelines*, which includes descriptions of terms (relating to, for example, competitive conditions) that are used throughout this Notice. The Notice and Guidance Notes include cross-references to relevant parts of that document where appropriate.

8 As noted in paragraph 8, where information requested in the Notice is not provided, a brief explanation should be provided setting out why this information is not relevant in the circumstances of the case.

9 For non-hostile acquisitions, the CMA would expect that an acquiring party should be able to access all relevant information relating to the target's activities through cooperation obligations between the transaction parties. Where notifying parties consider that they are unable to provide the information requested, they may be required to detail any steps taken by notifying parties to obtain that information.

10 As explained in paragraph 5 above, the period of 40 working days begins on the first working day after the day on which the CMA gives notice to notifying parties that it is satisfied that the Notice is in the prescribed form, contains the prescribed information and states that the existence of a proposed merger has been made public.

11 Section 99(5)(a) of the Act. Where appropriate, such situations could include where during market testing the CMA finds that notifying parties, when providing contact details, did not provide working email addresses and the false/incorrect information is material in any respect.

12 Section 117 of the Act.

PART I: GENERAL INFORMATION

[3.421]

1. Provide the name and contact details of:

(*a*) an individual within each of the merger parties
(*b*) any authorised representatives of each of the merger parties
(*c*) if not already provided in response to (a) and (b), the person(s) submitting the Notice[13]
(*d*) the person to whom the CMA should address any correspondence.

Guidance Note to question 1

Notifying parties can authorise a representative, for example, a firm of solicitors, to complete the Notice on their behalf and to act for them in further correspondence with the CMA.[14] If notifying parties do authorise someone to act in this way they must sign the authorisation at Part III of the Notice.

If an authorised representative ceases to act for notifying parties, the CMA must be advised of this immediately.

Notifying parties must give the name and address of a person who is authorised to accept all correspondence and accept service or take receipt on behalf of notifying parties. This may be a person within the company or notifying parties' authorised representative.

'Contact details' include full name, telephone number, UK address and email address where the CMA can make contact between 9.00am and 5.00pm on working days. If any such details change, notifying parties should notify the CMA immediately in writing.

NOTES

[13] That is, the notifying party or parties, as described in paragraph 2 of the Preamble above.

[14] Note, however, that the Notice must be signed by a person or persons with authority to bind each notifying party (see Part VI of this Notice and the associated Guidance Notes).

PART II: MERGER DETAILS

THE MERGER SITUATION

[3.422]

See chapter 4 of the Guidance and part 3 of *Merger Assessment Guidelines*.

2. Describe the arrangements by which the enterprises will cease/have ceased to be distinct (the merger), including:

- *(a)* the parties to the merger (the merger parties)
- *(b)* the type of transaction
- *(c)* the consideration
- *(d)* the key terms
- *(e)* the timing
- *(f)* the strategic and economic rationale for the transaction
- *(g)* whether it is being notified in any other jurisdictions and, if so, whether the merger parties are willing to offer a waiver to support coordination between the CMA and the competition authorities in those jurisdictions, and
- *(h)* the ownership structure pre and post-merger, including any pre-merger links between the merger parties.

Guidance Note to question 2

See chapter 4 of the Guidance and part 3 of *Merger Assessment Guidelines* text

Note to 2.a – When describing the merger parties, provide their full legal names and explain how this entity fits within a wider group structure if relevant, specifying the ultimate ownership. Identify any legal or natural person which, directly or indirectly, owns, controls, or has material influence over (together, referred to hereafter as 'controls')[15] any one of the merger parties and is active in any of the Candidate Markets identified in response to question 13 below, and any legal or natural person that any one of the merger parties controls and which is active in any of the Candidate Markets. If the acquiring party or group (where relevant) qualifies as 'small' or 'medium-sized' under the Companies Act 2006 (sections 382 and 465) please specify. Information responsive to question 2(a) may be given by way of a diagram.

Note to 2.b – When describing the type of transaction, indicate, for example, whether it is (a) a full merger, an agreed bid, or a full takeover, (b) the acquisition of assets, (c) the acquisition of a minority shareholding giving material influence, (d) a change of directorship giving material influence, or (e) the formation of or change of control in a joint venture.

Where the transaction gives rise to material influence, please describe in detail the aspects of the transaction that enable material influence to be exerted, including shareholding, voting patterns, board representation and other relevant factors.[16]

Note that where notifying parties submit that a minority shareholding does not give rise to material influence, where the CMA considers that the circumstances of the case are such that the determination of a lack of material influence is not clear cut, the CMA may nonetheless require information on the minority shareholder to be provided for the purposes of a Satisfactory Notification, and will inform notifying parties of this.

Where notifying parties are unsure as to whether or not information related to material influence is required for a Satisfactory Notification, they are encouraged to contact the CMA in pre-notification to discuss.

Note to 2.c – When describing the consideration, indicate its value as well as the form it will take.

Note to 2.d – The description of the key terms of the merger should include but should not necessarily be limited to any factors upon which completion of the merger is conditional together with the status of these factors.

Note to 2.e – On timing, for completed mergers, specify when the enterprises ceased to be distinct (within the meaning of sections 26 and 27 of the Act). For anticipated mergers, specify the expected time scale for exchange of contracts and completion of the merger as well as any other dates that notifying parties wish the CMA to be aware of.

Note to 2.g – The CMA considers that where mergers are subject to investigation in more than one jurisdiction, there can be substantial benefits to the merger parties and to the competition authorities in those jurisdictions from communication and cooperation between the competition authorities. If the merger has been or is being notified in other jurisdictions, please indicate whether notifying parties would be willing to provide the CMA with a confidentiality waiver allowing it to exchange confidential information with the relevant competition agencies in other jurisdictions in respect of the notified merger. A Satisfactory Notification will not be conditional on notifying parties' providing such a waiver. In any event, merger parties should be aware that there are circumstances where the Act permits the CMA to share information with other overseas agencies and sectoral regulators without prior consent (see *Transparency and Disclosure: statement of the CMA's policy and approach* (CMA6) and chapter 19 of the Guidance).

Guidance Note to question 2

Note to 2.h – If the structure of the proposed arrangements is complex, provide a diagram. Where appropriate, details of the ownership structure should include the identity and shareholdings, pre- and post-merger, of any persons holding 10% or more of the voting rights, issued share capital or other securities in the business that has been or will be acquired.

Include a description of any other links between the merger parties (either formal or informal). This should also include (but should not necessarily be limited to) any associated persons.

3. Provide a brief description of the businesses of the merger parties (and, where relevant, their groups).

Guidance Note to question 3

When describing the business or businesses over which control is being or has been acquired, if assets are being acquired, set out which assets – both tangible and intangible – form part of the acquisition and include a brief description of the main products and services supplied by the acquired business or businesses.

In the case of an acquisition, a brief description of the acquirer group's business should include a brief description of the main products and services provided, together with a corporate structure chart and an organisation chart (showing the names, job titles and areas of responsibility of the senior executives of the merger parties).[17]

Where the transaction involves a full merger or a joint venture, specify for each merger party the information identified in the preceding paragraph.

4. Provide brief details of any other transactions (merger, acquisition, disposal, joint venture) undertaken by:

(a) either of the merger parties in the last two years which involve the products or services in any Candidate Market identified in response to question 13,[18] and

(b) both or all merger parties in the last two years (that is, where the merger parties were party to the same transaction).

JURISDICTION

See chapter 4 of the Guidance and paragraphs 3.1.3 to 3.3.10 of *Merger Assessment Guidelines.*

5. Explain why:

(a) a relevant merger situation (as per section 23 of the Act) has been created, or

(b) arrangements are in progress or contemplation which will result in the creation of a relevant merger situation.

Guidance Note to question 5

See chapter 4 of the Guidance and paragraphs 3.1.3 to 3.3.10 of *Merger Assessment Guidelines*

Notifying parties should explain the reasons why they consider that:

(a) two or more enterprises have ceased to be distinct or arrangements are in progress or in contemplation which, if carried into effect, will result in two or more enterprises ceasing to be distinct (see chapter 4 of the Guidance), and

(b) the turnover or share of supply tests are met, including where relevant:

(i) the UK turnover associated with the enterprise being acquired (see section 28 of the Act and chapter 4 of the Guidance). If relevant, explain the methodology adopted to estimate such turnover, and/or

(ii) an estimate of the share of supply for any product or service of any description where the merging/merged businesses[19] combined have a share of supply in the UK, or in a substantial part of the UK, of 25% or more and where the merger causes an increment in such share (see section 23 of the Act and chapter 4 of the Guidance). Explain the methodology adopted to estimate such shares.

In particular, if a relevant merger situation has been created due to the acquisition of the ability to exercise material influence, the explanation should refer to the factors identified in paragraphs 4.14 to 4.27 of the Guidance and paragraphs 3.1.3 to 3.3.10 of Merger *Assessment Guidelines*, as well as any other factors notifying parties consider relevant to that assessment.

6. Indicate the annual UK, EEA, and worldwide turnover in the last financial year associated with each of:

(a) the acquirer (including group companies where relevant – see Annexe B of the Guidance), and

(b) the target (if not already provided under question 5).

Guidance Note to question 6

For turnover, provide details of sales exclusive of VAT and duty.

7. Explain why the transaction is not subject to the European Union Merger Regulation (EU Merger Regulation),[20] (highlighting whether it is notifiable in the UK by virtue of the 'two-thirds' rule in article 1(2) or 1(3) of that Regulation).

NOTES

15 Within the meaning of section 26 of the Act. See chapter 4 of the Guidance for further information on the meaning of ownership, control and material influence.

16 For the avoidance of doubt, the use of the term merger parties throughout the Notice should be construed as including any party which exercises material influence over the acquirer or the target enterprise.

17 If the acquirer is a conglomerate or multinational undertaking, notifying parties will not generally be expected to provide such details of senior executives with responsibility only for areas of the business that do not fall within any of the Candidate Markets identified in response to Question 13 below.

18 Where this involves a large number of transactions, notifying parties are encouraged to contact the CMA to discuss.

19 That is, the enterprises that will cease, or have ceased, to be distinct.

20 Council Regulation (EC) No 139/2004 of 20 January 2004.

PART III: SUPPORTING DOCUMENTS

[3.423]

8. Provide:

(*a*) a press release or report and details of all notifications to listing authorities (for example, for admission to the UK Listing Authority Official List and for admission to trading on the London Stock Exchange) or other documentation evidencing that the merger (or merger proposal) has been made public, and

(*b*) a copy of the documents bringing about the merger situation, including heads of terms, memorandum of understanding, sale and purchase agreement, business purchase agreement or equivalent. Where these are not in final form, please provide the latest draft and keep the CMA informed of subsequent changes to the document, if any.

(*c*) If the offer is subject to the City Code, copies of the Offer Document and Listing Particulars. If these are not yet available, provide copies of the latest drafts and supply the final versions as soon as they are issued.

Guidance Note to question 8c

For mergers governed by the City Code, the CMA does not envisage that the pre-notification timetable will raise significant difficulties in relation to the timing of public offers. Merger parties should however bear in mind the need to reconcile timing of submission of the Notice with the requirements of the City Code. If merger parties are seeking a decision by the first closing date of an offer (as defined in the City Code), the CMA will need to receive the Notice (following pre-notification) before the posting of the Offer Document. This will increase the likelihood of obtaining a Phase 1 decision by the first closing date. The CMA will take account of timing constraints relating to the City Code, or merger control regulation in other jurisdictions, when conducting its investigation and may, where the demands of the particular case and its existing caseload allow, seek to make its decision more quickly than the standard statutory timetable. The CMA cannot be bound by the first closing date however, and where it is not in a position to reach a decision by the first closing date, the consideration period under the City Code will need to be extended.

(*d*) for each of the acquirer and acquirer group (if relevant) and the target (or merger parties in the case of a full merger), the most recent annual report and accounts.

Guidance Note to question 8d

The CMA will usually need only the most recent annual report and accounts of the main parties to the merger. However, where the acquiring company is part of a larger group, the CMA will normally also need the most recent group annual report and accounts. It will not need group accounts for the target's parent company where the target is a subsidiary or associate company and separate accounts are prepared for that company. Where documents are submitted in electronic format, annual reports and accounts can be provided by way of a hyper-link.

It is important that the target's UK turnover for the preceding business year is provided. If no annual report or accounts are available, provide separate figures (audited if reasonably practicable) on annual turnover (including UK turnover), profits and assets. For turnover, provide details of sales exclusive of VAT and duty. For profit, provide the profit and loss accounts.

(*e*) copies of the most recent business plan of the acquirer and acquirer group (if relevant) and the target (or merger parties in the case of a full merger). Where a horizontal overlap or vertical relationship involves, for example, a specific division or brand of one or both of the merger parties, the most recent business plan for the relevant division or brand should be provided as well.

9. Provide copies of any documents in either of the merger parties' possession which:

(*a*) have been prepared by or for, or received by, any member of the board of directors (or equivalent body) or senior management or the shareholders' meeting of either merger party (whether prepared internally or by external consultants), and

(*b*) either:

(i) set out the rationale for the merger (including but not limited to the benefits of, and/or investment case for the acquisition), or

(ii) assess or analyse the merger with respect to competitive conditions, competitors (actual and potential), potential for sales growth or expansion into new product or geographic areas, market conditions, market shares and/or the price to be paid. This should include but not necessarily be limited to post-merger business plans or strategy (including integration plans and financial forecasts) and Information Memoranda prepared by or for the merger parties that specifically relate to the sale of the target. If no such Information Memoranda exist, explain what information or document(s) given to any of the merger parties is meant to serve the function of an Information Memorandum.

Indicate (if not contained in the document itself) the date of preparation and the identity and role of the author(s) within the merger parties or external consultants.

Guidance Note to question 9

The consideration of internal documents is an important element of the CMA's investigation and therefore a complete response to this question is necessary for a Satisfactory Notification.

The CMA encourages notifying parties to discuss the process for gathering these documents with the CMA in pre-notification discussions, particularly if notifying parties are unsure what documents may be responsive or if, in their case, the question may result in a large number of responsive documents.

The CMA expects that documents responsive to this question will typically include minutes of meetings, studies, reports, presentations, surveys, analyses or recommendations. In most cases, the CMA would not expect to receive documents such as emails, handwritten notes, or instant messages in response to this question.

If notifying parties consider that they have no or limited documents responsive to this question (or if the documents provided contain limited information of substance), the CMA may request a list of the key members of each merger party involved in the merger and decision-making process. It may then ask for documents prepared for or by them, including substantive emails that may contain the information it would expect to appear in the supporting documents described in this question.

Further, where no Information Memorandum exists, the CMA may then use the explanation of information or documents given to the acquirer or other merger party in place of an Information Memorandum to identify and specify any documents that it wishes notifying parties to provide

10. Provide copies of documents (including, but not necessarily limited to, reports, presentations, studies, internal analyses, industry/market reports or analysis, including customer research and pricing studies) in either merger parties' possession and prepared or published in the last two years which:

(a) have been prepared by or for, or received by, any member of the board of directors (or equivalent body) or senior management of either merger party (whether prepared internally or by external consultants), and

(b) set out the competitive conditions, market conditions, market shares, competitors, or the merging parties' business plans in relation to the product(s) or service(s) where the merger parties have a horizontal overlap as identified in response to question 12 below.

Guidance Note to question 10

As noted above, the consideration of internal documents is an important element of the CMA's investigation and therefore a complete response to this question is necessary for a Satisfactory Notification.

The CMA encourages notifying parties to discuss the process for gathering these documents with the CMA in pre-notification, particularly If notifying parties are unsure what may be responsive to this question or if, in their case, the question results in a large number of responsive documents (for example, because of a large number of overlaps).

As noted above, the CMA expects that the documents responsive to this question will typically include reports, presentations, studies, internal analyses, industry/market reports or analyses, including customer research and pricing studies. In most cases, the CMA would not expect to receive documents such as emails, handwritten notes, or instant messages in response to this question.

Where notifying parties consider that they have no or limited documents (or if the documents provided contain limited information of substance), the CMA may request other documents that may contain the information it would expect to appear in the supporting documents described in this question, for example, substantive emails to or from certain key individuals.

The CMA will typically not require documents responsive to this question to be provided for product(s) or (services), as identified in response to question 13, in which the merger parties' combined share of supply does not exceed 15%.

In some limited cases, the CMA may – having regard to the specific circumstances of the case at hand – require a broader set of documents to be produced in response to this question. This might include, for example, documents that have been prepared by or for, or received by, a broader set of custodians (other than the board of directors or senior management). Similarly, in some circumstances, the CMA may require the production of documents relating to product(s) or service(s) in which the merger parties' combined share of supply does not exceed 15%, or where there is a vertical relationship between the merger parties' activities. This should be discussed with the CMA in pre-notification.

PART IV: COMPETITION ASSESSMENT

COUNTERFACTUAL

[3.424]

11. If the notifying parties consider that the CMA should assess the competitive effects of the merger against a counterfactual other than the current or pre-existing competitive situation, please describe that counterfactual and explain why the notifying parties consider it should be used for that assessment.

Guidance Note to question 11

See paragraphs 4.3.1 to 4.3.29 of *Merger Assessment Guidelines*

Notifying parties may wish to submit an alternative counterfactual from the current or pre-existing competitive situation to the merger. Where notifying parties wish to do so, given the statutory time constraints on the CMA's Phase 1 investigation, the CMA requires this to be done at the time of filing in order for the Notice to be a Satisfactory Notification. Indeed, notifying parties are encouraged to discuss such alternatives with the case team at the earliest opportunity as part of pre-notification discussions. For the avoidance of doubt, in the event notifying parties do not put forward such arguments for the purposes of the CMA's Phase 1 investigation, they will not be prevented from doing so in the event of a reference for a Phase 2 investigation.

Where the notifying parties contend that the acquired firm and/or the acquirer would have exited or would exit the market absent the merger, they should submit detailed evidence (including internal documents) as to why such exit by the firm would be, or would have been, inevitable. These could include, but are not limited to:

(a) board documents (including those discussing what would happen absent the merger as well as alternative options to the merger and why these were discounted)

(b) statutory accounts for the last three years and monthly management accounts for the last 18 months

(c) cash flow forecasts (including underlying assumptions)

(d) balance sheet projections assumptions

(e) documents showing that underlying assumptions of these cash flow forecasts or balance sheet projections hold absent the merger

(f) details of current financial arrangements and any additional finance that would be required

(g) documents that show all avenues of operational and financial restructuring have been exhausted, and

(h) documents showing that the firm has sought additional finance and been rejected.

Notifying parties should also explain whether there would have been an alternative purchaser for the firm or its assets including, for example, (i) how, if at all, the exiting business was marketed to potential purchasers, (ii) to whom it was marketed, (iii) if any expressed an interest, and (iv) what bids were offered, and provide any internal documents assessing the bids.

Where notifying parties submit that the acquired firm and/or the acquirer would have exited or would inevitably exit the market absent the merger, they should provide the name and contact details (including address, email address and telephone number) for all relevant insolvency practitioners or company voluntary arrangement (CVA) practitioners working with the companies and for lenders (secured or unsecured) that have provided the exiting firm with financing.

MARKET DEFINITION

See section 5.2 of *Merger Assessment Guidelines*.

12. Describe the product(s) or service(s) and geographic area(s) where the merger parties overlap, where they have a vertical relationship, or where they supply related products/services.

Guidance Note to question 12

Horizontal overlaps include any business activity in which both merger parties are active. Standard Industrial Classification (SIC) codes should be provided for all overlapping products/services. For the latest version of the SIC codes, please consult the CMA's webpages.

Vertical relationships include any product/service or product/service types which one of the merger parties supplies, and which another merger party purchases (or could purchase as a substitute for other products), within the same geographic area. For the purposes of this Notice, it is not necessary for there to be a direct supply or purchase arrangement between the merger parties in order to constitute a vertical relationship (that is, the term vertical relationship also includes diagonal mergers).

Related products/services are those which do not lie within the same market, but which are nonetheless related in some way; for example, because they are complements (so that a fall in the price of one product/service increases the customer's demand for another), or because there are economies of scale in purchasing them (so that customers buy them together).

Notifying parties should provide an overview and explanation of the product/services and geographic areas the merger parties supply (where they overlap, or have a vertical relationship, or where the products/services are related). Where notifying parties consider it might be helpful for the CMA in understanding the products/services, provide any documents (for example, sales documentation) describing the products/services. It is not expected that this response will discuss market definition, which should be covered in question 13 below.

13. Identify (and explain the rationale for identifying):

(a) the narrowest candidate product/service and geographic market(s) where the merger parties overlap, and (if the parties have a vertical relationship or supply related products/services)[21] the narrowest candidate product/service and geographic market(s) at each level of the vertical supply chain and for each related product/service (the Narrowest Candidate Market(s)).

(b) any other plausible candidate product/service and geographic market(s)[22] where the merger parties overlap, have a vertical relationship, or supply related products/services (together with the Narrowest Candidate Market(s), the Candidate Market(s)).

Guidance Note to question 13

Notifying parties should explain (by reference, for example, to the market definition principles explained in section 5.2 of *Merger Assessment Guidelines*) why they consider that each Candidate Market would or would not be an appropriate market definition for the purposes of the CMA's assessment of the competitive effects of the merger, and provide supporting evidence where reasonably practicable. Notifying parties should refer, in particular, to demand-side and (if relevant) supply-side substitution considerations.

Notifying parties are encouraged also to refer to previous merger decisions published by the CMA and its predecessors.

Where relevant, the response should include a description of the catchment area (see *Merger Assessment Guidelines*, paragraph 5.2.25) or flows (where this is the basis on which the CMA or its predecessors have previously assessed mergers in the relevant sector) for the geographic area(s).[23]

SHARES OF SUPPLY

14. Provide the shares of supply (by value and, where appropriate, volume) for the merger parties and each of their principal competitors for the Candidate Markets (see question 13).

Guidance Note to question 14

See sections 5.4 to 5.5 of *Merger Assessment Guidelines*

The notifying parties should provide the share of supply of the merger parties and their principal competitors (typically competitors with a share of supply of 5% or more) for the Narrowest Candidate Market(s).

The CMA will also typically request the notifying parties to provide an estimate of each of the merger parties' share of supply in any other Candidate Market(s) in which they have a significant combined share of supply (eg more than 25%).

If the Narrowest Candidate Market is broader than the UK, the notifying parties should provide data based on shares of supply within the UK.

For the purposes of calculating shares of supply, notifying parties should use the merger parties' internal data and refer to third party data sources where available. Notifying parties should use the most recent figures available and specify the period that they cover (in most cases, annual data for the most recent complete year should be provided).

The notifying parties should identify the sources for their estimates and explain the methodology used to calculate shares of supply (ie how these have been derived and any underlying assumptions). Notifying parties should also provide a copy of any underlying third party data used in its original format and any working files used to produce the market share calculations.

In most cases, a Satisfactory Notification will require annual data for the most recent complete year. Where shares of supply may vary significantly from year to year, it may be required to provide share data for several years (typically three to five years).

Depending on the nature of the sector in which the merger parties operate, it may be necessary to supply figures only by value (ie share of total value of sales in the Candidate Market(s)) or volume (ie share of total units sold in the Candidate Market(s)). Notifying parties are encouraged to discuss this with the CMA during pre-notification if they think only one or the other will provide meaningful figures in their sector.

Where notifying parties are unsure about the data that should be provided in response to this question, this should be discussed with the CMA.

HORIZONTAL EFFECTS

15. Provide a description of how competition works in each Candidate Market where the merger parties overlap. The description of such competitive dynamics in the Candidate Market should include (but not necessarily be limited to):

(a) information on the competitive constraint posed by each of the merger parties on each other and on the competitive constraint posed by the other principal suppliers in the Candidate Market(s);

(b) an explanation of what drives customer choice for the overlap product/services. Where relevant, the response should include the identification of separate customer groups, if any, and an explanation of how the competitive dynamics differ across these customer groups (see 5.2.28 to 5.2.31 of *Merger Assessment Guidelines*);

(c) a description of the parameters of competition (for example, price, quality, service, innovation) and their importance relative to one another;

(d) an explanation of the role and significance of product/service differentiation (including an

Part 3 CMA and other Guidelines

explanation of the extent to which the merger parties' products/services are differentiated);

(e) an explanation of how pricing is determined (for example, whether set by suppliers, negotiated between suppliers and customers, or the result of a bidding process organised by customers), including, in appropriate cases (as explained below), supporting documentation; and

(f) an explanation of the supply chain (including distribution channels) for the product(s)/services(s), and of any differences between separate geographic areas, where the merger parties overlap, in relation to the supply of the same products/services.

Guidance Note to question 15

See sections 5.4 to 5.5 of *Merger Assessment Guidelines*

The extent and detail of information that the merger parties need to provide in response to this section for Satisfactory Notification will depend on the complexity of the merger and on the potential competition concerns on which the CMA is likely to focus its investigation, which will typically differ between cases and sectors.

For an indication of what this might include, notifying parties are encouraged to refer to previous merger decisions published by the CMA and its predecessors, as well as the *Merger Assessment Guidelines*. If the notifying parties are unsure as to what information may be responsive to this question in their case, the CMA encourages notifying parties to contact the CMA to discuss this in pre-notification.

Where the merger parties' activities overlap within many local geographic areas and they propose to undertake filtering analysis to identify specific areas for which to provide detailed competitive assessment, merger parties are encouraged to engage with the CMA in relation to the approach to filtering before providing those individual assessments.

In most cases, the CMA's assessment is likely to focus on potential horizontal unilateral effects (ie the post-transaction ability of the merged entity to raise prices on its own without needing to coordinate with its rivals). If the CMA considers that the merger could give rise to coordinated effects, the notifying parties may be required to provide additional information in relation to that potential theory of harm.

Supporting documentation on determination of pricing

Where the merger parties' combined share of supply in a Candidate Market does not exceed 15%, notifying parties will not typically have to provide supporting documentation in relation to how pricing is determined in that Candidate Market in order for the CMA to be able to confirm that the notification is satisfactory.

Where the merger parties' combined share of supply in a Candidate Market exceeds 15%, notifying parties are encouraged to consider the specifics of their case and, if appropriate, discuss with the CMA in pre-notification the extent to which any such supporting documentation is necessary for a Satisfactory Notification.

In some limited cases, the CMA may – having regard to the specific circumstances of the case at hand – consider that certain supporting documentation in relation to a Candidate Market is required in response to this question before it can confirm that a notification is satisfactory, even where the merger parties' combined share in that Candidate Market does not exceed 15%.

Any supporting documentation provided should include, where relevant, documentation outlining the merger parties' price setting process and any analysis used to set prices.

Capacity, switching data and variable profit margins

Where the merger parties' combined share in a Candidate Market does not exceed 15%, notifying parties will not typically have to provide information on capacity, switching data and variable profit margins in relation to that Candidate Market in order for the CMA to be able to confirm that the notification is satisfactory.

Where the merger parties' combined share of supply in a Candidate Market exceeds 15%, notifying parties are encouraged to consider the specifics of their case and, if appropriate, discuss with the CMA in pre-notification the extent of any information on capacity, switching data and variable profit margins in relation to that Candidate Market necessary for a Satisfactory Notification.

In some limited cases, the CMA may – having regard to the specific circumstances of the case at hand[24] – consider that, in relation to a Candidate Market, certain further information on substitutability, such as information on capacity, switching data and/or profit margins, is required in response to this question before it can confirm that the notification is satisfactory, even where the merger parties' combined share in that Candidate Market does not exceed 15%.

Any information on capacity, switching data and/or profit margins provided should include:

(a) an estimate of total capacity in each Candidate Market, the proportion of total capacity accounted for by each of the merger parties (including a description of the location and capacity of the manufacturing facilities of each of the merger parties) and their principal competitors, the respective rates of capacity utilisation for each of the merger parties and their principal competitors;

(b) if available, any data of customers switching between suppliers in the past three to five years or, more generally, information that points to the degree of competitive interaction between suppliers,[25] and

(c) variable profit margins (sales revenue minus direct cost of sales) for each of the products/services where the merger parties overlap. Provide details about the income and all of the costs for each product/service and an explanation of whether such costs are fixed (and therefore excluded) or variable costs

16. For Candidate Markets characterised by bidding processes and/or where customers typically issue requests for quotations, provide bidding data setting out any bids made by each of the merger parties to win business in the overlapping markets.

Guidance Note to question 16

Bidding data

Bidding data need only be provided for Candidate Markets characterised by bidding processes and/or where customers typically issue requests for quotations. In such cases, provide details of any bids made by each of the merger parties in the last one to five years to win business in the overlapping markets, indicating for each bid (to the extent available):

(a) whether the bid was won or lost;

(b) if known, the reason why the bid was won or lost;

(c) the suppliers that participated in the bid;

(d) the winner and the ranking of the other bidders;

(e) the date of the bid;

(f) the value of the bid, and

(g) the date and duration of the final contract.

The period for which bidding data are likely to depend on the circumstances of the case (but is, in practice, likely to vary between one and five years). For example, for markets in which bids are submitted relatively infrequently, the period for which bidding information should be provided is likely to be longer in order to provide a sufficiently representative sample size. Notifying parties are encouraged to use pre-notification discussions with the CMA to discuss the appropriate scope of bidding information in their case.

INCREASE IN THE MERGER PARTIES' BUYER POWER

See section 5.4.19 to 5.4.21 of *Merger Assessment Guidelines*.

17. If applicable, for any product(s) (including raw materials) or service(s) which the merger parties both purchase, provide details of the merger parties' ability to obtain more favourable commercial conditions from suppliers as a result of this merger and the effects, if any, of such increased ability on competition at any levels of the supply chain.

Guidance Note to question 17

See section 5.4.19 to 5.4.21 of *Merger Assessment Guidelines*.

Where the merger parties' combined share of procurement of the products/services they both purchase on a Candidate Market does not exceed 25%, notifying parties will not typically have to provide any details, in relation to that Candidate Market, on the merger parties' ability to obtain more favourable commercial conditions from suppliers as a result of the merger in order for the CMA to be able to confirm that the notification is satisfactory. In such cases, notifying parties should indicate that the merger parties' combined share of procurement is less than 25%.

Where the merger parties' combined shares of procurement on a Candidate Market exceed 25%, notifying parties are encouraged to consider the specifics of their case and, if appropriate, discuss with the CMA in pre-notification the extent to which, in relation to that Candidate Market, any information on the merger parties' ability to obtain more favourable commercial conditions from suppliers as a result of the merger is necessary for a Satisfactory Notification.

In some limited cases, the CMA may – having regard to the specific circumstances of the case at hand – consider that, in relation to a Candidate Market, certain information relating to merger parties' buyer power is required in response to this question before it can confirm that the notification is satisfactory, even where the merger parties' combined share in that Candidate Market does not exceed 25%.

In relevant cases, responses should include (but not necessarily be limited to):

(a) the merger parties' combined share of procurement from the market upstream to the product(s) or service(s) that they supply (that is, the procurement of product(s) or service(s) which are used as input to a product or to provide a service, or that are sold on as bought)

(b) an explanation of whether, in notifying parties' view, any such ability could result in the suppliers being forced or induced to offer less favourable conditions to the merger parties' competitors. For example, where the supplier incurs fixed costs, it may recover such costs by charging a larger proportion of them to the merger parties' competitors than to the merger parties, as a result of the merger parties' increased buyer power (known as the 'waterbed effect'), and

(c) details of the merger parties' ability and incentive to reduce demand in order to reduce the purchase price (known as 'demand withholding'), as a result of the merger parties' increased buyer power.

LOSS OF POTENTIAL COMPETITION

18. Describe whether any merger party has plans or has attempted in the last three years to start supplying product(s)/service(s)/geographic area(s) which it does not currently supply but which the other merger party is already supplying (or expected to supply). If so:

(a) Provide any internal documents setting out plans of any merger party to expand in the overlapping product(s), service(s) and/or geographic area(s) or to enter a market where another merger party is operating.

(b) Explain what barriers to entry or expansion exist for each merger party to start supplying product(s)/service(s)/geographic area(s) which it does not currently supply but which the

other merger party is already supplying (or expected to supply).

VERTICAL EFFECTS

See section 5.6 of *Merger Assessment Guidelines*.

19. If the merger parties operate at different levels of the supply chain (that is, a merger party is engaged in activities upstream or downstream of the activities in which the other merger party is engaged), describe the impact of the merger on the ability and incentive of the merged entity to foreclose rivals (including partial and/or full foreclosure) post-transaction, either by limiting the supply of key inputs or access to customers.

Guidance Note to question 19

Where the merger parties' individual and (where relevant) combined shares of supply do not exceed 30% in either of a pair of upstream and downstream Candidate Markets where they have a vertical relationship, responses to this question can typically be limited to:

(a) a description of the vertical supply chain (including each of the merger parties' and their key competitors' roles at each stage and the extent of pre and post-merger vertical integration); and

(b) for input foreclosure, a description of the general importance of relevant inputs to the downstream product or service; and/or

(c) for customer foreclosure, a description of the importance of the merged entity as a customer for the upstream product or service.

Where the merger parties' individual or combined shares of supply exceed 30% on either (or both) of a pair of upstream and downstream Candidate Markets where they have a vertical relationship, a more comprehensive response to this question is likely to be required.

In this case, notifying parties are encouraged to consider the specifics of their case and, if appropriate, discuss with the CMA in pre-notification the extent to which, in relation to that pair of Candidate Markets, any of the information indicated below or any other information may also be necessary for a Satisfactory Notification:

(a) a description of the pricing mechanism at any stage of the vertical supply chain where any of the merger parties operates (as well as in each other relevant stage);

(b) variable profit margins (sales revenue minus direct cost of sales) for each of the products/services supplied by each party in the vertical supply chain. Provide details about the income and all of the costs for each product/service and an explanation of whether such costs are fixed (and therefore excluded from the calculation of variable profit margin) or variable costs

(c) the ratio between average upstream and average downstream price for each of the products/services supplied by each merger party in each level of the vertical chain

(d) the degree of economies of scale or scope in the input product or service in vertical supply arrangements, if any, and the extent to which demand is characterised by network effects (that is, when the value of a product increases when the number of customers using the product increases)

(e) if available, an estimate of cost-pass through

(f) a list of exclusivity agreements (to which one or other of the merger parties is a party) relating to the upstream or downstream product(s) or service(s) in the vertical supply chain and internal documents discussing plans to put in place an exclusivity agreement regarding the same in the future, and

(g) supporting documents (as described in question 10) in relation to the products/services where the merger parties have a vertical relationship.[26]

CONGLOMERATE EFFECTS

See section 5.6 of *Merger Assessment Guidelines*.

20. If the merger parties are active in "related" markets (eg products that are complementary or that belong to a range of products generally purchased by the same set of customers) and their individual share in any such related Candidate Market exceeds 30%, describe the impact of the merger on the ability and incentive of the merged entity to foreclose rivals (including partial and/or full foreclosure) post-transaction, either by limiting the supply of inputs or access to customers.

Guidance Note to question 20

Where the merger parties have common customers in related Candidate Markets and their individual share in any such related Candidate Market exceeds 30%, notifying parties are encouraged to consider the specifics of their case and, if appropriate, discuss with the CMA in pre-notification the extent to which information on potential conglomerate effects is necessary for a Satisfactory Notification.

Where information on conglomerate effects is required, this is likely to include:

(a) each of the merger parties' share of supply in each of the related product(s) or service(s) and geographic area (to the extent not already provided in response to Question 14);

(b) the merger parties' variable profit margins (sales revenue minus direct cost of sales) for each of the products/services supplied by each merger party in each of the related product categories. Provide details about the income and all of the costs for each product/service and an explanation of whether such costs are fixed (and therefore excluded) or variable;

Guidance Note to question 20

(c) the extent to which customers purchase the products/services together as a bundle or from the same supplier;

(d) customer preferences for variety/range and one-stop shopping, and

(e) the costs to rivals of providing variety/range and one-stop shopping at a scale to enable them to compete effectively with the merged firm.

ENTRY OR EXPANSION

See section 5.8 of *Merger Assessment Guidelines*.

21. Where notifying parties would like the CMA to consider whether or not the merged entity will be subject to constraints from potential entry or expansion, provide a description of the barriers to entry and expansion with respect to the Candidate Market(s).

Guidance Note to question 21

See section 5.8 of *Merger Assessment Guidelines*.

Where notifying parties may wish the CMA to consider potential entry or expansion, notifying parties should provide the following information for the purposes of a Satisfactory Notification:

(a) how easy it is to start supplying the products/services in the appropriate geographical areas

(b) how easy it is for customers to switch between competitors' products or services, with an estimate of any switching costs

(c) an estimate of the capital expenditure and time required to enter the market on a scale necessary to gain a 5% share of supply, both as a new entrant and as a company which already has the necessary technology and expertise (for example, a company located overseas)

(d) an estimate of the scale of annual expenditure on advertising/promotion required to achieve a 5% share of supply

(e) details of any other factors affecting entry, for example, planning restraints, technology or research and development requirements, availability of raw materials, length of contracts including, where possible, actual or estimated time and cost necessary to overcome these factors

(f) an assessment of the ease of exit from the market (including an estimate of to what extent costs are recoverable), and

(g) an explanation as to whether entry would be timely, likely and sufficient.

22. If the notifying parties wish the CMA to consider potential entry or expansion in its competitive assessment, notifying parties should provide:

(a) details of any expansion, entry or exit in any of the Candidate Markets over the past five years, and

(b) details of any companies that the notifying parties believe are likely, post-merger, to enter or expand into any of the Candidate Markets in a sufficiently timely manner so as to adequately constrain the merged entity,

including, in either case, any available evidence for that submission and contact details for any companies named.

Guidance Note to question 22

Merger parties may wish to submit that one or more third parties, in particular, are likely to start supplying or expand their supply of products or services in competition with the merger parties in the near future to such an extent that any competition concern regarding the merger is mitigated or neutralised.

Where notifying parties wish the CMA to consider such potential entry or expansion, notifying parties should, for the purposes of a Satisfactory Notification:

(a) identify such entrant(s);

(b) explain whether such entrant(s) would have started supplying the products/services in the absence of the merger and the extent to which such entry would lead to greater competition

(c) provide evidence of any firms which do not currently supply the product(s) or service(s) but which, nevertheless, could readily enter

(d) provide evidence of any existing smaller suppliers that could readily expand, and

(e) explain whether any such entry would be timely, likely and sufficient.

COUNTERVAILING BUYER POWER

23. Where notifying parties would like the CMA to consider whether or not the merged entity will be subject to countervailing buyer power, explain, with evidence where available, how the merged entity will be subject to this constraint.

Guidance Note to question 23

See section 5.9 of *Merger Assessment Guidelines.*

The type of information that the notifying parties should provide if they would like the CMA to consider whether or not the merged entity will be subject to countervailing buyer power, they should, for the purposes of a Satisfactory Notification, include (but not necessarily be limited to) the following:

(a) whether there are single customers or groups of customers holding particular negotiating strength with the merger parties in any of the Candidate Markets (for example, where the customer(s) can easily switch its/their demand away from the supplier, can sponsor entry or supply the product(s) itself/themselves)

(b) whether and, if so, how customers outside such groups would be able to benefit from the negotiating strength of the customers within the group. For example, explain whether contracts are negotiated individually with single customers and the extent to which it is possible for the supplier to price discriminate across customers of varying negotiating strength, and

(c) how (and the extent to which) the merger will affect customers' negotiating strength.

EFFICIENCIES AND CUSTOMER BENEFITS

24. Where notifying parties would like the CMA specifically to consider at phase 1 any efficiencies or relevant customer benefits that the notifying parties believe will arise from the merger, describe such efficiencies and provide any documents prepared internally or by external consultants that discuss such expected efficiencies or relevant customer benefits.

Guidance Note to question 24

See section 5.7 of *Merger Assessment Guidelines* and paragraphs 4.1 to 4.13 of *Mergers: Exceptions to the duty to refer and undertakings in lieu of reference guidance.*

Where notifying parties would like the CMA to consider whether or not the merger gives rise to efficiencies, any description should include (but not necessarily be limited to) the following:

(a) a detailed explanation of how the merger would generate such efficiencies

(b) if reasonably practicable, a quantification of any such efficiencies, specifying the timeframe required to achieve them

(c) an explanation of the extent to which the efficiencies would be sufficient to prevent a substantial lessening of competition

(d) an explanation of the reasons why such efficiencies could not be achieved in the absence of this merger, and

(e) any documents prepared internally or by external consultants discussing the expected efficiencies.

Where notifying parties wish to submit that the merger gives rise to relevant customer benefits, any description should include (but not necessarily be limited to) the following:[27]

(a) a detailed explanation of how the merger would generate such relevant customer benefits

(b) if reasonably practicable, a quantification of any relevant customer benefits, specifying the timeframe required to achieve them

(c) an explanation of the extent to which the benefits generated by the merger are likely to be passed on to UK customers and UK final consumers

(d) an explanation of the reasons why such relevant customer benefits could not be achieved in the absence of this merger or a similar lessening of competition, and

(e) any documents prepared internally or by external consultants discussing the expected relevant customer benefits.

Guidance Note to questions 21 to 24

Notifying parties who intend to submit information responsive to questions 21 to 24are advised to do so during pre-notification in order to ensure that the CMA is able to fully verify the submissions made by the notifying parties within the 40 working-day statutory timeframe. Where the notifying parties submit information after the CMA has given notice of a Satisfactory Notification, the CMA may not be able to fully verify these claims during its Phase 1 investigation (and therefore may only be able to place limited weight on these submissions) For the avoidance of doubt, in the event notifying parties do not put forward such arguments for the purposes of the CMA's Phase 1 investigation, they will not be prevented from doing so in the event of a reference for a Phase 2 investigation.

OTHER INFORMATION

25. Provide any other information that the notifying parties consider may be relevant to the CMA's Phase 1 investigation.

Guidance Note to question 25

Notifying parties may, of course, provide any other information they consider relevant. For example, references to earlier decisional practice within the same markets, contacts with other government departments or regulators about the merger, either because they have responsibilities in the relevant areas or because they are customers, and any contacts with overseas competition authorities. This could also include, for example, submissions on the relevance of the 'de minimis' exception (see *Mergers: Exceptions to the duty to refer and undertakings in lieu of reference guidance* (OFT1122)).

Notifying parties are also welcome to give their own views on the competition implications or any other effects of the merger.

NOTES

21 These are products or services which do not lie within the same market, but which are nevertheless related in some way; for example, because they are complements (so that a fall in the price of one product/service increases the customer's demand for another), or because there are economies of scale in purchasing them (so that customers buy them together). See guidance note to Question 12.

22 This may include, for example, the products/services and geographic area(s) in the Narrowest Candidate Market(s) together with other products/services and geographic areas that might be considered substitutes with such products/services and geographic area(s).

23 Where local markets exist, the CMA strongly encourages notifying parties to discuss in pre-notification the method for identifying geographic area(s) of overlap and the data they use for the same.

24 For example, whether the parties' products are differentiated, whether the transaction would affect different customers in different ways, whether shares could have been calculated on a narrower basis, whether the merger involves a business with a promising pipeline product or whether shares are not an accurate reflection of market presence or power.

25 This information can take various different forms and may involve pricing and volume information over time and/or in different geographic areas or competitive contexts. Notifying parties may also be required to identify any relevant events (such as significant price changes) that can be illustrative, through the analysis of customers' behaviours in response to them, of customers' preferences for different suppliers. The CMA encourages notifying parties to engage with the case team in pre-notification to establish the information available that may allow for an assessment of the closeness of substitution between products/services.

26 If notifying parties are unsure what may be responsive, or if, in their case, the question results in a large number of responsive documents, the CMA recommends that notifying parties discuss the process for gathering these documents with the CMA in pre-notification. Where notifying parties provide no or limited documents (or if the documents provided contain limited information of substance), the CMA may request other documents that may contain the information it would expect to appear in the supporting documents described in question 10, for example, substantive emails to or from certain key individuals.

27 For example, in mergers involving NHS Foundation Trusts the CMA will liaise closely with Monitor as to whether the information received with respect to relevant customer benefits will allow Monitor to start its assessment of the same (see paragraph 6.43 of the Guidance). The CMA reserves the right to consider the Notice incomplete if this is not the case. See *CMA Guidance on the Review of NHS Mergers* (CMA29) for more information.

PART V: THIRD PARTY CONTACT DETAILS

[3.425]

26. Provide contact details for the relevant competitors and customers of the merger parties for (where applicable):

(*a*) each of the Candidate Markets in which they overlap;

(*b*) each of the Candidate Markets in which the merger parties have a vertical relationship (providing contact details for the relevant competitors and customers of the merger parties on the upstream and downstream markets on which each merger party is active); and

(*c*) each of the Candidate Markets in which each of the merger parties provides related products/services.

27. To the extent applicable, provide contact details for relevant suppliers providing an estimate of the annual value and/or volume of purchases.

28. To the extent applicable, provide contact details for each of the companies that the notifying parties consider are likely to enter and expand into any of the Candidates Markets.

29. Provide the name and contact details, including address, and email address and telephone number, of:

(*a*) any relevant regulatory authorities covering the industry in which the merger parties overlap, have a vertical relationship, or supply related product(s)/service(s).

(*b*) any trade associations which cover the industry in which the merger parties overlap, have a vertical relationship, or supply related product(s)/service(s).

Guidance Note to questions 26 and 29

Third party contact details to be provided

Contact details are used by the CMA principally for the purposes of, early in its investigation, testing the competitive effects of the merger with third parties in the sector.

Notifying parties are required to make their best efforts to provide those contacts and should be aware that providing incomplete or erroneous contact details may delay the CMA's investigation of the merger. In all cases:

Guidance Note to questions 26 and 29

(a) A specific contact person for each third party contact should be provided, along with the full contact details for that person;

(b) Such contact details must, in particular, include a specific and direct email address and telephone number for the named contact identified (eg john.smith@xyz.com and not info@xyz.com); and

(c) All contact details must be provided using the Excel template provided in Annex 1 to this Notice.

Notifying parties are encouraged to discuss with the CMA in pre-notification the number of contact details required for each category in their case for a Satisfactory Notification. The guidance provided below sets out the information that is likely to be required by the CMA in the majority of cases.

Customer and competitor contact details

Candidate Markets in which there is horizontal overlap between the merging parties' activities

The notifying parties are requested to provide named contact details for customers and competitors of each merger party in each Candidate Market where the merger parties overlap.

By way of guidance, in the majority of cases, this should include, for each party:[28]

(a) contact details for at least the top five competitors (by volume or value) (including overseas companies/importers) for each Candidate Market;

(b) contact details and estimated share of the merger party's business of at least the top ten customers (by volume or value) of each of the merger parties for each Candidate Market (including overseas customers if appropriate);

(c) to the extent that a Candidate Market is characterised by bidding processes (see question 16), the contact details for the entity or entities running each bidding process in which either of the merger parties have participated, or of which notifying parties are aware, in relation to that Candidate Market. If this means a larger number of responsive contact details (that is, more than ten such entities for each Candidate Market), notifying parties are encouraged to contact the CMA to discuss in pre-notification.

Where there are marked differences in the size or other features of the merger parties' customers, such that some customers may purchase goods or services by different means or in significantly different quantities, provide these same details for at least five representative customers (by value or volume) for each group of customers identified (for example, five large, five medium and five small customers). Where this may be relevant, notifying parties are encouraged to contact the CMA to discuss in pre-notification how to delineate each customer group.

The CMA may – having regard to the specific circumstances of the case at hand (in particular, the extent to which contacts for five competitors and/or ten customers would allow for adequate market testing) – consider that full contact details for further competitors or customers are required in response to this question before it can give notice that it has a Satisfactory Notification. The number of customers and competitors whose contact details are required will vary from case to case, depending on the total number of customers/competitors the merger parties have, how representative of the parties' overall customer/competitor set a given sample of such customer/competitors would be, and the extent to which the contact details would permit the CMA to carry out an adequate market test having regard to the specific circumstances in the case at hand.

Candidate Markets in which there is vertical relationship between the merging parties' activities

Where the merger parties do not have common customers in related Candidate Markets or where their individual shares of supply do not exceed 30% in any of the related Candidate Markets, notifying parties will not typically have to provide contact details of their customers and competitors in each upstream or downstream Candidate Market where they have a vertical relationship.

In some limited cases, the CMA may – having regard to the specific circumstances of the case at hand – consider that contact details are required in response to this question before it can confirm that the notification is satisfactory, even where the merger parties do not have common customers in related Candidate Markets or where their individual shares of supply do not exceed 30% in any of the related Candidate Markets.

Where the merger parties have common customers in related Candidate Markets and their individual share in any such related Candidate Market exceeds 30%, the notifying parties need to provide contact details of their customers and competitors in each upstream or downstream Candidate Market where they have a vertical relationship for a Satisfactory Notification.

By way of guidance, in the majority of cases, notifying parties should provide:[29]

(a) at least the top five competitors (by value or volume) of the merger parties in each upstream and downstream Candidate Market (to the extent they have not been provided as competitor operating in the same Candidate Market of the merger parties), and

(b) at least the top five customers (by value or volume) of the merger parties in each upstream and downstream Candidate Market. Where there are marked differences in the size or other features of the customers, such that some customers may purchase goods or services by different means or in significantly different quantities, provide these same details for five representative customers for each customer group identified (to the extent they have not been provided as competitor operating in the same Candidate Market of the merger parties). Where this may be relevant, notifying parties are encouraged to contact the CMA to discuss in pre-notification how to delineate each customer group.

Guidance Note to questions 26 and 29

In some limited cases, the CMA may – having regard to the specific circumstances of the case at hand[30] – consider that, in relation to an upstream or downstream Candidate Market, full contact details for more than five competitors or customers are required in response to this question before it can give notice that it has a Satisfactory Notification.

Candidate Markets in which conglomerate effects could arise

Where the merger parties do not have common customers in related Candidate Markets or where their individual shares of supply do not exceed 30% in any of the related Candidate Markets, notifying parties will not typically have to provide contact details in response to this question in order for the CMA to be able to confirm that the notification is satisfactory.

Where the merger parties have common customers in related Candidate Markets and their individual share in any such related Candidate Market exceeds 30%, notifying parties are encouraged to consider the specifics of their case and, if appropriate, discuss with the CMA in pre-notification the extent to which these contact details are necessary for a Satisfactory Notification.

In some limited cases, the CMA may – having regard to the specific circumstances of the case at hand – consider that contact details are required in response to this question before it can confirm that the notification is satisfactory, even where the merger parties do not have common customers in related Candidate Markets or where their individual shares of supply do not exceed 30% in any of the related Candidate Markets.

By way of guidance, in the majority of cases, merger parties should provide:[31]

(a) at least the top five competitors (by volume or value) of the merger parties in each related Candidate Market (to the extent they have not been provided as competitor operating in the same Candidate Market of the merger parties), and

(b) at least the top five customers (by value or volume) of the merger parties in each related Candidate Market (to the extent they have not been provided as competitor operating in the same Candidate Market of the merger parties). Where there are marked differences in the size or other features of the customers, such that some customers may purchase goods or services by different means or in significantly different quantities, provide these same details for five customers for each group of customers identified (to the extent not already provided in response to question 16). Where this may be relevant, notifying parties are encouraged to contact the CMA to discuss in pre-notification how to delineate each customer group.

In some limited cases, the CMA may – having regard to the specific circumstances of the case at hand[32] – consider that full contact details for further customers or competitors are required in response to this question before it can provide confirmation that it has a Satisfactory Notification

Supplier contact details

Circumstances in which supplier contact details may not be required

Where the merger parties' combined share of procurement of the products/services they both purchase on a Candidate Market does not exceed 25%, notifying parties will not typically have to provide, in relation to that Candidate Market, contact details of relevant suppliers in response to question 18 in order for the CMA to be able to confirm that the notification is satisfactory.

Where the merger parties' combined share of procurement on a Candidate Market exceeds 25%, notifying parties are encouraged to consider the specifics of their case and, if appropriate, discuss with the CMA in pre-notification the extent to which, in relation to that Candidate Market, contact details of relevant suppliers are necessary for a Satisfactory Notification.

In some limited cases, the CMA may – having regard to the specific circumstances of the case at hand – consider that certain contact details in relation to a Candidate Market are required in response to this question before it can confirm that the notification is satisfactory, even where the merger parties' combined share of procurement in relation to that Candidate Market does not exceed 25%.

Relevant suppliers

Relevant suppliers are generally those that supply the input for the overlap product or service (or of a product bought if sold on in the same state). However, they may include contact details for upstream suppliers other than the merger parties' suppliers (where this would be necessary in order for the CMA to carry out an adequate market test).

Number of supplier's contact details

Notifying parties are encouraged to contact the CMA to discuss in pre-notification what number of supplier contact details is appropriate in their case. However, by way of guidance, in the majority of cases, the response should include contact details for at least the top five (by value or volume) of each of the merger parties' suppliers.

However in some limited cases, the CMA may – having regard to the specific circumstances of the case at hand[33] – consider that full contact details for more than five suppliers are required in response to this question before it can provide confirmation that it has received a Satisfactory Notification.

New entrants

The merger parties should provide contact details for each company identified in response to question 22.

NOTES

[28] For the avoidance of doubt, where one or both of the merger parties have less than the 10 competitors or customers, the CMA will only require contact details for the amount of competitors and customers that they actually have.

[29] For the avoidance of doubt, where one or both of the merger parties have less than the five competitors or customers, the CMA will only require contact details for the amount of competitors and customers they actually have.

[30] Including, for example, if five competitor or customer contact details would not allow for an adequate market test.

[31] For the avoidance of doubt, where one or both of the merger parties have less than the five competitors or customers, the CMA will only require contact details for the amount of competitors and customers they actually have.

[32] Including, for example, if five competitor or customer contact details would not allow for an adequate market test.

[33] For example, if the contact details of five supplier would not allow for an adequate market test. This could be the case where the top five suppliers account for a very small proportion of suppliers.

PART VI: DECLARATION

DECLARATION

[3.426]

This Declaration must be signed by a duly authorised person or on behalf of each of the notifying parties:

I declare that, to the best of my knowledge and belief, the information given in response to the questions in this Notice is true, correct, and complete in all material respects.

I understand that:

It is a criminal offence under section 117 of the Enterprise Act 2002 for a person recklessly or knowingly to supply to the CMA information which is false or misleading in any material respect. This includes supplying such information to another person knowing that the information is to be used for the purpose of supplying information to the CMA;

The CMA may reject any Notice if it is suspected that it contains information which is false or misleading in any material respect;

The CMA conducts both Phase 1 and Phase 2 investigations. In the event that the merger is referred for a Phase 2 investigation, information provided to the CMA during the course of the Phase 1 investigation will also be used for the Phase 2 investigation; and

The CMA will bring the merger described in this Notice, and the fact that the Notice has been given, to the attention of interested parties.

Signed:

Name: (block letters)

Position: (block letters)

Date:

In addition to the above Declaration, the Declaration below should also be signed by a duly authorised person or on behalf of each of the notifying parties if the merger parties are appointing legal representatives:

I confirm that the representative(s) (if any) named in reply to question 1(b) is/are authorised for the purposes of proceedings related to the arrangements described under question 2 to act on behalf of the merger parties respectively specified in response to question 1(b) of this Notice. I hereby specify the address of the representatives named in reply to question 1(b) as an address at which [name of notifying party] will accept service or take receipt of documents in accordance with section 126(4) of the Enterprise Act 2002.

Signed:

Name: (block letters)

Position: (block letters)

Date:

Guidance Note to Part VI

As noted above, see the CMA's webpages for information on how to submit a Notice. The information required in this Notice must be complete and correct, to the best of the merger parties knowledge and belief, as confirmed in the declaration to be signed by the notifying parties at the end of the Notice.

The CMA will not accept a Notice unless the section 117 Declaration has been signed by a duly authorised person, by the notifying party or by each of the notifying parties in anticipated mergers. The authorised person is defined as any person carrying on an enterprise to which the notified arrangements relate. The Declaration must be signed by a person or persons with authority to bind each notifying party. An authorised person may use an electronic signature to sign the Declaration. Where a Notice is submitted jointly, each notifying party must sign the Declaration that the notice is true, correct and complete in all material respects.

The authorised persons may, appoint representatives (such as a firm of solicitors) to complete the Merger Notice on their behalf and to act for them in further correspondence with the CMA. If they wish to appoint such a representative, the authorised persons should also sign the confirmation of authorisation, ensuring that they comply with the requirements of section 126 of the Act when doing so. For the avoidance of doubt, where a notice is submitted jointly (anticipated merger) each notifying party may wish to sign the confirmation appointing a representative for the purpose of receiving service.

Guidance Note to Part VI

The Declaration draws notifying parties' attention to two important provisions of the Act.

- The first relates to the provision of false or misleading information. Under section 117 of the Act, it is an offence:
  - knowingly or recklessly to give to the CMA information that is false or misleading in a material respect, either in the Notice, or in reply to any additional questions raised by the CMA during the consideration period, or
  - knowingly or recklessly to supply information to a third party that is false or misleading in a material respect, for example an authorised representative or legal adviser, in the knowledge that they will then supply it to the CMA.

  The penalties for breach of this provision may include an unlimited fine or a maximum of two years' imprisonment, or both.

  The CMA also has powers to reject the Notice, at any time before the period for consideration expires, where it suspects that any information given in the Notice, or in response to further enquiries, is false or misleading.[34] The effect of rejection is that the proposal which is notified will remain liable for reference for a period of four months after the date of its completion (subject to any extension in some circumstances).[35]
- Secondly, the Declaration reminds notifying parties that the CMA will publicise the existence of the merger as notified in both completed and anticipated cases. The CMA will also draw the merger to the attention of third parties in order to seek their views. The CMA will have regard to the provisions of Part 9 of the Act in relation to disclosure of information in determining how much information should be disclosed. Its aim in publicising the merger is solely to ensure that those with an interest in the merger are given an opportunity to comment. The CMA is very aware of the need to protect commercially sensitive information it receives from parties. Whenever the CMA considers whether or not to disclose specified information it must have regard, amongst other considerations, to (a) the need to exclude from disclosure (so far as practicable) commercial information whose disclosure the CMA thinks might significantly harm the legitimate business interests of the to which it relates and (b) the extent to which the disclosure of the information is necessary for the purpose for which the CMA is permitted to make disclosure. The CMA's published reports commonly excise commercially sensitive information. Further information about the CMA's procedures and powers to disclose information is contained in the Chairman's Guidance on Disclosure of Information (CC7 Revised) and Transparency and disclosure: Statement of the CMA's policy and approach (CMA6).

The Declaration also confirms the authorisation of any representative named in the Notice to act on behalf of a notifying party and accept service in accordance with section 126 of the Act.

NOTES

34 Section 99(5)(a) of the Act.

35 Section 100 of the Act.

ANNEX 1 TO MERGER NOTICE TEMPLATE: THIRD PARTY CONTACT DETAILS

[3.427]

NOTES

September 2017.

Note: the original document is an Excel spreadsheet, and consists of four separate tabs. It has been reproduced here as four tables. The original document is available at: www.gov.uk/government/publications/mergers-forms-and-fee-information.

Customers

Organisation	Contact person	Position of contact person	Postal address	Postcode	Telephone number (of the contact person)	Email address (of the contact person)	Candidate market(s)

Competitors

Organisation	Contact person	Position of contact person	Postal address	Postcode	Telephone number (of the contact person)	Email address (of the contact person)	Candidate market(s)

Suppliers						
Organisation	Contact person	Position of contact person	Postal address	Postcode	Telephone number (of the contact person)	Email address (of the contact person)

Reg. Aut. and Trade Associations						
Organisation	Contact person	Position of contact person	Postal address	Postcode	Telephone number (of the contact person)	Email address (of the contact person)

ANNEX 2 TO MERGER NOTICE TEMPLATE: INDEX OF ANNEXES AND ATTACHMENTS TO THE MERGER NOTICE FORM IN [CASE NAME]

[3.428]

NOTES

November 2017.

Note: the original document is an Excel spreadsheet and is available at: www.gov.uk/government/publications/mergers-forms-and-fee-information. It has been reproduced here as a table.

Document / annex number	File name	Responsive to question	Document title	Purpose of document*	Date produced	Produced by (if applicable)	Produced for (if applicable)
Documents should be named and formatted in accordance with the guidance note "Providing documents to the CMA", available on the CMA website.							
* e.g. Presentation to board; board minutes; briefing paper to sales director to inform price negotiations with customer X; etc.							

GOOD PRACTICE IN THE DESIGN AND PRESENTATION OF CUSTOMER SURVEY EVIDENCE IN MERGER CASES REVISED (CMA78, MAY 2018)

[3.429]

NOTES

Note that all references to issues of jurisdiction or procedure in mergers cases must be read in the light of Mergers: Guidance on the CMA's jurisdiction and procedure (CMA2); in the case of conflict, CMA2 prevails.

1. INTRODUCTION

STATUS OF THIS DOCUMENT

[3.430]

1.1 During our merger casework, the Competition and Markets Authority (CMA) sometimes receives submissions of evidence derived from surveys of customers that have been commissioned by the merging organisations ('Parties') or their external advisors for the specific purpose of helping to understand aspects of a merger. We believe that the use of statistically robust customer survey research can be very important in reaching informed decisions, and we very much welcome this type of evidence.

1.2 This document sets out our general views on good practice in the design, conduct and reporting of such surveys. While the Parties and their advisors are the primary intended audiences for this document, it may also be of interest to market research agencies involved in designing and conducting surveys for merger cases.

1.3 Where appropriate, the CMA may commission its own survey research and, if so, the survey design, analysis and interpretation of results are informed by in-house statisticians who work closely with inquiry teams and the market research agencies commissioned to conduct the research on our behalf. The principles described in this document apply equally to these surveys.

1.4 This document focuses on surveys for merger cases, but many of the principles are applicable to other types of case which the CMA conducts, such as market studies and market investigations, Competition Act enforcement cases, super complaints or consumer protection enforcement cases. However, the uses of survey evidence and the nature of cases themselves can vary and assessments of fitness for purpose need to take this into account.

1.5 Generally speaking, the aim of a statistical sample survey is to interview a small proportion of people from a large population of interest (eg a few hundred customers from the many thousands who use a cinema chain) in such a way that robust inferences can be made from their responses about the population as a whole. Research to inform our investigations may be, alternatively or in addition, 'qualitative' in nature, for example, in the form of focus groups or in-depth interviews. Good practice for qualitative research methods is outside the scope of this guidance.

1.6 For brevity, this document 'Good practice in the design and presentation of customer survey evidence in merger cases' is referred to as 'this document'. It replaces the document published in 2011 by the then Office of Fair Trading (OFT) and Competition Commission (CC)[1]. It should be noted for the avoidance of any doubt that this document does not constitute guidance under section 106(1) of the Enterprise Act 2002.

1.7 This document is about customer survey research for merger cases. We use the term 'customer' here in a loose and non-technical sense. Usually the CMA will be interested in surveying the person (or an entity, such as a business) who buys a product or service directly from (one of) the merging Parties. However, this is not always the case. For example, sometimes the CMA is interested in surveying the end-customers of products or services even if they do not purchase the product or service directly from the Parties.

1.8 This document provides principles and examples for illustration, not hard and fast rules or bright-line tests. We recognise that circumstances vary and that knowledge of the relevant scenario, along with judgment and reason, will be required in applying customer survey research methods to a particular case. Where time and/or resource constraints mean that the research possible under particular circumstances cannot comply fully with all of the principles set out here, we will still consider its use to the case.

1.9 Submissions that follow the principles set out in this document are more likely to be given evidential weight in the CMA's merger investigations.

1.10 Customer survey research conducted by Parties in the normal course of their business, eg to inform strategy prior to a merger being considered, may also have evidential value for the purpose of a merger inquiry. The interpretation and use of such evidence, and weight to be given to it, will depend on the nature and purpose of the survey and the way in which it relates to the merger case. For example, there are some circumstances in which the CMA would take more account of a survey if it was clear the Party has acted on the results.

1.11 This document offers illustrations and examples drawn from recent experience in merger cases that are intended to assist in the design of good customer research. These illustrations are included by way of example and are not exhaustive, nor will they be applicable in all cases.

1.12 We would encourage Parties and their external advisors to use what they consider to be the most appropriate research techniques to generate robust evidence. The omission of a particular research technique from this document does not imply that it is invalid, or that the results would not be given evidential weight in appropriate circumstances.

1.13 This document is a technical resource to assist Parties in submitting customer survey research evidence that may be given weight in an inquiry. It is without prejudice to the provisions of the Enterprise Act 2002, as amended, and without prejudice to the advice and information in the Quick guide to UK merger assessment[2] and the Merger Assessment Guidelines originally published jointly by the OFT/CC[3].

USES OF SURVEYS IN MERGER CASES AND PROCEDURAL ISSUES

1.14 Survey evidence has been submitted to the OFT/CC/CMA in numerous merger cases, by the Parties themselves and by third parties. Most surveys conducted primarily for the merger case itself have been submitted by the Parties as part of phase 1 of a merger case. However, a small number of such surveys have been conducted at phase 2.

1.15 In contrast, all the surveys *commissioned* by the CMA have been run as part of phase 2 merger cases. A small number of surveys have been run by the CMA itself during phase 1 of a merger case, all of which (to date) have been online using customer lists with email addresses supplied by Parties.

1.16 The CMA considers a large number of factors when making a decision about whether to conduct a survey in a merger case. For any individual case these will include: the theories of harm to be tested, the range of evidence available (or planned) and anticipated evidential gaps, the nature and number of customers in the market, the practical options for contacting and surveying a sample of these customers, and the feasibility of obtaining survey results of sufficient quality to be fit for purpose within the time available. The CMA also has to be mindful of the cost of the research, to assess whether it would be a good use of public money.

1.17 The CMA is obliged, under the Merger Guidelines, to give Parties 24 hours to comment on a draft questionnaire for any survey that it intends to commission as part of a phase 2 merger inquiry. In practice, we always try to allow longer and also provide a description of the overall survey methodology (sample design, mode of interview, etc). We endeavour to provide Parties with a similar opportunity to comment if we conduct survey research as part of a phase 1 investigation.

1.18 When designing a survey, it is important to start with a clear view of the objectives of the research. From the Parties' point of view, it is desirable to give the CMA as much time as possible to consider details of the research planned in order to address any concerns the CMA has about it. However, discussions about the survey should not be seen as the CMA giving its approval for the survey.

1.19 Looking at merger cases over time, there are some commonly occurring ways in which survey evidence has been relevant to the inquiry and has had an impact on decision-making. These translate into the following topic areas for merger survey questionnaires:

(a) Demography – to understand the demographic characteristics (eg age, sex, education) of customers in the market. In some cases this can be useful in assessing the extent to which the Parties' customers are differentiated, for example, whether there is evidence that their products or services appeal to different types of people. Note that responses to demographic questions can also be used to evaluate whether the survey respondents are representative of the population of interest (particularly when benchmark population distributions are available to compare them against), and for weighting purposes.

(b) Choice attributes – to understand how customers make choices in the market of interest, including the relative importance of such factors as price, quality, range, service, location and brand. Other aspects of the purchase decision that may be of interest include the extent to which it was planned or made on impulse, search activity, brand awareness and level of knowledge about the market and competitor options.

(c) Geography – to understand the geographical aspects of the merger, eg how far customers travel (measured in distance and/or time) to obtain the product or service and the location of firms (particularly in cases with local area theories of harm). This is often done by asking customers how they have travelled to the Parties' premises, which mode(s) of transport they have used, how long it has taken, and where they have travelled from (including whether this is from, for example, home or work).

(d) Cross-channel substitution – to understand the extent to which customers switch between or make use of different purchase channels (usually in-store and online). This can be particularly important in cases where, for example, a bricks-and-mortar retail merger is the subject of the inquiry but it is important to assess the nature and strength of potential or actual online constraints on the bricks-and-mortar outlets[4].

(e) Closeness of competition – to estimate the closeness of competition between the Parties themselves, and between the Parties and competitor third parties. This is often the most influential part of the survey[5], using hypothetical diversion questions to elicit 'next best' options (alternatives/substitutes) from respondents[6].

1.20 The above does not provide an exhaustive list; there are many other potential topic areas that might be relevant to particular markets and, accordingly, form part of the questionnaire for a particular case.

1.21 Timing should be a key consideration for Parties and their external advisors when considering whether to conduct a survey. Survey evidence that is submitted too late or is of insufficient quality to be taken into consideration is a waste of time and resources. The general principle on timing is that the earlier the CMA receives survey evidence, the more time we will have to consider it and provide our assessment of the survey's quality and relevance to the case, along with our analysis and interpretation of results, to the Parties for comment.

1.22 For phase 1 mergers, the CMA ideally should receive survey evidence before the phase 1 clock starts. In practice, the CMA will not have sufficient time to fully consider new survey evidence received after the submission of a Party's response to the issues letter. This would be too late for the CMA to decide whether a survey is of sufficient quality to be given evidential weight, particularly if we have not had sight of the survey materials up to that point.

1.23 Parties wishing to conduct a survey for a merger case are strongly encouraged to contact the CMA in the early stages of the survey process to discuss their proposed design, including a draft questionnaire (if available) and wider aspects of the survey methodology.

1.24 Any discussion with the CMA would be on a 'without prejudice' basis and would not preclude developing or changing views on the evidential weight of a piece of customer survey research on either side. The discussion should not be seen as an alternative to rigorous testing and piloting by the Parties of the planned survey approach and research instruments. As part of its assessment of the quality of the survey, the CMA may ask to observe or listen to certain aspects of the operation of the survey, including the interviewer briefing ahead of fieldwork and/or live interviews once fieldwork is underway. The CMA expects the Parties to accommodate these requests. If, for whatever reason, the Parties are unable to accommodate the CMA's requests, the CMA may be unable to assure itself on the quality and reliability (and hence the evidential value) of the survey.

1.25 Where Parties do not discuss their survey design with the CMA in advance, and/or do not give the CMA an opportunity to monitor and assess the quality of fieldwork while it is underway, it is not necessarily the case that we will consider the survey findings to have no or only limited evidential weight. The weight to be given to such evidence will be assessed against the same principles and standards for conducting surveys described in this document. However, it has been our experience that survey designs not discussed with us in advance have tended to be of insufficient quality, and in the absence of first-hand experience of how fieldwork was conducted, it has been hard to conclude that the findings have genuine weight. In these circumstances, then, the onus will be on Parties to provide highly compelling information about the survey methodology and the steps taken to assure its quality.

1.26 We expect good surveys to be neutral and not biased towards one outcome or another. Given the nature of the phase 1 legal test, there is a particular risk to Parties that survey results beneficial to their case may be given little or no weight if they are perceived to have been led by a biased survey design.

1.27 We aim to be open and transparent in our work. We will consider requests from Parties in merger cases for the disclosure of underlying information and analyses derived from the CMA's own customer survey research. However, these requests may be subject to important legal and practical constraints on our ability to disclose such information. These include provisions of the Enterprise Act 2002, as amended, the Data Protection Act 1998 (soon to be replaced by the General Data Protection Regulation), and the statutory timetable for each merger inquiry.

WORKING WITH MARKET RESEARCH AGENCIES

1.28 The CMA commissions market research agencies to conduct most of its survey work. The choice of agency, and of the team within the agency, is a key decision affecting the survey quality achieved.

1.29 CMA research that provides evidence for merger cases is conducted to high quality standards, and in many cases we place requirements on agencies that go over-and-above standard practices. In particular, for the surveys we commission we take a keen interest in how the survey is conducted *after* the survey design and questionnaire have been agreed. For example, if interviews are to be conducted using a face-to-face or telephone methodology, then we would ask to see and make changes as appropriate to interviewer briefing materials. We like to participate in the interviewer briefing where possible, and check the quality of fieldwork ourselves (in addition to the agency's own monitoring), requesting changes where we think it appropriate. This might involve changing a question, the interviewer instructions and/or interviewing personnel, or asking for an interviewer re-briefing, additional supervisor checks or adjustments to interviewer schedules, as appropriate. Our involvement is aimed at driving up the quality of the survey fieldwork, as well as understanding how the survey has worked in the field, which we see as an important part of interpreting the results.

1.30 We encourage Parties and their external advisors to use the same hands-on approach to monitoring the merger-related customer surveys they commission. Survey data can only be as good as the fieldwork that generates it, and interviewer instructions and a survey questionnaire are often interpreted and implemented in unexpected ways by interviewers. Respondents' reactions, interpretations and answers can also differ from expectation, even when the survey has been extensively piloted.

1.31 If the Parties are able to demonstrate to the CMA that a survey has been conducted well, and show an understanding of how the survey has worked in practice, this will foster confidence in the survey results, and assist the CMA in assessing the evidential weight that may be attached to the findings.

1.32 We would expect market research agencies working for Parties and their external advisors to observe the MRS Code of Conduct, and to have appropriate qualifications to demonstrate their commitment to quality, for example, an ISO accreditation or similar. It is not considered good practice to sub-contract fieldwork without stringent and transparent processes to ensure high fieldwork standards.

NOTES

1 https://www.gov.uk/government/publications/mergers-consumer-survey-evidence-design-and-presentation CC2com1/OFT1230, March 2011

2 Quick guide to UK merger assessment, CMA, March 2014.

3 Merger Assessment Guidelines, September 2010, OFT1254 and CC2 (revised).

4 In these cases, we are interested in the behaviour of customers of bricks-and-mortar stores, eg would they switch to online channels.

5 As with all other survey findings, this depends on how robust the results are judged to be, and is only part of the evidence considered.

6 There can be some overlap between these questions and those used to address cross-channel substitution.

2. DESIGN

[3.431]

2.1 Sound statistical research requires that the survey design adheres to certain principles, in particular that:

(a) the population of interest is clearly defined;
(b) the sample source provides a representative coverage of the population;
(c) the sample is selected using random methods and the sample is of sufficient size to provide robust estimates;

(d) the interview method is appropriate for researching the audience and subject matter;
(e) the survey is notified to potential respondents in a neutral way that does not bias results;
(f) the questionnaire is well-designed, and is properly tested and piloted in advance;
(g) the fieldwork team is appropriately briefed, and interviewing quality monitored, as appropriate; and
(h) The design takes account of likely response rates, the need to minimise the potential for non-response bias and, where possible, incorporates metrics to measure and adjust for such bias[7].

TARGET POPULATION

2.2 Customer survey research involves defining a population of interest and then interviewing a sample from that population. This is done so that measures relating to the population may be estimated, and the sampling uncertainty in the estimates quantified.

2.3 In merger cases we are often interested in sub-populations, eg customers from specific geographic areas, or customers from each of the Parties separately, as well as an overall population of interest. Where such sub-populations of interest exist, these should be clearly set out in advance to inform the sample design.

SAMPLE SOURCE AND SURVEY MODE

2.4 Having defined the population of interest, the next task is to identify the best way of finding people who are in this population, ie the best source of sample to provide a representative coverage of the population. A variety of sample sources may be considered, including:
(a) intercepting customers close to the time of purchase, eg as they leave a store[8];
(b) customer lists provided by the Parties;
(c) external lists from reputable sources; and
(d) customers free-found using a random sampling technique[9] (eg random digit dialling or face-to-face omnibus interviews).

2.5 The following sections consider each of the four types of sample source listed above in more detail. Some problematic alternatives will then be discussed.

Intercepting customers at stores

2.6 One possible survey objective may be to investigate whether competition takes place locally and, if so, the extent of such competition, eg what are the locations of the firms that constrain each of the Parties' outlets. In these cases, ideally, customers should be surveyed from all of the Parties' outlets in areas of concern in order to determine the competitive constraints on them.

2.7 For this type of survey, a common approach is face-to-face interviewing with customers as they exit the store. This allows the interviewer to focus the interview on purchases just made, and to measure potential diversion accordingly.

2.8 Alternatively, customers may be recruited to the survey at the store (or bus stop, cinema, etc) by collecting postal, telephone and/or email contact details for a follow-up interview. This has the advantage of minimising the time demanded of customers 'there and then'. However, significant over-recruitment will usually be required to ensure that the required number of follow-up interviews is achieved.

2.9 Whichever approach is used, time and resource constraints often make such surveys difficult and so it is important to consider very carefully which outlets to survey. Where there are many outlets for which the CMA considers there to be a competition risk, then sometimes it is possible to eliminate a sufficient number by taking account of existing information, to leave a practicable number of outlets for surveying purposes[10].

2.10 If, following the application of this initial cut, the number of outlets is still too high to survey them all, then a number of strategies might be adopted to decide which outlets to sample. The context of each case will be different, but there is often a need for this sample to form the basis of inferences about Parties' outlets that have not been surveyed as well as providing direct survey estimates for those that have[11]. Approaches for the choice of outlets to survey may include:
(a) Random sample – randomly selecting either outlets or overlap areas.
(b) Stratified random sample – categorising outlets or overlap areas by characteristics that may have an impact on competition (eg competitor fascia count, whether rural/urban/London) and randomly selecting outlets or areas within each of these categories [eg Ladbrokes/Coral].
(c) Competition gradient – ordering outlets or overlap areas by a competition metric (eg distance between the Parties' outlets) and selecting outlets or overlap areas in a defined way (eg at fixed intervals) from the ranking [eg Celesio/Sainsbury's].
(d) Discriminative sample – selecting a set of outlets to survey that maximise the variety and combinations of different characteristics (eg size of outlet, type of outlet, distance to the nearest merger Party outlet, type of area, number and type of third-party competitors, etc) that might be relevant to an assessment of the nature and strength of the competitive constraint that the merger Party has on that outlet [eg Poundland/99p Stores].

2.11 Please note that the same issue of selecting a subset of outlets or areas to survey may arise while using other types of sample source, but we mention it specifically in relation to intercepting customers at stores because having a large number of outlets would make this particular type of survey prohibitively expensive.

2.12 It is important that the method employed is applied objectively, avoiding cherry-picking of outlets unless this is a clearly stated part of the interpretation of the results (eg choosing a subset of outlets most likely to create competition issues with the aim of showing that if the Parties are not close competitors in these outlets then they are unlikely to be anywhere else).

2.13 In exit surveys, it is important that interviewers approach potential respondents at random (rather than target those who they perceive to be more likely to take part). Sometimes, additional rules may need to be set to ensure that customers selected for interview at the outlet are representative of the population of customers at that outlet. For example, the survey design may require interview quotas if there are known characteristics of the customer population that should be reflected in the sample, or interviews may need to be carried out on specified days and at specified times of day to reflect the known footfall of customers using an outlet.

Customer lists provided by the Parties

2.14 Where they exist, customer lists supplied by the Parties may be used. Care must be taken to ensure that the list(s) match, as far as possible, the target population(s). Any under-coverage (particularly exclusion of specific sub-groups of customers) or over-coverage should be recorded and consideration given to any assumptions made about any inference from the survey population [eg Cineworld/City Screen where assumptions about under-coverage were tested with a small validation survey].

2.15 In many merger cases, all eligible customers in the list are included in the sample. However, if the number of customers in the list is very large, then a sample can be drawn from it at random. There may be other information about customers (eg demographic or categorisation characteristics) that may be expected to have an influence on their behaviours or attitudes with respect to the surveyed market. If so, the sample should have broadly the same composition by those characteristics as does the population. This may require stratification of the sample list before drawing the sample and/or interview quotas or post-stratification weighting to ensure that the achieved interviews are representative.

2.16 Where there are specific sub-populations of interest, the sample list should be stratified by those sub-populations to ensure that a sufficient number of respondents for each is obtained. Over-sampling of a sub-population may be necessary to achieve this.

2.17 While not exhaustive, the list below describes the methodological options typically considered in merger cases when interviewing from customer lists. Judgement is required as to which is the best approach, as there are advantages and disadvantages to each.

(a) **Telephone survey**. The response rate from a telephone survey can be higher than from an online survey, reducing the risks of non-response bias. This is particularly true when surveying businesses where there is the added advantage of being able to ensure that an appropriate person within the business is responding. Interaction with an interviewer also provides more opportunity to ensure that questions and response item lists are communicated in full and understood as intended. However, telephone surveys can be more expensive and time-consuming to conduct compared with other research methods and their usefulness depends upon having a good starting list of customer contact details.

(b) **Online survey (email or SMS invitation)**. Online surveys tend to be cheaper and faster to undertake, and may be a more natural method in some sectors, eg technology and online media, where the customer base is likely to be more responsive to an email survey. If the list of customer email addresses is very long (eg tens of thousands) then a large-scale online survey may be possible. In some circumstances, this can overcome the problem (discussed above) of needing to sample outlets to survey. However, response rates to online surveys are often low and the quality of responses is often not as high as when the respondent is interacting with an interviewer face-to-face or by telephone.

(c) **A combination of the above (mixed mode)**. A mixed interview method might be considered where, for example, the customer list contains both email and telephone contact details for each person and a follow-up telephone interview can be attempted with anyone who does not respond to the initial email invitation to participate in an online survey. Alternatively, where it is possible to contact some of the sample by email but not telephone, and others by telephone but not email, a mixed method approach may be appropriate.

2.18 However, particular care is needed in using mixed method approaches. Any solution which involves a mix of interviewer-administered (eg telephone) and self-completion (eg online) survey methods can be biased by modal effects, ie the results between the two methods are different *simply because of the method of interviewing*. Potential modal effects can be mitigated by ensuring that questions are asked in *exactly* the same way across each method. For example, if a question in a telephone survey is asked with an open-ended spontaneous response format, the online survey question should be asked in the same way.

2.19 This said, there are potential modal effects that may not be eliminated entirely even with the best questionnaire design. For example, in telephone interviewing the interviewer is typically instructed to prompt and probe respondents to capture full and considered responses, whereas there is no such parallel in an online survey. This explains why the number of answers to a question where multiple response is allowed (eg 'which brands have you used in the last three months'?) tends to be higher in a telephone survey than in an online survey.

2.20 Regardless of interview method, it is important that no systematic difference in response by customer type ensues. If one type of customer is more likely to respond to the survey than another, the achieved sample will misrepresent the population. So far as possible, therefore, the survey design should include strategies to maximise the response rate and to minimise the risk of significant non-response bias.

2.21 Where time permits for a telephone survey, and the appropriate contact details are held, a pre-notification letter or email outlining the purpose of the survey is likely to increase the response rate, as is a carefully worded survey introduction that explains the purpose of the research (see 2.39f).

2.22 For an online survey, again where time permits, it is usual to send a reminder to those customers who have not responded to the initial survey invitation within the first few days of fieldwork. Ideally, the fieldwork period should span at least one weekend, so that the opportunity for 'time poor' customers to respond is maximised.

2.23 Where there are no customer lists of sufficient quality, external lists from other reputable sources (eg Dun & Bradstreet for businesses) may be considered. Appropriate screening will be required to ensure that only genuine customers of the Parties are recruited, and it will be even more important to assess the extent to which the lists represent the target population.

Free-finding customers

2.24 Where no customer or reputable external lists exist, free-find sampling methods are possible (eg telephone random digit dialling or face-to-face omnibus surveys) but they can become expensive to use if the proportion of eligible individuals in the general population is low.

2.25 These are well-established research methods used within the research industry. However, it is important to ensure that the recruitment approach used with these methods is robust, with proper rules for the selection of households and individuals within them. As with external list sources, appropriate screening will be required to ensure that only genuine customers of the Parties are recruited.

2.26 Telephone numbers for random digit dialling should include mobile-only households, noting the increasing prevalence of households without a landline in the UK.

More problematic sources: street recruitment and online panels

2.27 Some customer sources that are used in commercial research are generally not considered sufficiently robust by the CMA for merger cases. In particular, we advise against recruiting customers:

(a) on the street; and

(b) from panels with non-random samples (ie most online panels).

2.28 On-street recruitment is likely to generate sample bias. For example, interviewers may not approach potential respondents at random as they should (tending to target those they perceive to be more 'willing' or likely to take part in a survey instead). Time and place of interviewing may also have a bearing on the type of people who are in the vicinity of the interviewer.

2.29 Sample bias is also a concern when respondents are drawn from a panel, in particular from an online panel, where sample recruitment does not rely on randomisation methods. Whilst a panel can be made to look like a random, representative cross-section of consumers in terms of its demographic profile, the characteristics of people who join a panel may be very different from other consumers. For example, evidence in the research literature suggests that those who join an online panel spend more time on the internet and engage more actively than other consumers in searching for better deals online. For a merger inquiry where channel substitution issues can be important, this could be a flaw. The CMA tends to place less evidential weight on surveys involving customer recruitment from panels, though each case is treated on its individual merits.

2.30 If panel sources are used, transparency and rigour of panel recruitment and data weighting methods will be factors in the CMA's evaluation of the survey results.

SAMPLE SIZE

2.31 In the surveys it commissions as part of a phase 2 merger inquiry, the CMA aims (as a general rule) to achieve a minimum of 100 completed interviews with any pre-defined group of interest for rigorous analysis (eg if analysis is required at an individual outlet level, a minimum of 100 interviews per outlet is needed). If there are other pre-defined sub-populations of interest within a more general population of customers, then the same threshold applies.

2.32 The target of 100 is not always met. Below this threshold, the CMA puts less reliance on statistical inferences about corresponding populations and will interpret and report results in a way that cannot be automatically applied to the whole population – for example, "23 of the 61 respondents who were customers of Party A said they would divert to Party B", not "38% . . . said . . . ".

2.33 In some cases, survey analysis might retrospectively reveal other groups with particular characteristics of interest. It is difficult to design a survey to ensure a sufficient number of interviews within all potential groups of interest, as these may only become evident at the analysis stage. The sample size requirements should be considered at the survey design stage, taking into account the implications of the likely response rates on the resulting numbers of interviews. Weighting a survey dataset reduces effective sample sizes, sometimes very considerably. It may be the case that the unweighted sample is above the threshold of 100, but the effective sample size of the weighted sample is below 100, in which case care should be taken to present results appropriately.

SURVEY VALIDATION ACROSS MODES

2.34 Where there is concern about potential for sample bias with a chosen method, a parallel validation survey using another research method may provide evidence as to whether or not such bias exists. For example, if the main survey is conducted online, a telephone survey conducted with a smaller sample, or within a specific sub-group, may be helpful in validating the results of the main survey[12].

INCENTIVES

2.35 There is no hard-and-fast rule about whether to use a respondent incentive (eg a gift voucher or entry into a prize draw) to increase the response rate to a merger inquiry survey. The CMA usually has no objection to their use, particularly where a low response rate is reasonably expected and would be a concern.

ADVANCE LETTERS/EMAILS AND INTRODUCTIONS TO RESPONDENTS

2.36 Care should be taken when drafting materials such as pre-notification letters/emails and survey introductions to ensure there is nothing in the wording that gives rise to an unplanned excessive level of participation in the survey by a type of customer with one view on the subject, in preference to another type of customer with a systematically different view.

2.37 Advance letters/emails should explain the purpose of the survey and how it will be conducted. Importantly, though, framing effects normally should be avoided so there must be no mention of a merger inquiry: the survey's purpose should be described as seeking customer views more generally.

2.38 In addition, such letters/emails will normally:
(a) Be on agency or commissioning organisation "letterhead" (as appropriate) signed by an appropriate authority;
(b) Be kept short and focused purely on the survey;
(c) Explain how the customer will be contacted, and when; and
(d) Include contact details (telephone and/or email) for potential respondents to use if they wish to opt out of the survey.

2.39 When designing introduction scripts for an interviewer-administered customer survey, an appropriate context needs to be established for the questions being put to respondents, so that respondents know what is being asked of them and why. Again, though, there normally should be no mention of a merger inquiry, and other information provided about the research should not be in any way pre-emptive of the survey questions.

2.40 Introductions should be delivered clearly in understandable blocks of plain English, but it is good practice to avoid long introductions which may serve to discourage survey participation. For interviewer-administered surveys, a useful technique to keep introductions short is to add scripts that can be used at the interviewer's discretion, to help clarify the task and reassure respondents. For example:
(a) *"This survey is purely for research purposes; no attempt will be made to sell you anything either during or after the survey."*
(b) *"Everything you say is confidential and no responses will be attributed to you individually."*
(c) *"Your views are important; this research is being used to find out what people like you think about . . ."*
(d) *"This survey will take about x minutes to complete."*
(e) *"This survey is being conducted according to the Market Research Society code of conduct."*
(f) *"You should have received a letter of introduction about the survey a week or so ago."* (Here, it is also helpful if interviewers have a copy of the letter to hand, which can be posted/emailed/read out to the respondent as appropriate.)

2.41 In interviewer-administered surveys, respondents should have an opportunity to ask questions of clarification before the main part of the interview begins. However, it is important that the interviewer adheres to the script provided in the survey introduction, and uses the reassurances exactly as written, to avoid any unintentional bias in respondent recruitment.

INTERVIEWER BRIEFING AND MONITORING

2.42 Strict adherence to the questionnaire script during interviewer-administered surveys is a key principle for merger inquiry research. Interviewers must follow interviewer instructions, including reading the questionnaire script verbatim, and not attempting to paraphrase anything. This can be difficult to achieve in practice, and based on its experience the CMA has come to the view that the following is the best way of ensuring that interviewers adhere to this principle.

2.43 Where questionnaires are interviewer-administered, either by telephone or face-to-face, there should be a full briefing of all interviewers scheduled to work on the survey before fieldwork starts. The purpose of the briefing is to ensure that all interviewers are familiar with the questionnaire script and routing, understand when to read out pre-codes, and prompt or probe responses as required.

2.44 Ideally, all field managers, supervisors and interviewers should be briefed directly by a member of the agency executive team. This is common practice for commercial telephone surveys where interviewers usually work together in one central location, but is less common for face-to-face surveys where interviewers may be geographically dispersed. However, personal briefing from a member of the agency executive team helps to ensure that interviewers understand and follow all the correct survey procedures[13] We recognise that a telephone briefing of interviewers may be more practical and cost-effective than asking interviewers to travel to a central location.

2.45 Normally, the briefing sessions will cover:
(a) A short background to the inquiry, highlighting the survey's importance and emphasising that the data will be subject to intense scrutiny, so the requirement is for the highest possible standards of fieldwork;
(b) The population of interest for the survey and the screening questions;

(c) Where the sample has been sourced from, and how to answer questions from respondents about how their personal details have been obtained (if applicable);
(d) The importance of screening properly, so that only eligible individuals are interviewed;
(e) The importance of a high response rate;
(f) The importance of, and rationale for, complete adherence to the questionnaire script;
(g) Whether each survey question allows one response (single code) or multiple responses (multi-code);
(h) At each question, whether potential response options should be read out (prompted) or whether responses should be captured spontaneously and probed to pre-codes;
(i) The use of any prompt material (eg maps, showcards, product descriptions);
(j) Routing/filtering protocols; and
(k) The importance, where applicable, of interviewing at the correct times and in the right places.

2.46 A separate *written* briefing note should also be given to interviewers working on the project. This should include all the instructions from the briefing session as well as a copy of the questionnaire with all routing instructions shown.

2.47 Research that is going to provide evidence for a merger inquiry requires particular attention to detail that often goes over-and-above the standards for commercial research, and this should be emphasised in both the verbal and written briefings.

2.48 A full and comprehensive briefing will mitigate the risk of poor quality fieldwork. However, it will not eliminate the risk entirely, and it is important that interviewing is monitored rigorously, with the agency executive team taking a keen interest in how the interviewing works in practice.

2.49 Good practice is for the agency project executive who conducted the briefing to listen to (telephone)/attend and observe (face-to-face) a selection of the interviews initially conducted post-briefing. Regardless of how well the questionnaire has been piloted (see 2.55ff), a number of details may need to be ironed out after the survey 'goes live'. Instructions and a survey questionnaire can be implemented in unexpected ways when entrusted to interviewers; and the reactions, interpretations and answers of respondents can differ from expectation.

2.50 Once mainstage fieldwork is fully underway, it is also good practice for the agency project executives to continue to monitor a proportion of interviews. Monitoring of interviewer performance in the field for face-to-face surveys is time-consuming (as it requires agency project executives and field managers/supervisors to travel with interviewers) but the CMA's experience is that it plays an important role in ensuring high standards of interviewing are maintained.

2.51 As a result of monitoring, questionnaire amendments, revised interviewer instructions and refresher briefings may be required (especially for any interviewers who fail to reach and maintain the required standards). Any adjustments needed should be documented and agreed with the client. If there is a systematic problem with the way that some interviewers have conducted interviews, these individuals should be replaced in the fieldwork team and new interviews conducted to replace any erroneous ones.

2.52 Telephone interviews are normally audio recorded as part of standard quality control procedures (although permission is required from the respondent to do so). These should be made available for scrutiny by the agency project executive and, if necessary, the client during the fieldwork period. Audio recording is less common for face-to-face surveys, but might be requested (by the agency executive team and/or the client) if felt necessary and the technology is available (subject to the same respondent permissions as for telephone).

2.53 The CMA generally likes to be given an opportunity to attend interviewer briefings and observe or listen to some fieldwork. Where possible our preference is to choose interviewing points and which interviewers to monitor for ourselves rather than the agency selecting them for us. All of this is subject to respondents being made aware that their interview is being recorded, or giving consent if the interview is being conducted face-to-face. This needs some prior planning and we encourage early communication with the CMA to facilitate it.

2.54 Where Parties are able to demonstrate that a survey has been conducted to a high standard, and show an understanding of how the survey has worked in practice in the field, this will assist the CMA in assessing the evidential weight of the data generated.

COGNITIVE TESTING/PILOTING

2.55 Where time allows, the soundness of any research design and questionnaire should be tested before the 'live' survey begins by conducting, monitoring and evaluating cognitive interviews and/or a survey pilot.

2.56 Undertaking a small number of cognitive interviews is often an effective way of identifying potential problems with a questionnaire. Usually, cognitive testing involves retrospective interviewing, where the researcher (usually one of the agency executive team responsible for the survey) – after conducting a full interview with an eligible respondent – then works back through the questionnaire asking them about their comprehension and interpretation of questions and discussing possible improvements[14]. Given the time involved in doing this, respondents are often offered a small incentive to participate.

2.57 Pilots are mini-versions of the full survey process, including and therefore testing the interviewer briefing, respondent contact/screening process and the questionnaire with customers drawn from the population of interest.

2.58 Members of the agency executive team responsible for the survey should be closely involved in the piloting process. This means conducting at least some of the pilot interviews themselves, or listening in and taking notes directly.

2.59 The extent of the pilot will depend upon the complexity of the survey design and the sensitivity or difficulty of the subject matter. Good practice involves the formal recruitment, interview and debrief of a number of pilot respondents, followed by a full design review.

2.60 Where there are particular sub-populations of interest, the pilot should cover each in turn, ideally. As a general rule, the CMA recommends conducting at least ten pilot interviews, with a minimum of two from each sub-population of interest. However, where time or sample is limited, the scale of the pilot may have to be cut back.

2.61 Parties should note that it is risky to put a survey into the field without proper piloting, and it is better to allow time in the project schedule to incorporate a full pilot rather than rushing the survey set-up and finding problems with survey quality at a later stage. However, the CMA recognises that time constraints sometimes make a more limited pilot necessary. In these circumstances the risks can be partly mitigated by testing a paper version of the questionnaire 'in-house' by interviewing colleagues, friends or family. The survey can also be 'soft launched', ie only a few interviews conducted on the first day or two of fieldwork with careful monitoring of how it is working, so that any mistakes can quickly be identified and rectified. If changes are made, it may be necessary to replace some or all of the interviews conducted beforehand.

NOTES

7 Many of the surveys considered as evidence in merger cases, including surveys commissioned by the CMA, suffer from low response rates and the consequent risk of a non-response bias which is difficult to quantify. This can affect the evidential weight that decision-makers place on the results of a survey. The effect of non-response bias can sometimes be partially mitigated by including a question in the survey from which the results of the survey can be benchmarked from another source. For example, if date of birth is held in the Parties' customer lists and age is asked in a customer survey, then the age distribution can be compared between the survey respondents and the customer lists and weights applied to adjust for any differences.

8 Often referred to as an 'exit survey'.

9 Quotas for sub-populations may be set; the important principle is that the selection of customers within each sub-population is random.

10 See section 3 of the Retail mergers commentary (CMA, 2017) for more details on filtering.

11 In some circumstances it may even be possible to use the survey dataset, or estimates derived from it, as inputs to an econometric model 'predicting' diversion ratios for non-surveyed outlets.

12 See the 'Discussion of survey method - cinema merger case' for a description of a research design incorporating this form of validation.

13 This is not the normal practice of many market research agencies. However, in the CMA's experience, problems often arise when briefing is delegated to/cascaded by field managers/supervisors, particularly for face-to-face surveys.

14 For example, "Would this question have been clearer to you if I had asked . . . ?"

3. QUESTIONNAIRE

INTRODUCTION

[3.432]

3.1 While there is a well-developed body of good practice in questionnaire design for social research, experience has shown that merger inquiry research requires particular attention to specific (and sometimes small) details to help obtain reliable and valid customer survey evidence. Any bias in response caused by imprecise or leading question wording, or ordering of the questions, can weaken the evidential value of a survey.

STRUCTURE

3.2 We start by describing an appropriate structure for a merger inquiry questionnaire. Responses to questions in each of these areas will provide key data for the exploration of competition in the market and the potential impact of a merger on customers' choices.

3.3 It is good practice to ask easily answered questions on matter-of-fact topics at the start of a survey to 'warm up' respondents, followed by matters of behaviour, then preferences and reasons for choice, and then responses to hypothetical questions. The best questionnaires flow naturally for the respondent, enabling them to give a narrative of their behaviour in the market of interest. Typically, a merger inquiry questionnaire might be structured to include the following sections:

(a) An introduction inviting potential respondents to take part in the survey;
(b) Screening questions (ie questions that establish the respondent's eligibility to take part in the survey[15]);
(c) General purchasing behaviour, eg nature of purchase(s), suppliers, frequency of purchases, channels used;
(d) Influences on purchasing behaviour/choice attributes;
(e) Geography of most recent purchase, eg distance travelled/time taken to get to purchase point, departure point, travel modes used, whether main reason for visit/journey;
(f) Aspects of most recent purchase, eg (as appropriate) what was purchased, when, who with, how much was spent, how many items;
(g) Response to hypothetical change in a Party's offering;

(h) Respondent demographics (if not covered during the screening of respondents).

3.4 It is important to carefully consider the order of individual questions within particular questionnaire sections as well, to avoid influencing answers to later questions by earlier ones within the section.

3.5 Questions should be introduced in such a way that clearly states the context in which they are to be answered and reminds customers of this, as necessary. Linking phrases such as 'Still thinking about the recent purchase you made . . . ' will be useful in this regard. This, and a structure such as the one above, should be used to help the respondent return to the mindset of their most recent purchase before answering the diversion questions.

3.6 Care should be taken not to burden the respondent with a survey that is too long. The quality of responses will deteriorate if the questionnaire is too detailed and time-consuming to answer. Adherence to the structure above will help in designing a questionnaire that is succinct and relevant both to the customer and to the merger analysis. Ideally, the questionnaire should take no more than 10-15 minutes of a customer's time to answer, although in some circumstances (eg store exit interviews) a shorter questionnaire may be necessary.

LANGUAGE

3.7 When designing a questionnaire it is important to use appropriate language that avoids ambiguity or confusion. Wording should be in plain English, to reflect a wide range of language comprehension skills (reading, speaking and/or listening).

3.8 In surveys of the general population, technical terms should be used only where these are widely used and understood or – if not widely used/understood but their use is unavoidable – carefully explained so that they are understood in the same way by all respondents. However, if there is any risk that they may be interpreted differently by respondents even with an explanation, they should not be used at all. In surveys of business audiences, the use of technical terms may be more appropriate, but care should still be taken to keep the wording as straightforward as possible.

3.9 There needs to be consistency in interpretation of the survey questions by respondents to ensure that the views they express are based on a common understanding of the questions being asked. Any scope for ambiguity or confusion in the phrasing of a customer survey question is likely to reduce its evidential weight. However, there is sometimes a fine balance to be struck between having sufficient detail in a question to avoid ambiguity and it becoming too long and difficult to remember. Where such tension exists, it is often better to split a long question into two (or more) shorter questions.

3.10 In addition, the questionnaire must not influence customers to give particular answers: it must not lead them to express an opinion or fact that is not a proper representation of their views or behaviours. It is important, therefore, to provide a sufficient range of response options at all questions so that customer views are represented properly.

3.11 A question that is presented in a way that leads customers to one answer in preference to another (irrespective of their actual view or behaviour) constitutes bias, and is likely to be of limited evidential value as a result. Some potential sources of bias that should be considered when drafting customer survey questions include:

(a) Acquiescence bias, where the customer thinks they should agree with a statement included in the question and therefore does so. For example, 'Have you been to the dentist in the last year?' contains an acquiescence bias to the response 'Yes'. A better, more neutral question would be: 'When, if at all, did you last go to the dentist?';

(b) Restrictive bias, where the question leads the customer to think only of certain options. For example, asking 'If you had known before you went there that this branch of X was closed for refurbishment for one year, what would you have done instead?' – without an explicit encouragement in the question wording to respondents to consider all options, such as 'Please imagine that you had known before you went there that this branch of X was closed for refurbishment for one year. *Thinking of all the options open to you*, what would you have done instead?' – may cause respondents to discount shopping online as an alternative source of supply;

(c) Hypothetical bias, where a customer may indicate a willingness to spend money or change behaviour which does not reflect their likely real response to the situation described[16];

(d) Inertia bias, where a customer over-states their likely reaction to a change in the market, eg by not taking into account switching costs, inconvenience, uncertainty of information, etc.

QUESTION TYPES

3.12 Selecting the correct question type(s) is an essential part of survey design, and the type(s) of question that can be used will be influenced by survey mode, typically whether this is:

(a) an interviewer-administered face-to-face interview, using paper and pen or computer-assisted personal interviewing (CAPI);

(b) an interviewer-administered telephone (CATI) interview;

(c) a scripted online questionnaire.

Pre-coded (closed) and open questions

3.13 Data collection and analysis is often facilitated by using questions where likely frequent answers are included in the questionnaire (closed questions) rather than leaving the customer or interviewer to write in the response (open questions). For interviewer-administered surveys, closed questions can be asked either as prompted (where the response codes are read out or shown to the customer) or as unprompted/spontaneous (where the interviewer codes the response from what the customer says, often probing to clarify what the customer means and how the response fits into the pre-codes on the questionnaire)[17].

3.14 However, care should be taken in the drafting of pre-coded responses. As an over-riding principle, the codes must cover what are likely to be the most frequent survey responses. Then:

(a) If potential responses are to be prompted (read out or shown to customers), the list should contain responses that can be easily understood and (if not shown) remembered by a typical customer (usually 6-8 possible answers at most).

(b) If (for an interviewer-administered survey) the pre-coded question is designed to collect responses in a spontaneous (unprompted) fashion, a longer list is feasible, but the response codes should be presented to the interviewer in a logical fashion, ideally with the most likely frequent response codes first on the list, alphabetically or in groups of related responses, and they should not extend over more than one page or screen.

3.15 Response codes should be drafted so that they are easily understood (by both respondent and interviewer), so good practice is to avoid any with too many words that make it difficult to interpret their meaning (and how they are differentiated from other codes).

3.16 When using pre-coded response questions in an interviewer-administered survey, it is important that there is a clear instruction on the questionnaire to say whether the list is to be read out (prompted) or not (spontaneous). If using a spontaneous approach, make clear in the instruction the extent to which interviewers should prompt for further answers or probe to clarify whether the response fits one pre-code or another. (It is also helpful to remind interviewers that they should not allow respondents to read the pre-codes over their shoulder on the page or screen). Standard practice with spontaneous pre-coded questions is to prompt the customer (eg 'Why else?', 'What else?', 'Anything else?') until he/she has nothing further to add, and to code the first mention separately from all other mentions. However, there may be occasions when the first 'top of mind' response is of most interest, in which case further prompting may be of less value.

3.17 Some surveys are designed with the inclusion of fully open-ended response questions, where there are no pre-codes and interviewers write in the answers given by the customer, or the customers themselves write in their answer. Fully unstructured responses can be highly informative, but this approach is not often used in merger inquiry surveys because open-ended questions can be time-consuming to ask and costly to analyse.

Scalar responses

3.18 Another often-used question technique in customer surveys is to capture responses via semantic or numeric scales. A semantic scale is labelled either at the end points or at every point on the scale (eg Strongly agree, Tend to agree, Neither agree nor disagree, Tend to disagree, Strongly disagree), while a numeric scale uses numbers as labels. The CMA's preference is to use semantic rather than numeric scales, because the former is easier to interpret by both respondent and analyst.

3.19 There is no standardised semantic scale approach used in merger cases, although bipolar scales normally include a neutral mid-point and allow customers to give 'Don't know' as an answer. However, in some cases it may be more appropriate to use an unbalanced scale without a neutral mid-point to unpick differentiation in customer attitudes where there is a natural tendency for customers to answer in a similar fashion. For example, importance scales are often used to identify the key factors that drive consumer choice in a market, by reading out a list of factors and asking customers to rate each of them in turn in terms of importance. Typically some customers will rate all factors as 'important' when presented with this task, and so it can be useful to have more granular distinctions at the 'important' end of the scale (such as 'essential', 'very important', 'fairly important') to help identify which are the most important factors. Alternatively, respondents could be asked to choose and rank, for example, the three attributes that are most important to them.

QUESTIONNAIRE DESIGN FOR DIFFERENT MODES

3.20 Different modes have particular strengths and weaknesses in terms of the way in which questions can be designed and presented to customers. These should be taken into account when deciding on the appropriate survey mode. For example:

(a) In CAPI, CATI and scripted online questionnaires (where the interviewing mode facilitates 'automated' or pre-scripted randomisation), it is good practice to vary the order in which item lists are read out to or displayed to customers when it is appropriate to do so (ie because possible answers are not in any way hierarchical), and to automatically reverse response scales for half the sample[18];

(b) CAPI, CATI and online self-completion modes also allow complex, conditional routing/filtering to be built into the questionnaire. Necessarily, the routing in paper and pen questionnaires must be simpler, but there remains a risk that customers will not answer questions they should, and answer questions that they should not. Clear interviewer instructions and a comprehensive briefing can help reduce this risk;

(c) In interviewer-administered isurveys, valid responses such as "Don't know" and "Not applicable" can be captured as spontaneous answers (ie without being read out). However, in online surveys, such answers are effectively prompted for all customers and this may increase the frequency with which they are selected;

(d) In interviewer-administered face-to-face interviews, a showcard can be used to minimise the amount of information that customers must retain to be able to give an answer. However, in a telephone survey, customers may be required to absorb/remember a considerable amount of detail before making their response which is why it is important that item lists are limited in length;

(e) Face-to-face and online questionnaires can include stimulus content (eg logos, fascia images) in a way that a telephone survey cannot.

CONTENT

Screening questions

3.21 In general, screening questions will be necessary at the start of a customer survey interview to ensure that only those within the population of interest are included in its scope. Occasionally, this will be all potential customers or businesses within the market[19], but is usually only the customers of one or both of the Parties.

3.22 Where customers are free-found using a random recruitment method (eg a face-to-face omnibus), the screening section may include a question(s) on previous purchasing behaviour to establish whether they are the customer of a merger Party. Importantly, such a question should not lead the customer to the identification of the other merger Party, as this may bias subsequent responses. Good practice is to ask for responses spontaneously or from a prompted list that includes all potential suppliers, as appropriate.

3.23 Screening questions are often used to ensure that the respondent was personally involved in the purchase decision. For example, a customer may have seen a film at a particular cinema but a friend or family member chose the cinema and booked the tickets. Timing of last purchase is also important. If the last purchase was a long time ago, then respondent recall may be a problem. Much depends on the product or service being purchased; recall is likely to be better regarding the purchase of laser eye surgery than about a visit to a convenience store. Piloting the survey can help to test recall and set a limit on how recently a relevant purchase needs to have been made to be eligible for the survey.

3.24 In many research surveys, screening questions are added to exclude customers who may have an informed/expert or vested interest in the subject because of their employment or personal connections, on the grounds that this may lead them to purposefully bias their responses in a particular way. The CMA's general view is that all members of the population of interest should be included within the eligible sample and any such questions should be crafted to exclude as few people as possible. For example, it is not our usual practice to exclude people working in the market research industry or journalism from responding to merger surveys. In the surveys we commission, the CMA would normally include customers who have opted out of marketing communications or who have been flagged as recent participants in other market research.

Customer demography

3.25 Demographic questions may be asked after the screening questions (by way of easy introduction to the survey) or right at the end of the interview. The latter approach is usually preferable when the information requested may be sensitive, eg respondent income. Where the survey sample is taken from a customer list/database and already includes key demographic information about potential respondents, it is better (where possible) to take these 'answers' from the database and not waste interviewing time to recapture them, unless there is a reason to believe that verification is desirable and their importance merits it.

3.26 Typical demographic information collected is:

(a) Sex (may be observed, not asked);

(b) (If not already covered during the screening) Age (ideally the customer's specific age, only asking them to indicate an age band if this is refused);

(c) Working status;

(d) Highest educational qualification.

3.27 We would not generally recommend asking a detailed social grade question in a merger inquiry survey: collecting sufficient information to enable an accurate classification takes time that is better spent on questions that are typically of more interest.

Previous purchase behaviour/consideration of other suppliers

3.28 Responses to hypothetical questions about what customers would do in the event of a change in a Party's offering should always be assessed in the context of other evidence about the customer and a general understanding of consumer behaviour in the market as gained from the survey. Questions on previous purchase behaviour provide this contextual understanding. Similarly, collecting information about whether customers have considered other suppliers in the market in the past, and whether they have actively searched out information about other suppliers, may help to give a better understanding of consumer behaviour and whether customers are actively engaged in the market.

3.29 Typical questions:

(a) Brands purchased in last day/week/month/year etc (depending upon typical purchase frequency)[20];

(b) Frequency with which brands are purchased;

(c) Purchase channels used (bricks-and-mortar outlet, online, telephone etc);

(d) Whether the customer has considered purchasing from another supplier(s) and/or been approached by another supplier(s);

(e) Whether the customer has searched for information about another supplier(s) or about the supplier they purchased from, and if so where and for how long they searched for information.

Choice attributes; purchase decision

3.30 Understanding why customers choose to buy from one supplier rather than another enables the identification of key drivers of consumer choice and helps us to draw inferences about how suppliers compete in the market. It also gives respondents an opportunity to think about the factors that are important to them, and makes it more likely that they will give a considered response to the subsequent diversion question(s).

3.31 Two different question approaches are commonly used to understand what drives customer choice:

(a) A choice attribute question that asks the customer to identify the most important reason(s) for choosing one product/service or supplier over another;

(b) Attribute importance questions (with a scalar response for each of several attributes) that asks how important each attribute is to the customer.

3.32 A choice attribute question may be asked either as a spontaneous (unprompted) question or as a prompted question. The advantage of asking reason(s) for choice spontaneously is that it captures the 'top of mind' differentiators; the disadvantage is that one or two attributes may dominate (price, for example) and then there is less evidence about the importance of other factors. The question may be asked just to capture the *single most important* reason or alternatively *all important* reasons (although here it is advisable to capture the first mention separately to help identify the key reason for choice). An option to capture and code 'other' responses is usually included.

3.33 Attribute importance questions should be prompted on a one-by-one basis, using a scale which is semantically defined. Here, the CMA often uses an Essential/Very important/Fairly important/Not important/Don't know scale because in our experience it generates results that discriminate effectively between attributes.

3.34 It is usually inadvisable to include both a *prompted* choice attribute question and attribute importance questions in the same survey, as this combination may introduce respondent fatigue. Instead, it will usually be better to ask reason(s) for choice spontaneously and then the prompted attribute importance questions (in that order so that spontaneous responses are captured first)[21].

3.35 The choice attribute question is usually the most informative in discerning parameters of competition from a customer perspective because it *differentiates* the Parties' offerings. Consequently, it is often (although not always) the more relevant question in a merger case compared with attribute importance questions. (The latter quantify the importance of component parts of the Parties' offerings but those revealed as most important are frequently common to both Parties[22]). For a fuller discussion of the interpretation of these types of question, illustrated with an example, see the hospital merger case study in Section 5.

Discrete choice; conjoint analysis

3.36 There are other well-established question approaches that use modelling techniques to understand the importance to customers of various attributes in the purchase decision (eg Choice Based Conjoint (CBC) or other forms of discrete choice analysis). These tend not to be used extensively in merger inquiry research due to time constraints – there is often insufficient time to design and test conjoint survey instruments extensively before fieldwork, to administer the necessary questions during the interview, or to undertake the modelling prior to presentation of results[23].

'Geography' of local competition

3.37 The collection of details about where a product or service was purchased, how the customer travelled to the purchase point, how long it took, and where they travelled from (their departure point), can be useful information to help identify the geographic scope of the competitive constraints on the Parties' products or services. Clearly this is not of relevance for purchases made online.

3.38 Typical questions are:

(a) Where the customer travelled from to get to the purchase point (home, workplace, somewhere else);

(b) Travel mode(s) used;

(c) Time taken to travel/distance travelled to purchase point;

(d) Whether the visit was the only/main reason for making the trip, or not the main reason.

3.39 This information can be used sometimes to map customers in terms of proximity to a particular purchase outlet, and to define the catchment area for a particular outlet[24].

3.40 The phrasing of these questions needs to be considered carefully to ensure they are meaningful to all customers in different purchase circumstances. For example, if the purchase is made on impulse or planned as part of a more general shopping or commuting trip (rather than being the sole or main reason for the trip), the question may need to focus on the travel from the relevant local point to the outlet, rather than from the home or workplace[25].

Diversion

3.41 In many merger cases, the main objective of the survey is to assess the closeness of competition between the Parties and their competitors. A key element of this assessment is the inclusion of a suite of questions asking customers what they would have done under various hypothetical scenarios on a previous purchase occasion from one of the Parties. The most common of these scenarios is that a given product/service/supplier (or a given supplier's outlet or website) was not available (forced diversion)[26], or a product/service was offered at a higher price (price diversion).

3.42 As indicated before, these questions should normally be asked in relation to the last purchase occasion, to put them in a specific and meaningful context. Thus, a price diversion question may take the form: "Thinking about [your most recent purchase from x], what would you have done if the price of this product/service had gone up by £1?"[27]

3.43 Conceptually, we are trying to measure the extent to which sales revenues lost through a deterioration in an aspect of one merger Party's offerings would be internalised as a result of the merger, because some customers would choose to divert some or all of their expenditure to purchases from the other merger Party. In more technical language, we are using a hypothetical question to capture the stated next best alternatives/substitutes of 'marginal' customers: customers whose demand is elastic in regard to the dimension of the offering that is being varied under the hypothetical scenario presented in the diversion question. This is usually a small increment in price, but can be a change in some other aspect such as frequency of service in transport markets.

3.44 In most circumstances only a small proportion of customers will be marginal in the sense described above. Subsequently, the sample of marginal customers for which we have diversion responses is likely to be too small to provide estimates of sufficient precision for robust analysis. To overcome this, we ask the forced diversion question, removing a Party's offering altogether, which results in all customers being asked what they would have done instead. When interpreting the findings, it is then necessary to make the assumption that the distribution of their responses is the same as for marginal customers. Note that this is equivalent to making the assumption that the diversion behaviour of marginal and non-marginal ("inframarginal") customers is the same[28].

3.45 In cases where both price diversion and forced diversion questions are asked of all customers, the CMA has found that the order in which the questions are asked makes little difference to the results, ie it does not matter whether the forced diversion question is asked before or after the price diversion question. However, it is usually more natural to ask the price diversion question first, as this will help to identify marginal customers in response to a specified price increase. It is also a more logical question sequence for respondents, particularly those who are inframarginal customers.

3.46 When asking customers about their response to price increases, it is usually better to frame questions in terms of absolute amounts (eg in pence or £s) based on an actual price recently paid for a product or service, or typical price. Information may need to be collected in the survey about the actual price paid, and then a calculation made (this can be done automatically in a computer-assisted interviewing script) of the new amount after, say, a 5% price increase. We try to avoid presenting a price increase to consumers within the general population as a percentage (eg "What would you do in the event of a 5% increase in the price you paid?"), because they may find it difficult to work out what a percentage increase means in monetary terms. This is less of a concern for business respondents.

3.47 Questions about diversion options should be designed and tested to ensure they cover all possibilities. The exact wording will depend upon the range of options specific to a given merger situation, but as a general rule the initial question should ask about hypothetical behaviour at the highest level, eg would the customer (a) not 'purchase' or (b) 'purchase' or (c) don't know[29]. Those who say 'purchase' should then be asked a follow-up question, ie what product/service/supplier[30] (or supplier's outlet or website) would they substitute.

3.48 When framing the follow-up question, consideration should be given to allowing a spontaneous (unprompted) answer, avoiding the risk that a non-exhaustive showcard or read-out list of options introduces bias (although there is no hard-and-fast rule here and prompted lists are usually needed in online surveys). However, care is required with this approach: it necessitates no prompted mentions of particular products/services/suppliers (or supplier's outlet or website) earlier in the survey, and interviewers must probe carefully to identify the correct product/service/supplier (or supplier's outlet or website) in circumstances where they are recording responses against a pre-code rather than capturing verbatim what the respondent says.

3.49 The interviewer can be given lists and maps to help validate responses to unprompted questions. However, it is important to brief interviewers not to show these materials to the respondent when first asking the question. Experience suggests that many respondents struggle to read maps so while they might be a useful aid for the interviewer, interviews should not be dependent upon them.

3.50 Where it might be difficult to collect sufficiently accurate details of the substitute that respondents have in mind, it may be better to prompt the customer with a showcard or read-out list. This style of question is more appropriate when there is a limited number of alternatives in the market, or where precise outlet location details are required. If a short prompted list is used, the order in which alternatives are listed can be randomised. Otherwise, the list should be ordered in a systematic way such as alphabetically by brand/supplier fascia or name (and location, if applicable), or product/service name, to ensure no order effect biases are introduced (and if appropriate the alphabetic start point could be rotated between interviews).

3.51 In some merger cases, attempts have been made to investigate the effect of hypothetical non-price changes such as reductions in quality. This is a difficult (but not impossible) survey task. The challenge is to find a quality measure where a hypothetical deterioration has a precise meaning to all customers. Harder measures such as 'waiting times for hospital appointments' are better in this context than softer measures like 'friendliness of staff'. As with price diversion, any question asking for a response to a hypothetical deterioration should be based on the actual product or service delivered on the last or most typical purchase occasion.

3.52 Diversion questions need to be worded in such a way that the customer puts themselves in the mindset of the original purchase decision. This purchase may have been planned or on impulse and it is sometimes appropriate to have different question wording to cover each of these situations[31].

3.53 There are some markets where one or both of the Parties have other products/services, outlets or websites, that customers may consider as alternatives. If a high proportion of own-party diversion (eg from one of the Party's products/services or outlets or websites to another) is anticipated, then a staged approach to the diversion questions may be desirable. In the first instance, the customer can be asked what they would have done instead if a particular product/service was unavailable or outlet was shut or website taken down and, for those saying that they would purchase another of the same Party's products/services or go to another of their outlets or websites, a follow-up question would ask the customer what they would do if none of that Party's products/services or outlets was available[32].

3.54 In some markets, it may be necessary to consider scenarios where the nature of a purchase presents several diversion possibilities. For example, during an exit survey, a customer may report that they have just purchased three items from a merger Party's store. When asked what they would have done if the store had been closed, they may say (1) they would not have bought any of the items or (2) they would have gone to one different store to buy all three. Equally, though, they may say they would have bought one of the items in one different store and not bought the other two, or bought one each of the items in three different stores, and so on. These are what we refer to as 'split basket' diversion options[33].

3.55 Theoretically, a customer survey should accommodate (where applicable) the potential for split basket diversion behaviour. In our experience, though, it is very difficult to do in practice, because keeping track of the various basket components creates confusion for the respondent. Generally, therefore, a more pragmatic approach is needed, and CMA surveys instead tend to direct respondents to state the alternative that covers all or the greater part of the items in their basket, recording this as their answer.

3.56 Where this simplified approach is taken, it needs to be considered carefully when interpreting the survey results. The avoidance of split basket options may steer respondents into limiting alternatives to those suppliers that offer all the items they have just purchased[34]. This may be a smaller set of suppliers than is available for individual items in the basket.

Cross-channel substitution

3.57 The investigation of customer searching and purchasing via the internet may be helpful in establishing the competitive constraint from online suppliers. Typical questions used to help assess this are:

(a) Whether the customer has looked online for information about product(s)/service(s) and/or suppliers;

(b) Use of digital comparison tools (DCTs) (eg a price comparison website) to investigate prices across different products/services and/or suppliers;

(c) Whether the customer has purchased product(s)/service(s) online previously;

(d) Potential diversion to an online source.

3.58 Care needs to be taken in placing these questions in the right part of the questionnaire. Context is key and in some circumstances they should be near the start of the survey, to ensure bias is not introduced and customers lead to a particular answer by questions about internet usage or online purchasing immediately before the diversion section.

3.59 In exit surveys, customers may be influenced by the physical context of being interviewed in or outside a store to think only of other bricks-and-mortar suppliers as an alternative. To this extent, it may be appropriate to position questions in a way that encourages respondents to consider all options, with potential answers not restricted to bricks-and-mortar substitutes. For example, it may be appropriate to ask about online alternatives in an earlier section of the interview. Parties and their external advisors should ensure that there is a fair balance to the survey and that question order does not lead customers to consider one channel over another in their diversion responses.

3.60 Where there is a realistic option for customers to divert purchases to an online supplier, the main (first) diversion question might include both 'purchase from an online supplier' and 'purchase from an offline supplier' pre-codes. This should ensure that both online and offline channels are presented as possible options when customers are considering what they would do (particularly as the pre-codes to the first diversion question are usually read out to respondents). It should also ensure that responses to the second diversion question (what product/service/supplier or supplier outlet or website would they substitute) can be identified as either the online or offline/bricks-and-mortar channel of the alternative supplier mentioned (if the supplier operates through both).

NOTES

15 For many surveys, it is important for the first question to determine the respondent's age. Parental permission is required to interview anyone under the age of 16, and those under the age of 16 should either be treated as ineligible to participate in the survey, or should not be asked anything further until parental permission is secured.

16 Hypothetical diversion questions are inevitably subject to this bias; this should always be carefully considered when interpreting findings based on them.

17 Note that the interpretation of responses may be different depending on whether the question is asked as prompted or unprompted. An example of this is provided in chapter 5.

18 Other, Don't know and Not applicable response options should not be randomised or reversed, always appearing at the end of item lists.

19 For example, in markets where branding is not very important. In a recent merger case involving two suppliers of

pay-to-use (PTU) automatic teller machines (ATMs), the survey design involved free-finding recent customers of any PTU ATM, because we knew from the outset that it would be difficult to establish whether they had used one of the merger Parties' machines specifically.

20 In some merger contexts, eg those involving the provision of an ongoing service, it might be more appropriate to ask about switching suppliers (including reasons why the respondent has, or has not, done so).

21 We note that in paper or online self-completion surveys, prompted versions of both types of question are likely to be unavoidable.

22 For example, it is essential that supermarkets provide lighting, trolleys and accept payments by cash or card, but these are 'hygiene factors' that customers will take for granted as being offered by all supermarkets and so are not differentiating factors in the way that prices or location might be.

23 The Authority for Competition and Markets in the Netherlands has conducted a number of surveys in merger cases in recent years that have used conjoint methods. See 'Using Conjoint Analysis in Merger Control' (ACM Working Paper, 2016).

24 To do this, additional data such as customer home or work postcode may be required.

25 In our experience, though, this is difficult to do unambiguously (eg Poundland/99p Stores, Celesio/Sainsbury's).

26 Either permanently, or for a reasonably extensive amount of time, so that the purchase cannot just be delayed.

27 Further examples of diversion questions are provided in section 5.

28 It is sometimes possible to test this assumption. For example, if a survey is being conducted in more than one area there may not be a sufficient number of respondents in any one area stating a change in behaviour as a result of a price increase, but responses can be aggregated across all areas to check the relationship between responses to the price and forced diversion questions. Where this has been done, the CMA has usually found them to be similar.

29 Each survey is different and the list of options is usually more complex than this in practice. For example, diversion may be from a bricks-and-mortar outlet to another bricks-and-mortar outlet or to an online outlet, and vice versa.

30 For example, own-Party supplier (OP) (= same supplier), other merger Party supplier (MP), third-party supplier (TP), or don't know.

31 For example, in the Poundland/99p Stores phase 2 merger case, the CMA's exit survey asked respondents early in the interview when they had decided to visit the store. Their answer determined which of the following two wordings of the diversion question they were subsequently asked, that is:

Where the visit was pre-planned: "Earlier, you told me you decided to visit [Party] today before you set out. If you had known before you set out today that [Party] was closed for several months for refurbishment . . . "

For those whose visit was on impulse: "If you had found today that [Party] was closed for several months for refurbishment . . ."

32 See the Ladbrokes/Coral merger case questions in section 5 of this document for a fully worked example.

33 Note that the examples given here are not exhaustive.

34 This is referred to as 'bundling' in the economics literature.

4. ANALYSIS, INTERPRETATION AND DISSEMINATION

SURVEY DATASET PROCESSING, CLEANING/EDITING AND PRESENTATION

[3.433]

4.1 As part of a merger inquiry, the CMA will request a copy of any respondent-level customer survey dataset(s) used by the Parties and/or their external advisors to support the arguments or contentions made in their submission (eg Parties' estimates of diversion). Datasets should be supplied to the CMA with all data validation, cleaning and editing (including coding) completed, and all quality assurance procedures carried out in line with ISO 20252:2012 data management and processing standards. A note detailing any changes made to the dataset(s) during this process should also be supplied.

4.2 In supplying the customer survey dataset(s) to the CMA, Parties and/or their external advisors must observe the requirements of the Data Protection Act 1998 (soon to be replaced by the General Data Protection Regulation) in regard to the processing of personal data. Where they have not obtained permission to pass on information that would allow individual survey respondents to be identified, Parties and/or their external advisors must anonymise the dataset(s) before they are transmitted to the CMA, for example, by:

(a) removing personal identifiers such as respondents' names, telephone numbers and email addresses;

(b) aggregating or reducing the precision of other variables, for example, by replacing a full postcode with a partial postcode, or by replacing geospatial point co-ordinates with wider (but still meaningful), non-disclosive geographical areas; and

(c) removing (or reducing the precision of) indirect identifiers that, if linked, might disclose the identity of an individual (eg, age + employer + detailed job title).

4.3 However, Parties and/or their external advisors should be mindful of not excluding individual responses to demographic questions where they are essential to the testing of an important hypothesis or theory of harm.

4.4 Data should be supplied to the CMA in the following software formats: Excel (as a minimum and not just in .pdf form) plus Stata and/or SPSS (if possible). It is worth noting that in the conversion of data from one format to another (eg from survey software into data processing software, or between different types of statistical software), changes may occur to some data or internal metadata (eg missing value definitions, variable labelling, decimal numbers, formulae etc). The dataset(s) should be fully checked, and any changes caused by the conversion process corrected, before the dataset(s) are shared with the CMA.

4.5 Each record in the dataset should be labelled with a unique reference (or identifier) number (URN). Where the survey data might be matched to other data (for example, transactional information on a customer database), each respondent's URN should be the same in both datasets.

4.6 Where the Parties' research has been undertaken using an interviewer-administered survey methodology (ie face-to-face or by telephone), the CMA also expects each record in the dataset to include the date and time of the interview and the ID number of the interviewer who conducted the interview (unless the inclusion of these details could allow individual respondents to be identified).

4.7 As far as possible, data codes should always be consistent. For example, if (at Question 1) yes = 1 and no = 2, use these codes for all Yes/No questions. Ideally, too, data codes that might be applicable to any question (such as Other, Don't know, Not applicable, Refused) should be standardised. For example, code 3 (at Question 1) and code 7 (at Question 2) should not both = Don't know. Instead, say, let 95 = Other, 97 = Don't know, 98 = Not applicable and 99 = Refused throughout the dataset.

4.8 With the customer survey dataset(s), Parties and/or their external advisors should supply documentation – or a data dictionary – that includes:

(a) a copy of the questionnaire(s), setting out the exact wording used for each question, any associated pre-codes and (where applicable) all interviewer instructions (read out/do not read out, etc), and clearly indicating all survey routing;
(b) names, labels and descriptions for variables, and their source (eg whether taken from the original sample file, from questionnaire responses, or appended from another dataset);
(c) for derived variables, a description of how they have been constructed;
(d) categorical and numeric variable value labels;
(e) codes of, and reasons for, missing values (and an explanation of any techniques applied to the dataset for dealing with missing values);
(f) an explanation of coding/classification schemes used;
(g) information on any weighting variables applied;
(h) a description of the algorithms or calculations used in the analysis of the data; and
(i) a summary of any selection, cleaning or other adjustments that have been applied to the original response data.

4.9 Survey results should be weighted where appropriate. These weights should be included as part of the survey dataset and their method of calculation provided. Decisions about weighting need to be made on an individual survey basis, but the following is a list of some of the common circumstances in which weighting might be considered:

(a) When the sample design intentionally under- or oversamples a particular sub-population (design weights).
(b) When the achieved sample is not representative of the target population, eg as a result of non-response bias. Note that this requires good quality benchmark data about the population, such as information contained within customer lists, to use for the weighting.
(c) Where weighting converts the units of the achieved sample onto the correct conceptual analytical basis (eg spend or frequency weighting).

4.10 Estimates based on the customer survey dataset(s) should always show the unweighted base size (the number of individual responses) on which they have been calculated and, if weighted, the effective sample size. The survey response rate (and the assumptions underlying the response rate calculation) should also be reported, where possible.

4.11 Finally, information that allows the CMA to verify the professional credentials of the market research agency/agencies that have conducted the customer survey(s) on behalf of the Parties and/or their external advisors should be provided (ie the agency's name and website address).

DIVERSION RATIOS

4.12 The diversion ratio is a measure of the proportion of sales lost as a result of a deterioration of one merger Party's offering that is recaptured by the other merger Party. Note that it is also possible to calculate diversion ratios to third-party competitors, ie the proportion of lost sales that are captured by a particular third party.

4.13 The calculation of a diversion ratio from a survey is based on the responses to the suite of diversion questions (see 3.41ff). In principle, the diversion ratio (to the merger Party) is calculated from the following equation:

$$\{M+[D*(M/(M+T))]\}/(M+T+D+N)$$

Where:

M = Number that would divert to the merger Party

T = Number that would divert to a named third party

D = Number that would switch supplier, but DK which supplier

N = Number that would not purchase the product or service nor purchase an alternative instead.

4.14 The calculations for forced diversion questions follow the same principles as those for price diversion questions, but typically involve more sample as all customers are, in effect, 'forced' to state a diversion intention[35].

Part 3 CMA and other Guidelines

4.15 However, these calculations are rarely straightforward and a description of the main elements of the CMA's usual approach to making them is explained in the following section. These are not hard-and-fast rules and there is often a need to make sensible decisions about the treatment of particular combinations of response that arise in a survey.

Analysis units

4.16 The first thing that needs to be considered for the calculation is the units of analysis. In most merger situations, the unit that we are conceptually most interested in is the value of *sales in monetary terms*. The diversion ratio therefore becomes the value of sales that are diverted to the merger Party over the total value of lost sales. However, it is often difficult to achieve this and care should be exercised in attempting to do so.

4.17 If a survey is run from a customer list, weights can be derived sometimes from total sales recorded by the Parties. This information is often held where the customers are businesses and sales revenues are recorded for each customer.

4.18 If no such information is available, then questions can be asked in the survey about spend per visit and frequency of visit to establish the total sales value of the customer. The visit spend can be captured by asking the respondent how much they have just spent (this can be verified with the receipt if the respondent is unsure). Care is required though, as diversion questions work best if asked about the most recent purchase occasion, and if this was atypical – particularly if more than usual was spent – this can create a very inflated estimate of total spend over a wider period. Also, the implicit assumption with this approach is that diversion would be the same for every purchase visit, and does not vary by the products(s) or service(s) purchased, the time of purchase or any other factors.

4.19 Weighting by spend can also be problematic in its impact on effective sample size. This may be a reflection of the true situation, in which only a small proportion of a large number of customers accounts for a high proportion of sales, or it may be a feature that is exaggerated by frequency weighting, as described in the previous paragraph.

4.20 In some circumstances it may be appropriate to show results that are weighted by spend as well as unweighted by spend. They are both potentially informative and have different interpretations.

4.21 If the survey is an exit survey, the sample of customers is effectively weighted already by frequency of visit in that it is customer visits that are being sampled; the more frequently a particular customer visits an outlet, the more likely they are to be interviewed for the survey. In these situations, frequency weighting is inappropriate[36].

4.22 Note that sales value, or price, is not always very well-defined. For example, in casinos and betting shops the 'price' is not the amount staked because some of this is returned as winnings, and in pharmacies the amount paid by the customer for the prescription does not reflect the income that the pharmacy receives. This problem has arisen in a number of CMA cases in recent years, including casinos, betting shops, pharmacies and hospitals, and also in transport, cinemas, and magazines cases where season tickets, membership schemes and subscription packages respectively complicate the concept of price. In these circumstances it usually does not make sense to ask a price diversion question and it may not be possible or appropriate to weight by 'spend'.

Treatment of 'don't know' responses

4.23 'Don't know' responses need to be considered very carefully. A response of don't know to the main (first) diversion question usually means that the respondent is not asked any further questions relating to that hypothetical scenario[37] and the response is not informative for the purpose of the diversion ratio calculation. Therefore, it can be ignored for this purpose and should not be included in the denominator of the calculation.

4.24 However, if the customer answers that they would divert to another supplier but in a subsequent question says they do not know *which* supplier, then this answer is partially informative because they have stated that they would have diverted their expenditure rather than staying with the merger Party or exiting the market. In these circumstances, usual practice is to allocate 'don't know' responses in the same proportions as those who have explicitly named the retailer to which they would divert.

Diversion ratio – with or without own-party diversion

4.25 There may be cases where the customer could divert to another of the Party's outlets (eg in a cinema case where the customer says they would go to another cinema in the same Party's chain). In these cases it is possible to calculate two variants of the diversion ratio: (i) diversion ratio not allowing own-party diversion (as per the equation at paragraph 4.13); and (ii) diversion ratio allowing own-party diversion which is calculated from the following equation:

$$\{M+[D*(M/(O+M+T))]\}/(O+M+T+D+N)$$

Where:

O = Number that would divert to another product/service/outlet of the same party

M = Number that would divert to the merger Party

T = Number that would divert to a named third party

D = Number that would switch supplier, but DK which supplier

N = Number that would not purchase the product or service nor purchase an alternative instead.

4.26 The interpretation and appropriateness of the two conceptual bases for diversion ratios is a complicated topic discussed at length in section 5 of the CMA's Retail mergers commentary (2017).

4.27 Note that in some cases we have included additional diversion questions asked of customers that would divert to another outlet of the same Party, to enable more information to be used in the calculation of diversion behaviour. For example, in a cinema case we asked those who said they would have diverted to another cinema in the same Party's chain what they would have done if, at the time they decided to go to the film, they had known that tickets at *all* cinemas in that Party's chain had gone up in price (or (in the forced diversion question) had closed).

Split basket

4.28 The inclusion of split basket options usually complicates the diversion calculation considerably. A full analysis of diversion employing split basket responses can be very time-consuming and complex. A good analysis of diversion should incorporate the following:

(a) **Clarity about the units of analysis**. This is even more important when there is a split basket as the basket may be split by value or by the number of items in the basket (usually with the simplifying assumption that all items are of similar value).

(b) **A thorough understanding of the questionnaire and the way that it has been scripted**, including the different routes through the diversion questions. Is there any validation within the questions to ensure that all items/values are accounted for in the diversion responses? What if these controls are not in place and the responses are partial (eg a customer has bought five items, but only stated diversion alternatives for three of them), or more diversion is indicated than the purchases they relate to (diversion alternatives are stated for seven)?

(c) **Good documentation**. It can be difficult to keep track of the variety of respondent routes through/combinations of response to the diversion questions, and of all the decisions that need to be made at the analysis stage in order to interpret these combinations in the context of a diversion ratio calculation. It is good practice to be as systematic as possible in structuring the analysis and to document it carefully.

Treatment of imprecise or missing data

4.29 The sections above illustrate some of the issues faced in the calculation of diversion ratios, and provide guidance on how to tackle them. However, there may be other circumstances, such as having imprecise or missing data, where there is a certain amount of discretion in the calculation of the diversion ratio. In these situations, the CMA tries to be fair in calculating what it considers to be a central best estimate. For example, if a customer states (in response to a diversion question) that they would divert to "x OR y", we would assign weights of 0.5 to x and 0.5 to y. The important principle is to avoid the introduction of undue bias into the calculation resulting in, for example, a diversion ratio estimate which is the lowest variant of a range of possible estimates that could be derived from the survey dataset.

Sampling errors

4.30 One of the main advantages of random probability sampling methods is that they enable sampling error – a key element of uncertainty associated with survey results – to be calculated. A standard textbook can be used to look up the various different measures, but the literature can become very complex and does not strictly apply as the standard formulae assume complete response. In practice, the CMA tends to use the achieved sample (ie the number of respondents)[38] as the 'sample' (the 'n' in the textbooks) and apply some simplifying approximations to sampling error calculations.

4.31 This is particularly true in the case of diversion ratios which are often derived using complicated calculations. In the CMA, we usually base the sampling error calculation on a simplifying conceptualisation of the diversion ratio as the result of binary response – either the customer diverts or does not divert to the merger Party. So, for example, if the diversion ratio is calculated to be 26% and is based on the responses of 200 people, then we ignore the fact that some of the 26% will have been built up from split basket responses, partially informative responses, assumptions about the allocation of don't know responses and so on.

This simplification enables us to calculate a simple 95% confidence interval using the formula for the normal approximation of the binomial distribution for large populations. So, denoting n as the sample size, and d as the diversion ratio, the 95% confidence interval is given by:

$$d \pm 1.96\sqrt{\frac{d(1-d)}{n}}$$

39 40

4.32 When weights have been applied to the data, this will reduce the effective sample size and widen confidence intervals. A simple and practical calculation that approximates[41] the effect of this is provided by the Kish adjustment, where the effective sample size is given by:

$$\frac{(\sum w)^2}{\sum w^2}$$

where w's are the weights for each sample record.

4.33 The effective sample size should be substituted into the confidence interval calculation above instead of the "n".

Further analysis and presentation

4.34 The CMA often calculates diversion ratios to the merger Party and to main third-party competitors. This should be done at an appropriate level of disaggregation (eg outlet, specialism, brand, local area) although care should be taken with sample sizes (see 2.31ff for a discussion of minimum sample sizes). A diversion table might look something like the following example from a recent CMA merger inquiry [VTech/Leapfrog]:

Table 6: Parties' survey, TEL toys diversion ratios – not allowing own-party diversion

LeapFrog consumers		***VTech consumers %***	
Not bought anything	22	Not bought anything	24
LeapFrog	N/A	VTech	N/A
VTech	13	LeapFrog	8
Fisher Price	25	Fisher Price	23
TOMY	10	TOMY	4
Chad Valley	7	Chad Valley	3
Early Learning Centre	4	Early Learning Centre	21
Chicco	3	Chicco	1
Disney	2	Hasbro	3
Baby Annabell	2	Golden Bear	1
Play Doh	2	Play Doh	1
Lego	2	Lego	3
Xbox	2	Little Tikes	3
Mothercare	1	LadyBird	1
Bruin	1	Fingerprint	3
Total	100	Total	100

Source: CMA calculations using data from Parties' consumer survey of TEL toys.

Base: LeapFrog 144, VTech 203.

4.35 Sample sizes are sometimes sufficiently high to enable further detailed analysis of sub-populations and, in local markets, it is often informative to make use of the geography of markets, presenting diversion ratios in maps. One useful type is maps marking all the diversion alternatives in the area (eg cinemas) by Party and with diversion percentages marked beside them.

4.36 Generally, the CMA does not consider responses to price diversion questions to be fit for the purpose of estimating own price elasticities. In our view, this calculation requires a degree of accuracy that is particularly sensitive to the bias introduced by the hypothetical nature of the question. The price diversion question is an approximate way of distinguishing 'more marginal' from 'less marginal' customers. However, it is unlikely that survey respondents will be able to judge reliably the likelihood of diverting in response to the particular calibration of price increment given in the question.

TECHNICAL REPORTING

4.37 For any merger investigation survey, it is important to provide a written technical report that describes the key aspects of how the survey was undertaken. This will provide transparency of process to the CMA. Typically, the technical report should include a description, as applicable, of the:

(a) population of interest (and any exclusions), including sub-populations of interest and actual or estimated population and sub-population size;
(b) sample source;
(c) sampling approach used to generate a representative sample;

(d) interview method (eg telephone, face-to-face, online) and use of any incentives/reminders;
(e) piloting approach, and any notable adjustments made as a consequence;
(f) survey notification/invitation letter and questionnaire (appended to the technical report);
(g) fieldwork briefing and monitoring approach;
(h) survey fieldwork dates;
(i) response rates;
(j) data cleaning/editing approach (including coding); and
(k) data weighting.

QUALITY ASSESSMENT AND EVIDENTIAL WEIGHT

4.38 The CMA takes many aspects into account when assessing the evidential weight that can be given to survey results. It is difficult to be prescriptive about these aspects, but the following sets out what we typically consider:
(a) Coverage – under- or over-coverage of the survey sampling frame with respect to the target population;
(b) Fieldwork method and quality;
(c) Representativeness of the achieved sample, scope for sample bias and non-response bias;
(d) Questionnaire – question wording, relevance of the questions, any biases that might arise from the ordering or framing of questions;
(e) Dataset – quality, consistency and cleaning;
(f) Inappropriate or missing weighting or analysis;
(g) Response rates – unless there is evidence that the achieved sample is representative of the target population, the CMA is generally cautious about giving full evidential weight to surveys that achieve a response rate below 5%;
(h) Precision – similarly, the CMA is cautious about giving full evidential weight to analysis of sub-populations for which the achieved (effective) sample size is less than 100.

4.39 The nature of any perceived problems will affect our interpretation of survey results and the evidential weight that can be given to them. Under-coverage is usually the most benign problem in this respect. As long as the survey coverage is understood, and the survey sample is representative of the eligible population falling within that coverage, then survey results should be interpreted as only relating to that population.

4.40 Problems with the questionnaire may lead to less, or no, account being taken of the results of a particular question or questions. This may also be true of other problems that are limited to only part of the survey questionnaire.

4.41 Many problems that arise affect the quality of the whole survey and in these circumstances the CMA's assessment generally concludes one of the following:
(a) The survey is of high quality and fit for making robust inferences about the population(s) from which the survey sample has been taken.
(b) The survey is sufficiently problematic that population inferences cannot be considered to be robust and the weight given to the survey's findings should be limited accordingly. In these circumstances, decision-makers might look for supporting evidence from other sources in the case before regarding the survey results as being reliable.
(c) The survey is sufficiently flawed that it cannot be taken into account as evidence in the case.

4.42 Judgements about the interpretation and weight given to survey evidence are complex ones. Ultimately, they are made by decision-makers taking into account many aspects of the case, market context, assessment of the quality of the survey itself and how its findings sit against or alongside other available evidence.

NOTES

35 Examples of diversion ratio calculations are provided in section 5.

36 However, note that it is usual to interview a customer once only for a survey and so frequent visitors to a store may be slightly under-represented in the achieved sample.

37 If this is a price diversion question, they may be asked a subsequent forced diversion question.

38 Unless the data is weighted.

39 A further approximation and simple rule of thumb is that the 95% confidence interval is given by:

$$d \pm \frac{1}{\sqrt{n}}$$

This results in slightly wider intervals but this is not problematic as there are potential sources of non-sampling error that have not been taken into account.

40 Where d is close to 0 or 1, and/or the (effective) sample size is less than 30, the simple approximation does not work as well and a Wilson interval should be used instead. The 95% confidence interval is given by:

$$\frac{n}{n+3.84}\left[d+\frac{1.92}{n}\pm 1.96\sqrt{\left(\frac{1}{n}d(1-d)+\frac{0.96}{n^2}\right)}\right]$$

41 Departures from these assumptions tend to narrow the confidence intervals. However, as noted above, the use of the formula as it stands is not problematic, as there are other sources of error that have not been taken into account.

5. ILLUSTRATIONS

DISCUSSION OF SURVEY METHOD – CINEMA MERGER CASE STUDY

[3.434]

5.1 To illustrate the choices that may be available for a merger case we can consider the example of a cinema merger, setting out and assessing a range of possible ways of surveying customers. In recent cinema cases, the CMA (and the CC and OFT previously) have focused on assessing the likelihood of a substantial lessening of competition in local areas where each of the Parties owns one or more cinemas. Evidence such as the location and number of merger Party and third-party competitor cinemas has been used to make an initial assessment of those areas of competition risk. In such cases, a survey of customers of the Parties' cinemas in these risk areas has then been considered.

5.2 There are three principal methods of finding eligible cinema customers to survey: free-find; customer lists provided by the Parties; and intercepting customers at the cinema venues.

Free-find method

5.3 This would involve interviewing members of the adult general population and using the first (screening) questions in the survey to establish whether they had recently seen a film at one of the cinemas within scope and so are eligible to take part in the survey. It is likely that most adults approached would not be eligible and the survey would therefore need to be efficient at finding and eliminating the ineligible so that costs could be kept in check.

5.4 If we free-find people on the street, location and times of interview may have a big impact on the survey results, underlining the fact that this is not a controlled or scientific way of sampling and is unlikely to result in an achieved sample that is representative. A better alternative would be to employ interviewers to knock on doors for a sample of dwellings within a certain distance of the cinema. This could be supplemented by putting a paper self-completion questionnaire through the door if there is no answer (an example of a so-called mixed mode approach), although this may result in a biased sample due to a low response rate and respondent self-selection.

5.5 The standard free-find method for a telephone survey is to use random digit dialling (RDD). Historically, the performance of RDD surveys has been reasonably good, although the duel challenges of falling response rates and the declining use of landline telephones/increase in mobile-only households is making them less effective. Costs can be considerable and RDD surveys work best when the eligibility incidence rate among the general population is high, something that is unlikely to be the case in a cinema customer survey of this type.

5.6 The low incidence rate would also be a problem for free-finding eligible respondents via a face-to-face omnibus survey. Omnibus surveys have the advantage that respondents are recruited using methods rooted in random sampling. However, they generate large samples only at a national level and are not designed to be representative of/to allow robust analysis at a defined local level. Therefore, the CMA is most likely to consider an omnibus survey in cases where we are interested in results at a national level.

Customer lists

5.7 The Enterprise Act 2002 gives the CMA data gathering powers that enables it, subject to certain conditions being met, to require Parties to provide customer lists. It also has the legal powers to share this data with a market research agency for survey taking. Customer lists avoid the problem of coverage encountered in the free-find methods described above, and this is particularly true in markets where incidence rates are low. However, the feasibility of a client list approach is highly dependent on the range and quality of data held by the Parties about their customers.

5.8 We know from experience that this varies by cinema chain. In theory, surveys could be run using telephone numbers, email addresses or postal addresses, or a combination of them, from customer information held by the Parties. Coverage tends to be the issue; some cinema chains capture very little information about their customers, whereas others have extensive membership discount and marketing schemes that result in fairly comprehensive lists. However, even in these latter cases, there will be a proportion of customers (such as walk-in customers purchasing tickets at the box office) who will not be included.

5.9 An additional problem is that customer details might only be held for those customers who are on a 'global' membership list (such as Cineworld's Unlimited Scheme which acts like a season ticket, providing free access to films at any Cineworld cinema for the duration of the membership). Such a ticket is not tied to a specific venue in a chain and so it would be necessary to first ascertain whether the customer had recently visited one of the cinemas of interest. Postcodes could be used to construct a subset of customers that might be within the catchment area of one of the cinemas of interest, to reduce screening costs. The postcode area should not be too narrowly defined.

5.10 In our experience, we have found that some cinema chains have email addresses for a reasonably high proportion of their customer base enabling an internet-based survey approach.

Intercepting customers at cinemas

5.11 A direct way of finding the customers of cinemas of interest is for interviewers to go to bricks-and-mortar venues around the times that films are showing. They could then: (i) conduct a face-to-face interview with cinema-goers as they enter or leave the cinema; or (ii) collect follow-up contact details (postal, telephone and/or email) from cinema-goers for an interview at a later date; or (iii) give cinema-goers a self-completion questionnaire that could be filled in and returned either to the interviewer on the day or later by post to the agency. A combination of these methods could also be employed (eg a face-to-face interview is conducted if the respondent has time for it, but otherwise follow-up contact details are collected for a later interview).

5.12 This approach has the advantage of capturing a range of eligible customers, regardless of how they bought their tickets or whether their details are held on a customer list. However, the logistical difficulties of recruiting respondents as they enter or leave the cinema may be challenging, and it might be the case that responses are obtained from visits only for a limited number of screenings (eg by film type/target audience, day of the week, time of day, etc).

Methods used in recent merger cases

5.13 Looking at approaches used in cinema merger cases, there are three recent examples. In the Cineworld/City Screen phase 2 merger case, the Parties held quite comprehensive information about their customers, particularly email addresses. The Competition Commission (CC) undertook an online survey using these lists which had a good response, enabling detailed analysis of the findings for individual cinemas. However, recognising possible under-coverage, the CC sought to test the assumption that responses of customers on the Parties' lists were the same as those not on their lists (particularly with respect to diversion behaviour) by conducting an RDD telephone survey in two (Brighton and Bury St. Edmonds) of the 10 areas covered by the main survey. This helped validate the findings from the main online survey. The CMA has also run an online survey using customer lists provided by the Parties in (to date) two phase 1 cinema merger cases.

IMPORTANCE OF FACTORS THAT INFLUENCE CUSTOMER CHOICE OF SUPPLIER – HOSPITAL MERGER CASE STUDY

5.14 To understand which factors were important in patients electing to have a treatment at the surveyed hospital rather than another, the following two questions were asked: the first a spontaneous reasons for choice question, the second a prompted choice attribute question.

A1 Why did you decide to go to {Text insert eligible hospital} for the condition you were originally referred for, rather than go to another hospital? PROMPT: Why else? PROMPT UNTIL NO FURTHER RESPONSE

(1) Close to your home
(2) Easy to get to by public transport
(3) Parking at the hospital
(4) {GP/Dentist/Optometrist} recommendation
(5) Expertise of consultants and other healthcare professionals
(6) Treatment outcomes e.g. lower infection rates, higher recovery rates
(7) Availability of specialist medical equipment at the hospital
(8) Quality of nursing care
(9) Waiting times for appointments
(10) Good previous experience at this hospital
(11) Bad previous experience at another hospital
(12) Other (Write In)
(13) Don't know/can't remember

A2 I am going to read out a list of features. For each one I'd like you to tell me how important it was when choosing a hospital for the condition you were originally referred for. Please use one of the phrases on the following scale to describe your answer.

READ OUT SCALE

ESSENTIAL

VERY IMPORTANT

FAIRLY IMPORTANT

NOT IMPORTANT

DON'T KNOW (NOT ON SHOWCARD)

So, first of all (READ OUT FIRST STATEMENT). How important was that to you, was it . . . ? INTERVIEWER: READ OUT EACH STATEMENT IN TURN. READ OUT SCALE FOR FIRST THREE ATTRIBUTES ONLY.

NOTE TO SCRIPTWRITER: ROTATE ORDER BETWEEN INTERVIEWS

(1) How close the hospital is to your home
(2) Ease of getting to the hospital by public transport
(3) Parking at the hospital
(4) {GP/Dentist/Optometrist} recommendation
(5) Expertise of consultants and other healthcare professionals
(6) Treatment outcomes e.g. lower infection rates, higher recovery rates
(7) Availability of specialist medical equipment at the hospital
(8) Quality of nursing care
(9) Waiting times for appointments
(10) Good experience at the hospital

(11) Bad experience at another hospital

5.15 There are a number of points to note in this example.

(a) First, the order of questions: the reasons for choice question which requires a spontaneous response was asked before the prompted choice attribute question. This ensured that we captured spontaneous reasons first.

(b) Secondly, at question A1, patients were prompted to continue mentioning reasons until they could think of no other. With prompting in this way we hoped to tease out all the factors that were important. Although it was not done in this survey, it might have been advisable to capture the first mention separately from all other mentions so that the most 'top of mind' response could be identified. There was also an 'Other (write in)' code that could be used by interviewers to capture any factors not already pre-coded on the questionnaire.

(c) The question wording used in A1 asked for reasons for going to the surveyed hospital (for the elected treatment) *rather than to another hospital*. This wording attempted to focus patients' attention on their reasons for choosing between different suppliers, and so to help identify the factors that differentiated the suppliers' offering.

(d) Turning now to question A2, an unbalanced importance scale was used, as we wanted to identify those factors that were most important in the choice of hospital. At the analysis stage, we concentrated on the percentage of respondents saying each feature was either essential or very important. The whole scale was read out to respondents for the first three attributes, to ensure that patients gave one of the responses on the scale (and if necessary read out again for the other attributes if the interviewer felt this was necessary). The order in which the attributes were read out was automatically randomised between interviews in the CATI script.

5.16 The survey results demonstrated how the combination of questions helped identify what was important for the patient. When asked reasons for choice spontaneously, patients at one of the Party locations (St. Peters) most often said proximity to home, while for patients at the other Party location (Royal Surrey County) previous good experience at the hospital was as important as proximity to home. No other factors were considered important to any marked extent.

5.17 However, when patients were asked the prompted choice attribute question, the priority order changed. Top in importance was the expertise of the consultants and other healthcare professionals (for both hospitals) followed by the quality of nursing care, good previous experience at the hospital, the availability of specialist medical equipment, and treatment outcomes.

5.18 These findings on first inspection appeared contradictory, but can be explained. While many of the (prompted) attributes were considered to be important in choosing a hospital, they were not necessarily the things that differentiated hospitals in the local area. For example, a high proportion of respondents stated that consultant/healthcare professional expertise was essential, but presumably assumed that this expertise was available in all their local hospitals (ie was a hygiene factor).

DIVERSION QUESTIONS – EXAMPLES

Example 1: price diversion questions (Cineworld/City Screen phase 2 merger case)

5.19 These questions were asked of Cineworld customers. Note that this version of the questionnaire was the one used by the programmers (scriptwriters) in the market research agency who set up the online version of the questionnaire.

D2 Suppose you had known beforehand that tickets at all Cineworld cinemas had gone up by . . . (NOTE TO SCRIPTWRITER: INSERT AMOUNT FROM BELOW), and the price at all other cinemas had stayed the same. Would you have . . . ?

PLEASE TICK ONE ANSWER

NOTE TO SCRIPTWRITER: RANDOMISE PRECODE ORDER BETWEEN INTERVIEWS (BUT ALWAYS END WITH DK/NOT SURE)

(1) Chosen not to go to the cinema at all
(2) Gone to another cinema to see this or another film
(3) Still have seen the film at the same cinema
(4) Don't know/not sure

NOTE TO SCRIPTWRITER: INSERT PRICES AS FOLLOWS

London, Full-price ticket = 75p
London, Discounted ticket = 50p
Outside London, Full-price ticket = 50p
Outside London, Discounted ticket = 30p

NOTE TO SCRIPTWRITER: ASK D3 IF WOULD HAVE CHOSEN TO GO TO ANOTHER CINEMA (CODE 2 AT D2)

D3 Which other cinema would you have gone to instead?

PLEASE TICK ONE ANSWER

NOTE TO SCRIPTWRITER: RANDOMISE ORDER (EXCEPT "OTHER" AND "DK" AT END).

(1) SCRIPTWRITER TO INSERT LIST PROVIDED OF LOCAL CINEMAS
(2) Other cinema
(3) Don't know/not sure

NOTE TO SCRIPTWRITER: PRECODE LIST INCLUDES ANY OTHER CINEMA FROM SAME FASCIA IN THE LOCAL AREA, IF RELEVANT

5.20 There is much to note in this example, which shows the start of a suite of diversion questions included in an online survey of cinema customers contacted via email addresses provided by the Parties.

(a) First, it should be mentioned that the preceding section had asked questions about customers' last visit to the Cineworld cinema of interest including how they travelled to the cinema, whether they came alone/with others and which film they saw. Responses to these questions were of interest in their own right, but they also helped respondents to get into the mind-set of when they last visited the cinema. This clearly established the visit that was the basis of the hypothetical question asked at question D2.

(b) Question D2 is a good example of a price diversion question. The amount of the price rise was determined by the type of ticket the customer said they had purchased and did not require the respondent to make any calculations themselves (which would have been the case if the question had suggested, eg, a 5% price rise). The order of the list of responses seen by the customer was randomised for each respondent to avoid any ordering biases that might arise. The wording of the responses is clear and they are mutually exclusive responses, covering all possibilities.

(c) Note also the inclusion of a 'don't know' option for the customer at question D2. This is always important in diversion questions and in this case it might be argued that many customers were unlikely to be certain, when responding, about which films were showing at which cinemas and when the showings began (unless they had a clear memory of any research they may have done before deciding on the original visit). The provision of the 'don't know' option prevents the forcing of customers into responses that might undermine some of the validity of the diversion analysis.

(d) Question D2 was designed to deter customers from saying they would divert to another Cineworld cinema by saying that prices had gone up at *all* cinemas in the chain. This approach was adopted (in this case) because a number of the surveyed cinemas had another cinema in the same chain close by. The disadvantage of the wording above is that it was not informative about the extent of diversion between Cineworld cinemas. An alternative, valid wording of question D2 (using the example of customers of the Queens Link Cineworld in Aberdeen) would have been "Suppose you had known before that tickets at the Aberdeen Queens Link Cineworld had . . .". This approach has the opposite disadvantage in that many respondents to this question would have been likely to divert to the other Cineworld cinema in Aberdeen, which would not have been informative for calculating the version of a diversion ratio that excludes this as an option (ie excludes own-party diversion).

(e) Question D3 presented those respondents who at D2 said they would divert to another cinema with a list of the 12 closest other cinemas in the area (including those of the same fascia, where present). Twelve was considered to be the longest list practicable for an online survey and the CC decided to make the choice of cinemas included in the list as objective as possible by making it rule-based. This worked well in all locations except perhaps in London, where West End cinemas were not captured well by this approach.

5.21 Subsequent questions in this survey asked the forced diversion question.

Example 2: forced diversion questions (Ladbrokes/Coral phase 2 merger case)

Q9. Imagine that this Ladbrokes betting shop was closed for refurbishment for 6 months. Thinking of all the options open to you, what would you have done instead of visiting this betting shop today?

Gone to another betting shop

Placed bets or gambled online

Gone to another gaming venue (e.g. bingo hall, casino, arcade)

Saved money or spent it on something else

Don't know

If 'gone to another betting shop' at Q9:

Q10. Which other betting shop would you have gone to?

If gone to another Ladbrokes at Q10:

Q11. Now imagine that all Ladbrokes betting shops were closed for refurbishment for 6 months. What would you have done instead of visiting this betting shop today?

Gone to another betting shop

Placed bets or gambled online

Gone to another gaming venue (e.g. bingo hall, casino, arcade)

Saved money or spent it on something else

Don't know

If gone to another betting shop at Q11:

Q12. Which other betting shop would you have gone to?

5.22 This set of questions formed part of the questionnaire of a survey conducted by face-to-face interviewers in some Ladbrokes and Coral betting shops (the version above is the one that was used in Ladbrokes betting shops). Q9 takes care to say that the betting shop is *closed for six months*[42] rather than just closed. This avoids respondents saying that they would 'come back later' (so-called 'temporal substitution') or something similar, which would not be informative for our purposes.

5.23 Many of the Coral and Ladbrokes betting shops sampled had another betting shop of the same group in the local area giving rise to a lot of 'own-party diversion' (eg diversion from one Ladbrokes betting shop to another Ladbrokes betting shop). The sequence of questions in the example above shows how these respondents were subsequently asked a further question in which they would have to choose a different alternative (Q11). The advantage of this approach is that it enables a full sample of responses for calculating diversion ratios in two forms: one that allows for own-party diversion and another that does not. These measures are both potentially helpful in interpreting competition.

Example 3: example of a poor diversion question

Q: What would you be most likely to do if you wanted to place a bet or play a poker or casino game (e.g. roulette, blackjack, slots, etc.) and before leaving home you were told your usual LBO was temporarily closed for refurbishment?

5.24 An analysis of responses to this question was used in evidence submitted to the CMA as part of a merger case. The question was included in both a telephone and an online survey. It does not follow the usual structure of a diversion question in which a particular visit to one of the Parties' stores/outlets (in this case local betting offices – LBOs) is the premise of the question and the respondent is asked what they would do instead, if this option were not available. We do not know how many of the respondents to the Parties' telephone and online surveys would have visited one of the Parties' or any of the other fascia's LBOs to gamble in the first place, as this had not been established in this or previous survey questions.

5.25 The preceding questions provided no context to enable the respondent to be thinking about a visit to a LBO. In fact, the questions immediately before asked if retail gamblers expect to spend more or less on retail gambling and, if less, a prompted list of possible reasons why this is the case including many options, almost all of which mentioned 'online'. This may have made the respondents think of online alternatives more than they would have done otherwise, possibly influencing their answers to the diversion question.

DIVERSION RATIO CALCULATION – HYPOTHETICAL EXAMPLE

5.27 As discussed above, the calculation of a diversion ratio using responses to a suite of diversion questions can be quite complex. Here we show the calculation from a *hypothetical example* of a cinema merger between Party A and Party B, with the results of an exit survey of cinema goers at Cinema A owned by Party A.

Q1 Suppose you had known beforehand that tickets at this cinema had gone up by £1. Would you have . . . ?

Responses from a sample of 956 customers:

10	Not gone to the cinema or done anything else instead
736	Gone to the same cinema
120	Gone to another cinema instead
50	Done something else instead
40	Don't know

Q2 Which cinema would you have gone to instead?

Responses from the subset of 120 customers who said that they would have 'gone to another cinema instead'

18	Cinema B (the merger Party's cinema)
30	Cinema C (owned by third party C)
48	Cinema D (owned by third party D)
4	Cinema E (owned by third party E)
20	Don't know

5.28 In this case the diversion ratio would be calculated as follows:

Diversion to the merger Party	= 18+20*(18/(18+30+48+4))	= 21.6
Total lost sales	= 10+120+50	= 180
Diversion ratio	= 100*21.6/180	= 12%

5.29 This example involves simplifications, one of which is that it does not consider the situation where some diversion is to another cinema owned by cinema chain A. We can consider the effect of this by reviewing the calculations in the alternative scenario in which cinema C is owned by cinema chain A. We can now calculate two different versions of the diversion ratio:

Diversion ratio allowing own-party diversion (as before)

Diversion to the merger Party	= 18+20*(18/(18+30+48+4))	= 21.6
Total lost sales	= 10+120+50	= 180

Diversion ratio	= 100*21.6/180	= 12%
Diversion ratio not allowing own-party diversion		
Diversion to the merger Party	= 18+20*(18/(18+30+48+4))	= 21.6 (as before)
Sales lost from cinema chain A	= 10+120+50 – {30+20*30/(18+30+48+4)}	= 144
Diversion ratio	= 100*21.6/144	= 15%

NOTES

Editorial note: the original version of this document does not contain a paragraph 5.26.

42 An alternative is to say 'permanently' closed. This may be appropriate in markets where, for example, large infrequent purchases are made.

COMPETITION AND MARKETS AUTHORITY MERGER FEES INFORMATION (NOVEMBER 2018)

[3.435]

NOTES

This document is available on the Competition and Markets Authority website at: www.gov.uk/government/publications/merger-fees-payment-information.

Subject to some limited exceptions (see below), all mergers that qualify for reference for a phase 2 investigation are subject to a fee, irrespective of whether a reference for a phase 2 investigation is made. The fee is collected by the Competition and Markets Authority (CMA) on behalf of HM Treasury.

For mergers which involve the acquisition of a controlling interest, the fee becomes payable on the announcement of the CMA's decision (or the Secretary of State's decision in public interest cases) whether or not to refer the merger for a phase 2 investigation. The CMA's practice is to send an invoice to the merger parties after the decision on reference has been announced. Payment must be made within 30 days of the date of the invoice.

Merger fees are also discussed at Chapter 20 of *Mergers: Guidance on the CMA's jurisdiction and procedure* (CMA2, January 2014), and, in respect of mergers between water enterprises, paragraphs 2.17–19 of *Water and sewerage mergers: Guidance on the CMA's procedure and assessment* (CMA49, 13 November 2015).[1]

LEVEL OF MERGER FEES

Fees vary according to the value of the UK turnover of the acquired enterprise(s) in the business year preceding the date of completion of the merger (for completed mergers) or the date of the CMA's (or the Secretary of State's) decision on reference (for anticipated mergers), or an earlier business year if the CMA (or Secretary of State) considers this appropriate. The following fees will apply:[2]

Fee	Charge Band
£40,000	Value of the UK turnover of the enterprises being acquired is £20 million or less
£80,000	Value of the UK turnover of the enterprises being acquired is over £20 million but not over £70 million
£120,000	Value of the UK turnover of the enterprises being acquired exceeds £70 million, but does not exceed £120 million
£160,000	Value of the UK turnover of the enterprises being acquired exceeds £120 million

CIRCUMSTANCES IN WHICH A MERGER FEE IS NOT PAYABLE

A merger fee is not payable if the merger involves the acquisition of an interest that is less than a controlling interest and the CMA investigated the acquisition on its own initiative.[3] This exception does not apply if the merger parties notified such an acquisition by submitting a merger notice.

Further, an acquirer is exempt from paying a merger fee if, in its most recent financial year before the time the fee would become payable, it meets the criteria for small or medium-sized enterprises, as defined by reference to certain provisions in the Companies Act 2006.[4] For financial years beginning on or after 1 January 2016 and, if the directors of the acquirer so decided, financial years beginning on or after 1 January 2015, the acquirer qualifies as small or medium-sized if it, or the group of which it is a member (as defined in section 474 of the Companies Act 2006), satisfies at least two of the following three criteria in its most recent financial year:[5]

Part 3 CMA and other Guidelines

	Turnover	Balance sheet total (aggregate amount of assets)	Number of employees
Small company	£10.2 million	£5.1 million	50
Small group	£10.2 million net (or £12.2 million gross)	£5.1 million net (or £6.1 million gross)	50
Medium-sized company	£36 million	£18 million	250
Medium-sized group	£36 million net (or £43.2 million gross)	£18 million net (or £21.6 million gross)	250

If the acquirer's directors did not decide to apply these criteria to the acquirer's financial year between 1 January 2015 and 1 January 2016, the acquirer qualifies as small or medium-sized if it, or the group of which it is a member (as defined in section 474 of the Companies Act 2006), satisfies at least two of the following three criteria in its most recent financial year:[6]

	Turnover	Balance sheet total (aggregate amount of assets)	Number of employees
Small company	£6.5 million	£3.26 million	50
Small group	£6.5 million net (or £7.8 million gross)	£3.26 million net (or £3.9 million gross)	50
Medium-sized company	£25.9 million	£12.9 million	250
Medium-sized group	£25.9 million net (or £31.1 million gross)	£12.9 million net (or £15.5 million gross)	250

PAYMENT OF MERGER FEES

Fees may either be paid by banker's draft, or cheque, payable to the Competition and Markets Authority and crossed 'AC Payee Only', or by Bankers Automated Clearing Systems (BACS) or Clearing House Automated Payments Systems (CHAPS). The fee must be paid in sterling. If payment is made by an electronic transfer the amount of payment received must be net of any service, transfer or wiring fees charged by any bank or financial institution.

Please use the following information if paying by BACS or CHAPS.

National Westminster Bank (NatWest)

Sort Code: 60-70-80

Account Number: 10018220

Account Name: CMA TRUST ACCOUNT

IBAN Number: GB97NWBK60708010018220

BIC/SWIFT Code: NWBKGB2L

Bank Address:

NatWest, Government Banking Service Branch,

2nd Floor, 280 Bishopsgate,

London

EC2M 4RB

Any cheque sent as payment should be accompanied by the payment slip at the end of the fees request letter. The BACS or CHAPS payment should contain the acquirer's name.

Please send an email giving the acquirer's name, the CMA's file reference and invoice number, if applicable, and the CHAPS / BACS reference number to MergerSupportTeam@cma.gsi.gov.uk so that the transfer can be matched to the relevant case.

NOTES

1 In respect of water mergers, see article 3(d) of the Enterprise Act 2002 (Merger Fees and Determination of Turnover) Order 2003 SI 2003/1370 (the 'Merger Fees Order'), as amended most recently by regulations 23 and 24 of the Water Mergers (Miscellaneous Amendments) Regulations 2015 SI 2015/1936.

2 Article 5 of the Merger Fees Order. The value of the UK turnover may be adjusted where, since the end of the preceding business year, the enterprises being acquired have been involved in an acquisition or divestment, or another relevant transaction or event has occurred (article (11(3) of the Merger Fees Order).

3 Article 4(1) and (3) of the Merger Fees Order. See Chapter 4 (in particular paragraph 4.30) of *Mergers: Guidance on the CMA's jurisdiction and procedure* for an explanation of the term 'controlling interest'.

4 Article 7 of the Merger Fees Order.

5 Sections 382(3) to (6), 383(4) to (7), 465(3) and 466(4) of the Companies Act 2006, as amended by Regulations 4 and

9 of the Companies, Partnerships and Groups (Accounts and Reports) Regulations 2015 SI 2015/980. These Regulations apply in respect of financial years beginning on or after 1 January 2016, but the directors of a company may instead decide to apply this aspect of the amended law to the company's financial year beginning on or after 1 January 2015 (but before 1 January 2016) (Regulation 2(2)).

6 Sections 382(3) to (6), 383(4) to (7), 465(3) and 466(4) of the Companies Act 2006 as applicable prior to the amendment of these sections by the Companies, Partnerships and Groups (Accounts and Reports) Regulations 2015 SI 2015/980.

MERGERS: EXCEPTIONS TO THE DUTY TO REFER (CMA64, DECEMBER 2018)

[3.436]

NOTES

INTRODUCTION - EXCEPTIONS TO THE DUTY TO REFER

[3.437]

1. If the Competition and Markets Authority (CMA) believes that it may be the case that a relevant merger situation may lead to a substantial lessening of competition (SLC), then it is under a duty to refer the merger for in-depth (phase 2) investigation.[1]

2. However, in certain circumstances the CMA has a discretion not to make a reference despite the fact that there is a realistic prospect that the merger will lead to a SLC in a market or markets in the United Kingdom.[2] These are:

- when the markets concerned are not of sufficient importance to justify a reference;
- in the case of anticipated mergers, when the arrangements concerned are insufficiently far advanced, or insufficiently likely to proceed, to justify a reference; or
- when any relevant customer benefits arising from the merger outweigh the SLC concerned and any adverse effects of the SLC concerned.

3. Each of these exceptions to the duty to refer is considered in further detail below.

4. This guidance forms part of the advice and information published by the CMA under section 106 of the Act. It should be read alongside Mergers: Guidance on the CMA's jurisdiction and procedure (CMA2) and the Office of Fair Trading (OFT)/Competition Commission (CC) publication Merger Assessment Guidelines (CC2/OFT1254).

5. This guidance updates and replaces Mergers: Exception to the duty to refer in markets of insufficient importance (CMA64); and Chapters 1, 3 and 4 of Mergers: Exceptions to the duty to refer and undertakings in lieu of reference guidance (OFT1122).

6. This guidance sets out the CMA's current practice (and intended future practice) but may be revised from time to time. Where there is any difference in emphasis or detail between this guidance and other guidance produced by the CMA, the most recently published guidance takes precedence.

NOTES

1 Sections 22(1) and 33(1) of the Enterprise Act 2002 (the Act).

2 Sections 22(2) and 33(2) of the Act.

MARKETS OF INSUFFICIENT IMPORTANCE ('DE MINIMIS')

INTRODUCTION

[3.438]

7. Under sections 22(2)(a) and 33(2)(a) of the Act the CMA may decide not to refer a merger for an in-depth 'phase 2' investigation if it believes that the market(s) to which the duty to refer applies is/are not of sufficient importance to justify a reference. This exception is designed to avoid references being made where the costs involved would be disproportionate to the importance of the market(s) concerned.

8. The CMA considers that the market(s) concerned will *generally* be of sufficient importance to justify a reference (such that the exception will not be applied) where the annual value in the UK, in aggregate, of the market(s) concerned is more than £15 million. The way this figure is calculated is explained at paragraph 36.

9. By contrast, where the annual value in the UK of the market(s) concerned is, in aggregate, less than £5 million, the CMA will *generally* not consider a reference justified unless a clear-cut undertaking in lieu of reference is in principle available.

10. Where the annual value in the UK, in aggregate, of the market(s) concerned is between £5 million and £15 million, the CMA will consider whether the expected customer harm resulting from the merger is materially greater than the average public cost of a phase 2 reference (currently around £400,000).

11. The CMA will base its assessment of expected customer harm on: the size of the market concerned; its view of the likelihood that a SLC will occur; its assessment of the magnitude of any competition that would be lost; and its expectation of the duration of that SLC.

12. The CMA will also take account of the wider implications of its decisions in this area, and will be less likely to exercise its discretion, and therefore more likely to refer, where the merger is one of a potentially large number of similar mergers that could be replicated across the sector in question.

13. Although the CMA considers that the primary purpose of the de minimis exception is to avoid disproportionate public expense following a finding that a merger gives rise to the realistic prospect of a SLC, the CMA also sets out at the end of this chapter a number of ways in which it may use the de minimis exception to reduce the burden of merger control at earlier stages of review (see paragraphs 51 to 60 below).

ADOPTION OF A BROAD COST/BENEFIT ANALYSIS FOR 'DE MINIMIS'

14. The primary purpose of the de minimis exception is to avoid references being made where the costs involved would be disproportionate to the importance of the market(s) concerned. The Act does not specify what criteria the CMA should consider in exercising this discretion, but leaves the matter to the judgment and expertise of the CMA.

15. The CMA applies the discretion with regard to a broad cost/benefit analysis. That is, the CMA takes the view that it is proportionate – and therefore justifiable – to refer a merger where the CMA considers that the benefits of that reference, in terms of preventing or remedying the customer harm that would otherwise result from the merger,, materially exceed the public costs of the reference.

16. When considering the cost of a reference, the CMA considers it appropriate to take account only of the public costs (ie the costs to the CMA) of a phase 2 reference, and not those costs that might be incurred by the parties.

17. The average public cost of a phase 2 reference is, at present around £400,000. The CMA therefore considers whether, in broad terms, the benefit of a reference in terms of the potential customer harm saved (taking account of the fact that not all references result in an anti-competitive finding) is materially greater than £400,000.

18. The expected customer harm that directly results from the individual merger under consideration will be a function of a number of factors: the size of the market, the likelihood that the SLC will actually occur (paragraph 37 below), the magnitude of competition that would be lost by the merger (paragraph 40below), and the duration of the SLC (paragraph 44 below). Prevention or remedy of an anti-competitive merger by the CMA at phase 2 would therefore avoid this harm. The CMA will also have regard to the wider implications for future cases of any decision that it takes to exercise its de minimis discretion.

GUIDELINES ON THE AVAILABILITY OF 'DE MINIMIS': APPLICABLE THRESHOLDS

19. The CMA takes into account a range of factors (discussed in this guidance) in using its judgment as to whether or not to exercise its discretion in a particular case. However, recognising the value of predictability, the CMA has sought to provide guidance on when the exception will generally not apply, and when it would be more likely to apply.

20. By way of upper threshold, the CMA considers that the market(s) concerned will generally be of sufficient importance to justify a reference (such that the exception will not generally be applied) where the annual value in the UK of the markets concerned is more than £15 million in aggregate. This is because the benefits of a phase 2 reference would be expected to outweigh the public costs where the market(s) concerned have an aggregated turnover above £15million.

21. Conversely, the CMA considers that where the annual value in the UK of the market(s) concerned is, in aggregate, less than £5 million (and where the CMA considers there are no clear-cut undertakings in lieu in principle available – see paragraph 27) a reference to phase 2 will generally not be justified.[3] The CMA would expect to refer a merger where the value of the market(s) concerned was less than £5 million only exceptionally, and where the direct impact of the merger in terms of customer harm was particularly significant and/or where the merger is one of a potentially large number of similar mergers that could be replicated across the sector in question (see paragraphs 46 and following below). Application of the cost/benefit analysis

22. In all cases where the value of the market(s) concerned is below £15 million, the CMA will consider whether a reference, overall, would be proportionate on the basis of a broad cost/benefit analysis.[4]

23. In making this assessment, the CMA will typically consider three issues:

- First, whether undertakings in lieu could in principle be offered by the merging parties to remedy in a clear-cut way any SLC concerns created by the merger.
- Second, whether the customer harm potentially resulting from the actual merger under investigation is likely materially to exceed the costs of a reference, taking account: the size of the market, the likelihood that the SLC will actually occur, the magnitude of competition that would be lost by the merger, and the duration of the SLC.
- Third, whether a reference would be proportionate when account is taken of the wider implications of the decision in question.

These three considerations are each discussed below.

24. Whilst the CMA believes that it is informative to consider the potential scale of customer harm that could result from the merger – and which would be prevented by a reference – the CMA is aware that the costs and benefits associated with merger references are inherently difficult to estimate accurately in advance. For this reason, although seeking broadly to estimate the customer harm that would be expected to result from a merger may be useful directionally, this cost/benefit assessment is ultimately a judgment for the CMA to make in a particular case depending on the relevant facts and circumstances.

INTERACTION BETWEEN 'DE MINIMIS' AND POTENTIAL UNDERTAKINGS IN LIEU OF REFERENCE[5]

25. This section explains how the CMA's exercise of its de minimis discretion is affected by its ability to accept undertakings in lieu of reference to phase 2.

Legislative framework

26. Sections 22 and 33 of the Act require the CMA to consider as a first question whether it is under a duty to make a reference to phase 2. If it is, the CMA must then decide whether to apply certain exceptions to the duty to refer, including the de minimis discretion. Only where it decides not to apply any available exception (such that it would otherwise actually make a reference), the CMA may alternatively accept undertakings in lieu of reference offered by the parties under section 73(2) of the Act.

27. Although the Act is clear on the sequence of questions that the CMA must ask itself, the Act leaves open to the CMA the considerations it may take into account in exercising its de minimis discretion. Consequently, it is open to the CMA, when exercising its de minimis discretion, to have regard to all relevant considerations, including whether the potential customer harm in the case in question could be avoided, without the need for a reference, by the provision of clear-cut undertakings in lieu.

Proportionality of a reference where undertakings in lieu of reference are in principle available

28. The CMA's general policy is not to apply the de minimis exception where clear-cut undertakings in lieu of reference could be offered by the parties to resolve the competition concerns identified, for the following reasons:

- The aim of the de minimis exception is to avoid the cost of a reference where this is not proportionate to the harm identified. Undertakings in lieu of reference avoid the risk of customer harm identified by the CMA – yet at the same time avoid in full the costs of a reference.
- Even where the market(s) concerned is/are small in size, parties should remain in centivised to offer clear-cut undertakings in lieu to remedy concerns or to design their transactions so as to avoid anti-competitive effects (sometimes known as a 'fix it first' approach).
- The costs of a reference in an individual case[6] are outweighed by the long-run, aggregated benefit of remedial action in similar cases at the phase 2 stage.
- In any given case where the prospect of a reference arises, it is ultimately for the parties to decide whether to offer undertakings in lieu or to pursue their case in phase 2. The CMA cannot impose a first-phase remedy via order (as it can in appropriate phase 2 cases) and the CMA's approach as to whether or not to apply the de minimis exception does not remove the parties' choice as to whether to offer undertakings in lieu.

CMA's assessment of when undertakings in lieu are in principle available

29. The CMA's judgment as to whether undertakings in lieu are available (at the time of considering the de minimis exception) is an 'in principle' one that does not depend on the actual offer, if any, of undertakings in lieu (or indeed whether the CMA believes they are likely to be offered). The actual offer of undertakings in lieu is a separate question relevant only to the subsequent exercise of the CMA's ability to accept undertakings under section 73(2) of the Act and is not relevant at this stage of the CMA's consideration.

30. In practical terms, therefore, the CMA will consider whether the de minimis exception should be applied before any consideration is given to whether or not the parties have in fact offered undertakings in lieu of reference to phase 2.[7]

31. Cases that the CMA considers are in principle suitable for resolution by undertakings in lieu are typically those where the part of the transaction that raises concerns can be divested to an independent third-party purchaser. The de minimis exception is therefore unlikely to be applied to this type of case.

32. By contrast, the CMA will not consider that undertakings in lieu are in principle available where the CMA's competition concerns relate to such an integral part of a transaction that to remedy them via a structural divestment would be tantamount to prohibiting the merger altogether.[8]

33. Nor will the CMA consider for these purposes that undertakings in lieu are in principle available where the minimum structural divestment that would be required to ensure the remedy was effective would be wholly disproportionate in relation to the concerns identified.[9] It is not the role of the undertakings in lieu process effectively to invite parties to abandon their own transactions. On the contrary, the logic of first-phase remedies is to resolve competition concerns clearly whilst allowing the transaction, albeit in modified form, to proceed.[10]

34. The CMA will take a conservative approach to assessing whether undertakings in lieu are in principle available. To the extent that there is any doubt as to whether undertakings in lieu would meet the 'clear-cut' standard, it will not be included in the 'in principle' assessment.[11] In other words, it must be clear that the competition concerns in the case in question are obviously such as to make the case a candidate for resolution by undertakings in lieu.[12]

ASSESSMENT OF THE EXPECTED CUSTOMER HARM FROM THE MERGER

35. Where the annual value in the UK of the market(s) concerned is in aggregate less than £15 million, and the CMA concludes that clear-cut undertakings in lieu of reference are not in principle available, it will consider whether the merger impact is expected materially to outweigh the public costs of a reference. In assessing the customer harm of an individual merger, the CMA will generally pay close attention to the interaction of four key variables:

- the size of the market;
- the likelihood that the SLC will actually occur;
- the magnitude of competition lost by the merger; and
- the duration of the SLC.

36. The fact that one of these factors may point towards or against exercise of the discretion should not be regarded as decisive in any individual case. The CMA considers these factors in the round as part of its overall assessment of whether the expected impact of the merger in terms of customer harm is likely to materially exceed the public costs of a reference.

Size of the market

37. In line with the wording of the Act, the starting point for the CMA's considerations is the size of the market(s) concerned.[13] For the purposes of applying the de minimis exception, the market concerned is the affected market.[14] The smaller the size of the market(s) concerned, the more likely it is that the CMA will apply the 'de minimis' exception (in any event the market(s) will be expected to fall within the £15 million threshold[15]). The CMA applies the following principles in determining the size of the market:

- Only markets in relation to which the CMA concludes there is a realistic prospect of a SLC qualify as 'markets concerned'.[16]
- The size of the market concerned is the sum of all suppliers' annual turnover in the UK in that market (and not solely the annual turnover of the parties).
- Where the test for reference is met in multiple markets, the relevant figure will be the aggregate size of all such markets.
- If the geographic scope of any market concerned is wider than the UK, turnover generated outside the UK will not be taken into account.[17]
- The CMA considers that, when considering market size for these purposes, it should not view the market statically, but should take into account any factors which indicate that the market size may be significantly expanding or contracting in the foreseeable future.[18]
- As a general statement, in lumpy markets,[19] the CMA considers it artificial to consider the value of contracts for one particular year only as the market size, as this may inflate or underestimate the true annual value of the overall market. In such circumstances, the CMA is likely to err on the side of caution in determining the annual size of the market and obtain a more representative figure by considering the annual value over a number of years.[20]

CMA's belief regarding the likelihood of a SLC

38. The CMA will take into account the strength of its belief regarding the likelihood that the merger will have an anti-competitive effect when deciding whether to exercise the de minimis exception. As the Court of Appeal ruled in IBA Health,[21] the CMA's duty to refer can in principle be triggered by a belief as the likelihood of a SLC that may be no higher than 'more than fanciful' atone end of the spectrum but may alternatively extend to, at the other extreme, a very high degree of confidence.

39. The CMA considers it appropriate to attach weight to the belief it holds regarding the likelihood of a SLC. This is because customers in the relevant market will receive no direct benefit if a benign merger is subject to in-depth scrutiny and is then cleared, a scenario which becomes increasingly likely the lower the likelihood that a SLC will occur.

40. In a number of cases in which the CMA has applied the de minimis exception to date, the CMA therefore attached weight to the fact that its belief as to the likelihood was merely on the 'may be the case' standard, rather than on the 'is the case' (more likely than not) standard.[22]

Magnitude of competition lost by the merger

41. In all cases in which the CMA has concluded that its duty to refer is met, it follows that it must believe that any lessening of competition is potentially 'substantial' in scale. However, above this threshold, the magnitude of the CMA's substantive competition concerns will vary between different cases.

42. The CMA's assessment of the magnitude of competition that could be lost by the merger essentially acts as a proxy for the extent of the price effect (for example, whether the merger could lead to a 5, 15 or 30% price increase) or equivalent non-price effect.[23] Where there are factors that would directly constrain any price increase in the market (even if insufficient to prevent a realistic prospect of a SLC from arising at all) these will be relevant in this context.[24]

43. By way of general illustration, where the CMA considers each merging party to be the only significant competitor to the other (a 'two to one' merger) or one of only two (a 'three to two' merger), the merger would typically be expected to lead (absent countervailing competitive constraints) to large price increases and/or quality or innovation cutbacks.

44. In considering the magnitude of competition concerns that could result from a merger, the CMA will take account of evidence of coordination between competitors (including hard-core breaches of Chapter I of the Competition Act 1998) in one or more of the markets in question and whether the merger may increase the impact of any such coordination. In addition, when considering the magnitude of competition lost by the merger, the CMA will have regard to whether a substantial proportion of the likely detriment would be suffered by vulnerable customers.

Durability of the merger's impact

45. The CMA will consider the likely durability of the merger effect as part of its assessment of the overall impact of the merger on the market in question.

46. The CMA may consider whether any barriers to entry into the market are substantial and durable. For example, the CMA may not be sufficiently confident that entry would be timely, likely and sufficient such as to prevent competition concerns from arising in the first place,[25] but may believe that barriers to entry are such that effective new entry is likely ultimately to occur.[26] Equally, the CMA may consider that the durability of a merger's impact will be limited because technological or market transformation will render merger effects relatively short-lived.[27]

Consideration of the wider implications of a 'de minimis' decision

47. The CMA believes that it is appropriate for it to take account of the wider implications of any decision that it takes to exercise its de minimis discretion for its treatment of future cases.

Replicability of merger and 'de minimis' decisions

48. The CMA will be less likely to apply the 'de minimis' discretion where it believes that the merger is one of a potentially large number of similar mergers that could be replicated across the sector in question.

49. Research for the OFT by Deloitte in 2007[28] clearly confirms the view that individual merger decisions (as well as the existence of the mergers regime as a whole) can have a significant impact in the relevant sector by determining whether future anti-competitive transactions are pursued.

50. Consistency of treatment requires that the application of the de minimis discretion by the CMA in one case should mean that the discretion is also applied to an analogous future case in the same sector where competitive conditions are comparable. Where the merger is one of a potentially large number of similar mergers that could be replicated across the sector in question, the CMA's de minimis decision could be 'replicable' also. This could mean that the exercise of the CMA's discretion in one case could cumulatively lead to aggregate customer harm far in excess of the costs of referring the individual problematic merger at hand.

Economic rationale

51. In considering the wider implications of a particular decision whether to exercise the de minimis discretion, the CMA may also have regard to the economic rationale behind an individual transaction.[29] In particular, the CMA will be less likely to apply the de minimis discretion where there is evidence that the merger in question is solely or primarily motivated by the acquisition of market power.[30] For example, a firm decides to acquire its only competitor active in one or more small local markets for the principal purpose of eliminating competition and reaping monopoly profits post-merger. The CMA will take into account factors such as whether the market in question is developing rapidly or has the potential to do so. Where the merger may have the effect of stifling nascent competition in such a market a reference may be appropriate even if the market size is very small.

USE OF THE 'DE MINIMIS' EXCEPTION TO REDUCE THE COSTS OF FIRST-PHASE REVIEW

52. The CMA considers that the primary aim of the de minimis discretion is to avoid the public cost of a phase 2 investigation where the market(s) concerned is/are not of sufficient importance to justify the making of a reference. However, the CMA is also mindful of the value of reducing the overall costs of first-phase review where this is possible without compromising the performance of the CMA's duties under the Act and/or the rights of private parties (merging parties and third parties).

53. The CMA considers that the availability of the de minimis discretion can, in some circumstances, also serve to eliminate, or reduce, the costs of a first-phase review in three ways:

- First, by the CMA taking into account the existence and operation of the discretion when deciding whether to send an enquiry letter.
- Second, through the provision of informal advice on the application of the discretion.
- Third, through consideration of whether the discretion is applicable in suitable cases at an early stage of the CMA's review.

These three measures are discussed below.[31]

Consideration of 'de minimis' when sending enquiry letters

54. The CMA will have regard to the potential applicability of its de minimis discretion in deciding whether or not to send an enquiry letter to trigger an own-initiative investigation.[32]

55. Where the CMA is confident on the basis of available information that any market(s) potentially concerned by a merger would be of insufficient importance to justify a reference, regardless of the magnitude, likelihood or duration of any SLC caused by the merger, and taking into account any wider effects of a decision whether or not to apply the de minimis exception to such a merger, then the CMA is likely to conclude that there is no sensible justification for it to call the case in for a first-phase review.

In practical terms, for the CMA to be confident this is the case, it would generally need to be very clear that the annual value of any market(s) potentially concerned would be below £5 million and that there would not be any clear-cut undertakings in lieu of reference available if the duty to refer were to be met.

56. This consideration does not eliminate the possibility of the CMA investigating a case of its own initiative and ultimately deciding to apply the de minimis discretion to it. As is clear from the discussion in paragraphs 22 and following above, whether to apply the de minimis discretion will – in markets of less than £15 million – often turn on factors that become clear only after an investigation by the CMA.

Availability of informal advice on 'de minimis'

57. The CMA (via the Mergers Group) will offer informal advice on the potential application of the de minimis exception, subject to the caveats generally applicable to such advice.[33]

58. Of particular relevance in the context of de minimis is the fact that the CMA relaxes its normal requirement that the request for informal advice relates to a transaction that raises a genuine issue as to referral where the party seeking informal advice is a private enterprise that is unable to afford external competition law advice.[34]

Consideration of de minimis at an early stage by the CMA

59. When a merger is notified to the CMA, either voluntarily by the parties or following receipt of an enquiry letter from the CMA, the CMA will consider at an early stage of its investigation whether the case is a candidate for application of the de minimis discretion. Indeed, where appropriate, the CMA will engage with parties during any pre-notification phase on what information might be helpful in following the CMA to assess whether a merger is appropriate for application of the de minimis exception.

60. In cases where it becomes clear to the CMA during its investigation that the market(s) concerned is/are of insufficient importance to justify a reference to phase 2, and that there would not be any clear-cut undertakings in lieu of reference available if the duty to refer were met, then the CMA is likely to move towards a decision not to refer on the basis of the de minimis exception.

61. This will include scenarios where it would obviously be quicker and more efficient to determine that the discretion would be applied than it would be for the CMA to reach the requisite level of belief that the transaction in question does not in fact trigger the duty to refer (that is, that it should be unconditionally cleared). In such circumstances, the CMA would discuss with the parties whether they would be willing to waive their procedural rights to a full investigation[35] (including an issues letter and issues meeting) to the extent that the CMA is minded to apply the de minimis discretion.[36] In such cases, the CMA would generally leave open the question of whether its duty to refer is met on the basis that its conclusion is that the merger should not be referred to phase 2, either because the duty to refer is not met or because, even if the duty to refer is met, then the discretion would be applied.[37]

NOTES

3 It is not possible, given the cost/benefit approach the CMA adopts, to identify a 'safe harbour' in terms of market size below which the de minimis exception will always be applied. Furthermore, providing a firm 'safe harbour' threshold risks being inconsistent with the CMA's proper exercise of its discretion in the light of the facts and circumstances of each case.

4 For examples of the application of the exception of the duty to refer see Universal Sealants (U.K.) Limited/ Ekspan Holdings Limited (23 March 2018); Integra LifeSciences Holdings Corporation/ Codman neurosurgery business (3 August 2017); GLO Dutch Bidco/ Mallinckrodt Nuclear Medicine and Mallinckrodt Netherlands Holdings (26 June 2017); IKO plc/ Pure Asphalt Company Limited (25 August 2016); DX Network Services Limited/ the businesses and assets of The Legal Post (Scotland) Limited and First Post Limited (21 October 2016); Kaplan International Holdings Limited/ Osborne Books Limited (9 February 2016); First TransPennine Express Limited/ TransPennine Express franchise (14 March 2016); Sheffield City Taxis Limited/ certain assets and business of Mercury Taxis (Sheffield) Limited (13 October 2015); Tattersalls Limited/ bloodstock auctioneering business of Brightwells Limited (15 September 2015); Key Publishing Limited/ certain assets of Kelsey Publishing Limited (2 March 2015); Xchanging Holdings Limited/ Total Objects Limited (9 December 2014); WGSN Inc. of Stylesight Inc (25 June 2014); Phonak AG of Comfort Audio I Halmstad AB (17 September 2014); and Diamond Bus Company Limited/ the bus business of Firstgroup plc in Redditch and Kidderminster (23 August 2013).

Examples of cases in which the CMA considered the exception but decided not to apply it include Nielsen Holdings PLC/ the AdIntel division of Ebiquity PLC (13 June 2018); Vanilla Group Limited (JLA)/ Washstation Limited (27 April 2018); Capita plc/ the one-way wide-area paging services business of Vodafone (30 May 2017); Reckitt Benckiser/ the K-Y brand (19 December 2014); Alliance Medical Limited/ the assets of IBA Molecular UK Limited used to manufacture Fluorodeoxyglucose 18f (24 March 2014).

5 See Dunfermline Press Limited/ the Berkshire regional newspapers business of Trinity Mirror plc (4 February 2008).

6 That is, in any given case where the CMA considers that undertakings in lieu of reference are 'in principle' available (such that the de minimis exception is not applied) but are not in fact offered by the parties (such that a reference actually follows and the public costs of a reference are incurred).

7 See CMA2, paragraphs 7.46 & 8.2.

8 See BOC Limited/ the packaged chlorine business and assets carried on by Ineos Chlor Limited (29 May 2008), paragraph 111; Idox plc/ Grantfinder Limited (2 September 2010), paragraph 100; and DX Network Services Limited/ the businesses and assets of The Legal Post (Scotland) Limited and First Post Limited (21 October 2016) at paragraph 70.

9 See Integra LifeSciences Holdings Corporation/ Codman neurosurgery business (3 August 2017) at paragraph 157; and GLO Dutch Bidco/ Mallinckrodt Nuclear Medicine and Mallinckrodt Netherlands Holdings (26 June 2017) at paragraphs 103–107.

10 See acquisition by General Healthcare Group of control of four Abbey hospitals and de facto control over Transform Holdings Limited, previously part of the Covenant Healthcare Group (14 September 2010), footnote 37; and Universal Sealants (U.K.) Limited/ Ekspan Holdings Limited (23 March 2018) at paragraphs 109–114.

11 For example, in Capita Group plc/ IBS OPENSystems plc (19 November 2008), paragraph 112, the OFT discounted as an 'in principle' remedy at this stage the divestment of IBS's revenue and benefits software services business on the basis that this would raise concerns as to whether it was clearly and effectively separable from the remainder of IBS (for example, by reason of shared software/codes). It recognised that such concerns might ultimately be surmountable, but considered it appropriate for it to take a cautious view of the workability of a structural remedy for these purposes. See also Xchanging Holdings Limited/ Total Objects Limited (9 December 2014) at paragraphs 201 – 204 and Reckitt Benckiser/ the K-Y brand (19 December 2014) at paragraphs 260–266.

12 As a result of this conservative approach, the CMA has on occasion considered seriously undertakings in lieu that have actually been offered by the merging parties having previously considered that, in its view, the case was not an obvious candidate for resolution by way of undertakings in lieu (such that it should not exclude application of de minimis on this ground). Clearly this situation can occur only where the CMA does not apply the de minimis exception, such that there would be a phase 2 reference absent acceptable undertakings in lieu. See BOC Limited/ the packaged chlorine business and assets carried on by Ineos Chlor (29 May 2008), paragraph 128 and footnote 54 and Reckitt Benckiser/ the K-Y brand (19 December 2014), paragraphs 260–266 and reference decision in the same case discussing undertakings in lieu offered by the Parties (7 January 2015).

13 For examples see Universal Sealants (U.K.) Limited/ Ekspan Holdings Limited (23 March 2018) - £4m; Integra LifeSciences Holdings Corporation/ Codman neurosurgery business (3 August 2017) - £6.6m; GLO Dutch Bidco/ Mallinckrodt Nuclear Medicine and Mallinckrodt Netherlands Holdings (26 June 2017) - £4.6m; IKO plc/ Pure Asphalt Company Limited (25 August 2016) – market size redacted; DX Network Services Limited/ the businesses and assets of The Legal Post (Scotland) Limited and First Post Limited (21 October 2016) - £3-5m; Kaplan International Holdings Limited/ Osborne Books Limited (9 February 2016) - £2-3m; First TransPennine Express Limited/ TransPennine Express franchise (14 March 2016) - <£1m; Sheffield City Taxis Limited/ certain assets and business of Mercury Taxis (Sheffield) Limited (13 October 2015) - <£3m; Tattersalls Limited/ bloodstock auctioneering business of Brightwells Limited (15 September 2015); Key Publishing imited/ certain assets of Kelsey Publishing Limited (2 March 2015) - £2.8m; Xchanging Holdings Limited/ Total Objects Limited (9 December 2014) - <£3m; WGSN Inc. of Stylesight Inc (25 June 2014) - <£10m; Phonak AG of Comfort Audio I Halmstad AB (17 September 2014); and Diamond Bus Company Limited/ the bus business of Firstgroup plc in Redditch and Kidderminster (23 August 2013) - £2-3m.

Examples of cases in which the CMA considered the exception but decided not to apply it include Nielsen Holdings PLC/the AdIntel division of Ebiquity PLC (13 June 2018) - >£11.3m; Vanilla Group Limited (JLA)/Washstation Limited (27 April 2018) close to £15m and growing; Capita plc/the one-way wide-area paging services business of Vodafone (30 May 2017) - £5-10m; Reckitt Benckiser/the K-Y brand (19 December 2014) - £5-10m; Alliance Medical Limited/the assets of IBA Molecular UK Limited used to manufacture Fluorodeoxyglucose 18f (24 March 2014) - £5-10m.

14 This may be a subset of the relevant market as defined for the purposes of the competition assessment (see the CMA's Merger Assessment Guidelines, paragraph 5.2.1) where it is clear that the size of any customer detriment will be experienced by only a proportion of the relevant market. See, for example, National Express Group/ Intercity East Coast Rail franchise (20 December 2007), paragraph 83 (where the OFT disregarded rail revenue given that the theory of harm related only to merger effects on coach services) and FMC corporation/ the alginates business of ISP holdings (U.K.) Limited (30 July 2008), paragraph 71 (where the exceptionally differentiated position of the largest customer meant that its purchases should not be included for calculation of the size of the market concerned for the purposes of the de minimis exception).

15 Where the annual value of the market(s) concerned only very marginally exceeds £15 million, the CMA may consider whether the de minimis exception should be applied: see Global Radio UK Limited/ GCap Media plc (8 August 2008), paragraph 232 where the OFT was considering the market size under the previous £10 million threshold.

16 For example, in Stagecoach Bus Holdings Limited/ Cavalier Contracts Limited (18 September 2008), paragraph 98, the market size for de minimis purposes was the projected revenue associated with the Cambridge Guided Busway (which was the only overlap in respect of which the OFT found a realistic prospect of a SLC).

17 This reflects the fact that the Act is concerned with a SLC within any market or markets in the UK for goods and services (sections 22 and 33 of the Act).

18 See Spectris plc/ Lochard Ltd (29 January 2009), paragraphs 120–126.

19 That is, where short-term fluctuations in market shares can be dramatic as large contracts are won and lost.

20 See Capita Group plc/ IBS OPENSystems plc (19 November 2008), paragraph 119, where the OFT stated that it was not persuaded that the number of contracts coming up for renewal in one particular year alone was the correct way to ascertain the annual market size for the purposes of de minimis. Although the OFT accepted that the relevant market could be characterised at the time of the merger by a relatively limited number of contracts expected to come up for renewal in the short term, it noted that this situation could change going forward.

21 IBA Health v OFT [2004] EWCA Civ 142.

22 See, for example, Prince Minerals Limited/ Castle Colours Limited (6 May 2009), paragraph 67. Contrast Reckitt Benckiser/ the K-Y brand (19 December 2014) at paragraphs 271–275.

23 In assessing the magnitude of competition that would be lost if the SLC posited actually materialises, the CMA will take into account evidence that the amount of competition between the parties has been more limited: see Orbital Marketing Services Group Ltd/ Ocean Park Ltd (14 November 2008), paragraph 81.

24 See Stagecoach Bus Holdings Limited/ Cavalier Contracts Limited (18 September 2008), paragraph 100, where the OFT considered that any price increases resulting from the merger may not be that significant given the limited ability of Stagecoach to cause a price increase on multi-operator tickets, the constraint on Stagecoach's own tickets posed by multi-operator tickets, and the role played by the Council in limiting and vetoing price increases.

25 See Merger Assessment Guidelines, paragraph 5.8.3.

26 See in this respect FMC corporation/ the alginates business of ISP Holdings (U.K.) Limited (30 July 2008), paragraph 74, in which the OFT stated that it was possible that entry could take place in the medium to long term, and as such it did not consider that the negative impact of the merger would definitely persist for the foreseeable future.

27 DX Network Services Limited/The Legal Post (Scotland) Limited and First Post Limited (21 October 2016) at paragraphs 80–84.

28 *The deterrent effect of competition enforcement by the OFT: a report prepared for the OFT by Deloitte* (OFT962, November 2007).

29 See Orbital Marketing Services Group Ltd/Ocean Park Ltd (14 November 2008), paragraph 85, where the OFT took into

account the fact that customers did not raise concerns about the merger and were, in some cases, supportive of it for reasons of ensuring security of supply.

30 See paragraph 78 of Stagecoach Group plc/ East Midlands Franchise (4 February 2008) (which focused on the particular nature of rail franchise awards and the general lack of an anti-competitive rationale for rail franchise bids), in contrast to paragraph 125 of BOC Limited/ packaged chlorine business and assets carried on by Ineos Chlor Limited (29 May 2008).

31 The procedures for the CMA's decision-making process, including application of the de minimis discretion, are set out in full in CMA2. However, the CMA considers it useful in this context to highlight these points that relate to the de minimis discretion.

32 For further information and guidance on the CMA's process for launching own-initiative investigations and the mergers intelligence functions relating to this see CMA2, paragraphs 6.5–6.8 and 6.15–6.19 and Guidance on the CMA's mergers intelligence function (17 June 2016, CMA56).

33 See CMA2, paragraphs 6.25–6.38.

34 See CMA2, paragraph 6.30.

35 Such consent would be without prejudice to the parties' views on whether the duty to refer was actually met.

36 For example, see Kaplan International Holdings Limited/ Osborne Books Limited (9 February 2016) at paragraph 89; First TransPennine Express Limited/ TransPennine Express franchise (14 March 2016) at paragraph 161; and Govia Limited/ South Central Rail Franchise (6 August 2009) at paragraph 8.

37 Such a conclusion might be particularly suitable in circumstances such as those arising in Chiral Technologies Europe SAS/ Chromtech Limited (24 September 2008), in which the target's UK turnover amounted to only £80,000 and the overall UK value of the market concerned amounted to substantially less than £10 million.

ARRANGEMENTS WHICH ARE INSUFFICIENTLY ADVANCED OR LIKELY TO PROCEED

[3.439]

62 This provision ensures that the CMA is not obliged to make a reference if a merger is insufficiently likely to proceed. This may arise where the CMA has issued a decision finding that a merger gives rise to a SLC (which ordinarily would give rise to a duty to make a reference absent an offer of satisfactory undertakings in lieu of reference) but the parties choose to abandon the merger during the 10-working day window for the consideration of undertakings in lieu of a reference.[38]

63. Another function of section 33(2)(b) of the Act is to avoid the unnecessary expense of a reference where it is still uncertain whether the parties will proceed with the merger (the "insufficiently far advanced" limb).

64. The CMA would usually expect a transaction to be sufficiently advanced to justify a reference where:

- the parties to a transaction have publicly announced an agreed merger or their intention to merge (in whole or in part), or
- one of the parties to a proposed transaction has announced a possible offer or a firm intention to make an offer for the other notwithstanding that this may be subject to conditions or be a hostile bid.

65. This exception may be appropriate for use in situations where commercial discussions between the parties are still ongoing at the time of the CMA's investigation, for example in anticipated joint venture situations where there remains material ambiguity about how the joint venture will be structured.

66. In practice, and where this is justified, the CMA would take a view soon after notification as to whether an investigation is appropriate in light of the early stage of proceedings and will not proceed with the investigation if the transaction is insufficiently far advanced.[39] This limb of the provision is therefore only likely to be used if the proposed merger suffers unexpected disruption after the CMA has started the 40-working day clock of the initial period and issued an invitation to comment.

NOTES

38 Section 73A of the Act. Examples of abandonment after the decision on SLC but before reference are Safetykleen/Puresolve (2016) and Capita/Vodafone (2017). The CMA is not obliged under section 107(1)(a) of the Act to publish a decision if it decides not to refer on the basis of this exception. Under article 4(2) of The Enterprise Act 2002 (Merger Fees and Determination of Turnover) Order 2003 no fee is payable in respect of a merger which is the subject of a decision under section 33(2)(b). In contrast, a fee is payable if the merger is referred and then abandoned.

39 See footnote 3 to the Case Team Allocation Form, available on the CMA's website, and paragraph 6.44 of CMA2.

RELEVANT CUSTOMER BENEFITS

INTRODUCTION

[3.440]

67. While mergers can harm competition, they can also give rise to efficiencies which enhance rivalry and/or produce relevant customer benefits.

68. If the efficiencies arising from the merger enhance rivalry within a market where a SLC finding might potentially arise, the CMA can take this into account in its assessment of the merger's impact on competition. For example, a merger of two of the smaller firms in a market resulting inefficiency gains might allow the merged entity to compete more effectively with the larger firms. Rivalry-enhancing efficiencies may lead the CMA to conclude (at Phase 1) that the merger does not give rise to a realistic prospect of an SLC in a particular market, or may mitigate the severity of any SLC caused by the merger.[40]

69. In addition, the CMA may conclude that the merger gives rise to a realistic prospect of a SLC in one market, but also gives rise to efficiencies in a different market. Moreover, the merger may give rise to an adverse effect on one set of customers but not on another set of customers. The CMA has the discretion not to refer a merger for a Phase 2 investigation, or not to accept remedies following a Phase 2 investigation, if the efficiencies arising from the merger result in relevant customer benefits which outweigh the SLC caused by the merger.

70. The CMA considers the likeliness, timeliness and merger specificity of relevant customer benefits, in establishing whether they exist, and considers both quantitative and qualitative evidence of their likelihood and probability in deciding whether they outweigh the adverse effects of the SLC.

71. Relevant customer benefits as a potential exception to the duty to refer a merger to Phase 2 are discussed further below. Relevant customer benefits can also be taken into account in the selection of remedies under section 73,82 or 84 of the Act.[41]

72. In practice, the CMA has rarely exercised its discretion to apply relevant customer benefits as an exception to the duty to refer.[42] Where merging parties expect relevant customer benefits to play a decisive role in the CMA's assessment of a merger, they should collect and present the relevant evidence to the CMA at the earliest possible opportunity during the pre-notification period. It may be difficult to consider claimed benefits in detail in a phase 1 investigation unless they are raised at an early stage. This applies in particular to cases, such as hospital mergers, which require the input of other regulators in assessing RCBs.

STATUTORY DEFINITION OF RELEVANT CUSTOMER BENEFITS

73. Relevant customer benefits are defined by section 30(1) of the Enterprise Act 2002 (the Act) to be benefits to relevant customers in the form of:

- lower prices, higher quality or greater choice of goods or services in any market in the United Kingdom, or
- greater innovation in relation to such goods or services.

74. Sections 30(2) and (3) of the Act provide that a benefit is only a relevant customer benefit if it has accrued or is expected to accrue to relevant customers within the UK within a reasonable period from the merger and would be unlikely to accrue without the merger or a similar lessening of competition. Relevant customers are customers at any point in the chain of production and distribution and are therefore not limited to final customers (section 30(4) of the Act).

ILLUSTRATIONS OF RELEVANT CUSTOMER BENEFITS

75. Illustrations of situations where relevant customer benefits (as defined by the Act) might be weighed against the identified loss of competition include the following.[43]

- Lower prices. A merger may, despite leading to a SLC, give clear scope for large cost savings through a reduction in marginal costs of production. In these circumstances, the merged firm – even if it is a monopolist – may therefore pass on some of this reduction in the form of lower prices to its customers such that it might outweigh the SLC.
- Greater innovation. A merger might, in rare cases, facilitate innovation through research and development that could only be achieved through a certain critical mass, especially where larger fixed (and) sunk costs are involved. Exceptionally, the benefits likely to be passed through to customers from such innovation might outweigh the SLC.
- Greater choice or higher quality. In unusual circumstances, a merger might bring together two companies' specialist resources in a way which would not be possible, absent the merger, and which would allow them to produce a higher quality product.

ASSESSING THE EXISTENCE OF RELEVANT CUSTOMER BENEFITS

76. Where potential relevant customer benefits have been identified, the CMA considers the likelihood, timeliness and merger specificity of the claimed benefits, to assess whether relevant customer benefits exist under section 30of the Act.

77. In assessing a claimed benefit's likelihood, the CMA considers the merging parties' incentives, and their ability to implement the claimed benefit, post-merger. The claimed relevant customer benefits must be clear, and the parties should be able to produce detailed and verifiable evidence that anticipated price reductions or other benefits will in fact emerge. Where relevant, the CMA may consider the views of a sector regulator.[44]

78. In considering the timeliness of a claimed benefit, what is a reasonable period will vary on a case-by-case basis and will depend on the complexity of the changes required to bring about the benefit. It may depend, for example, on the nature of the proposed benefit and the circumstances of its implementation.

79. To determine whether a claimed benefit is merger specific, the CMA will consider whether the merging parties had plans to take similar actions absent the merger (eg to undertake a given research project), and whether the merger parties would have the ability and incentive to achieve the benefits independently or through other arrangements, such as another merger or through an agreement which does not amount to a merger, that do not themselves give rise to competition issues of a similar magnitude.

80. In assessing the likelihood, timeliness and merger specificity of relevant customer benefits, the CMA may consider a wide range of evidence, including:

Part 3 CMA and other Guidelines

- The merging parties' plans to implement the relevant customer benefits (the more detailed, the better);
- The views of third party stakeholders (especially those which could delay or prevent of the realisation of relevant customer benefits); and
- The merging parties' track record in implementing similar initiatives in similar circumstances.

81. The provision of evidence by merging parties that relevant customer benefits will result from the merger in no way implies that they accept the existence of a SLC.

WEIGHING RELEVANT CUSTOMER BENEFITS AGAINST THE SLC

82. When it finds that relevant customer benefits exist, the CMA considers whether they outweigh the adverse effect from the merger's impact on competition.

83. To clear a case on the basis of relevant customer benefits, the CMA would need to believe that, on the specific facts of the case, customers overall would be better off with the merger, despite the fact that the CMA believes that the merger raises a realistic prospect of a SLC which will harm some customers. These will be rare cases since, ordinarily, the CMA would expect that a substantial loss of competition which leads to higher prices, lower quality, reduced service and/or reduced innovation in one or more markets would be unlikely to also present benefits to customers, whether in those or other markets.

84. To be counted, the claimed relevant customer benefits must accrue to customers of the merging parties (or to customers in a chain beginning with those customers), but need not necessarily arise in the market(s) where the SLC concerns have arisen. Sufficient relevant customer benefits may accrue in some market(s) as a result of the merger that outweigh a finding of realistic prospect of a SLC in other market(s).

85. In assessing the weight of the claimed relevant customer benefits, the CMA has regard to both the magnitude of the benefits and the probability of them occurring. This is set against the magnitude and probability of the identified anti-competitive effects. The more powerful and more likely the anti-competitive effects of the merger, the greater and more likely the relevant customer benefits must be to meet and overcome such concerns.[45]

86. The CMA may consider both qualitative and quantitative evidence in assessing the magnitude of relevant customer benefits. Merging parties should give careful thought to what quantitative evidence they can provide to substantiate claimed benefits. Quantitative evidence is particularly important in circumstances in which it is difficult to judge whether the scale of the relevant customer benefits is such that they outweigh the competition concerns.

RELEVANT CUSTOMER BENEFITS AND REMEDIES

87. It is not possible for the CMA both (i) to apply relevant customer benefits as an exception to the duty to refer, eg in relation to certain affected markets, and (ii) to accept an undertaking in lieu in respect of other affected markets.[46]

88. The CMA is exercising its discretion in deciding whether to apply an exception to the duty to refer the merger in question for a Phase 2 investigation. In exercising this discretion, the CMA has regard to the benefits of a Phase 2 investigation, including the possibility of remedies being obtained at Phase 2that could prevent a SLC while also capturing any relevant customer benefits.

NOTES

[40] *Merger Assessment Guidelines (CC2)*, section 5.7.

[41] Merger remedies

[42] As of April 2018, the CMA has only exercised this discretion in relation to the University Hospitals Birmingham NHS Foundation Trust/Heart of England NHS Foundation Trust (**UHB/HEFT**) and the Derby Teaching Hospitals NHS Foundation Trust/Burton Hospitals NHS Foundation Trust (**DTHFT/BHFT**). The CMA has also published *CMA guidance on the review of NHS Mergers (CMA29)*.

[43] Different types of efficiencies, which may be considered in some cases as relevant customer benefits, are discussed in the Merger Assessment Guidelines paragraphs 5.7.6 to 5.7.18.

[44] For example, in UHB/HEFT and DTHFT/BHFT, NHS Improvement (an expert regulator) advised the CMA, assisting in verifying the Parties' submissions on benefits.

[45] For example, in UHB/HEFT and DTHFT/BHFT, the merging parties were public service providers operating in a heavily regulated environment. The CMA therefore concluded that the role of competition was reduced (although not eliminated), and took this into account in weighing the benefits against the competition concerns.

[46] See Merger Remedies

MERGER REMEDIES (CMA87, DECEMBER 2018)

[3.441]

NOTES

This guidance seeks to provide a single source of guidance on remedies for Phase 1 and Phase 2 merger investigations. This guidance applies to any Phase 1 merger investigations commenced after 13 December 2018 and any Phase 1 merger investigations referred to Phase 2 after 13 December 2018 and supersedes the Competition Commission guidelines on merger remedies (CC8), Chapter 5 of the Office of Fair Trading guidelines on undertakings in lieu of reference (OFT1122), and Chapters 8 and 14 of the CMA's guidelines on merger jurisdiction and procedure (CMA2). For any Phase 2 merger investigations that commenced prior to 13 December 2018, the previous guidance remains applicable.

CONTENTS

1. PREFACE

[3.442]

1.1 This guidance forms part of the advice and information published by the Competition and Markets Authority (CMA) under section 106 of the Enterprise Act 2002, as amended (the Act).

1.2 This guidance is intended for merger parties and their advisers. The purpose of this guidance is to explain the CMA's approach and requirements in the selection, design and implementation of remedies in:

(a) Phase 1 merger investigations, where the CMA must decide whether there is a realistic prospect that the merger gives rise to a substantial lessening of competition (SLC) and therefore, whether the merger should be referred for an in-depth Phase 2 investigation; and

(b) Phase 2 merger investigations, where the CMA must decide whether the merger has resulted, or may be expected to result, in an SLC and therefore, whether action should be taken to remedy, mitigate or prevent the SLC or any adverse effect resulting from the SLC.

1.3 This document seeks to provide a single source of guidance on remedies for Phase 1 and Phase 2 merger investigations. It therefore supersedes the Competition Commission (CC) guidelines on merger remedies,[1] Chapter 5 of the Office of Fair Trading (OFT) guidelines on undertakings in lieu of reference (UILs)[2] and Chapters 8 and 14 of the CMA's guidelines on merger jurisdiction and procedure.[3]

1.4 The approach outlined in this document is consistent with these previous documents, but has been updated and extended to take account of the CMA's experience of merger investigations in recent years, judgments of the Competition Appeal Tribunal (CAT) and the CMA's research into the outcomes of remedies.[4] This guidance also takes into account the principles outlined by the International Competition Network, the work carried out by the Organisation for Economic Co-operation and Development and the European Competition Network and recent merger remedies guidance published by other international competition authorities.

1.5 This guidance reflects the views of the CMA at the time of publication and may be revised from time to time to reflect changes in best practice, legislation and the results of experience, legal judgements and research. Where there is any difference in emphasis or detail between this guidance and other guidance produced or adopted by the CMA, the most recently published guidance takes precedence.

1.6 The CMA will have regard to this guidance in considering remedial action in merger investigations. However, in each investigation, the appropriate remedy will be determined by having regard to the particular circumstances of the investigation. The CMA will therefore apply this guidance flexibly and may depart from the approach described in the guidance where there are appropriate reasons for doing so.[5]

NOTES

[1] Merger Remedies: Competition Commission Guidelines (CC8) was originally published by the CC and has been adopted by the CMA.

[2] Mergers: Exceptions to the duty to refer and undertakings in lieu of reference guidance (OFT1122) was originally published by the OFT and was adopted by the CMA. It was replaced by Mergers: Exceptions to the duty to refer (CMA64). Guidance on UILs (previously in Chapter 5 of OFT1122) is now included in this guidance on merger remedies.

[3] Mergers: Guidance on the CMA's jurisdiction and procedure (CMA2) was published by the CMA in January 2014. This guidance on merger remedies replaces Chapter 8 , Phase 1 remedies – undertakings in lieu of reference, and Chapter 14, Implementation of remedies, but the remainder of CMA2 remains applicable.

[4] See Understanding past merger remedies. Report on case study research, 6 April 2017.

[5] In Phase 1 merger investigations, the decision on whether to refer, including any decision on UILs, is made by either the Senior Director of Mergers or another senior member of CMA staff (the decision maker). In Phase 2 merger investigations, the final decision-making authority is an independent group of experts selected from a panel appointed by the Secretary of State (the Inquiry Group). In cases where a public interest intervention notice, special intervention notice or European intervention notice has been issued, the decision falls to the Secretary of State.

2. INTRODUCTION

[3.443]

Scope of the guidance

2.1 This guidance sets out the criteria that the CMA applies in determining the appropriate remedial action in Phase 1 and Phase 2 merger investigations.[6]

2.2 This guidance does not address whether the CMA has jurisdiction under the Act, and the policies and procedures that the CMA will use in discharging its functions under the Act.[7] It also does not address the substantive 'SLC' test against which the CMA assesses mergers.[8]

Structure of the guidance

2.3 This guidance explains the purpose of remedial action and the process for the selection, design, implementation and monitoring and enforcement of remedies. To this end, it is structured as follows:

(a) Chapter 3 explains the purpose and key principles of remedial action, including a summary of the various types of remedies available to the CMA.

(b) Chapter 4 outlines the process for remedial action in Phase 1 and Phase 2 merger investigations, from the merger parties' initial contact with the CMA (prior to the commencement of a Phase 1 merger investigation), through to the implementation, monitoring and review of remedies following the outcome of a Phase 2 merger investigation.[9]

(c) Chapters 5 to 7 provide more detailed guidance on divestiture remedies, intellectual property (IP) remedies and behavioural remedies respectively.

(d) Chapter 8 explains the CMA's approach in relation to the use of trustees and third-party monitors.

NOTES

6 Considerations regarding the use, design and implementation of interim measures, including interim orders, which are intended to prevent or unwind pre-emptive action which might prejudice the outcome of a reference and/or impede the CMA taking appropriate remedial action, are set out in Guidance on initial enforcement orders and derogations in merger investigations (CMA60).

7 CMA2 provides advice and general information on the procedures used by the CMA in operating the merger control regime set out in the Act, as amended, including guidance on when the CMA will have jurisdiction to review mergers under the Act.

8 Detailed information on the application of the substantive test for mergers is provided in Merger Assessment Guidelines (OFT1254/CC2), which has been adopted by the CMA.

9 The CMA's approach to the review of remedies is set out in Remedies: Guidance on the CMA's approach to the variation and termination of merger, monopoly and market undertakings and orders (CMA11).

3. PURPOSE AND PRINCIPLES OF REMEDIAL ACTION

[3.444]

Objectives of remedial action

3.1 At Phase 1, where the CMA decides that there is a realistic prospect that the merger gives rise to an SLC, the CMA has discretion to accept UILs instead of making a reference to Phase 2. In exercising this discretion, the CMA may accept from the merger parties undertakings to take such action as the CMA considers appropriate to remedy, mitigate or prevent the SLC concerned or any adverse effect resulting from it.[10]

3.2 At Phase 2, where the CMA concludes that a relevant merger situation has resulted, or may be expected to result, in an SLC, it is required to decide whether action should be taken to remedy, mitigate or prevent the SLC or any adverse effect resulting from the SLC.[11] The CMA is also required to decide whether such action should be taken by itself or recommended for others, such as Government, regulators or public authorities. In either case, the CMA must state in its final report the action to be taken and what it is designed to address.

3.3 At both Phase 1 and Phase 2, the Act requires that the CMA, when considering remedies, shall 'in particular, have regard to the need to achieve as comprehensive a solution as is reasonable and practicable to the SLC and any adverse effects resulting from it'.[12]

3.4 There are common principles that apply to the assessment of remedies at Phase 1 and Phase 2, although the application of these principles will take account of the relevant differences in the decisions to be taken at each phase. The CMA will seek remedies that are effective in addressing the SLC and its resulting adverse effects and will then select the least costly and intrusive remedy that it considers to be effective. The CMA will seek to ensure that no remedy is disproportionate in relation to the SLC and its adverse effects. The CMA may also have regard, in accordance with the Act, to any relevant customer benefits (RCBs) arising from the merger.[13] In the following paragraphs, we consider these factors and their interaction in greater detail.

Effectiveness

3.5 The CMA will assess the effectiveness of remedies in addressing the SLC and resulting adverse effects before going on to consider the costs likely to be incurred by the remedies. Assessing the effectiveness of a remedy will involve several distinct dimensions:

(a) Impact on SLC and resulting adverse effects. The CMA views competition as a dynamic process of rivalry between firms seeking to win customers' business over time. Restoring this process of rivalry through structural remedies, such as divestitures, which re-establish the structure of the market expected in the absence of the merger, should be expected to address the adverse effects at source. Such remedies are normally preferable to measures that seek to regulate the ongoing behaviour of the merger parties (so-called behavioural remedies, such as price caps, supply commitments or restrictions on use of long term contracts). Behavioural remedies are unlikely to deal with an SLC and its adverse effects as comprehensively as structural remedies and may result in distortions when compared with a competitive market outcome.

(b) Appropriate duration and timing. Remedies need to address the SLC effectively throughout its expected duration. Remedies that act quickly in addressing competitive concerns are preferable to remedies that are expected to have an effect only in the long term or where the timing of the effect is uncertain.

(c) Practicality. A practical remedy should be capable of effective implementation, monitoring and enforcement. To enable this to occur, the operation and implications of the remedy need to be clear to the merger parties and other affected parties. The practicality of any remedy is likely to be reduced if elaborate and intrusive monitoring and compliance programmes are required. Remedies regulating ongoing behaviour are generally subject to the disadvantage of requiring ongoing monitoring and compliance activity.

(d) Acceptable risk profile. The effect of any remedy is always likely to be uncertain to some degree. In evaluating the effectiveness of remedies, the CMA will seek remedies that have a high degree of certainty of achieving their intended effect. Customers or suppliers of merger parties should not bear significant risks that remedies will not have the requisite impact on the SLC or its adverse effects.

Cost of remedies and proportionality

3.6 Having decided which of the remedy options would be effective in addressing the SLC and resulting adverse effects, the CMA will then consider the costs of those remedies. In order to be reasonable and proportionate, the CMA will seek to select the least costly remedy, or package of remedies, of those remedy options that it considers will be effective. If the CMA is choosing between two remedies which it considers will be equally effective, it will select the remedy that imposes the least cost or that is least restrictive. The CMA will seek to ensure that no remedy is disproportionate in relation to the SLC and its adverse effects.

3.7 At Phase 1, where the CMA finds that there is a realistic prospect that the merger gives rise to an SLC on and its duty to refer is met, the CMA may accept UILs provided these remedy the competition concerns identified to the clear-cut standard. This means that the CMA may accept a more extensive remedy offer at Phase 1 through UILs than might be needed if the merger were to receive a detailed Phase 2 investigation.[14]

3.8 The costs of a remedy may be incurred by a variety of parties, including the merger parties, third parties, the CMA and other monitoring agencies. As the merger parties have the choice of whether or not to proceed with the merger, the CMA will generally attribute less significance to the costs of a remedy that will be incurred by the merger parties than the costs that will be imposed by a remedy on third parties, the CMA and other monitoring agencies.

3.9 In particular, for completed mergers, the CMA will not normally take account of costs or losses that will be incurred by the merger parties as a result of a divestiture remedy, as it is open to the merger parties to make merger proposals conditional on the approval of the relevant competition authorities.[15] It is for the merger parties to assess whether there is a risk that a completed merger would be subject to an SLC finding, and the CMA would expect this risk to be reflected in the agreed acquisition price. Since the cost of divestiture is, in essence, avoidable, the CMA will not, in the absence of exceptional circumstances, accept that the cost of divestiture should be considered when selecting remedies.

3.10 The costs of a remedy may arise in various forms. Remedies may result in costs through distortions in market outcomes. This is more likely to be the case where behavioural remedies are used, which intervene directly in market outcomes, especially over a long period. Remedies may also result in significant ongoing compliance costs. The CMA will endeavour to minimise such costs, subject to the effectiveness of the remedy not being reduced, and will have regard to the costs to the CMA and other monitoring agencies in ensuring compliance. At Phase 2, if remedies extinguish RCBs then, as we discuss below, the benefits foregone may be considered to be a relevant cost of the remedy.

3.11 In exceptional circumstances, even the least costly but effective remedy might be expected to incur costs that are disproportionate to the scale of the SLC and its adverse effects (eg if the costs incurred by the remedy on third parties are likely to be greater than the likely scale of adverse effects). In these exceptional circumstances, the CMA will not pursue the remedy in question.

3.12 In unusual situations, it is possible that all feasible remedies will only be partially effective in remedying an SLC. In such cases, the CMA will select the most effective remedy or package of remedies that is available, provided that the costs of this remedy are not disproportionate (as described above) in relation to the SLC.

3.13 At Phase 1, the voluntary nature of the UILs process means that the CMA will not reject an offer of UILs on the basis that it forms too great a proportion of the wider transaction. The CMA would, in principle, be prepared to accept the abandoning or complete unwinding of a transaction if this were offered by the merger parties.[16]

Relevant customer benefits

3.14 At Phase 1, the CMA has a discretion not to make a reference to Phase 2 if it believes that any RCBs in relation to the creation of the relevant merger situation outweigh the SLC concerned and any adverse effects of that SLC.[17],[18] In addition, the CMA may have regard to the effect of Phase 1 UILs on any RCBs.[19]

3.15 At Phase 2, in deciding the question of remedies, the CMA is permitted to have 'regard to the effects of any action on any RCBs in relation to the creation of the relevant merger situation concerned'.[20] At Phase 2, the CMA will normally take RCBs into account by considering the extent to which alternative remedies may preserve such benefits.[21]

3.16 RCBs that will be foregone due to the implementation of a particular remedy may be considered as costs of that remedy by the CMA. The CMA may modify a remedy to ensure retention of an RCB or it may change its remedy selection. For instance, it may decide to implement a remedy other than prohibition[22] or, in rare cases, it may decide that no remedy is appropriate.[23]

3.17 RCBs are limited by the Act to benefits to relevant customers in the form of:

(a) 'lower prices, higher quality or greater choice of goods or services in any market in the United Kingdom (whether or not in the market(s) in which the SLC has occurred or may occur) or

(b) greater innovation in relation to such goods or services'.[24]

3.18 Relevant customers for these purposes are direct and indirect customers (including future customers) of the merger parties at any point in the chain of production and distribution and are therefore not limited to final consumers.[25]

3.19 The Act provides that a benefit is only an RCB if it accrues from the creation of the relevant merger situation concerned or may be expected to accrue within a reasonable period from the creation of that merger situation and would be unlikely to accrue 'without the creation of that situation or a similar lessening of competition'.[26]

3.20 The merger parties will be expected to provide convincing evidence regarding the nature and scale of RCBs that they claim to result from the merger and to demonstrate that these fall within the Act's definition of such benefits.

3.21 The following paragraphs provide examples of possible RCBs and how these will be considered by the CMA.

3.22 A merger may lead to economies of scale, for example, in production or distribution, but if this benefit just accrued to the merged firm it would not constitute an RCB. To qualify as an RCB, the prospective cost reductions must be expected to result in lower prices (or better quality, service, choice or innovation) than if the merger did not take place. In many instances, this may not be the case, as the parties may have scope to charge higher prices, or not pass on cost reductions, due to the reduction in competitive pressures resulting from the merger.

3.23 Where there are network effects, an increase in the number of access points to the network may result in an increase in the value of the network to customers. However, given that this would also be likely to increase the barriers to entry and expansion, the CMA would need to weigh up the effects.

3.24 Vertical mergers involve the merging of firms at different levels of the supply chain of a particular good or service. Vertical mergers may generate efficiencies[27] that could potentially result in benefits to customers, such as lower prices, improved quality or greater innovation, even when the merger also substantially lessens competition. Examples include improved coordination, for instance, in marketing and product design between firms at different stages of the supply chain; lower transaction and inventory costs; and removal of possible 'double marginalisation' that may occur when two non-integrated firms both have significant market power.[28] However, as for all RCBs, it would be necessary for the CMA to be satisfied that these effects could not be achieved by plausible less anti-competitive alternatives to the proposed merger.

Undertakings in lieu of reference to Phase 2

3.25 Section 73(1) of the Act gives the CMA the power to accept UILs only where the CMA has concluded that the duty to refer is met and the CMA has decided not to apply any available exceptions to the duty to refer.[29] Any UILs accepted by the CMA must be for the purpose of remedying, mitigating or preventing the SLC concerned or any adverse effects identified.

3.26 The merger parties may be willing to resolve the problems identified by offering to divest part of the merged business (structural undertakings), or the acquirer may give a formal commitment about its future conduct (behavioural undertakings). However, it is always at the parties' discretion whether or not to offer UILs. The CMA cannot impose a remedy via an order at Phase 1.[30]

3.27 In order to accept UILs, the CMA must be confident that all of the potential competition concerns that have been identified at Phase 1 would be resolved by means of the UILs without the need for further investigation. The need for confidence reflects the fact that, once UILs have been accepted, section 74(1) of the Act precludes a reference after that point. UILs are therefore appropriate only where the remedies proposed to address any competition concerns raised by the merger are clear cut. Furthermore, those remedies must be capable of ready implementation.

3.28 The clear-cut requirement has two separate dimensions:

(a) In relation to the substantive competition assessment, it means that there must not be material doubts about the overall effectiveness of the remedy. The more extensive the competition concerns, in terms of magnitude of potential customer harm, the more significant the error costs of an ineffective remedy, and hence the greater the belief must be that the UILs will comprehensively resolve those concerns. Whilst the CMA will require that the clear-cut standard is applied to any remedy where the test for reference has been met, in those cases where the potential magnitude of harm is especially large, the CMA will be particularly cautious in its approach to accepting UILs.

(b) In practical terms, it means that UILs of such complexity that their implementation is not feasible within the constraints of the Phase 1 timetable are unlikely to be accepted. This practical requirement, in terms of assessment and implementation, may impact on the specifications of a divestment package, in order to ensure it remains practicable. Therefore, there is a greater need for early dialogue between the CMA and the merger parties on the specifications of the divestiture package.[31] Under these circumstances, the CMA case team may provide guidance to the merger parties on which of the possible remedies being considered by the parties might be suitable (see paragraph 4.4).

3.29 In some cases, there may remain some doubt over the precise nature of the SLC or how any merger effect would likely to be felt even though the test for reference is met.[32] This in itself will not exclude the possibility of UILs being acceptable. The question for the CMA is whether the remedy proposed would act in a clear-cut manner to remove all competition concerns meeting the test for reference caused by the merger.

3.30 Section 73(2) of the Act provides the CMA with the ability to accept UILs 'for the purpose of remedying, mitigating or preventing' competition concerns. At the same time, the Act refers to the obligation on the CMA 'to have regard to the need to achieve as comprehensive a solution as is reasonable and practicable' (section 73(3)). The CMA's starting point is to seek an outcome that restores competition to the level that would have prevailed absent the merger, thereby comprehensively remedying the SLC.[33] The objective is to ensure that competition following the implementation of the remedy is as effective as pre-merger competition.[34]

3.31 As a general rule, and in line with the CMA's starting point detailed above, the CMA considers that at Phase 1, it is appropriate for it to seek to remedy or prevent competition concerns rather than simply mitigate concerns. The CMA is mindful that at Phase 2, it has significant remedy powers under Schedule 8 of the Act, including the ability to prohibit a merger, and that it has increased time available in the context of a Phase 2 merger investigation to consider more detailed remedies. The CMA is therefore unlikely to accept an offer of UILs at Phase 1 where these do not comprehensively address the SLC unless it was abundantly clear that at Phase 2, it would be materially no better placed than it had been at Phase 1 to achieve a remedy that would restore the levels of competition that existed pre-merger.[35]

3.32 At Phase 1, the CMA is generally unlikely to consider that behavioural UILs will be sufficiently clear cut to address the identified competition concerns. Moreover, the CMA's experience (and that of its predecessor, the OFT) is that devising a workable and effective set of behavioural commitments within the context of a short, Phase 1 timetable is difficult. Nevertheless, despite its preference for structural remedies, the CMA does not inevitably refuse behavioural remedy offers, in particular where divestment would be clearly impractical or is otherwise unavailable.[36] Further, mergers raising vertical concerns are potentially more suitable to some form of behavioural undertaking, as are mergers in markets in which there already exists a significant degree of regulation.

3.33 The CMA may have regard to the effect of any UILs on any RCBs (see paragraphs 3.14 to 3.24). In practice, this means that where there is a choice of two UILs offers that are equally effective in terms of remedying the SLC identified, the CMA will prefer the remedy that preserves any RCBs.

Choice of remedies

Types of remedies

3.34 Figure 1 below outlines the possible types of merger remedy. Remedies are conventionally classified as either structural or behavioural. Structural remedies, such as prohibition and divestiture, are generally one-off measures that seek to restore or maintain the competitive structure of the market by addressing the market participants and/or their shares of the market. Behavioural remedies are normally ongoing measures that are designed to regulate or constrain the behaviour of merger parties. Some remedies, such as those relating to access to IP rights, may have features of structural or behavioural remedies depending on their particular formulation.

Figure 1: Possible remedies

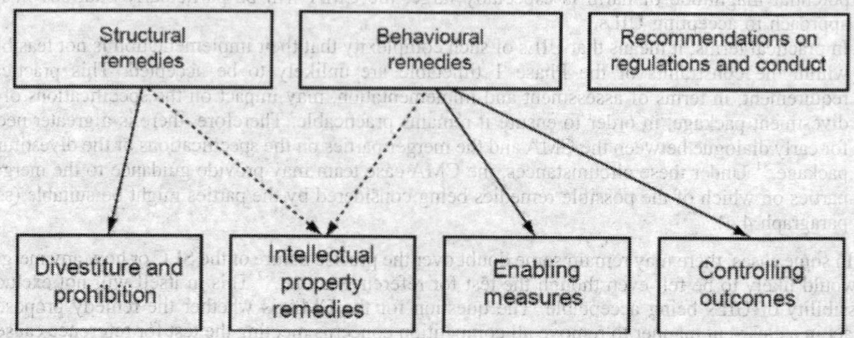

Prohibition

3.35 Full prohibition of an anticipated merger is an effective remedy as it necessarily maintains the competitive structure of a market that would have otherwise been changed by the merger. Partial rather than full prohibition may be appropriate, if feasible, where the merger parties carry out activities in a market or markets other than those that are expected to give rise to an SLC.[37]

3.36 In some mergers, a party to the merger may have built up a minority shareholding in the party to be acquired. In such instances, a decision to prohibit a merger may require the party to divest such a shareholding (or to reduce its shareholding to below a specified maximum level at which the CMA judges that the SLC will be remedied).[38] Such measures are rare at Phase 1.

Divestiture

3.37 The aim of divestiture is to address an SLC through the disposal of a business or assets from the merger parties to create a new source of competition (if sold to a new market participant) or to strengthen an existing source of competition (if sold to an existing participant independent of the merger parties).

3.38 A successful divestiture will effectively address at source the loss of rivalry resulting from the merger by changing or restoring the structure of the market. Divestitures will generally not require detailed monitoring following implementation, although, in some cases, an effective divestiture may require supplementary behavioural measures for a specified period (eg to secure supplies of an essential input or service from the merger parties to the divested business).[39] The design and implementation of divestiture remedies is considered in Chapter 5.

IP remedies

3.39 Remedies that provide access to IP by licensing or assignment of patents, brands, data or other IP rights may be viewed in general as a specialized form of asset divestiture. The parties acquiring the IP rights should be able to compete effectively with the merger parties as a result of the acquisition. Where the terms of an IP remedy result in a material ongoing link between the merger parties and the parties gaining the IP (eg providing access to new releases or upgrades of technology or data), the measure may take on some of the characteristics of a behavioural commitment, which requires ongoing monitoring and enforcement.[40] The design and implementation of IP remedies is considered in Chapter 6.

Enabling measures

3.40 Certain forms of behavioural remedy operate principally to enable competition by removing obstacles to competition or stimulating potential competition.[41] These include measures that seek to prevent merger parties from restricting access to their customers. Such measures may, for example, limit the merger parties' ability to:

(a) require their customers to enter into long term or exclusive contracts;
(b) create switching costs for customers; and/or
(c) bundle or tie the sale of particular products.

3.41 In the context of vertical mergers, if the merged entity controls key facilities or inputs required by other firms to compete effectively, then enabling measures may include:

(a) provisions governing access to and pricing of facilities and products (eg commitments from the merged entity not to discriminate in access to the facility or input as between itself and its competitors); and
(b) restrictions of access to confidential information ('firewall provisions') generated by competitors' use of the merged companies' facilities or products.

3.42 A key question in evaluating the expected effectiveness of enabling measures is whether the response to these measures is likely to be of sufficient scale and timeliness to restore adequately the rivalry lost as a result of the merger. Enabling measures are likely to require ongoing intervention and monitoring and, in some instances, this may involve highly complex issues (eg the pricing of access to facilities). The design and implementation of behavioural remedies is considered in Chapter 7.

Controlling outcomes

3.43 Certain types of behavioural remedy, such as price caps,[42] supply commitments and service level undertakings, control or restrict the outcomes of business processes. These remedies aim to control the adverse effects expected from a merger rather than addressing the source of the SLC. This type of remedy may not only be complex to implement and monitor, but may also create significant market distortions. The design and implementation of behavioural remedies is considered in Chapter 7.

Recommendations on regulations or conduct

3.44 In some situations, certain regulations or conduct may inhibit entry or restrict market outcomes (eg planning or certification requirements). In these rare situations, the CMA may recommend modifications of these requirements to the Government or other controlling body to help address an SLC or to control the adverse effects of a merger. For example, in a regulated sector, the CMA may seek to take steps to address the effects of a merger by recommending a modification to a licence condition.

Selection of remedies

3.45 The choice of remedies will reflect the particular circumstances of each investigation. The CMA will seek to select remedies that will effectively address the SLC and its resulting adverse effects in the least costly way.

3.46 The CMA prefers structural remedies, such as divestiture or prohibition, over behavioural remedies, because:

(a) structural remedies are more likely to deal with an SLC and its resulting adverse effects directly and comprehensively at source by restoring rivalry;

(b) behavioural remedies are less likely to have an effective impact on the SLC and its resulting adverse effects, and are more likely to create significant costly distortions in market outcomes; and

(c) structural remedies rarely require monitoring and enforcement once implemented.

3.47 In practice, therefore, the CMA and its predecessors, the CC and OFT, have selected structural remedies in most merger investigations that have required remedies under the Act.[43] In some of these investigations, behavioural remedies have, however, been required in a supporting role, for example, to protect the divested entity for a limited period or to ensure continuation of key contracts or inputs.

3.48 Behavioural remedies can operate satisfactorily in limited circumstances, especially where the company operates in a regulated environment and where there are expert monitors. In general, one or more of the following conditions will normally apply in the limited circumstances where the CMA selects behavioural remedies as the primary source of remedial action in a merger investigation:

(a) Divestiture and/or prohibition is not feasible, or the relevant costs of any feasible structural remedy far exceed the scale of the adverse effects of the SLC.

(b) The SLC is expected to have a relatively short duration (eg two to three years) due, for example, to the limited remaining term of a patent or exclusive contract.[44]

(c) RCBs are likely to be substantial compared with the adverse effects of the merger, and these benefits would be largely preserved by behavioural remedies but not by structural remedies.[45]

3.49 In general, in the above circumstances, the CMA will prefer to use enabling measures that 'work with the grain of competition', such as access remedies, and measures that remove obstacles to competition, rather than measures that control market outcomes, such as price caps. The latter measures tend to be onerous to operate and monitor, may create significant market distortions and do not address the causes of an SLC. Therefore, they are unlikely to be appropriate other than for a limited duration, unless there is no effective or practical alternative remedy.

3.50 Where behavioural remedies are needed, enabling measures may be expected to work relatively slowly in addressing an SLC. In these circumstances, measures that control market outcomes may be needed to supplement enabling measures for a limited period to provide protection to customers from the adverse effects of an SLC.

3.51 In relation to whether divestiture is feasible, substantial uncertainty as to whether a suitable purchaser will emerge will generally not be sufficient for the CMA to conclude that any form of divestiture remedy is not feasible. The CMA has found that it is normally possible to implement divestiture remedies, despite such uncertainties, given flexibility in the disposal price.

3.52 Where vertical mergers are expected to result in substantial RCBs, the CMA could select enabling measures, such as access remedies and/or firewall provisions, rather than structural remedies. However, such cases are rare, as enabling measures are likely to be highly complex to set up or monitor and may be rendered ineffective by possible behaviour of the merger parties.

3.53 It is possible that, in unusual circumstances, any effective remedy will result in disproportionate costs that far exceed the scale of the SLC or a disproportionate loss of RCBs. In such circumstances, the CMA will select the effective remedy that minimises the level of costs or loss of RCBs. In cases where all feasible remedies are likely to be disproportionate, the CMA may conclude that no remedial action should be taken. In practice, such instances are expected to be extremely rare.

Recommendations

3.54 In deciding whether to make a recommendation to Government or other controlling body for remedial action, the CMA will consider the likelihood of whether its recommendation will be adopted. In view of this uncertainty, the CMA will generally only make recommendations for action by others where it lacks the ability to carry out relevant measures itself, and only after consultation with the organisations possessing the relevant powers.[46]

International constraints

3.55 The CMA is permitted to impose remedies that extend to a person's conduct outside the UK if that person is a UK national, incorporated in the UK, or a person carrying out business in the UK.[47] This includes circumstances where that person is sufficiently involved in a business being carried on in the UK, despite being based overseas.[48]

3.56 Where competition authorities in other jurisdictions are considering a merger which the CMA is also investigating, the CMA will consult with some or all of these authorities to seek consistency and effectiveness in the approach to remedies where relevant.[49] It will normally be in the interests of the competition authorities and the merger parties for such consultation to take place at an early stage to prevent inconsistent approaches or outcomes. The consultation will also generally be more effective if the merger parties give their consent to sharing relevant information between the CMA and other competition authorities at an early stage.[50]

NOTES

10 Section 73(2) of the Act.

11 Sections 35 and 36 of the Act.

12 Section 73(3) of the Act at Phase 1 and Sections 35(4) and 36(3) of the Act at Phase 2.

13 Sections 22(2)(b) and 33(2)(c) of the Act at Phase 1 and Sections 35(5) and 36(4) of the Act at Phase 2.

14 The CMA is under a duty to refer where it believes that 'it is or may be the case that' a merger has resulted or may be expected to result in an SLC. See the OFT's investigation into the anticipated acquisition by Co-operative Group Limited of Somerfield Limited (2009), where the OFT took the view that 'it may be the case that' the merger may be expected to result in an SLC in '3 to 2' pharmacy overlap areas.

15 The CAT and the courts have upheld divestiture remedies in a number of investigations where this approach has been taken by the CC and the CMA. See Groupe Eurotunnel S.A. v Competition Commission [2013] CAT 30, Ryanair Holdings plc v Competition and Markets Authority [2014] CAT 3 and Intercontinental Exchange, Inc v Competition and Markets Authority [2017] CAT 6.

16 However, for the purposes of determining whether clear-cut UILs are 'in principle' available as part of a 'de minimis' assessment, the CMA will not take account of a hypothetical remedy that would amount to the prohibition of a transaction and will have regard to the proportionality of the remedy.

17 Sections 22(2)(b) and 33(2)(c) of the Act.

18 See the CMA's investigations into the anticipated merger between University Hospitals Birmingham NHS Foundation Trust and Heart of England NHS Foundation Trust (2017) and the anticipated merger between Derby Teaching Hospitals NHS Foundation Trust and Burton Hospitals NHS Foundation Trust (2018).

19 Section 73(4) of the Act.

20 Sections 35(5) and 36(6) of the Act.

21 Sections 35(5) and 36(4) of the Act.

22 See the CC's investigation into the completed acquisition by Macquarie UK Broadcast Ventures Limited of National Grid Telecoms Investment Limited, Lattice Telecommunications Asset Development Company Limited and National Grid Wireless No.2 Limited (2008). The CC concluded that a package of behavioural remedies had a high probability of being effective in addressing the adverse effects of the merger and would pass back to customers a significant proportion of the relevant merger synergies and substantial compensation in lieu of the loss of future competition.

23 See the CMA's investigation into the anticipated merger between Central Manchester University Hospitals NHS Foundation Trust and University Hospital of South Manchester NHS Foundation Trust (2017). The CMA found that the merger may be expected to give rise to an SLC in the provision of NHS elective and maternity services and NHS specialised services, and that prohibiting the merger was the only practicable and effective remedy. However, the CMA concluded that prohibition would result in the loss of substantial RCBs which may be expected to arise as a result of the merger. The CMA found that, when balanced against the nature of the SLC and its resulting adverse effects, the RCBs were likely to be more significant. The CMA therefore concluded that it would be disproportionate to prohibit the merger, and that it should be cleared.

24 Section 30 of the Act.

25 Section 30(4) of the Act.

26 Section 30(2) and 30(3) of the Act.

27 The extent to which efficiencies may also be taken into account by the CMA in determining whether a merger gives rise to an SLC is considered in OFT1254/CC2, adopted by the CMA.

28 Double marginalisation may occur because, in the absence of price discrimination, each non-integrated firm has the incentive to raise prices above cost without taking account of the fact that this lowers the output of the other. The result is lower output and profits (and higher prices) than if the two firms pursued a policy of joint profit maximization.

29 In making its decision as to whether its duty to refer applies, the CMA will also consider whether it should exercise its discretion to apply any available exceptions to that duty to refer, such as where the markets concerned are not of sufficient importance to justify the making of a reference.

30 Unless the CMA has previously accepted UILs and, for example, those undertakings are not being or will not be fulfilled, in which case the CMA gains order-making powers under section 75 of the Act.

31 See the UILs given by Boots Group plc to the OFT in relation to its acquisition of Alliance UniChem plc (2008), where the OFT required that 96 pharmacy stores be divested in no more than 25 packages, and the UILs given by Co-operative Group Limited to the OFT in relation to its acquisition of Somerfield Limited (2009), where the OFT required that 109 grocery stores be divested in no more than 25 packages.

32 This reflects the fact that the CMA's test for reference at Phase 1 is whether there is a realistic prospect of an SLC, rather than establishing an SLC on the balance of probabilities, which is the test at Phase 2.

33 See Co-operative Group (CWS) Limited v OFT [2007] CAT 24, where the CAT considered it was not unreasonable for the OFT to adopt as its starting point the objective of restoring competition to pre-merger levels.

34 This is without prejudice in any given case to the ability of the merger parties to persuade the CMA that a proposed remedy

that does not directly restore competition to pre-merger levels nevertheless clearly and comprehensively removes the SLC identified.

35 See the OFT's investigation into the anticipated acquisition by Co-operative Group Limited of Somerfield Limited (2009), where the OFT, in its decision to accept the proposed UILs, stated that it approved a purchaser for one store, notwithstanding that it was a grocery retailer from outside the effective competitor set (as defined in the decision), given the demonstrable absence of any purchaser from within the effective competitor set. The OFT stated that approving that purchaser provided the most satisfactory and comprehensive means of restoring competition to pre-merger levels. The OFT stated that its decision was influenced by the fact that, were the merger to be referred to the CC for a Phase 2 investigation, the CC would be no better placed than the OFT to identify an effective purchaser to resolve competition concerns in that local area.

36 See the CMA's investigations into the anticipated acquisition by Inter City Railways Limited of the InterCity East Coast rail franchise (2015), the completed acquisition by Regus Group Limited of Avanta Serviced Office Group plc (2016), and the award of the South Western rail franchise to FirstGroup plc and MTR Corporation (2017).

37 See the CC's investigations into the proposed acquisition by Stena AB of certain assets relating to the supply of ferry services operated by The Peninsular and Oriental Steam Navigation Company on the Irish Sea between Liverpool to Dublin and Fleetwood to Larne (2004), and the anticipated acquisition by The Rank Group Plc of Gala Casinos Limited (2013), where the CC found that in one local area, the least costly and least intrusive effective remedy was partial prohibition through the divestiture of a 'cold licence'.

38 See the CC's investigation into the acquisition by British Sky Broadcasting Group plc (BskyB) of 17.9 per cent of the shares in ITV plc (2008), where, in line with the CC's recommendation, the Secretary of State required the partial divestment of BSkyB's shares in ITV down to a level below 7.5%. See also the CC/CMA's investigation into the completed acquisition by Ryanair Holdings plc of a minority shareholding in Aer Lingus Group plc (2015), where the CMA required Ryanair to sell its 29.8% stake in Aer Lingus Group plc down to 5%.

39 See the UILs given by SRCL Limited to the OFT in relation to the anticipated acquisition by SRCL Limited of Cliniserve Holdings Limited (2009), and the UILs given by Global Radio UK Limited to the OFT in relation to the completed acquisition by Global Radio UK Limited of GCap Media plc (2008).

40 See the CMA's investigation into the anticipated acquisition by Reckitt Benckiser Group plc of the K-Y brand in the UK (2015), where the CMA decided that completion of the transaction would be conditional on Reckitt Benckiser Group plc agreeing a licensing agreement in line with criteria set out by the CMA.

41 See the CMA's investigation into the anticipated acquisition by Muller UK & Ireland Group LLP of the dairy operations of Dairy Crest Group plc (2015), where the CMA accepted UILs by Muller UK & Ireland Group LLP that included arrangements to provide for the expansion of an existing supplier to serve national grocery retailers with fresh liquid milk in the areas where the CMA had found competition concerns.

42 See the CC's investigations into the completed acquisition by Imerys Minerals Limited of the kaolin business of Goonvean Limited (2013), where the CC concluded that the most effective and proportionate remedy was a price control remedy for five years for kaolin supplied for use in performance-mineral applications to existing Goonvean and Imerys customers, and the completed acquisition by Breedon Aggregates Limited of certain assets of Aggregate Industries UK Limited (2014), where the CC implemented a price control for asphalt produced in the Inverness area.

43 As at October 2017, structural remedies involving prohibition or divestiture have been required by the CC and/or the CMA in 27 out of 34 Phase 2 merger investigations requiring remedies since the Act came into force. Almost all Phase 1 merger investigations involving UILs involve structural remedies.

44 See the CC's investigation into the completed acquisition by Nufarm Crop Products UK Limited of AH Marks Holdings Ltd (2009), where the CC concluded that a package of behavioural remedies, including supply agreements and the transfer of a registration of a product to a third party, would be more targeted in addressing the SLCs that the CC had identified than the divestiture of the AH Marks business. The CC concluded that the behavioural remedies would: (a) not affect other markets where no SLC had been found; (b) directly address the key barriers to entry; and (c) have a fixed duration, appropriate to the limited expected duration of the SLCs.

45 See the CC's investigations into the completed acquisition by Macquarie UK Broadcast Ventures Limited of National Grid Telecoms Investment Limited, Lattice Telecommunications Asset Development Company Limited and National Grid Wireless No.2 Limited (2008), where significant RCBs contributed to the selection of a behavioural remedy, and the completed acquisition by Imerys Minerals Limited of the kaolin business of Goonvean Limited (2013), where the CMA, in selecting a behavioural remedy, noted that to the extent that efficiencies existed, these would be eliminated if full divestiture had been required.

46 The CC's investigation into the proposed acquisition of certain assets representing the Air-Shields business of Hill-Rom, Inc, a subsidiary of Hillenbrand Industries (2004) is a rare example of the use of a recommendation.

47 Section 86(1) of the Act.

48 See the CC's investigation into the anticipated acquisition by Akzo Nobel N.V. of Metlac Holding S.r.l (2015) and the judgment of the Court of Appeal in Akzo v Competition Commission [2014] EWCA Civ 482.

49 See the CMA's investigation into the completed acquisition by Diageo plc of a shareholding and voting rights and other associated rights in United Spirits Limited (2014), a company based in India. The CMA accepted UILs from Diageo plc, which involved the divestment of its Whyte & Mackay business (apart from 2 malt distilleries, Dalmore and Tamnavulin, and their associated brands) and was subject to a regulatory review by the Reserve Bank of India and the approval of United Spirits Limited's shareholders in line with Indian law. The CMA did not accept the UILs until all other third party steps had been completed.

50 The International Competition Network has developed a model form that merger parties and competition authorities can use to facilitate waivers of confidentiality protection for information that merger parties submit during the merger review process.

4. REMEDIES PROCESS

Introduction

[3.445]

4.1 Figure 2 below provides an overview of the key Phase 1 and Phase 2 remedies processes.

Figure 2: Remedies process

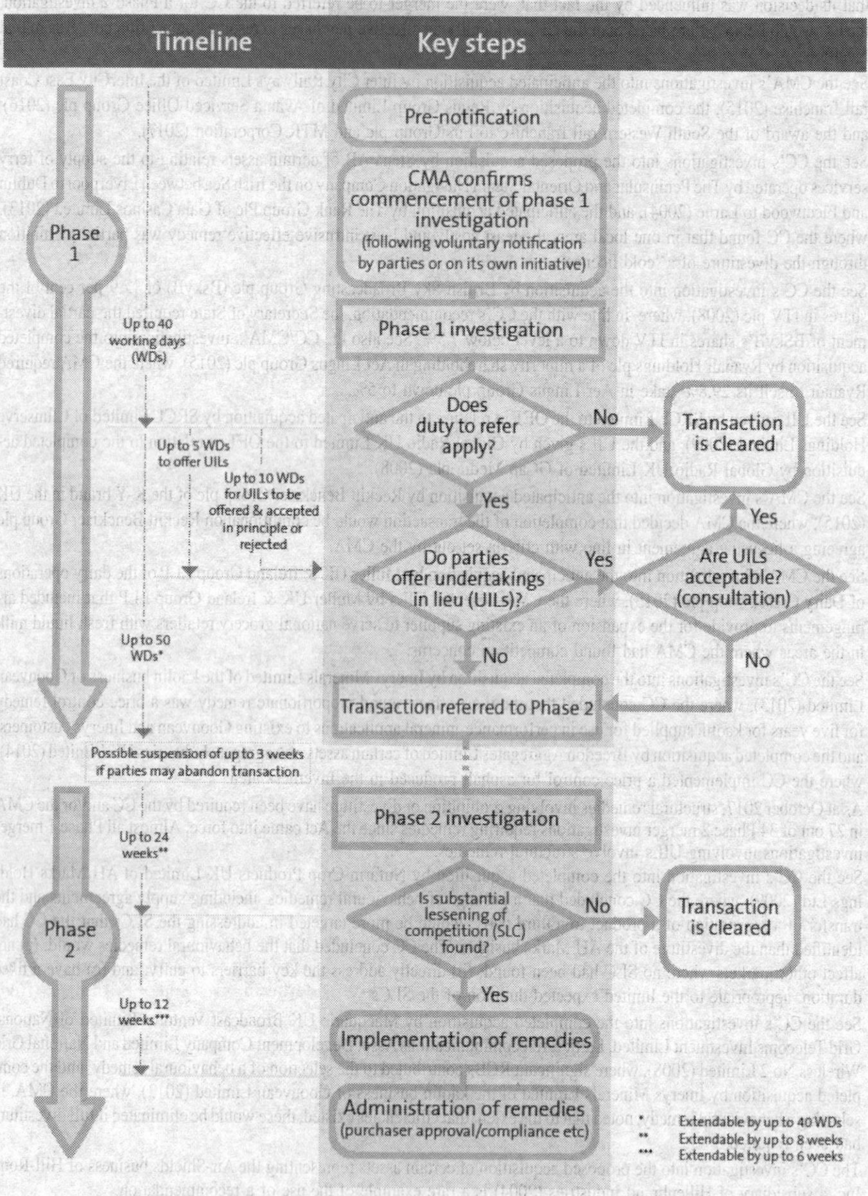

Phase 1

4.2 If the CMA finds that its duty to refer the merger for a Phase 2 investigation applies, section 73 of the Act allows the CMA (or the Secretary of State in public interest cases)[51] to accept from the parties concerned[52] binding UILs as an alternative to reference.

Procedure for submission of UILs

UILs proposals in advance of the SLC decision

4.3 Merger parties can put forward possible UILs to the CMA case team at any stage during the Phase 1 investigation or during pre-notification.[53] The CMA strongly recommends that merger parties and their legal advisers consider possible UILs early in the process, even if this is not communicated to the CMA. This ensures that, if an SLC decision is reached, the parties will be better able to submit their proposed UILs and engage in any related discussions with the CMA rapidly, maximising the chance of the CMA accepting UILs as an alternative to reference.

4.4 In advance of the SLC decision, the CMA case team will assist merger parties in understanding the function of UILs. They will also, where possible, provide guidance to parties on which of the possible remedies being considered by the parties might be suitable. However, these discussions will be conducted on a hypothetical basis, as the case team will not be able to inform the parties of the CMA's decision or direction of thinking on whether there is a realistic prospect that the merger gives rise to a SLC prior to the announcement of the decision. Any discussion of UILs prior to the SLC decision will not prejudice that decision.

4.5 The decision on the existence and scope of the SLC precedes and is independent of the decision on whether any UILs offered address the competition concerns identified. The decision maker will not typically be involved in any discussions concerning UILs until the decision on the existence and scope of SLC(s) has been made.[54] If a Phase 1 investigation case proceeds to an issues meeting, the merger parties will be invited to raise possible UILs with the case team at the end of the meeting after the decision maker has left the room.[55]

4.6 In exceptional circumstances (eg where the remedies are likely to be complex in design and/or implementation or where competition authorities in other jurisdictions are considering a merger which the CMA is also investigating),[56] or when requested by the merger parties, the decision maker may choose to be involved in discussions concerning UILs prior to taking the SLC decision. The merger parties will be informed if the decision maker deems that this is appropriate. In these circumstances, the decision maker will engage with the merger parties, in order to maximise the chance of the CMA achieving an effective remedy to any competition concerns which might arise from the merger. The merger parties are not obliged to engage with the decision maker. The CMA will consider on a case-by-case basis whether additional procedural safeguards are necessary to ensure that the early discussion of remedies does not prejudice the SLC decision.

UILs offers following the SLC decision

4.7 Merger parties may wish to see the SLC decision before discussing UILs with the CMA. The SLC decision will set out the CMA's competition concerns and should therefore provide the merger parties with sufficient information to assess whether they wish to offer UILs to provide a clear-cut remedy to those concerns.

4.8 Under the Act, notifying parties have up to five working days after receiving the CMA's reasons for its SLC decision to offer UILs formally in writing (the UILs offer).[57] During this period of time, the CMA case team will be available to discuss possible UILs with the parties (subject to the constraints described in paragraph 4.4). Although the parties will not have access to the decision maker, the case team will have, in advance of any discussions, an understanding of the decision maker's view on what might be an acceptable UILs offer.

4.9 Given that the period for making a UILs offer is short, merger parties should not expect to engage in iterative discussions or negotiations with the CMA. Parties may formally submit two or three versions of their offer,[58] if necessary, which the CMA will consider at the same time to select the least intrusive effective clear-cut remedy, but parties should be careful to include the offer they believe will address fully the competition concerns set out in the SLC decision.[59] Parties should also indicate clearly their preferred remedy, providing reasons.

4.10 The Act does not allow the CMA to consider new UILs offers made after the five-working day deadline for the UILs offer.

4.11 If parties do not wish to submit a UILs offer, they may wish to inform the CMA (in writing) before the end of the five-working day period so that it can proceed to make the reference to Phase 2 as soon as possible.

Remedies Form

4.12 UILs offers (accompanied by the merger parties' proposed draft text of their UILs) should be made formally in writing using the CMA's Remedies Form for Offers of Undertakings in Lieu of Reference (*Remedies Form*) and the CMA's *UIL template*.

4.13 The Remedies Form provides details of the information that will assist the CMA in understanding clearly what the merger parties are offering (or not offering) in their UILs offer. Parties should bear in mind the following points when completing the Remedies Form:

(a) A UILs offer merely to 'remedy the SLC', without specifying how this will be achieved, will be considered insufficiently clear-cut.

(b) A UILs offer which proposes a behavioural remedy rather than a structural remedy is generally less likely to be considered sufficiently clear-cut.

(c) A UILs offer to remedy the SLC through divestment of one of the overlapping businesses should make it clear which of the overlapping businesses the merger parties are proposing to divest. Where the merger parties are equally willing to divest either business, they should state this in their UILs offer. Parties should be aware that, in certain cases, the CMA may consider that divestment of one particular business may not be sufficient to remove the competition concerns, given the need for the divestment to be a viable business and to be capable of attracting a suitable purchaser. In this situation, a UILs offer might include a fall-back proposal to divest another business should a buyer not be found quickly for the first business.

(d) Where parties are offering a divestiture remedy, they should state in their UILs offer whether they are proposing an upfront buyer.[60]

4.14 The level of information required by the CMA will vary according to the type and structure of the remedy proposed. Merger parties are encouraged to discuss with the case team the likely requirements of the CMA before completing the Remedies Form.

4.15 Merger parties are not obliged to complete all aspects of the Remedies Form, but providing all relevant information will enhance the CMA's ability to assess effectively the UILs offer.

The UILs 'acceptable in principle' decision

4.16 Where merger parties offer UILs, the CMA has until the tenth working day after the merger parties received the reasons for its SLC decision to decide whether the UILs offer (or a modified version of it) might be acceptable as a suitable remedy to the SLC or the identified adverse effects arising from it.[61] This decision is taken by the Phase 1 decision maker.

4.17 Where the CMA decides that the UILs offer (or a modified version of it) might be acceptable as a suitable remedy, it will confirm this to the parties who offered the UILs, and issue a public announcement to that effect (the UILs 'acceptable in principle' decision).

CMA discretion to propose modifications to UILs offers

4.18 As the merger parties will have received the CMA's reasons for its SLC decision before submitting their UILs offer, the CMA expects that, in the vast majority of cases, the merger parties will be in a position to assess whether to make a UILs offer capable of providing a clear-cut remedy to the SLC within the five-working day deadline. However, the CMA is mindful of the significant public policy benefits achieved through the UILs process. Therefore, the CMA reserves the right, where appropriate, to revert to the merger parties following receipt of their UILs offer to inform them that it could be suitable to address the SLC identified, subject to specified modifications.[62] This can happen either before or after the UILs 'acceptance in principle' decision. These modifications will not amount to a different remedy, but minor modifications of the existing proposal.

4.19 Where the CMA proposes modifications to a UILs offer, it will ask the merger parties whether they agree to the proposed modifications. The merger parties will be given a short period[63] in which to state whether or not they wish to offer the modified UILs. This includes the opportunity to make written or oral representations if they do not agree to the proposed modifications (in full or part).

Procedure for acceptance of UILs

4.20 Having made the decision that the UILs offer (or a modified version of it) might be acceptable in principle as a suitable remedy, the CMA will then start the process of detailed consideration of the proposed UILs. This process also has statutory timeframes. Where the UILs involve a divestment remedy, the process will differ depending on whether or not the UILs offer includes an upfront buyer.

Timeframes

4.21 The CMA is required to decide whether to accept the offered UILs within 50 working days of the SLC decision.[64] This can be extended by up to 40 working days if the CMA considers that there are special reasons for doing so.[65]

4.22 In considering whether an extension for special reasons may be appropriate, the CMA will have regard to:

(a) whether any delay may increase the risk of anticompetitive outcomes from the merger (eg where there is a risk that the target business may deteriorate pending the outcome of the merger investigation, or where any consumer harm may be ongoing);[66]

(b) the ability of the CMA and the parties to conclude the UILs acceptance process within the 50 working days; and

(c) the likelihood that the CMA will be able to accept UILs from the parties if an extension is granted.

4.23 As UILs must be a clear-cut solution to the SLC identified, the CMA would not expect to have to extend the timeframe for final acceptance of UILs unless:

(a) the case involves an 'upfront buyer' (see paragraphs 4.30 to 4.34 below);

(b) it is necessary for the CMA to undertake a further consultation with interested third parties on a modified version of the UILs offer (see paragraph 4.28 below); or

(c) there is some other exceptional circumstance and the additional time will likely lead to the acceptance of UILs.[67]

4.24 Within the SLC decision, the CMA will, where necessary, under section 25(4) of the Act, extend its four-month statutory timetable for considering a completed merger. This period will end at the earliest of the following events:

(a) the final giving of the UILs;

(b) the expiry of a period of 10 working days beginning with the first day after the receipt by the CMA of a notice from the notifying party that it does not intend to give UILs; or

(c) the cancellation by the CMA of the extension.

4.25 Throughout the process, the CMA remains under a statutory duty, under section 103 of the Act, to have regard to the need to make a decision as soon as reasonably practicable. It will therefore aim to accept the final form of the UILs as quickly as possible. In all cases, a reference may still be made if the CMA is unable to accept UILs within the statutory deadlines under the Act.

4.26 The CMA will agree with the merger parties a timetable of milestones through the UILs process to ensure that the merger parties are making timely progress towards the ultimate signing of an agreement with a suitable purchaser. This timetable will not be made public. However, failure by the merger parties to progress according to the timetable will be taken into account should the CMA need to consider whether to extend the 50-working day timetable for accepting UILs.

Consultation

4.27 In order to give interested third parties an opportunity to comment, the Act provides for third parties to be consulted prior to the CMA's final acceptance of UILs.[68] The CMA will publish the draft of the provisionally agreed UILs[69] and will invite comments from third parties. The CMA is required by the Act[70] to give third parties a period of not less than 15 calendar days in which to respond with comments on the purpose and effect of the proposed UILs.

4.28 To the extent that, as a result of the consultation process or otherwise, the originally published UILs are modified, a second consultation period will be required unless such modifications are not material in any respect. In such cases, in accordance with the Act, the consultation period for third parties to respond will be no less than seven calendar days.[71]

Acceptance

4.29 Following the necessary consultations, the CMA will ask the merger parties to sign the final version of the UILs, after which they will be formally accepted by the CMA. The CMA will announce publicly that it has formally accepted the UILs, thereby ending its duty to refer, and will publish the final version of the accepted UILs on the CMA website.

Upfront buyer cases

4.30 Where the CMA decides that UILs will be accepted only where the merger parties have identified an upfront buyer, the CMA will not accept the UILs unless a sale agreement, generally conditional from the buyer's perspective only on acceptance of the UILs by the CMA (and the completion of the main transaction if it remains anticipated), has been agreed with a buyer for the divestment business and the CMA considers that the buyer would be acceptable.

4.31 Where merger parties wish to offer an upfront buyer in their UILs offer, they may either identify a proposed buyer straight away or make the offer on the basis that any divestiture would be to an upfront buyer. In the latter case, parties will be given a relatively short period[72] after the CMA's UIL 'acceptance in principle' decision in which to identify the upfront buyer. After the merger parties have proposed their upfront buyer, the CMA will assess the suitability of the proposed buyer. The CMA will gain information from the buyer and, in most cases, will meet with the buyer. The CMA will specify the proposed buyer in the public consultation.[73]

4.32 Once the merger parties have obtained provisional confirmation from the CMA that the buyer is likely to be acceptable, they will enter into a sale agreement on the terms set out in paragraph 4.30 above.

4.33 If, following the CMA's assessment and public consultation, the CMA considers that the proposed buyer is not suitable, the merger may either be referred to Phase 2 or the parties will be required to identify quickly a suitable alternative buyer. In either case, the principles set out in paragraph 4.28 above in relation to further public consultation will apply.

4.34 Given the statutory deadline by which UILs must be finally accepted, merger parties are advised to give early consideration to the possible need for, and identity of, an upfront buyer.

Following final acceptance of UILs in non-upfront buyer cases

4.35 Where no upfront buyer provision is required, the CMA will continue to have an active role to play after it has formally accepted the UILs from the parties.

4.36 Where the UILs are structural in nature, they will provide for a divestment period within which the merger parties must identify a suitable purchaser for the divestment business and conclude a sale agreement with that buyer. As for an upfront buyer case, the CMA will assess the suitability of the proposed purchaser.

4.37 The CMA will again agree with the merger parties a timetable of milestones for this period (see paragraph 4.26).

4.38 Once a purchaser has been formally approved by the CMA, the merger parties are able to proceed with the divestment. Depending on the terms of the UILs, the merger parties may be required to enter into the relevant contractual document for the divestment and/or to complete the divestment by a date specified in the UILs.

Assessing the suitability of a purchaser

4.39 In a divestiture remedy, the merger parties must satisfy the CMA that their proposed purchaser is independent of the merger parties; has the necessary capability to compete; is committed to competing in the relevant market(s); and that a divestiture to this purchaser will not create further competition or regulatory concerns. Please refer to paragraphs 5.20 to 5.27 for more information on the CMA's purchaser suitability criteria.

4.40 In assessing whether a proposed purchaser should be approved, the CMA will examine information presented by the merger parties carefully and impartially, but will only undertake a proportionate amount of investigation and analysis at this phase.[74] If approval of a proposed purchaser requires a detailed investigation, it is likely that the CMA will choose not to approve that purchaser rather than to undertake an in-depth analysis.[75]

4.41 In principle, divestitures as a result of UILs may result in the creation of a new relevant merger situation, which the CMA could investigate. However, in practice, where a proposed divestment to a purchaser raises competition concerns,[76] the CMA will notify the merger parties that the proposed purchaser does not satisfy the purchaser suitability criteria.

Monitoring trustee

4.42 The CMA will assess on a case-by-case basis whether a monitoring trustee should be appointed to oversee and report on the divestiture process.[77] The CMA may appoint a monitoring trustee at Phase 1 or Phase 2.

4.43 Monitoring trustees help ensure the CMA better understands the progress being made in a divestiture by reporting on the merger parties' compliance with the agreed timetable. A monitoring trustee can also be used to review the separation of a business and ensure the divestiture package is as described in the proposed UILs.

4.44 The need for a monitoring trustee will depend, among other things, upon the nature of the divestiture package and the risk profile of the remedy. The need for a monitoring trustee in an upfront buyer case is likely to be lower than in a non-upfront buyer case, as the incentives for the parties to complete the divestment in good time is likely to be greater. A monitoring trustee is more likely to be appointed where:
(a) the divestiture package is not an existing business;
(b) significant assets are to be excluded from the existing business;
(c) significant transitional arrangements are required; and/or
(d) purchaser risks are particularly high.

4.45 If parties consider that a monitoring trustee is not required, they should include reasons for this in their Remedies Form.

4.46 Please see Chapter 8 for more information on trustees and third party monitors.

Divestiture trustee and CMA intervention

4.47 In a non-upfront buyer case, if merger parties are unable to find a suitable purchaser capable of being approved by the CMA within the time period specified within the UILs, the UILs will typically provide for the CMA to be able to appoint a divestiture trustee to sell the divestment business on behalf of the merger parties at no minimum price, or for the CMA to direct the parties to sell at no minimum price.

4.48 Whether UILs are structural or behavioural in nature, if, after accepting the UILs, it becomes apparent to the CMA that the undertakings are not being or will not be fulfilled, section 75 of the Act gives the CMA the power to issue an order against the merger parties to ensure fulfilment of the UILs. Such orders are enforced in the High Court.

Ongoing role for the CMA in behavioural UILs

4.49 For behavioural UILs, under section 92 of the Act, the CMA has an ongoing monitoring role for the duration of the UILs.[78]

UILs in public interest cases

4.50 In public interest cases, which fall to the Secretary of State for decision, the CMA considers at Phase 1 whether the competition issues that arise are such that the CMA would recommend a reference if there were no public interest issues. If the CMA would recommend a reference, the CMA will consider, under section 44(4)(f) of the Act, whether or not these concerns could be resolved by UILs and will advise the Secretary of State accordingly. To the extent that merger parties make it clear that they are not prepared to offer UILs, the CMA is likely to advise that it would not be appropriate to deal with the competition concerns arising from the merger situation by way of undertakings under paragraph 3 of Schedule 7 to the Act (or in the equivalent provisions in the Protection of Legitimate Interests Order).[79]

4.51 The Secretary of State must have regard to the CMA's view on competition issues, but may decide that public interest issues require a different outcome to that which would be required to address the competition issues. This could include a decision to clear the merger, a decision to make a reference, or a decision to accept undertakings, which might be different from those proposed by the CMA to resolve any competition concerns.[80]

Remedies for breach of UILs

4.52 Once UILs have been accepted, the CMA is released from its duty to refer by section 74(1) of the Act. UILs therefore become the definitive solution to any SLC. Section 74(1) of the Act precludes a reference to Phase 2[81] even where UILs are not fulfilled. In that situation, the CMA must rely on its order-making power under section 75 of the Act and, if necessary, invoke civil proceedings, under section 94 of the Act, to enforce the UILs and/or the order.

4.53 Under section 94 of the Act, third parties have the right to bring an action for breach of statutory duty against a party to UILs where the third party has suffered loss or damage as a result of a failure to comply with the UILs. It is in part for this reason that it is important that the terms of UILs are clear and straightforward to assist with their enforceability.[82]

Phase 2

4.54 At Phase 2, the CMA will start to gather information on possible remedies and consider relevant options after the basis of a possible SLC has been identified. The Inquiry Group will generally only consider possible remedies after it has reached its provisional finding on whether the merger is likely to give rise to an SLC.

4.55 In exceptional circumstances (eg where the remedies are likely to be complex in design and/or implementation or where competition authorities in other jurisdictions are considering a merger which the CMA is also investigating) or when requested by the merger parties, the CMA may consider possible remedies prior to having identified the basis of a possible SLC. The merger parties will be informed if the CMA deems that this is appropriate. The early consideration of possible remedies will typically only involve the CMA case team, although the Inquiry Group may choose to be involved in these discussions. In these circumstances, the Inquiry Group will engage with the merger parties, in order to maximise the chance of the CMA achieving an effective remedy to any competition concerns which might arise from the merger. The merger parties are not obliged to engage with the Inquiry Group. The CMA will consider on a case-by-case basis whether additional procedural safeguards are necessary to ensure that the early discussion of remedies does not prejudice the SLC decision.

4.56 Where the Inquiry Group reaches a provisional finding of an SLC, at the same time as publishing its provisional finding (or as soon as practicable thereafter), the CMA will consult on possible remedies to address the SLC.[83] The CMA's notice of possible remedies is a starting point for discussion with the merger parties and other parties, including customers, competitors and any relevant sectoral regulator.

4.57 The CMA will consider remedy options proposed by the merger parties and others, in addition to its own proposals. Parties will be expected to demonstrate that their proposed remedy options will address effectively the provisional SLC and the resulting adverse effects. The merger parties will also be expected to provide evidence to support any claims concerning RCBs and their potential for pass through to relevant customers.

4.58 Where the Inquiry Group reaches a provisional finding of an SLC, response hearings will take place after the publication of the provisional findings and notice of possible remedies. Response hearings will be held with the merger parties and sometimes also with key third parties likely to provide useful evidence or views (eg potential buyers, significant customers or relevant sectoral regulators).[84]

4.59 Response hearings may take place where the provisional finding is that no SLC arises as a result of the merger, although merger parties can waive their right to a response hearing under these circumstances.[85]

4.60 The response hearing with the merger parties will be led by the Inquiry Group with case team support. Hearings with third parties may be led by the Inquiry Group or the case team and may be held face-to-face or by teleconference.

4.61 In a response hearing, parties are given the opportunity to comment orally on the provisional findings and the CMA may seek clarification on evidence previously provided. However, much of the focus of the hearing is on possible remedies.

4.62 A transcript of the hearing will be taken and will be sent to the relevant parties after the hearing for checking – the transcript is not published.[86] The CMA may sometimes prepare and publish a summary of evidence gathered through third party response hearings, but this will not typically be the case. The publication of a summary will depend on the circumstances of the case and will take into account confidentiality considerations. Where relevant, and subject to confidentiality considerations, comments from third parties will be incorporated into the remedies working paper that is disclosed to the merger parties (see paragraph 4.64).

4.63 Following the response hearings, the merger parties or other parties may submit further, or amended, proposals for remedies. Non-confidential versions of these proposals will be published on the CMA website. There may also be further meetings with the merger parties at case team level.

4.64 A remedies working paper, containing a detailed assessment of the different remedies options and setting out the CMA's provisional decision on remedies, will be sent to the merger parties for comment following the response hearings. This paper will also set out the CMA's views on whether the merger gives rise to RCBs, and if so, whether the proposed remedy should be modified in order to preserve those benefits. The merger parties will typically have at least five working days to respond to the remedies working paper. Third parties may also be consulted about the proposed scope of remedies and their views on any RCBs, and the remedies working paper may in some cases be published on the CMA website, but only if the CMA deems wider consultation to be necessary. In most cases, the remedies working paper is not published.

4.65 Following consultation on the remedies working paper and any further discussions and meetings with parties that the CMA considers necessary, the CMA will take its final decision on both the competition issues and any remedies.

4.66 The CMA will publish its final decision on the SLC and remedies, together with its supporting reasons and information, in a final report.[87] The report will contain sufficient detail on the nature and scope of remedies to provide a firm basis for subsequent implementation by the CMA.

4.67 Following publication of the final report, the CMA has the choice of implementing remedies by obtaining Final Undertakings from the relevant parties or making a Final Order, subject to the limitations set out in Schedule 8 of the Act. The CMA will consult with the merger parties and other parties affected by the remedies in determining the required Final Undertakings or Final Order. This will include a period of formal public consultation, as specified in Schedule 10 of the Act.

4.68 The CMA is subject to a statutory deadline of 12 weeks following its final report[88] to accept Final Undertakings[89] or to make a Final Order.[90] This period may be extended once by up to six weeks[91] if the CMA considers there are special reasons for doing so.[92] [93]

4.69 The CMA will normally seek to obtain Final Undertakings in an appropriate form from the merger parties. However, if agreement on Final Undertakings is not forthcoming on a timely basis, the CMA will have recourse to imposing a Final Order. The length of time required to obtain agreed Final Undertakings from the merger parties following the final report will reflect, inter alia, the complexity of the remedies involved and the variety of parties involved in the consultation.

4.70 The Inquiry Group will disband following its acceptance of Final Undertakings or the imposition of a Final Order to implement remedies. Responsibility within the CMA for any further implementation of remedies (eg overseeing any divestiture process) will pass to a Group appointed to oversee this part of the process (usually the original Inquiry Group).

4.71 The CMA will have an ongoing responsibility for the monitoring and enforcement of any behavioural remedies.[94]

4.72 The CMA will publish and update an administrative timetable regarding the implementation of remedies.

4.73 The action the CMA takes in implementing remedies must be consistent with the decisions in the final report unless there has been a material change of circumstances since the preparation of the report or the CMA has a special reason for acting differently.[95]

4.74 If a person fails to comply with any Final Undertakings that it has given or any Final Order imposed on it by the CMA, compliance may be enforced by means of civil proceedings brought by the CMA for an injunction or for interdict or for any other appropriate relief or remedy in one of the UK courts.[96] In addition to enforcement by the CMA, any person affected by the contravention of Final Undertakings or a Final Order who has sustained loss or damage as a result of such contravention may also bring an action against the party bound by the Final Undertakings or Final Order.

4.75 The CMA has a statutory duty to keep undertakings and orders under the Act under review.[97] From time to time, the CMA must consider whether, by reason of a change in circumstances (eg significant changes in market structure or changes in laws and regulations affecting a market), the undertaking or the order is no longer appropriate and should be varied or terminated.[98] Responsibility for deciding on variation or termination of undertakings or orders lies with the CMA in all but a very limited number of cases.[99] Please refer to the guidance on the CMA's approach to the variation and termination of merger, monopoly and market undertakings and orders (CMA11) for further information.

Remedies implementation during litigation

4.76 Merger parties have the right to apply to the CAT for a review of a decision by the CMA. However, such an application does not suspend the effect of the decision, except insofar as a direction to the contrary is made by the CAT.[100]

4.77 The effect of the statutory deadline for acceptance of Final Undertakings or the making or a Final Order is that, notwithstanding any such application, the CMA is required to accept Final Undertakings or make a Final Order whilst appeal proceedings are pending, unless there is some form of interim relief granted by the CAT or the courts.

4.78 The CMA will aim to work with the merger parties to progress as far as practicable the prompt implementation of remedies, while paying appropriate respect to merger parties' legitimate rights of defence and the role of the CAT and other courts.

Completed mergers

4.79 The CMA's approach to remedies will follow similar principles for anticipated mergers and completed mergers. However, the remedies process in completed merger investigations may often face circumstances which, in practice, increase the risks of not achieving an effective solution compared with anticipated merger investigations. For example, there may be greater difficulty in separating a divestiture package or the merger parties may have weaker incentives to pursue timely divestiture.

4.80 The CMA will take action to limit these risks and ensure an effective outcome. Completed merger cases therefore typically require interim measures, such as an interim enforcement order and the appointment of a monitoring trustee.[101] As noted in paragraph 3.9 , the CMA will not normally consider the cost of divestiture to the merger parties in selecting appropriate remedies.

NOTES

51 In public interest cases (described more fully in Chapter 16 of CMA2), the CMA will advise the Secretary of State whether UILs are appropriate to deal with the competition issues identified pursuant to section 44 of the Act. Any such UILs concerning competition issues are negotiated by the CMA and accepted by the Secretary of State. For mergers involving national security considerations, the Ministry of Defence will discuss any proposed public interest undertakings with the merger parties on the Secretary of State's behalf.

52 Section 73(2) of the Act provides the CMA with the power to accept undertakings from 'such of the parties concerned as it considers appropriate'. The Act does not give the CMA the power to accept undertakings from unconcerned third parties.

53 Such discussions with the case team will not impact on the prospect that the decision maker ultimately determines that the test for reference is not met; nor will they prejudice the merger parties' right to decide not to offer any UILs.

54 Section 73(1) of the Act.

55 The Phase 1 decision maker will not be informed of whether any UILs were discussed until after the decision on the SLC has been made.

56 At Phase 1, the CMA will look to proceed with its investigation in parallel with any investigations taking place in other jurisdictions.

57 Section 73A(1) of the Act.

58 Parties should submit their best offer. However, on occasion, there can be uncertainty about what exactly needs to be included for the remedy to be fully effective in addressing the competition concerns identified. To avoid the unnecessary rejection of a UIL offer, the CMA is willing to consider two or three versions of an offer (eg including a smaller or larger package of assets).

59 See the CMA's investigation into the anticipated acquisition by John Wood Group plc of Amec Foster Wheeler plc (2017),

where the CMA did not take up the option of an upfront buyer, as it did not consider that this was necessary.

60 This is a commitment to find a buyer which will be assessed and approved by the CMA, and to conclude an agreement with this buyer, prior to the CMA's final acceptance of UILs. Merger parties are able to offer two or three versions of their UILs offer, so they might, as their preference, submit a divestiture proposal with a non-upfront buyer offer, but say that, in the alternative, they would also be willing to offer a divestiture proposal with an upfront buyer.

61 Section 73A(2) of the Act.

62 Such modifications relate to the substance of the UIL offer, such as the specification of the divestment package or the requirement for an upfront buyer, and not to the text of the undertakings.

63 The length of this period will depend on the particular circumstances of the investigation, but would not typically be longer than a few days.

64 Section 73A(3) of the Act.

65 Section 73A(4) of the Act. The CMA may also extend the period for considering UILs if it considers that a relevant person has failed to comply with a notice requiring evidence issued under section 109 of the Act.

66 The CMA's assessment of this issue may be linked to the likelihood of it being able to agree acceptable UILs with the merger parties if an extension is granted. Where the CMA considers that there is sufficient likelihood of reaching agreement, it would be more likely to grant an extension, in order to avoid the delay associated with an in-depth Phase 2 investigation.

67 In relation to (a) and (b), see the CMA's investigation into the anticipated acquisition by Muller UK & Ireland Group LLP of the dairy operations of Dairy Crest Group plc (2015). In relation to (c), see the CMA's investigation into the completed acquisition by AMC (UK) Acquisition Limited of Odeon and UCI Cinemas Holdings Limited (2017), where the CMA extended the period to ensure that the parties could obtain a required consent from a third party.

68 Section 90 of, and Schedule 10 to, the Act.

69 The CMA may also publish non-confidential parts of the merger parties' Remedies Form alongside the draft UILs.

70 Paragraph 2(2) of schedule 10 to the Act.

71 Pursuant to paragraph 2(5) of schedule 10 to the Act.

72 The length of this period will depend on the particular circumstances of the investigation, but would not typically be longer than a few days.

73 The CMA will consult on both the draft of the provisionally agreed UILs and the proposed buyer.

74 This is consistent with the requirement that UILs should provide a clear cut solution to the SLC identified at Phase 1.

75 See Co-operative Group (CWS) Limited v Office of Fair Trading [2007] CAT 24.

76 The fact that the acquisition by a proposed purchaser would qualify for investigation pursuant to the share of supply test does not necessarily mean that it would create substantive competition concerns; this will depend on the circumstances of the case and the market(s) in question.

77 The parties will be responsible for the remuneration of the monitoring trustee. To ensure that the structure of such remuneration does not compromise the monitoring trustee's independence and provides sufficient incentive to perform the required function to an appropriate standard, the CMA must approve the remuneration agreement with the monitoring trustee.

78 Note, however, that behavioural undertakings will not generally (absent particular facts) be considered to be a credible, clear-cut remedy suitable for UILs at Phase 1.

79 See the anticipated acquisition by Lloyds TSB plc of HBOS plc, Report to the Secretary of State for Business Enterprise and Regulatory Reform, 24 October 2008, paragraph 381.

80 See Chapter 16 of CMA2 for further information on public interest mergers.

81 Unless material facts about the relevant arrangements or transactions in consequence of which the enterprises subject to the merger have or will cease to be distinct (or relevant proposed arrangements or transactions) were not notified to the CMA, or made public before the UILs were accepted (sections 74(2) to (4) of the Act).

82 See Administrative penalties: Statement of Policy on the CMA's approach (CMA4) for further information.

83 See CMA Rules for Merger, Market & Special Reference Groups (CMA17), Rule 12.

84 The hearings with the merger parties and third parties will be held separately.

85 Where the CMA reaches a provisional finding of no SLC, it will consider whether it is appropriate to have response hearings with any third parties.

86 Intentional or reckless provision of false or misleading information is a criminal offence, and this includes where the information is provided during a hearing (Section 117 of the Act).

87 Section 38 of the Act.

88 Section 41A(1) of the Act.

89 Section 82 of the Act.

90 Section 84 of the Act.

91 Section 41A(2) of the Act.

92 For example, due to extensive discussions relating to behavioural remedies or a complex partial divestiture.

93 These time limits may be further extended where a relevant party has failed to comply with the requirements of a notice requiring the submission of evidence issued under section 109 of the Act (Section 41A(3) of the Act).

94 Section 92 of the Act.

95 Section 41(3) of the Act.

96 Section 94 of the Act.

97 Under sections 92(2) and 162(2) of the Act. There is a similar legacy duty under sections 88(4) and (5) of the Fair Trading Act 1973 (as preserved in Schedule 24 to the Act).

98 The statutory language refers to the variation, release or superseding of undertakings and the variation or revocation of orders.

99 Certain undertakings and orders originally given to the Secretary of State under the Fair Trading Act 1973 remain the responsibility of the Secretary of State.

100 Section 120 of the Act.

101 Considerations regarding the use, design and implementation of interim measures, including interim orders, are set out

in CMA60.

5. DIVESTITURE REMEDIES

Introduction

[3.446]

5.1 A divestiture seeks to remedy an SLC by either creating a new source of competition, through disposal of a business or set of assets to a new market participant, or by strengthening an existing source of competition, through disposal to an existing market participant independent of the merger parties.

5.2 To be effective in restoring or maintaining rivalry in a market where the CMA has decided that there is an SLC, a divestiture remedy will involve the sale of an appropriate divestiture package to a suitable purchaser through an effective divestiture process.

Divestiture risks

5.3 Divestitures may be subject to a variety of risks that may limit their effectiveness in addressing an SLC. It is helpful to distinguish between three broad categories of risks that may impair the effectiveness of divestiture remedies, as follows:

(a) Composition risks: these are risks that the scope of the divestiture package may be too constrained or not appropriately configured to attract a suitable purchaser or may not allow a purchaser to operate as an effective competitor in the market.

(b) Purchaser risks: these are risks that a suitable purchaser is not available or that the merger parties will dispose to a weak or otherwise inappropriate purchaser.

(c) Asset risks: these are risks that the competitive capability of a divestiture package will deteriorate before completion of the divestiture, for example, through the loss of customers or key members of staff.

5.4 The incentives of merger parties may serve to increase the risks of divestiture. Although merger parties will normally have an incentive to maximise the disposal proceeds of a divestiture, they will also have incentives to limit the future competitive impact of a divestiture on themselves. Merger parties may therefore seek to sell their less competitive assets/businesses and target them to firms which they perceive as weaker competitors. They may also allow the competitiveness of the divestiture package to decline during the divestiture process.[102]

5.5 Divestiture risks can be overcome, at least in part, through the design of the divestiture package and by adopting protective measures, such as the appointment of a monitoring trustee (see paragraphs 5.37 to 5.39) and divestiture trustee (see paragraphs 5.43 to 5.44) and requiring an upfront buyer (see paragraphs 5.28 to 5.32).

Scope of divestiture packages

Package definition

5.6 In identifying a divestiture package, the CMA will take, as its starting point, divestiture of all or part of the acquired business.[103] This is because restoration of the pre-merger situation in the markets subject to an SLC will generally represent a straightforward remedy. The CMA will consider a divestiture drawn from the acquiring business if this is not subject to greater risk in addressing the SLC.[104, 105] In appropriate cases, the CMA may be willing to leave open to the merger parties which of the overlapping businesses they wish to sell, with the UILs or Final Undertakings stipulating that one of them must be sold.[106]

5.7 In defining the scope of a divestiture package that will satisfactorily address the SLC, the CMA will normally seek to identify the smallest viable, stand-alone business that can compete successfully on an ongoing basis and that includes all the relevant operations pertinent to the area of competitive overlap. This may comprise a subsidiary or a division or the whole of the business acquired. Following discussion with the merger parties, the CMA may modify the scope of the proposed divestiture package, provided that the parties can demonstrate, to the CMA's satisfaction, that the modified package addresses the SLC and the modification does not create significant composition, purchaser or asset risks after taking account of protective measures.

5.8 The divestiture may comprise the sale of all relevant assets in one package or the sale of assets grouped together in a limited number of packages. The scope of the package will reflect the particular circumstances of the case.[107]

5.9 The scope of a divestiture package will be outlined, with reasons, in the CMA's decision or final report, and will be specified in greater detail in the UILs accepted, the Final Undertakings accepted or the Final Order made by the CMA when implementing the remedy. The merger parties may subsequently add further assets to the specified package with the approval of the CMA, or may be required to do so by the CMA, to secure divestment to a suitable purchaser.

5.10 The merger parties will generally be prohibited from subsequently purchasing assets or shareholdings sold as part of a divestiture package or acquiring material influence over them. The CMA will normally limit this prohibition to a period of 10 years.

5.11 In appropriate cases, the CMA will consider other structural or quasi-structural remedies. A structural remedy other than divestiture might comprise, for example, an amendment to IP licences to grant a divestment purchaser a perpetual and royalty-free licence.[108]

Divestiture of an existing business or package of assets

5.12 The CMA will generally prefer the divestiture of an existing business, which can compete effectively on a stand-alone basis, independently of the merger parties, to the divestiture of part of a business or a collection of assets. This is because divestiture of a complete business is less likely to be subject to purchaser and composition risk and can generally be achieved with greater speed.

5.13 Where a proposed divestiture comprises part of a business or specified assets, such as IP rights, the capabilities and resources of prospective buyers are likely to be more critical to a successful outcome than for a standalone business. A package of assets proposed for divestiture may, for example, lack an established infrastructure and its viability may therefore be more dependent on an appropriate match with the capabilities of the purchaser.

5.14 A package of assets may also be far more difficult to define or 'carve out' from an underlying business,[109] and the CMA may have less assurance that the purchaser will be supplied with all it requires to operate competitively. In such circumstances, the CMA is likely to require additional protective measures, such as the identification of an upfront buyer (see paragraphs 5.28 and 5.32) to mitigate increased purchaser and composition risk.[110] Where a package of assets is proposed for divestiture, the CMA will require the merger parties to specify the composition and operation of the package in detail.

5.15 In particular circumstances, merger parties may propose a 'virtual divestiture' consisting of the divestiture of production capacity[111] for a specified period rather than the conventional disposal of a business or package of assets. Such a proposal may have higher risks and costs than a conventional divestiture and may require ongoing monitoring and compliance activity. The CMA would need to satisfy itself that there was good reason to justify such a proposal in preference to a conventional divestiture and that the risks of the proposal could be appropriately contained.

Preference for avoiding 'mix-and-match' divestitures

5.16 Divestiture of a mixture of assets from both merger parties (a so-called 'mix-and-match' approach) may create additional composition risks such that the divestiture package will not function effectively. Therefore, if divestiture of a set of assets or parts of a business is proposed, it will normally be preferable for all the assets to be provided by one of the merger parties unless it can be demonstrated to the CMA's satisfaction that there is no significant increase in risk from a mix-and-match alternative.

Alternative divestiture packages

5.17 In some circumstances, it may be appropriate to define a more extensive and/or more marketable divestiture package (an 'alternative divestiture package'), which the CMA would require the merger parties to sell if the initially proposed divestiture package were not sold within a specified period.[112]

5.18 Alternative divestiture packages may be appropriate if there is doubt as to the marketability of the initially proposed divestiture package or where a business is subject to major asset risks and the speed of divestiture is likely to be a critical requirement. In such circumstances, the prior identification of an alternative, more extensive and more marketable package may be the most effective means of facilitating rapid disposal if the initial package cannot be sold to a suitable purchaser within a specified period.[113] Alternatively, the CMA may require that, in the event that the merger parties' preferred divestiture does not proceed to its satisfaction within the timescales set out in the UILs, Final Undertakings or Final Order, a divestiture trustee may be appointed to ensure the sale of an alternative package.

5.19 The alternative divestiture package will include all the core assets necessary to remedy the SLC. The CMA will wish to satisfy itself that the purchaser of such a package is committed to operating the core assets to compete effectively in the market(s) affected by the SLC and is not primarily attracted by the additional assets. The CMA will identify the alternative package in its final report, but the existence of an alternative package will generally be excised from the published version of the final report to prevent the existence of the alternative package undermining the divestiture of the initial package.

Suitable purchasers

Criteria

5.20 The identity and capability of a purchaser will be of major importance in ensuring the success of a divestiture remedy. The merger parties will therefore need to obtain the CMA's approval of the prospective purchaser.

5.21 The CMA will wish to satisfy itself that a prospective purchaser is independent of the merger parties; has the necessary capability to compete; is committed to competing in the relevant market; and divestiture to the purchaser will not create further competition concerns. The relative importance that the CMA attributes to each of these criteria will depend on the circumstances of the investigation. These criteria are considered in more detail below:

(a) The acquisition by the proposed purchaser must remedy, mitigate or prevent the SLC concerned or any adverse effect resulting from it, achieving as comprehensive a solution as is reasonable and practicable.

(b) Independence. The purchaser should have no significant connection to the merger parties that may compromise the purchaser's incentives to compete with the merged entity (eg an equity interest, common significant shareholders, shared directors, reciprocal trading relationships or continuing financial assistance).[114] It may also be appropriate to consider links between the purchaser and other market players.[115]

(c) Capability. The purchaser must have access to appropriate financial resources, expertise (including managerial, operational and technical capability) and assets to enable the divested business to be an effective competitor in the market. This access should be sufficient to enable the divestiture package to continue to develop as an effective competitor. For example, a highly-

Part 3 CMA and other Guidelines

leveraged acquisition of the divestiture package which left little scope for competitive levels of capital expenditure or product development is unlikely to satisfy this criterion. The proposed purchaser will be expected to obtain in advance all necessary approvals, licences and consents from any regulatory or other authority.[116]

(d) Commitment. The CMA will wish to satisfy itself that the purchaser has an appropriate business plan and objectives for competing in the relevant market(s), and that the purchaser has the incentive and intention to maintain and operate the relevant business as part of a viable and active business[117] in competition with the merged party and other competitors in the relevant market.[118] [119];

(e) Absence of competitive or regulatory concerns. Divestiture to the purchaser should not create a realistic prospect of further competition or regulatory concerns.

5.22 Except in circumstances where a divestiture trustee is in place (see paragraphs 5.43 to 5.44), the merger parties are responsible for securing a prospective buyer and demonstrating that it satisfies the CMA's criteria for a suitable purchaser. However, the CMA will keep the progress of the divestiture under close scrutiny.

5.23 Where the merger parties receive interest in the divestiture package from multiple prospective buyers, they may ask the CMA to evaluate the suitability of a small set of short-listed purchasers. This is to avoid the merger parties progressing one prospective purchaser, possibly through lengthy due diligence, but this purchaser then being found not to satisfy the CMA's purchaser suitability criteria, and the merger parties having to start the assessment process afresh.

5.24 In requiring that the proposed purchaser be independent of and unconnected to the merger parties, the CMA will pay close attention to any links that would exist between the merger parties and the purchaser following divestment. This includes any proprietary interest that the merger parties would retain in or over the divested business that could impede the successful, independent operation of the divested business.[120]

5.25 Purchasers may require access to key inputs or services at appropriate terms from the merger parties, on an interim basis, in order to enable the divestiture to operate effectively. Such arrangements may be permitted by the CMA for a limited period.[121] The CMA may also permit or require non-solicitation clauses or other measures to protect the purchaser from the merger parties for a limited period (eg up to one year) to enable the purchaser to become established as an effective competitor in the relevant market(s).

5.26 In terms of determining whether the proposed purchaser has the financial resources, expertise, incentive and intention to maintain and operate the divestment business, the CMA is seeking to assess whether the purchaser will compete vigorously in the future on the basis of what it has acquired to address the SLC or the adverse effect resulting from it. The CMA will consider carefully the evidential basis on which the merger parties (and the proposed purchaser) assert that the proposed purchaser will have an incentive to compete going forward.[122]

5.27 On the basis that the CMA will approve a divestment purchaser only where it is confident that the acquisition by that proposed purchaser does not itself create a realistic prospect of an SLC within any market or markets in the UK, the CMA would not expect to investigate this transaction. This is regardless of whether or not the transaction constitutes a relevant merger situation under the Act.[123]

Upfront buyers

5.28 Where the CMA is in doubt as to the viability or attractiveness to purchasers of a proposed divestiture package (ie composition risk) or believes there may be only a limited pool of suitable purchasers (ie purchaser risk),[124] it may require the merger parties to obtain a suitable purchaser that is contractually committed[125] to the transaction before approving the UILs (at Phase 1) or it may accept Final Undertakings that the transaction will only proceed once a suitable purchaser is contractually committed (Phase 2).[126] This is because, while, at Phase 1 or Phase 2, undertakings given to the CMA without an upfront buyer will typically provide for the appointment of a divestiture trustee to sell the divestiture package (or greater if necessary) at no minimum price in the event that the parties do not achieve a sale within the stated divestment period, this is of limited benefit if there are no interested suitable purchasers.

5.29 The CMA generally adopts a more cautious approach with regard to these concerns at Phase 1 than at Phase 2. At Phase 1, the CMA will generally require an upfront buyer unless it considers that there are reasonable grounds for not doing so and, in particular, where the risk profile of the remedy does not require it. This may be the case where, for example, there is a liquid market for the assets or business; the assets or business are viable and profitable; there are a number of potential purchasers; and discussions with purchasers are at an advanced stage. To the extent that the merger parties are unable to identify a suitable purchaser at Phase 1 and so cannot offer an upfront buyer, the CMA can reactivate its duty to refer the merger to Phase 2, where the CMA has enhanced remedy powers.[127] This helps to align the interests of the merger parties with those of the CMA and customers, as the merger parties are motivated to achieve a sale swiftly to end their exposure to the possibility of a reference, minimising risks around deterioration of the divestiture package, and avoiding any continuation of the SLC in the market if the merger is completed.

5.30 At both Phase 1 and Phase 2, the use of an upfront buyer brings other advantages in reducing the risk of an unsuccessful remedy:

(a) The CMA is able to consult publicly on the identity and suitability of the proposed purchaser prior to accepting the UILs or Final Undertakings. This is particularly important where the identity of the purchaser is critical to the success of the divestment remedy (eg where the purchaser will need to apply its existing resources and capability to exploit the divestiture package). The CMA is more likely to be confident to approve such a purchaser in cases where third parties have been formally given an opportunity to comment on that proposed purchaser.

(b) The certainty provided for by an upfront buyer may provide latitude for the CMA to explore a remedy option that the CMA would not feel confident accepting in a non-upfront buyer context. Certainty around saleability becomes less important where this is going to be addressed prior to the UILs or Final Undertakings being accepted. For this reason, the CMA is likely to be less prescriptive where an upfront buyer is used, possibly providing merger parties with greater flexibility in determining, for example, which of the overlapping assets they wish to sell.

5.31 Where the CMA considers that the competitive capability of the divestiture package may deteriorate pending the divestiture (ie asset risk) or completion of the divestiture may be prolonged, it may also require that the upfront buyer completes the acquisition of the divestiture package before the merger may proceed or, in the case of a completed merger, before the merger parties may progress with integration.

5.32 In cases involving the divestment of multiple discrete assets or businesses, of which only a minority raise divestment risks justifying the use of an upfront buyer, the CMA may consider requiring a partial upfront buyer solution. In this situation, the merger parties may be required to sell to an upfront buyer those assets or businesses that raise concerns of the type listed in paragraph 5.28 above, whilst the CMA will permit the remainder of the assets or businesses to be sold following acceptance of the UILs or Final Undertakings.[128]

Effective divestiture process

Objective of process

5.33 An effective divestiture process will protect the competitive potential of the divestiture package before disposal and will enable a suitable purchaser to be secured in an acceptable timescale. The process should also allow prospective purchasers to make an appropriately informed acquisition decision.

Protecting the divestiture package

5.34 The merger parties may have significant incentives to run down or neglect the business or assets of a divestment package, in order to reduce its future competitive impact. The resulting asset risk may also be influenced by such factors as the length and complexity of the divestiture process and the pace at which customer goodwill and employee relations may erode.

5.35 To protect against asset risk, the CMA will generally impose an Initial Enforcement Order at Phase 1, which will continue at Phase 2, or seek Interim Undertakings or impose an Interim Order at Phase 2. This is to maintain the divestiture package and ensure the competitive position of the package is not undermined. Generally, it will require the divestiture package to be held and managed separately from the retained business.[129]

5.36 The appointment of a 'hold-separate' manager, or management team, may also be required to manage the assets/business to be divested, in order to maintain their competitiveness and separation from the retained assets.

Use of monitoring trustees

5.37 For completed mergers, where a monitoring trustee has not already been appointed at the point at which UILs, Final Undertakings or a Final Order are put in place, the CMA will normally require the appointment of a monitoring trustee to oversee the merger parties' compliance and, if applicable, the performance of the hold-separate manager. A monitoring trustee may also be required for anticipated mergers where the CMA determines that the risks associated with the divestment remedy warrant it.

5.38 The monitoring trustee will have an overall duty to act in the best interests of securing an appropriate divestiture. The monitoring trustee will monitor the ongoing management of the divestiture package and the conduct of the divestiture process. The CMA will have the right to propose and direct measures necessary to ensure compliance with the UILs, Final Undertakings or Final Order.

5.39 Please see paragraphs 4.42 to 4.45 and Chapter 8 for more information on the considerations regarding the appointment of trustees.

The divestiture period

5.40 At Phase 2, the CMA will state in its final report the period in which the merger parties should achieve effective disposal of a divestiture package to a suitable purchaser (ie the 'initial divestiture period'). However, this period may be excised from the final report if it is considered that disclosure to third parties may undermine the divestiture process.

5.41 The length of this period will depend on the circumstances of the merger, but will normally be a maximum period of six months. The CMA, when determining the divestiture period, will seek to balance factors which favour a shorter duration, such as minimising asset risk and giving rapid effect to the remedy, with factors that favour a longer duration, such as canvassing a sufficient selection of potential suitable purchasers and facilitating adequate due diligence. The divestiture period may be extended by the CMA where this is necessary to achieve an effective disposal.

5.42 While the merger parties are responsible for securing a suitable purchaser in the divestiture period, the CMA will keep the progress of the divestiture process under close review, through regular reporting and, where applicable, through the scrutiny of a monitoring trustee.

Use of divestiture trustees

5.43 If the merger parties cannot procure divestiture to a suitable purchaser within the terms of their UILs at Phase 1 in non-upfront buyer cases, or within the specified divestiture period at Phase 2, then, unless this period is extended by the CMA, the CMA may require the parties to appoint an independent divestiture trustee to dispose of the package within a specified period (the 'trustee's divestiture period'). The divestiture will be at the best available price in the circumstances, but subject to prior approval by the CMA of the purchaser and the divestiture arrangements.

5.44 The CMA may require that a divestiture trustee is appointed before the end of the initial divestiture period (eg if the CMA is not satisfied that divestiture is likely to take place within that period) or, in unusual cases, at the outset of the divestiture process.[130] The role of a divestiture trustee is distinct from that of a monitoring trustee, but the two roles may be performed by the same person.

Review of divestiture documentation

5.45 The CMA will wish to ensure, before providing its final approval of any divestiture, that the divestiture agreement and relevant supporting documentation include all assets required to be divested and contain no provisions that are inconsistent with the remedial objectives of the divestiture.

NOTES

102 See the Federal Trade Commission's A Study of the Commission's Divestiture Process (1999), DG COMP's Merger Remedies Study (2005) and the CC's Understanding past merger remedies: report on case study research (2007).

103 See Somerfield plc v Competition Commission [2006] CAT 4, where the CAT confirmed that it was reasonable for the CC, as a starting point, to consider that restoring the *status quo ante* would normally involve reversing the completed acquisition unless the contrary were shown.

104 See the CMA's investigation into the anticipated acquisition by Celesio AG of Sainsbury's Supermarkets Limited UK Pharmacy Business (2017), where the CMA concluded that, with the exception of Christchurch and Sandy, the divestiture of a particular Lloyds pharmacy in each of the areas where the CMA had found an SLC would be an effective and proportionate remedy to address the SLC that had been identified. The CMA found that in Christchurch and Sandy, the divestiture of either of two particular Lloyds pharmacies in these areas would be an effective and proportionate remedy to address the SLC that had been identified. The CMA also decided that a number of other safeguards were required to protect the pharmacies to be divested to ensure that there were no risks of asset deterioration occurring during the sale process.

105 The CMA will (in line with statements of the CAT in Somerfield PLC v Competition Commission) not seek to prevent an acquirer from 'trading up' by selling its own business, but will consider whether a sale of the acquirer's own business raises its own competition concerns or issues of achievability of divestment.

106 See the UILs given by MRH (GB) Limited to the CMA in relation to its acquisition of 78 petrol stations from Esso Petroleum Company Limited (2016).

107 See the anticipated acquisition by Heineken UK Limited of Punch Taverns Holdco (A) Limited (2017), where the CMA required the sale of the Divestment Businesses in no more than 4 packages.

108 See the OFT's investigations into the anticipated acquisition by Tetra Laval Group of part of Carlisle Process Systems (2006), where the OFT accepted UILs focused on an irrevocable, perpetual and exclusive licence of certain IP rights, and the completed acquisition by Unilever of Alberto Culver Company (2011), where the OFT accepted UILs from Unilever to divest the bar soap business of Alberto Culver, including the divestment of the Simple brand, which was effected by a perpetual and royalty-free licence covering UK, Ireland and the Channel Islands.

109 DG COMP's Merger Remedies Study found that carve out problems were a common cause of serious design and implementation issues in a significant proportion of divestiture remedies within its purview.

110 See the CMA's investigation into the anticipated merger between Ladbrokes plc and certain businesses of Gala Coral Group Limited (2016), where the CMA found there would be significant composition risk in the divestiture of several hundred licensed betting offices.

111 So-called 'virtual power plant' remedies are examples of this type of remedy.

112 Such packages are sometimes referred to as 'crown jewel' packages. However, in view of the wide variety of usage of this term, the CMA uses the more closely defined terminology of 'alternative divestiture packages'.

113 See the CMA's investigation into the completed acquisition by Euro Car Parts Limited of assets of the Andrew Page business (2018), where the CMA reserved its right in each overlap area to require divestment of an alternative depot to those nominated by the merger parties.

114 See Co-Operative Group (CWS) Limited v OFT [2007] CAT 24, paragraph 195.

115 See the CMA's investigation into the completed acquisition by Hain Frozen Foods UK Limited of Orchard House Foods Limited (2016).

116 This is because the CMA wishes to be satisfied that the divestment to the proposed purchaser will in fact go ahead. To the extent that a purchaser would face difficulties in obtaining such consents, this may call into question the suitability of the purchaser.

117 The CMA will routinely ask to see the proposed purchaser's annual accounts and business plan for the acquired business in assessing whether this criterion is satisfied.

118 This approach was upheld by the CAT in Somerfield plc v Competition Commission (2006). The CC excluded limited assortment discount retailers from acquiring Somerfield stores on the basis that these were insufficiently close competitors to conventional supermarkets.

119 The CMA will normally require the selling party to require from the divestment purchaser a warranty reflecting this obligation, or a variant of it, in its sale and purchase documentation. Such wording is included in the CMA's UIL template. See paragraph 2.5 and 3.1 of the UILs given by Vision Express (UK) Limited to the CMA on 15 November 2017 in relation to its acquisition of 209 Tesco Opticians outlets (2017).

120 The CMA may require that such links be severed or otherwise addressed as part of the remedy. See paragraph 2.5 of the UILs given by SRCL Limited and Cliniserve Holdings Limited to the OFT on 31 March 2009, and paragraph 10.2

of the UILs given by Co-operative Group Limited to the OFT in relation to its acquisition of Plymouth and South West Co-operative Limited on 26 March 2010.

121 See the CMA's investigation into the anticipated acquisition by Muller UK & Ireland Group LLP of the dairy operations of Dairy Crest Group plc (2015), where the CMA accepted UILs by Muller UK & Ireland Group LLP that included arrangements to provide for the expansion of an existing supplier to serve national grocery retailers with fresh liquid milk in the areas where the CMA found competition concerns.

122 The CMA will scrutinise the purchaser's incentives particularly carefully in a situation in which the purchaser is paying no compensation for the divested assets or business, or a price that is materially below market value.

123 The transaction could still require merger control filings outside the UK.

124 See the CC's investigation into the completed acquisition by Sports Direct International plc of a number of stores from JJB Sports plc (2010). In assessing the need for an upfront buyer, the CMA will often consider the number of potential purchasers that could reasonably be expected to be able and willing to acquire the divestment business. See the CMA's investigation into the completed acquisition by Immediate Media Company Bristol Limited of certain assets of Future Publishing Limited (2015), where the CMA, in deciding that an upfront buyer condition was required, noted that the proposed divestment packages were not standalone businesses and the number of possible buyers was reduced.

125 Contractual commitment may occur, for instance, through exchange of contracts, subject to limited conditions.

126 See, the CC's investigations into the anticipated joint venture between Kemira GrowHow Oyj and Terra Industries Inc (2007) and the proposed acquisition of a controlling interest in Academy Music Holdings Limited by Hamsard 2786 Limited (2007).

127 For the merger parties, the upfront buyer mechanism provides them with the option of terminating divestment discussions at Phase 1 and continuing their case at Phase 2 where they experience difficulty in agreeing satisfactory commercial terms with a potential divestment purchaser. This is in contrast to offering UILs without an upfront buyer where those undertakings will typically provide for divestment in these circumstances even at no minimum price.

128 See the OFT's investigation into the anticipated acquisition by Co-operative Group Limited of Somerfield Limited (2009), where the OFT required divestment to an upfront buyer only in relation to those stores in which there were expected to be a limited number of potential effective purchasers.

129 Considerations regarding the use, design and implementation of interim measures are set out in CMA60.

130 See the CC's investigations into the acquisition of the Co-operative Group (CWS) Limited's store at Uxbridge Road, Slough by Tesco plc (2007) and the completed acquisition by Ryanair Holdings plc of a minority shareholding in Aer Lingus Group plc (2015).

6. IP REMEDIES

Introduction

[3.447]

6.1 The licensing or assignment of IP, including patents, licences, brands and data, may be viewed generally as a specialised form of asset divestiture. However, in certain cases, the terms of a licence may contain ongoing behavioural elements such that the remedy is a structural/behavioural hybrid. The key element is the extent to which any material link between licensor and licensee will exist following award of the licence.

6.2 A remedy that requires an assignment or licence of an IP right that is exclusive, irrevocable and non-terminable with no performance-related royalties will effectively be treated by the CMA as structural in form and subject to similar consideration and evaluation as an asset divestiture. A licence that requires a licensee to rely on the licensor for updates of the technology or continuing access to specialist inputs or know-how will be regarded as a behavioural commitment, which is subject to significant risks of not being an effective remedy.

6.3 For licensing of IP alone to be effective as a remedy, it must be sufficient to enhance significantly the acquirer's ability to compete with the merger parties and thus address the SLC and any resulting adverse effects.[131] Such a remedy may not be effective if the IP needs to be accompanied by other resources (eg technical expertise and sales networks) to enable effective competition if these resources are unlikely to be available to the potential purchasers of the IP.

6.4 In view of the possible risks to effectiveness that may result from using IP remedies, the CMA will generally prefer to divest a business including IP rights, where this is feasible, rather than rely on licensing IP alone. This is because divestiture of a business including IP rights is more likely to include all that the purchaser needs to compete effectively with the merger parties.

Design factors

6.5 The appropriate design of an IP remedy may be influenced by a number of factors specific to the investigation, such as:

(a) the form and jurisdiction of the relevant IP (eg patent, exclusive licence and trademark). The CMA will wish to ensure that the IP to be divested is sufficient to enable a purchaser to compete effectively. This may sometimes include less easily transferable forms of IP (eg 'know-how').[132] Where there is uncertainty regarding the scope of a licence or its terms and conditions, the parties may be required to divest the underlying right and accept a licence back;

(b) the relative specialisation of the IP. Highly specialised IP may impose particular constraints on selecting a suitable purchaser, as there may be few parties competent to use the IP;

(c) the rate of innovation expected in the relevant market. A high rate of innovation may imply a shorter required duration for a licensing remedy than in a more stable market; and

(d) forms of payment for IP. The form of payment (eg one-off payment, royalties or profit shares) may have an effect on competitive incentives.

6.6 IP rights generally enable the remuneration of investment in innovation by granting time-limited exclusivity. In considering the design and scope of IP remedies, the CMA will recognise the need for preserving incentives for innovation while addressing competitive concerns.

6.7 Mergers critically dependent on IP rights may have international repercussions due, for instance, to international filing and licensing of patent rights. International cooperation with other competition authorities is therefore often particularly necessary in these cases.

NOTES

[131] See the CC's investigation into the completed acquisition of GV Instruments Limited by Thermo Electron Manufacturing Limited (2007), where the CC rejected a licensing remedy proposed by the merger parties on the basis that it would not adequately restore competition lost as a result of the merger.

[132] See the European Commission's investigation into the creation of a jointly controlled full function joint venture between Shell and BASF (2000), where the European Commission found that certain difficulties in transferring 'know-how' and other types of IP would have significantly reduced the scope and effectiveness of a licensing commitment.

7. BEHAVIOURAL REMEDIES

Introduction and general principles

[3.448]

7.1 Behavioural remedies are designed to address an SLC and/or its adverse effects by regulating the ongoing conduct of parties following a merger.

7.2 The CMA will generally only use behavioural remedies as the primary source of remedial action where:

(a) structural remedies are not feasible;
(b) the SLC is expected to have a short duration; or
(c) at Phase 2, behavioural measures will preserve substantial RCBs that would be largely removed by structural measures.

7.3 The CMA may also use behavioural measures as an adjunct to structural measures.

Design, monitoring and enforcement

7.4 Behavioural remedies seek to change aspects of business conduct from what may be expected, based on businesses' incentives and resources. The design of behavioural remedies should seek to avoid four particular forms of risk to enable these measures to be as effective as possible:

(a) Specification risks: these risks arise if the form of conduct required to address the SLC or its adverse effects cannot be specified with sufficient clarity to provide an effective basis for monitoring and compliance. The intended operation of the measure needs to be clear to the persons to whom it is directed and other relevant parties, so that it is apparent what conduct constitutes compliance and what does not. For example, a commitment to permit access 'on fair and reasonable' terms may create significant specification risk, as the provision may be insufficiently specific to allow effective enforcement. Markets that are subject to frequent change in products or supply arrangements may be particularly prone to specification risk if the definition of required conduct is vulnerable to such changes.
(b) Circumvention risk: as behavioural remedies generally do not deal with the source of an SLC, it is possible that other adverse forms of behaviour may arise if particular forms of behaviour are restricted.[133] For example, if prices are controlled, a firm may reduce product quality. To avoid or reduce these risks, behavioural measures need to deal with all the likely substantial forms in which enhanced market power may be applied. In practice, this may not be feasible or may make the behavioural measures too complex to monitor.
(c) Distortion risks: these are risks that behavioural remedies may create market distortions that reduce the effectiveness of these measures and/or increase their effective costs. Distortion risks may result from remedies overriding market signals or encouraging circumvention behaviour. For example, prohibiting the use of long-term contracts may result in a lack of incentives to compete for new business.
(d) Monitoring and enforcement risks: even clearly specified remedies may be subject to significant risks of ineffective monitoring and enforcement. This may be due to a variety of causes, such as the volume and complexity of information required to monitor compliance; limitations in monitoring resources; asymmetry of information between the monitoring agency and the business concerned; and the long timescale of enforcement relative to a rapidly moving market.

7.5 For behavioural remedies to have the desired impact, it is essential that there are effective and adequately resourced arrangements in place for monitoring and enforcement, so that there is a powerful threat that non-compliance will be detected and that action will be taken to enforce compliance where this is necessary.

7.6 The CMA is responsible for the monitoring and enforcing compliance of remedies under the Act.[134] Customers and competitors of the merged entity may be in a strong position to report to the CMA on instances of non-compliance where they have appropriate resources and incentives. However, such persons may be inhibited from fulfilling this reporting role by lack of resources and verifiable information, lack of understanding of the measures, fear of reprisals and other disincentives. The likelihood of effective monitoring will be significantly increased if it is possible to involve a sectoral regulator in the monitoring regime.

7.7 In view of the constraints on the CMA's resources and the possible limitations on the reliance that can be placed on the reporting role of customers and competitors, it may be necessary for the CMA to require the merger parties to appoint and remunerate a third-party monitor to enable the CMA to fulfil its monitoring responsibilities effectively.[135]

7.8 If the merged entity is considered to have a dominant market position, then certain types of conduct that behavioural remedies may seek to prevent (eg predation or foreclosure of access) may already be prohibited under section 18 of the Competition Act 1998 or under Article 102 of the Treaty on the Functioning of the European Union (TFEU). Similarly, a behavioural remedy may seek to prevent the making of agreements that may be prohibited under section 2 of the Competition Act 1998 or Article 101 of the TFEU.

7.9 The CMA recognises the importance of ex-post competition enforcement. However, the CMA has an obligation to achieve as comprehensive a solution to the SLC and its adverse effects as is reasonable and practicable. The CMA will therefore normally prefer to specify its own remedial measures rather than rely on the general provisions of competition law, as this has the advantages that the CMA's measures can be designed to take account of the particular circumstances of the investigation, and the provisions for monitoring and enforcement can be fully defined.

Duration

7.10 As behavioural remedies are designed to have ongoing effects on business conduct throughout the period they are in force, the duration of these measures is a material consideration.

7.11 The CMA may specify a limited duration if measures are designed to have a transitional effect. Where measures need to apply as long as an SLC persists and as this period can rarely be predicted during the course of an investigation, the CMA will generally rely on the merged parties applying for variation or cancellation of the measures on the basis of a significant change of circumstances[136] or possibly recommend that the CMA reviews the need for the measures after a given period. However, the CMA may, in addition, specify a long-stop date in a 'sunset clause' beyond which the measures will definitely not apply. The period used for the long-stop date will depend on the circumstances of the investigation.[137]

Types of behavioural remedy

7.12 Effective remedy packages may require both enabling measures, which address an SLC by seeking to remove obstacles to competition or stimulating competition, and measures that control outcomes, which restrict the adverse effects of an SLC rather than address the SLC itself. Enabling measures may be further subdivided between measures that restrain the impact of vertical mergers and measures that restrain market power in a horizontal market context.

7.13 The variety of circumstances, conduct and possible behavioural measures that may be encountered on individual investigations is extensive. This guidance therefore seeks to outline the CMA's general approach rather than deal with all possibilities.

Enabling measures

Restraining the impact of vertical mergers

7.14 A vertical merger involves the merger of firms at different levels of the supply chain of particular goods or services. Where a party to such a merger has significant market power at one or more levels of the supply chain, the resulting merger may result in an SLC, typically through the incentive and ability of the merged entity to disadvantage competitors by foreclosing access to key inputs, facilities or customers and/or exploiting access to confidential information.

7.15 For example, if, as illustrated in Figure 3 below, the manufacturer (Compco) of most of a key industry component acquired a major user of this component (Prodco1), the ability of other users (Prodco2 and Prodco3) to compete could be disadvantaged by the merged entity through restricting supply of this component to Prodco2 and Prodco3 or making use of information concerning component orders by Prodco2 and Prodco3.

Figure 3: Vertical merger configuration

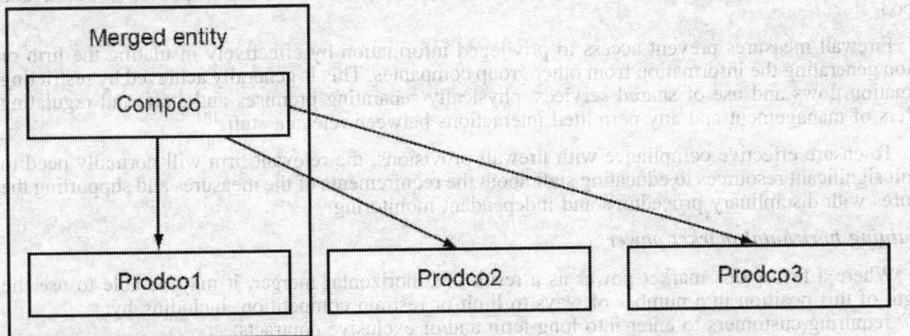

7.16 An SLC arising from a vertical merger may be remedied effectively by structural measures. Such measures might involve reversing the merger, but could also involve reducing the market power that the merged entity has at the critical stage of the supply chain (eg partial divestiture of Compco). However, if divestiture is not appropriate or feasible (see paragraph 7.2), then behavioural measures may enable continued access to necessary products or facilities on appropriate terms, or prevent the merged entity exploiting privileged access to information.

Access remedies

7.17 Access remedies seek to maintain or restore competition by enabling competitors to have access on appropriate terms to the products and facilities of a merged entity that they require to remain competitive.

7.18 An access remedy will normally need to specify an access commitment by the merged entity to customers in significant detail so that customers and monitoring agencies can enforce the commitment effectively. This will include details of the product or facility to be provided, including quality and technical parameters, and the terms of supply of the product or facility, including service levels and the basis of pricing. The latter may be particularly complex and will be subject to many of the same issues that are encountered with price caps. If the access commitment is not specified or monitored in sufficient detail, then the measure will be vulnerable to specification risk and the merged entity may be able to avoid its obligations. In such circumstances, the CMA will consider alternative forms of remedy (eg divestiture) that are likely to be more effective.

7.19 To overcome specification risk, the CMA will generally require that an access remedy should make explicit provision for accommodating future changes, for example, in product specifications or supply arrangements. Where a market is likely to be subject to frequent technological change or other wide-ranging market developments, there is likely to be a significant risk that an access remedy will become ineffective if the terms of the access commitment do not accommodate these changes. However, significant technological change might also reduce the market power that results in the SLC (eg effective substitutes are developed for the component supplied by Compco).

7.20 In some supply arrangements, certain factors may be particularly important for competitive access that are not easily specified (eg quality of product support, priority for system upgrades, or quality of management assigned to a customer's account). Such factors may result in 'soft biases' in access to supply that may generate significant circumvention risk and may significantly undermine the purpose and suitability of an access remedy.[138]

7.21 In certain circumstances, it may be possible to simplify the specification of an access remedy by obliging the merged entity to supply a particular product on fair, reasonable and non-discriminatory (FRAND) terms, where supplies to external customers are provided on the same or similar terms as apply to its own businesses. For this to be effective, the nature of FRAND terms must deal adequately with the circumstances of external customers and must be transparent to customers and monitoring agencies in sufficient detail to enable effective enforcement.

7.22 The use of FRAND terms may still leave competitors vulnerable to a margin-squeeze by the merged entity as it may have an incentive to charge all downstream businesses, including its own, a uniformly high price since reduced profitability in its downstream business can be offset by higher profitability in its upstream business. The CMA may therefore require that use of FRAND terms is accompanied by provisions to protect against a margin squeeze (eg submission of regular reports demonstrating full cost recovery in the downstream business).

7.23 Where it is necessary to preserve access to a key facility owned or controlled by a vertically merged company, and the usage and capacity of the facility is readily assessed, the CMA may determine that the most practical and effective means of providing access to competitors is to cap usage of the facility by the merged company and require it to auction remaining capacity to third parties.[139] This would be effectively a form of 'virtual divestiture' as considered in paragraph 5.15.

Firewall measures

7.24 Firewall measures[140] seek to prevent a vertically integrated company from accessing and using privileged information generated by competitors' use of the merged company's facilities or products. For example, in Figure 3, in the absence of firewall provisions, Prodco1 may be able to exploit privileged information regarding the orders and deliveries of key components from Compco to Prodco2 and Prodco3.

7.25 Firewall measures prevent access to privileged information by effectively insulating the firm or division generating the information from other group companies. This is generally achieved by restricting information flows and use of shared services, physically separating premises and staff, and regulating transfers of management and any permitted interactions between relevant staff.[141]

7.26 To ensure effective compliance with firewall provisions, the relevant firm will normally need to commit significant resources to educating staff about the requirements of the measures and supporting the measures with disciplinary procedures and independent monitoring.

Restraining horizontal market power

7.27 Where a firm gains market power as a result of a horizontal merger, it may be able to use the strength of this position in a number of ways to limit or restrain competition, including by:

(a) requiring customers to enter into long-term and/or exclusive contracts;
(b) creating switching costs for customers through, for example, volume discounts, contractual penalties or requiring complex switching procedures;
(c) bundling or tying the sale of particular products; and
(d) selective discounting or predation.

7.28 This category of remedies comprises measures that prohibit, restrict or discourage types of behaviour, such as those listed above, that may limit or restrain competition. The selection and design of these measures will depend critically on the circumstances revealed by the investigation and the need to avoid specification, circumvention, and monitoring and enforcement risks. Where circumstances point to the use of these measures, the CMA will follow the general approach of considering the likely anti-competitive behaviours that the merger parties may have an incentive and ability to engage in. It will then consider the measures that may be taken to prevent or limit these behaviours and the effectiveness and costs of these measures.

7.29 As an example of this approach, the use of long-term and/or exclusive contracts may create a significant barrier to entry or expansion. However, if, in the market in question, firms need to invest heavily to acquire new customers (eg by investing in new facilities or systems), then requiring that all contracts are short term in nature may generate significant distortion risks, as this would reduce incentives for firm to compete for new contracts due to insufficient opportunity to recoup their investment. In implementing a constraint on the use of long-term contracts, the CMA will therefore seek an appropriate balance between facilitating switching and permitting sufficient incentives to compete for new contracts.

7.30 Selective discounting or price discrimination can also have the effect of creating barriers to entry or expansion when used systematically to reduce prices to particular customers that are more likely to switch to other suppliers. Measures to restrict selective discounting or price discrimination may therefore be necessary where enabling entry and expansion is appropriate to address the SLC. However, such a restriction may only be necessary for a limited period until other sources of competition develop. Measures restricting selective discounting or price discrimination could generate significant distortion risk by adversely affecting the competitive dynamics of a market if maintained in the long term.

7.31 The CMA will have particular regard to avoiding circumvention risk in implementing measures limiting behaviour that would restrict competition. This is because firms with enhanced market power may readily evolve new forms of behaviour to replace restricted conduct.

Controlling outcomes

7.32 Remedies that control or restrict the outcomes of business processes, such as price caps, supply commitments and service level requirements, seek to prevent the merger parties from exercising the enhanced market power that they are likely to acquire from a merger. As such, these remedies seek to restrict the adverse effects expected from a merger rather than addressing the source of the SLC.

7.33 In order to overcome specification risk, remedies that control outcomes normally need to specify in significant detail the products or services that are subject to control and the basis of the control (eg the application of price indices to a price cap). The remedy will generally also need to specify how the control will deal with changes, such as the introduction of new products.

7.34 This class of remedy is subject to several significant disadvantages regarding its effectiveness and cost:

(a) Defining appropriate parameters for the control measure (eg the level of a price cap) may be complex and impractical and the measure may therefore be vulnerable to specification risks. This is especially likely where any of the following conditions apply:
   (i) Pricing in the relevant market is volatile.
   (ii) Products or services are differentiated rather than homogeneous.
   (iii) Prices are individually negotiated.
   (iv) Supply arrangements and products are subject to significant ongoing change.

(b) This class of remedy directly overrides market signals with the result that it may generate substantial distortion risks over time, increasing the effective cost of the remedy or reducing its effectiveness. For example, a price cap may deter entry or a supply commitment may discourage product innovation.

(c) The measure may be vulnerable to circumvention risks despite the addition of complex preventative provisions. For example, a price cap may be circumvented by a firm reducing the quality of controlled products or restricting the supply of controlled products.

(d) Monitoring and enforcement may be costly and intrusive and may lack effectiveness, especially where the form of remedy is complex.

7.35 In view of these disadvantages, the CMA will only use remedies that control outcomes where other, more effective, remedies are not feasible or appropriate. In addition, where this class of remedy is employed, it is most likely to be used on a temporary basis unless there is no alternative to a continuing regulatory solution.

Price caps

7.36 Price caps are likely to be the most common form of measure for controlling outcomes and illustrate many of the issues outlined above.

7.37 Different approaches may be adopted to defining the products and prices to be controlled depending on the circumstances of the investigation:

(a) Prices of all affected products may be individually capped. This may be impractical where a large number of products are involved and may be inflexible in dealing with product changes.

(b) The average price of a basket of products may be capped. This allows greater flexibility in taking account of shifts in demand between products, but the weighting of the constituents of the basket may be problematic and subject to distortion, for example, if revenue-weighting is used and the firm introduces a number of low cost product variants.

(c) The price cap may be restricted to key benchmark products. This approach could greatly simplify monitoring and compliance, but is only likely to be effective if a few key products continue to account for a large proportion of sales, and the pricing of other products is expected to remain closely related to the benchmark products.

7.38 The CMA will seek a basis for the price cap which will prevent the enhanced market power acquired through the merger from being reflected in prices. The basis of a price cap may take a variety of forms:

(a) Prices may be benchmarked to the prices of products in analogous markets that are determined by competition. In practice, this may only be feasible in limited circumstances due to the lack of an analogous market.

(b) Prices may be determined on the basis of input cost data and an approved return on capital. This resembles the approach adopted by many sectoral regulators, but generally requires a highly resource-intensive regulatory process backed by extensive information gathering and enforcement powers to be effective.

(c) The price cap may be indexed to pre-merger prices using an index that is representative of input cost changes after incorporating current productivity gains. The CMA will wish to use an index which has robust data sources and is constructed independently of the merger parties. Use of such an index may provide a broad approximation to a competitive price outcome in the short term, but is at risk of departing significantly from such an outcome in the medium to long term.

7.39 The CMA will generally require that price caps are accompanied by measures to prevent circumvention risk that may arise, for example, through the merged entity restricting the supply or service levels of price-controlled products or reducing product quality.

NOTES

133 This may be sometimes referred to as a 'waterbed effect'.

134 Section 92 of the Act.

135 See the OFT's investigation into the completed acquisition by Macquarie UK Broadcast Ventures Ltd of National Grid Telecoms Investment Ltd, Lattice Telecommunications Asset Development Company Ltd and National Grid Wireless No.2 Ltd (2007), where the merger parties undertook to remunerate an adjudicator responsible to the OFT to resolve contractual issues as part of a package of behavioural remedies.

136 Section 92 of the Act.

137 See the CMA's investigation into the anticipated acquisition by Mastercard UK Holdco Limited of Vocalink Holdings Limited (2017).

138 See the CC's investigation into the proposed acquisition of London Stock Exchange plc by Deutsche Börse AG or Euronext NV (2005), where the CC rejected a solely behavioural access commitment to clearing and settlement services due, in part, to the likely difficulty of 'soft biases'.

139 See the CC's investigation into the completed acquisition by Centrica of Dynegy Storage Ltd and Dynegy Onshore Processing UK Ltd (2006), where the CC required Centrica to restrict its usage of the Rough Gas Storage Facility to a percentage of total capacity to prevent foreclosure of access.

140 These may be referred to alternatively as 'Chinese wall' measures.

141 See the CC's investigation into the completed acquisition by Centrica of Dynegy Storage Ltd and Dynegy Onshore Processing UK Ltd (2006), which provides an example of the measures that may be required by the CMA to make firewalls effective.

8. TRUSTEES AND THIRD-PARTY MONITORS

Appointment and responsibilities

[3.449]

8.1 Trustees or third-party monitors (collectively 'trustees') may be used by the CMA in a variety of circumstances to assist in the monitoring and implementation of UILs, Final Undertakings or Final Orders.

8.2 Trustees should always be independent of the parties, have appropriate qualifications and capacity for the task, and should not be subject to conflicts of interest. Trustees may be part of an accounting firm, management consultancy or other professional organisation. Trustee candidates may be proposed by the merger parties, but can only be appointed by the parties following approval by the CMA.

8.3 The CMA may set a timetable for the appointment of trustees and would normally expect a trustee to be nominated and approved before UILs or Final Undertakings are accepted or a Final Order made. Typically, only the CMA can terminate the appointment of trustees before completion of their responsibilities. However, the merger parties can make representations to the CMA to replace the trustees if they have good cause.

8.4 The trustee's responsibilities will be specified in the trustee mandate/letter of engagement, which will be approved by the CMA. The trustee will perform the directions of the CMA in accordance with the mandate/letter and will not be permitted to accept instructions from the merger parties. The mandate/letter will also have appropriate clauses governing conflict of interest, trustee liability and confidentiality.

Remuneration

8.5 The merger parties are responsible for the remuneration of trustees. The structure of remuneration must not compromise a trustee's independence and must provide sufficient incentive to perform the required function to an appropriate standard. To ensure that this is so, the CMA must approve the remuneration agreement.

GUIDANCE ON REQUESTS FOR INTERNAL DOCUMENTS IN MERGER INVESTIGATIONS (CMA100, JANUARY 2019)

[3.450]

NOTES

1. INTRODUCTION

[3.451]

1. This guidance is primarily intended for merging parties and legal advisers advising on a transaction that may be subject to merger investigation by the CMA. The guidance should also be used by third parties that have been requested to provide information in merger investigations.

2. In some cases, the CMA will ask parties to provide internal documents (*i.e.*, documents that merging parties have generated internally in the ordinary course of business) to inform its investigation. The CMA requires certain internal documents, such as studies, reports, and presentations, to be produced as a matter of course as part of the merger notice (or in response to an enquiry letter where a merger is not voluntarily notified to the CMA). In some circumstances, other types of document – in particular emails sent or received by the merging parties' officers or employees that are relevant to the CMA's investigation – will be requested by the CMA. For the purposes of this guidance, all types of document in the merging parties' possession, which have been prepared, sent or received by an officer or employee of the merging parties, are referred to as '*internal documents*.'

3. Given the importance to businesses and consumers of the CMA's substantive decisions in mergers, and the need for such decisions to be taken in accordance with statutory timescales, it is vital for the CMA to be able to take decisions based on information that is accurate and complete, and to gather that information as quickly as possible. Internal documents can be an important source of evidence in a merger investigation and it is imperative that merging parties provide complete and accurate responses to document requests to enable the CMA to carry out its statutory functions. The CMA recognises, however, that requests for internal documents can be onerous for merging parties. The CMA (*i.e.*, inquiry groups and case teams) will therefore carefully consider the appropriate scope and nature of a document request in light of the circumstances of the case in order to ensure that such requests are proportionate.

4. The CMA can issue requests for information '*informally*' or using the powers provided by section 109 of the Enterprise Act 2002 (the Act). Section 109 of the Act provides the CMA with a mandatory information gathering tool for '*permitted purposes*' (including any aspect of its mergers-related functions).

5. This guidance is intended to provide further clarification in relation to the circumstances in which the CMA will request the production of internal documents, either through informal requests for information or under the statutory powers provided by section 109 of the Act.[1] The guidance also explains how CMA case teams may approach such requests and how merging parties are likely to be expected to respond.

6. The guidance should be read in conjunction with paragraphs 7.2 to 7.20 and 11.11 to 11.40 of Mergers: Guidance on CMA's Jurisdiction and Procedure (CMA2). Together with the guidance provided in CMA2, this guidance is intended to set out how the CMA will use requests for internal documents, including those requests made using section 109. The penalties for failure to comply with a section 109 request are set out in Administrative penalties: Statement of Policy on the CMA's approach (CMA4).

7. Where there is any difference in emphasis or detail between this guidance and other guidance produced or adopted by the CMA, the most recently published document will take precedence.

NOTES

1 As explained in further detail in paragraphs 12 to 16 below, section 109 of the Act provides the CMA with a mandatory information-gathering tool. Unless otherwise stated, references to 'requests' for internal documents within this guidance include notices requiring the production of documents under these mandatory powers.

2. THE USE AND SCOPE OF INTERNAL DOCUMENT REQUESTS

THE USE OF INTERNAL DOCUMENTS IN CMA MERGER INVESTIGATIONS

[3.452]

8. The CMA's merger notice requires merging parties to provide copies of certain documents in their possession that relate to the rationale and impact of the merger (under question 9 of the merger notice) and provide competitive analysis of the potential segments within which their activities overlap (under question 10 of the merger notice). As the guidance notes to questions 9 and 10 make clear, the CMA would not typically expect to receive documents such as emails, handwritten notes, or instant messages in response to those questions.

9. In cases where a merger is not voluntarily notified to the CMA, but where the CMA learns of it through another route, the CMA will consider whether to seek further information about the case by sending the acquiring party or parties an enquiry letter.[2] The enquiry letter sent by the CMA will typically request similar internal documents to those requested by the merger notice.

10. The principles set out in this guidance apply to requests for internal documents in both Phase 1 and Phase 2 merger investigations (although there is, in practice, likely to be some difference in the extent and type of information requested by the CMA in Phase 1 and Phase 2 proceedings). In most cases, merging parties are unlikely to be asked to provide material volumes of additional internal documents (*i.e.*, beyond those responsive to questions 9 and 10 of the merger notice or the equivalent questions in an enquiry letter in a Phase 1 investigation). Additional internal documents may, however, be requested depending on the circumstances of the case.

11. In Phase 1 investigations, additional documents (*i.e.*, beyond those referenced in paragraph 10 above) may be required, for example, where:

(a) The documents provided in response to questions 9 and 10 of the merger notice (or the equivalent questions in an enquiry letter) do not appear to fully capture the merging parties' analysis of the merger or their assessments of competitive conditions within the markets at issue. This might be the case, for example, where commercial decisions are taken via email (rather than at set-piece events such as meetings of a board of directors) or where internal reporting takes place via email (rather than in reports or presentations).

(b) The documents provided in response to questions 9 and 10 of the merger notice refer to other documents that the CMA considers may be material to its investigation.

(c) The merging parties submit that an exiting firm scenario is the appropriate counterfactual for competitive assessment.[3] In this circumstance, internal documents may be required (where not proactively provided by the merging parties) to substantiate whether the firm would have exited the market (whether through failure or otherwise) and whether there would have been an alternative purchaser for the firm or its assets to the acquisition under consideration.[4]

(d) There is an evidence 'gap' in relation to an issue (or relatively narrow set of issues) that is material to the CMA's Phase 1 investigation. This might be the case, for example, where the submissions and evidence provided by the merging parties on a given issue (which is material to the CMA's investigation) appear to be incomplete or inconsistent with other evidence obtained by the CMA in its investigation. In practice, where a material volume of further evidence (including evidence from internal documents) would be needed to dismiss competition concerns in relation to a broad range of substantive issues, it may be difficult for the CMA to undertake this kind of information-gathering within the context of a Phase 1 investigation.

12. In general, in keeping with the in-depth nature of a Phase 2 investigation, requests for internal documents are likely to be more extensive at Phase 2. Documentary evidence gathered in Phase 1 will also be used by the Inquiry Group in Phase 2. Questionnaires issued to the merging parties at the start of the Phase 2 investigation may request internal documents relating to the transaction (which might cover synergies, evaluations, alternative commercial options absent the merger *etc.*), customers, suppliers, product characteristics, competitor analysis, pricing, marketing, bidding strategy, and barriers to entry, expansion and exit. Follow-up document requests may then be issued where relevant to any of the matters under investigation.

THE USE OF STATUTORY POWERS TO REQUEST INTERNAL DOCUMENTS

13. The CMA can issue requests for information '*informally*' or using its section 109 powers. Section 109 provides the CMA with a mandatory information-gathering tool for 'permitted purposes' (including any aspect of its mergers-related functions). The definition of '*permitted purpose*' includes assisting the CMA in any aspect of its mergers-related functions, for any matter that is subject to a reference or a possible reference.[5] Under section 109(2) of the Act, the CMA can require, by a given deadline, the production of certain documents in a person's custody and control.[6]

14. Non-compliance with a notice sent under section 109 (a section 109 notice) can have a number of consequences. In particular:

(a) Where the CMA considers that a section 109 notice has not been complied with in the absence of a reasonable excuse, an administrative penalty may be imposed under section 110 (1) of the Act;[7]

(b) Where a merging party has not complied with a section 109 notice by the stated deadline, the CMA may 'stop the clock' and extend the statutory timetables for reviewing the merger;

(c) Where a section 109 notice is sent to merging parties who have notified their transaction by way of a merger notice (rather than responding to an enquiry letter), the CMA can reject the entire merger notice; and

(d) Under section 110(5) of the Act, it is a criminal offence to intentionally alter, suppress, or destroy any information that the CMA has required to be produced.

15. Separately to the consequences provided for by section 110 of the Act, it is, under section 117 of the Act, a criminal offence punishable by a fine or a maximum of two years' imprisonment (or both) either to knowingly or recklessly supply false or misleading information to the CMA, or to give false or misleading information to any third party knowing that they will then supply it to the CMA.[8]

16. The CMA's practice in relation to whether to request internal documents using informal or statutory requests has varied in previous investigations. To support the CMA's ability to carry out its statutory functions, which is dependent, in large part, on being able to rely on the accuracy and comprehensiveness of merging parties' submissions, the CMA is likely to use section 109 notices as standard in future investigations where internal documents are requested from main parties in both Phase 1 and Phase 2 merger investigations.

17. Section 109 notices can also be addressed to third parties, so long as the request is being made for a permitted purpose. The CMA will, however, typically request information from third parties informally in the first instance.[9] Section 109 notices will be used where the CMA has doubts about whether it will receive a full or timely response to informal requests and the evidence requested is material to the CMA's investigation.

THE LIKELY SCOPE OF INTERNAL DOCUMENT REQUESTS

18. The CMA may request any potentially relevant document. However, as noted above, the CMA will carefully consider the appropriate scope and nature of a document request in light of the circumstances of the case in order to ensure that such requests are proportionate.

19. The types of document included within the scope of requests for internal documents will be driven by the way in which a party conducts its commercial operations. To this end, the CMA may engage with merging parties to discuss their decision-making procedures and the way in which they gather, assess and disseminate competitive analysis. In practice, most requests for internal documents are likely to relate to specific categories of emails (including the files attached to those emails) and internal analyses (such as studies, presentations, spreadsheets, surveys etc). In some circumstances, the CMA may request the production of written materials (such as handwritten notes or notebooks). Similarly, where appropriate, the CMA may require the production of chats on instant messaging systems.

20. The identity of the custodians included within the scope of requests for internal documents is likely to be driven by involvement in or influence over commercial decision-making in relation to the matters under investigation. In advance of issuing a request for internal documents, the CMA may request information relating to the decision-making processes of the merging parties, or certain of their business activities (such as organisation charts and details of reporting lines and decision-making bodies and processes), in order to understand which business people are likely to hold potentially responsive documents.

21. The periods for which internal documents are requested will vary depending on the circumstances of the case and, in particular, on the history of the markets at issue. In most cases, the CMA would expect that the period covered by a request for internal documents would run from no earlier than three years before the date of the request (but notes that materially shorter or longer periods could be justified by the circumstances of a given case).[10]

APPROACH TO IT ISSUES

22. The CMA notes that the technology used by businesses in their day-to-day work and the technology used in document review and production processes tend to evolve rapidly. The CMA's approach to technical issues may therefore vary on a case-by-case basis to reflect these developments and the nature of the parties' IT systems. The CMA encourages the parties to engage at the earliest possible stage on these points.

23. While there may therefore be some differences between the IT systems used in different businesses, the CMA will typically expect parties responding to a request to internal documents to apply the following principles in preparing their response:

(a) *Responses should typically cover all of a custodian's IT 'environment.'* Responses to document requests will typically be expected to cover all parts of the custodian's IT environment where relevant documents might be stored. The CMA is therefore likely to seek to understand what IT facilities are available to custodians (e.g., in terms of email clients, instant messaging systems, document storage systems etc.) and what facilities custodians use in practice.

(b) *Appropriate measures should be taken to ensure that potentially responsive documents remain available for production.* The CMA may ask parties what measures have been taken to ensure that potentially responsive documents in the parties' custody or under their control on the date of the request remain available for production (e.g., whether the suspension of internal document deletion processes may be appropriate).

(c) *A robust search methodology should be used to identify responsive documents.* The CMA may ask parties to provide a full description of the search terms used (broken down by specific question and custodian where appropriate), including all Boolean searches used, as well as any technology-assisted review tools (such as predictive coding) that have been used. The CMA may also ask parties to explain to what extent documents were manually searched (and the approach adopted to such review).

(d) *Documents should be text-searchable.* All documents produced in response to requests for internal documents should be text-searchable. Where applicable (*i.e.*, in the relatively limited circumstances in which such documents fall within the scope of document requests), the CMA will ask how handwritten documents and scanned materials have been uploaded and whether they are searchable. Where such documents are not text-searchable, the CMA may request the manual review of these documents.

(e) *Parties may also be required to provide the metadata of digital material.* In most cases, the CMA is likely to require the merging parties to provide the metadata for responsive documents. If metadata for certain responsive documents are unlikely to be available (or if providing metadata is likely to be particularly burdensome), this should be discussed with the CMA as early as possible.

(f) *'Family' items will typically be considered as being responsive to the document request:* Parties should ensure that all 'family' attachments are included along with responsive documents.[11]

(g) *Responsive documents should be provided in their entirety.* Parties should ensure that documents are provided in their entirety, including the parts of a document that deal with matters that are not specified in the request. Emails should include the entire email chain (and should also, as described above, include all relevant attachments).

(h) *Parties may be expected to ensure that document submissions do not contain duplicate files.* The CMA may ask parties to ensure that duplicate files have been removed from a response to a document request. Depending on the circumstances of the case, the CMA may request 'case de-duplification' (*i.e.*, documents already provided to the CMA during the case in question should not be reproduced), 'custodian de-duplification' (*i.e.*, duplicate files within a set of responsive documents relating to the same custodian should be removed), and 'production de-duplification' (*i.e.*, duplicate files within the set of documents produced in response to the full information request should be removed).[12] The CMA may ask parties to provide an explanation of any steps taken to exclude duplicate files from the final production.

(i) *Parties may not be expected to produce draft documents.* Unless otherwise stated, requests for internal documents will cover the final (or most recent) versions of a responsive document and not any drafts (or previous versions) of the document.[13] In some circumstances, the CMA may request the production of draft files (*e.g.*, where the CMA has reason to believe that the content of certain draft documents may be material to its investigation). The CMA may ask parties to provide an explanation of any steps taken to exclude draft files from the final production.

(j) *Documents should be provided in the required format.* All documents should be submitted to the CMA in their native format.[14] Individual documents must not be password-protected.[15]

APPROACH TO LEGALLY PRIVILEGED MATERIALS

24. Where parties inform the CMA that privileged materials have been redacted or removed from the final production, the CMA is likely to ask the parties to describe the process used to identify and withhold privileged materials. Parties may also be requested to provide a privilege log describing the documents withheld from production (or produced in redacted form) in non-privileged terms. Merging parties are encouraged to engage with the CMA on the appropriate approach to privileged materials at an early stage of the evidence-gathering process.

NOTES

2 See paragraphs 6.15 to 6.19 of Mergers: Guidance on CMA's Jurisdiction and Procedure (CMA2).

3 See paragraphs 4.3.8 to 4.3.18 of the Merger Assessment Guidelines (CC2/OFT1254).

4 For the avoidance of doubt, the CMA does not consider that internal documents are the only source of 'compelling evidence' within the meaning of the Merger Assessment Guidelines to support an exiting firm counterfactual.

5 Section 109 can also be used by the CMA when assisting the Secretary of State in its merger functions under the Act. Given that this has limited relevance to the CMA's use of section 109 notices, this is not considered further in this document.

6 Through a section 109 notice, the CMA can also require the attendance of a named individual to give evidence (under section 109(1)) or the production of certain *"estimates, forecasts, returns or other information"* (under section 109(3)). This document is intended to provide guidance on the CMA's approach to the production of internal documents and therefore these powers are not considered further.

7 See Penalty notice under section 110 of the Enterprise Act 2002 – Addressed to Hungryhouse Holdings Limited, Anticipated acquisition by JUST EAT plc of Hungryhouse Holdings Limited, Case ME/6659-16, 24 November 2017.

8 Where an act is capable of constituting both a failure warranting an administrative penalty and a criminal offence, the CMA cannot impose an administrative penalty if the person who has failed to comply with a section 109 information request has been found guilty of the criminal offence (see sections 110(8) and 174A(7) of the Act). Similarly, a criminal offence is not committed by a person who has failed to comply with a section 109 information request where the CMA has imposed an administrative penalty in respect of the same act (see sections 110(6) and 174A(5) of the Act).

9 As noted in footnote 216 of Mergers: Guidance on the CMA's jurisdiction and procedure (CMA2), section 109 notices can be used, without first issuing an informal request, where parties request that the CMA require them to provide such information using its powers under section 109 of the Act, for example where they have regulatory concerns about providing the data voluntarily.

10 Unless otherwise agreed with the CMA, a document will be responsive if any of the following dates, as recorded in the document or its metadata, fall within the specified period: document creation date, document sending date, document last editing/modification date.

11 An email 'family' commonly refers to a 'parent' email and all attachments (*e.g.*, an email and a word document attached to that email). The same principle applies where the parent document is a different type of file (*e.g.*, where a word document or excel file is embedded in another word document).

12 For example, if production de-duplication is requested in relation to an information request in which A and B are relevant custodians, where a given email from A to B is produced because it has been sent by A, the same email should not be produced a second time within the same response because it has been received by B.

13 In keeping with the principle set out in paragraph 22(f), a draft document will typically be considered as a responsive document where attached to a responsive email (even where a final or most recent version of the attached document is also available).

14 The CMA may require a load file to be produced. The CMA's preferred load file format is available on the CMA's website (although, depending on the circumstances of the case, the metadata fields required may vary and therefore merging parties are encouraged to discuss the appropriate load file with the CMA).

15 If the parties consider that they are likely to encounter problems with encryption or password protection, they are encouraged to raise these concerns with the CMA as early as possible.

3. THE FORMAT OF INTERNAL DOCUMENT REQUESTS

[3.453]

25. As noted in paragraph 10 above, the scope and nature of a document request will vary in light of the circumstances of the case (in particular in order to ensure that such requests are appropriately targeted and proportionate). The specific questions included within requests for internal documents will therefore vary considerably from case-to-case. This section of the guidance explains other aspects of the likely format of document requests that are likely to arise in most cases.

ENGAGEMENT ON COMPLEX DOCUMENT REQUESTS IN DRAFT FORM

26. As the content of document requests is likely to vary considerably from case-to-case, it is not possible to provide further guidance on the specific questions likely to be included in document requests (beyond the general principles set out in paragraphs 17 to 20 above).

27. The CMA may, where it is practicable and appropriate, share document requests in draft with parties before issuing a notice under section 109.[16] This is particularly likely to be appropriate where the document request is complex or extensive (and therefore responding may impose a material burden on the parties). Sending document requests in draft can be helpful in prompting parties to identify whether any suggested questions (or other parameters of the request, such as the targeted custodians or the time period) are likely to be irrelevant. It can also be helpful in assessing the likely volume of responsive documents, as the CMA may consider whether it would be appropriate to narrow the scope of a document request if the volume of responsive documents is likely to be disproportionate.

28. It is ultimately the parties' responsibility to ensure that relevant material is produced in response to a document request. The CMA may engage with merging parties on whether the proposed approach is sensible and practical(and, in particular, seek to ensure that specific questions do not impose a disproportionate burden on the merging parties). The CMA may, in particular, engage with parties on the number of responsive documents generated by specific search terms in order to ensure that approach envisaged would not result in a disproportionate number of documents being produced. The CMA will not, however, be able to pre-emptively give assurances that no breach of the section 109 notice would occur in the event that relevant material later comes to light which parties could and should have provided.

STANDARD QUESTION FOR EXPLANATION OF METHODOLOGY

29. While the content of document requests will vary on a case-by-case basis, such requests will typically include a standard question intended to verify the approach adopted to document collection, search, and review. This standard methodology question is intended to help the CMA assess whether a party has adopted an appropriate approach to document collection, search, and review. The full version of the standard methodology question is set out in the box below (although, as explained in more detail below, it is not envisaged that the full version of the question should be used in all cases).

Provide a detailed description of the methodology used to identify and produce the documents and information responsive to Question [X]. This description should identify:

(a) *The relevant custodians whose documents have been reviewed;*

(b) *The time parameters used for the review of potentially responsive documents;*

(c) *The parts of the custodian's IT environment that have been searched (e.g., email, local folders, shared folders, cloud services, external media etc.), and the approach taken to retrieving this data;*

(d) *Any measures taken to ensure that potentially responsive documents remain available for production;*

(e) *The approach adopted (if applicable) to documents that are not text searchable;*

(f) *The approach adopted to family items (e.g. attachments) in responsive emails;*

(g) *The approach adopted to the transfer of metadata of digital material (such as document created dates etc);*

(h) *The search terms used to identify responsive documents (including any Boolean search terms used);*

(i) *The approach adopted (if applicable) to remove duplicate or draft files; and*

(j) *The approach adopted (if applicable) to redact or remove any privileged materials.*

30. The use of a methodology question is intended to ensure that the CMA has sufficient clarity about the approach adopted by parties in responding to requests for internal documents.

31. The CMA may request a party's proposed response to the methodology question to be submitted in draft before responsive documents are produced to the CMA. This may form part of the CMA's engagement with parties on document requests in draft form. The CMA may engage with merging parties on whether the proposed approach is sensible and practical but will not, as explained above, be able to pre-emptively give assurances that no breach of the section 109 notice would occur in the event that relevant material later comes to light which parties could and should have provided.

32. In keeping with the CMA's objective to adopt a proportionate approach to document requests, it will not use the full version of the methodology question in all cases. The CMA will also typically be willing to engage with parties to discuss whether the proposed approach is sensible and practical.

33. In this regard, it will typically be appropriate to ask merging parties to answer the main part of the methodology question – *i.e.*, how they have gathered the documents produced to the CMA – in all cases. Whether responses to these sub-questions intended to highlight specific aspects of the approach adopted by the respondent are required will be considered on a case-by-case basis. The CMA considers that it is likely that parts (a) to (c) of the question, along with part (j), would be used in almost all cases. Parts (d) to (i) of the question might only be appropriate in cases where a more extensive document production exercise is envisaged.

34. The standard methodology question should not be taken to suggest that an extensive document review should be undertaken to respond to all section 109 document requests. In particular, in some cases (*e.g.*, for smaller parties or where the information sought is less material to the matters that the CMA is investigating), it might be appropriate, for example, for a party simply to state that certain business people 'self-selected' potentially responsive documents(*e.g.*, based on searching their own email folders). As noted above, merging parties are encouraged to engage with the CMA on their envisaged approach at an early stage of the evidence-gathering process.

THE USE OF COMPLIANCE STATEMENTS

35. The CMA may include a request for the Chief Executive Officer or General Counsel (or equivalent) to sign a 'compliance statement' confirming that the business has complied with the section 109 notice when it provides its response to the document request. This is intended to ensure that the merging parties (and not just their external advisers) are appropriately aware of the nature of the request and the approach that has been adopted in responding to it. This is particularly important because a section 109 notice is typically addressed to the business, rather than the advisers, and therefore the consequences of an incomplete response to the request will fall on the business.

36. The production of a compliance statement is particularly likely to be appropriate in circumstances where a document request is extensive or where the CMA has encountered difficulties in its information-gathering within the case to date. It may also be appropriate where senior individuals have 'self-selected' relevant emails from their email inboxes and outboxes rather than documents having been produced through a more forensic document retrieval and review process.

NOTES

16 In paragraph 4.3 of Administrative Penalties: Statement of Policy on the CMA's approach (CMA4), the CMA notes that it may be more likely to impose a penalty for failure to comply with investigatory requirements where the CMA has provided a draft request.

INTERIM MEASURES IN MERGER INVESTIGATIONS

(CMA108, June 2019)

[3.454]

NOTES

See also the list of consultations and draft documents in the Appendix at **[A1]**.

CONTENTS

1. INTRODUCTION

ABOUT THIS GUIDANCE

[3.455]

1.1 This guidance is intended for merging parties and for legal advisers advising on a transaction where interim measures may be relevant. It should be read in conjunction with *Mergers: Guidance on the CMA's Jurisdiction and Procedure* (**CMA2**). Where there is any difference in emphasis or detail between this guidance and other Competition and Markets Authority (**CMA**) guidance, the most recently published guidance takes precedence.

1.2 This guidance reflects experience gained since the current system was introduced in April 2014, in particular, recent enforcement action. It replaces CMA60 (*Guidance on initial enforcement orders and derogations in merger investigations*) and those portions of CMA2 which dealt with interim measures.

WHAT ARE INTERIM MEASURES?

1.3 When the CMA is investigating a merger, the Enterprise Act 2002 (the **Act**) enables it to take steps to prevent or unwind pre-emptive action. Pre-emptive action is action which might prejudice the outcome of a reference or impede the taking of any appropriate remedial action.[1]

1.4 Measures to prevent or unwind pre-emptive action can take three forms (collectively referred to as **Interim Measures** for the purposes of this guidance), depending on the stage of the investigation and whether they are imposed on the merging parties or agreed:

(a) an initial enforcement order (IEO),[2] which is imposed at phase 1. IEOs can include orders to unwind pre-emptive action which has or may have been taken;[3]

(b) an interim order (**IO**),[4] which is imposed at phase 2 and replaces any IEO imposed in phase 1.[5] IOs can include orders to unwind pre-emptive action which has or may have been taken;[6] or

(c) interim undertakings,[7] which are agreed with the merging parties at phase 2 (typically after provisional findings in relation to an anticipated merger) and which replace any IEO imposed in phase 1.

THE IMPORTANCE OF COMPLYING WITH INTERIM MEASURES

1.5 The United Kingdom (**UK**) is unusual in having a voluntary, non-suspensory merger filing regime. Unlike most other jurisdictions, it allows merging parties to self-assess whether to complete a merger without first seeking clearance. The benefit of this approach is that it gives merging parties greater flexibility and reduces regulatory obstacles to those mergers which are clearly unproblematic.

1.6 However, the purpose of merger control is to regulate in advance the impact of mergers on the competitive structure of markets.[8] If the CMA decides that a merger does require scrutiny, it is essential to the functioning of the UK's voluntary, non-suspensory merger regime that Interim Measures to preserve the pre-merger competitive structure of markets should be effective.[9] The CMA's ability to impose Interim Measures on merging parties, and to impose penalties where these have not been complied with, are the necessary corollary of having a voluntary regime.

1.7 If the CMA has decided to investigate, it is critical that any business which has been acquired continues, during the CMA's investigation, to compete independently with the acquiring business and is maintained as a going concern. This is to ensure that the viability and competitive capability of each of the merging parties is not undermined pending the outcome of the CMA's investigation, as this would risk prejudicing the ability of the CMA to achieve an effective remedy if it were to find that the merger gives rise to a substantial lessening of competition (**SLC**). The emphasis of Interim Measures on preserving the viability and competitive capability of the acquired business reflects the extensive experience of the CMA and its predecessor bodies in operating the UK regime, including the results of evaluations of past merger remedies.[10]

1.8 The CMA will act proportionately in imposing Interim Measures, whilst having regard to the necessity of preventing pre-emptive action which might prejudice the outcome of a reference or impede the taking of any appropriate remedial action. What is necessary to achieve this in each case is judged on the basis of the facts available to the CMA at any given time. As the CMA's understanding and analysis evolves in a particular case it may be prepared to relax some of the requirements of the Interim Measures, for example, through derogations, variations or lifting the Interim Measures entirely.[11] Equally, the CMA will, if necessary, impose further requirements as its understanding and analysis evolves.

1.9 However, merging parties should expect all requests for derogations or other relaxation of Interim Measures to be scrutinised carefully. For the reasons set out above, the CMA will err on the side of caution in deciding whether specific provisions in Interim Measures are still required.

1.10 The CMA's role in regulating merger activity, and its ability to do so effectively, is a matter of public importance[12] and the CMA takes merging parties' compliance with their obligations under Interim Measures very seriously. Where the CMA considers that a person has, without reasonable excuse, failed to comply with Interim Measures, it may impose a penalty of such fixed amount as it considers appropriate, which shall not exceed 5% of the total value of the turnover (both in and outside the UK) of the enterprises owned or controlled by the person on whom the penalty is imposed.[13] The CMA will make full use of this power to deter activity which undermines the effectiveness of Interim Measures.

1.11 It is therefore of the utmost importance that merging parties take steps to understand fully their compliance obligations (including seeking legal advice as needed) and consider carefully the consequences of any action which may be in breach of Interim Measures.

NOTES

1 There is no exhaustive list of the kinds of conduct that may amount to pre-emptive action. Depending on the nature of the business, pre-emptive action might include actions such as closing or selling sites; selling or failing to maintain equipment; degrading service levels; failing to retain key employees; integrating IT systems; failing to compete at arm's length for tenders; integrating customer-facing functions; weakening the independence of brands; discontinuing competing products; or exchanging confidential commercially sensitive information. See sections 72(8) and 80(10) of the Act.

2 Section 72 of the Act. Following the amendments to the Act which took effect in April 2014 (including repeal of section 71 of the Act), the CMA no longer has the power to negotiate initial undertakings during the phase 1 process. Accordingly, while the OFT previously agreed initial undertakings with merging parties, IEOs may now be imposed without negotiation.

3 Sections 72(3A) and 72(3B) of the Act.

4 Section 81 of the Act.

5 The IEO ceases to be in force under section 72(6) of the Act when the CMA makes an IO under section 81 of the Act.

6 Section 81(2A) of the Act.

7 Section 80 of the Act.

8 See the discussion of this issue in *Société Coopérative de Production SeaFrance SA (Respondent) v The Competition and Markets Authority and another (Appellants)* [2015] UKSC 75 at paragraph 4.

9 The need for robust Interim Measures was recognised in the Enterprise and Regulatory Reform Act 2013, which significantly strengthened the CMA's powers in this regard.

10 See Merger Remedy Evaluations (CMA109) at paragraph 5.4: "*The case studies have demonstrated both the costs of putting in place inadequate interim measures and the benefits of putting in place effective interim measures. They have also illustrated how the UK competition agencies have learnt over time how to put in place stronger interim measures so as to allow effective remedies to be implemented if needed later on.*"

11 Interim Measures are only likely to be lifted entirely if the CMA is confident that the merger does not require remedial action.

[12] *Electro Rent Corporation v CMA* [2019] CAT 4 at paragraphs 120, 200, 201 and 206. The Court stated: "*[200] It is a matter of public importance that the merger control process, and the duties that it creates, are strictly, and conscientiously, observed . . . .[201] We do not regard it as a mitigating factor that Electro Rent considered that there were good commercial reasons for terminating the Lease or that termination would make the UK business more attractive to purchasers who did not want the Lease. That was not a judgement for Electro Rent to make and, in any event, was not relevant to the issue of whether the consent of the CMA was required. [206] . . . it is of the utmost importance that interim orders be scrupulously complied with, and that a party should not itself form judgments or reach decisions that are properly for the CMA.*"

[13] Section 94A of the Act. For further information on enforcement see section 7 of this document.

2. TIMING AND IMPLEMENTATION OF INTERIM MEASURES

TIMING FOR IMPOSING INTERIM MEASURES

[3.456]

2.1 Interim Measures may be imposed at any time during the CMA's review, including:

(a) before the completion of the merger, to take effect immediately (see the discussion of Interim Measures in anticipated mergers in paragraphs 2.15 to 2.22 below);

(b) before the completion of the merger, to take effect on completion (see the discussion of Interim Measures conditional on completion in paragraphs 2.23 to 2.24 below); or

(c) on or after completion of the merger, to take effect immediately (see the discussion of Interim Measures in completed mergers in paragraphs 2.25 to 2.28 below).

2.2 If a merger has been notified to the CMA then Interim Measures are likely to be put in place upon the completion of the merger (and, in some circumstances, in advance of completion). If the CMA investigates a completed merger which has not been notified to it, it is likely to impose an IEO very shortly after sending an initial enquiry letter.

2.3 Where the CMA has reasonable grounds for suspecting that pre-emptive action has been, or may have been, taken before any IEO or IO is imposed,[14] the CMA may order the persons concerned to restore the position to what it would have been had the pre-emptive action not been taken, or to otherwise mitigate its effects. (An IEO or IO with such an effect is referred to as an **Unwinding Order**).[15] The circumstances in which the CMA may consider this to be necessary are described in section 5 below.

2.4 At phase 1, under section 72 of the Act, an IEO can be made as soon as the CMA has reasonable grounds for suspecting that it is, or may be, the case that two or more enterprises have ceased to be distinct, or that arrangements are in progress or in contemplation which, if carried into effect, will result in two or more enterprises ceasing to be distinct.[16]

2.5 At phase 1 the CMA may impose an IEO to prevent pre-emptive action (or reverse it) but may subsequently grant a derogation giving consent to the merging parties to undertake certain actions that would otherwise be prohibited by the IEO. The extent to which derogations might be granted depends on the circumstances of the case. The CMA will balance the need to guard against pre-emptive action against the burdens that IEOs can place on merging parties.

2.6 Once a reference to phase 2 has been made, the IEO remains in force unless the CMA decides to impose an IO or accept an interim undertaking. In addition, statutory restrictions prevent merging parties from taking certain actions after a merger has been referred to phase 2 (see also paragraph 2.27).[17] At phase 2, an IO can be imposed or an interim undertaking can be accepted even if no IEO was imposed in phase 1.

2.7 During the course of its investigation, the CMA may also take additional steps, where appropriate, to prevent pre-emptive action, including issuing directions pursuant to the IEO or IO to ensure compliance with the Interim Measures, or accepting interim undertakings (typically after provisional findings in relation to an anticipated merger[18]).

2.8 The CMA keeps Interim Measures under review throughout the course of an investigation. Additional measures may replace, amend or supplement measures already in place at any stage of the process.[19]

2.9 IEOs, IOs and interim undertakings continue in force, subject to subsequent variation, release or revocation by the CMA,[20] until the final determination of the investigation (see section 6).[21]

TO WHOM DO THE INTERIM MEASURES APPLY?

2.10 In a completed merger, Interim Measures will usually be imposed on both the direct acquirer and the acquiring business's ultimate UK parent company. In the case of an anticipated merger, they will usually also be imposed on both the target business and the target business's ultimate UK parent. Where the acquiring or target business's ultimate parent company is an overseas company the Interim Measures will, to the extent appropriate, also be imposed on the overseas parent. The above will ensure that the target business is appropriately maintained and, if relevant, that no changes are made to the acquiring business if it is possible that it might form the basis of a divestment remedy package.[22]

ENSURING A SMOOTH PROCESS

2.11 If Interim Measures are in place, any person concerned who is subject to an order or undertaking should inform the CMA of any planned or past action which might constitute pre-emptive action. Failure to do so may lead the CMA to take action to ensure compliance with the Interim Measures, including (as applicable) issuing an Unwinding Order or formal directions; requiring the appointment of a monitoring trustee or a hold separate manager (see section 4);[23] or imposing a fine (see section 7).

2.12 Even where Interim Measures are not in place, the CMA suggests that parties to a merger which is under investigation should keep the CMA informed of planned actions which may be pre-emptive to avoid the disruption of an Unwinding Order.

2.13 In both completed and anticipated mergers, the CMA will request the merging parties to provide the CMA with the details of any actions taken before the Interim Measures came into force which would have been prohibited if the Interim Measures had been in force prior to such actions. Where pre-emptive action has, or may have, taken place before Interim Measures come into force, the CMA may consider it appropriate to use its powers to issue an Unwinding Order to reverse or mitigate the effect of such action. The circumstances in which the CMA may consider this to be appropriate are described in section 5 below.

2.14 Interim Measures generally require that the target business should be carried on separately, and at arm's length, from the acquiring business. Therefore, if Interim Measures are imposed on a completed merger, the merging parties should immediately consider whether the arrangements they have in place meet this requirement and take any steps necessary to ensure compliance with the Interim Measures. Compliance measures should be reviewed periodically to ensure that they are still adequate, for example, prior to submitting compliance statements. In particular, it must be clear to the person managing the target business while the Interim Measures are in effect what they can and should do without reference to the acquirer.[24] While it is for the merging parties to decide how to achieve compliance, the simplest way to achieve clarity is a written delegation of authority. For information on the restrictions on the target business which may be acceptable to the CMA see paragraphs 3.32 to 3.36. In addition, merging parties should ensure that all affected staff understand the Interim Measures and what they individually are required to do to ensure compliance.

INTERIM MEASURES IN ANTICIPATED MERGERS

When will Interim Measures be imposed prior to completion?

2.15 The risk of pre-emptive action in an anticipated merger is generally much lower than in a completed merger. Accordingly, the circumstances in which the CMA might consider that Interim Measures need to take effect before a merger completes (referred to as an anticipated IEO or IO) are relatively rare.[25]

2.16 In contrast, mergers which are to complete during the CMA's investigation are more likely to be subjected to Interim Measures conditional on completion and are considered below at paragraphs 2.23 to 2.24.

2.17 To assess whether Interim Measures are appropriate in cases which are not expected to complete during the CMA's investigation, the CMA may request the merging parties to an anticipated merger to provide the CMA with the relevant transaction documents (either in draft or final form) and the details of any actions which the merging parties have taken, or are planning to take prior to completion.

2.18 The CMA might consider Interim Measures necessary in relation to an anticipated merger where the steps which the parties are taking, or are about to take, would be prohibited if the standard template Interim Measures were in force. For example, where the merging parties have begun jointly to conduct commercial negotiations with customers or suppliers; or have otherwise affected the way in which one or both of the merging parties engage with, or are perceived by, customers or suppliers.

When might Interim Measures affect completion?

2.19 At phase 1, where the CMA does impose an IEO in relation to an anticipated merger, this will typically not prevent completion of the transaction from taking place (unless there are unusual circumstances which could mean that completion would necessarily result in pre-emptive action).[26] In other words, at phase 1, the CMA is typically concerned with limiting integration (maintaining pre-merger competitive conditions and ensuring the continued effective operation of the acquiring and target businesses) rather than preventing completion.

2.20 During a phase 2 investigation into an anticipated merger, the Act prevents the merging parties (or associated persons) from acquiring any interest in shares in a company to which the reference relates without the CMA's consent pending final determination of the reference.[27] In practice, given this statutory restriction and the fact that the reference test has been met, the CMA is unlikely to consent to the completion of an anticipated transaction during phase 2 proceedings. In some cases,[28] the CMA may be willing to consent to completion where this is necessary to allow the transaction to complete at a global level, subject to Interim Measures and sufficient safeguards (likely to include hold separate arrangements and a monitoring trustee) being put in place in order to prevent pre-emptive action.

2.21 If the CMA is concerned that an anticipated merger may complete during the CMA's phase 2 investigation and that this could prejudice the reference and/or its ability to remedy any SLC resulting from the merger, the CMA may prevent completion of the merger pending final determination of the reference.[29] This may be the case where there is no Interim Measure or statutory prohibition which would preclude completion, for example, because the transaction relates to the acquisition of assets rather than further shares in the target business or because of the exceptions to which the bar on transfer of shares is subject.

2.22 If, in relation to an anticipated merger, the CMA finds a SLC at phase 2, this may lead to a need for further Interim Measures (for example, the appointment of a monitoring trustee to oversee a divestiture process: see section 4 below).

INTERIM MEASURES CONDITIONAL ON COMPLETION

2.23 In cases where an anticipated merger is expected to complete during the CMA's investigation, but the CMA considers that the need for Interim Measures would arise only once completion has taken place, the CMA is likely to issue Interim Measures in advance of completion, but with the operative provisions only taking effect upon completion.[30]

2.24 In such cases the merging parties should keep the CMA appraised of their plans for completion and initiate early discussions in relation to the Interim Measures and any necessary derogations. This will enable the CMA to minimise the inconvenience to the merging parties resulting from Interim Measures by considering, and if appropriate granting, derogations prior to completion.

2.25 Interim Measures serve a particularly important function where the merger is completed before it is examined by the CMA.[31]

2.26 At phase 1, an IEO has a precautionary purpose, and the CMA would therefore normally impose an IEO in completed merger cases which it is investigating (given the immediate risk of pre-emptive action). The only exceptions to this approach are likely to arise where the CMA has been provided with compelling evidence that demonstrates that there is no risk of pre-emptive action[32] or there are self-evidently no competition concerns.[33] Merging parties who believe that they might satisfy the criteria for either of these exceptions are encouraged to discuss this with the CMA prior to completing their transaction.

2.27 At phase 2, during the course of an inquiry into a completed merger, the Act prohibits the merging parties from taking any further steps to integrate without the CMA's consent, where no Interim Measures have been put in place.[34] This statutory restriction in relation to completed mergers prevents the merging parties from 'completing any outstanding matters' or 'making further arrangements' in connection with the merger and from transferring the ownership or control of any enterprise to which the reference relates. Given the potential for pre-emptive action which falls outside the remit of these statutory restrictions,[35] the CMA will normally seek Interim Measures in relation to completed mergers at phase 2 to supplement the prohibitions set out in the Act.

2.28 An IEO or IO is an order and can therefore be imposed without negotiation with the merging parties (see paragraph 2.4).[36] An IEO or IO in a completed merger will take effect as soon as the order is made.[37]

FORM OF INTERIM MEASURE AND 'TAILORED' INTERIM MEASURES

2.29 Given the need to impose an IEO quickly in completed mergers, any IEO imposed in these circumstances will almost always take the form of the standard template available on the CMA's website, which will be updated from time to time. Discussions over the scope of the IEO in completed mergers will therefore almost always take the form of derogations (which the CMA may grant simultaneously with the IEO or after the IEO is imposed) rather than amendments to the standard form IEO. This approach is intended to ensure that effective IEOs can be put in place as quickly as possible and to provide greater factual and legal certainty around the initial scope of an IEO.

2.30 In completed merger cases, where practicable, the CMA will consider submissions on derogations from the merging parties before imposing an IEO or IO, and merging parties are encouraged to engage with the CMA as early as possible for this purpose. Where the merging parties have clearly demonstrated that some of the provisions are not relevant to a specific merger, the CMA will publish a derogation for those provisions simultaneously with the IEO or IO, provided that the merging parties have engaged with the CMA on such derogations on a timely basis.[38] Given the importance of speed, the CMA is unlikely to be able to engage in detailed discussions on proposed derogations at this point. Accordingly, where the CMA is unable to establish that a derogation is justified (eg because there is insufficient time available to review the merging parties' submissions or because insufficient information has been provided to support the derogations requested), an IEO or IO may be imposed without prior discussion of possible derogations. The CMA therefore encourages the merging parties to provide fully specified, reasoned and evidenced submissions to facilitate early discussions if the merging parties consider it necessary to have derogations in place on completion.

2.31 Where the CMA is investigating an anticipated merger and the merging parties begin discussions early with the CMA about the transaction completing, the CMA may consider creating a tailored IEO (rather than granting derogations to a standard form IEO).[39] The CMA will consider taking this approach where, on the facts of the case, this is likely to optimise procedural efficiency (for example, because it would minimise the number of derogation requests that may be required to be considered) and avoid unnecessary disruption to the merging parties' businesses.[40]

2.32 This may be the case where the CMA is able to conclude in advance of imposing an IEO that: *(a)* certain of the risks of pre-emptive action that the standard form IEO is designed to prevent do not arise; and/or *(b)* the provisions of the standard form IEO may lead to undesirable consequences.

2.33 As is the case for all material variations to the standard form IEO (whether through derogations or a tailored IEO) the CMA will only be able to reach such a view where sufficient time and information are available.[41] As explained in paragraph 2.29, a standard form IEO with relevant derogations is likely to be the appropriate approach in nearly all cases.

NOTES

14 Pre-emptive action is defined at 1.3 above.

15 This is done under section 72(3B) of the Act at phase 1 and under section 81(2A) of the Act at phase 2.

16 Following the amendments to the Act which took effect in April 2014, the CMA no longer has the power to negotiate

initial undertakings during the phase 1 process (the CMA retains the ability to negotiate interim undertakings under section 80 of the Act following a reference to phase 2). Accordingly, while the OFT previously agreed initial undertakings with merging parties, IEOs may now be imposed without negotiation. The CMA is no longer required to establish that the transaction gives rise to a relevant merger situation, or that the merging parties are contemplating pre-emptive action, or that there are preliminary indications of competition concerns, before imposing an IEO.

17 Sections 77 and 78 of the Act.

18 See, for example, Reckitt/KY (2015); Celesio/Sainsbury's Pharmacy Business (2016); Ladbrokes/Coral (2016).

19 Sections 72(6)(a)(i), 80(7) and 81(7) of the Act.

20 Sections 72(4), 80(5) and 81(5) of the Act.

21 Sections 72(6)(a), 72(6)(b), 80(8) and 81(8) of the Act. Final determination of an investigation occurs when the CMA decides not to refer, accepts undertakings in lieu of reference, (phase 1 outcomes) accepts final undertakings, makes a final order or, in the absence of a SLC finding, on publication of the final report (phase 2 outcomes).

22 See, for example, Celesio/Sainsbury's Pharmacy Business (2015), Euro Car Parts/Andrew Page (2016) and Motor Fuel Group (MFG)/MRH (2018).

23 Examples of other possible measures include requiring non-disclosure agreements or logs of communications between merging parties.

24 See the penalty notice issued to Ausurus and EMR (2018).

25 See, for example, Linergy/Ulster Farm (2015), Mole Valley Farmers/Countrywide Farmers (2018), Castle Water/Invicta Water (2018), Lakeland Dairies/LacPatrick Dairies (2018), CareTech/Cambian (2018) and Aer Lingus/Cityjet (2018). Most of these transactions completed after the IEO was put in place but before the CMA had concluded its investigation.

26 This might be the case, for example, where: (a) the act of completion would directly lead to the loss of key staff or management or operational capability (eg through the loss of customer or supplier contracts) for the target business. This is more likely to occur in an asset acquisition than where a functioning business is being acquired, which could be preserved through a post-completion IEO; (b) the act of completion would result in significant changes to the acquiring or target businesses, which would be difficult or costly to reverse, eg the loss of regulatory licences.

27 Sections 77 and 78 of the Act impose statutory restrictions on certain actions following a reference where no Interim Measures are in place. These include, in the case of anticipated mergers (as noted above), a restriction on the acquisition of the target business's shares, and, in the case of completed mergers, restrictions on the completion of any further matters in connection with the merger arrangements, or transferring ownership or control of the target business. Separate provisions apply where references are made on public interest grounds (see paragraphs 7 and 8 of Schedule 7 to the Act).

28 See, for example, Iron Mountain/Recall (2015).

29 This is most likely to occur following a provisional finding or final report that the merger in question may be expected to result in an SLC. For example, in Reckitt Benckiser/K-Y (2014), the CMA accepted undertakings from both merging parties following the publication of its phase 2 report, which prevented completion taking place prior to final undertakings being accepted by the CMA to remedy the SLC identified.

30 For example, Tobii/Smartbox (2018), (IEO imposed on 28 September 2018 and took effect on completion of the merger on 1 October 2018);PayPal/iZettle (2018–2019) (IEO imposed on 19 September 2018 and took effect on completion of the merger on 20 September 2018); and Global/Semper Veritas (2018–2019)(IEO imposed on 14 November 2018 to take effect on completion).

31 *Electro Rent Corporation v CMA* [2019] CAT 4 at paragraph 120.

32 The CMA may consider that there is no risk of pre-emptive action where there are factual circumstances that would prevent any integration of the merging parties' businesses for the duration of the CMA's investigation. This is very rare; however, it might be the case, for example, where the target business is active in a highly regulated sector in which the regulatory approvals required to make any material changes to the operation of the business will take many months to obtain.

33 The CMA may consider that a transaction self-evidently raises no competition concerns where it is clear that the reference test will not be met. This exception is unlikely to apply where the CMA has initiated an investigation on its own initiative through its mergers intelligence function.

34 Section 77 of the Act.

35 For example, the acquiring business may have significant incentives to run down or neglect the business or assets of one of the merging businesses (usually the target business), or to extract know-how and other commercially sensitive information from the target business in order to reduce its competitive capability should divestiture be required.

36 As noted in footnote 2, prior to the amendments to the Act that took effect in April 2014, the OFT agreed initial undertakings with merging parties, but the CMA no longer has this power at phase 1.

37 For this reason, the CMA will, where possible, provide merging parties (or their advisers) with advance notice of the imposition of an IEO or IO. The CMA generally seeks to avoid unnecessary inconvenience to the merging parties but will impose an order without notice if it considers it necessary to prevent pre-emptive action.

38 For example, if no IT systems have been acquired, the CMA may derogate from the provisions prohibiting the integration of IT systems.

39 In most cases, the CMA would expect this to be an abridged version of the standard form IEO, although the exclusion of particular provisions of the IEO, or the circumstances of the case, may require additional conditions (not included in the standard form IEO) to be added.

40 See, for example, Arriva Rail North/Northern rail franchise (2016) and Aer Lingus/Cityjet (2018).

41 Depending on the nature of the variation requested, the CMA may require a well-developed understanding of the merging parties; the product and geographic markets affected by the merger; the potential substantive issues; the likely practical consequences of the standard form IEO; and/or any additional other factors that may be relevant to an assessment of the risk of pre-emptive action (including, in particular, whether the merging parties are subject to other sources of regulation or governance that make particular provisions of the standard form IEO unnecessary). It may therefore be difficult for the CMA to make an informed decision on complex derogation requests early on in its investigation and a decision on such requests may be deferred until an understanding of the above factors has been developed.

3. DEROGATIONS

REQUESTING A DEROGATION

[3.457]

3.1 The CMA may (on written application by the merging parties) grant a derogation, giving consent to the merging parties to undertake certain actions that would otherwise be prohibited by Interim Measures.[42] Derogations will not be given retrospectively to approve actions that have already occurred and that may be in breach of Interim Measures, nor does the giving of a derogation preclude the CMA from taking action against any steps that were in breach of the Interim Measures prior to the derogation having been granted.

3.2 Merging parties should engage early with the CMA to discuss potential derogation requests that are considered urgent and necessary by the merging parties. Derogations are more likely to be granted if requests are fully specified, reasoned and supported by relevant evidence, including, for example:[43]

(a) a full and detailed explanation of the action the merging party wishes to take. For example, terms such as 'integration planning' should be explained fully in terms of what business functions any integration planning will cover; what types of information would be shared (and with whom);
(b) the relevant provisions of the Interim Measures against which the derogation request is made;
(c) why the derogation request is being made[44] - the purpose of the derogation should be as detailed and clear as possible;
(d) why the action proposed does not amount to pre-emptive action;[45]
(e) a full description of any proposed safeguards[46] (eg non-disclosure agreements or limits on the actions that the merging parties can take under the derogation) to ensure that the action proposed does not create any risk of pre-emptive action;
(f) why the action proposed would not be difficult or costly to reverse;
(g) whether the derogation request is urgent (and if so, how urgent it is and why it is strictly necessary to safeguard the viability and competitive capability of the target business in advance of the CMA's decision on the merger);
(h) proposed draft text for the derogation consent letter based on the CMA's standard derogation request template (as amended from time to time), which is available on the CMA's website; and
(i) any other information which may assist the CMA in considering the request. More detail is provided in the sections below regarding additional information that may be required based on the type of derogation request being sought.

3.3 Merging parties should note that the information provided to support a derogation request may also be used in the substantive analysis of the merger (including at phase 2 if the merger is referred). Furthermore, it is a criminal offence under section 117 of the Act for a person recklessly or knowingly to supply to the CMA information which is false or misleading in any material respect.[47] For further information on compliance and enforcement see section 7 of this document.

3.4 All derogations will be given in writing and published on the case page. Prior to publishing such a notice of consent, the CMA will provide the merging parties seeking consent with a reasonable opportunity (at least one working day) to revert with any requests for business secrets to be redacted from the published version of the document.

3.5 Where the CMA's fact-finding remains at an early stage (ie particularly within phase 1), the CMA is likely to adopt a cautious approach to granting derogations (typically granting narrow derogations that are closely calibrated to the justifications provided by the merging parties, and which are sufficiently evidenced). The involvement of a monitoring trustee (see section 4) may enable the CMA to grant more complex derogation requests, as well as speed up the CMA's decision on whether to grant derogation requests.

3.6 Where possible, it is preferable for merging parties to collate derogations sought within a single comprehensive written request. A drip-feed of multiple derogation requests can unnecessarily hamper the CMA's investigation. This may ultimately cause a delay in lifting the Interim Measures completely (see section 6).

3.7 When considering whether a derogation should be requested, merging parties should note that it is of the utmost importance that Interim Measures be scrupulously complied with, and that a merging party should not itself form judgements or reach decisions that are properly for the CMA.[48] Pre-emptive action is a broad concept. It concerns conduct which might prejudice the reference or which might impede action justified by the CMA's ultimate decision. The word 'might' means that it is the possibility of prejudice to the reference or an impediment to justified action which is prohibited. Interim Measures catch more than just actual prejudice or impediments, which is why the onus is on the addressee of the Interim Measure to seek consent from the CMA if their conduct creates the possibility of prejudice or an impediment.[49]

3.8 Merging parties that are subject to Interim Measures may make submissions to the CMA setting out reasons why there is no longer a risk of pre-emptive action. The CMA will then consider whether it would be appropriate to vary, revoke or release the Interim Measures. Given the precautionary purpose of Interim Measures, the CMA would expect to vary, revoke or release Interim Measures only where it has seen compelling evidence that the risk of pre-emptive action no longer arises. For further information on revocation see section 6 of this document.

EXCHANGE OF INFORMATION BETWEEN MERGING PARTIES PRIOR TO INTERIM MEASURES BEING IMPOSED

3.9 Acquiring parties have a legitimate need to conduct due diligence on potential acquisition targets prior to completing a merger. When merging parties exchange information prior to the imposition of

Interim Measures, it is incumbent on them (assisted by their legal advisers) to self-assess and ensure that they are complying with any relevant laws, in particular Chapter 1 of the Competition Act 1998 (**CA98**) and Article 101 of the Treaty on the Functioning of the European Union (**TFEU**).

3.10 Where information which is confidential, proprietary or otherwise commercially sensitive is shared between the merging parties (for example, for the purposes of due diligence) prior to Interim Measures coming into force and the exchange has the potential to impact competition, then safeguards are likely to include:

(a) taking steps to ensure that such information is fully ring-fenced (with appropriate IT firewalls in place and physical ring-fencing measures where needed); and

(b) restricting information to internal and/or external "clean teams" and requiring all individuals who had access to such information to enter into non-disclosure agreements.

3.11 If the recipient of the information wishes to continue to access it following the imposition of the Interim Measures, the parties, together with their legal advisers, should immediately re-assess the safeguards which have been put in place to ensure that the information flow is compliant with the Interim Measures, as explained in paragraphs 3.12 to 3.18.

EXCHANGE OF INFORMATION BETWEEN MERGING PARTIES DURING INTERIM MEASURES

3.12 As mentioned at paragraph 3.9 above, prior to the imposition of Interim Measures, merging parties have a legal duty to self-assess whether information exchanges are compliant with relevant laws, in particular the CA98 and the TFEU. The requirements of Interim Measures are in addition to these statutory requirements.

3.13 Interim Measures aim to preserve the stand-alone viability and competitive capability of each of the merging businesses, and therefore prohibit pre-emptive action.[50] Once Interim Measures are in place it is incumbent on the merging parties, assisted by their legal advisers, to assess whether information exchange might amount to pre-emptive action, and apply for a derogation if it might.

3.14 Records should be kept of communications between the merging parties. The CMA may check that, in self-assessing, the merging parties have taken appropriate steps to control the information flow. If it does so, it will expect to see that measures to avoid pre-emptive action, such as those mentioned in paragraphs 3.15 to 3.18, have been carefully considered.

3.15 The following are examples of what the merging parties, assisted by their legal advisers, should consider if confidential or proprietary information is to be exchanged between the merging parties; Interim Measures are in place; and there is a competitive nexus between the parties (for example, where the merging parties are actual or potential competitors or upstream and downstream of one another):

(a) the purpose of exchanging confidential or proprietary information and why it is strictly necessary for this exchange to take place;

(b) the types of information which need to be shared (and the frequency with which this information needs to be shared) with reasons for believing that this information is strictly limited to that which is necessary to achieve the purpose. Where the purpose relates to compliance with external obligations, the precise wording of the relevant provisions of the external obligation should be carefully considered; and

(c) the safeguards (procedural or otherwise) that need be put in place to ensure that any confidential or proprietary information is only shared to the extent strictly necessary.

3.16 Procedural safeguards, which should be clearly set out in writing, may, for example include:

(a) the information should be disclosed only to a set of named individuals (whose roles and functions should also be recorded). The CMA expects the merging parties to limit the recipients of the information to those with a strict need to receive that information. In particular, the merging parties should ensure that commercially sensitive information is not shared with, or used by, staff who have any control or influence over commercial strategy or decision-making (unless **strictly necessary**).[51] Any information shared with individuals with control or influence over commercial decision-making or commercial activities for the acquiring business (such as members of the acquiring business's senior management) should be sufficiently aggregated in nature to ensure that it is not commercially sensitive;

(b) any individual in receipt of such information should enter into a non-disclosure agreement that: (i) prevents them from sharing the information with any individual who does not strictly require access to the information for this purpose; (ii) strictly limits the uses to which the information may be put; and (iii) remains in place until the Interim Measures are revoked or the merger is cleared; and

(c) robust physical and IT firewalls should be put in place to prevent unauthorised individuals from accessing the disclosed information.

The CMA may request a copy of documents setting out the safeguards which were put in place before information was exchanged.

3.17 Where financial information is to be shared while Interim Measures are in place, the merging parties should create a reporting template detailing any information that is to be shared. While it is for the merging parties to self-assess, exchange of financial information is unlikely to be appropriate if it goes beyond:

(a) consolidated profit and loss account information which is limited to historic consolidated revenues and historic consolidated earnings before interest, tax, depreciation and amortisation (EBITDA); and

Part 3 CMA and other Guidelines

(b) historic and high-level consolidated balance sheets and cash flow information (eg which does not reveal a granular breakdown of capital expenditure).

3.18 In particular, while Interim Measures are in place it is unlikely to be appropriate to share the target business' consolidated gross margins; prices or margins of specific products or services; revenues or margins of individual retail or business units; granular cost data (or any information that would enable the acquiring business to deduce such granular data); or management commentary on the financial information. The CMA may request a copy of the reporting template to check that, in self-assessing, the merging parties have limited the exchange of financial information to what is appropriate.

INTEGRATION WHICH HAS COMPLETED PRIOR TO INTERIM MEASURES COMING INTO FORCE

3.19 The standard form Interim Measure requires the merging parties to disclose to the CMA any integration actions that occurred, or were completed, prior to the Interim Measure coming into force.[52] Integration that has already occurred or was completed prior to the Interim Measures coming into force will not be in breach of the Interim Measures.

3.20 If the merging parties enter into an obligation or take a decision before the Interim Measures take effect, but the obligation will be performed or the decision implemented, or continue to be implemented, after the Interim Measures have come into force, then the merging parties should make full disclosure of the situation to the CMA and seek a derogation if any further action might breach the Interim Measures.

3.21 The CMA has the power to issue an Unwinding Order to require integration to be unwound if it judges it necessary to preserve the CMA's ability to pursue its investigation and/or to implement effective remedies (see section 5).

ACTIONS TAKEN IN THE ORDINARY COURSE OF BUSINESS

3.22 The standard form Interim Measures allow, without the need for a derogation, action taken in the 'ordinary course of business' and define this as matters connected to the day-to-day supply of goods and/or services by each of the merging parties. It does not include matters involving significant changes to their respective organisational structure or to the post-merger integration of the merging parties or the whole or parts of their businesses.[53] By way of example, while the scope of 'ordinary course of business' will vary case-by-case, the CMA would generally not regard the termination of a significant head lease, major redundancy plans, or sales of assets that might impair either business's ability to compete independently as falling within the definition of 'ordinary course of business'.[54] Whilst a given course of action may be in the best interests of a business, this does not mean it will fall within the meaning of ordinary course of business as defined in the Interim Measures.[55]

3.23 If merging parties are uncertain as to whether an action falls within this definition they should consult the CMA.[56]

DEROGATIONS GENERALLY GRANTED BY THE CMA IN PREVIOUS CASES

3.24 The CMA will take into account the particular circumstances of the case when assessing the risks of pre-emptive action, and therefore the derogations granted by the CMA in previous cases may not apply across all future cases. The CMA has generally granted derogation requests (where sufficiently specified, reasoned, and evidenced) in relation to:

(a) the provision of certain essential services by the acquiring business to the target business;

(b) the delegation of authority for the target business which clearly set out the limited circumstances in which the acquiring business can take decisions over certain commercial or operational actions proposed by the target business; and

(c) access for the acquiring firm to certain financial information from the target business for the purpose of financial oversight.

3.25 Possible justifications for such derogations, and the safeguards that may be required to be put in place to support them, are described further below.

Provision of essential services by the acquiring business to the target business

3.26 Derogation requests are commonly received for the provision of certain essential services by the acquiring business to the target business, for example, the provision of back-office support, or the acquiring business granting the target business access to its group credit facilities or insurance coverage.

3.27 The potential provision of back-office support by the acquiring business to the target business immediately pre-completion often arises within the context of asset transactions where support functions, such as IT systems, are not part of the sale. In order to ensure the viability and competitive capability of the target business, the CMA may, in appropriate circumstances, allow the provision of some forms of administrative support to the target business by the acquiring business.

3.28 Within this context, the CMA is likely to pay particular consideration to the relevance to the target business's commercial activity of the back-office functions that the acquiring business proposes to provide. It will also consider the impact that the provision of such functions by the acquiring business might have on the potential transfer of all or parts of the target business if remedies were ultimately required.

3.29 A derogation in relation to back-office support to be provided by the acquirer is unlikely to be granted where the target business will continue to have access to its pre-existing back-office support functions. This may be the case, for example, where back-office functions form part of the target business transferred by the vendor (even if the acquiring business ultimately intends to use its own back-office functions to support the target business) or where a transitional services arrangement enables the target business to continue using the vendor's back-office functions. Where transitional services arrangements with the vendor are coming to an end, the CMA expects the merging parties first to explore the possibility of an extension of the transitional services arrangements before any derogation requests are considered. In situations where the merging parties plan to terminate some, or all, of the transitional services arrangements with the vendor early, the CMA would expect the merging parties to explain in detail the reasons for the early termination and why the target business cannot outsource such arrangements to a third-party provider that is independent of the acquiring business.

3.30 In previous cases, the CMA has granted derogation requests (where sufficiently specified, reasoned, and evidenced) in relation to certain essential services including the provision of:

(a) payroll, HR, and other back-office functions;[57]
(b) access to the acquiring business's group credit arrangements or funding;[58]
(c) access to the acquirer's group insurance coverage to the target business;[59] and
(d) legal services.[60]

3.31 By contrast, the CMA is unlikely to grant derogations in relation to the integration of IT systems, customer-facing functions such as sales and marketing, or R&D and technological support (eg software development and design), which are typically likely to have a material impact on the commercial activity of the target business and the development, manufacture, and sale of the target business's products or services.

Delegations of authority for the target business

3.32 In the context of a completed transaction, the CMA understands that, in some cases, the acquiring business may wish to exercise some oversight over the commercial activity of the target business in order ensure that the target business is being maintained as a going concern.[61]

3.33 In such cases, the CMA is willing to consider whether, in specified circumstances, it is appropriate to require the target business to seek approval from the acquiring business for a proposed course of action. Actions in relation to which a requirement for the acquirer's approval may be appropriate include:

(a) approval of capital expenditure and operating expenditure, which had not been budgeted for in the target business's pre-merger business plan and/or above a certain financial threshold;
(b) entering into customer/supplier contracts above a certain financial threshold;
(c) approval of expenses of the Managing Director of the target business; and
(d) entering into contracts with uncapped liability.

3.34 The merging parties must demonstrate, to the satisfaction of the CMA, that the proposed terms of the delegation of authority to the management of the target business do not significantly restrict the ability of the target business to operate independently from the acquiring business, or to pursue its pre-merger business plan.[62] In deciding on the appropriateness of the delegated authority levels, the merging parties should consider how frequently the delegated authority levels would be reached. The CMA is unlikely to accept a delegation of authority which requires the target business to approach the acquiring business for approval of a proposed expenditure or course of action on a regular basis.

3.35 The merging parties need to consider who within the acquiring business is the most appropriate person to be consulted by the target business on such matters. The merging parties should ensure that the person exercising such oversight of the target business does not have a commercial or strategic role at the acquiring business.

3.36 In addition, the CMA would also seek to ensure that the following safeguards are in place:

(a) the information shared with the selected individual at the acquiring business is no more than is strictly necessary to allow the individual to reach a view on the specific matter at hand and should not include any commercially sensitive information;
(b) the selected individual at the acquiring business must not consult with any other individual at the acquiring business in taking decisions on the specific matters where the target business's level of delegated authority has been exceeded;
(c) the CMA may, at its discretion, also request to be provided with a summary of the information shared with the selected individual at the acquiring business after a request for approval has been submitted by the target business;
(d) the CMA is notified of any proposed veto and the reasons for this in advance of any such veto being exercised; and
(e) the selected individual at the acquiring business who is to be consulted under the delegation of authority will be required to sign a non-disclosure agreement in a form agreed by the CMA.

Provision to the acquiring business of certain financial information relating to the target business

3.37 The CMA recognises that, in the context of a completed transaction,[63] there may be a need for the acquiring business to maintain high-level financial oversight of the target business in order to preserve its ongoing viability and competitive capability pending completion of the CMA's merger review process. The CMA may be willing to consider derogation requests from the merging parties for such limited purposes.[64]

3.38 The CMA is unlikely to grant derogations which require the target business to provide more than the financial information mentioned in paragraph 3.17, on the basis that such information should be considered sufficient for the limited purposes of financial oversight.

3.39 In the event that the merging parties consider that access to further, more granular financial information is strictly necessary, the merging parties should provide the CMA with compelling reasons (see also paragraph 3.18).

GUIDANCE ON MORE COMPLEX DEROGATIONS

3.40 The CMA may consider granting more complex derogations which concern:

(a) parts of one merging party's business that are not engaged in activities related to the other merging party's business;

(b) parts of the merging parties' businesses that have no relevance to their relevant activities in the UK; or

(c) the replacement of key staff or substantive changes to the merging parties' organisational or management structures.

3.41 Derogation requests that have the effect of excluding from the scope of any Interim Measure any part of the target business, generally carry higher risks of pre-emptive action. This is because:

(a) the overlapping and non-overlapping (or the UK and non-UK) parts of the target business may have complex operational and financial links and share certain assets. These may be difficult to separate comprehensively; and

(b) it would be difficult to reverse the effects of such derogations if it became necessary to do so as part of any effective divestment remedy.

3.42 Possible justifications for such derogations, and the safeguards that may be required to be put in place to support them, are described further below.

Parts of one merging party's business that are not engaged in activities related to the other merging party's business

3.43 In some cases, the CMA may be willing to grant derogations where it is clear that certain parts of the target business's activities are not related to those of the acquiring business. A derogation on this basis will only be granted where the CMA is able to establish clearly that this will not impede the CMA from taking any appropriate remedial action that might be required. For this reason, the CMA is likely to be particularly cautious about granting derogations on this basis at the earlier stages of its investigation where the full scope of the merging parties' activities may not yet have been fully analysed.

3.44 Merging parties requesting derogations on this basis will be required to delineate clearly the parts of the merging parties' businesses that respectively do, and do not, engage in activities related to each other. Derogation requests should therefore include clear descriptions of all relevant businesses, along with their functions and reporting lines. To this end, merging parties should be able to show, in particular, that:

(a) the viability or competitive capability of the 'related' business (which will remain subject to the Interim Measure) is not dependent on the 'non-related' business (for which a derogation is sought);

(b) staff from the 'related' business do not interact with staff from the 'non-related' business, nor do staff have dual responsibilities in respect of both the 'related' and 'non-related' businesses;

(c) the tangible and intangible assets (including intellectual property rights) of the 'related' business, are not also used by the 'non-related' business;

(d) there are no customers and/or supplier contracts/relationships which are common to both the 'related' and 'non-related' businesses;

(e) the provision of back-office support functions (eg accounting, legal, HR, procurement) to the 'related' and 'non-related' businesses does not give rise to a risk that commercially-sensitive, confidential or proprietary information of the 'related' business can flow back to the 'non-related' business;

(f) the 'related' and 'non-related' businesses operate on separate IT systems or that shared IT systems are otherwise capable of being effectively ring-fenced;

(g) there are, in practice, no other material links between the 'related' business and the 'non-related' business including, for example, that the services provided by these businesses are not purchased together by customers; and

3.45 In certain cases, the CMA has granted derogation requests (where sufficiently specified, reasoned, and evidenced) in relation to:

(a) Non-overlapping businesses: for example, where an investment company (or other multi-product company) has holdings in businesses active across multiple industries, it may be clear at a relatively early stage of the case that many of the businesses in which the acquiring business holds an interest are not active in (and could not enter) any markets relevant to the target business.[65]

(b) Non-overlapping sites: for example, where the CMA is conducting a local area analysis (eg in a retail merger case) and there are no wider (eg national) effects, it may be possible, as the CMA's investigation develops, to grant derogations exempting specific non-overlapping sites.[66]

(c) Non-overlapping products: for example, as the CMA's investigation develops, it may be possible to grant derogations exempting businesses that are active only in relation to products/services in which the CMA has been able to dismiss possible competition concerns.[67]

3.46 While the examples described above relate to circumstances in which there is no horizontal overlap between the merging parties, the CMA will also take any potential vertical relationships between the merging parties' activities into account when assessing whether derogations can be granted on this basis. As mentioned in paragraph 3.43, the CMA is likely to be particularly cautious about granting these types of derogations at the earlier stages of its investigation.

3.47 Where integration is permitted in relation to only part of the merging parties' business, the Interim Measures will generally prevent staff from the parts of the business that remain subject to the Interim Measures from contacting former colleagues who are no longer subject to the Interim Measures. Such contacts should also be subject to procedural safeguards (such as those described in paragraphs 3.15 to 3.16 above).

3.48 Merging parties requesting derogations on this basis should be able to show (supported by relevant evidence) why such contacts are strictly necessary (eg to fulfil existing customer agreements or maintain existing customer relationships). Such contacts should also be subject to procedural safeguards (such as those described in paragraph 3.15 to 3.16 above).

Parts of the merging parties' businesses that have no relevance to their relevant activities in the UK

3.49 The CMA may consider granting derogations that will facilitate the integration of the non-UK aspects of the merging parties' businesses, unless the continued separation of these businesses is necessary to guard against pre-emptive action.[68]

3.50 For example, the CMA has previously consented to a derogation that enabled identified employees in a target's UK business to be involved in certain activities, which were generally prohibited by the Interim Measure, in relation to markets outside the UK. The derogation was granted subject to the condition that their involvement in these activities should not have any impact on the development, manufacture, distribution and/or sale of the target business's products in the UK. The relevant employees were also required to enter into non-disclosure agreements in order to prevent the dissemination of commercially sensitive information to any non-authorised employees.

3.51 The CMA is likely to be particularly cautious about granting derogations on this basis at the earlier stages of its investigation where the merging parties' activities (and, in particular, the links between their UK and non-UK activities) have not yet been fully analysed.

3.52 In practice, therefore, it will be more straightforward to obtain derogations in relation to the non-UK aspects of the merging parties' businesses when the CMA's investigation is at a more advanced stage. It may then be clearer that these businesses have no material connection to the functioning of their respective UK businesses (see also paragraph 6.3).

3.53 Merging parties requesting derogations on this basis will be required to delineate clearly the parts of their businesses that respectively do, and do not, engage in activities relating to the UK. Derogation requests should therefore include clear descriptions of all relevant businesses, along with their functions and reporting lines (along the lines described in paragraph 3.44 above).

3.54 As the CMA's investigation develops, it may be possible to grant derogations in relation to non-UK aspects of the merging parties' businesses that do have some connection to their UK businesses. It may, in particular, be possible to grant derogations in relation to non-UK businesses that are active only in relation to products/services in which the CMA has been able to dismiss competition concerns or non-UK businesses that would not form part of any remedial action that might be justified by the CMA's decision on the reference.

3.55 The CMA will need to consider carefully whether it is appropriate to grant derogations in respect of non-UK businesses where the UK and non-UK businesses operate under common intellectual property rights and know-how, or share other important resources or personnel. The CMA is likely to take a cautious approach, particularly at the initial stages of its investigation.

3.56 Where a derogation has been granted to exclude the non-UK business of the target business from the scope of the Interim Measures, and the non-UK business of the target business has been integrated with the acquiring business, the guidance on access to key staff in paragraphs 3.47 to 3.48 applies.

Replacement of key staff or substantive changes to the merging parties' organisational or management structures

3.57 In general, the operation and management of the target business under Interim Measures should be entirely separate from that of the acquiring business. Steps should be taken to retain key staff in the target business during the course of the CMA's investigation and the management and organisational structure of the target business should not be subject to material change. What constitutes key staff or material change may depend on the nature of the business in question. If in doubt, this should be discussed with the CMA.

3.58 In exceptional cases, the CMA may, however, be willing to consider derogations allowing the replacement of key staff at the target business by staff from the acquiring business, for example, if certain of the target business's key staff have left on, or after, completion of the merger. The merging parties will need to demonstrate, to the satisfaction of the CMA, that there are no other reasonable options available to the merging parties (such as recruitment on the open market, temporary consultancy arrangements or secondments from other parts of the target business). The CMA may also be prepared to consider substantive changes to the merging parties' organisational or management structures, where these are strictly necessary for the effective running of the target business during the CMA's investigation.[69] The CMA is unlikely to grant derogations where such changes are not time-critical or otherwise are not strictly needed to safeguard the viability and competitive capability of the target business.

3.59 The replacement of the target business's employees by staff that previously worked at the acquiring business could lead to the disclosure of confidential information or the coordination of commercial conduct.[70] Accordingly, the CMA would expect this to happen only where strictly necessary (ie where all other reasonable options have been explored). Merging parties requesting derogations on this basis should therefore be able to show (supported by relevant evidence):

(a) the roles and responsibilities of the affected key staff of the target business;
(b) why these key staff intend to leave, or have left, the target business;
(c) what steps have been taken to encourage all key staff to remain with the target business;
(d) why it is not possible to replace these key staff (or otherwise carry out their functions) with other staff from within the target business; and
(e) why it is not possible to replace these key staff (or otherwise carry out their functions) with individuals who do not currently work for the acquiring business.

3.60 The replacement of target business key staff in this way is likely to be subject to a number of safeguards. Depending on the circumstances of the case, the safeguards required are likely to include appropriate non-disclosure agreements signed by the replacement staff, which may, for example, explicitly forbid contact with the acquiring business's staff during the CMA's review and confirm that these staff no longer have access to the acquiring business's IT systems. The CMA is unlikely to accept the transfer of staff from the acquiring business to fulfil a key commercial function at the target business.

3.61 The CMA may also be willing to grant derogations allowing other changes to the organisational structure of, or the management responsibilities within, the merging parties' businesses. This might be the case, for example, where certain of the target business's management have left on, or after, completion of the merger and the remaining management of the target business decides that the most effective way of carrying out certain of their functions would be to reallocate them to other members of the management team.

3.62 Changes to the organisational and management structure of the merging parties could have a material impact on the CMA's ability to achieve effective remedies. Merging parties requesting derogations on this basis should therefore be able to show (supported by relevant evidence) why these specific organisational or management changes are strictly necessary.

DEROGATION REQUESTS THAT ARE UNLIKELY TO BE GRANTED BY THE CMA

3.63 The CMA will typically not grant a derogation request unless it can be shown that the proposed derogation is:

(a) strictly necessary to safeguard the viability and competitive capability of the target business;
(b) both urgent and necessary in advance of the CMA's decision on the merger; and
(c) clearly unlikely to have any impact on the CMA's ability to achieve effective remedies.

3.64 The fact that integration could subsequently be unwound should a divestment remedy be required, is not, by itself, sufficient to justify a derogation. This is primarily because of the risk that information obtained and/or actions taken by the acquiring business could impact negatively on competition between the merging parties if the merger were to be ultimately prohibited and could undermine potential remedies if remedies were found to be necessary.

3.65 The CMA would be likely, in most cases, to reject derogation requests in relation to:

(a) the appointment of any staff of the acquiring business to board or management positions of the target business (see paragraphs 3.59 to 3.60 and section 4 below on hold separate managers);
(b) granting the acquiring business any observer rights at board meetings of the target business;
(c) the acquiring business having any influence over the commercial policy of the target business (subject to any derogations granted by the CMA concerning delegation of authorities (see also paragraphs 3.32 to 3.36);
(d) the transfer of sales or other customer-facing functions from the target business to the acquiring business;
(e) the acquiring business bidding or negotiating on behalf of the target business;
(f) any action that would likely have the effect of undermining the independence and separate operation of the target business from the acquiring business from the perspective of customers, eg joint-branding, joint-marketing or references to the target business's activities and locations on the acquiring business's website and/or marketing materials;
(g) the acquiring business and the target business amending any existing commercial agreements between them or entering into new agreements;
(h) the acquiring business having access to detailed strategic, operational and financial information, or any other commercially sensitive information, relating to the target business (including but not limited to information about contracts, detailed revenue, cost and profit margin information, customers, suppliers, products and services etc);
(i) the acquiring business and the target business dealing jointly with customers or suppliers;[71]
(j) the discontinuation of overlapping products and services;
(k) the closure of overlapping business functions; and
(l) any action during the CMA's investigation that is intended to extract or accelerate the realisation of any revenue, cost or other synergies which is not strictly necessary to safeguard the viability and competitive capability of the target business (for example, restructuring to achieve tax savings would not be considered strictly necessary in this context).

3.66 As noted throughout this section, the CMA's decision on a derogation request will be guided not only by the impact that the proposed derogation could have on the CMA's ability to achieve effective remedies but also by the strict necessity of measures to safeguard the viability and competitive capability of the target business. Where the CMA cannot clearly ascertain the impact of a proposed derogation or the CMA's ability to achieve effective remedies is uncertain, the CMA is likely either to not grant the derogation or defer the granting of that derogation until such time as its impact can be clearly determined.

3.67 In some circumstances (eg where the target business is in severe financial difficulty or where, in the case of an acquisition of assets or parts of business, the target business cannot operate as a going concern on a stand-alone basis), the CMA may permit the acquiring business to exercise direct control over the commercial policy of the target business or to appoint an independent manager to run that business (see section 4 below on hold separate managers). The CMA is likely to require intense monitoring in such circumstances (eg through a monitoring trustee) and may require explanations of any material actions taken (eg where expenditure requests are denied).

3.68 In such circumstances, the CMA may also be willing to grant derogation requests of the type set out in paragraph 3.65 above.

3.69 Merging parties requesting derogations on this basis will be required to demonstrate to the satisfaction of the CMA (supported by relevant evidence) that the measures requested are strictly necessary to safeguard the viability and competitive capability of the target business. Merging parties should also consider whether there are any alternative measures available that could achieve this objective with a less significant potential impact on competition. Any derogations granted are likely to be subject to strict safeguards and conditions (eg to ensure that commercially sensitive information is not disclosed more widely than is strictly necessary, and along the lines described in paragraphs 3.15 to 3.18).

NOTES

42 Sections 72(3C), 80(2B) and 81(2B) of the Act.

43 See also paragraph 3.63.

44 For example, this might be to safeguard the viability and competitive capability of the target business, which would otherwise be at significant risk, to ensure the effective operation of the Interim Measures as a whole, or to meet a regulatory, statutory or other obligation. Requests that relate solely to bringing forward merger synergies or to the acquiring business's plans for the target business are unlikely to be granted.

45 Sections 72(8) and 80(10) of the Act define pre-emptive action as action which might prejudice the reference concerned or impede the taking of any action which may be justified by the CMA's decisions on a reference.

46 In this regard, the large volume of derogation consent letters previously issued by the CMA, which are available (in non-confidential form) on the CMA's website, provide a useful source of the types of safeguards the CMA may require.

47 Parties requesting a derogation will be required to sign a declaration in the following form:

I declare that, to the best of my knowledge and belief, the information given in this request is true, correct, and complete in all material respects. I understand that: It is a criminal offence under section 117 of the Enterprise Act 2002 (Act) for a person recklessly or knowingly to supply to the CMA information which is false or misleading in any material respect. This includes supplying such information to another person knowing that the information is to be used for the purpose of supplying information to the CMA. The information provided may be used in the substantive analysis of this transaction. In the event that the merger is referred for a Phase 2 investigation, information provided to the CMA during the course of the Phase 1 investigation will also be used for the Phase 2 investigation. In accordance with section 100(1) of the Act the CMA may make a reference after the expiry of the statutory deadline if information provided is in any material respect incomplete, false or misleading.

48 *Electro Rent Corporation v CMA* [2019] CAT at 206. See also *Intercontinental Exchange Inc v CMA and Nasdaq Stockholm AB* [2017] CAT 6 at paragraph 223.

49 *Intercontinental Exchange Inc v CMA and Nasdaq Stockholm AB* [2017] CAT 6 at paragraph 220. See also *Electro Rent Corporation v CMA* [2019] CAT 4 at paragraph 200 and *Stericycle International LLC v Competition Commission* [2006] CAT 21 at 128-129.

50 Sections 72(8) and 80(10) of the Act define pre-emptive action as action which ***might*** prejudice the reference concerned or impede the taking of any action which may be justified by the CMA's decisions on a reference.

51 It may therefore be necessary for reporting lines within the merging parties to be adjusted. See, for example, VTech/LeapFrog (2016–2017).

52 Paragraph 4 of the standard form IEO.

53 *Electro Rent Corporation v CMA* [2019] CAT at 127: *'In our view, simply as a matter of the language of the definition, a reasonable person reading the definition "matters connected to the day-to-day supply of goods and/or services by the . . . Electro Rent Corporation business" would have concluded, at the very least, that it was possible that the proper view was that the definition was restricted to Electro Rent's trading operations and did not extend to the disposal of its only UK premises'*.

54 See the penalty notices in the Electro Rent and Vanilla Group cases.

55 *Electro Rent Corporation v CMA* [2019] CAT at 128.

56 *Electro Rent Corporation v CMA* [2019] CAT at 138: "*The decision as to whether [terminating the lease] would promote the divestment was not his to make . . . We accept the CMA's submission that, even if Mr Brown believed that serving the Break Notice would promote Electro Rent's commercial interests, he should have consulted the CMA and sought a derogation from the Interim Order.*" See also *Intercontinental Exchange v CMA* [2017] CAT 6 at 221-223.

57 See, for example, Euro Car Parts/Andrew Page (2016–2018) and Tayto Group/The Real Pork Crackling Company (2018).

58 See, for example, PayPal/iZettle (2018–2019), Valeo Foods/Tangerine Confectionery (2018), CareTech Holdings/Cambian Group (2018–2019), Rentokil Initial/MPCL (2018–2019), Tobii/Smartbox (2018–2019) and Global Radio Services/Semper Veritas (Exterion) (2018–2019).

59 See, for example, PayPal/iZettle (2018–2019) and CareTech Holdings/Cambian Group (2018–2019).

60 See, for example, Interserve/Initial Facilities merger inquiry (2014). The consent in this case was granted in relation to initial undertakings, rather than a derogation from an IEO, but nevertheless provides an example of the circumstances in which the CMA may consent to the provision of legal services to the target business by the acquiring business.

61 See, for example, CareTech Holdings/Cambian Group (2018–2019), Rentokil Initial/MPCL (2018–2019), Tobii/Smartbox (2018–2019) and Global Radio Services/Semper Veritas (Exterion) (2018–2019).

62 In technology sectors, competitive capability can depend on ongoing R&D expenditure and activity and the need to maintain a pipeline of new products to replace obsolete products.

[63] In rare circumstances, the CMA may be willing to consider whether it would be appropriate for such financial oversight to be afforded to the acquiring business in the context of an anticipated merger, subject to strict safeguards being in place.

[64] See, for example, CareTech Holdings/Cambian Group (2018–2019), Rentokil Initial/MPCL (2018–2019), Global Radio Services/Semper Veritas (Exterion) (2018–2019) and Core Assets Group/Partnership in Children's Services (2019).

[65] See, for example, Harman/Bang & Olufsen (2015) and Immediate Media Company Bristol/Future Publishing (2014–2015).

[66] See, for example, MRH (GB)/Esso Petroleum (2015–2016) and Pure Gym/LA Fitness (2014).

[67] See, for example, Hain Frozen Foods/Orchard House Foods (2016).

[68] See, for example, ProStrakan/Archimedes Pharma (2014) and VTech/LeapFrog (2016–2017).

[69] Changes to organisational structure or management responsibilities that are not substantive are not prohibited by the standard form IEO.

[70] Even when the replacement staff have no contact with the acquiring business while the Interim Measures are in force, they know the general commercial conduct of the acquiring business, and may wish to return to the acquiring business should the transaction not go ahead.

[71] By way of exception, the CMA may grant derogations permitting the target business to benefit from the acquiring business's back-office arrangements (eg in relation to insurance and credit arrangements) where these arrangements are not transferring with the target business.

4. MONITORING TRUSTEES AND HOLD SEPARATE MANAGERS

MONITORING TRUSTEE

[3.458]

4.1 A monitoring trustee may be required by the CMA, in order to monitor and report on the merging parties' compliance with the Interim Measures (including Unwinding Orders). The involvement of a monitoring trustee may also assist the CMA in considering more complex derogation requests, as well as speed up the CMA's decisions on whether to grant derogation requests.

4.2 A monitoring trustee's role will usually be to assess, in its first report, and report on:

(a) the extent of integration (and confirm to the CMA that this is consistent with the representations made by the merging parties in their submission to the CMA at the start of the phase 1 investigation) and to make recommendations as to how to mitigate the risk of pre-emptive action; and

(b) the extent of compliance with any the Interim Measures and the adequacy of existing Interim Measures.

4.3 Thereafter, the monitoring trustee will be tasked with monitoring compliance with the Interim Measures and assisting the CMA with the consideration of derogation requests. Merging parties may consult the monitoring trustee about derogation requests, but should note that derogations can only be granted by the CMA, and will always be granted in writing (see paragraph 3.4).

4.4 In the event that the CMA requires a remedy involving a divestiture, the monitoring trustee's role may be expanded to ensure that any divestiture process is carried out in compliance with the CMA's remedy decision and with any Interim Measures.

4.5 At phase 1, the CMA may consider it necessary to appoint a monitoring trustee where, based on the CMA's risk assessment, one or more of the risk factors in paragraph 4.6 apply[72] in particular, but not only, where the CMA is concerned about the ability or willingness of the merging parties to comply fully with the IEO. The CMA will routinely consider whether any of these considerations apply both at the beginning of phase 1 and when a decision is taken that the case raises more material or complex competition issues and therefore requires an issues meeting. In addition to considering the need for a monitoring trustee at these points in its investigation the CMA may appoint a monitoring trustee at any point in the investigation if a significant risk of pre-emptive action is identified.

4.6 At phase 2, the CMA will normally require a monitoring trustee to be appointed in completed mergers unless merging parties can provide compelling evidence as to why there is little risk of pre-emptive action and/or that none of the risk factors below are present:

(a) substantial integration of the two businesses prior to implementation of the Interim Measures;

(b) concerns that there may have been a breach or breaches of the Interim Measures;

(c) a need for further or continued integration of the business throughout the CMA's investigation, subject to the necessary consents from the CMA, for example if the target business is not a stand-alone business;

(d) a risk of deterioration of the business, for example through loss of key customers or members of staff; and/or

(e) the pre-merger senior management of the target business is absent and/or strong incentives exist for the senior management of the target business to operate the target business on behalf of the acquiring business.

This last risk factor, in particular, will also suggest the need for the appointment of a hold separate manager.

PROCEDURE FOR APPOINTMENT OF A MONITORING TRUSTEE

4.7 The CMA will inform the merging parties of its intention, or provisional decision, to require them to appoint a monitoring trustee. The CMA will offer the merging parties typically no more than 24 hours to comment on the proposed appointment of a monitoring trustee. If, having considered any submissions from the merging parties concerning the appointment of a monitoring trustee, the CMA decides to require the merging parties to appoint a monitoring trustee, the CMA will notify the merging parties of its final decision to require them to appoint a monitoring trustee by sending a letter containing draft directions and a roster of monitoring trustees who, to the knowledge of the CMA, currently provide monitoring trustee services. The merging parties will be given a short period to comment on the draft wording of the directions (typically no more than 24 hours) before they are finalised and published on the case page.

4.8 The CMA maintains a roster of monitoring trustees with whom it has either worked in the past or who currently provide monitoring trustee services.[73] The roster is supplied to merging parties at the same time as the letter requiring a monitoring trustee to be appointed. Merging parties are, however, entitled to nominate a monitoring trustee that is not on the roster. The roster provided by the CMA is not a list of monitoring trustees who have been pre-approved by the CMA, and therefore any monitoring trustee nominated by the merging parties will need to be approved separately by the CMA following an interview process to assess its suitability.

4.9 Merging parties will typically be given two working days from the date of the final directions to nominate a monitoring trustee who meets the suitability criteria set out in paragraph 4.10 (and a second monitoring trustee in reserve should the CMA not approve the merging parties' first nomination) with their proposed terms of appointment and a further three working days to appoint a monitoring trustee on terms approved by the CMA, although this timeframe may be altered depending on the facts of the case. The CMA reserves the right to select a monitoring trustee of its own choosing and require its appointment by the merging parties if a suitable monitoring trustee cannot be found within five working days of the date of the final directions.

4.10 Before approving the monitoring trustee, the CMA will typically conduct an interview with each nominated monitoring trustee to discuss its suitability for the appointment. When nominating a monitoring trustee to the CMA, merging parties and/or the nominated monitoring trustee should demonstrate the suitability of the monitoring trustee by providing evidence on:

(a) the independence of the monitoring trustee firm (and its affiliates if applicable) from the merging parties;

(b) the relevant experience and qualifications of individuals within the monitoring trustee team who will be engaged on the case;

(c) the monitoring trustee's capacity to take on the appointment for the entire duration of the CMA's investigation (including any possible remedies process); and

(d) the process followed, and checks carried out, by the monitoring trustee to confirm whether there are any actual or perceived conflicts of interest arising from the appointment of the monitoring trustee.

4.11 During the five working-day period described in paragraph 4.9, the CMA will consider the nomination of the monitoring trustee by the merging parties and will approve the appointment if the monitoring trustee meets the suitability criteria set out in paragraph 4.10, and a satisfactory draft mandate has been provided, including suitable arrangements for remuneration. The merging parties are required to keep the CMA closely informed should the timelines for the appointment of the monitoring trustee (as set out in the final directions) prove problematic. The appointment of a monitoring trustee is at the expense of the acquiring party.

4.12 The monitoring trustee is required to keep the CMA informed should it become aware of any developments or changes to the circumstances of the monitoring trustee that may have the effect of the monitoring trustee failing to meet the suitability criteria set out in paragraph 4.10 above.

HOLD SEPARATE MANAGER

4.13 The CMA may require the appointment of a hold separate manager with executive powers, in order to operate the target business separately from the acquiring business and in line with the Interim Measures for the duration of the investigation. The hold separate manager's role is a day-to-day management role in the target business, reporting to the CMA rather than the acquiring firm. This role is distinct from that of a monitoring trustee.[74]

4.14 The CMA will consider the need for the appointment of a hold separate manager, inter alia, at the start of phase 1; following the decision on whether the case requires an issues meeting; and, following the CMA's decision to accept undertakings in lieu of reference, to oversee a divestiture. It will also consider the need for a hold separate manager at the outset of a phase 2 investigation and review the issue throughout the phase 2 investigation. As is the case for a monitoring trustee, the appointment of a hold separate manager is at the expense of the acquiring business.

4.15 Hold separate managers can be either an internal or external appointee. Where appropriate, the CMA will require appointment of a hold separate manager external to the merging parties.[75] In other cases, it may not be necessary to require an external hold separate manager, but the CMA may require existing employees of the merged entities to act independently in key managerial roles in the target business.[76] The factors the CMA will consider when weighing up the choice between an external or internal hold separate manager are: the relative experience and suitability of existing employees; the independence of existing employees; and the complexity of the hold separate requirements. Typically, if a suitable internal hold separate manager is available, the CMA will seek to appoint this manager before exploring external options. However, the CMA will expect to be satisfied that the hold separate manager is sufficiently independent. For example, if the hold separate manager is employed by the acquiring business, the CMA may require an undertaking that he or she will not return to the acquiring business if the merger is prohibited, or if a divestment of the target business is later required, that the hold separate manager would transfer with the divestment business.

PROCEDURE FOR APPOINTMENT OF A HOLD SEPARATE MANAGER

4.16 The procedure for appointment of a hold separate manager will vary depending on the circumstances of the case and, in particular, the existing management arrangements at the target business. The CMA will issue directions requiring the appointment of a hold separate manager where appropriate.

4.17 The CMA will usually invite the merging parties to put forward candidates for the role of hold separate manager, but may also, or instead, look for candidates itself. Prior to appointment, the CMA will need to approve any candidate proposed by the merging parties, including the terms of the candidate's appointment. Depending on the circumstances of the case, the CMA may consider it appropriate to require the appointment of a hold separate manager according to the same process and timing as applies to the appointment of a monitoring trustee in paragraph 4.9 above.

NOTES

72 See, for example, Rentokil Initial/MPCL (2018–2019), Tobii/Smartbox (2018–2019), Nicholls/DCC ((2018) and Global Radio/GMG (2013), and, in relation to overseeing phase 1 divestitures following undertakings in lieu of reference, the OFT directions in Nakano/Premier Foods (2012); Rexel UK/Wilts Wholesale Electrical (2012); and Vue Entertainment/Apollo Cinemas (2012).

73 The CMA will periodically seek to update and expand the roster and meet with potential candidates.

74 See Trinity Mirror / Northern & Shell Media Group (2018) for an example of the appointment of a hold separate manager in phase 1.

75 For example, in the Competition Commission's merger investigations into Stericycle International LLC/Sterile Technologies Group Limited (2006), Clifford Kent Holdings Limited/Deans Food Group Limited (2007) and Stagecoach Group plc/Preston Bus Limited (2009).

76 For example, VTech/Leapfrog (2016–2017), and the Competition Commission's merger investigations into Booker Group plc/Makro Holding Limited (2013), Capita Group plc/IBS OPENSystems plc (2009) and Stagecoach Group plc/Eastbourne Buses Limited (2009).

5. UNWINDING INTEGRATION

[3.459]

5.1 In certain circumstances, the CMA may consider it necessary to use its powers to unwind integration that has already occurred prior to the Interim Measures coming into force.[77] This will be assessed on a case-by-case basis, where the CMA reasonably suspects that action has, or may have, been taken which constitutes pre-emptive action. If Interim Measures are breached the CMA may order the person responsible to unwind the breach in addition to imposing a penalty.

5.2 Pre-emptive action can extend beyond the integration of business functions and systems. It can also include the merging parties entering into arrangements or agreements in anticipation of the merger; closer collaboration between the merging parties; or actions that might undermine the independent competitive capabilities of either business.

5.3 Unwinding may be undertaken voluntarily following discussion with the CMA, pursuant to an Unwinding Order, or pursuant to directions under Interim Measures to ensure their compliance.

5.4 The CMA would typically expect to use its unwinding powers at both phase 1 and phase 2 in cases if, based on the CMA's own risk assessment one or more of the following factors applies:

(a) The integration affects the way in which the parties compete with each other or with third parties, or their ability to compete. For example, this may be the case if:
   (i) the merging parties have discontinued some of their pre-merger products or services in anticipation or as a result of the merger; or
   (ii) the merging parties are engaging in joint-branding (eg on their websites or communications to customers or suppliers); or
   (iii) the merging parties' customer call centres and sales teams share common contact details;
   (iv) the integration affects the way in which customers and suppliers engage with, or perceive the independence of, the merging parties; or

(b) if the risk of pre-emptive action significantly increases if immediate unwinding action is not taken.

5.5 Examples of measures to unwind integration that have been required in the past include requiring:

(a) by way of an Unwinding Order, the reversal of actions to discontinue products and development projects, and the termination of an agreement entered into between the merging parties prior to completion of the transaction;[78]

(b) reversal of any re-branding of the target business's assets with the acquiring business's branding (eg changing the livery of buses);

(c) the destruction of, or retention by a third party (eg legal advisers) of, confidential information relating to the target business (eg customer lists) that had passed to, or was accessible by, the acquiring business;

(d) the reversal of changes to an organisation's structure, for example, by requiring:
   (i) representatives from the acquiring business not to attend the target business's board meetings, or
   (ii) departed key staff to be replaced (eg a Finance Director) or a hold separate manager to be appointed to manage the target business;

(e) the separation of functions or decision-making processes, which have previously been integrated (eg sales forces or production lines); and

(f) the retraction of regulatory requests (eg bus route registrations and de-registrations).

NOTES

77 Pursuant to sections 72(3B), 80(2A) or 81(2A) of the Act.

78 Pursuant to section 81(2A) of the Act, the CMA issued on Unwinding Order in Tobii/Smartbox (2018–2019) at phase 2. The merging parties were ordered to unwind an agreement under which Smartbox acted as a reseller of Tobii products in the UK and Ireland. The Unwinding Order obliged Smartbox to stop accepting new orders under the reseller agreement (and eventually terminate this agreement), to restart its development projects and to restart supplying its discontinued products.

6. TIMING FOR REVOKING INTERIM MEASURES AND GRANTING DEROGATIONS

[3.460]

6.1 During the course of the CMA's investigation, the CMA may release merging parties from some, or all, of their obligations under the Interim Measures. This will be done as early as is appropriate in the circumstances of the case.

6.2 Where, following the internal state of play meeting at phase 1, the CMA has reached the provisional view (subject to any subsequent evidence or assessment to the contrary) that the merger does not give rise to competition concerns, the CMA will typically be willing to revoke the IEO in full.

6.3 Similarly, as soon as the CMA reaches the provisional view (subject to any subsequent evidence to the contrary) that only part of the merger is potentially of concern, either at phase 1 or phase 2, a derogation may be granted in relation to the parts of the merger that are no longer of concern provided also that they are unrelated to the potentiality problematic areas, and the derogation does not undermine the CMA's ability to impose effective remedies. At phase 1 the CMA will be mindful of the need not to prejudice a potential reference by releasing from the IEO parts of the merger which a phase 2 inquiry might subsequently find to be problematic, and therefore the CMA is likely to take a cautious approach. Merging parties may be required to provide additional evidence at this stage, along the lines described in paragraph 3.44 above, to establish that the parts of the target business that do not raise concerns can be clearly delineated from those that remain under investigation.

7. COMPLIANCE STATEMENTS AND ENFORCEMENT

COMPLIANCE

[3.461]

7.1 To help ensure compliance with Interim Measures, the CMA will normally require the Chief Executive Officers (or other persons agreed by the CMA) of each of the acquiring and target businesses subject to Interim Measures to provide a compliance statement separately certifying the compliance of the acquiring business and the target business with the Interim Measures on a fortnightly basis.[79] The CMA is likely to agree to a person other than the CEO (such as an alternative director or the General Counsel) signing the compliance statement where that individual has the actual authority to bind the enterprise and holds sufficient knowledge of its operations.

7.2 If the Interim Measures impose an obligation on the acquiring business to ensure that the target business is complying with the Interim Measures, then the acquiring business is not absolved of this responsibility by the fact that the person in charge of the target business is also supplying a compliance statement.

7.3 In addition, the CMA may require further information or a further statement of compliance to be provided on an ad hoc or periodic basis. In certain circumstances, the CMA may also require a representative of the target business (or enterprise) to prepare a periodic report to the CMA, in such form as may be directed by the CMA, for the purpose of monitoring compliance with any Interim Measures.

7.4 Merging parties subject to Interim Measures should ensure the retention of documents relating to compliance, including re-visiting their document retention policies and practices in light of the Interim Measures. Deletion of evidence relevant to compliance may be viewed as aggravating any breach which occurs.[80]

POTENTIAL CONSEQUENCES OF FAILING TO COMPLY

7.5 The CMA takes the merging parties' compliance with their obligations under Interim Measures very seriously. With this in mind, the person signing the compliance statement should note that it is a criminal offence recklessly or knowingly to supply to the CMA information which is false or misleading in any material respect.[81] Breach of this provision can result in fines, imprisonment for a term not exceeding two years, or both.

7.6 Failure to comply with Interim Measures without reasonable excuse may result in the CMA imposing a penalty of up to 5% of the total value of the turnover (both in and outside the United Kingdom) of the enterprises owned or controlled by the person on whom the penalty is imposed. To date the penalties imposed have been significantly less than the 5% cap.[82] However, given the importance of Interim Measures to the functioning of the regime, the CMA will not hesitate to make full use of its fining powers. The CMA will therefore impose proportionately larger penalties in future cases should this prove necessary in the interests of deterrence.

NOTES

79 The matters set out in the template compliance statement are a starting point for discussion between the CMA and the relevant merging party or parties. The template will be adapted to meet specific requirements on a case-by-case basis.

80 Penalty decision in relation to Vanilla Group at paragraphs 160-161.

Part 3 CMA and other Guidelines

[81] Section 117 of the Act.

[82] Section 94A of the Act. The CMA has imposed a number of penalties under this provision. These include penalties imposed on Electro Rent (£100,000 penalty imposed on 11 June 2018; upheld by the CAT on 11 February 2019 in *Electro Rent Corporation v CMA* [2019] CAT 4; a further £200,000 penalty imposed on 12 February 2019); European Metal Recycling (£300,000 penalty imposed on 20 December 2018); and Vanilla Group (£120,000 penalty imposed on 7 March 2019).

COMPETITION & MARKETS AUTHORITY: TEMPLATE INITIAL ENFORCEMENT ORDER (COMPLETED MERGER) ACQUISITION BY X OF Y

[3.462]

NOTES

See also the list of consultations and draft documents in the Appendix at **[A1]**.

INITIAL ENFORCEMENT ORDER MADE BY THE COMPETITION AND MARKETS AUTHORITY PURSUANT TO SECTION 72(2) OF THE ENTERPRISE ACT 2002 (THE ACT)

[3.463]

[Note: In this template X is the direct acquirer and Y is the target. The initial enforcement order is imposed on both the ultimate UK parent company of X (the UK Topco), which is referred to as A, and on X. If X is also the UK Topco then A can be read as X. Where the acquirer is an overseas company, the initial enforcement order will, to the extent appropriate, be imposed on both the Overseas Topco and the UK Topco (in which case, A refers to both).]

Whereas:

(a) the Competition and Markets Authority (CMA) has reasonable grounds for suspecting that it is or may be the case that X and Y ([definition of Y]) have ceased to be distinct;

(b) the CMA is considering, pursuant to section 22 of the Act, whether it is or may be the case that a relevant merger situation has been created and whether the creation of that situation has resulted or may be expected to result in a substantial lessening of competition in any market or markets in the United Kingdom (UK);

(c) the CMA wishes to ensure that no action is taken pending final determination of any reference under section 22 of the Act which might prejudice that reference or impede the taking of any action by the CMA under Part 3 of the Act which might be justified by the CMA's decisions on the reference; and

(d) the circumstances set out in section 72(6) of the Act do not apply and the reference has not been finally determined in accordance with section 79(1) of the Act.

Now for the purposes of preventing pre-emptive action in accordance with section 72(2) of the Act the CMA makes the following order addressed to [insert full registered name of UK Topco [and Overseas Topco] A] ([if necessary, definition of A]) and [insert full registered name of X] ([definition of X]) (Order).

COMMENCEMENT, APPLICATION AND SCOPE

1. This Order commences on the commencement date: [date of order].

2. This Order applies to [A and] X.

3. Notwithstanding any other provision of this Order, no act or omission shall constitute a breach of this Order, and nothing in this Order shall oblige [A or] X to reverse any act or omission, in each case to the extent that it occurred or was completed prior to the commencement date.

MANAGEMENT OF THE [A/X] AND Y BUSINESSES UNTIL DETERMINATION OF PROCEEDINGS

4. Except with the prior written consent of the CMA, [A and] X shall not, during the specified period, take any action which might prejudice a reference of the transaction under section 22 of the Act or impede the taking of any action under the Act by the CMA which may be justified by the CMA's decisions on such a reference, including any action which might:

(a) lead to the integration of the Y business with the [A/X] business;

(b) transfer the ownership or control of the [A/X] business or the Y business or any of their subsidiaries; or

(c) otherwise impair the ability of the Y business or the [A/X] business to compete independently in any of the markets affected by the transaction.

5. Further and without prejudice to the generality of paragraph 4 and subject to paragraph 3, [A and] X shall at all times during the specified period procure that, except with the prior written consent of the CMA:

(a) the Y business is carried on separately from the [A/X] business and the Y business's separate sales or brand identity is maintained;

(b) the Y business and the [A/X] business are maintained as a going concern and sufficient resources are made available for the development of the Y business and the [A/X] business, on the basis of their respective pre-merger business plans;

(c) except in the ordinary course of business, no substantive changes are made to the organisational structure of, or the management responsibilities within, the Y business or the [A/X] business;

(d) the nature, description, range and quality of [goods and/or services] supplied in the UK by each of the two businesses are maintained and preserved;

(e) except in the ordinary course of business for the separate operation of the two businesses:

(i) all of the assets of the Y business and the [A/X] business are maintained and preserved, including facilities and goodwill;

(ii) none of the assets of the Y business or the [A/X] business are disposed of; and

(iii) no interest in the assets of the Y business or the [A/X] business is created or disposed of;

(f) there is no integration of the information technology of the Y or [A/X] businesses, and the software and hardware platforms of the Y business shall remain essentially unchanged, except for routine changes and maintenance;

(g) the [customer and supplier] lists of the two businesses shall be operated and updated separately and any negotiations with any existing or potential [customers and suppliers] in relation to the Y business will be carried out by the Y business alone and for the avoidance of doubt the [A/X] business will not negotiate on behalf of the Y business (and vice versa) or enter into any joint agreements with the Y business (and vice versa);

(h) all existing contracts of the Y business and the [A/X] business continue to be serviced by the business to which they were awarded;

(i) no changes are made to key staff of the Y business or [A/X] business;

(j) no key staff are transferred between the Y business and the [A/X] business;

(k) all reasonable steps are taken to encourage all key staff to remain with the Y business and the [A/X] business; and

(l) no business secrets, know-how, commercially-sensitive information, intellectual property or any other information of a confidential or proprietary nature relating to either of the two businesses shall pass, directly or indirectly, from the Y business (or any of its employees, directors, agents or affiliates) to the [A/X] business (or any of its employees, directors, agents or affiliates), or vice versa, except where strictly necessary in the ordinary course of business (including, for example, where required for compliance with external regulatory and/or accounting obligations or for due diligence, integration planning or the completion of any merger control proceedings relating to the transaction) and on the basis that, should the transaction be prohibited, any records or copies (electronic or otherwise) of such information that have passed, wherever they may be held, will be returned to the business to which they relate and any copies destroyed.

COMPLIANCE

6. [A and] X shall procure that each of [its/their] subsidiaries complies with this Order as if the Order had been issued to each of them.

7. [A and] X shall provide to the CMA such information or statement of compliance as it may from time to time require for the purposes of monitoring compliance by [A and] X and its/their] subsidiaries with this Order. In particular, on [•] 201[•] and subsequently [every two weeks/month/specified date of the month] (or, where this does not fall on a working day, the first working day thereafter) the Chief Executive Officer of [A and] X or other persons of [A and] X as agreed with the CMA shall, on behalf of [A and] X, provide a statement to the CMA in the form set out in the Annex to this Order confirming compliance with this Order.

8. At all times, [A and] X shall, or shall procure that Y shall, actively keep the CMA informed of any material developments relating to the Y business or the [A/X] business, which includes but is not limited to:

(a) details of key staff who leave or join the Y business or the [A/X] business;

(b) any interruption of the Y or [A/X] business (including without limitation its procurement, production, logistics, sales and employee relations arrangements) that has prevented it from operating in the ordinary course of business for more than 24 hours;

(c) all substantial customer volumes won or lost or substantial changes to the customer contracts for the Y or [A/X] business including any substantial changes in customers' demand; and

(d) substantial changes in the Y or [A/X] business's contractual arrangements or relationships with key suppliers.

9. If [A or] X has any reason to suspect that this Order might have been breached it shall immediately notify the CMA and any monitoring trustee that [A and/or] X may be directed to appoint under paragraph 10.

10. The CMA may give directions to a specified person or to a holder of a specified office in any body of persons (corporate or unincorporated) to take specified steps for the purpose of carrying out, or ensuring compliance with, this Order, or do or refrain from doing any specified action in order to ensure compliance with the Order. The CMA may vary or revoke any directions so given.

11. [A and] X shall comply in so far as [it is/they are] able with such directions as the CMA may from time to time give to take such steps as may be specified or described in the directions for the purpose of carrying out or securing compliance with this Order.

INTERPRETATION

12. The Interpretation Act 1978 shall apply to this Order as it does to Acts of Parliament.

13. For the purposes of this Order:

'**A**' means [full registered name and company number (Companies House) of acquirer's UK parent and, if relevant, overseas parent];

'**the A business**' means the business of A and its subsidiaries carried on as at the commencement date;

'**the Act**' means the Enterprise Act 2002;

'**an affiliate**' of a person is another person who satisfies the following condition, namely that any enterprise (which, in this context, has the meaning given in section 129(1) of the Act) that the first person carries on from time to time and any enterprise that the second person carries on from time to time would be regarded as being under common control for the purposes of section 26 of the Act;

'**business**' has the meaning given by section 129(1) and (3) of the Act;

'**commencement date**' means [date of order];

'**control**' includes the ability directly or indirectly to control or materially to influence the policy of a body corporate or the policy of any person in carrying on an enterprise;

'**the decisions**' means the decisions of the CMA on the questions which it is required to answer by virtue of section 35 of the Act;

'**key staff**' means staff in positions of executive or managerial responsibility and/or whose performance affects the viability of the business;

'**the ordinary course of business**' means matters connected to the day-to-day supply of [goods and/or services] by Y or [A/]X and does not include matters involving significant changes to the organisational structure or related to the post-merger integration of Y and [A/]X;

'**specified period**' means the period beginning on the commencement date and terminating in accordance with section 72(6) of the Act;

'**subsidiary**', unless otherwise stated, has the meaning given by section 1159 of the Companies Act 2006;

'**the transaction**' means [the transaction by which X and Y have ceased to be distinct within the meaning of section 23 of the Act];

'**the two businesses**' means the [A/X] business and the Y business;

'**X**' means [full registered name and company number (Companies House) of acquirer];

'**the X business**' means the business of X and its subsidiaries but excluding the Y business, carried on as at the commencement date;

'**Y**' means [full registered name and company number (Companies House) of target, or description of the acquired business if asset transaction];

'**the Y business**' means the business of Y and its subsidiaries carried on as at the commencement date;

unless the context requires otherwise, the singular shall include the plural and vice versa.

ANNEX
COMPLIANCE STATEMENT FOR A/X

[3.464]

I [insert name] confirm on behalf of A/X that:

COMPLIANCE IN THE RELEVANT PERIOD

1. In the period from [insert date] to [insert date] (the Relevant Period):

(a) A/X has complied with the Order made by the CMA in relation to the transaction on [insert date of this Order] (the Order).

(b) A/X's subsidiaries have also complied with this Order.

2. Subject to paragraph 3 of the Order, and except with the prior written consent of the CMA:

(a) No action has been taken by A/X that might prejudice a reference of the transaction under section 22 of the Act or impede the taking of any action by the CMA which may be justified by its decision on such a reference, including any action which might:

(i) lead to the integration of the Y business with the [A/X] business;

(ii) transfer the ownership or control of the [A/X] business or the Y business or any of their subsidiaries; or

(iii) otherwise impair the ability of the Y business or the [A/X] business to compete independently in any of the markets affected by the transaction.

(*b*) The Y business has been carried on separately from the [A/X] business and the Y business's separate sales or brand identity has been maintained.

(*c*) The Y business and the [A/X] business have been maintained as a going concern and sufficient resources have been made available for the development of the Y business and the [A/X] business, on the basis of their respective pre-merger business plans.

(*d*) No substantive changes have been made to the organisational structure of, or the management responsibilities within, the Y business or the [A/X] business, except in the ordinary course of business.

(*e*) The nature, description, range and quality of [goods and/or services] supplied in the UK by the Y business and the [A/X] business have been maintained and preserved.

(*f*) Except in the ordinary course of business for the separate operation of the two businesses:

(*i*) all of the assets of the Y business and the [A/X] business, including facilities and goodwill, have been maintained and preserved as at the start of the Relevant Period;

(*ii*) none of the assets of the Y business or the [A/X] business have been disposed of; and

(*iii*) no interest in the assets of the Y business or the [A/X] business has been created or disposed of.

(*g*) There has been no integration of the information technology of the Y or [A/X] businesses, and the software and hardware platforms of the Y business have remained essentially unchanged, except for routine changes and maintenance.

(*h*) Subject to integration which had occurred prior to the commencement date, the [customer and supplier] lists of the two businesses have been operated and updated separately and any negotiations with any existing or potential [customers and suppliers] in relation to the Y business have been carried out by the Y business alone and, for the avoidance of doubt, the [A/X] business has not negotiated on behalf of the Y business (and vice versa) or entered into any joint agreements with the Y business (and vice versa).

(*i*) All existing contracts of the Y business and the [A/X] business have been serviced by the business to which they were awarded, except to the extent novated, assigned or subcontracted prior to the commencement date.

(*j*) No changes have been made to key staff of the Y business or the [A/X] business.

(*k*) No key staff have been transferred between the Y business and the [A/X] business.

(*l*) All reasonable steps have been taken to encourage all key staff to remain with the Y business and the [A/X] business.

(*m*) Except as permitted by the Order, no business secrets, know-how, commercially-sensitive information, intellectual property or any other information of a confidential or proprietary nature relating to either of the two businesses, has passed, directly or indirectly, from the Y business (or any of its employees, directors, agents or affiliates) to the [A/X] business (or any of its employees, directors, agents or affiliates), or vice versa.

(*n*) Except as listed in paragraph (o) below, there have been no:

(*i*) key staff that have left or joined the Y business or the [A/X] business;

(*ii*) interruptions of the Y business or the [A/X] business (including without limitation procurement, production, logistics, sales and employee relations arrangements) that have prevented it from operating in the ordinary course of business for more than 24 hours;

(*iii*) substantial customer volumes won or lost or substantial changes to the customer contracts for the Y business or the [A/X] business; or

(*iv*) substantial changes in the Y or [A/X] business's contractual arrangements or relationships with key suppliers.

(*o*) [*list of material developments*]

3. A/X and its subsidiaries remain in full compliance with the Order and will, or will procure that Y, continue actively to keep the CMA informed of any material developments relating to the Y or the [A/X] business in accordance with paragraph 8 of the Order.

INTERPRETATION

4. Terms defined in the Order have the same meaning in this compliance statement.

FOR AND ON BEHALF OF A/X

Signature . . . .

Name . . . .

Title . . . .

Date . . . .

COMPETITION & MARKETS AUTHORITY: TEMPLATE DEROGATION LETTER IN RESPECT OF INITIAL ENFORCEMENT ORDERS ISSUED PURSUANT TO SECTION 72(2) ENTERPRISE ACT 2002 – COMPLETED ACQUISITION

[3.465]

NOTES

Dear [insert name of legal representative on behalf of the merging parties]

Consent under section 72(3C) of the Enterprise Act 2002 to certain actions for the purposes of the Initial Enforcement Order made by the Competition and Markets Authority ('CMA') on [insert date of initial enforcement order (IEO)]

Completed acquisition by [X] of [Y] [Use the name of the acquirer [X] and target [Y] as identified in the IEO or if asset purchase use "Completed acquisition by [X] of the assets of the [Y] business"]

We refer to your email/letter/s [delete as appropriate] [and accompanying note[s]/ further information] dated [insert date/s] requesting that the CMA consents to derogations to the Initial Enforcement Order of [insert date] (the 'Initial Order'). The terms defined in the Initial Order have the same meaning in this letter.

Under the Initial Order, save for written consent by the CMA, [insert addressee of the IEO] and [insert any additional entities identified in the IEO, as appropriate] are required to hold separate the [insert] business from the [insert] business [Please use the definitions as set out in the IEO to describe the relevant businesses] and refrain from taking any action which might prejudice a reference under section 22 of the Act or impede the taking of any remedial action following such a reference. After due consideration of your request for derogations from the Initial Order, based on the information received from you and in the particular circumstances of this case, [insert addressee of the IEO] and [insert relevant target entities/business as appropriate] may carry out the following actions, in respect of the specific paragraphs:

1. Paragraphs [] and [] of the Initial Order [insert relevant paragraphs of the IEO from which a derogation is being requested]

[Insert brief explanation and reasons for derogation/s from the IEO and specify what the CMA is being requested to consent to and what specific actions are permitted within the terms of that consent. Include, if necessary, any specific actions such consent does *not* apply to and/or conditions that need to be additionally fulfilled as appropriate, eg entering into NDA's approved by the CMA. Please also provide any relevant evidence to support the submissions made in relation to the reasons for the derogation/s from the IEO.]

[The CMA notes, as set out in paragraphs 3.6 to 3.14 of its guidance on initial enforcement orders and derogations in merger investigations, that the passing of confidential or proprietary information from the target to the acquirer is not prohibited where 'strictly necessary in the ordinary course of business (including, for example, where required for compliance with external regulatory and/or accounting obligations or for due diligence, integration planning or the completion of any merger control proceedings relating to the transaction) [. . . .]'. The CMA therefore encourages merging parties and their advisers to 'self-assess' whether the passing of confidential or proprietary information requires a derogation from the IEO prior to submitting any request to the CMA.]

DEPARTMENT FOR BUSINESS, ENERGY & INDUSTRIAL STRATEGY ENTERPRISE ACT 2002: CHANGES TO THE TURNOVER AND SHARE OF SUPPLY TESTS FOR MERGERS

(Guidance 2020)

[3.466]

NOTES

CONTENTS

INTRODUCTION

[3.467]
The Government published a Green Paper, 'National Security and Infrastructure Investment Review',[1] on 17 October 2017. In this, the Government proposed short and long-term proposals to reform how Government can ensure that national security is not undermined by investments or mergers. Two consultations followed.

The first consultation, which closed on 14 November 2017, focused on the proposals that resulted in the changes to the Enterprise Act 2002. A summary of those changes is set out at the start of this guidance.

The second consultation, which closed on 9 January 2018, set out broad options for longer-term, more far-reaching reforms. It was followed by a White Paper in July 2018, which set out more detailed proposals. The National Security and Investment Bill making far-reaching reforms will be brought forward by the Government when Parliamentary time allows.

This guidance focuses on further changes made to the Enterprise Act 2002 to extend the Government's powers in intervening in mergers for public interest reasons. In particular, the Government has legislated in this area for the intention of tackling risks to our national security.

PURPOSE OF THIS GUIDANCE

This guidance was produced by the Department for Business, Energy and Industrial Strategy (BEIS) to accompany the Enterprise Act 2002 (Share of Supply Test) (Amendment) Order 2020 and the Enterprise Act 2002 (Turnover Test) (Amendment) Order 2020 ('the Orders'). It also consolidates guidance on previous amendments to the Act, the Enterprise Act 2002 (Share of Supply Test) (Amendment) Order 2018 and the Enterprise Act 2002 (Turnover Test) (Amendment) Order 2018.

The Orders amend the Enterprise Act 2002 ('the Act') to deal with the protection of critical sectors mergers in which it would otherwise not be able to intervene.

This guidance explains why the Government amended the Act, describes the legal and practical effect of the amendments, and offers advice to businesses and others about how they may be affected by the changes.

This guidance is not statutory guidance. It does not change, for example, the legal duties of the Competition and Markets Authority (the CMA). Nor does it impose legal duties on businesses or any other organisation.

Whilst the guidance is intended to provide an indication of how the public interest merger regime will operate in practice, and the approach the Secretary of State is likely to adopt in considering cases, each transaction will be looked at on its merits on a case by-case basis. Businesses should consider their own particular circumstances and, where necessary, seek their own legal advice.

The Government will keep this guidance under review, updating it to ensure it remains as relevant and as useful as possible. It welcomes comments from parties about any additions or clarifications that would be helpful.

NOTES

[1] Department for Business, Energy and Industrial Strategy (2017), 'National Security and Infrastructure Investment Review', https://www.gov.uk/government/consultations/national-security-and-infrastructure-investment-review.

EXECUTIVE SUMMARY

[3.468]
The Government is committed to fostering innovation in areas of advanced technology, not only for the economic benefits it brings, but also the potential of emerging technologies to enhance the lives of British citizens. The Government prides itself on advanced technology being one of the fastest growing sectors in the United Kingdom and welcomes the increase in research, development and investment. However, the Government will not hesitate to take the necessary actions to ensure that our national security is protected. As a result, it has amended the Enterprise Act 2002 to make targeted changes to ensure it has sufficient powers to act when necessary. The guidance focuses on the tests in the Act that determine whether the Government can intervene in mergers.

In 2018 the Government amended the tests in the Act that determine whether it can intervene in specific mergers. The Enterprise Act 2002 (Share of Supply Test) (Amendment) Order 2018 and the Enterprise Act 2002 (Turnover Test) (Amendment) 2018,[2] which came into force on 11 June 2018, amended the thresholds for the turnover and share of supply tests within the Act for three sectors: military and dual-use technologies, quantum technology and computing hardware.

For mergers which involve the takeover of businesses covered by section 23A, the two tests were amended as follows:

- the business being taken over must have a UK turnover of over £1 million, rather than £70 million; and,

- the requirement in the share of supply test to increase the share of supply was removed.

In 2020, the Enterprise Act 2002 (Share of Supply Test) (Amendment) Order 2020 and the Enterprise Act 2002 (Turnover Test) (Amendment) Order 2020 were made to add three more categories of enterprises, to which the lower share of supply and turnover thresholds applies. The three categories are: artificial intelligence, advanced materials and cryptographic authentication.

The Orders do not require any business to take any direct action. The UK operates a voluntary notification mergers system, both for competition and public interest, including national security considerations. The changes made by the Orders will also only relate to mergers that take place after they come into force.

NOTES

[2] Guidance to accompany the amendments https://www.gov.uk/government/publications/enterprise-act-2002-guidance-on-changes-to-the-turnover-and-share-of-supply-tests-for-mergers.

CHAPTER 1: CHANGES TO GOVERNMENT INTERVENTION IN MERGERS

[3.469]

Summary

Under the Enterprise Act 2002, the Government can only intervene in limited circumstances:

when a transaction constitutes a "relevant merger situation", i.e:

— it involves two or more enterprises ceasing to be distinct; and

— the merger meets tests related to specific turnover and/or share of supply; and

when the merger raises at least one of four specific public interest issues – national security, financial stability, media plurality, or to combat a public health emergency.

The only exception to the above is in relation to the limited circumstances prescribed by the Special Public Interest Regime.

INTRODUCTION

The tests for when and how Government can intervene in mergers are set out in the Enterprise Act 2002. As the Act's explanatory notes[3] described, a key change introduced by the Act was to provide that "final decisions on most mergers are to be taken by independent competition-focused authorities[4] rather than by the Secretary of State".

As a result, the Act deliberately limited the Secretary of State's ability to intervene in mergers to cases where they raised "public interest considerations". The Act ensured that the Secretary of State could only intervene in mergers that met certain turnover and/or share of supply tests.[5] These same thresholds permit the competition authorities to intervene in order to prevent a merger from substantially lessening competition.

As described in the next chapter, the Government concluded that the thresholds as set in 2002 were no longer working effectively as a threshold for intervention on national security grounds in certain areas of the economy. In 2018, the Government amended the turnover threshold and share of supply jurisdictional tests within the Enterprise Act 2002 in three sectors of the economy: the military and dual-use technologies; quantum technology; and computing hardware.

The Government assessed the impact of pursuing further secondary legislation to amend the jurisdictional tests for mergers for additional areas of advanced technology against the risk of not taking any action. Following this assessment, the Government made further secondary legislation in relation to the following sectors: artificial intelligence (AI); cryptographic authentication; and advanced materials. Chapter 3 and 4 respectively describe in more detail the areas of the economy concerned and the amendments to the thresholds for intervention.

THE TESTS SET OUT IN THE ENTERPRISE ACT 2002

Under the Enterprise Act 2002, there are a number of steps that must be met before the Government[6] can intervene:

- there must be a relevant merger situation; and
- the intervention can only be on 'public interest' grounds as described in Section 58 of the Act.

The Government can also intervene in a merger subject to the European Commission's jurisdiction.

a) a relevant merger situation

Section 23 of the Enterprise Act 2002 defines a relevant merger situation. The first limb of the definition provides that a relevant merger situation occurs when "two or more enterprises have ceased to be distinct enterprises". Section 26 of the Act goes on to define further what "ceasing to be distinct" means.

The CMA has published statutory guidance[7] describing and explaining these, and other issues, in more detail — including the meaning of "enterprise".

Before the 2018 Orders came into force, the second limb of the definition of a relevant merger situation under the Act was that:

- the acquired business must have an annual UK turnover of more than £70 million; and/or
- the merger must result in the creation of, or increase in, a 25% or more combined share of sales or purchases in the UK (or in a substantial part of it) of goods or services of a particular description.

The 2018 provisions amended the two tests mentioned in paragraph 1.9 in relation to specific areas of the economy, as follows:

- the 'target' business must have UK turnover over £1 million, rather than £70 million;
- either the existing share of supply test must be met, or the target must have a share of supply of 25% or more of relevant goods or services in the UK, i.e. goods or services connected with their activities in the three defined areas of the economy. It is therefore no longer a requirement that the merger must lead to an increase in the merging parties' share of supply to, or over, 25%.

The 'Special Public Interest Regime', which allows ministerial intervention in the absence of the requirements for a relevant merger situation being met in full so long as certain other conditions are satisfied, is described later in this chapter.

b) the intervention can only be on 'public interests' grounds

At present, under the Enterprise Act 2002, Ministers can only intervene in domestic and EU merger cases that raise the following public interest considerations:[8]

- national security (including public security);
- financial stability;
- media plurality; and
- to combat a public health emergency.

The Orders do not amend or extend these public interest considerations. The Government will only be able to intervene in additional mergers as a result of the amendments if they raise the existing public interest considerations listed in the Act. Indeed, the Government does not foresee instances when it would intervene in mergers brought into scope by the amendments for any other public interest ground than national security given the nature of the businesses described in Chapter 3.

NOTES

3 http://www.legislation.gov.uk/ukpga/2002/40/notes/division/4/3.

4 At the time of introduction, this was the Office of Fair Trading and the Competition Commission. These were replaced by the Competition and Markets Authority in 2014 following the Enterprise and Regulatory Reform Act 2013.

5 A limited exception to this applies in cases where a merger qualifies as a "special public interest merger". In such a case, Ministers can intervene where the threshold tests would not be met as described later in this chapter.

6 The Act actually permits a 'Secretary of State', a Government minister, to intervene in mergers.

7 Competition and Markets Authority (2014), 'Mergers – the CMA's jurisdiction and procedure: CMA2', https://www.gov.uk/government/publications/mergers-guidance-on-the-cmas-jurisdiction-and-procedure.

8 Prudential regulation is also recognised as a legitimate interest under the EU Merger Regulation but is not a public interest ground in the Enterprise Act 2002.

CHAPTER 2: WHY THE PROVISIONS ARE REQUIRED

[3.470]

Summary

From 2002 to 2018, the same tests (related to UK turnover and share of supply) applied to interventions on both competition and public interest grounds across the economy. The only exceptions have related to two specific instances under the Special Public Interest Regime.

Since 2002, there have been considerable technological advances, developments in local, national and global economic structures, and changes in the national security threat facing the UK. These mean that the thresholds in the Act were no longer effectively safeguarding our national security in all areas of the economy. The Government therefore concluded in 2018 that the thresholds needed to be amended for three sectors of the economy. Since then the Government has monitored the evolving situation and concluded that three further sectors should be subject to the amended thresholds.

TECHNOLOGICAL ADVANCES

Technological advances have changed the way in which people interact and businesses develop and grow. New products and services offer the potential to radically transform the way we live — computers are exponentially more powerful than in 2002, and internet connectivity has been integrated into daily lives and an ever-increasing range of goods. The Government is proud that British businesses have been at the forefront of this change — driving innovation that has brought huge benefits to the global economy and society.

However, these technological changes have also brought challenges. Some of these challenges are national security related. As described in more detail in relation to specific businesses to which the revised thresholds will apply, hostile intent and action can be multiplied in more ways than ever before.

The businesses that are driving the development of innovative goods and technological advances are not necessarily those with large turnovers. In fact, some of the most radical, far-reaching developments are made by enterprises with small turnovers. In addition, often a merger in this area will not raise the parties' combined share of supply because the target firm is undertaking a unique activity.

The Government wishes to ensure that it has sufficient powers to address national security threats that may arise from mergers involving these businesses.

ECONOMIC DEVELOPMENTS

The last eighteen years have also seen significant change in the global economic market which, while bringing enormous benefits, raise national security challenges for all countries. Since the Enterprise Act 2002 was introduced, the global market has become more connected and industries now have deeper, broader and more complicated supply chains.

As a result of this change, essential goods and services are provided by increasingly more diverse networks of businesses, including those with small turnovers. The Government wishes to ensure that it can address any national security concerns that can arise when these businesses are acquired.

THE CHANGING NATIONAL SECURITY THREAT

Foreign intelligence agencies continue to engage in hostile activity against the UK and our interests, and against many of our close allies. This includes human, technical and cyber operations at home and overseas to compromise the Government, diplomatic missions, Government-held information and critical national infrastructure; attempts to influence Government policy covertly; and operations to steal commercial secrets and disrupt the private sector. This could have significant negative consequences not just for particular businesses, but the entire UK economy and our national security as a whole.[9][10] It is especially important that Government maintain the UK's capability to act as a sovereign nation with its own capabilities in light of such developments.

NOTES

9 HM Government (2015), 'National Security Strategy and Strategic Defence and Security Review 2015', https://www.gov.uk/government/publications/national-security-strategy-and-strategic-defence-and-security-review-2015.

10 HM Government (2019), 'NSS and SDSR 2015: Third Annual Report', https://www.gov.uk/government/publications/nss-and-sdsr-2015-third-annual-report--2.

CHAPTER 3: THE RELEVANT ENTERPRISES TO WHICH THE AMENDED THRESHOLDS APPLY

[3.471]

Summary

The 2018 amendments to the Act related to businesses active in three areas of the economy:
- the development or production of items for military or military and civilian use ('dual use');
- the design and maintenance of aspects of computing hardware; and
- the development and production of quantum technology.

The 2020 amendments to the Act relate to businesses active in three additional areas of the economy:
- artificial intelligence,
- cryptographic authentication, and
- advanced materials.

Section 23A of the Act defines each of these. This guidance gives further details and examples to aid businesses and other parties.

The new provisions only relate to mergers which involve businesses in these areas of the economy being acquired.

THE 2018 AMENDMENTS: MILITARY AND DUAL-USE TECHNOLOGIES, COMPUTING HARDWARE AND QUANTUM TECHNOLOGY

In light of the developments and national security concerns described in Chapter 2, the amendments to the thresholds in the Act are focused on particular areas of the economy where the Government has concluded that (without these changes) the Act would not permit Government to intervene in mergers that might raise national security concerns.

The thresholds, which were amended in 2018, apply to "relevant enterprises" as defined in section 23A of the Act. Section 23A provides definitions of business activities which raise the clearest risks to national security.

This chapter describes how the revised thresholds are focused on the target of a merger or takeover (rather than on the business that is acquiring another). The chapter then considers each of the three business activity areas in more detail.

This guidance gives further practical advice about the types of business activities, goods and services which would make an enterprise a "relevant enterprise". However, this is not an exhaustive list, nor is it a definitive interpretation of the law. If you are unsure and wish to establish whether your business, or a business you are considering acquiring, is a relevant enterprise, you may wish to seek independent legal advice.

The amendments relate to the 'target' of a takeover

The thresholds only relate to mergers when enterprises in the relevant areas of the economy are taken over or are, for example, the subject of certain joint ventures. That means that mergers involving relevant enterprises acquiring non-relevant enterprises are not covered by the revised thresholds.

Example of how the thresholds relate only to the target in a takeover

Company A designs processing units. It is, therefore, a relevant enterprise for the purpose of the Orders.

A is considering acquiring Company B — a UK-based business that makes software. B is not a relevant enterprise (nor an enterprise covered by the Special Public Interest Regime). This transaction, therefore, is not covered by the amendments. As a result, the Government could only intervene (on national security or other specified public interest grounds) if B had a UK turnover of over £70 million or if the two businesses' merger led to an increase in share of supply of goods or services in the UK (or a substantial part thereof) to, or above, 25%.

A is also considering expanding into the quantum technology sector by acquiring company C which designs quantum sensors. This would be A's first venture in that sector and market. The target of this merger, C, is a relevant enterprise and so this transaction would be subject to the revised thresholds. Government could, therefore, intervene (on national security or other specified public interest grounds) if C had a UK turnover over £1 million or at least a 25% share of supply of those goods in the UK or a substantial part thereof.

A's Board concludes that its long-term interests would be better served by establishing a joint venture with B. New company D would be the result of an equal merger of A and B — that is to say, they would pool their resources and their respective previous owners would have 50% of D. Because one party (in this case, A) is a relevant enterprise, this merger would be covered by the tests.

In each case, the revised thresholds apply to businesses which undertake certain activities. This applies whether the activity is the business's entire field or only a part of it. However, the Government will only be able to intervene when a merger involves a change in material influence or control over that particular activity.

For example, the amendments would apply to the takeover of a business with several divisions, only one of which designs quantum sensors. However, if the merger were structured such that the division designing quantum sensors was not subject to the new acquirer's material influence or control (i.e. it was retained under the existing ownership and control), then Government intervention in the merger (on national security grounds) involving the other divisions would only be permitted if it met the existing tests, such as the enterprise being taken over having UK turnover in excess of £70 million[11]

MILITARY AND DUAL-USE ITEM TECHNOLOGIES

Government's national security interests

Military and dual-use technologies cover the design and production of military items (such as arms, military and paramilitary equipment) and so-called dual-use items which can be used for both military and civil purposes.

The national security interests in this sector are obvious — these items can, in the wrong hands, pose clear and immediate risks to the UK, our people and society. There are also 'indirect' national security interests — thanks to UK businesses' innovation, our military and defence forces have a clear operational advantage over others. The acquisition of items which provide this advantage can, therefore, raise legitimate and significant national security concerns.

Export control

The Government, like many others, controls the export of these items. Through the Export Control Joint Unit within the Department for International Trade, the Government assesses applications for export licences for so-called strategic items, delivering an efficient service for businesses while ensuring that the items do not end up in the wrong hands.

The items subject to strategic export control are set out in a number of lists, collectively known as Strategic Export Control Lists (SECLs).

The lists are derived, in large part, from various international commitments related to the non-proliferation of conventional arms and of weapons of mass destruction, as well as from concerns around national security and human rights. However, there are items on the control lists in which Government has no national security interests. Therefore, not all businesses which produce or design items subject to export control are subject to the amended thresholds.

Which businesses are covered by the provisions

Section 23A refers to the following lists which have national security aspects:

- the UK Military List (Schedule 2, last amended by SI 2019/989 (ECO 2008));
- the UK Dual-Use List (Schedule 3, last amended by S1 2019/1159) ECO 2008));
- the UK Radioactive Source List (Schedule to the Export of Radioactive Sources(Control) Order 2006); and,
- the EU Dual-Use List (Annexes I and IV of Council Regulation (EC) No. 428/2009, last amended by Regulation (EU) No. 2199/2019).

Part 3 CMA and other Guidelines

To ensure that the Government can adequately protect national security by preventing the acquisition of relevant enterprises, not just the export of controlled items, the provisions brought into scope of the amended tests under the Act businesses that:

- **develop or produce** these goods or services; or,
- **hold related information** (including but not limited to information comprised in software and documents such as blueprints, manuals, diagrams and designs) that is capable of use in connection with the development or production of these goods and the information is responsible for achieving or exceeding the performance levels, characteristics or functions of the good or service where 'these goods or services' are items on the lists set out in this chapter.

The revised thresholds do not apply to the development or production of equipment or components not on the above lists.

The development and production of military and dual-use items – example of what is covered

Ships

Waterborne vessels can, in theory, be used for military or civil purposes. However, the vast majority of boats do not fall under export control – nor, therefore, would the manufacturers or designers of that majority of boats come into scope of the 2018 provisions.

Specifically, the UK Military List includes only specific types of waterborne vessels. Under section ML9, it stipulates that only "vessels of war" and specially designed components for those vessels are subject to export control. It goes on to specify that this means, for example, vessels "specially designed or modified for military use" (ML9.a.1) and/or with "automatic weapons" integrated (ML9.a.2.a) are subject to export control. Manufacturers of non-military vessels, therefore, were unaffected by the changes made by the 2018 provisions.

How to check whether a business in this sector comes into scope of the provisions

A large proportion of the items are on the lists are clear and unambiguous. For example, existing businesses and would-be investors will be under no doubt as to whether they:

- produce semi-automatic type weapons (ML1.b.2.b);
- design rotor blades incorporating "variable geometry airfoils" for helicopters (7E004); or
- manufacture sensors specially designed for wind tunnels designed for speeds of Mach 1.2 or over (9B005.a).

If there had been doubt, the well-established and reasonable principle of export control, and the specific UK system for this, means the Government expects businesses will be reasonably aware that export of their goods is subject to export control, or would be subject to export control if they transferred them to other countries. This similarly applies to a business or entity giving serious consideration to acquiring (or merging with) a business.

However, the Government accepts that there may be some businesses or investors who may be unsure as to whether they are covered by the scope of provisions. This might be particularly the case if the business has not, to date, exported items. Equally, there may be investors interested in acquiring a business who may not be sufficiently familiar with its activities to have confidence about whether it would be covered by the provisions, and therefore the amended thresholds for Government intervention on national security grounds.

If a party would like assistance with this, the Government advises parties to use the Goods Checker Tool.[12] Guidance is also available about how parties should best use the tool.[13][14]

If parties have followed these steps and still require further advice as to whether particular businesses are subject to the revised thresholds, they can contact nsiireview@beis.gov.uk with specific queries. The Government will endeavour to provide clear, informal (non-binding) advice as quickly as possible. However, any such advice (like this guidance) is not legal advice. Businesses are encouraged to seek their own independent legal advice.

How changes to the SECLs will affect the amended thresholds

The Government will periodically lay further secondary legislation amending section 23A of the Act to reflect updates to the SECLs. This will ensure that as items are added to, or removed from, the list of what is subject to export control – the businesses which design or produce them will similarly be brought into, and out of, scope of the amendments to the Act. The process of amending the lists operates, and will continue to operate, independently from any consideration of whether or not a merger or takeover involving a company designing or manufacturing items on the lists should be subject to amended tests.

The majority of the items to which the revised tests will apply are controlled for export because they appear on lists agreed in the four international export control regimes.[15] Changes to these lists are agreed with partner countries in the regimes and implemented either via national legislation or by the EU (or by a combination thereof). Changes to controls on military items, and other items subject to national control, are implemented by way of a statutory instrument. Changes to controls on dual-use items are implemented by the EU through amendment to Council Regulation 428/2009. Updates are done on a regular basis — the UK lists are typically updated every six months, the EU lists on an annual basis.

Businesses or other interested parties can subscribe to the Export Control Joint Unit's Notices to Exporters[16] in order to keep updated about these or other related changes.

For the avoidance of doubt, businesses which design or manufacture items subject to temporary export controls will not be in scope of the new thresholds.

The Special Public Interest Regime

Some mergers involving businesses which produce military and dual-use items will remain covered by the scope of the Special Public Interest Regime. Specifically, mergers affecting relevant government contractors, as defined by section 59 of the Act, who have been informed that their business holds confidential defence-related information and whose turnover and share of supply does not meet the tests set out in the Act.

However, due to the provisions, some mergers that were previously covered by the scope of the Special Public Interest Regime, will now be covered by the tests introduced by the provisions.

Given the thresholds also apply to determine which mergers are subject to scrutiny on competition grounds, businesses which are in scope of the thresholds may wish to consider whether a merger they are contemplating raises competition issues.

COMPUTING HARDWARE

Government's national security concerns

Technological advances have changed the way in which people interact and businesses develop and grow. New products and services offer the potential to transform the way we live. Much of this depends on continuing advances in computing power and in connectivity, in and out of the home. These changes have also brought challenges. Advances in technology now mean that there are ubiquitous goods with the potential to be directed remotely should, for instance, a hostile actor obtain access or control. Mergers related to businesses that undertake these activities, therefore, have the potential to give hostile actors knowledge or expertise that could be used to undermine our national security.

Which computing hardware technology firms are subject to the provisions

Section 23A specifies two activities in this area of the economy:

- the ownership, creation or supply of intellectual property relating to the functional capability of:
  - computer processing units;
  - the instruction set architecture for such units;
  - computer code that provides low level control for such units
- the design, maintenance or provision of support for the secure provisioning or management of:
  - roots of trust of computer processing units;
  - computer code that provides low level control for such units

What are "roots of trust"?

"roots of trust" means hardware, firmware, or software components that are inherently trusted to perform critical security functions, (including, for example, cryptographic key material bound to a device that can identify the device or verify a digital signature to authenticate a remote entity).

This means that enterprises that own, create or supply intellectual property in relation to the way that processing units function will be in scope. Businesses that manage roots of trust in relation to processing units are also in scope. This could include businesses that design firmware containing the cryptographic material for a processing unit.

Computing hardware — example 1 of what is, and what is not, covered

Company A has a UK turnover of over £1 million, but under £70 million and has significant expertise in the production of processing units and firmware. Whilst they have ceased to produce processing units themselves, as a result of historic activity in this area, they have built up substantial intellectual property and they license this intellectual property to other companies who produce the units.

Party B is interested in acquiring A. The Government believes that this acquisition would raise national security concerns.

Because A is in scope of the turnover threshold, as it has a UK turnover of over £1 million, the Government is able to intervene in this transaction on national security grounds, regardless of the size of Company A (or whether there has been an increase in) the share of supply.

QUANTUM TECHNOLOGY

What is quantum technology?

Quantum theory arose in the first quarter of the 20th Century to explain how light and matter behave on a fundamental level.

While a conventional computer uses binary 'bits' which take the value 0 or 1, the fundamental unit of information in a quantum computer is the qubit, which can be in the state 0, 1 or a combination of both simultaneously.

A new generation of quantum technologies are now driving and enabling a new generation of devices and systems, from very powerful medical imaging devices to entirely new methods of computing to solve currently intractable problems – all made possible by the engineering of quantum effects into next-generation technologies.[17]

Government's national security concerns

The Government strongly supports the quantum technology sector in the UK. The Blackett review published in November 2016[18] highlighted the significant potential offered by new post-digital quantum technologies.

The Government is aware, however, that the huge potential offered by quantum technology also presents national security challenges. Quantum technology has the potential to break currently secure computer and telecommunications systems. It could also transform military power — giving vehicles and weapons systems substantial additional abilities.

Quantum technology — the areas covered by the changes made by the 2018 Orders

quantum computing or simulation means the study, simulation or realisation of systems that utilise certain properties of quantum mechanics, in particular superposition or entanglement, to process information, run algorithms or perform operations on data;

quantum imaging means utilising certain properties of quantum mechanics, in particular superposition or entanglement, to create images of objects with a resolution or other imaging criteria that is beyond what is possible in non-quantum optics;

quantum sensing means utilising certain properties of quantum mechanics, including measurements of suspensions of atoms or ions, to determine a property or rate of change in the property of an object, or the effect of an object on a measurable quantity, with a resolution or sensitivity that is beyond what is possible in non-quantum devices or systems;

quantum timing means utilising certain properties of quantum mechanics, including measurements of suspensions of atoms or ions, to provide a timing signal with a resolution or sensitivity that is beyond what is possible in non-quantum devices or systems;

quantum navigation means utilising certain properties of quantum mechanics, including measurements of suspensions of atoms or ions, to establish the location or movement of objects with a resolution or sensitivity that is beyond what is possible in non-quantum devices or systems;

quantum resistant cryptography means methods of securing information or data being transmitted or stored, including by non-quantum means, with a view to resisting attack by a quantum computer; (quantum computers make direct use of quantum-mechanical phenomena, such as superposition and entanglement, to perform operations on data);

quantum communications means the transmission of information, from one location to another (point-to-point) or across a network, utilising the properties of quantum mechanics, in particular superposition or entanglement and includes the establishment of cryptographic keys and the generation of true random numbers using a quantum physical process.

Quantum technology — example 1 of what is, and what is not, covered

Quantum computing

University A has been undertaking innovative research aimed at applying quantum phenomena to particular types of computing systems. Recognising the potential commercial application, researchers establish Company B, which holds the intellectual property and which provides commercial services based on this, with a view to commercialising the research.

B has more than 25% share of supply of the particular services underpinned by quantum technology (e.g. it provides consulting services in relation to quantum simulation). Party C, with no role in the UK quantum sector, is interested in acquiring B. The Government believes that this acquisition would raise national security concerns.

Because B is in scope of the thresholds, the Government is able to intervene in this transaction on national security grounds, notwithstanding that B has a UK turnover of less than £70 million (and, indeed, £1 million) and that the merger would not increase the parties' combined share of supply.

Which quantum technology firms are covered?

The definition of relevant enterprise in section 23A covers the following quantum technology activities:

- quantum computing or simulation;

- quantum imaging, sensing, timing or navigation;
- quantum communications; and
- quantum resistant cryptography.

The thresholds apply to businesses which research, develop, or produce goods designed for use in these activities or which supply services employing these activities. It is intended that "development" means all stages prior to production (e.g. design, assembly and testing of prototype). This would include the creation of intellectual property (even if not yet put to commercial use). Businesses supplying quantum technology components to other firms would, therefore, be covered by the definitions in section 23A. Similarly, businesses offering services (such as consultancy advice, or data analysis) which use quantum-based technology would also be within scope of the revised tests.

Businesses which provide non-quantum technology-related goods, or services, to quantum technology businesses are not covered by the definitions in section 23A unless covered in their own right. A firm providing accountancy services, for example, to a quantum technology business is not in scope of the changes.

The definitions for these activities come, in part, from the National Strategy for Quantum Technologies and have been informed by the Government's consultation in 2017. The Government considers that those businesses which undertake these activities, and any investors with a serious intent to acquire them, will be clear about the scope of the provisions.

Quantum technology — example 2 of what is, and what is not, covered

Companies using quantum technology

The provisions only apply to businesses which carry out research into, design or manufacture quantum technology. Those which use quantum goods or services provided by others are not in scope.

Pharmaceutical company A is developing a new drug. This requires substantial computing power in order to try various permutations of data. It employs quantum business B to use its quantum technology computers to significantly increase the speed at which these calculations can happen.

Company A is unaffected by the provisions. Any competition or national security-related intervention in the takeover of A would be subject to the £70 million UK turnover threshold, and the requirement for the merger to increase the share of supply to or over 25%.

THE 2020 AMENDMENTS: ARTIFICIAL INTELLIGENCE, CRYPTOGRAPHIC AUTHENTICATION AND ADVANCED MATERIALS

ARTIFICIAL INTELLIGENCE

Government's national security interests

Artificial intelligence (AI) technologies are transforming the global economy. They can be seen as new industries in their own right, but they are also transforming business models across many sectors. They deploy vast datasets to identify better ways of doing complex tasks.

AI devices or software have the potential to be directed remotely or in ways that raise national security concerns should, for instance, a hostile actor obtain access or control over them.

The opportunity to use AI positively across the UK economy can only be harnessed if sensitive and critical applications of AI, especially in defence and security and national infrastructure, can be protected from, for instance, the risk of hostile actors intending to do harm to the UK and its interests.

What is artificial intelligence?

'Artificial intelligence' refers to technology enabling the programming, or execution of a computational process capable of undertaking complex tasks commonly associated with human intelligence. These tasks are often data intensive, including but not restricted to analysis, decision making, image processing and recognition, natural language understanding, autonomous operation in complex domains, reflection or introspection.

AI can employ, for example, machine learning algorithms (algorithms with the ability to learn without being explicitly programmed) in order to deploy adaptable, automated decision-making models for complex tasks. This implies interaction with the digital and in some cases the physical environment.

Which AI firms are covered by the new provisions?

The Government intends to cover all businesses that produce, develop and design AI technologies, including components and service providers and all relevant intellectual property, where these products are reasonably expected to be used in systems critical for national security. This also includes technology which enables the training of a device or software to use or process external data (independent of any further input or programming). The Government does not intend to intervene in mergers or takeovers where enterprises whose goods and services that utilise AI which are generally available to the public and for use by the consumer , for example, virtual AI assistants that are capable of undertaking certain actions by voice commands. Other examples of widely available functions include traffic routing, SPAM removal, social networking applications, facial recognition for security and shopping recommendations.

AI is integral to the Government's Industrial Strategy and embedding AI across the UK will create thousands of good quality jobs and drive economic growth. This legislation is not intended to undermine the Government's commitment to fostering research, development and investment in AI; it is designed to strike the right balance between the priorities of championing economic prosperity and protecting national security. It is anticipated that only a small minority of mergers will raise national security concerns.

CRYPTOGRAPHIC AUTHENTICATION

Government's national security interests

Cryptographic technology enables information to be protected whilst in storage or in transit by making it inaccessible or unreadable by everyone except those who have the information needed to access or read it. The technology is integral to a well-functioning economy, for example, by enabling businesses to go about their work, secure in the knowledge that their important information is safe. The Government recognises the importance of these technologies to the UK and promotes research and innovation in cyber security through research grants and supporting the development of new cyber innovation centres.

A risk that may arise in this area is, for instance, a hostile actor being able to access critical systems and undermine national security by acquiring a business that produces, develops, designs, or provides services for technologies which are used to control access to these critical systems. Significant damage to the UK could result if authentication systems are compromised or bypassed, including through sabotage and espionage, to allow a hostile actor to gain unauthorised access to systems critical for national security.

Which firms are covered by the provisions?

The Government intends the proposed legislation will apply to businesses that develop products whose primary function is authentication using cryptographic means, where these products are reasonably expected to be used in systems critical for national security. This includes IT systems in critical infrastructure sectors. Such products may be used in the verification of the identity of an individual or user. The legislation also applies to include companies that provide services relating to cryptographic authentication.

Examples of technologies within scope of the proposed new amendments are systems that authenticate:

- the identity of a physical person using an access token to gain entrance to a civil nuclear site;
- the identity of a user to gain electronic access to the computer network of a power station;
- a biometric property of an individual to allow access to a restricted area of an industrial site;
- a credit/debit chip-and-pin card at an ATM or retail point of sale;
- facial recognition technology used in conjunction with CCTV footage; and
- the digital information held on an e-passport to determine whether to allow the holder into the country.

The Government does not intend to use its powers to intervene where authentication products and systems that are generally available to the public and for use by the consumer. The Government does not intend to intervene in businesses that develop products which have a primary function of encryption and not authentication.

Examples of technology firms which are unlikely to be subject to Government intervention:

- (a) username and password access to log on locally to computers running consumer operating systems;
- (b) username and password access to online services
- (c) multi-factor authentication technologies used to access online services
- (d) fingerprint and other biometric verification devices built into smart phones; and
- (e) chip-and-pin card readers used for access to online banking accounts.

Cryptographic technology — example of what is, and what is not, covered

Cryptographic authentication

University A has been undertaking innovative research aimed at applying cryptographic authentication to products in IT systems. Recognising the potential commercial application, researchers establish Company B, which holds the intellectual property and which provides commercial services based on this, with a view to commercialising the research.

B has more than 25% share of supply of the particular services underpinned by cryptographic technology. Party C, with no role in the UK technology sector, is interested in acquiring B. The Government believes that this acquisition would raise national security concerns.

Because B is in scope of the revised thresholds, the Government is able to intervene in this transaction on national security grounds, notwithstanding that B has a UK turnover of less than £70 million (and, indeed, £1 million) and that the merger would not increase the parties' combined share of supply.

ADVANCED MATERIALS

Government's national security interests

Materials sciences encompasses the discovery and development for example, of new classes of two-dimensional materials like graphene and new functional materials like metamaterials. However, advances in traditional classes of advanced materials science remain a dominant and important contribution.

Breakthroughs in advanced materials science are fundamental enablers across all areas of societal and economic development. They have underpinned and continue to underpin advances in the physical and digital world. These all stem from understanding, manipulating and exploiting the composition, arrangement and properties of matter.

The Government will act to maintain advantage in its defence and security capability and there may be a risk of loss in this advantage if UK companies (and the Intellectual Property that they generate) in this area are controlled by hostile actors.

An enterprise falls within this subsection if its activities consist in or include —

(a) research into;
(b) developing or producing;
(c) developing or producing anything designed as an enabler for use in;
(d) developing or producing anything designed to be used to make;
(e) owning, creating, supplying or exploiting intellectual property relating to, or
(f) provide know-how or services of enablers for use in —
  - (a) any materials that are capable of modifying (including in real time) the appearance, detectability, traceability or identification of any object to a human or to sensors within the range 1.5e13 Hz up to and including ultraviolet;
  - (b) any alloys that are formed by chemical or electrochemical reduction of feedstocks in the solid state;
  - (c) any manufacturing processes that are involved in the solid state formation of alloys in or into crude or semi-fabricated forms, or powders for additive manufacturing, where "additive manufacturing" means a process of joining materials to make parts from three-dimensional model data; or,
  - (d) any metamaterial that does not include-
    - fibre-reinforced plastics in structural components, products or coatings with completely random dispersion of pigment or other filler; or
    - any packaged device components that are designed for civil application.

Advanced materials – relevant definitions included in the 2020 Orders

"metamaterial" means a composite material in which the constituents are designed and spatially arranged through a rational design-led approach to change the manner in which electromagnetic, acoustic or vibrational energy interacts with the material, in order to achieve a property or performance that is not possible naturally and includes a metasurface; and for this purpose "composite material" means a solid material formed from two or more constituents and "constituent" includes a region containing a vacuum, gas or liquid;

"metasurface" means a two-dimensional form of metamaterial which includes one or more layers of material that are intentionally patterned or textured (irrespective of whether they are periodic or not) through a rational design-led approach.

BUSINESS OPERATING IN MORE THAN ONE AREA COVERED BY THE PROVISIONS

Businesses may operate in more than one area of the economy covered by new section 23A of the Act. This does not affect the provisions' applicability to them. Businesses only need to be undertaking activities in one of the described areas, for a relevant merger in which they are involved be subject to the provisions.

NOTES

[11] Under existing powers, the Government can intervene in certain limited categories of mergers that do not meet the normal UK turnover and share of supply tests (and which therefore do not amount to a relevant merger situation, whether

Part 3 CMA and other Guidelines

on the original thresholds or the new thresholds). This is set out in the Special Public Interest Regime as referred to in chapter 1 of this document.

12 https://www.ecochecker.trade.gov.uk/spirefox5live/fox/spire/.

13 https://www.spire.trade.gov.uk/docs/guidance/Goods%20Checker%20Guidance.pdf.

14 In using the checker tool parties should also bear in mind that there may have been updates to the SECLs which may not yet have been reflected in amendments to the Act — see paragraph 3.22 for details.

15 The regimes are the Wassenaar Arrangement (WA); Nuclear Suppliers Group (NSG); Missile Technology Control Regime (MTCR) and Australia Group (AG).

16 See https://www.gov.uk/government/collections/notices-to-exporters for further details.

17 See the National Strategy for Quantum Technologies (https://www.gov.uk/government/publications/national-strategy-for-quantum-technologies) for further information.

18 Government Office for Science (2016), 'The Quantum Age: technological opportunities', https://www.gov.uk/government/publications/quantum-technologies-blackett-review.

CHAPTER 4: THE TURNOVER AND SHARE OF SUPPLY TESTS

[3.472]

Summary

For mergers in relation to the relevant enterprises as set out in Chapter 3, the provisions mean that a relevant merger situation will arise if the target firm has UK turnover of over £1 million, or an existing share of supply of at least 25%. The existing share of supply test (where a relevant merger situation is created if a merger leads to an increase in the share of supply to or beyond 25%) will continue to apply.

The Government will be able to intervene in the transaction if at least one of these tests is met and it believes that the merger may raise national security concerns.

TURNOVER TEST

For those businesses active in the areas set out in Chapter 3 and 4, the provisions mean that a relevant merger situation will arise if the business being acquired is a relevant enterprise (or if there is a change of control over a relevant enterprise in any other scenario such as a pure merger) and the relevant enterprise has UK turnover of over £1 million, rather than £70 million. This still excludes the acquiring of micro-businesses from the scope of the revised thresholds, ensuring that the Government take as proportionate and focused approach as possible to delivering its policy intention.

The provisions do not change the definition of turnover or how the turnover of the enterprise being taken over is calculated, nor do they alter the fact the threshold relates only to UK turnover. As set out in the Enterprise Act 2002 (Merger Fees and Determination of Turnover) Order 2003 and the CMA's guidance, in essence this relates to sales to (or acquisitions from) UK customers or suppliers. In assessing whether a firm is active in the UK, the CMA will have regard to whether its sales or purchases are made directly or indirectly (via agents or traders) to UK customers. In the event that the Government wishes to intervene in a merger brought into scope by the amendments, the CMA retains its role in confirming whether the deal meets the relevant thresholds, including turnover.

The CMA's guidance[19] provides greater detail on how the turnover test is interpreted in various scenarios such as a straightforward acquisition, a full legal merger, or a joint venture.

SHARE OF SUPPLY TEST

The share of supply test means that (in the case of transactions in which a relevant enterprise is acquired or in a pure merger or other transaction involving a change of control or the acquisition of material influence over a relevant enterprise) the Government can intervene in a merger if those carrying on the relevant enterprise had an existing share of supply of at least 25% before the merger.

This approach is taken because the Government wishes to ensure that it can act when a merger or takeover raises national security concerns because it involves a business with a significant share of the supply of particular critical goods or services in the UK. Whether the other businesses involved in the merger have an overlapping share of supply in the UK, is immaterial to this national security risk. Indeed, there is a significant risk that hostile actors could invest via a 'clean' business, unconnected to the target's sector, in order to evade Government's scrutiny of national security implications.

The provisions adds to, rather than replaces, the previous share of supply tests in relation to the acquisition of relevant enterprises. That is to say that the Government could intervene in a merger where a relevant enterprise (with less than 25% share of supply) merges with another business and this transaction leads to an increase to, or over, a combined 25% share of supply.

WHEN THE PROVISIONS TAKE EFFECT

The provisions do not apply retrospectively. The Government cannot rely on the new provisions to intervene in mergers where the parties ceased to be distinct before the relevant order came into force. The Government can, however intervene on national security grounds in mergers which are underway (for example, are subject to ongoing negotiation) but where the parties have not yet ceased to be distinct at the time that the new provisions take effect.

THE ASSESSMENT OF WHETHER A PARTICULAR MERGER IS COVERED BY THE PROVISIONS

As the next chapter sets out in greater detail, mergers within scope of the amended thresholds will follow the same statutory process as those in any other area of the economy. That means that **it will be the CMA which will determine whether a relevant merger situation has arisen** and thus whether the Government can refer a merger for investigation on national security grounds. Following the issue of an intervention notice by the Government, the CMA is obliged to report to the Secretary of State (under section 44 of the Enterprise Act 2002) on a number of matters including whether a particular merger qualifies as a "relevant merger situation".

THE GROUNDS ON WHICH GOVERNMENT CAN INTERVENE

Because of the structure of the Enterprise Act 2002, following the amendments to the Act, the Government will in theory be able to intervene in mergers in the relevant sectors for any of the public interest criteria — namely:

- national security (including public security);
- financial stability;
- media plurality; and
- maintaining capability to combat a public health emergency.

The Government's rationale for the changes to the Act is related solely to national security. The Government does not foresee any circumstances where it would wish to, or need to, intervene in a merger brought into scope of its power by the new provisions, for reasons other than national security.

The Government believes that free, well-regulated markets remain the best way to develop economic growth and wealth. It has been free markets, with international flows of capital and investment that have transformed the global economy and lifted millions out of poverty. The provisions do not undermine this wider commitment. The UK will remain the strongest advocate for free trade.

NATIONAL SECURITY

National security is about protecting lives and protecting our way of life. Mergers and acquisitions can, in theory, put either of these at risk in three different manners:

- the greater opportunity to undertake **disruptive or destructive actions** or an increase in the impact of such action;
- the increase access (to businesses, physical assets, people, operations or data) and ability to undertake **espionage**; and
- the ability to exploit an investment to dictate or alter services or to utilise ownership or control as **inappropriate leverage** in other negotiations.

Businesses and others will appreciate that Government (cannot give detailed guidance about what factors might cause national security concerns in a particular merger (nor, for that matter, can the CMA). Doing so would, of course, help those determined to cause us harm.

However, it is the case that, in the broadest terms, foreign investment is more likely than domestic investment to raise national security concerns. Foreign investors are less likely to have the UK's interests at heart and may be controlled or influenced by hostile state actors who wish to undermine our country, society, military or way of life. However, the overwhelming majority of foreign investment poses no national security concerns — and Government would expect this to remain the case in relation to the businesses covered by the thresholds.

Any national security assessment must, necessarily, be undertaken on a case-by-case basis. An investor acquiring one business may pose no national security concerns but would in relation to a different company.

WHAT THE GOVERNMENT CAN DO AS A RESULT OF THE AMENDMENTS

The Government wishes to ensure that mergers can go ahead in such a way as to not undermine national security. The Government is clear that not all mergers or takeovers in the six areas of the economy, even those that meet the thresholds, raise national security-related concerns. It has amended the Act to ensure it has sufficient powers to intervene in the rare instances where national security concerns do arise.

For those deals that do raise national security concerns, the Government would follow the process set out in the Act, which it has followed for the previous seven instances when it has intervened on the basis of national security. This is set out in more detail in the following chapter.

If the Government intervenes formally in a deal, the CMA's first Phase 1 report to the Government will detail any undertakings voluntarily proposed by the parties in order to deal with any national security (or other public interest) concerns or will report that undertakings are being considered. In all seven national security-related interventions to date, this process has been sufficient. However, if this was to prove insufficient (and following a CMA-led Phase 2 investigation), the Government can issue orders to ensure that a merger does not undermine national security.

Whether proposed voluntarily in undertakings or imposed by order, remedies can take two broad forms – behavioural and structural. The first relates to parties doing, or not doing, certain activities to protect national security. Structural conditions relate to the organisational structure of enterprises or the merger.

An example of behavioural undertakings in relation to national security could include limiting access to certain physical sites, or other tangible or non-tangible assets of the target business to those with appropriate UK security clearances.

Structural undertakings, meanwhile, could include (but not be limited to) a requirement that control over a particular division or asset is not part of a wider merger. This might be the case where the acquired party undertakes a broad range of economic activity in addition to the activity subject to the revised thresholds. A suitable remedy might be that that activity is not part of the merger so does not change hands.

In the event that Government has intervened in a merger, it would welcome parties' suggestions at the earliest point as to acceptable undertakings which they consider could deal with the Government's concerns.

Before deciding whether to refer a merger for a Phase 2 investigation, the Secretary of State would consider whether any national security concerns could be adequately addressed by undertakings offered by the parties. Only when this process has been followed and any offered undertakings have been found to be insufficient to deal with national security concerns, would the Government refer a merger for a Phase 2 investigation20. Only following the Phase 2 investigation and as a last resort would the Government impose remedies or, when even this was insufficient to protect national security, would it block a deal altogether. The Government has never had to use the power to block for national security-related interventions since the Enterprise Act 2002 was introduced.

The Government's intervention in a deal and any decisions in relation to undertakings or remedies will, as with all powers, be reasonable and proportionate. Parties which consider that Government is acting otherwise can seek judicial review of its actions under section 120 of the Act, and as set out in the next chapter.

THE PROVISIONS' INTERACTION WITH THE COMPETITION REGIME

The provisions were introduced for these areas of business in order to permit the Government to intervene effectively in mergers, if necessary, on national security grounds. The provisions, and thus the thresholds, also apply to the assessment of whether the CMA has jurisdiction for the purpose of undertaking a competition assessment under the Act. As such, those mergers that Government can now intervene in for national security reasons could in principle also be investigated by the CMA for competition concerns. Therefore, the amendments do, in theory, also bring more mergers within scope of the CMA's jurisdiction.

While competition assessment remains a matter for the CMA, which is an independent body, the Government notes that the CMA is only concerned with relevant merger situations that raise competition concerns.[21] Neither the Government nor the CMA itself expects that there will be a consequential material change in the CMA's approach to competition scrutiny.

For further guidance on the impact of the provisions on the CMA's merger review function see the CMA's published 'Guidance on changes to the jurisdictional thresholds for UK merger control'.

SUMMARY OF WHAT THE PROVISIONS DO NOT CHANGE

The provisions made important changes to the Government's powers to protect national security. However, the changes do not affect a number of key tests, powers or processes as set out in the Act. This section summarises these in order, the Government hopes, to reassure all parties about the proportionate and focused amendments to the Act.

The amendments do not change:

- the definition of an enterprise as described in the Act
- the definition of what constitutes enterprises "ceasing to be distinct" which remains asset out in section 26 of the Act;
- what constitutes UK turnover;
- the way in which a share of supply is determined;
- the requirements on businesses set out in the EU Merger Regulation, including the requirement to notify relevant mergers to the European Commission;
- the process by which mergers subject to public interest interventions are scrutinised by the CMA to confirm they meet jurisdictional tests;
- the powers open to the Secretary of State in respect of relevant mergers; or
- the ability for affected parties to pursue a judicial review of all actions and decisions made by the Government under the public interest regime.

NOTES

19 CMA (2014), 'Mergers: Guidance on the CMA's jurisdiction and procedure': CMA2' https://www.gov.uk/government/publications/mergers-guidance-on-the-cmas-jurisdiction-and-procedure.

20 As described in more detail in chapter 5, the CMA can also refer cases to Phase 2 investigation on competition grounds.

21 See sections 3.1 to 3.6 of the CMA guidance 'Guidance on changes to the jurisdictional thresholds for UK merger control'.

CHAPTER 5: THE PROCESS FOR ANY GOVERNMENT INTERVENTIONS IN MERGERS

[3.473]

Summary

The process for Government intervention remains as set out in the Enterprise Act 2002.

This statutory process involves:

— The Government issuing (and publishing) a Public Intervention Notice.

— Following a call for evidence and a review, the CMA provides the Secretary of State with a Phase 1 report. This report includes its assessment as to whether the merger meets the relevant jurisdictional tests, including any relating to UK turnover or share of supply.

— The Secretary of State can decide i) there are no public interest concerns, ii) to accept (subject to consultation) voluntary undertakings provided by the parties, or iii) to refer the transaction for further investigation.

— In the event of further investigation being required, the CMA undertakes a Phase2 investigation before providing a report to the Secretary of State.

— The Secretary of State can then either decide there are no public interest concerns, accept undertakings, or impose an order to deal with the public interest concerns.

— Parties can pursue judicial review of any decision made by the Secretary of State.

THE STATUTORY PROCESS

The amendments to the Act do not change the statutory process by which mergers can be scrutinised for public interest, including national security, concerns. The Government wishes to retain the clarity, the transparency and fairness of the current process. The process is set out in detail in guidance.[22] This section of the guidance seeks only to summarise the process.[23]

The Public Intervention Notice

The first formal step for the Government's intervention in a merger is the issuing of a Public Intervention Notice. The Secretary of State issues an intervention notice to the CMA if he or she has "reasonable grounds for suspecting" that it is or may be the case that a relevant merger situation has been created or is in progress, and one of the public interest considerations in section 58 of the Act is relevant. This notice has to be published.

In the event of a merger that has already taken place, the CMA (under section 24 of the Enterprise Act 2002) can decide up to four months after it completed whether to refer the case to a Phase 2 investigation on competition grounds. The Secretary of State has the same four-month period in which to decide, having issued a Public Intervention Notice, whether to refer a completed merger for a Phase 2 investigation of whether it is likely to operate against the public interest. Where the CMA is investigating the merger, however, the Secretary of State must intervene before the CMA reaches a decision on whether to make a reference to Phase 2 on competition grounds.

Phase 1

Following an intervention notice, the CMA is obliged to prepare a report for the Secretary of State by a date specified by the Secretary of State. To enable it to produce this report, the CMA will carry out an investigation of the merger and will publicly seek third party views on the merger.

Following this investigation, the CMA will report on its views on the competition issues and whether, if it were not a public interest case, it would refer the matter for further investigation (a 'Phase 2' investigation) or accept undertakings in lieu of a reference. The report will also summarise the views received on the public interest aspects of the merger and, where relevant, it may refer to any undertakings offered by the parties to mitigate the public interest concerns.

Having received the report, the Secretary of State has three options:

- they may conclude that there are no relevant public interest concerns and the merger can proceed (assuming the CMA has not raised any competition-related concerns);
- they can (subject to a public consultation) accept undertakings offered by the parties in order to mitigate national security risks and/or any competition concerns raised by the CMA;
- refer the merger for further investigation.

There is no statutory deadline for the Secretary of State to respond to the CMA's Phase 1 report. They are likely to also receive advice from the MoD and/or other parts of Government in order to inform this decision.

Phase 2

In the event that the Secretary of State wishes the merger to be investigated further, it is referred to the CMA which will establish a group of independent panel members (not involved in the Phase 1 investigation) to look at the matter. This group will undertake a further investigation into whether the merger is likely to operate against the public interest, taking account of any competition issues and the public interest consideration. It will also consider whether any remedies are appropriate to deal with either or both considerations.

The CMA must submit its Phase 2 report to the Secretary of State within 24 weeks (with a possible extension for a further eight weeks). This report is published.

The Secretary of State has 30 days from receipt of the Phase 2 report to consider their decision. If they consider that there are relevant public interest considerations, they may choose to accept undertakings. Alternatively, the Secretary of State may make orders imposing conditions or, if they consider no remedies can adequately address the public interest concerns, they can block the deal entirely. If they conclude that there are no relevant any public interest considerations, the Secretary of State cannot make any finding at all on the competition issues (if there are any); any such decision will be the CMA's alone.

INTERVENTION IN AN EU MERGER

Where the Secretary of State believes that they may wish to exercise their powers under Article 21(3) of the EU Merger Regulation to protect legitimate interests, they will issue a European Intervention Notice under the Enterprise Act 2002. The process then broadly follows the procedure for public interest cases described above. However, the CMA would investigate and report solely on the public interest issues, as the competition aspects of the case fall within the competence of the European Commission.

JUDICIAL REVIEW

The Secretary of State's decisions at each stage of the process may be challenged by a judicial review.[24] Specifically, affected parties can request judicial review of the decision to serve (or not to serve) a Public Interest Notice, any decision that follows a Phase 1 report, or any decision that follows a Phase 2 report. In each case, the courts will scrutinise whether the Secretary of State acted in a reasonable and lawful manner.

INFORMATION SHARING

The Government may choose to share information provided by parties throughout the process with other parts of Government and with the CMA. However, this will always be done in accordance with its obligations under the Enterprise Act 2002 and other relevant legislation as regards the handling of confidential information.

NOTES

[22] CMA (2014), 'Mergers: Guidance on the CMA's jurisdiction and procedure: CMA2' https://www.gov.uk/government/publications/mergers-guidance-on-the-cmas-jurisdiction-and-procedure.

[23] The statutory process is slightly different for some media- and newspaper-related mergers where Ofcom has a role. This chapter does not seek to cover the process for such a merger.

[24] For applications to the CAT for review see section 120 of the Enterprise Act.

CHAPTER 6: WHAT YOU MIGHT WISH TO DO AS A RESULT OF THE NEW PROVISIONS

[3.474]

Summary

The process for Government intervention remains as set out in the Enterprise Act 2002.

No immediate action is required. However, relevant businesses or their advisors, may wish to familiarise themselves with the implications of the new public interest consideration so as to be well-placed in relation to any relevant merger or acquisition

ACTION NEEDED

The new provisions do not impose any legal obligations on any business or other private organisation or individual. Therefore, there is no need take any action as a direct consequence of the amendments coming into force.

Businesses and investors, or their advisers, may wish to familiarise themselves with the implications of the changes to the Act so as to be well placed in relation to any relevant merger or acquisition that might raise national security concerns.

PROCESS FOR ANY MERGER OR ACQUISITION BROUGHT INTO SCOPE BY THE NEW PROVISIONS

For mergers and acquisition brought into scope of Government intervention as a result of the Orders, parties may wish to voluntarily notify BEIS of the transaction (publicinterestandmergers@beis.gov.uk). The statutory process for Government public interest interventions will remain the same.

The Secretary of State will make intervention decisions on a case-by-case basis. To inform the Secretary of State's decisions, central government departments' officials will seek to work as closely as appropriate, as early as appropriate, with the parties. They will communicate directly with parties, recognising takeovers can be fast-moving. They will seek to understand and discuss (where appropriate) any concerns with a takeover, and how these might be mitigated.

Whilst the information needed to inform the Secretary of State's intervention decisions will differ from case to case, these are likely to be informed, in part, by the following types of information:

- which business, or part of a business, will change hands;
- who is acquiring an interest in the business or division — the individual or business name, and any existing holdings they have in these or other sectors;

- what influence or control that interest may give rise to — for example, how is any new business being structured, what share of voting rights will the acquirer have, or how many Board members can they appoint;
- how could that influence or control be manifested;
- any proposed mitigations that the parties propose in order to deal with Government's concerns; and,
- with whom Government should engage.

The process for public interest interventions has previously been set out by the CMA in its guidance "Mergers - the CMA's jurisdiction and procedure: CMA2".[25]

BEIS welcomes parties' notification of mergers and acquisitions which might raise concerns as early as possible. This can allow it to begin its assessment process. Where relevant, it can also allow Government to say that it has no present public interest concerns with a deal so that parties can choose to proceed subject to any competition assessment that may be relevant and other regulatory processes. However, parties should note that such an indication is subject to change as other information may come to light, or relevant circumstances may change.

Relevant enterprises, or their advisers, may wish to familiarise themselves with the implications of the changes to the Act so as to be well placed ahead of any relevant merger in future that might raise national security-related concerns. These parties should contact their existing government contact or the department that has responsibility for their area of the economy.

If businesses or investors wish to discuss the Orders they should contact NSIIReview@beis.gov.uk. Like this guidance, any such discussion cannot change the legal scope of the Orders and cannot be considered binding. If businesses or investors are considering a merger it may be advisable to seek independent legal advice.

NOTES

25 https://www.gov.uk/government/publications/mergers-guidance-on-the-cmas-jurisdiction-and-procedure.

ANNEX A — CONTACT DETAILS

[3.475]

Area(s)	Contact
Military	NSII-Defence@mod.gov.uk
Dual-use, Computing hardware, Quantum technologies, Artificial Intelligence, cryptographic authentication technology, advanced materials	Parties should contact their existing Government contact. Where there is not a clear email contact publicinterestandmergers@beis.gov.uk
Public interest and Mergers generally	publicinterestandmergers@beis.gov.uk
General queries	nsiireview@beis.gov.uk

DEPARTMENT FOR BUSINESS, ENERGY & INDUSTRIAL STRATEGY ENTERPRISE ACT 2002: CHANGES TO THE PUBLIC INTEREST GROUNDS FOR INTERVENTION IN MERGER CASES

(Guidance 2020)

[3.476]

NOTES

CONTENTS

INTRODUCTION

CONTEXT

[3.477]

1. The demands that the COVID-19 pandemic has placed on the United Kingdom (UK) and the resulting economic impact has led the Government to assess whether its powers of intervention under the Enterprise Act 2002 ("the Act") in respect of mergers and acquisitions are adequate to ensure that the UK is able to respond to public health emergencies.

Part 3 CMA and other Guidelines

2. The Government concluded that its powers were not sufficient, and as such the Government has amended the Act to include a new public interest consideration under which it can intervene in qualifying mergers and acquisitions: "The need to maintain in the UK the capability to combat, and to mitigate the effects of, public health emergencies".

PURPOSE OF THIS GUIDANCE

3. This guidance was produced by the Department for Business, Energy and Industrial Strategy (BEIS) to accompany The Enterprise Act 2002 (Specification of Additional Section 58 Consideration) Order 2020.

4. The Order amends section 58 of the Act to add an additional public interest consideration: "The need to maintain in the UK the capability to combat, and to mitigate the effects, of public health emergencies". This will enable the Government to address risks arising from mergers and acquisitions in which it would otherwise not be able to intervene.

5. This guidance is not statutory guidance. This guidance explains why the Government amended the Act, describes the practical effect of the amendments, and offers guidance to businesses and others about what they might wish to do as a result of these changes.

6. It should be borne in mind that, whilst the guidance is intended to provide an indication of how the new public interest consideration is likely to be applied, and the approach the Secretary of State is likely to adopt in considering cases, each transaction will be looked at on its merits on a case by-case basis. Businesses and investors should consider their own particular circumstances and, where necessary, seek their own legal advice.

7. The Government will keep this guidance under review, updating it to ensure it remains as relevant and as useful as possible. It welcomes comments about any additions or clarifications that would be helpful.

EXECUTIVE SUMMARY

[3.478]

8. The Government is committed to making the UK the best place in the world to do business. The UK is a strong advocate for free trade; this has helped drive growth and wealth in the UK and around the world. However, the Government must ensure that critical UK public health and crisis mitigation capabilities are preserved, in order to safeguard the welfare of the British people.

9. This public interest consideration helps the Government to meet this responsibility by enabling it to scrutinise and to take action in relation to qualifying mergers and acquisitions for the purpose of maintaining UK capability to combat, and to mitigate the effects of, public health emergencies. This could for example involve imposing conditions on a merger prohibiting any diminution of critical capabilities or even blocking the merger, where appropriate.

10. Whilst the vast majority of takeovers are done for genuine business reasons, the Government is attuned to the fact that some critical public health capabilities must be kept in the UK to ensure delivery, self-reliance and self-determination.

11. This guidance focuses on the new public interest consideration that provides a new basis for the Government to intervene in mergers.

12. The new public interest consideration is "the need to maintain in the UK the capability to combat, and to mitigate the effects, of public health emergencies". This adds to the three existing public interest considerations in the Act. To date, the Government has intervened 12 times under the national security consideration, 7 under media plurality and once under financial stability.

13. The Government considers that this new public interest consideration is a necessary and proportionate measure to address risks mergers and acquisitions may pose to the UK's ability to respond to the COVID-19 pandemic or future public health emergencies. Firstly, the Government must be able to ensure that companies related to COVID-19 (or any future public health emergency) response are not subject to mergers or acquisitions that are against the public interest. Secondly, when firms that can help mitigate against the effects of COVID-19 or future public health emergencies are taken over, Government must be able to intervene to ensure that the transaction does not undermine this capability. Finally, as a result of the economic uncertainty caused by the pandemic, usually stable businesses may be suffering a short-term impact to their share price or profitability. This could leave UK enterprises with critical capabilities more vulnerable to takeover.

14. The Government does not expect the new provisions to bring about any change in the Competition and Markets Authority's ("CMA") approach to the assessment of mergers on competition grounds.

15. The changes to the Act do not require any business or investor to take any direct action. They do not affect the fact that the UK retains a voluntary notification mergers system. The European Commission's powers are not affected. Parties whose merger meets the jurisdictional thresholds under the EU Merger Regulation are still required to notify (and obtain approval from) the Commission in advance of the transaction being completed.[1]

16. The amendments do not change any of the procedural provisions under the Act. As a result, any Government intervention under this new public interest consideration will follow the same clear and transparent process under the Act.

17. The Department for Business, Energy and Industrial Strategy ("BEIS") welcomes engagement with parties involved in qualifying mergers and acquisitions that could raise concerns. If businesses or investors consider it possible that a transaction might do so, they are encouraged to speak to the department as early as possible, in the manner set out in this guidance.

18. The Government has never blocked a merger under the Act, and this additional public interest consideration is a proportionate measure in light of the COVID-19 pandemic and does not reflect any substantial shift in Government policy.

NOTES

1 CMA guidance on the merger regime during the transition period can be found at: https://www.gov.uk/government/publications/uk-exit-from-the-eu-guidance-on-the-functions-of-the-cma-under-the- withdrawal-agreement.

CHAPTER 1: WHY THE NEW PROVISION IS REQUIRED

[3.479]

Summary

Since 2008, the same three public interest considerations have applied: national security, media plurality, and financial stability.

In light of the COVID-19 pandemic, the Government concluded that this arrangement poses risks to the UK and a fourth public interest consideration needed to be added to ensure that the Government can respond to risks relating to public health emergencies.

19. The UK has always valued the benefits that foreign investment creates. In 2018 alone, over 57,000 jobs were created as a result of foreign direct investment for example.

20. However, Government also has a duty to regularly review risks that the UK faces. In light of the COVID-19 pandemic, Government has assessed that some mergers and acquisitions may pose risks to the UK's ability to respond to and recover from public health emergencies, that it needs to be in a position to address.

21. The Government sees these risks arising in one of two ways. Firstly, risks arising from the takeover of companies that can combat public health emergencies. Secondly, risks arising from the takeover of businesses that can help mitigate the effects of public health emergencies. These risks, whilst not limited to the COVID-19 pandemic, are explored through the prism of the pandemic below.

22. As a result of the economic uncertainty caused by the pandemic, usually stable businesses may be suffering a short-term impact to their share price or profitability. This could leave UK enterprises with critical capabilities more vulnerable to takeover and is another reason why the Government is acting now.

RISKS TO COMPANIES CRUCIAL TO OUR COVID-19 RESPONSE

23. From vaccine researchers and ventilator manufacturers to delivery companies, UK firms have come together to combat COVID-19. As we continue the fight, many of these firms will continue to be crucial.

24. Mergers and acquisitions can be used to take ownership and control of these firms. This would pose a risk if the acquirer were to reduce the firm's critical capabilities in the UK, for example by transferring them abroad, or to assert their influence to render the capabilities less than fully effective. The Government therefore needs to be in a position to intervene to ensure that critical capabilities are protected and remain fully effective. Inmost cases, the Government would look to accept undertakings from the parties under the Act, that allow the transaction to proceed, whilst protecting the capabilities crucial to the UK's fight against the pandemic.

25. The UK is not alone in ensuring its own capability, and similar measures have been taken throughout Europe and the world.

Example of influence over UK firm that would be detrimental to the fight against COVID-19

A UK research company might create a high-accuracy, easy to administer COVID-19 antibody test. Whilst clearly it would be in the UK's best interest to ensure that this test could be accessed worldwide and by as many people as possible, the Government would have a duty to ensure that UK residents received the test first.

If, however, the research company was taken over by an overseas entity, that entity could assert pressure on the firm to first export its new test to its home country, before UK residents could benefit.

In this instance, the Government might wish to intervene, investigate, and potentially accept undertakings that UK residents would be the first to benefit from the test.

RISKS RELATED TO THE EFFECTS OF COVID-19

26. As a result of the economic uncertainty caused by the pandemic, usually stable businesses may be suffering a short-term impact to their share price or profitability. This could leave UK enterprises with critical capabilities more vulnerable to takeover.

27. In relation to maintaining the capability to mitigate the effects of the pandemic, the Government may for example need to intervene if an internet service provider or food supply chain company becomes the subject of a takeover, given the potential for increased demand for internet services in a lockdown situation or disruption to food supply.

CHAPTER 2: THE NEW PUBLIC INTEREST CONSIDERATION

[3.480]

Summary
Section 58 of the Act has been amended to include the new public interest consideration of "'the need to maintain in the UK the capability to combat, and to mitigate the effects, of public health emergencies".

THE 'NEED TO MAINTAIN . . . CAPABILITY'

28. The new consideration is concerned with preserving capability, that already exists in the UK, to combat, and to mitigate the effects of, public health emergencies.

29. For example, if a UK company that produces personal protective equipment has a capability of producing a certain number of facemasks per day, then this would clearly be a relevant capability that already exists in the UK.

30. The Government also considers repurposable capabilities to fall within the scope of the new consideration. So, for example, an engineering company that designs and makes parts for cars might have the engineering know-how and machinery which could be repurposed to design and make ventilators during a public health emergency. In making such a link, the Government would have to act reasonably, and it is not anticipated that intervention on these grounds would be frequent.

THE CAPABILITY TO COMBAT PUBLIC HEALTH EMERGENCIES

31. The Government expects that the new public interest consideration will most often be used with a view to maintaining UK capability to combat public health emergencies.

32. Relevant capability will be found in firms that are active in the public health sector, such as vaccine researchers, drug manufacturers, and medical supply companies. Other companies may also have relevant capability, for example companies that might help the UK model the spread of a public health emergency.

33. The Government appreciates that in some cases, preservation of capability to combat public health emergencies will amount to a national security issue, for example where the security of supply of a vaccine that is or might be needed to treat a significant section of the population is at risk. The Government does not wish to detract from that.

34. However, in other cases the threshold for action on national security grounds will not be met and the Government considers that intervention on a public health basis should be available. It also considers that some overlap in the public interest considerations is preferable to carving out national security cases from the new public interest consideration. Furthermore, the new public interest consideration provides more certainty to parties that the Government might intervene in takeovers of firms with relevant capabilities.

THE CAPABILITY TO MITIGATE THE EFFECTS OF PUBLIC HEALTH EMERGENCIES

35. The Government recognises that the vast majority of investment causes no concern and is overwhelmingly positive for the UK; it creates jobs, allows firms to innovate and improves productivity.

36. However, the Government may need to intervene in the takeover of a company that provides, or could provide, the UK with the ability to mitigate the effects of a present or future public health emergency, for example, an internet service provider or a food supply chain company, given the potential for increased demand for internet services in a lockdown situation or disruption to food supply.

SUMMARY OF WHAT THE NEW PROVISIONS DO NOT CHANGE

37. The changes do not affect a number of key tests, powers or processes as set out in the Act. This section summarises these in order, the Government hopes, to reassure all parties about the proportionate and focused amendments to the Act.

38. The amendments do not change:

- the definition of an enterprise as described in the Act;
- the definition of what constitutes enterprises "ceasing to be distinct" which remains as set out in section 26 of the Act;
- the turnover test or what constitutes UK turnover;
- the share of supply test or the way in which a share of supply is determined;
- the requirements on businesses set out in the EU Merger Regulation, including the requirement to notify relevant mergers to the European Commission;
- the process by which mergers subject to public interest interventions are scrutinised by the CMA to confirm they meet jurisdictional tests; and
- the ability for affected parties to pursue a judicial review of all decisions made by the Government under the public interest regime.

CHAPTER 3: WHAT YOU MIGHT WISH TO DO AS A RESULT OF THE NEW PROVISIONS

[3.481]

Summary
No immediate action is required. However, relevant businesses or their advisors, may wish to familiarise themselves with the implications of the new public interest consideration so as to be well-placed in relation to any relevant merger or acquisition.

ACTION NEEDED

39. The new provisions do not impose any legal obligations on any business or other private organisation or individual. Therefore, there is no need take any action as a direct consequence of the amendments coming into force.

40. Businesses and investors, or their advisers, may wish to familiarise themselves with the implications of the changes to the Act so as to be well placed in relation to any relevant merger or acquisition that might raise concerns regarding the UK's ability to combat, or to mitigate the effects of, public health emergencies.

PROCESS FOR ANY MERGER OR ACQUISITION BROUGHT INTO SCOPE BY THE NEW PROVISIONS

41. For mergers and acquisition brought into scope of Government intervention as a result of the new consideration, parties may wish to voluntarily notify BEIS of the transaction. The statutory process for Government public interest interventions will remain the same.

42. The Secretary of State will make intervention decisions on a case-by-case basis. To inform the Secretary of State's decisions, central government departments' officials will seek to work as closely as appropriate, as early as appropriate, with the parties. They will communicate directly with parties, recognizing takeovers can be fast-moving. They will seek to understand and discuss (where appropriate) any concerns with a takeover, and how these might be mitigated.

43. Whilst the information needed to inform the Secretary of State's intervention decisions will differ from case to case, these are likely to be informed, in part, by the following types of information:

- which business, or part of a business, will change hands;
- who is acquiring an interest in the business or division – the individual or business name, and any existing holdings they have in these or other sectors;
- what influence or control that interest may give rise to – for example, how is any new business being structured, what share of voting rights will the acquirer have, or how many Board members can they appoint;
- how could that influence or control be manifested;
- any proposed mitigations that the parties propose in order to deal with Government's concerns; and
- with whom Government should engage.

44. The process for public interest interventions has previously been set out by the CMA in its guidance "Mergers - the CMA's jurisdiction and procedure: CMA2".[2]

45. BEIS welcomes parties' notification of mergers and acquisitions which might raise concerns as early as possible. This can allow it to begin its assessment process. Where relevant, it can also allow Government to say that it has no present public interest concerns with a deal so that parties can choose to proceed subject to any competition assessment that may be relevant and other regulatory processes. However, parties should note that such an indication is subject to change as other information may come to light, or relevant circumstances may change.

46. Businesses and investors who wish to engage with the Government about transactions that they believe may have a public health emergency dimension should contact BEIS in the first instance, using PHEconsideration@beis.gov.uk.

NOTES

[2] https://www.gov.uk/government/publications/mergers-guidance-on-the-cmas-jurisdiction-and-procedure.

PROVIDING DOCUMENTS TO THE CMA
(Updated 23 December 2020)

[3.482]

NOTES

This document is available on the Competition and Markets Authority website at: www.gov.uk/government/publications/mergers-forms-and-fee-information.

All documents submitted to the CMA (eg, as annexes to the Merger Notice, in response to further information requests; additional analysis, etc.) must have a document number or annex number. Annexes should be numbered starting from 001, 002, 003 onwards. For example: Annex 001-Plan A; Annex 002-Plan B; Annex 003-Plan C. The numbering must be sequential and not overlap with numbers allocated to other annexes.

Please do not include special characters such as @, &, ‘, %, (,), <, or > ~ # in file names.

All documents submitted to the CMA must be submitted in a readable and searchable format. Documents must be classified and indexed using Annex 2 to the Merger Notice, available on the CMA website.

Documents must be sent to the CMA electronically or on discs or USB drives wherever practicable, either in a format compatible with Microsoft Office programs, or as tagged PDF files. If files are password protected, please provide the relevant passwords.

Please submit spreadsheets, charts and all other digital source data files, as far as possible, in Microsoft Excel or their equivalent original format, to facilitate the CMA's internal analysis. Should you submit spreadsheets without the underlying formulae, whether in hard copy or electronically, the CMA is likely to ask for such information.

When sending material electronically or making up discs/USB drives, please ensure that each file is given a succinct and self-explanatory title. Files should not be grouped into folders and sub-folders.

10MB is the limit for acceptance by our system of emailed material in any one message.

COMPETITION & MARKETS AUTHORITY MERGERS – CASE TEAM ALLOCATION FORM

(Updated 23 December 2020)

[3.483]

NOTES

To be sent by email to mergers@cma.gov.uk

1.	**Your contact details**	
	Name	
	Company/law firm	
	Telephone number	
	Email	

2.	**Merger parties**	
	Name of parties	1. 2. 3. 4.
	UK turnover of parties (indicate year)	1. 2. 3. 4.
	Describe the main products or services supplied by the parties[1]	
	Describe the overlapping or vertically related products or services	

3.	**Transaction**	
Brief description of the transaction (e.g. acquisition of entire issued share capital, or part of a business)		
	Is the transaction anticipated or completed?	
	Date of completion or expected date of completion	
	Evidence of good faith intention to proceed with the transaction[2]	
	Is the transaction conditional on CMA clearance?	
	Is the transaction subject to the City Code on Takeovers?	

4.	**Reason for the case team allocation request** [3] *If you are requesting a team because you intend to voluntarily notify a merger, please provide a brief overview of the markets involved and the expected complexity of the case.*

5. **Interaction with other processes**
Is the transaction being notified to other competition authorities? If so, please specify which authorities and explain the stage of the investigation reached with each authority.
Does the transaction affect any sector in which the Secretary of State may make a public interest intervention?[4]

6. **Confidentiality**
Information submitted in pre-notification is protected by Part 9 of the Enterprise Act 2002 and pre-notification contacts are kept confidential. Nevertheless, please indicate whether the transaction has been publicly announced.
Publicly announced: Yes/No
Date of announcement:
Please include a link to the announcement, or a copy of the announcement

7. **Expected date of first draft Merger Notice**
Date you expect the first draft Merger Notice Form to be submitted to the CMA[5]:

8.	**Coronavirus (COVID-19)** *When submitting a case team allocation form to the CMA, merging parties are asked to provide as much information as possible (and to be realistic) about the likely timing of the case. Merging parties are also expected to update the CMA on a regular basis regarding any changes in the timing of the merger under consideration or changes in the likelihood that this merger will proceed under current market conditions.*
Please also explain whether you expect that the current circumstances would have any material impact on the CMA's ability to engage with the merging parties, and their key staff, and/or to meaningfully engage with customers and competitors during the CMA's investigation within the CMA's standard timetables.	

9. Any other information you would like to submit at this stage

NOTES

[1] If applicable, please explain whether and how any of these products or services qualify as "relevant enterprises" as set out under section 23A of the Enterprise Act 2002.

[2] As explained in Chapter 6 of the Guidance on the CMA's Jurisdiction and Procedure (CMA2) (CMA Mergers Guidance), the pre-notification process is not available for transactions that remain hypothetical. The merger parties should therefore explain the basis upon which they can evidence a good faith intention to proceed with the transaction (eg because heads of terms have been concluded, adequate finance has been put in place, the transaction has been subject to board-level consideration etc).

[3] Where merger parties are uncertain about the extent of information or the nature of the evidence to submit in their merger notice, the CMA encourages them to engage in pre-notification discussions. In order to allocate resources efficiently, the CMA may not immediately allocate a full case team on receipt of every Case Team Allocation Form (depending on the likely timing of engagement and the nature of the issues that may need to be addressed in pre-notification discussions).

[4] See Chapter 16 of the CMA Mergers Guidance.

[5] Please provide a realistic assessment of the submission date. As the CMA will allocate its resources on the basis of the response provided to this question, an accurate estimate is particularly important to enable the CMA to deal with the case as quickly and effectively as possible. An unscheduled delay in the submission of a sufficiently developed notification may lead the CMA to re-allocate its staff resources to other cases and result in the need to submit a new case team allocation form.

COMPETITION & MARKETS AUTHORITY CONFIDENTIALITY WAIVER TEMPLATE

(Updated 23 December 2020)

[3.484]

NOTES

[TITLE OF CASE]

[entity giving consent], hereby gives its consent in accordance with section 239 of the Enterprise Act 2002 (the **Act**) to the disclosure of information which would otherwise be subject to the restrictions on disclosure set out in Part 9 of the Act. It also waives its rights under any other applicable laws restricting disclosure by the Competition and Markets Authority (**CMA**) of confidential information obtained from [entity giving consent] in connection with [acquirer's] [proposed] acquisition of [target] and consents to the disclosure of such information subject to the qualifications set out below.

Specifically, [entity giving consent] agrees that the staff of the CMA may share with the [receiving entity] documents, statements, data, and information the disclosure of which would otherwise be prohibited by the laws mentioned above.

This waiver is granted with respect to disclosures to the [receiving entity]. If statutory filings are made with other competition authorities in the future, [entity giving consent] shall notify the CMA of this and will be willing to discuss extension of this waiver to permit disclosure to such other competition authorities.

[Entity giving consent] acknowledges that this waiver is without prejudice to the CMA's powers to disclose information under Part 9 of the Act without the consent of the person providing the information.

This authorisation does not constitute a waiver of legal privilege in relation to any materials which in proceedings in the High Court or the Court of Session would be protected from disclosure on grounds of legal privilege, provided that [entity giving consent] has notified the CMA in writing that it wishes to assert legal privilege over such materials prior to any disclosure being made by the CMA to the [receiving entity].

A copy of this letter is being sent to the [receiving entity].

The signatory hereby confirms that he/she is duly authorised to sign this waiver.

SIGNED BY

....

AS DULY AUTHORISED SIGNATORY FOR AND ON BEHALF OF

....

MERGERS: GUIDANCE ON THE CMA'S JURISDICTION AND PROCEDURE (CMA2REVISED, DECEMBER 2020)

[3.485]

NOTES

CONTENTS

1 PREFACE

[3.486]

1.1 The CMA's merger control function is part of its duty to promote competition for the benefit of consumers.[1] Its merger control procedures are designed to fulfil this duty in an efficient manner, while ensuring that the merger parties' rights to due process are fully respected. The CMA is also required to balance the rights of the merger parties with those held by third parties.

1.2 This guidance forms part of the advice and information published by the Competition and Markets Authority (CMA) under section 106 of the Enterprise Act 2002, as amended (the Act). It is designed to provide general information and advice to companies and their advisers on the procedures used by the CMA in operating the merger control regime set out in the Act. It also includes guidance on when the CMA will have jurisdiction to review mergers under the Act, and it explains the respective roles of the CMA, the Secretary of State, and relevant sectoral regulators in UK merger control.[2]

1.3 This guidance reflects experience gained since the Act entered into force in 2003 and, in particular, since the CMA was established in April 2014. It replaces CMA2, which was published in 2014.

1.4 This guidance should be read alongside other CMA guidance including in particular: *Merger Assessment Guidelines* (OFT1254/CC2); *Merger Remedies* (CMA87); *Guidance on the CMA's mergers intelligence function* (CMA56); *Interim measures in merger investigations* (CMA108); *Mergers: Exceptions to the duty to refer* (CMA64); *Guidance on requests for internal documents in merger investigations* (CMA100); *Administrative Penalties: Statement of policy on the CMA's approach* (CMA4) and *Transparency and disclosure: Statement of the CMA's policy and approach* (CMA6). A full list of relevant guidance is provided in Annex B.

1.5 Where there is any difference in emphasis or detail between this guidance and other guidance produced or adopted by the CMA, the most recently published document takes precedence.

1.6 While the CMA will have regard to this guidance in handling mergers under the Act, it will apply this guidance flexibly and may depart from the approach described in the guidance where there is an appropriate and reasonable justification for doing so.

NOTES

1 Section 25(3) of the Enterprise and Regulatory Reform Act 2013 (the ERRA13).

2 At the date of publication of this guidance the relevant sectoral regulators for the purposes of this guidance are: the Office of Communications (Ofcom), the Gas and Electricity Markets Authority (Ofgem), the Oil and Gas Authority (OGA), the Water Services Regulation Authority (Ofwat), the Northern Ireland Authority for Utility Regulation (URegNI), the Office of Rail and Road (ORR), the Civil Aviation Authority (CAA), NHS Improvement (NHSI), the Financial Conduct Authority (FCA), and the Payment Systems Regulator (PSR).

2 INTRODUCTION

SCOPE OF THE GUIDANCE

[3.487]

2.1 This guidance describes the procedures used by the CMA in operating the merger control regime set out in the Act. In particular, this guidance discusses the criteria that the CMA applies to determine whether it has jurisdiction under the Act (chapter 4) and the policies and procedures that the CMA will use in discharging its functions under the Act (chapter 5 onwards).

2.2 This guidance does not address the substantive 'substantial lessening of competition' (SLC) test against which the CMA assesses whether a merger raises competition concerns. Detailed information on the application of the substantive test for mergers is provided in *Merger Assessment Guidelines* (OFT1254/CC2). This guidance also does not explain the CMA's approach and requirements in the selection, design and implementation of remedies in merger investigations, which is covered in *Merger Remedies* (CMA87).

2.3 Other aspects of the CMA's practice in merger control cases (for example in relation to the use of interim measures,[3] the approach taken to considering whether non-notified cases should be called in for investigation[4] and the approach taken to gathering internal documents[5]) are referred to in this guidance but explained more fully in separate guidance documents.

WHO DOES WHAT?

2.4 The Act assigns distinct roles in relation to merger control to the CMA, the Secretary of State, and certain sectoral regulators. The inter-relationship between these roles is summarised in the following paragraphs.

The CMA

2.5 The ERRA13 established the CMA as the UK's economy-wide competition authority responsible for ensuring that competition and markets work well for consumers. The CMA's primary duty is to seek to promote competition, both within and outside the UK, for the benefit of consumers.

2.6 Under the Act, the CMA has a function to obtain and review information relating to merger situations, and a duty to refer for an in-depth 'phase 2' investigation any relevant merger situation where it believes that it is or may be the case that the merger has resulted or may be expected to result in a substantial lessening of competition in a UK market.

2.7 Following a reference for a phase 2 investigation, the CMA conducts a more detailed analysis to determine whether: (i) there is a relevant merger situation falling within the UK merger control regime, (ii) that relevant merger situation has resulted, or may be expected to result, in an SLC, and (iii) it should take action to remedy any SLC identified.

2.8 At phase 2, those decisions are taken by an Inquiry Group, selected for each case from the independent experts appointed by the Secretary of State to the CMA's panel.

2.9 The CMA's role in relation to public interest merger cases is set out in chapter 16.

The Secretary of State

2.10 The Secretary of State has a role in certain public interest cases, as described more fully below in chapter 16. The decision on the competitive effects of a merger is, however, solely for the CMA under the Act. Outside the public interest interventions described in chapter 16, the UK merger control process is independent of government and the UK Government does not play any formal role within, or otherwise exercise any influence over, a CMA merger control investigation.

The sectoral regulators

2.11 The CMA routinely consults the sectoral regulators about any mergers in which they are likely to have industry-specific knowledge. This is described further in chapter 9 below. In addition, Ofwat, Ofcom, and NHSI have statutory roles in the assessment of, respectively, certain water mergers, media mergers, and mergers involving NHS foundation trusts. See chapters 9 and 17 below.

OVERVIEW OF THE CMA'S MERGER INVESTIGATION PROCESS

2.12 The diagram below provides a high-level summary of the principal stages in phase 1 and phase 2 merger investigations undertaken by the CMA, from initial contact with the CMA through to, in appropriate cases, the outcome of a full, two-phase investigation.[6] While this broad process applies in all CMA merger investigations, the approach adopted can (as explained further in this guidance) vary depending on the circumstances of the case.[7]

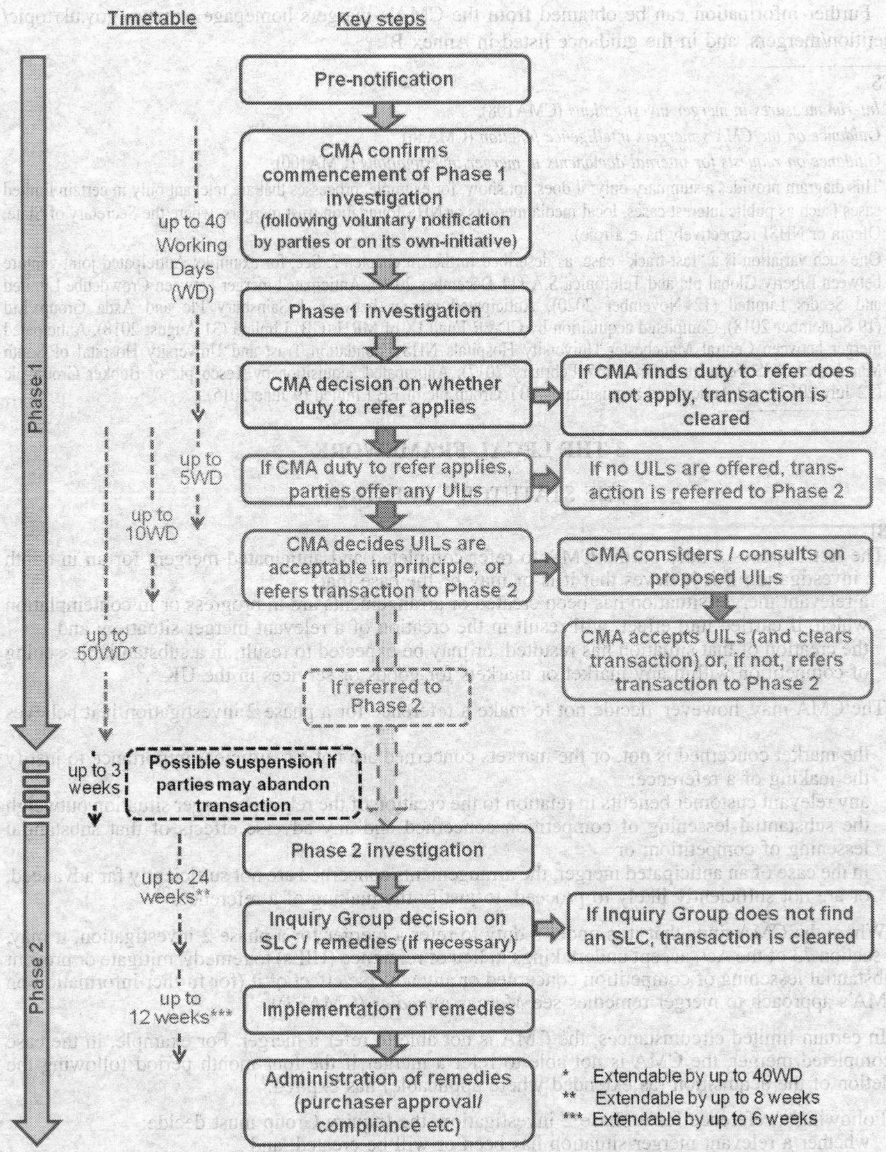

THE STRUCTURE OF THIS GUIDANCE

2.13 This guidance seeks to follow broadly the chronology of the UK merger process shown in the diagram above. To this end, it is structured as follows:

(a) **chapters 3 and 4** set out the legal framework for the UK merger control regime and provide guidance on the relevant merger situations which the CMA has jurisdiction to review;

(b) **chapters 5 to 9** provide guidance on the phase 1 process, from initial contact with the CMA, and covers the notification of mergers and 'calling in' of non-notified mergers;

(c) **chapters 10 to 15** provide guidance on the phase 2 process explaining the further information-gathering and assessment that the CMA may undertake as part of this more in-depth examination of the merger and the role of CMA panel members in the investigation and decision-making process. These chapters also explain the process followed in cancelling an investigation;

(d) **chapters 16 to 20** provide more general information on the different process applicable to public interest mergers, the interaction of the UK merger control regime with other regulatory processes, considerations relating to international (multi-jurisdictional) mergers, communication and publication of CMA merger decisions, and the payment of merger fees to the CMA following its phase 1 investigation; and

(e) finally, the **annexes** provide further information on the calculation of turnover, other published CMA guidance in relation to mergers, ancillary restraints, and relevant contact addresses.

FURTHER INFORMATION

2.14 Further information can be obtained from the CMA's mergers homepage at www.gov.uk/topic/competition/mergers, and in the guidance listed in Annex B.

NOTES

[3] *Interim measures in merger investigations* (CMA108).

[4] *Guidance on the CMA's mergers intelligence function* (CMA56).

[5] *Guidance on requests for internal documents in merger investigations* (CMA100).

[6] This diagram provides a summary only: it does not show, for example, processes that are relevant only in certain limited cases (such as public interest cases, local media mergers or NHS foundation trust mergers, where the Secretary of State, Ofcom or NHSI respectively have a role).

[7] One such variation is a "fast-track" case, as described further in chapter 7. See, for example: Anticipated joint venture between Liberty Global plc and Telefónica S.A (11 December 2020), Anticipated merger between Crowdcube Limited and Seedrs Limited (12 November 2020), Anticipated merger between J Sainsbury Plc and Asda Group Ltd (19 September 2018), Completed acquisition by CD&R Fund IX of MRH (GB) Limited (31 August 2018), Anticipated merger between Central Manchester University Hospitals NHS Foundation Trust and University Hospital of South Manchester NHS Foundation Trust (27 February 2017), Anticipated acquisition by Tesco plc of Booker Group plc (12 July 2017), and Anticipated acquisition by BT Group plc of EE Limited (9 June 2015).

3 THE LEGAL FRAMEWORK

THE STATUTORY QUESTIONS

[3.488]

3.1 The Act imposes a duty on the CMA to refer completed and anticipated mergers for an in-depth phase 2 investigation if it believes that it is or may be the case that:

(a) a relevant merger situation has been created or arrangements are in progress or in contemplation which, if carried into effect, will result in the creation of a relevant merger situation; and

(b) the creation of that situation has resulted, or may be expected to result, in a substantial lessening of competition within any market or markets for goods or services in the UK.[8],[9]

3.2 The CMA may, however, decide not to make a reference for a phase 2 investigation if it believes that:

(a) the market concerned is not, or the markets concerned are not, of sufficient importance to justify the making of a reference;

(b) any relevant customer benefits in relation to the creation of the relevant merger situation outweigh the substantial lessening of competition concerned and any adverse effects of that substantial lessening of competition; or

(c) in the case of an anticipated merger, the arrangements concerned are not sufficiently far advanced, or are not sufficiently likely to proceed, to justify the making of a reference.[10]

3.3 Where the CMA finds that it is under a duty to refer a merger for a phase 2 investigation, it may, under section 73 of the Act, accept undertakings in lieu of reference (UILs) to remedy, mitigate or prevent the substantial lessening of competition concerned or any adverse effect of it (for further information on the CMA's approach to merger remedies see *Merger remedies* (CMA87)).

3.4 In certain limited circumstances, the CMA is not able to refer a merger. For example, in the case of a completed merger, the CMA is not able to refer a merger if the four month period following the completion of the acquisition (as extended where applicable) has expired.[11]

3.5 Following a reference for a phase 2 investigation, the Inquiry Group must decide:

(a) whether a relevant merger situation has been or will be created; and

(b) if so, whether the creation of that situation has resulted, or may be expected to result, in a substantial lessening of competition within any market or markets in the UK for goods or services (where both limbs are satisfied, this is referred to as an 'anti-competitive outcome').[12]

3.6 If the Inquiry Group finds that there is an anti-competitive outcome, it must decide:

(a) whether action should be taken by it, or by others, to remedy, mitigate or prevent the substantial lessening of competition concerned or any adverse effect that has resulted from, or may be expected to result from, that substantial lessening of competition; and

(b) if action is to be taken, what action should be taken and what is to be remedied, mitigated or prevented.

3.7 While many mergers will not raise competition issues, the merger control process is designed to allow the CMA to identify those where such issues may arise, so that they may be properly investigated and, where necessary, resolved through appropriate remedies.

3.8 At phase 1, the CMA's test for reference (its 'duty to refer') will be met if the CMA has a reasonable belief, objectively justified by relevant facts, that there is a realistic prospect that the merger will lessen competition substantially. At phase 2, the Inquiry Group is then required to base its decisions on whether the merger will lessen competition substantially on the balance of probabilities. Further guidance on the application of these tests may be found in *Merger Assessment Guidelines* (OFT1254/CC2).

PUBLIC INTEREST INTERVENTIONS

3.9 The Act permits intervention by the Secretary of State in cases where public interest issues arise.[13] In such cases, the CMA is responsible for the competition assessment, but the Secretary of State may take public interest factors into account in deciding whether to make a reference to phase 2, accept UILs, or impose remedies following a phase 2 investigation. The public interest considerations that the Secretary of State may take into account are those relating to:[14]

(a) national security, including public security;
(b) media plurality and other considerations relating to newspaper and certain other media mergers;
(c) the stability of the UK financial system; and
(d) the need to maintain in the United Kingdom the capability to combat, and to mitigate the effects of, public health emergencies.[15]

3.10 The Secretary of State is able to intervene in special public interest cases where the standard jurisdictional thresholds relating to share of supply and turnover are not satisfied. The Secretary of State can only intervene in special public interest cases where one or more of the enterprises concerned is carried on in the UK, or by or under the control of a body corporate incorporated in the UK, and where one or more of the enterprises concerned is a relevant government contractor (as defined) in defence mergers, or where the merger involves certain newspaper or broadcasting companies.[16] These are known as special merger situations and are considered under the special public interest regime of the Act. There is no competition assessment in such cases.

NOTES

8 Crown dependencies (Jersey, Guernsey and the Isle of Man) are not part of the United Kingdom and may have separate merger control laws applicable in their respective jurisdictions (for example Jersey has a specific merger control regime: see the Jersey Competition Regulatory Authority, which forms part of the Channel Islands Competition and Regulatory Authorities, at www.cicra.gg).

9 Sections 22(1) and 33(1) of the Act.

10 Sections 22(2) and 33(2) of the Act.

11 Section 24(1) of the Act.

12 Section 35(2) of the Act.

13 Section 42 of the Act.

14 The Secretary of State has the power to add further public interest considerations by statutory instrument. See sections 58(3) and 58(4) of the Act.

15 Section 58 of the Act.

16 Section 59 of the Act.

4 JURISDICTION AND RELEVANT MERGER SITUATIONS

INTRODUCTION

[3.489]

4.1 The question of whether there is a 'relevant merger situation' under the Act or arrangements are in progress or contemplation that will give rise to such a relevant merger situation is relevant at both phase 1 and phase 2.[17]

4.2 The Act's definition of a 'relevant merger situation' covers several different kinds of transaction and arrangement. A company that buys or intends to buy a majority shareholding or a significant minority shareholding in another company is the most obvious example, but other arrangements such as the transfer or pooling of assets or employees, the creation of a joint venture, or outsourcing arrangements may, in certain circumstances, also give rise to relevant merger situations. The Act's provisions apply both to mergers that have already taken place (subject to time limits) and to those that are proposed or in contemplation.

4.3 Subject to the provisions described at paragraph 4.4 below in relation to certain specified sectors, a merger must meet all three of the following criteria to constitute a relevant merger situation for the purposes of the Act:[18,19]

(a) first, either:
  (i) two or more enterprises (broadly speaking, business activities of any kind)[20] must cease to be distinct; or
  (ii) there must be arrangements in progress or in contemplation which, if carried into effect, will lead to enterprises ceasing to be distinct;
(b) and second, either:
  (i) the UK turnover associated with the enterprise which is being acquired exceeds £70 million (this is referred to as 'the turnover test');[21] or
  (ii) the enterprises which cease to be distinct supply or acquire goods or services of any description and, after the merger, together supply or acquire at least 25% of all those particular goods or services of that kind supplied in the UK or in a substantial part of it. The merger must also result in an increment to the share of supply or acquisition (this is referred to as 'the share of supply test');[22]
(c) and third, either:
  (i) the merger must not yet have taken place; or

Part 3 CMA and other Guidelines

(ii) the date of the merger must be no more than four months before the day the reference is made, unless the merger took place without having been made public and without the CMA being informed of it (in which case the four-month period starts from the earlier of the time the merger was made public or the time the CMA was told about it).[23] This four-month deadline may be extended in certain circumstances.[24]

4.4 For mergers that involve an enterprise being taken over which is active in the areas specified under section 23A of the Act, (a **'relevant enterprise'**), there are also alternative jurisdictional thresholds which differ from those applicable to other mergers under the UK merger control regime (as set out in paragraph 4.3 above). These areas of specified activity are:
(a) the development or production of items for military or military and civilian use;
(b) the design and maintenance of aspects of computing hardware;
(c) the development and production of quantum technology;
(d) artificial intelligence;
(e) cryptographic authentication; and
(f) advanced materials.[25]

4.5 For mergers in which the enterprise being taken over (or part of it) is a relevant enterprise, the criteria at paragraph 4.3 apply. However, in addition, the turnover and share of supply tests can be met in the following ways:
(a) the turnover test is met if the relevant enterprise's annual UK turnover exceeds £1 million;
(b) the share of supply test is met if before the merger, the relevant enterprise being acquired or merged has a share of supply or purchase of 25% or more of relevant goods or services in the UK or in a substantial part of it.[26]

4.6 In other words, the test is met even if share of supply does not increase as a result of the merger so long as the relevant enterprise has a 25% share of supply. The relevant goods or services for the purposes of deciding whether the share of supply test is met are those by virtue of which the target enterprise qualifies as a relevant enterprise. This provision adds to, rather than replaces, the 'share of supply' test discussed at paragraph 4.3.

4.7 These thresholds are intended to enable the Secretary of State to be able to intervene on public interest national security grounds in transactions involving changes of control over relevant enterprises. They also enable the CMA to review a merger involving changes of control of relevant enterprises on competition grounds.

4.8 In the context of mergers that have not yet completed, at phase 1 the CMA will generally consider that 'arrangements are in progress or in contemplation' for the purposes of section 33 of the Act if a public announcement has been made by the merger parties concerned.[27]

ENTERPRISES CEASING TO BE DISTINCT

4.9 Two enterprises will 'cease to be distinct' if they are brought under common ownership or control.[28]

ENTERPRISES

4.10 The term 'enterprise' is defined in section 129 of the Act as the activities, or part of the activities, of a business. This does not mean that the enterprise in question need be a separate legal entity: it simply means that the activities in question could be carried on for gain or reward. However, there is no requirement that the transferred activities have generated,[29] or are expected to generate, a profit or dividend for shareholders: indeed, the transferred activities may be loss-making or conducted on a not-for-profit basis.[30]

4.11 In making a judgement as to whether or not the activities of a business, or part of a business, constitute an enterprise under the Act, the CMA will have regard to the substance of the arrangement under consideration, rather than merely its legal form.[31]

4.12 An 'enterprise' may comprise any number of components, most commonly including some combination of the assets and records needed to carry on certain activities of the business, employees working in the business, and existing contracts and/or goodwill. However, the Act does not require that a business (or part thereof) be of any minimum scale, or include any particular combination of components, in order to constitute an enterprise.[32]

4.13 In some cases, the transfer of assets or employees alone may be sufficient to constitute an enterprise: for example, where the facilities or site transferred, or a group of employees and their know-how, enables a particular business activity to be continued. A collection of 'bare assets' is unlikely to amount to an enterprise for the purposes of the Act.[33] An enterprise would generally require something more than bare assets, related to the fact that the assets being transferred were previously employed in combination in the activities of the business being acquired.[34] There is, however, no requirement for the business being transferred to include physical assets, or any particular category of asset, in order to constitute an enterprise under the Act.

4.14 The CMA's assessment of whether what is being acquired amounts to an enterprise will depend on the specific facts and circumstances of each case and the industry in question. No one single factor will necessarily be determinative. Rather, the CMA will make an assessment based on the totality of all relevant considerations.

4.15 Where a transaction results in the acquisition of parts of a business, in determining whether the activities or components of the business being acquired constitute an enterprise, the CMA will have particular regard to whether the transaction includes:

(a) The transfer of tangible or intangible assets. However, intangible assets such as intellectual property rights (including know-how) are unlikely, on their own, to constitute an enterprise unless it is possible to identify recently-generated turnover directly related to the transferred intangible assets (or expected revenues directly related to the assets being transferred without material further development).[35]
(b) The transfer of business data (including customer databases, lists or other customer relationships).[36]
(c) The transfer of employees, including under the TUPE[37] regulations.[38]
(d) Consideration for the goodwill obtained by the purchaser. The presence of a price premium being paid over the value of any assets being transferred would be indicative of goodwill being transferred.[39]
(e) The transfer of trademarks, trade names, or domain names.

4.16 The CMA will also consider, as an important factor, whether the combination of components results in a degree of economic continuity in the activities of the business being transferred.

4.17 Outsourcing arrangements involving ongoing supply arrangements will not generally result in enterprises ceasing to be distinct, but may do so where, for example, they involve the permanent (or long-term) transfer of assets, rights and/or employees to the outsourcing service supplier and where those may be used to supply services other than to the original owner/employer. The CMA will assess whether, overall, the assets, rights and employees transferred to the outsourcing service supplier are such as to constitute an enterprise under the principles set out above.[40]

4.18 The fact that a target business may no longer be, or has not yet started, actively trading does not in itself prevent it, or a combination of its assets, from being an enterprise for the purposes of the Act.[41] The CMA will consider whether what is being acquired amounts to more than 'bare assets', owing to the fact that the assets were previously employed in combination in the activities of a business (or would be employed in combination to commence active trading). In such cases, while the relevant criteria may vary according to the particular circumstances of a case, the CMA will consider, for example:
(a) the period of time elapsed since the business was last trading (if relevant);
(b) the extent and cost of the actions that would be required in order for the business to start trading;[42]
(c) the extent to which customers, investors and competitors would regard the assets transferred as, in substance, amounting to a business; and
(d) whether, despite the fact that the business is not trading, goodwill or other benefits may be acquired beyond the assets being transferred.[43]

4.19 None of these factors, individually, is necessarily conclusive. The CMA will assess all relevant circumstances, with a view to determining whether the target business constitutes an enterprise under the Act.

CONTROL

4.20 'Ceasing to be distinct' is defined in section 26 of the Act as two enterprises being brought under common ownership or common control. 'Control' is not limited to the acquisition of outright voting control but may include situations falling short of outright voting control. Section 26 of the Act distinguishes three levels of interest (in ascending order):
(a) material influence,
(b) de facto control, and
(c) a controlling interest (also known as 'de jure', or 'legal' control).

Material influence

4.21 The ability to exercise material influence is the lowest level of control that may give rise to a relevant merger situation. When making its assessment, the CMA focuses on the acquirer's ability materially to influence policy relevant to the behaviour of the target entity in the marketplace. The policy of the target in this context means the management of its business, and thus includes the strategic direction of a company and its ability to define and achieve its commercial objectives.[44]

4.22 The assessment of material influence requires a case-by-case analysis of the overall relationship between the acquirer and the target. In making its assessment, the CMA will have regard to all the circumstances of the case.

4.23 A finding of material influence may be based on the acquirer's ability to influence the target's policy through exercising votes at shareholders' meetings, together with, in some cases, any additional supporting factors (see paragraph 4.28 below). However, material influence may also arise as a result of the ability to influence the board of the target, and/or through other arrangements: that is, without the acquirer necessarily being able to block votes at shareholders' meetings.

4.24 Each of these potential sources of influence (shareholding, board representation, and other sources) is described further below. The variety of commercial arrangements entered into by firms makes it difficult to state categorically what will (or will not) constitute material influence. The following matters may be of particular relevance, although this list is by no means exhaustive.

Shareholdings

4.25 The size of the acquirer's minority shareholding in the target company will typically have a direct bearing on the extent of the acquirer's voting power at a shareholders' meeting, and thus on the acquirer's influence on the corporate and strategic decisions of the target company. For example, a shareholding conferring on the holder more than 25% of the voting rights in a UK company generally enables the holder to block special resolutions.

4.26 Given the nature of the decisions that typically will require a special resolution - and which the holder could therefore block - a share of voting rights of over 25% is likely to be seen as conferring the ability materially to influence policy - even when all the remaining shares are held by only one person.

4.27 Shareholdings of below 25% will typically be less likely to confer material influence. However, the CMA may examine any shareholding to determine whether the holder might be able materially to influence the company's policy. Even shareholdings of less than 15% might attract scrutiny where other factors indicating the ability to exercise material influence over policy are present.[45],[46]

4.28 In considering whether material influence may be present in a particular case, the CMA will consider not only whether the acquiring party has the right to block special resolutions but also whether, given other factors, it is able to do so as a practical matter.[47] This gives effect to the general principle that the purpose of UK merger control is to enable the CMA to consider the commercial realities and results of transactions and that the focus should be on substance and not legal form. Other factors relevant to whether special resolutions might be blocked in practice may include:

(a) the distribution and holders of the remaining shares, for example whether the acquiring entity's shareholding makes it the largest shareholder; and

(b) patterns of attendance and voting at recent shareholders' meetings based on recent shareholder returns,[48] and, in particular, whether voter attendance is such that a shareholder holding 25% of the voting rights or less would be able in practice to block special resolutions. In making this determination, the CMA may have regard to the votes of other shareholders that it considers may be expected to be voted with the acquirer against a special resolution.

4.29 In addition, an acquirer's shareholding, whilst insufficient in itself to enable the acquirer to defeat a special resolution (even as a practical matter), may still in some cases afford the acquirer special voting or veto rights over relevant policy or strategic matters sufficient to confer material influence.

4.30 The CMA may also have regard to the status and expertise of the acquirer, and its corresponding influence with other shareholders, and may consider whether, given the identity and corporate policy of the target company, the acquirer may be able materially to influence policy formulation through, for example, meetings with other shareholders.[49]

4.31 Where a company's appetite for pursuing certain strategies would be reduced because of a perception that these strategies would be likely to cause conflict with the acquirer, this may be an additional relevant factor in determining material influence.

Board representation

4.32 In addition to the ability materially to influence policy through the voting of shares, the CMA's determination may also, or alternatively, turn on whether the acquirer is able materially to influence the policy of the target entity through board representation.[50] Indeed, board representation alone may confer material influence.[51]

4.33 Whether as a free-standing basis for material influence or as a supporting factor in the context of a shareholding, the CMA will review a range of factors in relation to such board representation, including, for example, the corporate/industry expertise,[52] other relevant experience or incentives of the various members of the board.[53]

4.34 Where a party acquires the right or ability to obtain board representation, the CMA considers it appropriate to take this right or ability into account in its jurisdictional assessment (and potentially also in its substantive assessment), even where it has not yet been exercised and/or there is no certainty about when it will be exercised in future.

Other sources of material influence

4.35 The CMA may also consider whether any other factors, such as agreements with the target company, might enable the acquirer materially to influence policy. Whilst there are no fixed types of agreement that will (or will not) be relevant to this assessment, such arrangements might include the provision of consultancy services to the target and other relevant customer/supplier relationships.

4.36 Financial arrangements may in certain circumstances confer material influence where the conditions are such that one party becomes so dependent on the other that the latter gains material influence over the company's commercial policy (for example, where a lender could threaten to withdraw loan facilities if a particular policy is not pursued, or where the loan conditions confer on the lender an ability to exercise rights over and above those necessary to protect its investment, say, by options to take control of the company or veto rights over certain strategic decisions).[54]

De facto control

4.37 Merger arrangements may give rise to a position of 'de facto' control when an entity controls a company's policy, notwithstanding that it holds less than the majority of voting rights in the target company (that is, it does not have a controlling interest). De facto control requires the ability to unilaterally determine (as opposed to just materially influence) a company's policy.[55] De facto control is likely to include situations where the acquirer has in practice control over more than half of the votes actually cast at shareholder meetings. However, other factors may be relevant and there is no 'bright line' between factors which might give rise to material influence and those giving rise to de facto control. For instance, de facto control might also involve situations where an investor's industry expertise might lead to its advice being followed to a greater extent than its shareholding would seem to warrant.

4.38 The CMA has the ability under section 26(3) of the Act to decide whether or not to treat 'de facto' control as equivalent to 'control' for the purposes of establishing whether enterprises have been 'brought under common ownership or common control' within the meaning of the Act.

A controlling interest

4.39 A 'controlling interest' generally means a shareholding conferring more than 50% of the voting rights in a company. Only one shareholder can have a controlling interest, but it is not uncommon for a company to be subject to the control (in the wider senses described above) of two or more major shareholders at the same time - in a joint venture, for instance. Therefore, a significant minority shareholder may be seen as being able materially to influence a company's policy even though someone else owns a controlling interest.

ACQUIRING CONTROL BY STAGES

4.40 Under section 26(4) of the Act, should a shareholding (and/or a level of board representation) that confers the ability materially to influence a company's policy increase subsequently to a level that amounts to 'de facto' control or a controlling interest, that further acquisition may produce a new relevant merger situation (which is therefore potentially liable to reference for a phase 2 investigation and to the imposition of remedies at the end of the phase 2 process). The same applies to a move from 'de facto' control to a controlling interest.[56,57]

4.41 In principle, therefore, if Company A acquires Company B in stages, this could give rise to three separate relevant merger situations: first, as Company A acquires material influence; then to 'de facto' control; and, finally, to a controlling interest.[58] But further acquisitions of a company's shares by a person who already owns a controlling interest do not give rise to a new merger situation.

4.42 For the purposes of a merger reference, where a person acquires control of an enterprise (in any of the three senses described above) during a series of transactions or successive events within a single two-year period, sections 27(5) and 29 of the Act allow them to be treated as having occurred or occurring simultaneously on the date of the last transaction.[59] The CMA has discretion in whether to apply these sections. In exercising this discretion, the CMA will have regard to the nature and extent of any competition issues associated with the merger.[60] In giving effect to these provisions, the CMA may take into account transactions in contemplation (that is, where the last of the events has not yet occurred).[61]

4.43 A new merger situation would not arise directly from the fact that there has been a reduction in the level of a shareholder's control (for example from a controlling interest to 'de facto' control). However, it is possible in these circumstances that a merger situation could arise through a third party thereby acquiring material influence, 'de facto' control or a controlling interest.

TEMPORARY MERGER SITUATIONS

4.44 The Act does not define the period of time that a merger situation should last in order for it to qualify as a relevant merger situation under the Act.[62] In theory, therefore, acquisitions of control intended purely as a temporary step in a wider overall transaction might constitute a relevant merger situation. In practice, such arrangements might include break-up bids, stake-building in the context of a public bid[63], and 'warehousing' arrangements.[64]

4.45 Break-up bids occur where one or more entities purchase an enterprise pursuant to an agreement that the acquired enterprise will be divided up according to a pre-existing plan upon completion of the transaction. In some cases, the break-up bid is structured in anticipation of merger control concerns that would otherwise occur. The question therefore arises whether the CMA will consider the first step (that is, the initial acquisition of the target enterprise) as a separate relevant merger situation concerning the entire target enterprise, or whether it will examine the ultimate acquisitions in the second step (that is, after the target enterprise is split up).[65]

4.46 The nature of the voluntary regime under the Act means there is, as a starting point, no requirement on the party or parties acquiring control under the first step in the above scenario to notify the CMA about the initial acquisition.

4.47 In terms of whether the CMA will investigate the initial acquisition on its own initiative, the CMA will generally be unlikely to do so where it is clear that it will be merely an interim step in the context of a wider transaction and that the subsequent steps will occur within the four-month time period within which the CMA has the ability to refer the initial acquisition. Where it appears that the subsequent steps may not take place within four months of the completion of the initial acquisition, the CMA will not risk losing its ability to refer the initial acquisition simply on the basis that it is intended that the current situation will not be permanent.

4.48 Where the initial acquisition is notified to it (whether the initial acquisition is anticipated or completed), the CMA would not be able to clear the transaction unconditionally simply on the basis that the situation as notified was not intended to be permanent. To avoid any referral for a phase 2 investigation that would otherwise be required on the basis of the initial acquisition, the CMA would require UILs (potentially effectively formalising in undertakings the merger parties' intended break-up).

ASSOCIATED PERSONS

4.49 For the purposes of considering whether an enterprise has ceased to be distinct, section 127 of the Act requires the CMA to consider whether a number of persons acquiring an enterprise are in fact 'associated persons' and thus should be viewed as acting together.

4.50 This situation will most commonly arise where the acquiring persons are related or have a signed agreement to act jointly to make an acquisition.[66] The Act does not require that each of the acquiring parties should themselves individually have control over the acquired entity for them all to be regarded as being associated persons.[67] Separate groups of enterprises may be associated persons where a single member that is an associated person to each of those groups is common to both groups.[68]

TIME LIMITS FOR REFERENCE DECISIONS

4.51 After starting an investigation, the CMA is in most cases required to decide whether the test for reference is met within a timetable of 40 working days,[69] failing which it loses its ability to refer the merger to a phase 2 inquiry. Where merger parties notify the CMA using a Merger Notice, that timetable (referred to in the Act as the 'initial period') starts on the first working day after the CMA confirms to the merger parties that the Merger Notice is complete.[70] In other cases, the timetable starts on the first working day after the CMA confirms that it has received sufficient information to enable it to begin its investigation.[71] The 40 working day deadline is subject to extension in certain circumstances,[72] and does not apply to decisions by the Secretary of State to refer a merger after issuing an intervention notice.

4.52 In addition, for the CMA to be able to refer a merger either:

(a) the merger must not yet have taken place (that is, the parties must not yet have ceased to be distinct); or

(b) under section 24 of the Act, the completed merger must have taken place not more than four months before the reference is made, unless the merger took place without having been made public and without the CMA being informed of it (in which case the four-month period starts from the earlier of the time that material facts are made public or the time the CMA is told of material facts).

4.53 The test under the Act for when material facts are 'made public' is when they are 'so publicised as to be generally known or readily ascertainable'.[73] In interpreting these provisions of the Act, the CMA will have regard to the following factors:

(a) The CMA interprets 'material facts' as being the necessary facts that are relevant to the determination of the CMA's jurisdiction in terms of the four-month time period (but not facts relevant to other aspects of whether a relevant merger situation exists for the purposes of the Act). In practice, this means information on the identity of the merger parties and whether the transaction remains anticipated (including the status of any conditions precedent to completion) or has completed.[74]

(b) Where the merger parties do not notify the CMA, but 'make public' material facts about the transaction such that they are generally known or reasonably ascertainable, the CMA interprets this as meaning that such information could readily be ascertained by the CMA acting reasonably and diligently in accordance with its statutory functions. In practical terms, the CMA would consider that an acquiring party would normally be said to have 'made public' material facts where those facts had been publicised in the national[75] or relevant trade press in the UK and where the acquiring party had itself taken steps to publicise the transaction at large, normally by publishing and prominently displaying on its own website a press release about the transaction.[76]

4.54 The Act permits the CMA to extend the four-month time period in certain circumstances. When examining completed mergers, for example, the CMA may under section 25 of the Act extend that period if an information request issued by it under section 109 of the Act is not complied with (for example, information is not supplied within the stated deadline).[77]

4.55 As described at paragraph 4.42 above, section 27(5) of the Act allows the CMA to treat successive events within a period of two years between the same parties as occurring simultaneously on the date of the latest event.

THE TURNOVER TEST

4.56 The 'turnover test' is met where:

(a) the annual UK turnover of the enterprise being acquired exceeds £70 million[78]; or

(b) where the enterprise being taken over (or part of it) is a relevant enterprise, the relevant enterprise's annual UK turnover exceeds £1 million.

Enterprise being acquired

4.57 Under section 28 of the Act, two types of situation may be distinguished for the purposes of calculating turnover: those where one or more enterprises remain under the same ownership and control after the merger as they were under before it, and those where no enterprise remains under the same ownership and control after the merger.

4.58 Where one or more enterprises remain under the same ownership and control after the merger, turnover is calculated by taking the total value of all enterprises ceasing to be distinct (that is, the acquiring entities and target entities) and deducting the turnover of those enterprises that remain under the same ownership and control after the merger.

(a) This situation includes a straightforward acquisition, in which the acquirer (A) and the target (T) cease to be distinct from each other. The turnover of the acquirer is deducted as it remains under the same ownership and control after the merger. The relevant turnover is therefore that of the target. (See Figure 1 below.)

(b) It also includes a situation where two or more companies (A and B) form a joint venture incorporating their assets and businesses in a particular area of activity. In this situation, each parent with control ceases to be distinct from the target business contributed to the joint venture by the other parent.[79] As all the parent companies remain under the same ownership and control after the merger,[80] and therefore have their turnover deducted, the turnover is the sum of the turnover of each of the contributed enterprises (which are, effectively, the target enterprises) (TA and TB).[81] (See Figure 2 below.)

4.59 Where no enterprises remain under the same ownership and control after the merger, the relevant turnover is calculated by taking the total value of all enterprises ceasing to be distinct and deducting the turnover of the enterprise with the highest UK turnover.

(a) This includes a situation in which two enterprises (A and B) come together to form a full legal merger.[82] The relevant turnover would be that of the existing enterprise with the smaller UK turnover (B). (See Figure 3 below.)

(b) It also includes a situation in which two or more companies (A, B and C) form a joint venture (Newco) incorporating all of their assets and businesses. The relevant turnover would be that of all the existing companies, excluding the company with the largest UK turnover. (See Figure 4 below.)

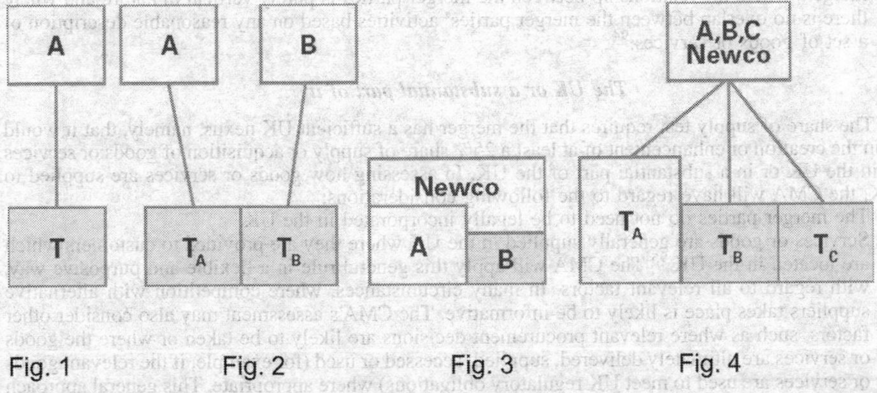

Fig. 1 Fig. 2 Fig. 3 Fig. 4

Shaded areas mark those businesses to be included in the turnover calculation

Calculation of turnover

4.60 In principle, the turnover test applies to the turnover of the acquired enterprise that was generated in relation to customers within the UK[83] in the business year preceding the date of completion of the merger or, if the merger has not yet taken place, the date of the reference for a phase 2 investigation.[84] The figures in the enterprise's latest published accounts will normally be sufficient to measure whether the turnover test is met, unless there have been significant changes since the accounts were prepared.[85] In this circumstance, more recent accounts would provide a better guide to the actual turnover of the enterprises concerned. Where company accounts do not provide a relevant figure, for example because only part of a business is being acquired or the accounts do not provide a suitable geographic breakdown of turnover, the CMA will consider evidence presented by the merger parties and other interested parties to form its own view as to what it believes to be the value of UK turnover for jurisdictional purposes.

4.61 The basic principles set out above are elaborated further in Annex A.

THE SHARE OF SUPPLY TEST

4.62 Under section 23 of the Act, the 'share of supply test' is satisfied if the merged enterprises:

(a) both[86] either supply or acquire goods or services of a particular description in the UK;[87] and

(b) will, after the merger,[88] supply or acquire 25% or more of those goods or services, in the UK as a whole or in a substantial part of it.

The supply or acquisition of goods or services of any description

4.63 The Act confers on the CMA a broad discretion to identify, for the purposes of applying the share of supply test, a specific category of goods or services supplied or acquired by the merger parties.[89] In applying the share of supply test, the CMA will have regard to the following considerations:

(a) The share of supply test is not an economic assessment of the type used in the CMA's substantive assessment; therefore, the group of goods or services to which the jurisdictional test is applied need not amount to a relevant economic market, and can aggregate, for example, intra-group and third party sales even if these might be treated differently in the substantive assessment.[90] As such, the description of goods or services to which the jurisdictional test is applied may differ from the relevant economic market used for the purposes of the substantive assessment of the merger.[91]

(b) The CMA will have regard to any reasonable description of a set of goods or services to determine whether the share of supply test is met. Whilst the share of supply used may correspond with a standard recognised by the industry in question, this need not necessarily be the case.

(c) The CMA will consider the commercial reality of the merger parties' activities when assessing how goods or services are supplied, focussing on the substance rather than the legal form of arrangements. Firms can engage in a variety of different business models and offer differentiated products or services, and the forms of supply which firms may offer in competition with one another can vary significantly. The CMA will consider whether there are sufficient elements of common functionality between the merger parties' activities.[92] Moreover, the CMA will take account of the life cycle of the supplies in question, noting that parties may have a material presence in the UK market by virtue of pipeline products or services,[93] or other factors.

(d) In applying the share of supply test, the CMA may, under section 23(8) of the Act, apply such criteria as it considers appropriate to decide whether certain goods or services should be treated as goods or services of a separate description (and therefore not taken into account in assessing whether the share of supply test is met) in any particular case. The same approach applies to whether goods or services are of the same description.

(e) The CMA cannot apply the share of supply test unless the merger parties together supply or acquire the same category of goods and services (of any description). The test cannot capture mergers where the relationship between the merger parties is purely vertical in nature and where there is no overlap between the merger parties' activities based on any reasonable description of a set of goods or services.[94]

The UK or a substantial part of it

4.64 The share of supply test requires that the merger has a sufficient UK nexus, namely, that it would result in the creation or enhancement of at least a 25% share of supply or acquisition of goods or services either in the UK or in a substantial part of the UK. In assessing how goods or services are supplied to the UK, the CMA will have regard to the following considerations:

(a) The merger parties do not need to be legally incorporated in the UK.

(b) Services or goods are generally supplied in the UK where they are provided to customers which are located in the UK.[95] The CMA will apply this general rule in a flexible and purposive way, with regard to all relevant factors. In many circumstances, where competition with alternative suppliers takes place is likely to be informative. The CMA's assessment may also consider other factors, such as where relevant procurement decisions are likely to be taken or where the goods or services are ultimately delivered, supplied, accessed or used (for example, if the relevant goods or services are used to meet UK regulatory obligations) where appropriate. This general approach also applies in the case of sales to multinational companies, irrespective of place of incorporation, domicile or principal place of business.

(c) The CMA will also have regard to the nature of the relationships between the merger parties and their customers (including as between different customer groups). While the CMA will consider direct contractual relationships, it may also consider customer relationships that are not governed by contract,[96] as well as other relevant factors. For example, under section 128 of the Act, the supply of services includes the provision of services by making them available to potential users,[97] and making arrangements for the use of computer software.[98]

Substantial part of the UK

4.65 The share of supply test may be applied to the UK as a whole or to a substantial part of it. The test may be satisfied on the basis of the share of supply or acquisition in a relatively wide geographic area (such as the UK, Great Britain, England, Scotland, Wales or Northern Ireland), even if the transaction's competitive impact is more likely to be regional or local in nature.[99]

4.66 There is no statutory definition of 'a substantial part'. The House of Lords (now the Supreme Court of the UK) ruled in the context of similar provisions in the Fair Trading Act 1973 that, while there can be no fixed definition, the area or areas considered must be of such size, character and importance as to make it worth consideration for the purposes of merger control.[100] The CMA will take such factors into account as: the size, population, social, political, economic, financial and geographic significance of the specified area or areas, and whether it is (or they are) special or significant in some way.[101]

4.67 There is no need in the application of the share of supply test for the substantial part of the UK to constitute an undivided geographic area. This interpretation gives effect to the purposes of the Act. The economic significance of a merger, in terms of a substantial lessening of competition, does not necessarily depend on whether several localities are contiguous or separated.[102]

The 25% Threshold

4.68 Under section 23(3) and (4) of the Act, the share of supply test is satisfied where the merger will result in a share of supply of 25% or more in relation to the supply of goods or services of any description in the UK or in a substantial part of the UK.

4.69 Accordingly, where an enterprise already supplies or acquires 25% of any particular goods or services, the test is satisfied so long as its share is increased as a result of the merger, regardless of the size of the increment.[103] Where there is no increment, the share of supply test is not met (subject to the exceptions and special regimes described below).

4.70 In applying the share of supply test, the CMA may under section 23(5) of the Act have regard to the value, cost, price, quantity, capacity, number of workers employed[104] or any other criterion, or combination of criteria, in determining whether the 25% threshold is met.[105]

EXCEPTIONS AND SPECIAL REGIMES

4.71 The following exceptions and special regimes apply in relation to the share of supply test:

(a) No increment is required in relation to the shares of supply of newspapers and/or broadcasting where the Secretary of State issues a special intervention notice (see paragraph 16.15 below).

(b) For mergers in which the enterprise being taken over (or part of it) is a relevant enterprise (see paragraphs 4.4 to 4.5 above), the share of supply test is met if, before the merger, the relevant enterprise being acquired or merged has a share of supply or purchase of 25% or more of relevant goods or services in the UK or in a substantial part of it. The test is met even if the share of supply does not increase as a result of the merger. The relevant goods or services for the purposes of deciding whether the share of supply test is met are those by virtue of which the target enterprise qualifies as a relevant enterprise. This provision adds to, rather than replaces, the share of supply test discussed in paragraph 4.62 above.

4.72 For mergers involving two or more 'water enterprises' the jurisdictional test is based on turnover only (see paragraph 17.1 below for further information).

4.73 The increase in the share of supply (referred to in paragraph 4.69) must result from the enterprises ceasing to be distinct. In the case of an acquisition, this requires calculation of the share of supply based on the activities of the acquirer and the target company. In joint venture situations, the share of supply is calculated by reference to the activities of the joint venture, although it will include shares of the controlling joint venture parents where they remain active in the same activities as the joint venture. For example, where two companies, Company A and Company B, form a joint venture incorporating their assets and businesses in a particular area of activity, enterprises TA and TB respectively, the share of supply test is applied with reference to whether there is an increase in the share of supply between A, B, TA and TB in relation to the areas of activity in which TA and/or TB are active. The CMA would therefore not apply the share of supply test as between A and B outside the areas of activity of the joint venture.

NOTES

17 See paragraphs 2.6 and 2.7 above in relation to the standard of proof required for these decisions at phase 1 and phase 2.

18 It may, in certain limited circumstances, be appropriate to treat a single commercial transaction as giving rise to more than one relevant merger situation. See, for example, CMA Decision: Completed acquisition by Circle Health Holdings of GHG Healthcare Holdings (8 April 2020); CMA Decision: Anticipated joint venture between Dawn Meats and Dunbia (12 October 2017); and the CC's Thomas Cook Group plc/Co-operative Group Limited/Midlands Co-operative Society Limited inquiry (2011). In contrast, in some circumstances it may be appropriate to treat more than one commercial transaction as a single relevant merger situation. See, for example, CMA Decision: Anticipated acquisition by Motor Fuel Limited of 90 petrol stations from Shell Service Station Properties Limited, Shell U.K. Limited and GOGB Limited (26 August 2015).

19 Section 23 of the Act.

20 See paragraphs 4.10 to 4.19 below.

21 See further paragraphs 4.56 to 4.61 below.

22 See further paragraphs 4.62 to 4.67below.

23 In this context, the date of the merger refers to the date when the enterprises cease to be distinct (see section 24(1) of the Act).

24 See for example sections 25, 42 and 122 of the Act.

25 BEIS Guidance: Enterprise Act 2002: changes to the turnover and share of supply tests for mergers (June 2020). This can be found at https://assets.publishing.service.gov.uk/government/uploads/system/uploads/attachment_data/file/902531/ Enterprise_Act_2002_guidance_on_changes_to_the_turnover_and_share_of_supply_tests_for_mergers__Orders_2020_.pdf.

26 As above.

27 In the case of a public bid, this will generally mean announcement of a possible offer or of a firm intention to make an offer.

28 Section 26 of the Act. In the case of a 'start-up' joint venture, the question under the Act will be whether the activities transferred to the joint venture by one or more parents (or acquired from a third party) are sufficient to constitute an enterprise.

29 See for example CMA Decision: Anticipated acquisition by Roche Holdings of Spark Therapeutics (16 December 2019).

30 See CMA Decision: Anticipated acquisition by Bupa Insurance Limited of Civil Service Healthcare Society Limited (24 September 2020). NHS Foundation Trusts may also constitute enterprises for this purpose - see CMA Guidance on the review of NHS mergers (CMA29). See also CMA Decision: Anticipated merger between The Royal Bournemouth and Christchurch Hospitals NHS Foundation Trust and Poole Hospital NHS Foundation Trust (27 April 2020).

31 For example, the fact that the merger was effected via two legal agreements rather than a single agreement did not mean that the target did not constitute one enterprise in CMA Decision: Completed acquisition by Rentokil Initial plc of MPCL Ltd (formerly Mitie Pest Control Ltd) (12 April 2019), and the fact that there was no direct sale agreement between the existing cinema operator and the new cinema operator did not preclude enterprises ceasing to be distinct for the purposes of the Act in the OFT Decision: Anticipated acquisition by Cineworld Group plc, through its subsidiary Cine-UK Limited, of the Cinema Business operating at the Hollywood Green Leisure Park, Wood Green (17 March 2008).

32 For instance, there is no requirement for the inclusion of physical assets. See CMA Decisions: Completed agreement between Aer Lingus Limited and CityJet designated Activity Company (21 December 2018); Anticipated acquisition by Arla Foods Limited of Yeo Valley Dairies Limited, including a licence to supply certain dairy products under the Yeo Valley brand (11 July 2018); and Completed acquisition by Medtronic plc of certain assets of Animas Corporation (30 May 2018).

33 *Société Cooperative De Production Seafrance SA (Respondent) v The Competition and Markets Authority and another (Appellants)* [2015] UKSC 75 *("Eurotunnel")* at paragraphs 39 and 40, endorsing the CAT's view in *Groupe Eurotunnel SA v Competition Commission* [2013] CAT 30 at paragraph 105.

34 *Société Cooperative De Production Seafrance SA (Respondent) v The Competition and Markets Authority and another (Appellants)* [2015] UKSC 75 *("Eurotunnel")* at paragraphs 39 and 40.

35 See the CC's inquiry into the Anticipated joint venture between The British Broadcasting Corporation, ITV Broadcasting Limited, Channel 4 Television Corporation, Channel 5 Broadcasting Limited, British Telecommunications plc, Talk Talk Telecoms Limited and Arqiva Limited – Project Canvas inquiry (2010) and OFT Decision: Completed supplier agreement between Guestlogix Inc and Panasonic Avionics in respect of a commercial arrangement to provide services in the devel-

opment of onboard point of sale payment facility integrated into in-flight entertainment systems (21 December 2012).

36 See CMA Decisions: Completed acquisition by Medtronic plc of certain assets of Animas Corporation (30 May 2018); Completed agreement between Aer Lingus Limited and CityJet designated Activity Company (21 December 2018).

37 The Transfer of Undertakings (Protection of Employment) Regulations 2006.

38 See, for example, CMA Decisions: Completed agreement between Aer Lingus Limited and CityJet designated Activity Company (21 December 2018); Anticipated acquisition by Arla Foods Limited of Yeo Valley Dairies Limited, including a licence to supply certain dairy products under the Yeo Valley brand (11 July 2018); and Completed acquisition by Medtronic plc of certain assets of Animas Corporation (30 May 2018).

39 See CMA Decision: Completed acquisition by Medtronic plc of certain assets of Animas Corporation (30 May 2018).

40 See CMA Decision: Anticipated acquisition by DHL Supply Chain Limited of the enterprise constituted by the secondary distribution assets of Carlsberg Supply Company UK Limited (13 January 2017), OFT Decisions: Anticipated contract award to Nuclear Management Partners Limited as the Parent Body Organisation for Sellafield Limited (22 October 2008), and Completed acquisition by AEG Facilities (UK) Limited of the contract to manage Wembley Arena (22 March 2013). Similar principles apply in relation to the award of contracts or concessions. See CMA decision: Acquisition by Keolis Amey Docklands Limited of the Docklands Light Railway Franchise (14 November 2014), OFT Decision: Anticipated acquisition by Tramlink Nottingham Consortium of NET Phase Two concession (12 September 2011).

41 Considered in *Société Coopérative de Production SeaFrance SA v Competition and Markets Authority* [2015] UKSC 75 at paragraph 37 ff. See also *Groupe Eurotunnel SA v Competition Commission* [2013] CAT 30, and *Groupe Eurotunnel SA v Competition and Markets Authority* [2015] CAT 1. Although these judgments considered the acquisition of assets from an entity that was no longer actively trading, the CMA considers that the principles are of broader application, including to cases in which the target business has not yet started actively trading.

42 See for example, OFT Decision: Completed acquisition by European Metal Recycling of five sites and certain assets of SITA Metal Recycling (7 March 2014). It is not essential for the purposes of the jurisdictional test for the buyer to use the business assets in the same manner as they were used before transfer (including, if relevant, before the target enterprise ceased trading). See also OFT Decisions: Completed acquisition by a consortium of Shell UK Limited, Greenergy International Limited and Vopak Holdings UK Limited of certain assets of former Petroplus Refining and Marketing Limited (24 May 2013); and Completed acquisition by Servisair UK Limited of the regional ground handling business of Aviance UK Limited (27 May 2010).

43 See OFT Decisions: Completed acquisition by European Metal Recycling of five sites and certain assets of SITA Metal Recycling (7 March 2014); The assignment of a lease to Tesco plc for the site of a former FreshXpress store at St Helens (21 April 2009); Anticipated acquisition by Cineworld Group plc, through its subsidiary Cine-UK Limited, of the cinema business operating at the Hollywood Green Leisure Park, Wood Green (17 March 2008); and Completed acquisition by Home Retail Group plc of 27 leasehold properties from Focus (DIY) Limited (15 April 2008).

44 The CMA does not consider that material influence is likely to arise in situations where a shareholder has no more than the rights normally accorded to minority shareholders, such as rights in the context of a liquidation.

45 See, for example, the factors discussed in paragraphs 4.35 and 4.36 below. In its past decisional practice, the CMA has only rarely found shareholdings of less than 15% to confer material influence on the acquirer.

46 This does not mean that all cases in which parties obtain material influence through minority shareholdings need to be notified to the CMA, or will be investigated by the CMA on its own initiative. In deciding whether to investigate any such merger situation on its own initiative, the CMA will have regard to whether, on the information available to it, there is a reasonable chance that the test for a reference under the Act will be met.

47 See CMA Decision: Anticipated acquisition by RWE AG of a 16.67% minority stake in E.On SE (5 April 2019); CMA Decision: Anticipated acquisition by Prosafe SE of Floatel International Limited (5 September 2019); OFT Report: Acquisition by British Sky Broadcasting Group plc of a 17.9% in ITV plc; Report to the Secretary of State for Trade and Industry (14 December 2007) and *British Sky Broadcasting Group plc v the CC and the Secretary of State* [2008] CAT 25; and OFT Decision: Anticipated acquisition by Centrica plc of a 20% stake in Lake Acquisitions Limited (a wholly owned subsidiary of EDF SA) (7 August 2009).

48 Given that any prediction of attendance and voting at shareholders' meetings is complex, involving a wide range of factors, the CMA considers that patterns of participation at recent shareholders' meetings of a particular company (for example over the last three years) are likely to be the best available indication of future participation.

49 See CMA Final Report: Anticipated acquisition by Amazon of a minority shareholding and certain rights in Deliveroo (4 August 2020); CMA Decision: Anticipated acquisition by RWE AG of a 16.67% minority stake in E.On SE (5 April 2019) and the CC's British Sky Broadcasting Group/ITV plc inquiry (2007).

50 See CMA Final Report: Anticipated acquisition by Amazon of a minority shareholding and certain rights in Deliveroo (4 August 2020). See OFT Decisions: Completed acquisition by JCDecaux UK Limited of rights in Concourse Initiatives Limited and Media Initiatives Limited (19 March 2012); and Anticipated acquisition by Centrica plc of a 20% stake in Lake Acquisitions Limited (a wholly owned subsidiary of EDF SA) (7 August 2009).

51 This does not mean that all cases in which parties obtain material influence through board representation need to be notified to the CMA. See footnote 46 above for analogous considerations in the context of minority shareholdings.

52 See CMA Decision: Anticipated acquisition by RWE AG of a 16.67% minority stake in E.On SE (8 April 2019). See the CC's report: Acquisition by British Sky Broadcasting Group of 17.9 per cent of the shares in ITV (14 December 2007).

53 See CMA Final Report: Anticipated acquisition by Amazon of a minority shareholding and certain rights in Deliveroo (4 August 2020). See OFT Decision: Completed acquisition by First Milk Limited of a 15% stake in Robert Wiseman Dairies plc (7 April 2005).

54 See OFT Decision: Completed acquisition by First Milk Limited of a 15% stake in Robert Wiseman Dairies plc (7 April 2005).

55 See CMA Final Report: Completed acquisition by Hunter Douglas N.V. of convertible loan notes and certain rights in 247 Home Furnishings Ltd. in 2013 and the completed acquisition by Hunter Douglas N.V. of a controlling interest in 247 Home Furnishings Ltd. in 2019 (14 September 2020).

56 See CMA Final Report: Completed acquisition by Hunter Douglas N.V. of convertible loan notes and certain rights in 247 Home Furnishings Ltd. in 2013 and the completed acquisition by Hunter Douglas N.V. of a controlling interest in 247 Home Furnishings Ltd. in 2019 (14 September 2020); and OFT Decision: Anticipated acquisition by Cavendish Square

Partners (General Partner) Limited of a controlling interest in each of Lakeside 1 Limited (Keepmoat) and Apollo Group Holdings Limited (Apollo) (24 November 2011).

57 Such cases may qualify on the share of supply test (as well as the turnover test) given that section 26(4) of the Act allows for the acquirer to be 'treated' as bringing the target under its control (notwithstanding that it already had material influence or 'de facto' control over the target) such that there would therefore (under such 'treatment') be an increment in the share of supply.

58 See OFT Decisions: Anticipated acquisition by The Coca-Cola Company of full control over Fresh Trading Limited (1 May 2013); Completed acquisition by Travis Perkins plc of a controlling interest in Toolstation Limited (29 March 2012); and Anticipated acquisition by Cavendish Square Partners (General Partner) Limited of a controlling interest in each of Lakeside 1 Limited (Keepmoat) and Apollo Group Holdings Limited (Apollo) (24 November 2011).

59 See CMA Decision: Completed acquisition by Co-operative Foodstores Limited of eight My Local grocery stores from ML Convenience Limited and MLCG Limited (19 October 2016); and OFT Decision: Completed acquisition by Dairy Crest Group plc of certain assets of Arla Foods UK plc (8 January 2007).

60 See OFT Decision: Completed acquisitions by Tesco plc of the Co-operative Group's stores in Uxbridge Road, Slough (2 February 2004), in which the OFT declined to exercise its discretion.

61 Article 3 of the Enterprise Act 2002 (Anticipated Mergers) Order 2003 SI2003/1595 (as amended).

62 See CMA Decision: Completed agreement between Aer Lingus Limited and CityJet designated Activity Company (21 December 2018).

63 In this situation, the CMA's decision if and when to investigate on its own initiative a minority interest will depend on all the circumstances of the case (including the likelihood of a public bid being launched), and in particular its belief as to the extent of the competition concerns that could potentially result from a minority shareholding.

64 'Warehousing' refers to a situation where a transferring business is temporarily acquired by an interim buyer, often a bank, on the basis of an agreement for the subsequent onward sale of the business to an ultimate acquirer.

65 The CMA will apply similar principles to those set out in paragraphs 4.47 to 4.48 in the context of joint acquisitions for a start-up period.

66 See *Lebedev Holdings Limited and Another v Secretary of State for Digital, Culture, Media and Sport* [2019] CAT 21, at paragraph 30.

67 See *Groupe Eurotunnel SA v Competition Commission* [2013] CAT 30 at paragraph 57, *Groupe Eurotunnel SA v Competition and Markets Authority* [2015] CAT 1 at paragraph 79(c), *Société Coopérative de Production SeaFrance SA v Competition and Markets Authority* [2015] UKSC 75 at paragraph 6.

68 See *Lebedev Holdings Limited and Another v Secretary of State for Digital, Culture, Media and Sport* [2019] CAT 21 at paragraphs 66-67; CMA Report to the Secretary of State for Digital, Culture, Media and Sport: Completed acquisition by Mr. Sultan Muhammad Abduljadayel and Wondrous Investment Holdings LP. of Independent Digital News and Media Limited and Lebedev Holdings Limited (28 June 2019); and OFT Decisions: Anticipated joint venture between The British Broadcasting Corporation, ITV Broadcasting Limited, Channel 4 Television Corporation, Channel 5 Broadcasting Limited, British Telecommunications plc, Talk Talk Telecoms Limited and Arqiva Limited - Project Canvas (19 May 2010); and Anticipated acquisition by Tramlink Nottingham Consortium of Net Phase 2 Concession (12 September 2011).

69 If parties choose not to notify a completed merger, the initial period for the CMA's Phase 1 investigation may be reduced to fewer than 40 working days by virtue of the four-month statutory deadline for a reference with which the CMA must also comply under the Act.

70 Section 34ZA(3)(a) of the Act. A Merger Notice must meet the requirements set out in section 96(2) of the Act. Further information on notifying mergers to the CMA is set out in chapter 6.

71 Section 34ZA(3)(b) of the Act.

72 Section 34ZB of the Act. These include where relevant parties have failed to comply with the requirements of a formal information request under section 109 of the Act and where the Secretary of State has served an intervention notice in relation to a merger which may raise public interest issues.

73 Section 24(3) of the Act.

74 See *Lebedev Holdings Limited and Another v Secretary of State for Digital, Culture, Media and Sport* [2019] CAT 21 at paragraphs 60, 64-68; CMA Report to the Secretary of State for Digital, Culture, Media and Sport: Completed acquisition by Mr. Sultan Muhammad Abduljadayel and Wondrous Investment Holdings LP. of Independent Digital News and Media Limited and Lebedev Holdings Limited (28 June 2019). See also CMA Final Report: Completed acquisition by Ecolab Inc. of the Holchem Group Limited (8 October 2019) at paragraph 4.6 where a public announcement by Ecolab shortly after the Merger completed did not constitute material facts about the Merger being made public because the press release erroneously indicated that the Merger had not completed. See also the CC's report: Icopal Holding A/S and Icopal a/s: A report on the merger situation (2001) at paragraph 2.50. That report concerned the application of the equivalent provisions of the Fair Trading Act 1973, but the result would not have differed under the Act.

75 See *Lebedev Holdings Limited and Another v Secretary of State for Digital, Culture, Media and Sport* [2019] CAT 21, at paragraph 53.

76 See OFT Decisions: Completed acquisition by Genus plc of Local Breeders Limited (14 May 2008) and Completed acquisition by Tesco Stores Limited of Brian Ford's Discount Store Limited (22 December 2008). For a discussion of steps which were not considered by the CMA to give rise to material facts being made public, see CMA Final Report: Completed acquisition by Bottomline Technologies (de), Inc. of Experian Limited's Experian Payments Gateway business and related assets (2020), at paragraph 5.26.

77 Other circumstances in which the CMA can extend the four month time period include, for example, by agreement with the merger parties and in certain circumstances following the giving of an intervention notice by the Secretary of State. See, in those respects, sections 25 and 42 of the Act.

78 See the Enterprise Act 2002 (Merger Fees and Determination of Turnover) Order 2003 SI 2003/1370 (as amended).

79 See CMA Decision: Anticipated joint venture between Anglian Water Group Ltd and Northumbrian Water Group Ltd (1 August 2017). See the CC's report: A report on the anticipated joint venture between BBC Worldwide Limited, Channel Four Television Corporation and ITV plc relating to the video on demand sector (2009), at paragraph 3.53.

80 In certain cases, the CMA may treat entry into a joint venture as giving rise to more than one relevant merger situation (see footnote 18 above). In such a case, the CMA will treat the turnover of the enterprise being taken over as being the turnover of the enterprises contributed to the joint venture by the other parent(s).

[81] See OFT Decision: Anticipated relevant joint venture between Goodrich Corporation and Rolls-Royce plc (8 December 2008).

[82] A full legal merger occurs where a full merger of A and B as equals is achieved by Newco C acquiring both. In this circumstance, neither A nor B survives the merger. Both firms are brought under common control, but neither remains under the same control as it was pre-merger. The turnovers to be considered are those of A and B.

[83] For the purpose of the geographic allocation of turnover, subject to complying with the Enterprise Act 2002 (Merger Fees and Determination of Turnover) Order 2003 SI 2003/1370 (as amended), the CMA will follow the approach set out in Annex A. Subject to the qualifications outlined in Annex A, the general rule is that turnover should be regarded as UK turnover for the purposes of the Act when the customer is located in the UK. The CMA will have regard to whether sales are made directly or indirectly (via agents or traders) to UK customers.

[84] In some cases, this may include intra-group sales (for example where a target business previously made intra-group sales, which would become external sales as a result of the acquisition of the target by a third party). See further Annex A. Such considerations were relevant in OFT Decision: Anticipated joint venture between Vodafone Limited and Telefonica UK Limited (28 September 2012).

[85] In line with Article 11(3) of the Enterprise Act 2002 (Merger Fees and Determination of Turnover) Order 2003 SI 2003/1370 (as amended), the CMA would regard acquisitions or divestments or other transactions or events as relevant for these purposes, but considers that the gain or loss of individual customers would, absent exceptional circumstances, be unlikely to be relevant.

[86] Where more than two enterprises cease to be distinct, at least two of them must supply or acquire such goods or services.

[87] See, for example, CMA Decision: Anticipated acquisition by Roche Holdings, Inc. of Spark Therapeutics, Inc (10 February 2020) where the CMA found that the share of supply test was satisfied (on an alternative basis) based on the number of patents procured by the merger parties.

[88] In accordance with section 23(9) of the Act, the CMA assesses whether the share of supply test is met at the time of its decision on reference, unless the reference of an anticipated merger is subsequently treated by the CMA as being a reference of a completed merger pursuant to section 37(2) of the Act (in which case, it is at such time as the CMA may determine).

[89] Section 23 of the Act.

[90] See CMA Decision: Anticipated acquisition by Roche Holdings, Inc. of Spark Therapeutics, Inc (10 February 2020) and OFT Decision: Anticipated acquisition by Montauban S.A. of Simon Group plc (21 August 2006).

[91] See CMA Decisions: Anticipated acquisition by Roche Holdings, Inc. of Spark Therapeutics, Inc (10 February 2020); Completed acquisition by ION Investment Group Limited of Broadway Technology Holdings LLC (7 July 2020); Anticipated acquisition by LN-Gaiety Holdings Limited of MCD Productions Unlimited Company (11 July 2019).

[92] See CMA Decision: Anticipated acquisition by Visa International Service Association of Plaid Inc (24 August 2020); CMA Final Report: Completed acquisition by Linergy of Ulster Farm By-Products (6 January 2016).

[93] See CMA Decision: Anticipated acquisition by Roche Holdings, Inc. of Spark Therapeutics, Inc (10 February 2020).

[94] In CMA Decision: Completed acquisition by Google LLC of Looker Data Sciences, Inc. (13 February 2020), the share of supply test was applicable where parties were active at the same level of the supply chain, in addition to being vertically related. See also OFT Decisions: Completed acquisition by GFI Group Inc of Trayport Limited (28 May 2008) and Completed acquisition by the BUPA Group of the Cromwell Hospital (24 June 2008).

[95] The mere fact that a supplier is located in the UK is therefore not conclusive that services are being supplied in the UK. Conversely, suppliers based overseas may be supplying services in the UK.

[96] In some cases, interactions between firms and their customers might not be reduced to single (formal) 'procurement' decisions giving rise to direct contractual relationships, and it may be necessary to consider the significance of commercial relationships in the round. See, for example, CMA Decision: Anticipated acquisition by Evolution Gaming Group AB of NetEnt AB (8 December 2020).

[97] Section 128(3) of the Act. See CMA Request pursuant to article 22 of Council Regulation (EC) 139/2004: Anticipated acquisition by Mastercard Incorporated of Parts of the Corporate Services Business of Nets A/S (16 March 2020).

[98] Section 128(4) of the Act. See CMA Decision: Completed acquisition by ION Investment Group Limited of Broadway Technology Holdings LLC (7 July 2020).

[99] See CMA Final Report: Anticipated acquisition by LN-Gaiety Holdings Ltd of MCD Productions Unlimited Company (19 December 2019).

[100] See *Regina v Monopolies and Mergers Commission and another ex parte South Yorkshire Transport Limited* [1993] 1 WLR 23, at paragraphs 31A to 32B: " . . . the epithet "substantial" is there to ensure that the expensive, laborious and time-consuming mechanism of a merger reference is not set in motion if the effort is not worthwhile . . . [To be a substantial part of the UK] "the part must be of such size, character and importance as to make it worth consideration for the purposes of the Act."

[101] See CMA Decisions: Completed acquisition by Novo Invest GmbH acting through Novomatic UK Ltd of Talarius Limited (28 October 2016); Completed acquisition by Co-operative Foodstores Limited of eight My Local grocery stores from ML Convenience Limited and MLCG Limited (19 October 2016); Anticipated acquisition by Co-operative Foodstores Limited of 15 Budgens grocery stores from Booker Retail Partners (GB) Limited (6 June 2016); Completed acquisition by LN-Gaiety Holdings Limited of MAMA & Company Limited (19 February 2016); Completed acquisition by Oasis Dental Care (Central) Limited of Total Orthodontics Limited (2 September 2015).

[102] See CMA Decisions: Completed acquisition by Henderson Retail Limited of part of the Martin McColl Limited portfolio (16 February 2018); Completed acquisition by Novo Invest GmbH acting through Novomatic UK Ltd of Talarius Limited (28 October 2016); See also the CC's report: A report on the acquisition by Archant Limited of the London newspapers of Independent News and Media Limited (22 September 2004).

[103] See, for example, CMA Final Report: Anticipated acquisition by LN-Gaiety Holdings Ltd of MCD Productions Unlimited Company (19 December 2019).

[104] See CMA Decision: Anticipated acquisition by Roche Holdings, Inc. of Spark Therapeutics, Inc (10 February 2020).

[105] In the CMA Decision: Anticipated acquisition by Roche Holdings, Inc. of Spark Therapeutics, Inc (10 February 2020), the CMA relied on the number of patents procured by the merger parties as an alternative basis to satisfy the share of supply test. In CMA Request pursuant to article 22 of Council Regulation (EC) 139/2004 in Anticipated acquisition by Mastercard Incorporated of Parts of the Corporate Services Business of Nets A/S (16 March 2020), the CMA considered that the share of supply test would be met based on the number of suppliers bidding to supply certain services.

5 THE PHASE 1 PROCESS: OVERVIEW

[3.490]

5.1 The table below shows the key stages - and indicative timing - of a typical phase 1 investigation by the CMA, together with a high level summary of the actions that are typically taken by the CMA[106] and by the merger parties (and, where relevant, third parties) at each stage.

5.2 As noted in the table, certain actions (for example, information gathering, the imposition of interim measures, or engagement with the CMA on potential remedies) may in practice occur at various stages of the phase 1 process, including prior to the formal commencement of the investigation timetable. The CMA will apply a reasonable and proportionate approach to these actions according to the complexity of the issues under investigation.

5.3 Each of the stages is described in more detail in chapters 6 to 9 below.

FIGURE: THE KEY STAGES OF A TYPICAL PHASE 1 INVESTIGATION

	Milestones	CMA	Parties
Stage 1: Initial discussions commence between merger parties and CMA (for parties wishing to submit a voluntary notification)			
Typically minimum of 2 weeks before initial submission of draft notification	Initial contact between parties and CMA	CMA allocates case team of CMA staff to review transaction and liaise with parties.	Merger parties engage in initial contact with CMA and submit a case team allocation request form.
STAGE 2A: Pre-notification discussions begin (where transaction is voluntarily notified by merger parties)[107]			
Duration of pre-notification process will differ on case-by-case basis; cases raising complex and/or *prima facie* competition concerns will typically entail a longer pre-notification period	Pre-notification process begins Merger parties submit voluntary notification (Merger Notice)	CMA case team engages with merger parties on the nature and scope of information and internal documents which the case team considers the merger parties will need to provide in their voluntary notification. For some mergers, it may also be appropriate for the case team to hold informal discussions on remedies with the merger parties at any point from the start of the pre-notification process onwards. CMA continues pre-notification discussions and reviews draft Merger Notice. CMA will typically issue information requests (including statutory requests under section 109 of the Act) to the merger parties to complete the notification and ensure that the CMA has sufficient information to commence its investigation. CMA is also likely to engage with third parties and may issue a public invitation to comment, inviting submissions about the potential competitive impact of the merger. Once CMA is satisfied that the Merger Notice is in the form, and contains the information, required by the Act, it confirms this to the merger parties, and confirms the consequent statutory deadline for its phase 1 decision. CMA considers whether interim measures are necessary to prevent or unwind pre-emptive action – in some cases, this may be before submission of the voluntary notification.[108]	Merger parties respond to CMA information requests. Merger parties may also wish to signal to the CMA at this stage that they wish to engage in early remedies discussions or pursue a 'fast-track' process (eg to proceed more quickly to offering remedies or to a phase 2 investigation). Merger parties submit a Merger Notice, usually in draft form. Merger parties respond to any information requests, and submit updated drafts of voluntary notification as appropriate. Merger parties submit completed Merger Notice. Third parties respond to requests for information (in writing or orally) and/or to any invitation to comment.
STAGE 2B: Own initiative investigation (where transaction is not voluntarily notified by the merger parties)			

	Milestones	CMA	Parties
	CMA becomes aware of a transaction that has not been voluntarily notified	CMA considers whether there is a reasonable chance that its duty to refer would be met if it investigated the transaction. Where appropriate, CMA sends an enquiry letter to the merger parties requesting further information about the transaction. CMA also likely to engage third parties and may issue a public invitation to comment, inviting submissions about the potential competitive impact of the merger. CMA considers whether interim measures are necessary to prevent or unwind pre-emptive action. When CMA has sufficient information to begin its investigation, it confirms this to the merger parties, and confirms the consequent statutory deadline for its phase 1 decision.	Merger parties respond to enquiry letter and provide CMA with requested information. Third parties respond to requests for information (in writing or orally) and/or to any invitation to comment.
Stage 3: Phase 1 assessment			
Working Day 1		The 40 working day initial period for the CMA's phase 1 investigation begins on the first working day after it confirms to the merger parties that it has received a complete Merger Notice or that it has sufficient information to begin its investigation.	
	Information-gathering	CMA continues to engage with merger parties as appropriate throughout the 40 working day period. CMA requests further information from merger parties (if necessary) during the 40 working day period. CMA may also directly contact third parties to seek views and information relevant to the assessment of the transaction.[109]	Ongoing liaison between case team and merger parties. Merger parties respond to any information requests. Third parties respond to any requests for information.
	Invitation to comment	CMA publishes invitation to comment notice, inviting views from interested third parties on the transaction under review. CMA assesses responses from third parties.	Third parties respond to invitation to comment.
Working Day 15 – 20	State of play discussion	CMA holds 'state of play' discussion with merger parties (typically by telephone call/videoconference).	Merger parties participate in state of play discussion.
Stage 4A: Phase 1 decision-making process (for cases raising no serious competition concerns)			
By Working Day 40	Phase 1 decision	CMA clears transaction. CMA drafts clearance decision and communicates this to the merger parties. CMA publicly announces clearance decision (full decision published at a later date following identification of confidential information).	
Stage 4B: Phase 1 decision-making process (for cases raising more complex or material competition issues)			

	Milestones	CMA	Parties
By Working Day 40	Issues Meeting (Typically held by Working Day 25)	CMA invites merger parties to issues meeting. CMA sends merger parties 'issues letter' stating core arguments for reference to phase 2. CMA holds 'issues meeting' with merger parties.	Merger parties may provide written response to issues letter (before and/or after issues meeting). Merger parties attend issues meeting, in person or via videoconference.
	Phase 1 decision	CMA holds internal 'Case Review Meeting'. CMA holds internal decision meeting. The CMA's phase 1 decision maker decides whether duty to refer has been met.	
	Notice of decision	CMA provides merger parties with its reasoned decision within statutory period. CMA publishes notice of decision (full decision published at a later date following identification of confidential information).	
Stage 5: Phase 1, potential remedies – where CMA decides duty to refer is met			
0-5 working days after merger parties given decision	Offer of undertaking in lieu of reference (UILs)		Merger parties decide whether to offer UILs to remedy identified concerns. Merger parties who do wish to offer UILs submit completed Remedies Form and draft UILs to CMA.
Up to 10 working days after merger parties given decision	Consideration of offered UILs	If no UILs offered within five working day period, CMA refers transaction to phase 2. CMA considers any UILs offered. CMA decides whether to provisionally accept UILs (or a modified version of them). If CMA rejects UILs, transaction is referred to phase 2.	Merger parties respond to any modifications to the UILs proposed by the CMA.
Within 50 working days of merger parties being given decision (subject to extension for special reasons)	Agreement and acceptance of UILs	CMA gives detailed consideration to terms of proposed UILs to determine if any modifications required before they can be finally accepted. CMA publishes draft UILs for third party comment. CMA considers whether to formally accept draft UILs (with possible further, shorter consultation if required following any material changes to the UILs). If UILs are considered sufficiently 'clear cut' and effective, the CMA publishes a notice of acceptance of UILs. If UILs are not agreed, transaction is referred to phase 2.	Merger parties discuss any necessary modifications to the UILs so as to agree a version for publication for third party consultation. Third parties submit comments on draft UILs within consultation period (at least 15 days for the initial consultation, and at least seven days for any subsequent consultation). If CMA agrees UILs, merger parties sign UILs.
	Implementation of UILs if agreed	CMA publishes final UILs. CMA assesses, and as appropriate approves, proposed purchaser(s) of the business(es) being divested by merger parties (will occur prior to acceptance of UILs in 'upfront buyer' cases).	Merger parties implement UILs, including (where no upfront buyer was required) submitting for CMA approval details of proposed purchasers of any divestments required under the UILs.

NOTES

106 The table does not show the statutory functions performed by Ofcom, NHSI or the Secretary of State in relation to, respectively, local media mergers, NHS mergers and public interest mergers nor does it show the responsibilities of the CMA in respect of these types of merger (see further chapters 9 and 16 below).

107 For information regarding submission of a "briefing note" to the CMA's mergers intelligence function, see *Guidance on the CMA's mergers intelligence function* (CMA56).

108 The Act permits the CMA to make initial enforcement orders (IEOs), including unwinding orders, at any stage of the phase 1 investigation process (including prior to the formal commencement of its phase 1 investigation), in order to prevent action which may prejudice any reference to phase 2 or impede any action by the CMA which may be justified by its findings following a phase 2 investigation.

109 In some cases, the CMA may contact third parties and/or publish an invitation to comment notice during the pre-notification stage.

6 NOTIFICATION OF MERGERS TO THE CMA

[3.491]

6.1 Under the Act, there is no requirement to notify mergers to the CMA. Notification to the CMA is therefore described as 'voluntary',[110] in contrast to the situation in most other jurisdictions. The CMA does not, for the purposes of substantive competition assessment, treat completed acquisitions any differently to anticipated transactions.[111] However, as described in this chapter, there can be significant benefits to merger parties notifying a merger to the CMA and/or engaging in early discussions with the CMA as to whether they should notify a merger, particularly in the case of transactions which may be notifiable across multiple jurisdictions.

6.2 In cases that constitute a relevant merger situation, but where competition concerns clearly do not arise, the merger parties may decide that notification to the CMA is not necessary.

6.3 However, in cases that do raise the possibility of competition concerns, parties should consider carefully whether to notify the merger to the CMA. In making this choice, they should be aware that:

(a) the CMA may well become aware of the transaction as a result of its own mergers intelligence functions (including through the receipt of complaints); and

(b) a decision not to notify the CMA carries particular risks once the merger has been completed.

These considerations are discussed in turn below.

THE CMA'S MERGERS INTELLIGENCE FUNCTION

6.4 The fact that a merger has not been voluntarily notified to the CMA does not mean that the CMA will not review it. The CMA has a duty to track merger activity to determine whether any unnotified merger may give rise to a substantial lessening of competition. The CMA will take a decision to investigate if it believes that there is a reasonable chance that the test for a reference to an in-depth phase 2 investigation will be met (ie there is a reasonable chance that an investigation will identify a relevant merger situation that gives rise to a realistic prospect of a substantial lessening of competition).

6.5 The CMA has dedicated mergers intelligence staff responsible for monitoring non-notified merger activity. Any interested party that wishes to make the CMA aware of a merger that it considers could raise competition concerns can also contact the CMA confidentially at Mergers.Intelligence@cma.gov.uk.

6.6 Further information about the operation of the CMA's mergers intelligence function is provided in the CMA's *Guidance on the CMA's mergers intelligence function* (CMA56).

RISKS TO THE MERGER PARTIES OF NOT NOTIFYING AND/OR COMPLETING MERGERS

6.7 The fact that a merger has been completed does not prevent the CMA from investigating and referring it for a phase 2 investigation for possible remedial action, or accepting UILs. For non-notified completed mergers, the CMA will generally seek to prevent pre-emptive action which might prejudice the reference or impede any action by the CMA which may be justified by its findings through its powers to make an initial enforcement order (IEO). Where it decides to make such an order, the CMA will notify the merger parties that it has made an IEO under section 72 of the Act that prevents them from starting integration (or undertaking further integration) at the same time as it sends the enquiry letter, or shortly thereafter.

6.8 In considering whether to notify a merger to the CMA, merger parties should note, in the context of completed mergers, that:

(a) First, the CMA will normally issue IEOs[112] in investigations where it has reasonable grounds for suspecting that two or more enterprises have ceased to be distinct.[113] An IEO is intended to prevent any action (for example, integration of the merging businesses) that might prejudice the reference to a phase 2 investigation and/or impede any action by the CMA which may be justified by its findings. An IEO will remain in force until the merger is cleared or remedial action is taken, unless varied, revoked or replaced.[114] In certain circumstances, the CMA may consider it necessary to use its powers to unwind integration that has already occurred prior to the IEO coming into force. This will also be assessed on a case-by-case basis, where the CMA reasonably suspects that action has, or may have, been taken which constitutes pre-emptive action. See *Interim measures in merger investigations* (CMA108) for further information about IEOs.

(b) Second, completing a merger without first obtaining clearance from the CMA carries the risk that the CMA may order the disposal of the acquired business (or otherwise the disposal of other businesses or assets) following an investigation. This has occurred under the Act in a number of cases.[115] The fact that a merger has been completed does not reduce the likelihood of the CMA referring the merger to phase 2 or of implementing remedies (which will typically be structural in nature). When considering remedies in the context of a completed merger, the CMA will not normally consider the costs of divestment to the merger parties as it is open to the merger parties to make merger proposals conditional on competition authorities' approval.[116]

INFORMING THE CMA ABOUT MERGERS

6.9 Companies and their advisers are strongly encouraged to contact the CMA at an early opportunity to discuss the application of the Act to a merger situation, particularly in cases where competition concerns cannot easily be ruled out. Contact details are available on the CMA website.[117]

6.10 There are two ways in which parties to a merger that is sufficiently advanced may voluntarily bring a merger to the attention of CMA. These are:

(a) Where merger parties wish to formally notify a merger to the CMA for investigation, they should first submit a request for a case team.[118] This request is made by submitting a Case Team Allocation Form (CTAF), available on the CMA website, and following up with a Merger Notice.

(b) Where merger parties do not intend to formally notify a merger to the CMA for investigation, they can submit a short briefing paper to the mergers intelligence function explaining why, in their view, the merger does not give rise to a relevant merger situation and/or does not give rise to a substantial lessening of competition. This may result in a decision to investigate, or the CMA may indicate that it has no further questions about the merger at that stage.[119] Further information relating to the mergers intelligence function is set out in the CMA's *Guidance on the CMA's mergers intelligence function* (CMA56).

6.11 As part of pre-notification, merger parties will be asked to provide information to the CMA in relation to whether they consider the merger to fall within the scope of a public interest consideration.

Submitting a Merger Notice

6.12 If merger parties wish to obtain a binding decision from the CMA, a formal investigation is required. This process is commenced by the submission of a CTAF, followed by a Merger Notice.[120] The submission of the final Merger Notice is typically preceded by a pre-notification process during which the CMA ensures that it has sufficient information to be able to begin its phase 1 investigation.

Case Team Allocation Form

6.13 The pre-notification process is available for all transactions regardless of whether or not they are in the public domain. The CMA does not make public the fact that it is in pre-notification discussions on a case. The submission of a CTAF enables the CMA to allocate a case team to lead the CMA's phase 1 investigation. The case team is the principal point of contact within the CMA for the merger parties and their representatives.

6.14 The pre-notification process is not available for transactions that remain hypothetical. Where the merger parties have not signed a share purchase agreement or equivalent, the CTAF should therefore set out evidence of a good faith intention to proceed with the transaction (such as because heads of terms have been concluded, adequate finance has been put in place, or the transaction has been subject to board-level consideration). In the case of a public bid, the CMA will expect at least a public announcement of a firm intention to make an offer or the announcement of a possible offer in order to open a phase 1 investigation.[121]

6.15 For completed mergers, the CMA is likely to impose an IEO and issue an information request to ascertain the extent of any integration.

6.16 Merger parties should keep the CMA informed of any material developments, in particular in relation to the timing or status of the transaction, following the submission of the original CTAF.

Pre-notification process

6.17 The case team will endeavour to review submissions and revert to the merger parties within a reasonable timeframe. Where the CMA considers that a pre-notification meeting or telephone call/videoconference is desirable, the case team will schedule one. In some cases, in pre-notification the CMA may issue an invitation to comment and/or engage with relevant third parties.

Benefits of pre-notification

6.18 Pre-notification is the process in which the CMA ensures that it has all the information it needs before formally starting its merger inquiry. It is intended to enable information-gathering and engagement on the issues that are likely to be the focus of the CMA's formal investigation. Depending on the circumstances of the case at issue, the pre-notification process is intended to facilitate:

(a) The clarification of the information and evidence the CMA will require for the purposes of the Merger Notice and is likely to require during the 40-working day investigation;

(b) The clarification of any types of information in the Merger Notice form that the CMA does not consider necessary for a complete notification in the case at hand; and

(c) Informal dialogue on the CMA's likely approach to the assessment of particular competition concerns (noting that the CMA's assessment of the substance of the case is ultimately arrived at by its formal investigation), including the approach to evidence-gathering to inform that assessment (including, for example, the approach to any local analysis that may be appropriate).[122]

6.19 In some cases, pre-notification may also be an opportunity for the case team and the merger parties to discuss, on an informal basis (and without prejudice to the CMA's competition assessment), potential remedy options if a competition concern is ultimately found. Such discussions will not usually be disclosed to the CMA decision maker in advance of his or her decision on competition issues.[123]

Formal commencement of the investigation

6.20 Once the Merger Notice is complete (which also requires the merger to be public knowledge), the CMA is able to commence its 40-working day investigation.[124]

6.21 The 40-working day period within which the CMA must decide whether the test for reference is met begins on the working day after the CMA has confirmed to the merger parties that:

Part 3 CMA and other Guidelines

(a) it is satisfied that it has received a complete Merger Notice meeting the requirements of the Act: that is, it is in the prescribed form and contains the prescribed information, and states that the existence of the proposed merger has been made public; or
(b) the CMA believes that it has sufficient information to enable it to begin its investigation.

6.22 The template Merger Notice[125], once completed to the satisfaction of the CMA, comprises the 'prescribed form' for the purposes of the Act. The template includes guidance notes to assist parties in identifying the information that is likely to be required by the CMA within the Merger Notice. In certain mergers, some of the information requested by the template Merger Notice may not be relevant (or may not be required to the full extent indicated in the guidance notes in the template Merger Notice).[126] Merger parties are encouraged to engage with the case team during pre-notification to discuss what information is likely to be required for a complete Merger Notice.

6.23 Parties are free to supply the requisite information in the format of the Merger Notice template, or to provide a submission in a written format of their choosing, accompanied by a signed and annotated version of the Merger Notice template completed to indicate clearly where in that bespoke submission the information responsive to each question in the Merger Notice can be found.

6.24 The CMA will endeavour to confirm that a submitted notice is complete as promptly as is practicable in the circumstances.[127] Similarly, where it considers that prescribed information is missing from a submitted Merger Notice, the CMA will inform the merger parties of this fact. The CMA may, in appropriate circumstances, use its compulsory information-gathering powers (described in chapter 9) to obtain the necessary information.

Rejection of a Merger Notice after commencement of the initial period

6.25 Even where the CMA has accepted a Merger Notice and confirmed that the 40-working day initial period has commenced, it can, at any time during that initial period, subsequently reject a Merger Notice for three reasons:[128]
(a) it suspects information given to the CMA, whether in the Merger Notice or otherwise, to be false or misleading;
(b) it suspects that the relevant parties do not propose to carry the notified arrangements into effect; or
(c) the merger parties fail to provide information which should in fact have been included in the Merger Notice, or fail, without reasonable excuse, to provide on time, any information requested by the CMA using its powers under section 109 of the Act.

6.26 The CMA's decision to reject a Merger Notice takes effect from the moment it is sent to the notifier or an authorised representative. The CMA will give notice in writing (including by email).

Withdrawal of a Merger Notice

6.27 A company can withdraw a Merger Notice at any time. The withdrawal must be made in writing by the notifier or an authorised representative.

6.28 Where a Merger Notice is withdrawn, but the CMA suspects that the merger parties nevertheless propose to carry the notified arrangements into effect, it will continue to examine the merger on its own initiative. In that scenario, the CMA will not be bound by its original statutory deadline to reach its decision as to whether its duty to refer applies.[129]

Reference after expiry of statutory deadlines

6.29 In some circumstances, a notified merger can still be referred for a phase 2 investigation after expiry of the statutory periods in section 34ZA of the Act within which the CMA must decide whether its duty to refer a merger is met.[130]

COMPETING BIDS AND PARALLEL INDUSTRY MERGERS

6.30 Where there are competing bids for the same company, the CMA tries, other factors being equal, to consider them simultaneously. As in the case of a single bidder, each case will be considered on its own merits. It does not necessarily follow that, because one is referred, the other or others will be also.

RESTRICTIONS DIRECTLY RELATED AND NECESSARY TO THE MERGER (ANCILLARY RESTRAINTS)

6.31 Mergers and ancillary restrictions to the merger are generally excluded from the prohibitions of the Competition Act 1998 under Schedule 1 of the Competition Act 1998.

6.32 The CMA's analytical approach to ancillary restrictions is described in Annex C.

NOTES

[110] The merger parties may, however, be asked to provide sufficient information for the CMA to be able to review the merger, if the CMA chooses to investigate on its own initiative.

[111] A number of cases referred by the CMA for a phase 2 investigation have been ones which the merger parties did not voluntarily notify, but which the CMA decided to investigate on its own initiative or following a complaint from a third party. See, for example, CMA Decisions: Completed acquisition by Tobii AB of Smartbox Assistive Technology Limited and Sensory Software International Ltd (25 January 2019) and Completed acquisition by Vanilla Group Limited (JLA) of Washstation Limited (3 April 2018).

[112] Section 72 of the Act. Such orders may also require the appointment, at the cost of the merger parties, of a hold separate manager and/or monitoring trustee to oversee the order.

113 This is a lower threshold than having reasonable grounds for suspecting that a relevant merger situation has been created, since it does not require the turnover or share of supply jurisdictional tests to be met (see chapter 4 above).

114 An IEO made at phase 1 will be reassessed in the event of a reference to phase 2, and additional or alternative safeguards may be put in place (for example, to prevent the target business from deteriorating during the phase 2 investigation).

115 See, for example, Completed acquisition by Tobii AB of Smartbox Assistive Technology Limited and Sensory Software International Ltd (25 January 2019); Completed acquisition by Danspin A/S of Lawton Yarns Limited (5 November 2019); Completed acquisition by Ecolab Inc. of Holchem Group Limited (8 October 2019); Completed acquisition by Vanilla Group Limited (JLA) of Washstation Limited (3 April 2018).

116 See *Merger Remedies* (CMA87).

117 https://www.gov.uk/guidance/mergers-how-to-notify-the-cma-of-a-merger.

118 See section 96 of the Act.

119 This does not preclude further questions at a later stage and, if further information comes to light, the CMA may open an investigation at any point until the expiry of the four-month statutory period set out in section 24 of the Act.

120 The relevant templates are available at https://www.gov.uk/government/publications/mergers-forms-and-fee-information.

121 Corresponding with Rules 2.7 and 2.4 of the City Code respectively.

122 This includes any primary data collection undertaken for the purposes of merger review, such as a consumer survey. The time and scale of work required to design and conduct reliable consumer surveys means that they are often more suited to use during an in-depth phase 2 process (although the CMA sometimes conducts its own surveys at phase 1). If merger parties consider that the gathering of survey evidence may allow the merger to be cleared at phase 1, the CMA encourages parties, prior to undertaking such a survey, to discuss the need for, and (as appropriate) design and scope of, the survey with the CMA during pre-notification discussions. This will increase the likelihood that the survey results will constitute robust evidence (although the final assessment of the evidence remains one for the decision maker at the end of the investigation).

The CMA has published *Good practice in the design and presentation of consumer survey evidence in merger cases* (CMA78) to provide further assistance to merger parties. Given, however, that the circumstances of each case vary considerably, parties are encouraged to discuss with the CMA in advance how the principles in that document should be applied in their case.

123 In exceptional circumstances (eg where the remedies are likely to be complex in design and/or implementation, or where competition authorities in other jurisdictions are considering a merger which the CMA is also investigating), or when requested by the merger parties, the decision maker may be involved in discussions concerning UILs prior to taking the SLC decision. The merger parties will be informed if the decision maker deems that this is appropriate. In these circumstances, the decision maker will engage with the merger parties, in order to maximise the chance of the CMA achieving an effective remedy to any competition concerns which might arise from the merger. The merger parties are not obliged to engage with the decision maker. The CMA will consider on a case-by-case basis whether additional procedural safeguards are necessary to ensure that the early discussion of remedies does not prejudice the SLC decision: see *Merger Remedies* (CMA87), at paragraph 4.6.

124 Under section 96(2)(b) of the Act, a Merger Notice must state that the existence of the proposed merger has been made public.

125 Available at https://www.gov.uk/government/publications/mergers-forms-and-fee-information.

126 The fact that the CMA has accepted a Merger Notice as complete without having received particular information from the merger parties does not prevent the CMA requesting that information at a later stage, should it consider it to be material to its review.

127 This will typically be within five (and no more than ten) working days of receipt of that Merger Notice, and is likely to depend on, for example, the volume and length of submissions, the extent to which the CMA has previously considered earlier drafts of the same submissions, and the available CMA resource. In general, the CMA is likely to be able to provide such confirmation more promptly in those cases in which parties have engaged in pre-notification.

128 Under section 99(5) of the Act.

129 Section 100(1)(f) of the Act. A fee will be payable on the publication of the CMA's decision as to whether its duty to refer applies.

130 Section 100(1) of the Act. These are where: the Merger Notice is rejected by the CMA prior to the end of the initial 40 working day period; the Merger Notice is withdrawn; before the merger covered by the Merger Notice is completed, any of the enterprises concerned enters into an unrelated merger with any other enterprise not covered by the Merger Notice; the merger covered by the Merger Notice is not completed within six months of the expiry of the consideration period; any information supplied by the notifier (or any associate or subsidiary) is in any material respect false or misleading; any material information which is, or ought to be, known to the notifier (or an associate or subsidiary) is not disclosed to the CMA (such information must be given in writing); or the merger parties have offered UILs to the CMA (or to the Secretary of State in public interest cases) but the CMA (or Secretary of State) has not accepted those UILs.

7 FAST TRACK PROCESSES AND CONCEDING AN SLC

[3.492]

7.1 In some circumstances, such as where a merger is subject to review in multiple jurisdictions, merger parties may wish to waive their rights in relation to certain procedural steps in order to enable a binding outcome to be arrived at more quickly.

7.2 As set out below, merger parties are able to request that a case should be 'fast tracked' to the consideration of UILs or to an in-depth phase 2 investigation.

7.3 Similarly, in a phase 2 investigation, merger parties are able to 'concede' that the relevant merger situation has resulted, or may be expected to result, in a substantial lessening of competition within a specified market or markets for goods or services in the UK.

7.4 The CMA expects that these cases will usually progress substantially more quickly than they would have done under the ordinary investigation timetable. As explained below, a request for a fast track process may not always be granted and such requests are therefore made on a 'without prejudice' basis.

The CMA will also consider on a case-by-case basis whether additional procedural safeguards are necessary to ensure that a request for a fast track process, or to concede an SLC, does not, in the event that it is declined, prejudice the CMA's SLC decision at phase 1 or phase 2.

FAST TRACK PROCESSES

7.5 Merger parties are able to request that a case should be 'fast tracked' where they accept that the CMA has evidence at an early stage in an investigation that objectively justifies a belief that the test for reference is met.

7.6 A case can be fast tracked for two purposes:

(a) To proceed more quickly to offering UILs, with the objective of reaching a phase 1 clearance with remedies;[131] or

(b) To proceed more quickly to an in-depth phase 2 investigation.[132]

7.7 As in any other case in which the CMA has decided to investigate, the CMA is required to publish a reasoned decision at the end of a phase 1 investigation in fast track cases.[133]

Fast track for the consideration of UILs

7.8 The merger parties can request a case to be referred for the consideration of UILs early during the phase 1 investigation or during pre-notification.

7.9 In this circumstance, the merging parties would typically have discussed possible UILs with the CMA case team early during the phase 1 investigation or during pre-notification.[134]

7.10 The merger parties are required to accept in writing that the test for reference is met (ie that there is sufficient evidence available to meet the CMA's statutory threshold for reference) and that they agree to waive their right to challenge that position during a phase 1 investigation. This process therefore differs from circumstances in which merging parties have hypothetical discussions with the CMA case team, on a without prejudice basis, on possible remedies in the event that the CMA decision maker decides that the merger gives rise to an SLC following the issues meeting process.[135]

7.11 The CMA will therefore not follow all of the normal procedural steps prior to reference (including an issues meeting). The CMA will generally reduce the time provided for third-party consultation, given that the merger parties have accepted that competition concerns arise and third parties will have an opportunity to present their views on whether the proposed remedies are effective during the consultation on UILs.

7.12 The CMA may decline a request for a fast track process where this would not be appropriate for the substantive assessment of the case (for example because there remains material uncertainty about the nature or scope of the potential competition concerns that the merger gives rise to) or for the efficient conduct of the CMA's investigation (including, for example, where this could hinder the ability of the CMA to align its proceedings with those in other jurisdictions).

7.13 Any UILs offered further to a fast-track process are subject to the same requirements as UILs in other phase 1 cases, as set out in the CMA's guidance on *Merger remedies* (CMA87). For the avoidance of doubt, this means that, even where the CMA has discussed possible UILs with the merger parties at an early stage, there remains the possibility that the transaction is referred to a phase 2 inquiry if the CMA ultimately decides that the UILs do not meet these requirements.

Fast track to phase 2 investigation

7.14 The merger parties can request a case to be referred for a phase 2 investigation early during the phase 1 investigation or during pre-notification. The merger parties are required to accept in writing that the test for reference is met (ie that there is sufficient evidence available to meet the CMA's statutory threshold for reference) and that they agree to waive their right to challenge that position during a phase 1 investigation. Further, the CMA must have evidence in its possession at an early stage in its investigation that it believes objectively justifies a belief that the test for reference is met.

7.15 The CMA will encourage merger parties to remedy competition concerns where possible by means of UILs (subject to the requirements for phase 1 UILs described in the CMA's remedies guidance).[136] Candidate cases for fast track reference for a phase 2 investigation are therefore likely to be cases where a phase 1 outcome is unlikely to be possible because any competition concerns ultimately established would, by their nature, impact on the whole or substantially all of the transaction, and not just one part.

7.16 Subject to these conditions being satisfied, in a fast track case, the CMA will not follow all of the normal procedural steps prior to reference (including an issues meeting). In cases fast tracked to a phase 2 investigation, the CMA will generally reduce the time provided for third-party consultation, given that third parties will have an opportunity to present their views during a phase 2 investigation.

7.17 The CMA may decline a request for a fast track procedure where: a significant amount of the CMA's information-gathering (in pre-notification or in a phase 1 investigation) has already been carried out; the CMA disagrees with the merger parties' assessment that the case is suitable to be fast-tracked; or it would not be appropriate to fast-track the case for the efficient conduct of the CMA's investigation (including, for example, where this could hinder the ability of the CMA to align its proceedings with those in other jurisdictions). The CMA may also ask the merger parties to formally request a fast-track procedure by a given point in proceedings, noting that the CMA would be unlikely to be minded to grant any request for a fast-track procedure received at a later date on the basis that it would not expect to be able to achieve the same administrative efficiencies.

CONCEDING AN SLC

7.18 In a phase 2 investigation, merger parties are able to request that they formally accept that the CMA has evidence that establishes, to the required legal standard, that the relevant merger situation has resulted, or may be expected to result, in an SLC within specified market or markets for goods or services in the UK.

7.19 In practice, merger parties may wish to consider this approach where it could facilitate the efficient conduct of the case. This might be, for example, where the 'concession' of an SLC would aid the alignment of the CMA's remedies process with proceedings in other jurisdictions or where it would enable the CMA and merger parties to focus their efforts during the remainder of the CMA's substantive assessment on other areas.

7.20 Where merger parties wish to 'concede' an SLC, they are required to accept in writing that an SLC arises within a specified market or markets for goods or services in the UK and that they agree to waive their right to challenge that position during a phase 2 investigation.

7.21 The CMA may decline a request to 'concede' an SLC where this would not be appropriate for the substantive assessment of the case (for example, because there remains material uncertainty about the nature or scope of the potential competition concerns that the merger gives rise to or competition concerns in different areas might be linked) or for the assessment of effective and proportionate remedies. The CMA will also consider whether 'conceding' an SLC would support the efficient conduct of the CMA's investigation (including, for example, whether this could in fact hinder the ability of the CMA to align its proceedings with those in other jurisdictions).

NOTES

131 See, for example, CMA Decisions: Anticipated acquisition by Stryker Corporation of Wright Medical Group N.V. (30 June 2020); Completed acquisition by CD&R Fund IX of MRH (GB) Limited (31 August 2018); Completed acquisition by GTCR of PR Newswire (20 June 2016).

132 Cases which have been fast-tracked to an in-depth phase 2 investigation include: Anticipated acquisition by J Sainsbury Plc of Asda Group Ltd (2018); Anticipated merger between Central Manchester University Hospitals NHS Foundation Trust (CMFT) and University Hospital of South Manchester NHS Foundation Trust (UHSM) (2017); Anticipated acquisition by Tesco plc of Booker Group plc (2017); Anticipated merger between Ladbrokes plc and certain businesses of Gala Coral Group Limited (2016); Anticipated acquisition by BT Group plc of EE limited (2015); Completed acquisition by Global Radio Holdings Limited of GMG Radio Holdings Limited (2012); and Anticipated joint venture between Thomas Cook Group plc, the Co-operative Group Limited and the Midlands Co-operative Society Limited (2011).

133 Section 107 of the Act.

134 For further information on the UIL process, see *Merger remedies* (CMA87).

135 See *Merger remedies* (CMA87) at paragraph 4.4.

136 *Merger remedies* (CMA87).

8 INTERACTIONS WITH OTHER PROCEEDINGS

[3.493]

8.1 The CMA recognises that merger parties may be subject to other regulatory processes in addition to UK merger control, such as the City Code governing public takeovers, or merger control regulation in other jurisdictions. Parties should inform the CMA if the merger is subject to such processes and any associated timing constraints for the merger.

8.2 The CMA will take account of such constraints when conducting its review and may, where the demands of the particular case and its existing caseload allow, seek to make its decision more quickly than the standard statutory timetable. If merger parties wish to request that a decision is taken more quickly than the statutory timetable, the case team allocation request should clearly explain why the case is urgent, with evidence if available, and why the merger parties did not commence pre-notification discussions earlier. In such cases, the CMA would expect the merger parties to be particularly alert to the importance of a full and complete merger submission and to the need for very prompt responses to additional requests for information.

8.3 In deciding whether to open an investigation on its own initiative, the CMA may take into account any merger control proceedings in other jurisdictions. The CMA may decide not to open an investigation if any remedies imposed or agreed in those proceedings would be likely to address any competition concerns that could arise in the UK. This could be the case, for example, where all of the markets that are relevant to the transaction are broader than national in scope.

8.4 In this circumstance, merger parties may be invited to update the CMA on the progress of proceedings in other jurisdictions and to provide the necessary waivers for the CMA to discuss these proceedings with other competition authorities (and, where appropriate, waivers to other competition authorities to allow them to discuss the proceedings with the CMA). The CMA may consider whether to open a formal investigation at any point before expiry of the four-month statutory period and merging parties run the risk that remedies in other jurisdictions that would not fully eliminate any competition concerns relating to the UK would result in the CMA opening a formal investigation at a later stage.

8.5 For more information in relation to the CMA's approach to multi-jurisdictional mergers, see chapter 18 below.

9 THE PHASE 1 ASSESSMENT PROCESS

[3.494]

9.1 This chapter of the guidance provides a more detailed summary of certain aspects of the

CMA's typical phase 1 assessment process (chapters 10 to 14 provide equivalent information on the phase 2 process). It first explains how the CMA may gather information from the merger parties and from third parties. It sets out the penalties for failure to comply with the CMA's investigatory powers. It also sets out interactions with the merger parties, as well as with other bodies. It then sets out the decision-making process followed in determining where the duty to refer is met, both in cases which do not raise material competition concerns and in more complex cases.

9.2 The CMA aims to conduct its investigations flexibly within the applicable legal framework in light of the circumstances of the transaction under review. While the CMA will ensure that the procedural rights of merger parties and third parties are fully respected in all circumstances, it may be that certain of the steps set out below are not applied in all cases.

9.3 The CMA may also decide to adapt its typical phase 1 process where a transaction may be subject to merger review processes in other jurisdictions. In these cases, the CMA may coordinate certain stages of its investigation timetable with those of other competition agencies. For further information on the CMA's general approach to multi-jurisdictional mergers, see chapter 18.

INFORMATION GATHERING

9.4 The CMA will often require additional information from the merger parties than provided in the initial Merger Notice,[137] or than is requested via an enquiry letter (ie where the CMA's mergers intelligence function has 'called-in' a merger), to inform its decision on reference. In practice, the CMA asks for any such additional data, information or documents as soon as it is clear this will be necessary, but, given the nature of the statutory timescales within which the CMA operates, responses will often be requested within a relatively short (but reasonable) period.

9.5 For both information requests made using the CMA's formal section 109 powers and for informal requests, it is important that recipients, as soon as possible after receiving a request for information, inform the CMA of any difficulties they may have in meeting the deadline for providing the information or in submitting the information in the requested format. Such discussions may enable the CMA to vary the information request or the stipulated response date (where appropriate).

Informal requests for information

9.6 The CMA may request information about the transaction from merger parties or third parties without using its formal powers. This may include via questionnaires, telephone or videoconference calls,[138] and in-person meetings.[139]

9.7 The intentional or reckless provision of false or misleading information in response to an informal request for information (or during discussions with the CMA) is a criminal offence.[140]

Formal requests for information

9.8 The CMA has the power under section 109 of the Act to issue a notice requiring a person to provide information or documents, or to give evidence as a witness (a section 109 notice):

(a) ***Internal documents.*** The CMA regularly asks parties to provide internal documents (ie documents that merger parties or third parties have generated internally in the ordinary course of business) to inform its investigation. When requesting internal documents from the merger parties, the CMA will use a section 109 notice as standard.[141] When requesting internal documents from third parties, the CMA may decide to request such documents informally in the first instance or may decide to use section 109 notices if it considers this appropriate, depending on the materiality of that evidence to its investigation, and/or if it has doubts about whether it will receive a full or timely response to an informal request. More information on the CMA's approach to requests for internal documents in merger investigations is provided in the CMA's *Guidance on requests for internal documents in merger investigations* (CMA100).

(b) ***Other information.*** The CMA regularly asks parties to provide a wide variety of views, information and data to inform its investigation. Depending on the nature of the evidence being requested, the materiality of the evidence to the investigation, and/or whether the CMA has doubts about whether it will receive a full or timely response to an informal request, the CMA may request this evidence informally or through a section 109 notice.[142]

(c) ***Interviews.*** In some cases, the CMA may also issue a section 109 notice requiring an individual to give evidence in person (or by telephone or videoconference) in a formal interview with the CMA.[143] This is a more formal process than an ordinary information-gathering call with the merging parties (or third parties), and a failure to comply with such a notice can result in enforcement action under section 110 of the Act.

9.9 The failure to comply without reasonable excuse with a notice under section 109 of the Act can cause delay to the review timetable. If a relevant party[144] fails to comply with a section 109 notice, this permits the CMA to extend the relevant statutory timetable (including, where relevant, the four-month statutory deadline for referring completed mergers) until the party has produced the documents and/or supplied the information and the CMA has assessed whether the documents and/or information form a satisfactory response to its section 109 notice (commonly known as 'stopping the clock').

9.10 The failure to comply with a section 109 notice can also result in the imposition of a fine (as explained further below).

9.11 The intentional or reckless provision of false or misleading information in response to a section 109 notice is a criminal offence.[145]

Third-party submissions

9.12 The CMA invites comments on any public merger situation under review from interested third parties by means of an invitation to comment notice published through the Regulatory News Service and on its website.[146]

9.13 The CMA recognises that, in some cases, third parties may have commercial incentives to raise concerns in relation to a merger. The CMA will always scrutinise any views submitted by third parties carefully and consider the available evidence, such as internal documents prepared in the ordinary course of business, to support these views. The CMA also recognises that third parties may have concerns about the confidentiality of information and/or documents which are provided to the CMA.[147] The CMA's general approach to confidentiality is set out in chapter 19 below.

PENALTIES FOR FAILURE TO COMPLY WITH THE CMA'S INVESTIGATORY POWERS

9.14 There are penalties for parties (including third parties) who supply false or misleading information. It is an offence punishable by a fine or a maximum of two years imprisonment (or both) to:

(a) knowingly or recklessly to supply false or misleading information to the CMA, Ofcom, NHSI or the Secretary of State in connection with any of their merger control functions under Part 3 of the Act, or to give false or misleading information to any third party knowing that they will then supply it to the CMA, Ofcom, NHSI or the Secretary of State;[148] or

(b) intentionally alter, suppress, or destroy any information that the CMA has required to be produced under an information request notice under section 109 of the Act.[149]

9.15 In addition, the CMA may impose a fine[150] where a person has:

(a) without a reasonable excuse, failed to comply with any requirement of an information request notice under section 109 of the Act;[151] or

(b) intentionally obstructed or delayed a CMA official or other person in the exercise of their powers under section 109(6) of the Act to take a copy of information produced pursuant to such a notice.[152]

9.16 This is in addition to the CMA's powers to, for example, suspend the statutory timetables for reviewing mergers where information required under a section 109 notice is not provided by a relevant person or is found to be false or misleading.

9.17 Further guidance on the CMA's approach to penalties is set out in *Administrative Penalties: Statement of policy on the CMA's approach* (CMA4).

INTERACTIONS WITH MERGER PARTIES

9.18 The CMA encourages merger parties and their advisers to liaise closely with the case team during the lifetime of the case. The level of interaction required between merger parties and their advisers and the CMA's case team will depend on the individual circumstances of the case in question.

9.19 In all cases, the CMA will have a 'state of play' discussion with the merger parties, typically 'remotely' ie by telephone call or video-conference. This will generally take place in the period between working days 15 and 20 but may occur earlier depending on the circumstances of the case. The purpose of this discussion is to inform merger parties about any competition concerns that have been raised in the CMA's investigation to date, including feedback from the CMA's market test, and whether or not the CMA is to proceed to an issues letter. The case team will provide an update on the likely timetable for the case going forward.

9.20 If the CMA does intend to proceed to an issues letter, the CMA will also provide an overview of the theories of harm that the CMA proposes to include in the issues letter.

CONTACTS WITH OTHER BODIES

9.21 The CMA may also contact other governmental bodies, regulators (including the sectoral regulators), industry associations and consumer bodies for their views on merger cases where appropriate. Sectoral regulators may also carry out their own public consultation before providing comments to the CMA. The CMA will take any views it receives into account, although it is ultimately for the CMA to decide whether there is a realistic prospect that the merger will gives rise to substantial lessening of competition.[153]

9.22 Where a merger is being investigated by competition authorities in other jurisdictions, the CMA will typically seek a confidentiality waiver from the merger parties. This is intended to enable the CMA and the relevant competition authorities (for example, the European Commission and/or national competition authorities) to discuss any competition concerns that may arise from the merger, exchange confidential information and evidence related to the merger, discuss any potential or actual remedies and, where appropriate, gather information to facilitate coordinating certain stages of the investigation timetables.

Media mergers

9.23 In local media mergers involving newspaper publishing and/or commercial radio or television broadcasting, where the case raises *prima facie* competition concerns, the CMA will ask Ofcom to provide it with an assessment in order further to inform the CMA's decisions on the reference test and on the application of any available exceptions to the duty to refer. Drawing on Ofcom's understanding of media markets, this assessment may include information relating to:

(a) the overall market context;
(b) the relevant counterfactual to the merger (including the risk of the asset or business in question failing);
(c) the scope of relevant product and geographic markets;
(d) the competitive effects of the merger; and
(e) exceptions to the duty to refer, and in particular Ofcom's views on whether the markets are of insufficient importance (de minimis) to warrant reference and whether there are 'relevant customer benefits' (RCBs) that might be weighed against an identified substantial lessening of competition.

9.24 For further information on the role of Ofcom in relevant mergers where the Secretary of State has issued a Public Interest Intervention Notice (PIIN), see chapter 16 below.

National Health Service mergers

9.25 For mergers involving NHS foundation trusts, the CMA must notify NHSI where it decides to carry out an investigation into the merger. NHSI is then required to provide advice to the CMA on relevant benefits for NHS users arising from the merger, and any other matters relating to the investigation that NHSI considers appropriate to bring to the CMA's attention.[154] The CMA retains responsibility for making the decision under the Act, but in doing so, will take NHSI's advice into account in reaching its conclusions within the context and timeframe of its normal review processes. Further information is provided in *CMA guidance on the review of NHS mergers* (CMA 29).

THE PHASE 1 DECISION MAKING PROCESS

9.26 This section sets out the procedure typically followed by the CMA when it is deciding whether the test for reference for a phase 2 investigation is met ('the SLC decision').

9.27 In cases that raise no serious competition issues, the decision to clear the merger is made by a staff member of the CMA (at the Assistant Director level or above). The decision will then be adopted by the CMA, relayed to the merger parties or their advisers and announced publicly. See chapter 19 for the process around publishing the CMA's decisions.

9.28 In cases that raise more complex or material competition issues, a different process is followed. As noted above, the CMA will have a 'state of play' discussion with the merger parties in which it will indicate whether or not the CMA is minded to proceed to an issues meeting. The merger parties will be invited to attend an issues meeting.[155]

9.29 An issues letter is sent to the merger parties to help them prepare for the issues meeting. The issues letter sets out the core arguments in favour of a reference in the case so that merger parties have an opportunity to make representations on these concerns during the issues meeting and in a written response to the issues letter.

9.30 The issues letter is not a provisional decision or a statement of objections. Rather, the issues letter sets out hypotheses which the CMA is still evaluating in the light of the evidence put to it by the merger parties and gathered from third parties. The issues letter will therefore typically not consider in detail the arguments in favour of clearance.

9.31 The CMA will provide the merger parties with a short interval of two working days (at least 48 hours, not counting weekends or public holidays) between receipt of the issues letter and the issues meeting to allow them time to prepare. Although this is a relatively short time period, the description of the competition concerns provided by the case team in the state of play discussion should ensure that the merger parties understand the theories of harm that the issues letter outlines at an earlier stage and can already start to prepare their representations to the CMA on these points.[156]

9.32 Parties to a merger may either respond to the issues letter in writing, or orally at an issues meeting, or both.[157] The case team will advise the merger parties on the deadline within which responses must be received in order to be considered within the statutory time limits for the SLC decision. The period to make written submissions will typically be longer than the period of two working days (at least 48 hours, not counting weekends or public holidays) to prepare for the issues meeting.

9.33 Third parties will not normally be informed as to whether an issues meeting has been held (or will be held) in a particular case and will not be given a copy of the issues letter.

9.34 Issues meetings will generally be chaired by a member of the case team and, absent exceptional circumstances, the phase 1 decision maker (either the Senior Director of Mergers or another senior member of CMA staff) will attend.[158]

9.35 To further enhance the level of scrutiny to which the case team's recommendations are subject, and to assist the phase 1 decision maker in making the SLC decision, a member of CMA staff from outside the case team is charged specifically with acting as a 'devil's advocate' to comment critically on the case team's recommended outcome (whether that is for or against reference). The 'devil's advocate' will also attend the issues meeting wherever possible.

9.36 At the issues meeting, the CMA will wish to speak to senior management in the businesses affected by the merger. The CMA will inform the merger parties if it wishes specified individuals or representatives of particular business areas to attend the issues meeting. Merger parties may wish to provide a presentation for the issues meeting, particularly where they have not yet responded in writing to the issues letter.

9.37 In exceptional circumstances (eg where the remedies are likely to be complex in design and/or implementation or where competition authorities in other jurisdictions are considering a merger which the CMA is also investigating), or when requested by the merger parties, the decision maker may choose to be involved in discussions concerning UILs prior to taking the SLC decision. The merger parties will be informed if the decision maker deems that this is appropriate. In these circumstances, the decision maker will engage with the merger parties, in order to maximise the chance of the CMA achieving an effective remedy to any competition concerns which might arise from the merger. The merger parties are not obliged to engage with the decision maker. The CMA will consider on a case-by-case basis whether additional procedural safeguards are necessary to ensure that the early discussion of remedies does not prejudice the SLC decision.[159]

9.38 After the issues meeting, the phase 1 decision maker will meet with members of the case team and the devil's advocate to consider the case and to decide on whether or not the reference test is met.

9.39 In cases where the decision maker concludes that the test for reference is met, the decision maker will then consider whether any of the available exceptions to the duty to refer (such as the 'de minimis' exception) should be applied.[160]

9.40 Once the decision maker has considered whether any of these exceptions apply, the decision will be adopted by the CMA, relayed to the merger parties or their advisers and announced publicly. See chapter 19 for the process around publishing the CMA's decisions.

UNDERTAKINGS IN LIEU OF REFERENCE (UILS)

9.41 If the CMA finds that its duty to refer the merger for a phase 2 investigation applies, the merger parties may have an opportunity to avoid that outcome by offering binding undertakings in lieu of reference (UILs) for the CMA (or the Secretary of State in public interest cases)[161] to accept.

9.42 UILs may be accepted by the CMA only where it has concluded that the merger should be referred for a phase 2 investigation. Any UILs accepted by the CMA must be for the purpose of remedying, mitigating or preventing the substantial lessening of competition concerned or any adverse effects identified.

9.43 For further information on the CMA's approach to remedies, please see *Merger remedies* (CMA87). Merger parties and their advisers are advised to review this Guidance in detail (see in particular, paragraphs 4.2 to 4.53) for further information on the UILs process applicable at phase 1.

NOTES

137 This is usually the case even where the information received was sufficient for the CMA to be satisfied that the Merger Notice was complete for the purposes of commencing the CMA's review and its 40 working day timetable.

138 Where appropriate, the CMA will record telephone/videoconference calls, having informed the counterparty before doing so. The CMA will generally not transcribe these interactions but may also take a written note where practicable.

139 The CMA will usually take a written note of any in-person meetings.

140 Section 117 of the Act.

141 As stated in paragraph 16 of the CMA's *Guidance on requests for internal documents in merger investigations* (CMA100).

142 See section 109 (3) of the Act.

143 For example, in the phase 1 inquiry concerning the anticipated acquisition by Amazon of a minority shareholding and certain rights in Deliveroo (29 January 2020) the CMA requested representatives of Amazon to provide information to the CMA by means of an interview.

144 In this context, this does not include third parties who are not connected to the merger parties.

145 Section 117 of the Act.

146 In some cases the CMA will publish the invitation to comment notice during the pre-notification period.

147 Where the CMA intends to rely on third-party submissions as part of the case for reference in a phase 1 investigation, it will inform the merger parties of the nature of the concerns expressed by the third-parties (but not of their identity) in sufficient detail to enable the merger parties to respond to those concerns.

148 Section 117 of the Act and section 73(6) of the Health and Social Care Act 2012.

149 Section 110(5) of the Act.

150 Fines may be of a fixed amount or calculated by reference to a daily rate. The amount of the fine is determined by the CMA, up to a maximum of £15,000 per day or £30,000 for a fixed amount, or such lower maximum as the Secretary of State may impose by statutory instrument.

151 Section 110(1) of the Act. The CMA has imposed fines in a number of merger cases for failure to comply with the requirements of section 109 notices. See penalty notices related to CMA Decisions: Anticipated acquisition by Just Eat.co.uk Limited of Hungryhouse Holdings Limited (24 November 2017); Anticipated acquisition by AL-KO Kober Holdings Limited of Bankside Patterson Limited (28 May 2019); Completed acquisition by Rentokil Initial plc of MPCL Limited (14 August 2019); and Anticipated acquisition by Sabre Holdings Corporation of Farelogix Inc. (11 October 2019).

152 Section 110(3) of the Act.

153 The operation of the public interest intervention regime in mergers is described below in chapter 16.

154 This is a requirement under section 79 of the Health and Social Care Act 2012.

155 Given the statutory deadlines for the phase 1 investigation that apply to the CMA, the CMA may be limited in its ability to accommodate requests from the merger parties for the issues meeting to be held at a time or date other than that suggested by the CMA.

156 However, due to the timing constraints of a phase 1 investigation, the CMA is not in a position to provide any written information in relation to these theories of harm ahead of the issues letter.

157 There is no obligation to respond to an issues letter and/or to attend an issues meeting.

158 If, for exceptional reasons, it is not practicable for the phase 1 decision maker to attend the issues meeting, he or she will in any event be informed of the discussion at the issues meeting by those who were present at that meeting, and will consider this alongside the other (written and oral) evidence in the case.

159 *Merger Remedies* (CMA87), at paragraph 4.6.
160 See *Mergers: Exceptions to the duty to refer* (CMA64).
161 See chapter 16 of this Guidance.

10 PHASE 2 INQUIRIES: OVERVIEW

[3.495]
10.1 The following chapters set out the typical phase 2 process. Chapter 10 sets out the role and responsibilities of the Inquiry Group and CMA staff team; it also summarises, at a high-level, the phase 2 process. Chapters 11 to 14 then provide greater detail on various aspects of the process.

THE PHASE 2 INQUIRY GROUP AND CASE TEAM

10.2 An Inquiry Group is appointed for each inquiry, supported by a case team of CMA staff. The duties and powers of Inquiry Groups conducting a phase 2 inquiry are set out in the Act.[162]

10.3 The Chair of the CMA is responsible for identifying and appointing the Inquiry Group that will conduct a particular inquiry and for selecting one of them to act as chair of the Inquiry Group (the Inquiry Group Chair). In practice, the Chair of the CMA will delegate these responsibilities to the CMA Panel Chair (or one of the CMA Deputy Panel Chairs).[163] Until the Inquiry Group is appointed, the Chair of the CMA (or his/her delegate, in practice usually the CMA Panel Chair) may act in its place.[164]

10.4 The CMA's panel members come from a variety of backgrounds and expertise in different areas including law, economics, business and consumer policy. For a phase 2 inquiry, an Inquiry Group will comprise at least three members, including the Inquiry Group Chair.

10.5 Before appointing a member to an Inquiry Group, the CMA will assess (by reference to the CMA's conflicts of interest policy[165]) whether the proposed member has any outside interests that could give rise to a conflict of interest which would affect, or be seen to affect, the Group's impartiality (a potential conflict of interest). The CMA's practice is not to appoint a member to an Inquiry Group where a conflict of interest is likely to arise. In limited cases, the CMA may contact the merger parties to disclose an outside interest ahead of appointing a member even though the CMA believes that the potential conflict of interest would not affect, nor be seen to affect, the Group's impartiality. Where appropriate, particular interests may also be disclosed on the relevant case page.

10.6 Phase 2 Inquiry Groups are appointed for the duration of the inquiry, up to the point at which the reference is finally determined.[166] In cases where a merger is found to give rise to a substantial lessening of competition (SLC), the merger is finally determined when remedy undertakings[167] are accepted by the CMA or a final remedy order is made; and if no SLC is found, the reference is finally determined when the final report is published.[168]

10.7 The appointed Inquiry Group are the decision makers on phase 2 inquiries. Their role is to set the overall direction of the inquiry, review the appropriate evidence and analysis, and answer the statutory questions on the case (see chapter 3). They also hear directly from the merger parties in a formal hearing during the assessment phase of the case (the 'main party hearing': see paragraphs 12.4 to 12.6), and will attend any site visit (see paragraph

11.32). Inquiry Groups are required by law to act independently of the CMA Board,[169] and therefore make their own independent decisions, based on the objective evidence before them. The appointment of an independent group is intended to provide a 'fresh pair of eyes' in relation to the CMA's phase 1 investigation, in which a member of CMA staff decides whether the test for reference is met.

10.8 Inquiry Groups are supported by a case team. The phase 2 case team will include a combination of both:

(a) project delivery staff, responsible for the day-to-day running of the inquiry, and ensuring that inquiry procedures are followed correctly and that the inquiry progresses according to the published timetable; and

(b) specialist staff, who will provide advice to the Inquiry Group in particular areas of expertise and are responsible for analysing, and advising the Inquiry Group on, the substantive issues that arise during the inquiry. There are usually one or more economists, lawyers, and business/financial advisors assigned to each phase 2 inquiry as well as other experts as appropriate (for example, statisticians).

THE KEY STAGES OF A PHASE 2 INQUIRY

10.9 The key stages of a typical phase 2 inquiry are shown in the table on the following pages. This indicates the steps the CMA will usually take and what the merger and third parties will usually need to do at each key stage of a phase 2 inquiry. Although indicative timings for each stage have been set out, the steps described may not, in practice, always take place or may not take place sequentially and may sometimes overlap. In particular, information-gathering takes place throughout the inquiry.

10.10 Further, subject to agreement with the CMA, it may be possible to omit certain stages of the process where to do so would lead to greater efficiency.[170] There may also be reason to adjust the typical process where the merger may be subject to review in other jurisdictions (see further, chapter 18 below). In all cases, merger parties and their advisers are encouraged to speak to the CMA to discuss.

FIGURE: THE KEY STAGES OF A TYPICAL PHASE 1 INQUIRY

	Milestones	CMA	Parties
Following Referral: Possible suspension of reference (anticipated mergers only)			
Following reference to phase 2	Possible abandonment of transaction	CMA considers, in response to any request by merger parties, whether transaction may be abandoned and whether to suspend the phase 2 investigation for up to three weeks. If transaction is abandoned, CMA cancels reference. CMA publishes notice of suspension (and termination of any suspension if merger is not abandoned).	Merger parties may request suspension of reference in light of any possible abandonment of transaction.
Stage 1: Phase 2 information gathering		**Weeks 1–6[171]**	
	Reference	CMA issues phase 2 opening letter to merger parties.	Where appropriate, merger parties attend case management meeting and data meeting with CMA case team (which will usually be by telephone/videoconference).
		CMA considers need for modified interim measures	Merger parties discuss with the CMA any ongoing phase 1 IEOs or if necessary phase 2 interim measures and reporting on compliance. CMA makes interim order or merger parties accept interim undertakings. CMA may also consider unwinding integration.
		CMA creates administrative timetable. Timetable is published after it is shared with the merger parties.	Merger parties comment on administrative timetable.
	Initial information-gathering	CMA issues information requests to merger parties under section 109 of the Act (and to third parties, usually on a voluntary basis) as necessary.	Merger parties (and third parties) respond to information requests.
		CMA develops any consumer surveys.	Merger parties provided opportunity to comment on any draft consumer survey.[172]
		CMA attends site visit (if being held).	Merger parties organise site visit.
		CMA conducts calls and meetings with third parties to the extent necessary to supplement existing evidence base.	Third parties give oral evidence.
	Publication of issues statement, reflecting theories of harm on which the CMA is focusing	CMA publishes issues statement and considers responses to it.	Merger parties (and third parties) respond to issues statement.
Stage 2: Phase 2 assessment		**Weeks 7–15**	

	Milestones	CMA	Parties
		CMA conducts analysis of evidence. CMA holds a 'main party hearing' with each merger party. An annotated issues statement is sent to the merger parties in advance of the main party hearing setting out the Inquiry Group's emerging thinking by reference to the matters outlined in the issues statement. Key working papers (or extracts of them) may also be disclosed to the merger parties as appropriate in advance of the main party hearing.	Merger parties attend main party hearing. Merger parties comment on annotated issues statement and any working papers (or extracts of working papers) disclosed to them.
		Put-back of material to parties where appropriate.	Parties check put-back.[173]
Around week 15	Publication of Notice of provisional findings, provisional findings and (if relevant) Notice of Possible Remedies.	The provisional findings report is the main means the CMA uses to satisfy its duty to consult under section 104 of the Act, by disclosing its provisional decisions, and the underlying reasoning.	
Stage 3: After provisional findings		**Weeks 16–24**	
		CMA considers responses to provisional findings and (if relevant) Notice of Possible Remedies	Merger parties (and third parties) comment on provisional findings and (if relevant) any Notice of Possible Remedies.
		Where new evidence has been obtained after provisional findings, and to the extent not previously commented on, put-back of material to parties for checking for factual accuracy and to identify confidential information prior to publication of final report.	Parties check put-back.
		Where relevant the CMA will conduct subsequent hearings ('response hearings') to receive evidence on any remedies proposals and brief submissions on the provisional findings.	Merger parties (and sometimes third parties, if appropriate) attend response hearings.
		CMA produces remedies working paper and discloses this to merger parties for comment.	Merger parties comment on remedies working paper.
Week 24	Statutory deadline for publication of the final report	CMA publishes final report by the end of week 24 (subject to any extension of statutory deadline).	
STAGE 4: Implementation of remedies – after publication of the CMA's final report		Weeks 24 –36	
		CMA considers whether any variation to interim measures is necessary.	CMA varies interim order or merger parties accept revised or additional interim undertakings if appropriate. CMA may also consider unwinding any integration.
		CMA creates timetable for implementation of undertakings/order, and informs merger parties of key milestones.	

	Milestones	CMA	Parties
		CMA consults merger parties (and, where relevant, third parties) on draft undertakings/order.	Merger parties (and, where relevant, third parties) comment on draft undertakings/order and request excisions (if any) prior to publication.
		CMA consults publicly on draft undertakings/order.	Merger parties (and third parties) comment further on draft undertakings/order.
Week 36	Statutory deadline for implementation of remedies (subject to any extensions of statutory deadlines)	CMA accepts final undertakings/makes final order within statutory 12 week deadline (subject to extension by six weeks if there are special reasons to do so). Responsibility for further implementation is assigned to a Group appointed to oversee this part of the process (usually the original Inquiry Group).	

SUSPENSION OF THE REFERENCE

10.11 Following the reference of an anticipated merger for a phase 2 investigation and within three weeks of the reference date, the CMA can suspend its phase 2 inquiry for a period of up to three weeks if the merger parties request it and the CMA reasonably believes that the merger may be abandoned by the merger parties.[174] This prevents wasted or unnecessary work by the CMA (and the need for merger parties and third parties to respond to initial information requests).

10.12 If the CMA suspends the investigation, it will publish, at the end of the suspension period (or earlier if the merger parties themselves announce publicly that the investigation has been suspended), a notice stating that the power was used and (if the merger was not abandoned) the date by which the CMA's phase 2 report will be published.

NOTES

162 See parts 3 and 9 of, and Schedules 8 and 10 to, the Act and Schedule 4 to the ERRA13.

163 The CMA Panel Chair is a member of the CMA Board.

164 Paragraph 46, Schedule 4 to the ERRA13.

165 CMA Board Rules of Procedure.

166 Sections 79(1) and (2) of the Act.

167 Section 82 of the Act.

168 Section 84 of the Act.

169 See paragraph 49, Schedule 4 to the ERRA13.

170 For example, merger parties may decide that a 'main party hearing' is unnecessary where the CMA's emerging thinking is such that the merger may not be expected to result in an SLC.

171 Information gathering continues to some extent throughout the inquiry. However, this initial phase (around weeks 1 to 6) is the period during which parties should expect information gathering to be most intensive (although the precise extent of necessary information gathering during this period will vary from case to case, depending on the extent, and ongoing relevance to the CMA's investigation, of information previously gathered at phase 1).

172 The CMA does not typically share its customer or competitor questions with the merger parties.

173 The CMA will typically not 'put back' text from written submissions or agreed oral evidence with parties. See further paragraph 12.8 below.

174 Section 39(8A) of the Act. See chapter 15 for the process of cancelling a reference. For abandonment after the SLC decision has been issued but before a reference is made, see paragraph 15.3.

11 PHASE 2 INQUIRIES: KEY STAGES PRIOR TO PROVISIONAL FINDINGS

PREPARATORY WORK FOR THE PHASE 2 INQUIRY

[3.496]

11.1 Shortly after a merger is referred, the CMA will publish the terms of its reference for a phase 2 investigation.[175] These terms of reference specify the transaction which is to be investigated, and summarise at a high level the basis on which the reference is made (that is, the market or markets in which the phase 1 decision maker believes there is an SLC).

11.2 In its phase 2 investigation, the CMA will use the evidence and information gathered in phase 1. In some cases, it may not be necessary to significantly expand this evidence base in order for the CMA to reach a properly informed decision on the phase 2 statutory competition questions.[176] In other cases, it will be necessary to expand this evidence base, but the CMA will seek to do so in a proportionate and targeted manner.

11.3 At an early stage in its phase 2 inquiry the CMA also considers the 'theories of harm' which will frame its substantive assessment of the phase 2 statutory competition question (see above) and focus any further information-gathering and analysis. Typically, the 'starting point' at phase 2 will be the theories of harm on which the CMA determined at phase 1 that the statutory test for reference was met. The CMA's theories of harm will be outlined in the issues statement when it is published (see paragraphs 11.30 to 11.31), and may evolve during the course of the inquiry in light of further evidence received and analysis undertaken.

11.4 The CMA also considers how best to conduct the phase 2 inquiry and draws up an administrative timetable which reflects the statutory time limits for investigations. The merger parties are sent a draft of the administrative timetable for comment. The final version of the administrative timetable is published on the case page.

CONTACT WITH THE MERGER PARTIES AT THE OUTSET OF THE PHASE 2 PROCESS

11.5 Following a reference from phase 1, the CMA will send the parties to the merger a phase 2 'opening letter'. This letter marks the formal start of the phase 2 inquiry. The phase 2 opening letter:

(a) covers important administrative details, for example, requesting information about the availability of the merger parties and any advisers during the inquiry period;

(b) in some cases, may include an information request under section 109 of the Act. The scope of any such information request will be determined primarily by the nature of information already gathered by the CMA at phase 1, on which it seeks to build. Where the CMA considers any information already provided at phase 1 to be sufficient for the purposes of starting a phase 2 inquiry, it will not ask merger parties to submit it again, but may (where relevant) ask for it to be updated to cover the time period (and any relevant developments or changes) since its original submission;

(c) invites the merger parties to participate, usually by telephone or videoconference and where the CMA considers it will be useful, in:
   (i) a 'case management meeting' with the case team. This meeting is an opportunity for merger parties to discuss the phase 2 timetable and administrative arrangements[177] and to ask the CMA questions about the phase 2 process; and
   (ii) a data meeting. This is an opportunity for the case team to discuss what (if any) relevant additional or updated data, internal documents and other information sources, not already drawn on during the phase 1 investigation, may be available to the merger parties. This helps to focus subsequent information requests, which will usually be sent under section 109 of the Act. The CMA will therefore request that representatives of the merger party who are familiar with that party's data and internal records/documents attend this meeting; and

(d) refers:
   (i) to the ongoing applicability and effect of any IEOs made during the phase 1 investigation, including any variation that may be required to such order(s);[178] and
   (ii) in the case of anticipated mergers, to section 78 of the Act, which prohibits the acquiring company from acquiring, without the CMA's consent, an interest in shares in a company if any enterprise to which the reference relates is carried on by or under the control of that company.

PHASE 2 INFORMATION-GATHERING

11.6 The theories of harm (see paragraph 11.3 above) form the framework for any subsequent information gathering by the CMA from both the merger parties and third parties. Information may be gathered by various means, including questionnaires, submissions, hearings, telephone or videoconference calls, surveys and site visits. Information-gathering takes place throughout the phase 2 inquiry. However, as set out in 11.2 above, the CMA's 'starting point' will be the evidence base obtained at phase 1 and, in some cases, it may not be necessary to significantly expand this evidence base.

11.7 As soon as practicable after the start of the phase 2 inquiry, the CMA is likely to issue the merger parties with questionnaires requesting any additional information to supplement the phase 1 evidence base.

11.8 Third parties will generally not be subject to the same degree of information-gathering in the phase 2 inquiry process as the merger parties.[179] However, some will receive information requests (which may be under section 109 of the Act where appropriate) and may be invited to give oral evidence to the case team (see paragraphs 11.23 to 11.24 below).

11.9 It is very important that merger parties (and third parties) respond to information requests fully and accurately. As at all other stages of the CMA's investigation, intentional or reckless provision of false or misleading information is a criminal offence, regardless of whether that information has been required by a notice under section 109 of the Act or has been provided voluntarily.[180] Intentional alteration, suppression or destruction of any documents a person is required to produce by a notice under section 109 of the Act is also an offence.[181] (See also paragraphs 9.14 to 9.17 above.)

11.10 Because of the strict phase 2 statutory deadlines that the CMA has to meet, it is essential that the CMA gathers the bulk of any additional information that it may require for its phase 2 analysis early in the process (notwithstanding that it may need to make further requests for information as the inquiry progresses).

11.11 Requests for information may be made informally or using the CMA's formal powers (see paragraphs 9.5 to 9.10 above). Requests for information from third parties will typically be issued on a voluntary basis but the CMA will use its section 109 information-gathering powers in relation to third parties where appropriate - for example, where delay or failure to respond to a voluntary request affects the ability of the CMA to progress its investigation. Whether information is requested on an informal or formal basis, it is important that recipients, as soon as possible after receiving a request for information, inform the CMA of any difficulties they may have in meeting the deadline for providing the information or in submitting the information in the requested format. Such discussions may enable the CMA to vary the information request or the stipulated response date (where appropriate).

Submissions

Key points where merger parties are invited to make written submissions

11.12 The merger parties are invited to make written submissions at several different stages in the process. The main opportunities to make written submissions on the substance of the case are, first, in response to the issues statement (see paragraphs 11.30 to 11.31), second, in response to the annotated issues statement (and any working papers disclosed at the same time) and, third, in response to the provisional findings. Where an SLC has been provisionally found, and remedies are envisaged, further opportunities to make written submissions are provided in response to a Notice of Possible Remedies and the CMA's remedies working paper[182] (see chapter 13 below).

11.13 A CMA phase 2 investigation is formal in nature and the process is not well suited to accommodating unsolicited submissions at other times. Parties and their advisers may wish to take into account that focusing their submissions on the key stages described in paragraph 11.12 above is the optimal means of engaging with the Inquiry Group. Parties are, of course, generally encouraged to bring new information or new circumstances to the attention of the CMA as soon as possible. While the CMA will seek to take other submissions provided outside the key stages into account, to the extent possible within the applicable statutory timescales, it may not do so where this would risk undermining the effective functioning of the CMA's investigation (for example by unnecessarily delaying the completion of the investigation).

11.14 In making submissions to the CMA, parties should provide the reasoning and evidence (including supporting documents) necessary to support the arguments or contentions made. Parties can, if they wish, provide this evidence by reference to previous submissions to the CMA (including submissions at phase 1). The CMA will generally publish submissions it receives (see paragraphs 11.18 to 11.22 below).

Submissions of technical economic analysis

11.15 When making submissions of technical economic analysis, parties should refer to the principles set out in the CC publication *Suggested best practice for submissions of technical economic analysis from parties to the CC* (CC2com3), which the CMA has adopted. Parties are encouraged to inform the CMA in advance of any proposed technical economic analysis but should be aware that the CMA will form its own independent assessment of the appropriate weight to be placed on any analysis and should not expect the CMA to agree the analytical approach in advance. Parties should also be aware that the timing of submission may also affect the weight that can be placed on any analysis due to the statutory timescales for a phase 2 inquiry.

Submissions of evidence based on surveys

11.16 In some cases, merger parties submit to the CMA evidence derived from surveys, for example, of consumers, customers, or suppliers; the CMA may also or alternatively commission its own surveys. In such cases, it is important that the research is statistically robust and the design and implementation of the survey is effective. If considering a survey, merger parties should refer to the principles set out in the CMA's *Good practice in the design and presentation of customer survey evidence in merger cases* (CMA78).

11.17 As with technical economic analysis, merger parties are encouraged to inform the CMA in advance of any proposed survey but should be aware that the CMA will form its own independent assessment of the appropriate weight to be placed on any survey evidence and should not expect the CMA to agree the survey approach in advance. Merger parties should also be aware that the timing of submission may also affect the weight that can be placed on any survey evidence due to the statutory timescales for a phase 2 inquiry.

Publication of submissions

11.18 The CMA generally publishes written submissions it receives in phase 2 investigations. Parties should provide non-confidential versions of all submissions for publication at the same time as their full submissions. If this is not possible, parties should submit a non-confidential version as soon as possible and agree a time-frame with the case team (which will be no more than five working days from the date that the full submission was provided).

11.19 The non-confidential version of the submission must set out the fundamentals of the relevant party's case, with a sufficient description of the evidence relied upon to enable other parties to understand and, if appropriate, make representations in relation to the inferences drawn from this evidence. Requests for confidential treatment of information should be limited to information that is genuinely sensitive, the disclosure or publication of which would be likely to cause significant harm to a party's legitimate business interests or to the interests of any individual to whom the information relates.[183] Parties should therefore accompany the non-confidential version with a detailed explanation of why they consider that particular parts of their submissions should not be disclosed, including explaining the nature of the information, the harm that could be caused, and the likelihood and magnitude of that harm. Where appropriate, it should also identify information which may be confidential as between the merger parties - for example, where external advisers have combined confidential information from both parties.

11.20 The final decision on disclosure lies with the Inquiry Group, having regard to the CMA's powers and duties under the Act.[184] The publication of a non-confidential version of a party's submission should not be taken to mean that the CMA necessarily accepts that all the material excised in that version of the document should not be published or disclosed at some future stage of the inquiry, if such disclosure becomes necessary to fulfil the CMA's functions under the Act.[185]

11.21 In practice, it may be possible to avoid disclosure of sensitive information by, for example, publishing an anonymous version of the submission or publishing the confidential information in a way that mitigates the sensitivity of this information, for example replacing specific figures with ranges.

11.22 In the event of a disagreement on the treatment of purportedly confidential information with the Inquiry Group, parties may make representations to the CMA's Procedural Officer within one working day (at least 24 hours, not counting weekends or public holidays) of the Inquiry Group's decision. The Procedural Officer will advise the Inquiry Group following consideration of the parties' representations.[186] The Inquiry Group will have all due regard to that advice, but the final decision remains with the Inquiry Group.

Third party oral evidence

11.23 Where a third party is asked to give oral evidence (which will usually be by telephone/videoconference call but may occasionally be in person) the discussion will typically be led by the case team, although Inquiry Group members may also participate. The CMA will record the telephone/videoconference call, having informed the counterparty before doing so. In some circumstances (for example, a merger which has attracted significant public interest), the CMA may consider that it is appropriate to publish a summary of third-party oral evidence on the CMA's website.[187]

11.24 In the case of completed mergers, the CMA may wish to seek views on the merger from those associated with the acquired business, separately from any submissions or oral evidence from the acquirer. For example, senior management of the acquired business, who have transferred to the acquirer, may be asked to give evidence separately from the acquirers. In addition, the seller, including any senior management of the acquired business that have left the organisation and professional advisers to the business (such as financial or insolvency advisers), may be required to provide information or give evidence to the CMA during the course of its inquiry.

Open and joint hearings

11.25 Early in the phase 2 inquiry, the CMA will consider whether one or more public hearings should be held. Given the timescales in a phase 2 inquiry, it is unusual in practice to hold an open hearing. Private, multi-party hearing (for example, involving industry commentators or a group of industry participants, sometimes under the auspices of a trade association) may occasionally be held.[188] These hearings are inquisitorial in nature and the aim is to allow the CMA to put questions to the parties, probe responses and test the strength of the submissions and evidence previously provided to the CMA by the parties.

Surveys and consultants

11.26 Where an inquiry involves a significant number of third-party suppliers or customers, or where the market is one directly affecting consumers, a survey may be a useful part of the phase 2 information-gathering process. If the CMA decides to conduct a survey, the merger parties will be consulted[189] on the draft survey design and survey questions.[190]

11.27 Before any contract to conduct the survey is awarded, the merger party or parties will, where practicable, be asked if they have any objections to the proposed market research organisations (for example, due to a possible conflict of interest). Any objections will be considered by the CMA prior to any appointment being made.

11.28 In cases where a survey is to be conducted, the CMA will sometimes need to obtain relevant contact details from those individuals or businesses who will be surveyed and will seek these details directly from the merger parties (and in some cases, from third parties as well).[191]

11.29 In some merger inquiries, the CMA may wish to employ a consultant to provide specialist advice on the sector concerned. Where possible, before any contract is awarded, the merger party or parties will be informed and allowed a short time to inform the CMA of any objections to the proposed consultants, which the CMA will consider prior to any appointment being finalised.

The issues statement

11.30 At an early stage of the phase 2 inquiry the CMA publishes an issues statement. The issues statement sets out one or more theories of harm which will form the framework for the CMA's competitive analysis at phase 2 and outlines the issues which the inquiry will be exploring. The issues statement will invite comments from parties, setting a deadline for their receipt. The issues statement will be sent to the merger party or parties shortly before publication.

11.31 Later in the inquiry, the issues statement will be annotated to indicate the current state of the CMA's thinking on the issues and provided to the merger parties in advance of the main party hearing (see paragraphs 12.4 to 12.6 below). The annotated issues statement is not published.

Site visit

11.32 During the early weeks of the phase 2 inquiry the case team may arrange a 'site visit' for the Inquiry Group and a selection of the case team.[192] This 'site visit' may be an 'in-person' event or it may be by videoconference. The 'site visit' is an opportunity for the CMA to gain a greater understanding of the merger parties' businesses and to engage with key commercial and operational staff. Merger parties are encouraged to organise a short presentation on their businesses in order to explain the nature of the businesses, followed by a tour of the relevant business areas (where appropriate and possible) and to provide an opportunity for the CMA to ask questions.[193] The CMA may also ask the merger parties to present on particular issues of relevance in the inquiry to help inform its understanding of these issues.

NOTES

[175] Pursuant to either section 22 (completed mergers) or section 33 (anticipated mergers) of the Act. In certain cases raising public interest considerations the reference is made by the Secretary of State; see chapter 16.

[176] That is, firstly, whether or not a relevant merger situation has been (or will be) created and second, if so, whether or not the relevant merger situation has resulted, or may be expected to result, in an SLC within any market or markets in the United Kingdom for goods or services.

[177] For example, suggestions for site visits.

[178] On referral to a phase 2 investigation, the CMA will consider whether any or additional interim measures are necessary. For further information on the CMA's approach to interim measures, please see *Interim measures in merger investigations* (CMA108).

[179] In cases where third parties have a significant role in the industry affected by the merger, third party input may be more substantial.

Part 3 CMA and other Guidelines

[180] Section 117 of the Act.

[181] Section 110(5) of the Act.

[182] The remedies working paper is typically only disclosed to the merger parties.

[183] Section 244 of the Act.

[184] As described in this guidance, as well as in *Transparency and disclosure: Statement of the CMA's policy and approach* (CMA6) and *Chairman's Guidance on Disclosure of Information in Merger Inquiries, Market Investigations and Reviews of Undertakings and Orders accepted or made under the Enterprise Act 2002 and Fair Trading Act 1973* (CC7).

[185] Parties will be informed of any decision to publish previously excised material that remains unpublished and given an opportunity to make representations.

[186] The Procedural Officer is intended to provide a swift, efficient supplementary mechanism for resolving disputes relating to the confidentiality of information in a party's submission proposed to be published by the CMA. The procedure followed by the Procedural Officer in this regard will be flexible, and will be tailored to the nature of the dispute at hand and, in particular, to any specific timing constraints to which the CMA's investigation is subject.

[187] If a summary of third party oral evidence is to be published then, prior to its publication, the summary will be sent to the relevant third party for checking of factual accuracy and for the identification of any confidential material. The CMA will then consider whether the material is within the scope of Part 9 of the Act.

[188] See, for example, the CMA Final Report: Anticipated acquisition by 21st Century Fox of shares in Sky plc (5 June 2018), during which the CMA held a roundtable on issues concerning media plurality, as well as a multi-party hearing with various interested third parties.

[189] The CMA's timing constraints at this stage of its investigation means that, in some cases, the time available for this consultation will be necessarily short and merging parties may only be given one working day (at least 24 hours, not counting weekends or public holidays) to submit any comments.

[190] See *Tobii AB (PUBL) v CMA* [2020] CAT 1, at paragraphs 291 and 220, where the CAT found that the CMA's *Good practice in the design and presentation of consumer survey evidence in merger cases* (CMA78)) is targeted at commissioned statistical sample research surveys rather than qualitative research methods. In contrast to its stated approach regarding statistical sample research surveys, the CMA will typically not consult the merger parties on or disclose questions put to third parties as part of its evidence gathering or requests for information that are issued during the course of its investigation.

[191] Parties may request that the CMA require them to provide such information pursuant to its powers under section 109 of the Act, where they have regulatory or other concerns about providing the data voluntarily.

[192] Where this is appropriate, given the nature of the businesses involved. If the nature of the business does not lend itself to a site visit, a presentation by the merger parties on the relevant industry may take place instead.

[193] Although these are intended to be scene-setting meetings, where appropriate, the CMA may disclose to other parties non-confidential versions of material presented to it.

12 PROVISIONAL FINDINGS

DEVELOPING THE ANALYSIS

[3.497]

12.1 Following any submissions in response to the issues statement and its continued information-gathering, the CMA will develop its analysis on the case prior to the main party hearing.

ANNOTATED ISSUES STATEMENT

12.2 In advance of a main party hearing, the CMA will provide the merger parties with an annotated issues statement which sets out its emerging thinking on the matters outlined in the issues statement. In addition to the annotated issues statement, the CMA may also decide to disclose a limited number of key 'working papers' covering matters it wishes to discuss with the merger parties at the hearing (although the number and nature of working papers that the CMA discloses will vary depending on the circumstances of the case at issue).

12.3 Merger parties will be given the opportunity to comment in writing on the annotated issues statement (and any key working papers which have been disclosed). Typically, the deadline for any comments will be shortly after the main party hearing.

THE MAIN PARTY HEARINGS

12.4 Towards the end of the information-gathering phase, the CMA will typically hold hearings with each of the merger parties.[194] A hearing agenda will give an indication of the topics that the CMA wishes to explore in the main party hearing. The hearings will be attended by the Inquiry Group[195] and members of the case team. The CMA will wish to speak to senior management in the businesses affected by the merger. The CMA will inform the merger parties if it wishes specified individuals or representatives of particular business areas to attend the hearing. In the case of a completed merger, the CMA may wish to hold a separate hearing with the sellers/former management of the acquired company (see paragraph 11.24). For an anticipated merger, the CMA is likely to want to hear from the acquirer and the target business separately.

12.5 The primary purpose of the main party hearing is to enable the CMA to test certain evidence and explore key issues with the merger parties. The hearings therefore take place at a stage in the investigation at which Inquiry Group members have absorbed sufficient evidence to produce an annotated issues statement and to frame challenging questions based on the evidence[196] and the annotated issues statement/any working papers which have been disclosed to the merger parties. It also provides an opportunity for the merger parties to explain their position on these issues orally and directly to the phase 2 decision makers.

12.6 At the hearing, the merger party is given the opportunity to make brief opening and/or closing statements.[197] The CMA will then ask the merger party a series of questions. These questions will be led by the Inquiry Group but members of the case team are also likely to ask questions. A transcript of the hearing will be taken, and will be sent to the relevant merger party after the hearing for checking (the transcript is not published). The intentional or reckless provision of false or misleading information during a hearing is a criminal offence.[198] While a merger party may be accompanied by its legal or other professional advisers, the CMA will expect to hear primarily from the representatives of the business themselves. The CMA may direct its questioning at specific individuals. If merger parties are unable to provide specific information requested at the hearing, this may be provided subsequently in writing, usually with a short deadline for response.[199]

'PUT-BACK'

12.7 Towards the end of the information-gathering phase, and prior to its provisional findings, the CMA may, where appropriate, send extracts - from its working papers and/or its draft provisional findings - to merger parties and third parties to identify potentially confidential material, prior to disclosure of the material.

12.8 The CMA will typically not 'put back' draft text to parties to verify factual accuracy where the draft text is taken directly from information already provided to the CMA, whether in phase 1 or in phase 2 - for example, from previous written submissions, responses to written questions, or from agreed notes of oral evidence. In these cases, put back will be limited to the purpose of identifying potentially confidential information (to the extent parties have not previously been given the opportunity to indicate whether or not the information may be confidential).

12.9 Parties should give reasons for any requests they make for material to be excised from CMA documents that are to be published (for example, its provisional findings), by reference to section 244 of the Act (see also paragraphs 11.18 to 11.22 above).

12.10 As the put-back process is intended to be limited to identifying confidential information (and occasionally, and typically mainly with third parties, any factual inaccuracies), the relevant parties will be given a relatively brief period to respond to put-back requests.

12.11 When the Inquiry Group has made its decision on excisions from its provisional findings (see paragraphs 12.12 to 12.13 below), parties will be informed of any requests the Inquiry Group has rejected. The party has the right to make further representations to the Procedural Officer, although the final decision remains with the Inquiry Group.

PROVISIONAL FINDINGS

12.12 After considering all of the relevant evidence, the CMA publishes its provisional findings which represents a provisional decision on first, whether or not a relevant merger situation has been (or will be) created and second, if so, whether or not the relevant merger situation has resulted, or may be expected to result, in an SLC within any market or markets in the United Kingdom for goods or services.

12.13 The provisional findings report sets out the core background details necessary for an understanding of the inquiry (for example, details of the merger parties, the principal features of the industry where relevant and a description of the transaction) and a full explanation of the CMA's reasoning in reaching its provisional findings. The provisional findings report is therefore the main means the CMA uses to satisfy its duty to consult under section 104 of the Act, by disclosing its provisional decisions, and the underlying reasoning. Alongside the provisional findings report, the CMA will publish a Notice of provisional findings[200] and will generally issue a press release. For further information on the CMA's approach to communicating and publishing the provisional findings report see chapter 19 below.

NOTICE OF POSSIBLE REMEDIES

12.14 Where the CMA has provisionally found an SLC (or SLCs), it will publish a Notice of Possible Remedies which acts as a formal starting point for discussion of remedies. The Notice of Possible Remedies will set out one or more options to remedy the SLC (or SLCs) that the CMA provisionally expects to arise as a result of the merger, and will usually set out the CMA's initial thoughts on the relative merits of these options. If merger parties wish to propose potential remedies in advance of publication of provisional findings, details of the proposals should be provided in writing and may be discussed with the case team (and the Inquiry Group, in certain circumstances) without prejudice to the CMA's provisional findings. Where relevant, the Notice of Possible Remedies will include any options put forward by the merger parties (although generally these will not be identified as such in the Notice). The Notice of Possible Remedies will invite comments by a given date from all interested parties on the remedies set out in the Notice, and will also invite parties to suggest alternatives.

NOTES

194 The CMA may compel specified persons to attend to give evidence and may also take evidence under oath using its powers under section 109 of the Act.

195 The merger parties will be informed if members of the Inquiry Group are unable to attend the main party hearing.

196 The CMA will give the merger parties advance notice of any evidence it wishes to discuss at the main party hearing.

197 Merger parties must inform the case team in advance if they wish to make an opening or closing statement and discuss the appropriate length of such statements given the timing constraints of the hearing (typically no more than 15 minutes will be available for such statements). Where relevant, merger parties should provide copies in advance of any presentation materials they wish to use when making those statements. As the CMA will have received and considered written submissions from the merger parties, as well as other evidence, it is not necessary for the merger parties to restate in detail all aspects of their case.

[198] Section 117 of the Act.

[199] In such circumstances, the CMA may recall specified persons to give further evidence (whether voluntarily or pursuant to a notice issued under section 109 of the Act).

[200] *CMA Rules for Merger, Market and Special Reference Groups,* (CMA 17), Rule 11.

13 AFTER PROVISIONAL FINDINGS

PUBLIC CONSULTATION ON PROVISIONAL FINDINGS AND NOTICE OF POSSIBLE REMEDIES

[3.498]

13.1 The Notice of provisional findings identifies a period (of at least 21 days[201]) in which parties can comment on the provisional findings. Where the CMA has provisionally found an SLC arising from the merger, consideration of possible remedies to the SLC proceeds in parallel with consultation on the provisional findings. Responses to the Notice of Possible Remedies are typically requested within 14 days of publication of that Notice (and in any event, no less than seven days) so that they can be considered before any 'response hearings' (see paragraph 13.16 below).[202]

13.2 Responses from parties to the provisional findings and the Notice of Possible Remedies are published on the CMA's inquiry web-page. For further information on the CMA's approach to communicating and publishing the provisional findings report see chapter 19 below.

13.3 The CMA will consider all responses it receives, and whether the provisional findings should be altered in the light of these.

DISCLOSURE IN PROVISIONAL FINDINGS REPORT

13.4 The CMA has a statutory duty to consult any party whose interests are likely to be adversely affected by the CMA's proposed decision on the outcome of a merger and to give reasons for that proposed decision.[203] Consistent with settled precedent,[204] the provisional findings are the means by which the CMA fulfils this duty,[205] enabling merger parties to have an opportunity to respond to, challenge, and correct[206] the CMA.

13.5 However, the Act also imposes a general restriction on the disclosure of 'specified information'; that is, information the CMA receives during the course of a merger inquiry which relates to the affairs of an individual or business of an undertaking.[207]

13.6 Both of these duties are qualified under the Act. The CMA's obligation to consult is subject to any need to keep what is proposed, or the reasons for it, confidential,[208] while the obligation to keep confidential specified information can be overridden for the purpose of facilitating the exercise by the CMA of its functions under the Act.[209] In balancing these potentially conflicting obligations, the CMA must ensure that it discloses confidential specified information[210] only insofar as it is necessary to do so.[211]

13.7 In accordance with settled precedent, the disclosure of confidential information will be deemed necessary where it forms part of the 'gist of the case' the merger parties have to answer.[212] In other words, the merger parties need to be provided with sufficient information in order to be able to make informed submissions in response to the CMA's provisional findings.

13.8 What constitutes the 'gist' of a case is context-sensitive.[213] In most cases, the 'gist' of the case will be provided in the provisional findings report.

13.9 There is therefore no general right of 'access to file' within CMA merger control proceedings,[214] and the CMA is not, as a general principle, obliged to disclose all inculpatory or exculpatory material.[215]

Additional Disclosure

13.10 Where the CMA considers that it must disclose highly confidential third party information as part of the gist of the case, it may choose to impose additional safeguards to the disclosure of such information, most commonly by disclosing the information into a confidentiality ring or data room.

13.11 It is in the CMA's discretion to decide whether this is appropriate in a particular case.[216] Disclosure may take the form of unredacted sections of the provisional findings or of information contained in separate documents (eg a summary of third party views or unredacted data sets).

13.12 Confidentiality rings and disclosure rooms provide access to confidential information held by the CMA in a restricted manner. They limit the number and/or category of persons having access (and the use of the information being accessed). Strict rules relating to access and onward disclosure will be applied and recipients, likely to be restricted to the merger parties' external advisers only, will be required to acknowledge that they understand the basis on which such disclosure is made and that they will comply with these restrictions.[217]

13.13 Breaching the terms of the confidentiality ring or data room carries serious consequences and may result in criminal penalties (up to 2 years imprisonment and/or a fine with no upper limit),[218] referral of the advisors to their professional regulator for disciplinary action, and potential exclusion from the current data room and any future CMA data access.

13.14 The CMA will engage in advance with other parties (including third parties where relevant) prior to disclosing information in this way. The CMA may also anonymise and/or aggregate information and take any other steps it considers are reasonable in relation to the disclosed information.

13.15 The disclosure of information into a confidentiality ring or data room to the merger parties' external advisers remains subject to Part 9 of the Act. The CMA will at all times seek to uphold its duty of maintaining confidentiality where possible, and the possibility of using a confidentiality ring or disclosure room to share confidential information will not result in the disclosure of confidential information beyond that necessary to provide the 'gist' of the case.

RESPONSE HEARINGS

13.16 Where the CMA has provisionally found an SLC arising from the merger, response hearings with the merger parties will take place. Response hearings will usually take place after the deadline for responses to the Notice of Possible Remedies but before the deadline for responses to the CMA's provisional findings.

13.17 The response hearing will be led by the Inquiry Group with case team support. Parties will be given the opportunity at the beginning to briefly comment orally on the provisional findings and the CMA may seek clarification of particular points made in written submissions or at the hearing. However, the hearing will focus on possible remedies. The format of the response hearing is otherwise similar to that of the main party hearing (see paragraph 12.6 above).

REMEDIES WORKING PAPER

13.18 A remedies working paper, containing a detailed assessment of the different remedies options and setting out a provisional decision on remedies, will be sent to the merger parties for comment following the response hearings.[219] The remedies working paper will also set out the CMA's views on whether the merger gives rise to RCBs,[220] and if so, whether the proposed remedies should be modified in order to preserve those benefits. A period of typically no less than five working days would normally be allowed for the merger parties to submit their comments. Third parties may also be consulted about the proposed scope of remedies and their views on any RCBs. The remedies working paper is not usually published.

13.19 Following consultation with the merger parties on the remedies working paper and any further discussions and meetings with them that the CMA considers necessary, the CMA takes its final decisions on both the competition issues and any remedies.

13.20 The CMA's final report must normally be published[221] within 24 weeks of the date of the reference.[222] The inquiry can be extended, once only, by up to eight weeks if the CMA considers there are special reasons why a report cannot be prepared and published within the statutory deadline.[223] In addition to an extension for special reasons, the inquiry period can be extended if one of the merger parties fails (with or without reasonable excuse) to provide information in response to a formal section 109 notice within the time stated in the notice.[224] In this case the inquiry timetable is extended until the information is provided to the satisfaction of the CMA or the CMA decides to cancel the extension. If the inquiry timetable is extended for any reason a notice of extension will be published[225] and the administrative timetable will be revised and republished.

13.21 Where the CMA changes its provisional decisions on the statutory questions (or, exceptionally, where the 'gist' of the CMA's case fundamentally evolves) as a result of evidence received following publication of its provisional findings, it may be appropriate for the CMA to publish on its website, or otherwise disclose to the merger parties and relevant third parties, a description of its reasons for changing its provisional decision in order to provide parties with an opportunity to comment prior to publication of the final report. In such cases, the requirement for a minimum 21-day period for consultation on provisional findings does not apply and an appropriate period for response will be set depending on the circumstances of the case in question.[226] In deciding whether it is necessary to publish or otherwise disclose such an update to its provisional findings, the CMA will in particular have regard to its statutory duties to consult where it proposes to make a relevant decision that is likely to be adverse to the interests of the merger parties.[227]

THE FINAL REPORT

13.22 The CMA is required to publish its conclusions on the statutory questions (see paragraphs 3.1 to 3.8 above) in a report which must contain the reasons for the decisions and such information as the CMA considers appropriate for a proper understanding of the decision and the reasons.[228] The report will also contain the CMA's final decisions on remedies if there is an SLC finding. For further information on the CMA's approach to communicating and publishing the final report see chapter 19 below.

13.23 If there is no SLC finding in the CMA's final report, this is the final stage in the phase 2 inquiry process.

13.24 Following publication of the final report, if the CMA has concluded that a merger would give rise to an SLC and that remedial action should be taken by it to remedy that SLC, the CMA will take steps to implement such remedies.

NOTES

201 Note that these are calendar days and run from the date on which the merger parties are notified of the provisional findings, and not the date of publication on the CMA's website.

202 In the interests of keeping the inquiry to schedule, response hearings will usually be held before the 21-day consultation period on the provisional findings has expired. In such cases, the merger parties are still able to provide their written comments in response to the provisional findings at any time within the period specified in the Notice of provisional findings.

203 Section 104 of the Act.

204 *Tobii AB (Pulb) v CMA* [2020] CAT 1, at paragraph 117; *Ryanair v Competition Commission* [2014] CAT 3, at

Part 3 CMA and other Guidelines

paragraph 128; *BMI Healthcare Limited v Competition Commission* [2013] CAT 24, at paragraph 20.

205 *Chairman's guidance on disclosure of information in merger and market inquiries* (CC7) (Revised), paragraph 7.1.

206 *Ryanair v Competition Commission* [2014] CAT 3, at paragraph 133.

207 Sections 237 and 238 of the Act. The CMA also notes that section 104 of the Act refers to the need to protect confidentiality.

208 Section 104(4)(b) of the Act. It is also qualified by the practical restrictions imposed by the CMA's investigation timetable (under section 104(4)(a) of the Act).

209 Section 241 of the Act. Other gateways are set out in sections 239 to 244 of the Act.

210 That is, commercial information whose disclosure the CMA thinks might significantly harm the legitimate business interests of an undertaking or information relating to the private affairs of an individual whose disclosure the CMA thinks might significantly harm the individual's interests.

211 Section 244 of the Act.

212 *R v Secretary of State for the Home Department, Ex parte Doody* [1993] UKHL 8 ("**Doody**"), page 14.

213 *BMI Healthcare Ltd v. Competition Commission* [2013] CAT 24 ("**BMI**"), at paragraph 39(7).

214 *BMI Healthcare Ltd v. Competition Commission* [2013] CAT 24 ("**BMI**"), at paragraph 4.

215 *Groupe Eurotunnel SA v Competition Commission* [2013] CAT 30 at paragraph 221.

216 *BMI Healthcare (No.1) v Competition Commission* [2013] CAT 24, at paragraph 46.

217 The CMA has published confidentiality ring and disclosure room undertakings templates.

218 A breach of Part 9 of the Act constitutes a criminal offence under s.245 of the Act.

219 *Merger Remedies* (CMA87) explains how the CMA conducts its substantive assessment of remedies options, and how it takes RCBs into account in this assessment.

220 As defined in section 30 of the Act.

221 The CMA is responsible for publishing all its reports of merger inquiries that are not public interest cases (as to which, see chapter 16).

222 Section 39(1) of the Act. The statutory deadline for publication will normally, for convenience, be stated in the phase 1 reference and will also be shown in the administrative timetable and on the inquiry page for the relevant inquiry at https://www.gov.uk/cma-cases.

223 Section 39(3) of the Act. The CMA is required also to publish the reasons for any such extension (section 107(2)(c) and 107(4) of the Act).

224 Section 39(4) of the Act. For further information on section 109 notices, see paragraphs 11.10 to 11.11; and paragraphs 18. 1 to 18.7 concerning multi-jurisdictional mergers.

225 Section 107(2)(c) of the Act.

226 See, for example, CMA revised provisional findings: Anticipated acquisition by Amazon of certain rights and a minority shareholding in Deliveroo (1 July 2020).

227 Section 104 of the Act.

228 Section 38 of the Act.

14 IMPLEMENTATION OF PHASE 2 REMEDIES

[3.499]

14.1 Following publication of the final report, if the CMA has concluded that a merger would give rise to an SLC and that remedial action should be taken by it to remedy that SLC, the CMA will take steps to implement such remedies.

14.2 The CMA will also consider whether interim measures should be put in place (where none are already in place) or existing interim measures varied (for example, allowing for the appointment of a monitoring trustee), pending the implementation of final remedies.

14.3 The CMA will agree draft undertakings with the merger parties, or produce a draft order, which will then be consulted on publicly. Taking into account any responses to its consultation, the CMA will then publish a 'notice of acceptance of undertakings' or a 'notice of making an order'. At this point, the inquiry will be finally determined.

14.4 The CMA is subject to a statutory deadline of 12 weeks following its final report, extendable once by up to six weeks if the CMA considers there are special reasons for doing so, to implement its phase 2 remedies.[229]

14.5 The process of agreeing undertakings or making an order is set out fully in the CMA's guidance on *Merger remedies* (CMA87).

NOTES

229 These time limits may be further extended where a relevant party has failed to comply with the requirements of a notice requiring the submission of evidence issued under section 109 of the Act.

15 THE ABANDONMENT PROCESS

[3.500]

15.1 In some cases an anticipated merger may be abandoned by the merger parties during the course of the CMA's review.

15.2 In order to be satisfied that the merger parties have abandoned the merger, the CMA will require sufficient evidence that this is the case. The CMA may seek written assurances directly from the merger parties (from persons of suitable seniority and with authority to bind the acquirer).

15.3 If an anticipated merger is abandoned before the CMA takes a decision at phase 1, the CMA can issue a decision finding that its duty to refer does not arise because there is no relevant merger situation.[230] If an anticipated merger is abandoned after an SLC has been found at phase 1 but before reference (during the period when the CMA is waiting to receive a UIL offer) then the duty to refer has arisen, but the CMA may exercise its discretion not to refer on the basis that the merger is insufficiently likely to proceed.[231]

15.4 Section 37(1) of the Act requires the CMA to cancel a phase 2 reference if it considers that the proposal to make arrangements of the kind mentioned in the reference has been abandoned.[232] Where it is claimed that the arrangements have been abandoned and new arrangements are proposed or contemplated, the CMA must be satisfied that the arrangements that are described in the terms of reference have, in fact, been abandoned and that the new arrangements are not merely an amended form of the arrangements that were referred.[233]

15.5 If an Inquiry Group has not been constituted, or an Inquiry Group has not held its first meeting, the Chair of the CMA is able to cancel a reference where he or she is satisfied that arrangements have been abandoned.[234] If an Inquiry Group has been appointed and has held its first meeting, it falls to the Inquiry Group to cancel the reference.

15.6 Merger parties may seek cancellation of a reference at any time prior to final determination of that reference.

15.7 The CMA has no power to cancel an investigation of a completed merger.[235 229] These time limits may be further extended where a relevant party has failed to comply with the requirements of a notice requiring the submission of evidence issued under section 109 of the Act.

NOTES

230 See, for example, CMA Decision: Anticipated acquisition by Non-Standard Finance PLC of Provident Financial PLC (11 June 2019).

231 Section 33(2)(b) of the Act. The Act does not require such decisions to be published, but the outcome will be indicated on the case page. See, for example, CMA Decision: Anticipated acquisition by Safetykleen UK Ltd of Pure Solve UK Limited (11 May 2016).

232 As discussed in paragraphs 10.11 and 10.12 above, the CMA may also, within three weeks of the reference and at the request of a relevant person connected to the merger parties, suspend the phase 2 timetable for up to three weeks if the CMA reasonably believes that an anticipated merger might be abandoned (section 39(8A) of the Act). If during this suspension the merger parties abandon the merger, the CMA will cancel the reference.

233 *R v MMC and SoS for Trade and Industry ex parte Argyll Group* [1986] 2 All ER 257.

234 Paragraph 47, Schedule 4 to ERRA13.

235 In circumstances where only part of the arrangements under consideration have been abandoned, it may be appropriate for the CMA to continue its investigation.

16 PUBLIC INTEREST MERGERS

INTRODUCTION TO PUBLIC INTEREST MERGERS

[3.501]

16.1 The Act provides that (as the default position) the CMA decides whether or not to refer the merger for a phase 2 investigation, and that the phase 2 Inquiry Group makes the final decision as to whether any competition issues arise and whether any remedies are required, based purely on whether the merger has caused or may cause a substantial lessening of competition (SLC). However, the Act also allows for the Secretary of State to assume responsibility for determining whether or not to refer a merger when defined public interest considerations are potentially relevant by issuing a public interest intervention notice (PIIN). If the Secretary of State has referred a merger on such public interest grounds, he or she also takes the final decision on whether the merger operates or may be expected to operate against the public interest, and on any remedies for identified public interest concerns.

16.2 The UK Government has published guidance on the operation of the public interest merger regime, which includes contact information for interested parties.[236]

16.3 Section 42 of the Act therefore provides that the Secretary of State may issue a PIIN in the case of mergers that meet the Act's jurisdictional thresholds (set out in paragraph 4.5 above), that have public interest implications[237], and which the CMA has not referred for a phase 2 investigation.

16.4 To facilitate this, the CMA has an obligation under section 57 of the Act to inform the Secretary of State where it is investigating a merger (at phase 1) that it believes raises material public interest considerations.

PUBLIC INTEREST CONSIDERATIONS

16.5 Section 58 of the Act details the public interest considerations on which the Secretary of State may intervene in a merger case. These are:

(a) national security, including public security;[238, 239]

(b) plurality and other considerations relating to newspapers and other media, specifically[240]

  (i) the need for accurate presentation of news and free expression of opinion in newspapers

  (ii) the need for, to the extent that it is reasonable and practicable, a sufficient plurality of views in newspapers in each market for newspapers in the UK or a part of the UK

  (iii) the need, in relation to every different audience in the UK or in a particular area or locality of the UK, for there to be a sufficient plurality of persons with control of the media enterprises serving that audience

  (iv) the need for the availability throughout the UK of a wide range of broadcasting which (taken as a whole) is both of high quality and calculated to appeal to a wide variety of tastes and interests

(v) the need for persons carrying on media enterprises, and for those with control of such enterprises, to have a genuine commitment to the attainment in relation to broadcasting of the standards objectives set out in section 319 of the Communications Act 2003;[241]

(c) the interest of maintaining the stability of the UK financial system;[242],[243] and

(d) the need to maintain in the UK the capability to combat, and to mitigate the effects of, public health emergencies.[244]

16.6 In addition to the specified considerations outlined above, section 42(3) of the Act also allows the Secretary of State to intervene on the basis of a consideration which is not specified but which the Secretary of State believes ought to be specified. To the extent that the Secretary of State intervenes on the basis of a consideration that he or she believes ought to be specified, he or she is required by section 42 of the Act to seek to have that consideration subsequently inserted into section 58 of the Act by means of an order approved by both Houses of Parliament.

PROCESS FOR PUBLIC INTEREST CASES

Phase 1

16.7 If a PIIN is issued, the case is handled in the following way:

(a) The CMA will publish an invitation to comment seeking third party views on both competition and public interest issues.

(b) As well as generally issuing an invitation for comment, the CMA will actively contact other governmental departments, sectoral regulators, industry associations and consumer bodies for their views on public interest issues where appropriate. For example, in a case raising national security issues relating to security of energy supply, the CMA would seek submissions from Ofgem and would pass these on in full to the Secretary of State. For cases raising national security issues relating to defence, this would be the Ministry of Defence, and for national security issues relating to the police, this would be the Home Office. In media public interest cases, section 44A of the Act provides expressly for a report by Ofcom.[245]

(c) The CMA will carry out its review of the jurisdictional and competition issues in a similar way as it would for any other case, with the caveat that its process and timetable will be adapted in order to enable it to provide its report to the Secretary of State by the deadline specified in the PIIN.

(d) The CMA then provides advice to the Secretary of State on jurisdictional and competition issues, which must be accepted (section 46 of the Act). The CMA is also required to pass to the Secretary of State a summary of any representations it has received that relate to the public interest matters.[246] The Act allows the CMA to provide advice and recommendations on the public interest consideration to the Secretary of State; however, given the CMA's role as a competition agency, the CMA would not normally provide its advice on public interest issues at phase 1. (By contrast, following a reference on public interest grounds, the independent phase 2 Inquiry Group will report to the Secretary of State about whether the merger operates or may be expected to operate against the public interest: see further paragraph 16.9 below.)

(e) The CMA will also inform the Secretary of State about the applicability of any of the exceptions to the duty to refer and as to whether it would be appropriate to deal with any competition concerns by way of UILs.[247]

(f) The Secretary of State then makes a decision on the outcome of the case in the light of the CMA's advice.[248] References for a phase 2 investigation can be made under section 45 of the Act either:

(i) because the Secretary of State believes that a relevant merger situation has been created or arrangements are in progress or in contemplation which, if carried into effect, will result in the creation of a relevant merger situation and it is or may be the case that the merger has resulted, or may be expected to result, in an SLC and, combined with the relevant public interest consideration(s), the merger operates or may be expected to operate against the public interest; or

(ii) while there is no realistic prospect of an SLC arising from the merger, because the public interest considerations are such that it is or may be the case that the merger operates or may be expected to operate against the public interest.[249]

(g) Alternatively, the Secretary of State may decide under section 45(6) of the Act not to make a reference on the basis that an anti-competitive outcome in the form of a CMA finding of a realistic prospect of an SLC is justified by one or more public interest considerations.[250]

(h) Where the Secretary of State is minded to refer the case for a phase 2 investigation, he or she will also consider whether UILs are justified.

16.8 If the Secretary of State concludes, after receipt of the CMA's report, that there are no public interest issues that are relevant to the PIIN, the CMA will be instructed under section 56 of the Act to deal with the merger as an ordinary merger case.[251],[252]

Phase 2

16.9 If a reference is made on public interest grounds (whether or not there are any competition concerns), the CMA conducts a phase 2 inquiry and reports to the Secretary of State. If the CMA considers that the merger operates or may be expected to operate against the public interest, it makes recommendations as to the action the Secretary of State (or others) should take to remedy any adverse effects. The Secretary of State will make the final decision on the public interest test and take whatever remedial steps he or she considers necessary to address the competition and public interest issues.

16.10 The CMA's phase 2 procedures for public interest inquiries are similar to those for ordinary merger references. The principal differences are that the CMA provides its report to the Secretary of State and the final decision on public interest matters lies with the Secretary of State. The CMA has to prepare a report and give it to the Secretary of State within 24 weeks (subject to a possible eight-week extension) from the date of the reference.

The Act does not require the CMA to consult the Secretary of State in the event that the CMA proposes to extend the inquiry.

16.11 Once the Secretary of State has received the CMA's report, he or she has 30 days in which to make and publish his or her decision.[253] The Secretary of State is bound by the CMA's decision on whether there is a merger situation and its findings on whether or not there is an SLC, but must decide on whether there is a concern in relation to the specified public interest issue. The Secretary of State must have regard to the findings in the CMA's report regarding remedies, but can also decide on remedies other than those the CMA has recommended. If the Secretary of State decides that the public interest issue does not raise a concern, the case will be sent back to the CMA to decide how to remedy any competition issue identified.[254]

16.12 There may also be further procedural differences applicable to a PIIN case and a typical merger investigation focussing purely on competition grounds, to reflect the different statutory questions at issue, differences in the assessment which is required to answer the statutory questions at issue, as well as differences in the CMA's approach to engagement with the merger parties and third parties. As part of its inquiry, the CMA will typically engage other governmental departments as relevant third parties. The degree to which the CMA seeks information and views from governmental departments, relative to other parties, will depend on the nature and scope of the phase 2 inquiry. There may also be particular sensitivities around the confidentiality of information which may include national security considerations (if applicable) that would require the CMA to amend its typical approach to an ordinary merger investigation.

PUBLICATION OF DECISIONS

16.13 When the Secretary of State has made a decision as to whether or not to refer the case for a phase 2 investigation, the Secretary of State is required under section 107 of the Act to publish a non-confidential version of the CMA's phase 1 report. At phase 2, the Secretary of State must publish a non-confidential version of the CMA's final report no later than the publication of his or her decision on the case[255] (that is, within 30 days). The final decision on the material to be excised from the published report is made by the Secretary of State.[256]

FEES

16.14 A merger fee is calculated in respect of cases in which a PIIN has been issued in the same way as for normal competition cases (see chapter 20 below).

PUBLIC INTEREST IN SPECIAL MERGER SITUATIONS

16.15 Section 59 of the Act also allows the Secretary of State to intervene in a very limited number of cases that do not qualify under the Act's general merger regime but where a specified consideration is relevant to the merger. These special merger situations may arise in defence industry mergers if at least one of the enterprises concerned is carried on in the UK by, or under the control of, a body corporate incorporated in the UK and where one or more of the enterprises concerned is a relevant government contractor.[257] In addition, following the Communications Act 2003, a special merger situation may also arise where the merger involves a supplier or suppliers of at least 25% of any description of newspapers or broadcasting in the UK or in a substantial part of the UK. Unlike the standard jurisdictional test, no increment to this share of supply is required. The CMA will not conduct a competition assessment in such cases.

16.16 In cases where the Secretary of State has issued a special public interest intervention notice (SPIIN), the CMA will prepare a report under section 61 of the Act for the Secretary of State advising on whether a special merger situation has been created. The SPIIN will set out the time period within which the CMA must provide this report to the Secretary of State. The CMA will also summarise representations that it has received relating to the considerations in the SPIIN. Given that the CMA is not expert in the considerations that would be expected to be specified in the SPIIN, it is likely to confine itself at phase 1 to summarising and commenting on the representations received by relevant third party experts, such as the Ministry of Defence or Ofcom as applicable.[258]

16.17 The Secretary of State may make a reference for a phase 2 investigation under section 62 of the Act if he or she believes that it is or may be the case that, taking account only of the public interest consideration, the creation of the special merger situation operates or may be expected to operate against the public interest. The CMA's phase 1 report is published by the Secretary of State at the time the reference decision is announced. The final decision on the material to be excised from the published report is made by the Secretary of State.

16.18 Following a reference on special public interest grounds, the CMA is responsible for the conduct of the inquiry and reports its findings to the Secretary of State. The CMA would apply similar procedures to those outlined for normal mergers subject to the procedural differences set out in paragraphs 16.9 to 16.12 above relating to public interest mergers, although its assessment would be confined to the public interest issues specified in the intervention notice.

16.19 No merger fee is payable in special public interest cases.

NOTES

236 See BEIS Guidance: Enterprise Act 2002: changes to the turnover and share of supply tests for mergers (June 2020). This can be found at https://assets.publishing.service.gov.uk/government/uploads/system/uploads/attachment_ data/file/902531/Enterprise_Act_2002_guidance_on_changes_to_the_turnover_and_share_of_supply_tests_for_mergers__Orders_2020_.pdf.

237 The Secretary of State may also intervene in certain public interest cases where the jurisdictional thresholds are not met (see 'public interest in special merger situations' below; paragraph 16.15 *et seq.).*

238 Different jurisdictional thresholds for certain mergers involving a 'relevant enterprise' (see paragraph 4.4 above) were introduced by the Government principally to enable the Secretary of State to intervene on public interest national security grounds in transactions involving changes of control of 'relevant enterprises.' See BEIS Guidance: Enterprise Act 2002: changes to the turnover and share of supply tests for mergers (June 2020). This can be found at https://assets.publishing.service.gov.uk/government/uploads/system/uploads/attachment_data/file/902531/Enterprise_Act_2002_guidance_on_changes_to_the_turnover_and_share_of_supply_tests_for_mergers__Orders_2020_.pdf.

239 See, for example, CMA Decisions: Anticipated acquisition of Sepura plc by Hytera Communications Corporation Ltd (12 May 2017); Anticipated acquisition of Northern Aerospace Limited by Gardner Aerospace Holdings Limited (20 July 2018); Anticipated acquisition by Connect Bidco Limited of Inmarsat plc (20 October 2019); Anticipated acquisition of Impcross Ltd by Gardner Aerospace Holdings Ltd (9 September 2019); Anticipated acquisition of Mettis Aerospace by Aerostar (26 February 2020).

240 See, for example, OFT Decisions: Acquisition by British Sky Broadcasting of a 17.9% stake in ITV plc (27 April 2007); Completed acquisition by Global Radio Holdings Limited of GMG Radio Holdings Limited (2012); CMA Decisions: Completed acquisition by Trinity Mirror plc of certain assets of Northern & Shell Media Group Limited (20 June 2018); Completed acquisition by DMG Media Limited of JPIMedia Publications Limited (17 April 2020); and CMA Final Report: Anticipated acquisition of Sky plc by Twenty-First Century Fox, Inc. (5 June 2018).

241 The media considerations were added by the Communications Act 2003. See also BEIS (formerly DTI) Guidance: Enterprise Act 2002: Public Interest Intervention in Media Mergers: Guidance on the operation of the public interest merger provisions relating to newspaper and other media mergers (May 2004). This can be found at https://assets.publishing.service.gov.uk/government/uploads/system/uploads/attachment_data/file/595816/file14331 __1_.pdf.

242 Added by the Enterprise Act 2002 (Specification of Additional Section 58 Consideration) Order 2008 SI 2008/2645.

243 See, for example, OFT Decision: Anticipated acquisition by Lloyds TSB plc of HBOS plc (31 October 2008).

244 Added by the Enterprise Act 2002 (Specification of Additional Section 58 Consideration) Order 2020 SI 2020/627. See also BEIS Guidance Enterprise Act 2002: Changes to the public interest grounds for intervention in merger cases (June 2020). This can be found at https://assets.publishing.service.gov.uk/government/uploads/system/uploads / attachment_data/file/902531/Enterprise_Act_2002_guidance_on_changes_to_the_turnover_and_share_of_supply_tests_for_mergers__Orders_2020_.pdf.

245 In phase 1 cases in which the Secretary of State has intervened on media public interest grounds, Ofcom will advise the Secretary of State on the public interest aspects of the case under section 44A of the Act. Ofcom may also advise the Secretary of State at phase 2, following receipt of the CMA's phase 2 report.

246 The position is different in cases raising media public interest issues where Ofcom will provide a separate report on issues of media plurality and diversity. See, for example, OFT Decision: Acquisition by British Sky Broadcasting Group plc of 17.9% per cent stake in ITV plc (27 April 2007); and see CMA Final Report: Anticipated acquisition by 21st Century Fox, Inc of Sky plc (1 May 2018). The CMA may also summarise any representations it has received that relate to the media public interest.

247 Sections 44(4) and 44(5) of the Act.

248 Section 45 of the Act does not provide a specific time limit within which this decision must be taken.

249 See OFT Decision: Anticipated acquisition by News Corporation of British Sky Broadcasting Group plc (2011).

250 See OFT Decision: Anticipated acquisition by Lloyds TSB plc of HBOS plc (31 October 2008).

251 See, for example, CMA Decision: Completed acquisition by Trinity Mirror plc of certain assets of Northern & Shell Media Group Limited (20 June 2018).

252 Under section 34ZB(4) of the Act, the CMA may in those circumstances extend the 'standard' 40 working day deadline to decide whether its duty to make a reference for a Phase 2 investigation applies.

253 Section 54(5) of the Act.

254 See *Merger remedies* (CMA87) for more information on the CMA's approach to remedies in the context of public interest mergers.

255 Section 107(9)(b) of the Act.

256 Accordingly, parties are not able to apply to the CMA's Procedural Officer if they disagree with any decisions in relation to excisions.

257 See OFT Decision: Anticipated acquisition by Atlas Elektronik UK Ltd of the underwater systems Winfrith division of Qinetiq plc (25 June 2009).

258 By contrast, as described in paragraph 16.18 below, following a reference on special public interest grounds the independent phase 2 Inquiry Group will report to the Secretary of State about whether the merger operates or may be expected to operate against the public interest.

17 INTERACTIONS WITH OTHER REGULATORY PROCESSES

MERGERS OF WATER OR SEWERAGE UNDERTAKINGS

[3.502]

17.1 Mergers involving two or more water and sewerage or water-only companies are in certain circumstances subject to a special water merger regime. For guidance on water and sewerage mergers, see *Water and sewerage mergers: Guidance on the CMA's procedure and assessment* (CMA 49) and the statement of intent setting out an agreement on the working arrangements between the CMA and Ofwat for the special water merger regime.[259]

REGULATED UTILITIES

17.2 There are no special provisions under UK merger legislation for regulated utilities such as electricity, gas, telecommunications, postal services, rail,[260] airports and air traffic services. A merger in these industries, however, may require the modification of an operating licence or give rise to other issues falling within the ambit or experience of the relevant sectoral regulator. For this reason, the CMA and the sectoral regulators work closely together on such mergers. In some cases, the sectoral regulator may issue a consultation document in respect of the merger, the responses to which will inform the views offered to the CMA. The CMA is not bound by the sectoral regulator's views but will consider them carefully.

NOTES

[259] See *Water and sewerage mergers: Guidance on the CMA's procedure and assessment* (CMA49).

[260] Entering into a rail franchise agreement constitutes an acquisition of control of an enterprise by virtue of section 66(3) of the Railways Act 1993. For guidance on rail franchise mergers, see *Rail franchise mergers - Review of methodologies and guidance* (CMA74).

18 MULTI-JURISDICTIONAL MERGERS

[3.503]

18.1 Some mergers qualify for merger control review in more than one jurisdiction (these mergers are referred to as 'multi-jurisdictional' mergers for the purposes of this guidance). For multi-jurisdictional mergers, there can be substantial benefits (to merging parties and competition authorities, and therefore, in turn, to consumers) from communication and cooperation between the competition authorities that have jurisdiction to investigate the merger.

18.2 In practice, communication and cooperation between competition authorities in such circumstances typically relates to both the substantive assessment of the merger (eg through the sharing of evidence and analysis), as well as any remedies that might be put in place to address competition concerns (eg to ensure that potential remedies in different jurisdictions are consistent, or at least mutually compatible, while meeting the applicable statutory requirements).

18.3 In carrying out its merger investigations, the CMA frequently cooperates with other competition authorities. More broadly, the CMA actively seeks to promote best practice in merger control through networks such as the International Competition Network (ICN) and the Competition Committee of the Organisation for Economic Co-operation and Development (OECD).

18.4 In relation to multi-jurisdictional mergers, communication and cooperation between competition authorities typically takes place within formal multilateral or bilateral arrangements or through the use of waivers. The CMA will, as standard, ask merger parties whether they have also notified or intend to notify the merger to other competition authorities. Where this is the case, the CMA will typically ask the merger parties to provide a confidentiality waiver[261] allowing the CMA to exchange confidential information with the relevant competition authorities specified in that waiver in respect of the merger. The CMA will then typically contact the relevant officials at the other competition authorities to discuss and share information on the merger as appropriate.

18.5 Multi-jurisdictional mergers, being subject to different merger control requirements across multiple jurisdictions (and processes that have different timelines), can raise several additional considerations that the CMA, and merger parties, may seek to reflect in the CMA's approach to those mergers. In some circumstances, it may be beneficial for the CMA, in executing its duties under the Act, to be able to communicate and coordinate extensively with other authorities in reaching decisions on the competition assessment and remedies. There may also be circumstances in which it is appropriate for the CMA to take account of developments in other jurisdictions in assessing what action the CMA is required to take in relation to a given merger.

18.6 Merger parties are encouraged to discuss the process and timing of the review of a multi-jurisdictional merger with the CMA at an early stage (and to provide confidentiality waivers expediently to facilitate early-stage discussions with other competition authorities). This may, in some cases, include discussing with the CMA the timing of any pre-notification discussions and the commencement of formal proceedings before the CMA and/or other competition authorities to ensure, so far as possible, the alignment of the respective timetables.

18.7 In addition, the following aspects of this guidance may be particularly relevant in multi-jurisdictional mergers:

(a) As noted in paragraph 8.3 above, the CMA might decide not to open an investigation immediately where a transaction is subject to review by a competition authority outside the UK and any remedies imposed or agreed in those proceedings would be likely to address any competition concerns that could arise in the UK. This could be the case, for example, where all of the markets that are relevant to the transaction are broader than national in scope. In this circumstance, merger parties may be invited to update the CMA on the progress of proceedings in other jurisdictions and to provide waivers to the CMA to discuss these proceedings with other competition authorities. The CMA may consider whether to open a formal investigation at any point before expiry of the four-month statutory period and merger parties run the risk that remedies in other jurisdictions that would not fully eliminate any competition concerns relating to the UK would result in the CMA opening a formal investigation at a later stage.

(b) As noted in paragraph 1.6 above, the CMA will generally apply this guidance flexibly and may depart from the approach described in the guidance where there is an appropriate and reasonable justification for doing so, which may include the alignment of the CMA's investigation with the

Part 3 CMA and other Guidelines

processes of other competition authorities. Merger parties may wish to give early consideration to the potential process variations set out in this guidance where that might help to support alignment between the processes in different competition authorities in multi-jurisdictional mergers.[262]

(c) For example, as noted in paragraph 7.2 above, merger parties are able to request that a case should be 'fast tracked' to the consideration of UILs or to an in-depth phase 2 investigation. In some circumstances, this may aid the alignment of the CMA's substantive assessment and/or remedies process with proceedings in other jurisdictions.

(d) Moreover, as noted in paragraph 7.17 above, merger parties are, in a phase 2 investigation, able to request that they formally accept that the CMA has evidence that establishes, to the required legal standard, that the relevant merger situation has resulted, or may be expected to result, in a substantial lessening of competition within a specified market or markets for goods or services in the UK. In some circumstances, the 'concession' of an SLC (which might involve business activities that may be within the scope of remedies being put in place in other jurisdictions) may aid the alignment of the CMA's remedies process with proceedings in other jurisdictions.

(e) As noted in paragraph 9.37 above, the fact that competition authorities are considering a merger that the CMA is also investigating is one of the circumstances in which the CMA decision maker at phase 1 (or the Inquiry Group, at phase 2) may choose to become involved in remedies discussions before the SLC decision. The merger parties will be informed if the decision maker deems that this is appropriate. The merger parties are also able to request that the decision maker should become involved in remedies discussions before any SLC decision.

NOTES

261 The CMA's template waiver is available at: https://www.gov.uk/government/publications/confidentiality-waiver-template.

262 See, for example, CMA Decision: Anticipated acquisition by Stryker Corporation of Wright Medical Group N.V. (30 June 2020).

19 COMMUNICATION AND PUBLICATION OF DECISIONS, UNDERTAKINGS AND ORDERS

GENERAL APPROACH TO PUBLICATION

[3.504]

19.1 The CMA is mindful of the need to respect the confidentiality of commercially-sensitive information provided to it (by the merger parties and third parties). At the same time, it is required by section 107 of the Act to publish its decisions and the reasons for them. Accordingly, it will ensure that the 'gist' of the evidence that is key to the reasoning and outcome of a decision is included in the public version of the decision.[263] Therefore, when parties make requests for excision of confidential information, they are expected to justify each of those requests. The CMA will not accept blanket claims that particular classes of information are confidential.

19.2 In the event of a disagreement with the CMA as to the confidentiality of specific information relating to a party that the CMA proposes to publish in its decision, parties should seek in the first instance to resolve the matter with the CMA case team.[264] If, thereafter, the parties' concerns remain unresolved, they may make representations to the CMA's Procedural Officer, who will consider those representations and reach a determination on the issue in relation to a phase 1 inquiry or provide advice to the Inquiry Group in relation to a phase 2 inquiry who will make the final decision.[265]

PHASE 1

19.3 Section 34ZA(1)(b) of the Act requires the CMA to provide the merger parties with the reasons for its decision whether its duty to refer applies. Section 107 of the Act requires the CMA to publish its decisions, including decisions that a transaction is not a relevant merger situation and decisions not to refer (including findings that the market is of insufficient importance to justify a reference). However, this publication obligation does not apply to decisions where the CMA decides not to make a reference because it believes that the arrangements concerned are not sufficiently far advanced, or are not sufficiently likely to proceed, to justify the making of a reference.[266]

19.4 Where the CMA finds that its duty to refer applies, and considers that there are reasonable grounds for believing that any UILs offered by the merger parties (or a modified version of them) might be accepted by the CMA, it will also publish a notice of that decision.[267]

19.5 On the day that the decision is finalised and adopted, the outcome of the CMA's decision is communicated to the merger parties and announced publicly. The CMA may also issue a press release (and/or a short summary of its findings) in relation to its decision. The text of the reasoned decision is provided to the merger parties and subsequently published on https://www.gov.uk/cma-cases following the excision of confidential information (see paragraph 19.6 below).

19.6 Publication is generally a two-step process:

(a) The first step is the announcement of the nature of the CMA's decision, done through the Regulatory News Service and placed on https://www.gov.uk/cma-cases. Before publicly announcing the decision, the CMA will seek to notify the merger parties of the precise timing and nature of the decision. The exact timing of this communication will vary from case-to-case but typically the timing of this communication may be the day before, or on the same day as, the date of the announcement.[268] Where a press release is issued and/or where a summary of the decision will be published at the same time as announcement of the decision, these documents will also normally be sent to the merger parties at the same time.[269],[270] The purpose of sending these documents to the merger parties/their advisers is solely to identify, ahead of publication, any information which may be protected by Part 9 of the Act (see paragraphs 19.12 to 19.14 below). On the day the CMA announces its decision, it will also provide the merger parties with the text of its decision, having redacted any information which may relate to a third party.

(b) The second step, usually sometime later, is the publication of the non-confidential text of the decision or notice on https://www.gov.uk/cma-cases, which will be announced on the Regulatory News Service, following engagement with the merger parties and any third parties to identify any information which may be protected by Part 9 of the Act.

PHASE 2

Provisional findings

19.7 The CMA's usual practice is to provide to the merger parties (and any external advisers[271]) the following materials shortly before publication: a copy of the CMA's press release (where one will be issued); the Notice of provisional findings; the summary of provisional findings; and, where relevant, the Notice of Possible Remedies. These are finalised documents that are provided on an embargoed basis until publication solely to enable the merger parties to prepare their external and/or internal communications and to identify any information which may be protected under Part 9 of the Act. The merger parties are therefore not invited to make submissions on the substantive content of these documents. The CMA will publish these documents after a short delay.[272]

19.8 At around the same time (or shortly thereafter), the merger parties will also be given the redacted version of the full provisional findings report. The redacted provisional findings report will typically be published once the merger parties have had an opportunity to make final representations on the CMA's treatment of information which may be protected under Part 9 of the Act. This period will be brief and may, in some cases, be as short as only a few hours (given that CMA will have taken steps earlier in the process to identify any confidential material). However, if the CMA is fully satisfied that all confidential material has been treated appropriately within the provisional findings report, it may publish the full decision at the same time as the Notice of provisional findings.

Final report

19.9 The CMA will send the final report, including a summary, to the merger parties in the form in which it will be published, that is, with excisions. The final report and summary are embargoed until publication. At this stage, the merger parties are not generally invited to make a final check of the text because most excision requests will have been resolved ahead of publication of provisional findings (see paragraphs 19.7 to 19.8 above) or through a 'put-back' process of any additional submissions/evidence prior to production of the final report.

PUBLICATION OF UNDERTAKINGS AND ORDERS

19.10 The CMA publishes the details of all merger undertakings and orders that have been agreed and accepted or imposed under the Act on the relevant case page of the CMA website.[273] Publication is designed to ensure that interested third parties are aware of the undertakings and, in the event of a breach of undertakings, they may take action in the courts under section 94 of the Act.

19.11 Once they are in place, undertakings and orders are monitored by the CMA under section 92 of the Act in order to ensure compliance and so that the CMA may consider whether they should be amended or replaced, or, where relevant, so that the CMA may advise the Secretary of State as to such issues (see *Remedies: Guidance on the CMA's approach to the variation and termination of merger, monopoly and market undertakings and orders* (CMA11)). Any changes that are agreed are published in the same way as the original undertakings.

FREEDOM OF INFORMATION ACT

19.12 The Freedom of Information Act 2000 (the FOIA) creates a general right of access to information held by public bodies, including the CMA.[274] A request for information under the FOIA will be dealt with within 20 working days of receipt.

19.13 There are a number of exemptions from disclosure under the FOIA of potential relevance to a request for information held by the CMA, including where disclosure would be prohibited under any statutory bar to disclosure including under the Act.[275] Part 9 of the Act, under which information relating to the affairs of an individual (a sole trader, for example) or any business of an undertaking which has come to the CMA may not be disclosed during the lifetime of the individual or while the undertaking continues in existence unless the disclosure is permitted under one of the gateways in the Act, therefore continues to apply. In addition, the CMA may rely on section 31(1)(g) of the FOIA (for the purposes at section 31(2)) in withholding information if it considers its disclosure would, or would be likely to, prejudice the exercise by the CMA of its statutory merger control functions and there are public interest arguments for maintaining the exemption outweighing the public interest in disclosing the information. Other exemptions may also be engaged, depending on the facts.

19.14 Further information on exchanges of confidential information in the context of multi-jurisdictional mergers is provided in chapter 18 above.

NOTES

263 For guidance on the CMA's wider approach to such issues of confidentiality, see *Transparency and disclosure: Statement of the CMA's policy and approach* (CMA6).

264 If the matter in disagreement arises in relation to a phase 2 inquiry the staff team will liaise with the Inquiry Group as necessary.

265 The Procedural Officer is intended to provide a swift, efficient supplementary mechanism for resolving disputes relating to the confidentiality of information proposed to be published by the CMA.

266 ie decisions under section 33(2)(b) of the Act; see section 107(1)(aa).

267 The final decision on whether to accept the UILs would be made following further consideration and public consultation - see *Merger Remedies Guidance* (CMA87).

268 In cases where one or more of the merger parties is a UK-listed company, the CMA will contact the merger parties/their advisers after the London Stock Exchange has closed on the day before publication, normally after 5pm. By 7.00am (when the London Stock Exchange opens) the following day, the decision will be announced (and any press release/summary of the decision will be published) on www.gov.uk/cma. Where the merger parties are listed companies in other jurisdictions, the CMA will, where possible, seek to avoid announcing its decision during stock exchange hours in those jurisdictions.

269 Before prior notice of any announcement is given to the merger parties, an email will be sent to the merger parties or their advisers that sets out the terms on which any price-sensitive information is being provided. The merger parties must agree to these terms before the price-sensitive information will be provided. The same terms regarding price-sensitive information will also apply in the event that the case is referred for a phase 2 investigation.

270 In some circumstances, the CMA may consider it is inappropriate to provide advance copies of any or some of the documents to the merger parties and/or their external advisers. For example, where the CMA has concerns as to the ability of merger parties and/or their external advisers to keep the contents of documents confidential before publication; or where there are issues of confidentiality which cannot be sufficiently protected under the terms of any embargo.

271 As noted above, there may be circumstances in which the CMA considers it is inappropriate to provide advance copies of any or some of the documents to the merger parties and/or their external advisers.

272 Where the merger parties are not UK-listed companies, this delay will generally be a matter of a few hours. In cases where one or more of the merger parties is a UK-listed company, a copy of the Notice of provisional findings, summary of provisional findings and, where relevant, Notice of Provisional Remedies is made available to the merger parties on an embargoed basis after the London Stock Exchange has closed on the day before publication, normally after 5pm. By 7.00am (when the London Stock Exchange opens) the following day, these documents are published on www.gov.uk/cma. Where the merger parties are listed companies in other jurisdictions, the CMA will, where possible, seek to avoid publication during stock exchange hours in those jurisdictions.

273 See https://www.gov.uk/cma-cases. The CMA is also required by section 107 of the Act to publish any IEO or interim order made by it under section 72 or 76 of, or paragraph 2 of Schedule 7 to, the Act.

274 More information on the FOIA can be found at www.gov.uk/cma, including contact details should you require further information. More detailed information on the FOIA is available on the Information Commissioner's website at www.ico.org.uk.

275 Section 44(1)(a) of the FOIA.

20 FEES

[3.505]

20.1 Subject to some limited exceptions[276], any merger that qualifies as a relevant merger situation (including on the 'may be the case' standard)[277] and in which the CMA (or Secretary of State in public interest cases) reaches a decision on whether or not to refer the merger for a phase 2 investigation, is subject to a fee irrespective of whether a reference is made.[278] That fee is collected by the CMA on behalf of HM Treasury. The main exception is where the interest acquired or being acquired is less than a controlling interest and a merger notice has not been submitted in relation to that acquisition.[279] In addition, there is an exemption from paying a fee where the acquirer and any group of which it is a member qualify as small or medium sized. This is defined by reference to qualifying conditions in the Companies Act 2006 (see paragraph 20.6 below).

20.2 Where a fee is due, that fee is payable by the person filing the Merger Notice, or - in cases in which no Merger Notice is filed - the person acquiring control. The fee becomes payable on the publication by the CMA of either a reference decision or any decision not to make a reference. No fee is payable if the CMA finds that the case does not qualify as a relevant merger situation. For cases resolved through UILs, the fee becomes payable when the CMA loses its duty to refer as a result of its formal acceptance of UILs. In the case of public interest cases decided by the Secretary of State, the fee becomes payable to the CMA when the Secretary of State publishes a reference decision under section 45 of the Act or publishes any decision not to make such a reference. In all cases, an invoice will be issued by the CMA when the fee becomes payable. Payment must be made within 30 days of the date of the invoice.

20.3 Given that a fee is payable in all cases in which the CMA reaches a decision whether or not to refer in respect of a relevant merger situation, a fee will be payable in cases where the CMA decides to investigate the merger on its own initiative and proceeds to publish such a decision (save, as noted above, in cases where the interest acquired is less than a controlling interest).

20.4 Information on how to pay the fee (including the CMA's account details and the forms of payment that it will accept) is available on https://www.gov.uk/government/publications/merger-fees-payment-information.

20.5 Fees vary according to the type and size of the merger. Details of the current fee scales are available from the case team and on https://www.gov.uk/government/publications/merger-fees-payment-information.

20.6 Where the acquirer qualifies as small or medium sized as defined (by reference to provisions of the Companies Act 2006[280]) in the Enterprise Act 2002 (Merger Fees and Determination of Turnover) Order 2003 (as amended) it is exempt from paying the above fees.

20.7 Fees are payable on the making of a merger reference under the Water Industry Act 1991 (see chapter 17). In such cases, the level of the fee is determined depending on the value of the turnover of the water enterprise being acquired in England and Wales.[281]

NOTES

276 A fee shall not be payable in relation to arrangements that are in progress or in contemplation which, if carried into effect, will result in the creation of a relevant merger situation, where the CMA decides pursuant to section 33(2)(b) of the Act that the arrangements concerned are not sufficiently far advanced, or are not sufficiently likely to proceed, to justify the making of a merger reference.

277 This therefore excludes 'found-not-to-qualify' cases (where the transaction is found not to give rise to a relevant merger situation). In those cases, no fee is payable.

278 Full details in respect of the payment of fees are, pursuant to section 121 of the Act, set out in the Enterprise Act 2002 (Merger Fees and Determination of Turnover) Order 2003 SI 2003/1370 (as amended).

279 Chapter 4 explains further the meaning of the term 'controlling interest'. It should be noted, however, that multiple parties may be treated as one person for the purposes of determining whether fees are payable, potentially as a result of the application of the 'associated persons' provision, in which case they are jointly and severally liable for the fee under Article 6(4) of the Enterprise Act 2002 (Merger Fees and Determination of Turnover) Order 2003 SI 2003/1370 (as amended).

280 At the time of writing, 'small enterprises' under section 382 of the Companies Act 2006 are those satisfying two or more of the following criteria: (i) turnover of not more than £10.2 million; (ii) balance sheet total of not more than £5.1 million; (iii) number of employees not more than 50. 'Medium enterprises' under section 465 of the Companies Act 2006 are those satisfying two or more of the following criteria: (i) turnover of not more than £36 million; balance sheet total of not more than £18 million; (iii) number of employees of not more than 250. Full details are set out in sections 382 and 465 of the Companies Act 2006, most recently amended by the Companies, Partnerships and Groups (Accounts and Reports) Regulations SI 2015/980. Where the acquirer is a member of a group as defined in section 474 of the Companies Act, it will qualify as small if the group qualifies as small under section 383 of the Companies Act, or medium sized if the group qualifies as medium-sized under section 466 of the Companies Act.

281 The Enterprise Act 2002 (Merger Fees and Determination of Turnover) Order 2003 SI 2003/1370 (as amended).

ANNEXES

ANNEX A

GUIDANCE ON THE CALCULATION OF TURNOVER FOR THE PURPOSES OF PART 3 OF THE ENTERPRISE ACT 2002

[3.506]

A.1 This annex provides guidance on the calculation of turnover for the purposes of Chapter 1 of Part 3 of the Act.

A.2 While this annex is intended to help explain the detailed provisions of the law concerning turnover calculation, it should not be regarded as a substitute for the Act and secondary legislation made under it. Nor should it be regarded as a substitute for expert legal advice on the interpretation of the Act and secondary legislation.

Background

A.3 Under the turnover test in the Act, a relevant merger situation will arise if two or more enterprises cease to be distinct and the turnover in the UK of the enterprise being taken over exceeds £70 million (or for certain mergers which give rise to potential public interest considerations, £1 million) (see chapters 4 and 16 above).[282]

A.4 The turnover of the enterprise being taken over is, for these purposes, calculated by taking together the total value of the UK turnover of all the enterprises ceasing to be distinct and deducting either:

(a) the UK turnover of any enterprise which continues to be carried on under the same ownership and control, or

(b) if no enterprise continues to be carried on under the same ownership or control, the UK turnover of the enterprise whose turnover has the highest value.[283]

A.5 In most relevant merger situations, this means in practice that the applicable turnover for mergers within (i) above - which is most takeovers and acquisitions - will be the UK turnover of the target enterprise. For mergers falling within (ii) above - a full legal merger or a joint venture combining all of the merger parties' assets and businesses, for example - the applicable UK turnover will be that of the enterprise having the lower turnover (or, put another way, in this scenario both enterprises must have UK turnover exceeding £70 million).

A.6 The method of calculating the applicable turnover is set out in the Enterprise Act 2002 (Merger Fees and Determination of Turnover) Order 2003 SI 2003/1370 (as amended) (referred to in this annex as the Order).

Period over which turnover is calculated

A.7 The relevant period used for the purposes of determining turnover under Part 3 of the Act is the business year preceding either the date the enterprises ceased to be distinct (in the case of a completed merger); or, the date of the CMA's decision whether or not to make a reference (in the case of a proposed

Part 3 CMA and other Guidelines

merger). However, in either case, the CMA may substitute such earlier date as it considers appropriate.[284] In practice, the CMA will usually consider the turnover for the last completed 'business year' preceding either the date the enterprises ceased to be distinct (for a completed merger) or the date of notification (in the case of a proposed merger).

A.8 A 'business year' for these purposes is any period of more than six months for which accounts have been or will be prepared.[285] In general, this will, of course, be a 12-month period. Where (perhaps because the enterprise has been newly formed) there is a period for which there is no preceding business year then the applicable turnover is the turnover for that shorter period.[286]

A.9 If the preceding business year is not a period of 12 months, then turnover, for the purposes of Chapter 1 of Part 3 of the Act, is arrived at by adjusting the applicable turnover received in that period by the same proportion as 12 months bears to that period.[287] Thus, if the preceding business year for an enterprise ceasing to be distinct is a nine-month period during which the applicable turnover was £54 million, then turnover for this purpose (that is, for determining whether the jurisdictional threshold is met) would be £72 million (£54 million ÷ 9 × 12).

A.10 In determining the applicable turnover of an enterprise, the CMA may take into account events which have occurred since the end of the business year and which may have a significant impact on the turnover of the enterprise ceasing to be distinct.[288] This allows the CMA to take account of acquisitions or divestments or other transactions which have had, or will potentially have, a continuing positive or negative effect on the turnover of the enterprise. The CMA would only expect to exercise this discretion in cases where the effect may impact upon the question of jurisdiction or the fee due.

Applicable turnover

A.11 The applicable turnover of an enterprise is the turnover of the enterprise arising during the previous business year. It comprises the amounts derived from the sale of products and the provision of services which it makes in the ordinary course of its business activities to customers (businesses or consumers) in the UK, net of any sales rebate, value added tax and other taxes directly related to that turnover.[289] The calculation of turnover for these purposes should be interpreted in accordance with accounting principles and practices that are generally accepted in the UK.[290] Turnover includes any aid granted by a public body to a business which is directly linked to the sale of products or the provision of services by the business and therefore reflected in the price of those products/services.[291] Special provisions, described below, apply to an enterprise which is (in whole or in part) a credit institution, financial institution or insurance undertaking.

Credit institutions and financial institutions

A.12 The applicable turnover of an enterprise which, in whole or in part, is a credit institution or financial institution is the sum of certain specified income received by the branch or division of that institution in the UK, after the deduction of value added tax and other taxes directly related to those items.[292] The types of income specified for these purposes are:

(a) interest income and similar income
(b) income from securities:
(c) income from shares and other variable yield securities
(d) income from participating interests
(e) income from shares in affiliated undertakings
(f) commissions receivable
(g) net profit on financial operations, and
(h) other operating income.

Insurance undertakings

A.13 The applicable turnover of an enterprise which, in whole or in part, is an insurance undertaking is the value of the gross premiums received from residents of the UK after deduction of taxes and certain other premium-related deductions.[293] Gross premiums received comprises all amounts received together with all amounts receivable in respect of insurance contracts issued by or on behalf of an insurance undertaking, including outgoing reinsurance premiums.

Enterprises treated as under common ownership or control

A.14 Where an enterprise ceasing to be distinct consists of two or more enterprises which are under common ownership or common control the applicable turnover is calculated by adding together the applicable turnover of each of those enterprises.[294] For the purposes of determining whether enterprises are treated as being under common control when calculating the applicable turnover, the provisions of section 26(2) and (3) (as reproduced in paragraphs 5 and 6 of the Schedule to the Order) and section 127 of the Act apply as they apply in the Act for the purposes of determining whether enterprises have ceased to be distinct.[295]

A.15 As a result, applicable turnover may include not only the applicable turnover of the particular enterprise ceasing to be distinct but also that of certain other enterprises to which it is 'linked'. In particular, this might include the applicable turnover of any enterprise over which the enterprise ceasing to be distinct has control for the purposes of section 26(3) (as reproduced at paragraph 6 of the Schedule) of the Act – that is where the interest held confers, at least, the ability materially to influence policy. Where applicable turnover includes the applicable turnover of a linked enterprise, in which the enterprise ceasing to be distinct has less than a controlling interest, the whole of the applicable turnover of the linked enterprise is included in assessing whether the jurisdictional test is met. There is no reduction simply because the interest is less than a controlling interest.

A.16 For example:

(a) Company A acquires Company B and also its subsidiaries B1 and B2: B and B1 and B2 are enterprises of interconnected bodies corporate which are treated as being under common control and their turnover is taken together in arriving at the applicable turnover of the enterprises ceasing to be distinct.

(b) Company A acquires Company C which also has a significant shareholding – conferring at least material influence – in Company D. The turnover of Company C and Company D is taken together in determining the applicable turnover.

(c) Partnerships A, B and C act together to secure control of Partnership D and form Partnership E. Partnerships A, B and C are associated persons and their turnover is added together. To determine the applicable turnover, the higher of the two turnover figures (that is, of A, B and C together or of D) is deducted from the combined turnover figure (of A, B, C and D).

A.17 In the case of some joint ventures, none of the enterprises will remain under the same ownership or control. For example, Company A and Company B may form a 50:50 joint venture (Newco) incorporating all their assets and businesses. In this case, neither enterprise A or B will remain under the same ownership or control as previously. In determining the relevant applicable turnover, the highest turnover (of A or B) would therefore, effectively, be ignored. By contrast, where Company A and Company B form a joint venture incorporating their assets and businesses in a particular area of activity, each parent with control ceases to be distinct from the target business contributed to the joint venture by the other parent, but the parent companies themselves remain under the same ownership and control after the merger. Therefore, the parent companies have their turnover deducted and the relevant turnover is the sum of the turnover of each of the contributed enterprises.

Treatment of intra-group transactions

A.18 To avoid double counting, applicable turnover does not include amounts that are derived from transactions involving the sale of goods or provision of services between enterprises that are and will remain, post-merger, under the same common ownership or common control.[296] In other words, external sales only are taken into account.

A.19 However, in certain cases the CMA may take into account sales that were previously internal to a group and may attribute an appropriate value to such sales. This is to allow the CMA to make a sensible assessment of the turnover for jurisdictional purposes of the business being sold.

A.20 Where, as a result of the merger, one or more enterprises will cease to be under the same common ownership or common control – that is, where what was an intra-group transaction pre-merger would, post-merger, be regarded as an external transaction – then the CMA may treat the amounts derived from the previously internal transactions as applicable turnover. In these cases, if such transactions have not resulted in any turnover, or the CMA believes that the turnover attributed to them does not reflect open market value, then the CMA may attribute an appropriate value to those transactions for inclusion in the applicable turnover.[297]

Example:

The enterprise ceasing to be distinct is part of a vertically integrated process, a mill supplying flour to a downstream baking operation. It is possible that, pre-merger, the raw material (flour) may be supplied by the mill to the baking operation at a nil value or less than market price. If only the mill was being taken over, the turnover attributed to the milling operation may, as a result, be artificially low. In these circumstances the CMA might exercise its discretion to take into account the pre-merger supplies of raw materials (flour) to the baking operation in calculating the applicable turnover, and to attribute a more appropriate value for those supplies. In seeking to re-value the turnover attributed to the supply of such goods so that it more accurately reflects an open market value, the CMA might have regard to the terms of any future supply agreement that might be part of the transaction as well as market prices more generally. Again, it is likely that the CMA would only seek to exercise this discretion in those cases where the effect may impact upon the question of jurisdiction or the fee due.

Treatment of foreign currencies

A.21 The turnover test is expressed in terms of pounds sterling. If it is necessary to convert foreign currencies in order to arrive at this figure then the CMA would usually be content to accept the approved exchange rate applicable at the date of the accounts.

NOTES

282 Section 23(1)(b) of the Act.

283 Section 28(1) of the Act.

284 Article 10(2)(a) and (b) of the Order.

285 Article 2(c) of the Order.

286 Article 10(4) of the Order.

287 Article 2(b) of the Order.

288 Article 10(3) of the Order.

289 Paragraph 3 of the Schedule to the Order.

290 Paragraph 2 of the Schedule to the Order.

291 Paragraph 13 of the Schedule to the Order.

[292] Paragraphs 10 and 11 of the Schedule to the Order.
[293] Paragraphs 10 and 12 of the Schedule to the Order.
[294] Paragraph 4 of the Schedule to the Order.
[295] Paragraphs 5, 6 and 7 of the Schedule to the Order.
[296] Paragraph 8 of the Schedule to the Order.
[297] Paragraph 9 of the Schedule to the Order.

ANNEX B
GUIDANCE AND COMMENTARY IN RELATION TO THE CMA'S ASSESSMENT OF MERGERS

[3.507]

B.1 In addition to this guidance, the CMA (or its predecessor organisations) has published a number of other pieces of guidance and commentary in relation to the assessment of mergers, namely:

(a) Merger assessment guidelines (OFT1254/CC2)
(b) Suggested best practice for submission of technical economic analysis to the CC (CC2com3)
(c) Chairman's guidance on disclosure of information in merger and market inquiries (CC7) (Revised)
(d) Remedies: Guidance on the CMA's approach to the variation and termination of merger, monopoly and market undertakings and orders (CMA11)
(e) Rules of procedure for merger, market and special reference groups (CMA17)
(f) Quick guide to UK merger assessment (CMA18)
(g) CMA guidance on the review of NHS mergers (CMA29)
(h) Water and sewerage mergers: Guidance on the CMA's procedure and assessment (CMA49)
(i) Guidance on the CMA's mergers intelligence function (CMA56)
(j) Retail mergers commentary (CMA62)
(k) Mergers: Exceptions to the duty to refer (CMA64)
(l) Rail franchise mergers: Review of methodologies and guidance (CMA74)
(m) Good practice in the design and presentation of customer survey evidence in merger cases (CMA78)
(n) Merger remedies (CMA87)
(o) Guidance on requests for internal documents in merger investigations (CMA100)
(p) Interim measures in merger investigations (CMA108)
(q) Mergers and markets remedies – guidance on reporting, investigation and enforcement of potential breaches (CMA123)
(r) Guidance on the functions of the CMA after the end of the Transition Period (CMA126)

B.2 The following guidance has been withdrawn:

(a) Guidance on changes to the jurisdictional thresholds for UK merger control (CMA90)

B.3 Interested parties should refer to those documents listed above where relevant, subject in particular to the following general limitations:

(a) all references to issues of jurisdiction or procedure in mergers cases must be read in the light of this guidance
(b) in the case of conflict between this guidance and any other guidance produced or adopted by the CMA, the most recently published document takes precedence
(c) the original text of any guidance issued by one of its predecessor organisations and adopted by the CMA ('adopted guidance') has been retained unamended: as such, that text does not reflect or take account of developments in case law, legislation or practice since its original publication, and
(d) all the adopted guidance should be read subject to the following cross-cutting amendments:
    (i) references to the 'OFT' or 'CC' (except where referring to specific past OFT or CC practice or case law), should be read as referring to the CMA
    (ii) references to 'referral to the CC' or 'a reference to the CC' should be read as referring to the referral of a case by the CMA (or Secretary of State) of a case for a phase 2 investigation involving an Inquiry Group of CMA panel members
    (iii) certain OFT or CC departments, teams or individual roles may not be replicated in the CMA, or may have been renamed. A copy of the CMA's organisational chart is available on www.gov.uk/cma, and
    (iv) parties should check any contact details against those listed on www.gov.uk/cma, which will be the most up to date.

ANNEX C
ANCILLARY RESTRAINTS

Introduction

[3.508]

C.1 Mergers and ancillary restrictions to the merger are generally excluded from the prohibitions of the Competition Act 1998 (CA98), as amended by the Enterprise and Regulatory Reform Act 2013 (ERRA13), under Schedule 1 of the CA98. This extends to any provision directly related and necessary to the implementation of the merger provisions (referred to in this guidance as 'ancillary restraints').[298]

C.2 The CMA considers that it is, in principle, no better placed than the merger parties and their advisers in most cases to determine whether contractual arrangements and agreements are ancillary to a merger and, therefore, automatically excluded from the Chapter I and Chapter II prohibitions of the Competition Act 1998. Accordingly, the CMA will not ordinarily give a view in its published decision (or to the merger parties confidentially) on whether or not a restriction is ancillary.[299]

C.3 This Annex sets out the CMA's analytical approach to ancillary restraints. It sets out the principles for assessing whether, and to what extent, the most common types of agreements are considered to be ancillary restraints.

General Principles

C.4 The criteria of direct relation and necessity set out under Schedule 1 of the CA98 are objective in nature. Restrictions are not directly related and necessary to the implementation of a merger simply because the merger parties regard them as such.

C.5 For restrictions to be considered 'directly related to the implementation of the merger', they must be closely linked to the merger itself. It is not sufficient that an agreement has been entered into in the same context or at the same time as the merger.[300] Restrictions which are directly related to the merger are economically related to the main transaction and intended to allow a smooth transition to the changed company structure after the merger.

C.6 Agreements must be 'necessary to the implementation of the merger provisions'[301], which means that, in the absence of those agreements, the merger could not be implemented or could only be implemented under considerably more uncertain conditions, at substantially higher cost, over an appreciably longer period or with considerably greater difficulty. Agreements necessary to the implementation of a merger are typically aimed at protecting the value transferred, maintaining the continuity of supply after the break-up of a former economic entity, or enabling the start-up of a new entity. In determining whether a restriction is necessary, it is appropriate not only to take account of its nature, but also to ensure that its duration, subject matter, and geographical field of application does not exceed what the implementation of the merger reasonably requires. If equally effective alternatives are available for attaining the legitimate aim pursued, the merger parties must choose the one which is objectively the least restrictive of competition.

C.7 For acquisitions which are carried out in stages, the contractual arrangements relating to the stages before the establishment of control[302] within the meaning of section 26 of the Act cannot normally be considered directly related and necessary to the implementation of the merger. However, an agreement to abstain from material changes in the target's business until completion is considered directly related and necessary to the implementation of the merger.[303] The same applies, in the context of a joint bid, to an agreement by the joint purchasers of an enterprise to abstain from making separate competing offers for the same enterprise, or otherwise acquiring control.

C.8 Agreements which serve to facilitate the acquisition of any level of control over a target by more than one enterprise are to be considered directly related and necessary to the implementation of the merger. This will apply to arrangements between the merger parties for the acquisition of control aimed at implementing the division of assets in order to divide the production facilities or distribution networks among themselves, together with the existing trademarks of the acquired enterprise.

C.9 To the extent that such a division involves the break-up of a pre-existing economic entity, arrangements that make the break-up possible under reasonable conditions are to be considered directly related and necessary to the implementation of the merger, under the principles set out below.

Principles applicable to commonly encountered ancillary restraints in cases of acquisition of an enterprise

C.10 Restrictions agreed between the merger parties in the context of a transfer of an enterprise may be to the benefit of the purchaser or of the seller. In general terms, the need for the purchaser to benefit from certain protection is more compelling than the corresponding need for the seller. It is the purchaser who needs to be assured that she/he will be able to acquire the full value of the acquired business. Thus, as a general rule, restrictions which benefit the seller are either not directly related and necessary to the implementation of the merger at all, or their scope and/or duration need to be more limited than that of clauses which benefit the purchaser.

Non-competition clauses

C.11 Non-competition obligations which are imposed on the seller in the context of the transfer of an enterprise can be directly related and necessary to the implementation of the merger. In order to obtain the full value of the enterprise transferred, the purchaser must be able to benefit from some protection against competition from the seller in order to gain the loyalty of customers and to assimilate and exploit the know-how. Such non-competition clauses guarantee the transfer to the purchaser of the full value of the assets transferred, which in general include both physical assets and intangible assets, such as goodwill or know-how. These are not only directly related to the merger but are also necessary to its implementation because, without them, there would be reasonable grounds to expect that the sale of the enterprise could not be accomplished.

C.12 However, such non-competition clauses are only justified by the legitimate objective of implementing the merger when their duration, their geographical field of application, their subject matter, and the persons subject to them do not exceed what is reasonably necessary to achieve that end.

C.13 Non-competition clauses are justified for periods of up to three years, when the transfer of the enterprise includes the transfer of customer loyalty in the form of both goodwill and know-how. When only goodwill is included, they are justified for periods of up to two years.

C.14 By contrast, non-competition clauses cannot be considered necessary when the transfer is in fact primarily physical assets (such as land, buildings or machinery) or exclusive industrial and commercial property rights (the holders of which could immediately take action against infringements by the transferor of such rights).

C.15 The geographical scope of a non-competition clause must be limited to the area in which the seller has offered the relevant products or services before the transfer, since the purchaser does not need to be protected against competition from the seller in territories not previously penetrated by the seller. That geographical scope can be extended to territories which the seller was planning to enter at the time of the transaction, provided that it had already invested in preparing this move.

C.16 Similarly, non-competition clauses must remain limited to products (including improved versions or updates of products as well as successor models) and services forming the economic activity of the enterprise transferred. This can include products and services not yet fully developed or marketed at the time of the transaction.

C.17 The seller may bind itself and its subsidiaries and commercial agents. However, an obligation to impose similar restrictions on others would not be regarded as directly related and necessary to the implementation of the merger. This applies, in particular, to clauses which would restrict the freedom of resellers or users to import or export.

C.18 Clauses which limit the seller's right to purchase or hold shares in a company competing with the business transferred shall be considered directly related and necessary to the implementation of the merger under the same conditions as outlined above for non-competition clauses, unless they prevent the seller from purchasing or holding shares purely for financial investment purposes, without granting it, directly or indirectly, management functions or any material influence in the competing company.

C.19 Non-solicitation and confidentiality clauses have a comparable effect and are therefore evaluated in a similar way to non-competition clauses.

Licence agreements

C.20 The transfer of an enterprise can include the transfer to the purchaser, with a view to the full exploitation of the assets transferred, of intellectual property rights or know-how. However, the seller may remain the owner of the rights in order to exploit them for activities other than those transferred. In these cases, the usual means for ensuring that the purchaser will have the full use of the assets transferred is to conclude licensing agreements in its favour. Likewise, where the seller has transferred intellectual property rights with the business, it may still want to continue using some or all of these rights for activities other than those transferred; in such a case the purchaser will grant a licence to the seller.

C.21 Licences of patents, of similar rights, or of know-how, can be considered necessary to the implementation of the merger. They may equally be considered an integral part of the merger and, in any event, need not be limited in time. These licences can be simple or exclusive and may be limited to certain fields of use, to the extent that they correspond to the activities of the enterprise transferred.

C.22 However, territorial limitations on manufacture reflecting the territory of the transferred activity are not necessary to the implementation of the operation. As regards licences granted by the seller of a business to the buyer, the seller can be made subject to territorial restrictions in the licence agreement under the same conditions as laid down for non-competition clauses in the context of the sale of a business.

C.23 Restrictions in licence agreements going beyond the above provisions, such as those which protect the licensor rather than the licensee, are not necessary to the implementation of the merger.

C.24 Similarly, in the case of licences of trademarks, business names, design rights, copyrights or similar rights, there may be situations in which the seller wishes to remain the owner of such rights in relation to activities retained, but the purchaser needs those rights in order to market the goods or services produced by the enterprise transferred. Here, the same considerations as set out above apply.

Purchase and supply obligations

C.25 In many cases, the transfer of an enterprise can entail the disruption of traditional lines of purchase and supply which have existed as a result of the previous integration of activities within the economic unity of the seller. In order to enable the break-up of the economic unity of the seller and the partial transfer of the assets to the purchaser under reasonable conditions, it is often necessary to maintain, for a transitional period, the existing or similar links between the seller and the purchaser. This objective is normally attained by purchase and supply obligations for the seller and/or the purchaser of the enterprise. Taking into account the particular situation resulting from the break-up of the economic unity of the seller, such obligations can be recognised as directly related and necessary to the implementation of the merger. They may be in favour of the seller as well as the purchaser, depending on the particular circumstances of the case.

C.26 The aim of such obligations may be to ensure the continuity of supply to either of the merger parties of products necessary for carrying out the activities retained by the seller or taken over by the purchaser. However, the duration of purchase and supply obligations must be limited to a period reasonably necessary for the replacement of the relationship of dependency by autonomy in the market. Thus, depending on the circumstances of the market at issue (including, for example, the typical length of contracts entered into by market participants in the ordinary course of business), purchase or supply obligations aimed at guaranteeing the quantities previously supplied may be justified for a transitional period of up to five years.

C.27 Both supply and purchase obligations providing for fixed quantities, possibly with a variation clause, are recognised as directly related and necessary to the implementation of the merger. However, obligations providing for unlimited quantities, exclusivity, or conferring preferred-supplier or preferred-purchaser status, are not necessary to the implementation of the merger.

C.28 Service and distribution agreements are equivalent in their effect to supply arrangements; consequently the same considerations as set out above apply.

Principles applicable to commonly encountered restrictions in cases of joint ventures

Non-competition obligations

C.29 A non-competition obligation between the parent companies and a joint venture may be considered directly related and necessary to the implementation of the merger where such obligations correspond to the products, services, and territories covered by the joint venture agreement or its by-laws. Such non-competition clauses reflect, inter alia, the need to ensure good faith during negotiations; they may also reflect the need to fully utilise the joint venture's assets or to enable the joint venture to assimilate know-how and goodwill provided by its parents; or the need to protect the parents' interests in the joint venture against competitive acts facilitated, inter alia, by the parents' privileged access to the know-how and goodwill transferred to or developed by the joint venture. Such non-competition obligations between the parent companies and a joint venture can be regarded as directly related and necessary to the implementation of the merger for the lifetime of the joint venture.

C.30 The geographical scope of a non-competition clause must be limited to the area in which the parents offered the relevant products or services before establishing the joint venture. That geographical scope can be extended to territories which the parent companies were planning to enter at the time of the transaction, provided that they had already invested in preparing this move.

C.31 Similarly, non-competition clauses must be limited to products and services constituting the economic activity of the joint venture. This may include products and services at an advanced stage of development at the time of the transaction, as well as products and services which are fully developed but not yet marketed.

C.32 If the joint venture is set up to enter a new market, reference will be made to the products, services and territories in which it is to operate under the joint venture agreement or by-laws. However, the presumption is that one parent's interest in the joint venture does not need to be protected against competition from the other parent in markets other than those in which the joint venture will be active from the outset.

C.33 Additionally, non-competition obligations between investors whose level of control falls below material influence and a joint venture are not directly related and necessary to the implementation of the merger.

C.34 The same principles as for non-competition clauses apply to non-solicitation and confidentiality clauses.

Licence agreements

C.35 A licence granted by the parent companies to the joint venture may be considered directly related and necessary to the implementation of the merger. This applies regardless of whether or not the licence is an exclusive one and whether or not it is limited in time. The licence may be restricted to a particular field of use which corresponds to the activities of the joint venture.

C.36 Licences granted by the joint venture to one of its parents, or cross-licence agreements, can be regarded as directly related and necessary to the implementation of the merger under the same conditions as in the case of the acquisition of an enterprise. Licence agreements between the parents are not considered directly related and necessary to the implementation of a joint venture.

Purchase and supply obligations

C.37 If the parent companies remain present in a market upstream or downstream of that of the joint venture, any purchase and supply agreements, including service and distribution agreements are subject to the principles applicable in the case of the transfer of an enterprise.

NOTES

298 Competition Act 1998, Schedule 1, section1(2).

299 In exceptional cases raising novel or unresolved questions, the CMA may agree to provide guidance on the ancillary nature of a restriction. In these rare cases, the CMA may need to seek the views of third parties, and it will include its assessment of the restriction in its published decision on the merger. As a result, the CMA will not be able to express a view as to whether the restrictions are ancillary if the merger parties consider that the arrangements are confidential, or if there is insufficient time to consider these matters within the statutory deadlines of an investigation

300 Likewise, a restriction could, if all other requirements are fulfilled, be 'directly related' even if it has not been entered into at the same time as the agreement carrying out the main object of the merger.

301 Section 1(2), Schedule 1 to the Competition Act 1998.

302 For the purposes of this Annex, 'control' is defined as comprising any level of control set out under Section 26 of the Act, including material influence.

303 The CMA may put in place interim measures to prevent the merger parties from giving effect to such ancillary restraints where the CMA considers it necessary to prevent or unwind pre-emptive action.

ANNEX D
CONTACT ADDRESSES

[3.509]
Contact for further information about the application of competition law to mergers in the UK:

The Mergers Unit

Competition and Markets Authority

The Cabot

25 Cabot Square

London

E14 4QZ

CMA switchboard: 020 3738 6000

Email: general.enquiries@cma.gov.uk.

CMA website: www.gov.uk/cma.

Additional contact details are available on https://www.gov.uk/guidance/mergers-how-to-notify-the-cma-of-a-merger.

For further information about public interest mergers, contact:

Consumer and Competition Policy Directorate

Department for Business, Energy and Industrial Strategy

1 Victoria Street

London

SW1H 0ET

BEIS switchboard: 020 7215 5000

Email: enquiries@beis.gov.uk.

BEIS website:

www.gov.uk/government/ organisations/department-for-business-energy-and-industrial-strategy.

GUIDANCE ON THE CMA'S MERGERS INTELLIGENCE FUNCTION (CMA56REVISED, DECEMBER 2020)

[3.510]

NOTES

CONTENTS

1 INTRODUCTION

[3.511]

1.1 This guidance is concerned with the mergers intelligence function of the Competition and Markets Authority (CMA). It is intended for legal advisers advising on a merger. For more general information on how the CMA deals with mergers, see the *Quick guide to UK merger assessment* (CMA18) and *Mergers: Guidance on the CMA's jurisdiction and procedure* (CMA2).

1.2 In the interests of avoiding an excessive regulatory burden, the Enterprise Act 2002 (the Act) does not oblige merger parties to notify the CMA of a merger. However, the CMA has a duty to track merger activity to determine whether any unnotified merger may give rise to a substantial lessening of competition. The CMA therefore has mergers intelligence staff who scan sources of information on mergers[1] and present potential candidates for investigation to the mergers intelligence committee, which meets weekly. The mergers intelligence committee is chaired by a Director of Mergers who also oversees the CMA's mergers intelligence function. The CMA will take a decision to investigate if it believes that there is a reasonable chance that the test for a reference to an in-depth phase 2 investigation will be met. The threshold for the CMA to open an investigation is therefore lower than the threshold for reference. The CMA may investigate and take action against mergers that have completed provided the completed merger has taken place not more than four months before the reference is made.[2]

1.3 Under section 105 of the Act, there is a distinction between deciding whether to investigate a matter (which the CMA does through its mergers intelligence function) and deciding whether to make a reference (which the CMA does following a phase 1 investigation). If the CMA decides to investigate, then it must publish an invitation to comment. In addition, once the CMA has decided to investigate, section 107 of the Act generally requires it to publish a reasoned decision setting out why it has decided to make a reference or decided not to make a reference. Neither the duty to publish an invitation to comment nor the duty to publish a reasoned decision applies while the CMA is still deciding whether to investigate.

1.4 This guidance explains how the mergers intelligence function operates in the light of the distinction drawn in section 105 of the Act.

NOTES

1 The CMA also maintains an active dialogue with Governmental departments and other regulatory bodies (including UK regulators and other international competition agencies) to obtain intelligence about merger activity.

2 See section 24 of the Act. If the merger took place without having been made public and without the CMA being informed of it, the four-month period starts from the earlier of the time that material facts are made public or the time the CMA is told of material facts.

2 INFORMATION REQUESTS TO THE PARTIES TO THE MERGER OR TO THIRD PARTIES

[3.512]

2.1 Where the CMA believes that an investigation is warranted, it will often open an investigation without any prior engagement with either the merger or third parties.

2.2 Where the CMA has identified a transaction that may qualify for investigation and raises potential concerns, it may ask parties to provide information to help it determine whether to open an investigation. These requests will usually be to the parties involved in the transaction but can also be to third parties. They are made under section 5 of the Act, which gives the CMA a general power to obtain information about matters relating to the carrying out of its functions. One of these functions is determining whether it should investigate a transaction (so as to enable it to decide whether to make a reference). The CMA will typically send such requests for information to a publicly available email address for the relevant companies in the first instance (but can use specific contact details where these have previously been provided by the company in question).[3]

2.3 Requests to merger parties will usually relate to the turnover and share of supply tests set out in section 23 of the Act, but may also relate to whether the target is an enterprise, when the transaction completed, and/or preliminary information to explain the businesses of the merger parties or the sectors in which they operate. Where a merger is subject to review by a competition authority outside of the UK, requests may also relate to the current status of those proceedings. If the initial response to these questions is insufficient, the CMA might ask supplementary clarifying questions without opening an investigation, but the CMA will not typically engage in more than two rounds of questions before taking a decision whether or not to investigate.

2.4 Requests to third parties will be made rarely. Where requests to third parties occur, they are likely to relate to understanding the nature of the businesses of the merger parties and the sectors in which they operate and any overlap for the purpose of applying the share of supply test. The CMA will only contact third parties in relation to transactions that are in the public domain and have either completed or been signed and announced.

2.5 If the CMA determines that there is a reasonable chance that the test for a reference to an in-depth phase 2 investigation will be met after asking these questions, then it will take a decision to investigate so as to enable the CMA to decide whether to make a reference under section 22 or 33 of the Act.

NOTES

3 Recipients who wish to check the veracity of an email purportedly from the CMA can do so by contacting general.enquiries@cma.gov.uk.

3 HOW THE CMA WILL RESPOND TO PARTIES CONTACTING THE CMA

[3.513]

3.1 The CMA invites parties to provide it with intelligence in relation to merger activity that affects UK markets, and welcomes both short briefings from merger parties about their transactions and complaints from concerned third parties.[4]

3.2 Merger parties are welcome to submit a short briefing note[5] to the CMA, explaining why they do not propose to submit or have not submitted a Merger Notice to the CMA. The note may address:

(a) Whether there may be a relevant merger situation;

(b) Whether any relevant merger situation may give rise to a substantial lessening of competition;

(c) Whether the merger has been or is being investigated by any competition authority outside of the UK and, if so, whether the parties intend to offer (or otherwise expect to be subject to) remedies in those proceedings that the merger parties consider would prevent any substantial lessening of competition in the UK;[6]

(d) With respect to completed mergers, the note should include when the merger was completed. With respect to anticipated mergers, the note should also include details of the likely completion date and the key remaining steps prior to completion.

3.3 As a general rule, the CMA will only consider a briefing note after there is a signed merger agreement.[7] This is to ensure that the CMA's mergers intelligence function does not commit resources to transactions that may not ultimately be agreed and reviews only those transactions which have not been or are not going to be notified on the basis of the parties' self-assessment.[8] The submission of a briefing note does not attract a merger fee, although a fee may be payable if the CMA subsequently opens an investigation.

3.4 Third parties are welcome to set out their concerns about a merger to the CMA. Complainants should explain clearly why they believe the merger raises competition concerns and, where possible, provide supporting evidence.

3.5 The CMA may then follow up with the person submitting the briefing note or complaint to understand the submission better. In these cases, the questions raised by the CMA may relate either to jurisdiction or to the overlaps between the merger parties, but typically remain short as they are still only for the purpose of deciding whether to investigate.

NOTES

4 To be sent by email to mergers.intelligence@cma.gov.uk.

5 The initial note should be 5 pages. The Parties may subsequently be invited to make follow-up submissions, particularly when the merger is being investigated by other competition authorities outside of the UK.

6 The CMA would encourage parties to such transactions to contact the mergers intelligence team at an early stage to discuss the transaction and their proposed approach.

7 The CMA does not wish its willingness to review a briefing note to change the duty on parties to self-assess, which is a key feature of a voluntary merger regime. However, there may be exceptional circumstances in which the CMA will consider a briefing note prior to a signed merger agreement – eg when the potential acquirer has made an announcement pursuant to Rule 2.7 of the UK Takeover Code in the context of a UK public bid. Where a signed merger agreement has not yet been concluded, the merger parties should set out the evidence which demonstrates their binding intention to merge or, in the case of a public offer, the binding nature of the offer. The CMA would typically not review a briefing note where the merger parties (or at least the offeror, in the case of a public bid) have not yet entered into a binding commitment but merely have a good faith intention to proceed.

8 For this reason, the appropriate point at which to provide a briefing note to the mergers intelligence committee is later than the appropriate point at which to submit a case team allocation form (see CMA2, paragraphs 6.12 to 6.19).

4 WHAT THE CMA WILL DO FOLLOWING ENGAGEMENT WITH THE MERGER PARTIES

[3.514]

4.1 Where, following engagement with the merger parties, either at the CMA's own initiative or as a result of a briefing note from the parties, the CMA decides to open an investigation to decide whether to make a reference, it will generally inform the parties of this decision within a week of the last contact. If the merger is anticipated the CMA will typically provide the merger parties with the option to notify the transaction.[9] Alternatively, the CMA will send the merger parties an enquiry letter under section 109 of the Act.[10] The extent of information requested by the CMA in its enquiry letter will vary depending on the circumstances of the case in question.

4.2 Alternatively, the CMA might decide not to open an investigation immediately. In such cases the CMA will contact the merger parties and indicate that it has no further questions at this stage. This does not preclude further questions at a later stage and, if further information comes to light, the CMA may open an investigation at any point until the expiry of the four-month statutory period set out in section 24 of the Act. This period commences when enterprises have ceased to be distinct and that fact becomes public or is drawn to the attention of the CMA.[11]

4.3 One circumstance in which the CMA might decide not to open an investigation immediately is where a transaction is subject to review by a competition authority outside the UK and any remedies imposed or agreed in those proceedings, in the event that competition concerns are found, would be likely to address any competition concerns that could arise in the UK. This could be the case, for example, where all of the markets that are relevant to the transaction are broader than national in scope. In this circumstance, merger parties are encouraged to engage with the CMA at an early stage, and may be invited to update the CMA on the progress of proceedings in other jurisdictions and to provide waivers to the CMA to discuss these proceedings with other competition authorities.

4.4 The CMA may consider whether to open a formal investigation at any point before expiry of the four-month statutory period, and merger parties run the risk that, where remedies in other jurisdictions do not fully eliminate any competition concerns relating to the UK, the CMA opens a formal investigation at a later stage. Where, following receipt of a briefing note and/or discussions with the merger parties the CMA decides not to open an investigation immediately in light of parallel proceedings, the CMA will specifically inform the merger parties that this decision has been made based on the existence of parallel proceedings.

4.5 If the parties consider it is important to have complete certainty as to whether their transaction might be the subject of a reference before expiry of the four-month statutory period set out in section 24 of the Act, then they should submit a case team allocation request form and a Merger Notice requesting the CMA to open a formal investigation.

NOTES

9 In this circumstance, the merger parties will typically be expected to commit to submitting a draft merger notice to the CMA within 10 working days, although the CMA may agree to a longer timeline following discussion with the merger parties.

[10] The template used as the starting point for the enquiry letter used by the CMA when initiating investigation of a non-notified merger is available on the government publications website: https://www.gov.uk/government/publications/merger-enquiry-letter-template.

[11] Where the mergers intelligence committee has considered a briefing note submitted by the merger parties and taken no immediate action, this does not exclude that the CMA will open an investigation until the expiry of the four-month statutory period.

MERGER ASSESSMENT GUIDELINES (CMA129, 18 MARCH 2021)

[3.515]

NOTES

CONTENTS

1. INTRODUCTION

[3.516]

1.1 This publication explains the substantive approach of the Competition and Markets Authority (CMA) to its analysis when investigating mergers and supersedes the Merger Assessment Guidelines from 2010.[1]

PURPOSE OF MERGER CONTROL AND THE CMA'S ROLE

1.2 The CMA's primary duty is to promote competition for the benefit of consumers. Part of this responsibility is to investigate mergers between organisations, to ensure that they do not result in a substantial lessening of competition.[2]

1.3 The protection of the welfare of consumers is at the heart of what the CMA does, including its role with regard to merger control.[3] Mergers have the potential to have a significant impact on consumers and their welfare, including an impact on the prices they pay for goods and services, and the range and quality of those goods and services that they have available to them. Consumers' interests are taken into account at every stage of the CMA's assessment of mergers, and is therefore implicit throughout these Guidelines, from considering the effect that any particular theory of harm might have on consumers, to weighing up relevant customer benefits that may arise as a result of a merger.[4] It is important that the CMA continues to adapt its approach to merger control as appropriate to ensure that it is fulfilling its statutory duty. It is also important that the CMA provides appropriate guidance to businesses considering entering into transactions which may have an impact on competition in the UK. It is with these two aims in mind that the CMA has produced these Merger Assessment Guidelines.

BACKGROUND TO THESE GUIDELINES

1.4 While the CMA's role and the legal tests that it applies remain the same,[5] since the previous Merger Assessment Guidelines were published in 2010, the UK economy has changed and with it the type of mergers that the CMA reviews. For example, digital technologies have changed, and will continue to change, the way goods and services are sold, delivered and used by consumers and the way that businesses compete. These changes have not introduced new theories of harm or economic principles in the field of merger control, but nevertheless require the CMA to consider carefully its approach to the assessment of mergers in such digital markets, to ensure that it is delivering on its duties to promote competition for the benefit of consumers. For example, in dynamic markets,[6] firms that may not compete head-to-head today might do so in the future. The threat of future disruption may inspire incumbent suppliers to improve their offer in the present, for the benefit of consumers. Fast-changing and evolving markets make predicting the future uncertain. The CMA needs to be prepared for these challenges and to be able to take effective decisions for the benefit of consumers.

1.5 To help it improve its decision making, the CMA continues to learn from various studies into its merger case work.[7] The Merger Assessment Guidelines also reflect the CMA's merger control casework, as well as the work undertaken by other teams within the CMA, such as the CMA's Market Studies and Market Investigations regime.

1.6 The courts of England and Wales have also clarified the meaning of some aspects of the applicable legislation since 2010. References to the relevant case law have been included in these Guidelines where appropriate.

1.7 In addition to the learnings from recent CMA cases and case law, as described above, the CMA has also benefited from the experience of other competition authorities around the world, as well as the large number of expert reports and academic literature that has been produced in recent years, including Unlocking digital competition, the Report of the Digital Competition Expert Panel, March 2019 (the Furman report);[8] and the Ex-post Assessment of Merger Control Decisions in Digital Markets, Final Report, May 2019 (the Lear report).[9] A theme in each of these reports is the risk of under-enforcement, particularly in relation to digital markets (including the loss of potential competition in these markets), by competition authorities such as the CMA. These two reports have suggested concrete changes to the CMA's Merger Assessment Guidelines to address this risk of under-enforcement.

1.8 Indeed, the Furman report noted that over the 10 years to 2018 the five largest digital firms have collectively made over 400 acquisitions globally. None has been blocked and very few have had conditions attached to approval, in the UK or elsewhere, or even been scrutinised by competition authorities.[10] The Stigler Center has noted that, in dealing with digital markets that have high levels of uncertainty and move quickly, competition authorities need to recalibrate how they assess some mergers because under-enforcement can be very costly.[11]

1.9 In light of all the valuable insights gleaned over the past 10 years, we have updated our Merger Assessment Guidelines in order to provide greater clarity and guidance to our merger work in future. The findings as set out in the reports referred to above have been carefully considered (and largely adopted) in the updates to these Guidelines.

1.10 In the years immediately following the introduction of the previous Merger Assessment Guidelines there were 70-100 Phase 1 cases a year. Over the past five years the number of Phase 1 cases reviewed has been around 55 to 65 per year. Despite this decline in overall case numbers, there has not been a corresponding decline in the number of mergers being referred for in-depth Phase 2 investigation (meaning a greater proportion of cases are referred for Phase 2 investigation). There has also been an increase in the proportion of cases requiring remedies (including prohibition and unwinding) at both Phase 1 and Phase 2. The large majority of cases that the CMA investigates are horizontal mergers, where the firms compete head-to-head. In recent years non-horizontal mergers have accounted for less than 20% of the CMA's Phase 1 cases.

PURPOSE OF THESE GUIDELINES

1.11 The Merger Assessment Guidelines are applicable to the CMA's Phase 1 and Phase 2 investigations. It is guidance that forms part of the advice and information published by the CMA under section 106 of the Enterprise Act 2002 (the Act).[12]

1.12 The CMA will have regard to the Merger Assessment Guidelines when conducting Phase 1 and Phase 2 investigations. The CMA will also follow relevant judgments of the Competition Appeal Tribunal (CAT) and other courts in its application of the merger provisions in Part 3 of the Act. However, merger assessment is inevitably case specific and must take account of the particular transaction and the markets being analysed. The methodologies employed in merger analysis should not be applied in a rigid and mechanistic way. The CMA will therefore consider each merger with due regard to the particular circumstances of the case,[13] including the information available and the time constraints applicable to the case. The particular analytical methods used by the CMA may vary across investigations, even across cases in the same industry. The review of any merger, particularly in fast-changing and evolving markets, will be largely case-specific. Whilst these Merger Assessment Guidelines provide a framework for merger analysis, the particular circumstances of a sector, market or business and the consumers who will be affected by the merger, are the critical factors in any case. The CMA will apply the Merger Assessment Guidelines flexibly, departing from them where it considers it appropriate to do so.[14] While past case references are included in the Merger Assessment Guidelines for illustrative purposes, decisional practice naturally evolves over time and the cases referenced will not constrain the approach of the CMA.

NOTES

1 The Enterprise and Regulatory Reform Act 2013 established the CMA as the UK's economy-wide competition authority responsible for ensuring that competition and markets work well for consumers.

2 What amounts to a substantial lessening of competition is set out in further detail in Chapter 2 below.

3 Of course, not all mergers involve businesses that are consumer-facing. In these guidelines customers of merger firms are sometimes used as proxies for consumers.

4 The CMA will also have particular regard to vulnerable consumers and the extent to which they may be impacted by a merger.

5 Further discussion of the standard of proof that the CMA will apply at Phase 1 and Phase 2 is provided in Chapter 2 below.

6 Dynamic markets are typically those which are growing and/or evolving and in which competition revolves around bringing new and innovative products to market.

7 For example, Lear, Ex-post Assessment of Merger Control Decisions in Digital Markets, May 2019; and KPMG, Entry and expansion in UK merger cases: an ex-post evaluation, April 2017.

8 Unlocking Digital Competition: Report of the Digital Competition Expert Panel, March 2019.

9 Ex-post Assessment of Merger Control Decisions in Digital Markets, Final Report, May 2019.

10 Unlocking Digital Competition: Report of the Digital Competition Expert Panel, March 2019, page 12.

11 Chicago Booth Stigler Center for the Study of the Economy and the State, Stigler Committee for Digital Platforms: Final Report, 2019.

12 A list of the CMA's Mergers Guidance (including these Merger Assessment Guidelines) can be found on the following

webpage, and at Annex 2 to the CMA's Guidance on Jurisdiction and procedure (CMA2).

13 *Ecolab Inc. v Competition and Markets Authority* [2020] CAT 12, paragraph 93: 'merger decisions of the CMA do not constitute precedents and it is axiomatic that each case turns on its own facts and that the characteristics of one market may be very different from those of another. Consistency is achieved by the CMA applying its statutory guidance . . . '.

14 The CMA will typically set out its reasons for departing from guidance.

2. A SUBSTANTIAL LESSENING OF COMPETITION

WHAT IS AN SLC?

[3.517]
2.1 If the CMA finds that a relevant merger situation has been created (or arrangements are in progress or in contemplation which, if carried into effect, will result in the creation of a relevant merger situation), it must decide whether the creation of that situation has resulted, or may be expected to result, in an SLC within any market or markets in the UK for goods or services.[15] Although the CMA is required to determine whether a merger it investigates will lead to an SLC, the term 'substantial lessening of competition' is not defined in the Act. How the CMA understands and typically applies the term is set out below.

2.2 The CMA views competition as a process of rivalry between firms seeking to win customers' business over time by offering them a better deal. Rivalry creates incentives for firms to cut price, increase output, improve quality, enhance efficiency, or introduce new and better products. This is because rivalry provides the opportunity for successful firms to take business away from competitors, and poses the threat that firms will lose business to others if they do not compete successfully.

2.3 In its merger assessments, the CMA will develop a general understanding of the competitive process, including of the competitive parameters that are most important to the process of competition in the relevant industry. The nature of competition may influence the theories of harm the CMA considers, or the frameworks it applies to assess it.

2.4 Both price and non-price aspects of competition are often important parts of the competitive process. In some cases, non-price competition may be the primary focus: for example, when customers do not pay a monetary price for consuming digital services or content, where firms compete mainly by innovating, or where prices are regulated.[16] The fact that customers do not pay a monetary price for a good or service does not preclude competitive effects from arising.[17]

2.5 The range of possible non-price aspects of competition that firms may use to win customers is wide, and terms such as 'quality' should be interpreted broadly. Examples might include, for example, staffing levels in store; speed and responsiveness to customer queries; the level of privacy offered to users of digital services; the benefits to users of a platform being able to interact with a large base of other users actively using the same platform; the reassurance afforded to customers by a well-known brand or good reputation; the sustainability of a product or service; and the ability to enjoy content without being served with advertisements. Innovation will play a key role in some merger investigations.

2.6 The CMA will consider any merger in terms of its effect on rivalry over time in the market or markets affected by it. When levels of rivalry are reduced, firms' competitive incentives may be dulled, to the detriment of customers.

2.7 Some mergers will lessen competition but not substantially so, because sufficient post-merger competitive constraints will remain to ensure that rivalry continues to discipline the commercial behaviour of the merger firms. However, some mergers lead to a lessening of competition that is substantial. Since merger assessments are prospective, an element of judgement is necessary in deciding whether any loss of competition is substantial rather than any exact quantitative measurement.[18]

2.8 The CMA does not apply any thresholds to market share, number of remaining competitors or on any other measure to determine whether a loss of competition is substantial. The CMA will decide whether a loss of competition is substantial under the applicable legal standard.[19]

2.9 Substantial in the context of an SLC does not necessarily mean *'large'*, *'considerable'* or *'weighty'* in absolute terms. Rather, it can encompass a range of meanings and will depend on the facts of the case.[20] A lessening of competition in a market (or in a particular segment of a market) may be considered substantial even if that segment or market is small in total size or value.[21] In considering whether a lessening of competition is substantial, the CMA may also take into account whether the market to which it applies is large or is otherwise important to UK customers,[22] or whether there is only limited competition in the market to begin with.[23]

2.10 While all merger assessments are prospective, there can be a higher degree of uncertainty in some markets, such as those characterised by potentially significant changes in competitive conditions. The CAT has previously held that all mergers should be assessed on a case-by-case basis to the same evidential standard regardless of the theory of harm being considered. There is, therefore, no special elevated evidential burden for particular theories of harm,[24] including theories of harm that involve changes in future competitive conditions. The fact that there may be some uncertainty in how the market is likely to develop in future is a relevant consideration, but may not be determinative. It does not, by itself, reduce the likelihood that a merger could give rise to competition concerns, and the presence of some uncertainty therefore does not in itself preclude the CMA from finding competition concerns on the basis of all the available evidence where the CMA is satisfied that the relevant standard of proof is met.

HOW AN SLC MIGHT ARISE

2.11 The CMA assesses the potential competitive effects of mergers by reference to 'theories of harm'. A theory of harm is a hypothesis about how the process of rivalry could be harmed as a result of a merger. Theories of harm provide a framework for assessing the effects of a merger and whether or not it could lead to an SLC relative to the counterfactual.

2.12 In formulating theories of harm, the CMA will consider how a merger might affect rivalry between firms seeking to win customers' business over time by offering them a better deal. The theories of harm will depend on the levels of the supply chain at which the merger firms operate; the links between the merger firms and with their rivals; the nature of competition and how firms go about winning customers from each other; and any long-run dynamics in the relevant sectors.

2.13 The theories of harm may also depend on the level of control that one merger firm is acquiring over the other.[25] For example, a theory of harm with respect to a firm that is acquiring material influence over another may be different -and require different analyses - to that involving a firm that is acquiring full legal control over another.[26] Although each level of control can encompass a range of shareholdings or other abilities to influence the target firm, in general the CMA will assess the merger on the basis of the specific shareholding or influence that results from the relevant merger situation. However, in some rare instances, if the CMA has evidence that a merger firm has another transaction in contemplation that will further increase its shareholding or influence in the target firm but still remain within the same overall level of control, the CMA may take that into account in its analysis of competition and any consideration of remedy options.[27]

2.14 The CMA will generally take a forward-looking approach to the assessment of any theories of harm, considering the effects of the merger both now, and in the future.

2.15 Theories of harm are commonly classified according to whether the merger in question is horizontal or non-horizontal. Horizontal mergers - discussed in Chapters 4, 5 and 6 - combine firms that are currently active, or absent the merger would be active in the future, at the same level of the supply chain and compete to supply products that are substitutable for each other. Chapter 4 discusses the possibility that horizontal mergers can give rise to unilateral effects from losses of existing competition, and Chapter 5 discusses unilateral effects from losses of potential competition. Chapter 6 discusses the possibility for coordinated effects as a result of a merger. Non-horizontal mergers - discussed in Chapter 7 - combine firms that offer products that are not substitutable but operate in related markets; for example, at different levels of the supply chain, or selling products that are complementary.

2.16 The theories of harm discussed in Chapters 4 to 7 are not exhaustive - the CMA may consider any theory of harm involving a potential SLC that could arise as the result of a merger. For some mergers, the CMA may consider several theories, sometimes affecting the same market.[28] The CMA may revise the theories of harm as its assessment progresses.

EXAMPLES OF WHEN A MERGER CAN RESULT IN AN SLC

2.17 When considering whether a merger gives rise to an SLC, the CMA will consider the characteristics of each merger on a case-by-case basis. These Merger Assessment Guidelines discuss how the CMA approaches its assessment of mergers under its main theories of harm, which are whether a merger would lead to:

(a) the merged entity being able to profitably and unilaterally raise its prices, worsen its quality or service and non-price factors of competition, or reduce innovation efforts at one or more of the pre-merger businesses;

(b) coordination occurring between some remaining suppliers or becoming more stable as a result of the merger; or

(c) the foreclosure of rivals when the merger is between firms at different levels of a supply chain or when the merger is between firms in different markets which are nevertheless related in some way.

2.18 When considering whether a loss of competition is substantial under any theory of harm, the CMA will consider each merger on its merits. Given the case-specific nature of the competitive dynamics and evidence, it is not possible to provide a comprehensive list of scenarios of when the CMA will find an SLC. As such, the following are examples of scenarios in which the CMA may be more likely to find an SLC and do not constitute a threshold for the CMA finding (or not finding) an SLC:

(a) the merger involves the market leader and the number of significant competitors is reduced from four to three;[29]

(b) the merger firms are close competitors in a differentiated market;[30]

(c) absent the merger, one of the merger firms would have entered or expanded and could be expected to become a strong competitor to the other firm or would have made efforts to enter or expand and thereby threatened the other firm;[31]

(d) innovation is a key aspect of competition between the merger firms and the level or pace of future innovation or product development is threatened by a merger;[32]

(e) a merger prevents effective competition emerging in other markets or services, even if these markets or services are new or nascent at the time of the merger;

(f) a merger strengthens one or more of the conditions for coordination in a market which is susceptible to coordination or where there is evidence of pre-existing coordination; or

(g) when a merger between firms at different levels of a supply chain, or a merger between firms in otherwise related markets, is expected to lead to the foreclosure of one important rival.[33]

HOW THE CMA ASSESSES EVIDENCE

2.19 The CMA does not have a prescriptive list of evidence that it will take into account in its assessments. Instead, the CMA will in each case undertake reasonable evidence gathering, consider the relevant available evidence and decide the weight to place on that evidence in its decision-making. The evidence gathered and used will depend on factors such as the theories of harm being investigated, the nature of competition in the marketplace and what evidence is available. In general, after reasonable evidence gathering, where the evidence supporting competition concerns is strong at an early stage, especially if there is little evidence to the contrary, the CMA will expect to undertake less detailed further analysis in deciding whether there is an SLC.

2.20 The CMA must take reasonable steps to acquaint itself with the relevant information to enable it to answer each of the statutory questions including whether the merger will lead to an SLC.[34] Where the CMA has persuasive evidence of a particular proposition to answer a statutory question, there may be little additional value of gathering further evidence on the same proposition and evidence submitted on those points may need to be more persuasive to counter it. In considering appeals of CMA decisions, the CAT has said that it will not intervene merely because it considers that further inquiries would have been desirable or sensible, but will assess whether the CMA has a sufficient basis in light of the totality of the evidence available to it for making the assessments and in reaching the decisions it did.[35]

2.21 The CMA also has a wide margin of appreciation in its use of evidence.[36] Given the case-specific nature of merger investigations, the CMA may apply different analytical methodologies and approaches in different cases.[37] In assessing the evidence, the CMA is not required to make precise predictions about the future such as whether any particular innovations will take place or whether a specific price rise or particular degrading of service quality will take place after a merger.[38]

2.22 Nor will the CMA normally quantify the expected loss of competition or detriment to customers. The CAT has confirmed that the CMA is not required to quantify any SLC, although there may be occasions when the CMA will estimate some quantification of the SLC or adverse effect.[39] Notwithstanding this position, any direct evidence that price increases, deteriorations in non-price competitive parameters or losses of innovation would occur as a result of the merger may be considered as evidence that the merger is likely to give rise to an SLC. However, the CMA is not required to separately assess the expected impact of a merger on each parameter of competition in order to identify an SLC.[40]

2.23 The CMA does not normally consider specific pieces of evidence in isolation when considering the question of an SLC, although it is common for the CMA to weight pieces of evidence differently.

2.24 The previous experience of the CMA is that the evidence it uses and the weights it attaches to different types of evidence evolve over time with the CMA's decisional practice. For example, the CMA has increasingly interrogated the merger firms' internal documents as a part of its merger investigations and has more closely scrutinised evidence on deal valuation, for example when considering losses of actual and potential competition or when seeking to understand the rationale for and synergies arising from mergers.[41]

2.25 In attaching weight to different pieces of evidence, there is no set hierarchy between quantitative evidence, such as consumer surveys or statistical or econometric analysis, and qualitative evidence, such as internal documents or the statements or conduct of market participants, and the CMA may attach greater weight to one or the other as appropriate in the circumstances, depending on the relative quality of such evidence.[42]

2.26 The CMA may take into account any evidence of an explicit intention on the part of the merger firms to take a particular course of action that would be consistent with an SLC, such as raising prices, foreclosing a rival, reducing their efforts to innovate, or to enter or expand in a market absent a merger. However, there is no requirement for the CMA to find any such direct evidence of explicit intentions, and the CMA will often rely on an assessment of the firms' economic incentives.

2.27 Merger assessments involve the CMA assessing the likely development of markets several years into the future. Some aspects of the CMA's assessment may be subject to a large degree of uncertainty. Whilst the degree of uncertainty will be appropriately weighted in the CMA's assessment of whether the relevant standard of proof is met, the presence of some uncertainty will not in itself preclude the CMA from concluding that the SLC test is met on the basis of all the available evidence.

2.28 In the context of sectors that are characterised by fast-moving technological and commercial developments or assessments of potential or dynamic effects that are particularly dependent on the evolution of competitive conditions, the types of evidence that are available to the CMA may be more restricted (for example, in many instances recent evidence from the pre-merger period will be a good indicator of future competitive conditions without the merger, however this is unlikely to be the case in nascent markets with dynamic effects). In such cases, the CMA may place particular weight on evidence such as internal documents, the expected number of competitors after the merger, similarities between the characteristics of the products or services that are under development, and the views and expansion plans of market participants. As with uncertainty, the absence of certain types of evidence such as historical data will not in itself preclude the CMA from concluding that the SLC test is met on the basis of all the available evidence assessed in the round.

2.29 The CMA will maintain an open mind regarding the assessment of evidence, including internal documents, in each case, and its interpretation of that evidence will be affected by the context in which it was generated. For example:

(a) Where internal documents support claims being made by merger firms or third parties that have an interest in the outcome of the CMA's investigation, the CMA may be likely to attach more evidentiary weight to such documents if they were generated prior to the period in which those firms were contemplating or aware of the merger, or if they are consistent with other evidence.

(b) In the context of completed mergers, the CMA may not attach weight to evidence that the merged entity has not changed its behaviour post-completion, as merger firms may have an incentive to delay any change in behaviour until the CMA has completed its investigation or is no longer able to investigate the transaction.

(c) The decision by a merger firm to enter or expand through a merger (ie inorganically) may supplant any efforts or plans the firm would otherwise have made towards organic entry or expansion. Therefore, when considering whether a merger firm may have entered or expanded absent the merger, the CMA may consider the incentives and ability of the firm to enter or expand and other available evidence. Where the CMA is satisfied that there is sufficient evidence of incentive and ability of a firm to enter or expand, a lack of direct evidence of efforts or explicit entry or expansion plans made available to the CMA may not be sufficient to demonstrate that the firm would not have entered absent the merger.

(d) An absence of internal documents pointing to, for example, competitive interactions between the merger firms may not be probative if the merger firms do not normally generate documents in the ordinary course of business or where merger firms have document retention policies whereby documents are regularly deleted.

2.30 The CMA may also consider the purpose and effect of the internal document (for example, whether it was a document for the board or executive decisionmaking). When considering the weight to place on internal document evidence the CMA will consider that evidence alongside all of the evidence that it has.

STANDARD OF PROOF

2.31 Under the UK's two-phase merger control regime, the CMA is required to apply different evidential thresholds when answering the statutory questions in the Act at Phase 1 and Phase 2. At Phase 1, the CMA applies a 'realistic prospect' threshold, whereas at Phase 2, the CMA applies a 'balance of probabilities' threshold.[43] The approach described in these guidelines is applicable to both phases of investigation.

2.32 When answering the statutory questions, it is not necessary for the CMA to assess whether the applicable evidential threshold is met at each step of the analytical process.[44] The standard of proof applies to the CMA's overall conclusions on the statutory questions which it has to decide, given the totality of evidence available to it.[45] Accordingly, the CMA may form a view that the SLC test is met based on a single theory of harm or based on several theories of harm affecting the same market.[46] At Phase 1, in keeping with the nature of the realistic prospect threshold (paragraphs 2.33 to 2.34), the CMA may find that multiple theories of harm each individually give rise to the realistic prospect of an SLC (based on the requisite legal standard), even where the conditions under which those theories of harm may lead to an SLC are different (such that it would be unlikely for both theories of harm to materialise, and give rise to an SLC, at the same time).

Phase 1

2.33 At Phase 1, the CMA examines mergers that are notified to it and mergers in relation to which it decides to initiate an investigation.[47] The CMA has a duty to refer for further investigation in Phase 2 any relevant merger situation where it believes, objectively justified on the evidence, that it is or may be the case that the relevant merger situation has resulted or may be expected to result in an SLC.[48] If the CMA believes that the relevant likelihood of an SLC is greater than fanciful, but below 50%, it has a wide margin of appreciation in exercising its judgement whether to refer. At the end of its Phase 1 investigation, the CMA might clear a merger unconditionally, decide the test for reference is met and therefore refer the merger for Phase 2 investigation or accept undertakings in lieu of reference to remedy the competition concerns it has identified.[49]

2.34 The realistic prospect threshold at Phase 1 is intentionally a lower and more cautious threshold for an SLC finding than that applied by the CMA after more extensive investigation at Phase 2.

Phase 2

2.35 By law, Phase 2 inquiries are conducted by an inquiry group of independent panel members, supported by CMA staff. The inquiry group is the decisionmaking body for Phase 2 merger inquiries.[50]

2.36 At Phase 2 investigation, the inquiry group decides whether: (i) there is a relevant merger situation falling within the UK merger control regime, (ii) that relevant merger situation has resulted, or may be expected to result, in an SLC, and (iii) it should take action to remedy any SLC identified. At Phase 2, the CMA will apply a 'balance of probabilities' threshold to its analysis, ie is it more likely than not that an SLC will result?[51] The CMA must therefore form an expectation which has a higher level of probability than that required of the CMA at Phase 1. Phase 2 investigations are more in-depth than those carried out at Phase 1.

NOTES

15 Sections 22 and 35 of the Act for completed mergers and sections 33 and 36 of the Act for anticipated mergers.

16 Nevertheless, price may still be relevant in all of these cases, including when prices are zero. A price of zero may be higher than the price level that would prevail in the presence of greater competition if customers could plausibly be paid for access to their private data. Examples of cases where non-price competition was the primary focus include: Celesio AG/Sainsbury's Pharmacy Business, Experian Limited/Credit Laser Holdings (ClearScore) (Provisional Findings), Illumina Inc/Pacific Biosciences of California Inc. (Provisional Findings), and Future Plc/TI Media Limited.

17 In Future Plc/TI Media Limited, the CMA considered the impact of the merger on the supply of technology websites on the readers of those websites. While readers of website content often do not pay a fee for consuming that content, websites can monetise readers' attention through advertising.

18 The meaning of substantial lessening of competition is considered in *Global Radio Holdings Limited v CC* [2013] CAT 26, paragraphs 18 to 25. That the likelihood of an SLC varies with the facts of a case and is prospective is discussed in

Intercontinental Exchange, Inc. v CMA and Nasdaq Stockholm AB [2017] CAT 6, paragraphs 115 and 246.

19 At Phase 1, the CMA must meet the 'realistic prospect' standard (paragraphs 2.33 to 2.34). At Phase 2, the decision is made on a balance of probabilities standard (paragraph 2.36).

20 The meaning of the word substantial in the context of an SLC is considered in *Global Radio Holdings Limited v CC* [2013] CAT 26; and *R v Monopolies and Mergers Commission ex p South Yorkshire Transport Ltd* [1993] 1 WLR 23.

21 For example, in Rentokil Initial plc/Cannon Hygiene Limited, the CMA found that an SLC would be likely to arise in relation to two segments within a more broadly defined market.

22 In J Sainsbury's Plc/Asda Group Ltd., in assessing what may constitute 'substantial' for the purposes of its assessment of in-store groceries, the CMA had regard to the fact that groceries were a non-discretionary expenditure that accounted for a significant share of household spend.

23 For example, in Celesio AG/Sainsbury's Pharmacy Business, the CMA found that regulation inhibited to some extent the degree of competition, but the amount of competition was still sufficiently significant that its loss would be a matter of concern.

24 *Intercontinental Exchange, Inc. v CMA and Nasdaq Stockholm AB* [2017] CAT 6, paragraph 114.

25 See Mergers: Guidance on the CMA's jurisdiction and procedure (CMA2 revised) for a discussion on the levels of control that exist under the Act.

26 Amazon.com NV Investment Holdings LLC/Roofoods Ltd (Deliveroo).

27 Section 29(2)(a)(ii) of the Act and Mergers: Guidance on the CMA's jurisdiction and procedure (CMA2 revised), paragraph 4.42.

28 These may include different effects on the same aspect of competition (for example, unilateral and coordinated effects on price), the same effects on different competitive aspects (for example, unilateral effects on price and on quality), or different effects on different aspects (for example, unilateral effects on price and coordinated effects on innovation). These theories of harm may apply over different time periods—for example, short-run unilateral effects on price and long-run coordinated effects on innovation.

29 *Tobii AB v Competition and Markets Authority* [2020] CAT 1, paragraph 353. The Competition Appeal Tribunal upheld the CMA's finding that the loss of competition could be expected to be substantial in a merger involves the market leader and the number of significant suppliers in a market is reduced from four to three. For the avoidance of doubt, this judgment does not preclude the CMA from finding an SLC in markets where there is a higher number of suppliers, for example if the merger reduced the number of suppliers from five to four.

30 For example, in both Ecolab Inc/The Holchem Group Limited and Hunter Douglas NV/247 Home Furnishing Ltd, the CMA found that the merger firms were close competitors in differentiated markets.

31 For example, the CMA considered the expansion of the merger firms in the Provisional Findings of Illumina Inc/Pacific Biosciences of California Inc.

32 For example, the Provisional Findings in Illumina Inc/Pacific Biosciences of California Inc and Experian Limited/Credit Laser Holdings (ClearScore) considered innovation as a key aspect of competition.

33 *Intercontinental Exchange, Inc. v CMA and Nasdaq Stockholm AB* [2017] CAT 6, paragraph 114: 'It is clear that vertical mergers can and do raise competition concerns'.

34 *BAA Limited v Competition Commission* [2012] CAT 3, paragraph 20(3); *Secretary of State for Education and Science v Tameside Metropolitan Borough Council* [1977] AC 1014, at 1065B; *Barclays Bank plc v Competition Commission* [2009] CAT 27, at [24].

35 *BAA Limited v Competition Commission* [2012] CAT 3, paragraph 20; *R v Royal Borough of Kensington and Chelsea, ex p. Bayani* (1990) 22 HLR 406, at 415.

36 See *Société Coopérative de Production SeaFrance SA v CMA* [2015] UKSC 75 paragraph 44.

37 *JD Sport Fashion plc v Competition and Markets Authority* [2020] CAT 24, paragraph 97.

38 *BSkyB and Virgin Media v Competition Commission and BERR* [2010] EWCA. Civ 2, paragraph 69. See also *Intercontinental Exchange, Inc. v CMA and Nasdaq Stockholm AB* [2017] CAT 6, paragraph 246.

39 *Tobii AB v Competition and Markets Authority* [2020] CAT 1, paragraphs 392-393.

40 *JD Sport Fashion plc v Competition and Markets Authority* [2020] CAT 24, paragraphs 95-100.

41 Lear, Ex-post Assessment of Merger Control Decisions in Digital Markets, May 2019; and Unlocking Digital Competition: Report of the Digital Competition Expert Panel, March 2019.

42 *Aberdeen Journals v OFT* [2003] CAT 11, paragraphs 126-127.

43 The 'realistic prospect' formulation is shorthand for more complex statutory language. The Court of Appeal clarified the meaning of 'is or may be the case that . . . may be expected to result' used in sections 22 and 33 in its judgment dated 19 February 2004 in *IBA Health Limited v OFT* [2004] EWCA Civ 142.

44 Clarity about the application of the threshold applicable to the CMA when answering the SLC question was provided by the Court of Appeal in *BSkyB and Virgin Media v Competition Commission and BERR* [2010] EWCA. Civ 2, paragraph 69. See also *Intercontinental Exchange, Inc. v CMA and Nasdaq Stockholm AB* [2017] CAT 6, paragraph 246.

45 *BSkyB and Virgin Media v Competition Commission and BERR* [2010] EWCA. Civ 2, paragraph 69.

46 For example, the CMA may consider vertical foreclosure effects and horizontal effects affecting the same market.

47 Further information on the CMA's mergers intelligence function can be found in the Guidance on the CMA's mergers intelligence function (CMA56).

48 Sections 22 and 33 of the Act.

49 Mergers: exceptions to the duty to refer (CMA64) and Merger remedies (CMA87).

50 Section 34C of the Act.

51 The Court of Appeal has endorsed the approach of expressing an expectation as a more than 50% chance, *IBA Health Ltd v OFT* [2004] EWCA Civ 142, paragraph 46.

3. THE COUNTERFACTUAL

WHAT IS THE COUNTERFACTUAL?

[3.518]

3.1 Applying the SLC test involves a comparison of the prospects for competition with the merger

Part 3 CMA and other Guidelines

against the competitive situation without the merger. The latter is called the 'counterfactual'.[52] The counterfactual is not a statutory test but rather an analytical tool used in answering the question of whether the merger gives rise to an SLC.[53]

3.2 The counterfactual may consist of the prevailing, or pre-merger, conditions of competition, or conditions of competition that involve stronger or weaker competition between the merger firms than under the prevailing conditions of competition.[54] The appropriate counterfactual may increase or reduce the prospects of an SLC finding by the CMA.

3.3 The CMA's conclusion on the counterfactual does not seek to ossify the market at a particular point in time. For example, an assessment based on the prevailing conditions of competition might reflect that, absent the merger under review, a merger firm would have continued making investments in improvements, innovations or new products.

3.4 Only events that would have happened in the absence of the merger under review—and are not a consequence of it—can be incorporated into the counterfactual.[55]

3.5 The CMA will not use as a counterfactual a competitive dynamic that involves violations of competition law, eg a cartel.[56]

THE CMA'S APPROACH TO THE COUNTERFACTUAL

3.6 In determining the counterfactual, the depth of analysis in the CMA's assessment is usually not to the same level as in its competitive assessment. Indeed, in many cases the counterfactual assessment is likely to be brief, although this will vary across cases.

3.7 The counterfactual is not intended to be a detailed description of the conditions of competition that would prevail absent the merger. Those conditions are better considered in the competitive assessment.

3.8 The counterfactual assessment will often focus on significant changes affecting competition between the merger firms, such as entry into new markets in competition with each other, significant expansion by the merger firms in markets where they are both present, or exit by one of the merger firms.[57]

3.9 Moreover, the CMA is likely to only focus on significant changes where there are reasons to believe that those changes would make a material difference to its competitive assessment. For example, where a firm that is being acquired could, in the counterfactual, have remained an independent competitor by raising external funding, or alternatively could have remained an independent competitor by being acquired by a firm with no current or potential activities in the relevant sector, the CMA would be unlikely to seek to consider the relative likelihood of those scenarios arising since both lead to the same conditions of competition. The CMA will generally conclude on the counterfactual conditions of competition broadly - that is, prevailing or premerger conditions of competition, conditions of stronger competition or conditions of weaker competition. If two or more possible counterfactual scenarios lead to broadly the same conditions of competition the CMA may not find it necessary to select the particular scenario that leads to its counterfactual.[58]

3.10 Significant changes affecting competition from third parties which would occur with or without the merger (and therefore form a part of the counterfactual) are unlikely to be assessed in any depth as part of the CMA's counterfactual assessment. This includes entry or expansion by a third party. Likewise, where there is evidence to indicate that entry and/or expansion may be likely in reaction to any adverse effects from the merger, this will be considered in the countervailing factors part of the CMA's SLC assessment (Chapter 8).

3.11 The CMA seeks to avoid predicting the precise details or circumstances that would have arisen absent the merger. For example, the CMA might assess, as part of the counterfactual, the likelihood that one of the merger firms would have entered or significantly expanded (see paragraph 3.17), but not the precise characteristics of the product or service it would have introduced or the level of sales it would have achieved. Similarly, the CMA (at Phase 1 or Phase 2) will not have as its counterfactual a sale of the target firm to a purchaser that is likely to result in a referral for an in-depth Phase 2 investigation, given the uncertainty over whether such an acquisition would, ultimately, be cleared or subject to subsequent remedial action.[59] In this scenario, the counterfactual will often be the prevailing or pre-merger conditions of competition.

3.12 In its assessment of mergers at Phase 1, the CMA is required to assess whether the merger creates a realistic prospect of an SLC. While the counterfactual is not a statutory test, the 'is or may be the case' standard in the Phase 1 SLC test also has implications for its approach to the counterfactual. In Phase 1 investigations, if the CMA must consider multiple potential counterfactual scenarios where each of those scenarios is a realistic prospect, it will choose the one where the merger firms exert the strongest competitive constraint on each other, and where third parties exert the weakest competitive constraints on the merger firms.

3.13 At Phase 2, the CMA has to make an overall judgement as to whether or not an SLC has occurred or is likely to occur.[60] To help make this assessment the CMA will select the most likely conditions of competition as its counterfactual against which to assess the merger. In some instances, the CMA may need to consider multiple possible scenarios before identifying the relevant counterfactual (eg a merger firm being purchased by alternative acquirers). In doing this, the CMA will consider whether any of the possible scenarios make a significant difference to the conditions of competition and, if any do, the CMA will find the most likely conditions of competition absent the merger as the counterfactual.

3.14 Establishing the appropriate counterfactual to assess the merger against is an inherently uncertain exercise and evidence relating to future developments absent the merger may be difficult to obtain.

Uncertainty about the future will not in itself lead the CMA to assume the pre-merger situation to be the appropriate counterfactual. As part of its assessment, the CMA may consider the ability and incentive (including but not limited to evidence of intention) of the merger firms to pursue alternatives to the merger, which may include reviewing evidence of specific plans where available.[61]

3.15 The time horizon that the CMA considers when describing the counterfactual will depend on the context. In some markets, relevant developments may not take place for some years while in others the relevant time horizon for the counterfactual will be shorter.[62] For example, when considering entry by a merger firm, becoming successful can take longer than two years in some instances (although the CMA will maintain a reasonable period).[63] In contrast, the time horizon over which a firm may exit the market could be significantly shorter than two years. The time horizon for considering the counterfactual will be consistent with the time horizon used in the CMA's competitive assessment (for example, but not exhaustively, entry or expansion by third parties and whether a merger is expected to result in efficiencies).

3.16 Three specific examples of situations where the CMA may use a different counterfactual which are discussed below are:

(a) entry or expansion by one of the merger firms;
(b) the exiting firm scenario; and
(c) where there are competing bids.

Entry or expansion by one of the merger firms

3.17 The CMA will consider whether the counterfactual situation should include the entry by one of the merger firms into the market of the other firm or, if already within the market, whether the firm would have expanded had the merger not taken place. One example of when this is likely to be relevant is where one merger firm is a start-up company or newly active in a market. Another example is where an established firm decides to enter a new market through acquisition, where it otherwise would have invested in organic entry by developing its own product or service.[64] In both scenarios, a merger may eliminate potential competition between the firms.

3.18 The CMA will consider evidence on the likelihood of the merger firms' entry or expansion. This may include direct evidence of their intentions to enter or expand, which could include their broader commercial strategy and the rationale for the merger.[65] The CMA may also take into account any history of entry into closely related markets. Responses by existing competitors to the threat of entry or expansion by the merger firms may also be relevant to the likelihood it will occur. Further, the CMA may consider evidence on the ability and incentive of merger firms to enter or expand in competition with each other.[66]

3.19 The CMA will consider the timeliness and strength of entry or expansion (and whether, taking this into account, it would be sufficient for the merger would give rise to an SLC) in its competitive assessment.[67] In markets which have a lengthy but prescribed set of steps to go through in order to develop products, get regulatory approval and supply them to customers, for example, the period for considering entry may be longer than it would otherwise be. Notwithstanding this, entry would also have to be sufficiently likely in those circumstances.

3.20 Where the CMA's competitive assessment considers a loss of dynamic competition (see paragraphs 5.17 to 5.24) where the merger firms compete by making efforts or investments towards entry or expansion (or respond to such efforts made by potential entrants), the CMA may not conclude in the counterfactual on whether entry or expansion would ultimately occur, but rather may conclude on whether or not such efforts would have continued absent the merger.

The exiting firm scenario

3.21 The CMA may consider whether, absent the merger, one of the merger firms is likely to have exited the market.[68] In forming a view on an exiting firm scenario, the CMA, in both its Phase 1 and Phase 2 investigations, will use the following framework of cumulative conditions:

(a) the firm is likely to have exited (through failure or otherwise); and, if so
(b) there would not have been an alternative, less anti-competitive purchaser for the firm or its assets to the acquirer in question.

3.22 The exiting firm scenario is most commonly considered when one of the firms is said to be failing financially. However, exit may also be for other reasons, for example because the target firm's corporate strategy has changed.

3.23 For the CMA to accept an exiting firm argument at Phase 1, it would need to see compelling evidence that it was inevitable that the considerations listed in paragraph 3.21 would be met. At Phase 2, the CMA will consider what is most likely. Where the CMA concludes that one of the merger firms would exit absent the merger and there would have been no alternative, less anticompetitive purchaser for the firm or its assets, it will not find an SLC.

3.24 When considering any exiting firm argument, the CMA will usually attach greater weight to evidence that has not been prepared in contemplation of the merger. It may be particularly important in the context of an exiting firm scenario for the CMA to understand the rationale for the transaction under review (ie to consider why the purchaser is acquiring a firm or its assets in the context of claims that it would have exited from the market).

3.25 If the CMA finds that the merger firm would not be likely to exit absent the merger, it does not follow that it may instead decide that the firm would be a weaker competitor in the counterfactual.

However, if the CMA does consider that the firm will be a weaker competitor in the future it is likely to assess the strength of competition between the merger firms in its competitive assessment.

Limb 1 - likelihood of exit

3.26 The first question the CMA will consider is whether one of the firms would have exited the market absent the Merger.

3.27 The CMA is likely to be mindful that if a firm has entered administration, although the financial position of the firm would be serious, being in administration may not be sufficient to demonstrate that exit is inevitable or likely.

3.28 Where a firm may be exiting because of financial failure, consideration is given both to whether the firm is unable to meet its financial obligations in the near future and to whether it is unable to restructure itself successfully. In practice, the CMA will carefully examine the firm's profitability over time, its cash flows and its balance sheet in order to determine the profile of assets and liabilities.[69] It may consider the action the management has taken to address the firm's position and will review contemporaneous internal documents such as board minutes, management accounts and strategic plans.[70] The CMA will also typically request and consider contemporaneous analysis provided by external legal, financial and insolvency advisers, as well as external auditors, in relation to the position of the company.[71] The CMA may also request evidence from the company's debt or equity providers, such as the banks that provide its financial facilities. If the firm is part of a larger corporate group, the CMA will also consider the parent company's ability and incentive to provide continued financial support.[72]

3.29 A merger firm may exit for strategic rather than financial reasons absent the merger. The CMA would need to be satisfied that the business would have ultimately exited for strategic reasons unrelated to the transaction in question.

Limb 2 - alternative purchasers

3.30 When considering if there were alternative purchasers, the CMA will seek to identify who the alternative purchaser(s) might have been and take this into account when determining the counterfactual. The CMA may consider the marketing process for the target firm as well as offers received for it.[73] The CMA will not restrict its analysis to alternative purchasers who were willing to pay the same or similar price that was agreed in the merger under investigation, but rather if there was an alternative purchaser willing to acquire the firm at any price above liquidation value.[74] Importantly, the CMA will consider alternative purchasers that would have operated the business as a competitor.

3.31 If the CMA considers that a more competitive realistic counterfactual or the most likely counterfactual (as applicable) would have involved an alternative purchaser for the firm or its assets, it will conduct its analysis of the impact on competition of the merger on the basis of that counterfactual (ie whether the effect of the merger under review would be substantially less competitive than the effect of an acquisition by that alternative purchaser).

3.32 Where there are multiple alternative purchasers, including one or more which is not active in the same markets as the exiting firm, the CMA will normally consider the most likely counterfactual to involve the target being under independent ownership that maintains (or, in some instances, increases) the competitive constraint of the exiting firm.[75] As set out above (see paragraph 3.6), the depth of analysis undertaken by the CMA with respect to the counterfactual will not be at the same level of detail as the competitive assessment and the CMA will not conduct a full competitive assessment of each alternative purchaser. In an assessment of the competitiveness of the exiting firm (or its assets) under different alternative purchasers, the CMA may therefore only differentiate between purchasers when this could make a material difference to competitive conditions.

Competing bids

3.33 Where there is more than one bidder with an active or 'live' bid for a target business at the time of the CMA's assessment, the CMA will examine each competing bid separately, if the CMA has jurisdiction to do so.[76]

3.34 At Phase 1 the CMA will consider whether each proposed merger would create a realistic prospect of an SLC as against the scenario in which competition between the merger firms is strongest, as long as it believes that scenario is realistic. Such a scenario will not include competing bids.

3.35 At Phase 2 the appropriate counterfactual will depend on the circumstances of the case. If only one merger is referred, the counterfactual used by the CMA may be the prevailing or pre-merger competitive situation or the sale of the target firm to one of the alternative purchasers.

3.36 If two or more merger situations involving competing bids are referred for Phase 2 investigation, but there are other merger situations involving other bids that are not, the counterfactual is more likely to involve a merger that is not referred than one of the referred mergers or the prevailing conditions of competition.

3.37 The CMA will not take into account the possibility of remedies being implemented to address competition concerns raised by the alternative mergers, ie a sale to a 'remedied bidder' would not become the counterfactual situation.

3.38 Where mergers involving all the bids are referred, the counterfactual will often be the prevailing or pre-merger conditions of competition.

NOTES

52 Developments which have arisen or are likely to arise as a result of the merger will not form part of the counterfactual assessment but will be examined as part of the competitive assessment.

53 Because of the particular nature of rail franchises, the CMA's approach to the counterfactual in rail franchises is set out in its rail franchise guidance: Rail Franchise Mergers: review of methodologies and guidance.

54 The conditions of competition before a merger in anticipated acquisitions are generally referred to as the 'prevailing conditions of competition' and in completed acquisitions as 'pre-merger conditions of competition'. The discussion of the counterfactual in these guidelines is equally applicable to both anticipated and completed acquisitions and therefore the terms 'pre-merger' and 'prevailing' are interchangeable.

55 For example, if the merged entity has plans to close down stores or redirect investment funding after the merger but such actions would not have occurred without the merger, then the CMA would not incorporate these in the counterfactual.

56 For example, in Fenland Laundries Limited/Fishers Services Limited, the CMA considered whether a JV agreement contained horizontal partitioning of the market. In that case, the CMA found that it was not clear that the JV agreement infringed competition law and the CMA did not disregard the existence of the JV agreement in its counterfactual analysis (paragraph 29).

57 See for example PayPal Holdings Inc/iZettle AB.

58 For example, in Rentokil Initial/Cannon Hygiene, the CMA considered that absent the merger the target firm would have been sold to another purchaser but did not consider it necessary to specify which of the alternative bidders would have been most likely to acquire it since any of the alternative bidders would have resulted in premerger conditions of competition. In PayPal Holdings Inc/iZettle AB, the CMA did not consider it necessary to assess the likelihood of each alternative scenario occurring since the most likely counterfactual was that PayPal would have sought to improve its offline payment service capabilities through one, or a mix of, the potential scenarios. In BT Group plc/EE Limited, the merger took place when a parallel merger was being assessed by the European Commission. In that case the CMA considered a counterfactual of the prevailing conditions of competition was appropriate given the most likely scenario was that either the parallel transaction did not proceed, or the European Commission would require remedies in clearing the merger.

59 This is consistent with the CMA's approach to considering competing bids in the counterfactual (paragraphs 3.37-3.39). See also the Final Report in Bauer Media Group/Celador Entertainment Limited/Lincs FM Group/Wireless Group Limited/UKRD Group Limited, paragraph 16 and the Final Report in PayPal/iZettle at paragraph 7.37.

60 '[it] is not necessary for the [CMA] to isolate each step in the analytical process and to apply the balance of probability separately at each stage [of the SLC assessment]', *BSkyB and Virgin Media v Competition Commission and BERR* [2010] EWCA. Civ 2, paragraph 55.

61 PayPal Holdings Inc/iZettle AB.

62 The CMA considered the relevant time horizon for the counterfactual in PayPal Holdings Inc/iZettle AB; and Amazon.com NV Investment Holdings LLC/Roofoods Ltd (Deliveroo).

63 For example, Lear, Ex-post Assessment of Merger Control Decisions in Digital Markets, May 2019.

64 The CMA considered the prospect of entry by the acquiring firm in Illumina Inc/Pacific Biosciences of California Inc.

65 The CMA considered the intention of the merger firms to enter or expand, including their broader commercial strategy and rationale for the merger, in Amazon.com NV Investment Holdings LLC/Roofoods Ltd (Deliveroo).

66 In PayPal Holdings Inc/iZettle AB, the CMA considered PayPal's incentives to improve its offline payment services capabilities absent the merger, in light of evidence on the importance of these services to customers, PayPal's valuation of the synergies it would realise from the ability to cross-sell offline services, and the resources available to PayPal to pursue such expansion. See also, Amazon.com NV Investment Holdings LLC/Roofoods Ltd (Deliveroo), where the CMA considered whether, absent the merger, Amazon would choose to re-enter the supply of online restaurant platforms in the UK.

67 See, for example, paragraph 4.15 or Chapter 5 on potential competition.

68 The CMA has considered the exiting firm scenario in, for example, East Coast Buses Limited/First Scotland East Limited; Poundland Group plc/99p stores Limited; Chemring Group plc/Wallop Defence Systems Limited; Alliance Medica Group Limited/IBA Molecular UK Limited; and Amazon.com NV Investment Holdings LLC/Roofoods Ltd (Deliveroo).

69 For example, in Poundland Group plc/99p stores Limited, the CMA rejected the exiting firm scenario after an in-depth Phase 2 investigation and following a detailed assessment of the financial and operational performance of the target 99p. The CMA's review of Chemring Group plc/Wallop Defence Systems Limited also contained detailed assessment of Wallop's profitability and balance sheet.

70 See for example, the CMA's assessment of Limb 1 in East Coast Buses Limited/First Scotland East Limited; Poundland Group plc/99p stores Limited; and Chemring Group plc/Wallop Defence Systems Limited.

71 In Alliance Medical Group Limited/IBA Molecular UK Limited, the CMA considered (amongst other factors) the financial due diligence carried out by PwC and the analysis of the performance of IBA by the Monitoring Trustee.

72 In Chemring Group plc/Wallop Defence Systems Limited, the CMA found that limb 1 had not been met because the parent company would have been able to provide continued financial support to the target business that was experiencing financial difficulties.

73 In Chemring Group plc/Wallop Defence Systems Limited, the CMA considered the sales process undertaken and the acceptability of alternative offers received.

74 In East Coast Buses Limited/First Scotland East Limited the CMA concluded that an operator should not be considered as offering a realistic prospect of being a less anti-competitive purchaser as the operator's estimate of the value to it of the depot alone (without the employees associated with it) would have fallen considerably below the liquidation value of the property.

75 In Euro Car Parts Limited/Andrew Page Limited, the CMA adopted the alternative purchaser that was not present in the market, over alternative purchasers that were already present.

76 Considering alternative bidders may be relevant in other counterfactual considerations. For example, see the discussion on the exiting firm scenario and footnote 55.

4. HORIZONTAL UNILATERAL EFFECTS

[3.519]

4.1 Unilateral effects can arise in a horizontal merger when one firm merges with a competitor that previously provided a competitive constraint, allowing the merged entity profitably to raise prices or degrade non-price aspects of its competitive offering (such as quality, range, service and innovation) on its own and without needing to coordinate with its rivals.[77] Unilateral effects giving rise to an SLC can occur in relation to customers at any level of a supply chain, for example at a wholesale level or retail level (or both), and is not limited to end consumers.

4.2 The competitive constraint eliminated by a merger may be an existing constraint, or a potential or future constraint. The following sections discuss the CMA's approach to losses of existing competition, including issues relating to differentiated products (including two-sided platforms and local mergers) and undifferentiated products.[78] The assessment of mergers involving losses of potential competition is discussed in Chapter 5.

4.3 Horizontal unilateral effects are the most common type of theory of harm that gives rise to competition concerns in mergers considered by the CMA. While the following sections discuss the theory of harm in greater detail, the concern under horizontal unilateral effects essentially relates to the elimination of a competitive constraint by removing an alternative that customers could switch to. The CMA's main consideration is whether there are sufficient remaining good alternatives to constrain the merged entity post-merger. Where there are few existing suppliers, the merger firms enjoy a strong position or exert a strong constraint on each other, or the remaining constraints on the merger firms are weak, competition concerns are likely. Furthermore, in markets with a limited likelihood of entry or expansion, any given lessening of competition will give rise to greater competition concerns.

4.4 One way in which the CMA may assess whether there are sufficient remaining alternatives is through a consideration of measures of concentration. Concentration can be measured in different ways, and the relevance of different measures to a given assessment will depend on the specific circumstances of a case. Measures of concentration might include, for example: shares of supply (by volume, by value, of capacity, or other measures), counts of the number of competitors, or the Herfindahl-Hirschman Index (HHI).[79]

4.5 While the following sections discuss certain aspects of the CMA's approach in the context of horizontal mergers, many will also be relevant to non-horizontal mergers (which are discussed further in Chapter 7).

DIFFERENTIATED PRODUCTS

4.6 Unilateral effects may arise in differentiated product markets because a price increase becomes less costly when the products of the two firms are brought under common ownership or control. Absent the merger, firms face a trade-off when considering whether to raise prices or reduce quality, range or service. On the one hand, the firm will incur a cost because some customers will switch away, and the firm will lose the profits they would have earned on those customers. On the other hand, the firm also gains, because it makes a bigger profit on the customers that remain (because of the higher price, or the lower cost associated with reduced quality, range or service).

4.7 After the merger, it would no longer be as costly for the merged entity to raise prices or reduce quality: it would recoup the profit on recaptured sales from those customers who would switch to the products of the other merger firm.

4.8 In differentiated markets, horizontal unilateral effects are more likely where the merger firms are close competitors or where their products are close substitutes. The more closely the merger firms compete the greater the likelihood of unilateral effects because the merged entity will recapture a more significant share of the sales lost in response to a price increase (or another worsening in the offering), making the price rise more profitable. The merger firms need not be each other's closest competitors for unilateral effects to arise. It is sufficient that the merger firms compete closely and that the remaining competitive constraints are not sufficient to offset the loss of competition between them resulting from the merger.[80]

4.9 The concept of close competition is not limited to products or services that have similar characteristics. A firm may be a close competitor if it represents a significant competitive force or exerts a strong constraint on other firms. For example, a firm that has a particular reputation or incentive to compete aggressively or behave as a 'maverick', or that is actively disrupting the status quo using a new technology or business model, may represent a close competitor to other firms, even if their respective offerings are quite different.

4.10 Closeness of competition is a relative concept. Where there is a degree of differentiation between the merger firms' products, they may nevertheless still be close competitors if rivals' products are more differentiated, or if there are few rivals. The CMA will consider the overall closeness of competition between the merger firms in the context of the other constraints that would remain post-merger. For example, where the CMA finds evidence that competition mainly takes place among few firms, any two would normally be sufficiently close competitors that the elimination of competition between them would raise competition concerns, subject to evidence to the contrary.[81] The smaller the number of significant players, the stronger the prima facie expectation that any two firms are close competitors. In such a scenario, the CMA will require persuasive evidence that the merger firms are not close competitors in order to allay any competition concerns.

4.11 The constraints exerted by the merger firms on each other may be asymmetric, such that one merger firm may be a close competitive constraint on the other, without the reverse being the case.[82]

4.12 Some factors may make horizontal unilateral effects more or less likely in the context of a differentiated market. For example:

(a) **Market power.** While the focus of the CMA's assessment is on the *change* in the competitive constraints on the merger firms arising from the merger, where one merger firm has a strong position in the market, even small increments in market power may give rise to competition concerns. Conversely, evidence that firms are price takers may suggest that the incremental change from a merger between two firms is unlikely to have an effect. Evidence relevant to market power may include the level and stability of market shares; the number and strength of competitive constraints; the extent of past entry or exit; or the impact of past changes in concentration on prices.

(b) **Profit margins**. Where incremental profit margins are high,[83] unilateral effects are more likely because the value of sales recaptured by the merged entity will be greater, making it less costly to raise prices or worsen non-price aspects of the competitive offering.[84]

(c) **Capacity.** Where firms have significant spare capacity, they may be better able to compete. Conversely, firms facing capacity constraints may not be able to serve customers switching away from rivals and may provide a less effective constraint.

4.13 The types of evidence the CMA may rely on to assess closeness of competition are diverse and will vary from case to case. Examples include evidence on products' characteristics or their intended use, which might be indicative of their substitutability. The CMA often gathers the views of customers or competitors. The CMA may review firms' internal documents, which can describe their perceptions of the competitive importance of rivals or reflect which competitors they monitor or respond to. The CMA might gather evidence on customer switching or diversion, for example from the data held by firms or from customer surveys.[85] Past competitive interactions, such as to each other's offers in tenders or negotiations, reactions to each other's innovations, or through other responses to each other's competitive offering generally, may also be informative. Evidence of an impact on competitive outcomes following previous comparable mergers, or previous entry or exit, may also provide relevant evidence. The CMA will normally not gather evidence from every possible source and will decide which sources to prioritise, and the CMA may consider evidence not described here. The CMA's broader approach to assessing evidence is described in paragraphs 2.18 to 2.28.

4.14 Measures of concentration such as shares of supply can be useful evidence when assessing closeness of competition, particularly when there is persuasive evidence on demand- and supply-side substitution as to which potential substitutes should be included or excluded, and when, although differentiated, the degree of differentiation between firms is more limited. In such circumstances, a firm with a higher share of supply is more likely to be a close competitor to its rivals, and therefore merger that removes the competitive constraint such a firm exerts on its rivals would be more likely to raise competition concerns. In cases such as this, market shares can represent a readily available source of evidence on which the CMA can base its assessment of closeness.

4.15 In other cases, such as where the boundaries of the market are not as clear-cut, where reliable estimates of shares of supply are not readily available, or where there is a high degree of differentiation, the CMA may rely to a greater extent on other sources of evidence on closeness of competition. Where products are more differentiated or customer preferences are more diverse, shares of supply may not provide evidence on the closest alternatives available to the merger firms' customers, as these may be different from the products that achieve the greatest sales across a wider body of customers. Market definition is discussed in paragraphs 9.1 to 9.15.[86]

4.16 The CMA's assessment is generally forward-looking and will seek to account for the future evolution of competitive conditions, including constraints from rival entry or expansion. Entry or expansion by rivals may be accounted for in two broad scenarios:

(a) **Entry that would have occurred irrespective of the merger.** In such circumstances, even though such entry or expansion would form part of the counterfactual, the CMA will often consider such entry or expansion as a constraint on the merged entity in its competitive assessment.[87]

(b) **Entry triggered by the merger.** In this scenario, the CMA will consider whether such entry would replace the constraint eliminated by the merger. This is discussed as a countervailing factor (see paragraphs 8.1 to 8.43).

4.17 Where new entry or expansion by rivals is unlikely, for example because barriers to entry are high, or because the chance of successful and profitable entry is low, any given lessening of competition is likely to be longer lasting, and is more likely to result in an SLC, given the lower likelihood that it will be diminished by the emergence of new entry or expansion in the long run.

4.18 While the constraint from rivals may increase as a result of the merger by triggering entry or expansion, it can potentially also decrease. Competing suppliers may respond to a price rise by the merged entity by increasing their own prices, reducing the risk of losing sales to them and thereby making such a price increase more profitable.

4.19 Where a customer has the ability and incentive to trigger new entry, it may be able to restore competitive conditions to the levels that would have prevailed absent the merger. The two main ways customers may be able to trigger new entry - sponsored entry and self-supply - are assessed under the same framework that the CMA applies to other forms of countervailing entry and expansion (see paragraphs 8.41 to 8.43).

4.20 Most other forms of buyer power that do not result in new entry - for example, buyer power based on a customer's size, sophistication, or ability to switch easily - are unlikely to prevent an SLC that would otherwise arise from the elimination of competition between the merger firms. This is because a customer's buyer power depends on the availability of good alternatives they can switch to, which in the context of an SLC will have been reduced. In that sense, market power and buyer power are two sides of the same coin, and an SLC can be interpreted as a substantial lessening of customers' buyer power.

TWO-SIDED PLATFORMS

4.21 Some firms operate two-sided (or multi-sided) platforms which supply services to two distinct but related customer groups.[88] Examples include media publishers or social media platforms, which serve consumers on one side and advertisers on the other; shopping centres, which serve both retail tenants and shoppers; and online food delivery platforms, which serve both restaurants and consumers.[89] Two-sided platforms are typically differentiated products, but have some specific characteristics that may affect the CMA's approach to the assessment. These are discussed below.

4.22 Two-sided platforms are often characterised by network effects, where the value of the product for customers on one side of the platform depends on the volume of users either on the same side (direct network effects) or on the other side (indirect network effects). Network effects may operate in one direction (eg a social network will be more attractive to advertisers if it has more users, but not vice versa) or both directions (eg a food delivery platform will be more attractive to users if it has more restaurants and vice versa).[90]

4.23 Where network effects are strong, the growth of a two-sided platform may be self-reinforcing: growth in customer numbers increases network effects; increased network effects attract more customers; more customers lead to greater network effects, and so on. In some circumstances, this may lead to a 'tipping' effect, where one platform becomes dominant and smaller platforms exert only a weak constraint and find it difficult to expand.

4.24 When assessing competitive effects in mergers involving two-sided platforms, the CMA may consider each side of the platform separately, or it may consider the overall competition between the platforms (incorporating both sides in one assessment). The CMA's approach will depend on:

(a) **How competition works.** Where competition primarily involves platform operators improving aspects of their offer that affect one side of the platform (for example, charges applied or service levels offered to users on one side), the CMA may assess each side separately.[91] Where competition is focused on aspects of the platform that affect both sides (for example, improvements to technology that benefit the overall efficiency of the platform), the CMA may assess both sides together.[92]

(b) **Competitive conditions.** Where competitive conditions (such as the number and strength of alternatives available) are different on the two sides of the platform, a platform operator may have different incentives as regards what it offers to users on either side, and the CMA may therefore assess each side separately.[93]

(c) **Network effects.** Where indirect network effects are strong, the platform operator's incentive to compete for users on each side of the platform are more likely to be influenced by competitive conditions on the other side of the platform. When they are strong in both directions, the assessment of the two sides may be sufficiently closely linked that a single assessment would be appropriate.

4.25 Network effects and the risk of tipping may influence the CMA's competitive assessment of two-sided platforms. Network effects mean that mergers among platforms are more likely to give rise to competition concerns because network effects mean that:

(a) **Mergers are more likely to induce a tipping effect.** Mergers may harm customers if they accelerate the market towards tipping, whereas customers would have benefited from a longer period of competition between platforms vying to be the 'winning platform' prior to tipping occurring. Mergers may also award network effects to a platform with lower relative merit, and cause demand to 'tip' to that weaker platform.

(b) **Platform mergers are more likely to have a strong effect on incentives**. Lost sales are more significant in the presence of network effects because in addition to the profits lost directly on those lost sales, the platform may also lose further profits as their platform becomes less attractive and additional customers switch away. The platform may also suffer a reduction in the chance that demand will 'tip' to their platform. The recapture of sales between two merging platforms may therefore have a more substantial impact on the incentive to raise prices or reduce quality, range, service levels or innovation.

(c) **Larger platforms are more likely to exert a strong constraint on rivals**. Where network effects are important, larger platforms with more significant network effects may represent a more attractive option for users.

(d) **Barriers to entry are likely to be high**. Barriers to entry may also be increasing for each successive entrant: as the pool of available users shrinks, the cost of building sufficient network efficiencies to compete may rise. Moreover, incumbent platform operators that have market power derived from network effects may be able to amplify their effect, for example by limiting interoperability with rival platforms. Multi-homing by users of platforms may increase the ability of new entrants to acquire customers and build up network effects, but existing network effects may nevertheless still represent a barrier to doing so.

LOCAL MERGERS

4.26 Firms that compete in many different local areas may take different approaches to how they adjust different parameters of competition depending on conditions in each local area. This section discusses how the different approaches taken by firms active across local areas may affect the CMA's approach to the competitive assessment. However, the broad principles set out in this section may also apply to the analysis of mergers involving firms that are active across multiple markets or segments of other types (such as product segments, customer groups, or distribution channels).[94]

Flexing of parameters of competition

4.27 There are three broad approaches that firms typically take when competing in many different local areas:

(a) firms may set their competitive offering uniformly across all of the local areas they operate in - for example, a national retail chain offering a broadly consistent price, quality, range and service level in every store they operate in the UK;

(b) firms may 'flex' or tailor their offering to suit the specific conditions in each different area - for example, a chain of petrol stations setting a different price at each location depending on the prices set by local competitors;[95] or

(c) firms may take a mixed approach - for example, a retailer offering the same price in every store, but adjusting its range or level of service at individual stores depending on local competition.[96]

4.28 In practice, the CMA will seek to ensure that its assessment reflects the reality of how firms compete in a market or markets. Where firms mainly compete by improving aspects of their offer in a uniform way at the national level, the incentives of the firm to improve prices or non-price aspects of its competitive offer will depend on the aggregate conditions of competition across the geographic areas in which its stores are active. In such circumstances, the CMA will conduct its competitive assessment at the aggregate level, reflecting the aggregate effect of the loss in the competitive constraints on the merger firms across those different local areas.

4.29 Even where there is material variation in the merger firms' competitive offerings across different local areas, the CMA may nevertheless conduct its assessment at the aggregate level where there is evidence that such variation is not driven by differences in competitive conditions (but rather, for example, by differences in local demand).

4.30 Where firms mainly compete by flexing aspects of their competitive offering that are tailored for the specific competitive conditions within each local area, the CMA's assessment may focus on competition at this narrower level.[97] The CMA will typically only carry out an assessment at both the local and the aggregate national level where important aspects of competition take place at each level.

4.31 The CMA may consider how a merger might change the merger firms' incentives to set their competitive offering uniformly across different local areas.[98] For example, a merger firm may decide to move away from having a uniform competitive offering if a merger creates profitable opportunities to raise prices in individual local areas. The CMA will tend to consider this only where there is evidence of the merger firms considering changing their approach, other firms already taking a different approach to the merger firms, or firms changing their approach over time.

Filtering and decision rules

4.32 Where the merger firms do tailor their offering to each specific local area, this may result in the CMA having to consider a large number of overlaps between the merger firms. In such cases, the CMA may employ a filtering approach. Filtering generally involves identifying some areas as requiring no further consideration based on systematic information that is relatively easy to gather. For example, the CMA might gather information on the number of stores operated by effective competitors within a certain drive time of each of the merger firms' stores, and eliminate some areas from further consideration where sufficient competition would remain based on this information. By eliminating these areas, the CMA may make it feasible to gather further information for a more manageable number of areas (ie those that 'failed' the filter) and give them further consideration.[99]

4.33 Where a filter has been applied and local areas remain for further consideration, there may be limited time available (or it may not be compatible with the efficient conduct of the CMA's investigation) to conduct a detailed competitive assessment of a large number of local areas. Therefore, the competitive assessment of local areas that fail a filter will typically be based on an assessment of factors that can be systematically analysed across all local areas (rather than an in-depth assessment of the varied indicators of competition). Where the merger firms conduct a non-systematic review of competitive conditions in individual local areas (ie considering different factors in different areas), it may be difficult for the CMA to verify whether the material presented to it provides a balanced picture of each particular area, or whether it presents a partial view which is favourable to the interests of the merger firms. The CMA may be better able to attach weight to reviews that have been conducted systematically, such that the same factor is taken into account across all local areas.

4.34 In some cases, a filtering approach may not be capable of reducing the number of local areas under consideration to a sufficiently small number to allow the CMA to review a wider range of evidence on an area-by-area basis. In such cases, the CMA may apply a 'decision rule' approach. This involves developing a systematic measure or set of measures that can be used to describe the impact of the merger on competition in each area, and comparing that measure or measures to a threshold above which the CMA considers the SLC test would be met.[100]

UNDIFFERENTIATED PRODUCTS

4.35 In markets involving undifferentiated products, such as raw materials or mass-produced commodities, firms select the volume of output they supply to the market and receive the market price.

For some firms - especially large ones -the volume they decide to supply to the market can have a material impact on total supply and, therefore, may influence the market price.

4.36 Mergers in undifferentiated product markets may give rise to unilateral effects.[101] Without a merger, it is costly for one of the merger firms to cut its volumes, as it will lose the margins on the volumes it no longer sells. However, to the extent a volume reduction reduces total supply and results in an increase in market prices, the firm will earn greater profits on the volumes it continues to sell.

4.37 After a merger, it may become more attractive for the merger firms to restrict volumes, as they will benefit not only from the increased profits on their own volumes, but also the increased profits on the volumes of the other merger firm.

4.38 Some factors may make horizontal unilateral effects more or less likely in the context of an undifferentiated market:

(a) **Concentration of rivals.** Where the market is concentrated among few rivals, price increases may be more likely.

(b) **Shares of supply.** The merged entity may have a greater incentive to restrict volumes to the extent it has a large share of supply, as the benefits of a higher price would apply to a greater volume than would be the case for a smaller firm.

(c) **Spare capacity of rivals**. If rivals have spare capacity, they may be expected to respond to a reduction in volumes by expanding their own production. This may prevent an increase in price levels.

(d) **The merger involves a marginal supplier.** Suppliers that are less efficient earn lower margins, and therefore the loss from withholding volumes from a small and less profitable plant may be smaller.

(e) **Competitive fringe.** Firms that currently do not supply significant volumes, but could rapidly and profitably begin doing so if prices were to rise, may act as a constraint on prices. Evidence of firms actively monitoring prices, or evidence of entry or expansion in response to past price fluctuations, may be relevant to assessing the credibility of the competitive fringe as a constraint. When considering the constraint of a competitive fringe, the CMA may consider evidence on the reasons why they are currently not supplying significant volumes, and whether these may have implications for their ability to constrain the merged entity.

4.39 Paragraphs 4.15 to 4.19, which related to third party entry and expansion and buyer power in differentiated markets, are also relevant to undifferentiated markets. As in differentiated markets, where one merger firm has a strong position in the market, even small increments in market power may give rise to competition concerns (see paragraph 4.12(a)).

NOTES

77 In these guidelines, the CMA may use 'price' as shorthand for other forms of competitive parameter, including quality, range, or service. For example, instead of raising prices post-merger, a merged entity may find it profitable to degrade quality, reduce range or lower service levels.

78 The large majority of mergers that the CMA examines involve products or services that are differentiated along at least some dimensions.

79 The HHI is a measure of market concentration that takes account of the differences in the sizes of market participants, as well as their number. The HHI is calculated by adding together the squared values of the percentage market shares of all firms in the market. The change in the HHI (known as the 'delta') can be calculated by subtracting the market's pre-merger HHI from its expected post-merger HHI.

80 See for example Tobii AB/Smartbox Assistive Technology Limited and Sensory Software International Ltd, paragraph 6.72. The CMA has frequently found competition concerns in relation to close competitors that were not each other's closest competitors, including for example Diebold Incorporated/Wincor Nixdorf AG, and the Provisional Findings in Illumina Inc/Pacific Biosciences of California Inc.

81 The CMA has found or provisionally found competition concerns in concentrated markets with few significant players in previous cases, including for example Tobii AB/Smartbox Assistive Technology Limited and Sensory Software International Ltd; Diebold Incorporated/Wincor Nixdorf AG; Prosafe SE/Floatel International Limited (Provisional Findings); Ecolab Inc/The Holchem Group Limited; Experian Limited/Credit Laser Holdings (ClearScore) (Provisional Findings); Rentokil Initial plc/Cannon Hygiene Limited; and JLA New Equityco Limited/Washstation Limited.

82 For example, large supermarkets may be a good alternative for customers of convenience stores, while convenience stores may be a poor alternative for customers of large supermarkets.

83 That is, the profits earned on marginal customers that may be lost in the event of a price increase or other deterioration in the competitive offering.

84 Incremental profits may include not only the profits earned directly on sales, but also any associated profits arising from sales, for example because sales have strategic value or contribute to a firm's ability to make greater future profits - for example, by contributing to the firm's reputation, brand awareness, customer loyalty, or network effects.

85 A diversion ratio between Product A and Product B represents the proportion of sales that would divert to Product B (as opposed to Products C, D, E etc) as customers' second choice in the event of a price increase for Product A. The cross-price elasticity of demand of Product A to Product B is a measure of the percentage change in the quantity of Product A sold when the price of Product B rises by 1 per cent. Higher diversion ratios are associated with closer competition between two firms. Diversion ratios may be combined with other evidence to generate 'pricing pressure indices', which may be used by the CMA to judge whether the merged entity would be likely to find a price rise profitable.

86 Shares of supply may also be a useful indicator when there are limitations on the evidence the CMA can gather during its investigation—for example, when the number of overlaps between the merger firms is very large.

87 For example, a merger may be characterised as reducing the number of existing competitors from two to one. To the extent the CMA finds evidence that a rival would have entered absent the merger, the merger may be characterised as reducing the number of competitors from three to two. In this scenario, the merger may be concerning even if the entrant

was broadly equivalent to the firm eliminated by the merger - unlike where entry is triggered by the merger.

88 Firms can also operate multi-sided platforms that intermediate between more than two customer groups. The guidance set out in this section relating to two-sided markets can be extended to multi-sided platforms.

89 The CMA has considered two-sided platforms in a number of cases including Just-Eat plc/Hungryhouse Holdings Limited, Taboola.com Ltd/Outbrain Inc; and Future Plc/TI Media Limited.

90 Two-sided platforms sometimes also involve users on one side of the platform being offered a product or service at a zero price. As discussed in paragraph 2.4, users may pay a non-monetary price, such as providing personal data, advertising space, or even their attention (for example, as a reader of a news feed).

91 For example, in Taboola.com Ltd/Outbrain Inc, the CMA considered the impact of the merger for publishers separately from the impact on advertisers.

92 The CMA took this approach in PUG LLC (Viagogo)/StubHub.

93 The CMA took this approach in Taboola.com Ltd/Outbrain Inc.

94 Other examples might include firms that compete across temporal markets (such as 'peak' and 'off peak ticket sales), or across the supply of standalone and bundled services.

95 For example, J Sainsbury's Plc/Asda Group Ltd (fuel), and Cellnex UK Limited/Arqiva Services Limited, where parameters of competition were flexed locally.

96 J Sainsbury's Plc/Asda Group Ltd (groceries).

97 Examples of this include competition for specific customer groups that would be affected to a greater extent by a loss of competition between the merger firms (for example, because of a stronger preference or requirement to use the merger firms' products, or because of less availability of good alternatives) and where the merged entity could tailor its competitive offering for those customers (for example, by setting separate, higher prices).

98 The CMA considered the incentive of firms to move from nationally uniform offering to a varied local offering in Poundland Group plc/99p stores Limited.

99 For example, in the Motor Fuel Limited/Murco Petroleum Limited, following a filtering exercise, the CMA identified just six local areas which required a more detailed local competitive assessment.

100 The CMA applied a decision rule approach to its assessment of unilateral effects in the supply of in-store groceries, online groceries and fuel in J Sainsbury's Plc/Asda Group Ltd.

101 For example, Breedon Group plc/Cemex Investments Limited.

5. POTENTIAL AND DYNAMIC COMPETITION

[3.520]
5.1 Unilateral effects may also arise from the elimination of potential or dynamic competition. In this chapter, the term 'potential competition' is used to refer to competitive interactions involving at least one firm that has the potential to enter or expand in competition with other firms. Potential competition is relevant to the potential for a merger to substantially lessen competition where, absent the merger, entry or expansion by either or both merger firms may have resulted in new or increased competition between them.

5.2 Mergers involving a potential entrant can lessen competition in different ways. First, a merger involving a potential entrant may imply a loss of the future competition between the merger firms after the potential entrant would have entered or expanded.

5.3 Second, existing firms and potential competitors can interact in an ongoing dynamic competitive process, and a merger could lead to a loss of dynamic competition. Firms that are making efforts or investments that may eventually lead to their entry or expansion will do so based on the opportunity to win new sales and profits, which may in part be 'stolen' from the other merger firm. Incumbent firms that are making efforts to improve their own competitive offering may do so to mitigate the risk of losing future profits to potential entrants. In this sense, potential entrants can be thought of as dynamic competitors, even before they effectively enter and begin supplying customers. A merger may reduce the incentives of dynamic competitors to continue with efforts to enter or expand, or the incentive of incumbent firms to mitigate the threat of future rival entry or expansion. The impact of such a reduction in efforts would affect customers in the present, rather than solely from the future point in time when entry or expansion has occurred.

5.4 Losses of dynamic competition are more relevant when the investments involved in entering or expanding represent an important part of the competitive process, in industries where the process of entering markets takes place over a long period of time and involves significant costs or risks, or where key aspects of the competitive offering are set during the investment phase rather than flexed on an ongoing basis. Examples might include digital platforms, where the costs and time required to build up a significant user base and achieve network efficiencies might involve years of losses (with ongoing uncertainty about whether the platform would eventually be successful), or pharmaceutical mergers where investments in new products might involve years of investment in products that may never come to fruition.

5.5 The following paragraphs discuss aspects of how the CMA approaches losses of future and dynamic competition in mergers involving potential entrants.[102] While this section discusses competitive interactions with potential entrants, similar reasoning may apply to competitive interactions with firms that are already active in the market but have the potential to expand significantly.

5.6 The guidance set out in relation to losses of existing competition (see paragraphs 4.1 to 4.37) is also relevant to the assessment of potential competition, and therefore the following paragraphs should be read in conjunction with that section.

LOSS OF FUTURE COMPETITION

5.7 In assessing whether a merger involving a potential entrant leads to a loss of future competition between the merger firms, the CMA will consider evidence on:

(a) whether either merger firm would have entered or expanded absent the merger; and
(b) whether the loss of future competition brought about by the merger would give rise to an SLC, taking into account other constraints and potential entrants.

5.8 The following paragraphs set out the CMA's approach to assessing the prospect and impact of potential entry.

Assessment of whether either merger firm would enter or expand

5.9 Entry by the merger firms will typically be considered as part of the counterfactual (paragraph 3.17). In some cases, evidence relevant to the counterfactual and evidence relevant to the competitive assessment will be overlapping.

5.10 The CMA may consider a range of evidence on the prospect of entry by the merger firms. Entry may be considered more likely where a merger firm has the incentive and ability to enter; has well-developed plans or has already taken significant steps towards entry; where incumbent firms are taking action in anticipation of its entry; or where it has a past history of entry into related markets.[103]

5.11 The decision to pursue a merger may supplant the creation of detailed business plans assessing alternative routes to enter or expand. Therefore, the CMA is likely to consider the merger firms' ability and incentive to enter.

5.12 For example, the CMA may conclude on the prospect that one of the merger firms would have entered absent the merger, without concluding on the precise characteristics of the product it would launch, or which particular assets (out of a set of possible options) it might acquire in order to enter.

Assessment of the loss of future competition

5.13 If one of the merger firms is a potential entrant, then the merger will remove any future competition between them.

5.14 The CMA's assessment of competitive effects from the loss of the future competition between the merger firms is similar to its assessment when the merger firms are existing suppliers (see Chapter 4), except that the CMA's assessment will reflect the future competitive conditions expected after entry or expansion by the merger firms has taken place.

5.15 The impact of a potential entrant on competition is likely to be more significant when there are fewer strong existing competitive constraints on the other merger firm; where the other merger firm would already have market power absent the merger (with greater market power being associated with a greater likelihood of an entrant having a bigger impact on competition); and/or where there are few other potential constraints. In line with paragraph 4.12(a), where one merger firm has a strong position in the market and there are few significant potential competitors, even small increments in market power may give rise to competition concerns. Therefore, the acquisition by any such firm of a potential entrant may be concerning even if that potential entrant is expected to be small. The CMA will take into account entry or expansion by non-merging rivals over a similar time horizon as the merger firms' entry or expansion.

5.16 Evidence relevant to the CMA's assessment of the loss of future competition brought about by the merger might include, firms' internal documents, business forecasts or valuation models. The CMA may consider the likely characteristics of the potential entrant's future product or service, in particular any that would make it attractive to customers, for example if it is planning to introduce a disruptive new business model or technology.[104] The CMA may also consider whether the potential entrant has any features that would affect how well-placed it is to enter, such as existing customer relationships from related products that could enable it to cross-sell or bundle them to gain scale quickly.[105] Any commercial responses made by existing firms in anticipation of rival entry may also be indicative of the entrant's expected impact.

LOSS OF DYNAMIC COMPETITION

5.17 In some sectors, an important aspect of how firms compete involves efforts or investments aimed at protecting or expanding their profits in the future. This includes efforts that may give firms the ability to compete in entirely new areas (ie to enter), or the ability to compete more effectively in areas where they are already active (ie to expand). Examples of the types of efforts or investments firms might make include developing new products or improving existing ones; introducing more efficient or disruptive business models; introducing new features that benefit customers but also increase customer stickiness; or sacrificing short-run margins (or even operating at a loss) in order to attract users to their platform and benefit from network efficiencies, to achieve a minimum efficient scale, to scale up a distribution network, or to establish a reputation.

5.18 Where investment and innovation efforts represent an important part of the competitive process itself, this can lead to dynamic competitive interactions between existing competitors and potential entrants that are making efforts to enter or expand (ie, dynamic competitors). Existing firms may invest in the present in order to protect future sales from dynamic competitors. Dynamic competitors making investments in the present will do so in order to win new sales in the future, including by winning sales from other suppliers.

5.19 Mergers can reduce the dynamic competitive interactions between an existing supplier and a dynamic competitor, or between two dynamic competitors:[106]

(a) A merger involving an existing supplier and a dynamic competitor may lead the existing supplier to reduce its efforts in the present to protect against the possible impact of the dynamic competitor, as any future loss of sales to the dynamic competitor would not reduce the profits of the merged entity.

(b) A merger involving a dynamic competitor making efforts towards entry or expansion may lead the merged entity to reduce those efforts. After a merger, any profits that the dynamic competitor would expect to 'steal' from the other merger firm would no longer contribute to an incentive to enter, as these profits would already be captured by the merged entity.

5.20 There may be some uncertainty about the outcome of investments and innovation efforts absent the merger, including whether the investments being made by merger firms would ultimately result in products or services being made available to customers. However, uncertainty about the outcome of a dynamic competitive process does not preclude the CMA from assessing the impact of the merger on that dynamic process.[107] A process of dynamic competition can increase the likelihood of new innovations or products being made available, and therefore has economic value in the present.

5.21 Accordingly, while the CMA's assessment of dynamic competition may, in some cases, focus on entry and expansion in relation to specific products, in others, it may consider a broader pattern of dynamic competition in which the specific overlaps may not be identified easily at the point in time of the CMA's assessment. Examples might include two digital platforms exhibiting a pattern of using their existing platforms or suites of integrated services as a launchpad to enter into new, overlapping services; two pharmaceutical companies engaging in research programmes that are likely to treat the same illnesses; or two firms with geographic expansion strategies that are likely to target similar local areas.[108] Where this is the case, the CMA may assess a broader loss of competition arising from a reduction in the merger firms' incentives to continue investing in these competing programmes or strategies, rather than focusing on individual future overlaps.[109]

5.22 When assessing losses of dynamic competition, the CMA may consider evidence on any direct response of an incumbent merger firm to the threat of entry or expansion by the other merger firm or may consider evidence on the incumbent's incentive to respond to any such threat.

5.23 The likelihood of successful entry by a dynamic competitor and the expected closeness of competition between a dynamic competitor and other firms are both relevant to the constraint exerted by a dynamic competitor on other firms and the CMA will take this into account. The elimination of a dynamic competitor that is making efforts towards entry or expansion may lead to an SLC even where entry by that entrant is unlikely and may ultimately be unsuccessful. This may be the case if, for example, there is evidence that the competitor's entry or expansion would have a significant impact on other firms' future profits. In such circumstances, the removal of the threat of entry may lead to a significant reduction in innovation or efforts by other firms to protect those future profits.

5.24 Firms may use different levers to respond to dynamic competition. For example, firms may be more likely to flex their prices (which may be changed rapidly in the short-run) in response to competition from existing competitors, while using investment and innovation efforts to protect their profits from long-run, dynamic threats from potential entrants. Therefore, competition concerns may arise in relation to losses of existing competition despite the presence of dynamic constraints from potential entrants. Conversely, a loss of dynamic competition may be significant even though there are sufficient constraints to protect existing competition on aspects of competition that can be flexed in the short run.

NOTES

102 Losses of future competition and losses of dynamic competition are interrelated, as they both involve the constraint from potential entrants. As both depend on the likelihood of entry or expansion by a potential entrant, and the impact of such entry or expansion on competition, the CMA's assessment of each may to an extent rely on overlapping evidence. The CMA may therefore consider them together or separately.

103 The CMA has considered the likelihood of entry in a number of recent cases including: Amazon.com NV Investment Holdings LLC/Roofoods Ltd (Deliveroo); PayPal Holdings Inc/iZettle AB; Roche Holdings, Inc./Spark Therapeutics, Inc.; and the Provisional Findings in Illumina Inc/Pacific Biosciences of California Inc.

104 For example, the Provisional Findings in Experian Limited/Credit Laser Holdings (ClearScore).

105 In Amazon.com NV Investment Holdings LLC/Roofoods Ltd (Deliveroo), the CMA considered that Amazon would be well-placed to be an effective entrant.

106 Antitrust and Innovation: Welcoming and Protecting Disruption, by Carol Shapiro, Giulio Federico, and Fiona Scott Morton. Innovation Policy and the Economy, Volume 20 and Ioannis K, Valletti T, 2020, Innovation considerations in horizontal merger control, *Journal of Competition Law and Economics,* Vol: 16, Pages: 220-261, ISSN: 1744-6414.

107 For example, the European Commission case of COMP/M.7275 - Novartis/GlaxoSmithKline Oncology Business. The CMA also considered the impact of uncertainty on the assessment of dynamic competition in its Provisional Findings in Illumina Inc/Pacific Biosciences of California Inc.

108 For example, two retail firms may have a strategy involving opening new stores and tend to open stores in the same types of local areas, leading to greater competition; or two pharmaceutical firms may have research programmes that have are likely to develop products with similar applications.

109 For example, in Pure Gym Limited/The Gym Limited, the CMA found at Phase 1 that in the absence of one of the merger firms, the other may not have the same incentive to maintain policies such as a uniform network-wide price-for-life policy or 24/7 opening. The CMA also found that the merger is likely to materially alter the incentives of the merger firms to expand their networks. See also, European Commission cases M.7932 - Dow/DuPont, M.8084 - Bayer/Monsanto, and COMP/M.7275 - Novartis/GlaxoSmithKline Oncology Business.

6. COORDINATED EFFECTS

[3.521]

6.1 Coordination occurs when firms operating in the same market act on a common understanding to limit their rivalry.

6.2 Coordination may take different forms and can affect any aspect of competition. For example, firms may coordinate by fixing prices, by dividing up the market between them, such as by geographic area or customer characteristics, or by allocating contracts among themselves in bidding competitions. Firms which operate across a number of related markets may coordinate on avoiding launching competing products. Coordination may also involve firms reaching a collective understanding that they will avoid taking an overly aggressive stance in terms of their competitive offering. Regardless of the mechanism used, in many instances, coordination will result in firms keeping prices higher than they would otherwise have been in a more competitive market.

6.3 Coordination can be explicit or tacit. Explicit coordination is achieved through communication and agreement between the parties involved. Tacit coordination is achieved through implicit understanding between the parties, but without any formal arrangement. Both can be germane to an assessment of the effects of a merger although explicit coordination is caught by the Chapter 1 prohibition of the Competition Act 1998 and may be subject to sanction regardless of whether a merger takes place.

6.4 A merger may give rise to an SLC through coordinated effects. Coordinated effects arise when a merger enables or strengthens coordination.

6.5 Coordinated effects have been considered by the CMA relatively infrequently in the past. Some commentators have argued that enforcement in this area should be strengthened,[110] based partly on evidence which, they suggest, demonstrates that coordination in concentrated markets is common and has the effect of restricting competition and raising prices, even when imperfect. As it has in recent cases, the CMA will consider seriously the impact of mergers in concentrated markets on the potential for firms to coordinate, including tacitly through the recognition of their interdependence and avoidance of competition.[111]

PRE-EXISTING COORDINATION

6.6 When assessing coordinated effects, the CMA will consider whether firms in the market were coordinating pre-merger. In those instances where there is evidence of pre-existing coordination, this will indicate that the necessary conditions for coordination are met pre-merger.[112] However, pre-existing coordination is not a necessary condition for a coordinated effects SLC finding.

6.7 The CMA will consider a range of evidence on whether there was coordination in the market before the merger. For example, pre-merger trends in competitive parameters such as prices, market shares, entry, capacity or margins may be consistent with coordinated behaviour. There may also be evidence that firms are aware of their strategic interdependence or seek to facilitate such an understanding through, for example, information sharing, public or private communications, or structural links.

6.8 Evidence of some competition between some or all market participants is not inconsistent with also finding evidence of coordination, as rivals may not coordinate over all competitive parameters or in all regions, coordination may not include all firms in the market and coordination may be characterised by periods during which the coordinating group reverts to fully competing.

6.9 If the pre-merger market shows evidence of coordinated outcomes, the CMA will consider whether the conditions for coordination have been strengthened or weakened as a result of the merger.[113] In general, a horizontal merger in a market already showing evidence of coordinated outcomes is likely to make coordination more sustainable or more effective, unless the structure and scale of the merged entity is so different from those of its predecessors that the incentive to coordinate has been removed. Where the CMA has not found evidence of pre-existing coordination, it will consider to what extent the merger may enable future coordination.

FRAMEWORK FOR ASSESSING COORDINATION

6.10 When considering whether a merger increases the likelihood of coordination or makes it more effective (more stable or profitable for example), the CMA will analyse the extent to which the following three conditions are met:

(a) Firms are able to reach a common understanding of the terms of coordination.

(b) Coordination is internally sustainable among the coordinating group, ie firms find it in their individual interests to adhere to the coordinated outcome.

(c) Coordination is externally sustainable, ie it is unlikely that coordination will be undermined by competition from outside the coordinating group.

6.11 The CMA will assess the extent to which these conditions are met in relation to the form (or forms) of coordination that it considers to be most likely in the particular market on the basis of the available evidence.

Ability to reach the terms of coordination

6.12 For coordination to emerge, the firms involved need to be able to reach a common understanding about their objectives (for example, a price below which they would not sell or customers they will not target). This includes firms recognising their interdependence and avoiding competitive actions. For example, where firms have different geographic strengths, they may be able to reach an understanding that they will avoid competing strongly outside their core areas. Such an understanding need not involve a precise outcome but needs to be sufficiently clear to enable their behaviour to be aligned. It need not involve explicit communication; for example, the terms of coordination might emerge over time through repeated competitive interaction.

6.13 Factors that may be relevant to assessing whether the firms in a market would be able to reach an understanding on the terms of coordination may include:

(a) **Number of coordinating firms.** The fewer firms in the coordinating group, the lower the complexity and the easier it will be to reach a common understanding.

(b) **Suitable focal point for coordination.**[114] This may be more challenging in a complex environment, for example where products are differentiated, firms sell a large number of products or differ in their capabilities, product portfolios, customer mix and strategies. However, even in these circumstances, firms may be able to come to a common understanding through simplifying the parameters of competition or focusing on a subset of parameters such as coordinating on known pricing points. Market division may be an easier means of coordinating than fixing prices. For example, firms may be able to reach an understanding to avoid targeting each other's customers, areas of geographic strength or areas of product development.

(c) **Symmetry**. Firms may find it easier to reach a common understanding if they are relatively symmetric, for example in terms of cost structures, market shares, capacity levels and extent of vertical integration.

(d) **Structural links.** The existence of significant structural links between firms in the market (such as being each other's customers or suppliers, holding cross-shareholdings or belonging to trade associations) may also assist in reaching a common understanding on the terms of coordination.

Internal sustainability

6.14 Coordination will be sustainable where the incentive to coordinate is higher than the incentive to deviate from the coordinated outcome for each coordinating firm. Deviating may include, for example, offering discounts to the coordinated price, targeting another firm's customers or failing to match a price rise. Typically, deviating firms will make a short-term gain from having a more competitive offer than the coordinating firms so for coordination to be internally sustainable, the gain to firms from deviation must be outweighed by the costs of future reduced profits.

6.15 The size of the gain from deviation will depend on the characteristics of the industry. This may be relatively low in some cases, for example where there is strong customer loyalty or where many customers are already committed to long-term contracts. On the other hand, there will be a greater incentive to deviate where there are more coordinating firms since the profits from coordination are shared between a greater number of participants, lowering the relative payoff from coordination compared to the profit from deviating (although this assumes that a deviating firm has correspondingly greater spare capacity relative to its current sales). The gain from deviation may also be higher for some firms than others where firms have very different incentives; for example, if a firm particularly values having a reputation for offering the lowest price in the market. Such a firm is sometimes termed a 'maverick'. If it is unable to price discriminate, a large firm may have a lower incentive to deviate than smaller firms if it will have to offer lower prices to its whole customer base.

6.16 Where there is an incentive to deviate, in order to sustain coordination firms must be able to detect and respond to deviation in a timely manner.

6.17 In assessing whether this is likely, the CMA will consider evidence on the ease with which firms can detect the choices of their rivals. Factors which may enhance the ability to detect rivals' choices are:

(a) **Observability of rivals' behaviour.** Transparency around firm's strategic choices and market outcomes will typically assist coordination, particularly where it enables timely detection of deviations. Online markets may be particularly transparent. Where there are firms outside the coordinating group, it may also be important to be able to observe whether any changes to market outcomes are a result of competition from these firms.

(b) **Market stability.** Where demand is predictable, it is easier for firms to detect deviation from coordination.

(c) **Practices which enhance transparency.** These may include public announcements or the exchange of information through trade associations.

6.18 The aspects of firms' commercial strategies where transparency is required will depend on the form of coordination at issue. For example, an understanding in relation to the allocation of customers may be feasible even if the firms in the market cannot observe each other's prices. Publicly available information on firms' pricing, product portfolio or investment decisions may enable the detection of deviation. The CMA may also consider whether firms can infer their rivals' actions from market outcomes even if they cannot observe them directly. For example, a firm's knowledge of its own or competitors' sales volumes and capacities might, in some contexts, provide enough information to determine whether or not deviation from coordination is taking place.

6.19 In assessing whether other firms' responses would be sufficient to disincentivise deviation and thus sustain coordination, the CMA may consider, for example:

(a) **Swiftness of response**. How swiftly any response would follow on from deviation. For example, in a market where prices are set using algorithms, the response to deviation may be automatic and almost immediate. Customers may be able to encourage deviation by offering long-term contracts (which prevent an immediate response by fixing the terms of firms' competitive offers during the period of the contract). Conversely, most-favoured customer clauses may raise the expected cost of deviation by guaranteeing a competitive response.

(b) **Effectiveness of response.** Whether other firms' responses would be sufficient to disincentivise deviation. A more severe response may be more likely to discourage deviation but may also be less credible, as it is more costly to the responding firms. Often the response will take the form of a reversion to more intense competition by the other firms rather than a deliberate punitive strategy, particularly where coordination is tacit.

External sustainability

6.20 It is not necessary for all firms in the market to be involved in coordination but those firms which coordinate need to be able collectively to exercise a degree of market power.

6.21 In assessing whether coordination would be externally sustainable, the CMA may consider:

(a) **Existing competition.** Coordination will be less sustainable where existing competitors outside the coordinating group (the competitive 'fringe') make up a significant proportion of the market or are able to impose a strong competitive constraint.

(b) **Dynamic competition.** External sustainability will typically be easier where entry is unlikely and any existing competitive fringe is unlikely to be able to expand. It will be more difficult if there is a firm with the capacity to take significant share from any group of firms that tried to coordinate without its participation (eg a 'maverick').[115]

EFFECT OF THE MERGER

6.22 The CMA will consider the impact of the merger on the likelihood and effectiveness of coordination. In doing so, the CMA will consider the extent to which the three conditions for coordination in paragraph 6.10 are met premerger and whether the merger strengthens these conditions.

6.23 These conditions could be strengthened in a number of ways. For example, in relation to each of the three conditions set out above:

(a) as the number of firms in the market reduces, it may become easier to reach and monitor an understanding;

(b) the incentives to sustain coordination are likely to be higher in markets with fewer firms, as the payoff from coordinating is shared between a smaller number of participants, raising the relative payoff from coordination compared to the profit from deviating; and

(c) if the firm being acquired is a fringe competitor which could disrupt coordination, this may make external sustainability more likely post-merger.

6.24 However, the merger does not need to strengthen all of these three conditions in order to lead to an SLC. If some or all conditions are met pre-merger then the merger may need to have only a limited impact in order to enable or strengthen coordination.[116]

NOTES

110 Jonathan B. Baker and Joseph Farrell. 'Oligopoly Coordination, Economic Analysis, and the Prophylactic Role of Horizontal Merger Enforcement.' *University of Pennsylvania Law Review,* 168 U. Pa. L. Rev. 1985 (2020); John Kwoka, 'Reviving Merger Control: a comprehensive plan for reforming policy and practice', October 9 2018.

111 See for example Breedon Group plc/Cemex Investments Limited, J Sainsbury's Plc/Asda Group Ltd and Yorkshire Purchasing Organisation/Findel Education Limited.

112 Although the CMA will nevertheless assess the preconditions for coordination and whether the merger materially changes any of them. In Breedon Group plc/Cemex Investments Limited, the CMA considered the findings of a 2013 Market Investigation that three cement producers (including one of the merger firms) had recognised and exploited the structural susceptibility of the market to coordination. The CMA found that the features of the market had not materially changed since that Market Investigation.

113 In J Sainsbury's Plc/Asda Group Ltd, the CMA found that while there was not sufficient evidence to support a finding of pre-existing coordination in online delivered groceries, there was some evidence of retailers recognising their mutual independence which was relevant to the assessment of the conduciveness of the relevant markets to coordination and the likelihood of coordination emerging post-Merger. The CMA ultimately concluded that the Merger would make coordination more likely than not as the merger would impact on two of the three conditions for coordination and all three conditions were likely to be met post-merger.

114 In J Sainsbury's Plc/Asda Group Ltd, the CMA found that there would be significant challenges for the hypothetical coordinating group to reach a common understanding, in spite of the high levels of transparency and sophistication in the market, in relation to each of the different potential focal points for coordination, due to factors such as the volatility of pricing, interdependencies with other products, and differing underlying data on sales.

115 In Yorkshire Purchasing Organisation/Findel Education Limited, the CMA found at Phase 1 that there were few external constraints which could destabilise coordination due to high barriers to entry and expansion. The CMA did not conclude on the external sustainability of coordination in its Provisional Findings at Phase 2, as its provisional conclusion was that coordination was unlikely to be internally sustainable.

116 In J Sainsbury's Plc/Asda Group Ltd, the CMA found that the Merger would impact on two of the three conditions for coordination and that all three conditions are likely to be met post-Merger such that the Merger would make coordination over delivery pricing in online delivered groceries more likely than not.

7. VERTICAL AND CONGLOMERATE EFFECTS

[3.522]

7.1 Non-horizontal mergers combine firms that do not directly compete, but that operate in related markets. The CMA typically distinguishes between two types:

(a) Vertical mergers are those between firms active at different levels in the same industry (ie an upstream firm and a downstream firm), so competition in one market could be directly affected by outcomes in the other.

(b) Conglomerate mergers are those between firms that are not active within the same supply chain, and so cannot directly affect each other's markets, but which are nevertheless related in some way. For example, this may be because their products target similar customers or may be purchased alongside each other. These mergers raise the possibility that competition in one market may be indirectly affected by actions in the other.

7.2 Non-horizontal mergers do not involve a direct loss of competition between the merger firms. Instead, a common concern is that they may result in the foreclosure of current or potential rivals - that the merged entity will be able to use its position in one market to harm the competitiveness of its rivals in the other. This would weaken the constraints that the merged entity faces and as a result harm competition and therefore customers.

7.3 Another possible concern is that the merged entity may gain access to commercially sensitive information of its rivals through its role as their supplier or customer. Depending on the industry context, this could include data on specific sales and bids, overall pricing strategies and algorithms, technical product specifications or innovation plans. This could allow the merged entity to compete less aggressively, eg with prices or product specifications only marginally better than its rivals and may also deter rivals from innovating. The CMA may assess this concern as a separate theory of harm, or as part of a broader foreclosure theory of harm.

7.4 In certain circumstances these mergers may also give rise to other concerns. For example, they may directly incentivise an increase in the downstream party's prices, if any lost sales from customers switching to rivals would be mitigated by increased sales of inputs to these downstream rivals. Alternatively, the merger may facilitate coordination between the merged entity and its rivals, for example by facilitating flows of information between rivals.

7.5 Non-horizontal mergers can also give rise to potential and dynamic competition issues if, in the absence of the transaction, the merger firms may have launched competing products. In some cases, the fact that they are in closely related markets may mean they have an enhanced ability and incentive to expand in this way. The framework for the assessment of these issues is set out in Chapter 5.

7.6 Non-horizontal mergers may also result in efficiencies, such as reduced prices or better product integration. We discuss the framework for assessing them in more detail in Chapter 8.

7.7 The CMA has frequently investigated vertical mergers, and in several cases found that these give rise to competition concerns, in particular when one of the merger firms had a degree of pre-existing market power which it would be able to use to foreclose its rivals.[117] However, a number of commentators continue to warn of the substantial risks of under-enforcement against vertical mergers.[118]

7.8 The rest of this section discusses the three main foreclosure theories of harm:

(a) Input foreclosure: where a merger involves one party that supplies an input to rivals of the other party, the merged entity may restrict these rivals' access to this input or offer it on worse terms, directly harming the rival's competitiveness and therefore competition in the downstream market.

(b) Customer foreclosure: where a merger involves one party that buys inputs from rivals of the other party, the merged entity may restrict these rivals' access to this customer, which would in turn harm the rival's competitiveness and therefore competition in the upstream market.

(c) Conglomerate effects: where a merger involves two parties in adjacent markets, the merged entity may link the sales of the two products and thereby restrict its rivals' access to customers, which would in turn harm the rival's competitiveness and therefore competition.

INPUT FORECLOSURE

7.9 The concern with an input foreclosure theory of harm is that the merged entity may use its control of an important input to harm its downstream rivals' competitiveness, for example by refusing to supply the input (total foreclosure) or by increasing the price or worsening the quality of the input supplied to them (partial foreclosure). This might then harm overall competition in the downstream market, to the detriment of customers. This may occur irrespective of whether the merger firms have a pre-existing commercial relationship.

7.10 In assessing this concern, the CMA will consider whether three cumulative conditions are satisfied.[119]

(a) Would the merged entity have the ability to use its control of inputs to harm the competitiveness of its downstream rivals?

(b) Would it have the incentive to actually do so, ie would it be profitable?

(c) Would the foreclosure of these rivals substantially lessen overall competition?

7.11 The CMA may use the same framework in similar situations where the merged entity could use its presence in one market to directly harm the competitiveness of its rivals in another, even if there is not a conventional supplier/customer relationship. For example, it could do this by using control of a complementary product to deteriorate its interoperability with competitors, or a distribution channel to make it harder for rivals to attract customers. These situations give rise to the same three questions: would the merged entity have the ability to harm its rivals' competitiveness, would it have the incentive to do this and would this harm overall competition?

Ability to foreclose rivals

7.12 In assessing the ability of the merged entity to foreclose its rivals, the CMA will go beyond examining simply whether it could supply its inputs to them on worse terms and will consider whether it would be able to harm their competitiveness by doing so.

7.13 The CMA may consider a wide range of mechanisms through which the merged entity could potentially harm its rivals when supplying inputs. These may include, for example: refusing or restricting supply, increasing prices, reducing quality or service levels, deteriorating product interoperability, slowing the rollout of upgrades, restricting licensing of intellectual property, shutting down APIs,[120] reprioritising R&D spending, or limiting access to data. The CMA's focus will be on understanding if collectively these would allow the merged entity to foreclose its rivals, not on predicting the precise actions it would take.[121]

7.14 When assessing whether the merged entity will have the ability to foreclose its rivals, the CMA will typically focus on two issues.

(a) **Market power upstream**. If downstream rivals can easily switch away from the upstream party to a range of effective alternative suppliers, then they will be less likely to suffer harm than if the merged entity occupies an important position upstream. The starting point for this assessment will

Part 3 CMA and other Guidelines

be the structure of the upstream market. The CMA may also investigate if there are features that may limit the constraint from upstream rivals, such as economies of scale, switching costs, direct or indirect network effects, brand and reputation, high fixed costs, control of intellectual property, access to data or integration into wider ecosystems. It may also consider whether any attempt at foreclosure would be accommodated by rival suppliers also competing less aggressively.[122]

(b) **Importance of the input**. The merged entity could only harm the competitiveness of its rivals if the input it supplies plays an important role in shaping downstream competition.[123] In assessing this the CMA will have regard to all foreclosure mechanisms, so will consider not only the proportion of rivals' costs that the input accounts for, but also for example the role it plays as a determinant of product quality or the rate of innovation. Its focus will be not on predicting the precise impact of each possible deterioration on rivals' businesses, but on the overall question of whether in aggregate they could be foreclosed.

7.15 The CMA's assessment of the ability of the merged entity to foreclose its rivals is unlikely to place material weight on contractual protections, for example, to continue supplying both the current version and future upgrades of the input. In practice, such contracts may not completely remove a firm's ability to harm its rivals, given that certain rivals might not be covered by these contracts, the contracts might not protect all ways in which the competitiveness of rivals could be harmed, and the contracts may be of limited duration. Moreover, over time contracts may be renegotiated or terminated, and firms may waive their rights to enforce any breaches in light of their overall bargaining position (reflecting the change in market structure brought about by a merger). However, the CMA may consider any financial or reputational costs of terminating contracts in its assessment of foreclosure incentives.[124]

Incentive to foreclose rivals

7.16 Even where the merged entity would have the ability to foreclose its rivals, it may not have the incentive to do so. This is because while foreclosure may result in additional profits downstream, it may also result in costs such as a loss of sales upstream. If these costs are greater than the benefits, the merged entity will not have the incentive to engage in input foreclosure. The CMA will therefore consider whether the merged entity would have the incentive to pursue a foreclosure strategy, in particular through a consideration of the magnitude and likelihood of the costs and benefits.

7.17 Where the CMA is considering several possible ways in which the merged entity may foreclose its rivals, it may either undertake one common assessment of incentives or several related assessments. It will be more likely to undertake distinct assessments where there are major differences in how these foreclosure strategies may affect the market and the merged entity.

7.18 The assessment of incentives typically involves a combination of quantitative and qualitative evidence, though the balance will vary between cases. The CMA may undertake more extensive quantitative analysis in simple markets with high quality data, but focus on a qualitative assessment in complex and dynamic markets, where firms' current positions and margins may not be a good guide to the future, and strategic considerations may play a greater role. In any event, its focus will be on the relative magnitude of the overall cost and benefit of foreclosure, not on predicting the exact size of each element.[125]

7.19 The CMA's assessment of incentives may consider the following factors:

(a) **Business strategy**. The purpose of the incentives analysis is to predict the merged entity's behaviour, and it may be possible to understand this directly from its past conduct, business strategy and deal rationale. For example, if the merger firms' internal documents show that it would be strategically beneficial to stop supplying rivals, it may not be necessary to try to infer their behaviour from their financial incentives.

(b) **Gain in downstream sales**. This will be greater if the merged entity has a more successful downstream offering, and if this competes closely with the rivals that may be foreclosed. It is also likely to be greater if the merged entity has a particularly strong ability to foreclose, as this would likely result in substantial switching away from the affected rivals. These additional sales may in turn enable it to increase downstream prices.

(c) **Loss of upstream sales**. This is likely to be lower if the merged entity has strong market power upstream, and if it can engage in price discrimination or similar targeted deterioration of supply. This would allow it to hinder specific rivals in competing for customers that its downstream division is best placed to win, whilst minimising the risk to its upstream sales by otherwise continuing to offer its input on competitive terms.

(d) **Relative profit margins**. Foreclosure is more likely to be profitable if margins downstream are relatively large compared to those upstream.

(e) **Other costs and benefits**. Particularly in complex and dynamic markets, firms may not focus on short term margins but may pursue other objectives to maximise their long-run profitability, which the CMA may consider. This may include eliminating a possible long-term threat, increasing the stickiness of existing customers, positioning themselves strongly in high-growth markets, gaining customers to obtain direct or indirect network effects, obtaining access to customer data or enabling cross-selling within a broader ecosystem.

Effect on competition

7.20 In this part of the assessment the CMA will consider whether the harm to competitors it has identified will result in substantial harm to overall competition in the downstream market. This will include through raising barriers to entry for potential entrants, where the negative impact on customers may take some time to materialise.

7.21 In practice, this will build on the same evidence as the assessment of the ability and incentive to foreclose. When it has been established that there will be harm to competitors this will often directly imply there will be harm to overall competition, where the foreclosed firms play a sufficiently important role in the competitive process on the downstream market. Competition concerns may be particularly likely to arise if one of the merger firms has a degree of pre-existing market power in the downstream market, and already faced limited competitive constraints pre-merger.

7.22 However, if sufficient credible rivals to the downstream party would be unaffected, for example because they are vertically integrated, then foreclosure of some marginal competitors may not harm competition.

CUSTOMER FORECLOSURE

7.23 The concern with a customer foreclosure theory of harm is that the merged entity may use its control of a downstream firm to switch purchases from rivals to itself, and thereby restrict its competitors' access to customers. While a loss of sales by competitors is not problematic in and of itself, and a firm using its own inputs can result in efficiencies, this may be a concern if it would result in these rival suppliers becoming less effective competitors for other customers. The merged entity would then face less competition in the upstream market, resulting in higher prices and lower quality.

7.24 In addition to explicit reductions in purchases, the CMA may also consider other actions that may result in a loss of sales by its upstream rivals. For example, if a phone manufacturer pre-installed its own social networking app into its handsets, this may reduce the usage of alternative social networks and therefore the size of their user bases, making them less effective competitors.

7.25 In assessing a customer foreclosure theory of harm, the CMA will again typically use the ability, incentive and effect framework.

Ability to foreclose rivals

7.26 The assessment of the merged entity's ability to foreclose will consider not only whether it could restrict its rivals' access to customers, but whether it could harm their competitiveness by doing so. It will typically focus on two issues.

(a) **Size of the customer**. The merger may only have a significant impact on rivals' volumes if the downstream party is an important customer that accounts for a substantial proportion of purchases. The CMA will consider this in the context of the full range of alternative sales opportunities that rivals have, including different channels, customer segments, uses and geographies.

(b) **Importance of scale upstream**. A loss of sales would typically only result in other firms becoming less effective rivals if there is a link between volumes and competitiveness. For example, fewer sales could lead to an increase in costs if economies of scale are substantial. It may also result in a reduction in product quality through the loss of direct or indirect network effects, a reduction in customer data, or a diminished incentive to innovate, if these are important. Most significantly, it could reduce the total number of rivals, either through driving firms to exit or deterring potential entrants, if they are financially marginal.

Incentive to foreclose rivals

7.27 In assessing the incentive to foreclose, the CMA will consider whether the benefit of additional sales upstream, as a result of foreclosing rivals, would exceed the potential cost of losing sales downstream, as a result of a deteriorated offering. It may consider the following factors.

(a) **Business strategy**. The merger firms may be more likely to pursue customer foreclosure if their broader strategy or deal rationale involves self-supply, or where either party has considered or used customer foreclosure strategies in the past, in which case it may not be necessary to try to infer their behaviour from their financial incentives.

(b) **Gain in upstream sales**. This will be greater if the merged entity has a more successful upstream offering, and if this competes closely with the rivals that may be foreclosed. It is also likely to be greater if the merged entity has a particularly strong ability to foreclose, as this would likely result in a large volume of switching away from the affected rivals.

(c) **Loss of downstream sales**. Switching purchases from rivals to the upstream merger firm could reduce the competitiveness of the downstream party's offering and result in it losing customers. For example, if rivals offer inputs that are significantly lower cost or higher quality than those of the upstream party.

(d) **Relative profit margins**. Foreclosure will be more profitable if margins are larger upstream, where the merger firms may gain sales, than downstream, where they may lose them.

(e) **Other costs and benefits**. These may include increasing the stickiness of existing customers of the upstream party, positioning it strongly if the upstream market is growing rapidly, gaining customers to obtain direct or indirect network effects or obtaining access to customer data.

Effect on competition

7.28 The CMA will consider whether the harm to competitors it has identified will result in substantial harm to overall competition in the upstream market.

7.29 This will again largely build on the evidence considered under ability and incentive, and when it has been established that there will be harm to competitors this will often directly imply there will be harm to overall competition, where the foreclosed firms play a sufficiently important role in the upstream market. The CMA will also consider the impact of foreclosure on potential competitors through raising barriers to entry, where the negative impact on customers may take some time to materialise.

CONGLOMERATE EFFECTS

7.30 The concern with a conglomerate theory of harm is that the merged entity may restrict its rivals in one 'focal' market from accessing customers using its strong position in an 'adjacent' market.[126] The merged entity could do this through linking the sales of the two products in some way, thereby encouraging customers who want its product in the adjacent market to also purchase its product in the focal market, at the expense of rivals. For example, it may only offer the products as a bundle, integrate them within a digital ecosystem, or offer customers of the adjacent product a discount if they also purchase its focal product, potentially through increasing the stand-alone price of the adjacent product.

7.31 This loss of sales by competitors is not problematic in and of itself, and linked sales of related products can result in efficiencies. However, competition concerns may arise if such a strategy would result in rivals in the focal market becoming less effective competitors, which may result in higher prices or lower quality in the longer term. Particularly in digital markets, this may take place through denying entrants growth opportunities, ie a loss of sales relative to the counterfactual, thereby protecting and reinforcing the power of incumbents.

7.32 The CMA will again typically use the ability, incentive and effect framework to analyse this theory of harm.

Ability to foreclose rivals

7.33 The CMA's assessment of the merged entity's ability to foreclose its rivals will focus not only on whether it would be able to link the sales of the two products in some way, but whether it could harm its rivals' competitiveness by doing so. The CMA may consider the following factors:

(a) **Market power in an adjacent market**. The merged entity will only be able to have a substantial impact in the focal market if it occupies an important position in an adjacent market. If it does not, then any attempt to make customers take the focal product alongside the adjacent one may result in customers buying the adjacent product from rivals. This assessment will typically begin with a consideration of the structure of the adjacent market, and may also consider if it has any features that limits the constraint from rivals.

(b) **Feasibility of a combined offering**. The CMA may consider whether customers have an incentive to buy the two products together, or if it would be realistic for the merger firms to link sales of the two products in some way, for example through bundling or tying. In assessing this the CMA may have regard to how the market, products and business models may evolve in future.

(c) **Loss of sales by rivals**. Competitors in the focal market are more likely to be foreclosed if the merged entity can deprive them of a substantial volume of sales. This will be the case if a sufficiently large number of customers in the focal market are or could be customers in the adjacent market, and if their behaviour can be easily influenced by the combination. It is less likely if rivals can realistically mitigate any loss, for example by developing or partnering to create their own combined offering.

(d) **Importance of scale**. A loss of customers in the focal market would typically only result in other firms becoming less effective rivals if there is a link between volumes and competitiveness. This could be through economies of scale, direct or indirect network effects, access to data, incentives to innovate - if these factors are important. Alternatively, this could be by driving them to exit or deterring potential entrants, if they are financially marginal.

Incentive to foreclose rivals

7.34 In assessing the incentive to foreclose, the CMA may consider whether any potential gain in sales from foreclosing rivals in the focal market would be outweighed by any loss of sales in the adjacent market.

(a) **Business strategy**. The merged entity may be more likely to pursue a combined offering if its business strategy involves this approach, it has a history of doing this with similar products or its deal rationale involves plans to do so post-merger, in which case it may not be necessary to try to infer their behaviour from their financial incentives.

(b) **Gain in sales in focal market**. This may be greater if the merged entity has a more attractive offering in the focal market, and if this competes closely with the rivals that may be foreclosed. It is also likely to be greater if the merged entity has a particularly strong ability to foreclose, as this would likely result in a large volume of switching from the affected rivals.

(c) **Loss of sales in adjacent market**. These are likely to be greater if many customers of the adjacent product have little interest in purchasing the focal product, and if the merged entity would need to pursue an aggressive strategy to foreclose competitors, such as by tying sales. These losses may be lower if the merged entity can provide the combined offering on a targeted basis to only those customers who would be likely to accept it.

(d) **Relative profit margins**. Foreclosure may be more profitable if margins are relatively higher in the focal market than the adjacent one.

(e) **Other costs and benefits**. These may include the merger firms increasing the stickiness of existing customers in the focal market, positioning themselves strongly if the focal market is rapidly growing, gaining customers to obtain direct or indirect network effects, obtaining access to customer data or enabling cross-selling within a broader ecosystem.

Effect on competition

7.35 The CMA will consider whether the harm to competitors it has identified will result in substantial harm to overall competition in the focal market.

7.36 This will again largely build on the evidence considered under ability and incentive, and when it has been established that there will be harm to competitors this will often directly imply that there will be harm to overall competition, where the foreclosed firms play a sufficiently important role in the focal market. The CMA will also consider the impact of foreclosure on potential competitors through raising barriers to entry, where the negative impact on customers may take some time to materialise.

7.37 Conglomerate effect concerns may be greatest in nascent and digital markets, as new customers may be more easily diverted between firms, scaling particularly critical, competitors more easily marginalised, and the future benefits of controlling these markets especially large. However, these anticompetitive effects may not emerge in full until after the market has reached maturity, so in assessing these mergers the CMA may focus on their impact on the structure of the market and competition over the longer term. Such an assessment will likely be subject to a degree of uncertainty, but this will not in itself preclude the CMA from concluding that the SLC test is met on the basis of all the available evidence (paragraph 2.10).

NOTES

117 Recent examples of cases where the CMA has assessed vertical mergers in detail include: Thermo Fisher Scientific / Roper Technologies (Gatan) (Provisional Findings), Tobii AB/Smartbox Assistive Technology Limited and Sensory Software International Ltd, BT Group plc/EE Limited, Tesco plc/Booker Group plc, Intercontinental Exchange Inc/Trayport; LN-Gaiety Holdings/MCD Productions.

118 For example, see Steven C Salop (2018), 'Invigorating Vertical Merger Enforcement', The Yale Law Journal, and Jonathan B. Baker, Nancy L. Rose, Steven C Salop and Fiona Scott Morton (2020), 'Recommendations and Comments on the Draft Vertical Merger Guidelines'. In addition, the CMA's own study into digital advertising found that Google has previously undertaken a number of vertical mergers with firms throughout the digital advertising value chain, mostly notably acquiring DoubleClick, and has subsequently been able to leverage its wider ecosystem to preference its own activities and further reinforce its market power.

119 In practice, the CMA is likely to apply this framework flexibly and consider these as overlapping analyses, rather than as distinct chronological stages.

120 Application Programming Interface.

121 *British Sky Broadcasting Group PLC v The Competition Commission and The Secretary of State for Business, Enterprise and Regulatory Reform* [2008] CAT 25, paragraph 80; *Intercontinental Exchange, Inc. v CMA and Nasdaq Stockholm AB* [2017] CAT 6, paragraphs 245 and 268.

122 For example, if an increase in the price of the input by the upstream party was followed by other upstream suppliers also increasing their prices, this would further limit the ability of downstream rivals to switch away from it to get a good deal. These accommodating responses by rivals could arise because they have a unilateral incentive to act in this way, or potentially as part of a coordinated arrangement if they are also vertically integrated.

123 *Tobii AB v Competition and Markets Authority* [2020] CAT 1, paragraph 426.

124 For example, see the discussion of this point in the CMA's Provisional Findings in Thermo Fisher Scientific inc/Roper Technologies (Gatan), paragraph 10.125.

125 *Intercontinental Exchange, Inc. v CMA and Nasdaq Stockholm AB* [2017] CAT 6 , paragraph 246.

126 This can also apply to leveraging between different segments of the same market as well as between different markets.

8. COUNTERVAILING FACTORS

[3.523]

8.1 In some instances, there may be countervailing factors that prevent or mitigate any SLC arising from a merger. There are two main ways in which this could happen: through merger efficiencies or through the entry and/or expansion of third parties in reaction to the effects of a merger. The CMA's experience is that it is uncommon for a merger to be cleared on the basis of countervailing factors alone.

MERGER EFFICIENCIES

8.2 In some instances, mergers can give rise to efficiencies. Examples of efficiencies might include cost savings; the elimination of double marginalisation through vertical integration; greater innovation or quality arising from the combination of unique assets; or better meeting customers' needs by enabling the integration or interoperability of complementary products.

8.3 Merger efficiencies fall into two categories:

(a) **Rivalry-enhancing efficiencies:** Efficiencies that change the incentives of the merger firms and induce them to act as stronger competitors to their rivals—for example, by reducing their marginal costs giving them the incentive to provide lower prices or a better quality, range or service.

(b) **Relevant customer benefits:** Benefits to UK customers resulting from a merger, other than through improved competition in the market related to the SLC finding—for example, greater levels of innovation resulting from the combination of unique assets of the merger firms applying to products other than those where the firms compete, or reduced carbon emissions (to the extent firms do not normally compete on sustainability).

8.4 Rivalry-enhancing efficiencies may prevent an SLC by offsetting any anticompetitive effects. The CMA will generally first consider whether there is scope for an SLC and, if there is, it will consider rivalry-enhancing efficiency claims from the merger firms. In some cases, the CMA may consider efficiencies and the evidence for an SLC together.

8.5 While relevant customer benefits do not prevent an SLC, they may outweigh an SLC and any adverse effects of the SLC. While the CMA does not take relevant customer benefits into account in its competitive assessment, it may take them into account when considering whether to refer a merger for a Phase 2 investigation and the overall benefit to consumers of having such an investigation. Relevant customer benefits may also be taken into account when the CMA considers options to remedy competition concerns and whether any of the remedy options would result in relevant customer benefits being unrealised. These are discussed at the end of this section.

8.6 Cost and revenue synergies often form part of the rationale for mergers, and it is not uncommon for firms to make efficiency claims in merger proceedings. Many efficiency claims by merger firms are not accepted by the CMA because the evidence supporting those claims is difficult to verify and substantiate. Some studies have found that firms often do not fully realise the expected synergies from their mergers and, even for the synergies that they do realise, firms do not always pass on the benefits to their customers.[127] This indicates the difficulty involved in accepting prospectively that a merger is likely to lead to efficiencies.

8.7 Most of the information relating to the synergies and cost reductions resulting from a merger is held by the merger firms. Merger firms who do wish to make efficiency claims are encouraged to provide verifiable evidence to support their claims in line with the CMA's framework (paragraph 8.8) early in the CMA's merger review process.

Framework for assessing merger efficiencies

8.8 This section discusses an assessment of efficiencies that result in stronger rivalry in a market. The CMA will use the following criteria when it assesses whether merger efficiencies mean that the merger does not result in an SLC. The merger efficiencies must:

(a) enhance rivalry in the supply of those products where an SLC may otherwise arise;
(b) be timely, likely and sufficient to prevent an SLC from arising;
(c) be merger-specific; and
(d) benefit customers in the UK.[128]

Merger efficiencies must enhance rivalry

8.9 Because the CMA has a duty to consider whether a merger will lead to an SLC in a market, if merger efficiencies are to be relevant in its assessment those efficiencies must be expected to affect competition in order to counter what would otherwise be an SLC finding. To do this, efficiencies need to enhance rivalry in a way that counteracts the effects on competition identified in the SLC assessment.[129] Efficiencies due to the merger must be likely to strengthen the ability and incentive of the merged entity to act pro-competitively for the benefit of consumers.

8.10 The CMA will generally view reductions in the merger firms' marginal or variable costs as being more likely to result in an incentive to reduce price or make short-run improvements in quality than reductions in fixed costs. Some fixed cost savings or other efficiencies from a merger may enhance the ability of firms profitably to innovate or invest in entry or expansion, although cost reductions from a reduction in output will not be considered as efficiencies.

8.11 However, efficiencies are not restricted to price competition. It may be that some mergers result in efficiencies pertaining to (for example) product or service quality or innovation. For example, a merger might bring together complementary assets in research and development activities or otherwise reduce incremental costs in innovation.

Merger efficiencies must be timely, likely and sufficient to prevent an SLC

8.12 The CMA will assess whether the claimed efficiencies are to be realised (and the resultant rivalry-enhancing effects felt) within the same timeframe as the CMA has adopted in the rest of its analysis. However, usually the longer the time period necessary for efficiencies to be realised, the greater will be the level doubt that efficiencies will be realised at all.

8.13 The merger efficiencies must be likely to be realised. This means that the evidence supporting efficiencies needs to be verifiable. Merger firms may, for example, wish to submit evidence of efficiencies realised from previous mergers or mergers in analogous markets.

8.14 The greater the expected adverse effect of a merger, the greater the expected efficiencies must be.

8.15 At Phase 1, the evidence must be sufficient to satisfy the CMA within the time available in an initial investigation that efficiencies would prevent the realistic prospect of an SLC. At Phase 2, the CMA must be satisfied that the evidence shows that that the criteria are met. As noted above, it is for the merger firms to demonstrate that the merger will result in efficiencies.

Merger efficiencies must be merger-specific

8.16 The CMA will assess whether the merger efficiencies are reliant on the merger in question or whether they would be brought about by other means. The CMA may, for example, investigate whether there are significant barriers to the merger firms achieving the same improvements without the merger.

8.17 It may be relevant to the CMA's assessment whether the merged entity has a greater incentive to achieve the same improvements absent the merger than as a result of the merger. For example, efficiencies arising from greater scale may need to be significant when the merger itself substantially lessens competition and therefore lessens the incentive to compete to achieve greater scale.[130]

8.18 Examples of actions that may result in efficiencies without a merger might include a firm investing in innovation (eg by investing in staff or R&D capability), entering into a licensing agreement or using a buying group. In the case of vertical mergers, alternative means to achieve the reduction of double marginalisation include contractual agreement and non-merger expansion along the supply chain.

8.19 In addition, the CMA will consider ways in which customers and consumers are able to access benefits without the merger. For example, claims by merger firms that efficiencies will arise by one merger firm getting access to the cutting-edge technology or innovation of the other merger firm will not be accepted by the CMA if customers can get the benefit by switching to the other merger firm.

Merger efficiencies must benefit customers in the UK

8.20 The CMA will consider whether, even if the merger does give rise to efficiencies, the merged entity would have the incentive to allow customers in the UK to benefit from the efficiencies. The CMA may consider the strength of competition that is likely to exist after the merger when evaluating this incentive.

Relevant customer benefits

8.21 The Act allows relevant customer benefits to be taken into account.[131] These benefits are defined as being lower prices, higher quality or greater choice of goods or services in any market in the UK, or greater innovation in relation to the goods or services. What constitutes higher quality, greater choice or greater innovation will depend on the facts of individual cases. It might be, for example, that benefits in the form of environmental sustainability and supporting the transition to a low carbon economy are relevant customer benefits in some circumstances. A merger may lead to lower energy costs and some benefits that customers may value (such as a lower carbon footprint of the firm's products).

8.22 The Act defines customers for the purpose of considering relevant customer benefits as being both direct and indirect customers of the merged entity and future customers.[132] In this way the CMA is able to take into account a broader range of efficiencies and benefits from a merger to consumers and to society more generally.

8.23 Rivalry-enhancing efficiencies, as discussed above, are concerned with the question of whether a merger will lead to an SLC. They therefore must be relevant to the process of rivalry in the market in which the CMA is considering the SLC question. Relevant customer benefits, on the other hand, can be taken into account even if they are expected to be realised in markets other than the one subject to an SLC finding.

8.24 Because a merger may realise significant benefits to customers (which may not affect rivalry in an SLC market) the CMA is able to take into account relevant customer benefits in one of two ways.

8.25 First, in its Phase 1 investigation as an exception to the duty to refer a merger for Phase 2 investigation (if the efficiencies arising from the merger result in relevant customer benefits which outweigh the SLC and any adverse effects caused by the merger).[133]

8.26 Second, in considering remedy options. If any of the effective remedy options preserves relevant customer benefits that any of the alternative effective remedy options do not, the CMA may select the remedy option that allows for relevant customer benefits to be realised.[134] At Phase 2, the CMA may modify a remedy to ensure that relevant customers benefits can be realised.[135] In rare cases, the CMA may decide that no remedy is appropriate.[136]

8.27 How the CMA takes relevant customer benefits into account - as an exception to its the duty to refer a merger for Phase 2 investigation as well as in its consideration of remedies - is considered in separate guidance.[137] As with rivalry-enhancing efficiencies, the CMA's experience to date is that has been rare for a merger to be cleared on the basis relevant customer benefits.[138]

ENTRY AND EXPANSION

8.28 In its competitive assessment, the CMA may take into account entry and/or expansion plans of rivals who will enter or expand irrespective of whether the merger proceeds. However, any analysis of a possible SLC includes consideration of the direct responses to the merger by rivals, potential rivals and customers. If effective entry and/or expansion occurs as a result of the merger and any consequent adverse effect (for example, a price rise), the effect of the merger on competition may be mitigated. In these situations, the CMA might conclude that no SLC arises as a result of the merger.

8.29 The CMA therefore considers the possibility of entry and/or expansion as a countervailing measure to what might otherwise be an SLC finding. If the CMA considers that an SLC would not arise from the merger, it may not conclude on the evidence regarding entry and expansion or even consider it. This means that when the CMA does consider the evidence on effective entry or expansion, it will be doing so in cases which have features that might lead to competition concerns (eg the market is concentrated). The CMA considers that entry and/or expansion preventing an SLC from arising would be rare. The CMA's evaluation of a selection of some of its past cases has shown that in some instances, when it has relied on entry or expansion to clear mergers, that entry or expansion did not in fact materialise.[139]

8.30 The CMA will seek to ensure that the evidence is robust when confronted with claims of entry or expansion being timely, likely and sufficient to prevent an SLC from arising. It is likely to place greater weight on detailed consideration of entry or expansion and previous experience of entry and expansion (including how frequent and recent it has been).

Framework for assessing entry and expansion

8.31 The CMA will use the following framework to determine whether entry or expansion would prevent an SLC. The entry or expansion must be:

(a) timely;
(b) likely; and
(c) sufficient to prevent an SLC.

8.32 These conditions are cumulative and must be satisfied simultaneously. If, for example, it is likely that entry by a rival would occur rapidly after a merger, but to achieve sufficient expansion to offset the adverse effects of the merger the rival would need a period of time further in the future (which would not be timely within the context of the markets at issue), then the CMA may conclude that entry and expansion would not prevent an SLC.

Timeliness of entry or expansion

8.33 The CMA will consider whether the effect on competition and the market will be timely. It is not just a case of entry or expansion occurring in a timely manner but the effectiveness of that entry or expansion on market outcomes must be timely. What is considered to be timely in order to prevent or mitigate the adverse effects of a merger will depend on the industry and the characteristics and dynamics of the market, and the timeframe over which the CMA expects an SLC to result from a merger. Typically, entry or expansion being effective within two years of an SLC arising would be considered by the CMA to be timely although, depending on the nature of the market, the CMA may consider a period of time shorter or longer than this (for example, see paragraph 3.15).[140]

8.34 Generally, the further out in time that entry or expansion is expected to occur the less certainty the CMA can attach to whether such entry or expansion would occur.

Likelihood of entry or expansion

8.35 In considering whether any potential rivals will enter or existing rivals will expand in response to a merger, the CMA must be satisfied that the rivals will have both the ability and incentive to do so. The CMA will consider the scale of any barriers to entry and/or expansion. In a market characterised by low barriers to entry and/or expansion, potential entrants may nevertheless be discouraged from entering by the small size of the available market (for example because the market itself is small or declining),[141] or the credible threat of retaliation by incumbents (whether in the same market as the merged entity or another market where that new entrant is already present).[142]

8.36 The circumstances around potential entry or expansion may fall into three broad categories:

(a) A firm with the potential to enter or expand may find it profitable to enter (or expand) at pre-merger prices. In such cases, the CMA might expect to see evidence that the firm was actively planning to enter or expand premerger. In such cases, the CMA may assess the impact of such entry as part of its competitive assessment.
(b) A firm may only find it profitable to enter or expand if prices remain above pre-merger levels. Such cases of entry or expansion are unlikely to restore pre-merger prices and are unlikely to prevent an SLC from arising.
(c) A firm may find that it would be profitable to operate (or add capacity) at pre-merger prices, but nevertheless would not find it profitable to enter or expand because its entry or expansion would push prices down below pre-merger levels. In such cases, a merger that causes prices to rise may introduce the buffer that the firm needs in order be able to enter and expand and subsequently compete at pre-merger prices. Therefore, when considering countervailing entry and expansion, the CMA may be particularly interested in evidence that entrants or incumbents were actively monitoring the opportunity to enter or expand prior to the merger, that such entrants could operate (or expand) profitably at pre-merger prices, and/or that entry or expansion would quickly become attractive if prices were to start rising.

Sufficiency of entry or expansion

8.37 Entry or expansion should be of sufficient scope and effectiveness to prevent an SLC from arising as a result of the merger. Entry or expansion needs to be successful over a sustained period of time. Sufficiency to constrain the merged entity may come from a single entrant or firm expanding or from several, in aggregate.

8.38 Expansion is unlikely to constrain the merged entity where that expansion results from a rival simply gaining some sales from a merged entity which has raised prices. The CMA may therefore examine evidence as to whether any entry or expansion would increase the competitive constraint that rivals exert on the merged entity, for example by introducing additional capacity, or new or better competitive offerings. The CMA may consider the history and experience of past entry or expansion.

8.39 Small-scale entry that is not comparable to the constraint eliminated by the merger is unlikely to prevent an SLC. In a differentiated market, entry into a market niche may be possible, but to the extent the niche product may not necessarily compete strongly with other products in the overall market, it may not constrain incumbents effectively.

Barriers to entry and expansion

8.40 Potential or actual competitors may encounter barriers which reduce or even severely hamper their ability to enter or expand in the market. Barriers to entry and expansion are specific features of the market that give incumbent firms advantages over potential competitors. Barriers to entry and expansion hinder the ability of potential entrants or firms looking to expand to constrain the exercise of market power by incumbents. The CMA will therefore identify barriers to entry and/or expansion in its analysis. Where barriers are low, and the costs of entry or expansion are not substantial relative to the profits that are available, entry and/or expansion might be expected to occur in order to capture sales from the merged entity if it were to increase prices and/or worsen non-price factors of competition. Conversely, this is less likely where barriers are substantial relative to available profits.

8.41 Often barriers to entry or expansion are related to the nature of the market. While it is not possible to provide a comprehensive list of barriers to entry and expansion (given that such barriers are liable to vary between different sectors and over time), common barriers include:

(a) Initial set-up costs and costs associated with investment in specific assets are more likely to deter entry or expansion where a significant proportion of them are sunk.[143]

(b) Customers may place a high value on the reputation and track record of suppliers.[144] This might be especially true where the product or service being provided is important for the customer, and where the quality of the product is difficult to ascertain in advance.

(c) Consumers may demonstrate a high level of brand loyalty, be tied into long contracts or exclusivity agreements, or face other significant switching costs, which may make entry or expansion more difficult and require investment. For example, in some digital markets switching might involve giving up access to an ecosystem of products and services.

(d) Economies of scale may be present.[145] These may prevent small-scale entry from acting as an effective competitive constraint in the market. Further, in the presence of economies of scale, large-scale entry or expansion will generally be successful only if it expands the total market significantly, or substantially replaces one or more existing firm; and if the entrant can afford the risk that such investment will involve, especially in terms of sunk costs. Many markets exhibit economies of scale.[146]

(e) Network effects.[147] In such circumstances, the need to attract a large number of customers to one or both sides of the entrant's platform in order to be an effective constraint may make sufficient entry and expansion both costly and risky, particularly in the presence of larger incumbents.[148] Many digital markets are characterised by considerable network effects as well as non-digital markets.[149]

(f) The technology and production methods used in the market may themselves present barriers to an entrant. For example, intellectual property rights of rivals and interoperability requirements may need to be taken into account by entrants.

(g) Early mover advantages. Incumbents may have early mover advantages as a result of branding or creating switching costs. The data held by many digital market firms allow them to hone, improve and personalise their products and services, and this may be difficult for an entrant to replicate in a timely manner.[150] Early mover advantages may be strengthened by the combination of the merger firms.

(h) Regulations, licensing arrangements, intellectual property rights and trade barriers may also form considerable barriers to entry.[151]

8.42 Barriers to entry and expansion might be particularly high if some of these factors are present in combination. For example, an incumbent might have a large cost advantage from its scale and/or data while also benefitting from network effects.

8.43 Finally, when considering the likelihood of successful entry by third parties, the CMA may consider the strategic behaviour of the merged entity or other incumbents which itself might create or strengthen a barrier to entry or limit the ability of a new entrant to gain a foothold in the market. This might involve strategic, temporary price cuts, entering into exclusive dealing arrangements or long contracts, or otherwise increasing customer stickiness, for example. The merged entity's ability to engage in this behaviour may be increased through the merger.

Self-supply and sponsored entry

8.44 The above discussion focuses on entry or expansion by third party rivals to constrain the merged entity. However, there may be instances in which third party rivals do not enter or expand solely on the market signals of a post-merger price rise or quality degradation but instead either the customer itself enters (self-supply) or a third party is encouraged and supported by customers to enter or expand (sponsored entry).[152] Although the above considerations are applicable to these scenarios, we discuss these specific types of entry and expansion below.

8.45 In these circumstances the CMA will consider whether:

(a) entry or expansion meets the timely, likely and sufficient requirements discussed above; and

(b) after entry or expansion occurs, supply will be available to the market (thereby potentially preventing an SLC from arising in the market) or only to the individual customer. Even if self-supply or sponsored entry protects particular customers, it may not prevent the merged entity from raising prices or worsening quality of service for other customers.

8.46 In addition, the CMA is also likely to consider whether such mitigating strategies by customers will be effective in addressing the SLC and its adverse effects in a dynamic context. A customer self-supplying may be far less effective than a third party over time, especially if the self-supply activity is not the customer's core business. For example, if product innovation or ongoing efficiencies to reduce costs (especially, but not only, if substantial economies of scale are present) are important elements of competition self-supply is unlikely to be an effective countervailing measure.

NOTES

127 John Kwoka, 'Reviving Merger Control: a comprehensive plan for reforming policy and practice', October 9 2018.

128 See, for example, J Sainsbury's Plc/Asda Group Ltd, in which the CMA considered rivalry-enhancing efficiencies might lead to an incentive to reduce some grocery and general merchandising prices but not fuel prices.

129 Efficiencies do not only need to affect the market which is the subject to the CMA's SLC assessment. For example, R&D efficiencies may affect multiple markets.

130 Joseph Farrell and Carl Shapiro (2000), 'Scale economies and synergies in horizontal merger analysis', UC Berkeley, Center for Competition Working Paper No. CPC00-15

131 Relevant customer benefits are defined in section 30 of the Act.

132 Section 30(4) of the Act. 'Indirect customers' means customers of a customer of the merged entity (or a customer further down the chain of customers).

133 In the investigations into the anticipated merger between Derby Teaching Hospitals NHS Foundation Trust and Burton Hospitals NHS Foundation Trust (2018), the CMA found that the relevant customer benefits in relation to the creation of the relevant merger situation outweighed the SLC and any adverse effects of the SLC Therefore, the CMA applied the relevant customer benefit exception under section 33(2)(c) of the Act.

134 Section 73(4) relating to undertakings in lieu at the end of a Phase 1 investigation and section 41(5) in relation to remedies after a Phase 2 investigation; In Macquarie UK Broadcast Ventures Limited/National Grid Wireless Group, significant relevant customer benefits contributed to the selection of a behavioural remedy; also in Imerys Minerals Limited/Goonvean Limited, when selecting a behavioural remedy, the CMA noted that to the extent that efficiencies existed, these would be eliminated if full divestiture had been required, but possible relevant customer benefits would not be affected by the chosen price control remedy.

135 Merger remedies (CMA87) paragraph 3.16.

136 Merger remedies (CMA87) paragraph 3.16; In Central Manchester University Hospitals NHS Foundation Trust/ University Hospital of South Manchester NHS Foundation Trust, the CMA found that the merger may be expected to give rise to an SLC However, the prohibition would result in the loss of substantial relevant customer benefits which may be expected to arise as a result of the merger. The CMA found that, when balanced against the nature of the SLC and its resulting adverse effects, the relevant customer benefits were likely to be more significant. The CMA, therefore, concluded that it would be disproportionate to prohibit the merger, and that it should be cleared.

137 Mergers: Exceptions to the duty to refer (CMA64) and Merger remedies (CMA87).

138 At the time of publishing the Merger Assessment Guidelines the CMA has only ever cleared three cases on the basis of relevant customer benefits: Central Manchester University Hospitals NHS Foundation Trust/South Manchester NHS Foundation Trust, University Hospitals Birmingham NHS Foundation Trust/Heart of England NHS Foundation Trust and Derby Teaching Hospitals/Burton Hospitals.

139 KPMG, Entry and expansion in UK merger cases: an ex-post evaluation, April 2017.

140 In general, the same standard of evidence, and the relevant time period, of entry or expansion by one of the merger firms in the counterfactual will be applied to entry or expansion by a third party, whether in the CMA's assessment of countervailing factors or in its assessment of the theory of harm(s).

141 In Prosafe SE/Floatel International Limited (Provisional Findings), the CMA found evidence that value of contracts were small relative to the cost of entry for firms operating outside North-West Europe.

142 In Arriva Rail North/Northern rail franchise, the CMA considered incumbent's ability to credibly threaten to retaliate against operators seeking to enter their 'core territories'.

143 ie the costs cannot be recovered when exiting from the market. The CMA considered the upfront costs required for entry in Tobii AB/Smartbox Assistive Technology Limited and Sensory Software International Ltd, and its Provisional Findings in Illumina Inc/Pacific Biosciences of California Inc.

144 In Ecolab Inc/The Holchem Group Limited, the CMA found that customers had low switching rates and placed value on reputation, reliability and a proven track record.

145 These arise where average costs fall as the level of output rises over a range of output volume.

146 For example, many digital and software markets as well as other markets such as pharmaceutical markets.

147 See the section on *Nature of competition,* in Chapter 9.

148 See the Final Report of Intercontinental Exchange Inc/ Trayport, in particular paragraphs 7.112-7.170 and 9.4-9.16.

149 For example, card payment systems.

150 Early mover advantages are also present in non-digital markets.

151 For example, in Bauer Media Group/Celador Entertainment Limited/Lincs FM Group/Wireless Group Limited/UKRD Group Limited the CMA found that the lack of available radio spectrum was a barrier to entry; in Ladbrokes plc/Gala Coral Group Limited planning approval was considered to be a barrier to entry; and in the Provisional Findings of Illumina Inc/Pacific Biosciences of California Inc intellectual property rights were provisionally viewed as a barrier to entry.

152 For example, in John Menzies plc/Airline Service Limited the CMA found that self-supply of de-icing services at London Heathrow was a credible option for airlines with a large presence but not a credible option for airlines with relatively few airlines movements.

9. THE MARKET IN WHICH AN SLC ARISES

THE ROLE OF MARKET DEFINITION

[3.524]

9.1 Where the CMA makes an SLC finding, this must be 'within any market or markets in the United Kingdom for goods or services'.[153] The CMA is therefore required to identify the market or markets within which an SLC exists. An SLC can affect the whole or part of a market or markets. Within that context, the assessment of the relevant market is an analytical tool that forms part of the analysis of the competitive effects of the merger and should not be viewed as a separate exercise.

9.2 Market definition involves identifying the most significant competitive alternatives available to customers of the merger firms and includes the sources of competition to the merger firms that are the immediate determinants of the effects of the merger. While market definition can be an important part of the overall merger assessment process, the CMA's experience is that in most mergers, the evidence gathered as part of the competitive assessment, which will assess the potentially significant constraints on the merger firms' behaviour, captures the competitive dynamics more fully than formal market definition. Consequently, while the appropriate approach will reflect the circumstances in each case, the CMA anticipates that in future, merger assessments will place more emphasis on the competitive assessment as opposed to static market definition.

9.3 Market definition can sometimes be helpful in developing certain types of evidence that may be relevant for the competitive assessment. For example, the relevant market can be used as the basis for calculating market shares or for constructing other measures of concentration, which may be helpful in some cases (especially where products are homogenous). On the other hand, measures of concentration can often be interpreted without concluding on a bright-line market definition. For example, the CMA may calculate concentration measures on multiple different bases, including and excluding different firms, depending on which firms the CMA wishes to compare. The CMA may then attach greater weight to concentration measures that include firms whose products are more substitutable, and less weight to concentration measures that include firms whose products are less substitutable. In some cases, market definition may be a less relevant part of the competitive assessment. Evidence on closeness of competition can often be interpreted without having defined the relevant market, for example: internal documents discussing competitors; views from customers or competitors on the closest substitutes for the merger firms' products; analyses of bidding data; evidence on diversion between the firms; and data on customers won and lost.

9.4 While market definition can sometimes be a useful tool, it is not an end in itself. The outcome of any market definition exercise does not determine the outcome of the CMA's analysis of the competitive effects of the merger in any mechanistic way. In assessing whether a merger may give rise to an SLC, the CMA may take into account constraints outside the relevant market, segmentation within the relevant market, or other ways in which some constraints are more important than others. In many cases, especially those involving differentiated products, there is often no 'bright line' that can or should be drawn. Rather, it can be more helpful to describe the constraint posed by different categories of product or supplier as sitting on a continuum between 'strong' and 'weak'. The CMA will generally not need to come to finely balanced judgements on what is 'inside' or 'outside' the market. Not every firm 'in' a market will be equal and the CMA will assess how closely two merger firms compete. The constraint posed by firms 'outside' the market will also be carefully considered.

9.5 There may be no need for the CMA's assessment of competitive effects to be based on a highly specific description of any particular market definition (including, for example, descriptions of the precise boundaries of the relevant markets and bright-line determinations of whether particular products or services fall within the relevant market). The CMA may take a simple approach to defining the market - for example, by describing the market as comprising the most important constraints on the merger firms that have been identified in the CMA's assessment of competitive effects.

DEFINING MARKETS

Product markets

9.6 Product market definition starts with the relevant products of the merger firms.[154] In identifying what other significant competitive alternatives should be included in the relevant market, the CMA will pay particular regard to demand- side factors (the behaviour of customers). The CMA may also consider supply-side factors.

Demand-side factors

9.7 The relevant product market is identified primarily by reference to demand-side substitution. One framework the CMA may use for considering substitution that the CMA may use involves considering evidence on the response of customers to a small but significant increase in price (or equivalent reduction in the value offered to customers in terms of quality, range or service) of the products of the merger firms. The CMA will often consider qualitative evidence on demand- and supply-side responses and often will not seek to produce quantitative estimates of what customers would do in response to price increases or how such responses would affect the profitability of a supplier or suppliers. Types of evidence the CMA might consider when evaluating the closeness of substitution between products are described at paragraph 4.13 of the chapter on *Horizontal unilateral effects.*

Supply-side factors

9.8 The boundaries of the relevant product market are generally determined by reference to demand-side substitution alone. However, there are circumstances where the CMA may aggregate several narrow relevant markets into one broader market based on considerations about the response of suppliers to changes in prices. The CMA may aggregate markets when:

(a) firms routinely use their existing production assets to supply a range of different products that are not demand-side substitutes[155] and there is evidence that firms in practice shift their existing capacity between these different products depending on demand for each; and

(b) the same firms compete to supply these different products and the conditions of competition between the firms are the same for each product; in this case aggregating the supply of these products and analysing them as one market does not affect the CMA's decision on the competitive effects of the merger.

Part 3 CMA and other Guidelines

9.9 These conditions are cumulative. Examples of cases where the two conditions may be satisfied might include:

(a) a merger between two retailers that compete with a set of retailers that all offer the same broad range of products (eg different types of outdoor clothing), where each retailer shifts between offering different specific products simply by changing the products in stock, without any significant adjustments to their supply chain, distribution network, retail stores or brand, and none has a particular strength in any subset of products;

(b) in a market where suppliers bid competitively to supply services which are bespoke to the customer and are therefore not demand-side substitutes, but where those suppliers use the same production assets to compete across tenders, and competitive conditions are similar across those tenders; or

(c) a two-sided market between two social media platforms where the services provided to the two customer groups are different (and therefore not substitutable), but competitive conditions are very similar on both sides because, for example, the same set of social media platforms compete for both sets of customers, and both platforms are similarly competitive for both groups.

9.10 In cases where firms do not currently shift their capacity across different products as a matter of routine, it may be more appropriate for the CMA to consider the prospect that they may start doing so using the CMA's framework for assessing entry by rivals (see paragraphs 8.28 to 8.43).

Parameter flexing

9.11 Where multiple product markets cannot be aggregated on the basis of demand-side or supply-side considerations, the CMA may aggregate them if the main parameters of competition are set uniformly across those markets.

Two-sided markets

9.12 The CMA's approach to market definition in two-sided markets is likely to reflect its approach to conducting the competitive assessment (paragraph 4.24). To the extent the CMA assesses the two sides separately, it may be more likely to define two separate markets.

Geographic markets

9.13 As with product markets, the CMA's focus in defining geographic markets is on demand-side factors and identifying the most important competitive alternatives to the merger firms. The CMA may consider evidence such as:

(a) information on the competitive performance of firms supplying from different geographic areas or over different distances;

(b) information on differences in pricing, sales, advertising and marketing strategies by area, as well as information on delivery costs or barriers to entry when supplying into an area or over different distances or across borders;

(c) the views of market participants on consumer preferences; and

(d) product characteristics such as perishability.

9.14 When determining whether supply-side substitution is sufficient to aggregate geographic markets, the CMA will have reference to the same conditions set out at paragraph 9.8.

9.15 When assessing mergers involving a large number of local geographic markets—for example, mergers of grocery retailers operating in multiple localities—the CMA may examine the geographic catchment area within which the great majority of a store's custom is located. Catchment areas are a pragmatic approach to identifying the most significant competitive alternatives available to customers of the merger firms.

9.16 Where multiple geographic markets cannot be aggregated on the basis of demand-side or supply-side considerations, the CMA may aggregate them if the main parameters of competition are set uniformly across those markets.

NOTES

[153] Sections 22(1)(b) and 33(1)(b) of the Act for Phase 1 and sections 35(1)(b) and 36(1)(b) of the Act for Phase 2.

[154] The outcome of any market definition exercise will depend on the starting point, ie the overlapping products of the merger firms. Therefore, there is no one market definition that can be expected to apply across all cases in a similar area.

[155] Production assets may include traditional physical assets such as premises and equipment, it may also include other assets. Some examples might include human capital, know-how or intellectual property, technology, reputation and experience.

2. SECTOR SPECIFIC

(I) COMMUNICATIONS

DTI GUIDANCE ON THE OPERATION OF THE PUBLIC INTEREST MERGER PROVISIONS RELATING TO NEWSPAPER AND OTHER MEDIA MERGERS ENTERPRISE ACT 2002: PUBLIC INTEREST INTERVENTION IN MEDIA MERGERS

(May 2004)

[3.525]

NOTES

Note: the DTI is now the Department for Business, Energy & Industrial Strategy. This guidance has been adopted by the Department for Digital, Culture, Media & Sport.

CONTENTS

EXECUTIVE SUMMARY

[3.526]

Merger law was reformed by the Enterprise Act 2002, which came into force on 20 June 2003. This took Ministers out of the decision-making process for the vast majority of merger cases and left them to be dealt with by the competition authorities – the Office of Fair Trading and the Competition Commission – on the basis of a competition test. However, the Act allows Ministers to intervene in merger cases which raise public interest considerations specified in the Act. The only consideration specified at that time was national security.

The Communications Act 2003 amended the Enterprise Act 2002, specifying new public interest considerations which can be applied to mergers involving newspaper enterprises and broadcasting enterprises (as well as, amongst other things, repealing the newspaper merger provisions of the Fair Trading Act 1973 and making changes to the media ownership and regulation rules). The Enterprise Act procedures allowing for intervention by Ministers can now therefore be used where the media public interest considerations may be relevant to a merger. The assessment of mergers on competition grounds will continue to be the responsibility of the competition authorities.

The Secretary of State may publish advice and information explaining the media public interest considerations specified in sections 58(2A) to (2C) of the Act and indicating how these provisions are expected to operate. Accordingly, this guidance seeks to explain the media public interest considerations and provide an indication of how the Secretary of State expects the provisions to operate in relation to mergers involving newspapers or broadcast media enterprises, and to cross-media mergers involving both broadcast media enterprises and newspaper enterprises.

This guidance sets out the background to the new regime, explains when intervention in media mergers by the Secretary of State is possible, and the process for considering mergers on media public interest grounds. The newspaper sections of the guidance emphasise the continuity of assessment of newspaper mergers on public interest grounds between the current regime and the old regime (the Fair Trading Act 1973), notwithstanding the fact that the procedures are very different. As regards the broadcasting and cross-media public interest considerations, the guidance confirms that, as Ministers indicated to Parliament when bringing forward the relevant amendments to the Communications Bill, intervention will only normally take place where media ownership rules have been completely removed by the Communications Act 2003.

SECTION 1
INTRODUCTION

[3.527]

1.1 This guidance gives advice and information on how certain media mergers may be considered by the Secretary of State in so-called media public interest cases.

1.2 The framework for the assessment of mergers under UK domestic law is set out in the Enterprise Act 2002 (the Act), which came into force on 20 June 2003. The Act requires the Office of Fair Trading (the "OFT") to obtain and keep under review information relating to its functions, including its merger functions, and imposes a duty on the OFT, except in certain specified circumstances, to refer to the Competition Commission (the "CC") for further investigation any relevant merger situations that it believes have resulted, or may be expected to result, in a substantial lessening of competition. Guidance on the roles of the OFT and the CC in relation to mergers is given in the OFT's publications "Mergers: Procedural Guidance (May 2003)" and "Mergers: Substantive Assessment Guidance (May 2003)" (available at www.oft.gov.uk/) and in the CC's publications "Rules of Procedure (June 2003)" and "Merger References: Competition Commission Guidelines (June 2003)" (available at www.competition-commission.org.uk), amongst others.

1.3 The Act also permits intervention by the Secretary of State (in practice, the Secretary of State for Trade and Industry) in certain mergers. For mergers which meet the standard jurisdictional criteria for investigation on competition grounds the Secretary of State may issue an "intervention notice". In these cases, the Secretary of State may take into account public interest factors specified in the Act other than the OFT's competition assessment in deciding whether or not to refer a merger to the CC or to remedy any adverse effects of a merger. The Secretary of State is also able to intervene in special public interest cases where the standard merger jurisdictional thresholds relating to share of supply and turnover are not satisfied. She does this by issuing a "special intervention notice". There is no competition assessment in these special public interest cases. The Secretary of State can also intervene on public interest grounds in cases which fall to the European Commission under the provisions of the EC Merger Regulation. In this case she issues a "European intervention notice" (see chapter 11 for further details). The only public interest considerations that the Secretary of State may take into account are specified in the Act. The Secretary of State retains the power to add further public interest considerations by statutory instrument.

1.4 The only public interest consideration specified when the Act completed its Parliamentary passage was national security, which includes public security (section 58(2)). However, the Communications Act 2003 amended the Act by adding further public interest considerations relating to mergers involving media and newspaper enterprises. These new public interest considerations (referred to collectively in the legislation as the "media public interest considerations") are set out in section 58(2A) to (2C) of the Act. The public interest considerations set out in section 58(2A) and (2B) may apply in the context of mergers involving newspapers; these considerations are referred to in this guidance as the "newspaper public interest considerations". The public interest considerations set out in section 58(2C) may apply in the context of mergers involving broadcast media enterprises or cross-media mergers involving both broadcast media enterprises and newspaper enterprises. For present purposes these public interest considerations are referred to as the "broadcasting and cross-media public interest considerations". The term "media public interest considerations" is used, as in the legislation, to cover all the new public interest considerations.

1.5 The new regime also provides an advisory role for the Office of Communications ("OFCOM") after the Secretary of State intervenes in a case on the grounds of media public interest considerations. OFCOM does not advise the Secretary of State on whether to intervene in a merger on media public interest grounds.

1.6 New section 106A of the Act provides for the publication by the Secretary of State of advice and information explaining the media public interest considerations specified in sections 58(2A) to (2C) of the Act and indicating how the Secretary of State expects these provisions to operate. Accordingly, the policies and procedures that will apply to mergers raising media public interest considerations form the subject matter of this guidance.

1.7 Although it is provided under statutory provisions and has authority as such, this guidance is not a substitute for the provisions of the Act or the Communications Act 2003. Anyone in any doubt about whether and how they may be affected by the legislation should seek legal advice. It should also be borne in mind that, whilst the guidance is intended to provide an indication of how the media public interest merger regime will operate in practice, and the approach the Secretary of State is likely to adopt in considering cases, each transaction will be looked at on its merits on a case-by-case basis. The guidance may be revised from time to time in the light of experience in operating the media public interest regime.

SECTION 2
BACKGROUND TO THE MEDIA PUBLIC INTEREST CONSIDERATIONS

NEWSPAPER MERGERS

[3.528]

2.1 A regulatory system for newspaper mergers was first introduced by the Monopolies and Mergers Act 1965, following the Report of the Royal Commission on the Press in 1962,[1] which concluded that control of the Press was a matter of particular public sensitivity and that the increasing concentration of newspaper ownership in too few hands could stifle the expression of opinion and argument and distort the presentation of news. The Secretary of State considers that these concerns continue to underlay the special consideration that can be given to newspaper mergers.

2.2 The regime in the Monopolies and Mergers Act 1965, which was largely replicated in the Fair Trading Act 1973 (the "FTA"), subjected most newspaper mergers to a stricter system of control than other mergers. A transfer of a newspaper that met the criteria for the application of the regime was unlawful and void if it proceeded without the prior consent of the Secretary of State. With certain limited exceptions the Secretary of State could not consent to qualifying newspaper transfers without a reference to the CC.[2] Criminal penalties attached to breach of the consent requirements.

2.3 The FTA newspaper merger regime imposed significant costs on the industry and yet the vast majority of cases considered by the Secretary of State were given unconditional consent, whether following or without a CC reference.[3] Nonetheless, there have been a small number of cases where Ministers have intervened in newspaper mergers over concerns other than competition. These cases indicate a continued need, now met by the new newspaper public interest considerations, to address these concerns.

THE NEW REGIME FOR NEWSPAPER MERGERS

2.4 The new regime for newspaper mergers[4] takes elements from the FTA newspaper merger regime whilst integrating the assessment of newspaper mergers into the general merger regime of the Act. The new regime seeks to secure the continued protection of the particular public interests related to newspapers while lifting much of the regulatory burden on the industry and on the regulatory authorities.

2.5 In consequence, whilst the newspaper merger procedures under the new regime are radically different from the old, the Secretary of State expects there to be considerable continuity in the substantive assessment of the public interest issues. Indeed, the newspaper public interest considerations now specified in the Act are based on public interest detriments that have been found to exist in previous newspaper mergers examined under the FTA regime. Consequently, decisions under the old regime and previous reports of the CC or Monopolies and Mergers Commission (the "MMC") are expected by the Secretary of State often to be relevant to the consideration of public interest issues under the new regime.

OTHER MEDIA MERGERS

2.6 In common with other modern democracies, the UK has for some time regulated the communications industry. Media ownership rules have applied because market forces alone, even regulated by competition law, cannot necessarily provide the market-place of ideas[5] that enables democracy to prosper. Nevertheless, developments in technology and the desire to promote a more competitive communications industry that will attract greater investment have encouraged the deregulation of the industry. The broadcasting and cross-media public interest considerations were introduced into the Act by the Communications Act 2003, which at the same time relaxed certain ownership rules that have applied to broadcast media and to cross-media ownership. Notwithstanding this relaxation, the media and cross-media public interest regime provides a safeguard to prevent media mergers bringing about undue concentrations of ownership, which may operate against the public interest. It will enable the Secretary of State to intervene in certain mergers involving media enterprises so as to ensure a sufficient plurality of media ownership, to protect the availability of a wide range of high quality broadcasting and to ensure that those with control of media enterprises have a genuine commitment to the broadcasting standards objectives set out in the Communications Act 2003.

NOTES

1 Cmnd 1811.

2 The Competition Commission replaced the Monopolies and Mergers Commission on 1 April 1999.

3 Of the 191 applications considered under the FTA regime between November 1973 (when the FTA came into force) and December 2003, only ten were refused consent or were granted subject to conditions.

4 Introduced into the Enterprise Act 2002 by the Communications Act 2003.

5 The phrase is usually traced to Justice Holmes' dissenting opinion in Abrams v. United States, in 1919.

SECTION 3
ESTABLISHING JURISDICTION

"STANDARD" JURISDICTION

[3.529]

3.1 In order to provide consistency with the procedures and scope of the mainstream merger provisions of the Act, the jurisdictional criteria established in that Act are also used to identify the scope of the standard jurisdiction for the media public interest merger regime.

3.2 Under the Act, the Secretary of State is able to intervene under the public interest regime where she believes a merger may raise a public interest consideration specified in section 58 of the Act and the transaction constitutes a "relevant merger situation".[6] A "relevant merger situation" is created where two or more enterprises cease to be distinct[7] and where at least one of the following thresholds is met, namely:

- the value of the turnover in the UK of the enterprise being taken over exceeds £70 million (the "turnover test"); or
- the merger would result in the creation or enhancement of at least a 25% share of supply of goods or services of any description in the UK or in a substantial part of the UK (the "share of supply test").

3.3 Thus, the Secretary of State will be able to intervene where she believes that a media public interest consideration is or may be relevant to the "relevant merger situation". If she intervenes then the merger will be looked at on competition grounds and against the specified public interest grounds.

EXTENSION OF SPECIAL PUBLIC INTEREST REGIME FOR MEDIA MERGERS

3.4 The jurisdictional thresholds of the mainstream merger regime in the Act focus on transactions that (a) involve acquisitions of enterprises with relatively high overall economic significance (the turnover test) and/or (b) will have a consolidating impact which could reduce direct competition (the share of supply test).

3.5 However, media public interest concerns are not necessarily so limited. For example, where the concern relates to the likely impact of a change of owner of a newspaper on accurate presentation of the news or free expression of opinion, it may not be relevant whether the acquisition has a consolidating effect. Similarly, change of ownership of broadcast media enterprises may give rise to concerns regarding the commitment of the new owner to a broad range of high quality programming even if there is no consolidation. It is also the case that a £70 million turnover threshold in the context of the newspaper industry is a relatively high one; many local newspapers fall below this level and yet such newspapers can be of key significance for their local communities, which if small may not be able to support a great diversity of newspaper titles.

3.6 As a result, the legislation provides that mergers that may raise media public interest considerations can be scrutinized on these grounds under the special public interest regime in circumstances where the standard jurisdictional criteria (set out in paragraph 3.2) are not met. In such "special merger situations",[8] the review will be on specified public interest grounds only – there will be no assessment of competition issues. However, it is also important that regulatory burdens are not imposed on the very smallest transactions, where any impact on competition or plurality would be de minimis.

3.7 Accordingly, in order to strike a balance between looking at transactions of concern and not imposing regulatory burdens on the very smallest transactions, the media public interest considerations are not restricted to transactions leading to the *creation* or *enhancement* of a 25% share of supply (as is the case under the mainstream share of supply provisions). So long as one of the parties to the merger has an existing 25% or more share of supply of newspapers of any description in the UK or in a substantial part of the UK, the Secretary of State may intervene in order to protect a newspaper public interest consideration.[9] Similarly, the Secretary of State can only intervene under the public interest regime to protect broadcasting and cross-media public interest considerations where one of the parties to the merger has an existing share of provision of broadcasting of any description of at least 25% in the UK or in a substantial part of the UK.[10]

3.8 Transactions where the UK turnover of the company acquired does not exceed £70 million and there is neither an existing share of supply of newspapers or provision of broadcasting of 25% or more in the UK or in a substantial part of the UK,[11] nor is such a share created by the merger, are completely excluded from merger scrutiny in the UK. In these circumstances the Secretary of State is not able to intervene.

3.9 It should be noted that no consequences will flow from the fact that a merger falls within the special public interest regime unless and until the Secretary of State exercises her discretion to intervene in a particular case.

SHARE OF SUPPLY IN THE SPECIAL PUBLIC INTEREST REGIME FOR MEDIA MERGERS

3.10 In order to avoid too many transactions falling within the scope of the special merger regime for media mergers the generic sector to which the special merger jurisdiction applies is specified – ie the supply of newspapers[12] or provision of broadcasting.[13] This may be broken down more specifically by identifying the category of goods or services in relation to which the 25% share of supply is held in any particular case. This is consistent with, and calculated in the same way as, the share of supply test applied under the mainstream merger regime of the Act. Thus, the criteria for determining whether the share of supply has been fulfilled would be up to the decision-making authorities to determine in each case and could, for example, be based on circulation, share of viewers or listeners, value, cost or advertising revenue.[14]

CONCEPT OF A "NEWSPAPER"

3.11 The scope of the term "newspaper" is set out in the legislation[15] and is the same as that applied in the, now repealed, FTA newspaper merger regime.[16] A newspaper is defined as "a daily, Sunday or local (other than daily or Sunday) newspaper circulating wholly or mainly in the United Kingdom or in a part of the United Kingdom". The effect of this is that the newspaper public interest considerations potentially apply to mergers involving daily and Sunday newspapers, whether national or local, and local periodical newspapers (subject of course to the jurisdictional criteria described above applying). The regime does not apply to newspapers circulated predominantly outside the UK.

3.12 Whether or not a publication is a "newspaper" will depend on an examination of the particular publication. The Secretary of State takes the view that the definition of "newspaper" starts with the ordinary and a natural meaning of the word and includes a publication regardless of whether or not it is paid for. To be a newspaper, the publication should contain some news content. Publications consisting wholly or almost wholly of advertising are not, in the Secretary of State's view, newspapers.

3.13 In considering whether or not a publication is a "newspaper" for the purposes of the newspaper public interest considerations, the following questions are in the opinion of the Secretary of State relevant:

- Is there any real attempt at news coverage? News coverage is not limited to actual reporting of events but includes editorials and articles of interest.
- Does it contain advertisements that should properly appear in a newspaper? For instance certain statutes require matters to be advertised in a newspaper and not in an advertising free sheet.

- What is the proportion of the publication that contains advertisements or advertorials as compared with news content?

3.14 In considering whether a newspaper is a local newspaper for the purposes of the newspaper public interest regime, the factors to which the Secretary of State will have regard include the geographic distribution of the newspaper and the nature of the news content and whether it deals with local issues. The definition of a newspaper may be changed by order.[17]

3.15 As noted in paragraph 2.5 above, the Secretary of State expects there to be considerable continuity between the assessment of the substantive issues under the FTA regime and under the new regime.

CONCEPT OF "BROADCASTING"

3.16 Broadcasting is defined in the legislation[18] as the provision of services the provision of which is required to be licensed under Part 1 or 3 of the Broadcasting Act 1990 or Part 1 or 2 of the Broadcasting Act 1996 or would be required to be so licensed if provided by a person subject to licensing under the Part in question.

3.17 The latter part of the definition is intended to include services provided by the BBC or the Welsh Authority, or by broadcasters established abroad and broadcasting into the UK under European Union licences. This broad definition allows the Secretary of State to take account of the existence of, for example, the services of the BBC or the Welsh Authority when carrying out the assessment of the sufficiency of plurality of controllers of media enterprises in new section 58(2C).

ACQUISITIONS OF "CONTROL" OF NEWSPAPERS

3.18 The FTA newspaper merger regime applied only to direct or indirect acquisitions of a 25% voting interest,[19] whereas the standard merger provisions of the Act apply where enterprises come under common ownership or common control[20] (so long as the share of supply or turnover thresholds are satisfied). This includes acquisitions of "material influence" over an enterprise,[21] which can arise at lower levels of interest and conceivably in the absence of an equity interest.[22]

NO PRE-NOTIFICATION REQUIREMENT

3.19 Under the FTA newspaper merger regime a transfer of a newspaper or newspaper assets to a newspaper proprietor required the prior written consent of the Secretary of State where the newspapers of the proprietor to whom the transfer is made (including the titles being acquired) have an average paid for circulation of 500,000 copies or more per day. Subject to certain statutory exceptions, the Secretary of State could not give this consent without a CC report. Under the new merger regime, merger parties will have the option to proceed to close the transaction before clearance is obtained (albeit at their own risk). As is the case with all UK relevant mergers situations, the merger may be referred to the CC after the completion of the transaction. In the event of an adverse public interest finding in such a case, the transaction may have to be unwound if no other remedies are appropriate. The power to refer a completed media merger to the CC on competition or public interest grounds (under the standard, special or European intervention schemes) is subject to the standard longstop on reference of four months.[23]

NOTES

6 Section 23(1) and (2) Enterprise Act 2002 – see OFT guidance "*Mergers: Substantive Assessment Guidance*", Chapter 2.

7 See section 26 Enterprise Act 2002.

8 Section 59(1) Enterprise Act 2002.

9 Section 59(3C) Enterprise Act 2002.

10 Section 59(3D) Enterprise Act 2002.

11 In the context of the Fair Trading Act 1973, the meaning of "a substantial part of the UK" has been clarified by case law as meaning the part must be of "such a size, character and importance as to make it worthy of consideration for the purposes of the Act" (Nourse LJ in *South Yorkshire Transport Ltd v. MMC* [1983] 1 All. E.R. 289). In the first instance it is for the OFT to determine jurisdiction; additional guidance can be found at paragraph 2.25 of their publication "*Mergers – Substantive Assessment Guidance (May 2003)*".

12 As defined in section 44(10) Enterprise Act 2002.

13 As defined in section 44(9) Enterprise Act 2002.

14 Section 59A Enterprise Act 2002. In the first instance it is for the OFT to determine jurisdiction; additional guidance can be found at paragraph 2.24 of their publication "*Mergers – Substantive Assessment Guidance (May 2003)*".

15 Section 44(10) Enterprise Act 2002.

16 Section 57(1)(a) Fair Trading Act 1973.

17 Section 44(11) Enterprise Act 2002.

18 Section 44 (9) Enterprise Act 2002. The definition of broadcasting may be amended by order pursuant to section 44(11) of the Act.

19 Section 57 Fair Trading Act 1973.

20 Section 26(1) Enterprise Act 2002.

21 Section 26(3) Enterprise Act 2002.

22 On this subject, see in particular OFT *Mergers: Substantive Assessment Guidance* (paragraphs 2.9 to 2.12), the OFT press release on BSkyB/Leeds Sporting (PN8/00, 3 February, 2000) and the Competition Commission report on NTL Communications Corporation/Newcastle United (Cm 4411, July 1999).

23 From the date on which the enterprises cease to be distinct, or, if later, the date on which material facts about the transaction under which they ceased to be distinct is made public – section 24 Enterprise Act 2002. For the time when enterprises are to be regarded as ceasing to be distinct, see section 27 Enterprise Act 2002.

SECTION 4
PROCEDURES

[3.530]

4.1 The procedure for examination of transactions raising media public interest considerations is largely aligned with the mainstream merger provisions in the Act, with certain modifications to take account of OFCOM's advisory role where the Secretary of State has intervened on media public interest grounds. The processes and possible timescales are set out in diagrammatic form in Annexes A and B.

MARKET MONITORING

4.2 Consistent with its obligations as the body responsible for the operation of the mainstream merger provisions, the OFT has responsibility for carrying out the initial market monitoring activity in relation to media merger cases, with the obligation to inform the Secretary of State of cases that it believes raise any specified media public interest considerations.[24] In addition, the Secretary of State retains the ability to look at cases on her own initiative, and it would equally be open to OFCOM or anyone else to draw cases to her attention.

NOTIFICATION OF MERGER SITUATIONS INVOLVING NEWSPAPERS AND BROADCASTING

4.3 Parties to a merger which potentially raises media public interest considerations have a number of options for approaching OFT, OFCOM and DTI to discuss the merger.

4.4 Parties may make OFT, OFCOM and DTI aware informally of an anticipated transaction ahead of its announcement. By doing so they can ensure that any notification is more focused on the information OFT, OFCOM and DTI will require to make their assessments of the merger.

INFORMAL ADVICE AND CONFIDENTIAL GUIDANCE

4.5 Parties may seek informal advice or confidential guidance from the OFT on competition issues and (in certain circumstances) DTI, on likelihood of intervention, and OFCOM, for a likely view on public interest issues. Informal advice or confidential guidance on public interest grounds will only be offered in broadcasting and cross-media mergers where media ownership rules have been removed, as the Secretary of State has said she will only consider intervening in these cases save in exceptional circumstances (see paragraph 8.8 below). It will be open to the parties to put a case to officials as to why their merger might be an "exceptional circumstance", in which case officials would offer views on the parties' reasoning. Informal advice or confidential guidance will also be available for newspaper mergers where a party to the merger thinks that a media public interest issue arises.

INFORMAL ADVICE

4.6 The informal advice process basically follows the procedure set out in the OFT's Merger Guidance.[25] This involves submitting a paper outlining the anticipated transaction at least 48 hours ahead of a meeting with officials, who then give their non-binding and confidential view, based purely on the information provided. In such cases the OFT will act as the primary contact point for parties. The paper should be submitted to OFT, and copied to OFCOM and DTI.

4.7 In cases for which informal advice is available, DTI officials will advise on the likelihood of intervention in the merger on public interest grounds. Informal advice is given by officials, and not by the Secretary of State or any other Minister. If officials indicate they would be likely to recommend intervention, OFCOM officials will offer advice on the likely media public interest considerations arising out of the prospective media merger situation.[26] OFT officials will provide their usual view of the competition aspects of the prospective merger situation.

CONFIDENTIAL GUIDANCE

4.8 Parties may also seek confidential guidance on anticipated transactions that have yet to be announced. Again this follows the procedure set out in the OFT's Merger Guidance and OFCOM's guidance.[27] The Secretary of State will provide confidential guidance on whether, on the information available to her, she would be minded to intervene on public interest grounds, on the case. If she concluded that should would be minded to intervene then OFCOM would advise on whether it is likely to recommend referral on media public interest grounds should the Secretary of State at the public stage issue an intervention notice. None of these views, which are sent to parties as a letter stating the conclusion reached and offering a joint meeting in which the OFT, OFCOM and DTI can expand upon their conclusion, is binding. The OFT will relay its views, along with those of DTI and (if appropriate) OFCOM, within a specified administrative timetable.

NOTIFICATION OF A MERGER

4.9 Once a merger has been announced, and before it is completed, the parties can notify it using a merger notice (also known as a formal submission) to the OFT and copying it to OFCOM. The procedures for this are outlined in the OFT Merger Guidance and the information should be supplemented with such details as required by OFCOM (see their guidance for further details). The parties have the alternative of making an informal submission.

4.10 A merger notice can only be used if the merger qualifies under the standard merger regime. If an intervention notice is not issued the OFT will make a decision on the competition aspects within the statutory deadline of 20 working days, although the OFT can extend this by 10 working days, and the

Secretary of State's ability to issue an intervention notice will lapse once the OFT makes a reference decision within that statutory deadline. If an intervention notice is issued the statutory deadline for the Secretary of State to make a decision on reference following advice from OFT and OFCOM may be extended by the OFT by a further 10 working days – so if the Secretary of State intervenes in a case subject to a merger notice the maximum timescale for a decision on reference is 40 working days.[28]

4.11 Parties can also choose to make an informal submission for anticipated or completed mergers, sent to OFT, and copied to OFCOM and DTI if the parties think media public interest issues may arise. If an intervention notice is issued the Secretary of State will aim to make a decision on reference (or to seek undertakings in lieu of a reference) within 10 working days of receiving the OFT and OFCOM reports.

INTERVENTION BY THE SECRETARY OF STATE

4.12 Where a transaction is identified as giving rise to a media public interest consideration, the Secretary of State will be able to intervene through issuing an "intervention notice", or a "special intervention notice", or a "European intervention notice", specifying the relevant public interest consideration(s).[29]

4.13 A merger may come to the Secretary of State's attention or it may be brought to her attention as set out in paragraph 4.2 above. If the Secretary of State is going to take a view on whether or not to intervene in the case on public interest grounds, the parties to the merger will be informed of this and invited to submit any views they have on this in writing. In taking a view on whether to intervene the Secretary of State will have regard to all available information which, depending on the case, may include:

- submissions from the parties to the merger (as invited by the Secretary of State);
- complaints made to the Press Complaints Commission and judgments made;
- any previous regulatory decisions which include relevant information or judgments;
- published articles raising matters of relevance; and
- any third party representations received; but
- she will not receive advice from OFCOM on whether to intervene (though she may receive and / or seek information from them in order to inform her decision).

4.14 The Secretary of State can issue an intervention notice at any time until the OFT makes a reference decision, and can issue a special intervention notice at any point up to 4 months after completion of the merger. However, as a matter of policy, in order to prevent undue uncertainty, the Secretary of State will aim to take an initial decision on whether to intervene within 10 working days of the later of: the transaction being notified to the OFT, or the transaction being brought to her attention. Because of this timescale, parties to the merger will only be given typically 3–4 working days to make a written representation on whether the Secretary of State should intervene. The Secretary of State will not normally conduct a public consultation on whether she should intervene in a case, but will welcome and take account of any representations she receives. She may also seek the views of a few interested parties if time permits.

4.15 If the Secretary of State decides to intervene, she will make this fact known by issuing a press notice announcing her decision, and publishing the intervention notice or special intervention notice. If her initial decision is not to intervene, the parties will be informed of this in a non-confidential letter; this letter will be without prejudice to her ability to intervene (within the timescales set out in the Act) if new or additional information subsequently comes to her attention. However, she will not herself make public any decision not to intervene, as this might cause uncertainty as to her role in mergers on which she has not made a public announcement because they have not been brought to her attention.

4.16 If she intervenes, the Secretary of State will then be able to consider whether to:

- refer the transaction to the CC for examination of any media public interest considerations together with any competition issues that are identified by the OFT (in the case of mergers meeting the standard jurisdictional criteria);
- clear the merger; or
- direct the OFT to seek undertakings in lieu of a reference.

4.17 Both the OFT and OFCOM must provide advice to the Secretary of State within the deadline set by the Secretary of State[30] and, in the context of a merger notice,[31] in sufficient time for an informed decision to be made within the statutory timetable.[32]

INTERVENTION NOTICE

4.18 OFCOM will carry out the consultation seeking third party views on the impact of the transaction on the media public interest considerations specified in the intervention notice,[33] with OFT taking responsibility only for the competition and jurisdiction aspects of the transaction (although if representations are made to the OFT relating to any of the media public interest considerations, it may include a summary of these representations in its report). The Secretary of State will publish a non-confidential version of any such report made by the OFT or OFCOM.[34]

4.19 If the Secretary of State wishes to add a further public interest consideration to the list in section 58 of the Act, she must bring forward an order specifying the consideration in section 58 and seek Parliament's approval of it ('finalise' the consideration) as soon as practicable.

4.20 The Secretary of State may, where she believes there is a realistic prospect of the new public interest consideration being finalised, delay taking the decision on reference for up to 24 weeks from the date of the intervention notice so that she might be able to take a newly approved consideration into account in making that decision. There are currently no plans to introduce additional public interest considerations

Part 3 CMA and other Guidelines

4.21 In the event that the Secretary of State decides that the specified media public interest considerations are not relevant to a transaction, the case will revert to a competition-only assessment and the OFT will make the reference decision, which will be published.[35] Otherwise the Secretary of State will balance any competition detriment identified along with the specified media public interest considerations in making the decision as to reference,[36] whether to accept undertakings in lieu of a reference,[37] or whether to clear the merger.

4.22 The Secretary of State will not be able to dispute the OFT's finding as to jurisdiction or competition.[38] If no competition concerns are identified the Secretary of State will not be able to make a competition reference, but she will still be able to make a reference to the CC on the media public interest consideration aspects alone.

4.23 Where a competition problem has been identified by the OFT this must be treated as being adverse to the public interest unless the Secretary of State considers this to be outweighed in the overall assessment.[39] However, the Secretary of State may not clear a merger where the OFT has identified competition concerns if the public interest consideration that she wishes to base that decision on has not been approved by Parliament.[40]

SPECIAL INTERVENTION NOTICE

4.24 In relation to special merger situations, broadly the same procedures will apply as for media mergers under the standard jurisdiction.[41] The Secretary of State can issue a special intervention notice specifying a media public interest consideration, and the OFT and OFCOM will provide her with advice within a timescale specified by the Secretary of State. However, in the context of a special merger situation the OFT will assess only jurisdiction and will not carry out any competition analysis.[42] In addition, unlike the case for relevant merger situations, it is not possible for the Secretary of State to specify new public interest considerations in a special intervention notice whilst a case is being considered. She can only invoke those public interest considerations specified in section 58 of the Act at the time the special intervention notice is given.

COMPETITION COMMISSION PROCEDURES

4.25 Once a merger where a media public interest consideration has been specified in the reference has been referred to it, the CC will be required:[43]

- to decide whether a "relevant merger situation" within the mainstream merger regime has been or will be created or, in the alternative, whether a "special merger situation" has been or will be created;
- where specified in the reference, to consider whether the merger has resulted or may be expected to result in a substantial lessening of competition;
- taking account only of competition aspects (if referred) and the identified public interest consideration, to decide whether the transfer operates or may be expected to operate against the public interest;
- if the CC has decided that the merger operates or may be expected to operate against the public interest, to decide (a) whether any action should be taken by the Secretary of State or (b) whether to recommend the taking of any action by the Secretary of State or by others to remedy the identified effects adverse to the public interest;
- if the CC has decided there is or may be a substantial lessening of competition, to decide whether it should take action, or whether it should recommend the taking of action by others, to remedy the substantial lessening of competition, or any adverse effects resulting from it.

4.26 As indicated above, in cases falling to the standard merger regime the Secretary of State has the power to add additional public interest considerations to those specified in section 58. However, if a new public interest consideration mentioned in the reference is not approved by Parliament within 24 weeks of the intervention notice having been served, the CC must disregard that consideration when drawing up its report.

4.27 Where the CC investigates a special merger situation, it may have regard only to the public interest considerations specified in the reference – no competition assessment is carried out.

4.28 On completion of its investigation, the CC will deliver the report to the Secretary of State, and at the same time will supply a copy to OFCOM.[44]

CONSULTATION OBLIGATIONS

4.29 In general, the CC will be able to adopt its own procedures, within the limits prescribed for public interest consideration cases in the Act. However, where a reference is made to the CC specifying a media public interest consideration there is a specific requirement on the CC to have regard to the need to consult with a view to obtaining a representative cross section of opinion of those who may be affected by the media merger.[45]

NEWSPAPER PANELS

4.30 The CC has a specialist newspaper panel.[46] The Chairman of the CC must appoint one or more members from the newspaper panel to the group constituted to deal with a newspaper merger reference where the reference is made specifying a newspaper public interest consideration. If the Chairman selects three such members, the group may consist entirely of those members.[47]

4.31 The Chairman cannot select a newspaper panel member to be a member of the group where a reference is made which does not specify a newspaper public interest consideration (unless the newspaper panel member in question is also a member of the general reporting panel[48]). Cases that are not subject to intervention will therefore be dealt with under the general merger regime in the same way as any other transaction.

SECRETARY OF STATE'S OBLIGATIONS

4.32 On receipt of the report, the Secretary of State will:

- publish her decision on whether to make an adverse public interest finding, or make no finding at all (in which case the case will revert back to the CC who will make the final decision), within 30 working days of receipt of the report.[49] She will accept the CC's conclusions on jurisdiction and competition (where applicable).[50] OFCOM can advise the Secretary of State following the receipt of a CC report;[51]
- consider the question of remedies where the decision made is that there is an adverse public interest (see chapter 9 for more details on remedies). She must have regard to the report of the CC, but the final question on remedies will rest with her;[52] and
- publish the report,[53] subject to any excisions that may be required.[54]

MIXED TRANSACTIONS

4.33 An acquisition may involve both newspaper/broadcasting and non-newspaper/ non-broadcasting assets and once the Secretary of State intervenes in relation to a merger on the basis of a media public interest consideration, the whole transaction (not just the newspaper or broadcasting aspects) will be examined under the public interest consideration procedures. However, because the Secretary of State will be bound by the findings of both the OFT and the CC as to the competition analysis, it is anticipated that the substantive outcome for the non-newspaper/non-broadcasting aspects of the transaction will be unchanged.[55]

4.34 In the case of a cross-media merger involving both a newspaper enterprise and a broadcast media enterprise, both the newspaper public interest considerations and the broadcasting and cross-media public interest considerations may be relevant.

NOTES

24 Sections 5, 57 and 119B Enterprise Act 2002.

25 See OFT publication "Mergers: Procedural Guidance (May 2003)" paragraphs 3.4–3.10.

26 See OFCOM publication "Ofcom Guidance For The Public Interest Test For Media Mergers (May 2004)" paragraphs 28–34.

27 See OFT publication "Mergers: Procedural Guidance (May 2003)" paragraphs 3.11–3.18, and OFCOM publication "Ofcom Guidance For The Public Interest Test For Media Mergers (May 2004)" paragraphs 35–44.

28 The OFT can also extend the statutory timetable for a merger subject to a merger notice – and for a completed merger – if additional information is requested by statutory notice but not received by the deadline stipulated in the notice – see paragraph 5.3 of the OFT publication "Mergers: Procedural Guidance (May 2003)". A further extension can also be made if the OFT or the Secretary of State is seeking undertakings in lieu of a reference – see section 97(7) Enterprise Act 2002.

29 Section 42(2), 59(2), 67(2) Enterprise Act 2002.

30 Sections 44 and 44A Enterprise Act 2002.

31 The merger notice may only be used to notify relevant merger situations and is not appropriate in the case of special merger situations.

32 See OFT Publication "*Mergers: Procedural Guidance (May 2003)*" Annex A.

33 See OFCOM publication "*Ofcom Guidance For The Public Interest Test For Media Mergers (May 2004)*" paragraphs 58–70 for further information on OFCOM's role.

34 Section 107(3) Enterprise Act 2002.

35 Section 56 Enterprise Act 2002

36 Section 45 Enterprise Act 2002.

37 Paragraph 3 of Schedule 7 Enterprise Act 2002.

38 Section 46(2) Enterprise Act 2002.

39 Section 45(6) Enterprise Act 2002

40 Section 46(4) Enterprise Act 2002

41 Sections 59 to 66 Enterprise Act 2002 – note that sections 96 to 102 concerning merger notices do not apply in relation to special merger situations.

42 Section 61 Enterprise Act 2002.

43 Sections 47 and 63 Enterprise Act 2002.

44 Sections 50(2A) and 65(2A) Enterprise Act 2002.

45 Section 104A Enterprise Act 2002.

46 Paragraph 22 of Schedule 7 to the Competition Act 1998 as amended and see the definition of "newspaper merger reference" in paragraph 1 of the Schedule.

47 Paragraph 15(5) of Schedule 7 to the Competition Act 1998 as amended.

48 Paragraph 2 Schedule 7 Competition Act 1998 as amended.

49 Sections 54(5) and 66(3) Enterprise Act 2002.

50 Section 54(7)(a) Enterprise Act 2002.

51 Section 106B Enterprise Act 2002.

52 Sections 55 and 66 Enterprise Act 2002.

53 Section 107(3) Enterprise Act 2002

54 Section 118 Enterprise Act 2002

55 But note that as regards remedies following a reference, the Secretary of State will be able to balance competition and public interest aspects in deciding on the appropriate remedies.

SECTION 5
SCOPE OF THE NEWSPAPER PUBLIC INTEREST CONSIDERATIONS

[3.531]

5.1 Relevant merger situations and special merger situations in relation to which an intervention notice specifying a newspaper public interest consideration is served will be assessed by reference to the newspaper public interest considerations specified in that notice.[56]

5.2 The newspaper public interest considerations set out in section 58(2A) and (2B) Enterprise Act 2002 encompass the public interest in the need for:

- accurate presentation of the news in newspapers;
- free expression of opinion in newspapers; and
- to the extent reasonable and practicable, a sufficient plurality of views in newspapers in each market for newspapers in the UK or a part of the UK.

5.3 These newspaper public interest considerations are derived from concerns identified in particular cases examined by the CC and MMC under the FTA newspaper merger regime. Under that regime, the CC was required to look at "whether the transfer in question may be expected to operate against the public interest, taking into account all matters which appear in the circumstances to be relevant and, in particular, the need for accurate presentation of the news and free expression of opinion".[57] As explained in paragraph 2.5 above, for the purposes of assessing the newspaper public interest considerations under the Act, the Secretary of State expects there to be considerable continuity between the analysis of cases under the FTA newspaper regime and under the new regime. The following section of this guidance therefore draws out precedents from the treatment of newspaper mergers under the FTA as a guide to how similar cases are likely to be looked at under the new regime. However, although in practice the CC considers its previous relevant cases when making a decision on a matter referred to it, it is not under an obligation to do so and is not bound by precedent.

5.4 Of the 50 newspaper cases referred to it since 1973 under the FTA special newspaper merger regime, the CC[58] has made adverse findings (in relation to all or part of the transfers in question), in ten published reports.[59] Of these, editorial issues relating to free expression of opinion and the accurate presentation of news were relevant to five decisions. Further details of the way in which these tests have been applied in practice in the past are set out below.

ACCURATE PRESENTATION OF THE NEWS

5.5 The impact of a relevant merger situation on accurate presentation of the news is likely to be assessed by reference to evidence of past behaviour by the enterprises in question, or by the persons with control of such enterprises, in relation to that or other enterprises, including but not limited to newspapers. However, the Secretary of State expects that behaviour in sectors more closely related to newspapers, such as magazines, is likely to be more relevant than behaviour in sectors with a less direct connection.

5.6 In the 1990 case of David Sullivan and the Bristol Evening Post the MMC concluded that evidence of David Sullivan's connection with the Daily Star (plus his holdings in the Sport and the Sunday Sport) suggested that he would seek to influence editorial policy and the character and content of the newspapers in a manner which would harm both the accurate presentation of news and the free expression of opinion.

FREE EXPRESSION OF OPINION

5.7 In considering the impact of a newspaper merger on free expression of opinion, the CC (and before it the MMC) has focused on the potential impact on editorial decision-making of the transfer of newspapers in question ie the extent to which the transaction would affect the freedom of editors to operate without interference from the proprietor.

5.8 The CC (and before it the MMC) has generally been of the view that to maintain or increase circulation, regional or local newspapers must reflect the views and concerns of readers in their area, and that local editors are best placed to judge this.[60] Market forces therefore tend to ensure a significant degree of independence for local editors, whether the owner is a national publisher or a local publisher. However, there are exceptional cases – for example the Sullivan case referred to above – where the CC has been of the view that these forces were insufficient to prevent a newspaper proprietor from seeking to influence editorial policy.

5.9 Similarly, in George Outram & Company Ltd/The Observer (June 1981) the MMC recommended that conditions be attached to the Secretary of State's consent to safeguard editorial independence against a potential conflict of interest arising out of the extensive business interests of Lonrho (the parent company of the purchaser George Outram & Company Ltd).

5.10 Issues of editorial interference were also examined in the CC report on Johnston Press plc/Trinity Mirror plc (May 2002), where an allegation of editorial interference was raised part way through the reference and was investigated by the CC. Although the concern was ultimately not upheld (the partial block was on the basis of competition concerns) paragraphs 2.122–2.136 of the CC's report on that case describe the manner in which it conducted this aspect of the inquiry and illustrate how they concluded whether there was evidence of editorial interference rather than normal management issues and relationships.

PLURALITY OF VIEWS

5.11 The concept of "a sufficient plurality of views" is in the Secretary of State's view intended to encompass the need for a diversity of viewpoints exhibited in the relevant sector of the press. In particular, it allows consideration of the structural impact of a transaction on the overall range of views and distribution of voice within the relevant market. The test of a sufficient plurality of views is intended to enable regard to be had not only to the need for a sufficient number of views to be expressed, but also to the need for variety in those views and for there to be a variety of outlets and publications in which they can be expressed. There is a qualitative element to the plurality assessment that requires account to be taken of the context in which titles circulate and the nature of those titles – for example, one title in a particular area may be of greater significance for plurality purposes than another.

5.12 The plurality consideration in section 58(2B) of the Act is qualified by the reference to reasonableness and practicability. In the Secretary of State's view, this reflects the fact that although plurality of views in each and every market us the ideal goal of the regime, it may not be reasonable to require this in relation to a particular part of the market, for example because of associated costs. Moreover the level of plurality of views that may be considered reasonable in a large urban area may differ from the level practicable in a small rural community. In making this assessment the Secretary of State expects to take into account all relevant circumstances, for example the size and nature of the relevant area, and the extent to which other newspapers in the same area contribute to the level of plurality of views.

5.13 The plurality newspaper public interest consideration is aimed at identifying issues such as those arising in the MMC's report on the proposed merger of Century Newspapers and TRN (April 1989). In that case, the merged entity would have owned both the *News Letter* (a publication with a strong Unionist emphasis) and the *Belfast Telegraph* (which also expressed Protestant views but was considered to be a more middle of the road publication read by both Protestants and Roman Catholics). Consent was refused by the then Secretary of State as the merger would lead to the *News Letter* joining the *Belfast Telegraph* in the middle ground, leading to a loss of a distinctive viewpoint in representing Unionist opinion in Northern Ireland.

5.14 Similar concerns were raised in the context of the merger of the CC's report on Trinity plc/Mirror Group plc and Regional Independent Media Holdings Ltd/Mirror Group plc (July 1999). In relation to the proposed acquisition of Mirror plc by Trinity plc, the CC was concerned that the common ownership of two Northern Irish publications with a unionist stance was likely to lead to convergence in the perspectives of the two papers and the loss of a distinctive voice in representing unionist opinion. The CC recommended that the two newspapers should remain in separate ownership, so that the existing distinctness of view and opinion would be maintained. The then Secretary of State accepted this but also considered that the transfer would damage the ability of the *Irish News* (the Roman Catholic title) to generate advertising revenue, which would threaten the viability of that title and the expression of a Roman Catholic viewpoint in the press.[61] The then Secretary of State's consent to the transfer merger was conditional on the disposal of certain titles in Northern Ireland, including the *Belfast Telegraph*.

5.15 Whilst plurality concerns may be more likely to arise in relation to mergers between existing newspaper proprietors, when assessing the impact of a merger on the newspaper public interest considerations it is not intended to replicate or import aspects of the substantial lessening of competition test that applies in relation to mergers raising competition concerns. This test will be applied separately by the competition authorities, where appropriate. An example of concerns regarding the impact of consolidation on the need for a plurality of views in newspapers in the UK can be seen in the MMC's report on the proposed acquisition by Daily Mail & General Trust of *Nottingham Evening Post*.[62] In that case, the CC concluded that the increase in regional concentration of ownership could be expected to pose a risk to the maintenance of diversity of opinion in the region and would in turn jeopardize accurate presentation of news and free expression of opinion.

NOTES

56 A special intervention notice may only specify public interest considerations that have been approved by Parliament and are set out in section 58 of the Enterprise Act 2002 at the time of intervention.

57 Section 59(3) Fair Trading Act 1973.

58 The CC replaced the Monopolies and Mergers Commission with effect from 1 April 1999.

59 Bristol United Press/West Somerset Free Press (April 1980); Reed International/Berrows Organisation (April 1981); George Outram & Company Ltd/The Observer (June 1981); TR Beckett Ltd/EMAP plc (February 1989); Century Newspapers/TRN (April 1989); Bristol Evening Post/David Sullivan (May 1990); DMGT/T Bailey Forman Ltd (October 1994); Trinity plc/Mirror Group plc (March 1999); Johnston Press/Trinity Mirror (May 2002); Newsquest (London)Ltd/Independent News and Media (October 2003). Note that conditions were also attached to the consent for transfer of The Times and the Sunday Times to News International in 1981, without a reference to the MMC.

60 See paragraph 2.22 of the Trinity/Mirror Group/ Regional Independent Media Holdings Competition Commission report.

61 The CC considered this issue but did not believe that the risk was likely to materialise. The Secretary of State disagreed with this. Unlike the general merger regime, under the FTA special newspaper merger regime the Secretary of State was not bound by the findings of the CC as to whether or not the merger would operate against the public interest. This remains the case under the public interest merger process set out in the Enterprise Act 2002 where the final decision on whether a merger gives rise to public interest issues rests with the Secretary of State.

62 DMGT/T Bailey Forman Ltd (October 1994).

SECTION 6
POLICY ON INTERVENTION IN NEWSPAPER PUBLIC INTEREST CASES

[3.532]

6.1 The approach the Secretary of State will take in deciding whether or not to intervene in a particular case will develop in the light of experience in operating the new newspaper public interest merger regime.

This is not an area suited to generalisation; each case will need to be considered on its own facts and merits. However, the Secretary of State can give some indications of the general approach she expects to adopt.

6.2 The initial decision to intervene will inevitably be taken when only basic information is known about a given transaction. It will be informed by general knowledge and experience as to the types of transaction that can raise newspaper public interest concerns and any third party comments that may be available. OFCOM will not have an advisory role at this stage, but will be obliged to provide any relevant information the Secretary of State may need to reach her decision. The Secretary of State will also have regard to the intention that the new regime should be no more burdensome than necessary.

6.3 The rationale for having a special regime to deal with public interest considerations arising in the context of newspaper mergers is that historically there have been a small number of cases that have raised issues beyond those that would be considered as part of a competition assessment. Such cases have generally been fairly easily identifiable from the outset: – the contentious acquirer (eg David Sullivan's proposed acquisition of the *Bristol Evening Post*), the contentious case involving national newspapers (*The Times, The Observer*) or cases involving areas of particular cultural or political sensitivity (such as the cases involving newspaper titles in Northern Ireland[63]). The small number of cases that have resulted in adverse public interest findings other than on competition grounds under the FTA newspaper merger regime suggests that the number of cases in which the Secretary of State will find it necessary to intervene on the basis of newspaper public interest considerations under the new regime is likely to be small.

6.4 The Secretary of State has considered a range of factors that might be identified in a particular case, and the weight that these should carry in deciding whether or not to intervene. Set out below is a summary of these factors with an indication of the approach that the Secretary of State is currently minded to take. However, this is no more than a preliminary and general analysis that may need to be refined in the light of further experience in operating the regime. It should also be noted that fewer newspaper mergers will be referred to the CC than are initially reported on by OFCOM as a reference would only be made where, having received relevant reports from the OFT and OFCOM, the Secretary of State had concerns regarding the impact of a merger on the newspaper public interest considerations that warranted further investigation.

ACQUISITION OF A NON-NEWSPAPER BUSINESS BY AN EXISTING NEWSPAPER OWNER

6.5 Although this type of transaction may qualify for intervention, that is likely to be extremely rare. Circumstances which may lead the Secretary of State to *consider* intervention in such cases include those where for corporate structuring or tax reasons the form of a transaction does not reflect the reality of the situation (ie the transaction really involves a change of control of a newspaper), or cases where a transaction has unusual features raising particular plurality issues.

THIRD PARTY COMMENTS

6.6 Where a transaction gives rise to a significant volume of adverse third party comments regarding the impact or potential impact of the transaction on newspaper public interest considerations, it may be appropriate to *consider* intervention. However, the specificity of the concerns raised in such cases and evidence in support of the concerns will be significant factors. Intervention is more likely where comments are received raising and substantiating a *specific* newspaper public interest concern.

NEWSPAPER TO NEWSPAPER MERGERS

6.7 The likelihood of intervention in a newspaper to newspaper merger will depend upon the identity of the parties and the extent and nature of any overlaps between their newspaper activities (although the competition effects of the merger can be examined by the OFT if the standard jurisdictional tests are satisfied). However, there is a recognisable correlation between high levels of concentration and the potential for newspaper ownership concerns to arise. Thus, where a merger leads to market overlaps (eg a merger of two newspapers in the same market, in neighbouring markets, or within a cluster) it may be appropriate for the Secretary of State to *consider* in more detail whether newspaper ownership concerns may arise. Whilst no firm indication can be given regarding the level of consolidation that might in itself lead to intervention by the Secretary of State to protect the newspaper public interest considerations, such intervention is likely in local newspaper transfers at a threshold above the level at which a potential competition issue would commonly be identified. However, for a transfer of a national newspaper to another newspaper proprietor, intervention may be appropriate at a lower threshold, depending on a number of factors including how the market may be defined for competition purposes.

ACQUISITIONS OF NEWSPAPERS BY PERSONS WITH EXISTING INTERESTS IN OTHER (NON-NEWSPAPER) MEDIA

6.8 The mere fact that a newspaper would come into common ownership with other media in the relevant area is not of itself an issue for the purposes of the newspaper public interest considerations. Nonetheless, there are circumstances in which the fact that a newspaper would become part of a group with other media interests in the same geographic market as the newspaper in question might be a relevant factor in assessing the impact of the transaction on the newspaper public interest considerations (for example, this may provide an indication of the likely editorial policy of the new owner in relation to newspapers). Where such geographic cross media overlaps occur, and the newspaper in question has a significant market share, the Secretary of State may wish to *consider* whether the transaction potentially gives rise to newspaper public interest concerns that would merit intervention.

6.9 In such cases, it is possible that the broadcasting and cross-media public interest considerations set out in section 58(2C) of the Act may also be relevant.

ACQUISITIONS BY PERSONS WITH NO EXISTING NEWSPAPER INTERESTS

6.10 Such acquisitions are only likely to raise newspaper public interest concerns in exceptional circumstances where the identity of the acquirer gives rise to concerns (as was the case in relation to the proposed acquisition of *Bristol Evening Post* by David Sullivan in 1990, although in that case Mr Sullivan did have existing newspaper interests) or where the acquirer is already present in other media in the same geographic area as the newspaper(s) in question (see above). However, in the absence of a significant volume of third party comments raising newspaper public interest concerns, or evidence of previous conduct that gives rise to such concerns (such as editorial interference in a periodical that is not a newspaper for the purposes of the newspaper public interest regime), the Secretary of State is unlikely to intervene in relation to acquisitions of local newspapers by persons with no existing newspaper interests. Where a national newspaper is being acquired, the same circumstances – the contentious acquirer, or the acquirer's presence in other media in the same geographic area – may well give rise to concerns, and might lead to intervention, even in the absence of a significant volume of third party comments.

NOTES

[63] Century Newspapers/TRN (April 1989), Trinity plc/Mirror Group plc and Regional Independent Media Holdings Ltd/Mirror Group plc (July 1999).

SECTION 7
SCOPE OF THE BROADCASTING AND CROSS-MEDIA PUBLIC INTEREST CONSIDERATIONS

[3.533]

7.1 The broadcasting and cross-media public interest considerations specified in section 58(2C) of the Act are:

- the need, in relation to every different audience in the UK, or in a particular area or locality of the UK, for there to be a sufficient plurality of persons with control of media enterprises serving that audience;
- the need for the availability throughout the UK of a wide range of broadcasting which (taken as a whole) is both of high quality and calculated to appeal to a wide variety of tastes and interests; and
- the need for persons carrying on media enterprises, and for those with control of such enterprises, to have a genuine commitment to the attainment in relation to broadcasting of the standards objectives set out in section 319 of the Communications Act 2003.

7.2 For these purposes, a media enterprise is an enterprise consisting of or involved in broadcasting. However, where a relevant merger situation or special merger situation involves both a broadcast media enterprise and a newspaper enterprise, the newspaper enterprise is also considered to be a media enterprise for the purposes of the plurality public interest consideration specified in section 58(2C)(a) (that is the first consideration above). Thus plurality can be considered across a wide range of newspaper and media audiences, which may include readership, and shares held by an enterprise through ownership of broadcasting and newspaper enterprises may be aggregated for the purpose of making the assessment of sufficiency of plurality. Considerations of range and quality, and of standards specified in 58(2C)(b) and (c), relate to broadcasting only. However, in considering how such a merger may impact on the range and quality, or the standards, of UK broadcasting, the Secretary of State considers it is reasonable to have regard to any relevant information as to the track record both of the enterprise seeking to acquire a broadcaster and of those who control it. In particular, where a relevant merger or special merger situation involves a broadcast media enterprise and a newspaper enterprise, she may look at any relevant information as to how either the broadcasting or newspaper enterprise have run their affairs. Examples of information that may be relevant are given later on in this guidance.

7.3 These media public interest considerations invoked by the Secretary of State are distinct from the competition-based test applied by the competition authorities. The aim of this competition analysis is to prevent a level of concentration of ownership which could give rise to a substantial lessening of competition. However, there is a recognisable overlap between this competition assessment and at least the first of the broadcasting and cross-media public interest considerations, which posits the need for there to be a sufficient plurality of persons controlling media enterprises.

7.4 Although she will remain conscious of the distinctions between the competition and the public interest regimes, the Secretary of State anticipates that in some cases she may take the view that action to safeguard competition in a market will by itself be likely to provide a sufficient plurality of control. Such a view would be unlikely to be taken in cross-media mergers if the competition authorities considered that advertising in newspapers and in the broadcast media did not represent a sufficient competitive restraint on each other – that is, they are not in the same market.

7.5 This view of the relationship between competition control and the public interest regime may also inform the Secretary of State's exercise of her powers of intervention (for more details of which see the following section). At that point, however, information on the approach of the competition authorities to the relevant markets may be limited, so the Secretary or State may err on the side of caution in deciding to issue an intervention notice where the definition of the relevant markets are unclear.

7.6 The Secretary of State recognizes that, in applying the broadcasting and cross-media public interest considerations, it will be necessary to analyse and consider all the relevant circumstances at the time, on a case-by-case basis. Analysis of these considerations is different from the economic analysis of competition issues, notwithstanding the overlap mentioned above. Nevertheless, the Secretary of State will expect OFCOM's report following an intervention notice, the role of which is explained in paragraphs 4.10–11 above, to be evidence based, to reflect market research and to take account of stakeholders' views. The Secretary of State will then take this report, together with the OFT's report on the competition issues, into account in deciding whether to refer the particular media merger to the CC.

PLURALITY OF PERSONS WITH CONTROL OF MEDIA ENTERPRISES

7.7 The first of the broadcasting and cross-media public interest considerations set out in section 58(2C) refers to the need for a sufficient plurality of persons with control of media enterprises serving the same audience in any given area of the UK. This public interest consideration is concerned primarily with ensuring that control of media enterprises is not overly concentrated in the hands of a limited number of persons. It would be a concern for any one person to control too much of the media because of their ability to influence opinions and control the agenda. This broadcasting and cross-media public interest consideration, therefore, is intended to prevent unacceptable levels of media and cross-media dominance and ensure a minimum level of plurality.

7.8 In considering the impact of a merger on this consideration, the Secretary of State may assess the effect of the merger on a range of factors.

7.9 First and foremost, the Secretary of State may consider the impact of the merger on the number of persons controlling media enterprises serving the relevant audiences in any given area of the UK, with the object of securing that control of media enterprises continues to be spread across a sufficient number of persons. When assessing the number of persons controlling media enterprises post-merger, it would be relevant to take into account the number of other players serving that audience. This would include BBC and the Welsh Authority, where relevant, as well as owners of broadcasters established abroad and broadcasting into the UK under European Union licences.

7.10 However, bare numbers may not tell the whole story. It might be relevant to consider the audience shares of the media enterprises brought under common control by the merger and the audience shares of other media enterprises. This is because the Secretary of State considers that what constitutes a sufficient number of owners controlling media enterprises in a given case may be affected by the relative audience shares that these enterprises hold. Audience shares can be assessed in relation to every different audience in the UK or locality of the UK served by these media enterprises. In assessing audience shares, it might also be relevant to consider the audience shares of other players serving the same audience.

7.11 Thus, the Secretary of State considers that sufficient plurality in this context refers to the number of persons controlling media enterprises, taking into account as appropriate relative audience shares. The Secretary of State will assess whether there is likely to be a significant reduction in plurality in relation to any relevant audience as a result of the merger.

7.12 For these purposes, the Secretary of State may define an audience in relation to a media enterprise in the manner she considers appropriate. In particular, she can define an audience: as any one of the audiences served by that enterprise, taking them separately; as all of the audiences served by that enterprise, taking them together; as a number of those audiences taken together in such group as the Secretary of State considers appropriate; or as any part of any of these audiences.[64] This enables the Secretary of State to treat different audiences as separate or group them together. The audience could, therefore, include cross media coverage and could include newspaper readership.[65] The criteria for deciding the composition of an audience shall be such as the Secretary of State considers appropriate and may include potential members of that audience.[66]

7.13 When assessing plurality, where a merger situation (ie a relevant merger situation or a special merger situation) involves two media enterprises serving the same audience as defined by the Secretary of State, then there is deemed to be a reduction in the number of media enterprises serving that audience for the purposes of the plurality assessment in subsection (2C).[67] All such mergers, including those involving an increase in levels of control of such media enterprises, may be examined for the purposes of subsection (2C). This means that the Secretary of State can assess whether, as a result of the merger, there will still be a sufficient plurality of persons with control of enterprises serving the relevant audience even though the number of enterprises serving that audience may be unchanged.

7.14 Where a number of media enterprises would fall to be treated as under common ownership or common control for the purposes of section 26 of the Act,[68] they are treated as being controlled by one person for the purpose of determining whether there is sufficient plurality of control of media enterprises.[69] This is because in assessing the effect of a merger on the sufficiency of plurality of persons with control of media enterprises, the Secretary of State needs to assess the total number of persons with control of media enterprises and what effect the merger will have on the plurality of media as a whole. Apart from the merging media enterprises, when looking across the spectrum to assess who has control of the remaining media enterprises, it is important to be able to look not just at the owners of those entities, but the controllers of those entities to get an accurate picture in relation to plurality in order to carry out the assessment relating to sufficiency of plurality.

7.15 A person can have common control over two or more enterprises under section 26 of the Act if, in respect of each of the enterprises, he (amongst other things) owns the enterprise; he has a controlling interest in the enterprise (ie more than 50% of the voting rights); he has control of the policy of the enterprise; or he has material influence over the policy of the enterprise.

7.16 When determining whether enterprises are under common control for the purposes of section 58(2C) of the Act, associated persons are treated as one person.[70] This provision enables interests held by family members, business partners etc to be aggregated.[71]

RANGE OF BROADCASTING

7.17 The second of the broadcasting and cross-media public interest considerations specified in section 58(2C) relates to the impact of a merger on broadcasting content in the UK. It refers to the need for the availability, throughout the UK, of a wide range of television and radio services which (taken as a whole) are both of high quality and calculated to appeal to a variety of tastes and interests.

7.18 This consideration is concerned with safeguarding the quality and range of broadcasting when mergers take place in order to ensure a diversity of programming and protect the interests of viewers and listeners. Assessment of whether a particular merger will reduce the range and quality of broadcasting in the UK may take into account a range of factors.

7.19 It might involve an assessment of the impact of the merger on the availability of broadcasting services which secure programmes dealing with a wide range of subject matters; which are likely to meet the needs and satisfy the interests of as many different audiences as practicable; which are properly balanced in nature and subject matter for meeting the needs and satisfying the interests of the available audiences; and which maintain high general standards with respect to the contents of the programmes included in them, the quality of the programme making and the professional skill and editorial integrity applied in the making of the programmes.[72] The primary focus of the test will be on an assessment of future plans of the acquirer. The media owner's plans for the broadcasting enterprise, including proposals for programme origination, programme content, genre or style of programming, as well as the overall innovation and ambition of the media owner's plans might all be considered relevant.

7.20 In making this assessment, the Secretary of State may nevertheless also wish to take into account the media owner's past compliance with requirements on his other broadcasting enterprises to deliver a sufficient range and/or quality of broadcasting services in the UK. For example, she might consider compliance with qualitative public service broadcasting rules and radio format or localness obligations where relevant. The assessment might also include the media owner's record in respect of more quantitative obligations such as independent origination and European quotas. In particular, the media owner's past compliance with programme origination obligations might be relevant. All other material factors will also be taken into consideration.

COMMITMENT TO THE BROADCASTING STANDARDS OBJECTIVES

7.21 The third broadcasting and cross-media public interest consideration specified in section 58(2C) refers to the need for those carrying on media enterprises and those with control of such enterprises to have a genuine commitment to the broadcasting standards objectives set out in the Communications Act 2003. Under that Act OFCOM is required to secure the application, in the case of all television and radio services, of standards that provide adequate protection to members of the public.

7.22 In the Secretary of State's view, the intention behind this consideration is to assess whether persons controlling or carrying on media enterprises post-merger are likely to comply with the spirit as well as the letter of the broadcasting standards set down in the Communications Act 2003. These standards objectives relate to the protection of minors; the prohibition of material likely to encourage crime or disorder; the due impartiality and accuracy of television and radio news services, and impartiality requirements more generally; the exercise of responsibility with respect to the content of religious programmes; the protection of the public from offensive and harmful material; the exclusion of prohibited political advertising; the prevention of misleading, harmful or offensive advertising and unsuitable sponsorship; the fulfilment of the international obligations of the United Kingdom in respect of broadcast advertising; the prevention of undue discrimination between advertisers; and the prohibition of broadcasts of subliminal material.[73]

7.23 In considering the effect of a merger on the genuine commitment to broadcasting standards of those controlling or carrying on media enterprises, the Secretary of State may take into account a range of factors. They include the following.

7.24 First and foremost, the Secretary of State will consider the likelihood that there will be a genuine commitment to broadcast standards by the person or persons who will control the merged media enterprise. The Secretary of State may wish to consider the past compliance of any other broadcasting enterprises controlled by this media owner with broadcasting standards in the UK; an assessment of this would be qualitative rather than focusing simply on the question of how many infringements, however minor, may have occurred. The media owner's previous compliance with OFCOM's broadcasting standards might therefore be relevant. In particular, it might be appropriate to consider the due impartiality and accuracy of news offered by the media owner's other broadcasting enterprises. Evidence of breaches of UK broadcasting standards may be taken into account. Another factor relevant to the acquiring media owner's commitment to standards objectives might be the compliance of any other broadcasting enterprises it controls with broadcasting standards in other geographic regions or jurisdictions. This may add usefully to the overall assessment of the extent to which an enterprise is truly committed to broadcasting standards, wherever it operates. Similarly, the record of any non-broadcasting media enterprise's compliance with standards applicable to those media enterprises might also be considered, as adding to the overall assessment of an enterprise's commitment to standards in markets where it operates. This would include standards imposed under self-regulatory regimes.

7.25 All other material factors will also be taken into account. This might include comments, statements and any other plans made by the acquiring media owner which give an indication as to its commitment to UK broadcasting standards post-merger.

NOTES

[64] Section 58A(6) Enterprise Act 2002.

[65] Section 59A(8) Enterprise Act 2002.

66 Section 58(A)(7) Enterprise Act 2002
67 Section 58A(4) Enterprise Act 2002
68 See OFT publication "*Merger: Substantive Assessment Guidance*" (May 2003) paragraphs 2.6 to 2.12.
69 Section 58A(5).
70 Section 127(1)(aa) Enterprise Act 2002.
71 See OFT publication "*Mergers: Substantive Assessment Guidance*" (May 2003) paragraphs 2.16 and 2.17.
72 cf section 264(4), Communications Act 2003.
73 Section 319(2) Communications Act 2003.

SECTION 8
POLICY ON INTERVENTION IN BROADCASTING AND CROSS-MEDIA PUBLIC INTEREST CASES

[3.534]

8.1 In principle, the Secretary of State may intervene in any relevant or special merger situations involving media enterprises, including cross media mergers, where she believes that the broadcasting and cross-media public interest considerations are relevant.

8.2 The Secretary of State's policy is that, save in exceptional circumstances, she will consider intervention only in cases where media ownership rules have been removed by the Communications Act 2003. These are:

- mergers involving national newspapers with more than 20% of the market and the Channel 5 licence holder;
- mergers involving national newspapers with more than 20% of the market and a national radio service;
- mergers involving a change in control of one or more Channel 3 licences such that the acquirer would control licences accounting for an audience share of greater than 15% (though such acquisitions are less likely to raise concerns where the acquirer is already an existing ITV licence holder in view of ITV's proven track record as a public service broadcaster);
- mergers involving two Channel 3 licences for the same area;
- mergers involving a Channel 3 licence holder and the Channel 5 licence holder;
- mergers involving the national ITV licence holder and the Channel 5 licence holder;
- mergers involving the national Channel 3 licence holder and a national radio service;
- mergers involving the Channel 5 licence holder and a national radio service;
- mergers involving two or more national radio services;
- mergers involving owners from outside the European Economic Area (except where prior to the Communications Act 2003 there were no restrictions on non-European Economic Area ownership).

8.3 If some of the remaining restrictions on media ownership were to be lifted in future, the Secretary of State would expect to consider intervention in these areas as well.

8.4 In addition, the Secretary of State's policy is that, save in exceptional circumstances, she will not intervene in respect of mergers in areas where there are no media ownership restrictions and none were removed by the Communications Act 2003 (eg mergers involving satellite and cable television and radio services).

8.5 In relation to areas where there continue to be media ownership rules, the Secretary of State's policy is as follows.

8.6 For media owners within the European Economic Area, it would not normally be sensible or desirable to intervene on the grounds of the broadcasting and cross-media public interest considerations since the continuing rules will protect plurality (eg ownership of local sound broadcasting licences).

8.7 However, for media owners from outside the European Economic Area, the Secretary of State believes it would be sensible to consider intervening on the grounds of the broadcasting and cross-media public interest considerations, even where media ownership rules continue to apply, since foreign media ownership rules have now been removed completely.

8.8 In exceptional circumstances, the Secretary of State may consider it necessary to intervene in mergers in areas where there continue to be media ownership rules or where there have never been such rules. The Secretary of State will only consider intervening in such a merger where she believes that it may give rise to serious public interest concerns in relation to any of the three considerations. During Parliamentary debate of these provisions, Ministers suggested that these might include circumstances where a large number of news or educational channels would be coming under single control, or if someone were to take over all the music channels. The Secretary of State may consider intervention if a prospective new entrant to local radio ownership has not shown a genuine commitment to broadcasting standards in other media or countries. The Secretary of State is not currently aware of any other types of cases in which exceptional circumstances might arise. She has also taken the view that an adverse public interest finding by a previous regulatory authority into a proposed merger is not necessarily in itself an exceptional circumstance meriting intervention; such cases should be considered in light of the reasons for the adverse finding and if the law has been changed to allow the sort of concentration resulting from the merger.

SECTION 9
ENFORCEMENT

[3.535]

9.1 Under the FTA newspaper merger regime, the primary means of enforcement was through the requirement for prior consent, with criminal sanctions and nullity of the transaction applying in the event of a breach. With the removal of pre-notification requirements and criminal sanctions, more extensive provision has been made in relation to remedies and enforcement powers in relation to the newspaper mergers. However, for the most part, the enforcement powers of the Secretary of State in relation to media public interest cases mirror the powers of the decision-making authority in relation to the mainstream merger regime.

INTERIM MEASURES

9.2 The OFT and the Secretary of State have interim powers that are intended to ensure that the effectiveness of a reference or subsequent remedies is not prejudiced by action taken by the parties in the period of consideration of a merger.[74]

FINAL MEASURES

9.3 Where the Secretary of State has made an adverse public interest finding, the final decision on remedies will be hers, although the CC must make recommendations in its report where it has decided that the merger operates, or may be expected to operate against the public interest,[75] and OFCOM may also give advice to the Secretary of State.[76]

9.4 The powers that will be available to the Secretary of State in the event of an adverse public interest finding are essentially equivalent to those applying to the mainstream Enterprise Act 2002 merger regime.[77] However, remedies to an adverse finding on the basis of a newspaper public interest consideration, or a broadcasting and cross-media public interest consideration in the case of cross media mergers involving newspapers, may be different in character to the remedies directed at competition detriments with which the Act provisions are principally concerned. As a result, specific provision has been made to allow all remedies that have been considered appropriate in the past in cases involving newspapers to continue to be used in the future.[78] The non-exhaustive list of such remedies[79] includes provisions:

- altering the constitution of a body corporate (whether in connection with the appointment of directors, the establishment of an editorial board or otherwise);
- requiring the agreement of the Secretary of State before the taking of a particular action (including the appointment or dismissal of an editor, journalist or directors or acting as a shadow director);
- attaching conditions to the operation of a newspaper;
- prohibiting consultation or co-operation between subsidiaries.

APPEALS

9.5 Any person aggrieved by a decision of the Secretary of State in relation to a merger raising a media public interest consideration may appeal to the Competition Appeal Tribunal, which must apply the same principles as would be applied by a court on an application for judicial review.[80]

NOTES

74 Paragraph 2, Schedule 7 Enterprise Act 2002.

75 Section 47(7) Enterprise Act 2002.

76 Section 106B(1) Enterprise Act 2002.

77 See Schedule 8 to the Enterprise Act 2002.

78 See for example the conditions imposed on the consent given following the 1994 DMGT plc/T Bailey Forman Ltd Report (P/94/730, 5 December, 1994). See also the press release P/2002/203 of 28 March 2002 announcing the revocation of all but one of the conditions. The provisions relating to the editorial board were retained.

79 See Paragraph 20A(4) of Schedule 8 to the Enterprise Act 2002.

80 Section 120 Enterprise Act 2002.

SECTION 10
TRANSITIONAL PROVISIONS FOR NEWSPAPER MERGERS

[3.536]

10.1 The newspaper merger provisions of the Act, introduced by the Communications Act 2003, came into force on 29th December 2003. The transitional arrangements that will apply to newspaper mergers are set out in paragraphs 59 to 62 of Schedule 18 to that Act.

10.2 Paragraph 59 provides that the new provisions will not apply to any transfer of a newspaper or of newspaper assets that has already taken place as at the commencement date of these provisions.

10.3 Paragraph 62 sets out provisions applying to conditional consents that have been given under the FTA. Existing consents are unaffected and will continue in effect as consents given under the FTA. However, where these consents have conditions attached to them, such that the party concerned is subject to ongoing obligations, paragraph 62 provides that the Secretary of State may accept undertakings in lieu of the conditions on the consent. Acceptance of an undertaking will be at the Secretary of State's discretion but, if accepted, any such undertaking would then be treated as equivalent to an undertaking given to the Secretary of State in a public interest case under the Act. Such undertakings could relate to competition or to general public interest obligations or both and so in deciding whether to accept such undertakings the Secretary of State can, in particular, consult with the OFT or OFCOM or both.

SECTION 11
EC MERGER REGULATION

[3.537]

11.1 The assessment of the competition aspects of large international mergers which satisfy certain jurisdictional criteria falls to be considered by the European Commission's Competition Directorate under the EC Merger Regulation.[81] In any such qualifying case involving newspapers or broadcast media enterprises, therefore, the competition assessment would be made by the European Commission, rather than by the UK competition authorities under the merger provisions of the Act. However, Member States may take appropriate measures to protect their legitimate interests, including plurality of the media,[82] and accordingly the public interest merger regime set out in the Act may still apply in relation to the assessment of the impact of such transactions on the media public interest considerations.[83]

11.2 A European intervention notice may be issued by the Secretary of State if the merger meets the standard jurisdictional thresholds and she believes that a specified public interest consideration is relevant to the case.[84]

11.3 If a European intervention notice is issued citing a media public interest consideration the competition aspects of the case remain with the European Commission, but OFCOM will report to the Secretary of State on the relevant media public interest consideration and OFT on jurisdiction[85] within the time period specified by the Secretary of State. The Secretary of State can only refer the merger to the CC, or seek undertakings in lieu of reference, on public interest grounds.

11.4 The Secretary of State may issue a European intervention notice where the case has been referred to the European Commission under article 4(5) of the EC Merger Regulation. If there is no relevant merger situation, and the case falls to the EC Merger Regulation, the Secretary of State may nevertheless issue a special intervention notice if the relevant jurisdictional criteria are satisfied; again, the Secretary of State does not receive a report on the competition aspects of the case, which remain with the European Commission.

11.5 In deciding whether to intervene on media public interest grounds in a case which falls to the European Commission the Secretary of State will consider the factors set out in the section "Intervention by the Secretary of State" in Chapter 4 above. She will aim to take an initial decision on intervention in the timescale set out in chapter 4.

11.6 In certain circumstances the OFT can seek the repatriation of the competition aspects of a case, using Article 9 of the EC Merger Regulation[86] and the parties to the merger may also ask for the merger to be considered domestically notwithstanding the fact that it falls to the EC Merger Regulation, under article 4(4) of that Regulation. If an article 9 or 4(4) request is successful, the OFT will be carry out the competition assessment under the Act.

11.7 If a European intervention notice is in force in a case where an article 9 or 4(4) request is successful, it will no longer be applicable (as a reference under either section 22 or 33 of the Enterprise Act is now possible).[87] The Secretary of State would then be able to issue an intervention notice which would trigger a competition and public interest report.

11.8 If the OFT is considering whether to seek repatriation of the case under Article 9 the Secretary of State may consider delaying intervention to avoid issuing both a European intervention notice and an intervention notice on the same case.

11.9 If the case has been referred back to the UK under article 9 or article 4(4) and an intervention notice is in force the Secretary of State will decide whether to make a reference or seek or accept undertakings in lieu of a reference within 45 European Commission working days.[88]

NOTES

81 Council Regulation 139/2004/EC

82 Article 21(4) Council Regulation 139/2004/EC

83 See in particular section 67 Enterprise Act 2002 and the Enterprise Act 2003 (Protection of Legitimate Interests) Order 2003, as amended by the Enterprise Act 2002 and Media Mergers (Consequential Amendments) Order 2003 which will apply where there is a relevant merger situation.

84 Section 67(1) and (2).

85 See the Enterprise Act 2002 (Protection of Legitimate Interests) Order 2003, as amended.

86 See OFT Publication "*Mergers: Procedural Guidance (May 2003)*" paragraph 9.11

87 Section 67(1)(b) Enterprise Act 2002.

88 See section 46A Enterprise Act 2002, as inserted by the EC Merger Control (Consequential Amendments) Regulations 2004.

ANNEX A
PUBLIC INTEREST INTERVENTION ON MEDIA PUBLIC INTEREST GROUNDS – PROCESS

[3.538]

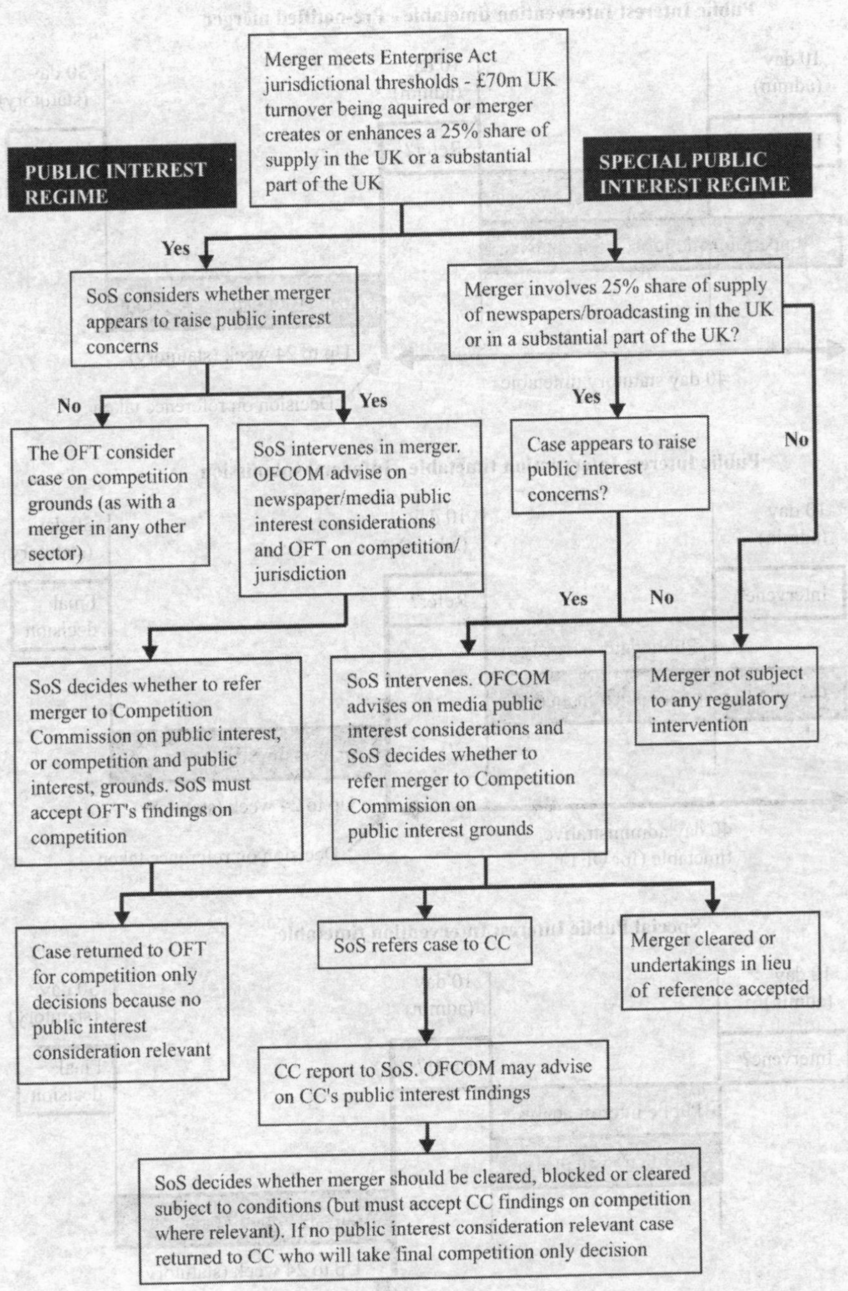

ANNEX B
TIMETABLES FOR INTERVENTION

[3.539]

Public Interest Intervention timetable - Pre-notified merger

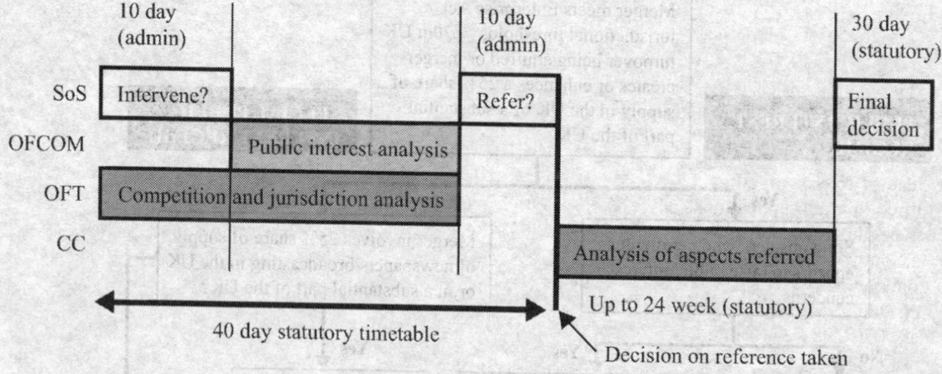

Public Interest Intervention timetable - Informal submission

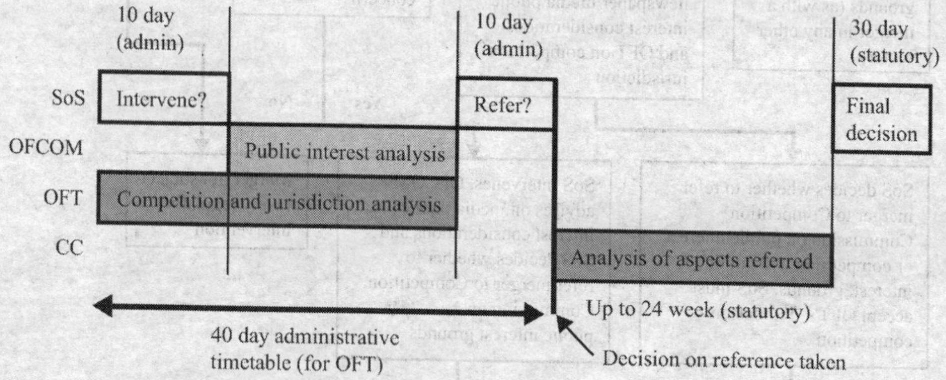

Special Public Interest Intervention timetable

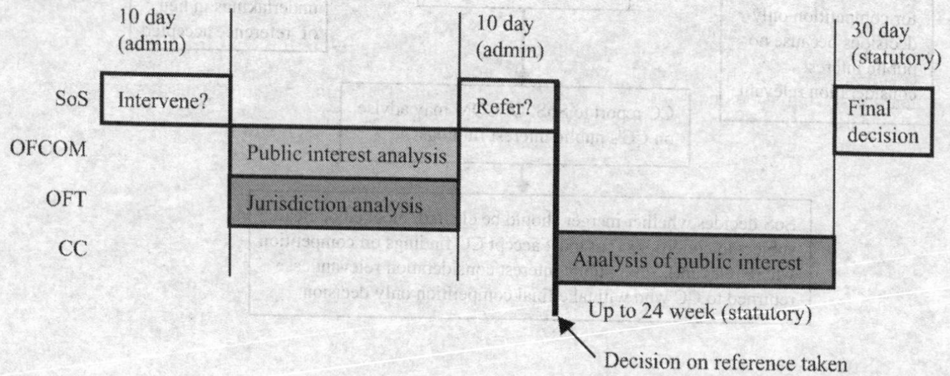

ANNEX C
CONTACT DETAILS

[3.540]
For further information about the media mergers public interest regime, contact:

Consumer and Competition Policy Directorate,
Department of Trade and Industry,
1 Victoria Street
London SW1H 0ET
Tel: 020 7215 6954/5009
Fax: 020 7215 6565
DTI switchboard: 020 7215 5000
www.dti.gov.uk/ccp/topics2/mergers.htm

or

Head of Market Intelligence
Office of Communications
Riverside House
2a Southwark Bridge Road
London SE1 9HA
Tel: 020 7981 3476
Fax: 020 7981 3406
www.ofcom.org.uk/

For ordinary merger inquiries, or to obtain copies of the merger notice form or common notification form, contact:

The Mergers Branch
Office of Fair Trading
Fleetbank House
2-6 Salisbury Square
London EC4Y 8JX
Tel: 020 7211 8915/8917/8918
Fax: 020 7211 8916
OFT switchboard: 020 7211 8000
www.oft.gov.uk

OFCOM: LOCAL MEDIA ASSESSMENT GUIDANCE
(December 2010)

[3.541]

NOTES

BACKGROUND

[3.542]
1. In January 2009 the Government published the Digital Britain Interim Report.[1] It noted the views of local media groups who felt there were strong pressures on them to consolidate in order to make the transition to digital business models.[2] It also noted arguments that the current media merger regime did not take into account the potential for competition across boundaries between newspapers and other media. In response to this, the Digital Britain Interim Report invited the OFT to undertake an exploratory review across the local and regional media sector and to make appropriate recommendations.

2. The OFT's subsequent Review of the Local and Regional Media Merger Regime report[3] was published alongside the Government's Digital Britain Final Report[4] in June 2009. It concluded that the existing merger regime is "flexible and evidence-based", and thus able to take into account the various considerations raised.[5]

3. Similarly, the Government's final Digital Britain Report, published in June 2009, concluded that:

> "*. . . the existing framework provides an adequate mechanism for considering the importance of having a source of independent news and reporting at a local and regional level across the UK.*"[6]

4. Nonetheless, in recognition of the benefit available from Ofcom's knowledge of the media sector, the OFT proposed to amend its merger guidance. This meant that in local media merger cases raising *prima facie* competition concerns, the OFT would ask Ofcom to provide them with a Local Media Assessment (LMA) covering relevant factors arising from Ofcom's understanding of media markets.

5. The OFT's revised Jurisdictional and Procedural Merger Guidance,[7] published in June 2009, confirmed that:

> "*In media mergers involving newspaper publishing and/or commercial radio or television broadcasting, where the case raises prima facie competition concerns, the OFT will ask Ofcom to provide*

Part 3 CMA and other Guidelines

it with a local media assessment in order further to inform the OFT's decisions on the reference test and on the application of any available exceptions to the duty to refer".[8]

6. The OFT's Jurisdictional and Procedural Merger Guidance explains that:

"*. . . Drawing on Ofcom's understanding of media markets, the [local media] assessment would be likely to include Ofcom's views on:*

— *the relevant counterfactual to the merger (including the risk of the asset or business in question failing),*
— *the scope of relevant product and geographic markets,*
— *the competitive effects of the merger, and*
— *exceptions to the duty to refer, and in particular Ofcom's views on whether the markets are of insufficient importance (de minimis) to warrant reference and whether there are 'relevant customer benefits' – such as higher quality (which, in the context of newspapers, could for example reflect the range and quality of news reporting) or greater choice of products – which might be weighed against an identified substantial lessening of competition."*[9]

7. This LMA Guidance sets out the approach that Ofcom intends to take in carrying out an LMA. In particular it covers:

- the objectives of an LMA;
- the circumstances in which Ofcom will carry out an LMA;
- how the timing of the Ofcom LMA will fit into the OFT's merger process and timescales;
- the issues that are likely to be covered by an LMA; and
- arrangements for information sharing.

8. A separate Memorandum of Understanding (MOU) published alongside this LMA Guidance sets out the working arrangements and describes the relationship between Ofcom and the OFT in relation to LMAs.

NOTES

1 Digital Britain Interim Report, www.culture.gov.uk/images/publications/digitalbritain interimreportian09.pdf
2 Digital Britain Interim Report, section 3.3, p. 47
3 OFT: Review of the Local and Regional Media Merger Regime, www.oft.gov.uk/shared oft/mergers ea02/oft1091.pdf
4 Digital Britain Final Report, www.culture.gov.uk/images/publications/digitalbritain-finalreport-jun09.pdf
5 OFT: Review of the Local and Regional Media Merger Regime, paragraph 4.71
6 Digital Britain Final Report, chapter 5, paragraph 71
7 OFT: Mergers – Jurisdictional and Procedural Guidance, www.oft.gov.uk/shared oft/mergers ea02/oft527.pdf
8 OFT: Mergers – Jurisdictional and Procedural Guidance, paragraph 6.15
9 OFT: Mergers – Jurisdictional and Procedural Guidance, paragraph 6.15

THE OBJECTIVES OF AN LMA

[3.543]

9. Media industries have undergone profound changes over recent years and there is no indication that the pace of change is slowing down. While different media sectors are inevitably subject to their own individual pressures, the traditional distinctions between them are beginning to blur. Furthermore, it is important to recognise that media services are generally two-sided, providing services to consumers, and also to advertisers.

10. This has potential implications for whether mergers between local media companies are to be regarded as pro- or anti-competitive. The current merger regime, as the OFT report concluded, is sufficiently flexible to take account of these factors in assessing the impact of a merger on competition.[10] The LMA will provide a means for Ofcom, using its sectoral knowledge, to provide views on these issues to assist the OFT in evaluating mergers.

11. Ofcom's LMAs will not reach binding decisions on the competition impact of a media merger. Ofcom's aim in providing an independent LMA is to assist the OFT in evaluating the relevant merger and reaching its decision on whether to make a reference to the Competition Commission (CC). The final conclusion on all aspects of the competitive analysis (including, for example, the scope of the relevant market) remains one for the OFT, as does the ultimate conclusion on whether the merger creates a realistic prospect of a substantial lessening of competition.

12. The central objective of an LMA is, therefore, that it should add value to the OFT's investigation into a local media merger, by providing additional evidence and argumentation. This added value will come from two sources:

- Ofcom will be in a position to provide an independent view informed by its existing knowledge of the media sector concerned.
- Ofcom will aim to assist the OFT by considering certain arguments that potentially have an important bearing on the OFT's competition assessment.

NOTES

10 OFT: Review of the Local and Regional Media Merger Regime, paragraph 4.71

IN WHAT CIRCUMSTANCES WILL OFCOM CONDUCT AN LMA?

[3.544]

13. The OFT's merger guidance states that the OFT will request an LMA "*where the case raises prima* *facie competition concerns"*.[11] In practice this is likely to mean that an LMA will be requested as soon as the OFT believes that it is appropriate to send an Issues Letter to the parties and to consider the case at a Case Review Meeting (CRM), in line with the OFT's Jurisdictional and Procedural Merger Guidance.[12] The decision to send an Issues Letter is typically communicated to the merging parties by the OFT at the 'state of play' discussion.[13]

14. Ofcom will use its discretion as to whether to commence work on an LMA in respect of a particular local media merger prior to the OFT's formal request. In any event Ofcom will only submit its LMA when it is clear that the LMA is likely to add value to the overall merger process and when the analysis carried out by Ofcom could materially aid the OFT's merger assessment. Ofcom and the OFT will liaise as appropriate in all relevant cases, even where an LMA is not ultimately required.

15. Ofcom will be mindful of the need to use its resources efficiently and of the pressures an LMA may place on stakeholders. These considerations will be an important factor in Ofcom's decision whether or not to commence an LMA.

16. Ofcom will in any event make an initial assessment at an early point as to whether an LMA is likely to provide additional material that might significantly aid the OFT's merger decision in a particular case. This will rely, not just on whether the merger potentially raises any competition concerns, but also on whether the analysis that Ofcom can provide in an LMA has the potential materially to affect the OFT's competition assessment. This will depend, not least, on the merging parties' ability to provide Ofcom with relevant information at a suitably early juncture.

17. An LMA will also not be undertaken when a merger solely involves UK-wide media. There is no generally accepted definition of "local", or indeed "regional" media, and Ofcom will consequently interpret the scope of the LMA broadly to cover any sub-UK media presence.

18. Ofcom may therefore provide an LMA in cases of mergers between local newspapers, radio or television broadcasters, including cross-media mergers. It may also provide an LMA in cases where only one merging party is a local media firm while the other is a UK wide media firm, or any other firm.

NOTES

11 OFT: Mergers – Jurisdictional and procedural guidance, paragraph 6.15
12 OFT: Mergers – Jurisdictional and procedural guidance, paragraph 6.49
13 OFT: Mergers – Jurisdictional and procedural guidance, paragraph 6.8

TIMING OF AN LMA

[3.545]

19. The OFT's *Jurisdictional and procedural merger guidance* distinguishes between its procedures depending on whether notification is made by way of informal submission or statutory merger notice. The OFT's administrative timescales generally allow it 40 working days to reach a decision from the date that it receives a satisfactory submission.[14] The statutory merger procedure provides that an anticipated merger in the public domain must be considered by the OFT within 20 working days, with a maximum extension of 10 working days at the OFT's discretion.[15]

20. Where the merger is notified under the administrative timetable, the OFT aims to hold a "state of play" discussion with the parties between working days 15 and 20, depending on the type of case,[16] at which the OFT will aim to inform the parties whether an Issues Letter will be sent and a CRM is required. The Issues Letter is generally sent soon after the "state of play" discussion.

21. Where the merger is notified under the statutory timetable, the "state of play" discussion will take place between days 10 and 15 of the process. The Issues Letter is generally sent soon after the "state of play" discussion. Given the shorter timescales, the OFT's guidance states that the statutory merger notice procedure is *"most suitable for transactions that do not raise material anticompetitive concerns but where the certainty of regulatory clearance is required within a fixed time period"*.[17]

22. In either event, Ofcom would aim to produce its LMA in time for it to be considered by the OFT in advance of the Issues Letter being sent to the parties. Ofcom would ordinarily not begin working on an LMA before the merger is formally notified. The timing for Ofcom to produce an LMA is therefore potentially very short. Furthermore, it will not be clear whether the OFT is of the view that an Issues Letter (and therefore an LMA) is needed until well into its timescale. The OFT will inform Ofcom of any potentially relevant merger at the earliest opportunity and Ofcom will need to take a view on whether to commence preparing an LMA for a particular merger at the earliest possible juncture. Ofcom will inform the merging parties at the point it will commence working on an LMA

23. An LMA is likely to be required approximately half way through the OFT's merger process. The potential benefits of Ofcom's LMA to the merger process depend on Ofcom's ability to provide additional analysis. This is more likely to be the case if Ofcom is allowed sufficient time. Ofcom therefore encourages parties to engage in discussion ahead of formal notification of the merger. The more this is possible, the more it is likely that an LMA will add value to the overall process. This also implies that for mergers notified by way of a statutory merger notice and in cases where the merging parties choose not to engage in pre-notification discussions with Ofcom, it is less likely that Ofcom would be able to provide an LMA.

NOTES

14 OFT: Mergers – Jurisdictional and procedural guidance, paragraph 4.65
15 OFT: Mergers – Jurisdictional and procedural guidance, paragraph 4.52
16 OFT: Mergers – Jurisdictional and procedural guidance, paragraph 6.8

[17] OFT: Mergers – Jurisdictional and procedural guidance, paragraph 4.54

WHAT WILL AN LMA COVER?

[3.546]

24. Given the objectives of the LMA set out above, Ofcom will focus on the areas that it believes will add value to the OFT's decision making. This is likely to centre on three broad issues:

- the overall sectoral context;
- the competitive constraints acting on the market (or markets);
- the potential for a merger to produce relevant customer benefits, such as an increase in "quality".

25. In line with the objective that an LMA should add value to the OFT's decision-making process, Ofcom is unlikely to need to cover all these issues to a similar extent for all mergers. Rather, it will focus on those areas that have a greater bearing on the OFT's assessment.

26. Similarly, LMAs may vary substantially in terms of the level of attention paid to each set of issues. Ofcom will make an assessment of which issues to focus on, and to what extent, on a case by case basis. In addition, there may be issues, aside from those covered by the broad areas set out above, that Ofcom may decide should be included in a particular LMA.

27. The scope of an LMA will in part be determined by what is feasible in the timescales and given the available information, as set out above. It may be limited by time constraints, especially in cases where the merging parties do not engage in pre-notification with Ofcom before submitting the merger notification and/or where they elect to use a statutory merger notice.

SECTORAL CONTEXT

28. Ofcom will set out a view of the overall context to the merger drawing on its existing knowledge of the relevant sector. It will outline the central trends affecting the sector and relate these to the merger being considered.

29. A central argument behind some local media mergers (in particular local newspapers) has been the need to consolidate to ensure long term financial viability and growth. An LMA will provide Ofcom's view on the sectoral context and will also seek to relate this to the stated rationale for the merger.

30. In particular, the OFT's assessment of the merger is based against a counterfactual situation of what would happen if the merger did not take place. Generally, as set out in the Merger Assessment Guidelines,[18] the OFT will take the pre-merger situation as the best approximation of the counterfactual to a merger. In dynamic sectors, however, as recognised by the OFT, the OFT's competitive assessment may need to take into account the sectoral context.

COMPETITIVE CONSTRAINTS

31. A major issue affecting the assessment of any merger is how widely to define the market. In local media mergers, this is relevant both in the product sense (whether the merging firms experience wider competitive pressures from other products or services that would limit their ability to raise prices after a merger) and in the geographical sense (what is the geographic area over which the market spreads).

32. In respect of product markets, an LMA will examine the extent to which competitive pressure is exerted by other forms of media (e.g. radio on newspapers etc). A key feature in the development of media markets has been the potential for greater substitutability between different media, due in particular to the growth of the internet and its use as a means of advertising.

33. An LMA will, consequently, seek to provide views on whether there are broader competitive constraints from other products that potentially limit the merged entity's ability to raise prices. In doing this, Ofcom will seek to provide views on product substitutability between different forms of media and between different platforms. These will be based on an assessment of generic trends applied to the particular merger under consideration.

34. In a similar way, Ofcom may also provide views on the nature of geographic competition in respect to the particular merger. The issue of geographic market definition will inevitably be specific to the merger in question, depending on which parts of the country the merging companies operate in. Ofcom will seek to provide views on whether competitive pressures from areas outside the geographic market definition initially posited by the OFT can be expected to affect post-merger competition.

RELEVANT CUSTOMER BENEFITS – QUALITY

35. Under the Enterprise Act 2002 section 22(2)(b), 33(2)(c) and 30, where the OFT believes that there are *"relevant customer benefits"* that outweigh the potential substantial lessening of competition concerned and any adverse effects of the substantial lessening of competition, the OFT may exercise its discretion not to refer a merger to the CC. The Enterprise Act 2002 section 30(1) indicates that amongst such customer benefits is the potential for greater innovation and higher quality.

36. An LMA will consider whether potential improvements in quality exist and whether any such benefits might be weighed against the potential customer harm arising from an identified substantial lessening of competition.

37. When a merger takes place, in addition to the benefits accruing to the merging parties, there may be a number of wider benefits that result from the transaction. These benefits can be considered in two broad ways:

- a "public interest" perspective; and
- private consumer benefits.

38. The "public interest" perspective is where "quality" is the level of contribution that the media makes to the life of consumers as democratic citizens. This viewpoint captures the positive externalities and wider social value of media. It would also include issues such as plurality of views and the coverage of democratic proceedings (e.g. local council meetings). A related view of the "quality" of media makes this synonymous with the quantity and depth of "worthwhile" journalism, whether or not this is what consumers would themselves choose if left to their own devices. In economic terms, quality in this sense is a "merit good". "Quality" can also be seen in terms of the depth of "worthwhile" journalism, i.e. the quality of writing, the level of analysis of issues, etc.

39. On the other hand, "quality" can also be seen from a private consumer demand perspective — "quality" is what consumers consider it to be; specifically how an individual personally values the content of the media. That is, "quality" can be measured by whether the media satisfies consumer demand for particular types of content.

40. The public interest and merit good arguments are in essence "public values" whereas the private consumer benefits viewpoint focuses purely on the "private value" to an individual. Because the LMA is intended to inform the OFT's assessment under the Enterprise Act 2002, the LMA will focus on the private value of media. This means that Ofcom will focus on the specific elements of the particular media involved that consumers themselves directly value, i.e. what they themselves enjoy and value.

41. While private consumer benefits might potentially fall within the definition of relevant customer benefits under section 30 of the Act, public values, on the other hand, would be more relevant if the Secretary of State has issued a public interest intervention notice under section 42 of the Enterprise Act (see section below.)

OTHER ISSUES

42. In addition to the issues described above, an LMA may also cover further issues that Ofcom sees as potentially relevant to the OFT's assessment. These may include the impact of media specific regulations on competition, and the overall importance of the merger. In particular an LMA may include views on whether the value of the affected markets is sufficiently low that they might be seen as being of insufficient importance (*"de minimis"*) to warrant a reference to the CC.

REMEDIES

43. Because an LMA will cover specific aspects as set out above, it is not a full assessment of the impact of the merger. As such, Ofcom will not generally focus on potential remedies to the merger within LMA.

44. Nonetheless, the issues raised by an LMA may affect the OFT's view of what undertakings in lieu it might be willing to consider. Ofcom will therefore provide views as and when it is valuable to do so.

NOTES

18 Office of Fair Trading /Competition Commission: Merger Assessment Guidelines 2010 (OFT1254), paragraph 4.3.5, www.competition-commission.org.uk/about_us/our_organisation/workstreams/analysis/pdf/100916_merger_assessment guidelines.pdf

PUBLIC INTEREST TEST AND LOCAL MEDIA ASSESSMENT

[3.547]

45. In addition to LMAs, Ofcom has an existing role in providing advice in relation to media mergers, namely to assist the Secretary of State in assessing the public interest impact of media mergers.

46. Section 42 of the Enterprise Act 2002 allows for the Secretary of State to assume responsibility for determining whether or not to refer a merger to the CC, and what action to take in relation to the merger, by issuing a public interest intervention notice (PIIN). A PIIN may be issued when certain public interest considerations may be relevant to a particular media merger. In cases where the Secretary of State decides to intervene on media public interest grounds, Ofcom will provide an initial report with advice and recommendations to inform the Secretary of State on the public interest aspects of the case under section 44A of the Enterprise Act 2002.

47. An LMA is distinct from any assessment that Ofcom may carry out in relation to the broader public interest implications of a merger. It operates under a different framework and considers different issues.

48. Ofcom's role in advising the Secretary of State on the public interest aspects of the merger is to allow for considerations of, for example, the need for the accurate presentation of news and free expression of opinion (in newspapers) and the need for a sufficient plurality of persons with control of media enterprises. Parliament considered these to be necessary for a healthy functioning democracy and they allow for other wider social value to be taken into account if the merger is seen as raising issues in this regard. In assessing the public interest considerations, Ofcom will not consider any competition effects of the merger.

49. The role of an LMA, on the other hand, as set out above, is to assist the OFT in making its decision on the competition effects of the merger (and potentially any relevant exceptions to the duty to refer, including relevant customer benefits). As set out in the OFT's merger guidance, in cases where a PUN has been issued, the OFT will carry out its review in the same way as it would for any other case.[19] The LMA is undertaken to advise the OFT on competition issues, whereas a public interest assessment is undertaken to advise the Secretary of State on public interest issues which are wider than those recognised in the OFT's review. The two exercises are therefore distinct, even though Ofcom may be required to undertake both exercises in relation to a single case.

NOTES

[19] OFT: Mergers: Jurisdictional and Procedural Guidance, paragraph 9.7

INFORMATION GATHERING AND SHARING

[3.548]

50. Ofcom provides an LMA to the OFT on an advisory basis, given that the decisions in relation to the assessment of the substantial lessening of competition test fall to the OFT. Nonetheless Ofcom will need information from the merging parties to conduct an LMA. This information may include:

- the rationale for merging;
- the parties' future plans for the new business;
- any information on what the likely future consumer benefits could be;
- evidence relevant to the counterfactual;
- any research conducted relating to consumer and supplier views of substitution;
- information relating to pricing policies (this is to get an understanding about demand elasticities);
- views (consumer, supplier and merging parties) of characteristics and functionality of products; and
- details of products produced by target (e.g. if newspaper merger, number of titles, circulation, ad revenues, profitability overtime, geographic coverage).

51. As outlined in the OFT Jurisdictional and Procedural Merger Guidance,[20] the OFT would also require similar information and Ofcom would therefore encourage the parties to provide this information to both the OFT and Ofcom.

52. Recognising the potential burden on parties, Ofcom will seek not to duplicate the information requested by the OFT. Ofcom encourages parties to provide copies of all material provided to the OFT to Ofcom at the same time to facilitate Ofcom's assessment.[21]

53. Ofcom may also engage with the parties directly in order to obtain any additional information that might be needed for an LMA. This information may relate to any of the elements being considered under an LMA. Ofcom will notify merging parties what information it thinks it will need as early as possible. Any information provided to Ofcom in relation to a specific merger will also be shared with the OFT.

54. In preparing an LMA, Ofcom may take into consideration unsolicited submissions received from third parties. Any information provided by third parties will be shared with the OFT.

55. Ofcom will treat all commercially confidential information sensitively, in line with its statutory responsibilities in this regard.

NOTES

[20] OFT: Mergers: Jurisdictional and Procedural Guidance, chapter 5

[21] It should be noted that there is a statutory gateway under Section 241 (1) Enterprise Act 2002 pursuant to which the OFT may be able to pass information that it receives to Ofcom for the purpose of facilitating the exercise by the OFT of its merger control function.

(II) WATER

OFWAT'S APPROACH TO MERGERS AND STATEMENT OF METHODS

October 2015

[3.549]

NOTES

CONTENTS

ABOUT THIS DOCUMENT

[3.550]
This document sets out our approach to mergers under the revised special merger regime following the changes introduced as part of the Water Act 2014. It also sets out our statement of methods for the assessment of mergers. It takes account of responses received to our consultation in May 2015. We have published a separate summary of these, our consideration of them and changes made to them.

OVERVIEW

[3.551]
A water merger occurs where two or more water companies[1] cease to be distinct by coming under common ownership or control. As each water company is a regional monopoly, we use comparative information to ensure that customers are paying a fair price for their water, to identify good performance and to set incentives for companies to improve. This need for comparative information is recognised through a special merger regime which examines whether water sector mergers may prejudice our ability to carry out our functions by impacting on our ability to make comparisons.

Our approach to regulation will evolve over time. For example the development of the retail market for non-household customers in April 2017 and our proposals for upstream activities in Water 2020. This will change our need for comparative information in a dynamic way. Our approach to mergers will also change as a result and this document should be read in that context.

Following the introduction of changes set out in the Water Act 2014, the special merger regime will be amended[2] to allow a process whereby a decision on a water merger can be achieved during the first stage (Phase 1) of a merger investigation rather than automatic referral to an in-depth (Phase 2) investigation. This aims to reduce the disincentives for companies to merge and the level of regulatory uncertainty when a merger is proposed.

The revised special merger regime provides a role for the Water Services Regulation Authority (Ofwat) during Phase 1 of a merger inquiry and requires us to provide an opinion to the Competition and Markets Authority (CMA) on: the impact of a merger on our ability to make comparisons and relevant customer benefits; and whether undertakings in lieu (UILs) would remedy, mitigate or prevent the prejudicial effect on our ability to make comparisons. We are also required to consult on and prepare a statement of methods, which sets out the criteria we will use to assess the impact on our ability to make comparisons and the weighting applied to those criteria.[3]

This document sets out our approach to mergers under the revised special merger regime and our statement of methods.

We consulted on our draft Statement of Methods in May 2015.[4] We have published a separate document which sets out our assessment of consultation responses and the changes we have made to address responses to the consultation.[5, 6]

WATER ACT 2014 AMENDMENTS TO THE SPECIAL MERGER REGIME

When the relevant sections are in force,[7] the Water Act 2014 introduces a revised Phase 1 process to the special mergers regime. In the revised Phase 1 process, in addition to the existing tests on applicability and turnover, the CMA can decide not to refer a qualifying water merger to a six month inquiry group-led investigation if the:

Part 3 CMA and other Guidelines

- merger is not likely to prejudice Ofwat's ability to make comparisons;
- likely prejudice is outweighed by relevant customer benefits; or
- company has offered appropriate UILs of a reference which remedy, mitigate or prevent the prejudicial effect on our ability to make comparisons.

The amendments to the Water Act 2014 do not affect the Phase 2 merger process. Figure 1 sets out the Phase 1 process and our role in the revised special merger regime.

Figure 1 Phase 1 merger process following the Water Act 2014

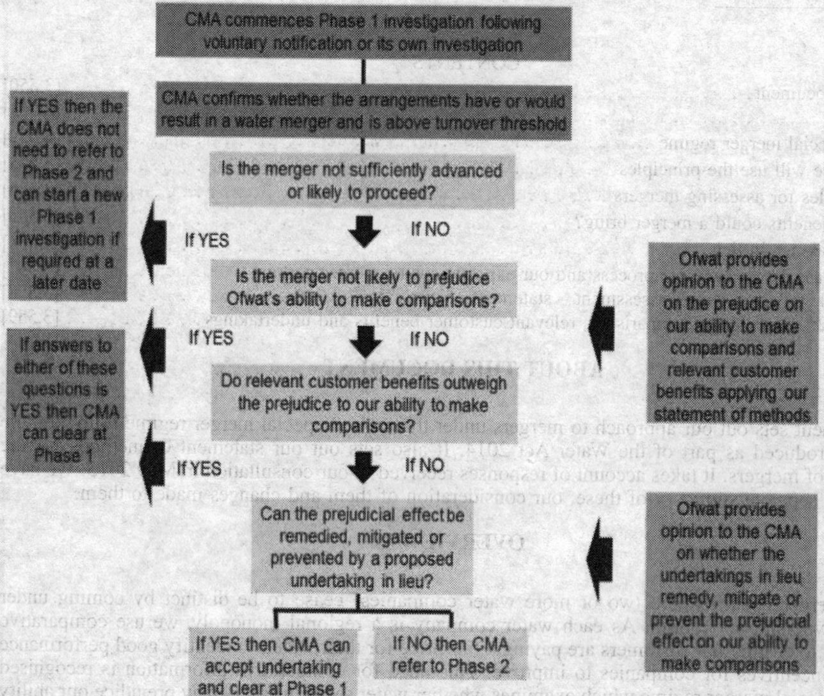

WHY COMPARISONS ARE IMPORTANT

Under the revised special merger regime, before deciding on whether to refer a merger to a Phase 2 inquiry, the CMA will consider whether a merger is likely to prejudice our ability to make comparisons. We are required to provide an opinion to the CMA on whether and to what extent we consider this is the case.

Water companies are regional monopolies, so comparisons between water companies have underpinned the way we have regulated the sector since privatisation. We make use of comparisons both during the price review process – for example, in setting price limits or service quality requirements, and between price reviews, for monitoring and enforcement and spreading best practice. While our approach to making comparisons has changed over time, without the ability to make comparisons between water companies then it is likely that we would not have been able to set the same stretching cost and service targets. This, in turn, would have been a detriment to customers through higher bills or lower service quality.

Particular areas where we have recently made use of comparisons include:

- risk based assessment of company business plans and the categorisation of companies' business plans, which introduced rivalry between companies to obtain enhanced status at the 2014 price review;
- wholesale and retail cost modelling in the 2014 price review where we used information on individual water company costs to develop our cost models, cost benchmarks and cost allowances;
- outcome delivery incentives (ODIs) which were set at the 2014 price review where, for five cross-company ODIs we used comparisons across water companies to identify upper quartile performance and intervened to ensure that companies were only able to access financial rewards for genuinely stretching performance;
- service incentive mechanism (SIM) which uses qualitative and quantitative measures of customer satisfaction to financially reward or penalise companies based on their performance relative to the rest of the industry; and

- standards of board leadership, transparency and governance across companies where we highlighted and shared best practice to encourage all companies to meet our principles in this area.

The 2014 price review introduced changes to the way that we regulate, for example the setting of separate price limits for wholesale and retail elements. The way we regulate is likely to change further going forwards, for example the introduction of competition into non-household retail and the creation of separate price controls in new areas. While this is likely to reduce the importance of direct comparisons between water companies in some areas, for example retail, there are other areas which will still be regional monopolies, such as companies' water and wastewater networks, where we will still need to make use of comparisons. If we set price limits at a more granular level it is also possible that our use of comparisons in some of these areas might become more important.

OUR PRINCIPLES FOR ASSESSING MERGERS

We are moving our overall regulatory approach to a regime that is more ex post, framework-based, pro-market, proportionate and targeted. It continues to evolve for example as highlighted by the work on Water 2020. We recognise that it is important for the market for corporate control to work well and we would not want to present barriers to this. Consistent with the changes in our regulatory approach, our approach to mergers has evolved. We approach our assessment of the impacts of each merger on a case by case basis. We value mergers where it can be demonstrated that customers will benefit from greater innovation and/or efficiency.

Our approach to assessing mergers is guided by a set of high-level principles.

- Each merger will be considered on its merits, taking full account of its benefits.
- Any merger has the potential to prejudice Ofwat's ability to make comparisons.
- A merger between companies whose scope of activities does not overlap is unlikely to prejudice our ability to make comparisons.
- A merger of a high performing company in terms of efficiency/service could prejudice our ability to set cross industry benchmarks. But we recognise that company positions in our benchmarking analysis do not remain static.
- Each merger may permanently reduce the number of independent comparators in the monopoly parts of the value chain; and as a result the detriment to the comparative regime may increase for each successive merger.
- A merger could lead to the loss of a company which had important similarities to other companies, for example operating in similar conditions facing similar issues.
- A merger could lead to the loss of a company which had important differences from other companies, which for example could reduce the scope of the development of best practice.
- It might be possible for us to amend our approach to offset, to an extent, the impact of the loss of a comparator.
- A merger has the potential to create customer benefits which could outweigh the prejudice to our ability to make comparisons. These benefits can encompass price reductions, service improvements, greater choice and increased innovation.
- UILs may be appropriate to remedy, mitigate or prevent the prejudicial effect on our ability to make comparisons.

WHAT BENEFITS COULD A MERGER BRING?

Under the revised special merger regime, the CMA does not need to refer a merger to a Phase 2 investigation if relevant customer benefits from the merger outweigh the likely prejudice to our ability to make comparisons. We are required to provide our opinion to the CMA on whether relevant customer benefits outweigh the prejudice to our ability to make comparisons.

Relevant customer benefits can take the form of:

- lower prices, which could result from operational cost savings (reduced head office costs), improved water resource management (from contiguous companies sharing/better planning of resources) or reduced financing costs (from the ability of a larger company to obtain more favourable terms);
- higher service quality, for example by improving security of supply;
- greater choice, for example through the greater availability of special tariffs; and
- greater innovation, for example the creation of innovative new structures from the merger itself (such as a very large water only company or a wastewater only company) or through greater effectiveness of research and development.

Relevant customer benefits can only be considered if they would be unlikely to be realised without the merger or a similar prejudice to our ability to make comparisons.

UNDERTAKINGS IN LIEU

Under the revised special merger regime, the CMA may accept undertakings in lieu of making a reference for a Phase 2 inquiry. The CMA will consider whether the proposed undertakings would remedy, mitigate or prevent the prejudicial effect of the merger on our ability to make comparisons. We are required to provide our opinion to the CMA on the effect of the proposed undertakings, including the extent to which they would remedy, mitigate or prevent the prejudicial effect.

Our advice to the CMA on whether a UIL is acceptable will depend on the circumstances involved and the level of prejudice created. When assessing potential UILs we will consider the prejudice to our ability to make comparison now, but also what measures might assist our ability to make comparisons to regulate more effectively in the future. When considering UILs, we will be particularly concerned about the degree of independence of any new comparators that might be created. For example, we would have a preference for ownership independence over management independence, and for accounting separation over separate reporting.

In Phase 1 of a merger investigation, we will want to be confident that the likely prejudice will be resolved by the UILs offered without the need for Phase 2 investigation. We consider that UILs are only appropriate where there are clear cut remedies proposed to address the prejudice caused by the merger. This mirrors the CMA's approach to UILs in the general merger regime. We would not expect that every merger will be resolved at Phase 1. It should be emphasised that the final decision to accept UILs rests with the CMA, after considering Ofwat's opinion.

UILs could include:

- divesture – for example, the sale of a non-contiguous part of the water company, which could create an additional independent comparator;
- partial divestures – for example, a reduction in the equity stake and therefore the degree of control, which in some circumstances, could create management independence and restore our ability to make comparisons;
- separate administration – for example, an undertaking to maintain or create separate management, accounting or reporting arrangements, for either the company taken over or for particular services within the merged entity. This could include offering to create a separate retail company, or separate management of water resources and networks. This could also include the adoption of innovative structures that allow for new or different forms of comparisons to be made to help set stretching benchmarks in the future; and/or
- amending licences – for example the creation of modular licences for separate services within the merged entity, in particular where such licence amendments could be adopted by other companies where they represent a useful direction of travel for the industry.

Each of the examples above has the potential to mitigate, prevent or remedy the prejudicial effect on our ability to make comparisons. Consistent with the view set out by the CMA, we do not consider price reductions qualify for consideration as undertakings in lieu as undertakings at Phase 1 must directly address any prejudice that would otherwise occur. We consider price reductions may, however, be considered as a remedy in Phase 2 as remedies may be broader in scope.

THE PHASE 1 PROCESS AND OUR EXPECTATIONS OF MERGER PARTIES

The Water Act 2014 does not specify a timetable for water mergers. If the CMA's general merger regime timetable is applied to Phase 1 water mergers, and taking into account the statutory requirements, there are up to three main stages to the Phase 1 process, as shown in figure 2.

- **Pre-notification.** During pre-notification merger parties will need to develop a merger impact assessment, which will set out the expected impact of the merger. In undertaking the merger impact assessment merger parties should have regard to our statement of methods which sets out how we will assess mergers. Prior to formally submitting a merger notification to the CMA, merger parties are encouraged to discuss the proposed merger and any UILs with both Ofwat and the CMA. There is no formal time limit on these discussions, so merger parties are encouraged to open dialogue with Ofwat and the CMA at the earliest opportunity to enable all parties to consider their positions ahead of any formal Phase 1 investigation.
- **Phase 1 investigation.** The will not start the investigation until it has sufficient information and Ofwat has the necessary information it requires to carry out the assessment. CMA will have up to 40 working days to conduct the Phase 1 investigation. During this period the CMA will consider whether the merger will prejudice Ofwat's ability to make comparisons and where relevant, whether customer benefits arising from the merger would outweigh this prejudice. In Phase 1, the CMA will issue an invitation to comment on the merger – this is the part of the process which provides the opportunity for third parties to provide their submissions on the merger. The Statement of intent[8] confirms the views the CMA receives from this process will be shared with Ofwat. The CMA must request and consider Ofwat's opinion on these issues within this time period. Ofwat must provide its advice in accordance with its statement of methods. If merger parties have raised UILs by this stage of the process, the CMA must also consider Ofwat's opinion on the effect of those UILs. Merger parties should note that the CMA is the body that makes the final decisions at Phase 1, which includes whether UILs should be accepted and whether the merger should be referred to a Phase 2 investigation. The Statement of intent confirms that the CMA will place significant weight on Ofwat's opinion when making decisions in relation to prejudice, to our ability to make comparisons, relevant customer benefits and UILs.[9] The prospect of clearance at Phase 1, on the basis of a lack of prejudice, that relevant benefits outweigh the prejudice or acceptance of UILs is likely to be higher where the views of the parties and Ofwat on the impact of the merger are broadly aligned.
- **Consideration of UILs of a Phase 2 reference.** If the CMA concludes that a merger prejudices Ofwat's ability to make comparisons between water companies and that this prejudice is not outweighed by relevant customer benefits, the merger parties will have the opportunity to propose UILs to offset that prejudice. If UILs are proposed the CMA must request and consider Ofwat's opinion on these undertakings before determining whether the UILs offered are sufficient to offset the prejudice.

Figure 2 Potential timings for Phase 1

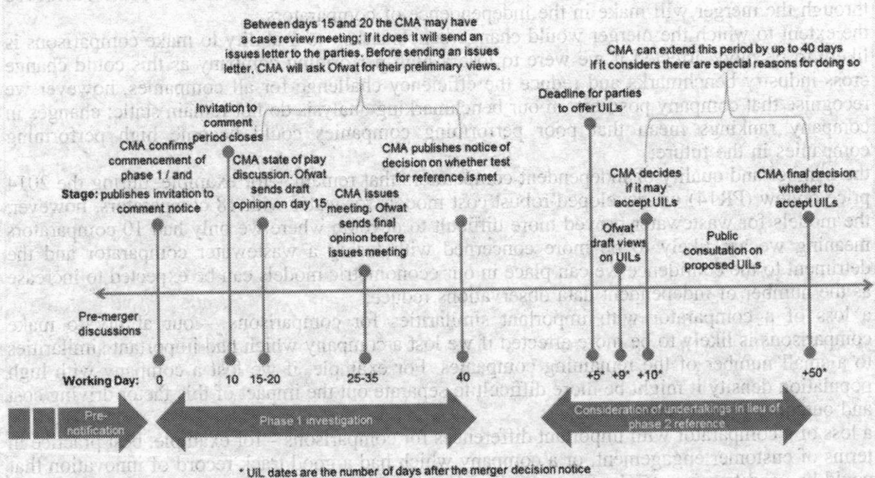

One of Parliament's objectives of the revised special merger regime is to allow for some mergers to proceed following a Phase 1 investigation as the automatic referral of all mergers to an in-depth Phase 2 investigation under the previous regime was viewed as a disincentive to potentially beneficial mergers. The short timescales for the formal Phase 1 investigation place importance on the quality of the evidence provided by merger parties during the pre-notification and Phase 1 process.

Consistent with our strategy of companies taking responsibility for the relationships with their customers, we expect merger parties to have a good understanding of the potential impact of the merger, particularly in terms of relevant customer benefits. We expect companies to set out in their merger impact assessment submission (submitted at the start of the Phase 1 process), their views on:

- the impact of the merger on our ability to make comparisons;
- the relevant customer benefits that arise directly from the merger, and whether these outweigh the impact on our ability to make comparisons; and, if they do not,
- any UILs that would prevent, mitigate or remedy the prejudicial effect on our ability to make comparisons.

To provide the best opportunity of us recommending to the CMA that the merger is cleared at Phase 1, merger parties should develop their submission in line with our statement of methods and take account of the report that we have commissioned into valuation methods by Europe Economics.[10] As set out above, due to the short timetable in Phase 1 and the importance of the merger impact assessment submission, merger parties are encouraged to discuss their proposed submission with us during the pre-notification phase of the process.

OUR STATEMENT OF METHODS

Our statement of methods is required to set out the criteria and the weighting of those criteria we will use to assess whether a merger is likely to prejudice our ability to make comparisons, and whether relevant customer benefits outweigh that prejudice. In defining the criteria we have taken account of:

- our statutory duties;
- our principles for assessing mergers;
- the requirements of the revised special merger regime introduced by the Water Act 2014; and
- the approach taken by the Competition Commission, the CMA and Ofwat in previous merger cases.

Our assessment of the impact of a merger will be based on evidence provided by merger parties, where appropriate taking into account our own analysis. The assessment will be based on a comparison between the factual (with merger) and counterfactual (without merger) situation. We will also use a scenario-based approach to take into account future uncertainty. This approach will include potential changes to regulatory policy, based on public statements about where and how our approach might change. Further, we will consider the loss of a comparator in each of the areas where we use comparisons: setting price limits, service quality and our ongoing role in monitoring, enforcement and spreading best practice.

Our criteria for assessing whether a merger would prejudice our ability to make comparisons are:

- the extent to which the merger involves overlaps in functions – if it does not then we will take the view that there is no prejudice – for example, a water only company taking over sewerage functions would not prejudice our ability to make comparisons in these areas;

- whether the merger involves the loss of an independent comparator – if it does not then we will take the view that there is no prejudice. For example, if the companies are already under common control, then our ability to make comparisons would not be prejudiced. Where there is a degree of control pre-merger but the level of that control is less than complete (for example, as a result of a minority shareholding) we will assess what difference the additional level of control achieved through the merger will make in the independence of comparators.;
- the extent to which the merger would change benchmarks – our ability to make comparisons is likely to be more affected if we were to lose a high performing company as this could change cross-industry benchmarks and reduce the efficiency challenge for all companies, however we recognise that company positions in our benchmarking analysis do not remain static; changes in company rankings mean that poor performing companies could become high performing companies in the future;
- the number and quality of independent comparators that remain – for example, during the 2014 price review (PR14) we developed robust cost models for water with 18 comparators, however, the models for wastewater proved more difficult to develop where we only had 10 comparators meaning we are likely to be more concerned with losing a wastewater comparator and the detriment to the confidence we can place in our econometric models can be expected to increase as the number of independent data observations reduce;
- a loss of a comparator with important similarities for comparisons – our ability to make comparisons is likely to be more affected if we lost a company which had important similarities to a small number of the remaining companies. For example, if we lost a company with high population density it might be more difficult to separate out the impact of this factor driving cost and outcome performance;
- a loss of a comparator with important differences for comparisons – for example, best practice in terms of customer engagement, or a company which had a good track record of innovation that could be used to raise standards across the sector; and
- are there alternative approaches available to us to offset the loss of this comparator? – that is, could we amend our regulatory approach to offset the loss of this comparator? We note however that changes that could be made to improve the way we regulate to reflect good regulatory practice absent the merger should not be seen as offsetting the prejudice – they should be included in the baseline assessment.

The assessment of the first two criteria will be based on yes/no response, although we accept that this can sometimes be a matter of degree. If the answer to either question is no, then we are unlikely to take the view that the merger would cause prejudice to our ability to make comparisons. If this is the case then we would not proceed with the assessment against the other criteria and would provide our opinion to the CMA on that basis.

We will apply equal weights to each of the other criteria. Where possible we will monetise impacts against these criteria, that is convert impacts (both detriment and benefits) into a £m impact. This will identify the scale of impact and the relative weight of that impact against other criteria.

We will take account of the impact over time by discounting future values to present values. We will calculate the present value both over the long term, for example, 30 years (to reflect the long term impact of the loss of a comparator where we are certain similar regulatory approaches will persist in the future) and a shorter term view, for example, five to ten years (where impacts are more certain). In undertaking this assessment we will consider the likelihood that current regulatory practices will persist in the future – for example, it is more likely that benchmarking analysis of network costs will continue in the long term as network activities are a natural monopoly. However, in other areas we may be less certain that current regulatory approaches will persist in the future. For example, retail is an area where we may be able to make greater use of comparators that are external to the sector in the future and so it may be reasonable to focus on the impacts over a shorter time period.

Where the criteria concern the use of comparators for setting price controls, the impacts assessment will consider both a 'static' approach (that is what the impact would have been if the merger had occurred prior to the last price control) and a 'forward looking' approach (that is by taking account of the possible impacts in future price controls). We will apply greatest weight to the forward looking approach as price limits under the 'static' approach will have already been set.

Where monetisation is not possible, we will undertake a quantitative or qualitative assessment of the impact on our ability to make comparisons and indicate the severity of the impact. When assessing impacts we will take into account the certainty around whether the impacts would occur, for example through changes in regulation, for example by including ranges around impacts.

In preparing our opinion on whether prejudice has occurred we will bring together the monetised, quantitative and qualitative impacts. After summing all monetised impacts, we will consider whether, in the round, the non-monetised impacts would change the balance of the decision and whether the overall impact constituted a prejudice to our ability to make comparisons.

The criteria for relevant customer benefits will be based on the legislation, as follows.

- Are there relevant customer benefits? These must be in terms of lower prices, higher quality or greater choice of services or greater innovation in relation to such services and must accrue to customers of merger parties.
- How likely or certain are the benefits to be achieved?
- Are the benefits merger specific? The benefits must be a direct result of the merger (and unlikely to occur otherwise).

- Are benefits likely to accrue in a reasonable period of time?
- Are benefits likely to be sustained?

As with the impacts on comparators, we will weight impacts against the criteria based on their monetised impacts. Where monetisation is not possible we will consider non-monetised impacts. We will attach most weight to customer benefits which are certain.

When determining whether the prejudice is outweighed by relevant customer benefits we will consider both monetised and non-monetised impacts. When undertaking this assessment we will be conscious that, there is the potential for a Phase 2 investigation. We will therefore need compelling evidence to recommend to the CMA that in our view customer benefits outweigh the likely prejudice from the impact of the merger on our ability to make comparisons. When undertaking this assessment we will be mindful that merger-specific relevant customer benefits might be short lived as they could be eroded by non-merger specific efficiency improvements (such as via the regulatory process). Conversely, merger benefits could also include the acceleration of benefits that would otherwise occur at a later time.

When assessing evidence provided by parties on the impact on our use of comparators and relevant customer benefits, we will use the following criteria.

- Clarity and transparency around the approach and assumptions;.
- Completeness of the description of the analysis.
- Ability of Ofwat to replicate results.
- Robustness and independent assurance.
- Evidence of customer support.

In assessing the impacts of the merger on our ability to make comparisons and the customer benefits, the greatest weight will be placed on merger party assessments which are complete, robust, certain, clear, independently assured and which provide evidence of customer support.

To provide clarity to parties subject to future mergers, we confirm that Ofwat's costs in relation to mergers will be funded through normal licence fees. Ofwat will appoint a Director as senior responsible officer and a project manager for day to day contact.

STRUCTURE OF THE REST OF THIS DOCUMENT

The rest of this document is structured as follows.

- Chapter 1 sets out the legal background to the special mergers regime.
- Chapter 2 sets out why water sector comparisons are important for the regulation of water companies.
- Chapter 3 sets out our principles for assessing mergers.
- Chapter 4 sets out the potential benefits that a merger could bring.
- Chapter 5 sets out potential undertakings that might be acceptable in lieu of a Phase 2 merger reference.
- Chapter 6 sets out the Phase 1 process in the revised special merger regime introduced by the Water Act 2014 and our expectations of merger parties.
- Appendix 1 sets out our statement of methods.
- Appendix 2 provides background to our assessment of mergers and gives examples of how we use comparators and highlights relevant customer benefits and undertakings and remedies in previous water merger cases.

NOTES

1 We use the term 'water companies' to mean companies holding appointments as water and/or sewerage undertakers under Chapter 1 of Part 2 of the Water Industry Act 1991.

2 Ofwat's Statement of methods is being published before the new regime is put in place. At the time of writing it is anticipated the new merger regime will be put in place in November 2015.

3 See section 33C of the Water Industry Act 1991 (inserted by section 14(2) of the Water Act 2014).

4 'Consultation on Ofwat's approach to future mergers and statement of method' – www.ofwat.gov.uk/regulating/pap_con201505mergers.pdf

5 Ofwat (2015), 'Consideration of responses to Ofwat's proposed approach to mergers and draft statement of methods'.

6 Ofwat (2015), 'Consultation on Ofwat's approach to future mergers and statement of methods'.

7 At the time of publication of the Statement of methods, it is anticipated the relevant sections of the Water Act will be commenced in November 2015.

8 The Statement of intent, which sets out the working relationships between the CMA and Ofwat in relation to water mergers was published in Appendix C of the CMA's 2015 consultation 'Water and sewerage mergers: Guidance on the CMA's procedure and assessment – draft for consultation'. It will be place on the Ofwat and CMA websites when the CMA has finalised its guidance.

9 Statement of intent, paragraph 4(d).

10 Europe Economics (2015) Valuing the Impact of Mergers in the Water and Sewerage Sectors and Identifying Undertakings in Lieu. This document can be accessed at: www.ofwat.gov.uk/rpt_com20151021mergers.pdf

1. THE SPECIAL MERGER REGIME

1.1 WHY IS THERE A SPECIAL MERGER REGIME FOR THE WATER SECTOR?

[3.552]
The water sector in England and Wales comprises 18 incumbent regional monopoly companies, including

10 water and sewerage companies with between 1.2 million and 8.5 million customers each and 8 main water only companies with between 0.1 and 3.1 million customers each. There are also 6 small water companies with around 2000 customers each providing either water or sewerage services or both and more than 10 water supply licensees offering water services to large use customers. The 18 main incumbent water companies and 6 small water companies are all subject to the special merger regime.

A merger occurs when enterprises will cease, or have ceased, to be distinct because they come under common ownership or common control.[11] The special merger regime applies when two or more water enterprises[12] merge with each other.[13] The special merger regime does not apply to water supply licensees (or between a water company and a water supply licensee), which are covered by the general merger regime.[14] Where a water company merges with another business outside of the industry it is known as a change in ownership and these mergers are not subject to the special merger regime.

A special merger regime applies to the water sector in England and Wales because the lack of competition in the sector means that we need to use comparisons in the regulation of the sector. As each of the water companies is effectively a regional monopoly we use comparative information to ensure that customers are paying a fair price for their water, identify good performance and set incentives for companies to improve. The special merger regime recognises that mergers between companies within the water sector may prejudice our ability to carry out these functions.

Automatic merger inquiries have been a feature of the water sector since privatisation. Since 2004 any merger has to be referred to an in-depth Phase 2 inquiry if it would bring together two or more appointed companies whose relevant turnover exceeds £10 million.[15] This is effectively an automatic reference for all incumbent water company mergers because only the six small water companies currently have annual regulated turnovers of less than £10 million.

1.2 THE SPECIAL MERGER REGIME UNDER THE WATER ACT 2014

In the Government's view the existing special merger regime within the Water Industry Act 1991 acts as a disincentive to potential beneficial mergers between undertakers and creates uncertainty when a merger is proposed or has taken place.[16] In its Water for Life White Paper, which proposed changes to the special merger regime, Defra stated that:

- mergers can be a strong driver for improving the efficiency of companies, leading to improved service and lower costs that can be passed on to customers;[17] and
- requiring that all water industry mergers to be subject to an (expensive) in-depth investigation reduced the likelihood of potential mergers between water companies and the scope for water companies to be taken over by more efficient operators and any resulting benefits.[18]

The Water Act 2014 addresses these issues by amending the Water Industry Act to allow the CMA to determine in Phase 1 of a merger inquiry whether to make a merger reference to Phase 2, or to accept undertakings to compensate for the loss of a comparator in lieu of a reference. This will mean that not all qualifying mergers will need to be referred to the in-depth Phase 2 CMA inquiry group-led review.[19] The CMA can conclude that a Phase 2 review is not necessary if:

- the merger arrangements are not sufficiently far advanced, or not sufficiently likely to proceed to justify making a reference; or
- the merger is not likely to prejudice Ofwat's ability, in carrying out its functions by virtue of the Water Industry Act 1991, to make comparisons between water enterprises;[20] or
- the merger is likely to prejudice that ability, but the prejudice in question is outweighed by relevant customer benefits relating to the merger; or
- there are appropriate UILs from the merger parties which remedy, mitigate or prevent the prejudicial effect on Ofwat's ability to make comparisons between water enterprises resulting from the merger.[21]

Relevant customer benefits are defined in the Water Industry Act 1991 as lower prices, higher quality or greater choice of goods or services or greater innovation.[22] These benefits must accrue to the customers of the merger parties[23] within a reasonable period as a result of the merger and be unlikely to accrue without the merger.[24] The Water Act 2014 changes will also require the CMA to keep under review the £10 million turnover threshold and condition where water companies should not be referred to a Phase 2 merger investigation, and to advise the Secretary of State from time to time whether this threshold is still appropriate.[25] Figure 3 sets out the Phase 1 process following the Water Act 2014.

Figure 3 Phase 1 merger regime process (following the Water Act 2014)

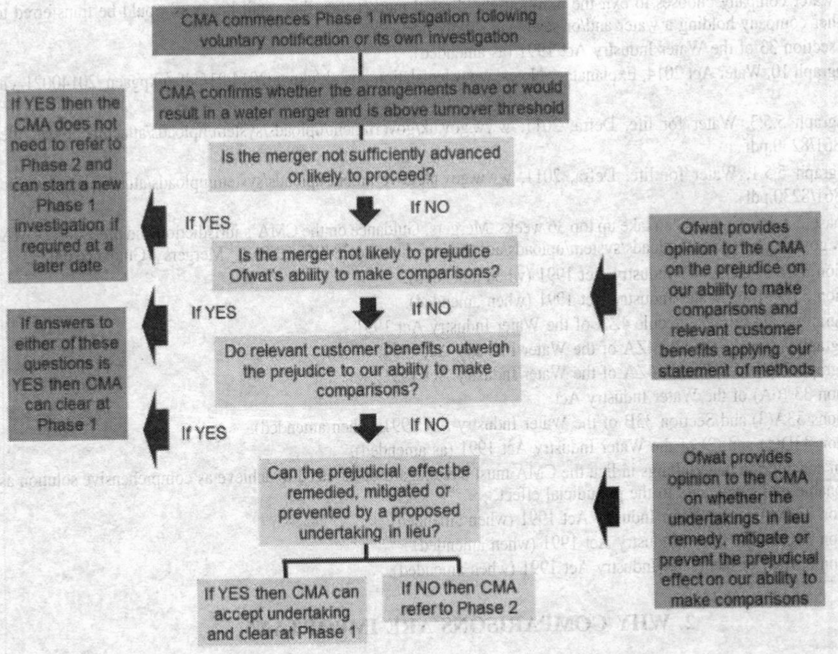

1.3 OFWAT'S ROLE UNDER THE SPECIAL MERGER REGIME

We have an important role under the revised special merger regime as revised by the Water Act 2014. Within Phase 1 of the merger inquiry, the CMA must request, and Ofwat must provide, its opinion on:

- whether the merger is likely to prejudice Ofwat's ability, in carrying out its functions, to make comparisons between water enterprises; and if so,
- whether the prejudice in question is outweighed by any relevant customer benefits relating to the merger.[26]

If, after considering Ofwat's opinion, the CMA considers it is under a duty to make a merger reference it may instead accept UILs which remedy, mitigate or prevent the prejudicial effect on Ofwat's ability to make comparisons.[2728] Before deciding whether or not to accept an undertaking, the CMA must request and consider Ofwat's opinion on the effect of the undertakings.[29]

The Statement of intent, which sets out the working relationships between the CMA and Ofwat in relation to water mergers confirms that the CMA will place significant weight on Ofwat's opinion when making decisions in relation to prejudice, to our ability to make comparisons, relevant customer benefits and UILs. The prospect of clearance at Phase 1, on the basis of a lack of prejudice, that relevant customer benefits outweigh the prejudice or acceptance of UILs is likely to be higher where the views of the parties and Ofwat on the impact of the merger are broadly aligned.

Further detail on the respective roles of the CMA and Ofwat in respect of a water merger investigation was set out paragraphs 1.11 to 1.22 of the CMA's consultation, 'Water and sewerage mergers: Guidance on the CMA's procedure and assessment – Draft for consultation'. We anticipate these will also be stated in the CMA's final, published guidance.

1.4 STATEMENT OF METHODS

The changes made by the Water Act 2014 also state that Ofwat must prepare and keep under review a statement of methods.[30] The statement of methods must in particular set out:

- the criteria to be used for assessing the impact of a merger on Ofwat's ability to make comparisons; and
- the relative weight to be given to the criteria.

Ofwat must use this statement of methods when providing an opinion to the CMA of the likely prejudice to Ofwat's ability to make comparisons and whether the prejudice is outweighed by relevant customer benefits.[31]

NOTES

11 See Mergers: Guidance on the CMA's jurisdiction and procedures, CMA (chapter 4).

12 A 'water enterprise' is defined in the Water Industry Act 1991 as an enterprise carried on by a water undertaker or a sewerage undertaker.

13 See section 32 of the Water Industry Act 1991 (as amended).

14 If a water company chooses to exit the non-household retail market then that retail business would be transferred to another company holding a water and/or sewerage supply licence.

15 See section 33 of the Water Industry Act 1991 (as amended).

16 Paragraph 10, Water Act 2014, Explanatory Notes. www.legislation.gov.uk/ukpga/2014/21/pdfs/ukpgaen_20140021_en.pdf

17 Paragraph 5.5.3, Water for life, Defra, 2011. www.gov.uk/government/uploads/system/uploads/attachment_data/file/228861/8230.pdf

18 Paragraph 5.5.1, Water for life, Defra, 2011. www.gov.uk/government/uploads/system/uploads/attachment_data/file/228861/8230.pdf

19 A Phase 2 merger inquiry can take up top 36 weeks. Mergers: Guidance on the CMA's jurisdiction and procedure, CMA. www.gov.uk/government/uploads/system/uploads/attachment_data/file/384055/CMA2__Mergers__Guidance.pdf

20 Section 33A of the Water Industry Act 1991 (when amended).

21 Section 33D of the Water Industry Act 1991 (when amended).

22 Paragraph 7 (1) (a) of Schedule 4ZA of the Water Industry Act 1991.

23 Paragraph 7 (4) of Schedule 4ZA of the Water Industry Act 1991.

24 Paragraph 7 (2) of Schedule 4ZA of the Water Industry Act 1991.

25 Section 33 (6A) of the Water Industry Act.

26 Sections 33A(3) and Section 33B of the Water Industry Act 1991 (when amended).

27 Section 33D(1) and (2) of the Water Industry Act 1991 (as amended).

28 When considering undertakings in lieu the CMA must have regard of the need to achieve as comprehensive solution as reasonable and practicable to the prejudicial effect.

29 Section 33D(6) of the Water Industry Act 1991 (when amended).

30 Section 33C of the Water Industry Act 1991 (when amended).

31 Section 33B(2) of the Water Industry Act 1991 (when amended).

2. WHY COMPARISONS ARE IMPORTANT

[3.553]

This chapter sets out:

- why comparisons are important to the regulation of the water sector;
- how we currently use comparators; and
- how our use of comparators could change in the future.

2.1 WHY COMPARISONS ARE IMPORTANT

Water companies are regional monopolies. They are therefore not subject to the same market forces as companies in competitive sectors. The Water Industry Act 1991 provides us with powers and duties to regulate water companies. We regulate water companies in line with our statutory duties, in particular to further the customer objective, to secure that water companies carry out their functions and are able to finance their activities (and long term resilience for English water companies). We also have other duties which include promoting efficiency and contributing to sustainable development.[32]

Comparative regulation has underpinned the way we have regulated the water and sewerage sector since privatisation. We use comparisons both during the price review process, for example in setting wholesale and retail price limits or service quality requirements, and between price reviews, for monitoring and enforcement and spreading best practice. Making comparisons between companies is one of the key tools we have, and it is recognised as such in the Water Industry Act 1991.

Comparative regulation provides a number of benefits:[33]

- It can improve cost estimation as we are better able to assess the true costs of water companies, as we are able to compare costs across a number of independent firms operating in similar circumstances.
- It can provide an impartial view of the performance of water companies by allowing comparisons to be made across the sector.
- It helps us overcome imperfect information, better allowing customers, investors, us and other stakeholders to assess the performance of companies.
- It provides a greater incentive for independent companies and their management to outperform their peers in the water sector.
- It provides greater incentives for innovation by facilitating a variety of different approaches to attempting to outperform price controls and other companies in the sector.

Losing an independent company through a merger could reduce the number of comparators we have available. Having fewer comparators could make it more difficult for us to make meaningful comparisons.

The first question that we must consider is the impact of the merger on our ability to carry out our functions. Specifically, we must consider whether the water merger is likely to prejudice our ability, in carrying out our functions, to make comparisons between water enterprises.

The loss of a comparator from a merger can affect our ability to make comparisons in a number of ways.

- It can remove a high performing company from our comparisons, which could impact on our benchmarks, reducing the scale of challenge for the industry as a whole.
- It would reduce the number of independent observations in our benchmarking, potentially impacting on the confidence that we can have in this benchmarking, which may be made worse with each successive merger as the number of independent comparators reduces.
- It could remove companies with important similarities or differences to other companies, making comparisons with other companies more difficult.

Mergers could also have a beneficial effect. For example they could remove a poorly performing company or they could create new innovative structures.

2.2 OUR CURRENT USE OF COMPARATORS

We currently use comparators across three main areas of activity.

- To set price limits.
- To monitor and incentivise service quality.
- To carry out ongoing monitoring, enforcement and spreading best practice.

2.2.1 Comparisons used to set price limits

One of our primary functions is to set price control limits, which determine the amount of revenue water companies receive during the subsequent price control period. The price control protects customers from excessive prices, while incentivising companies to make efficiency improvements and enables efficient companies to finance their activities. As an example Figure 2.1 sets out the overall approach to setting price control in the PR14 which set revenues for the period 2015-20.

FIGURE 4 THE OVERALL APPROACH TO THE 2014 PRICE REVIEW OF THE PRICE CONTROL

Wholesale controls		Retail controls	
Water	**Wastewater**	**Household**	**Non-household**
Monopoly service		Monopoly service	Competition introduced in 2017
Total revenue control set for five years		Total revenue control set for five years	Average revenue controls per customer type set for two years
Cost assessment based on upper quartile performance using econometric modelling. supplemented by special factor cost claims for areas not covered.		Cost assessment based on average cost to serve (adjusted for special factors such as bad debt)	Companies must offer default tariffs which comply with control but not all customers have to remain on these
Expenditure split into money recovered in period (through Pay as you go (PAYG) and run-off of the regulatory capital value (RCV)) and money recovered over time (though the RCV)		Companies receive a margin on costs	Revenue control based on average cost to serve with a retail margin
Companies receive a return on the RCV based on the weighted average cost of capital (debt and equity)			

One of the most important aspects in the determination of revenue limits is identifying the level of allowed expenditure. At PR14, for the first time, we set separate price controls for wholesale and retail activities, meaning separate assessments of wholesale water, wholesale wastewater, non-household retail and household retail costs were made. Each water company will know more than the regulator about its future costs and efficiency and so we used comparisons between water companies for each price control to help overcome the information asymmetry and identify an efficient expenditure allowance. Some detailed examples of our use of comparators in the development of price limits are as follows.

- **Comparisons through econometric modelling.** We used a suite of econometric and unit cost models to determine wholesale cost allowances at PR14.[34] Water and wastewater wholesale costs were assessed separately. For water, we used econometric models to assess total expenditure (totex) using panel data from 18 companies over a five-year period. For wastewater, we used econometric models to assess base expenditure (for ten companies over seven years) and unit cost models to assess enhancement expenditure.
- **Comparisons in assessing special factor claims.** In determining the totex allowance we considered a number of special factor claims from companies, some of which were assessed through comparisons between companies. For example, we assessed one company's claim for additional energy cost allowances by comparing its pumping head and energy costs as a percentage of totex across the industry.
- **Comparisons using retail average cost to serve.** Our assessment of household retail price limits used an industry-wide average cost to serve (ACTS) as its starting point.[35] Drawing on data from each of the 18 companies we calculated separate ACTS for different customer types – that is, for

measured and unmeasured water-only, wastewater-only and water-and-wastewater customers.[36] We also considered whether any company-specific (or special factor) adjustments should be made, including for bad debt costs, input price pressure claims and new costs. Our assessment of bad debt cost related adjustments included comparisons of companies' bad debt management practices and the relative deprivation of the areas served by each company.

- **Comparisons made in our risk based review of company business plans.** This process introduced reputational, procedural and financial incentives for companies' Boards to produce high-quality business plans. It was designed to encourage companies to compete with each other, to deliver good business plans at an early stage and submit high-quality 'best offers'. In assessing company business plans, we drew qualitative comparisons across a broad range of areas and companies were able to learn from the best practice approaches of other companies in submitting their revised business plans.

Appendix 2 provides further examples of our use of comparators for assessing costs and setting price limits at PR14. Further details of our price control methodology are set out on our website.[37]

2.2.2 COMPARISONS USED TO MONITOR AND INCENTIVISE SERVICE QUALITY

At PR14, in addition to setting price limits we also considered the service quality and outcomes that companies would deliver over the 2015-20 period. To incentivise companies to meet or exceed the expectations of their customers we set two main types of incentive mechanism.

- **ODIs and performance commitments.** Companies' performance commitments set out target performance levels. While some performance commitments were reputational, other commitments had financial ODIs which set out the implications, in terms of rewards and penalties, of exceeding, meeting or failing to meet these commitments.
- **The SIM** comprises quantitative and qualitative components which measure customers' overall satisfaction with the service levels they receive from companies. Under the SIM companies are rewarded or penalised financially for their performance relative to the rest of the industry. The SIM is incorporated into the household retail price control for all English and Welsh companies. In the absence of the opening of retail activities to competition for all non-household customers in Wales, we use a separate SIM to measure and incentivise non-household retail performance of the two Welsh water companies. This uses comparisons of the performance of the Welsh companies to those in England.

We also currently annually monitor and publish company performance against a range of service quality and other measures. While as a consequence of PR14 and recent decisions, the performance measures we require companies to publish is likely to change, the performance measures companies reported in 2010-15 include:

- customer experience: the SIM score, internal sewer flooding incidents and water supply interruptions;
- environmental impact: greenhouse gas emissions, sewerage pollution incidents, serious sewerage pollution incidents, discharge permit compliance and satisfactory sludge disposal;
- reliability and availability: water non-infrastructure serviceability, water infrastructure serviceability, sewerage non-infrastructure serviceability, sewerage infrastructure serviceability, leakage and security of supply index.[38][39]

Appendix 2 presents some examples of our use of comparisons in monitoring and incentivising service quality.

2.2.3 Comparisons used to carry out ongoing activities in relation to monitoring, enforcement and spreading of best practice

We make comparisons in our on-going activities to monitor performance, undertake enforcement action and identify and spread best practice. Some examples of Ofwat's use of comparators in these areas include the following.

- **Board leadership and transparency.** Following the publication of a set of principles in January 2014,[40] we published a commentary in June 2014 on all companies' codes including a breakdown of whether or not the proposed codes would allow companies to meet the principles in each area.[41] This highlighted the companies that performed well in this area and we encouraged other companies to move towards this best practice.
- **Social tariffs.** We undertook a survey of companies' approaches to social tariffs in 2013, following which instances of best practice were identified and highlighted to the industry (through an industry workshop). This work contributed to the high take of up social tariffs by companies in their business plans.
- **Customer redress.** Through the qualitative use of comparators we were able to identify which companies were 'leaders of the pack' with respect to the implementation of alternative dispute resolution (ADR) processes. These companies were then asked to take a prominent role in taking the industry forward.
- **Interim determinations of K (IDoKs).** Where we use comparators to assess the robustness of company claims for changes to price limits during a control period. When assessing these claims we aim to identify the change in costs which an efficient company would have incurred as a result of the change in circumstances and if so whether that justifies a change in a company's price

control. As part of this we make comparisons across the industry to understand whether a company has been particularly affected by the circumstances which it has claimed have given rise to the additional costs incurred and whether the company has taken appropriate steps to mitigate the effects of those circumstances on its costs.

- **Bad debt and revenue recognition.** As companies had approached this in different ways, we published a note identifying best practice approaches.
- Accounting separation. We have carried out a targeted review of accounting separation data[42] and published best practice guidance for reporting upstream services.[43]

Appendix 2 sets out examples of where we use comparisons for on-going monitoring, enforcement and spreading best practice.

2.3 HOW OUR USE OF COMPARATORS COULD CHANGE IN THE FUTURE

Our approach to regulation and therefore how we use comparators is likely to change going forwards. We have already set out some of the changes that we would do – for example the introduction of non-binding sub-limits for network plus during the 2015-20 period;[44] whereas some are facilitated by changes introduced by the Water Act 2014, such as upstream competition from 2019; and some we may consider for the next or subsequent price controls, such as binding sub-limits for different services.

Our approach to regulation and our use of comparators could change from:

- changes in key elements to the PR14 price control – for example a move from an average to efficient cost to serve for retail;[45]
- changes introduced during the 2015-20 period – for example the introduction of non-household retail competition,[46] the abstraction incentive mechanism and network plus sub-limits;[47] and
- potential longer term changes from upstream competition (that is, competition in some of the non-retail elements of the control)[48] and binding service level sub-limits (where sub-limits could be introduced for individual services, such as water resources, water storage, water distribution, water treatment, sewerage collection, sewerage treatment and sludge treatment and sludge disposal).

Further details of possible regulatory changes and the potential impact on our use of comparisons are given in appendix 2.

NOTES

32 Water companies are also subject to regulation from other bodies such as the Environment Agency and the Drinking Water Inspectorate.

33 Adapted from benefits of comparative regulation set out in the Sale of Gas Networks by National Grid, NAO.

34 Ofwat (2014), 'Final price control determination notice: policy chapter A3 – wholesale water and wastewater costs and revenues'.

35 Ofwat (2014), 'Final price control determination notice: policy chapter A5 – household retail costs and revenues'.

36 The average cost to serve a water-only customer was calculated as the simple unweighted arithmetic average of all 18 companies' cost to serve a water-only customer, but the average cost to serve a sewerage-only customer was calculated as the simple unweighted arithmetic average of the ten water and sewerage companies' cost to serve a sewerage only customer.

37 Further details on the approach taken at PR14 are available on Ofwat's website, see ofwat.gov.uk/pricereview/pr14

38 See, for example, www.ofwat.gov.uk/regulating/casework/reporting/rpt_los2013-14performance

39 We also monitor and publish data on financial performance

40 See Ofwat (2014), 'Board leadership, transparency and governance – principles', January, www.ofwat.gov.uk/regulating/gud_pro20140131leadershipregco.pdf

41 See Ofwat (2014), 'Ofwat's commentary on water companies' governance codes', June, www.ofwat.gov.uk/regulating/pap_res201406govcodecomment.pdf

42 See www.ofwat.gov.uk/publications/rags/rpt_com1306costallocey

43 See 'Best practice guidance upstream services – methodology statement disclosures' www.ofwat.gov.uk/publications/rags/gud_pro201504upstream.pdf

44 Page 160, Ofwat (2014), 'Setting price controls for 2015-20 –final methodology and expectations for companies business plans'.

45 Page 97, Ofwat (2013), 'Setting price controls for 2015-20 – final methodology and expectations for companies business plans'.

46 Non-household retail competition – introduces retail competition to all non-households in England and non-households above 50Ml/d in Wales.

47 Network plus – introduces non-binding sub-limits for:

- water; covering raw water distribution, water treatment and treated water distribution, but not water resources; and
- wastewater; covering sewerage collection and treatment but not sludge treatment, recycling and disposal.

48 Upstream covers storing, treating and distributing water and collecting and disposing of sewerage.

3. PRINCIPLES FOR ASSESSING MERGERS

[3.554]
The way we regulate has changed and will continue to change in the future as we embed our new strategy. We have developed a set of high level principles which will guide our approach to mergers. These principles have been developed based on our use of comparators and the potential impact of a merger on those comparisons. We have used these principles as the basis for the development of the criteria in our statement of methods, which is set out in appendix 1.

Part 3 CMA and other Guidelines

- Each merger will be considered on its merits, taking full account of its benefits.
- Any merger has the potential to prejudice Ofwat's ability to make comparisons.
- A merger between companies whose scope of activities does not overlap is unlikely to significantly prejudice our ability to make comparisons.
- A merger involving a high performing company in terms of efficiency/service can prejudice our ability to set cross industry benchmarks. But we recognise that company positions in our benchmarking analysis do not remain static.
- Each merger may permanently reduce the number of independent comparators in the monopoly parts of the value chain; and as a result the detriment to the comparative regime may increase for each successive merger.
- A merger can lead to the loss of a company with important similarities to the remaining companies. It might, for example, operate in similar conditions and face similar issues.
- A merger can lead to the loss of a company with important differences to the remaining companies, which for example could reduce the scope of the development of best practice.
- It might be possible for us to amend our approach to offset, to an extent, the impact of the loss of a comparator.
- A merger has the potential to create customer benefits which could outweigh the prejudice to our ability to make comparisons. These benefits can encompass price reductions, service improvements, greater choice and increased innovation.
- UILs may be appropriate to remedy, mitigate or prevent the prejudice to our ability to make comparisons.

Our first principle is that we will consider each merger on its merits but below we discuss what types of issues we think will be important.

3.1 TYPE OF COMPANIES MERGING

Any reduction to the number of comparators can have an impact on the robustness of our analysis by reducing the number of independent observations. We currently have a higher number of water comparators so the loss of a water comparator is likely to have less impact than the loss of a sewerage comparator. Therefore the potential detriment on the robustness of our analysis will be greater for a merger which would reduce the number of sewerage companies than one that reduces the number of water companies. It follows that a whole company merger between two water and sewerage companies has the greatest detriment to Ofwat's ability to make comparisons. This is because it will cause us to lose both a water comparator and a sewerage comparator. We expect the detriment from the loss of a comparator to increase for each successive merger as fewer comparators would remain.

3.2 PERFORMANCE OF MERGING COMPANIES

If at least one of the merging companies is leading/high performing in some areas, there is a greater risk of detriment for customers than if both companies are poor performers. This is because there is a risk that a high performing comparator might be lost as a result of the merger which would have a detrimental impact on cross industry benchmarks, reducing the scale of challenge for other companies in the sector. However, we recognise that company positions in our benchmarking analysis do not remain static; changes in company rankings mean that poor performing companies could become high performing companies in the future.

3.3 LOSS OF A COMPANY WITH IMPORTANT SIMILARITIES

A merger can lead to the loss of a company with important similarities to the remaining companies, or a sub-set of the remaining companies. A company might, for example, operate in similar conditions to other companies, or face similar issues that make it particularly useful as a comparator. For example such comparisons could be useful when assessing claims put forward by companies for operating in particularly rural or urban areas, in respect of proposals put forward by companies to address issues related to supply and demand, or a merger between contiguous companies could affect our ability to make comparisons across companies that are operating in similar circumstances facing similar issues.

3.4 LOSS OF A COMPANY WITH IMPORTANT DIFFERENCES

A merger can lead to the loss of a company with important differences from the remaining companies, or a sub-set of the remaining companies. These differences can arise in terms of developing best practice in some areas or the adoption of innovative approaches. This could, for example, reduce the scope for the development of best practice or the scope for innovation if a company had demonstrated a good track record of innovation that is used to raise standards across the sector.

3.5 IT MIGHT BE POSSIBLE FOR US TO AMEND OUR APPROACH TO REDUCE THE IMPACT OF THE LOSS OF A COMPARATOR

The loss of a comparator could have a detrimental impact on the way that we currently regulate. It might be possible to change the way that we regulate to offset, to some extent, the potential detriment of the loss of a comparator. However, for the purposes of assessing the impacts, we consider any changes to improve the way we regulate to reflect good regulatory practice absent the merger, should not be seen as offsetting the prejudice - they should be included in the baseline assessment.

3.6 A MERGER HAS THE POTENTIAL TO CREATE CUSTOMER BENEFITS

A merger has the potential to create customer benefits which could outweigh the prejudice to our ability to make comparisons. These customer benefits can take many forms but can include price reductions which result from operating synergies, reductions in financing costs, improved water resource management, higher service quality, greater choice or increased innovation – for example, the creation of new or different company structures, such as a very large water only company or a wastewater only company.

3.7 UILS MAY BE APPROPRIATE TO REMEDY, MITIGATE OR PREVENT A PREJUDICE TO OUR ABILITY TO MAKE COMPARISONS

UILs could, in some circumstances, remedy, mitigate or prevent a prejudice to our ability to make comparisons. For example, UILs could create the ability to make new comparisons, for example by committing to greater separation between the provision of different services and providing more detailed disaggregated data, which could facilitate more detailed or new forms of comparisons to be undertaken.

4. WHAT BENEFITS COULD A MERGER BRING?

[3.555]
If we consider that a merger is likely to prejudice our ability to make comparisons between water companies, we will then consider whether the prejudice is outweighed by relevant customer benefits relating to the merger.

The Water Industry Act 1991 (as amended by the Water Act 2014) provides the CMA with the discretion not to make a reference for a Phase 2 CMA investigation if the prejudice is outweighed by the relevant customer benefits related to the merger.[49]

This chapter sets out the key issues that we will consider when providing our advice to the CMA on whether the prejudice to our ability to make comparisons is outweighed by relevant customer benefits. Our understanding of potential benefits is based in part on previous water merger cases (see appendix 2) and will develop over time as we gain greater experience of the new regime.

This chapter:

- sets out what is, and what is not, a relevant customer benefit;
- identifies possible relevant customer benefits in terms of lower prices, higher quality, greater choice and greater innovation;
- sets out how relevant customer benefits need to be merger specific; and
- identifies how relevant customer benefits might change in the future.

4.1 RELEVANT CUSTOMER BENEFITS

Under the Water Industry Act 1991, relevant customer benefits are limited to benefits to relevant customers in the form of **lower prices, higher quality, increased choice or greater innovation** in relation to goods or services.[50]

Relevant customers[51] are customers of the merging enterprises at any point lower in the chain of production and distribution. Therefore they might not necessarily be the final consumers and can include future customers. For example, it would be a relevant benefit of a merger if, as a result of the merger, a customer in an intermediate market obtained lower prices (or higher quality) whether or not final consumers were likely to benefit. The term customer is defined in accordance with Part 3 of the Enterprise Act[52] which makes clear that the definition of a customer includes a customer who is not a consumer.[53] We note that relevant customer benefits can only accrue to customers (and customers of customers) of merger parties whereas the impacts of the merger on our ability to make comparisons will have wider effects on customers across the industry.

In addition to falling within the description of customer benefits described above we must be satisfied[54] that the benefit has **accrued as a result of the merger**,[55] or is expected to accrue within a **reasonable time period** as a result of the merger, and that the benefit was, or is, unlikely to accrue without the merger or a similar prejudice.[56] Merger benefits can also include the acceleration of benefits that would otherwise occur at a later time.

We expect the merger parties to set out the time period over which they expect merger benefits will accrue. Where merger parties provide evidence that provides certainty that the merger benefits will arise, it may be reasonable to assume that benefits will take one to two years to be implemented and achieved.[57] We would also expect there to be some costs associated with the implementation of the benefits. We can have greatest confidence in the benefits that may arise before the next price review; while it may be possible to assess the impact of merger benefits beyond the current price control period, there will be less certainty that such benefits are relevant customer benefits arising from the merger as these would need to be over and above the benefits customers would otherwise receive, for example as a result of efficiency challenges at the next price review.

4.2 RELEVANT CUSTOMER BENEFITS FROM PAST MERGER PROPOSALS

Mergers themselves can lead to a range of benefits but for benefits to be relevant customer benefits they must be:

- lower prices, higher quality or greater choice of goods or services in any market in the United Kingdom; or

Part 3 CMA and other Guidelines

- greater innovation in relation to such goods or services.[58]

Some of the benefits which have been considered and/or proposed in past water merger proposals are set out in appendix 2.

4.3 POSSIBLE RELEVANT CUSTOMER BENEFITS

Companies who are proposing a merger should consider the different types of customer benefit that the merger gives rise to. The list of historical benefits described in past water mergers is illustrative of the types of benefits that could be proposed. It should not be assumed that each of these benefits will be regarded as acceptable and is not meant to be exhaustive. We encourage merger parties to bring forward innovative proposals for benefits arising from their specific case although we expect them to be credible and securable. The following sections categorise potential relevant customer benefits that we might consider when providing our advice to the CMA.

4.3.1 Lower prices

There are several ways in which a merger could result in a reduction in costs which could lead to lower prices which we discuss below.

We would expect companies to present a clear mechanism for how any cost savings will be passed on to customers in the form of reduced prices. We will attach a high degree of certainty if, for example, companies agreed to licence modifications which, if the merger was cleared, reduced prices in the current control period and/or at the next periodic review. We will place less weight on cost reductions which are less certain to be passed on to customers in the form of lower prices for example through totex cost sharing mechanisms, this is because we consider it is necessary to ensure that the management of the merged company is clearly incentivised to deliver the proposed savings. In addition the further into the future adjustments take place the less certainty and weight we are likely to place on them.

In general merger cases, savings in fixed costs might not be assumed to pass through to customers as they would not affect companies' optimal short-run pricing. However as water companies are monopolies, where we set prices based on average costs, savings in both fixed and marginal costs could be passed on to customers, although companies should be clear on the mechanism for how cost reductions would result in lower prices.

Operational cost savings

Operational cost savings comprise production and/or administrative efficiencies that can arise as a result of a merger. These efficiencies are usually understood through the concepts of economies of scale and economies of scope.

Economies of scale are where the average cost of production decreases with the scale of production. For example a merged company that had increased in size might not require a proportionate increase in the size of support functions and consequently the overhead costs per unit of production would decrease.

By rationalising such support functions and avoiding a duplication of shared activities, a merger may also be able to reduce the staff, IT and other infrastructure costs of the merged party. Cost savings were cited as a benefit in the 1990 merger of Three Valleys arising from staff reductions and also in the SAUR/Mid Kent/General Utilities merger in 1997 relating to head office savings and reduced infrastructure development needs.

Economies of scope describes a situation where the joint production cost of different goods or services is less than the sum of the production costs of the goods or services by separate specialised firms. In the context of the water industry, economies of scope would refer to the potential for cost savings due to the joint supply of:

- water and sewerage services as a whole;
- household and non-household customers; or
- upstream and downstream services in either water or sewerage.

Economies of scope may come from the use of common inputs in the supply of water and sewerage services or reduced overhead costs through, for example, shared network management and common billing.

The use of common inputs may also increase buyer power and thereby generate further cost savings, for example a small water only company (WoC) may increase its buying power on merging with a larger water and sewerage company (WaSC) as together they represent a larger customer for third party suppliers which may be able to negotiate better rates.

The evidence on economies of scale and economies of scope from previous empirical studies is dependent on the size and type of the merging firms. We would therefore expect clear direct evidence of economies, for example post-merger implementation plans, rather than relying solely on models which predict cost savings.

Mergers and acquisitions can provide benefits through an increased focus on the delivery of efficiencies, which could provide benefits to customers, including those of companies not the subject of the merger. Where merger parties propose such benefits should be taken into account, they will need to set out how these relevant customer benefits will reasonably be expected to occur and why they would not occur otherwise.

Improved water resource management (from contiguous companies sharing/better planning of resources)

Mergers may lead to improved water resource management (or reduced wastewater treatment) where companies can benefit from either sharing resources or planning them better. This is especially true of contiguous companies. This can lead to relevant customer benefits by reducing costs and customer charges. For these benefits to be included we would need to understand why this improvement in resource planning was only possible following a merger and not through other means.

Water resource management improvements and associated enhancements to security of supply were given as potential benefits in the South East/Mid Kent merger in 2006 and the SAUR/Mid Kent/General Utilities merger in 1997 which identified a range of water resource related benefits including integrating the network, leakage reduction and enhanced resource planning). Similarly Wessex/South West proposed a merger in 1996 which considered the more flexible use of an existing reservoir to be a benefit of the merger.

Reduced financing costs (from the ability to obtain more favourable terms as a larger company)

A merger could lead to reduced financing costs, or financial synergies from the ability of the companies post-merger to raise finance more cheaply than they could pre-merger. In PR14 we identified that small WoCs (Bristol Water, Dee Valley Water, Portsmouth Water, Sembcorp Bournemouth Water, Sutton and East Surrey Water and South Staffordshire Water) had higher debt costs of 25 basis points[59] which increased their weighted average cost of capital by 15 basis points. While a merger might not impact on embedded debt costs, it could reduce the costs of new debt for these companies.

4.3.2 Higher quality goods or services

A merger could increase service quality, for example by improving the security of supply, better customer service or reduced leakage rates. The SAUR/Mid Kent/General Utilities merger of 1997 cited improved service standards as a possible benefit, while Wessex/South West proposed improved customer service and enhanced customer confidence as potential benefits.

Improved service quality could be driven by sharing best practices where one company has better customer service practices and procedures and the other company could benefit from adopting those procedures post-merger. For these benefits to be included we would need to understand why this introduction of best practice was only possible following a merger and not through other means.

It may also be possible for two contiguous companies to increase their service quality for example by increasing their security of supply, through a better sharing of water resources. This was cited as a benefit to the 1996 proposed merger between South West Water and Wessex Water with the:

- potential merged company having flexible use of the Wimbleball reservoir;
- linking of Wessex Water Services and South West Water trunk mains; and
- completion of South West Water's water grid. Again we would need to understand why these customer benefits would only be possible through a merger.

4.3.3 Greater choice of goods or services

Choice for customers in the water sector is limited. Household customers cannot change supplier and so their choice of retail services is limited. The range of tariffs and terms and conditions available to household customers is largely influenced by companies' statutory obligations such as providing a vulnerable customer tariff or through steers from our incentives such as SIM. However it is possible that if each company had different tariffs and terms and conditions pre-merger, post-merger the new entity may keep both sets of tariffs and terms and conditions resulting in a greater choice of for their customers (as customers may have a greater range of tariffs to choose from).

There is currently some limited choice for non-household customers consuming at least 5 Ml of water per year (50 Ml for customers of Welsh water companies) and in terms of differing products for large industrial customers (for example, different grades of water quality, non-potable, potable and polished).

Choice is likely to improve for non-household customers after April 2017 when all business customers and public sector, charitable and not-for-profit organisations served by English water companies will be able to choose their water supplier and sewerage service provider. This may result in companies offering a greater range of goods and services and therefore may increase potential merger benefits if the merged entity offers all the goods and services of both pre-merged companies.

4.3.4 Greater innovation in relation to such goods or services

A merger can also impact on the level of innovation. Two ways this may occur are discussed below.

Research and development (R&D) spending on innovation

A merger can impact on the effectiveness of R&D spending in a number of ways.

Firstly, the returns from R&D could be higher the more widely the results are applied. Consequently a merger could increase the returns to the R&D process. This could increase incentives for, and investment in, R&D. For example the effectiveness of R&D could be increased by encouraging employees of the merged firm to share information. This would improve the chances of finding innovative solutions and allow lessons on operational efficiencies to be shared across operating regions. Horizontal mergers – that is, mergers of companies providing the same services such as water companies – could be particularly conducive to such R&D complementarities. However, it should be noted that as water companies effectively provide similar services with similar production processes there may little additional innovation to be realised from merging.[60]

A merger could also be detrimental to R&D if there are diminishing marginal returns to R&D investment – that is, for every extra unit of R&D, the expected returns on that extra unit fall. In theory, a merging party that combines two existing R&D programmes (without tempering the scale of the R&D investment) might be expected to reach diminishing marginal returns quicker than two separate R&D departments. The extent to which diminishing marginal returns would materialise would depend on how far away each merging firm is from the minimum efficient scale of R&D, and where the merged firm will lie in relation to this threshold. Potentially of greater consequence are other factors such as differing cultures and internal rivalries which can often lead to R&D failures in mergers.

Creation of more innovative structures

A merger could itself lead to more innovative structures, such as a very large water only company or a wastewater only company. These could provide customer benefits by producing greater efficiency than created by existing industry structures.

4.4 MERGER SPECIFICITY

Before we are satisfied that a benefit is a relevant customer benefit, we will have to be satisfied that the benefit would be unlikely to accrue without the merger and could not be achieved through other forms of permitted agreement between the parties. For example, in the Mid Kent/South East merger inquiry in 2007, the Competition Commission considered whether or not the water resource benefits put forward by the merger parties could be replicated by using flexible bulk supply agreements. We will look at any evidence submitted by the merger parties which indicates that the benefits from the merger could not be generated in any other way.

Where a benefit may have occurred absent the merger but taken longer to be realised, the accelerated benefits can be taken into account as a relevant customer benefit.

4.5 HOW MIGHT RELEVANT CUSTOMER BENEFITS CHANGE IN THE FUTURE?

There are a number of changes and challenges which may affect our views of future relevant customer benefits. We discuss these below.

4.5.1 Improved resilience

Particularly given our new duty (in relation to English water companies) to secure the long-term resilience of water supply and wastewater systems, we expect water companies to take steps to enable them, in the long term, to meet the need for water supplies and wastewater services. Improved resilience from a merger could take the form of increased security of supply from having greater availability of a range of water resources. This could result in relevant customer benefits from improved service quality, such as a reduction in the possibility of hosepipe bans.

4.5.2 Impact of abstraction reform on water resource management

Some undertakers have surplus water resources under their licences that they do not abstract. However, as the licence has been given and may be used in full if the company decided to, no further licences can be issued. This has an adverse effect on new entrants to the upstream markets as they have limited or no access to incumbent's surplus water supplies. We are considering abstraction reform which may address this issue.

Any future abstraction reform would need to be taken into account when considering the benefits of merging. For example abstraction reform could reduce the potential future customer benefits of a company with scarce water resources merging with a contiguous company with surplus water resources.

4.5.3 Creating more competitive markets could reduce scope for benefits from mergers

As set out above in relation to the impact on comparators, there may be a number of changes to the way that we regulate. These could have an impact on relevant customer benefits.

- Changes introduced during the 2015-20 period – non-household retail competition[61] network plus sub-limits.[62]
- Potential longer term changes from upstream competition (that is, competition in some of the non-retail elements of the control)[63] and binding service level sub-limits (where sub-limits could be introduced for individual services such as water resources, water storage, water distribution, water treatment, sewerage collection, sewerage treatment and sludge treatment and sludge disposal).

Where competition or more disaggregated price limits are introduced, we would expect this to increase the pressure on water companies to be more efficient and increase service quality. Relevant customer benefits must be unlikely to accrue without a merger. Changes to the way we regulate could erode some of the potential relevant customer benefits from a merger as improvements in efficiency or quality would take place without a merger.

NOTES

49 See sections 33A(1)(c) for anticipated mergers and 33A(2)(b) for completed mergers.

50 See paragraph 7(1) of Schedule 4ZA of the Water Industry Act 1991, as inserted by the Enterprise Act 2002.

51 Schedule 4ZA paragraph 7 of the Water Industry Act 1991 as inserted by the Enterprise Act 2002.

52 See Schedule 4ZA paragraph 7(8) of the Water Industry Act 1991 as inserted by the Enterprise Act 2002.

53 See section 129 Enterprise Act 2002. A consumer means any person who is (a) a person to whom goods are or are sought to be supplied (whether by way of sale or otherwise) in the course of a business carried on by the person supplying or seeking to supply them; or (b) a person for whom services are sought to be supplied in the course of a business carried on by the person supplying or seeking to supply them; and who does not receive or seek to receive the goods or services in the course of a business carried on by him.

54 See Schedule 4ZA paragraph 7(2) and 7(3) of the Water Industry Act 1991 as inserted by the Enterprise Act 2002 respectively for anticipated and completed mergers.

55 This is sometimes called the test of 'merger specificity'.

56 See Schedule 4ZA paragraph 7(2) and 7(3) of the Water Industry Act 1991.

57 This is consistent with the guidance adopted by Monitor for mergers in the health sector. See page 11 of 'Supporting NHS providers: guidance on merger benefits' – www.gov.uk/government/uploads/system/uploads/attachment_data/file/340823/Monitor_mergerbenefits_guidance.pdf

58 See Schedule 4ZA paragraph 7(1) of the Water Industry Act 1991.

59 This was based on a notional capital structure and typical debt costs and so does not match precisely their individual actual debt costs, see section a.7.4.2.www.ofwat.gov.uk/pricereview/pr14/det_pr20141212riskreward.pdf

60 60 Davidson, C. and Ferrett, B. (2006) 'Mergers in Multidimensional Competition'. Economica, vol. 74, pp695-712.

61 Non-household retail competition – introduces retail competition to all non-household customers of English water companies (non-household customers of Welsh water companies consuming at least 50Ml/d will continue to be able to switch supplier).

62 Network plus – introduces non-binding sub-limits for:

- water; covering raw water distribution, water treatment and treated water distribution, but not water resources; and
- wastewater; covering sewerage collection and treatment but not sludge treatment, recycling and disposal.

63 Upstream covers storing, treating and distributing water and collecting and disposing of sewerage.

5. UNDERTAKINGS IN LIEU

[3.556]
As set out in the Water Act 2014, if relevant customer benefits from a merger do not outweigh the likely prejudice to our ability to make comparisons, then the CMA may accept UILs instead of making a reference for a Phase 2 inquiry.[64] UILs must remedy, mitigate or prevent the prejudice to our ability to make comparisons from a merger. Before deciding on whether to accept UILs the CMA must request and consider our opinion on the effect of the undertakings offered.[65]

This chapter sets out the key issues that we will consider when providing our advice to the CMA on the effect of the undertakings offered. This chapter describes:

- the background to UILs;
- the principles of a 'good' UIL;
- potential types of UIL;
- undertakings and remedies in previous water merger cases; and
- our approach in the future.

5.1 BACKGROUND TO UILS

UILs are for remedying, mitigating or preventing the prejudicial effect of a merger on our ability to make comparisons.[66] When considering undertakings the CMA must have regard to the need to achieve as comprehensive a solution as reasonable and practicable to the prejudicial effect on our ability to make comparisons.[67] The CMA may also have regard to the effect of undertakings on relevant customer benefits from the merger.[68]

Once an undertaking is in place and a merger has proceeded it may be varied, replaced or released by the CMA.[69] The CMA must consider any representations made to make a change to or vary an undertaking as soon as reasonably practicable.[70]

5.2 UNDERTAKINGS AND REMEDIES IN PREVIOUS WATER MERGER CASES

UILs have not previously formed part of Phase 1 of a water merger inquiry. However, the Competition Commission (one of the CMA's predecessors) has previously considered remedies as part of a Phase 2 water merger inquiry. Remedies and undertakings proposed in previous mergers or potential mergers have included:

- prohibition – Severn Trent/Wessex and South West;
- divestment – Vivendi/Southern – divestment of Three Valleys Water and stake in South Staffordshire Water (did not proceed); and
- customer cost savings – South East/Mid Kent (one off rebate and opex reduction in PR09).

Appendix 2 provides further details of remedies and undertakings proposed in previous mergers or potential mergers.

5.3 PRINCIPLES OF A 'GOOD' UIL

We consider that a good UIL (or package of undertakings) should provide as comprehensive a solution as possible to the prejudicial effect on our ability to make comparisons as a result of a merger. However, it will not necessarily restore us to exactly the same position in terms of our ability to make comparisons which we were in pre-merger. We consider that an undertaking should adhere to the following key principles. It should:

- provide a clear cut solution in addressing the prejudice caused by losing a comparator (that is, there should be no material doubts on the effectiveness of the UILs). Ofwat, and therefore water customers, should not bear significant risks that UILs will have the requisite impact on our ability to make comparisons (but with the understanding that it not always possible to fully anticipate all effects of the UILs). UILs should therefore have a high degree of certainty that they will work;
- be able to be assessed and implemented with the resources available at Phase 1;
- cause minimal adverse effects;
- have the appropriate duration and timing (addressing the adverse effects quickly is preferable);
- be practical, that is, if monitoring and enforcement is required it must be effective and clear to us, the CMA and merger parties what is going to be done and the implications;
- be proportionate to the prejudicial harm identified; and
- maintain any relevant customer benefits as far as possible.

In Phase 1 of a merger investigation, we will want to be confident that the likely prejudice will be resolved by means of the UILs offered without the need for a Phase 2 investigation. We consider that UILs are only appropriate where the remedies proposed to address them are clear cut – that is, without material doubts about their overall effectiveness and capable of ready implementation within the timeframes of a Phase 1 investigation. This mirrors the CMA's approach to UILs in the general merger regime. We would not expect that every merger will be resolved at Phase 1. It should be emphasised that the final decision to accept UILs rests with the CMA, after considering Ofwat's opinion.

5.4 POTENTIAL TYPES OF UNDERTAKINGS

UILs can be structural such as the divestment of part of the merged business or behavioural such as a formal commitment from merger parties about future conduct. The CMA has stated that in line with its general merger guidance it will consider behavioural remedies for mergers in markets in which there already exists a significant degree of regulation (such as water).[71]

The acceptability of an undertaking to Ofwat will depend on the circumstances involved and the level of prejudice that a merger is likely to cause to our ability to make comparisons. When assessing potential undertakings we will consider both the prejudice to our ability to make comparisons now, but also what measures might assist our ability to make comparisons in the future. This could include creating the ability to make comparisons in new areas, by for example creating separate management, licencing, accounting or reporting of specific water or wastewater services. For example, an undertaking could separate out retail or water resources from treatment and networks. The greater the degree of independence and separation of these services, the greater benefit this is likely to bring in providing comparisons in the future.

The following are provided as an indication of potential undertakings and are not intended to be comprehensive. We would particularly welcome undertakings that created new or innovative comparators.

UILs could comprise:

- divestiture – for example the sale of a non-contiguous part of the water company, which could create an additional independent comparator;
- partial divestitures – for example a reduction in the equity stake and therefore the degree of control, which in some circumstances, could create management independence and restore our ability to make comparisons;
- separate administration – for example an undertaking to maintain or create separate management, accounting or reporting arrangements, for either the company taken over or for particular services within the merged entity. This could include, for example, offering to create a separate retail company, or separate management of water resources and networks. This could also include the adoption of innovative structures that allow for new or different forms of comparisons to be made to help set stretching benchmarks in the future; and/or
- amending licences – for example the creation of modular licences for separate services within the merged entity. Such licence amendments could subsequently be adopted by other companies.

Each of the examples above have the potential to mitigate, prevent or remedy the prejudicial effect on our ability to make comparisons. Consistent with the view set out by the CMA,[72] we do not consider price reductions qualify for consideration as undertakings in lieu as undertakings at Phase 1 must directly address any prejudice that would otherwise occur. Price reductions may, however, be considered as a remedy in Phase 2 as remedies may be broader in scope.

5.4.1 Divestiture of other water enterprises

A merging party could undertake to divest itself of a holding in one or more other water enterprises. Where this would appropriately restore our ability to make comparisons (that is, it creates an additional independent comparator) it could provide an effective and proportionate remedy.

5.4.2 Partial divestitures

Undertakings to divest part of a water enterprise (rather than full divestiture) could, in some instances, provide an effective and proportionate remedy to the identified prejudice from the merger. This would be the case when our ability to make comparisons would be restored by divestiture of part of one of the merging companies. A partial divestiture might be of a stand-alone, going-concern business or of physical assets, for instance those serving part of a company's licence area or divestiture of water or sewerage activities. A partial divesture could also involve the reduction in the equity holding of a company, however such a reduction would need to give the water company management independence where this was not previously the case.

5.4.3 Separate administration

Separate administration could involve an undertaking to maintain separate management or separate accounting arrangements of the company taken over or to create separate management or accounting arrangements within the merged entity. The greater the degree of independence or separation of the company or services then the greater the comparator benefits. Maintaining separate data points from companies under common ownership can provide value to the regulatory regime,[73] although we consider comparators that are fully independent (that is, under independent ownership) have the greatest value. This is because companies operating under common ownership or control are likely to adopt the same management structures and operational structures over time. A lesser but related benefit may also be created by having separate cost information (for example split by upstream services) within the merged company.

UILs could also include the creation of innovative structures that would allow new or different forms of comparisons to be undertaken, which would help us to continue to adopt stretching benchmarks in the future.

5.4.4 Amending licences

An undertaking to agree to amend one or both of the company's licences could amount to a structural undertaking (for example introducing conditions which require the separation of certain activities into separate business units), or a behavioural undertaking (for example, the provision of information). As with other areas, the greater the level of independent data created, the greater the benefit.

NOTES

64 Section 33D (1) of the Water Industry Act 1991 as amended.

65 Section 33D (6) of the Water Industry Act 1991 as amended.

66 Section 33D (2) of the Water Industry Act 1991 as amended.

67 Section 33D (4) of the Water Industry Act 1991 as amended.

68 Section 33D (6) of the Water Industry Act 1991 as amended.

69 Section 33D (8) of the Water Industry Act 1991 as amended.

70 Section 33D (10) of the Water Industry Act 1991 as amended.

71 See paragraph 6.12 CMA (2015), Water and sewerage mergers: Guidance on the CMA's procedure and assessment.

72 CMA 2015, 'Water and sewerage mergers: Guidance on the CMA's procedure and assessment – draft for consultation'.

73 There are circumstances where separate reporting is necessary for the purposes of monitoring against the final determination, for example in relation to ODIs.

6. THE PHASE 1 WATER MERGER PROCESS AND OUR EXPECTATIONS OF MERGER PARTIES

[3.557]

This chapter sets out the Phase 1 water merger process following the Water Act 2014, including our expectations of merger parties and the process we expect to follow.

6.1 LEGAL REQUIREMENTS

The Water Act 2014 introduces a 'two stage' process for water mergers. This will mean that not all qualifying mergers will need to be referred to the in-depth Phase 2 CMA inquiry group-led review.[74] The existing Phase 1 merger inquiry process assesses whether the merger is a water merger and whether at least one of the water companies meets a minimum turnover threshold of £10 million. If these tests are met then the merger is referred to a detailed Phase 2 investigation. The Water Act 2014 adds in additional tests to allow the CMA to conclude within Phase 1 that it would not need to refer the merger for a more detailed investigation if:

- the merger is anticipated and the arrangements are not sufficiently advanced or unlikely to proceed;
- the merger is not likely to prejudice our ability, in carrying out its functions, to make comparisons between water enterprises;[75] or
- the merger is likely to prejudice that ability, but the prejudice in question is outweighed by relevant customer benefits relating to the merger; or
- there are appropriate UILs from the merger parties which remedy, mitigate or prevent the prejudicial effect on our ability to make comparisons between water enterprises from the merger.[76]

The ultimate decision on whether there is a requirement to undertake a Phase 2 investigation, and which (if any) undertakings to accept, rests with the CMA after considering our advice.

6.2 OVERVIEW OF PHASE 1 PROCESS

Based on the general merger regime and the requirements under the Water Act 2014 there are potentially three main stages to the Phase 1 process.

- **Pre-notification.** In the pre-notification phase, merger parties are encouraged to discuss the proposed merger with both Ofwat and the CMA. There is no formal time limit on these discussions, so merger parties are encouraged to open dialogue with Ofwat and the CMA at the earliest opportunity in respect of merger impacts and undertakings in lieu to enable all parties to consider their positions ahead of any formal Phase 1 investigation. As stated in section 6.2.3, if requested, we may provide informal advice on a potential transaction, but this will not endorse any particular view put forward by the merger parties, nor be binding on Ofwat.

- **Phase 1 investigation.** In the Phase 1 investigation the CMA will consider whether the merger will prejudice Ofwat's ability to make comparisons and whether relevant customer benefits arising from the merger would outweigh this prejudice. The CMA must request and consider Ofwat's opinion on these issues. Ofwat must provide its advice in accordance with its statement of methods. If merger parties have raised UILs by this stage of the process the CMA must also consider Ofwat's opinion on the effect of those UILs.
- **Consideration of UILs of a Phase 2 reference.** If the CMA concludes that a merger prejudices Ofwat's ability to make comparisons between water companies, and that this prejudice is not outweighed by relevant customer benefits, the merger parties will have the opportunity to propose UILs to offset that prejudice. If UILs are proposed the CMA must request and consider Ofwat's opinion on these undertakings before determining whether the UILs offered are sufficient to offset the prejudice.

6.2.1 Our expectations of merger parties

Following the introduction of changes set out in the Water Act 2014, the special merger regime will be amended[77] to allow a process whereby a decisions on a water merger can be achieved during Phase 1 of a merger investigation rather than automatic referral to an in-depth, Phase 2, investigation.

Given the short timescales for the formal Phase 1 investigation and the need for robust analysis, this places significant importance on evidence provided by merger parties during the pre-notification and Phase 1 process.

Consistent with our strategy of companies taking responsibility for their relationship with their customers,[78] we expect merger parties to have a good understanding of the potential impact of a merger, particularly in terms of relevant customer benefits. In their submission to us, we expect merger parties to set out:

- the rationale for the merger;
- the impact of the merger on our ability to make comparisons;
- the relevant customer benefits from the merger, and whether these outweigh the impact on our ability to make comparisons; and, if they do not;
- any UILs that would prevent, mitigate or remedy the impact our ability to make comparisons.

Our statement of methods sets out the criteria and weightings that we would apply to the assessment of a merger on our ability to make comparisons and relevant customer benefits. Our statement of methods also sets out the criteria on which we would expect to assess evidence provided by merger parties. We have also commissioned a report by Europe Economics into techniques for assessing the impact of mergers. To provide the best opportunity for assessment at Phase 1, merger parties should develop their submission in line with our statement of methods and take account of the report into evaluation methods developed by Europe Economics.

Consistent with our wider commitment to transparency, we expect to publish non-confidential versions of our spreadsheets that are used to assess merger impacts where these do not contain confidential information. We consider that sufficient information will be available in the pre-notification phase in order to carry out the assessment, with the main uncertainties being those associated with synergy savings and other benefits to customers that might arise direct as a result of the merger.

6.2.2 The potential timetable for the Phase 1 process

The Water Act 2014 does not specify a Phase 1 timetable for water mergers.[79] Table 1 sets out the expected timetable based on the application of the CMA's general merger regime timetable to water mergers. This is based on the CMA's published guidance on jurisdiction and procedure.[80] In the light of the revised water merger regime the CMA has consulted on revisions to its guidance on water mergers. The timetable is consistent with the timetable the CMA set out in its consultation.[81]

TABLE 1 THE POTENTIAL TIMETABLE FOR THE PHASE 1 PROCESS

Timing	Party	Action
Pre-notification		
During pre-notification period	Merger parties	Merger parties contact Ofwat to identify potential merger and discuss merger process and Ofwat's information requirements. Merger parties are encouraged to contact the CMA at the same time.
	Merger parties	Merger parties submit draft of evidence to Ofwat.
Phase 1 investigation		

Timing	Party	Action
Day 1	CMA	The CMA will not start the investigation until it has sufficient information and Ofwat has the necessary information required to carry out the assessment. Ofwat expects to receive a complete **merger impact assessment** from the merger parties to have sufficient information to begin its assessment and expects that merger parties share this with the CMA. Merger parties should provide confidential and non-confidential versions of the merger impact assessment
Day 1	CMA	The CMA start the assessment stage of the investigation by publishing an invitation to comment notice on their website (which is open for ten working days) in order to understand third parties views on the merger.
Before state of play discussion	Ofwat	Ofwat sends draft opinion to the CMA on whether the merger would prejudice its ability to make comparisons and whether relevant customer benefits outweigh this prejudice.
Day 15–20	CMA	CMA holds **state of play discussion** with merger parties (typically by phone) which will set out whether it has no serious concerns and can clear the transaction of whether it has identified issues which require a subsequent issues meeting. Ofwat will attend the state of play discussion.
Before Day 40	CMA	For cases which raise no serious concerns CMA can clear the transaction and issue a clearance decision.
No earlier than day 25	CMA	Where CMA has not cleared the transaction, the CMA invites merger parties to an **issues meeting** and sends merger parties an issues letter stating core arguments for reference to Phase 2 and holds an issues meeting with the parties where parties have an opportunity to respond to the outlined concerns. Ofwat will attend the issues meeting.
Before issues meeting	Ofwat	Ofwat sends its final opinion on the issues raised by the merger
Before or after issues meeting	Merger parties	Merger parties may provide comments on the issues statement either before or after the issues meeting.
After issues meeting	Ofwat	Where appropriate Ofwat will provide the CMA with its reply to the parties' response to the issues letter and issues meeting.
By Day 40	CMA	CMA publishes **notice of decision** (with full decision published at a later date)
Consideration of UILs of a Phase 2 reference		
Before day 40	Merger parties	Merger parties are encouraged to engage in early discussion with Ofwat and the CMA on UILs.
0–5 working days after parties given decision	Merger parties	Merger parties who wish to make offer of UILs provide these to the CMA, unless already provided. The CMA provides UILs to Ofwat.
By day 9 after parties given decision	Ofwat	Ofwat provides draft opinion to the CMA on the UILs
Up to 10 workings days after parties given decision	CMA	If no UIL is provided within 5 working days then CMA refers to Phase 2. CMA decides whether to provisionally accept UILs, taking into account Ofwat's opinion on the offered UILs. If CMA rejects UILs then it refers the transaction to Phase 2 investigation.
Before CMA decision on UILs	Ofwat	Ofwat provides its final opinion on UILs to the CMA.
Within 50 working days of parties being given decision	CMA	CMA gives detailed consideration to terms of proposed UILs. CMA publishes draft UILs for third party comment. CMA decides whether to formally accept UILs, and either publishes notice of acceptance or refers the transaction to Phase 2.

6.2.3 The pre-notification discussions

Pre-notification discussions take place when parties to a merger have decided to notify a merger and wish to engage with Ofwat and the CMA in advance of its formal notification.[82] The formal process for Ofwat will be different to that of the CMA in that it will focus on the parties' submission on the impact of the merger and the subsequent provision of its opinion to the CMA. It is in the interests of both Ofwat and the merger parties that the parties' formal merger impact assessment submission to Ofwat is as well formed as possible as this will provide the best opportunity for parties to avoid an in-depth Phase 2 investigation. Given the short timescale for the Phase 1 investigation, pre-notification discussions will provide merger parties the best opportunity of providing a well formed submission.

We recognise that discussions with the merger parties will be commercially sensitive throughout the merger investigation. Consistent with the CMA's guidance,[83] we expect the merger parties will work closely and openly with both us and the CMA throughout the merger investigation, including in the pre-notification phase. During this period and throughout the investigation information may be shared between the CMA and Ofwat, as set out in information requests below.

The pre-notification process can assist both us and merger parties in a number of ways.

- It provides us with details on the merger, including its rationale and potential benefits.
- It allows merger parties to clarify our process and to take account of our views on the information we require as part of the formal merger impact assessment submission by the merger parties on the impact on our ability to make comparisons and relevant customer benefits.
- It allows merger parties to provide drafts of the evidence they intend to submit, and allow us to provide informal advice on these submissions, to allow the formal submission to be well formed. Any informal advice will be:
  - made on an informal 'without prejudice basis' and will not fetter our discretion to make an appropriate formal submission to the CMA;
  - made on a strictly confidential basis;
  - dependent on the information provided by the merger parties, and as there will not be time to test parties submissions, will assume the information provided is accurate;
  - any advice will not provide agreement in principle on a merger, nor endorse a particular view put forward by advisers, nor will it be binding; and
  - restricted to a limited number of occasions so that informal advice is not iterative although other informal pre-notification discussions are not limited:
- It allows merger parties to discuss with us any potential UILs that could prevent, remedy or mitigate any prejudice to our ability to make comparisons. We are particularly ready to engage with parties who acknowledge that the merger might create potential issues and wish to seek advice on how to resolve these.

6.2.4 Phase 1 investigation

The start of the Phase 1 investigation

The CMA has indicated that Phase 1 will begin when we and the CMA have sufficient information to begin our respective investigations. For us this will mean that we have all information that the merging companies wish to be considered in the Phase 1 investigation.

Merger parties merger impact assessment submission

We set out our expectations for the content of the merger impact assessment in section 6.2.1.

When making their submission, merger parties should be aware that we will assess the impact of the merger on our ability to make comparisons and relevant customer benefits based on our statement of methods, which is set out in Appendix 1. Merger parties should also take account of the evaluation techniques set out in the Europe Economics report.

Merger party submissions that comply with our statement of methods are likely to have the most weight. To this end companies should consider the loss of a comparator and the resulting prejudice on our ability to regulate in terms of:

- setting price limits – for example, setting cost benchmarks and comparing expenditure and financing costs across companies;
- service quality – for example, comparing performance commitments and service quality across companies; and
- our ongoing role in monitoring, enforcement and spreading best practice – for example, comparisons of company Board leadership, transparency and reporting.

Companies should have regard to our statement of methods and address:

- whether the merger involves overlaps in the merger parties' scope of services;
- whether the merger involves the loss of an independent comparator;
- whether the merger leads to a loss of a comparator which changes benchmarks;
- the number and quality of independent observations that will remain after the merger;
- whether the merger leads to a loss of a comparator with important similarities for comparisons;
- whether the merger leads to a loss of a comparator with important differences for comparison; and
- whether there are alternative approaches available to Ofwat to offset the loss of this comparator.

Companies should consider relevant customer benefits, which are benefits that:

- lower prices;
- increase service quality;
- lead to a greater choice of services;
- lead to greater innovation;
- are a direct result of the merger (and unlikely to occur otherwise);
- accrue to customers (and their customers) of merger parties; and
- accrue within a reasonable period of time.

Merger parties should monetise impacts where possible over the long term, for example, 30 years and a shorter term view, for example, five to ten years, consistent with the statement of methods. Where monetised impacts are not possible merger parties should quantify or qualitatively assess impacts and provide an indication of scale, for example how these non-monetised impacts compare with the monetised impacts, together with supporting evidence.

To inform our assessment of the proposed benefits of a merger, merger parties should provide detailed evidence about the types of benefits which they anticipate will accrue, when those benefits will accrue, how likely these benefits are to accrue to customers, how long the benefits will last and which customers will benefit.

As a part of developing an evidence base, merger parties may wish to seek to demonstrate that customers support the proposed means of delivering benefits to them, and also that the proposed means of delivering benefits is customers' most preferred option – that is, that some alternative approach is not preferred by customers.

Merger parties should also describe how the benefits will be generated – that is, how the operation of the companies will be changed and how that will create the proposed benefits. For example, where cost savings are proposed, we will consider evidence on the details of how those cost savings may be achieved by the merging companies, for example in terms of clear and detailed post-merger implementation plan. This will help to show how likely it is that those cost savings will be secured and whether or not cost savings are likely to continue beyond the initial price control period. Likewise, if a merger is anticipated to give rise to improvements in quality of service or water resource management, merger parties should set out how those benefits will arise. It is important for merger parties to provide evidence that benefits can only be gained as a result of the merger and not through any other means. For example improved security of supply could be a benefit of merging but it could also potentially be realised through a flexible bulk supply agreement.

Merger parties should also set out how benefits, for example reductions in costs would flow through to benefits to customers. We will attach most weight to customer benefits which are certain.

To support their analysis merger parties should provide supporting data, spreadsheets, conclusions and evidence of customer support. We will place the most weight on evidence which

- is clear and transparent around approach and assumptions;
- is a complete description of the analysis;
- we able are to replicate;
- is robust and includes independent assurance; and
- has evidence of customer support.[84]

Information should be provided in both confidential and non-confidential formats where applicable along with reasons for confidentiality where necessary.

The Statement of intent, which sets out the working arrangements between Ofwat and the CMA in relation to water mergers, confirms the CMA will not commence a merger review until it considers the merger parties have provided sufficient information required for the respective assessments of both Ofwat and the CMA. If suitable information is not included in the merger parties' merger impact assessment submission, then we will inform the CMA not to start Phase 1 of the merger investigation until such time as suitable information is presented to us.

Where merger parties analysis indicates that there may be prejudice to our ability to make comparisons we encourage companies to consider, evaluate and provide evidence for potential UILs which would mitigate any prejudicial effect.

The onus is on merger parties to provide enough evidence and a robust and through analysis to justify why merger should not proceed to Phase 2.

Further information from merger parties

We may need additional, or more comprehensive, information from the merger parties than is provided in the initial merger impact assessment submission (even though the information we have received is sufficient for the CMA to start its investigation). In this case we will ask for any such additional data, information or documents as soon as it is clear they will be necessary. However, given the short timescales replies also have to be supplied quickly which might be as short as one business day where necessary.

Information requests

Water companies are required to provide Ofwat with information that we reasonably require for the purposes of carrying out our functions under the Water Industry Act 1991, including our functions of advising the CMA.[85]

We would expect to share relevant information provided to Ofwat with the CMA. Given the short timescales in the Phase 1 process we encourage companies to send all information to Ofwat and the CMA at the same time. Sharing of information (including data) between Ofwat and the CMA is crucial for the effective fulfilment of our respective duties. It should reduce the burden on merger parties which would otherwise arise. Any disclosure of information between Ofwat and the CMA, and any use by the recipient of such information, shall only be to the extent permitted by law, including by reference to the provisions of section 206 of the Water Industry Act 1991 and Part 9 of the Enterprise Act 2002.

Discussions with merger parties

We will continue to engage with and request information from merger parties as appropriate until we make our final submission to the CMA. We will also continue to engage with merger parties throughout the Phase 1 process on potential UILs of a reference to Phase 2.

We encourage merger parties and their advisers to liaise closely with our merger team during the lifetime of the case. Ideally, this process should start with pre-notification discussions.

The level of interaction required between merger parties and their advisers and our merger team will depend on the individual circumstances of the merger in question. It may be sufficient for the parties to liaise with the merger team by email on a periodic basis, alternatively it may be helpful for parties and our merger team to have conference calls and/or meetings. There is no fixed timetable as to when such contacts should occur. Merger parties may suggest such contacts if they consider they would be useful and we will agree to a meeting if we consider it appropriate.

The Phase 1 decision making process

We will assess the merger based on our statement of methods, taking into account the evidence provided by merger parties and the valuation techniques set out in the Europe Economics report. We will provide our evidence to the CMA.

The decision on whether to refer a merger to Phase 2 rests with the CMA.

We will publish our advice after the CMA makes its decision on whether the merger should be referred to Phase 2.

6.2.5 Undertakings in lieu

UILs are for the purpose of remedying, mitigating or preventing the prejudicial effect of the merger on Ofwat's ability to make comparisons.

Under the general merger regime after the publication of the CMA's merger decision notice, merger parties have 5 working days to provide UILs to avoid a Phase 2 review.[86] However, notifying parties can provide draft UILs as part of the merger impact assessment submission or during the Phase 1 investigation. We strongly recommend that where notifying parties consider that there may be concerns with the impact of the merger on our ability to make comparisons then they should consider possible UILs during the pre-notification phase and include proposals as part of the merger impact assessment submission. This ensures that, if UILs are formally proposed following the merger decision, parties will be able to submit their proposed UILs rapidly, maximising the chance of acceptance.

In advance of the merger decision, our merger team can assist merger parties in understanding the functioning of UILs. Our merger team will also, where possible, provide guidance to parties on which of the possible remedies being considered by the parties might be more suitable. However our merger team is not able to formally agree with the parties whether a formal package of UILs would be acceptable to us. **It should be emphasised that although we must provide our opinion to the CMA on any UILs offered by the parties, the final decision on whether the UILs are acceptable rests with the CMA and not with Ofwat.** For this reason, we would be willing to consider, and provide our opinion to the CMA on, undertakings put forward that are conditional on the CMA clearing the merger at Phase 1.

If the CMA finds that its duty is to refer the merger for a Phase 2 investigation, merger parties have 5 working days after the CMA's merger decision notice, to provide UILs of a Phase 2 reference. We would then have to provide an opinion to the CMA on the effect of the UILs offered. Within 10 days of the decision notice the CMA will publish its provisional view on whether the proposed UILs can remedy the detriment caused by the merger.

There is then a period of a further 40 working days (that is a total of 50 working days after the merger decision notice) where the CMA will consider the proposed UILs in detail. Consistent with the Statement of intent, which sets out the agreed working practices between Ofwat and the CMA in respect of a merger investigation, Ofwat will provide its opinion on the UIL no later than the ninth working day after the parties have received the CMA's duty to refer the decision. Consistent with the Statement of intent, this may be considered a provisional decision; if the CMA decides to consult on the UILs, Ofwat will provide its final decision on the UILs at least two days before the start of the consultation period. Third parties will also have the opportunity to comment on the CMA's consultation on the proposed undertakings. The CMA then makes the final decision as to whether the proposed UIL is appropriate and publishes a note of acceptance or refers the merger to Phase 2. In special cases the CMA may extend the period of 50 working days by a maximum of a further 40 working days.

6.2.6 Our approach to licence modifications

Companies that merge may come to Ofwat to seek a single appointment or licence. The instrument of appointment sets out the area for which the appointment is held, that is, the geographical area the monopoly water company operates in, and the conditions of that appointment. These conditions include charges, charges schemes, codes of practice, accounting information, ring fencing and service standards.

We consider that the introduction of a merged licence provides an opportunity to include standard licence conditions, where appropriate, and introduce other measures that are expected to improve our ability to make comparisons in the future. We might also seek these changes even if merged parties do not ask for a single licence. We would therefore expect updated licence conditions to include the following.

- Standard licence conditions where these are not already in the merging companies' licences, including – for example, the introduction of the full suite of ring-fencing licence conditions.
- A requirement that prices in the acquired area are no higher than they otherwise would have been under the current price control.
- Any provisions which would ensure that the customers of the acquired company do not receive deterioration in service.
- Any requirements that will be placed on the merger parties in respect of separate accounting and outcome reporting between water or sewerage supply regions.
- Where appropriate, a modular licence and licence conditions which reflect the way that we regulate (we are developing a suite of modular licence conditions as part of our published 2015-16 forward programme).
- Any licence amendments required as part of undertakings, for example reductions in price limits.

Where merger parties agree to a set of licence amendments, such as the introduction of modular licences as an undertaking in lieu, such licence amendments could subsequently be adopted by other companies. We do recognise however that companies might be operating in different circumstances and so licence conditions might need amending in certain circumstances.

The licence modification process will commence following the decision not to prohibit a merger by the CMA following the process required under the Water Industry Act 1991.

If companies are not proposing to accept these conditions to a merged licence then merger parties should indicate this, together with the reasons why in the merger impact assessment submission. The less certain that the benefits of the merger will be transferred to customer benefits, the less likely we will be able provide an opinion to the CMA that relevant customer benefits would outweigh the prejudicial effect on our ability to make comparisons.

NOTES

74 A Phase 2 merger inquiry can take up top 36 weeks. Mergers: Guidance on the CMA's jurisdiction and procedure, CMA. www.gov.uk/government/uploads/system/uploads/attachment_data/file/384055/CMA2__Mergers__Guidance.pdf

75 Section 33A of the Water Industry Act 1991 (as amended).

76 Section 33D of the Water Industry Act 1991 (as amended).

77 Ofwat's Statement of Methods must be published before the new regime is put in place. At the time of writing, it is anticipated the new merger regime will be put in place in November 2015.

78 Cathryn Ross, March 2015, Regulating modern utilities: the future approach.

79 The introduction of statutory deadlines for water mergers will require secondary legislation.

80 CMA, 2014, Mergers: Guidance on the CMA's jurisdiction and procedure.

81 CMA 2015, 'Water and sewerage mergers: Guidance on the CMA's procedure and assessment – draft for consultation'.

83 CMA (2015), 'Water and sewerage mergers: Guidance on the CMA's procedure and assessment – draft for consultation'.

84 The first three of these criteria follow CMA guidance on the submission of evidence and the last two are in line with the principles used in PR14.

85 See licence condition M.

86 See CMA (2014) Mergers: Guidance on the CMA's jurisdiction and procedure.

APPENDIX A1: OFWAT'S MERGER ASSESSMENT – STATEMENT OF METHODS

[3.558]

The Water Industry Act 1991 (as amended) requires Ofwat to publish a statement of methods which we must apply when forming an opinion on mergers.[87] The statement of methods must include the criteria we will use for assessing the effect of any particular water merger on our ability, in carrying out our functions by virtue of the Water Industry Act 1991, to make comparisons between water enterprises and the relative weight to be given to the criteria.

Our statement of methods is based on our duties, our strategy (which puts the focus on company ownership), our principles for assessing mergers and takes into account CMA merger guidelines.

Based on our general duties we would normally expect that, if a company was able to carry out and finance its functions pre-merger, then it should be able to do so post-merger. Consequently the assessment of the impact of the loss of a comparator is likely to be focused on the customer impact and, where relevant, our resilience duty.

This statement of methods sets out the:

- basis for our assessment (the counterfactual and the impact of our regulatory approach);
- criteria for determining the impact on our ability to make comparisons and for the assessment of customer benefits;
- weighting given to each criterion; and
- approach for determining whether the prejudice is substantially outweighed by the relevant customer benefits.

A1.1 THE COUNTERFACTUAL

Our assessment of the impact of a merger is based on both the factual (with the merger) and counterfactual (without the merger).

The counterfactual can be defined in a number of ways. At Phase 1, we will consider the effect of the merger compared with the counterfactual that creates the most detriment, that is, the counterfactual against which the merger would do most harm to our ability to make comparisons as long as we consider that scenario to be a realistic prospect. The aim in doing so at Phase 1 is to make sure that problematic mergers are not missed.[88]

In practice, we will normally use the prevailing conditions for the foreseeable future as the counterfactual against which to assess the impact of the merger – that is, both firms operating under independent ownership.

A1.2 IMPACT OF OUR REGULATORY APPROACH

When considering the impact of a merger we will also need to consider the regulatory regime under which the use of comparators or customer benefits needs to be evaluated. Typically we will use the prevailing form of regulation as the main basis for our assessment. However, we may use alternative scenarios where we believe conditions might change for example if we have made public statements about where our future regulatory approach might change whether this change has been implemented or not. Where there is less certainty about the evolution of the use of comparators we will use a scenario approach to the assessment, to assess whether future regulatory changes would have a material impact on our ability to use comparisons or customer benefits.

A1.3 CRITERIA FOR DETERMINING WHETHER THE MERGER WOULD PREJUDICE OUR ABILITY TO MAKE COMPARISONS

We will consider the loss of a comparator and the resulting prejudice on our ability to regulate in three key areas.

- Setting price limits – for example, setting cost benchmarks and comparing expenditure and financing costs across companies.
- Improving service quality – for example, comparing performance commitments and service quality across companies.
- Our on-going role in monitoring, enforcement and spreading best practice – for example, comparisons of company Board leadership, transparency and reporting.

When considering the impact of a merger, we will measure it against the criteria below. The criteria are based on the harm that a merger might do to our ability to make comparisons:

Criterion 1: The extent to which the merger involves overlaps

We consider that the greater the degree of overlap in merger parties' scope of activities, the more likely a merger is to prejudice our ability to make comparisons between undertakers. For example, a WaSC merging with another WaSC has a large degree of overlap (water, sewerage and retail services are all provided by both companies) and so is more likely to prejudice our ability to make comparisons. Conversely a WoC taking over the wastewater activities of a WaSC would have no overlap in the scope of services and so we would be less concerned about potential prejudice.

Criterion 2: Whether the merger involves the loss of an independent comparator

A water merger brings under common ownership or common control two or more undertakers. The merging undertakers continue to operate under separate licences (referred to in the Water Industry Act 1991 as the appointments) unless their licences are modified, which would require our approval. In the absence of licence changes, we can continue to receive separate information from each of the merging water enterprises and this can provide value in making comparisons. However, in general, we believe that companies under common ownership may behave in similar ways; we consider comparators that provide fully independent data points provide greatest value to the regime and therefore a water merger may reduce the value of comparisons made by Ofwat.

Criterion 3: The extent to which the merger will change benchmarks

We will consider the relative performance of the pre-merger companies. If at least one of the merging companies is leading or high performing in some areas, there is a greater risk of detriment for customers than if both companies are poor performers. This is because there is a risk that a high performing comparator might be lost as a result of the merger, for example if the high performing company is taken over. In addition even if two high performing companies merge then a high performing comparator would be lost which would have a detrimental impact on cross industry benchmarks, reducing the scale of challenge for other companies in the sector. We acknowledge that a take-over by high performing company might improve the performance of a poorer performing company by providing improved efficiency or service to a greater number of customers, although we will need evidence to demonstrate why this would be the case. We also note that relative company performance changes over time and so poor performing companies could become high performing companies in the future and so our analysis will take this into account. We will consider the impact of the merger in each of the areas where we use cross industry benchmarks, and how these benchmarks might change if the merger takes place.

Criterion 4: The number and quality of independent observations that remain

We will consider the number and quality of independent companies that would remain after the merger. Any reduction to the number of comparators can have an impact on the robustness of our analysis by reducing the number of independent observations. We currently have 18 water comparators and only 10 sewerage comparators, so the loss of a water comparator is likely to have less impact than losing a sewerage comparator. So the potential detriment on the robustness of our analysis will be greater from a sewerage merger than a water merger. It follows that a whole company merger between two water and sewerage companies has the greatest detriment to Ofwat's ability to make comparisons. This is because it will cause us to reduce the number of independent comparators in wholesale water and sewerage and retail. We will consider the impact of the merger on the number and quality of comparators and whether this is likely to make our analysis less robust, for example by reducing the precision of our cost modelling, or make our ability to regulate more difficult, for example as there are insufficient companies to create effective competition for enhanced business plan status. We expect the detriment from the loss of a comparator to increase for each successive merger as fewer comparators would remain.

Criterion 5: A loss of a comparator with important similarities for comparisons

We will consider the extent to which the pre-merger companies are in similar circumstances to a limited number of other companies in the industry. If at least one of the merger parties are valuable comparators for the regulatory regime– perhaps for a subset of other companies in the industry, or in respect of one or more specific areas of operation, this would have potential for a greater detriment. For example such comparisons could be useful when assessing claims put forward by companies for operating in particularly rural or urban areas, in respect of proposals put forward by companies to address issues related to supply and demand, or a merger between contiguous companies could affect our ability to make comparisons across companies that are operating in similar circumstances facing similar issues. We will look at evidence where we have used or might use information about the merger parties to challenge or validate information from other companies.

Criterion 6: A loss of a comparator with important differences for comparison

We will also consider the extent to which a loss of differences between the merger parties and other undertakers is important for performing our functions. If one or more of the merger parties takes an approach which is different from other companies, it can be useful to us when making comparisons, for example in terms of spreading best practice or the adoption of innovative approaches. This could, for example, reduce the scope of the development of best practice or the scope of innovation if a company had demonstrated a good track record of innovation that is used to raise standards across the sector. If there is a reasonable prospect that the different approach would be lost as a result of the merger, then this would produce a detriment.

Criterion 7: are there alternative approaches available to us to offset the loss of this comparator?

We will consider whether we could we amend our regulatory approach to offset the loss of this comparator. This could include using different econometric techniques or a different choice of a benchmark within the sample (for example upper quintile rather than upper quartile) which could offset, to some extent, the detriment to our ability to make comparisons. However, changes that could be made to improve the way we regulate to reflect good regulatory practice absent the merger should not be seen as offsetting the loss of a comparator – they should be included in the baseline assessment.

A1.3.1 Weighting of the criteria on the loss of comparators

We will assess criterion 1 and 2 on the basis of a yes/no response, although we accept that this can sometimes be a matter of degree. If the answer to either question is no then it is unlikely that the merger would cause prejudice to our ability to make comparisons. If this is the case then we would not proceed with the assessment against the other criteria and would provide our opinion to the CMA on this basis. We will apply equal weights to each of the other criteria. That is, a customer loss of £1 million under criterion 3 will be weighted the same as customer loss of £1 million under criterion 4, 5, 6 and 7. The size of the impact of a merger under some criteria could be larger than others. To take account of this we will monetise impacts where possible – that is, convert impacts into a £m impact. This will identify the scale of impact and the relative weight of that impact against other criteria.

We will take account of the impact over time. To allow impacts to be compared over time we will discount future impacts to reflect the fact that individuals generally prefer to receive reductions in prices now than in the future. We will use the Treasury social discount rate of 3.5% to discount future impact to calculate present values. We will calculate the present value both over the long term, for example, 30 years (to reflect the long term impact of the loss of a comparator) and a shorter term view, for example, 5 to 10 years (where impacts are more certain). In undertaking this assessment we will consider the likelihood that current regulatory practices will persist in the future – for example, it is more likely that benchmarking analysis of network costs will continue in the long term as network activities are a natural monopoly. However, in other areas we may be less certain that current regulatory approaches will persist in the future. For example, retail is an area where we may be able to make greater use of comparators that are external to the sector in the future and so it may be reasonable to focus on the impacts over a shorter time period.

Where the criteria concern the use of comparisons for setting price controls, the impacts assessment will consider both a 'static' approach (that is what the impact would have been if the merger had occurred prior to the last price control) and a 'forward looking' approach (that is by taking account of the possible impacts in future price controls). We will apply greatest weight to the forward looking approach as price limits under the 'static' approach will have already been set.

Where monetisation is not possible, we will undertake a quantitative or qualitative assessment of the impact on our ability to make comparisons and indicate the severity of the impact. Qualitative assessments are more likely in some areas than others, for example where we make more qualitative uses of comparisons. For example it might not be possible to monetise the impact under criterion 5 (the loss of a comparator with important differences or similarities), however we would expect to monetise most but possibly not all the impacts under criterion 3 (impact on benchmarks).

When assessing impacts we will take into account the certainty around whether the impacts would occur, for example through changes in regulation, for example by including ranges around impacts.

A1.3.2 Our assessment on whether the merger is likely to prejudice our ability to make comparisons

Our assessment of whether a merger is likely to prejudice our ability to make comparisons will be based on an overall assessment, taking into account both monetised and non-monetised impacts. In particular we will first consider the monetised impacts, taking into account the certainty that they will occur, and then consider whether the non-monetised impacts would change the balance of the decision. When making this decision we will be conscious that the CMA has the ability to make a more detailed investigation with a Phase 2 reference and so we would want to be reasonably certain that a merger would not prejudice our ability to make comparisons.

A1.4 CRITERIA FOR ASSESSING RELEVANT CUSTOMER BENEFITS

We will evaluate the evidence put forward by merger parties on relevant customer benefits against the following criteria:

Criterion 1: Are there relevant customer benefits?

We will consider whether the proposed benefits meet the test laid out in the Water Industry Act 1991 (as amended by the Water Act 2014). That is does the proposed merger lead to lower prices, higher quality or greater choice of goods or services in any market in the United Kingdom, or greater innovation in relation to such goods or services for customers, including future customers, at any point in the chain of production and distribution (not just final consumers).

Criterion 2: How likely or certain are the benefits to be achieved?

Not all proposed cost-savings from mergers are achieved and so we will consider how certain the relevant customer benefits are to be achieved. All else equal, benefits which are more likely to accrue to customers, for example licence modifications or undertakings to allow immediate reductions in price limits, baseline adjustments to wholesale totex or improvements in outcome commitments, will be more likely to be considered to be relevant. We consider licence modifications or commitments that confirm the proposed benefits will be delivered provide the greatest certainty and incentives on management to ensure that customers will share in the benefits that are cited by the merger parties.

We will also consider how easy is it to monitor that the benefits are actually achieved. The more difficult it is for companies to demonstrate compliance with the delivery of the benefits and/or the more difficult it is for us to monitor that the benefits have been secured, the less likely we will be of the opinion that benefits should be considered relevant customer benefits.

Criterion 3: Are the benefits merger specific?

We will consider whether the benefits are unlikely to accrue without the merger. Only benefits which are unlikely to accrue without the merger will be Relevant customer benefits. Relevant customer benefits can include the time gained if customer benefits would have taken longer than a reasonable period to occur in the absence of a merger. Relevant customer benefits are only considered if we identify a prejudice to our ability to make comparisons.

Criterion 4: Are the benefits expected to accrue within a reasonable time period of the merger?

Benefits which will accrue immediately (or at least in the short term) and which are easy to secure, for example result from immediate changes to licences, are more likely to be considered relevant customer benefits. While the time period that we might expect benefits will vary from case to case, we would generally expect benefits to start to accrue within 1 to 2 years of the merger. We expect the merger parties to set out the time period over which they expect merger benefits will accrue. Where merger parties provide evidence that provides certainty that the merger benefits will arise (Criterion 1), these can be assessed until the next price determination. It may be possible to assess the impact of merger benefits beyond the current price control period, but there will be less certainty that such benefits are relevant customer benefits arising from the merger as these would need to be over and above the benefits customers would otherwise receive, for example as a result of efficiency challenges at the next price review.

Criterion 5: Are the benefits likely to be sustained?

As a part of that assessment, it will be relevant to consider how sustainable the benefits are. We will apply most weight to those benefits that are likely to be sustained as they are more likely to outweigh the prejudice to our ability to make comparisons arising from the merger.

A1.4.1 Weighting of relevant customer benefits

We would expect to weight relevant customer benefits, where possible based on their monetised impacts. We will discount future monetised impacts based on the Treasury Green Book social discount rate of 3.5%. Where monetised impacts are not possible we will consider quantitative and qualitative evidence on relevant customer benefits, taking into account supporting evidence on the potential scale. We will place less weight on relevant customer benefits that are less certain, do not accrue over a reasonable period of time or are less likely to be sustained. We will give less weight to relevant customer benefits that are a long way in the future, for example beyond ten years, due to the potential that these incremental benefits will be eroded by improvements elsewhere in the industry as other water companies catch-up with the performance of the merged entity.

A1.4.2 Determining whether the likely prejudice is outweighed by the relevant customer benefits

When determining whether the prejudice is outweighed by relevant customer benefits we would first consider the monetised impacts. In particular we will consider whether the monetised relevant customer benefits outweigh the likely prejudice, taking into account the certainty around potential impacts. In forming our opinion, we will then consider whether, in the round the non-monetised impacts would change the balance of the decision based on the monetised impacts. When undertaking this assessment we will be conscious that, the CMA can exercise discretion if it decides not to refer the merger in question for a Phase 2 investigation. In exercising that discretion, the CMA would consider the benefits of a CMA Phase 2 investigation, including the possibility of remedies being obtained that seek to preserve any relevant customer benefits.[89] We will therefore need compelling evidence that customer benefits outweigh the likely prejudice from the impact of the merger on our ability to make comparisons.[90] When undertaking this assessment we will be mindful that merger-specific relevant customer benefits might be short lived (and therefore of lower value) as they could be eroded by underlying efficiency improvements created by the regulatory framework.

A1.5 COMPANY EVIDENCE

We will expect companies to submit evidence on the impact of the merger on both our ability to make comparisons and relevant customer benefits. When examining the evidence we have received for the assessment of a merger we will place the greatest weight on assessments which are complete, robust, certain, clear and independently assured, and specifically on benefits with evidence of customer support.

We will evaluate evidence on both prejudice and relevant customer benefits based the criteria below:

Criterion 1: Clarity and transparency around approach and assumptions

Submissions by the merger parties should clearly present the results and conclusions of any analysis undertaken as well as the methodology used, any assumptions made, the justification for the methodology and the robustness of the results to any assumptions made. For example any estimated impacts of the merger on our ability to make comparisons should be submitted with a practical explanation of how the characteristics of the two merger parties affect this impact. This explanation might consider relevant differences between the two parties, such as the environmental conditions in which they operate or the different customer bases served.

Criterion 2: Completeness of the description of the analysis

Submissions should contain a complete description of any analysis undertaken. Relevant assumptions should be discussed and choice of any valuation techniques explained. We should be able to fully understand the results and also any modelling behind them, without having to seek more information from the submitting party.

Criterion 3: Ability of Ofwat to replicate results

We should be able to replicate the results of analysis that has been submitted. This means that merger parties should be prepared to respond promptly to a request, at very short notice, for all relevant information, models and supporting data necessary for us to reproduce the results presented in the parties' submissions.

Criterion 4: Robustness and independent assurance,

We expect evidence to be robust. We will have more confidence in analysis which uses sensitivity analysis to demonstrate the robustness of its impacts. Similarly we will also have more confidence if both the methodology employed and the results of applying that methodology have been subject to expert review in relevant fields. The degree of independent assurance merger parties wish to provide is a matter for those parties. However we will adopt a proportionate approach and would expect evidence which is significant to the merger parties' case may require a higher degree of independent assurance.

Criterion 5: Evidence of customer support

Ofwat has a duty to protect the interests of consumers. As a result, evidence which suggests that customers support the proposed merger, or the proposed benefits from the merger would play an important role in our assessment.

NOTES

[87] Section 33C of the Water Industry Act 1991 as amended by the Water Act 2014.

[88] This sentence mirrors the CMA's Merger Assessment Guidelines at paragraph 4.3.1;www.gov.uk/government/uploads/system/uploads/attachment_data/file/284449/OFT1254.pdf

[89] This paragraph mirrors paragraph 4.5 of the CMA's 'Mergers: Exceptions to the duty to refer and undertakings in lieu of reference guidance'. See:www.gov.uk/government/uploads/system/uploads/attachment_data/file/284397/oft1122.pdf. At Phase one, only undertakings are considered whereas the CMA has order making powers, and hence potentially more flexibility in remedy design, at Phase 2.

[90] Office of Fair Trading (2010), 'Mergers: exceptions to the duty to refer and undertakings in lieu of a reference'.

APPENDIX A2: EXAMPLES OF COMPARISONS, RELEVANT CUSTOMER BENEFITS AND UNDERTAKINGS

[3.559]

This appendix provides examples of our use of comparators to:

- set price limits in PR14 (table A2.1);
- incentivise monitor and incentivise service quality (table A2.2); and
- monitor, enforce and spread best practice (table A2.3).

The potential impact on our use of comparators of possible regulatory changes is set out in table A2.4.

This appendix also provides examples from previous water merger references.

- Relevant customer benefits (table A2.5.
- Remedies imposed or considered (table A2.6).

TABLE A2.1 EXAMPLES OF OUR USE OF COMPARATORS TO SET PRICE LIMITS IN PR14

Area	How we use comparators
Business planning process	The move to a risk based review with the best business plans qualifying for enhanced status relied extensively on comparisons.
Wholesale cost modelling	As data points in totex models and unit cost models.
Retail average cost to serve	As data points in retail average cost to serve calculation.
Bad debt	In PR14 we compared bad debt claims across companies as well as levels of deprivation.
Pensions	At PR09 we compared pension deficit levels to help us set our policy. We used the same policy at PR14.
Wholesale special cost factor claims	For some claims (for example energy) we made comparisons across the industry to establish if a company was different from others.
Cost allocation	We compared approaches to cost allocation between wholesale and retail and household and non-households to highlight areas where companies are not following guidelines.
PAYG and RCV run-off	We compared PAYG and RCV run-off rates to identify whether to challenge company proposals.
Accounting policies and assumptions	For PR14 we compared the accounting treatments across companies for example on Infrastructure Renewals Expenditure under IFRS accounting standards.
Tax allowances	We compared the tax treatment of capital expenditure across the industry to allow us to challenge companies that appeared to be in a different position.
Cost of capital	We compared actual gearing levels across companies to inform our notional gearing structure, we also compared debt costs across companies to corporate benchmarks
Credit rating	We compared target credit ratings and forecast financial ratios across companies to identify whether there were any financeability issues.

TABLE A2.2 EXAMPLES OF OUR USE OF COMPARATORS TO MONITOR AND INCENTIVISE SERVICE QUALITY

Area	How Ofwat uses comparators
Outcome delivery incentives (ODIs) and performance commitments (PCs)	Companies proposed ODIs and PCs across a wide range of areas, some of which were company-specific and some of which were common across the industry. Those ODIs and PCs which were common across the industry were assessed through comparative analysis. For five ODIs (supply interruptions; water quality customer contacts, water quality standards, sewerage pollution incidents; and internal sewer flooding) we used comparative assessment to identify upper quartile performance commitments and to intervene to ensure that companies were only able to access rewards for genuinely stretching performance. Our assessment of company specific ODIs was informed by comparisons to similar ODIs proposed by other companies and/or historic performance data (where available). We also used cross company comparisons to identify gaps where we intervened to introduce additional ODIs. We assessed performance commitments proposed by companies as a part of the risk based review. Scoring criteria included an assessment of the value for money of the performance commitments proposed, justification of the level of the performance commitment and the processes and procedures for measuring, reporting and governance of the performance commitments. Companies with a score of more evidence required or significantly more evidence required for criteria assessed in the risk based review of company business plans were able to learn from the best practice approaches adopted by those companies scored as exceptional.
Service incentive mechanism (SIM)	All companies have the SIM as an outcome incentive (for retail). The SIM comprises quantitative and qualitative components which measure customers' overall satisfaction with the service levels they receive from companies. Under this mechanism companies are rewarded or penalised financially for their performance relative to the rest of the industry. Comparisons are therefore critical to the operation of the SIM.[91]
Company performance measures	We monitor and publish comparative company performance against a range of customer experience, environmental and reliability and availability performance measures. Company performance is assessed on a red, amber green scale depending whether expectations are met, and identifies companies which raise concerns.

TABLE A2.3 EXAMPLES OF OUR USE OF COMPARATORS TO MONITOR, ENFORCE AND SPREAD BEST PRACTICE

Area	How Ofwat uses comparators
Customer issues	
Customer Engagement	Compared proposals across companies to identify best practice and encouraged other companies to adopt. As part of PR14, we assessed the information companies had provided on customer engagement and willingness to pay. In some cases, companies that received a score of more evidence required or significantly more evidence required were able to learn from the best practice approaches adopted by the companies rated as exceptional.
Codes of practice and compensation schemes	When companies publish these documents it drives reputational incentives to be at least as good as their peers.
Social tariffs and affordability measures	We compared proposals across companies to identify best practice and encouraged other companies to adopt (including affordability measures as part of PR14).
Tariff structures and innovation	In the past we have used comparative cost information to derive tariff policies (especially on more innovative tariffs). We have moved away from detailed scrutiny of charges schemes, companies have to assure us their tariffs comply with our policies; as a result of our assessment of companies' charges for 2015-16, companies were allocated to three assurance categories according to the issues identified with the information provided.
Company behaviour and operating practices	
Board leadership, transparency and governance	We compare performance across companies which feeds into our view of overall company performance and management capability (and was also used as part of PR14).
Approach and response to consultations, including proposals for future regulation and market reform	We get a wide selection of viewpoints and contributions from different, independent, management styles and approaches that contribute to the development of policy.
Compliance with market rules	We compare across companies to identify companies which need additional input.

Part 3 CMA and other Guidelines

Area	How Ofwat uses comparators
Challenge in the case of Interim Determination of K (IDoK) claims	We have made use of industry comparisons to challenge the costs submitted and the companies' approach (including management practices) to incurring the costs.
Innovation	By identifying new approaches and ideas (for example, responding creatively to new requirements) we may be able to identify which companies have been innovative.
Accounting and reporting of data	
Assurance in respect of information provided to us	We compare level and nature of assurance provided by companies and challenge companies with least assurance; companies are graded into one of three categories which affects the expectations we place on them in respect of the assurance required on information reported to us under our assurance framework. This formed part of PR14.
Transparency and approach to reporting	We have compared across companies to highlight best practice and encourage others to adopt it. Also part of PR14, we expected companies to be transparent about their business plans and established a high bar in respect of the publication of information that was used in making our decisions in the price review. In some instances, we made use of comparisons where companies set out that publication of a specific piece of information might seriously or prejudicially affect their interests.
Financial metrics and credit rating	On-going monitoring of credit ratings and key financial metrics based on actual company structure (collected as part of company performance measures).

TABLE A2.4 POTENTIAL IMPACT ON OUR USE OF COMPARATORS OF POSSIBLE REGULATORY CHANGES

Regulatory change	Impact on our use of comparators
Continuation of key elements of PR14 methodology	
Wholesale costs	Water sector comparisons are likely to continue to be important for assessing wholesale costs. While it might be expected that water companies would converge to the frontier over time, this has not been the case for water sector costs so far, although efficiency improvements have reduced since the early price controls. Convergence to the frontier might reduce if more focused wholesale controls are introduced, which will lead to improved understanding of the costs associated with the delivery of individual services and allow more specific efficiency challenges to be set (see below).
Retail cost to serve	At PR14 we set the retail efficiency challenge based on average costs to serve, however we said that this was part of an evolutionary approach and we hope to move to an efficient cost to serve over future price controls.[92] In the PR14 methodology impact assessment we assumed that companies would eliminate 75% of the difference between their cost and that of the most efficient company within 20 years.[93] This implies a move towards upper quartile and then potentially frontier efficiency benchmarking over time.
Outcome delivery incentives	In PR14 we used comparators to set our performance requirements in our horizontal ODIs. In our work on the company specific uplift we stated that " . . . by the middle of the 2015-20 period we expect all companies to reach current upper quartile performance. Consequently it is unclear on what basis we would set any horizontal ODIs for subsequent control periods at the start of the next period . . . ".[94] Horizontal ODIs were an important development as part of this price control and so our use of them is likely to continue, however our approach is likely to change. For example we could set a dynamic upper quartile target for service and efficiency.[95]
Service incentive mechanism	Comparative performance measures such as the SIM are good at continuing to drive improvements in less well performing companies. However they are less good at driving improvements to the frontier.[96] While we stated that we considered the SIM was appropriate to drive improvements for 2015 onwards.[97] We have also stated that water companies are unlikely to provide as much value as retail comparators beyond 2015-20 as Ofwat could offset the loss of a water company benchmark by greater reference to other sectors.[98] In our work on the company specific uplift we assumed that there would be no benefits from SIM beyond 2025 as it would be speculative to make assumption on what might replace the SIM. We continue to consider that this is a reasonable assumption.

Regulatory change	Impact on our use of comparators
Regulatory changes that will impact between 2015-20	
Non-household retail competition (from 2017)	Effective competition would remove the need to use comparisons to assess non-household retail costs and other elements of the non-household control. While competition is developing there is likely to be a continuing need for reporting, transparency and monitoring. Hence the focus of comparisons would move from an ex-ante to ex-post basis. If competition develops sufficiently it may be possible to remove regulatory reporting requirements and monitoring.
Abstraction incentive mechanism	The objective of the abstraction incentive mechanism will be to incentivise companies to reduce abstractions at low flows at environmentally sensitive sites compared to baseline historic levels. It is expected that the abstraction incentive mechanism will be introduced in 2015[99] as a reputational incentive based on a ranking in a league table.[100] This will introduce an additional area of comparison going forwards.
Network plus non-binding sub-limits (from 2015-20)	As set out in the PR14 methodology impact assessment when describing the move to split wholesale and retail controls, we expect the introduction of separate controls to encourage efficiency by improving transparency of costs and revenues.[101] Consequently, if network plus sub-limits were used for subsequent controls then the importance of water sector comparators in wholesale cost assessment, could if anything, increase. However a move to more focused controls could lead to better specified models, and therefore more robust results, which might reduce the reliance on individual comparators (although this seems less likely for sewerage where it was not possible to specify a robust full totex model). The impact of network plus sub-limits on the use of comparators is therefore unclear.
Potential longer term regulatory changes	
Upstream competition (feasible from 2019)	The introduction of upstream competition could allow individual parts of the upstream value chain, for example sludge, to be subject to competition. The introduction of competition in specific areas could require the allocation of the RCV across the value chain. While competition would provide a greater customer focus on price and service, this could increase the need for ex-post comparisons and monitoring in the short term as competition developed (to ensure that customers were being protected). However over the longer term the introduction of competition, when sufficiently developed, could reduce the need for comparators.
Binding service level sub-limits (future price controls)	The impact of binding sub-limits is likely to be similar to network plus non-binding sub-limits, although the introduction of binding sub-limits would if anything increase the need for robust models.

TABLE A2.5 TYPES OF BENEFITS IDENTIFIED IN PAST WATER MERGER REFERENCES

Merging firms	Year	Potential benefits from merger
South East; Mid Kent	2006	Reduced pumping costs from proposed interconnections. Sale or lease of newly redundant office space. Improved planning of water resources enabling postponement of investment projects.
Vivendi; Southern	2002	Access to expertise and worldwide experience of Vivendi group. Ability to pool and share best practice. Improved management of water resources, and hence in security of supply. Some cost savings (though not specified). Better retention and morale of Southern staff, due to improved career prospects.
South Staffordshire; Cambridge	2012	Operating cost savings, primarily at Cambridge.
SAUR; Mid Kent; General Utilities	1997	Alleviate water resource imbalance. Integrated supply network which would optimise water resource usage and improve security of supply. Long-term resource planning. Leakage reduction and metering. Generation of additional water resources. Resource management and water conservation programme. Deferment of need for major new resource development. Efficiency gains relating to head office costs and savings on infrastructure development. Improved service standards. Creation of better circumstances for genuine competition in the region.

Merging firms	Year	Potential benefits from merger
Wessex; South West	1996	Cost savings in the South West Water Services (SWWS) region. The creation of a strong regional company and increased opportunities for employees of the merged entity. Improved customer service and increased confidence by SWWS customers in their water and sewerage service. The flexible use of Wimbleball reservoir, the linking of Wessex Water Services (WWS) and SWWS trunk mains and the completion of SWWS's water grid. Improvements in water quality in the SWWS region and improved sewage treatment. The removal of planning embargoes and the greater use of local contractors in the SWWS area. Price reductions for water and sewerage services to SWWS's customers.
Severn Trent; South West	1996	Cost savings and an improvement in SWWS's operating efficiency, leading to price reductions in water and sewerage services for SWWS customers. Radical transformation of SWWS's management, leading to the restoration of trust in drinking water quality and the improved management of water supplies. Introduction of a more effective sewage treatment programme. Increased responsiveness to customer needs. Strengthening of the water supply grid. More effective and accelerated investment programme.
Lyonnaise des Eaux; Northumbrian	1995	Direct savings due to rationalisation of head office and technical management functions.
Colne Valley; Lee Valley; Rickmansworth	1990	Operational cost savings, mainly on staff costs. Interest savings as a result of improved cash flows and ability to achieve more favourable finance terms. One-off benefits from sales of surplus properties. Benefits from cancellation and deferral of capital projects.
Southern Water; Mid Sussex Water	1990	Opportunities for reducing duplication of effort in: • customer billing; • telemetry; • engineering design; • training; • digital mapping; and • legal expertise
General Utilities/Mid Kent	1990	Access by Mid Kent Water to water technology and know-how. Access to French water industry's extensive water industry research on an arms-length basis, enabling more effective and cost-efficient solutions to problems to be achieved. Facilitate opportunities for further informal exchanges on technical matters.

TABLE A2.6 REMEDIES IMPOSED/CONSIDERED IN PREVIOUS WATER MERGER REFERENCES

Merging firms	Year	Remedies or undertakings imposed/considered
Post Enterprise Act cases		
South Staffordshire; Cambridge	2012	No prejudice was found in this case and so remedies were not considered.
South East; Mid Kent	2006	One-off rebate of £4 million distributed between customers An efficiency adjustment of £3.1 million annual operating expenditure savings (equal to the value of merger synergies specified by merging firms) was required as part of PR09. Divestiture of one company was also considered but found disproportionate to the prejudice resulting from the merger.
Pre-Enterprise Act cases (final decision by Secretary of State – SoS)		

Merging firms	Year	Remedies or undertakings imposed/considered
Vivendi; Southern[102]	2002	Undertakings offered by Vivendi to Ofwat:[103] a) Establish a new comparator in the form of separate business unit for Hampshire and the Isle of Wight under a separate license granted by Ofwat: and b) Commitment to sell interest in Bristol Water Under these proposals the merger of Folkestone and Dover (F&D) with Southern Water would also have been subject to a Phase 2 reference and investigation. Prior to a Phase 2 reference, the minority interest (24.6%) in Bristol Water was sold. At Phase 2, the panel found that a prohibition would be disproportionate to the detriment found. A less intrusive remedy considered was divestment of Three Valleys, by far the largest of Vivendi's three majority owned WoCs but this was also found disproportionate by a majority of the panel since there was no prejudice on the sewerage side. F&D or Tendring Hundred were deemed too small for a divestment to be relevant in the context of the loss of the much larger Southern's independence. The divestment of F&D also had the disadvantage that it would involve the loss of relevant benefits from bringing southern and F&D under common control. Four of the Phase 2 panel found that divestment of the minority stake in South Staffordshire Water would be sufficient. However one member of the panel, and subsequently the Secretary of State (SoS), believed that a more intrusive remedy was required – that Vivendi should also be required to sell Three Valleys Water.
SAUR; Mid Kent; General Utilities	1997	General Utilities (GU) and SAUR Water plc, owner of South East Water, bid for Mid Kent. Proposed merger was prohibited.
Severn Trent or Wessex and South West	1996	This merger case considered competing bids by two WaSCs Severn Trent plc and Wessex Water plc for a third WaSC, South West Water. Both bids were prohibited on the basis that no remedy would be sufficient to remedy loss of comparator
Lyonnaise des Eaux;Northumbrian[104]	1995	A Phase 2 investigation recommended that the bid should be allowed if substantial price reductions were agreed, sufficient to move the merged company to the efficiency frontier. The SoS permitted the merger on the basis that prices to water customers of the merging companies would be reduced by 15% over the following six years.
Colne Valley; Lee Valley; Rickmansworth	1990	Merged company was required to co-operate fully with DGWS for setting of new efficiency factor. Savings resulting from the merger were to be 'wholly' applied to users. Merged company had to agree that for ten years after the merger no class of customer would be charged more than they would have been if the merger had not taken place. The merging companies had to continue as separate profit centres and information on those profit centres had to be available for the DGWS as required.
Southern Water; Mid Sussex Water	1990	Merger allowed with no remedies.
General Utilities/Mid Kent	1990	General Utilities and Parent company CGE were required to undertake to: • have no involvement in management of the merging companies, including having no access to financial or commercial information from Mid Kent Holdings or Mid Kent Water which could be relevant to the DGWS's functions in relation to Mid Kent Water; • not be represented on the board of Mid Kent Water or Mid Kent Holdings; and • not use its power to block special resolutions of Mid Kent Holdings. Alternately GU required to divest holding to level "at which it would not have the ability materially to influence policy".

NOTES

91 At PR14 we used SIM scores from 2011-14 (that is, a three-year period) to determine industry average performance, to which each company was then compared.

92 Page 97, Ofwat (2013), 'Setting price controls for 2015-20 – final methodology and expectations for companies business plans'.

93 Page 43, PwC (2013), 'Updated price limits impact assessment'.

94 Page 44, Ofwat (2014), 'Final price control determination notice: policy chapter A7 – Annex 3: benefits assessment of an uplift to the cost of capital'.

95 'Uncharted waters: A forward look at managing change in the water sector', Jonson Cox, March 2015.

96 Page 13, 'Service incentive mechanism (SIM) for 2015 onwards – a consultation'.

97 Page 3, 'Service incentive mechanism (SIM) for 2015 onwards – conclusions'.

98 Page 35, 'Final price control determination notice: policy chapter A7 – Annex 3: benefits assessment of an uplift on the cost of capital'.

99 Page 29, Setting price controls for 2015-20 – policy and information notice

100 Page 25, 'Setting price controls for 2015-20 – final methodology and expectations for companies business plans'.

101 Page 6, PwC (2013), 'Updated price limits impact assessment'.

102 This merger would have brought together Southern Water (a WaSC) and a variety of WoCs: Three Valleys Water; Folkstone and Dover (F&D) Water; Tendring Hundred Water; a 24.6% minority stake in Bristol Water and a 31.4% minority stake in South Staffordshire Water.

103 See webarchive.nationalarchives.gov.uk/20140402141250/http://www.competition-commission.org.uk/rep_pub/reports/2002/fulltext/472a3.13.pdf

104 Lyonnaise owned North East Water Ltd, a WoC which it wished to merge with a neighbouring WaSC, Northumbrian under a single appointment and thereby achieve significant cost savings.

WATER AND SEWERAGE MERGERS: GUIDANCE ON THE CMA'S PROCEDURE AND ASSESSMENT (CMA49, NOVEMBER 2015)

13 November 2015

[3.560]

NOTES

CONTENTS

1. INTRODUCTION

SCOPE OF THE GUIDANCE

[3.561]

1.1 This guidance is concerned with the merger control regime for mergers involving two or more water and sewerage or water-only companies (either of which are referred to as 'water enterprises' in this guidance)[1] in England and Wales under the Water Industry Act 1991 (WIA) as amended by the Water Act 2014 (WA14).[2] Mergers between water enterprises (water mergers) are in certain circumstances subject to a special water merger regime. This guidance is concerned with the policies, procedure and methodology that the Competition and Markets Authority (CMA) will use in discharging its functions under the WIA.

1.2 This guidance should be read alongside other detailed guidance that the CMA has published or adopted in relation to merger control provisions of the Enterprise Act 2002 (EA02). This guidance cross-refers to other CMA guidance extensively and the CMA strongly recommends that merger parties make themselves familiar with these guides. Where this guidance is different from the CMA's other merger control guidance, this reflects the specific merger control regime applicable to water mergers and this guidance takes precedence.

1.3 This guidance replaces the previous CMA's guidance on water mergers.[3] While the CMA is not bound to follow the approach taken by the Competition Commission (CC) in water merger investigations, this guidance cites previous relevant CC decisions to illustrate how it will apply the provisions of the WIA.

1.4 This guidance does not consider any competition issues which might arise as a result of mergers involving water enterprises that the CMA may be investigating under the EA02. While the water and sewerage market is largely regulated and each water enterprise is a regional monopolist for water and/or waste water services, there are certain aspects of the market that are not subject to regulation, or have some degree of competition. If water enterprises with such activities have merged or will merge as part of a merger involving non-water enterprises as well as water enterprises, the CMA will consider the transaction, excluding the water enterprises, under the general merger provisions of the EA02. If, in such a case, a merger is likely to give rise to competition issues, interested parties should refer to the CMA general merger guidance.[4] The CMA will consider these issues on a case-by-case basis, however, to minimise the burden on the parties, where a transaction is being considered under both the special water merger regime and the general merger regime, the CMA will endeavour to investigate the cases together.

1.5 For future water merger transactions that may give rise to competition issues, in line with the general merger regime, the CMA's informal advice procedure is available. For further advice on this procedure please see paragraphs 6.25 to 6.38 of the CMA general merger guidance *Mergers: Guidance on the CMA's jurisdiction and procedure* (CMA2).

1.6 This guidance reflects the views of the CMA at the time of publication and may be revised from time to time to reflect changes in best practice, legislation and the results of experience, legal judgments and research. It may in due course be supplemented, revised or replaced. The CMA's webpages will always display the latest version of the guidance. Where there is any conflict, or difference in emphasis or detail between this guidance and other guidance produced or adopted by the CMA, the most recently published guidance takes precedence.

1.7 For merger cases that are referred for an in-depth phase 2 investigation, the final decision-making authority is an independent group of experts selected from a panel appointed by the Secretary of State (the inquiry group). Where this guidance is expressed to apply to the CMA's policy when making decisions at phase 1 whether to refer a merger for an in-depth phase 2 investigation, this does not bind the independent inquiry group when undertaking its assessment at phase 2.

PURPOSE OF THE SPECIAL WATER MERGER REGIME

1.8 Under the EA02 the CMA has a general duty to review and obtain information related to mergers. Where the CMA believes that it is or may be the case that a merger qualifies as a relevant merger situation[5] and has resulted, or may be expected to result, in a substantial lessening of competition (SLC), it has a duty to refer it for an in-depth phase 2 investigation (the general merger regime). Mergers of two or more water enterprises are an exception this regime. In certain circumstances, the merger of two or more water enterprises is subject to a special merger regime which has been in place since the water industry was privatised in 1989 (the special water merger regime).

1.9 The intention of the special water merger regime is to ensure that a merger between two or more water or sewerage enterprises in England and Wales will not prejudice the Water Services Regulation Authority's (Ofwat) ability to make comparisons for the purpose of carrying out its statutory functions (such as setting price controls on regulated water enterprises and other regulatory functions).

1.10 The WIA (as amended) enables the CMA to clear a merger between two or more water enterprises in England and Wales (referred to in this guidance as a 'water merger') after a phase 1 investigation, either unconditionally or by accepting undertakings in lieu of a reference (UILs). The CMA must, during a phase 1 investigation, request and consider Ofwat's opinion on the water merger.[6]

1.11 The following chapters in this guidance document outline in more detail the policies, procedure and methodology used by the CMA to operate the special water merger regime.

WHO DOES WHAT?

1.12 The WIA assigns specific roles to the CMA and Ofwat in the special water merger regime during the phase 1 investigation process. The CMA is the UK's primary competition authority and is responsible for the merger control regime in the UK. However, under the WIA Ofwat has a statutory role in the phase 1 assessment of water mergers. The following section provides a brief overview of how these roles interrelate and the role of the European Commission (the Commission).

Role of the CMA

1.13 In line with the general mergers regime the WIA provides for a two stage process for water mergers. The CMA has a duty to refer a water merger for an in-depth phase 2 investigation (a phase 2 reference) unless the CMA believes that:

(a) the merger arrangements for anticipated mergers are not sufficiently advanced or are unlikely to proceed;

(b) the merger is not likely to prejudice Ofwat's ability, in carrying out its functions, to make comparisons between water enterprises; and

(c) the merger is likely to prejudice Ofwat's ability to make comparisons, but the prejudice is outweighed by relevant customer benefits (RCBs).

1.14 Before the CMA makes a decision on whether there is a duty to refer it must request and consider Ofwat's opinion on considerations (*b*) and (*c*) above. See paragraphs 1.18 to 1.23 on Ofwat's role.

1.15 The WIA also gives the CMA the power to accept UILs of a phase 2 reference in relation to water mergers, as it can with general mergers. In relation to water mergers the UILs must remedy, mitigate or prevent the merger's prejudicial effect on Ofwat's ability to make comparisons.[7] When considering whether to accept UILs the CMA must request and consider Ofwat's opinion on the effect of the undertakings offered.

1.16 Where the CMA refers the merger for an in-depth phase 2 investigation, it conducts a more detailed analysis and the inquiry group must decide:

- whether a water merger has been created or will be created;

- whether the water merger has prejudiced, or may be expected to prejudice, the ability of Ofwat to make comparisons between water enterprises; and
- where there is a prejudicial outcome, on the appropriate remedy.[8]

1.17 The inquiry group are an independent group of experts and are the final decision makers in phase 2.

Role of Ofwat

1.18 Ofwat is the independent economic regulator for water and sewerage services in England and Wales. Water enterprises are regional monopolies and are regulated by Ofwat in line with its statutory duties, in particular to further the customer objective, to secure that water companies carry out their functions and are able to finance their activities (and long-term resilience for England water companies).[9] Ofwat compares information between water companies to regulate prices, identify good performance to incentivise best practice, and set incentives for water companies to improve their quality of service.

1.19 Before the CMA forms a view on whether or not to refer a water merger for a phase 2 investigation the CMA must request and Ofwat must give its opinion on:

- the impact of the merger on its ability to make comparisons between water enterprises; and
- where Ofwat forms the view that the merger is likely to prejudice its ability to make comparisons, whether this prejudice is outweighed by the RCBs of the merger.

1.20 When forming its opinion on these points, Ofwat must apply the methods set out in its statement of methods.[10] The statement of methods sets out the criteria it will use in its assessment of the effect of the merger on its ability to make comparisons, and the relevant weight that it will place on each criterion.[11]

1.21 Where merger parties have offered UILs, the CMA must request and Ofwat must give its opinion on the effect of the UILs offered. The CMA must consider Ofwat's opinion.

1.22 Detailed information on Ofwat's approach to water mergers and its statement of method is provided in its publication: *Consultation on Ofwat's approach to future mergers and statement of method*.[12]

1.23 Ofwat does not have a statutory role in a CMA phase 2 investigation and the final decision on whether to allow the merger to proceed is made by the inquiry group. Based on past experience from the CC's and the CMA's phase 2 investigations, the CMA expects that Ofwat's views and submissions will play an important role in those investigations.[13]

The European Union Merger Regulation

1.24 The Commission has jurisdiction over all mergers, including those between water enterprises, which have an 'EU dimension' as defined in the European Union Merger Regulation (EU Merger Regulation).[14] Mergers have an EU dimension where they satisfy one of two alternative sets of jurisdictional thresholds:

(a) either:
 (i) the combined aggregate worldwide turnover of all the undertakings concerned is more than €5 billion; and
 (ii) the aggregate EU-wide turnover of each of at least two of those undertakings is more than €250 million;

(b) or:
 (i) the combined aggregate worldwide turnover of all the undertakings concerned is more than €2.5 billion; and
 (ii) in each of at least three member states, the combined aggregate turnover of all those undertakings is more than €100 million; and
 (iii) in each of at least three of the member states included for the purposes above, the aggregate turnover of each of at least two of the undertakings concerned is more than €25 million; and
 (iv) the aggregate EU-wide turnover of at least two of the undertakings concerned is more than €100 million;

(c) unless in relation to either situation above, each of the undertakings concerned achieves more than two-thirds of its aggregate EU-wide turnover within one and the same member state.

1.25 Those mergers that satisfy one of these two sets of jurisdictional thresholds must be notified to, and cleared by the Commission prior to their implementation, which is, in essence, prior to the merger being completed. There is no specific deadline within which a merger must be notified to the Commission.

1.26 There are a number of circumstances in which a merger falling within the Commission's jurisdiction may be referred to the CMA for investigation by the Commission. For example, a case may be referred by virtue of either Article 4(4) or Article 9 of the EU Merger Regulation, on the basis that the main competition issues of the merger are limited to the UK.[15]

1.27 In addition, a national authority (in the UK, the Secretary of State) may take appropriate action to protect legitimate interests where they would be impacted by a merger with an EU dimension.[16] As a result a merger may be referred to the CMA (in part or in its entirety) for investigation on public interest grounds. Any competition aspects of the merger will in that situation continue to be investigated by the Commission.

1.28 In 1995 the Commission published a decision recognising the legitimate interest of the UK in applying a special water merger regime.[17] This decision was taken in the context of the takeover by Lyonnaise des Eaux SA of Northumbrian Water Group plc. The UK authorities conducted their assessment on the public interest aspects of the merger[18] and the wider competition aspects of the merger were reserved for the Commission. This guidance takes into account this approach taken by the Commission in that case.

1.29 Given the flexibility in allocation between the CMA and the Commission for mergers with an EU dimension the CMA would encourage merger parties to keep the CMA and Ofwat informed of any intention to notify to the Commission.

1.30 For more information about the time limits and procedures for those mergers with an EU dimension see CMA2, Chapters 16 and 18.

NOTES

1 A water enterprise is an enterprise carried on by a company appointed under section 6 of the WIA to be a water and/or sewerage undertaker.

2 The general merger regime (merger control provisions in the EA02) applies to water enterprises in Northern Ireland and Scotland. However, water merger parties in Northern Ireland must notify the Republic of Ireland Competition and Consumer Protection Commission if the overall turnover of the merging parties in Ireland exceeds €50 million, and the turnover of at least two of the parties in Ireland exceeds €3 million.

3 *Water Merger References: Competition Commission Guidelines* (CC9), December 2004.

4 For further information on competition issues please see the CMA's general merger guidance documents on *our webpages*.

5 As defined by section 23(1) and (2) of the EA02.

6 From 2004 to November 2015 the CMA had a mandatory duty to refer any water mergers for a phase 2 investigation provided that: the anticipated or completed arrangements will result or have resulted in a merger of two or more water enterprises; and the turnover of the water enterprises being taken over, or of those already belonging to the acquirer, each is greater than £10 million.

7 Before the CMA decides whether or not to accept UILs, it will request and consider Ofwat's opinion on the effect of the UILs. See section 33D(6) WIA.

8 This may include behavioural, intellectual property and/or divestiture remedies.

9 Section 2 of WIA.

10 Section 33B(2) of WIA.

11 Section 33C of WIA.

12 See Ofwat (2015), *Consultation on Ofwat's approach to future mergers and statement of method*.

13 The CMA took over a number of functions formally performed by the Office of Fair Trading and the CC when it was formed on 1 April 2014. The CC was previously responsible for conducting phase 2 investigations, including those involving water enterprises.

14 Council Regulation (EC) No. 139/2004 of 20 January 2004 on the control of concentrations between undertakings, OJ 2004 L24/1, Articles 1 and 3. See further CMA2, Chapter 18.

15 See CMA2 for further guidance.

16 Article 21(4) of the EU Merger Regulation limits the legitimate interests on the basis of which the Secretary of State may intervene to public security, plurality of the media and prudential rules. Further, Article 21(4) allows EU member states to communicate other public interests to the Commission, which may recognise these after an assessment of their compatibility with the general principles and other provisions of EU law.

17 Case M.567, Lyonnaise des Eaux/Northumbrian Water, Commission decision of 21 December 1995. The Commission took this decision under Article 21(3) of Regulation (EEC) 4064/89, the forerunner of the current EU Merger Regulation, which for these purposes is similar to Article 21(4) of the EU Merger Regulation. The Commission also noted that a new application for recognition of the UK's legitimate interest would be necessary should any amendment be made to the regulatory legislation.

18 Lyonnaise des Eaux SA and Northumbrian Water Group PLC report (1995) by the Monopolies and Mergers Commission (the forerunner of the CC).

2. THE LEGAL FRAMEWORK

INTRODUCTION

[3.562]

2.1 The following chapter provides an overview of the statutory questions the CMA is required to answer in relation to water mergers.

STATUTORY QUESTIONS

2.2 The WIA imposes a duty on the CMA to refer completed and anticipated water mergers for an in-depth phase 2 investigation unless the CMA believes that:

(a) for anticipated mergers, the arrangements are not sufficiently far advanced or not sufficiently likely to proceed to justify a reference;

(b) the water merger has not prejudiced, or is not likely to prejudice, Ofwat's ability in carrying out its functions to use comparative regulation; or

(c) the water merger has prejudiced, or is likely to prejudice, Ofwat's ability to make comparisons between water enterprises, but that this prejudice is outweighed by RCBs relating to the merger.[19]

2.3 Before forming a view about the exceptions set out at (*b*) and (*c*), the CMA must request and consider Ofwat's opinion about both the likely prejudice and whether such prejudice is outweighed by RCBs.[20] In view of the two-phase structure of the merger control regime, the CMA considers that for the purposes of the exception in (b) its duty to refer will apply if it believes that there is a realistic prospect of prejudice to Ofwat's ability to make comparisons between water enterprises resulting from the water merger.

2.4 Where the CMA is under a duty to refer a water merger for a phase 2 investigation it may accept UILs to remedy, mitigate or prevent the merger's prejudicial effect on Ofwat's ability to make comparisons between water enterprises.[21] When forming a view on UILs the CMA must consider the need to achieve as comprehensive a solution to that effect on Ofwat as is reasonable and practicable. Moreover, the CMA must request and consider Ofwat's opinion on the effect of the offered UILs.

2.5 Following a reference for a phase 2 investigation, the inquiry group must:

(a) confirm that a water merger has taken place or that arrangements are in progress which, if carried into effect, will result in a water merger; and

(b) determine whether the water merger has prejudiced, or may be expected to prejudice, the Ofwat's ability to make comparisons between different water enterprises.[22]

2.6 If the inquiry group decides that there is a prejudicial outcome, it must decide the following additional questions:

(a) whether the CMA should take action for the purpose of remedying, mitigating or preventing the prejudice or any adverse effect that has resulted, or may be expected to result, from this prejudice;

(b) whether the CMA should recommend the taking of action by others for this purpose; and

(c) in either case, what action should be taken and what is to be remedied, mitigated or prevented.[23]

2.7 In deciding whether action should be taken and, if so, what action, the inquiry group may in particular have regard to the effect of any such action on any RCBs in relation to the merger, provided that this would not prevent a solution to the prejudice concerned or the benefits are substantially more important than the prejudice.[24,25]

JURISDICTION

2.8 The CMA has jurisdiction to examine a water merger under the special water merger regime where:

- arrangements are in progress which, if carried into effect, will result in a merger of any two or more water enterprises (anticipated merger), or that such a merger has taken place;[26]
- the turnover of the water enterprise being taken over, and at least one of the water enterprises already belonging to the person making the takeover, are greater than £10 million (the turnover test);[27] and
- where the merger has taken place, the merger completed not more than four months before the reference for a phase 2 investigation, unless completion took place without this having been made public and without the CMA being informed of it.[28]

The merger of two or more water enterprises

2.9 To establish if the transaction will result or has resulted in a merger of two or more water enterprises the CMA must determine if the merger parties are water enterprises. Both parties (or where the merger is between more than two parties, at least two of those parties) must be water enterprises for the special water merger regime to apply. Where only one party is a water enterprise the transaction will be assessed under the EA02 and follow the general merger regime.

2.10 The CMA must also determine whether the water enterprises will cease or have ceased to be distinct. This concept has the same meaning as in the general merger regime, and hence the CMA must identify whether the water enterprises are being brought under common ownership or control.[29] Further guidance on this concept can be found in Chapter 4 of CMA2.

The turnover test

2.11 For water mergers the CMA cannot make a reference for a phase 2 investigation where the value of the turnover of the water enterprises being taken over, or already belonging to the acquirer, are each less than £10 million.[30]

2.12 The jurisdictional test is based on turnover only. This differs from the general merger regime where mergers may qualify for investigation based on a turnover test or a share of supply test.[31]

2.13 The relevant turnover is limited to the provision of services as a water or water and sewerage company, ie the 'regulated' turnover. Consequently, any turnover attributed to other services/products, offered by the water company other than water and sewerage services, should be excluded from the calculation of the relevant turnover for the purposes of the turnover test.[32]

2.14 The WIA also places a duty on the CMA to keep the thresholds for the turnover test in water mergers under review and periodically advise the Secretary of State on whether such thresholds are still appropriate.[33]

Time limits for reference decisions

2.15 After starting an investigation, the CMA is required to decide within a timetable of 40 working days whether its duty to refer is met. As in the general merger regime, this timetable starts on the first working day after the CMA confirms to the merger parties that it has received sufficient information to enable it to begin its investigation.[34]

2.16 In addition, as in the general merger regime, for the CMA to be able to refer a completed merger, the reference must take place within four months from the date of completion or, where completion was not made public and the CMA was not informed of it, within four months from the earlier of the time that material facts are made public or the time the CMA is told of material facts.[35] Further guidance on this concept can be found in paragraphs 4.42 to 4.46 of CMA2.

Merger fees

2.17 Subject to some limited exceptions, any water merger where the CMA reaches a decision on whether or not to refer the merger for a phase 2 investigation. This fee is applicable irrespective of whether a reference is made.[36]

2.18 The merger fee for water mergers is currently calculated by reference to the value of the turnover in England and Wales of the water enterprise being taken over and is payable to the CMA when the decision on whether or not to refer the merger for a phase 2 investigation is announced. The bands for this fee are, as for other mergers, as follows:

- £40,000 where the value of the UK turnover of the enterprise being acquired is £20 million or less.
- £80,000 where the value of the UK turnover of the enterprise being acquired is over £20 million but less than £70 million.
- £120,000 where the value of the UK turnover of the enterprise being acquired is over £70 million but less than £120 million.
- £160,000 where the value of the UK turnover of the enterprise being acquired is over £120 million.

2.19 For further information on merger fees please see Merger fees payment information on the CMA webpages and paragraphs 20.1 to 20.7 of CMA2.

NOTES

19 Sections 32 and 33A(1) of WIA.

20 Section 33A(3) of WIA.

21 Section 33D of WIA.

22 Sections 35(1) and 36(1) of EA02 as modified by regulation 11 of the Water Mergers (Modification of Enactments) Regulations 2004 (SI 2004/3202) (the Water Mergers Regulations).

23 Sections 35(5) and 36(4) of EA02 as modified by regulation 11 of the Water Mergers Regulations.

24 Further discussion on RCBs can be found in Chapter 6.

25 Sections 35(7) and 36(6) of EA02 as modified by regulation 11 of the Water Mergers Regulations.

26 Section 32 of WIA.

27 Section 33 of WIA.

28 Section 24 of EA02 as modified by regulation 4 of the Water Mergers Regulations.

29 Section 35(2) of WIA and section 26 of EA02.

30 Section 33 of WIA.

31 The share of supply test is where the enterprises that cease to be distinct supply or acquire goods or services of any description and, after the merger, together supply or acquire at least 25% of all those particular goods or services of that kind supplied in the UK or in a substantial part of it. The merger must also result in an increment to the share of supply or acquisition.

32 Section 33(4) WIA states that the applicable turnover is calculated in accordance with the provisions specified in regulations published by the Secretary of State (The Water Mergers Determination of Turnover Regulations, SI 2004/3206), and Schedule of the SI 2004/3206. Paragraph 3 of the Schedule, the applicable turnover of a water enterprise 'shall be limited to the amounts derived from the sale of products and the provision of services falling within the appointed business of the water enterprise to businesses or consumers in England and Wales after deduction of sales rebates, value added tax and other taxes directly related to turnover'.

33 Section 33(6A) of WIA.

34 SI [to be confirmed]/2015. The regulations will come into force on [date to be confirmed] 2015.

35 Section 24 of EA02 as modified by regulation 4 of the Water Mergers Regulations.

36 [To be confirmed by Defra] Full details in respect of the payment of fees are, pursuant to section 121 of the, EA02 (Merger Fees and Determination of Turnover) Order [to be confirmed] (as amended [to be confirmed]).

3. THE MERGER PROCESS

INTRODUCTION

[3.563]

3.1 This chapter of the guidance provides more detail on certain aspects of the phase 1 and phase 2 water merger process. Annex A provides an overview of the principal stages and timings in a phase 1 and a phase 2 investigation. Annex B outlines the key interactions between the CMA and Ofwat in the phase 1 investigation.

PHASE 1 PROCESS

Notifying water mergers

3.2 The UK merger regime is a voluntary notification regime. This means that there is no legal requirement to notify the CMA of a water merger even if it meets the jurisdictional threshold. However the CMA keeps merger activity under review and it may investigate mergers on its own initiative if a merger has not been notified.[37]

3.3 Where the CMA learns of a water merger, it may decide to send merger parties an enquiry letter requesting information about the transaction, in particular, to understand if the jurisdiction thresholds

Part 3 CMA and other Guidelines

have been met. Once the CMA is satisfied that the information it has received in response to its enquiry letter is complete, and if it appears that the jurisdictional threshold is met, it will, if appropriate, commence its investigation.

3.4 Where merger parties have decided to make a voluntary notification to the CMA of the water merger, they are encouraged to enter into pre-notification discussions with the CMA and Ofwat.[38]

Information exchange between the CMA and Ofwat

3.5 To minimise the burden on merger parties, where appropriate, Ofwat and the CMA will coordinate information requests. The CMA will request a waiver from the merger parties to allow disclosure of information to Ofwat. The CMA expects that the merger parties will work closely and openly with both itself and Ofwat throughout the entire phase 1 and phase 2 processes including any UIL process.

3.6 Sharing of information (including data) between the CMA and Ofwat is crucial for the effective fulfilment of their respective duties under the special water merger regime and should reduce the burden on merger parties that could otherwise arise, for example from duplicative information requests. The CMA and Ofwat may, where appropriate, discuss with each other water merger issues that the merging parties bring to their attention; informal advice they will be providing or have provided; pre-notification drafts; and information obtained throughout the phase 1 investigation.

3.7 Any disclosure of information between the CMA and Ofwat, and any use by the recipient of such information, shall only be to the extent permitted by law, including by reference to the provisions of Part 9 of the EA02 and to section 206 of the WIA.[39]

Pre-notification

3.8 In line with the general merger regime the 40 working day timetable will not start until the CMA has confirmed it has sufficient information to start its investigation. In the case of water mergers, this will include the information Ofwat requires, in the form of a merger impact assessment submission, to start its assessment of the merger required for the purpose of providing its opinion to the CMA.[40] Merger parties should allow sufficient time in their planning for this and should approach Ofwat at the earliest opportunity to start this process.

3.9 In addition to working with Ofwat before making a voluntary notification to the CMA, merger parties are strongly encouraged to discuss the merger and the notification with the CMA.

3.10 Pre-notification can benefit both the merger parties and the CMA in a number of ways. For example:

- The water and sewerage sector is complex and features a high degree of specialised regulation. Pre-notification discussions can help the CMA case team better understand those issues and provide more time for the case team to develop their understanding of the sector.
- Discussions in advance can be used to clarify the information that the CMA and Ofwat require from the merger parties in order to start the investigation. This can help reduce the amount of information that is provided at notification and streamline subsequent information requests to the merger parties during the investigation.
- The CMA is not able to stop the clock once the water merger investigation has started to allow a more in-depth consideration of any complex issues or particularly large volumes of new information, except in some limited circumstances where information from the parties remains outstanding. More detailed pre-notification discussions maximise the opportunity the CMA and Ofwat have to consider the impact on Ofwat's ability to use comparative regulation and therefore the appropriateness of a decision that an exception to the duty to refer applies.
- In certain cases it may be appropriate to discuss potential UILs during pre-notification, particularly where the merger parties acknowledge that the merger may prejudice Ofwat's ability to use comparative regulation.

3.11 For further information on the benefits of pre-notification, please see CMA2, Chapter 5, paragraphs 6.39 to 6.43.

3.12 The CMA will not make any pre-notification discussions public. However, during this period and throughout the investigation information may be shared between Ofwat and the CMA. Please see paragraph 3.5 to 3.7 above, and the statement of intent.

Fast track reference cases

3.13 In some circumstances the CMA may accelerate a case to a phase 2 investigation where there is sufficient evidence of an adverse impact on Ofwat's ability to make comparisons for a reference and where this reflects the wishes of the merger parties.

3.14 For a case to be fast-tracked the CMA must have evidence in its possession at an early stage of the investigation that it believes that the test for a reference to phase 2 is met and the notifying parties must have requested and given consent for the use of the procedure. For more information about fast track references please see CMA2, Chapter 6, paragraphs 6.61 to 6.65.

Water merger assessment

3.15 A detailed discussion of the CMA's phase 1 merger assessment process in the general merger regime is in CMA2. This discussion also applies to water mergers except as set out below.

3.16 The assessment phase starts by the CMA issuing notice of commencement of the case on its webpages. An 'invitation to comment' to invite interested third parties to submit their views to the CMA on the transaction will also be issued around that time. The CMA will also contact and interact with third parties directly to obtain their views on the merger, this may include other governmental bodies, industry, customer and consumer groups, to understand their views and request evidence to support them.

3.17 The CMA will liaise closely with both the merger parties and Ofwat during the lifetime of the case. The CMA will take account of the evidence provided by these third parties, including the merger parties and Ofwat, when forming its decision on the merger.

3.18 There may be a need for additional or more comprehensive information from merger parties beyond what is provided to the CMA in order to start its investigation.[41] Where the CMA identifies a need for further information it will ask for the data, information or documents as soon as it is clear that they are necessary.

3.19 CMA has 40 working days to complete the initial phase 1 process.[42] Ofwat and the CMA will work closely together throughout the phase 1 investigation.[43] Ofwat has a statutory role in phase 1 to provide the CMA with its opinion at key stages of the investigation. A table in Annex B lists the principal stages in phase 1 and an overview of the responsibilities of Ofwat and the CMA at each stage. Ofwat will input into the merger process at the following stages:

- **Pre-notification**: The CMA expects that the merger parties will engage with both Ofwat and the CMA during pre-notification.
- **Day 1**: The CMA will not start the investigation until it has sufficient information and Ofwat has the necessary information it requires to carry out its assessment.
- **No later than day 15**: Before the CMA's internal state of play meeting, Ofwat will provide the CMA with its draft opinion on whether the merger has prejudiced or is likely to prejudice its ability to make comparisons and its view of whether any such prejudice is outweighed by any RCBs of the merger.[44]
- **No earlier than day 25**: If the CMA decides to hold a case review meeting,[45] Ofwat will attend the issues meeting with the merger parties and will submit its final opinion to the CMA no later than two working days before the CMA sends the issues letter to the merger parties. Ofwat and the CMA will discuss the issues letter before it is sent to the parties.[46] The merger parties will be sent a non-confidential version of Ofwat's opinion with the issues letter.
- **By day 40**: The CMA will decide whether to refer the water merger for a phase 2 investigation and provide the reasons for its decision to the merger parties. The full non-confidential decision will be published on the CMA's webpages at a later date. Unless otherwise agreed with the CMA, Ofwat will not publish its opinion or comment on the merger until after the CMA has published its full non-confidential decision. See paragraph 3.23 below for further information.

3.20 If the CMA finds that it is under a duty to refer the merger for a phase 2 investigation the merger parties have an opportunity to avoid this outcome by offering the CMA UILs at phase 1. The CMA cannot impose remedies on the merger parties at phase 1.

3.21 Merger parties can discuss potential UILs with the case team or decide to offer UILs at any stage of the phase 1 investigation. The statutory framework means that the CMA will only formally consider UILs after a decision has been taken. Notwithstanding this, the CMA strongly recommends that where merger parties believe a merger has the potential to raise concerns they consider possible UILs during pre-notification and in the early stages of the investigation and discuss these with the CMA case team and Ofwat. These discussions can help merger parties to identify if the UILs being discussed might be suitable to address any concerns. These early discussions also help to ensure that if the CMA reaches a decision to provisionally refer the case for a phase 2 investigation the merger parties will be able to formally propose UILs quickly and maximise the chances of the UILs being accepted.[47]

3.22 The latest the parties can offer such UILs is five working days after receiving the CMA's reasons for its decision that the duty to refer is met.[48] Where the parties make such an offer, the CMA must decide within ten days of the decision, taking account of Ofwat's views, whether there are reasonable grounds for believing that the UILs offer or a modified version of them might be accepted by the CMA. If so, the CMA must reach a final decision on acceptance of the UILs within 50 working days from the date of the parties' receipt of the CMA's decision that the duty to refer is met. The CMA can extend this period by a further 40 working days if it considers there are special reasons for doing so.[49] The CMA strongly encourages merger parties to discuss possible UILs as soon as possible after they receive the CMA's reasoned decision. The high-level process and indicative timings following the receipt of the duty to refer decision are:

- **UILs day 0-5**: During the five-day period that the parties have to offer UILs following receipt of the CMA's decision Ofwat may attend meetings or calls with the CMA and merger parties on UILs.
- **UILs by day 9**: Ofwat submits its provisional view on the UILs offered to the CMA by the ninth day following the CMA's decision.
- **UILs by day 10**: The CMA considers Ofwat's view and the evidence submitted by the merger parties and decides whether there are reasonable grounds for believing that the UILs offered (or a modified version of them) might be accepted by the tenth day following the CMA's decision.
- **UILs consultation**: Where merger parties offer UILs, and the CMA considers that these might be suitable, the CMA will invite comments from third parties on the UILs before its final acceptance of any such UILs. If the CMA decides to consult on the UILs offered Ofwat will give detailed consideration to the UILs offered and submits its final opinion to the CMA two days before the start of the consultation.
- **UILs by day 50**: After the public consultation the CMA decides whether or not to accept the UILs offered and publishes its decision.

Publication

3.23 By working day 40 of the phase 1 investigation the CMA is required to publish a notice of its decision and provide the reasons for its decision to the merger parties.[50] In some cases this is accompanied by a press release. Following discussions with the merger parties and Ofwat a non-confidential version of the full CMA decision will be published at a later date. Ofwat will provide the CMA with a confidential version of its opinion for the purpose of the CMA's decision on the merger. For publication purposes, the CMA may request Ofwat to provide it with a non-confidential version of its opinion.

3.24 A link to the CMA's and Ofwat's publications related to the merger will be provided on each organisation's respective websites.

PHASE 2 PROCESS

3.25 If the CMA refers a water merger for a phase 2 investigation, in line with the general merger regime the CMA has 24 weeks for this investigation. This may be extended by up to eight weeks if it considers that there are special reasons why a report cannot be prepared and published within the deadline.[51] A diagram outlining the process and the expected timelines that apply to general mergers can be found in Annex A.

3.26 All the CMA's functions in a phase 2 investigation are carried out by inquiry groups and they are the decision makers for the water merger. Their role is to set the direction of the inquiry, review the evidence and analysis, and answer the statutory questions (which are outlined in paragraphs 2.5 to 2.7 above). The inquiry groups are supported by a CMA case team.

3.27 In contrast to a phase 1 investigation, Ofwat does not have a statutory role in a phase 2 merger. However, it is likely that the CMA will continue to work closely with Ofwat throughout a phase 2 investigation.

3.28 The process for phase 2 water merger investigations will follow the same procedure as general merger investigations. For more information about the phase 2 process and procedure see Chapters 10 to 14 of CMA2.

NOTES

37 Further information can be found in CMA2, in particular paragraphs 6.5–6.21 and 6.59 & 6.60.

38 Further information can be found in CMA2, in particular paragraphs 6.39–6.58.

39 For further information about information sharing between the CMA and Ofwat please see *Statement of intent: An agreement on the working arrangements between the CMA and Ofwat for the special water merger regime* (the statement of intent).

40 For further information on the merger impact assessment submission, see Ofwat (2015), *Ofwat's approach to mergers and statement of methods.*

41 The CMA has the power under section 109 of the EA02 to issue a notice to require a person to provide information and documents or to give evidence. However, the CMA is likely to request information informally where possible. Section 109 of the EA02 applies to the CMA's investigations of water mergers in both phase 1 and phase 2 pursuant to regulation 30 of the Water Mergers Regulations and paragraph 22(19) of Schedule 1 to the Enterprise and Regulatory Reform Act 2013 (Competition) (Consequential, Transitional and Saving Provisions) (No. 2) Order 2014 (SI 2014/549).

42 SI [to be confirmed]/2015.

43 For information on how the CMA and Ofwat will work together in practice, see the statement of intent.

44 This is no later than 15 working days after the investigation has started.

45 See CMA2, paragraphs 7.34–7.49.

46 In line with the general merger regime, while the CMA will interact with third parties, in light of the short timescales of a phase 1 investigation and the confidentiality constraints, it is not CMA practice to provide third parties with an opportunity to comment on the issues letter provided to the merger parties.

47 For further information see CMA2, Chapter 8, paragraphs 8.7–8.9.

48 SI [to be confirmed]/2015.

49 For further information see CMA2, Chapter 8, paragraphs 8.23–8.26.

50 See further CMA2, Chapter 9.

51 Section 39(3) of EA02, which applies to water mergers pursuant to paragraph 1 of Schedule 4ZA of WIA.

4. ANALYTICAL APPROACH AND METHODOLOGIES

INTRODUCTION

[3.564]

4.1 The question of substance that the CMA has to consider in its decision on water mergers is whether the merger may prejudice Ofwat's ability to make comparisons between water enterprises, and if so, to what extent. The basic analytical framework on this question applies across both phases 1 and 2 of the CMA's investigation.

4.2 There are different legal tests that apply at phase 1 and phase 2 and as a consequence of this, there are different evidential thresholds on prejudice between the two phases. The question for the CMA at phase 1 is whether the merger is **not likely** to prejudice Ofwat's ability to make comparisons between water enterprises. At phase 2 the question for the CMA is whether the merger **has or may be expected to** prejudice Ofwat's ability to make comparisons. Given these different legal tests, and the time constraints, the amount and complexity of analysis conducted by the CMA is likely to differ between the two phases.

4.3 The section below explains briefly the main areas where Ofwat makes comparisons, and the factors that the CMA may take into account in its assessment of prejudice, which make reference to Ofwat's statement of method.[52]

USE OF COMPARATORS BY OFWAT

4.4 Ofwat is responsible for the economic regulation of the water sector in England and Wales. The WIA imposes duties and confers powers on Ofwat to regulate water enterprises in line with its statutory objectives, in particular to further customer interests, and to secure that water enterprises can carry out their functions and are able to finance their activities. Other duties include promoting efficiency and contributing to sustainable development.

4.5 As each water enterprise is effectively a regional monopoly, comparative regulation has underpinned the way Ofwat has regulated the water and sewerage sector since privatisation in 1989. Ofwat uses comparisons both during the price review process, for example in setting price limits or service quality requirements, and between price reviews, for monitoring and enforcement, and spreading best practice.

4.6 One of Ofwat's primary functions is to set price control limits, which determine the amount of revenue water enterprises can receive during the subsequent price control period. Ofwat sets these limits for a five-year period following a price review, the latest of which (PR14) set revenues for the period 2015 to 2020. The price control protects customers from excessive prices, while incentivising companies to make efficiency improvements, and enables efficient companies to finance their activities.

4.7 Ofwat's determination of revenue limits requires (among other things) identifying the level of allowed expenditure (costs). For example, at PR14 Ofwat set separate price controls for wholesale and retail activities, meaning separate assessments of wholesale water, wholesale wastewater, non-household retail and household retail costs were made. It used comparisons between companies for each price control to maximise the information available to it on likely future costs and to identify an efficient expenditure allowance. Comparisons help it overcome issues of imperfect and asymmetric information, to better allow it and other stakeholders to assess company performance.

4.8 Within the wholesale price control process Ofwat uses econometric modelling and other benchmarking approaches to determine the level of efficient costs.[53] This comparative approach can improve cost estimation, as Ofwat is better able to assess the true costs of water enterprises by comparing costs across a number of independent firms operating in similar circumstances, and to control for differences between companies. The number and quality of comparators is of particular importance to econometric modelling since its statistical robustness depends on the number, independence, and degree of variation of observations. Comparisons between companies can also be used to consider special factor claims for areas not otherwise covered in the cost assessment. To ensure that identified cost thresholds represented reasonably efficient costs, at PR14 Ofwat adjusted the costs forecast by its models to reflect upper quartile performance, thereby using comparators for benchmarking purposes.

4.9 As well as its econometric modelling, Ofwat typically uses comparisons between companies in a range of other ways in determining price controls. For example, at PR14 comparisons were used in:

- assessment of household retail price limits;
- cost of capital and financeability; and
- business planning processes.

4.10 Ofwat also uses comparisons to monitor and incentivise performance and service quality. For example:

(a) As part of PR14 Ofwat conducted comparative analysis of companies' performance commitment and outcome delivery incentive proposals, covering aspects such as: duration of supply interruptions; number of contacts from customers regarding quality of water; number of sewerage pollution incidents; and leakages.

(b) Ofwat has in recent price controls set a service incentive mechanism, which comprises quantitative and qualitative components that measure customers' overall satisfaction with service levels. Companies are rewarded or penalised financially for their performance relative to the rest of the industry.

4.11 The CMA notes that beyond the use of comparators at periodic price reviews, Ofwat also makes comparisons between approaches taken by different companies to aid ongoing activities in relation to monitoring and enforcement activities, and to spread best practice. Examples of Ofwat's use of comparators in these areas include its review of companies' approaches to: board leadership and transparency; social tariffs; customer redress; and claims for interim changes in price limits during a control period.

4.12 Ofwat's approach to regulation and therefore how it uses comparators may change in future in response to developments in the sector. For example, the introduction of non-household retail competition may affect the use of comparisons to assess elements of the non-household control. Cost to serve benchmarks used by Ofwat in its retail price controls may also change in future. The CMA will have regard to foreseeable prospective changes in the use of comparators in its assessment of prejudice, in particular as Ofwat proceeds in developing its approach to the next price review.

IMPACT OF A MERGER ON OFWAT'S ABILITY TO MAKE COMPARISONS

4.13 The CMA considers that an increase in common ownership or control across one or more companies has the potential to affect the ability of Ofwat to make comparisons. A merger may have an adverse impact on Ofwat's ability to:

(a) set price controls (whether at the wholesale or retail level);
(b) monitor and incentivise service quality; and
(c) use comparisons to carry out ongoing monitoring and enforcement activities, and to identify and spread best practice.

4.14 The loss of a comparator resulting from a merger could affect Ofwat's ability to make comparisons in a number of ways:
(a) It may remove a high performing company from Ofwat's set of comparators, which could impact on regulatory benchmarks used by Ofwat and reduce the scale of the efficiency challenge to the wider industry.
(b) It would reduce the number of independent observations in Ofwat's econometric and other models, and consequently could reduce the precision of those estimates or their susceptibility to outliers. To the extent that Ofwat can place less reliance on efficiency comparisons, water companies may expect future price caps to be based to a greater extent on factors related to their own costs and to a lesser extent on factors independent of their own costs, and consequently may have less incentive to achieve costs savings.
(c) It may remove companies with important similarities or differences to other companies, where these aspects can be valuable in making comparisons between companies or in identifying best practice or the use of innovative approaches.

4.15 Some examples of the type of factors that the CMA will consider (consistent with Ofwat's statement of methods) when assessing the impact of the merger on the value of Ofwat's comparisons are listed below and discussed further in paragraphs 4.16 to 4.22. These factors are:
- the extent to which the merger involves overlaps (discussed in paragraph 4.16);
- whether the merger involves the loss of an independent comparator (discussed in paragraph 4.17);
- the extent to which the merger will change benchmarks (discussed in paragraph 4.18);
- the number and quality of independent observations that remain (discussed in paragraph 4.19);
- whether the merger leads to the loss of a company with important similarities for comparisons (discussed in paragraph 4.20);
- whether the merger leads to the loss of a company with important differences for comparisons (discussed in paragraph 4.21); and
- whether Ofwat could amend its approach to reduce the impact of the loss of a comparator (discussed in paragraph 4.22).

4.16 Extent to which merger involves overlaps. As a general principle, the greater the degree of overlap in the scope of merging parties' activities, the more likely a merger is to prejudice Ofwat's ability to make comparisons.

4.17 Loss of an independent comparator. A water merger brings under common ownership or control two or more water enterprises. In general, it is anticipated that companies under common ownership may behave in similar ways, and therefore a water merger may reduce the value of comparisons made by Ofwat. However, if a merger involves a water enterprise that Ofwat does not use to make comparisons, for example a small water company, Ofwat might not in practice lose an independent comparator.

4.18 Extent to which the merger will change benchmarks. If at least one of the merging companies is high performing in some areas, there is a greater risk of detriment for customers than if both companies are poor performers. This is because there is a risk that a high performing comparator might be lost as a result of the merger, which would have an adverse impact on cross-industry benchmarks, reducing the scale of challenge for other companies in the sector. At the same time there may be potential benefits of a high performing company taking over a poorer performing company, since it might improve the performance of a poorer performing company by providing improved efficiency or service to a greater number of customers, though this would need to be evidenced. When assessing whether one or both merger parties is high performing the CMA will examine their performance at the last price determination and their expected ranking at the next determination.

4.19 Number and quality of independent observations that remain. Any reduction to the number of comparators can have an impact on the robustness of Ofwat's analysis by reducing the number of independent observations. Ofwat currently has a higher number of water comparators 18 than sewerage comparators 10, so the loss of a water comparator is likely to have less impact than the loss of a sewerage comparator. The CMA will consider the impact of a merger on the number and quality of comparators, and whether this is likely to make Ofwat's analysis less robust, for example by reducing the precision of its cost modelling. Other things equal, the impact from the loss of a comparator may be expected to increase for each successive merger that occurs, as fewer comparators would remain.

4.20 Loss of a company with important similarities. A merger can lead to the loss of a company with important similarities to the remaining companies. For example a merger between contiguous companies could affect Ofwat's ability to make comparisons across companies that are operating in similar circumstances facing similar issues.

4.21 Loss of a company with important differences. A merger can lead to the loss of a company with important differences from the remaining companies. These differences can take the form of best practice in some areas, or the use of innovative approaches. The loss of these important differences in approach as a result of the merger can have an adverse impact on Ofwat's use of comparators.

4.22 A change to Ofwat's approach. It may be possible for Ofwat to change the way that it regulates to offset, at least to some extent, the potential detriment from the loss of a comparator. This could include using different econometric techniques or a different choice of benchmark within the sample.

4.23 In considering the impact of a merger on Ofwat's ability to make comparisons the CMA will take into account all the factors set out above. Hence the impact depends on the circumstances of the merger under consideration and it is not possible to state, for example, a minimum number of comparators below which Ofwat's ability to make comparisons would be prejudiced.

4.24 Where possible and appropriate, the CMA will seek to quantify the adverse effect of the merger. For example, the CMA may seek to estimate the net present value of cumulative customer detriment if there is expected to be a lowering of the efficiency benchmark as a result of the merger. The CMA's decisions will be based on an assessment of both quantified and non-quantified impacts.

4.25 In reaching its decision at phase 1 the CMA will place significant weight on Ofwat's opinion on whether the merger is likely to prejudice its ability, in carrying out its functions, to make comparisons between water enterprises. The prospect of a clearance at phase 1, on the basis of a lack of prejudice, or acceptance of UILs is likely to be higher when the views of the parties and Ofwat on the impact of the merger are relatively aligned. In particular, where Ofwat considers that a merger is likely to lead to prejudice, but the parties disagree with its analysis, and a detailed analysis is required for the CMA to take a decision, the CMA would typically expect the case to progress to phase 2.[54]

4.26 To ensure that there is no need to refer the case for a phase 2 investigation, the CMA needs to be able to make a decision that the merger is not likely to prejudice Ofwat's ability to make comparisons within the phase 1 timetable. Therefore, even where there is agreement in principle between Ofwat and the parties on whether the merger is not likely to lead to prejudice, the CMA may conclude that the issues are sufficiently complex that a referral is necessary to come to a conclusion. This would need to be considered on a case-by-case basis, based on a review of the specific circumstances of the evidence provided.

NOTES

52 See also Ofwat (2015), *Ofwat's approach to mergers and statement of methods*.

53 At PR14 Ofwat used a range of econometric models and unit cost models to determine wholesale cost allowances for water and wastewater, which were assessed separately. For water, it used econometric models to assess total expenditure (totex) using panel data from 18 companies over a five-year period. For wastewater, it used econometric models to assess base expenditure (for ten companies over seven years) and unit cost models to assess enhancement expenditure.

54 The time and resource constraints of the phase 1 merger process imply that the CMA will not be able to undertake extensive analysis at phase 1 in order to arbitrate between widely differing estimates of a merger's impact provided by the parties and Ofwat.

5. RELEVANT CUSTOMER BENEFITS

INTRODUCTION

[3.565]

5.1 At phase 1, one of the exceptions to the CMA's duty to refer water mergers for an in-depth phase 2 investigation applies if the RCBs in relation to the water merger outweigh any prejudice to Ofwat's ability to make comparisons. Further, the CMA may also have regard to RCBs in deciding on any remedies in a phase 2 investigation.

5.2 This chapter provides further information on potential RCBs and their role in water merger investigations.

RELEVANT CUSTOMER BENEFITS

5.3 RCBs may be taken into account during both phase 1 and phase 2 of the special water merger regime. RCBs are limited to benefits to 'relevant' customers in the form of:

- lower prices, higher quality or greater choice of goods or services in any market in the UK; or
- greater innovation in relation to such goods and services.[55]

5.4 Relevant customers are customers of the merging enterprises at any point in the chain of production and distribution and are therefore not limited to final consumers, and include future customers.

5.5 In addition to falling within the description of RCBs, the CMA must believe that the benefit has accrued as a result of the merger, or is expected to accrue within a reasonable time period as a result of the merger, and that the benefit was, or is, unlikely to accrue otherwise.

5.6 The CMA will disregard any benefits that might arise from commitments that the parties may wish to offer but that do not meet the criteria of a relevant customer benefit.

5.7 The paragraphs below provide examples of possible RCBs followed by an explanation of how they will be taken into account when considering whether a merger should be referred.

POSSIBLE RELEVANT CUSTOMER BENEFITS IN WATER MERGERS

5.8 Mergers that lead to cost savings may generate RCBs if they lead to lower prices. A water merger might lead to cost savings due to economies of scale or scope in the supply of water and/or sewerage services. There may also be costs savings arising from improved water resource management, particularly if contiguous companies are involved.

5.9 The CMA will assess both the expected cost savings and the extent to which any such cost savings can be expected to lead to RCBs by being passed on to the merged company's customers. In assessing RCBs the CMA will have regard to the timing and relative certainty of the proposed benefits, including the mechanism by which cost reductions would result in lower prices.[56]

5.10 An RCB may also arise from higher quality. Possible examples of higher quality may arise from improved security of supply due to improved coordination between companies in sharing water resources, or improved service standards due to sharing of best practices. Before deciding that such a benefit is an RCB, the CMA would have to be satisfied that it would be unlikely to accrue without the merger, for example that it could not be achieved through investment by one or both of the parties on an individual basis.

5.11 In addition, an RCB could take the form of greater choice of goods or services, or greater innovation. Possible such other customer benefits that might be put forward by parties could include:

- Greater choice of tariffs or services. Although choice for customers in the water sector is limited, a merger could lead to greater availability of special tariffs. Other elements of choice of goods and services may become relevant once non-household retail competition is introduced.
- Positive impact on the level of innovation. A merger could in principle impact on the level of innovation, for example through greater effectiveness of research and development or the creation of innovative new company structures.

5.12 As above, the CMA would have to be persuaded on the basis of compelling evidence that such benefits were merger-specific, realistic, and would be passed through to customers. The CMA's approach to assessing RCBs is set out in detail in its general merger guidance.[57]

CMA APPROACH TO RELEVANT CUSTOMER BENEFITS IN PHASE 1

5.13 Where the CMA concludes that a merger may prejudice Ofwat's ability to make comparisons, it will further consider whether the likely prejudice is outweighed by RCBs in reaching its decision on whether the reference test is met. Quantitative and qualitative measures of both the prejudice and the RCBs may be considered. It is not sufficient that there are merely some theoretical benefits to customers: the merging parties must demonstrate that benefits will be passed on to customers and that those benefits will outweigh the identified prejudice.

5.14 In reaching its decision on whether a merger should be referred to phase 2 the CMA will place significant weight on Ofwat's opinion on whether the prejudice identified is outweighed by any RCBs relating to the merger.

5.15 At phase 1 the CMA may have regard to the effect of (or action on) any UIL in relation to any RCBs.[58] In practice, this means that where the CMA may have a choice of two UILs that are equally effective in terms of remedying the prejudice on Ofwat's ability to make comparisons, the CMA will prefer a remedy that preserves the RCBs. Where a benefit may have occurred absent the merger but would have taken longer than a reasonable period, the CMA may take into account the time gained as an RCB. For further information on UILs see Mergers: Exceptions to the duty to refer and undertakings in lieu of a reference guidance (OFT1122), Chapter 3, paragraph 3.23 and Chapter 6, paragraph 6.9 to 6.16

CMA APPROACH TO RELEVANT CUSTOMER BENEFITS IN PHASE 2

5.16 At phase 2, in deciding on remedies the CMA may have regard to the effect of any such action on any RCBs in relation to the merger, provided that: (a) a consideration of those benefits would not prevent a solution to the prejudice concerned; or (b) the benefits that may be expected to accrue are substantially more important than the prejudice concerned.[59] If the first circumstance is applicable, the CMA will, wherever possible, seek to choose remedial action that would not adversely affect the RCBs.[60] If the second circumstance is applicable it may be taken into account in the CMA's decision on whether remedial action should be taken, and if so, what action that should be.

NOTES

55 Paragraph 7 of Schedule 4ZA to WIA (which applies in phase 1 pursuant to section 33A(5) of WIA), and section 30 of EA02 as modified by regulation 6 of the Water Mergers Regulations.

56 In its South East Water/Mid Kent Water report (in 2007) the CC thought it likely that the acquirer would achieve savings in operating expenditure of at least £3.1 million a year, as well as further savings in capital expenditure. The CC expected customers to receive these benefits in the foreseeable future, but was not persuaded that, in the absence of an imposed remedy, they would be fully reflected in the price determination at PR09 (in 2009). See CC (2007), South East Water Limited and Mid Kent Water Limited report, paragraph 35.

57 OFT1122.

58 33D (5) of the WIA.

59 Sections 35(7) and 36(6) of EA02 as modified by regulation 11 of the Water Mergers Regulations.

60 This was the approach followed by the CC in the South East Water/Mid Kent Water inquiry, in choosing a price reduction remedy in preference to a full divestiture remedy. The CC explained in its final report in paragraph 37: 'We noted that full divestiture would result in the loss of all relevant customer benefits arising from the merger. We thought that a price reduction remedy would effectively mitigate the adverse effects we expect to result from the limited prejudice that we have identified, and would at the same time allow relevant customer benefits to be realised.'

6. APPROACH TO REMEDIES

INTRODUCTION

[3.566]

6.1 The general aim of remedies in water mergers is to remedy, mitigate or prevent the prejudicial effect of the merger on Ofwat's ability to make comparisons.

6.3 The changes introduced to the special water merger regime by the WA14 create the possibility of voluntary remedies at the phase 1 stage if the merger parties offer UILs, which may be of a comparable form to remedies that the CMA would be expected to implement in phase 2.

6.3 The principles for remedies at both phase 1 and phase 2 in water mergers as well as guidance on what may constitute an effective remedy is discussed below. Further general merger guidance on remedies is given in the CMA's exceptions to the duty to refer guidance[61] and the merger remedies guidance.[62] In addition, general process guidance is set out in Chapter 8 of CMA2.

6.4 The procedure for the CMA's engagement with Ofwat during the remedy process (at phase 1) is in Chapter 2.

RANGE OF POTENTIAL REMEDIES

6.5 Remedies may be either structural or behavioural.

6.6 Structural remedies are intended to restore all or part of the industry structure prior to the merger, for example:

- Partial prohibition or divestiture (covering part of one or more of the merging companies' businesses, for example either through a reduced equity stake; or through the sale of a non-contiguous part of the water company, which could create an additional independent comparator).
- Prohibition of a proposed merger.
- Divestiture of a completed acquisition.

6.7 For divestitures at either phase 1 or phase 2 the CMA will approve the purchaser before the divestiture is allowed to be completed. Further guidance on purchaser approval is in Chapter 8 of CMA2, in particular paragraphs 8.32 to 8.49.

6.8 Behavioural remedies are intended to reduce the prejudice to Ofwat's ability to make comparisons and any adverse effect resulting from the prejudice. An example might be an amendment to the company's licence which could include:

- a requirement to maintain separate management and/or separate accounting and reporting arrangements that are subject to external assurance assessments (this could, for example, involve the creation of a separate company to manage particular parts of the supply chain such as retail, water resources or networks); and
- changes to prices and/or service quality commitments for customers of one or both companies. In such circumstances the time period that such commitments would apply must be clearly identified.

PHASE 1 – UNDERTAKINGS IN LIEU OF A REFERENCE

6.9 Where the CMA decides in phase 1 that the reference test is met, the parties may offer UILs.[63] The CMA will consider whether the proposed UILs would remedy, mitigate or prevent the prejudicial effect of the merger on Ofwat's ability to make comparisons. When considering UILs the CMA must have regard to the need to achieve as comprehensive a solution as reasonable and practicable to the prejudicial effect on Ofwat's ability to make comparisons. The CMA may have regard to the effect of accepting UILs on any RCBs in relation to the merger. Where UILs are offered by the merger parties the CMA must consider Ofwat's opinion on the effectiveness of the UILs offered.[64] Guidance on the CMA's general policies on UILs is available in OFT1122 and Chapter 8 of CMA2.

6.10 In order to accept UILs the CMA must be confident that the potential concerns regarding prejudicial effect that have been identified in its investigation would be resolved by means of the UILs without the need for further investigation. UILs are therefore appropriate only where the remedies proposed to address any concerns are both clear cut and capable of ready implementation.[65]

6.11 The CMA will generally expect UILs to restore Ofwat's ability to make comparisons between water enterprises to a level similar to that which existed pre-merger.

6.12 Structural remedies are capable of being clear-cut solutions in water mergers as they are in the wider economy and in line with its general merger guidance the CMA will consider behavioural remedies for mergers in markets in which there already exists a significant degree of regulation (such as water mergers).[66]

6.13 This reflects the need to identify UILs that can be implemented. Structural undertakings can satisfy these conditions and can be implemented in all markets. Within regulated sectors, an agreement to clear cut and enforceable licence modifications may be similarly effective. However, there would need to be a binding commitment to any such licence modifications, and the form would need to be clear and unambiguous.

6.14 Whilst this provides flexibility to consider both behavioural and structural remedies on a case-by-case basis, the CMA will nevertheless expect UILs to remedy, mitigate or prevent the prejudicial effects to meet the test that no reference to phase 2 is required. The CMA would not accept behavioural remedies that are solely for the purpose of providing RCBs (ie benefits to the customers of the merging companies) in phase 1, where there is evidence of likely prejudice arising from the merger, and the behavioural remedies do not address that prejudice. This is comparable to the general merger regime, where RBCs are a potential exception to the duty to refer a merger to phase 2 however any RCBs must outweigh the SLC and any adverse effects of the SLC in all affected markets at phase 1.[67] A phase 2 investigation allows the CMA to take a balanced view of the way in which any RCBs might form part of the remedial action required, the phase 1 process should not attempt to pre-empt this if at phase 1 it is identified that a prejudice is likely to be arising from the water merger.

6.15 The CMA would expect parties to engage with both the CMA and Ofwat at the earliest opportunity to discuss potential UILs.

PHASE 2 – REMEDIAL ACTION

The remedy questions

6.16 If the CMA has decided on a reference under section 32 of the WIA that the water merger results in a prejudicial outcome to Ofwat's ability to make comparisons, the CMA has to decide whether to take action to remedy, mitigate or prevent the prejudice, or any adverse effect that might result, and to decide what action to take. In deciding what action to take, the CMA may have regard to the effect of any action on RCBs.

6.17 The CMA should first consider whether the CMA itself should take remedial action to remedy the prejudice to Ofwat or any adverse effect which has resulted from, or may be expected to result from, the prejudice to Ofwat's ability to make comparisons. This would take the form of either using its order-making powers or accepting undertakings from the parties (see paragraphs 6.19 and 6.20 below). The second question is whether the CMA should recommend that remedial action should be taken by others, such as ministers and regulators, including Ofwat. Such recommendations cannot bind the person to whom they are addressed. They can be additional or alternative to any remedial action taken by the CMA. The third question specifically asks the CMA to address what action should be taken and what it is designed to address.

6.18 In deciding these questions, the CMA shall 'in particular have regard to the need to achieve as comprehensive a solution as is reasonable and practicable to the prejudice to Ofwat and any adverse effects resulting from it'.[68]

6.19 In general, the CMA's decision as to which form of remedy to use will be determined by issues of practicality. When the particular circumstances of the case point to the need for action to be taken speedily, the CMA may choose to implement the remedy by way of an order to avoid delay while undertakings are negotiated.

6.20 The CMA welcomes the possibility of accepting undertakings that the parties put forward as being those they are willing to enter into and which the CMA considers would provide a comprehensive solution. However, even if the parties do propose undertakings, the CMA may consider alternative remedies.

Consideration of appropriate remedies

6.21 Although the CMA must always consider the appropriateness of any remedial action, it is likely that it would decide to take remedial action if it has decided that a merger results or is expected to result in a prejudicial outcome. Examples of exceptional circumstances where the CMA might conclude that no action was appropriate might be where the costs of any practicable remedy seemed disproportionate in the light of the extent of the prejudice to Ofwat. However, even in these circumstances, the CMA, having decided that no action should be taken by it, might recommend action to be taken by others.

6.22 The WIA enables the CMA, under certain circumstances, to take into account, any RCBs that arise from the merger, when deciding upon remedial action. Those circumstances are: first, when the consideration of those benefits would not prevent a solution to the prejudice concerned; and second, when the benefits that may be expected to accrue are substantially more important than the prejudice concerned.[69] This consideration too might lead to the decision that no action should be taken. The circumstances in which RCBs can be considered, and what constitutes an RCB, are described above in Chapter 5.

6.23 The remedial action that the CMA will decide should be taken will always depend on the facts and circumstances of the case. The CMA will consider remedy options proposed by the merger parties and others in addition to its own options. When deciding what an appropriate remedy is, it will consider the effectiveness of different remedies and their associated costs and will have regard to the principle of proportionality. These are discussed in the next sections.

The cost of remedies and proportionality

6.24 The CMA must have regard to the reasonableness of any remedy, and this will include consideration of the costs of any action it might decide is appropriate. It will not require a remedy that it considers is disproportionate in relation to the prejudice to Ofwat's ability to make comparisons or any adverse effects resulting or expected to result from such prejudice. If it is choosing between two remedies that it considers would be equally effective, it will choose the remedy that imposes the least cost to the parties or that is least restrictive.

6.25 The CMA will generally include in its consideration of parties' costs the costs of implementing a remedy. However, for completed mergers it will not normally consider the costs of divestiture to the parties as it is open to the parties to make merger proposals conditional on competition authorities' approval. It is for the parties concerned to assess whether there is a risk that a completed merger would be prohibited subsequently, and the CMA will normally expect this risk to have been reflected already in the acquisition price.

6.26 The CMA will endeavour to minimise any ongoing compliance costs to the parties, subject to the effectiveness of the remedy not being reduced, and will have regard to the costs to the CMA and/or Ofwat in implementing, and monitoring compliance with, any remedies that the CMA may put in place or recommend.

Effectiveness of remedies

6.27 Before the several types of remedy are considered in more detail, a few general observations can be made about the effectiveness of remedies.

6.28 First, a factor bearing on the effectiveness of any remedy is whether the remedy is clear to the person to whom it is directed and also to other relevant interested parties, for example the CMA, which has responsibility for monitoring compliance, and Ofwat. Other examples of interested parties include consumer groups (notably the Consumer Council for Water), other regulators including the Environment Agency and the Drinking Water Inspectorate, competitors, suppliers and customers, each of whom may have an interest in ensuring compliance and may bring to the CMA's attention any concern that a remedy is not being complied with.

6.29 A second consideration is the prospect of the remedial action being implemented and complied with. Some remedies are a commitment as to future behaviour or to a standard of acceptable future behaviour. There may be less certainty with some remedies compared with others that the remedies will have the desired effect. A relevant factor will be the ease of monitoring notwithstanding the possibility of establishing a compliance programme. The effectiveness of any remedy is reduced if elaborate, and possibly costly, monitoring and compliance programmes are required. One-off remedies that change the structure of the market (so-called structural remedies) are (subject to the proportionality test as described in paragraph 6.26) likely to be preferable to remedies that impinge upon the behaviour or conduct of firms (so-called behavioural remedies) as they address the effect of the merger directly and, once implemented, will require comparatively little, if any, monitoring or enforcement of compliance.

6.30 A third consideration is the timescale within which the effects of any remedial action will occur. Some remedies will have a more or less immediate effect, for example in eradicating any prejudice to Ofwat's ability to make comparisons, while the effects of others will be delayed. There may be particular uncertainty about the timescale within which results can be expected when the remedy calls for action by some other person, for example a recommendation to government to change regulations. The CMA will tend to favour a remedy that can be expected to show results in a relatively short time period – provided it is satisfied that the remedy is both reasonable and practicable and has no adverse long-run consequences.

Types of remedies

6.31 A summary of the potential types of remedies that the CMA will consider is set out in paragraphs 6.5 to 6.8 above.

Addressing the prejudice to Ofwat's ability to make comparisons

6.32 In addressing the question of whether a particular remedy would be appropriate, and would provide as comprehensive a solution as is reasonable and practicable to address the prejudice to Ofwat's ability to make comparisons and any adverse effects resulting from the prejudice, the CMA will take account of how adequately the action would remedy, prevent or mitigate the concerns caused by the merger.

6.33 The CMA's starting point will be to choose remedial action that will prevent the prejudice to Ofwat's ability to make comparisons and any resulting adverse effects. Given that the effect of the merger is to change the structure of the industry, remedies that aim to restore all or part of the status quo ante industry structure are likely to be a direct way of addressing the adverse effects. However, issues such as the effectiveness of the remedy, the costs associated with the remedy and RCBs that would be forgone may mean that other types of remedy need to be considered. The CMA may decide to impose more than one type of remedy.

Prohibition and divestiture

6.34 With a proposed merger, the most effective remedy will often be the prohibition of the merger. A complication may be that the potential acquirer has invested in a partial shareholding in the target company that it is seeking to increase through a proposed further transaction. This may need to be reduced to a specified maximum level, below which the CMA judges there could be no possibility of material influence, within a specified and reasonable time period.

6.35 For mergers that have already completed, the most effective remedy may be divestiture of the acquired business. The CMA would expect remedial action, including divestiture, to occur within a specified and reasonable time after the CMA has published its decision. The length of the period will depend on the circumstances but will normally be a maximum of six months. Until the divestiture is complete, measures intended to safeguard the competitiveness of the business, including the appointment of a trustee or other person to monitor the process, may be implemented. The CMA will generally insist on having the right to approve the prospective purchaser and the divestiture agreement before the parties may proceed with the divestiture.

6.36 As an alternative to either prohibition or divestiture of the acquired business, the CMA may consider divestiture of the acquirer's holdings in other water enterprises, where this would appropriately restore Ofwat's ability to make robust comparisons.

Partial prohibition and divestiture

6.37 Partial prohibition and divestiture (rather than outright prohibition or full divestiture) may be an appropriate remedy in some cases. This would be the case when Ofwat's ability to make comparisons would be restored by divestiture of part of one of the merging companies. A partial divestiture might be of a stand-alone, going-concern business or of physical assets, for instance those serving part of a company's licence area or the retail operation (separated from its wholesale operation). The *Merger Remedies: Competition Commission Guidelines (CC8)* outlines the CMA's general approach to defining divestiture packages (see Part 3: Divesture and intellectual property).

6.38 There are two key questions that will help to determine whether partial divestiture can be an effective remedy in a water merger case:

- whether the business or assets to be divested provide the basis of a viable business that can operate independently of the merging firms and, in a reasonably short time, say within one year, can be expected to provide an effective comparator to Ofwat; and
- whether there is a suitable purchaser of the assets who will be capable of operating the assets and running a viable, independent and competitive business.

6.39 As with other remedies, the CMA will have regard to RCBs in considering partial prohibition and divestiture.

Behavioural remedies

6.40 The CMA will also consider whether to recommend that action be taken by others, in particular Ofwat. This could include changes to the merging companies' price caps; performance commitments and incentives; business separation; and licence conditions requiring the provision of information to Ofwat. Paragraph 6.8 of this guidance reviews a range of potential behavioural remedies.

NOTES

61 OFT1122.

62 *Merger Remedies: Competition Commission Guidelines November 2008* (CC8).

63 Section 33D of WIA.

64 See Chapter 3, paragraph 2.4 for further information.

65 For further detail see OFT1122, paragraphs 5.6 & 5.7.

66 For further detail see OFT1122, paragraph 5.43.

67 Paragraph 5.13 of OFT1122 states that: 'the [CMA] will not accept undertakings in lieu that do not address the identified competition effects but which are designed instead to 'lock in' sufficient customer benefits to outweigh the risks of a substantial lessening of competition arising'.

68 Sections 35(6) and 36(5) of the EA02.

69 Sections 35(7) and 36(6) as modified by regulation 11.

ANNEX A: PRINCIPAL STAGES AND INTERACTION BETWEEN THE CMA AND OFWAT DURING A PHASE 1 INVESTIGATION

[3.567]

Day[70]	Stage	CMA	Ofwat
Typically at least two weeks before notification	Pre-notification	The CMA and Ofwat discuss the transaction with the parties, including the relevant information required from the parties necessary to start the investigation.	
1	Commencement of phase 1	The CMA publishes on its webpages the notice of commencement of the initial period of investigation	
1	Information gathering	The CMA and Ofwat will continue to liaise with the parties throughout the 40 working day period and request further information as appropriate.	
1-10	Invitation to comment	The CMA will publish an invitation to comment notice on its webpages inviting views from third parties. The CMA will provide Ofwat with any responses received by third parties that are relevant for its assessment.	
15–20	State of play meeting	The CMA will hold a 'state of play' discussion with the merger parties	Ofwat will attend the state of play meeting. Ofwat will provide the CMA with a draft opinion on the transaction no later than day 15.
Phase 1 decision (for cases raising no serious concerns)			
By day 40	Phase 1 decision (for cases raising no serious concerns)	CMA clears the transaction and issues a clearance decision.	
Phase 1 decision process (for cases raising more complex or serious concerns)			
By day 40 but typically no earlier than day 25	Issues letter	CMA will share and discuss the issues letter with Ofwat before sending it to the merger parties. CMA sends an issues letter to the parties. CMA organises an issues meeting	Ofwat provides the CMA with its final opinion on the issues raised by the merger no later than two working days before the issues letter is sent to the parties. Ofwat provides the CMA with a confidential and non-confidential version of its opinion; the parties will receive the non-confidential version when they receive the issues letter.

Day[70]	Stage	CMA	Ofwat
	Issues meeting	The CMA will consider any response Ofwat subsequently makes to the parties response to the issues letter. The CMA may ask Ofwat to provide supplementary information in relation to its opinion or additional evidence submitted by the parties.	Ofwat will attend the issues meeting. Ofwat will be available to meet the CMA case team and explain the reasoning and analysis in its advice. Where appropriate Ofwat will provide the CMA with its reply to the parties' response to the issues letter and issues meeting.
By day 40	Phase 1 decision (for cases raising more complex or serious concerns)	CMA holds an internal case review meeting.	
	Publication of the decision	CMA publishes notice of its decision (whether the test for reference has been met).	
After day 40		At a later date the CMA will publish a full non-confidential decision.	Ofwat will issue a non-confidential version of its advice to the CMA following the publication of the CMA's full decision.
Undertakings in lieu of a reference			
Before day 40	Preliminary discussion on UILs	The CMA will inform Ofwat as soon as practical of any material discussions on UILs. The CMA will share with Ofwat any relevant information provided by the parties on potential UILs.	(Where appropriate) Ofwat may attend meetings and/or calls between the CMA and the merging parties when discussing UILs. Ofwat will provide the CMA with a written or oral provisional review[71] on any potential UILs that have been raised by the parties.
0–5 days after reference decision	Parties offer UILs	If no UILs are offered within 5 days of the decision the CMA will refer the merger for a phase 2 inquiry. CMA will share with Ofwat UILs offered.	
0–10 days after reference decision	Consideration of the UILs	The CMA considers the UILs and makes a decision whether to provisionally accept or reject the UILs offered.[72]	Ofwat provides the CMA with a provisional view on the UILs offered by the parties no later than 9 days after the reference decision.
Within 50 days of the reference decision	Agreement and acceptance	The CMA gives detailed consideration to the UILs offered and publishes draft UILs for comment. If UILs are agreed the CMA publishes notice of acceptance; if not the transaction is referred to phase 2.	Ofwat submits its final views to the CMA on the UILs offered by the parties no later than two days before the consultation period begins.[73]

NOTES

70 Working days.

71 This provisional review may not reflect Ofwat's final formal view and may not have approval from its board.

72 Where there is a disagreement between the CMA and Ofwat on the UILs offered, the CMA will inform Ofwat before it takes its final decision. Where UILs proposed by the merger parties are rejected by the CMA the merger will proceed for a phase 2 investigation.

73 For further information please see the statement of intent.

ANNEX B: PRINCIPAL STAGES OF A CMA MERGER INVESTIGATION

[3.568]

1. Figure 1 below provides a high-level summary of the principal stages in phase 1 and phase 2 merger investigations undertaken by the CMA under the EA02 from initial contact with the CMA, through to a full phase 2 investigation.

Figure 1: CMA merger investigations – principal stages

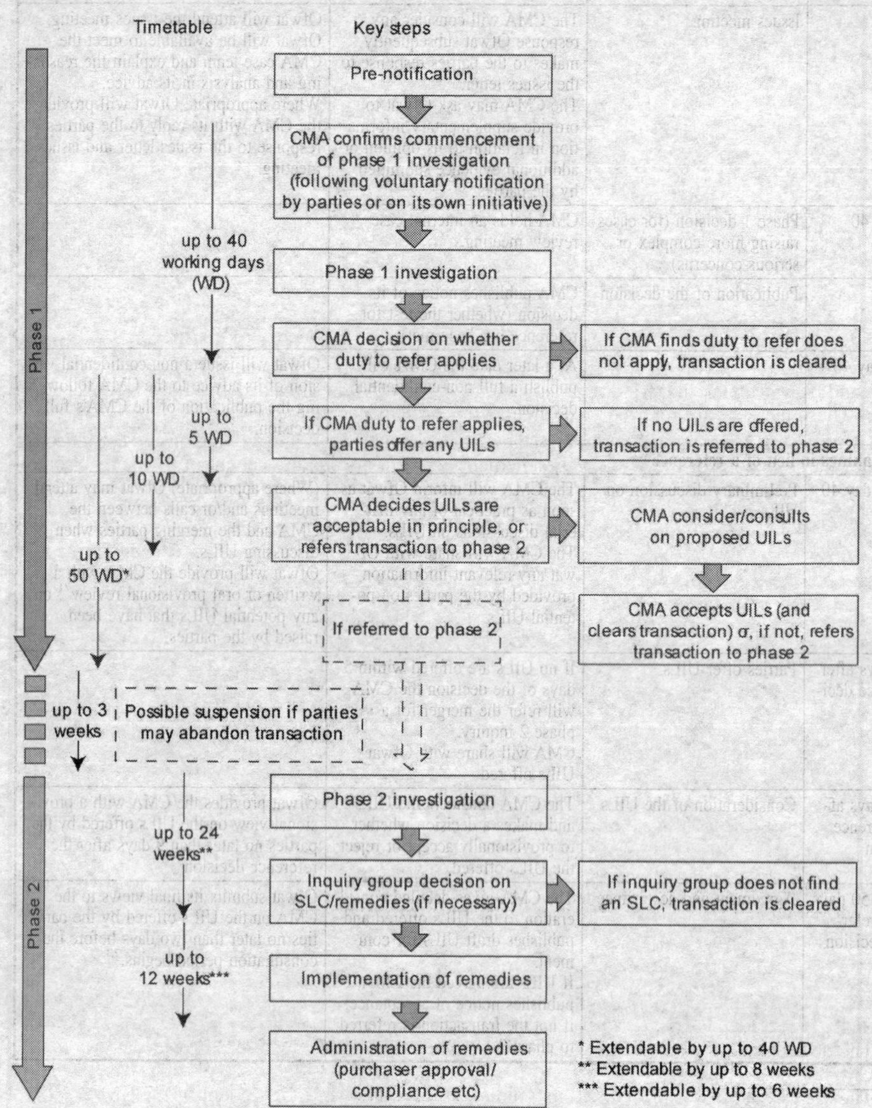

STATEMENT OF INTENT
AN AGREEMENT ON THE WORKING ARRANGEMENTS BETWEEN THE CMA AND OFWAT FOR THE SPECIAL WATER MERGER REGIME

(November 2015)

[3.569]

NOTES

INTRODUCTION

[3.570]

1. The purpose of this statement of intent is to set out the working arrangements between the Water Services Regulation Authority (Ofwat) and the Competition and Markets Authority (CMA) in relation to the review of mergers involving water and sewerage or water only companies (water enterprises) in England and Wales under the Water Industry Act 1991 (WIA) as amended by the Water Act 2014 (WA14).[1] These mergers are referred to in this document as water mergers.

2. The working arrangements set out in this statement of intent are not legally binding and are reflective of the relevant provisions of the WIA. This statement of intent also takes account of the merger control provisions of the Enterprise Act 2002 (EA02) as amended by the Enterprise and Regulatory Reform Act 2013. This statement of intent is restricted to Ofwat's role in giving an opinion to the CMA in phase 1 assessments of mergers between water enterprises and does not consider any competition issues resulting from these mergers that the CMA may also be investigating under the EA02. The CMA routinely consults with regulators about mergers that they are likely to have sector specific knowledge. This is equally the case during a phase 2 water merger investigation. For further information please see *Mergers: Guidance on the CMA's jurisdiction and procedures* (CMA2).

3. These working arrangements should be considered alongside *Water and sewerage mergers: Guidance on the CMA's procedure and assessment* (CMA49) and the existing memorandum of understanding between the CMA and Ofwat in relation to their concurrent competition law powers in the water and sewerage sector.[2]

NOTES

1 A water enterprise is an enterprise carried on by a company appointed under section 6 of the WIA to be a water and/or sewerage undertaker.

2 CMA and Ofwat memorandum of understanding (2014).

GENERAL PRINCIPLES

[3.571]

4. Ofwat and the CMA will observe the following general principles in relation to Ofwat's opinion regarding prejudice to its ability to make comparisons, relevant customer benefits (RCBs) and undertakings in lieu (UILs):

(a) The CMA and Ofwat will cooperate with each other in the exercise of their respective functions under Part 3 of the EA02 and sections 32 to 35 of the WIA.

(b) The decision as to whether the CMA refers a water merger for a phase 2 investigation is for the CMA alone.

(c) The views that Ofwat presents in its opinion will be its own, independent of the CMA.

(d) Ofwat's opinion is not binding on the CMA, but the CMA will give significant weight to it when making decisions in relation to prejudice to Ofwat's ability to make comparisons, RCBs and UILs.

(e) The CMA and Ofwat will work in close contact throughout the investigation, and will have particular regard to the timing requirements placed on both the CMA and Ofwat in phase 1 of the inquiry.

PRE-NOTIFICATION PERIOD

5. Ofwat and the CMA will liaise with each other as to whether they are satisfied that the information submitted by the merger parties is sufficient to start their respective assessments.

6. The CMA will liaise closely with Ofwat as to whether the information received with respect to Ofwat's ability to make comparisons and RCBs will allow it to start its assessment and provide an opinion to the CMA within the CMA's phase 1 timetable. This information is required to be provided in the merger notice form of the CMA.

7. If the merger parties decide not to make submissions in relation to the information required for Ofwat's assessment, or aspects of the required information, and they indicate their decision in writing to Ofwat, then Ofwat will inform the CMA of the merger parties' decision as soon as reasonably practicable.

8. The CMA will not commence a merger review until it considers that the merger parties have provided sufficient information required for the respective assessments of both Ofwat and the CMA.

ASSESSMENT PERIOD

9. In the special merger regime the CMA has a statutory period of 40 working days for phase 1 of the investigation (after the CMA has confirmed with the merger parties that their merger notice form is complete or, when such a form was not provided, the CMA has sufficient information to begin its investigation). These are the same time periods that apply by statute to the general merger regime.

10. In general the CMA will apply to the special merger regime the same procedures used in the general merger regime except for any differences set out in this statement of intent and CMA49. The CMA starts the assessment stage of its phase 1 investigation by publishing a notice of commencement of the initial period on its webpages. The CMA will also publish an invitation to comment, which is typically open for a period of ten working days. The invitation to comment will make clear that the CMA will provide Ofwat with any comments received regarding prejudice to Ofwat's ability to carry out its regulatory functions and/or RCBs and/or UILs. During this period the CMA and Ofwat continue to progress their respective assessments. Ofwat and the CMA will discuss respective views on an ongoing basis.

11. The CMA will have a 'state of play' discussion with the merger parties around days 15 to 20 of the statutory timetable of a phase 1 investigation. The purpose of this discussion is to give the merger parties information on any comparative regulation concerns, whether or not the CMA is to take the merger to a case review meeting and send the merger parties an issues letter and, if so, the theories of harm that the CMA proposes to include in the issues letter.[3] The CMA will invite Ofwat to attend the state of play discussion.

12. To inform the state of play discussion with the merger parties Ofwat will provide the CMA with a draft opinion in writing on the matters listed in paragraphs 2.2 (b) and (c) of CMA49 by no later than working day 15 of the phase 1 investigation.

13. For cases that raise no serious issues, it is possible that the CMA, taking account of Ofwat's opinion, may decide to clear the merger on the grounds that one of the circumstances described in paragraph 2.2 of CMA49 applies. The CMA will then issue its clearance decision within the phase 1 deadline.

14. In cases where the CMA intends to proceed to a case review meeting, and consequently sends an issues letter to the merger parties the CMA will notify Ofwat of that as soon as practicable and share and discuss the draft issues letter with Ofwat before it is sent to the parties.

15. Ofwat will then provide its final opinion on the issues raised by the merger to the CMA as soon as practicable but no later than two working days before the issues letter is provided to the parties. The issues letter will normally be sent on or after day 25. Ofwat will provide the CMA with a confidential and non-confidential version of its opinion. The merger parties will then be provided with Ofwat's opinion alongside the issues letter. The CMA will share with Ofwat the issues letter (or a non-confidential version of it) at the same time as it is sent to the parties.[4] The CMA will consider any response Ofwat subsequently makes to the parties' response to the issues letter.

16. Ofwat staff involved in producing the opinion will make all reasonable effort to be available to meet the CMA case team to explain the reasoning and analysis underlying the opinion provided. The CMA may ask Ofwat to provide further information in relation to arguments it raised or in relation to additional evidence provided by the merger parties in response to the issues letter.

MEETINGS WITH THE MERGER PARTIES

17. Meetings with the merger parties will generally be held separately by Ofwat and the CMA. However, both Ofwat and the CMA expect the merger parties to be transparent with the information that is shared between the parties and the respective authorities. Where appropriate, joint meetings may be held between the merger parties, the CMA and Ofwat in order to facilitate the phase 1 investigation and ensure administrative efficiency.

18. Ofwat will attend the state of play call and issues meetings between the CMA and the parties. Moreover, Ofwat will be given the same time period as the parties to submit any further written responses to the CMA as a result of evidence submitted or discussion at the issues meeting.

19. If necessary, both Ofwat and the merger parties will be given individual access to the phase 1 decision maker during the issues meeting.

NOTES

[3] This process is described in CMA2, Chapter 7. In the state of play discussion the CMA will also raise any competition concerns arising from the merger of the parties' non-water activities.

UNDERTAKINGS IN LIEU OF A REFERENCE TO PHASE 2

[3.572]

20. The CMA has the ability to accept UILs offered by the merger parties at phase 1 of the investigation but cannot impose remedies on the merger parties. Both the CMA and Ofwat will strongly encourage merging parties to consider the possibility of offering UILs early in the investigation and to liaise with both the CMA and Ofwat as soon as possible if the merger parties are considering undertakings.[5]

21. The merger parties can offer UILs at any point during the phase 1 investigation; however the latest the parties can offer such UILs is five working days after receiving the CMA's decision that the duty to refer is met (the 'duty to refer decision').

22. In the special water merger regime, the CMA can accept UILs in order to remedy, mitigate or prevent the water merger's prejudicial effect on Ofwat's ability to make comparisons between water enterprises that the merger has had, may have had or may be likely to have. When forming a view on UILs the CMA must have regard to the need to achieve as comprehensive a solution as is reasonable and practicable to the prejudicial effect on Ofwat's ability to make comparisons. The CMA may also have regard to the effect of any action on any RCBs in relation to the merger.[6]

23. Before the CMA makes a decision on any UILs offered, the CMA must request and consider Ofwat's opinion on the effect of the UILs.[7]

24. Within the statutory timetable the CMA has until the tenth working day after the parties have received the CMA's duty to refer decision to decide whether there are reasonable grounds for believing that the UILs offered might be accepted by the CMA. The CMA must reach a final decision on acceptance of the UILs within 50 working days from the date of the parties' receipt of the CMA's duty to refer decision, although the CMA can extend this by a further 40 working days if it considers there are special reasons for doing so.

25. The CMA will take into account Ofwat's opinion in deciding whether to accept the UILs, to extend the period in which the decision will be made, or to reject the UILs and proceed to phase 2.

26. Where the merger parties are willing to initiate discussion on potential UILs before the CMA duty to refer decision has been taken, the CMA will inform Ofwat as soon as practicable about any material discussions on UILs with the merger parties and will endeavour to include Ofwat in any substantive discussions with the merger parties. In any case, it will share with Ofwat any relevant information provided by the parties on potential UILs.

27. If the parties offer UILs after receiving the CMA's duty to refer decision, the CMA will share with Ofwat any formal offer in writing (or, if appropriate, a non-confidential version of it).

28. In these circumstances, Ofwat will provide its opinion to the CMA as soon as practicable after the merger parties' submission of their formal offer and in any case Ofwat will provide its opinion no later than the ninth working day after the parties have received the CMA's duty to refer decision. In light of the CMA's timetable to make a decision on the UILs offered Ofwat may consider this its provisional decision and if the CMA decides to consult on the UILs offered Ofwat will provide its final opinion on the UILs at least two days before the start of the consultation period. In previous general merger cases consultations have been launched between three to four weeks after the reference decision. The CMA will notify Ofwat as soon as it can as to when it intends to begin the public consultation.

29. If the CMA does not agree with Ofwat's opinion on the UILs offered by the parties, it will inform Ofwat before making its final decision and take into account Ofwat's representations before making its final decision.

NOTES

4 Whether Ofwat receives all of the issues paper or an excised version of it will depend on disclosure gateways available to the CMA including Part 9 of the EA02.

5 See also CMA2, paragraph 8.7.

6 Sections 33D(2), (4) and (5) of WIA.

7 Section 33(6) of WIA.

PUBLICATION OF THE DECISION AND RELATED DOCUMENTS[8]

[3.573]

30. By working day 40 of the phase 1 investigation the CMA publicly announces its decision. In some cases this is accompanied by a press release. The CMA's communications team will liaise with Ofwat to provide it with advance notice of when the press release will be issued and its content, in strict confidence. Ofwat will not issue any press release or announcement on the merger prior to the public announcement of a CMA decision.

31. Following discussions with the merger parties and Ofwat, a non-confidential version of the full CMA decision will be published at a later date. Ofwat will provide the CMA with a confidential version of its opinion for the purpose of the CMA's decision on the merger. For publication purposes, Ofwat will also provide the CMA with a non-confidential version of its opinion.

32. The publication of Ofwat's opinion will not occur until after the non-confidential decision is published by the CMA unless otherwise agreed with the CMA.

33. Ofwat's opinion may contain information that is confidential (either as regards the merger parties or other confidential information known to Ofwat). As set out above, Ofwat may share such information with the CMA. To the extent that the merger parties consider that information they provide to Ofwat should not be included in the published version of Ofwat's opinion, they should submit a non-confidential version of such submission to Ofwat and state clearly what information should remain confidential to Ofwat, together with the reasons for this.

34. A link to publications related to the merger will be provided on each organisation's respective websites.

NOTES

8 See also CMA2, Chapter 9.

REQUESTING AND SHARING INFORMATION

[3.574]

35. To minimise the burden on merger parties, where appropriate, Ofwat and the CMA will coordinate information requests. The CMA will request a waiver from the parties to facilitate disclosure of information between the CMA and Ofwat.

36. Sharing of information (including data) between the CMA and Ofwat is crucial for the effective fulfilment of their respective duties under the special water merger regime and should reduce the burden on merger parties which could otherwise arise, for example from duplicative information requests. The CMA and Ofwat may, where appropriate, discuss with each other water merger issues that the merging parties bring to their attention; informal advice they will be providing or have provided; pre-notification drafts; and information obtained throughout the phase 1 investigation.

37. Any disclosure of information between the CMA and Ofwat, and any use by the recipient of such information, shall only be to the extent permitted by law, including by reference to the provisions of section 206 of the WIA and Part 9 of the EA02. The information and data sharing from the CMA to Ofwat will include information that the CMA considers will facilitate the exercise of its statutory functions under the WIA. If either or both of the merger parties request that the CMA should not share with Ofwat some or all of the information or data submitted to it, they should submit a non-confidential version of such submission and state clearly what information should remain confidential to the CMA, together with the reasons for this. However, in certain circumstances, whilst having regard to the confidentiality requests, the CMA may nonetheless decide to disclose information to Ofwat without the consent of the merger parties. This may occur, for example, where it considers that disclosure is necessary to enable the CMA to exercise its statutory functions, including the need to have regard to Ofwat's opinion.[9] This is likely to include the parties' written response to the CMA's issues letter.

38. Information with respect to any particular business which has been obtained by virtue of any of the provisions of the WIA and relates to the affairs of any individual or to any particular business is subject to the restriction on disclosure in section 206 of the WIA. Such information may only be disclosed by Ofwat or the CMA where permitted by section 206 of the WIA or as otherwise allowed by law. For example, the CMA and Ofwat may share such information between them for the purpose of facilitating the carrying out by Ofwat or the CMA of any of their functions by virtue of the WIA or for the purpose of facilitating the carrying out by the CMA of any of its functions under the EA02. Where the CMA shares with Ofwat information and data to which Part 9 of the EA02 applies, it will only be used by Ofwat for the purposes necessary to carry out its functions in relation to the review of the water merger, and (unless it is already publicly available) will not be further disclosed by Ofwat. If Ofwat requires any of the information held by the CMA to facilitate the exercise of its other functions it can request the information from the CMA for disclosure specifically for that purpose, in which case the CMA will conduct a separate assessment of the disclosure of confidential information.[10]

NOTES

9 The CMA's obligations and policy as to confidentiality generally in phase 1 merger investigations are set out in CMA2, paragraphs 7.21–27.

10 Sections 241(3) and 244 of the EA02.

(III) TRANSPORT

RAIL FRANCHISES: A GUIDE FOR POTENTIAL BIDDERS (MARCH 2018)

[3.575]

NOTES

See also CMA74 – Rail franchise mergers: Review of methodologies and guidance (March 2018) at www.gov.uk/government/publications/rail-franchises-questions-and-answers.

This updated guide (which supersedes the document *Rail Franchises: Q&As*, last updated in April 2014) is published to assist franchise bidders and other stakeholders by explaining the Competition and Market Authority's (CMA) approach to reviewing the award of rail franchises under its merger control duties. This updated guide reflects developments to streamline the CMA's review process and ensure close coordination between the CMA and the franchise awarding body. Alongside this guide, the CMA is publishing guidance on its methodology for reviewing franchise awards.

CONTENTS

1. THE CMA'S ROLE IN FRANCHISE AWARDS

[3.576]

The CMA is an independent non-ministerial department with a statutory duty to promote competition for the benefit of consumers.

Under section 66(3) of the Railways Act 1993, entering into a rail franchise agreement constitutes an acquisition of control of an enterprise under the merger control provisions of the Enterprise Act 2002 (EA02). The CMA therefore has a statutory role in reviewing the award of rail franchises, which it aims to complete prior to the start of a new franchise.

The CMA's role is to assesses whether a franchise award could give rise to competition concerns. Its review seeks to protect passengers from fare increases and/or degradation of services which might arise where the successful bidder for a rail franchise already operates rail, bus or coach services on the same routes. For example, in relation to rail services, franchisees compete on certain routes by offering cheaper dedicated tickets to passengers and these fares may be increased or withdrawn once the services come under common ownership.

Passenger rail services in the UK are procured under a variety of models. In some cases, the franchisee retains the fare revenue and has significant freedom in setting unregulated fares (such as the Northern or South Western franchises). In others, the franchisee may bear little or no revenue risk (such as the Thameslink, Southern and Great Northern franchise in which the DfT takes almost all the fare revenue and imposes significant restrictions on the operator's commercial freedom, with the operator being paid a management fee). Concessions may also be awarded, under which the awarding body retains control over price and operational service levels, as well as customer-facing and marketing activities (such as Crossrail[1]).

Models closer to the latter end of the spectrum may not qualify for investigation, and are likely to raise fewer competition concerns, other things being equal.

The CMA has published a guide to UK Merger Assessment, available on Gov.uk.

NOTES

[1] MTR Corporation (Crossrail) / Crossrail merger inquiry (2015).

2. HOW AND WHEN BIDDERS OR PROSPECTIVE BIDDERS FOR RAIL FRANCHISES SHOULD CONTACT THE CMA

[3.577]

All bidders are encouraged to enter into pre-notification discussions with the CMA shortly after having submitted their bids. The CMA has a standing rail mergers team, and is open to having preliminary discussions with bidders at an earlier stage, particularly around the review timetable or the CMA's process.

Although the CMA will only ultimately conduct a formal merger investigation into the winning bid, pre-notification with all bidders will allow the investigation timetable to commence as soon as the winner is announced.[2] The CMA believes that, in practice, this process is necessary, given the relatively short timescale between selecting the winning bid and the start of operations. Bidders should commence formal pre-notification four to six weeks prior to the expected date of the award.[3]

Generally, pre-notification will involve bidders providing the CMA with a draft Merger Notice for discussion, with the aim of producing a final Merger Notice that allows the CMA's investigation to begin in the event the bidder is awarded the franchise.

General guidance on the CMA's procedures and a template Merger Notice for parties to complete are available on Gov.uk: Mergers - the CMA's jurisdiction and procedure: CMA2.

In order to limit the information required and to assist the CMA's preliminary analysis, the CMA encourages each individual bidder to discuss with it as early as possible what information should be provided in the Merger Notice about the overlaps between the bidder's existing bus, coach and train services and the rail franchise route(s), taking account of the specific facts of each bidder's case.4 For example, it may be possible for bidders to provide detailed information only for the overlaps which are more likely to raise competition concerns.

Where there are no overlaps between a bidder's existing services and the rail franchise routes, the bidder is asked to inform the CMA of this position in writing. If the franchise is awarded to this bidder, the bidder is free to decide whether to formally notify the franchise award to the CMA given the voluntary merger regime in the UK.[5] For example, the CMA did not investigate the 2016 award of the East Anglia franchise to Abellio.

The CMA is conscious that some bidders are potential new entrants to the UK or have not been awarded a franchise in the current bidding round. The CMA is particularly keen to engage with such bidders as part of its work to ensure a healthy franchise bidding market.

NOTES

[2] Where the winning bid meets the jurisdictional thresholds for notification under the European Merger Regulation, the CMA's timetable will not begin before the European Commission has taken a decision on reference to the UK (see Question 6 below).

[3] In some cases, there may be sufficient time between the announcement and the commencement to conduct part of the pre-notification in this period, but this depends on the timing of the various stages of the award and the extent of potential competition concerns. Therefore the CMA does not consider there to be an appropriate 'one size fits all' timetable; bidders are encouraged to discuss this with the CMA.

[4] The CMA notes that, for the purposes of making their bid as requested in the invitation to tender, bidders will generally already have conducted an assessment of the possible competition concerns their bid could give rise to. The CMA expects that this assessment will further reduce the burden on bidders in pre-notification discussions with the CMA.

[5] This does not apply to notification to the European Commission where the winning bid meets the jurisdictional thresholds under the EU Merger Regulation.

3. THE CMA'S MERGER REVIEW PROCESS

[3.578]

The CMA aims to engage with bidders on competition issues as part of the pre-award process (ie pre-notification) to allow sufficient time for a Phase 1 review to be completed prior to the start of the franchise. Depending on timetables, this may mean that a complete Merger Notice needs to be submitted as soon as the winning bid is announced. In other cases, some elements of the pre-notification process may take place post-award depending on the time period between award of the franchise and commencement. Once the CMA deems that a Merger Notice is complete, with all relevant data provided, the CMA will start its statutory 40 working day review period.

During the review, the CMA will assess the impact of the franchise award on competition (details of the approach to the assessment are set out in Question 4 below).

The CMA will seek the views of local authorities, competitors and customer groups in the course of its review. As set out at Question 5 below, the CMA will work closely with Department for Transport (DfT), Transport Scotland (TS) or Transport for Wales (TfW) as well as devolved regional administrations with a role in the franchising process. If additional information is required, the CMA will send further information requests to the franchisee during the course of the investigation.

The franchisee will be provided with a 'state of play' update between days 15 and 20 of the investigation. If the CMA has identified potential competition concerns, an 'issues meeting' will be held with the franchisee around day 25 of the investigation. The CMA will announce its decision by no later than day 40 of the investigation.[6]

If the CMA finds that there is a realistic prospect of a substantial lessening of competition at the end of its Phase 1 review, the franchisee has the opportunity to offer undertakings in lieu of being referred to a Phase 2 inquiry.[7] In order to be accepted, any offered undertaking must address the competition concerns identified in a clear-cut and readily implementable manner. For example, in the CMA's 2017 review of the award of the South Western Franchise, a fare cap on the rail route between London and Exeter was agreed with the winning bidder in lieu of being referred for a Phase 2 inquiry.

The CMA is fully aware of the tight timescales involved in the rail franchise process, especially between the announcement of the winning bid and the start of the services. The CMA recommends that, where relevant, bidders and their legal advisers consider possible undertakings in lieu of a reference to Phase 2 as early as possible in the process and ideally during pre-notification. The CMA case team is open to engage in early discussions with bidders on possible undertakings. This will maximise the chances of acceptance of undertakings that are offered at the end of the CMA's Phase 1 investigation, should the franchise award give rise to competition concerns.[8]

If undertakings cannot be agreed in circumstances where competition concerns arise, a Phase 2 inquiry will take place.

NOTES

6 Where the review of a franchise award is referred back to the UK by the European Commission, the CMA is required to reach its decision by day 45 (see question 6 below).

7 See *Mergers: Guidance on the CMA's jurisdiction and procedure* (CMA2), chapter 8.

8 See *Mergers: Guidance on the CMA's jurisdiction and procedure* (CMA2), paragraph 8.7.

4. HOW THE CMA ASSESSES THE EFFECT OF A RAIL FRANCHISE AWARD ON COMPETITION

[3.579]

As a starting point for the analysis, the CMA will identify point-to-point journeys (described as 'flows') on which the rail services of new franchise overlap with the existing transport services provided by the winning bidder.

The CMA will examine whether fare increases and/or degradation of services might arise where the successful bidder for a rail franchise already operates rail, bus, tram or coach services on the same flows and routes.[9]

Where a significant number of overlaps are identified, the CMA will apply a series of filters for prioritisation purposes in order to focus its analysis on the flows most likely to raise competition concerns.

The analysis of flows prioritised for further assessment will consider factors including how closely the overlapping services competed prior to the franchise award, the extent to which pricing and service decisions are constrained by regulation, the number of current and potential competing operators and local factors affecting competition.

Competition concerns are more likely to arise where the transport services coming under common ownership competed closely prior to the franchise award, where there are few competitors and where regulation provides only a limited constraint on fare setting and service provision.

Detailed guidance on the CMA's methodology for reviewing franchise awards is published alongside this guide. This is a draft for consultation, and the CMA welcomes comments on it.

NOTES

9 Flows form part of longer routes and the CMA will consider whether competition is affected at the route level as well as the flow level.

5. INFORMATION SHARING BETWEEN THE CMA AND DFT, TS AND TFW, AND THE CONFIDENTIALITY OF A BIDDER'S COMMERCIALLY SENSITIVE INFORMATION

[3.580]

It is important for the CMA and the franchise awarding body to work closely together to ensure that the CMA merger review and franchise award timetables are aligned as far as possible, to enable industry knowledge to be shared and to avoid duplication in the information requested from bidders.

The CMA and the franchise awarding bodies have therefore taken a number of steps in recent investigations to ensure that they coordinate closely, enabling the effective sharing of industry knowledge and a faster and less burdensome investigation process. Where relevant, the CMA will also engage with relevant regional devolved bodies with a role in the franchise award process. All discussions between the CMA and the franchise awarding bodies and the sharing of any commercially sensitive information is on a confidential basis. In particular, as a competition authority, the CMA is concerned to ensure the integrity of bidding processes and so would treat information it receives from bidders/and the franchise awarding bodies in that context as being especially commercially sensitive.

6. CIRCUMSTANCES IN WHICH BIDDERS SHOULD NOTIFY THE EUROPEAN COMMISSION OF A RAIL FRANCHISE BID

[3.581]

In some cases, bidders for rail franchises will also currently meet the jurisdictional thresholds for mandatory notification to the European Commission under the EU Merger Regulation (EUMR).[10] It is the responsibility of bidders to consider whether the EUMR applies in their respective cases and to contact the European Commission for pre-notification discussions where appropriate.

As stated in the CMA's jurisdictional and procedural guidance,[11] mergers with an EU dimension that might be considered to have a particular impact on competition in the UK should be brought directly to the attention of the CMA at the earliest possible stage, in addition to making the mandatory notification to the European Commission. The CMA considers this to apply to any UK rail franchise.

The CMA expects that there will be strong reasons for a referral of rail franchise mergers back to the UK where they may have a significant impact on competition, since rail franchises concern only the UK and remedies may not be open to the European Commission given that the affected markets may not be a substantial part of the common market. Bidders may therefore wish to consider making a pre-notification request under Article 4(4) EUMR for referral back to the CMA, in cases where the appropriate tests are satisfied. The CMA is willing to discuss the possibility of such a request in more detail on an individual basis.

NOTES

10 This situation is likely to change following the UK's exit from the European Union.

11 *Mergers: Guidance on the CMA's jurisdiction and procedure* (CMA2), paragraph 18.12.

7. INFORMATION THAT BIDDERS SHOULD PROVIDE TO THE CMA

[3.582]

The winning bidder will be expected to notify the CMA using the Merger Notice template (see Question 3 above). The template sets out the categories of information required for the purposes of a merger investigation and should be read in conjunction with the CMA's guidance on its assessment of rail franchise awards, which provides more detail on the information required. Parties are free to supply the required information using the Merger Notice template or to provide a submission in a written format of their choosing, accompanied by a completed Merger Notice indicating clearly where in that submission the required information can be found.[12]

The CMA is conscious that the information required for it to conduct its assessment is likely to vary depending on the case. As set out in Question 2, the CMA therefore welcomes informal discussions on an individual basis in pre-notification to determine the information required in order to conduct its assessment.

NOTES

12 See paragraph 17 of the preamble to the Merger Notice.

8. WHEN INTERIM MEASURES ARE NECESSARY

[3.583]

The CMA has the power to impose initial enforcement orders (IEO) in both anticipated and completed mergers.[13] An IEO requires merging parties to hold their business activities separate during the course of the CMA's investigation.

An IEO will only be necessary in circumstances where the franchise commences prior to the conclusion of the CMA's merger investigation (for example, if the award is referred for a Phase 2 inquiry). As set out in Question 2, the CMA intends that engagement with bidders on competition issues as part of the pre-award process (ie pre-notification) will allow sufficient time for a Phase 1 review to be completed prior to commencement of the franchise.

In circumstances where an IEO is required, the CMA will ensure that the IEO will not prevent the franchisee from meeting its obligations under the franchise agreement[14] upon commencement of the franchise.[15] The IEO will instead focus on ensuring that there is no unnecessary integration nor any alteration to the supply terms for the overlapping franchise network and the franchisee's activities unless in the ordinary course of business. In light of the exceptional circumstances presented by rail franchise cases, the CMA will tailor its template IEO to ensure that the franchisee is able to meet its obligations under the franchise agreement. The CMA will also consider on a case by case basis any derogation requests to ensure that the franchise can be run on the most efficient basis provided that the granting of any such request will not hinder the CMA's ability to remedy any competition concerns identified.[16]

NOTES

13 Section 72 of EA02 (as amended by the Enterprise and Regulatory Reform Act 2013). Further information on the CMA's approach to initial enforcement orders is in paragraphs 7.28 to 7.31 and Annexe C of *Mergers: Guidance on the CMA's jurisdiction and procedure* (CMA2).

14 'Obligations' in this context includes all provisions under the franchise agreement to which the franchisee is subject.

15 For example, Arriva commenced the operation of the Northern franchise during the CMA's Phase 2 inquiry in 2016.

16 For example, see the IEO issued for Arriva's award of the Northern Rail Franchise. footnotes 13 to 16 here

9. CONTACTING THE CMA TO DISCUSS THE MERGER INVESTIGATION PROCESS AS IT APPLIES TO RAIL FRANCHISES

[3.584]

Please contact the Merger Unit's Rail franchise team.

Competition and Markets Authority

Victoria House, 37 Southampton Row

London, WC1B 4AD

Email: mergers@cma.gsi.gov.uk

Telephone: 020 3738 6586

(IV) HEALTHCARE

CMA GUIDANCE ON THE REVIEW OF NHS MERGERS (CMA29, JULY 2014)

[3.585]

NOTES

See also:

(i) Monitor Briefing Note on the application of merger control rules to pathology service reconfigurations (June 2013) at www.gov.uk/government/publications/merger-rules-how-they-affect-pathology-service-reconfigurations;

(ii) Competition Review of NHS mergers: A short guide for mergers to NHS providers (July 2014) at www.gov.uk/government/publications/supporting-nhs-providers-considering-transactions-and-mergers;

CONTENTS

1. PREFACE

[3.586]

1.1 This guidance provides an overview of the approach of the Competition and Markets Authority (CMA) when reviewing mergers involving a National Health Service (NHS) foundation trust and mergers between NHS trusts and other enterprises in England (NHS mergers).

1.2 The CMA recognises that there are many drivers for NHS mergers and these include financial savings, sharing of best practices, better delivery of integrated care and service reconfiguration to generate better outcomes for patients or value for money for the taxpayer. The CMA acknowledges that mergers in the NHS may bring benefits and address some of the significant financial challenges that NHS providers face as well as assist with their continual strive to improve clinical quality, service and safety.

1.3 The CMA's role in reviewing NHS mergers has arisen due to the gradual introduction of choice and competition in the NHS. The NHS has evolved from centrally organised to a system where providers and commissioners have increased autonomy to drive delivery of high-quality services to patients. The initiatives leading to this started with the purchaser/provider split in 1991 and further initiatives introduced in the 2000s to facilitate more effective competition and increased quality, including: payment-by-results, the establishment of foundation trusts, the provision of some NHS services by independent sector treatment centres and the introduction of patient choice. These developments have facilitated choice for patients and commissioners. They have also led to a greater focus by providers of healthcare services to improve services to attract patients.

1.4 Therefore, whilst collaboration and integrated care remain important to delivering effective healthcare services to patients, these developments mean that competition also plays an important role in incentivising providers to improve quality for patients and efficiency.

1.5 Many mergers will not affect an NHS provider's incentives to improve services for patients. However, some may impact improving clinical quality and safety and therefore adversely affect patient interests by reducing incentives for the providers to maintain and improve services for patients thereby leading to reduced quality or choice for patients or commissioners. Specifically, the aspects of quality which may be impacted by a reduction in incentives to compete include clinical factors such as infection rates, mortality rates, ratio of nurses or doctors to patients, equipment, best practice and non-clinical factors such as waiting times, patient experience, cleanliness and parking facilities.

1.6 The CMA recognises the benefits that the exercise of patient choice and competition can deliver, one of a number of incentives on providers to continually improve care, but also the benefits a merger can bring, such that it may nevertheless be the best way of delivering certain benefits to patients in a timely manner.

1.7 In this context, the merger review process is designed to examine the potential (i) adverse effects for patients and/or commissioners arising from a loss of competition and (ii) benefits of a merger for patients and commissioners. The CMA is seeking to ensure that the merger is in the overall interest of patients. To assess the merger, it gathers and considers evidence from various sources including the merging providers, the Department of Health, Monitor (the sector regulator for health services in England), NHS England, the Care Quality Commission, commissioners, local patient representatives, third party providers and others. In its assessment, the CMA takes into account the structure and the regulatory regime that providers are subject to.

1.8 UK merger control applies to any transactions leading to a change of control over the activities (or a part of the activities) of one or more providers. In the NHS context, the term 'merger' includes, among other types of transactions, those as set out in section 56 of the NHS Act 2006 as amended, 'acquisitions' regardless of whether any financial consideration is payable; joint ventures; the transfer of individual services or activities to another provider; and asset swaps.

1.9 Many NHS mergers will not raise competition concerns and therefore may not require review by the CMA. As explained in this guidance, the CMA and Monitor are willing to aid and advise the providers contemplating a merger. However, it is up to providers to decide whether or not to notify. This guidance explains how the CMA will approach its assessment of NHS mergers both procedurally and substantively in order to assist merging providers seeking to analyse whether their NHS merger may raise competition concerns.

2. SCOPE OF THE GUIDANCE

[3.587]

2.1 This guidance is concerned with those mergers involving at least one foundation trust or NHS trust (or a part of it, if related to specific services) of NHS services in England, such as NHS hospitals (acute, community and mental health), ambulance trusts or other trusts (collectively referred to throughout as providers) or part of their organisation, which are covered by the provisions of the Enterprise Act 2002, as amended by the Enterprise and Regulatory Reform Act 2013 (ERRA13) (the Act).[1] Mergers between NHS trusts only are not covered by the Act. However, mergers involving NHS trusts and other organisations will be covered by the Act. Chapter 5 provides more detail on the types of transactions that are covered by the Act. This guidance does not concern transactions between clinical commissioning groups (CCGs), general practitioners (GPs), dentists and pharmacies, between other providers of healthcare services to the NHS or commercial suppliers in the healthcare sector, for example suppliers of pharmaceuticals or medical equipment.

2.2 This guidance forms part of the advice and information published by the CMA under section 106 of the Act. This guidance should be read alongside the other detailed guidance that the CMA has published or adopted in relation to merger review and the CMA's procedures (see Chapter 9 on further information). Readers may also find it helpful to read Monitor's guidance on relevant customer benefits.[2]

2.3 This guidance reflects the views of the CMA at the time of publication and may be revised from time to time to reflect changes in best practice, legislation and the results of experience, legal judgments and research. It may in due course be supplemented, revised or replaced. The CMA's webpages will always display the latest version of the guidance. Where there is any difference in emphasis or detail between this guidance and other guidance produced or adopted by the CMA, the most recently published guidance takes precedence. While the CMA is not bound to follow the approach taken by the Office of Fair Trading (OFT) or Competition Commission (CC) in merger investigations under the Act prior to the coming into force of the ERRA13, this guidance cites previous relevant OFT and CC decisions to illustrate how it will apply the provisions of the Act. Similarly, whilst not bound by their advice, the CMA has referred to advice by the Cooperation and Competition Panel, in relation to relevant customer benefits in particular, where it has felt this would be useful despite the different legal test they applied.[3]

2.4 This guidance is not intended to be comprehensive. It cannot, therefore, be seen as a substitute for the Act or the Health and Social Care Act 2012 (HSCA), the ERRA13 and the regulations and orders made under these statutes, nor can it be cited as a definitive interpretation of the law. Anyone in any doubt about whether they may be affected by the legislation should consider seeking legal advice.

2.5 Furthermore, although the CMA will have regard to this guidance in handling NHS mergers under the Act, the CMA will apply this guidance flexibly and may depart from the approach described in the guidance where there is an appropriate and reasonable justification for doing so.

2.6 In addition, the merger control regime in England provides that, in cases referred for an in-depth 'Phase 2' investigation, the final decision-making authority is an independent group of experts selected from a panel appointed by the Secretary of State (the Inquiry Group). Where this guidance is expressed to apply to the CMA's policy when making decisions whether to refer a merger for an in-depth Phase 2 investigation, this does not bind the independent Phase 2 Inquiry Group when undertaking its assessment.

NOTES

1 The guidance does not apply to Scotland, Wales and Northern Ireland. The healthcare sector is somewhat different in Scotland, Wales and Northern Ireland. For example, they do not have foundation trusts and Monitor does not have a role. However, if there were to be a merger of a public provider within those countries that fell within the CMA's jurisdiction (the same provisions of the Act apply throughout the UK), merging providers in those jurisdictions may find this guidance helpful.

2 see www.monitor.gov.uk/ for Monitor Guidance on Merger Benefits.

3 The Cooperation and Competition Panel previously considered mergers against the Principles and Rules for Cooperation and Competition and provided advice to the Department of Health and Monitor.

3. NHS MERGER REVIEW IN ENGLAND

INTRODUCTION

[3.588]
3.1 Merger review in England is primarily the responsibility of the CMA, which is an independent non-ministerial government department.

3.2 The merger control regime applies to all sectors of the economy. While the competition test is the same for nearly all mergers reviewed by the CMA, the CMA's assessment takes into account all of the particular characteristics and specificities of the sector. In relation to NHS mergers, for example:

- NHS providers may compete on quality in addition to or instead of price (as discussed in detail in Chapter 6 below)
- Monitor has a statutory role as part of the merger regime to provide advice to the CMA on the relevant customer benefits of the merger
- the CMA will consider how any regulation that providers are subject to may affect the competitive assessment of the merger.

ROLE OF THE CMA

3.3 The CMA is the UK's competition authority responsible for ensuring that competition and markets work well for consumers.[4] In the healthcare context, this means that the CMA is working for the benefit of patients and taxpayers.

3.4 The CMA has a function to obtain and review information relating to merger situations.

3.5 The UK has a two-phase merger control regime. The Act imposes a duty on the CMA to refer completed and anticipated mergers for an in-depth 'Phase 2' investigation if it believes that it is or may be the case that:

- a relevant merger situation has been created or arrangements are in progress or in contemplation which, if carried into effect, will result in the creation of a relevant merger situation
- the creation of that situation has resulted, or may be expected to result, in a substantial lessening of competition (SLC)[5]

3.6 This is subject to the exceptions to the duty to refer, where the CMA may exercise its discretion as to whether to refer to a Phase 2 inquiry, and undertakings that the CMA may accept in lieu of reference (see Chapters 7 and 8).

3.7 If a reference to Phase 2 is made, the CMA conducts a more detailed analysis and the Inquiry Group must decide:

- whether a relevant merger situation has been or will be created
- if so, whether the creation of that situation has resulted, or may be expected to result, in an SLC with worse outcomes for patients and/or commissioners within any market or markets in the UK for goods or services (where both limbs are satisfied, this is referred to as an 'anti-competitive outcome').[6]

3.8 If the Inquiry Group finds that there is an anticompetitive outcome it must decide:

- whether action should be taken by it, or by others, to remedy, mitigate or prevent the SLC concerned or any adverse effect that has resulted from, or may be expected to result from, that SLC
- if action is to be taken, what action should be taken and what is to be remedied, mitigated or prevented.

ROLE OF MONITOR

3.9 Monitor is the sector regulator for health services in England. Monitor's job is to make the health sector work better for patients. As well as making sure that independent NHS foundation trusts are well led so that they can deliver quality care on a sustainable basis, Monitor makes sure that: essential services are maintained if a provider gets into serious difficulties; the NHS payment system promotes quality and efficiency; and patients do not lose out through restrictions on their rights to make choices, through poor purchasing on their behalf, or through inappropriate anticompetitive behaviour by providers and commissioners.

Monitor arrangements to support NHS foundation trusts

3.10 Monitor's role includes assessing NHS providers' compliance with the provider licence. As part of this role, Monitor will review certain transactions (such as mergers) to ensure that foundation trusts comply with the governance and continuity of service conditions of their provider licence. This is separate from the CMA merger control review process; Monitor does not have the power to prohibit mergers to which the Act applies on the basis that they are expected to give rise to an SLC.

3.11 NHS foundation trusts engage with Monitor in most transactions in connection with Monitor's other regulatory obligations. In addition to conducting a risk assessment of mergers, Monitor, as sector regulator, will also be active in engaging with those NHS foundation trusts considering a merger, for example by reviewing the strategic rationale for the transaction to help the NHS foundation trust ensure it is robust. Such discussions may assist merging providers to identify at an early stage if the merger raises competition issues and so help the merging providers when considering whether to notify the merger to the CMA. They might also assist merging providers to identify at an early stage whether a merger will lead to benefits for patients. The CMA expects this to benefit providers as they will take into account any competition issues at the outset of their proposals. Further information on how NHS foundation trusts can engage with Monitor is set out in Monitor's Transactions Guide.

3.12 Ultimately, the CMA is responsible for deciding whether an NHS merger falls within its jurisdiction.[7] The CMA is also responsible for deciding whether an NHS merger may lessen competition leading to worse outcomes for patients/commissioners and Monitor's role is an advisory one to the merging providers. Therefore, if in doubt as to whether the NHS merger may fall within CMA jurisdiction or raise competition concerns, merging providers may wish to approach the CMA directly for informal advice.[8] Where they have decided to notify the CMA, it is particularly helpful to the merging providers to engage with the CMA early in pre-notification discussions to help identify the information that should be included in the Merger Notice (see Chapter 4).

The role of Monitor within the CMA merger review process

3.13 The CMA must notify Monitor as soon as reasonably practicable where it decides to carry out an investigation of a merger involving an NHS foundation trust. The CMA will do so as soon as possible after it has sent notice to the relevant merging provider(s):

- either informing them that it is satisfied that the Merger Notice is satisfactory or
- informing them that it has sufficient information for it to begin an investigation.

3.14 Once notified, Monitor is under a duty to provide advice to the CMA on:[9]

- benefits[10] arising from the merger (for people who use healthcare services provided for the purposes of the NHS)
- such other matters relating to the matter under investigation, as Monitor considers appropriate.

3.15 Monitor's advice is not binding on the CMA. However, the CMA will place significant weight, given Monitor's role and expertise as sectoral regulator, on its views and opinion on relevant customer benefits of a merger. A flow chart setting out the various steps and interrelationship between the CMA merger control review and Monitor processes is set out in Annex A.

ROLE OF THE NHS TRUST DEVELOPMENT AUTHORITY

3.16 The NHS Trust Development Authority (TDA) is responsible for providing leadership and support to the non-foundation-trust sector of NHS providers. The TDA will oversee the performance management of these NHS trusts, ensuring they provide high-quality sustainable services, and will provide guidance and support on their journey to achieving foundation trust status.

3.17 The TDA has a role in agreeing mergers involving NHS trusts and will act as the seller in mergers involving NHS trusts. The CMA will therefore engage with and seek views from the TDA where relevant.

NOTES

4 In some markets, for example pathology, other customers who may suffer adverse effects from a loss of competition could also include hospitals. However, patients and commissioners are used as proxy for all customers throughout this guidance.

5 Sections 22(1) and 33(1) of the Act.

6 Sections 35 & 36 of the Act.

7 See Chapter 5 below.

8 See paragraph 4.4ff.

9 Section 79 of the HSCA.

10 See section 30(1)(a) of the EA02.

4. PROCEDURE AND CONTACTING THE CMA

THE VOLUNTARY REGIME

[3.589]

4.1 Under the Act there is no requirement to notify[11] mergers to the CMA, regardless of whether or not the CMA would have jurisdiction to review the merger. In the UK, merging providers decide whether or not to notify the CMA. The merger control regime is therefore described as 'voluntary'.[12]

4.2 The CMA has a responsibility to keep merger activity under review and may investigate, on its own initiative, mergers that have not been notified.[13] The CMA has four months from the merger being made public or it being completed (whichever is the later) to decide whether or not to make a Phase 2 reference.

4.3 Merging providers should determine for themselves whether to notify the CMA. If providers are unsure as to whether the CMA has jurisdiction to review their NHS merger or as to whether it may raise competition concerns, providers can contact the CMA for informal advice (see paragraphs 4.4 to 4.10 below). Providers are encouraged to notify the CMA about their merger before completing where the merger could give rise to possible competition concerns.[14]

APPROACH TO ENGAGING WITH THE CMA

Informal engagement and advice

4.4 In planning mergers, it is for merging providers to assess whether transactions might give rise to competition concerns and whether to notify the NHS merger to the CMA. As noted in paragraph 3.11, the CMA expects that merging providers which fall within Monitor's regulatory regime may find it helpful to discuss their plans with Monitor and their independent advisers. Such engagement with Monitor should generally take place before either advice is sought from the CMA or a notification is made to the CMA. However, merging providers are ultimately free to contact the CMA or to notify a transaction to the CMA at a time of their own choosing. The section below explains how providers may choose to engage with the CMA in addition and the advice the CMA can offer.

CMA's advice on the merger review process

4.5 The CMA is willing to assist NHS providers before they have decided whether or not to notify their merger.

4.6 Merging providers may wish to contact the CMA either for general advice on how it assesses jurisdiction or undertakes its competitive assessment.

CMA's advice on specific proposed transactions

4.7 The CMA also offers Informal Advice on specific proposed transactions in line with its *Mergers: Guidance on the CMA's approach to jurisdiction and procedure (CMA2)*.

4.8 The content of the Informal Advice will differ depending on the case and information received. However, the CMA will not be in a position to provide a definitive view on whether or not a merger raises competition concerns, given that it will not have undertaken any market testing, for example. Therefore the CMA will generally explain how it conducts its assessment, what considerations may be relevant and what type of evidence it would be looking for.

4.9 Where merging providers have obtained Informal Advice on a particular transaction (rather than obtained generic advice), they will be requested to inform the CMA Mergers Unit if and when the proposed transaction goes ahead (where key steps are taken for the proposed transaction to go ahead). Informing the case officer is different from submitting a Merger Notice and does not mean that the CMA will necessarily investigate the transaction. Nevertheless, where the CMA considers that it is a case it would want to review, it may encourage the merging providers to engage in pre-notification discussions.

4.10 Any advice (including Informal Advice) provided is not a decision of the CMA and cannot bind the CMA. Therefore, both the content of the advice and the fact that a merging provider has contacted the CMA is strictly confidential to the provider(s) seeking that advice and their advisers, even after the transaction becomes public. The CMA would be concerned by any intentional or accidental breach of confidence in this respect – either by the providers concerned or by their advisers – and might take the view that it could not offer those responsible any such advice in the future. This restriction applies even where only one provider to a transaction seeks advice, as the advice should not be revealed by the recipient to the other provider. The CMA will, however, normally be willing on request to inform orally the other provider of the terms of the advice given. In all cases, the guidance given by the CMA is confidential and is only for the board members, senior executive officers and the general counsel of the provider making the request and any advisers that are privy to the request.[15]

Pre-notification

4.11 As soon as merging providers have decided to notify the CMA (following initial discussions with Monitor and/or based on their and their adviser(s)' assessment) and before submitting a Merger Notice, providers are strongly encouraged to approach the CMA to discuss their merger (and any drafts of the providers' Merger Notice).

4.12 At the pre-notification stage the CMA is able to discuss mergers on a confidential basis, which means the CMA will not disclose that it is in pre-notification without the providers' consent. Pre-notification of an NHS merger may happen before or after the merger proposal has been announced. The benefits of pre-notification, especially in the context of NHS mergers, are as follows:

(a) help to reduce the amount of information that is provided to the CMA by clarifying what information the CMA needs. The CMA can assist the merging providers to understand how to complete the Merger Notice and what specific evidence will assist it to assess the merging providers' claims

(b) allow more time for the CMA to develop its understanding of the relevant local health economy (such as services provided by the merging providers and their competitors in the area) and consider in more depth submissions from the merging providers

(c) allow merging providers to engage in early discussions with the CMA on areas that may raise competition concerns (such as particular services where the merging providers are particularly close competitors)

(d) where the merging providers consent, allow the CMA to contact certain third parties, such as commissioners, for their views. This may allow merging providers to address some issues raised by others upfront in the Merger Notice

(e) facilitate early engagement with the CMA and Monitor on any relevant customer benefits of the merger from an early stage

(f) lessen pressures on the statutory timelines and reduce information requests during the CMA's assessment process

Notification

4.13 Where merging providers decide to notify formally an NHS merger to the CMA, they must do so by completing a Merger Notice. A template Merger Notice, available at www.gov.uk/government/publications/mergers-forms-and-fee-information, sets out the categories of information required by the CMA, together with guidance notes to assist merging providers in identifying the specific nature and extent of information required in their case. The CMA webpage also sets out how to submit the Merger Notice. Merging providers cannot formally submit a Merger Notice until the merger (whether anticipated or completed) has been made public.

Information exchange between the CMA and Monitor

4.14 Sharing of information (including data) between the CMA and Monitor is crucial for the effective fulfilment of their respective duties and should reduce the burden on merging providers which could otherwise arise, for example from duplicative information requests. The CMA may, where appropriate, wish to discuss with Monitor mergers that merging providers bring to its attention; informal advice it will be providing or has provided; pre-notification drafts; and information it obtains throughout its investigation.

4.15 The information and data sharing from the CMA to Monitor will include any confidential information which the CMA considers will facilitate the effective fulfilment of its merger control statutory functions. If either or both of the merging providers request that the CMA should not share with Monitor some or all of the information or data submitted to it, they should submit a non-confidential version of such submission and state clearly what information should remain confidential to the CMA, together with the reasons for this. However, in certain circumstances, whilst having regard to the confidentiality requests, the CMA may nonetheless decide to disclose information to Monitor without the consent of the merging providers. This may occur, for example, where it considers that disclosure is necessary to enable the CMA to exercise its statutory functions, including the need to have regard to Monitor's advice on relevant customer benefits.

4.16 Monitor's advice may contain information that is confidential (either as regards the merging providers or other confidential information known to Monitor). Monitor may share such information with the CMA. To the extent that the merging providers consider that information they provide to Monitor should not be included in the published version of Monitor's advice, they should submit a non-confidential version of such submission to Monitor and state clearly what information should remain confidential to Monitor, together with the reasons for this.

4.17 For further information on the treatment of confidential information by the CMA, see *Transparency and disclosure: Statement of the CMA's policy and approach (CMA6)*, which also explains how the CMA will deal with a request under the Freedom of Information Act 2000.

Timescales for the merger review process

4.18 A flow chart setting out an overview of the process is set out in Annex B. The CMA has a statutory deadline of 40 working days in which to complete the initial merger review process (Phase 1). That statutory period starts on the first working day after the CMA confirms *(a)* that it has received a satisfactory Merger Notice, containing the information it requires for its review, or *(b)* in the case of an investigation started on the CMA's initiative, that it has received sufficient information to enable it to begin its investigation. The CMA may 'stop the clock' where information the CMA has formally requested from the merging parties remains outstanding. The CMA will notify Monitor that it has started its investigation into a merger involving a foundation trust as soon as possible once the statutory period begins.

4.19 There is also a statutory deadline, of 24 weeks for Phase 2 investigations. This may be extended by up to eight weeks if the CMA considers there are special reasons why a report cannot be prepared and published within the statutory deadline[16] and the CMA is also able to stop the clock where information requested from the merging providers, using its statutory powers, is outstanding (see below). If it determines in its final report that a merger is expected to result in an SLC, the CMA has a statutory period of 12 weeks (extendable by up to six weeks for special reasons) in which to implement remedies by either making an order or accepting undertakings.

INFORMATION-GATHERING POWERS

4.20 The CMA's decisions are evidence-based. The information provided with the initial Merger Notice will enable the CMA to commence its investigation and request information and views from third parties. Sometimes the CMA may need additional, or more comprehensive, information from merging providers than is provided in the Merger Notice to allow it to make a decision on whether or not to make a reference or, if at Phase 2, for the purposes of the Phase 2 investigation. The CMA asks for any such additional data, information or documents as soon as it is clear it will be necessary. For the timetables to be met, requests for such information normally identify a short deadline for a full response. However, in all cases the CMA ensures that its requests are tailored to the case at hand and appropriate for its investigation.

4.21 The CMA has the power under section 109 of the Act to issue a notice requiring a person to provide information or documents, or to give evidence at a specified time and place (a section 109 notice). While the CMA may issue requests for information informally,[17] it is likely to use the section 109 power where (i) it considers there to be a risk that it will not receive the information sufficiently in advance of its statutory deadline for the information to be analysed and taken into account in its decision(s), (ii) it has doubts that the recipient will comply with an informal request and/or the recipient has previously failed to respond to such an informal request, or (iii) the CMA believes that there is a risk that relevant evidence may be destroyed.[18]

4.22 If a merging provider fails to comply with a section 109 notice, this permits the CMA to extend the relevant statutory timetable (including, where relevant, the four-month statutory deadline for referring completed mergers – see paragraph 4.2) for as long as the response to the information requested is overdue. If the merging providers have notified the merger to the CMA using a Merger Notice, the CMA may also reject the Merger Notice.

4.23 In addition to causing delay to the review timetable, failure to comply without reasonable excuse with a notice under section 109 of the Act can have more serious consequences, including in some circumstances the imposition of a fine.

4.24 The CMA will also contact other governmental departments, regulators (including Monitor), NHS England, commissioners, industry associations and patient groups for their views on merger cases where appropriate.

PUBLICATION

4.25 At Phase 1, the CMA will be mindful of the need to respect the confidentiality of commercially sensitive information provided to it (by the merging providers and third parties). At the same time, it is required by section 107 of the Act to publish its decisions and in respect of SLC decisions it will try to ensure that evidence that is key to the reasoning and outcome of its decision is included within the public version of the decision.[19]

4.26 At Phase 2 the CMA will publish various documents including key submissions of the merging providers and third parties, and key documents (that is issues statement, provisional findings, notice of possible remedies).[20] Parties should provide non-confidential versions of all submissions for publication at the same time as their full submissions. If this is not possible, parties should discuss timing of submission of the non-confidential version with the case team. Parties should accompany the non-confidential version with a detailed explanation of why they consider that particular parts of their submissions should not be disclosed, including explaining the nature of the information, the harm that could be caused, and the likelihood and magnitude of that harm.

4.27 In the event of a disagreement concerning a proposal by the CMA to publish information, parties may make representations to the CMA's Procedural Officer.

INTERIM ORDERS

4.28 The CMA will normally make interim orders in Phase 1 where it has reasonable grounds for suspecting that two or more enterprises have ceased to be distinct (for example, the transaction is completed). An interim order is intended to prevent any pre-emptive action (for example, implementation of the NHS merger including the merging of functions or consolidation of decision-making of the merging providers) that might prejudice the reference and/or impede the taking of any remedial action by the CMA.[21]

4.29 The risk of pre-emptive action in an anticipated merger is generally lower than in a completed merger. However, in anticipated mergers at Phase 1 the CMA would expect to make an interim order in those cases that it considers raise concerns about pre-emptive action that is difficult or costly to reverse. This could occur, for example, where merging providers are coordinating commercial strategies for the next few years, for example regarding recruitment, bed closures and targeted marketing of service. In anticipated cases, the CMA would normally expect to use tailored interim orders which have greater focus on specific concerns rather than the template interim order.[22] In anticipated mergers, interim orders would not typically prohibit collaboration between the merging providers that pre-date discussions on the merger.[23]

MERGER FEES

4.30 A fee is payable for the CMA's review by the provider who gives the Merger Notice or, in the event of a CMA own initiative case, by the acquiring provider, subject to some limited exceptions (including where the merger is found to be outside the CMA's jurisdiction). The amount of the fee and exemptions are set out in the Enterprise Act 2002 (Merger Fees and Determination of turnover) Order 2003 (SI 2003/1370), as amended. The amount of the fees can also be found in Merger Fee Information. There is no specific exemption for NHS providers.

FURTHER INFORMATION

4.31 Further information is available in *Mergers: Guidance on the CMA's approach to jurisdiction and procedure (CMA2)*.

NOTES

11 Notification means submitting a Merger Notice to the CMA.

12 The merging providers may, however, be asked to provide sufficient information for the CMA to be able to review the merger if the CMA chooses to investigate on its own initiative.

13 The CMA obtains information about anticipated and completed mergers from a range of sources, including through dedicated Mergers Intelligence staff responsible for monitoring non-notified merger activity, from Monitor and third parties. Where the CMA learns of a merger that it thinks might have adverse effects on patients or commissioners due to a loss of competition, the CMA may open an investigation on its own initiative. The CMA may contact the merging providers in order to establish whether the thresholds which trigger its jurisdiction are met and to obtain information about the merger.

14 Completing a merger without notifying the CMA can result in additional costs for merging providers: (i) the CMA has powers to impose restrictions (known as interim measures) on merging providers to prevent them taking actions (for example, merging of functions or consolidation of decision making) that might pre-empt the CMA's exercise of its merger review powers and (ii) costs can arise from having to undo the merger if the merger is prohibited.

15 In case of doubt, providers should confirm with the CMA the identity of the persons with whom they are permitted to share the advice received.

16 Section 39(3) of the Act.

[17] Where the CMA requests information from third parties, it will typically request that information informally in the first instance.

[18] Such notices may also be issued before the CMA's investigation formally opens, for example the CMA may issue enquiry letters under its formal section 109 powers.

[19] For guidance on the CMA's wider approach to such issues of confidentiality, see *Transparency and disclosure: Statement of the CMA's policy and approach (CMA6)*.

[20] For further information about disclosure during Phase 2, see *Chairman's guidance on disclosure of information in merger and market inquiries (CC7)*.

[21] Section 72 of the Act.

[22] See the CC Notice of Acceptance of Interim Undertakings pursuant to section 80 of the Act in the anticipated merger of The Royal Bournemouth and Christchurch Hospitals NHS Foundation Trust and Poole Hospital NHS Foundation Trust.

[23] The CMA notes that it is the merging providers' responsibility to consider how the competition law rules apply to information exchanges. For assistance, see Monitor Guidance on the application of the Competition Act 1998 in the healthcare sector.

5. WHAT IS A RELEVANT MERGER SITUATION?

THE CMA'S JURISDICTION

[3.590]

5.1 The CMA has jurisdiction to examine a merger where:

- two or more enterprises cease to be distinct
- and
  - either the UK turnover of the acquired enterprise exceeds £70 million
  - or the enterprises which cease to be distinct supply or acquire goods or services of any description and, after the merger, together supply or acquire at least 25% of all those particular goods or services of that kind supplied in the UK or in a substantial part of it. The NHS merger must also result in an increment to the share of supply or acquisition.[24]

5.2 UK merger control applies to any transactions leading to a change of control over the activities (or a part of the activities) of one or more providers. In the NHS context, the term 'merger' includes, among other types of transactions, those as set out in section 56 of the NHS Act 2006 as amended,[25] 'acquisitions' regardless of whether any financial consideration is payable; joint ventures; the transfer of individual services or activities to another provider;[26] and asset swaps. The terms 'acquirer' and/or acquired assets or target are interpreted widely and refer to the acquisition of control in all of these scenarios.

Enterprise

5.3 'Enterprise'[27] in the context of UK merger control may refer to an entire organisation or a part of it, whether or not it operates for profit. An 'enterprise' may comprise any number of components, most commonly including the employees working in the service and the assets and records needed to carry on that activity, together with the benefit of existing contracts and/or goodwill. In healthcare, entire organisations such as NHS foundation trusts and NHS trusts controlling hospitals, ambulance services, mental health services, community services and individual services or specialities may be enterprises for the purpose of UK merger control.

5.4 The CMA assesses, on a case by case basis, whether the combination of staff, assets (for example, equipment, patient records), rights and liabilities (for example, NHS contracts) each provider contributes to a transaction is sufficient to form an 'enterprise'. In this assessment, the CMA takes account of the substance of the transaction and the features of the sector. In the case of NHS mergers, it considers what is necessary to operate the relevant service or clinical specialty (considered against the background of the acquiring provider's pre-existing activities). It is not always necessary for the transaction to include the transfer of an NHS contract.[28] An enterprise may be acquired even without the transfer of a contract if, for example, the acquiring provider is already able to supply the services without requiring the NHS contract to transfer and acquires staff and assets.

5.5 See *Mergers: Guidance on the CMA's approach to jurisdiction and procedure (CMA2)* for further information on the CMA's approach to enterprise.

Change of control

5.6 Two enterprises cease to be distinct if they are brought under common ownership or control.[29] There must be a change in the level of control over the activities of one or more enterprises for UK merger control to apply.[30]

5.7 A merger between two NHS trusts is not deemed to create a relevant merger situation because, under the existing legislation, both merging providers are already under the common control of the Secretary of State for Health. Monitor continues to assess mergers between NHS trusts only and will advise the TDA on the competition aspects of such transactions.

5.8 The changes in the level of control are assessed on a case-by-case basis taking into account the features of the sector and the substance of the NHS merger. Ownership or control include situations falling short of full control, such as where one enterprise has material influence over the policy of the other.[31]

5.9 The ability to exercise 'material influence' is the lowest level of control that may give rise to a relevant merger situation. In assessing material influence, the CMA focuses on the acquiring provider's ability materially to influence policy relevant to the behaviour of the target entity in its provision of NHS healthcare services. The policy of the target in this context means the management of the provider, in particular in relation to its competitive conduct, and thus includes the strategic direction of an organisation and its ability to achieve its strategic and commercial objectives. In the case of a full merger or joint ventures, it relates to the ability of each member of the joint venture to gain the ability materially to influence policy relevant to the behaviour of the other providers' activities in the provision of relevant NHS services.

5.10 Other levels of control set out in the Act are 'de facto control' and holding a 'controlling interest' in the organisation. A 'controlling interest' would occur, for example, where an NHS foundation trust acquires all of the rights over all or part of the activities of another NHS provider.

5.11 The Act will apply to situations of 'shared' control by several providers over another. Only one party can have a controlling interest over an organisation but other entities might have lower levels of control over the same organisation. For example, while an NHS foundation trust may have a controlling interest over the activities of all its services, another provider (such as another NHS foundation trust) may gain material influence over one or more services of the first NHS foundation trust by way of entering into a management contract transferring a material amount of control over the running of those services.

5.12 Any increase in the level of control over the target (or in the case of a merger of equals or joint ventures over the other merging providers' activities) may give rise to a relevant merger situation.

5.13 See *Mergers: Guidance on the CMA's approach to jurisdiction and procedure (CMA2)* for further information on the CMA's approach to jurisdiction to change of control.

Turnover test

5.14 The relevant turnover is calculated by adding the UK turnover of all the enterprises involved in the transaction and either deducting the UK turnover of those enterprises which remain under the same ownership and control after the merger or, where no enterprises remain under the same ownership after the merger, by deducting the lower of them.[32] In practice, in an acquisition where only two merging providers are involved, the target's UK turnover (either in its entirety or of the relevant service being acquired) will be the relevant turnover.

5.15 See *Mergers: Guidance on the CMA's approach to jurisdiction and procedure (CMA2)* for further information on the CMA's approach to jurisdiction on turnover.

Share of supply

5.16 The merging providers' share of supply or acquisition must be 25% or more in the UK or a substantial part of the UK for the share of supply test to be met. For the test to be satisfied, the share of supply must lead to an increment. In other words, the merging providers must supply or acquire the same category of services or goods (of any description). The test cannot capture mergers where the merging providers are solely active at different levels of the supply/procurement chain.

5.17 The Act expressly provides the CMA with a wide discretion in describing the relevant services or goods, requiring only that, in relation to that description, the merging providers' share of supply or acquisition is 25% or more.[33] The share of supply may differ from the market share, which is determined through an economic analysis of market definition. The share of supply can relate to any reasonable description of services or goods. It can include a wide variety of specialties (such as the provision of outpatient consultations) or a narrow description of a specialty or sub-specialty measured by a reasonable criteria. Also, the CMA has a wide discretion when determining what criteria can be relevant to quantify the estimated share of supply of the merger parties.[34] For example, two pathology providers may have a small market share when considering the routine tests they provide within a 1-hour drive. However, they may still meet the share of supply test if they both provide routine pathology tests and these account for 25% or more of routine pathology services to the nearest CCGs to them (they need not both supply the same CCGs), if these areas are sufficient to form a substantial part of the UK.

5.18 See *Mergers: Guidance on the CMA's approach to jurisdiction and procedure (CMA2)* for further information on the CMA's approach to what constitutes a substantial part of the UK, including reference to relevant jurisprudence.

APPLICABILITY OF THE UK MERGER CONTROL REGIME TO NHS MERGERS

5.19 In practice, this means that the Act applies to mergers between NHS foundation trusts, between NHS foundation trusts and NHS trusts and between NHS foundation trusts and other 'enterprises'.[35] It also applies to mergers between NHS trusts and other 'enterprises'.[36] All types of NHS foundation trusts and NHS trusts may be subject to UK merger control, including those managing hospitals, community, mental health or ambulance services. Transactions between individual services, controlled prior to the merger by two different entities, may also trigger a merger review if all jurisdictional criteria explained above are met.[37,38]

APPLICABILITY OF THE UK MERGER CONTROL REGIME TO NHS SERVICE RECONFIGURATIONS

5.20 The merger control regime may apply to NHS service reconfigurations in certain circumstances. Where those with control over providers[39] decide to merge two or more enterprises, the transaction may qualify for investigation if it meets the jurisdictional thresholds set out above.

5.21 NHS service reconfigurations can take many forms and may involve the transfer of an 'enterprise' depending on the circumstances. In some cases, NHS commissioners and providers enter into multi-party

Part 3 CMA and other Guidelines

agreements that lead to the transfer of staff and/or assets. Sometimes providers agree between themselves to transfer assets and/or staff and other rights and liabilities. In other cases, providers decide to merge following an NHS commissioner's independent decision to change who provides services. For example, following the award for the provision of a particular service to a sole provider, other providers might agree to transfer their assets and staff to the new chosen provider or a third party. In all these cases, if the combination of assets, staff, and rights transferred is sufficient to form an enterprise (see paragraphs 5.3 and 5.4 above) and the other jurisdictional criteria are met, these types of transfer can create a relevant merger situation reviewable under UK merger control.

5.22 The award of a contract for the provision of a clinical service, that was not previously commissioned, to a provider by any NHS commissioner does not imply any change of control of an existing 'enterprise' leading to a relevant merger situation. In addition, the CMA's jurisdiction to review mergers does not extend to the award of a contract following a competitive process to provide particular services, provided that there is nothing more attached to the contract award (that is, no transfer of assets such as equipment or staff from one provider to the winning provider, for example).

5.23 NHS service reconfigurations can also be relevant when deciding on the most appropriate counterfactual against which the impact of an NHS merger must be assessed. This is considered in paragraphs 6.10 to 6.35 below. NHS service reconfigurations can also be relevant to the assessment of relevant customer benefits (for example, where merging providers propose to deliver higher-quality services through service reconfiguration). This is considered in Chapter 7.

NOTES

24 Transactions which do not give rise to a relevant merger situation are still subject to general competition provisions contained in the Act and the Competition Act 1998.

25 See the report on the anticipated merger of The Royal Bournemouth and Christchurch Hospitals NHS Foundation Trust and Poole Hospital NHS Foundation Trust, 17 October 2013, paragraph 3.3.

26 See the OFT's decision in the acquisition by University College London Hospitals NHS Foundation Trust of Royal Free London NHS Foundation Trust's neurosurgery services, ME/5574/12, dated 21 February 2013, and the OFT's decision on anticipated pathology joint venture between University College London Hospitals NHS Foundation Trust, Royal Free London NHS Foundation Trust and The Doctors Laboratory Limited, ME/6094/13, dated 8 November 2013.

27 The term enterprise is defined in section 129 of the Act.

28 NHS contracts refer to the supply of goods and services to the NHS.

29 Section 26 of the Act.

30 See OFT decision on the anticipated pathology joint venture between University College London Hospitals NHS Foundation Trust, Royal Free London NHS Foundation Trust and The Doctors Laboratory Limited, ME/6094/13, dated 8 November 2013. For an example of a case in which none of the assets contributed to the joint venture came under common control of any of the other joint venture partners, see the OFT's decision on the anticipated Pathology Joint Venture between Cambridge University Hospitals NHS Foundation Trust, Colchester Hospital University NHS Foundation Trust, East and North Hertfordshire NHS Trust, Hinchingbrooke Health Care NHS Trust, The Ipswich Hospital NHS Trust and West Suffolk NHS Foundation Trust, ME/6427/14, dated 27 March 2014.

31 Section 26 of the Act.

32 See paragraph 4.47ff and Annex B of the CMA Mergers Guidance on how to calculate the relevant turnover for the jurisdictional test. In the context of NHS mergers, an enterprise may include a service (part of a service) only. See further paragraph 5.19 below.

33 Section 23 of the Act.

34 See, for example, the OFT's decision of 21 February 2013 on the acquisition by University College London Hospitals NHS Foundation Trust of Royal Free London NHS Foundation Trust's neurosurgery services.

35 Section 23 of the Act.

36 The CMA considers that NHS trusts are capable of being enterprises. While NHS services are 'free for the patient at the point of delivery', the primary care trusts (and/or commissioning organisations) procure and pay a consideration for the provision of such services.

37 See, for example, OFT's decision of 21 February 2013 on the acquisition by University College London Hospitals NHS Foundation Trust of Royal Free London NHS Foundation Trust's neurosurgery services. Also the OFT's decision of 8 November 2013 on the creation of a joint venture in relation to pathology services only between University College London Hospitals NHS Foundation Trust, Royal Free London NHS Foundation Trust and the Doctors Laboratory Limited.

38 See paragraphs 5.1–5.17 above.

39 This can be the board of an NHS foundation trust or the Secretary of State for Health in the case of NHS trusts.

6. MERGER ASSESSMENT

[3.591]

6.1 While many mergers that take place in the UK do not raise competition issues which lead to worse outcomes for patients and/or commissioners, the merger control process is designed to allow the CMA to identify those where such issues may arise, so that they may be properly investigated and, where necessary, resolved through appropriate remedies.

6.2 This section should be read alongside the *Merger assessment guidelines (CC2 (revised)/OFT1254).*

THE SUBSTANTIAL LESSENING OF COMPETITION TEST

6.3 Competition occurs between providers seeking to obtain more commissioner contracts and/or patients by providing them with a better offering. An SLC occurs when competition is substantially less after the merger than would otherwise have been the case, resulting in a worse outcome for patients and/or commissioners (through, for example, higher prices, a reduction in range, quality and/or choice or less innovation).

6.4 At Phase 1, the CMA's test for reference (see paragraph 3.5) will be met if the CMA has a reasonable belief, objectively justified by relevant facts, that there is a realistic prospect that the merger will lessen competition substantially.[40] If the reference test is met, the question as to whether there is a relevant merger situation and SLC is one for resolution by the Inquiry Group on the basis of a detailed Phase 2 investigation.[41] At Phase 2, the Inquiry Group decides whether in its view an SLC is likely to arise.[42]

COMPETITION IN THE NHS IN ENGLAND

6.5 There are, broadly speaking, two different models of competition in the provision of NHS healthcare services. These are competition to attract patients (that is, competition in the market) and competition to attract contracts to provide services (that is, competition for the market).

6.6 Competition to attract patients occurs where patients have a choice between providers of the same service. Payments for these services are commonly made according to the payment-by-results rules, at nationally mandated prices across England. Providers are motivated to compete on quality in order to attract patient referrals and hence income.

6.7 The effect of competition to attract patients is to focus provider decisions on factors that matter to patients and GPs. The number and quality of alternative providers in a local area has an impact on the strength of the providers' incentives to focus on delivering those aspects of quality that are important to the providers' patients and their GPs. Examples of benefits of competition include focusing on waiting times, implementing best practice guidance, delivering innovative models of care, extending expertise and enhanced service provision and improving facilities to attract patients.[43]

6.8 Competition to attract contracts to provide services occurs because commissioners have to select which provider or providers are best placed to provide services to patients. Providers therefore have incentives to maintain their reputations for quality and value and perform well under existing contracts, as well as to demonstrate that they can deliver high quality and excellent value for money when commissioners select which provider or providers are best placed to provide services to patients.

6.9 The loss of actual competition between providers may manifest itself in a reduction (or lack of improvement) in quality in services in which competition would be removed, or in a reduction in quality at the provider level. For services where the price is not fixed, commissioners may also benefit from competition in the form of lower prices and greater choice.

IDENTIFYING THE APPROPRIATE COUNTERFACTUAL

6.10 The application of the SLC test involves a comparison of the merger scenario against the competitive situation without the merger. The competitive situation that would likely exist if the merger did not take place is referred to as 'the counterfactual'. The counterfactual may be either more or less competitive than the prevailing conditions of competition.[44] As such, selection of the appropriate counterfactual is an important step in determining whether or not there is an SLC.

6.11 The CMA will consider the merging providers' submissions on the counter-factual together with any relevant views of third parties (including commissioners, the TDA and Monitor). With regard to documentation from the merging providers, the CMA will be particularly interested in evidence that has not been prepared in contemplation of the merger.

6.12 At Phase 1, the CMA considers the effects of the merger compared with the most competitive counterfactual providing always that it considers that situation to be a realistic prospect. In practice, the CMA generally adopts the pre-merger situation as the counterfactual. An alternative counterfactual to the prevailing (pre-merger) conditions may be used at Phase 1, where there is compelling evidence that the prospect of prevailing conditions continuing is not realistic.

6.13 At Phase 2, the CMA may examine several possible scenarios but only the most likely scenario will be selected as the counterfactual. Typically only developments that appear likely on the basis of the facts available to it and the extent of its ability to foresee future developments will be incorporated in the counterfactual.

6.14 Examples of possible counterfactuals are:

- the prevailing conditions of competition (or the pre-merger situation in the case of completed mergers)
- a provider ceasing to provide services (this could be either ceasing to provide certain services (we refer to this as exiting services) or ceasing to provide all services (we refer to this as exiting provider)) (see paragraphs 6.16 to 6.33 below)[45]
- loss of a potential entrant
- parallel transactions[46]
- another merger than the one under review (involving one of the merging providers)
- it is also possible that new legislation or policy developments will affect the way that merging providers would have competed absent the merger.

This section addresses some of these possible counterfactuals in more detail.

Providers ceasing to provide all or certain services

6.15 Future events significant for the assessment of the most appropriate counter-factual can relate to certain or all services of one or more of the merging and/or other providers. Due to financial and clinical difficulties faced, providers may submit that they are not viable in their current form. The counterfactual whereby providers cease to provide all services (exiting provider) is discussed below. However, previous cases have also required the CMA to consider changes to (including the possible closure of) certain services. These possible counterfactuals are considered separately below. In both cases, where the evidence is not sufficient for the CMA to adopt an exiting provider/service counterfactual, it will take into account any evidence from the merging parties on financial and/or clinical difficulties in its competitive assessment.

Exiting provider scenario

6.16 Where merging providers consider that either of them would have exited the market (that is, been dissolved) absent the merger, they should submit evidence (including internal documents) as to why such exit would occur. They should also explain, in the event of such exit, what would happen to the assets used to provide the services, for example whether the services would be provided in the same location by another provider, or if patients/commissioners would use services of another provider elsewhere.

6.17 When assessing whether the appropriate counterfactual is that either of the merging providers would exit the market, the CMA will consider such factors as the providers' current and forecast financial positions, internal documents, reports and/or the view of the Care Quality Commission (CQC), Monitor's views, its risk ratings and any action taken by Monitor.

6.18 In forming a view on an exiting provider scenario, the CMA will consider the following three limbs:

(a) whether the provider would exit (through failure or otherwise) and, if so

(b) whether there would be an alternative acquirer for the provider's assets to the acquirer under consideration; and

(c) where the patients and the commissioner contracts of the provider would go in the event of the provider's exit.

6.19 For the CMA to accept at Phase 1 an exiting provider argument, it would need compelling evidence to believe that it was inevitable that the provider would exit and be confident that there was no substantially less anticompetitive acquirer for the provider or its assets. The CMA would then consider whether the result of the exit of the provider and its assets would be a substantially less anticompetitive outcome than the merger. Where the CMA finds that all three limbs of the exiting provider test are met (see paragraph 6.18 above), the merger will not lead to an SLC.

6.20 At Phase 2 the three limbs described in paragraph 6.18 above are also relevant to the CMA's consideration. If the CMA considers that there were alternative acquirers, it will try to identify who the alternative acquirer(s) might have been and take this into account when determining the counterfactual. Having identified the most appropriate counterfactual, the CMA at Phase 2 will generally consider the implications of that counterfactual as part of the SLC analysis.

Would the provider exit?

6.21 When considering whether or not the provider would exit, the CMA will consider the inevitability (at Phase 1) or likelihood (at Phase 2) of the relevant entity being dissolved.

6.22 When considering this limb, the CMA would have regard to the regulatory regime that is in place to ensure that NHS hospitals and other providers meet certain regulatory obligations including those in provider licences relating to, among other things, financial and clinical measures. If an NHS provider is found not to meet certain obligations, it may be placed in 'special measures'. If, following further investigation and analysis undertaken by Monitor and the CQC, it is found to be significantly failing against its obligations, it may be placed into the Trust Special Administration (TSA) process by Monitor or the Secretary of State, which is a statutory process triggered by an NHS provider being unable to pay its debts when they fall due.[47] The TSA process may lead to dissolution of a provider. This regulatory context and the treatment of an NHS provider plays a role in the assessment of the counterfactual.

Would there be an alternative acquirer for the provider's assets?

6.23 The CMA will consider whether the provider would go through the TSA process and be dissolved absent the merger. In so doing, it will consider the relevant provider's financial position, reports and/or the views of the CQC and action taken by Monitor or the TDA, as relevant. In the vast majority of instances where NHS providers face financial difficulties, there is little or no risk that these providers would go through the TSA process and exit the market in the short to medium term. The TSA process is only expected to arise in exceptional circumstances and the CMA envisages that the cases where exit is inevitable or likely in the short or medium term may be small in number. However, the CMA will take into account any evidence of the strength of a provider in its competitive assessment where relevant.

6.24 Dissolution of a provider is only one outcome of a TSA process. If the TSA process is significantly advanced (that is, at draft report stage) and dissolution is the likely recommendation, this will be relevant evidence of dissolution. If the likely recommendation involves changes to specific services rather than dissolution, this will be assessed in accordance with the CMA's approach to exiting services outlined below.

6.25 In the event that dissolution of the relevant entity appears inevitable (Phase 1) or the most likely outcome (Phase 2), the CMA would then consider the alternative options that were available to the trust special administrator. When considering the prospects for an alternative acquirer of the provider's assets, the CMA will look at available evidence supporting any claims that the merger under consideration was the only possible merger, including evidence from the TSA process, the merging providers, Monitor or the TDA, as relevant. The CMA will take into account any submissions as to why another provider would not have delivered safe clinical services or not done so on a financially viable basis.

Where would the patient and commissioner contracts of the provider go?

6.26 If there was no alternative or less anticompetitive acquirer, the CMA will consider what would happen to the commissioner contracts and patients of that provider in the event that the entity was dissolved and in the absence of any merger. It will consider whether these would be redistributed among a number of remaining providers and, if so, how. If patients and commissioner contracts are likely to have been dispersed across several providers, the merger, by transferring most or all of the commissioner contracts and patients to the acquiring provider, may have a significant impact on competition. If, on the other hand, the majority of the commissioner contracts and patients were expected to switch to the acquiring provider, the merger may have little effect on competition.

Exiting services

6.27 Where the merging providers consider that either of them would, absent the merger, cease to provide specific services[48] or if their service offering would change in other ways (for example, due to financial or other constraints or commissioners' plans), they should submit detailed evidence (including internal documents) as to why this would happen. The CMA will then consider the service offering that the provider could be expected to provide in the absence of the merger.

6.28 Changes to services can be:

(a) led by commissioners
(b) led by the provider[49]
(c) required by the CQC[50]
(d) recommended by the Trust Special Administrator.

6.29 In each case the CMA would consider the reasons for the proposed service variation or exit, whether exit is dependent on other factors (for example, where the service exit is provider led but requires commissioner approval, the CMA would take into account whether this being granted will be inevitable – at Phase 1 – or likely – at Phase 2), what other options were considered and what would happen to the commissioner contracts and patients in the absence of the service exit.

6.30 The CMA will examine evidence provided by the merging providers and/or third parties relating to why the provider would have exited the service.

6.31 Any proposals for substantial development or variation of the healthcare service (whether led by commissioners or providers) will be subject to public consultation.[51] The fact that consultation has not yet taken place would not in itself preclude the CMA from concluding that a service change was inevitable at Phase 1 or likely at Phase 2. However, the CMA would require a robust evidence base in support of the proposed change being likely to go ahead absent the merger.

6.32 In the absence of sufficient evidence relating to exit, merging providers may wish to consider making submissions as to whether one of the providers is less likely to be a strong alternative choice for patients or commissioners due to clinical or financial difficulties and therefore less likely to exercise a strong competitive constraint on the other merging provider. This would be taken into account in the overall substantive assessment of the case (see paragraph 6.58 below).

Loss of potential entrant

6.33 Absent the merger, one or more of the merger providers may be most likely to increase capacity to provide existing services or begin providing new services in an area served by the other merger provider. This counterfactual suggests that without the merger competition between the merging providers will be stronger than in the prevailing situation without the merger.

Parallel transactions

6.34 The CMA may be required to assess an NHS merger at a time when there is the realistic prospect of another NHS merger proceeding in the same market.[52] The CMA will assess whether an SLC arises both independently of the parallel transaction proceeding and on the assumption that the parallel transaction proceeds (unless the parallel transaction can clearly be ruled out as too speculative).

IDENTIFYING THE RELEVANT MARKETS

6.35 In examining whether an SLC is likely to occur, the CMA needs to identify the market that is relevant to the merger. Identifying the relevant market involves an element of judgement.

6.36 The purpose of market definition is to provide a framework for the CMA's analysis of the competitive effects of the merger. The relevant market contains the most significant competitive alternatives available to the patients and/or commissioners of the merging providers. We note that market definition is a useful tool, but not an end in itself, and that the boundaries of the market do not determine the outcome of our competitive assessment in any mechanistic way.

Product market definition

6.37 The CMA generally considers the narrowest market (where the merging providers overlap) and then whether this can be widened through substitution on the demand side or supply side.[53]

6.38 Product market definition is specific to each case. However, in relation to mergers of NHS hospital and clinical services, the CMA may adopt the following product market definitions:

- Markets no wider than an individual specialty.[54] Where there are limits to supply-side substitution within specialties, the CMA may take into account constraints at sub-specialty level in its competitive effects assessment.

- Within each specialty:
  - — The CMA may treat outpatient and inpatient[55] activities as separate markets. There is an asymmetric constraint between inpatient and outpatient services, with inpatient providers readily capable of providing outpatient services but not vice versa.
  - — Outpatient (and to a lesser extent inpatient) services are not generally likely to be further separated according to whether or not the services can be provided in community settings.[56] However, where certain services are provided only in the community, these community services may be viewed as separate markets.
  - — Non-elective and elective activities may be separate markets,[57] although the provision of elective activities may be constrained to some extent by non-elective providers.
- Privately-funded healthcare services are likely to be separate markets from NHS services. Within private services, each specialty likely constitutes a separate market and within each specialty, markets may be defined along inpatient and outpatient lines (as with NHS services).[58]

6.39 There are other services where it may be appropriate to consider different markets according to patient characteristics or type. For example, mental health services could be segmented according to whether they are for adults, elderly people, children or adolescents.[59]

Geographic market definition

6.40 In publicly funded healthcare services the relevant geographic market may be based on the location of providers and will be informed by an assessment of the willingness of patients to travel for consultation or treatment (the 'catchment area').[60] The geographic market may not necessarily be the same for all services or for all competition concerns ('theories of harm') under investigation.

6.41 In particular, the CMA may find it appropriate to define different geographic markets when considering competition in the market and for the market. The CMA will be guided by the needs and behaviour of those who make choices about the service. Patients and GPs may in practice tend to choose from a smaller set of providers than those considered by a commissioner seeking to establish a limited number of providers in an area.

6.42 As part of the assessment the CMA will consider whether the merging providers are constrained by providers located outside the relevant geographic market.

MEASURES OF CONCENTRATION: MARKET SHARES

6.43 Market shares of providers can give an indication of the potential extent of market power. The combined market shares of the merging providers, when compared with their respective pre-merger market shares, may provide an indication of the change in market power resulting from the merger.

6.44 As part of its assessment of the merger, the CMA may consider market shares of the merging providers and other providers. If so, the CMA will seek to define what the relevant market is on which these shares are calculated (as discussed above).[61]

6.45 The CMA will generally look at shares at the specialty level across the relevant geographic area, consistent with its general approach to defining markets. However, on the basis that there may be some differences within specialties, the CMA may also take constraints at sub-specialty level into account by analysing the level of activity of relevant providers within specialties at treatment level. The CMA may also look at shares across a wider or narrower geographic area (for example, GP surgeries or sets of surgeries), if these are informative for the competitive assessment. The CMA may consider shares of volume and/or shares of revenue.

EXAMINING THE EFFECTS ON COMPETITION

Unilateral effects

6.46 One way a horizontal merger[62] can harm competition is if it removes an important current or potential[63] competitor, resulting in a reduced incentive for the merged provider to maintain and provide better-quality services to patients and value for money for commissioners. This effect is known as a 'unilateral effect' and is the effect that the CMA considers most frequently.

6.47 The depth and breadth of analysis undertaken is different between Phase 1 and Phase 2. However, the framework within which that assessment takes place is broadly similar.

Competition to attract patients

6.48 In relation to competition to attract patients of NHS services, competition is almost always on quality,[64] rather than on price,[65] as the majority of services are covered by national prices and the payment-by-results rules. The same basic framework applies to elective, non-elective, specialised and community services.[66] Specifically, the aspects of quality which may be impacted by a reduction in competition include clinical factors, such as infection rates, mortality rates, ratio of nurses or doctors to patients, equipment, best practice, and non-clinical factors such as waiting times, access cleanliness and parking facilities.

6.49 The CMA will assess the extent and nature of current (or pre-merger) competition. The CMA's approach will generally be to identify which services are provided by both merging providers (the overlap services), then ask whether, in respect of each of the overlap services:

(a) patients and/or GPs have and exercise choice of provider
(b) quality and/or price influences that choice

(c) the merging providers would have an incentive to compete to attract patients absent the merger
(d) the merging providers are close competitors.

6.50 The CMA will assess the merging providers' incentives to compete and how they have responded to them. In this respect, the CMA will consider submissions from the merging providers and internal documents together with third party views on the market.

6.51 The CMA may take into account the extent to which the merging providers' incentives to compete might have been affected by factors including, but not limited to:
(a) the profitability of increasing activity given the tariff and cost structures
(b) capacity constraints
(c) the relationships the merging providers have with CCGs.

6.52 In previous merger inquiries, providers have submitted that:
(a) the contracts the merging providers had with each other for sharing clinical staff meant that they had reduced incentives to compete with each other and limited ability to differentiate themselves from each other
(b) there was no scope for the merger to reduce quality due to the regulation around quality which existed in relation to the merging providers' services.

Whilst the CMA will consider each case and arguments on their merits, the CMA's predecessor found on the first point that (i) where the provider supplying treatment, rather than the provider lending the doctor, would be paid for the treatment, each provider still had an incentive to attract patients and (ii) the consultant is one factor among many in patient choice or in quality. On the second point, although regulation plays an important role in ensuring minimum standards of quality in the provision of elective services, it does not lead to all providers providing the same levels of quality and does not remove the incentive for providers to compete on quality.[67] That is, providers can strive to exceed minimum regulation standards, which is in the interest of patients.

6.53 When assessing closeness of competition, the CMA's starting point will be to consider referral patterns and the overlaps between the catchment areas of the merging providers together with those of any other local providers,[68] given that location is usually important in patients' choice of hospitals. The CMA may also survey patients[69] or use existing evidence on diversion ratios (for example, evidence of where patients went in the event of a temporary closure).[70] This may provide evidence of how patients and GPs are choosing between providers in the local area.

6.54 Ultimately the CMA is assessing whether there are geographical areas where the merging providers appear to be each other's closest competitors or where patients have little or no choice of other providers for any services.[71] The larger this geographical area and the greater the number of services relative to the merging providers' overall activity, the greater the likely effect of the merger on the merging providers' incentives to compete.

Competition to attract contracts to provide services

6.55 Providers compete for the market when they are (or may be) competing to be one of a limited number of providers of a service. This is often the case for specialised services, where there is an expectation of a small number of providers of services that are often costly to provide, and pathology services, where routine tests are commissioned for GPs by clinical commissioning groups, for example. Providers may compete on quality and, in some cases, price.[72]

6.56 There are generally two concerns in a merger when competition is 'for the market':
(a) in the event of a competitive tender the merger could lead to worse outcomes because there would be fewer bidders (which may be reflected in commissioners receiving reduced value for money, including lower-quality services or higher prices where services are not subject to a national price)
(b) providers on existing contracts might provide lower-quality services, knowing that commissioners have fewer alternative possible providers of those services, and therefore commissioners would be less likely to switch away from the existing provider.

6.57 Where there is competition to attract contracts to provide services, the CMA's assessment will consider whether the merging providers would be close competitors to supply these services and what other providers would constrain them.

Weakened competitive constraint

6.58 When considering the competitive constraint that the merging providers exercise on each other, the CMA may take into account whether one or both of the merging providers faces clinical or financial challenges (and whether this is expected to continue to be the case absent the merger). The CMA is likely to take into account, among other evidence, CQC reports on quality over time, Monitor governance ratings over time and any turnaround plan(s).[73]

Coordinated effects

6.59 A horizontal merger may also lessen competition by enabling or encouraging post-merger coordinated interaction among providers in the market that has adverse effects on patients and/or commissioners by diminishing the incentive to provide high-quality services or value for money.

6.60 Coordination may arise when providers operating in the same market recognise that they can provide less value for money without the threat of losing revenue or patients if they limit the extent to which they compete against each other.

6.61 Such coordination need not be explicit (that is, no anticompetitive agreement is required) but might emerge through implicit understandings and can take a number of forms. Providers may be able to keep quality lower or provide less value for money than they would otherwise, if there is an implicit understanding between those providers that they will not compete strongly against each other, for example by dividing up the services they provide or the geographic areas they provide services in between them or allocating contracts among themselves in bidding competitions. For anticompetitive coordination to be effective, the following conditions need to be met:

- providers need to be able to reach a common understanding and monitor compliance with such an understanding
- providers must have the incentive to stick to the coordinated outcome
- there must be little chance of such an understanding being disrupted by other factors, such as entry or expansion by other providers or action by the commissioners.

6.62 See *Merger assessment guidelines (CC2 (revised)/OFT1254)*[74]for further information on coordinated effects.

6.63 The CMA is aware that NHS providers have a duty to cooperate to improve services and deliver care to patients. There are many ways in which providers can do so (for example, by ensuring the patient experiences seamless care along a care pathway) whilst complying with competition law. However, they should not reach agreements which restrict choice and competition if they operate against patients' and commissioners' interests.[75]

Vertical and conglomerate mergers

6.64 Mergers are not always between providers of the same set of services.[76] In general, vertical and conglomerate mergers are less likely than horizontal mergers to give rise to an SLC. In a vertical merger, the merging providers may benefit from efficiencies that give them a greater incentive to compete (and therefore, for example, to offer better quality or lower prices).

6.65 Nevertheless, vertical mergers may occasionally damage competition if the merged provider restricts downstream competitors' access to a key input or restricts upstream competitors from a key 'route to market'. For example, a merger may distort the pattern of onward referrals from one merger provider to the other at the expense of other providers of the same set of services who might compete on quality for referrals absent the merger.

6.66 Conglomerate mergers may occasionally damage competition and thereby adversely affect patients and/or commissioners if the merged provider can link the services or products in the separate markets.

6.67 These harmful effects of vertical or conglomerate mergers on competition and therefore patients and/or commissioners will only arise if the merged provider would have the ability and incentive to act this way. Such a strategy results in harm to competition and therefore adversely affects patients and/or commissioners, and such harm outweighs any beneficial effects on competition through efficiencies achieved by the merger.

6.68 See *Merger assessment guidelines (CC2 (revised)/OFT1254)* for further information on vertical and conglomerate effects.

ASSESSING COUNTERVAILING FACTORS

6.69 The CMA will also consider any factors that might prevent or significantly reduce any harmful impact of the merger. There are three main factors – efficiencies, entry and expansion in the market, and countervailing buyer power.

Efficiencies

6.70 While mergers can harm competition and thereby adversely affect patients, they can also give rise to efficiencies that make the merged provider a more effective competitor (for example, if the merger itself gives the merging providers incentives to increase quality of services or reduce prices). If these merger-specific efficiencies are large and timely enough, they can enhance rivalry and prevent a merger giving rise to an SLC. Efficiencies that do not enhance rivalry can also be taken into account as relevant customer benefits, provided that they are likely to arise within a reasonable period (see Chapter 7).

6.71 However, claimed efficiencies can be hard for the CMA to verify because most of the information is held by the merging providers. As a result, for the CMA to give weight to efficiency arguments, it must have compelling evidence that such efficiencies not only result directly from the merger itself, but also that they will be timely, likely and sufficient to prevent an SLC from arising.

6.72 Further information on types of efficiencies are set out in the *Merger assessment guidelines (CC2 (revised)/OFT1254)*.

Entry and expansion

6.73 In some cases, entry by new providers or expansion by providers already in the market may be timely enough and sufficient in scope and likelihood to prevent any harmful impact of the merger.

6.74 In order for entry or expansion to be a constraint post-merger, it is necessary that (i) other providers can profitably begin or expand activity in response to a reduction in quality or increase in price by the merging providers, and (ii) patients or commissioners would be willing to switch to those providers in sufficient numbers to make the quality reduction or price increase by the merged provider unprofitable.

6.75 However, there may be barriers to entry or expansion in the market. These barriers may be absolute, for example a patent; structural, for example economies of scale; or strategic, for example the advantage of being the first mover or pioneer in a market.

6.76 To determine whether entry or expansion is most likely, the CMA will consider factors such as how the investment in new services or service expansion will be financed; the profitability of entry and expansion; and the likely demand for the services from patients and commissioners.

6.77 The CMA considers that barriers to entry for inpatient services are high and generally entry into inpatient services by anyone other than an existing acute hospital is unlikely.[77] Barriers to entry into outpatient services are generally lower, especially for services which are not capital intensive and do not require specific equipment (for example, many consultations would fall into this category); however, the availability of consultants may still make entry difficult.

6.78 The CMA will consider the likelihood and effectiveness of new entry and expansion on a case-by-case basis. The CMA will seek evidence from merging providers and/or third parties of planned entry and expansion by a specific provider.

Countervailing buyer power

6.79 A customer has countervailing buyer power when it has the negotiating strength to limit a provider's ability to raise prices or lower quality. An SLC is less likely to occur where all customers have countervailing buyer power post-merger than where only some customers do. A customer's negotiating strength is greater if it can easily switch its demand away from the merged provider.

6.80 NHS services are free at the point of use. Therefore, in the provision of NHS services there is a split between those exercising choice and using services (the patients), and those who pay for the services (the commissioners). In relation to the users of NHS services, individual GPs and patients are unlikely in the majority of cases to have negotiating strength sufficient to require the merged provider to maintain and improve quality levels. This is because no GP/practice or patient is likely to account for a substantial proportion on an ongoing basis of either provider's income in relation to any specific service (even at the level of inpatient elective services provided in a particular specialty, it is unlikely that a GP or practice would persistently account for a significant proportion of those services). Therefore in relation to competition in the market, individual GPs and patients are unlikely to have negotiating strength.

6.81 When looking at whether the commissioners would be likely to have the ability to prevent the merged provider from reducing quality or increasing price in respect of those specialties where it was less constrained by a competitor, the CMA will consider whether in these circumstances the commissioner would be able easily to switch (or threaten to switch) its demand to another provider or otherwise constrain the merged provider. The CMA would be looking at whether the commissioners could act to prevent a decrease in quality or increase in price at the margins, in particular in an area where, for example, the merging providers both provided services of a high quality, at levels over and above key regulatory requirements or in areas where the merged provider would not consider a decrease in quality such that it lost Commissioning for Quality and Innovation (CQUIN) payments or fell below a quality regulatory threshold to be a significant issue.

NOTES

40 At Phase 1, the decision on reference is taken by a senior staff member of the CMA.

41 Subject to the CMA exercising the exceptions to the duty to refer or accepting undertakings in lieu of a reference (see Chapters 7 and 8).

42 The statutory questions the CMA must decide at Phase 2 are summarised in Chapter 3.

43 See the CC report on the anticipated merger of The Royal Bournemouth and Christchurch Hospitals NHS Foundation Trust and Poole Hospital NHS Foundation Trust, 17 October 2013, paragraph 6.122.

44 For a discussion of whether or not to apply a more competitive counterfactual than the prevailing conditions of competition, see OFT decision on the anticipated pathology joint venture between University College London Hospitals NHS Foundation Trust, Royal Free London NHS Foundation Trust and The Doctors Laboratory Limited, ME/6094/13, dated 8 November 2013.

45 See the CC report on the anticipated merger of The Royal Bournemouth and Christchurch Hospitals NHS Foundation Trust and Poole Hospital NHS Foundation Trust, 17 October 2013, for a discussion of exiting provider and the OFT decision on acquisition by University College London Hospitals NHS Foundation Trust of Royal Free London NHS Foundation Trust's neurosurgery services, ME/5574/12, dated 21 February 2013, for a discussion of exiting services.

46 For a discussion of parallel transactions, see the OFT decision on anticipated pathology joint venture between University College London Hospitals NHS Foundation Trust, Royal Free London NHS Foundation Trust and The Doctors Laboratory Limited, ME/6094/13, dated 8 November 2013.

47 The Care Act 2014 allows the TSA process to be triggered if there is a serious failure by an NHS foundation trust to provide services that are of sufficient quality. Whilst a number of NHS providers have been placed into 'special measures' and in some cases have been successfully turned around such that they have come out of 'special measures', there have to date been only two instances of NHS providers going through the TSA process, which was established in 2009.

48 There are some limitations to a provider's ability to make changes to its services. Where a provider is an NHS foundation trust, under its licence conditions, it is required to deliver Commissioner Requested Services, unless agreement is obtained from the commissioner. For all providers (both NHS foundation trusts and NHS trusts), even where commissioners support a proposed change, clinical interdependencies between services may restrict the service reconfiguration options available to it.

49 See the OFT decision on acquisition by University College London Hospitals NHS Foundation Trust of Royal Free London NHS Foundation Trust's neurosurgery services, ME/5574/12, dated 21 February 2013.

50 The CQC has the power to suspend or cancel registration for some or all services, thereby preventing a provider from providing these services.

[51] There is no definition of what constitutes a substantial development/variation; this is something on which the commissioner and local authority are encouraged to reach agreement. See: Department of Health, Local Authority Health Scrutiny, Proposals for consultation, 12 July 2012, paragraph 42.

[52] A parallel transaction is considered as part of the counterfactual on the basis that it would occur whether or not the merger happens. In this context, a parallel transaction is one which is either anticipated or which has been completed but remains subject to merger review by the CMA under the Act.

[53] See the OFT decision on the anticipated pathology joint venture between University College London Hospitals NHS Foundation Trust, Royal Free London NHS Foundation Trust and The Doctors Laboratory Limited, ME/6094/13, dated 8 November 2013.

[54] The CMA will endeavour to ensure that specialties are defined consistently across providers and, where appropriate, may combine individual specialties which are substitutes. See, for example, the report on the anticipated merger of The Royal Bournemouth and Christchurch Hospitals NHS Foundation Trust and Poole Hospital NHS Foundation Trust, 17 October 2013 (paragraph 6.297), where the CC noted that certain activities common to the merging providers (including births) were classified as obstetrics by one provider and as midwifery by the other, and the CC therefore combined these two specialties to give a total figure for maternity.

[55] The CMA is likely to treat day cases as part of inpatient activity.

[56] The CMA may further segment services where the community setting does not constrain the outpatient services. The CMA is more likely to segment between outpatient services and services provided in a community setting in the case of a merger involving one or a few services rather than a full hospital merger.

[57] See the CC report on the anticipated merger of The Royal Bournemouth and Christchurch Hospitals NHS Foundation Trust and Poole Hospital NHS Foundation Trust, 17 October 2013, paragraphs 5.44–5.47, in which the CC found that non-elective and elective activities are separate markets. Elective providers are unlikely to be able to expand quickly to provide non-elective services in the same specialties, and it is unlikely that a provider will be supplying non-elective services without also providing elective services in the same specialty. Therefore in practice the two types of service are unlikely to constrain each other.

[58] See the CC report on the anticipated merger of The Royal Bournemouth and Christchurch Hospitals NHS Foundation Trust and Poole Hospital NHS Foundation Trust, 17 October 2013, paragraphs 5.7–5.53.

[59] See, for example, the decision of the Cooperation and Competition Panel (which previously considered mergers against the Principles and Rules for Cooperation and Competition and provided advice to the Department of Health and Monitor) in the Merger of Norfolk and Waveney Mental Health NHS Foundation Trust and Suffolk Mental Health Partnership NHS Trust.

[60] See the CC report on the anticipated merger of The Royal Bournemouth and Christchurch Hospitals NHS Foundation Trust and Poole Hospital NHS Foundation Trust, 17 October 2013, where the CC looked at the distances travelled by patients to reach the providers, and the geographic areas where the merging providers attracted a large share of patients. See also OFT decision on the anticipated pathology joint venture between University College London Hospitals NHS Foundation Trust, Royal Free London NHS Foundation Trust and The Doctors Laboratory Limited, ME/6094/13, dated 8 November 2013, where the OFT defined geographic markets on the basis of drive-times from each customer's location, while noting that the conditions of competition are similar across the particular customers in question in that case.

[61] This relevant market will represent a technical market and may differ from what providers refer to as the market that they operate in.

[62] That is, a merger between providers of the same (or similar) services.

[63] See paragraphs 5.4.13–5.4.18 of *Merger assessment guidelines (CC2 (revised)/OFT1254)* for further information on the treatment of potential competition in the review of mergers generally.

[64] See the CC report on the anticipated merger of The Royal Bournemouth and Christchurch Hospitals NHS Foundation Trust and Poole Hospital NHS Foundation Trust, 17 October 2013, paragraphs 6.72–6.77.

[65] However, it is possible for there to be variations from the national tariff.

[66] Different types of tariffs apply to different services. For example, national prices do not apply to some community services.

[67] See the CC report on the anticipated merger of The Royal Bournemouth and Christchurch Hospitals NHS Foundation Trust and Poole Hospital NHS Foundation Trust, 17 October 2013, paragraphs 6.133–6.142 & 6.179–6.184.

[68] When undertaking the competitive assessment, the CMA will look primarily at providers offering a similar or broader service than the merging providers. This means that if some specialties or major treatments are only provided by a subset of providers, including the merging providers, the CMA will consider whether there is a different competitive constraint on the merging providers in those specialties/treatments.

[69] This is more likely to take place in a Phase 2 investigation.

[70] A diversion ratio between Service A and Service B represents the proportion of revenues that would divert to Service B (as opposed to Services C, D, E) as patients' second choice in the event of a price increase for Service A (or the temporary unavailability of Service A).

[71] This is because providers may be able to flex certain aspects of quality at a local level (such as through services provided at outpatient clinics), depending on the conditions of competition. For example, see paragraphs 72–80 of the report on the anticipated merger between Heatherwood and Wexham Park Hospitals NHS Foundation Trust and Frimley Park Hospital NHS Foundation Trust.

[72] Any Qualified Provider services do not typically restrict the number of providers, so these will not generally feature in an assessment of the effect of the merger on competition to attract contracts to provide services.

[73] See the OFT's decision in the acquisition by University College London Hospitals NHS Foundation Trust of Royal Free London NHS Foundation Trust's neurosurgery services, ME/5574/12, dated 21 February 2013, paragraphs 80–81.

[74] Adopted by the CMA.

[75] See Monitor Guidance on the application of the Competition Act 1998 in the healthcare sector.

[76] Vertical and conglomerate mergers bring services or products together that do not themselves compete but may be related. For example, a vertical merger in the NHS would include a merger of provider services at different stages of a patient pathway.

[77] See the CC report on the anticipated merger of The Royal Bournemouth and Christchurch Hospitals NHS Foundation Trust and Poole Hospital NHS Foundation Trust, 17 October 2013, paragraphs 7.12–7.17.

7. EXCEPTIONS TO THE DUTY TO REFER AT PHASE 1

[3.592]

7.1 Where the CMA believes at the end of a Phase 1 assessment that it is or may be the case that the merger results or may be expected to result in an SLC, the CMA has a discretion to clear the merger where:

- any relevant customer benefits in relation to the creation of the relevant merger situation concerned outweigh the SLC concerned and any adverse effects of the SLC
- the market concerned is not, or the markets concerned are not, of sufficient importance to justify the making of a reference to Phase 2
- for anticipated mergers, the arrangements concerned are not sufficiently far advanced, or are not sufficiently likely to proceed, to justify the making of a reference to Phase 2.[78]

7.2 The sections below explain how the CMA applies its discretionary exceptions to the duty to refer at Phase 1.

RELEVANT CUSTOMER BENEFITS

7.3 Where the CMA believes that it is or may be the case that the merger results or may be expected to result in an SLC which would result in worse outcomes for patients and/or commissioners,[79] the CMA may take relevant customer benefits arising from a merger into account when deciding whether to refer a merger for a Phase 2 investigation. In the context of NHS mergers, this means benefits to patients and/or commissioners.

7.4 The CMA takes account of relevant customer benefits in different ways at Phase 1 and Phase 2 (see paragraphs 8.4 to 8.6 for a discussion of how these are taken into account at Phase 2). At Phase 1, relevant customer benefits provide a potential exception to the duty to refer a merger where they outweigh adverse effects on patients and/or commissioners of the SLC. This is discussed in more detail below.

Process and Monitor involvement

7.5 Where a foundation trust is involved, Monitor must provide the CMA in Phase 1 with advice on relevant customer benefits of the merger (see below what constitutes a relevant customer benefit) for people who use health services provided for the purposes of the NHS, as soon as reasonably practicable after receiving notice that the CMA has decided to investigate the merger.[80] In practice, this will be done as soon as possible after the CMA informs the merging providers that it is starting the statutory timetable for Phase 1 merger review.

7.6 Monitor's advice is not binding on the CMA. However, the CMA will place significant weight on Monitor's expert advice on the relevant customer benefits of a merger.

7.7 It is open to merging providers to decide not to claim relevant customer benefits.[81] As explained in Chapter 4, where merging providers intend to claim that the merger gives rise to relevant customer benefits, they are encouraged to engage in pre-notification discussions with Monitor and the CMA on these at the earliest opportunity. This can be done in parallel to discussing the substantive assessment and evidence for inclusion in the Merger Notice with the CMA during the pre-notification period. If merging providers do not make claims on relevant customer benefits until after filing the Merger Notice, it is unlikely that the CMA will have time to consider fully the claims made by the merging providers within the 40 working day statutory time frame for merger review.

7.8 Monitor is likely to be the primary point of contact in relation to relevant customer benefits, and merging providers should expect to engage extensively with Monitor on the evidence required in this respect.[82] Merging providers are encouraged to provide the CMA with copies of draft submissions provided to Monitor in relation to relevant customer benefits (once they have decided to notify the CMA). The CMA will not commence an investigation until it considers that the merging providers have provided sufficient information on relevant customer benefits or indicated in the Merger Notice that they will not be submitting any in Phase 1. Therefore, if the CMA is not provided with drafts of the relevant customer benefits submission, this may delay the start of the CMA review. The CMA will liaise closely with Monitor as to whether the information received with respect to relevant customer benefits will allow Monitor to start its assessment of relevant customer benefits.

7.9 Monitor will share its thinking (written or oral) with the CMA in order for the CMA to be able to refer to it on the 'state of play' call with the merging providers as well as reflect it in the issues letter.[83]

7.10 Monitor and the CMA will discuss Monitor's views in relation to relevant customer benefits on an ongoing basis and in any event prior to the issues meeting and case review meeting.[84] The CMA may ask Monitor to provide further advice in relation to additional evidence provided by the merging providers in response to the issues letter. Monitor will provide written advice on relevant customer benefits to the CMA, which it will have shared with the merging providers, and which will be published alongside the full text of the decision.

7.11 See *Monitor Guidance on Merger Benefits* for further information on the process for Monitor providing advice to the CMA.[85]

What constitutes a relevant customer benefit?

7.12 First, relevant customer benefits are limited to be benefits in the form of:[86]

(a) lower prices, higher quality or greater choice of services or goods in any market in the UK, or
(b) greater innovation in relation to such services or goods.

Part 3 CMA and other Guidelines

7.13 The types of benefits providers have previously submitted, either to the Cooperation and Competition Panel, Monitor or the OFT/CC, include:

(a) Higher-quality services through implementing a particular model of care. The Cooperation and Competition Panel found that implementing a particular model of care across a merged provider would improve the quality of services, for example by reducing the length of stay,[87] providing round-the-clock access to a dedicated treatment room,[88] reducing mortality rates and delivering higher-quality stroke services.[89] The CMA will take into account such factors as any previous experience the merging providers or other providers may have of successfully implementing a particular model of care and whether the specific model of care will improve quality for patients and what issues it is looking to address.

(b) Higher-quality services through service reconfiguration.[90] The CMA will consider, for example, how the quality of those services will improve and any effect on interdependent services and whether the reconfigurations lead to any disadvantages for some patients and/or commissioners. In particular, where quality is expected to improve due to volume, the CMA will consider the evidence between minimum volumes and quality outcomes in the relevant services.

(c) Higher-quality services through increased consultant or staff cover.[91] The CMA will consider, for example, the extent to which existing services suffer from staffing problems and how staff increases will result in clinical improvements to patients.

(d) Higher-quality services through access to equipment. The CMA will consider how the equipment leads to better outcomes for patients.

(e) Greater innovation through research and development and greater ability to attract funding for research and development.[92] The CMA will consider what improvements in research and development will arise as a result of the merger.

(f) Financial savings.[93] Benefits could arise from efficiencies from having a large-scale operation (through, for example, making more efficient use of clinical staff or equipment or sharing back-office functions), supplying a broader scope of service (for example, by making the care pathway more efficient or making the treatment of patients with multiple healthcare needs more efficient) and from using the more efficient processes or working methods of one of the merging providers. Merging providers may also avoid costs that would otherwise have been incurred.

— Financial savings could be retained by the health service providers in which case the CMA would typically expect the monies to be reinvested in healthcare services and so give benefits to patients and/or they could be passed on to commissioners and in either case they could qualify as relevant customer benefits. Merging providers should explain what savings can be expected and how the savings will benefit patients and/or commissioners (and whether there are any disbenefits, for example if staff savings led to a decrease in the number of nurses as well as the costs of implementation).

7.14 Whether or not any of these benefits constitute relevant customer benefits will need to be assessed on a case-by-case basis. In addition to evidence provided by the merging providers and Monitor's advice, the CMA may also take into account relevant evidence such as reports by commissioning entities, clinical studies, Royal College guidance, academic papers and/or patient surveys.

7.15 Secondly, a benefit is only a relevant customer benefit if it has accrued or is expected to accrue to relevant patients (and/or commissioners) within the UK within a reasonable period from the merger and would be unlikely to accrue without the merger or a similar lessening of competition.[94]

7.16 What is a reasonable period will vary on a case-by-case basis, depending, for example, on the nature of the proposed benefit and the circumstances of its implementation. For example, a large-scale building project or merger of a maternity[95] or A&E service may reasonably require a longer implementation period – with benefits possibly not accruing to patients for a number of years – than a small project. In addition to the timeliness consideration, the CMA needs sufficient evidence to form a belief that the benefits will accrue (see paragraph 7.18).

7.17 In determining whether the benefit is merger specific, the CMA will consider whether it was likely to occur in any event (for example, if the benefit was in any event likely to arise through a commissioner-led reconfiguration) and whether the merging providers would have the ability and incentive to achieve the benefits independently or through arrangements (such as another merger) that do not give rise to competition issues.

7.18 The CMA will consider whether it believes the benefits are likely to be realised. The CMA will review implementation plans, and the more detailed and advanced these are, the more persuasive they are likely to be. The merging providers' incentives to implement the benefits will also be relevant to the likelihood of implementation. When considering incentives, the CMA will take into account the competitive constraints post-merger.

7.19 The CMA recognises that providers going through an NHS merger are required to go through a number of regulatory approvals. The CMA appreciates that the timing and sequencing may mean that certain reconfiguration plans which are relevant for the merging providers to put forward a benefits case may not have been fully developed. While this may be the case when assessing benefits, the CMA must reach a degree of confidence that the planned action gives rise to a benefit.

7.20 In this context, the level of information required to demonstrate a benefit will vary on a case-by-case basis. When submitting benefits, the evidence required to prove the planned action will give rise to a benefit will vary depending on the nature of the action put forward. The CMA understands that in order to effect reconfigurations, providers need to go through a number of steps. Not all of them need to have been completed for the CMA to accept a benefit. The absence of the merging providers having completed the following steps may not prevent the CMA from concluding that the benefit is expected to arise:

(a) undertaken or started a public consultation on the benefits (in respect of changes where consultation would be required for reconfiguration)
(b) taken a firm decision to proceed with them
(c) implemented or started to implement them

7.21 However, for the more extensive benefit proposals (for example, accident and emergency reconfiguration), the CMA expects that for each benefit the merging providers put forward, the merging providers will have satisfied themselves that the proposed customer benefits are likely to occur and have taken the first in a series of steps, namely:

(a) determined what the preferred proposal is (the CMA would look at, among other evidence, the merging providers' internal documents) and, where relevant, provided evidence for the need for change (for example, if the current service does not comply with relevant quality and safety standards or recommendations)
(b) discussed plans with clinicians of the merging providers and relevant commissioners
(c) developed a model of care (a plan for the way in which services will be delivered following reconfiguration) by engaging with clinicians of the merging providers, relevant commissioners, as well as any clinical experts and any relevant advisory group as appropriate
(d) produced an assessment of the clinical advantages (and any disadvantages) as well as a robust assessment of the financial or economic viability of the plans[96]

7.22 The CMA will also contact relevant third parties such as commissioners for their views on the benefits. Third parties will be contacted at the beginning of the Phase 1 inquiry (likely within the first week) for their views on the merger with the potential for more detailed follow-up questions throughout the inquiry.

7.23 See Monitor *Guidance on Merger Benefits* for further information on what might constitute a benefit and the evidence required.

Weighing up the benefits against the SLC at Phase 1

7.24 In order for the CMA to decide not to refer a merger to Phase 2 on the basis of the relevant customer benefits, it must believe that any such relevant customer benefits concerned outweigh the SLC and any adverse effects of the SLC in all affected markets.[97] The relevant customer benefits need not necessarily arise in the market(s) where the SLC has arisen. It is therefore open to the merging providers to show that sufficient relevant customer benefits might accrue in one market as a result of the merger that would outweigh the finding of an SLC in another market(s).

7.25 The CMA will examine the evidence put forward by the merging parties, together with Monitor's advice on the benefits accruing to patients as a result of the merger. If the evidence received is sufficient for the CMA to establish that there are relevant customer benefits, it will then consider if these outweigh the likely adverse effects of the merger on patients and/or commissioners.

7.26 Weighing up the benefits against the adverse effects on patients involves consideration of the facts and circumstances of an individual case. In exercising its discretion to decide whether the claimed relevant customer benefits are such as to outweigh the SLC concerned and any adverse effects of the SLC, the CMA has regard both to the magnitude of the benefits and the probability of them occurring, and sets this against the scale of the identified anticompetitive effects and the probability of them occurring.

7.27 The more powerful and more likely the anticompetitive effects of the merger, the greater and more likely the relevant customer benefits must be to meet and overcome such concerns.[98]

7.28 Whilst the framework differs, the analysis set out above from paragraph 7.12 to 7.22 is also relevant to Phase 2 merger decisions (see Chapter 8).

MARKETS OF INSUFFICIENT IMPORTANCE ('DE MINIMIS')

7.29 The CMA may decide not to refer a merger if it believes that the market(s) to which the duty to refer applies is/are not of sufficient importance to justify a reference.

7.30 The CMA considers that the market(s) concerned (as opposed to the merging providers' turnover in the relevant market(s) concerned) will generally be of sufficient importance to justify a reference (such that the exception will not be applied) where its/their annual value in the UK, in aggregate, is more than £10 million. By contrast, where the annual value in the UK of the market(s) concerned is, in aggregate, less than £3 million, the CMA will generally not consider a reference justified provided that there is in principle not a clear-cut undertaking in lieu of reference available.

7.31 Where the annual value in the UK, in aggregate, of the market(s) concerned is between £3 million and £10 million, the CMA will consider whether the expected adverse effect on patients and/or commissioners resulting from the merger is materially greater than the average public cost of a reference. The CMA will base its assessment of expected harm on: the size of the market concerned; its view of the likelihood that an SLC will occur; its assessment of the magnitude of any competition that would be lost and therefore adverse effects on patients; and its expectation of the duration of that SLC.

7.32 The CMA will also take account of the wider implications of its decisions in this area, and will be less likely to exercise its discretion, and therefore more likely to refer, where the merger is potentially replicable across a number of similar markets in a particular sector.

7.33 The CMA may also have regard to the rationale behind an individual merger. In so doing, the CMA may take into account the clinical and financial position of the providers as well as any benefits expected from the merger, even where the CMA did not find that these constituted relevant customer benefits.

ARRANGEMENTS INSUFFICIENTLY FAR ADVANCED/INSUFFICIENTLY LIKELY TO PROCEED

7.34 The CMA may decide not to refer a merger if it believes that the arrangements concerned are not sufficiently far advanced or are not sufficiently likely to proceed to justify a reference. This exception therefore only applies to anticipated mergers.

7.35 The intention of this exception to the duty to refer under section 33(2)(b) of the Act is to avoid the unnecessary expense of a reference where it is still uncertain whether the merging providers will proceed with the merger.

7.36 This provision also ensures that the duty to refer is not triggered when the CMA is informed of potential transactions on a confidential basis in order for the merging providers to seek informal advice.

7.37 The CMA would usually expect a merger to be sufficiently advanced to justify a reference where the providers to a merger have publicly announced an agreed merger or their intention to merge (in whole or in part).[99]

7.38 This exception may be appropriate for use in situations where commercial discussions between the merging providers are still ongoing at the time of the CMA's investigation, for example in anticipated joint venture situations where there remains material ambiguity about how the joint venture will be structured.

7.39 In practice, the CMA would take a view soon after notification as to whether this exception applies.

7.40 The fact that further approval is required, for example from Monitor, for the merger to proceed would not be sufficient to justify the use of this exception.

NOTES

78 Sections 22(2) & 33((2) of the Act.

79 The CMA will not take relevant customer benefits into account where it does not identify an SLC. In such cases, the merger is cleared without the need to assess relevant customer benefits.

80 Section 79(5) of the HSCA.

81 If merging providers decide not to make reasoned submissions in relation to relevant customer benefits, this should be noted in the Merger Notice and the decision indicated in writing to Monitor. There is no requirement on the merging providers to explain their decision in this respect. In order to comply with its statutory duty, Monitor will then inform the CMA of the providers' decision as soon as reasonably practicable.

82 It is envisaged that Monitor and the CMA will liaise closely in relation to the information provided in relation to relevant customer benefits. Wherever possible the CMA and Monitor will consolidate questions on relevant customer benefits for the merging providers to avoid two information requests on these.

83 In all cases, the CMA commits that, generally in the period between working days 15 and 20, it will have a 'state of play' discussion with the merging providers, typically by conference call. The purpose of this discussion is to give the merging providers information on any competition concerns, including feedback from the CMA's market test, whether or not the CMA is to send the merging providers an issues letter, and the theories of harm that the CMA proposes to include in the issues letter. The case team will also provide an update on the likely timetable for the case going forward.

84 The case review meeting is an internal meeting following the issues meeting held with the merging providers.

85 The draft guidance which was consulted on can be found at www.monitor.gov.uk/. The CMA understands that Monitor will shortly be publishing the final version of that guidance.

86 Section 30(1) of the Act.

87 See the Cooperation and Competition Panel advice on the merger of Barts and the London NHS Trust, Newham University Hospital NHS Trust and Whipps Cross University Hospital NHS Trust.

88 See the Cooperation and Competition Panel advice on the merger of acute services between University Hospitals Bristol NHS Foundation Trust and North Bristol NHS Trust.

89 See the Cooperation and Competition Panel advice on the merger of Northumbria Healthcare NHS Foundation Trust with North Cumbria University Hospitals NHS Trust.

90 See the CC report on the anticipated merger of The Royal Bournemouth and Christchurch Hospitals NHS Foundation Trust and Poole Hospital NHS Foundation Trust, 17 October 2013, Section 9 & Appendix M, and the Cooperation and Competition Panel advice on the merger of Nuffield Orthopaedic Centre NHS Trust and Oxford Radcliffe Hospitals NHS Trust.

91 See the CC report on the anticipated merger of The Royal Bournemouth and Christchurch Hospitals NHS Foundation Trust and Poole Hospital NHS Foundation Trust, 17 October 2013, Section 9 & Appendix M.

92 See the Cooperation and Competition Panel advice on the merger of Nuffield Orthopaedic Centre NHS Trust and Oxford Radcliffe Hospitals NHS Trust.

93 See the CC report on the anticipated merger of The Royal Bournemouth and Christchurch Hospitals NHS Foundation Trust and Poole Hospital NHS Foundation Trust, 17 October 2013, Section 9 & Appendix M, and the Cooperation and Competition panel advice on the merger of Nuffield Orthopaedic Centre NHS Trust and Oxford Radcliffe Hospitals NHS Trust.

94 Section 30(2) & (3) of the Act. Where a benefit may have occurred absent the merger but taken longer than a reasonable period, the CMA may take into account the time gained as a relevant customer benefit.

95 See the CC report on the anticipated merger of The Royal Bournemouth and Christchurch Hospitals NHS Foundation Trust and Poole Hospital NHS Foundation Trust, 17 October 2013, paragraph 9.84.

96 See the CC report on the anticipated merger of The Royal Bournemouth and Christchurch Hospitals NHS Foundation Trust and Poole Hospital NHS Foundation Trust, 17 October 2013, Section 9.

97 Sections 22(2) & 33(2) of the Act. It is not possible to apply an exception to the duty to refer on the basis of relevant customer benefits in relation to certain affected markets, whilst accepting an undertaking in lieu in respect of other markets.

98 Paragraph 4.10 of *Mergers: Exceptions to the duty to refer and undertakings in lieu of reference guidance* (OFT1122).

99 The CMA requires the merger or merger proposal to be in the public domain before it starts its investigation. In practice, the CMA will also ask for evidence of heads of agreement or similar for the agreed merger or evidence of board-level approval in principle.

8. REMEDIES

PROCEDURE AND FRAMEWORK

Undertakings in lieu at Phase 1

[3.593]

8.1 If the CMA finds that its duty to refer the merger for a Phase 2 investigation applies, the merging providers may be able to avoid that outcome by offering binding undertakings in lieu of reference (UILs) for the CMA to accept. See *Mergers: Guidance on the CMA's approach to jurisdiction and procedure (CMA2)* for further information on the UIL process.

8.2 In order to accept UILs under section 73 of the Act, the CMA must be confident that the competition concerns identified will be resolved by means of the UILs offered without the need for further investigation. UILs are therefore appropriate only where the competition concerns raised by the merger and the remedies proposed to address them are clear-cut, and those remedies are effective and capable of ready implementation. Any UILs accepted by the CMA must be for the purpose of remedying, mitigating or preventing the SLC concerned or any adverse effects identified.

8.3 Given the complexity of remedies in healthcare cases, where merging providers are looking to obtain a Phase 1 clearance by offering UILs, the CMA is particularly ready to engage in early dialogue with merging providers on the availability and design of remedies with the case team throughout the case, including in pre-notification. Such discussion will not be disclosed to the CMA decision-maker in advance of their decision on competition issues.

Remedies and relevant customer benefits at Phase 2

8.4 If, following a Phase 2 assessment, the CMA decides that a merger gives rise to an SLC, it must consider whether action should be taken by it, or by others, to remedy, mitigate or prevent the SLC concerned or any adverse effect that has resulted from, or may be expected to result from, that SLC. If action is to be taken, the CMA then considers what action should be taken and what is to be remedied, mitigated or prevented.

8.5 The CMA at Phase 2 will normally take relevant customer benefits into account, as permitted by the Act, by considering the extent to which effective alternative remedies may preserve such benefits.[100] The CMA may modify a remedy to ensure retention of a relevant customer benefit or it may change its remedy selection, for instance it may decide to implement a remedy other than prohibition or it may decide that no remedy is appropriate. See paragraphs 7.12 to 7.22 for a discussion of what constitutes a relevant customer benefit, which also applies to Phase 2.

8.6 Merging providers may either submit further evidence on relevant customer benefits at Phase 2 to the CMA or, in the event that they did not submit any relevant customer benefits during the Phase 1 inquiry, make such submissions for the first time in Phase 2. The CMA will seek Monitor's views regarding the Phase 2 relevant customer benefits proposal recognising its expertise as a sectoral regulator. Where the CMA has been provided with advice in Phase 1, the CMA will attach such weight to that advice in Phase 2 as it considers appropriate in the light of any changes to the proposed customer benefits and/or relevant evidence gathered and analysis undertaken during the course of its investigation.

CATEGORIES OF REMEDIES

8.7 Remedies fall into two categories:

(a) structural remedies, which are generally one-off measures that seek to restore or maintain the competitive structure of the market (such as divestment of all or part of the acquired assets to a suitable purchaser who can provide effective competition for a completed merger, or prohibition for an anticipated merger)

(b) behavioural remedies, which are normally ongoing measures that are designed to regulate or constrain the behaviour of merger parties. Behavioural undertakings may be accepted or imposed in addition to, or instead of, divestiture

8.8 At Phase 1 the CMA is more likely to accept structural undertakings as UILs than behavioural undertakings because they address the change to the market structure that gives rise to the competition concerns.

8.9 Behavioural undertakings and remedies may bring a number of risks which can reduce their effectiveness or create competition concerns elsewhere. In terms of monitoring and enforceability, behavioural remedies can raise significant concerns: it is difficult to design them so that there are no loopholes and, even if this is achieved, requires monitoring and may be liable to circumvention.

8.10 As such, the CMA will therefore typically expect UILs offered by merging providers to be structural, rather than behavioural, in nature.[101] As discussed above, where merging parties wish to obtain clearance for the merger at Phase 1 by offering UILs, they are encouraged to engage early with the case team in their design.

8.11 See *Mergers: Exceptions to the duty to refer and undertakings in lieu of reference guidance (OFT1122)* for more information on how the CMA will assess UILs in Phase 1.

8.12 Similarly, at Phase 2, the CMA will generally prefer structural remedies to behavioural remedies because:

(a) structural remedies are likely to deal with an SLC and its resulting adverse effects directly and comprehensively at source by restoring rivalry (they address the change to the market structure that gives rise to competition concerns);

(b) behavioural remedies may not have an effective impact on the SLC and its resulting adverse effects, and may create significant costly distortions in market outcomes; and

(c) structural remedies do not normally require monitoring and enforcement once implemented.

See *Merger remedies (CC8)* for more detail on the assessment of remedies in Phase 2.[102]

NOTES

100 Sections 35(5) & 36(6) of the Act.

101 See further *Mergers: Exceptions to the duty to refer and undertakings in lieu of reference guidance* (OFT1122). Experience has indicated that UILs are accepted most frequently in cases where, first, the problematic overlaps represent a small proportion of the merger and, second, those overlaps involve asset packages – such as stand-alone operations in separate local markets – that are severable from the remainder of the transaction without materially affecting the overall rationale for the merger.

102 The CC report on the anticipated merger of The Royal Bournemouth and Christchurch Hospitals NHS Foundation Trust and Poole Hospital NHS Foundation Trust, 17 October 2013, paragraph 9.162ff, discusses behavioural remedies, including those previously accepted by the Cooperation and Competition Panel.

9. FURTHER INFORMATION

CMA PUBLICATIONS

[3.594]

Mergers: Guidance on the CMA's approach to jurisdiction and procedure (CMA2)

Administrative penalties: Statement of Policy on the CMA's approach (CMA4)

Merger Notice for use by business for notifying an anticipated or completed merger to the CMA under Section 96 of the Enterprise Act 2002 (as amended)

Transparency and disclosure: Statement of the CMA's policy and approach (CMA6)

OFT/CC PUBLICATIONS ADOPTED BY THE CMA[103]

Merger assessment guidelines (CC2 (revised)/OFT1254)

Mergers: Exceptions to the duty to refer and undertakings in lieu of reference guidance (OFT1122)

Merger Remedies: Competition Commission Guidelines (CC8)

Chairman's Guidance on Disclosure of Information in Merger and Market Inquiries (CC7)

CMA publications and OFT/CC publications adopted by the CMA are available at www.gov.uk/cma.

NOTES

103 As the documents were published prior to the amendments introduced to the Act by the ERRA13, they should be read subject to guidance CMA2 and to the notes in Annex D of that guidance.

ANNEX A

[3.595]

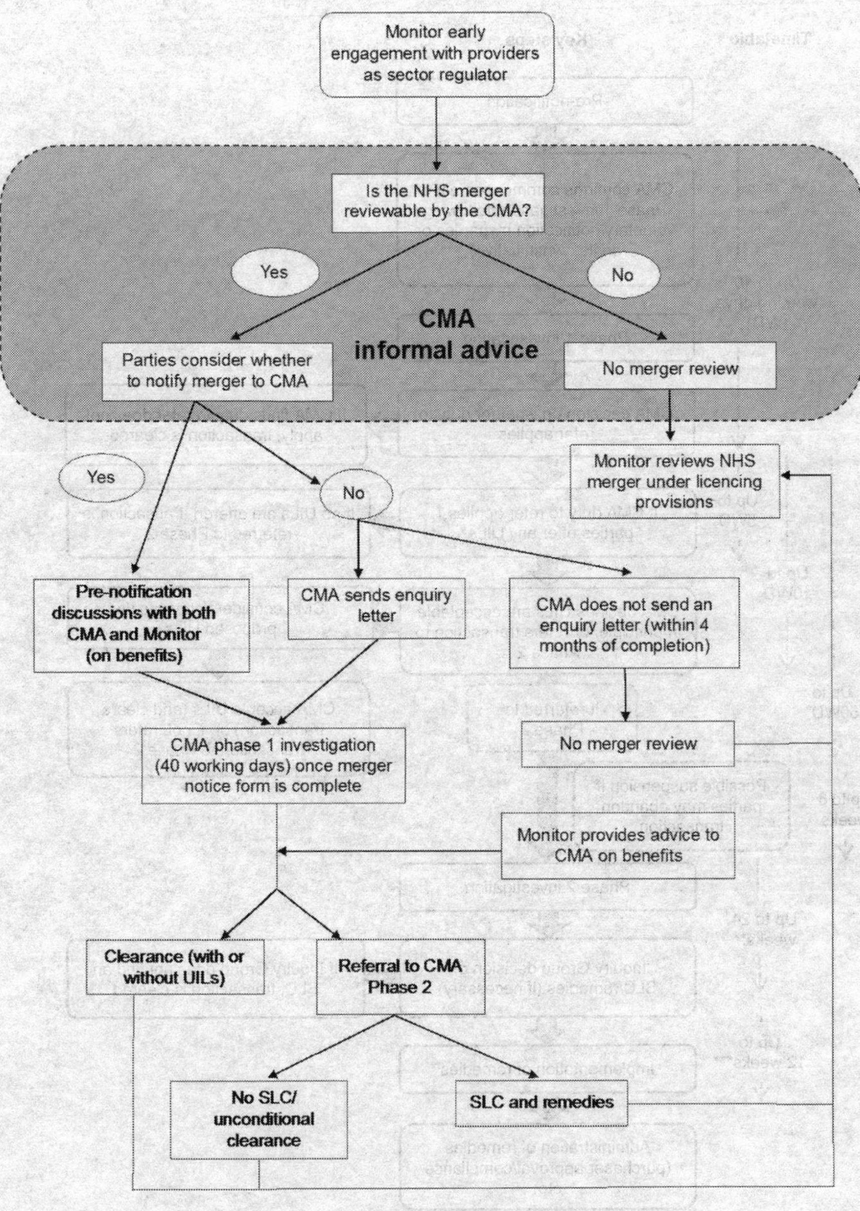
Principal stages and interaction of CMA and Monitor processes
Monitor early engagement with providers as sector regulator
Is the NHS merger reviewable by the CMA?
Yes
No
CMA informal advice
Parties consider whether to notify merger to CMA
No merger review
Monitor reviews NHS merger under licencing provisions
Yes
No
Pre-notification discussions with both CMA and Monitor (on benefits)
CMA sends enquiry letter
CMA does not send an enquiry letter (within 4 months of completion)
CMA phase 1 investigation (40 working days) once merger notice form is complete
No merger review
Monitor provides advice to CMA on benefits
Clearance (with or without UILs)
Referral to CMA Phase 2
No SLC/ unconditional clearance
SLC and remedies

ANNEX B

[3.596]

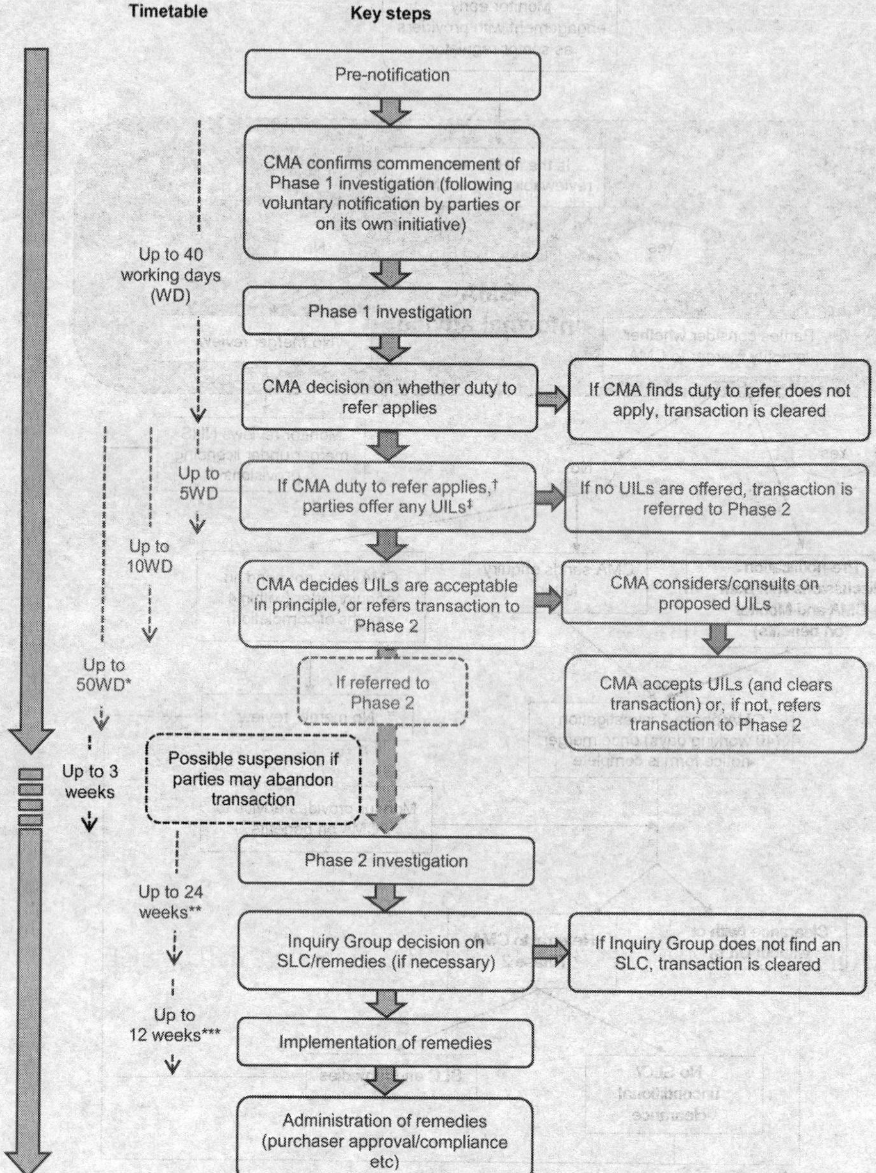

*Extendable by up to 40 working days. **Extendable by up to eight weeks. ***Extendable by up to six weeks.
†Exceptions to the duty to refer considered including relevant customer benefits.
‡Undertakings in lieu of reference to Phase 2.

GLOSSARY

[3.597]

Act	Enterprise Act 2002, as amended, which sets out the legislation governing the CMA's review of mergers.
Buyer power	This can arise where commissioners enjoy significant negotiating power, for example because they account for a significant proportion of revenues of the provider and have good alternatives.
Conglomerate merger	Merger between two providers which are not active in the same market but which are nevertheless related in some way.
Counterfactual	CMA examines the likely effects of the merger against what would happen without the merger (this is known as the counterfactual).
Enterprise	The activities or part of the activities of a business.
Entry/expansion	Where other providers are able and have incentives to begin supplying or expanding their service offering such that it limits the risk of harm from the merger.
ERRA13	The Enterprise and Regulatory Reform Act 2013, which amended the Enterprise Act 2002 and created the CMA.
HSCA	Health and Social Care Act 2012, which confirmed the CMA's jurisdiction over mergers involving a foundation trust and set out Monitor's role.
Integrated care	Mergers arising from integrated care initiatives can be subject to merger control. Typically, mergers between providers that supply different parts of the patient care pathway (for example, GPs and acute hospitals) are less likely to give rise to competition concerns. However, they may do so if they distort patient choice (for example, by enabling the merged provider to direct referrals to itself to the detriment of competitors).
Market definition	The purpose of market definition is to provide a framework for the CMA's analysis of the competitive effects of the merger. The relevant market contains the most significant competitive alternatives available to the customers of the merging providers.
Relevant customer benefits	Benefits to patients and/or commissioners arising as a result of the merger within a reasonable period.
Service reconfigurations	Mergers arising from service reconfigurations can be subject to merger control. The CMA will have regard to the context of the service reconfiguration in its assessment (for example, it may be relevant to the counterfactual or benefits of the merger). The CMA's jurisdiction to review mergers does not extend to the award of a contract by a commissioner, provided that there is nothing more attached to the contract award (that is, no transfer of assets such as equipment or staff from one provider to another).
Share of supply	Share of supply of any particular goods or services.
UILs	Undertakings in lieu. Undertakings offered by the merging providers, which the CMA may accept instead of referring the merger for a Phase 2 investigation.
Vertical merger	Merger between two providers supplying services at a different point in time of a patient's pathway.

MONITOR: SUPPORTING NHS PROVIDERS: GUIDANCE ON MERGER BENEFITS
(August 2014)

[3.598]

NOTES

Note that Monitor became part of NHS Improvement in April 2016.

See also "Monitor: Supporting NHS providers: guidance on transactions for NHS foundation trusts" (March 2015) at www.gov.uk/government/publications/supporting-nhs-providers-considering-transactions-and-mergers.

CONTENTS

ABOUT MONITOR

[3.599]
As the sector regulator for health services in England, our job is to make the health sector work better for patients. As well as making sure that independent NHS foundation trusts are well led so that they can deliver quality care on a sustainable basis, we make sure: essential services are maintained if a provider gets into serious difficulties; the NHS payment system promotes quality and efficiency; and patients do not lose out through restrictions on their rights to make choices, through poor purchasing on their behalf, or through inappropriate anti-competitive behaviour by providers or commissioners.

INTRODUCTION

[3.600]
In the current challenging financial climate, healthcare mergers can benefit patients by helping providers to deliver safe, high quality and sustainable care. However, some mergers can work against patients' best interests by reducing choice, and by curbing the drive to improve quality and value for money and to innovate that choice encourages. This is why proposed NHS mergers must be carefully considered by all parties concerned, with the patient firmly in mind.

As health sector regulator, one of our core responsibilities is to ensure that co-operation and competition work in the best interests of patients. When a merger involving an NHS foundation trust is reviewed, we have a duty to provide advice[1] to the Competition and Markets Authority (the CMA)[2] on the benefits of the merger for patients and commissioners. We also review mergers and other transactions involving foundation trusts as part of our on-going overall assessment of whether they meet the conditions of their provider licence.[3]

THE PURPOSE OF THIS GUIDANCE

The guidance you are about to read is one of a set of documents explaining how we exercise our co-operation and competition functions, first published in March 2013 for a 12-week public consultation. We are grateful for all the feedback we received to help us further develop the guidance.

This guidance[4] is designed to help you make the best decisions for patients and will be helpful to any NHS organisation planning a merger. It should be read alongside other guidance explaining our new approach to transactions (see below).

HOW THIS GUIDANCE WORKS WITH OUR NEW APPROACH TO TRANSACTIONS

Since our consultation on transactions in 2014, we have listened to the sector and looked more comprehensively at our approach to transactions, including mergers. We have been working with the CMA to develop a joint approach that will make sure patients' interests are at the heart of assessing merger proposals.

We are now implementing our new approach, which seeks to:

- better support NHS foundations trusts contemplating a merger or acquisition to navigate the relevant regulatory processes, from an earlier stage
- change the rules for reporting and reviewing transactions involving NHS foundation trusts (as part of our approach to risk assessing transactions to ensure compliance with licence conditions).

To support providers, we are publishing a range of complementary guidance documents that cover our new approach, comprising:

- this revised guidance on merger benefits
- Supporting NHS providers: Guidance on transactions for NHS foundation trusts' that updates and consolidates all our previous guidance on transactions; provides further detail and clarity on the new arrangements to assist NHS foundation trusts contemplating a merger or acquisition; and sets out our risk assessment process for transactions
- 'Competition review of NHS mergers: A short guide for managers of NHS providers', co-published with the CMA, explaining how statutory merger control applies to NHS mergers.

You may also find the 'CMA guidance on the review of NHS mergers' helpful.

FURTHER HELP

If you have queries about this guidance, or about our new approach to transactions, please contact us at: cooperationandcompetition@monitor.gov.uk

NOTES

[1] We are required to provide advice to the CMA by section 79(5) of the Health and Social Care Act 2012.

[2] The CMA is the UK's primary competition and consumer authority. It is an independent non-ministerial government department with responsibility for carrying out investigations into mergers, markets and the regulated industries and enforcing competition and consumer law. From 1 April 2014 it took over the functions of the Competition Commission and the competition and certain consumer functions of the Office of Fair Trading (OFT).

[3] See 'Supporting NHS providers: Guidance on transactions for NHS foundation trusts'.

[4] This guidance reflects our views at the time of publication and may be revised from time to time to reflect changes in best practice, legislation and the results of experience, legal judgments and research. It may in due course be supplemented, revised or replaced. Our website will always display the latest version of the guidance. Within this document we cover most of the points about merger benefits likely to be of interest to NHS organisations and their advisers, but it is not comprehensive or a definitive interpretation of the law.

HOW TO USE THIS GUIDANCE

[3.601]

This guidance explains how we will assess and provide advice to the CMA on the benefits of mergers involving NHS foundation trusts. It covers:

- our role in relation to merger benefits
- what is a relevant customer benefit
- how the CMA will take our advice into account
- our approach to assessing merger benefits
- examples of types of merger benefits.

The appendices contain supporting information on what should go into submissions to us, how we advise the CMA and the statutory framework around relevant customer benefits.

WHAT IS OUR ROLE IN RELATION TO MERGER BENEFITS?

[3.602]

We expect NHS foundation trusts to engage with us early on when they are considering their strategic options (such as a merger). We will advise them on the competition implications of proposed mergers and conduct a preliminary review of their approach to assessing and demonstrating merger benefits. Our guide 'Supporting NHS providers: Guidance on transactions for NHS foundation trusts' contains more information on how we will engage with NHS foundation trusts contemplating mergers.

As part of our early engagement with NHS foundation trusts contemplating mergers, we can help merging providers understand whether their merger is reviewable by the CMA. There is further information on which mergers the CMA will review in 'Competition review of NHS mergers: A short guide for managers of NHS providers' (published by the CMA and Monitor) and the CMA's guidance on the review of NHS mergers. If the CMA reviews a merger involving an NHS foundation trust, we have a statutory duty to provide advice to the CMA on the following matters:

- the effect of the merger on benefits (in the form of those defined in the Enterprise Act as 'relevant customer benefits')[5] for people who use NHS healthcare services and
- such other matters relating to the merger as we consider appropriate.

NOTES

[5] The term 'relevant customer benefit' is defined in Section 30 of the Enterprise Act 2002.

WHAT IS A 'RELEVANT CUSTOMER BENEFIT'?

[3.603]

'Customer' is a term used in the Enterprise Act in relation to all the economic activities it covers.[6] In relation to the health sector, the term 'customer' means a current or future user of healthcare services (often but not always referred to as a 'patient') or a commissioner. In this guidance we use the terms 'merger benefits' and 'relevant customer benefits' interchangeably.

The Enterprise Act defines a 'relevant customer benefit' as one which:[7]

- is a benefit to relevant customers in the form of: lower prices, higher quality or greater choice of goods or services in any market in the United Kingdom,[8] or greater innovation in relation to such goods or services and
- the CMA believes has accrued, or may be expected to accrue, within a reasonable period as a result of the merger and
- the CMA believes was or is unlikely to accrue without the merger or a similar lessening of competition.

Appendix 3 contains more detail on the statutory framework for relevant customer benefits.

NOTES

[6] 'Relevant customers', as defined in the Enterprise Act, are customers at any point in the chain of production and distribution and are therefore not limited to final consumers. Relevant customers include customers of the merger parties, customers of such customers, any other customers in a chain of customers beginning with the customers of the merger parties, and future customers.

[7] Section 30 of the Enterprise Act.

[8] Whether or not the market or markets in which the substantial lessening of competition concerned has, or may have, occurred or (as the case may be) may occur.

HOW WILL THE COMPETITION AND MARKETS AUTHORITY TAKE OUR ADVICE INTO ACCOUNT?

[3.604]

The CMA assesses whether a merger is likely to have adverse effects on patients by reducing competition

Part 3 CMA and other Guidelines

between providers. This reduction is known as a 'substantial lessening of competition'. The CMA's approach to this assessment is set out in 'Competition review of NHS mergers: A short guide for managers of NHS providers' and its guidance on the review of NHS mergers. If the CMA finds that a merger is likely to substantially lessen competition, it will consider whether the merger gives rise to any relevant customer benefits. There is a two phase process for merger review, and the CMA takes account of benefits in different ways at Phase 1 and Phase 2:

- At Phase 1 the CMA weighs the benefits of the merger against the substantial lessening of competition. If the benefits of the merger outweigh the adverse effects, the CMA can clear the merger (that is, decide not to refer the merger for a Phase 2 investigation).
- At Phase 2 the CMA takes benefits into account when deciding what remedies are appropriate.[9] The CMA will consider the impact of a remedy on the benefits expected to arise from the merger, and may modify or select a particular remedy to preserve these benefits.

In reaching its view on relevant customer benefits, the CMA will place significant weight on our advice.[10]

HOW WILL THE COMPETITION AND MARKETS AUTHORITY WEIGH BENEFITS AGAINST THE SUBSTANTIAL LESSENING OF COMPETITION AT PHASE 1?

The merger benefits need not necessarily arise in the market(s) where the competition concerns have arisen. It is possible that a merger might lead to benefits for one set of patients but adverse effects as a result of a substantial lessening of competition for a different set of patients. An example of this could be a merger that substantially lessens competition in relation to urology services but leads to benefits in relation to maternity services. For the CMA to clear such a merger at Phase 1, the benefits in maternity services would need to outweigh the adverse effects on patients in urology services.

Weighing up the benefits against the adverse effect on patients involves a consideration of the facts and circumstances of an individual case. The CMA's approach to this assessment is explained in its guidance on the review of NHS mergers.

NOTES

[9] The CMA will select a remedy it believes is effective and proportionate to address the adverse effects of the merger. The CMA can impose remedies such as prohibiting the merger, or requiring the merger parties to sell a business or assets, or to give supply commitments.

[10] Our statutory obligation to provide advice on relevant customer benefits applies at Phase 1 of the merger review process. We are not separately required to advise again at Phase 2 but the CMA will take account of any advice we have already provided at Phase 2.

OUR APPROACH TO ASSESSING MERGER BENEFITS

[3.605]

In this section, we explain the framework we apply when assessing whether proposals submitted by merger parties meet the statutory test for relevant customer benefits.[11] The illustrations and examples come from previous merger cases considered by us, the Competition Commission and the Co-operation and Competition Panel (CCP).[12] They are intended to be helpful but whether or not a proposal constitutes a relevant customer benefit within the meaning of the Enterprise Act will ultimately depend on the particular facts of the case.

In our assessment of merger benefits, we examine the following questions:

- Is the proposed change likely to represent a real improvement in quality, choice or innovation of services for patients[13] or in value for money for commissioners?
- Is the proposed change likely to be realised within a reasonable period as a result of the merger?
- Is the proposed change unlikely to accrue without the merger or a similar lessening of competition? (This is sometimes referred to as the benefit being merger dependent or merger specific.)

When an NHS foundation trust is considering its strategic options, and as soon as it believes there is a significant likelihood that it might want to undertake a merger, we suggest it enter into discussion with us. We will offer advice at this stage to ensure the robustness of the underlying strategy. We can also offer advice on the competition issues that might arise.

We expect parties to a merger to be able to identify and describe the improvements arising from their proposed merger, and present well thought through plans as to how these benefits will be realised. Parties should be able to explain the steps they will take to implement the proposed changes and the expected timing of these, the proposed staffing arrangements, the anticipated cost of delivery and how this will be funded, and any risks to delivery and how these will be mitigated.

This approach reflects the fact that the merger parties, as the main actors in the transaction, are the organisations responsible for ensuring that the intended improvements are realised. It is consistent with the CMA's approach, which requires merger parties to produce detailed and verifiable evidence of any anticipated benefits.[14]

In addition to considering the evidence presented by the merger parties, we may gather further information from the merger parties and others, such as commissioners, local patients and/or their representatives and other providers. We will base our advice on evidence we receive from the merger parties and others and will pay particular attention to the informed views of clinicians and local commissioners on the specific improvements proposed by the parties (and the plans for local implementation of these).

We would generally expect improvements for patients and commissioners to be key drivers for merger proposals, so parties should be able to show that they have, from an early stage, identified and planned for the delivery of such improvements. We recognise that implementation plans are likely to be refined and developed as planning for the merger progresses. However, if there is apparent uncertainty in information we receive from merger parties (for example, about where services will be located after the merger), we may take this into account in our assessment of whether the improvement is likely to be realised.

Once a trust has decided to proceed with a merger that is subject to review by the CMA, it may wish to provide us with a submission on merger benefits that will form the basis of our advice to the CMA. The submission should include information about the transaction and a description of what improvements for patients and commissioners the parties expect to arise from the merger. Appendix 1 provides guidance on what to include in submissions and Appendix 2 explains how we provide advice to the CMA. The type of evidence we would expect parties to provide to demonstrate that proposed changes fall within the Enterprise Act's definition of relevant customer benefits is discussed in detail below.

There may be cases where merger parties decide not to provide a submission to us on relevant customer benefits. This might be because, for example, the parties have decided not to notify the CMA of the merger or the parties' view is that the merger is unlikely to substantially lessen competition and so an analysis of benefits is unnecessary. In such a case, we would still be required to provide advice to the CMA if it decides to review the merger, but our advice would generally be that without information from the parties we have not identified relevant customer benefits. We would still need to conduct a risk assessment of the merger from the perspective of foundation trust governance and continuity of services in accordance with our role of monitoring compliance with the NHS provider licence.

NOTES

11 As discussed above, the CMA decides whether the relevant customer benefits of the merger outweigh the substantial lessening of competition.

12 Before 1 April 2013, CCP was responsible for reviewing NHS mergers under the Principles and Rules for Co-operation and Competition. Unlike Monitor and the CMA, CCP did not apply the Enterprise Act test for relevant customer benefits. Nevertheless, CCP cases provide helpful illustrations of the types of benefits that may be identified.

13 'Patients' in this context refer to people who use healthcare services provided for the purposes of the NHS. See section 79(5)(a) of the Health and Social Care Act.

14 The CMA will consider evidence of benefits if it finds that a merger is likely to substantially lessen competition. See the CMA's guidance on the review of NHS mergers.

IS THE SUBMITTED BENEFIT A REAL IMPROVEMENT?

[3.606]

Parties should provide information to demonstrate that the proposed intervention or change will lead to improvements for patients and/or commissioners. Such evidence may include clinical studies, Royal College guidance, academic papers and/or patient surveys. In assessing submissions we will also consider whether or not the proposed changes appear to be seen as improvements by patients and commissioners themselves.

For us to conclude that an improvement attributed to a merger represents a real improvement[15] in quality, choice or innovation of services for patients, or value for money for commissioners, parties to the merger should be able to describe in sufficient detail the existing situation that the merger will improve.[16] Implementing a particular model of care, for example, could lead to reduced length of stay, increased consultant cover or reduced mortality rates.

Where the delivery of proposed improvements may involve some reduction of access to the services available to patients, for example because it involves the rationalisation of services, we would consider the potential impact of these changes on quality of service. If some patients will have to travel further because of the consolidation of services, for example, we would consider factors such as the number of patients affected and the increase in travel time for these patients. The merger parties should conduct an assessment to understand the impact of these potential disadvantages.

NOTES

15 We will consider whether this represents an improvement compared with the likely situation if the merger does not happen.

16 We will also take account of any evidence demonstrating there is likely to be some change to the existing situation if the merger does not proceed.

REALISING THE BENEFIT WITHIN A REASONABLE PERIOD

[3.607]

We will have greater confidence that a particular improvement is likely to be realised where the parties to a merger have a clear and detailed post-merger implementation plan that sets out how the merging providers' existing structures, processes and practices will be modified along with proposed timeframes.[17] Parties should also provide evidence that funds are available to implement the proposed changes. We are likely to place greater weight on the credibility of post-merger implementation plans where they have been scrutinised by clinicians and/or other experts, and where they have been developed for broader purposes than the CMA's or our consideration of the merger.

In assessing the credibility of any plans we will also look at the experience of the merger parties and their management teams in previous transactions and their success in realising improvements from those transactions.[18] We will consider the incentives that the merged organisation has to carry out the implementation plans. We may also look at other similar transactions and consider whether the parties to those transactions have been successful in realising similar improvements.

Where one or both of the merger parties is clinically or financially challenged this may have an impact on the merged organisation's ability to achieve substantial changes to models of care and service delivery while it implements the merger. Therefore it will be important in such a case for the parties to show that they have identified the risks of a merger involving a challenged provider or providers and planned effectively to mitigate these.

What is a reasonable period will vary case by case, depending for example on the nature of the proposed change and the circumstances of its implementation. We are likely to have greater confidence that improvements will be realised where their implementation is planned to take place soon after the merger. In previous merger cases, Monitor and CCP have typically found that a 1–2 year period to implement clinical changes or achieve cost savings following the merger is reasonable, although in some cases a longer period may be needed. For example, in its assessment of the merger of The Royal Bournemouth and Christchurch Hospitals NHS Foundation Trust and Poole Hospital NHS Foundation Trust ('the Bournemouth and Poole merger'), the Competition Commission found that five years would, in the circumstances of that case, be a reasonable period for the construction of a new maternity unit.[19]

Where merger parties and/or commissioners submit that relevant customer benefits will be delivered by a reconfiguration of services which is subject to consultation, we will not expect the parties to have started or completed public consultation on the proposed reconfiguration, taken a firm decision to proceed with the reconfiguration, or implemented the service reconfiguration. However, for the more extensive proposals (for example, accident and emergency reconfiguration), we would expect the parties to have taken a number of steps as outlined below:

- determined what the preferred proposal is and, where relevant, provided evidence of the need for change; for example, if the current service does not comply with relevant quality and safety standards or recommendations
- discussed plans with clinicians of the merger parties and relevant commissioners
- developed a model of care (a plan for the way in which services will be delivered following the reconfiguration) by engaging with clinicians of the merger parties and relevant commissioners, as well as any clinical experts and relevant advisory groups as appropriate
- produced an assessment of the clinical advantages (and any disadvantages) as well as a robust assessment of the financial or economic viability of the plans.[20]

NOTES

17 We also look at the credibility and robustness of the merger parties' post-merger integration plan as part of our risk assessment of the transaction.

18 For example, where there have been changes in circumstances (such as a change in management) which mean that the merger parties' previous experience should not be relied on, we will take that into account.

19 A report on the anticipated 'Bournemouth and Poole merger', Competition Commission, 17 October 2013, paragraph 9.84.

20 See also a report on the anticipated 'Bournemouth and Poole merger', Competition Commission, 17 October 2013, paragraphs 9.51 to 9.54.

DOES THE BENEFIT DEPEND ON THE MERGER?

[3.608]

To constitute relevant customer benefits under the Enterprise Act, improvements must be unlikely to occur without the merger or a similar lessening of competition. To determine whether or not this is the case we will examine whether there is evidence that the proposed changes are likely to occur in any event, for example if the merger parties have the ability and the incentive to deliver the proposed changes independently or together through an arrangement other than the merger.

Where there is evidence that services are likely to change as a result of commissioner-led or other centrally led changes (for example, to meet government recommendations), we will consider whether this action would have the same effect as the merger parties' proposals and how soon that action is likely to occur. If we find that the change to services could be realised within a reasonable period without the merger, it is likely that the proposed change will not meet the Enterprise Act test.

In our assessment of the benefits of the Bournemouth and Poole merger, for example, we found that improvements arising from the consolidation of haematology services were likely to be achieved by commissioner-led reconfiguration and therefore were not specific to the merger.[21]

In the context of healthcare mergers, many kinds of improvements for patients may be realisable without a merger. This is because NHS organisations have a legal duty to co-operate.[22] The culture of co-operation means that parties should think carefully about whether a particular improvement is really dependent on the merger. On the other hand, sometimes it may be possible to realise a particular improvement more quickly or more cost effectively because of a merger. If so, the time gained or money saved is the benefit that can be attributed specifically to the merger. If this is the case, merger parties should explain why a particular improvement will be realised more quickly with the merger than without, identify the time or money that will be saved, and the impact this will have on patients or commissioners.

NOTES

21 Our advice to the OFT under section 79(5) of the Health and Social Care Act on the anticipated 'Bournemouth and Poole merger', Monitor, 11 February 2013. In its report on the anticipated 'Bournemouth and Poole merger, Competi-

tion Commission, 17 October 2013, the Competition Commission determined that benefits were not likely to be achieved in this area, but on the basis of different reasoning due to a change in the evidence regarding this service between the period between our report on relevant customer benefits and its own review.

22 Section 72, National Health Service Act 2006.

TYPES OF MERGER BENEFITS

[3.609]
Below are examples of the types of improvements for patients and commissioners which merger parties have submitted would arise from healthcare mergers in previous cases. We set out the relevant issues and the type of evidence that would be required for us to advise the CMA whether there are relevant customer benefits in a particular case.

The examples are not exhaustive, nor are they suggestions of what we would expect to see in parties' submissions. Whether or not there are merger benefits in a particular case will depend on the facts of the case. These examples are for illustrative purposes only. We may adapt or build on them as our experience grows.

HIGHER QUALITY SERVICES THROUGH IMPLEMENTING A PARTICULAR MODEL OF CARE

To demonstrate that implementing a particular model of care or a particular working practice will improve the quality of services for patients, merger parties will need to:

- describe the model of care or working practices that will be implemented and any issues with the existing service provision that will be addressed
- identify the services and categories of patients that will be affected by the change
- provide evidence (such as clinical studies) demonstrating that the model of care or working practices will lead to better quality outcomes.

Merger parties should provide a plan showing how the changes will be implemented and the anticipated timeframe for delivering the model of care. They should also explain why the model has not or will not be implemented independently by the parties without the merger, or will be delivered faster and/or more effectively with the merger. Where the proposal is likely to disadvantage some patients (for example, by reducing their access to services), the merger parties should be able to explain what work has been done to assess and weigh the impact of the proposal.

In several previous cases, CCP accepted that implementing a particular model of care across a merged trust would improve the quality of services, for example, by reducing length of stay,[23] providing round-the-clock access to a dedicated treatment room,[24] reducing mortality rates, and delivering higher quality stroke services.[25]

In its assessment of the merger of North Cumbria University Hospitals NHS Trust (North Cumbria Trust) and Northumbria Healthcare NHS Foundation Trust (Northumbria Trust), CCP accepted that the merger would lead to quicker improvement of services at North Cumbria Trust by applying Northumbria Trust's models of care for various services. The parties submitted convincing evidence in support of their case including information about quality issues at North Cumbria Trust, Northumbria Trust's track record of high performance and experience in successfully implementing a service model to turn around a troubled trust across multiple sites, and a detailed implementation plan. CCP accepted that Northumbria Trust was uniquely placed to expedite implementation of the changes on the basis of its skills and experience, the rural nature of the areas served by the merger parties, and the ability for staff to move regularly between the parties' sites.

By contrast, in a different case CCP did not accept that delivering a particular new model for breast-care diagnostic outpatient services was a merger-specific benefit.[26] In particular, CCP noted that the proposed new model of care could have been adopted by the parties independently without the merger if it was likely to deliver significant quality improvements. It also did not appear that the model of care used before the merger was adversely affecting the quality of services for patients.

In its assessment of another merger, CCP examined whether the merger would be likely to lead to higher quality services through the parties implementing a particular model of care but found that the information provided by the parties was not sufficient to reach a view. In particular, the parties had not explained what each organisation did well and what they would roll out in terms of best practice improvement.[27]

HIGHER QUALITY SERVICES THROUGH SERVICE RECONFIGURATION

To show that service reconfiguration will improve the quality of services for patients, merger parties will need to provide details of the reconfiguration proposed, identify the patients and services affected, including any effects on interdependent services, and explain the quality improvements arising from the reconfiguration and the timeframe for implementation. It will also be necessary to explain why the improvements in quality depend on, or will be realised more quickly or more effectively through, the merger and why these have not been or will not be implemented by the merger parties without the merger (either independently or together, for example, through a service level agreement between them).

In some previous cases merger parties have submitted that the merger provides them with a sufficient volume of patients to enable them to reconfigure services. This is linked to the expectation that improved outcomes can be achieved in certain treatment groups where a larger volume of patients is treated in a particular centre. In order for this to constitute a relevant customer benefit, the merger parties will need to provide evidence of the link between minimum volumes and quality outcomes applicable to the services the parties have described. They will also need to provide evidence of the predicted outcome improvements for the group of patients who will benefit.

In our view it would not be appropriate to make a service viable artificially by distorting patient choice through a merger if the service is not valued by patients and commissioners. We will therefore consider whether a service improvement that depends on an increased number of patients could be achieved by one of the parties independently providing a high quality service that would attract a sufficient volume of patients. If it appears that a service operated by one of the merger parties could not be expected to attract sufficient referrals, this may indicate either that the demand for that local service is not sufficient or that patients and commissioners do not value the service.

As discussed under 'Is the submitted benefit a real improvement?', if the proposed reconfiguration is likely to disadvantage some patients (for example, by reducing their access to services), we would consider factors such as the number of patients affected and the increase in travel time for these patients. In its assessment of the Bournemouth and Poole merger, the Competition Commission found that reconfiguring accident and emergency services could create both benefits and disadvantages for local patients and that the scope and nature of these was likely to differ depending on where the service would be located. The Competition Commission did not find that the proposal was an overall benefit to patients as the merger parties had not yet undertaken an assessment of the impact of the proposal.[28]

If the proposed reconfiguration of services is subject to consultation, we would expect the parties to demonstrate that they have taken the steps outlined in the section on 'Realising the benefit within a reasonable period' above. In particular, where consultation will be required, evidence that commissioners and clinicians have been involved in the development of the proposal will be important.

In previous cases, CCP and Monitor have found that reconfiguring services may improve quality of care for patients by reducing or eliminating transfers of patients between hospitals,[29] or by providing a comprehensive service enabling patients to be treated closer to home.[30]

In some cases, rationalising services without a merger may be better for patients because it will preserve choice in relation to other services and the associated incentives on providers to improve quality and value for money. It is therefore important to show that improvements arising from service rationalisation or consolidation are merger specific. In some previous cases, Monitor and CCP have found that improvements arising from service reconfiguration were not specific to the merger, for example because they were likely to be achieved by commissioner-led reconfiguration even without a merger[31] or by the wider London programme to improve cancer care.[32] In another case CCP found that a proposed co-location of diagnostic outpatient services and the associated improvement in quality of services could have been carried out by one of the parties independently without needing the merger.[33]

HIGHER QUALITY SERVICES THROUGH INCREASED CONSULTANT OR STAFF COVER

Where parties submit that a merger will improve staffing and provide better coverage of staff absences, they should be able to explain the way in which existing services are provided and the impact and extent of any staffing problems, as well as how improvements to staffing levels and staff coverage will result in clinical improvements to patients. Without this information we will not be able to assess the existence or size of any improvement in services. Parties should also be able to explain whether they have explored other ways to achieve the same improvements, for example by agreeing staff sharing arrangements or joint rotas.

The Competition Commission, OFT, Monitor and CCP have previously considered cases in which merger parties submitted that establishing a dedicated rota for a particular service (for example, a cardiology rota,[34] an upper gastrointestinal bleed rota,[35] a spinal rota[36]) would provide increased consultant cover (in terms of hours of cover or the number of consultants in attendance) and improve quality outcomes for patients. Due to the prevalence of staff sharing and other co-operative arrangements (such as service level agreements) in the healthcare sector, parties will need to think carefully about whether any benefits arising from a joint rota could be achieved without a merger.

To demonstrate that increased consultant or staff cover will be realised it will be necessary for merger parties to provide details of the number of relevant clinical staff pre- and post-merger, the number of clinical staff that would be required to establish a joint rota for a given service, and details of current gaps in the rota. It will also be necessary to explain why improvements to rotas could not otherwise be achieved by service level agreements, other staff-sharing arrangements or by employing more staff. Where parties submit that a merger will improve their ability to recruit staff, we note that there are several ways to attract and retain staff, including offering more attractive terms of employment, and therefore it will be important to demonstrate why recruitment could not be improved without a merger.

Factors we may take into account when considering whether increased consultant or staff cover could be achieved without the merger include: previous attempts by the parties to enter into a service level agreement or other staff sharing arrangement; whether such arrangements are in place (either with each other or other providers) with respect to other services; and the feasibility of establishing a joint rota (and the parties' financial incentives to do so) in the absence of the merger.

Even if we find that increased consultant or staff cover could be achieved without the merger, we would still take into account any costs that would be avoided by merging. In that context, it will be important for parties to show that these cost savings will not be achieved in a way which would have an adverse impact on the quality of services.

HIGHER QUALITY SERVICES THROUGH ACCESS TO EQUIPMENT

To demonstrate that a merger will improve access to equipment, and thereby deliver higher quality services, the parties will need to explain what the equipment is used for and provide evidence (such as clinical studies) that this leads to better outcomes for patients. The parties should provide a plan showing how the merger will enable the purchase of new equipment, or better utilisation of existing equipment, and explain why this could not be achieved without the merger.

CCP previously considered cases in which parties submitted that the merger would enable them to share equipment and thereby improve the quality of services for patients. In the merger of parts of University Hospitals Bristol NHS Foundation Trust and North Bristol NHS Trust, the parties submitted that the quality of a breast screening service would be improved by having two mammography machines in one location instead of in separate locations. The CCP did not accept that this constituted a relevant benefit because the merger parties did not explain how the machines would be staffed, and how additional capacity would be created by having both mammography machines in the same place.

In the merger of Dartford and Gravesham NHS Trust (Dartford and Gravesham Trust) and Medway NHS Foundation Trust (Medway Foundation Trust), the parties submitted that patients at Dartford and Gravesham Trust would benefit from having access to a specialist gamma camera that Medway Foundation Trust was planning to purchase. However, Medway Foundation Trust had committed to the investment regardless of the merger and the service would be provided anyway. Patients would be able to choose to go to Medway Foundation Trust if they wanted to receive the service. CCP therefore concluded that the improvement in services for patients could be achieved without the merger.

GREATER INNOVATION THROUGH RESEARCH AND DEVELOPMENT

Merger parties may submit that the increased size of the merged organisation will improve their ability to attract research and development funding. To demonstrate this is a relevant customer benefit, they will need to identify the improvements in research and development that will result from the merger and explain why these could not be achieved without the merger.

We note that research and development can often be facilitated or co-ordinated by local research networks. Therefore it will be necessary for parties to demonstrate that the merger will bring some improvement which would not be achieved this way, for example, due to the complementary nature of the different research expertise of the parties and the patients or clinical areas affected by the merger.

In CCP's assessment of the merger of the Nuffield Orthopaedic Centre NHS Trust and Oxford Radcliffe Hospitals NHS Trust, some of the improvements in research and development were not specific to the merger, since they flowed from collaboration between the parties' research centres, which was already occurring before the merger.

FINANCIAL SAVINGS

There are a number of ways in which financial savings may arise from a merger, as outlined below.

- The merged organisation may be able to achieve efficiencies from having a larger scale of operation, for example by making more efficient use of clinical staff and equipment or sharing back office functions.
- The merged organisation may be able to achieve efficiencies from supplying a broader scope of services, for example by making the care pathway more efficient or making the treatment of patients with multiple healthcare needs more efficient.
- The merged organisation may be able to achieve efficiencies across its portfolio of services from the more efficient clinical or managerial processes or working methods of one of the merger parties.
- Other possible savings may be generated by improved recruitment and retention of staff.
- By merging, the merger parties may be able to avoid costs which would otherwise be incurred.

To be treated as merger benefits, financial savings generated by the merger parties must be used for the benefit of patients or commissioners. We would generally expect any savings made by a foundation trust to be reinvested in healthcare services, for example through lower prices to commissioners or investment in services for current and future patients (leading to higher quality, greater choice or innovation of services). Nevertheless, where merger parties can explain how they will use any financial savings this will help to demonstrate that the benefit to patients will be realised. For example, identifying which aspects of services would benefit from improvement, and providing details of the work undertaken to identify this and what would happen without the investment, will enable merger parties to make a stronger case that the identified cost savings from the merger are in practice likely to be realised within a reasonable time period. In addition, an explanation of how savings will be reinvested will help the parties make a stronger case that the identified cost saving is likely to represent a real improvement for patients or commissioners.

The parties will also need to quantify any savings and explain how these will be achieved. We would expect parties to be able to provide a business case or implementation plan that describes and explains how the savings will be achieved. The parties' plans will also need to take into account any costs associated with implementing financial savings (eg redundancy costs). If savings involve service rationalisation, the parties will also need to consider whether there is any associated reduction in quality for patients, for example as a result of reduced access or increased waiting times, and may wish to conduct a quality impact assessment to enable any potential impact on quality to be understood and assessed (see above in relation to reconfiguration).[37]

We will consider whether the savings could be achieved without the merger, for example through service level agreements or the merger parties independently investing in or rationalising services. Monitor and CCP have found in some previous cases back office savings did not depend on the merger in question because they could have been delivered by a merger with another provider which would not have given rise to competition concerns, or a shared services arrangement.[38] Where parties submit that savings could be achieved by improving the care pathway or the way that patients with multiple healthcare needs are treated, we note that there are many initiatives in the sector intended to ensure the delivery of more integrated care to patients and many of these are also intended to generate cost savings. Many of these initiatives do not depend on the services in question being delivered by a single organisation so the parties will need to explain why the savings from their proposals would not be achieved without the merger.

NOTES

23 Merger of Barts and the London NHS Trust, Newham University Hospital NHS Trust and Whipps Cross University Hospital NHS Trust, CCP, 15 December 2011.

24 Merger of parts of University Hospitals Bristol NHS Foundation Trust and North Bristol NHS Trust, CCP, 20 September 2013.

25 Merger of North Cumbria University Hospitals NHS Trust with Northumbria Healthcare NHS Foundation Trust, CCP, 21 December 2012.

26 Merger of parts of University Hospitals Bristol NHS Foundation Trust and North Bristol NHS Trust, CCP, 20 September 2013.

27 Merger of Dartford and Gravesham NHS Trust with Medway NHS Foundation Trust, CCP, 10 October 2012.

28 A report on the anticipated 'Bournemouth and Poole merger' merger, Competition Commission, 17 October 2013, paragraphs 9.105 to 9.111.

29 Our advice to OFT under section 79(5) of the Health and Social Care Act on the anticipated 'Bournemouth and Poole merger', Monitor, 11 February 2013, paragraph 44(a). In its advice to OFT, we found that this would be a relevant customer benefit. However, when the merger was reviewed by the Competition Commission the merger parties indicated that they no longer intended to reconfigure the relevant service in the way they had originally proposed and which we had found to be a benefit to patients (see report on the anticipated 'Bournemouth and Poole merger', Competition Commission, 17 October 2013, paragraphs 9.92 to 9.100); See also Merger of parts of University Hospitals Bristol NHS Foundation Trust and North Bristol NHS Trust, CCP, 20 September 2013.

30 Merger of Nuffield Orthopaedic Centre NHS Trust and Oxford Radcliffe Hospitals NHS Trust, CCP, 30 September 2011.

31 Our advice OFT under section 79(5) of the Health and Social Care Act on the anticipated 'Bournemouth and Poole merger', Monitor, 11 February 2013. In its report on the anticipated 'Bournemouth and Poole merger', Competition Commission, 17 October 2013, the Competition Commission determined that benefits were not likely to be achieved in this area, but on the basis of different reasoning due to a change in the evidence regarding this service between the period between our report on relevant customer benefits and its own review.

32 Merger of Barts and the London NHS Trust, Newham University Hospital NHS Trust and Whipps Cross University Hospital NHS Trust, CCP, 15 December 2011.

33 Merger of parts of University Hospitals Bristol NHS Foundation Trust and North Bristol NHS Trust, CCP, 20 September 2013.

34 Our advice to OFT under section 79(5) of the Health and Social Care Act on the anticipated 'Bournemouth and Poole merger', Monitor, 11 February 2013; a report on the anticipated 'Bournemouth and Poole merger', Competition Commission, 17 October 2013.

35 Merger of Dartford and Gravesham NHS Trust with Medway NHS Foundation Trust, CCP, 10 October 2012.

36 Our advice to OFT under section 79(5) of the Health and Social Care Act on the transfer of neurosurgery services from the Royal Free London NHS Foundation Trust to University College London Hospitals NHS Foundation Trust, Monitor, 6 March 2013.

37 A report on the anticipated 'Bournemouth and Poole merger', Competition Commission, 17 October 2013, paragraphs 9.119 to 9.128.

38 Our advice to OFT under section 79(5) of the Health and Social Care Act on the anticipated 'Bournemouth and Poole merger', Monitor, 11 February 2013; Merger between Norfolk and Waveney Mental Health NHS Foundation Trust and Suffolk Mental Health Partnership NHS Trust, CCP, 8 March 2011.

APPENDIX 1: GUIDANCE ON THE CONTENT OF SUBMISSIONS

[3.610]

Once a trust has decided to proceed with a merger that is reviewable by the CMA, they may wish to provide us with a submission on merger benefits that will form the basis of our advice to the CMA. Merger benefits will be considered by the CMA if it finds that a merger is likely to substantially lessen competition. This appendix is intended to assist merger parties preparing submissions to Monitor in relation to relevant customer benefits that may arise from a merger.

BACKGROUND INFORMATION

In their submission merger parties should provide the following background information:

- parties to the merger, including their status
- structure of the merger
- services, assets and liabilities transferring
- rationale for the merger.

BENEFITS CASE

As well as the background information set out above, the merger parties should identify and describe the improvements for patients and commissioners arising from the merger and include the information outlined below. For each benefit the parties attribute to the merger the benefits case should explain:

- how the change represents a real improvement in quality, choice or innovation of services for patients or value for money for commissioners. This should include:
  - an explanation of the existing situation that the merger will improve, including the nature and scale of current problems, if any, that the changes are expected to address
  - evidence of why this represents an improvement (eg clinical studies, Royal College guidance, academic papers, patient surveys, views from patients and commissioners)
  - an identification of the services and categories of patients that will be affected by the proposed changes including any effects on interdependent services
  - when and how the benefit will be realised as a result of the merger and whether the benefit has a degree of longevity (rather than a temporary or one-off gain). This should include a well-developed post-merger implementation plan setting out the steps that will be taken to implement the benefit, and how the merging providers' existing structures, processes and practices will be modified
  - the expected timing of these steps
  - proposed staffing arrangements
  - anticipated cost of delivery and how this will be funded
  - any risks to delivery and how these will be mitigated
- why, in the merging providers' view, the period in which the changes will be implemented is a reasonable period.
- why the improvement is unlikely to be delivered without the merger. This should include an explanation of why the change would not be implemented without the merger (by the merger parties either independently or in co-operation, or by a third party).

Where the delivery of the proposed changes may have an adverse impact on some patients (for example, because it involves rationalisation of services), the merger parties should do further work to understand these disadvantages and the impact on patients.

For the more extensive proposals (for example, accident and emergency reconfiguration), the merger parties should provide evidence that they have:

- determined what the preferred proposal is and, where relevant, provided evidence for the need for change; for example, if the current service does not comply with relevant quality and safety standards or recommendations
- discussed plans with clinicians of the merger parties and relevant commissioners
- developed a model of care (a plan for the way in which services will be delivered following the reconfiguration) by engaging with clinicians of the merger parties and relevant commissioners, as well as any clinical experts and relevant advisory groups as appropriate
- produced an assessment of the clinical advantages (and any disadvantages) as well as a robust assessment of the financial or economic viability of the plans.

The merger parties should submit any documentary evidence supporting the assessment and/or quantification of the benefits outlined in the benefits case.

APPENDIX 2: PROCESS FOR OUR PROVISION OF ADVICE TO THE COMPETITION AND MARKETS AUTHORITY

[3.611]

If the CMA decides to carry out a Phase 1 review of a merger involving an NHS foundation trust, it must notify us as soon as reasonably practicable. We will then provide our advice to the CMA as soon as reasonably practicable after receiving that notification.

We will provide the CMA with our assessment of the relevant customer benefits identified by the merger parties, in line with our statutory obligations. Where appropriate, we will also share our views on the potential competition issues.

We expect NHS foundation trusts to engage with us early on when they are contemplating strategic options (such as a merger). We can help merging providers understand whether their merger needs to be reviewed by the CMA.

If providers decide to formally notify the CMA of their merger, they should engage in pre-notification discussions with both the CMA on the competition aspects and Monitor on the benefits of the merger. These discussions will help them identify the information they will need to provide to the CMA on the competition aspects and Monitor on the benefits of the merger, and so help ensure the merger review proceeds efficiently. Pre-notification discussions usually involve providing a draft submission to the CMA on the competition effects of the merger and a draft submission to us on the benefits of the merger. Guidance on the content of submissions can be found above (in relation to us) and in the CMA's guidance on the review of NHS mergers (in relation to the CMA).

We will provide comments on the draft submission on benefits including on its completeness. We will gather further information from the merger parties and relevant third parties such as commissioners by sending information requests and/or holding meetings (by phone or in person). We will keep a record of these meetings. Meetings with the merger parties and relevant third parties will generally be held separately by Monitor and the CMA.

We expect that the merger parties will provide their final submission on benefits and any additional information requested by us before submitting a merger notice to the CMA. In order to address any potential issues early and constructively, we will endeavour for this process to be as open as possible and encourage merger parties to remain open and co-operative throughout.

We will share our thinking (written or oral) with the CMA in order for the CMA to be able to refer to it on the 'state of play' call with the merger parties as well as reflect it in the issues letter.[39] The CMA may ask us to provide further advice in relation to additional evidence provided by the merger parties in response to the issues letter.

We will discuss our views in relation to relevant customer benefits with the CMA on an on-going basis and in any event prior to the CMA's issues meeting and case review meeting.[40]

Before providing our written advice to the CMA, we expect to provide the merger parties and the CMA with our provisional view on the relevant customer benefits arising from the merger. The merger parties will be invited to comment on this provisional view. The merger parties will be given an appropriate period of time to comment depending on the nature of the advice (generally no less than 48 hours). We will take responses to the provisional view into account when producing our final advice.

Our advice may contain information that is confidential (either as regards the merger parties or other confidential information known to us). We may share such information with the CMA. To the extent that the parties consider that information they provide to us should not be included in the published version of our advice, they should submit a non-confidential version of such submission and state clearly what information should remain confidential to us, together with the reasons for this.

We will provide the CMA with a confidential version of our advice for the purpose of the CMA's decision on the merger. Following the CMA's decision we will generally publish a non-confidential version of our advice on our website.

Before it is published, the text of our advice will be circulated to the parties or their advisers to enable them to request the redaction of sensitive confidential information from the text, if necessary to protect confidentiality.

The non-confidential version of our advice must clearly set out the reasons for our advice and as such, we would expect to describe the nature of any benefits that the parties submit are likely to arise from the merger. We therefore ask that, when parties make requests on the redaction of sensitive confidential information from the text, they justify each of those requests and do not make blanket claims that particular classes of information are confidential.

NOTES

39 In all cases, the CMA commits that, generally in the period between working days 15 and 20 of Phase 1 of its review, it will have a 'state of play' discussion with the merger parties, typically by conference call. The purpose of this discussion is to give the merger parties information on any competition concerns, including feedback from the CMA's market test, whether or not the CMA is to send the merger parties an issues letter, and the theories of harm that the CMA proposes to include in the issues letter. The case team will also provide an update on the likely timetable for the case going forward.

40 The case review meeting is an internal meeting held by the CMA following its issues meeting with the merger parties.

APPENDIX 3: RELEVANT CUSTOMER BENEFITS – STATUTORY FRAMEWORK

[3.612]

Section 30(1)(a) of the Enterprise Act provides that for the purposes of Part 3 of the Enterprise Act (which deals with mergers), a benefit is a relevant customer benefit if it is a benefit to relevant customers in the form of:

- lower prices, higher quality or greater choice of goods or services in any market in the United Kingdom (whether or not the market or markets in which the substantial lessening of competition concerned has, or may have, occurred or (as the case may be) may occur); or
- greater innovation in relation to such goods or services.

For the purposes of section 30(1) of the Enterprise Act, 'relevant customers' are defined as:

- customers of any person carrying on an enterprise which, in the creation of the relevant merger situation concerned, has ceased to be, or (as the case may be) will cease to be, a distinct enterprise[41]
- customers of such customers[42] and
- any other customers in a chain of customers beginning with the customers mentioned in section 30(4)(a).[43]

For the purposes of section 30(1) of the Enterprise Act, 'customers' includes future customers.[44]

In order to constitute a relevant customer benefit within the meaning of section 30 of the Enterprise Act, the CMA must believe that the benefit:[45]

- has accrued as a result of the creation of the relevant merger situation concerned or may be expected to accrue within a reasonable period as a result of the creation of that situation and
- the benefit was, or is, unlikely to accrue without the creation of that situation or a similar lessening of competition.

Under section 79(5) of the Health and Social Care Act, we are required to provide the CMA with advice in relation to mergers involving NHS foundation trusts that are investigated by the CMA. In particular, we must provide advice on:

- the effect of the matter under investigation on benefits (in the form of those within section 30(1)(a) of the Enterprise Act 2002 (relevant customer benefits)) for people who use health care services provided for the purposes of the NHS[46] and
- such other matters relating to the matter under investigation as Monitor considers appropriate.[47]

NOTES

41 Section 30(4)(a) of the Enterprise Act.
42 Section 30(4)(b) of the Enterprise Act.
43 Section 30(4)(c) of the Enterprise Act.
44 Section 30(4) of the Enterprise Act.
45 Section 30(1)(b) of the Enterprise Act.
46 Section 79(5)(a) of the Health and Social Care Act.
47 Section 79(5)(b) of the Health and Social Care Act.

MONITOR GUIDANCE: TRANSACTIONS INVOLVING NEW CARE MODELS
(August 2015)

[3.613]

NOTES

Note that Monitor became part of NHS Improvement in April 2016.

1. THREE STAGE REVIEW: EARLY ENGAGEMENT TO IDENTIFY RISKS AND TAILOR OUR WORK PROGRAMME

[3.614]

1.1 Stage 1

Similar to our approach at Stage 1 of a proposed merger, as soon as you believe it is likely that you will enter into a transaction involving a new care model you should discuss this with your relationship team to help you determine whether it is a relevant transaction for review.

At this stage, we will offer informal support and advice on the underlying strategy and analysis of relevant patient benefits. We will also advise whether the transaction might give rise to any competition issues and, if so, what you should do to determine more precisely their nature and extent.

1.2 Stage 2

If the transaction meets the 'material' or 'significant' threshold as set out in the risk assessment framework or requires more detailed review from a competition perspective, we would at Stage 2 meet with you, the parties to the transaction and the relevant commissioners, including your relationship team and their relevant colleagues from our Provider Appraisal and Co-operation and Competition Directorates. This meeting would take place at the outline business case stage or once the preferred bidder for a new contract has been selected.

To prepare for this meeting, we will review available information regarding the proposed transaction, particularly from a competition perspective if relevant. The scale and scope of this review will be determined on a case by case basis but should take no longer than one month. At the meeting, all pertinent aspects of the model can then be discussed, including:

- further consideration and challenge of the strategic rationale for the transaction (recognising that a key test will often be that the proposed transaction represents a material improvement over the next best alternative or "do nothing" counterfactual)
- the foundation trust's approach to assessing relevant patient benefits, including plans to realise those benefits and the fit with commissioning intentions in the local area
- the proposed legal structure, contracting and risk sharing arrangements (financial, clinical and demand management risks)
- where relevant, comparison of the foundation trust's own assessment of any competition issues resulting from the proposed transaction with Monitor's assessment of them.

Following this meeting, we will write to you (copying your commissioners) giving our views on the quality and robustness of the underlying business case and the assessment of patient benefits. We will highlight any areas we think could impede the successful implementation of the model as well as likely risks you will need to mitigate before our detailed review, should the transaction meet the 'significant' threshold.

We will also set out a clear timetable and scope for this review to reflect the risks of the transaction. We will aim to ensure that we do our work and provide the final risk rating in line with your planned timescales. Through this early engagement you should also be well placed to decide whether to notify the Competition and Markets Authority of the proposed transaction.

To determine whether the transaction meets the significant threshold (and therefore requires a Stage 3 review) we will take into account the risk factors associated with the new care model and the relative size of the transaction.

Further details of our approach are provided below.

1.3 Stage 3 (final detailed review)

Should the new care model be deemed a 'significant' transaction, a detailed transaction review will be undertaken. This review will look at the extent to which you can demonstrate the proposed model represents a better balance of risk and benefit in clinical (patient benefit) and financial terms than the next best alternative, with a particular focus on the foundation trust's level of exposure to risk in early years and the associated cash profile in a reasonable downside case.

Such a review typically takes a minimum of 3 months from the point at which a trust submits to Monitor a board-approved final full business case and the associated financial model (in Monitor's Long Term Financial Model format). However, we will seek to be as flexible as possible, streamlining our approach and minimising the timetable for review in line with the amount of information gathered and the level of risk identified during our early engagement. In planning your transactions we would ask that you ensure your timetable reflects our process and that you do not sign any legally binding agreements before we complete our review and issue a transaction risk rating.

'Supporting NHS providers: guidance on transactions for NHS foundation trusts' provides further guidance on our review of transactions. This autumn, we will update this guidance with more examples of the 'major risk factors' associated with a new model of care and add detail to the timeline for early engagement.

Please keep us informed

If you are contemplating a new care model in the next 12 months, whether involving an acquisition, a new legal entity or a new type of contract, it would help to let us know what the stage of development is. Please do this by informing your relationship manager.

2. WHAT MAKES NEW CARE MODELS 'SIGNIFICANT' TRANSACTIONS?

[3.615]

There are 3 particular aspects of new models of care that make them inherently risky:

New and innovative delivery models

For example creative solutions to deliver care may involve a number of NHS organisations and Local Authorities with varying cultures coming together to deliver integrated patient care.

Unusual or unfamiliar legal structures

NHS parties may wish to utilise novel legal structures including setting up a new legal entity or jointly entering into an arrangement to deliver a new service.

Outside core competencies/normal areas of business

As new models may make greater use of clinical networks across nearby sites, involve joint ventures between NHS organisations (eg to take on social services), or the delivery of specialist single services across a number of different providers, some organisations may begin to deliver services that are outside their historic competencies or normal course of business.

Aspects of transactions we are likely to want to understand in some detail include, but are not limited to:

- risk sharing arrangements (financial, clinical and demand management risks)
- potential exit provisions and associated costs
- payment arrangements, including the use of capitated contracts/capitation-based funding
- commissioning to sub-contractors
- system pressure to accelerate delivery
- changes to workforce structures or terms and conditions
- value added tax implications
- timing, amount and certainty of transformation funding

Having understood these aspects in more detail we will determine whether there are any major risk factors associated with the transaction. Then, taking account of the relative size of the transaction we will consider whether it meets the requirements to be classified as a significant transaction under the definitions set out in the risk assessment framework. If this is the case it will require a detailed (Stage 3) review.

D. MARKETS

1. GENERAL

SUPER-COMPLAINTS – GUIDANCE FOR DESIGNATED CONSUMER BODIES (OFT 514, JULY 2003)

[3.616]

NOTES

As to the construction of this document (following the abolition of the OFT and Competition Commission), see further the note "The Competition and Markets Authority (references to the OFT and Competition Commission etc)" in the introductory notes to Part 3 preceding **[3.1]**.

Note also that all references to market studies or investigations must be read in the light of Market studies and market investigations: Supplemental guidance on the CMA's approach (CMA3); in the case of conflict, CMA3 prevails.

1. INTRODUCTION

THIS GUIDANCE

[3.617]

1.1 This guidance is designed to help those making super-complaints to the Office of Fair Trading (the OFT), the Director General of Telecommunications,[1] the Gas and Electricity Markets Authority, the Northern Ireland Authority for Energy Regulation, the Director General of Water Services, the Rail Regulator and the Civil Aviation Authority (the Regulators).[2] It explains what activates the super-complaint process, confirms who can make super-complaints, who can accept them and how they will be dealt with.

1.2 This guidance is indicative rather than definitive. The super-complaints process is new and the guidance will be amended in the light of further experience in handling super-complaints.

WHO IS THIS GUIDANCE FOR?

1.3 It has been written for those consumer bodies who will be designated by the Department of Trade and Industry (the DTI) and thus be entitled to make super-complaints. In addition others, such as businesses or trade associations, may find it useful to know what is expected from a super-complainant and how the complaint is then managed.

WHY ISSUE GUIDANCE?

1.4 We want the new provision for super-complaints to work successfully and contribute to our aim of making markets work well for consumers.

1.5 The OFT has a commitment to transparency. We want to explain clearly our procedures and the reasons behind them. Section 11(7) of the Enterprise Act 2002 (the Act) also places upon the OFT a duty to issue guidance as to the presentation by the complainant of a reasoned case for the complaint.

WHAT IS IN THE GUIDANCE?

1.6 This guidance seeks to guide complainants on the presentation of a reasoned case for complaint. It also describes the processes and procedures the OFT and Regulators will apply in dealing with any super-complaint.

1.7 The guidance is organised as follows:

- **Chapter 2** sets out the super-complaint process in more detail. It provides a general explanation of what a super-complaint is and who will be able to make one. It also describes the factors the OFT and the Regulators will take into account when considering a super-complaint and sets out how super-complaints will be dealt with.
- **Chapter 3** explains the role of the OFT and the Regulators.
- **Chapter 4** lists contacts for further advice and information.
- The annexe provides guidance as to the kind of evidence that should be provided by super-complainants.

NOTES

[1] The text reflects the situation at July 2003. It is likely that the roles currently fulfilled by OFTEL, ITC and other bodies will be transferred to OFCOM in the future.

[2] See chapter 3 for further details on concurrency.

2. SUPER-COMPLAINTS

WHAT IS A SUPER-COMPLAINT?

[3.618]

2.1 A super-complaint, as defined in section 11(1) of the Act, is a complaint submitted by a designated consumer body that 'any feature, or combination of features, of a market in the UK for goods or services is or appears to be significantly harming the interests of consumers'.[3]

2.2 For the purposes of making a super-complaint a consumer is an individual who is supplied, or sought to be supplied, goods or services in the course of a business carried on by the person supplying or seeking to supply them. In other words the end consumer.[4]

2.3 A feature of a market has the same meaning as in section 131(2) of the Act. It may be:

- the structure of the market concerned or any aspect of that structure
- any conduct (whether or not in the market concerned) of one or more than one person who supplies or acquires goods or services in the market concerned, or
- any conduct relating to the market concerned of customers of any person who supplies or acquires goods or services. The market in question may be regional, national or supranational (where the UK forms part of the market) although the authority can only consider the effects within the UK.

2.4 The super-complaint process is intended to be a fast-track system for designated consumer bodies to bring to the attention of the OFT and the Regulators, market features that appear to be significantly harming the interests of consumers. When deciding whether or not to make a super-complaint, careful thought should be given as to whether the super-complaint process is the most effective route. It may be that specific competition or consumer legislation would provide a more immediate and/or effective means of satisfying and addressing the issue. For example when the feature of a market that is, or appears to be, significantly harming the interests of consumers relates to single firm conduct. Given the definition of consumer outlined at 2.2, super-complainants assessing the impact of a market feature should focus on the effect on end consumers and not business intermediaries.

WHO CAN MAKE A SUPER-COMPLAINT?

2.5 Only designated consumer bodies can make a super-complaint. Under section 11(5) of the Act it is specified that a consumer body has to be designated by the Secretary of State for Trade and Industry by order. The Secretary of State can make any organisation a designated consumer body provided it appears to her to represent the interests of consumers of any description and also meets any other criteria published by the Secretary of State which are applied when determining whether to make or revoke a designation. It is expected that those designated will be informed bodies who are in a strong position to represent the interests of groups of consumers and able to provide solid analysis and evidence in support of any super-complaint they may make.

2.6 The DTI has issued separate guidance for consumer bodies wishing to apply for designated status to make super-complaints. This guidance sets out the criteria for achieving designated status and the application process. The full text of the guidance is available at www.dti.gov.uk/enterpriseact/pdfs/superguide.pdf

2.7 Consumer bodies wishing to apply for designated status or those with general enquiries on the designation process should contact the DTI for further information. Contact details are given in chapter 4 of this guidance.

TO WHOM SHOULD A SUPER-COMPLAINT BE MADE?

2.8 A super-complaint should be made in writing to any authority with the duty to respond to super-complaints.[5] Information on these authorities is set out at chapter 3 and current contact details are at chapter 4.

2.9 Prior to submission, designated consumer bodies should ascertain the most appropriate recipient for each complaint. This will depend on the market that the complaint is concerned with. Complaints about markets regulated by the Regulators listed in chapter 3 should be sent to the Regulator responsible for that market. All other complaints should be sent to the OFT. In some circumstances it may not be clear who should receive a particular complaint. In these cases the complainant should contact the authorities most likely to be concerned for further advice.

2.10 Sending a complaint to the wrong authority or simultaneously to several authorities with concurrent duties could delay consideration of the complaint.

WHAT NEEDS TO BE IN A SUPER-COMPLAINT?

2.11 When making a complaint the super-complainant should provide a paper setting out the reasons why in its view a UK market for goods or services has a feature or combination of features which is or appears to be significantly harming the interests of consumers and should therefore be investigated. This paper should be supported, wherever possible, by documented facts and evidence.

2.12 The objective of presenting the case is to help the receiving authority undertake a full appraisal of whether any feature or combination of features of a UK market is or appears to be significantly harming consumer interests and what action, if any, should be taken. Super-complainants are not expected to provide the level of evidence necessary for the OFT or a Regulator to decide that immediate action is appropriate. However, they should present a reasoned case for further investigation. Complaints that are, or that appear to be, frivolous or vexatious will be rejected.

2.13 The annexe sets out the kind of evidence that designated consumer bodies should consider providing when deciding whether to make a super-complaint.

2.14 Complaints raised by individuals or bodies about specific instances of anti-competitive behaviour or infringements of consumer protection legislation will continue to be considered under other legislation as at present. Procedural safeguards that ensure fairness for those who may be the subject of enforcement action are unaffected by super-complaints.

HOW WILL SUPER-COMPLAINTS BE HANDLED?

2.15 Super-complaints will be given fast-track consideration. Those with the duty to respond to super-complaints are required to publish a reasoned response within 90 calendar days from the day after a complaint is received.[6]

2.16 On receipt of a complaint the super-complainant will be contacted within five working days to acknowledge receipt and let them know who within the OFT or relevant Regulator will be the main contact during the 90 day period.

2.17 The assigned official and supporting team will examine the contents of the complaint in more detail to see if it meets the criteria set out in section 11. All the criteria contained in section 11(1) must be satisfied for the complaint to receive super-complaint status.

2.18 If the complaint satisfies the criteria contained in section 11(1) the team will assess the quality of information and evidence supplied. They will decide whether it is possible to proceed on the basis of the information provided or if further evidence or clarification is required. In parallel the team will also form a view as to whether the super-complaint is frivolous or vexatious, in which case it will reject the complaint.

2.19 The team will also consider whether the complaint raises issues that may fall within the remit of another authority with concurrent duties. If this is the case the team will liaise with the relevant authority so an early decision can be made on how to progress the complaint.

2.20 Where the team finds that a reasoned case for complaint has not been made or that it requires clarification of the super-complaint, they will contact the super-complainant as soon as possible, setting out the further information or clarification that is required. The team will only request further information at this stage where it considers that the super-complainant is the best placed person to provide it. If the OFT or the relevant Regulator is better placed to obtain this information itself, it will do so. Where a request for clarification or further information is made, the super-complainant will be given a set time in which to respond to such a request. If it fails to do so, the team may consider making a formal response that no action will be taken with regard to the complaint. It is not possible to extend the 90 day response time if the complainant is not able to respond within the set time.

2.21 If appropriate, a meeting will be arranged between the team and the super-complainant to discuss any immediate questions about the evidence submitted and to indicate the broad lines of enquiry that will be taken to establish whether the super-complaint is well founded.

2.22 The team will then carry out wider enquiries with a view to testing the evidence provided and obtaining any further information it considers necessary in order to form a reasoned view on whether the super-complaint justifies further action. Exactly how it does this will be determined on a case by case basis but may involve:

- internal research
- public requests for information
- approaching any relevant businesses or trade associations for information
- approaching consumer organisations, trading standards departments, government departments and/or other public bodies for information, or
- any other necessary action.

2.23 The super-complainant will be kept informed of progress and may be contacted for clarification of issues or for further information as appropriate.

2.24 Within 90 days after the day on which it received the super-complaint, the OFT or the Regulator concerned has a duty to publish a public response stating what action, if any, it intends to take in response to the complaint. This 90 day period is the maximum time allowed for a response. Clearly, for some of the outcomes listed below a swifter decision may be made. The published response must also state the reasons for the decision taken.

WHAT ACTION WILL RESULT FROM A SUPER-COMPLAINT?

2.25 The possible outcomes of a super-complaint include:

- enforcement action by the OFT's competition or consumer regulation divisions
- finding that another authority with concurrent duties is better placed to deal with the complaint
- launching a market study into the issue
- making a market investigation reference to the Competition Commission (CC) if there is a competition problem
- action by a sectoral regulator with concurrent duties
- referring the complaint to a sectoral regulator without concurrent duties
- referring the complaint to the OFT for action (if the complaint was sent to a regulator with concurrent duties)
- referring the complaint to another consumer enforcement body
- finding the complaint requires no action
- finding the complaint to be unfounded
- dismissing the complaint as frivolous or vexatious.

2.26 The above list is not exhaustive. It should also be noted that a super-complaint could generate more than one outcome depending on the issues raised.

MARKET STUDIES

2.27 The market studies referred to above are distinct from market investigations, also referred to above, that are undertaken by the CC under Part 4 of the Act. Further details on when an issue is considered suitable by the OFT for reference to the CC can be found in the OFT's published guidance *Market Investigation References*.[7]

PUBLICITY FOR SUPER-COMPLAINTS

2.28 It is for a super-complainant to decide whether or not to issue a press notice recording that it has made a super-complaint. However, super-complainants should consult with the authority they intend to receive the complaint to avoid jeopardising investigations that could be hampered by prior disclosure of the complaint. In such circumstances, the agreement of the super-complainant may be sought to keep the existence of the super-complaint confidential for a period.

2.29 In some circumstances the receiving authority will take the view that it would be appropriate to issue a press notice itself, for example if the announcement of the complaint was to be combined with a public request for information. This will be decided on a case by case basis.

2.30 Super-complainants may be encouraged to create a public summary of their complaint, where not already in the public domain, to assist the submission of relevant information from interested parties.

FORMAL RESPONSES TO SUPER-COMPLAINTS

2.31 When making its decision on a super-complaint, the receiving authority is required by the Act to publish its decision on further action, if any, giving reasons for that decision.[8] As a minimum, this will be to place a copy of the response on its website to achieve publication. If considered appropriate, a press notice may also accompany the response.

NOTES

[3] Section 11(9)(a) of the Act says that "references to a feature of a market in the United Kingdom for goods or services have the same meaning as if contained in Part 4". A feature of a market is defined in section 131(2).

[4] See section 11(9)(b).

[5] At the time of writing these authorities are those listed in paragraph 1.1.

[6] By virtue of section 11(2) of the Act.

[7] OFT 511, March 2003.

[8] Section 11(2) and 11(3) of the Act.

3. CONCURRENT SUPER-COMPLAINT DUTIES

[3.619]

3.1 Under section 205 of the Act the Secretary of State for Trade and Industry has the power to provide by order for specified sectoral regulators to have concurrent duties in relation to super-complaints.[9] By virtue of the Enterprise Act 2002 (Super-complaints to Regulators) Order 2003 (SI 2003/1368) super-complaint duties have been given to: the Director General of Telecommunications,[10] the Gas and Electricity Markets Authority, the Northern Ireland Authority for Energy Regulation, the Director General of Water Services, the Rail Regulator and the Civil Aviation Authority.

AREAS OF RESPONSIBILITY

3.2 The following is a brief overview of the scope of the OFT and each Regulator to receive super-complaints. These authorities are able to respond to super-complaints using any of their competition enforcement and consumer protection powers, unless otherwise stated. This section is not exhaustive and further information can be obtained from the contact points listed in chapter 4.

- **The OFT:** The OFT's role is to make markets work well for consumers. It is responsible for promoting and protecting consumer interests throughout the UK, while ensuring that businesses are fair and competitive. It must respond to super-complaints made to it concerning any UK market.
- **The Civil Aviation Authority (the CAA):** The CAA is the regulator for the UK aviation industry. It must respond to super-complaints made to it on air traffic services in relation to its functions under the Transport Act 2000.
- **The Office of Gas and Electricity Markets (OFGEM):** OFGEM is the regulator for Britain's gas and electricity industries. It must respond to super-complaints made to it in relation to its functions provided under the Gas Act 1986 and the Electricity Act 1989, as amended by the Utilities Act 2000.
- **The Office of Telecommunications (OFTEL):** OFTEL is the regulator for the UK telecommunications industry. It must respond to super-complaints made to it in relation to its functions under the Telecommunications Act 1984.
- **The Office of Communications (OFCOM):** OFCOM will consider super-complaints in relation to communications markets after the enactment of the Communications Bill. Until then super-complaints on current telecommunications issues should be made to OFTEL.
- **The Northern Ireland Authority for Energy Regulation (OFREG-NI):** OFREG-NI is the regulator the Northern Ireland electricity and natural gas industries. It must respond to super-complaints made in relation to its functions provided under the Energy (Northern Ireland) Order 2003.
- **The Office of Water Services (OFWAT):** OFWAT is the regulator for the water and sewerage industry in England and Wales. It must respond to super-complaints made to it in relation to its functions under the Water Industry Act 1991.

- **The Office of the Rail Regulator (ORR):** The Rail Regulator is the economic regulator of the monopoly and dominant elements of the rail industry in Great Britain and must respond to super-complaints made to him in relation to his functions under the Railways Act 1993 as amended by the Transport Act 2000.

HOW WILL CONCURRENCY WORK?

3.3 Before making a super-complaint, a designated consumer body should first consider carefully which authority is best placed to deal with the complaint. The factors considered in determining which of the OFT or the Regulators deals with the issue include such matters as the sectoral knowledge of a Regulator and any previous contacts between the designated body and a Regulator, or with the OFT. In cases of uncertainty, further information can be obtained from the contact points listed at chapter 4.

3.4 It is recognised that there may be circumstances where it is not easy to decide the most appropriate recipient of a complaint; for example where the super-complaint raises issues with potentially overlapping responsibilities between Regulators and/or the OFT. The OFT and the Regulators have put in place suitable coordination procedures to ensure that complaints are addressed by the most appropriate authority and to ensure consistency of approach. These procedures are operated through the Concurrency Working Party (CWP). The CWP was set up to coordinate concurrent functions of the OFT and the Regulators under the Competition Act 1998. Its work has been extended to include the coordination of concurrent super-complaint duties. The procedures for coordinating concurrent super-complaints are completely separate from the concurrency provisions under the Competition Act 1998. Super-complaint Terms of Reference for the CWP are currently being finalised. A copy will be placed on the OFT's website in the near future.

NOTES

[9] Section 205(3) specifies that regulators have the meaning given in section 54(1) of the Competition Act 1998 (CA98). Only regulators listed in that section may be specified.

[10] The text reflects the situation at July 2003. It is likely that the roles currently fulfilled by OFTEL and other bodies will be transferred to OFCOM in the future.

4. CONTACT POINTS

[3.620]

4.1 Anyone with any queries regarding super-complaints, or designated consumer bodies considering making a complaint, should contact, in the first instance:[11]

OFT
Simone Collins
Office of Fair Trading
Fleetbank House
2–6 Salisbury Square
London EC4Y 8JX
Telephone: 020 7211 8558
Fax: 020 7211 8391
Email: supercomplaints@oft.gsi.gov.uk
www.oft.gov.uk

CAA
Paul Taylor
Civil Aviation Authority
45–49 Kingsway
London WC2B 6TE
Telephone: 020 7453 6232
Fax: 020 7453 6244
Email: paul.taylor@caaerg.org.uk
www.caa.co.uk

OFGEM
Andrew MacFaul
Office of Gas and Energy Markets
9 Millbank
London SW1P 3GE
Telephone: 020 7901 7083
Fax: 020 7901 7066
Email: andrew.macfaul@ofgem.gov.uk
www.ofgem.gov.uk

OFTEL
Michael Knowles
Office of Telecommunications
50 Ludgate Hill
London EC4M 7JJ
Telephone: 020 7634 8706
Fax: 020 7634 8949

Email: michael.knowles@oftel.gov.uk
www@oftel.gov.uk

OFCOM
Office of Communications
Riverside House
2A Southwark Bridge Road
London SE1 9HA
Telephone: 020 7981 3000
Fax: 020 7981 3333
www.ofcom.org.uk

OFREG-NI
Gerry Donnelly
Northern Ireland Authority for Energy Regulation
Brookmount Buildings
42 Fountain Street
Belfast BT1 5EE
Telephone: 028 90 311 575
Fax: 028 90 311 740
Email: gerry.donnelly@ofregni.gov.uk
www.ofreg.nics.gov.uk

OFWAT
Paul Hope
Head of Tariffs
Office of Water Services
Centre City Tower
7 Hill Street
Birmingham B5 4UA
Telephone: 0121 325 3612
Fax: 0121 625 1359
Email: paul.hope@ofwat.gsi.gov.uk
www.ofwat.gov.uk

ORR
Competition Team
Office of the Rail Regulator
1 Waterhouse Square
138–142 Holborn
London EC1N 2TQ
Telephone: 020 7282 2000
Fax: 020 7282 2043
Email: contact.cct@orr.gsi.gov.uk
www.rail-reg.gov.uk

4.2 Anyone interested in applying for designation status to make super-complaints or with general queries on the designation process should contact:

DTI
Marie Cawley
Department of Trade and Industry
Consumer and Competition Policy Directorate
Bay 417
1 Victoria Street
London, SW1H 0ET
Telephone: 020 7215 6771
Fax: 020 7215 0339
Email: marie.cawley@dti.gsi.gov.uk
www.dti.gov.uk

NOTES

11 This list will be revised from time to time and an up-to-date version placed on the OFT's website.

ANNEXE: GUIDANCE AS TO EVIDENCE TO BE PROVIDED BY SUPER-COMPLAINANTS

[3.621]

Complainants should consider whether any of the types of information listed below might be relevant to asserting that a feature or combination of features of the UK market in question is or appears to be harming the interests of consumers.[12]

Only some might be relevant in any given complaint but the list gives an indication of the kind of information the recipient might expect a super-complaint to contain depending on the nature of the problem identified by the complainant.

1. Details of the market (nature of the good or service) to which the complaint relates and whether there are particular aspects of the good or service relevant to potential problems for consumers such as infrequency or high cost of purchase.

2. Details of the nature of the complaint.

3. Whether the complaint relates to the market as a whole or only to certain suppliers or parts of the market.

4. How consumers' interests are harmed and an indication of the scale of detriment.

5. Whether all or only certain consumers of the relevant good or service are affected by the aspect(s) of the market to which the complaint relates.

6. Whether there is disproportionate purchase of the good or service by particular vulnerable groups of consumers such as the elderly or those on low incomes.

7. Available information on market shares by volume and value of suppliers in the relevant market for the good or service. Any information on changes in market shares over the past few years.

8. Evidence of barriers to entry to the market by existing or new suppliers.

9. Information on the level and impact of buying power in the relevant market and whether any benefits from exercising buyer power are passed onto consumers.

10. Details or information on:

- current retail/wholesale prices (as relevant) for the good or service
- discounts to some or all customers
- different prices charged to different classes or categories of customer
- levels of price dispersion in the market more generally
- price trends over the past few years
- comparative information on different suppliers' prices and the timing of price changes.

11. Information (if available) on the general level of profitability of suppliers in the relevant sector for the good or service.

12. Any evidence of practices by suppliers in the sector that may be restricting or distorting competition.

13. Any evidence of high-pressure selling techniques or other sales practices that could be having detrimental effects on consumers.

14. Whether there are complex contractual terms for the good or service.

15. Whether the relevant good or service is only supplied together with other goods or services (rather than separately).

16. Details of any costs incurred by consumers as a direct result of switching to alternative suppliers of the relevant good or service. Evidence of the degree of switching.

17. Any available indicators of the general level of quality of goods or services in the relevant sector.

18. Any available indicators showing how well informed consumers in the sector are relative to suppliers about the quality and prices of goods and services offered by different suppliers.

19. Information relating to whether complex aspects of the good or service, the way in which it is supplied, or difficulties in assessing quality, presents particular problems for consumers.

20. Details of means of redress available to consumers of the good or service who have complaints, and their effectiveness.

21. Details of any codes of practice, whether or not approved by the OFT, that apply to the good or service.

22. Details of relevant policies and legislation undertaken by local or central government, EU or other public bodies.

23. Details of organisations, such as governing bodies, interest and lobby groups that may affect and/or be affected by the market in question.

NOTES

[12] This section is not exhaustive and complainants may wish to consider other factors when making a reasoned case for the complaint.

SUPER-COMPLAINT CONCURRENT DUTIES: TERMS OF REFERENCE OF THE CONCURRENCY WORKING PARTY (OFT 548, NOVEMBER 2003)

[3.622]

NOTES

As to the construction of this document (following the abolition of the OFT and Competition Commission), see further the note "The Competition and Markets Authority (references to the OFT and Competition Commission etc)" in the introductory notes to Part 3 preceding **[3.1]**.

Note also that all references to market studies or investigations must be read in the light of Market studies and market investigations: Supplemental guidance on the CMA's approach (CMA3); in the case of conflict, CMA3 prevails.

A. INTRODUCTION

[3.623]

1 Super-complaints are made by designated consumer bodies under section 11 of the Enterprise Act 2002 (EA02). Section 11 of the EA02 is applied by the Office of Fair Trading (OFT) concurrently with the Director General of Telecommunications,[1] the Gas and Electricity Markets Authority, the Northern Ireland Authority for Energy Regulation, the Director General of Water Services, the Rail Regulator and the Civil Aviation Authority (the Regulators).[2] These are the same Regulators as those who have concurrent powers under the Competition Act 1998 (CA98).

2 The Concurrency Working Party (CWP) was formed in 1997 to co-ordinate concurrent functions of its members in relation to the CA98. In 2003 the remit of the CWP was extended to include the co-ordination of super-complaint duties. The CWP is chaired by a representative of the OFT. Membership currently consists of the OFT and the Regulators with concurrent CA98 and EA02 powers, and includes the Independent Television Commission (ITC), Postcomm and OFCOM who sit as observers but do not have concurrent powers.

3 The aims of the CWP in relation to section 11 of the EA02 are:

- to facilitate, to the greatest extent possible, a consistent approach by the OFT and the Regulators to the requirement to publish a response to a super-complaint made under section 11 of the EA02
- to consider practical working arrangements between them
- to provide a vehicle for the discussion of matters of common interest, and the sharing of information where appropriate and where legally permitted
- to co-ordinate the provision of guidance on section 11 of the EA02 to the public, and
- to agree and implement procedures for joint working on super-complaints.

NOTES

[1] The text reflects the situation now. The role currently fulfilled by OFTEL in relation to super-complaints will be undertaken by OFCOM once the Communications Act commences although it will be in relation to activities connected with communications matters.

[2] The various Regulators are given their concurrent powers to deal with super-complaints by virtue of section 205 EA02 and the 2003 Regulations (see below).

B. LEGAL REQUIREMENTS

[3.624]

4 It is desirable that duties under section 11 should be exercised so as to ensure consistency of approach in relation to super-complaint handling and outcomes. This document represents a commitment by the members of CWP to work together to achieve this goal.

SECTION 11: THE OFT'S DUTY TO RESPOND TO SUPER-COMPLAINTS

5 A super-complaint is a complaint made by a designated consumer body that any feature, or combination of features, of a market in the United Kingdom for goods or services is or appears to be significantly harming the interests of consumers.

6 Sections 11(2) & (3) impose a duty on the OFT to publish a response to any super-complaint received, stating how it proposes that the complaint be dealt with. This response must be published within 90 days from the day after the complaint is received by the OFT.

THE ENTERPRISE ACT 2002 (SUPER-COMPLAINTS TO REGULATORS) ORDER 2003 (THE REGULATIONS)

7 Regulation 2 of the Regulations imposes on the Regulators a duty to respond to super-complaints made to them in the same manner as the OFT under section 11(2) & (3) of the EA02 if the complaint concerns a market in relation to which that Regulator has functions.

SECTION 11: ISSUING OF GUIDANCE

8 The OFT is required by section 11(7) of the EA02 to issue guidance as to the presentation by the complainant of a reasoned case for the complaint. The Regulators do not have this duty but to facilitate a consistent approach this guidance has been published by the OFT after consultation with (and endorsement by) the Regulators through the CWP as *Guidance for designated consumer bodies making super-complaints.*

9 The OFT and the Regulators may also issue such other guidance as appears to be appropriate for the purpose of section 11.

C. AREAS OF CO-OPERATION

[3.625]

10 The Regulations do not make provision for the co-ordination of the performance of the duty to respond to super-complaints under section 11. Therefore the co-ordination of super-complaint duties will be based on policies agreed and applied through the CWP.

11 The OFT and the Regulators believe that the CWP is a means by which concurrent application of section 11 can be delivered, to meet the objective of achieving, as far as possible, a consistent approach to handling super-complaints. The OFT and the Regulators recognise that there are benefits to be derived from co-operation and consistency of approach, where possible, in administering a new legal framework.

12 Any CWP member receiving a super-complaint has the responsibility for identifying that it meets the legal criteria of a super-complaint under section 11 and identifying areas of concurrent jurisdiction. All members of the CWP will be informed of the receipt, substance (as permitted)[3] and proposed response of any super-complaint. Any CWP member who may have an interest in a super-complaint that has been received by another CWP member will inform the recipient of their interest as soon as possible. Only CWP members who declare an interest will have the option to be kept informed either of the day to day administrative matters or just the significant developments of each complaint.

13 Appropriate procedures will be agreed to ensure application of section 11 by CWP members and to facilitate efficient case handling.

NOTES

[3] The level of detail that can be shared with any CWP members including those without concurrent jurisdiction is subject to legal restrictions on the disclosure of information.

WHERE A SUPER-COMPLAINT IS MADE EITHER TO ONE REGULATOR OR THE OFT

14 In many cases where a super-complaint is made to either one Regulator or the OFT the cause for complaint will only concern the authority who must respond to it. The complaint can then be progressed with little if any input required from other CWP members.

15 However it is possible that a super-complaint made to either one Regulator or the OFT could span the jurisdiction of other CWP members. It is envisaged that normally in such cases the relevant authorities will agree areas of concurrent jurisdiction and will work together to produce a joint response, but recognising that only the authority to which the super-complaint was made has the duty to respond.

16 Other possible outcomes include:[4]

- advising the complainant to make the same super-complaint to another more appropriate CWP member with a duty to respond to super-complaints[5]
- advising the complainant that the super-complaint has been transferred to another CWP member or other (non CWP member) authority better placed to investigate the complaint.[6]

17 The recipient of the super-complaint will acknowledge the contributions made by other actively involved CWP members in its public response.

NOTES

[4] This list is not exhaustive and other outcomes may be identified.

[5] The complaint remains a super-complaint and the new recipient must respond accordingly.

[6] At this point the complaint will cease to be a super-complaint.

WHERE A SUPER-COMPLAINT IS MADE SIMULTANEOUSLY TO MORE THAN ONE CWP MEMBER

18 Such super-complaints must be responded to by each CWP member because each will have a duty to respond in this situation. In these cases it is envisaged that the relevant authorities will agree areas of concurrent jurisdiction and where necessary establish which part of the complaint each recipient will focus on.

19 It is desirable that when the same super-complaint is sent simultaneously to more than one CWP member that the published responses from those in receipt of the complaint are consistent with each other or that a joint response is made. To achieve this it will be necessary for the authorities to consult with one another to identify main issues and agree working arrangements, and to share knowledge and expertise where appropriate.

20 Possible outcomes include:[7]

- only the better placed CWP member in receipt of the super-complaint publishes a full response, and any other member in receipt of the same complaint advises the complainant that this will be the case
- those in receipt of the super-complaint publish a joint response
- advising the complainant to make the same super-complaint to another more appropriate CWP member with a duty to respond to super-complaints[8]
- advising the complainant that the super-complaint has been transferred to another CWP member or other (non CWP member) authority better placed to investigate the complaint.[9]

21 Where a joint response is not possible or preferable, each individual response will refer to any additional responses made by other CWP recipients of the super-complaint.

INFORMATION SHARING

22 The CWP will share information with regard to general policy and precedent relating to the application and interpretation of section 11 in order to facilitate a consistency of approach. At CWP meetings the OFT and each Regulator will provide where possible and in an appropriate form, having regard to any legal restrictions on disclosure, a brief summary of policy issues arising from current super-complaints. Where a complaint raises new issues of general policy or of precedent in respect of the application or interpretation of section 11, the CWP member who received the complaint will endeavour to bring these issues to the attention of the CWP for discussion before publicly responding to the super-complaint. Where a super-complaint has been responded to, the CWP may wish to discuss any issues of common interest arising from the complaint.

23 CWP members may use their discretion (subject to legal restrictions on the disclosure of information) in identifying issues within a super-complaint that could be usefully shared with any other members of the CWP.

24 The OFT and the Regulators between them have considerable knowledge, experience and expertise across a wide range of sectors and this should be shared where appropriate and possible. The particular sectoral knowledge of the ITC, Postcomm and OFCOM are noted.

NOTES

7 This list is not exhaustive and other outcomes may be identified.

8 The complaint remains a super-complaint and the new recipient must respond accordingly.

9 At this point the complaint will cease to be a super-complaint.

WORKING ARRANGEMENTS

25 The CWP will normally meet every two months but super-complaints need not be discussed at every meeting. To aid efficient handling of business attendance will generally be limited to one or two persons from each authority. There will be flexibility to ensure that additional meetings to deal with specific issues can be called at short notice where necessary. Ad hoc groups may be formed where appropriate and where there is a need for the discussion of super-complaint issues to take place separately from the main CWP meetings.

26 It may be necessary for staff of the OFT and the Regulators to work together on a particular super-complaint. In particular this may be required when one authority is the recipient of a super-complaint that in part spans the jurisdiction of another. It is desirable in these situations that the relevant authorities share their knowledge and expertise so that the outcome identified in a published response is based on the most appropriate use of available resources.

27 Best practice for joint working procedures, information sharing and providing guidance will be agreed. Any proposed changes will be discussed and agreed by the CWP.

DISPUTE RESOLUTION

28 If CWP members with joint jurisdiction are not able to agree over areas of responsibility on a super-complaint, the matter will be put before the CWP forum for further guidance and resolution.

29 In the unlikely event that the CWP is evenly split and agreement cannot be reached the OFT will have the casting vote. (However, it will only be used as a last resort.)

MARKET INVESTIGATION REFERENCES (OFT 511, MARCH 2006)

Guidance About the Making of References Under Part 4 of the Enterprise Act

[3.626]

NOTES

As to the construction of this document (following the abolition of the OFT and Competition Commission), see further the note "The Competition and Markets Authority (references to the OFT and Competition Commission etc)" in the introductory notes to Part 3 preceding **[3.1]**.

Note also that all references to issues of jurisdiction or procedure in mergers cases or to market studies or investigations must be read in the light of Mergers: Guidance on the CMA's jurisdiction and procedure (CMA2) and Market studies and market investigations: Supplemental guidance on the CMA's approach (CMA3); in the case of conflict, CMA2 or CMA3 prevail.

See further CMA 3 Market Studies and Market Investigations: Supplemental guidance on the CMA's approach (revised July 2017). The Annex to the Guidance (at **[3.655]**) lists changes to this Guidance consequential on the revision of CMA 3.

CONTENTS

PART I
THE REFERENCE PROCESS

PART II
APPLICATION OF THE REFERENCE TEST

PART I
THE REFERENCE PROCESS

1. INTRODUCTION

[3.627]
1.1 UK competition law was strengthened by the Competition Act 1998 (CA98) which came into force on 1 March 2000. CA98 prohibits anti-competitive agreements and concerted practices, and conduct amounting to the abuse of a dominant position, where UK trade is affected. However, the government retained the monopoly reference provisions of the Fair Trading Act 1973 (FTA) on the grounds that these powers, particularly complex monopoly references, allowed market-wide investigations by the Competition Commission (CC).

1.2 The market investigation reference provisions of the Enterprise Act (the Act) replace these FTA provisions. It will primarily be for the Office of Fair Trading (OFT) to make market investigation references, but, as with CA98 and the monopoly reference provisions of the FTA, certain sectoral regulators have concurrent jurisdiction with the OFT to make references within their regulated sectors. The sectoral regulators are the Office of Communications (OFCOM), the Gas and Electricity Markets Authority (OFGEM), the Director General of Water Services (OFWAT), the Northern Ireland Authority for Energy Regulation (OFREG NI), the Office of Rail Regulation (ORR), and the Civil Aviation Authority (CAA).[1] In specified circumstances the appropriate minister will also be able to make a market investigation reference.

1.3 The purpose of this guidance is to indicate how the OFT intends to apply the provisions of the Act relating to the making of market investigation references. It does not deal with ministerial references.

1.4 The OFT will apply the principles of the Enforcement Concordat to its work on market investigation references (as to its other enforcement activities) and this guidance is based on these principles.[2] It is not binding, but will help business, its advisers and consumers to understand the grounds on which the OFT may decide that a market investigation reference is justified. It is not intended to provide a prescriptive framework for analysis nor do the various issues discussed constitute an exhaustive list of factors that may prevent, restrict or distort (adversely affect) competition, not least because markets and thinking about competition continue to evolve. The guidance will be updated as and when necessary.

1.5 The guidance is structured as follows: the remainder of this chapter sets out the OFT's powers to make references (referred to elsewhere in the guidance as 'the reference test'); the rest of Part I describes other aspects of the reference process, such as when references will be made and various procedural points; and Part II explains how the OFT will apply the reference test.

Power to make references

1.6 Under section 131 of the Act, the OFT may make a market investigation reference to the CC where it has reasonable grounds for suspecting that any feature, or combination of features, of a market in the United Kingdom for goods or services prevents, restricts, or distorts competition in connection with the supply or acquisition of any goods or services in the UK or a part of the UK. However, a reference cannot be made by the OFT where an undertaking has been accepted in lieu of a reference or where a ministerial reference of the same matter has been made but not determined by the CC.

1.7 Section 131(2) states that a feature of a market is to be construed as a reference to:
- the structure of the market concerned or any aspect of that structure
- any conduct (whether or not in the market concerned) of one or more than one person who supplies or acquires goods or services in the market concerned, or
- any conduct relating to the market concerned of customers of any person who supplies or acquires goods or services.

1.8 Section 131(3) adds that 'conduct' includes any failure to act (whether intentional or not) and any other unintentional conduct.

1.9 It may not always be clear whether a feature of a market that affects competition is best described as structural or as an aspect of conduct; for example, a firm's supply contracts or distribution arrangements (a matter of conduct) may add to entry barriers in a market (a structural feature). Provided the relevant feature is clearly identified, categorising it as conduct or structure is a semantic issue. The separate references to structure and conduct in section 131 do not require the OFT to state whether particular features of a market that are the subject of a reference are to be considered structural features or some aspect of conduct.

1.10 The OFT has the discretion rather than a duty to make a market investigation reference where the statutory criteria appear to be met. Before making a reference, it must therefore consider:
- whether it has reasonable grounds to suspect that competition is prevented, restricted or distorted in some market in the UK or in a part of the UK
- whether it is a feature, or combination of features, of a market that gives rise to this adverse effect on competition, and
- whether a market investigation reference to the CC would be the most appropriate way of proceeding.

The first two points are considered in Part II of this guidance, the third point is discussed in the next chapter of Part I.

1.11 Following a reference it will be for the CC to decide whether competition is indeed prevented, restricted or distorted, and (if so) what, if any, action should be taken to remedy the adverse effect on competition or any detrimental effect on customers resulting from it (in the form of higher prices, lower quality or less choice of goods or services, or less innovation in relation to goods or services in any market in the UK).

NOTES

Note that para 1.6 above should be read in conjunction with paragraphs 1.21 to 1.24 of the revised CMA 3 which explain how the reference process is changed to take account of the formation of the CMA. See Annex A of CMA 3 at **[3.655]**.

Note that para 1.7 above should be read in conjunction with paragraph 2.32 of the revised CMA 3 which explains that only features relating to conduct can be the subject of a cross-market reference. See Annex A of CMA 3 at **[3.655]**.

1 References to the OFT in this guidance are to be interpreted as applying to these regulators with concurrent jurisdiction, unless the text indicates otherwise.

2 Further details of the Concordat and its principles can be found at www.cabinet-office.gov.uk/regulation/publicsector/enforcement/enforcement.htm

2. WHEN REFERENCES MAY BE MADE

[3.628]

2.1 The OFT will only make references to the CC when the reference test set out in section 131 of the Act and, in its view, each of the following criteria have been met:

- it would not be more appropriate to deal with the competition issues identified by applying CA98 or using other powers available to the OFT or, where appropriate, to sectoral regulators
- it would not be more appropriate to address the problem identified by means of undertakings in lieu of a reference
- the scale of the suspected problem, in terms of its adverse effect on competition, is such that a reference would be an appropriate response to it
- there is a reasonable chance that appropriate remedies will be available.

These points are discussed in the remainder of this chapter and the OFT's application of the reference test in Part II.

Relationship with CA98

2.2 CA98 prohibits agreements, which have the object or effect of preventing, restricting or distorting competition, and abuses of a dominant position. These two prohibitions are described in the Competition Act Guidance *The Chapter I Prohibition* (OFT 401) and *The Chapter II Prohibition* (OFT 402). Market investigations are concerned with something different from particular anti-competitive agreements or abuses of dominance. Their purpose is to determine whether the process of competition is working effectively in markets as a whole. They will provide a framework for identifying, analysing and, where appropriate, remedying industry-wide or market-wide competition problems which there is no adequate basis for addressing under CA98.

2.3 When dealing with a suspected competition problem it is the OFT's policy always to consider first whether it may involve an infringement of one or both of the CA98 prohibitions and to investigate accordingly. It will only go on to consider a reference to the CC in one of two circumstances:

- when it has reasonable grounds to suspect that there are market features, which prevent, restrict or distort competition, but not to establish a breach of the CA98 prohibitions
- when action under CA98 has been or is likely to be ineffective for dealing with the adverse effect on competition identified.

Sectoral regulators may, in addition, wish to exercise their discretion and consider whether it would be more appropriate to deal with a competition problem under any sector specific legislation or rules.

2.4 Adverse effects on competition that do not involve either agreements between undertakings or abuses of dominance are beyond the reach of CA98. Market investigation references are therefore likely to focus on competition problems arising from uncoordinated parallel conduct by several firms or industry-wide features of a market in cases where the OFT does not have reasonable grounds to suspect the existence of anti-competitive agreements or dominance. Such problems may have a variety of sources such as competition-dampening common practices whose origins have long been forgotten, customers who are poorly informed relative to suppliers (information asymmetries), and sheer inertia on the part of ostensible competitors.

2.5 Oligopolistic markets in which firms engage in apparently parallel behaviour while falling short of actually concerting their actions (often referred to as tacit collusion) present a more complicated issue. The OFT recognises that EC case law has confirmed that the concept of collective dominance may be applicable in these circumstances, which would bring the conduct involved within the ambit of CA98. But this case law does not at present cover all types of coordinated parallel behaviour that may have an adverse effect on competition. Indeed, the judgement of the Court in the **Airtours** case appears to limit the applicability of the concept of collective dominance.[3] Market features that can lead to adverse effects on competition in an oligopolistic market can be wider than the conditions that the case law has found to be necessary for collective dominance, that is, for oligopolists successfully to engage in tacit collusion. Furthermore, what qualifies as an abuse of collective dominance is underdeveloped in the case law. For these reasons a market investigation reference will be able to address wider competition concerns than could be addressed by a CA98 case and might, therefore, be a better way of proceeding.

2.6 Market investigation references may, in certain circumstances, also be relevant for dealing with possible competition problems arising from vertical agreements. Such agreements, unless they involve price fixing, are currently excluded from the Chapter I prohibition of CA98. Although it is possible for the OFT to withdraw the benefit of the CA98 exclusion from a particular agreement this might not be the best way of dealing with the consequences of a network of parallel agreements involving many firms, particularly when the question of penalties does not arise. A market investigation reference may be the most appropriate way to proceed where vertical agreements are prevalent in a market and have the effect of preventing the entry of new competitors, but there is no evidence of collusion between the firms involved that might have caused this situation to arise. For the treatment of networks of vertical agreements which affect trade between European Union Member States (and hence may be caught by Articles 81 and 82 of the EC Treaty), see paragraphs 2.17 to 2.18.

2.7 The problems referred to in the previous three paragraphs involve industry-wide market features or multi-firm conduct. It is likely that the great majority of references the OFT makes will be of that type. Generally speaking single-firm conduct will, where necessary and possible, be dealt with under CA98 or appropriate sectoral legislation or rules. It is not the present intention of the OFT to make market references based on the conduct of a single firm, whether dominant or not, where there are no other features of a market that adversely affect competition.

2.8 This general principle is subject to the following comments and qualifications:

- In many cases anti-competitive conduct by a single firm may be associated with structural features of the market, for example barriers to entry or regulation and government policies, or conduct by customers which have adverse effects on competition. These other market features are discussed in sections 5 and 7 of this guidance. Where they are present a market investigation reference may be more appropriate than action under CA98 even though only a single firm appears to be conducting itself anti-competitively.
- The principle will be reviewed should the development of case law relating to the CA98 Chapter II prohibition give good grounds for believing that the prohibition is inadequate to deal with conduct by a single firm which has an adverse effect on competition.
- The OFT might decide to make a market investigation reference when there has been an abuse of a dominant position and it is clear that nothing short of a structural remedy going beyond what is appropriate under CA98 would be effective in dealing with the consequential adverse effect on competition. This position will be reviewed in the light of changes to CA98 arising from the implementation in the UK of the modernisation of EC competition law (see paragraphs 2.9 to 2.18).

Relationship with EC competition law

2.9 The European Community has revised the main regulation implementing Articles 81 and 82 of the EC Treaty (Regulation 17/62/EEC), a process widely known as 'modernisation'. The new regulation[4] will apply from 1 May 2004.

2.10 The modernisation regulation gives the competition authorities and courts in Member States the responsibility, shared with the European Commission, for the application and enforcement of Articles 81 and 82.[5] It imposes an obligation on competition authorities and courts to apply Articles 81 and 82 where they apply national competition law to agreements or practices which may affect trade between Member States. It also imposes certain limits on the use of national competition law.

2.11 When the modernisation regulation comes into force, where the OFT applies national competition law such as the Enterprise Act to agreements, decisions or concerted practices within the meaning of Article 81(1) which may affect trade between Member States it must also apply Article 81. In addition, national competition law cannot prohibit agreements which may affect trade between Member States:

- that do not restrict competition law within the meaning of Article 81(1)
- that fulfil the conditions of Article 81(3), or
- that are covered by an EC block exemption.

The modernisation regulation does not prevent the application of stricter national law to pursue behaviour by an undertaking not involving an agreement or concerted practice where that behaviour falls short of an abuse of dominance.

2.12 In the context of a market investigation by the CC, the obligation to apply Articles 81 or 82 in parallel with national competition law will arise only at the stage where remedies are imposed by the CC following a reference. The obligation does not affect any investigation carried out by the OFT to determine whether to make a reference, the making of a reference to the CC or the investigation by the CC.

2.13 When the modernisation regulation has come into force, the OFT will adapt its current procedure to ensure that it applies Articles 81 and 82 in parallel with national competition law. When dealing with a suspected competition problem, the OFT will consider first both whether it might involve an infringement of CA98 and whether it might involve any infringement of Article 81 and/or 82.

2.14 For this reason it is likely to be rare that a reference to the CC will include agreements within the meaning of Article 81(1) except in the special circumstances discussed in paragraphs 2.17 to 2.18. The CC would be unable to impose remedies addressing such agreements without parallel proceedings being opened under Article 81 and the OFT would take this into account when considering whether to make a reference. If an agreement within the meaning of Article 81(1) is uncovered during the course of the CC's investigation the CC would consider whether to remit the agreement back to the OFT for consideration under Article 81.

2.15 It is possible that a reference could be made that included conduct which the CC investigation showed was in fact conduct that amounted to an abuse of a dominant position prohibited by Article 82.

Part 3 CMA and other Guidelines

In such cases, the CC would complete its investigation and impose remedies under the Act. The OFT would then take these remedies into account when carrying out an Article 82 investigation.

2.16 As a general rule the OFT will avoid actually investigating a suspected infringement of Articles 81 or 82 simultaneously with a CC investigation of the same agreement, decision, concerted practice or conduct, both to reduce undue burdens on business and as a matter of administrative good practice. For the same reasons it will not normally refer a market to the CC when a significant feature of that market is being investigated by the European Commission under Articles 81 or 82.

2.17 Many vertical agreements fall within the terms of the EC block exemption regulation on vertical agreements (Regulation 2790/99/EC). Article 29 of the modernisation regulation permits the competition authorities of Member States to withdraw the benefit of any block exemption regulation from specified agreements within their own territory if both of the following conditions are met:

- the territory of the Member State, or a part of it, has all the characteristics of a distinct geographic market, and
- the agreements in question have effects incompatible with Article 81(3) in the territory of the Member State.

These provisions also apply to agreements that fall within the block exemption regulation on motor vehicles (Regulation 1400/2002/EC).

2.18 Where the OFT has reasonable grounds to suspect that these conditions apply to one or more markets in the UK, it may decide to refer the relevant markets to the CC for investigation. It will be open to the CC, if it finds that competition has been prevented, restricted or distorted by the network of similar vertical agreements and that the conditions as set out above have been met, to recommend to the OFT that it withdraw the benefit of the relevant block exemption regulation. If the OFT accepts this recommendation and the benefit of the exemption is withdrawn it may then take action against the agreements in question under Article 81 or CA98.

OFT market studies

2.19 The OFT proactively studies markets that appear not to be working well for consumers.[6] Where competition or consumer regulation enforcement action (including a reference to the CC) does not appear, initially, to be the appropriate response, an OFT market study is undertaken. The decision to launch such a study is made public and the report prepared at its conclusion is published. The possible outcomes of these studies, dealt with in the reports, include:

- enforcement action by the OFT's competition and consumer regulation divisions
- a reference to the Competition Commission (provided the criteria described in paragraph 2.1 are met)
- recommendations for changes in laws and regulations
- campaigns to promote consumer education and awareness, and
- a clean bill of health.

Where a reference to the CC is considered by the OFT and rejected, it will explain in its report why it reached this decision.

Undertakings in lieu

2.20 Section 154 of the Act gives the OFT the power to accept undertakings instead of making a reference to the CC. In exercising this power the OFT must have regard to the need to achieve as comprehensive a solution, as is reasonable and practicable, to any adverse effects on competition identified (and any detrimental effects on customers so far as they result or may be expected to result from such adverse effects). It may also have regard, as appropriate, to the effect of the possible undertakings on any relevant customer benefits arising from a feature or features of the markets concerned.

2.21 Undertakings in lieu of a reference are unlikely to be common. In many cases the OFT will not have done a sufficiently detailed investigation of a competition problem, prior to making a reference to the CC, to be able to judge with any certainty whether particular undertakings will achieve as comprehensive a solution as is reasonable and practicable. This is particularly likely to be the case when the adverse effects on competition arise from market features involving several firms or industry-wide practices. Moreover, trying to negotiate undertakings with several parties, in circumstances in which possible adverse effects on competition have not been comprehensively analysed, is likely to pose serious practical difficulties. By contrast, where an adverse effect on competition arises from the conduct of a very few firms there may be more scope for accepting undertakings in lieu, provided that the OFT is confident that they will achieve a comprehensive solution.

2.22 In assessing customer benefits the OFT will take into account the same factors as the CC discusses in its guidance.[7] Such benefits comprise lower prices, higher quality or greater choice of goods or services in any UK market, or greater innovation in relation to such goods or services.

2.23 Before accepting any undertaking in lieu the OFT must publish the proposed undertaking in a notice which, among other things, states the purpose and effect of the undertaking and identifies the adverse effect on competition and any resulting detrimental effect on customers identified by the OFT that the proposed undertaking is intended to remedy (the list of all the points to be included in such notices is given in section 155(2) of the Act). The OFT must consider any representations arising from the publication of the notice. There is a power for the Secretary of State to intervene at this stage if he believes that wider public interest matters are relevant to the case. The Secretary of State is able to block the acceptance of undertakings in lieu when he believes that a public interest consideration specified in the legislation (currently only national security) is relevant. In such a case, the outcome may be other undertakings in lieu or a reference.

2.24 When an undertaking in lieu is accepted, the OFT may not make a market investigation reference involving the same goods or services for a period of 12 months unless it considers the undertaking has been breached or it has been given false or misleading information by the person responsible for giving the undertaking.

2.25 The FTA was amended in 1994 to give the Director General of Fair Trading the power to accept undertakings in lieu of a monopoly reference to the CC. These powers have never been used for monopoly references though on a few occasions informal assurances (rather than statutory undertakings) have been accepted. The absence of the use of powers to accept undertakings in lieu in the past suggests that their use in future will not be extensive.

2.26 In line with existing policy the OFT will keep under review all undertakings given in lieu of a reference and orders or undertakings arising from CC reports. It will also consider any representations received from interested parties that undertakings should be varied or their signatories released from them. In the absence of such representations reviews will be conducted at five yearly intervals.

Scale of the problem

2.27 The OFT will only make a reference when it has reasonable grounds to suspect that the adverse effects on competition of features of a market are significant. In making this assessment it will consider whether these suspected adverse effects are likely to have a significant detrimental effect on customers through higher prices, lower quality, less choice or less innovation. Where it seems likely that this effect is not significant the OFT will normally take the view that the burden on business, particularly in terms of management time, and the public expenditure costs of an investigation by the CC are likely to be disproportionate in relation to any benefits that may be obtained from remedying the adverse effects.

2.28 It is not possible to make a definitive statement about the circumstances in which adverse effects on competition, or the customer detriments arising from them, will be regarded as not significant. However, the following factors are relevant and will be taken into account by the OFT:

- **The size of the market**. Generally speaking, the cost of a CC investigation into a very small market would not be justified.[8] However, problems in some relatively small specialised or local markets could have a significant detrimental impact on customers affected by them, in which case a reference may be justified.
- **The proportion of the market affected by the feature giving rise to adverse effects on competition**. When this proportion is small the adverse effects will be unlikely to lead to significant customer detriment. The OFT does not think that it would be appropriate to specify a figure for the proportion of the market affected below which it would not make a reference, not least because the precise definition of the market (or markets) concerned and the extent of the market features having an adverse affect on competition may not be clearly established until after the CC has conducted its investigation. However, where possible the OFT will act in a way that is broadly consistent with its practice when applying its powers under CA98. In relation to the Chapter I prohibition (on anti-competitive agreements), it has said that such agreements generally have no appreciable effect on competition if the parties' combined share of the relevant market does not exceed 25 per cent, although there will be circumstances in which this is not the case particularly where agreements involve price fixing.
- **The persistence of the feature giving rise to adverse effects on competition**. If the feature concerned seems likely to be short-lived (for example, because of an expected change in regulations) or clearly relates to a one-off incident, and there are no other market features giving cause for concern, then a reference to the CC is not likely to be justified.

2.29 In some cases the market features that adversely affect competition may also produce offsetting customer benefits. Such benefits might arise, for example, where customers gain when more of them use the same good or service (network effects) or where there are substantial economies of scale. Where the OFT is confident that offsetting customer benefits exceed the likely detriment from the adverse effect on competition it will not make a reference. However, where there is uncertainty the OFT will normally wish to leave the weighing of benefits and detriments to the CC.

Availability of remedies and value of CC reports

2.30 The OFT will also take into account the likely availability of appropriate remedies in the event that the suspected adverse effects on competition were found by the CC to exist. Where the OFT has not investigated a market in sufficient depth to be confident that it is in a position to identify the possible remedies it will not give this factor much weight. However, where the OFT has a reasonably good understanding of a market, perhaps because it has already performed a market study, or because a reference is being considered following an investigation under CA98, it may decide not to make a reference when it believes that no appropriate remedies by means of direct action by the CC are likely to be available. For example, it may have established that a particular market is global in scope, or at least goes much wider than the UK, and that any remedy for the UK (which would be all that was available under the Act) would have no discernible impact on the way the market operated even in the UK. The OFT will have regard, however, to situations in which a CC investigation and report with recommendations for action (including recommendations for action by the European Commission or other bodies) is likely to make a useful contribution.

2.31 Similarly, where the OFT is satisfied that adverse effects on competition arise primarily from laws, regulations, or government policies it will have regard to the fact that the CC will not be able directly to remedy such adverse effects. In such circumstances, the OFT itself may submit a report to the Government as an outcome of a market study (see paragraph 2.19 and note 6) or it may make a reference when it considers a CC investigation and report would be more appropriate, for example because the CC has greater resources, stronger legal powers to require information, or more formal evidence gathering procedures. In either case, in the event of an adverse finding, the reporting body would make reasoned recommendations for changes to the relevant laws or regulations, and advise on policy options as appropriate.

2.32 Although the availability of remedies and the prospective value of CC investigations and reports will be the most important practical issues taken into account by the OFT when considering a reference, it will also consider others where relevant. In particular, it may take into account whether the evidence that would enable the CC to reach a conclusion is likely to be available.

NOTES

Note that para 2.19 above should be read in conjunction with paragraphs 2.6 to 2.10 of the revised CMA 3 which explain the requirement to publish a market study notice and the applicable timescales for the market study stage. See Annex A of CMA 3 at **[3.655]**.

3 Case T-342/99 *Airtours v Commission* [2002] 5 CMLR 317. The Court stated (paragraph 62) that three conditions were necessary for a finding of collective dominance: each member of the dominant oligopoly must have the ability to know how the others are behaving in order to monitor whether or not they are adopting a common policy; tacit collusion must be sustainable over time, which requires that retaliation against firms deviating from the common policy is feasible; and the foreseeable reaction of current and future competitors, and of consumers, must not jeopardise the results expected from the common policy.

4 Council Regulation (EC) No 1/2003 of 16 December 2002 (OJ L1, 4.1.2003, p 1), referred to in the guidance as the 'modernisation regulation'.

5 The CA98 prohibitions are based on Articles 81 and 82 and apply to agreements or conduct which may affect trade within the UK. Articles 81 and 82 apply to agreements and conduct which may affect trade between Member States.

6 This responsibility is specific to the OFT. Sectoral regulators do not necessarily engage in a similar activity for their own sectors (see www.oft.gov.uk/NR/rdonlyres/03AD31EC-3533-40BE-AE79-2A83424E9C9B/0/OFT519.pdf).

7 *Market Investigation References: Competition Commission Guidelines* paragraphs 4.26 to 4.38.

8 The Director General of Water Services, in particular, is of the view that for the water and sewerage industries market investigation references may often not be appropriate because there are a number of small regional markets each with a few players.

3. POWERS AND PROCEDURES

The OFT's powers of investigation

[3.629]
3.1-3.3 . . .

3.4 Where the OFT is considering a reference to the CC following a CA98 investigation in which it used its powers under that Act, the information it has obtained from the earlier investigation may be used as a basis for making a reference. Conversely, when the OFT has used its investigatory powers under the Act but subsequently decides to proceed by means of a CA98 investigation rather than by a reference to the CC, the information it has obtained under Enterprise Act powers can be used for the purposes of the CA98 investigation. Sectoral regulators may similarly use information obtained under Enterprise Act powers in connection with their functions under sectoral legislation, in particular for the purpose of investigating possible licence breaches.

3.5 However, the OFT will use its powers of investigation in good faith and will not use powers available under one piece of legislation if it has already decided to proceed under another.

Consultation and publicity

3.6 Where the OFT is proposing to make a reference to the CC it must first consult, so far as practicable, any person on whose interests the reference is likely to have a substantial impact (section 169 of the Act).

3.7 In undertaking this consultation the OFT must, so far as practicable, give its reasons for the proposed reference. The content of any statement of reasons will vary from case to case but the OFT expects that it would normally cover the following points:

- a description of the goods or services concerned
- the identity of the main parties affected by the reference, whether as suppliers or as customers; or this may involve the identification of categories of persons rather than individuals
- a view as to the possible definition of the market (or markets) affected
- a summary of the evidence that has led the OFT to have a reasonable suspicion that competition has been prevented, restricted or distorted, including the possible market features that may be relevant.

Market definition, the prevention, restriction or distortion of competition, and market features are all discussed in Part II of this guidance.

3.8 The OFT will not attempt to make more than a preliminary analysis of these points in its statement of reasons. It will be for the CC to produce a definitive analysis if a reference is made.

3.9 The length of the formal consultation period, following the issue by the OFT of a statement of its reasons for a proposed reference, will depend upon the complexity of the issues and the extent to which discussions have already taken place with the parties affected. In general, the OFT expects to have discussed the issues thoroughly with the parties concerned, where they have been identified, before the start of the formal consultation period. In such cases a relatively short formal consultation may be appropriate. However, the OFT will ensure that the length of total consultation period, formal and informal, is sufficient to enable parties to put their concerns and arguments to it. At the end of this period the OFT will take account of representations received before making a final decision about whether to make a reference. Any reference that it makes must be published together with the reasons for it. It is likely that the published reasons for making a reference will cover the same ground as the reasons for a proposed reference, taking account of any relevant points that have arisen from the consultation on the proposal.

3.10 . . .

Content of references

3.11 Section 133 of the Act requires that a market investigation reference shall specify the enactment under which it is made, the date on which it is made, and the description of the goods or services to which the feature or combination of features concerned relates. In order to avoid the CC being led into an investigation of markets that do not involve the adverse effect on competition that has given rise to the reference, the OFT may describe the goods or services in the reference in terms of the persons to whom they are supplied (or by whom they are acquired) or the places where they are supplied (or acquired). The formal reference is likely to be limited to the matters specified in section 133, but (as indicated in paragraph 3.9) the statement of the reasons for the reference will give much more detail, including the possible markets affected and the possible features that could give rise to an adverse effect on competition.

3.12 A single reference may involve several different markets or several different features provided that they all relate to the specified goods or services. This will occur, for example, when the supply of goods involves a chain with several links (such as manufacturer to wholesaler, wholesaler to retailer, and retailer to consumer) and features giving rise to competition concerns exist at each level.

3.13 The content of references gives the CC scope to identify markets affected which differ from those that were considered by the OFT when making the reference, and to identify features giving rise to adverse effects on competition of which the OFT was not aware. Notwithstanding this scope, it may be that the goods and services described in the reference are sufficiently complicated that as the CC proceeds with its investigations it discovers that the description of the goods or services in the reference needs modification. For example, it may find that certain related goods and services are affected by the same market features as those it is investigating or, conversely, that some of the goods or services specified are not affected by these features and need not be investigated further. In those circumstances it may wish to ask the OFT to vary the reference. It is very likely that the OFT would respond positively to such requests provided it was satisfied that there was still sufficient time to enable all interested parties to make representations to the CC.

3.14 It may be that a deficiency in the original reference is brought to the OFT's attention by someone other than the CC. If the OFT believes that the reasons for varying a reference are sound it must consult the CC before proceeding further. It is likely that, when deciding whether to make a variation, the OFT will follow the advice of the CC.

Concurrency

3.15 The Act makes provision for the market investigation functions exercised by the OFT (with the exception of maintaining a register of undertakings and orders) also to be exercised by sectoral regulators with concurrent powers (see paragraph 1.2). These regulators have the power to make references in relation to the supply of some or all of the goods or services which fall within their regulated sectors.

3.16 When either a sectoral regulator or the OFT is considering a reference of such goods and services they must consult the other. As a matter of practice, where a market investigation reference is appropriate for goods or services which are unambiguously part of a regulated industry and are the subject of concurrent powers, the reference would normally be made by the sectoral regulator. In ambiguous cases it would be made by whichever authority is better placed to do so. The factors to be considered in determining which authority deals with the matter include the extent to which sectoral knowledge is relevant and recent experience of dealing with the markets concerned.

NOTES

Paras 3.1 to 3.3 have been superseded by paragraphs 2.11 to 2.16 of the revised CMA 3 which explain the investigatory powers available to the CMA and when they are available in relation to market studies. See Annex A of CMA 3 at **[3.655]**.

Para 3.10 has been superseded by paragraphs 2.18 to 2.30 of the revised CMA 3 which explain the changes made to the procedure for making public interest interventions. See Annex A of CMA 3 at **[3.655]**.

Note that paras 3.6 to 3.9 above should be read in conjunction with paragraph 2.9 of the revised CMA 3 which sets out the statutory timescales and consultation process that apply when the CMA proposes to make a reference. See Annex A of CMA 3 at **[3.655]**.

PART II
APPLICATION OF THE REFERENCE TEST

4. PREVENTION, RESTRICTION OR DISTORTION OF COMPETITION

[3.630]
4.1 The OFT views competition as a process of rivalry between firms seeking to win customers' business. Competition will be effective and markets will work well when firms engaged in the market are subject to competitive constraints from other firms already in the market and/or from firms that could readily enter it, perhaps with new products, and from their customers.

4.2 The phrase 'prevention, restriction or distortion of competition' is familiar from the complex monopoly provisions of the FTA, section 2 of CA98 and Article 81(1) of the European Community Treaty. The past practice of the CC and EC case law both indicate that the phrase should be interpreted broadly to encompass any reduction or dampening of actual or potential competition. The OFT will use this interpretation when considering references. Conduct that adversely affects the opportunity for others to compete is not the only thing that could prevent, restrict or distort competition. Where other features of a market create a situation in which suppliers do not need to compete to the extent that they would in a competitive market, those features may be found to restrict competition.

4.3 The OFT's enquiries into a possible market investigation reference may embrace several levels of a supply chain. It might be, for example, that competition appeared to be prevented, restricted and distorted in some way by the structure of the market or the conduct of firms at the manufacturing stage, yet further examination of the situation suggested that practices at the downstream level could also have an adverse effect on competition. A market investigation reference could require that the effectiveness of competition at various levels of a supply chain should be assessed.

4.4 Although section 131 of the Act sets out the three types of market feature that could have an adverse effect on competition, in practice there may not be a clear divide between structural features and those relating to conduct. For example, exclusionary conduct by firms in the market will affect structure to the extent that it raises entry barriers. In most cases, the OFT's assessment that a reference would be appropriate is likely to be based on a combination of features and will include evidence about both structure and conduct. It may also include evidence about the performance of firms in the market.

4.5 Information on prices and profitability, in particular, can sometimes be a useful supplement to the OFT's evidence on structural features of a market and on firms' market conduct. Indeed, evidence on prices and profitability might be the beginning of the OFT's interest in a particular market. This is because complaints of anti-competitive conduct will often focus on excessive prices and high levels of profitability, perhaps making comparisons with prices or the profitability of firms in other similar markets or in other countries. Other performance indicators such as the level of costs or efficiency measures may, on occasions, also be a useful supplement to analyses of market features.

4.6 The OFT is well aware of the limitations of such information for its purpose. Performance indicators in isolation yield little useful information about the state of competition in a market. At best they should be used as an indirect indicator that a competition problem may exist. For example, profits in dynamic markets, where technological advances are important, can be lumpy so a snapshot of profitability will not give a good indication of a firm's performance. Furthermore, identifying the concept of excessive prices and profits and the 'normal' rate of return is extremely difficult. There is a need for care before any inferences about competition are drawn. Nevertheless, the OFT will consider any available and reliable information on the dynamics of prices, profitability and other performance indicators in its assessment of the case for a market investigation reference.

4.7 In short, in any competition assessment, the OFT will usually wish to consider a combination of features and their inter-relationships and will look at various types of information and sources of evidence. However, it is not required to reach firm conclusions before making references and it would be inappropriate for it to engage in extensive research. Provided it has reasonable grounds for suspecting that there are market features that adversely affect competition, the reference test has been met and further investigation can be left to the CC.

Market definition

4.8 In making a market investigation reference to the CC, the OFT must specify the goods or services for whose supply or acquisition competition is adversely affected. This will require some consideration of the definition of the relevant market. Market definition can be a useful step along the way to an analysis of market structure and an assessment of the extent to which firms may have market power, but it need not always be a necessary step. The effects on competition of some feature may be clear enough that firm conclusions on the definition of the relevant market by the OFT are unnecessary.

4.9 That said, the OFT's approach to market definition in enquiries into a possible market investigation reference will conceptually be the same as in other competition cases.[9] A market definition will usually comprise two dimensions, the product dimension and the geographic dimension. The product dimension comprises those products (or services) that are close enough substitutes for the price of one of the products to be constrained by the prices of the other products comprising the market. Products are close substitutes if a significant number of customers are able and prepared to switch their purchasing from one to the other on a change in their relative prices. This is referred to as demand-side substitutability.

4.10 A market may also be defined from the supply side, recognising the fact that a competitive constraint will apply wherever firms who do not currently supply a particular product could speedily, and at little cost, switch their facilities to the production of that product, should it become profitable to do so on a change in relative prices.

4.11 The geographical area that constitutes the relevant market will also be determined by reference to demand-side substitutability and, where it is appropriate, supply-side substitutability. This geographic market may be a lesser or a wider area than that of the UK, though where it is wider the reference to the CC will be concerned only with the UK part of it.

4.12 In all cases, the OFT's purpose in defining markets will be to achieve a sufficient understanding of the competitive constraints that apply to firms supplying or acquiring the goods or services that would be the subject of a possible market investigation, so as to enable it to reach a view on whether any effects on the competitive process are of sufficient significance to justify a reference.

NOTES

9 For a detailed guide to the OFT's approach to market definition, see the Competition Act 1998 Guideline, *Market Definition, OFT 403*. For some caveats about the use of market definition see the report *Innovation and competition policy*, OFT 377, paragraphs 4.43–4.59.

5. STRUCTURAL FEATURES OF A MARKET

[3.631]

5.1 Structure describes the environment within which firms operate in a particular market. The OFT interprets it broadly to include such matters as government regulations and any information asymmetries that are inherent in the nature of the market. Any assessment of the working of competition in a market will begin with an analysis of market structure and the implications of this structure for the conduct of the firms engaged in the market. A wider range of structural features can give rise to concern under the market investigation reference provisions of the Act than would normally arise in considering whether a firm or firms had infringed one of the CA98 prohibitions.

5.2 This part of the guidance gives a brief account of the more important structural features. Readers may also find it useful to refer to various Competition Act Guidelines, particularly OFT 402, *The Chapter II Prohibition*, OFT 415, *Assessment of Market Power*, and OFT 414 *Assessment of Individual Agreements and Conduct*.

Concentration

5.3 Market concentration is about the number and size distribution of firms in a particular market. It is generally accepted that, other things being equal, the larger the market share of a firm, the greater its market power is likely to be, particularly if its high market share has persisted over a period of time and is relatively stable. This applies to both sellers and buyers. Market shares are not conclusive indicators of a firm's market power of course. Other factors can be relevant. Notable among these are entry barriers. Markets in which firms have high market shares are often, though not necessarily, markets with high entry barriers. In assessing the degree of concentration it is important for the market to be correctly defined as too narrow a definition will overstate concentration (and vice versa).

5.4 A firm may have market power, and the capacity to act in ways that may prevent, restrict or distort competition, with a market share below that usually regarded as necessary to suggest dominance for the purposes of CA 98.[10] Much will depend upon the effectiveness of the constraints exerted by its competitors or its customers. Generally speaking, a firm with a stable market share will be more likely to have market power than one whose share fluctuates from year to year.

5.5 In markets comprising a small number of firms (oligopolies) each firm might find it relatively easy to predict the reaction of its competitors to any action it might take. This could provide an opportunity for firms to coordinate their behaviour for mutual advantage or it could simply dull the incentive to compete, leading to a situation in which rivalry to attract new customers becomes muted. By no means all oligopolistic market structures produce these results. Among the more important of the market features that may assist the coordination of behaviour are:

- the existence of substantial barriers to entry
- the homogeneity of the firms' products
- the similarity (symmetry) of the firms with respect to their market shares, their cost structures, the time horizons of their decisions and their strategies
- the stability of market conditions on both the demand and the cost side
- the degree of excess capacity
- the extent to which prices, outputs and market shares are transparent so that competitors can be well-informed about each other's behaviour
- the awareness by firms that their competitors have the ability to respond quickly and effectively to any price reductions they make
- the structure of the buying side of the market (if the issue is possible co-ordination among sellers), and
- the extent of any multi-market contacts.

5.6 This list is not exhaustive nor are any of the items on it necessary conditions for competition dampening to take place. It also is quite possible for a market displaying many of these factors to be competitive. Nevertheless, the more symmetrical the firms in the oligopoly, the more homogeneous their products, and the more stable the market conditions, the more likely it is that an understanding on, say, a particular price can be reached and sustained. It can be difficult to sustain a coordinated price where buyers are large and may encourage sellers to offer special and secret deals.

5.7 A view on the likelihood of coordination or the existence of muted rivalry can only be reached after a close study of the market concerned, not least because the influence of some of the features listed in paragraph 5.5 can be ambiguous. Therefore, product homogeneity makes it easier for oligopolists to reach a tacit understanding, but it also makes it easier for customers to compare the offerings of different firms, possibly encouraging greater keenness on price. However, research suggests as a generalisation that firm symmetries, market transparency and relatively stable demand and cost conditions appear to be the combination of market characteristics most conducive to coordination.[11]

Vertical integration

5.8 A structural market feature that can have a bearing on market conduct and the effectiveness of competition is the degree (if any) of vertical integration of firms engaged in the market. Although vertical

Part 3 CMA and other Guidelines

integration may often be efficient or pro-competitive, a vertically integrated firm can have adverse effects on competition if it can foreclose non-integrated competitors from a significant part of their market either by refusing to supply or to deal with them or by discriminating against them in its pricing. Vertical integration may also add to entry barriers if a potential competitor would have to enter at both stages in order to be able to compete effectively with incumbent firms, and if the riskiness of the necessary investment is thereby increased.

5.9 For vertical integration to have any of these effects, the vertically integrated firm(s) will need to have a sizeable share of either of the vertically linked markets. Where only a single firm is vertically integrated adverse effects on competition will usually arise only if it is dominant in terms of CA98. A market investigation reference might be appropriate, however, if a number of firms in a market are vertically integrated and they engage in some common form of anti-competitive conduct, for example, discrimination against any non-integrated competitors.

Conditions of entry, exit and expansion

5.10 Entry conditions are always a crucial part of any competition assessment. If there are no significant barriers or impediments to entry into the market under consideration, so that there is a realistic possibility that a new entrant could establish itself in the market on a viable basis within a reasonably short period of time, the established suppliers will have no lasting market power. However, while there can be such contestable markets, more often than not, in markets in which the OFT is interested there will be some significant entry barriers facing any potential entrant.

5.11 One definition of entry barriers is any feature of the market that gives incumbent suppliers a cost or other advantage over efficient potential entrants. The strength of entry barriers may then be measured by the extent of the cost (or other) disadvantage that the entrant must bear.

5.12 There are various sources of entry barriers and they can be classified in a number of ways, but it is helpful to distinguish between three types:[12]

- **absolute advantages** such as access to a scarce input, intellectual property rights, and regulatory barriers that limit the number of market participants
- **strategic or 'first-mover' advantages of incumbents**. An entrant will be concerned to make a return on the commitment it makes in entering the market. This will depend on the response to entry of the incumbents and the size of the commitment the entrant has to make. First-mover advantages can be particularly potent in an industry where economies of scale are important or in a market where incumbents have built up brand loyalty through advertising and promotion
- **exclusionary behaviour by incumbents**. For example, predatory price cuts directed at an entrant, or restrictive distribution arrangements which raise entrants' distribution costs.

5.13 Strategic entry barriers will tend to be more important the greater are the sunk costs of entry (costs that will be incurred on entry but cannot be recovered on exit from the market) and therefore the commitment that any potential entrant would have to make. Sunk costs can include the set-up costs in entering the market (market research, finding a location and getting planning permission, attracting and training staff etc), investment in specific assets and advertising and promotion costs.

5.14 Some entry barriers are 'natural' in that they arise from the technology of the industry such as economies of scale, from statutory provisions such as exclusive rights under intellectual property law or from government regulations (see next section). Other entry barriers can more readily be loosened by action under the competition legislation. These are entry barriers created by the conduct of incumbent firms. Sometimes such barriers involve actions by a dominant firm, such as a refusal to supply essential inputs to a downstream competitor or to grant access to an essential facility, and can be dealt with under CA98. On other occasions they may involve several incumbent firms, for example where there are networks of restrictive distribution agreements or the exploitation of information advantages to deter the entry of new competitors, and these may be more suited to investigation by means of a market investigation reference.

5.15 Barriers to expansion determine how easy it is for an entrant to grow once they have entered a market, thereby gaining customers and market share from the incumbents. This could be closely related to the degree of switching by consumers and the information asymmetry inherent in the market: the sunk costs for entry may be small but if customers are unwilling to switch (due to brand loyalty for example) then price competition may not provide a basis for expansion.

5.16 Barriers to exit relate to the cost of exit from the market if the business does not go according to plan. This is closely related to the degree of sunk costs incurred on entry and the extent to which investment can be recovered on exit. Where the barriers to exit are high, the firms in the market have burnt their bridges which provides them with a credible threat that they will not consider exiting the market easily. This could lead to situations where tacit collusion becomes the optimal strategy rather than intense price competition.

Regulations and government policies

5.17 Government regulations can have a direct effect upon competition when they limit the number of firms that can operate in a market. This might be achieved by a licensing system or by specified entry criteria, for example a minimum capital funds requirement as in much of the financial sector. However, It does not follow that such entry barriers will necessarily have significantly adverse effects upon competition. That will depend upon how seriously the regulations limit the number of firms in the market, for example, whether the restrictions are quantitative or qualitative, and how active the competition is between those that are in the market.

5.18 Regulations can also affect firms' conduct. Often they will be innocuous in competition terms, such as regulations on product labelling, emissions of pollutants and hiring and firing of employees, although they will raise firms' costs and can bear more heavily on small firms than on their larger competitors. Sometimes the effects on competition will be more significant, for example the imposition of demanding product standards, restrictions on trading hours or the restrictions on advertising tobacco products or marketing drugs. The circumstances in which markets affected by regulation might be suitable for a reference to the CC were mentioned in paragraph 2.31.

5.19 Government policies can affect markets in other ways, for example by influencing the way in which public sector bodies act as providers or purchasers of services. Where such policies have a significant effect on competition they will be among the market features that OFT takes into account when considering a reference.

5.20 Competition can also be affected by the rules emanating from systems of self-regulation, for example, those applicable to financial services and to a number of occupations and professions. In many cases this can be adequately addressed using CA98 or sector-specific legislation. Where it cannot, the market affected might be suitable for a reference to the CC.

Information asymmetries

5.21 Where customers are well informed, they can make efficient choices and their purchases will provide useful information to sellers about customers' preferences. Sellers then have the incentive to provide the goods and services that customers most value. Without such information, the incentives to compete on price, quality and other terms are likely to be diminished. In short, adequate information available to customers is one of the pre-requisites for markets to work well. If customers have inadequate information, or are unwilling or unable to search for the best deal, firms may be able to exercise a degree of market power, even if there are many firms supplying the market.

5.22 In many markets, suppliers will have more information than their customers about the quality and other attributes of their products. This will not necessarily adversely affect competition, particularly if suppliers have an incentive to provide their customers with relevant information. However, where the quality of products is difficult for customers to assess, either because of their complexity or the infrequency with which they are purchased, information asymmetries can have a significant impact on the nature and degree of competition in the market for the product or service. Information asymmetries can restrict competition by adding to customers' switching costs.

Switching costs

5.23 For competition to work effectively, it is often necessary that customers are readily able to switch their patronage if a competing supplier is found to offer better value for money. Where customers face difficulties in switching between suppliers, whether because of the monetary costs, administrative hurdles or inconvenience, competition can be affected. If firms find it difficult to persuade customers to switch their incentive to compete with each other may be reduced and rivalry between them dulled.

5.24 Switching costs allow firms potentially to charge high prices to 'captive' customers. Firms face conflicting incentives. They want to offer low prices to attract new customers but to charge high prices to their existing customers. Even if the firm is unable to discriminate between the two types of customer, it is still possible that the existence of switching costs will permit firms to charge higher prices than they would set in the absence of these costs.

5.25 Firms may engage in practices that increase switching costs, for example, by not releasing information needed for a switch to be feasible or by not doing so in a timely fashion. In its report on *Banking Services to Small and Medium Sized Enterprises*, the CC identified the 'hassle in moving direct debits, standing orders etc and a fear that crucial payments could be missed whilst a switch was in progress' as a factor discouraging switching between banks. It also found that banks reduced charges selectively and in a discriminatory way to enterprises likely to switch to another bank. Marketing devices such as loyalty cards, often seen as pro-competitive, can have the effect of increasing switching costs. Negative advertising may also be used to reduce switching by creating doubts in customers' minds about the acceptability of competitors' offerings.

5.26 In some markets, the problem may be that the customer is unaware of the existence of competing products. For example a consumer may not be aware of a generic pharmaceutical product having the same medicinal properties as a more expensive branded product.

Countervailing power

5.27 The structure of the buying side of the market can also be relevant to the assessment of the effectiveness of competition between suppliers. It may suggest that any market power of suppliers would be countervailed by the bargaining power of customers, or that any attempt of suppliers not to compete on price would be eroded by the temptation to negotiate special terms with large buyers.

5.28 The effectiveness of buyer power as a constraint on suppliers will depend upon a number of factors, particularly upon the relative dependence of seller and buyer on the business of the other and the credibility of any threat by the buyer to switch its business to an alternative supplier.

Summary

5.29 There are many dimensions of market structure. In its assessment of a possible market investigation reference, the OFT will examine any structural feature that, on its own, or more likely in combination with other market features, could enable suppliers (or buyers) to behave in ways that significantly prevent, restrict or distort competition, or that exploit the absence of effective competition in a market. Where there is no abuse of a dominant position but structural features of the market nevertheless appear to affect the competitive process adversely, then a market investigation reference will be a possibility.

NOTES

10 The Competition Act 1998 Guideline, The Chapter II Prohibition, OFT 402, para 3.13 states that the OFT 'considers it unlikely that an undertaking will be individually dominant if its market share is below 40 per cent although dominance could be established below that figure if other relevant factors (such as the weak position of competitors in that market) provided strong evidence of dominance'.

11 See European Commission, *Assessment criteria for distinguishing between competitive and dominant oligopolies, Enterprise papers No 6, 2001* (A report prepared by Europe Economics, London).

12 This follows the treatment of entry barriers in the Competition Act 1998 Guideline, *The Assessment of Market Power*, OFT 415.

6. FIRMS' CONDUCT

[3.632]

6.1 The conduct of firms refers to their behaviour and practices in the broadest sense including what decisions they take, how they make them and the resulting action or lack of it. Section 131(3) of the Act states that conduct includes failure to act and unintentional conduct. A significant part of the evidence on which the OFT will base its case for a market investigation reference will normally concern the conduct of firms (as sellers or buyers) who, because of structural or other features of the market, are in a position to exercise a degree of market power.

6.2 The conduct of the firms in a market may affect competition in that market (horizontal effects), competition in the (upstream) market of its suppliers or in the (downstream) market of its customers (vertical effects). It is also possible for conduct adversely to affect competition in a market for some related good or service.

6.3 As stated in paragraph 2.7, most market investigation references are likely to involve markets where the conduct of a number of firms (whether sellers or buyers) appears to have the effect of preventing, restricting or distorting competition (without an agreement or concerted practice that would be unlawful under Chapter I of CA98). This part of the guidance give a number of examples of such conduct. However, these should not be regarded in any way as exhaustive or exclusive.

Conduct of oligopolies

6.4 Many of the markets in which the OFT is likely to be interested will be oligopolistic. These are markets comprising very few firms (or few firms of any significance) where those firms are aware of the mutual interdependence of their actions. Each firm's strategy is therefore determined at least partly by its beliefs about its rivals' likely reactions. These strategies can take various forms, ranging from competitive rivalry to conduct that is tantamount to collusion, even without an explicit agreement not to compete. With either of these extremes, the outcome can be parallel behaviour. The task will then be to determine whether the oligopolists' conduct reflects a restriction of effective competition and would be an appropriate ground for an OFT investigation.

6.5 It is a common feature of oligopolistic markets that competition takes forms other than competition in price. These include competitive advertising and promotional activity, rebates and discounts linked to purchases, and more explicit customer loyalty-inducing schemes. These forms of conduct are often pro-competitive but they may have effects, that, especially when combined with other market features, blunt the competitive process, for example by adding to entry barriers.

6.6 Where firms in an oligopolistic market reach a tacit understanding to pursue their joint interests by coordinating their behaviour (tacit collusion) the adverse effects on competition are likely to be severe. The OFT will not need to establish conclusively that any observed parallel conduct reflects coordinated rather than competitive behaviour by oligopolists. However, it will need to establish that the market features that make tacit collusion a feasible strategy are present (see paragraph 5.5 for an indicative list) and will need to have a reasonable suspicion that the oligopolists are not competing effectively with consequences that are likely to be detrimental to their customers.

6.7 Among the evidence that the OFT might examine in this regard are:

- the pattern of price changes over time, with a view to establishing the degree of parallelism in the face of any changes in demand or cost conditions, and whether the pattern seems more consistent with collusive than competitive behaviour
- price inertia, such as when sustained exchange rate advantages are not exploited by importers
- any evidence that, notwithstanding evidence of parallelism in, say, published prices, the oligopolists compete in discounts or other concessions off the published price, and
- the oligopolists' rates of return compared to returns in comparable markets or to the cost of capital (since the expected outcome of tacit collusion is that the level of prices will be higher than could be sustained in a competitive market). However, where there is persistent excess capacity, excessive prices may not be reflected in high rates of return.

6.8 Even if the conditions necessary for tacit collusion are not met, other market features such as switching costs and informational inadequacies may limit the effectiveness of competition, especially price competition. Competition can be muted in oligopolistic markets without any coordination of firms' decisions. In its report on Supermarkets, for example, the CC concluded that the market was 'broadly competitive' with no suggestion of collusion, but that competition was concentrated on certain products or in certain areas and was less than fully effective elsewhere. This was held to distort the competitive process.

6.9 The OFT will therefore be concerned to consider, in contemplating a reference, whether there are any steps that could be taken to facilitate entry into an oligopolistic market and whether there is any conduct that serves to reinforce the market features that are conducive to tacit collusion and that could, if appropriate, be struck down. One such possibility is facilitating practices.

Facilitating practices

6.10 Facilitating practices are the conduct of firms that make it easier for oligopolists to arrive tacitly at a coordinated outcome and to maintain it in the face of the temptation of all the firms involved to cheat on the other participants. Examples would be a practice of announcing price increases well in advance of the date of implementation, most-favoured-customer clauses in contracts, uniform systems for reflecting transport charges in prices, and information exchanges, for example, on costs.

6.11 There can be objective justifications for such practices and they do not necessarily have the effect of restricting competition. However, where other market features appear conducive to tacit collusion, practices of firms that appear to facilitate such conduct will be closely scrutinised by the OFT. They could even be the focus of a market investigation in their own right.

Custom and practice

6.12 Practices that may restrict competition can be adopted widely in a market as a custom of the trade and with no apparent agreement or understanding between firms. A good example is provided by the CC report on *Underwriting Fees*. Custom and practice appeared to be the reason why underwriting fees for new share issues were charged on a common basis virtually throughout the industry.

6.13 Another example could be the practice of manufacturers' recommended retail prices. While the practice can be innocuous, its widespread use in a market can have the effect of restricting competition in the downstream (retail) market by dampening price competition, should retailers generally choose to follow the recommended price; or of restricting competition in the upstream market, by making it easier for a manufacturer to monitor competitors' prices and thereby to detect, and hence to deter, competitive price cutting. Examples of anti-competitive effects of the practice are to be found in the CC's reports on *Domestic Electrical Goods*.

6.14 Any common practices in a market, that appear to reflect a restriction of competition and to have no objective justification, could be the subject of a market investigation reference.

Networks of vertical agreements

6.15 Vertical agreements of one kind or another are commonplace in industry and are frequently pro-competitive or neutral. Agreements between manufacturers and distributors (wholesalers or retailers) will often include terms that restrict the freedom of action of one or other party, as will agreements between a manufacturer and suppliers of its inputs. Such restrictions could in some circumstances adversely affect competition. Where several firms in a market have agreements with their distributors or suppliers that contain restrictions which, taken together, have an adverse effect on competition in the market of one or other party, for example, by foreclosing the market to competitors or adding to entry barriers, a market investigation reference could be justified. It is not necessary for there to be any horizontal agreement to engage in particular vertical arrangements (indeed, if there was such an agreement it would have to be considered under Chapter I of CA98). Such networks of vertical agreements can result from the independent decisions of the firms concerned, or even from long custom in a trade.

6.16 Types of vertical agreement that have been the subject of FTA monopoly references in the past and may be suitable for market investigation references in the future include exclusive purchasing (ie where the retailer or other downstream party is tied to a single supplier), exclusive or selective distribution (where a supplier only sells to certain downstream outlets), and tie-in sales and product bundling. For a fuller discussion of the various types of vertical agreement and their effects see the Competition Act Guideline, *Assessment of Individual Agreements and Conduct*, OFT 414.

6.17 The effect on competition of vertical agreements will depend not just on the foreclosure and entry barrier-enhancing effects but also on the effectiveness of competition between suppliers and the willingness of consumers to shop around among competing suppliers' products. Where inter-brand competition is strong, the effects may not be significant. On the other hand, inter-brand competition can be weakened if consumers find that particular retailers are effectively tied to particular suppliers (or vice versa) and they are unwilling for one reason or another to shop around and switch to another retailer (brand) if it is found to offer better value for their money.

6.18 Vertical agreements are frequently efficiency enhancing so that even where the OFT suspects that they adversely affect competition it will need to consider the trade-off. A reference will only be appropriate where there are reasonable grounds to suspect that the net effect of the agreement is detrimental to the interests of customers.

Summary

6.19 The conduct of firms can affect competition in various ways. For the OFT to have any concern, it is the process of competition that needs to be affected not the fortunes of individual competitors.

Adverse effects are less likely to be a concern where there are no structural features of the market that give rise to market power, either for an individual firm or a number of firms in a market. Single firm conduct will usually not be the cause of a market investigation reference in the absence of such features. Conduct that embraces a number of firms engaged in a market and appears to prevent, restrict or distort competition is more likely to lead to a market investigation reference to the CC.

7. CONDUCT OF CUSTOMERS

[3.633]

7.1 Section 131(2)(c) of the Act identifies the conduct of customers as a market feature that could give rise to adverse effects on competition and be the subject of a market investigation reference. The customers concerned may be businesses or final consumers. It may seem rather unlikely that the conduct of consumers could affect the competitive process until it is recalled that 'conduct' includes failures to act. One feature of consumers' conduct that can then affect competition is the search process.

Search costs

7.2 Competition requires customer choice. In order to make informed choices customers need to spend at least some time and effort finding out what alternative products are available to them. Where such search costs are perceived to be high searching is likely to be curtailed. Customer sensitivity about a product may also limit the amount of search that will be contemplated. Depending on other features of the market, reduced searching may blunt sellers' incentives to compete.

7.3 Even if a proportion of customers do engage in search activity there may remain enough uninformed customers with high search costs, who purchase from the first firm they encounter, for the seller to be able to charge prices without regard to competition. In this situation, the profit foregone by losing informed consumers who buy elsewhere is more than offset by the increase in profits accruing from uninformed consumers who do not shop around. Markets serving both tourists (with high search costs) and local residents (with low search costs) may be an example.

7.4 Firms may engage in practices that increase search costs (or fail to engage in practices that would reduce search costs). For example, firms may choose not to display prices prominently. An example of price display reducing search costs is the prominent display of petrol prices at filling stations. Restrictions on advertising in the rules of many professional bodies in the past also served to increase the difficulties of search.

7.5 Firms may fail to make available all the product information needed by consumers to make an informed choice. Customers may be ignorant of all the product attributes that they should consider in choosing between competing products. This is likely to be the case with many financial products, extended warranties on electrical products, certain professional services and some consumer durables. Where one-off purchases are involved, with no repeat sales, there will be little incentive for a firm to provide consumers with the information that they need. Indeed, there may be an incentive for the firm deliberately to provide consumers with partial and potentially misleading information.

7.6 Search costs are therefore a market feature that could be a factor pointing to a market investigation reference, especially when associated with sellers' conduct that is likely to have adverse effects on competition in its own right. Structural features of the market would also be relevant, but it is noteworthy that the effect of high search costs on prices will be greater the more firms that there are in the industry.

7.7 The effects of search costs on the competitive process are likely to be compounded when they are combined with high switching costs. A good example of such a combination of market features is durable goods where the consumer needs information on the availability and costs of aftermarket services, such as spare parts and maintenance, if an informed choice is to be made between competing products. A competition problem can arise where consumers are unable to factor in to their purchase decisions all the aftermarket costs of the products or where the aftermarket is not competitive. For some durable products such as new motor cars there are adequate sources of information on lifetime aftermarket costs for any customer willing to take a little trouble. For other products such information is inherently difficult to obtain. Suppliers are well placed to take advantage of customers who are short of relevant aftermarket information with little risk of losing sales to competitors.

7.8 High search and/or switching costs will therefore be features of markets that could justify a market investigation reference. They can feed into other market features by facilitating anti-competitive or exploitative conduct by suppliers and by adding to market entry barriers. But the OFT will need to be convinced that market behaviour is affected. It is not necessary for all customers to be well informed and quick to switch suppliers in response to price differences for markets to work well.

7.9 Indicators that market behaviour may be little affected by search or switching costs with little risk of detriment to customers at large include:

- prices clustering together (in the absence of resale price maintenance or recommended retail prices)
- advertising of prices by all or most suppliers
- customary and inexpensive comparison shopping
- inability of suppliers to discriminate between informed and uninformed customers.

Summary

7.10 Customers' conduct on its own is unlikely to be sufficient to justify a market investigation reference. However, when combined with other features of the market, a failure or the inability of customers to engage in meaningful search activity can add to firms' opportunities for anti-competitive conduct.

MARKET STUDIES (OFT 519, JUNE 2010)

Guidance on the OFT approach

[3.634]

NOTES

As to the construction of this document (following the abolition of the OFT and Competition Commission), see further the note "The Competition and Markets Authority (references to the OFT and Competition Commission etc)" in the introductory notes to Part 3 preceding **[3.1]**.

Note also that all references to issues of jurisdiction or procedure in mergers cases or to market studies or investigations must be read in the light of Mergers: Guidance on the CMA's jurisdiction and procedure (CMA2) and Market studies and market investigations: Supplemental guidance on the CMA's approach (CMA3); in the case of conflict, CMA2 or CMA3 prevail.

See further CMA 3 Market Studies and Market Investigations: Supplemental guidance on the CMA's approach (revised July 2017). The Annex to the Guidance (at **[3.655]**) lists changes to this Guidance consequential on the revision of CMA 3.

CONTENTS

1. INTRODUCTION TO THE GUIDANCE

[3.635]

1.1 This guidance is designed to inform stakeholders – businesses and their advisers, consumer groups, and other interested parties – how the OFT conducts market studies. The guidance is divided into five sections answering the following questions:

- Why does the OFT conduct market studies?
- How does the OFT choose markets to study?
- How does the OFT manage market studies?
- What are the outcomes of market studies?
- How does the OFT evaluate market studies?

1.2 This guidance is not intended to be comprehensive in that it cannot cover every possible set of circumstances. It aims to set out the general framework the OFT uses to conduct market studies so that businesses that have an interest in the markets we study, and other stakeholders including consumer bodies and the Government, will be aware of the processes and principles that will be followed.

1.3 This guidance should not be regarded as a legal authority. While it does set out certain legal requirements that must be adhered to, many of the processes described are not subject to detailed regulations. The OFT's approach is to be proportionate and, wherever possible, open. However, where the law allows flexibility, the OFT reserves the right to depart from the general principles set out in this guidance. The OFT may also revise and reissue this guidance in the light of experience and other developments in law and practice.

1.4 This guidance is part of a series of guidance on the Enterprise Act 2002. This series includes guidance on market investigation references and super-complaints.

1.5 Information about the OFT's current and completed market studies can be found on the OFT website: www.oft.gov.uk/OFTwork/markets-work/

1.6 The OFT welcomes ideas for market studies from stakeholders. You can provide your ideas by completing and sending us a form that can be downloaded from our website: www.oft.gov.uk/OFTwork/markets-work/market-studies-further-info/

2. WHY DOES THE OFT CONDUCT MARKET STUDIES?

THE PURPOSE OF MARKET STUDIES

[3.636]

2.1 The OFT aims to make markets work well for consumers. It achieves this by promoting and protecting consumer interests throughout the United Kingdom (UK), while ensuring that businesses are fair and competitive.

2.2 Typically, market studies are examinations into the causes of why particular markets are not working well for consumers, leading to proposals as to how they might be made to work better. They take an overview of regulatory and other economic drivers in a market and patterns of consumer and business behaviour.

2.3 As well as taking a look at particular markets, market studies can relate to practices across a range of goods and services, for example, doorstep selling. The term 'market studies' is therefore not limited to markets in the economic sense. The OFT may also conduct market studies to improve its knowledge of markets or practices, or to look at developing markets, for example where the potential risks to consumers may be high, or where there may be potential barriers to entry.

2.4 The geographic scope of many market studies will be the UK. However, there may be some cases where a market study focuses on a particular part of the UK.

2.5 When markets are working well, firms compete to win business by achieving the lowest level of cost and prices, developing better products and services or exploiting their strengths, skills, and other advantages to meet consumers' needs more effectively than their rivals. This process encourages innovation and provides consumers with increased choice. Competition is enhanced when consumers are empowered to shop around through access to readily available and accurate information about products and services.

2.6 Markets that are not working well can result in serious negative effects for consumers, businesses and the economy. For example, consumers may be unable to make informed choices about prospective purchases, businesses may be deterred from improving their products or entering the market, and productivity in the sector may be undermined.

2.7 Through gathering intelligence from a range of sources, the OFT can identify markets which appear not to be working well. A market study can then examine whether there is a problem. If it finds there is, the study looks at its effects, and the causes of those effects, and considers how those causes may be best addressed by the most proportionate means.

2.8 As well as investigating adverse effects on competition caused by business and consumer behaviour, market studies can also examine restrictions on competition that can arise through Government regulation or public policy. Whether intentionally or not, public sector restrictions may create barriers to entry into markets, distort the conditions under which market players compete, prevent competitive markets from developing, and even take markets or sectors outside the scope of competition scrutiny altogether.

2.9 Market studies can also be used to examine issues in markets in which public sector bodies operate as suppliers. Market studies can also investigate markets where the public sector acts as a customer, where greater competition can lead to better value for money for the taxpayer.

2.10 In the White Paper *Productivity and Enterprise: a world class competition regime*, the Government stated its wish for competition authorities to take on a high profile advocacy role, both by advising on the impact of the Government's own laws and regulations on competition and by promoting competition.[1] The Government saw strong competition contributing to long-run national economic benefits by improving productivity as well as delivering more direct consumer benefits.

2.11 By identifying ways of making markets more competitive and improving consumer welfare, market studies not only benefit consumers, they can also have positive effects on productivity. Competition is a driver of productivity. By encouraging markets to be more competitive, market studies can enhance markets' long-run efficiency.[2]

2.12 Market studies lead to a range of outcomes. They may conclude that, at the time of the report, a market can be given a clean bill of health in that the initial concerns about consumer detriment are not substantiated by the information collected over the course of the study. Where the market is found not to be working well, there are a number of options the OFT will consider to address the causes. These may include:

- improving the quality and accessibility of information for consumers
- encouraging businesses in the market to self-regulate
- making recommendations to the Government to change regulations or public policy
- taking competition or consumer enforcement action, or
- making a market investigation reference to the Competition Commission (CC).

These outcomes are discussed in Chapter 5.

MARKET STUDIES AND THE OFT'S OTHER TOOLS

2.13 Market studies are conducted under the OFT's general function in section 5 of the Enterprise Act 2002, which includes the functions of obtaining information and conducting research. Market studies are one of a number of tools at the OFT's disposal to address competition or consumer protection problems, alongside its enforcement and advocacy activities. The OFT may also use its functions under section 5 to carry out research into markets-related issues which is not covered by this guidance. This is because the outcomes of such work do not directly affect stakeholders, so that the same level of transparency and stakeholder engagement is not appropriate.[3]

2.14 Where there is a clear case of a breach of competition or consumer protection law by an individual business, taking enforcement action will usually be preferred over starting a market study. In many cases it will be evident from the outset of the OFT's work that enforcement action is the most appropriate way of dealing with conduct that comes to the attention of the OFT, provided that the issue is sufficiently serious to warrant intervention. There may also be cases where market studies uncover evidence, or provide a clearer understanding of the level and nature of any harm, or of how legal principles should be applied to it, such that enforcement action may be taken following the study.

2.15 It may be the case, however, that enforcement action appears impractical, or may be ineffective, so that a market study is a better way of identifying a remedy to a perceived problem. Enforcement action may not address all of the root causes of any problem, or behaviour across a whole market or markets.

Market studies can look beyond individual abuses of dominance, agreements that reduce competition, or breaches of specific consumer protection legislation, and consider all aspects of market structure and conduct. This holistic perspective allows for the examination of whole markets to assess the best way of remedying problems. Looking at the whole market also provides the opportunity to address factors that may affect productivity which are beyond the scope of enforcement tools.

2.16 Market studies are also the tool that best links the OFT's competition and consumer protection responsibilities. Market studies consider the relationship between consumer behaviour in a market, the behaviour of firms in that market, and the market's structure. By looking at these relationships, the OFT can determine whether action that will encourage changes to consumer behaviour, business behaviour, or both, will best address market problems.

2.17 As government regulation and policy are not typically susceptible to enforcement action, market studies can be the best response to concerns regarding markets where public restrictions may be distorting a market or chilling competition. The Government welcomes advice from the OFT on the impact of laws and regulations on competition. It has made a commitment to consider the advice presented in the OFT's market study reports and to respond to that advice within 90 days.[4]

2.18 Diagram 2.1 shows the central role that market studies play in the work of the OFT. Market studies complement the OFT's enforcement and non-enforcement work and occupy the interface between competition and consumer protection policy.

2.19 The OFT's aim is for market studies work to drive a virtuous circle to the benefit of consumers. On the one side, informed consumers have the confidence to engage more proactively in markets, helping to drive competition between firms. On the other, vigorous competition drives firms to deliver higher quality, increased choice, greater innovation and lower prices.

Diagram 2.1 Market studies and the work of the OFT

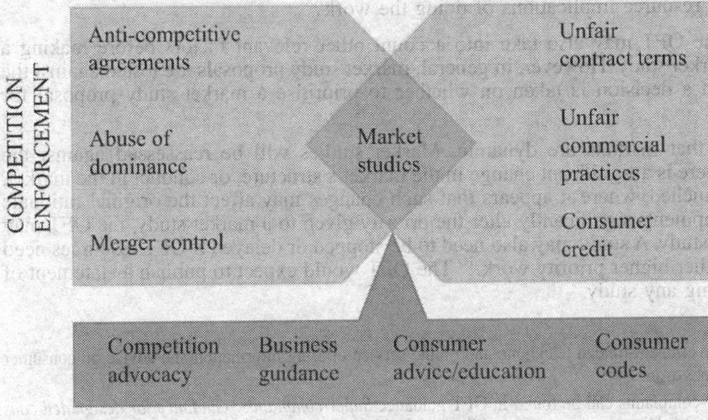

NOTES

1 *Productivity and Enterprise: a world class competition regime* (White Paper) Department of Trade and Industry, 2001. www.dti.gov.uk/ccp/topics2/ukcompref.htm

2 The OFT paper *Productivity and Competition* provides a detailed examination of the relationship between productivity and competition: www.oft.gov.uk/shared_oft/economic_research/oft887.pdf

3 See, for example, the economic and other research reports at: www.oft.gov.uk/advice_and_resources/publications/reports/

4 *Productivity and Enterprise: a world class competition regime* (White Paper) Department of Trade and Industry, 2001.

3. HOW DOES THE OFT CHOOSE MARKETS TO STUDY?

[3.637]

3.1 The OFT makes use of a range of sources to identify possible markets to study. These may include:

- complaints from businesses and trade associations
- consumer complaints data from Consumer Direct[5]
- suggestions from organisations representing consumer interests
- super-complaints from designated consumer bodies[6]
- suggestions made by other Government departments, local authority Trading Standards Services (TSS) and regulatory bodies
- OFT concerns based on information acquired in the course of enforcement and advocacy work
- intelligence gathering from publicly available sources, and
- OFT research.

3.2 The leads provided by stakeholders, the monitoring of complaints from businesses and consumers, and the OFT's concerns will typically be cross-checked against other information about the market in question. The OFT may carry out an initial assessment of the market by, for example, researching productivity levels, concentration, or the numbers of businesses entering and exiting the market. It may review the market's history of consumer complaints using information from its local authority TSS partners and Consumer Direct. It may also assess information about the market from other Government departments and public bodies and review relevant past OFT research.

3.3 Following this initial research phase, market study proposals are prepared. A market study proposal typically includes a description of the market and a theory of harm (an identification of the possible problems in the market and an explanation of their possible causes). A proposal typically considers possible remedies, assesses the potential impact the market study may have on consumer welfare, and estimates the OFT resources required to carry out the study.

3.4 As well as estimating the cost of the study for the OFT, in selecting studies, the OFT takes into account the fact that market study outcomes may involve costs to business. As these costs will, in all likelihood, be passed on to consumers, the OFT takes into account whether the net effect on consumer welfare of a market study is likely to be positive.[7]

3.5 Market study proposals are then considered against the OFT's prioritisation principles. These principles ensure that OFT resources are used to produce the greatest benefits for consumers. The principles can be summarised as:

- impact
  - — what is the likely direct or indirect impact on consumers?
  - — what are the wider economic benefits?
- strategic significance
  - — does the work tie in with the OFT's strategy and objectives?
  - — is the OFT best placed to act?
  - — how would the balance of the OFT's portfolio be affected?
- risks
  - — what is the likelihood of a successful outcome?
- resources
  - — what are the resource implications of doing the work?[8]

3.6 Where appropriate, the OFT may also take into account other relevant factors before making a decision to commence a market study. However, in general, market study proposals are tested against the prioritisation principles and a decision is taken on whether to prioritise a market study proposal for action.[9]

3.7 The OFT recognises that markets are dynamic. Market studies will be reassessed against the prioritisation principles if there is a significant change in the market's structure, or conduct in the market, after the study has been launched, where it appears that such changes may affect the original rationale for the study. If such developments significantly alter the priority given to a market study, the OFT may decide to curtail or stop the study. A study may also need to be stopped or delayed if OFT resources need to be diverted urgently to other higher priority work.[10] The OFT would expect to publish a statement of its reasons for not completing any study.

NOTES

5 Consumer Direct is the Government-funded telephone and online service offering information and advice on consumer issues: www.consumerdirect.gov.uk

6 More information on super-complaints can be found in OFT guidance *Super-complaints: Guidance for designated consumer bodies*: www.oft.gov.uk/advice_and_resources/publications/guidance/enterprise_act/oft514

7 The OFT will bear in mind that many of the costs are 'one-offs' whereas the benefits will be felt on an ongoing basis following implementation of any remedies, and may have knock-on effects on other markets. Even market studies that lead to a 'clean bill of health' can bring about benefits to the market in question, for example by removing regulatory uncertainty or promoting consumer confidence.

8 The OFT has published a document that provides a detailed description of each of the OFT's prioritisation principles and how they are used: www.oft.gov.uk/advice_and_resources/publications/corporate/general/oft953

9 Applying relevant OFT governance rules, including the OFT Board's Rules of Procedure www.oft.gov.uk/shared_oft/board/rules.pdf and authorisations under Schedule 1, paragraph 12 of the Enterprise Act 2002.

10 Such decisions would be taken according to relevant OFT governance rules (see footnote 9).

4. HOW DOES THE OFT MANAGE MARKET STUDIES?

PROJECT MANAGEMENT, TRANSPARENCY AND STAKEHOLDER ENGAGEMENT

[3.638]

4.1 Although market studies differ greatly in terms of subject matter, they are all managed according to the same set of project management principles. The OFT's project management framework is informed by the OFT's public service objectives and project management best practice. Key aspects of the framework are robust planning, clear roles and responsibilities for project team members, a structured project lifecycle, and a system for monitoring progress.

4.2 The OFT is committed to the principle of transparency. In the context of market studies, transparency means providing timely and useful information to stakeholders. Transparency also means being clear about why a market is being studied, how we intend to study the market, and providing accessible explanations about our findings and recommendations to stakeholders and the general public.

4.3 Stakeholder engagement means actively consulting, and taking into account the views of, interested parties such as businesses, organisations representing business, consumer groups and Government departments over the course of the market study. In most cases this will be done informally, rather than consulting formally on findings and recommendations. Engagement gives the OFT the opportunity to be clear about the issues we are considering, allowing for more focused submissions from stakeholders. It also helps the project team gain a better understanding of the market, and increases the likelihood that any recommendations will be accepted by stakeholders.

STAGES OF MARKET STUDY PROJECTS

4.4 In general, once a market study has been prioritised for action, there are four project stages that lead to the publication of the market study report. These stages are:

- pre-launch
- launch
- data collection and analysis, and
- informal consultation on findings and recommendations.

The duration of a study depends on many factors including the scale and complexity of the market. The average length of OFT market studies from launch to publication of the report has been around 12 months, but some studies have been as short as five months.

PRE-LAUNCH

4.5 Having decided to prioritise a market study proposal for action, a project team is formed. Market study project teams vary in size depending on the size and scope of the study. A typical team might consist of three to five staff, with input from OFT's legal and economic staff. The size and composition of the team will, however, vary according to the scale of the project and the specific skills required.

4.6 In the pre-launch period, the project team will generally work on the following:

- refining the scope of the project by describing the goods and services that make up the market, and developing the theory of harm and possible remedies
- reviewing the project proposal assumptions concerning the potential impact the project will have on reducing consumer detriment, and making an impact estimation plan[11]
- producing a project plan
- developing a stakeholder management and communication strategy
- identifying and assessing the risks affecting the study and agreeing the actions required to mitigate those risks, and
- depending on the significance of the study, forming an internal consultative steering committee to offer high level advice to the project team.

4.7 Where the OFT considers that it may be helpful to seek the views of stakeholders in advance of the formal launch of a market study, for example because there are questions around the appropriate scope, it may announce its intentions in a press release on its website, following which it will contact key stakeholders directly as well as inviting submissions from other interested parties.

LAUNCH

4.8 To launch a market study, the OFT will usually publish a press release. The press release will often be accompanied by a short document describing the study in more detail. This may include information on one or more of the following:

- the scope of what the project team intends to study and questions it is considering
- an invitation to make submissions
- contact details for the project team, and
- a timetable and high level milestones for the project.

This material is published on the OFT's website.

4.9 Stakeholders are free to contact, and make submissions to or seek clarification from, the OFT throughout the course of a market study. Such approaches should be made in the first instance to the contact point named on the OFT's website, who will arrange for them to be handled by the appropriate member of the project team.

DATA COLLECTION AND ANALYSIS

4.10 During this phase of the market study, the project team gathers detailed information about the market in order to test the theory of harm and possible remedies.[12]

4.11 Project teams collect data from businesses, consumers and organisations through a variety of means. Questionnaires, surveys and focus groups for businesses and consumers are used when appropriate. They may also hold meetings with individual stakeholders either in person or by telephone. Site visits to businesses may also be arranged. To find out about consumers' experience in the market, project teams may conduct 'mystery shopping' exercises.

4.12 Project teams may undertake further literature reviews to obtain additional information. They may also obtain information about similar markets in other sectors or countries. This comparative work can help inform analysis and provide ideas for how to address any problems which may be identified, although the OFT recognises the need to treat it with caution and to take account of differences in market structure and other features.

4.13 Quantitative data about the market is used in most market studies. This may be supplemented by qualitative data. Qualitative data can provide insights into the market and therefore lead to better analysis on the part of the project team. Examples drawn from stakeholders' experience may also be published in market study reports for illustrative purposes where these will promote a better understanding for readers.

4.14 For market studies dealing with public bodies acting as suppliers or customers, or projects focusing on the impact of regulations on competition, the project team will usually collect information from the relevant public bodies by questionnaires and through meetings.

4.15 Project teams aim to gather information in a way that imposes the minimum cost to business, and welcome early discussions with parties on alternative ways of collecting necessary data. Where a market study interacts with related work by other regulators and public bodies, the OFT will seek, as far as possible, to work with them to avoid overlaps and duplication, and, where possible, to coordinate information requests.

4.16 Market studies may require external consultants to provide additional resource for particular project activities, for example, conducting a survey. External consultants may also be used if specialist skills are required. In selecting consultants, the project team will have regard to potential conflicts of interest, and will also ensure that consultants who are awarded contracts are required to deal with sensitive information in accordance with the Official Secrets Act 1989, Data Protection Act 1998 and Enterprise Act 2002.

4.17 Project teams analyse the results of their data collection and test their theory of harm against the information. Based on this analysis, they will begin to determine what measures might be most appropriate to address any competition and consumer issues in the market.

INFORMAL CONSULTATION ON FINDINGS AND OUTCOMES

4.18 In most market studies, the project team will informally discuss its findings and proposed outcomes with stakeholders who will be affected by them. If a large number of stakeholders have been involved, only key stakeholders may be approached to ensure an efficient consultation, although any representations received at this stage will be considered. This informal consultation process provides an opportunity for the project team to test its analysis of the market and the recommendations it plans to make. Feedback can help the project team refine its recommendations so that they are effective and appropriately targeted.

4.19 For studies focused on the impact of regulations, team members will meet the relevant Government department or public body to discuss proposed recommendations and how they might best be implemented.

4.20 At this stage, the project team may approach those who have provided information to discuss the need for exclusion of potentially sensitive information prior to publication.[13]

PUBLICATION

4.21 Generally, market study reports give a description of the market or practice under consideration and the reasons for carrying out the study, describe the methodologies used to collect and analyse the data, set out the OFT's conclusions on the issues considered, and propose remedies to address any problems which may be identified. The research supporting the report will usually be annexed to it.

4.22 The report is published on the OFT website. Publication will usually be accompanied by a press release. Project team members and OFT officials may give media interviews about the study.[14]

DISCLOSURE OF INFORMATION OBTAINED DURING A MARKET STUDY

4.23 In terms of disclosing information the OFT acquires during a market study, Part 9 of the Enterprise Act 2002 and the Data Protection Act 1998 restrict the ability of the OFT to disclose information it receives in the course of its work. The Enterprise Act 2002 provides[15] a general restriction on disclosure of information relating to the affairs of an individual or the business of an undertaking if it has come to the OFT in the exercise of listed functions[16] unless disclosure is otherwise permitted under Part 9. Part 9 sets out a number of permitted gateways for disclosure, including, for example, disclosure for the purpose of facilitating the exercise of a statutory function.

4.24 Prior to making any disclosure, the OFT must have regard to the considerations in section 244 of the Enterprise Act 2002.[17] Where necessary, in order to reach an informed view on the application of section 244, the OFT will consult relevant individuals and businesses prior to publication of its report to seek their views on the level and nature of harm that might result from publication of certain information that they have supplied.

NOTES

The words omitted from footnote 12 below have been superseded by the revised CMA 3 (Market Studies and Market Investigations: Supplemental guidance on the CMA's approach), paras 2.11–2.16. See Annex A of CMA 3 at **[3.655]**.

Note that para 4.4 above should be read (with the exception of the pre-launch stage) in conjunction with paragraphs 2.6 to 2.10 of the revised CMA 3 which explain the requirement to publish a market study notice and the applicable timescales for the market study stage. See Annex A of CMA 3 at **[3.655]**.

Note that para 4.8 above should be read in conjunction with paragraph 2.6 of the revised CMA 3 which explains the requirement to publish a market study notice. From 1 April 2014 market studies are launched within the meaning of paragraph 4.8 by publication of a market study notice. See Annex A of CMA 3 at **[3.655]**.

Note that paras 4.21 and 4.22 above should be read in conjunction with paragraph 2.9 of the revised CMA 3 which explains the requirement on the CMA to publish a market study report within the statutory timeframe. See Annex A of CMA 3 at **[3.655]**.

[11] Chapter 6 gives more information on impact estimation.

[12] Section 5 of the Enterprise Act 2002 provides the legal basis for requests for information during the course of a market study. Section 5(1) states that 'the OFT has the function of obtaining, compiling, and keeping under review information relating to the carrying out of its functions.' These include the functions in sections 6 to 8 of the Enterprise Act 2002,

namely providing information to the public, providing information and advice to Ministers, and promoting good consumer practice. . . .

13 In particular, commercial information or information relating to the private affairs of an individual which, if disclosed, the OFT thinks might significantly harm the legitimate business interests of a business or the interests an individual (section 244(3) of the Enterprise Act 2002).

14 The legal basis on which the OFT publishes its market study reports is section 4(4) of the Enterprise Act 2002. This section states that the OFT 'may: prepare other reports in respect of matters relating to any of its functions, and arrange for any such report to be published'. In addition, the OFT can rely on its functions of providing information and advice for the benefit of the public and of promoting good consumer practice (sections 6 and 8 of the Enterprise Act 2002). When market study reports relate to markets involving Government regulations or public bodies, the OFT relies on its function of making proposals or giving other information or advice to Ministers or other public authorities (section 7 of the Enterprise Act 2002).

15 Section 237 of the Enterprise Act 2002.

16 Including functions under the Enterprise Act 2002.

17 The considerations the OFT must have regard to are as follows: the need to exclude from disclosure (so far as practicable) any information whose disclosure the OFT thinks is contrary to the public interest (section 244(2)); the need to exclude from disclosure (so far as practicable) (a) commercial information whose disclosure the OFT thinks might significantly harm the legitimate business interests of the undertaking to which it relates, or (b) information relating to the private affairs of an individual whose disclosure the OFT thinks might significantly harm the individual's interests (section 244(3)); the extent to which the disclosure of information subject to the second consideration is necessary for the purpose for which the OFT is permitted to make the disclosure (section 244(4)).

5. WHAT ARE THE OUTCOMES OF MARKET STUDIES?

[3.639]

5.1 The principal outcomes of a market study are one or more of the following:
- a clean bill of health for the market
- consumer-focused action
- recommendations to business
- recommendations to Government
- investigation and enforcement action, and
- a market investigation reference to the CC.

5.2 Except in the event of a clean bill of health, the outcomes of market studies generally require follow-up work, either to implement actions which are for the OFT to pursue, or to monitor the implementation of recommendations addressed to others, such as business or Government. This work may be carried out by the original project team, or passed to another team in the OFT.

A CLEAN BILL OF HEALTH

5.3 A market study may conclude that on balance, at the time of the report, the market, or aspects of the way it functions, can be given a clean bill of health. A clean bill of health will mean that some or all of the potential consumer detriment identified during the project proposal stage is not substantiated by the information obtained, or that intervention would not be proportionate to the detriment. Giving a clean bill of health can address public interest or concerns about a market. However, it does not preclude the OFT from revisiting the market at a later date should new information, or a change in market circumstances, suggest that there are concerns about the functioning of the market, and the OFT's prioritisation principles are met.

CONSUMER-FOCUSED ACTION

5.4 Consumer-focused action may take the form of an OFT-led information campaign. The objective of such campaigns is to raise consumer awareness so that consumers are able to make better purchasing decisions. The campaign may stress factors that consumers should consider when making a purchase, or inform consumers of their rights when transacting with businesses.

5.5 Consumer-focused action may involve the OFT working in partnership with organisations that assist consumers and other Government bodies. If the market involves a particular group of consumers, the OFT may work with the most appropriate organisation to help ensure that the campaign is successful.

RECOMMENDATIONS TO BUSINESS

5.6 Where market problems can be addressed through changes to business behaviour, the OFT may make recommendations to business. Recommendations may address a range of issues. Examples include improving how, when and what information on after-sales services is made available to consumers, changes to the standard terms and conditions of consumer contracts, and improving avenues for consumer redress in the event of problems or disputes.

5.7 The OFT can recommend that businesses in the market develop a code of conduct or improve an existing one. Codes of conduct may be appropriate if the market study finds a significant number of consumer complaints and problems having those complaints resolved. As codes are voluntary, the OFT will be more likely to recommend a code if the businesses concerned want to make improvements for consumers. The OFT may follow up recommendations on codes of conduct by providing support to trade bodies to ensure their codes address the issues identified in the market study report. Where appropriate, the OFT may work with relevant trade bodies to give OFT approval to a code of practice under its Consumer Codes Approval Scheme.[18]

RECOMMENDATIONS TO THE GOVERNMENT

5.8 When the OFT concludes that changes in the law, Government policy, and/or regulatory practice are necessary to remedy any problems which may be identified in the market, it will make recommendations to Government departments and/or other public agencies or regulators.

5.9 Recommendations to the Government are the likely outcome of market studies that examine the effect of regulations in a market, or markets where a public sector agency is a supplier or major customer. Recommendations to the Government may also be made when a market study concludes that consumers will benefit from additional protection, especially in markets where the risks of consumer harm are significant.

5.10 To promote its recommendations to the Government, the OFT will meet relevant agencies and departments to present findings and answer questions. The Government has committed to responding to the OFT's recommendations within 90 days of the market study report being published.[19]

5.11 The Department for Business Innovation and Skills (BIS) is responsible for coordinating the Government's responses where market studies make regulatory recommendations.[20] The OFT liaises closely with BIS[21] and, where appropriate, other interested Government departments, to monitor how actions on recommendations are progressing.

INVESTIGATION AND ENFORCEMENT ACTION

5.12 The appropriateness of enforcement action as a means of addressing the harm envisaged is considered at the selection stage, and such a course of action could, if appropriate, be followed at that point rather than as the outcome of a market study. Enforcement action may, however, follow a market study should evidence or understanding obtained through conducting the study indicate possible breaches of competition law or consumer protection legislation, or if it is concluded that enforcement action is in fact necessary to address the issues identified.[22] A study may help inform potential enforcement action, or identify alternative or additional outcomes.

MARKET INVESTIGATION REFERENCE TO THE COMPETITION COMMISSION

5.13 When the findings of a market study by the OFT give rise to reasonable grounds to suspect that a feature or combination of features of a market in the UK prevents, restricts or distorts competition, and a market investigation reference appears to be an appropriate and proportionate response, the OFT is able to make such a reference to the CC.[23] Decisions to make market investigation references are made in accordance with relevant OFT governance rules.[24] The OFT has a duty to consult on making a market investigation reference.[25] . . .

NOTES

The words omitted from para 5.13 have been superseded by CMA 3 (Market Studies and Market Investigations: Supplemental guidance on the CMA's approach), paras 2.9, 2.10 which set out the statutory timescales and consultation process that apply when the CMA proposes to make a reference. See Annex A of CMA 3 at **[3.655]**.

18 Information on OFT's code approval scheme can be found on the OFT's website: www.oft.gov.uk/consumer-advice/approved-codes-explained/

19 The 90 day response time to market studies is a Government commitment made in the White Paper, *Productivity and Enterprise: a world class competition regime*, Department of Trade and Industry, 2001.

20 The Department for Business Innovation and Skills' responses to market studies can be found on the Department's website: www.bis.gov.uk/policies/business-law/competition-matters/market-studies

21 Where recommendations are to the devolved administrations, the OFT works with the relevant bodies to promote the recommendations and monitor how they are acted upon.

22 Guidance and policy statements describing how the OFT uses its powers to enforce consumer protection and competition law are available on the OFT website: www.oft.gov.uk/OFTwork

23 The OFT's guidance *Market Investigation References* describes the legal test applied by the OFT when making a decision to refer a market, the process for making that decision and how the test is applied: www.oft.gov.uk/advice_and_resources/publications/guidance/enterprise_act/oft511

The CC's guidelines describe how it conducts its market investigations once a reference has been made. These guidelines can be found on the CC's website: www.competition-commission.org.uk

24 See footnote 9.

25 Section 169 of the Enterprise Act 2002.

6. HOW DOES THE OFT EVALUATE ITS MARKET STUDIES?

INDIVIDUAL MARKET STUDIES

[3.640]

6.1 Impact estimation measures the effect which interventions by the OFT are envisaged to have on reducing consumer detriment, and is a component of all market studies.[26] By estimating the impact of market studies, the OFT can assess if they are providing value for money.

6.2 As impact is an OFT prioritisation principle, an initial assessment of impact is presented in the market study project proposal.

6.3 In its annual reports, the OFT publishes estimates of consumer savings from completed market studies whose recommendations were implemented in the year.

MARKET STUDIES IN GENERAL

6.4 The OFT also runs a more in-depth evaluation programme for its work including market studies.[27] This programme currently commits the OFT to evaluating at least one market study a year. A key objective of the evaluation programme is to improve the effectiveness of the OFT by providing learning points that will inform how it prioritises its work and its choice of intervention methods. Comprehensive evaluations on past market studies provide information that will help the OFT:

- focus on markets where a market study is likely to make the most impact
- maximise the impact of each market study, and
- decide if further action should be taken in markets the OFT has studied.

6.5 Where appropriate, evaluations of individual market studies will consider whether their effect would have been different had a different approach been taken to implementation of their recommendations.

NOTES

[26] Further details of the principles and processes used to estimate impact can be found in the OFT publication *Approach to calculating direct benefits to consumers*: www.oft.gov.uk/advice_and_resources/publications/reports/Evaluating/oft955

[27] Further details on how market studies are evaluated can be found in the OFT publication *Evaluation strategy for market studies*: www.oft.gov. uk/shared_oft/about_oft/oft862.pdf

GUIDELINES FOR MARKET INVESTIGATIONS: THEIR ROLE, PROCEDURES, ASSESSMENT AND REMEDIES (CC3 (REVISED), APRIL 2013)

[3.641]

NOTES

As to the construction of this document (following the abolition of the OFT and Competition Commission), see further the note "The Competition and Markets Authority (references to the OFT and Competition Commission etc)" in the introductory notes to Part 3 preceding **[3.1]**.

Note also that all references to issues regarding the variation and termination of undertakings and orders or of jurisdiction or procedure in mergers cases or to market studies or investigations must be read in the light of Mergers: Guidance on the CMA's jurisdiction and procedure (CMA2), Market studies and market investigations: Supplemental guidance on the CMA's approach (CMA3) and Remedies: Guidance on the CMA's approach to the variation and termination of merger, monopoly and market undertakings and orders (CMA11); in the case of conflict, CMA2, CMA3 or CMA11 prevail.

See further CMA3 Market Studies and Market Investigations: Supplemental guidance on the CMA's approach (revised July 2017). The Annex to the Guidance (at **[3.655]**) lists changes to this Guidance consequential on the revision of CMA 3.

CONTENTS

INTRODUCTION

[3.642]

1. Market investigations were introduced by the Enterprise Act 2002 (the Act). In June 2003, the Competition Commission (CC) published *CC3, Market Investigation References: Competition Commission Guidelines* as one of the series of documents which it is required to publish under section 171(3) of the Act. Since the inception of the regime the CC has learnt much from its practical experience of conducting cases, and has progressively refined its policies, practices and procedures. These Guidelines distil the lessons the CC has absorbed since the introduction of the new regime and replace the 2003 version.

2. The Guidelines are in four parts, plus two annexes:

- Part 1 outlines the nature of competition and sets market investigations within the context of the overall regime for the promotion of competition within the UK. It describes how references are made to the CC and the statutory questions the terms of reference put to the CC.
- Part 2 provides guidance on the way the CC gathers evidence and the range and depth of its analysis, and outlines the processes and procedures the CC typically follows in conducting a market investigation and, if necessary, implementing remedies.
- Part 3 addresses the three issues the CC looks at in applying the AEC test:
  - the characteristics of the market and the outcomes of competition within it;
  - the definition of the market; and
  - the state of competition in the market; specifically, whether there are any features harming competition.

- Part 4 discusses the remedial action the CC may prescribe, if it has found there to be an AEC; this may include divestiture, behavioural remedies or recommendations for action by Government or other agencies.
- Annexes:
  - (A) Market characteristics and outcomes:
    - (1) Measuring market shares and concentration.
    - (2) Measuring profitability.
  - (B) Remedial action.

3. The types of markets referred to the CC vary widely, making it impossible to cover in these Guidelines all issues and aspects that might be encountered during investigations. The CC's assessment of markets has inevitably to be case-specific. The Guidelines cannot therefore be applied in a rigid and mechanistic way. While the CC will always have regard to these Guidelines in conducting market investigations, it will apply them flexibly and may sometimes depart from them, explaining its reasons for doing so, if it considers that the particular circumstances of the case (including the information available and the time constraints applicable) justify doing so. Past case references are included in the Guidelines for illustrative purposes only and do not constrain the CC's approach.

4. The Guidelines reflect the views of the CC and the competition regime in place at the time of publication. However, markets, economic theory, the legal background and best practice may develop and these Guidelines may be revised from time to time to reflect such developments.

5, 6. . . .

A BRIEF NOTE ON TERMINOLOGY

7. All references to statute, unless otherwise stated, relate to the Enterprise Act 2002 — referred to throughout as 'the Act' — and all references to 'section(s)', unless otherwise specified, relate to the Act. The term 'referring body' refers to the body making the reference (see paragraph 22).

8. Several terms used in the context of market investigations are 'terms of art', having specific and limited, rather than literal, meanings: notably, 'theory of harm' (see paragraph 163), 'relevant market' (see paragraph 26), 'efficiencies' (see paragraph 174) and 'a well-functioning market' (see paragraphs 30 and 320).

9. Throughout this publication also:

- unless otherwise specified, the term 'price' is used as shorthand for all aspects of a supplier's competitive offer; a change in price should be read as incorporating any comparable change in any element of the competitive offer;
- the term 'customers' includes 'consumers';[1]
- the term 'products' is used to apply to goods and/or services;
- 'market participants' are sellers, buyers and intermediaries, such as distributors, agents and platforms in multi-sided markets;
- the term 'market power' is used to denote the ability of a firm to influence aspects of competition (see paragraphs 178 to 204: unilateral market power); there are gradations of market power, with many firms having limited or transitory market power but only some having 'significant market power' which endures over time and gives them the ability to maintain prices above the competitive level, or restrict output or quality below competitive levels, without the consequent loss of sales becoming unprofitable; and
- the phrase 'to harm' competition is often used in the Guidelines as shorthand for the statutory language of 'prevents, restricts or distorts' competition.

NOTES

Paras 5, 6 (omitted) have been superseded by the revised CMA 3 (Market Studies and Market Investigations: Supplemental guidance on the CMA's approach). See Annex A of CMA 3 at **[3.655]**.

[1] See section 183(1).

PART 1: THE PROMOTION OF COMPETITION IN THE UK

[3.643]

10. Competition is a process of rivalry as firms seek to win customers' business. It creates incentives for firms to meet the existing and future needs of customers as effectively and efficiently as possible—by cutting prices, increasing output, improving quality or variety, or introducing new and better products, often through innovation; supplying the products customers want rewards firms with a greater share of sales. Beneficial effects may also come from expansion by efficient firms and the entry into the market of new firms with innovative products, processes and business models, and the exit of less successful ones.

11. In some instances firms compete for a market, rather than in a market, for example, by competing to be the first to claim a patent in a key area, the first to achieve scale in a new market, or to win a public procurement contract or franchise to supply a public service.

12. Vigorous competition between firms also fosters economic growth, as firms respond to competitive pressure by striving for efficiency and directing their resources to customers' priorities. Customers have an important part to play in stimulating rivalry between suppliers by making informed decisions which reward those firms that best satisfy their needs or preferences. Markets work best when both the supply side (the firms) and the demand side (the customers) interact effectively.

THREATS TO COMPETITION

13. There are many different ways—and combinations of ways—competition may be impeded in a market. Some instances are given in the following two paragraphs.

14. One or more firms may exhibit significant market power[2] when the market is highly concentrated, potentially adversely affecting not only price, cost and profits levels but also competition in the more dynamic sense of innovation and product development. There may be barriers to entry and expansion of various kinds, giving incumbent firms an advantage over potential market entrants as a result of, for example, scale economies, technological expertise, a strong customer network or regulatory requirements.

15. Other ways in which competition can be threatened include: rival firms may adopt, in some cases only tacitly, a coordinated approach to the market; vertical relationships among firms may enable them to foreclose markets or customers to rival firms, or otherwise to exert a dampening effect on competition; and customers may lack information about what product to choose, may not be able to judge between different products on offer or may be locked into one supplier and unable to switch to another.

RESPONDING TO THE THREATS TO COMPETITION

16. Regulators, competition authorities and governments have an important role to play in making sure competition is as effective as possible. They do so in various ways. Sometimes the Government may intervene directly in specific markets with this aim (for example, in the programme of liberalizing public utilities in the 1980s and 1990s). The merger control regime limits the ability of firms to avoid competing with their rivals by gaining control of them. Economic regulation of certain sectors involves measures to assist customers to make informed choices and to encourage new entry and investment, promoting the emergence of competition in markets where it has been historically weak. Regulators can also intervene directly to prevent or mitigate the harmful effects of a lack of competition in the short term.

17. Legal prohibitions play a particularly important role in limiting the extent to which firms are able to restrict competition between them or win customers in non-competitive ways. Specifically, the prohibitions under the Treaty on the Functioning of the European Union (TFEU)[3] and the Competition Act 1998 (CA98)[4] are designed to prevent and penalize collusive conduct among rival firms or abusive practices by a dominant firm.[5] Enforcement of these prohibitions falls, not to the CC, but to the European Commission and the OFT together with certain ('concurrent') sectoral regulators,[6] respectively.

THE MARKET INVESTIGATION REGIME

18. The CC's market investigation regime sits within the broad spectrum of competition law, operating alongside other regulatory mechanisms, including prohibitions (see paragraph 17), by allowing the competition authorities the opportunity to assess whether competition in a market is working effectively, where it is desirable to focus on the functioning of the market as a whole rather than on a single aspect of it or the conduct of particular firms within it. A market investigation may examine any competition problem and identify the feature causing the problem. It aims only to see if competition within the particular market under review is working well or can be improved and is not seeking to establish general rules and obligations for firms.

19. Its overarching framework allows the investigation to tackle adverse effects on competition (AECs) from any source. As well as being able to look into the conduct of firms, the CC can probe for other causes of possible AECs, such as structural aspects of the market (including barriers to entry and expansion) or the conduct of customers. However, the focus of an investigation is always on competition. There may be other problems in the market—for example, 'externalities', such as air or water pollution, the cost or benefit of which is not transmitted through prices—which fall outside the ambit of a market investigation.

20. Having established a competition problem, and identified its causes, the CC is able to impose a wide range of legally enforceable remedies that typically focus on making the market more competitive in the future and make recommendations for remedial action by other public bodies.

21. The identification of anticompetitive features in a market investigation or the imposition of remedies does not mean that market participants[7] have infringed the law. The process is investigative and inquisitorial, not accusatorial. To be required to give evidence in a market investigation or be subject to remedial action following an investigation does not imply that market participants are suspected of wrongdoing.

THE MAKING OF REFERENCES TO THE CC

22. The CC does not select markets for investigation. The referring bodies—the OFT, a sector regulator[8] or, exceptionally, a Minister[9]—make market investigation references to the CC when they have reasonable grounds for suspecting that a feature or combination of features of a market in the UK is preventing, restricting or distorting competition.[10] However, once a reference is received, the CC proceeds wholly independently of the referring body; a CC market investigation casts a 'fresh pair of eyes' able to look more deeply at new evidence and analysis of the market. Regardless of the views of the referring body, it may conclude that there are no adverse effects in the market.

23. Before a case reaches the CC the referring body will have looked into the market in question, either on its own initiative or in response to a complaint, which may include a 'super-complaint' from certain designated consumer bodies.[11] The Act[12] allows the OFT to study markets that appear not to be working well for customers. There is no statutory definition of a 'market study' but it was envisaged from the inception of the Act that the OFT should use market studies as a way to promote competition. The Enterprise White Paper *A World Class Competition Regime* (July 2001) said that the OFT 'should scrutinize markets to assess whether strong competition pressures are at work . . . in some cases . . . it will need to refer the market to the Competition Commission for further study'. The other sectoral regulators having powers concurrently with the OFT (see paragraph 22) can also study markets coming within their purview. Where a market study suggests that a market is not working well, the referring body has several options open to it. It may recommend legislation, or actions by customers; it may proceed to investigate any suspected breaches of consumer protection legislation or the competition law prohibitions; and/or, where it has reasonable grounds for suspecting there are features which prevent, restrict or harm competition, make a market investigation reference. (But the referring body may also accept undertakings in lieu of making a reference if appropriate undertakings are offered.) Where a market study leads to a reference to the CC, it thus serves as the first phase in a two-phase investigation process.

24. When faced with a choice on how to deal with a perceived competition problem, the approach the OFT or sectoral regulator takes will depend on many factors, some of which may suggest that a market investigation reference is the appropriate course:[13]

- A market investigation might be preferred when, for example, the facts and issues underlying a perceived competition problem are complex and other forms of intervention by the Government or regulatory body might have to be too tightly focused to benefit the overall operation of the market.
- The range of remedies available under the market investigation regime can also make a market investigation a more appropriate instrument than relying on the system of prohibitions (see paragraph 17). Prohibitions on using market power to exploit customers or exclude rivals, or on coordinating with the few rivals that remain, may not be sufficient to address issues in a market whose characteristics and structure limit the ability or incentive of firms to compete effectively. There are markets, for example, in which the root cause of a problem lies within the regulatory framework; or it may lie within the way the market operates, with weak competition resulting, for example, from network effects,[14] customer inertia or imperfect information flows between market participants.

25. . . .

TERMS OF REFERENCE AND THE STATUTORY QUESTIONS

26. In its terms of reference (ToR) for the CC investigation, the referring body describes the goods or services in the UK that the CC is to investigate. The ToR will indicate the sources (the feature or features, see paragraph 28) the referring body suspects are giving rise to an AEC (see paragraphs 19 and 29). When making the reference, the referring body may also require the CC to confine its investigation to either the supply or the acquisition of the goods or services described in the ToR, in particular by reference to the place where the goods and services are supplied or acquired or the persons by or to whom they are supplied or acquired or by or from whom they are acquired.[16] The 'relevant market' is defined in the Act to mean the market for the goods or services described in the ToR given to the CC for investigation.[17] The market definition(s) used by the CC (see paragraphs 130 to 153) need not always correspond with the 'relevant market(s)' as used in the Act.[18]

27. The Act enables the ToR to be varied, either at the instigation of the referring body, after consultation with the CC, or at the request of the CC. In principle this could be to widen or narrow the scope of the investigation while it is in progress, It will also be for the CC to reach its own conclusions on whether or not there is any AEC. [19] although it would be likely to raise procedural and timing issues. A variation would not affect the statutory timetable.

An AEC

28. The CC is required to decide 'whether any feature, or combination of features, of each relevant market prevents, restricts or distorts competition in connection with the supply or acquisition of goods or services in the United Kingdom or a part of the United Kingdom'.[20]

29. If that proves to be the case, under the Act this constitutes an AEC (see paragraphs 19 and 26).[21] The CC interprets the phrase 'prevents, restricts or distorts' in the Act broadly to cover any adverse effect on competition, whether actual or potential. It will therefore consider features that affect potential competition in a market (for example, by preventing entry and expansion) as well as those that affect the existing market situation.

30. The Act does not specify a theoretical benchmark against which to measure an AEC. In its market investigation reports the CC uses the term 'a well-functioning market' in the sense, generally, of a market without the features causing the AEC, rather than to denote an idealized, perfectly competitive market. The criteria the CC applies in coming to a view on the existence of an AEC are discussed in paragraphs 319 and 320, below.

Features

31. The Act states that the following may be taken to be a 'feature' of a market:[22]

(a) the structure of the market concerned or any aspect of that structure;

(b) any conduct (whether or not in the market concerned) of one or more than one person who supplies or acquires goods or services in the market concerned; or

(c) any conduct relating to the market concerned of customers of any person who supplies or acquires goods or services.

32. How the CC identifies features that prevent, restrict or distort competition is described in paragraphs 155 to 162.

Remedial action

33. Where the CC decides that there is an AEC, it is required to decide additional questions relating to remedial action, which are set out in paragraph 325.

NOTES

Para 25 (and the associated footnote) have been superseded by paragraphs 3.15 to 3.19 of the revised CMA 3 which explain the changes made in relation to how cases raising specified public interest considerations are handled during the market investigation stage. See Annex A of CMA 3 at **[3.655]**.

Note also that para 22 should be read in conjunction with paragraphs 1.23 to 1.27 of the revised CMA 3 which explain how the reference process and appointment of the reference group are changed to take account of the formation of the CMA. See Annex A of CMA 3 at **[3.655]**.

2 See paragraph 9.

3 Articles 101(1) and 102.

4 See The Chapter I Prohibition (OFT401) and Chapter II Prohibition (OFT402).

5 The relationship between Articles 101 and 102 TFEU and national competition law is provided for in Article 3 of Council Regulation 1/2003/EC. Under Article 1 of that regulation, where national competition authorities apply national competition law to agreements, decisions by associations of undertakings or concerted practices within the meaning of Article 101(1) which may affect trade between member states or to any abuse prohibited by Article 102 they shall also apply Article 101 or 102 respectively. Under Article 2 the application of national competition law may not lead to the prohibition of agreements, decisions by associations of undertakings or concerted practices which may affect trade between member states but which are not prohibited under Article 101(1) or which fulfil the conditions of Article 101(3) or are covered by an EC block exemption, although they may prohibit or sanction unilateral conduct engaged in by undertakings which is not prohibited by Article 102. Article 3 of the regulation provides that, without prejudice to the general principles and other provisions of Community law, Articles 1 and 2 do not preclude the application of provisions of national law that predominantly pursue an objective different from that pursued by Articles 101 and 102. In the context of a market investigation these provisions do not affect the exercise by the CC of its powers of investigation, but may be relevant at the remedies stage (ie the CC would have to consider whether it was limited or prevented from taking remedial action). If during the course of its investigation the CC uncovered a potential breach of Article 101(1), it would consider whether that matter should be referred to the authorities responsible for enforcing Article 101 but would also expect to continue with its investigation and then take the application of Regulation 1 into account when determining whether to take remedial action and if so, what action to take. If the CC found evidence suggesting a breach of Article 102 it would normally continue its investigation and, when appropriate, implement remedies under the Act. The OFT would then be able to take such action into account when carrying out any Article 102 investigation it considered appropriate.

6 The following bodies have concurrent powers with the OFT in designated areas to apply and enforce CA98 and Articles 101 and 102 of the TFEU: Office of Communications (Ofcom) (communications); Water Services Regulation Authority (Ofwat) (water and sewerage in England and Wales); Office of Rail Regulation (ORR) (railways); Gas and Electricity Markets Authority (Ofgem) (gas and electricity); Northern Ireland Authority for Utility Regulation (NIAUR) (gas and electricity in Northern Ireland); Civil Aviation Authority (CAA) (air traffic services); and Monitor (healthcare services in England).

7 See paragraph 9.

8 The powers of the concurrent regulators (see footnote 6) apply also to the making of market investigation references under section 131 of the Act.

9 Section 132. Ministers have the ability to make market references as a reserve power; in addition to applying the same criteria set out in the Act for the making of a reference by the OFT or other referring body, a minister must either be 'not satisfied' with an OFT decision not to make a reference or, having brought information to the attention of the OFT, will decide whether to make a reference in the period that the minister considers is reasonable, As at the date of publication of these Guidelines, this power had never been used.

10 As at the time of publication of these Guidelines, the OFT had been responsible for 13 of the 15 references made since the Act came into force.

11 Section 11 of the Act allows a consumer body (acting collectively on behalf of consumers), that has been designated by Ministers, to make a 'super-complaint' to the OFT about features of a market that appear to be significantly harming the interests of consumers. See: www.oft.gov.uk/advice_and_resources/resource_base/super-complaints/ and www.oft.gov.uk/advice_and_resources/resource_base/market-studies/.

12 Section 5.

13 For further details see OFT511, www.oft.gov.uk/shared_oft/business_leaflets/enterprise_act/oft511.pdf.

14 See paragraph 179.

16 Section 133.

17 Section 134(3). An alternative description could be 'reference market'.

18 In these Guidelines, 'relevant market' is used in two contexts: first, when referring to the statutory test, it has the meaning as defined in section 134(3) (see footnote 17); secondly, when referring to market definition, the relevant market is the market defined by the CC (an alternative description of which could be 'economic market').

19 The ToR in March 2004 for the investigation of *(a)* store card credit and related services to retailers, and *(b)* consumer credit through store cards were, for example, varied in March the following year to include insurance services, related to store cards, for retailers, and insurance for consumer credit associated with store cards (see *Store cards market investigation*, 7 March 2006).

20 Section 134(1).

21 Section 134(2).

22 Section 131(2).

Part 3 CMA and other Guidelines

PART 2: THE CONDUCT OF A MARKET INVESTIGATION

[3.644]

34. This part of the Guidelines begins by outlining the ways the CC gathers evidence and the range and depth of the analysis it conducts (paragraphs 35 to 41). A second section outlines the processes and procedures typically followed in the conduct of market investigations and in the implementation of remedies (paragraphs 42 to 93); the latter section discusses: (A) statutory obligations and rules for Inquiry Groups; (B) the appointment of Inquiry Groups and staff; (C) overarching procedural issues; and (D) the main stages of an investigation.

1. THE GATHERING AND ANALYSIS OF EVIDENCE

35. In collecting and analysing evidence on the way the market under investigation operates, the CC will particularly try to assemble evidence on the impact possible features have on the market's operation.

Range of analysis

36. The CC only carries out analysis that it considers necessary so as to reach a decision on the statutory questions. As the CC scrutinizes evidence, it will prioritise the uses of its resources to undertake as wide and as deep analyses as appropriate.[23]

37. The CC's analysis covers all relevant aspects of competition. It often assesses the ability or incentives firms have to offer better prices or terms to customers and to strive for efficiency, better ways of operating and improved products.

38. Whatever forms competition takes, the CC considers its effects and expected development over time. Although there may be circumstances in which analysis can be conducted only on the basis of the current state of the market, the CC always considers how a market may evolve. The prospect of gaining a lasting advantage over rivals can be a spur to competition, and the CC may in some circumstances consider assessing the effectiveness of competition for the market as well as, or rather than, within the market (see paragraph 11).

Qualitative and quantitative analysis

39. The CC applies a range of analytical techniques, both qualitative and quantitative, so as to understand the nature of competition in the market under investigation as well as the impact of any features. The CC will seek data and information about a range of factors, including the pricing and quality of goods and services supplied in the market under investigation. It often commissions surveys, normally on customer behaviour and attitudes, at an early stage of an investigation (see paragraph 67). It will use various other means of collecting evidence, including questionnaires to parties, requests for internal company documents (including management information), and discussions with customers, investors and other market participants. (See paragraphs 63 to 69 on the procedures for information-gathering).

40. Parties may also choose to provide the CC with any information they consider relevant to the investigation. When making submissions involving technical economic analysis, parties should adhere to the principles set out in the CC's publication *Suggested best practice for submissions of technical economic analysis from parties to the Competition Commission.*[24] A joint CC/OFT good practice guide for parties wishing to submit evidence based on consumer surveys in merger inquiries[25] is also relevant to market investigations.

41. The extent to which the CC will seek to quantify particular effects (eg on the adverse effects on competition or the effects of remedies)—and the degree of precision with which this is attempted—is likely to vary from case to case. Relevant considerations in determining the extent and nature of quantification that the CC will carry out in a particular case may include:

(a) The scale of any particular effect: if it is clear from an initial assessment that a particular effect is unlikely to be material, it may not be necessary to quantify its magnitude with great precision to reach a view about the scale of any harm to competition. Similarly, when it considers that the harm is material, the CC may decide that quantification would not add value to its assessment.

(b) The practicality of conducting quantitative analysis: whether reliable data is available and the extent to which it is possible to quantify a particular effect with any degree of accuracy. (In general, it is likely to be more straightforward to estimate the effects on prices in the shorter term than to quantify the longer-term effects on dynamic and non-price competition.)

(c) The resource implications: the costs in terms of time and resources to acquire and process the data, to apply a suitable methodology and to test the robustness of the results would not be justified if the outcome would not significantly help the CC to reach a decision on the statutory questions.

2. PROCESSES AND PROCEDURES

42. The procedures the CC follows in market investigations have been developed to fulfil and balance different demands. It is imperative that investigations are concluded within the statutory time limit, and the time and resources of both the CC and the parties must consequently be used efficiently. At the same time, the CC recognizes that market investigations can result in significant interventions in markets and that its investigations must not only be thorough and disciplined but also fair. The requirement for fairness includes giving the parties opportunities to understand the CC's analysis affecting them; the CC accordingly aims to be open and transparent in its work.[26]

43. The following sections:

(A) outline the statutory obligations and rules with which Inquiry Groups must comply (paragraphs 44 and 45);
(B) explain how Inquiry Groups and staff teams are appointed (paragraphs 46 to 49);
(C) discuss some of the overarching procedural issues in conducting a market investigation (paragraphs 50 to 61); and
(D) provide a guide to the main stages in a typical investigation (paragraphs 62 to 93).

A. Statutory obligations and rules for Inquiry Groups

44. The CC has a statutory duty to consult on its proposed decisions on the AEC test and the remedy questions when it considers a decision likely to have a substantial impact on any parties' interests.[27] The Chairman of the CC is also required to issue Rules of Procedure for market reference Inquiry Groups. The current Rules of Procedure[28] are published on the CC website and may be revised from time to time. The Rules include requiring Inquiry Groups to:
(a) draw up and notify the parties of the administrative timetable for each investigation (and to prepare a revised timetable if required);
(b) decide the forms of hearings (public or private, joint or individual) and who should attend them;
(c) notify the main parties of their provisional findings on the statutory questions (on the AEC issue) and allow them at least 21 days to comment on the provisional findings; and
(d) notify main parties of actions which may be taken to remedy the AEC and give the parties the chance to make representations about the Inquiry Group's proposed actions.

45. Subject to complying with the Rules of Procedure, and having regard to any guidance issued by the CC Chairman, Inquiry Groups are free to decide how they conduct a market investigation.[29]

B. Appointment of Inquiry Groups and staff

46. Market investigations are performed by Inquiry Groups of independent CC members[30] (commonly between four and six), normally chaired by the Chairman of the CC or by one of the Deputy Chairmen.[31] An Inquiry Group conducting an investigation provides its strategic direction, weighs the evidence and considers the arguments from parties, both received in writing and given orally, and directs and assesses the analysis produced by the staff team. It makes the final decisions on whether or not there are features of a market that give rise to an AEC and if so on the remedies to be applied.

Appointment of Inquiry Groups

47. As soon as practical after receiving the reference, the CC Chairman identifies and appoints an Inquiry Group. The composition of the Inquiry Group and biographical details of its members are sent to parties and published on the CC inquiry webpage. The appointment of the Inquiry Group is made for the duration of the investigation, up to the point at which the reference is 'finally determined.'[32]

48. Before deciding to appoint a member to a particular Inquiry Group, the CC will consider whether there might be a risk that a member's outside interests could affect, or could be perceived as affecting, the impartiality of the CC. [33] In some cases the CC may inform parties of specific interests and give them the opportunity to comment before deciding whether to make a proposed appointment. Relevant outside interests of appointed members are disclosed on the CC website. In addition, the CC may take action to deal with any relevant and significant changes in members' interests that may arise during the course of the investigation.[34]

Staff team

49. Each Inquiry Group is supported by a staff team. The team is led by an Inquiry Director and includes both inquiry management and specialist staff. The inquiry management team is responsible for the day-to-day running of the investigation; the key point of contact at the CC for the parties is likely to be the Inquiry Manager. The specialist staff provide advice to the Inquiry Group in their areas of expertise (including economics, law, business and finance). They conduct the analysis on the substantive issues that arise during the investigation and develop remedies where needed. The staff team may sometimes be supplemented by academic specialists or other advisers.

50-61 . . .

D. The main stages of an investigation

62-87 . . .

Implementation of remedies

88. Following publication of the final report, if the CC has determined to take action itself, the CC has the choice of implementing remedies by accepting undertakings from the relevant parties and/or by making an order (see paragraphs 92 and 93 for a discussion of the considerations relevant to this choice).

89. The CC will publish an administrative timetable for the implementation of those remedies where it has decided to take action itself. For straightforward remedies, the CC expects to make an order or accept undertakings within around six months of publication of its final report. The implementation of more complex remedies may take longer, though the CC expects to make an order or accept undertakings within ten months from publication of its final report, other than in exceptional circumstances.[53] The CC consults all parties affected by the remedies in determining the required undertakings or order. This includes a period of formal public consultation.[54]

90. The action the CC takes in implementing remedies must be consistent with the decisions in the final report unless there has been a material change of circumstances since the preparation of the report or the CC has a special reason for acting differently.[55]

91. An Inquiry Group will normally be disbanded following its acceptance of Final Undertakings or the imposition of an order to implement remedies. Responsibility for overseeing any further implementation activity that falls to the CC, such as the implementation of any divestiture remedy, falls to either the CC's Remedies Standing Group or to a specifically-appointed Group. A Group specifically appointed to oversee further implementation activity may include some or all members of the original Inquiry Group (see footnote 32). The identity of the Group charged with this activity is determined in light of factors such as the availability and expertise of members, the type of remedy to be implemented and the extent to which implementation is expected to be resource- and/or time-intensive. If all remedies are being implemented by means of recommendations to other bodies, the Inquiry Group originally appointed is normally disbanded following publication of the final report. The OFT is normally responsible for monitoring and enforcement of behavioural remedies[56] following acceptance of undertakings or the imposition of an order by the CC. Compliance with undertakings or an order is enforceable in the courts.[57]

Undertakings and Orders

92. The CC's decision whether to implement remedies by means of accepting undertakings or making an order is determined case by case, primarily by practical issues including the number of parties concerned, and their willingness to negotiate and agree undertakings. Another consideration is the scope of the CC's order-making powers and whether the remedy it is considering falls within those powers.

93. The content of any orders made by the CC is limited by the Act.[58] In contrast, the subject matter of an undertaking is not similarly limited.[59] This, and the process involved in agreeing undertakings, can help the CC and the parties, in terms of flexibility and suitability, in implementing remedies. However, because market investigations are likely to be market-wide rather than focused on the conduct of one firm, it may be more practical to implement remedies by order rather than through undertakings, so as to avoid the likely delay and complexity of negotiating undertakings with several parties.[60] In regulated sectors, if the CC decides to modify licence conditions to give effect to, or take account of, any provision of a proposed remedy, it will make an order.[61]

NOTES

Paras 50 to 87 described the process for undertaking market investigations, and are superseded by paragraphs 3.24–3.64 of the revised CMA 3. See Annex A of CMA 3 at **[3.655]**. Note also that the first sentence of para 54 is superseded by paragraphs 3.5 to 3.7 of the revised CMA 3 which explain the shorter statutory timescales that apply to the market investigation stage.

Note that paras 46 to 48 above should be read in conjunction with paragraphs 1.23 to 1.27 which explain how the reference process and appointment of the reference group are changed to take account of the formation of the CMA. See Annex A of CMA 3 at **[3.655]**.

Note that para 49 above should be read in conjunction with paragraph 1.22 which explains the reference process at an operational (staff) level. See Annex A of CMA 3 at **[3.655]**.

Note that para 89 above should be read in conjunction with paragraphs 4.5 to 4.7 of the revised CMA 3 which explain the statutory timescales applicable to the remedies implementation period. See Annex A of CMA 3 at **[3.655]**.

23 The need for the CC to focus on the bigger issues in reaching a decision on the statutory questions has been underlined in Competition Appeal Tribunal (CAT) judgments: in *Barclays Bank plc v Competition Commission* (2009), CAT 27 (paragraph 21); citing *Tesco v Competition Commission* (2009), CAT 6 (paragraph 139), the CAT wrote: 'the depth and sophistication called for in relation to any particular relevant aspect of the inquiry needs to be tailored to the importance or gravity of the issue within the general context of the Commission's task.' This proposition was labelled 'double proportionality' in the CAT judgments.

24 Suggested best practice for submissions of technical economic analysis from parties to the CC, www.competitioncommission.org.uk/rep_pub/corporate_documents/corporate_policies/best_practice.pdf.

25 www.competition-commission.org.uk/assets/competitioncommission/docs/2011/consultations/good_practice_guide.pdf.

26 As explained in *CC7 (Revised), Chairman's Guidance on Disclosure of Information in Merger Inquiries, Market Investigations and Reviews of Undertakings and Orders accepted or made under the Enterprise Act 2002 and Fair Trading Act 1973* (April 2013), an important aim of transparency is to ensure that 'by having a better understanding of the CC's analysis affecting them, the main parties in inquiries are treated fairly' (paragraph 2.2(a)).

27 Section 169 of the Act.

28 *CC1, Competition Commission Rules of Procedure*, 2006: www.competition-commission.org.uk/assets/competitioncommission/docs/pdf/non-inquiry/rep_pub/rules_and_guide/pdf/cc1.pdf.

29 CA98, Schedule 7, paragraph 19 (see paragraph 17 above).

30 A pool of members—currently (March 2013) around 40—is appointed by the Department for Business, Innovation and Skills (BIS) for eight years, following open competition. Members are selected for their experience, ability and diversity of skills in competition economics, law, finance and industry. All except the CC Chairman and Deputy Chairmen work part-time for the CC.

31 Occasionally, a member who is neither the Chairman nor one of the Deputy Chairmen will be asked to chair an Inquiry Group conducting a market investigation.

32 Generally a reference is finally determined, as defined in section 183(3)-(6) of the Act, when the final report is published or, if remedial action is to be taken by the CC, when the remedies are implemented (ie either by the making of an Order or acceptance of Final Undertakings). Paragraph 17 of Schedule 7 to CA98 provides that the CC Chairman may appoint replacements to the Inquiry Group if necessary. Members may be reappointed to deal with matters arising from the reference following final determination, for example to consider any ongoing remedy implementation or post-litigation issues (see paragraph 91).

33 See guidance on outside interests on the CC website: www.competition-commission.org.uk/our_peop/members/

conflicts_interest/110407_Conflicts_guidance_for_publication.pdf. The guidance categorizes the most common interests that could put the CC's impartiality at risk as: financial interests, organisational relationships, personal relationships and pre-judgement.

34 If at any time during an investigation it appears to the Chairman that, because of a particular interest of a member, it is inappropriate for him or her to remain in the Inquiry Group, the Chairman may appoint a replacement. CA98, Schedule 7, paragraph 17(1)(c).

35 An upstream firm provides raw materials or manufactures inputs for processing and/or distribution by a downstream firm.

36 See paragraph 23.

38 Rule 6.4 provides that the administrative timetable should be produced having regard to the views of the main parties *(CC1)*.

39 Section 109 of the Act, which applies to market investigations by virtue of section 176 of the Act. For further details see *CC5, Statement of Policy on Penalties, June 2003*.

40 Section 180 of the Act deals with the provision of false or misleading information and the commission of offences by bodies corporate. Section 125 states that offences of bodies corporate may be an offence of the secretary, director or other officer of the body corporate.

41 Part 9 of the Act, in particular section 245, provides that a person commits an offence if he or she discloses or uses specified information unless in the circumstances permitted by the Act or the information is already in the public domain in the circumstances described by section 237(3).

42 Section 244.

43 For example, to enable disclosure of some data used in its analysis, the CC might set up a data room in which the parties' economic advisers can review it. Rules relating to access, use and non-disclosure are applied and participants are required to sign undertakings that they will comply with the restrictions.

44 *CC7 (Revised)* and *CC6, Chairman's Guidance to Groups*, March 2006, paragraphs 19–26.

45 On possible variations in the timing and content of procedures see paragraph 55.

46 Section 170 of the Act stipulates that the referring body provide the CC with: *(a)* such information in its possession as the CC might reasonably require; *(b)* any other assistance which the CC may reasonably require to carry out its investigation and which the body has the power to give, and; *(c)* information in its possession which, although not requested by the CC, is appropriate for the referring body to give the CC to assist it in carrying out its functions.

47 See paragraph 23.

48 See paragraphs 23 & 52.

49 The survey results will usually be disclosed through publication (accompanied by an explanation of the methodology) but there may be instances when it is inappropriate to publish the whole report. The Inquiry Group will consider whether other information relating to the survey should be disclosed, for example cross-tabulations of the survey results.

50 See *CC7 (Revised)*, paragraphs 7.1–7.3. Disclosed working papers provide a snapshot of the issues, analysis and views that are relevant at the time of disclosure and may change.

51 Section 136.

52 Following appeals against CC decisions, the CAT ordered the CC to reconsider parts of the remedies packages in the final reports on *Groceries* (April 2008) and *Payment Protection Insurance (PPI)* (January 2009). These aspects were, respectively, the competition test applied to grocery retail planning applications and the inclusion of a prohibition of the issuing of PPI at the point of sale.

53 The period envisaged for the implementation of remedies by the CMA (see paragraph 5) is limited to six months, with the possibility of a four-month extension.

54 As specified in Schedule 10 to the Act.

55 Section 138. For example, following the Court of Appeal's judgment on 13 October 2010 to reinstate the CC's findings on the *BAA airports* investigation (March 2009), the CC invited representations from all interested parties as to whether there had been any developments since the publication of the CC's report which constituted a material change of circumstances or a special reason within the scope of section 138(3) of the Act, to the extent that it should amend the remedy package set out in the report, for example the timing of proposed airport divestitures. In its decision of July 2011, the CC found that while the change in government policy on building new runway capacity in south-east England represented a significant change of circumstances, it did not remove the scope for, and the need for, competition between airports in south-east England as claimed by BAA. Consequently, the CC did not change its decision on the appropriate remedy.

56 Section 162.

57 If a person fails to comply with any undertakings that it has given or any order imposed on it by the CC, compliance may be enforced by means of civil proceedings brought by the OFT or the CC (section 167). In addition to enforcement by the OFT or the CC, any person affected by the contravention of undertakings or an order who has sustained resulting loss or damage may also bring an action against the relevant party.

58 Schedule 8 sets out the types of provisions that could be included in an order and Part 1 of Schedule 9 enables the CC to modify, by order, licence conditions in various regulated markets.

59 Section 164(1).

60 For example, in *Home Credit* and *PPI*, the remedies applied to a large number of parties and this was a reason for implementing these measures by means of an order. By contrast, in *Classified Directories*, the remedies applied to only one party and undertakings were preferred. In other cases (eg *Groceries*, *Rolling Stock Leasing market (ROSCOs)*), some measures were implemented by means of an order, while others were implemented through undertakings.

61 The CC has the power to make such changes by Order through the amendments made to sector specific legislation by Part 1 of Schedule 9 to the Act.

PART 3: THE AEC TEST

[3.645]

94. In assessing whether or not an AEC has arisen the CC looks at three basic issues:

(a) the main characteristics of the market and the outcomes of the competitive process;

(b) the composition of the relevant market[62] within which competition may be harmed (market definition); and

Part 3 CMA and other Guidelines

(c) the features, if any, which are harming competition in the relevant market (the competitive assessment—which the CC frames using 'theories of harm'), considering also possible countervailing factors, such as efficiencies, which may remove or mitigate the competitive harm of the features.

95. Analyses of these issues are not conducted as distinct chronological stages of the investigation but as overlapping and continuous pieces of work, which often feed into each other. For example, the CC may take an initial view about the scope of the relevant market but the competitive assessment may suggest that this initial view of the market was either too broad or too narrow. Evaluation of outcomes continues throughout the investigation.

96. Part 3, Sections 1 to 3, below, deal with each of these issues in turn, and are followed by a short section on the conclusion of the AEC test.

PART 3: SECTION 1—MARKET CHARACTERISTICS AND OUTCOMES

97. To develop robust findings on whether or not features in a market are harming competition, the CC needs to understand how a market operates and reach a view about its performance. A part of its investigation is therefore the collection and analysis of information about the main characteristics of the market referred and the outcomes of the competitive process within that market. The CC's evaluation of characteristics and outcomes goes on throughout an investigation and continuously informs its assessment of what might be causing any adverse effects in the market.

MARKET CHARACTERISTICS

98. Reviewing evidence and observations on the main characteristics of the markets that it investigates helps the CC to frame the analysis of market definition and competitive effects, as well as to assess the practicability of remedy options, should an AEC be found.

99. Any assessment of the working of competition usually begins with an overview of market structure and the possible implications of this structure for the conduct of the firms within the market. The CC studies the profiles and performances of the suppliers (or, where relevant, acquirers) of the goods or services referred for investigation.

Market share data

100. The CC calculates the market shares of the suppliers of the reference products (and sometimes other measures of market concentration), if possible over several years, using the methodologies set out in Annex A (The measurement of: market shares and concentration; profitability).

101. The calculation of market concentration measures can provide background data for the assessment of the levels of firms' market power (see paragraphs 9, 14 and 186 to 195)[63] and may be relevant for the assessment of other sources of potential competitive harm, for example coordinated conduct. In many cases, the weight the CC places in its competitive assessment on market concentration measures will be influenced by its ability to define with confidence the boundaries of that market (see paragraph 195) so as to ensure that these are neither too narrow nor too wide (paragraph 137). However, there are some measures of market concentration, such as the Logit Competition Index (LOCI), which can be used, if relevant information is available, without relying on establishing market boundaries (see Annex A, paragraph 8).

Other background market characteristics

102. The other market characteristics most relevant to the CC's investigation will vary from case to case. However, the CC normally looks at the following:

(a) The nature and characteristics of the products or services included in the terms of reference and of any potential substitutes for these products.

(b) The nature of the customer base—for example, whether customers are businesses or final consumers, the extent of customer segmentation in a market, the demographic profile of the customer base or, where relevant, the extent to which they are informed about the products in the market subject to investigation.

(c) The legal and regulatory framework that applies to the reference market. Laws and regulations can determine the nature of competition within a market and may also be relevant to the CC's consideration of remedies.

(d) Industry practices, for example the way in which products are sold and how prices are set and communicated to customers.

(e) The history of the market, including recent competitive developments such as any recent examples of entry, expansion or exit and any significant changes that are anticipated in the market in the foreseeable future.

MARKET OUTCOMES

103. Outcomes of the competitive process in their different forms in a market—eg prices and profitability, levels of innovation, product range and quality—can also provide evidence about its functioning. Evaluating these outcomes helps the CC determine whether there is an AEC and, if so, the extent to which customers may be harmed by it, ie the degree and nature of 'customer detriment'. This can be an important factor in any later consideration of possible remedies.

104. Prices and costs are among the more observable and measurable outcomes and an analysis of these may be useful in quantifying the extent and nature of competition and can be helpful in measuring customer detriment. However, the other, less-quantifiable factors, such as quality and innovation, are no less important to customers.

105. Although the outcomes of the competitive process may differ in character, there may be linkages between them, and the CC does not therefore consider each in isolation. The extent to which prices respond to changes in costs and the question of whether those costs are at an efficient level, for example, may have implications for a firm's profitability, and the level of investment may have implications for efficiency and product or service quality.

106. The following paragraphs in this section deal in turn with:
(A) Prices and profitability.
(B) Quality, innovation and other non-price indicators.

A. Prices and profitability

107. The types of analysis the CC may undertake on prices and profitability depend on the nature of the markets and the theories of harm the CC has postulated (see paragraphs 163 to 169). Four possible types of analysis are considered below: pricing patterns; price cost margins; price comparisons; and profitability.

Price patterns

108. In markets subject to effective competition prices are likely to respond to changing supply and demand conditions and firms will seek to win business by improving their prices and other aspects of their offer. The pattern of prices over time can therefore indicate the nature of competition (see, for example, paragraph 246). However, the CC recognizes that there may be several factors affecting prices and will take this into account when considering inferences from this type of analysis. Taken in conjunction with other evidence and in the absence of other explanatory factors, such as cost increases:
(a) static or continually rising prices may indicate a lack of competition; and
(b) parallel pricing—ie the practice by a seller of varying prices in a similar way and at about the same time as competitors—may be a symptom of coordinated effects (see paragraphs 249 and 189).

109. The pricing strategies adopted by firms in the market can also be indicative of competitive conditions. For example:
(a) introductory discounts followed by price increases might indicate high switching costs or customer inertia (see section on weak customer response, paragraphs 295 to 318); and
(b) a wide range of prices for similar goods or services might indicate the presence of search costs (see section on weak customer response, paragraphs 295 to 318).

110. Another type of analysis in this category, price concentration studies, looks at the extent to which prices may vary with market concentration. This is relevant to the assessment of unilateral market power (paragraphs 186 to 195). For example, if there were several local geographic markets, higher prices being charged in more concentrated areas may indicate limitations in the competitive process in those areas.[64] This type of analysis may also examine the relationship between prices, margins and concentration over time.

Price-cost margins

111. The analysis of prices will in many cases be complemented by an analysis of costs, because these may explain price changes over time or differentials between areas. Therefore when analysing patterns of prices over time or geography, the CC may consider price-cost margins. Typically a price-cost margin is calculated by subtracting some measure of marginal cost from revenue and expressing the difference as a percentage of revenue.[65]

112. Price-cost margins can also provide useful information about the effectiveness of competition in the short run (ie for a current range of products), including about the willingness and ability of customers to switch between alternatives. Vigorous competition may be expected to lead firms to price towards marginal cost. The CC may therefore consider the pattern of price-cost margins across geographic markets or customer segments or over time. A pattern of sustained high price-cost margins may, for example, indicate an unwillingness or inability to switch because of, for example, switching costs, search costs, limited customer information or significant product differentiation (see section on 'weak customer response', paragraphs 295 to 318). But the CC interprets price-cost margins with caution: margins may be a misleading indicator in some industries[66] and in many circumstances a gap between price and marginal cost can be consistent with robust competition.[67] A fuller analysis of profitability may be required to establish whether prices are on average above the competitive level, as described below.

Price comparisons

113. Comparisons of prices with those of other markets, such as markets for similar products in other countries or in markets for comparable products in the UK, are sometimes made in CC market investigations. Such comparisons can be relevant where market conditions are similar. In the Home Credit investigation (November 2006), for example, the CC found that prices in that market were high in comparison with the prices of other credit products and were higher than prices in the Republic of Ireland, where similar products were offered to customers.

Profitability

114. One approach to the question of whether prices are above competitive levels is to consider the profitability of the business activity being investigated. In many cases, the CC's focus will be on the largest incumbent firms in the market or market sector. However, the CC may also consider the profitability of less well established firms with smaller market shares, eg for comparative purposes. Where the business activity being investigated is only one part of the firms' activities, it will be necessary to take this into account.

115. In its analysis the CC is concerned with economic profits and these can differ in important respects from accounting profits. The CC will generally derive the profitability of the relevant business activity by identifying the relevant revenues and costs for that business activity, including an appropriate value for capital employed and an allowance for the cost of capital. More information about the CC's approach to the calculation of profitability is in Annex A (The measurement of profitability).

116. Firms in a competitive market would generally earn no more than a 'normal' rate of profit—the minimum level of profits required to keep the factors of production in their current use in the long run, ie the rate of return on capital employed for a particular business activity would be equal to the opportunity cost of capital for that activity. The profitability of firms representing a substantial part of the market can therefore be a useful indicator of competitive conditions in a market (see paragraphs 118 and 119).

117. In practice, a competitive market would be expected to generate significant variations in profit levels between firms and over time as supply and demand conditions change, but with an overall tendency towards levels commensurate with the cost of capital of the firms involved. At particular points in time the profitability of some firms may exceed what might be termed the 'normal' level. There could be several reasons, including cyclical factors, transitory price or other marketing initiatives, and some firms earning higher profits as a result of past innovation, or superior efficiency.

118. However, a situation where profitability of firms representing a substantial part of the market has exceeded the cost of capital over a sustained period could be an indication of limitations in the competitive process.

119. The ability to earn profits persistently above the competitive level could indicate the presence of entry barriers (see paragraph 231). A situation where a firm with a large market share has earned profits that have been persistently above the competitive level may indicate significant market power (see paragraph 180). A situation where levels of profitability have remained persistently high and stable over time across several incumbent firms may indicate coordinated conduct (see paragraph 247).

120. The extent to which the results of profitability analysis indicate limitations in the competitive process may depend on both the size of the gap between the level of profitability and the cost of capital and the length of the period over which the gap persists.

121. The appropriate time period over which to examine the persistence of the gap between profitability and the cost of capital may therefore vary according to the specific market. The pattern of investment and the nature of sources of competitive advantage (advertising, research and development (R&D), more efficient production) may affect the CC's view of the relevant timescales over which it would expect to see competition playing out in the market. Where large and risky investments have been made, the CC would expect to see a normal level of profitability restored over a relatively long timescale.

122. In cases where a persistent gap is not unequivocally substantial, it is particularly important for the CC to consider the analysis in conjunction with other information about the operation and nature of the market concerned.

123. Moreover, as with other forms of analysis, the CC's interpretation of profitability analysis may be affected by the quality of the data available (see section on the gathering and analysis of evidence, paragraphs 35 to 41).

124. The trend in profits will be an important consideration and the CC will seek to understand the reasons for the observed trend. Where the size of the gap between the level of profitability and the cost of capital has grown over a period the competitive situation may have worsened. Where that gap has narrowed competitive conditions may have improved. Where that gap has fluctuated the CC may consider whether, on average for firms representing a substantial part of the market, profits have exceeded the cost of capital.

125. A CC finding of low profitability would not necessarily signify that competition is working well. Low profitability may be concealing ineffective competition. Reasons for this may include:

(a) A period of low profitability may occur during the course of a downturn in trading conditions, regardless of the state of competition in the affected market.

(b) Weak competition as a result of customers not responding effectively to competing offers may sometimes result in an inefficient market structure in which operators have higher costs and set higher prices than would be the case in a competitive market[68] (see section on weak customer response, paragraphs 295 to 318).

(c) Incumbent firms, despite being protected from new entry, are not earning high profits because they are inefficient and operate with higher costs than would be sustainable with stronger competition in the market (see section on barriers to entry, paragraphs 205 to 236).

In some cases, the CC may be able to compare actual costs with efficient costs when looking at the level of profitability achieved by firms but this may not always be practical.

Indicators—not features

126. In summary, the CC will consider prices and profitability in the context of its overall assessment of the market. While useful, findings that price-cost margins are wide or profitability is high in a market do not on their own provide conclusive evidence that the market could be more competitive. Such findings are not in themselves causes of competitive harm—they are not features of the market for the purpose of the AEC test.

B. Quality, innovation and other non-price indicators

127. As indicated above, prices and costs are not the sole indicators of the level of competition in a market. Poor quality, lack of innovation, or limited product ranges are prominent among other indicators of weak competition in a market. Evidence about this kind of indicator tends to be qualitative, coming particularly from surveys, questionnaires or discussions with customers, investors, or other market observers. In several past market investigations, such analysis has spotlighted various negative non-price factors as important indicators of weak competition.

128. In the investigation into Northern Irish personal banking, the CC chose a range of indicators on which information was readily obtainable and readily comparable and, analysing responses to questionnaires, made a comparison between banks within Northern Ireland and some of the large banks based in Great Britain. This evidence indicated several non-price indicators of a lack of competition between Northern Irish banks in relation to branch opening hours, functionality of Internet banking and product innovation.[69] In its investigation into PPI, the CC considered evidence it had obtained so as 'to identify: any new PPI policies which had been introduced, whether there had been any innovations within existing policies, the rationale for product change or innovation, and whether, and if so how, distributors advertised and marketed their policies'. The CC concluded that there was less choice (and possibly less innovation), as well as higher prices, 'than would be expected in a well-functioning market'.[70]

129. In its investigation into BAA airports, the CC compared Aberdeen Airport with other regional airports and found slower development of routes; lack of ambition in development; underinvestment and poor facilities. In relation to the South-East of England airports the CC found a lack of responsiveness to the interests of airlines and passengers that would not be expected in a well-functioning market;[71] weaknesses in the approach to planning and consulting on capital expenditure; and deficiencies in the level and quality of service.[72]

PART 3: SECTION 2—MARKET DEFINITION

130. A market is a collection of goods and services provided in particular geographic areas (or in some cases to particular groups of customers or at particular times), connected by a process of competition. The process is one in which firms seek to win customers' business over time by improving their portfolios of products and the terms on which these are offered, so as to increase demand for the products (see paragraph 10). The willingness of customers to switch to other products is a driving force of competition. In forming its views on market definition, the CC will therefore consider the degree of demand substitutability. In some markets, supply-side constraints will also be important (see paragraph 134).

131. In considering the substitutability of goods or services or areas of supply set out in the ToR, the CC may (as stated above, paragraph 26) conclude that the market definition goes wider or narrower than those goods and services.

THE ROLE AND DETERMINANTS OF MARKET DEFINITION

132. In defining the relevant market (see paragraph 26), the CC identifies the participating firms and customers and the traded products in the market(s) that are the subject of the reference. This enables the CC to focus on the sources of any market power[73] and provides a framework for its assessment of the effects on competition of features of a market (see paragraph 31).[74]

133. Market definition is thus a useful tool, but not an end in itself, and identifying the relevant market involves an element of judgement. The boundaries of the market do not determine the outcome of the CC's competitive assessment of a market in any mechanistic way. The competitive assessment will take into account any relevant constraints from outside the market, segmentation within it, or other ways in which some constraints are more important than others.

134. While the composition of a relevant market is usually determined by the degree of demand substitutability (see paragraph 130), the CC will where relevant include supply-side factors in defining the market. There might, for example, be a possibility that firms supplying non-substitute products have the capabilities and assets to redirect production to goods and services that would be substitutes for those in the market.[75] (For further detail on substitutability, see paragraphs 198 to 204.) Alternatively, the same firms might compete to supply the non-substitute products under similar conditions of competition; in that case aggregating the supply of these products and analysing it as one market does not affect the competitive assessment (for example, in markets characterized by bidding and tendering processes).[76]

135. The nature of competition in a particular market (and the theories of harm[77] under consideration) may require that the CC identify more than one market for the same product so as to understand different aspects of competition. For example, in some industries certain aspects of competition are determined at a national level, while others occur at a local level. Looking at how competition operates at both levels, and at how the levels interact, could produce important insights.[78]

136. Substitutability in the short run may, moreover, be different in the longer term. In the short run firms compete on the basis of the products in their existing portfolios and the current geographical footprint of their distribution systems. In assessing short-run competition the CC will therefore usually define markets on the basis of substitutability between existing products and areas. However, in the longer term firms may compete by improving their product portfolios, or extending the geographical scope of their operations. The CC's assessment of this sort of competition may be concerned with identifying groups of firms that have the capability to introduce new or improved substitute products, or open new outlets in a more broadly defined product category or areas.

Assessing substitutability

137. In defining a market it is important to ensure that the pool of products identified as effective substitutes for the relevant product(s) is not unrealistically small. If the market is drawn too narrowly there is a risk that a party is incorrectly viewed as holding significant market power,[79] whereas in reality that position is undermined by constraints from alternative suppliers that should be included in the market. (Conversely, defining a market too widely carries the risk that market participants, in seeming to be in weaker positions, are inferred to have less market power than they actually enjoy.)

138. The hypothetical monopolist test (HMT) is a tool which can be used to identify effective substitutes and to check that the market is not defined too narrowly. The principle behind it rests on defining a market as a product, or collection of products, a sole supplier of which could hypothetically impose a small but significant non-transitory increase in price (sometimes referred to as the SSNIP test). The test can help to identify the constraints that would prevent a hypothetical monopolist from exercising market power. In practice it may often be used, not quantitatively, but as a conceptual framework.[80]

139. There are some practical difficulties in using the HMT in market investigations. If significant market power is already being exercised, using prevailing prices can lead to defining markets too broadly and possibly to an incorrect inference that significant market power does not exist.[81] In theory, the HMT could be implemented in the presence of significant market power using notional competitive prices, but in many cases it is difficult to assess what those prices would be. There is also a risk that using a notional benchmark in effect assumes the existence of significant market power as part of the framework within which the competitive assessment is being undertaken.[82]

140. The CC will consider the pros and cons of using the HMT depending on the particular facts and circumstances of the case, including whether the practical difficulties mentioned above can be avoided and how informative its use would be.

141. In practice, the HMT is more likely to be used to check that the market has not been defined too narrowly in cases where the CC's findings include a finding that high concentration is a feature harming competition (see paragraph 195).

DIMENSIONS OF THE MARKET

142. The different dimensions of the market are discussed in the following sections. These are (as indicated in paragraph 130): the product dimension, the geographic dimension, and markets defined with reference to customer group or temporal factors.

Product market

143. The CC may consider the following types of information, where available, when assessing whether products are substitutes:

(a) Product characteristics, such as physical properties and intended use that can indicate similarities (from the purchaser's perspective) between different products.

(b) Relative price levels and the extent to which prices of products within the possible relevant market are correlated with each other, as compared with the prices of products outside that market.

(c) Prices and sales volumes over time or across areas that permit analysis of the way that customers respond to changes in prices or to firms entering or leaving the market.

(d) Responses from customers, competitors and interested and informed third parties to questions—sometimes posed in surveys—about customer behaviour.

(e) Firms' view of the products, drawing on internal documents such as marketing studies, consumer surveys prepared in the normal course of business, market analyses prepared for investors, and internal business analyses (eg board papers, business plans and strategy documents).

144. The existence of a market for secondary products has sometimes to be considered in fixing the dimensions of a market. Secondary (or aftermarket) products are those that are purchased only as a result of the customer having purchased a primary product. An example is the market for printer cartridges, a secondary market linked to the primary market for printers. The CC may sometimes consider primary and secondary products to be in separate markets. However, it may consider the products to be in the same market where customers take into account the cost of the secondary product when purchasing the primary product (see also paragraphs 291 to 293). Whichever of the two definitions is chosen will not determine the outcome of the CC's competitive assessment, since the competitive constraint from other suppliers will be taken into account in either case.[83]

Geographic market

145. Geographic markets may be based on the location of either suppliers or customers. In the case of the former, the geographic market is an area covering a set of firms or outlets which compete closely because enough customers consider them to be substitutes (as in the case of retail markets and some industrial markets). In the latter case, a geographic market is an aggregation of customers paying individually negotiated prices but enjoying sufficiently similar purchasing options (ie in effect many customers in industrial markets).

146. The geographic market: may be local, regional, national or wider. Imports may be taken into account as well as UK products. Depending on the circumstances of the case and the theory of harm posited, the CC may examine geographic markets at more than one level in the same investigation, eg at both national and local levels.

147. The key to defining both supplier-based and customer-based geographic markets, as to defining the product market, is the degree of substitutability, ie the extent to which suppliers can switch their areas of supply and the extent to which customers in one area may be served in another area.

148. In the case of supplier-based markets the geographic scope may be described as a set of competing outlets. In identifying these sets the CC may consider the following information on:
(a) the catchment areas from which the bulk of an outlet's customers is drawn;
(b) differences in pricing, sales, advertising and marketing strategies by area;
(c) which outlets customers consider to be substitutes for each other; and
(d) natural experiments which show the effect on one outlet's sales arising from entry, exit or expansion by other outlets nearby.

149. The CC may consider the following when identifying the boundaries of customer-based markets:
(a) product characteristics such as perishability;
(b) differences in pricing, sales, advertising and marketing strategies by area;
(c) information enabling the estimation of switching costs (which can include additional delivery costs) that customers might incur in changing to products currently supplied in other geographic areas, relative to the value of the products and the length of time taken to make the switch; and
(d) the flows of goods between regions or into the UK and any barriers to entry, whether legislative, natural or strategically created.

OTHER ISSUES

Customer groups

150. Many markets serve a diverse customer base, for example suppliers may have both business and personal customers. One set of customers may be more affected than others by any particular feature. Where such diversity exists, and where suppliers can charge different prices to different groups (ie price discriminate), the CC will recognize these differences. In terms of market definition, depending on the market and the evidence presented, the CC may choose either to treat these different groups as separate markets, or as segments within one market, noting the scope for price discrimination between different groups within the market (see also the discussion of the hypothetical monopolist test at paragraph 139).

Temporal dimensions

151. When customers are not able to substitute products between periods, there may be a temporal dimension to the market, for example seasonality, peak and off-peak services. A typical example concerns commuters and leisure travellers on trains. Commuters constrained by their hours of work have little choice but to travel at 'peak' times, during which the train companies charge more than at other times. On the other hand, leisure travellers may be less concerned about the time of travel and more willing to travel at off-peak times and are charged less. In such instances, depending on the circumstances of the case, the CC may decide to define two or more markets, or it may decide to define only one market and note the scope for price discrimination within the market, for instance identifying a market for rail travel with different prices charged to peak and off-peak travellers.

Grouping markets together

152. In some cases, the CC may treat a group of product, geographic or other types of markets together for the purposes of assessing competitive effects. This can be the case where a feature manifests itself in a similar way across several different markets (for example, the need for an operating licence may be an aspect of many local markets) and the CC is able to reach a view about the effects of the feature on competition across the group of markets as a whole. In the investigation into home credit,[84] for example, the CC was satisfied that the conditions of competition were sufficiently similar to justify a conclusion that applied throughout the reference area, without looking at every geographic area in detail.

Effects outside the relevant market

153. The CC may also consider effects in neighbouring markets, including those which are upstream or downstream of the relevant market (see paragraph 26). For example, one firm's advantage as a buyer in an input market may protect it from competitive pressures when supplying a downstream market for manufactured goods relying on that input. If the input market has been referred to it, the CC may consider effects in the downstream output market.

PART 3: SECTION 3—THE COMPETITIVE ASSESSMENT

154. In deciding whether or not there is an AEC, the CC's core task—given the statutory questions (paragraphs 28 and 29)—is to assess the effects of possible features on competition. In conducting this assessment, the CC will seek to establish whether or not any of the possible features, or any combination of them, can be expected to harm competition when measured against a theoretical benchmark (see paragraphs 30, 319 and 320). The emphasis on assessing the competitive effects of features means that any AEC finding will be grounded in a clear understanding of why competition in a market may be harmed.

IDENTIFYING FEATURES THAT HARM COMPETITION

155. As noted in paragraph 31, a market feature may be intrinsic to the structure of the market or may arise from the conduct of any market participant (whether supplier, acquirer or customer and whether or not in the reference goods or services market). The Act does not require the CC to state whether particular features of a market are to be considered structural features or an aspect of conduct. Provided the relevant feature falls within at least one of these categories, the categorization is of little practical importance. Since the concept of a feature is broad, the CC has the flexibility to investigate a wide range of possible market features, each of which may have effects on the different aspects of competition (see paragraphs 13 to 15). Moreover, how far any feature identified by the CC is along a causal chain resulting in harm to competition may vary (ie some may be directly causing harm and others may be doing so indirectly).

156. It has been emphasized (see paragraph 22) that the CC, on receiving a market investigation, makes no presumption that there are market features that harm competition. A CC investigation may find that there are no such features giving rise to an AEC in the relevant market (as was the case in the investigation into Movies on Pay TV).[85]

Structural features

157. Structural features may include high levels of market concentration, high entry barriers, common ownership of competing facilities and buyer power.[86] For example, market concentration was identified as a feature harming competition, in the market investigations into classified advertising services[87] and the supply of groceries by retailers;[88] high barriers to entry in the cases of the supply of groceries and domestic bulk liquefied petroleum gas (LPG)[89] and the ROSCOs[90] investigation; common ownership in the case of BAA airports;[91] and buyer power in the case of the supply of groceries investigation.

158. Specific structural features identified in past investigations to be harming competition include aspects of the planning system, government policy and the regulatory system (in the BAA airports investigation and, with regard to the planning regime, in the grocery retailing market); the criteria applied for the award of franchises (in the ROSCOs market investigation); information asymmetries between incumbents and entrants (in the home credit market investigation);[92] and a point-of-sale advantage for credit providers selling PPI (in the PPI market investigation).[93]

Conduct features

159. 'Conduct' of a market participant includes any failure to act, whether intentional or not, and any other unintentional conduct.[94]

160. Conduct features by sellers identified in past investigations as harming competition include: a failure of Northern Irish banks sufficiently to explain their charging structures and practices for personal current accounts;[95] and the failure of distributors and intermediaries in the market for PPI to try to win customers by setting competitive price or quality levels for their policies.[96] 'Exclusionary behaviour' — for example, by bus companies deliberately obstructing the services of competitors[97]— also falls within the category of a conduct feature. The conduct of firms which supply the market when acting in other markets can be a feature of the market. For example, if the market investigation concerned competition to supply a particular manufactured good, the conduct of vertically integrated suppliers in the market for the input might be a conduct feature.

161. The behaviour of customers can also sometimes be a feature limiting competition between firms. (As noted in paragraph 19, market investigations allow the competition authorities to look at customer behaviour and customer vulnerability in relation to their implications for competition, instead of just looking at them as consumer protection issues; see also paragraphs 295 to 318). The insensitivity of customers to measures of price other than the level of weekly repayment was found to be a feature detrimental to competition in the home credit market.[98] Similarly, the low sensitivities of customers to store card APRs[99] and late payment charges were identified as features harming competition between store card credit services.[100] A customer behaviour feature—failure to investigate alternative accounts or banks— was also found in the market for personal current accounts in Northern Ireland.[101]

A combination of features

162. In some circumstances, several features may in combination harm competition. In the PPI investigation,[102] for example, competition was found to be adversely affected by several interconnected features, including barriers to searching and switching, which hindered customers' ability to compare PPI policies or to switch to alternatives, as well as the point-of-sale advantage credit providers enjoyed. Barriers to searching included product complexity, the perception that taking PPI would increase a customer's chances of being given credit, the bundling of PPI with credit and the limited scale of stand-alone provision. Barriers to switching included contract terms which made switching expensive or which risked leaving customers uninsured.

THEORIES OF HARM

163. To provide focus and structure to its assessment of the way competition is working in a market the CC sets out one or more 'theories of harm'. A theory of harm is a hypothesis of how harmful competitive effects might arise in a market and adversely affect customers. The use of the term does not imply any prejudgement of an AEC in a given market.

164. Focusing the competitive assessment on the testing of theories of harm helps the CC to understand the market and to evaluate evidence so as to be able to decide the statutory question of whether or not there is a prevention, restriction or distortion of competition and, if so, identify what features are causing it. The use of theories of harm also helps the parties by identifying the issues that will be addressed and indicating the information that will be gathered.

Formulating and reviewing theories of harm

165. The starting point for formulating theories of harm in market investigations is the work already done by the referring body, particularly the terms of reference (paragraph 26) and decision documents.[103] These will not only include observations on the structure of the market but will also have described the products the referring body considers are affected and the features it has grounds for suspecting may be the cause of harm to competition. At this stage, the CC supplements the analysis carried out by the referring body with its own initial consideration and may formulate theories of harm involving other possible aspects of the market on the basis of its own analysis (see paragraphs 98 to 105 on market characteristics and outcomes).

166. The initial theories are set out in the issues statement published at an early stage in an investigation (see paragraph 68). In the market investigation into local bus services, for example, the CC noted in the issues statement (4 February 2010): 'It appears from the OFT investigation that in many (local bus) markets there is limited head-to-head competition. The OFT's report also suggests that concentration is high.' It went on to list hypotheses as to why this might be so, including theories derived from barriers to entry, supplier behaviour and aspects of the tendering and bidding systems.

167. Although the CC aims to focus on those aspects of the market that appear most likely to influence competition directly, these are not always clear at the outset of an investigation. At this early stage, one or more theories may often therefore be set out in broad, generic terms.

168. As the CC investigates the interlinked issues of market characteristics and outcomes, market definition and the operation of competition within that market, it reviews its theories. The theories often become increasingly specific to the investigation. Some may be dropped and others put forward (see paragraph 72 for information on how substantial changes in theories of harm are communicated to the parties).

169. Several different hypotheses may be put forward for investigation. They need not be mutually exclusive. One or more theories may be linked to different outcomes, may in combination produce a single outcome, or may relate to different markets. On the other hand, several competing theories may sometimes be advanced linking features with observed market outcomes, and in that case the CC has to consider which theory, if any, best explains the outcome.

POTENTIAL SOURCES OF COMPETITIVE HARM

170. Individual theories of harm are numerous and specific to different market investigations. However, most draw on a limited number of common potential sources of competitive harm. These reflect the nature of competition as set out in Part 1 (paragraphs 10 to 15), which explained that the constraints helping to ensure that competition is effective mainly come: first, from other firms already in the market; secondly, from firms that could readily enter it; and, thirdly, from their customers; conversely, competitive harm can flow from five main sources:

(a) unilateral market power (including market concentration);
(b) barriers to entry and expansion;
(c) coordinated conduct;
(d) vertical relationships; and
(e) weak customer response.

171. The list is not exhaustive. While the majority of theories of harm flow from these five sources, other theories may be identified that do not do so.

172. Moreover, the five sources are not mutually exclusive. Individual features identified in a market investigation have been associated with more than one of them. Some may have mutually reinforcing effects. Barriers to entry and expansion, in particular, have been found to be features, sometimes in combination with other features, in many investigations.

Countervailing factors

173. In assessing the potential sources of harm, the CC considers aspects of the competitive situation that may, on the other hand, benefit competition and operate to the benefit of customers.

174. In some circumstances, for example, the positive effects of *efficiencies* on competition associated with a particular market feature may outweigh the harmful effects of that feature, which would otherwise cause an AEC. Efficiencies can enhance rivalry when they induce one or more firms to follow a course of action of benefit to customers (eg lowering prices or increasing innovation) in response to actual or expected actions by rivals. Examples of such rivalry-enhancing efficiencies are given within each of the following sections on the potential sources of competitive harm. Should the CC decide that, despite the existence of some efficiencies that benefit customers, there is still an AEC in the market, these efficiencies may be taken into account as RCBs when the CC considers possible remedies (see paragraphs 355 to 366).

175. The prospect of *entry or expansion* (see paragraphs 205 to 236)—and therefore of stronger competition in the longer term—may also sometimes offset competitive harm that may otherwise arise, if there are no significant barriers to entry or expansion and the CC judges that:

(a) actual entry or expansion is likely, of sufficient scale and swift enough to constrain incumbent firms in the near future; or
(b) the threat of potential entry or expansion is sufficient to exercise a constraint even though no actual entry of sufficient scale has been observed in the recent past (small-scale past entry does not demonstrate the absence of entry barriers see paragraph 234); such a constraint could arise when entry would be swift and low-cost so as to exploit any commercial opportunity in the market.

176. Countervailing buyer power may also be taken into account in the CC's competitive assessment. In some markets prices are in effect determined by the relative bargaining power of sellers and buyers. The exercise of buyer power can sometimes be a feature harming competition (see paragraph 157 and footnote 86). However, in other circumstances 'countervailing buyer power' can have the positive effect of preventing the exercise of a supplier's market power in the bargaining process. The presence of large buyers relative to the size of the suppliers does not necessarily guarantee that the buyers can exert countervailing buyer power. The relative importance to each buyer and supplier of its business with the other party[104] is a key factor, and the strength of the buyers' 'outside options', ie their alternative strategies in relation to the relevant product, is often the crucial determinant of countervailing buyer power. Whether or not suppliers have the ability to offer different prices that discriminate between customers and customer groups, and thereby reduce any potential impact of buyer power, can sometimes be an important issue in the CC's assessment. The CC will also assess the extent to which the benefits of any countervailing buyer power are passed on to customers in lower prices.

The five potential sources of competitive harm

177. The following subsections deal with each of the five sources of potential competitive harm identified above (see paragraph 170) by considering first the nature of the mechanism involved, and secondly its potential impact on the market, including any positive effects, and the CC's approach to testing this impact.

1. UNILATERAL MARKET POWER

178. As explained in Part 1 of these Guidelines (see paragraph 14), competition within a market may be weak when one or more market participants[105] enjoys significant market power,[106] and is therefore able to influence market outcomes and other important aspects of competition. The features that give rise to significant market power may cause an AEC to arise. When exerted by a single firm, or by several firms acting independently in a market, such power is termed 'unilateral market power', distinguishing it from the market power that arises as a result of coordinated conduct.

179. A single firm's level of market power will be related to the elasticity of demand for its product and its rivals' elasticity of supply for that product. The market power of a firm will be strong if the level of demand for its product is insensitive to an increase in price of that product and if its rivals are unlikely to step up their supplies in response to a price rise. Significant market power may also be conferred on one or more firms operating in markets with particular characteristics. Such cases include:

(a) monopolies, where a single firm or group supplies all or nearly all of a market for a product or service;
(b) oligopolies, where a concentrated market or industry is dominated by a small number of sellers (see paragraph 189);
(c) network or two-sided markets providing services over a network or through a platform;[107] and
(d) secondary or after-markets (where the products are purchased only as a result of the customer having purchased another (primary) product; see paragraph 144 and paragraphs 291 to 293).

Indicators of unilateral market power

180. The CC may sometimes observe indicators of unilateral market power, such as high profits (see paragraphs 114 to 126), high price-cost margins (see paragraph 112), low single-firm demand elasticities (see paragraph 179) or other evidence of adverse effects in the form of high prices, low quality and limited choice (see paragraphs 127 to 129).

181. The way a firm behaves—for example, in relation to its customers or competitors— may also give an indication of the market power it may enjoy. However, actions apparently indicating the exercise of unilateral market power may be benign or even beneficial practices. For example, a supplier pitching prices below cost may be predatory action, but may alternatively be part of an introductory offer which will expand future demand for the product and therefore increase competition in the longer term.

Innovation and new product development

182. One important outcome of unilateral market power can be to stifle incentives on firms to innovate or invest in product development and thereby prevent the gains in productive efficiency and customer benefits that innovation or new products bring over time. When firms face competition—whether from other incumbents or from the threat of entry—the possibility of generating high profits encourages them to discover new products and processes. In contrast, firms that do not face competitive pressures may choose not to invest significantly in R&D (see paragraph 121).

183. However, the relationship between market power and innovation is not always clear cut. Large incumbent firms may benefit from significant economies of scale in the innovative process.[108] On the other hand, an incumbent firm with unilateral market power may have a lower incentive to innovate than a smaller competitor or new entrant because it has less to gain.[109] In some markets innovators may expect to benefit only to a small extent but, even in such markets innovation incentives may be strong if rivalry is intense.

184. In assessing market power in high-technology industries, the CC will pay particular attention to the number of products and/or technologies that are being developed. Another useful indicator in high-technology industries is R&D spending relative to sales. High R&D spending to sales ratios provide a clear indication that competition takes place through innovation. Where R&D investment is high, market power may be vulnerable to future innovations by rivals or new entrants. Substantial shifts in market share over time are also positive signs of a high level of rivalry in innovative or high-technology industries.

Assessing sources of unilateral market power

185. Generally, the most common reasons for one or more firms to possess unilateral market power are:
(a) high concentration (see paragraphs 186 to 195);
(b) capacity constraints (see paragraphs 196 and 197);
(c) lack of substitutability (see paragraphs 198 and 199); and
(d) absence of supply-side constraints (see paragraphs 200 to 204).

(a) High concentration

186. An examination of market structure, including the initial calculation of market shares and sometimes other concentration measures (as discussed above, paragraph 101 and in Annex A), often provides a starting point for the assessment of firms' market power.

187. In general, a highly concentrated market—as indicated by, for example, persistently high market shares held by one or more firms—might be an indicator that one or more firms hold unilateral market power. If a firm has a high market share it might have less incentive to compete vigorously with its rivals (particularly if there are barriers to entry). For example, if a price reduction aimed at new customers would also apply to existing customers, a firm with a large market share may be more reluctant to implement a price reduction than might one with a small share. The firm with a large market share may feel little pressure to reduce price even if a smaller rival does so.

188. A large market share could also confer advantages in bargaining with suppliers upstream, or buyers downstream (see paragraph 50), and a firm may be able to control prices in its favour or impose conditions in the negotiation process that restrict competition in one or more markets.

189. As explained in paragraph 179, market concentration and the exercise of market power are not necessarily linked to the position of a single firm. A market with a small number of suppliers which are protected by barriers to entry (an oligopoly), for example, may be characterized by significant market power. One mechanism by which this market power can manifest itself is through coordinated conduct (see paragraphs 237 to 294). However, unilateral market power can be enjoyed by a number of firms even where they act independently, albeit aware of each other's presence—so-called 'non-coordinated oligopolies'.[110] In such situations, each firm knows that it can affect market prices and hence its rivals' profits. This awareness conditions the way in which competition occurs, although the precise way it does so will depend on the specific characteristics of the market in question.

190. A large market share does not always indicate that competition within the market is weak. It may simply indicate that the firm(s) possessing it is capable and relatively efficient, having low costs, an attractive product, or both. Moreover, a firm with a large market share could be vulnerable to entry and expansion which might constrain its market power (see paragraphs 175), or face countervailing buyer power (see paragraph 176).

191. Conversely, since a firm's level of market power will be related to the elasticity of demand for its product, and to its rivals' elasticity of supply for that product (see paragraph 179), even a firm with a low share of sales of a product may have significant market power if both measures of elasticity are low.

192. Observed changes in market share over time (see paragraph 101) may help interpret the implication of high concentration in a market. For example, when market shares have been stable over time, especially in the face of historical changes in prices or costs, high concentration may indicate that competition within the market is weak. However, a highly concentrated market may be competitive if market shares fluctuate over short periods in response to changes in competitive offers; such volatility may indicate the existence of effective competitive constraints, such as successful entry and innovative developments.

193. In markets characterized by bidding and tendering processes (see paragraph 134 and footnote 76), market shares may fluctuate only when tenders occur and a firm may have a high market share at any given point, as a result of winning several recent tenders, without necessarily possessing significant market power.

194. In some cases, recent or ongoing changes in market conditions may indicate that the current market share of a particular firm either understates or overstates the firm's expected competitive significance in the near future. Predictable effects of such changes—for example, the spreading of new technologies, the longevity of patents and the prospective development of new products—may be taken into account when calculating and interpreting market share data.

195. In some circumstances, the CC will find that high concentration is a feature causing harm to competition. It has been so identified in several market investigations (see paragraph 157). As explained in paragraphs 101 and 137, the CC will consider how confident it is that it has defined the market neither too widely nor too narrowly before identifying market concentration as a feature harming competition. The CC would generally expect to find this in conjunction with other features, such as barriers to entry.

(b) Capacity constraints

196. In markets involving relatively undifferentiated products, one or more market participants may find it profitable unilaterally to reduce output and increase the market price (eg by leaving capacity idle or diverting production to another market). Such a strategy is more likely to be profitable when any rival is limited by capacity constraints or a relatively low elasticity of demand in the market (see paragraph 179). In some markets, therefore, share of capacity may be more important than share of supply.

197. In assessing the power of a firm to suppress output unilaterally in this way the CC focuses on the degree of spare capacity other firms in the market may possess, the ease with which these firms could expand existing capacity, and their commercial incentive to counteract any overall output shortfall.

(c) Lack of substitutability of products

198. A firm may also enjoy unilateral market power because it controls a group of close substitute products, for which its customers have limited alternatives. In differentiated product markets, while some products can be close substitutes and compete strongly with each other, others are more distant substitutes and compete less strongly. Branding, quality, product characteristics or geographical location will have effects on the extent to which a product competes with another; one high-end product, for example, may compete more directly with another high-end product than with a low-end product.

199. Assessing the extent of direct competition between close and distant substitute products may involve calculations of diversion ratios and of cross-price elasticities of demand.[111] The higher the cross-price elasticity of demand between two products the closer substitutes they are in the eyes of customers.

(d) Weak supply-side constraints

200. Unilateral market power can only be sustained if potential market participants will not respond to a price rise by expanding their production facilities to produce the goods and services concerned,[112] ie 'supply-side substitutes' do not come into the market.

201. Two products are considered to be supply-side substitutes if the supplier of one of the products already owns the key assets needed to produce and market the other, without incurring additional sunk (ie non-recoverable) costs.[113] An incumbent firm may be able to do so, and sometimes new entrant firms may exert a competitive constraint if they can easily and rapidly begin selling in the market without incurring significant sunk costs. This may be the case when, for example, a firm has idle capacity or when it produces the relevant product but sells it in a neighbouring geographic market—or to customers in another market. Similarly some firms, even producing relatively distant substitutes, may have access to the know-how, and may have assets (physical and human) that can be easily and rapidly adjusted to produce and distribute close substitute goods.

202. So as to assess the extent to which suppliers of potential supply-side substitutes enhance competition in the market (or whether the absence of supply-side constraints restricts competition), the CC considers whether:

- there are economic incentives to engage in production of the relevant goods/services;
- the suppliers are able to divert production to the relevant goods or services, or conversely are contractually tied to continue production of existing products; and
- the suppliers possess unused plant capacity that can be brought into production at a reasonable cost.[114]

203. The CC will also consider whether the existence of supply-side substitutes influences the market behaviour of incumbent firms which otherwise would enjoy significant market power (seeking evidence, for example from internal documents, past episodes of successful rapid entry and exit, and from customers about the credibility of rapid entrants).[115]

204. In assessing the prospects of expansion, repositioning, and mobility, the CC will consider in particular, the timing of the likely supply response, possible legal restrictions, access to distribution channels, and commercial risks and incentives on account of such factors as customer loyalty, brand reputation or managerial expertise.

2. BARRIERS TO ENTRY AND EXPANSION

205. Entry or expansion by firms will often stimulate competition and, as noted in paragraph 175, the prospect of entry and expansion within a short time can sometimes countervail against a prospective AEC decision. The possibilities of entry by outside firms or the expansion of incumbent firms have featured in most findings on whether or not there is an AEC in a market.

206. Firms can enter a market or expand within it in several ways. Firms coming into a market may build new capacity or take over existing capacity to use it in new or more productive ways. Incumbent firms may expand by building new plants or capacity, developing new products or expanding into neighbouring markets. Incumbent firms may invest in upstream or downstream companies to supply materials and process their output, respectively (see paragraph 50). Entry or expansion, or just the threat of it, can:

- upset established patterns of market conduct, particularly by making it difficult for an incumbent firm to continue wielding significant market power;
- promote efficient firms at the expense of inefficient ones;
- introduce new technology and fresh approaches to product design, marketing and delivery; the impact of entry and expansion on innovation within an industry has been observed above (see paragraph 182); and
- lead to more competitive prices as well as greater choice and quality to the benefit of customers.

207. A major source of competitive discipline is therefore generally eliminated or reduced if there is any barrier to market entry and expansion, whether an absolute barrier[116] or some other form of restriction such as aspects of the market that deter entry.[117] Barriers to entry and expansion give at least some incumbent firms an advantage over efficient potential firms or rival incumbent firms, either by reducing the expected profits, or increasing the expected costs, of entry or expansion. They may therefore constitute a feature, often in combination with other features, that harm competition.

208. The main focus of the CC's assessment of the conditions for entry and expansion in a market is generally on the ability and incentive of new or relatively small incumbent firms to enter into or expand in a market. However, the prospects for larger incumbent firms, which can also in some cases be an important driver of competition, will also be evaluated.

209. A barrier to entry, as well as denoting different levels of restrictions (paragraph 207), takes various forms. The following sections of these Guidelines, first, outline the different types of barriers to entry and, secondly, describe the CC's approach to assessing the impact of these barriers. The barriers surveyed are mostly entry barriers but some are barriers to expansion; the same analytical principles apply in assessing both sorts of barrier.

Types of entry barriers

210. There are three broad categories of barriers to entry: natural or intrinsic barriers; strategic and other 'first mover' advantages (including the endogenous costs of investing in market entry);[118] and regulatory barriers. Other factors will also help determine an entrant's decision to move into a market, for example, the possession of the necessary production facilities, and the economic prospects for the market. Barriers to exit—the cost of exit from the market if the business venture fails—have also to be considered. Barriers to entry or exit can interact with and magnify each other's effects.[119]

Natural or intrinsic barriers to entry

211. Firms entering a market unavoidably incur costs, These costs can sometimes in effect be 'natural' or 'intrinsic' barriers to entry, and may include the cost of putting the production process in place, gaining access to essential facilities or inputs and the acquisition of any necessary intellectual property rights (IPRs). Important considerations in evaluating the effects of such costs on the ability of firms to enter the market are the nature of the costs and the extent to which the costs are 'sunk', ie investments that cannot be recovered upon exit and hence would serve to commit a firm or firms to staying in the market. Sunk costs may include, for example, some specific asset investments, advertising, R&D and, in some markets, the costs of acquiring a reputation (eg for producing quality products).[120] (Non-sunk costs, in contrast, are recoverable if production ceases, and do not therefore pose the same risk.)

212. Economies of scale, in combination with sunk investment costs, can constitute a barrier in cases where these relate to the cost of getting into or expanding in the market.

213. In industries where economies of scale are significant, entry on a small scale may not be profitable unless the firm is aiming at a 'niche' in the market or can develop a new production strategy which offsets the disadvantages of small-scale production. Entry on a large scale will often entail a high risk (that sunk investment costs may not be recovered) because it will generally be successful only if the firm can expand the total market significantly, or substantially replace one or more existing firms.[121]

214. Entrant firms may also face disadvantages relative to incumbents where production costs decrease as the cumulative quantity produced increases (ie through 'learning by doing'). Similar considerations apply to economies of scope, which arise where producing two (or more) products is less costly for a single firm than for two (or more) firms each to produce the products separately. Where economies of scope are significant, an entrant, if it is to be successful, might have to produce a range of products from the outset, adding to the costs of entry.

215. Other disadvantages to entrants, imposed by natural or intrinsic barriers to entry, may arise simply because incumbents are already in the market. Switching costs for customers may be such an intrinsic barrier, as well as other demand-side factors (see also strategic and 'first-mover' advantages, paragraphs 217 to 222).

216. Network effects—where other customers committing to a particular product or service makes it more attractive to new customers (see paragraph 179)—may constitute a barrier to entry.[122] This is because incumbents with an existing customer base have an automatic advantage over entrants. However, when demand is growing fast, or innovation is rapid, the barrier might not be as high as when demand or technological change is more static.

Strategic advantages of incumbents

217. Some forms of investments by incumbents, although they may often be pro-competitive and/or benefit customers, may sometimes have the effect of deterring market entry by increasing the sunk costs of entry. Such barriers are termed strategic and can have the effects of:

(a) lowering the incumbents' costs relative to those of potential entrants (for example, by increasing capacity);
(b) altering the cost structure of rivals (for example, by vertical arrangements); and
(c) altering demand conditions in their favour (for example, by brand and product proliferation).

218. Such strategic entry barriers may increase the risks faced by new entrants. For example, vertical arrangements may in some cases make it difficult for an entrant to gain sufficient distribution outlets, because existing sellers are largely tied up with existing suppliers, or to gain access to vital components (see also paragraph 269).

219. The risks will be proportionately higher if the sunk costs of entry are high and the difference between the incumbent's profitability and the rival's post-entry profitability is substantial. In general, the greater the financial investment needed by a potential entrant the greater becomes the risk associated with entry.

220. The existence of significant switching costs for customers may act as a barrier to entry. These may be intrinsic to the market (see paragraph 215), but firms may also act strategically to increase them, for example by offering fidelity discounts or agreeing long-term contracts with customers, accompanied by penalties for early termination. Moreover, incumbent firms producing complementary goods may tie or bundle them together, potentially raising the costs for an entrant producing only one of the complementary goods (see paragraphs 286 to 290).

221. The incumbent firms may also be able to deter entry by signalling that they would respond aggressively to entry, including by over-investing in spare capacity, or seek to target entrants specifically to discourage them from entering the market.

'First mover' advantages

222. Other entry barriers may result simply from the established position of the incumbent firms in the market. Such so-called 'first-mover' advantages may make it difficult for other firms to enter a particular industry because experience or an established reputation is necessary to compete effectively. Relevant factors in this context include customer loyalty to a particular brand, the closeness of the relationships between suppliers and customers, and the role of promotion or advertising in the particular industry.

Regulatory barriers to entry

223. The ability of firms to enter a market can be affected by the market's regulatory framework, broadly defined as including any applicable legislation (for example, intellectual property law and planning law), voluntary or compulsory standards and codes of practice, and other applicable sectoral regulations.

224. Regulations may be beneficial for a variety of reasons ranging from ensuring the stability of the financial system to protecting the environment, but they may inhibit the extent to which competition can flourish in certain circumstances. Some types of regulations may concern the production process and the characteristics of the finished product, for instance health and safety standards. Others may limit the number of competitors in the market directly, for example by requiring that only firms with a licence or permit may operate within it.[123]

225. With regard to their effect on competition, a distinction can be drawn between regulations that impose costs proportionately on all firms and those that hit new entrants harder than incumbent firms. Subsidies, tax reliefs and preferential purchasing may raise barriers to entry in a market if potential entrants are not equally eligible for them. Barriers that raise fixed costs can more easily be absorbed by an incumbent firm than by an entrant (because of the former's larger sales in the market); however, barriers that raise variable costs would fall more evenly on both firms. Planning policies and regulations can also constitute a barrier to potential entrants into a market to the advantage of incumbent firms. IPRs such as patents, trademarks and copyrights give the owners of such rights exclusive use of them and the ability to control their use by others, though the period of such exclusivity or control varies according to the nature of the property right. IPRs can act as barriers to entry when access to the rights owned by an incumbent may be vital for entry.[124]

226. Quality, environmental, and health and safety standards that apply to all the firms in a market may on occasions adversely affect entry despite making no formal distinction between incumbents and new entrants. For example, they might favour the technology the incumbent owns and therefore raise the costs of a new entrant. Some regulations may give advantage to incumbents by not requiring them to comply with the same standards as new entrants.[125]

Assessing the impact of entry barriers

227. To test a theory of harm based on the effects on competition of any barriers to entry, the CC has to assess the impact that the entry barriers identified have had, are having or may have in the future.

Current competitive climate

228. The CC considers how the competitive climate within a market affects the decisions of individual firms to enter or invest in that market, taking into account the advantages of established sellers. This entails examining the factors influencing entry decisions, while recognizing that these will be accorded different weights by different firms.

229. The post-entry profitability that a firm can expect—and therefore the degree of attractiveness to that firm of entering a market—is affected, not only by the extent to which entry costs are sunk (see paragraph 211) but also by its assessment of the likely intensity of competition post-entry. The expectation of a tough competitive regime post-entry leads entrants to anticipate lower prices, reducing the profitability of entry and making it less attractive. If, on the other hand, growth in demand is likely to be large and rapid, barriers to entry are less likely to have a lasting effect. Similarly, in markets characterized by innovation, product cycles are likely to be shorter and barriers less likely to have a lasting effect. Entry decisions are often influenced by a range of other factors, including payback periods, the effect on other business segments (eg possible cannibalization, ie creation of competition to a firm's existing business), and the risk of the project. The risk will in turn be affected by various factors influencing the certainty or otherwise of forecast future cash flows: for example, the management team's level of experience, the predictability of demand, and likely competitor reactions.

230. In assessing the factors influencing entry decisions, the CC therefore may consider:

- the costs involved in entry and in operating at the minimum efficient scale necessary to achieve a reasonably competitive level of costs;

- the likelihood of entry within a timescale that would bear on the incentives and decisions of the existing firms in the market;
- the cost of exiting the market; and
- the likely response to entry by incumbent firms.

Past and prospective entry

231. Evidence of persistent profits above the competitive level within the industry or among large incumbents could suggest there may be entry barriers in the market. But such evidence is neither necessary nor sufficient. Conversely, data showing that incumbents consistently fail to earn high profits may be consistent with low entry barriers, but it does not prove that barriers are low and that competition is working dynamically (see paragraph 125).

232. The CC will examine the history of entry and evidence of planned entry. This assessment will include the extent to which past entrants and smaller firms have successfully gained market share (see paragraphs 100 and 101) and, more generally, the cost of gaining a significant share of the market.

233. In considering historical evidence, the CC may consider: survival rates, ie how long any entrants traded in the market; the effects that entry or expansion had on competition in the market, in particular whether past entry or expansion modified the pattern of behaviour and competition; and if so, whether this would be relevant for the present analysis. The CC may also consider the price effects, if any, from past episodes of entry, the viability of the entrant and its experience in trying to gain market share.

234. Although evidence of past entry (or the lack of it) can be helpful in assessing the significance of entry barriers in a market, previous episodes of entry do not necessarily prove that it was easy, that it was competitively significant, that it is likely to take place again, or that the possibility of entry is imposing a competitive constraint (see also paragraph 175). Moreover, current potential entrants may not face the same market conditions that previous entrants faced. Similarly, although an absence of actual or meaningful entry in the past may indicate the presence of entry barriers, it does not necessarily prove that significant entry is unlikely in the future.

The positive effects of a barrier

235. In some circumstances barriers to entry may have a positive impact:

- Entry barriers may sometimes increase incentives to innovate. While new entrants can often lead to innovative competition, the effect of entry barriers, or the prospect of creating them, may also increase the incentives for incumbents to create new products and services. IPRs, for example, provide an incentive to innovate because they prevent rivals 'free-riding'[126] on other firms' innovations. Given these conflicting factors, the CC will assess the incentives of incumbents relative to those of potential entrants to engage in innovative activities in the presence of entry barriers. The CC will also sometimes assess whether or not potential technological change and innovation could affect the nature and effectiveness of current barriers to entry.
- Some regulations which restrict entry may achieve important social goals outside the scope of competition policy (see paragraphs 224 and 226). Safety regulations, for example, may make it more difficult to switch suppliers of domestic liquified gas in the UK, but the CC recognized in its investigation of the LPG market that regulation in that industry was necessary.[127]

236. Such positive impacts could be taken into account at different stages of an investigation. First, they may be considered as part of the competitive assessment, for example, a restriction on short-run competition might be tolerated so as to preserve incentives to compete in longer-term ways. Secondly, they may be considered during the remedies process as RCBs (see paragraphs 355 to 366).

3. COORDINATED CONDUCT BY FIRMS

237. The successful adoption by rival firms of a coordinated course of action is a third way in which competition in a market may be harmed to the detriment of customers.

Forms of coordination

238. Coordination typically involves repeated interaction, aimed at increasing or protecting profits, between firms in the market. But coordination can take different forms across a wide spectrum of behaviour.

239. At one end of the spectrum, direct and unambiguous communication among competitors can lead to explicit agreements to fix prices, share markets or allocate customers. At the other end of the spectrum, when a market is sufficiently stable and rival firms interact repeatedly they may be able to anticipate each other's future actions, enabling them tacitly to establish a coordinated course of action without communicating directly or sharing information. Coordination does not have to be 'perfect' at all times to affect a market. For example, it may be intermittent; ie periods of coordination may be interspersed with periods of greater competition when not all competitors see it in their interest to cooperate.

240. The sole focus of any market investigation is upon the effects on competition of possible features of the market (whether through coordinated conduct or otherwise) and it is not the CC's role to ascertain whether one or more parties have been acting unlawfully. While enforcement action on some cases of coordinated behaviour may fall within Article 101 of the TFEU or Chapter 1 of CA98,[128] the CC may investigate all forms of coordination. Any form of coordination has the potential to reduce strategic uncertainty among competitors to the detriment of their customers and, depending on the degree, may thereby result in an AEC.

Impact of coordinated conduct

241. Coordination may have an impact on any dimension of competition, including price and output levels, the scope of firms' geographic operations, investment or innovation.

242. Not all cooperation will be harmful. It may sometimes also bring about pro-competitive effects, which benefit customers. For example:

- In some financial markets, credit providers and insurers routinely share certain data (eg about customers' repayment or claim history) that facilitates the efficient operation of those markets. The CC found that the absence of such data sharing was a feature harming competition in the market for home credit and required lenders above a certain size to provide credit reference agencies with full data on the payment records of customers.[129]
- In its investigation into local bus markets, the CC found that effective multi-operator ticketing schemes could reduce barriers to entry and expansion associated with network effects and made various recommendations to facilitate the development of such schemes.[130]

243. However, in many cases coordination between rivals has harmful effects on both competition and customers. Prices may be higher than they would have been if firms had taken unilateral decisions. In other cases, coordination may involve limiting production or innovation. Firms may divide up the market between them, for example by geographic area or customer characteristics, or by allocating contracts between themselves. Joint action may be taken to foreclose access to markets, inputs or customers. In these ways, coordination between rivals can worsen the terms on which products are offered to customers, reduce customer choice and hold back efficiency and innovation.

Assessing potential concerns about coordination

244. In assessing whether coordination gives rise to an AEC, the CC will examine the evidence of the behaviour of firms in the market, structural characteristics of the market and market outcomes. In doing so, the CC considers whether market conditions are conducive to coordination, seeks to understand the way in which the firms in the market operate and comes to a view on whether the observed outcomes are best explained by coordinated or non-coordinated behaviour.[131]

Observed market outcomes

245. The CC will consider whether observed market outcomes may suggest coordinated behaviour. A range of market outcomes may be relevant to this assessment. Some examples are given below (paragraphs 246 to 248).

246. Certain forms of pricing behaviour can be possible outcomes of coordination. For example, information on demand elasticities (see paragraph 179) and variable profit margins (sales revenue minus costs of sales) may suggest that prices are higher than would be expected if firms were acting unilaterally since each firm would stand to profit by undercutting the current market price.

247. It has also been noted (see paragraph 119) that a situation where levels of profitability have remained high and stable over time across several incumbent firms could indicate coordinated behaviour.

248. The absence of a provider serving an area where there are potential customers that it would be economic to supply may also be an indication of coordination by firms over the scope of geographic operations.

249. The CC will generally look at a range of market outcomes in combination. A single outcome looked at in isolation may often be consistent with both coordinated and non-coordinated behaviour. For example, whilst coordination may result in price parallelism (see paragraph 108(b)), intense price competition often also does so. Non-coordinated behaviour may be the more likely explanation if parallel pricing is explained by common movements in costs, and the CC will therefore consider information about changes in variable costs alongside price movements.

Market conditions and characteristics

250. Three conditions are necessary for coordination to be sustainable in a market:

(a) Firms need to be able to reach an understanding and monitor the terms of coordination. Where there is no explicit agreement, firms need to have sufficient awareness of each other and be able to anticipate each other's reactions so as to identify a mutually beneficial outcome.

(b) Coordination needs to be internally sustainable among the coordinating group— ie firms have to find it in their individual interests to adhere to the coordinated outcome; the firms must lack an incentive, or have a positive disincentive, to compete because they appreciate how each other will react. However, coordination does not need to be perfect or continuous to fulfil this criterion (see paragraph 239).

(c) Coordination also needs to be externally sustainable, in that coordination is unlikely to be undermined by competition from outside the coordinating group or from the reactions of customers.

251. An important part of the CC's investigation is therefore to establish whether or not the specific characteristics of the market—structural characteristics and the way firms behave—create the conditions in which coordination can arise and be sustained.[132] These characteristics are described below. Which of them the CC will consider as potentially facilitating coordination will depend on the facts of the individual case.

(A) Structural characteristics of the market

252. Structural characteristics that may help firms reach an understanding and monitor terms of coordination, include:

(a) *A non-complex and stable economic environment* can help firms to reach an understanding on the terms of coordination. For example: where markets are concentrated, firms are more likely to be aware of the behaviour of individual competitors; it is often easier to coordinate on a price when demand and supply conditions are relatively stable than when they are continually changing.
(b) *Simple and relatively undifferentiated products* are more easily subject to the coordinated setting of prices than situations in which each firm's offering is different from the offerings of its rivals.[133]
(c) *Customers with easily identifiable characteristics* help firms coordinate by way of market segmentation (based on geography or customer type or simply on customers who typically buy from one supplier).
(d) Firms that are relatively *symmetric*, for example in terms of cost structures, market shares or spare capacity levels, may more easily respond to incentives to reach an understanding with each other.[134]
(e) Firms with cross-shareholdings, participating in joint ventures with each other or in reciprocal supplier/buyer relationships may also find it easier to reach an understanding.

253. Other structural characteristics that may help firms reach an understanding and monitor terms include the need for firms to make a long-term market commitment, and the existence of institutions (eg trade associations) or regulations that may facilitate the sharing of information.

254. The following market characteristics can help increase the *internal sustainability* of coordination:
(a) A *concentrated market* is the foremost factor in helping to sustain coordination internally. It allows deviations to be spotted quickly. (In a less concentrated market with many companies coordinating, deviation may be more likely because a larger market share can be gained through undercutting.)
(b) *Market transparency* also allows coordinating firms to monitor whether one or more of them are deviating from a coordinated outcome. The way transactions are conducted will often determine the degree of transparency in a market; price transparency will, for example, be higher on a public exchange, than when transactions are negotiated confidentially and bilaterally. Nonetheless, even where price transparency is limited, other aspects of transparency (eg of sales or production volumes or customer relationships) may help increase internal sustainability.
(c) *Transparency* in the market also affects the speed, and hence effectiveness, of any deterrent mechanism used against a deviating firm or strengthens firms' ability to anticipate each other's conduct.
(d) *Factors that make it easier to respond quickly to deviation from a coordinated outcome* may make coordination easier to sustain. For example, firms could use excess capacity as a credible threat against deviation. Likewise a response to a perceived deviation from a coordinated outcome need not necessarily take place in the same market as the deviation; if coordinating firms have commercial interactions in several markets, these may offer various ways of responding to deviations, such as cancellation of joint ventures or selling shares in jointly-owned companies.

255. The *external sustainability* of coordination may be affected by the following characteristics:
(a) *Barriers to entry or expansion* facilitate coordination. If barriers to entry or expansion are low, the threat of entry or expansion by non-coordinating competitors will tend to undermine coordination.
(b) *The number and size* of the non-coordinating (or fringe)[135] rivals, their *cost* and *profit margins* and, critically, their scope to *expand output* in relation to their current levels and to the output of the coordinating firms will determine the extent to which non-coordinating firms act as a competitive constraint.
(c) If a firm has the capacity to take significant share from any group of firms that tried to coordinate without its participation but also has substantially different incentives from those of the coordinating group, it can undermine a coordination strategy. (Such a firm is sometimes referred to as 'a maverick'.)[136]
(d) *Countervailing buyer power* of customers (see paragraph 176) can similarly undermine the stability of coordination. For example, a large buyer may do so by concentrating its purchases on one supplier or by offering long-term contracts and tempting one of the coordinating firms to break ranks to gain substantial new business.

(B) Practices of firms operating in the market

256. In addition to investigating structural characteristics of the market that may be conducive to coordination and considering evidence of outcomes that might be indicative of coordinated conduct, the CC will look at whether would-be competitors have taken any actions[137] to reach, sustain or enhance coordination. Such actions may involve exchanges of information or specific types of arrangements.

• *Availability of information*

257. The ease with which firms can obtain information about their competitors tends to facilitate coordination. Readily available information or exchanges of information increase transparency between firms and help firms interpret the choices their competitors have made. Information availability can facilitate coordination by:
(a) generating mutually consistent expectations among rival firms regarding their conduct and beliefs, making it easier for firms to reach an *understanding on the terms of coordination* (paragraph 250(a));

Part 3 CMA and other Guidelines

(b) giving an indication of rivals' past and present conduct and enabling rival firms to monitor deviations and, potentially, to retaliate, thereby increasing *internal sustainability* of coordination (paragraph 250(b)); and

(c) increasing transparency making it easier for coordinating companies to monitor where and when other companies are trying to enter the market, allowing the coordinating companies to target the new entrant. This can increase the *external sustainability* of coordination (paragraph 250(c)).

258. The means by which companies may obtain or exchange information, other than by the many forms of direct communication, include most-favoured customer clauses (MFCs, see paragraphs 261 and 272), voluntary publication of information, price announcements, or information shared—even anonymously—through trade associations. Cross-directorships, joint ventures, supplier/buyer relationships and similar arrangements may also make monitoring and retaliation easier.

259. Less obvious means and practices may also increase the transparency or predictability of the environment in which firms operate. These may include the adoption of rules of conduct, ethics codes, product standardization, regulatory disclosures, joint marketing or buying agreements, price computation manuals and R&D joint ventures. Such practices may sometimes be justifiable on efficiency or customer-benefit grounds, but they could also create market conditions favourable for coordination.

260. These Guidelines cannot be prescriptive about the type of information that may be associated with coordinated conduct. The likely effects of the availability of particular items of information on competition are analysed by the CC on a case-by-case basis. The assessment compares the likely effect of the information flow with the competitive situation that would prevail in its absence.

• *Specific arrangements made by firms*

261. The specific types of arrangements firms make, which, although sometimes benign from a competition viewpoint, can sometimes facilitate coordination, include:

- *Best price policies* (or low-price guarantee);[138] they can increase transparency, facilitating consensus and the detection and punishment of cheating.
- *Most favoured customer (MFC) clauses*;[139] although generally benign, these provisions can in some circumstances deter competitive price cutting, reduce the incentive to deviate from established terms of coordination, and deter a firm from offering discounts to its smaller customers.
- *Minimum advertised price agreements*[140] can be conducive to coordination at both retail and manufacturing levels since they can control the pricing strategies of several competing retailers and are visible to competing manufacturers.
- *Resale price maintenance (RPM)*[141] can be used to facilitate coordination between suppliers and retailers, making it easier to detect whether a supplier deviates from a coordinated price; strong or well-organized distributors may be able to use RPM to influence one or more suppliers to fix their resale price above the competitive price. Instances of RPM may sometimes fall to CA98 and TFEU investigation (see paragraph 17). However, depending on the circumstances, manufacturers can use RPM to promote effective competition by preventing 'free-riding'[142] at the distribution level.

4. VERTICAL RELATIONSHIPS

262. Market outcomes may sometimes be the result of vertical integration or other vertical arrangements within the market (collectively known as 'vertical relationships').

- 'Vertical integration' means that activities at upstream and downstream levels of the supply chain have been brought under common ownership and control (see paragraph 50).
- 'Vertical arrangements' fall short of vertical integration and may involve agreed pricing schemes or other contractual provisions between companies at different levels of the supply chain.

263. Vertical relationships will often have been established when upstream and downstream firms in a trading relationship (see paragraph 50) consider that it is more efficient and economical for transactions to be organized within firms.[143] Arm's length supply contracts between such firms may be imprecise, incomplete and/or difficult to enforce and in practice may give one of the contracting firms leverage over the other. To avoid this risk one or other of the firms may decide to bring the transaction 'in house', either through internal growth or external acquisition.

264. Alternatively, firms may make vertical arrangements with each other, either via legally enforceable contracts or commitments by each firm not to behave opportunistically against the interests of the other. By restricting each other's actions, vertical arrangements may give both parties a mutual incentive to invest in their relationship. A wide variety of vertical arrangements are employed by firms. Among the most prominent are exclusive purchasing, tying and bundling, franchising, selective distribution systems and pricing arrangements. Some examples of vertical arrangements, and the CC's approach to assessing their effects, are discussed in paragraphs 271 to 294.

Impacts of vertical relationships

265. Vertical relationships often have beneficial effects. They can improve the coordination of activities at different stages of the supply chain and deliver savings in transaction and inventory costs.[144] With vertical integration, the benefits are achieved by bringing 'in-house' activities which would otherwise be carried out in separately-owned businesses.[145] The benefits of other vertical arrangements flow from a closer alignment of the incentives of firms within a supply chain (eg the supplier and its distributor), towards the achievement of complementary objectives. Vertical relationships may also help to resolve the 'free-rider' problem[146] in markets where suppliers require their distributors to incur certain costs if advice and other pre-sale services are to be provided in a sustained way.

266. Since vertical relationships involve complementary products, services or activities, each firm would like the other to lower the price of its product. Such a relationship can therefore have the effect of lowering prices that would be charged to customers if the firms acted independently and in this way can sometimes benefit customers.

267. However, despite their potential to enhance efficiency and consumer welfare, vertical relationships can also sometimes lead to an AEC in a market, particularly by allowing the firms to:
(a) foreclose rivals' access to inputs and customers; and/or
(b) otherwise have a dampening effect on competition.

(a) Foreclosure

268. For a vertically related firm, foreclosure may be achieved by practices that restrict access to essential inputs or raise rivals' costs, or limit rivals' ability to acquire sufficient customers to benefit from economies of scale, learning effects[147] and/or network effects.

269. Foreclosure can be total (where rivals are forced to exit from the market or are prevented from entering) or partial (where rivals or potential entrants—are materially disadvantaged and consequently compete less effectively).

270. Foreclosure of access to key inputs ('input foreclosure') may lead to a reduced competitive constraint on a vertically related firm. When deciding whether to supply its competitors downstream with key inputs, a vertically integrated firm may take into account how these sales would affect the profits of its own downstream division. If it has significant market power in the upstream market, the firm may have an incentive to refuse access to the input or to raise its price, and consequently increase the costs of competing downstream firms. By being subjected to higher input prices—of which an extreme form is a 'margin squeeze'[148] — downstream competitors may be unable to compete effectively. As a result of such foreclosure effects a vertically integrated firm may be able to maintain high prices and/or increase the prices charged to customers relative to the prices obtained in the absence of vertical integration.

(b) Dampened competition

271. Since the rationale for vertical relationships is often unconnected to competition issues (see paragraph 263), a widespread network of overlapping vertical relationships may develop within an industry. While such arrangements may address market failures, they can have far-reaching effects on the operational structure of the upstream and downstream markets, reducing the incentives on firms to compete vigorously against each other and possibly leading to an increased likelihood of coordinated conduct by firms at the same level of the supply chain and to a greater incidence of entry barriers.

272. Pricing relationships especially, notably MFC and RPM arrangements (see section on coordinated conduct, paragraph 261) may sometimes harm competition in some industries because a commitment to apparently less vigorous conduct may lead rivals to see that their best interest lies in allowing prices to rise. Such practices have greatest impact when the arrangements have been adopted by most or all of the firms in an industry.

Assessment of vertical relationships

273. In reaching a judgement on whether a particular vertical relationship has an adverse effect on competition, the CC will evaluate its overall impact on competition, taking into account rivalry-enhancing, as well as adverse, effects. This will normally require an assessment of the impact of the vertical relationship on rivalry at different stages of the supply chain.[149]

274. For vertical relationships to result in foreclosure of rivals, the firms involved must have significant market power in one or more markets along the supply chain. They will also need to have both the ability and an incentive to seek to foreclose rivals (this will not necessarily be the case, even if the firms enjoy significant market power).[150]

275. In conducting its assessment of the overall impact of vertical relationships on competition, the CC will look at a variety of evidence. Economic modelling may be used to test whether or not different vertical relationships have a harmful effect on the evolution of competition in a market. The CC will also assess the conduct and strategic interactions of relevant market participants. This may involve comparing relevant industry characteristics and firm behaviour over time or across geographical locations, making comparisons with other similar sectors or examining and drawing inferences from any observed natural experiment, where available.

276. Analysis of profitability and financial data can help provide an insight into whether foreclosure would be a profitable strategy.

277. The profitability of input foreclosure will depend on:
(a) the integrated firm's ability to refuse to supply or to increase the price of an essential input, or limit access to an asset, facility or platform;
(b) the competitiveness of upstream and downstream markets (lower competition leads to higher profitability);
(c) the size of any cost asymmetry[151] it can create on the downstream market (higher cost asymmetries lead to higher profitability); and
(d) counter-measures by rivals such as vertical integration, or other factors (such as switching costs) which could reduce the profitability of foreclosure.

278. The following paragraphs survey some of the more prominent among the wide range of vertical arrangements and discuss how the CC approaches an assessment of their effects on competition. Some arrangements, such as exclusive purchasing arrangements, tying and bundling and RPM can sometimes come within the jurisdiction of the TFEU and CA98 (see paragraph 17).

Exclusive purchasing obligations

279. Exclusive purchasing obligations may effectively require the customer to purchase all or a significant part of its requirements from a particular upstream supplier.[152] If the customers make up a large part of the market, this has the effect of foreclosing the upstream supplier's competitors from the market. Similar foreclosure effects may derive from conditional rebates and other inducements that levy switching costs on any buyer seeking to switch from an incumbent. Exclusive purchasing may thus be used in some situations as a substitute for vertical integration and have similar effects as a refusal to deal.

280. Foreclosure may lead to an AEC where, without the exclusive purchasing obligations, an important competitive constraint could be exercised by competitors that either were not present in the market at the time the obligations were concluded, or that were not in a position to compete for the full supply of the customers.

281. In general, the longer the duration of the obligation, the stronger the likely foreclosure effect, in particular if new entrants are affected. Foreclosure of this type will be more likely if the exclusive purchasing obligation has been tied selectively to buyers of particular relevance to new entrants. In such cases an anticompetitive foreclosure effect may result even though the market share involved is modest.

282. The existence of exclusive purchasing arrangements in a market does not necessarily suggest that competition is harmed. For example, when an upstream supplier faces significant inter-brand competition,[153] it may need to compensate buyers, in whole or in part, for the loss in choice resulting from the possible foreclosure. Such compensation could, for instance, take the form of lower prices or other benefits.

283. Moreover, competitors may have counter-strategies at their disposal allowing them to protect themselves against exclusive purchasing strategies and to prevent any harm to competition. Such counter-strategies could, for instance, include: *(a)* concentrating their sales on certain customers; *(b)* building up stronger 'ex-ante' competition for the customers, as foreclosure is less likely if customers, before entering into exclusive purchasing obligations, have had access to several alternative competitive offers; and *(c)* ensuring new entry in the downstream market, either by sponsoring entry or by integrating vertically.

Exclusive supply obligations

284. Exclusive supply obligations—by which a supplier is obliged to sell exclusively or to a large extent to an incumbent downstream firm—may also be used to try to foreclose the downstream market to new entry if an incumbent downstream firm has sufficient market power to induce all input suppliers to make such arrangements. Exclusive supply obligations may be found to lead to an AEC if they have tied most of the efficient input suppliers and rival buyers have been unable to find alternative sources of input supply. The foreclosure effects would be likely to be stronger if there were significant scale economies or network effects in the downstream market (see paragraph 179) or if there were significant entry barriers for input suppliers.

285. Exclusive supply incentives may have similar effects to exclusive supply obligations. Under such arrangements, for example, an incumbent firm with significant buyer power offers to pay a higher price if the supplier sells it a higher percentage of its output, or the supplier may be required to pay a lump sum so as to get its goods on to the shelves of the incumbent buyer.

Tying and bundling

286. Tying and bundling are common commercial practices, frequently having no anticompetitive consequences but with the potential sometimes to foreclose markets and harm customers.

287. Tying occurs when the supplier makes the sale of one product (the tying product) conditional upon the purchase of another distinct product (the tied product) from the supplier or a firm designated by that supplier. Bundling relates to situations where a package of two or more goods is offered in fixed proportions.[154] Tying and bundling may also be achieved in indirect ways, eg by offering discounts or rebates to customers using both products or limiting guarantees to customers using only one of the products.

288. Tying and bundling can benefit customers by enabling firms to provide better products or offerings in cost-effective ways. They can lead to significant savings in production, distribution and transaction costs.

289. However, a firm with significant market power in the tying market can harm customers through tying by foreclosing the tied market and, indirectly, the tying market. In the case of the tied market, competition may be harmed if the tying has led to less competition for customers buying the tied good but not the tying good; if there are not enough of these customers to sustain competitors of the tying firm in the tied market, these customers may face higher prices. In the tying market such foreclosure may constrain market entry by rivals, which would have been likely in the absence of the tie. Similar effects may arise from pure and mixed bundling. (Paragraph 220 discusses tying and bundling as a potential barrier to entry and expansion.)

290. The factors the CC considers in assessing the extent of the foreclosure effect of tying and bundling in a market, include: the nature of the restriction applied, eg whether tying or bundling, and its effects on the choices of customers and the commercial strategies of firms; the tied percentage of total sales on the tied market; the overall strength of the tying firm on both the tying and the tied markets; the identity of the tied customers; the level of sales of the tied product to customers not buying the tying product and, in the case of bundling, the extent to which a firm is bundling goods, and whether the items within the bundle may also be purchased separately. In considering whether foreclosure of the tying market had deterred market entry, the CC may examine previous attempts to enter it.

Aftermarket arrangements

291. In those aftermarkets where secondary products can be used with one brand of primary product but not easily with another brand (although the primary products may be substitutable), the supplier of the primary product may reserve the secondary product for itself by excluding competitors, for example through tying or a refusal to deal (eg to supply necessary information, licences, IPRs or spare parts). In other cases, the supplier of the primary product may have a point-of-sale advantage in relation to the secondary product that restricts the ability of other potential suppliers of the secondary product to serve its customers.[155]

292. In assessing the effects of aftermarket arrangements, the CC will typically first consider the nature of the relationship between the primary and secondary markets. This may constrain the extent of, or in some cases remove, any market power enjoyed in the secondary market by the supplier of the primary product. In particular, if the primary market is competitive and if customers anticipate the likely cost of secondary products when making decisions about which primary product to buy, competition in the primary market may constrain suppliers' ability to raise prices of the secondary product. Competition in the primary market may in this way ensure that the overall price of the 'bundle' of goods and services comprising the primary product and the secondary product(s) is set at a competitive level.

293. The extent to which competition in the primary market may constrain market power in the secondary market is determined by:

(a) The amount of information available to customers, together with the use customers make of this information when buying a primary product. These are important factors in assessing the extent to which customers calculate the overall cost of the bundle over the expected life cycle of the primary product. For this competitive constraint from the primary market to function effectively, a sufficient number of customers must engage in life-cycle cost calculations, and the supplier(s) concerned must not be able to discriminate between customers that make such calculations and those that do not.

(b) Whether the suppliers, even if customers have not based their choice on accurate life-cycle calculations, make their own assessment of the profitability of a customer relationship over the life cycle of a product and compete vigorously in the primary market so as to enjoy profits on subsequent aftermarket sales.[156] The CC may consider the extent to which customers benefit from lower prices of the primary product as part of its assessment of RCBs (see paragraphs 355 to 366).[157]

Wider competition-dampening effects

294. As explained (see paragraphs 271 and 272) in some circumstances vertical relationships can have far-reaching effects on the operational structure of a market. These potential effects, for example the possibilities of coordination or entry barriers arising from competition-dampening relationships are assessed in the ways described in the relevant sections on coordinated conduct and entry barriers.

5. WEAK CUSTOMER RESPONSE

295. Competition (as emphasized in Part 1, paragraph 15) may be threatened if customers respond weakly to competitive offers. A weakness of customer response may be variously caused by customers' behaviour, actions by suppliers or a structural feature of the market (for example, affecting the availability of information). A market investigation is well placed among competition policy instruments to analyse and remedy undesirable patterns of customer responses which result in a lack of competition.[158]

Impacts and assessment of weak customer response

296. To drive effective competition customers need to be both willing and able to: access information about the various offers available in the market; assess these offers to identify the good or service that provides the best value for them; and act on this assessment by switching to purchasing the good or service from their preferred supplier.

297. Theories of harm that competition is adversely affected by weak customer response are therefore generally examined in relation to these three issues so as to establish what may be restricting customers from exercising effective choice. The following sections of the Guidelines examine barriers to:

(a) accessing information;
(b) identifying best value offers; and
(c) switching suppliers.

(a) Barriers to accessing information

298. When customers face significant impediments or costs in their search for—and comparison of—alternatives, sellers may be able to set prices with only limited regard to competition.

299. Firms can enjoy some market power (see paragraph 9) if customers cannot easily or effectively compare their products with others on offer, because of the difficulty or cost (including the opportunity cost of customers' time) of finding better deals.[159]

300. Where it is difficult to obtain information, or where the cost of obtaining information is high, customers may not search the market but simply choose a firm randomly; firms may respond by charging a high price to these customers. Search costs are likely to be substantial in cases where the information that could possibly affect purchasing decisions is relatively complex, or difficult to obtain or process.

301. Firms may be able to charge high prices even where some customers search for information but a significant number of less well-informed customers remain; a seller's profit foregone by losing informed customers who buy elsewhere may be more than offset by the higher profits accruing from less well-informed customers who do not shop around.[160] An increase in the proportion of informed customers will generally increase the level of effective competition in a market.

302. Prices in the market tend to increase with the cost of acquiring information (although there is no general formulation for the relationship between prices and customers' search costs). This is because the higher the search costs, the lower the net gain for customers from searching for a lower price and the higher the degree of market power that firms can exploit.

303. Firms may sometimes engage in practices that increase search costs so as to obtain market power (or fail to engage in practices that would reduce search costs). They may do so, for example, by:

(a) charging different prices for the same good at various locations or under different brand names, making it difficult to find the low-priced brand;

(b) not clearly displaying prices or referring to some prices (eg special offers) which are not necessarily available to all customers; and

(c) failing to make available all the product information needed by customers to make an informed choice, in particular of one-off purchases.[161]

304. Other reasons buyers—in particular end-consumers—may have difficulty acquiring knowledge of substitutes or of the quality and prices of goods on offer might include:

(a) information may vary in availability or may become dated;

(b) customers' knowledge about their requirements may be imprecise;

(c) customers may have limited capabilities to search for products and compare alternatives, for example they can remember and readily recall only a limited amount of information; and

(d) customers may be sensitive or embarrassed about the product for which they are searching.

305. Advertising and other freely available information on products (eg online price comparison sites or organizations conducting product reviews) might be expected to reduce search costs. However, their influence may be limited in this respect, for example because:

(a) Advertising, while a 'free' resource reducing buyers' search costs to some degree, may not tell customers everything that they want or need to know about a product.

(b) Third party providers of information may have a legitimate commercial interest in protecting the IPRs (see paragraph 211) to the information they collect and distribute—for example, to prevent its use to publicize only the 'bottom' line (eg which brand is most or least reliable overall), or to benefit those who have not produced or paid for information.[162]

(c) The large fixed costs typically associated with the creation of information, and the small marginal costs of distributing it, may prevent fully efficient pricing and may give sellers an incentive to limit the information they provide.

(b) Barriers to identifying best value offers

306. Even if customers are able to access several offers, their assessment of those offers may be handicapped by two main factors:

(a) the susceptibility of some customers to behavioural biases and the potential for exploitation of these biases by providers (see paragraphs 307 to 310); and

(b) the potential for asymmetries of information to exist between suppliers and their customers (see paragraphs 311 to 315).

Behavioural bias

307. There are many explanations of the biases customers apply when making purchasing decisions. The main biases identified in the literature on the subject[163] are:

(a) Processing power biases including: choice overload (faced with too many choices, customers have difficulties making a purchasing decision); representational biases (customers use visible value as a reliable indicator of hidden value); and rules of thumb (for example, customers imitate what other customers do rather than make their own decisions).

(b) Framing biases including: relative utility (a customer's choice is affected by reference points such as past actions); default biases (customers adopt the default option); and placement biases (customers' choices depend on where goods are placed on a list—for example, they may tend to choose the first).

(c) Time inconsistency biases including: projection bias (customers expect that they will feel the same tomorrow as they do today); overoptimism (customers overestimate how much they will use a good, or underestimate how much it will cost them); and hyperbolic discount biases (customers value a reward today disproportionately more than one tomorrow).

(d) Loss aversion biases including endowment biases (customers value something more once they have owned it than before they own it).

308. In practice it can be difficult to predict how a customer will react in a particular situation. Empirical evidence is normally required to identify behavioural biases and any possible impact on competition in particular markets. The persistence of a bias is also hard to predict. Customers can learn from their biases and become more sophisticated, for example in markets where they make frequent purchases (or can benefit from the learning of others via word of mouth).[164] Advisers, intermediaries, consumer organizations and the media can also act as catalysts in improving customer decision-making, where there are customer biases.[165]

309. As well as influencing their purchasing decisions, the behavioural biases of customers can have a bearing on suppliers' behaviour. Where such biases exist, firms can act to exploit them at every stage in the decision-making process. They can potentially increase their profits by playing to these biases in certain ways, for example, unilaterally or jointly restricting the information provided to customers or by failing to highlight the add-on costs of a service.

310. In some markets there will be a proportion of 'active' customers who recognize their biases and correct for them and a proportion of more 'passive' customers who do not do so. Competition in these markets will work most effectively where there is a high proportion of 'active' customers and it is difficult for suppliers to discriminate between 'active' and 'passive' customers.

Information asymmetries

311. Information asymmetries between suppliers and customers might have adverse effects on competition, particularly in markets for goods or services where customers are not able to gauge the quality of a service when acquiring it.

312. Buyers may not know, for example, how quality varies across brands. Markets where customers may be unsure about quality include those for professional services, used goods and complex mechanical or electronic products. When, as a result of information asymmetries, customers are unable to form an accurate assessment of product quality (eg if they consistently underestimate the probability of product failure), a market may operate inefficiently. Imperfect information about quality can be a particularly severe problem for infrequently purchased goods or goods the quality of which cannot be verified even after purchase—so-called 'credence' goods.

• *Potential adverse effects on competition*

313. In extreme cases, asymmetric information about quality may lead to only the lowest quality product being offered, effectively meaning that a true market may not exist. This could arise where sellers of low-quality products are able to make their products appear indistinguishable from higher-quality products, and consequently sellers of the higher-quality products are unable to convince customers of their products' worth. In this situation, customers are only willing to pay the price of the average quality product, which is not enough to cover the cost of the higher quality products, leading to these products not being supplied. Even if information asymmetries do not lead to all higher-quality products being forced out of the market, quality levels are lower than they would be in the absence of any asymmetry.

314. A related issue (the so called *'principal-agent'* problem) arises where a provider (the agent) acts on behalf of another party (the principal), thereby providing a service to it. If the agent has better information than the principal about how well it is providing the service, the principal may be prevented from exercising effective choice. Moreover, where the two parties' interests are not aligned, the agent may act against the interests of the principal if information asymmetries allow it to do so undetected by the principal.[166]

315. These effects of asymmetric information are generally commensurate with the degree of asymmetry: the greater the asymmetry of information, the greater the effect. However, the potential effects of asymmetric information may be mitigated in various ways:

(a) The Government, consumer groups, industry groups or others may provide information in the form of standards (defining a metric, or scale, for evaluating a particular product) and certification (that a particular product has been found to meet a standard)—for example, relating to the licensing of new drugs, car safety regulations and rules for financial fund managers.

(b) Liability laws may serve the same function as explicit warranties, forcing the manufacturer to make good any defective products.

(c) Professional and other bodies can regulate entry into, and ongoing participation in, the profession and require that practitioners obtain certain qualifications, thus guaranteeing quality of service to some degree (see also discussion of entry barriers, paragraphs 223 and 224).

(d) A disinterested expert may be able to provide customers with reliable information, for example, a mechanic in the case of a used car.

(e) Warranties or guarantees may eliminate problems due to limited information or act as a signal of the item's quality at the time of purchase, for example 'satisfaction guarantees' might be offered by holiday providers.

(c) Barriers to switching suppliers

316. Switching from one supplier or provider to another, so as to respond to attractive offers, may be made difficult for customers by the costs of doing so.

317. In investigating switching costs, the CC recognizes that they can sometimes have both detrimental and beneficial effects on different groups of customers.

(a) On the one hand, switching costs allow firms potentially to charge high prices to 'captive' customers. Even if the firm is unable to discriminate between 'captive' and new customers, switching costs may enable it to charge higher prices in what would in other respects be a competitive market.

(b) On the other hand, the presence of switching costs may benefit some customers by intensifying the competition for new customers, particularly if there is scope to charge different prices to new as opposed to existing customers. In other situations, some limited constraint on switching (eg for a fixed period after signing a contract) may enable providers to recoup upfront costs of supplying a customer and may in that way facilitate customer-specific investments (eg in the equipment needed to receive a particular product).

318. Among the causes of high switching costs the CC may consider are:

(a) Lack of information on the part of the customer about alternative products; in some markets the customer may be unaware of the existence of competing products, possibly because of a lack of access to information or high search costs (see paragraph 300 above). The latter in particular magnify switching costs.[167]

(b) Inconvenience and administrative obstacles: the CC's report on banking services to small and medium-sized enterprises[168] identified the 'hassle in moving direct debits, standing orders etc and a fear that crucial payments could be missed whilst a switch was in progress' as a factor discouraging switching between banks.

(c) The presence of network effects (see paragraph 179 and footnote 107), which gives rise to collective switching costs, locking customers into existing standards and the firms that control them.

(d) If customers have made a large investment in a piece of equipment or in product-specific skills they may be deterred from switching if it involves a further substantial investment;[169] the CC found that such high switching costs were features harming competition in the markets for domestic LPG.[170]

(e) Contractual terms (eg low early settlement rebates)[171] or marketing devices, such as loyalty cards, and negative advertising can have the effect of increasing switching costs or influencing switching decisions.

PART 3: SECTION 4—CONCLUDING THE AEC TEST

319. Having considered evidence of all kinds, the CC comes to a rounded judgement on what may be causing any adverse effects on competition. This judgement entails the CC reaching a finding on whether there is a feature, or combination of features, of a relevant market that prevents, restricts or distorts competition in connection with the supply or acquisition of any goods or services in the UK or part of the UK. If so, it will find that there is an AEC. In forming its judgement the CC will apply a 'balance of probabilities' threshold to its analysis, ie it addresses the question: is it more likely than not that features or a combination of features lead to an AEC?

320. In identifying some features or combination of features of the market that may give rise to an AEC, the CC has to find a benchmark against which to determine how the market may be judged to be performing. In the absence of a statutory benchmark, the CC defines such a benchmark as 'a well-functioning market' (see paragraph 30)—ie one that displays the beneficial aspects of competition as set out in paragraphs 10 to 12 but not an idealized perfectly competitive market.[172] The benchmark will generally be the market envisioned without the features. But there may sometimes be reasons to depart from that general concept, for example, if features are intrinsic to the market but nevertheless have anticompetitive effects (as in the case of a natural monopoly) or if the nature of competition in the market is defined by arrangements put in place by Government, eg as in rolling stock leasing.[173]

321. If the CC decides that there are features in the market leading to an AEC, it moves on to consider appropriate remedies.

NOTES

62 The term 'relevant market' is used throughout these Guidelines in two contexts, see paragraph 26.

63 Examples of investigations in which the CC found that high concentration was a feature of the market that prevented, limited or distorted competition are given in paragraph 157.

64 The suitability of this technique will vary on a case by case basis. For examples of where the CC has applied the technique see *The supply of groceries in the UK market investigation*, 30 April 2008 (paragraphs 4.106–4.113) and *Local bus services market investigation*, 20 December 2011 (paragraph 7.37). In the latter investigation, an analogous performance concentration study was also undertaken (paragraphs 7.35 & 7.36 and Appendix 7.1).

65 Typically, this analysis is feasible only if it is possible accurately to measure price and some version of marginal cost, usually average incremental cost.

66 Those in which marginal cost is below average cost and capacity constraints are not binding.

67 For example, where there are no entry barriers, fixed costs are present and products are differentiated. Customers might be unwilling to switch between highly differentiated products, but nonetheless competition on the basis of development efforts to introduce new products could be robust.

68 Hotels near airports, for example, may exhibit a form of monopolistic competition characterized by low entry barriers, in which customers do not compare offers effectively, and hence there are more operators, with excess capacity, charging higher prices than would otherwise be the case. Individual operators may be observed to have normal profitability in this example.

69 *Northern Irish personal banking*, 15 May 2007, paragraphs 4.193–4.206.

70 *PPI market investigation*, 29 January 2009, paragraphs 4.12 & 9.4. For the concept of a 'well-functioning' market, see paragraph 30 and paragraphs 319 & 320.

71 See paragraph 30.

72 *BAA airports market investigation*, 19 March 2009.

73 See paragraph 9.

74 Market definition in a market investigation flows from the statutory questions the investigation is required to address (see

paragraphs 26–28. Markets defined in answering other statutory questions under other regimes may not necessarily be comparable.

75 Manufacturers of fast-moving consumer goods may use their expertise in marketing and product development to compete by expanding their portfolios of products. The CC may therefore identify such a supply-side market when, for example: *(a)* at least some suppliers supply a range of different products in the same broad category, using the same set of assets and capabilities; or *(b)* these suppliers regularly introduce new products or reposition existing ones within the category.

76 In markets characterized by bidding and tendering processes firms bid on the basis of the service they can offer to supply customers with bespoke products. The competitive constraint on firms in these markets comes from a customer's willingness to award a contract to a rival rather than to switch to a different bespoke product. Aggregating a range of contracts where the same set of firms would have been credible bidders can provide more useful information about the competitive constraints on each firm than is available from focusing on just one bespoke product.

77 See paragraph 164.

78 See, for example, *Local bus services market investigation*, 7 January 2010, Summary, paragraph 23: We found that local markets will generally be at the level of particular flows. However, competition between bus operators may occur on a number of different geographic levels including at the level of specific flows, routes or across a wider local area. The appropriate geographic area for the assessment of competition depends on the nature of the constraints faced by local bus operators. Regardless of the precise geographic boundaries of the market, we therefore assessed competition between bus operators at a number of geographic levels, including at the route and depot level. We also used Urban Areas to measure concentration and to consider the constraints of supply-side substitution from different operators.

79 Unilateral market power is discussed in paragraphs 178–184.

80 In these Guidelines, references to the 'use' of the HMT applies to its use both quantitatively and as a conceptual framework.

81 This problem is known as the 'Cellophane Fallacy' because it arose in a US Supreme Court case involving cellophane, in which the issue was whether the relevant market was cellophane or all flexible packaging materials.

82 Competitive price levels that are clearly below current levels will usually be an indicator of an AEC. Alternatively, the competitive assessment may provide some insight into an appropriate competitive benchmark to feed into the HMT.

83 Other types of markets are described in paragraphs 179 & 193.

84 *Home credit market investigation*, 28 April 2006.

85 *Movies on pay TV market investigation*, 2 August 2012.

86 Buyer power is the ability of a firm to secure from its supplier(s) prices or other terms in its favour.

87 *Classified Directory Advertising Services market investigation*, 21 December 2006.

88 *The supply of groceries in the UK market investigation*, 30 April 2008.

89 *Market investigation into supply of bulk liquefied petroleum gas for domestic use*, 29 June 2006.

90 *ROSCOs market investigation*, 7 April 2009.

91 *BAA airports market investigation*, 19 March 2009.

92 *Home credit market investigation*, 28 April 2006.

93 *PPI market investigation*, 29 January 2009.

94 Section 131(2).

95 *Northern Irish personal banking*, 15 May 2007.

96 *PPI market investigation*, 29 January 2009.

97 *Local bus services market investigation*, 7 January 2010, paragraphs 8.263–8.277.

98 *Home credit market investigation*, 28 April 2006.

99 Annual Percentage Rate of the Total Charge for Credit.

100 *Store cards market investigation*, 7 March 2006.

101 *Northern Irish personal banking*, 15 May 2007.

102 *PPI market investigation*, 29 January 2009.

103 But, as noted in paragraph 22, the CC proceeds wholly independently of the referring body.

104 In retailing, for example, a supplier may be more dependent on its sales to a large retailer than is the retailer on its purchases from that supplier. (This may be the case even if the supplier has a larger share of its market than the retailer has of the retail market.)

105 See paragraph 9.

106 See paragraphs 9 & 14.

107 107 Customers value the network or platform more highly when it is used by a greater number of other customers; for example, in newspaper (and other media) markets both readers (or viewers, or listeners) and advertisers are served and the value of the product (eg an advertisement) to one group of customers (advertisers) is affected by the number of customers served in the other group (the number of readers of a newspaper, listeners to a radio station or viewers of a television channel).

108 108 Large-scale firms that undertake large amounts of R&D may be able to employ more specialized resources; they will face smaller average total costs because they can average the fixed costs of their innovative effort over a greater level of output; and they may be able to support a larger portfolio of R&D efforts, increasing the likelihood that this will develop an improved product or process likely to be applicable to at least one of its businesses.

109 A strong incumbent company might be deterred from investing because it could not be confident that it would increase its sales or its already large share of the market. In contrast, a new entrant or small incumbent supplier might have a strong incentive to invest because, having only a small or no presence in the market, its investment would have greater potential to gain business there.

110 It may on occasions be difficult to assess whether a particular market outcome has been driven by coordinated conduct or is the result of a non-coordinated oligopoly.

111 A *diversion ratio* between Product A and Product B represents the proportion of sales that would divert to Product B (as opposed to Products C, D, E etc) as customers' second choice in the event of a price increase for Product A. The *cross-price elasticity of demand* of Product A to Product B is a measure of the percentage change in the quantity of Product A sold when the price of Product B rises by 1 per cent.

112 As noted in paragraph 179.

Part 3 CMA and other Guidelines

113 See also paragraph 211.

114 The extent of intra-market rivalry may depend on whether firms' cost structures are similar, and how low-cost firms utilize this advantage.

115 Situations in which firms compete with products that are currently available may be distinguished from situations where firms compete by producing to order or on the basis of blueprints or where firms define their businesses in terms of the skills of their employees. In the latter situations the extent to which substitution exists is likely to be particularly important.

116 Absolute barriers to entry may include, for example, the constraints on entering a network market (paragraph 216).

117 Factors that delay entry may include licensing, certification, or product registration requirements that involve little or no costs but take significant amounts of time to satisfy. Other examples include the time required to obtain contracts (ie where the market's products are sold via long-term contracts) or to gain a market share large enough to influence the behaviour of incumbents significantly. Sometimes these market aspects can apply for such a long period as to be tantamount to an absolute barrier.

118 Endogenous costs are those located within a firm's organization—human capital, innovation, knowledge and so forth.

119 Economists distinguish between 'stand-alone' and 'ancillary' barriers. The former is a cost that constitutes a barrier to entry by itself. An 'ancillary' barrier to entry is a cost that does not constitute a barrier by itself but reinforces other barriers that may be present. A group of small stand-alone barriers may constitute a significant barrier but a group of small ancillary barriers cannot do so.

120 Three important aspects of sunk costs may influence entry and exit decisions. First, sunk costs increase the risk of entering an industry because they cannot be recouped on exiting. Secondly, sunk costs create a cost asymmetry between entrants and incumbents. Once costs are sunk they are no longer a portion of the opportunity costs of production, and hence an incumbent will require a lower return on costs so as to stay in an industry than will be required to enter. Thirdly, sunk costs can serve as a commitment by incumbent firms not to exit the industry.

121 Economies of scale may constitute a particular barrier to entry if the size of the market is small relative to the minimum efficient scale.

122 On telephone networks, for example, customers pay less to call other people on the network than they pay to contact those on other networks. If most existing customers (and therefore likely recipients of calls from new customers) are on the same network, it is harder for a rival to attract new customers.

123 Although sometimes in a competitive market licences and permits can be traded and a potential entrant is able to enter the market by buying a licence, depending on how frequently such opportunities arise.

124 In some such cases it might be appropriate to assess the impact of IPRs on competition for the market rather than within it.

125 For example, existing high pollution factories often have 'grandfather' rights to pollute, which are not enjoyed by entrants, because the factory existed before the relevant regulation came into force.

126 See paragraph 261 and footnote 142.

127 *Market investigation into supply of bulk liquefied petroleum gas for domestic use*, 29 June 2006.

128 See footnotes 3, 4 and 5.

129 *Home credit market investigation*, 28 April 2006, paragraphs 26, 9.36–9.40, and Appendix 2.1.

130 *Local bus services market investigation*, 20 December 2011, paragraph 15.11 and Appendix 9.2.

131 'Non-coordinated behaviour' in this context refers to the interaction of firms acting unilaterally.

132 For an example of the CC's approach see, for example, the *Local bus services market investigation*, 20 December 2011 (paragraphs 8.239-8.243 and 8.261). The CC had identified as a conduct feature of some bus markets that 'operators avoid competing with other operators in "Core Territories" (certain parts of an operator's network which it regards as its "own" territory') leading to geographic market segregation' (final report, paragraph 5). The CC found evidence of contacts between operators and actions which had the effect of segregating areas of operation. These behaviours reduced or eliminated head-to-head competition and diminished the constraint from potential competition. Finding conditions facilitating coordination caused the CC to be concerned that geographic market segregation might be a more widespread feature than was identified.

133 Coordination can become more complex—and may be more difficult to sustain—if important characteristics of the product are changed over time or if new products are introduced. However, coordination through, for example, simple pricing rules may overcome problems stemming from complex economic environments. One example of such a rule is the setting of only a small number of pricing points. The more complex the market environment the more transparency or communication is needed to reach an understanding of coordination arrangements.

134 Coordination is also possible where markets display elements of asymmetry: for example, one participant (say, the largest) may act as a market leader.

135 The term 'competitive fringe' is often used by economists to describe a group of relatively small firms in a market containing larger firms.

136 For example, a firm might value having a reputation for offering the lowest price in the market, and might consider itself likely to sacrifice profits in the long term if it were to lose that reputation by coordination.

137 Equivalent, in economic parlance, to 'facilitating practices'.

138 Best price policy is a commitment made by a firm (frequently a retailer) either to match or beat the lower price charged by other firms—a price-matching guarantee (PMG) and price-beating guarantee (PBG)—or by the same firm to other current or future customers—MFC clause. Such policies may be adopted unilaterally or through agreement or they may simply become accepted practice.

139 An MFC clause is a provision in a sales contract, under which the seller agrees to give the buyer the benefit of any more favourable contract terms it may later negotiate with some other purchaser.

140 Under minimum advertised price agreements, the manufacturers set the price of a product and the distributor enforces it; retailers may spend cooperative advertising allowances they receive from the product manufacturers.

141 RPM is the practice whereby a manufacturer and its distributors agree that the latter will sell the former's product at certain prices.

142 'Free-riding' is where other parties benefit from the provision of a good or service without paying for its provision.

143 In economists' parlance, the relationships often result from attempts to resolve a market failure.

144 For example, by helping guarantee stability of supplies, improve coordination on product design, production process and the way in which the products are sold).

145 In the absence of vertical coordination, if both producers and distributors add mark-ups over their costs, the resulting 'double' mark-up — or 'double marginalization' — may lead to inefficiently high prices. This is because each partner, when setting its price (the wholesale price for the producer and the retail price for the distributor) takes no account of the effect of this price on the other's profit. By aligning incentives, vertical relationships may lead to a coordinated reduction of the mark-ups at different levels in the supply chain, both increasing firms' profits and benefiting consumers.

146 See paragraph 261 and footnote 142.

147 'Learning effects' relate to firms becoming more efficient as they gain experience of providing a good or service (average cost falls over time spent in the market); see paragraph 214.

148 A margin squeeze occurs when downstream competitors are charged such a high price for the upstream input of the upstream firm that they cannot compete downstream since their operating costs plus the wholesale prices exceed retail prices.

149 Vertical arrangements normally relate to competition between brands (inter-brand competition) but some arrangements can affect competition between the same brands sold in different outlets (intra-brand competition). While the latter could potentially lead to an AEC, the CC is more likely to identify an AEC if vertical relationships result in a reduction in inter-brand competition.

150 For instance, an upstream monopolist may have limited incentive to leverage its upstream power to monopolize the downstream market since monopoly profits can be taken only once along a vertically linked chain; moreover, suppliers often have an incentive to expand their distribution networks and to expand sales.

151 ie the difference between the costs of an affiliated downstream firm and those of its downstream rivals. If the costs of an affiliated downstream firm are lower than those of its downstream rivals it makes commercial sense for the upstream firm to supply its downstream affiliate since it increases the profitability of the overall relationship. If, on the other hand, the costs of downstream rival firms are significantly lower than those of the affiliate, this will reduce the profitability of the relationship.

152 Obligations, such as stocking requirements that appear to fall short of requiring exclusive purchasing, may in practice lead to exclusivity.

153 See paragraph 273 and footnote 149.

154 With 'pure bundling' only the bundle, and not the components, is made available. 'Mixed bundling' allows both the sale of the bundle and at least some of the separate components. 'Technical bundling' is where the tied product is physically integrated in the tying product.

155 For example, in its investigation into PPI, the CC found that suppliers of credit (the primary product) enjoyed a point-of-sale advantage in relation to the supply of PPI (the secondary product) to their own credit customers and that, in combination with other features, this feature of PPI markets harmed competition.

156 This pattern of low pricing for primary products and high pricing for secondary products is sometimes referred to as a 'waterbed effect'.

157 This was the approach adopted in the *PPI* market investigation (29 January 2009).

158 While strengthened competition plays an important role in solving some customer-related problems, others can only be tackled by means of consumer protection policies.

159 If, for example, one store raises its price for a commonly-available good above the level of other stores, and all customers know this and switch to rivals, that store would lose all its business. In contrast, if some or all customers do not know that other stores charge lower prices and hence do not switch, the store may be able to raise its price without losing all its sales, ie the store has some degree of market power.

160 For example, markets serving both tourists (with high search costs) and local residents (with low search costs).

161 For example, in the case with many financial products, extended warranties on electrical products, certain professional services and some consumer durables.

162 The 'positive externalities' associated with the provision of information in consumer markets affect both buyers and sellers: buyers because, for example, search by some individuals tends to improve the market for all customers; and sellers because, for example, advertised information that applies to more than a single brand may help sellers of competing brands or other competing products.

163 There is a wide economic literature on the influence of bias—cognitive, emotional or reflexive—on economic decision-making. See, for example, Steffen Huck, Jidong Zhou and London Economics (Charlotte Duke), *Consumer Behavioural Bias in Competition: a Survey* (OFT1324), OFT, 2011.

164 When purchases are infrequent or large value (for example, when entering into a sale and rent back arrangement), learning may not provide the constraint required. There will also be circumstances where biases are hardwired (for example, limits to computation capabilities cannot be overcome) or where customers cannot learn from others.

165 The reach and effectiveness of intermediaries have been greatly extended with the advent of the Internet and price-comparison websites and the consequent ability to compare prices and terms across different sellers. However, there may be cases when incentives of the intermediaries are not always aligned with customers. For example, when firms pay intermediaries for their advice to customers their impartiality may be questioned.

166 Similarly, where a service (eg liability insurance) is provided to one party, while another party is liable to pay for it, a service provider may not have an incentive to compete as fiercely on price, or quality, as where the party receiving the service also pays for it.

167 In purchasing durable goods, for example, the customer needs information on the availability and costs of spare parts, other aftermarket services and maintenance. A competition problem can arise where customers are unable to factor into their purchase decisions all the aftermarkets costs of the product or where the aftermarket is not competitive.

168 *The supply o f banking services by clearing banks to small and medium-sized enterprises*, CC, 2002 under the Fair Trading Act 1973.

169 However, such a cost may not reduce competition if customers are able to make a fully informed choice about the lifetime costs of all the alternatives at the time of the initial investment.

170 *Market investigation into supply of bulk liquefied petroleum gas for domestic use*, 29 June 2006 (see, for example, paragraphs 4.47-4.52.)

171 For example. *PPI market investigation*, paragraph 53: 'The final barrier to switching we identified was the rebate policy on single-premium policies. Rebates are not given on a pro-rata basis . . . if a consumer cancels a PPI policy, the

rebate given is not enough to take out an identical policy . . . .'

172 See, for example, the CC report on the *PPI* market investigation. Referring to this in its judgment in *Barclays Bank v CC* (October 2009) the CAT wrote (paragraph 104): 'On a fair reading, the Commission concluded that a well-functioning market for PPI (ie a market without the AEC) was consistent with the continuation of some incumbency or POSA being enjoyed by distributors and intermediaries. There is, in our view, a clear distinction between a properly functioning market unaffected by an AEC and an ideal market, in which every potential supplier of the relevant product competes on a precisely level playing field.'

173 *ROSCOs market investigation*, 7 April 2009.

PART 4: REMEDIAL ACTION

[3.646]

322. When identifying and implementing a remedy to an AEC the CC may have to intervene directly in the structure of established markets and/or address the conduct of firms and their customers. Consideration of whether remedies are necessary and identification of the right remedy are highly dependent on the facts and context of the investigation and require the exercise of judgement by the Inquiry Group conducting the reference.[174] The starting point for the CC's remedies assessment is its finding of features that give rise to an AEC and the related findings of fact. More broadly, the CC will have developed, through the course of its investigation, a detailed understanding of the market and an appreciation of the way in which it is capable of working.

323. In choosing a remedy the CC will normally have to consider the interaction of a range of legal, factual and economic considerations.

324. This part of the Guidelines first sets out the framework for consideration of remedies (paragraphs 325 to 369). It then provides an overview of the different types of remedy and their characteristics (paragraphs 371 to 380) before setting out some of the main considerations that go into the selection of remedies from the options available (paragraphs 381 to 393. A more detailed discussion of particular types of remedy is included in Annex B.

FRAMEWORK FOR CONSIDERATION OF REMEDIES

The remedy questions

325. Where the CC decides that there is an AEC, it is required to decide the following additional questions:[175]

(a) whether action should be taken by [the CC] . . . for the purpose of remedying, mitigating or preventing the adverse effect on competition concerned or any detrimental effect on customers so far as it has resulted from, or may be expected to result from, the adverse effect on competition;

(b) whether it should recommend the taking of action by others for the purpose of remedying, mitigating or preventing the adverse effect on competition concerned or any detrimental effect on customers so far as it has resulted from, or may be expected to result from, the adverse effect on competition; and

(c) in either case, if action should be taken, what action should be taken and what is to be remedied, mitigated or prevented.

326. A detrimental effect on customers is defined as one taking the form of:[176]

(a) higher prices, lower quality or less choice of goods or services in any market in the UK (whether or not the market to which the feature or features concerned relate); or

(b) less innovation in relation to such goods or services.

327. Whether action should be taken therefore involves consideration of both the action the CC can take and the action the CC can recommend others to take. The CC may act itself through exercising its order-making powers or through accepting undertakings from parties (see paragraphs 92 and 93). Alternatively or in addition, the CC may recommend that remedial action should be taken by others, such as government, regulators and public authorities. Such recommendations do not bind the person to whom they are addressed, although the UK Government has committed to respond to any recommendation made to it within 90 days of publication of the CC's final report.[177] When deciding on certain remedial actions in regulated sectors the CC has to have regard to the relevant statutory functions of the sectoral regulator concerned.[178] In all cases, the CC will state the action that should be taken and what it is designed to address.

328. In practice, the CC may decide to take several actions itself and/or make several recommendations. This combination of actions and/or recommendations is sometimes referred to as a 'package' of measures. Unless otherwise specified, reference to a remedy or a remedy option in this section encompasses the package of measures the CC is taking and/or recommending.

329. The Act requires the CC, in considering these questions, 'in particular to have regard to the need to achieve as comprehensive a solution as is reasonable and practicable to the adverse effect on competition and any detrimental effects on customers so far as resulting from the adverse effect on competition'.[179] To fulfil this requirement, the CC will consider how comprehensively possible remedy options address the AEC and/or its detrimental effects and whether they are effective and proportionate. The CC may also have regard, in accordance with the Act, to any RCBs of the market feature(s) giving rise to the AEC[180] (see paragraph 83). Paragraphs 330 to 333 provide greater detail about these factors and their interaction, the ways in which the CC seeks to assess the impact of remedies and the possible outcomes that may arise from balancing these factors.

A comprehensive solution to the AEC and/or detrimental effects

330. Remedies can remedy, mitigate or prevent the AEC or its detrimental effects on customers. The clear preference of the CC is to deal comprehensively with the cause or causes of AECs wherever possible, and by this means significantly increase competitive pressures in a market within a reasonable period of time.

331. AECs are likely to result in costs to the UK economy in general and to customers in particular. Remedies that are effective in generating competition are likely to deliver substantial benefits, by driving down prices and costs and increasing innovation and productivity, thereby facilitating economic growth and increasing the choice available to customers.

332. In deciding what action to take, the CC will typically consider whether tackling some or all of the features it has identified (see paragraphs 154 to 162) will remedy, mitigate or prevent the AEC. In some situations, for example where an AEC arises from a combination of features, it may be necessary to devise a package of remedies to address the AEC, generally by addressing its causes. However, the remedy that is ultimately selected need not directly address every feature identified, if for example, tackling a subset of features directly would be sufficient to generate effective competition and thereby remedy the AEC.

333. While generally preferring to address the causes of the AEC, the CC will consider introducing measures which mitigate the harm to customers created by competition problems, for example if other measures are not available, or as an interim solution while other measures take effect.[181] Such measures to control outcomes may be able to reduce the harm to customers associated with high prices, for example, but are unlikely to generate the dynamic benefits, such as innovation, that are normally associated with competitive markets. These measures are therefore likely to represent a less comprehensive remedy to the AEC and any detrimental effects.

Effectiveness

334-341. . . .

Reasonableness and proportionality

342. In considering the reasonableness of different remedy options the CC will have regard to their proportionality.

343. The CC's assessment of proportionality will depend on the particular facts and circumstances of the case. It often depends on what other remedy options are also being considered and on judgements about the respective merits of each option, including whether or not a remedy option is likely to be effective in practice.

344. In making an assessment of proportionality, the CC is guided by the following principles. A proportionate remedy is one that:
(a) is effective in achieving its legitimate aim;
(b) is no more onerous than needed to achieve its aim;
(c) is the least onerous if there is a choice between several effective measures; and
(d) does not produce disadvantages which are disproportionate to the aim.[187]

345. Applying these principles to the circumstances of particular cases usually involves consideration of remedy options both relative to other effective measures as well as relative to taking no action

346. The CC will apply these principles to the evaluation of individual measures within a package of remedies as well as to the package taken as a whole (see paragraph 332).

347. Where the CC is considering whether to modify licence conditions in a regulated sector would be proportionate it will have regard to the relevant statutory functions of the regulator concerned.[188]

Assessing the impact of remedies

348. In reaching a judgement about whether to proceed with a particular remedy, the CC will consider its potential effects—both positive and negative—on those persons most likely to be affected by it. The CC will pay particular regard to the impact of remedies on customers. The CC will also have regard to the impact of remedies on those businesses subject to them and on other affected parties, such as other businesses (eg potential entrants, or firms active in upstream or downstream markets),[189] government and regulatory bodies, the OFT and other monitoring agencies.

349. The CC will explain what effects it expects to result from a remedy option and will form a view of their significance. As in its assessment of competition in a market (see paragraphs 35 to 41), the CC may take into account a variety of evidence and use a variety of techniques—both qualitative and, where appropriate, quantitative—to analyse effects of remedy options. Similarly to its prioritisation of resources in conducting the AEC test (see paragraph 36), the level of detail in which the CC investigates particular effects of a remedy will be influenced by their importance to the CC's overall assessment. For example, if it is clear that the costs of a particular remedy are likely to be very small—both in absolute terms and relative to its likely benefits—the CC may not seek to establish these costs with greater precision.[190]

350. The extent to which the CC will seek to quantify particular effects of remedies, and the degree of precision with which such quantification is attempted, are likely to vary from case to case. The CC will not carry out quantitative analysis that it considers unnecessary or otherwise not justified by the need to identify a remedy that meets the statutory tests. The general principles the CC follows in its use of evidence are set out in paragraphs 35 to 41.

351. The CC will assess the potential beneficial effects of its interventions. In considering how markets may develop with remedies in place, the CC will consider both benefits that are relatively easy to quantify (such as lower prices) and benefits that are more difficult to quantify (for example, the dynamic benefits of increased rivalry on productivity and innovation). Both are important. The more an AEC reflects longer-term and structural problems within a market, the greater the significance the CC is likely to accord to the long-term development of competition in the market and to the less quantifiable consequences of an improvement in the competitive pressures in the market.[191] Conversely, if addressing the AEC requires a remedy focused on achieving relatively predictable changes to outcomes in the shorter term, quantification of these changes is more likely to be a material aspect of the CC's assessment of the beneficial effects of the remedy.

352. Similarly, the CC will consider the potential negative effects of a remedy including the costs to business. Such negative effects may arise in various forms, for example:

(a) A remedy may result in unintended distortions to market outcomes. This is more likely to be the case where behavioural remedies are used which intervene directly in market outcomes, especially over a long period. Such distortions may reduce economic efficiency (including dynamic incentives to invest and innovate) and adversely affect the economic interests of customers over the longer term.

(b) A remedy may result in implementation costs (for example, modifying a distribution system), ongoing compliance costs (for example, providing the OFT with periodic information on prices or reporting to the OFT on other aspects of compliance), and monitoring costs (for example, the costs of the OFT or other agencies in monitoring compliance). The CC will normally collect information from parties about the potential cost of implementing and complying with its remedies. In evaluating such information, the CC will bear in mind that it has less information than the parties have about how such potential costs have been estimated and that there might be incentives for parties to overstate the cost of those remedies that they do not support. The CC is likely to place most weight on estimates of implementation and compliance costs where parties have provided a clear explanation of how the estimate was reached, together with supporting evidence as to the assumptions used to derive those estimates.

(c) If remedies extinguish RCBs, the amount of RCBs foregone may be considered to be a relevant cost of the remedy (see discussion of RCBs, paragraphs 355 to 366).

353. To avoid imposing unnecessary burdens on business, the CC will seek (as stated in paragraph 344) to ensure that its remedies are no more onerous than is necessary to remedy the AEC it has identified. In selecting and designing remedies, the CC will also have regard to the potential for more competitive markets to create profitable opportunities for new and innovative competitors as well as the cost of remedial measures on established businesses. However, where businesses have been found to be earning profits persistently in excess of their cost of capital as a direct result of a feature of the market (see paragraphs 114 to 126), and are likely to continue to do so in the absence of intervention, the CC will not usually give any significant weight to the anticipated reduction of such profits as a negative effect of a remedy.

Possible remedy outcomes

354. In reaching a decision on what remedial action to take, the CC will seek a comprehensive solution to the AEC and resulting customer detriment. In so doing, it will have regard to the need for the solution to be both reasonable and practicable. A consequence of balancing these considerations is that there may be circumstances where the CC judges, for example on the basis of considerations of proportionality, that it should not pursue an effective remedy option that is potentially available to it. There may also be rare cases where, having found an AEC, the CC chooses not to take any remedial action, for example:

(a) Where there are no practicable remedy options available to the CC, including any possible recommendations to others.

(b) Where the cost of each practicable remedy option is disproportionate compared with the extent that the remedy option resolves the AEC. This might be the case, for example, if the market in which the AEC was found was small in relation to the costs of each practicable remedy option and/or if it was only practicable to mitigate some of the negative consequences of an AEC and the costs of doing so were prohibitively high.

(c) Where RCBs accruing from the market features are both large in relation to the AEC and would be lost as a consequence of any practicable remedy (see paragraphs 355 to 359).

RELEVANT CUSTOMER BENEFITS

355. The CC, in deciding the question of remedies, may in particular 'have regard to the effect of any action on any relevant customer benefits of the feature or features of the market concerned'.[192, 193]

356. RCBs are limited to benefits to relevant customers in the form of:[194]

(a) lower prices, higher quality or greater choice of goods or services in any market in the UK (whether or not the market to which the feature or features concerned relate); or

(b) greater innovation in relation to such goods or services.

357. The Act provides that a benefit is only an RCB if the CC believes that:

(a) the benefit has accrued as a result (whether wholly or partly) of the feature or features concerned or may be expected to accrue within a reasonable period of time as a result (whether wholly or partly) of that feature or those features; and

(b) the benefit was, or is, unlikely to accrue without the feature or features concerned.[195]

358. In considering potential RCBs, the CC will therefore need to ascertain that the market feature(s) with which it has been concerned results, or is likely to result, in lower prices, higher quality, wider choice or greater innovation, and that such benefits are unlikely to arise in the absence of the market feature(s) concerned. RCBs may include benefits to customers in the market in which the CC has found an AEC and to customers in other markets within the UK,[196] provided these benefits meet the criteria set out in paragraphs 356 and 357.

359. In general, the CC would expect parties to put forward for the CC's consideration any RCBs they think relevant. Parties doing so will be expected to provide convincing evidence regarding the nature and scale of any RCB that they claim to result from the market feature(s) concerned and to demonstrate that these fall within the Act's definition of such benefits.

Possible relevant customer benefits

360. Whether a particular claimed benefit to customers is found to be an RCB will depend on the facts of the case and the characteristics of a particular market.

361. It would normally be expected that market features that have been found to adversely affect competition—after consideration of any potential rivalry-enhancing efficiencies (see paragraph 174)—would also have detrimental effects on customers. For example, one usual consequence of a failure of competition is that prices will be higher than they would otherwise be. Nevertheless, it is possible that features that adversely affect competition could result in beneficial effects on customers, either in the market in which competition is adversely affected, or in other related markets. The potential loss of such beneficial effects on customers may therefore be taken into account by the CC in its consideration of remedies. In the following paragraphs, examples of possible RCBs are given. In all instances the CC will need to consider whether the criteria set out in paragraphs 356 and 357 are met.

362. Aspects of market structure that could adversely affect competition, such as a high level of concentration, might enable economies of scale and/or scope to be obtained that would not be available if there were a larger number of firms in the market. Whether scale or scope economies would constitute an RCB in a particular case would depend partly on the extent to which, in practice, any cost economies were being passed on to customers as lower prices, improved quality, greater innovation or more choice.

363. Similarly, on the demand side, network effects and the operation of multi-sided markets or platforms (see paragraph 179) may lead to barriers to entry and sustained market concentration, but may also bring benefits to customers of being able to participate in a larger and/or better integrated network or platform.[197] In determining whether a particular form of network effects constitutes an RCB, the CC will consider whether customers benefit in practice from such effects and whether such benefits are unlikely to arise in the absence of the AEC resulting from the network effects.[198]

364. Generally, customers are unlikely to enjoy any benefits as a direct result of entry barriers. However, some entry barriers may indirectly secure other kinds of benefit (see paragraph 235). For example, regulations that limit entry to persons of proven competence or with adequate capital resources may lead to an improvement in product or service quality. Likewise regulations that protect IPRs (see paragraph 211), while potentially restricting access to markets, may lead to improvements in innovation by enabling innovative companies to benefit from the new ideas that they generate. The CC will generally have regard to the wider purpose of such regulations in considering their effects on customers. In the absence of clear, countervailing customer benefits from barriers to entry, the CC would normally expect customers to benefit from any reduction of entry barriers as this would be expected to facilitate dynamic competition and better market outcomes (see paragraphs 205 and 206).

365. As set out in paragraphs 265 and 266, vertical relationships can often have beneficial effects, for example through better coordination of activities at different stages in the supply chain, resolving 'free-rider' problems between producers and distributors and creating incentives to reduce the price of complementary products, Where an AEC has nonetheless arisen from vertical relationships within a market (see paragraph 267), the CC will consider whether these relationships have resulted in RCBs.

366. The CC will similarly consider, when AECs have arisen from the many forms of business conduct that can also have either positive or negative effects, depending on the context, whether these conducts have resulted in RCBs. Tie-in sales or product bundling (see paragraphs 286 to 290), for example, may sometimes be convenient to customers, reduce transaction costs or provide quality assurance.

Relevant customer benefits and remedies

367. If the CC is satisfied that there are RCBs deriving from a market feature that has resulted in an AEC, the CC will consider whether to modify the remedy that it might otherwise have imposed or recommended. The CC will consider several factors including the size and nature of the expected RCB, what proportion of the benefit will be preserved through the modification, and how long the RCB may be sustained. The CC will also consider the different impacts of the features on different customers or groups of customers.

368. It is possible that the RCBs are of such significance compared with the effects of the market feature(s) on competition that the CC will decide that no remedy is called for (see paragraph 354). This might occur if no remedies can be identified that are able to preserve the RCBs whilst also remedying or mitigating the AEC and/or the resulting customer detriment. This situation has not arisen on a market investigation to date.

369. Alternatively, the CC, as a result of identifying RCBs, may choose a different remedy, for example a behavioural remedy rather than a structural remedy (see paragraph 371 for an explanation of this distinction). In this case, the CC will have to weigh the disadvantage of a less comprehensive solution to the competition problem against the preservation of the RCBs that result from the feature concerned.[199]

CHOICE OF REMEDY

370. Paragraphs 371 to 380 provide an overview of the various types of remedy and their characteristics. Paragraphs 381 to 393 consider the selection from these types of remedy by applying the decision framework outlined in paragraph 384.

Remedies universe

371. A diagrammatic representation of the universe of possible remedies is shown in Figure 1. Remedies are conventionally classified as either structural or behavioural. Structural remedies are generally one-off measures that seek, in market investigations, to increase competition by altering the competitive structure of the market. Behavioural remedies are generally ongoing measures that are designed to regulate or constrain the behaviour of parties in a market and/or empower customers to make effective choices. Some remedies, such as those relating to access to IPRs, may have characteristics of structural or behavioural remedies depending on their particular formulation. Likewise, recommendations to others may be either structural or behavioural in nature, depending on their content. Further discussion of the different categories of remedy may be found in Annex B.

FIGURE 1

Overview of the universe of possible remedies

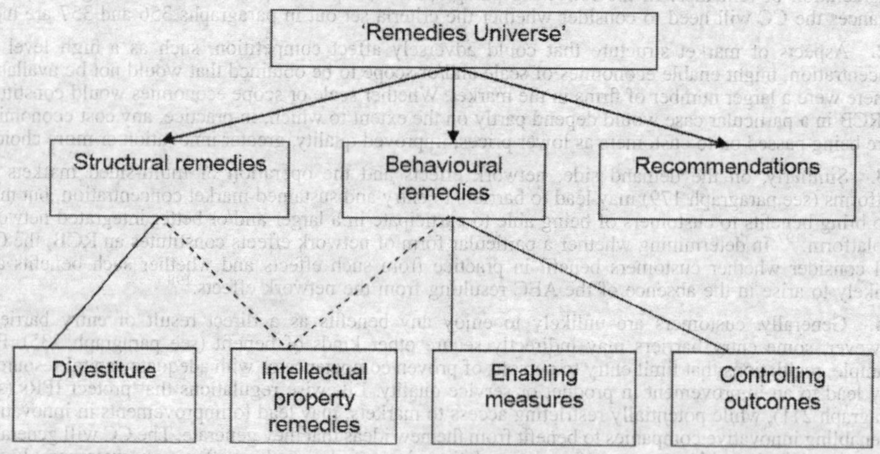

Divestiture

372. The aim of divestiture in market investigations will generally be to address competition problems resulting from structural features of a market.[200] This may be done by either creating a new source of competition through disposal of a business or assets to a new market participant, or by strengthening an existing source of competition through disposal of a business or assets to an existing market participant that is independent of the divesting party (or parties).

373. A successful divestiture will address at source the lack of rivalry resulting from structural features of a market. Divestiture remedies will generally not require detailed ongoing monitoring beyond the completion of the disposal of the business or assets in question, although, in some cases, an effective divestiture may require supplementary behavioural measures for an interim period (eg to secure supplies of an essential input or service from the divesting party to the divested business). The requirements for design and implementation of divestiture remedies are considered in detail in Annex B, paragraphs 3 to 30.

Intellectual property remedies

374. A remedy that provides access to intellectual property (IP) by licensing or assignment of those rights may be viewed as a specialized form of divestiture remedy.[201] The aim of such a remedy is that the party or parties acquiring the IPRs should thereby be able to compete effectively with other companies in the market. Where the terms of an IP remedy result in a material ongoing link between the original owner of the IP and the parties gaining the IP (eg providing access to new releases or upgrades of technology) an IP remedy may take on some of the characteristics of a behavioural commitment, which may require ongoing monitoring and enforcement. As with other types of remedies, the CC will assess the extent to which specific interventions in relation to IPRs may risk creating distortions, for example by reducing incentives to innovate (see paragraphs 225 and 235). Considerations regarding the design and implementation of IP remedies are outlined in Annex B, paragraphs 31 to 36.

Enabling measures

375. Certain forms of behavioural remedy operate principally to enable competition by removing obstacles to competition or stimulating actual or potential competition.

376. Within the category of enabling measures, there are further distinctions between:

(a) market-opening measures, which are intended to open up a market to new sources of competition by removing or reducing barriers to entry, expansion or switching. Such measures may, for instance, limit parties' ability to require their customers to enter into long-term or exclusive contracts or to otherwise create switching costs for customers (see Annex B, paragraphs 46 to 60);[202]

(b) informational remedies, which are aimed at giving customers information to help them make choices and thereby increase competitive pressure on firms in the market (see Annex B, paragraphs 61 to 71).[203] Where an AEC results from coordinated effects (see paragraphs 241 to 243) the CC may consider remedies that prevent the sharing of information between firms, if sharing such information has been found to facilitate coordination; and

(c) remedies that restrict the adverse effects of vertical relationships (see paragraphs 267 to 272). Such measures may include restriction of access to confidential information ('firewall provisions'), or obligations to provide access to facilities on fair, reasonable and non-discriminatory (FRND) terms (see Annex B, paragraphs 72 to 85).[204]

377. Enabling measures are generally likely to require ongoing intervention and monitoring. In some instances this may involve complex issues, for instance the pricing of access to facilities that are subject to rapid technological change. Further considerations regarding the design and implementation of enabling measures are outlined in Annex B, paragraphs 46 to 85.

Controlling outcomes

378. Certain forms of behavioural remedy seek to prevent the exercise of significant market power and thereby control the detrimental effects arising from an AEC. For example, price caps, supply commitments and service level undertakings all control the way a business can operate to limit any possible detrimental effects on a customer.[205] Such measures are often used in regulated sectors, where it may not be feasible to introduce effective competition. However, this type of behavioural remedy can be complex to implement and monitor, given informational asymmetries between the parties and the authorities and the associated risk of circumvention. There is also a risk that such controls create market distortions, particularly if they are kept in place over a long period. Ensuring that measures to control outcomes remain fit for purpose in the light of market developments may involve costs for monitoring and enforcement agencies as well as for the parties subject to them. Further considerations regarding this type of remedy are outlined in Annex B, paragraphs 86 to 93.

Recommendations

379. The CC can decide to make recommendations to other bodies, rather than taking action itself. Such recommendations can be thought of as falling into one of two categories:

(a) In some cases, the legal framework, regulations or conduct applicable to a market may be a structural feature giving rise to an AEC; for example, planning or certification requirements may inhibit entry or restrict market outcomes (see paragraphs 223 to 226). In such cases the CC may recommend modifications of these requirements to the Government or other controlling body to help address the AEC or control its detrimental effects. For example, the CC may recommend the removal or reform of regulatory requirements that have been found to constitute a barrier to entry.

(b) The CC may also make recommendations in situations where it is more practicable, or otherwise preferable, to implement a remedy by means of a recommendation.[206]

380. It will, of course, be for the Government or other person to whom a recommendation is addressed to decide whether to act on the recommendation and the CC will consult with the relevant body prior to making the recommendation. Further considerations regarding this type of remedy are outlined in Annex B, paragraphs 94 to 102.

SELECTION OF REMEDIES

381. As set out in paragraphs 88 to 93, the identification of the Group's preferred remedy is an iterative process in which a potentially wide range of remedy options are progressively narrowed down until a solution has been found that enables the CC to meet its statutory duties. This process involves public consultation on those remedy options that appear to the Inquiry Group to have the best chance of being both effective and proportionate. Some of the key considerations that affect the selection of remedies are set out in the remainder of these Guidelines.

382. As set out in paragraph 330, in deciding what remedial action should be taken, the CC will first look for a remedy that would effectively address the causes of the AEC directly and thereby deal with any detrimental effects on customers of the AEC.

383. The type of action that will be effective in increasing competition will depend on the nature of the AEC concerned. The range of potential competition problems that may be identified as giving rise to an AEC is wide, as is the range of potential remedies. The relative merits of different remedy options will be determined by the facts of the case and, in particular, the nature of the underlying competition problem that gives rise to the need for remedial action.

384. Table 1 illustrates some possible approaches to remedying some of the different types of competition problem that may give rise to an AEC.

TABLE 1. ILLUSTRATION OF POSSIBLE REMEDY APPROACHES TO DIFFERENT TYPES OF COMPETITION PROBLEM

Example of problem arising	*Possible remedy approaches*
Restrictions on competitive entry or expansion reduce dynamic competition and slow technological progress and introduction of new products.	• **Market-opening measures** to reduce barriers to entry and promote dynamic competition. • **Recommendations to Government or regulatory bodies** to address any barriers to entry which are caused or created by government laws or regulatory actions (eg planning rules).
Concentrated market structure means that the market is dominated by one player, or a small number of players, whose position is protected by high barriers to entry and/or expansion.	• **Structural measures** (eg divestiture, IP licensing) to create directly a less concentrated market structure. • **Market-opening measures** (eg reduction of entry barriers) to increase the competitive constraint from entry, addressing market structure indirectly and thereby increase competitive threat to incumbents. • **Recommendations to Government or regulatory bodies** to address regulatory barriers to entry or expansion. • **Measures to control outcomes** (eg price caps) possibly on an interim basis to mitigate the harm to customers until market-opening measures become effective. Measures to control outcomes might also be used if market concentration is very difficult or very costly to alter in practice (eg in a natural monopoly) and/or if concentration gives rise to very substantial RCBs (eg network effects) that would be lost in a more fragmented market structure and market-opening measures are unlikely to be successful.
Coordination between rivals means that competition is restricted and customers are made worse off.	• **Structural measures** (eg divestiture, IP licensing) to make it harder to achieve, monitor and sustain a coordinated outcome, by increasing the number of significant market participants. • **Market-opening measures** (eg reduction of entry barriers) to increase the competitive constraint from entry and thereby increasing competitive threat to incumbents. • **Restrictions on supplier conduct or other market features that have the effect of facilitating coordination**—for example, remedies might be aimed at limiting the availability of information held by suppliers about their rivals. • **Recommendations to Government or regulatory bodies** to ensure that government laws or regulatory actions do not facilitate coordination or cause unnecessary barriers to entry or expansion.
Vertical effects. Competition problems can arise where a single firm operates at a number of levels of the supply chain or where there are other vertical arrangements between firms active at different levels of a supply chain.	• **Structural measures**—for example, to separate 'natural monopoly' activities from potentially competitive activities, or to reduce market power at one or other stage of the supply chain. • **Remedies to restrict the effects of vertical relationships** to ensure access to key services, products or facilities; prevent discrimination; or prohibit vertical arrangements that restrict competition. • **Measures to control outcomes**—for example, to mitigate the detrimental effects in 'natural monopoly' activities and/or if vertical relationships give rise to substantial RCBs (eg network effects) that would be lost with other measures.
Information shortfalls and behavioural biases. Competition can be weak, when customers find it hard to identify good value products in a market or switch between providers, or are subject to behavioural biases.	• **Market-opening measures** to address the source of switching costs and/or encourage entry and expansion by firms with incentives to reduce search costs (eg by advertising). • **Informational remedies** to make it easier for customers to find out about products in the market and to facilitate comparisons; to address 'customer' barriers to switching (eg inertia, or lack of familiarity with the switching process) and/or to encourage whole-life costing (eg upfront disclosure of 'hidden' charges). Such measures might involve an element of product regulation to simplify the choices facing customers and/or to protect customer interests, where customer search for information on a particular aspect is unlikely to occur.

385. As Table 1 shows, structural remedies such as divestiture are a potential solution where horizontal market concentration, coordinated effects or vertical integration are among the principal market features that give rise to an AEC (see Annex B, paragraphs 3 to 30). Likewise, IP licensing may be used to remedy AECs that result from highly concentrated markets, if, by virtue of an IP remedy, new or expanding suppliers would be able to provide an effective competitive constraint on powerful incumbents (see Annex B, paragraphs 31 to 36).

386. Enabling measures may also remedy structural problems. Market-opening measures, for example, may remove or reduce barriers to entry (see Annex B, paragraphs 47 to 60) or measures may be introduced to restrict the adverse effects of vertical relationships (see Annex B, paragraphs 72 to 85).

387. In choosing between structural remedies and enabling measures that impact on market structure indirectly, the CC will consider whether the market response to either type of remedy will be timely and of sufficient scale to represent a comprehensive solution to the AEC. In remedying competition problems arising from high concentration structural remedies have some important advantages over other measures. Once implemented, structural remedies may be expected to increase competitive constraints on the behaviour of firms in the market within a short timescale and without requiring ongoing detailed monitoring by the OFT and/or any other body such as the relevant sector regulator. The underlying cause of high concentration may also be relevant. For example, if certain features of a market (eg network advantages or other barriers to entry and expansion) result in a tendency towards high levels of concentration, enabling measures that address the underlying causes of high concentration (eg by lowering barriers to entry or expansion) might be preferred. The costs of different remedy approaches, including the extent to which any RCBs are retained (see paragraphs 355 to 366) may also be relevant to this choice.

388. In other circumstances, structural remedies may not address the features giving rise to the AEC and behavioural remedies are likely to be preferred. An important difference between remedies in merger and market investigations is that structural remedies, even if they are feasible in a market investigation, may not be an appropriate solution to a particular AEC because of the wide range of features, including non-structural features, that can give rise to an AEC. For example, enabling measures are more likely to be chosen where:

(a) the conduct of firms has given rise to an AEC—for example, by raising barriers to entry or facilitating coordination. In such situations the CC may consider restrictions on firms' behaviour that constrain firms' future ability to engage in such conduct (see Annex B, paragraphs 49 to 53);

(b) switching costs or barriers to entry or expansion are among the features that give rise to an AEC. Here, the CC may consider market-opening measures that address the main barriers to switching, entry or expansion that it has identified (see Annex B, paragraphs 54 to 60); or

(c) search costs and other information shortfalls are among the features giving rise to an AEC. In such situations, informational remedies that make it easier for customers to search and switch may be an appropriate response (see Annex B, paragraphs 61 to 71).

389. Remedial action may also be required to address customer detriment directly, for example where effective remedies aimed at introducing competition by addressing the AEC are unavailable or will not bear fruit in the short term (see Annex B, paragraphs 86 to 93). Price controls are the most obvious example. However, such measures to control outcomes are not likely, by their nature, to provide a solution to the underlying problem and may also give rise to distortion risks, if retained over a long period. For these reasons (as stated in paragraph 330), remedial action to control outcomes will not generally be preferred as a long-term solution.

390. As stated in paragraph 379, recommendations may be considered where an aspect of regulation or government behaviour is itself giving rise to an AEC or where it would be more practicable (or otherwise preferable) for the CC to implement a remedy by means of a recommendation rather than taking action itself. This may include situations in which other bodies have powers that are unavailable to the CC[207] or where a recommendation enables a remedy to be better integrated with existing interventions in a sector.[208] It may also include cases where a remedy to increase competition in a market has the potential to come into conflict with other important public policy objectives and it is more appropriate for Government, rather than the CC, to balance these conflicting objectives.[209]

391. In deciding whether to make a recommendation rather than take action itself, the CC will form a view as to the likelihood that the recommendation will be acted upon and, if so, over what time period. In reaching this view, the CC will have regard both to the stated policy of the body to which the recommendation is to be directed and to the possibility that that stated policy may change, either in light of the CC's recommendation or subsequent events (see Annex B, paragraphs 94 to 102). The likelihood of a recommendation being implemented is therefore relevant to the timeliness and effectiveness of such a recommendation. However, the CC may sometimes make recommendations that may not be implemented immediately, where it judges that these are nonetheless likely to be more effective than other possible remedies.

392. In looking for remedies that would be likely to increase competition in the relevant market(s), the CC will give attention to the time period within which the remedy can be expected to show results. If a remedy is not likely to have rapid results, the CC may choose an alternative remedy or implement additional remedies such as measures to address the detrimental effects on customers during the interim period. Otherwise, not only might there be uncertainty as to whether the beneficial effects of the remedy would materialize, but, in the meantime, customers would continue to suffer from the consequences of the AEC.

393. The CC's experience to date suggests that remedies in market investigations may take the form of a 'package' of measures, rather than the implementation of a single measure (see paragraph 332). This may be because there are several features giving rise to an AEC, and consequently an individual measure may be incapable of addressing the AEC in its entirety. For example, to deal with problems associated with a lack of customer switching it may be necessary both to remove contractual barriers to switching and also to put in place informational remedies that raise customer awareness of the potential benefits of switching. Where more than one measure is being introduced, the CC will consider the way in which the measures are expected to interact with each other. As a general rule (as stated in paragraph 341), measures which share the aim of introducing competition into a market will tend to be mutually reinforcing.

NOTES

Paras 334–341 and the associated footnotes 182–186 have been superseded by paragraphs 4.15 to 4.24 of the revised CMA 3 which explain the CMA's new procedure relating to sunset clauses and reviews of remedies. See Annex A of CMA 3 at **[3.655]**.

174 See paragraph 46 for information on Inquiry Groups.

175 Section 134(4).

176 Section 134(5). The reference to customers includes future customers.

177 The Enterprise White Paper, *A World Class Competition Regime*, Department of Trade and Industry, July 2001 Cm 5233, p12.

178 Section 168.

179 Section 134(6).

180 Section 134(7).

181 Section 138(6). However, the CC is prevented from taking action to address future detrimental effects on customers if no detrimental effects on customers currently exist and the CC is not remedying the AEC (that is, the source of the problem).

187 These principles have been referred to by the CAT in various judgments including *Tesco v CC* (4 March 2009), the PPI appeal *(Barclays and others v CC*, 16 October 2009) and *BAA v CC* (21 December 2009 and 1 February 2012). See Tesco judgment, paragraph 137:

A useful summary of the proportionality principles is contained in the following passage from the judgment of the ECJ in Case C-331/88 R v Ministry of Agriculture, Fisheries and Food and Secretary of State for Health, ex parte Fedesa [1990] ECR I-4023, paragraph [13], to which we were referred by the Commission: 'By virtue of that principle, the lawfulness of the prohibition of an economic activity is subject to the condition that the prohibitory measures are appropriate and necessary in order to achieve the objectives legitimately pursued by the legislation in question; when there is a choice between several appropriate measures recourse must be had to the least onerous, and the disadvantages caused must not be disproportionate to the aims pursued'.

188 Section 168.

189 See paragraph 50.

190 For further discussion of this principle, see the judgment of the CAT in *Tesco v Competition Commission* (2009), CAT 6, (paragraph 139): 'it may well be sensible for the Commission to apply a 'double proportionality' approach: for example, the more important a particular factor seems to be in the overall proportionality assessment, or the more intrusive, uncertain in its effect, or wide-reaching a proposed remedy is likely to prove, the more detailed or deeper the investigation of the factor in question may need to be'; see also the CAT judgment in *Barclays Bank plc v Competition Commission* (2009), CAT 27 (paragraph 21), and footnote 23, above.

191 For example, in the *BAA airports* market investigation (March 2009), the CC concluded that the main benefits from the divestitures of Gatwick and Stansted airports would result from the dynamic aspects of competition, for example in relation to the delivery and allocation of airport capacity. While it was not possible to quantify the benefits of divesting these airports, given among other factors the interaction with the regulatory regime, the CC was confident that the expected benefits would outweigh the costs of divestiture.

192 Section 134(7).

193 As noted in paragraph 173, in reaching a judgement about a particular theory of harm, the CC will evaluate its overall impact on rivalry, taking into account rivalry-enhancing as well as adverse effects.

194 Section 134(8)(a).

195 Section 134(8)(b).

196 For example, in the *PPI* market investigation (January 2009), the CC found that credit prices, and credit cut-off scores, were lower than they otherwise would be because of PPI income generated at the credit point of sale and that this was an RCB.

197 For example, in the *Stagecoach/Preston Bus* merger inquiry the CC took into account an RCB associated with integrated ticketing brought about by the merger.

198 For example, it may be possible for network benefits to be preserved through requiring interoperability between competing networks.

199 For example, in the *Macquarie UK Broadcast Ventures/National Grid Wireless Group* merger inquiry (March 2008), the CC required the merged company to agree a package of measures with the CC, including price reductions for customers on new and existing contracts and the appointment of an adjudicator to resolve disputes. The CC decided that these measures would be effective in addressing the adverse effects of the acquisition, whilst preserving the RCBs that could arise from the acquisition, including reducing the risks associated with the digital switchover process and passing back cost savings to customers.

200 For example, in the *BAA airports* market investigation (March 2009), the CC required the divestiture of Gatwick and Stansted airports and a Scottish airport as part of its package of remedies.

201 At the time of publication of these Guidelines, the CC had not used an IP remedy in any market investigation. The package of remedies applied in the *Nufarm/AH Marks* merger inquiry (February 2009) had some characteristics of an IP remedy.

202 For example, the remedies introduced following the *LPG* market investigation (June 2006) included measures designed to facilitate the transfer of tank ownership when a customer wishes to switch supplier and other measures to make the switching process easier.

203 For example, the remedies introduced following the *Home Credit* market investigation (November 2006) included an obligation to publish price and other information on a comparative website www.lenderscompared.org.uk.

204 In the *Local bus services* market investigation, the CC decided to introduce by means of an Order a requirement for bus operators to provide access on FRND terms to privately-owned and operated bus stations. This type of remedy is also sometimes used in merger cases. For example, the *Centrica/Dynegy Storage* merger inquiry (2003) was a case in which firewall provisions and an access remedy were introduced to restrict the adverse effects of vertical relationships following a merger.

205 In the *Classified Directories* market investigation, the CC found that prices of Yell, the largest provider, had been largely constrained by an existing price cap rather than competition. Were it not for the price cap, customers of Yell would be paying more for advertisements in Yellow Pages than they would if the market was functioning well. However, the CC expected that growing competition would increasingly constrain Yell's prices and that Yell would feel more pressure due to the Internet. The CC's remedies included a revised price control to prevent Yell from exploiting its market power and other measures designed to preserve developing competition from actions that could be targeted at competitors.

206 For example, in the *Local bus services* market investigation the CC decided to make a series of recommendations (eg in relation to multi-operator ticketing schemes) which would enable the implementation of these measures to take account of specific local conditions.

207 For example, in the *Local bus services* market investigation the CC made several recommendations to the OFT about the operation of existing competition law mechanisms that are the responsibility of the OFT rather than the CC.

208 For example, in the *PPI* market investigation, the CC made a recommendation to the Consumer Financial Education Body— now known as the Money Advice Service—to publish information on its existing price comparisons website, rather than requiring the creation of a new price comparison site.

209 For example, in the *ROSCOs* market investigation, the CC made recommendations in relation to the operation of the rail franchising system to increase competition in the supply of rolling stock. In making these recommendations, the CC was mindful of the Government's wider public policy objectives in relation to rail franchising.

ANNEX A: MARKET CHARACTERISTICS AND OUTCOMES

1. MEASURING MARKET SHARES AND CONCENTRATION

Market shares

[3.647]

1. Subject to the availability of data, the CC normally calculates market shares for all firms currently producing products in the relevant market or in any market the CC considers relevant to its investigation. It does so on the basis of the available indicators of firms' future competitive significance in the market. These may depend upon the nature of competition in the market as well as on the availability of data. In many cases, the CC will calculate market shares on the basis of several indicative measures (see paragraph 2) so as to understand fully how a market is operating. The CC may use information from a variety of sources including established sellers, potential entrants, customers, buyers, suppliers, trade associations and market research reports.

2. Market shares can be measured in terms of revenues, volumes, production capacities or inputs:

- *Revenues*. In most contexts, the CC uses actual or projected revenues in the market as the bases for measurement. They are the best 'real world' measure and are particularly pertinent when products differ in quality. But in some cases, unit sales (eg when a new, less expensive product has entered the market) or revenues earned just from recently acquired customers (when long-term contracts or high switching costs are involved) may be better measures of competitive significance than total revenues.
- *Capacities*. In markets for homogeneous products, the level of readily available capacity or reserves to serve the market can be an appropriate measure if that capacity is efficient enough to make expansion profitable in response to a price rise or to reduced output by competitors. If this measure is used, market participants that are not current producers may sometimes be assigned positive market shares to reflect their impact on competition.

3. Typically, annual data is used, but where individual transactions are large and infrequent, annual data may be unrepresentative, and in these cases the CC may measure market shares over a longer period of time.

Concentration measures

4. The degree of concentration in a market may be measured in different ways, depending on the nature of competition and availability of data. A numerical count of the firms in a market is the basic measure. It does not take into account differences in market shares and the size distribution of firms, but can be useful when there is a gap in market share between significant competitors and smaller rivals or when it is difficult to measure revenues in the market. The CC attaches particular weight to a numerical count of firms when considering coordinated conduct.

5. Two other commonly used measures are the concentration ratio and the Herfindahl-Hirschman Index (HHI).

6. The concentration ratio measures the combined market share of the largest firms in a market. For example, the 'five firm' concentration ratio is simply the sum of the market shares of the five largest firms in the market. It does not provide any information on the relative size of the firms nor on the number, or size, of the smaller firms.

7. The HHI potentially reflects both the number of firms in the industry and their relative size. It is defined as the sum of the squares of all the market shares in the market, and thus gives proportionately greater weight to the larger market shares. The CC is likely to regard any market with an HHI in excess of 2,000 as highly concentrated, and any market with an HHI in excess of 1,000 as concentrated. However, the CC will have regard to these threshold levels—if considered relevant—only as one factor in its wider assessment of competition.

8. The calculations of market shares, numbers of firms, concentration ratios and the HHI generally depend on being able to identify the boundaries of the market concerned. However, one technique, which is closely related to other traditional concentration measures, but does not rely on pre-defined boundaries, is the Logit Competition Index, sometimes referred to as LOCI. LOCI can be computed as (one minus) a firm's weighted average market share across the submarkets within which it operates. The weights are calculated according to the importance to the firm of each submarket, and the definition of a submarket depends on the particular application. In practical terms, LOCI requires that a much greater amount of information be available than is required for computing the traditional concentration measures described in paragraphs 4 to 7 above.

2. MEASURING PROFITABILITY

9. In measuring profitability the CC's approach will often be to start with accounting profit produced in line with UK Generally Accepted Accounting Principles (GAAP) and then to make adjustments to arrive at an economically meaningful measure of profitability, usually in terms of rates of return on capital.[1] The CC will often inform its judgement on what is an 'economically meaningful measure of profitability' by examining the management accounting records of the firms in question. The manner by which industry participants, including firms, analysts, and investors, assess profitability for the purposes of monitoring and reporting performance may well inform our view as to what is an appropriate measure for the industry in question.[2] For example, in the financial sector the CC has previously considered return on equity over a five-year period as its primary measure of profitability. In other industries the CC has considered return on capital employed over a similar period.[3]

10. The appropriateness of a given measure will also depend on the nature of the industry and the pattern of investment. Where investment is characterized by large one-off expenditure, or the industry has experienced a period of growth, it may be desirable to consider profitability over a relatively long period of time or on a project appraisal basis. For example, it may be appropriate to use a cash-flow-based model to compute a measure of the internal rate of return (IRR) where reliable data is available on this basis.[4]

11. An important factor to consider when selecting an appropriate model will be data availability. Where possible, the CC will base its calculations on financial data that can be reconciled to audited financial statements, albeit with appropriate adjustments. For example, where the market of interest is a division or segment of a company it may not be possible to obtain reliable cash flow data at this level and the CC may therefore adopt a return on capital approach for this reason.

12. Whatever measure of profitability is used, the calculation of profitability for the purposes of competition analysis is often not straightforward because of the need to obtain an appropriate value for capital employed, as described below. In industries with a relatively low level of tangible assets, such as service and knowledge-based industries, the book value of capital employed may bear little relationship to the economic value because of the presence of significant intangibles. In some cases, the replacement cost of assets may be different from historical costs due to the length of time elapsed and changes in asset prices and efficient technologies over time.

13. Obtaining a value for capital employed can present difficulties irrespective of the choice of model. For example, the use of a truncated IRR requires the assets to be valued appropriately at the beginning and end of the period selected. Similarly, a return on capital approach, whether return on equity or return on capital employed (ROCE), requires an economically meaningful value for the capital base which may not accord with the value ascribed in the financial records.

14. Hence, it may be necessary to make adjustments to accounting data produced in line with UK GAAP. In particular, the following adjustments may be considered:

- Under current accounting standards, most assets are held at historical cost and this may differ substantially from the 'replacement cost' or 'Modern Equivalent Asset value',[5] which the CC considers to be the economically meaningful measure for its purposes in most cases. In these circumstances, and where this would be likely to have a material effect on its calculations, the CC will consider whether replacement cost values can be derived reliably.
- Secondly, the CC may consider the inclusion of certain intangible assets where the following criteria[6] are met:
  - — it must comprise a cost that has been incurred primarily to obtain earnings in the future;
  - — this cost must be additional to costs necessarily incurred at the time in running the business; and
  - — it must be identifiable as creating such an asset separate from any arising from the general running of the business.

  In establishing a value for intangible assets meeting the above criteria, the CC will have regard to similar principles as for other types of assets.
- Other adjustments may be considered on a case-specific basis.

15. In situations where capital employed cannot be reliably valued the CC may consider alternative measures, such as the return on sales or other relevant financial ratios. For instance, comparisons with businesses operating in different but similar markets may on occasions be helpful.

16. In assessing levels of profitability the CC will have regard to its view of firms' cost of capital. The CC will generally look to the capital asset pricing model (CAPM) when considering the cost of capital, since this is a widely understood technique with strong theoretical foundations. However, the CC will have regard to alternative models where appropriate.

NOTES

1. Where the capital base is valued appropriately. See, for example, the reports on *Store Cards* (March 2006), *Home Credit* (November 2006) and *PPI* (January 2009).
2. See, for example, *PPI*.
3. See *BAA Airports*.
4. In *Movies on Pay TV* the CC used a cash-flow-based truncated IRR in conjunction with a return on capital employed (ROCE) approach.
5. These terms are used interchangeably to mean the current cost of acquiring assets which yield equivalent services to those currently used by the firm, based on the most efficient technology and optimal configuration.
6. These criteria were originally set down in the CC report, *The supply o f banking services by clearing banks to small and medium-sized enterprises* (March 2002).

ANNEX B: REMEDIAL ACTION

TYPES OF REMEDY

[3.648]

1. This annex summarizes some of the key considerations relevant to the evaluation, design and implementation of different classes of remedies. It is structured as follows:

(a) Section 1 discusses divestiture and IP remedies.
(b) Section 2 discusses behavioural remedies.
(c) Section 3 discusses recommendations.

SECTION 1: DIVESTITURE AND INTELLECTUAL PROPERTY REMEDIES

2. This section deals with issues relating to divestiture and IP remedies. These types of remedy are sometimes referred to as 'structural remedies', though as set out in paragraph 31, IP remedies can have both structural and behavioural aspects. Divestiture remedies are discussed in paragraphs 3 to 30 and IP remedies in paragraphs 31 to 36.

Divestiture remedies

Introduction

3. In essence, a divestiture seeks to remedy an AEC by either creating a new source of competition through disposal of a business or set of assets to a new market participant or strengthening an existing source of competition through disposal to an existing market participant independent of the divesting party (or parties).

4. The CC has required divestiture in one market investigation to report to date (BAA Airports). This guidance reflects the CC's experience in that case and also, where relevant, the experience of designing and implementing divestiture remedies in merger inquiries, where divestiture is the most frequently used remedy option.[1]

5. The design of a divestiture remedy will seek to address the underlying cause of an AEC and will take account of any risks of not addressing the AEC and any RCBs that may be affected by the form of divestiture.

Divestiture risks

6. Divestitures may be subject to a variety of risks that may limit their effectiveness in addressing an AEC. It is helpful to distinguish between three broad categories of risks that may impair the effectiveness of divestiture remedies as follows:

(a) *Composition risks*—these are risks that the scope of the divestiture package may be too constrained or not appropriately configured to attract suitable purchasers or may not allow a purchaser to operate as an effective competitor in the market.
(b) *Purchaser risks*—these are risks that a suitable purchaser is not available or that the divesting party (or parties) will dispose to a weak or otherwise inappropriate purchaser.
(c) *Asset risks*—these are risks that the competitive capability of a divestiture package will deteriorate before completion of divestiture, for example through loss of customers or key members of staff.

7. The incentives of divesting parties may serve to increase the risks of divestiture. Although divesting parties will normally have an incentive to maximize the disposal proceeds of a divestiture they will also have incentives to limit the future competitive impact of a divestiture on themselves. Parties may therefore have, on balance, an incentive to make divestitures to weaker competitors of less competitive assets or businesses and may also allow the competitiveness of divestiture packages to decline during the divestiture process.[2]

8. Divestiture risks can be overcome, at least in part, through the design of the divestiture and by adopting protective measures such as appointment of monitoring and divestiture trustees and alternative divestiture packages as shown later in this section. To be effective in increasing rivalry—and managing divestiture risks—a divestiture remedy should involve the sale of an appropriate divestiture package to a suitable purchaser through an effective divestiture process. These critical elements of the design of a divestiture remedy are discussed in detail in the following sections.

Scope of divestiture packages

Package definition

9. In defining the scope of a divestiture package that will satisfactorily address an AEC, the CC will normally seek to identify a divestiture package that comprises a viable, stand-alone business that can compete successfully on an ongoing basis and is of sufficient scale and scope to enable its acquirer to become an effective competitor. This may comprise a division or the whole of an operating company functioning in the market affected by the AEC. Depending on the nature of the AEC, it may be necessary to identify more than one divestiture package to achieve a comprehensive solution—for example, if several distinct businesses under common ownership need to be divested to remedy the AEC.[3]

10. In order to achieve a proportionate solution, the CC will seek to identify the smallest such package (or packages) that is likely to be a viable competitor and satisfactorily addresses the AEC. Following

Part 3 CMA and other Guidelines

discussion with parties, the CC may modify the scope of the proposed divestiture package (or packages) provided that the parties can demonstrate, to the CC's satisfaction, that the modified package (or packages) addresses the AEC and the modification does not create significant additional new costs or composition, purchaser or asset risks after taking account of protective measures.

11. The scope of a divestiture package will be outlined, with reasons, in the CC's report. The package will generally be specified in greater detail in the undertakings accepted or orders made by the CC when implementing the remedy. The divesting parties may also add further assets to the specified package at their request with the approval of the CC, or may be required to do so by the CC, to secure divestment to a suitable purchaser. The divesting parties will generally be prohibited from subsequently purchasing assets or shareholdings sold as part of a divestiture package or acquiring material influence over them. The CC will normally limit this prohibition to a sunset clause period of ten years.

Divestiture of an existing business or package of assets

12. The CC will generally prefer divestiture of an existing business that can compete effectively on a stand-alone basis independently of the divesting party (or parties), to divestiture of part of a business or a collection of assets. This is because divestiture of a complete business is less likely to be subject to purchaser and composition risk and can generally be achieved more quickly.

13. Where a proposed divestiture comprises part of a business or specified assets, such as IPRs, the capabilities and resources of prospective buyers are likely to be more critical to a successful outcome than for a stand-alone business. A package of assets proposed for divestiture may, for example, lack an established infrastructure and its viability may therefore be more dependent on an appropriate match with the capabilities of the purchaser. A package of assets may also be far more difficult to define or 'carve out' from an underlying business[4] and the CC may have less assurance that the purchaser will be supplied with all it requires to operate competitively. In such circumstances, the CC is likely to require additional protective measures such as identification of an alternative divestiture package (see paragraphs 15 and 16) to mitigate increased purchaser and composition risk. Where a package of assets is proposed for divestiture, the CC will require the divesting parties to specify the composition and operation of the package in detail.

14. In particular circumstances, parties may propose a 'virtual divestiture' consisting of divestiture of production capacity[5] for a specified period rather than conventional disposal of a business or package of assets. Such a proposal may have higher risks and costs than a conventional divestiture, and require continuing monitoring and compliance activity. The CC would need to satisfy itself that there was good reason to justify such a proposal in preference to a conventional divestiture and that the risks of the proposal could be appropriately contained.

Alternative divestiture packages

15. In some circumstances, it may be appropriate to define a more extensive and/or more marketable divestiture package ('alternative divestiture package')[6] which the CC would require the parties to sell if the initially proposed divestiture package were not sold within a specified period. Alternative divestiture packages may be appropriate if there is doubt as to the marketability of the initially proposed divestiture package or where a business is subject to major asset risks and speed of divestiture is likely to be a critical requirement.[7] In such circumstances, prior identification of a more extensive, more marketable package may be the most effective means of facilitating rapid disposal if the initial package cannot be sold to a suitable purchaser within a specified period.[8] In specifying an alternative divestiture package the CC would wish to satisfy itself that divestiture of such a package would be effective and (in the event that the proposed divestiture package had not been disposed to a suitable purchaser) proportionate.

16. The alternative divestiture package will include all the core assets necessary to remedy the AEC. The CC will wish to satisfy itself that the purchaser of such a package is committed to operate the core assets so as to compete effectively in the market(s) affected by the AEC and not primarily attracted by the additional assets. The CC will identify the alternative package in its report but the precise nature, and in some cases the existence, of an alternative package may be excised from the published version of the report to prevent the existence of the alternative package undermining divestiture of the initial package.

Suitable purchasers

Criteria

17. The identity and capability of a purchaser will be of major importance in ensuring the success of a divestiture remedy. The divesting party (or parties) will therefore need to obtain the CC's approval of the prospective purchaser(s). The CC will wish to satisfy itself that a prospective purchaser is independent of the divesting parties, has the necessary capability to compete, is committed to competing in the relevant market(s) and that divestiture to the purchaser will not create further competition concerns. The relative importance that the CC attributes to each of these criteria will depend on the circumstances of the inquiry. These criteria are considered in more detail below:

(a) *Independence.* The purchaser should have no significant connection to the divesting parties that may compromise the purchaser's incentives to compete with them or, where relevant, with other major suppliers in the relevant market(s). Significant connections may include, for example, an equity interest, shared directors, reciprocal trading relationships or continuing financial assistance. The CC will seek to understand the significance of such connections in the context of the overall relationship between the parties concerned, in order to form a view of their cumulative effect on incentives to compete.

(b) *Capability.* The purchaser must have access to appropriate financial resources, expertise and assets to enable the divested business to be an effective competitor in the market. This access should be sufficient to enable the divestiture package to continue to develop as an effective competitor. For example, a highly leveraged acquisition of the divestiture package that left little scope for competitive levels of capital expenditure or product development is unlikely to satisfy this criterion. Where the purchaser takes the form of a consortium, the CC will wish to satisfy itself that the structure and governance arrangements of the consortium will permit appropriate access to expertise and finance.[9]

(c) *Commitment to relevant market.* The CC will wish to satisfy itself that the purchaser has an appropriate business plan and objectives for competing in the relevant market(s).[10]

(d) *Absence of competitive or regulatory concerns.* Divestiture to the purchaser should not create a realistic prospect of further competition or regulatory concerns. Moreover, the CC's approval of a purchaser may be subject to clearance by the OFT or other regulatory authority.

18. Except in circumstances, as specified below, where a divestiture trustee is in place, the divesting parties are responsible for securing a prospective buyer which is able to demonstrate that it satisfies the CC's criteria for a suitable purchaser. However, the CC will keep the progress of the divestiture under close scrutiny.

19. Where divesting parties receive interest from more than one prospective buyer, the CC will generally wish to evaluate whether purchasers fulfil the criteria before any purchaser is granted exclusivity to undertake detailed due diligence. This is to avoid situations where a prospective purchaser undertakes lengthy due diligence on an exclusive basis but is then found not to satisfy the CC's criteria.

20. In certain cases, for example where the effectiveness of a divestiture remedy is particularly dependent on the long-term development of the divested entity, the CC may require a purchaser to provide it with undertakings that it will not sell on the divested entity within a limited period other than with the CC's approval that the new purchaser satisfies the same purchaser criteria as applied in the initial divestiture. Whether such a restriction is necessary and the time period over which any such restriction will apply will be determined by the facts of the case.[11]

Continuing links and purchaser protection

21. A purchaser should not have continuing links with the divesting party (or parties) after divestiture that may compromise the purchaser's incentives to compete with these parties, for example financial, ownership or management links. However, purchasers may require access to key inputs or services at appropriate terms from the divesting party (or parties), on an interim basis, in order to enable the divestiture to operate effectively. Such transitional service arrangements may be permitted by the CC for a limited period. The timescale over which transitional service arrangements will be permitted is likely to vary from case to case, depending on the time that it may reasonably be expected to take potential purchasers to develop their own independent access to the inputs or services in question.

22. The CC may also permit or require non-solicitation clauses or other measures to protect the purchaser from the divesting party (or parties) for a limited period to enable the purchaser to become established as an effective competitor in the relevant market(s). In order to ensure a timely remedy, the CC will seek to ensure that any period of purchaser protection is no longer than necessary and can be justified by reference to the steps necessary for the purchaser to become established as an effective competitor. In any event, given the desirability of achieving a timely remedy, the CC would not normally expect to permit or require such measures for more than two years.

Effective divestiture process

Objective of process

23. An effective divestiture process will protect the competitive potential of the divestiture package before disposal and will enable a suitable purchaser to be secured in an acceptable timescale. The process should also allow prospective purchasers to make an appropriately informed acquisition decision.

Protecting the divestiture package

24. Divesting parties may have significant incentives to run down or neglect the business or assets of a divestment package, and/or continue to extract know-how and other commercially sensitive information from the divestment package. Such incentives, if acted upon, are likely to reduce the future competitive impact of the divestment package. The resulting asset risk may also be influenced by such factors as the length and complexity of the divestiture process and the pace at which customer goodwill and employee relations may erode.

25. To protect against these forms of asset risk, the CC will generally seek undertakings from the relevant parties which impose a general duty to maintain the divestiture package in good order and not to undermine the competitive position of the package. The CC may also require 'hold-separate' undertakings to mitigate asset risk. These will require the divestiture package to be held and managed separately from the retained business. Protection measures specified in final undertakings may sometimes continue existing measures specified in any interim undertakings that have been accepted by the CC (although interim undertakings can only be accepted in market investigations following publication of the final report). The appointment of a hold-separate manager or management team may also be required to manage the assets/business to be divested so as to maintain their competitiveness and establish separation from the retained assets.[12] Establishing separation may be a more complex issue than in merger inquiries.

Part 3 CMA and other Guidelines

Use of monitoring trustees

26. Where divestiture undertakings are in place, the CC will normally require the appointment of an independent monitoring trustee to oversee the parties' compliance with the undertakings and, if applicable, the performance of the hold-separate manager. The trustee will have an overall duty to perform in accordance with his or her agreed mandate and the directions of the CC. The trustee will monitor the ongoing management of the divestiture package and the conduct of the divestiture process. The CC will have the right to propose and direct measures necessary to ensure compliance with the undertakings. The trustee will report to the CC at regular intervals.

The divestiture period

27. The CC will state in its report the period in which the parties should achieve effective disposal of a divestiture package to a suitable purchaser (ie the 'initial divestiture period'). However, this period will normally be excised from the report if it is considered that disclosure to third parties may undermine the divestiture process. The length of this period will depend on the circumstances of the case but will normally have a maximum duration of six months in relatively straightforward divestiture cases. The CC, when determining the initial divestiture period, will seek to balance factors which favour a shorter duration, such as minimizing asset risk and giving rapid effect to the remedy, with factors that favour a longer duration such as canvassing a sufficient selection of potential suitable purchasers to facilitate effective disposal and adequate due diligence. In general, the CC would expect that the period permitted for divestiture in market investigations would be sufficient for the divesting company to realize an approximation-to-fair market value for the divestiture package. The initial divestiture period may be extended by the CC where this is necessary to achieve an effective disposal.

28. While the divesting parties are responsible for securing a suitable purchaser in the initial divestiture period, the CC will keep the progress of the divestiture process under close review through regular reporting and, where applicable, the scrutiny of a monitoring trustee.

Use of divestiture trustees

29. If the divesting parties cannot procure divestiture to a suitable purchaser within the initial divestiture period, then, unless this period is extended by the CC, an independent divestiture trustee may be mandated to dispose of the package within a specified period (the trustee's divestiture period) at the best available price in the circumstances, subject to prior approval by the CC of the purchaser and the divestiture arrangements. If the CC has reason to expect that parties will not procure divestiture to a suitable purchaser within the initial divestiture period, the CC may require that a divestiture trustee is appointed before the end of the initial divestiture period, or in unusual cases, at the outset of the divestiture process.[13] The role of a divestiture trustee is distinct from that of a monitoring trustee, but the two roles may be performed by the same person subject to consideration of any potential conflict of interest. The CC may require a divestiture trustee to be selected and made ready prior to the end of a divestiture period in order to prevent any delay in appointment following the end of the divestiture period.

Review of divestiture documentation

30. The CC will wish to ensure, before providing its final approval of the divestiture at the end of the divestiture process, that the divestiture agreement and relevant supporting documentation convey all assets required to be divested, and contain no provisions that are inconsistent with the remedial objectives of the divestiture. For example, continuing links between the purchaser and the parties, as outlined in paragraph 21, may undermine competitive incentives.

Intellectual property remedies

Introduction

31. The licensing or assignment of IP, including patents, licences and brands, may be viewed generally as a specialized form of asset divestiture. However, in certain cases, the terms of a licence may contain ongoing behavioural elements such that the remedy is a structural/behavioural hybrid. The key element is the extent to which any material link between licensor and licensee will exist following award of the licence. A remedy that requires an assignment or licence of an IP right that is exclusive, irrevocable and non-terminable with no performance-related royalties will effectively be treated by the CC as structural in form and subject to similar consideration and evaluation as an asset divestiture. A licence that requires a licensee to rely on the licensor for updates of the technology or continuing access to specialist inputs or know-how will be regarded as a behavioural commitment and is generally subject to greater risks of not being an effective remedy.

32. For licensing of IP alone to be effective as a remedy, it must be sufficient to enhance significantly the acquirer's ability to compete with other parties in the market and thus address the AEC.[14] Such a remedy may not be effective if the IP needs to be accompanied by other resources (for example, technical expertise and sales networks) to enable effective competition if these are unlikely to be available in potential acquirers of the IP.

33. In view of the possible risks to effectiveness, as outlined in paragraph 32, that may result from using IP remedies, the CC will generally prefer to divest a business including IPRs, where this is feasible, rather than rely on licensing narrowly defined IP alone. This is because divestiture of a business including IPRs is more likely to include all that the acquirer needs to compete effectively with other parties in the market.

Design factors

34. The appropriate design of an IP remedy may be influenced by several case-specific factors such as:

(a) *The form and jurisdiction of the relevant IP (eg patent, exclusive licence, trade mark etc).* The CC will wish to ensure that the IP to be divested is sufficient to enable a purchaser to compete effectively. This may sometimes include less easily transferable forms of IP (eg 'know-how').[15] Where there is uncertainty regarding the scope of a licence or its terms and conditions, the parties may be required to divest the underlying right and accept a licence back.

(b) *The relative specialization of the IP.* Highly specialized IP may impose particular constraints on selecting a suitable acquirer as there may be few parties competent to use the IP.[16]

(c) *The rate of innovation expected in the relevant market.* A high rate of innovation may imply a shorter required duration for a licensing remedy than in a more stable market.

(d) *Forms of payment for IP.* The form of payment (eg one-off payment, royalties or profit shares) may have an effect on competitive incentives.

35. IPRs generally enable the remuneration of investment in innovation by granting time-limited exclusivity. In considering the design and scope of IP remedies, the CC will recognize the need for preserving incentives for innovation while addressing competitive concerns.

36. Remedies relating to the transfer of IPRs may have international repercussions due, for instance, to international filing and licensing of patent rights. International cooperation with other competition authorities is therefore often particularly necessary in these cases.

SECTION 2: BEHAVIOURAL REMEDIES

Introduction

37. Behavioural remedies are designed to regulate the ongoing conduct of parties so as to address an AEC and/or its adverse effects. In market investigations the CC may use behavioural measures as a main remedy or as an adjunct to other measures (eg structural measures or recommendations).

38. The variety of market features and possible behavioural measures that may be encountered on individual investigations is extensive. This guidance therefore seeks to outline the CC's general approach to behavioural remedies, making reference to the types of measure that have been implemented in investigations to date, rather than dealing with all possibilities.

39. In the rest of this section some general issues are first considered relating to the design, monitoring and enforcement of behavioural remedies and their duration (paragraphs 40 to 45). The two main categories of behavioural remedies are then considered, namely enabling measures (paragraphs 46 to 85) and measures to control outcomes (paragraphs 86 to 93). The former address an AEC by seeking to remove obstacles to competition or otherwise stimulating competition within a market, whereas the latter seek to prevent the exercise of significant market power and thereby control the detrimental effects arising from an AEC rather than remedy the AEC itself. A comprehensive and timely solution to an AEC may require both categories of remedy.

General issues

Design, monitoring and enforcement

40. Behavioural remedies seek to change aspects of business conduct from what may be expected based on businesses' incentives and resources. The design of behavioural remedies should seek to avoid four particular forms of risk to enable these measures to be as effective as possible:

(a) *Specification risks*—These risks arise if the form of conduct required to address the AEC or its detrimental effects cannot be specified with sufficient clarity to provide an effective basis for monitoring and compliance. The intended operation of the measure needs to be clear to the persons to whom it is directed and other relevant parties, so that it is apparent what conduct constitutes compliance and what does not. For example, a commitment to permit access on FRND terms, without further clarification of what this means in practice, may create significant specification risk as the provision may be insufficiently specific to allow effective enforcement. Markets that are subject to frequent change in products or supply arrangements may be particularly prone to specification risk if the definition of required conduct is vulnerable to such changes.

(b) *Circumvention risks*—It is possible that other adverse forms of behaviour may arise if particular forms of behaviour are restricted.[17] For example, if prices are controlled a firm may reduce product quality. To avoid or reduce these risks, behavioural measures will generally need to deal with all the likely substantial forms in which enhanced market power may be applied. In some cases this may not be feasible or may make the behavioural measures too complex to monitor and/or enforce.

(c) *Distortion risks*—These are risks that behavioural remedies may create market distortions that reduce the effectiveness of these measures and/or increase their effective costs. Distortion risks may result from remedies overriding market signals or encouraging circumvention behaviour. For example, prohibiting the use of long-term contracts may result in a lack of incentives to compete for new business.

(d) *Monitoring and enforcement risks*—Even clearly specified remedies may be subject to significant risks of ineffective monitoring and enforcement. This may be due to a variety of causes such as the volume and complexity of information required to monitor compliance, limitations in monitoring resources, asymmetry of information between the monitoring agency and the business concerned and the long timescale of enforcement relative to a rapidly moving market.

41. For behavioural remedies to have the desired impact it is important that there are effective and adequately resourced arrangements in place for monitoring and enforcement so that there is a powerful threat that non-compliance will be detected and that action will be taken to enforce compliance where this is necessary.

42. The OFT, or the relevant sectoral regulator where appropriate, is responsible for monitoring and enforcing compliance of remedies under the Act.[18] Customers and competitors of the firms subject to behavioural remedies may be in a strong position to report to the OFT, or the relevant sectoral regulator, on instances of noncompliance where they have appropriate resources and incentives to do so. However, such persons may be inhibited from fulfilling this reporting role by lack of resources and verifiable information, lack of understanding of the measures, fear of reprisals and other disincentives.

43. In view of constraints on the OFT's resources and the possible limitations in the reliance that can be placed on the reporting role of customers and competitors, it may be necessary for the CC to seek undertakings from the relevant parties to appoint and remunerate a third party monitor to enable the OFT, or the relevant sectoral regulator, to fulfil its monitoring responsibilities effectively.[19] Alternatively monitoring may be facilitated by the CC making an order requiring the relevant parties to publish certain information[20] or to produce compliance reports that have been verified by an independent third party.[21] The likelihood of effective monitoring will be significantly increased if it is possible to involve a sectoral regulator in the monitoring regime.

44. A behavioural remedy may seek to prevent certain conduct that may be prohibited under the CA98's Chapter II Prohibition or under Article 102 TFEU. Similarly, a behavioural remedy may seek to prevent the making of agreements that may be prohibited under the CA98's Chapter I Prohibition or Article 101 TFEU. The CC recognizes the importance of ex post competition enforcement. However, the CC has an obligation to achieve as comprehensive a solution to the AEC and its detrimental effects as is reasonable and practicable. The CC will therefore normally prefer to specify its own remedial measures rather than rely on the general provisions of competition law, as this has the advantages that the CC measures can be designed to take account of the circumstances of the case and the provisions for monitoring and enforcement can be fully defined.

Duration

45. . . .

Enabling measures

46. Enabling measures aim to remedy an AEC by removing obstacles to competition or otherwise stimulating competition. Most enabling measures that have been introduced by the CC to date may be classified as:[23]

(a) market-opening measures;
(b) informational remedies; or
(c) measures to restrain the impact of vertical relationships.

Market-opening measures

47. Market-opening measures are aimed at removing impediments to effective competition, such as barriers to entry, expansion and/or switching. Such impediments may result from structural features of the market (eg barriers to entry) or from the behaviour of individual firms in that market (eg exclusionary conduct).

48. This is a diverse category of remedies. The specific aim of any market-opening measure and the particular mechanism that is used in any case, will depend on the market features that have been identified as preventing, restricting or distorting competition and the practical opportunities available for addressing those features. Market-opening measures can be further subdivided into the following two categories:

(a) Firm-specific measures to restrain horizontal market power.
(b) Market-wide measures to reduce barriers to entry, expansion and switching.

Firm-specific measures to restrain horizontal market power

49. Where a firm enjoys significant market power it may be able to use the strength of this position in a number of ways to limit or restrain competition. These may include:

(a) requiring customers to enter into long-term and/or exclusive contracts;
(b) creating switching costs for customers through, for example, volume discounts or contractual penalties;
(c) bundling or tying the sale of particular products; and
(d) selective discounting or exclusionary conduct.

50. Remedies may be introduced that prohibit, restrict or discourage types of behaviour, such as those listed above, where these have been found to prevent, restrict or distort competition. The selection and design of these measures will depend critically on the circumstances revealed by the inquiry and the need to manage specification, circumvention, monitoring and enforcement risks. Where circumstances point to the use of these measures, the CC will follow the general approach of considering the anticompetitive conduct that has been identified as having an AEC. It will then consider the measures that may be taken to prevent or limit this conduct and the effectiveness and costs of these measures.

51. As an example of the types of consideration relevant to this approach, the use of long-term and/or exclusive contracts by a firm with significant market power may create a barrier to entry or expansion.

However, if, in the relevant market, firms need to invest heavily to acquire new customers (for example, by investing in new facilities or systems) requiring a firm with significant market power to have contracts that are short term in nature may generate distortion risks as this could reduce incentives to compete for new contracts if firms do not have sufficient opportunity to recoup their initial investment. In implementing a constraint on the use of long-term contracts, the CC will therefore seek an appropriate balance between facilitating switching and permitting sufficient incentives to compete for new contracts.

52. Likewise, selective discounting or price discrimination by a firm with market power can also have the effect of creating barriers to entry or expansion when used systematically to reduce prices to particular customers that are more likely to switch to other suppliers.[24] Measures to restrict selective discounting or price discrimination may therefore sometimes be necessary to address an AEC. However, measures restricting selective discounting or price discrimination may themselves generate significant distortion risk by adversely affecting the competitive dynamics of a market if maintained in the long term. They may therefore be most appropriate as a transitional measure until other sources of competition develop.

53. The CC will have particular regard to avoiding circumvention risk in implementing measures limiting the behaviour of firms with significant market power that has been found to prevent, distort or restrict competition. This is because firms with significant market power may readily evolve new forms of behaviour to replace prohibited or restricted conduct.

Market-wide measures to reduce barriers to entry, expansion and switching

54. Market-opening measures may also be applied where incumbency advantages and other barriers to entry or switching have been found to prevent, restrict or distort competition. In this type of situation, market-opening measures to address these features may be applied to a market as a whole or, if this is not necessary and/or practicable, to the largest suppliers within the market.

55. The selection and design of these measures will depend critically on the specific features that have been identified as preventing, restricting or distorting competition. The types of measures that might be considered by the CC include:

(a) measures to address barriers to switching; and

(b) measures to reduce incumbency advantages and other barriers to entry and expansion.

56. In some markets, customers may be put off switching suppliers by a perception that switching is costly, complex, time consuming and/or risky. This perception may be grounded in customers' own experience. Where barriers to switching have been identified as causing competition problems, measures may be introduced to make it easier for customers to switch.[25] For example, the CC may introduce obligations on a customer's existing supplier to cooperate with the proposed new supplier to ensure that costs and disruption to customers are minimized. Generally a new supplier will have significant incentives to make the switching process as easy as possible for the customer and will not normally require corresponding obligations.

57. Another factor that can deter customers from switching is if an important attribute of their current service is not transferable (or 'portable') from one provider to another and this leads them to remain loyal to their current supplier. For example, customers may wish to retain their existing telephone number if they change suppliers and may be deterred from doing so if this were not possible. Interventions to increase the portability of product attributes are most likely to be beneficial when the attribute that customers value is easily identifiable and the ownership rights of the attribute are easily transferable to rival firms or customers. In assessing remedies of this type, the CC is likely to evaluate the extent of any material benefits to customers associated with non-portability such as, for example, being able to identify the network to which a call is being made.

58. Remedies may also be introduced to address competition problems in markets where some existing providers have significant incumbency advantages over other providers (eg potential entrants), which are found to act as a barrier to entry and/or expansion. In some cases, 'incumbency advantages' may result from good commercial decisions made in the past (eg to invest in and patent a successful new technology) and interventions to overcome these sources of competitive advantage may risk undermining dynamic incentives to invest and innovate. In other situations the source of incumbency advantages may result from firms having preferential access to key resources, information or customers and it may be possible to intervene to promote competition without adversely affecting dynamic incentives.[26]

59. A further potential source of incumbency advantage, which may sometimes require intervention, is the 'point-of-sale advantage'. This occurs when a particular supplier has systematically better access to customers than potential rivals. A range of possible approaches might be taken to remedying competition problems resulting from a point-of-sale advantage. For example:

- customers may be encouraged to search for alternatives (eg through informational remedies) before they reach a particular point of sale;
- providers who enjoy a point-of-sale advantage may be prohibited from completing a sale until a customer has an opportunity to shop around;[27] or
- providers who enjoy a point-of-sale advantage may be required to offer customers a choice of products at the point of sale.[28]

60. In considering such alternatives, the CC will consider the effectiveness and proportionality of different approaches, for example their impact on the behaviour of customers and suppliers as well as whether there are benefits to customers associated with purchasing a product at a particular point of sale.[29]

Information remedies

61. Informational remedies can be used to address competition problems that are caused by shortfalls in the information that customers have to enable them to make informed purchasing or switching decisions. Informational remedies can lead to changes in customer behaviour, for example by reducing search costs, increasing customers' awareness of alternatives and making it easier for customers to make comparisons between products when making an initial purchase or when switching suppliers. Informational remedies can also lead to changes in suppliers' behaviour— for example, suppliers may improve their offering, in order that their products appear attractive in terms of the information that customers receive. Information remedies may also facilitate new entry, if a lack of awareness by customers of alternatives was a factor that was restricting entry.[30]

62. The CC has introduced informational remedies in six market investigations completed to date (April 2013) under the Act,[31] as well as in complex monopoly investigations under the Fair Trading Act 1973, such as *Extended Warranties.*[32] Informational remedies put in place by the CC include:

(a) obliging firms to submit information about their products for publication on price comparisons sites (eg *Home Credit, PPI);*

(b) standardization of pricing structures[33] *(eg PPI* single-premium prohibition);

(c) mandatory disclosure of price and other key messages at the point of sale and in marketing materials (eg *Extended Warranties, Northern Irish personal banking*);

(d) requirement to offer written quotations that remain valid for a fixed period (eg *Extended Warranties, PPI);*

(e) requirement to provide information to existing customers in regular statements (eg *Store Cards, Northern Irish personal banking, PPI);*

(f) requirements to provide information to customers about their rights to switch and the switching process *(LPG, Northern Irish personal banking, PPI);*

(g) requirements to provide or extend 'cooling-off' periods (eg *Extended Warranties);* and

(h) requirements to provide financial information underpinning the pricing of products and services to potential franchise operators (eg *ROSCOs*).

63. The CC's starting point for the selection of appropriate informational remedies will generally be the identification of the particular barrier to search or other information shortfall which is causing the AEC. This will help identify the information or message that needs to be communicated to customers: for example, if switching is suppressed because many customers have a mistaken belief that they are unable to switch suppliers, then an informational remedy could focus on correcting this misperception.

64. The CC will also consider how information may best be communicated to customers (eg via a website, through companies' marketing material, or by periodic statements to customers). The choice between these options may depend on a number of factors, including:

(a) *The ways in which customers currently obtain information about the product.* It may be more practicable to introduce informational remedies that build on existing sources of information used by customers.[34]

(b) *Customers' ability to access particular information channels.* For example, the level of Internet access among a customer base is likely to be relevant to consideration of whether to require firms to disclose prices on a price-comparison website.

(c) *The nature of the information to be provided to customers.* For example, the CC will generally consider whether information needs to be tailored to individual customers (eg via a customer statement) or whether a common message needs to be communicated to all customers (eg in marketing materials).[35]

65. Any obligation to provide information to customers will usually fall on the providers of the product under investigation.[36] If information is to be provided using a medium over which providers have control, the CC may find it necessary to specify in some detail what information is to be provided and how. This is particularly likely to be the case if:

(a) the disclosure is intended to help customers make comparisons between providers and a standard format for disclosure will help achieve this objective;[37] or

(b) providers have incentives to conceal or marginalize information that presents them in an unfavourable light or which encourages their customers to switch or shop around.

66. The CC will also have regard to the potential benefits of taking a less prescriptive approach. The cost to firms of complying with informational remedies will generally be lower if they have some flexibility as to how they meet their requirements. It may also be necessary to allow some flexibility, in order to 'future proof' the remedy, so that it is still effective in relation to new or unusual situations or products.

67. In considering the design of informational remedies, the CC will generally be mindful of how the remedy is likely to interact with existing obligations on firms relating to information provision. For example, the content of advertisements may already be regulated (as was the case in *Home Credit*) or firms may already be required to give various disclosures to customers at the point of sale (as was the case in PPI). The CC will look, where possible, to exploit positive synergies between existing regulations and CC proposed remedies.[38] It may sometimes be possible to implement informational remedies by building on existing mechanisms for communication with customers. Where this is the case, this may be a lower cost option than requiring the establishment of a new form of communication.[39]

68. In specifying information remedies, the CC will look to ensure that information is provided at a time that the recipient can make use of it. For example, informational remedies that are intended to help customers search the market and compare products will tend to be most effective when customers see this information *before* they have made their main purchase decision. So, for example, providing price and product information in writing after a sale has been concluded—while sometimes required for consumer protection—may only have a limited impact on search behaviour.[40]

69. Informational remedies that are intended to facilitate switching will tend to be most effective if they are targeted at those customers who are able to switch, at a time when they are likely to be interested in switching (eg on invoices or statements setting out how much they have paid over a period).[41]

70. The CC may consider whether introducing an information remedy might have the unintended consequence of facilitating coordination between suppliers. As not all markets are conducive to coordination and as suppliers will generally have better information than customers about the prices charged by their competitors, this is most likely to be a material risk if the conditions for coordination are met and if prices are opaque to competitors in the absence of the remedy (eg because prices are subject to individually negotiated discounts).[42]

71. The CC will consider carrying out specific customer research into informational remedies (or 'road-testing') before they are put in place.[43] Road-testing may be carried out during a market investigation to inform choices between alternative remedy options and the design of individual options. The CC has also carried out road-testing after publication of the CC's final report, to fine-tune the detail of particular remedies prior to final implementation.[44]

Restraining the impact of vertical relationships

72. Competition problems can sometimes arise where individual firms are active at different levels of the supply chain of particular goods or services (vertical integration). Similar problems can arise from contractual arrangements between firms active at different levels of the supply chain (vertical arrangements). Where a party has significant market power at one or more levels of the supply chain, vertical integration and/or vertical arrangements (collectively, vertical relationships) may contribute to an AEC, typically through the firm's incentive and ability to disadvantage competitors by foreclosing access to key inputs, facilities or customers and/or exploiting access to confidential information.

73. For example, if, as illustrated below, the manufacturer (Compco) of most of a key industry component also owned a major user of this component (Prodco1) then the ability of other users (Prodco2 and Prodco3) to compete could be disadvantaged by the combined entity through restricting supply of this component to Prodco2 and Prodco3 or making use of information concerning component orders by Prodco2 and Prodco3.

FIGURE 1: Illustration of vertical configuration

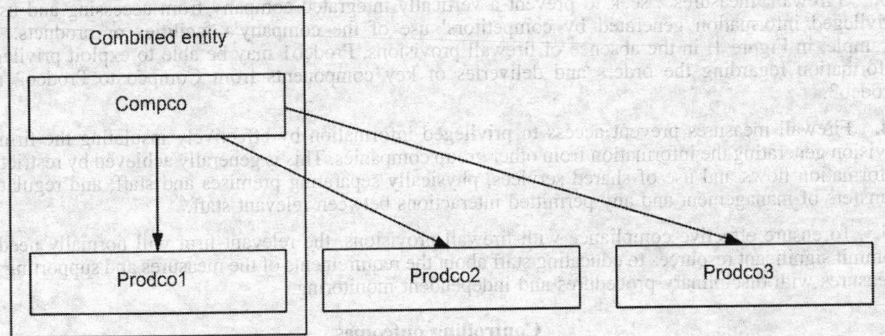

74. An AEC resulting from vertical relationships might be remedied by structural measures. Such measures might involve vertical separation (eg requiring divestiture of ProdCo1),[45] but could also involve reducing the significant market power that the combined entity has at the critical stage of the supply chain (eg partial divestiture of Compco).

75. If vertical relationships produce substantial RCBs that would be largely reduced by structural measures, or if divestiture is otherwise not appropriate or feasible, then behavioural measures may be selected by the CC that enable continued access to necessary products or facilities on appropriate terms and/or measures that prevent the combined entity exploiting privileged access to information.

Access remedies

76. Access remedies seek to address competition problems resulting from vertical relationships by enabling competitors to have access on appropriate terms to the products and facilities of a combined entity that they require to be an effective competitor.

77. An access remedy will normally need to specify an access commitment by the firm concerned to third parties in sufficient detail so that third parties and monitoring agencies can enforce the commitment effectively. This will include details of the product or facility to be provided, including quality and technical parameters, and the terms of supply of the product or facility, including service levels and the basis of pricing. The latter may be particularly complex and may be subject to some of the same issues that are encountered with price caps, as discussed in paragraphs 90 to 93. If the access commitment is not specified or monitored in sufficient detail then the measure may be vulnerable to specification risk and the combined entity may be able to avoid its obligations readily. In such circumstances the CC may need to consider alternative forms of remedy (eg divestiture) that are likely to be more effective.

78. To overcome specification risk, the CC will also generally require that an access remedy should make explicit provision for accommodating future changes, for example, in product specifications or supply arrangements. Where a market is likely to be subject to frequent technological change or other wide-ranging market developments, there is likely to be a significant risk that an access remedy will become ineffective if the terms of the access commitment do not accommodate these changes. However, significant technological change might also reduce the market power that results in the AEC (eg if—see Figure 1—effective substitutes are developed for the component supplied by Compco).

79. In some supply arrangements, certain factors that are not easily specified may be particularly important for competitive access, for example quality of product support, priority for system upgrades, and quality of management assigned to a customer's account. Such factors may result in 'soft biases' in access to supply that may generate significant circumvention risk and may significantly undermine the purpose and suitability of an access remedy.[46]

80. In certain circumstances it may be possible to simplify the specification of an access remedy by obliging the combined entity to supply a particular product on FRND terms where supplies to external customers are provided on the same or similar terms as apply to its own businesses (see paragraph 40). For this to be effective, the nature of FRND terms must deal adequately with the circumstances of external customers and must be transparent to customers and monitoring agencies in sufficient detail to enable effective enforcement.

81. The use of FRND terms may still leave competitors vulnerable to a margin squeeze by the combined entity as it may have an incentive to charge all downstream businesses, including its own, a uniformly high price since reduced profitability in its downstream business can be offset by higher profitability in its upstream business. The CC may therefore require that use of FRND terms is accompanied by provisions to protect against a margin squeeze (eg submission of regular reports demonstrating full cost recovery in the downstream business).

82. Where it is necessary to preserve access to a key facility owned or controlled by a vertically integrated company and the usage and capacity of the facility is readily assessed, the CC may determine that the most practical and effective means of providing access to competitors is to cap usage of the facility by the combined entity and require it to auction remaining capacity to third parties.[47] This would be effectively a form of 'virtual divestiture' as considered in paragraph 14.

'Firewall' measures

83. 'Firewall' measures[48] seek to prevent a vertically integrated company from accessing and using privileged information generated by competitors' use of the company's facilities or products. For example, in Figure 1, in the absence of firewall provisions, Prodco1 may be able to exploit privileged information regarding the orders and deliveries of key components from Compco to Prodco2 and Prodco3.

84. Firewall measures prevent access to privileged information by effectively insulating the firm or division generating the information from other group companies. This is generally achieved by restricting information flows and use of shared services, physically separating premises and staff, and regulating transfers of management and any permitted interactions between relevant staff.[49]

85. To ensure effective compliance with firewall provisions, the relevant firm will normally need to commit significant resources to educating staff about the requirements of the measures and supporting the measures with disciplinary procedures and independent monitoring.

Controlling outcomes

86. Remedies that control or restrict the outcomes of business processes, such as price caps, supply commitments and service level agreements, seek to prevent firms from exercising market power. As such, these remedies seek to restrict the customer detriment arising from an AEC, rather than addressing its cause.

87. In order to overcome specification risk, remedies that control outcomes normally need to specify in significant detail the products or services that are subject to control and the basis of the control, for example, the application of price indices to a price cap. The remedy will generally also need to specify how the control will deal with changes, such as the introduction of new products.

88. Measures to control outcomes are often used in regulated sectors, where it may not be feasible to introduce effective competition. The introduction of such measures is also a potential outcome of market investigations, particularly where it is not possible to identify effective ways of addressing the causes of the AEC or where competition-enhancing measures are likely to take a long time to remove the customer detriment that results from the AEC. However, such measures are vulnerable to the main risks associated with behavioural remedies (see paragraph 40) and this can have a negative impact on their effectiveness and cost. Specifically:

(a) Defining appropriate parameters for the control measure—for example, the level of a price cap—may be complex and, in some cases impractical, and the measure may therefore be vulnerable to specification risks. This is especially likely where any of the following conditions apply:
   (i) Pricing in the relevant market is naturally volatile, for example because of variability in input costs.
   (ii) Products or services are differentiated rather than homogeneous; this may increase the complexity of any control in order to capture adequately the diversity of products offer.
   (iii) Prices are individually negotiated, which may also increase the complexity of any control measure.

(iv) Supply arrangements and products are subject to significant ongoing change, which require the control measure to change to reflect new developments.

(b) This class of remedy directly overrides market signals with the result that it may generate distortion risks over time that increase the effective cost of the remedy or reduce its effectiveness. For example, a supply commitment for a particular product may discourage product innovation. While it may sometimes be possible to design measures to minimize distortion risk (sometimes referred to as 'incentive regulation') this may be at the expense of increasing the complexity of the control.

(c) The control may be vulnerable to circumvention risks. For example, a price cap may be circumvented by a firm reducing the quality of controlled products or restricting the supply of controlled products. It may be sometimes possible to add preventative provisions to reduce the risk of circumvention, though this may be at the expense of increasing the complexity of the control.

(d) Monitoring and enforcement may be costly and intrusive and, in the absence of an industry-specific adjudicator or regulator,[50] may lack effectiveness, especially where the form of remedy is complex.

89. In view of these risks the CC will not generally use remedies that control outcomes unless other, more effective, remedies are not feasible or appropriate.[51] In addition, where this class of remedy is employed, it is most likely to be used on a temporary basis unless there is no alternative to a continuing regulatory solution.

Price caps

90. Price caps are likely to be the most common form of measure for controlling outcomes and illustrate many of the issues outlined above.

91. Different approaches may be adopted to defining the products and prices to be controlled depending on the circumstances of the case:

(a) Prices of all affected products may be individually capped. This may be impractical where a large number of products are involved and may be inflexible in dealing with product changes.[52]

(b) The average price of a basket of products may be capped. This allows greater flexibility in taking account of shifts in demand between products but the weighting of the constituents of the basket may be problematic and subject to distortion, for example, if revenue-weighting is used and the firm introduces a number of low-cost product variants.[53]

(c) The price cap may apply to key benchmark products. This approach could greatly simplify monitoring and compliance but is only likely to be effective if a few key products are likely to continue to account for a large proportion of sales and the pricing of other products is expected to remain closely related to the benchmark products.

(d) The price cap may be to particular product terms (eg 'hidden charges'). Again, this approach could simplify monitoring and compliance and may increase the overall level of price transparency for customers, though it may result in a 'waterbed effect' whereby other charges increase.[54]

92. The CC will seek a basis for the price cap which will restrict the extent to which a firm's market power is reflected in prices. The basis of a price cap may take a variety of forms:

(a) Prices may be benchmarked to the prices of products in analogous markets that are determined by competition. In practice, this may only be feasible in limited circumstances due to the lack of an analogous market.

(b) Prices may be determined on the basis of input cost data and an approved return on capital. This resembles the approach adopted by many sectoral regulators but generally requires a highly resource-intensive regulatory process backed by extensive information-gathering and enforcement powers to be effective.

(c) A hybrid approach may be taken whereby an initial price reduction is determined on the basis of input cost data and an approved return on capital, with subsequent changes to the level of the price cap being updated by reference to an index that is representative of input cost changes after incorporating current productivity gains.[55] The CC will wish to use an index which has robust data sources which cannot be influenced by the parties subject to the price control. Use of such an index may provide a broad approximation to a competitive price outcome in the short term but is at risk of departing significantly from such an outcome in the medium to long term.

93. The CC will generally require that price caps are accompanied by measures to prevent circumvention risk that may arise, for example, through the merged entity restricting the supply or service levels of price-controlled products or reducing product quality.

SECTION 3: RECOMMENDATIONS

94. The CC can decide to make recommendations to others, either on their own or in combination with other measures as part of a solution to an AEC. The most common instances where the CC is likely to use recommendations are where it does not have jurisdiction to implement undertakings or orders directly, for instance where the area concerned is governed by a regulator or government department. Recommendations may also be included as a 'fallback' remedy, if it is uncertain whether the CC will be able to achieve its preferred remedy itself—for example, if this depends on parties being prepared to offer satisfactory undertakings.[56]

95. Recommendations will be directed to the party that is best able to implement the necessary action. It will, of course, be for the person to whom a recommendation is addressed to decide whether to act on the recommendation. The Government has made a commitment to give a public response to any recommendation made to it within 90 days of the publication of a CC report. In its response, the Government will set out where it does or does not propose to make changes in light of the report, or where it proposes to consult on options. The Government will take into account all public policy and welfare considerations, including considerations of Better Regulation, in making its assessment.

96. The CC has made recommendations in five market investigations to report to date (April 2013)—*Home Credit, ROSCOs, PPI, Groceries, BAA Airports*. Recommendations have been used to address a diverse range of market features and have had structural and behavioural elements, for example:

(a) Improvements to the information provided to customers. For example, in *Home Credit*, the CC made a recommendation to BIS to require additional information on the Annual Statement that already had to be produced by lenders subject to the Consumer Credit Act.

(b) Changes to the policy and regulatory framework applying to a market. In *BAA Airports*, the CC made recommendations to the Department for Transport (DfT) and CAA about future airport regulation and airports policy.

(c) Changes to the operation of rail franchising. In *ROSCOs*, the CC made recommendations to the DfT and to Transport Scotland about the operation of the rail franchise system, for example the introduction of longer rail franchise periods.

(d) Changes to the operation of the planning regime. In *Groceries*, one element of the remedies package was a recommendation to the Department for Communities and Local Government (CLG) that a competition test for grocery store developments should be introduced into the planning system.

97. The fact that recommendations are not binding on the party to which they are addressed represents an intrinsic risk to their effectiveness as a remedy. A recommendation may not be accepted, may not be implemented in a way that is consistent with the CC's intentions, or may become redundant following a change of policy. There may be a risk to the effectiveness of a wider package of remedies, if the success of other measures in the package is dependent on a recommendation being followed.

98. In evaluating the effectiveness of a recommendation as a potential remedy, the CC will form a view on the likelihood that the recommendation will be acted on and the timescale over which this might be expected to occur. In reaching this view, the CC will have regard both to the stated policy of the body to which the recommendation is to be directed and to the possibility that that stated policy may change, either in light of the CC's recommendation or subsequent events.

99. Before making a recommendation, the CC will consult with the body to which the recommendation may be directed as well as parties likely to be affected by it. This will enable the CC to understand the benefits and risks of implementing the recommendation, to inform decisions about the specification of any recommendation, as well as informing the CC's judgement about the likelihood of the recommendation being accepted.

100. When considering the specification of a recommendation, the CC will normally consider a range of factors including:

(a) what change is required to remove or reduce the obstacle to competition that has been identified;

(b) who is best placed to take the action necessary to effect the necessary change;

(c) how that change might be best achieved by the party to which the recommendation is addressed; and

(d) the likelihood of a recommendation being implemented, the timescale within this would happen under different assumptions and the likelihood that change, if implemented, would be sustained.

101. In relation to these factors, the CC will have regard to the degree of complexity and the number of institutions involved in making the change. Recommendations that are relatively straightforward to specify and to introduce are generally more likely to be implemented than recommendations which are more complex or which require closely coordinated action by a large number of bodies.

102. There may sometimes be a trade-off between these factors. For example, the ideal outcome from a competition perspective might be very difficult to achieve in a reasonable timescale, whereas it may be possible to achieve a material improvement in competition by means of a recommendation that can be implemented more quickly. In such circumstances, the CC will weigh up the relative merits of increased certainty of implementation against the possibility of achieving a better outcome, but with less certainty or over a longer timescale.

NOTES

Para 45 and the associated footnote 22 (omitted) have been superseded by paragraph 4.25 of the revised CMA 3 which explains the CMA's new procedure relating to sunset clauses and reviews of remedies. See Annex A of CMA 3 at **[3.655]**.

1 As a consequence, many of the examples cited in this section relate to divestitures in merger inquiries, where these examples illustrate a point that is also relevant to market investigations.

2 See, for example, the *SCR Sibelco/Fife Silica Sands* inquiry (2001) as discussed in the CC's report *Understanding past merger remedies; report on case study research* (2010). See also the Federal Trade Commission's *A Study of the Commission's Divestiture Process* (1999) and DG COMP's *Merger Remedies Study* (2005) (for example, paragraph 44 of Summary and Conclusions).

3 As was the case in the *BAA Airports* market investigation.

4 DG COMP's *Merger Remedies Study* (2005) found that carve-out problems were a common cause of serious design and implementation issues in a significant proportion of divestiture remedies within its purview—see section 6 of Summary and Conclusions (pp152–155, public version).

5 So-called 'virtual power plant' remedies are examples of this type of remedy. See, for example, the Nuon/Reliant Energy

case in the Netherlands, outlined in Appendix J of the ICN's Merger Remedies Review Project.

6 Such packages are sometimes referred to as 'Crown Jewel' packages; however, in view of the wide variety of usage of this term, the CC uses the more closely defined terminology of 'alternative divestiture packages'.

7 Other measures are also available to the CC to manage the risk that a divestiture is not implemented to the timescales set out by the CC in its final report. These include the ability to appoint a monitoring or divestiture trustees (see paragraphs 26 & 29). The specification of an alternative divestiture package may be used in conjunction with such measures.

8 The EWS *Railway Holdings/Marcroft Engineering* (2006), *Sterilised International LLC/Sterile Technologies Group Limited* (2006) and *Capita/IBS* (2009) merger inquiries provide examples of the use of alternative divestiture packages.

9 The CC reviewed consortium arrangements in the divestiture of Gatwick Airport (BAA *Airports*).

10 This approach was upheld by the CAT in the *Somerfield v Competition Commission* case [2006] where the CC excluded limited assortment discount retailers from acquiring Somerfield stores on the basis that these were insufficiently close competitors to conventional supermarkets, paragraph 183.

11 This restriction was required in the BAA divestitures, for which a period of five years was specified. This is the only instance to date in which the CC has specified a restricted period of this type in either a merger inquiry or a market investigation.

12 The appointment of a hold-separate manager is particularly likely where strong incentives exist for the current senior management of the divestiture package to operate the divestiture package on behalf of the divesting party and/or if there is a high risk of deterioration of the business, for example through loss of key customers or members of staff.

13 The *Tesco/Co-op* store acquisition inquiry (2008) is an instance where the CC has required the appointment of a divestiture trustee from the outset of the divestiture period.

14 In the *Thermo Electron Manufacturing/GV Instruments* merger inquiry (2007) the CC rejected a licensing remedy proposed by the parties on the basis that it would not adequately restore competition lost by the merger.

15 See, for example, the Shell/BASF case in which the EC found that difficulties in transferring 'know-how' and other types of IP could have significantly reduced the scope and effectiveness of a licensing commitment (as outlined in Appendix D of the ICN's Merger Remedies Review Project).

16 The *Nufarm/AH Marks* merger inquiry is an example of an IP-style remedy where the field of suitable acquirers was particularly constrained.

17 This general phenomenon may be sometimes referred to as a 'waterbed effect'.

18 Section 162.

19 For example, in *Northern Irish personal banking* the Lending Standards Board (LSB) played an important role in monitoring compliance with the CC's remedies. The duties of a third party monitor might include arbitrating disputes and advising the CC and/or OFT of relevant market developments as well as monitoring compliance.

20 The *Home Credit* market investigation provides an example where parties were required to publish product and pricing information on a website.

21 The *PPI* market investigation provides an example where the largest providers were required to produce compliance reports and to have these verified by an independent third party.

23 This is not an exhaustive classification. For example, in a situation where the CC found an AEC resulting from tacit coordination, remedy options might include enabling measures designed to prevent or restrict the flow of information between market participants, alongside other measures (eg structural remedies or measures to facilitate new entry).

24 The CC considered introducing measures designed to reduce the scope for selective discounting in the *LPG* market investigation.

25 For example, in the *LPG* market investigation, the CC found that a major barrier to switching was the requirement to replace a customer's existing tank with one owned and operated by the new supplier. This was costly and disruptive to customers. To overcome this barrier to switching the CC developed and implemented a 'tank transfer' remedy requiring suppliers to transfer the ownership of the LPG tank from one supplier to another when a customer switched. The tank transfer remedy was accompanied by other measures aimed at preventing contract terms that acted as a barrier to switching and informational remedies to raise customers' awareness of the options available to them.

26 For example, in the *Home Credit* market investigation, the CC found that an existing home credit lender had a critical incumbency advantage in lending to its existing customer base over all other potential lenders. This was its knowledge of its customers' repayment history in relation to loans taken out with it. This acted as a barrier to customer switching and as a barrier to entry and expansion. It also served to restrict competition from mainstream lenders. As part of a package of measures, the CC required the largest home credit lenders to share their repayment data with other lenders by entering into agreements with at least two credit reference agencies.

27 For example, the point-of-sale prohibition in the *PPI* market investigation.

28 For example, the so-called 'guest beer' provision in the 'Beer Orders'.

29 For example, in the *PPI* market investigation and the subsequent remittal, the CC considered the implications of any loss of convenience for the assessment of the proportionality of including the point-of-sale prohibition in the remedy package.

30 A survey of the economic literature on different types of informational remedies may be found in Garrod et al, *Assessing the effectiveness of potential remedies in consumer markets*, OFT research paper 994, April 2008.

31 *Store Cards, LPG, Home Credit, Northern Irish personal banking, PPI, ROSCOs.*

32 *Extended warranties on domestic electrical goods* (2003).

33 This type of remedy is more prescriptive than most informational remedies as it can constrain the type of product that can be offered. It therefore has some characteristics of a measure that controls outcomes.

34 For example, in the *Home Credit* market investigation, some of the informational remedies required information to be included on customers' payment books as this was a document that customers were likely to retain and look at regularly.

35 For example, in *Store Cards*, information on the option to pay by direct debit and any APR that was over 25 per cent was provided to customers on statements; and in *Northern Irish personal banking*, information on charges relating to overdrafts was required to be communicated in marketing materials. Similarly, in *PPI* the CC is requiring PPI providers to provide existing customers with a personalized annual review and to include a small number of 'key messages' (which are not customer-specific) in their marketing material.

36 In some circumstances (eg an obligation to publish information on an existing website) a third party may control the final presentation of information to customers. In such cases the CC would need to be satisfied that the way in which information was provided by a third party would be effective in addressing the competition problem identified. This may

give rise to a recommendation to the third party concerned.

37 See, for example, *Consumers and mortgage disclosure documentation*, September 2006, FSA, p9 and Insight Research PPI forms consumer testing, April 2009, CC, p4.

38 For example, the recent review on the Northern Ireland Personal Current Account Banking Order took into account the information obligations banks face under two European Directives (the Payment Services Directive and the Consumer Credit Directive) and under other UK regulations (eg the FSA's Banking Conduct of Business Sourcebook).

39 For example, in *PPI*, the CC is obliging firms to provide information to the Money Advice Service for publication in its comparative tables, rather than developing a new site.

40 There is evidence from the academic literature that consumers can display a 'status quo' bias, which makes them more reluctant to change decisions that they have already made than to consider alternatives when making an initial choice. See, for example, FSA, *Financial Capability: A Behavioural Economics Perspective*, July 2008.

41 For example, in *Northern Irish personal banking*, a switching leaflet was required to be provided alongside customers' annual summaries.

42 For an example of how such a risk might materialize, see 'Government-Assisted Oligopoly Coordination? A Concrete Case', S Albæk, P Møllgaard and PB Overgaard, 1997, *Journal of Industrial Economics*, 45(4), pp429–443. The CC considered the possibility that informational remedies could facilitate coordination in the *LPG* and *Home Credit* market investigations.

43 See *Road Testing of Consumer Remedies*, London Economics, July 2009.

44 For example, in *PPI*, the CC appointed market researchers after the final report to conduct focus groups with PPI customers, to see how customers reacted to different specifications of personal PPI quote and annual review forms. The findings of this research informed the development of the two forms, which were used as the basis for schedules to the resulting Order.

45 Or in the case of vertical arrangements, prohibiting the commercial arrangements between Compco and Prodco1.

46 In the *London Stock Exchange plc* merger inquiry (2005), the CC rejected a solely behavioural access commitment to clearing and settlement services due, in part, to the likely difficulty of 'soft biases'.

47 In the *Centrica/Dynegy Storage* merger inquiry (2003), the CC required Centrica to restrict its usage of the Rough Gas Storage Facility to a percentage of total capacity to prevent foreclosure of access.

48 These may be referred to alternatively as 'Chinese wall' measures.

49 The *Centrica/Dynegy Storage* merger inquiry provides an example of the measures that may be required by the CC to make firewalls effective.

50 Monitoring and enforcement of measures to control outcomes may be facilitated by the existence or appointment of a sufficiently resourced monitoring or adjudication body and/or a specialist industry regulator. For example, in the *Macquarie UK Broadcast Ventures/National Grid Wireless Group* merger inquiry, an independent adjudicator was appointed to resolve disputes arising in relation to the commitments that formed the package of behavioural remedies in this case. The adjudicator is paid for by the parties but is accountable to the OFT and under the guidance of Ofcom. In reaching its decision in this case, the CC had regard to the fact that Ofcom already had regulatory responsibilities for the relevant market.

51 Measures to control outcomes have been considered but rejected in a number of market investigations to report to date, including, for example, *ROSCOs* and *Store Cards*.

52 For example, in the *Classified Directories* market investigation, consideration was given to how new local and re-scoped directories should be taken into account in order to avoid circumvention of the price control. The final remedies package included a provision within the price cap which set maximum prices that Yell could charge in new directories created as a result of re-scoping.

53 For example, in the *Classified Directories* market investigation it was noted that although a basket may be preferable for regulated monopolies, its use on an incumbent facing emerging competition may not be beneficial. In this instance it was considered that the greater flexibility that a basket mechanism would give to Yell would enable it to target price-sensitive customers of its competitors and so undermine emerging competition. It would also enable it to target less price-sensitive Yell customers with price increases. Finally, it was also noted that a basket control introduced greater complexity, making it more difficult for customers and the OFT to monitor compliance.

54 For example, in the *Home Credit* market investigation, the CC increased the value of the rebates paid to customers when they settled a loan early.

55 For example, variation to the original FirstBus/SBH Undertakings was made to allow revenue to rise by a hybrid index calculated using costs from the Confederation of Passenger Transport UK (CPT) Scotland index, rather than the original 1997 fare cap which was based on increases to RPI. This was because there was concern that the previous method was distorting competition by restricting fare increases below increases in bus industry costs.

56 For example, in *Groceries*, a recommendation was made to BIS that if the CC did not receive satisfactory undertakings from the parties in relation to the establishment of an Ombudsman then BIS should take action to establish the Ombudsman.

MARKET STUDIES AND MARKET INVESTIGATIONS: SUPPLEMENTAL GUIDANCE ON THE CMA'S APPROACH (CMA3, REVISED JULY 2017)

[3.649]

NOTES

PREFACE

[3.650]

The Enterprise and Regulatory Reform Act 2013 (ERRA13) established the Competition and Markets

Authority (CMA) as the UK's economy-wide competition authority responsible for ensuring that competition and markets work well for consumers. On 1 April 2014, the functions of the Competition Commission (CC) and many of the functions of the Office of Fair Trading (OFT) were transferred to the CMA and those bodies abolished. The CMA's primary duty is to promote competition, both within and outside the UK, for the benefit of consumers.

The ERRA13 also made a number of changes to the markets regime by amending the Enterprise Act 2002 (EA02).[1]

This guidance is being issued in order to explain the changes introduced to the markets regime by the ERRA13. It supplements the existing guidance on the markets regime[2] and should be read in conjunction with that guidance. Where sections of the three existing main markets guidance documents are significantly amended or superseded by the changes that are outlined in this guidance, these are listed in Annexe A to this guidance. Annexe B indicates which existing markets-related guidance documents have been adopted by the CMA Board. To the extent that any conflict arises between the content of such existing guidance and this guidance, the content of this guidance will prevail.

This guidance sets out the CMA's practice (and intended future practice) as from 1 April 2014. The new powers and procedures set out in it will apply to all cases, subject to the transitional arrangements provided for by the Secretary of State for market studies and market investigations that are ongoing as at 1 April 2014.[3]

This guidance reflects the views of the CMA as at 1 April 2014 and may be revised from time to time to reflect changes in best practice, legislation and the results of experience, legal judgments and research. This guidance may in due course be supplemented, revised or replaced. The CMA's webpages will always display the latest version of the guidance.

Although it covers most of the points likely to be of immediate concern to businesses and their advisers, this guidance makes no claim to be comprehensive. It cannot, therefore, be seen as a substitute for the EA02 and the ERRA13 and the regulations and orders made under these Acts, nor can it be cited as a definitive interpretation of the law. Anyone in any doubt about whether they may be affected by the legislation should consider seeking legal advice.

The CMA will apply this guidance flexibly. This means that the CMA will have regard to the guidance when handling market studies and market investigations under the EA02, but that, when the facts of a case reasonably justify it, the CMA may adopt a different approach.

NOTES

1 References in this guidance are to the EA02 as amended by the ERRA13 unless otherwise stated.

2 There are three main existing guidance documents that relate to the markets regime: *Market studies: Market Studies: Guidance on the OFT approach* (OFT519), *Market investigation references* (OFT511), and *Guidelines for market investigations* (CC3 (revised)). Other guidance documents also contain information relevant to markets cases, including: *Super-complaints: guidance for designated consumer bodies* (OFT514) and *Chairman's Guidance on Disclosure of Information in Merger Inquiries, Market Investigations and Reviews of Undertakings and Orders accepted or made under the Enterprise Act 2002 and Fair Trading Act 1973* (CC7 (revised)). See further Annexes A and B, which explain the status of OFT and CC markets-related guidance.

3 For information on the transitional arrangements that apply to market studies and market investigations, see *Transitional Arrangements: Guidance on the CMA's approach - Part 1* (CMA14).

1. INTRODUCTION

SCOPE OF THIS GUIDANCE

[3.651]

1.1 This guidance provides an overview of the changes to the markets regime introduced by the ERRA13. It outlines:

- the legal framework that applies to market studies and market investigations, including the roles of the CMA, the Secretary of State, and sectoral regulators
- the ERRA13 provisions on the CMA's governance and decision making structure, and
- key procedural aspects of market studies and market investigations.

1.2 The main body of this guidance is structured to reflect the key stages of a market study that results in undertakings in lieu (UIL) of a market investigation or in a market investigation. Chapter 2 addresses the market study stage and the reference process; chapter 3 addresses the in-depth market investigation stage that follows a reference; and chapter 4 addresses the remedies implementation stage following a finding of an adverse effect on competition (AEC).

1.3 The CMA Board has adopted, amongst others, the three main existing markets guidance documents, namely:

- *Market studies: Guidance on the OFT approach* (OFT519)
- *Market investigation references* (OFT511), and
- *Guidelines for market investigations* (CC3 (revised)).

1.4 Where sections of these guidance documents are significantly amended or superseded by the changes that are outlined in this guidance, these are listed in Annexe A to this guidance. Annexe B explains which existing OFT or CC guidance documents containing information relevant to markets cases have been adopted by the CMA Board, and which documents have been replaced or rendered obsolete by CMA guidance or publication.

WHAT IS A MARKET STUDY?

1.5 Market studies are one of a number of tools at the CMA's disposal to address competition or consumer protection problems, alongside its enforcement and advocacy activities. They are examinations into the causes of why particular markets may not be working well, taking an overview of regulatory and other economic drivers and patterns of consumer and business behaviour.[4]

1.6 Market studies may lead to a range of outcomes, including:[5]

- a clean bill of health
- actions which improve the quality and accessibility of information to consumers
- encouraging businesses in the market to self-regulate
- making recommendations to the Government to change regulations or public policy
- taking competition or consumer enforcement action, and
- making a market investigation reference, or accepting a UIL.

1.7 Market studies are conducted under the CMA's general review function in section 5 of the EA02.[6] The ERRA13 introduced a formal requirement for a market study to be commenced by the issuing of a market study notice when the CMA exercises its function under section 5 for certain specified purposes.[7] This guidance explains the process for issue of a market study notice and the consequences that follow from it. These include statutory time limits and formal investigatory powers for the CMA. Further information on the management of market studies is contained in chapter 4 of *Market Studies: Guidance on the OFT approach* (OFT519).

OTHER WORK CARRIED OUT UNDER SECTION 5 OF THE EA02

1.8 The CMA may carry out a range of other work under its general review function in section 5 of the EA02. Such work enables the CMA to assess markets and it may, but need not be a pre-cursor to a market study. The form such work may take will vary from desktop research only through to engagement with market participants and other interested persons. This may include seeking views of stakeholders in advance of the launch of a market study on such matters as the potential issues identified and scope of a possible market study. These types of work enable the CMA to decide whether further consideration of an issue or market is or is not appropriate and so facilitates the efficient and effective use of the resources of the CMA and other persons. For example, where the CMA decides to undertake a market study in relation to a matter that it has previously considered under its general review functions in section 5 of the EA02, this may enable it to reduce the time taken to complete the market study or to focus the scope of the market study.

1.9 Unless the CMA has issued a market study notice, when conducting work under its general review function in section 5 of the EA02, it is not bound by statutory time limits nor does it have any of the compulsory information gathering powers set out in section 2 of this guidance.

1.10 If the CMA engages with stakeholders as part of these types of work, for example, by seeking their views and requesting information (sometimes referred to as 'Calls for Information') the CMA will also inform them of the scope and purpose of the work on which it engages with them. It will also provide them with an indicative timetable of next steps in the work (although there is no associated statutory time period). If part of pre launch work in advance of a possible market study, the timetable will cover the period up to the decision being taken on whether to launch a market study.

WHAT IS A MARKET INVESTIGATION?

1.11 Market investigations are more detailed examinations into whether there is an AEC in the market(s) for the goods or services referred. If so, the CMA must decide what remedial action, if any, is appropriate. Section 131 of the EA02 sets out the power of the CMA to make references (see paragraphs 1.21 to 1.22 on the identity of the decision makers).

1.12 When the findings of a market study give rise to reasonable grounds for suspecting that a feature or combination of features[8] of a market or markets in the UK prevents, restricts or distorts competition, and a market investigation reference appears to be an appropriate and proportionate response, the CMA is able to make such a reference. However, a market study is not a prerequisite to a reference: references may be made of matters which have not been the subject of a market study,[9] provided the statutory reference thresholds are satisfied and the CMA has consulted in accordance with section 169 of the EA02.[10]

TYPES OF MARKET INVESTIGATION REFERENCE

1.13 The following types of market investigation reference may be made by the CMA:

- **ordinary references** (these are references which are not cross-market references and do not raise public interest issues),[11] and
- **cross-market references** (this is a new type of reference in respect of specific features or combinations of features that exist in more than one market).[12]

1.14 The following types of market investigation reference may be made by the Secretary of State in cases that raise defined public interest issues:

- **restricted public interest references** (these are references that require the CMA to investigate competition issues, while the Secretary of State investigates defined public interest issues in relation to the matter referred),[13] and
- **full public interest references** (this is a new type of reference requiring the CMA to investigate defined public interest issues alongside competition issues in relation to the matter referred).[14]

WHO DOES WHAT

1.15 The ERRA13 assigns distinct roles to the CMA, the Secretary of State and the sectoral regulators in relation to the markets regime. These roles are summarised in the following paragraphs.

The CMA

1.16 The CMA replaced the OFT and the CC on 1 April 2014 as part of the reforms to the UK competition regime introduced by the ERRA13. The CMA is responsible for conducting both market studies and market investigations.

1.17 The ERRA13 makes provision for the governance and decision making structure to take account of the formation of the CMA. These are described further below.

Sectoral regulators

1.18 Under Part 4 of the EA02, the CMA and the Sector Regulators may, in the respective sectors for which they have responsibility, undertake market studies, and make market investigation references to the Chair of the CMA for the constitution of a CMA group to conduct an in-depth market investigation into single or multiple markets for goods or services in the UK.[15]

1.19 As at the date of publication the regulators are the Civil Aviation Authority (CAA), the Financial Conduct Authority (FCA), NHS Improvement (NHSI),[16] Northern Ireland Authority for Utility Regulation (NIAUR), the Office of Communications (Ofcom), the Office of Rail and Road (ORR), the Gas and Electricity Markets Authority (Ofgem), the Water Services Regulation Authority (Ofwat), and the Payment Systems Regulator (PSR)

The Secretary of State

1.20 The Secretary of State has the power to intervene in certain markets cases which raise defined public interest issues (see chapters 2 and 3). The Secretary of State is also able to modify by order certain provisions of the EA02, for example, the time limits that apply to market studies, market investigations and the remedies implementation period.

1.21 Ministers also have a reserve power to make ordinary and cross-market references under section 132 of the EA02.[17] In addition to applying the same criteria set out in the EA02 for the making of a reference, a minister must either be 'not satisfied' with a CMA decision not to make a reference or, having brought information to the attention of the CMA, that the CMA will decide whether to make a reference in such period that the minister considers is reasonable.

DECISION-MAKING BY THE CMA IN MARKETS CASES

1.22 The ERRA13 makes provision for the governance and decision making structure of the CMA to take account of the fact that the CMA is responsible for the conduct of both market studies and market investigations. These processes are outlined below. They ensure that key decisions in market studies and subsequent market investigations are made by separate groups within the CMA.

1.23 At operational (staff) level, in order to avoid unnecessary duplication and to facilitate an efficient end-to-end markets process, the CMA would normally expect to have a degree of case team continuity by retaining at least some of the market study case team to work on the larger market investigation case team when a matter is referred.[18]

Market studies and market investigation references

1.24 The CMA Board is responsible for key decisions relating to market studies and the making of market investigation references. These decisions cannot be delegated. They include decisions as to:[19]

- whether the duty to publish a market study notice applies[20]
- whether to propose to make, or to make, a market investigation reference
- the CMA's obligation to consult relevant persons in specified circumstances on such a proposal,[21] and
- whether to accept an UIL instead of making a reference, or whether to vary, supersede or release an UIL that has been given.

1.25 If the CMA Board decides that a market investigation reference is to be made, it refers the matter to the CMA Chair, who is responsible under the ERRA13 for constituting the market reference group that will undertake the market investigation. In practice, the CMA Chair will delegate these responsibilities to the CMA Panel Chair (or one of the Deputy Panel Chairs).[22] The CMA Panel Chair must ensure that any Board member who might reasonably be expected to be a member of the market reference group does not participate in the Board's consideration of whether to refer the matter.[23]

Market investigations

1.26 The market reference group appointed by the CMA Panel Chair is responsible for the conduct of a market investigation. The group must consist of at least three members selected from the CMA panel.[24]

1.27 The market reference group is required to decide whether there is an AEC in the market(s) referred and, if so, whether and what remedial action is appropriate.[25] In order to make a valid finding of an AEC that can be subject to remedial action, a decision must be taken by at least a two-thirds majority of the market reference group.[26] The group oversees the implementation of remedies up to the point at which the reference is finally determined.[27]

1.28 The CMA Board is required to make rules of procedure for market reference groups (the Rules). Subject to these Rules, groups can decide their own procedures.[28] The CMA Board may also issue guidance on market investigation procedures, to which market reference groups must have all due regard when conducting market investigations.[29]

NOTES

4 For a more detailed explanation of the purpose of market studies, see chapter 2 of *Market Studies: Guidance on the OFT approach* (OFT519).

5 This guidance focuses on the changes to the markets regime introduced by the ERRA13 and therefore does not cover all the various possible outcomes of a market study. For information on the possible outcomes of a market study see chapter 5 in *Market Studies: Guidance on the OFT approach* (OFT519).

6 See chapter 3 of *Market Studies: Guidance on the OFT approach* (OFT519) for an explanation of how market studies are chosen.

7 See paragraph 2.6.

8 Section 131(2) of the EA02 sets out what is to be construed as a feature for the purposes of Part 4 of the EA02.

9 For example, following a super-complaint under section 11 of the EA02, the CMA may make a market investigation reference. For further information on super-complaints, see *Super-complaints: guidance for designated consumer bodies* (OFT514).

10 For further information on the consultation process, see paragraphs 3.6–3.10 in *Market investigation references* (OFT511).

11 This is a form of reference that existed under the EA02 prior to 1 April 2014.

12 Cross-market references are considered further in paragraphs 2.31–2.37 and 3.20–3.23.

13 This is a form of public interest reference that existed under the EA02 prior to 1 April 2014.

14 Public interest references may be made on an ordinary or cross-market basis. Public interest cases are considered further in paragraphs 2.18–2.30 and 3.8–3.19.

15 Further information on the concurrency regime is contained in *Regulated Industries: Guidance on concurrent application of competition law to regulated industries* (CMA10).

16 NHS Improvement is the operational name for the organisation that brings together Monitor, NHS Trust Development Authority, Patient Safety, the National Reporting and Learning System, the Advancing Change Team and the Intensive Support Teams.

17 Under Part 5 Section 63 of the Scotland Act 2016, the Scottish Ministers now also have the power to make such references acting jointly with the Secretary of State, or the Secretary of State and one or more than one other Minister of the Crown.

18 In the case of a market investigation referred to the CMA by a regulator, some of the market study case team may be seconded to the CMA to be part of the relevant market investigation case team.

19 Paragraph 29 of Schedule 4 to the ERRA13.

20 The CMA must publish a market study notice when it proposes to carry out its functions under section 5 of the EA02 for certain specified purposes. This is explained further in paragraph 2.6.

21 For further information see paragraphs 29(2)(c) and (f) of Schedule 4 to the ERRA13.

22 The CMA Panel Chair is a member of the CMA Board.

23 Paragraph 33 of Schedule 4 to the ERRA13.

24 Paragraph 38 of Schedule 4 to the ERRA13. The CMA panel is a panel of persons available for selection as members of a group in accordance with Part 3 of Schedule 4 to the ERRA13.

25 The statutory questions that the group must decide on an ordinary reference (as defined in section 131(6)(b) of the EA02) are explained at paragraphs 28 and 325 of *Guidelines for market investigations* (CC3 (revised)). See paragraphs 3.10, 3.12 and 3.21 in relation to the questions that the group must decide on restricted public interest references, full public interest references and cross-market references respectively.

26 Paragraphs 55–58 of Schedule 4 to the ERRA13.

27 See paragraph 91 of *Guidelines for market investigations* (CC3 (revised)) which explains the process for any further remedies implementation that may be required once the group has been disbanded. Section 183 of the EA02 explains when a reference is 'finally determined'. For example, depending upon the circumstances, it may be when the final report is published or, if remedial action is to be taken, when the remedies are implemented (that is, either by the making of an order or acceptance of final undertakings).

28 Paragraph 51 of Schedule 4 to the ERRA13.

29 Paragraph 52 of Schedule 4 to the ERRA13.

2. MARKET STUDIES

[3.652]

2.1 Market studies are examinations into the causes of why particular markets may not be working well, taking an overview of regulatory and other economic drivers and patterns of consumer and business behaviour. Guidance on the conduct of market studies is contained in *Market studies: Guidance on the OFT approach* (OFT519). OFT519 remains applicable after 1 April 2014, subject to the changes set out in the ERRA13 that are explained in this guidance. Annexe A to this guidance lists the parts of OFT519 that are significantly amended, or superseded, by those changes.

2.2 This chapter explains the changes to the market study process.[30] These are, in summary:

- changes to the requirements for commencing a market study
- the introduction of a statutory time limit within which market studies must be completed, and
- changes to the powers of investigation available to the CMA in relation to market studies, and to the sanctions for non-compliance.

2.3 As explained in chapter 1, one possible outcome of a market study is a market investigation reference. Guidance on the market investigation reference process is contained in *Market investigation references* (OFT511). OFT511 remains applicable after 1 April 2014, subject to the changes set out in the

ERRA13 that are explained in this guidance. Annexe A to this guidance lists the parts of OFT511 that are significantly amended, or superseded, by those changes.

2.4 Accordingly, this chapter also explains the changes to the market investigation reference process.[31] These are, in summary:

- changes to the way in which cases raising public interest issues are handled, and
- the introduction of a new power to make cross-market references.

2.5 Each of these changes to market studies and market investigation references is explained below.

MARKET STUDY NOTICES

2.6 A market study formally begins with publication of a market study notice by the CMA.[32] A market study notice must be published where the CMA is proposing to carry out its functions under section 5 of the EA02 for the following purposes:

- to consider the extent to which a matter in relation to the acquisition or supply of goods or services of one or more than one description in the UK has or may have effects adverse to the interests of consumers, and
- to assess the extent to which steps can and should be taken to remedy, mitigate or prevent any such adverse effects.[33]

2.7 The CMA Board is responsible for deciding whether the duty to publish a market study notice applies in a particular case. It is therefore the CMA Board that will decide whether to launch a market study in a particular case.

2.8 A market study notice must contain the following information:

- the scope of the market study
- the period during which representations may be made to the CMA in relation to the study, and
- the timescales within which the study will be completed.[34]

Time limits for proposals and market study report

2.9 Publication of a market study notice triggers the following statutory time limits:[35]

- where the CMA proposes to make a market investigation reference in relation to the subject matter of a market study, it must publish notice of its proposed decision and begin the process of consulting relevant persons within six months of publication of the market study notice[36]
- where the CMA does not propose to make a market investigation reference, but has received (non-frivolous) representations in response to a market study notice arguing that a reference should be made, it must, within six months of publication of the market study notice, publish notice of its proposed decision and begin the process of consulting relevant persons[37]
- where the CMA does not propose to make a market investigation reference and no representations have been made in response to a market study notice arguing that a reference should be made, it must publish notice of its decision not to make a reference within six months of publication of the market study notice[38]
- the CMA must within 12 months of publication of a market study notice publish a market study report setting out its findings and the action (if any) it proposes to take.[39] When the CMA's decision is to make a reference, not to make a reference (when non frivolous representation have been received to the effect a reference should be made) or to accept undertakings in lieu of a reference, the market study report must in particular contain the decision, the reasons for the decision and such information the CMA considers appropriate for facilitating a proper understanding of its reasons for the decision,[40] and
- where a market study report sets out a decision to make a market investigation reference, the reference must be made at the same time as the report is published.[41]

2.10 The statutory upper time limits[42] that apply to the market study process leading to a market investigation reference are set out below in simplified diagrammatic form.[43]

Investigatory powers for market studies

2.11 Publication of a market study notice triggers the CMA's ability to exercise statutory investigatory powers to assist it in carrying out its functions under section 5 of the EA02.[44] The powers are:

- to give notice requiring any person to attend a specified place to give evidence to the CMA or a person nominated for the purpose
- to give notice requiring any person to produce specified documents or categories of documents that are in that person's custody or under his control, and
- to give notice requiring any person carrying on business to supply specified forecasts, estimates, returns or other information in a specified form and manner.[45]

2.12 The CMA has the same investigatory powers available to assist it in monitoring and enforcing compliance with any UIL that it has accepted instead of making a reference.[46] These powers are also available during the market investigation and remedies implementation stages (see chapters 3 and 4).[47]

2.13 Where the CMA considers that a person has, without reasonable excuse, failed to comply with any requirement of a notice issued by the CMA using its statutory investigatory powers or intentionally obstructed or delayed another person in the exercise of its powers under section 174(7) of the EA02, the CMA has the power to impose an administrative penalty (non-compliance includes failures to attend interviews or meetings with the CMA, failure to provide evidence, and failure to produce documents required by the CMA).[48]

2.14 It is a criminal offence for a person intentionally to alter, suppress or destroy any document which the person has been required by notice to produce.[49] Where an act is capable of constituting both (a) a failure warranting an administrative penalty and (b) a criminal offence, the CMA cannot impose a financial penalty if the CMA has brought criminal proceedings against the person. Similarly, criminal proceedings cannot be brought against the person if an administrative penalty has been imposed in respect of the same act.[50]

2.15 Administrative penalties may be imposed in the form of a fixed amount, by reference to a daily rate, or using a combination of the two. Maximum penalty amounts are set by order and are, as at 1 April 2014, £30,000 (in the case of a fixed amount) and £15,000 (in the case of a daily penalty).[51] Persons committing a criminal offence are liable, on summary conviction, to a fine not exceeding the statutory maximum, and on conviction on indictment, to imprisonment for a term not exceeding two years or to a fine, or to both.[52]

2.16 The CMA aims to be fair and reasonable in its requests for information and the deadlines it sets for parties to respond to such requests. The CMA will use its statutory investigatory powers where necessary to ensure that information requests are answered completely and in a timely manner. It will adopt a flexible approach – the form of engagement with parties may differ depending on the individual circumstances (for example, the extent of informal co-operation achieved or the nature of the information requested) may affect the CMA's decision whether to proceed initially on an informal basis or formally.

MARKET INVESTIGATION REFERENCES

2.17 The ERRA13 makes changes to the reference process in certain cases, by:

- amending the process for intervention by the Secretary of State in cases raising public interest issues, and
- introducing a new power to make cross-market references.

The remainder of the chapter explains these changes.

Cases raising public interest considerations

2.18 The Secretary of State may intervene in markets cases that raise one or more specified public interest considerations but is expected to do so rarely. In these cases, where the CMA decides that a reference (ordinary or cross-market) should be made on competition grounds, the Secretary of State shall decide whether one or more than one specified public interest consideration is relevant to the case and, if so, the type of public interest reference that should be made.[53]

2.19 There are two types of public interest reference, both of which are initiated by the Secretary of State giving a public interest intervention notice to the CMA before a reference is made:

- a **full public interest reference**, where the Secretary of State requests the CMA to investigate the defined public interest issues alongside the competition issues, and
- a **restricted public interest reference**, where the Secretary of State retains the ability to consider the defined public interest issues him/herself whilst requesting the CMA to investigate the competition issues.[54]

2.20 The ability of the Secretary of State to make full public interest references gives the Government the option of drawing on the CMA's investigative expertise to look across markets cases at issues that relate to competition and go wider, rather than having to create independent inquiry bodies.

2.21 The interests of national security is currently the only specified public interest consideration in relation to the markets regime. The Secretary of State may by order introduce new public interest considerations.[55]

Issuing intervention notices

2.22 The Secretary of State may give an intervention notice to the CMA if he/she believes that it is or may be the case that one or more than one specified public interest consideration is relevant to the matter being investigated by the CMA.[56] The CMA has a corresponding duty to bring to the attention of the Secretary of State any case that it believes raises a specified public interest consideration.[57]

2.23 The intervention notice must be issued:

- when a market study notice has been published, within the period commencing on the publication by the CMA of a market study notice[58] and ending once a reference has been made, UIL accepted, the CMA's decision not to make a reference has been published or on the expiry of the time limit for publishing a market study report if the CMA has not published such a report,[59]
- if no market study notice has been published, within the period commencing with the CMA's consultation under section 169(6)(a)(i) of the EA02 on whether to make a market investigation reference and ending once a reference has been made, UIL accepted or where the CMA's decision not to make a reference has been published.[60]

Intervention notices cannot be issued after these periods.

2.24 Intervention notices must contain certain prescribed information:

- if a market study notice has been published, this includes:[61]
  - the subject matter of the market study notice
  - the date of publication of the market study notice, and
  - the public interest consideration(s) that are, or may be, relevant to the case,
- if a market study notice has not been published, this includes:[62]
  - the subject matter of the consultation under section 169 of the EA02
  - the date on which the process of consultation began, and
  - the public interest consideration(s) that are, or may be, relevant to the case.

2.25 Intervention notices must be published by the Secretary of State.[63]

2.26 Where an intervention notice is in force and the CMA proposes to make a market investigation reference, the CMA cannot itself make the reference or publish its market study report.[64] In such cases, the CMA is instead required to provide its market study report to the Secretary of State within 12 months from the date of publication of the market study notice. In a case where no market study notice has been issued the CMA must instead provide to the Secretary of State a document containing the CMA's decision and the reasons for its decision and such information as the CMA considers appropriate for facilitating a proper understanding of the reasons for its decision.[65] In such cases, the 12-month time limit does not apply.

2.27 The Secretary of State decides whether the public interest consideration stated in the intervention notice is relevant to the matter and, if so, whether to make a restricted public interest reference or a full public interest reference.[66] If the Secretary of State decides to make a full public interest reference, he/she must also decide whether to appoint one or more persons with relevant expertise in relation to the public interest issue in question (public interest expert(s)) to advise the CMA during the market investigation stage.[67]

2.28 If the Secretary of State decides that the public interest consideration stated in the intervention notice is not relevant to the matter, he/she will make a market investigation reference which will follow the normal procedure. In this case the CMA will conduct its investigation into the competition issues with no further involvement of the Secretary of State.[68]

2.29 The reference made by the Secretary of State must be published, together with the market study report of the CMA or in a case where no market study notice has been issued, the document which contains the CMA's reasons for its decision.[69]

2.30 The procedures that apply to the CMA's conduct of cases during the market investigation stage following a restricted or full public interest reference are outlined in chapter 3.

Cross-market references

2.31 The ERRA13 gives the CMA the power to make a cross-market reference: that is, to refer a specific feature (or combination of features) existing in more than one market without also having to refer the whole of each market concerned.[70]

2.32 In order to make a cross-market reference the CMA must have reasonable grounds for suspecting that a feature, or combination of features, of more than one market in the UK prevents, restricts or distorts competition in connection with the supply or acquisition of goods or services in the UK or a part of the UK.[71] Only features that relate to conduct can be the subject of a cross-market reference.[72]

2.33 A cross-market reference must specify:

- the enactment under which it is made
- the date on which it is made, and
- the feature or features concerned and the descriptions of goods or services to which it or they relate.[73]

2.34 The same procedural provisions apply to market studies which result in cross-market references as they do to market studies which result in ordinary references. These provisions include: the requirement to publish a market study notice, statutory time-limits, decision-making structure, and the CMA's investigatory and enforcement powers. Public interest interventions may also be made in relation both to cross-market references and to ordinary references.

2.35 Where the CMA accepts an UIL in a case instead of making a cross-market reference, no ordinary or cross-market reference can be made for a period of 12 months that relates to or includes the same feature(s) in relation to the same market(s) as those covered by the UIL.[74]

2.36 The types of issue for which cross-market references are likely to be most useful include:

- features that do not fit neatly within one market (for example, the collective licensing of public performance and broadcasting rights in sound recordings), and
- recurring sources of consumer complaint or identified detriment which have the potential to affect competition adversely across multiple, distinct markets (for example, the sale of secondary products at particular points of sale).

2.37 The CMA will seek to ensure a targeted use of the cross-market reference power with a clear delineation of scope in each case, in order that its interventions across markets are made only where they are needed, and to avoid imposing unnecessary burdens on businesses involved while wishing to ensure that the ability to take effective and appropriate action is not restricted by the scope of the reference.

NOTES

30 For information on the transitional arrangements see *Transitional Arrangements: Guidance on the CMA's approach – Part 1* (CMA14).

31 For information on the transitional arrangements see *Transitional Arrangements: Guidance on the CMA's approach – Part 1* (CMA14).

32 Chapter 4 of *Market studies: Guidance on the OFT approach* (OFT519) explains the typical project stages of a market study.

33 Section 130A of the EA02.

34 Section 130A(3) of the EA02.

35 The procedures and time limits differ in a case where a public interest intervention notice has been issued by the Secretary of State. See paragraphs 2.18–2.30. The statutory time periods are upper time limits and may be adjusted downwards by order. If the Secretary of State proposes to make an order adjusting these periods, he/she must consult the CMA and other relevant persons before doing so.

36 Section 131B(1) of the EA02.

37 Section 131B(1) of the EA02.

38 Section 131B(2) and (3) of the EA02.

39 Section 131B(4) of the EA02.

40 Section 131B(5) of the EA02.

41 Section 131B(6) of the EA02.

42 The CMA aims to complete the market study process in a shorter period of time, if possible.

43 The procedures and time limits differ in a case where a public interest intervention notice has been issued by the Secretary of State. See paragraphs 2.18–2.30.

44 Section 174(1)(a) of the EA02.

45 Sections 174(3) to (5) of the EA02.

46 Sections 174(1)(b) and (c) of the EA02. Further information on the process for acceptance of UIL is contained in chapter 2 of OFT511.

47 Sections 174(1)(b) and (c) of the EA02.

48 Section 174A(1) to (3) of the EA02.

49 Section 174A(4) of the EA02.

50 Sections 174A(4) and (5) of the EA02.

51 See The Competition and Markets Authority (Penalties) Order 2014 and *Administrative Penalties: Statement of policy on the CMA's approach* (CMA4).

52 Section 174A(6) of the EA02.

53 See section 139 of the EA02.

54 Under the provisions of the EA02 that applied prior to 1 April 2014 the Secretary of State only had the ability to investigate public interest issues him/herself, under what is now termed the restricted public interest reference procedure. The ERRA13 introduced the full public interest reference procedure.

55 Section 153 of the EA02.

56 Section 139(1) of the EA02.

57 Section 152(1) of the EA02.

58 Section 139(1A) of the EA02.

59 Section 139(1A) of the EA02. For time limits for the making of decisions about references see section 131B of the EA02.

60 Section 139(1B) of the EA02.

61 Section 140(1) of the EA02. When a market study notice has not been published, the Secretary of State is nevertheless under a duty to consult on his decision after making an intervention notice. In such a case, the intervention notice must specify the subject matter of the consultation; the date on which the consultation process began and the public interest consideration(s) that are, or may be, relevant to the case.

62 Section 140(1) of the EA02.

63 Section 172(3)(c) of the EA02.

64 Section 140A(3) of the EA02. Where an intervention notice has been issued but the CMA proposes not to make a market investigation reference, the intervention notice ceases to be in force when the matter is finally determined as defined in section 140(5) of the EA02. This is when the CMA either accepts UIL, publishes notice that it has otherwise decided not to make a market investigation reference or the period for making the market study report has expired and the CMA has not prepared a report or taken action (see section 140 of the EA02).

65 Section 140A(3) of the EA02.

66 Under section 140B the Secretary of State can (having consulted with the CMA if applicable) vary a restricted public interest reference or a full public interest reference.

67 Sections 140A(4) to (12) of the EA02.

68 Section 140A(5) of the EA02.

69 Sections 140A(10), 140A(11) and 172(3)(da) of the EA02.

70 Sections 131(2A) and (6) of the EA02.

71 Section 131 of the EA02.

72 Sections 131(1) and 131(2A) of the EA02.

73 Section 133(1) of the EA02.

74 Section 156 of the EA02. The prohibition on reference does not apply where there has been a breach of an UIL, or where false or misleading information has been supplied by the person giving the UIL.

3. MARKET INVESTIGATIONS

[3.653]

3.1 Market investigations are detailed examinations into whether there is an AEC in the market(s) referred and, if so, what remedial action may be appropriate.

3.2 As explained in chapters 1 and 2, a market investigation is one possible outcome of a market study. It is commenced by the making of a market investigation reference. The CMA may make a reference where it has reasonable grounds for suspecting that any feature, or combination of features, of a market or markets in the UK for goods or services prevents, restricts or distorts competition in connection with the supply or acquisition of any goods or services in the UK or a part of the UK.[75]

3.3 When a competition problem is identified, a wide range of legally enforceable remedies are available, aimed at making the market(s) more competitive in the future. Guidance on the substantive aspects of market investigations and possible outcomes is contained in *Guidelines for market investigations* (CC3 (revised)). CC3 (revised) remains applicable after 1 April 2014, subject to the changes set out in this guidance. Annexe A to this guidance lists the parts of CC3 (revised) that are significantly amended, or superseded, by those changes.

3.4 This chapter explains the changes to the market investigation stage following reference.[76] These are, in summary:

- changes to the statutory time limits within which market investigations must be completed
- changes to the way in which cases raising public interest issues are handled
- the introduction of a new power to conduct investigations following a cross-market reference, and
- changes to market investigation procedures.

Each of these changes is explained below.

TIME LIMITS AND PROCEDURE

3.5 The CMA publishes an administrative timetable setting out the key stages in the market investigation process. There is also a statutory time limit on completion of this process. A market investigation must be completed and the report published within 18 months of the date of reference.[77]

3.6 The CMA may extend this period by up to a further six months if it considers that there are special reasons why the investigation cannot be completed and the report published within 18 months.[78] Only one extension is possible. A decision to extend the timetable must be published.[79]

3.7 The power to extend the timetable is most likely to be used in complex cases (for example, where there are multiple parties, issues and/or markets), in order to ensure a thorough and fair consideration of the issues raised and proper engagement with parties. It should generally be clear by the time of the provisional findings (contained in the Provisional Decision Report) how likely it is that an extension will be needed. The CMA is required also to publish the reasons for any such extension (section 172(5) of the EA02).[80]

CASES RAISING PUBLIC INTEREST CONSIDERATIONS

3.8 As outlined in chapter 2, if the Secretary of State decides that one or more specified public interest consideration(s) is relevant to a matter, he/she may decide to make a restricted public interest reference or a full public interest reference. A restricted public interest reference follows a similar procedure to the public interest reference procedure before ERRA13. Under a full public interest reference the CMA is required to consider the public interest issues alongside the competition issues.[81] The questions the CMA must answer are explained below.

3.9 A market investigation on a public interest reference follows the same main procedural steps as a market investigation that addresses competition issues only.[82] There are however certain differences in relation to the questions that must be decided by the CMA following a public interest reference, and the subsequent reporting and remedies implementation processes that must be followed. These differences are outlined below.

Questions to be decided on a restricted public interest reference

3.10 Following a restricted public interest reference, the CMA is required to decide:

- whether any feature, or combination of features, of each relevant market prevents, restricts or distorts competition in connection with the supply or acquisition of any goods or services in the United Kingdom or a part of the United Kingdom[83] and
- if the CMA finds that there is an AEC, the CMA must decide on two sets of questions concerning the taking of remedial action. First, the CMA must decide what action (if any) should be taken by the Secretary of State, or it should recommend others take for the purpose of remedying the AEC or any detrimental effect on customers resulting from the AEC.[84] Secondly, the CMA must decide what action (if any) should be taken by it, or it should recommend others to take for the same purpose.[85]

3.11 When answering both sets of remedial questions, the CMA, must have regard to the need to achieve as comprehensive a solution as is reasonable and practicable to the AEC concerned and any detrimental effects on customers resulting from the AEC.[86] Similarly the CMA will have regard to the effect of any action on any relevant customer benefits.[87]

Questions to be decided on a full public interest reference

3.12 Following a full public interest reference, the CMA is required to decide:

- whether any feature, or combination of features, of each relevant market prevents, restricts or distorts competition in connection with the supply or acquisition of any goods or services in the UK or a part of the UK[88]
- if there is an AEC, whether, taking into account only any AEC and the admissible public interest consideration(s),[89] any feature or combination of features which gave rise to an AEC operate(s) or may be expected to operate against the public interest,[90] and
- if the CMA finds that there is an adverse effect on the public interest, it must decide on what (if any) action should be taken by the Secretary of State, or it should recommend others take for the purpose of remedying the adverse effect on the public interest,[91] or
- if the CMA does not find any adverse effect on public interest but finds an AEC, it must decide what (if any) action should be taken by it or it should recommend others take for the purposes of remedying the AEC or any resulting detrimental effects on customers.[92]

3.13 When answering the remedial questions the CMA must have regard to the need to achieve as comprehensive a solution as is reasonable and practicable to the public interest consideration or the AEC (as appropriate) and any resulting detrimental effects on customers.[93] Similarly the CMA will have regard to the effect of any action on any relevant customer benefits.[94]

3.14 If the Secretary of State has appointed a public interest expert the CMA must, when deciding whether there is an adverse effect on the public interest and if so, what action should be taken to remedy it, have regard, in particular, to the views of the expert.[95]

Reporting procedure following a public interest reference

3.15 Following its investigation, the CMA prepares a market investigation report containing its conclusions on both competition issues and public interest issues. If, in the case of a full public interest reference, the Secretary of State has appointed a public interest expert to assist the CMA, the CMA must include a summary of the expert's views in the report.[96]

3.16 Where the CMA decides that action should be taken by the Secretary of State, it is required to provide the report to the Secretary of State.[97] The report must be provided to the Secretary of State within the 18-month reporting period.[98]

3.17 Having received the report, the Secretary of State is required to decide:

- on a restricted public interest reference, whether any eligible public interest consideration is relevant; or any eligible public interest considerations are relevant to any remedial action mentioned in the report and which the CMA should take for the purpose of remedying, mitigating or preventing any AEC or any detrimental effect on customers, and[99]
- on a full public interest reference, whether to make an adverse public interest finding and, if so, how the adverse effects should be remedied, taking into account the recommendations included in the CMA's report on the matter.[100] The Secretary of State must accept the CMA's findings and remedies in relation to competition issues.[101]

3.18 The Secretary of State's decision must be made and published within 90 days of receipt of the CMA's market investigation report.[102]

3.19 If the CMA reaches any decision on the reference which does not require action to be taken by the Secretary of State, it publishes the market investigation report itself.[103] In those circumstances, the remedies implementation process (if necessary) follows the normal procedure with no further involvement of the Secretary of State.

CROSS-MARKET REFERENCES

3.20 As explained in chapter 2, the CMA has the power to refer a specific feature (or combination of features)[104] existing in more than one market without also having to refer the whole of each market concerned. This is called a cross-market reference.

3.21 The statutory questions to be decided by the CMA in a cross-market investigation differ from the questions to be decided following an ordinary reference. In a cross-market investigation, the CMA must decide:

- in relation to each feature and each combination of the features specified in the reference
- whether the feature or combination of features, as it relates to goods or services of one or more than one of the descriptions so specified, prevents, restricts or distorts competition in connection with the supply or acquisition of any goods or services in the UK or a part of the UK.[105]

3.22 If the CMA reaches an adverse finding following a cross-market reference, it must also consider remedies (see chapter 4 and Part 4 and Annex B of *Guidelines for market investigations* (CC3 (revised)).

3.23 The same procedural provisions (including statutory time limits) apply to cross-market investigations as to ordinary market investigations, and the CMA's investigatory and enforcement powers are the same in relation to both reference types.

MARKET INVESTIGATION PROCEDURES

3.24 The following paragraphs provide an overview of the procedures for a market investigation and replace the relevant paragraphs of the *Guidelines for market investigations* (CC3 (revised)) as outlined in Annex B. In practice, some aspects of the procedures used in a particular case may vary from those set out below. This is inevitable because no two market investigations are alike in all respects. The sectors under investigation can range in size from small, highly specialised industries to large-scale multi-faceted sectors.[106] Some references can encompass both upstream and downstream markets. Moreover, the numbers of parties with an interest in the investigation may vary from a few to several hundred.

Managing investigations with a large number of parties

3.25 All providers of the goods or services in a market under investigation are potentially main parties to an investigation. However, the degree of each party's engagement with the CMA may vary, particularly where there are substantial numbers of main parties. The CMA may need more information and evidence from some than from others. Some firms may choose to engage more with the CMA than others. Differences in communication by the CMA with different main parties may consequently reflect the different levels of party engagement.

3.26 In addition, there will be parties which are not providers of the goods or services in the market but which may be materially affected by the investigation (including super-complainants, customers and consumer groups, upstream suppliers, and trade and professional bodies). Levels of engagement with these parties will also vary. For example, the CMA may seek information from some of them, while others may volunteer information and views to the CMA.

3.27 The CMA makes extensive use in market investigations of its website to communicate or to make disclosures, enabling any number of parties to follow the progress of an investigation (as far as possible the CMA notifies parties when relevant material is posted). While the detail of its processes might vary, the CMA will ensure that its procedures are fair and give parties the opportunity to participate appropriately in an investigation.

Timescales

3.28 The EA02, as amended by the ERRA13, requires the CMA to publish its report on a market investigation within 18 months of the reference.[107] There is scope to extend the investigation by up to a further six months if the CMA considers there are special reasons for doing so.[108]

3.29 The timescales for the different stages of a market investigation will be decided by the Group on a case-by-case basis. The following timetable shows the stages of a typical 18-month investigation. In practice, some of the stages may overlap and developments in the investigation, for example a revision of the Provisional Decision Report and a consequent need for additional consultations, may require adjustments to the timings and procedures.

Stage of process	Timing within 18-month investigation
Reference	Pre-reference sharing of appropriate information with the CMA by the CMA market study team/the referring body

Part 3 CMA and other Guidelines

Stage of process	Timing within 18-month investigation
'First day letter'/initial information requests Publication of initial Issues Statement (setting out theories of harm and inviting views on possible remedies) Initial submissions from main and third parties	Months 1–2
Site visits and hearings	Month 3
Further interaction with parties and consultation on analysis: eg roundtables, confidentiality rings, disclosure rooms, working papers	Months 2–11
Final deadline for all parties' submissions before the Provisional Decision Report	Month 11
Publication of Provisional Decision Report on the AEC and remedies (if needed)	**Month 12**
Consideration of responses to Provisional Decision Report Response hearings with parties	Months 12–16
Final deadline for all parties' submissions before Final Report	Month 16
Publication of Final Report	**Month 18**

3.30 The CMA draws up and publishes an administrative timetable at an early stage in the investigation. A draft is sent to main parties for comment. The administrative timetable is updated as necessary during the investigation.

Information provision and disclosure

3.31 While the time taken to conclude a market investigation depends on several factors, including the complexity of the investigation and the number of parties involved, a key factor is the timely provision of information to the CMA. The CMA aims to be reasonable in its requests for information and the deadlines it sets for parties to respond to such requests. It expects parties to meet the timescales set. The CMA is empowered to require information and the attendance of witnesses and may impose financial penalties under section 174A of the EA02 for failures to comply without reasonable excuse.[109] Failure to comply includes failures to answer questions asked by the CMA, failures to produce documents required by the CMA, or failures to provide adequate or accurate information in response to any requirement imposed (including the deadline) on a person under section 174 of the EA02. The provision of false or misleading information to the CMA is a criminal offence, regardless of whether that information has been provided voluntarily or in response to a statutory notice.[110]

3.32 In pursuing its aim to conduct investigations in a fair and transparent manner, the CMA discloses its key documents, mainly by publishing them (in particular an Issues Statement, key results from its analysis, a Provisional Decision Report and Final Report). Typically, it also publishes a large amount of other documentation, for example non-confidential versions of key submissions from parties, including their submissions on the Issues Statement, the Provisional Decision Report and responses to other publications, key submissions of third parties, details of points arising in hearings, survey reports and some working papers.

3.33 Part 9 of the EA02 provides for the protection of confidential information relating to individuals and businesses.[111] But the CMA may disclose information under certain circumstances and having taken into account the considerations specified in the EA02.[112]

3.34 Where issues arise as to the confidentiality of some information in the CMA's possession that underlies a decision or a piece of analysis, but the CMA nevertheless considers that disclosure of some sort is necessary to allow a party to comment on it, the CMA may decide on some form of limited disclosure.[113]

3.35 For further details on the statutory provisions relating to the information obtained during the course of an investigation and to its disclosure, see the Chairman's guidance on disclosure (CC7 Revised) and the CMA's guidance on transparency and disclosure (CMA6).

The main stages of an investigation

3.36 The following paragraphs describe the main stages of a market investigation and outline the key interactions which the CMA has with parties and their advisers in the course of a typical investigation. However, market investigations vary significantly and the CMA may adapt its procedures to take account of the particular circumstances of an investigation.

Handover between a market study and a market investigation

3.37 Where the CMA (as opposed to one of the other referring bodies) undertakes the market study, the CMA's market study team considers the appropriate scope of the market investigation following consultation on a possible reference. It will also consider whether remedies are potentially available as part of its decision to make the market investigation reference (and sometimes also in the context of an offer of undertakings in lieu of a reference from the parties).[114]

3.38 To ensure an efficient handover, the CMA begins preparatory work on a market investigation on a contingency basis before the final decision on whether or not to make a reference is taken. This will include consideration of the further information-gathering and analysis likely to be required in the market investigation. A preparatory market investigation team of staff and members is normally established to prepare for the reference and they receive briefings on the work undertaken in the market study and the key concerns underpinning any anticipated reference.

3.39 In addition to drafting the formal terms of reference for the market investigation, the CMA Board may append an advisory steer to the reference decision setting out its expectations regarding the scope of the market investigation and the issues that could be the focus of the investigation. The Inquiry Group would be expected to take this into account. However, the Inquiry Group will continue, as required by the legislation, to make its statutory decisions independently of the CMA Board.

3.40 Where another referring body undertakes the market study, the CMA's preparatory market investigation team will seek to engage with the referring body to share information and analysis and understand the key concerns underpinning any anticipated reference.

Information-gathering

3.41 Once the market investigation reference has been made, the CMA formally launches its investigation with a 'first day letter' to key main parties. The letter includes information on the terms of the reference, the statutory deadline for the CMA's report, relevant guidance material, the key CMA staff working on the investigation, and the next steps to be taken. The first day letter also takes forward the information-gathering process by requesting specified information.

3.42 At an early stage, informal meetings are held between the staff team and selected main parties (and, where relevant, with other parties such as the super-complainant). Such meetings usually cover the procedures to be adopted for the conduct of the investigation, and seek information and views on the market. In addition, the CMA holds 'data meetings' as early as possible with appropriate main parties to discuss the organisation and availability of technical data. There may be subsequent staff meetings as the investigation progresses – see, for example, paragraph 3.53.

3.43 A detailed market and financial questionnaire is next sent to the main parties; and, in many cases, other information is collected from a wider range of parties. The information-gathering will be informed by the developing 'theories of harm'. When practicable, parties are consulted on questionnaires to facilitate efficient collection of useful and consistent information, whilst as far as possible minimising the burden to business.

3.44 The CMA may decide to conduct one or more surveys as part of the information-gathering process.[115] If the decision is taken to conduct a survey, relevant parties are consulted on the draft survey design and content. In some cases, so as to construct the sample for questioning, parties may be required to provide contact details for some or all of their customers or suppliers.

3.45 In many cases, the CMA organises early site visits to several parties. These are designed to be helpful to both the CMA and the parties involved. A site visit offers a chance for the Inquiry Group members and staff to gain a greater understanding of the party's business by visiting key facilities and meeting key operational staff. A party receiving a site visit is encouraged to organise a short presentation, and take some questions, on its business so as to explain its nature and the market context in which it is operating. In some cases, a site visit may be combined with a hearing.

Issues Statement

3.46 An Issues Statement is published by the CMA at an early stage in the investigation process. This generally discusses the theories of harm framing the analysis the CMA intends to pursue, as well as welcoming views on potential remedies. Where the CMA conducted the market study, the Issues Statement is likely to be a short document that cross refers to the market study report and (if applicable) the Board's advisory steer. Parties are invited to provide submissions commenting on the issues and possible remedies set out in the statement.

Hearings

3.47 The Inquiry Group holds a round of hearings with parties (individually or multi-party where appropriate) at an early stage in the investigation. The primary purpose of these hearings is to enable the CMA to understand the market, discuss the parties' submissions, and discuss the issues and possible remedies with the parties. They also provide an opportunity for the parties to explain their views in person directly to the decision-makers as their thinking is developing. The CMA aims to ensure that hearings are held with a range of parties. However, decisions on which main and third parties to invite to hearings, and the format and sequencing of any hearings, rest with the CMA.

3.48 Although the format of hearings varies, parties are normally given an opportunity to make brief opening and/or closing statements, and should expect to respond to the CMA's questions. A transcript of the hearing will be taken and will be sent to the relevant party for checking. Additionally, staff-led hearings (sometimes via teleconferencing) are conducted with some parties not attending hearings with the Inquiry Group, including some main parties when there are large numbers of them. Some members of the Inquiry Group may also participate. Transcripts or written notes are taken and sent to the relevant party for checking.

3.49 A summary of the key points raised at a hearing may be prepared by the CMA or a transcript may be published, as deemed appropriate by the Inquiry Group. The parties involved are given the opportunity to comment on both content and confidentiality before these are published. The party is also invited to follow up in correspondence any issue raised during the hearing.

Assessment

3.50 Using the information gathered and the theories of harm postulated, the CMA progresses the competition assessment. The issues addressed will be diverse, covering the many aspects raised by the investigation: for example, background on the market, the operation of the market or the performance of parties, market definition and assessments of the relevant competition issues set out in the Issues Statement. The CMA will also consider possible remedies at the same time as assessing the problems, and provisional decisions on both are included in the Provisional Decision Report. In practice this means the CMA will consider and discuss potential remedies alongside working on understanding what features of the market give rise to adverse effects. The consideration of possible remedies is always contingent on an AEC finding having been reached.

3.51 The staff and the Inquiry Group work together on these issues, and many internal working papers/presentations are typically prepared on the various aspects of the investigation. Generally, internal documents are not disclosed.

3.52 The Inquiry Group's provisional analysis is included in the Provisional Decision Report (see paragraph 3.59). However, the Inquiry Group will disclose key elements of its analysis before publication of the Provisional Decision Report through, for example, the use of confidentiality rings where appropriate or disclosure rooms, and/or it may disclose some of the working papers, or parts of working papers, often through publication.[116]

3.53 On occasions, specific pieces of technical analysis merit discussion between a party and the CMA on the methodology used and, possibly, the results found. The CMA arranges meetings or roundtables with one or more parties for this purpose. These are generally attended by CMA staff (together, on occasion, with members of the Inquiry Group), the party and its technical advisers.

3.54 The administrative timetable will include a deadline for the receipt of all parties' responses and submissions for consideration by the Inquiry Group in forming its provisional decision.

Put-back

3.55 The CMA may also send ('put back') text to parties for the purpose of enabling them to:

- verify the factual correctness of certain content (usually information supplied by them); and
- identify any confidential material, prior to publication; parties are asked to provide reasons for any requests for excisions of the material from published documents.

3.56 The put-back process is separate from disclosure of the CMA's developing thinking.

Provisional Decision Report

3.57 When the Inquiry Group has provisionally formed a view on whether or not there are features of the market(s) that give rise to an AEC, its provisional findings will be published in the Provisional Decision Report, and a public consultation on them will be held.

3.58 If an AEC has provisionally been found, the Provisional Decision Report will also contain the CMA's provisional decision on remedies. The Provisional Decision Report will contain details of remedies the CMA has identified as addressing the AEC effectively, and may also outline details of remedies the CMA considers unlikely to be effective and the reasons why it has reached this provisional decision.

3.59 As set out in the Rules, the time allowed for the consultation will be no less than 21 days and the CMA applies some flexibility in setting reasonable deadlines case by case in light of the relevant circumstances.

Response hearings

3.60 Once the CMA has published the Provisional Decision Report, response hearings (individually or multi-party where appropriate) will take place with main parties and potentially with key third parties. At a response hearing, parties will be given the opportunity to comment orally on the provisional decision on the AEC and remedies, and the CMA may seek clarification of particular points made in written submissions or at the hearing. Transcripts, or alternatively notes, of response hearings will be taken and, in most cases, summaries prepared and both will be processed in a similar way to those relating to hearings held earlier in the investigation (see paragraphs 3.47 to 3.49).

3.61 Having considered the responses from parties, the CMA may undertake additional consultations with parties as required. If further consultation is not needed, the CMA will proceed to publishing its final decision on the AEC and remedies in its Final Report.

3.62 Separately, a deadline will have been set in the administrative timetable for the receipt of all parties' responses and submissions for consideration by the Inquiry Group ahead of reaching its final decision.

Final Report

3.63 The CMA will publish its final decision on the competition question and (if necessary) remedies together with supporting reasons and information in a Final Report.[117] The report will, if it confirms the finding of an AEC, contain an explanation of the AEC finding and sufficient detail on the nature and scope of remedies to provide a firm basis for subsequent implementation of remedies by the CMA.

3.64 Parties may, during the two months following the notification of the Final Report, lodge an appeal with the Competition Appeal Tribunal (CAT) against the decisions. If a judgment of the CAT upholds an aspect of an appeal, this could lead to the investigation or a part of it being remitted to the CMA for reconsideration.[118] Appeals against CAT judgments can, if allowed, go forward to the Court of Appeal or, in Scotland, the Court of Session and, ultimately, to the Supreme Court.

NOTES

75 Section 131(1) of the EA02.

76 For information on the transitional arrangements see *Transitional Arrangements: Guidance on the CMA's approach – Part 1* (CMA14).

77 Section 144 of the EA02. Under the provisions of the EA02 that applied prior to 1 April 2014 the statutory time limit was 24 months. This time limit differs for full public interest references where the Secretary of State proposes to appoint a public interest expert to assist the CMA. In such cases, the 18-month period runs from the earliest of: the date of the expert's appointment, the Secretary of State giving notice that he/she does not intend to appoint an expert, or the period ending two months from the date of reference.

78 Section 137 of the EA02.

79 Section 172(2)(za) of the EA02.

80 The 18-month and additional six-month periods set out above are upper limits, and may be adjusted downwards by order. If the Secretary of State proposes to make an order adjusting those periods, he/she must consult the CMA and other relevant persons before doing so.

81 See paragraph 1.14.

82 The main stages of an investigation are explained in paragraphs 3.24–3.64 of this document.

83 Section 141(2) of the EA02.

84 Section 141(3) of the EA02.

85 Section 141(4) of the EA02.

86 Section 141(5) of the EA02.

87 Section 141(6) of the EA02.

88 Section 141A(2) of the EA02. This relates to an ordinary reference (as defined in section 131(6)(b) of the EA02). The first question that the CMA is required to decide differs slightly in relation to a cross-market reference, as explained in paragraph 3.21.

89 Defined in section 141A(11) of the EA02.

90 Section 141A(4) of the EA02.

91 Section 141A(5) of the EA02.

92 Section 141A(6) of the EA02.

93 Sections 141A(8) and 141A(9) of the EA02.

94 Section 141A(10) of the EA02.

95 Section 141A(7) of the EA02.

96 Section 142(2)(d) of the EA02.

97 Sections 143(3) and 143A(3) of the EA02. In other circumstances the CMA publishes the report.

98 Subject to the possibility of an extension of up to six months as explained in paragraph 3.6. The starting date for the 18-month period may be later in cases where the Secretary of State has proposed to appoint a public interest expert, as explained in footnote 77.

99 Section 146(2) of the EA02.

100 Sections 146A(1) and 146A(2) of the EA02.

101 Section 146A(5) of the EA02.

102 Sections 143(4), 143A(4), 146(3) and 146A(6) of the EA02. The Secretary of State must also publish the CMA's market investigation report (given to the Secretary of State under section 143(3) or section 143A(3) of the EA02 no later than publication of the Secretary of State's decision under sections 146(2) or 146A(2) of the EA02 in relation to the case).

103 Sections 143(1) or 143A(2) of the EA02.

104 Only features that relate to conduct can be the subject of a cross-market reference. See paragraph 2.32.

105 Section 134(1A) of the EA02.

106 An upstream firm provides raw materials or manufactures inputs for processing and/or distribution by a downstream firm.

107 Section 137(1) of the Act.

108 Section 137(2A) of the Act. See also paragraphs 3.5–3.7.

109 See also paragraphs 2.13–2.15 where the same provisions are discussed in relation to market studies.

110 For more information on potential financial penalties for failing to comply with the CMA's powers of investigation see Administrative Penalties: Statement of policy on the CMA's approach (CMA4).

111 Part 9 of the Act, in particular section 245, provides that a person commits an offence if he or she discloses or uses specified information unless in the circumstances permitted by the Act or the information is already in the public domain in the circumstances described by section 237(3).

112 Section 244.

113 For example, to enable disclosure of some data used in its analysis, the CMA might set up a disclosure room or confidentiality ring in which the parties' external legal and economic advisers can review it. Rules relating to access, use and non-disclosure are applied and participants are required to sign undertakings that they will comply with the restrictions. See the CMA's guidance and templates for confidentiality rings and disclosure rooms.

114 See OFT511, paragraphs 2.20–2.26 and 2.30–2.31.

115 The survey results will usually be disclosed through publication (accompanied by an explanation of the methodology) but there may be instances when it is inappropriate to publish the whole report. The Inquiry Group will consider whether other information relating to the survey should be disclosed, for example cross-tabulations of the survey results.

116 See CC7 (Revised), paragraphs 7.1–7.3. Disclosed working papers provide a snapshot of the issues, analysis and views that are relevant at the time of disclosure and may change.

117 Section 136.

118 For example, following appeals against CC decisions, the CAT ordered the CC to reconsider parts of the remedies

packages in the Final Reports on Groceries (April 2008) and Payment Protection Insurance (PPI) (January 2009). These aspects were, respectively, the competition test applied to grocery retail planning applications and the inclusion of a prohibition of the issuing of PPI at the point of sale.

4. IMPLEMENTATION OF REMEDIES

[3.654]

4.1 If, following any type of market investigation, the CMA finds an AEC, it is required to consider whether remedies are appropriate. In ordinary and cross-market references it must decide the following questions:

- whether action should be taken by it for the purpose of remedying, mitigating or preventing the AEC concerned or any detrimental effect on customers so far as it has resulted from, or may be expected to result from, the AEC
- whether it should recommend the taking of action by others for the purpose of remedying, mitigating or preventing the AEC concerned or any detrimental effect on consumers so far as it has resulted from, or may be expected to result from, the AEC, and
- in either case, if action should be taken, what action should be taken and what is to be remedied, mitigated or prevented.[119]

4.2 If the CMA has decided to take action itself to remedy, mitigate or prevent an adverse effect on competition, it has the choice of accepting undertakings from the relevant parties and/or of making an order.

4.3 The period following publication of the final report during which the CMA puts in place its remedies is known as the remedies implementation stage.

4.4 This chapter explains the changes to the remedies implementation stage following a market investigation report finding an AEC.[120] These changes are, in summary:

- the introduction of statutory time limits within which remedies must be implemented by the CMA
- the introduction of mandatory investigatory powers for the CMA during the remedies implementation and subsequent monitoring periods
- changes to the powers available to the CMA to impose remedies by order, and
- clarification of the powers available to the CMA following a report to reverse pre-emptive action that has been taken.

Each of these changes is explained below.

TIME LIMITS AND PROCEDURE

4.5 The CMA publishes an administrative timetable for the implementation of those remedies where it has decided to take action itself. The ERRA13 introduced statutory time limits for the implementation of remedies by the CMA to address findings from a market investigation. The CMA must accept final undertakings or make a final order within six months of the date of publication of the market investigation report.[121] This six-month period includes a period of formal public consultation.

4.6 The CMA may extend the six-month period by up to a further four months if it considers that there are special reasons why final undertakings cannot be accepted or a final order made within the statutory deadline. Only one extension is possible.[122] A decision to extend the timetable must be published.[123]

4.7 The power to extend the timetable is most likely to be used where the remedies themselves are more complex, for example where consumer testing of the detailed implementation of remedies is necessary, where proposed remedies give rise to complex practical issues, or where an additional consultation is required to address material changes arising from comments made in earlier consultations.

4.8 During the period covered by the statutory timetable for remedies implementation, the CMA has investigatory powers.[124] In addition to the ability to impose penalties in some circumstances, the CMA has the ability to 'stop the clock' if it considers that any person has failed (whether with or without reasonable excuse) to comply with any requirement of a notice issued by the CMA using its statutory investigatory powers (for example, a notice requiring the production of specified documents).[125] In this case, the time limits set out above are extended. In effect, the timetable is suspended either until the documents or information requested is provided to the satisfaction of the CMA, or until the CMA publishes a notice to cancel the extension. The extension periods described in this paragraph and in paragraph 4.6 can be used together if necessary, in which case the extension periods are added together.[126]

4.9 The process to be followed in the event of an appeal to the CAT will depend upon the circumstances and will therefore be considered on a case-by-case basis. Subject to any directions made by the CAT the CMA will, when considering the process to be followed, consider the prevailing circumstances including the terms of any remittal. It will also have regard to the statutory time limits that applied to its inquiry to which the challenged CMA decision related.

SCOPE OF THE CMA'S ORDER-MAKING POWERS

4.10 The CMA's decision as to whether to implement remedies by means of accepting undertakings or making an order is determined on a case-by-case basis. It is informed both by the scope of the CMA's order-making powers under Schedule 8 to the EA02 and by practical issues such as the number of parties concerned and their willingness to negotiate and agree undertakings.

4.11 The CMA has additional flexibility and stronger enforcement powers under Schedule 8 in two respects:

- parties may be required to publish certain non-price information without also being required to publish price information,[127] and
- parties may be required to appoint and remunerate an independent third party to monitor and/or implement remedies and to deal with disputes.[128]

INTERIM MEASURES

4.12 After the CMA has published its final report but before the reference has been finally determined (by final undertakings being accepted or a final order made), the CMA has the power to prevent pre-emptive action that might impede the taking of final action in relation to the investigation.[129] It may do so by accepting from the parties concerned interim undertakings to take such action as the CMA thinks is appropriate or by making an interim order.[130]

4.13 The CMA can take steps to require parties to reverse any action that has already occurred before any interim measures have been put in place.[131] This will enable the CMA, once a report has been published, to prevent the effectiveness of any ultimate remedy being jeopardised through pre-emptive action by the parties.

SUNSET CLAUSES AND REVIEWS OF REMEDIES

4.14 As a single competition authority, the CMA is responsible for the entire remedies lifecycle and has sought to capitalise on potential benefits arising from institutional reform in this area. As a result, it has developed its guidance to commit more clearly to considering the use of sunset clauses and to reviewing the ongoing need for remedies, with a view to ensuring that remedies do not remain in force where they are no longer necessary to achieve the purposes for which they were imposed. The paragraphs below will replace the relevant paragraphs of the *Guidelines for market investigations* (CC3 (revised)) as outlined in Annex B.

Effectiveness

4.15 The CMA will assess the extent to which different remedy options are likely to be effective in achieving their aims, including their practicability.

4.16 The effect of any remedy is always uncertain to some degree. In evaluating the effectiveness of potential remedies, the CMA will consider the risks associated with different remedy options and will tend to favour remedies that have a higher likelihood of achieving their intended effect. Assessing the effectiveness and practicability of a remedy may involve consideration of several dimensions discussed further below.

4.17 First, a remedy should be capable of effective implementation, monitoring and enforcement. To facilitate this, the operation and implications of the remedy need to be clear to the persons to whom it is directed and also to other interested persons. Other interested persons may include customers, other businesses that may be affected by the remedy, sectoral regulators, and any other body that has responsibility for monitoring compliance. The effectiveness of any remedy may be reduced if elaborate monitoring and compliance programmes are required.[132] Remedies regulating behaviour generally have the disadvantage of requiring ongoing monitoring of compliance and may also constrain beneficial aspects of competitive rivalry.

4.18 Secondly, the timescale over which a remedy is likely to have effect will be considered. The CMA will generally look for remedies that prevent an AEC by extinguishing its causes, or that can otherwise be sustained for as long as the AEC is expected to endure. The CMA will also tend to favour remedies that can be expected to show results within a relatively short time. Some remedy options may have an almost immediate impact, while the effects of others will be delayed. In such instances the CMA may select a remedy package combining both types of measure, taking into account both when each measure would take effect and how long it would endure. Where an AEC is expected to be short-lived (for example, because a specific future event is expected to bring it to an end) and the timescale for implementation of a particular remedy option would extend significantly into this period, the CMA will consider whether an alternative measure would be more appropriate.

4.19 When designing remedies the CMA will consider whether to specify a finite duration – for example, by means of a long-stop date in a 'sunset clause' – as part of the design of individual measures.[133] A sunset clause will generally specify when individual measures cease to have effect, whether by reference to a specific date or a clearly defined future event (for example the expiry of an intellectual property right or concession). A measure which is the subject of a sunset clause will cease to have effect on the specific date or defined event and will not be enforceable or reviewable beyond that specific date or defined event. Some measures, for example an obligation to implement a divestiture within a specified period of time, take effect when they are completed and therefore a sunset clause may not be necessary for these measures.[134]

4.20 A number of considerations may be relevant to the CMA's decision whether to specify a finite duration for a measure and the duration of any such 'sunset clause',[135] including:

(a) The length of time over which the AEC is expected to persist. For example – if the CMA considered that an AEC and/or its detrimental effects would not endure beyond a particular date or event, then there would not need to be ongoing remedial action beyond that point, and the CMA may adopt a sunset clause linked to that date or event.

(b) The role that the measure is expected to play in tackling the AEC and/or resulting customer detriment. For example, some measures are intended to be a temporary arrangement to deliver improvements in the short term, while other longer-term measures

take effect. Such a transitional measure might be suitable for a relatively short sunset clause – for example, of less than five years – which might be linked to the length of time it was expected to take for the longer-term measures to take effect.[136] Other measures may be intended to work as a catalyst to introduce greater competition into a market – for example, by promoting new entry, or removing obstacles to competition – such that, once this change has become established there is no longer a need for ongoing intervention. For such a measure the CMA might consider adopting a sunset clause that might be linked to achievement of the desired change or the timescale within which it expects such a change to occur. Where remedies are intended to create enduring characteristics of how the market operates, the CMA might adopt a relatively long sunset period or not have a sunset period.[137]

(c) The extent to which the measure is expected to become obsolete over time. This might sometimes be anticipated if prospective changes in technology, the policy and regulatory framework applying to the sector, consumer behaviour or other aspects of the competitive environment (for example, the way in which information is provided to consumers) mean that a measure is unlikely to serve its original purpose after a period of time. While the CMA will generally seek to 'future-proof' its remedies to prolong their effectiveness, all markets are subject to evolution and some more than others. The CMA might therefore adopt a sunset clause in some cases to reflect this, taking into account the characteristics of the market and remedy concerned.

4.21 Whether to include a sunset clause and the period used for any sunset date will therefore depend on the circumstances of the case and will be matters for the CMA to decide on a case-by-case basis. The duration of an AEC in the absence of an effective intervention by the CMA cannot always be predicted and there will similarly be some uncertainty about the precise timescale over which remedies will take effect. However, the CMA may nonetheless be able to identify a date or event beyond which it considers it would not be necessary to retain a remedy in force and, in these circumstances, the CMA would typically expect to adopt a sunset clause as part of the design of the remedy.

4.22 In addition to the upfront consideration that the CMA gives to duration in designing its remedies, the CMA is obliged to keep remedies under review[138] and may remove or revise those that are no longer appropriate. Such reviews might take place as a result of parties applying for variation or revocation of remedies on the basis of a change of circumstances.[139] Alternatively, the CMA might identify a change of circumstances following a review conducted on its own initiative. Consistent with the CMA's objective to avoid retaining remedies in force when they are no longer needed, when introducing a remedy without a sunset clause (or if the sunset clause substantially exceeds ten years), the CMA would normally expect to initiate an assessment of whether the remedy remains appropriate within ten years of the remedy coming into force. In some cases, the CMA may recommend consideration of the continued need for particular measures within a shorter timescale and/or specify the types of future circumstances which might be expected to trigger such a review – for example significant new entry.[140]

4.23 Thirdly, remedies may need to take account of existing laws or regulations either currently applicable or expected to come into force in the near future. Such other legislation may include both UK and EU legislation and could cover any aspect, for example competition law, health and safety, or data protection. Where there is a tension between existing laws or regulations and the actions that the CMA considers necessary to achieve an effective remedy, the CMA may make recommendations to the body responsible for the laws or regulations in question. Remedies will also need to take into account the extent to which the prohibitions on anti-competitive agreements and abuses of market power are applicable to the market concerned and what impact, if any, these have on the need and ability to impose remedies (see paragraph 17).[141]

4.24 Fourthly, where more than one measure is being introduced as part of a remedy package, the CMA will consider the way in which the measures are expected to interact with each other. As a general rule, measures that have a shared aim of introducing or strengthening competition within a market will tend to be mutually reinforcing. For example, where market-opening measures are being introduced that increase customer choice by facilitating entry or removing barriers to switching, these may be accompanied by information remedies that help customers choose the best product available to them.[142]

Duration [of behavioural remedies]

4.25 As behavioural remedies are designed to have ongoing effects on business conduct throughout the period they are in force, the duration of these measures is a material consideration. The CMA may specify a finite duration, for example, if measures are designed to have a transitional effect or are otherwise expected to become obsolete within a specified period. In such circumstances, the CMA might consider setting a finite duration or 'sunset clause' beyond which the measures will definitely not apply. The period the CMA adopts for the sunset clause date will depend on the circumstances of the case. Where no sunset date or event has been set, or if the period is for substantially longer than ten years, the CMA would normally expect to assess the continued need for the remedy within ten years. Relevant parties remain able to apply for variation or revocation of the remedies on the basis of a change of circumstances rather than awaiting an own-initiative review or the expiry of a sunset clause.[143]

NOTES

119 Section 134(4) of the EA02. In full public interest references, the CMA is additionally required to decide whether (and, if so, what) action should be taken by the Secretary of State to remedy, mitigate or prevent any adverse public interest effects that have been identified. In cases where the Secretary of State makes an adverse public interest finding, he/she may take action to remedy, mitigate or prevent any of the adverse effects identified.

120 For information on the transitional arrangements see *Transitional Arrangements: Guidance on the CMA's approach – Part 1* (CMA14).

121 Section 138A of the EA02. These time limits do not apply to any further implementation required after final undertakings have been accepted or a final order made.

122 The six-month and additional four-month periods set out above are upper time limits, and may be adjusted downwards by order. If the Secretary of State proposes to make an order adjusting those periods, he/she must consult the CMA and other relevant persons before doing so.

123 Section 172(2)(zb) of the EA02. The CMA is required also to publish the reasons for any such extension (section 172(5) of the EA02).

124 Section 174(1)(b) of the EA02. The scope of these powers and sanctions for non-compliance are explained in paragraphs 2.11–2.16. The powers remain available to the CMA in relation to the enforcement and monitoring of remedies that have been implemented, and in relation to its remedies monitoring function.

125 Sections 138A(3) to (5) of the EA02.

126 Section 138B of the EA02.

127 Under the EA02 prior to amendment a remedy implemented by means of order could require publication of non-price information only together with price information.

128 Under the provisions of the EA02 that applied prior to 1 April 2014 the appointment of third parties and the terms of such appointment relied on the parties' agreement.

129 In the case of a restricted public interest reference or a full public interest reference, this power is exercisable by the Secretary of State (section 157(6) of the EA02).

130 Sections 157 and 158 of the EA02.

131 Sections 157(2B) and 158(2B) of the EA02.

132 The CMA will also consider the costs of compliance as part of its assessment of the impact of remedies and their proportionality (see Guidelines for market investigations (CC3 (revised)), paragraph 352).

133 While consideration may be given to the individual duration of elements of a remedy package; the CMA may also give consideration to applying a sunset clause across a package of measures.

134 Some ancillary measures accompanying divestitures – eg not to reacquire the divestiture package – may themselves involve ongoing obligations on parties, and these ancillary measures may themselves be subject to a sunset clause (see Guidelines for market investigations (CC3 (revised)), paragraph 27 of Annex B).

135 Some of these considerations may also be relevant to decisions about whether to initiate a review of a remedy.

136 For example, in the report on Veterinary Medicines (April 2003) under the FTA, the package of remedies included an obligation on veterinary surgeons not to charge for writing prescriptions for a period of three years.

137 For example, in the statutory audit services market investigation, the CMA introduced a requirement for FTSE 350 companies to put their statutory audit engagement out to tender at least every ten years. This type of longer-term remedy is less well-suited for a sunset clause, as it will take at least a decade to fully take effect.

138 A statutory duty under section 92(1), (2) and (3) and section 162 (1), (2) and (3) of the EA02; sections 88(4) and (5) of the FTA (as preserved in Schedule 24 of the EA02).

139 For example, in 2012, the CC decided to remove the Domestic Electrical Goods Order (the DEGs Order) (and certain associated undertakings). The DEGs Order, which was introduced in 1998, prevented suppliers of goods such as televisions and washing machines from recommending resale prices or making agreements that restricted the resale prices of wholesalers and retailers, and from restricting or withholding supply from particular retailers. In deciding to lift the DEGs Order, the CC found that a number of changes since the Order was introduced had significantly increased competition in the market and removed the need for the safeguards provided by the Order. The CC also considered that the enactment of the Competition Act 1998 provided an effective mechanism to address attempts to fix prices or restrict supply unfairly. A memorandum of understanding set out how the OFT and CC approached their respective roles on reviews of undertakings and orders.

140 For example, in the 2002 report on the supply of banking services by clearing banks to small and medium-sized enterprises under the FTA, the CC recommended that, three years after implementation of the remedies, the OFT should review whether further measures were needed or, on the other hand, in the light of market developments, whether any or all of the measures in the CC's package of remedies could be modified or discontinued. Following a review by the OFT, the CC decided in 2007 to release the UK's four largest clearing banks from most of the Transitional Undertakings given by them in 2002.

141 Of Guidelines for market investigations (CC3 (revised)).

142 For example, the packages of remedies in the market investigations into home credit (November 2006), domestic bulk liquefied petroleum gas (June 2006) and payment protection insurance (January 2009) each included a combination of market-opening measures and information remedies.

143 Section 162 of the EA02. For example, in 2007, acting on the basis of advice from the OFT, the CC decided to release the UK's four largest clearing banks from most of the Transitional Undertakings given by them in 2002 following the investigation into supply of banking services by clearing banks to small and medium-sized enterprises under the FTA.

ANNEXE(S)

A. KEY CHANGES TO EXISTING MARKETS GUIDANCE

[3.655]

A.1 The following table lists those sections of the three existing main markets guidance documents[144] that are significantly amended or superseded by the changes that are outlined in this guidance. It is not intended to provide a comprehensive list of all changes, nor does it address all existing guidance documents which may be of relevance to the markets regime. Note also the following general limitations which apply to all existing OFT and CC markets-related guidance documents that are listed in Annexe B as having been adopted by the CMA Board (the adopted guidance):

- in the case of conflict between this guidance and the adopted guidance, this guidance prevails

Part 3 CMA and other Guidelines

- the original text of the adopted guidance has been retained unamended: as such, that text does not reflect or take account of developments in case law, legislation or practice since its original publication, and
- all existing guidance documents should be read subject to the following cross-cutting amendments:
  - references to the OFT or CC (except where referring to specific past OFT or CC practice or case law) should be read as referring to the CMA
  - references to 'referral to the CC' or 'a reference to the CC' should be read as referring to the referral of a case by the CMA (or Secretary of State) for a market investigation by a market reference group of CMA panel members
  - references to articles of the EC Treaty should be read as referring to the equivalent articles of the Treaty on the Functioning of the European Union (TFEU)
  - certain OFT or CC departments, teams or individual roles may not be replicated in the CMA, or may have been renamed. A copy of the CMA's organisational chart is available on www.gov.uk/cma, and
  - parties should check any contact details against those listed on www.gov.uk/cma, which will be the most up to date.

Existing guidance reference	Supplemental guidance reference
Market studies: Guidance on the OFT approach (OFT519)	
Paragraph 4.4	Should be read (with the exception of the pre-launch stage) in conjunction with paragraphs 2.6 to 2.10 which explain the requirement to publish a market study notice and the applicable timescales for the market study stage
Paragraph 4.8	Should be read in conjunction with paragraph 2.6 which explains the requirement to publish a market study notice. From 1 April 2014 market studies are launched within the meaning of paragraph 4.8 by publication of a market study notice
Paragraph 4.10 (footnote 12)	The last two sentences of footnote 12 are superseded by paragraphs 2.11 to 2.16 which explain the investigatory powers available to the CMA and when they are available in relation to market studies
Paragraphs 4.21 and 4.22	Should be read in conjunction with paragraph 2.9 which explains the requirement on the CMA to publish a market study report within the statutory timeframe
Paragraph 5.13	The last two sentences of this paragraph are superseded by paragraphs 2.9 and 2.10 which sets out the statutory timescales and consultation process that apply when the CMA proposes to make a reference
Market investigation references (OFT511)	
Paragraph 1.6	Should be read in conjunction with paragraphs 1.21 to 1.24 which explain how the reference process is changed to take account of the formation of the CMA
Paragraph 1.7	Should be read in conjunction with paragraph 2.32 which explains that only features relating to conduct can be the subject of a cross-market reference
Paragraph 2.19	Should be read in conjunction with paragraphs 2.6 to 2.10 which explain the requirement to publish a market study notice and the applicable timescales for the market study stage
Paragraphs 3.1 to 3.3	These paragraphs are superseded by paragraphs 2.11 to 2.16 which explain the investigatory powers available to the CMA and when they are available in relation to market studies
Paragraphs 3.6 to 3.9	Should be read in conjunction with paragraph 2.9 which sets out the statutory timescales and consultation process that apply when the CMA proposes to make a reference
Paragraph 3.10	This paragraph is superseded by paragraphs 2.18 to 2.30 which explain the changes made to the procedure for making public interest interventions
Guidelines for market investigations (CC3 (revised))	
Paragraphs 5 and 6	These paragraphs explain the reforms introduced by the ERRA13 and therefore are superseded by this guidance
Paragraphs 22 and 46 to 48	Should be read in conjunction with paragraphs 1.23 to 1.27 which explain how the reference process and appointment of the reference group are changed to take account of the formation of the CMA

Existing guidance reference	Supplemental guidance reference
Paragraph 25	This paragraph is superseded by paragraphs 3.15 to 3.19 which explain the changes made in relation to how cases raising specified public interest considerations are handled during the market investigation stage
Paragraph 49	Should be read in conjunction with paragraph 1.22 which explains the reference process at an operational (staff) level.
Paragraphs 50 - 87	These paragraphs describe the process for undertaking market investigations, and are superseded by paragraphs 3.24–3.64.
Paragraph 54	The first sentence of this paragraph is superseded by paragraphs 3.5 to 3.7 which explain the shorter statutory timescales that apply to the market investigation stage
Paragraph 89	Should be read in conjunction with paragraphs 4.5 to 4.7 which explain the statutory timescales applicable to the remedies implementation period
Paragraphs 334 to 341	These paragraphs are superseded by paragraphs 4.15 to 4.24 which explain the CMA's new procedure relating to sunset clauses and reviews of remedies.
Paragraph 45 of Annex B	This paragraph is superseded by paragraph 4.25 which explains the CMA's new procedure relating to sunset clauses and reviews of remedies.

NOTES

144 *Market studies: Guidance on the OFT approach* (OFT519), *Market investigation references* (OFT511) and *Guidelines for market investigations* (CC3 (revised)).

B. ANNEXE B: STATUS OF EXISTING OFT AND CC GUIDANCE

[3.656]

B.1 The table below indicates the status of OFT and CC markets-related guidance documents and publications that had been published and were in effect prior to the transfer of their market study and market investigation functions to the CMA on 1 April 2014. Certain of those documents have been adopted by the CMA Board in order to facilitate transition to the new UK markets regime, and to minimise disruption to the parties and the CMA.

OFT/CC code	Title	Status of document	
		Replaced/obsolete[1]	Adopted by the CMA Board[2]
OFT511	Market investigation references	-	✔
OFT514	Super-complaints: guidance for designated consumer bodies	-	✔
OFT518	Overview of the Enterprise Act	✔	-
OFT519	Market studies: Guidance on the OFT approach	-	✔
OFT530	Practical information – everything you need to know about the Enterprise Act	✔	-
OFT548	Super-complaint concurrent duties	-	✔
OFT1060	Memorandum of understanding between the OFT and the CC on the variation and termination of merger and market undertakings and orders	✔	-
OFT1308	Practice on consultation on proposed decisions in relation to market investigation references	✔	-
CC1	Competition Commission rules of procedure for merger reference groups, market reference groups and special reference groups	✔	-
CC3 (revised)	Guidelines for market investigation	-	✔
CC4	Competition Commission: general advice and information	✔	-
CC5	Statement of policy on penalties	✔	-
CC6	Competition Commission: guidance to merger reference groups, market reference groups and special reference groups	✔	-

OFT/CC code	Title	Status of document	
		Replaced/obsolete[1]	Adopted by the CMA Board[2]
CC7 (revised)	Chairman's guidance on disclosure of information in merger and market inquiries	-	✔
CC12	Disclosure of information by the CC to other public authorities	✔	-
	Competition Commission: suggested best practice for submissions of technical economic analysis	-	✔
	Competition Commission: guidance on outside interests of members, staff and external advisers	✔	-

NOTES

[1] OFT and CC publications listed in this column have, with effect from 1 April 2014, been replaced, or rendered obsolete, by CMA guidance or publications.

[2] OFT and CC publications listed in this column have been adopted by the CMA Board (subject to any guidance prepared by the CMA in the future). See Annexe A above for the general limitations that apply to the adopted guidance.

2. SECTOR SPECIFIC

(I) FINANCIAL SERVICES

FINANCIAL CONDUCT AUTHORITY FINALISED GUIDANCE FG15/9: MARKET STUDIES AND MARKET INVESTIGATION REFERENCES (NOTE)

A guide to the FCA's powers and procedures

July 2015

[3.657]

NOTES

This document describes:

— the FCA's powers to carry out market studies under the Financial Services and Markets Act 2000 (FSMA2000), or under its concurrent functions and the provisions of the Enterprise Act 2002 (EA2002), and explains how it chooses which powers to use;

— how the FCA will carry out studies under FSMA2000 and the remedies that may follow;

— how the FCA will carry out market studies under its concurrent functions and the provisions of EA2002 and the remedies that may follow;

— how the FCA will make market investigation references (MIRs) or accept undertakings in lieu of making an MIR

— the FCA's policies regarding disclosure and the use of information in market studies.

See the FCA website at www.fca.org.uk/publications/finalised-guidance/fg15-9-market-studies-and-market-investigation-references.

MARKET REVIEWS, MARKET STUDIES AND MARKET INVESTIGATION REFERENCES (PSR PS15/2.2) A GUIDE TO THE PSR'S POWER AND PROCEDURES (MARKET GUIDANCE)

(August 2015)

[3.658]

NOTES

This Guidance is available on the PSR's website at: www.psr.org.uk/markets-guidance.

1 INTRODUCTION

[3.659]

- Market reviews and market studies are the principal ways in which we investigate the market for payment systems or the markets for services provided by payment systems.
- We may carry out market reviews under the Financial Services (Banking Reform) Act 2013 (FSBRA) or we may carry out market studies under our concurrent competition law functions and the provisions of the Enterprise Act 2002 (EA02).
- We have a range of powers which we can use if we need to take action to advance our statutory objectives.

1.1 Market reviews and market studies are the principal ways in which we investigate the market for payment systems, or the markets for services provided by payment systems, to see how well they are working for service users (i.e. those who use, or are likely to use, services provided by payment systems). They are in line with our competition, innovation and service-user objectives (see paragraph 2.2). If we find that the markets we review or study could be made to work better, we have a range of powers to take appropriate action.

1.2 As from 1 April 2014, under the concurrency provisions in FSBRA relating to the EA02,[1] we have competition law powers under the EA02 to carry out market studies and make market investigation references (MIRs) which relate to participation in payment systems to the Competition and Markets Authority (CMA) for detailed investigation.[2] These competition law powers may also be exercised by the CMA, whose powers extend to all sectors of the UK economy. Accordingly, we are a 'concurrent regulator' having concurrent competition law functions (concurrent functions).

1.3 We can also use our information-gathering power under section 81 FSBRA to carry out market reviews.

1.4 This document describes:

- our powers to carry out market reviews under FSBRA or market studies under our concurrent functions and the provisions of EA02, and explains how we choose which powers to use (section 2)
- how we carry out market reviews under FSBRA and the outcomes that may follow (section 3)
- how we carry out market studies under our concurrent functions and the provisions of EA02 and the outcomes that may follow (section 4)
- how we will make MIRs or accept undertakings in lieu of making an MIR (section 5)
- our approach to disclosure and use of information in market reviews and market studies (section 6)

NOTES

1 Section 59 FSBRA

2 As from 1 April 2015, we also have powers to enforce the Competition Act 1998.

2 OUR POWERS TO CARRY OUT MARKET REVIEWS AND MARKET STUDIES

[3.660]

- We may carry out market reviews under FSBRA or market studies under our concurrent functions and the provisions of EA02.
- We have a broad choice as to which tool to use.
- We will choose which markets to review/study based on several factors, but broadly we aim to have the greatest impact with our limited resources.
- We will think carefully about what it is that might be preventing the market from working well for service users, and what we will need to do to investigate this, before launching a market review/study.

THE PSR'S POWERS TO CARRY OUT MARKET REVIEWS AND STUDIES

2.1 We may conduct market reviews using our information-gathering power under section 81 FSBRA or we may conduct market studies under our concurrent functions and the provisions of EA02.

FSBRA market reviews

2.2 Under FSBRA, the PSR has three statutory objectives:

- to promote effective competition in the market for payment systems and the markets for services provided by payment systems in the interests of service users ('the competition objective')[3]
- to promote the development of, and innovation in, payment systems in the interests of service users ('the innovation objective')[4]
- to ensure that payment systems are operated and developed in a way that takes account of, and promotes, the interests of service users ('the service-user objective')[5]

2.3 We have a range of regulatory powers including:

- the power to give directions to participants in regulated payment systems, either generally or in relation to a specific participant or category of participant[6]
- the power to require operators of regulated payment systems, either generally or in relation to a specific operator or category of operator, to take certain steps in relation to the rules for the operation of a regulated payment system[7]
- the powers to require an operator or a direct member payment service provider (PSP) to grant access to a payment system, or to vary the fees, charges and terms and conditions of agreements relating to a payment system[8]
- the power to require a person who has an interest in the operator of a regulated payment system or an infrastructure provider to dispose of all or part of that interest[9]

2.4 Under FSBRA, we have various powers to gather information and to conduct investigations,[10] and we can obtain information for the purposes of carrying out a market review using our information-gathering power under section 81 FSBRA (FSBRA market reviews). We can also use information we routinely receive from participants in regulated payment systems, or request within the framework of pursuing our objectives, to support our functions and to inform ourselves with a view to deciding whether or not to use our powers. We see FSBRA market reviews as one of our principal tools for advancing our competition, innovation and service-user objectives.

NOTES

3 Section 50 FSBRA

4 Section 51 FSBRA

5 Section 52 FSBRA

6 Section 54 FSBRA

7 Section 55 FSBRA

8 Sections 56 and 57 FSBRA

9 Section 58 FSBRA

10 These are described in detail in paragraphs 25.1 to 29.4 of the PSR's *Powers and Procedures Guidance* (PPG), available at www.psr.org.uk/powers-and-procedures-guidance

EA02 market studies

2.5 For the purpose of our concurrent functions[11] we have the function of keeping under review the market for payment systems, and the markets for services provided by payment systems,[12] and we may carry out market studies under the provisions of EA02 (EA02 market studies).[13] We may do this when we need to:

- consider the extent to which a matter in relation to the participation in payment systems used to provide services in the United Kingdom has or may have effects adverse to the interests of consumers (including any person who uses, or is likely to use, services provided by payment systems in the course of a business carried on by that person)[14]
- assess the extent to which steps can and should be taken to remedy, mitigate or prevent any such adverse effects[15]

2.6 The concurrent function of keeping the market under review is to be carried out with a view to ensuring we have sufficient information to take informed decisions and to carry out our other functions effectively.[16]

NOTES

[11] That is, our functions under EA02 (section 59 FSBRA) and the Competition Act 1998 (section 61 FSBRA).

[12] Section 64 FSBRA

[13] Section 59 FSBRA

[14] Section 130A EA02 and sections 59(4)(c) and 59(6)(a) FSBRA

[15] Section 130A EA02

[16] Section 64(2) FSBRA

FSBRA market review or EA02 market study?

2.7 At the outset of any review/study, we have an open mind as to whether a market is in fact working well for service users or not, and accordingly, we do not have a decided view as to whether we need to take action to make the market work better. Only once we have gathered evidence, analysed it and sought the views of interested parties can we form a view of what the outcome of a review/study should be.

2.8 We have a broad choice as to which procedure to follow. We have a broadly similar range of powers to take action available to us under both FSBRA and EA02 procedures. In particular, we may:

- make an MIR whether or not we have first conducted an EA02 market study, as long as the statutory test for making an MIR is met (see paragraph 5.1)
- use our powers under FSBRA to take action in respect of participants in regulated payment systems (see paragraphs 3.16 to 3.26) whether we have followed either a FSBRA or an EA02 process

2.9 Accordingly, we will decide on a case-by-case basis whether to pursue a FSBRA market review or an EA02 market study. In considering whether to conduct a FSBRA market review or an EA02 market study, we would take account of the aim(s) of the review/study. An EA02 market study can be used to consider the extent to which there are adverse effects on consumers and how these might be remedied. A FSBRA market review might have a similar aim, or might instead (or also) be focused on advancing our competition, innovation or service-user objectives in other ways (for example, by considering the extent to which there could be untapped potential for innovations or improvements in the experience of service users).

2.10 There are different procedural requirements and timetables for FSBRA market reviews and EA02 market studies (described in sections 3 and 4). One difference is that we have different sets of powers under FSBRA and EA02 to gather information (see section 6) and this may influence our choice of tool.

CHOOSING WHICH MARKETS TO REVIEW OR STUDY

2.11 We identify markets for payment systems and the services they provide that appear not to be working well for service users and/or matters concerning those markets that may be impeding competition, using information from a range of sources, such as:

- own-initiative desk research or intelligence-gathering, including from previous market reviews/studies
- our regulatory activities under FSBRA in respect of participants in regulated payment systems
- internal papers and analyses
- complaints, including super-complaints from bodies designated under section 68 FSBRA[17]
- applications made under sections 56 and 57 FSBRA
- general market intelligence
- other regulators

2.12 We welcome information from industry participants, representative groups and the public about markets for payment systems and the services they provide that appear not to be working well or where there may be competition concerns. You can bring such concerns or complaints to our attention by contacting: Payment Systems Regulator

25 The North Colonnade
Canary Wharf
London E14 5HS
Email: PSRcomplaints@psr.org.uk

2.13 Based on the information we have about the market(s) identified, we may form an initial view of how well the market is working in the interests of service users. However, understanding properly the functioning of any market is complex, and we cannot study every market. We must therefore choose which markets or aspects of markets to review/study. We decide on a case-by-case basis whether to open a market review/study and will have regard to our Administrative Priority Framework.[18] Under that framework, we might have regard to factors including, but not limited to:

- The prospects for and likely impact of any intervention in the market, having regard to such factors as market size and the number of participants and/or service users affected.
- The scope for the PSR to take effective action (taking into account, for example, domestic versus international issues, the impact of harmonising EU legislation and the PSR's regulatory perimeter).
- The prospects for intervention to have a wider impact (e.g. clear read-across to other markets).
- How the issue in question fits in with any upcoming regulatory developments or ongoing activity at a domestic, EU or wider international level. For example, are there other current competition investigations taking place that are considering the issue?
- Any expected change in regulation that will affect the relevant market behaviour.
- Whether the market has been subject to recent significant non-regulatory change that has not had sufficient time to bed in, but might have an important impact on the relevant issues, or whether market changes or forces are anticipated in the future that might serve to address any issues identified.
- How a market review/study would affect the PSR's current portfolio of work, including any resource implications.
- Whether the issue might be better addressed by another form of PSR action (such as enforcement, including under CA98, or FSBRA regulatory action), or by another authority (FCA/PRA/Bank of England/CMA/European Commission/other).
- The likelihood of a successful outcome (e.g. in terms of being able to take action to make the market work better for service users).

2.14 As part of the process of deciding whether or not to launch a market review/study, we may choose publicly to call for evidence and/or consult stakeholders.

NOTES

17 We have produced guidance on how designated bodies can bring a super-complaint (*Super-Complaints Guidance*). See: www.psr.org.uk/how-psr-regulates/complaints-and-disputes/super-complaints.

18 See: www.psr.org.uk/administrative-priority-framework

THE PRE-LAUNCH STAGE

2.15 Before launching a market review/study, we consider what might be preventing the market working well for service users. We consider what information, data and analysis might indicate whether or not the market is working well, in order to shape our investigation and help us to decide what information to seek. We may consult third parties regarding the availability of such information. We may engage external parties on particular aspects of the market review/study. We produce an initial project plan and establish the resources we need. In some cases, it may be necessary to undertake some preliminary work to define the scope of our FSBRA market reviews (given that they may involve competition, innovation and/or service-user interest issues). We may do so through consultation on draft terms of reference, for example.

2.16 We decide whether to launch a FSBRA market review or an EA02 market study. In either case, we will consult the CMA,[19] and we will also consult with the FCA as appropriate.[20] We cannot launch an EA02 market study if the CMA or FCA has launched such a study into the same matter.[21] The CMA and FCA are subject to reciprocal obligations.[22] If the CMA or FCA has launched or is about to launch an EA02 market study, we will take this into account in deciding whether or not to launch a FSBRA market review. We will aim to avoid duplication, and may work jointly with the CMA or FCA on an EA02 market study.

NOTES

19 In line with the general principle of cooperation set out in our Memorandum of Understanding (MoU) with the CMA, and our duty under section 60(1) FSBRA for EA02 market studies. [*Note: Our website will be updated with the MoU agreed and adopted by the CMA and the PSR. See:* www.psr.org.uk/how-psr-regulates/memorandums-understanding]

20 Under section 60(4) FSBRA, we must consult with the FCA before exercising our concurrent functions under EA02.

21 Sections 60(2) and 60(5) FSBRA

22 Sections 60(1), 60(2), 60(4) and 60(5) FSBRA

3 HOW WE CARRY OUT FSBRA MARKET REVIEWS

OVERVIEW

[3.661]

3.1 The following table illustrates the stages of a typical FSBRA market review following the prelaunch stage (which is described at paragraphs 2.15 and 2.16 above).

Phase	Detail
Launch	• Announce publicly the intentions of the market review and the issues under consideration

Phase	Detail
	• Indicate the scope of the matters on which views and evidence are sought • Engage with relevant stakeholders, including, as appropriate, Operators, PSPs, trade bodies, service users, consumer bodies, government departments and other regulators
Research	• Fully define the data requirements for the market review • Collect and request data and information • Carry out market research, business model analysis, interviews, roundtables and other research as appropriate
Analysis and Interim Report	• Assess how well the market is working for service users and any evidence of issues/market failures • Assess extent of any service-user/consumer detriment • Publish interim report outlining analysis, preliminary conclusions and, where practicable and appropriate, proposed solutions for addressing any concerns identified
Report	• Publish final report including analysis, conclusions and, where appropriate, the action we propose to take
Outcomes	• Use existing powers and processes to develop and implement proposed actions (including, for example, making directions, publishing guidance and making proposals for enhanced industry action) • If required, conduct formal consultation on proposed actions

LAUNCH

3.2 We announce the launch of any market reviews we carry out under FSBRA on our website and via a regulatory information service. We will generally set out:

- The information-gathering powers which we may exercise in conducting the market review.
- The scope of the market review (which may be through the publication of final terms of reference). The scope may include the questions we are seeking to answer or the hypotheses we are trying to test (such as ways in which the market might be made to work better for service users).
- The period during which initial representations may be made to the PSR in relation to the review.
- The timescales within which we expect to complete the review. This will usually be one year from launch to report, but may vary depending on the specific circumstances of the review.[23]

3.3 In launching the review publicly, we invite all relevant participants in payment systems, trade bodies, service users (including consumers) and representative bodies, government departments and other regulators (UK and international) to provide us with information and data. In line with the PSR's general policy on responses to formal consultations, we will seek to publish views or submissions in full or in part (see section 6 regarding our treatment of information). Respondents should seek to limit claims for confidential treatment to the minimum necessary. If respondents include extensive tracts of confidential information in their submissions, we would ask that they submit non-confidential versions which they consent for us to publish. We will also not accept blanket claims of confidentiality, and will require respondents to identify specific information over which confidentiality is claimed, and to explain the basis for this claim.

3.4 For each market review, we will provide a clear point of contact for stakeholders.

NOTES

[23] Unlike EA02 market studies, there are no statutory deadlines within which we must complete a FSBRA market review. See paragraph 4.4.

RESEARCH

3.5 We gather information about the market to see how well it is working for service users. A market review may involve gathering specific information from a broad set of stakeholders (e.g. participants in payment systems, trade bodies, service users (including consumers) and representative bodies, government departments and other regulators (UK and international)). We will also use our own data, past reviews/studies, other papers and any previous analysis we have conducted, in order to limit the information-gathering burden on stakeholders.

3.6 We gather this information through questionnaires, desk research, surveys and working with other regulators. We may also meet with stakeholders to discuss issues raised by the review.

3.7 We may ask for information on an informal basis without using our statutory information-gathering power under section 81 FSBRA. We would typically expect regulated participants to assist us with such a request, in line with their duty of cooperation and disclosure under General Direction 1, thus: '*A participant must deal with the PSR in an open and cooperative way, and must disclose to the PSR appropriately anything relating to the participant which could materially adversely impact advancement of the PSR's statutory objectives and duties*'. We may also ask for information from organisations and individuals that we do not regulate.' Alternatively, we may use our power under section 81 FSBRA to formally require persons to provide us with information or documents (see paragraphs 6.2 to 6.5).[24]

3.8 In order to reach well-evidenced decisions, we may need detailed information and data. We recognise that providing this can be onerous for the parties that supply it to us. Accordingly, before making requests for information and documents, we scope our requests carefully in light of the purpose for which the information is sought, the availability of relevant information from other sources, including information held by the PSR already, and the ease with which respondents can provide the information we need. The PSR as a whole aims to coordinate its various activities regarding data requests, in order to be proportionate and manage the burden on any given respondent, and this also applies to our market review activity. Section 6 describes how we must treat information we receive.

3.9 Where appropriate, we may also share data and coordinate with other authorities, such as the CMA, the FCA and the Prudential Regulation Authority (PRA), subject to complying with the provisions governing disclosure under FSBRA (as set out in section 6).

NOTES

24 The PSR's information-gathering and investigation powers are described in detail in paragraphs 25.1 to 29.4 of the PSR's *Powers and Procedures Guidance* (PPG), available at www.psr.org.uk/powers-and-procedures-guidance.

ANALYSIS AND INTERIM REPORT

3.10 We use the information and data we collect to examine how the market functions, and to assess whether the market is working well for service users. We consider the evidence and views we receive with reference to the issues identified. We investigate our initial views in the review, taking into account the feedback from stakeholders and information gathered during the review.

3.11 When assessing competition, we consider all the features of the market, including the competitive constraints that suppliers of payment systems or the services they provide face from current rivals, the ability of new suppliers to enter the market (and how this entry might be constrained by costs, applicable regulation and other factors), and the ability of service users (including consumers) to obtain, assess and act on information relevant to their usage decisions.

3.12 We will publish an interim report (other than in exceptional circumstances – for example, where we have decided not to proceed with the market review), presenting our analysis and preliminary conclusions and, where practicable and appropriate, include possible remedies to address any concerns identified. The timing and form of these interim reports and statements on possible remedies vary according to the needs of particular reviews.

3.13 We set a deadline for interested parties to make submissions on our interim report and any possible remedies, which will usually be a minimum of 15 days, depending on what is appropriate in a specific case. Again, in line with the PSR's general policy on responses to formal consultations, we will seek to publish views or submissions in full or in part and respondents should seek to limit claims for confidential treatment to the minimum necessary (see further paragraph 3.3 above). See also section 6 regarding our treatment of information.

REPORT

3.14 The duration of a market review depends on many factors, such as the scale and complexity of the market. However, we aim to complete a market review from launch to final report stage within approximately a year. Once complete, we publish a market review report, including:

- a description of the market(s) and issue(s) we considered
- the reasons for carrying out the review
- a description of the methodologies used to collect and analyse the data
- our analysis and, as appropriate, our responses to feedback received
- our conclusions on the issues considered

3.15 If appropriate, we will also publish our proposals for the action we will take to address any issues that we have identified.

OUTCOMES

3.16 We may conclude that no action is necessary following a market review. However, if we conclude that the market is not working well for service users, we may take any of the following action:

- General action, including (but not restricted to):
  - Directions and Requirements. This includes giving general directions under section 54 FSBRA, or imposing generally-imposed requirements under section 55 FSBRA.
  - Publishing general guidance. This covers guidance issued under section 96 FSBRA about the operation of FSBRA or specified parts of it, about any directions we have given, or requirements we have imposed, using our FSBRA powers, or guidance about any of the PSR's functions or any other matter about which it appears to the PSR to be desirable to give advice or information.
  - Proposing enhanced industry action. This refers to providing the payments industry an opportunity to develop measures that promote the interests of service users.
- Specific action, including giving specific directions or imposing specifically-imposed requirements, or taking enforcement action against compliance failures (where existing directions or requirements have not been complied with).[25]

- Making an MIR to the CMA. The purpose of an MIR is typically to investigate markets where it appears that competition is adversely affected by the structure of a market, by the businesses operating in the market or by conduct of their customers or suppliers. We may also accept undertakings in lieu of making a reference (see section 5 for more detail).

3.17 Alternatively, we may decide to take no further action for the time being. This could be because our concerns are likely to be satisfied by upcoming legislative measures, action by the relevant participants or other circumstances. In such cases, we may continue to monitor the market in case our concerns are not addressed.

3.18 We may seek to implement a package of actions. For instance, we might make an MIR, but deal with a discrete issue identified in our market review if it can be addressed appropriately through use of our other tools.

3.19 We will have regard to the principles of proportionality in relation to the action we take. The nature of any action we take depends on the individual circumstances of each case, and could include:

- Measures that affect how participants engage with service users – for example, determining the information to be provided to service users or the terms and conditions of agreements relating to payment systems.
- Market-opening measures to reduce barriers to entry and expansion.
- Measures to control outcomes.
- Structural measures where behavioural remedies (or other less intrusive options) would not adequately address our concerns (for example, the disposal of an interest in the operator of a payment system or an infrastructure provider) provided that these are proportionate measures.

3.20 The process involved in implementing regulatory actions will depend on the specific power we select to exercise.

NOTES

25 The PSR also has powers to take enforcement action against infringements of the Competition Act 1998 which might be identified in the course of its market review. The CMA has concurrent functions in this respect.

General action

3.21 General action such as giving general directions, imposing generally-imposed requirements or publishing general guidance will usually entail a consultation exercise.[26] More information on the consultation process in such cases can be found in the PSR's *Powers and Procedures Guidance* (PPG).[27]

3.22 We may also encourage self-regulation within the payments industry, e.g. implementing codes of conduct. Such measures aid our efforts in promoting the interests of service users. The aim is to establish a partnership with the payments industry where participants may be better placed to develop solutions that can be easily implemented and are tailored to our concerns.

NOTES

26 However, we are not required to conduct a public consultation on a draft direction or requirement if we consider that the delay involved would be prejudicial to the interests of service users.

27 See paragraphs 5.1 to 5.5 of the PPG.

Specific action

3.23 Specific action such as giving specific directions or imposing specifically-imposed requirements, on the other hand, may or may not entail a public consultation process. We will normally send the specific addressees a notice of a proposed direction or requirement and seek their representations. Where a proposed direction or requirement is likely to have wider implication or relevance beyond the specific addressees, we might decide to share the draft direction or requirement more widely and seek the views of other stakeholders. More information on the representation and consultation processes in the case of specific directions and specifically-imposed requirements can be found in the PPG.[28]

3.24 In the case of proposed disposal requirements (under section 58 FBSRA), we will normally publish a draft of the disposal requirement and invite representation on it from all affected stakeholders, including stakeholders other than the affected operator/infrastructure provider and the person holding an interest (who will be sent a notice of the proposed disposal requirement).We would have previously engaged with the operator/infrastructure provider and the person holding an interest before we propose to exercise the relevant power.[29]

3.25 Additionally, we may also open investigations into the nature, conduct or state of business of any participant in a regulated payment system.[30] We may also open investigations into suspected compliance failures.[31] If we take the view that a warning notice should be issued in relation to any compliance failure, we will recommend such action to the Enforcement Decisions Committee (EDC). More information on enforcement action (including EDC warning notices and decision notices) can be found in the PPG.[32]

3.26 We also have the option to apply to the civil courts for injunctive relief to enforce certain of our regulatory decisions. Our powers to seek injunctions apply in relation to the same compliance failures that give rise to our powers to publish details or impose a financial penalty.[33]

3.27 It is also possible that during a market review, we identify potential infringements of other laws, such as competition law, and we may open an investigation accordingly, or refer the matter to other enforcement agencies.

NOTES

28 See paragraphs 4.1 to 4.5 of the PPG.

29 See paragraphs 16.1 to 16.5 of the PPG.

30 Section 83(1) FSBRA

31 Section 83(2) FSBRA

32 See, in particular, paragraphs 21.1 to 21.27 of the PPG.

33 See further paragraphs 24.1 to 24.4 of the PPG.

Market investigation references

3.28 Where we have reasonable grounds to suspect that features of a market are adversely affecting competition, we can refer a market or a feature of several markets to the CMA for an in-depth investigation, or accept undertakings in lieu of making a reference. If we wish to make such a market investigation reference, we must consult any persons whose interests we consider may be substantially impacted by this proposed decision. See section 5.

Effectiveness and proportionality, equality and diversity

3.29 We aim to ensure that any action we take is effective and proportionate to the concerns identified.[34] We must have regard to the regulatory principles in section 53 FSBRA when exercising our general functions relating to payment systems, including giving general directions, and determining the general policy and principles by reference to which the PSR performs its particular functions.[35] We consider that these regulatory principles are also relevant when we are carrying out market reviews under FSBRA, and also when we carry out market studies under EA02. There are eight principles, three of which in particular will generally be relevant when considering intervention:

- the efficiency principle – the need to use the resources of each regulator in the most efficient and economical way
- the proportionality principle – that a burden or restriction which is imposed on a person, or on the carrying on of an activity, should be proportionate to the benefits, considered in general terms, which are expected to result from the imposition of that burden or restriction
- the transparency principle – the principle that the regulators should exercise their functions as transparently as possible

3.30 In addition, we will be mindful, as appropriate, of the five high-level 'better regulation' principles in the Legislative and Regulatory Reform Act 2006, including proportionality and transparency, and the additional requirements of the Regulators' Code.[36] Accordingly, we carry out an assessment of the proportionality of our proposed actions and will consult on the draft measures as appropriate.

3.31 We consider Equality and Diversity Implications as part of our decision-making processes in line with our public sector equality duty under the Equality Act 2010. In particular, we will assess the likely equality and diversity impacts and rationale of our proposals to assess whether they give rise to any concerns as a result of any protected characteristic.[37]

NOTES

34 We note what the CMA has said regarding effectiveness and proportionality in the context of its assessment of possible remedies following a market investigation: CC3 (revised) April 2014. See: www.gov.uk/government/uploads/system/uploads/attachment_data/file/284390/cc3_revised.pdf (Part 4 in general and paragraphs 334 to 347 in particular).

35 Section 49(3)(c) FSBRA states that in discharging our general functions relating to payment systems, we must have regard to the regulatory principles found in section 53 FSBRA.

36 See the Legislative and Regulatory Reform Act 2006 (LRRA) principles around the exercise of regulatory functions at www.legislation.gov.uk/ukpga/2006/51/contents, and the 6 April 2014 Regulators' Code at www.gov.uk/government/uploads/system/uploads/attachment_data/file/300126/14-705-regulators-code.pdf.

37 Our website provides more information: www.psr.org.uk/corporate-responsibility

Ongoing review

3.32 We have ongoing duties under FSBRA to promote effective competition, innovation and the interests of service users in payment systems and the services they provide (see paragraph 2.2). We will continue to monitor the effectiveness and proportionality of any action that we take following a FSBRA market review or indeed following an EA02 market study.

URGENT ACTION

3.33 In the majority of circumstances we complete the market review procedures outlined above (paragraphs 3.1 to 3.15) before taking any action. However, in exceptional circumstances, where we identify a need to act more quickly, we may take action early to prevent harm to or to protect the interests of service users – for example, we may give a specific direction or impose a specifically-imposed requirement.

4 HOW WE CARRY OUT EA02 MARKET STUDIES

[3.662]

- The stages of an EA02 market study are similar to those of a FSBRA market review.
- There are statutory deadlines and an EA02 market study must be complete within 12 months of formal launch.

- There are also different formal powers for gathering information.
- Our powers to take action following an EA02 market study are similar to those following a FSBRA market review.

4.1 The stages of an EA02 market study are similar to those of a FSBRA market review (section 3). However, there are some key differences, described below.

LAUNCH AND TIMESCALE

4.2 When we formally launch an EA02 market study, we must publish a 'market study notice'. This sets out:

- the scope of the market study
- the period during which representations may be made to the PSR in relation to the study, and
- the timescales within which the study will be completed[38]

4.3 In line with the PSR's general policy on responses to formal consultations, we will make submissions available for public inspection unless the respondent requests otherwise and we accept its request. See further section 6 regarding our treatment of information.

4.4 Publication of a market study notice triggers the following statutory deadlines:

- Where we propose to make an MIR in relation to the subject matter of a market study, we must publish notice of our proposed decision and begin the process of consulting relevant persons within six months of publication of the market study notice.[39]
- Where we do not propose to make an MIR, but have received (non-frivolous) representations in response to a market study notice arguing that a reference should be made, we must, within six months of publication of the market study notice, publish notice of our proposed decision and begin the process of consulting relevant persons.[40]
- Where we do not propose to make an MIR and no representations have been made in response to a market study notice arguing that a reference should be made, we must publish a notice of our decision not to make a reference within six months of publication of the market study notice.[41]
- We must publish a market study report setting out our findings and the action (if any) we propose to take, within 12 months of publication of a market study notice.[42] When our decision is (a) to make an MIR, (b) not to make an MIR (when non-frivolous representations have been received to the effect a reference should be made) or (c) to accept undertakings in lieu of an MIR, the market study report must in particular contain the decision, the reasons for the decision and such information we consider appropriate for facilitating a proper understanding of our reasons for the decision.[43]
- Where a market study report sets out a decision to make an MIR, the reference must be made at the same time as the report is published.[44]

NOTES

38 Section 130A(3)EA02
39 Section 131B(1)EA02
40 Section 131B(1) EA02
41 Sections 131B(2) and (3) EA02
42 Section 131B(4) EA02
43 Section 131B(5) EA02
44 Section 131B(6) EA02

RESEARCH AND INFORMATION GATHERING

4.5 We will carry out research for an EA02 market study in the same way as for a FSBRA market review. However, we have a different set of formal powers with which we can require information (see section 6).

ANALYSIS AND INTERIM REPORT

4.6 We anticipate conducting similar types of analysis for EA02 market studies as we do for FSBRA market reviews. However, the binding legal obligation on us to reach a preliminary view and make a proposal as to whether or not to make an MIR within six months of launching an EA02 market study may affect the amount of information we can gather and the extent of the analysis that we may carry out before deciding whether or not a market should be referred for investigation by the CMA (see section 5).

4.7 As noted, where we propose to make an MIR, or not to make an MIR where we have received non-frivolous submissions urging such a reference, we must consult on this within six months of publication of the market study notice (paragraph 4.4). We will do this in an interim report. We must consult any persons on whose interests we consider making an MIR would have a substantial impact.[45]

4.8 When consulting, we must give our reasons so far as practicable, having regard to the restrictions imposed by the timetable for making the decision, and any need to keep the proposal or the reasons for it, confidential.[46] We will make any responses to our proposal to make or not to make an MIR available for public inspection unless the respondent requests otherwise and we accept its request. See further section 6 regarding our treatment of information.

NOTES

45 Sections 131A(2)(b) and (4) EA02
46 Sections 131A(5) and (6) EA02

FINAL REPORT

4.9 If we receive no submissions urging an MIR and are not ourselves minded to make such a reference, we must publish that decision within six months of the market study notice (see paragraph 4.4).[47]

4.10 We must within 12 months of publication of a market study notice publish a market study report setting out our findings and the action (if any) we propose to take (see paragraph 4.4).[48] In particular, we must decide whether or not to make an MIR (see section 5). The report will contain our reasons for this decision.

4.11 Following an EA02 market study we may use our FSBRA regulatory powers (see paragraphs 3.16 to 3.26), and any such proposed action will be set out in the EA02 market study report (see paragraph 4.4).

NOTES

47 Section 131B(3) EA02

48 Section 131B(4) EA02

5 MARKET INVESTIGATION REFERENCES AND UNDERTAKINGS IN LIEU OF A REFERENCE

[3.663]

- We can refer a market, or a feature of several markets, to the CMA for in-depth investigation.
- We may do this where we have reasonable grounds to suspect that features of the market are adversely affecting competition.
- It is possible for us to accept undertakings in lieu of making a reference, if we think they would address our competition concerns.

THE PSR'S POWER TO REFER MARKETS OR FEATURES OF MORE THAN ONE MARKET TO THE CMA

5.1 We have the power to refer a market to the CMA where we have reasonable grounds to suspect that any feature, or combination of features, of a market or markets for payment systems and the services they provide in the UK prevents, restricts or distorts competition (an 'ordinary reference').[49] The task of the CMA on a reference is focused on competition, while our market reviews/studies may explore broader issues (see paragraphs 2.2 to 2.6). The CMA has 18 months to complete its investigation (extendable by 6 months), which is a more detailed examination into whether there is an adverse effect on competition in the markets referred.

5.2 A 'feature' of a market may be:[50]

- the structure of the market concerned or any aspect of that structure
- any conduct (whether or not in the market concerned) of one or more than one person who supplies or acquires goods or services in the market concerned[51]
- any conduct relating to the market concerned of customers of any person who supplies or acquires goods or services

5.3 'Conduct' includes any failure to act (whether intentional or not) and any other unintentional conduct.[52]

5.4 We may also make a 'cross-market reference': that is, to refer a specific feature (or combination of features) existing in more than one market without also having to refer the whole of each market concerned.[53] The legal criteria for an ordinary reference or a cross market reference are the same (see paragraph 5.1), although only features that relate to conduct can be the subject of a cross-market reference.[54]

5.5 We have the power to make an MIR if the applicable legal test is met, even without having completed an EA02 market study. However, if we propose to do this, we must consult any persons on whose interests we consider making an MIR would have a substantial impact.[55]

NOTES

49 Section 131(1)EA02

50 Section 131(2)EA02

51 We understand the reference to 'one or more than one person who supplies or acquires goods or services' to include one or more than one participant in a payment system or payment systems used to provide services in the United Kingdom.

52 Section 131(3)EA02

53 Sections 131(2A) and (6) EA02

54 Sections 131(1) and (2A) EA02

55 Section 169 (2) EA02

FACTORS THE PSR WILL TAKE INTO ACCOUNT WHEN CONSIDERING WHETHER TO MAKE AN MIR

5.6 A market investigation entails detailed examination by the CMA of whether there is an adverse effect on competition in the market(s) referred and, if so, what remedial action may be appropriate. Following its investigation, the CMA has a duty to take such action as it considers reasonable and practicable to remedy any adverse effect on competition it identifies, which may include behavioural and/or structural remedies.

5.7 While we have powers under FSBRA, they do not extend beyond participants in regulated payment systems.[56] Accordingly, a key factor in deciding whether to make an MIR will be whether we foresee the need to implement remedies affecting persons that are not participants in regulated payment systems.

5.8 Otherwise, we intend to follow the CMA's own approach as set out in *Market Investigation References* (OFT511)[57] in deciding whether or not to make an MIR, i.e. we expect to make an MIR where all of the following criteria are met:

- It would not be more appropriate to deal with the competition issues identified by applying CA98 or using other powers available to us.
- It would not be more appropriate to address the problem identified by means of undertakings in lieu of a reference (see paragraphs 5.9 to 5.12).
- The scale of the suspected problem, in terms of its adverse effect on competition, is such that a reference would be an appropriate response to it.
- There is a reasonable chance that appropriate remedies will be available.[58]

NOTES

[56] That is, those payment systems designated as regulated payment systems by the Treasury. See further sections 43 to 48 FSBRA.

[57] *Market Investigation References: Guidance about the making of references under Part 4 of the Enterprise Act*, paragraph 2.1. www.gov.uk/government/uploads/system/uploads/attachment_data/file/284399/oft511.pdf

[58] The CMA's powers to impose remedies are described in the *CMA's Market investigations guidelines*, CC3, Part 4. www.gov.uk/government/publications/market-investigations-guidelines

UNDERTAKINGS IN LIEU OF A REFERENCE

5.9 Section 154 EA02 gives the PSR the power to accept undertakings instead of making an MIR. In exercising this power we must have regard to the need to achieve as comprehensive a solution as is reasonable and practicable to any adverse effects on competition identified (and any detrimental effects on customers so far as they result or may be expected to result from such adverse effects). We may also have regard to the effect of the possible undertakings on any relevant customer benefits arising from a feature or features of the markets concerned.

5.10 In practice, we expect that undertakings in lieu of a reference are unlikely to be common. We may not have completed a sufficiently detailed investigation of a competition problem to be able to judge whether particular undertakings will achieve 'as comprehensive a solution as is reasonable and practicable'. Seeking to negotiate undertakings with several parties with different interests is likely to pose serious practical difficulties, especially within the 12 months provided under an EA02 market study.

5.11 Before accepting any undertaking in lieu of a reference, we must publish the proposed undertaking in a notice. This must state the purpose and effect of the undertaking and identify the adverse effect on competition and any resulting detrimental effect on customers that the proposed undertaking is intended to remedy.[59] We must consider any representations arising from the publication of the notice. There is a power for the Secretary of State to intervene at this stage if he or she believes that wider public interest matters are relevant to the case. The Secretary of State is able to block the acceptance of undertakings in lieu when he or she believes that a public interest consideration specified in the legislation (currently only national security) is relevant. In such a case, the outcome may be other undertakings in lieu of a reference.

5.12 When an undertaking in lieu is accepted, we may not make an MIR involving the same services for a period of 12 months unless we consider the undertaking has been breached or we have been given false or misleading information by the person responsible for giving the undertaking.[60]

NOTES

[59] The list of all the points to be included in such notices is given in section 155(2) EA02.

[60] Section 156(1) EA02

6 INFORMATION GATHERING, USE AND DISCLOSURE IN MARKET REVIEWS AND MARKET STUDIES

[3.664]

- We have different sets of powers under FSBRA and EA02 to gather information.
- In exercising our functions we may use information we have gathered regardless of its source.
- We can only disclose information in accordance with the applicable legal regime.
- We will make submissions available for public inspection unless the respondent requests otherwise and we accept its request, and may publish working papers and other relevant documents.

INFORMATION GATHERING

6.1 Although we expect parties to respond to our requests that information be provided on an informal basis, we have formal powers with which we can gather information under FSBRA and EA02.[61]

NOTES

[61] See paragraphs 3.7 and 3.8.

FSBRA

6.2 Under section 81 FSBRA, the PSR may by notice in writing require a person to provide the PSR with information or documents that it requires in connection with its functions under Part 5 FSBRA. The PSR can also apply, in certain circumstances, to a justice of the peace for a warrant to enter premises where documents or information are held.[62]

6.3 The PSR may also appoint investigators who will have the power to require a person to attend and answer questions, or to provide any information or document required by the investigator.[63] These requirements can only be imposed so far as the investigator reasonably considers the questions, or the provision of information or production, to be relevant to the purposes of the investigation.[64]

6.4 Failure to comply, without reasonable excuse, with an information requirement, or other requirement imposed by an investigator, may be treated as a contempt of court.[65] Furthermore, if a person knows or suspects that an investigation is being conducted,[66] it is a criminal offence for that person to falsify, conceal, destroy or otherwise dispose of documents[67] which he knows or suspects to be relevant to the investigation,[68] unless he can show that he had no intention to hide the facts disclosed in those documents from the investigator.[69] A person could also be guilty of a criminal offence if, in purported compliance with a requirement, he knowingly or recklessly provides information that is false or misleading in a material particular.[70]

6.5 A detailed description of the PSR's information-gathering and investigation powers can be found in the PPG.[71]

NOTES

62 Section 88 FSBRA
63 Sections 83 and 85 FSBRA
64 Section 85(4) FSBRA
65 Sections 90(1) and 90(2) FSBRA
66 Or is likely to be conducted.
67 Or to cause or permit this to occur.
68 Section 90(4) FSBRA
69 Section 90(5) FSBRA
70 Section 90(6) FSBRA
71 See paragraphs 25.1 to 29.4 of the PPG.

EA02

6.6 Under our concurrent functions, we have powers under EA02:

- to give notice requiring any person to attend a specified place to give evidence to the PSR or a person nominated for the purpose
- to give notice requiring any person to produce specified documents or categories of documents that are in that person's custody or under his control
- to give notice requiring any person carrying on business to supply specified forecasts, estimates, returns or other information in a specified form and manner[72]

6.7 Like section 81 FSBRA, we can use these powers against any person.[73]

6.8 Where the PSR considers that a person has, without reasonable excuse, failed to comply with any requirement of a notice issued by the PSR using its EA02 investigatory powers or intentionally obstructed or delayed another person in copying documents produced to that other person, the PSR has the power to impose an administrative penalty.[74]

6.9 It is a criminal offence for a person intentionally to alter, suppress or destroy any document which the person has been required by notice to produce.[75] Where an act is capable of constituting both (a) a failure warranting an administrative penalty and (b) a criminal offence, the PSR cannot impose a financial penalty if it has brought criminal proceedings against the person. Similarly, criminal proceedings cannot be brought against the person if an administrative penalty has been imposed in respect of the same act.[76]

6.10 Administrative penalties may be imposed in the form of a fixed amount, by reference to a daily rate, or using a combination of the two. Maximum penalty amounts are set by order and are, as at 1 April 2014, £30,000 (in the case of a fixed amount) and £15,000 (in the case of a daily penalty).[77] Persons committing a criminal offence are liable, on summary conviction, to an unlimited fine, and on conviction on indictment, to imprisonment for a term not exceeding two years or to a fine, or to both.[78]

6.11 The PSR is under a statutory obligation to issue its own statement of policy for penalties under section 174A(1) to (3) EA02. For the sake of consistency with the CMA, the practice of other concurrent regulators in relation to such penalties[79] and with the PSR's approach to penalties for failure to comply with information-gathering powers in CA98 investigations, the PSR has adopted the CMA's penalty policy (CMA4: *Administrative penalties: Statement of Policy on the CMA's approach*, January 2014) as its policy on penalties under sections 174(1) to (3) EA02.[80]

NOTES

72 Section 174(1)(a) and sections 174(3) to (5) EA02
73 Section 174 EA02
74 Sections 174A(1) to (3) EA02
75 Section 174A(4) EA02
76 Sections 174A(4) and (5) EA02

77 Competition and Markets Authority (Penalties) Order 2014 (SI 2014/559)
78 Section 174A(6) EA02
79 All other concurrent regulators (other than the FCA) are obliged to have regard to the CMA's statement of policy on such penalties.
80 The CMA's statement of policy also relates to penalties imposed in CA98 investigations for failure to comply with information-gathering powers. The PSR is required to have regard to this guidance in relation to such penalties in CA98 investigations.

USE AND DISCLOSURE OF INFORMATION BY THE PSR

6.12 We can use information we receive in the course of undertaking a FSBRA market review or an EA02 market study for our other functions, such as FSBRA regulatory action, including compliance failure proceedings, or enforcement of the prohibitions in the Competition Act 1998.[81]

6.13 The applicable legal framework for the disclosure of information is determined by the statutory context in which it was received by. In particular, whether we carry out a FSBRA market review or an EA02 market study will determine the legal framework for disclosure of information received by us in the context of that review/study.

NOTES

81 However, there may be restrictions on our use of information if we receive it from other authorities.

FSBRA

6.14 When we receive information for the purposes of, or in discharge of, our statutory functions under FSBRA (for example, during a FSBRA market review) which is not in the public domain and relates to a person's business or other affairs, the information will be 'confidential information' under section 91 FSBRA. Information which is already publicly available, or which is in aggregated form so that it is not possible to ascertain from it information relating to a particular person, is not considered confidential information under FSBRA.

6.15 However, when we receive information for the purposes of, or in discharge of, our concurrent functions, the disclosure of this information is expressly excluded from the FSBRA regime and will instead be dealt with under the regime set out in EA02. In other words, information received by the PSR for the purposes of or in discharge of its concurrent functions can only be disclosed by the PSR under Part 9 EA02, not under FSBRA (see paragraphs 6.18 to 6.21).[82]

6.16 Where we have obtained information under FSBRA rather than in connection with our concurrent competition functions (see paragraph 6.18), FSBRA provisions on disclosure will apply. Section 91 FSBRA restricts the disclosure of confidential information unless we have the consent of the person who provided the information (and the person to whom the information relates, if different) or a gateway applies. A gateway is an exception to the restriction on disclosure, allowing the disclosure of confidential information to third parties in certain prescribed circumstances. If a gateway is not applicable, we may not release confidential information without the requisite consent(s).

6.17 The full set of gateways is set out in Regulations made under FSBRA.[83] They include disclosure to assist the PSR in the discharge of its functions, and disclosure to the FCA, the Prudential Regulation Authority and the CMA to assist them in the discharge of their functions. When we disclose information pursuant to a gateway, we may restrict the use to which it may be put.

NOTES

82 Section 91(6) FSBRA
83 Financial Services (Banking Reform) Act 2013 (Disclosure of Confidential Information) Regulations 2014 (SI 2014/8820)

EA02

6.18 When we receive information in connection with the exercise of our concurrent functions, including EA02 market studies, Part 9 EA02 will apply to any disclosure of such information.[84] This imposes a general restriction on the disclosure of information relating to the affairs of an individual or any business of an undertaking which we obtain during the exercise of our EA02 functions (referred to as 'specified information') to other persons.[85] The restriction applies during the lifetime of an individual or while the undertaking continues in existence (for the individual or business to which the specified information relates, respectively). Disclosure is permitted if it falls within one of the 'information gateways', as set out in sections 239 to 243 EA02. These gateways include where we obtain the required consents[86] or where the disclosure is made for the purpose of facilitating the exercise of any of our statutory functions.[87]

6.19 Even when Part 9 EA02 and one of its information gateways apply, we must have regard to certain considerations before making a disclosure. In particular, we must have regard to the three considerations set out in section 244 EA02:

- The need to exclude from disclosure (so far as it is practicable to do so) any information whose disclosure we consider to be contrary to the public interest.
- The need to exclude from disclosure (so far as practicable) commercial information we consider might significantly harm the legitimate business interests of the undertakings; or information relating to the private affairs of an individual which we think might significantly harm that individual's interests.

- The extent to which the disclosure of information relating to the private affairs of an individual or of commercial information is necessary for the purpose for which we are permitted to make the disclosure.

6.20 We will apply these three considerations on a case-by-case basis when we are considering disclosure of specified information.

6.21 Where we disclose information to another person, there are restrictions on the further disclosure or use of the information by that person.[88]

NOTES

[84] Section 91(6) FSBRA
[85] Section 237 EA02
[86] Section 239 EA02
[87] Section 241 EA02
[88] Section 241(1) and (4) EA02

TRANSPARENCY

6.22 We have noted throughout this document that we will make submissions available for public inspection unless the respondent requests otherwise (see paragraphs 3.3, 3.13, 4.3 and 4.8). We will seek parties' views on which parts of their submission are confidential before deciding if, and if so how much, information should be redacted prior to making them publicly available. We will apply the relevant legislation in making this decision: for FSBRA market reviews, see paragraphs 6.14 to 6.17; for EA02 market studies, see paragraphs 6.18 to 6.21.

6.23 We may in addition publish working papers or other relevant documents, in the interests of transparency and to allow interested parties to make better-informed submissions. Again, we will apply the relevant legislation when considering disclosure of information, depending on how we gathered the information.

(II) TRANSPORT

ORR'S APPROACH TO MONITORING AND REVIEWING MARKETS

(January 2017)

[3.665]

NOTES

CONTENTS

1. INTRODUCTION

[3.666]

1.1 The Office of Rail and Road (**ORR**) is the combined economic and health and safety regulator for Great Britain's rail network[1] and the monitor for England's strategic road network. As the designated sectoral regulator for rail, we must keep the provision of railway services[2] under review. We are also required to monitor the competitive situation in the rail services markets.[3]

1.2 We have a number of powers to address issues which we identify in the rail services markets.

1.3 The purpose of this guidance is to outline our approach to discharging our monitoring and reviewing responsibilities in relation to rail markets. This guidance also sets out the range of potential outcomes which may result from our monitoring and reviewing activities, and the range of tools we may utilise. These include our power to undertake market studies under the Enterprise Act 2002 (the **Enterprise Act**) and our power to make directions under the Access and Management Regulations.[4]

1.4 In undertaking our market monitoring and review functions we must, at all stages, have regard to our statutory duties.[5]

1.5 Other bodies also review markets. These bodies include the Competition & Markets Authority (the **CMA**), other sectoral regulators with concurrent competition powers[6] and the European Commission.[7] We liaise with concurrent regulators[8] and the European Commission to ensure that our work does not duplicate theirs[9] and in order to decide, in certain circumstances (such as in a cross market investigation), who is best placed to act.[10]

1.6 This document replaces our earlier guide *ORR's approach to reviewing markets* which we published in 2009. We may revise and reissue this guidance in the light of experience and other developments in law and practice.

NOTES

1 Upon the implementation in Northern Ireland of Directive 2012/34/EU of the European Parliament and of the Council of 21 November 2012 establishing a single European railway (the **Recast Directive**) ORR will also be the economic regulator for the Northern Ireland rail network

2 Section 69(1) of the Railways Act 1993 (the **Railways Act**)

3 Regulation 34 of the Railways (Access, Management and Licensing of Railway Undertakings) Regulations 2016 (the **Access and Management Regulations**), which implement the Recast Directive

4 As defined in footnote 3 above

5 Under section 4 of the Railways Act

6 The other sectoral regulators are CAA (Civil Aviation Authority), Ofcom (Office of Communications), Ofgem (the Gas and Electricity Markets Authority), Ofwat (the Water Services Regulation Authority), FCA (the Financial Conduct Authority), PSR (Payment Systems Regulator), and the Northern Ireland Authority for Utility Regulation. Monitor (the regulator of healthcare services in England), has concurrent competition powers but not a statutory duty to promote competition; Monitor is not a member of the UKCN but attends its meetings with an observer status

7 The European Commission may decide to conduct an inquiry into a particular sector of the economy or into particular types of agreements across various sectors (Sector Inquiries), "*where the trend of trade between Member States, the rigidity of prices or other circumstances suggest that competition may be restricted or distorted within the common market*", Council Regulation 1/2003/EC on the implementation of the rules on competition laid down in Articles 81 and 82 of the Treaty, Article 17(1). Examples include Sector Inquiries into e-commerce, pharmaceuticals, energy, roaming and media. These inquiries tend to last around 15 to 24 months from inception to final report and include stakeholder consultation. Outcomes from Sector Inquiries may include; pursuing individual cases under competition rules; informing the European Commission's view in merger cases; and/or changing the regulatory framework

8 See the Memorandum of Understanding between CMA and ORR: www.gov.uk/government/uploads/system/uploads/attachment_data/file/318909/MoU_-_CMA_and_the_ORR.pdf (**Memorandum of Understanding**)

9 As an example, in March 2016, the CMA published its conclusions in relation to the possibilities for greater competition

Part 3 CMA and other Guidelines

between train operators in passenger rail services: assets.digital.cabinet-office.gov.uk/media/56ddc41aed915d037600000d/Competition_in_passenger_rail_services_in_Great_Britain.pdf

10 The CMA has the power to decide which competition authority will lead on a case: see Annex B of CMA1: 'Towards the CMA', July 2013: www.gov.uk/government/uploads/system/uploads/attachment_data/file/212285/CMA1_-_Towards_the_CMA.pdf

2. MONITORING MARKETS

[3.667]

2.1 As the economic and safety regulator we have significant day to day interaction with the railway industry. We use intelligence gained in this way to monitor the competitive situation in railway markets and to keep under review the delivery of railway services.

2.2 We receive intelligence through, amongst other things:

- regulating health and safety for the entire mainline rail network in Great Britain, as well as London Underground, light rail, trams and the heritage sector;
- approving and directing access agreements for rail operators to track, stations and light maintenance depots;
- receiving accounting information from railway operators; and
- monitoring Network Rail and holding it to account for delivering its regulated outputs set as part of its five year price control.[11]

2.3 We also gain intelligence from other engagement with industry and with users of railway services, for example:

- through our freight panel[12] and consumer watchdogs;
- through complaints and appeals which we receive through our role as an appeal body under certain parts of the Network Code,[13] which regulates the interaction between Network Rail and its access beneficiaries, and under the Access and Management Regulations;[14]
- through interaction with the Rail Delivery Group;[15] and
- from those providing funding to the sector.

2.4 Information provided to us by market participants is very important. Our assessment of how markets are working has to be informed by the experience and knowledge of those operating within those markets (both suppliers and customers). We remain open, therefore, to suggestions on what areas of the railway we should prioritise for review. In particular we welcome suggestions regarding markets which may not be covered by our day to day interaction with the industry. Please use the form at Annex C to make any suggestions to us.

2.5 As part of our duty to monitor the competitive situation in the rail services markets under European legislation, we must, in particular, look for and prevent discrimination against applicants with an interest in obtaining capacity on railway infrastructure (**Applicants**). This entails controlling arrangements for: access to railway infrastructure and relevant network services; the allocation of such access; the charges levied for access; schemes for charging for access; and, the content of network statements[16] produced by managers of railway infrastructure (**Infrastructure Managers**). In fulfilling this responsibility we must, in particular:

- control such matters on our own initiative with a view to preventing discrimination against Applicants,[17] for example, by considering making a direction (see Chapter 4, below); and
- check that network statements do not contain discriminatory clauses or give infrastructure managers discretionary powers that may be used to discriminate against Applicants.

2.6 From time to time, and where our monitoring brings to our attention a potential competition or consumer issue, we will seek further information typically by researching what is publicly available, and sometimes by conducting interviews with a small number of relevant stakeholders. Alternatively if our market monitoring identifies potential competition issues or other market issues which require more specific or urgent action, we may:

- consider moving into a research stage, which is described in more detail at paragraphs 2.7 to 2.10 below;
- progress immediately to undertaking a formal market study if this is appropriate – the process for market studies is set out at paragraphs 3.1 to 3.15 below;
- consider it appropriate to move directly to giving directions under the Access and Management Regulations, the procedure for which we set out at paragraphs 4.1 to 4.4 below; or
- in certain circumstances, proceed directly to enforcement action using our statutory powers.

RESEARCH STAGE

2.7 During the research stage typically we will gather information from our own records and from governmental and public sources to assess how a market is functioning and assess whether there appear to be market problems that warrant further attention. The research stage may take up to three months, but can be shorter, for example, if we receive a detailed submission or complaint or if sufficient information is readily available. The research stage is not typically public.

2.8 We seek to impose the minimum burden on stakeholders at the research stage, but it may be the case that only industry participants can provide us with the information we need to come to a robust view on next steps in a particular case. Where a suggestion is made by an industry party we may consider it necessary to contact that party to explore the matter they have raised to ensure we fully understand it. We are conscious however that involving one party may necessitate involving others to provide a balanced perspective.

2.9 There are several outcomes which are possible as a result of the research stage. We may decide to give a clean bill of health to a market where the results of our research do not suggest that there are any issues of significant concern. Where we think there is an issue which requires further analysis we may choose to progress to a more in depth review of the market which could take the form of a market review or a market study (see Chapter 3). The latter is more likely where:

- we already have significant information at our disposal, perhaps by way of a well-articulated complaint; and
- that information is highly indicative of a matter which could result in a market investigation reference and benefit from being investigated using formal investigation powers.

2.10 Alternatively, there are several other options following the research stage:

- we may decide that the issues we identify are not ones that we should prioritise under our prioritisation criteria – see Annex A;
- we may progress to an investigation under the Competition Act 1998 (the **Competition Act**)[18] or take action under consumer law[19] where we have identified a specific potential breach of competition or consumer law which would appropriately be addressed through direct enforcement action; or
- we may decide that there are matters which are capable of resolution under our sector-specific powers, for example licence enforcement.

MARKET REVIEWS

2.11 A market review is a more formal stage of enquiry, which is likely to impose burdens on industry to some extent. For example, we may issue information requests with set deadlines or publish a call for evidence from other interested stakeholders. As described above, we may initiate a market review as an outcome of the research stage or as the result of a complaint from an interested party.

2.12 We may also initiate a market review in response to a super-complaint under the Enterprise Act.[20]

2.13 Although there is no statutory timescale for the conduct of market reviews we will endeavour to conclude the process within six months. Our ability to do so will, however, be highly dependent on the information available to us and, therefore, the response of stakeholders to our information gathering.

INFORMATION GATHERING

2.14 We may choose to gather information from market participants and other parties, for example other public bodies and consumer groups. We may gather information in a number of ways including:

- making requests for information or issuing questionnaires;
- conducting our own market research (for example, telephone surveys);
- holding industry-wide seminars, meetings and/or interviews; and/or
- commissioning research from external consultants where we require specific technical expertise and advice.

2.15 In conducting market reviews we will typically seek to gather information on a cooperative basis, i.e. without using statutory powers to compel the production of information or documents from parties. We do have statutory powers to compel the production of information from licence holders,[21] however we anticipate only using these powers where the particular circumstances of a matter render it proportionate to do so. An example of where we may consider using our formal powers would be where a business refused to provide us with key information on a cooperative basis.

OUTCOMES

2.16 Although there is no formal requirement to do so, we may decide to consult the industry in relation to the outcome of a market review. Whether or not we undertake public consultation in a particular case, we will publish the outcomes of all market reviews in an appropriate manner, most likely in a report or in a public letter to stakeholders. The manner in which we communicate the outcomes of market reviews will be determined on a case by case basis.

2.17 Following a market review, we may decide any of the following:[22]

- that the issues we identify are not ones that we should prioritise under our prioritisation criteria – see Annex A;
- to progress to an investigation under the Competition Act[23] or take action under consumer law[24] where we have identified a specific potential breach of competition or consumer law which would appropriately be addressed through direct enforcement action;
- that there are matters which are capable of resolution under our sector specific powers, for example licence enforcement;
- to commence a market study[25] (see Chapter 3);
- to engage with industry to develop an industry-led solution to an issue which we identify, for example, a Code of Practice, or, we may ask the industry to review established industry mechanisms which have been created to deal with similar issues but which may not be entirely effectual in addressing the facts identified during our review;
- that there are issues which could be more effectively dealt with elsewhere, for example, by Government, a franchising authority or other public body. We may in such a circumstance write to the relevant authority setting out recommendations on how our competition concerns could be met; or
- that there is a significant issue or a pattern of behaviour identified for which a remedy is not available and the matter is one which would not be suitable for a Market Investigation Reference. In such a circumstance we may make a detailed report to Government. The report may, for example, include recommendations for changes to laws or regulations.

NOTES

11 For more information in relation to our regulation of Network Rail and five year control periods, please see: http://orr.gov.uk/what-and-how-we-regulate/regulation-of-network-rail/how-we-regulate-network-rail/periodic-review-2018/about-periodic-review-18-pr18

12 This panel comprises freight customers who represent a wide range of expertise and interest from across the rail freight community. This panel forms part of our work to ensure that our policies and regulatory decisions take into account the commercial environment in which freight customers work

13 The Network Code is a set of rules which is incorporated into, and therefore forms part of, each bilateral access contract between Network Rail and holders of rights of access to the track owned and operated by Network Rail

14 Regulation 32 of the Access and Management Regulations

15 http://www.raildeliverygroup.com/

16 Network statements are produced by Infrastructure Managers and set out in detail the general rules, deadlines, procedures and criteria for charging and capacity-allocation schemes, including such other information as is required to enable applications for infrastructure capacity. Infrastructure Managers are required to produce a network statement by Regulation 13 of the Access and Management Regulations

17 The particular issues we must control as part of our duty to monitor the railway are the same as those to which Applicants have a right of appeal to us under Regulation 32(1) of the Access and Management Regulations in the event that they believe that they have been unfairly treated, discriminated against or otherwise aggrieved. An explanation of how our power to give directions overlaps with our roles as an appeals body, together with a list of the matters which may be subject to an appeal, is set out at paragraph 4.7 to 4.9, below

We have produced separate guidance on how we will discharge our function as an appeals body. This guidance is also subject to consultation and is available on our website.

18 http://orr.gov.uk/__data/assets/pdf_file/0019/21367/competition-act-guidance.pdf

19 We are a designated enforcer of consumer law under Part 8 of the Enterprise Act, so that we are a civil enforcer of the Consumer Protection from Unfair Trading Regulations 2008. We will also be a designated enforcer under Part 8 of the Enterprise Act for the purposes of the Consumer Rights Act 2015 when that takes effect in relation to railway transport services

20 Under section 205 of the Enterprise Act designated consumer bodies may make super-complaints to sectoral regulators, about market features that may be harming consumers. A super-complaint may be made to us in relation to the rail industry. Under section 11 of the Enterprise Act, we must respond to a super-complaint within 90 days after receipt stating whether we will take action and if so what that action will be. There is a statutory duty obliging us to consider the complaint, but this does not extend to requiring us to take any action following that initial review. We would typically characterise this initial review as equivalent, or at least comparable, to a market review

21 Under section 80 of the Railways Act

22 We note that a number of the potential outcomes following a market review are the same as those following the research stage. However, we would expect that the outcomes listed in paragraph 2.17 are more likely to follow as a result of a market review than following the research stage, given the additional information gathering and analysis that we would have been able to undertake in the market review process

23 See footnote 17 above

24 See footnote 18 above

25 Where we identify an issue which we anticipate may lead us to proceed to a market study, we would expect to liaise with the CMA and keep them informed as to the issue we have identified

3. MARKET STUDIES AND MARKET INVESTIGATION REFERENCES

MARKET STUDIES

[3.668]

3.1 Market studies are examinations into the causes of why particular markets may not be working well, taking an overview of regulatory and other economic drivers and patterns of consumer and business behaviour.[26] Through gathering intelligence from a range of sources, we can identify markets which appear not to be working well. A market study can then examine whether there is a problem, in which case the study looks at its effects, the causes of those effects, and considers how those causes may be best addressed by the most appropriate means.

3.2 We will consult with the CMA before exercising any of our concurrent powers in relation to markets.[27]

Market study notices

3.3 Market studies are conducted under our general function to keep under review the provision, both in Great Britain and elsewhere, of railway services. In the course of market studies we may utilise formal investigation powers in order to gather evidence from relevant parties.

3.4 Market studies are commenced through the publication of a market study notice (a **Market Study Notice**). When we are carrying out our functions to monitor markets[28] and we consider it appropriate to use formal investigation powers,[29] we may publish a Market Study Notice.

3.5 The legal test for deciding whether to publish a Market Study Notice requires us to consider whether an issue is one where the use of formal information gathering powers is appropriate with a view to deciding whether to make a Market Investigation Reference (**MIR**) to the CMA,[30] who would then conduct an in-depth examination of the relevant markets (see below). In assessing whether a matter is 'appropriate' under this test, we will have regard to our prioritisation principles and the feasibility of using other tools.[31] Market studies are resource intensive processes and can create significant burdens on industry. We will therefore carefully consider whether the legal test has been met and consider our duties under section 4 of the Railways Act before making a decision to publish a Market Study Notice.

3.6 A Market Study Notice will set out:

- the scope of the market study;
- the period during which representations can be made to us in relation to the market study; and
- the timescales within which the market study will be completed.[32]

Statutory time limits for market studies

3.7 When we publish a Market Study Notice, this initiates the following statutory timetable,[33] which is illustrated below:

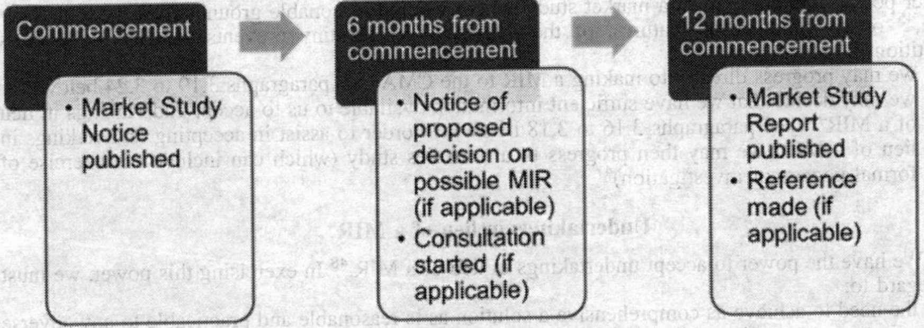

3.8 **Within six months** of the date of publication of the Market Study Notice:

- **where we propose to make a MIR**[34] in relation to the subject matter of the market study, we must publish a notice of our proposed decision and begin the process of consulting relevant persons;[35] or
- **where we do not propose to make a MIR** -
  - if we have received representations in response to the Market Study Notice which suggest that we should make a MIR,[36] we must publish a notice of our proposed decision and begin a process of consultation; or
  - if we have not received any representations to the contrary, we must publish a notice of our decision.[37]

3.9 **Within 12 months** of the date of publication of the Market Study Notice:

- We must publish a report setting out our findings and our reasoning on any action which we propose to take.[38] Where we have decided:
  - to make a MIR;
  - not to make a MIR, where we have received representations to the contrary; or
  - to accept undertakings in lieu of a MIR.

  then the report must contain our decision, the reasons for such decision and such information as we consider appropriate for facilitating a proper understanding of the reasons for our decision.[39] Where our report sets out a decision to make a MIR, we must make that reference at the same time as publishing the report.[40]

3.10 Through the consultation which we undertake as part of a market study, stakeholders will be given the opportunity to comment on matters such as the criteria being used to assess competition in the particular market(s) under review and on our proposed methodology.

Cases raising public interest considerations

3.11 The Secretary of State has a power[41] to intervene in a markets case where the case raises public interest considerations, by giving us a notice that one or more than one public interest consideration is relevant to the matter. At present, the interests of national security constitute the only specified public interest consideration, although the Secretary of State has the power to introduce other specified public interest considerations. As such, we would not anticipate the power to make public interest interventions to be commonly used in the rail sector. Further guidance in relation to this power can be found in the CMA's guidance.[42]

Investigatory powers

3.12 Once we publish a Market Study Notice, we are able to use certain formal investigatory powers to assist us in carrying out our functions[43] and we would expect to use them. These powers are:

- to give notice to require any person to attend at a time and place specified in the notice to give evidence to a person nominated by us for the purpose;
- to give notice to any person requiring that person to produce specified documents or categories of documents which are in that person's custody or control; and
- to give notice to any person carrying on business to supply us with specified estimates, forecasts, returns or other information in a specified form and manner.

3.13 These information gathering powers will enable us to make a fuller assessment of any concerns identified during the market review stage. The overarching principle we follow during a market study is to reach a decision as quickly as practicable so as to limit the perception of risk and uncertainty in the industry and the imposition of disproportionate burdens on businesses. We aim to be fair and reasonable in the use of our information gathering powers and in setting the deadlines which we set for parties to provide information to us.

3.14 Where we consider that a person has, without reasonable excuse, failed to comply with any requirement of a notice issued by us using our investigatory powers under the Enterprise Act, we have the power to impose an administrative penalty.[44]

Outcomes of a market study

3.15 Following a market study, we may reach any of the same outcomes as we might reach following a research study or a market review, as set out in paragraphs 2.09, 2.10 and 2.17, above. There is also a further possible outcome from a market study, where we find reasonable grounds to suspect that any feature,[45] or combination of features, of the market under scrutiny prevents, restricts or distorts competition, in which case:

- we may progress directly to making a MIR to the CMA (see paragraphs 3.19 to 3.24 below); or
- we may decide that we have sufficient information available to us to accept undertakings in lieu of a MIR[46] (see paragraphs 3.16 to 3.18 below). In order to assist in accepting undertakings in lieu of a MIR, we may then progress to a remedies study (which can include the exercise of formal powers of investigation)[47].

Undertakings in lieu of a MIR

3.16 We have the power to accept undertakings in lieu of a MIR.[48] In exercising this power, we must have regard to:

- the need to achieve as comprehensive a solution as is reasonable and practicable to any adverse effects on competition identified; and
- any detrimental effects on customers so far as they result or may be expected to result from such adverse effects.

3.17 We may also have regard to the effect of the undertakings on any relevant customer benefits arising from a feature or features of the markets concerned.

3.18 Before accepting undertakings in lieu of a MIR, we are obliged to publish a notice of the proposed undertakings, which must state the purpose and effect of the undertaking and identify the situation which the undertaking is seeking to deal with, as well as setting out any other facts which we consider justify the acceptance of the undertaking. We must consider any representations we receive which are made in accordance with the notice in relation to the undertakings before accepting them.

MAKING A MARKET INVESTIGATION REFERENCE

3.19 As set out above, one of the possible outcomes of a market study is that we make a MIR to the CMA.[49] A MIR can be either:

- an 'ordinary reference', where we have reasonable grounds for suspecting that any feature, or combination of features, of a market for goods or services relating to railways in the UK prevents, restricts or distorts competition; or
- a 'cross-market reference', where the feature or each of the features concerned exists in more than one market.[50]

3.20 Before making a decision to make a MIR we will apply our duties as set out in section 4 of the Railways Act and take into account a number of factors including:

- the nature and significance of the competition problems that we believe exist in the market(s) concerned;
- whether a MIR would be a proportionate response to the scale of the competition problems identified;
- whether it would be possible to accept commitments/undertakings in lieu of a MIR (see paragraphs 3.16 to 3.18 above); and/or
- whether appropriate remedies are likely to be available to the CMA, or in the absence of appropriate remedies, whether a CMA report might provide a useful alternative contribution.

3.21 In some cases we may have direct regulatory powers which may be used to address issues raised by a market study. In such cases we will carefully weigh the advantages and disadvantages of the possible approaches prior to making a decision whether or not to make a MIR.

3.22 If we make a MIR, it must specify:[51]

- the enactment under which it is made;
- the date on which it is made; and
- the description of goods and services to which the feature or combination of features concerned relates.

3.23 More information in relation to the CMA's procedure for undertaking a Market Investigation can be found on the CMA's website.[52]

3.24 Upon receiving a MIR, the CMA will conduct a detailed investigation and reach its own conclusions about the market. The CMA has the power to impose remedies which may include divestiture, behavioural remedies or recommendations for action by Government or other agencies. Further details of the UK market investigation regime and remedies available to the CMA can be found in the CMA's guidance.[53]

NOTES

26 Market studies should not be confused with market investigations carried out by the CMA or sector inquiries carried out by the European Commission as described at paragraph 1.5, above

27 Memorandum of Understanding, paragraph 78

28 Section 69(1) of the Railways Act

29 Under section 174 of the Enterprise Act

30 This consideration is made in accordance with the legal test set out at section 130A of the Enterprise Act as applied by section 67(2C) of the Railways Act. Namely we make this assessment in circumstances where we are proposing to carry out our functions under section 69(1) of the Railways Act for the purposes of:

– considering the extent to which a matter in relation to services related to railways has or may have effects adverse to the interests of consumers; and

– assessing the extent to which steps can and should be taken to remedy, mitigate or prevent any such adverse effects

31 See Annex A

32 Section 130A(3) of the Enterprise Act

33 Under section 131C of the Enterprise Act, the Secretary of State has a power to amend the time limits set out in section 131B of the Enterprise Act

34 See paragraphs 3.19 to 3.24

35 Section 131B(1) of the Enterprise Act

36 Section 131B(1) of the Enterprise Act

37 Section 131B(3) of the Enterprise Act

38 Section 131B(4) of the Enterprise Act

39 Section 131B(5) of the Enterprise Act

40 Section 131B(6) of the Enterprise Act

41 Under section 139 of the Enterprise Act

42 CMA3 - "Market Studies and Market Investigations: Supplemental guidance on the CMA's approach", January 2014, paragraphs 2.18 to 2.30

43 Section 174 of the Enterprise Act

44 Sections 174A(1) to (3) of the Enterprise Act. See also section 174 of the Enterprise Act. For more information on penalties, see the Competition and Markets Authority (Penalties) Order 2014

45 Section 131(2) of the Enterprise Act defines a "feature" of a market as: the structure of the market concerned or any aspect of that structure; any conduct (whether or not in the market concerned) of one or more than one person who supplies or acquires goods or services in the market concerned; or any conduct relating to the market concerned of customers of any person who supplies or acquires goods or services. Conduct is described as including "any failure to act (whether or not intentional) and any other unintentional conduct"

46 Section 154 of the Enterprise Act

47 As set out in section 174 of the Enterprise Act

48 Section 154 of the Enterprise Act

49 Section 131(1) of the Enterprise Act

50 Under sections 131(2A) and (6) of the Enterprise Act. In such a case, there is no statutory requirement to refer the whole of each market as a MIR, but we would consider the wider implications of doing so on a case by case basis

51 Section 133 of the Enterprise Act

52 See footnote 46 above

53 This can be found at: www.gov.uk/government/uploads/system/uploads/attachment_data/file/284390/cc3_revised.pdf and www.gov.uk/government/uploads/system/uploads/attachment_data/file/462715/CMA3_Markets_Guidance_-_updated_September_2015.pdf

4. DIRECTIONS IN RELATION TO MARKETS

POWER TO MAKE DIRECTIONS

[3.669]

4.1 Under the Access and Management Regulations we must, where appropriate, give appropriate directions in order to correct:

- discrimination against applicants for access to the rail network;
- market distortion; or
- undesirable developments in relation to the competitive situation in the rail services markets.[54]

4.2 We may exercise this power on our own initiative, for example as a result of an issue which we have identified through our monitoring activities. We may also choose to exercise this power in response to an issue raised by an interested or affected party.

4.3 Any party to whom a direction is given must comply with and give effect to that direction. We have a power to impose a financial penalty for a failure to comply with a direction.[55]

4.4 Our power to issue directions is separate from our concurrent competition power to undertake market studies under the Enterprise Act. This power is designed specifically to address issues we identify in the functioning of the rail services market and allows us to swiftly intervene to correct such issues.

WHEN WE MAY USE THIS POWER

4.5 In determining whether issuing a direction is appropriate in any particular case we will have regard to the need to act proportionately.

4.6 Subject to consideration of our prioritisation principles (set out in Annex A), typically we consider that giving directions is likely to be appropriate in cases where:

- swift targeted intervention is an optimal approach to correct relatively straightforward and easily identifiable market issues, without the need for in-depth investigation; and
- there are no established regulatory means such as a licensing or access solution which would be equally as effective and expedient in resolving the issue.

Overlap between appeals function and power to give directions

4.7 An appeal can be submitted to us under the Access and Management Regulations, relating to:[56]

- the network statement produced in accordance with regulation 13 of the Access and Management Regulations, in its provisional and final versions;
- the information which must be included in that network statement;
- the allocation process for infrastructure capacity;
- the charging scheme and charging system and the Channel Tunnel charging framework;
- the level or structure of infrastructure fees which an applicant is or may be required to pay;
- the arrangements for access under Part 2 of the Access and Management Regulations;[57] and
- access to and charging for services provided under Part 2 of the Access and Management Regulations.

4.8 The Access and Management Regulations allow for the possibility that we may be required to consider an issue under the appeal function[58] which may also be appropriately addressed through our power to make directions.[59] Where we receive an appeal under the Access and Management Regulations, our power to make a decision extends only as far as the matters which are brought to us as part of the appeal. Our power to issue directions, however, is more wide reaching and allows us to address related issues which may not have been brought directly as part of an appeal but which we nonetheless consider need to be addressed.

4.9 If applicants have a preference as to which function is applied, then reasons for this should be submitted to us. Ultimately we will determine, having considered representations received, which function should be utilised in each case. We may, in certain circumstances, determine that it is most appropriate to operate the appeal and directions functions in parallel. We will endeavour to keep interested parties informed of the approach being adopted in each particular case.

PROCESS AND TIMESCALES

4.10 If we are considering making a direction under regulation 34 in relation to an issue which has been appealed under regulation 32 (i.e. exercising the functions in parallel), we will seek to exercise both powers, so far as possible, to the same timescales; namely, we will publish our final decision in relation to both the appeal and whether we consider it appropriate to issue directions within a maximum of 6 weeks of the date of receipt of all relevant information.

4.11 In all other circumstances we will endeavour to complete our enquiries and make a determination on whether directions are appropriate within a 6 week timeframe. If it is apparent that we are likely to require significantly longer than this, we may consider whether it is more appropriate to undertake a market review (see paragraphs 2.11 to 2.17 above), or publish a Market Study Notice under the Enterprise Act (see paragraphs 3.4 to 3.6 above).

4.12 When exercising this power we will have regard to the principles of good regulation which are proportionality, transparency, accountability, consistency and targeting.[60] Before issuing a direction we will consult with the relevant parties and consider their representations.[61]

DIRECTIONS

4.13 Given the nature of the power to issue directions and the timescales within which it will be used, we expect directions given under the Access and Management Regulations to constitute straightforward actions required of individual persons or businesses. We do not anticipate issuing directions which require changes in business structures or on-going monitoring by ORR. If it is apparent that such intervention may be appropriate to resolve the relevant issues, we may consider whether it would be more appropriate to use alternative regulatory powers available to us (such as licensing) or we could proceed to the issue of a Market Study Notice. Either course of action could be preceded by a market review.

NOTES

54 Regulation 34 of the Access and Management Regulations

55 Regulation 38 of the Access and Management Regulations. We will be amending our Enforcement Policy and Penalties Statement to reflect this power. The current version is available here: http://orr.gov.uk/__data/assets/pdf_file/0018/4716/economic-enforcement-statement.pdf

56 Regulation 32(2) of the Access and Management Regulations. This list is also the list of matters which we have a duty to control, on our own initiative and with a view to preventing discrimination, under Regulation 34(2)(a) of the Access and Management Regulations

57 Part 2 of the Access and Management Regulations covers access to railway infrastructure and services

58 Regulation 32 of the Access and Management Regulations

59 Regulation 34(3) of the Access and Management Regulations

60 These principles are set out here: www.google.co.uk/url?url=http://webarchive.nationalarchives.gov.uk/20100407162704/http:/archive.cabinetoffice.gov.uk/brc/upload/assets/www.brc.gov.uk/principlesleaflet.pdf&rct=j&frm=1&q=&esrc=s&sa=U&ved=0ahUKEwjfksLw4dbLAhWEVhQKHfsVAlwQFggUMAA&usg=AFQjCNED8JAFFYVj3Z6mEpBhM4QbKkgFAA

61 This includes consultation with the Secretary of State where the decision in question affects a rail link or, as the case may be, the operation of the development agreement

ANNEX A: PRIORITISATION CRITERIA AND CHOICE OF TOOL

PRIORITISATION CRITERIA

[3.670]

1. We apply prioritisation principles at regular intervals during our internal projects and formal investigations, in order to help us focus our resource in a way that delivers most value from our interventions. When applying the prioritisation principles in the context of our market monitoring powers we will afford particular weight to prioritising the protection of consumers and other users of railway services. The weight attached to each of the criteria will also be influenced by our strategic priorities. Otherwise, the criteria below are not ordered by priority or significance.[62]

2. Our prioritisation criteria are:

- **Strategic significance** – We will consider how our intervention will deliver outcomes which are in line with our strategic objectives; for example to secure value for money from the railway, for users and funders.
- **Is ORR better/best placed to act** – We will examine whether a particular course of action is best carried out by ORR. We work in partnership with a number of concurrent competition and consumer protection authorities. Consideration of this criterion will typically involve determining whether other organisations are better or best placed to address the issue in question.
- **Impact** – We will consider the likely impact of our intervention. Factors which we will take into consideration in measuring that impact include:
  - the actual or potential level of harm (which, depending on the circumstances, could be harm to passengers, taxpayers or other users of the railways);
  - evidence to suggest a systemic issue, rather than an isolated incident;
  - whether conduct is recurrent and/or on-going;
  - whether the issue in question is leading or could lead to inefficiencies in the market, either in terms of costs or end prices to consumers; and
  - other indirect benefits such as deterrence or raised awareness amongst consumers. This impact could be in the market in question or in related markets.
- **Costs** – We will estimate the internal and external costs attached to our intervention. The internal costs will include any opportunity costs (for example, knock-on effects on ORR's current and future portfolio of work). It is important that the costs of our intervention are proportionate to the impact that we are seeking.
- **Risks** – We will adopt a risk-based approach when assessing whether or not a matter constitutes a priority. The risks that we will consider include:
  - the probability of a successful outcome particularly in terms of better outcomes for taxpayers, passengers or other users of the railways;
  - the legal risks, notably the strength of the evidence available or likely to become available during the investigation; and
  - the impact of our decisions on our reputation, since credibility plays an important role in the overall effectiveness of the regime.

3. The list of criteria set out above is not exhaustive and we may consider other factors where appropriate. We will keep our prioritisation assessment of any particular intervention under review throughout the course of such intervention.

CHOICE OF TOOL

4. As set out in Chapters 3 and 4, we have a statutory power to undertake market studies and to make MIRs, and, to make directions under the Access and Management Regulations. However, ORR's monitoring toolkit encompasses a number of other tools to address competition and/or consumer protection issues. This means that in some circumstances we may have to make a decision as to which tool is more appropriate to deal with a particular issue.

5. In practice we will, at an early stage, determine which tool is most appropriate to deal with the particular issues being raised. The appropriateness of the tool being utilised to address a particular issue will be kept under review.

6. The overriding principle is that we will seek to use the most effective, efficient and expeditious solution where an issue is found to exist. In order to make this assessment we will have regard to our prioritisation criteria with particular consideration of:

- the resource and timing implications of the tool being used;
- the potential outcomes which may be achieved; and
- any other advantages or disadvantages between using particular tools, for example potential deterrent effect and establishing case precedent.

7. Where ORR is confronted with a serious and clear breach of the law, taking enforcement action will usually be the most appropriate response rather than launching a market review. However, in certain circumstances we might consider that there are issues with the way that the market is working and there would be merit in looking at the issue from a whole market rather than individual conduct perspective. In such circumstances we will consider the use of our market review or study functions.

NOTES

62 It should be noted that our prioritisation criteria solely apply to areas of work in respect of which ORR has discretion to intervene. Therefore, the criteria do not apply where we have a duty to take action (e.g. ORR appeal function under Regulation 32 of the Access and Management Regulations).

ANNEX B: HANDLING INFORMATION

[3.671]

1. The Freedom of Information Act 2000 (**FOIA**) gives any person the right to request non-published information from us. However, we recognise that we will obtain information in the context of market studies and competition investigations that should not be widely disclosed. There are certain exemptions in the FOIA that could be relevant to information held by us through the exercise of our functions. The application of exemptions in the FOIA will be considered on a case by case basis.

2. Part 9 of the Enterprise Act restricts our ability to disclose information we receive in the course of our work. In particular, Part 9 of the Enterprise Act contains a general prohibition against disclosure of information that relates to the affairs of a business or an individual, unless disclosure is otherwise permitted (for example where the parties have given their consent, or where the disclosure is for the purpose of facilitating the exercise of a public authority's statutory function). It is a criminal offence to disclose information in breach of those provisions.

3. Section 145(1) of the Railways Act restricts the disclosure by ORR of information it has obtained under or by virtue of the Railways Act. However, section 145(2) of the Railways Act allows disclosure for the purpose of facilitating our carrying out of our functions under the Railways Act, the Transport Act 2000 and the Railways Act 2005, including our concurrent competition powers. Therefore, we can use or disclose information gathered under the Railways Act to facilitate our Enterprise Act functions. Any disclosure in breach of section 145 is a criminal offence.

4. Similarly, section 71 of the Railways Act allows us to publish such information and advice as appears to us expedient to give to users or potential users of railway services. This is subject to a requirement for us to exclude from publication any matter which relates to the affairs of an individual or body of persons, where publication would or might seriously and prejudicially affect the interests of that individual or body of persons.

5. Where information we have obtained in the course of investigations falls within the prohibitions of disclosure contained in sections 71 or 145 of the Railways Act or Part 9 of the Enterprise Act, it would be exempt from disclosure under section 44 of the FOIA. There are also exemptions from disclosure, for example, for information that would prejudice any civil proceedings (including competition or consumer proceedings) if disclosed.

ANNEX C: MARKET STUDY PROPOSAL FORM

[3.672]

Office of Rail and Road market study proposal form	
Name **Organisation** **Contact details**	Please state whether you think your or your organisation's identity should be kept confidential and give reasons for this. We will consider your representations before making a decision.
Proposed market for review	This need not be an economic market defined according to competition law but can be anything relating to railways within Great Britain.
Description of problems	Please set out the problems and how they are likely to lead to significant harm to users of the railways.
Market importance	Please explain why this is an important area for us to look at, with reference to our prioritisation criteria at Annex A to our guide to ORR's approach to reviewing markets. Please be as specific as possible and include details such market turnover or the significance of the service/product to the railways and views on where this would fit within ORR's strategic objectives: http://orr.gov.uk/about-orr/what-we-do/our-strategic-obiectives.
Supporting information	Please either attach the evidence you have to support this proposal, or provide your sources if these are easily accessible, such as internet hyperlinks to reference documents.
Further assistance	Please state the level of further assistance that you or your organisation would be able offer us if we prioritise your proposal for review.
Please note that we normally assess and identify areas to review on an annual basis, to inform corporate planning for the forthcoming business year. This means your proposal will usually be assessed alongside other proposals in the Autumn for review from the following Spring. However, please indicate if there is any degree of urgency to your proposal, giving reasons.	

(III) HEALTHCARE

MONITOR'S APPROACH TO MARKET INVESTIGATION REFERENCES: GUIDANCE FOR PROVIDERS

(September 2014)

[3.673]

NOTES

Note that Monitor became part of NHS Improvement in April 2016.

FOREWORD

[3.674]

Monitor's job as regulator is to protect and promote the interests of patients by ensuring that the whole healthcare sector works for their benefit. We recognise that providers and commissioners have challenging roles on the front line of healthcare: our philosophy is to help people do the right thing rather than punishing them for doing the wrong thing.

This guidance has been written to help you, as healthcare providers, make the best decisions for patients. It is one of a set of documents explaining how we apply competition rules, first published in March 2013 for a 12-week public consultation. We are grateful for all the support and engagement we received to help us develop our guidance, and we have acted on feedback.[1]

The full set of finalised guidance comprises this document, alongside:

- how we apply the choice and competition conditions of the licence for providers of NHS healthcare services
- how the Competition Act 1998 applies to the healthcare sector.

As an extra aid we have published (and will continue to publish) hypothetical scenarios on our website, which help illustrate how the choice and competition conditions of the provider licence and competition law work in practice.

We have previously published guidance both to support NHS providers considering transactions[2] and to assist commissioners using the Procurement, Patient Choice and Competition Regulations.[3]

To help you use this guidance most fully and identify when it might be necessary to work with us, we briefly explain what we mean by choice and competition and set out how and why we are working in this area below.

NOTES

1 Please see the consultation response document at: www.gov.uk/government/publications/nhs-healthcare-providers-working-with-choice-and-competition

2 www.gov.uk/government/publications/supporting-nhs-providers-considering-transactions-and-mergers

3 www.gov.uk/government/publications/procurement-patient-choice-and-competition-regulations-guidance

OUR ROLE IN CHOICE AND COMPETITION

Choice and competition have existed in the NHS in England for many years and are powerful tools for improving the quality of care provided to patients. They enable patients and commissioners to select the providers which offer quality services that best meet the needs of patients.

Choice and competition are governed by specific rules which seek to make sure that:

- they operate in the best interests of patients
- procurement decisions by commissioners achieve the best results
- all providers are treated fairly
- no-one behaves anti-competitively to the disadvantage of patients.

Our role is to make sure that this all works the way it is meant to: that the rules are applied taking into account the specific circumstances of the health sector, and above all that they are applied in the best interest of patients.

We take this responsibility seriously. We will enforce the competition rules affecting healthcare services to ensure that they operate fairly in the interests of patients, and to help both NHS providers and NHS commissioners meet the needs of patients.

To achieve this, we will explain in documents like this one how any breach of these rules might have negative effects on patients, and how we expect our intervention to maintain or improve service quality or innovation, or deliver better value for money.

INTRODUCTION TO THIS GUIDANCE

[3.675]

The aim of this guidance[4] is to inform patients, healthcare providers, commissioners, patient groups and other interested parties of how we approach our powers to make market investigation references under

Part 4 of the Enterprise Act 2002 (EA02).[5] It also provides an overview of changes made by the Enterprise and Regulatory Reform Act 2013 (ERRA13)[6] to the way market investigation references and market studies are conducted.

It is structured as follows:

- examining markets
- our approach
- undertakings in lieu of a market investigation reference
- consulting on proposed market investigation references and on accepting undertakings in lieu
- market investigations.

As we gain more experience examining markets, we expect to update this guidance from time to time.

NOTES

4 This guidance reflects the views of Monitor at the time of publication and may be revised from time to time to reflect changes in best practice, legislation and the results of experience, legal judgments and research. This guidance may in due course be supplemented, revised or replaced. Monitor's website will always display the latest version of the guidance. Although this guidance covers most of the points likely to be of interest to organisations and their advisers, it makes no claim to be comprehensive and cannot be cited as a definitive interpretation of the law.

5 References to the Competition and Markets Authority in Part 4 of EA02, except in sections 166, 171 and 174E of EA02, shall be construed as including references to Monitor – see section 73(2) of the Health and Social Care Act 2012.

6 The ERRA13 established the Competition and Markets Authority (CMA) as the UK's economy-wide competition authority with an obligation to promote competition for the benefit of consumers. On 1 April 2014, the functions of the Competition Commission and many of the functions of the Office of Fair Trading (OFT) were transferred to the CMA, and the OFT and Competition Commission were abolished.

EXAMINING MARKETS

[3.676]

We undertake a range of work to examine whether healthcare services are working well for patients, including whether choice and competition is working effectively. This includes reviews of the provision of services,[7] calls for evidence,[8] research[9] and market studies.

The work may lead to a range of outcomes including a clean bill of health for the market, making recommendations to the government to change regulations or public policy, taking enforcement action, accepting commitments from parties to take certain actions, or making a market investigation reference to the Competition and Markets Authority (CMA).

NOTES

7 See, for example, our review of NHS walk-in centre services in England: www.gov.uk/government/publications/nhs-walk-in-centre-services-in-england-review

8 See, for example, the call for evidence on the general practice services sector in England: www.gov.uk/government/publications/nhs-walk-in-centre-services-in-england-review

9 See, for example, our research project on NHS adult hearing loss services in England: www.gov.uk/government/consultations/nhs-adult-hearing-services-in-england-how-any-qualified-provider-is-working-for-patients and our research on how NHS commissioners are working to improve community services for patients: www.gov.uk/government/publications/how-nhs-commissioners-are-working-to-improve-community-services-for-patients.

MARKET INVESTIGATION REFERENCES

We can make a market investigation reference when we want the CMA to conduct a detailed examination to determine whether there is an adverse effect on competition in the market(s) referred.

We have concurrent (shared) powers with the CMA to make market investigation references under Part 4 of EA02 in relation to activities concerning the provision of healthcare services in England.[10] Our concurrent powers are not limited to NHS-funded services but apply to all healthcare[11] services in England.

We can make a market investigation reference if we have reasonable grounds for suspecting that any feature, or combination of features, of a market in the UK prevents, restricts or distorts competition in connection with the supply or acquisition of any goods or services in the UK or part of the UK.

A feature of a market means:

- the structure of the market concerned or any aspect of that structure
- any conduct (whether or not in the market concerned) of one or more than one person who supplies or acquires goods or services in the market concerned or
- any conduct relating to the market concerned of customers or any person who supplies or acquires goods or services.[12]

Conduct in this context includes any failure to act (whether intentional or not) and any other unintentional conduct.[13]

Under Part 4 of EA02 we have investigatory powers to require parties to give evidence in person and/or to supply specified documents and information (including estimates or forecasts).[14] If a person fails to comply with these requirements without reasonable excuse, we have the power to impose a penalty.[15]

If we consider that it would be appropriate to use these investigatory powers in connection with deciding whether to make a market investigation reference[16] we must publish a market study notice.

NOTES

[10] That is, in respect of healthcare services in England, either we or the CMA may make such a reference (Section 73 of the Health and Social Care Act 2012).

[11] Section 64(3) of the Health and Social Care Act 2012 defines 'healthcare' as all forms of healthcare provided for individuals, whether relating to physical or mental health.

[12] Section 131(2) of EA02

[13] Section 131(3) of EA02

[14] Section 174 of EA02

[15] Administrative penalties may be imposed in the form of a fixed amount, by reference to a daily rate, or using a combination of the two. Maximum penalty amounts are set by order and are, as at August 2014, £30,000 (in the case of a fixed amount) and £15,000 (in the case of a daily penalty). It is a criminal offence for someone intentionally to alter, suppress or destroy any document which they have been required by notice to produce. People committing a criminal offence are liable, on summary conviction, to a fine not exceeding the statutory maximum, and on conviction on indictment, to imprisonment for a term not exceeding two years or to a fine, or to both. See the Competition and Markets Authority (Penalties) Order 2014 and 'Administrative penalties: statement of policy on the CMA's approach' (CMA4).

[16] And we are proposing to carry out our functions under paragraph 14 of Schedule 8 to the Health and Social Care Act 2012 in relation to a matter for the purposes mentioned in section 130A(2) of EA02.

MARKET STUDY NOTICE

Publishing a market study notice triggers statutory time limits as outlined below:

- We must complete the market study and publish a report setting out our findings and actions (if any) which will be taken as a result of the market study within 12 months of publishing the market study notice.[17]
- Within six months of publishing a market study notice, we must publish notice of whether we propose to make a market investigation reference. We are required to consult relevant people on our proposed decision in the following circumstances:
  - if we propose to make a market investigation reference or
  - if we do not propose to make a market investigation reference but we have received (non-frivolous) representations in response to a market study notice arguing that a reference should be made.

Market studies are one of several tools we use to examine whether a particular market is working well and, if not, why. We undertake a range of work that may lead to the launch of a market study or market investigation reference, or form the basis of other action by us. Such work, for example, a review of the provision of a service, economic research, or a call for evidence on a particular issue, does not itself constitute a market study. We can make a market investigation reference without conducting a market study.

We will publish information about market studies and other work that we undertake on our website.

NOTES

[17] Section 131B, EA02

OUR APPROACH

[3.677]
We will initially launch a market study or making a market investigation reference based on information coming from a wide range of sources, for example a complaint or information acquired during an informal review of a market.

In relation to healthcare services in England, the CMA and Monitor will always consult each other before:

- publishing a market study notice
- using our investigatory powers under Part 4 of EA02
- making a market investigation reference or
- accepting undertakings in lieu (undertakings in lieu are described below).

The general principle is that the relevant functions will be exercised by whichever authority is better placed to do so. In determining which authority that is, they will consider factors including the extent to which sectoral knowledge is relevant and recent experience of dealing with the markets concerned.

When determining whether the statutory criteria for a market investigation reference are met, we will have regard to the CMA's Market studies and market investigations: supplemental guidance on the CMA's approach,[18] taking into account the specific characteristics of the healthcare sector. Where we do not follow this guidance, we will explain why not.

We have discretion to decide whether to make a market investigation reference where the statutory criteria appear to be met. In deciding whether to do so, we will take into account the following factors:

- the nature and the seriousness of the competition issues we believe exist in the market in question
- whether a market investigation reference would be a proportionate response to the competition issues identified
- whether we could accept undertakings in lieu[19]
- whether, alternatively, we have other powers to address the issues identified and
- there is a reasonable chance that appropriate remedies will be available.

ERRA13 changes the way in which market investigation references are made in certain cases. This includes a new power to make a cross-market reference; that is, refer a specific feature (or combination of features) in more than one market without also having to refer the whole of each market concerned.[20]

NOTES

18 See 'Market studies and market investigations: supplemental guidance on the CMA's approach' (CMA3).

19 See section 154 of EA02.

20 For example, a cross-market reference may be made where features do not fit neatly within one market.

UNDERTAKINGS IN LIEU OF A MARKET INVESTIGATION REFERENCE

[3.678]

We can accept undertakings instead of making a market investigation reference (undertakings in lieu). In doing this, we must take into account the need to achieve a solution to the adverse effect on competition.[21] We may also have regard to the effect of any action on any relevant customer benefits[22] of a feature or features of the market concerned.[23]

When considering whether to accept undertakings in lieu, we will have regard to the Office of Fair Trading (OFT) guidance on market investigation references which has been adopted by the CMA,[24] taking into account the specific characteristics of the health sector. Where we do not follow this guidance, we will explain why not.

Prior to accepting undertakings in lieu, we must publish a notice stating, among other things, that we propose to accept the undertakings, the purpose and effect of the undertakings, and the adverse effect on competition and any resulting detrimental effect on patients identified by us that the undertakings are seeking to deal with. The notice must also mention any other facts which we consider justify the acceptance of the undertakings.[25] We must take into account any representation arising from the publication of the notice. Further information on the CMA's concurrent power to accept undertakings instead of making a market investigation reference is set out at paragraphs 2.20 to 2.24 of their guidance.[26]

NOTES

21 Section 154 of EA02 requires us to have regard to the need to achieve as comprehensive a solution as is reasonable and practicable to the adverse effect on competition concerned and any detrimental effect on customers so far as they result or may be expected to result from such adverse effects.

22 In relation to the health sector, the term 'customer' means a current or future user of healthcare services (often but not always referred to as a 'patient') or a commissioner.

23 Section 154(4) of EA02.

24 'Market investigation references' (OFT511): www.gov.uk/government/uploads/system/uploads/attachment_data/file/284399/oft511.pdf

25 See section 155(2) of EA02 which details all the points to be included in the notice.

26 'Market investigation references' (OFT511).

CONSULTING ON PROPOSED MARKET INVESTIGATION REFERENCES AND ON ACCEPTING UNDERTAKINGS IN LIEU

[3.679]

When we propose to make a market investigation reference or to accept undertakings in lieu, we are required under EA02,[27] so far as is practicable, to consult the people whose interests we consider are likely to be substantially affected by our decision. We must consult before making the decision and, so far as is practicable, we must give our reasons for our proposed decision.

Where we have published a market study notice and we are required to consult on a proposed decision about whether to make a market investigation reference or not, we will publish notice of the proposed decision within six months of the market study notice being published.

We will publish information about market investigation references and undertakings in lieu on our website www.gov.uk/monitor.

We have a duty, when considering whether to make a market investigation reference, to bring to the attention of the Secretary of State any case that we consider raises public interest issues relating to national security. National security is currently the only specified public interest consideration in the legislation but others may be specified in future.[28]

NOTES

27 Section 169 of EA02. The ERRA13 amended section 169 of EA02 so there is no duty to consult on decisions not to make a market investigation reference, except where there has been a request for a reference to be made during a market study.

28 Section 153 of EA02. Currently the Secretary of State has the ability to intervene in market investigations to investigate defined public interest issues that are relevant to the case, while the CMA investigates the competition issues. The ERRA13 gives the Secretary of State the power to request the CMA to investigate public interest issues alongside competition issues as part of its market investigation.

MARKET INVESTIGATIONS

[3.680]

Once a market investigation reference is made, the CMA's market reference group is required to investigate and decide whether any feature, or combination of features, of each relevant market prevents, restricts or distorts competition in connection with the supply or acquisition of goods or services in the UK or a part of the UK.[29]

Where the CMA's market reference group decides there is an adverse effect on competition, it is required to decide what action should be taken by the CMA or others to remedy, mitigate or prevent the adverse effect on competition concerned or any resulting detrimental effect on customers.[30] These detrimental effects can take the form of higher prices, lower quality or less choice of goods or services, or less innovation in relation to goods or services in any market in the UK.[31]

The CMA's market reference group may decide on remedies, such as structural remedies (for example, divestiture of assets), behavioural remedies (such as enabling measures to open up a market or give customers more information), or making recommendations to other bodies.

The CMA is required to publish its report within 18 months of the reference,[32] with a possible six-month extension in special circumstances.[33]

Guidance on the substantive and procedural aspects of market investigations and possible outcomes is set out in the CMA's guidance[34] and in the Competition Commission's guidelines for market investigation which have been adopted by the CMA Board.

NOTES

29 Section 134(1) of EA02

30 Section 134(4) of EA02: in relation to the health sector, the term 'customer' means a current or future user of healthcare services (often but not always referred to as a 'patient') or a commissioner.

31 Section 134 of EA02

32 Section 144 of EA02

33 Section 137 of EA02.

34 Market studies and market investigations: supplemental guidance on the CMA's approach (CMA3). www.gov.uk/government/publications/market-studies-and-market-investigations-supplemental-guidance- on-the-cmas-approach

E. NATIONAL SECURITY AND INVESTMENT

DEPARTMENT FOR BUSINESS, ENERGY & INDUSTRIAL STRATEGY GUIDANCE NATIONAL SECURITY AND INVESTMENT ACT: PREPARE FOR NEW RULES ABOUT ACQUISITIONS WHICH COULD HARM THE UK'S NATIONAL SECURITY

(Originally published 20 July 2021; updated 15 November 2021)

[3.681]

NOTES

This Guidance is available on the BEIS collection of materials dealing with the National Security and Investment Act 2021 at: https://www.gov.uk/government/collections/national-security-and-investment-act.

CONTENTS

INTRODUCTION

[3.682]

Under new rules starting on 4 January 2022, the government will be able to scrutinise and intervene in certain acquisitions made by anyone, including businesses and investors, that could harm the UK's national security. The government will be able to impose certain conditions on an acquisition. In rare instances, the government may unwind or block an acquisition completely.

These new rules fall under the National Security and Investment (NSI) Act which will come into force on 4 January 2022. The Act is administered by the Investment Security Unit within the Department for Business, Energy and Industrial Strategy (BEIS) and the decision maker will be the Secretary of State for BEIS.

The government can call in an acquisition for assessment if it reasonably suspects that it is a qualifying acquisition (this guidance explains what these are) that has given rise to, or may give rise to, a risk to national security. This applies whether the acquisition has been completed or is still in progress or contemplation. However, it will not be possible to call in and scrutinise acquisitions completed before 12 November 2020.

If you are planning an acquisition of a qualifying entity in one of 17 defined sensitive areas of the UK economy, you may need to get approval from the government before you can complete it. This is called a notifiable acquisition. Completing a notifiable acquisition without approval will mean the acquisition is void and may mean that the acquirer is subject to civil or criminal penalties.

This guidance tells you how to prepare for the new rules. It covers:

- what types of acquisitions are covered by the new rules
- whether you need to tell the government about an acquisition
- how the government will scrutinise the acquisition

HOW THE NEW RULES WILL WORK

[3.683]

1. Check if the rules will apply to your acquisition. This will depend on what you are acquiring and how much control you have over it.

2. Check if you will need to tell the government about your acquisition. You will be legally required to inform the government about certain acquisitions of entities if your acquisition is in a sensitive area of the UK economy.

3. Tell the government about your acquisition. You can do this online by submitting a notification.

4. The government will review your acquisition. It can either clear your acquisition, impose certain conditions, or block or unwind it.

CHECK IF THE NEW RULES WILL APPLY TO YOUR ACQUISITION

[3.684]
The new rules only apply to qualifying acquisitions. These are referred to as trigger events in the National Security and Investment Act.

Your acquisition is a qualifying acquisition if all of the following apply:

- the acquisition is of a right or interest in, or in relation to, a qualifying asset or qualifying entity (these terms are explained below)
- the entity or asset you are acquiring is from, in, or has a connection to the UK
- the level of control you acquire over the qualifying entity or qualifying asset meets or passes a certain threshold (for example, your stake or voting rights in a qualifying entity becomes higher than 25%)

If the government reasonably suspects that an acquisition meets these criteria and that it has given rise to, or may give rise to, a risk to national security, it can be scrutinised by the government. The rules do not apply to acquisitions that were completed before 12 November 2020.

In addition, if this qualifying acquisition is of an entity in one of the 17 defined sensitive areas of the economy it may need to be notified to the government. Qualifying acquisitions outside the 17 defined areas do not need to be notified to the government.

CHECK IF YOU ARE ACQUIRING A QUALIFYING ENTITY OR ASSET

A qualifying entity is any entity other than an individual, including:

- a company
- a limited liability partnership
- any other body corporate
- a partnership
- an unincorporated association
- a trust

Qualifying assets include:

- land
- tangible moveable property
- ideas, information or techniques which have industrial, commercial or other economic value ('intellectual property')

Entities and assets might be qualifying entities and qualifying assets if they are outside or not from the UK but have a connection to the UK.

ACQUISITIONS OF ENTITIES OR ASSETS OUTSIDE OR NOT FROM THE UK

If an entity is formed or recognised under the law of a country or territory outside the UK, it is a qualifying entity if it either:

- carries on activities in the UK
- supplies goods or services to people in the UK.

For land or tangible moveable property situated outside the UK or its territorial sea, or for any intellectual property, it is a qualifying asset if it is either:

- used in connection with activities carried on in the UK
- used in connection with the supply of goods or services to people in the UK.

Read further on how the new rules will work for entities and assets outside or not from the UK.
[**Editorial note:** See the BEIS Guidance *How the National Security and Investment Act could affect people or acquisitions outside the UK* at **[3.692]**.]

CHECK THE LEVEL OF CONTROL YOU HAVE ACQUIRED, OR WILL ACQUIRE, OVER THE QUALIFYING ENTITY OR ASSET

If you are acquiring a qualifying entity or asset that is from, in, or has a connection to the UK, you will then need to check if the level of control you have acquired, or will acquire, over it could bring it in scope of the new rules.

Your acquisition will be in scope of the new rules if you acquire a right or interest in, or in relation to, a qualifying entity or asset, and the level of control you acquire meets any of the following thresholds:

- your shareholding stake or voting rights in a qualifying entity meets or crosses certain percentage thresholds (for example, it becomes higher than 25%)
- you acquire voting rights in a qualifying entity that allow you to pass or block resolutions governing the affairs of the entity

- you are able to materially influence the policy of a qualifying entity, for example acquiring the right to appoint members of the board of the entity that enables you to influence the strategic direction of the entity
- you are able to use a qualifying asset, or direct or control its use, or you are able to do so more than you could prior to the acquisition.

If your qualifying acquisition takes place over more than one day, the acquisition will be treated as having taken place on the last day of the period.

Further details of each threshold are outlined below.

If your shareholding stake or voting rights meet or cross certain percentage thresholds

Your acquisition will be in scope of the new rules if your shareholding stake or voting rights increase:

- from 25% or less to more than 25%
- from 50% or less to more than 50%
- from less than 75% to 75% or more

If the entity has a share capital, the thresholds describe holding shares comprised in the issued share capital of a nominal value (in aggregate) of that percentage of the share capital.

If the entity does not have a share capital, the thresholds describe holding a right to that percentage share of the capital or profits of the entity.

If the entity is a limited liability partnership, the thresholds describe holding a right to that percentage share of any surplus assets of the partnership on its winding up. Where this is not expressly provided for, each member will be treated as having an equal share.

Example

Investor A owns 20% of Entity B and acquires shares comprising 10% more, leaving Investor A with 30% in total. This is a qualifying acquisition because it takes Investor A's shareholding from 25% or less to more than 25%, which is a qualifying acquisition threshold set out in the NSI Act.

Investor A then acquires an additional 10%, leaving them with 40% of the shares. This is not a qualifying acquisition because Investor A's shareholding has not met or passed any of the three thresholds.

Investor A then acquires an additional 15%, leaving them with 55% of the shares. This is a qualifying acquisition because it takes Investor A's shareholding from 50% or less to more than 50%, which is a qualifying acquisition threshold.

If you acquire voting rights that allow you to pass or block resolutions governing the affairs of the entity

Such an acquisition is in scope of the new rules, regardless of the percentage of voting rights you may already hold, or the percentage of your shareholding, or taking into account other voting rights you hold as well as your acquisition. Any voting rights you already held before the acquisition are taken into account when assessing whether the acquisition meets this threshold.

Voting rights means rights that are given to shareholders or members to vote at general meetings on all, or substantially all, matters.

If the entity does not have general meetings at which matters are decided by such votes, voting rights includes any rights in relation to the entity that are of the equivalent effect.

In the case of minority veto rights, the voting rights only count where they provide the holder with a right to vote on all or substantially all matters governing the affairs of the entity.

Example

Person A owns 20% of an entity's voting rights and acquires a preferential share which provides them with the ability to pass, by themselves, ordinary resolutions. This is a qualifying acquisition because the acquisition gives Person A the ability to pass resolutions governing the affairs of the entity.

If you acquire a right or interest in, or in relation to, a qualifying entity which provides you with 'material influence' over the entity's policy

The Competition and Markets Authority has produced guidance on its assessment of material influence when operating the merger control regime under the Enterprise Act 2002. [**Editorial note:** the guidance referred to in this paragraph is *CMA2 (Revised) – Mergers: Guidance on the CMA's jurisdiction and procedure (2020)*. See paragraph **[3.485]** *ante*.]

When making its assessment, the CMA focuses on the acquirer's ability materially to influence policy relevant to the behaviour of the target entity in the marketplace. The policy of the target in this context means the management of its business, and thus includes the strategic direction of a company and its ability to define and achieve its commercial objectives. Any assessment by the government of an acquisition of material influence under the NSI Act will be considered in the light of the relevant section on material influence in the CMA guidance but applying the concept in the context of the NSI Act, so far as is appropriate.

The material influence threshold in the NSI Act does not apply if:

- you are acquiring an asset
- you already hold a right or interest enabling you to materially influence the policy of the entity.

Example

Investor A acquires a 20% shareholding in Entity B, and, in this instance, this makes Investor A the largest single shareholder of the entity. Taking into account Investor A's status and expertise in the sector and resulting influence over the actions of other shareholders, Investor A may be judged to have acquired material influence over the entity and, in such circumstances, this would be a qualifying acquisition.

If you acquire a right or interest in, or in relation to, a qualifying asset and as a result you are able to use, or to direct or control how the asset is used, or can do so to a greater extent than before the acquisition

This could include acquiring a right or interest that gives you the ability to use, or to direct or control the use of an asset, even if you do not acquire the asset itself.

Qualifying assets include land, tangible moveable property and intellectual property, and these may be within or outside the UK. If an asset is outside the UK, or is intellectual property, it must have a sufficient connection to the UK. Read further on how the new rules will work for entities and assets outside or not from the UK. **[Editorial note:** see the BEIS Guidance *How the National Security and Investment Act could affect people or acquisitions outside the UK* at **[3.692]** *post*.]

Example

Company A's sole business is to manufacture equipment. Party B operates in a similar area for a range of clients. Party B does not acquire Company A but does acquire its equipment.

This is a qualifying acquisition because Party B acquires the assets and as a result can use or direct or control the use of these assets. If Party B signed a contract with Party A providing it with rights to use the assets, that would also be a qualifying acquisition.

If your qualifying acquisition is part of a corporate restructure or reorganisation

Qualifying acquisitions that are part of a corporate restructure or reorganisation may be covered by the new rules. This is the case even if the acquisition takes place within the same corporate group. This means that even within corporate restructures, it may be mandatory to notify.

Example

Two parties share the same ultimate owner but are run separately from each other. One of the parties acquires part of the other which takes its control over one of the thresholds to make it a qualifying acquisition. The ultimate owner remains the same, but their ownership now goes through a different corporate chain. This means there has been a change of control under the NSI Act. This is true even though the ultimate owner remains the same.

IF YOU ARE PLANNING A QUALIFYING ACQUISITION BUT IT HAS NOT YET TAKEN PLACE

The government can assess a potential qualifying acquisition that has not yet happened if it reasonably suspects it may cause a national security risk. The government can call in a qualifying acquisition that has already happened, or is in progress or contemplation.

Example

Entity A is negotiating an agreement for the purchase of 100% of UK Company B and has signed heads of terms. This is likely to be interpreted as a qualifying acquisition that is in contemplation. Even though the acquisition has not yet happened, the government may still be able to call it in.

INTERESTS AND RIGHTS

Interests and rights count as acquired if you begin to hold them in any of the following ways:

- hold an interest or right jointly with someone else
- have a joint arrangement with someone else that means you will exercise all, or substantially all, of the rights or interests in a way pre-determined by the arrangement. The Act has a broad definition of 'arrangement' which means most types of arrangement count under these rules
- hold a majority stake in an entity that holds the interest or right, or is part of a chain of entities which each hold majority stakes through the chain and the last one holds the interest or right
- a nominee holds an interest for you
- control a right that is owned by another party (unless the owner also controls the right)
- hold a right exercisable only under certain circumstances, when the circumstances have arisen or you control whether those circumstances exist. This does not apply to administrators or creditors, who are not regarded as holding those rights while an entity is in relevant insolvency proceedings in certain circumstances, hold a right attached to shares which are held as security by a lender. The owner, not the

lender, is treated as owning or acquiring the rights where the rights are exercisable only in accordance with the owner's instructions (apart from exercising the rights for the purpose of preserving the value of the security, or of realising the value). It is also the case where the shares are held in connection with loans as part of normal business activities and the rights are exercisable only in the owner's interest (apart from exercising the rights for the purpose of preserving the value of the security, or of realising it)

• hold combined rights or interests with another person by virtue of being connected (for example, a spouse or relative or two or more undertakings in one group)

• hold rights or interests with another person or more people, with whom you share a common purpose (for example, coordinating influence on an entity's activities)

Check Schedule 1 of the Act for full details. This includes some specific limitations of what is considered as acquired such as whether an acquisition has taken place when shares are given as security for a loan.

CHECK IF YOU WILL NEED TO TELL THE GOVERNMENT ABOUT YOUR ACQUISITION

[3.685]
You will be legally required to tell the government about certain acquisitions of qualifying entities in 17 sensitive areas of the economy subject to certain criteria. These are mandatory notification requirements, known as 'notifiable acquisitions' and you must get approval from the government before you complete the acquisition otherwise the acquisition will be void.

You will be able to do this by submitting an online form to the government (called a 'mandatory notification form').

The government will then review your acquisition to see if it could cause a national security risk. If the government clears the acquisition, it cannot assess it again, unless false or misleading information was submitted.

WHEN YOU WILL BE LEGALLY REQUIRED TO TELL THE GOVERNMENT ABOUT YOUR ACQUISITION (MANDATORY NOTIFICATION)

If you are a party acquiring a qualifying entity, you will be legally required to tell the government about certain acquisitions in 17 sensitive areas of the economy. These are called 'mandatory notification' requirements and cover areas which are considered more likely to give rise to national security risks.

The 17 areas of the economy are:

- Advanced Materials
- Advanced Robotics
- Artificial Intelligence
- Civil Nuclear
- Communications
- Computing Hardware
- Critical Suppliers to Government
- Cryptographic Authentication
- Data Infrastructure
- Defence
- Energy
- Military and Dual-Use
- Quantum Technologies
- Satellite and Space Technologies
- Suppliers to the Emergency Services
- Synthetic Biology
- Transport

You will need to tell the government about a notifiable acquisition by submitting a mandatory notification online. Qualifying acquisitions which are subject to mandatory notification requirements are called 'notifiable acquisitions'. The requirement to notify the government about notifiable acquisitions will come into force on 4 January 2022.

If you are notifying, you will be asked to provide information on the structure and share ownership of the qualifying entity, the acquirer and the acquisition. Further guidance will be available on how to submit a notification form and the information required.

Mandatory notification requirements only apply to the acquisition of qualifying entities. These requirements do not apply to the acquisition of qualifying assets.

Your acquisition is a 'notifiable acquisition' if it meets the following criteria:

1. You are acquiring a qualifying entity that carries out certain activities in the UK within one of 17 sensitive areas of the economy.

2. And any of the following apply:

i) Your shareholding stake or voting rights increase:

- from 25% or less to more than 25%
- from 50% or less to more than 50%
- from less than 75% to 75% or more

ii) Your acquisition is of voting rights and this will enable you to secure or prevent the passage of any class of resolution governing the affairs of the entity.

Read further guidance about the activities of qualifying entities in the 17 areas of the economy that will be subject to mandatory notification. [**Editorial note:** see the BEIS Guidance National Security and Investment Act: guidance on notifiable acquisitions at **[3.725]**.]

CHECK IF YOUR ACQUISITION IS A NOTIFIABLE ACQUISITION WHEN THE ENTITY IS OUTSIDE THE UK

For notifiable acquisitions, a qualifying entity falls within the scope of mandatory notification requirements only if it carries out the activity specified in the regulations in the UK.

If a qualifying entity is formed or recognised under the law of a country or territory outside the UK and carries on activities in the UK which are specified in the notifiable acquisition regulations then the acquisition of such an entity may be a notifiable acquisition.

Example

Company A undertakes notifiable acquisition activities in Germany, but also undertakes activities within the UK which are not in scope of the notifiable acquisition regulations. An acquisition of company A would not constitute a notifiable acquisition as it does not undertake the specified activities within the notifiable acquisitions within the UK.

Example

Company B is a US-based company that supplies robotics parts to the UK. It does not undertake any activities within the UK besides supplying parts of the UK. This would not constitute a notifiable acquisition as Company B does not undertake the specified activities in the UK.

IF YOU DO NOT TELL THE GOVERNMENT ABOUT A NOTIFIABLE ACQUISITION

The acquisition is void if you complete a notifiable acquisition without notifying and gaining approval from the government. You will be able to apply for retrospective validation online.

There are civil and criminal penalties for completing a notifiable acquisition without gaining the necessary approval. A civil penalty could require you to pay up to 5% of your organisation's global turnover or £10 million, whichever is greater.

IF YOU HAVE AN ACQUISITION THAT IS NOT COVERED BY MANDATORY NOTIFICATION

You are not legally required to tell the government about your qualifying acquisition if it is not covered by a mandatory notification. You can submit a voluntary notification if you are a party to a completed or planned qualifying acquisition that is not covered by mandatory notification and want to find out if the government is going to call it in.

Even if you do not notify an acquisition, if the government reasonably suspects it may give rise to a national security risk it may still be called in for a national security assessment. The government can assess acquisitions up to 5 years after they have taken place and up to 6 months after becoming aware of them if they have not been notified.

HOW TO SUBMIT A NOTIFICATION AND WHAT TO EXPECT WHEN IT IS BEING REVIEWED AND ASSESSED

[3.686]
Once you have confirmed that you are required, or wish, to submit a notification, you should follow this guidance.

This guidance tells you how the process of submitting a notification form will work, the process following the acceptance of the notification, and the government's potential responses.

SUBMITTING A NOTIFICATION FORM

[3.687]
There are three different forms that can be used to notify the government about an acquisition:

- mandatory notification form: as explained above, you will be legally required to tell the government about notifiable acquisitions in 17 sensitive areas of the economy

Part 3 CMA and other Guidelines

• voluntary notification form: as explained above, you can submit a voluntary notification if you are a party to a completed or planned qualifying acquisition that is not covered by mandatory notification;

• retrospective validation application form: as explained above, an acquisition is void if you complete a notifiable acquisition (which is subject to mandatory notification) without notifying and gaining approval from the government. You can apply for retrospective validation if you have completed a notifiable acquisition without notifying

You will be able to submit an online notification form which asks for all of the relevant information. Information given will be held in a secure and confidential manner.

You will be able to use the online notification form service from 4 January 2022.

Further guidance on how to register for the online notification form service and complete notification forms will be published closer to full commencement of the NSI Act on 4 January 2022.

WHAT TO EXPECT ONCE YOU'VE SUBMITTED A NOTIFICATION FORM

ACCEPTING OR REJECTING A NOTIFICATION FORM

[3.688]

After a notification form has been submitted, the government will give you a case reference number and will confirm whether the form has been accepted or rejected as soon as is reasonably practicable after receiving it.

The notification form will only be accepted for consideration if it complies with the notification requirements and includes all the necessary information. Only then will the government process your notification form to the timescales set out in the NSI Act.

A notification form that is rejected will not progress to the next stage and will be returned with the reasons why it was not accepted. This applies to all types of notification form, whether mandatory, voluntary or retrospective.

The government may ask you to resubmit a notification form before it is accepted if more information is needed.

ONCE A NOTIFICATION FORM HAS BEEN ACCEPTED

The consideration of notifications is divided into 2 parts:

• the review period (applies to all notified acquisitions)

• the assessment period (applies only if an acquisition is 'called in')

The processes for review and, if required, assessment are the same for each type of notification, whether mandatory, voluntary or retrospective.

The review period and the assessment period each last up to 30 working days. The government may extend the assessment period by an additional period of 45 working days, subject to certain tests being met. Any further extension beyond those 45 working days must be with the written agreement of the acquirer (known as the 'voluntary period'). In calculating these days, a working day is any day other than a Saturday, Sunday or a Bank Holiday anywhere in the UK.

REVIEW PERIOD

The government will email you telling you it has accepted your notification form. The 30 working day period for the government's review begins on the day this email is sent.

WITHIN 30 WORKING DAYS OF ACCEPTANCE OF THE NOTIFICATION FORM

The government will either:

• clear the acquisition and tell you it can go ahead

• call in the acquisition for a full national security assessment

• require further information, which you should provide as soon as possible, to help complete the assessment (known as an 'information notice')

• require you or people involved in the acquisition to attend a meeting (known as an 'attendance notice')

We expect that most notifications will be cleared rather than called in, and you will be informed of the outcome of the government's decision during the first 30 working day review period.

If the government wishes to call in the acquisition to investigate further, you will be informed by email on or before the final day of the review period.

Information or attendance notices issued during the review period do not change the 30 working day deadline. This is different from information notices and attendance notices issued during the assessment period, which have the legal effect of "stopping the clock".

ASSESSMENT PERIOD

The government will tell you by email if it needs to carry out a full assessment of your acquisition for a national security risk. This is known as 'call in'. The assessment will last up to 30 working days (subject to any extensions).

During this period, the government will carry out a detailed assessment of the potential national security risks and decide what, if any, action it considers necessary and proportionate to address any of these risks.

The government may extend the assessment period for an additional period of 45 working days (known as the 'additional period'). Any further extension must be with the written agreement of the acquirer (known as the 'voluntary period').

WHAT THE GOVERNMENT CAN ASK YOU TO DO DURING THE ASSESSMENT PERIOD

During the 30-working day assessment period, the government can:

- put in place immediate and temporary controls to prevent you taking action that might undermine conditions the Secretary of State might seek to put in place (known as an 'interim order')
- require you to provide further information to help complete its assessment (known as an 'information notice')
- require you or people involved in the acquisition to attend a meeting (known as an 'attendance notice')

Information notices and attendance notices issued during the assessment period have the legal effect of "stopping the clock". This is different from information notices and attendance notices issued during the review period. More detail is set out in the sections below.

INTERIM ORDERS

An interim order may be issued at any time during the assessment period. Interim orders are intended to prevent you or other parties to the acquisition taking any steps which might undermine any conditions the Secretary of State may seek to put in place at the end of the assessment period through a final order.

Interim orders could include (but are not limited to) preventing the exchange of confidential information and access to sensitive sites or assets, pending the outcome of the assessment, and may include compliance monitoring requirements. Interim orders will be communicated to you by email.

The government may issue an interim order to any person (or to the holder of a position in the company), where provisions of the order are necessary and proportionate. Interim orders can apply to people outside the UK. You will be informed of the order's details and rationale. The government will not routinely make interim orders public.

If you are required to comply with an interim order but wish to request that it be varied or revoked, the government must consider your request as soon as practicable after receiving it. The best way to make requests is by contacting the ISU by email.

INFORMATION NOTICES

During the assessment period, the government may need more information. If this is the case, the government may issue an information notice, setting out the reason for requiring the information, how it should be provided, a time limit for providing the information and the potential consequences of not doing so. The "clock" for assessing your acquisition stops until this information has been provided or the deadline for providing the information has passed. The clock will restart the day after the government has confirmed that either of these two things has happened.

Information notices can also be issued during the review period (i.e. the first 30 working days after your notification is accepted), but these will not result in a 'clock stop'.

ATTENDANCE NOTICES

The government may also need to hear from people involved in the acquisition to inform its decision making. This will be required through an attendance notice, setting out the time and place of the meeting, and the purpose of the meeting. This could include you (the representative of a party involved in the acquisition), people in specific positions in one of the companies involved (for example someone with technical knowledge of the business), or others as required.

You and/or others whose attendance is requested must attend this meeting. If the attendance notice is issued during the assessment period, the "clock" for assessing your acquisition stops until the meeting has taken place and the required information has been provided or the deadline for complying with the attendance notice has passed. The clock will restart the day after the government has confirmed that either of these two things has happened.

Attendance notices can also be issued during the review period (i.e. the first 30 working days after your notification is accepted), but these will not result in a 'clock stop'.

BY THE 30TH WORKING DAY OF THE ASSESSMENT PERIOD

By the 30th working day, the government will inform you of one of the following:

- your acquisition is cleared and can carry on (the final notification)
- your acquisition can go ahead subject to certain conditions (the final order)
- your acquisition is blocked and cannot carry on (the final order)
- the assessment period needs to be extended for another 45 working days

A called in acquisition may be cleared by the government at any time during the assessment period. You will be informed by email.

If the government determines there are national security risks raised by your acquisition, representatives of the parties may be contacted at any stage during the assessment period to be informed of conditions the government may put in place through a final order. The purpose of these conditions is to mitigate risk (as determined by the government) and allow the acquisition to proceed.

You will be issued a 'final order' if the government imposes conditions on your acquisition, or if your acquisition is blocked. Relevant parties will be provided with information about the decision, including details of any conditions imposed and the consequence of any breach of these conditions, once a national security assessment has been concluded.

Before making a final order, the government must consider any representations made. Representations should be made to the government by contacting the ISU at investment.screening@beis.gov.uk.

Notices of final orders made by the government will be published on GOV.UK. The government will remove sensitive information.

IF THE ASSESSMENT PERIOD IS EXTENDED

The assessment period may be extended for another 45 working days where it is reasonably believed that a qualifying acquisition raises or would raise a national security risk and an additional period is required to further assess the acquisition. Any further extension beyond this must be with the written agreement of the acquirer (known as the 'voluntary period').

CARRYING ON AN ACQUISITION WHILST REVIEW AND ASSESSMENT IS ONGOING

You can continue to progress an acquisition during the review and assessment periods up to the point of completion unless the government has told you not to through an interim order. Interim orders can only be issued during the assessment period, and may place immediate and temporary controls on the parties to prevent any action which could have the effect of undermining conditions the Secretary of State may seek to put in place through a final order.

In the case of mandatory notification, you must not complete the acquisition until you have received clearance from the government. If you do complete without clearance, the acquisition will be legally void.

In the case of a voluntary notification, you may choose to continue your acquisition (unless the government has told you not to do so through an interim order). However, if you choose to complete your acquisition before the government has made its decision, the acquisition can later be unwound if the government finds that there are national security concerns.

CONFIDENTIALITY WHILST REVIEW AND ASSESSMENT IS ONGOING

The government will not routinely make public that it has called in an acquisition for national security assessment or that it has issued an interim order and will inform you if it intends to do so.

Throughout the review and assessment periods, and in any interactions with the ISU, you should remain mindful of the other legislative obligations that you may be under. For example, if you are a relevant issuer, you will still need to comply with applicable transparency and disclosure obligations such as the obligation under the UK Market Abuse Regulation to disclose inside information to the public as soon as possible.

If your disclosure obligations give rise to any doubts or concerns about your ability to comply with any specific requirements raised during the review and assessment process, or as a result of interim or final orders you are subject to, you can contact the ISU by email at investment.screening@beis.gov.uk.

Find further information on the UK Market Abuse Regulation on the Financial Conduct Authority's website. [**Editorial note:** see https://www.fca.org.uk/markets/market-abuse/regulation.]

AFTER THE ASSESSMENT PERIOD

If no further action is being taken following the full national security assessment, you will be informed by the government that the acquisition has been cleared. That decision cannot be revisited. The only exception is if it is established that false or misleading information was provided in a notification form or in response to an information notice or attendance notice.

Where you are subject to interim orders or final orders, the government has a duty to keep these under review and to vary and/or revoke them, where appropriate. This would generally happen in discussion with the parties, who can also request that the order be reviewed.

COMPLIANCE AND ENFORCEMENT

[3.689]

Through compliance and enforcement the government's aim is to support you in meeting your obligations under the NSI Act. The approach to compliance and enforcement aims to be risk-based, proportionate and consistent. The government seeks to minimise burdens on business throughout.

The NSI Act specifies offences may be committed in respect of:

- completing a notifiable acquisition without approval [**Editorial note:** see s 32 of the National Security and Investment Act 2021]
- failing to comply with an interim or final order [**Editorial note:** see s 33 of the National Security and Investment Act 2021]
- failing to comply with an information notice or attendance order, and various associated offences [**Editorial note:** see s 34 of the National Security and Investment Act 2021]
- using or disclosing information in contravention of disclosure of information provisions [**Editorial note:** see s 35 of the National Security and Investment Act 2021]

The responses available to the government in dealing with non-compliance and offences range from supportive intervention through to penalties for individuals or businesses. These may include:

- advice, guidance and warnings
- agreeing actions with parties
- applying for civil injunctions
- imposing civil penalties
- instituting criminal proceedings

Further guidance will be published on the government's approach to compliance and enforcement closer to full commencement of the NSI Act on 4 January 2022.

FURTHER GUIDANCE

[3.690]
For businesses seeking investment, considering potential security issues early in your investment planning can protect both your company and the UK's national security. Read guidance on Informed Investment for practical advice on how to reduce potential risks associated with investment. [**Editorial note:** see https://www.cpni.gov.uk/informed-investment.]

CONTACT THE INVESTMENT SECURITY UNIT

[3.691]
For general enquiries or informal discussion around future acquisitions or a specific notification, please contact the ISU at investment.screening@beis.gov.uk.

DEPARTMENT FOR BUSINESS, ENERGY & INDUSTRIAL STRATEGY GUIDANCE HOW THE NATIONAL SECURITY AND INVESTMENT ACT COULD AFFECT PEOPLE OR ACQUISITIONS OUTSIDE THE UK

(Published 20 July 2021)

[3.692]

NOTES

This Guidance is available on the BEIS collection of materials dealing with the National Security and Investment Act 2021 at: https://www.gov.uk/government/collections/national-security-and-investment-act.

CONTENTS

INTRODUCTION

[3.693]
The government will be able to scrutinise and intervene in acquisitions made by anyone, including businesses and investors, that could harm the UK's national security. The government will be able to impose certain conditions on an acquisition, unwind it or if necessary, block it completely, but expects to do this rarely.

The new rules under the National Security and Investment (NSI) Act will come into force on 4 January 2022.

Only acquisitions completed on or after 12 November 2020 can be called in and scrutinised by the government, once the Act is in force.

Under the National Security and Investment Act 2021, there are new rules that apply to certain acquisitions of entities or assets that are outside, but have a connection to, the UK.

This guidance tells you:

- what type of acquisitions outside of the UK are covered by the new rules
- common circumstances that would put an acquisition in scope of the new rules
- examples of how the rules may affect parties not based in the UK.

TYPES OF ACQUISITIONS THAT ARE COVERED BY THE NEW RULES

[3.694]
An acquisition might be covered by the new rules if a qualifying entity or qualifying asset is being or has been acquired, and if that acquisition meets other tests in the Act that would make it a trigger event. If the entity or asset being acquired qualifies, the government may be able to call in that acquisition to investigate it.

Read more about how the NSI Act will work. [**Editorial note:** the guidance referred to is the BEIS Guidance *National Security and Investment Act: Prepare for new rules about acquisitions which could harm the UK's national security* at **[3.681]** *ante*.]

ENTITIES

If an entity is formed or recognised under the law of a country or territory outside the UK, it is a qualifying entity if it either:

- carries on activities in the UK
- supplies goods or services to people in the UK

There are additional requirements about acquisitions of entities that are engaged in particularly sensitive activities in the UK. The acquirers of such entities may be legally required to notify the government and receive clearance before completing the acquisition. Detail on what those sensitive activities are will be published separately.

An entity carrying on activities in the UK

For an entity, such as a company, to be carrying on activities in the UK, there needs to be an activity (such as a business) being carried on in, or partly in, the UK. In addition, the entity must be sufficiently involved in that activity to be said to be carrying it on, whether alone or with others.

For example, this would be treated as including an overseas company that does business from a regional office or a research and development facility in the UK.

An entity supplying goods or services to people in the UK

For an entity, such as a company, to be supplying goods or services to the UK, there need to be goods or services being provided from one person to another, and the recipient needs to be in the UK. The entity would need to be sufficiently involved in that supply to be said to be making the supply, whether alone or with others.

For example, this would generally be treated as including an overseas company that produces goods for exporting to a company in the UK or is responsible for distributing them to the UK company.

ASSETS

For land or tangible moveable property situated outside the UK or its territorial sea, or for any intellectual property, it is a qualifying asset if it is either:

- used in connection with activities carried on in the UK or
- used in connection with the supply of goods or services to people in the UK.

An asset being used in connection with activities carried on in the UK

For an asset to be used in connection with activities carried on in the UK, there needs to be an activity carried on in the UK (regardless of who is carrying on that activity, or where they are based), and that asset needs to be used in connection with that activity.

For example, this would include an asset such as machinery located overseas used to produce equipment that is used in the UK.

An asset being used in connection with the supply of goods or services to people in the UK

For an asset to be used in connection with the supply of goods or services to people in the UK, there needs to be a supply of goods or services to people in the UK and the asset must be used in connection with that supply.

For example, this would include an offshore wind farm which is used to generate electricity which is supplied to the UK.

COMMON CIRCUMSTANCES THAT COULD ALLOW THE GOVERNMENT TO INVESTIGATE AN ACQUISITION

[3.695]
This section tells you how these rules might apply to some common circumstances.

CHARACTERISTICS OF ENTITIES FORMED OR RECOGNISED OUTSIDE THE UK THAT ARE LIKELY TO BE IN SCOPE OF THE NEW RULES

The entity being acquired is likely to be classed as a qualifying entity if any of the following apply. The entity:

- supplies goods or services to the UK
- carries out research and development in the UK
- has an office in the UK from which it carries on activities
- oversees the activities of a subsidiary that carries on activities in the UK (unless it is independent from the parent entity being acquired)
- supplies goods to a UK hub which sends the goods onto other countries (unless the UK hub only places orders for goods to be sent to other countries).

If the entity has staff who travel to the UK for business

The entity is likely to be a qualifying entity if its staff undertake business activities similar to working in a regional office (for example, by performing services for a UK client on a regular basis).

The entity is likely not to be a qualifying entity if its staff are solely doing work such as conducting market research or are part of a sales team seeking new clients.

If the entity supplies goods that pass through the UK while travelling to other destinations

The entity would be a qualifying entity if the goods are modified or used while in the UK.

The entity may also be a qualifying entity if the goods passed through the UK as part of a wider journey. This would depend on the specific arrangements in place.

CHARACTERISTICS OF ENTITIES FORMED OR RECOGNISED OUTSIDE THE UK THAT ARE UNLIKELY TO BRING THEM IN SCOPE OF THE NEW RULES

The entity being acquired is not likely to be a qualifying entity just because it does any of the following:

- has staff who work remotely for a non-UK office, but are based in the UK
- has owners or investors who are based in the UK
- buys goods or services from UK-based suppliers
- has a parent company that also has other subsidiaries that carry on activities in the UK
- lists securities on a regulated or exchange-regulated market in the UK.

Assets that are either land or moveable property situated outside the UK or its territorial sea, or intellectual property

The asset you are acquiring is likely to be a qualifying asset if any of the following apply. The asset is used:

- by someone in the UK
- by someone outside the UK to supply goods or services to the UK or
- to generate energy or materials that are used in the UK.

If an asset was originally brought from the UK by a previous owner or had at some point been in the UK, this would not, on its own, make it a qualifying asset.

Investigations of asset acquisitions are expected to be rare. You are not legally required to notify the government about asset acquisitions. We will publish a statement on how the government expects to use its call-in power in due course. Read and respond to our consultation on a draft of this statement. **[Editorial note:** see www.gov.uk/government/consultations/national-security-and-investment-act-2021-statement-on-the-use-of-the-power-to-call-in-acquisitions.]

WHEN THE GOVERNMENT CAN CALL IN AND ASSESS ACQUISITIONS

[3.696]
The government can call in and investigate an acquisition – whether it is in contemplation, in progress or completed – of a qualifying entity or asset if the control being acquired meets any of the following thresholds:

- the acquisition of shares or voting rights in a qualifying entity passes any of the following thresholds:
  - from 25% or less to more than 25%
  - from 50% or less to more than 50%
  - from less than 75% to 75% or more
- the acquisition of voting rights in a qualifying entity that allow the acquirer to block or secure any class of resolution governing how the entity operates
- the acquisition of a right or interest in the entity that allows the acquirer to materially influence the policy of the entity, for example acquiring the right to appoint members of the board of the entity that enables the acquirer to influence the strategic direction of the entity
- the acquisition of a right or interest in a qualifying asset to use it, or use it to a greater extent than prior to the acquisition
- the acquisition of a right or interest in a qualifying asset to direct or control how the asset is used, or direct or control how it is used to a greater extent than prior to the acquisition.

WHEN THE GOVERNMENT CAN ASK YOU FOR INFORMATION IF YOU ARE OUTSIDE THE UK

[3.697]
If relevant to the functions of the Act, the government can require you to provide information or to give evidence if any one of the following applies:

- you carry on business in the UK, even if you are not directly involved in an acquisition being investigated
- you are a UK national
- you are an individual ordinarily resident in the UK
- you are a body incorporated or constituted under the law of any part of the UK
- you have acquired, or are in the process of or contemplating acquiring, a qualifying entity or qualifying asset.

The government can do this by issuing information and attendance notices.

The definition of 'carrying on business in the UK' is narrower than carrying on activities in the UK. A business may include having a professional practice, an undertaking that is carried on for gain or reward, or an undertaking in which goods or services are supplied otherwise than free of charge.

For example, if you run a trade body or pure research institution in the UK, you are carrying on activities in the UK, but this would not mean you are carrying on business in the UK.

WHEN THE GOVERNMENT CAN REQUIRE YOU TO TAKE FURTHER ACTION IF YOU ARE OUTSIDE THE UK

[3.698]
The government can require you to take certain actions relating to an acquisition if it is in scope of the Act and meets other tests within the Act, if you are either in or outside the UK. For example, it can require you to stop progressing the acquisition until the assessment of it is complete.

To help you prepare for the new rules, you should read further guidance on how the Act works. **[Editorial note:** see the BEIS Guidance *National Security and Investment Act: Prepare for new rules about acquisitions which could harm the UK's national security* at **[3.681]**.]

The government will publish further information on how it expects to use its call-in power in the Section 3 Statement. Read a draft of the statement. [**Editorial note:** now the BEIS Notice: National Security and Investment Act 2021: Statement for the purposes of section 3 (November 2021) at **[3.715]**.]

IF YOU BREACH THE ACT AND ARE OUTSIDE THE UK

[3.699]
The government can take legal action against you if you breach the Act, even if you are outside the UK. This could either be through civil or criminal penalties and can, depending on the severity of the offence, include fines and custodial sentences.

EXAMPLES OF HOW OVERSEAS COMPANIES COULD BE AFFECTED BY THE NATIONAL SECURITY AND INVESTMENT ACT

SUPPLIERS TO A UK COMPANY

[3.700]
Company A is incorporated outside the UK and does not carry on any activities in the UK. It does however export critical components to Company B, which is located in the UK. Company B works in a highly sensitive area of the UK economy that falls under the mandatory notification requirements. Company A works in the same sensitive area, but overseas.

Company C, also incorporated overseas and with no UK operations, is contemplating acquiring a 75% stake in Company A, and the government considers that that acquisition could give rise to a risk to national security due to the control this could give Company C over Company A's operations. The government would be able to call in that acquisition for scrutiny, as Company A is supplying goods to the UK. It does not need to wait until the acquisition takes place – it can call it in while it is in contemplation.

Because Company B is located in the UK, the government could, if necessary and proportionate, then require actions to be taken by Company B through an interim order or final order. For example, this may include requiring Company B to put in place additional checks if it continues to purchase from Company A. In this scenario, notification and pre-approval of the acquisition would not be mandatory since Company A, as the target entity, does not come under the mandatory notification rules, not least because it does not carry on activities in the UK; it only provides goods or services to the UK.

REQUIRING INFORMATION

Company D is not incorporated in the UK. It is acquiring Company E which is incorporated in the UK. Company F is a company in Company D's supply chain incorporated abroad and does not carry on any activities in the UK.

The government may in certain circumstances require Company D and Company E to provide information. However, it could not require Company F to take any action or provide information, even if Company F held information about Company D that could aid the government's decision-making.

PARENT COMPANIES AND SUBSIDIARIES

Company G is incorporated abroad. It does business out of a regional office in the UK but most of its operations are overseas. A multinational, Company H, owns 90% of Company G's shares and voting rights and oversees Company G's activities. A further company, Company I, sits within Company H's portfolio and has no links to the UK.

Company I is acquired by a company in another country. While Company H does carry on activities in the UK as a result of overseeing Company G's activities, the company being bought (Company I) does not. Simply being part of the same group of companies does not mean that Company I comes under the scope of the NSI Act. The government therefore could not call in this acquisition.

However, if Company G were to be bought, this acquisition could be called in, as it does carry on activities in the UK. If instead Company H itself were bought, the government could call this in, as any party that owns Company H would then also acquire control over Company G.

REMEDIES

Company J is headquartered and incorporated overseas but has a large R&D facility in the UK conducting research into advanced military technologies, and it supplies the UK armed forces. Company K notifies the government that it wishes to acquire 60% of Company J's shares, which are currently owned by Company J. Company K has previously attempted to carry out actions in the past that could harm the UK's national security.

The government calls in the acquisition due to the risk to national security from Company K gaining access to Company J's R&D facility, and decides that remedies are needed to mitigate these risks before the acquisition can go ahead. Due to the risks to the UK's national security from the proposed acquisition, the government judges that it is necessary and proportionate to require the parties to make changes to the proposed acquisition, including:

- requiring Company J to not sell more than a certain percentage of its shares to Company K
- ensuring Company K cannot access certain intellectual property
- requiring Company J to report regularly to the government on compliance
- government checks on Company J's compliance with its agreed actions.

NO CONDITIONS IMPOSED ON AN ENTITY ACQUISITION

Company L is headquartered and incorporated overseas and does not carry on any activities in the UK. It does however supply sensitive government-run facilities in the UK with specialist equipment. It also provides a sensitive government-run UK infrastructure provider with access through a licensing arrangement to specialist services, using assets situated outside the UK and intellectual property registered outside the UK. It is not the only potential provider of such services.

Company M notifies the government that it wishes to acquire 70% of Company L's shares and a license to use the same specialist services as the UK infrastructure provider. Company M is known to have previously tried to gain access to the supply chain of this area of the UK's infrastructure in a way that could harm national security.

However, due to the limited nature of Company L's links to the UK, the government does not judge that it would be able to, or wish to, impose limits on the acquisitions or the activities of Company L and Company M, and so decides not to call in the acquisitions, and instead clears them to proceed.

Instead, in this instance, the government decides to stop importing certain equipment from Company L and to stop using its services, and to instead seek alternative suppliers.

NO CONDITIONS IMPOSED ON AN ASSET ACQUISITION

Company N is incorporated overseas and does not carry on any activities in the UK. Company O is a company incorporated in the UK that supplies a sensitive piece of critical national infrastructure in the UK. Company O has a factory outside the UK that uses specialist machinery owned by Company N before moving its now-processed goods back into the UK for use in the piece of infrastructure. Company N is considering selling that machinery.

Company N decides to notify the government because the machinery is an asset used in connection with the supply of goods to the UK in a sensitive area of the economy. After considering potential national security risks, the government decides that the sale of the machinery would not give rise to a national security risk, because the owners of the infrastructure would have other options if that machinery was no longer available due to the sale. The government therefore confirms that it will not call in the acquisition for scrutiny and so it is cleared to proceed as planned.

CONDITIONS IMPOSED ON AN ASSET ACQUISITION

Company P is a multinational company that is incorporated overseas and has several R&D facilities in the UK. It holds unique software that is used under license by Company Q. Company Q is based in the UK and uses Company P's software to carry out essential functions in a sensitive sector of the UK economy. The original decision to use Company P's software followed due diligence by Company Q and the government to ensure this licensing arrangement did not give rise to national security concerns.

Company P is considering a proposal to allow other parties to use its software through a licensing agreement, and notifies the government due to its work with Company Q. The government identifies potential risks to national security from such licensing and so calls it in for further scrutiny.

Following that scrutiny, the government judges that it is necessary and proportionate to impose conditions on the proposal before it can be enacted. In particular, Company P must not allow other parties to access the software's source code, to ensure that other parties do not gain sensitive insights into the sensitive sector.

DEPARTMENT FOR BUSINESS, ENERGY & INDUSTRIAL STRATEGY GUIDANCE THE NATIONAL SECURITY AND INVESTMENT ACT ALONGSIDE REGULATORY REQUIREMENTS

(Published 20 July 2021)

[3.701]

NOTES

This Guidance is available on the BEIS collection of materials dealing with the National Security and Investment Act 2021 at: https://www.gov.uk/government/collections/national-security-and-investment-act.

CONTENTS

OVERVIEW

[3.702]

The National Security and Investment (NSI) Act comes into force on 4 January 2022. This guidance tells you how the NSI Act interacts with other regulators and codes.

The government understands that acquisitions may require consideration by multiple bodies, and it may need to manage the interactions with other regulators as appropriate. Unless specified, operating under the NSI Act does not change regulatory requirements that already apply to acquisitions imposed by other regulators.

You can contact the Investment Security Unit (ISU) for general enquiries or advice about the Act on investment.screening@beis.gov.uk.

ENTERPRISE ACT 2002 – PUBLIC INTEREST INTERVENTIONS

[3.703]

The Enterprise Act 2002 (EA02) allows the government to intervene in mergers and acquisitions on public interest grounds.

Under the EA02, the government will maintain the power to intervene in mergers and acquisitions that raise public interest concerns in relation to the stability of the UK financial system, maintaining the

UK's capability to combat, and to mitigate the effects of, public health emergencies, and media plurality. The public interest provisions of the Enterprise Act will continue in force, but the NSI Act replaces the national security consideration of the EA02.

Cases can only be called in for a national security assessment once, unless false or misleading information has been provided. Any merger which has previously been subject to a national security intervention under the EA02 – either through an intervention notice, a special intervention notice, or a European intervention notice – cannot be called in under the NSI Act.

COMPETITION ASSESSMENT

[3.704]
The Competition and Markets Authority (CMA) is responsible for investigating competition issues raised by mergers and acquisitions under the EA02. The CMA remains the independent and expert authority responsible for competition assessments.

A CMA merger control investigation assesses the impact of a transaction on competition to protect consumers. If there are grounds for an acquisition to be considered for both competition and national security reasons, the Investment Security Unit will work closely with the CMA to manage the case.

Where a final order is in force or a final notification that no further action is to be taken has been given under the NSI Act, the government can issue a direction to the CMA to do or not do anything under Part 3 of the Enterprise Act, as long as the government reasonably considers that the direction is necessary and proportionate for the purpose of preventing, remedying or mitigating a risk to national security.

Prior to issuing any direction, the government will consult with the CMA (and with other parties where appropriate).

EXPORT CONTROL

[3.705]
The Export Control Joint Unit (ECJU) administers the UK's system of export controls and licensing for military and dual-use items. It remains a key method of regulating trade in strategic goods and only covers the export of certain military and dual-use assets.

Export control and the NSI Act have the shared objective of safeguarding national security but with different remits and factors considered. Export control operates with specific regard to the exporting of items specified on a 'control list'. These export control lists form the basis of determining whether any products, software or technology that are intended for export are 'controlled' and therefore require an export license. Additionally, there are some circumstances in which export controls can apply to non-listed items.

Asset acquisitions are not subject to the mandatory notification requirements under the NSI Act and so you are not required to submit a notification in relation to the acquisition of an asset. However, the government may call in an asset acquisition if there is reasonable suspicion that it has given rise to or may give to a risk to national security. For more detail on how the government will decide whether to call in an asset acquisition please refer to the Section 3 Statement. [**Editorial note:** now the BEIS Notice: National Security and Investment Act 2021: Statement for the purposes of section 3 (November 2021) at **[3.715]**.]

In the case where the two systems both consider the same asset, the government, when using the powers under the NSI Act, will take account of any controls and licenses issued by the ECJU.

The ECJU does not have the ability to screen acquisitions of UK entities, nor the ability to intervene in the acquisition of sensitive assets outside the control list, unlike the NSI Act.

TAKEOVER CODE

[3.706]
The Takeover Code is a set of rules, administered by the Takeover Panel, that apply to publicly traded companies and certain other public and private companies. The Takeover Panel has no current plans to amend the Takeover Code as a result of the NSI Act. However, acquirers will need to consider any existing requirements under the Takeover Code, before proceeding with an acquisition. [**Editorial note:** see www.thetakeoverpanel.org.uk/the-code/download-code.]

The Takeover Code currently provides the framework to allow acquirers (offerors) awaiting a decision under the NSI Act to suspend or pause the offer timetable prescribed by the Code. Further details can be found in the Code Committee's Response Statement to the consultation on 'Conditions to offers and the offer timetable'. [**Editorial note:** see www.thetakeoverpanel.org.uk/wp-content/uploads/2021/03/RS-2020_1-FINAL-31-March-2021.pdf.]

FINANCIAL CONDUCT AUTHORITY AND PRUDENTIAL REGULATION AUTHORITY

[3.707]
The Financial Conduct Agency (FCA) and Prudential Regulation Authority (PRA) are regulatory bodies responsible for regulating financial services. They operate independently of the government and maintain the integrity of the UK financial markets. The PRA is part of the Bank of England.

Under the NSI Act, the government's powers to intervene in an acquisition take the form of orders, which may put certain conditions on an acquisition.

The NSI Act sits alongside regulatory bodies that may place obligations on entities, including requirements from the FCA and PRA. It is possible, but highly unlikely, that orders under the NSI Act could have an impact on other obligations, and the NSI Act is not intended to prevent persons complying with their statutory obligations, for example with the FCA and PRA. In the rare event that you have any concerns that an order under the NSI Act may conflict with other regulatory obligations please make the ISU aware.

DEPARTMENT FOR BUSINESS, ENERGY & INDUSTRIAL STRATEGY GUIDANCE NATIONAL SECURITY AND INVESTMENT ACT: GUIDANCE FOR THE HIGHER EDUCATION AND RESEARCH-INTENSIVE SECTORS

(Published 20 July 2021)

[3.708]

NOTES

This Guidance is available on the BEIS collection of materials dealing with the National Security and Investment Act 2021 at: https://www.gov.uk/government/collections/national-security-and-investment-act.

CONTENTS

INTRODUCTION

[3.709]

This guidance helps Higher Education Institutions, other research organisations and investors in this area to understand the scope of the National Security and Investment Act 2021 ("NSI Act") and how to prepare for the new rules.

It covers:

- a summary of the NSI Act
- examples of assets and entities within the scope of the NSI Act (qualifying assets and entities) within the higher education and research-intensive sectors
- how you may be required to notify the government about an acquisition of a qualifying entity in one of the specified 17 sensitive areas of the UK economy, and get approval from the government before you can complete it
- when you can voluntarily notify the government about other qualifying acquisitions
- hypothetical scenarios of qualifying acquisitions of entities and assets in the higher education and research-intensive sectors.

Higher Education Institutions and other research organisations should be aware of the NSI Act when collaborating with other parties to acquire, sell or develop qualifying entities or assets.

SUMMARY OF THE NSI ACT

[3.710]

The government will be able to scrutinise and intervene in certain acquisitions made by anyone, including businesses and investors, that could harm the UK's national security. The government will be able to impose certain conditions on an acquisition, or, if necessary, unwind or block it, although the government expects to do this rarely.

These new rules fall under the National Security and Investment (NSI) Act which will come into force on 4 January 2022.

The new rules cover qualifying acquisitions of certain entities and assets, known as qualifying entities and assets, and examples for the higher education and research-intensive sectors are given in this guidance.

The government can call in an acquisition for assessment if it reasonably suspects that it is a qualifying acquisition that has given rise to, or may give rise to, a risk to national security. This applies whether the acquisition has been completed or is still in progress or contemplation. However, it will not be possible to call in and assess acquisitions completed before 12 November 2020.

HOW THE NEW RULES WILL WORK

[3.711]
The new rules only apply to qualifying acquisitions. These are referred to as trigger events in the National Security and Investment Act.

Your acquisition is a qualifying acquisition if all of the following apply:

- the acquisition is of a right or interest in, or in relation to, a qualifying asset or qualifying entity (these terms are explained below)
- the entity or asset you are acquiring is from, in, or has a connection to the UK
- the level of control you acquire over the qualifying entity or qualifying asset meets or passes a certain threshold (for example, your stake or voting rights in a qualifying entity becomes higher than 25%).

Read the guidance on how the NSI Act will work and what these thresholds are. [**Editorial note:** see the BEIS Guidance *National Security and Investment Act: Prepare for new rules about acquisitions which could harm the UK's national security* at **[3.681]**.]

If you are planning an acquisition of a qualifying entity in one of the defined sensitive areas of the UK economy, you may be legally required to get approval from the government before you can complete it. This is called a notifiable acquisition, and Higher Education Institutions and other research organisations work within many of these areas. Completing a notifiable acquisition without approval will mean the acquisition is void and may mean that the acquirer is subject to civil or criminal penalties.

There is no legal requirement to notify the government of acquisitions of control over assets. However, the government can assess qualifying asset acquisitions if it is reasonably suspected that the acquisition gives rise to, or may give rise to, a risk to national security. All cases will be considered on an individual basis.

You can submit a voluntary notification if you are a party to a completed or planned qualifying acquisition that is not covered by mandatory notification and want to find out if the government is going to call it in.

WHAT IS A QUALIFYING ENTITY AND QUALIFYING ASSET?

Entities and assets might be qualifying entities and qualifying assets if they are from, in or have a connection to the UK.

Read further guidance on the acquisition of entities or assets outside the UK. [**Editorial note:** see the BEIS Guidance *How the National Security and Investment Act could affect people or acquisitions outside the UK* at **[3.692]**.]

A qualifying entity is any entity other than an individual, including a company, a limited liability partnership, any other body corporate, a partnership, or an unincorporated association or trust.

In the higher education and research-intensive sectors, a qualifying entity could include, but is not limited to, a foreign or UK:

- university, which is registered as a charitable organisation
- private university
- trust
- university spin-out
- university subsidiary (for example a company that a university has incorporated and carries out specific activities that the university operates)
- research organisation
- private company or corporation doing contractual work with a higher education institution or research organisation.

Qualifying assets include land, tangible, moveable property, and ideas, information or techniques which have industrial, commercial or other economic value ('intellectual property').

In the higher education and research-intensive sectors a qualifying asset could include but is not limited to:

- designs
- plans, drawings and specifications
- software
- trade secrets
- databases
- source code
- algorithms
- formulae

- land
- tangible moveable property e.g. laboratory equipment.

THE LEVEL OF CONTROL YOU HAVE ACQUIRED, OR WILL ACQUIRE, OVER THE QUALIFYING ENTITY OR ASSET

Your acquisition is a qualifying acquisition if you acquire a right or interest in, or in relation to, a qualifying entity or asset, and the level of control you acquire meets any of the following thresholds:

- your shareholding stake or voting rights in a qualifying entity meets or crosses certain percentage thresholds (for example, it becomes higher than 25%)
- you acquire voting rights in a qualifying entity that allow you to pass or block resolutions governing the affairs of the entity
- you are able to materially influence the policy of a qualifying entity, for example by acquiring the right to appoint members of the board of the entity that enables you to influence the strategic direction of the entity
- you are able to use a qualifying asset, or you are able to direct or control its use, or you are able to do so more than you could prior to the acquisition.

Read the guidance on how the NSI Act will work for further details of each threshold. [**Editorial note:** see the BEIS Guidance *National Security and Investment Act: Prepare for new rules about acquisitions which could harm the UK's national security* at [**3.681**].]

MANDATORY NOTIFICATION

If you are a party acquiring a qualifying entity, you will be legally required to tell the government about certain acquisitions in 17 sensitive areas of the economy as these areas are considered more likely to give rise to national security risks.

Acquisitions of entities in these areas which meet certain thresholds of control and other conditions (to be specified in notifiable acquisition regulations) are called notifiable acquisitions and will need to be notified, and approved, before proceeding.

Acquisition of assets are not subject to mandatory notification.

Further guidance for each of these areas and the thresholds for notifiable acquisitions will be made available separately.

The areas of the economy are:

- Advanced Materials
- Advanced Robotics
- Artificial Intelligence
- Civil Nuclear
- Communications
- Computing Hardware
- Critical Suppliers to Government
- Cryptographic Authentication
- Data Infrastructure
- Defence
- Energy
- Military and Dual-Use
- Quantum Technologies
- Satellite and Space Technologies
- Suppliers to the Emergency Services
- Synthetic Biology
- Transport

The regulations specifying the acquisitions within the 17 areas of the economy listed above which will be subject to mandatory notification, will be published later this year.

Read a draft of the regulations. [**Editorial note:** now see the National Security and Investment Act 2021 (Notifiable Acquisition) (Specification of Qualifying Entities) Regulations 2021, SI 2021/1264 at [**2.205**].]

You will need to tell the government about a notifiable acquisition by submitting a notification online. The requirement to notify the government about notifiable acquisitions will come into force on 4 January 2022.

If you complete a notifiable acquisition without gaining approval from the government, the acquisition is void. There are civil and criminal penalties for proceeding with a notifiable acquisition without gaining the necessary approval.

Mandatory notification only applies to the acquisition of entities and not assets (such as intellectual or tangible movable property).

VOLUNTARY NOTIFICATION

You can submit a voluntary notification if you are a party to a qualifying acquisition that is not covered by mandatory notification and want to gain clarity as to whether the government is going to call in the acquisition. You are not legally required to tell the government about your qualifying acquisition. However, if the government reasonably suspects it may give rise to a national security risk it may still be called in.

Once a complete notification has been accepted, the government has 30 working days to review the acquisition and provide clearance or call in the acquisition for a national security assessment. If the acquisition is called in, the government has 30 working days to complete its national security assessment, although this can be extended by a further 45 working days if more time is needed. After this, any further extensions must be agreed by the acquirer. If the Government clears your acquisition, it cannot investigate it again, unless you have submitted false or misleading information.

In deciding whether to voluntarily notify, parties may be assisted by the NSI Section 3 Statement which will provide further information on how the government expects to use its call-in power and assess qualifying acquisitions. The statement is currently out for consultation. [**Editorial note:** now the BEIS Notice: National Security and Investment Act 2021: Statement for the purposes of section 3 (November 2021) at **[3.715]**.]

Market guidance notes will also be published within 6 months of commencement of the Act and will draw on analysis of notifications received over time, as well as market monitoring intelligence, to help parties in deciding whether to voluntarily notify.

You can contact the Investment Security Unit for general enquiries or advice about the Act on investment.screening@beis.gov.uk.

IF THE GOVERNMENT DECIDES TO ASSESS YOUR QUALIFYING ACQUISITION FOR A NATIONAL SECURITY RISK (CALLING IN)

[3.712]
You will be told by the government if it is assessing your acquisition for a national security risk. This is known as 'calling in' the acquisition. A qualifying acquisition may be called in after you have submitted a notification or because it comes to the attention of the government through market monitoring. The government will only be able to do this if it has a reasonable suspicion that the acquisition may pose a risk to national security.

SCENARIOS OF ACQUISITIONS

[3.713]
The hypothetical examples below show qualifying acquisitions which the government will be able to call in for assessment if it reasonably suspects the acquisition has given rise, or may give rise, to a national security risk.

The NSI Section 3 Statement will provide further information on how the government expects to use its call-in power and assess qualifying acquisitions. Read our consultation on the draft statement. [**Editorial note:** now the BEIS Notice: National Security and Investment Act 2021: Statement for the purposes of section 3 (November 2021) at **[3.715]**.]

INVOLVEMENT IN UNIVERSITY RESEARCH

Private companies, governments and other organisations are frequently involved in universities' and other organisations' research at early stages, often at a pre-commercial stage.

This can be done through a collaborative, or other, agreement involving:

- contract or sponsored research
- sponsoring a research position (for example, a chair)
- sponsoring a research theme

If through these agreements a person gains control over a university or research organisation's qualifying assets, which can include both tangible moveable and intellectual property, for example where such assets are licensed out (exclusively or non-exclusively) by a university, then this is a qualifying acquisition under the NSI Act.

It will also be a qualifying acquisition if a party gains control over a qualifying asset generated by the research it has funded. Any agreement that provides for this will also be in scope of the NSI Act as a contemplated qualifying acquisition.

Qualifying asset acquisitions do not have mandatory notification requirements and the government can only call in a completed or contemplated qualifying acquisition for assessment if it reasonably suspects the acquisition has given rise, or may give rise, to a national security risk.

Example 1

A foreign corporation provides funding for a UK university to carry out a research project on the foreign corporation's behalf. The foreign corporation sits on the steering board for the research project. The foreign corporation will also be entitled to all intellectual and tangible moveable property generated from the research.

The government may be able to call in this contemplated acquisition for assessment if it reasonably suspects the acquisition may give rise to a risk to national security. This is because this scenario is a contemplated qualifying asset acquisition as the funding gives the corporation control over any intellectual or tangible moveable property generated through this project.

You are not legally required to notify the government in this scenario as the research project is not a qualifying entity and mandatory notification only applies to certain acquisitions of qualifying entities.

Example 2

A private company acquires 30% of the shares in a university subsidiary which undertakes research work in one of the 17 sensitive areas of the economy and is specified in the notifiable acquisition regulations.

This scenario is a notifiable acquisition of a qualifying entity.

If you are the private company (the acquirer) you will be legally required to notify the government of your planned investment and obtain approval before proceeding, otherwise your acquisition will be void. You may also be liable to criminal or civil penalties if the acquisition is completed without prior approval.

Example 3

A company sponsors a professorship in a UK university. The company can influence the direction of the research the professor leads but has no agreed access to any assets.

This scenario is not a qualifying acquisition and not in scope of the NSI Act as the company has not gained control over any qualifying entity or asset.

Example 4

Academic Institution A acquires the right to use the background intellectual property of Academic Institution B through a collaborative agreement.

The government may be able to call in this acquisition for assessment if it reasonably suspects the acquisition has given rise, or may give rise, to a national security risk. This is because this scenario is a qualifying asset acquisition as Academic Institution A has acquired control over Academic Institution B's intellectual property.

You are not legally required to notify the government in this scenario because mandatory notification requirements do not apply to acquisitions of intellectual property.

Example 5

A private company enters a collaborative research project with an academic institution in the UK. The collaborative agreement stipulates an option for the private company to enter into a non-exclusive license agreement for any intellectual property generated by the project. The private company decides to exercise this option and enter into a non-exclusive license agreement to use the intellectual property which has been generated by the academic institution and is being used to conduct further research.

The government may be able to call in this qualifying acquisition for assessment if it reasonably suspects the acquisition has given rise, or may give rise, to a risk to national security. This is because the granting of the license is an acquisition of control over a qualifying asset. Through the licence the private company has acquired control over intellectual property.

You are not legally required to notify the government in this scenario as intellectual property is not a qualifying entity and mandatory notification only applies to certain acquisitions of qualifying entities.

DEVELOPING OR FORMING RESEARCH CENTRES

Research centres are often collaborative projects between different research organisations and public and private partners.

If, in the development or founding of a research centre, control over qualifying assets or entities is acquired, the government can call in such a qualifying acquisition for assessment if it reasonably suspects the acquisition has given rise, or may give rise, to a risk to national security.

Example 1

A foreign research centre, which is a collaboration of private and public partners, acquires 50% of the shares in a UK research organisation which will become part of the centre. The acquired research organisation conducts research in one of the 17 sensitive areas of the economy that are specified in the notifiable acquisition regulations.

The foreign research centre (the acquirer) will be legally required to notify the government of its planned acquisition and obtain approval before proceeding, otherwise the acquisition will be void. This is because this acquisition is a notifiable acquisition of a qualifying entity which is specified in the notifiable acquisition regulations.

The foreign research centre and certain employees may also be liable to criminal or civil penalties if the acquisition is completed without prior approval.

Example 2

A UK research organisation partners with a UK research centre (which is owned by a foreign research organisation and a private UK company) and carries out research in one of the 17 sensitive areas of the economy specified in the notifiable acquisition regulations. Through the terms of the partnership, the research centre gains control over the laboratory equipment and software of the UK research organisation.

The government may be able to call in this acquisition for assessment if it reasonably suspects the acquisition has given rise, or may give rise, to a national security risk. This is because this acquisition is an acquisition of control over a qualifying asset. The research centre can now use the UK research organisation's laboratory and software.

You are not legally required to notify the government in this scenario because mandatory notification requirements do not apply to acquisitions of assets such as the laboratory equipment and software. This applies even if the assets are held by a qualifying entity that operates in areas of the economy specified in the notifiable acquisition regulations, such as in this scenario.

DEVELOPING UNIVERSITY OR RESEARCH ORGANISATION SPIN-OUT COMPANIES

A university or research organisation spin-out company is a company which is created to develop a university's research for commercial application. The spin-out is a private company but often the university will retain shares in the company or retain some ownership of the intellectual property.

If a spin-out company is acquired or the spin out gains control of qualifying assets of a university or research organisation, this could be called in by the government for assessment if it reasonably suspects this has given rise, or may give rise, to a risk to national security.

If an established spin-out is subsequently acquired by another party, for example by trade sale, merger, or investment, this could also be in scope of the NSI Act. If the spin-out operates in one of the 17 sensitive areas of the economy specified in notifiable acquisition regulations, there may be a legal requirement to notify the government of the acquisition.

Example 1

A number of investors establish a university spin-out in the UK in order to commercialise a UK university's patented technology. The investors and the university receive equity stakes in the spin-out and the technology is licensed to the spin-out through the university's Technology Transfer Office.

The government may be able to call in this acquisition for assessment if it reasonably suspects the acquisition has given rise, or may give rise, to a risk to national security. This is because in this scenario there is a qualifying acquisition of a qualifying asset as the spin-out has gained control over the use of the technology as a licensee.

You are not legally required to notify the government of the grant of the licence as intellectual property is not a qualifying entity and mandatory notification only applies to certain acquisitions of qualifying entities.

Example 2

A venture capital fund that is backed by multiple investors invests in an established university spin-out, in return for a 27% equity stake. The university spin out carries out research and produces goods in one of the 17 sensitive areas of the economy that are specified in the notifiable acquisition regulations.

The venture capital fund (the acquirer) will be legally required to notify the government of its planned acquisition and obtain approval before completing it, otherwise the acquisition will be void. This is because this investment is a notifiable acquisition of a qualifying entity which is specified in the notifiable acquisition regulations.

The fund and certain employees may also be liable to criminal or civil penalties for completing the acquisition without approval. Within the notification form the venture capital fund will be asked to provide the ownership details of the fund.

FUNDING EMPLOYEES OR STUDENTS IN UNIVERSITY PROGRAMMES

Funding for PhDs and other academic placements can come from various sources including industry, academic institutions and public and charitable funders. Companies fund employees or students to carry out research projects including PhDs at universities.

The ownership of the intellectual property generated in academic placements can vary depending on the agreement, and can include the following scenarios:

- the student has rights over the intellectual property generated
- the intellectual property rights reside with the university
- the intellectual property generated is assigned to the company who is funding an employee to do research at a university and the terms are stipulated through the employee's contract.

If a company or other person acquires control over intellectual property generated in the UK, for example the right to use the intellectual property, this is a qualifying acquisition under the NSI Act. Any agreement that provides for control to be acquired over any future intellectual property generated in the UK will also be in scope of the NSI Act as a contemplated qualifying acquisition. However, the government will only be able call in a completed or contemplated qualifying acquisition if it reasonably suspects the acquisition has given, or may give, rise to a national security risk.

Example 1

A private foreign company funds an employee through an academic placement which results in a PhD. As part of the employee's contract, all intellectual property generated is assigned to the company.

The government may be able to call in this contemplated acquisition for assessment if it reasonably suspects the acquisition may give rise to a risk to national security. This is because this scenario is a contemplated acquisition of control over a qualifying asset because the private company has contractual rights over any intellectual property generated by the employee during their PhD.

You are not legally required to notify the government in this scenario as no party has acquired a qualifying entity and mandatory notification only applies to certain acquisitions of qualifying entities.

DONATING TO AN ACADEMIC INSTITUTION

Many alumni and other parties donate to universities and related organisations. Universities have due diligence processes for accepting donations, which are often stated publicly.

Donations differ and may include a grant or sponsorship. They generally must meet the following criteria: the donation will result in no commercial value for the donor, and the initiative for the project is driven by the recipient university which will retain ownership of any research or IP that is generated.

Donations and donations for research are not covered by the NSI Act as no control is gained over a qualifying asset or entity. It is for universities to ensure robust and transparent procedures for accepting donations.

Example 1

A private company donates a large sum to a university for the development of a new research laboratory. The private company is later awarded contracts as an equipment supplier at the same university in line with the necessary contracts regulations.

This scenario is not a qualifying acquisition and is not in scope of the NSI Act as the private company has not gained control over the use of the laboratory or any intellectual property. The company has won contracts through the university's standard tender process.

OTHER RESOURCES TO ENSURE BEST PRACTICE IN YOUR APPROACH TO PROTECTING YOUR RESEARCH

[3.714]

The Centre for the Protection of National Infrastructure (CPNI) and the National Cyber Security Centre (NCSC) have produced guidance on how to collaborate securely with international research partners. The guidance includes downloadable checklists and a strategic guide for senior leaders. [**Editorial note:** see www.cpni.gov.uk/trusted-research.]

Universities UK (UUK) has published detailed guidance for institutions on the considerations and measures they should take to guard against hostile interference and promote academic freedom. [**Editorial note:** see www.universitiesuk.ac.uk/what-we-do/policy-and-research/publications/managing-risks-internationalisation.]

DEPARTMENT FOR BUSINESS, ENERGY & INDUSTRIAL STRATEGY NOTICE NATIONAL SECURITY AND INVESTMENT ACT 2021: STATEMENT FOR THE PURPOSES OF SECTION 3

(Published 2 November 2021)

[3.715]

NOTES

This Guidance is available on the BEIS collection of materials dealing with the National Security and Investment Act 2021 at: https://www.gov.uk/government/collections/national-security-and-investment-act.

CONTENTS

INTRODUCTION

[3.716]

1. This statement is made under section 3 of the National Security and Investment Act 2021 ('the NSI Act'). It sets out how the Secretary of State expects to exercise the power to give a call-in notice. An acquisition can be called in for assessment if the Secretary of State reasonably suspects the acquisition has given, or may give, rise to a risk to national security or arrangements are in progress or contemplation which, if carried into effect, will result in an acquisition that may give rise to a risk to national security. The acquisition must also meet certain criteria to be a qualifying acquisition under the NSI Act. The Secretary of State may then clear the acquisition or, if necessary and proportionate, impose certain conditions, block or unwind it completely.

2. This statement gives as much detail as is possible on how the Secretary of State expects to use the call-in power, given the sensitivity of national security. The call-in power will be used solely to safeguard the UK's national security and not to promote any other objectives. This statement must be reviewed by the Secretary of State every five years and may be reviewed more frequently.

3. This statement refers to 'qualifying acquisitions', which means those acquisitions that the Act defines as 'trigger events'. It is hoped that this will aid readability and general understanding. See separate guidance on the scope of qualifying acquisitions. [**Editorial note:** this guidance is at **[3.681]**.]

NATIONAL SECURITY AND INVESTMENT ACT 2021 AND THE CALL-IN POWER

[3.717]

4. The Act intentionally does not set out the circumstances in which national security is, or may be, considered at risk. This reflects longstanding government policy to ensure that national security powers are sufficiently flexible to protect the nation.

5. Each qualifying acquisition will be assessed on a case-by-case basis, taking account of all relevant considerations and with regard to the risk factors set out below. This applies to all qualifying acquisitions, whether they involve parties only within the UK or involve parties overseas.

6. The call-in power will not be used to interfere arbitrarily with investment. The UK has a proud record as one of the most open economies in the world and the Secretary of State's use of the call-in power will not change that. The UK remains firmly open to investment and the government wants the UK to be the best place in the world to work and do business.

AREAS OF THE ECONOMY IN WHICH QUALIFYING ACQUISITIONS ARE MORE LIKELY TO GIVE RISE TO A RISK TO NATIONAL SECURITY AND MORE LIKELY TO BE CALLED IN

[3.718]

7. Qualifying acquisitions across the whole economy are in scope of the NSI Act but the call-in power may only be used in respect of qualifying acquisitions that the Secretary of State reasonably suspects give rise to or may give rise to a risk to national security. The NSI Act is not a system for screening all acquisitions in the economy.

8. Some qualifying acquisitions of target entities in the 17 areas of the economy listed below are subject to mandatory notification because of their particular sensitivity. As a result, such acquisitions are more likely to be called in, as the activities in which these entities are engaged are more likely to give rise to risks to national security.

9. The National Security and Investment Act 2021 (Notifiable Acquisition) (Specification of Qualifying Entities) Regulations 2021 ('the Notifiable Acquisition Regulations') describe these target entities and the activities in which they are engaged.

10. The 17 areas of the economy are:

- Advanced Materials
- Advanced Robotics
- Artificial Intelligence
- Civil Nuclear
- Communications
- Computing Hardware
- Critical Suppliers to Government
- Cryptographic Authentication

- Data Infrastructure
- Defence
- Energy
- Military and Dual-Use
- Quantum Technologies
- Satellite and Space Technologies
- Suppliers to the Emergency Services
- Synthetic Biology
- Transport

11. While not subject to mandatory notification, acquisitions of control through material influence over such target entities are also more likely to be called in.

12. In addition, qualifying acquisitions of entities which undertake activities closely linked to the activities in these 17 areas of the economy (for example, they are related to transport but are not within the definition of transport in the regulations) are more likely to be called in than those that are not closely linked.

13. Qualifying acquisitions which occur outside the above areas of the economy subject to mandatory notification are unlikely to be called in as national security risks are expected to occur less frequently in these areas.

14. Where a qualifying acquisition is not subject to mandatory notification, the parties may choose to notify the Secretary of State, so as to be certain whether the acquisition will be called in.

15. Parties should be aware that loans, conditional acquisitions, futures, and options are unlikely to pose a risk to national security and so are unlikely to be called in.

WHAT THE SECRETARY OF STATE IS SEEKING TO PROTECT BY USING THE CALL-IN POWER

[3.719]

16. The powers granted to the Secretary of State under the NSI Act seek to protect the UK's national security and are one of many tools and pieces of legislation that do this. The government intentionally does not set out the exhaustive circumstances in which national security is, or may be, considered at risk. This is longstanding policy to ensure that national security powers are sufficiently flexible to protect the nation. Therefore nothing in this statement should be interpreted as a definition of national security.

17. The Secretary of State is likely to use the call-in power where there may be a potential for immediate or future harm to UK national security. This includes risks to governmental and defence assets (infrastructure, technologies and capabilities), such as disruption or erosion of military advantage; the potential impact of a qualifying acquisition on the security of the UK's critical infrastructure; and the need to prevent actors with hostile intentions towards the UK building defence or technological capabilities which may present a national security threat to the UK. The call-in power will not be used when the acquisition of infrastructure or technological capabilities does not present a national security risk to the UK.

18. Under the Act, the call-in power can only be used for the purpose of dealing with risks to national security.

FACTORS THE SECRETARY OF STATE WILL TAKE INTO ACCOUNT WHEN DECIDING WHETHER TO EXERCISE THE CALL-IN POWER

RISK FACTORS

[3.720]

19. Decisions on whether to exercise the call-in power will be made on a case-by-case basis. In order to assess the likelihood of a qualifying acquisition giving rise to a risk to national security (and therefore whether to call in the acquisition), the Secretary of State expects to consider primarily three risk factors, explained below.

20. The risk factors are:

a. Target risk. This concerns whether the target of the qualifying acquisition (the entity or asset being acquired) is being used, or could be used, in a way that raises a risk to national security.

b. Acquirer risk. This concerns whether the acquirer has characteristics that suggest there is, or may be, a risk to national security from the acquirer having control of the target.

c. Control risk. This concerns the amount of control that has been, or will be, acquired through the qualifying acquisition. A higher level of control may increase the level of national security risk.

21. The Secretary of State expects that, when calling in an acquisition, all 3 risk factors will be present, but does not rule out calling in an acquisition on the basis of fewer risk factors.

22. For most qualifying acquisitions, the overall consideration of these risks is expected to indicate a low risk to national security.

RISK FACTORS EXPLAINED

TARGET RISK

[3.721]

23. The target of a qualifying acquisition is the qualifying entity or qualifying asset that has been or will be acquired. In assessing the target risk, the Secretary of State will consider what the target does, is used for, or could be used for, and whether that has given rise to, or may give rise to, a risk to national security. Assessment of the target risk may also involve consideration of any national security risks arising from the target's proximity to sensitive sites.

24. The Secretary of State considers that qualifying entities which undertake activities in the 17 areas of the economy listed in paragraph 10, or closely linked activities, are more likely to raise a target risk than other qualifying entities.

ACQUIRER RISK

25. The Secretary of State will consider whether the acquirer poses a risk to national security. Characteristics of the acquirer such as the sector(s) of activity, technological capabilities and links to entities which may seek to undermine or threaten the national security of the UK, are likely to be considered in order to understand the level of risk the acquirer may pose.

26. Some characteristics, such as a history of passive or long-term investments, may indicate low or no acquirer risk. The Secretary of State does not regard state-owned entities, sovereign wealth funds or other entities affiliated with foreign states, as being inherently more likely to pose a national security risk.

27. In assessing an acquirer, the Secretary of State may consider several factors, including:

a. the ultimate controller of an acquirer, or if the acquirer can be readily exploited;

b. whether the acquirer may pose a risk to national security in the light of their pre-existing holdings;

c. whether the acquirer, or their ultimate controller, has committed, or is linked to, criminal or illicit activities that are related to national security, or activities that have given rise to or may give rise to a risk to national security.

28. If an acquirer has links to entities which may seek to undermine or threaten the national security of the UK, this does not automatically mean that the acquisition will be called in.

29. The Secretary of State will not make judgements based solely on an acquirer's country of origin. However, an acquirer's ties or allegiance to a state or organisation which is hostile to the UK will be considered when assessing whether their qualifying acquisition has given, or may give, rise to a risk to the UK's national security.

CONTROL RISK

30. The control risk refers to the amount of control the acquirer gains of an entity's activities or strategy. It also concerns the amount of control over an asset, which includes controlling or directing its use, as well as using it.

31. The Secretary of State will consider the control that has been or will be acquired through the qualifying acquisition. A greater degree of control may increase the possibility of a target being used to harm national security. Additionally, a large amount of control may enable parties to reduce the diversity of a market, or influence the market's behaviour, in a way that may give rise to a risk to national security. In such cases, the acquisition is more likely to be called in.

32. The control risk will be assessed alongside the target and acquirer risk. This is because when the target and/or acquirer risk is low, the level of control acquired is less likely to give rise to a risk to national security and so the Secretary of State is less likely to call in that acquisition.

Example 1: Qualifying acquisition of a qualifying entity that is likely to be called in

Company A is undertaking activities in the UK which include the development of cryptographic authentication for the purpose of activities that would be in scope of mandatory notification in the sector. Party B acquires shares in Company A that are below a 25% acquisition of shareholding stake or voting rights but which enable Party B materially to influence the policy of Company A. The UK government has concerns that the activities of Party B may be linked to hostile activity.

The target risk is high. The activities of Company A are in an area of the economy likely to give rise to risks to national security, as the cryptographic authentication technology could be used for malicious purposes.

The acquirer risk is high as the activities of Party B may be linked to hostile activity and requires an assessment by the government to identify possible national security risks.

While material influence is the lowest form of control over entities, there is a control risk as the acquisition enables Party B materially to influence how Company A's technology could be used or sold.

Therefore, this acquisition is likely to be called in.

Example 2: Qualifying acquisition of a qualifying entity that is unlikely to be called in

Investor C is a non-UK based entity that increases its share of the voting rights in Company D from 15% to 26%. Company D is a financial services company which holds public contracts with the UK government. Investor C is well-known to the UK government and there is no existing activity that would give rise to concerns around national security.

Part 3 CMA and other Guidelines

The target risk is low as, while Company D is a supplier to the UK government, it undertakes activities that do not require mandatory notification nor are they closely linked to the activities which require mandatory notification.

The acquirer risk is low as Investor C's activities are well known to the UK government and there has been no history of activity by Investor C that would give rise to national security concerns.

Despite the acquisition increasing Investor C's share of the voting rights in Company D from 25% or less to more than 25%, the control risk is unlikely to increase materially the risk to national security as the target risk and acquirer risk are low.

Therefore, this acquisition is unlikely to be called in.

ASSETS

[3.722]

33. Acquisitions of control over qualifying assets are also in scope of the call-in power. This is principally so that acquisitions may be called in if control of an asset is acquired instead of an entity that owns it, or in the event that an asset, such as land, is located near a sensitive site, which may give rise to a national security risk.

34. Asset acquisitions are not subject to the mandatory notification requirements and so no one is required to submit a notification in relation to a qualifying acquisition of an asset. Parties may make a voluntary notification to the Secretary of State about an acquisition if they wish to be certain whether the acquisition will be called in. The Secretary of State may call in a qualifying acquisition of an asset if they have reasonable suspicion that it has given rise to or may give rise to a risk to national security. The Secretary of State will consider what the asset could be used for and whether that use could give rise to a risk to national security.

35. The call-in power is more likely to be used for qualifying acquisitions of assets that are or could be, used in connection with the activities set out in the Notifiable Acquisition Regulations or closely linked activities. This is because these acquisitions are more likely to pose a risk to national security.

36. Land is mainly expected to be an asset of national security interest where it is, or is proximate to, a sensitive site. Examples of such sensitive sites include critical national infrastructure sites or government buildings. However the Secretary of State may also take into account the intended use of the land.

37. The Secretary of State expects to call in rarely acquisitions of assets which do not fall into the above categories.

38. Overall, the Secretary of State expects to call in rarely acquisitions of assets compared to acquisitions of entities.

Example 3: Qualifying acquisition of a tangible asset that is unlikely to be called in

Company A has bought Building B located in the UK for residential use. Building B is a house adjacent to a sensitive military site. Company A is an overseas pharmaceutical company that is known to the UK government with no evidence of ties to hostile activity in the UK.

The target risk is medium as there is a proximity risk as the target to a sensitive site. However, it is unlikely that owning the adjacent property for residential use could pose a risk to national security, given other security protections in place at the military site.

The acquirer risk is low as there is no evidence to suggest that the acquirer, Company A, is linked to hostile activity, so the possibility of the target being used to threaten the UK's national security is low. Company A has also demonstrated that it intends to use the asset as a place of residence, which does not pose a national security risk.

As Company A has purchased the asset outright, enabling Company A to use or to control or direct Building B's use, this represents a higher level of control risk.

Nonetheless, this acquisition is unlikely to be called in because of the levels of target and acquirer risk.

Example 4: Qualifying acquisition of a tangible asset that is likely to be called in

Company C seeks to acquire Machinery D. Company C is based in the UK but owned by an organisation based overseas and is of concern to UK security organisations. Machinery D is specialised and used in the manufacture of military hardware.

The target risk is high since this is specialised hardware with a military purpose.

The acquirer risk is high because the acquirer is owned by an organisation with potentially concerning behaviour.

This acquisition would result in a high level of control as it would enable Company C to use or to control or direct the use of Machinery D and is therefore likely to increase the level of national security risk.

Therefore, this acquisition is likely to be called in.

Example 5: Qualifying acquisition of an intellectual property asset that is likely to be called in

Asset F is the underlying source code used by Business E in its computer programmes, which are used by UK air traffic control operators – an area of the economy in which certain acquisitions of entities are covered by mandatory notification. Business E is approached by Party G who wishes to acquire the right to access and use Asset F. Party G is known by the government to have existing ties to an organisation that is hostile to the UK.

The target risk is high as the source code may be used to identify vulnerabilities in the programmes used to monitor and communicate with aircraft in UK airspace.

The acquirer risk is high as the acquirer, Party G, has existing ties to an organisation that is of concern to the UK government.

There is a control risk as the acquisition of the right to access and use Asset F means that Party G could use the asset for malicious purposes. However, Party G does not have full ownership over the asset and so does not have full control over the asset.

Nonetheless, this acquisition is likely to be called in.

EXTRATERRITORIAL USE OF THE CALL-IN POWER

[3.723]
39. Acquisitions of qualifying entities that are outside the UK and assets that are outside the UK and the territorial sea are less likely to give rise to national security risks than those within the UK and so these are less likely to be called in. Similarly, the risk to national security will be related to how strongly the entity or asset is connected to the UK. The Secretary of State will consider to what extent people in the UK rely on qualifying entities and assets outside the UK and how this may affect national security risks.

40. There is separate guidance on the application of the NSI Act in relation to entities and assets outside the UK. [**Editorial note:** this guidance is at **[3.692]**.]

RETROSPECTIVE USE OF THE CALL-IN POWER

[3.724]
41. The Secretary of State may call in qualifying acquisitions after they have taken place. This power is set out in section 1(1)(a) of the Act.

42. When deciding whether to call in a qualifying acquisition that has already taken place, the same assessment of risk factors will be applied as for qualifying acquisitions that have not already taken place.

43. The decision whether to call in a qualifying acquisition after it has taken place will be made according to the risk to national security at the point of the decision rather than the risk to national security at the point that the qualifying acquisition took place.

DEPARTMENT FOR BUSINESS, ENERGY & INDUSTRIAL STRATEGY GUIDANCE NATIONAL SECURITY AND INVESTMENT ACT: GUIDANCE ON NOTIFIABLE ACQUISITIONS

(Published 15 November 2021)

[3.725]

NOTES

This Guidance is available on the BEIS collection of materials dealing with the National Security and Investment Act 2021 at: https://www.gov.uk/government/collections/national-security-and-investment-act.

CONTENTS

OVERVIEW

[3.726]
The National Security and Investment Act comes into force on 4 January 2022. It allows the government to scrutinise and intervene in certain acquisitions made by anyone, including businesses and investors, that could harm the UK's national security.

From 4 January 2022, subject to certain criteria, you will be legally required to tell the government about acquisitions of certain entities in 17 sensitive areas of the economy (called 'notifiable acquisitions').

The 17 areas of the economy are:

- Advanced Materials
- Advanced Robotics
- Artificial Intelligence
- Civil Nuclear
- Communications
- Computing Hardware
- Critical Suppliers to Government
- Cryptographic Authentication
- Data Infrastructure
- Defence
- Energy
- Military and Dual-Use
- Quantum Technologies
- Satellite and Space Technologies
- Suppliers to the Emergency Services
- Synthetic Biology
- Transport

If an entity you are acquiring performs a certain activity, it could put you in scope of the National Security and Investment Act and you may be legally required to tell the government about it (known as a 'mandatory notification'). This guidance tells you what these activities are.

Before reading this guidance, you should read guidance on preparing for the National Security and Investment Act to understand the wider rules around acquisitions and check what you need to do from 4 January 2022. [**Editorial note:** this guidance is at **[3.681]**.]

You can contact the Investment Security Unit (ISU) at investment.screening@beis.gov.uk for further support.

ADVANCED MATERIALS

[3.727]
The development and utilisation of Advanced Materials across Defence as well as civil sectors is rapidly growing and is crucial to help transform important industrial sectors and underpin key areas of high-value manufacturing.

The risk to national security posed by Advanced Materials is also clear. Advanced Materials offer significant benefits to military capability, through increased functionality, improved survivability, enhanced maintainability and reduced through-life cost.

The cross-cutting and dual-use nature of Advanced Materials also means that emerging technologies using advanced materials are likely to have defence and security applications and implications; irrespective of the application or sector that is driving their development.

AM I IN SCOPE OF THE ADVANCED MATERIALS PART OF THE REGULATIONS?

You will be legally required to submit a mandatory notification to the government if the qualifying entity you are acquiring carries out activities in relation to advanced materials.

Generally, Advanced Materials cover the following:

- advanced composites
- metals and alloys
- engineering and technical polymers
- engineering and technical ceramics
- technical textiles
- metamaterials

- semiconductors
- photonic and optoelectronic materials and devices
- graphene and related 2D materials
- nanotechnology
- critical materials
- other materials

The activities covered are:

- research
- development or production
- development or production of anything designed as an enabler
- development or production of anything designed to be used for the purpose of production
- the provision of qualified or certified designs, materials, parts or products
- owning, creating, supplying or exploiting intellectual property
- the provision of know-how or services of enablers
- recycling or re-using

CHECK WHICH ADVANCED MATERIALS ARE COVERED

The material is an 'advanced material' if it is listed in either of the following documents:

- the Advanced Materials section of the regulations. You should read all the sections of the Advanced Materials regulations as the categories overlap with one another
- the Strategic Export Control List (SECL) [**Editorial note:** see https://www.gov.uk/guidance/uk-strategic-export-control-lists-the-consolidated-list-of-strategic-military-and-dual-use-items.]

You must check both documents to see if your acquisition is in scope.

The following sections of the SECL are of relevance to the requirement to notify the UK government in relation to Advanced Materials:

- UK Military List [Schedule 2 to the Export Control Order 2008]
- EU Dual-Use List [Annex I to Council Regulation (EC) No. 428/2009]
- EU Dual-Use List [Annex IV to Council Regulation (EC) No. 428/2009]

Further information about semiconductors

Application-specific integrated circuit (ASICs) are a type of chip included in the Advanced Materials and not the Computing Hardware part of the regulations. This is because ASICs can be an important component in these other technological applications, whereas they are not for central processing units and provision of memory.

For further information on semiconductors and what is meant by the terms 'fabrication' and 'packaging' you should review the Computing Hardware guidance.

ADVANCED ROBOTICS

[3.728]
Robots are no longer limited to factory or laboratory settings, with increasingly capable, mobile and autonomous robots providing new services and capabilities on land (for example, self-driving cars or fruit-picking robots), in the air (drones), on or under the sea and in space. While these capabilities, including the ability to operate independently and to work safely alongside humans, will unlock important business and public benefit applications, even where an entity develops or produces robots or services specifically for civilian applications, these could potentially be adapted for use in military or national security relevant applications.

AM I IN SCOPE OF THE ADVANCED ROBOTICS PART OF THE REGULATIONS?

You will be legally required to submit a mandatory notification if the qualifying entity you are acquiring either:

- develops or produces advanced robotics
- develops or produces core components specially designed or modified for use in advanced robotics

'Advanced robotics' are defined as meeting both of the following criteria:

- it's a physical machine that can interact with its environment and can move itself or its 'limbs' or tools
- it has either a meaningful degree of autonomy, and/or the ability to use sensors to carry out sophisticated surveillance and data collection

'Autonomy' means the capability to operate independently of human control, either fully or partially. Where the autonomy is partial, this may be in addition to remote control or tele-operation or though pre-programming of operations or responses.

Autonomy therefore includes the ability to sense, reason (for example, using forms of artificial or machine intelligence) and respond or adapt to its surroundings. This may include but is not limited to:

- the ability to self-navigate and react to changing circumstances, such as a self-driving vehicle navigating the roads and responding to traffic lights

- the ability to autonomously make changes to improve performance, for example adapting or learning through iteration and experience, and/or

- the ability to self-repair, self-heal or adapt to their surroundings, including, for example, through the use of compliant or flexible materials that mimic the natural world, known as 'soft robotics'

'Advanced robotics' also includes the ability to use sensors to carry out sophisticated surveillance and data collection. This does not include simple data capture such as CCTV cameras (or other static devices) but includes robots with the ability to capture high fidelity data from their environment, including those that may be entirely pre-programmed or remotely controlled. This would include reconnaissance activities by drones, satellites, underwater vessels or other forms of mobile robot.

You will also be legally required to submit a mandatory notification to the government if you are acquiring a qualifying entity that develops or produces core components specially designed or modified for use in advanced robotics.

These core components include:

- sensors which give advanced robotics the ability to accurately sense their environment, the objects around them or their own position

- end-effectors such as grippers, manipulator arms, magnetic, pneumatic or vacuum tools that enable them to physically interact and deliver their capability with the intended precision and effect

- bespoke means of locomotion for use in advanced robotics, including for example, wheels, propellors or fins

- bespoke energy sources for use in advanced robotics and

- control systems (including forms of artificial intelligence for use in advanced robotics) and communications systems (including components that enable the advanced robotics to communicate with other robots or a central artificial intelligence system that, for example, controls a swarm of robots).

Example: autonomy

Company A is considering acquiring Company B, which designs and builds a mobile fruit picking robot equipped with AI, sensors and a new form of dextrous soft gripper. The AI and sensors enable the robot to demonstrate a meaningful degree of autonomy and it therefore meets the relevant test for being considered advanced robotics. Company A must notify the UK government of this acquisition, as Company B is a qualifying entity that develops and produces advanced robotics.

Example: components specially designed or modified for advanced robotics

Company A specialises in the provision of machine learning software for robotic control systems, to optimise picking and packing of a range of physical products. Company A does not itself produce any physical machines, but sells this capability to Company B, which Company B integrates into a broader automated robotic warehouse and stock-picking management solution. If Company C wishes to acquire either Company A or Company B it would be required to notify the UK government. This is because the integration of the standalone software capability into the broader automated robotic solution constitutes the development or production of advanced robotics capabilities.

In the event that Company A provides the systems integration capability to Company B, and Company B is therefore a consumer not involved in developing or producing the broader advanced robotics solution, then the acquisition of Company B would be out of scope.

WHAT IS OUT OF SCOPE OF THE ADVANCED ROBOTICS PART OF THE REGULATIONS?

The following are out of scope of the Advanced Robotics regulations:

- robotics that are widely available consumer goods including robotic toys and smart appliances (such as vacuum cleaning or lawnmowing robots)

- consumers of advanced robotics who purchase 'complete systems' or standalone devices or equipment and use them as they are intended, for example to perform their farming, surveying or logistics operations. By 'complete systems' we mean systems whose core technical capabilities cannot be altered, in contrast to technology or equipment that will be used in production or development activities relating to advanced robotics. If a qualifying entity purchases specific components or advanced robotics systems that it then integrates into or alters to deliver new advanced robotic functions or capabilities as part of a wider system, that qualifying entity is in scope and would need to notify

- robots performing pre-programmed repetitive tasks, most frequently seen in the older generation of industrial robotics, for example the machining, lifting or pressing operations of a manufacturing process or assembly line. This includes mechanical robotic tools performing repetitive functions with basic or no sensory or cognitive abilities

• automated parking and lane departure warning capabilities for cars or other mobile robotics, which are now commonplace across the market. However, self-driving cars and the core capabilities of autonomy underpinning them are in scope of the regulations

• basic, static, sensing, imaging or computing devices such as temperature monitors, cameras or smart speakers

• entities in the supply chain producing components intended for use more broadly than advanced robotics, including basic or generic hardware or electrical components, for example, industry standard electronics such as Complementary Metal Oxide Semiconductor (CMOS) sensors or radio transmitters.

Example: an acquisition that isn't in scope

Company A, an audit company, purchases from Company B an advanced, high-definition drone services contract, to survey and report on the activities of a range of infrastructure and construction sector clients with high specificity. Company A uses the drone in a range of different environments and uses the data it finds as part of its own business but has no expertise in developing or producing the drone itself. If Company C acquires Company A at a future date, it would not be required to notify the UK government, as it is merely a consumer / user of the products and services of Company B.

If you do not think your acquisition is covered by the Advanced Robotics guidance, you should read guidance for the following areas:

Artificial Intelligence

Computing Hardware - activities relating to 'a specialist processor for artificial intelligence applications'. You are advised to consider if the qualifying entity's work covers a) the ownership, creation or supply of intellectual property to or b) the fabrication or packaging of specialist processors for artificial intelligence applications

Defence

Military and Dual-Use

Satellite and space technologies

ARTIFICIAL INTELLIGENCE

[3.729]
The development of artificial intelligence (AI) technologies is growing rapidly and transforming the global economy. The development and application of these technologies is an industry in its own right, but AI is also transforming business models across many sectors.

AI can optimise the efficiency, precision, and performance of many existing technologies.

AI is also inherently dual-use and potentially easy to repurpose. There is increasing interest by military and law enforcement organisations to advance the use of AI in their domains. There is potential for other actors to deploy AI applications for malicious and harmful uses. This means technologies that are used for the commercial market and consumers could also be repurposed and used in manners which could give rise to national security concerns. The opportunity to use AI positively across the UK economy can only be harnessed if sensitive and critical applications of AI can be protected.

As AI technologies are often general purpose and used across sectors, this regulation will capture entities that do not necessarily identify as 'AI companies'. Whether a qualifying entity is focused solely on AI, or incorporates or develops AI as part of a wider approach to their sector or business, it is the specific work being undertaken that is most important to consider.

AM I IN SCOPE OF THE ARTIFICIAL INTELLIGENCE PART OF THE REGULATIONS?

To determine if a qualifying entity you are seeking to acquire is in scope of the AI part of the regulations, you will need to consider 2 questions:

• does the qualifying carry on entity research into, or develop or produce goods, software or technology that use AI?

• is the AI work of the qualifying entity used for one of the following applications: identification or tracking, advanced robotics or cyber security?

If the answer is yes to both questions for the qualifying entity being acquired, you will be legally required to submit a mandatory notification to the government.

There are two steps to considering the entity you are acquiring is in scope.

1. Confirm the use of AI.
2. Confirmation application of AI.

STEP 1: CONFIRM THE USE OF AI

You first need to consider if the qualifying entity researches into, or develops or produces goods, software or technology that use 'artificial intelligence'.

'Artificial Intelligence' is defined in the regulations as:

"technology enabling the programming or training of a device or software to:

i) perceive environments through the use of data

ii) interpret data using automated processing designed to approximate cognitive abilities and

iii) make recommendations, predictions or decisions

with a view to achieving a specific objective".

'Cognitive abilities' means reasoning, perception, communication, learning, planning, problem solving, abstract thinking, decision-making or organisation.

STEP 2: CONFIRM APPLICATION OF AI

If you believe the qualifying entity does fit the definition of AI, you then need to consider how this is being applied.

Three categories of application are in scope of the new rules. You will be legally required to submit a mandatory notification if the qualifying entity does any of the following:

- identification or tracking
- advanced robotics
- cyber security

Identification

Examples of 'identification' may include, but are not limited to:

Human identification:

- audio and speech recognition
- data re-identification
- emotion recognition
- facial recognition
- gait analysis

Object identification:

- automated vehicle parking systems
- image classification
- image retrieval
- machine inspection
- object localisation
- object detection and object segmentation
- surveillance (human and object)

Event identification:

- activities captured in 'real time' (i.e. video analysis to track an individual moving)
- tracking and processing

Advanced robotics

"Advanced robotics" has the same meaning as in Schedule 2 of the National Security and Investment Act 2021 (Notifiable Acquisition) (Specification of Qualifying Entities) Regulations 2021.

Examples of 'advanced robotics' may include, but are not limited to:

- autonomous vehicles
- digital twinning
- path or action execution
- path or action planning
- sensor data processing.

Cyber security

"Cyber security" means the activities necessary to protect network and information systems, the users of such systems, and other persons affected by cyber threats.

"Cyber threat" means any potential circumstance, event or action that could damage, disrupt or otherwise adversely affect network and information systems, the users of such systems and other persons".

Examples of 'cyber security' may include, but are not limited to:

- authentication
- behaviour analysis

- predictive analysis
- threat detection and classification
- vulnerability discovery

If you do not think your acquisition is covered by the AI guidance, you are advised to read guidance for the following areas:

- Advanced Robotics - where the application of the qualifying entity's work relates to robotics.
- Computing Hardware - this covers activities relating to 'a specialist processor for artificial intelligence applications'. You are advised to consider if the qualifying entity's work covers a) the ownership, creation or supply of intellectual property to or b) the fabrication or packaging of specialist processors for artificial intelligence applications.

CIVIL NUCLEAR

[3.730]
The UK's civil nuclear sector is among the most advanced in the world, from fuel production, generation, new build, research through to decommissioning, waste management and transportation and our world class regulatory system.

The civil nuclear sector is also part of the UK's Critical National Infrastructure (CNI). It generates essential baseload, low carbon electricity critical to families and businesses, providing around 17% of the UK's current electricity needs.

As well as generating electricity, the civil nuclear sector also stores, processes and transports radioactive material, and nuclear safety and nuclear security are essential to any nuclear operation.

AM I IN SCOPE OF THE CIVIL NUCLEAR PART OF THE REGULATIONS?

In the UK, certain types of nuclear material, information and technology are regulated for safety and/or security, and the Civil Nuclear part of the regulations specifically references some of the notifiable acquisition regulations and relevant legislation.

As a first step when self-assessing whether your proposed acquisition will fall into the scope of the mandatory notification requirement, you should find out whether the qualifying entity you are seeking to acquire holds any licences or certifications in relation to nuclear activities, as this may be helpful in identifying whether an acquisition needs to be notified.

This guidance is structured to reflect each individual criterion of the regulations. To identify whether you need to submit a notification, you should find out if the qualifying entity you are seeking to acquire meets any of the criteria below.

You will be legally required to notify if the qualifying entity you are acquiring is involved in any of the following.

The qualifying entity either:

- holds a nuclear site licence for non-military purposes
- is a tenant on a non-military licensed nuclear site
- holds Category I, II or III nuclear material
- holds a Class A or Class B licence to transport nuclear material
- is planning to build a nuclear reactor
- is awaiting the outcome of a relevant assessment by the Office for Nuclear Regulation
- holds equipment, software or information relevant to enrichment of uranium
- holds Sensitive Nuclear Information (SNI)
- is receiving relevant public funding in relation to fission nuclear reactors.

THE QUALIFYING ENTITY HOLDS A NUCLEAR SITE LICENCE FOR NON-MILITARY PURPOSES

You should review whether the qualifying entity you are seeking to acquire holds a nuclear site licence for non-military purposes, and if you conclude that it does you will be legally required to submit a mandatory notification to the government. In the UK, nuclear site licences are issued by the Office for Nuclear Regulation (ONR). The activities for which a site licence is required are described in Section 1 of the Nuclear Installations Act 1965, and include things such as operating a nuclear power plant, producing nuclear fuel, or enriching uranium.

THE QUALIFYING ENTITY IS A TENANT ON A NON-MILITARY LICENCED NUCLEAR SITE

Licensed civil nuclear sites may have tenants. When assessing whether your acquisition will fall into the scope of mandatory notification, you should review whether the qualifying entity you are seeking to acquire holds a tenancy agreement for premises on the type of licensed nuclear site described above. If you conclude that it does, you will be legally required to submit a mandatory notification.

THE QUALIFYING ENTITY HOLDS CATEGORY I, II OR III NUCLEAR MATERIAL

You should check whether the qualifying entity you are seeking to acquire holds any Category I, II or III nuclear material. If you assess that it does, you will be legally required to submit a mandatory notification to the government. Categories I, II and III of nuclear material are described in the Nuclear Industries Security Regulations 2003. This includes certain types of plutonium, uranium, neptunium, americium, and other types of reactor fuel or irradiated nuclear material.

THE QUALIFYING ENTITY HOLDS A CLASS A OR CLASS B LICENCE TO TRANSPORT NUCLEAR MATERIAL

In order for an entity to transport nuclear material of Category I, II or III, it must be approved as either a Class A or Class B carrier by the Office for Nuclear Regulation. You should review whether the qualifying entity you are seeking to acquire holds a relevant licence to transport nuclear material, and if you conclude that it does you will be legally required to submit a mandatory notification to the government.

THE QUALIFYING ENTITY IS PLANNING TO BUILD A NUCLEAR REACTOR

You should check whether the qualifying entity you are seeking to acquire intends to build certain types of infrastructure defined as a Nationally Significant Infrastructure Project in the Planning Act 2008, for example, certain types of large-scale electricity generation projects. If so, you should find out whether it has received development approval from the Secretary of State for Business, Energy & Industrial Strategy (BEIS), or has submitted an application for this. If you conclude that it has and that the development consent or application relates to a nuclear reactor, you will be legally required to submit a mandatory notification to the government. A nuclear reactor is as defined in the Nuclear Installations Act 1965.

THE QUALIFYING ENTITY IS AWAITING THE OUTCOME OF A RELEVANT ASSESSMENT BY THE OFFICE FOR NUCLEAR REGULATION

Some entities may be required to pay a fee to the Office for Nuclear Regulation in relation to an assessment of a design proposal, or the preparation of a relevant assessment agreement. These purposes are defined in the relevant section of the Health and Safety and Nuclear (Fees) Regulations 2021 and include, for example, a Generic Design Assessment. You should check whether the qualifying entity you are seeking to acquire has asked ONR to carry out this type of assessment, and if you conclude that it has and that this assessment is on-going you will be legally required to submit a mandatory notification to the government.

THE QUALIFYING ENTITY HOLDS EQUIPMENT, SOFTWARE OR INFORMATION RELEVANT TO ENRICHMENT OF URANIUM

Some entities may hold equipment, software or information relevant to enrichment of uranium as defined in the Uranium Enrichment Technology (Prohibition on Disclosure) Regulations 2004. You should check whether the qualifying entity you are seeking to acquire holds any equipment, software or information defined in this legislation, and if you conclude that it does you will be legally required to submit a mandatory notification to the government. Enrichment of uranium refers to the process of treating uranium to increase the proportion of the isotope 235 contained in the uranium.

THE QUALIFYING ENTITY HOLDS SENSITIVE NUCLEAR INFORMATION (SNI)

Sensitive Nuclear Information (SNI) is a type of officially classified information and is defined in the Anti-Terrorism, Crime and Security Act 2001. Within the UK, holders of SNI outside of nuclear facilities are regulated by the Office for Nuclear Regulation (ONR) under Regulation 22 of the Nuclear Industries Security Regulations (NISR) 2003. Regulation 22 duty holders may be placed on 'List N'. Further information on SNI is available on the ONR website [**Editorial note:** see https://www.onr.org.uk/cnss/regulation-of-sensitive-nuclear-information-list-n.htm]. You should review whether the qualifying entity you are seeking to acquire holds any SNI, and if you conclude that it does you will be legally required to submit a mandatory notification to the government.

THE QUALIFYING ENTITY IS RECEIVING CERTAIN PUBLIC FUNDING IN RELATION TO FISSION NUCLEAR REACTORS

Some entities receive public funding for research and development purposes – such as funding from UK Research and Innovation - under the Science and Technology Act 1965 or the Higher Education and Research Act 2017.

You should review whether the qualifying entity you are seeking to acquire is directly receiving funding from a public organisation under either of these Acts in relation to fission nuclear reactors (including Small Modular Reactors and Advanced Modular Reactors). If you conclude that it is, then you will be legally required to submit a mandatory notification to the government. The financial support arrangements will usually state the legislation under which funding has been awarded.

COMMUNICATIONS

[3.731]
The communications sector is a diverse, technologically advanced and constantly evolving. It is integral

to national security, the economy and society as it supports the operations of businesses, public safety organisations, government, the wider public sector, other critical national infrastructure and citizens. The mandatory notification requirements include many of the most significant providers within the sector.

As a regulated sector, the mandatory notification requirements in the Communications part of the regulations are informed by existing legislation, primarily the Communications Act 2003, in order to provide clarity and consistency across the regulatory frameworks.

AM I IN SCOPE OF THE COMMUNICATIONS PART OF THE REGULATIONS?

You will be legally required to submit a mandatory notification if any of the following apply. The entity you are acquiring either:

- is a public electronic communications network or service (PECN/S) with a UK turnover of at least £50 million
- makes available an 'associated facility' to a PECN/S with a turnover of at least £50 million (exceptions apply, see below)
- owns a building where its main purpose is to host active telecommunications equipment
- owns a submarine cable system with a UK turnover of at least £50 million
- owns a cable landing station which is used by a PECN/S with UK turnover at least £50 million
- owns a repair or maintenance service for submarine cable systems or cable landing stations which is used by PECN/S with UK turnover at least £50 million
- has a top-level domain name registry, domain name system resolver, authoritative hosting service or internet exchange points subject to certain thresholds
- provides broadcast infrastructure for either:

  — the BBC

  — Channel 3 (ITV PLC and STV)

  — Channel 4

  — Channel 5

  S4C

  — national commercial radio (analogue or digital).

TELECOMMUNICATIONS

Public electronic communications providers

The qualifying entity you are acquiring is in scope if it is a public electronic communications network or service (PECN/S) with a turnover of at least £50 million, or is a provider of certain associated facilities by reference to such a PECN/S.

A PECN refers to an electronic communications network that is provided wholly or mainly for the purpose of making electronic communications services available for use by members of the public.

A PECS refers to an electronic communications service that is either:

- an internet access service
- a number-based interpersonal communications service
- any other service consisting in, or having as its principal feature, the conveyance of signals, such as a transmission service used for machine-to-machine services or for broadcasting - provided so as to be available for use by members of the public

Social media services (such as Facebook and Instagram) or messenger/video services (such as WhatsApp and Zoom) are not in scope when they are only providing content or number-independent interpersonal communications services.

Private electronic communications networks and services (for example, those used on transport systems) are not in scope. However, private networks used by emergency services and some private networks used within the defence sector are in scope of the regulations.

The turnover threshold

Providers of PECN/S are only included if the annual turnover of their specific business activity that involves the provision of a PECN/S conducted in the UK is at least £50 million during the relevant period. This applies to those who own, or have controlling interests in, such providers of PECN/S and other associated entities. If you are seeking to acquire a qualifying entity which falls above this threshold, you will be legally required to notify the government.

Associated facilities

An 'associated facility' refers to a facility, element or service used in association with an electronic communications network or service for specified purposes.

Your acquisition is in scope if the qualifying entity you are acquiring makes available an associated facility to a qualifying PECN/S. There are exceptions for 'passive infrastructure' and 'support infrastructure' (see below).

A facility can be physical infrastructure such as a data centre used to provide the core network function of a PECN/S, or a satellite ground station. It can be a service provided to communications service providers such as businesses who provide billing services or managed service providers. Businesses who provide more general services to communications service providers such as cleaning or HR services would not be included here, as these services do not specifically enable or support the provision of communications networks or services.

A qualifying entity making available an associated facility would not include a supply chain vendor of equipment or software if the qualifying entity simply sells its product onwards and does not also operate or retain control over it when in use. However, if the contractual relationship allowed a supply chain vendor to retain an element of control over the use of the equipment, then they might be included in mandatory notification.

Your acquisition is in scope of mandatory notification if you are seeking to acquire an operator of an associated facility that is used by a PECN/S with a UK turnover of at least £50 million. If you are acquiring a qualifying entity that operates an associated facility with a UK turnover of over £50 million, but the entity only provides that facility to a PECN/S with a turnover below £50 million, then your acquisition would not be in scope of mandatory notification.

Passive infrastructure

Your acquisition is not in scope of mandatory notification if the associated facility is a 'passive' network element. This means it has equipment which transmits information but does not convert or process it and is unlikely to consume electrical power. Examples of passive infrastructure for the purposes of these regulations include pipes, ducts, cables and wires.

Support infrastructure

Some elements within a network are used to support or "host" other elements. The term "host" refers to support infrastructure which houses, protects, guides or supports other network elements, which are themselves active or passive.

If you are seeking to acquire a qualifying entity which meets the turnover threshold and makes available network elements which are passive, but hosts active network elements, then you will be legally required to submit a mandatory notification to the government.

Passive network elements that host other passive elements are not in scope for mandatory notification. For instance, street cabinets are passive support infrastructure that may host active equipment, whereas telephone poles are passive infrastructure which may only host passive equipment (cables).

Some types of equipment such as antenna can be active or passive depending on the specific piece of equipment and how it is used. Similarly, masts and towers may host active or passive equipment and therefore the operators of masts and/or towers will only be exempt from mandatory notification if their masts/towers only host passive equipment such as cables and not any active equipment such as active antenna.

Building owners and landowners

Entities which own or make available buildings that host telecommunications equipment, including on the roof of the building, are excluded from mandatory notification. The only exception to this is if the main purpose of that building is to host active telecommunications equipment, and where that active equipment is used by a PECN/S with a UK turnover of at least £50 million. Owners of residential properties or unrelated commercial properties which have active telecommunications equipment on their roofs, such as 5G small cells, are not in scope of mandatory notification, as the main purpose of those buildings is not to host active telecommunications equipment. Owners of cable landing stations, satellite ground stations and relevant data centres are in scope of mandatory notification, as the specific purpose of these buildings is to host active telecommunications equipment.

Owners of land upon which a qualifying associated facility is located (whether that is active, passive or support infrastructure) are not in scope of mandatory notification. Exceptions to this include when the landowner is also carrying out other activities which are in scope of the regulations, such as owning/operating the telecommunications infrastructure on its land, which would mean it would be making available an associated facility or if they were also providing a PECN/S within the turnover threshold.

Submarine cable systems and cable landing stations

If you are seeking to acquire a qualifying entity which owns a submarine cable system which has a UK turnover at least £50 million then you will be legally required to submit a notification to the government as these are considered to be PECN/S.

Cable landing stations are considered to be associated facilities therefore, if you are seeking to acquire a qualifying entity which owns a cable landing station which is used by a PECN/S with UK turnover at least £50 million, then your acquisition will be in scope.

Please note: The explicit reference to submarine cable systems and cable landing stations have been included in the Communications part of the regulations for completeness. They should not be read as meaning that they would otherwise necessarily fall outside the scope of the Communications Act 2003 definitions of PECN/S and associated facilities.

If you are seeking to acquire a repair and maintenance service for submarine cable systems and cable landing stations, which is used by a PECN/S with UK turnover above £50 million, you will be required to submit a notification to the government too.

Information systems

If you are seeking to acquire a top-level domain name registry, domain name system resolver, authoritative hosting services and internet exchange points then (subject to the thresholds below) your acquisition is in scope of the mandatory notification requirements. These terms are defined in the Network and Information Systems Regulations 2018 (as amended) (NIS Regulations).

The thresholds reflect those in the NIS Regulations, and are as follows:

- top-level domain name registry: services 14 billion or more queries from any UK device in a consecutive 168-hour period for domains registered within the Internet Corporation for Assigned Names and Numbers
- domain name system resolver service: services 500,000 or more different Internet Protocol addresses used by persons in the UK in any consecutive 168-hour period
- domain name system authoritative hosting service: services 100,000 or more domains registered to persons with an address in the UK
- internet exchange points: has 30% or more market share for such services in the UK in terms of interconnected autonomous systems

It is important to note that qualifying entities that operate internet exchange points (those that are involved or operate infrastructure which is provided for the exchange of digital data) are also in scope of the Data Infrastructure part of the regulations, where no threshold is applied.

Supply chain

Entities in the supply chain which sell equipment and software, but do not subsequently operate that equipment and do not have any control over its use, are excluded from the Communications part of the regulations.

BROADCASTING

Providers of broadcast infrastructure for the BBC, national commercial radio (analogue or digital) or television services for the UK's public service broadcasters (holders of Channel 3 licenses, Channel 4, Channel 5 and S4C) are also included. However, the definition of a PECS service excludes services that are content services, meaning that providers of broadcasting content services (including television and radio) are not included and therefore not subject to the mandatory notification requirements. Enterprises which provide both broadcasting infrastructure and content are covered by the Communications part of the regulations.

COMPUTING HARDWARE

[3.732]

Computing hardware is essential to all digital devices. Technological advances in computing hardware have changed the way in which people can use digital devices to interact and the way businesses develop and grow. Digital technologies are used in our day to day lives, but they are also important to the UK's national security, underpinning critical UK infrastructure, and are now just as intrinsic to defence uses as they are to our daily lives.

The Computing Hardware part of the regulations focus on specific activities, products and functions that take place within the supply chain for these products. As the process for creating computing hardware is advancing all the time, risks can emerge upstream of the final product, including vulnerabilities that could cause harm.

AM I IN SCOPE OF THE COMPUTING HARDWARE PART OF THE REGULATIONS?

To determine if a qualifying entity you are seeking to acquire is in scope of the Computing Hardware part of the regulations, you will need to consider 2 questions:

- is the qualifying entity involved with any of the activities set out in the definition?
- if so, do these activities apply to any of the corresponding products or functions as listed in the definition?

If the qualifying entity you are seeking to acquire falls into both categories, then you will be legally required to submit a mandatory notification to the UK government.

You will need to check if the qualifying entity you are acquiring is involved in any of the following activities:

- the ownership, creation, supply or exploitation of intellectual property of certain products or functions
- design, maintenance or delivery of a service for secure provisioning or management
- fabrication of packaging.

THE OWNERSHIP, CREATION, SUPPLY OR EXPLOITATION OF INTELLECTUAL PROPERTY OF CERTAIN PRODUCTS OR FUNCTIONS

An acquisition is likely to be in scope if the qualifying entity is involved in the ownership, creation, supply or exploitation of intellectual property of any of the following products or functions:

- computer processing units
- architectural, logical or physical designs for such units
- the instruction set architecture for such units
- code, written in a low-level language, that can control how such units operate
- integrated circuits with the purpose of providing memory

Computer processing units include field central processing units (CPUs), programmable gate arrays (FPGA), microcontrollers, system on chips, graphics processor units and specialist processors for Artificial Intelligence applications.

DESIGN, MAINTENANCE OR DELIVERY OF A SERVICE FOR SECURE PROVISIONING OR MANAGEMENT

Your acquisition is likely to be in scope if the qualifying entity is involved in the design, maintenance or delivery of a service for the secure provisioning or management of any of the following products or functions:

- roots of trust of computer processing units
- code, written in a low level language, that can control how such units operate.

FABRICATION OR PACKAGING

Your acquisition is likely to be in scope if the qualifying entity is involved in the fabrication or packaging of any of the following products or functions:

- central processing units (CPU)
- integrated circuits with the principal purpose of providing memory

Fabrication means the process of producing a microelectronic circuit on a semiconductor substrate or using other advanced materials.

Examples of fabrication include, but are not limited to:

- deposition
- etching
- ion implantation
- lithography
- wafer preparation

Packaging means the process of turning a microelectronic circuit on an appropriate substrate into a package suitable for use in an electronic circuit but does not include the assembly and packaging of chips and devices into circuit boards.

Example of packaging include, but are not limited to:

- bonding
- die preparation
- encapsulation.

FURTHER DETAILS ON TERMS USED

Artificial Intelligence

The Computing Hardware part of the regulations references 'a specialist processor for artificial intelligence applications', a definition of 'Artificial intelligence' is provided in the Artificial Intelligence part of the regulations.

'Artificial intelligence' means technology enabling the programming or training of a device or software to—

i) perceive environments through the use of data

ii) interpret data using automated processing designed to approximate cognitive abilities and

iii) make recommendations, predictions or decisions

with a view to achieving a specific objective.

Products and functions

The following are examples of terms used in the definition. These are for example only and should not be seen as an exhaustive list.

Architectural, logical or physical designs

Examples include, but are not limited to:

- electronic Design Automation (EDA) software
- layout / schematic designs
- microarchitecture
- register transfer language (RTL)

Instruction set architecture

Examples include, but are not limited to:

- instruction set architectures
- formal definitions of these
- instruction set extensions

Code, written in a low level language, that can control how such units operate

Examples include, but are not limited to:

- microcode
- drivers
- firmware for roots of trust

Roots of trust of computer processing units - means hardware, firmware or software components that are inherently trusted to perform critical security functions

Examples include, but are not limited to:

- cryptographic key material bound to a device that can identify the device or verify a digital signature to authenticate a remote entity)

Integrated circuits with the purpose of providing memory

An example could include, but is not limited to:

- a chip developed to provide volatile or non-volatile memory to an external computer processing unit, using either well developed memory technologies (e.g. SRAM, DRAM, flash) or newer memory technologies (e.g. PCM, RRAM, FRAM, MRAM)

A specialist processor for artificial intelligence applications

Examples include, but are not limited to:

- approximate processors and other architectures with a similar purpose of accelerating artificial intelligence
- machine learning applications
- neuromorphic processors

If you do not think your acquisition is covered by the Computing Hardware guidance, you should read guidance for the following areas:

- Artificial Intelligence - if the entity works with 'a specialist processor for artificial intelligence applications'.
- Advanced Materials - If the entity uses application-specific integrated circuit (ASICs), or an electronic component not captured under the Computing Hardware regulations

CRITICAL SUPPLIERS TO GOVERNMENT

[3.733]

The purpose of this part of the regulations is to help protect the government supply chain from potential national security risks. The regulations focus on the most sensitive government information, assets or estates where the risk to national security is the greatest were they subject to compromise.

AM I IN SCOPE OF THE CRITICAL SUPPLIERS TO GOVERNMENT PART OF THE REGULATIONS?

For the purpose of these regulations, Critical Suppliers to Government are those contracted to access very sensitive government data, assets or estates, all of which might be subject to attack from adversaries.

The critical suppliers to government part of the regulations only applies to suppliers that hold direct contracts with government (sometimes referred to as prime suppliers). It does not apply to subcontractors.

The regulations define government as being equivalent to "contracting authorities" as outlined in the Public Contracts Regulations 2015. A contracting authority includes:

"the State, regional or local authorities, bodies governed by public law or associations formed by one or more such authorities or one or more such bodies governed by public law, and includes central government authorities but does not include Her Majesty in her private capacity."

You will be legally required to submit a mandatory notification if the qualifying entity you are seeking to acquire holds a public contract with government which includes any of the following features:

- processing and/or storing SECRET or TOP SECRET material
- a requirement to have list X accreditation
- a requirement for employees to be vetted at or above Security Check (SC) level.

PROCESSING AND/OR STORING SECRET OR TOP SECRET MATERIAL

Government information is classified to indicate sensitivity, with SECRET and TOP SECRET being the most sensitive. Visit the government security classifications page (https://www.gov.uk/government/publications/government-security-classifications) to understand how the government classifies information assets.

You will be legally required to submit a mandatory notification if the qualifying entity you are seeking to acquire has both of the following features:

- a public contract with government
- processes or stores SECRET or TOP SECRET material.

LIST X ACCREDITATION

List X (sometimes referred to as Facility Security Clearance) applies to companies operating in the UK which have government contracts which require them to hold information on site that is classified as:

- SECRET and above or
- international partners' information classified as CONFIDENTIAL and above

Further information can be found on the international classified information page (https://www.gov.uk/government/publications/international-classified-information).

The UK government does not publish the names or locations of List X facilities, but the Ministry of Defence is the contracting authority for the majority of these sites.

List X contractors are also required to notify the Ministry of Defence of potential changes in ownership. Check the guidance for security requirements for List X contractors (https://www.gov.uk/government/publications/security-requirements-for-list-x-contractors).

You will be legally required to submit a mandatory notification if the qualifying entity you want to acquire has both of the following features:

- a public contract with government
- a contractual requirement to have a list X accreditation.

VETTING EMPLOYEES TO SECURITY CHECK LEVEL OR ABOVE

There are currently 5 levels of national security vetting in the UK:

- Counter Terrorist Check (CTC)
- Security Check (SC)
- Enhanced Security Check (eSC)
- Developed Vetting (DV)
- Enhanced Developed Vetting (eDV)

View guidance from UK Security Vetting for more information on clearance levels (https://www.gov.uk/government/publications/united-kingdom-security-vetting-clearance-levels).

As a general rule, those who need frequent access to SECRET material will require Security Check clearance. Individuals who need unsupervised access to TOP SECRET material will require Developed Vetting clearance.

You will be legally required to submit a mandatory notification if the qualifying entity you want to acquire has both of the following features:

- a public contract with government
- a requirement for their employees to be vetted at SC level or above.

CRYPTOGRAPHIC AUTHENTICATION

[3.734]

Authentication is the process of verifying the identity of a person or device. Where the technical method depends on cryptography, rather than a non-technical method such as checking the signature of an individual or that their face matches their driving licence, it is deemed to be a sensitive technology.

Companies that provide cryptographic authentication operate across much of the economy, providing software and hardware tools for businesses to enable a number of key capabilities, including:

- verification of user identity through passwords, two-factor or multi-factor authentication (such as a hardware token or software application)
- authentication of a human-operated or automated device to a network to allow access to the network, data and other resources
- verification of the origin and integrity of an email, message or document through digital certificates, and security protocols

These functions can be enablers of further security steps, such as management of access, and help to prevent unauthorised access to data, network resources, personal information, physical spaces, intellectual property and other assets. This might include use or ownership of a device containing a cryptographic key. It can include determining the identity or some attributes of the device owner asserted by an authoritative third party or recognising the user as a repeat visitor or as the owner of a previously established account.

AM I IN SCOPE OF THE CRYPTOGRAPHIC AUTHENTICATION PART OF THE REGULATIONS?

You will be legally required to notify the government if the qualifying entity you are acquiring is involved in one, or more, of the following activities:

- research into any product(s)
- developing any product(s)
- producing any product(s)

Where that product(s) meets the following 3 criteria:

- has authentication as a primary function
- employs cryptography in performing the authentication function and
- is a product that is not ordinarily supplied to or made available for acquisition by consumers

Examples of technologies within scope, but are not limited to, are systems that authenticate:

- the identity of a physical person using an access token to gain entrance to a restricted area at a critical national infrastructure site
- the identity of a user to gain electronic access to the computer network of a power station
- a biometric property of an individual to allow access to a restricted area of an industrial site
- a credit/debit chip-and-pin card at an ATM or retail point of sale; and
- the digital information held on an e-passport to determine whether to allow the holder into the country.

DATA INFRASTRUCTURE

[3.735]
Data infrastructure provides the ability to store, process and transmit data. The government has a responsibility to ensure that data and its supporting infrastructure is secure, resilient and trustworthy in the face of established, new and emerging risks, protecting the economy as it grows.

Data infrastructure is physical or virtualised infrastructure used for storing, processing or transmitting data in digital form or infrastructure that is provided for peering, interconnection or exchange of digital data

AM I IN SCOPE OF THE DATA INFRASTRUCTURE PART OF THE REGULATIONS?

Qualifying entities in the Data Infrastructure part of the regulations could include:

- data centre operators
- cloud storage service providers
- managed service providers
- specialist or technical service providers with physical access to relevant data infrastructure
- software providers whose product gives the software provider ongoing privileged access to customer data

Types of entities not in scope of the Data Infrastructure part of the regulations include:

- a data centre storing exclusively paper records
- an entity that sells off-the-shelf software to customers with no ongoing configuration, integration or maintenance support or

• an entity that provides a public electronic communications service or network but does not provide any dedicated infrastructure or facilities to its customers for storing, processing, or transmitting data in addition to the provision of that electronic communications network or service.

You may need to submit a mandatory notification if the qualifying entity you are acquiring stores, processes or transmits data in a digital form.

To find out if you need to submit a mandatory notification to the government, you will need to:

• 1. Check if the qualifying entity you are acquiring is involved in 'relevant data infrastructure'.

• 2. Check if the qualifying entity performs a 'qualifying activity'.

If you meet both criteria, you will be legally required to notify the government about your planned acquisition.

STEP 1: CHECK IF THE ENTITY IS INVOLVED IN 'RELEVANT DATA INFRASTRUCTURE'

A qualifying entity must perform any one of the activities listed below in relation to relevant data infrastructure in order to be in scope of mandatory notification.

'Relevant data infrastructure' is physical or virtualised infrastructure which does any of the following:

• stores, processes or transmits data in digital form which is used in connection with the administration and operation of certain public sector authorities

• is provided for peering, interconnection or exchange of digital data between providers of public electronic communications networks and/or services but which is not owned by a provider of public electronic communications networks or service or

• enables the interconnection of one or more public electronic communications networks with an electronic communications network where part of that network is provided by means of a submarine cable system.

If you provide data infrastructure services to a public authority, check which public authorities are covered by the regulations

You may need to notify if the qualifying entity that you want to acquire has a relationship with certain public sector authorities to perform relevant activity – that is, to store, process or transmit data in digital form.

This could be a direct contract or an indirect relationship, such as a subcontractor to the qualifying entity which has the direct contract with the public sector authority. If the qualifying entity is a subcontractor, it is only in scope if it has been made aware at or before the time that the acquisition took place that it is storing, processing or transmitting data for certain public sector authorities, or providing an activity that would fulfil or contribute towards the fulfilment of the main contract with the public sector authority.

Example

Company A is a colocation data centre and has a direct contractual relationship with Company B, a web hosting company. Company B has a direct contractual relationship with Company C, a public sector authority, whose data is stored in Company A's facilities. However, Company A does not have a direct contract with Company C and has not been notified that it is a subcontractor in the contractual relationship between Company B and C. Company A is therefore not in scope of mandatory notification.

The scope of the definition of relevant activity may include a public communications provider (PCP) that owns or operates infrastructure which stores, processes or transmits public sector authority data. PCPs should also review the Communications guidance to determine if their acquisition is in scope of mandatory notification.

View a list of the public sector authorities that are covered by the regulations (https://assets.publishing.service.gov.uk/government/uploads/system/uploads/attachment_data/file/1033352/public-sector-authorities-covered-by-nsi-regulations.ods).

Peering and interconnection infrastructure

Peering infrastructure that is owned or operated by a provider of public electronic communications networks or a provider of a public electronic communications service itself is not in scope of mandatory notification. The infrastructure which is provided by a third party - such as a data centre – and which provides the facilities for public network and service providers to interconnect with each other is in scope of mandatory notification. Any qualifying entity carrying out a qualifying activity in relation to this third party provided peering infrastructure is in scope of mandatory notification. It is also advised that you review the Communications guidance to determine if your acquisition is in scope of mandatory notification.

Infrastructure which is used to connect a public electronic communications network as defined in the Communications Act 2003 to a network transmitting data into the UK via a submarine cable is in scope of mandatory notification. This infrastructure could be located at a cable landing station. The infrastructure may also be located inside inland facilities, such as a data centre.

STEP 2: CHECK WHAT ACTIVITIES ARE COVERED BY THE RULES

You may need to notify your acquisition if the qualifying entity you are seeking to acquire does any one of the following activities. It is not necessary for the qualifying entity to perform all of the activities to be in scope. The activities are as follows:

- owns or operates relevant data infrastructure
- manages relevant data infrastructure on behalf of other entities
- manages facilities where relevant data infrastructure is located
- provides specialist or technical services to entities involved in any of the above activities
- produces or develops software for entities involved in any of the above activities and
- is given administrative access to relevant data infrastructure.

Further information on these terms is outlined below.

Specialist or technical services

You may need to notify if you are seeking to acquire a qualifying entity which provides specialist or technical services to entities which:

- own or operate relevant data infrastructure
- manage relevant data infrastructure on behalf of other entities or
- manage facilities where relevant data infrastructure is located

and where the provision of those services enables physical access to relevant data infrastructure. For example:

- a qualifying entity performing specialist or technical services that has physical access to infrastructure used for peering, interconnection or exchange of digital data between providers of public communications networks and services
- a qualifying entity performing specialist or technical services that has physical access to infrastructure used to enable the interconnection of one or more public communications networks with a network which is part of a submarine cable system
- a qualifying entity performing specialist or technical services with physical access to infrastructure storing, processing or transmitting data in digital form is only in scope if it could be expected to know that the infrastructure is used for "relevant activity"

The type of services that are captured by the regulation are installation, equipment repair or maintenance.

Example

If Company A's business activities include installation of cooling equipment to Company B and Company B is an owner/operator of relevant data infrastructure, then Entity A is in scope of the regulations.

If Company C is performing maintenance on cables located in a facility where relevant data infrastructure is located, then Company C will also be in scope of the regulations.

Administrative access

"Administrative access" is used to describe logical access to virtualised data infrastructure. It refers to either or both authorisation or access granted via either or both logical or administrative access controls by virtue of which an entity may access relevant data infrastructure or control access to relevant data infrastructure where such access would otherwise be restricted or compartmented and where such access would permit the modification of the relevant data infrastructure in a way that was not authorised.

The scope of the administrative access definition has several caveats to ensure that it is capturing only those entities that could present risks to national security, for example:

- "would otherwise be restricted or compartmented" - this captures a service provider whose service is of a type that gives it unrestricted rights and permissions to data and its underlying infrastructure that would not be available to a standard user and
- "would permit the modification of the relevant data infrastructure in a way that was not authorised" - this captures a service provider whose service gives it a level of authorisation that would enable it to effectively bypass controls intended to protect the confidentiality, integrity and availability of the relevant data and its underlying infrastructure. It does not mean that the service provider is in scope of mandatory notification only if and when it bypasses controls rather, it means that if the service provider has the access to enable it to bypass such controls if it wished to, then it would be in scope of mandatory notification

Producing or developing software

You may need to notify the government if a qualifying entity that you are acquiring produces, designs or develops software that could be used by a qualifying entity to provide services which give it administrative access to virtualised data infrastructure.

A qualifying entity that sells off-the-shelf software to customers with no ongoing configuration, integration or maintenance support is not in scope. However, the entity that you are acquiring may be in scope if it provides any such support to customers.

The qualifying entity does not need to know whether the software it is producing, designing or developing is used or is going to be used in relation to "relevant data infrastructure", only whether the software is of a type that could be used to configure or manage the provision of administrative access to virtualised infrastructure which hosts, processes or transmits data.

A qualifying entity which produces, designs or develops software should also be aware of the type of activities carried out by customers for whom it is producing, designing or developing the software. Where those customer activities involve providing a service the provision of which requires administrative access to virtualised data infrastructure, the qualifying entity is in scope of mandatory notification.

You are advised to read the guidance for these other areas of the regulations.

A qualifying entity might be in scope of more than one part of the regulations as some areas of the economy are closely related and may overlap. If you are an acquirer considering whether you are in scope of the Data Infrastructure guidance, you are advised to read guidance for the following areas:

- Communications
- Suppliers to Emergency Services
- Artificial Intelligence.

GUIDANCE FOR PROCUREMENT AND SUPPLY CHAINS

The Notifiable Acquisition Regulations will provide the government with a strong lever to mitigate national security risks while minimising the impact on businesses in the sector. However, the NSI Act does not negate the need for businesses to take a proactive approach toward mitigating risk in their procurement and supply chains, particularly around the protection and security of data.

Supply chains can be large and complex, involving many suppliers undertaking many different activities. Effectively securing the supply chain can be challenging because vulnerabilities can be inherent or introduced and exploited at any point in the supply chain.

The National Cyber Security Centre (NCSC) and Centre for the Protection of National Infrastructure (CPNI) have produced Supply Chain Security Guidance (https://www.cpni.gov.uk/system/files/documents/2e/87/Supply_Chain_Security_Collection_Jan2018.pdf) with 12 principles designed to help entities establish effective control and oversight of supply chains. The guidance will provide organisations with an improved awareness of supply chain security, as well as helping to raise the baseline level of competence in this regard, through the continued adoption of good practice.

The NCSC has also produced Supplier Assurance Questions (https://www.ncsc.gov.uk/guidance/supplier-assurance-questions), which will help entities to gain confidence in suppliers' cyber security practices. You are advised to understand who has responsibility for cyber security at the supplier organisation and what policies the organisation has in place.

DEFENCE

[3.736]

A robust defence sector is vital to our national security. It provides defence capabilities that are critical to our national security and prosperity, it sustains jobs and skills, contributes to research and development programmes, supports manufacturing and offers export opportunities.

The government recognises that inward investment creates a dynamic industry, promotes innovation and supports the development of first-class military capabilities that enable us to protect our people, territories, values and interests at home and overseas. Given its importance to our national security the defence sector must remain resilient to a wide range of evolving threats.

AM I IN SCOPE OF THE DEFENCE PART OF THE REGULATIONS?

All suppliers to the Ministry of Defence (MOD) will be covered by the regulations. This includes companies at all tiers, including sub-contractors and those in the chain of sub-contractors, where the goods or service that they research, develop, design, produce, create or apply are provided or used for defence or national security purposes.

You will be legally required to submit a mandatory notification to the government if:

- you are seeking to acquire a qualifying entity whose UK activities include the research, development, production, creation or application of goods or services which are used or provided for defence or national security purposes

and either of the following apply. The qualifying entity you are acquiring either:

- is a government contractor, or any subcontractor in a chain of sub-contractors which begins with the government contractor, which provides such goods or services, or
- has been notified by the government that they hold, or may come into possession of, classified material

Contracts which provide access to defence facilities may still give rise to potential national security risks. The obligation to notify extends to contractors or subcontractors who provide goods or services without clear 'military' applications, such as catering or cleaning.

The meaning of "defence" and "government contractor" (Section 3 of the regulation) can be found in section 2(4) and section 12, respectively, of the Official Secrets Act 1989.

CONTRACTORS AND SUB-CONTRACTORS

The government expects that most suppliers who are providing goods and services for defence and national security purposes will be aware of the nature of their contractual arrangements. The MOD has a standing contractual requirement for providers to notify the department of a change of control of a contractor, including any sub-contractors, through Defence Contractual Condition (DEFCON) 566 - Change of Control of Contractor.

The mandatory notification requirement in the regulations reinforces this standing requirement and the entities with a statutory obligation to notify will be clearly identifiable by virtue of their contractual arrangements.

CLASSIFIED MATERIAL

The government has an established Security Policy Framework Security policy framework: protecting government assets (https://www.gov.uk/government/publications/security-policy-framework) and entities which are subject to that framework are notified that they are involved in the handling of classified material. This notification may be issued in different ways, depending on the nature of the activity concerned, but most commonly through the issuing of a Security Aspects Letter or the designation of a facility as a List X (Facility Security Clearance) site.

Defence Contractual Condition (DEFCON 566 – Change of Control of Contractor)

The obligation contained in Defence Contractual Condition (DEFCON) 566, requires companies within the defence supply chain (i.e. those with a contract with the MOD) to provide the MOD with prior notice of a change in control. This obligation remains extant.

This requirement goes beyond the NSI screening process (with its focus on national security) and extends to wider due diligence that allows the MOD to make informed decisions on such issues as the conduct of extant competitions or negotiations, future contract award and other such issues. The contractual obligation does, however, provide an important indicator as to whether a company satisfies the first condition of the notification obligation as set out.

DEFCON 566 can be found within the Commercial section of the Knowledge in Defence guidance (https://www.gov.uk/guidance/knowledge-in-defence-kid). To access the website, interested parties must register via the KiD portal - which is a free and straight-forward process.

ENERGY

[3.737]
Energy is a diverse sector that is rapidly developing to deliver the UK's 2050 net zero goal. The energy sector produces and uses a wide range of products and services in its operation and new and innovative technologies are being integrated all the time.

The government believes that there are certain areas within the sector that are sufficiently sensitive that they should be included in the mandatory notification requirement. The regulations covers upstream oil and gas, downstream gas, downstream oil and electricity entities.

AM I IN SCOPE OF THE ENERGY PART OF THE REGULATIONS?

The regulations cover:

- upstream oil and gas
- downstream gas
- electricity
- downstream oil

UPSTREAM OIL AND GAS

The Upstream Oil and Gas sector refers to companies involved with upstream petroleum facilities, i.e. upstream petroleum pipelines (including subsea pipelines), terminals and infrastructure necessary to a petroleum production project. A "petroleum production project" means a project carried out under a relevant licence (e.g. under section 3 Petroleum Act 1998) to search for, bore for and get petroleum (i.e. oil and gas).

You will be legally required to submit a mandatory notification if the qualifying entity carries on at least one of the following activities onshore in the UK:

- it owns an upstream petroleum facility
- it operates an upstream petroleum facility
- it develops an upstream petroleum facility (for "new" facilities only, i.e. those still being constructed, or which only began operations less than 12 months before the date of the proposed acquisition)
- it enables the operation of an upstream petroleum facility
- it enables the development of an upstream petroleum facility (for "new" facilities only) or

• it holds a Petroleum Act licence for an upstream petroleum facility (under s3 of the Petroleum Act 1998 or s2 of the Petroleum (Production) Act 1934)

In each case, the relevant facility must also:

• meet the 3,000,000-tonne throughput threshold (see below) and

• be either:

— onshore in the UK

— offshore and used in connection with the supply of oil and gas to people in the UK

Calculation of the throughput thresholds for Upstream oil and gas

If the qualifying entity you are acquiring has a throughput of more than 3,000,000-tonnes in their facility for the 12 months calculated as below, you will be legally required to submit a mandatory notification to the government.

The throughput threshold for existing facilities is calculated over the 12 calendar months preceding the month in which a person gains control.

The throughput threshold for "new" facilities is calculated by the expected throughput in its first 12 calendar months of operation.

Example

Facility A is owned by Company A and began operating three years ago. Facility A is therefore an "existing" facility. Someone intends to acquire Company A on 15 June this year. The throughput of Facility A would be assessed for the period between 1 June of the previous year and 31 May of this year.

DOWNSTREAM GAS

Downstream Gas activity refers to the onshore processing, transportation or distribution of gas across Great Britain (GB) (but not Northern Ireland). It contributes, either directly or indirectly, to the supply of gas to domestic and/or commercial properties.

You will be legally required to submit a mandatory notification if the qualifying entity you are acquiring does any of the following. The qualifying entity:

• holds a Transmission licence or exemption under the Gas Act 1986: this captures owners and operators of GB's gas transmission network

• holds a Distribution licence or exemption under the Gas Act 1986: this captures the owners and operators of GB's Gas Distribution Networks (GDNs)

• holds a Gas Interconnector licence or exemption under the Gas Act 1986: this captures the owners and operators of gas interconnectors. For these purposes, a gas interconnector means any pipeline used to transfer gas between GB and another country or territory

• owns or operates a gas processing facility: this captures the operators and owners of onshore facilities in GB that treat imported gas and bring it within the prescribed quality specifications for safe use in homes and businesses. This only applies if the gas processing facility has the technological capacity to carry on gas processing operations in relation to greater than 6 million cubic metres of gas per day

• owns or operates a Liquefied Natural Gas (LNG) import or export facility: this captures the owners and operators of onshore terminals in GB which are used for the importation, offloading, re-gasification or export of Liquid Natural Gas. This only applies if the export facility which has the technological capacity to carry on the importation, regasification or liquefaction of greater than 6 million cubic metres of gas per day

Example

Company B plans to acquire Company C. Company C operates a gas processing facility in the East of England. The facility is able to process up to 10 million cubic metres of gas per day. Therefore, Company C's facility has the technological capacity to carry on gas processing operations in relation to greater than 6 million cubic metres of gas per day. Company B must submit a mandatory notification to government.

ELECTRICITY

Electricity activity refers to the onshore and offshore generation, storage, aggregation, transmission or distribution of electricity across GB (but not Northern Ireland). It contributes, either directly or indirectly, to the supply of power to homes and business.

You will be legally required to submit a mandatory notification if the qualifying entity you are acquiring holds any of the following types of licence or exemption under the Electricity Act 1989:

• a transmission licence or exemption: this captures owners and operators of GB's electricity transmission networks which transport electricity from onshore or offshore generators to onshore substations, regional distribution networks or directly to large industrial users

• a distribution licence or exemption: this captures the owners and operators of GB's Electricity Distribution Networks, which transport electricity from the transmission network to domestic and commercial properties. It includes smaller networks owned and operated by Independent Distribution Networks Operators (IDNOs) which are located within the areas covered by the larger distribution networks

- an interconnector licence or exemption this captures the owners and operators of electricity interconnectors that allow the transfer of electricity across GB borders, or
- a Generation licence or exemption this includes all technology types capable of generating or storing electricity for the purpose of enabling supply

You will also be legally required to submit a mandatory notification if the qualifying entity you are acquiring conducts the following activity:

- aggregates electricity this activity includes combining multiple customer loads or generated electricity for sale, purchase or auction in the electricity market of GB

The mandatory notification requirement only applies to substantial generators or aggregators of electricity. These activities are therefore subject to the following thresholds:

- the qualifying entity you are acquiring owns or operates a single generating asset (onshore or offshore) with a capacity of 100MW or more or
- you, your group companies and the qualifying entity you are acquiring together have a cumulated generation or aggregation capacity of 1GW or more

Example

Company D holds a generation licence and owns several power generating assets in Wales with a total generation capacity of 800MW. Company E manages the demand of 500MW of customer load for sale in the GB electricity market. Therefore, Company E is carrying on aggregation. The combined "relevant capacity" of Company D and Company E is 1,300MW which is greater than one gigawatt. A mandatory notification must be submitted to the government if Company D acquires Company E or if Company E acquires Company D.

DOWNSTREAM OIL

Downstream oil sector activity is that which is carried out in the UK in the course of a business, and which contributes, either directly or indirectly, to the supply of crude oil-based fuels to UK consumers.

You will be legally required to submit a mandatory notification if the qualifying entity you are acquiring has a capacity in excess of 500,000 tonnes of oil or owns a facility in the UK that has capacity in excess of 50,000 tonnes, and carried on at least one of the following activities, in at least one of the three previous calendar years:

- storing oil: this captures activities associated with the storage of crude oil and oil products.
- handling oil: this captures activities associated with the receipt, production, storage, transport and sale of crude oil and oil products
- the carriage of oil by sea or inland water: this captures activities associated with the transport of crude and oil products via waterways
- transporting oil by road: this captures activities associated with the distribution of oil feedstocks and products in road tankers, generally by haulage firms
- conveying oil by pipes: this captures activities associated with the distribution of oil products via the network of underground pipelines across the UK or
- refining or otherwise processing oil: this captures activities associated with the conversion of crude oil or oil feedstocks into finished products through large scale processing plants (including refineries)

Example

Company F intends to gain control of Company G. Company G supplies petrol to the UK market. To determine whether a mandatory notification is required we need to look at the volume of petrol handled in the UK by Company G over a 3 year period:

- *in 2020, it imported 300,000 tonnes of finished fuel*
- *in 2021, it imported 400,000 tonnes of finished fuel and produced a further 200,000 tonnes of finished fuel through blending*
- *in 2022, it imported 100,000 tonnes of finished fuel*

In 2021, Company G therefore had a capacity of 600,000 tonnes, so a mandatory notification must be submitted for the acquisition.

MILITARY AND DUAL-USE

[3.738]
Military and dual-use items can, in the wrong hands, pose immediate and direct threats to the UK.

Military items are goods, software and technology (including for example documents and diagrams) and include arms, military and paramilitary equipment used for a military purpose. Dual-use items are goods, software and technology which can be used for both civil and military applications. Dual-use items can range from raw materials to components to complete systems, for example aluminium alloys, bearings, or lasers. Dual-use items could also be used in the production or development of military goods or chemical, biological or nuclear weapons, for example machine tools, chemical/manufacturing equipment and computers.

The Military and Dual-use part of the regulations purposefully relates to goods and technology which are already 'controlled' due to their military or dual-use characteristics under the export control regime.

The Department for International Trade maintains the Strategic Export Control Lists, which form the basis for determining whether any products, software or technology intended for export are 'controlled' and therefore require an export licence. A "Consolidated list of strategic military and dual-use items that require export authorisation"' can be found on the gov.uk website (see link below). It is compiled from several lists of controlled goods from a number of legislative sources.

AM I IN SCOPE OF THE MILITARY AND DUAL-USE PART OF THE REGULATIONS?

You will be legally required to submit a mandatory notification if you are seeking to acquire a qualifying entity that researches, develops or produces restricted goods or technology that are controlled by the aspects of the export control legislation which concern national security controls.

View the list of restricted goods and technology in the consolidated list of strategic military and dual-use items that require export authorisation (https://www.gov.uk/government/publications/uk-strategic-export-control-lists-the-consolidated-list-of-strategic-military-and-dual-use-items-that-require-export-authorisation).

The relevant lists are:

- UK Military List [taken from Schedule 2 to the Export Control Order 2008]
- UK Dual-Use List [taken from Schedule 3 to the Export Control Order 2008]
- UK Radioactive Sources List [taken from the Schedule to the Export of Radioactive Sources (Control) Order 2006]
- Dual-Use List [taken from Annex I to Council Regulation (EC) No. 428/2009].

You will not need to submit a mandatory notification if the activities of the qualifying entity concern goods or technology which appear on the Human Rights Strategic Export Control Lists and the Non-Military Firearms List - unless they also appear on the Military and Dual-Use Lists.

TECHNOLOGY

The Military and Dual-Use regulations adopt the definition of technology which is used within the export control regime.

Technology means specific 'information' necessary for the development, production or use of goods or software.

'Information' may take forms including, but not limited to: blueprints, plans, diagrams, models, formulae, tables, 'source code', engineering designs and specifications, manuals and instructions written or recorded on other media or devices (for example disk, tape read-only memories).

'Source code' (or source language) is a convenient expression of one or more processes which may be turned by a programming system into equipment executable form.

'Information' is not Restricted Technology where it is in the public domain, i.e. when it is realistically accessible to a member of the general public.

QUANTUM TECHNOLOGIES

[3.739]
The increasing understanding and control of what are known as 'quantum effects' (for example superposition and entanglement) are leading to a new wave of advances in areas such as sensing, data transmission and encryption, timing and computing that will have significant civil, defence and national security applications. These are often referred to as 'second generation' quantum technologies.

All areas of second generation quantum technology production and development are of potential importance for national security. This is predicated on the dual-use potential that all quantum technologies hold.

AM I IN SCOPE OF THE QUANTUM TECHNOLOGIES PART OF THE REGULATIONS?

To determine if the qualifying entity you are seeking to acquire is in scope of the quantum technologies part of the regulations, you will need to consider whether the qualifying entity develops or produces a quantum technology.

If the qualifying entity you are seeking to acquire is in scope then you will be legally required to submit a mandatory notification to the UK government.

For the purposes of these regulations, development and production mean as follows:

- '**development**' means all stages prior to production, including design, design research, design analyses, design concepts, assembly and testing of prototypes, pilot production schemes, design data, process of transforming design data into goods or software, configuration design, integration design, layouts and

- '**production**' means all production stages, including product engineering, manufacture, integration, assembly (mounting), inspection, testing and quality assurance

'**Quantum technologies**' employ the mathematical theory of quantum mechanics to describe the physical world and process information in new ways. Quantum technologies cover the following technology groups:

- quantum communications
- quantum connectivity
- quantum imaging, sensing, timing or navigation
- quantum resistant cryptography
- quantum information processing, computing or simulation

QUANTUM COMMUNICATIONS

This includes:

- transmitting information using quantum effects, such as superposition (the fundamental principle of quantum mechanics allowing a single quantum property to be in more than one quantum state at the same time), entanglement (when two quantum objects – an object at the atomic scale which is described by the physical laws of quantum mechanics, such as an electron or photon - are entangled together, their state can only be described as a whole system not for the components separately), or conjugate variable technologies (technologies that store, process or transmit information using the quantum effect of conjugate variables, meaning pairs of variables which are subject to the uncertainty principle in quantum mechanics)
- using a communication network to send information that is encoded in a quantum state (a mathematical representation of a physical system, such as an atom, that provides the basis for processing quantum information)
- the use of quantum effects to create and send a digital key that can then be used to encrypt data, as well as to create truly random (i.e. unpredictable) numbers to secure and authenticate data

QUANTUM CONNECTIVITY

This covers the preservation of a quantum superposition state (see definition above) as it is shared between separate devices. In this context, coherence refers to the time a quantum superposition state can survive before beginning to degrade.

QUANTUM IMAGING, SENSING, TIMING OR NAVIGATION

This includes devices that use quantum effects to offer, for example, increased resilience, enhanced situational awareness, higher sensitivity, accuracy and speed, to perform a function. This function could include:

- creating images of objects
- sensing the size, shape or movement of an object
- establishing the location of and guide objects
- providing a timing signal

In the case of imaging, 'the phase or amplitude properties of quantum mechanics' refers to the measurement of the properties of the wave-like characteristics of quantum objects – such as an electron or a photon. Quantum imaging includes 'sub-Poissonian sources or detectors', which are quantum light sources such as those capable of emitting single photons, or detectors (devices capable of detecting single photons and their properties).

QUANTUM INFORMATION PROCESSING, COMPUTING OR SIMULATION

This covers systems that harness quantum effects to perform computation. This includes all levels or layers of software (operating system, system utilities, development tools and software tools, e.g. mathematical functions) as well as quantum emulation (a classical computer representing the operation of a quantum computer) and the hosting of quantum computing as a cloud-based service.

QUANTUM RESISTANT CRYPTOGRAPHY

This covers methods of securing information or data with the purpose of protecting against the threat of quantum computers to break current encryption techniques. If you are seeking to acquire a qualifying entity that 'develops' or 'produces' one of the above quantum technologies, then you will be legally required to submit a mandatory notification to the government

Example 1

Company A is considering acquiring company B, which designs and builds quantum sensors for the purposes of underground surveying. Company A is required by law to notify the government of this acquisition, as company B is a qualifying entity that develops and produces a specified quantum technology.

WHAT IS NOT IN SCOPE OF THE QUANTUM TECHNOLOGIES PART OF THE REGULATION?

If you are seeking to acquire a qualifying entity which fits into the following, then you are unlikely to fall within the scope of the mandatory notification requirement in relation to quantum technology:

- an entity undertaking solely fundamental research into quantum information science
- an entity which uses use quantum goods or services provided by others, without having played a part in developing or producing the technology. For example, an energy company that purchases a quantum sensor to detect emissions of greenhouse gases
- an entity that supplies a component for use in a quantum technology system, for example a company that provides a dilution refrigerator for use in the development of quantum computing technology. Please note, however, that the Advanced Materials regulations capture technology with relevance to quantum, such as photonics and semiconductors. You are advised to review the Advanced Materials guidance.

Example 2

Company A, a pharmaceutical company, is developing a new drug. It procures the services of Company B to access its quantum computer to speed up the processing of information. If Company C acquires Company A at a future date, it would not be required by law to notify the government as Company A would in scope of mandatory notification.

Example 3

Company A, a bank, employs the services of Company B, a quantum company, to explore the use of quantum computing technology to improve its operations. Company A has an in-house team that is tasked with developing an algorithm to run on a quantum computer to help speed up financial trading. If Company C acquires Company A at a future date, it would be required to notify the Government, as Company A has played a role in the development of a quantum technology (namely quantum algorithms that enable the functionality of the overall system).

SATELLITE AND SPACE TECHNOLOGY

[3.740]

Space is a rapidly developing sector that delivers a broad range of services and capabilities. By nature, all space-based services have crossover and affect other Critical National Infrastructure (CNI) sectors. The range of products and technologies available can vary hugely depending on the service (for example, earth observation, position, navigation, and timing).

The ease with which satellite and space technology can be used for both civilian and military purposes – either in the UK or internationally – is a growing concern and is something that the government will continue to monitor closely. This concern is nuanced, and the main issue is the potential for adversaries to use what seem to be predominantly civil capabilities to meet military objectives.

AM I IN SCOPE OF THE SATELLITE AND SPACE TECHNOLOGY PART OF THE REGULATIONS?

'Carrying on activities' in the Satellite and Space Technology part of the regulations means the qualifying entity you are acquiring is carrying on activities that consist of or include operating, developing, producing, creating, or using any of these activities:

- space debris management
- in-orbit activities
- satellite communication links
- secure facilities
- manufacture or testing
- space-derived data for any defence purpose
- space infrastructure operational control facilities
- provision or processing of space situational awareness data (SSA)

SPACE DEBRIS MANAGEMENT

This includes 'clean-up services' - sending an object into outer space to remove or manage space debris or using an object that is already in outer space to remove or manage space debris.

IN-ORBIT ACTIVITIES

This covers servicing and robotic activities carried out while the satellite is in orbit. This includes:

- making satellites that are already in orbit last longer (for example, by repairing or refuelling them)
- inspection services (for example, checking a satellite to see what condition it is in)
- performing maintenance
- moving a satellite while it is in orbit

• any technology or system that could be used to disrupt, change or interfere with other satellites. Changing a satellite includes, but is not limited to, repairs, relocation and refuelling of a satellite

SATELLITE COMMUNICATIONS LINKS

Satellite communications links are the links that enable and facilitate communication between various objects in space and from space to earth. This includes radio frequency and optical links. Optical links are communications links that provide a data connection between two points and that use optical (light) signals instead of traditional radio frequencies. Satellite communications links are provided:

- between satellites that are in orbit
- between spacecraft and satellites that are in orbit
- between satellites and celestial bodies (for example the Moon and Mars), or
- from earth to outer space, and from outer space to earth

SECURE FACILITIES

Secure facilities (including secure ground infrastructure, such as command-and-control stations and ground sites, and secure systems) are required for the smooth operation of satellite and space technologies. Any of these secure facilities and systems that relate to space activity or sub-orbital activity, or to services that are derived from space activity, will be in scope of the mandatory notification requirement.

Any operation or maintenance of the capability of these secure facilities is covered by mandatory notification. Capability covers anything that ensures the safe and secure access to services that are derived from space activity. For example, services such as general cleaning services would not be in scope, because they would not contribute to maintaining the secure nature of the facilities – but control rooms would be, because they provide and maintain the secure capability of the facilities that allow secure access to services derived from space activity.

'Space activity' has the same meaning as set out in section 1(4) of the Space Industry Act 2018.

MANUFACTURE OR TESTING

If the qualifying entity you intend to acquire is involved in testing or manufacturing any of the below, then you will be legally required to submit a mandatory notification. This includes the manufacturing or testing of:

- spacecraft (the meaning of which can be found in Section 2(6) of the Space Industry Act 2018)
- launch vehicles
- satellites
- planetary probes (spacecrafts that explore outer space and planets/bodies other than Earth – for example the Moon or Mars)
- orbital stations (space stations), or
- ground support equipment (ground support means all ground-based parts of a spacecraft system – so for example, ground stations or launch facilities)

Included are any materials, component parts or materials used for the manufacturing and/or testing of any of the items listed above.

'Testing' means that the qualifying entity provides quality assurance assessments of equipment or systems for space activity (including engines, component parts, radio frequency, software and systems), launch site equipment and facilities and equipment and facilities for the transport of satellites, launch vehicles or their major parts between sites.

SPACE-DERIVED DATA FOR ANY DEFENCE PURPOSE

Space-derived data are data that are obtained from space activity, or from ground stations that receive data from outer space, or from both space activity and ground stations receiving data from outer space, and include:

- position, navigation and timing services
- earth observation
- space situational awareness (which includes space surveillance tracking, space weather monitoring and forecasting, mapping or detection of near-earth objects and space debris)
- telecommunications
- signal intelligence (this means the gathering of intelligence through the interception of signals – for example, through radar or electronic systems)
- remote sensing (this is the science of gathering data about objects (for example, satellites or planetary bodies) from a distance using remote sensors)
- research and development

If the qualifying entity that you are seeking to acquire uses space-derived data for defence purposes, then you will be legally required to submit a mandatory notification. You must notify the government regardless of how you wish to use the data as an acquirer.

'Defence' has the same meaning that is given to it in the Official Secrets Act 1989 in Section 2(4).

SPACE INFRASTRUCTURE OPERATIONAL CONTROL FACILITIES

If the qualifying entity you intend to acquire provides space infrastructure operational control facilities, then you will be legally required to submit a mandatory notification. Here, 'infrastructure' includes:

- command and control stations
- ground stations, ground sites and ground segment equipment
- software (which includes any analysis software)
- information technology and telecommunications networks (including fibre cables)
- uplink and downlink terminals (uplink is the portion of the link that transmits signals from earth to space, and downlink is from space to earth)
- data processing and storage facilities (which includes databases)
- satellites
- technological systems or equipment that are deployed either in space or on earth.

PROVISION/PROCESSING OF SPACE SITUATIONAL AWARENESS DATA (SSA)

Space situational awareness includes:

- the mapping or detection of near-earth objects and space debris
- space surveillance and tracking
- space weather monitoring and forecasting

If the qualifying entity you are seeking to acquire provides or processes any of these SSA data, either on earth, or by space activity, you will be legally required to submit a mandatory notification. You will also be required to notify the government if the qualifying entity provides or processes SSA data for any of the following:

- orbital or sub-orbital activity (the definition for which can be found in section 1(4) of the Space Industry Act 2018)
- the mapping or detection of near-earth and space weather events
- defence purposes

SUPPLIERS TO THE EMERGENCY SERVICES

[3.741]
The emergency services are essential to the safety and security of citizens in the UK. They use a wide variety of tools, goods and services to achieve their goals. The government believes that there are certain services provided within the sector that are sufficiently sensitive that inclusion is justified in the mandatory notification requirement.

The government does not seek to include goods and services that, while important, are non-essential to the execution of key emergency service functions, such as general office supplies or non-emergency IT infrastructure.

AM I IN SCOPE OF THE EMERGENCY SERVICES PART OF THE REGULATIONS?

If you are acquiring all or part of a qualifying entity that supplies the emergency services with one or more of the goods and services which are used for the operational delivery of that emergency service, you will be required to submit a mandatory notification to the government.

The Emergency Services include:

- Border Force
- The British Transport Police Force
- The Civil Nuclear Constabulary
- a fire and rescue authority
- the Ministry of Defence Police
- the National Crime Agency
- a police body, including a Police Force

Ambulance Service Providers are only covered in the sections that relate to electronic communications networks or electronic communications services.

UNMANNED AIRCRAFT

If the qualifying entity you are acquiring provides unmanned aircraft, or drones, and their associated technology and equipment to the Emergency Services, then you will be required to submit a mandatory notification to the government. Unmanned aircraft for these purposes means "any aircraft operating or designed to operate autonomously or to be piloted remotely without a pilot on board".

This includes associated technologies such as (but not limited to):

- Global Positioning Systems (GPS)
- transmission equipment
- cameras
- software related to the control or operation of unmanned aircraft
- remote controls
- technology designed to detect, track and identify drones
- equipment designed to disrupt the systems of unmanned aircraft

Unmanned aircraft, such as drones, supplied to the general public are not covered.

FIREARMS

This category covers firearms and ammunition that are subject to mandatory notification. The College of Policing has helpful summaries of the legal definition of firearms in the Authorised Professional Practice for Armed Policing (https://www.app.college.police.uk/app-content/armed-policing/weapons-and-equipment/).

If the qualifying entity you are acquiring provides any of the following you will be legally required to submit a mandatory notification:

- firearms, defined in section 57(1) of the Firearms Act 1968:

  — prohibited weapons

  — any equipment that attaches to firearms or has been designed to diminish the noise and the flash by firing the weapon, for example sound moderators (silencers) and flash suppressors.

- ammunition, defined in section 57(2) of the Firearms Act 1968:

  — specialist munitions – including those designed to have a non-lethal effect on an individual, or those munitions where there is no designed effect on an individual, but collateral damage may occur

Items that are not covered include (but are not limited to):

- telescopic truncheons
- batons (straight, side-handled or friction-lock)
- pepper sprays and other self-defence sprays.

OTHER GOODS AND SERVICES

If you are acquiring a qualifying entity that provides the below goods and services to the Emergency Services, you will be legally required to submit a mandatory notification.

Maintenance and Supply

Supply, maintenance or support in the following categories:

- Border Force vessels, including the supply of electronic aids to navigation, repairs and certification, and
- unmanned aircraft, including any component, part or product of an unmanned aircraft as well as any electronic device relating to the unmanned aircraft

Entities that supply or maintain the following services are not covered:

- any other marine vessels used by the emergency services
- other emergency services vehicles including police vehicles, and
- any parties who provide maintenance and repairs of unmanned aircraft for the general public are outside the scope of the regulations

Fuel cards

You will be legally required to submit a mandatory notification if the qualifying entity you are acquiring supplies any card to the emergency services which is specifically designed to enable the holder to pay for fuel, discharging their obligation to a supplier of fuel in respect of payment for that fuel with the supplier being reimbursed by a third party.

Part 3 CMA and other Guidelines

Security access to buildings

You will be legally required to submit a mandatory notification if the qualifying entity you are acquiring provides an access control system to a building used by the emergency services.

This could be in the form of (but is not limited to):

- pin access keypad
- proximity card/card readers (key fobs)
- fingerprints and other biometrics and
- covert systems used to secure entry and egress from buildings.

Security alarms designed to detect intruders are not included.

Communications and Storage of Electronic Data

The emergency services use a variety of electronic systems which can be split into two broad categories:

- electronic communications, which refers to any information sent between parties over a phone line or internet connection. This includes phone calls, faxes, text messages, video messages, emails and internet messaging
- a range of physical infrastructure, cloud-based solutions and platforms that store electronic data

If you are acquiring a qualifying entity that supplies any of the following you will be legally required to submit a mandatory notification:

- a private electronic communications network that is used by the emergency service for the purposes of:

  — the prevention or detection of crime

  — fulfilling the functions of a fire and rescue authority

- maintenance to a private electronic communications network that is used by the emergency service for the purposes of:

  — the prevention or detection of crime and

  — fulfilling the functions of a fire and rescue authority.

- hardware, systems or platforms to facilitate the storage of electronic data, used exclusively or primarily by the emergency service for the purposes of:

  — the prevention or detection of crime

  — fulfilling the functions of a fire and rescue authority or

  — the storage of personal data, including personnel data.

This may include:

- private networks, their connections and devices used by individual police force and law enforcement organisations' systems, national policing systems and force-managed systems for the policing community
- communication and processing devices and network infrastructure, including information exchange communication services
- information systems and data centres
- systems which hold and store local and national emergency services records and crime and intelligence records and
- the resilience direct system, helplines, and email for assisting in crime investigation holding personal information.

The following are not covered:

- any public electronic communications network or public electronic communications service.
- generally available information such as the content of web pages or broadcast programming. Read more information on electronic communications (https://ico.org.uk/for-organisations/guide-to-pecr/key-concepts-and-definitions/).

Ambulance Service Providers

The only notification required in relation to Ambulance Services Providers is where a qualifying entity is acquired that supplies an Ambulance Services Provider with:

- an electronic communications network or electronic communications service that:

  — is not a public electronic communications network or a public electronic communications service and

  — is used by the ambulance services provider for the purposes of fulfilling its functions

Contingency labour against strike action

If you are acquiring a qualifying entity which has a contract with a fire and rescue authority to provide frontline personnel in the event of a strike, then you will be legally required to submit a mandatory notification.

The provision of any other contractual service to the emergency services during a strike is not included.

SYNTHETIC BIOLOGY

[3.742]
Synthetic biology is a rapidly evolving and developing technology that delivers an increasingly broad range of services and capabilities. It has high dual use potential and will overlap with other Critical National Infrastructure (CNI) sectors. The range of products and technologies available varies hugely depending on the application.

Synthetic biology can be used for both civilian and military purposes. The challenge is identifying an offensive capability interest over legitimate industry and research. It is the capability that the synthetic biology technology may enable that will decide a national security concern rather than the specific approach. Undertaking the activities listed in the scope section below may appear innocuous but given their dual-use potential, they could present a national security concern in the wrong hands. There are increasingly lower barriers to entry as the enabling technology and knowledge becomes more accessible, meaning that identifying offensive capabilities in the synthetic biology sector is a concern.

AM I IN SCOPE OF THE SYNTHETIC BIOLOGY PART OF THE REGULATIONS?

You will be legally required to submit a mandatory notification if you are acquiring a qualifying entity that carries out any of the activities described in the regulations:

- carrying out basic scientific research into synthetic biology
- involved in the development of synthetic biology
- produces goods using synthetic biology
- uses synthetic biology to enable the degradation of materials, or
- the provision of services that enable these activities

MEANING OF SYNTHETIC BIOLOGY AND THE DEFINITIONS OF OTHER RELATED TERMS

Synthetic biology is defined in the regulations as the process of applying engineering principles to biology to design, redesign or make biological components or systems that do not exist in the natural world.

Synthetic biology includes but is not limited to the following:

- the design and engineering of biological-based parts of:
  - — enzymes
  - — genetic circuits and cells
  - — novel devices and systems
- redesigning existing natural biological systems
- using microbes to template materials
- cell-free systems
- gene editing and gene therapy
- the use of DNA for data storage, encryption, and bio-enabled computing. This includes approaches which may be adapted to permit cryptography. It also includes using nucleic acids as part of an overall computing system alongside, for example, silicon and quantum computing approaches

DEFINITIONS

"Basic scientific research" means experimental or theoretical work undertaken principally to acquire new knowledge of the fundamental principles of phenomena or observable facts and not primarily directed towards a specific practicable aim or objective.

"Core" synthetic biology refers to those activities without which experiments cannot be conducted, such as DNA synthesis and cloning.

"Medicine" means:

- any substance or combination of substances presented as having properties of preventing or treating disease in human beings or animals
- any substance or combination of substances that may be used by or administered to human beings or animals with a view to:

Part 3 CMA and other Guidelines

— restoring, correcting or modifying a physiological function by asserting a pharmacological, immunological or metabolic action

— making a medical diagnosis

"Services" are the routine synthetic biology processes that are outsourced to specialist providers for completion before being re-integrated into the original workstream to assemble into an experiment or product. This includes making a specific strand of DNA or running a proprietary algorithm on a dataset but does not include maintenance of equipment.

EXEMPT ACTIVITIES IN THE SYNTHETIC BIOLOGY PART OF THE REGULATIONS

You will not need to submit a mandatory notification if the qualifying entity you are seeking to acquire carries out activities in one of the following areas:

- general services and servicing not related to core synthetic biology
- the use of microorganisms to remove harmful contaminants, pollutants, and toxins from the environment (known as bioremediation), including bio-based reagents that allow for testing for contaminants
- gathering clinical information for the purpose of making a clinical decision or making a diagnosis, known as diagnostics. However, the storage or ownership of sensitive human genetic information that enables the identification of an individual is not exempt and is in scope of mandatory notification
- industrial biotechnology research, development and production using enzymes or organisms that have not been modified through the application of systematic biodesign techniques, including the approaches described in the synthetic biology definition
- the production of substances ordinarily consumed as food or used as feed, including any ingredient or component thereof. However, delivery systems employing synthetic biology approaches to deliver compounds including chemicals, drugs or nucleic acids to multiple plants or animals in the environment simultaneously, are in scope of mandatory notification
- gene therapy where it is used solely for the purpose of replacing missing or defective genes to restore phenotypes to achieve a therapeutic effect. However, the addition of new genes (beyond the replacement of missing or defective genes), and deleting or inactivating genes are not exempt
- cell therapy where cells are modified by genetic engineering and then introduced into a patient to treat disease or
- the ownership, including of intellectual property, or development of both human or veterinary medicines and immunomodulatory approaches that employ synthetic biology at any stage of development or production. However, these are not exempt from mandatory notification if they have a synthetic biology technology that could be employed or modified to produce and/or deliver:

— toxic chemicals to achieve an incapacitating or lethal effect, or

— uses materials, substances, or pathogens set out in Schedule 5 to the Anti-terrorism Crime and Security Act 2001

For example, a company developing antibody-drug-conjugates would not be exempt from mandatory notification since these products contain highly potent toxins and use a linker technology that enable antibodies to deliver toxins to specific tissues. However, a company developing standard monoclonal antibody therapies would be exempt from submitting a mandatory notification.

TRANSPORT

[3.743]
The transport sector keeps the country moving and is an enabler of increased prosperity, security and a higher quality of life. Our transport sector therefore needs to be secure.

Only certain entities are sensitive enough to be subject to mandatory notification, therefore we have not included all transport-related entities. The transport part of the regulations focuses on key transport infrastructure in the maritime, aviation and air traffic control sectors. In some cases, the regulations will supplement existing notification requirements under the existing regulatory regimes, in which notification to the government is already either a requirement or unavoidable due to public ownership.

AM I IN SCOPE OF THE TRANSPORT PART OF THE REGULATIONS?

The regulations apply to:

- ports and harbours
- airports
- air traffic control

PORTS AND HARBOURS

You will be legally required to submit a mandatory notification to the government if either:

- the qualifying entity you are acquiring owns or operates a port or harbour in the UK that handled at least 1 million tonnes of cargo in the year preceding the year in which the acquisition is due to be completed, or

- the qualifying entity you are acquiring owns and operates terminals, wharves or other infrastructure situated in a port or harbour that handled at least 1 million tonnes of cargo in the year preceding the year in which the acquisition is due to be completed

Check the Port Freight Annual Statistics to see how much cargo is handled in each port and harbour (https://www.gov.uk/government/collections/maritime-and-shipping-statistics).

A port refers to an area of land and water made up of infrastructure, facilities, and equipment that permits the following activity:

- the receiving and departing of ships
- the loading and unloading of ships
- the storage of cargo
- the receipt and delivery of cargo, or
- the embarkation and disembarkation of passengers, crew and other persons

A harbour refers to estuaries, navigable rivers, piers, jetties, and other works in, via or at which ships can obtain shelter or ship and unship goods or passengers. This meaning is set out in section 313(1) of the Merchant Shipping Act 1995.

AIRPORTS

You will be legally required to submit a mandatory notification to the government if the qualifying entity you are acquiring owns or has overall responsibility for the management of an airport in the UK that handled either:

- 6 million passenger movements or more in 2018, or
- 100,000 tonnes of freight or more in 2018

To help assess whether your qualifying entity is in scope, you can:

- check passenger movements at airports in 2018 (https://www.caa.co.uk/uploadedFiles/CAA/Content/Standard_Content/Data_and_analysis/Datasets/Airport_stats/Airport_data_2018_annual/Table_08_Air_Pax_by_Type_and_Nat_of_Op.pdf)
- check the tonnes of freight handled at airports in 2018 (https://www.caa.co.uk/uploadedFiles/CAA/Content/Standard_Content/Data_and_analysis/Datasets/Airport_stats/Airport_data_2018_annual/Table_13_2_Freight.pdf)

2018 figures are used as a benchmark due to reduced demand for travel since 2020 due to the COVID-19 pandemic.

The definition of airport is the same as set out in section 66(1) of the Civil Aviation Act 2012. In summary an airport comprises an aerodrome which contains other land, buildings and structures used for the purposes of:

- the landing and taking off of aircraft
- the manoeuvring, parking, or servicing of aircraft
- the arrival or departure of persons as passengers, together with their baggage
- the arrival or departure of cargo
- the processing of such persons, baggage, and cargo between their arrival and departure and
- the arrival or departure of persons who work at the airport

The meaning of aerodrome is set out in section 105(1) of the Civil Aviation Act 1982. An aerodrome includes any area of land or water designed, equipped, set apart or commonly used for affording facilities for the landing and departure of aircraft.

For the purposes of the regulations the entities that are to be regarded as owning an airport are the company which owns the airport as well as any parent undertaking of that company. Parent undertaking has the same meaning as in section 1162 of the Companies Act 2006.

AIR TRAFFIC CONTROL

You will be legally required to submit a mandatory notification to the government if the qualifying entity you are acquiring either:

- provides en route air traffic control services in the UK or
- owns a provider of en route air traffic control services in the UK

A provider of these services will hold a licence for air traffic services under section 6 of the Transport Act 2000 and will be providing en route air traffic control services pursuant to that licence.

Air traffic control services, means the giving of instructions or advice to aircraft, whether in flight or on the manoeuvring area or apron of an aerodrome, for the purpose of: (a) preventing, or assisting in the prevention of, collisions between aircraft and (b) managing the flow of air traffic for the purpose of expediting and maintaining an orderly flow of air traffic. (See further the definition of air traffic control services in condition 1 interpretation and construction of the air traffic services licence for NATs (En Route) Plc).

For the purposes of the regulations the entities which are to be regarded as owning a provider of en route air traffic control services are the company which owns the provider as well as any parent undertaking of that company. As noted above parent undertaking has the same meaning as in section 1162 of the Companies Act 2006.

PART 4
EU & RETAINED EU MATERIALS

A. GENERAL

NOTES

Note that the United Kingdom left the European Union at 11pm on 31 January 2020. The implementation period provided for by Article 126 of the EU-UK Withdrawal Agreement came to an end at 11pm on 31 December 2020. As to the incorporation of "direct EU legislation" into domestic law, see the European Union (Withdrawal) Act 2018, s 3 at **[7.5]**.

CONSOLIDATED VERSION OF THE TREATY ON THE FUNCTIONING OF THE EUROPEAN UNION

[4.1]

NOTES

Date of publication in OJ: OJ C202, 7.6.2016, p 47.

Formerly titled the "Treaty Establishing the European Community" (Treaty of Rome). This is the Treaty currently in force, as consolidated following the amendments to, and the renaming of, the Treaty of Rome by the Treaty of Lisbon (which came into force on 1 December 2009). The abbreviation "TEC" refers to the Treaty Establishing the European Community.

PART THREE UNION POLICIES AND INTERNAL ACTIONS

TITLE VII COMMON RULES ON COMPETITION, TAXATION AND APPROXIMATION OF LAWS

CHAPTER 1 RULES ON COMPETITION

Section 1
Rules Applying to Undertakings

[4.2]

Article 101

1. The following shall be prohibited as incompatible with the internal market: all agreements between undertakings, decisions by associations of undertakings and concerted practices which may affect trade between Member States and which have as their object or effect the prevention, restriction or distortion of competition within the internal market, and in particular those which:

(a) directly or indirectly fix purchase or selling prices or any other trading conditions;
(b) limit or control production, markets, technical development, or investment;
(c) share markets or sources of supply;
(d) apply dissimilar conditions to equivalent transactions with other trading parties, thereby placing them at a competitive disadvantage;
(e) make the conclusion of contracts subject to acceptance by the other parties of supplementary obligations which, by their nature or according to commercial usage, have no connection with the subject of such contracts.

2. Any agreements or decisions prohibited pursuant to this Article shall be automatically void.

3. The provisions of paragraph 1 may, however, be declared inapplicable in the case of:

— any agreement or category of agreements between undertakings,
— any decision or category of decisions by associations of undertakings,
— any concerted practice or category of concerted practices,

which contributes to improving the production or distribution of goods or to promoting technical or economic progress, while allowing consumers a fair share of the resulting benefit, and which does not:

(a) impose on the undertakings concerned restrictions which are not indispensable to the attainment of these objectives;
(b) afford such undertakings the possibility of eliminating competition in respect of a substantial part of the products in question.

NOTES

Formerly Article 81 TEC.

[4.3]

Article 102

Any abuse by one or more undertakings of a dominant position within the internal market or in a substantial part of it shall be prohibited as incompatible with the internal market in so far as it may affect trade between Member States.

Such abuse may, in particular, consist in:

(a) directly or indirectly imposing unfair purchase or selling prices or other unfair trading conditions;
(b) limiting production, markets or technical development to the prejudice of consumers;
(c) applying dissimilar conditions to equivalent transactions with other trading parties, thereby placing them at a competitive disadvantage;
(d) making the conclusion of contracts subject to acceptance by the other parties of supplementary obligations which, by their nature or according to commercial usage, have no connection with the subject of such contracts.

NOTES
Formerly Article 82 TEC.

[4.4]
Article 103
1. The appropriate regulations or directives to give effect to the principles set out in Articles 101 and 102 shall be laid down by the Council, on a proposal from the Commission and after consulting the European Parliament.
2. The regulations or directives referred to in paragraph 1 shall be designed in particular:
(a) to ensure compliance with the prohibitions laid down in Article 101(1) and in Article 102 by making provision for fines and periodic penalty payments;
(b) to lay down detailed rules for the application of Article 101(3), taking into account the need to ensure effective supervision on the one hand, and to simplify administration to the greatest possible extent on the other;
(c) to define, if need be, in the various branches of the economy, the scope of the provisions of Articles 101 and 102;
(d) to define the respective functions of the Commission and of the Court of Justice of the European Union in applying the provisions laid down in this paragraph;
(e) to determine the relationship between national laws and the provisions contained in this Section or adopted pursuant to this Article.

NOTES
Formerly Article 83 TEC.

[4.5]
Article 104
Until the entry into force of the provisions adopted in pursuance of Article 103, the authorities in Member States shall rule on the admissibility of agreements, decisions and concerted practices and on abuse of a dominant position in the internal market in accordance with the law of their country and with the provisions of Article 101, in particular paragraph 3, and of Article 102.

NOTES
Formerly Article 84 TEC.

[4.6]
Article 105
1. Without prejudice to Article 104, the Commission shall ensure the application of the principles laid down in Articles 101 and 102. On application by a Member State or on its own initiative, and in cooperation with the competent authorities in the Member States, which shall give it their assistance, the Commission shall investigate cases of suspected infringement of these principles. If it finds that there has been an infringement, it shall propose appropriate measures to bring it to an end.
2. If the infringement is not brought to an end, the Commission shall record such infringement of the principles in a reasoned decision. The Commission may publish its decision and authorise Member States to take the measures, the conditions and details of which it shall determine, needed to remedy the situation.
3. The Commission may adopt regulations relating to the categories of agreement in respect of which the Council has adopted a regulation or a directive pursuant to Article 103(2)(b).

NOTES
Formerly Article 85 TEC.

[4.7]
Article 106
1. In the case of public undertakings and undertakings to which Member States grant special or exclusive rights, Member States shall neither enact nor maintain in force any measure contrary to the rules contained in the Treaties, in particular to those rules provided for in Article 18 and Articles 101 to 109.
2. Undertakings entrusted with the operation of services of general economic interest or having the character of a revenue-producing monopoly shall be subject to the rules contained in the Treaties, in particular to the rules on competition, in so far as the application of such rules does not obstruct the performance, in law or in fact, of the particular tasks assigned to them. The development of trade must not be affected to such an extent as would be contrary to the interests of the Union.
3. The Commission shall ensure the application of the provisions of this Article and shall, where necessary, address appropriate directives or decisions to Member States.

NOTES
Formerly Article 86 TEC.

Section 2
Aids Granted by States

[4.8]
Article 107
1. Save as otherwise provided in the Treaties, any aid granted by a Member State or through State resources in any form whatsoever which distorts or threatens to distort competition by favouring certain undertakings or the production of certain goods shall, in so far as it affects trade between Member States, be incompatible with the internal market.
2. The following shall be compatible with the internal market:

(a) aid having a social character, granted to individual consumers, provided that such aid is granted without discrimination related to the origin of the products concerned;
(b) aid to make good the damage caused by natural disasters or exceptional occurrences;
(c) aid granted to the economy of certain areas of the Federal Republic of Germany affected by the division of Germany, in so far as such aid is required in order to compensate for the economic disadvantages caused by that division. Five years after the entry into force of the Treaty of Lisbon, the Council, acting on a proposal from the Commission, may adopt a decision repealing this point.

3. The following may be considered to be compatible with the internal market:
(a) aid to promote the economic development of areas where the standard of living is abnormally low or where there is serious underemployment, and of the regions referred to in Article 349, in view of their structural, economic and social situation;
(b) aid to promote the execution of an important project of common European interest or to remedy a serious disturbance in the economy of a Member State;
(c) aid to facilitate the development of certain economic activities or of certain economic areas, where such aid does not adversely affect trading conditions to an extent contrary to the common interest;
(d) aid to promote culture and heritage conservation where such aid does not affect trading conditions and competition in the Union to an extent that is contrary to the common interest;
(e) such other categories of aid as may be specified by decision of the Council on a proposal from the Commission.

NOTES

Formerly Article 87 TEC.

Cessation of Treaty Rights in the UK (Article 107(1)): see the State Aid (Revocations and Amendments) (EU Exit) Regulations 2020, SI 2020/1470, reg 3 at **[7.81]**.

[4.9]
Article 108

1. The Commission shall, in cooperation with Member States, keep under constant review all systems of aid existing in those States. It shall propose to the latter any appropriate measures required by the progressive development or by the functioning of the internal market.

2. If, after giving notice to the parties concerned to submit their comments, the Commission finds that aid granted by a State or through State resources is not compatible with the internal market having regard to Article 107, or that such aid is being misused, it shall decide that the State concerned shall abolish or alter such aid within a period of time to be determined by the Commission.

If the State concerned does not comply with this decision within the prescribed time, the Commission or any other interested State may, in derogation from the provisions of Articles 258 and 259, refer the matter to the Court of Justice of the European Union direct.

On application by a Member State, the Council may, acting unanimously, decide that aid which that State is granting or intends to grant shall be considered to be compatible with the internal market, in derogation from the provisions of Article 107 or from the regulations provided for in Article 109, if such a decision is justified by exceptional circumstances. If, as regards the aid in question, the Commission has already initiated the procedure provided for in the first subparagraph of this paragraph, the fact that the State concerned has made its application to the Council shall have the effect of suspending that procedure until the Council has made its attitude known.

If, however, the Council has not made its attitude known within three months of the said application being made, the Commission shall give its decision on the case.

3. The Commission shall be informed, in sufficient time to enable it to submit its comments, of any plans to grant or alter aid. If it considers that any such plan is not compatible with the internal market having regard to Article 107, it shall without delay initiate the procedure provided for in paragraph 2. The Member State concerned shall not put its proposed measures into effect until this procedure has resulted in a final decision.

4. The Commission may adopt regulations relating to the categories of State aid that the Council has, pursuant to Article 109, determined may be exempted from the procedure provided for by paragraph 3 of this Article.

NOTES

Formerly Article 88 TEC.

Cessation of Treaty Rights in the UK (Article 108(3)): see the State Aid (Revocations and Amendments) (EU Exit) Regulations 2020, SI 2020/1470, reg 3 at **[7.81]**.

[4.10]
Article 109

The Council, on a proposal from the Commission and after consulting the European Parliament, may make any appropriate regulations for the application of Articles 107 and 108 and may in particular determine the conditions in which Article 108(3) shall apply and the categories of aid exempted from this procedure.

NOTES

Formerly Article 89 TEC.

PART SIX INSTITUTIONAL AND FINANCIAL PROVISIONS

TITLE I INSTITUTIONAL PROVISIONS

CHAPTER 1 THE INSTITUTIONS

Section 5
The Court of Justice of the European Union

[4.11]

Article 263

The Court of Justice of the European Union shall review the legality of legislative acts, of acts of the Council, of the Commission and of the European Central Bank, other than recommendations and opinions, and of acts of the European Parliament and of the European Council intended to produce legal effects *vis-à-vis* third parties. It shall also review the legality of acts of bodies, offices or agencies of the Union intended to produce legal effects *vis-à-vis* third parties.

It shall for this purpose have jurisdiction in actions brought by a Member State, the European Parliament, the Council or the Commission on grounds of lack of competence, infringement of an essential procedural requirement, infringement of the Treaties or of any rule of law relating to their application, or misuse of powers.

The Court shall have jurisdiction under the same conditions in actions brought by the Court of Auditors, by the European Central Bank and by the Committee of the Regions for the purpose of protecting their prerogatives.

Any natural or legal person may, under the conditions laid down in the first and second paragraphs, institute proceedings against an act addressed to that person or which is of direct and individual concern to them, and against a regulatory act which is of direct concern to them and does not entail implementing measures.

Acts setting up bodies, offices and agencies of the Union may lay down specific conditions and arrangements concerning actions brought by natural or legal persons against acts of these bodies, offices or agencies intended to produce legal effects in relation to them.

The proceedings provided for in this Article shall be instituted within two months of the publication of the measure, or of its notification to the plaintiff, or, in the absence thereof, of the day on which it came to the knowledge of the latter, as the case may be.

NOTES

Formerly Article 230 TEC.

[4.12]

Article 267

The Court of Justice of the European Union shall have jurisdiction to give preliminary rulings concerning:

(a) the interpretation of the Treaties;

(b) the validity and interpretation of acts of the institutions, bodies, offices or agencies of the Union;

Where such a question is raised before any court or tribunal of a Member State, that court or tribunal may, if it considers that a decision on the question is necessary to enable it to give judgment, request the Court to give a ruling thereon.

Where any such question is raised in a case pending before a court or tribunal of a Member State against whose decisions there is no judicial remedy under national law, that court or tribunal shall bring the matter before the Court.

If such a question is raised in a case pending before a court or tribunal of a Member State with regard to a person in custody, the Court of Justice of the European Union shall act with the minimum of delay.

NOTES

Formerly Article 234 TEC.

PART SEVEN GENERAL AND FINAL PROVISIONS

[4.13]

Article 346

1. The provisions of the Treaties shall not preclude the application of the following rules:

   (a) no Member State shall be obliged to supply information the disclosure of which it considers contrary to the essential interests of its security;

   (b) any Member State may take such measures as it considers necessary for the protection of the essential interests of its security which are connected with the production of or trade in arms, munitions and war material; such measures shall not adversely affect the conditions of competition in the internal market regarding products which are not intended for specifically military purposes.

2. The Council may, acting unanimously on a proposal from the Commission, make changes to the list, which it drew up on 15 April 1958, of the products to which the provisions of paragraph 1(b) apply.

NOTES

Formerly Article 296 TEC.

Cessation of Treaty Rights in the UK (Article 346(1), in so far as Article 346(1) relates to Article 107(1) or Article 108(3)): see the State Aid (Revocations and Amendments) (EU Exit) Regulations 2020, SI 2020/1470, reg 3 at **[7.81]**.

COMMISSION NOTICE

(97/C372/03)

on the definition of relevant market for the purposes of Community competition law

[4.14]

NOTES

Date of publication in OJ: OJ C372, 9.12.1997, p 5.

Note: with effect from 1 December 2009, the EC Treaty was replaced by the Treaty on the Functioning of the European Union. References in this document to provisions of the EC Treaty should be construed accordingly.

See also the list of consultations and draft documents in the Appendix at **[A1]**.

I. INTRODUCTION

[4.15]

1. The purpose of this notice is to provide guidance as to how the Commission applies the concept of relevant product and geographic market in its ongoing enforcement of Community competition law, in particular the application of Council Regulation 17/62 and (EEC) 4064/89, their equivalents in other sectoral applications such as transport, coal and steel, and agriculture, and the relevant provisions of the EEA Agreement.[1] Throughout this notice, references to Articles 85 and 86 of the Treaty and to merger control are to be understood as referring to the equivalent provisions in the EEA Agreement and the ECSC Treaty.

2. Market definition is a tool to identify and define the boundaries of competition between firms. It serves to establish the framework within which competition policy is applied by the Commission. The main purpose of market definition is to identify in a systematic way the competitive constraints that the undertakings involved[2] face. The objective of defining a market in both its product and geographic dimension is to identify those actual competitors of the undertakings involved that are capable of constraining those undertakings' behaviour and of preventing them from behaving independently of effective competitive pressure. It is from this perspective that the market definition makes it possible inter alia to calculate market shares that would convey meaningful information regarding market power for the purposes of assessing dominance or for the purposes of applying Article 85.

3. It follows from point 2 that the concept of "relevant" market is different from other definitions of market often used in other contexts. For instance, companies often use the term "market" to refer to the area where it sells its products or to refer broadly to the industry or sector where it belongs.

4. The definition of the relevant market in both its product and its geographic dimensions often has a decisive influence on the assessment of a competition case. By rendering public the procedures which the Commission follows when considering market definition and by indicating the criteria and evidence on which it relies to reach a decision, the Commission expects to increase the transparency of its policy and decision-making in the area of competition policy.

5. Increased transparency will also result in companies and their advisers being able to better anticipate the possibility that the Commission may raise competition concerns in an individual case. Companies could, therefore, take such a possibility into account in their own internal decision-making when contemplating, for instance, acquisitions, the creation of joint ventures, or the establishment of certain agreements. It is also intended that companies should be in a better position to understand what sort of information the Commission considers relevant for the purposes of market definition.

6. The Commission's interpretation of "relevant" market is without prejudice to the interpretation which may be given by the Court of Justice or the Court of First Instance of the European Communities.

NOTES

1 The focus of assessment in State aid cases is the aid recipient and the industry/sector concerned rather than identification of competitive constraints faced by the aid recipient. When consideration of market power and therefore of the relevant market are raised in any particular case, elements of the approach outlined here might serve as a basis for the assessment of State aid cases.

2 For the purposes of this notice, the undertakings involved will be, in the case of a concentration, the parties to the concentration, in investigations within the meaning of Article 86 of the Treaty, the undertaking being investigated or the complainants; for investigations within the meaning of Article 85, the parties to the Agreement.

II. DEFINITION OF RELEVANT MARKET

DEFINITION OF RELEVANT PRODUCT MARKET AND RELEVANT GEOGRAPHIC MARKET

[4.16]

7. The Regulations based on Articles 85 and 86 of the Treaty, in particular in section 6 of Form A/B with respect to Regulation No 17, as well as in section 6 of Form CO with respect to Regulation (EEC) 4064/89 on the control of concentrations having a Community dimension have laid down the following definitions. "Relevant product markets" are defined as follows—

> "A relevant product market comprises all those products and/or services which are regarded as interchangeable or substitutable by the consumer, by reason of the products' characteristics, their prices and their intended use."

8. "Relevant geographic markets" are defined as follows—

"The relevant geographic market comprises the area in which the undertakings concerned are involved in the supply and demand of products or services, in which the conditions of competition are sufficiently homogeneous and which can be distinguished from neighbouring areas because the conditions of competition are appreciably different in those areas".

9. The relevant market within which to assess a given competition issue is therefore established by the combination of the product and geographic markets. The Commission interprets the definitions in paragraphs 7 and 8 (which reflect the case law of the Court of Justice and the Court of First Instance as well as its own decision-making practice) according to the orientations defined in this notice.

CONCEPT OF RELEVANT MARKET AND OBJECTIVES OF COMMUNITY COMPETITION POLICY

10. The concept of relevant market is closely related to the objectives pursued under Community competition policy. For example, under the Community's merger control, the objective in controlling structural changes in the supply of a product/service is to prevent the creation or reinforcement of a dominant position as a result of which effective competition would be significantly impeded in a substantial part of the common market. Under the Community's competition rules, a dominant position is such that a firm or group of firms would be in a position to behave to an appreciable extent independently of its competitors, customers and ultimately of its consumers.[3] Such a position would usually arise when a firm or group of firms accounted for a large share of the supply in any given market, provided that other factors analysed in the assessment (such as entry barriers, customers' capacity, etc) point in the same direction.

11. The same approach is followed by the Commission in its application of Article 86 of the Treaty to firms that enjoy a single or collective dominant position. Within the meaning of Regulation No 17, the Commission has the power to investigate and bring to an end abuses of such a dominant position, which must also be defined by reference to the relevant market. Markets may also need to be defined in the application of Article 85 of the Treaty, in particular, in determining whether an appreciable restriction of competition exists or in establishing if the condition pursuant to Article 85(3)(b) for an exemption from the application of Article 85(1) is met.

12. The criteria for defining the relevant market are applied generally for the analysis of certain types of behaviour in the market and for the analysis of structural changes in the supply of products. This methodology, though, might lead to different results depending on the nature of the competition issue being examined. For instance, the scope of the geographic market might be different when analysing a concentration, where the analysis is essentially prospective, from an analysis of past behaviour. The different time horizon considered in each case might lead to the result that different geographic markets are defined for the same products depending on whether the Commission is examining a change in the structure of supply, such as a concentration or a cooperative joint venture, or examining issues relating to certain past behaviour.

NOTES

3 Definition given by the Court of Justice in its judgment of 13 February 1979 in Case 85/76 [1979] ECR 461 *Hoffmann La Roche*, and confirmed in subsequent judgments.

BASIC PRINCIPLES FOR MARKET DEFINITION

COMPETITIVE CONSTRAINTS

13. Firms are subject to three main sources of competitive constraints: demand substitutability, supply substitutability and potential competition. From an economic point of view, for the definition of the relevant market, demand substitution constitutes the most immediate and effective disciplinary force on the suppliers of a given product, in particular in relation to their pricing decisions. A firm or a group of firms cannot have a significant impact on the prevailing conditions of sale, such as prices, if its customers are in a position to switch easily to available substitute products or to suppliers located elsewhere. Basically, the exercise of market definition consists in identifying the effective alternative sources of supply for the customers of the undertakings involved, in terms both of products/services and of geographic location of suppliers.

14. The competitive constraints arising from supply side substitutability other than those described in paras 20–23 and from potential competition are in general less immediate and in any case require an analysis of additional factors. As a result such constraints are taken into account at the assessment stage of competition analysis.

DEMAND SUBSTITUTION

15. The assessment of demand substitution entails a determination of the range of products which are viewed as substitutes by the consumer. One way of making this determination can be viewed as a speculative experiment, postulating a hypothetical small, lasting change in relative prices and evaluating the likely reactions of customers to that increase. The exercise of market definition focuses on prices for operational and practical purposes, and more precisely on demand substitution arising from small, permanent changes in relative prices. This concept can provide clear indications as to the evidence that is relevant to define markets.

16. Conceptually, this approach means that, starting from the type of products that the undertakings involved sell and the area in which they sell them, additional products and areas will be included in, or excluded from, the market definition depending on whether competition from these other products and areas affect or restrain sufficiently the pricing of the parties' products in the short term.

17. The question to be answered is whether the parties' customers would switch to readily available substitutes or to suppliers located elsewhere in response to a hypothetical small (in the range 5%–10%) but permanent relative price increase in the products and areas being considered. If substitution were enough to make the price increase unprofitable because of the resulting loss of sales, additional substitutes and areas are included in the relevant market. This would be done until the set of products and geographical areas is such that small, permanent increases in relative prices would be profitable. The equivalent analysis is applicable in cases concerning the concentration of buying

power, where the starting point would then be the supplier and the price test serves to identify the alternative distribution channels or outlets for the supplier's products. In the application of these principles, careful account should be taken of certain particular situations as described within paragraphs 56 and 58.

18. A practical example of this test can be provided by its application to a merger of, for instance, soft-drink bottlers. An issue to examine in such a case would be to decide whether different flavours of soft drinks belong to the same market. In practice, the question to address would be whether consumers of flavour A would switch to other flavours when confronted with a permanent price increase of 5% to 10% for flavour A. If a sufficient number of consumers would switch to, say, flavour B, to such an extent that the price increase for flavour A would not be profitable owing to the resulting loss of sales, then the market would comprise at least flavours A and B. The process would have to be extended in addition to other available flavours until a set of products is identified for which a price rise would not induce a sufficient substitution in demand.

19. Generally, and in particular for the analysis of merger cases, the price to take into account will be the prevailing market price. This might not be the case where the prevailing price has been determined in the absence of sufficient competition. In particular for the investigation of abuses of dominant positions, the fact that the prevailing price might already have been substantially increased will be taken into account.

Supply Substitution

20. Supply-side substitutability may also be taken into account when defining markets in those situations in which its effects are equivalent to those of demand substitution in terms of effectiveness and immediacy. This requires that suppliers be able to switch production to the relevant products and market them in the short term[4] without incurring significant additional costs or risks in response to small and permanent changes in relative prices. When these conditions are met, the additional production that is put on the market will have a disciplinary effect on the competitive behaviour of the companies involved. Such an impact in terms of effectiveness and immediacy is equivalent to the demand substitution effect.

21. These situations typically arise when companies market a wide range of qualities or grades of one product; even if, for a given final customer or group of consumers, the different qualities are not substitutable, the different qualities will be grouped into one product market, provided that most of the suppliers are able to offer and sell the various qualities immediately and without the significant increases in costs described above. In such cases, the relevant product market will encompass all products that are substitutable in demand and supply, and the current sales of those products will be aggregated so as to give the total value or volume of the market. The same reasoning may lead to group different geographic areas.

22. A practical example of the approach to supply-side substitutability when defining product markets is to be found in the case of paper. Paper is usually supplied in a range of different qualities, from standard writing paper to high quality papers to be used, for instance, to publish art books. From a demand point of view, different qualities of paper cannot be used for any given use, ie an art book or a high quality publication cannot be based on lower quality papers. However, paper plants are prepared to manufacture the different qualities, and production can be adjusted with negligible costs and in a short time-frame. In the absence of particular difficulties in distribution, paper manufacturers are able therefore, to compete for orders of the various qualities, in particular if orders are passed with sufficient lead time to allow for modification of production plans. Under such circumstances, the Commission would not define a separate market for each quality of paper and its respective use. The various qualities of paper are included in the relevant market, and their sales added up to estimate total market value and volume.

23. When supply-side substitutability would entail the need to adjust significantly existing tangible and intangible assets, additional investments, strategic decisions or time delays, it will not be considered at the stage of market definition. Examples where supply-side substitution did not induce the Commission to enlarge the market are offered in the area of consumer products, in particular for branded beverages. Although bottling plants may in principle bottle different beverages, there are costs and lead times involved (in terms of advertising, product testing and distribution) before the products can actually be sold. In these cases, the effects of supply-side substitutability and other forms of potential competition would then be examined at a later stage.

Potential Competition

24. The third source of competitive constraint, potential competition, is not taken into account when defining markets, since the conditions under which potential competition will actually represent an effective competitive constraint depend on the analysis of specific factors and circumstances related to the conditions of entry. If required, this analysis is only carried out at a subsequent stage, in general once the position of the companies involved in the relevant market has already been ascertained, and when such position gives rise to concerns from a competition point of view.

NOTES

4 That is such a period that does not entail a significant adjustment of existing tangible and intangible assets (see para 23).

III. EVIDENCE RELIED ON TO DEFINE RELEVANT MARKETS

THE PROCESS OF DEFINING THE RELEVANT MARKET IN PRACTICE

Product Dimension

[4.17]

25. There is a range of evidence permitting an assessment of the extent to which substitution would take place. In individual cases, certain types of evidence will be determinant, depending very much on the characteristics and specificity of the industry and products or services that are being examined. The same type of evidence may be of no importance in other cases. In most cases, a decision will have to be based on the consideration of a number of criteria

and different items of evidence. The Commission follows an open approach to empirical evidence, aimed at making an effective use of all available information which may be relevant in individual cases. The Commission does not follow a rigid hierarchy of different sources of information or types of evidence.

26. The process of defining relevant markets may be summarised as follows: on the basis of the preliminary information available or information submitted by the undertakings involved, the Commission will usually be in a position to broadly establish the possible relevant markets within which, for instance, a concentration or a restriction of competition has to be assessed. In general, and for all practical purposes when handling individual cases, the question will usually be to decide on a few alternative possible relevant markets. For instance, with respect to the product market, the issue will often be to establish whether product A and product B belong or do not belong to the same product market. It is often the case that the inclusion of product B would be enough to remove any competition concerns.

27. In such situations it is not necessary to consider whether the market includes additional products, or to reach a definitive conclusion on the precise product market. If under the conceivable alternative market definitions the operation in question does not raise competition concerns, the question of market definition will be left open, reducing thereby the burden on companies to supply information.

Geographic dimension

28. The Commission's approach to geographic market definition might be summarised as follows: it will take a preliminary view of the scope of the geographic market on the basis of broad indications as to the distribution of market shares between the parties and their competitors, as well as a preliminary analysis of pricing and price differences at national and Community or EEA level. This initial view is used basically as a working hypothesis to focus the Commission's enquiries for the purposes of arriving at a precise geographic market definition.

29. The reasons behind any particular configuration of prices and market shares need to be explored. Companies might enjoy high market shares in their domestic markets just because of the weight of the past, and conversely, a homogeneous presence of companies throughout the EEA might be consistent with national or regional geographic markets. The initial working hypothesis will therefore be checked against an analysis of demand characteristics (importance of national or local preferences, current patterns of purchases of customers, product differentiation/brands, other) in order to establish whether companies in different areas do indeed constitute a real alternative source of supply for consumers. The theoretical experiment is again based on substitution arising from changes in relative prices, and the question to answer is again whether the customers of the parties would switch their orders to companies located elsewhere in the short term and at a negligible cost.

30. If necessary, a further check on supply factors will be carried out to ensure that those companies located in differing areas do not face impediments in developing their sales on competitive terms throughout the whole geographic market. This analysis will include an examination of requirements for a local presence in order to sell in that area the conditions of access to distribution channels, costs associated with setting up a distribution network, and the presence or absence of regulatory barriers arising from public procurement, price regulations, quotas and tariffs limiting trade or production, technical standards, monopolies, freedom of establishment, requirements for administrative authorisations, packaging regulations, etc. In short, the Commission will identify possible obstacles and barriers isolating companies located in a given area from the competitive pressure of companies located outside that area, so as to determine the precise degree of market interpenetration at national, European or global level.

31. The actual pattern and evolution of trade flows offers useful supplementary indications as to the economic importance of each demand or supply factor mentioned above, and the extent to which they may or may not constitute actual barriers creating different geographic markets. The analysis of trade flows will generally address the question of transport costs and the extent to which these may hinder trade between different areas, having regard to plant location, costs of production and relative price levels.

Market integration in the Community

32. Finally, the Commission also takes into account the continuing process of market integration, in particular in the Community when defining geographic markets, especially in the area of concentrations and structural joint ventures. The measures adopted and implemented in the internal market programme to remove barriers to trade and further integrate the Community markets cannot be ignored when assessing the effects on competition of a concentration or a structural joint venture. A situation where national markets have been artificially isolated from each other because of the existence of legislative barriers that have now been removed will generally lead to a cautious assessment of past evidence regarding prices, market shares or trade patterns. A process of market integration that would, in the short term, lead to wider geographic markets may therefore be taken into consideration when defining the geographic market for the purposes of assessing concentrations and joint ventures.

The process of gathering evidence

33. When a precise market definition is deemed necessary, the Commission will often contact the main customers and the main companies in the industry to enquire into their views about the boundaries of product and geographic markets and to obtain the necessary factual evidence to reach a conclusion. The Commission might also contact the relevant professional associations, and companies active in upstream markets, so as to be able to define, in so far as necessary, separate product and geographic markets, for different levels of production or distribution of the products/services in question. It might also request additional information to the undertakings involved.

34. Where appropriate, the Commission will address written requests for information to the market players mentioned above. These requests will usually include questions relating to the perceptions of companies about reactions to hypothetical price increases and their views of the boundaries of the relevant market. They will also ask for provision of the factual information the Commission deems necessary to reach a conclusion on the extent of the relevant market. The Commission might also discuss with marketing directors or other officers of those companies to

gain a better understanding on how negotiations between suppliers and customers take place and better understand issues relating to the definition of the relevant market. Where appropriate, they might also carry out visits or inspections to the premises of the parties, their customers and/or their competitors, in order to better understand how products are manufactured and sold.

35. The type of evidence relevant to reach a conclusion as to the product market can be categorised as follows:

EVIDENCE TO DEFINE MARKETS—PRODUCT DIMENSION

36. An analysis of the product characteristics and its intended use allows the Commission, as a first step, to limit the field of investigation of possible substitutes. However, product characteristics and intended use are insufficient to show whether two products are demand substitutes. Functional interchangeability or similarity in characteristics may not, in themselves, provide sufficient criteria, because the responsiveness of customers to relative price changes may be determined by other considerations as well. For example, there may be different competitive constraints in the original equipment market for car components and in spare parts, thereby leading to a separate delineation of two relevant markets. Conversely, differences in product characteristics are not in themselves sufficient to exclude demand substitutability, since this will depend to a large extent on how customers value different characteristics.

37. The type of evidence the Commission considers relevant to assess whether two products are demand substitutes can be categorised as follows:

38. *Evidence of substitution in the recent past.* In certain cases, it is possible to analyse evidence relating to recent past events or shocks in the market that offer actual examples of substitution between two products. When available, this sort of information will normally be fundamental for market definition. If there have been changes in relative prices in the past (all else being equal), the reactions in terms of quantities demanded will be determinant in establishing substitutability. Launches of new products in the past can also offer useful information, when it is possible to precisely analyse which products have lost sales to the new product.

39. There are a number of *quantitative tests* that have specifically been designed for the purpose of delineating markets. These tests consist of various econometric and statistical approaches estimates of elasticities and cross-price elasticities[5] for the demand of a product, tests based on similarity of price movements over time, the analysis of causality between price series and similarity of price levels and/or their convergence. The Commission takes into account the available quantitative evidence capable of withstanding rigorous scrutiny for the purposes of establishing patterns of substitution in the past.

40. *Views of customers and competitors.* The Commission often contacts the main customers and competitors of the companies involved in its enquiries, to gather their views on the boundaries of the product market as well as most of the factual information it requires to reach a conclusion on the scope of the market. Reasoned answers of customers and competitors as to what would happen if relative prices for the candidate products were to increase in the candidate geographic area by a small amount (for instance of 5%–10%) are taken into account when they are sufficiently backed by factual evidence.

41. *Consumer preferences.* In the case of consumer goods, it may be difficult for the Commission to gather the direct views of end consumers about substitute products. *Marketing studies* that companies have commissioned in the past and that are used by companies in their own decision-making as to pricing of their products and/or marketing actions may provide useful information for the Commission's delineation of the relevant market. Consumer surveys on usage patterns and attitudes, data from consumers' purchasing patterns, the views expressed by retailers and more generally, market research studies submitted by the parties and their competitors are taken into account to establish whether an economically significant proportion of consumers consider two products as substitutable, also taking into account the importance of brands for the products in question. The methodology followed in consumer surveys carried out ad-hoc by the undertakings involved or their competitors for the purposes of a merger procedure or a procedure pursuant to Regulation No 17 will usually be scrutinised with utmost care. Unlike pre-existing studies, they have not been prepared in the normal course of business for the adoption of business decisions.

42. *Barriers and costs associated with switching demand to potential substitutes.* There are a number of barriers and costs that might prevent the Commission from considering two prima facie demand substitutes as belonging to one single product market. It is not possible to provide an exhaustive list of all the possible barriers to substitution and of switching costs. These barriers or obstacles might have a wide range of origins, and in its decisions, the Commission has been confronted with regulatory barriers or other forms of State intervention, constraints arising in downstream markets, need to incur specific capital investment or loss in current output in order to switch to alternative inputs, the location of customers, specific investment in production process, learning and human capital investment, retooling costs or other investments, uncertainty about quality and reputation of unknown suppliers, and others.

43. *Different categories of customers and price discrimination.* The extent of the product market might be narrowed in the presence of distinct groups of customers. A distinct group of customers for the relevant product may constitute a narrower, distinct market when such a group could be subject to price discrimination. This will usually be the case when two conditions are met: (a) it is possible to identify clearly which group an individual customer belongs to at the moment of selling the relevant products to him, and (b) trade among customers or arbitrage by third parties should not be feasible.

EVIDENCE FOR DEFINING MARKETS—GEOGRAPHIC DIMENSION

44. The type of evidence the Commission considers relevant to reach a conclusion as to the geographic market can be categorised as follows:

45. *Past evidence of diversion of orders to other areas.* In certain cases, evidence on changes in prices between different areas and consequent reactions by customers might be available. Generally, the same quantitative tests used for product market definition might as well be used in geographic market definition, bearing in mind that international comparisons of prices might be more complex due to a number of factors such as exchange rate movements, taxation and product differentiation.

46. *Basic demand characteristics.* The nature of demand for the relevant product may in itself determine the scope of the geographical market. Factors such as national preferences or preferences for national brands, language, culture and life style, and the need for a local presence have a strong potential to limit the geographic scope of competition.

47. *Views of customers and competitors.* Where appropriate, the Commission will contact the main customers and competitors of the parties in its enquiries, to gather their views on the boundaries of the geographic market as well as most of the factual information it requires to reach a conclusion on the scope of the market when they are sufficiently backed by factual evidence.

48. *Current geographic pattern of purchases.* An examination of the customers' current geographic pattern of purchases provides useful evidence as to the possible scope of the geographic market. When customers purchase from companies located anywhere in the Community or the EEA on similar terms, or they procure their supplies through effective tendering procedures in which companies from anywhere in the Community or the EEA submit bids, usually the geographic market will be considered to be Community-wide.

49. *Trade flows/pattern of shipments.* When the number of customers is so large that it is not possible to obtain through them a clear picture of geographic purchasing patterns, information on trade flows might be used alternatively, provided that the trade statistics are available with a sufficient degree of detail for the relevant products. Trade flows, and above all, the rationale behind trade flows provide useful insights and information for the purpose of establishing the scope of the geographic market but are not in themselves conclusive.

50. *Barriers and switching costs associated to divert orders to companies located in other areas.* The absence of trans-border purchases or trade flows, for instance, does not necessarily mean that the market is at most national in scope. Still, barriers isolating the national market have to be identified before it is concluded that the relevant geographic market in such a case is national. Perhaps the clearest obstacle for a customer to divert its orders to other areas is the impact of transport costs and transport restrictions arising from legislation or from the nature of the relevant products. The impact of transport costs will usually limit the scope of the geographic market for bulky, low-value products, bearing in mind that a transport disadvantage might also be compensated by a comparative advantage in other costs (labour costs or raw materials). Access to distribution in a given area, regulatory barriers still existing in certain sectors, quotas and custom tariffs might also constitute barriers isolating a geographic area from the competitive pressure of companies located outside that area. Significant switching costs in procuring supplies from companies located in other countries constitute additional sources of such barriers.

51. On the basis of the evidence gathered, the Commission will then define a geographic market that could range from a local dimension to a global one, and there are examples of both local and global markets in past decisions of the Commission.

52. The paragraphs above describe the different factors which might be relevant to define markets. This does not imply that in each individual case it will be necessary to obtain evidence and assess each of these factors. Often in practice the evidence provided by a subset of these factors will be sufficient to reach a conclusion, as shown in the past decisional practice of the Commission.

NOTES

5 Own-price elasticity of demand for product X is a measure of the responsiveness of demand for X to percentage change in its own price. Cross-price elasticity between products X and Y is the responsiveness of demand for product X to percentage change in the price of product Y.

IV. CALCULATION OF MARKET SHARE

[4.18]

53. The definition of the relevant market in both its product and geographic dimensions allows the identification of the suppliers and the customers/consumers active on that market. On that basis, a total market size and market shares for each supplier can be calculated on the basis of their sales of the relevant products in the relevant area. In practice, the total market size and market shares are often available from market sources, ie companies' estimates, studies commissioned from industry consultants and/or trade associations. When this is not the case, or when available estimates are not reliable, the Commission will usually ask each supplier in the relevant market to provide its own sales in order to calculate total market size and market shares.

54. If sales are usually the reference to calculate market shares, there are nevertheless other indications that, depending on the specific products or industry in question, can offer useful information such as, in particular, capacity, the number of players in bidding markets, units of fleet as in aerospace, or the reserves held in the case of sectors such as mining.

55. As a rule of thumb, both volume sales and value sales provide useful information. In cases of differentiated products, sales in value and their associated market share will usually be considered to better reflect the relative position and strength of each supplier.

V. ADDITIONAL CONSIDERATIONS

[4.19]

56. There are certain areas where the application of the principles above has to be undertaken with care. This is the case when considering primary and secondary markets, in particular, when the behaviour of undertakings at a point in time has to be analysed pursuant to Article 86. The method of defining markets in these cases is the same, ie assessing the responses of customers based on their purchasing decisions to relative price changes, but taking into account as

well, constraints on substitution imposed by conditions in the connected markets. A narrow definition of market for secondary products, for instance, spare parts, may result when compatibility with the primary product is important. Problems of finding compatible secondary products together with the existence of high prices and a long lifetime of the primary products may render relative price increases of secondary products profitable. A different market definition may result if significant substitution between secondary products is possible or if the characteristics of the primary products make quick and direct consumer responses to relative price increases of the secondary products feasible.

57. In certain cases, the existence of chains of substitution might lead to the definition of a relevant market where products or areas at the extreme of the market are not directly substitutable. An example might be provided by the geographic dimension of a product with significant transport costs. In such cases, deliveries from a given plant are limited to a certain area around each plant by the impact of transport costs. In principle, such an area could constitute the relevant geographic market. However, if the distribution of plants is such that there are considerable overlaps between the areas around different plants, it is possible that the pricing of those products will be constrained by a chain substitution effect, and lead to the definition of a broader geographic market. The same reasoning may apply if product B is a demand substitute for products A and C. Even if products A and C are not direct demand substitutes, they might be found to be in the same relevant product market since their respective pricing might be constrained by substitution to B.

58. From a practical perspective, the concept of chains of substitution has to be corroborated by actual evidence, for instance related to price interdependence at the extremes of the chains of substitution, in order to lead to an extension of the relevant market in an individual case. Price levels at the extremes of the chains would have to be of the same magnitude as well.

EUROPEAN PARLIAMENT AND COUNCIL REGULATION

(1049/2001/EC)

of 30 May 2001

regarding public access to European Parliament, Council and Commission documents

[4.20]

NOTES

Date of publication in OJ: OJ L145, 31.5.2001, p 43.

Repeal of this Regulation in relation to the UK: this Regulation is repealed, in relation to the UK, by the European Institutions and Consular Protection (Amendment etc) (EU Exit) Regulations 2018, SI 2018/1391, reg 12, Schedule, as from IP completion day (as defined in the European Union (Withdrawal Agreement) Act 2020, s 39).

Note: with effect from 1 December 2009, the EC Treaty was replaced by the Treaty on the Functioning of the European Union. References in this document to provisions of the EC Treaty should be construed accordingly.

THE EUROPEAN PARLIAMENT AND THE COUNCIL OF THE EUROPEAN UNION,

Having regard to the Treaty establishing the European Community, and in particular Article 255(2) thereof,

Having regard to the proposal from the Commission[1],

Acting in accordance with the procedure referred to in Article 251 of the Treaty[2],

Whereas:

(1) The second subparagraph of Article 1 of the Treaty on European Union enshrines the concept of openness, stating that the Treaty marks a new stage in the process of creating an ever closer union among the peoples of Europe, in which decisions are taken as openly as possible and as closely as possible to the citizen.

(2) Openness enables citizens to participate more closely in the decision-making process and guarantees that the administration enjoys greater legitimacy and is more effective and more accountable to the citizen in a democratic system. Openness contributes to strengthening the principles of democracy and respect for fundamental rights as laid down in Article 6 of the EU Treaty and in the Charter of Fundamental Rights of the European Union.

(3) The conclusions of the European Council meetings held at Birmingham, Edinburgh and Copenhagen stressed the need to introduce greater transparency into the work of the Union institutions. This Regulation consolidates the initiatives that the institutions have already taken with a view to improving the transparency of the decisionmaking process.

(4) The purpose of this Regulation is to give the fullest possible effect to the right of public access to documents and to lay down the general principles and limits on such access in accordance with Article 255(2) of the EC Treaty.

(5) Since the question of access to documents is not covered by provisions of the Treaty establishing the European Coal and Steel Community and the Treaty establishing the European Atomic Energy Community, the European Parliament, the Council and the Commission should, in accordance with Declaration No 41 attached to the Final Act of the Treaty of Amsterdam, draw guidance from this Regulation as regards documents concerning the activities covered by those two Treaties.

(6) Wider access should be granted to documents in cases where the institutions are acting in their legislative capacity, including under delegated powers, while at the same time preserving the effectiveness of the institutions' decision-making process. Such documents should be made directly accessible to the greatest possible extent.

(7) In accordance with Articles 28(1) and 41(1) of the EU Treaty, the right of access also applies to documents

relating to the common foreign and security policy and to police and judicial cooperation in criminal matters. Each institution should respect its security rules.

(8) In order to ensure the full application of this Regulation to all activities of the Union, all agencies established by the institutions should apply the principles laid down in this Regulation.

(9) On account of their highly sensitive content, certain documents should be given special treatment. Arrangements for informing the European Parliament of the content of such documents should be made through interinstitutional agreement.

(10) In order to bring about greater openness in the work of the institutions, access to documents should be granted by the European Parliament, the Council and the Commission not only to documents drawn up by the institutions, but also to documents received by them. In this context, it is recalled that Declaration No 35 attached to the Final Act of the Treaty of Amsterdam provides that a Member State may request the Commission or the Council not to communicate to third parties a document originating from that State without its prior agreement.

(11) In principle, all documents of the institutions should be accessible to the public. However, certain public and private interests should be protected by way of exceptions. The institutions should be entitled to protect their internal consultations and deliberations where necessary to safeguard their ability to carry out their tasks. In assessing the exceptions, the institutions should take account of the principles in Community legislation concerning the protection of personal data, in all areas of Union activities.

(12) All rules concerning access to documents of the institutions should be in conformity with this Regulation.

(13) In order to ensure that the right of access is fully respected, a two-stage administrative procedure should apply, with the additional possibility of court proceedings or complaints to the Ombudsman.

(14) Each institution should take the measures necessary to inform the public of the new provisions in force and to train its staff to assist citizens exercising their rights under this Regulation. In order to make it easier for citizens to exercise their rights, each institution should provide access to a register of documents.

(15) Even though it is neither the object nor the effect of this Regulation to amend national legislation on access to documents, it is nevertheless clear that, by virtue of the principle of loyal cooperation which governs relations between the institutions and the Member States, Member States should take care not to hamper the proper application of this Regulation and should respect the security rules of the institutions.

(16) This Regulation is without prejudice to existing rights of access to documents for Member States, judicial authorities or investigative bodies.

(17) In accordance with Article 255(3) of the EC Treaty, each institution lays down specific provisions regarding access to its documents in its rules of procedure. Council Decision 93/731/EC of 20 December 1993 on public access to Council documents[3], Commission Decision 94/90/ECSC, EC, Euratom of 8 February 1994 on public access to Commission documents[4], European Parliament Decision 97/632/EC, ECSC, Euratom of 10 July 1997 on public access to European Parliament documents[5], and the rules on confidentiality of Schengen documents should therefore, if necessary, be modified or be repealed,

NOTES

Repeal of this Regulation in relation to the UK: this Regulation is repealed in relation to the UK (as from IP completion day); see the introductory notes to this Regulation *ante*.

1 OJ C177 E, 27.6.2000, p 70.

2 Opinion of the European Parliament of 3 May 2001 (not yet published in the Official Journal) and Council Decision of 28 May 2001.

3 OJ L340, 31.12.1993, p 43. Decision as last amended by Decision 2000/527/EC (OJ L212, 23.8.2000, p 9).

4 OJ L46, 18.2.1994, p 58. Decision as amended by Decision 96/ 567/EC, ECSC, Euratom (OJ L247, 28.9.1996, p 45).

5 OJ L263, 25.9.1997, p 27.

HAVE ADOPTED THIS REGULATION:

[4.21]

Article 1 Purpose

The purpose of this Regulation is:

(a) to define the principles, conditions and limits on grounds of public or private interest governing the right of access to European Parliament, Council and Commission (hereinafter referred to as 'the institutions') documents provided for in Article 255 of the EC Treaty in such a way as to ensure the widest possible access to documents,

(b) to establish rules ensuring the easiest possible exercise of this right, and

(c) to promote good administrative practice on access to documents.

NOTES

Repeal of this Regulation in relation to the UK: this Regulation is repealed in relation to the UK (as from IP completion day); see the introductory notes to this Regulation *ante*.

[4.22]

Article 2 Beneficiaries and scope

1. Any citizen of the Union, and any natural or legal person residing or having its registered office in a Member State, has a right of access to documents of the institutions, subject to the principles, conditions and limits defined in this Regulation.

2. The institutions may, subject to the same principles, conditions and limits, grant access to documents to any natural or legal person not residing or not having its registered office in a Member State.

3. This Regulation shall apply to all documents held by an institution, that is to say, documents drawn up or received by it and in its possession, in all areas of activity of the European Union.

4. Without prejudice to Articles 4 and 9, documents shall be made accessible to the public either following a written application or directly in electronic form or through a register. In particular, documents drawn up or received in the course of a legislative procedure shall be made directly accessible in accordance with Article 12.

5. Sensitive documents as defined in Article 9(1) shall be subject to special treatment in accordance with that Article.

6. This Regulation shall be without prejudice to rights of public access to documents held by the institutions which might follow from instruments of international law or acts of the institutions implementing them.

NOTES

Repeal of this Regulation in relation to the UK: this Regulation is repealed in relation to the UK (as from IP completion day); see the introductory notes to this Regulation *ante*.

[4.23]

Article 3 Definitions

For the purpose of this Regulation:

(a) 'document' shall mean any content whatever its medium (written on paper or stored in electronic form or as a sound, visual or audiovisual recording) concerning a matter relating to the policies, activities and decisions falling within the institution's sphere of responsibility;

(b) 'third party' shall mean any natural or legal person, or any entity outside the institution concerned, including the Member States, other Community or non-Community institutions and bodies and third countries.

NOTES

Repeal of this Regulation in relation to the UK: this Regulation is repealed in relation to the UK (as from IP completion day); see the introductory notes to this Regulation *ante*.

[4.24]

Article 4 Exceptions

1. The institutions shall refuse access to a document where disclosure would undermine the protection of:

(a) the public interest as regards:

- *public security,*
- *defence and military matters,*
- *international relations,*
- *the financial, monetary or economic policy of the Community or a Member State;*

(b) privacy and the integrity of the individual, in particular in accordance with Community legislation regarding the protection of personal data.

2. The institutions shall refuse access to a document where disclosure would undermine the protection of:

- *commercial interests of a natural or legal person, including intellectual property,*
- *court proceedings and legal advice,*
- *the purpose of inspections, investigations and audits,*

unless there is an overriding public interest in disclosure.

3. Access to a document, drawn up by an institution for internal use or received by an institution, which relates to a matter where the decision has not been taken by the institution, shall be refused if disclosure of the document would seriously undermine the institution's decision-making process, unless there is an overriding public interest in disclosure.

Access to a document containing opinions for internal use as part of deliberations and preliminary consultations within the institution concerned shall be refused even after the decision has been taken if disclosure of the document would seriously undermine the institution's decision-making process, unless there is an overriding public interest in disclosure.

4. As regards third-party documents, the institution shall consult the third party with a view to assessing whether an exception in paragraph 1 or 2 is applicable, unless it is clear that the document shall or shall not be disclosed.

5. A Member State may request the institution not to disclose a document originating from that Member State without its prior agreement.

6. If only parts of the requested document are covered by any of the exceptions, the remaining parts of the document shall be released.

7. The exceptions as laid down in paragraphs 1 to 3 shall only apply for the period during which protection is justified on the basis of the content of the document. The exceptions may apply for a maximum period of 30 years. In the case of documents covered by the exceptions relating to privacy or commercial interests and in the case of sensitive documents, the exceptions may, if necessary, continue to apply after this period.

NOTES

Repeal of this Regulation in relation to the UK: this Regulation is repealed in relation to the UK (as from IP completion day); see the introductory notes to this Regulation *ante*.

[4.25]

Article 5 Documents in the Member States

Where a Member State receives a request for a document in its possession, originating from an institution, unless it is clear that the document shall or shall not be disclosed, the Member State shall consult with the institution concerned in order to take a decision that does not jeopardise the attainment of the objectives of this Regulation. The Member State may instead refer the request to the institution.

NOTES

Repeal of this Regulation in relation to the UK: this Regulation is repealed in relation to the UK (as from IP completion day); see the introductory notes to this Regulation *ante*.

[4.26]
Article 6 Applications

1. Applications for access to a document shall be made in any written form, including electronic form, in one of the languages referred to in Article 314 of the EC Treaty and in a sufficiently precise manner to enable the institution to identify the document. The applicant is not obliged to state reasons for the application.

2. If an application is not sufficiently precise, the institution shall ask the applicant to clarify the application and shall assist the applicant in doing so, for example, by providing information on the use of the public registers of documents.

3. In the event of an application relating to a very long document or to a very large number of documents, the institution concerned may confer with the applicant informally, with a view to finding a fair solution.

4. The institutions shall provide information and assistance to citizens on how and where applications for access to documents can be made.

NOTES

Repeal of this Regulation in relation to the UK: this Regulation is repealed in relation to the UK (as from IP completion day); see the introductory notes to this Regulation *ante*.

[4.27]
Article 7 Processing of initial applications

1. An application for access to a document shall be handled promptly. An acknowledgement of receipt shall be sent to the applicant. Within 15 working days from registration of the application, the institution shall either grant access to the document requested and provide access in accordance with Article 10 within that period or, in a written reply, state the reasons for the total or partial refusal and inform the applicant of his or her right to make a confirmatory application in accordance with paragraph 2 of this Article.

2. In the event of a total or partial refusal, the applicant may, within 15 working days of receiving the institution's reply, make a confirmatory application asking the institution to reconsider its position.

3. In exceptional cases, for example in the event of an application relating to a very long document or to a very large number of documents, the time-limit provided for in paragraph 1 may be extended by 15 working days, provided that the applicant is notified in advance and that detailed reasons are given.

4. Failure by the institution to reply within the prescribed time-limit shall entitle the applicant to make a confirmatory application.

NOTES

Repeal of this Regulation in relation to the UK: this Regulation is repealed in relation to the UK (as from IP completion day); see the introductory notes to this Regulation *ante*.

[4.28]
Article 8 Processing of confirmatory applications

1. A confirmatory application shall be handled promptly. Within 15 working days from registration of such an application, the institution shall either grant access to the document requested and provide access in accordance with Article 10 within that period or, in a written reply, state the reasons for the total or partial refusal. In the event of a total or partial refusal, the institution shall inform the applicant of the remedies open to him or her, namely instituting court proceedings against the institution and/or making a complaint to the Ombudsman, under the conditions laid down in Articles 230 and 195 of the EC Treaty, respectively.

2. In exceptional cases, for example in the event of an application relating to a very long document or to a very large number of documents, the time limit provided for in paragraph 1 may be extended by 15 working days, provided that the applicant is notified in advance and that detailed reasons are given.

3. Failure by the institution to reply within the prescribed time limit shall be considered as a negative reply and entitle the applicant to institute court proceedings against the institution and/or make a complaint to the Ombudsman, under the relevant provisions of the EC Treaty.

NOTES

Repeal of this Regulation in relation to the UK: this Regulation is repealed in relation to the UK (as from IP completion day); see the introductory notes to this Regulation *ante*.

[4.29]
Article 9 Treatment of sensitive documents

1. Sensitive documents are documents originating from the institutions or the agencies established by them, from Member States, third countries or International Organisations, classified as 'TRÈS SECRET/TOP SECRET', 'SECRET' or 'CONFIDENTIEL' in accordance with the rules of the institution concerned, which protect essential interests of the European Union or of one or more of its Member States in the areas covered by Article 4(1)(a), notably public security, defence and military matters.

2. Applications for access to sensitive documents under the procedures laid down in Articles 7 and 8 shall be handled only by those persons who have a right to acquaint themselves with those documents. These persons shall also, without prejudice to Article 11(2), assess which references to sensitive documents could be made in the public register.

3. Sensitive documents shall be recorded in the register or released only with the consent of the originator.

4. An institution which decides to refuse access to a sensitive document shall give the reasons for its decision in a manner which does not harm the interests protected in Article 4.

5. Member States shall take appropriate measures to ensure that when handling applications for sensitive documents the principles in this Article and Article 4 are respected.

6. The rules of the institutions concerning sensitive documents shall be made public.

7. The Commission and the Council shall inform the European Parliament regarding sensitive documents in accordance with arrangements agreed between the institutions.

NOTES

Repeal of this Regulation in relation to the UK: this Regulation is repealed in relation to the UK (as from IP completion day); see the introductory notes to this Regulation *ante*.

[4.30]

Article 10 Access following an application

1. The applicant shall have access to documents either by consulting them on the spot or by receiving a copy, including, where available, an electronic copy, according to the applicant's preference. The cost of producing and sending copies may be charged to the applicant. This charge shall not exceed the real cost of producing and sending the copies. Consultation on the spot, copies of less than 20 A4 pages and direct access in electronic form or through the register shall be free of charge.

2. If a document has already been released by the institution concerned and is easily accessible to the applicant, the institution may fulfil its obligation of granting access to documents by informing the applicant how to obtain the requested document.

3. Documents shall be supplied in an existing version and format (including electronically or in an alternative format such as Braille, large print or tape) with full regard to the applicant's preference.

NOTES

Repeal of this Regulation in relation to the UK: this Regulation is repealed in relation to the UK (as from IP completion day); see the introductory notes to this Regulation *ante*.

[4.31]

Article 11 Registers

1. To make citizens' rights under this Regulation effective, each institution shall provide public access to a register of documents. Access to the register should be provided in electronic form. References to documents shall be recorded in the register without delay.

2. For each document the register shall contain a reference number (including, where applicable, the interinstitutional reference), the subject matter and/or a short description of the content of the document and the date on which it was received or drawn up and recorded in the register. References shall be made in a manner which does not undermine protection of the interests in Article 4.

3. The institutions shall immediately take the measures necessary to establish a register which shall be operational by 3 June 2002.

NOTES

Repeal of this Regulation in relation to the UK: this Regulation is repealed in relation to the UK (as from IP completion day); see the introductory notes to this Regulation *ante*.

[4.32]

Article 12 Direct access in electronic form or through a register

1. The institutions shall as far as possible make documents directly accessible to the public in electronic form or through a register in accordance with the rules of the institution concerned.

2. In particular, legislative documents, that is to say, documents drawn up or received in the course of procedures for the adoption of acts which are legally binding in or for the Member States, should, subject to Articles 4 and 9, be made directly accessible.

3. Where possible, other documents, notably documents relating to the development of policy or strategy, should be made directly accessible.

4. Where direct access is not given through the register, the register shall as far as possible indicate where the document is located.

NOTES

Repeal of this Regulation in relation to the UK: this Regulation is repealed in relation to the UK (as from IP completion day); see the introductory notes to this Regulation *ante*.

[4.33]

Article 13 Publication in the Official Journal

1. In addition to the acts referred to in Article 254(1) and (2) of the EC Treaty and the first paragraph of Article 163 of the Euratom Treaty, the following documents shall, subject to Articles 4 and 9 of this Regulation, be published in the Official Journal:

- *(a) Commission proposals;*
- *(b) common positions adopted by the Council in accordance with the procedures referred to in Articles 251 and 252 of the EC Treaty and the reasons underlying those common positions, as well as the European Parliament's positions in these procedures;*
- *(c) framework decisions and decisions referred to in Article 34(2) of the EU Treaty;*
- *(d) conventions established by the Council in accordance with Article 34(2) of the EU Treaty;*
- *(e) conventions signed between Member States on the basis of Article 293 of the EC Treaty;*
- *(f) international agreements concluded by the Community or in accordance with Article 24 of the EU Treaty.*

2. As far as possible, the following documents shall be published in the Official Journal:

- *(a) initiatives presented to the Council by a Member State pursuant to Article 67(1) of the EC Treaty or pursuant to Article 34(2) of the EU Treaty;*
- *(b) common positions referred to in Article 34(2) of the EU Treaty;*
- *(c) directives other than those referred to in Article 254(1) and (2) of the EC Treaty, decisions other than those referred to in Article 254(1) of the EC Treaty, recommendations and opinions.*

3. Each institution may in its rules of procedure establish which further documents shall be published in the Official Journal.

NOTES

Repeal of this Regulation in relation to the UK: this Regulation is repealed in relation to the UK (as from IP completion day); see the introductory notes to this Regulation *ante*.

[4.34]

Article 14 Information

1. Each institution shall take the requisite measures to inform the public of the rights they enjoy under this Regulation.

2. The Member States shall cooperate with the institutions in providing information to the citizens.

NOTES

Repeal of this Regulation in relation to the UK: this Regulation is repealed in relation to the UK (as from IP completion day); see the introductory notes to this Regulation *ante*.

[4.35]

Article 15 Administrative practice in the institutions

1. The institutions shall develop good administrative practices in order to facilitate the exercise of the right of access guaranteed by this Regulation.

2. The institutions shall establish an interinstitutional committee to examine best practice, address possible conflicts and discuss future developments on public access to documents.

NOTES

Repeal of this Regulation in relation to the UK: this Regulation is repealed in relation to the UK (as from IP completion day); see the introductory notes to this Regulation *ante*.

[4.36]

Article 16 Reproduction of documents

This Regulation shall be without prejudice to any existing rules on copyright which may limit a third party's right to reproduce or exploit released documents.

NOTES

Repeal of this Regulation in relation to the UK: this Regulation is repealed in relation to the UK (as from IP completion day); see the introductory notes to this Regulation *ante*.

[4.37]

Article 17 Reports

1. Each institution shall publish annually a report for the preceding year including the number of cases in which the institution refused to grant access to documents, the reasons for such refusals and the number of sensitive documents not recorded in the register.

2. At the latest by 31 January 2004, the Commission shall publish a report on the implementation of the principles of this Regulation and shall make recommendations, including, if appropriate, proposals for the revision of this Regulation and an action programme of measures to be taken by the institutions.

NOTES

Repeal of this Regulation in relation to the UK: this Regulation is repealed in relation to the UK (as from IP completion day); see the introductory notes to this Regulation *ante*.

[4.38]

Article 18 Application measures

1. Each institution shall adapt its rules of procedure to the provisions of this Regulation. The adaptations shall take effect from 3 December 2001.

2. Within six months of the entry into force of this Regulation, the Commission shall examine the conformity of Council Regulation (EEC, Euratom) No 354/83 of 1 February 1983 concerning the opening to the public of the historical archives of the European Economic Community and the European Atomic Energy Community[1] with this Regulation in order to ensure the preservation and archiving of documents to the fullest extent possible.

3. Within six months of the entry into force of this Regulation, the Commission shall examine the conformity of the existing rules on access to documents with this Regulation.

NOTES

Repeal of this Regulation in relation to the UK: this Regulation is repealed in relation to the UK (as from IP completion day); see the introductory notes to this Regulation *ante*.

[1] OJ L43, 15.2.1983, p 1.

[4.39]

Article 19 Entry into force

This Regulation shall enter into force on the third day following that of its publication in the Official Journal of the European Communities.

It shall be applicable from 3 December 2001.

NOTES

Repeal of this Regulation in relation to the UK: this Regulation is repealed in relation to the UK (as from IP completion day); see the introductory notes to this Regulation *ante*.

COUNCIL REGULATION

(1/2003/EC)

of 16 December 2002

on the implementation of the rules on competition laid down in Articles 81 and 82 of the Treaty

(Text with EEA relevance)

[4.40]

NOTES

Date of publication in OJ: OJ L1, 4.1.2003, p 1.

Repeal of this Regulation in relation to the UK: this Regulation is repealed, in relation to the UK, by the Competition (Amendment etc) (EU Exit) Regulations 2019, SI 2019/93, reg 63, Sch 3, para 1, as from IP completion day (as defined in the European Union (Withdrawal Agreement) Act 2020, s 39) (for transitional provisions and savings in relation to the operation of the 2019 Regulations, see Sch 4 to those Regulations at **[7.69]** et seq).

Note: with effect from 1 December 2009, the EC Treaty was replaced by the Treaty on the Functioning of the European Union. References in this document to provisions of the EC Treaty should be construed accordingly. As to Articles 81 and 82 of the EC Treaty, see now Articles 101 and 102 of the Treaty on the Functioning of the European Union.

THE COUNCIL OF THE EUROPEAN UNION,

Having regard to the Treaty establishing the European Community, and in particular Article 83 thereof,

Having regard to the proposal from the Commission,[1] Having regard to the opinion of the European Parliament,[2]

Having regard to the opinion of the European Economic and Social Committee,[3]

Whereas—

(1) In order to establish a system which ensures that competition in the common market is not distorted, Articles 81 and 82 of the Treaty must be applied effectively and uniformly in the Community. Council Regulation No 17 of 6 February 1962, First Regulation implementing Articles 81 and 82[4] of the Treaty,[5] has allowed a Community competition policy to develop that has helped to disseminate a competition culture within the Community. In the light of experience, however, that Regulation should now be replaced by legislation designed to meet the challenges of an integrated market and a future enlargement of the Community.

(2) In particular, there is a need to rethink the arrangements for applying the exception from the prohibition on agreements, which restrict competition, laid down in Article 81(3) of the Treaty. Under Article 83(2)(b) of the Treaty, account must be taken in this regard of the need to ensure effective supervision, on the one hand, and to simplify administration to the greatest possible extent, on the other.

(3) The centralised scheme set up by Regulation No 17 no longer secures a balance between those two objectives. It hampers application of the Community competition rules by the courts and competition authorities of the Member States, and the system of notification it involves prevents the Commission from concentrating its resources on curbing the most serious infringements. It also imposes considerable costs on undertakings.

(4) The present system should therefore be replaced by a directly applicable exception system in which the competition authorities and courts of the Member States have the power to apply not only Article 81(1) and Article 82 of the Treaty, which have direct applicability by virtue of the case-law of the Court of Justice of the European Communities, but also Article 81(3) of the Treaty.

(5) In order to ensure an effective enforcement of the Community competition rules and at the same time the respect of fundamental rights of defence, this Regulation should regulate the burden of proof under Articles 81 and 82 of the Treaty. It should be for the party or the authority alleging an infringement of Article 81(1) and Article 82 of the Treaty to prove the existence thereof to the required legal standard. It should be for the undertaking or association of undertakings invoking the benefit of a defence against a finding of an infringement to demonstrate to the required legal standard that the conditions for applying such defence are satisfied. This Regulation affects neither national rules on the standard of proof nor obligations of competition authorities and courts of the Member States to ascertain the relevant facts of a case, provided that such rules and obligations are compatible with general principles of Community law.

(6) In order to ensure that the Community competition rules are applied effectively, the competition authorities of the Member States should be associated more closely with their application. To this end, they should be empowered to apply Community law.

(7) National courts have an essential part to play in applying the Community competition rules. When deciding disputes between private individuals, they protect the subjective rights under Community law, for example by awarding damages to the victims of infringements. The role of the national courts here complements that of the competition authorities of the Member States. They should therefore be allowed to apply Articles 81 and 82 of the Treaty in full.

(8) In order to ensure the effective enforcement of the Community competition rules and the proper functioning of the co-operation mechanisms contained in this Regulation, it is necessary to oblige the competition authorities and courts of the Member States to also apply Articles 81 and 82 of the Treaty where they apply national competition law to agreements and practices which may affect trade between Member States. In order to create a level playing field for agreements, decisions by associations of undertakings and concerted practices within the internal market, it is also necessary to determine pursuant to Article 83(2)(e) of the Treaty the relationship between national laws and Community competition law. To that effect it is necessary to provide that the application of national competition laws to agreements, decisions or concerted practices within the meaning of Article 81(1) of the Treaty may not lead to the prohibition of such agreements, decisions and concerted practices if they are not also prohibited under Community

competition law. The notions of agreements, decisions and concerted practices are autonomous concepts of Community competition law covering the coordination of behaviour of undertakings on the market as interpreted by the Community Courts. Member States should not under this Regulation be precluded from adopting and applying on their territory stricter national competition laws which prohibit or impose sanctions on unilateral conduct engaged in by undertakings. These stricter national laws may include provisions which prohibit or impose sanctions on abusive behaviour toward economically dependent undertakings. Furthermore, this Regulation does not apply to national laws which impose criminal sanctions on natural persons except to the extent that such sanctions are the means whereby competition rules applying to undertakings are enforced.

(9) Articles 81 and 82 of the Treaty have as their objective the protection of competition on the market. This Regulation, which is adopted for the implementation of these Treaty provisions, does not preclude Member States from implementing on their territory national legislation, which protects other legitimate interests provided that such legislation is compatible with general principles and other provisions of Community law. In so far as such national legislation pursues predominantly an objective different from that of protecting competition on the market, the competition authorities and courts of the Member States may apply such legislation on their territory. Accordingly, Member States may under this Regulation implement on their territory national legislation that prohibits or imposes sanctions on acts of unfair trading practice, be they unilateral or contractual. Such legislation pursues a specific objective, irrespective of the actual or presumed effects of such acts on competition on the market. This is particularly the case of legislation which prohibits undertakings from imposing on their trading partners, obtaining or attempting to obtain from them terms and conditions that are unjustified, disproportionate or without consideration.

(10) Regulations such as 19/65/EEC,[6] (EEC) No 2821/71,[7] (EEC) No 3976/87,[8] (EEC) No 1534/91,[9] or (EEC) No 479/92[10] empower the Commission to apply Article 81(3) of the Treaty by Regulation to certain categories of agreements, decisions by associations of undertakings and concerted practices. In the areas defined by such Regulations, the Commission has adopted and may continue to adopt so called "block" exemption Regulations by which it declares Article 81(1) of the Treaty inapplicable to categories of agreements, decisions and concerted practices. Where agreements, decisions and concerted practices to which such Regulations apply nonetheless have effects that are incompatible with Article 81(3) of the Treaty, the Commission and the competition authorities of the Member States should have the power to withdraw in a particular case the benefit of the block exemption Regulation.

(11) For it to ensure that the provisions of the Treaty are applied, the Commission should be able to address decisions to undertakings or associations of undertakings for the purpose of bringing to an end infringements of Articles 81 and 82 of the Treaty. Provided there is a legitimate interest in doing so, the Commission should also be able to adopt decisions which find that an infringement has been committed in the past even if it does not impose a fine. This Regulation should also make explicit provision for the Commission's power to adopt decisions ordering interim measures, which has been acknowledged by the Court of Justice.

(12) This Regulation should make explicit provision for the Commission's power to impose any remedy, whether behavioural or structural, which is necessary to bring the infringement effectively to an end, having regard to the principle of proportionality. Structural remedies should only be imposed either where there is no equally effective behavioural remedy or where any equally effective behavioural remedy would be more burdensome for the undertaking concerned than the structural remedy. Changes to the structure of an undertaking as it existed before the infringement was committed would only be proportionate where there is a substantial risk of a lasting or repeated infringement that derives from the very structure of the undertaking.

(13) Where, in the course of proceedings which might lead to an agreement or practice being prohibited, undertakings offer the Commission commitments such as to meet its concerns, the Commission should be able to adopt decisions which make those commitments binding on the undertakings concerned. Commitment decisions should find that there are no longer grounds for action by the Commission without concluding whether or not there has been or still is an infringement. Commitment decisions are without prejudice to the powers of competition authorities and courts of the Member States to make such a finding and decide upon the case. Commitment decisions are not appropriate in cases where the Commission intends to impose a fine.

(14) In exceptional cases where the public interest of the Community so requires, it may also be expedient for the Commission to adopt a decision of a declaratory nature finding that the prohibition in Article 81 or Article 82 of the Treaty does not apply, with a view to clarifying the law and ensuring its consistent application throughout the Community, in particular with regard to new types of agreements or practices that have not been settled in the existing case-law and administrative practice.

(15) The Commission and the competition authorities of the Member States should form together a network of public authorities applying the Community competition rules in close co-operation. For that purpose it is necessary to set up arrangements for information and consultation. Further modalities for the co-operation within the network will be laid down and revised by the Commission, in close co-operation with the Member States.

(16) Notwithstanding any national provision to the contrary, the exchange of information and the use of such information in evidence should be allowed between the members of the network even where the information is confidential. This information may be used for the application of Articles 81 and 82 of the Treaty as well as for the parallel application of national competition law, provided that the latter application relates to the same case and does not lead to a different outcome. When the information exchanged is used by the receiving authority to impose sanctions on undertakings, there should be no other limit to the use of the information than the obligation to use it for the purpose for which it was collected given the fact that the sanctions imposed on undertakings are of the same type in all systems. The rights of defence enjoyed by undertakings in the various systems can be considered as sufficiently equivalent. However, as regards natural persons, they may be subject to substantially different types of sanctions across the various systems. Where that is the case, it is necessary to ensure that information can only be used if it has been collected in a way which respects the same level of protection of the rights of defence of natural persons as provided for under the national rules of the receiving authority.

(17) If the competition rules are to be applied consistently and, at the same time, the network is to be managed in the best possible way, it is essential to retain the rule that the competition authorities of the Member States are automatically relieved of their competence if the Commission initiates its own proceedings. Where a competition

authority of a Member State is already acting on a case and the Commission intends to initiate proceedings, it should endeavour to do so as soon as possible. Before initiating proceedings, the Commission should consult the national authority concerned.

(18) To ensure that cases are dealt with by the most appropriate authorities within the network, a general provision should be laid down allowing a competition authority to suspend or close a case on the ground that another authority is dealing with it or has already dealt with it, the objective being that each case should be handled by a single authority. This provision should not prevent the Commission from rejecting a complaint for lack of Community interest, as the case-law of the Court of Justice has acknowledged it may do, even if no other competition authority has indicated its intention of dealing with the case.

(19) The Advisory Committee on Restrictive Practices and Dominant Positions set up by Regulation No 17 has functioned in a very satisfactory manner. It will fit well into the new system of decentralised application. It is necessary, therefore, to build upon the rules laid down by Regulation No 17, while improving the effectiveness of the organisational arrangements. To this end, it would be expedient to allow opinions to be delivered by written procedure. The Advisory Committee should also be able to act as a forum for discussing cases that are being handled by the competition authorities of the Member States, so as to help safeguard the consistent application of the Community competition rules.

(20) The Advisory Committee should be composed of representatives of the competition authorities of the Member States. For meetings in which general issues are being discussed, Member States should be able to appoint an additional representative. This is without prejudice to members of the Committee being assisted by other experts from the Member States.

(21) Consistency in the application of the competition rules also requires that arrangements be established for co-operation between the courts of the Member States and the Commission. This is relevant for all courts of the Member States that apply Articles 81 and 82 of the Treaty, whether applying these rules in lawsuits between private parties, acting as public enforcers or as review courts. In particular, national courts should be able to ask the Commission for information or for its opinion on points concerning the application of Community competition law. The Commission and the competition authorities of the Member States should also be able to submit written or oral observations to courts called upon to apply Article 81 or Article 82 of the Treaty. These observations should be submitted within the framework of national procedural rules and practices including those safeguarding the rights of the parties. Steps should therefore be taken to ensure that the Commission and the competition authorities of the Member States are kept sufficiently well informed of proceedings before national courts.

(22) In order to ensure compliance with the principles of legal certainty and the uniform application of the Community competition rules in a system of parallel powers, conflicting decisions must be avoided. It is therefore necessary to clarify, in accordance with the case-law of the Court of Justice, the effects of Commission decisions and proceedings on courts and competition authorities of the Member States. Commitment decisions adopted by the Commission do not affect the power of the courts and the competition authorities of the Member States to apply Articles 81 and 82 of the Treaty.

(23) The Commission should be empowered throughout the Community to require such information to be supplied as is necessary to detect any agreement, decision or concerted practice prohibited by Article 81 of the Treaty or any abuse of a dominant position prohibited by Article 82 of the Treaty. When complying with a decision of the Commission, undertakings cannot be forced to admit that they have committed an infringement, but they are in any event obliged to answer factual questions and to provide documents, even if this information may be used to establish against them or against another undertaking the existence of an infringement.

(24) The Commission should also be empowered to undertake such inspections as are necessary to detect any agreement, decision or concerted practice prohibited by Article 81 of the Treaty or any abuse of a dominant position prohibited by Article 82 of the Treaty. The competition authorities of the Member States should co-operate actively in the exercise of these powers.

(25) The detection of infringements of the competition rules is growing ever more difficult, and, in order to protect competition effectively, the Commission's powers of investigation need to be supplemented. The Commission should in particular be empowered to interview any persons who may be in possession of useful information and to record the statements made. In the course of an inspection, officials authorised by the Commission should be empowered to affix seals for the period of time necessary for the inspection. Seals should normally not be affixed for more than 72 hours. Officials authorised by the Commission should also be empowered to ask for any information relevant to the subject matter and purpose of the inspection.

(26) Experience has shown that there are cases where business records are kept in the homes of directors or other people working for an undertaking. In order to safeguard the effectiveness of inspections, therefore, officials and other persons authorised by the Commission should be empowered to enter any premises where business records may be kept, including private homes. However, the exercise of this latter power should be subject to the authorisation of the judicial authority.

(27) Without prejudice to the case-law of the Court of Justice, it is useful to set out the scope of the control that the national judicial authority may carry out when it authorises, as foreseen by national law including as a precautionary measure, assistance from law enforcement authorities in order to overcome possible opposition on the part of the undertaking or the execution of the decision to carry out inspections in non-business premises. It results from the case-law that the national judicial authority may in particular ask the Commission for further information which it needs to carry out its control and in the absence of which it could refuse the authorisation. The case-law also confirms the competence of the national courts to control the application of national rules governing the implementation of coercive measures.

(28) In order to help the competition authorities of the Member States to apply Articles 81 and 82 of the Treaty effectively, it is expedient to enable them to assist one another by carrying out inspections and other fact-finding measures.

(29) Compliance with Articles 81 and 82 of the Treaty and the fulfilment of the obligations imposed on

undertakings and associations of undertakings under this Regulation should be enforceable by means of fines and periodic penalty payments. To that end, appropriate levels of fine should also be laid down for infringements of the procedural rules.

(30) In order to ensure effective recovery of fines imposed on associations of undertakings for infringements that they have committed, it is necessary to lay down the conditions on which the Commission may require payment of the fine from the members of the association where the association is not solvent. In doing so, the Commission should have regard to the relative size of the undertakings belonging to the association and in particular to the situation of small and medium-sized enterprises. Payment of the fine by one or several members of an association is without prejudice to rules of national law that provide for recovery of the amount paid from other members of the association.

(31) The rules on periods of limitation for the imposition of fines and periodic penalty payments were laid down in Council Regulation (EEC) No 2988/74,[11] *which also concerns penalties in the field of transport. In a system of parallel powers, the acts, which may interrupt a limitation period, should include procedural steps taken independently by the competition authority of a Member State. To clarify the legal framework, Regulation (EEC) No 2988/74 should therefore be amended to prevent it applying to matters covered by this Regulation, and this Regulation should include provisions on periods of limitation.*

(32) The undertakings concerned should be accorded the right to be heard by the Commission, third parties whose interests may be affected by a decision should be given the opportunity of submitting their observations beforehand, and the decisions taken should be widely publicised. While ensuring the rights of defence of the undertakings concerned, in particular, the right of access to the file, it is essential that business secrets be protected. The confidentiality of information exchanged in the network should likewise be safeguarded.

(33) Since all decisions taken by the Commission under this Regulation are subject to review by the Court of Justice in accordance with the Treaty, the Court of Justice should, in accordance with Article 229 thereof be given unlimited jurisdiction in respect of decisions by which the Commission imposes fines or periodic penalty payments.

(34) The principles laid down in Articles 81 and 82 of the Treaty, as they have been applied by Regulation No 17, have given a central role to the Community bodies. This central role should be retained, whilst associating the Member States more closely with the application of the Community competition rules. In accordance with the principles of subsidiarity and proportionality as set out in Article 5 of the Treaty, this Regulation does not go beyond what is necessary in order to achieve its objective, which is to allow the Community competition rules to be applied effectively.

(35) In order to attain a proper enforcement of Community competition law, Member States should designate and empower authorities to apply Articles 81 and 82 of the Treaty as public enforcers. They should be able to designate administrative as well as judicial authorities to carry out the various functions conferred upon competition authorities in this Regulation. This Regulation recognises the wide variation which exists in the public enforcement systems of Member States. The effects of Article 11(6) of this Regulation should apply to all competition authorities. As an exception to this general rule, where a prosecuting authority brings a case before a separate judicial authority, Article 11(6) should apply to the prosecuting authority subject to the conditions in Article 35(4) of this Regulation. Where these conditions are not fulfilled, the general rule should apply. In any case, Article 11(6) should not apply to courts insofar as they are acting as review courts.

(36) As the case-law has made it clear that the competition rules apply to transport, that sector should be made subject to the procedural provisions of this Regulation. Council Regulation No 141 of 26 November 1962 exempting transport from the application of Regulation No 17[12] *should therefore be repealed and Regulations (EEC) No 1017/68,*[13] *(EEC) No 4056/86*[14] *and (EEC) No 3975/87*[15] *should be amended in order to delete the specific procedural provisions they contain.*

(37) This Regulation respects the fundamental rights and observes the principles recognised in particular by the Charter of Fundamental Rights of the European Union. Accordingly, this Regulation should be interpreted and applied with respect to those rights and principles.

(38) Legal certainty for undertakings operating under the Community competition rules contributes to the promotion of innovation and investment. Where cases give rise to genuine uncertainty because they present novel or unresolved questions for the application of these rules, individual undertakings may wish to seek informal guidance from the Commission. This Regulation is without prejudice to the ability of the Commission to issue such informal guidance,

NOTES

Repeal of this Regulation in relation to the UK: this Regulation is repealed in relation to the UK (as from IP completion day); see the introductory notes to this Regulation *ante*.

1 OJ C365E, 19.12.2000, p 284.

2 OJ C72E, 21.3.2002, p 305.

3 OJ C155, 29.5.2001, p 73.

4 The title of Regulation No 17 has been adjusted to take account of the renumbering of the Articles of the EC Treaty, in accordance with Article 12 of the Treaty of Amsterdam; the original reference was to Articles 85 and 86 of the Treaty.

5 OJ 13, 21.2.1962, p 204/62. Regulation as last amended by Regulation (EC) No 1216/1999 (OJ L148, 15.6.1999, p 5).

6 Council Regulation No 19/65/EEC of 2 March 1965 on the application of Article 81(3) (The titles of the Regulations have been adjusted to take account of the renumbering of the Articles of the EC Treaty, in accordance with Article 12 of the Treaty of Amsterdam; the original reference was to Article 85(3) of the Treaty) of the Treaty to certain categories of agreements and concerted practices (OJ 36, 6.3.1965, p 533). Regulation as last amended by Regulation (EC) No 1215/1999 (OJ L148, 15.6.1999, p 1).

7 Council Regulation (EEC) No 2821/71 of 20 December 1971 on the application of Article 81(3) (The titles of the Regulations have been adjusted to take account of the renumbering of the Articles of the EC Treaty, in accordance with Article 12 of the Treaty of Amsterdam; the original reference was to Article 85(3) of the Treaty) of the Treaty to categories of agreements, decisions and concerted practices (OJ L285, 29.12.1971, p 46). Regulation as last amended by the Act of Accession of 1994.

8 Council Regulation (EEC) No 3976/87 of 14 December 1987 on the application of Article 81(3) (The titles of the

Regulations have been adjusted to take account of the renumbering of the Articles of the EC Treaty, in accordance with Article 12 of the Treaty of Amsterdam; the original reference was to Article 85(3) of the Treaty) of the Treaty to certain categories of agreements and concerted practices in the air transport sector (OJ L374, 31.12.1987, p 9). Regulation as last amended by the Act of Accession of 1994.

9 Council Regulation (EEC) No 1534/91 of 31 May 1991 on the application of Article 81(3) (The titles of the Regulations have been adjusted to take account of the renumbering of the Articles of the EC Treaty, in accordance with Article 12 of the Treaty of Amsterdam; the original reference was to Article 85(3) of the Treaty) of the Treaty to certain categories of agreements, decisions and concerted practices in the insurance sector (OJ L143, 7.6.1991, p 1).

10 Council Regulation (EEC) No 479/92 of 25 February 1992 on the application of Article 81(3) (The titles of the Regulations have been adjusted to take account of the renumbering of the Articles of the EC Treaty, in accordance with Article 12 of the Treaty of Amsterdam; the original reference was to Article 85(3) of the Treaty) of the Treaty to certain categories of agreements, decisions and concerted practices between liner shipping companies (Consortia) (OJ L55, 29.2.1992, p 3). Regulation amended by the Act of Accession of 1994.

11 Council Regulation (EEC) No 2988/74 of 26 November 1974 concerning limitation periods in proceedings and the enforcement of sanctions under the rules of the European Economic Community relating to transport and competition (OJ L319, 29.11.1974, p 1).

12 OJ 124, 28.11.1962, p 2751/62; Regulation as last amended by Regulation No 1002/67/EEC (OJ 306, 16.12.1967, p 1).

13 Council Regulation (EEC) No 1017/68 of 19 July 1968 applying rules of competition to transport by rail, road and inland waterway (OJ L175, 23.7.1968, p 1). Regulation as last amended by the Act of Accession of 1994.

14 Council Regulation (EEC) No 4056/86 of 22 December 1986 laying down detailed rules for the application of Articles 81 and 82 (The title of the Regulation has been adjusted to take account of the renumbering of the Articles of the EC Treaty, in accordance with Article 12 of the Treaty of Amsterdam; the original reference was to Articles 85 and 86 of the Treaty) of the Treaty to maritime transport (OJ L378, 31.12.1986, p 4). Regulation as last amended by the Act of Accession of 1994.

15 Council Regulation (EEC) No 3975/87 of 14 December 1987 laying down the procedure for the application of the rules on competition to undertakings in the air transport sector (OJ L374, 31.12.1987, p 1). Regulation as last amended by Regulation (EEC) No 2410/92 (OJ L240, 24.8.1992, p 18).

HAS ADOPTED THIS REGULATION—

CHAPTER I PRINCIPLES

[4.41]

Article 1 Application of Articles 81 and 82 of the Treaty

1. Agreements, decisions and concerted practices caught by Article 81(1) of the Treaty which do not satisfy the conditions of Article 81(3) of the Treaty shall be prohibited, no prior decision to that effect being required.

2. Agreements, decisions and concerted practices caught by Article 81(1) of the Treaty which satisfy the conditions of Article 81(3) of the Treaty shall not be prohibited, no prior decision to that effect being required.

3. The abuse of a dominant position referred to in Article 82 of the Treaty shall be prohibited, no prior decision to that effect being required.

NOTES

Repeal of this Regulation in relation to the UK: this Regulation is repealed in relation to the UK (as from IP completion day); see the introductory notes to this Regulation *ante*.

[4.42]

Article 2 Burden of proof

In any national or Community proceedings for the application of Articles 81 and 82 of the Treaty, the burden of proving an infringement of Article 81(1) or of Article 82 of the Treaty shall rest on the party or the authority alleging the infringement. The undertaking or association of undertakings claiming the benefit of Article 81(3) of the Treaty shall bear the burden of proving that the conditions of that paragraph are fulfilled.

NOTES

Repeal of this Regulation in relation to the UK: this Regulation is repealed in relation to the UK (as from IP completion day); see the introductory notes to this Regulation *ante*.

[4.43]

Article 3 Relationship between Articles 81 and 82 of the Treaty and national competition laws

1. Where the competition authorities of the Member States or national courts apply national competition law to agreements, decisions by associations of undertakings or concerted practices within the meaning of Article 81(1) of the Treaty which may affect trade between Member States within the meaning of that provision, they shall also apply Article 81 of the Treaty to such agreements, decisions or concerted practices. Where the competition authorities of the Member States or national courts apply national competition law to any abuse prohibited by Article 82 of the Treaty, they shall also apply Article 82 of the Treaty.

2. The application of national competition law may not lead to the prohibition of agreements, decisions by associations of undertakings or concerted practices which may affect trade between Member States but which do not restrict competition within the meaning of Article 81(1) of the Treaty, or which fulfil the conditions of Article 81(3) of the Treaty or which are covered by a Regulation for the application of Article 81(3) of the Treaty. Member States shall not under this Regulation be precluded from adopting and applying on their territory stricter national laws which prohibit or sanction unilateral conduct engaged in by undertakings.

3. Without prejudice to general principles and other provisions of Community law, paragraphs 1 and 2 do not apply when the competition authorities and the courts of the Member States apply national merger control laws nor do they preclude the application of provisions of national law that predominantly pursue an objective different from that pursued by Articles 81 and 82 of the Treaty.

NOTES

Repeal of this Regulation in relation to the UK: this Regulation is repealed in relation to the UK (as from IP completion day); see the introductory notes to this Regulation *ante*.

CHAPTER II POWERS

[4.44]

Article 4 Powers of the Commission

For the purpose of applying Articles 81 and 82 of the Treaty, the Commission shall have the powers provided for by this Regulation.

NOTES

Repeal of this Regulation in relation to the UK: this Regulation is repealed in relation to the UK (as from IP completion day); see the introductory notes to this Regulation *ante*.

[4.45]

Article 5 Powers of the competition authorities of the Member States

The competition authorities of the Member States shall have the power to apply Articles 81 and 82 of the Treaty in individual cases. For this purpose, acting on their own initiative or on a complaint, they may take the following decisions—

— *requiring that an infringement be brought to an end,*
— *ordering interim measures,*
— *accepting commitments,*
— *imposing fines, periodic penalty payments or any other penalty provided for in their national law.*

Where on the basis of the information in their possession the conditions for prohibition are not met they may likewise decide that there are no grounds for action on their part.

NOTES

Repeal of this Regulation in relation to the UK: this Regulation is repealed in relation to the UK (as from IP completion day); see the introductory notes to this Regulation *ante*.

[4.46]

Article 6 Powers of the national courts

National courts shall have the power to apply Articles 81 and 82 of the Treaty.

NOTES

Repeal of this Regulation in relation to the UK: this Regulation is repealed in relation to the UK (as from IP completion day); see the introductory notes to this Regulation *ante*.

CHAPTER III COMMISSION DECISIONS

[4.47]

Article 7 Finding and termination of infringement

1. Where the Commission, acting on a complaint or on its own initiative, finds that there is an infringement of Article 81 or of Article 82 of the Treaty, it may by decision require the undertakings and associations of undertakings concerned to bring such infringement to an end. For this purpose, it may impose on them any behavioural or structural remedies which are proportionate to the infringement committed and necessary to bring the infringement effectively to an end. Structural remedies can only be imposed either where there is no equally effective behavioural remedy or where any equally effective behavioural remedy would be more burdensome for the undertaking concerned than the structural remedy. If the Commission has a legitimate interest in doing so, it may also find that an infringement has been committed in the past.

2. Those entitled to lodge a complaint for the purposes of paragraph 1 are natural or legal persons who can show a legitimate interest and Member States.

NOTES

Repeal of this Regulation in relation to the UK: this Regulation is repealed in relation to the UK (as from IP completion day); see the introductory notes to this Regulation *ante*.

[4.48]

Article 8 Interim measures

1. In cases of urgency due to the risk of serious and irreparable damage to competition, the Commission, acting on its own initiative may by decision, on the basis of a prima facie finding of infringement, order interim measures.

2. A decision under paragraph 1 shall apply for a specified period of time and may be renewed in so far this is necessary and appropriate.

NOTES

Repeal of this Regulation in relation to the UK: this Regulation is repealed in relation to the UK (as from IP completion day); see the introductory notes to this Regulation *ante*.

[4.49]

Article 9 Commitments

1. Where the Commission intends to adopt a decision requiring that an infringement be brought to an end and the undertakings concerned offer commitments to meet the concerns expressed to them by the Commission in its preliminary assessment, the Commission may by decision make those commitments binding on the undertakings. Such a decision may be adopted for a specified period and shall conclude that there are no longer grounds for action by the Commission.

2. The Commission may, upon request or on its own initiative, reopen the proceedings—

(a) where there has been a material change in any of the facts on which the decision was based;

(b) where the undertakings concerned act contrary to their commitments; or

(c) where the decision was based on incomplete, incorrect or misleading information provided by the parties.

NOTES

Repeal of this Regulation in relation to the UK: this Regulation is repealed in relation to the UK (as from IP completion day); see the introductory notes to this Regulation *ante*.

[4.50]

Article 10 Finding of inapplicability

Where the Community public interest relating to the application of Articles 81 and 82 of the Treaty so requires, the Commission, acting on its own initiative, may by decision find that Article 81 of the Treaty is not applicable to an agreement, a decision by an association of undertakings or a concerted practice, either because the conditions of Article 81(1) of the Treaty are not fulfilled, or because the conditions of Article 81(3) of the Treaty are satisfied.

The Commission may likewise make such a finding with reference to Article 82 of the Treaty.

NOTES

Repeal of this Regulation in relation to the UK: this Regulation is repealed in relation to the UK (as from IP completion day); see the introductory notes to this Regulation *ante*.

CHAPTER IV CO-OPERATION

[4.51]

Article 11 Co-operation between the Commission and the competition authorities of the Member States

1. The Commission and the competition authorities of the Member States shall apply the Community competition rules in close co-operation.

2. The Commission shall transmit to the competition authorities of the Member States copies of the most important documents it has collected with a view to applying Articles 7, 8, 9, 10 and Article 29(1). At the request of the competition authority of a Member State, the Commission shall provide it with a copy of other existing documents necessary for the assessment of the case.

3. The competition authorities of the Member States shall, when acting under Article 81 or Article 82 of the Treaty, inform the Commission in writing before or without delay after commencing the first formal investigative measure. This information may also be made available to the competition authorities of the other Member States.

4. No later than 30 days before the adoption of a decision requiring that an infringement be brought to an end, accepting commitments or withdrawing the benefit of a block exemption Regulation, the competition authorities of the Member States shall inform the Commission. To that effect, they shall provide the Commission with a summary of the case, the envisaged decision or, in the absence thereof, any other document indicating the proposed course of action. This information may also be made available to the competition authorities of the other Member States. At the request of the Commission, the acting competition authority shall make available to the Commission other documents it holds which are necessary for the assessment of the case. The information supplied to the Commission may be made available to the competition authorities of the other Member States. National competition authorities may also exchange between themselves information necessary for the assessment of a case that they are dealing with under Article 81 or Article 82 of the Treaty.

5. The competition authorities of the Member States may consult the Commission on any case involving the application of Community law.

6. The initiation by the Commission of proceedings for the adoption of a decision under Chapter III shall relieve the competition authorities of the Member States of their competence to apply Articles 81 and 82 of the Treaty. If a competition authority of a Member State is already acting on a case, the Commission shall only initiate proceedings after consulting with that national competition authority.

NOTES

Repeal of this Regulation in relation to the UK: this Regulation is repealed in relation to the UK (as from IP completion day); see the introductory notes to this Regulation *ante*.

[4.52]

Article 12 Exchange of information

1. For the purpose of applying Articles 81 and 82 of the Treaty the Commission and the competition authorities of the Member States shall have the power to provide one another with and use in evidence any matter of fact or of law, including confidential information.

2. Information exchanged shall only be used in evidence for the purpose of applying Article 81 or Article 82 of the Treaty and in respect of the subject matter for which it was collected by the transmitting authority. However, where national competition law is applied in the same case and in parallel to Community competition law and does not lead to a different outcome, information exchanged under this Article may also be used for the application of national competition law.

3. Information exchanged pursuant to paragraph 1 can only be used in evidence to impose sanctions on natural persons where—

— the law of the transmitting authority foresees sanctions of a similar kind in relation to an infringement of Article 81 or Article 82 of the Treaty or, in the absence thereof,

— the information has been collected in a way which respects the same level of protection of the rights of defence of natural persons as provided for under the national rules of the receiving authority. However, in this case, the information exchanged cannot be used by the receiving authority to impose custodial sanctions.

NOTES

Repeal of this Regulation in relation to the UK: this Regulation is repealed in relation to the UK (as from IP completion day); see the introductory notes to this Regulation *ante*.

[4.53]

Article 13 Suspension or termination of proceedings

1. Where competition authorities of two or more Member States have received a complaint or are acting on their own initiative under Article 81 or Article 82 of the Treaty against the same agreement, decision of an association or practice, the fact that one authority is dealing with the case shall be sufficient grounds for the others to suspend the proceedings before them or to reject the complaint. The Commission may likewise reject a complaint on the ground that a competition authority of a Member State is dealing with the case.

2. Where a competition authority of a Member State or the Commission has received a complaint against an agreement, decision of an association or practice which has already been dealt with by another competition authority, it may reject it.

NOTES

Repeal of this Regulation in relation to the UK: this Regulation is repealed in relation to the UK (as from IP completion day); see the introductory notes to this Regulation *ante*.

[4.54]

Article 14 Advisory Committee

1. The Commission shall consult an Advisory Committee on Restrictive Practices and Dominant Positions prior to the taking of any decision under Articles 7, 8, 9, 10, 23, Article 24(2) and Article 29(1).

2. For the discussion of individual cases, the Advisory Committee shall be composed of representatives of the competition authorities of the Member States. For meetings in which issues other than individual cases are being discussed, an additional Member State representative competent in competition matters may be appointed. Representatives may, if unable to attend, be replaced by other representatives.

3. The consultation may take place at a meeting convened and chaired by the Commission, held not earlier than 14 days after dispatch of the notice convening it, together with a summary of the case, an indication of the most important documents and a preliminary draft decision. In respect of decisions pursuant to Article 8, the meeting may be held seven days after the dispatch of the operative part of a draft decision. Where the Commission dispatches a notice convening the meeting which gives a shorter period of notice than those specified above, the meeting may take place on the proposed date in the absence of an objection by any Member State. The Advisory Committee shall deliver a written opinion on the Commission's preliminary draft decision. It may deliver an opinion even if some members are absent and are not represented. At the request of one or several members, the positions stated in the opinion shall be reasoned.

4. Consultation may also take place by written procedure. However, if any Member State so requests, the Commission shall convene a meeting. In case of written procedure, the Commission shall determine a time-limit of not less than 14 days within which the Member States are to put forward their observations for circulation to all other Member States. In case of decisions to be taken pursuant to Article 8, the time-limit of 14 days is replaced by seven days. Where the Commission determines a time-limit for the written procedure which is shorter than those specified above, the proposed time-limit shall be applicable in the absence of an objection by any Member State.

5. The Commission shall take the utmost account of the opinion delivered by the Advisory Committee. It shall inform the Committee of the manner in which its opinion has been taken into account.

6. Where the Advisory Committee delivers a written opinion, this opinion shall be appended to the draft decision. If the Advisory Committee recommends publication of the opinion, the Commission shall carry out such publication taking into account the legitimate interest of undertakings in the protection of their business secrets.

7. At the request of a competition authority of a Member State, the Commission shall include on the agenda of the Advisory Committee cases that are being dealt with by a competition authority of a Member State under Article 81 or Article 82 of the Treaty. The Commission may also do so on its own initiative. In either case, the Commission shall inform the competition authority concerned.

A request may in particular be made by a competition authority of a Member State in respect of a case where the Commission intends to initiate proceedings with the effect of Article 11(6).

The Advisory Committee shall not issue opinions on cases dealt with by competition authorities of the Member States. The Advisory Committee may also discuss general issues of Community competition law.

NOTES

Repeal of this Regulation in relation to the UK: this Regulation is repealed in relation to the UK (as from IP completion day); see the introductory notes to this Regulation *ante*.

[4.55]

Article 15 Co-operation with national courts

1. In proceedings for the application of Article 81 or Article 82 of the Treaty, courts of the Member States may ask the Commission to transmit to them information in its possession or its opinion on questions concerning the application of the Community competition rules.

2. Member States shall forward to the Commission a copy of any written judgment of national courts deciding on the application of Article 81 or Article 82 of the Treaty. Such copy shall be forwarded without delay after the full written judgment is notified to the parties.

3. Competition authorities of the Member States, acting on their own initiative, may submit written observations to the national courts of their Member State on issues relating to the application of Article 81 or Article 82 of the Treaty. With the permission of the court in question, they may also submit oral observations to the national courts of their

Member State. Where the coherent application of Article 81 or Article 82 of the Treaty so requires, the Commission, acting on its own initiative, may submit written observations to courts of the Member States. With the permission of the court in question, it may also make oral observations.

For the purpose of the preparation of their observations only, the competition authorities of the Member States and the Commission may request the relevant court of the Member State to transmit or ensure the transmission to them of any documents necessary for the assessment of the case.

4. This Article is without prejudice to wider powers to make observations before courts conferred on competition authorities of the Member States under the law of their Member State.

NOTES

Repeal of this Regulation in relation to the UK: this Regulation is repealed in relation to the UK (as from IP completion day); see the introductory notes to this Regulation *ante*.

[4.56]

Article 16 Uniform application of Community competition law

1. When national courts rule on agreements, decisions or practices under Article 81 or Article 82 of the Treaty which are already the subject of a Commission decision, they cannot take decisions running counter to the decision adopted by the Commission. They must also avoid giving decisions which would conflict with a decision contemplated by the Commission in proceedings it has initiated. To that effect, the national court may assess whether it is necessary to stay its proceedings. This obligation is without prejudice to the rights and obligations under Article 234 of the Treaty.

2. When competition authorities of the Member States rule on agreements, decisions or practices under Article 81 or Article 82 of the Treaty which are already the subject of a Commission decision, they cannot take decisions which would run counter to the decision adopted by the Commission.

NOTES

Repeal of this Regulation in relation to the UK: this Regulation is repealed in relation to the UK (as from IP completion day); see the introductory notes to this Regulation *ante*.

CHAPTER V POWERS OF INVESTIGATION

[4.57]

Article 17 Investigations into sectors of the economy and into types of agreements

1. Where the trend of trade between Member States, the rigidity of prices or other circumstances suggest that competition may be restricted or distorted within the common market, the Commission may conduct its inquiry into a particular sector of the economy or into a particular type of agreements across various sectors. In the course of that inquiry, the Commission may request the undertakings or associations of undertakings concerned to supply the information necessary for giving effect to Articles 81 and 82 of the Treaty and may carry out any inspections necessary for that purpose.

The Commission may in particular request the undertakings or associations of undertakings concerned to communicate to it all agreements, decisions and concerted practices.

The Commission may publish a report on the results of its inquiry into particular sectors of the economy or particular types of agreements across various sectors and invite comments from interested parties.

2. Articles 14, 18, 19, 20, 22, 23 and 24 shall apply mutatis mutandis.

NOTES

Repeal of this Regulation in relation to the UK: this Regulation is repealed in relation to the UK (as from IP completion day); see the introductory notes to this Regulation *ante*.

[4.58]

Article 18 Requests for information

1. In order to carry out the duties assigned to it by this Regulation, the Commission may, by simple request or by decision, require undertakings and associations of undertakings to provide all necessary information.

2. When sending a simple request for information to an undertaking or association of undertakings, the Commission shall state the legal basis and the purpose of the request, specify what information is required and fix the time-limit within which the information is to be provided, and the penalties provided for in Article 23 for supplying incorrect or misleading information.

3. Where the Commission requires undertakings and associations of undertakings to supply information by decision, it shall state the legal basis and the purpose of the request, specify what information is required and fix the time-limit within which it is to be provided. It shall also indicate the penalties provided for in Article 23 and indicate or impose the penalties provided for in Article 24. It shall further indicate the right to have the decision reviewed by the Court of Justice.

4. The owners of the undertakings or their representatives and, in the case of legal persons, companies or firms, or associations having no legal personality, the persons authorised to represent them by law or by their constitution shall supply the information requested on behalf of the undertaking or the association of undertakings concerned. Lawyers duly authorised to act may supply the information on behalf of their clients. The latter shall remain fully responsible if the information supplied is incomplete, incorrect or misleading.

5. The Commission shall without delay forward a copy of the simple request or of the decision to the competition authority of the Member State in whose territory the seat of the undertaking or association of undertakings is situated and the competition authority of the Member State whose territory is affected.

6. At the request of the Commission the governments and competition authorities of the Member States shall provide the Commission with all necessary information to carry out the duties assigned to it by this Regulation.

NOTES

Repeal of this Regulation in relation to the UK: this Regulation is repealed in relation to the UK (as from IP completion day); see the introductory notes to this Regulation *ante*.

[4.59]

Article 19 Power to take statements

1. In order to carry out the duties assigned to it by this Regulation, the Commission may interview any natural or legal person who consents to be interviewed for the purpose of collecting information relating to the subject matter of an investigation.

2. Where an interview pursuant to paragraph 1 is conducted in the premises of an undertaking, the Commission shall inform the competition authority of the Member State in whose territory the interview takes place. If so requested by the competition authority of that Member State, its officials may assist the officials and other accompanying persons authorised by the Commission to conduct the interview.

NOTES

Repeal of this Regulation in relation to the UK: this Regulation is repealed in relation to the UK (as from IP completion day); see the introductory notes to this Regulation *ante*.

[4.60]

Article 20 The Commission's powers of inspection

1. In order to carry out the duties assigned to it by this Regulation, the Commission may conduct all necessary inspections of undertakings and associations of undertakings.

2. The officials and other accompanying persons authorised by the Commission to conduct an inspection are empowered—

(a) to enter any premises, land and means of transport of undertakings and associations of undertakings;

(b) to examine the books and other records related to the business, irrespective of the medium on which they are stored;

(c) to take or obtain in any form copies of or extracts from such books or records;

(d) to seal any business premises and books or records for the period and to the extent necessary for the inspection;

(e) to ask any representative or member of staff of the undertaking or association of undertakings for explanations on facts or documents relating to the subject matter and purpose of the inspection and to record the answers.

3. The officials and other accompanying persons authorised by the Commission to conduct an inspection shall exercise their powers upon production of a written authorisation specifying the subject matter and purpose of the inspection and the penalties provided for in Article 23 in case the production of the required books or other records related to the business is incomplete or where the answers to questions asked under paragraph 2 of the present Article are incorrect or misleading. In good time before the inspection, the Commission shall give notice of the inspection to the competition authority of the Member State in whose territory it is to be conducted.

4. Undertakings and associations of undertakings are required to submit to inspections ordered by decision of the Commission. The decision shall specify the subject matter and purpose of the inspection, appoint the date on which it is to begin and indicate the penalties provided for in Articles 23 and 24 and the right to have the decision reviewed by the Court of Justice. The Commission shall take such decisions after consulting the competition authority of the Member State in whose territory the inspection is to be conducted.

5. Officials of as well as those authorised or appointed by the competition authority of the Member State in whose territory the inspection is to be conducted shall, at the request of that authority or of the Commission, actively assist the officials and other accompanying persons authorised by the Commission. To this end, they shall enjoy the powers specified in paragraph 2.

6. Where the officials and other accompanying persons authorised by the Commission find that an undertaking opposes an inspection ordered pursuant to this Article, the Member State concerned shall afford them the necessary assistance, requesting where appropriate the assistance of the police or of an equivalent enforcement authority, so as to enable them to conduct their inspection.

7. If the assistance provided for in paragraph 6 requires authorisation from a judicial authority according to national rules, such authorisation shall be applied for. Such authorisation may also be applied for as a precautionary measure.

8. Where authorisation as referred to in paragraph 7 is applied for, the national judicial authority shall control that the Commission decision is authentic and that the coercive measures envisaged are neither arbitrary nor excessive having regard to the subject matter of the inspection. In its control of the proportionality of the coercive measures, the national judicial authority may ask the Commission, directly or through the Member State competition authority, for detailed explanations in particular on the grounds the Commission has for suspecting infringement of Articles 81 and 82 of the Treaty, as well as on the seriousness of the suspected infringement and on the nature of the involvement of the undertaking concerned. However, the national judicial authority may not call into question the necessity for the inspection nor demand that it be provided with the information in the Commission's file. The lawfulness of the Commission decision shall be subject to review only by the Court of Justice.

NOTES

Repeal of this Regulation in relation to the UK: this Regulation is repealed in relation to the UK (as from IP completion day); see the introductory notes to this Regulation *ante*.

[4.61]

Article 21 Inspection of other premises

1. If a reasonable suspicion exists that books or other records related to the business and to the subject matter of the inspection, which may be relevant to prove a serious violation of Article 81 or Article 82 of the Treaty, are being kept in any other premises, land and means of transport, including the homes of directors, managers and other members of staff of the undertakings and associations of undertakings concerned, the Commission can by decision order an inspection to be conducted in such other premises, land and means of transport.

2. The decision shall specify the subject matter and purpose of the inspection, appoint the date on which it is to begin and indicate the right to have the decision reviewed by the Court of Justice. It shall in particular state the reasons that have led the Commission to conclude that a suspicion in the sense of paragraph 1 exists. The Commission shall take such decisions after consulting the competition authority of the Member State in whose territory the inspection is to be conducted.

3. A decision adopted pursuant to paragraph 1 cannot be executed without prior authorisation from the national judicial authority of the Member State concerned. The national judicial authority shall control that the Commission decision is authentic and that the coercive measures envisaged are neither arbitrary nor excessive having regard in particular to the seriousness of the suspected infringement, to the importance of the evidence sought, to the involvement of the undertaking concerned and to the reasonable likelihood that business books and records relating to the subject matter of the inspection are kept in the premises for which the authorisation is requested. The national judicial authority may ask the Commission, directly or through the Member State competition authority, for detailed explanations on those elements which are necessary to allow its control of the proportionality of the coercive measures envisaged.

However, the national judicial authority may not call into question the necessity for the inspection nor demand that it be provided with information in the Commission's file. The lawfulness of the Commission decision shall be subject to review only by the Court of Justice.

4. The officials and other accompanying persons authorised by the Commission to conduct an inspection ordered in accordance with paragraph 1 of this Article shall have the powers set out in Article 20(2)(a), (b) and (c). Article 20(5) and (6) shall apply mutatis mutandis.

NOTES

Repeal of this Regulation in relation to the UK: this Regulation is repealed in relation to the UK (as from IP completion day); see the introductory notes to this Regulation *ante*.

[4.62]

Article 22 Investigations by competition authorities of Member States

1. The competition authority of a Member State may in its own territory carry out any inspection or other fact-finding measure under its national law on behalf and for the account of the competition authority of another Member State in order to establish whether there has been an infringement of Article 81 or Article 82 of the Treaty. Any exchange and use of the information collected shall be carried out in accordance with Article 12.

2. At the request of the Commission, the competition authorities of the Member States shall undertake the inspections which the Commission considers to be necessary under Article 20(1) or which it has ordered by decision pursuant to Article 20(4). The officials of the competition authorities of the Member States who are responsible for conducting these inspections as well as those authorised or appointed by them shall exercise their powers in accordance with their national law.

If so requested by the Commission or by the competition authority of the Member State in whose territory the inspection is to be conducted, officials and other accompanying persons authorised by the Commission may assist the officials of the authority concerned.

NOTES

Repeal of this Regulation in relation to the UK: this Regulation is repealed in relation to the UK (as from IP completion day); see the introductory notes to this Regulation *ante*.

CHAPTER VI PENALTIES

[4.63]

Article 23 Fines

1. The Commission may by decision impose on undertakings and associations of undertakings fines not exceeding 1% of the total turnover in the preceding business year where, intentionally or negligently—

(a) they supply incorrect or misleading information in response to a request made pursuant to Article 17 or Article 18(2);

(b) in response to a request made by decision adopted pursuant to Article 17 or Article 18(3), they supply incorrect, incomplete or misleading information or do not supply information within the required time-limit;

(c) they produce the required books or other records related to the business in incomplete form during inspections under Article 20 or refuse to submit to inspections ordered by a decision adopted pursuant to Article 20(4);

(d) in response to a question asked in accordance with Article 20(2)(e),

- *they give an incorrect or misleading answer,*
- *they fail to rectify within a time-limit set by the Commission an incorrect, incomplete or misleading answer given by a member of staff, or*
- *they fail or refuse to provide a complete answer on facts relating to the subject matter and purpose of an inspection ordered by a decision adopted pursuant to Article 20(4);*

(e) seals affixed in accordance with Article 20(2)(d) by officials or other accompanying persons authorised by the Commission have been broken.

2. The Commission may by decision impose fines on undertakings and associations of undertakings where, either intentionally or negligently—

(a) they infringe Article 81 or Article 82 of the Treaty; or

(b) they contravene a decision ordering interim measures under Article 8; or

(c) they fail to comply with a commitment made binding by a decision pursuant to Article 9.

For each undertaking and association of undertakings participating in the infringement, the fine shall not exceed 10% of its total turnover in the preceding business year.

Where the infringement of an association relates to the activities of its members, the fine shall not exceed 10% of the sum of the total turnover of each member active on the market affected by the infringement of the association.

3. In fixing the amount of the fine, regard shall be had both to the gravity and to the duration of the infringement.

4. When a fine is imposed on an association of undertakings taking account of the turnover of its members and the association is not solvent, the association is obliged to call for contributions from its members to cover the amount of the fine.

Where such contributions have not been made to the association within a time-limit fixed by the Commission, the Commission may require payment of the fine directly by any of the undertakings whose representatives were members of the decision-making bodies concerned of the association.

After the Commission has required payment under the second subparagraph, where necessary to ensure full payment of the fine, the Commission may require payment of the balance by any of the members of the association which were active on the market on which the infringement occurred.

However, the Commission shall not require payment under the second or the third subparagraph from undertakings which show that they have not implemented the infringing decision of the association and either were not aware of its existence or have actively distanced themselves from it before the Commission started investigating the case.

The financial liability of each undertaking in respect of the payment of the fine shall not exceed 10% of its total turnover in the preceding business year.

5. Decisions taken pursuant to paragraphs 1 and 2 shall not be of a criminal law nature.

NOTES

Repeal of this Regulation in relation to the UK: this Regulation is repealed in relation to the UK (as from IP completion day); see the introductory notes to this Regulation *ante*.

[4.64]

Article 24 Periodic penalty payments

1. The Commission may, by decision, impose on undertakings or associations of undertakings periodic penalty payments not exceeding 5% of the average daily turnover in the preceding business year per day and calculated from the date appointed by the decision, in order to compel them—

- *(a) to put an end to an infringement of Article 81 or Article 82 of the Treaty, in accordance with a decision taken pursuant to Article 7;*
- *(b) to comply with a decision ordering interim measures taken pursuant to Article 8;*
- *(c) to comply with a commitment made binding by a decision pursuant to Article 9;*
- *(d) to supply complete and correct information which it has requested by decision taken pursuant to Article 17 or Article 18(3);*
- *(e) to submit to an inspection which it has ordered by decision taken pursuant to Article 20(4).*

2. Where the undertakings or associations of undertakings have satisfied the obligation which the periodic penalty payment was intended to enforce, the Commission may fix the definitive amount of the periodic penalty payment at a figure lower than that which would arise under the original decision. Article 23(4) shall apply correspondingly.

NOTES

Repeal of this Regulation in relation to the UK: this Regulation is repealed in relation to the UK (as from IP completion day); see the introductory notes to this Regulation *ante*.

CHAPTER VII LIMITATION PERIODS

[4.65]

Article 25 Limitation periods for the imposition of penalties

1. The powers conferred on the Commission by Articles 23 and 24 shall be subject to the following limitation periods—

- *(a) three years in the case of infringements of provisions concerning requests for information or the conduct of inspections;*
- *(b) five years in the case of all other infringements.*

2. Time shall begin to run on the day on which the infringement is committed. However, in the case of continuing or repeated infringements, time shall begin to run on the day on which the infringement ceases.

3. Any action taken by the Commission or by the competition authority of a Member State for the purpose of the investigation or proceedings in respect of an infringement shall interrupt the limitation period for the imposition of fines or periodic penalty payments. The limitation period shall be interrupted with effect from the date on which the action is notified to at least one undertaking or association of undertakings which has participated in the infringement. Actions which interrupt the running of the period shall include in particular the following—

- *(a) written requests for information by the Commission or by the competition authority of a Member State;*
- *(b) written authorisations to conduct inspections issued to its officials by the Commission or by the competition authority of a Member State;*
- *(c) the initiation of proceedings by the Commission or by the competition authority of a Member State;*
- *(d) notification of the statement of objections of the Commission or of the competition authority of a Member State.*

4. The interruption of the limitation period shall apply for all the undertakings or associations of undertakings which have participated in the infringement.

5. Each interruption shall start time running afresh. However, the limitation period shall expire at the latest on the day on which a period equal to twice the limitation period has elapsed without the Commission having imposed a fine or a periodic penalty payment. That period shall be extended by the time during which limitation is suspended pursuant to paragraph 6.

6. The limitation period for the imposition of fines or periodic penalty payments shall be suspended for as long as the decision of the Commission is the subject of proceedings pending before the Court of Justice.

NOTES

Repeal of this Regulation in relation to the UK: this Regulation is repealed in relation to the UK (as from IP completion day); see the introductory notes to this Regulation *ante*.

[4.66]

Article 26 Limitation period for the enforcement of penalties

1. The power of the Commission to enforce decisions taken pursuant to Articles 23 and 24 shall be subject to a limitation period of five years.

2. Time shall begin to run on the day on which the decision becomes final.

3. The limitation period for the enforcement of penalties shall be interrupted—

(a) by notification of a decision varying the original amount of the fine or periodic penalty payment or refusing an application for variation;

(b) by any action of the Commission or of a Member State, acting at the request of the Commission, designed to enforce payment of the fine or periodic penalty payment.

4. Each interruption shall start time running afresh.

5. The limitation period for the enforcement of penalties shall be suspended for so long as—

(a) time to pay is allowed;

(b) enforcement of payment is suspended pursuant to a decision of the Court of Justice.

NOTES

Repeal of this Regulation in relation to the UK: this Regulation is repealed in relation to the UK (as from IP completion day); see the introductory notes to this Regulation *ante*.

CHAPTER VIII HEARINGS AND PROFESSIONAL SECRECY

[4.67]

Article 27 Hearing of the parties, complainants and others

1. Before taking decisions as provided for in Articles 7, 8, 23 and Article 24(2), the Commission shall give the undertakings or associations of undertakings which are the subject of the proceedings conducted by the Commission the opportunity of being heard on the matters to which the Commission has taken objection. The Commission shall base its decisions only on objections on which the parties concerned have been able to comment. Complainants shall be associated closely with the proceedings.

2. The rights of defence of the parties concerned shall be fully respected in the proceedings. They shall be entitled to have access to the Commission's file, subject to the legitimate interest of undertakings in the protection of their business secrets. The right of access to the file shall not extend to confidential information and internal documents of the Commission or the competition authorities of the Member States. In particular, the right of access shall not extend to correspondence between the Commission and the competition authorities of the Member States, or between the latter, including documents drawn up pursuant to Articles 11 and 14. Nothing in this paragraph shall prevent the Commission from disclosing and using information necessary to prove an infringement.

3. If the Commission considers it necessary, it may also hear other natural or legal persons. Applications to be heard on the part of such persons shall, where they show a sufficient interest, be granted. The competition authorities of the Member States may also ask the Commission to hear other natural or legal persons.

4. Where the Commission intends to adopt a decision pursuant to Article 9 or Article 10, it shall publish a concise summary of the case and the main content of the commitments or of the proposed course of action. Interested third parties may submit their observations within a time limit which is fixed by the Commission in its publication and which may not be less than one month. Publication shall have regard to the legitimate interest of undertakings in the protection of their business secrets.

NOTES

Repeal of this Regulation in relation to the UK: this Regulation is repealed in relation to the UK (as from IP completion day); see the introductory notes to this Regulation *ante*.

[4.68]

Article 28 Professional secrecy

1. Without prejudice to Articles 12 and 15, information collected pursuant to Articles 17 to 22 shall be used only for the purpose for which it was acquired.

2. Without prejudice to the exchange and to the use of information foreseen in Articles 11, 12, 14, 15 and 27, the Commission and the competition authorities of the Member States, their officials, servants and other persons working under the supervision of these authorities as well as officials and civil servants of other authorities of the Member States shall not disclose information acquired or exchanged by them pursuant to this Regulation and of the kind covered by the obligation of professional secrecy. This obligation also applies to all representatives and experts of Member States attending meetings of the Advisory Committee pursuant to Article 14.

NOTES

Repeal of this Regulation in relation to the UK: this Regulation is repealed in relation to the UK (as from IP completion day); see the introductory notes to this Regulation *ante*.

CHAPTER IX EXEMPTION REGULATIONS

[4.69]

Article 29 Withdrawal in individual cases

1. Where the Commission, empowered by a Council Regulation, such as Regulations 19/65/EEC, (EEC) No 2821/71, (EEC) No 3976/87, (EEC) No 1534/91 or (EEC) No 479/92, to apply Article 81(3) of the Treaty by regulation, has declared Article 81(1) of the Treaty inapplicable to certain categories of agreements, decisions by associations of undertakings or concerted practices, it may, acting on its own initiative or on a complaint, withdraw the benefit of such an exemption Regulation when it finds that in any particular case an agreement, decision or concerted practice to which the exemption Regulation applies has certain effects which are incompatible with Article 81(3) of the Treaty.

2. Where, in any particular case, agreements, decisions by associations of undertakings or concerted practices to which a Commission Regulation referred to in paragraph 1 applies have effects which are incompatible with Article 81(3) of the Treaty in the territory of a Member State, or in a part thereof, which has all the characteristics of a distinct geographic market, the competition authority of that Member State may withdraw the benefit of the Regulation in question in respect of that territory.

NOTES

Repeal of this Regulation in relation to the UK: this Regulation is repealed in relation to the UK (as from IP completion day); see the introductory notes to this Regulation *ante*.

CHAPTER X GENERAL PROVISIONS

[4.70]

Article 30 Publication of decisions

1. The Commission shall publish the decisions, which it takes pursuant to Articles 7 to 10, 23 and 24.

2. The publication shall state the names of the parties and the main content of the decision, including any penalties imposed. It shall have regard to the legitimate interest of undertakings in the protection of their business secrets.

NOTES

Repeal of this Regulation in relation to the UK: this Regulation is repealed in relation to the UK (as from IP completion day); see the introductory notes to this Regulation *ante*.

[4.71]

Article 31 Review by the Court of Justice

The Court of Justice shall have unlimited jurisdiction to review decisions whereby the Commission has fixed a fine or periodic penalty payment. It may cancel, reduce or increase the fine or periodic penalty payment imposed.

NOTES

Repeal of this Regulation in relation to the UK: this Regulation is repealed in relation to the UK (as from IP completion day); see the introductory notes to this Regulation *ante*.

Article 32 *(Repealed by Council Regulation 1419/2006/EC, Art 2.)*

[4.72]

Article 33 Implementing provisions

1. The Commission shall be authorised to take such measures as may be appropriate in order to apply this Regulation. The measures may concern, inter alia—

(a) the form, content and other details of complaints lodged pursuant to Article 7 and the procedure for rejecting complaints;

(b) the practical arrangements for the exchange of information and consultations provided for in Article 11;

(c) the practical arrangements for the hearings provided for in Article 27.

2. Before the adoption of any measures pursuant to paragraph 1, the Commission shall publish a draft thereof and invite all interested parties to submit their comments within the time-limit it lays down, which may not be less than one month. Before publishing a draft measure and before adopting it, the Commission shall consult the Advisory Committee on Restrictive Practices and Dominant Positions.

NOTES

Repeal of this Regulation in relation to the UK: this Regulation is repealed in relation to the UK (as from IP completion day); see the introductory notes to this Regulation *ante*.

CHAPTER XI TRANSITIONAL, AMENDING AND FINAL PROVISIONS

[4.73]

Article 34 Transitional provisions

1. Applications made to the Commission under Article 2 of Regulation No 17, notifications made under Articles 4 and 5 of that Regulation and the corresponding applications and notifications made under Regulations (EEC) No 1017/68, (EEC) No 4056/86 and (EEC) No 3975/87 shall lapse as from the date of application of this Regulation.

2. Procedural steps taken under Regulation No 17 and Regulations (EEC) No 1017/68, (EEC) No 4056/86 and (EEC) No 3975/87 shall continue to have effect for the purposes of applying this Regulation.

NOTES

Repeal of this Regulation in relation to the UK: this Regulation is repealed in relation to the UK (as from IP completion day); see the introductory notes to this Regulation *ante*.

[4.74]

Article 35 Designation of competition authorities of Member States

1. The Member States shall designate the competition authority or authorities responsible for the application of Articles 81 and 82 of the Treaty in such a way that the provisions of this regulation are effectively complied with. The measures necessary to empower those authorities to apply those Articles shall be taken before 1 May 2004. The authorities designated may include courts.

2. When enforcement of Community competition law is entrusted to national administrative and judicial authorities, the Member States may allocate different powers and functions to those different national authorities, whether administrative or judicial.

3. The effects of Article 11(6) apply to the authorities designated by the Member States including courts that exercise functions regarding the preparation and the adoption of the types of decisions foreseen in Article 5. The effects of Article 11(6) do not extend to courts insofar as they act as review courts in respect of the types of decisions foreseen in Article 5.

4. Notwithstanding paragraph 3, in the Member States where, for the adoption of certain types of decisions foreseen in Article 5, an authority brings an action before a judicial authority that is separate and different from the prosecuting authority and provided that the terms of this paragraph are complied with, the effects of Article 11(6) shall be limited to the authority prosecuting the case which shall withdraw its claim before the judicial authority when the Commission opens proceedings and this withdrawal shall bring the national proceedings effectively to an end.

NOTES

Repeal of this Regulation in relation to the UK: this Regulation is repealed in relation to the UK (as from IP completion day); see the introductory notes to this Regulation *ante*.

Articles 36–43 *(Art 36 amended Council Regulation 1017/68/EEC (repealed). Art 37 amended Council Regulation 2988/74/EEC (repealed). Art 38 amended Council Regulation 4056/86/EEC (repealed). Art 39 repeals Council Regulation 3975/87/EEC, Arts 3–19 (subject to savings as regards Art 6(3)). Art 40 repeals Council Regulation 19/65/EEC, Art 7, Council Regulation 2821/71/EEC, Art 7, and Council Regulation 1534/91/EEC, Art 7. Art 41 substituted Council Regulation 3976/87/EEC, Art 6 (repealed) and repealed Art 7. Art 42 substituted Council Regulation 479/92/EEC, Art 5 (repealed) and repealed Art 6. Art 43 repeals Council Regulation 17/62/EEC (with the exception of Art 8(3) which continues to apply to decisions adopted pursuant to Art 81(3) of the Treaty prior to 1 May 2004, until the date of expiration of those decisions), and Council Regulation 141/62/EEC. In so far as they still have any effect, all were repealed in relation to the UK, as from IP completion day, as noted in the introductory notes to this Regulation ante.)*

[4.75]

Article 44 Report on the application of the present Regulation

Five years from the date of application of this Regulation, the Commission shall report to the European Parliament and the Council on the functioning of this Regulation, in particular on the application of Article 11(6) and Article 17.

On the basis of this report, the Commission shall assess whether it is appropriate to propose to the Council a revision of this Regulation.

NOTES

Repeal of this Regulation in relation to the UK: this Regulation is repealed in relation to the UK (as from IP completion day); see the introductory notes to this Regulation *ante*.

[4.76]

Article 45 Entry into force

This Regulation shall enter into force on the 20th day following that of its publication in the Official Journal of the European Communities.

It shall apply from 1 May 2004.

NOTES

Repeal of this Regulation in relation to the UK: this Regulation is repealed in relation to the UK (as from IP completion day); see the introductory notes to this Regulation *ante*.

COMMISSION RECOMMENDATION

(2003/361/EC)

of 6 May 2003

concerning the definition of micro, small and medium-sized enterprises

(notified under document number C(2003) 1422)

(Text with EEA relevance)

[4.77]

NOTES

Date of publication in OJ: OJ L124, 20.05.2003, p 36.

Note: with effect from 1 December 2009, the EC Treaty was replaced by the Treaty on the Functioning of the European Union. References in this document to provisions of the EC Treaty should be construed accordingly.

THE COMMISSION OF THE EUROPEAN COMMUNITIES,

Having regard to the Treaty establishing the European Community, and in particular Article 211, second indent, thereof,

Whereas:

(1) In a report submitted to the Council in 1992 at the request of the "Industry" Council held on 28 May 1990, the Commission had proposed limiting the proliferation of definitions of small and medium-sized enterprises in use at Community level. Commission Recommendation 96/280/EC of 3 April 1996 concerning the definition of small and medium-sized enterprises[1] was based on the idea that the existence of different definitions at Community level and at national level could create inconsistencies. Following the logic of a single market without internal frontiers, the treatment of enterprises should be based on a set of common rules. The pursuit of such an approach is all the more necessary in view of the extensive interaction between national and Community measures assisting micro, small and medium-sized enterprises (SME), for example in connection with Structural Funds or research. It means that situations

in which the Community focuses its action on a given category of SMEs and the Member States on another must be avoided. In addition, it was considered that the application of the same definition by the Commission, the Member States, the European Investment Bank (EIB) and the European Investment Fund (EIF) would improve the consistency and effectiveness of policies targeting SMEs and would, therefore, limit the risk of distortion of competition.

(2) Recommendation 96/280/EC has been applied widely by the Member States, and the definition contained in the Annex thereto has been taken over in Commission Regulation (EC) No 70/2001 of 12 January 2001 on the application of Articles 87 and 88 of the EC Treaty to State aid to small and medium-sized enterprises.[2] Apart from the need to adapt Recommendation 96/280/EC to economic developments, pursuant to Article 2 of the Annex thereto, consideration must be given to a number of difficulties of interpretation which have emerged in its application, as well as the observations received from enterprises. In view of the number of amendments now requiring to be made to Recommendation 96/280/EC, and for the sake of clarity, it is appropriate to replace the Recommendation.

(3) It should also be made clear that, in accordance with Articles 48, 81 and 82 of the Treaty, as interpreted by the Court of Justice of the European Communities, an enterprise should be considered to be any entity, regardless of its legal form, engaged in economic activities, including in particular entities engaged in a craft activity and other activities on an individual or family basis, partnerships or associations regularly engaged in economic activities.

(4) The criterion of staff numbers (the "staff headcount criterion") remains undoubtedly one of the most important, and must be observed as the main criterion; introducing a financial criterion is nonetheless a necessary adjunct in order to grasp the real scale and performance of an enterprise and its position compared to its competitors. However, it would not be desirable to use turnover as the sole financial criterion, in particular because enterprises in the trade and distribution sector have by their nature higher turnover figures than those in the manufacturing sector. Thus the turnover criterion should be combined with that of the balance sheet total, a criterion which reflects the overall wealth of a business, with the possibility of either of these two criteria being exceeded.

(5) The turnover ceiling refers to enterprises engaged in very different types of economic activity. In order not to restrict unduly the usefulness of applying the definition, it should be updated to take account of changes in both prices and productivity.

(6) As regards the ceiling for the balance sheet total, in the absence of any new element, it is justified to maintain the approach whereby the turnover ceilings are subjected to a coefficient based on the statistical ratio between the two variables. The statistical trend requires a greater increase to be made to the turnover ceiling. Since the trend differs according to the size-category of the enterprise, it is also appropriate to adjust the coefficient in order to reflect the economic trend as closely as possible and not to penalise microenterprises and small enterprises as opposed to medium-sized enterprises. This coefficient is very close to 1 in the case of microenterprises and small enterprises. To simplify matters, therefore, a single value must be chosen for those categories for the turnover ceiling and balance sheet total ceiling.

(7) As in Recommendation 96/280/EC, the financial ceilings and the staff ceilings represent maximum limits and the Member States, the EIB and the EIF may fix ceilings lower than the Community ceilings if they wish to direct their measures towards a specific category of SME. In the interests of administrative simplification, the Member States, the EIB and the EIF may use only one criterion — the staff headcount — for the implementation of some of their policies. However, this does not apply to the various rules in competition law where the financial criteria must also be used and adhered to.

(8) Following the endorsement of the European Charter for Small Enterprises by the European Council of Santa Maria da Feira in June 2000, microenterprises — a category of small enterprises particularly important for the development of entrepreneurship and job creation — should also be better defined.

(9) To gain a better understanding of the real economic position of SMEs and to remove from that category groups of enterprises whose economic power may exceed that of genuine SMEs, a distinction should be made between various types of enterprises, depending on whether they are autonomous, whether they have holdings which do not entail a controlling position (partner enterprises), or whether they are linked to other enterprises. The current limit shown in Recommendation 96/280/EC, of a 25% holding below which an enterprise is considered autonomous, is maintained.

(10) In order to encourage the creation of enterprises, equity financing of SMEs and rural and local development, enterprises can be considered autonomous despite a holding of 25% or more by certain categories of investors who have a positive role in business financing and creation. However, conditions for these investors have not previously been specified. The case of "business angels" (individuals or groups of individuals pursuing a regular business of investing venture capital) deserves special mention because — compared to other venture capital investors — their ability to give relevant advice to new entrepreneurs is extremely valuable. Their investment in equity capital also complements the activity of venture capital companies, as they provide smaller amounts at an earlier stage of the enterprise's life.

(11) To simplify matters, in particular for Member States and enterprises, use should be made when defining linked enterprises of the conditions laid down in Article 1 of Council Directive 83/349/EEC of 13 June 1983 based on Article 54(3)(g) of the Treaty on consolidated accounts,[3] as last amended by Directive 2001/65/EC of the European Parliament and of the Council,[4] in so far as these conditions are suitable for the purposes of this Recommendation. To strengthen the incentives for investing in the equity funding of an SME, the presumption of absence of dominant influence on the enterprise in question was introduced, in pursuance of the criteria of Article 5(3), of Council Directive 78/660/EEC of 25 July 1978 based on Article 54(3)(g) of the Treaty on the annual accounts of certain types of companies,[5] as last amended by Directive 2001/65/EC.

(12) Account should also be taken, in suitable cases, of relations between enterprises which pass through natural persons, with a view to ensuring that only those enterprises which really need the advantages accruing to SMEs from the different rules or measures in their favour actually benefit from them. In order to limit the examination of these situations to the strict minimum, the account taken of such relationships has been restricted to the relevant market or to adjacent markets — reference being had, where necessary, to the Commission's definition of "relevant markets" in the Commission notice on the definition of relevant market for the purposes of Community competition law.[6]

(13) In order to avoid arbitrary distinctions between different public bodies of a Member State, and given the need for legal certainty, it is considered necessary to confirm that an enterprise with 25% or more of its capital or voting rights controlled by a public body is not an SME.

(14) In order to ease the administrative burden for enterprises, and to simplify and speed up the administrative handling of cases for which SME status is required, it is appropriate to allow enterprises to use solemn declarations to certify certain of their characteristics.

(15) It is necessary to establish in detail the composition of the staff headcount for SME definition purposes. In order to promote the development of vocational training and sandwich courses, it is desirable, when calculating staff numbers, to disregard apprentices and students with a vocational training contract. Similarly, maternity or parental leave periods should not be counted.

(16) The various types of enterprise defined according to their relationship with other enterprises correspond to objectively differing degrees of integration. It is therefore appropriate to apply distinct procedures to each of those types of enterprise when calculating the quantities representing their activities and economic power,

NOTES

1 OJ L107, 30.4.1996, p 4.
2 OJ L10, 13.1.2001, p 33.
3 OJ L193, 18.7.1983, p 1.
4 OJ L283, 27.10.2001, p 28.
5 OJ L222, 14.8.1978, p 11.
6 OJ C372, 9.12.1997, p 5.

HEREBY RECOMMENDS—

[4.78]
Article 1

1. This Recommendation concerns the definition of micro, small and medium-sized enterprises used in Community policies applied within the Community and the European Economic Area.
2. Member States, the European Investment Bank (EIB) and the European Investment Fund (EIF), are invited:
   (a) to comply with Title I of the Annex for their programmes directed towards medium-sized enterprises, small enterprises or microenterprises;
   (b) to take the necessary steps with a view to using the size classes set out in Article 7 of the Annex, especially where the monitoring of their use of Community financial instruments is concerned.

[4.79]
Article 2

The ceilings shown in Article 2 of the Annex are to be regarded as maximum values. Member States, the EIB and the EIF may fix lower ceilings. In implementing certain of their policies, they may also choose to apply only the criterion of number of employees, except in fields governed by the various rules on State aid.

[4.80]
Article 3

This Recommendation will replace Recommendation 96/280/EC as from 1 January 2005.

[4.81]
Article 4

This Recommendation is addressed to the Member States, the EIB and the EIF.

They are requested to inform the Commission by 31 December 2004 of any measures they have taken further to it and, no later than 30 September 2005, to inform it of the first results of its implementation.

ANNEX

TITLE I DEFINITION OF MICRO, SMALL AND MEDIUM-SIZED ENTERPRISES ADOPTED BY THE COMMISSION

[4.82]
Article 1 Enterprise

An enterprise is considered to be any entity engaged in an economic activity, irrespective of its legal form. This includes, in particular, self-employed persons and family businesses engaged in craft or other activities, and partnerships or associations regularly engaged in an economic activity.

Article 2 Staff headcount and financial ceilings determining enterprise categories

1. The category of micro, small and medium-sized enterprises (SMEs) is made up of enterprises which employ fewer than 250 persons and which have an annual turnover not exceeding EUR 50 million, and/or an annual balance sheet total not exceeding EUR 43 million.
2. Within the SME category, a small enterprise is defined as an enterprise which employs fewer than 50 persons and whose annual turnover and/or annual balance sheet total does not exceed EUR 10 million.
3. Within the SME category, a microenterprise is defined as an enterprise which employs fewer than 10 persons and whose annual turnover and/or annual balance sheet total does not exceed EUR 2 million.

Article 3 Types of enterprise taken into consideration in calculating staff numbers and financial amounts

1. An "autonomous enterprise" is any enterprise which is not classified as a partner enterprise within the meaning of paragraph 2 or as a linked enterprise within the meaning of paragraph 3.

2. "Partner enterprises" are all enterprises which are not classified as linked enterprises within the meaning of paragraph 3 and between which there is the following relationship: an enterprise (upstream enterprise) holds, either solely or jointly with one or more linked enterprises within the meaning of paragraph 3, 25% or more of the capital or voting rights of another enterprise (downstream enterprise).

However, an enterprise may be ranked as autonomous, and thus as not having any partner enterprises, even if this 25% threshold is reached or exceeded by the following investors, provided that those investors are not linked, within the meaning of paragraph 3, either individually or jointly to the enterprise in question:

(a) public investment corporations, venture capital companies, individuals or groups of individuals with a regular venture capital investment activity who invest equity capital in unquoted businesses ("business angels"), provided the total investment of those business angels in the same enterprise is less than EUR 1,250,000;
(b) universities or non-profit research centres;
(c) institutional investors, including regional development funds;
(d) autonomous local authorities with an annual budget of less than EUR 10 million and fewer than 5000 inhabitants.

3. "Linked enterprises" are enterprises which have any of the following relationships with each other:

(a) an enterprise has a majority of the shareholders' or members' voting rights in another enterprise;
(b) an enterprise has the right to appoint or remove a majority of the members of the administrative, management or supervisory body of another enterprise;
(c) an enterprise has the right to exercise a dominant influence over another enterprise pursuant to a contract entered into with that enterprise or to a provision in its memorandum or articles of association;
(d) an enterprise, which is a shareholder in or member of another enterprise, controls alone, pursuant to an agreement with other shareholders in or members of that enterprise, a majority of shareholders' or members' voting rights in that enterprise.

There is a presumption that no dominant influence exists if the investors listed in the second subparagraph of paragraph 2 are not involving themselves directly or indirectly in the management of the enterprise in question, without prejudice to their rights as stakeholders.

Enterprises having any of the relationships described in the first subparagraph through one or more other enterprises, or any one of the investors mentioned in paragraph 2, are also considered to be linked.

Enterprises which have one or other of such relationships through a natural person or group of natural persons acting jointly are also considered linked enterprises if they engage in their activity or in part of their activity in the same relevant market or in adjacent markets.

An "adjacent market" is considered to be the market for a product or service situated directly upstream or downstream of the relevant market.

4. Except in the cases set out in paragraph 2, second subparagraph, an enterprise cannot be considered an SME if 25% or more of the capital or voting rights are directly or indirectly controlled, jointly or individually, by one or more public bodies.

5. Enterprises may make a declaration of status as an autonomous enterprise, partner enterprise or linked enterprise, including the data regarding the ceilings set out in Article 2. The declaration may be made even if the capital is spread in such a way that it is not possible to determine exactly by whom it is held, in which case the enterprise may declare in good faith that it can legitimately presume that it is not owned as to 25% or more by one enterprise or jointly by enterprises linked to one another. Such declarations are made without prejudice to the checks and investigations provided for by national or Community rules.

Article 4 Data used for the staff headcount and the financial amounts and reference period

1. The data to apply to the headcount of staff and the financial amounts are those relating to the latest approved accounting period and calculated on an annual basis. They are taken into account from the date of closure of the accounts. The amount selected for the turnover is calculated excluding value added tax (VAT) and other indirect taxes.
2. Where, at the date of closure of the accounts, an enterprise finds that, on an annual basis, it has exceeded or fallen below the headcount or financial ceilings stated in Article 2, this will not result in the loss or acquisition of the status of medium-sized, small or microenterprise unless those ceilings are exceeded over two consecutive accounting periods.
3. In the case of newly established enterprises whose accounts have not yet been approved, the data to apply is to be derived from a bona fide estimate made in the course of the financial year.

Article 5 Staff headcount

The headcount corresponds to the number of annual work units (AWU), ie, the number of persons who worked full-time within the enterprise in question or on its behalf during the entire reference year under consideration. The work of persons who have not worked the full year, the work of those who have worked part-time, regardless of duration, and the work of seasonal workers are counted as fractions of AWU. The staff consists of:

(a) employees;
(b) persons working for the enterprise being subordinated to it and deemed to be employees under national law;
(c) owner-managers;
(d) partners engaging in a regular activity in the enterprise and benefiting from financial advantages from the enterprise.

Apprentices or students engaged in vocational training with an apprenticeship or vocational training contract are not included as staff. The duration of maternity or parental leaves is not counted.

Article 6 Establishing the data of an enterprise

1. In the case of an autonomous enterprise, the data, including the number of staff, are determined exclusively on the basis of the accounts of that enterprise.

2. The data, including the headcount, of an enterprise having partner enterprises or linked enterprises are determined on the basis of the accounts and other data of the enterprise or, where they exist, the consolidated accounts of the enterprise, or the consolidated accounts in which the enterprise is included through consolidation.

To the data referred to in the first subparagraph are added the data of any partner enterprise of the enterprise in question situated immediately upstream or downstream from it. Aggregation is proportional to the percentage interest in the capital or voting rights (whichever is greater). In the case of cross-holdings, the greater percentage applies.

To the data referred to in the first and second subparagraph is added 100% of the data of any enterprise, which is linked directly or indirectly to the enterprise in question, where the data were not already included through consolidation in the accounts.

3. For the application of paragraph 2, the data of the partner enterprises of the enterprise in question are derived from their accounts and their other data, consolidated if they exist. To these is added 100% of the data of enterprises which are linked to these partner enterprises, unless their accounts data are already included through consolidation.

For the application of the same paragraph 2, the data of the enterprises which are linked to the enterprise in question are to be derived from their accounts and their other data, consolidated if they exist. To these is added, pro rata, the data of any possible partner enterprise of that linked enterprise, situated immediately upstream or downstream from it, unless it has already been included in the consolidated accounts with a percentage at least proportional to the percentage identified under the second subparagraph of paragraph 2.

4. Where in the consolidated accounts no staff data appear for a given enterprise, staff figures are calculated by aggregating proportionally the data from its partner enterprises and by adding the data from the enterprises to which the enterprise in question is linked.

TITLE II SUNDRY PROVISIONS

Article 7 Statistics

The Commission will take the necessary measures to present the statistics that it produces in accordance with the following size-classes of enterprises:

(a) 0 to 1 person;
(b) 2 to 9 persons;
(c) 10 to 49 persons;
(d) 50 to 249 persons.

Article 8 References

1. Any Community legislation or any Community programme to be amended or adopted and in which the term "SME", "microenterprise", "small enterprise" or "medium-sized enterprise", or any other similar term occurs, should refer to the definition contained in this Recommendation.

2. As a transitional measure, current Community programmes using the SME definition in Recommendation 96/280/EC will continue to be implemented for the benefit of the enterprises which were considered SMEs when those programmes were adopted. Legally binding commitments entered into by the Commission on the basis of such programmes will remain unaffected.

Without prejudice to the first subparagraph, any amendment of the SME definition within the programmes can be made only by adopting the definition contained in this Recommendation in accordance with paragraph 1.

Article 9 Revision

On the basis of a review of the application of the definition contained in this Recommendation, to be drawn up by 31 March 2006, and taking account of any amendments to Article 1 of Directive 83/349/EEC on the definition of linked enterprises within the meaning of that Directive, the Commission will, if necessary, adapt the definition contained in this Recommendation, and in particular the ceilings for turnover and the balance-sheet total in order to take account of experience and economic developments in the Community.

COMMISSION REGULATION

(773/2004/EC)

of 7 April 2004

relating to the conduct of proceedings by the Commission pursuant to Articles 81 and 82 of the EC Treaty

(Text with EEA relevance)

[4.83]

NOTES

Date of publication in OJ: OJ L123, 27.04.2004, p 18.

Repeal of this Regulation in relation to the UK: this Regulation is repealed, in relation to the UK, by the Competition (Amendment etc) (EU Exit) Regulations 2019, SI 2019/93, reg 63, Sch 3, para 2, as from IP completion day (as defined in the European Union (Withdrawal Agreement) Act 2020, s 39) (for transitional provisions and savings in relation to the operation of the 2019 Regulations, see Sch 4 to those Regulations at **[7.69]** et seq).

Note: with effect from 1 December 2009, the EC Treaty was replaced by the Treaty on the Functioning of the European Union. References in this document to provisions of the EC Treaty should be construed accordingly. As to Articles 81 and 82 of the EC Treaty, see now Articles 101 and 102 of the Treaty on the Functioning of the European Union.

THE COMMISSION OF THE EUROPEAN COMMUNITIES,

Having regard to the Treaty establishing the European Community,

Having regard to the Agreement on the European Economic Area,

Having regard to Council Regulation (EC) No 1/2003 of 16 December 2002 on the implementation of the rules on competition laid down in Articles 81 and 82 of the Treaty,[1] *and in particular Article 33 thereof,*

After consulting the Advisory Committee on Restrictive Practices and Dominant Positions,

Whereas:

(1) Regulation (EC) No 1/2003 empowers the Commission to regulate certain aspects of proceedings for the application of Articles 81 and 82 of the Treaty. It is necessary to lay down rules concerning the initiation of proceedings by the Commission as well as the handling of complaints and the hearing of the parties concerned.

(2) According to Regulation (EC) No 1/2003, national courts are under an obligation to avoid taking decisions which could run counter to decisions envisaged by the Commission in the same case. According to Article 11(6) of that Regulation, national competition authorities are relieved from their competence once the Commission has initiated proceedings for the adoption of a decision under Chapter III of Regulation (EC) No 1/2003. In this context, it is important that courts and competition authorities of the Member States are aware of the initiation of proceedings by the Commission. The Commission should therefore be able to make public its decisions to initiate proceedings.

(3) Before taking oral statements from natural or legal persons who consent to be interviewed, the Commission should inform those persons of the legal basis of the interview and its voluntary nature. The persons interviewed should also be informed of the purpose of the interview and of any record which may be made. In order to enhance the accuracy of the statements, the persons interviewed should also be given an opportunity to correct the statements recorded. Where information gathered from oral statements is exchanged pursuant to Article 12 of Regulation (EC) No 1/2003, that information should only be used in evidence to impose sanctions on natural persons where the conditions set out in that Article are fulfilled.

(4) Pursuant to Article 23(1)(d) of Regulation (EC) No 1/2003 fines may be imposed on undertakings and associations of undertakings where they fail to rectify within the time limit fixed by the Commission an incorrect, incomplete or misleading answer given by a member of their staff to questions in the course of inspections. It is therefore necessary to provide the undertaking concerned with a record of any explanations given and to establish a procedure enabling it to add any rectification, amendment or supplement to the explanations given by the member of staff who is not or was not authorised to provide explanations on behalf of the undertaking. The explanations given by a member of staff should remain in the Commission file as recorded during the inspection.

(5) Complaints are an essential source of information for detecting infringements of competition rules. It is important to define clear and efficient procedures for handling complaints lodged with the Commission.

(6) In order to be admissible for the purposes of Article 7 of Regulation (EC) No 1/2003, a complaint must contain certain specified information.

(7) In order to assist complainants in submitting the necessary facts to the Commission, a form should be drawn up. The submission of the information listed in that form should be a condition for a complaint to be treated as a complaint as referred to in Article 7 of Regulation (EC) No 1/2003.

(8) Natural or legal persons having chosen to lodge a complaint should be given the possibility to be associated closely with the proceedings initiated by the Commission with a view to finding an infringement. However, they should not have access to business secrets or other confidential information belonging to other parties involved in the proceedings.

(9) Complainants should be granted the opportunity of expressing their views if the Commission considers that there are insufficient grounds for acting on the complaint. Where the Commission rejects a complaint on the grounds that a competition authority of a Member State is dealing with it or has already done so, it should inform the complainant of the identity of that authority.

(10) In order to respect the rights of defence of undertakings, the Commission should give the parties concerned the right to be heard before it takes a decision.

(11) Provision should also be made for the hearing of persons who have not submitted a complaint as referred to in Article 7 of Regulation (EC) No 1/2003 and who are not parties to whom a statement of objections has been addressed but who can nevertheless show a sufficient interest. Consumer associations that apply to be heard should generally be regarded as having a sufficient interest, where the proceedings concern products or services used by the end-consumer or products or services that constitute a direct input into such products or services. Where it considers this to be useful for the proceedings, the Commission should also be able to invite other persons to express their views in writing and to attend the oral hearing of the parties to whom a statement of objections has been addressed. Where appropriate, it should also be able to invite such persons to express their views at that oral hearing.

(12) To improve the effectiveness of oral hearings, the Hearing Officer should have the power to allow the parties concerned, complainants, other persons invited to the hearing, the Commission services and the authorities of the Member States to ask questions during the hearing.

(13) When granting access to the file, the Commission should ensure the protection of business secrets and other confidential information. The category of "other confidential information" includes information other than business secrets, which may be considered as confidential, insofar as its disclosure would significantly harm an undertaking or person. The Commission should be able to request undertakings or associations of undertakings that submit or have submitted documents or statements to identify confidential information.

(14) Where business secrets or other confidential information are necessary to prove an infringement, the Commission should assess for each individual document whether the need to disclose is greater than the harm which might result from disclosure.

(15) In the interest of legal certainty, a minimum time-limit for the various submissions provided for in this Regulation should be laid down.

(16) This Regulation replaces Commission Regulation (EC) No 2842/98 of 22 December 1998 on the hearing of parties in certain proceedings under Articles 85 and 86 of the EC Treaty,[2] *which should therefore be repealed.*

(17) This Regulation aligns the procedural rules in the transport sector with the general rules of procedure in all sectors. Commission Regulation (EC) No 2843/98 of 22 December 1998 on the form, content and other details of applications and notifications provided for in Council Regulations (EEC) No 1017/68, (EEC) No 4056/86 and (EEC) No 3975/87 applying the rules on competition to the transport sector[3] *should therefore be repealed.*

(18) Regulation (EC) No 1/2003 abolishes the notification and authorisation system. Commission Regulation (EC) No 3385/94 of 21 December 1994 on the form, content and other details of applications and notifications provided for in Council Regulation No 17[4] *should therefore be repealed,*

NOTES

Repeal of this Regulation in relation to the UK: this Regulation is repealed in relation to the UK (as from IP completion day); see the introductory notes to this Regulation *ante*.

[1] OJ L1, 4.1.2003, p 1. Regulation as amended by Regulation (EC) No 411/2004 (OJ L68, 6.3.2004, p 1).

[2] OJ L354, 30.12.1998, p 18.

[3] OJ L354, 30.12.1998, p 22.

[4] OJ L377, 31.12.1994, p 28.

HAS ADOPTED THIS REGULATION:

CHAPTER I SCOPE

[4.84]

Article 1 Subject-matter and scope

This regulation applies to proceedings conducted by the Commission for the application of Articles 81 and 82 of the Treaty.

NOTES

Repeal of this Regulation in relation to the UK: this Regulation is repealed in relation to the UK (as from IP completion day); see the introductory notes to this Regulation *ante*.

CHAPTER II INITIATION OF PROCEEDINGS

[4.85]

Article 2 Initiation of proceedings

[1. The Commission may decide to initiate proceedings with a view to adopting a decision pursuant to Chapter III of Regulation (EC) No 1/2003 at any point in time, but no later than the date on which it issues a preliminary assessment as referred to in Article 9(1) of that Regulation, a statement of objections or a request for the parties to express their interest in engaging in settlement discussions, or the date on which a notice pursuant to Article 27(4) of that Regulation is published, whichever is the earlier.]

2. The Commission may make public the initiation of proceedings, in any appropriate way. Before doing so, it shall inform the parties concerned.

3. The Commission may exercise its powers of investigation pursuant to Chapter V of Regulation (EC) No 1/2003 before initiating proceedings.

4. The Commission may reject a complaint pursuant to Article 7 of Regulation (EC) No 1/2003 without initiating proceedings.

NOTES

Para 1: substituted by Commission Regulation 622/2008/EC, Art 1(1).

Repeal of this Regulation in relation to the UK: this Regulation is repealed in relation to the UK (as from IP completion day); see the introductory notes to this Regulation *ante*.

CHAPTER III INVESTIGATIONS BY THE COMMISSION

[4.86]

Article 3 Power to take statements

1. Where the Commission interviews a person with his consent in accordance with Article 19 of Regulation (EC) No 1/2003, it shall, at the beginning of the interview, state the legal basis and the purpose of the interview, and recall its voluntary nature. It shall also inform the person interviewed of its intention to make a record of the interview.

2. The interview may be conducted by any means including by telephone or electronic means.

3. The Commission may record the statements made by the persons interviewed in any form. A copy of any recording shall be made available to the person interviewed for approval. Where necessary, the Commission shall set a time-limit within which the person interviewed may communicate to it any correction to be made to the statement.

NOTES

Repeal of this Regulation in relation to the UK: this Regulation is repealed in relation to the UK (as from IP completion day); see the introductory notes to this Regulation *ante*.

[4.87]

Article 4 Oral questions during inspections

1. When, pursuant to Article 20(2)(e) of Regulation (EC) No 1/2003, officials or other accompanying persons authorised by the Commission ask representatives or members of staff of an undertaking or of an association of undertakings for explanations, the explanations given may be recorded in any form.

2. A copy of any recording made pursuant to paragraph 1 shall be made available to the undertaking or association of undertakings concerned after the inspection.

3. In cases where a member of staff of an undertaking or of an association of undertakings who is not or was not authorised by the undertaking or by the association of undertakings to provide explanations on behalf of the undertaking or association of undertakings has been asked for explanations, the Commission shall set a time-limit within which the undertaking or the association of undertakings may communicate to the Commission any rectification, amendment or supplement to the explanations given by such member of staff. The rectification, amendment or supplement shall be added to the explanations as recorded pursuant to paragraph 1.

NOTES

Repeal of this Regulation in relation to the UK: this Regulation is repealed in relation to the UK (as from IP completion day); see the introductory notes to this Regulation *ante*.

[4.88]

[Article 4a The Commission's Leniency Programme

1. The Commission may set the requirements and cooperation conditions under which it may reward undertakings that are or have been party to secret cartels, for their cooperation in disclosing the cartel and facilitating the establishment of an infringement, with immunity from fines or a reduction in fines which would otherwise be imposed under Article 23(2) of Regulation (EC) No 1/2003 (the Commission leniency programme).

Immunity from fines may be granted to the undertaking that is the first to submit evidence which in the Commission's view would enable it to carry out a targeted inspection or find an infringement of Article 101 of the Treaty in connection with the alleged cartel. A reduction in fines may be granted to undertakings which provide the Commission with evidence of the alleged infringement which represents significant added value with respect to the evidence already in the Commission's possession.

The Commission will only grant immunity from or a reduction of the fine under its leniency programme if, at the end of the administrative proceedings, the undertaking has met the requirements and cooperation conditions set out in the leniency programme. Those may cover, among others, the type of information and evidence the undertakings are required to submit and the further cooperation expected from the undertakings during the administrative proceedings.

2. In order to qualify for immunity from or reduction of the fine which would otherwise be imposed, undertakings shall provide the Commission with voluntary presentations of their knowledge of a secret cartel and their role therein, which may be also in the form of voluntary presentations of the knowledge of former or current employees or representatives of the undertaking (leniency corporate statements). Such leniency corporate statements shall be drawn up specifically for submission to the Commission with a view to obtaining immunity from or reduction of fines under the Commission's leniency programme.

3. The Commission will offer parties appropriate methods of providing leniency corporate statements other than by written submission, including orally. Oral corporate statements may be recorded and transcribed at the Commission's premises. The undertaking shall be granted an opportunity to check the technical accuracy of the recording of its oral statement at the Commission's premises, and, where necessary, to correct the substance of the statement without delay. The rules in this Regulation on leniency corporate statements shall apply to such statements irrespective of the medium on which they are stored. Pre-existing information, ie evidence that exists irrespective of the Commission proceedings and that is submitted to the Commission by an undertaking in the context of its application for immunity from or reduction of the fine, is not part of a leniency corporate statement.]

NOTES

Inserted by Commission Regulation 1348/2015/EU, Art 1(1).

Repeal of this Regulation in relation to the UK: this Regulation is repealed in relation to the UK (as from IP completion day); see the introductory notes to this Regulation *ante*.

CHAPTER IV HANDLING OF COMPLAINTS

[4.89]

Article 5 Admissibility of complaints

1. Natural and legal persons shall show a legitimate interest in order to be entitled to lodge a complaint for the purposes of Article 7 of Regulation (EC) No 1/2003.

Such complaints shall contain the information required by Form C, as set out in the Annex. The Commission may dispense with this obligation as regards part of the information, including documents, required by Form C.

2. Three paper copies as well as, if possible, an electronic copy of the complaint shall be submitted to the Commission. The complainant shall also submit a non-confidential version of the complaint, if confidentiality is claimed for any part of the complaint.

3. Complaints shall be submitted in one of the official languages of the Community.

NOTES

Repeal of this Regulation in relation to the UK: this Regulation is repealed in relation to the UK (as from IP completion day); see the introductory notes to this Regulation *ante*.

[4.90]

Article 6 Participation of complainants in proceedings

[1. Where the Commission issues a statement of objections relating to a matter in respect of which it has received a complaint, it shall provide the complainant with a copy of the non-confidential version of the statement of objections, except in cases where the settlement procedure applies, where it shall inform the complainant in writing of the nature and subject matter of the procedure. The Commission shall also set a time limit within which the complainant may make known its views in writing.]

2. The Commission may, where appropriate, afford complainants the opportunity of expressing their views at the oral hearing of the parties to which a statement of objections has been issued, if complainants so request in their written comments.

NOTES

Para 1: substituted by Commission Regulation 622/2008/EC, Art 1(2).

Repeal of this Regulation in relation to the UK: this Regulation is repealed in relation to the UK (as from IP completion day); see the introductory notes to this Regulation *ante*.

[4.91]

Article 7 Rejection of complaints

1. Where the Commission considers that on the basis of the information in its possession there are insufficient grounds for acting on a complaint, it shall inform the complainant of its reasons and set a time-limit within which the complainant may make known its views in writing. The Commission shall not be obliged to take into account any further written submission received after the expiry of that time-limit.

2. If the complainant makes known its views within the time-limit set by the Commission and the written submissions made by the complainant do not lead to a different assessment of the complaint, the Commission shall reject the complaint by decision.

3. If the complainant fails to make known its views within the time-limit set by the Commission, the complaint shall be deemed to have been withdrawn.

NOTES

Repeal of this Regulation in relation to the UK: this Regulation is repealed in relation to the UK (as from IP completion day); see the introductory notes to this Regulation *ante*.

[4.92]

Article 8 Access to information

1. Where the Commission has informed the complainant of its intention to reject a complaint pursuant to Article 7(1) the complainant may request access to the documents on which the Commission bases its provisional assessment. For this purpose, the complainant may however not have access to business secrets and other confidential information belonging to other parties involved in the proceedings.

2. . . .

NOTES

Para 2: repealed by Commission Regulation 1348/2015/EU, Art 1(2).

Repeal of this Regulation in relation to the UK: this Regulation is repealed in relation to the UK (as from IP completion day); see the introductory notes to this Regulation *ante*.

[4.93]

Article 9 Rejections of complaints pursuant to Article 13 of Regulation (EC) No 1/2003

Where the Commission rejects a complaint pursuant to Article 13 of Regulation (EC) No 1/2003, it shall inform the complainant without delay of the national competition authority which is dealing or has already dealt with the case.

NOTES

Repeal of this Regulation in relation to the UK: this Regulation is repealed in relation to the UK (as from IP completion day); see the introductory notes to this Regulation *ante*.

CHAPTER V EXERCISE OF THE RIGHT TO BE HEARD

[4.94]

Article 10 Statement of objections and reply

[1. The Commission shall inform the parties concerned of the objections raised against them. The statement of objections shall be notified in writing to each of the parties against whom objections are raised.]

2. The Commission shall, when notifying the statement of objections to the parties concerned, set a time-limit within which these parties may inform it in writing of their views. The Commission shall not be obliged to take into account written submissions received after the expiry of that time-limit.

3. The parties may, in their written submissions, set out all facts known to them which are relevant to their defence against the objections raised by the Commission. They shall attach any relevant documents as proof of the facts set out. They shall provide a paper original as well as an electronic copy or, where they do not provide an electronic copy, [31] paper copies of their submission and of the documents attached to it. They may propose that the Commission hear persons who may corroborate the facts set out in their submission.

NOTES

Para 1: substituted by Commission Regulation 622/2008/EC, Art 1(3).

Para 3: figure in square brackets substituted by Commission Regulation 519/2013/EU, Art 1, Annex.

Repeal of this Regulation in relation to the UK: this Regulation is repealed in relation to the UK (as from IP completion day); see the introductory notes to this Regulation *ante*.

[4.95]

[Article 10a Settlement procedure in cartel cases

1. After the initiation of proceedings pursuant to Article 11(6) of Regulation (EC) No 1/2003, the Commission may set a time limit within which the parties may indicate in writing that they are prepared to engage in settlement discussions with a view to possibly introducing settlement submissions. The Commission shall not be obliged to take into account replies received after the expiry of that time limit.

If two or more parties within the same undertaking indicate their willingness to engage in settlement discussions pursuant to the first subparagraph, they shall appoint a joint representation to engage in discussions with the Commission on their behalf. When setting the time limit referred to in the first subparagraph, the Commission shall indicate to the relevant parties that they are identified within the same undertaking, for the sole purpose of enabling them to comply with this provision.

2. Parties taking part in settlement discussions may be informed by the Commission of:

(a) the objections it envisages to raise against them;

(b) the evidence used to determine the envisaged objections;

(c) *non-confidential versions of any specified accessible document listed in the case file at that point in time, in so far as a request by the party is justified for the purpose of enabling the party to ascertain its position regarding a time period or any other particular aspect of the cartel; and*

(d) *the range of potential fines.*

This information shall be confidential vis-à-vis third parties, save where the Commission has given a prior explicit authorisation for disclosure.

[Should settlement discussions progress, the Commission may set a time limit within which the parties may commit to follow the settlement procedure by introducing settlement submissions reflecting the results of the settlement discussions and acknowledging their participation in an infringement of Article 101 of the Treaty as well as their liability. These settlement submissions shall be specifically drawn up by the undertakings concerned as a formal request to the Commission to adopt any decision in their case following the settlement procedure. Before the Commission sets a time limit for the introduction of settlement submissions, the parties concerned shall be entitled to have the information specified in the first subparagraph, disclosed to them, upon request, in a timely manner. The Commission shall not be obliged to take into account settlement submissions received after the expiry of that time limit.

The Commission will offer parties appropriate methods of providing settlement submissions other than by written submission, including orally. Oral settlement submissions may be recorded and transcribed at the Commission's premises. The undertaking shall be granted an opportunity to check the technical accuracy of the recording of its oral submission at the Commission's premises, and, where necessary, to correct the substance of their submission without delay. The rules in this Regulation on settlement submissions shall apply to settlement submissions irrespective of the medium on which they are stored.]

3. When the statement of objections notified to the parties reflects the contents of their settlement submissions, the written reply to the statement of objections by the parties concerned shall, within a time limit set by the Commission, confirm that the statement of objections addressed to them reflects the contents of their settlement submissions. The Commission may then proceed to the adoption of a Decision pursuant to Article 7 and Article 23 of Regulation (EC) No 1/2003 after consultation of the Advisory Committee on Restrictive Practices and Dominant Positions pursuant to Article 14 of Regulation (EC) No 1/2003.

4. The Commission may decide at any time during the procedure to discontinue settlement discussions altogether in a specific case or with respect to one or more of the parties involved, if it considers that procedural efficiencies are not likely to be achieved.]

NOTES

Inserted by Commission Regulation 622/2008/EC, Art 1(4).

Para 2: words in square brackets substituted by Commission Regulation 1348/2015/EU, Art 1(3).

Repeal of this Regulation in relation to the UK: this Regulation is repealed in relation to the UK (as from IP completion day); see the introductory notes to this Regulation *ante*.

[4.96]

Article 11 Right to be heard

[1. The Commission shall give the parties to whom it addresses a statement of objections the opportunity to be heard before consulting the Advisory Committee referred to in Article 14(1) of Regulation (EC) No 1/2003.]

2. The Commission shall, in its decisions, deal only with objections in respect of which the parties referred to in paragraph 1 have been able to comment.

NOTES

Para 1: substituted by Commission Regulation 622/2008/EC, Art 1(5).

Repeal of this Regulation in relation to the UK: this Regulation is repealed in relation to the UK (as from IP completion day); see the introductory notes to this Regulation *ante*.

[4.97]

[Article 12 Right to an oral hearing

1. The Commission shall give the parties to whom it addresses a statement of objections the opportunity to develop their arguments at an oral hearing, if they so request in their written submissions.

2. However, when introducing their settlement submissions the parties shall confirm to the Commission that they would only require having the opportunity to develop their arguments at an oral hearing, if the statement of objections does not reflect the contents of their settlement submissions.]

NOTES

Substituted by Commission Regulation 622/2008/EC, Art 1(6).

Repeal of this Regulation in relation to the UK: this Regulation is repealed in relation to the UK (as from IP completion day); see the introductory notes to this Regulation *ante*.

[4.98]

Article 13 Hearing of other persons

1. If natural or legal persons other than those referred to in Articles 5 and 11 apply to be heard and show a sufficient interest, the Commission shall inform them in writing of the nature and subject matter of the procedure and shall set a time-limit within which they may make known their views in writing.

2. The Commission may, where appropriate, invite persons referred to in paragraph 1 to develop their arguments at the oral hearing of the parties to whom a statement of objections has been addressed, if the persons referred to in paragraph 1 so request in their written comments.

3. The Commission may invite any other person to express its views in writing and to attend the oral hearing of the parties to whom a statement of objections has been addressed. The Commission may also invite such persons to express their views at that oral hearing.

NOTES

Repeal of this Regulation in relation to the UK: this Regulation is repealed in relation to the UK (as from IP completion day); see the introductory notes to this Regulation *ante*.

[4.99]

Article 14 Conduct of oral hearings

1. Hearings shall be conducted by a Hearing Officer in full independence.

2. The Commission shall invite the persons to be heard to attend the oral hearing on such date as it shall determine.

3. The Commission shall invite the competition authorities of the Member States to take part in the oral hearing. It may likewise invite officials and civil servants of other authorities of the Member States.

4. Persons invited to attend shall either appear in person or be represented by legal representatives or by representatives authorised by their constitution as appropriate. Undertakings and associations of undertakings may also be represented by a duly authorised agent appointed from among their permanent staff.

5. Persons heard by the Commission may be assisted by their lawyers or other qualified persons admitted by the Hearing Officer.

6. Oral hearings shall not be public. Each person may be heard separately or in the presence of other persons invited to attend, having regard to the legitimate interest of the undertakings in the protection of their business secrets and other confidential information.

7. The Hearing Officer may allow the parties to whom a statement of objections has been addressed, the complainants, other persons invited to the hearing, the Commission services and the authorities of the Member States to ask questions during the hearing.

8. The statements made by each person heard shall be recorded. Upon request, the recording of the hearing shall be made available to the persons who attended the hearing. Regard shall be had to the legitimate interest of the parties in the protection of their business secrets and other confidential information.

NOTES

Repeal of this Regulation in relation to the UK: this Regulation is repealed in relation to the UK (as from IP completion day); see the introductory notes to this Regulation *ante*.

CHAPTER VI ACCESS TO THE FILE AND TREATMENT OF CONFIDENTIAL INFORMATION

[4.100]

Article 15 [Access to the file]

1. If so requested, the Commission shall grant access to the file to the parties to whom it has addressed a statement of objections. Access shall be granted after the notification of the statement of objections.

[1a. After the initiation of proceedings pursuant to Article 11(6) of Regulation (EC) No 1/2003 and in order to enable the parties to introduce settlement submissions, the Commission shall disclose to them the evidence and documents described in Article 10a(2) upon request and subject to the conditions established in the relevant subparagraphs. In view thereof, when introducing their settlement submissions, the parties shall confirm to the Commission that they will only require access to the file pursuant to paragraph 1 after the receipt of the statement of objections, if the statement of objections does not reflect the contents of their settlement submissions. Where settlement discussions have been discontinued with one or more of the parties, such party shall be granted access to the file pursuant to paragraph 1 when a statement of objections has been addressed to it.]

[1b. Access pursuant to paragraph 1 or 1a to a leniency corporate statement within the meaning of Article 4a(2) or to a settlement submission within the meaning of Article 10a(2), shall only be granted at the premises of the Commission. The parties and their representatives shall not copy the leniency corporate statements or settlement submissions by any mechanical or electronic means.]

2. The right of access to the file shall not extend to business secrets, other confidential information and internal documents of the Commission or of the competition authorities of the Member States. The right of access to the file shall also not extend to correspondence between the Commission and the competition authorities of the Member States or between the latter where such correspondence is contained in the file of the Commission.

3. Nothing in this Regulation prevents the Commission from disclosing and using information necessary to prove an infringement of Articles 81 or 82 of the Treaty.

4. . . .

NOTES

Article heading: substituted by Commission Regulation 1348/2015/EU, Art 1(4)(a).

Para 1a: inserted by Commission Regulation 622/2008/EC, Art 1(7); substituted by Commission Regulation 1348/2015/EU, Art 1(4)(b).

Para 1b: inserted by Commission Regulation 1348/2015/EU, Art 1(4)(c).

Para 4: repealed by Commission Regulation 1348/2015/EU, Art 1(4)(d).

Repeal of this Regulation in relation to the UK: this Regulation is repealed in relation to the UK (as from IP completion day); see the introductory notes to this Regulation *ante*.

[4.101]

Article 16 Identification and protection of confidential information

1. Information, including documents, shall not be communicated or made accessible by the Commission in so far as it contains business secrets or other confidential information of any person.

2. Any person which makes known its views pursuant to Article 6(1), Article 7(1), Article 10(2) and Article 13(1) and (3) or subsequently submits further information to the Commission in the course of the same procedure, shall clearly identify any material which it considers to be confidential, giving reasons, and provide a separate non-confidential version by the date set by the Commission for making its views known.

3. Without prejudice to paragraph 2 of this Article, the Commission may require undertakings and associations of undertakings which produce documents or statements pursuant to Regulation (EC) No 1/2003 to identify the documents or parts of documents which they consider to contain business secrets or other confidential information belonging to them and to identify the undertakings with regard to which such documents are to be considered confidential. The Commission may likewise require undertakings or associations of undertakings to identify any part of a statement of objections, a case summary drawn up pursuant to Article 27(4) of Regulation (EC) No 1/2003 or a decision adopted by the Commission which in their view contains business secrets.

The Commission may set a time-limit within which the undertakings and associations of undertakings are to:

(a) substantiate their claim for confidentiality with regard to each individual document or part of document, statement or part of statement;

(b) provide the Commission with a non-confidential version of the documents or statements, in which the confidential passages are deleted;

(c) provide a concise description of each piece of deleted information.

4. If undertakings or associations of undertakings fail to comply with paragraphs 2 and 3, the Commission may assume that the documents or statements concerned do not contain confidential information.

NOTES

Repeal of this Regulation in relation to the UK: this Regulation is repealed in relation to the UK (as from IP completion day); see the introductory notes to this Regulation *ante*.

[CHAPTER VIA LIMITATIONS TO THE USE OF INFORMATION OBTAINED IN THE COURSE OF COMMISSION PROCEEDINGS

[4.102]

Article 16a

1. Information obtained pursuant to this Regulation shall only be used for the purposes of judicial or administrative proceedings for the application of Articles 101 and 102 of the Treaty.

2. Access to leniency corporate statements within the meaning of Article 4a(2) or to settlement submissions within the meaning of Article 10a(2) shall be granted only for the purposes of exercising the rights of defence in proceedings before the Commission. Information taken from such statements and submissions may be used by the party having obtained access to the file only where necessary for the exercise of its rights of defence in proceedings:

(a) before the European Union courts reviewing Commission decisions; or

(b) before the courts of the Member States in cases that are directly related to the case in which access has been granted, and which concern:

(i) the allocation between cartel participants of a fine imposed jointly and severally on them by the Commission; or

(ii) the review of a decision by which a competition authority of a Member State has found an infringement of Article 101 TFEU.

3. The following categories of information obtained pursuant to this Regulation shall not be used in proceedings before national courts until the Commission has closed its proceedings against all parties under investigation by adopting a decision pursuant to Article 7, 9 or 10 of Regulation (EC) No 1/2003 or has otherwise terminated its proceedings:

(a) information that was prepared by other natural or legal persons specifically for the proceedings of the Commission; and

(b) information that the Commission has drawn up and sent to the parties in the course of its proceedings.]

NOTES

Chapter VIa (Art 16a) inserted by Commission Regulation 1348/2015/EU, Art 1(5).

Repeal of this Regulation in relation to the UK: this Regulation is repealed in relation to the UK (as from IP completion day); see the introductory notes to this Regulation *ante*.

CHAPTER VII GENERAL AND FINAL PROVISIONS

[4.103]

Article 17 Time-limits

[1. In setting the time limits provided for in Article 3(3), Article 4(3), Article 6(1), Article 7(1), Article 10(2), Article 10a(1), Article 10a(2), Article 10a(3) and Article 16(3), the Commission shall have regard both to the time required for preparation of the submission and to the urgency of the case.]

2. The time-limits referred to in Article 6(1), Article 7(1) and Article 10(2) shall be at least four weeks. However, for proceedings initiated with a view to adopting interim measures pursuant to Article 8 of Regulation (EC) No 1/2003, the time-limit may be shortened to one week.

[3. The time limits referred to in Article 4(3), Article 10a(1), Article 10a(2) and Article 16(3) shall be at least two weeks. The time limit referred to in Article 3(3) shall be at least two weeks, except for settlement submissions, for which corrections shall be made within one week. The time limit referred to in Article 10a(3) shall be at least two weeks.]

4. Where appropriate and upon reasoned request made before the expiry of the original time-limit, time-limits may be extended.

NOTES

Paras 1, 3: substituted by Commission Regulation 622/2008/EC, Art 1(8).

Repeal of this Regulation in relation to the UK: this Regulation is repealed in relation to the UK (as from IP completion day); see the introductory notes to this Regulation *ante*.

[4.104]

Article 18 Repeals

Regulations (EC) No 2842/98, (EC) No 2843/98 and (EC) No 3385/94 are repealed.

References to the repealed regulations shall be construed as references to this regulation.

NOTES

Repeal of this Regulation in relation to the UK: this Regulation is repealed in relation to the UK (as from IP completion day); see the introductory notes to this Regulation *ante*.

[4.105]

Article 19 Transitional provisions

Procedural steps taken under Regulations (EC) No 2842/98 and (EC) No 2843/98 shall continue to have effect for the purpose of applying this Regulation.

NOTES

Repeal of this Regulation in relation to the UK: this Regulation is repealed in relation to the UK (as from IP completion day); see the introductory notes to this Regulation *ante*.

[4.106]

Article 20 Entry into force

This Regulation shall enter into force on 1 May 2004.

NOTES

Repeal of this Regulation in relation to the UK: this Regulation is repealed in relation to the UK (as from IP completion day); see the introductory notes to this Regulation *ante*.

ANNEX

FORM C

COMPLAINT PURSUANT TO ARTICLE 7 OF REGULATION (EC) NO 1/2003

[4.107]

I. Information regarding the complainant and the undertaking(s) or association of undertakings giving rise to the complaint

1. Give full details on the identity of the legal or natural person submitting the complaint. Where the complainant is an undertaking, identify the corporate group to which it belongs and provide a concise overview of the nature and scope of its business activities. Provide a contact person (with telephone number, postal and Email-address) from which supplementary explanations can be obtained.

2. Identify the undertaking(s) or association of undertakings whose conduct the complaint relates to, including, where applicable, all available information on the corporate group to which the undertaking(s) complained of belong and the nature and scope of the business activities pursued by them. Indicate the position of the complainant vis-à-vis the undertaking(s) or association of undertakings complained of (eg customer, competitor).

II. Details of the alleged infringement and evidence

3. Set out in detail the facts from which, in your opinion, it appears that there exists an infringement of Article 81 or 82 of the Treaty and/or Article 53 or 54 of the EEA agreement. Indicate in particular the nature of the products (goods or services) affected by the alleged infringements and explain, where necessary, the commercial relationships concerning these products. Provide all available details on the agreements or practices of the undertakings or associations of undertakings to which this complaint relates. Indicate, to the extent possible, the relative market positions of the undertakings concerned by the complaint.

4. Submit all documentation in your possession relating to or directly connected with the facts set out in the complaint (for example, texts of agreements, minutes of negotiations or meetings, terms of transactions, business documents, circulars, correspondence, notes of telephone conversations . . .). State the names and address of the persons able to testify to the facts set out in the complaint, and in particular of persons affected by the alleged infringement. Submit statistics or other data in your possession which relate to the facts set out, in particular where they show developments in the marketplace (for example information relating to prices and price trends, barriers to entry to the market for new suppliers etc).

5. Set out your view about the geographical scope of the alleged infringement and explain, where that is not obvious, to what extent trade between Member States or between the Community and one or more EFTA States that are contracting parties of the EEA Agreement may be affected by the conduct complained of.

III. Finding sought from the Commission and legitimate interest

6. Explain what finding or action you are seeking as a result of proceedings brought by the Commission.

7. Set out the grounds on which you claim a legitimate interest as complainant pursuant to Article 7 of Regulation (EC) No 1/2003. State in particular how the conduct complained of affects you and explain how, in your view, intervention by the Commission would be liable to remedy the alleged grievance.

IV. Proceedings before national competition authorities or national courts

8. Provide full information about whether you have approached, concerning the same or closely related subject-matters, any other competition authority and/or whether a lawsuit has been brought before a national court. If so, provide full details about the administrative or judicial authority contacted and your submissions to such authority.

Declaration that the information given in this form and in the Annexes thereto is given entirely in good faith.

Date and signature.

NOTES

Repeal of this Regulation in relation to the UK: this Regulation is repealed in relation to the UK (as from IP completion day); see the introductory notes to this Regulation *ante*.

COMMISSION NOTICE

(2004/C101/07)

Guidelines on the effect on trade concept contained in Articles 81 and 82 of the Treaty

(Text with EEA relevance)

[4.108]

NOTES

Date of publication in OJ: OJ C101, 27.4.2004, p 81.

Note: it appears that internal cross-referencing between paragraphs in this Notice was not completed before the publication this Notice in the English language version in Official Journal. Missing paragraph numbers have been added to this Notice by comparing it to the French version as published in the OJ. Those numbers are reproduced in italics and a Note to the provision concerned indicates their presence.

Note: with effect from 1 December 2009, the EC Treaty was replaced by the Treaty on the Functioning of the European Union. References in this document to provisions of the EC Treaty should be construed accordingly. As to Articles 81 and 82 of the EC Treaty, see now Articles 101 and 102 of the Treaty on the Functioning of the European Union.

1. INTRODUCTION

[4.109]

1. Articles 81 and 82 of the Treaty are applicable to horizontal and vertical agreements and practices on the part of undertakings which "may affect trade between Member States".

2. In their interpretation of Articles 81 and 82, the Community Courts have already substantially clarified the content and scope of the concept of effect on trade between Member States.

3. The present guidelines set out the principles developed by the Community Courts in relation to the interpretation of the effect on trade concept of Articles 81 and 82. They further spell out a rule indicating when agreements are in general unlikely to be capable of appreciably affecting trade between Member States (the non-appreciable affectation of trade rule or NAAT-rule). The guidelines are not intended to be exhaustive. The aim is to set out the methodology for the application of the effect on trade concept and to provide guidance on its application in frequently occurring situations. Although not binding on them, these guidelines also intend to give guidance to the courts and authorities of the Member States in their application of the effect on trade concept contained in Articles 81 and 82.

4. The present guidelines do not address the issue of what constitutes an appreciable restriction of competition under Article 81(1). This issue, which is distinct from the ability of agreements to appreciably affect trade between Member States, is dealt with in the Commission Notice on agreements of minor importance which do not appreciably restrict competition under Article 81(1) of the Treaty[1] (the de minimis rule). The guidelines are also not intended to provide guidance on the effect on trade concept contained in Article 87(1) of the Treaty on State aid.

5. These guidelines, including the NAAT-rule, are without prejudice to the interpretation of Articles 81 and 82 which may be given by the Court of Justice and the Court of First Instance.

NOTES

[1] OJ C368, 22.12.2001, p 13

2. THE EFFECT ON TRADE CRITERION

2.1. GENERAL PRINCIPLES

[4.110]

6. Article 81(1) provides that "the following shall be prohibited as incompatible with the common market: all agreements between undertakings, decisions of associations of undertakings and concerted practices which may affect trade between Member States and which have as their object or effect the prevention, restriction or distortion of competition within the common market". For the sake of simplicity the terms "agreements, decisions of associations of undertakings and concerted practices" are collectively referred to as "agreements".

7. Article 82 on its part stipulates that "any abuse by one or more undertakings of a dominant position within the common market or in a substantial part thereof shall be prohibited as incompatible with the common market insofar as it may affect trade between Member States." In what follows the term "practices" refers to the conduct of dominant undertakings.

8. The effect on trade criterion also determines the scope of application of Article 3 of Regulation 1/2003 on the implementation of the rules on competition laid down in Articles 81 and 82 of the Treaty.[2]

9. According to Article 3(1) of that Regulation the competition authorities and courts of the Member States must apply Article 81 to agreements, decisions by associations of undertakings or concerted practices within the meaning of Article 81(1) of the Treaty which may affect trade between Member States within the meaning of that provision, when they apply national competition law to such agreements, decisions or concerted practices. Similarly, when the

competition authorities and courts of the Member States apply national competition law to any abuse prohibited by Article 82 of the Treaty, they must also apply Article 82 of the Treaty. Article 3(1) thus obliges the competition authorities and courts of the Member States to also apply Articles 81 and 82 when they apply national competition law to agreements and abusive practices which may affect trade between Member States. On the other hand, Article 3(1) does not oblige national competition authorities and courts to apply national competition law when they apply Articles 81 and 82 to agreements, decisions and concerted practices and to abuses which may affect trade between Member States. They may in such cases apply the Community competition rules on a stand alone basis.

10. It follows from Article 3(2) that the application of national competition law may not lead to the prohibition of agreements, decisions by associations of undertakings or concerted practices which may affect trade between Member States but which do not restrict competition within the meaning of Article 81(1) of the Treaty, or which fulfil the conditions of Article 81(3) of the Treaty or which are covered by a Regulation for the application of Article 81(3) of the Treaty. Member States, however, are not under Regulation 1/2003 precluded from adopting and applying on their territory stricter national laws which prohibit or sanction unilateral conduct engaged in by undertakings.

11. Finally it should be mentioned that Article 3(3) stipulates that without prejudice to general principles and other provisions of Community law, Article 3(1) and (2) do not apply when the competition authorities and the courts of the Member States apply national merger control laws, nor do they preclude the application of provisions of national law that predominantly pursue an objective different from that pursued by Articles 81 and 82 of the Treaty.

12. The effect on trade criterion is an autonomous Community law criterion, which must be assessed separately in each case. It is a jurisdictional criterion, which defines the scope of application of Community competition law.[3] Community competition law is not applicable to agreements and practices that are not capable of appreciably affecting trade between Member States.

13. The effect on trade criterion confines the scope of application of Articles 81 and 82 to agreements and practices that are capable of having a minimum level of cross-border effects within the Community. In the words of the Court of Justice, the ability of the agreement or practice to affect trade between Member States must be "appreciable".[4]

14. In the case of Article 81 of the Treaty, it is the agreement that must be capable of affecting trade between Member States. It is not required that each individual part of the agreement, including any restriction of competition which may flow from the agreement, is capable of doing so.[5] If the agreement as a whole is capable of affecting trade between Member States, there is Community law jurisdiction in respect of the entire agreement, including any parts of the agreement that individually do not affect trade between Member States. In cases where the contractual relations between the same parties cover several activities, these activities must, in order to form part of the same agreement, be directly linked and form an integral part of the same overall business arrangement.[6] If not, each activity constitutes a separate agreement.

15. It is also immaterial whether or not the participation of a particular undertaking in the agreement has an appreciable effect on trade between Member States.[7] An undertaking cannot escape Community law jurisdiction merely because of the fact that its own contribution to an agreement, which itself is capable of affecting trade between Member States, is insignificant.

16. It is not necessary, for the purposes of establishing Community law jurisdiction, to establish a link between the alleged restriction of competition and the capacity of the agreement to affect trade between Member States. Non-restrictive agreements may also affect trade between Member States. For example, selective distribution agreements based on purely qualitative selection criteria justified by the nature of the products, which are not restrictive of competition within the meaning of Article 81(1), may nevertheless affect trade between Member States. However, the alleged restrictions arising from an agreement may provide a clear indication as to the capacity of the agreement to affect trade between Member States. For instance, a distribution agreement prohibiting exports is by its very nature capable of affecting trade between Member States, although not necessarily to an appreciable extent.[8]

17. In the case of Article 82 it is the abuse that must affect trade between Member States. This does not imply, however, that each element of the behaviour must be assessed in isolation. Conduct that forms part of an overall strategy pursued by the dominant undertaking must be assessed in terms of its overall impact. Where a dominant undertaking adopts various practices in pursuit of the same aim, for instance practices that aim at eliminating or foreclosing competitors, in order for Article 82 to be applicable to all the practices forming part of this overall strategy, it is sufficient that at least one of these practices is capable of affecting trade between Member States.[9]

18. It follows from the wording of Articles 81 and 82 and the case law of the Community Courts that in the application of the effect on trade criterion three elements in particular must be addressed:

(a) The concept of "trade between Member States",
(b) The notion of "may affect", and
(c) The concept of "appreciability".

2.2. THE CONCEPT OF "TRADE BETWEEN MEMBER STATES"

19. The concept of "trade" is not limited to traditional exchanges of goods and services across borders.[10] It is a wider concept, covering all cross-border economic activity including establishment.[11] This interpretation is consistent with the fundamental objective of the Treaty to promote free movement of goods, services, persons and capital.

20. According to settled case law the concept of "trade" also encompasses cases where agreements or practices affect the competitive structure of the market. Agreements and practices that affect the competitive structure inside the Community by eliminating or threatening to eliminate a competitor operating within the Community may be subject to the Community competition rules.[12] When an undertaking is or risks being eliminated the competitive structure within the Community is affected and so are the economic activities in which the undertaking is engaged.

21. The requirement that there must be an effect on trade "between Member States" implies that there must be an impact on cross-border economic activity involving at least two Member States. It is not required that the agreement or practice affect trade between the whole of one Member State and the whole of another Member State. Articles 81 and 82 may be applicable also in cases involving part of a Member State, provided that the effect on trade is appreciable.[13]

22. The application of the effect on trade criterion is independent of the definition of relevant geographic markets. Trade between Member States may be affected also in cases where the relevant market is national or sub-national.[14]

2.3. THE NOTION "MAY AFFECT"

23. The function of the notion "may affect" is to define the nature of the required impact on trade between Member States. According to the standard test developed by the Court of Justice, the notion "may affect" implies that it must be possible to foresee with a sufficient degree of probability on the basis of a set of objective factors of law or fact that the agreement or practice may have an influence, direct or indirect, actual or potential, on the pattern of trade between Member States.[15,16] As mentioned in paragraph 20 above the Court of Justice has in addition developed a test based on whether or not the agreement or practice affects the competitive structure. In cases where the agreement or practice is liable to affect the competitive structure inside the Community, Community law jurisdiction is established.

24. The "pattern of trade" test developed by the Court of Justice contains the following main elements, which are dealt with in the following sections:

(a) "A sufficient degree of probability on the basis of a set of objective factors of law or fact",
(b) An influence on the "pattern of trade between Member States",
(c) "A direct or indirect, actual or potential influence" on the pattern of trade.

2.3.1. A SUFFICIENT DEGREE OF PROBABILITY ON THE BASIS OF A SET OF OBJECTIVE FACTORS OF LAW OR FACT

25. The assessment of effect on trade is based on objective factors. Subjective intent on the part of the undertakings concerned is not required. If, however, there is evidence that undertakings have intended to affect trade between Member States, for example because they have sought to hinder exports to or imports from other Member States, this is a relevant factor to be taken into account.

26. The words "may affect" and the reference by the Court of Justice to "a sufficient degree of probability" imply that, in order for Community law jurisdiction to be established, it is not required that the agreement or practice will actually have or has had an effect on trade between Member States. It is sufficient that the agreement or practice is "capable" of having such an effect.[17]

27. There is no obligation or need to calculate the actual volume of trade between Member States affected by the agreement or practice. For example, in the case of agreements prohibiting exports to other Member States there is no need to estimate what would have been the level of parallel trade between the Member States concerned, in the absence of the agreement. This interpretation is consistent with the jurisdictional nature of the effect on trade criterion. Community law jurisdiction extends to categories of agreements and practices that are capable of having cross-border effects, irrespective of whether a particular agreement or practice actually has such effects.

28. The assessment under the effect on trade criterion depends on a number of factors that individually may not be decisive.[18] The relevant factors include the nature of the agreement and practice, the nature of the products covered by the agreement or practice and the position and importance of the undertakings concerned.[19]

29. The nature of the agreement and practice provides an indication from a qualitative point of view of the ability of the agreement or practice to affect trade between Member States. Some agreements and practices are by their very nature capable of affecting trade between Member States, whereas others require more detailed analysis in this respect. Cross-border cartels are an example of the former, whereas joint ventures confined to the territory of a single Member State are an example of the latter. This aspect is further examined in section 3 below, which deals with various categories of agreements and practices.

30. The nature of the products covered by the agreements or practices also provides an indication of whether trade between Member States is capable of being affected. When by their nature products are easily traded across borders or are important for undertakings that want to enter or expand their activities in other Member States, Community jurisdiction is more readily established than in cases where due to their nature there is limited demand for products offered by suppliers from other Member States or where the products are of limited interest from the point of view of cross-border establishment or the expansion of the economic activity carried out from such place of establishment.[20] Establishment includes the setting-up by undertakings in one Member State of agencies, branches or subsidiaries in another Member State.

31. The market position of the undertakings concerned and their sales volumes are indicative from a quantitative point of view of the ability of the agreement or practice concerned to affect trade between Member States. This aspect, which forms an integral part of the assessment of appreciability, is addressed in section 2.4 below.

32. In addition to the factors already mentioned, it is necessary to take account of the legal and factual environment in which the agreement or practice operates. The relevant economic and legal context provides insight into the potential for an effect on trade between Member States. If there are absolute barriers to cross-border trade between Member States, which are external to the agreement or practice, trade is only capable of being affected if those barriers are likely to disappear in the foreseeable future. In cases where the barriers are not absolute but merely render cross-border activities more difficult, it is of the utmost importance to ensure that agreements and practices do not further hinder such activities. Agreements and practices that do so are capable of affecting trade between Member States.

2.3.2. An influence on the "pattern of trade between Member States"

33. For Articles 81 and 82 to be applicable there must be an influence on the "pattern of trade between Member States".

34. The term "pattern of trade" is neutral. It is not a condition that trade be restricted or reduced.[21] Patterns of trade can also be affected when an agreement or practice causes an increase in trade. Indeed, Community law jurisdiction is established if trade between Member States is likely to develop differently with the agreement or practice compared to the way in which it would probably have developed in the absence of the agreement or practice.[22]

35. This interpretation reflects the fact that the effect on trade criterion is a jurisdictional one, which serves to distinguish those agreements and practices which are capable of having cross-border effects, so as to warrant an examination under the Community competition rules, from those agreements and practices which do not.

2.3.3. A "direct or indirect, actual or potential influence" on the pattern of trade

36. The influence of agreements and practices on patterns of trade between Member States can be "direct or indirect, actual or potential".

37. Direct effects on trade between Member States normally occur in relation to the products covered by an agreement or practice. When, for example, producers of a particular product in different Member States agree to share markets, direct effects are produced on trade between Member States on the market for the products in question. Another example of direct effects being produced is when a supplier limits distributor rebates to products sold within the Member State in which the distributors are established. Such practices increase the relative price of products destined for exports, rendering export sales less attractive and less competitive.

38. Indirect effects often occur in relation to products that are related to those covered by an agreement or practice. Indirect effects may, for example, occur where an agreement or practice has an impact on cross-border economic activities of undertakings that use or otherwise rely on the products covered by the agreement or practice.[23] Such effects can, for instance, arise where the agreement or practice relates to an intermediate product, which is not traded, but which is used in the supply of a final product, which is traded. The Court of Justice has held that trade between Member States was capable of being affected in the case of an agreement involving the fixing of prices of spirits used in the production of cognac.[24] Whereas the raw material was not exported, the final product — cognac — was exported. In such cases Community competition law is thus applicable, if trade in the final product is capable of being appreciably affected.

39. Indirect effects on trade between Member States may also occur in relation to the products covered by the agreement or practice. For instance, agreements whereby a manufacturer limits warranties to products sold by distributors within their Member State of establishment create disincentives for consumers from other Member States to buy the products because they would not be able to invoke the warranty.[25] Export by official distributors and parallel traders is made more difficult because in the eyes of consumers the products are less attractive without the manufacturer's warranty.[26]

40. Actual effects on trade between Member States are those that are produced by the agreement or practice once it is implemented. An agreement between a supplier and a distributor within the same Member State, for instance one that prohibits exports to other Member States, is likely to produce actual effects on trade between Member States. Without the agreement the distributor would have been free to engage in export sales. It should be recalled, however, that it is not required that actual effects are demonstrated. It is sufficient that the agreement or practice be capable of having such effects.

41. Potential effects are those that may occur in the future with a sufficient degree of probability. In other words, foreseeable market developments must be taken into account.[27] Even if trade is not capable of being affected at the time the agreement is concluded or the practice is implemented, Articles 81 and 82 remain applicable if the factors which led to that conclusion are likely to change in the foreseeable future. In this respect it is relevant to consider the impact of liberalisation measures adopted by the Community or by the Member State in question and other foreseeable measures aiming at eliminating legal barriers to trade.

42. Moreover, even if at a given point in time market conditions are unfavourable to cross-border trade, for example because prices are similar in the Member States in question, trade may still be capable of being affected if the situation may change as a result of changing market conditions.[28] What matters is the ability of the agreement or practice to affect trade between Member States and not whether at any given point in time it actually does so.

43. The inclusion of indirect or potential effects in the analysis of effects on trade between Member States does not mean that the analysis can be based on remote or hypothetical effects. The likelihood of a particular agreement to produce indirect or potential effects must be explained by the authority or party claiming that trade between Member States is capable of being appreciably affected. Hypothetical or speculative effects are not sufficient for establishing Community law jurisdiction. For instance, an agreement that raises the price of a product which is not tradable reduces the disposable income of consumers. As consumers have less money to spend they may purchase fewer products imported from other Member States. However, the link between such income effects and trade between Member States is generally in itself too remote to establish Community law jurisdiction.

2.4. THE CONCEPT OF APPRECIABILITY

2.4.1. General principle

44. The effect on trade criterion incorporates a quantitative element, limiting Community law jurisdiction to agreements and practices that are capable of having effects of a certain magnitude. Agreements and practices fall outside the scope of application of Articles 81 and 82 when they affect the market only insignificantly having regard to the weak position of the undertakings concerned on the market for the products in question.[29] Appreciability can be appraised in particular by reference to the position and the importance of the relevant undertakings on the market for the products concerned.[30]

45. The assessment of appreciability depends on the circumstances of each individual case, in particular the nature of the agreement and practice, the nature of the products covered and the market position of the undertakings concerned. When by its very nature the agreement or practice is capable of affecting trade between Member States, the appreciability threshold is lower than in the case of agreements and practices that are not by their very nature capable of affecting trade between Member States. The stronger the market position of the undertakings concerned, the more likely it is that an agreement or practice capable of affecting trade between Member States can be held to do so appreciably.[31]

46. In a number of cases concerning imports and exports the Court of Justice has considered that the appreciability requirement was fulfilled when the sales of the undertakings concerned accounted for about 5% of the market.[32] Market share alone, however, has not always been considered the decisive factor. In particular, it is necessary also to take account of the turnover of the undertakings in the products concerned.[33]

47. Appreciability can thus be measured both in absolute terms (turnover) and in relative terms, comparing the position of the undertaking(s) concerned to that of other players on the market (market share). This focus on the position and importance of the undertakings concerned is consistent with the concept "may affect", which implies that the assessment is based on the ability of the agreement or practice to affect trade between Member States rather than on the impact on actual flows of goods and services across borders. The market position of the undertakings concerned and their turnover in the products concerned are indicative of the ability of an agreement or practice to affect trade between Member States. These two elements are reflected in the presumptions set out in paragraphs *52* and *53* below.

NOTES

Missing paragraph references in the English language version of this Notice: see the introductory note to this Notice.

48. The application of the appreciability test does not necessarily require that relevant markets be defined and market shares calculated.[34] The sales of an undertaking in absolute terms may be sufficient to support a finding that the impact on trade is appreciable. This is particularly so in the case of agreements and practices that by their very nature are liable to affect trade between Member States, for example because they concern imports or exports or because they cover several Member States. The fact that in such circumstances turnover in the products covered by the agreement may be sufficient for a finding of an appreciable effect on trade between Member States is reflected in the positive presumption set out in paragraph *53* below.

NOTES

Missing paragraph references in the English language version of this Notice: see the introductory note to this Notice.

49. Agreements and practices must always be considered in the economic and legal context in which they occur. In the case of vertical agreements it may be necessary to have regard to any cumulative effects of parallel networks of similar agreements.[35] Even if a single agreement or network of agreements is not capable of appreciably affecting trade between Member States, the effect of parallel networks of agreements, taken as a whole, may be capable of doing so. For that to be the case, however, it is necessary that the individual agreement or network of agreements makes a significant contribution to the overall effect on trade.[36]

2.4.2. Quantification of Appreciability

50. It is not possible to establish general quantitative rules covering all categories of agreements indicating when trade between Member States is capable of being appreciably affected. It is possible, however, to indicate when trade is normally not capable of being appreciably affected. Firstly, in its notice on agreements of minor importance which do not appreciably restrict competition in the meaning of Article 81(1) of the Treaty (the de minimis rule)[37] the Commission has stated that agreements between small and medium-sized undertakings (SMEs) as defined in the Annex to Commission Recommendation 96/280/EC[38] are normally not capable of affecting trade between Member States. The reason for this presumption is the fact that the activities of SMEs are normally local or at most regional in nature. However, SMEs may be subject to Community law jurisdiction in particular where they engage in cross-border economic activity. Secondly, the Commission considers it appropriate to set out general principles indicating when trade is normally not capable of being appreciably affected, ie a standard defining the absence of an appreciable effect on trade between Member States (the NAAT-rule). When applying Article 81, the Commission will consider this standard as a negative rebuttable presumption applying to all agreements within the meaning of Article 81(1) irrespective of the nature of the restrictions contained in the agreement, including restrictions that have been identified as hardcore restrictions in Commission block exemption regulations and guidelines. In cases where this presumption applies the Commission will normally not institute proceedings either upon application or on its own initiative. Where the undertakings assume in good faith that an agreement is covered by this negative presumption, the Commission will not impose fines.

51. Without prejudice to paragraph *53* below, this negative definition of appreciability does not imply that agreements, which do not fall within the criteria set out below, are automatically capable of appreciably affecting trade between Member States. A case by case analysis is necessary.

NOTES

Missing paragraph references in the English language version of this Notice: see the introductory note to this Notice.

52. The Commission holds the view that in principle agreements are not capable of appreciably affecting trade between Member States when the following cumulative conditions are met:

(a) The aggregate market share of the parties on any relevant market within the Community affected by the agreement does not exceed 5%, and

(b) In the case of horizontal agreements, the aggregate annual Community turnover of the undertakings concerned[39] in the products covered by the agreement does not exceed 40 million euro. In the case of agreements concerning the joint buying of products the relevant turnover shall be the parties' combined purchases of the products covered by the agreement.

In the case of vertical agreements, the aggregate annual Community turnover of the supplier in the products covered by the agreement does not exceed 40 million euro. In the case of licence agreements the relevant turnover shall be the aggregate turnover of the licensees in the products incorporating the licensed technology and the licensor's own turnover in such products. In cases involving agreements concluded between a buyer and several suppliers the relevant turnover shall be the buyer's combined purchases of the products covered by the agreements.

The Commission will apply the same presumption where during two successive calendar years the above turnover threshold is not exceeded by more than 10% and the above market threshold is not exceeded by more than 2 percentage points. In cases where the agreement concerns an emerging not yet existing market and where as a consequence the parties neither generate relevant turnover nor accumulate any relevant market share, the Commission will not apply this presumption. In such cases appreciability may have to be assessed on the basis of the position of the parties on related product markets or their strength in technologies relating to the agreement.

53. The Commission will also hold the view that where an agreement by its very nature is capable of affecting trade between Member States, for example, because it concerns imports and exports or covers several Member States, there is a rebuttable positive presumption that such effects on trade are appreciable when the turnover of the parties in the products covered by the agreement calculated as indicated in paragraphs 52 and 54 exceeds 40 million euro. In the case of agreements that by their very nature are capable of affecting trade between Member States it can also often be presumed that such effects are appreciable when the market share of the parties exceeds the 5% threshold set out in the previous paragraph. However, this presumption does not apply where the agreement covers only part of a Member State (see paragraph 90 below).

54. With regard to the threshold of 40 million euro (cf. paragraph 52 above), the turnover is calculated on the basis of total Community sales excluding tax during the previous financial year by the undertakings concerned, of the products covered by the agreement (the contract products). Sales between entities that form part of the same undertaking are excluded.[40]

55. In order to apply the market share threshold, it is necessary to determine the relevant market.[41] This consists of the relevant product market and the relevant geographic market. The market shares are to be calculated on the basis of sales value data or, where appropriate, purchase value data. If value data are not available, estimates based on other reliable market information, including volume data, may be used.

56. In the case of networks of agreements entered into by the same supplier with different distributors, sales made through the entire network are taken into account.

57. Contracts that form part of the same overall business arrangement constitute a single agreement for the purposes of the NAAT-rule.[42] Undertakings cannot bring themselves inside these thresholds by dividing up an agreement that forms a whole from an economic perspective.

NOTES

2 OJ L1, 4.1.2003, p 1.

3 See eg Joined Cases 56/64 and 58/64, *Consten and Grundig*, [1966] ECR p 429, and Joined Cases 6/73 and 7/73, *Commercial Solvents*, [1974] ECR p 223.

4 See in this respect Case 22/71, *Béguelin*, [1971] ECR p 949, paragraph 16.

5 See Case 193/83, *Windsurfing*, [1986] ECR p 611, paragraph 96, and Case T-77/94, *Vereniging van Groothandelaren in Bloemkwekerijprodukten*, [1997] ECR II-759, paragraph 126.

6 See paragraphs 142 to 144 of the judgment in *Vereniging van Groothandelaren in Bloemkwekerijprodukteten* cited in the previous footnote.

7 See eg Case T-2/89, *Petrofina*, [1991] ECR II-1087, paragraph 226.

8 The concept of appreciability is dealt with in section 2.4 below.

9 See in this respect Case 85/76, *Hoffmann-La Roche*, [1979] ECR p 461, paragraph 126.

10 Throughout these guidelines the term "products" covers both goods and services.

11 See Case 172/80, *Züchner*, [1981] ECR p 2021, paragraph 18. See also Case C-309/99, *Wouters*, [2002] ECR I-1577, paragraph 95, Case C-475/99, *Ambulanz Glöckner*, [2001] ECR I-8089, paragraph 49, Joined Cases C-215/96 and 216/96, *Bagnasco*, [1999] ECR I-135, paragraph 51, Case C-55/96, *Job Centre*, [1997] ECR I-7119, paragraph 37, and Case C-41/90, *Höfner and Elser*, [1991] ECR I-1979, paragraph 33.

12 See eg Joined Cases T-24/93 and others, *Compagnie maritime belge*, [1996] ECR II-1201, paragraph 203, and paragraph 23 of the judgment in *Commercial Solvents* cited in footnote.

13 See eg Joined Cases T-213/95 and T-18/96, *SCK and FNK*, [1997] ECR II-1739, and sections 3.2.4 and 3.2.6 below.

14 See section 3.2 below.

15 See eg the judgment in *Züchner* cited in footnote 11 and Case 319/82, *Kerpen & Kerpen*, [1983] ECR 4173, Joined Cases 240/82 and others, *Stichting Sigarettenindustrie*, [1985] ECR 3831, paragraph 48, and Joined Cases T-25/95 and others, *Cimenteries CBR*, [2000] ECR II-491, paragraph 3930.

16 In some judgments mainly relating to vertical agreements the Court of Justice has added wording to the effect that the agreement was capable of hindering the attainment of the objectives of a single market between Member States, see eg Case T-62/98, *Volkswagen*, [2000] ECR II-2707, paragraph 179, and paragraph 47 of the *Bagnasco* judgment cited in footnote 11, and Case 56/65, *Société Technique Minière*, [1966] ECR 337. The impact of an agreement on the single market objective is thus a factor which can be taken into account.

17 See eg Case T-228/97, *Irish Sugar*, [1999] ECR II-2969, paragraph 170, and Case 19/77, *Miller*, [1978] ECR 131, paragraph 15.

18 See eg Case C-250/92, *Gøttrup-Klim* [1994] ECR II-5641, paragraph 54.

19 See eg Case C-306/96, *Javico*, [1998] ECR I-1983, paragraph 17, and paragraph 18 of the judgment in *Béguelin* cited in footnote 4.

20 Compare in this respect the judgments in *Bagnasco* and *Wouters* cited in footnote 11.

21 See eg Case T-141/89, *Tréfileurope*, [1995] ECR II-791, Case T-29/92, *Vereniging van Samenwerkende Prijsregelende Organisaties in de Bouwnijverheid (SPO)*, [1995] ECR II-289, as far as exports were concerned, and Commission Decision in Volkswagen (II) (OJ L264, 2.10.2001, p 14).

22 See in this respect Case 71/74, *Frubo*, [1975] ECR 563, paragraph 38, Joined Cases 209/78 and others, *Van Landewyck*, [1980] ECR 3125, paragraph 172, Case T-61/89, *Dansk Pelsdyravler Forening*, [1992] ECR II-1931, paragraph 143, and Case T-65/89, *BPB Industries and British Gypsum*, [1993] ECR II-389, paragraph 135.

23 See in this respect Case T-86/95, *Compagnie Générale Maritime and others*, [2002] ECR II-1011, paragraph 148, and paragraph 202 of the judgment in *Compagnie maritime belge* cited in footnote 12.

24 See Case 123/83, *BNIC v Clair*, [1985] ECR 391, paragraph 29.

25 See Commission Decision in Zanussi, OJ L322, 16.11.1978, p 36, paragraph 11.

26 See in this respect Case 31/85, *ETA Fabrique d'Ébauches*, [1985] ECR 3933, paragraphs 12 and 13.

27 See Joined Cases C-241/91P and C-242/91P, *RTE (Magill)*, [1995] ECR I-743, paragraph 70, and Case 107/82, *AEG*, [1983] ECR 3151, paragraph 60.

28 See paragraph 60 of the *AEG* judgment cited in the previous footnote.

29 See Case 5/69, *Völk*, [1969] ECR 295, paragraph 7.

30 See eg paragraph 17 of the judgment in *Javico* cited in footnote 19, and paragraph 138 of the judgment in *BPB Industries and British Gypsum* cited in footnote 22.

31 See paragraph 138 of the judgment in *BPB Industries and British Gypsum* cited in footnote 22.

32 See eg paragraphs 9 and 10 of the *Miller* judgment cited in footnote 17, and paragraph 58 of the *AEG* judgment cited in footnote 27.

33 See Joined Cases 100/80 and others, *Musique Diffusion Française*, [1983] ECR 1825, paragraph 86. In that case the products in question accounted for just above 3% of sales on the national markets concerned. The Court held that the agreements, which hindered parallel trade, were capable of appreciably affecting trade between Member States due to the high turnover of the parties and the relative market position of the products, compared to those of products produced by competing suppliers.

34 See in this respect paragraphs 179 and 231 of the Volkswagen judgment cited in footnote 16, and Case T-213/00, *CMA CGM and others*, [2003] ECR I-, paragraphs 219 and 220.

35 See eg Case T-7/93, *Langnese-Iglo*, [1995] ECR II-1533, paragraph 120.

36 See paragraphs 140 and 141 of the judgment in *Vereniging van Groothandelaren* in *Bloemkwekerijprodukten* cited in footnote 5.

37 See Commission Notice on agreements of minor importance which do not appreciably restrict competition under Article 81(1) of the Treaty (OJ C368, 22.12.2001, p 13, paragraph 3).

38 OJ L107, 30.4.1996, p 4. With effect from 1.1.2005 this recommendation will be replaced by Commission Recommendation 2003/361/EC concerning the definition of micro, small and medium-sized enterprises (OJ L124, 20.5.2003, p 36).

39 The term "undertakings concerned" shall include connected undertakings as defined in paragraph 12.2 of the Commission's Notice on agreements of minor importance which do not appreciably restrict competition under Article 81(1) of the Treaty establishing the European Community (OJ C368, 22.12.2001, p 13).

40 See the previous footnote.

41 When defining the relevant market, reference should be made to the notice on the definition of the relevant market for the purposes of Community competition law (OJ C372, 9.12.1997, p 5).

42 See also paragraph 14 above.

3. THE APPLICATION OF THE ABOVE PRINCIPLES TO COMMON TYPES OF AGREEMENTS AND ABUSES

[4.111]

58. The Commission will apply the negative presumption set out in the preceding section to all agreements, including agreements that by their very nature are capable of affecting trade between Member States as well as agreements that involve trade with undertakings located in third countries (cf. section 3.3 below).

59. Outside the scope of negative presumption, the Commission will take account of qualitative elements relating to the nature of the agreement or practice and the nature of the products that they concern (see paragraphs *29* and *30* above). The relevance of the nature of the agreement is also reflected in the positive presumption set out in paragraph 53 above relating to appreciability in the case of agreements that by their very nature are capable of affecting trade between Member States. With a view to providing additional guidance on the application of the effect on trade concept it is therefore useful to consider various common types of agreements and practices.

NOTES

Missing paragraph references in the English language version of this Notice: see the introductory note to this Notice.

60. In the following sections a primary distinction is drawn between agreements and practices that cover several Member States and agreements and practices that are confined to a single Member State or to part of a single Member State. These two main categories are broken down into further subcategories based on the nature of the agreement or practice involved. Agreements and practices involving third countries are also dealt with.

3.1. AGREEMENTS AND ABUSE COVERING OR IMPLEMENTED IN SEVERAL MEMBER STATES

61. Agreements and practices covering or implemented in several Member States are in almost all cases by their very nature capable of affecting trade between Member States. When the relevant turnover exceeds the threshold set out in paragraph *53* above it will therefore in most cases not be necessary to conduct a detailed analysis of whether trade between Member States is capable of being affected. However, in order to provide guidance also in these cases and to illustrate the principles developed in section 2 above, it is useful to explain what are the factors that are normally used to support a finding of Community law jurisdiction.

NOTES

Missing paragraph references in the English language version of this Notice: see the introductory note to this Notice.

3.1.1. Agreements concerning imports and exports

62. Agreements between undertakings in two or more Member States that concern imports and exports are by their very nature capable of affecting trade between Member States. Such agreements, irrespective of whether they are restrictive of competition or not, have a direct impact on patterns of trade between Member States. In *Kerpen & Kerpen*, for example, which concerned an agreement between a French producer and a German distributor covering more than 10% of exports of cement from France to Germany, amounting in total to 350,000 tonnes per year, the Court of Justice held that it was impossible to take the view that such an agreement was not capable of (appreciably) affecting trade between Member States.[43]

63. This category includes agreements that impose restrictions on imports and exports, including restrictions on active and passive sales and resale by buyers to customers in other Member States.[44] In these cases there is an inherent link between the alleged restriction of competition and the effect on trade, since the very purpose of the restriction is to prevent flows of goods and services between Member States, which would otherwise be possible. It is immaterial whether the parties to the agreement are located in the same Member State or in different Member States.

3.1.2. Cartels covering several Member States

64. Cartel agreements such as those involving price fixing and market sharing covering several Member States are by their very nature capable of affecting trade between Member States. Cross-border cartels harmonise the conditions of competition and affect the interpenetration of trade by cementing traditional patterns of trade.[45] When undertakings agree to allocate geographic territories, sales from other areas into the allocated territories are capable of being eliminated or reduced. When undertakings agree to fix prices, they eliminate competition and any resulting price differentials that would entice both competitors and customers to engage in cross-border trade. When undertakings agree on sales quotas traditional patterns of trade are preserved. The undertakings concerned abstain from expanding output and thereby from serving potential customers in other Member States.

65. The effect on trade produced by cross-border cartels is generally also by its very nature appreciable due to the market position of the parties to the cartel. Cartels are normally only formed when the participating undertakings together hold a large share of the market, as this allows them to raise price or reduce output.

3.1.3. Horizontal cooperation agreements covering several Member States

66. This section covers various types of horizontal cooperation agreements. Horizontal cooperation agreements may for instance take the form of agreements whereby two or more undertakings cooperate in the performance of a particular economic activity such as production and distribution.[46] Often such agreements are referred to as joint ventures. However, joint ventures that perform on a lasting basis all the functions of an autonomous economic entity are covered by the Merger Regulation.[47] At the level of the Community such full function joint ventures are not dealt with under Articles 81 and 82 except in cases where Article 2(4) of the Merger Regulation is applicable.[48] This section therefore does not deal with full-function joint ventures. In the case of non-full function joint ventures the joint entity does not operate as an autonomous supplier (or buyer) on any market. It merely serves the parents, who themselves operate on the market.[49]

67. Joint ventures which engage in activities in two or more Member States or which produce an output that is sold by the parents in two or more Member States affect the commercial activities of the parties in those areas of the Community. Such agreements are therefore normally by their very nature capable of affecting trade between Member States compared to the situation without the agreement.[50] Patterns of trade are affected when undertakings switch their activities to the joint venture or use it for the purpose of establishing a new source of supply in the Community.

68. Trade may also be capable of being affected where a joint venture produces an input for the parent companies, which is subsequently further processed or incorporated into a product by the parent undertakings. This is likely to be the case where the input in question was previously sourced from suppliers in other Member States, where the parents previously produced the input in other Member States or where the final product is traded in more than one Member State.

69. In the assessment of appreciability it is important to take account of the parents' sales of products related to the agreement and not only those of the joint entity created by the agreement, given that the joint venture does not operate as an autonomous entity on any market.

3.1.4. Vertical agreements implemented in several Member States

70. Vertical agreements and networks of similar vertical agreements implemented in several Member States are normally capable of affecting trade between Member States if they cause trade to be channelled in a particular way. Networks of selective distribution agreements implemented in two or more Member States for example, channel trade in a particular way because they limit trade to members of the network, thereby affecting patterns of trade compared to the situation without the agreement.[51]

71. Trade between Member States is also capable of being affected by vertical agreements that have foreclosure effects. This may for instance be the case of agreements whereby distributors in several Member States agree to buy only from a particular supplier or to sell only its products. Such agreements may limit trade between the Member States in which the agreements are implemented, or trade from Member States not covered by the agreements. Foreclosure may result from individual agreements or from networks of agreements. When an agreement or networks of agreements that cover several Member States have foreclosure effects, the ability of the agreement or agreements to affect trade between Member States is normally by its very nature appreciable.

72. Agreements between suppliers and distributors which provide for resale price maintenance (RPM) and which cover two or more Member States are normally also by their very nature capable of affecting trade between Member States.[52] Such agreements alter the price levels that would have been likely to exist in the absence of the agreements and thereby affect patterns of trade.

3.1.5. Abuses of dominant positions covering several Member States

73. In the case of abuse of a dominant position it is useful to distinguish between abuses that raise barriers to entry or eliminate competitors (exclusionary abuses) and abuses whereby the dominant undertaking exploits its economic power for instance by charging excessive or discriminatory prices (exploitative abuses). Both kinds of abuse may be carried out either through agreements, which are equally subject to Article 81(1), or through unilateral conduct, which as far as Community competition law is concerned is subject only to Article 82.

74. In the case of exploitative abuses such as discriminatory rebates, the impact is on downstream trading partners, which either benefit or suffer, altering their competitive position and affecting patterns of trade between Member States.

75. When a dominant undertaking engages in exclusionary conduct in more than one Member State, such abuse is normally by its very nature capable of affecting trade between Member States. Such conduct has a negative impact on competition in an area extending beyond a single Member State, being likely to divert trade from the course it would have followed in the absence of the abuse. For example, patterns of trade are capable of being affected where the dominant undertaking grants loyalty rebates. Customers covered by the exclusionary rebate system are likely to purchase less from competitors of the dominant firm than they would otherwise have done. Exclusionary conduct that aims directly at eliminating a competitor such as predatory pricing is also capable of affecting trade between Member States because of its impact on the competitive market structure inside the Community.[53] When a dominant firm engages in behaviour with a view to eliminating a competitor operating in more than one Member State, trade is capable of being affected in several ways. First, there is a risk that the affected competitor will cease to be a source of supply inside the Community. Even if the targeted undertaking is not eliminated, its future competitive conduct is likely to be affected, which may also have an impact on trade between Member States. Secondly, the abuse may have an impact on other competitors. Through its abusive behaviour the dominant undertaking can signal to its competitors that it will discipline attempts to engage in real competition. Thirdly, the very fact of eliminating a competitor may be sufficient for trade between Member States to be capable of being affected. This may be the case even where the undertaking that risks being eliminated mainly engages in exports to third countries.[54] Once the effective competitive market structure inside the Community risks being further impaired, there is Community law jurisdiction.

76. Where a dominant undertaking engages in exploitative or exclusionary abuse in more than one Member State, the capacity of the abuse to affect trade between Member States will normally also by its very nature be appreciable. Given the market position of the dominant undertaking concerned, and the fact that the abuse is implemented in several Member States, the scale of the abuse and its likely impact on patterns of trade is normally such that trade between Member States is capable of being appreciably affected. In the case of an exploitative abuse such as price discrimination, the abuse alters the competitive position of trading partners in several Member States. In the case of exclusionary abuses, including abuses that aim at eliminating a competitor, the economic activity engaged in by competitors in several Member States is affected. The very existence of a dominant position in several Member States implies that competition in a substantial part of the common market is already weakened.[55] When a dominant undertaking further weakens competition through recourse to abusive conduct, for example by eliminating a competitor, the ability of the abuse to affect trade between Member States is normally appreciable.

3.2. AGREEMENTS AND ABUSES COVERING A SINGLE, OR ONLY PART OF A, MEMBER STATE

77. When agreements or abusive practices cover the territory of a single Member State, it may be necessary to proceed with a more detailed inquiry into the ability of the agreements or abusive practices to affect trade between Member States. It should be recalled that for there to be an effect on trade between Member States it is not required that trade is reduced. It is sufficient that an appreciable change is capable of being caused in the pattern of trade between Member States. Nevertheless, in many cases involving a single Member State the nature of the alleged infringement, and in particular, its propensity to foreclose the national market, provides a good indication of the capacity of the agreement or practice to affect trade between Member States. The examples mentioned hereafter are not exhaustive. They merely provide examples of cases where agreements confined to the territory of a single Member State can be considered capable of affecting trade between Member States.

3.2.1. Cartels covering a single Member State

78. Horizontal cartels covering the whole of a Member State are normally capable of affecting trade between Member States. The Community Courts have held in a number of cases that agreements extending over the whole territory of a Member State by their very nature have the effect of reinforcing the partitioning of markets on a national basis by hindering the economic penetration which the Treaty is designed to bring about.[56]

79. The capacity of such agreements to partition the internal market follows from the fact that undertakings participating in cartels in only one Member State, normally need to take action to exclude competitors from other Member States.[57] If they do not, and the product covered by the agreement is tradable,[58] the cartel risks being undermined by competition from undertakings from other Member States. Such agreements are normally also by their very nature capable of having an appreciable effect on trade between Member States, given the market coverage required for such cartels to be effective.

80. Given the fact that the effect on trade concept encompasses potential effects, it is not decisive whether such action against competitors from other Member States is in fact adopted at any given point in time. If the cartel price is similar to the price prevailing in other Member States, there may be no immediate need for the members of the cartel to take action against competitors from other Member States. What matters is whether or not they are likely to do so, if market conditions change. The likelihood of that depends on the existence or otherwise of natural barriers to trade in the market, including in particular whether or not the product in question is tradable. In a case involving certain retail banking services[59] the Court of Justice has, for example, held that trade was not capable of being appreciably affected because the potential for trade in the specific products concerned was very limited and because they were not an important factor in the choice made by undertakings from other Member States regarding whether or not to establish themselves in the Member State in question.[60]

81. The extent to which the members of a cartel monitor prices and competitors from other Member States can provide an indication of the extent to which the products covered by the cartel are tradable. Monitoring suggests that competition and competitors from other Member States are perceived as a potential threat to the cartel. Moreover, if there is evidence that the members of the cartel have deliberately fixed the price level in the light of the price level prevailing in other Member States (limit pricing), it is an indication that the products in question are tradable and that trade between Member States is capable of being affected.

82. Trade is normally also capable of being affected when the members of a national cartel temper the competitive constraint imposed by competitors from other Member States by inducing them to join the restrictive agreement, or if their exclusion from the agreement places the competitors at a competitive disadvantage.[61] In such cases the agreement either prevents these competitors from exploiting any competitive advantage that they have, or raises their costs, thereby having a negative impact on their competitiveness and their sales. In both cases the agreement hampers the operations of competitors from other Member States on the national market in question. The same is true when a cartel agreement confined to a single Member State is concluded between undertakings that resell products imported from other Member States.[62]

3.2.2. Horizontal cooperation agreements covering a single Member State

83. Horizontal cooperation agreements and in particular non-full function joint ventures (cf. paragraph 66 above), which are confined to a single Member State and which do not directly relate to imports and exports, do not belong to the category of agreements that by their very nature are capable of affecting trade between Member States. A careful examination of the capacity of the individual agreement to affect trade between Member States may therefore be required.

84. Horizontal cooperation agreements may, in particular, be capable of affecting trade between Member States where they have foreclosure effects. This may be the case with agreements that establish sector-wide standardisation and certification regimes, which either exclude undertakings from other Member States or which are more easily fulfilled by undertakings from the Member State in question due to the fact that they are based on national rules and traditions. In such circumstances the agreements make it more difficult for undertakings from other Member States to penetrate the national market.

85. Trade may also be affected where a joint venture results in undertakings from other Member States being cut off from an important channel of distribution or source of demand. If, for example, two or more distributors established within the same Member State, and which account for a substantial share of imports of the products in question, establish a purchasing joint venture combining their purchases of that product, the resulting reduction in the number of distribution channels limits the possibility for suppliers from other Member States of gaining access to the national market in question. Trade is therefore capable of being affected.[63] Trade may also be affected where undertakings which previously imported a particular product form a joint venture which is entrusted with the production of that same product. In this case the agreement causes a change in the patterns of trade between Member States compared to the situation before the agreement.

3.2.3. Vertical agreements covering a single Member State

86. Vertical agreements covering the whole of a Member State may, in particular, be capable of affecting patterns of trade between Member States when they make it more difficult for undertakings from other Member States to penetrate the national market in question, either by means of exports or by means of establishment (foreclosure effect). When vertical agreements give rise to such foreclosure effects, they contribute to the partitioning of markets on a national basis, thereby hindering the economic interpenetration which the Treaty is designed to bring about.[64]

87. Foreclosure may, for example, occur when suppliers impose exclusive purchasing obligations on buyers.[65] In Delimitis,[66] which concerned agreements between a brewer and owners of premises where beer was consumed whereby the latter undertook to buy beer exclusively from the brewer, the Court of Justice defined foreclosure as the absence, due to the agreements, of real and concrete possibilities of gaining access to the market. Agreements normally only create significant barriers to entry when they cover a significant proportion of the market. Market share and market coverage can be used as an indicator in this respect. In making the assessment account must be taken not only of the particular agreement or network of agreements in question, but also of other parallel networks of agreements having similar effects.[67]

88. Vertical agreements which cover the whole of a Member State and which relate to tradable products may also be capable of affecting trade between Member States, even if they do not create direct obstacles to trade. Agreements whereby undertakings engage in resale price maintenance (RPM) may have direct effects on trade between Member States by increasing imports from other Member States and by decreasing exports from the Member State in question[68]. Agreements involving RPM may also affect patterns of trade in much the same way as horizontal cartels. To the extent that the price resulting from RPM is higher than that prevailing in other Member States this price level is only sustainable if imports from other Member States can be controlled.

3.2.4. Agreements covering only part of a Member State

89. In qualitative terms the assessment of agreements covering only part of a Member State is approached in the same way as in the case of agreements covering the whole of a Member State. This means that the analysis in section 2 applies. In the assessment of appreciability, however, the two categories must be distinguished, as it must be taken into account that only part of a Member State is covered by the agreement. It must also be taken into account what proportion of the national territory is susceptible to trade. If, for example, transport costs or the operating radius of equipment render it economically unviable for undertakings from other Member States to serve the entire territory of another Member State, trade is capable of being affected if the agreement forecloses access to the part of the territory of a Member State that is susceptible to trade, provided that this part is not insignificant.[69]

90. Where an agreement forecloses access to a regional market, then for trade to be appreciably affected, the volume of sales affected must be significant in proportion to the overall volume of sales of the products concerned inside the Member State in question. This assessment cannot be based merely on geographic coverage. The market share of the parties to the agreement must also be given fairly limited weight. Even if the parties have a high market share in a properly defined regional market, the size of that market in terms of volume may still be insignificant when compared to total sales of the products concerned within the Member State in question. In general, the best indicator of the capacity of the agreement to (appreciably) affect trade between Member States is therefore considered to be the share of the national market in terms of volume that is being foreclosed. Agreements covering areas with a high concentration of demand will thus weigh more heavily than those covering areas where demand is less concentrated. For Community jurisdiction to be established the share of the national market that is being foreclosed must be significant.

91. Agreements that are local in nature are in themselves not capable of appreciably affecting trade between Member States. This is the case even if the local market is located in a border region. Conversely, if the foreclosed share of the national market is significant, trade is capable of being affected even where the market in question is not located in a border region.

92. In cases in this category some guidance may be derived from the case law concerning the concept in Article 82 of a substantial part of the common market.[70] Agreements that, for example, have the effect of hindering competitors from other Member States from gaining access to part of a Member State, which constitutes a substantial part of the common market, should be considered to have an appreciable effect on trade between Member States.

3.2.5. Abuses of dominant positions covering a single Member State

93. Where an undertaking, which holds a dominant position covering the whole of a Member State, engages in exclusionary abuses, trade between Member States is normally capable of being affected. Such abusive conduct will generally make it more difficult for competitors from other Member States to penetrate the market, in which case patterns of trade are capable of being affected.[71] In Michelin,[72] for example, the Court of Justice held that a system of loyalty rebates foreclosed competitors from other Member States and therefore affected trade within the meaning of Article 82. In Rennet[73] the Court similarly held that an abuse in the form of an exclusive purchasing obligation on customers foreclosed products from other Member States.

94. Exclusionary abuses that affect the competitive market structure inside a Member State, for instance by eliminating or threatening to eliminate a competitor, may also be capable of affecting trade between Member States. Where the undertaking that risks being eliminated only operates in a single Member State, the abuse will normally not affect trade between Member States. However, trade between Member States is capable of being affected where the targeted undertaking exports to or imports from other Member States[74] and where it also operates in other Member States.[75] An effect on trade may arise from the dissuasive impact of the abuse on other competitors. If through repeated conduct the dominant undertaking has acquired a reputation for adopting exclusionary practices towards competitors that attempt to engage in direct competition, competitors from other Member States are likely to compete less aggressively, in which case trade may be affected, even if the victim in the case at hand is not from another Member State.

95. In the case of exploitative abuses such as price discrimination and excessive pricing, the situation may be more complex. Price discrimination between domestic customers will normally not affect trade between Member States. However, it may do so if the buyers are engaged in export activities and are disadvantaged by the discriminatory pricing or if this practice is used to prevent imports.[76] Practices consisting of offering lower prices to customers that are the most likely to import products from other Member States may make it more difficult for competitors from other Member States to enter the market. In such cases trade between Member States is capable of being affected.

96. As long as an undertaking has a dominant position which covers the whole of a Member State it is normally immaterial whether the specific abuse engaged in by the dominant undertaking only covers part of its territory or affects certain buyers within the national territory. A dominant firm can significantly impede trade by engaging in abusive conduct in the areas or vis-à-vis the customers that are the most likely to be targeted by competitors from other Member States. For example, it may be the case that a particular channel of distribution constitutes a particularly important means of gaining access to broad categories of consumers. Hindering access to such channels can have a substantial impact on trade between Member States. In the assessment of appreciability it must also be taken into account that the very presence of the dominant undertaking covering the whole of a Member State is likely to make market penetration more difficult. Any abuse which makes it more difficult to enter the national market should therefore be considered to appreciably affect trade. The combination of the market position of the dominant undertaking and the anti-competitive nature of its conduct implies that such abuses have normally by their very nature an appreciable effect on trade. However, if the abuse is purely local in nature or involves only an insignificant share of the sales of the dominant undertaking within the Member State in question, trade may not be capable of being appreciably affected.

3.2.6. Abuse of a dominant position covering only part of a Member State

97. Where a dominant position covers only part of a Member State some guidance may, as in the case of agreements, be derived from the condition in Article 82 that the dominant position must cover a substantial part of the common market. If the dominant position covers part of a Member State that constitutes a substantial part of the common market and the abuse makes it more difficult for competitors from other Member States to gain access to the market where the undertaking is dominant, trade between Member States must normally be considered capable of being appreciably affected.

98. In the application of this criterion regard must be had in particular to the size of the market in question in terms of volume. Regions and even a port or an airport situated in a Member State may, depending on their importance, constitute a substantial part of the common market.[77] In the latter cases it must be taken into account whether the

infrastructure in question is used to provide cross-border services and, if so, to what extent. When infrastructures such as airports and ports are important in providing cross-border services, trade between Member States is capable of being affected.

99. As in the case of dominant positions covering the whole of a Member State (cf. paragraph 95 above), trade may not be capable of being appreciably affected if the abuse is purely local in nature or involves only an insignificant share of the sales of the dominant undertaking.

3.3. AGREEMENTS AND ABUSES INVOLVING IMPORTS AND EXPORTS WITH UNDERTAKINGS LOCATED IN THIRD COUNTRIES, AND AGREEMENTS AND PRACTICES INVOLVING UNDERTAKINGS LOCATED IN THIRD COUNTRIES

3.3.1. GENERAL REMARKS

100. Articles 81 and 82 apply to agreements and practices that are capable of affecting trade between Member States even if one or more of the parties are located outside the Community.[78] Articles 81 and 82 apply irrespective of where the undertakings are located or where the agreement has been concluded, provided that the agreement or practice is either implemented inside the Community,[79] or produce effects inside the Community.[80] Articles 81 and 82 may also apply to agreements and practices that cover third countries, provided that they are capable of affecting trade between Member States. The general principle set out in section 2 above according to which the agreement or practice must be capable of having an appreciable influence, direct or indirect, actual or potential, on the pattern of trade between Member States, also applies in the case of agreements and abuses which involve undertakings located in third countries or which relate to imports or exports with third countries.

101. For the purposes of establishing Community law jurisdiction it is sufficient that an agreement or practice involving third countries or undertakings located in third countries is capable of affecting cross-border economic activity inside the Community. Import into one Member State may be sufficient to trigger effects of this nature. Imports can affect the conditions of competition in the importing Member State, which in turn can have an impact on exports and imports of competing products to and from other Member States. In other words, imports from third countries resulting from the agreement or practice may cause a diversion of trade between Member States, thus affecting patterns of trade.

102. In the application of the effect on trade criterion to the above mentioned agreements and practices it is relevant to examine, inter alia, what is the object of the agreement or practice as indicated by its content or the underlying intent of the undertakings involved.[81]

103. Where the object of the agreement is to restrict competition inside the Community the requisite effect on trade between Member States is more readily established than where the object is predominantly to regulate competition outside the Community. Indeed in the former case the agreement or practice has a direct impact on competition inside the Community and trade between Member States. Such agreements and practices, which may concern both imports and exports, are normally by their very nature capable of affecting trade between Member States.

3.3.2. ARRANGEMENTS THAT HAVE AS THEIR OBJECT THE RESTRICTION OF COMPETITION INSIDE THE COMMUNITY

104. In the case of imports, this category includes agreements that bring about an isolation of the internal market.[82] This is, for instance, the case of agreements whereby competitors in the Community and in third countries share markets, eg by agreeing not to sell in each other's home markets or by concluding reciprocal (exclusive) distribution agreements.[83]

105. In the case of exports, this category includes cases where undertakings that compete in two or more Member States agree to export certain (surplus) quantities to third countries with a view to co-ordinating their market conduct inside the Community. Such export agreements serve to reduce price competition by limiting output inside the Community, thereby affecting trade between Member States. Without the export agreement these quantities might have been sold inside the Community.[84]

3.3.3. OTHER ARRANGEMENTS

106. In the case of agreements and practices whose object is not to restrict competition inside the Community, it is normally necessary to proceed with a more detailed analysis of whether or not cross-border economic activity inside the Community, and thus patterns of trade between Member States, are capable of being affected.

107. In this regard it is relevant to examine the effects of the agreement or practice on customers and other operators inside the Community that rely on the products of the undertakings that are parties to the agreement or practice.[85] In Compagnie maritime belge,[86] which concerned agreements between shipping companies operating between Community ports and West African ports, the agreements were held to be capable of indirectly affecting trade between Member States because they altered the catchment areas of the Community ports covered by the agreements and because they affected the activities of other undertakings inside those areas. More specifically, the agreements affected the activities of undertakings that relied on the parties for transportation services, either as a means of transporting goods purchased in third countries or sold there, or as an important input into the services that the ports themselves offered.

108. Trade may also be capable of being affected when the agreement prevents re-imports into the Community. This may, for example, be the case with vertical agreements between Community suppliers and third country distributors, imposing restrictions on resale outside an allocated territory, including the Community. If in the absence of the agreement resale to the Community would be possible and likely, such imports may be capable of affecting patterns of trade inside the Community.[87]

109. However, for such effects to be likely, there must be an appreciable difference between the prices of the products charged in the Community and those charged outside the Community, and this price difference must not be eroded by customs duties and transport costs. In addition, the product volumes exported compared to the total market for those products in the territory of the common market must not be insignificant.[88] If these product volumes are insignificant

compared to those sold inside the Community, the impact of any re-importation on trade between Member States is considered not to be appreciable. In making this assessment, regard must be had not only to the individual agreement concluded between the parties, but also to any cumulative effect of similar agreements concluded by the same and competing suppliers. It may be, for example, that the product volumes covered by a single agreement are quite small, but that the product volumes covered by several such agreements are significant. In that case the agreements taken as a whole may be capable of appreciably affecting trade between Member States. It should be recalled, however (cf. paragraph 49 above), that the individual agreement or network of agreements must make a significant contribution to the overall effect on trade.

NOTES

43 See paragraph 8 of the judgment in *Kerpen & Kerpen* cited in footnote 15. It should be noted that the Court does not refer to market share but to the share of French exports and to the product volumes involved.

44 See eg the judgment in Volkswagen cited in footnote 16 and Case T-175/95, *BASF Coatings*, [1999] ECR II-1581. For a horizontal agreement to prevent parallel trade see Joined Cases 96/82 and others, *IAZ International*, [1983] ECR 3369, paragraph 27.

45 See eg Case T-142/89, *Usines Gustave Boël*, [1995] ECR II-867, paragraph 102.

46 Horizontal cooperation agreements are dealt with in the Commission Guidelines on the applicability of Article 81 of the EC Treaty to horizontal cooperation agreements (OJ C3, 6.1.2001, p 2). Those guidelines deal with the substantive competition assessment of various types of agreements but do not deal with the effect on trade issue.

47 See Council Regulation (EC) No 139/2004 on the control of concentrations between undertakings (OJ L24, 29.1.2004, p 1).

48 The Commission Notice on the concept of full-function joint ventures under the Merger Regulation (OJ C66, 2.3.1998, p 1) gives guidance on the scope of this concept.

49 See eg the Commission Decision in Ford/Volkswagen (OJ L20, 28.1.1993, p 14).

50 See in this respect paragraph 146 of the *Compagnie Générale Maritime* judgment cited in footnote 23 above.

51 See in this respect Joined Cases 43/82 and 63/82, *VBVB and VBBB*, [1984] ECR 19, paragraph 9.

52 See in this respect Case T-66/89, *Publishers Association*, [1992] ECR II-1995.

53 See in this respect the judgment in *Commercial Solvents* cited in footnote 3, in the judgment in *Hoffmann-La Roche*, cited in footnote, paragraph 125, and in *RTE and ITP* cited in footnote, as well as Case 6/72, *Continental Can*, [1973] ECR 215, paragraph 16, and Case 27/76, *United Brands*, [1978] ECR 207, paragraphs 197 to 203.

54 See paragraphs 32 and 33 of the judgment in *Commercial Solvents* cited in footnote 3.

55 According to settled case law dominance is a position of economic strength enjoyed by an undertaking which enables it to prevent effective competition being maintained on the relevant market by affording it the power to act to an appreciable extent independently of its competitors, its customers and ultimately of the consumers, see eg paragraph 38 of the judgment in *Hoffmann-La Roche* cited in footnote 9.

56 See for a recent example paragraph 95 of the *Wouters* judgment cited in footnote 11.

57 See eg Case 246/86, *Belasco*, [1989] ECR 2117, paragraph 32–38.

58 See paragraph 34 of the *Belasco* judgment cited in the previous footnote and more recently Joined Cases T-202/98 a.o., *British Sugar*, [2001] ECR II-2035, paragraph 79. On the other hand this is not so when the market is not susceptible to imports, see paragraph 51 of the *Bagnasco* judgment cited in footnote 11.

59 Guarantees for current account credit facilities.

60 See paragraph 51 of the *Bagnasco* judgment cited in footnote 11.

61 See in this respect Case 45/85, *Verband der Sachversicherer*, [1987] ECR 405, paragraph 50, and Case C-7/95P, *John Deere*, [1998] ECR I-3111. See also paragraph 172 of the judgment in Van Landewyck cited in footnote 22, where the Court stressed that the agreement in question reduced appreciably the incentive to sell imported products.

62 See eg the judgment in *Stichting Sigarettenindustrie*, cited in footnote 15, paragraphs 49 and 50.

63 See in this respect Case T-22/97, *Kesko*, [1999] ECR II-3775, paragraph 109.

64 See eg Case T-65/98, *Van den Bergh Foods*, [2003] ECR II- . . . , and the judgment in *Langnese-Iglo*, cited in footnote 35 paragraph 120.

65 See eg judgment of 7.12.2000, Case C-214/99, *Neste*, ECR I-11121.

66 See judgment of 28.2.1991, Case C-234/89, *Delimitis*, ECR I-935.

67 See paragraph 120 of the *Langnese-Iglo* judgment cited in footnote 35.

68 See eg Commission Decision in Volkswagen (II), cited in footnote 21, paragraphs 81 et seq.

69 See in this respect paragraphs 177 to 181 of the judgment in *SCK and FNK* cited in footnote 13.

70 See as to this notion the judgment in *Ambulanz Glöckner*, cited in footnote 11, paragraph 38, and Case C-179/90, *Merci convenzionali porto di Genova*, [1991] ECR I-5889, and Case C-242/95, *GT-Link*, [1997] ECR I-4449.

71 See eg paragraph 135 of the judgment in *BPB Industries and British Gypsum* cited in footnote.

72 See Case 322/81, *Nederlandse Banden Industrie Michelin*, [1983] ECR 3461

73 See Case 61/80, *Coöperative Stremsel-en Kleurselfabriek*, [1981] ECR 851, paragraph 15.

74 See in this respect judgment in *Irish Sugar*, cited in footnote 17 paragraph 169.

75 See paragraph 70 of the judgment in *RTE (Magill)* cited in footnote 27.

76 See the judgment in *Irish Sugar* cited in footnote 17.

77 See eg the case law cited in footnote 70.

78 See in this respect Case 28/77, *Tepea*, [1978] ECR 1391, paragraph 48, and paragraph 16 of the judgment in *Continental Can* cited in footnote 53.

79 See Joined Cases C-89/85 and others, *Ahlström Osakeyhtiö (Woodpulp)*, [1988] ECR 651, paragraph 16.

80 See in this respect Case T-102/96, *Gencor*, [1999] ECR II-753, which applies the effects test in the field of mergers.

81 See to that effect paragraph 19 of the judgment in *Javico* cited in footnote 19.

82 See in this respect Case 51/75, *EMI v CBS*, [1976] ECR 811, paragraphs 28 and 29.

83 See Commission Decision in Siemens/Fanuc (OJ L376, 31.12.1985, p 29).

84 See in this respect Joined Cases 29/83 and 30/83, *CRAM and Rheinzinc*, [1984] ECR 1679, and Joined Cases 40/73 and others, *Suiker Unie*, [1975] ECR 1663, paragraphs 564 and 580.

[85] See paragraph 22 of the judgment in *Javico* cited in footnote 19.

[86] See paragraph 203 of the judgment in *Compagnie maritime belge* cited in footnote 12.

[87] See in this respect the judgment in *Javico* cited in footnote 19.

[88] See in this respect paragraphs 24 to 26 of the *Javico* judgment cited in footnote 19.

COMMUNICATION FROM THE COMMISSION

(2004/C101/08)

Guidelines on the application of Article 81(3) of the Treaty

(Text with EEA relevance)

[4.112]

NOTES

Date of publication in OJ: OJ C101, 27.4.2004, p 97.

Note: with effect from 1 December 2009, the EC Treaty was replaced by the Treaty on the Functioning of the European Union. References in this document to provisions of the EC Treaty should be construed accordingly. As to Article 81 of the EC Treaty, see now Article 101 of the Treaty on the Functioning of the European Union.

1. INTRODUCTION

[4.113]

1. Article 81(3) of the Treaty sets out an exception rule, which provides a defence to undertakings against a finding of an infringement of Article 81(1) of the Treaty. Agreements, decisions of associations of undertakings and concerted practices[1] caught by Article 81(1) which satisfy the conditions of Article 81(3) are valid and enforceable, no prior decision to that effect being required.

2. Article 81(3) can be applied in individual cases or to categories of agreements and concerted practices by way of block exemption regulation. Regulation 1/2003 on the implementation of the competition rules laid down in Articles 81 and 82[2] does not affect the validity and legal nature of block exemption regulations. All existing block exemption regulations remain in force and agreements covered by block exemption regulations are legally valid and enforceable even if they are restrictive of competition within the meaning of Article 81(1).[3] Such agreements can only be prohibited for the future and only upon formal withdrawal of the block exemption by the Commission or a national competition authority.[4] Block exempted agreements cannot be held invalid by national courts in the context of private litigation.

3. The existing guidelines on vertical restraints, horizontal cooperation agreements and technology transfer agreements[5] deal with the application of Article 81 to various types of agreements and concerted practices. The purpose of those guidelines is to set out the Commission's view of the substantive assessment criteria applied to the various types of agreements and practices.

4. The present guidelines set out the Commission's interpretation of the conditions for exception contained in Article 81(3). It thereby provides guidance on how it will apply Article 81 in individual cases. Although not binding on them, these guidelines also intend to give guidance to the courts and authorities of the Member States in their application of Article 81(1) and (3) of the Treaty.

5. The guidelines establish an analytical framework for the application of Article 81(3). The purpose is to develop a methodology for the application of this Treaty provision. This methodology is based on the economic approach already introduced and developed in the guidelines on vertical restraints, horizontal co-operation agreements and technology transfer agreements. The Commission will follow the present guidelines, which provide more detailed guidance on the application of the four conditions of Article 81(3) than the guidelines on vertical restraints, horizontal co-operation agreements and technology transfer agreements, also with regard to agreements covered by those guidelines.

6. The standards set forth in the present guidelines must be applied in light of the circumstances specific to each case. This excludes a mechanical application. Each case must be assessed on its own facts and the guidelines must be applied reasonably and flexibly.

7. With regard to a number of issues, the present guidelines outline the current state of the case law of the Court of Justice. However, the Commission also intends to explain its policy with regard to issues that have not been dealt with in the case law, or that are subject to interpretation. The Commission's position, however, is without prejudice to the case law of the Court of Justice and the Court of First Instance concerning the interpretation of Article 81(1) and (3), and to the interpretation that the Community Courts may give to those provisions in the future.

NOTES

[1] In the following the term "agreement" includes concerted practices and decisions of associations of undertakings.

[2] OJ L1, 4.1.2003, p 1.

[3] All existing block exemption regulations and Commission notices are available on the DG Competition web-site: ec.europa.eu/competition/index_en.html

[4] See paragraph 36 below.

[5] See Commission Notice on Guidelines on vertical restraints (OJ C291, 13.10.2000, p 1), Commission Notice on Guidelines on the application of Article 81 of the Treaty to horizontal cooperation agreements (OJ C3, 6.1.2001, p 2), and Commission

Notice on Guidelines on the application of Article 81 of the Treaty to technology transfer agreements, not yet published.

2. THE GENERAL FRAMEWORK OF ARTICLE 81 EC

2.1. The Treaty provisions

[4.114]

8. Article 81(1) prohibits all agreements between undertakings, decisions by associations of undertakings and concerted practices which may affect trade between Member States[6] and which have as their object or effect the prevention, restriction or distortion of competition.[7]

9. As an exception to this rule Article 81(3) provides that the prohibition contained in Article 81(1) may be declared inapplicable in case of agreements which contribute to improving the production or distribution of goods or to promoting technical or economic progress, while allowing consumers a fair share of the resulting benefits, and which do not impose restrictions which are not indispensable to the attainment of these objectives, and do not afford such undertakings the possibility of eliminating competition in respect of a substantial part of the products concerned.

10. According to Article 1(1) of Regulation 1/2003 agreements which are caught by Article 81(1) and which do not satisfy the conditions of Article 81(3) are prohibited, no prior decision to that effect being required.[8] According to Article 1(2) of the same Regulation agreements which are caught by Article 81(1) but which satisfy the conditions of Article 81(3) are not prohibited, no prior decision to that effect being required. Such agreements are valid and enforceable from the moment that the conditions of Article 81(3) are satisfied and for as long as that remains the case.

11. The assessment under Article 81 thus consists of two parts. The first step is to assess whether an agreement between undertakings, which is capable of affecting trade between Member States, has an anti-competitive object or actual or potential[9] anti-competitive effects. The second step, which only becomes relevant when an agreement is found to be restrictive of competition, is to determine the pro-competitive benefits produced by that agreement and to assess whether these pro-competitive effects outweigh the anti-competitive effects. The balancing of anti-competitive and pro-competitive effects is conducted exclusively within the framework laid down by Article 81(3).[10]

12. The assessment of any countervailing benefits under Article 81(3) necessarily requires prior determination of the restrictive nature and impact of the agreement. To place Article 81(3) in its proper context it is appropriate to briefly outline the objective and principal content of the prohibition rule of Article 81(1). The Commission guidelines on vertical restraints, horizontal co-operation agreements and technology transfer agreements[11] contain substantial guidance on the application of Article 81(1) to various types of agreements. The present guidelines are therefore limited to recalling the basic analytical framework for applying Article 81(1).

2.2. The prohibition rule of Article 81(1)

2.2.1. General remarks

13. The objective of Article 81 is to protect competition on the market as a means of enhancing consumer welfare and of ensuring an efficient allocation of resources. Competition and market integration serve these ends since the creation and preservation of an open single market promotes an efficient allocation of resources throughout the Community for the benefit of consumers.

14. The prohibition rule of Article 81(1) applies to restrictive agreements and concerted practices between undertakings and decisions by associations of undertakings in so far as they are capable of affecting trade between Member States. A general principle underlying Article 81(1) which is expressed in the case law of the Community Courts is that each economic operator must determine independently the policy, which he intends to adopt on the market.[12] In view of this the Community Courts have defined "agreements", "decisions" and "concerted practices" as Community law concepts which allow a distinction to be made between the unilateral conduct of an undertaking and co-ordination of behaviour or collusion between undertakings.[13] Unilateral conduct is subject only to Article 82 of the Treaty as far as Community competition law is concerned. Moreover, the convergence rule set out in Article 3(2) of Regulation 1/2003 does not apply to unilateral conduct. This provision applies only to agreements, decisions and concerted practices, which are capable of affecting trade between Member States. Article 3(2) provides that when such agreements, decisions and concerted practices are not prohibited by Article 81, they cannot be prohibited by national competition law. Article 3 is without prejudice to the fundamental principle of primacy of Community law, which entails in particular that agreements and abusive practices that are prohibited by Articles 81 and 82 cannot be upheld by national law.[14]

15. The type of co-ordination of behaviour or collusion between undertakings falling within the scope of Article 81(1) is that where at least one undertaking vis-à-vis another undertaking undertakes to adopt a certain conduct on the market or that as a result of contacts between them uncertainty as to their conduct on the market is eliminated or at least substantially reduced.[15] It follows that co-ordination can take the form of obligations that regulate the market conduct of at least one of the parties as well as of arrangements that influence the market conduct of at least one of the parties by causing a change in its incentives. It is not required that co-ordination is in the interest of all the undertakings concerned.[16] Co-ordination must also not necessarily be express. It can also be tacit. For an agreement to be capable of being regarded as having been concluded by tacit acceptance there must be an invitation from an undertaking to another undertaking, whether express or implied, to fulfil a goal jointly.[17] In certain circumstances an agreement may be inferred from and imputed to an ongoing commercial relationship between the parties.[18] However, the mere fact that a measure adopted by an undertaking falls within the context of on-going business relations is not sufficient.[19]

16. Agreements between undertakings are caught by the prohibition rule of Article 81(1) when they are likely to have an appreciable adverse impact on the parameters of competition on the market, such as price, output, product quality, product variety and innovation. Agreements can have this effect by appreciably reducing rivalry between the parties to the agreement or between them and third parties.

2.2.2.
The basic principles for assessing agreements under Article 81(1)

17. The assessment of whether an agreement is restrictive of competition must be made within the actual context in which competition would occur in the absence of the agreement with its alleged restrictions.[20] In making this assessment it is necessary to take account of the likely impact of the agreement on inter-brand competition (ie competition between suppliers of competing brands) and on intra-brand competition (ie competition between distributors of the same brand). Article 81(1) prohibits restrictions of both inter-brand competition and intra-brand competition.[21]

18. For the purpose of assessing whether an agreement or its individual parts may restrict inter-brand competition and/or intra-brand competition it needs to be considered how and to what extent the agreement affects or is likely to affect competition on the market. The following two questions provide a useful framework for making this assessment. The first question relates to the impact of the agreement on inter-brand competition while the second question relates to the impact of the agreement on intra-brand competition. As restraints may be capable of affecting both inter-brand competition and intra-brand competition at the same time, it may be necessary to analyse a restraint in light of both questions before it can be concluded whether or not competition is restricted within the meaning of Article 81(1):

(1) Does the agreement restrict actual or potential competition that would have existed without the agreement? If so, the agreement may be caught by Article 81(1). In making this assessment it is necessary to take into account competition between the parties and competition from third parties. For instance, where two undertakings established in different Member States undertake not to sell products in each other's home markets, (potential) competition that existed prior to the agreement is restricted. Similarly, where a supplier imposes obligations on his distributors not to sell competing products and these obligations foreclose third party access to the market, actual or potential competition that would have existed in the absence of the agreement is restricted. In assessing whether the parties to an agreement are actual or potential competitors the economic and legal context must be taken into account. For instance, if due to the financial risks involved and the technical capabilities of the parties it is unlikely on the basis of objective factors that each party would be able to carry out on its own the activities covered by the agreement the parties are deemed to be non-competitors in respect of that activity.[22] It is for the parties to bring forward evidence to that effect.

(2) Does the agreement restrict actual or potential competition that would have existed in the absence of the contractual restraint(s)? If so, the agreement may be caught by Article 81(1). For instance, where a supplier restricts its distributors from competing with each other, (potential) competition that could have existed between the distributors absent the restraints is restricted. Such restrictions include resale price maintenance and territorial or customer sales restrictions between distributors. However, certain restraints may in certain cases not be caught by Article 81(1) when the restraint is objectively necessary for the existence of an agreement of that type or that nature.[23] Such exclusion of the application of Article 81(1) can only be made on the basis of objective factors external to the parties themselves and not the subjective views and characteristics of the parties. The question is not whether the parties in their particular situation would not have accepted to conclude a less restrictive agreement, but whether given the nature of the agreement and the characteristics of the market a less restrictive agreement would not have been concluded by undertakings in a similar setting. For instance, territorial restraints in an agreement between a supplier and a distributor may for a certain period of time fall outside Article 81(1), if the restraints are objectively necessary in order for the distributor to penetrate a new market.[24] Similarly, a prohibition imposed on all distributors not to sell to certain categories of end users may not be restrictive of competition if such restraint is objectively necessary for reasons of safety or health related to the dangerous nature of the product in question. Claims that in the absence of a restraint the supplier would have resorted to vertical integration are not sufficient. Decisions on whether or not to vertically integrate depend on a broad range of complex economic factors, a number of which are internal to the undertaking concerned.

19. In the application of the analytical framework set out in the previous paragraph it must be taken into account that Article 81(1) distinguishes between those agreements that have a restriction of competition as their object and those agreements that have a restriction of competition as their effect. An agreement or contractual restraint is only prohibited by Article 81(1) if its object or effect is to restrict inter-brand competition and/or intra-brand competition.

20. The distinction between restrictions by object and restrictions by effect is important. Once it has been established that an agreement has as its object the restriction of competition, there is no need to take account of its concrete effects.[25] In other words, for the purpose of applying Article 81(1) no actual anti-competitive effects need to be demonstrated where the agreement has a restriction of competition as its object. Article 81(3), on the other hand, does not distinguish between agreements that restrict competition by object and agreements that restrict competition by effect. Article 81(3) applies to all agreements that fulfil the four conditions contained therein.[26]

21. Restrictions of competition *by object* are those that by their very nature have the potential of restricting competition. These are restrictions which in light of the objectives pursued by the Community competition rules have such a high potential of negative effects on competition that it is unnecessary for the purposes of applying Article 81(1) to demonstrate any actual effects on the market. This presumption is based on the serious nature of the restriction and on experience showing that restrictions of competition by object are likely to produce negative effects on the market and to jeopardise the objectives pursued by the Community competition rules. Restrictions by object

such as price fixing and market sharing reduce output and raise prices, leading to a misallocation of resources, because goods and services demanded by customers are not produced. They also lead to a reduction in consumer welfare, because consumers have to pay higher prices for the goods and services in question.

22. The assessment of whether or not an agreement has as its object the restriction of competition is based on a number of factors. These factors include, in particular, the content of the agreement and the objective aims pursued by it. It may also be necessary to consider the context in which it is (to be) applied and the actual conduct and behaviour of the parties on the market.[27] In other words, an examination of the facts underlying the agreement and the specific circumstances in which it operates may be required before it can be concluded whether a particular restriction constitutes a restriction of competition by object. The way in which an agreement is actually implemented may reveal a restriction by object even where the formal agreement does not contain an express provision to that effect. Evidence of subjective intent on the part of the parties to restrict competition is a relevant factor but not a necessary condition.

23. Non-exhaustive guidance on what constitutes restrictions by object can be found in Commission block exemption regulations, guidelines and notices. Restrictions that are black-listed in block exemptions or identified as hardcore restrictions in guidelines and notices are generally considered by the Commission to constitute restrictions by object. In the case of horizontal agreements restrictions of competition by object include price fixing, output limitation and sharing of markets and customers.[28] As regards vertical agreements the category of restrictions by object includes, in particular, fixed and minimum resale price maintenance and restrictions providing absolute territorial protection, including restrictions on passive sales.[29]

24. If an agreement is not restrictive of competition by object it must be examined whether it has restrictive effects on competition. Account must be taken of both actual and potential effects.[30] In other words the agreement must have likely anti-competitive effects. In the case of restrictions of competition by effect there is no presumption of anti-competitive effects. For an agreement to be restrictive by effect it must affect actual or potential competition to such an extent that on the relevant market negative effects on prices, output, innovation or the variety or quality of goods and services can be expected with a reasonable degree of probability.[31] Such negative effects must be appreciable. The prohibition rule of Article 81(1) does not apply when the identified anti-competitive effects are insignificant.[32] This test reflects the economic approach which the Commission is applying. The prohibition of Article 81(1) only applies where on the basis of proper market analysis it can be concluded that the agreement has likely anti-competitive effects on the market.[33] It is insufficient for such a finding that the market shares of the parties exceed the thresholds set out in the Commission's *de minimis* notice.[34] Agreements falling within safe harbours of block exemption regulations may be caught by Article 81(1) but this is not necessarily so. Moreover, the fact that due to the market shares of the parties, an agreement falls outside the safe harbour of a block exemption is in itself an insufficient basis for finding that the agreement is caught by Article 81(1) or that it does not fulfil the conditions of Article 81(3). Individual assessment of the likely effects produced by the agreement is required.

25. Negative effects on competition within the relevant market are likely to occur when the parties individually or jointly have or obtain some degree of market power and the agreement contributes to the creation, maintenance or strengthening of that market power or allows the parties to exploit such market power. Market power is the ability to maintain prices above competitive levels for a significant period of time or to maintain output in terms of product quantities, product quality and variety or innovation below competitive levels for a significant period of time. In markets with high fixed costs undertakings must price significantly above their marginal costs of production in order to ensure a competitive return on their investment. The fact that undertakings price above their marginal costs is therefore not in itself a sign that competition in the market is not functioning well and that undertakings have market power that allows them to price above the competitive level. It is when competitive constraints are insufficient to maintain prices and output at competitive levels that undertakings have market power within the meaning of Article 81(1).

26. The creation, maintenance or strengthening of market power can result from a restriction of competition between the parties to the agreement. It can also result from a restriction of competition between any one of the parties and third parties, eg because the agreement leads to foreclosure of competitors or because it raises competitors' costs, limiting their capacity to compete effectively with the contracting parties. Market power is a question of degree. The degree of market power normally required for the finding of an infringement under Article 81(1) in the case of agreements that are restrictive of competition by effect is less than the degree of market power required for a finding of dominance under Article 82.

27. For the purposes of analysing the restrictive effects of an agreement it is normally necessary to define the relevant market.[35] It is normally also necessary to examine and assess, inter alia, the nature of the products, the market position of the parties, the market position of competitors, the market position of buyers, the existence of potential competitors and the level of entry barriers. In some cases, however, it may be possible to show anti-competitive effects directly by analysing the conduct of the parties to the agreement on the market. It may for example be possible to ascertain that an agreement has led to price increases. The guidelines on horizontal cooperation agreements and on vertical restraints set out a detailed framework for analysing the competitive impact of various types of horizontal and vertical agreements under Article 81(1).[36]

2.2.3.
Ancillary restraints

28. Paragraph 18 above sets out a framework for analysing the impact of an agreement and its individual restrictions on inter-brand competition and intra-brand competition. If on the basis of those principles it is concluded that the main transaction covered by the agreement is not restrictive of competition, it becomes relevant to examine whether individual restraints contained in the agreement are also compatible with Article 81(1) because they are ancillary to the main non-restrictive transaction.

29. In Community competition law the concept of ancillary restraints covers any alleged restriction of competition which is directly related and necessary to the implementation of a main non-restrictive transaction and proportionate to it.[37] If an agreement in its main parts, for instance a distribution agreement or a joint venture, does not have as its object or effect the restriction of competition, then restrictions, which are directly related to and necessary for the implementation of that transaction, also fall outside Article 81(1).[38] These related restrictions are called ancillary restraints. A restriction is directly related to the main transaction if it is subordinate to the implementation of that transaction and is inseparably linked to it. The test of necessity implies that the restriction must be objectively necessary for the implementation of the main transaction and be proportionate to it. It follows that the ancillary restraints test is similar to the test set out in paragraph 18(2) above. However, the ancillary restraints test applies in all cases where the main transaction is not restrictive of competition.[39] It is not limited to determining the impact of the agreement on intra-brand competition.

30. The application of the ancillary restraint concept must be distinguished from the application of the defence under Article 81(3) which relates to certain economic benefits produced by restrictive agreements and which are balanced against the restrictive effects of the agreements. The application of the ancillary restraint concept does not involve any weighing of pro-competitive and anti-competitive effects. Such balancing is reserved for Article 81(3).[40]

31. The assessment of ancillary restraints is limited to determining whether, in the specific context of the main non-restrictive transaction or activity, a particular restriction is necessary for the implementation of that transaction or activity and proportionate to it. If on the basis of objective factors it can be concluded that without the restriction the main non-restrictive transaction would be difficult or impossible to implement, the restriction may be regarded as objectively necessary for its implementation and proportionate to it.[41] If, for example, the main object of a franchise agreement does not restrict competition, then restrictions, which are necessary for the proper functioning of the agreement, such as obligations aimed at protecting the uniformity and reputation of the franchise system, also fall outside Article 81(1).[42] Similarly, if a joint venture is not in itself restrictive of competition, then restrictions that are necessary for the functioning of the agreement are deemed to be ancillary to the main transaction and are therefore not caught by Article 81(1). For instance in TPS[43] the Commission concluded that an obligation on the parties not to be involved in companies engaged in distribution and marketing of television programmes by satellite was ancillary to the creation of the joint venture during the initial phase. The restriction was therefore deemed to fall outside Article 81(1) for a period of three years. In arriving at this conclusion the Commission took account of the heavy investments and commercial risks involved in entering the market for pay-television.

2.3. The exception rule of Article 81(3)

32. The assessment of restrictions by object and effect under Article 81(1) is only one side of the analysis. The other side, which is reflected in Article 81(3), is the assessment of the positive economic effects of restrictive agreements.

33. The aim of the Community competition rules is to protect competition on the market as a means of enhancing consumer welfare and of ensuring an efficient allocation of resources. Agreements that restrict competition may at the same time have pro-competitive effects by way of efficiency gains.[44] Efficiencies may create additional value by lowering the cost of producing an output, improving the quality of the product or creating a new product. When the pro-competitive effects of an agreement outweigh its anti-competitive effects the agreement is on balance pro-competitive and compatible with the objectives of the Community competition rules. The net effect of such agreements is to promote the very essence of the competitive process, namely to win customers by offering better products or better prices than those offered by rivals. This analytical framework is reflected in Article 81(1) and Article 81(3). The latter provision expressly acknowledges that restrictive agreements may generate objective economic benefits so as to outweigh the negative effects of the restriction of competition.[45]

34. The application of the exception rule of Article 81(3) is subject to four cumulative conditions, two positive and two negative:

(a) The agreement must contribute to improving the production or distribution of goods or contribute to promoting technical or economic progress,
(b) Consumers must receive a fair share of the resulting benefits,
(c) The restrictions must be indispensable to the attainment of these objectives, and finally
(d) The agreement must not afford the parties the possibility of eliminating competition in respect of a substantial part of the products in question.

When these four conditions are fulfilled the agreement enhances competition within the relevant market, because it leads the undertakings concerned to offer cheaper or better products to consumers, compensating the latter for the adverse effects of the restrictions of competition.

35. Article 81(3) can be applied either to individual agreements or to categories of agreements by way of a block exemption regulation. When an agreement is covered by a block exemption the parties to the restrictive agreement are relieved of their burden under Article 2 of Regulation 1/2003 of showing that their individual agreement satisfies each of the conditions of Article 81(3). They only have to prove that the restrictive agreement benefits from a block exemption. The application of Article 81(3) to categories of agreements by way of block exemption regulation is based on the presumption that restrictive agreements that fall within their scope[46] fulfil each of the four conditions laid down in Article 81(3).

36. If in an individual case the agreement is caught by Article 81(1) and the conditions of Article 81(3) are not fulfilled the block exemption may be withdrawn. According to Article 29(1) of Regulation 1/2003 the Commission is empowered to withdraw the benefit of a block exemption when it finds that in a particular case an agreement covered by a block exemption regulation has certain effects which are incompatible with Article 81(3) of the Treaty. Pursuant to Article 29(2) of Regulation 1/2003 a competition authority of a Member State may also withdraw the benefit of a Commission block exemption regulation in respect of its territory (or part of its territory), if this territory has all the characteristics of a distinct geographic market. In the case of withdrawal it is for the competition authorities concerned to demonstrate that the agreement infringes Article 81(1) and that it does not fulfil the conditions of Article 81(3).

37. The courts of the Member States have no power to withdraw the benefit of block exemption regulations. Moreover, in their application of block exemption regulations Member State courts may not modify their scope by extending their sphere of application to agreements not covered by the block exemption regulation in question.[47] Outside the scope of block exemption regulations Member State courts have the power to apply Article 81 in full (cf. Article 6 of Regulation 1/2003).

NOTES

6 The concept of effect on trade between Member States is dealt with in separate guidelines.

7 In the following the term "restriction" includes the prevention and distortion of competition.

8 According to Article 81(2) such agreements are automatically void.

9 Article 81(1) prohibits both actual and potential anti-competitive effects, see eg Case C-7/95P, *John Deere*, [1998] ECR I-3111, paragraph 77.

10 See Case T-65/98, *Van den Bergh Foods*, [2003] ECR II . . . , paragraph 107 and Case T-112/99, *Métropole télévision (M6) and others*, [2001] ECR II-2459, paragraph 74, where the Court of First Instance held that it is only in the precise framework of Article 81(3) that the pro- and anti-competitive aspects of a restriction may be weighed.

11 See note above.

12 See eg Case C-49/92P, *Anic Partecipazioni*, [1999] ECR I-4125, paragraph 116; and Joined Cases 40/73 to 48/73 and others, *Suiker Unie*, [1975] ECR page 1663, paragraph 173.

13 See in this respect paragraph 108 of the judgment in *Anic Partecipazioni* cited in the previous note and Case C-277/87, *Sandoz Prodotti*, [1990] ECR I-45.

14 See in this respect eg Case 14/68, *Walt Wilhelm*, [1969] ECR 1, and more recently Case T-203/01, *Michelin (II)*, [2003] ECR II . . . , paragraph 112.

15 See Joined Cases T-25/95 and others, *Cimenteries CBR*, [2000] ECR II-491, paragraphs 1849 and 1852; and Joined Cases T-202/98 and others, *British Sugar*, [2001] ECR II-2035, paragraphs 58 to 60.

16 See to that effect Case C-453/99, *Courage v Crehan*, [2001] ECR I-6297, and paragraph 3444 of the judgment in *Cimenteries CBR* cited in the previous note.

17 See in this respect Joined Cases C-2/01P and C-3/01P, *Bundesverband der Arzneimittel-Importeure*, [2004] ECR I . . . , paragraph 102.

18 See eg Joined Cases 25/84 and 26/84, *Ford*, [1985] ECR 2725.

19 See in this respect paragraph 141 of the judgment in *Bundesverband der Arzneimittel-Importeure* cited in note.

20 See Case 56/65, *Société Technique Minière*, [1966] ECR 337, and paragraph 76 of the judgment in *John Deere*, cited in note 9.

21 See in this respect eg Joined Cases 56/64 and 58/66, *Consten and Grundig*, [1966] ECR 429.

22 See in this respect eg Commission Decision in Elopak/Metal Box–Odin (OJ 1990 L209, p 15) and in TPS (OJ 1999 L90, p 6).

23 See in this respect the judgment in *Société Technique Minière* cited in note 20 and Case 258/78, *Nungesser*, [1982] ECR 2015.

24 See rule 10 in paragraph 119 of the Guidelines on vertical restraints cited in note above, according to which inter alia passive sales restrictions — a hardcore restraint — are held to fall outside Article 81(1) for a period of 2 years when the restraint is linked to opening up new product or geographic markets.

25 See eg paragraph 99 of the judgment in *Anic Partecipazioni* cited in note 12.

26 See paragraph 46 below.

27 See Joined Cases 29/83 and 30/83, *CRAM and Rheinzink*, [1984] ECR 1679, paragraph 26, and Joined Cases 96/82 and others, *ANSEAU-NAVEWA*, [1983] ECR 3369, paragraphs 23–25.

28 See the Guidelines on horizontal cooperation agreements, cited in note, paragraph 25, and Article 5 of Commission Regulation 2658/2000 on the application of Article 81(3) of the Treaty to categories of specialisation agreements (OJ L304, 5.12.2000, p 3).

29 See Article 4 Commission Regulation 2790/1999 on the application of Article 81(3) of the Treaty to categories of vertical agreements and concerted practices (OJ L336, 29.12.1999, p 21) and the Guidelines on Vertical Restraints, cited in note, paragraph 46 et seq. See also Case 279/87, *Tipp-Ex*, [1990] ECR I-261, and Case T-62/98, *Volkswagen v Commission*, [2000] ECR II-2707, paragraph 178.

30 See paragraph 77 of the judgment in *John Deere* cited in note 9.

31 It is not sufficient in itself that the agreement restricts the freedom of action of one or more of the parties, see paragraphs 76 and 77 of the judgment in *Métropole television (M6)* cited in note10. This is in line with the fact that the object of Article 81 is to protect competition on the market for the benefit of consumers.

32 See eg Case 5/69, *Völk*, [1969] ECR 295, paragraph 7. Guidance on the issue of appreciability can be found in the Commission Notice on agreements of minor importance which do not appreciably restrict competition under Article 81(1) of the Treaty (OJ C368, 22.12.2001, p 13) The notice defines appreciability in a negative way. Agreements, which fall outside the scope of the de minimis notice, do not necessarily have appreciable restrictive effects. An individual assessment is required.

33 See in this respect Joined Cases T-374/94 and others, *European Night Services*, [1998] ECR II-3141.

34 See note 32.

35 See in this respect Commission notice on the definition of the relevant market for the purposes of Community competition law (OJ C372, 9.12.1997, p 1).

36 For the reference in the OJ see note 5.

37 See paragraph 104 of the judgment in *Métropole télévision (M6) and others*, cited in note 10.

38 See eg Case C-399/93, *Luttikhuis*, [1995] ECR I-4515, paragraphs 12 to 14.

39 See in this respect paragraphs 118 et seq of the *Métropole télévision* judgment cited in note 10.

40 See paragraph 107 of the judgment in *Métropole télévision* judgement cited in note 10.

41 See eg Commission Decision in Elopak/Metal Box–Odin cited in note 22.

42 See Case 161/84, *Pronuptia*, [1986] ECR 353.

43 See note 22. The decision was upheld by the Court of First Instance in the judgment in *Métropole télévision (M6)* cited in note 10.

44 Cost savings and other gains to the parties that arise from the mere exercise of market power do not give rise to objective benefits and cannot be taken into account, cf. paragraph 49 below.

45 See the judgment in *Consten and Grundig*, cited in note 21.

46 The fact that an agreement is block exempted does not in itself indicate that the individual agreement is caught by Article 81(1).

47 See eg Case C-234/89, *Delimitis*, [1991] ECR I-935, paragraph 46.

3. THE APPLICATION OF THE FOUR CONDITIONS OF ARTICLE 81(3)

[4.115]

38. The remainder of these guidelines will consider each of the four conditions of Article 81(3).[48] Given that these four conditions are cumulative[49] it is unnecessary to examine any remaining conditions once it is found that one of the conditions of Article 81(3) is not fulfilled. In individual cases it may therefore be appropriate to consider the four conditions in a different order.

39. For the purposes of these guidelines it is considered appropriate to invert the order of the second and the third condition and thus deal with the issue of indispensability before the issue of pass-on to consumers. The analysis of pass-on requires a balancing of the negative and positive effects of an agreement on consumers. This analysis should not include the effects of any restrictions, which already fail the indispensability test and which for that reason are prohibited by Article 81.

3.1. General principles

40. Article 81(3) of the Treaty only becomes relevant when an agreement between undertakings restricts competition within the meaning of Article 81(1). In the case of non-restrictive agreements there is no need to examine any benefits generated by the agreement.

41. Where in an individual case a restriction of competition within the meaning of Article 81(1) has been proven, Article 81(3) can be invoked as a defence. According to Article 2 of Regulation 1/2003 the burden of proof under Article 81(3) rests on the undertaking(s) invoking the benefit of the exception rule. Where the conditions of Article 81(3) are not satisfied the agreement is null and void, cf. Article 81(2). However, such automatic nullity only applies to those parts of the agreement that are incompatible with Article 81, provided that such parts are severable from the agreement as a whole.[50] If only part of the agreement is null and void, it is for the applicable national law to determine the consequences thereof for the remaining part of the agreement.[51]

42. According to settled case law the four conditions of Article 81(3) are cumulative,[52] ie they must all be fulfilled for the exception rule to be applicable. If they are not, the application of the exception rule of Article 81(3) must be refused.[53] The four conditions of Article 81(3) are also exhaustive. When they are met the exception is applicable and may not be made dependant on any other condition. Goals pursued by other Treaty provisions can be taken into account to the extent that they can be subsumed under the four conditions of Article 81(3).[54]

43. The assessment under Article 81(3) of benefits flowing from restrictive agreements is in principle made within the confines of each relevant market to which the agreement relates. The Community competition rules have as their objective the protection of competition on the market and cannot be detached from this objective. Moreover, the condition that consumers[55] must receive a fair share of the benefits implies in general that efficiencies generated by the restrictive agreement within a relevant market must be sufficient to outweigh the anti-competitive effects produced by the agreement within that same relevant market.[56] Negative effects on consumers in one geographic market or product market cannot normally be balanced against and compensated by positive effects for consumers in another unrelated geographic market or product market. However, where two markets are related, efficiencies achieved on separate markets can be taken into account provided that the group of consumers affected by the restriction and benefiting from the efficiency gains are substantially the same.[57] Indeed, in some cases only consumers in a downstream market are affected by the agreement in which case the impact of the agreement on such consumers must be assessed. This is for instance so in the case of purchasing agreements.[58]

44. The assessment of restrictive agreements under Article 81(3) is made within the actual context in which they occur[59] and on the basis of the facts existing at any given point in time. The assessment is sensitive to material changes in the facts. The exception rule of Article 81(3) applies as long as the four conditions are fulfilled and ceases to apply when that is no longer the case.[60] When applying Article 81(3) in accordance with these principles it is necessary to take into account the initial sunk investments made by any of the parties and the time needed and the restraints required to commit and recoup an efficiency enhancing investment. Article 81 cannot be applied without taking due account of such ex ante investment. The risk facing the parties and the sunk investment that must be committed to implement the agreement can thus lead to the agreement falling outside Article 81(1) or fulfilling the conditions of Article 81(3), as the case may be, for the period of time required to recoup the investment.

45. In some cases the restrictive agreement is an irreversible event. Once the restrictive agreement has been implemented the ex ante situation cannot be re-established. In such cases the assessment must be made exclusively on the basis of the facts pertaining at the time of implementation. For instance, in the case of a research and development agreement whereby each party agrees to abandon its respective research project and pool its capabilities with those of another party, it may from an objective point of view be technically and economically impossible to revive a project once it has been abandoned. The assessment of the anti-competitive and pro-competitive effects of the agreement to abandon the individual research projects must therefore be made as of the time of the completion of its implementation. If at that point in time the agreement is compatible with Article 81, for instance because a sufficient number of third parties have competing research and development projects, the parties' agreement to abandon their individual projects remains compatible with Article 81, even if at a later point in time the third party projects fail. However, the prohibition of Article 81 may apply to other parts of the agreement in respect of which the issue of

irreversibility does not arise. If for example in addition to joint research and development, the agreement provides for joint exploitation, Article 81 may apply to this part of the agreement if due to subsequent market developments the agreement becomes restrictive of competition and does not (any longer) satisfy the conditions of Article 81(3) taking due account of ex ante sunk investments, cf. the previous paragraph.

46. Article 81(3) does not exclude a priori certain types of agreements from its scope. As a matter of principle all restrictive agreements that fulfil the four conditions of Article 81(3) are covered by the exception rule.[61] However, severe restrictions of competition are unlikely to fulfil the conditions of Article 81(3). Such restrictions are usually black-listed in block exemption regulations or identified as hardcore restrictions in Commission guidelines and notices. Agreements of this nature generally fail (at least) the two first conditions of Article 81(3). They neither create objective economic benefits[62] nor do they benefit consumers.[63] For example, a horizontal agreement to fix prices limits output leading to misallocation of resources. It also transfers value from consumers to producers, since it leads to higher prices without producing any countervailing value to consumers within the relevant market. Moreover, these types of agreements generally also fail the indispensability test under the third condition.[64]

47. Any claim that restrictive agreements are justified because they aim at ensuring fair conditions of competition on the market is by nature unfounded and must be discarded.[65] The purpose of Article 81 is to protect effective competition by ensuring that markets remain open and competitive. The protection of fair conditions of competition is a task for the legislator in compliance with Community law obligations[66] and not for undertakings to regulate themselves.

3.2. First condition of Article 81(3): Efficiency gains

3.2.1. General remarks

48. According to the first condition of Article 81(3) the restrictive agreement must contribute to improving the production or distribution of goods or to promoting technical or economic progress. The provision refers expressly only to goods, but applies by analogy to services.

49. It follows from the case law of the Court of Justice that only objective benefits can be taken into account.[67] This means that efficiencies are not assessed from the subjective point of view of the parties.[68] Cost savings that arise from the mere exercise of market power by the parties cannot be taken into account. For instance, when companies agree to fix prices or share markets they reduce output and thereby production costs. Reduced competition may also lead to lower sales and marketing expenditures. Such cost reductions are a direct consequence of a reduction in output and value. The cost reductions in question do not produce any pro-competitive effects on the market. In particular, they do not lead to the creation of value through an integration of assets and activities. They merely allow the undertakings concerned to increase their profits and are therefore irrelevant from the point of view of Article 81(3).

50. The purpose of the first condition of Article 81(3) is to define the types of efficiency gains that can be taken into account and be subject to the further tests of the second and third conditions of Article 81(3). The aim of the analysis is to ascertain what are the objective benefits created by the agreement and what is the economic importance of such efficiencies. Given that for Article 81(3) to apply the pro-competitive effects flowing from the agreement must outweigh its anti-competitive effects, it is necessary to verify what is the link between the agreement and the claimed efficiencies and what is the value of these efficiencies.

51. All efficiency claims must therefore be substantiated so that the following can be verified:

(a) The *nature* of the claimed efficiencies;
(b) The *link* between the agreement and the efficiencies;
(c) The *likelihood* and *magnitude* of each claimed efficiency; and
(d) *How* and *when* each claimed efficiency would be achieved.

52. Letter (a) allows the decision-maker to verify whether the claimed efficiencies are objective in nature, cf. paragraph 49 above.

53. Letter (b) allows the decision-maker to verify whether there is a sufficient causal link between the restrictive agreement and the claimed efficiencies. This condition normally requires that the efficiencies result from the economic activity that forms the object of the agreement. Such activities may, for example, take the form of distribution, licensing of technology, joint production or joint research and development. To the extent, however, that an agreement has wider efficiency enhancing effects within the relevant market, for example because it leads to a reduction in industry wide costs, these additional benefits are also taken into account.

54. The causal link between the agreement and the claimed efficiencies must normally also be direct.[69] Claims based on indirect effects are as a general rule too uncertain and too remote to be taken into account. A direct causal link exists for instance where a technology transfer agreement allows the licensees to produce new or improved products or a distribution agreement allows products to be distributed at lower cost or valuable services to be produced. An example of indirect effect would be a case where it is claimed that a restrictive agreement allows the undertakings concerned to increase their profits, enabling them to invest more in research and development to the ultimate benefit of consumers. While there may be a link between profitability and research and development, this link is generally not sufficiently direct to be taken into account in the context of Article 81(3).

55. Letters (c) and (d) allow the decision-maker to verify the value of the claimed efficiencies, which in the context of the third condition of Article 81(3) must be balanced against the anti-competitive effects of the agreement, see paragraph 101 below. Given that Article 81(1) only applies in cases where the agreement has likely negative effects on competition and consumers (in the case of hardcore restrictions such effects are presumed) efficiency claims must be substantiated so that they can be verified. Unsubstantiated claims are rejected.

56. In the case of claimed cost efficiencies the undertakings invoking the benefit of Article 81(3) must as accurately as reasonably possible calculate or estimate the value of the efficiencies and describe in detail how the amount has been computed. They must also describe the method(s) by which the efficiencies have been or will be achieved. The data submitted must be verifiable so that there can be a sufficient degree of certainty that the efficiencies have materialised or are likely to materialise.

57. In the case of claimed efficiencies in the form of new or improved products and other non-cost based efficiencies, the undertakings claiming the benefit of Article 81(3) must describe and explain in detail what is the nature of the efficiencies and how and why they constitute an objective economic benefit.

58. In cases where the agreement has yet to be fully implemented the parties must substantiate any projections as to the date from which the efficiencies will become operational so as to have a significant positive impact in the market.

3.2.2.
The different categories of efficiencies

59. The types of efficiencies listed in Article 81(3) are broad categories which are intended to cover all objective economic efficiencies. There is considerable overlap between the various categories mentioned in Article 81(3) and the same agreement may give rise to several kinds of efficiencies. It is therefore not appropriate to draw clear and firm distinctions between the various categories. For the purpose of these guidelines, a distinction is made between cost efficiencies and efficiencies of a qualitative nature whereby value is created in the form of new or improved products, greater product variety etc.

60. In general, efficiencies stem from an integration of economic activities whereby undertakings combine their assets to achieve what they could not achieve as efficiently on their own or whereby they entrust another undertaking with tasks that can be performed more efficiently by that other undertaking.

61. The research and development, production and distribution process may be viewed as a value chain that can be divided into a number of stages. At each stage of this chain an undertaking must make a choice between performing the activity itself, performing it together with (an)other undertaking(s) or outsourcing the activity entirely to (an)other undertaking(s).

62. In each case where the choice made involves cooperation on the market with another undertaking, an agreement within the meaning of Article 81(1) normally needs to be concluded. These agreements can be vertical, as is the case where the parties operate at different levels of the value chain or horizontal, as is the case where the firms operate at the same level of the value chain. Both categories of agreements may create efficiencies by allowing the undertakings in question to perform a particular task at lower cost or with higher added value for consumers. Such agreements may also contain or lead to restrictions of competition in which case the prohibition rule of Article 81(1) and the exception rule of Article 81(3) may become relevant.

63. The types of efficiencies mentioned in the following are only examples and are not intended to be exhaustive.

3.2.2.1.
Cost efficiencies

64. Cost efficiencies flowing from agreements between undertakings can originate from a number of different sources. One very important source of cost savings is the development of new production technologies and methods. In general, it is when technological leaps are made that the greatest potential for cost savings is achieved. For instance, the introduction of the assembly line led to a very substantial reduction in the cost of producing motor vehicles.

65. Another very important source of efficiency is synergies resulting from an integration of existing assets. When the parties to an agreement combine their respective assets they may be able to attain a cost/output configuration that would not otherwise be possible. The combination of two existing technologies that have complementary strengths may reduce production costs or lead to the production of a higher quality product. For instance, it may be that the production assets of firm A generate a high output per hour but require a relatively high input of raw materials per unit of output, whereas the production assets of firm B generate lower output per hour but require a relatively lower input of raw materials per unit of output. Synergies are created if by establishing a production joint venture combining the production assets of A and B the parties can attain a high(er) level of output per hour with a low(er) input of raw materials per unit of output. Similarly, if one undertaking has optimised one part of the value chain and another undertaking has optimised another part of the value chain, the combination of their operations may lead to lower costs. Firm A may for instance have a highly automated production facility resulting in low production costs per unit whereas B has developed an efficient order processing system. The system allows production to be tailored to customer demand, ensuring timely delivery and reducing warehousing and obsolescence costs. By combining their assets A and B may be able to obtain cost reductions.

66. Cost efficiencies may also result from economies of scale, ie declining cost per unit of output as output increases. To give an example: investment in equipment and other assets often has to be made in indivisible blocks. If an undertaking cannot fully utilise a block, its average costs will be higher than if it could do so. For instance, the cost of operating a truck is virtually the same regardless of whether it is almost empty, half-full or full. Agreements whereby undertakings combine their logistics operations may allow them to increase the load factors and reduce the number of vehicles employed. Larger scale may also allow for better division of labour leading to lower unit costs. Firms may achieve economies of scale in respect of all parts of the value chain, including research and development, production, distribution and marketing. Learning economies constitute a related type of efficiency. As experience is gained in using a particular production process or in performing particular tasks, productivity may increase because the process is made to run more efficiently or because the task is performed more quickly.

67. Economies of scope are another source of cost efficiency, which occur when firms achieve cost savings by producing different products on the basis of the same input. Such efficiencies may arise from the fact that it is possible to use the same components and the same facilities and personnel to produce a variety of products. Similarly, economies of scope may arise in distribution when several types of goods are distributed in the same vehicles. For instance, a producer of frozen pizzas and a producer of frozen vegetables may obtain economies of scope by jointly distributing their products. Both groups of products must be distributed in refrigerated vehicles and it is likely that there are significant overlaps in terms of customers. By combining their operations the two producers may obtain lower distribution costs per distributed unit.

68. Efficiencies in the form of cost reductions can also follow from agreements that allow for better planning of production, reducing the need to hold expensive inventory and allowing for better capacity utilisation. Efficiencies of this nature may for example stem from the use of "just in time" purchasing, ie an obligation on a supplier of components to continuously supply the buyer according to its needs thereby avoiding the need for the buyer to maintain a significant stock of components which risks becoming obsolete. Cost savings may also result from agreements that allow the parties to rationalise production across their facilities.

3.2.2.2. *Qualitative efficiencies*

69. Agreements between undertakings may generate various efficiencies of a qualitative nature which are relevant to the application of Article 81(3). In a number of cases the main efficiency enhancing potential of the agreement is not cost reduction; it is quality improvements and other efficiencies of a qualitative nature. Depending on the individual case such efficiencies may therefore be of equal or greater importance than cost efficiencies.

70. Technical and technological advances form an essential and dynamic part of the economy, generating significant benefits in the form of new or improved goods and services. By cooperating undertakings may be able to create efficiencies that would not have been possible without the restrictive agreement or would have been possible only with substantial delay or at higher cost. Such efficiencies constitute an important source of economic benefits covered by the first condition of Article 81(3). Agreements capable of producing efficiencies of this nature include, in particular, research and development agreements. An example would be A and B creating a joint venture for the development and, if successful, joint production of a cell-based tyre. The puncture of one cell does not affect other cells, which means that there is no risk of collapse of the tyre in the event of a puncture. The tyre is thus safer than traditional tyres. It also means that there is no immediate need to change the tyre and thus to carry a spare. Both types of efficiencies constitute objective benefits within the meaning of the first condition of Article 81(3).

71. In the same way that the combination of complementary assets can give rise to cost savings, combinations of assets may also create synergies that create efficiencies of a qualitative nature. The combination of production assets may for instance lead to the production of higher quality products or products with novel features. This may for instance be the case for licence agreements, and agreements providing for joint production of new or improved goods or services. Licence agreements may, in particular, ensure more rapid dissemination of new technology in the Community and enable the licensee(s) to make available new products or to employ new production techniques that lead to quality improvements. Joint production agreements may, in particular, allow new or improved products or services to be introduced on the market more quickly or at lower cost.[70] In the telecommunications sector, for example, cooperation agreements have been held to create efficiencies by making available more quickly new global services.[71] In the banking sector cooperation agreements that made available improved facilities for making cross-border payments have also been held to create efficiencies falling within the scope of the first condition of Article 81(3).[72]

72. Distribution agreements may also give rise to qualitative efficiencies. Specialised distributors, for example, may be able to provide services that are better tailored to customer needs or to provide quicker delivery or better quality assurance throughout the distribution chain.[73]

3.3. Third condition of Article 81(3): Indispensability of the restrictions

73. According to the third condition of Article 81(3) the restrictive agreement must not impose restrictions, which are not indispensable to the attainment of the efficiencies created by the agreement in question. This condition implies a two-fold test. First, the restrictive agreement as such must be reasonably necessary in order to achieve the efficiencies. Secondly, the individual restrictions of competition that flow from the agreement must also be reasonably necessary for the attainment of the efficiencies.

74. In the context of the third condition of Article 81(3) the decisive factor is whether or not the restrictive agreement and individual restrictions make it possible to perform the activity in question more efficiently than would likely have been the case in the absence of the agreement or the restriction concerned. The question is not whether in the absence of the restriction the agreement would not have been concluded, but whether more efficiencies are produced with the agreement or restriction than in the absence of the agreement or restriction.[74]

75. The first test contained in the third condition of Article 81(3) requires that the efficiencies be specific to the agreement in question in the sense that there are no other economically practicable and less restrictive means of achieving the efficiencies. In making this latter assessment the market conditions and business realities facing the parties to the agreement must be taken into account. Undertakings invoking the benefit of Article 81(3) are not required to consider hypothetical or theoretical alternatives. The Commission will not second guess the business judgment of the parties. It will only intervene where it is reasonably clear that there are realistic and attainable alternatives. The parties must only explain and demonstrate why such seemingly realistic and significantly less restrictive alternatives to the agreement would be significantly less efficient.

76. It is particularly relevant to examine whether, having due regard to the circumstances of the individual case, the parties could have achieved the efficiencies by means of another less restrictive type of agreement and, if so, when they would likely be able to obtain the efficiencies. It may also be necessary to examine whether the parties could have achieved the efficiencies on their own. For instance, where the claimed efficiencies take the form of cost reductions resulting from economies of scale or scope the undertakings concerned must explain and substantiate why the same efficiencies would not be likely to be attained through internal growth and price competition. In making this assessment it is relevant to consider, *inter alia*, what is the minimum efficient scale on the market concerned. The minimum efficient scale is the level of output required to minimise average cost and exhaust economies of scale.[75] The larger the minimum efficient scale compared to the current size of either of the parties to the agreement, the more likely it is that the efficiencies will be deemed to be specific to the agreement. In the case of agreements that produce substantial synergies through the combination of complementary assets and capabilities the very nature of the efficiencies give rise to a presumption that the agreement is necessary to attain them.

77. These principles can be illustrated by the following hypothetical example:

A and B combine within a joint venture their respective production technologies to achieve higher output and lower raw material consumption. The joint venture is granted an exclusive licence to their respective production technologies. The parties transfer their existing production facilities to the joint venture. They also transfer key staff in order to ensure that existing learning economies can be exploited and further developed. It is estimated that these economies will reduce production costs by a further 5%. The output of the joint venture is sold independently by A and B. In this case the indispensability condition necessitates an assessment of whether or not the benefits could be substantially achieved by means of a licence agreement, which would be likely to be less restrictive because A and B would continue to produce independently. In the circumstances described this is unlikely to be the case since under a licence agreement the parties would not be able to benefit in the same seamless and continued way from their respective experience in operating the two technologies, resulting in significant learning economies.

78. Once it is found that the agreement in question is necessary in order to produce the efficiencies, the indispensability of each restriction of competition flowing from the agreement must be assessed. In this context it must be assessed whether individual restrictions are reasonably necessary in order to produce the efficiencies. The parties to the agreement must substantiate their claim with regard to both the nature of the restriction and its intensity.

79. A restriction is indispensable if its absence would eliminate or significantly reduce the efficiencies that follow from the agreement or make it significantly less likely that they will materialise. The assessment of alternative solutions must take into account the actual and potential improvement in the field of competition by the elimination of a particular restriction or the application of a less restrictive alternative. The more restrictive the restraint the stricter the test under the third condition.[76] Restrictions that are black listed in block exemption regulations or identified as hardcore restrictions in Commission guidelines and notices are unlikely to be considered indispensable.

80. The assessment of indispensability is made within the actual context in which the agreement operates and must in particular take account of the structure of the market, the economic risks related to the agreement, and the incentives facing the parties. The more uncertain the success of the product covered by the agreement, the more a restriction may be required to ensure that the efficiencies will materialise. Restrictions may also be indispensable in order to align the incentives of the parties and ensure that they concentrate their efforts on the implementation of the agreement. A restriction may for instance be necessary in order to avoid hold-up problems once a substantial sunk investment has been made by one of the parties. Once for instance a supplier has made a substantial relationship-specific investment with a view to supplying a customer with an input, the supplier is locked into the customer. In order to avoid that ex post the customer exploits this dependence to obtain more favourable terms, it may be necessary to impose an obligation not to purchase the component from third parties or to purchase minimum quantities of the component from the supplier.[77]

81. In some cases a restriction may be indispensable only for a certain period of time, in which case the exception of Article 81(3) only applies during that period. In making this assessment it is necessary to take due account of the period of time required for the parties to achieve the efficiencies justifying the application of the exception rule.[78] In cases where the benefits cannot be achieved without considerable investment, account must, in particular, be taken of the period of time required to ensure an adequate return on such investment, see also paragraph 44 above.

82. These principles can be illustrated by the following hypothetical examples:

P produces and distributes frozen pizzas, holding 15% of the market in Member State X. Deliveries are made directly to retailers. Since most retailers have limited storage capacity, relatively frequent deliveries are required, leading to low capacity utilisation and use of relatively small vehicles. T is a wholesaler of frozen pizzas and other frozen products, delivering to most of the same customers as P. The pizza products distributed by T hold 30% of the market. T has a fleet of larger vehicles and has excess capacity. P concludes an exclusive distribution agreement with T for Member State X and undertakes to ensure that distributors in other Member States will not sell into T's territory either actively or passively. T undertakes to advertise the products, survey consumer tastes and satisfaction rates and ensure delivery to retailers of all products within 24 hours. The agreement leads to a reduction in total distribution costs of 30% as capacity is better utilised and duplication of routes is eliminated. The agreement also leads to the provision of additional services to consumers. Restrictions on passive sales are hardcore restrictions under the block exemption regulation on vertical restraints[79] and can only be considered indispensable in exceptional circumstances. The established market position of T and the nature of the obligations imposed on it indicate this is not an exceptional case. The ban on active selling, on the other hand, is likely to be indispensable. T is likely to have less incentive to sell and advertise the P brand, if distributors in other Member States could sell actively in Member State X and thus get a free ride on the efforts of T. This is particularly so, as T also distributes competing brands and thus has the possibility of pushing more of the brands that are the least exposed to free riding.

S is a producer of carbonated soft drinks, holding 40% of the market. The nearest competitor holds 20%. S concludes supply agreements with customers accounting for 25% of demand, whereby they undertake to purchase exclusively from S for 5 years. S concludes agreements with other customers accounting for 15% of demand whereby they are granted quarterly target rebates, if their purchases exceed certain individually fixed targets. S claims that the agreements allow it to predict demand more accurately and thus to better plan production, reducing raw material storage and warehousing costs and avoiding supply shortages. Given the market position of S and the combined coverage of the restrictions, the restrictions are very unlikely to be considered indispensable. The exclusive purchasing obligation exceeds what is required to plan production and the same is true of the target rebate scheme. Predictability of demand can be achieved by less restrictive means. S could, for example, provide incentives for customers to order large quantities at a time by offering quantity rebates or by offering a rebate to customers that place firm orders in advance for delivery on specified dates.

3.4. Second condition of Article 81(3): Fair share for consumers

3.4.1.

General remarks

83. According to the second condition of Article 81(3) consumers must receive a fair share of the efficiencies generated by the restrictive agreement.

84. The concept of "*consumers*" encompasses all direct or indirect users of the products covered by the agreement, including producers that use the products as an input, wholesalers, retailers and final consumers, ie natural persons who are acting for purposes which can be regarded as outside their trade or profession. In other words, consumers within the meaning of Article 81(3) are the customers of the parties to the agreement and subsequent purchasers. These customers can be undertakings as in the case of buyers of industrial machinery or an input for further processing or final consumers as for instance in the case of buyers of impulse ice-cream or bicycles.

85. The concept of "*fair share*" implies that the pass-on of benefits must at least compensate consumers for any actual or likely negative impact caused to them by the restriction of competition found under Article 81(1). In line with the overall objective of Article 81 to prevent anti-competitive agreements, the net effect of the agreement must at least be neutral from the point of view of those consumers directly or likely affected by the agreement.[80] If such consumers are worse off following the agreement, the second condition of Article 81(3) is not fulfilled. The positive effects of an agreement must be balanced against and compensate for its negative effects on consumers.[81] When that is the case consumers are not harmed by the agreement. Moreover, society as a whole benefits where the efficiencies lead either to fewer resources being used to produce the output consumed or to the production of more valuable products and thus to a more efficient allocation of resources.

86. It is not required that consumers receive a share of each and every efficiency gain identified under the first condition. It suffices that sufficient benefits are passed on to compensate for the negative effects of the restrictive agreement. In that case consumers obtain a fair share of the overall benefits.[82] If a restrictive agreement is likely to lead to higher prices, consumers must be fully compensated through increased quality or other benefits. If not, the second condition of Article 81(3) is not fulfilled.

87. The decisive factor is the overall impact on consumers of the products within the relevant market and not the impact on individual members of this group of consumers.[83] In some cases a certain period of time may be required before the efficiencies materialise. Until such time the agreement may have only negative effects. The fact that pass-on to the consumer occurs with a certain time lag does not in itself exclude the application of Article 81(3). However, the greater the time lag, the greater must be the efficiencies to compensate also for the loss to consumers during the period preceding the pass-on.

88. In making this assessment it must be taken into account that the value of a gain for consumers in the future is not the same as a present gain for consumers. The value of saving 100 euro today is greater than the value of saving the same amount a year later. A gain for consumers in the future therefore does not fully compensate for a present loss to consumers of equal nominal size. In order to allow for an appropriate comparison of a present loss to consumers with a future gain to consumers, the value of future gains must be discounted. The discount rate applied must reflect the rate of inflation, if any, and lost interest as an indication of the lower value of future gains.

89. In other cases the agreement may enable the parties to obtain the efficiencies earlier than would otherwise be possible. In such circumstances it is necessary to take account of the likely negative impact on consumers within the relevant market once this lead-time has lapsed. If through the restrictive agreement the parties obtain a strong position on the market, they may be able to charge a significantly higher price than would otherwise have been the case. For the second condition of Article 81(3) to be satisfied the benefit to consumers of having earlier access to the products must be equally significant. This may for instance be the case where an agreement allows two tyre manufacturers to bring to market three years earlier a new substantially safer tyre but at the same time, by increasing their market power, allows them to raise prices by 5%. In such a case it is likely that having early access to a substantially improved product outweighs the price increase.

90. The second condition of Article 81(3) incorporates a sliding scale. The greater the restriction of competition found under Article 81(1) the greater must be the efficiencies and the pass-on to consumers. This sliding scale approach implies that if the restrictive effects of an agreement are relatively limited and the efficiencies are substantial it is likely that a fair share of the cost savings will be passed on to consumers. In such cases it is therefore normally not necessary to engage in a detailed analysis of the second condition of Article 81(3), provided that the three other conditions for the application of this provision are fulfilled.

91. If, on the other hand, the restrictive effects of the agreement are substantial and the cost savings are relatively insignificant, it is very unlikely that the second condition of Article 81(3) will be fulfilled. The impact of the restriction of competition depends on the intensity of the restriction and the degree of competition that remains following the agreement.

92. If the agreement has both substantial anti-competitive effects and substantial pro-competitive effects a careful analysis is required. In the application of the balancing test in such cases it must be taken into account that competition is an important long-term driver of efficiency and innovation. Undertakings that are not subject to effective competitive constraints-such as for instance dominant firms-have less incentive to maintain or build on the efficiencies. The more substantial the impact of the agreement on competition, the more likely it is that consumers will suffer in the long run.

93. The following two sections describe in more detail the analytical framework for assessing consumer pass-on of efficiency gains. The first section deals with cost efficiencies, whereas the section that follows covers other types of efficiencies such as new or improved products (qualitative efficiencies). The framework, which is developed in these two sections, is particularly important in cases where it is not immediately obvious that the competitive harms exceed the benefits to consumers or vice versa.[84]

94. In the application of the principles set out below the Commission will have regard to the fact that in many cases it is difficult to accurately calculate the consumer pass-on rate and other types of consumer pass-on. Undertakings are only required to substantiate their claims by providing estimates and other data to the extent reasonably possible, taking account of the circumstances of the individual case.

3.4.2.
Pass-on and balancing of cost efficiencies

95. When markets, as is normally the case, are not perfectly competitive, undertakings are able to influence the market price to a greater or lesser extent by altering their output.[85] They may also be able to price discriminate amongst customers.

96. Cost efficiencies may in some circumstances lead to increased output and lower prices for the affected consumers. If due to cost efficiencies the undertakings in question can increase profits by expanding output, consumer pass-on may occur. In assessing the extent to which cost efficiencies are likely to be passed on to consumers and the outcome of the balancing test contained in Article 81(3) the following factors are in particular taken into account:

(a) The characteristics and structure of the market,
(b) The nature and magnitude of the efficiency gains,
(c) The elasticity of demand, and
(d) The magnitude of the restriction of competition.

All factors must normally be considered. Since Article 81(3) only applies in cases where competition on the market is being appreciably restricted, see paragraph 24 above, there can be no presumption that residual competition will ensure that consumers receive a fair share of the benefits. However, the degree of competition remaining on the market and the nature of this competition influences the likelihood of pass-on.

97. The greater the degree of residual competition the more likely it is that individual undertakings will try to increase their sales by passing on cost efficiencies. If undertakings compete mainly on price and are not subject to significant capacity constraints, pass-on may occur relatively quickly. If competition is mainly on capacity and capacity adaptations occur with a certain time lag, pass-on will be slower. Pass-on is also likely to be slower when the market structure is conducive to tacit collusion.[86] If competitors are likely to retaliate against an increase in output by one or more parties to the agreement, the incentive to increase output may be tempered, unless the competitive advantage conferred by the efficiencies is such that the undertakings concerned have an incentive to break away from the common policy adopted on the market by the members of the oligopoly. In other words, the efficiencies generated by the agreement may turn the undertakings concerned into so-called "mavericks".[87]

98. The nature of the efficiency gains also plays an important role. According to economic theory undertakings maximise their profits by selling units of output until marginal revenue equals marginal cost. Marginal revenue is the change in total revenue resulting from selling an additional unit of output and marginal cost is the change in total cost resulting from producing that additional unit of output. It follows from this principle that as a general rule output and pricing decisions of a profit maximising undertaking are not determined by its fixed costs (ie costs that do not vary with the rate of production) but by its variable costs (ie costs that vary with the rate of production). After fixed costs are incurred and capacity is set, pricing and output decisions are determined by variable cost and demand conditions. Take for instance a situation in which two companies each produce two products on two production lines operating only at half their capacities. A specialisation agreement may allow the two undertakings to specialise in producing one of the two products and scrap their second production line for the other product. At the same time the specialisation may allow the companies to reduce variable input and stocking costs. Only the latter savings will have a direct effect on the pricing and output decisions of the undertakings, as they will influence the marginal costs of production. The scrapping by each undertaking of one of their production lines will not reduce their variable costs and will not have an impact on their production costs. It follows that undertakings may have a direct incentive to pass on to consumers in the form of higher output and lower prices efficiencies that reduce marginal costs, whereas they have no such direct incentive with regard to efficiencies that reduce fixed costs. Consumers are therefore more likely to receive a fair share of the cost efficiencies in the case of reductions in variable costs than they are in the case of reductions in fixed costs.

99. The fact that undertakings may have an incentive to pass on certain types of cost efficiencies does not imply that the pass-on rate will necessarily be 100%. The actual pass-on rate depends on the extent to which consumers respond to changes in price, ie the elasticity of demand. The greater the increase in demand caused by a decrease in price, the greater the pass-on rate. This follows from the fact that the greater the additional sales caused by a price reduction due to an increase in output the more likely it is that these sales will offset the loss of revenue caused by the lower price resulting from the increase in output. In the absence of price discrimination the lowering of prices affects all units sold by the undertaking, in which case marginal revenue is less than the price obtained for the marginal product. If the undertakings concerned are able to charge different prices to different customers, ie price discriminate, pass-on will normally only benefit price-sensitive consumers.[88]

100. It must also be taken into account that efficiency gains often do not affect the whole cost structure of the undertakings concerned. In such event the impact on the price to consumers is reduced. If for example an agreement allows the parties to reduce production costs by 6%, but production costs only make up one third of the costs on the basis of which prices are determined, the impact on the product price is 2%, assuming that the full amount is passed-on.

101. Finally, and very importantly, it is necessary to balance the two opposing forces resulting from the restriction of competition and the cost efficiencies. On the one hand, any increase in market power caused by the restrictive agreement gives the undertakings concerned the ability and incentive to raise price. On the other hand, the types of cost efficiencies that are taken into account may give the undertakings concerned an incentive to reduce price, see paragraph 98 above. The effects of these two opposing forces must be balanced against each other. It is recalled in this regard that the consumer pass-on condition incorporates a sliding scale. When the agreement causes a substantial reduction in the competitive constraint facing the parties, extraordinarily large cost efficiencies are normally required for sufficient pass-on to occur.

3.4.3.
Pass-on and balancing of other types of efficiencies

102. Consumer pass-on can also take the form of qualitative efficiencies such as new and improved products, creating sufficient value for consumers to compensate for the anti-competitive effects of the agreement, including a price increase.

103. Any such assessment necessarily requires value judgment. It is difficult to assign precise values to dynamic efficiencies of this nature. However, the fundamental objective of the assessment remains the same, namely to ascertain the overall impact of the agreement on the consumers within the relevant market. Undertakings claiming the benefit of Article 81(3) must substantiate that consumers obtain countervailing benefits (see in this respect paragraphs 57 and 86 above).

104. The availability of new and improved products constitutes an important source of consumer welfare. As long as the increase in value stemming from such improvements exceeds any harm from a maintenance or an increase in price caused by the restrictive agreement, consumers are better off than without the agreement and the consumer pass-on requirement of Article 81(3) is normally fulfilled. In cases where the likely effect of the agreement is to increase prices for consumers within the relevant market it must be carefully assessed whether the claimed efficiencies create real value for consumers in that market so as to compensate for the adverse effects of the restriction of competition.

3.5. Fourth condition of Article 81(3): No elimination of competition

105. According to the fourth condition of Article 81(3) the agreement must not afford the undertakings concerned the possibility of eliminating competition in respect of a substantial part of the products concerned. Ultimately the protection of rivalry and the competitive process is given priority over potentially pro-competitive efficiency gains which could result from restrictive agreements. The last condition of Article 81(3) recognises the fact that rivalry between undertakings is an essential driver of economic efficiency, including dynamic efficiencies in the shape of innovation. In other words, the ultimate aim of Article 81 is to protect the competitive process. When competition is eliminated the competitive process is brought to an end and short-term efficiency gains are outweighed by longer-term losses stemming *inter alia* from expenditures incurred by the incumbent to maintain its position (rent seeking), misallocation of resources, reduced innovation and higher prices.

106. The concept in Article 81(3) of elimination of competition in respect of a substantial part of the products concerned is an autonomous Community law concept specific to Article 81(3).[89] However, in the application of this concept it is necessary to take account of the relationship between Article 81 and Article 82. According to settled case law the application of Article 81(3) cannot prevent the application of Article 82 of the Treaty.[90] Moreover, since Articles 81 and 82 both pursue the aim of maintaining effective competition on the market, consistency requires that Article 81(3) be interpreted as precluding any application of this provision to restrictive agreements that constitute an abuse of a dominant position.[91,92] However, not all restrictive agreements concluded by a dominant undertaking constitute an abuse of a dominant position. This is for instance the case where a dominant undertaking is party to a non-full function joint venture,[93] which is found to be restrictive of competition but at the same time involves a substantial integration of assets.

107. Whether competition is being eliminated within the meaning of the last condition of Article 81(3) depends on the degree of competition existing prior to the agreement and on the impact of the restrictive agreement on competition, ie the reduction in competition that the agreement brings about. The more competition is already weakened in the market concerned, the slighter the further reduction required for competition to be eliminated within the meaning of Article 81(3). Moreover, the greater the reduction of competition caused by the agreement, the greater the likelihood that competition in respect of a substantial part of the products concerned risks being eliminated.

108. The application of the last condition of Article 81(3) requires a realistic analysis of the various sources of competition in the market, the level of competitive constraint that they impose on the parties to the agreement and the impact of the agreement on this competitive constraint. Both actual and potential competition must be considered.

109. While market shares are relevant, the magnitude of remaining sources of actual competition cannot be assessed exclusively on the basis of market share. More extensive qualitative and quantitative analysis is normally called for. The capacity of actual competitors to compete and their incentive to do so must be examined. If, for example, competitors face capacity constraints or have relatively higher costs of production their competitive response will necessarily be limited.

110. In the assessment of the impact of the agreement on competition it is also relevant to examine its influence on the various parameters of competition. The last condition for exception under Article 81(3) is not fulfilled, if the agreement eliminates competition in one of its most important expressions. This is particularly the case when an agreement eliminates price competition[94] or competition in respect of innovation and development of new products.

111. The actual market conduct of the parties can provide insight into the impact of the agreement. If following the conclusion of the agreement the parties have implemented and maintained substantial price increases or engaged in other conduct indicative of the existence of a considerable degree of market power, it is an indication that the parties are not subject to any real competitive pressure and that competition has been eliminated with regard to a substantial part of the products concerned.

112. Past competitive interaction may also provide an indication of the impact of the agreement on future competitive interaction. An undertaking may be able to eliminate competition within the meaning of Article 81(3) by concluding an agreement with a competitor that in the past has been a "maverick".[95] Such an agreement may change the competitive incentives and capabilities of the competitor and thereby remove an important source of competition in the market.

113. In cases involving differentiated products, ie products that differ in the eyes of consumers, the impact of the agreement may depend on the competitive relationship between the products sold by the parties to the agreement. When undertakings offer differentiated products the competitive constraint that individual products impose on each other differs according to the degree of substitutability between them. It must therefore be considered what is the degree of substitutability between the products offered by the parties, ie what is the competitive constraint that they impose on each other. The more the products of the parties to the agreement are close substitutes the greater the likely restrictive effect of the agreement. In other words, the more substitutable the products the greater the likely change brought about by the agreement in terms of restriction of competition on the market and the more likely it is that competition in respect of a substantial part of the products concerned risks being eliminated.

114. While sources of actual competition are usually the most important, as they are most easily verified, sources of potential competition must also be taken into account. The assessment of potential competition requires an analysis of barriers to entry facing undertakings that are not already competing within the relevant market. Any assertions by the parties that there are low barriers to market entry must be supported by information identifying the sources of potential competition and the parties must also substantiate why these sources constitute a real competitive pressure on the parties.

115. In the assessment of entry barriers and the real possibility for new entry on a significant scale, it is relevant to examine, *inter alia*, the following:

(i) The regulatory framework with a view to determining its impact on new entry.

(ii) The cost of entry including sunk costs. Sunk costs are those that cannot be recovered if the entrant subsequently exits the market. The higher the sunk costs the higher the commercial risk for potential entrants.

(iii) The minimum efficient scale within the industry, ie the rate of output where average costs are minimised. If the minimum efficient scale is large compared to the size of the market, efficient entry is likely to be more costly and risky.

(iv) The competitive strengths of potential entrants. Effective entry is particularly likely where potential entrants have access to at least as cost efficient technologies as the incumbents or other competitive advantages that allow them to compete effectively. When potential entrants are on the same or an inferior technological trajectory compared to the incumbents and possess no other significant competitive advantage entry is more risky and less effective.

(v) The position of buyers and their ability to bring onto the market new sources of competition. It is irrelevant that certain strong buyers may be able to extract more favourable conditions from the parties to the agreement than their weaker competitors.[96] The presence of strong buyers can only serve to counter a prima facie finding of elimination of competition if it is likely that the buyers in question will pave the way for effective new entry.

(vi) The likely response of incumbents to attempted new entry. Incumbents may for example through past conduct have acquired a reputation of aggressive behaviour, having an impact on future entry.

(vii) The economic outlook for the industry may be an indicator of its longer-term attractiveness. Industries that are stagnating or in decline are less attractive candidates for entry than industries characterised by growth.

(viii) Past entry on a significant scale or the absence thereof.

116. The above principles can be illustrated by the following hypothetical examples, which are not intended to establish thresholds:

Firm A is brewer, holding 70% of the relevant market, comprising the sale of beer through cafés and other on-trade premises. Over the past 5 years A has increased its market share from 60%. There are four other competitors in the market, B, C, D and E with market shares of 10%, 10%, 5% and 5%. No new entry has occurred in the recent past and price changes implemented by A have generally been followed by competitors. A concludes agreements with 20% of the on-trade premises representing 40% of sales volumes whereby the contracting parties undertake to purchase beer only from A for a period of 5 years. The agreements raise the costs and reduce the revenues of rivals, which are foreclosed from the most attractive outlets. Given the market position of A, which has been strengthened in recent years, the absence of new entry and the already weak position of competitors it is likely that competition in the market is eliminated within the meaning of Article 81(3).

Shipping firms A, B, C, and D, holding collectively more than 70% of the relevant market, conclude an agreement whereby they agree to coordinate their schedules and their tariffs. Following the implementation of the agreement prices rise between 30% and 100%. There are four other suppliers, the largest holding about 14% of the relevant market. There has been no new entry in recent years and the parties to the agreement did not lose significant market share following the price increases. The existing competitors brought no significant new capacity to the market and no new entry occurred. In light of the market position of the parties and the absence of competitive response to their joint conduct it can reasonably be concluded that the parties to the agreement are not subject to real competitive pressures and that the agreement affords them the possibility of eliminating competition within the meaning of Article 81(3).

A is a producer of electric appliances for professional users with a market share of 65% of a relevant national market. B is a competing manufacturer with 5% market share which has developed a new type of motor that is more powerful while consuming less electricity. A and B conclude an agreement whereby they establish a production joint venture for the production of the new motor. B undertakes to grant an exclusive licence to the joint venture. The joint venture combines the new technology of B with the efficient manufacturing and quality control process of A. There is one other main competitor with 15% of the market. Another competitor with 5% market share has recently been acquired by C, a major international producer of competing electric appliances, which itself owns efficient technologies. C has thus far not been active on the market mainly due to the fact that local presence and servicing is desired by customers. Through the acquisition C gains access to the service organisation required to penetrate the market. The entry of C is likely to ensure that competition is not being eliminated.

NOTES

48 Article 36(4) of Regulation 1/2003 has, inter alia, repealed Article 5 of Regulation 1017/68 applying rules of competition to transport by rail, road and inland waterway. However, the Commission's case practice adopted under Regulation 1017/68 remains relevant for the purposes of applying Article 81(3) in the inland transport sector.

49 See paragraph 42 below.

50 See the judgment in *Société Technique Minière* cited in note 20.

51 See in this respect Case 319/82, *Kerpen & Kerpen*, [1983] ECR 4173, paragraphs 11 and 12.

52 See eg Case T-185/00 and others, *Métropole télévision SA (M6)*, [2002] ECR II-3805, paragraph 86, Case T-17/93, *Matra*, ECR [1994] II-595, paragraph 85; and Joined Cases 43/82 and 63/82, *VBVB and VBBB*, [1984] ECR 19, paragraph 61.

53 See Case T-213/00, *CMA CGM and others*, [2003] ECR II . . . , paragraph 226.

54 See to that effect implicitly paragraph 139 of the *Matra* judgment cited in note 52 and Case 26/76, *Metro (I)*, [1977] ECR 1875, paragraph 43.

55 As to the concept of consumers see paragraph 84 below where it is stated that consumers are the customers of the parties and subsequent buyers. The parties themselves are not "consumers" for the purposes of Article 81(3).

56 The test is market specific, see to that effect Case T-131/99, *Shaw*, [2002] ECR II-2023, paragraph 163, where the Court of First Instance held that the assessment under Article 81(3) had to be made within the same analytical framework as that used for assessing the restrictive effects, and Case C-360/92P, *Publishers Association*, [1995] ECR I-23, paragraph 29, where in a case where the relevant market was wider than national the Court of Justice held that in the application of Article 81(3) it was not correct only to consider the effects on the national territory.

57 In Case T-86/95, *Compagnie Générale Maritime and others*, [2002] ECR II-1011, paragraphs 343 to 345, the Court of First Instance held that Article 81(3) does not require that the benefits are linked to a specific market and that in appropriate cases regard must be had to benefits "for every other market on which the agreement in question might have beneficial effects, and even, in a more general sense, for any service the quality or efficiency of which might be improved by the existence of that agreement". Importantly, however, in this case the affected group of consumers was the same. The case concerned intermodal transport services encompassing a bundle of, *inter alia*, inland and maritime transportation provided to shipping companies across the Community. The restrictions related to inland transport services, which were held to constitute a separate market, whereas the benefits were claimed to occur in relation to maritime transport services. Both services were demanded by shippers requiring intermodal transport services between northern Europe and South-East and East Asia. The judgment in CMA CGM, cited in note 53 above, also concerned a situation where the agreement, while covering several distinct services, affected the same group of consumers, namely shippers of containerised cargo between northern Europe and the Far East. Under the agreement the parties fixed charges and surcharges relating to inland transport services, port services and maritime transport services. The Court of First Instance held (cf. paragraphs 226 to 228) that in the circumstances of the case there was no need to define relevant markets for the purpose of applying Article 81(3). The agreement was restrictive of competition by its very object and there were no benefits for consumers.

58 See paragraphs 126 and 132 of the Guidelines on horizontal co-operation agreements cited in note 5 above.

59 See the *Ford* judgment cited in note 18.

60 See in this respect for example Commission Decision in TPS (OJ L90, 2.4.1999, p 6). Similarly, the prohibition of Article 81(1) also only applies as long as the agreement has a restrictive object or restrictive effects.

61 See paragraph 85 of the *Matra* judgment cited in note 52.

62 As to this requirement see paragraph 49 below.

63 See eg Case T-29/92, *Vereniging van Samenwerkende Prijsregelende Organisaties in de Bouwnijverheid (SPO)*, [1995] ECR II-289.

64 See eg Case 258/78, *Nungesser*, [1982] ECR 2015, paragraph 77, concerning absolute territorial protection.

65 See in this respect eg the judgment in *SPO* cited in note 63.

66 National measures must, inter alia, comply with the Treaty rules on free movement of goods, services, persons and capital.

67 See eg the judgment in *Consten and Grundig* cited in note 21.

68 See in this respect Commission Decision in Van den Bergh Foods (OJ 1998 L246, p 1).

69 See in this respect Commission Decision in Glaxo Wellcome (OJ 2001 L302, p 1).

70 See eg Commission Decision in GEAE/P& W (OJ 2000 L58, p 16); in British Interactive Broadcasting/Open (OJ 1999 L312, p 1) and in Asahi/Saint Gobain (OJ 1994 L354, p 87).

71 See eg Commission Decision in Atlas (OJ 1996 L239, p 23), and in Phoenix/Global One (OJ 1996 L239, p 57).

72 See eg Commission Decision in Uniform Eurocheques (OJ 1985 L35, p 43).

73 See eg Commission Decision in Cégétel + 4 (OJ 1999 L88, p 26).

74 As to the former question, which may be relevant in the context of Article 81(1), see paragraph 18 above.

75 Scale economies are normally exhausted at a certain point. Thereafter average costs will stabilise and eventually rise due to, for example, capacity constraints and bottlenecks.

76 See in this respect paragraphs 392 to 395 of the judgment in *Compagnie Générale Maritime* cited in note 57.

[77] See for more detail paragraph 116 of the Guidelines on Vertical Restraints cited in note 5.

[78] See Joined Cases T-374/94 and others, *European Night Services*, [1998] ECR II-3141, paragraph 230.

[79] See Commission Regulation No 2790/1999 on the application of Article 81(3) of the Treaty on categories of vertical agreements and concerted practices (OJ 1999 L336, p 21).

[80] See in this respect the judgment in *Consten and Grundig* cited in note 21, where the Court of Justice held that the improvements within the meaning of the first condition of Article 81(3) must show appreciable objective advantages of such a character as to compensate for the disadvantages which they cause in the field of competition.

[81] It is recalled that positive and negative effects on consumers are in principle balanced within each relevant market (cf. paragraph 43 above).

[82] See in this respect paragraph 48 of the *Metro (I)* judgment cited in note 54.

[83] See paragraph 163 of the judgment in *Shaw* cited in note 56.

[84] In the following sections, for convenience the competitive harm is referred to in terms of higher prices; competitive harm could also mean lower quality, less variety or lower innovation than would otherwise have occurred.

[85] In perfectly competitive markets individual undertakings are price-takers. They sell their products at the market price, which is determined by overall supply and demand. The output of the individual undertaking is so small that any individual undertaking's change in output does not affect the market price.

[86] Undertakings collude tacitly when in an oligopolistic market they are able to coordinate their action on the market without resorting to an explicit cartel agreement.

[87] This term refers to undertakings that constrain the pricing behaviour of other undertakings in the market who might otherwise have tacitly colluded.

[88] The restrictive agreement may even allow the undertakings in question to charge a higher price to customers with a low elasticity of demand.

[89] See Joined Cases T-191/98, T-212/98 and T-214/98, *Atlantic Container Line (TACA)*, [2003] ECR II- . . . , paragraph 939, and Case T-395/94, *Atlantic Container Line*, [2002] ECR II-875, paragraph 330.

[90] See Joined Cases C-395/96P and C-396/96P, *Compagnie maritime belge*, [2000] ECR I-1365, paragraph 130. Similarly, the application of Article 81(3) does not prevent the application of the Treaty rules on the free movement of goods, services, persons and capital. These provisions are in certain circumstances applicable to agreements, decisions and concerted practices within the meaning of Article 81(1), see to that effect Case C-309/99, *Wouters*, [2002] ECR I-1577, paragraph 120.

[91] See in this respect Case T-51/89, *Tetra Pak (I)*, [1990] ECR II-309, and Joined Cases T-191/98, T-212/98 and T-214/98, *Atlantic Container Line (TACA)*, [2003] ECR II- . . . , paragraph 1456.

[92] This is how paragraph 135 of the Guidelines on vertical restraints and paragraphs 36, 71, 105, 134 and 155 of the Guidelines on horizontal cooperation agreements, cited in note 5, should be understood when they state that in principle restrictive agreements concluded by dominant undertakings cannot be exempted.

[93] Full function joint ventures, ie joint ventures that perform on a lasting basis all the functions of an autonomous economic entity, are covered by Council Regulation (EEC) No 4064/89 on the control of concentrations between undertakings (OJ 1990 L257, p 13).

[94] See paragraph 21 of the judgment in *Metro (I)* cited in note 54.

[95] See paragraph 97 above.

[96] See in this respect Case T-228/97, *Irish Sugar*, [1999] ECR II-2969, paragraph 101.

COMMISSION NOTICE

(2005/C325/07)

on the rules for access to the Commission file in cases pursuant to Articles 81 and 82 of the EC Treaty, Articles 53, 54 and 57 of the EEA Agreement and Council Regulation (EC) No 139/2004

(Text with EEA relevance)

[4.116]

NOTES

Date of publication in OJ: OJ C325, 22.12.2005, p 7.

This Notice is reproduced as amended by Commission Communication 2015/C256/03 (OJ C256, 5.8.2015, p 3).

Note that Council Regulation (EC) No 139/2004 on the control of concentrations between undertakings is repealed, in relation to the UK, by the Competition (Amendment etc) (EU Exit) Regulations 2019, SI 2019/93, reg 63, Sch 3, para 1, as from IP completion day (as defined in the European Union (Withdrawal Agreement) Act 2020, s 39) (for transitional provisions and savings in relation to the operation of the 2019 Regulations, see Sch 4 to those Regulations at **[7.69]** et seq).

Note: with effect from 1 December 2009, the EC Treaty was replaced by the Treaty on the Functioning of the European Union. References in this document to provisions of the EC Treaty should be construed accordingly. As to Articles 81 and 82 of the EC Treaty, see now Articles 101 and 102 of the Treaty on the Functioning of the European Union.

I. INTRODUCTION AND SUBJECT-MATTER OF THE NOTICE

[4.117]

1. Access to the Commission file is one of the procedural guarantees intended to apply the principle of equality of arms and to protect the rights of the defence. Access to the file is provided for in Article 27(1) and (2) of Council Regulation (EC) No 1/2003,[1] Article 15(1) of Commission Regulation (EC) No 773/2004 ("the Implementing Regulation"),[2] Article 18(1) and (3) of the Council Regulation (EC) No 139/2004 ("Merger Regulation")[3] and Article 17(1) of Commission Regulation (EC) No 802/2004 ("the Merger Implementing Regulation").[4] In accordance with these provisions, before taking decisions on the basis of Articles 7, 8, 23 and 24(2) of Regulation (EC) No 1/2003

and Articles 6(3), 7(3), 8(2) to (6), 14 and 15 of the Merger Regulation, the Commission shall give the persons, undertakings or associations of undertakings, as the case may be, an opportunity of making known their views on the objections against them and they shall be entitled to have access to the Commission's file in order to fully respect their rights of defence in the proceedings. The present notice provides the framework for the exercise of the right set out in these provisions. It does not cover the possibility of the provision of documents in the context of other proceedings. This notice is without prejudice to the interpretation of such provisions by the Community Courts. The principles set out in this Notice apply also when the Commission enforces Articles 53, 54 and 57 of the EEA Agreement.[5]

2. This specific right outlined above is distinct from the general right to access to documents under Regulation (EC) No 1049/2001,[6] which is subject to different criteria and exceptions and pursues a different purpose.

3. The term access to the file is used in this notice exclusively to mean the access granted to the persons, undertakings or association of undertakings to whom the Commission has addressed a statement of objections. This notice clarifies who has access to the file for this purpose.

4. The same term, or the term access to documents, is also used in the above-mentioned regulations in respect of complainants or other involved parties. These situations are, however, distinct from that of the addressees of a statement of objections and therefore do not fall under the definition of access to the file for the purposes of this notice. These related situations are dealt with in a separate section of the notice.

5. This notice also explains to which information access is granted, when access takes place and what are the procedures for implementing access to the file.

6. As from its publication, this notice replaces the 1997 Commission notice on access to the file.[7] The new rules take account of the legislation applicable as of 1 May 2004, namely the above referred Regulation (EC) No 1/2003, Merger Regulation, Implementing Regulation and Merger Implementing Regulation, as well as [Decision 2011/695/EU of the President of the European Commission of 13 October 2011 on the function and terms of reference of the hearing officer in certain competition proceedings].[8] It also takes into account the recent case law of the Court of Justice and the Court of First Instance of the European Communities[9] and the practice developed by the Commission since the adoption of the 1997 notice.

NOTES

Para 6: words in square brackets substituted by Commission Communication 2015/C256/03, paras 1, 2.

1 Council Regulation (EC) No 1/2003 of 16 December 2002 on the implementation of the rules on competition laid down in Articles 81 and 82 of the Treaty, OJ L1, 4.1.2003, p 1.

2 Commission Regulation (EC) No 773/2004 of 7 April 2004 relating to the conduct of proceedings by the Commission pursuant to Articles 81 and 82 of the EC Treaty, OJ L123, 27.4.2004, p 18.

3 Council Regulation (EC) No 139/2004 of 20 January 2004 on the control of concentrations between undertakings, OJ L24, 29.1.2004, p 1.

4 Commission Regulation (EC) No 802/2004 of 21 April 2004 implementing Council Regulation (EC) No 139/2004 on the control of concentrations between undertakings, OJ L133, 30.4.2004, p 1. Corrected in the OJ L172, 6.5.2004, p 9.

5 References in this Notice to Articles 81 and 82 therefore apply also to Articles 53 and 54 of the EEA Agreement.

6 Regulation (EC) No 1049/2001 of the European Parliament and of the Council of 30 May 2001 regarding public access to European Parliament, Council and Commission documents, OJ L145, 31.5.2001, p 43. See for instance Case T-2/03, *Verein für Konsumenteninformation v Commission*, judgment of 13 April 2005, not yet reported.

7 Commission notice on the internal rules of procedure for processing requests for access to the file in cases under Articles 85 and 86 [*now 81 and 82*] of the EC Treaty, Articles 65 and 66 of the ECSC Treaty and Council Regulation (EEC) No 4064/89, OJ C23, 23.1.1997, p 3.

8 OJ L275, 20.10.2011, p 29.

9 In particular Joint Cases T-25/95 et al, *Cimenteries CBR SA et al v Commission*, [2000] ECR II-0491.

II. SCOPE OF ACCESS TO THE FILE

A. WHO IS ENTITLED TO ACCESS TO THE FILE?

[4.118]

7. Access to the file pursuant to the provisions mentioned in paragraph 1 is intended to enable the effective exercise of the rights of defence against the objections brought forward by the Commission. For this purpose, both in cases under Articles 81 and 82 EC and in cases under the Merger Regulation, access is granted, upon request, to the persons, undertakings or associations of undertakings,[10] as the case may be, to which the Commission addresses its objections[11] (hereinafter, "the parties").

B. TO WHICH DOCUMENTS IS ACCESS GRANTED?

1. The content of the Commission file

8. The "Commission file" in a competition investigation (hereinafter also referred to as "the file") consists of all documents,[12] which have been obtained, produced and/or assembled by the Commission Directorate General for Competition, during the investigation.

[9. In the course of competition investigations, the Commission may obtain a number of documents, some of which may, following a more detailed examination, prove to be unrelated to the subject matter of the case in question.[12A] Such documents may be returned to the undertaking from which they have been obtained. Upon return, these documents will no longer constitute part of the file.]

2. ACCESSIBLE DOCUMENTS

10. The parties must be able to acquaint themselves with the information in the Commission's file, so that, on the basis of this information, they can effectively express their views on the preliminary conclusions reached by the Commission in its objections. For this purpose they will be granted access to all documents making up the Commission file, as defined in paragraph 8, with the exception of internal documents, business secrets of other undertakings, or other confidential information.[13]

11. Results of a study commissioned in connection with proceedings are accessible together with the terms of reference and the methodology of the study. Precautions may however be necessary in order to protect intellectual property rights.

3. NON-ACCESSIBLE DOCUMENTS

3.1.
Internal documents

3.1.1
General principles

12. Internal documents can be neither incriminating nor exculpatory.[14] They do not constitute part of the evidence on which the Commission can rely in its assessment of a case. Thus, the parties will not be granted access to internal documents in the Commission file.[15] Given their lack of evidential value, this restriction on access to internal documents does not prejudice the proper exercise of the parties' right of defence.[16]

13. There is No obligation on the Commission departments to draft any minutes of meetings[17] with any person or undertaking. If the Commission chooses to make notes of such meetings, such documents constitute the Commission's own interpretation of what was said at the meetings, for which reason they are classified as internal documents. Where, however, the person or undertaking in question has agreed the minutes, such minutes will be made accessible after deletion of any business secrets or other confidential information. Such agreed minutes constitute part of the evidence on which the Commission can rely in its assessment of a case.[18]

14. In the case of a study commissioned in connection with proceedings, correspondence between the Commission and its contractor containing evaluation of the contractor's work or relating to financial aspects of the study, are considered internal documents and will thus not be accessible.

3.1.2
Correspondence with other public authorities

15. A particular case of internal documents is the Commission's correspondence with other public authorities and the internal documents received from such authorities (whether from EC Member States ("the Member States") or non-member countries). Examples of such non-accessible documents include:

— correspondence between the Commission and the competition authorities of the Member States, or between the latter;[19]
— correspondence between the Commission and other public authorities of the Member States;[20]
— correspondence between the Commission, the EFTA Surveillance Authority and public authorities of EFTA States;[21]
— correspondence between the Commission and public authorities of non-member countries, including their competition authorities, in particular where the Community and a third country have concluded an agreement governing the confidentiality of the information exchanged.[22]

16. In certain exceptional circumstances, access is granted to documents originating from Member States, the EFTA Surveillance Authority or EFTA States, after deletion of any business secrets or other confidential information. The Commission will consult the entity submitting the document prior to granting access to identify business secrets or other confidential information.

This is the case where the documents originating from Member States contain allegations brought against the parties, which the Commission must examine, or form part of the evidence in the investigative process, in a way similar to documents obtained from private parties. These considerations apply, in particular, as regards:

— documents and information exchanged pursuant to Article 12 of Regulation (EC) No 1/2003, and information provided to the Commission pursuant to Article 18(6) of Regulation (EC) No 1/2003;
— complaints lodged by a Member State under Article 7(2) of Regulation (EC) No 1/2003.

Access will also be granted to documents originating from Member States or the EFTA Surveillance Authority in so far as they are relevant to the parties' defence with regard to the exercise of competence by the Commission.[23]

3.2.
Confidential information

17. The Commission file may also include documents containing two categories of information, namely business secrets and other confidential information, to which access may be partially or totally restricted.[24] Access will be granted, where possible, to non-confidential versions of the original information. Where confidentiality can only be assured by summarising the relevant information, access will be granted to a summary. All other documents are accessible in their original form.

3.2.1
Business secrets

18. In so far as disclosure of information about an undertaking's business activity could result in a serious harm to the same undertaking, such information constitutes business secrets.[25] Examples of information that may qualify as business secrets include: technical and/or financial information relating to an undertaking's know-how, methods of assessing costs, production secrets and processes, supply sources, quantities produced and sold, market shares, customer and distributor lists, marketing plans, cost and price structure and sales strategy.

3.2.2
Other confidential information

19. The category "other confidential information" includes information other than business secrets, which may be considered as confidential, insofar as its disclosure would significantly harm a person or undertaking. Depending on the specific circumstances of each case, this may apply to information provided by third parties about undertakings which are able to place very considerable economic or commercial pressure on their competitors or on their trading partners, customers or suppliers. The Court of First Instance and the Court of Justice have acknowledged that it is legitimate to refuse to reveal to such undertakings certain letters received from their customers, since their disclosure might easily expose the authors to the risk of retaliatory measures.[26] Therefore the notion of other confidential information may include information that would enable the parties to identify complainants or other third parties where those have a justified wish to remain anonymous.

20. The category of other confidential information also includes military secrets.

3.2.3
Criteria for the acceptance of requests for confidential treatment.

21. Information will be classified as confidential where the person or undertaking in question has made a claim to this effect and such claim has been accepted by the Commission.[27]

22. Claims for confidentiality must relate to information which is within the scope of the above descriptions of business secrets or other confidential information. The reasons for which information is claimed to be a business secret or other confidential information must be substantiated.[28] Confidentiality claims can normally only pertain to information obtained by the Commission from the same person or undertaking and not to information from any other source.

23. Information relating to an undertaking but which is already known outside the undertaking (in case of a group, outside the group), or outside the association to which it has been communicated by that undertaking, will not normally be considered confidential.[29] Information that has lost its commercial importance, for instance due to the passage of time, can No longer be regarded as confidential. As a general rule, the Commission presumes that information pertaining to the parties' turnover, sales, market-share data and similar information which is more than 5 years old is No longer confidential.[30]

24. In proceedings under Articles 81 and 82 of the Treaty, the qualification of a piece of information as confidential is not a bar to its disclosure if such information is necessary to prove an alleged infringement ("inculpatory document") or could be necessary to exonerate a party ("exculpatory document"). In this case, the need to safeguard the rights of the defence of the parties through the provision of the widest possible access to the Commission file may outweigh the concern to protect confidential information of other parties.[31] It is for the Commission to assess whether those circumstances apply to any specific situation. This calls for an assessment of all relevant elements, including:

— the relevance of the information in determining whether or not an infringement has been committed, and its probative value;
— whether the information is indispensable;
— the degree of sensitivity involved (to what extent would disclosure of the information harm the interests of the person or undertaking in question)
— the preliminary view of the seriousness of the alleged infringement.

Similar considerations apply to proceedings under the Merger Regulation when the disclosure of information is considered necessary by the Commission for the purpose of the procedure.[32]

25. Where the Commission intends to disclose information, the person or undertaking in question shall be granted the possibility to provide a non-confidential version of the documents where that information is contained, with the same evidential value as the original documents.[33]

C. WHEN IS ACCESS TO THE FILE GRANTED?

26. Prior to the notification of the Commission's statement of objections pursuant to the provisions mentioned in paragraph 1, the parties have No right of access to the file.

1. In antitrust proceedings under Articles 81 and 82 of the Treaty

27. Access to the file will be granted upon request and, normally, on a single occasion, following the notification of the Commission's objections to the parties, in order to ensure the principle of equality of arms and to protect their rights of defence. As a general rule, therefore, No access will be granted to other parties' replies to the Commission's objections.

A party will, however, be granted access to documents received after notification of the objections at later stages of the administrative procedure, where such documents may constitute new evidence – whether of an incriminating or of an exculpatory nature –, pertaining to the allegations concerning that party in the Commission's statement of objections. This is particularly the case where the Commission intends to rely on new evidence.[33A]

2. IN PROCEEDINGS UNDER THE MERGER REGULATION

28. In accordance with Article 18(1) and (3) of the Merger Regulation and Article 17(1) of the Merger Implementing Regulation, the notifying parties will be given access to the Commission's file upon request at every stage of the procedure following the notification of the Commission's objections up to the consultation of the Advisory Committee. In contrast, this notice does not address the possibility of the provision of documents before the Commission states its objections to undertakings under the Merger Regulation.[34]

NOTES

Para 9: substituted, together with associated footnote, by Commission Communication 2015/C256/03, paras 1, 3.

Para 13: text of footnote numbered "17" substituted by Commission Communication 2015/C256/03, paras 1, 4.

Para 27: footnote 33A inserted by Commission Communication 2015/C256/03, paras 1, 5.

10 In the remainder of this Notice, the term "undertaking" includes both undertakings and associations of undertakings. The term "person" encompasses natural and legal persons. Many entities are legal persons and undertakings at the same time; in this case, they are covered by both terms. The same applies where a natural person is an undertaking within the meaning of Articles 81 and 82. In Merger proceedings, account must also be taken of persons referred to in Article 3(1)(b) of the Merger Regulation, even when they are natural persons. Where entities without legal personality which are also not undertakings become involved in Commission competition proceedings, the Commission applies, where appropriate, the principles set out in this Notice *mutatis mutandis*.

11 Cf. Article 15(1) of the Implementing Regulation, Article 18(3) of the Merger Regulation and Article 17(1) of the Merger Implementing Regulation.

12 In this notice the term "document" is used for all forms of information support, irrespective of the storage medium. This covers also any electronic data storage device as may be or become available.

12A [Judgment in *Aalborg Portland and others v. Commission*, C-204/00 P, C-205/00 P, C-211/00 P, C-213/00 P, C-217/00 P and C-219/00 P, EU:C:2004:6, paragraph 126.]

13 Cf. Article 27(2) of Regulation (EC) No 1/2003, Articles 15(2) and 16(1) of the Implementing Regulation, and Article 17(3) of the Merger Implementing Regulation. Those exceptions are also mentioned in Case T-7/89, *Hercules Chemicals v Commission*, [1991] ECR II-1711, paragraph 54. The Court has ruled that it does not belong to the Commission alone to decide which documents in the file may be useful for the purposes of the defence (Cf. Case T-30/91 *Solvay v Commission*, [1995] ECR II-1775, paragraphs 81–86, and Case T-36/91 *ICI v Commission*, [1995] ECR II-1847, paragraphs 91–96).

14 Examples of internal documents are drafts, opinions, memos or notes from the Commission departments or other public authorities concerned.

15 Cf. Article 27(2) of Regulation (EC) No 1/2003, Article 15(2) of the Implementing Regulation, and Article 17(3) of the Merger Implementing Regulation.

16 Cf. paragraph 1 above.

17 [Cf. Judgment of 30 September 2003, *Atlantic Container Line and others v Commission*, T-191/98 and T-212/98 to T-214/98, ECR, EU:T:2003:245, paragraphs 349-359. See also the Commission Notice on best practices for the conduct of proceedings concerning Articles 101 and 102 TFEU (OJ C 308, 20.10.2011, p. 6) point 44.]

18 Statements recorded pursuant to Article 19 or Article 20(2)(e) of Regulation 1/2003 or Article 13(2)(e) of Merger Regulation will also normally belong to the accessible documents (see paragraph 10 above).

19 Cf. Article 27(2) of Regulation (EC) No 1/2003, Article 15(2) of the Implementing Regulation, Article 17(3) of the Merger Implementing Regulation.

20 Cf. Order of the Court of First Instance in Cases T-134/94 et al *NMH Stahlwerke and Others v Commission* [1997] ECR II-2293, paragraph 36, and Case T-65/89, *BPB Industries and British Gypsum* [1993] ECR II-389, paragraph 33.

21 In this notice the term "EFTA States" includes the EFTA States that are parties to the EEA Agreement.

22 For example, Article VIII.2 of the Agreement between the European Communities and the Government of the United States of America regarding the application of their competition laws (OJ No L95, 27.4.1995, p 47) stipulates that information provided to it in confidence under the Agreement must be protected "to the fullest extent possible". That Article creates an international-law obligation binding the Commission.

23 In the merger control area, this may apply in particular to submissions by a Member State under Article 9(2) of the Merger Regulation with regard to a case referral.

24 Cf. Article 16(1) of the Implementing Regulation and Article 17(3) of the Merger Implementing Regulation; Case T-7/89 *Hercules Chemicals NV v Commission*, [1991] ECR II-1711, paragraph 54; Case T-23/99, *LR AF 1998 A/S v Commission*, [2002] ECR II-1705, paragraph 170.

25 Judgement of 18.9.1996 in Case T-353/94, *Postbank NV v Commission*, [1996] ECR II-921, paragraph 87.

26 The Community Courts have pronounced upon this question both in cases of alleged abuse of a dominant position (Article 82 of the EC Treaty) (Case T-65/89, *BPB Industries and British Gypsum* [1993] ECR II-389; and Case C-310/93P, *BPB Industries and British Gypsum* [1995] ECR I-865), and in merger cases (Case T-221/95 *Endemol v Commission* [1999] ECR II-1299, paragraph 69, and Case T-5/02 *Laval v Commission* [2002] ECR II-4381, paragraph 98 et seq).

27 See paragraph 40 below.

28 See paragraph 35 below.

29 However, business secrets or other confidential information which are given to a trade or professional association by its members do not lose their confidential nature with regard to third parties and may therefore not be passed on to complainants. Cf. Joined Cases 209 to 215 and 218/78, *Fedetab*, [1980] ECR 3125, paragraph 46.

30 See paragraphs 35–38 below on asking undertakings to identify confidential information.

31 Cf. Article 27(2) of Regulation (EC) No 1/2003 and Article 15(3) of the Implementing Regulation.

32 Article 18(1) of the Merger Implementing Regulation.

33 Cf. paragraph 42 below.

33A [See also the Commission Notice on best practices for the conduct of proceedings concerning Articles 101 and 102 TFEU (OJ C 308, 20.10.2011, p. 6) point 103.]

34 This question is dealt with in the Directorate General Competition document "DG COMP Best Practices on the conduct

of EC merger control proceedings", available on the web-site of the Directorate General for Competition: ec.europa.eu/competition/index_en.html.

III. PARTICULAR QUESTIONS REGARDING COMPLAINANTS AND OTHER INVOLVED PARTIES

[4.119]

29. The present section relates to situations where the Commission may or has to provide access to certain documents contained in its file to the complainants in antitrust proceedings and other involved parties in merger proceedings. Irrespective of the wording used in the antitrust and merger implementing regulations,[35] these two situations are distinct — in terms of scope, timing, and rights — from access to the file, as defined in the preceding section of this notice.

A. PROVISION OF DOCUMENTS TO COMPLAINANTS IN ANTITRUST PROCEEDINGS

30. The Court of First Instance has ruled[36] that complainants do not have the same rights and guarantees as the parties under investigation. Therefore complainants cannot claim a right of access to the file as established for parties.

31. However, a complainant who, pursuant to Article 7(1) of the Implementing Regulation, has been informed of the Commission's intention to reject its complaint,[37] may request access to the documents on which the Commission has based its provisional assessment.[38] The complainant will be provided access to such documents on a single occasion, following the issuance of the letter informing the complainant of the Commission's intention to reject its complaint.

32. Complainants do not have a right of access to business secrets or other confidential information which the Commission has obtained in the course of its investigation.[39]

B. PROVISION OF DOCUMENTS TO OTHER INVOLVED PARTIES IN MERGER PROCEEDINGS

33. In accordance with Article 17(2) of the Merger Implementing Regulation, access to the file in merger proceedings shall also be given, upon request, to other involved parties who have been informed of the objections in so far as this is necessary for the purposes of preparing their comments.

34. Such other involved parties are parties to the proposed concentration other than the notifying parties, such as the seller and the undertaking which is the target of the concentration.[40]

NOTES

35 Cf. Article 8(1) of the Implementing Regulation, which speaks about "access to documents" to complainants and Article 17(2) of Merger Implementing Regulation which speaks about "access to file" to other involved parties "in so far as this is necessary for the purposes of preparing their comments".

36 See Case T-17/93 *Matra-Hachette SA v Commission*, [1994] ECR II-595, paragraph 34. The Court ruled that the rights of third parties, as laid down by Article 19 of the Council Regulation No 17 of 6.2.1962 (now replaced by Article 27 of Regulation (EC) No 1/2003), were limited to the right to participate in the administrative procedure.

37 By means of a letter issued in accordance with Article 7(1) of the Implementing Regulation.

38 Cf. Article 8(1) of the Implementing Regulation.

39 Cf. Article 8(1) of the Implementing Regulation.

40 Cf. Article 11(b) of the Merger Implementing Regulation.

IV. PROCEDURE FOR IMPLEMENTING ACCESS TO THE FILE

A. PREPARATORY PROCEDURE

[4.120]

35. Any person which submits information or comments in one of the situations listed hereunder, or subsequently submits further information to the Commission in the course of the same procedures, has an obligation to clearly identify any material which it considers to be confidential, giving reasons, and provide a separate non-confidential version by the date set by the Commission for making its views known:[41]

a) In antitrust proceedings
   - an addressee of a Commission's statement of objections making known its views on the objections;[42]
   - a complainant making known its views on a Commission statement of objections;[43]
   - any other natural or legal person, which applies to be heard and shows a sufficient interest, or which is invited by the Commission to express its views, making known its views in writing or at an oral hearing;[44]
   - a complainant making known his views on a Commission letter informing him on the Commission's intention to reject the complaint.[45]

b) In merger proceedings
   - notifying parties or other involved parties making known their views on Commission objections adopted with a view to take a decision with regard to a request for a derogation from suspension of a concentration and which adversely affects one or more of those parties, or on a provisional decision adopted in the matter;[46]
   - notifying parties to whom the Commission has addressed a statement of objections, other involved parties who have been informed of those objections or parties to whom the Commission has addressed objections with a view to inflict a fine or a periodic penalty payment, submitting their comments on the objections;[47]
   - third persons who apply to be heard, or any other natural or legal person invited by the Commission to express their views, making known their views in writing or at an oral hearing;[48]
   - any person which supplies information pursuant to Article 11 of the Merger Regulation.

36. Moreover, the Commission may require undertakings,[49] in all cases where they produce or have produced documents, to identify the documents or parts of documents, which they consider to contain business secrets or other confidential information belonging to them, and to identify the undertakings with regard to which such documents are to be considered confidential.[50]

37. For the purposes of quickly dealing with confidentiality claims referred to in paragraph 36 above, the Commission may set a time-limit within which the undertakings shall: (i) substantiate their claim for confidentiality with regard to each individual document or part of document; (ii) provide the Commission with a non-confidential version of the documents, in which the confidential passages are deleted.[51] In antitrust proceedings the undertakings in question shall also provide within the said time-limit a concise description of each piece of deleted information.[52]

38. The non-confidential versions and the descriptions of the deleted information must be established in a manner that enables any party with access to the file to determine whether the information deleted is likely to be relevant for its defence and therefore whether there are sufficient grounds to request the Commission to grant access to the information claimed to be confidential.

B. TREATMENT OF CONFIDENTIAL INFORMATION

39. In antitrust proceedings, if undertakings fail to comply with the provisions set out in paragraphs 35 to 37 above, the Commission may assume that the documents or statements concerned do not contain confidential information.[53] The Commission may consequently assume that the undertaking has No objections to the disclosure of the documents or statements concerned in their entirety.

40. In both antitrust proceedings and in proceedings under the Merger Regulation, should the person or undertaking in question meet the conditions set out in paragraphs 35 to 37 above, to the extent they are applicable, the Commission will either:

— provisionally accept the claims which seem justified; or
— inform the person or undertaking in question that it does not agree with the confidentiality claim in whole or in part, where it is apparent that the claim is unjustified.

41. The Commission may reverse its provisional acceptance of the confidentiality claim in whole or in part at a later stage.

42. Where the Directorate General for Competition does not agree with the confidentiality claim from the outset or where it takes the view that the provisional acceptance of the confidentiality claim should be reversed, and thus intends to disclose information, it will grant the person or undertaking in question an opportunity to express its views. In such cases, the Directorate General for Competition will inform the person or undertaking in writing of its intention to disclose information, give its reasons and set a time-limit within which such person or undertaking may inform it in writing of its views. If, following submission of those views, a disagreement on the confidentiality claim persists, the matter will be dealt with by the Hearing Officer according to the applicable Commission terms of reference of Hearing Officers.[54]

43. Where there is a risk that an undertaking which is able to place very considerable economic or commercial pressure on its competitors or on its trading partners, customers or suppliers will adopt retaliatory measures against those, as a consequence of their collaboration in the investigation carried out by the Commission,[55] the Commission will protect the anonymity of the authors by providing access to a non-confidential version or summary of the responses in question.[56] Requests for anonymity in such circumstances, as well as requests for anonymity according to point 81 of the Commission Notice on the handling of complaints[57] will be dealt with according to paragraphs 40 to 42 above.

C. PROVISION OF ACCESS TO FILE

44. The Commission may determine that access to the file shall be granted in one of the following ways, taking due account of the technical capabilities of the parties:

— by means of a CD-ROM(s) or any other electronic data storage device as may become available in future;
— through copies of the accessible file in paper form sent to them by mail;
— by inviting them to examine the accessible file on the Commission's premises.

The Commission may choose any combination of these methods.

45. In order to facilitate access to the file, the parties will receive an enumerative list of documents setting out the content of the Commission file, as defined in paragraph 8 above.

46. Access is granted to evidence as contained in the Commission file, in its original form: the Commission is under No obligation to provide a translation of documents in the file.[58]

47. If a party considers that, after having obtained access to the file, it requires knowledge of specific non-accessible information for its defence, it may submit a reasoned request to that end to the Commission. If the services of the Directorate General for Competition are not in a position to accept the request and if the party disagrees with that view, the matter will be resolved by the Hearing Officer, in accordance with the applicable terms of reference of Hearing Officers.[59]

[48. Access to the file in accordance with this notice is granted on the condition that the information thereby obtained may only be used for the purposes of judicial or administrative proceedings for the application of the Union competition rules.[60] The use of this information in breach of the limitations set out in Article 16a of Regulation (EC) No 773/2004 is in certain situations subject to penalties under national law.[60A] If the use for a different purpose or the breach of the said limitations occurred with the involvement of an outside counsel, the Commission may report the incident to the bar of that counsel, with a view to disciplinary action.]

49. With the exception of paragraphs 45 and 47, this section C applies equally to the grant of access to documents to complainants (in antitrust proceedings) and to other involved parties (in merger proceedings).

NOTES

Para 42: text of footnote numbered "54" substituted by Commission Communication 2015/C256/03, paras 1, 6.
Para 47: text of footnote numbered "59" substituted by Commission Communication 2015/C256/03, paras 1, 7.
Para 48: substituted, together with associated footnotes, by Commission Communication 2015/C256/03, paras 1, 8.

41 Cf. Article 16(2) of the Implementing Regulation and Article 18(2) of the Merger Implementing Regulation.

42 pursuant to Article 10(2) of the Implementing Regulation.

43 pursuant to Article 6(1) of the Implementing Regulation.

44 pursuant to Article 13(1) and (3) of the Implementing Regulation.

45 pursuant to Article 7(1) of the Implementing Regulation.

46 Article 12 of the Merger Implementing Regulation.

47 Article 13 of the Merger Implementing Regulation.

48 pursuant to Article 16 of the Merger Implementing Regulation.

49 In merger proceedings the principles set out in the present and subsequent paragraphs also apply to the persons referred to in Article 3(1)(b) of Merger Regulation.

50 Cf. Article 16(3) of the Implementing Regulation and Article 18(3) of the Merger Implementing Regulation. This also applies to documents gathered by the Commission in an inspection pursuant to Article 13 of the Merger Regulation and Articles 20 and 21 of Regulation (EC) No 1/2003.

51 Cf. Article 16(3) of the Implementing Regulation and Article 18(3) of the Merger Implementing Regulation.

52 Cf. Article 16(3) of the Implementing Regulation.

53 Cf. Article 16 of the Implementing Regulation.

54 [Cf. Articles 3(7) and 8 of Decision 2011/695/EU of the President of the European Commission of 13 October 2011 on the function and terms of reference of the hearing officer in certain competition proceedings (OJ L275, 20.10.2011, p 29).]

55 Cf. paragraph 19 above.

56 Cf. Case T-5/02, *Tetra Laval v Commission*, [2002] ECR II-4381, paragraph 98, 104 and 105.

57 Commission Notice on the handling of complaints by the Commission under Articles 81 and 82 of the EC Treaty, OJ C101, 27.4.2004, p 65.

58 Cf. Case T-25/95 et al *Cimenteries*, paragraph 635.

59 [Cf. Articles 3(7) and 7 of Decision 2011/695/EU of the President of the European Commission of 13 October 2011 on the function and terms of reference of the hearing officer in certain competition proceedings (OJ L275, 20.10.2011, p 29).]

60 Article 16a(1) of Regulation (EC) No 773/2004, as amended by Commission Regulation (EU) 2015/1348 (OJ L208, 5.8.2015, p 3)

60A See, with respect to limitations of use in damages actions of certain categories of evidence, Articles 7 and 8 of Directive 2014/104/EU of the European Parliament and of the Council of 26 November 2014 on certain rules governing action for damages under national law for infringements of the competition law provisions of the Member States and of the European Union, OJ L349, 5.12.2014, p 1.

COMMUNICATION FROM THE COMMISSION

(2009/C45/02)

Guidance on the Commission's enforcement priorities in applying Article 82 of the EC Treaty to abusive exclusionary conduct by dominant undertakings

(Text with EEA relevance)

[4.121]

NOTES

Date of publication in OJ: OJ C45, 24.2.2009, p 7.

Note: with effect from 1 December 2009, the EC Treaty was replaced by the Treaty on the Functioning of the European Union. References in this document to provisions of the EC Treaty should be construed accordingly. As to Article 82 of the EC Treaty, see now Article 102 of the Treaty on the Functioning of the European Union.

I. INTRODUCTION

[4.122]

1. Article 82 of the Treaty establishing the European Community ("Article 82") prohibits abuses of a dominant position. In accordance with the case-law, it is not in itself illegal for an undertaking to be in a dominant position and such a dominant undertaking is entitled to compete on the merits. However, the undertaking concerned has a special responsibility not to allow its conduct to impair genuine undistorted competition on the common market. Article 82 is the legal basis for a crucial component of competition policy and its effective enforcement helps markets to work better for the benefit of businesses and consumers. This is particularly important in the context of the wider objective of achieving an integrated internal market.

II. PURPOSE OF THIS DOCUMENT

[4.123]

2. This document sets out the enforcement priorities that will guide the Commission's action in applying Article 82 to exclusionary conduct by dominant undertakings. Alongside the Commission's specific enforcement decisions, it is intended to provide greater clarity and predictability as regards the general framework of analysis which the Commission employs in determining whether it should pursue cases concerning various forms of exclusionary conduct and to help undertakings better assess whether certain behaviour is likely to result in intervention by the Commission under Article 82.

3. This document is not intended to constitute a statement of the law and is without prejudice to the interpretation of Article 82 by the Court of Justice or the Court of First Instance of the European Communities. In addition, the general framework set out in this document applies without prejudice to the possibility for the Commission to reject a complaint when it considers that a case lacks priority on grounds of lack of Community interest.

4. Article 82 applies to undertakings which hold a dominant position on one or more relevant markets. Such a position may be held by one undertaking (single dominance) or by two or more undertakings (collective dominance). This document only relates to abuses committed by an undertaking holding a single dominant position.

5. In applying Article 82 to exclusionary conduct by dominant undertakings, the Commission will focus on those types of conduct that are most harmful to consumers. Consumers benefit from competition through lower prices, better quality and a wider choice of new or improved goods and services. The Commission, therefore, will direct its enforcement to ensuring that markets function properly and that consumers benefit from the efficiency and productivity which result from effective competition between undertakings.

6. The emphasis of the Commission's enforcement activity in relation to exclusionary conduct is on safeguarding the competitive process in the internal market and ensuring that undertakings which hold a dominant position do not exclude their competitors by other means than competing on the merits of the products or services they provide. In doing so the Commission is mindful that what really matters is protecting an effective competitive process and not simply protecting competitors. This may well mean that competitors who deliver less to consumers in terms of price, choice, quality and innovation will leave the market.

7. Conduct which is directly exploitative of consumers, for example charging excessively high prices or certain behaviour that undermines the efforts to achieve an integrated internal market, is also liable to infringe Article 82. The Commission may decide to intervene in relation to such conduct, in particular where the protection of consumers and the proper functioning of the internal market cannot otherwise be adequately ensured. For the purpose of providing guidance on its enforcement priorities the Commission at this stage limits itself to exclusionary conduct and in, particular, certain specific types of exclusionary conduct which, based on its experience, appear to be the most common.

8. In applying the general enforcement principles set out in this Communication, the Commission will take into account the specific facts and circumstances of each case. For example, in cases involving regulated markets, the Commission will take into account the specific regulatory environment in conducting its assessment.[1] The Commission may therefore adapt the approach set out in this Communication to the extent that this would appear to be reasonable and appropriate in a given case.

NOTES

[1] See for instance paragraph 82.

III. GENERAL APPROACH TO EXCLUSIONARY CONDUCT

A. MARKET POWER

[4.124]

9. The assessment of whether an undertaking is in a dominant position and of the degree of market power it holds is a first step in the application of Article 82. According to the case-law, holding a dominant position confers a special responsibility on the undertaking concerned, the scope of which must be considered in the light of the specific circumstances of each case.[2]

10. Dominance has been defined under Community law as a position of economic strength enjoyed by an undertaking, which enables it to prevent effective competition being maintained on a relevant market, by affording it the power to behave to an appreciable extent independently of its competitors, its customers and ultimately of consumers.[3] This notion of independence is related to the degree of competitive constraint exerted on the undertaking in question. Dominance entails that these competitive constraints are not sufficiently effective and hence that the undertaking in question enjoys substantial market power over a period of time. This means that the undertaking's decisions are largely insensitive to the actions and reactions of competitors, customers and, ultimately, consumers. The Commission may consider that effective competitive constraints are absent even if some actual or potential competition remains.[4] In general, a dominant position derives from a combination of several factors which, taken separately, are not necessarily determinative.[5]

11. The Commission considers that an undertaking which is capable of profitably increasing prices above the competitive level for a significant period of time does not face sufficiently effective competitive constraints and can thus generally be regarded as dominant.[6] In this Communication, the expression "increase prices" includes the power to maintain prices above the competitive level and is used as shorthand for the various ways in which the parameters of competition — such as prices, output, innovation, the variety or quality of goods or services — can be influenced to the advantage of the dominant undertaking and to the detriment of consumers.[7]

12. The assessment of dominance will take into account the competitive structure of the market, and in particular the following factors:

— constraints imposed by the existing supplies from, and the position on the market of, actual competitors (the market position of the dominant undertaking and its competitors),
— constraints imposed by the credible threat of future expansion by actual competitors or entry by potential competitors (expansion and entry),
— constraints imposed by the bargaining strength of the undertaking's customers (countervailing buyer power).

(A) Market position of the dominant undertaking and its competitors

13. Market shares provide a useful first indication for the Commission of the market structure and of the relative importance of the various undertakings active on the market.[8] However, the Commission will interpret market shares in the light of the relevant market conditions, and in particular of the dynamics of the market and of the extent to which products are differentiated. The trend or development of market shares over time may also be taken into account in volatile or bidding markets.

14. The Commission considers that low market shares are generally a good proxy for the absence of substantial market power. The Commission's experience suggests that dominance is not likely if the undertaking's market share is below 40% in the relevant market. However, there may be specific cases below that threshold where competitors are not in a position to constrain effectively the conduct of a dominant undertaking, for example where they face serious capacity limitations. Such cases may also deserve attention on the part of the Commission.

15. Experience suggests that the higher the market share and the longer the period of time over which it is held, the more likely it is that it constitutes an important preliminary indication of the existence of a dominant position and, in certain circumstances, of possible serious effects of abusive conduct, justifying an intervention by the Commission under Article 82.[9] However, as a general rule, the Commission will not come to a final conclusion as to whether or not a case should be pursued without examining all the factors which may be sufficient to constrain the behaviour of the undertaking.

(B) Expansion or entry

16. Competition is a dynamic process and an assessment of the competitive constraints on an undertaking cannot be based solely on the existing market situation. The potential impact of expansion by actual competitors or entry by potential competitors, including the threat of such expansion or entry, is also relevant. An undertaking can be deterred from increasing prices if expansion or entry is likely, timely and sufficient. For the Commission to consider expansion or entry likely it must be sufficiently profitable for the competitor or entrant, taking into account factors such as the barriers to expansion or entry, the likely reactions of the allegedly dominant undertaking and other competitors, and the risks and costs of failure. For expansion or entry to be considered timely, it must be sufficiently swift to deter or defeat the exercise of substantial market power. For expansion or entry to be considered sufficient, it cannot be simply small-scale entry, for example into some market niche, but must be of such a magnitude as to be able to deter any attempt to increase prices by the putatively dominant undertaking in the relevant market.

17. Barriers to expansion or entry can take various forms. They may be legal barriers, such as tariffs or quotas, or they may take the form of advantages specifically enjoyed by the dominant undertaking, such as economies of scale and scope, privileged access to essential inputs or natural resources, important technologies[10] or an established distribution and sales network.[11] They may also include costs and other impediments, for instance resulting from network effects, faced by customers in switching to a new supplier. The dominant undertaking's own conduct may also create barriers to entry, for example where it has made significant investments which entrants or competitors would have to match,[12] or where it has concluded long-term contracts with its customers that have appreciable foreclosing effects. Persistently high market shares may be indicative of the existence of barriers to entry and expansion.

(C) Countervailing buyer power

18. Competitive constraints may be exerted not only by actual or potential competitors but also by customers. Even an undertaking with a high market share may not be able to act to an appreciable extent independently of customers with sufficient bargaining strength.[13] Such countervailing buying power may result from the customers' size or their commercial significance for the dominant undertaking, and their ability to switch quickly to competing suppliers, to promote new entry or to vertically integrate, and to credibly threaten to do so. If countervailing power is of a sufficient magnitude, it may deter or defeat an attempt by the undertaking to profitably increase prices. Buyer power may not, however, be considered a sufficiently effective constraint if it only ensures that a particular or limited segment of customers is shielded from the market power of the dominant undertaking.

B. FORECLOSURE LEADING TO CONSUMER HARM ("ANTI-COMPETITIVE FORECLOSURE")

19. The aim of the Commission's enforcement activity in relation to exclusionary conduct is to ensure that dominant undertakings do not impair effective competition by foreclosing their competitors in an anti-competitive way, thus having an adverse impact on consumer welfare, whether in the form of higher price levels than would have otherwise prevailed or in some other form such as limiting quality or reducing consumer choice. In this document the term "anti-competitive foreclosure" is used to describe a situation where effective access of actual or potential competitors to supplies or markets is hampered or eliminated as a result of the conduct of the dominant undertaking whereby the dominant undertaking is likely to be in a position to profitably increase prices[14] to the detriment of consumers. The identification of likely consumer harm can rely on qualitative and, where possible and appropriate, quantitative evidence. The Commission will address such anti-competitive foreclosure either at the intermediate level or at the level of final consumers, or at both levels.[15]

20. The Commission will normally intervene under Article 82 where, on the basis of cogent and convincing evidence, the allegedly abusive conduct is likely to lead to anti-competitive foreclosure. The Commission considers the following factors to be generally relevant to such an assessment:

— *the position of the dominant undertaking*: in general, the stronger the dominant position, the higher the likelihood that conduct protecting that position leads to anti-competitive foreclosure,

— *the conditions on the relevant market*: this includes the conditions of entry and expansion, such as the existence of economies of scale and/or scope and network effects. Economies of scale mean that competitors are less likely to enter or stay in the market if the dominant undertaking forecloses a significant part of the relevant market. Similarly, the conduct may allow the dominant undertaking to "tip" a market characterised by network effects in its favour or to further entrench its position on such a market. Likewise, if entry barriers in the upstream and/or downstream market are significant, this means that it may be costly for competitors to overcome possible foreclosure through vertical integration,

— *the position of the dominant undertaking's competitors*: this includes the importance of competitors for the maintenance of effective competition. A specific competitor may play a significant competitive role even if it only holds a small market share compared to other competitors. It may, for example, be the closest competitor to the dominant undertaking, be a particularly innovative competitor, or have the reputation of systematically cutting prices. In its assessment, the Commission may also consider in appropriate cases, on the basis of information available, whether there are realistic, effective and timely counterstrategies that competitors would be likely to deploy,

— *the position of the customers or input suppliers*: this may include consideration of the possible selectivity of the conduct in question. The dominant undertaking may apply the practice only to selected customers or input suppliers who may be of particular importance for the entry or expansion of competitors, thereby enhancing the likelihood of anti-competitive foreclosure.[16] In the case of customers, they may, for example, be the ones most likely to respond to offers from alternative suppliers, they may represent a particular means of distributing the product that would be suitable for a new entrant, they may be situated in a geographic area well suited to new entry or they may be likely to influence the behaviour of other customers. In the case of input suppliers, those with whom the dominant undertaking has concluded exclusive supply arrangements may be the ones most likely to respond to requests by customers who are competitors of the dominant undertaking in a downstream market, or may produce a grade of the product — or produce at a location — particularly suitable for a new entrant. Any strategies at the disposal of the customers or input suppliers which could help to counter the conduct of the dominant undertaking will also be considered,

— *the extent of the allegedly abusive conduct*: in general, the higher the percentage of total sales in the relevant market affected by the conduct, the longer its duration, and the more regularly it has been applied, the greater is the likely foreclosure effect,

— *possible evidence of actual foreclosure*: if the conduct has been in place for a sufficient period of time, the market performance of the dominant undertaking and its competitors may provide direct evidence of anti-competitive foreclosure. For reasons attributable to the allegedly abusive conduct, the market share of the dominant undertaking may have risen or a decline in market share may have been slowed. For similar reasons, actual competitors may have been marginalised or may have exited, or potential competitors may have tried to enter and failed,

— *direct evidence of any exclusionary strategy*: this includes internal documents which contain direct evidence of a strategy to exclude competitors, such as a detailed plan to engage in certain conduct in order to exclude a competitor, to prevent entry or to pre-empt the emergence of a market, or evidence of concrete threats of exclusionary action. Such direct evidence may be helpful in interpreting the dominant undertaking's conduct.

21. When pursuing a case the Commission will develop the analysis of the general factors mentioned in paragraph 20, together with the more specific factors described in the sections dealing with certain types of exclusionary conduct, and any other factors which it may consider to be appropriate. This assessment will usually be made by comparing the actual or likely future situation in the relevant market (with the dominant undertaking's conduct in place) with an appropriate counterfactual, such as the simple absence of the conduct in question or with another realistic alternative scenario, having regard to established business practices.

22. There may be circumstances where it is not necessary for the Commission to carry out a detailed assessment before concluding that the conduct in question is likely to result in consumer harm. If it appears that the conduct can only raise obstacles to competition and that it creates no efficiencies, its anti-competitive effect may be inferred. This could be the case, for instance, if the dominant undertaking prevents its customers from testing the products of competitors or provides financial incentives to its customers on condition that they do not test such products, or pays a distributor or a customer to delay the introduction of a competitor's product.

C. PRICE-BASED EXCLUSIONARY CONDUCT

23. The considerations in paragraphs 23 to 27 apply to price-based exclusionary conduct. Vigorous price competition is generally beneficial to consumers. With a view to preventing anti-competitive foreclosure, the Commission will normally only intervene where the conduct concerned has already been or is capable of hampering competition from competitors which are considered to be as efficient as the dominant undertaking.[17]

24. However, the Commission recognises that in certain circumstances a less efficient competitor may also exert a constraint which should be taken into account when considering whether particular price-based conduct leads to anti-competitive foreclosure. The Commission will take a dynamic view of that constraint, given that in the absence of an abusive practice such a competitor may benefit from demand-related advantages, such as network and learning effects, which will tend to enhance its efficiency.

25. In order to determine whether even a hypothetical competitor as efficient as the dominant undertaking would be likely to be foreclosed by the conduct in question, the Commission will examine economic data relating to cost and sales prices, and in particular whether the dominant undertaking is engaging in below-cost pricing. This will require that sufficiently reliable data be available. Where available, the Commission will use information on the costs of the dominant undertaking itself. If reliable information on those costs is not available, the Commission may decide to use the cost data of competitors or other comparable reliable data.

26. The cost benchmarks that the Commission is likely to use are average avoidable cost (AAC) and long-run average incremental cost (LRAIC).[18] Failure to cover AAC indicates that the dominant undertaking is sacrificing profits in the short term and that an equally efficient competitor cannot serve the targeted customers without incurring a loss. LRAIC is usually above AAC because, in contrast to AAC (which only includes fixed costs if incurred during the period under examination), LRAIC includes product specific fixed costs made before the period in which allegedly abusive conduct took place. Failure to cover LRAIC indicates that the dominant undertaking is not recovering all the (attributable) fixed costs of producing the good or service in question and that an equally efficient competitor could be foreclosed from the market.[19]

27. If the data clearly suggest that an equally efficient competitor can compete effectively with the pricing conduct of the dominant undertaking, the Commission will, in principle, infer that the dominant undertaking's pricing conduct is not likely to have an adverse impact on effective competition, and thus on consumers, and will therefore be unlikely to intervene. If, on the contrary, the data suggest that the price charged by the dominant undertaking has the potential to foreclose equally efficient competitors, then the Commission will integrate this in the general assessment of anti-competitive foreclosure (see Section B above), taking into account other relevant quantitative and/or qualitative evidence.

D. OBJECTIVE NECESSITY AND EFFICIENCIES

28. In the enforcement of Article 82, the Commission will also examine claims put forward by a dominant undertaking that its conduct is justified.[20] A dominant undertaking may do so either by demonstrating that its conduct is objectively necessary or by demonstrating that its conduct produces substantial efficiencies which outweigh any anti-competitive effects on consumers. In this context, the Commission will assess whether the conduct in question is indispensable and proportionate to the goal allegedly pursued by the dominant undertaking.

29. The question of whether conduct is objectively necessary and proportionate must be determined on the basis of factors external to the dominant undertaking. Exclusionary conduct may, for example, be considered objectively necessary for health or safety reasons related to the nature of the product in question. However, proof of whether conduct of this kind is objectively necessary must take into account that it is normally the task of public authorities to set and enforce public health and safety standards. It is not the task of a dominant undertaking to take steps on its own initiative to exclude products which it regards, rightly or wrongly, as dangerous or inferior to its own product.[21]

30. The Commission considers that a dominant undertaking may also justify conduct leading to foreclosure of competitors on the ground of efficiencies that are sufficient to guarantee that no net harm to consumers is likely to arise. In this context, the dominant undertaking will generally be expected to demonstrate, with a sufficient degree of probability, and on the basis of verifiable evidence, that the following cumulative conditions are fulfilled:[22]

— the efficiencies have been, or are likely to be, realised as a result of the conduct. They may, for example, include technical improvements in the quality of goods, or a reduction in the cost of production or distribution,
— the conduct is indispensable to the realisation of those efficiencies: there must be no less anti-competitive alternatives to the conduct that are capable of producing the same efficiencies,
— the likely efficiencies brought about by the conduct outweigh any likely negative effects on competition and consumer welfare in the affected markets,
— the conduct does not eliminate effective competition, by removing all or most existing sources of actual or potential competition. Rivalry between undertakings is an essential driver of economic efficiency, including dynamic efficiencies in the form of innovation. In its absence the dominant undertaking will lack adequate incentives to continue to create and pass on efficiency gains. Where there is no residual competition and no foreseeable threat of entry, the protection of rivalry and the competitive process outweighs possible efficiency gains. In the Commission's view, exclusionary conduct which maintains, creates or strengthens a market position approaching that of a monopoly can normally not be justified on the grounds that it also creates efficiency gains.

31. It is incumbent upon the dominant undertaking to provide all the evidence necessary to demonstrate that the conduct concerned is objectively justified. It then falls to the Commission to make the ultimate assessment of whether the conduct concerned is not objectively necessary and, based on a weighing-up of any apparent anti-competitive effects against any advanced and substantiated efficiencies, is likely to result in consumer harm.

NOTES

[2] Case 322/81 *Nederlandsche Banden Industrie Michelin (Michelin I) v Commission* [1983] ECR 3461, paragraph 57; Case T-83/91 *Tetra Pak v Commission (Tetra Pak II)* [1993] ECR II-755, paragraph 114; Case T-111/96 *ITT Promedia v Commission* [1998] ECR II-2937, paragraph 139; Case T-228/97 *Irish Sugar v Commission* [1999] ECR II-2969, paragraph 112; and Case T-203/01 *Michelin v Commission (Michelin II)* [2003] ECR II-4071, paragraph 97.

[3] See Case 27/76 *United Brands Company and United Brands Continentaal v Commission* [1978] ECR 207, paragraph 65; Case 85/76 *Hoffmann-La Roche & Co. v Commission* [1979] ECR 461, paragraph 38.

[4] See Case 27/76 *United Brands Company and United Brands Continentaal v Commission* [1978] ECR 207, paragraphs 113 to 121; Case T-395/94 *Atlantic Container Line and Others v Commission* [2002] ECR II-875, paragraph 330.

[5] Case 27/76 *United Brands and United Brands Continentaal v Commission* [1978] ECR 207, paragraphs 65 and 66; Case C-250/92 *Gøttrup-Klim e.a. Grovvareforeninger v Dansk Landbrugs Grovvareselskab* [1994] ECR I-5641, paragraph 47; Case T-30/89 *Hilti v Commission* [1991] ECR II-1439, paragraph 90.

[6] What is a significant period of time will depend on the product and on the circumstances of the market in question, but normally a period of two years will be sufficient.

[7] Accounting profitability may be a poor proxy for the exercise of market power. See to that effect Case 27/76 *United Brands Company and United Brands Continentaal v Commission* [1978] ECR 207, paragraph 126.

[8] Case 85/76 *Hoffmann-La Roche & Co. v Commission* [1979] ECR 461, paragraph 39-41; Case C-62/86 *AKZO v Commission* [1991] ECR I-3359, paragraph 60; Case T-30/89 *Hilti v Commission* [1991] ECR II-1439, paragraphs 90, 91 and 92; Case T-340/03 *France Télécom v Commission* [2007] ECR II-107, paragraph 100.

[9] As to the relationship between the degree of dominance and the finding of abuse, see Joined Cases C-395/96 P and C-396/96 P *Compagnie Maritime Belge Transports, Compagnie Maritime Belge and Dafra-Lines v Commission* [2000] ECR I-1365, paragraph 119; Case T-228/97 *Irish Sugar v Commission* [1999] ECR II-2969, paragraph 186.

[10] Case T-30/89 *Hilti v Commission* [1991] ECR II-1439, paragraph 19.

[11] Case 85/76 *Hoffmann-La Roche v Commission* [1979] ECR 461, paragraph 48.

[12] Case 27/76 *United Brands v Commission* [1978] ECR 207, paragraph 91.

[13] See Case T-228/97 *Irish Sugar v Commission* [1999] ECR II-2969, paragraphs 97 to 104, in which the Court of First Instance considered whether the alleged lack of independence of the undertaking vis-à-vis its customers should be seen as an exceptional circumstance preventing the finding of a dominant position in spite of the fact that the undertaking was responsible for a very large part of the sales recorded on the industrial sugar market in Ireland.

[14] For the meaning of the expression "increase price" see paragraph 11.

[15] The concept of "consumers" encompasses all direct or indirect users of the products affected by the conduct, including intermediate producers that use the products as an input, as well as distributors and final consumers both of the immediate product and of products provided by intermediate producers. Where intermediate users are actual or potential competitors of the dominant undertaking, the assessment focuses on the effects of the conduct on users further downstream.

[16] Case T-228/97 *Irish Sugar v Commission* [1999] ECR II-2969, paragraph 188.

[17] Case 62/86 *AKZO Chemie v Commission* [1991] ECR I-3359, paragraph 72: in relation to pricing below average total cost (ATC) the Court of Justice stated: "Such prices can drive from the market undertakings which are perhaps as efficient as the dominant undertaking but which, because of their smaller financial resources, are incapable of withstanding the competition waged against them". See also Judgment of 10 April 2008 in Case T-271/03 *Deutsche Telekom v Commission* not yet reported, paragraph 194.

[18] Average avoidable cost is the average of the costs that could have been avoided if the company had not produced a discrete amount of (extra) output, in this case the amount allegedly the subject of abusive conduct. In most cases, AAC and the average variable cost (AVC) will be the same, as it is often only variable costs that can be avoided. Long-run average incremental cost is the average of all the (variable and fixed) costs that a company incurs to produce a particular product. LRAIC and average total cost (ATC) are good proxies for each other, and are the same in the case of single product undertakings. If multi-product undertakings have economies of scope, LRAIC would be below ATC for each individual product, as true common costs are not taken into account in LRAIC. In the case of multiple products, any costs that could have been avoided by not producing a particular product or range are not considered to be common costs. In situations where common costs are significant, they may have to be taken into account when assessing the ability to foreclose equally efficient competitors.

[19] In order to apply these cost benchmarks it may also be necessary to look at revenues and costs of the dominant company and its competitors in a wider context. It may not be sufficient to only assess whether the price or revenue covers the costs for the product in question, but it may be necessary to look at incremental revenues in case the dominant company's conduct in question negatively affects its revenues in other markets or of other products. Similarly, in the case of two sided markets it may be necessary to look at revenues and costs of both sides at the same time.

[20] See Case 27/76 *United Brands v Commission* [1978] ECR 207, paragraph 184; Case 311/84 *Centre Belge d'études de marché — Télémarketing (CBEM) v Compagnie luxembourgeoise de télédiffusion (CLT) and Information publicité Benelux (IPB)* [1985] ECR 3261, paragraph 27; Case T-30/89 *Hilti v Commission* [1991] ECR II-1439, paragraphs 102 to 119; Case T-83/91 *Tetra Pak International v Commission (Tetra Pak II)* [1994] ECR II-755, paragraphs 136 and 207; Case C-95/04 P *British Airways v Commission* [2007] ECR I-2331, paragraphs 69 and 86.

[21] See, for instance, Case T-30/89 *Hilti v Commission* [1991] ECR II-1439, paragraph 118-119; Case T-83/91 *Tetra Pak International v Commission (Tetra Pak II)* [1994] ECR II-755, paragraphs 83 and 84 and 138.

[22] See, in the different context of Article 81, the Communication from the Commission — Notice — Guidelines on the application of Article 81(3) of the Treaty (OJ C101, 27.4.2004, p 97).

IV. SPECIFIC FORMS OF ABUSE

A. EXCLUSIVE DEALING

[4.125]

32. A dominant undertaking may try to foreclose its competitors by hindering them from selling to customers through use of exclusive purchasing obligations or rebates, together referred to as exclusive dealing.[23] This section sets out the circumstances which are most likely to prompt an intervention by the Commission in respect of exclusive dealing arrangements entered into by dominant undertakings.

(A) EXCLUSIVE PURCHASING

33. An exclusive purchasing obligation requires a customer on a particular market to purchase exclusively or to a large extent only from the dominant undertaking. Certain other obligations, such as stocking requirements, which appear to fall short of requiring exclusive purchasing, may in practice lead to the same effect.[24]

34. In order to convince customers to accept exclusive purchasing, the dominant undertaking may have to compensate them, in whole or in part, for the loss in competition resulting from the exclusivity. Where such compensation is given, it may be in the individual interest of a customer to enter into an exclusive purchasing obligation with the dominant undertaking. But it would be wrong to conclude automatically from this that all exclusive purchasing obligations, taken together, are beneficial for customers overall, including those currently not purchasing from the dominant undertaking, and the final consumers. The Commission will focus its attention on those cases where it is likely that consumers as a whole will not benefit. This will, in particular, be the case if there are many customers and the exclusive purchasing obligations of the dominant undertaking, taken together, have the effect of preventing the entry or expansion of competing undertakings.

35. In addition to the factors mentioned in paragraph 20, the following factors will generally be of particular relevance in determining whether the Commission will intervene in respect of exclusive purchasing arrangements.

36. The capacity for exclusive purchasing obligations to result in anti-competitive foreclosure arises in particular where, without the obligations, an important competitive constraint is exercised by competitors who either are not yet present in the market at the time the obligations are concluded, or who are not in a position to compete for the full supply of the customers. Competitors may not be able to compete for an individual customer's entire demand because the dominant undertaking is an unavoidable trading partner at least for part of the demand on the market, for instance because its brand is a "must stock item" preferred by many final consumers or because the capacity constraints on the other suppliers are such that a part of demand can only be provided for by the dominant supplier.[25] If competitors can compete on equal terms for each individual customer's entire demand, exclusive purchasing obligations are generally unlikely to hamper effective competition unless the switching of supplier by customers is rendered difficult due to the duration of the exclusive purchasing obligation. In general, the longer the duration of the obligation, the greater the likely foreclosure effect. However, if the dominant undertaking is an unavoidable trading partner for all or most customers, even an exclusive purchasing obligation of short duration can lead to anti-competitive foreclosure.

(B) CONDITIONAL REBATES

37. Conditional rebates are rebates granted to customers to reward them for a particular form of purchasing behaviour. The usual nature of a conditional rebate is that the customer is given a rebate if its purchases over a defined reference period exceed a certain threshold, the rebate being granted either on all purchases (retroactive rebates) or only on those made in excess of those required to achieve the threshold (incremental rebates). Conditional rebates are not an uncommon practice. Undertakings may offer such rebates in order to attract more demand, and as such they may stimulate demand and benefit consumers. However, such rebates — when granted by a dominant undertaking — can also have actual or potential foreclosure effects similar to exclusive purchasing obligations. Conditional rebates can have such effects without necessarily entailing a sacrifice for the dominant undertaking.[26]

38. In addition to the factors already mentioned in paragraph 20, the following factors are of particular importance to the Commission in determining whether a given system of conditional rebates is liable to result in anti-competitive foreclosure and, consequently, will be part of the Commission's enforcement priorities.

39. As with exclusive purchasing obligations, the likelihood of anti-competitive foreclosure is higher where competitors are not able to compete on equal terms for the entire demand of each individual customer. A conditional rebate granted by a dominant undertaking may enable it to use the "non-contestable" portion of the demand of each customer (that is to say, the amount that would be purchased by the customer from the dominant undertaking in any event) as leverage to decrease the price to be paid for the "contestable" portion of demand (that is to say, the amount for which the customer may prefer and be able to find substitutes).[27]

40. In general terms, retroactive rebates may foreclose the market significantly, as they may make it less attractive for customers to switch small amounts of demand to an alternative supplier, if this would lead to loss of the retroactive rebates.[28] The potential foreclosing effect of retroactive rebates is in principle strongest on the last purchased unit of the product before the threshold is exceeded. However, what is in the Commission's view relevant for an assessment of the loyalty enhancing effect of a rebate is not simply the effect on competition to provide the last individual unit, but the foreclosing effect of the rebate system on (actual or potential) competitors of the dominant supplier. The higher the rebate as a percentage of the total price and the higher the threshold, the greater the inducement below the threshold and, therefore, the stronger the likely foreclosure of actual or potential competitors.

41. When applying the methodology explained in paragraphs 23 to 27, the Commission intends to investigate, to the extent that the data are available and reliable, whether the rebate system is capable of hindering expansion or entry even by competitors that are equally efficient by making it more difficult for them to supply part of the requirements of individual customers. In this context the Commission will estimate what price a competitor would have to offer in order to compensate the customer for the loss of the conditional rebate if the latter would switch part of its demand ("the relevant range") away from the dominant undertaking. The effective price that the competitor will have to match is not the average price of the dominant undertaking, but the normal (list) price less the rebate the customer loses by switching, calculated over the relevant range of sales and in the relevant period of time. The Commission will take into account the margin of error that may be caused by the uncertainties inherent in this kind of analysis.

42. The relevant range over which to calculate the effective price in a particular case depends on the specific facts of each case and on whether the rebate is incremental or retroactive. For incremental rebates, the relevant range is normally the incremental purchases that are being considered. For retroactive rebates, it will generally be relevant to assess in the specific market context how much of a customer's purchase requirements can realistically be switched to a competitor (the "contestable share" or "contestable portion"). If it is likely that customers would be willing and able to switch large amounts of demand to a (potential) competitor relatively quickly, the relevant range is likely to be relatively large. If, on the other hand, it is likely that customers would only be willing or able to switch small amounts incrementally, then the relevant range will be relatively small. For existing competitors their capacity to expand sales to customers and the fluctuations in those sales over time may also provide an indication of the relevant range. For potential competitors, an assessment of the scale at which a new entrant would realistically be able to enter may be undertaken, where possible. It may be possible to take the historical growth pattern of new entrants in the same or in similar markets as an indication of a realistic market share of a new entrant.[29]

43. The lower the estimated effective price over the relevant range is compared to the average price of the dominant supplier, the stronger the loyalty-enhancing effect. However, as long as the effective price remains consistently above the LRAIC of the dominant undertaking, this would normally allow an equally efficient competitor to compete profitably notwithstanding the rebate. In those circumstances the rebate is normally not capable of foreclosing in an anti-competitive way.

44. Where the effective price is below AAC, as a general rule the rebate scheme is capable of foreclosing even equally efficient competitors. Where the effective price is between AAC and LRAIC, the Commission will investigate whether other factors point to the conclusion that entry or expansion even by equally efficient competitors is likely to be affected. In this context, the Commission will investigate whether and to what extent competitors have realistic and

effective counterstrategies at their disposal, for instance their capacity to also use a "non-contestable" portion of their buyers' demand as leverage to decrease the price for the relevant range. Where competitors do not have such counterstrategies at their disposal, the Commission will consider that the rebate scheme is capable of foreclosing equally efficient competitors.

45. As indicated in paragraph 27, this analysis will be integrated in the general assessment, taking into account other relevant quantitative or qualitative evidence. It is normally important to consider whether the rebate system is applied with an individualised or a standardised threshold. An individualised threshold — one based on a percentage of the total requirements of the customer or an individualised volume target — allows the dominant supplier to set the threshold at such a level as to make it difficult for customers to switch suppliers, thereby creating a maximum loyalty enhancing effect.[30] By contrast, a standardised volume threshold — where the threshold is the same for all or a group of customers — may be too high for some smaller customers and/or too low for larger customers to have a loyalty enhancing effect. If, however, it can be established that a standardised volume threshold approximates the requirements of an appreciable proportion of customers, the Commission is likely to consider that such a standardised system of rebates may produce anti-competitive foreclosure effects.

(C) EFFICIENCIES

46. Provided that the conditions set out in Section III D are fulfilled, the Commission will consider claims by dominant undertakings that rebate systems achieve cost or other advantages which are passed on to customers.[31] Transaction-related cost advantages are often more likely to be achieved with standardised volume targets than with individualised volume targets. Similarly, incremental rebate schemes are in general more likely to give resellers an incentive to produce and resell a higher volume than retroactive rebate schemes.[32] Under the same conditions, the Commission will consider evidence demonstrating that exclusive dealing arrangements result in advantages to particular customers if those arrangements are necessary for the dominant undertaking to make certain relationship-specific investments in order to be able to supply those customers.

B. TYING AND BUNDLING

47. A dominant undertaking may try to foreclose its competitors by tying or bundling. This section sets out the circumstances which are most likely to prompt an intervention by the Commission when assessing tying and bundling by dominant undertakings.

48. "Tying" usually refers to situations where customers that purchase one product (the tying product) are required also to purchase another product from the dominant undertaking (the tied product). Tying can take place on a technical or contractual basis.[33] "Bundling" usually refers to the way products are offered and priced by the dominant undertaking. In the case of pure bundling the products are only sold jointly in fixed proportions. In the case of mixed bundling, often referred to as a multi-product rebate, the products are also made available separately, but the sum of the prices when sold separately is higher than the bundled price.

49. Tying and bundling are common practices intended to provide customers with better products or offerings in more cost effective ways. However, an undertaking which is dominant in one product market (or more) of a tie or bundle (referred to as the tying market) can harm consumers through tying or bundling by foreclosing the market for the other products that are part of the tie or bundle (referred to as the tied market) and, indirectly, the tying market.

50. The Commission will normally take action under Article 82 where an undertaking is dominant in the tying market[34] and where, in addition, the following conditions are fulfilled: (i) the tying and tied products are distinct products, and (ii) the tying practice is likely to lead to anti-competitive foreclosure.[35]

(A) DISTINCT PRODUCTS

51. Whether the products will be considered by the Commission to be distinct depends on customer demand. Two products are distinct if, in the absence of tying or bundling, a substantial number of customers would purchase or would have purchased the tying product without also buying the tied product from the same supplier, thereby allowing stand-alone production for both the tying and the tied product.[36] Evidence that two products are distinct could include direct evidence that, when given a choice, customers purchase the tying and the tied products separately from different sources of supply, or indirect evidence, such as the presence on the market of undertakings specialised in the manufacture or sale of the tied product without the tying product[37] or of each of the products bundled by the dominant undertaking, or evidence indicating that undertakings with little market power, particularly in competitive markets, tend not to tie or not to bundle such products.

(B) ANTI-COMPETITIVE FORECLOSURE IN THE TIED AND/OR TYING MARKET

52. Tying or bundling may lead to anti-competitive effects in the tied market, the tying market, or both at the same time. However, even when the aim of the tying or bundling is to protect the dominant undertaking's position in the tying market, this is done indirectly through foreclosing the tied market. In addition to the factors already mentioned in paragraph 20, the Commission considers that the following factors are generally of particular importance for identifying cases of likely or actual anti-competitive foreclosure.

53. The risk of anti-competitive foreclosure is expected to be greater where the dominant undertaking makes its tying or bundling strategy a lasting one, for example through technical tying which is costly to reverse. Technical tying also reduces the opportunities for resale of individual components.

54. In the case of bundling, the undertaking may have a dominant position for more than one of the products in the bundle. The greater the number of such products in the bundle, the stronger the likely anti-competitive foreclosure. This is particularly true if the bundle is difficult for a competitor to replicate, either on its own or in combination with others.

55. The tying may lead to less competition for customers interested in buying the tied product, but not the tying product. If there is not a sufficient number of customers who will buy the tied product alone to sustain competitors of the dominant undertaking in the tied market, the tying can lead to those customers facing higher prices.

56. If the tying and the tied product can be used in variable proportions as inputs to a production process, customers may react to an increase in price for the tying product by increasing their demand for the tied product while decreasing their demand for the tying product. By tying the two products the dominant undertaking may seek to avoid this substitution and as a result be able to raise its prices.

57. If the prices the dominant undertaking can charge in the tying market are regulated, tying may allow the dominant undertaking to raise prices in the tied market in order to compensate for the loss of revenue caused by the regulation in the tying market.

58. If the tied product is an important complementary product for customers of the tying product, a reduction of alternative suppliers of the tied product and hence a reduced availability of that product can make entry to the tying market alone more difficult.

(C) MULTI-PRODUCT REBATES

59. A multi-product rebate may be anti-competitive on the tied or the tying market if it is so large that equally efficient competitors offering only some of the components cannot compete against the discounted bundle.

60. In theory, it would be ideal if the effect of the rebate could be assessed by examining whether the incremental revenue covers the incremental costs for each product in the dominant undertaking's bundle. However, in practice assessing the incremental revenue is complex. Therefore, in its enforcement practice the Commission will in most situations use the incremental price as a good proxy. If the incremental price that customers pay for each of the dominant undertaking's products in the bundle remains above the LRAIC of the dominant undertaking from including that product in the bundle, the Commission will normally not intervene since an equally efficient competitor with only one product should in principle be able to compete profitably against the bundle. Enforcement action may, however, be warranted if the incremental price is below the LRAIC, because in such a case even an equally efficient competitor may be prevented from expanding or entering.[38]

61. If the evidence suggests that competitors of the dominant undertaking are selling identical bundles, or could do so in a timely way without being deterred by possible additional costs, the Commission will generally regard this as a bundle competing against a bundle, in which case the relevant question is not whether the incremental revenue covers the incremental costs for each product in the bundle, but rather whether the price of the bundle as a whole is predatory.

(D) EFFICIENCIES

62. Provided that the conditions set out in Section III D are fulfilled, the Commission will look into claims by dominant undertakings that their tying and bundling practices may lead to savings in production or distribution that would benefit customers. The Commission may also consider whether such practices reduce transaction costs for customers, who would otherwise be forced to buy the components separately, and enable substantial savings on packaging and distribution costs for suppliers. It may also examine whether combining two independent products into a new, single product might enhance the ability to bring such a product to the market to the benefit of consumers. The Commission may also consider whether tying and bundling practices allow the supplier to pass on efficiencies arising from its production or purchase of large quantities of the tied product.

C. PREDATION

63. In line with its enforcement priorities, the Commission will generally intervene where there is evidence showing that a dominant undertaking engages in predatory conduct by deliberately incurring losses or foregoing profits in the short term (referred to hereafter as "sacrifice"), so as to foreclose or be likely to foreclose one or more of its actual or potential competitors with a view to strengthening or maintaining its market power, thereby causing consumer harm.[39]

(A) SACRIFICE

64. Conduct will be viewed by the Commission as entailing a sacrifice if, by charging a lower price for all or a particular part of its output over the relevant time period, or by expanding its output over the relevant time period, the dominant undertaking incurred or is incurring losses that could have been avoided. The Commission will take AAC as the appropriate starting point for assessing whether the dominant undertaking incurred or is incurring avoidable losses. If a dominant undertaking charges a price below AAC for all or part of its output, it is not recovering the costs that could have been avoided by not producing that output: it is incurring a loss that could have been avoided[40] Pricing below AAC will thus in most cases be viewed by the Commission as a clear indication of sacrifice.[41]

65. However, the concept of sacrifice does not only include pricing below AAC.[42] In order to show a predatory strategy, the Commission may also investigate whether the allegedly predatory conduct led in the short term to net revenues lower than could have been expected from a reasonable alternative conduct, that is to say, whether the dominant undertaking incurred a loss that it could have avoided.[43] The Commission will not compare the actual conduct with hypothetical or theoretical alternatives that might have been more profitable. Only economically rational and practicable alternatives will be considered which, taking into account the market conditions and business realities facing the dominant undertaking, can realistically be expected to be more profitable.

66. In some cases it will be possible to rely upon direct evidence consisting of documents from the dominant undertaking which clearly show a predatory strategy,[44] such as a detailed plan to sacrifice in order to exclude a competitor, to prevent entry or to pre-empt the emergence of a market, or evidence of concrete threats of predatory action.[45]

(B) ANTI-COMPETITIVE FORECLOSURE

67. If sufficient reliable data are available, the Commission will apply the equally efficient competitor analysis, described in paragraphs 25 to 27, to determine whether the conduct is capable of harming consumers. Normally only pricing below LRAIC is capable of foreclosing as efficient competitors from the market.

68. In addition to the factors already mentioned in paragraph 20, the Commission will generally investigate whether and how the suspected conduct reduces the likelihood that competitors will compete. For instance, if the dominant undertaking is better informed about cost or other market conditions, or can distort market signals about profitability, it may engage in predatory conduct so as to influence the expectations of potential entrants and thereby deter entry. If the conduct and its likely effects are felt on multiple markets and/or in successive periods of possible entry, the dominant undertaking may be shown to be seeking a reputation for predatory conduct. If the targeted competitor is dependent on external financing, substantial price decreases or other predatory conduct by the dominant undertaking could adversely affect the competitor's performance so that its access to further financing may be seriously undermined.

69. The Commission does not consider that it is necessary to show that competitors have exited the market in order to show that there has been anti-competitive foreclosure. The possibility cannot be excluded that the dominant undertaking may prefer to prevent the competitor from competing vigorously and have it follow the dominant undertaking's pricing, rather than eliminate it from the market altogether. Such disciplining avoids the risk inherent in eliminating competitors, in particular the risk that the assets of the competitor are sold at a low price and stay in the market, creating a new low cost entrant.

70. Generally speaking, consumers are likely to be harmed if the dominant undertaking can reasonably expect its market power after the predatory conduct comes to an end to be greater than it would have been had the undertaking not engaged in that conduct in the first place, that is to say, if the undertaking is likely to be in a position to benefit from the sacrifice.

71. This does not mean that the Commission will only intervene if the dominant undertaking would be likely to be able to increase its prices above the level persisting in the market before the conduct. It is sufficient, for instance, that the conduct would be likely to prevent or delay a decline in prices that would otherwise have occurred. Identifying consumer harm is not a mechanical calculation of profits and losses, and proof of overall profits is not required. Likely consumer harm may be demonstrated by assessing the likely foreclosure effect of the conduct, combined with consideration of other factors, such as entry barriers.[46] In this context, the Commission will also consider possibilities of re-entry.

72. It may be easier for the dominant undertaking to engage in predatory conduct if it selectively targets specific customers with low prices, as this will limit the losses incurred by the dominant undertaking.

73. It is less likely that the dominant undertaking engages in predatory conduct if the conduct concerns a low price applied generally for a long period of time.

(C) EFFICIENCIES

74. In general it is considered unlikely that predatory conduct will create efficiencies. However, provided that the conditions set out in Section III D are fulfilled, the Commission will consider claims by a dominant undertaking that the low pricing enables it to achieve economies of scale or efficiencies related to expanding the market.

D. REFUSAL TO SUPPLY AND MARGIN SQUEEZE

75. When setting its enforcement priorities, the Commission starts from the position that, generally speaking, any undertaking, whether dominant or not, should have the right to choose its trading partners and to dispose freely of its property. The Commission therefore considers that intervention on competition law grounds requires careful consideration where the application of Article 82 would lead to the imposition of an obligation to supply on the dominant undertaking.[47] The existence of such an obligation — even for a fair remuneration — may undermine undertakings' incentives to invest and innovate and, thereby, possibly harm consumers. The knowledge that they may have a duty to supply against their will may lead dominant undertakings — or undertakings who anticipate that they may become dominant — not to invest, or to invest less, in the activity in question. Also, competitors may be tempted to free ride on investments made by the dominant undertaking instead of investing themselves. Neither of these consequences would, in the long run, be in the interest of consumers.

76. Typically competition problems arise when the dominant undertaking competes on the "downstream" market with the buyer whom it refuses to supply. The term "downstream market" is used to refer to the market for which the refused input is needed in order to manufacture a product or provide a service. This section deals only with this type of refusal.

77. Other types of possibly unlawful refusal to supply, in which the supply is made conditional upon the purchaser accepting limitations on its conduct, are not dealt with in this section. For instance, halting supplies in order to punish customers for dealing with competitors or refusing to supply customers that do not agree to tying arrangements, will be examined by the Commission in line with the principles set out in the sections on exclusive dealing and tying and bundling. Similarly, refusals to supply aimed at preventing the purchaser from engaging in parallel trade[48] or from lowering its resale price are also not dealt with in this section.

78. The concept of refusal to supply covers a broad range of practices, such as a refusal to supply products to existing or new customers,[49] refusal to license intellectual property rights,[50] including when the licence is necessary to provide interface information,[51] or refusal to grant access to an essential facility or a network.[52]

79. The Commission does not regard it as necessary for the refused product to have been already traded: it is sufficient that there is demand from potential purchasers and that a potential market for the input at stake can be identified.[53] Likewise, it is not necessary for there to be actual refusal on the part of a dominant undertaking; "constructive refusal" is sufficient. Constructive refusal could, for example, take the form of unduly delaying or otherwise degrading the supply of the product or involve the imposition of unreasonable conditions in return for the supply.

80. Finally, instead of refusing to supply, a dominant undertaking may charge a price for the product on the upstream market which, compared to the price it charges on the downstream market,[54] does not allow even an equally efficient competitor to trade profitably in the downstream market on a lasting basis (a so-called "margin squeeze"). In margin squeeze cases the benchmark which the Commission will generally rely on to determine the costs of an equally efficient competitor are the LRAIC of the downstream division of the integrated dominant undertaking.[55]

81. The Commission will consider these practices as an enforcement priority if all the following circumstances are present:

— the refusal relates to a product or service that is objectively necessary to be able to compete effectively on a downstream market,
— the refusal is likely to lead to the elimination of effective competition on the downstream market, and
— the refusal is likely to lead to consumer harm.

82. In certain specific cases, it may be clear that imposing an obligation to supply is manifestly not capable of having negative effects on the input owner's and/or other operators' incentives to invest and innovate upstream, whether ex ante or ex post. The Commission considers that this is particularly likely to be the case where regulation compatible with Community law already imposes an obligation to supply on the dominant undertaking and it is clear, from the considerations underlying such regulation, that the necessary balancing of incentives has already been made by the public authority when imposing such an obligation to supply. This could also be the case where the upstream market position of the dominant undertaking has been developed under the protection of special or exclusive rights or has been financed by state resources. In such specific cases there is no reason for the Commission to deviate from its general enforcement standard of showing likely anti-competitive foreclosure, without considering whether the three circumstances referred to in paragraph 81 are present.

(A) Objective necessity of the input

83. In examining whether a refusal to supply deserves its priority attention, the Commission will consider whether the supply of the refused input is objectively necessary for operators to be able to compete effectively on the market. This does not mean that, without the refused input, no competitor could ever enter or survive on the downstream market.[56] Rather, an input is indispensable where there is no actual or potential substitute on which competitors in the downstream market could rely so as to counter — at least in the long-term — the negative consequences of the refusal.[57] In this regard, the Commission will normally make an assessment of whether competitors could effectively duplicate the input produced by the dominant undertaking in the foreseeable future.[58] The notion of duplication means the creation of an alternative source of efficient supply that is capable of allowing competitors to exert a competitive constraint on the dominant undertaking in the downstream market.[59]

84. The criteria set out in paragraph 81 apply both to cases of disruption of previous supply, and to refusals to supply a good or service which the dominant company has not previously supplied to others (de novo refusals to supply). However, the termination of an existing supply arrangement is more likely to be found to be abusive than a de novo refusal to supply. For example, if the dominant undertaking had previously been supplying the requesting undertaking, and the latter had made relationship-specific investments in order to use the subsequently refused input, the Commission may be more likely to regard the input in question as indispensable. Similarly, the fact that the owner of the essential input in the past has found it in its interest to supply is an indication that supplying the input does not imply any risk that the owner receives inadequate compensation for the original investment. It would therefore be up to the dominant company to demonstrate why circumstances have actually changed in such a way that the continuation of its existing supply relationship would put in danger its adequate compensation.

(B) Elimination of effective competition

85. If the requirements set out in paragraphs 83 and 84 are fulfilled, the Commission considers that a dominant undertaking's refusal to supply is generally liable to eliminate, immediately or over time, effective competition in the downstream market. The likelihood of effective competition being eliminated is generally greater the higher the market share of the dominant undertaking in the downstream market. The less capacity-constrained the dominant undertaking is relative to competitors in the downstream market, the closer the substitutability between the dominant undertaking's output and that of its competitors in the downstream market, the greater the proportion of competitors in the downstream market that are affected, and the more likely it is that the demand that could be served by the foreclosed competitors would be diverted away from them to the advantage of the dominant undertaking.

(C) Consumer harm

86. In examining the likely impact of a refusal to supply on consumer welfare, the Commission will examine whether, for consumers, the likely negative consequences of the refusal to supply in the relevant market outweigh over time the negative consequences of imposing an obligation to supply. If they do, the Commission will normally pursue the case.

87. The Commission considers that consumer harm may, for instance, arise where the competitors that the dominant undertaking forecloses are, as a result of the refusal, prevented from bringing innovative goods or services to market and/or where follow-on innovation is likely to be stifled.[60] This may be particularly the case if the undertaking which requests supply does not intend to limit itself essentially to duplicating the goods or services already offered by the dominant undertaking on the downstream market, but intends to produce new or improved goods or services for which there is a potential consumer demand or is likely to contribute to technical development.[61]

88. The Commission also considers that a refusal to supply may lead to consumer harm where the price in the upstream input market is regulated, the price in the downstream market is not regulated and the dominant undertaking, by excluding competitors on the downstream market through a refusal to supply, is able to extract more profits in the unregulated downstream market than it would otherwise do.

(D) EFFICIENCIES

89. The Commission will consider claims by the dominant undertaking that a refusal to supply is necessary to allow the dominant undertaking to realise an adequate return on the investments required to develop its input business, thus generating incentives to continue to invest in the future, taking the risk of failed projects into account. The Commission will also consider claims by the dominant undertaking that its own innovation will be negatively affected by the obligation to supply, or by the structural changes in the market conditions that imposing such an obligation will bring about, including the development of follow-on innovation by competitors.

90. However, when considering such claims, the Commission will ensure that the conditions set out in Section III D are fulfilled. In particular, it falls on the dominant undertaking to demonstrate any negative impact which an obligation to supply is likely to have on its own level of innovation.[62] If a dominant undertaking has previously supplied the input in question, this can be relevant for the assessment of any claim that the refusal to supply is justified on efficiency grounds.

NOTES

23 The notion of exclusive dealing also includes exclusive supply obligations or incentives with the same effect, whereby the dominant undertaking tries to foreclose its competitors by hindering them from purchasing from suppliers. The Commission considers that such input foreclosure is in principle liable to result in anti-competitive foreclosure if the exclusive supply obligation or incentive ties most of the efficient input suppliers and customers competing with the dominant undertaking are unable to find alternative efficient sources of input supply.

24 Case T-65/98 *Van den Bergh Foods v Commission* [2003] ECR II-4653. In this case the obligation to use coolers exclusively for the products of the dominant undertaking was considered to lead to outlet exclusivity.

25 Case T-65/98 *Van den Bergh Foods v Commission* [2003] ECR II-4653, paragraphs 104 and 156.

26 In this regard, the assessment of conditional rebates differs from that of predation, which always entails a sacrifice.

27 See Case T-203/01 *Michelin v Commission (Michelin II)* [2003] ECR II-4071, paragraphs 162 and 163. See also Case T-219/99 *British Airways v Commission* [2003] ECR II-5917, paragraphs 277 and 278.

28 Case 322/81 *Nederlandsche Banden Industrie Michelin v Commission (Michelin I)* [1983] ECR 3461, paragraphs 70 to 73.

29 The relevant range will be estimated on the basis of data which may have varying degrees of precision. The Commission will take this into account in drawing any conclusions regarding the dominant undertaking's ability to foreclose equally efficient competitors. It may also be useful to calculate how big a share of customers' requirements on average the entrant should capture as a minimum so that the effective price is at least as high as the LRAIC of the dominant company. In a number of cases the size of this share, when compared with the actual market shares of competitors and their shares of the customers' requirements, may make it clear whether the rebate scheme is capable to have an anti-competitive foreclosure effect.

30 See Case 85/76 *Hoffmann-La Roche & Co. v Commission* [1979] ECR 461, paragraphs 89 and 90; Case T-288/97 *Irish Sugar v Commission* [1999] ECR II-2969, paragraph 213; Case T-219/99 *British Airways v Commission* [2003] ECR II-5917, paragraphs 7 to 11 and 270 to 273.

31 For instance, for rebates see Case C-95/04 P *British Airways v Commission* [2007] ECR I-2331, paragraph 86.

32 See, to that effect, Case T-203/01 *Michelin v Commission (Michelin II)* [2003] ECR II-4071, paragraphs 56 to 60, 74 and 75.

33 Technical tying occurs when the tying product is designed in such a way that it only works properly with the tied product (and not with the alternatives offered by competitors). Contractual tying occurs when the customer who purchases the tying product undertakes also to purchase the tied product (and not the alternatives offered by competitors).

34 The undertaking should be dominant in the tying market, though not necessarily in the tied market. In bundling cases, the undertaking needs to be dominant in one of the bundled markets. In the special case of tying in after-markets, the condition is that the undertaking is dominant in the tying market and/or the tied after-market.

35 Case T-201/04 *Microsoft v Commission* [2007] ECR II-3601, in particular paragraphs 842, 859 to 862, 867 and 869.

36 Case T-201/04 *Microsoft v Commission* [2007] ECR II-3601, paragraphs 917, 921 and 922.

37 Case T-30/89 *Hilti v Commission* [1991] ECR II-1439, paragraph 67.

38 In principle, the LRAIC cost benchmark is relevant here as long as competitors are not able to also sell bundles (see paragraphs 23 to 27 and paragraph 61).

39 The Commission may also pursue predatory practices by dominant undertakings on secondary markets on which they are not yet dominant. In particular, the Commission will be more likely to find such an abuse in sectors where activities are protected by a legal monopoly. While the dominant undertaking does not need to engage in predatory conduct to protect its dominant position in the market protected by legal monopoly, it may use the profits gained in the monopoly market to cross-subsidize its activities in another market and thereby threaten to eliminate effective competition in that other market.

40 In most cases the average variable cost (AVC) and AAC will be the same, as often only variable costs can be avoided. However, in circumstances where AVC and AAC differ, the latter better reflects possible sacrifice: for example, if the dominant undertaking had to expand capacity in order to be able to predate, then the sunk costs of that extra capacity should be taken into account in looking at the dominant undertaking's losses. Those costs would be reflected in the AAC, but not the AVC.

41 In Case 62/86 *AKZO Chemie v Commission* [1991] ECR I-3359, paragraph 71, the Court held, in relation to pricing below average variable cost (AVC), that: "A dominant undertaking has no interest in applying such prices except that of eliminating competitors so as to enable it subsequently to raise its price by taking advantage of its monopolistic position, since each sale generates a loss . . . ".

42 If the estimate of cost is based on the direct cost of production (as registered in the undertaking's accounts), it may not adequately capture whether or not there has been a sacrifice.

43 However, undertakings should not be penalised for incurring ex post losses where the ex ante decision to engage in the conduct was taken in good faith, that is to say, if they can provide conclusive evidence that they could reasonably expect that the activity would be profitable.

44 See Case T-83/91 *Tetra Pak International v Commission* (Tetra Pak II) [1994] ECR II-755, paragraphs 151 and 171, and Case T-340/03 *France Télécom v Commission* [2007] ECR II-107, paragraphs 198 to 215.

45 In Case 62/86 *AKZO Chemie v Commission* [1991] ECR I-3359, the Court accepted that there was clear evidence of AKZO threatening ECS in two meetings with below cost pricing if it did not withdraw from the organic peroxides market. In addition there was a detailed plan, with figures, describing the measures that AKZO would put into effect if ECS would not withdraw from the market (see paragraphs 76 to 82, 115, and 131 to 140).

46 This was confirmed in Case T-83/91 *Tetra Pak International v Commission (Tetra Pak II)* [1994] ECR II-755, upheld on appeal in Case C-333/94 P *Tetra Pak International v Commission* [1996] ECR I-5951, where the Court of First Instance stated that proof of actual recoupment was not required (paragraph 150 in fine). More in general, as predation may turn out to be more difficult than expected at the start of the conduct, the total costs to the dominant undertaking of predating could outweigh its later profits and thus make actual recoupment impossible while it may still be rational to decide to continue with the predatory strategy that it started some time ago. See also COMP/38.233 Wanadoo Interactive, Commission Decision of 16 July 2003, paragraphs 332 to 367.

47 Joined Cases C-241/91 P and C-242/91 *Radio Telefis Eireann (RTE) and Independent Television Publications (ITP) v Commission (Magill)* [1995] ECR I-743, paragraph 50; Case C-418/01 *IMS Health v NDC Health* [2004] ECR I-5039, paragraph 35; Case T-201/04 *Microsoft v Commission* [2007] ECR II-3601, paragraphs 319, 330, 331, 332 and 336.

48 See Judgment of 16 September 2008 in Joined Cases C-468/06 to C-478/06 *Sot. Lélos kai Sia and Others v GlaxoSmithKline*, not yet reported.

49 Joined Cases 6/73 and 7/73 *Istituto Chemioterapico Italiano and Commercial Solvents v Commission* [1974] ECR 223.

50 Joined Cases C-241/91 P and C-242/91 P *Radio Telefis Eireann (RTE) and Independent Television Publications Ltd (ITP) v Commission (Magill)* [1995] ECR 743; Case C-418/01 *IMS Health v NDC Health* [2004] ECR I-5039. Those judgments show that in exceptional circumstances a refusal to license intellectual property rights is abusive.

51 See Case T-201/04 *Microsoft v Commission* [2007] ECR II-3601.

52 See Commission Decision 94/19/EC of 21 December 1993 in Case IV/34.689 *Sea Containers v Stena Sealink* — Interim Measures (OJ L15, 18.1.1994, p 8) and Commission Decision 92/213/EEC of 26 February 1992 in Case IV/33.544 *British Midland v Aer Lingus* — (OJ L96, 10.4.1992, p 34).

53 Case C-418/01 *IMS Health v NDC Health* [2004] ECR I-5039, paragraph 44.

54 Including a situation in which an integrated undertaking that sells a "system" of complementary products refuses to sell one of the complementary products on an unbundled basis to a competitor that produces the other complementary product.

55 In some cases, however, the LRAIC of a non-integrated competitor downstream might be used as the benchmark, for example when it is not possible to clearly allocate the dominant undertaking's costs to downstream and upstream operations.

56 Case T-201/04 *Microsoft v Commission* [2007] ECR II-3601, paragraphs 428 and 560 to 563.

57 Joined Cases C-241/91 P and C-242/91 *Radio Telefis Eireann (RTE) and Independent Television Publications LTD (ITP) v Commission (Magill)* [1995] ECR 743, paragraphs 52 and 53; Case 7/97 *Oscar Bronner v Mediaprint Zeitungs- und Zeitschriftenverlag, Mediaprint Zeitungsvertriebsgesellschaft and Mediaprint Anzeigengesellschaft* [1998] ECR I-7791, paragraphs 44 and 45; Case T-201/04 *Microsoft v Commission* [2007] ECR II-3601, paragraph 421.

58 In general, an input is likely to be impossible to replicate when it involves a natural monopoly due to scale or scope economies, where there are strong network effects or when it concerns so-called "single source" information. However, in all cases account should be taken of the dynamic nature of the industry and, in particular whether or not market power can rapidly dissipate.

59 Case 7/97 *Oscar Bronner v Mediaprint Zeitungs- und Zeitschriftenverlag, Mediaprint Zeitungsvertriebsgesellschaft and Mediaprint Anzeigengesellschaft* [1998] ECR I-7791, paragraph 46, Case C-418/01 *IMS Health v NDC Health* [2004] ECR I-5039, paragraph 29.

60 Case T-201/04 *Microsoft v Commission* [2007] ECR II-3601, paragraphs 643, 647, 648, 649, 652, 653 and 656.

61 Case C-418/01 *IMS Health v NDC Health* [2004] ECR I-5039, paragraph 49; Case T-201/04 *Microsoft v Commission* [2007] ECR II-3601, paragraph 658.

62 Case T-201/04 *Microsoft v Commission* [2007] ECR II-3601, paragraph 659.

DG COMPETITION BEST PRACTICES FOR THE SUBMISSION OF ECONOMIC EVIDENCE AND DATA COLLECTION IN CASES CONCERNING THE APPLICATION OF ARTICLES 101 AND 102 TFEU AND IN MERGER CASES (OCTOBER 2011)

[4.126]

NOTES

This document is available on the European Commission's website at: https://ec.europa.eu/competition-policy/antitrust/legislation_en.

1 SCOPE AND PURPOSE

[4.127]

1. Economic analysis plays a central role in competition enforcement. Economics as a discipline provides a framework to think about the way in which each particular market operates and how competitive interactions take place. This framework further allows formulating the possible consequences of the practices under review, whether a merger, an agreement between firms, or single firm conduct. In certain cases it may also provide tools to identify the direction and magnitude of these effects empirically, if appropriate and relevant. In a number of cases, economic analysis may involve the production, handling and assessment of voluminous sets of quantitative data, including, when appropriate, the development of econometric models.[1]

2. Economic analysis needs to be framed in such a way that the Commission and the EU Courts can understand and evaluate its relevance and significance. As an administrative authority the Commission is required to take a decision within an appropriate or sometimes a statutory time limit. It is therefore necessary to: (i) ensure that economic analysis meets certain minimum technical standards at the outset, (ii) facilitate the effective gathering and exchange of facts and evidence, in particular any underlying quantitative data, and (iii) use in an effective way reliable and relevant evidence obtained during the administrative procedure, whether quantitative or qualitative.

3. In order to determine the relevance and significance of an economic analysis for a particular case, it is first necessary to assess its intrinsic quality from a technical perspective, ie, whether it has been generated and presented in a way that meets adequate technical requirements prevalent in the profession. This involves, in particular, an evaluation of whether the hypothesis to be tested is formulated without ambiguity and clearly related to facts, whether the assumptions of the economic model are consistent with the institutional features and other relevant facts of the industry, whether economic models are well established in the relevant literature, whether the empirical methods and the data are appropriate, whether the results are properly interpreted and robust and whether counter-arguments have been given adequate consideration.

4. Second, one must assess the congruence and consistency of the economic analysis with other pieces of quantitative and qualitative evidence (such as customer responses, or documentary evidence).[2]

5. The present document formulates best practices concerning the generation as well as the presentation of relevant economic and empirical evidence that may be taken into account in the assessment of a case concerning the application of Articles 101 and 102 of the Treaty on the Functioning of the European Union (TFEU)[3] or merger case.[4] These Best Practices are organised along two themes.

i) First of all, it provides recommendations regarding the content and presentation of economic or econometric analysis. This is meant to facilitate its assessment and the replication of any empirical results by the Commission and/or other parties.
ii) Second, the document provides guidance to respond to Commission requests for quantitative data[5] to ensure that timely and relevant input for the investigation can be provided.

6. The desire to ensure transparency and accountability, these Best Practices apply to all parties involved in proceedings concerning the application of Articles 101 and 102 TFEU and mergers, that is the parties to the case and interested third parties (including complainants), as well as the Commission.

7. These Best Practices do not create any new rights or obligations, nor alter the rights and obligations which arise from the TFEU, secondary EU law and the case-law of the Court of Justice of the European Union. The Best Practices also do not alter the Commission's interpretative notices and established decisional practice.

8. The principles contained here may be further developed and refined by the Commission in individual cases when appropriate in light of future developments. The specificity of an individual case or particular circumstances may require an adaptation of, or deviation from, these Best Practices. The recommendations contained in this document should be interpreted in light of procedural and resource constraints.

NOTES

1 The assessment of mergers and potential infringements "by effect" often requires a complex economic assessment by the Commission, as well as the use of statistical or econometric analysis.

2 Economic models or econometric analysis, as is the case with other types of evidence will rarely, if ever, prove conclusive by themselves. The Commission can always take into account different items of evidence. The General Court has held that "*It is the Commission's task to make an overall assessment of what is shown by the set of indicative factors used to evaluate the competitive situation.*

It is possible, in that regard, for certain items of evidence to be prioritised and other evidence to be discounted. That examination and the associated reasoning are subject to a review of legality which the Court carries out in relation to Commission decisions on concentrations". See Case T-342/07, Ryanair v Commission, [2010] paragraph 136

3 Proceedings before the European Commission concerning Articles101 and 102 TFEU, in accordance with Council Regulation (EC) No 1/2003 of 16 December 2002 on the implementation of the rules on competition laid down in Articles 81 and 82 of the Treaty (OJ L1, 4.1.2003, p 1, as amended).

4 Proceedings under the Council Regulation (EC) No 139/2004 of 20 January 2004 on the control of concentrations between undertakings (OJ L24, 29.1.2004, p 1).

5 Quantitative data means, generally, observations or measurements, expressed as numbers. For the purposes of these Best Practices, this concept is used to refer to large sets of quantitative data submitted and/or obtained for the purposes of the conduct of an assessment of an economic (and often econometric) nature.

2 BEST PRACTICES REGARDING THE CONTENT AND PRESENTATION OF ECONOMIC AND ECONOMETRIC SUBMISSIONS

[4.128]

9. Economic reasoning is employed in competition cases notably in order to develop in a consistent manner or, conversely, to rebut because of its inconsistency, the economic evidence and arguments in a given case.

10. Any economic model which explicitly or implicitly supports a theoretical claim must rely on assumptions that are consistent with the facts of the industry under consideration. These assumptions should be carefully laid out and the sensitivity of its predictions to changes to the assumptions should be made explicit. While it is not necessary for economic submissions to actually formalize verbal arguments in a model, this will sometimes be helpful to clearly spell out the assumptions underlying an argument, to check its logic consistency, to assess effects of a high degree of complexity, or to use the model as the theoretical basis for an empirical estimation.[6]

11. An economic analysis may support an assessment of the anticompetitive or procompetitive effects of a merger. Such analysis usually involves a comparison of the actual or likely future situation in the relevant market with the absence of the proposed merger.

12. By their very nature, economic models and arguments are based on simplifications of reality. It is therefore normally not sufficient to disprove a particular argument or model, to point out that it is "based on seemingly unrealistic assumptions". It is also necessary to explicitly identify which aspects of reality should be better reflected in the model or argumentation, and to indicate why this would alter the conclusions.

13. In many cases, economic theory is used to develop a testable hypothesis that is later checked against the data. In that case, the economic analysis makes predictions about reality that can be tested by observations and potentially rejected or verified. Thus, whenever feasible, an economic model should be accompanied by an appropriate empirical model — ie, a model which is capable of testing the relevant hypotheses given the data available.

14. Very often simple but well focused measurement of economic variables (prices, cost, margins, capacity constraints, R&D intensity) will provide important insights into the significance of particular factors. Occasionally, more advanced statistical and econometric techniques may provide more useful evidence.[7] In any case, otherwise valid economic analysis may not always produce unambiguous results when applied to the facts of a competition or merger case. Contradictions may result from differences in the data, differences in the approach to economic modelling or in the assumptions used to interpret the data or differences in the empirical techniques and methodologies.

15. The following sections provide practical advice on the generation and communication of economic and econometric analyses. The goal of these recommendations is to ensure that every economic or econometric analysis developed by any party involved submitted for consideration in a case states to the largest possible extent the economic reasoning and the observations on which it relies and explains the relevance of its findings and the robustness of the results. This should allow the Commission and all interested parties to scrutinise the economic evidence submitted during the proceedings so as to avoid that empirical results that are not robust be disguised as such and key assumptions in theoretical reasoning be presented as innocuous. Economic or econometric analysis that does not strictly meet the standards set out in these Best Practices will normally be attached less probative value than otherwise and may not be taken into consideration.

2.1 FORMULATING THE RELEVANT QUESTION

16. The first step in any economic analysis, theoretical or empirical, is the formulation of a question that is relevant to the case at hand.

17. The question of interest should be:

(a) precisely formulated so that its answer can be interpreted without ambiguity,

(b) properly motivated taking into account the nature of the competition or merger case, the institutional features of the markets under consideration and the relevant economic theory.[8]

18. An economic or econometric report should explicitly formulate not only the hypothesis to be tested (the "null hypothesis"[9]) but also the alternative hypothesis (or hypotheses) under consideration, so that rejection of the null hypothesis can be properly interpreted.[10]

19. Sometimes, an empirical exercise which is being carried out may provide only partial verification of an accompanying economic model or theory of competitive effects. This evidence may be nonetheless useful but should be properly qualified.[11]

2.2 DATA RELEVANCE AND RELIABILITY

20. The intrinsic quality of an economic theory depends on the extent to which the underlying assumptions match the corresponding economic facts. Likewise, empirical analysis depends on the relevance and the reliability of the underlying data.

21. First, it is necessary to identify the relevant facts to validate the theoretical assumptions and employ data which is appropriate to respond to the empirical question under investigation.[12]

22. Second, not all facts can be observed or measured with high accuracy and most datasets are incomplete or otherwise imperfect. Hence, parties and/or the Commission should become familiar with the facts and data and acknowledge its limitations explicitly. As regards quantitative data, for example, this requires (i) a thorough inspection of the data, including summary statistics and graphs, and (ii) a sufficient understanding of how the data were gathered, the sample selection process, the measurement of the variables and whether they bear a close relationship with their theoretical counterparts. Quantitative data may contain anomalies because of miscoding or other errors, which should be discussed with the data providers to decide how to best adjust the data to address these problems.

23. Failure to observe and validate all key assumptions or deficiencies in the data should not prevent an economic analysis to be given weight, though caution must be exercised before relying on its conclusions.[13] Furthermore, statistical techniques have been developed to deal with measurement errors, missing observations and sample selection problems. While these techniques may not be able to improve the data, they may help to deal with some of its imperfections.

2.3 CHOICE OF EMPIRICAL METHODOLOGY

24. The choice of methodology to empirically test a hypothesis or to validate the predictions of an economic model should be properly motivated, and its pros and cons should be made explicit, including potential identification problems.[14]

25. Identification can be understood as clarifying the basis upon which one theory can be preferred to another. Similarly, the term can be used to refer to any situation where an econometric model will invariably have more than one set of parameters which generate the same distribution of observations.

26. One should explain how the chosen methodology exploits the variation in the data, to at least partially discriminate between the tested (or null) hypothesis and the alternative hypotheses. At the very least, an economic model or argument should generate predictions that are consistent with a significant number of relevant observed facts.

27. The choice of methodology must take due account of (a) the dataset and its potential limitations, (b) the features of the market under investigation, and (c) the economic issues under consideration — ie, it should be designed to test the hypothesis of interest (see also section 2.1 above).

28. If statistical and/or econometric methods are used, it is strongly recommended that important methodological choices are explicitly justified, in particular:

i) specification (what is the range of sensible general forms for the relationship under evaluation, including the relevant variables, the way they could interact, and the nature of errors or uncertainty?).
ii) observation (how well do the measurements approximate the variables they are intended to represent?).
iii) estimation (what do the data in the sample suggest as to the range of plausible relationships among variables?).

29. Moreover, a reasoned justification should be given when applying statistical techniques that deviate from generally accepted methods commonly used to assess the question of interest. In particular, one should motivate the changes, describe the modified technique or model, and document the likely biases, if any, that the new or adapted method is likely to introduce.

30. In general, it is recommended to follow a "bottom-up" approach. In the context of multiple regression analysis, this would mean estimating simple models first and then engage in more refined estimation exercises if necessary in order to avoid bias.[15] Large-scale surveys of final consumers may usefully supplement qualitative or other documentary evidence obtained from targeted requests of information to market participants. Whilst the evidential value of replies to information requests from market participants lies in the substance of the information provided by players with intrinsic industry or market knowledge, the specific purpose of large-scale surveys of final consumers is to obtain statistically relevant data in order to estimate the characteristics, behaviour and views of a larger group of final consumers from the responses received from a smaller sample. The objectives of a high quality sample survey should be specific, clear-cut and unambiguous. Further, the definition of the relevant population of consumers (and the associated sampling frame) is crucial because there may be systematic differences in the responses of various differentiated consumer segments. Identification of a survey population must be followed by selection of a sample that accurately represents that population. The researcher can apply probability sampling in large-scale surveys of final consumers to some aspects of respondent selection to reduce the likelihood of biased selection.[16]

31. The use of probability sampling techniques in large-scale surveys of final consumers enhances both the reliability and representativeness of the survey results and the ability to assess the accuracy of quantitative estimates obtained from the survey as regards the relevant population of consumers. Probability sampling in large-scale surveys of final consumers offers two important advantages over other types of sampling. First, the sample can provide an unbiased quantitative estimate of the responses of the relevant consumers from which the sample was drawn; that is, the expected value of the sample estimate is the population value being estimated. Second, the researcher can calculate a confidence interval that describes explicitly how reliable the sample estimate of the population is likely to be.

32. If possible, given time and data constraints, conducting multiple empirical analyses relying on different methodologies would help determine whether the conclusions of the empirical investigation are robust to different tests or models (see also section 2.5 below).

2.4 REPORTING AND INTERPRETING THE RESULTS

33. The results of economic and econometric analysis must be presented clearly, taking the reader through each step of the reasoning.[17] All empirical analysis, even descriptive statistics of relevant variables (eg, price series) should be accompanied by all the documentation needed to allow timely replication, as well as a deep understanding of the methodology of any prior data management efforts. Reports which do not allow for replication and in particular econometric analysis not including the code and data in electronic form will receive less consideration and are consequently unlikely to be given much weight.

34. An empirical submission should not only discuss the statistical significance of the results but also their practical relevance. In general, with very large samples coefficients may be statistically significant even if they are of trivial magnitude.[18] This creates the potentially misleading impression that certain variables are important. Therefore, the magnitude of the coefficients must always be examined and discussed. This requires interpreting the results in connection with the hypothesis that is being tested, so as to draw implications for the case under investigation.

35. Commonly, results from economic analysis and statistical information are presented in tables. Although it is not necessary to comment on or restate every piece of information that a table contains an interpretation of the data in it must be provided.

36. The results of the empirical analyses should be reported in the standard format found in academic papers. For example, when reporting multiple regression results, one should report on the statistical significance[19] of the parameter estimates by following the convention of reporting coefficients, p-values, standard errors and the size of the sample. Where the coefficient of interest is economically significant, the emphasis should be on statistically significant findings, for example to the 5% or 10% level (ie, p-value<0.05 or 0.10). However, just because some hypothesis cannot be rejected in a statistical sense does not necessarily mean that the empirical analysis has no evidentiary value.

37. It may be that a particular analysis can be criticized in terms of its accuracy. However, it is often possible to evaluate that inaccuracy, for example by providing confidence intervals around an estimate. Also, depending on the question of interest, an approximate economic or econometric result can be informative if, for example, it is the direction of the effects rather than its magnitude that are most relevant. Similarly a particular estimate may be criticized because some facet of the methodology introduces bias. However, it is often the case that an estimate is biased in a particular direction; if this is the case it may be known that the estimate is too large, or too small. This may not matter in the context of a particular case. If it is known that the estimate is too large, and yet it is insufficient in size to reach some critical value, then the bias does not invalidate the conclusion that the critical value will not be reached. Detailed information should also be provided on all other specification tests and statistical diagnoses (see also section 2.5 on robustness).

38. The results of any statistical or econometric analysis should also be assessed with respect to the relevant economic theory.[20] When discussing the results of a multiple regression analysis, this requirement includes assessing not only the coefficient(s) of direct interest, but also the coefficients of all other explanatory variables, as they often provide a signal on the reliability of the analysis. For example, a finding that the sign of a particular coefficient is counter to what would be expected by economic theory[21] may be an indication of an omitted-variable problem,[22] a selection bias,[23] or some other identification problem.[24]

39. In the case of large-scale surveys of final consumers the report should disclose essential information about how the research was conducted to allow judging the reliability and validity of the results. All data must be fully documented and made available (subject to appropriate safeguards to maintain privacy and confidentiality). Non-sampling error, in particular the non-response rate and response bias[25] should also be taken into account in the analysis. Conclusions from large-scale surveys of final consumers should be carefully distinguished from the factual findings.

2.5 ROBUSTNESS (NON IMPLEMENTED PROPOSAL: PLACE ROBUSTNESS BEFORE REPORTING)

40. Economic and econometric analysis should to the greatest possible extent be accompanied by a thorough robustness analysis, except where its absence is appropriately justified. In any event, any formal economic model or econometric analysis needs to be generally consistent and reasonably predict observed past outcomes and behaviour.

41. Other common robustness checks that may be appropriate include assessing whether empirical results are sensitive to changes in (a) the data, (b) the choice of empirical method, and (c) the precise modelling assumptions.[26] Similarly, the relevance and credibility of an economic model can be significantly enhanced if accompanied by a sensitivity analysis with respect to the key variables.

42. It is strongly recommended to address explicitly (i) to what extent, the results of the analysis are in line with past results using similar methods, and whether the results can be generalised.[27] Congruent and convergent results based on methods supported by academic and practitioners' are likely to be given greater significance than widely divergent results.

2.6 FURTHER RECOMMENDATIONS

43. The credibility of an economic submission may be enhanced when the limitations with regards to accuracy or explanatory power of the underlying data and methodology are explicitly acknowledged. In this regard it is often advisable to address rather than minimize uncertainty.

44. The parties rely sometimes on data that they do not have the means to audit and verify. Hence, they should be careful not to misleadingly present economic opinions as statements of fact. The sources of information should be carefully acknowledged, and the facts properly documented and described without ambiguity. This applies whether the economic or econometric analysis is a stand alone report or part of a broader submission.

45. It is advisable that the parties consult DG Competition regarding the types of empirical analyses that they consider useful in testing the anticompetitive and/or efficiencies theories. In particular, the parties can suggest potential analyses which may be easier for DG Competition to conduct, given its access to data from third parties. DG Competition, in turn, may propose analyses it believes might be useful for the parties to conduct. Similarly, it is recommended that the parties consult the DG Competition regarding the most suitable robustness checks for a given methodology. Experience suggests that such consultation can be most effective if the parties are prepared to share any relevant preliminary results in advance of a formal submission.

46. Where economic submissions rely on quantitative data the parties should provide the data and codes timely, in an appropriate format and in accordance with the criteria laid down in section 3 of this document. In particular, the absence of all the necessary elements needed for replication and assessment of an economic submission can constitute grounds for not taking it further into consideration.

47. When granting access to the file, the Commission may provide upon request the data and codes underlying its final economic analysis or, to the extent that they have been made available to the Commission, that of third parties on which it intends to rely or take into account. Where necessary to protect the confidentiality of other parties' data, access to the data and codes will be granted only at Commission premises in a so-called data room procedure,[28] subject to strict confidentiality obligations and secure procedures.[29] Third parties or complainants are equally expected to submit all the underlying data used in the analysis. They are also expected to authorise the Commission, where appropriate, to offer data room access to the parties upon request.

48. When conducting large-scale surveys of final consumers to address a case-specific issue the parties might want to involve the Commission in the questionnaire development and design.[30] Subject to time and resource constraints it is often desirable to conduct a pre-test or pilot.[31]

NOTES

6 If an economic submission is well-reasoned, then the fact that a particular argument is "theoretical" or "general" is often a strength rather than a weakness of the submission. This is the case when one has deduced a general conclusion (which holds irrespective of the precise magnitudes of the parameters of the analysis) from a set of assumptions that are considered consistent with the facts of the case. For instance, an economic submission may try to substantiate that irrespective of the size or existence of efficiencies, a particular conduct cannot possibly harm consumers.

7 For instance, an econometric analysis of the extent to which prices of an undertaking have been affected by the observed entry of a competitor may provide evidence of the competitive constraint exercised by that entrant. In turn this could provide insights with respect to the likely degree of harm, that would result if an incumbent dominant undertaking were to engage in practices resulting in anticompetitive foreclosure in that or related markets.

8 Occasionally the parties might submit a literature survey or review regarding an economic question of particular relevance for the case. A literature review may be useful when it is accompanied by an explanation on the merits and shortcomings, of the existing studies and explains how the party's own reasoning or analysis relates to past research, academic or otherwise.

9 The null hypothesis is generally that which is presumed to be true initially. A null hypothesis is a hypothesis set up to be nullified or refuted in order to support an alternative hypothesis.

10 For example, consider an empirical project aimed at testing whether certain conduct would lead to higher prices. One could define as the null hypothesis that prices did not increase in which case a rejection of the null hypothesis would imply that the agreement had a positive price impact. Alternatively, one could have defined as the null hypothesis that prices did not change as a result of the agreement. A rejection of the null hypothesis in that case would be harder to interpret: did prices rise or fall as a result of the specific relationship between buyer and seller?

11 For example, the analysis of scanner data (retail prices and quantities) may provide valuable evidence in the context of a merger between producers of fast moving consumption goods, even when the direct impact of the transaction would be felt at the wholesale level and not at the consumer level.

12 For example when discounts are important, the analysis of the price impact of a merger, agreement or practice must focus on prices paid by consumers rather than on list prices.

13 For example, assumptions regarding firms' expectations regarding the identity of the market leader may be inferred indirectly through observation of which firm first announces its future prices.

14 Problems of inference can be separated into statistical and identification problems. Studies of identification seek to characterize the conclusions that could be drawn if one could use the sampling process to obtain an unlimited number of observations. Studies of statistical inference seek to characterize the generally weaker conclusions that can be drawn from a finite number of observations.

15 For example, it is sound practice to estimate an Ordinary Least Squares (OLS) regression first and then, to the extent endogeneity is suspected to be a problem in the case at hand, move on to an instrumental variable (IV) estimation.

16 Probability samples range from simple random samples to complex multistage sampling designs that use stratification, clustering of population elements into various groupings, or both. In simple random sampling, the most basic type of probability sampling, every element in the population has a known, equal probability of being included in the sample, and all possible samples of a given size are equally likely to be selected. In all forms of probability sampling, each element in the relevant population has a known, nonzero probability of being included in the sample.

17 Any mathematical notation should either (a) follow the standard notation in the literature or (b) be very self-explanatory.

18 Statistical significance is determined, in part, by the number of observations in the data set. The more observations used to calculate the regression coefficients, the smaller the standard error of each coefficient. A smaller standard error reflects less random variability in the estimated coefficient (or estimate). Other things being equal, the statistical significance of a regression coefficient increases as the sample size increases. If the data set is sufficiently large, results that are economically significant are often also statistically significant. However, when the sample size is small it is not uncommon to obtain results that are economically significant but statistically insignificant.

19 A statistically significant result is one that is unlikely to have occurred by chance. In hypothesis testing, the significance level is the criterion used for rejecting the null hypothesis. The p-value is the probability of obtaining a test statistic at least as extreme as the one that was actually observed, assuming that the null hypothesis is true. If the obtained p-value is smaller than or equal to the significance level, then the null hypothesis is rejected and the outcome is said to be statistically significant.

20 For example, econometric estimates of the elasticity of demand for a given product implying an upward sloping demand curve should be discarded in almost all cases, unless the product in question can be shown to be a Giffen good — ie, a product for which a rise in price of this product makes people buy even more of the product.

21 For example, a study showing that an increase in the marginal costs of production of a given good is associated with lower prices for that product should, ceteris paribus, be discarded automatically.

22 That is, when a relevant explanatory variable, which is correlated with the dependent variable has been omitted from the analysis, so that the coefficients of some or all other explanatory variables suffer from a bias of a priori unknown sign or magnitude.

23 The bias that arises when the selection process influences the availability of data in a way that is related to the dependent variable.

24 See note 13 *supra*.

25 Response bias refers to situations were, for a host of reasons, respondents fail to answer questions truthfully, fully and/or were influenced by the interviewer.

26 For example, in a multiple regression analysis, one should indicate whether the results are severely affected by how the variables were defined, by the set of explanatory variables incorporated to the analysis, or the functional form.

27 For example, if the elasticity of demand for a given product has been estimated for a given country, where data is available, but the case at hand would require estimates of the elasticity of demand for various countries, one should consider whether or not, and under which assumptions, her results for one country apply to the others. Similarly, if an economic model assumes that firms make take-it-or-leave-it offers when interacting with intermediate buyers with certain characteristics, it may be necessary to assess whether such assumption extends to all types of intermediate buyers.

28 See Commission Notice on Best Practices for the conduct of proceedings concerning Articles 101 and102, paragraphs 97 and 98.

29 Similarly, the Commission will endeavour to organise access to a data room, normally to the parties' economic advisors and external counsel, if necessary to ensure their rights of defence are fully respected.

30 Occasionally, the Commission may take the initiative to commission its own large scale consumer survey. In that case, it will normally consult the parties and interested third parties on the questionnaire design and instruments of data collection, subject to confidentiality safeguards and to the extent such consultation does not delay or otherwise jeopardize the investigation.

31 All questions should be pretested to ensure that (i) questions are understood by respondents, (ii) can be properly administered by interviewers, and (iii) do not adversely affect survey cooperation

3 BEST PRACTICES ON RESPONDING TO REQUESTS FOR QUANTITATIVE DATA

[4.129]

49. Pursuant to Article 18 of Regulation 1/2003 and Article 11 of the Merger Regulation, the Commission is empowered, in order to carry out its duties, to require undertakings and associations of undertakings to provide it with all necessary information. It is the Commission that defines the scope and the format of requests for information.

50. Most competition or merger investigations involve (1) collecting data, (2) analysing data, and (3) drawing inferences from data. In most antitrust and merger cases, the Commission will gather evidence by sending targeted requests for information pursuant to Article 11 of the Merger Regulation and Article 18 of Regulation 1/2003 to the main players in the market (eg, competitors, direct customers and other parties with specific knowledge of the market). This document, however, provides specific guidance to respond to a request for quantitative data.[32] However, many of the principles here identified apply, more generally, to responses to any request for economic information, quantitative or qualitative.

51. Quantitative data may help the Commission to conduct statistical analysis to define markets, establish a counterfactual, assess the potential anti-competitive effects of a notified merger, validate efficiency claims or predict the impact of remedies. In order to do that the Commission needs to get accurate data, with sufficient time to analyse it.

52. The Commission is aware of the costs that its procedures may impose on undertakings. An important objective of this section is, therefore, to provide recommendations to reduce the burden on the involved parties and on the Commission posed by the production and processing of quantitative data, while at the same time ensuring and enhancing the effectiveness of the Commission's substantive review.

53. These best practices are intended as general guidance and do not supersede any specific instructions in any Data Request issued by the Commission in specific cases.

3.1 GENERAL MOTIVATION FOR DATA REQUESTS

54. The primary objective of a Data Request is to obtain accurate information concerning quantitative variables such as prices, turnover, capacity and entry or exit decisions within the possible relevant markets over a reasonable period. Quantitative data may be necessary to understand current market conditions and competitive dynamics. In some cases, reliable quantitative data may allow to conduct statistical or econometric analysis to be submitted as evidence in an antitrust or merger investigation.

55. The Commission will endeavour to ask for the appropriate amount of data to carry out the required analyses. The Commission is mindful of time constraints and must balance the usefulness of each request against the time left before any legal or procedural deadline. In appropriate cases, DG Competition may discuss in advance with the addressees or other affected parties the scope and the format of the Data Request. DG Competition may also explain the analysis that it intends to perform with the requested data in order to improve the efficiency of the data collecting process and to ensure the data is of adequate quality. This is particularly the case in the later stages of an investigation as early requests could be of a more general nature and aimed primarily at better understanding the functioning of the market in question.

56. The Commission will carefully consider what the proper sample to characterize a population is. Inferences from the part to the whole are justified only when the sample is representative.[33]

57. A further issue that may influence the scope of the Data Request is whether third party data will be necessary and available to conduct any meaningful analysis.

3.2 COMMON ELEMENTS OF A DATA REQUEST

58. Examples of data necessary for a competition investigation include data on costs, output, sales, prices, capacity, product characteristics, delivery flows, customer characteristics, tender details, entry barriers, business strategies, and market shares of the parties involved and of the other participants in the relevant market.

59. The source of the information can be the parties involved in the procedure, third parties, trade associations, trade press, independent consultants, survey information or government sources.

60. Data may be costly to collect or hardly accessible in the relevant time frame. Often, however, requests for quantitative data in merger proceedings seek data that is readily available to the involved parties. Readily available data refers to data that is routinely collected and maintained for a reasonable period as part of the firm's normal business operations, for example to inform business strategy or for internal reporting. Readily available data also includes data that is regularly purchased from third parties, such as scanner data or survey data.[34] In any event, in its investigations, the Commission is not limited to request only data that is readily available to the parties (see point 77 below). Deadlines for submitting data which is difficult or costly to retrieve will be decided by the Commission on a case-by-case basis.

61. A Data Request often includes the following sections, but each request will be tailored to the specific information needs and circumstances of the case:

(i) a glossary of terms, in particular key variables;
(ii) a list of the variables;
(iii) for each variable: the units of measurement; the level of aggregation over time (eg, monthly); the time range (eg, the last three fiscal years) and the geographic scope (eg, countries, regions or cities);
(iv) the preferred electronic format (stata file, excel file, etc);
(v) suggestions or specific requests on data formatting, variable classification and tests to detect data inconsistencies;
(vi) deadline for compliance with the request.

62. In some instances, particularly where data is requested from different parties, DG Competition may provide a template to ensure all submissions are compatible and can be efficiently combined with minimal risk of error.

3.3 MAIN CRITERIA TO CONSIDER WHEN RESPONDING TO A DATA REQUEST

63. Responses to a Data Request must be: (i) complete, (ii) correct, and (iii) timely.

64. The Commission may impose on undertakings and associations of undertakings fines where, intentionally or negligently, they supply incorrect or misleading information or when, in response to a request made by decision, they supply incomplete information or do not supply information within the required time-limit.[35] Furthermore, in merger

cases, the relevant time limits for initiating proceedings and for the adoption of decisions may exceptionally be suspended where, owing to circumstances for which one of the undertakings involved in the concentration is responsible, the Commission has had to request information by decision or to order an inspection.[36]

3.3.1 COMPLETENESS

65. The parties should provide all data requested, in any of the stated formats and follow indications regarding presentation and consistency checks. Subsidiary data that is necessary to construct or to understand any variable requested should also be provided, except when adequately justified and with prior approval by the Commission.

66. It is strongly encouraged that problems of missing data are flagged to the Commission well in advance of the deadline for compliance with the Data Request to allow, if appropriate, for either a modification of the request or an extension of the deadline. Any data missing from the original Data Request must be adequately justified. In any event, a response to a Data Request may not be considered complete unless accompanied by a memo:

(i) describing the data compilation process: from raw data through aggregation and merging operations to the final database submitted. How was the sample selected and was it necessary to eliminate certain kinds of observations;
(ii) identifying all relevant sources;
(iii) labelling and thoroughly describing all variables;
(iv) reporting on the reasons for potential measurement error such as missing information or any changes in the collection process;
(v) describing any assumptions and estimations used to fill incomplete data; and
(vi) reporting on consistency checking and all data cleaning operations.

3.3.2 CORRECTNESS

67. It is up to interested parties to ensure the correctness of the data submitted. Tests for accuracy of all variables should always be undertaken and reported.[37]

68. In order to detect incorrectness in data it will be expected that consistency checks are performed and documented prior to submission. In particular:

i) Responses to the Data Request should be consistent with responses provided to other requests for information (eg, turnover, market shares, etc);
ii) Individual values within a variable must be consistent with the economic reality;[38]
iii) When aggregation of raw data is necessary, one needs to ensure the aggregation algorithm is sensible and applied consistently;
iv) Coherence between different variables is necessary;[39]
v) Over time consistency across and within variables must also be ensured.

3.3.3 TIMELY SUBMISSION

69. Deadlines for responses to Data Requests must be strictly respected. Where parties plan to submit data in connection with an empirical analysis conducted at their own initiative, it is useful to warn in advance DG Competition of the planned timing and scope of such a submission. Results that the parties intend to rely upon or discuss in a meeting with DG Competition should be submitted, including data and code to facilitate replication, at least 2 working days before the said meeting.

3.4 OTHER RECOMMENDATIONS

70. This section sets down further recommended best practices concerning responses to a Data Request.

3.4.1 COOPERATION IN GOOD-FAITH

71. Data production is an area where cooperation between the parties and the Commission is especially important. The parties will need to explain clearly the complexities that can be associated with requests that the Commission may regard as simple.[40] The Commission endeavours to define its requests as specifically and quickly as possible so the parties can understand what is being sought. This dialogue may help both sides deal more efficiently with data issues. In any event, it is for the Commission to decide the scope, format and timing of the Data Request.

72. It is important to emphasise in that regard that the integrity and efficiency of the process are undermined if, inter alia, the parties make representations about what data exist without reasonably diligent efforts to confirm their accuracy, if they ignore a carefully drafted and limited Data Request and produce large amounts of data points disregarding the submission format, scope, or data processing requirements, if they use non-obvious "definitions" of common terms in construing requests, or if they make unilateral and undisclosed inferences about what the Commission is effectively seeking.

3.4.2 EARLY CONSULTATION WITH THE COMMISSION TO INFORM ABOUT WHAT TYPE OF DATA IS AVAILABLE

73. In some cases, the burden of compliance with Data Requests may be significantly reduced if the parties inform the Commission at the earliest opportunity on the availability of quantitative data. Early consultation allows to determine not only what data is available and its suitability, but also in what form it can be provided, thereby making it easier and faster for the parties to provide the data, in the event the Commission makes a Data Request. However, the Commission is not limited to request only data that is readily available to the parties.

74. To make these early discussions fruitful, parties must be prepared to thoroughly explain their information management systems and should be prepared to discuss certain issues such as: every field of information captured, how the underlying data is collected and formatted, the frequency of collection, what software is used, the size of the data set, what reports are routinely generated from that database, etc. It is recommended that the involved firms provide any written documentation and/or training materials to the Commission in advance of any discussion. It is

also generally useful that parties create a diagram to show how the relevant data is distributed throughout the organization. In any event, as a general rule, parties should provide relevant documents to support their contentions concerning the availability, scope and production time of quantitative data.

75. Preliminary meetings or telephone conversations with those responsible for data collection or analysis in the firms are often quite useful. Parties are advised to make such personnel available as early as possible. These discussions should involve descriptions of the type of electronic (or other) data that the parties maintain (both in the ordinary course of business and what is archived, and in what form).

76. In the case of mergers, pre-notification discussions should routinely deal with data issues. Although, the Commission will endeavour to identify all issues that may require a Data Request as soon as possible, certain issues may not be identified until later in the proceedings.

3.4.3 Consultation on a Draft Data Requests and data samples

77. When appropriate and useful, DG Competition will send a "draft" Data Request for quantitative data in order to facilitate a better identification of the format, and to allow for basic consistency checks (see section 3.3.2). The purpose of the draft Data Request is to invite parties to propose any modifications that could alleviate the compliance burden while producing the necessary information. Any reduction on the scope of the Data Request can only be accepted if it does not risk harming the investigation and may trigger, particularly in merger cases, a reduction in the deadline for response initially anticipated.

78. In this connection, providing samples of the data is generally very helpful as it helps the Commission to determine what data is available and would be useful. As a result, on the basis of the sample it may be possible to draft a more focused Data Request, limiting the eventual burden on the parties.

3.4.4 Transparency regarding data collection, formatting and submission

79. A transparent process allows for all parties involved to be aware of any incidences during the data collection process and thus react more rapidly and effectively.

80. The parties are advised to submit quantitative data in a format that minimises the time and manipulation required to process the data for analysis. Parties should always be able to answer all the following questions:

i) How applicable is the data to the analyses under consideration;
ii) How reliable or "clean" is the data;
iii) Is it enough to conduct a meaningful analysis;
iv) What institutional factors specific to the industry setting and/or company may impact the proper interpretation of the data?

81. The involved parties should draw the Commission's attention early on to any limitations in the data. They should make clear how raw data has been compiled and what steps have been taken to ensure its reliability.[41]

82. The involved parties are also strongly encouraged to conduct their own descriptive analysis to detect data problems before submitting the data to the Commission. Also the Commission may sometimes welcome efforts by the involved parties to deal with any remaining data imperfections using statistical analysis. In some cases statistics allow in various ways to average out errors in measurement and yield statistically sound estimates. All such statistical analysis should be adequately reported. In any event, raw data should be provided wherever possible because the aggregation and cleaning of data may have a significant impact on the outcome of statistical or econometric analysis. Also parties should provide the program files that manipulate, clean and complete the raw data in preparation for the analysis.

3.4.5 Direct access

83. In some instances, the Commission will accept that as part of its response to a Data Request the involved parties provide direct electronic access to the underlying data. This alternative can provide an inexpensive and fast way to provide access to large amounts of data. Limited direct access can also provide a means to assess the value of certain corporate information.

84. The terms and conditions for direct access can be discussed in advance, addressing issues such as the availability of technical assistance, the ability to print or otherwise retrieve the data, the number of log-ins the company should provide, assurances that the activities of the services of the Commission will not be tracked, that underlying data will not be removed without agreement of the Commission and, most importantly, continued access throughout the entire course of the investigation. In limited instances, when providing direct access to corporate resources is unworkable, the Commission may submit a set of queries to the firm so that reports can be generated.

NOTES

32 For statistical purposes, "quantitative data" means a series of observations or measurements, expressed as numbers. A statistic may refer to a particular numerical value, derived from the data. For example, an HHI measure and a correlation coefficient are statistics.

33 For example, in certain circumstances it may be appropriate to limit the data request to a certain representative subset of the involved firms' customers, or to a particular geographic market which stands out for a valid given reason.

34 Where econometric analyses are to be conducted, the sample needs to be of sufficient size for meaningful inference. For instance, in the absence of cross-section variability, requests would generally cover at least a three year period of monthly observations.

35 Article 23(1)(a) and (b) of Regulation 1/2003 and Article 14(1)(a), (b) and (c) of the Merger Regulation.

36 Article 10(4) of the Merger Regulation, but see also Article 8(6) thereof.

37 For example, negative sales volumes or zero transaction prices are normally inaccurate and are often indicative of data extraction errors, systematic measurement errors or inadequate accounting of rebates or taxes.

38 For example, transaction prices (net of discounts) should generally be positive, missing or unexpected values (ie, sales not in line with historical levels) should be checked.

39 For example, shipments of one product must be related to shipments of any by-products. Also, charged prices should generally remain above transportation costs (ie, ex-works negative prices cast doubts on either the correctness of the charged price and/or the transportation cost).

40 Why, for example, it may be difficult, impossible or useless to simply "turn over" a "database," or the burdens and costs associated with providing data in the manner the Commission seeks.

41 For example, if the raw data is based on a sample of individual customer accounts, an explanation of how these accounts have been chosen and why they are representative of all customers should also be provided.

ANNEX 1
STRUCTURE AND BASIC ELEMENTS OF A SOUND EMPIRICAL SUBMISSION

[4.130]
This Annex briefly describes how to structure an empirical submission in a competition or merger case according with the principles set out in the preceding sections (esp. section 2 above). A sound economic or econometric submission should contain the following sections and elements:

A. THE RELEVANT QUESTION

– The research question must be: (i) formulated unambiguously and (ii) properly motivated, taking into account both the nature of the competition issue, the institutional features of the markets and industries under consideration, and the relevant economic theory.

– The hypothesis to be tested (or null hypothesis) must be clearly spelled out as well as the alternative hypothesis or hypotheses under consideration.

B. THE DATA

– A clear description of data sources must be provided as well as hard copies of the databases employed in the analysis. Normally, an accompanying memo would describe how previous intermediate data sets and programs were employed to create the final dataset as well as the software code employed to generate the final dataset. All efforts made to correct for anomalies in the data should be clearly explained.

– One should also report how the data were gathered, the sample selection process, the measurement of the variables and whether they match with their theoretical counterparts, etc.

– In addition, the data should be thoroughly described. This includes reporting the sample time frame and the statistical population under consideration, the units of observation, a clear definition of each variable, any data cleaning procedures, etc. This information should be accompanied by descriptive statistics (including means, standard errors, maximums, minimums, correlations, and histograms, residual plots, etc) of all relevant variables.

C. METHODOLOGY

– The choice of empirical methodology should be properly motivated. One should discuss their methodological choices in light of: (a) their data limitations, (b) the features of the market under investigation, and (c) the economic issues under consideration (the relevant question).

– Alternative methodologies should also be discussed and if possible, given time and data constraints, employed to verify the robustness of the results to the choice of model. An economic model or argument must generate predictions that are consistent with a significant number of relevant observed facts.

D. RESULTS AND IMPLICATIONS

– Parties should explain the details of their models, and share any documentation needed to allow timely replication (eg, the programming code used to run the analysis).

– The results of the empirical analyses should be reported in the standard format found in academic papers. For example, when reporting multiple regression results, one should report both the estimated coefficients and their standard errors for all relevant variables. They should also provide detailed information on all other specification tests and statistical diagnoses.

– One should discuss not only the statistical significance of their results but also their practical relevance. This requires interpreting the results in connection with the hypothesis that is being tested, so as to draw implications for the case under investigation. The results of the statistical and econometric analyses should also be assessed with respect to the relevant economic theory.

E. ROBUSTNESS TESTS

– All empirical work should be accompanied by a thorough robustness analysis that (i) checks whether the empirical results are sensitive to changes in the data, the choice of empirical method, and the precise modelling assumptions; (ii) tests whether the results of the analysis can be generalised; and (iii) compares the results of the empirical work in question with previous results in the relevant literature.

– An economic model should generally be accompanied by a sensitivity analysis with respect to the key variables, to the extent only the plausible but not the exact value of each variable can be determined. All results from the sensitivity analysis conducted should also be reported and not only those that support the argument.

DG COMPETITION INFORMAL GUIDANCE PAPER ON CONFIDENTIALITY CLAIMS

(March 2012)

[4.131]

NOTES

This Guidance is available on the European Commission website at: https://ec.europa.eu/competition-policy/antitrust/procedures/access-file_en.

INTRODUCTION

[4.132]

The European Commission can address requests for information to undertakings and associations of undertakings, to governments and competent authorities of the Member States, in order to obtain the information necessary to conduct its investigations.

If the investigation leads to the adoption of a Statement of Objections, the Commission will make available documents that it has obtained during the course of its investigation, as part of the "Access to file" procedure. Access is given to the parties of the proceeding to the nonconfidential version of the submissions and documents.

This document drafted by DG Competition staff sets informal guidance for the recipients of a request for information, on how to claim confidentiality for information contained in their submission.

Please note that this informal document does not replace the provisions in EU law concerning professional secrecy and claims for confidentiality[1] that apply to the submissions/documents.

NOTES

[1] Article 339 TFEU; Regulation No 1/2003; and the Notice on access to file. This guide complements the Annex on Business secrets and other confidential information that is enclosed in all requests for information sent by the Commission. All documents are available on the Competition website of the European Commission (see Antitrust): ec.europa.eu/competition/index_en.html.

DO'S AND DON'TS – PRACTICAL ISSUES

1. IN GENERAL

[4.133]

(a) In order to claim confidentiality for information in your submissions/documents that you regard as business secrets or otherwise confidential, provide a non-confidential version of such documents in which you black out the information considered confidential. From the non-confidential version it has to be clear where information has been deleted. If necessary to understand where redactions have been made, add indications such as "business secret", "confidential" or "confidential information".

(b) In general, confidentiality cannot be claimed for the entire or whole sections of the document as it is normally possible to protect confidential information with limited redactions.

(c) The non-confidential document should keep the same format as the original version. So, if you claim confidentiality for only some parts of a document, you are requested to provide an accessible non-confidential version of the entire document.

(d) For administrative efficiency, the Commission may ask you to provide first a draft non-confidential version of your submissions/documents in which you only highlight the information you claim to be confidential in a way that it remains legible.

(e) A final non-confidential version in which information is blacked out will then only be submitted after the Commission has provisionally accepted your confidentiality claims.

2. SPECIFIC EXAMPLES

(a) If necessary to understand where redactions have been made, add indications such as "business secret", "confidential" or "confidential information".

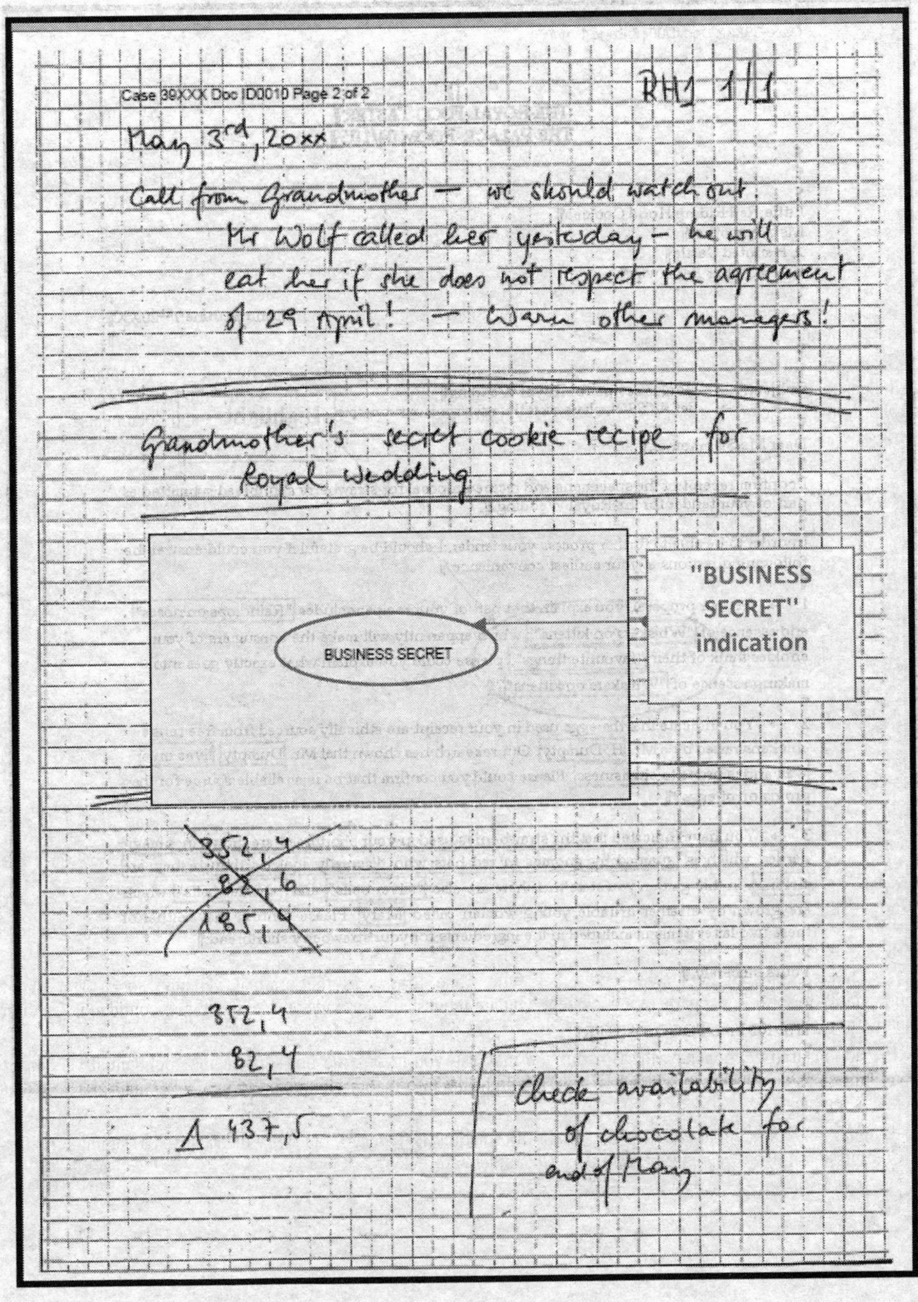

(b) For administrative efficiency, the Commission may ask you to provide first a draft non-confidential version of your submissions/documents in which you only highlight the information you claim to be confidential in a way that it remains legible.

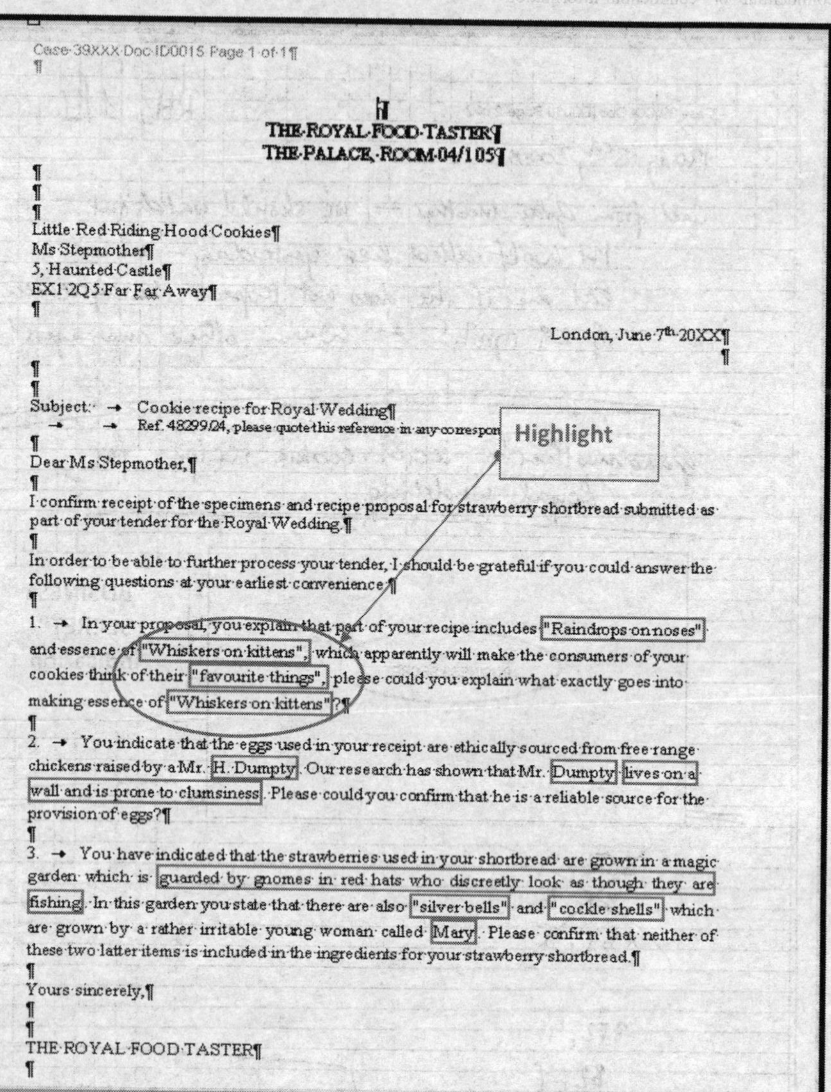
Case 39XXX Doc ID0015 Page 1 of 1

THE ROYAL FOOD TASTER
THE PALACE, ROOM 04/105

Little Red Riding Hood Cookies
Ms Stepmother
5, Haunted Castle
EX1 2Q5 Far Far Away

London, June 7th 20XX

Subject: Cookie recipe for Royal Wedding
Ref. 48299/24, please quote this reference in any correspon

Dear Ms Stepmother,

I confirm receipt of the specimens and recipe proposal for strawberry shortbread submitted as part of your tender for the Royal Wedding.

In order to be able to further process your tender, I should be grateful if you could answer the following questions at your earliest convenience.

1. In your proposal, you explain that part of your recipe includes "Raindrops on noses" and essence of "Whiskers on kittens", which apparently will make the consumers of your cookies think of their "favourite things", please could you explain what exactly goes into making essence of "Whiskers on kittens"?

2. You indicate that the eggs used in your receipt are ethically sourced from free range chickens raised by a Mr. H. Dumpty. Our research has shown that Mr. Dumpty lives on a wall and is prone to clumsiness. Please could you confirm that he is a reliable source for the provision of eggs?

3. You have indicated that the strawberries used in your shortbread are grown in a magic garden which is guarded by gnomes in red hats who discreetly look as though they are fishing. In this garden you state that there are also "silver bells" and "cockle shells" which are grown by a rather irritable young woman called Mary. Please confirm that neither of these two latter items is included in the ingredients for your strawberry shortbread.

Yours sincerely,

THE ROYAL FOOD TASTER

(c) If you received a registered version with internal reference number of your document by DG Competition, indicate this internal reference (ID) number in the list justifying the request for confidentiality.

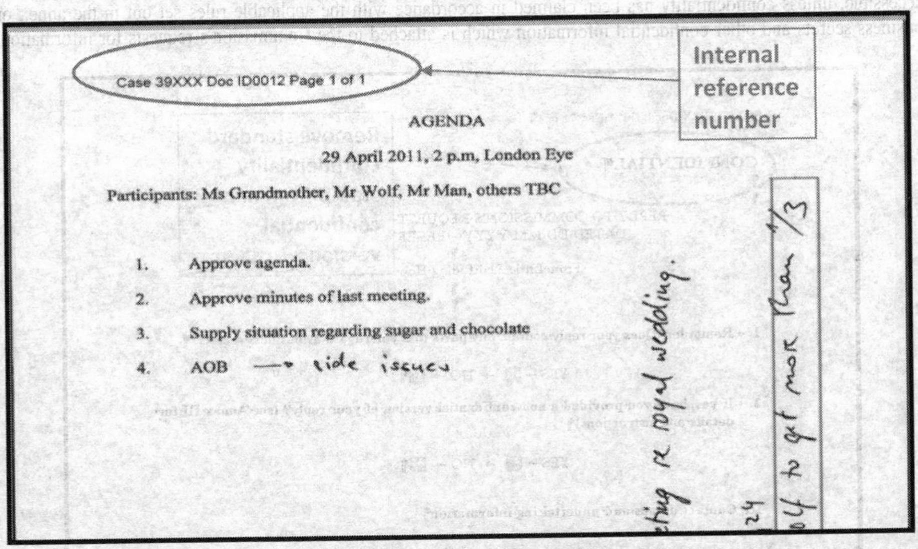

Case 39XXX Doc ID0012 Page 1 of 1

AGENDA

29 April 2011, 2 p.m, London Eye

Participants: Ms Grandmother, Mr Wolf, Mr Man, others TBC

1. Approve agenda.
2. Approve minutes of last meeting.
3. Supply situation regarding sugar and chocolate
4. AOB —→ side issues

(d) Provide a comprehensive justification for your claim, as well as, a meaningful nonconfidential description of the highlighted or already blacked-out/replaced information. Please use the list below:

ID # (if available)/Page # of original confidential version/paragraph # (please indicate annex # where relevant)	Reasons for confidentiality request	Suggested summary version
ID0015, point 1	Business secret: ingredients and their properties which are not known to third parties. If disclosed our company is likely to suffer significant losses since our competitors would be able to manufacture similar products. Our knowhow is not legally protected.	Company strategy
ID0015, points 2 and 3	Our supplier's identity is not known to third parties and it would give a competitive advantage to our competitors if details of individual recent business relations were disclosed. This is likely to cause serious harm to us and our supplier.	Suppliers' details

(e) Standard confidentiality stamps in letterheads from law firms, or automatic disclaimers in e-mails, are not regarded as a properly justified request for confidential treatment. The Commission will make such documents accessible, unless confidentiality has been claimed in accordance with the applicable rules set out in the annex on business secrets and other confidential information which is attached to the Commission's requests for information.

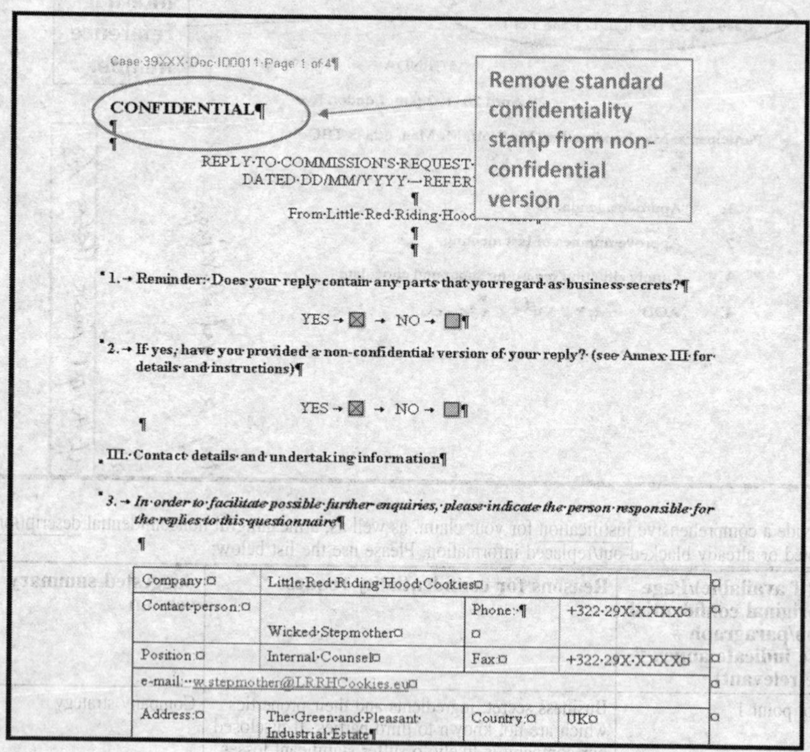

Case 39XXX Doc ID0011 Page 1 of 4

CONFIDENTIAL

REPLY TO COMMISSION'S REQUEST
DATED DD/MM/YYYY — REFER

From Little Red Riding Hood

1. Reminder: Does your reply contain any parts that you regard as business secrets?

YES → ☒ → NO → ☐

2. If yes, have you provided a non-confidential version of your reply? (see Annex III for details and instructions)

YES → ☒ → NO → ☐

III. Contact details and undertaking information

3. In order to facilitate possible further enquiries, please indicate the person responsible for the replies to this questionnaire

Company:	Little Red Riding Hood Cookies		
Contact person:	Wicked Stepmother	Phone:	+322 29X XXXX
Position:	Internal Counsel	Fax:	+322 29X XXXX
e-mail: w.stepmother@LRRHCookies.eu			
Address:	The Green and Pleasant Industrial Estate	Country:	UK

(f) Do not redact the headings of the documents and/or the headings of the columns, nor empty columns or spaces, contained in tables and pictures.

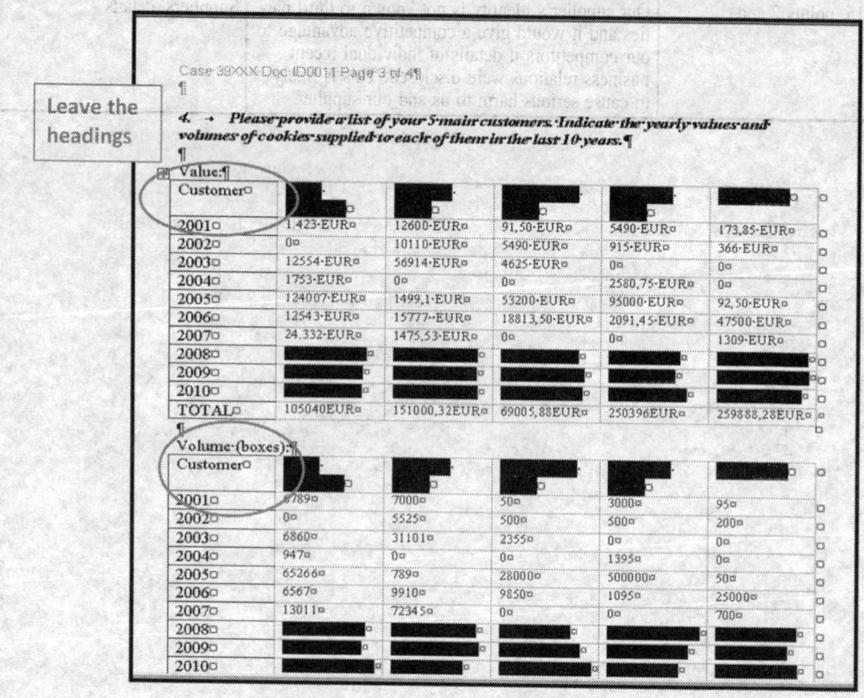

Case 39XXX Doc ID0011 Page 3 of 4

4. Please provide a list of your 5 main customers. Indicate the yearly values and volumes of cookies supplied to each of them in the last 10 years.

Value:

Customer					
2001	1.423 EUR	12600 EUR	91,50 EUR	5490 EUR	173,85 EUR
2002	0	10110 EUR	5490 EUR	915 EUR	366 EUR
2003	12554 EUR	56914 EUR	4625 EUR	0	0
2004	1753 EUR	0	0	2580,75 EUR	0
2005	124007 EUR	1499,1 EUR	53200 EUR	95000 EUR	92,50 EUR
2006	12543 EUR	15777 EUR	18813,50 EUR	2091,45 EUR	47500 EUR
2007	24.332 EUR	1475,53 EUR	0	0	1309 EUR
2008					
2009					
2010					
TOTAL	105040EUR	151000,32EUR	69005,88EUR	250396EUR	259888,28EUR

Volume (boxes):

Customer					
2001	6789	7000	50	3000	95
2002	0	5525	500	500	200
2003	6860	31101	2355	0	0
2004	947	0	0	1395	0
2005	65266	789	28000	500000	50
2006	6567	9910	9850	1095	25000
2007	13011	72345	0	0	700
2008					
2009					
2010					

DO'S AND DON'TS – SUBSTANTIAL ISSUES

[4.134]
1) The Commission does not accept confidentiality claims in oral corporate statements made in the framework of the Leniency Notice.

Case 39XXX Doc ID0018 Page 1 of 2

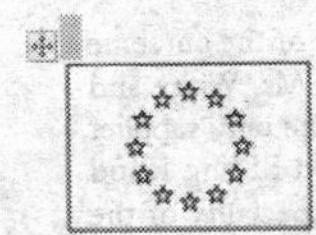

EUROPEAN COMMISSION
DG Competition

Brussels, 10/02/20XX

Case COMP/XXXXX
LITTLE RED RIDING HOOD COOKIES Inc.

Submission 1

This document records an oral corporate statement made in the context of an application for immunity or/and reduction of fines under the Commission Notice on immunity from fines and reduction of fines in cartel cases[1]. This document is the property of the Commission of the European Communities. Any mechanical or electronic reproduction of this document or any part of it is prohibited. The information obtained from this document may only be used for the purposes of judicial or administrative proceedings for the application of the Community competition rules at issue in the related administrative proceedings.

QUOTE

Following an internal investigation, and interviews with Ms. S. White, Head of Sales, Little Red Riding Hood Cookies has discovered the following:

1. Telephone conference call on 15th March 20XX conducted with the following competitors:

Big Bad Wolf Industries Inc (BE) (represented by Mr. Wolf)
Muffin Man Bakeries (NL) (represented by Mr. Man)

Ms. White informs us that party to the call were also three of her sales team of seven, and Ms. F. Grandmother, CEO of Grandmother Biscuits Inc.

Mr. Wolf of Big Bad Wolf Industries Inc indicated that he was extremely eager to secure at least part of the tender for the Royal Wedding, as he wished to extend his range of fine chocolate biscuits into the UK market. It was indicated that should Big Bad Wolf Industries Inc. secure a large part of this tender, it would mean that Grandmother Biscuits Inc. would be given priority for future tenders for the supply of cookies in other parts of Europe. Mr. Man indicated that his company was more inclined to secure the tender for the delivery of bread for the Royal Wedding. The cookie side of their company is quite small. They were willing to forego bidding on the cookie tender in this instance, in return for securing the tender for the

[1] OJ C298 of 8.12.2006

Case 39XXX Doc ID0018 Page 2 of 2

supply of bread which Big Bad Wolf and Grandmother were also scheduled to bid on. A further meeting was scheduled to be held in a pod in the London Eye on 29th March.

2. Meeting in a pod in the London Eye – 29th March

Having conducted further interviews with Ms. White, we can now inform you of the outcome of this meeting. Present at the meeting were, Ms. Grandmother, Mr. Wolf, Ms. White and Mr. Man. During this meeting it was decided that Big Bad Wolf would be the only supplier of cookies, and would tender for the supply of chocolate biscuits. Little Red Riding Hood Cookies would submit a tender for the supply of strawberry shortbread – a speciality of the company, and one which The Palace had indicated they would require. In this way, Big Bad Wolf would acquire at least 65% of the value of the tender, and Little Red Riding Hood either the rest of the tender or a smaller part. Muffin Man Bakeries would bid for the tender for the supply of bread. Grandmother Biscuits would also bid for this tender, but at a higher price.

Having agreed to the above, it was decided that collusion would take place between these four competitors in the future as and when similar tenders in the future arose.

We hereby supply at annexes 6, 7, 8, 9 and 10 an agenda and minutes of the meeting of 29th March, along with copies of Ms. White's diary entry for that day and a handwritten note made following a phone call with Ms. Grandmother. As the travel arrangements from Belgium and the Netherlands to London for this meeting were organised by Ms. White's office, we also include travel documents for Mr. Wolf and Mr. Man.

2) Public information as well as evidence pertaining to the alleged infringement cannot be accepted as confidential.

CONFIDENTIAL

REPLY TO COMMISSION'S REQUEST FOR INFORMATION
DATED DD/MM/YYYY – REFERENCE D/XXXX

From Little Red Riding Hood Cookies

1. Reminder: Does your reply contain any parts that you regard as business secrets?

YES ☒ NO ☐

2. If yes, have you provided a non-confidential version of your reply? (see Annex III for details and instructions)

YES ☒ NO ☐

III. Contact details and undertaking information

3. In order to facilitate possible further enquiries, please indicate the person responsible for the replies to this questionnaire

Company: Little Red Riding Hood Cookies	
Contact person: Wicked Stepmother	Phone: +322 29X XXXX
Position: Internal Counsel	Fax: +322 29X XXXX
e-mail: w.stepmother@LRRHCookies.eu	
Address: The Green and Pleasant Industrial Estate	Country: UK
Company web-site: www.LRRHCookies.com	

4. Please provide a short description of your undertaking. What are the most important activities of your business and the countries in which you are active? Does your undertaking belong to a group of undertakings?

Little Red Riding Hood Cookies is a wholly-owned subsidiary of Grandmother Biscuits Inc. Both the parent company and subsidiary are based in the UK. Our main areas of activity

Case 39XXX DocID0011 Page 2 of 4

involve the baking and supply of cookies. We are also active in researching new flavours and recipes.

5. ***Which corporate structure and organisation does your undertaking have? Which are the most significant developments that occurred in it since 1 January 20XX?***

Please see attached graph

Red Riding Hood Cookies was originally a small family-owned business which was purchased by Grandmother Biscuits Inc. in June 20XX upon the retirement of its founder, Miss Hood.

Answers to Section IV: Questions relating to the Royal Wedding Tender:

Please provide the following information:

1. ***Any documentation received from The Palace, along with any correspondence of your undertaking to The Place in relation to the offer of supply of cookies.***

See attached annexes 2 through 5

2. ***Please provide a detailed description of the procedure followed with regards to the composition and submission of your offer and any delivery of cookies.***

The Royal Wedding Tender was a public tender, announced officially on the Palace's website. All offers had to be submitted by 17h00 on 30th May 20XX directly and by hand to the Palace. Little Red Riding Hood Inc. submitted its tender on time and in the manner requested (sealed in a double envelope and hand delivered to a Palace Official).

Our offer dealt solely with the supply of strawberry shortbread, a speciality of Little Red Riding Hood Cookies. We were granted a tender for part supply (25%) of the cookies for the Royal Wedding. The other 75% of the cookies were eventually supplied by Big Bad Wolf Industries Inc, a company based in Belgium, which specialises in fine chocolate biscuits. Big Bad Wolf Industries Inc. is the largest of our competitors in the EU market.

3. ***The Commission is in possession of information which indicates that your undertaking had contact with competitors on 15th March 20XX and on 29th April 20XX regarding the Royal Wedding tender. Please specify the type of contact (meetings, telephone conversations); where such contacts took place and who participated in them. If possible provide travel expense records, agendas, invitations, minutes, diary entries, hand written notes.***

We have undertaken a full internal investigation with regards to the alleged contact with competitors which you indicate took place on 15th March 20XX and on 29th April 20XX regarding the Royal Wedding tender. After extensive interviews with colleagues, in particular, Ms. S. White, Head of Sales. This information has been provided in an oral statement under the Commission's Leniency programme.

3) The Commission presumes that information pertaining to the parties' turnover, sales, market share data and similar information which has lost its commercial sensitivity, for example, due to the passage of time can no longer be considered as confidential.

Case 39XXX DocID0011 Page 3 of 4

4. ***Please provide a list of your 5 main customers. Indicate the yearly values and volumes of cookies supplied to each of them in the last 10 years.***

Value:

Customer	Little mermaid	The first piglet	The second piglet	The third piglet	Frau Holle
2001	1.422 EUR	12600 EUR	91,50 EUR	5490 EUR	173,85 EUR
2002	0	10110 EUR	5490 EUR	915 EUR	366 EUR
2003	12554 EUR	56914 EUR	4625 EUR	0	0
2004	1753 EUR	0	0	2580,75 EUR	0
2005	124007 EUR	1499,1 EUR	53200 EUR	95000 EUR	92,50 EUR
2006	12543 EUR	15777 EUR	18813,50 EUR	2091,45 EUR	47500 EUR
2007	24.332 EUR	1475,53 EUR	0	0	1309 EUR
2008	0	0	0	0	179629,80 EUR
2009	0	44865,90 EUR	22737,93 EUR	1045 EUR	0
2010	1889 EUR	0	0	0	0

Volume (boxes):

Customer	Little mermaid	The first piglet	The second piglet	The third piglet	Frau Holle
2001	6789	7000	50	3000	95
2002	0	5525	500	500	200
2003	6860	31101	2355	0	0
2004	947	0	0	1395	0
2005	65266	789	28000	500000	50
2006	6567	9910	9850	1095	25000
2007	13011	72345	0	0	700
2008	0	0	0	0	94542
2009	0	2340	23423	98345	0
2010	983	0		0	0

5. ***Please explain your undertaking's internal decision making procedure for the submission of a tender for cookies.***

In this instance it was decided to make up a special recipe for the supply of the strawberry shortbread. This was finally called "Royal Strawberry Shortbread". Ms. Goldie Locks is head of Research and Recipe Testing, and she is assisted by three staff members, Mr, Mrs and Master Bear. The "Royal Strawberry Shortbread" recipe was made into cookies, which were then sampled by Mr. Charming (Head of Distribution) and Ms. White (Sales Director). The final decision is always taken by Ms. Magic Mirror, a senior employee of Grandmother Biscuits Inc. in whom our CEO Ms. Stepmother puts a lot of trust, and apparently consults on many issues, including pricing, distribution and exports.

Once the recipe was established, the tender was packaged and sealed and forwarded to the palace. The documents were signed by our CEO Ms. Stepmother. Upon request from the "Royal Taster" a sample of the "Royal Strawberry Shortbread" was hand delivered to The Palace about a week after the original tender was delivered.

Case 39XXX DocID0011 Page 4 of 4

6. ***Please provide the estimated market share of your company in the following geographical areas:***

Far Far Away
Never Never Land
No-Man's Land
FairyLand

AREA	ESTIMATED MARKET SHARE
Far Far Away	15%
Never Never Land	23.2%
No-Man's Land	17.5%
Fairy Land	28%

4) Possible corroborating evidence and information, the disclosure of which would not cause serious harm cannot be considered as confidential.

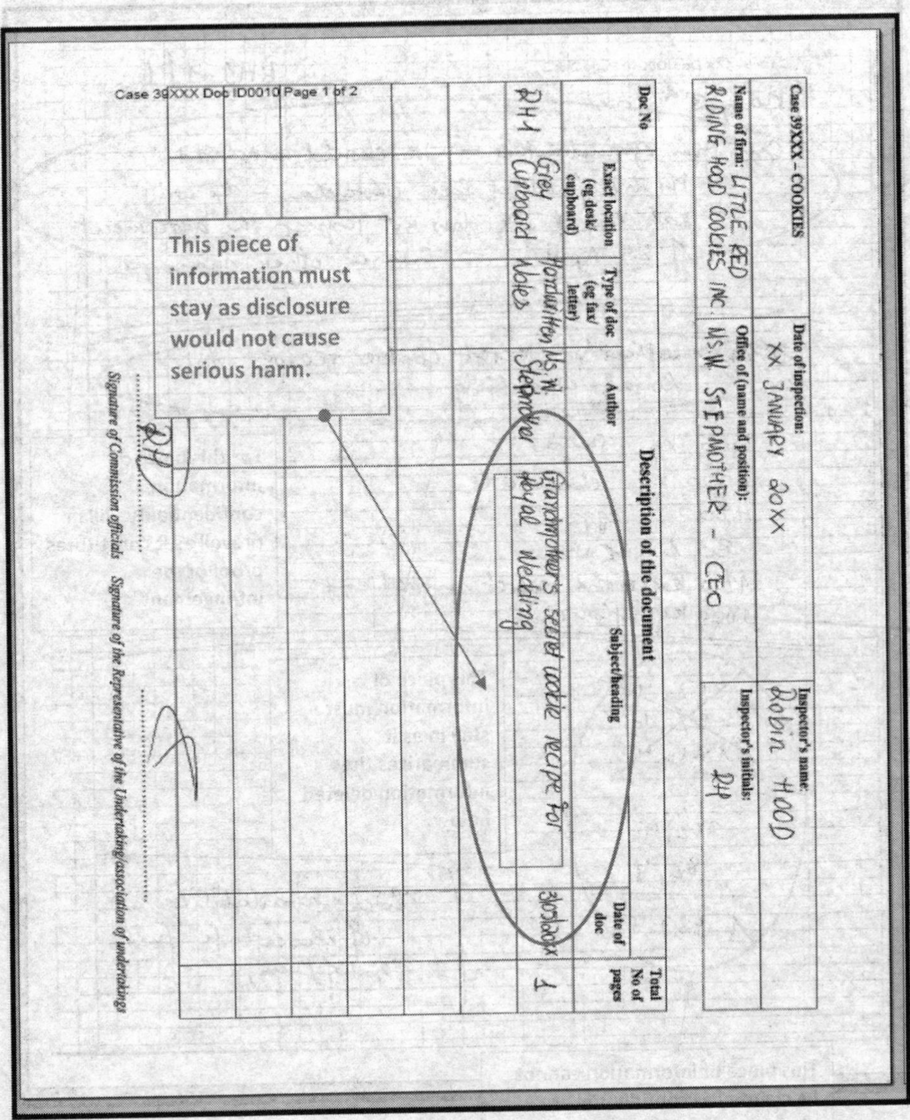

Case 39XXX – COOKIES

Name of firm: LITTLE RED RIDING HOOD COOKIES INC.	Date of inspection: XX JANUARY 20XX	Inspector's name: Robin HOOD
	Office of (name and position): MS.W. STEPMOTHER - CEO	Inspector's initials: RH

Doc No	Description of the document					Total No of pages
	Exact location (eg desk/ cupboard)	Type of doc (eg fax/ letter)	Author	Subject/heading	Date of doc	
RH1	Grey Cupboard	Handwritten Notes	Ms. W. Stepmother	Grandmother's secret cookie recipe for Royal Wedding	30/5/20XX	1

This piece of information must stay as disclosure would not cause serious harm.

.......RH....... Signature of Commission officials

.... Signature of the Representative of the Undertaking/association of undertakings

Case 39XXX Doc ID0010 Page 1 of 2

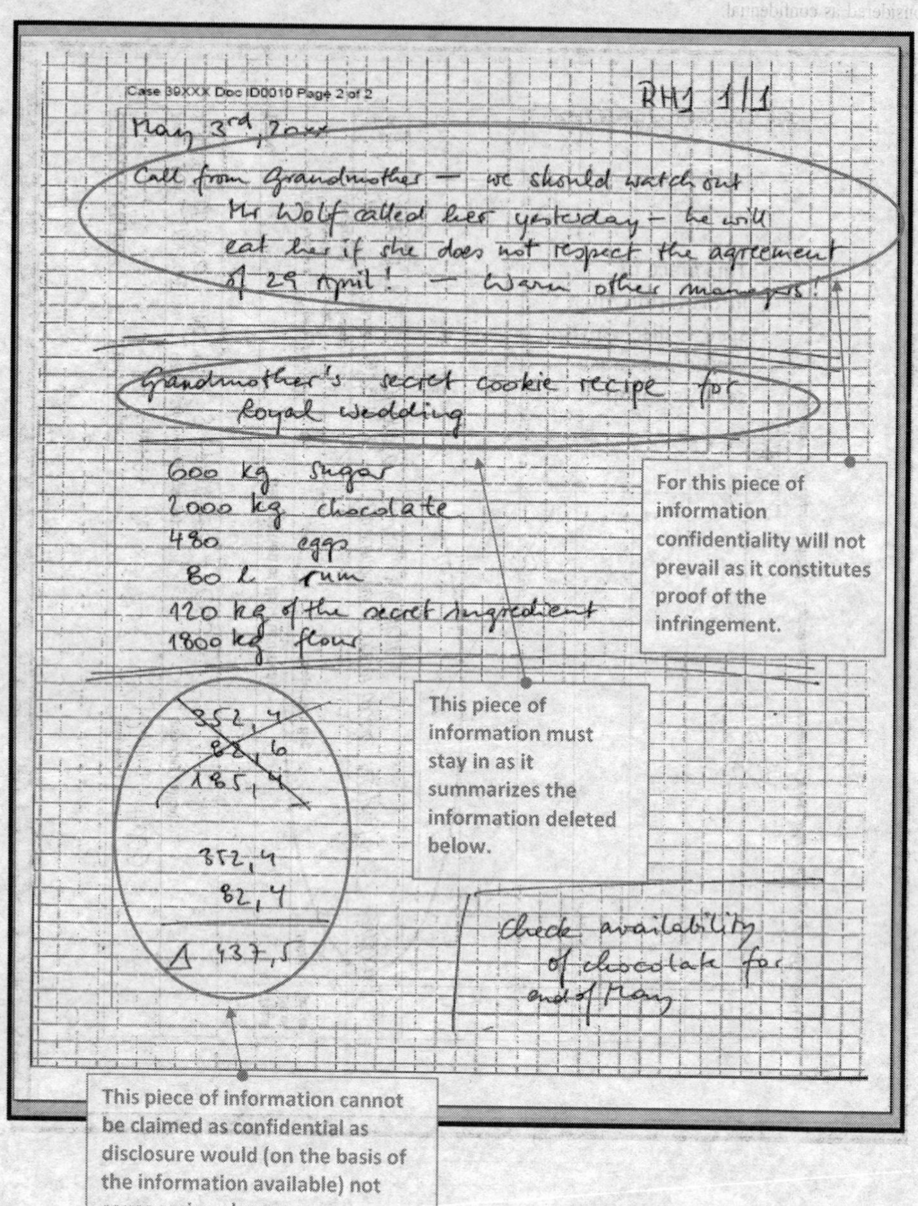

Case 39XXX Doc ID0010 Page 2 of 2

RH1 1/1

May 3rd, 20xx

Call from Grandmother – we should watch out
Mr Wolf called her yesterday – he will
eat her if she does not respect the agreement
of 29 April! – Warn other managers!

Grandmother's secret cookie recipe for
Royal wedding

600 kg sugar
2000 kg chocolate
480 eggs
80 l rum
120 kg of the secret ingredient
1800 kg flour

352,4
82,6
185,4

352,4
82,4
437,5

Check availability
of chocolate for
end of May

For this piece of information confidentiality will not prevail as it constitutes proof of the infringement.

This piece of information must stay in as it summarizes the information deleted below.

This piece of information cannot be claimed as confidential as disclosure would (on the basis of the information available) not cause serious harm.

5) Employees' names involved in the alleged infringement cannot be considered as confidential.

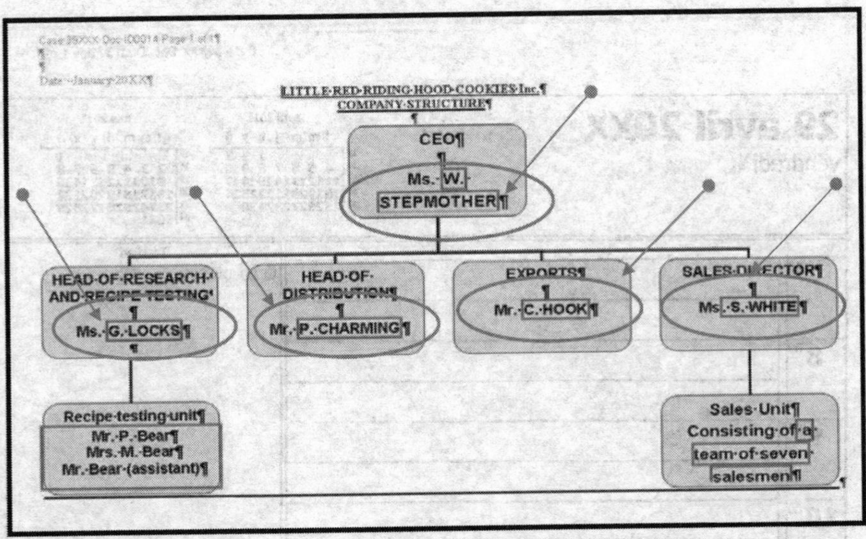

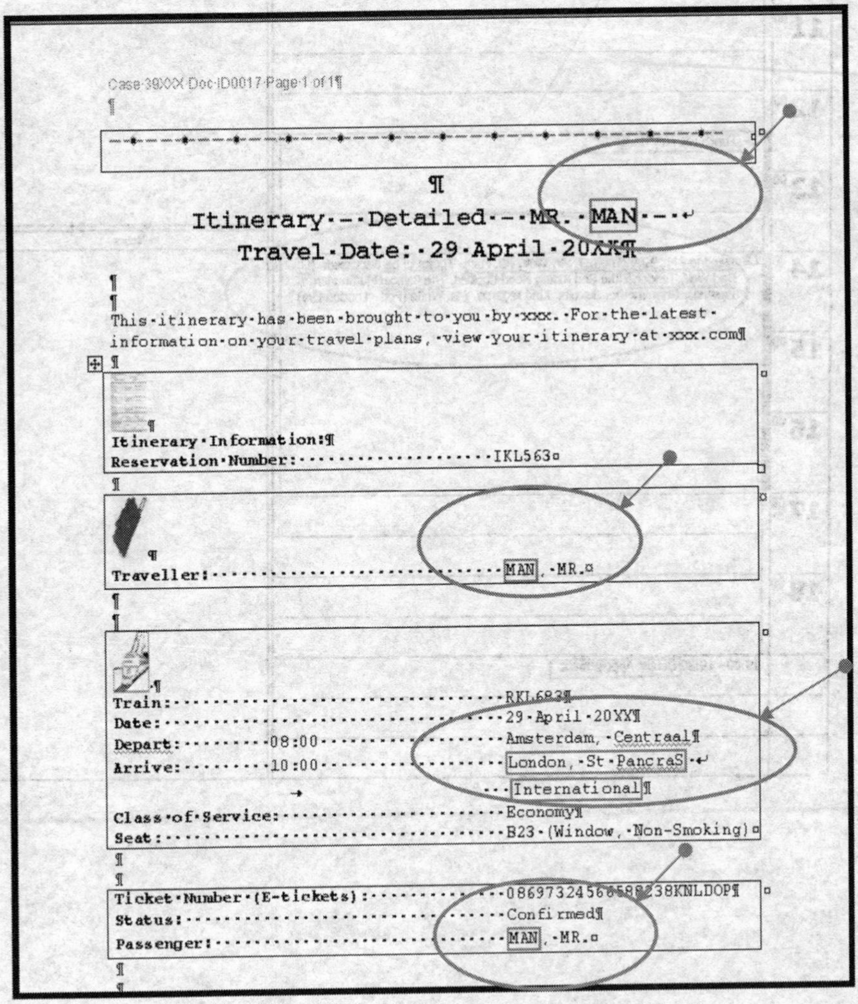

Case 39XXX Doc ID0017 Page 1 of 1

Itinerary – Detailed – MR. MAN –
Travel Date: 29 April 20XX

This itinerary has been brought to you by xxx. For the latest information on your travel plans, view your itinerary at xxx.com

Itinerary Information:
Reservation Number: IKL563

Traveller: .... MAN, MR.

Train: RKL683
Date: .... 29 April 20XX
Depart: .... 08:00 .... Amsterdam, Centraal
Arrive: .... 10:00 .... London, St Pancras International
Class of Service: .... Economy
Seat: .... B23 (Window, Non-Smoking)

Ticket Number (E-tickets): 08697324566588238KNLDOP
Status: .... Confirmed
Passenger: .... MAN, MR.

6) Possible proof of an infringement under investigation cannot be considered as confidential.

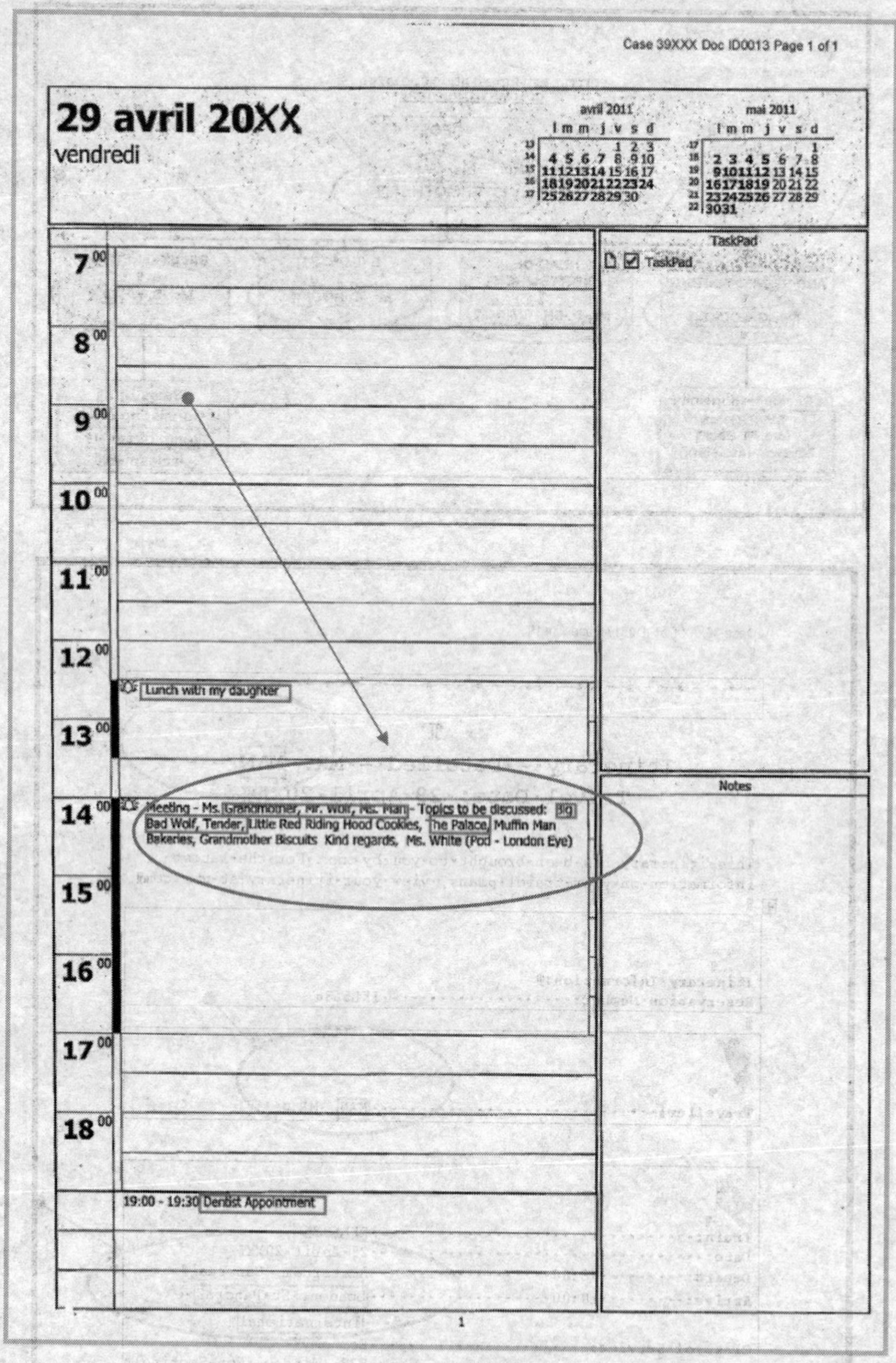
Case 39XXX Doc ID0013 Page 1 of 1

29 avril 20XX
vendredi

avril 2011 / mai 2011

Lunch with my daughter

Meeting - Ms. Grandmother, Mr. Wolf, Ms. Man - Topics to be discussed: Big Bad Wolf, Tender, Little Red Riding Hood Cookies, The Palace, Muffin Man Bakeries, Grandmother Biscuits Kind regards, Ms. White (Pod - London Eye)

19:00 - 19:30 Dentist Appointment

TaskPad

Notes

1

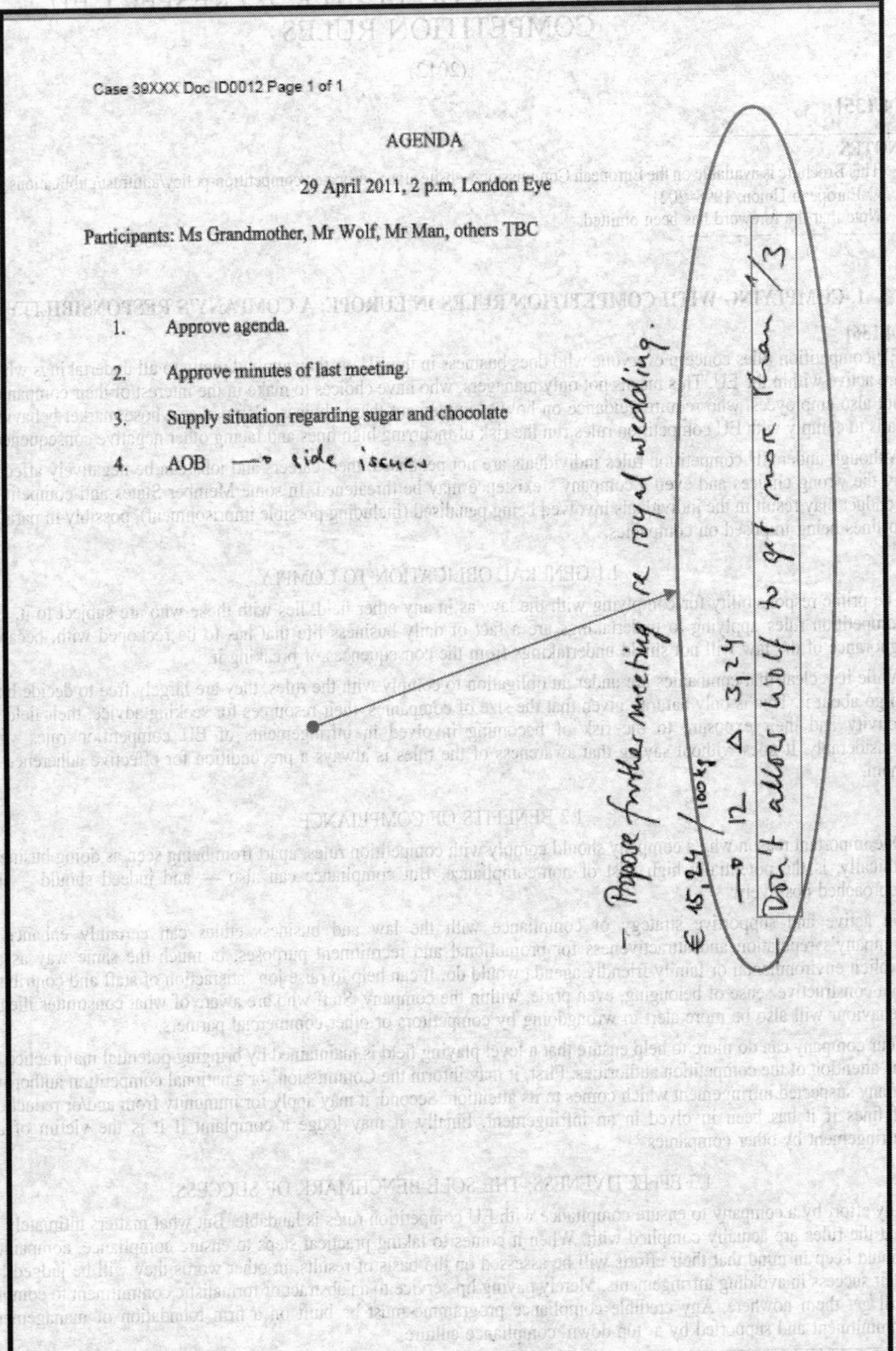

Case 39XXX Doc ID0012 Page 1 of 1

AGENDA

29 April 2011, 2 p.m, London Eye

Participants: Ms Grandmother, Mr Wolf, Mr Man, others TBC

1. **Approve agenda.**
2. **Approve minutes of last meeting.**
3. **Supply situation regarding sugar and chocolate**
4. **AOB** → side issues

COMMISSION BROCHURE: COMPLIANCE MATTERS – WHAT COMPANIES CAN DO BETTER TO RESPECT EU COMPETITION RULES

(2012)

[4.135]

NOTES

This Brochure is available on the European Commission website at: ec.europa.eu/competition-policy/antitrust/publications_en.

Note that the foreword has been omitted.

1. COMPLYING WITH COMPETITION RULES IN EUROPE: A COMPANY'S RESPONSIBILITY

[4.136]

EU competition rules concern everyone who does business in the EU, as they apply directly to all undertakings which are active within the EU. This means not only managers, who have choices to make in the interest of their companies, but also employees, who require guidance on how to implement these choices. Companies whose market behaviour fails to comply with EU competition rules run the risk of incurring high fines and facing other negative consequences.

Although under EU competition rules individuals are not penalised, their careers and jobs can be negatively affected by the wrong choices and even a company's existence may be threatened. In some Member States anti-competitive conduct may result in the individuals involved being penalised (including possible imprisonment), possibly in parallel to fines being imposed on companies.

1.1 GENERAL OBLIGATION TO COMPLY

The prime responsibility for complying with the law, as in any other field, lies with those who are subject to it. EU competition rules applying to undertakings are a fact of daily business life that has to be reckoned with, because ignorance of the law will not shield undertakings from the consequences of breaking it.

While it is clear that companies are under an obligation to comply with the rules, they are largely free to decide how to go about it. This is only natural, given that the size of companies, their resources for seeking advice, their field of activity and their exposure to the risk of becoming involved in infringements of EU competition rules vary considerably. It goes without saying that awareness of the rules is always a precondition for effective adherence to them.

1.2 BENEFITS OF COMPLIANCE

One important reason why a company should comply with competition rules, apart from being seen as doing business ethically, is the potentially high cost of non-compliance. But compliance can also — and indeed should — be approached positively.

An active and supportive strategy of compliance with the law and business ethics can certainly enhance a company's reputation and attractiveness for promotional and recruitment purposes, in much the same way as an explicit environmental or family-friendly agenda would do. It can help to raise job satisfaction of staff and contribute to a constructive sense of belonging, even pride, within the company. Staff who are aware of what constitutes illegal behaviour will also be more alert to wrongdoing by competitors or other commercial partners.

Your company can do more to help ensure that a level playing field is maintained by bringing potential malpractice to the attention of the competition authorities. First, it may inform the Commission[1] or a national competition authority[2] of any suspected infringement which comes to its attention. Second, it may apply for immunity from and/or reduction of fines if it has been involved in an infringement. Finally, it may lodge a complaint if it is the victim of an infringement by other companies.[3]

1.3 EFFECTIVENESS: THE SOLE BENCHMARK OF SUCCESS

Any effort by a company to ensure compliance with EU competition rules is laudable. But what matters ultimately is that the rules are actually complied with. When it comes to taking practical steps to ensure compliance, companies should keep in mind that their efforts will be assessed on the basis of results, in other words they will be judged by their success in avoiding infringements. Merely paying lip-service to an abstract or formalistic commitment to comply will get them nowhere. Any credible compliance programme must be built on a firm foundation of management commitment and supported by a 'top-down' compliance culture.

NOTES

1 Concerns can by reported to the Commission by email to comp-market-information@ec.europa.eu. Please indicate your name and address, identify the companies and products concerned and describe the practice you have observed. This will help the European Commission to detect problems in the market and can be the starting point for an investigation.

2 The link to contact details of the national competition authorities of the EU Member States, members of the European Competition Network, is provided at the end of this brochure.

3 Citizens and/or companies may want to lodge a formal complaint if they are directly affected by a practice which they suspect restricts competition and are able to provide specific information. Certain requirements which must be fulfilled are explained in detail in the Commission Notice on the handling of complaints (OJ C101/65 of 27.04.2004), a summary of which can be found at europa.eu/legislation_summaries/competition/companies/l26111_en.htm. You can also send an email to comp-market-information@ec.europa.eu if you want more information on how to lodge a formal complaint.

2. THE COSTS OF NON-COMPLIANCE FOR A COMPANY

2.1 FINES ON COMPANIES

[4.137]
The fines which the European Commission imposes on companies that infringe EU competition rules can be very substantial, even as high as 10% of a company's annual worldwide turnover. It should be noted that fines may be imposed even where the illegal purpose of an infringement was not actually achieved.

For example, members of a cartel that are found to have fixed prices will face high fines irrespective of whether or not the price levels rose as intended.

Several years ago the Commission set out its fining policy in writing,[4] so as to make companies fully aware of the financial risk which they run if they do not comply with EU competition rules.

The risk of engaging in anti-competitive behaviour is thus considerable for a company, as evidenced particularly by the number of anti-cartel decisions in recent years, causing substantial fines to be imposed.

CARTELS

Despite the Commission's and national competition authorities' determined fight against them, cartels still appear in many sectors, from basic industries to service markets, and companies of all sizes are involved in these infringements, from big multinational groups to small businesses.

In most of the cases investigated, unlawful behaviour had been encouraged and often directly perpetrated at the highest levels of responsibility. This shows that in certain circles, infringing the most essential rules of a market economy is still considered a rational way of doing business and maximising revenue.

In recent years, and in particular since 2001, the Commission has increased the frequency of its decisions prohibiting and fining cartels, imposing several billions of euros in fines overall. Most of these decisions have been upheld on appeal.

THE *INTERNATIONAL REMOVALS* CARTEL

In 2008, the Commission fined international removal companies a total of more than €31 million for having participated in a cartel in Belgium.

Between 1984 and 2003 the companies fixed prices, shared the market and manipulated the procedures for submission of tenders, in particular by issuing false quotes ('cover quotes') to customers and through a compensation system for rejected offers.

The Commission started the investigation on its own initiative with surprise inspections which proved particularly successful and abundant evidence of cartel activities was obtained.

One company received a reduction of 50% of its fine under the Commission's Leniency Notice for providing the Commission with evidence of significant added value.

THE *INDUSTRIAL SEWING THREAD* CARTEL

In 2005, the Commission fined thread producers from Germany, Belgium, the Netherlands, France, Switzerland and the United Kingdom over € 43 million for their participation in different cartels.

Industrial thread is used in a variety of industries to sew or embroider various products such as clothes, home furnishings, motor vehicle seats and seat-belts, leather products, mattresses, footwear and ropes.

Between 1990 and 2001, these companies took part in regular meetings and had bilateral contacts to agree on price increases and/or target prices, to exchange sensitive information on price lists or prices charged to various consumers, to avoid undercutting the incumbent supplier's prices, and to arrange customer allocation.

National competition authorities have also targeted similar types of cartel behaviour in such sectors as coffee roasters, bath and personal care products, contact lenses, and flour.

Abusive behaviour by dominant companies is also of great — and indeed growing — concern for the Commission. This has led to a number of decisions imposing fines in the last few years relating to the ICT sector and to recently liberalised or partially liberalised markets, such as the energy, telecommunication and postal sectors. However, other sectors are not devoid of abusive practices by dominant companies.

2.2 SANCTIONS ON INDIVIDUALS

In addition to imposing fines on undertakings, a number of Member States provide for sanctions on individuals (eg, fines, director disqualification). The laws of some countries even allow custodial sanctions for individuals involved in general competition law infringements and/or in certain pre-defined types of infringements (eg, bid-rigging). Such sanctions can be separate or cumulatively applied on top of pecuniary sanctions. Company managers who behave in an unlawful way therefore run the risk of jail in certain Member States.

2.3 ILLEGAL AGREEMENTS ARE VOID AND MAY ATTRACT DAMAGES

Restrictive agreements which are incompatible with EU competition rules are automatically void and therefore cannot be enforced in court by the parties involved.

This means that a party cannot be obliged to honour an agreement which is illegal. Negative consequences for business can be considerable.

If an infringement of EU competition rules causes or has caused harm to a third party, the victim may bring a claim for damages before a national court against the perpetrator. For example, in the air freight cartel case,[5] damages claims were filed even before the Commission had fined 11 air cargo carriers for fixing prices.

2.4 BAD PRESS FOR LAWBREAKERS AND OTHER COLLATERAL CONSEQUENCES

The Commission issues a press release whenever it has made a finding of illegal conduct and has fined the companies involved.

The resulting media coverage, both general and specialised, could have a detrimental impact on the reputation of those companies. Moreover, they may face hostility from clients and consumers who feel cheated.

Investigations by competition authorities can be time-consuming and costly for companies. Managers may become embroiled in lengthy legal discussions, thereby distracting attention from the core business activity.

NOTES

4 Guidelines on the method of setting fines imposed pursuant to Article 23(2) (a) of Regulation No 1/2003, published in the Official Journal of the EU under number OJ C 210 of 1.9.2006, p 2.

5 See also Commission *Press Release IP/10/1487 of 9.11.2010.*

3. COMPLIANCE WITH EU COMPETITION RULES — ARE YOU CERTAIN YOU HAVE COVERED THE RISK?

[4.138]

Two main provisions of the Treaty on the Functioning of the European Union (TFEU) deal with the market behaviour of companies. **Article 101** prohibits agreements between companies which restrict competition, unless they produce substantial benefits to customers and consumers, while **Article 102** outlaws abuses by dominant companies.

These fundamental rules and prohibitions are further clarified by legal texts adopted by the Council or the European Commission, as the case may be, spelling out how the basic principles are applied to particular sectors or to particular types of agreements or behaviour by companies. Note that at national level behaviour purely affecting competition within a Member State is similarly prohibited.

3.1 EU COMPETITION RULES ARE DIRECTLY APPLICABLE TO YOUR COMPANY

EU rules are about the competitive behaviour of companies and they apply directly in all EU Member States. No transposition into national law is required. This makes it all the more important for companies to be aware of them, as they are directly enforceable by both the European Commission and national competition authorities and courts.

It is worth noting that EU competition rules apply to 'undertakings', a term which encompasses any entity engaged in an economic activity. Groupings of undertakings, such as trade associations and other industry groupings, while generally pursuing legitimate purposes and operating as a useful business forum, also have an obligation to comply with EU competition rules.

As indicated above, there are two basic types of behaviour in which companies may feel tempted to engage in the marketplace, but which are prohibited by EU competition law:

ILLEGAL CONTACTS AND AGREEMENTS BETWEEN COMPANIES

Anti-competitive contacts between companies which, irrespective of their form, may distort the normal play of competitive forces are prohibited. Such contacts can take many forms and do not require the formal acceptance by the companies involved through an agreement. Even informal arrangements among business representatives can be considered illegal.

The most striking examples of anticompetitive contacts between companies include price fixing, sharing markets or customer allocation, production or output limitation, whether through bid rigging or otherwise. Such practices are often kept secret and generally referred to as 'cartels'. They are qualified as 'hardcore' restrictions of competition in legal jargon as they are by their very nature most likely to restrict competition. These hardcore infringements are vigorously pursued by the Commission and can result in companies being heavily fined.

Private exchanges between competing companies of individualised information concerning their intended future prices or quantities can also amount to a hardcore infringement. More generally all exchanges of confidential, strategic information between competitors can give rise to competition concerns.

This concerns all types of information that reduces strategic uncertainty in the market, for example relating to production costs, customer lists, turnover, sales, capacities, qualities, marketing plans, etc.

Furthermore, even the unilateral disclosure of strategic information by one company via mail, email, phone calls or meetings to its competitor(s) can be considered problematic.

Agreements between companies at different levels of the supply chain, typically distribution agreements between suppliers and re-sellers, which aim at fixing prices or artificially partitioning the internal market, are also illegal.

For instance, a supplier may not oblige its distributors to refuse to sell goods to customers residing outside of a given territory. In addition, it may not impose on its distributors a resale price for a given product.

In short, the following basic 'DON'Ts' should always be kept in mind by managers and employees of companies when they deal with competitors:

DON'T fix purchase or selling prices or other trading conditions;

DON'T limit production, markets, technical development or investment;

DON'T share markets or sources of supply;

DON'T exchange individualised information on intended future prices or quantities or other strategic information.

It is important to keep in mind that agreements between competitors and companies at different levels of the supply chain can also have anticompetitive effects even if they do not contain any of the above-mentioned hardcore restrictions.

For example, the agreement might have a negative impact on one of the parameters of competition, namely price, output, innovation, or the quality or variety of goods and services.

Such restrictive effects also need to be assessed by companies. A detailed framework for analysing the competitive impact of such agreements is provided by the Commission in specific guidelines.

ABUSE OF A DOMINANT POSITION

If companies have a large proportion of the business in a particular market, they are likely to hold a dominant position in that market. Such companies have a special responsibility not to engage in behaviour which is considered abusive. They should not act in a way that prevents competitors from competing effectively or drives them out of the market.

Examples of abusive conduct on the part of dominant companies are: charging unreasonably high prices which may exploit customers; charging unrealistically low prices which may be used to drive competitors out of the market; unjustified discrimination between customers; and forcing unjustified trading conditions on trading partners.

WHAT ABOUT SMALL & MEDIUM ENTERPRISES?

All companies are subject to competition rules, with no differentiation according to their size. Being small is no excuse for not complying with the applicable EU or national competition rules.

3.2 ACTIVITIES BY PUBLIC AUTHORITIES

It falls to both European and national competition authorities and courts to ensure that EU competition rules are complied with.

ENFORCEMENT AGAINST ILLEGAL PRACTICES

The European Commission ensures effective application of these rules throughout the EU. It investigates suspected infringements and addresses binding decisions to companies in order to bring established infringements to an end. The Commission also has the power to impose fines on companies which have been found to infringe EU competition law.

The enforcement activity by national competition authorities, which are equally empowered to apply EU competition rules, needs to be added to that of the Commission.

National courts also play an important role. They may declare an agreement void if it is in breach of EU competition rules. They may also hear claims for damages resulting from a company's infringement of EU competition rules and award compensation to plaintiffs.

FURTHER EXPLAINING THE RULES

The Commission endeavours to make it easier for companies to acquaint themselves with and know the rules which they must respect.

Certain types of agreements are exempted from general prohibition if their restrictive nature can be justified by benefits for consumers and the economy as a whole. The hardcore practices mentioned above are very unlikely to bring such benefits.

Companies have to assess for themselves whether their behaviour complies with competition rules and in doing so they might consider seeking legal advice.

General guidance as to whether an agreement is deemed exempted or not is provided by the Commission in particular by way of so-called Block Exemption Regulations. Mostly, such Regulations exempt restrictions in certain categories of agreements (eg, Research & Development, Specialisation or Distribution agreements) up to a certain level of market power, defined in terms of market share, providing there are no 'hardcore' restrictions and certain conditions are met.

Outside the 'safe harbour' of the block exemption, guidelines such as those on horizontal cooperation agreements[6] or on vertical restraints[7] also set out the Commission's policy and decision-making practice on a variety of competition issues.

As regards abusive behaviour, the Commission has published guidance on its enforcement priorities in applying Article 102 TFEU.[8]

Furthermore, formal Commission decisions[9] and Court judgments are publicly available, and the Commission publishes the formal opening and closing of proceedings on its website and/or by issuing a press release.[10]

Finally, the Commission also publishes an annual report on competition policy and a number of informative brochures.[11]

NOTES

6 Commission Guidelines on the applicability of Article 101 of the Treaty on the Functioning of the European Union to horizontal cooperation agreements, OJ C11 of 14.1.2011, p1.

7 Commission Guidelines on vertical restraints, OJ C130 of 19.5.2010, p1.

8 Communication from the Commission, OJ C45 of 24.2.2009, p 7.

9 Article 30 of Council Regulation 1/2003.

10 The same applies in cases where proceedings have not been formally opened but DG Competition has already made public the fact that it is investigating a case (eg, by having publicly confirmed certain inspections). See Commission Notice on Best Practices for the conduct of proceedings concerning Articles 101 and 102 TFEU, OJ C308 of 20.10.2011, p 6.

11 See last section of this brochure « Where to find further relevant information ».

4. HOW CAN YOUR COMPANY ENSURE COMPLIANCE?

4.1 A CLEAR STRATEGY

[4.139]

In order to ensure effective compliance with EU competition rules, companies should think ahead, develop an approach tailor-made for their particular situation and set it out in writing, rather than react to problems only when they occur.

The ultimate goal of such a strategy is to raise awareness of potential conflicts with EU competition law and disseminate adequate knowledge of how to avoid them at all levels of the company, from employees to middle and top management.

IDENTIFYING THE OVERALL RISK AND INDIVIDUAL EXPOSURE

A successful company's compliance strategy would be based on a comprehensive analysis of the areas in which it is most likely to run a risk of infringing EU competition rules.

These areas will depend on factors such as:

— the sector of activity; for example a history of previous infringements in the sector indicates a need for particular attention.

— (frequency/level of) the company's interaction with competitors; for example in the course of industry meetings or within trade associations, but also in day-to-day commercial dealings.

— the characteristics of the market; position of the company and its competitors, barriers to entry ... If a company holds a dominant position in a market, the preventive measures to be taken will differ from those where the risk factor is more in the nature of 'cartelisation'.

But the exposure to that risk may vary greatly according to the position held by each member of staff. Employees whose specific areas of responsibility cause them to be particularly exposed (for example, employees who frequently interact with competitors as part of their job or through trade associations) would be made aware of what is at stake and of the basic principles to keep in mind.

MAKING THE STRATEGY EXPLICIT

In the interest of genuine compliance it is also important to disseminate the company's compliance strategy throughout its entire organisational structure. For the sake of internal clarity the strategy would preferably be laid down in writing, plainly worded and in all the working languages of the company, so that it is understood by everyone. It could for example take the form of a manual.

Such internal guidance would ideally contain a general description of EU competition law and its purpose, explain the way it is enforced and highlight the potential costs of non-compliance for the company. In this way, employees will better understand the reason behind the compliance strategy and its importance.

In addition, guidance in particular risk areas would be provided. For instance, a company which mainly deals in homogeneous products or has management or employee level contacts with competitors on a regular basis could stress the ban on cartels.

A practical set of 'DON'Ts' and 'RED FLAGS' can be a useful tool:

— A list of 'DON'Ts' could include clearly illegal conduct such as price-fixing agreements, the exchange of future pricing intentions, allocation of production quotas and the fixing of market shares;

— 'RED FLAGs' are warning signs which serve to identify situations in which infringements of competition rules can be suspected. They would encourage managers and employees to exercise particular caution in seeking to avoid any infringement on the part of their own company.

VISIBLE AND LASTING COMMITMENT TO THE COMPLIANCE STRATEGY BY SENIOR MANAGEMENT

Apart from choosing the right strategy and making it accessible to all staff, unequivocal senior management support is vital. The message that compliance with the law is a fundamental policy of a company needs to be clearly endorsed. This is an essential element of creating a culture of respect for the law within the company.

Designating an individual member of the senior management to take overall responsibility for compliance is considered advisable to ensure lasting commitment to and visibility for this objective.

Small and medium-sized companies have the advantage that the 'tone from the top' can more easily be disseminated to the employees, who are fewer in number.

Whilst the Commission does not wish to be prescriptive, a company should devote sufficient resources – appropriate to its size and the risks it faces – to ensure it has a credible programme.

4.2 FORMAL ACTS OF ACKNOWLEDGEMENT BY STAFF AND CONSIDERATION OF COMPLIANCE EFFORTS IN STAFF EVALUATION

Backup measures taken by companies as regards adherence of their staff to the adopted compliance strategy might include:

— asking staff for written acknowledgement of receipt of relevant information on compliance with EU competition law, for example when providing them with a manual or after dedicated training sessions. This form of explicit recognition helps to make individual staff members more aware that compliance concerns each and every one of them;

— putting in place positive incentives for employees to consider this objective with utmost seriousness. Compliance duties could for instance be part of job descriptions. A particularly vigilant attitude in that respect may also form part of the staff evaluation criteria.

— penalties for breach of the internal compliance rules. Such penalties would however have to be consistent with national employment law and double-checked with legal advisers first.

PROPER INTERNAL REPORTING MECHANISMS

A further essential feature of a successful compliance strategy is the inclusion of clear reporting mechanisms. Staff must not only be aware of potential conflicts with EU competition law, but also need to know whom to contact and in what form when concrete situations of conflict arise.

A company may for example consider appointing a compliance officer who directly reports to the company's management. The communication channels should in any event allow management to take swift action. Time is usually of the essence, irrespective of whether or not competition authorities are already aware of the particular problem.

If an employee or manager discovers or even suspects an infringement, the compliance strategy should provide her/him with concrete guidance on how to proceed.

An environment that encourages employees to speak up when they are confronted with questionable situations can be decisive for the effectiveness of the compliance strategy.

4.3 CONSTANT UPDATE, CONTACT POINTS FOR ADVICE AND TRAINING

Obviously it is not enough just to put down a strategy on paper. Where a manual is made available to staff, it should be reviewed regularly. There should also be a clearly identified contact point where advice can be sought by staff in case of doubts about the compatibility of certain types of behaviour or agreements with EU competition law.

Training on applicable EU competition rules also plays an important role. Many companies already offer their staff, in particular newcomers, an ambitious training programme. In such cases the development of a module on competitive behaviour would be advisable. Where a company's analysis has indicated particular risk areas, training should be provided to those staff members who are most likely to be confronted with situations that could lead to the company becoming involved in infringements, for example sales personnel and sales managers as regards price agreements between competitors and anyone attending trade associations or industry events.

The specific details will vary from one business to another, depending on available resources and expertise. In any case, a compliance strategy will be more effective if it incorporates a clear mechanism for ensuring that updates of the written policy can be obtained by staff at any time and that all employees and managers are kept informed about new developments.

4.4 MONITORING/AUDITING

Monitoring and auditing can serve as effective tools to prevent and detect anti-competitive behaviour inside the company. Monitoring, for instance by verifying the company's own behaviour in the competitive process in bidding markets, would mean a more preventive approach.

Auditing would tend to discover anticompetitive behaviour only after it had already occurred.

Both mechanisms can also be combined. The appropriate procedure depends on the specific needs of the undertaking, but some form of control is surely important to underpin the internal credibility of a compliance strategy.

4.5 THE STRATEGY HAS FAILED TO ENSURE FULL COMPLIANCE? IT MAY STILL SERVE TO LIMIT EXPOSURE!

An effective compliance strategy will be expected to simply prevent any infringement from happening. Yet it may prove insufficient to ensure compliance, and there may nevertheless be instances of wrongdoing.

STOPPING THE INFRINGEMENT AT THE EARLIEST POSSIBLE STAGE

In such a case, the existence of a compliance strategy – on condition that it incorporates appropriate reporting mechanisms – will allow mishaps to be nipped in the bud.

It will enable the company to take appropriate measures without delay, so that any potential infringement is swiftly brought to an end. This will contribute to limiting damage to competition and minimising the company's exposure.

COOPERATING UNDER THE LENIENCY PROGRAMME AND THE SETTLEMENT PROCEDURE: LIMITING THE DAMAGE OF CARTEL BEHAVIOUR

The detection mechanisms provided by an effective compliance strategy can also help to get the best out of the Commission's leniency programme. Aimed at enabling the detection of secret agreements between competitors – some of the most egregious infringements of competition law – it offers a unique opportunity, for companies willing to cooperate with the Commission (or with the national competition authorities), to receive immunity from fines or to get a fine reduced.

Full immunity can be granted to the company that is the first to denounce a secret cartel to the Commission or to provide the Commission with sufficient corroborative evidence. Companies which, despite their willingness to cooperate, file their leniency application after another competitor has qualified for immunity, can only hope to obtain a reduction of up to 50% of any fine imposed on them.

However, remember that competition authorities are also on constant lookout for markets showing signs of distorted competition. When such signs appear, they may launch investigations themselves.

The exact conditions under which immunity from or reduction of fines in cartel cases is granted are explained in the corresponding Commission Notice.[12]

Therefore, if you believe your company is or has been involved in a cartel, you might consider filing an application under the Commission's leniency programme and seeking legal advice in that respect.

Initial contact with the Commission should be made through the following dedicated fax number:

+ 32 2 299 45 85

Or through the following dedicated telephone numbers:

+ 32 2 298 41 90

+ 32 2 298 41 91

Further information on the Commission's leniency programme is available on the Internet at ec.europa.eu/competition/cartels/leniency/leniency.html[13]

Finally, if companies are prepared to acknowledge their participation in a cartel, the Commission may invite them to participate in a swifter conclusion of the procedure. The companies' cooperation in this "settlement" procedure is rewarded with a 10% reduction of the fine in addition to any reductions for leniency.

4.6 THE COMMISSION WELCOMES COMPLIANCE EFFORTS BY COMPANIES

The Commission welcomes and supports all compliance efforts by companies as they contribute to the firm rooting of a truly competitive culture in all sectors of the European economy.

Companies, supported by the legal profession, have already contemplated and indeed implemented schemes to ensure compliance with EU competition law. These schemes are usually referred to as 'business compliance programmes' or just 'compliance programmes'.

In practice, they are often developed in reaction to past infringements or even after fines have been imposed. Increasingly such programmes are seen as an essential element of good corporate governance.

The Commission would advocate a more proactive approach that avoids infringements of EU competition rules from the outset. It cannot be overemphasised that a compliance programme worthy of the name must ensure that companies do not infringe competition law.

As has already been pointed out, it is not so much the effort made, but the result achieved, which counts once competition authorities become involved and launch an investigation. The quality of a compliance programme stands or falls by its effectiveness.

The Commission's attitude towards compliance programmes can, therefore, be summarised as follows:

— **Compliance programmes need to be tailor-made to the company concerned.** The range of situations that a compliance programme may need to address is wide. Equally the type, size and resources of companies which may find it useful to adopt a compliance programme vary considerably.
Consequently, there is **no 'one size fits all' model:** an exhaustive all-encompassing model would not be adequate. It is for each company to reflect on its needs to ensure compliance and develop its own strategy. Further legal advice can be sought if considered appropriate.

— **Access to useful information can be provided by the Commission but there will be no endorsement of any individual compliance programme**. While the Commission constantly seeks to improve the accessibility of relevant legislation and information on EU competition rules, it considers it not to be the task of competition authorities to formally advise on or approve individual compliance programmes.
Indeed, companies know best what is required for their own compliance strategy. This brochure provides companies with food for thought about the nature of their own compliance strategy. This includes for example creating the necessary positive and negative incentives to ensure compliance.

— Although all compliance efforts are welcomed, **the mere existence of a compliance programme is not enough to counter the finding of an infringement of competition rules**[14] — companies and their employees must, in fact, comply. If a company which has put a compliance programme in place is nevertheless found to have committed an infringement of EU competition rules, the question of whether there is any positive impact on the level of fines frequently arises. The answer is: No.
Compliance programmes should not be perceived by companies as an abstract and formalistic tool for supporting the argument that any fine to be imposed should be reduced if the company is 'caught'. The purpose of a compliance programme should be to avoid an infringement in the first place.
For the purpose of setting the level of fines, the specific situation of a company is duly taken into account. But **the mere existence of a compliance programme will not be considered as an attenuating circumstance.**[15]
Nor will the setting-up of a compliance programme be considered as a valid argument justifying a reduction of the fine in the wake of investigation of an infringement. It would nevertheless be encouraged by competition authorities as a preventive means to avoid the occurrence and possible repetition of illegal behaviour in the first place.
It goes without saying that **the existence of a compliance programme will not be considered an aggravating circumstance** if an infringement is found by the enforcement authorities: if the programme has failed to deliver results, the sanction will come in the form of the fine imposed. In other words: a credible competition compliance programme can only deliver benefits to a company.

NOTES

12 OJ C45 of 19.2.2002.

13 See also Commission *Press Release IP/06/1705* and *Memo MEMO/06/469 of 7.12.2006.*

14 See, for example, Case C-189/02 P Dansk Rørindustri, paragraph 373.

15 See, for example, Joined Cases T-101/05 and T-111/05, BASF and UCB, paragraph 52, and Case T-138/07, Schindler Holding, paragraph 282.

5. WHERE TO FIND FURTHER RELEVANT INFORMATION

[4.140]
Competition website on 'Europa', the Internet site of the European Commission:

ec.europa.eu/competition/

On this site, easy access to relevant legislative texts, Commission decisions, Press Releases, Annual Reports, sector-specific and other background information is provided. Links to other important sources of information, like the website of the Court of Justice of the European Union and the General Court, are equally available.

Publications on competition matters published by the European Commission:

ec.europa.eu/competition/publications/

Contact details of European Competition Authorities/members of the European Competition Network, available via:

ec.europa.eu/competition/ecn/competition_authorities.html

Website on compliance:

ec.europa.eu/competition/antitrust/compliance/

COMMISSION COMMUNICATION

(2014/C291/01)

Notice on agreements of minor importance which do not appreciably restrict competition under Article 101(1) of the Treaty on the Functioning of the European Union (De Minimis Notice)

[4.141]

NOTES

Date of publication in OJ: OJ C291, 30.8.2014, p 1.

I.

[4.142]
1. Article 101(1) of the Treaty on the Functioning of the European Union prohibits agreements between undertakings which may affect trade between Member States and which have as their object or effect the prevention, restriction or distortion of competition within the internal market. The Court of Justice of the European Union has clarified that that provision is not applicable where the impact of the agreement on trade between Member States or on competition is not appreciable.[1]

2. The Court of Justice has also clarified that an agreement which may affect trade between Member States and which has as its object the prevention, restriction or distortion of competition within the internal market constitutes, by its nature and independently of any concrete effects that it may have, an appreciable restriction of competition.[2] This Notice therefore does not cover agreements which have as their object the prevention, restriction or distortion of competition within the internal market.

3. In this Notice the Commission indicates, with the help of market share thresholds, the circumstances in which it considers that agreements which may have as their effect the prevention, restriction or distortion of competition within the internal market do not constitute an appreciable restriction of competition under Article 101 of the Treaty. This negative definition of appreciability does not imply that agreements between undertakings which exceed the thresholds set out in this Notice constitute an appreciable restriction of competition. Such agreements may still have only a negligible effect on competition and may therefore not be prohibited by Article 101(1) of the Treaty.[3]

4. Agreements may also fall outside Article 101(1) of the Treaty because they are not capable of appreciably affecting trade between Member States. This Notice does not indicate what constitutes an appreciable effect on trade between Member States. Guidance to that effect is to be found in the Commission's Notice on effect on trade,[4] in which the Commission quantifies, with the help of the combination of a 5 % market share threshold and a EUR 40 million turnover threshold, which agreements are in principle not capable of appreciably affecting trade between Member States.[5] Such agreements normally fall outside Article 101(1) of the Treaty even if they have as their object the prevention, restriction or distortion of competition.

5. In cases covered by this Notice, the Commission will not institute proceedings either upon a complaint or on its own initiative. In addition, where the Commission has instituted proceedings but undertakings can demonstrate that they have assumed in good faith that the market shares mentioned in points 8, 9, 10 and 11 were not exceeded, the Commission will not impose fines. Although not binding on them, this Notice is also intended to give guidance to the courts and competition authorities of the Member States in their application of Article 101 of the Treaty.[6]

6. The principles set out in this Notice also apply to decisions by associations of undertakings and to concerted practices.

7. This Notice is without prejudice to any interpretation of Article 101 of the Treaty which may be given by the Court of Justice of the European Union.

NOTES

1 See Case C-226/11 Expedia, not yet reported, paragraphs 16 and 17.
2 See Case C-226/11 Expedia, in particular paragraphs 35, 36 and 37.

3 See, for instance, Joined Cases C-215/96 and C-216/96 Bagnasco and Others [1999] ECR I-135, paragraphs 34 and 35.

4 Commission Notice – Guidelines on the effect on trade concept contained in Articles 81and 82 of the Treaty (OJ C101, 27.4.2004, p 81), in particular points 44 to 57.

5 It should be noted that agreements between small and medium sized undertakings (SMEs), as defined in the Commission Recommendation of 6 May 2003 concerning the definition of micro, small and medium-sized enterprises or any future recommendation replacing it (OJ L124, 20.5.2003, p 36), are also not normally capable of affecting trade between Member States. See in particular point 50 of the Notice on effect of trade.

6 In particular, in order to determine whether or not a restriction of competition is appreciable, the competition authorities and the courts of Member States may take into account the thresholds established in this Notice but are not required to do so. See Case C-226/11 Expedia, paragraph 31.

II.

[4.143]

8. The Commission holds the view that agreements between undertakings which may affect trade between Member States and which may have as their effect the prevention, restriction or distortion of competition within the internal market, do not appreciably restrict competition within the meaning of Article 101(1) of the Treaty:

(a) if the aggregate market share held by the parties to the agreement does not exceed 10% on any of the relevant markets affected by the agreement, where the agreement is made between undertakings which are actual or potential competitors on any of those markets (agreements between competitors);[1] or

(b) if the market share held by each of the parties to the agreement does not exceed 15% on any of the relevant markets affected by the agreement, where the agreement is made between undertakings which are not actual or potential competitors on any of those markets (agreements between non-competitors).

9. In cases where it is difficult to classify the agreement as either an agreement between competitors or an agreement between non-competitors the 10% threshold is applicable.

10. Where, in a relevant market, competition is restricted by the cumulative effect of agreements for the sale of goods or services entered into by different suppliers or distributors (cumulative foreclosure effect of parallel networks of agreements having similar effects on the market), the market share thresholds set out in point 8 and 9 are reduced to 5%, both for agreements between competitors and for agreements between non-competitors. Individual suppliers or distributors with a market share not exceeding 5%, are in general not considered to contribute significantly to a cumulative foreclosure effect.[2] A cumulative foreclosure effect is unlikely to exist if less than 30% of the relevant market is covered by parallel (networks of) agreements having similar effects.

11. The Commission also holds the view that agreements do not appreciably restrict competition if the market shares of the parties to the agreement do not exceed the thresholds of respectively 10%, 15% and 5% set out in points 8, 9 and 10 during two successive calendar years by more than 2 percentage points.

12. In order to calculate the market share, it is necessary to determine the relevant market. This consists of the relevant product market and the relevant geographic market. When defining the relevant market, reference should be had to the Notice on the definition of the relevant market.[3] The market shares are to be calculated on the basis of sales value data or, where appropriate, purchase value data. If value data are not available, estimates based on other reliable market information, including volume data, may be used.

13. In view of the clarification of the Court of Justice referred to in point 2, this Notice does not cover agreements which have as their object the prevention, restriction or distortion of competition within the internal market. The Commission will thus not apply the safe harbour created by the market share thresholds set out in points 8, 9, 10 and 11 to such agreements.[4] For instance, as regards agreements between competitors, the Commission will not apply the principles set out in this Notice to, in particular, agreements containing restrictions which, directly or indirectly, have as their object: a) the fixing of prices when selling products to third parties; b) the limitation of output or sales; or c) the allocation of markets or customers. Likewise, the Commission will not apply the safe harbour created by those market share thresholds to agreements containing any of the restrictions that are listed as hardcore restrictions in any current or future Commission block exemption regulation,[5] which are considered by the Commission to generally constitute restrictions by object.

14. The safe harbour created by the market share thresholds set out in points 8, 9, 10 and 11 is particularly relevant for categories of agreements not covered by any Commission block exemption regulation.[6] The safe harbour is also relevant for agreements covered by a Commission block exemption regulation to the extent that those agreements contain a so-called excluded restriction, that is a restriction not listed as a hardcore restriction but nonetheless not covered by the Commission block exemption regulation.[7]

15. For the purpose of this Notice, the terms 'undertaking', 'party to the agreement', 'distributor' and 'supplier' include their respective connected undertakings.

16. For the purpose of the Notice 'connected undertakings' are:

(a) undertakings in which a party to the agreement, directly or indirectly:

  (i) has the power to exercise more than half the voting rights, or

  (ii) has the power to appoint more than half the members of the supervisory board, board of management or bodies legally representing the undertaking, or

  (iii) has the right to manage the undertaking's affairs;

(b) undertakings which directly or indirectly have, over a party to the agreement, the rights or powers listed in (a);

(c) undertakings in which an undertaking referred to in (b) has, directly or indirectly, the rights or powers listed in (a);

(d) undertakings in which a party to the agreement together with one or more of the undertakings referred to in (a), (b) or (c), or in which two or more of the latter undertakings, jointly have the rights or powers listed in (a);

(e) undertakings in which the rights or the powers listed in (a) are jointly held by:
  (i) parties to the agreement or their respective connected undertakings referred to in (a) to (d), or
  (ii) one or more of the parties to the agreement or one or more of their connected undertakings referred to in (a) to (d) and one or more third parties.

17. For the purposes of point (e) in point 16, the market share held by these jointly held undertakings is apportioned equally to each undertaking having the rights or the powers listed in point (a) in point 16.

NOTES

1 On the definition of actual or potential competitors, see the Communication from the Commission — Guidelines on the applicability of Article 101 of the Treaty on the Functioning of the European Union to horizontal cooperation agreements (OJ C 11, 14.1.2011, p. 1),point 10. Two undertakings are treated as actual competitors if they are active on the same relevant market. An undertaking is treated as a potential competitor of another undertaking if, in the absence of the agreement, in case of a small but permanent increase in relative prices it is likely that the former, within a short period of time, would undertake the necessary additional investments or other necessary switching costs to enter the relevant market on which the latter is active.

2 See also the Guidelines on Vertical Restraints (OJ C 130, 19.5.2010, p. 1, in particular points 76, 134 and 179. While in the Guidelines on Vertical Restraints in relation to certain restrictions reference is made not only to the total but also to the tied market share of a particular supplier or buyer, in this Notice all market share thresholds refer to total market shares.

3 Notice on the definition of the relevant market for the purposes of Community competition law (OJ C372, 9.12.1997, p 5).

4 For these agreements, the Commission will exercise its discretion in deciding whether or not to institute proceedings.

5 For supply and distribution agreements between non-competitors see in particular Article 4 of Commission Regulation (EU) No 330/2010 of 20 April 2010 on the application of Article 101(3) of the Treaty on the Functioning of the European Union to categories of vertical agreements and concerted practices (OJ L102, 23.4.2010, p 1) and for licensing agreements between non-competitors see in particular Article 4(2) of Commission Regulation (EU) No 316/2014 of 21 March 2014 on the application of Article 101(3) of the Treaty on the Functioning of the European Union to categories of technology transfer agreements (OJ L93, 28.3.2014, p 17). For agreements between competitors see in particular Article 5 of Commission Regulation (EU) No 1217/2010 of 14 December 2010 on the application of Article 101(3) of the Treaty on the Functioning of the European Union to certain categories of research and development agreements (OJ L335, 18.12.2010, p 36), and Article 4 of Commission Regulation (EU) No 1218/2010 of 14 December 2010 on the application of Article 101(3) of the Treaty on the Functioning of the European Union to certain categories of specialisation agreements (OJ L335, 18.12.2010, p 43) as well as Article 4(1) of Regulation (EU) No 316/2014.

6 For instance, trade mark licence agreements and most types of agreements between competitors, with the exception of research and development agreements and specialisation agreements, are not covered by any block exemption regulation.

7 For excluded restrictions see in particular Article 5 of Regulation (EU) No 330/2010, Article 5 of Regulation (EU) No 316/2014 and Article 6 of Regulation (EU) No 1217/2010.

COMMISSION STAFF WORKING DOCUMENT: GUIDANCE ON RESTRICTIONS OF COMPETITION "BY OBJECT" FOR THE PURPOSE OF DEFINING WHICH AGREEMENTS MAY BENEFIT FROM THE DE MINIMIS NOTICE

SWD(2014) 198 final, Brussels 25.6.2014
REVISED VERSION OF 03/06/2015

Accompanying the document COMMUNICATION FROM THE COMMISSION Notice on agreements of minor importance which do not appreciably restrict competition under Article 101(1) of the Treaty on the Functioning of the European Union (De Minimis Notice) {C(2014) 4136 final}

[4.144]

NOTES

This document is available on the European Commission website at: ec.europa.eu/competition/antitrust/legislation/deminimis.html.

1. FINDING GUIDANCE ON RESTRICTIONS OF COMPETITION "BY OBJECT"

[4.145]

The Commission's De Minimis Notice[1] provides a safe harbour for agreements between undertakings which the Commission considers to have non-appreciable effects on competition. This safe harbour applies on condition that the market shares of the undertakings concluding those agreements do not exceed the market share thresholds set out in that Notice and provided that the agreements do not have as their object to restrict competition. For the purposes of the application of the De Minimis Notice, hardcore restrictions listed in the Commission block exemption regulations are generally considered to constitute restrictions by object.[2] Therefore, agreements containing restrictions listed as hardcore restrictions in any current or future Commission block exemption regulation cannot benefit from the market share safe harbour set out in that Notice.[3]

Article 101(1) of the Treaty on the Functioning of the European Union (the Treaty) prohibits agreements between undertakings which may affect trade between Member States and which have as their object or effect the prevention, restriction or distortion of competition within the internal market.[4] The distinction between "restrictions by object" and "restrictions by effect" arises from the fact that certain forms of collusion between undertakings reveal such a sufficient degree of harm to competition that there is no need to examine their actual or potential effects.[5] Such types of coordination between undertakings can be regarded, by their very nature, as being harmful to the proper functioning of normal competition.[6] These are restrictions which in the light of the objectives pursued by the Union competition rules are so likely to have negative effects on competition, in particular on the price, quantity or quality of goods or services, that it is unnecessary to demonstrate any actual or likely anti-competitive effects on the market.[7] This is due to the serious nature of the restriction and experience showing that such restrictions are likely to produce negative effects on the market and to jeopardise the objectives pursued by the EU Union competition rules.

In order to determine with certainty whether an agreement reveals a sufficient degree of harm to competition that it may be considered a restriction of competition "by object", regard must, according to the case law of the Court of Justice of the European Union, be had to a number of factors, such as the content of its provisions, its objectives and the economic and legal context of which it forms a part.[8] In addition, although the parties' intention is not a necessary factor in determining whether an agreement restricts competition "by object", the Commission may nevertheless take this aspect into account in its analysis.[9]

The types of restrictions that are considered to constitute restrictions "by object" differ depending on whether the agreements are entered into between actual or potential competitors or between non-competitors (for example between a supplier and a distributor). In the case of agreements between competitors (horizontal agreements), restrictions of competition by object include, in particular, price fixing, output limitation and sharing of markets and customers. As regards agreements between non-competitors (vertical agreements), the category of restrictions by object includes, in particular, fixing (minimum) resale prices and restrictions which limit sales into particular territories or to particular customer groups.[10]

The fact that an agreement contains a restriction "by object", and thus falls under Article 101(1) of the Treaty, does not preclude the parties from demonstrating that the conditions set out in Article 101(3) of the Treaty are satisfied. However, practice shows that restrictions by object are unlikely to fulfil the four conditions set out in Article 101(3).[11]

In exceptional cases, a restriction "by object" may also be compatible with Article 101 of the Treaty not because it benefits from the exception provided for in Article 101(3) of the Treaty, but because it is objectively necessary for the existence of an agreement of a particular type or nature or for the protection of a legitimate goal, such as health and safety, and therefore falls outside the scope of Article 101(1) of the Treaty.[12]

Types of practices that generally constitute restrictions of competition "by object" can be found in the Commission's guidelines, notices and block exemption regulations. These refer to restrictions by object or contain lists of so-called "hardcore" restrictions that describe certain types of restrictions which do not benefit from a block exemption on the basis of the nature of those restrictions and the fact that those restrictions are likely to produce negative effects on the market. Those so called "hardcore" restrictions are generally restrictions "by object" when assessed in an individual case. Agreements containing one or more "by object" or hardcore restrictions cannot benefit from the safe harbour of the De Minimis Notice.

For the purpose of assisting undertakings in their assessment of whether agreements can benefit from the market share safe harbour of the De Minimis Notice, this document lists the restrictions of competition that are described as "by object" or "hardcore" in the various Commission regulations, guidelines and notices, supplemented with some particularly illustrative examples taken from the case law of the Court of Justice of the European Union and the Commission's decisional practice.[13]

This document is without prejudice to any developments in the case law and in the Commission's decisional practice. It does not prevent the Commission from finding restrictions of competition by object that are not identified below. DG Competition intends to regularly update the examples listed below in the light of such further developments that may expand or limit the list of restrictions "by object".

NOTES

1 Notice on agreements of minor importance which do not appreciably restrict competition under Article 101(1) of the Treaty on the functioning of the European Union (De Minimis Notice) OJ C291, 30.08. 2014.

2 See point 23 of the Guidelines on the application of Article 81(3) of the Treaty (OJ C101, 24.4.2004, p 97), (the General Guidelines).

3 See point 13 of the De Minimis Notice.

4 For the purposes of this document, the term "agreements" also includes concerted practices and decisions by associations of undertakings.

5 Judgments of the Court of Justice in Case C-67/13 P *Groupement des Cartes Bancaires v. Commission*, ECLI-:EU:C:2014:2204, paragraph 49; Case C-286/13 P *Dole v Commission*, ECLI:EU:C:2015:184, paragraph 113.

6 See for example the judgments of the Court of Justice in Case C-67/13 P *Groupement des Cartes Bancaires v. Commission*, ECLI:EU:C:2014:2204, paragraph 50; Case C-286/13 P *Dole v Commission*, ECLI:EU:C:2015:184, paragraph 114; Case C-226/11 Expedia ECLI:EU:C:2012:795, paragraph 36 and case law cited.

7 Judgments in Case C-67/13 P *Groupement des Cartes Bancaires v. Commission*, ECLI:EU:C:2014:2204, paragraph 51; Case C-286/13 P *Dole v Commission*, ECLI:EU:C:2015:184, paragraph 115.

8 See the judgments of the Court of Justice in Case C-67/13 P *Groupement des Cartes Bancaires v. Commission*, ECLI:EU:C:2014:2204, paragraph 53; Case C-286/13 *P Dole v Commission*, ECLI:EU:C:2015:184, paragraph 117; Joined Cases C-501/06 P, C-513/06 P, C-515/06 P and C-519/06 P GlaxoSmithKline, ECLI:EU:C:2008:738, paragraph 58; Joined Cases 96/82 to 102/82, 104/82, 105/82, 108/82 and 110/82 IAZ International Belgium and Others ECLI:EU:C:1983:310, paragraph 25; Case C-209/07 Beef Industry Development Society ECLI:EU:C:2008:643, paragraph 16 and Case C-32/11 Allianz Hungária Biztosító Zrt and Others, ECLI:EU:C:2013:160, paragraph 36. For further guidance, see points 19 to 22 of the General Guidelines.

9 See for example the judgments of the Court of Justice in Case C-67/13 P *Groupement des Cartes Bancaires v. Commission*, ECLI:EU:C:2014:2204, paragraph 54; judgment of the Court of Justice in Case C-286/13 P *Dole v Commission*, ECLI:EU:C:2015:184, paragraph 118; Joined Cases C-501/06 P and Others GlaxoSmithKline ECLI:EU:C:2009:610, paragraph 58 and Case C-209/07 Beef Industry Development Society (BIDS) ECLI:EU:C:2008:643, paragraphs 15 et seq.

10 See point 23 of the General Guidelines.

11 See point 46 of the General Guidelines. For an example of how Article 101(3) of the Treaty applies to restrictions by object, see point 225 of the Guidelines on Vertical Restraints (OJ C130, 19.5.2010, p1), (the Vertical Guidelines).

12 See e.g. point 18 of the General Guidelines and points 60, 61 and 62 of the Vertical Guidelines.

13 All Commission's decisions are available at DG Competition's webpage: http://ec.europa.eu/competition under their respective case number. For cases decided by the Court of Justice (case numbers beginning with C- . . .) or the General Court (case numbers beginning with T- . . .), see http://curia.europa.eu. Judgements of national courts and decisions of national competition authorities have not been included in this document.

2. "BY OBJECT" RESTRICTIONS IN AGREEMENTS BETWEEN COMPETITORS

[4.146]
The three classical "by object" restrictions in agreements between competitors are price fixing, output limitation and market sharing (sharing of geographical or product markets or customers).

However, restrictions of that kind may not constitute restrictions "by object" where they are part of a wider cooperation agreement between two competitors in the context of which the parties combine complementary skills or assets. For example, in the context of production agreements, it is not considered a "by object" restriction where the parties agree on the output directly concerned by the production agreement (for example, the capacity and production volume of a joint venture or the agreed amount of outsourced products), provided that other parameters of competition are not eliminated. Another example is a production agreement that also provides for the joint distribution of the jointly manufactured products and envisages the joint setting of the sales prices for those products, and only those products, provided that the restriction is necessary for producing jointly, meaning that the parties would not otherwise have an incentive to enter into the production agreement in the first place. In those scenarios the agreement on output or prices will not be assessed separately, but will be assessed in the light of the overall effects of the entire production agreement on the market.[14]

NOTES

14 For example, in the context of a joint-venture created by competitors, a non-compete clause with respect to the parties' activities after the expiry of the joint-venture agreement in markets where the joint-venture was not active has been considered a restriction "by object" infringing Article 101 of the Treaty, whereas proportionate and objectively necessary non-compete clauses preventing the parties from competing on activities falling within the scope of joint-venture may be considered as not infringing Article 101 (See Case 39736 Siemens/Areva).

2.1. PRICE FIXING

[4.147]

2.1.1. General Principles

Restrictions whereby competitors agree to fix prices of products which they sell or buy are, as a matter of principle, restrictions by object. It is not necessary that the agreement expressly or directly fixes the selling or purchasing price: it is sufficient if the parties agree on certain parameters of the price composition, such as the amount of rebates given to customers.

Joined Cases C-238/99 P, C-244/99 P, C-245/99 P, C-247/99 P, C-250/99 P to C- 252/99 P and C-254/99 P ICI v Commission A cartel in which target prices and target quotas were fixed, and there were concerted initiatives to raise price levels and monitor the operation of the collusive arrangements.
Joined Cases C-125/07 P, C-133/07 P, C-135/07 P and C-137/07 P Österreichische Volksbanken v Commission A cartel in which banks fixed deposit and lending rates.
Case T-208/08 Gosselin Group v Commission A cartel on the international removal services market that related to the direct or indirect fixing of prices, market sharing and the manipulation of the procedure for the submission of tenders.
Joined Cases T-217/03 and T-245/03 French Beef Agreement concluded by federations representing farmers and federations representing slaughterers aimed at fixing minimum prices for the purchase of cows by slaughterers and suspending beef imports.
Case 38549 Architectes Belges Recommended minimum fees (i.e. recommended minimum prices) of a national association of architects. Like fixed prices, recommended prices reduce competition because they facilitate price coordination.

2.1.2. Price Fixing Which Can Benefit from the De Minimis Notice

The following restrictions do not prevent an agreement from benefitting from the safe harbour of the De Minimis Notice:

– In the context of joint purchasing agreements (that is to say, a number of competitors openly coming together to make joint purchases on the market), where the parties agree on the purchasing price that their "joint purchasing arrangement" may pay to its suppliers for the products subject to the supply contract.[15]
– In the context of specialisation agreements (including joint production agreements) covered by Commission Regulation (EU) No 1218/2010, where the parties agree on the fixing of prices charged to immediate customers in the context of joint distribution.[16]

– In the context of research and development (R&D) agreements[17] covered by Commission Regulation (EU) No 1217/2010, where the parties agree on the fixing of prices or the licence fee charged to immediate customers or immediate licensees[18] in those cases where the parties' joint exploitation of the results of the joint R&D includes certain forms of joint distribution of the products, or joint licensing of the technologies or processes, arising out of the joint R&D.[19]

NOTES

15 See point 206 of the Guidelines on the applicability of Article 101 of the Treaty on the Functioning of the European Union to horizontal cooperation guidelines (OJ C11, 14.1.2011, p1), (the Horizontal Guidelines).

16 See Commission Regulation (EU) No 1218/2010 of 14 December 2010 on the application of Article 101(3) of the Treaty on the Functioning of the European Union to certain categories of specialisation agreements (OJ L335, 18.12.2010, p43), Article 4(a).

17 As regards R&D agreements it should be noted that the same hardcore restrictions and exceptions apply regardless of whether the parties are competitors or not.

18 See Commission Regulation (EU) No 1217/2010 of 14 December 2010 on the application of Article 101(3) of the Treaty on the Functioning of the European Union to certain categories of research and development agreements (OJ L335, 18.12.2010, p36), Article 5(c).

19 This only applies to joint distribution or joint licensing as described in Article 1(1) point (m) (i) and (ii) of Commission Regulation (EU) No 1217/2010.

2.2. MARKET SHARING

[4.148]

2.2.1. General principles

Any arrangement by which competitors allocate markets (geographic markets or product markets) or customers is considered a restriction by object if it takes place in the context of a pure market sharing agreement between competitors (that is to say, a cartel not linked to any wider cooperation between the parties). If the conduct of the parties to an agreement (for example, a distribution agreement between actual or potential competitors) shows that their objective was to share the market, that objective may be taken into account in deciding whether the agreement is a restriction by object.[20] Allocation of markets can also be achieved through restrictions on where the parties may sell (actively and/or passively)[21] or through restrictions on production.

Case C-41/96 ACF Chemie farma NV v Commission
A cartel in which undertakings agreed to retain their respective domestic markets and fix prices and quotas for the export of quinine.
Joined cases 29/83 and 30/83 CRAM v Commission
Concerted action on market sharing with a view to protect markets against parallel imports of certain products in the market for zinc (cartel).
Cases T-370/09 GDF Suez v Commission and T-360/09 E.ON Ruhrgas and E.ON v Commission
In the context of an agreement to jointly build a pipeline to import gas into EU Member States, competitors agreed not to sell gas transported over this pipeline in each other's home markets and maintained that market sharing agreement after the liberalisation of the gas market.
Case 39226 Lundbeck
An agreement whereby a competitor pays a significant amount to an actual (or potential) competitor to stay out of a particular market was considered to be a form of market sharing.
Case 39839 Telefónica and Portugal Telecom
A non-compete clause between competitors (in this case a clause between the parties to stay out of each other's activities in a certain geographic area) was seen as market sharing.
Case 39685 Fentanyl
Potential competitors concluded a "co-promotion" agreement (where very little or nothing was done to promote the drug) which provided for significant payments on a monthly basis for as long as the competitor stayed out of the market. This practice was considered a form of market sharing ("market exclusion") since the aim of the agreement was to keep the potential competitor out of the market.

2.2.2. Market sharing which can benefit from the De Minimis Notice

The following restrictions do not prevent an agreement from benefitting from the safe harbour of the De Minimis Notice:

– In the context of R&D agreements covered by Commission Regulation (EU) 1217/10, where parties allocate between them individual tasks (such as production or distribution) or impose restrictions on each other regarding the exploitation of the results (such as restrictions in relation to certain territories or customers), this is not considered a hardcore restriction.[22] Another example would be where the parties agree on the limitation of active sales of the contract products[23], or contract technologies[24], in territories (or to customers) which have been exclusively allocated to one of the parties by way of specialisation in the context of exploitation.[25]

Although passive sales restrictions agreed between the parties to an R&D agreement are considered hardcore restrictions, the requirement to exclusively license the results of the joint R&D to another party is not.[26] The parties may also restrict their freedom to sell, assign or license products, technologies or processes which compete with the contract products or contract technologies during the period for which the parties have agreed to jointly exploit the results.[27]

– As to technology transfer agreements[28] covered by Commission Regulation (EU) 316/2014, the limitation of active and passive sales of the contract products in territories (or to customers) which have been exclusively allocated to one of the parties, if it is part of a non-reciprocal agreement, is not considered a hardcore restriction.[29] Another example would be, in a non-reciprocal agreement, prohibiting a party from producing within the exclusive territory of the other party.[30]

A licensor may have several licensees, where some were already a competitor of the licensor at the time of concluding their license while others were not. In such a scenario, it is not considered a hardcore restriction if, in a non-reciprocal agreement, active sales by a licensee are restricted in order to protect the exclusive territory (or customer group) allocated to another licensee which was not a competitor of the licensor when it concluded its licence.[31] Finally, an obligation on the licensee to produce the contract products only for its own use (provided that the licensee is not restricted in selling the contract products as spare parts for its own products) is not considered a hardcore restriction.[32] The same is true for an obligation on the licensee, in a non-reciprocal agreement, to produce the contract products only for a particular customer, where the licence was granted in order to create an alternative source of supply for that customer (so-called dual sourcing).[33]

NOTES

20 See for example point 236 of the Horizontal Guidelines, describing the competition concerns concerning distribution agreements between competitors in the context of commercialisation agreements.

21 "Active" sales mean actively approaching individual customers by for instance direct mail, including the sending of unsolicited e-mails, or visits; or actively approaching a specific customer group or customers in a specific territory through advertisement in media, on the internet or other promotions specifically targeted at that customer group or targeted at customers in that territory. "Passive" sales mean responding to unsolicited requests from individual customers including delivery of goods or services to such customers. General advertising or promotion that reaches customers in other distributors' (exclusive) territories or customer groups but which is a reasonable way to reach customers outside those territories or customer groups, for instance to reach customers in one's own territory, are considered passive selling. See point 51 of the Vertical Guidelines.

22 Commission Regulation (EU) 1217/10, Article 5(b)(iii). This practice is referred to as "specialisation in the context of exploitation".

23 See Commission Regulation (EU) No 1217/10 Article 1(1)(f), which defines "contract product" as a product arising out of the joint research and development or manufactured or provided applying the contract technologies.

24 See Commission Regulation (EU) No 1217/10 Article 1(1)(e), which defines "contract technology" as a technology or process arising out of the joint research and development.

25 Commission Regulation (EU) No 1217/10, Article 5(e) in conjunction with Article 1(1)(o).

26 Commission Regulation (EU) No 1217/10, Art. 5(d).

27 Commission Regulation (EU) No 1217/10, Art. 5(b)(iv).

28 Technology transfer agreements are agreements whereby a licensor licenses out intellectual property rights to a licensee for the purpose of producing goods or services. See Commission Regulation (EU) No 316/2014 of 21 March 2014 on the application of Article 101(3) of the Treaty on the Functioning of the European Union to categories of technology transfer agreements, (OJ L93, 28/03/2014, p 17), Article 1(c).

29 Article 4(1)(c)(i) of Commission Regulation (EU) No 316/2014. Article 1(d) of Commission Regulation 316/2014 defines "non-reciprocal agreement" as a technology transfer agreement where one undertaking grants another undertaking a technology rights licence, or where two undertakings grant each other such a licence but where those licences do not concern competing technologies and cannot be used for the production of competing products.

30 Article 4(1)(c)(i) of Commission Regulation (EU) No 316/2014.

31 Article 4(1)(c)(ii) of Commission Regulation (EU) No 316/2014.

32 Article 4(1)(c)(iii) of Commission Regulation (EU) No 316/2014.

33 Article 4(1)(c)(iv) of Commission Regulation (EU) No 316/2014.

2.3. OUTPUT RESTRICTIONS

[4.149]

2.3.1. General principles

Competitors agreeing to restrict the volume of their supply or production capacity (either for one or both of the parties) is seen as a restriction of output, which in turn is considered a restriction by object.

Case C-209/07 Beef Industry Development Society (BIDS)
Agreement to reduce production capacity within the context of a cartel on the market for beef and veal

2.3.2. Output restrictions which can benefit from the De Minimis Notice

The following restrictions do not prevent an agreement from benefitting from the safe harbour of the De Minimis Notice:

– As regards production agreements covered by Commission Regulation (EU) No 1218/2010, where the parties agree on the output directly concerned by the production agreement (for example, the capacity and production volume of a joint venture or the agreed amount of outsourced products).[34]

– As regards specialisation (and joint production) agreements covered by Commission Regulation (EU) 1218/2010, provisions on the agreed amount of products in the context of unilateral or reciprocal specialisation agreements or the setting of the capacity and production volume in the context of a joint production agreement. Another example would be the setting of sales targets where the parties have agreed to jointly distribute the products covered by their cooperation.[35]

- As regards R&D agreements covered by Commission Regulation (EU) 1217/2010, the setting of production targets where the contract products are jointly produced,[36] and setting of sales targets where the parties agreed on certain forms of joint distribution of the contract products or joint licensing of the contract technologies.[37]
- For consortia agreements between liner shipping companies covered by Commission Regulation (EU) 906/2009, certain capacity adjustments.[38]
- In technology transfer agreements covered by Commission Regulation (EU) 316/2014, the limitation of output of contract products imposed only on the licensee (either on the licensee in a non-reciprocal agreement or on only one of the licensees in a reciprocal agreement).[39]

NOTES

34 See point 160 of the Horizontal Guidelines.

35 See Commission Regulation (EU) No 1218/2010, Article 4(b).

36 See Commission Regulation (EU) No 1217/2010, Article 5(b)(i).

37 See Commission Regulation (EU) No 1217/2010, Article 5(b) (ii); this only applies for joint distribution or joint licensing as described in Article 1(1) point (m) (i) and (ii) of this regulation.

38 See Commission Regulation (EC) No 906/2009 on the application of Article 81(3) of the Treaty to certain categories of agreements, decisions and concerted practices between liner shipping companies (consortia), Articles 4(2) and 3(2).

39 See Commission Regulation (EU) No 316/2014, Article 4(1)(b).

2.4. BID RIGGING

[4.150]

Bid-rigging occurs when two or more companies agree that, in response to a call for bids or tenders, one or more of them will not submit a bid, withdraw a bid or submit a bid at artificially high prices arrived at by agreement. This form of collusion is generally considered to restrict competition by object. It is a form of price fixing and market allocation which may, for example, take place in the case of public procurement contracts.

Case T-21/99 Dansk Rorindustri v Commission
A cartel agreement between producers of district heating pipes allocating individual projects to designated producers and manipulating the bidding procedure to ensure that the designated producer was awarded the assigned project.

2.5. COLLECTIVE BOYCOTT AGREEMENTS

[4.151]

A collective boycott occurs when a group of competitors agree to exclude an actual or potential competitor. This practice generally constitutes a restriction by object.

Case C-68/12 Protimonopolný úrad Slovenskej republiky v Slovenská sporiteľňa a.s.
Three banks monitored a competitor's activity, conferred with each other and decided, by common agreement, to terminate in a coordinated manner the contracts they had concluded with that competitor.
Case IV/35.691 Pre-insulated pipes
Competitors used norms and standards (agreed on by the industry) to prevent or delay the introduction of new technology which would result in price reductions.
Case T-90/11 Ordre national des pharmaciens (ONP) and Others v European Commission
The association for pharmacists sanctioned groups of laboratories in the market for clinical laboratory testing with the aim of hindering the development of a new business format.

2.6. INFORMATION SHARING – FUTURE PRICES AND QUANTITIES

[4.152]

Information exchanges between competitors of individualised data regarding intended future prices or quantities are considered a restriction by object.[40]

Where information exchange is part of a monitoring or implementation mechanism for an existing cartel it will be assessed as part of that cartel (irrespective of whether it covers current/past or future prices or quantities).

Joined Cases T-25/95, T-26/95, T-30/95 to T-32/95, T-34/95 to T-39/95, T-42/95 to T- 46/95, T-48/95, T-50/95 to T-65/95, T-68/95 to T-71/95, T-87/95, T-88/95, T-103/95 and T-104/95 Cimenteries CBR and Others
Information exchange facilitating implementation of cartel – market for cement.
Case C-286/13 P Dole v Commission
Pre-pricing communications in which undertakings discussed price setting factors relevant to the setting of future quotation prices for bananas.
Case T-380/10 Wabco Europe and Others v Commission
Coordination of price increases and exchange of sensitive business information in a cartel - bathroom fixtures and fittings market.
Case C-8/08 T-Mobile Netherlands BV, KPN Mobile NV, Orange Nederland NV, Vodafone Libertel NV
Information exchange between competitors on future prices to be paid to sales representatives.

NOTES

40 See point 72 to 74 of the Horizontal Guidelines.

2.7. RESTRICTIONS ON CARRYING OUT R&D OR USING OWN TECHNOLOGY

[4.153]

2.7.1. GENERAL PRINCIPLES

Restrictions in agreements between competitors which aim at restricting the parties' ability to carry out R&D or to continue to use their own technology for further R&D are also hardcore restrictions and generally considered a restriction by object.[41]

2.7.2. RESTRICTIONS ON CARRYING OUT R&D OR USING OWN TECHNOLOGY WHICH CAN BENEFIT FROM THE DE MINIMIS NOTICE

The following restrictions do not prevent an agreement from benefitting from the safe harbour of the De Minimis Notice:

– In the context of R&D agreements covered by Commission Regulation (EU) 1217/2010, where the parties agree to restrict their freedom, during the period of the agreement, to carry out, independently or in cooperation with third parties, research and development in the field covered by the R&D cooperation.[42]
– In the context of technology transfer agreements covered by Commission Regulation (EU) No 316/2014, where the parties agree to restrict the licensee's ability to exploit its own technology or the ability of any of the parties to carry out research and development when this is indispensable to prevent disclosure of know-how to third parties.[43]

NOTES

41 Commission Regulation (EU) No 1217/2010, Article 5(a); Commission Regulation (EU) No 316/2014, Article 4(1)(d).
42 Commission Regulation (EU) No 1217/2010, Article 5(a).
43 Commission Regulation (EU) No 316/2014, Article 4(1)(d).

3. "BY OBJECT" RESTRICTIONS IN AGREEMENTS BETWEEN NON-COMPETITORS

[4.154]

Restrictions by object in agreements between non-competitors can be distinguished as to whether they relate to market partitioning by territory and/or customer group or to limitations on the buyer's ability to determine its resale price. The first category can be further divided into restrictions limiting the buyer's freedom to sell and restrictions limiting the supplier's freedom to sell. Moreover, the restrictions by object differ depending on whether they are agreed between a supplier and a buyer or between a licensor and a licensee.

3.1. SALES RESTRICTIONS ON BUYERS

[4.155]

3.1.1. GENERAL PRINCIPLES

A restriction on a buyer as to where (the territory) or to whom (the customers) the buyer can sell the contract products, actively and/or passively,[44] is a hardcore restriction and generally considered a restriction by object.[45] Such a restriction may result from direct obligations on the buyer but also from indirect measures aimed at inducing the buyer not to sell to particular customers or territories, such as refusal or reduction of bonuses or discounts, termination of supply, reduction of supplied volumes, requiring a higher price for products to be exported, limiting the proportion of sales that can be exported, etc.[46] However restrictions which restrict the buyer's place of establishment are not hardcore restrictions.[47]

Case C-70/93 BMW v ALD Autoleasing
A motor vehicle manufacturer with a selective distribution system was prohibiting its authorized dealers from delivering vehicles to independent leasing companies if those companies would make them available to lessees outside the contract territory of the dealer in question.
Joined Cases 32, 36 and 82/78 BMW Belgium v Commission
A motor vehicle manufacturer issued circulars prohibiting its dealers from exporting vehicles to authorized dealers in other countries.
Case C-439/09 Pierre Fabre
A manufacturer of cosmetics and personal care products with a selective distribution system was prohibiting its authorised distributors from selling via the internet.
Case C-551/03 P General Motors BV v Commission
A distribution agreement restricting or prohibiting dealers in one Member State from exporting to consumers in another Member State, not only through direct export prohibitions but also through indirect measures such as a restrictive supply or a bonuses policy which excludes exports to final consumers from retail bonus campaigns.
Case 37975 Yamaha
An obligation on authorised dealers operating in different Member States to sell exclusively to final consumers, with the object of preventing cross supplies within the network of dealers. This restricted dealers from competing for sales to other dealers and impeded trade within the selective distribution network.
Case C-501/06 P GlaxoSmithKline Services v Commission

Part 4 EU & Retained EU Materials

A pharmaceutical company's dual pricing policy according to which higher prices were charged to wholesalers for products to be exported to other Member States was considered to limit parallel trade and partition markets.

3.1.2. Sales restrictions on buyers which can benefit from the De Minimis Notice

The following restrictions do not prevent an agreement from benefitting from the safe harbour of the De Minimis Notice:

- Where a supplier operates an exclusive distribution system and does not at the same time operate a selective distribution system for the same product, it is not a hardcore restriction to prohibit the buyer from actively selling in the territory or to the customer group allocated exclusively to another distributor or reserved for the supplier.[48]
- Within selective distribution systems it is not a hardcore restriction to prohibit authorized distributors, within the territory where the selective distribution system operates, from selling to distributors who are not members of the selective distribution system.[49] This does not apply to restrictions on selected distributors on reselling spare parts for motor vehicles to independent repairers.[50]
- As regards restrictions on the resale of components[51] it is not a hardcore restriction if the buyer is prohibited from selling components, supplied for the purpose of incorporation in another product, to customers who would use them to manufacture the same type of goods as those produced by the supplier. An example would be a situation in which a producer of photocopiers supplies components to a producer of printers for the purpose of incorporating those components into the printers. The producer of photocopiers can prohibit the producer of printers from reselling the components to producers of photocopiers without the risk that the prohibition will be seen as a restriction by object.
- Similarly, it is not a hardcore restriction to prohibit a buyer, who operates as a wholesaler, from reselling passively or actively to end users.[52]

NOTES

44 See footnote 21 for a definition of active and passive sales. See also point 51 of the Vertical Guidelines.

45 See Article 4(b)(i) of Commission Regulation (EU) No 330/2010 of 20 April 2010 on the application of Article 101(3) of the Treaty on the Functioning of the European Union to categories of vertical agreements and concerted practices (OJ L102, 23.4.2010, p1).

46 For further examples, see point 50 of the Vertical Guidelines.

47 This means that the buyer can be required to restrict its distribution outlet(s) and warehouse(s) to a particular address, place or territory. See point 50 of the Vertical Guidelines.

48 See Article 4(b)(i) of Commission Regulation (EU) No 330/2010 and point 51 of the Vertical Guidelines.

49 See Article 4(b)(iii) of Commission Regulation (EU) No 330/2010.

50 See Article 5(a) of Commission Regulation (EU) No 461/2010 of 27 May 2010 on the application of Article 101(3) of the Treaty on the Functioning of the European Union to categories of vertical agreements and concerted practices in the motor vehicle sector (OJ L129, 28.5.2010, p52).

51 The term "component" includes any intermediate goods and the term 'incorporation' refers to the use of any input to produce goods. See Article 4(b)(iv) of Commission Regulation No (EU) 330/2010 and point 55 of the Vertical Guidelines.

52 See Article 4(b)(ii) of Commission Regulation (EU) No 330/2010 and point 55 of the Vertical Guidelines.

3.2. SALES RESTRICTIONS ON LICENSEES

[4.156]

3.2.1. General principles

In the case of technology transfer agreements, it is only restrictions of the licensee's passive sales (and not of its active sales) to a particular territory or customer group that are hardcore restrictions and which are generally considered restrictions by object.[53] However, when the licensee is a member of a selective distribution system and operates at the retail level, restrictions of both the licensee's active and passive sales to end users are hardcore restrictions, without prejudice to the possibility of prohibiting a member of the system from operating out of an unauthorised place of establishment.

Joined Cases C-403/08 and C-429/08 Football Association Premier League and Others

Licence agreement prohibiting or limiting broadcasters from supplying decoder cards to television viewers seeking to watch the broadcasts outside the Member State for which the licence was granted. Such clauses prohibit the broadcasters from effecting any cross-border provision of services and enable each broadcaster to be granted absolute territorial exclusivity in the area covered by its licence.

3.2.2. Sales restrictions on licensees which can benefit from the De Minimis Notice

The following restrictions do not prevent an agreement from benefitting from the safe harbour of the De Minimis Notice:

- to restrict the licensee's passive sales into an exclusive territory or to an exclusive customer group reserved for the licensor.[54]
- to agree with the licensee that the contract products may only be produced for its own use (provided that the licensee is not restricted in selling the contract products actively and passively as spare parts for its own products).[55]
- to agree that the licensee may only produce the contract products for a particular customer, where the licence was granted in order to create an alternative source of supply for that customer (so called dual sourcing).[56]
- to prohibit a licensee operating at the wholesale level from selling to end-users.[57]

– to prohibit members of a selective distribution system from selling to unauthorised distributors.[58]

NOTES

53 However, licensing of copyright for the purpose of reproduction and licensing of trademarks are subject to the rules applicable to vertical restraints.

54 Article 4(2)(b)(i) of Commission Regulation (EU) No 316/2014.

55 Article 4(2)(b)(ii) of Commission Regulation (EU) No 316/2014.

56 Article 4(2)(b)(iii) of Commission Regulation (EU) No 316/2014.

57 Article 4(2)(b)(iv) of Commission Regulation (EU) No 316/2014.

58 Article 4(2)(b)(v) of Commission Regulation (EU) No 316/2014.

3.3. SALES RESTRICTIONS ON THE SUPPLIER

[4.157]
Restrictions, agreed between a supplier of components and a buyer who incorporates those components, on the supplier's ability to sell the components as spare parts to end-users or to repairers or other service providers not entrusted by the buyer with the repair or servicing of its goods, are hardcore restrictions which are generally considered to be restrictions by object.[59]

Certain hardcore restrictions are specific to the motor vehicle sector. A first type may arise in the context of an agreement between a manufacturer of motor vehicles which uses components for the initial assembly of motor vehicles, and a supplier of such components. In this context, restrictions on the supplier's ability to place its trade mark or logo effectively and in an easily visible manner on the components supplied or on spare parts are hardcore restrictions and generally considered restrictions by object.[60] A second type of restrictions specific to the motor vehicle sector may arise in the context of an agreement between a supplier of spare parts, repair tools or diagnostic tools or other equipment and a manufacturer of motor vehicles. In this context, restrictions of the supplier's ability to sell those goods to authorised or independent distributors or to authorised or independent repairers or end users are considered hardcore restrictions.[61]

NOTES

59 Article 4(e) of the Commission Regulation (EU) No 330/2010.

60 Article 5(c) of Commission Regulation (EU) No 461/2010.

61 Article 5(b) of Commission Regulation (EU) No 461/2010.

3.4. RESALE PRICE MAINTENANCE

[4.158]
Restrictions of a buyer's ability to determine its minimum sale price generally constitute restrictions by object. Restrictions imposing maximum sale prices or recommending sale prices are not restrictions by object, provided that they do not amount to fixed or minimum sale prices as a result of pressure from, or incentives offered by, any of the parties.[62]

As regards technology transfer agreements, any restrictions on the licensor's or the licensee's ability to determine their sale prices are hardcore restrictions which are generally considered to be restrictions by object, without prejudice to the possibility of imposing a maximum sale price or recommending a sale price.[63]

Fixing of prices or setting a minimum sale price may be directly imposed by means of a contractual provision but may also result from indirect measures. For example, an agreement may oblige the buyer to add a specific amount or percentage on top of its purchase price to establish its sale price. Similarly, an agreement may require that the buyer complies with maximum discount levels. Such indirect means of vertical price fixing also constitute restrictions by object.

Case 243/83 SA Binon Cie v SA Agence et Messageries de la Presse

Provisions which fix the prices to be observed in contracts with third parties.

Case 37975 Yamaha

Imposition of minimum resale prices on distributors selling musical instruments either directly, by a prohibition on publishing, advertising or announcing prices different from the official price lists, or indirectly, by providing dealers with a formula for calculating their resale prices and with guidelines on recommended retail prices while making clear that advertising and promotion actions with more than 15% rebates would not be considered normal, which *de facto* amounted to an obligation to respect minimum prices.

NOTES

62 Article 4(a) of Commission Regulation (EU) No 330/2010.

63 Article 4(2)(a) of Commission Regulation (EU) No 316/2014.

DG COMPETITION BEST PRACTICES ON THE DISCLOSURE OF INFORMATION IN DATA ROOMS IN PROCEEDINGS UNDER ARTICLES 101 AND 102 TFEU AND UNDER THE EU MERGER REGULATION (JUNE 2015)

[4.159]

NOTES

This document is available on the European Commission website at: ec.europa.eu/competition-policy/antitrust/procedures/data-rooms-and-confidentiality-rings_en.

Note that Council Regulation (EC) No 139/2004 (the EU Merger Regulation) is repealed, in relation to the UK, by the Competition (Amendment etc) (EU Exit) Regulations 2019, SI 2019/93, reg 63, Sch 3, para 1, as from IP completion day (as defined in the European Union (Withdrawal Agreement) Act 2020, s 39) (for transitional provisions and savings in relation to the operation of the 2019 Regulations, see Sch 4 to those Regulations at **[7.69]** et seq).

1 SCOPE AND PURPOSE OF THE DATA ROOM BEST PRACTICES

[4.160]

(1) The purpose of this document (the "Data Room Best Practices") is to provide practical guidance on when and how to use data rooms to disclose in a restricted manner business secrets and other confidential information obtained during proceedings under Articles 101 and 102 TFEU (the "EU Antitrust Rules") and Council Regulation (EC) No 139/2004[1] (the "Merger Regulation"). The document aims at increasing transparency and predictability of the process within the existing legal and procedural framework,[2] thereby enhancing the efficiency of antitrust and merger investigations.

(2) The Data Room Best Practices make no claim to be comprehensive. They are based on the experience that DG Competition has acquired to date and are intended to reflect its current practice. The specific features of an individual case may require an adaptation of, or deviation from this guidance document. The Data Room Best Practices do not create or alter any rights or obligations as set out in the TFEU or relevant secondary legislation as interpreted by the case law of the Union Courts, nor does it alter the Commission's interpretative notices. The Commission may revise the Data Room Best Practices from time to time to reflect changes in legislation, jurisprudence and practice.

(3) The specific legal framework and constraints in proceedings under the Merger Regulation must be taken into account when deciding on when and how to use data rooms to disclose business secrets and other confidential information obtained during such proceedings. Merger proceedings are characterised in particular by their purely administrative nature and the need for speed, given the short and legally binding time limits under which merger investigations must be conducted.

(4) The organisation of data rooms in proceedings under the EU Antitrust Rules is not necessarily subject to the same considerations.[3] The Antitrust Best Practices provide some guidance on the circumstances where, and the conditions under which, a data room may be organised to disclose business secrets and other confidential information obtained in proceedings under the EU Antitrust Rules.[4] The present Data Room Best Practices complement the Antitrust Best Practices and set out further details on the rules applicable to data room procedures.

NOTES

1 Council Regulation (EC) No 139/2004 of 20 January 2004 on the control of concentrations between undertakings, OJ L24, 29.1.2004, p 1-22.

2 The Data Room Best Practices should be read in conjunction with the Merger Regulation, Commission Regulation (EC) No 802/2004 of 21 April 2004 implementing Council Regulation (EC) No 139/2004 on the control of concentrations between undertakings (OJ L133, 30.04.2004, p 1) as amended (the "Merger Implementing Regulation"), the DG Competition Best Practices on the conduct of EC merger proceedings ("Merger Best Practices"), Council Regulation (EC) No 1/2003 of 16 December 2002 on the implementation of the rules on competition laid down in Articles 81 and 82 of the Treaty, OJ L1, 4.1.2003, p 1-25 ("Regulation 1/2003"), Commission Regulation (EC) No 773/2004 of 7 April 2004 relating to the conduct of proceedings by the Commission pursuant to Articles 81 and 82 of the EC Treaty, OJ L123, 27.4.2004, p 18-24 ("Antitrust Implementing Regulation"), the Commission notice on best practices for the conduct of proceedings concerning Articles 101 and 102 TFEU, OJ C308, 20/10/2011, p 6-32 ("Antitrust Best Practices"), the Best Practices for the submission of economic evidence and data collection in cases concerning the application of Articles 101 and 102 TFEU and in merger cases ("Best Practices for the submission of economic evidence"), the Decision 2011/695/EU of the President of the European Commission on the function and terms of reference of the hearing officer in certain competition proceedings (OJ L275, 20.10.2011, p 29) ("Hearing Officers' Terms of Reference") and the Commission Notice on the rules for access to the Commission file in cases pursuant to Articles 81 and 82 of the EC Treaty, Articles 53, 54 and 57 of the EEA Agreement and Council Regulation (EC) No 139/2004 (OJ C325, 22.12.2005, p 7) ("Access to File Notice").

3 These proceedings take place pursuant to Regulation 1/2003 and the Antitrust Implementing Regulation.

4 Point 97 of the Antitrust Best Practices.

2 GENERAL PRINCIPLES ON DATA ROOMS

[4.161]
(5) As part of their procedural guarantees intended to protect the rights of defence, addressees of a Statement of Objections[5] have the right to access the non-confidential version of the Commission's file.[6] The rationale behind access to the Commission's file is to allow the addressees of the Statement of Objections an opportunity, before a decision is taken, to examine the evidence in the Commission's file so that they are in a position to express their views on the conclusions reached in the Statement of Objections on the basis of that evidence and defend themselves against these objections.

(6) In principle, access to the Commission's file is granted by giving the addressees of a Statement of Objections access to an electronic version of all documents contained in the Commission's file, with the exception of internal documents and confidential information (i.e. business secrets and other confidential information).[7]

(7) DG Competition obtains, in the course of its investigation, both quantitative and qualitative information, some of which may serve as evidence underpinning the reasoning in the Commission's Statement of Objections. Data collected from third parties (e.g. cost and price data, sales data, bidding data, margins etc.) often constitute business secrets which are by nature confidential. In particular, if the data are of a quantitative nature, it may not be possible to provide, in a timely manner,[8] a meaningful non-confidential version. Exceptionally, this may also be true for qualitative information (e.g. internal strategy documents of competitors). However, granting access to such data may be necessary in certain circumstances for an effective exercise of the rights of defence.

(8) In accordance with Article 339 TFEU, the Commission has a general duty to protect confidential information that could seriously harm the undertaking if disclosed.[9] Notwithstanding this, in antitrust proceedings confidential information may exceptionally be disclosed when such disclosure is necessary to prove an infringement of Articles 101 or 102 TFEU,[10] or to safeguard the rights of defence of the parties.[11] As regards merger proceedings, pursuant to Article 18(1) of the Merger Implementing Regulation, the Commission may exceptionally consider the disclosure of confidential information necessary for the purpose of the procedure. In merger cases, taking into account the administrative nature of the procedure and the need for speed, the Commission has usually considered such disclosure exceptionally necessary only in relation to information that the Commission relied upon in the Statement of Objections. In antitrust and merger proceedings, confidential information will not be disclosed when the rights of defence of the parties may be effectively exercised on the basis of non-confidential versions of the documents in the Commission's file.

(9) Data rooms are an exceptional tool which can – depending on the circumstances of the individual case – safeguard the rights of defence while respecting the legitimate interests of confidentiality of the undertakings or persons from which the Commission has obtained the information (the "Data Providers"). By means of a data room, documents in the Commission's file are made accessible to an addressee of a Statement of Objections in a restricted manner, i.e. by limiting the number and/or category of persons having access and the use of the information being accessed to the extent strictly necessary for the exercise of the rights of defence.

(10) It is in DG Competition's discretion to decide whether a data room is appropriate in a particular case. DG Competition decides to offer a data room, either on its own motion or upon a request from an addressee of a Statement of Objections, where it considers it to be necessary and proportionate in view of the principles set out above and provided that any legal and practical difficulties can be resolved swiftly in agreement with the addressees of the Statement of Objections and the Data Providers.

(11) In deciding whether a particular case is suitable for a data room procedure, DG Competition will also take into account whether it is appropriate to provide access at that moment in time, having regard to the circumstances of the case at hand, the nature and degree of sensitivity of the information, the progress of the case, the resource implications of operating data rooms, risk of information leaks, and the need for speed.[12] The latter is particularly important in proceedings under the Merger Regulation, in which DG Competition is subject to short, legally binding time limits under which merger proceedings must be conducted.

(12) Access to a data room is subject to compliance with the data room rules, confidentiality undertakings and sanctions in case of non-compliance (see Annex A for the standard data room rules (the "Data Room Rules"), and Annex B for the standard non-disclosure agreement (the "Non-Disclosure Agreement")).

NOTES

5 Issued pursuant to Article 13(2) of the Merger Implementing Regulation or Article 10(1) of the Antitrust Implementing Regulation.

6 See Article 18(1) and (3) of the Merger Regulation, Article 17(1) of the Merger Implementing Regulation, Article 27(2) of Regulation 1/2003 and Article 15(1) and (2) of the Antitrust Implementing Regulation. Throughout the Data Room Best Practices, the term "Commission file" is used as defined in point 8 of the Access to File Notice.

7 See Article 18(3) of the Merger Regulation, Article 27(2), 3rd sentence of Regulation 1/2003 and Article 15(2), 1st sentence of the Antitrust Implementing Regulation.

8 Taking into account the need for an effective application of the competition rules in light of the different legal and procedural frameworks for antitrust and merger proceedings, in particular the need for speed in the latter proceedings.

9 This principle is also endorsed by case law, for instance, in Case T-210/01, General Electric Company v Commission, [2005] ECR II-05575, paragraphs 631 and 650.

10 See Article 15(3) of the Antitrust Implementing Regulation.

11 See also in this context point 24 of the Access to File Notice.

12 See footnote 9.

3 SCOPE OF THE DATA INCLUDED IN THE DATA ROOM

[4.162]

(13) The Commission has organised data rooms in a number of cases, mostly for the disclosure of quantitative data (e.g. individual sales data, price data, cost data, bidding data, margins, etc.) on which the Commission has relied directly or indirectly in its Statement of Objections. In a few exceptional cases, data rooms have also been organised for the disclosure of qualitative data (e.g. internal strategy documents). The same basic principles in terms of purpose and scope apply to both quantitative and qualitative data rooms.

(14) Quantitative data are frequently confidential as they typically comprise sensitive internal strategic information. In addition to confidentiality concerns, an exchange of strategic data between competitors can lead to a reduction of competition, for example, by facilitating collusive practices, by harming consumers or by other means. Furthermore, it often proves impossible or very burdensome for the Data Provider to provide meaningful non-confidential versions in a timely manner,[13] due to the volume of the data and/or the difficulty of producing a non-confidential version with sufficient evidentiary value.

(15) Quantitative data included in a data room should enable the addressees of a Statement of Objections, through their external advisors (the "External Advisors"), to verify the methodology used by the Commission to collect, check the consistency of, manage and analyse, the data used in a Statement of Objections, as well as to replicate and check the robustness of the Commission's analysis. Therefore, software codes that may be necessary for the effective exercise of the rights of defence, in particular insofar as they have been used by the Commission for the purpose of the analysis set out in a Statement of Objections, may be included in a data room upon review by DG Competition.[14]

(16) As set out in Paragraph (13), exceptionally, qualitative confidential documents may also be disclosed to the External Advisors of the addressees of a Statement of Objections through a data room procedure. A qualitative data room may be organised where it is not possible or it is very burdensome for the Data Provider to provide meaningful non-confidential versions of such qualitative documents (for instance internal strategy documents) with sufficient evidentiary value and in a timely manner.[15] The organisation of a data room in these circumstances enables the addressees of the Statement of Objections, through their External Advisors, to verify the evidence in the Commission's file where the disclosure of such confidential information may be necessary for the effective exercise of the rights of defence, in particular insofar as such confidential information is relied upon in the Statement of Objections.

(17) Depending on the specific circumstances of the case, DG Competition may anonymise certain data included in the data room by, for example, translating all documents into the same language,[16] removing their document IDs, changing the currency of economic values, redacting countries and territories, partially aggregating figures or taking any other measure deemed necessary in order to protect the identity and confidentiality of Data Providers and minimise the risk of possible retaliatory measures.

NOTES

13 See footnote 9.

14 Insofar as the software codes are not confidential, they would be disclosed in the ordinary course of access to the Commission's file. The full confidential version of the software codes would also be provided in the data room environment so as to enable replication and verification of the Commission's analysis.

15 See footnote 9.

16 The Commission is under no obligation to provide a translation of documents in the Commission's file (see case T-25/95 et al., Cimenteries, Paragraph 635, and point 46 of the Access to File Notice).

4 ORGANISATION OF DATA ROOMS

4.1 TIMING OF A DATA ROOM

[4.163]

(18) A data room can be organised at any point of time at which access to the Commission's file may be granted (i.e. after the notification of the Commission's Statement of Objections to the parties and before the Advisory Committee).[17] Normally, a data room is organised before the oral hearing.

4.2 DATA ROOM PARTICIPANTS

(19) Because of the sensitive and confidential nature of the data contained in the data room, access to the data room is limited to a restricted group of persons on an "External Advisor only" basis.

(20) The External Advisors are in principle limited to the external economic advisors and/or the external legal counsel of the addressees of a Statement of Objections, depending on the quantitative or qualitative nature of the data room. A predefined number of External Advisors are granted access to the data room, in particular for the purpose of verifying the validity and soundness of the Commission's quantitative analyses adopted in a Statement of Objections, or whether the qualitative evidence on the Commission's file supports the conclusions drawn and the objections raised by it. The purpose of providing access to the data room is strictly limited to enabling the External Advisors to advise their clients, i.e. the addressees of a Statement of Objections, in exercising their rights of defence effectively without however disclosing to their client the confidential information they were able to see.

4.3 DATA ROOM RULES

(21) Every data room organised by DG Competition is subject to DG Competition's Data Room Rules, which must be accepted by the addressees of a Statement of Objections and signed by the External Advisors prior to getting access to the data room.

(22) The Data Room Rules provide that access to the data room is granted under strict confidentiality obligations, increased security measures and appropriate supervision. The standard Data Room Rules are provided in Annex A.

(23) External Advisors shall neither remove data, information or documents from the data room, nor disclose confidential information obtained within the framework of a data room procedure to the addressees of the Statement of Objections or any third party. It is in the first place for the External Advisors to ensure that they comply with any relevant professional conduct rules and that they are able to operate on this basis, including obtaining waivers in relation to such rules from their clients where necessary.

(24) Similarly, an addressee of a Statement of Objections must never request nor receive any confidential information derived from the data room by its External Advisor(s). Only a non-confidential data room report may be provided by the External Advisors to the addressees of a Statement of Objections (see section 4.4 below).

(25) DG Competition will make available to the External Advisors the technical equipment to enable the latter to prepare the data room report. The External Advisors will have a predefined number of secure computer workstations at their disposal, managed by DG Competition and equipped with the necessary software and the relevant data sets, as the case may require. The computer workstations will be backed-up daily to ensure business continuity. To facilitate collaboration among External Advisors in the data room, a secured, shared collaborative space is set up in the PC workstations provided by DG Competition. The data room is open for the number of days and during the working hours agreed with DG Competition (taking into account the need for speed), and set out explicitly in the Data Room Rules.

(26) External Advisors may bring additional computer codes, paper material or text in electronic format in the data room (e.g. handwritten, printed notes or electronic text files, a copy of the Statement of Objections etc.), that may be necessary for the verification of the Commission's analysis and the preparation of the data room report. Paper material brought into the data room by the External Advisors may be reviewed by DG Competition's officials at any time. Such documents may not, under any circumstances, be taken out of the data room and shall be destroyed at the end of the data room procedure.

(27) During the course of the data room procedure, External Advisors may (i) take notes on, copy or otherwise replicate the data, and (ii) print documents, on pre-numbered blank pages provided by DG Competition. All printouts and notes may be reviewed by DG Competition's officials at any time. Any such printouts and notes may not, under any circumstances, be taken out of the data room and shall be destroyed at the end of the data room procedure.

(28) No external communication in any form is allowed. The data room will be monitored at all times. External Advisors may not carry any electronic device, camera, mobile phone or other communication or recording device while they are in the data room.

(29) In addition, the Data Room Rules determine:

— the scope of the data included in the data room and any potential restrictions on its use,
— the equipment that will be made available,
— the duration and opening hours of the data room,
— the premises where the data room will be organised,
— the conditions under which access to the data room will be granted,
— the sanctions for non-respect of the Data Room Rules, and
— any other terms to which the data room will be subject in the individual case.

(30) Prior to getting access to the data room, the External Advisors must also sign the Non-Disclosure Agreement. The Non-Disclosure Agreement sets out the obligations and liabilities of the persons accessing the data room. In particular, by signing the Non-Disclosure Agreement, the External Advisors undertake, inter alia, to use the confidential data only for the purpose of verifying the Commission's analysis set out in a Statement of Objections, as described in paragraphs (15)–(16), and of drafting a non-confidential report in that respect.

4.4 DATA ROOM REPORT

(31) After having obtained access to the data room, and only during access to the data room, External Advisors may prepare a data room report (the "Data Room Report"). The Data Room Report is the only means through which the External Advisors may communicate to and discuss the data in the data room with the addressees of the Statement of Objections (their clients), to which the latter would not have otherwise obtained access.[18]

(32) The Data Room Report contains the findings and conclusions of the External Advisors regarding their assessment of data relevant for the exercise of their client's rights of defence, as described in paragraphs (15)–(16). As a general rule, the analysis of quantitative data carried out by the External Advisors must be replicable by the Commission.[19] In particular, any analysis underlying findings or conclusions in the Data Room Report shall be documented and identified by the External Advisors.

(33) The Data Room Report must only contain non-confidential information. At the end of the data room procedure, DG Competition will review and approve the Data Room Report that has been prepared and finalised by the External Advisors to ensure that it does not contain any business secrets and other confidential information.[20] Only upon its approval, DG Competition will send each addressee of the Statement of Objections the individual Data Room Report prepared by their respective External Advisors.

(34) The External Advisors shall not remove any data, information or documents from the data room, even if such data, information or documents do not contain business secrets and other confidential information.

(35) It is not possible to claim Legal Professional Privilege or other kind of privilege protection vis-à-vis any part of the Data Room Report to be provided to the addressees of the Statement of Objections.

(36) During access to the data room, the External Advisors may decide to prepare and address to the Commission a non-redacted, confidential version of the Data Room Report for the sole purpose of explaining in more detail how the External Advisors have conducted their calculations and have reached their findings and conclusions contained in the Data Room Report. In such case, the External Advisors shall explain the differences between both versions of the Data

Room Report, highlighting in the non-redacted, confidential version of the Data Room Report any confidential information or results. The non-redacted, confidential version of the Data Room Report will be registered in the Commission's file, will remain in the sole possession of the Commission, and will not be made accessible to the addressees of the Statement of Objections.

4.5 SANCTIONS FOR NON-RESPECT OF THE DATA ROOM RULES

(37) By signing the Non-Disclosure Agreement and agreeing to the Data Room Rules, the External Advisors recognise their rights and obligations stemming from the data room procedure. If any of the rules or obligations are not respected by any of the External Advisors, all of the relevant party's External Advisors will be immediately requested to leave the data room.

(38) In addition, the Commission and the Data Providers may take all appropriate legal action in case of breach of the Data Room Rules and/or the Non-Disclosure Agreement, including but not limited to damage actions. The Commission may also inform the relevant law bar associations or other professional associations, as appropriate, of a violation of the applicable deontological or professional conduct rules.[21]

NOTES

17 See points 26 to 28 of the Access to File Notice, Article 15(1) of the Antitrust Implementing Regulation and Articles 53, 54 and 57 of the Merger Regulation.

18 For the avoidance of doubt, where External Advisors acting for multiple addressees of the Statement of Objections are granted access to a data room, only one Data Room Report may be prepared for each of the addressees of the Statement of Objections by their respective External Advisors during access to the Data Room.

19 It is the External Advisor's responsibility to ensure replicability as described by the Commission's Best practices. See Best Practices for the Submission of Economic Evidence and Data Collection in Cases Concerning the Application of Articles 101 and 102 TFEU and in Merger cases.

20 During the review of the Data Room Report, further redactions may be made by DG Competition to protect third party business secrets and other confidential information, before the Data Room Report is approved by DG Competition.

21 See point 48 of the Access to File Notice.

5 INVOLVEMENT OF DATA PROVIDERS IN A DATA ROOM PROCEDURE

[4.164]

(39) Following a request to organise a data room by the addressees of a Statement of Objections, DG Competition will inform the Data Providers in writing and seek to obtain their consent. DG Competition will identify the information to be disclosed and provide the reasons for the proposed disclosure. The Commission will set a time period during which the Data Provider may submit any written comments.[22]

(40) Data Providers will be able to express any potential concerns in relation to the data room procedure, for example concerns about potential retaliatory measures from the addressees of a Statement of Objections, having the opportunity to consult the Data Room Rules and the Non-Disclosure Agreement and provide feedback, as well as to review the list of External Advisors for the purpose of identifying any potential conflicts of interest.

(41) DG Competition may implement measures to address such concerns. For instance, if the Data Providers are concerned about potential retaliatory measures from the addressees of a Statement of Objections, DG Competition may anonymise relevant variables,[23] or aggregate certain data to the extent that such altered data would still afford the addressees of a Statement of Objections an adequate opportunity to exercise their rights of defence.

(42) DG Competition aims at reconciling the opposing interests of the addressees of a Statement of Objections and those of Data Providers in good faith, while expediting the proceedings to the extent possible.

(43) At any point during the course of the data room, the Data Providers' legal counsel, at their request, may be allowed access to the data room for the sole purpose of ensuring that appropriate safeguards are in place.

NOTES

22 See Article 8(1) of Hearing Officers' Terms of reference.

23 See Paragraph (17).

6 ROLE OF THE HEARING OFFICER

[4.165]

(44) In case of persisting disagreement between DG Competition and the addressees of a Statement of Objections,[24] or the Data Provider,[25] in relation to the disclosure of confidential information, including via a data room, the matter may be brought before the Hearing Officer.[26] Addressees of a Statement of Objections can, if they believe that further access is necessary for exercising their right to be heard, address the matter to the Hearing Officer, after DG Competition has first dealt with it.[27] This is also the case for Data Providers, should they object to the disclosure of information which they consider to be confidential.

(45) The Hearing Officer may take a decision on the basis of Articles 7 and 8 of the Hearing Officers' Terms of Reference, respectively, including the ordering of the disclosure of confidential information in a data room under the conditions laid down in Article 8(4) of the Hearing Officers' Terms of Reference.

NOTES

24 See Article 7(1) of the Hearing Officers' Terms of Reference.

25 See Article 8(2) of the Hearing Officers' Terms of Reference.

26 As set out in recitals 8 and 15 to the Hearing Officers' Terms of Reference, the Hearing Officer acts as an independent arbiter between DG Competition and the respective parties to solve disputes about access to the Commission's file and the protection of business secrets and other confidential information.

27 See Article 3(7) of the Hearing Officers' Terms of Reference.

ANNEX A: STANDARD DATA ROOM RULES

TERMS OF DISCLOSURE OF BUSINESS SECRETS AND OTHER CONFIDENTIAL INFORMATION ON "EXTERNAL ADVISOR ONLY" BASIS ("DATA ROOM RULES")

[4.166]

Case [M.XXXX/AT.XXXXX] - [CASE NAME]

Within the framework of access to the Commission's file granted to [Names of Party/Parties to which data room access is granted through their External Advisors] in Case [M.XXXX/AT.XXXXX] - [CASE NAME] pursuant to [Article 27(1) and (2) of Council Regulation (EC) No 1/2003[1] / Article 18(3) of Council Regulation (EC) No 139/2004 (the "Merger Regulation")],[2] DG Competition makes available a room at its premises at Place Madou / Madouplein 1, 1210 Saint-Josse-ten-Noode / Sint-Joost-ten-Node, Brussels (the "Data Room") to the [external economic advisors and/or external legal counsel] (the "External Advisors") instructed by [Names of Party/Parties to which data room access is granted through their External Advisors] (the "[Party/Parties]") to the investigation in Case [M.XXXX/AT.XXXXX]. The [Party/Parties], [requested/accepted the] data room procedure by email dated [Date of email].

The Data Room contains information which DG Competition considers to constitute business secrets and other confidential information within the meaning of Article 339 TFEU, [Article 27(2) of the Council Regulation (EC) 1/2003, and Articles 15(2) and 16(1) of the Commission Regulation (EC) 773/2004[3] / Article 18(3) of the Merger Regulation and Article 17(3) of the Commission Implementing Regulation (EU) No 1269/2013[4]] (the "Data", as specified in Annex 1 of these Data Room Rules), and therefore will exceptionally be made available within the framework of the data room procedure and under the strict conditions set out in these Data Room Rules.

As set out in the Data Room Best Practices,[5] DG Competition may exceptionally, having balanced the effective exercise of the Parties' rights of defence with the legitimate confidentiality interests of Data Providers, disclose specific information for the sole purpose of allowing the External Advisors an opportunity to better understand the evidence relied upon by DG Competition relating to [Explanation of data contained in data room] so that they can respond to DG Competition's Statement of Objections on behalf of [Name of the Party]. Further disclosure of the Data seen in the Data Room without the written prior agreement of DG Competition is strictly forbidden.

It remains at DG Competition's absolute discretion to conduct a data room, as an exceptional tool of granting access to the Commission's file, in very limited circumstances where it is not possible or very burdensome for the Data Provider to provide meaningful non-confidential versions of part of the Commission's file with sufficient evidentiary value in a timely manner.[6] Business secrets and other confidential information that is not necessary for the exercise of the rights of defence or whose evidentiary value can be disclosed in an alternative way shall be left outside the scope of data included in a data room to avoid unnecessary exposure of the Data Provider's confidential information.

The Data Room Rules apply to the External Advisors and are set up in order to ensure the legitimate protection of the [Data Provider(s)]'s business secrets and other confidential information collected by the Commission within the framework of its on-going investigation in the above referenced case.

The External Advisors and any person who belongs to the team of such External Advisors are required to agree to these Data Room Rules and sign the attached Non-Disclosure Agreement prior to obtaining access to the data room and the Data thereof. The External Advisors and any person who belongs to the team of such External Advisors commit to respect the letter and the spirit of the following conditions.

Prior to obtaining access to the Data, the External Advisors will make available to the case team (contact: contact person, tel: +xxxxx) the name, the number of a valid identity document (passport or identity card), the job title and employer of each member of the External Advisors team who will access the data room. The External Advisors shall not exceed [number of persons] persons. The identity of the External Advisors will be disclosed to Data Providers before access is given to the Data Room.

These persons only will be allowed access to the Data Room. The usual rules for access to Commission buildings apply. A visitor's badge will have to be worn visibly at all times. In order to speed up the access procedures, the Parties will have to inform the DG Competition case team in advance and in writing (preferably by e-mail) of the composition of the External Advisors team that will be present on a specific date.

Entry to the Data Room, conduct within it and use of the Data are subject to these rules and to suitable undertakings being given to DG Competition, to which these rules will be attached:

1 EQUIPMENT

(1) In the Data Room, [number] PC workstation[s] will be made available with the following technical specifications:

(a) [Word Processing Software (with an equation editor) / Spreadsheet Processing Software / PDF Reader Software].

(b) [Data Analysis and Statistical Software].

(2) [This/These] PC workstation[s] [is/are] made available for the purpose of allowing the External Advisors an opportunity to [verify the evidence in the Commission's file where the disclosure of such confidential information may be necessary for the effective exercise of the rights of defence, in particular insofar as such confidential information is relied upon in the Statement of Objections/verify the methodology used by the Commission to collect, check the consistency of, manage and analyse, the data used in a Statement of Objections, as well as to replicate and check the robustness of the Commission's analysis] and of drafting the Report for the Parties (see section 3 of these Data Room Rules).

(3) No external storage medium will be available to the External Advisors.

Part 4 EU & Retained EU Materials

(4) A local printer with numbered blank pages [and a local network connecting the PC workstations and the printer] will also be made available.

2 THE CONDITIONS OF ACCESS TO THE DATA

(5) The Data will be made available to the External Advisors in electronic form. The PC workstation[s] will have access to a specific folder in which there will be a number of read-only files for review by the External Advisors. The computer workstations will be backed-up daily to ensure business continuity. To facilitate collaboration among External Advisors in the data room, a secured, shared collaborative space is set up in the PC workstations provided by DG Competition.

(6) External Advisors may bring additional computer codes, paper material or text in electronic format in the data room (e.g. handwritten, printed notes or electronic text files, a copy of the Statement of Objections etc.), that may be necessary for the verification of the Commission's analysis and the preparation of the data room report. Paper material brought into the data room by the External Advisors may be reviewed by DG Competition's officials at any time. Such documents may not, under any circumstances, be taken out of the data room and shall be destroyed at the end of the data room procedure.

(7) During the course of the data room procedure, External Advisors may (i) take notes on, copy or otherwise replicate the data and (ii) print documents, on pre-numbered blank pages provided by DG Competition. All printouts and notes may be reviewed by DG Competition's officials at any time. Any such printouts and notes may not, under any circumstances, be taken out of the data room and shall be destroyed at the end of the data room procedure.

(8) The External Advisors shall proactively activate and in any event not obstruct the logging functionality of the software made available to them in the Data Room. An automatically generated log with all manipulations and related actions performed on the Data shall be kept in the hard drive of the computer where such manipulations and related actions were performed. Furthermore, any file created/edited in the context of all manipulations and related actions performed on the Data shall be left stored in the hard drive of the computer where such manipulations and related actions were performed.

(9) No external communication in any form is allowed. The External Advisors are not allowed to carry any electronic device, camera, mobile phone or other communication or recording device while they are in the data room. The External Advisors agree that they can be searched at any time between each entry in and exit from the Data Room. Any device, such as mobile phones or other handheld/mobile wireless devices, laptops, PDAs, voice recorders, cameras, CDs, DVDs, USB sticks and the like, will be locked away and returned upon exit from the Data Room (or at the end of the day).

(10) The data room will be monitored at all times. Anyone leaving the Data Room, while on DG Competition premises will be accompanied by Commission staff.

3 REPORTING TO THE [PARTY/PARTIES] OR TO THE COMMISSION

(11) A non-confidential data room report (the "Data Room Report") is the only means through which the External Advisors may communicate to and discuss the data in the data room with the addressees of the Statement of Objections ([Party/Parties]).[7]

(12) The Data Room Report contains the findings and conclusions of the External Advisors regarding their assessment of the data consulted, which are relevant for the exercise of their client's rights of defence, as described in paragraph (2).

(13) The Data Room Report must only contain non-confidential information. At the end of the data room procedure, DG Competition will review and approve the Data Room Report that has been prepared and finalised by the External Advisors to ensure that it does not contain any business secrets and other confidential information.[8] Only upon its approval, DG Competition will send each addressee of the Statement of Objections the individual Data Room Report prepared by their respective External Advisors.

(14) The External Advisors shall not remove any data, information or documents from the data room, even if such data, information or documents do not contain business secrets and other confidential information.

(15) It is not possible to claim Legal Professional Privilege or other kind of privilege protection vis-à-vis any part of the Data Room Report to be provided to the addressees of the Statement of Objections.

(16) During access to the data room, the External Advisors may decide to prepare and address to the Commission a non-redacted, confidential version of the Data Room Report for the sole purpose of explaining in more detail how the External Advisors have conducted their calculations and reached their findings and conclusions contained in the Data Room Report. In such case, the External Advisors shall explain the differences between both versions of the Data Room Report, highlighting in the non-redacted, confidential version of the Data Room Report any confidential information or results included in the non-redacted, confidential version of the Data Room Report. The non-redacted, confidential version of the Data Room Report will be registered in the Commission's file, will remain in the sole possession of the Commission, and will not be made accessible to the addressees of the Statement of Objections.

4 DURATION OF THE DATA ROOM ACCESS

(17) The Data Room will be open for an initial period of [XX] working day[s] from 9h00 to 18h00 CET.

5 POSSIBLE PRESENCE OF [DATA PROVIDER]'S LEGAL COUNSEL

(18) At any point during the course of the Data Room procedure, [Data Provider(s)]'s legal counsel, at their request, may be allowed access to the Data Room for the sole purpose of verifying that appropriate safeguards are in place.

6 SANCTIONS

(19) By signing the Non-Disclosure Agreement and agreeing to the Data Room Rules, the Notifying Parties' External Advisors recognise their rights and accept the obligations stemming from the data room procedure. In case any of the rules or obligations is not respected by any of the Notifying Parties' External Advisors, all Data Room participants of the relevant party will be immediately requested to leave the data room.

(20) In addition, the Commission and the Data Providers shall take all appropriate legal action in case of breach of these Data Room Rules and/or Non-Disclosure Agreement, including but not limited to damage actions. The Commission shall also inform the relevant law bar associations or other professional associations, as appropriate, of a violation of the applicable deontological or professional conduct rules.

Date...... Name...... Signature......

NOTES

1 Council Regulation (EC) No 1/2003 of 16 December 2002 on the implementation of the rules on competition laid down in Articles 81 and 82 of the Treaty, OJ L 1, 4.1.2003, p 1-25.

2 Council Regulation (EC) No 139/2004 of 20 January 2004 on the control of concentrations between undertakings, OJ L 24, 29.1.2004, p 1-22.

3 Commission Regulation (EC) No 773/2004 of 7 April 2004 relating to the conduct of proceedings by the Commission pursuant to Articles 81 and 82 of the EC Treaty, OJ L 123, 27.4.2004, p 18 -24.

4 Commission Implementing Regulation (EU) No 1269/2013 of 5 December 2013 amending Regulation (EC) No 802/2004 implementing Council Regulation (EC) No 139/2004 on the control of concentrations between undertakings, OJ L 336, 14.12.2013, p 1-36.

5 Best Practices on the disclosure of information in data rooms in proceedings under Articles 101 and 102 TFEU and under the EU Merger Regulation (the "Data Room Best Practices").

6 Taking into account the need for an effective application of the competition rules in light of the different legal and procedural frameworks for antitrust and merger proceedings, in particular the need for speed in the latter.

7 For the avoidance of doubt, where External Advisors acting for multiple addressees of the Statement of Objections are granted access to a data room, only one Data Room Report can be prepared for each of the addressees of the Statement of Objections by their respective External Advisors during the Data Room access period.

8 During the review of the Data Room Report, further redactions may be made by DG Competition to protect third party business secrets and other confidential information, before the Data Room Report is approved by DG Competition.

ANNEX B: STANDARD NON-DISCLOSURE AGREEMENT

NON-DISCLOSURE AGREEMENT

[4.167]

Case [M.XXXX/AT.XXXXX] - [CASE NAME]

Whereas I, the undersigned,

Declare that I have been engaged as an external advisor by [Names of Party/Parties to which data room access is granted through their External Advisors] (the "[Party/Parties]") in connection with the Case [M.XXXX/AT.XXXXX] - [CASE NAME] and I am duly authorised by the same to make the below undertakings;

Whereas the Commission has, for the sole purpose of enabling the external [economic advisor/legal consultant] of the [Party/Parties] to verify the validity of its data analysis, made available a data room containing data collected from [Names of Data Provider(s)] (the "Data [Provider/Providers]") during the course of its investigation that have been used by the Commission in the analysis presented in the Statement of Objections (the "Data", as specified in Annex 1 of the Terms of Disclosure of Business Secrets and other Confidential Information on "External Advisor Only" basis (the "Data Room Rules"));

Whereas, for the purpose of verifying the validity of the Commission's analysis in the Statement of Objections, the [Party has/Parties have] released me from my professional duties and obligations I have towards the Notifying Parties, as their appointed external [economic advisor/legal consultant] in the above referenced proceeding, to disclose all relevant Data to my clients;

Whereas the Data constitute business secrets and other confidential information and must not be disclosed under any circumstances to the [Party/Parties] or to any other third party;

Therefore, I solemnly undertake:

(i) to use the Data solely for the preparation of a data room report (the "Data Room Report") addressed to the [Party/Parties], and if necessary of a non-redacted, confidential version of the Data Room Report addressed to the Commission (according to Section 3 of the Data Room Rules) containing my findings and conclusions on [the validity and soundness of the Commission's quantitative analyses adopted in the Statement of Objections / whether the qualitative evidence on the Commission's file supports the objections raised by it];

(ii) not to copy (in any format, physical, digital or otherwise) or remove any Data from the data room, and to fully abide by the procedures set forth in the attached Data Room Rules;

(iii) not to disclose, transmit, communicate or make the Data provided by the Data Providers or contained in the Data Room Report (or any observations, comments, inferences or conclusions drawn from such Information or such Data Room Report) available in any manner, shape or form to any other person (including the [Party/Parties]) other than as provided in paragraph (v) below;

(iv) to ensure that the Data Room Report does not contain any business secrets and other confidential information supplied by the Data Providers, and does not in any way reveal any such business secrets and other confidential information, whether directly, indirectly or by implication;

(v) to provide the Data Room Report to DG Competition, prior to its communication to the [Party/Parties], in order to verify that no business secrets and other confidential information have been copied or otherwise revealed;

(vi) to duly and promptly inform DG Competition of any breaches of these undertakings, whether as a result of my actions or failings or the actions of others, as soon as I become aware of them; and

(vii) to procure the full compliance with the terms of this agreement by any and all persons who work with me in any capacity in reviewing and analysing the Data in the data room and/or preparing the Data Room Report, and to provide a list of all such persons to DG Competition and their signed acceptance of the terms of this agreement.

Name:

Function:

Date:

Place:

COMMISSION STANDARD ANNEX: GUIDANCE ON CONFIDENTIALITY CLAIMS DURING COMMISSION ANTITRUST PROCEDURES[1]

(Version 2018)

[4.168]

NOTES

This document is available on the European Commission website at: ec.europa.eu/competition-policy/antitrust/procedures/access-file_en. See *Standard annex on business secrets and other confidential information.*

1 This guidance concerns confidentiality claims vis à vis parties of the proceedings. Note that there is distinct guidance on confidentiality in view of preparation of public versions of Commission decisions and related publications. With effect from 1 December 2009, Articles 81 and 82 of the EC Treaty have become Articles 101 and 102, respectively, of the Treaty on the Functioning of the European Union ("TFEU"). The two sets of provisions are, in substance, identical. In regulations and notices adopted before the 1 December 2009, references to Articles 81 and 82 of the EC Treaty should be understood as references to Articles 101 and 102 of the TFEU.

[4.169]

(1) If an investigation leads to adoption of a Statement of Objections, the Commission grants access to documents that DG Competition has obtained, produced and/or assembled during the course of its investigation. Access to that file is granted upon request and only to those undertakings/associations of undertakings to which a Statement of Objections is addressed.[2] If the Commission has decided in a cartel case to pursue a settlement procedure, the Commission will disclose information in its file to the parties that are engaged with it in settlement discussions.[3]

(2) The right of access to the file does not extend to the parts of the file that contain business secrets or other confidential information, or to internal documents of the Commission or of the competition authorities of the Member States (nevertheless, see also paragraph (26) below).[4]

(3) Access to the file is granted on condition that the information thereby obtained may be used only for the purposes of judicial or administrative proceedings for the application of Article 101 or 102 TFEU.[5]

(4) Undertakings, associations of undertakings and persons must indicate business secrets and other confidential information in submissions and/or documents in the Commission's file that originate from them.[6] This obligation extends also to observations that addressees of a Statement of Objections may submit.

(5) In certain circumstances the Commission may decide to grant access to documents in the file also at other stages of the proceedings. In particular the Commission may decide to grant access to key submissions in antitrust proceedings other than cartel proceedings, or to written replies to the Statement of Objections. If that would be the case, the Commission would take into account genuine concerns regarding confidentiality, including fears of retaliation, before granting any access.[7]

(6) This document provides guidance for identifying business secrets and other confidential information and outlines the manner in which the non-confidential versions must be submitted. If you do not to comply with this guidance, the Commission may assume that your submissions/documents do not contain any business secrets or other confidential information[8] and, that therefore you have no objections to the disclosure of that information.

(7) This guidance document does not replace the respective provisions in EU law concerning professional secrecy and claims for confidentiality.[9]

NOTES

2 Article 15 of Commission Regulation (EC) No 773/2004, OJ L123, 27.4.2004, p 18.

3 Article 10(a)(2) of Regulation 773/2004; paragraphs 15 and 16 of the Commission Notice on the conduct of settlement procedures in cartel cases, OJ C167, 2.7.2008, p 1.

4 Articles 27 and 28 of Council Regulation (EC) No 1/2003, OJ L1, 4.1.2003, p 1; Articles 15(2) and 16 of Regulation No 773/2004; point 10 of the Commission Notice on the rules for access to the Commission file in cases pursuant to Articles 81 and 82 of the EC Treaty, Articles 53, 54 and 57 of the EEA Agreement and Council Regulation (EC) No 139/2004, OJ C325, 22.12.2005, p 7 ("Notice on access to file"). See also Joined Cases C-204/00 P, C-205/00 P, C-211/00 P,

C-213/00 P, C-217/00 P and C-219/00 P Aalborg Portland and Others/Commission, EU:C:2004:6, [2004] ECR I-123, paragraph 68.

5 See Articles 16(a) of Regulation No 773/2004, as modified by Regulation 2015/1348; Point 48 of the Notice on access to file.

6 Article 16 of Regulation No 773/2004.

7 See in this regard paragraphs 71-74 and 103 of the Commission Notice on best practices for the conduct of proceedings concerning Articles 101 and 102 TFEU, OJ C308, 20.10.2011 ("Best Practices"), p 6–32.

8 Article 16(4) of Regulation No 773/2004.

9 Article 339 TFEU, Regulation No 1/2003, Regulation No 773/2004 and the Notice on access to file.

I. WHAT MAY CONSTITUTE BUSINESS SECRETS AND OTHER CONFIDENTIAL INFORMATION

[4.170]

(8) EU legislation on proceedings pursuant to Articles 101 and 102 of the TFEU foresees that information shall not be communicated or made accessible by the Commission in so far as it contains **business secrets** or **other confidential information** of a person.[10]

(9) **Business secrets** are confidential information about an undertaking's business activity of which not only disclosure to the public but also mere transmission to a person other than the one that provided the information may seriously harm the latter's interests.[11] Examples of information that may qualify as business secrets include: technical and/or financial information relating to an undertaking's know-how, methods of assessing costs, production secrets and processes, supply sources, quantities produced and sold, market shares, customer and distributor lists, marketing plans, cost and price structure and sales strategy.[12]

(10) **Other confidential information** is information other than business secrets, insofar as its disclosure would significantly harm a person or undertaking. Depending on the specific circumstances of each case, this may apply to information provided by third parties about undertakings which are able to place very considerable economic or commercial pressure on their competitors or on their trading partners, customers or suppliers. The Court of Justice of the European Union has acknowledged that it is legitimate to refuse to reveal to such undertakings certain letters received from their customers, since their disclosure might easily expose the authors to the risk of retaliatory measures.[13] Therefore, the notion of other confidential information may include information that would enable the parties to identify complainants or other third parties where those have a justified wish to remain anonymous. The category of other confidential information also includes military secrets.[14]

(11) In the context of the publication of competition law decisions, it emerges from the case law that, for **information to be regarded as confidential, all the following conditions must be met**: i) such information must be known only to a limited number of persons; ii) its disclosure must be liable to cause serious harm to the person who has provided it or to third parties; and iii) the interests liable to be harmed by the disclosure must be objectively worthy of protection.[15] These principles are applied also in the assessment of confidentiality claims in the context of Statements of Objections, access to the file and final decisions.

(12) Finally, the names of people not involved in the infringement may be considered confidential information to the extent that they constitute personal data which cannot be transferred. As with all redactions, it is up to the undertaking that provided the document to make such confidentiality claims. If such a name remains in a non-confidential version of a document because there was no confidentiality claim with respect to it, the Commission is entitled to infer that 'there is no reason to assume that the data subject's legitimate interests might be prejudiced' pursuant to Article 8 of Regulation no. 45/2001.[16]

NOTES

10 Article 16(1) of Regulation No 773/2004.

11 Case T-353/94 *Postbank NV/Commission*, EU:T:1996:119, [1996] ECR II-921, paragraph 87.

12 Point 18 of the Notice on access to file.

13 The EU Courts have pronounced upon this question both in cases of alleged abuse of a dominant position (Article 102 of the TFEU) (Case T-65/89, *BPB Industries and British Gypsum/Commission*, EU:T:1993:31, [1993] ECR II-389; of the TFEU) (Case T-65/89, *BPB Industries and British Gypsum/Commission*, EU:C:1995:101, [1995] ECR I-865), and in and Case C-310/93P, *BPB Industries and British Gypsum/Commission*, EU:C:1995:101, [1995] ECR I-865), and in merger cases (Case T-221/95 *Endemol v Commission*, EU:T:1999:85, [1999] ECR II-1299, paragraph 69, and Case T-5/02 *Laval/Commission* [2002], EU:T:2002:264, ECR II-4381, paragraph 98 et seq).

14 Points 19-20 of the Notice on access to file.

15 Case T-198/03 *Bank Austria Creditanstalt AG/Commission*, EU:T:2006:136, [2006] ECR II-1429, paragraph 71.

16 OJ L8, 12.1.2001, p 1.

II. WHAT IS NOT CONSIDERED TO BE A BUSINESS SECRET OR OTHER CONFIDENTIAL INFORMATION

[4.171]

(13) The assessment of whether given information contains business secrets or other confidential information has to be done on a case-by-case basis. Information in your submissions/documents that is not covered by the definitions of "business secrets and other confidential information" (see paragraphs (9)-(11)) will not be considered confidential.

(14) In particular, information relating to an undertaking that is already known outside the undertaking (in case of a group, outside the group), or outside the association to which it has been communicated by that undertaking, will usually not be considered as confidential. For information to lose its confidential nature, it is sufficient for it to be available to specialist circles or capable of being inferred from publicly available information.[17]

(15) Information that has lost its commercial importance, for instance due to the passing of time, can also no longer be regarded as confidential. The General Court has considered and ECJ confirmed a period of five years in itself to be sufficient for information to lose its qualification as business secrets or other confidential information.[18] Confidential treatment of information may only be granted to such data exceptionally, if it can be shown that, they still constitute essential elements of the commercial position of the undertaking concerned, notwithstanding their historical nature.[19]

(16) By way of example, the following type of information is usually not regarded as a business secret or other confidential information, unless duly justified (showing the need for their deletion from the accessible part of the file):[20]

— data from and about another undertaking (such as price announcements, sales data, etc). Exceptionally, however, data received pursuant to a contract with another undertaking, which envisages confidentiality, may be considered confidential. General references to a non-disclosure agreement are insufficient to justify the confidentiality of such data;

— information made known outside your undertaking (such as price targets, price increases, dates of implementation of such increases and customer names, especially when these are undertakings);

— facts relating to an application for immunity or a reduction of fines, where these facts aim to provide evidence of an alleged infringement, unless the disclosure of such facts could harm the Commission's leniency policy;

— names and positions of individuals related to the subject matter of the investigation. If the individuals in question were allegedly involved in or received information about the suspected infringement, their names and positions cannot be redacted from accessible versions of the submissions/documents.

(17) It should be noted that **oral corporate statements** that have been supplied in an application for immunity from or a reduction of fines under the Leniency Notice[21] **cannot by definition contain any business secrets or other confidential information**, as they are a presentation of undertaking's knowledge of a cartel and its role therein.[22]

NOTES

17 Order in Case T-89/96 *British Steel/Commission*, EU:T:1997:77, [1997] ECR II-835, paragraphs 26 and 27.

18 See Case T-341/12 *Evonik Degussa GmbH v Commission*, EU:T:2015:51, paragraphs 84-85 and Case C-162/15 P *Evonik Degussa GmbH v Commission*, paragraphs 64-67.

19 See, for example, Order in Case T-271/03 *Deutsche Telekom/Commission*, EU:T:2006:163, [2006] ECR II-1747, paragraph 45.

20 See, for example, point 19 of the Notice on access to file.

21 Commission notice on immunity from fines and reduction of fines in cartel cases, OJ C298, 8.12.2006, p 17 ("the Leniency Notice").

22 See paragraph 31 of the Leniency Notice. The Commission requires leniency applicants to make a declaration to that effect at the time of their leniency application.

III. HOW TO CLAIM CONFIDENTIALITY

[4.172]

(18) For reasons of administrative efficiency, the Commission may ask you to provide first a draft non-confidential version of the submissions/documents, in which the information claimed to be confidential is highlighted but remains legible. After the Commission has provisionally accepted your confidentiality claims, you will be asked to submit a final non-confidential version in which confidential information is blacked out. The Commission reserves the right to reconsider at a later stage in the proceedings its initial evaluation of your confidentiality claims.

— Submit complete non-confidential version to each document on which you have confidentiality claims

(19) You must submit a non-confidential version for each submission/document on which you claim confidentiality.[23] Standard confidentiality stamps in letterheads from law firms, or automatic disclaimers in e-mails, are not regarded as requests for confidential treatment.

(20) The non-confidential version of your submissions/documents must **mirror the confidential version in terms of the number of pages and its format**. If you claim confidentiality for any parts of a document, you are requested **to provide a non-confidential version of the ENTIRE document.**

— Limit redactions to specific pieces of information

(21) In general, you cannot claim confidentiality for an entire document or whole sections of it. It is normally possible to protect confidential information with limited redactions. Entirely blank or blacked-out pages will not be accepted. As a minimum, leave the headings of the documents and/or the headings of the columns contained in tables and pictures as well as any list of annexes intact.

— Provide reasons for your confidentiality claims and non-confidential summaries

(22) You are required to provide the Commission with all relevant details in order to enable it to assess the confidentiality of a piece of information. Therefore, you are requested to

a. **support each claim** for confidentiality in writing, explaining:

— the reasons why the information in question constitutes a business secret or other confidential information;

— in particular, how the disclosure of this information would cause serious harm to your undertaking or would significantly harm a person or undertaking.

b. **provide a concise but meaningful non-confidential summary** of each piece of information claimed to be confidential.

Standard justifications such as 'business secret' or 'information not known to other party' without any justification will not be accepted. When redacting figures such as market shares or turnover figures you are asked to indicate ranges. Regarding sales and/or turnover data, provide ranges not wider than 20% of the respective total amounts. Relative figures such as market shares (in %) should be indicated in ranges not wider than 5%.

(23) The justifications and the non-confidential summaries for each piece of information claimed to be confidential should be presented in the form of a list. Please see the format below:

EXAMPLE: LIST OF CONFIDENTIALITY CLAIMS[24] [ACCESSIBLE TO ADDRESSEES OF THE SO!]

ID # (if available)	Deletions on page # of original confidential version/paragraph # (please indicate annex # where relevant)	Reasons for confidentiality request	Non-confidential summary

(24) The non-confidential versions of the submissions/documents and the summaries of the redacted information must be drafted in a way as to enable a party entitled to access the non-confidential versions to determine whether the information deleted is likely to be relevant for its defence. **It is therefore very important to provide accurate descriptions, on the basis of which other parties can assess the information and make, if they deem necessary, well-motivated request to the Commission to grant access to information you have claimed to be confidential**.

(25) Please note that, in line with the non-confidential versions of submissions/documents, also the non-confidential summaries and the justifications of your confidentiality claims will need to be made accessible to the parties that are entitled to have access to the file. Therefore, **ensure that the table containing the summaries and the justifications of your confidentiality claims does not contain any confidential information**. Check also that the properties of your electronic documents do not contain any confidential information. The Commission will assume that the summaries and the justifications of your confidentiality claims as well as the properties of your submitted non-confidential versions are non-confidential.

(26) Please note that a piece of information which is considered to be confidential may nevertheless be disclosed, if such disclosure **is necessary to prove an alleged infringement or could be necessary to exonerate a party**.[25]

— Ensure that your non-confidential versions are technically reliable

(27) In access to the Commission's file, the non-confidential versions of your submissions/documents will be made accessible to the parties to the proceedings in the same format in which they were submitted by you. It is your responsibility to ensure that the non-confidential versions provided by you are technically reliable and redacted information cannot be retrieved by any means, including forensic tools. The Commission does not take any responsibility for insufficiently blacked-out non-confidential versions.

— Assessment of further access to file requests, disclosure of confidential information and comparison with your own confidentiality claims regarding your submissions/documents

(28) If you are granted access to the file and thereafter submit a reasoned request for further access to confidential information provided by other undertakings, the Commission will assess whether the need to safeguard the rights of the defence of the parties outweighs the concern to protect confidential information of other parties. In accordance with points 24 and 47 of the Access to File Notice, the Commission will assess whether such information is necessary to prove an alleged infringement ('inculpatory document') or could be necessary to exonerate a party ('exculpatory document').

(29) In assessing any requests you make for further access to information claimed by other parties to be confidential, the Commission will take account of whether these requests are consistent with any claims that you make with respect to your own information.

(30) Where the Commission intends to disclose information that you have claimed to be confidential, you will be granted the possibility to provide a non-confidential version of the document where that information is contained, with the same evidential value as the original document.[26] You can also propose the use of a negotiated disclosure procedure or a data room procedure if you think that such a procedure would better safeguard confidentiality and facilitate the exchange of such confidential information.[27]

NOTES

23 Article 16(2) of Regulation 773/2004.

24 For more details see below "Examples of confidentiality claims: how to provide reasons and non-confidential summaries".

25 Points 24-25 and 42 of the Notice on access to file.

26 Point 25 of the Notice on access to file.

27 Points 95-98 of the Best Practices.

EXAMPLES OF CONFIDENTIALITY CLAIMS: HOW TO PROVIDE REASONS AND NON-CONFIDENTIAL SUMMARIES

[4.173]

During antitrust proceedings companies are requested to provide reasoning for all of their confidentiality claims, along with non-confidential summaries, in a table format containing the headings set out in the table below.

This table provides examples of reasoning for confidentiality request and of non-confidential summaries. Please note that this table is provided as an example and is non-exhaustive.

ID # (if available)	Deletions on page # of original confidential version/ paragraph # (indicate annex # where relevant)	Reasons for confidentiality request	Non-confidential summary
ID 548-34[28]	Pages 1-3	A has ongoing price negotiations with B. Knowledge of its pricing strategy by B would seriously undermine A negotiation positions in ongoing negotiations and for future supply contracts.	Board meeting of [DATE] regarding price strategy towards B
ID 548-39	Page 6	Potential project with competitor of B. Project is still viable. Knowledge of the details of these discussions would impair current and future business opportunities of A.	Internal e-mail correspondence of [DATE] regarding supply in [NAME OF A COUNTRY/ GEOGRAPHIC AREA]
ID 549-22	Page 18	Recent information on production costs, profits or other financial information which are relevant for the current business strategy and commercial relations.	Strategic and commercial information on company A's operations, that includes information on production costs, profits and other financial information
ID 549-22	Page 54-57	Document contains details of A's business strategy and sensitive information on key commercial data which are not publicly known and whose knowledge by supplier B would seriously harm A's business interests and reveal its strategy for B, which would affect A's position in future supply discussions with B.	Internal Management Summary- Chart of [DATE] on volumes, pricing, contract structure and business strategy in [PRODUCT AND GEOGRAPHIC AREA CONCERNED]
ID 549-25	Pages 2-6	Names and/or role/title and/or other personal information enabling the identification of an individual that is not related to the investigation. The disclosure may harm the personal interests of these persons.	"Name of an individual" or "Employee of Company A" or "personal information"
ID 550	-	No confidentiality claimed.[29]	-
ID 551	Pages 2, 5 and 8	The deletions concern an internal assessment of minutes of meetings with B. A has ongoing business relations with B. If revealed, the information will give B insight into A's negotiation strategies, internal assumptions and seriously harm A's position in future supply discussions with B.	Minutes of meetings with B of [DATE]
ID 555	Page 5	Private discussions with individuals not related to the investigation.	Private discussions
ID 600	Pages 2, 4, 5 and 8	Private appointments in the personal agenda of a company's employee.	Private appointments
ID 603	Page 3	Identification details of an employee of a customer who is not related to the investigation.	Identification details of customers' employees not related to the investigation

ID # (if available)	Deletions on page # of original confidential version/ paragraph # (indicate annex # where relevant)	Reasons for confidentiality request	Non-confidential summary
ID 650	Page 1	Names of individuals (other than CEO, brand manager and marketing officer) having participated in an internal meeting where only incidentally it was discussed about issues related to the investigation.	Identification details of employees not related to the investigation
ID 717	Page 12	Internal strategic planning information on quantity and costs of raw materials, contractual obligations, technical processes, patents etc..	Internal strategic planning information
ID 1204	Page 1	Internal discussion on company's financial situation (debt/assets policy terms of finances, salary policy, etc.).	Internal discussion on company's financial situation
ID 1212	Page 18	Information regarding products/services that are not related to the current investigation.	Information regarding [PRODUCT X; SERVICES Z] that are not related to the current investigation
ID 1581	Page 14	Information regarding bilateral commercial relations with a customer (a meeting report), that was not disclosed to other competitors.	Information regarding bilateral commercial relations with a customer

NOTES

28 This is an example of reference to so called collection ID, which contains under one ID number (here 5480) all documents received in the same submission, where each document has received its own individual identification number (here 34).

29 In case you do not claim confidentiality for a document, this should also be explicitly stated in the table as shown above. Alternatively, you can list separately all documents for which you do not claim confidentiality. In any event, you are requested to make an explicit confidentiality waiver for all documents in which you have no confidentiality redactions.

EUROPEAN COMMISSION: THE USE OF CONFIDENTIALITY RINGS IN ANTITRUST ACCESS TO FILE PROCEEDINGS (DECEMBER 2018)

[4.174]

NOTES

This document is available on the European Commission website at: ec.europa.eu/competition-policy/antitrust/procedures/data-rooms-and-confidentiality-rings_en.

1. INTRODUCTION

[4.175]

1. In several recent proceedings, DG Competition has used confidentiality rings and data rooms as a means of providing access to file.[1] The guidance on confidentiality rings set out in this document is based on the experience that DG Competition has acquired to date and is intended to reflect its current practice. It includes a template for a negotiated disclosure agreement for use in confidentiality ring procedures. The specific features of an individual case may require an adaptation of, or deviation from what is set out in this document and the template.

2. This guidance does not create or alter any rights or obligations as set out in the Treaty or relevant secondary legislation as interpreted by the case law of the Union Courts, nor does it alter the Commission's interpretative notices. DG Competition may update this guidance document from time to time to reflect changes in legislation, case law and practice.

NOTES

1 In 2015, DG Competition published Best Practices on the disclosure of information in data rooms on its website. Available via http://ec.europa.eu/competition/mergers/legislation/disclosure_information_data_rooms_en.pdf. These Best Practices are accompanied by standard data room rules: http://ec.europa.eu/competition/mergers/legislation/data_room_rules_en.pdf and a standard non-disclosure agreement: http://ec.europa.eu/competition/mergers/legislation/non_disclosure_agreement_en.pdf

2. ACCESS TO FILE

[4.176]

3. Access to the Commission's file is one of the procedural guarantees intended to protect the rights of the defence.[2]

4. Therefore, before taking decisions on the basis of Articles 7, 8, 23 and 24(2) of Council Regulation (EC) No 1/2003, DG Competition will give addressees of its Statements of Objections (SO) an opportunity to have access to the Commission's file.

5. The Commission Notice on access to file explains the practicalities of access to file.[3] According to this Notice, the SO addressees will be granted access to all documents making up the Commission's file, with the exception of internal documents and confidential information. Access to the file is granted to the addressees after an SO has been notified.

6. Traditionally, DG Competition requests any person providing information for the Commission's file (the information provider) to prepare a non-confidential version of the original documents. In some instances, it may not be possible for the information provider to provide, in a timely manner, a meaningful non-confidential version. However, granting access to such information may be necessary for an effective exercise of the rights of defence.

NOTES

2 Article 41(2)(b) of the Charter of Fundamental Rights, OJ C83, 30.3.2010, p 389 (hereafter "the Charter"); The right of the parties to have access to file is also laid down in Article 27 (1) and (2) of Regulation (EC) No 1/2003 on the implementation of the rules on competition laid down in Articles 81 and 82 of the Treaty, OJ L1, 4.1.2003, p 1 (hereafter "Regulation No. 1/2003"); and Article 15 of Regulation (EC) No 773/2004 relating to the conduct of proceedings by the Commission pursuant to Articles 81 and 82 of the EC Treaty, OJ L123, 27.4.2004, p 18 (hereafter "Regulation No 773/2004"), as amended by Commission Regulation (EU) 2015/1348 of 3 August 2015, OJ L208, 5.8.2015.

3 Commission Notice on the rules for access to the Commission file in cases pursuant to Articles 81 and 82 of the EC Treaty, Articles 53, 54 and 57 of the EEA Agreement and Council Regulation (EC) No 139/2004, OJ C325, 22.12.2005, p 7-15

3. CONFIDENTIALITY RINGS AS A MEANS OF PROVIDING ACCESS TO FILE

[4.177]

7. In accordance with Article 339 TFEU, the Commission has a general duty to protect confidential information. Notwithstanding this, in antitrust proceedings confidential information may exceptionally be disclosed when such disclosure is necessary to prove an infringement of Articles 101 or 102 TFEU,[4] or to safeguard the rights of defence of the parties.[5]

8. Confidentiality rings are a form of negotiated disclosure set out in point 96 of the Commission notice on best practices for the conduct of proceedings concerning Articles 101 and 102 TFEU (hereafter "the Antitrust Best Practices").[6] Through confidentiality rings, DG Competition can safeguard the rights of defence while respecting the legitimate interests in confidentiality of the information providers. In addition, confidentiality rings remove or reduce the burden of preparing non-confidential versions of documents.

9. In a confidentiality ring, an SO addressee, who is entitled to access to documents in the Commission's file, agrees with the information provider to receive all or some of the information which the latter has provided to the Commission, including confidential information. The SO addressee limits access to the information to a restricted circle of persons (the members of the confidentiality ring).

10. The procedure can be used irrespective of whether the information provider is a party to the proceedings or a third party.

11. An information provider may agree to a confidentiality ring vis-à-vis some parties but not others.

NOTES

4 See Article 15(3) of Regulation No 773/2004.

5 See also in this context point 24 of the Access to File Notice

6 Commission notice on best practices for the conduct of proceedings concerning Articles 101 and 102 TFEU, OJ C308, 20.10.2011, p 6.

4. ROLE OF DG COMPETITION

[4.178]

12. DG Competition may facilitate the conclusion of an agreement between information provider and SO addressee to establish a confidentiality ring.

13. DG Competition has discretion to decide whether a confidentiality ring is appropriate in a particular case. As is the case with data rooms, DG Competition may decide to propose a confidentiality ring, either on its own motion or upon a request from an SO addressee or an Information Provider. This means that an SO addressee or information provider may propose that DG Competition facilitates a confidentiality ring, but DG Competition has discretion to accept the proposal or not. DG Competition may also suggest that an SO addressee or information provider make such a proposal but they have no obligation to agree to it.

14. To facilitate a confidentiality ring, DG Competition may:

a. Help the SO addressee and the information provider to consent to the use of a confidentiality ring by proposing a suitable draft negotiated disclosure agreement. This includes supervising the parties' efforts to define the members of the confidentiality ring;

b. Prepare the DVDs/USB sticks or any other form of electronic media which contain the documents that form part of the confidentiality ring.

15. Once the SO addressee, the information provider and DG Competition agree on the principle of using a confidentiality ring for some (or all) documents subject to access to file, they can start discussing the text of the negotiated disclosure agreement. This document must be signed before the confidentiality ring starts. Until the negotiated disclosure agreement is signed, DG Competition, the SO addressee and the information provider may decide to discontinue the process and revert to the normal access to file procedure.

5. THE NEGOTIATED DISCLOSURE AGREEMENT

[4.179]
16. The negotiated disclosure agreement (including its annexes) must be agreed upon by both the SO addressee and the information provider. The template may require some adjustments to take account of the specific circumstances of each case.

17. By signing the negotiated disclosure agreement, the SO addressee agrees with:

a. The fact that the confidentiality ring procedure satisfies its access to file rights with respect to the documents covered by the confidentiality ring.

b. The fact that its external counsel who is also member of the confidentiality ring is released from any obligation to disclose to it information contained in the documents included in the confidentiality ring.

18. By signing the negotiated disclosure agreement, the information provider agrees with:

a. A disclaimer stating that DG Competition's communication of the documents to the members of the confidentiality ring respects Article 339 TFEU and Article 28 of Regulation No. 1/2003.

b. A disclaimer stating that in case of a breach of the negotiated disclosure agreement by a member of the confidentiality ring, the European Commission cannot be held liable under Article 340 TFEU for any unauthorised disclosure by the members of the confidentiality ring.

c. The fact that the inclusion of documents in the confidentiality ring procedure does not necessarily imply that these documents contain confidential information.

19. The negotiated disclosure agreement will contain a provision on the destruction of the documents included in the confidentiality ring after a certain time limit.

20. In case of violation of the negotiated disclosure agreement by an external counsel, the Commission may report the incident to the bar association of the lawyer concerned with a view to disciplinary action.

6. THE MEMBERS OF THE CONFIDENTIALITY RING

[4.180]
21. A confidentiality ring would usually comprise the external counsel of the SO addressee and persons under the direction, control or supervision of the external counsel. It may include certain agreed representatives of the SO addressee or economic advisers. The members of the confidentiality ring will be listed in an enclosure to the negotiated disclosure agreement and must sign an appropriate undertaking to respect confidentiality.

7. TYPES OF NEGOTIATED DISCLOSURE FACILITATED BY DG COMPETITION

[4.181]
22. So far, DG Competition has used two types of confidentiality rings:

a. A confidentiality ring whereby the external counsel selects from the documents included in the ring only those documents that are considered potentially exculpatory. For these documents a non-confidential version is prepared by the information provider that can be shared with the SO addressee (client access). The non-confidential versions can also be used in the reply to the SO, the Oral Hearing and in possible further Court submissions.

b. A confidentiality ring whereby the external counsel of an SO addressee selects from the documents included in the ring those documents that are considered potentially exculpatory but no non-confidential versions are prepared of these documents. In this case, special arrangements will be sought to protect the confidential nature of the information from disclosure to the SO addressee and others in the reply to SO, the Oral Hearing as well as in possible further Court submissions. An optional clause may provide a possibility for the external counsel to apply for client access for some of the information if required by the rights of defence.

23. Details on both options are included in the template negotiated disclosure agreement and can be further negotiated between the information provider, the SO addressee and DG Competition.

8. THE ROLE OF THE HEARING OFFICER

[4.182]
24. If an SO addressee considers that further access to file is necessary for the proper exercise of its right to be heard and the issue cannot be resolved with DG Competition, that SO addressee may refer the matter to the Hearing Officer under Article 7 of the Hearing Officer's Terms of Reference.[7]

25. If the Commission intends to disclose information the information provider considers confidential, DG Competition must inform the information provider of the reasons for that intention and invite the information provider's comments. Where the information provider objects to the planned disclosure, it can refer the matter to the Hearing Officer under Article 8 of the Hearing Officer's Terms of Reference. Where appropriate, the Hearing Officer may decide that the information concerned may be made accessible in a restricted manner to the SO addressee requesting access.

NOTES

7 See Articles 3(7) and 7(1) of Decision 2011/695/EU of the President of the European Commission on the function and terms of reference of the hearing officer in certain competition proceedings, OJ L275, 20.10.2011, p 29. ("Hearing Officers' Terms of Reference").

ANNEX 1 – TEMPLATE NEGOTIATED DISCLOSURE AGREEMENT: TEMPLATE FOR NEGOTIATED DISCLOSURE/CONFIDENTIALITY RING

[4.183]

[NAME SO ADDRESSEE], a [PLACE OF ESTABLISHMENT] corporation, with its principal place of business at [ADDRESS], duly represented by [AUTHORIZED REPRESENTATIVE] ("**NAME**"); and

[NAME INFORMATION PROVIDER], an [PLACE OF ESTABLISHMENT] corporation, with its principal place of business at [ADDRESS], duly represented by [AUTHORIZED REPRESENTATIVE] (the "**Information Provider**")

(together: the "**Parties**")

On [DATE] entered into this

NEGOTIATED DISCLOSURE AGREEMENT

Whereas:

(1) On [DATE], the European Commission (the "Commission") issued a Statement of Objections ("SO") in Case AT [NUMBER] ("the Case") to [SO Addressee] (the "**SO Addressee**").

(2) The SO Addressee has engaged [EXTERNAL COUNSEL, FIRM] as external legal counsel in relation to the Case (the "**External Counsel**").

(3) The Commission [has/will] provide(d) the SO Addressee access to the file [on [DATE]]. Access to the file [will be/was] provided on the basis of Article 27(2) of Council Regulation (EC) No 1/2003,[8] Articles 15 and 16a of Commission Regulation (EC) No 773/2004[9] and the Commission Notice on Access to File.[10]

(4) In principle, the Commission grants the SO Addressee access to all documents contained in the Commission file, with the exception of internal documents, business secrets of other undertakings, and other confidential information.[11] In this Case, the Commission's file includes documents that are claimed to contain business secrets and other confidential information.

(5) A [third] party in an EU antitrust procedure can waive, *vis-à-vis* the Commission, its right to the protection of its business secrets and other confidential information.[12]

(6) The Commission has agreed to facilitate a negotiated disclosure of [ALL/PART] of the documents contained in the file. These documents are listed in Enclosure I to this Agreement (the "**Documents**"). The Commission obtained these Documents from the Information Provider. The Documents are claimed to contain business secrets or other confidential information. The SO Addressee has [not yet] received access to non-confidential versions of the documents or to summaries thereof [on DATE].

(7) This Agreement together with all of its Annexes is intended to facilitate disclosure of the Documents through a confidentiality ring comprising the External Counsel [and persons under the direction, control or supervision of the External Counsel and bound by confidentiality obligations towards his/her law firm] [and certain agreed representatives of the SO Addressee]. The members of the confidentiality ring are listed in the Enclosure II to this Agreement (the "**Members**").

(8) The SO Addressee has declared to the Commission that access to the Documents in accordance with this Agreement will satisfy the Commission's obligations towards the SO Addressee as regards the exercise of its right to access to file.

(9) In contemplation of the Commission providing the Members with the Documents pursuant to this Agreement, the Information Provider has waived its right to the protection of its business secrets and other confidential information by the Commission.

The Parties therefore conclude the following agreement:

1. Access to the Documents is granted on the condition that the information thereby obtained may only be used by the External Counsel for the purposes of the proceedings before the Commission in the Case and in any judicial review of a possible future Commission Decision in the Case before the Court of Justice of the European Union. External Counsel may use the information contained in the Documents only for the purposes stated above under the conditions set out in this Agreement.

2. The Information Provider hereby waives, *vis-à-vis* the Members, its right to protection of business secrets and other confidential information contained in the Documents. This waiver is solely for the purpose of enabling the Commission to disclose the Documents to the Members in accordance with the terms of this Agreement and is granted to that extent only.

Negotiated disclosure ring procedure

3. The Information Provider has provided the Documents to the Commission in an unredacted form. The Information Provider has consented that the Commission will provide the External Counsel with a password protected electronic storage device containing electronic copies of the Documents upon receipt of the following documents:
   a. Agreement duly executed by all the Parties; and
   b. Acknowledgements of Negotiated Disclosure Agreement signed by the External Counsel and each and every other Member in the form of Annex A.

[ALTERNATIVE I: NEGOTIATED DISCLOSURE TO GRANT FULL ACCESS (delete when using alternative II)

4. The SO Addressee agrees that the External Counsel
   — redacts or removes any information acquired from the Documents from written submissions pertaining to the Case made to the Commission and the Court of Justice of the European Union, and/or
   — places information acquired from the Documents in a confidential Annex to the Reply to the SO or Court submission which remains non-accessible to the SO Addressee.

— excludes information acquired from the Documents from any oral submission in the proceedings before the Commission and the Court of Justice of the European Union pertaining to the Case (save where arrangements have been made to prevent improper disclosure of information acquired from the Documents, or where ordered by the Court)

5. [OPTIONAL The Information Provider agrees that in the event that the External Counsel considers that SO Addressee's defence cannot properly be assured without information in certain of the Documents (or parts thereof) being disclosed in full to the SO Addressee, permission for such disclosure to the SO addressee shall be sought from the Information Provider. Where such permission is not granted within 10 working days, the External Counsel may address the Commission according to Article 3(7) and 7 of the Decision of the President of the European Commission of 13 October 2011 on the functions and terms of reference of the Hearing Officer in certain competition proceedings[13] seeking the provision by the Commission of (part(s) of) the Document(s) concerned.]]

[ALTERNATIVE II: NEGOTIATED DISCLOSURE AS A FILTER –delete when using alternative I

6. If the External Counsel identifies the information in the Documents as exculpatory and intends to use this information for the purposes identified in Article 1 of this Agreement, the External Counsel is required to:

a. clearly identify the Documents or parts thereof which are concerned; and
b. submit to the Commission a reasoned request for client access in the form of a list (the "**List**") including (i) clear identification of the relevant Documents or parts thereof and (ii) explanation of why the information in the identified Documents or parts thereof is considered exculpatory. General or vague justifications such as "*the information could be exculpatory*" or "*the information could be necessary to understand the context*" will not be considered as sufficient. The justification must clearly explain the specific reasons why the particular information is necessary for the exercise of the SO Addressee's rights of defence and what the External Counsel intends to show by it; and
c. provide the Commission with the List within 15 working days as of the receipt of the password protected electronic storage device containing electronic copies of the Documents.

7. If the External Counsel fails to provide the Commission with the List in accordance with and within the deadline set in Article 4 of this Agreement, it shall be considered that the SO Addressee's rights to access to file with respect to the Documents have been fully exercised by the SO Addressee and the External Counsel shall return the Access to File DVD to the Commission.

8. Upon receipt of the List, the Commission will contact the Information Provider and assess whether the information identified in the List can be disclosed. To the extent that the Information Provider does not object to the disclosure of the information, the Information Provider shall prepare and deliver it to the Commission within 10 working days from the Commission submitting the List to the Information Provider. If the Information Provider fails to deliver to the Commission non-confidential versions of any of the Documents identified in the List within the deadline set in this Article, the Commission may presume that the information contained in the Documents concerned should be accessible. The Commission will disclose the Documents to the SO Addressee in accordance with this agreement.]

9. To the extent that the Information Provider objects to disclosure of some of the information by showing that disclosure could cause serious commercial harm to the Information Provider, the procedure set out in Article 8 of the Decision of the President of the European Commission of 13 October 2011 on the functions and terms of reference of the Hearing Officer in certain competition proceedings applies.[14] This means that, with regard to that information, the Commission services will then assess whether the Information Provider's claim to confidential treatment of information outweighs the reasons provided by the External Counsel for making such information available to the SO Addressee in view of its rights of defence.

10. The Documents will not be copied or otherwise reproduced except to the extent such copying or reproduction is reasonably necessary for permitted uses under this Agreement, and all such copies or reproductions will be subject to the terms of this Agreement. If the duplication process by which copies or reproductions of the Documents are made does not itself preserve the possible confidentiality designations that may appear on the original Documents, all such copies or reproductions will be appropriately marked with those confidentiality designations. For the purposes of this Agreement and its Annexes, the expression "the Documents" covers, in addition to originals, any copies or reproductions of the Documents, even if made in contravention of this paragraph.

Liability

11. Members will take all necessary measures to ensure that the Documents are kept so as to avoid unauthorised disclosure. The Information Provider has a right to claim damages and such other relief as may be available from the Members and their firm or employer for any unlawful disclosure of the Documents or parts thereof in contravention of this Agreement.

12. Disclosure pursuant to and to the extent required under the terms of an order issued by a court of a competent jurisdiction or by a competent regulatory authority shall not constitute a violation of the Members' obligations under this Agreement.

Waiver of lawyer-client disclosure duty

13. The SO Addressee hereby releases any External Counsel who are Members and their law firms from any professional duties and obligations to disclose to it information contained in the Documents subject to the negotiated disclosure procedure. The SO Addressee will undertake any required or advisable action and execute any required or advisable document to effect the release described in this Article. The SO Addressee shall refrain from issuing any instruction to any Members which may result in the violation of this Agreement.

14. This Agreement will be governed by and construed in accordance with the [LAW]. All disputes arising out of or in connection with the Agreement shall be finally settled under the Rules of Arbitration of the International Chamber of Commerce by three (3) arbitrators appointed in accordance with the said Rules. The place of arbitration is [PLACE]. The language of the arbitral proceedings is [LANGUAGE]

On behalf of [SO ADDRESSEE]	On behalf of [INFORMATION PROVIDER]
....	....
Name:	Name:
Function:	Function:
Date:	Date:
Place:	Place:

DECLARATION OF [SO ADDRESSEE(S)] VIS-A-VIS THE EUROPEAN COMMISSION

[NAME], a [PLACE OF ESTABLISHMENT] corporation, with its principal place of business at [ADDRESS], duly represented by [AUTHORIZED REPRESENTATIVE] ("**[NAME]**")

Hereby declares with regard to the procedure in the Case AT.[NUMBER] – [NAME]:

[NAME] agrees to exercise its rights to access to file as regards the Documents as defined below solely in accordance with the terms set out in the draft Negotiated Disclosure Agreement annexed hereto, which, further to this Declaration, [SO ADDRESSEE(S)] intends to enter into with [NAME INFORMATION PROVIDER] a [PLACE OF ESTABLISHMENT] corporation, with its principal place of business at [ADDRESS] (the "**Information Provider**"). [NAME] agrees that the Commission, by acting in accordance with the disclosure procedure set out in the draft Negotiated Disclosure Agreement would comply with its obligation to provide access to the file as set out in Council Regulation (EC) No 1/2003, Commission Regulation (EC) No 773/2004 and the Commission Notice on Access to File, as regards the Documents.

The term "**Documents**" means [NUMBER] documents totalling around [NUMBER] pages received by the European Commission in the course of its investigation of the Case AT.[NUMBER] – [NAME]. The documents are listed in Enclosure I to the draft Negotiated Disclosure Agreement.

On behalf of [NAME].

....

Name:

Function:

Date:

Place:

WAIVER DECLARATION OF [INFORMATION PROVIDER] VIS-A-VIS THE EUROPEAN COMMISSION

[NAME], an [PLACE OF ESTABLISHMENT] corporation, with its principal place of business at [ADDRESS], duly represented by [AUTHORIZED REPRESENTATIVE] (the "**Information Provider**")

Hereby declares with regard to the procedure in the Case AT.[NUMBER] – [NAME]:

The Information Provider hereby waives with respect to the European Commission its right to the protection of business secrets and other confidential information contained in the Documents. This waiver is granted solely for the purpose of enabling the European Commission to disclose the Documents in accordance with the terms of the draft Negotiated Disclosure Agreement which, further to this Declaration, [INFORMATION PROVIDER] intends to enter into with [SO ADDRESSEE], a [PLACE OF ESTABLISHMENT] corporation, with its principal place of business at [ADDRESS] and the Information Provider.

The Information Provider agrees that disclosure of the Documents in accordance with the terms of the draft Negotiated Disclosure Agreement would satisfy the Commission's duty to respect professional secrecy under Article 339 TFEU and/or Article 28 of Regulation (EC) No 1/2003 and/or any other applicable rules. Accordingly, the Information Provider agrees not to pursue any claim against the Commission and its staff in respect of any damage that might result from a possible breach of the Negotiated Disclosure Agreement.

The term "**Documents**" means [NUMBER] documents totalling around [NUMBER] pages received by the European Commission in the course of its investigation of the Case AT.[NUMBER] – [NAME]. The documents are listed in Enclosure I to the draft Negotiated Disclosure Agreement.

On behalf of [INFORMATION PROVIDER]

....

Name:

Function:

Date:

Place:

ANNEX A

UNDERTAKING TO BE ENTERED INTO BY MEMBERS OF THE CONFIDENTIALITY RING

I am a [POSITION – *employee, partner, associate, in house counsel*] of [FIRM/SO ADDRESSEE] and I hereby acknowledge that:

1. I have read the Negotiated Disclosure Agreement of [DATE OF THE AGREEMENT] entered into by and between [SO ADDRESSEE], a [PLACE OF ESTABLISHMENT] corporation, with its principal place of business at [ADDRESS] and [INFORMATION PROVIDER], a [PLACE OF ESTABLISHMENT] corporation, with its principal place of business at [ADDRESS] (the "**Agreement**"), understand the terms thereof, and agree to be bound by it and by the following commitments:

a. I will not use any of the Documents for any purpose other than that authorized by the Agreement;

b. Subject to the exceptions provided in the Agreement, I will not disclose, transmit, communicate or make available the information contained in the Documents (or any observations or comments that repeat any parts of the Documents) in any manner, shape or form to anyone other than to the other Members;

c. I will take all appropriate measures necessary to ensure that the Documents are not unlawfully disclosed and notably to ensure that the password protected electronic storage device containing the Documents (and copies containing information extracted therefrom on any medium) [and copies of the List] will be stored in a manner that prevents their non-authorised use;

d. I will process the personal data contained in the Documents in accordance with applicable law, and accept responsibility as controller for any personal data thus processed by the Members or by the SO Addressee in case of disclosure to the SO Addressee allowed in accordance with this Agreement.

e. I will destroy all hard copies of the Documents and to take all reasonable steps to remove, destroy or render otherwise inaccessible any electronic copies of any parts of the Documents, irrespective of the storage medium used, within 60 days of the conclusion of the Commission Proceedings in the Case or within 60 days of the conclusion of any litigation before the Court of Justice of the European Union that might arise in relation to the Case whichever 60-day period expires later, and to certify (by way of affidavit) compliance with this requirement to the Commission and the Information Provider upon their request

f. I will make only such copies or notes as are required to enable me to render assistance in connection with the matters for which I am engaged;

g. I will inform the Commission and the Information Provider of any non-authorised disclosure of the Documents in breach of this Agreement and the circumstances of such disclosure as soon as they become aware thereof unless required not to do so by any applicable law or by any competent Court or regulatory or police authority.

h. I acknowledge [on behalf of the External Counsel's law firm/economists or in-house lawyers' employer] to assume liability for losses or damages incurred by the Information Provider for any damages which are caused by any breach of the terms of the Agreement attributable to me.

i. [FOR LAWYERS I acknowledge that if the information from the Documents is used at any time for a purpose other than the purposes identified in Article 1 of this Agreement, then the Commission may report the incident to the my Bar association with a view to disciplinary action].

The term "**Documents**" means [NUMBER] documents totalling around [NUMBER] pages received by the European Commission in the course of its investigation of the Case AT.[NUMBER] – [NAME]. These documents were submitted by to [INFORMATION PROVIDER], a [PLACE OF ESTABLISHMENT] corporation, with its principal place of business at [ADDRESS]. The documents are listed in Enclosure I to the Negotiated Disclosure Agreement of [DATE OF THE AGREEMENT].

In [PLACE], on [DATE] Name: ....

Signature: ....

ENCLOSURE I

[LIST OF DOCUMENTS]

ENCLOSURE II

[LIST OF MEMBERS, INDICATING NAME, FUNCTION AND A FIRM]

NOTES

8 Council Regulation (EC) No 1/2003 of 16 December 2002 on the implementation of the rules on competition laid down in Articles 81 and 82 of the Treaty, OJ L1, 4.1.2003, p 1.

9 Commission Regulation (EC) No 773/2004 of 7 April 2004 relating to the conduct of proceedings by the Commission pursuant to Articles 81 and 82 of the Treaty, OJ L123, 27.4.2004, p 18, as amended by Commission Regulation (EU) 2015/1348 of 3 August 2015, OJ L208, 5.8.2015..

10 Commission Notice on the rules for access to the Commission file in cases pursuant to Articles 81 and 82 of the EC Treaty, Articles 53, 54, 57 of the EEA Agreement and Council Regulation (EC) No 139/2004, OJ C325 22.12.2005, p 7.

11 Commission Notice on the rules for access to the Commission file in cases pursuant to Articles 81 and 82 of the EC Treaty, Articles 53, 54 and 57 of the EEA Agreement and Council Regulation (EC) No 139/2004, point 10.

12 See by analogy Case T-45/98, *Krupp Thyssen Stainless v Commission*, EU:T:2001:288, paragraph 63.

13 Decision of the President of the European Commission of 13 October 2011 on the functions and terms of reference of the hearing officer in certain competition proceedings OJ L275, 20.10.2011, p 29.

14 Decision of the President of the European Commission of 13 October 2011 on the functions and terms of reference of the hearing officer in certain competition proceedings OJ L275, 20.10.2011, p 29.

COMMISSION DECISION

(2018/1927/EU)

of 5 December 2018

laying down internal rules concerning the processing of personal data by the European Commission in the field of competition in relation to the provision of information to data subjects and the restriction of certain rights

[4.184]

NOTES

Date of publication in OJ: OJ L313, 10.12.2018, p 39.

Application of this Decision to the United Kingdom: in accordance with the European Union (Withdrawal) Act 2018, s 3 at **[7.5]**, this Decision became domestic law on IP completion day (as defined in the European Union (Withdrawal Agreement) Act 2020, s 39).

THE EUROPEAN COMMISSION,

Having regard to the Treaty on the Functioning of the European Union, and in particular Article 249(1) thereof,

Whereas:

(1) The Commission conducts administrative investigations for the purpose of enforcing the competition rules in accordance with the Treaty and secondary legislation as well as international agreements adopted for that purpose.[1] To that end, it exercises powers of investigation and enforcement (including related operational activities) in the fields of antitrust, merger control and State aid control conferred on the Commission by the relevant Union acts.

(2) Commission investigations and enforcement activities in the field of competition target undertakings or Member States which are subject to the competition rules of the Treaty, and not natural persons as such. Nevertheless, during competition investigations, personal data within the meaning of Article 3(1) of Regulation (EU) 2018/1725 of the European Parliament and of the Council[2] are inevitably processed within the meaning of Article 3(3) of Regulation (EU) 2018/1725. The Commission needs to process such personal data in order to fulfil the tasks assigned to it as the public authority enforcing Union competition rules. Investigation in the field of antitrust, merger control and State aid control, and enforcement of competition rules constitute monitoring, inspection or regulatory functions connected to the exercise of official authority in the cases referred to in Article 25(1)(c) and (g) of Regulation (EU) 2018/1725. Those activities serve the promotion and protection of a competitive internal market, thereby safeguarding an important economic and financial interest of the Union and of the Member States.

(3) For the purpose of its investigation and enforcement activities in the fields of antitrust, merger control and State aid control, the Commission processes personal data acquired or received from legal persons, natural persons, Member States and other entities (such as National Competition Authorities, regulatory bodies and other public bodies and authorities), competition authorities of third countries and international bodies and organisations. During competition investigations and enforcement activities, whether acting on its own initiative or on the basis of received input, the Commission may also process personal data acquired or received from publicly available sources (for example, in the context of market monitoring or screening activities), from anonymous sources (for example, whistle-blowers/informants) or identified sources (for example, complainants) that require protection of their identity.

(4) The Commission may, in turn, transmit personal data to legal or natural persons (for example, in the context of the access to file procedure), to National Competition Authorities and other authorities and bodies in the context of bilateral or multilateral cooperation with Member States or third country authorities and organisations, as necessary and appropriate to exercise its powers, to safeguard the rights of defence of parties subject to Commission proceedings and to ensure the efficient and effective application of Union competition rules.

(5) Personal data processing activities, within the meaning of Article 3(3) of Regulation (EU) 2018/1725, carried out in the course of investigation and enforcement activities in the field of competition, may take place even before the Commission formally initiates proceedings, continue throughout the handling of the investigation and may continue even after the formal closure of the investigation (for example, for the purposes of market or compliance monitoring or screening activities, assessing the need for initiating new investigative activities, legal proceedings, etc.).

(6) The personal data processed by the Commission are, for example, identification data, contact data, professional data and data related to or brought in connection with the subject matter of the investigation or procedure. The personal data are stored in a secured electronic environment to prevent unlawful access or transfer of data to persons who do not have a need to know. The personal data are retained in the services of the Commission in charge of the investigation for the time necessary for the investigation, for assessing the need to initiate new investigative activities, during the administrative procedure, and throughout any subsequent judicial review proceedings, and the administrative retention period that follows the definitive closure of the file. At the end of the retention period, the case related information including personal data is transferred to the historical archives of the Commission.[3]

(7) While carrying out its tasks, the Commission is bound to respect the rights of natural persons in relation to the processing of personal data recognised by Article 8(1) of the Charter of Fundamental Rights of the European Union and by Article 16(1) of the Treaty. At the same time, the Commission is

responsible for enforcing competition rules, which requires the Commission to conduct investigations in a timely manner, while respecting rules of confidentiality and professional secrecy[4] as well as the rights of defence of parties subject to its investigations,[5] and the rights of individuals that require protection of their identity.

(8) In certain circumstances, it is necessary to reconcile the rights of data subjects pursuant to Regulation (EU) 2018/1725 with the needs of investigations and enforcement activities, as well as with full respect for fundamental rights and freedoms of other data subjects. To that effect, Article 25 of Regulation (EU) 2018/1725 provides the Commission with the possibility to restrict the application of Articles 14 to 22 and 35, as well as Article 4 thereof, insofar as its provisions correspond to the rights and obligations provided for in Articles 14 to 22 of that Regulation.

(9) These internal rules should cover all processing operations carried out by the Commission in the performance of its powers of investigation, whether acting on its own initiative or on the basis of received input, and enforcement and related operational activities in the fields of antitrust, merger control and State aid control whenever the exercise of data subjects' rights may jeopardise the conduct of investigations or enforcement activities. These rules should apply to processing operations carried out prior to the formal initiation of proceedings, during the handling of investigations as well as after the formal closure of investigations, including processing in the context of bilateral or multilateral cooperation with National Competition Authorities, Member States or third country authorities and organisations.

(10) In order to comply with Articles 14, 15 and 16 of Regulation (EU) 2018/1725, the Commission should inform all individuals of its activities involving processing of their personal data and of their rights in a transparent and coherent manner in the form of the data protection notices published on the Commission's website.

(11) Without prejudice to Articles 14(5) and 16(5) of Regulation (EU) 2018/1725, the Commission is also able on the basis of Article 25 of that Regulation to restrict the provision of information to data subjects and the application of other rights of data subjects in order to protect its own competition investigations and enforcement of competition rules, investigations and proceedings of competition authorities of the Member States, the investigation tools and methods, as well as the rights of other persons related to its investigations.

(12) In addition, in order to maintain effective cooperation it may be necessary for the Commission to restrict the application of data subjects' rights in order to protect processing operations of other Union institutions, bodies, offices and agencies or of Member States' authorities. To that effect, the Commission should consult those services, institutions, bodies, offices, agencies, and authorities on the relevant grounds for imposing restrictions and the necessity and proportionality of the restrictions.

(13) The Commission may also have to restrict the provision of information to data subjects and the application of other rights of data subjects in relation to personal data received from third countries or international organisations, in order to cooperate with those countries or organisation and thus safeguard an important objective of general public interest of the Union. However, in some circumstances the interest or fundamental rights of the data subject may override the interest of international cooperation.

(14) The Commission has therefore identified the grounds listed in Article 25(1)(c), (g) and (h) of Regulation (EU) 2018/1725 as grounds for restrictions under Article 25 of the Regulation that may be necessary to apply to data processing operations carried out in the framework of the Commission's investigative and enforcement activities in the area of competition, encompassing antitrust, merger control and State aid control.

(15) The Commission should handle all restrictions in a transparent manner and register each application of restrictions in the corresponding record system.

(16) Pursuant to Article 25(8) of Regulation (EU) 2018/1725, controllers may defer or refrain from providing information on the reasons for the application of a restriction to the data subject if providing that information would in any way compromise the purpose of the restriction. This is, in particular, the case of restrictions to the rights provided for in Articles 16 and 35 of Regulation (EU) 2018/1725. In order to ensure that the data subject's rights under Articles 16 and 35 of Regulation (EU) 2018/1725 are restricted only as long as the reasons for the restriction last, the Commission should review its position regularly and at the closure of the relevant investigation.

(17) Where a restriction of other rights of data subjects is applied, the controller should assess on a case-by-case basis whether the communication of the restriction would compromise its purpose. The controller is the service in charge of the competition policy within the Commission.

(18) The Data Protection Officer of the Commission should carry out an independent review of the application of restrictions, with a view to ensuring compliance with this Decision.

(19) This Decision is adopted for the purposes of Article 25 of Regulation (EU) 2018/1725 and should enter into force at the same time as that Regulation in order to ensure legal certainty.

(20) The European Data Protection Supervisor has been consulted.

NOTES

1 See in particular for antitrust Council Regulation (EC) No 1/2003 of 16 December 2002 on the implementation of the rules on competition laid down in Articles 81 and 82 of the Treaty (OJ L1, 4.1.2003, p 1), for merger control Council Regulation (EC) No 139/2004 of 20 January 2004 on the control of concentrations between undertakings (the EC Merger Regulation) (OJ L24, 29.1.2004, p 1) and for State aid Council Regulation (EU) 2015/1589 of 13 July 2015 laying down detailed rules for the application of Article 108 of the Treaty on the Functioning of the European Union (OJ L248, 24.9.2015, p 9).

2 Regulation (EU) 2018/1725 of the European Parliament and of the Council of 23 October 2018 on the protection of natural persons with regard to the processing of personal data by the Union institutions, bodies, offices and agencies and

on the free movement of such data, and repealing Regulation (EC) No 45/2001 and Decision No 1247/2002/EC (OJ L295, 21.11.2018, p 39). Processing within the meaning of Article 3(3) of Regulation (EU) 2018/1725 also includes a situation where the Commission receives personal data voluntarily submitted to it.

3 Retention of files in the Commission is regulated by the Common retention list, a regulatory document (the last version is SEC(2012)713) in the form of a retention schedule that establishes the retention periods for the different types of Commission files.

4 See, in particular, Article 339 of the Treaty, as well as Article 28 of Regulation (EC) No 1/2003; Article 15(4) of Commission Regulation (EC) No 773/2004 of 7 April 2004 relating to the conduct of proceedings by the Commission pursuant to Articles 81 and 82 of the EC Treaty (OJ L123, 27.4.2004, p 18); Article 17 of Regulation (EC) No 139/2004 and Article 18 of Commission Regulation (EC) No 802/2004 of 21 April 2004 implementing Council Regulation (EC) No 139/2004 on the control of concentrations between undertakings (OJ L133, 30.4.2004, p 1); Articles 30 and 31 of Regulation (EU) 2015/1589; required declarations on confidential information in State aid notification forms as annexes to Regulation (EC) No 794/2004 in its amended form.

5 Implementation of the rights of data subjects under the Regulation (EU) 2018/1725 and compliance with the obligations of data controllers under that Regulation does not affect the Commission's handling of the rights of defence of parties subject to the competition proceedings. The integrity and authenticity of evidence on file collected in the course of competition investigations can therefore not be compromised by modifying documents received or collected in conformity with the applicable procedural rules in the competition field.

HAS ADOPTED THIS DECISION:

[4.185]
Article 1
Subject-matter and scope

1. This Decision lays down the rules to be followed by the Commission to inform data subjects of the processing of their data in accordance with Articles 14, 15 and 16 of Regulation (EU) 2018/1725, in the framework of its activities in the field of competition.

It also lays down the conditions under which the Commission may restrict the application of Articles 4, 14 to 17, 19, 20 and 35 of Regulation (EU) 2018/1725, in accordance with Article 25 thereof.

2. This Decision applies to the processing of personal data by the Commission for the purpose of or in relation to the activities carried out in order to fulfil its tasks pursuant to Articles 101 to 109 of the Treaty.

[4.186]
Article 2
Applicable exceptions and restrictions

1. Where the Commission exercises its duties with respect to the data subjects' rights pursuant to Regulation (EU) 2018/1725, it shall consider whether any of the exceptions laid down in that Regulation apply.

2. Subject to Articles 3 to 7 of this Decision, the Commission may restrict the application of Articles 14 to 17, 19, 20 and 35 of Regulation (EU) 2018/1725, as well as the principle of transparency laid down in Article 4(1)(a) in so far as its provisions correspond to the right and obligations provided for in Articles 14 to 17, 19, 20 and 35 of the Regulation (EU) 2018/1725 where the exercise of those rights and obligations would jeopardise the purpose of the Commission's investigative and enforcement activities, including by revealing its investigative tools and methods, or would adversely affect the rights and freedoms of other data subjects.

3. Subject to Articles 3 to 7, the Commission may restrict the rights and obligations referred to in paragraph 2 of this Article in relation to personal data obtained from other Union institutions, bodies, agencies and offices, competent authorities of Member States or third countries or from international organisations, in the following circumstances:

(a) where the exercise of those rights and obligations could be restricted by other Union institutions, bodies, agencies and offices on the basis of other acts provided for in Article 25 of Regulation (EU) 2018/1725 or in accordance with Chapter IX of that Regulation or in accordance with Regulation (EU) 2016/794 of the European Parliament and of the Council[1] or Council Regulation (EU) 2017/1939;[2]

(b) where the exercise of those rights and obligations could be restricted by competent authorities of Member States on the basis of acts referred to in Article 23 of Regulation (EU) 2016/679 of the European Parliament and of the Council,[3] or under national measures transposing Articles 13(3), 15(3) or 16(3) of Directive (EU) 2016/680 of the European Parliament and of the Council;[4]

(c) where the exercise of those rights and obligations could jeopardise the Commission's cooperation with third countries or international organisations in the conduct of competition investigations or enforcement of competition decisions.

Before applying restrictions in the circumstances referred to in points (a) and (b) of the first subparagraph, the Commission shall consult the relevant Union institutions, bodies, agencies, offices or competent authorities of the Member States unless it is clear to the Commission that the application of a restriction is provided for by one of the acts referred to in those points.

Point (c) of the first subparagraph shall not apply where the interest of the Commission to cooperate with third countries or international organisation is overridden by the interests or fundamental rights and freedom of the data subjects.

4. Paragraphs 1, 2 and 3 are without prejudice to the application of other Commission decisions laying down internal rules concerning the provision of information to data subjects and the restriction of certain rights under Article 25 of Regulation (EU) 2018/1725 and to Article 23 of the Rules of Procedure of the Commission.

NOTES

1 Regulation (EU) 2016/794 of the European Parliament and of the Council of 11 May 2016 on the European Union Agency for Law Enforcement Cooperation (Europol) and replacing and repealing Council Decisions 2009/371/JHA, 2009/934/JHA, 2009/935/JHA, 2009/936/JHA and 2009/968/JHA (OJ L135, 24.5.2016, p 53).

2 Council Regulation (EU) 2017/1939 of 12 October 2017 implementing enhanced cooperation on the establishment of the European Public Prosecutor's Office ('the EPPO') (OJ L283, 31.10.2017, p 1).

3 Regulation (EU) 2016/679 of the European Parliament and of the Council of 27 April 2016 on the protection of natural persons with regard to the processing of personal data and on the free movement of such data, and repealing Directive 95/46/EC (General Data Protection Regulation) (OJ L119, 4.5.2016, p 1).

4 Directive (EU) 2016/680 of the European Parliament and of the Council of 27 April 2016 on the protection of natural persons with regard to the processing of personal data by competent authorities for the purposes of the prevention, investigation, detection or prosecution of criminal offences or the execution of criminal penalties, and on the free movement of such data, and repealing Council Framework Decision 2008/977/JHA (OJ L119, 4.5.2016, p 89).

[4.187]
Article 3
Provision of information to data subjects

1. The Commission shall publish on its website data protection notices that inform all data subjects of its activities involving processing of their personal data.
2. Without prejudice to Articles 14(5) and 16(5) of Regulation (EU) 2018/1725, where the Commission restricts, wholly or partly, the provision of information to data subjects, whose data are processed for purposes of competition investigation or enforcement (including related operational activities) it shall record and register the reasons for the restriction in accordance with Article 6.

[4.188]
Article 4
Right of access by data subject, right of erasure and to restriction of processing

1. Where the Commission restricts, wholly or partly, the right of access to data by data subjects, the right of erasure, or the right to restriction of processing as referred to in Articles 17, 19 and 20 respectively of Regulation (EU) 2018/1725 it shall inform the data subject concerned, in its reply to the request for access, erasure or restriction of processing, of the restriction applied and of the principal reasons thereof, and of the possibility of lodging a complaint with the European Data Protection Supervisor or of seeking a judicial remedy in the Court of Justice of the European Union.
2. The provision of information concerning the reasons for the restriction referred to in paragraph 1 may be omitted for as long as it would undermine the purpose of the restriction.
3. The Commission shall record and register the reasons for the restriction in accordance with Article 6.
4. Where the right of access is wholly or partly restricted, the data subject shall exercise his or her right of access through the intermediary of the European Data Protection Supervisor, in accordance with paragraphs 6, 7 and 8 of Article 25 of the Regulation (EU) 2018/1725.

[4.189]
Article 5
Communication of personal data breaches to data subjects

Where the Commission restricts the communication of a personal data breach to the data subject, as referred to in Article 35 of Regulation (EU) 2018/1725, it shall record and register the reasons for the restriction in accordance with Article 6 of this Decision.

[4.190]
Article 6
Recording and registering of restrictions

1. The Commission shall record the reasons for any restriction applied pursuant to this Decision, including an assessment of the necessity and proportionality of the restriction.
2. To that end, the record shall state how the exercise of the right would jeopardise the purpose of the Commission's investigation and enforcement activities, or of restrictions applied pursuant to Article 2(2) or (3), or would adversely affect the rights and freedoms of other data subjects.
3. The record and, where applicable, the documents containing underlying factual and legal elements shall be registered. They shall be made available to the European Data Protection Supervisor on request.

[4.191]
Article 7
Duration of restrictions

1. Restrictions referred to in Articles 3, 4 and 5 shall continue to apply as long as the reasons justifying them remain applicable.
2. Where the reasons for a restriction referred to in Article 3 or 5 no longer apply, the Commission shall lift the restriction and provide the reasons for the restriction to the data subject. At the same time, the Commission shall inform the data subject of the possibility of lodging a complaint with the European Data Protection Supervisor at any time or of seeking a judicial remedy in the Court of Justice of the European Union.
3. The Commission shall review the application of the restrictions referred to in Articles 3 and 5 every year and at the closure of the relevant investigation.

[4.192]
Article 8
Review by the Data Protection Officer

1. The Data Protection Officer shall be informed, without undue delay, whenever data subjects' rights are restricted in accordance with this Decision. Upon request, the Data Protection Officer shall be provided with access to the record and any documents containing underlying factual and legal elements.
2. The Data Protection Officer may request a review of the restriction. The Data Protection Officer shall be informed about the outcome of the requested review.

[4.193]
Article 9
Entry into force

This Decision shall enter into force on the date of entry into force of Regulation (EU) 2018/1725.

B. COOPERATION AGREEMENTS

COUNCIL REGULATION

(2821/71/EEC)
of 20 December 1971

on application of Article 85(3) of the Treaty to categories of agreements, decisions and concerted practices

[4.194]

NOTES

Date of publication in OJ: OJ L285, 29.12.1971, p 46 (S edn 1971 (III), p 1032).

Repeal of this Regulation in relation to the UK: this Regulation is repealed, in relation to the UK, by the Competition (Amendment etc) (EU Exit) Regulations 2019, SI 2019/93, reg 63, Sch 3, para 1, as from IP completion day (as defined in the European Union (Withdrawal Agreement) Act 2020, s 39) (for transitional provisions and savings in relation to the operation of the 2019 Regulations, see Sch 4 to those Regulations at **[7.69]** et seq). See also Sch 3, para 2 to the 2019 Regulations which provides that, despite the repeal of this Regulation, Level 2 Regulations made under it are not repealed.

Note: the reference to Article 85(3) of the Treaty in the title of this Regulation is a reference to Article 85(3) of the Treaty establishing the European Economic Community which, in due course, was replaced by Article 81(3) of the EC Treaty. With effect from 1 December 2009, the EC Treaty was replaced by the Treaty on the Functioning of the European Union. References in this document to provisions of the EEC Treaty should be construed accordingly. As to Article 81 of the EC Treaty, see now Article 101 of the Treaty on the Functioning of the European Union.

THE COUNCIL OF THE EUROPEAN COMMUNITIES,

Having regard to the Treaty establishing the European Economic Community, and in particular Article 87 thereof;

Having regard to the proposal from the Commission;

Having regard to the Opinion of the European Parliament;

Having regard to the Opinion of the Economic and Social Committee;

Whereas Article 85(1) of the Treaty may in accordance with Article 85(3) be declared inapplicable to categories of agreements, decisions and concerted practices which fulfil the conditions contained in Article 85(3);

Whereas the provisions for implementation of Article 85(3) must be adopted by way of regulation pursuant to Article 87;

Whereas the creation of a common market requires that undertakings be adapted to the conditions of the enlarged market and whereas cooperation between undertakings can be a suitable means of achieving this;

Whereas agreements, decisions and concerted practices for co-operation between undertakings which enable the undertakings to work more rationally and adapt their productivity and competitiveness to the enlarged market may, in so far as they fall within the prohibition contained in Article 85(1), be exempted therefrom under certain conditions; whereas this measure is necessary in particular as regards agreements, decisions and concerted practices relating to the application of standards and types, research and development of products or processes up to the stage of industrial application, exploitation of the results thereof and specialisation;

Whereas it is desirable that the Commission be enabled to declare by way of regulation that the provisions of Article 85(1) do not apply to those categories of agreements, decisions and concerted practices, in order to make it easier for undertakings to co-operate in ways which are economically desirable and without adverse effect from the point of view of competition policy;

Whereas it should be laid down under what conditions the Commission, in close and constant liaison with the competent authorities of the Member States, may exercise such powers;

Whereas under Article 6 of Regulation No 17[1] *the Commission may provide that a decision taken in accordance with Article 85(3) of the Treaty shall apply with retroactive effect; whereas it is desirable that the Commission be empowered to issue regulations whose provisions are to the like effect;*

Whereas under Article 7 of Regulation No 17 agreements, decisions and concerted practices may by decision of the Commission be exempted from prohibition, in particular if they are modified in such manner that Article 85(3) applies to them; whereas it is desirable that the Commission be enabled to grant by regulation like exemption to such agreements, decisions and concerted practices if they are modified in such manner as to fall within a category defined in an exempting regulation;

Whereas the possibility cannot be excluded that, in a specific case, the conditions set out in Article 85(3) may not be fulfilled; whereas the Commission must have power to regulate such a case in pursuance of Regulation No 17 by way of decision having effect for the future;

NOTES

Repeal of this Regulation in relation to the UK: this Regulation is repealed in relation to the UK (as from IP completion day); see the introductory notes to this Regulation *ante*.

[1] OJ 13, 21.2.62, p 204/62.

HAS ADOPTED THIS REGULATION—

Part 4 EU & Retained EU Materials

[4.195]
Article 1

1. Without prejudice to the application of Regulation No 17 the Commission may, by regulation and in accordance with Article 85(3) of the Treaty, declare that Article 85(1) shall not apply to categories of agreements between undertakings, decisions of associations of undertakings and concerted practices which have as their object—

(a) the application of standards or types;

(b) the research and development of products or processes up to the stage of industrial application, and exploitation of the results, including provisions regarding industrial property rights and confidential technical knowledge;

(c) specialisation, including agreements necessary for achieving it.

2. Such regulation shall define the categories of agreements, decisions and concerted practices to which it applies and shall specify in particular—

(a) the restrictions or clauses which may, or may not, appear in the agreements, decisions and concerted practices;

(b) the clauses which must be contained in the agreements, decisions and concerted practices or the other conditions which must be satisfied.

NOTES

Repeal of this Regulation in relation to the UK: this Regulation is repealed in relation to the UK (as from IP completion day); see the introductory notes to this Regulation *ante*.

[4.196]
Article 2

1. Any regulation pursuant to Article 1 shall be made for a specified period.

2. It may be repealed or amended where circumstances have changed with respect to any of the facts which were basic to its being made; in such case, a period shall be fixed for modification of the agreements, decisions and concerted practices to which the earlier regulation applies.

NOTES

Repeal of this Regulation in relation to the UK: this Regulation is repealed in relation to the UK (as from IP completion day); see the introductory notes to this Regulation *ante*.

[4.197]
Article 3

A regulation pursuant to Article 1 may provide that it shall apply with retroactive effect to agreements, decisions and concerted practices to which, at the date of entry into force of that regulation, a decision issued with retroactive effect in pursuance of Article 6 of Regulation No 17 would have applied.

NOTES

Repeal of this Regulation in relation to the UK: this Regulation is repealed in relation to the UK (as from IP completion day); see the introductory notes to this Regulation *ante*.

[4.198]
Article 4

1. A regulation pursuant to Article 1 may provide that the prohibition contained in Article 85(1) of the Treaty shall not apply, for such period as shall be fixed by that regulation, to agreements, decisions and concerted practices already in existence on 13 March 1962 which do not satisfy the conditions of Article 85(3), where—

— within six months from the entry into force of the regulation, they are so modified as to satisfy the said conditions in accordance with the provisions of the regulation; and

— the modifications are brought to the notice of the Commission within the time limit fixed by the regulation.

[A regulation adopted pursuant to Article 1 may lay down that the prohibition referred to in Article 85(1) of the Treaty shall not apply, for the period fixed in the same regulation, to agreements and concerted practices which existed at the date of accession and which, by virtue of accession, come within the scope of Article 85 and do not fulfil the conditions set out in Article 85(3).]

[The provisions of the preceding sub-paragraph shall apply in the same way in the case of the accession of the Hellenic Republic, the Kingdom of Spain and of the Portuguese Republic.]

[The provisions of the preceding subparagraphs shall apply in the same way in the case of the accession of Austria, Finland and Sweden.]

2. Paragraph 1 shall apply to agreements, decisions and concerted practices which had to be notified before 1 February 1963, in accordance with Article 5 of Regulation No 17, only where they have been so notified before that date.

[Paragraph 1 shall be applicable to those agreements and concerted practices which, by virtue of the accession, come within the scope of Article 85(1) of the Treaty and for which notification before 1 July 1973 is mandatory, in accordance with Articles 5 and 25 of Regulation 17, only if notification was given before that date.]

[Paragraph 1 shall not apply to agreements and concerted practices to which Article 85(1) of the Treaty applies by virtue of the accession of the Hellenic Republic and which must be notified before 1 July 1981, in accordance with Articles 5 and 25 of Regulation 17, unless they have been so notified before that date.]

[Paragraph 1 shall not apply to agreements and concerted practices to which Article 85(1) of the Treaty applies by virtue of the accession of the Kingdom of Spain and the Portuguese Republic and which must be notified before 1 July 1986, in accordance with Articles 5 and 25 of Regulation 17, unless they have been so notified before that date.]

[Paragraph 1 shall not apply to agreements and concerted practices to which Article 85(1) of the Treaty applies by virtue of the accession of Austria, Finland and Sweden and which must be notified within six months of accession, in

accordance with Articles 5 and 25 of Regulation No 17, unless they have been so notified within that period. The present paragraph shall not apply to agreements and concerted practices which at the date of accession already fall under Article 53(1) of the EEA Agreement.]

3. The benefit of the provisions laid down pursuant to paragraph 1 may not be claimed in actions pending at the date of entry into force of a regulation adopted pursuant to Article 1; neither may it be relied on as grounds for claims for damages against third parties.

NOTES

Para 1: words in first pair of square brackets added by Council Regulation 2743/72/EEC, Art 1; words in second pair of square brackets originally added by AA2, and substituted by AA3; words in third pair of square brackets added by AA4, as adjusted by Council Decision 95/1/EC, Annex I(III)(A)(2).

Para 2: words in first pair of square brackets added by Council Regulation 2743/72/EEC, Art 1; words in second pair of square brackets added by AA2; words in third pair of square brackets added by AA3; words in final pair of square brackets added by AA4, as adjusted by Council Decision 95/1/EC, Annex I(III)(A)(2).

Repeal of this Regulation in relation to the UK: this Regulation is repealed in relation to the UK (as from IP completion day); see the introductory notes to this Regulation *ante*.

[4.199]

Article 5

Before making a regulation, the Commission shall publish a draft thereof to enable all persons and organisations concerned to submit their comments within such time limit, being not less than one month, as the Commission shall fix.

NOTES

Repeal of this Regulation in relation to the UK: this Regulation is repealed in relation to the UK (as from IP completion day); see the introductory notes to this Regulation *ante*.

[4.200]

Article 6

1. The Commission shall consult the Advisory Committee on Restrictive Practices and Monopolies—

(a) before publishing a draft regulation;

(b) before making a regulation.

2. Paragraphs 5 and 6 of Article 10 of Regulation No 17, relating to consultation with the Advisory Committee, shall apply by analogy, it being understood that joint meetings with the Commission shall take place not earlier than one month after dispatch of the notice convening them.

NOTES

Repeal of this Regulation in relation to the UK: this Regulation is repealed in relation to the UK (as from IP completion day); see the introductory notes to this Regulation *ante*.

Article 7 *(Repealed by Council Regulation 1/2003/EC, Art 40.)*

COMMISSION REGULATION

(1217/2010/EU)

of 14 December 2010

on the application of Article 101(3) of the Treaty on the Functioning of the European Union to certain categories of research and development agreements

(Text with EEA relevance)

[4.201]

NOTES

Date of publication in OJ: OJ L335, 18.12.2010, p 36.

Application of this Regulation in relation to the UK: in accordance with the European Union (Withdrawal) Act 2018, s 3 at **[7.5]**, this Regulation became domestic law on IP completion day (as defined in the European Union (Withdrawal Agreement) Act 2020, s 39). In so far as applying to the UK, this Regulation is amended by the Competition (Amendment etc) (EU Exit) Regulations 2019, SI 2019/93, as from IP completion day. The amendments are set out below. With regard to these amendments, note that Articles that are repealed are reproduced in italics and, in the case of other amendments, the amending provision from SI 2019/93 is set out in full in the Notes to the amended Article, and the text of the amended Article has not been altered. For transitional provisions and savings in relation to the operation of the 2019 Regulations, see Sch 4 to those Regulations at **[7.69]** et seq.

Note also that Regulation 2821/71/EEC (under which this Regulation was made) is repealed, in relation to the UK, by the Competition (Amendment etc) (EU Exit) Regulations 2019, SI 2019/93, reg 63, Sch 3, para 1, as from IP completion day (as defined in the European Union (Withdrawal Agreement) Act 2020, s 39) (for transitional provisions and savings in relation to the operation of the 2019 Regulations, see Sch 4 to those Regulations at **[7.69]** et seq). However, see Sch 3, para 2 to those Regulations (at **[7.67]**) which provides for the continued application of this Regulation despite the repeal of Regulation 2821/71/EEC.

THE EUROPEAN COMMISSION,

Having regard to the Treaty on the Functioning of the European Union,

Having regard to Regulation (EEC) No 2821/71 of the Council of 20 December 1971 on application of Article 85(3) of the Treaty to categories of agreements, decisions and concerted practices[1],

Having published a draft of this Regulation,

After consulting the Advisory Committee on Restrictive Practices and Dominant Positions,

Whereas:

(1) Regulation (EEC) No 2821/71 empowers the Commission to apply Article 101(3) of the Treaty on the Functioning of the European Union[*] by regulation to certain categories of agreements, decisions and concerted practices falling within the scope of Article 101(1) of the Treaty which have as their object the research and development of products, technologies or processes up to the stage of industrial application, and exploitation of the results, including provisions regarding intellectual property rights.

(2) Article 179(2) of the Treaty calls upon the Union to encourage undertakings, including small and medium-sized undertakings, in their research and technological development activities of high quality, and to support their efforts to cooperate with one another. This Regulation is intended to facilitate research and development while at the same time effectively protecting competition.

(3) Commission Regulation (EC) No 2659/2000 of 29 November 2000 on the application of Article 81(3) of the Treaty to categories of research and development agreements[2] defines categories of research and development agreements which the Commission regarded as normally satisfying the conditions laid down in Article 101(3) of the Treaty. In view of the overall positive experience with the application of that Regulation, which expires on 31 December 2010, and taking into account further experience acquired since its adoption, it is appropriate to adopt a new block exemption regulation.

(4) This Regulation should meet the two requirements of ensuring effective protection of competition and providing adequate legal security for undertakings. The pursuit of those objectives should take account of the need to simplify administrative supervision and the legislative framework to as great an extent as possible. Below a certain level of market power it can in general be presumed, for the application of Article 101(3) of the Treaty, that the positive effects of research and development agreements will outweigh any negative effects on competition.

(5) For the application of Article 101(3) of the Treaty by regulation, it is not necessary to define those agreements which are capable of falling within Article 101(1) of the Treaty. In the individual assessment of agreements under Article 101(1) of the Treaty, account has to be taken of several factors, and in particular the market structure on the relevant market.

(6) Agreements on the joint execution of research work or the joint development of the results of the research, up to but not including the stage of industrial application, generally do not fall within the scope of Article 101(1) of the Treaty. In certain circumstances, however, such as where the parties agree not to carry out other research and development in the same field, thereby forgoing the opportunity of gaining competitive advantages over the other parties, such agreements may fall within Article 101(1) of the Treaty and should therefore be included within the scope of this Regulation.

(7) The benefit of the exemption established by this Regulation should be limited to those agreements for which it can be assumed with sufficient certainty that they satisfy the conditions of Article 101(3) of the Treaty.

(8) Cooperation in research and development and in the exploitation of the results is most likely to promote technical and economic progress if the parties contribute complementary skills, assets or activities to the co-operation. This also includes scenarios where one party merely finances the research and development activities of another party.

(9) The joint exploitation of results can be considered as the natural consequence of joint research and development. It can take different forms such as manufacture, the exploitation of intellectual property rights that substantially contribute to technical or economic progress, or the marketing of new products.

(10) Consumers can generally be expected to benefit from the increased volume and effectiveness of research and development through the introduction of new or improved products or services, a quicker launch of those products or services, or the reduction of prices brought about by new or improved technologies or processes.

(11) In order to justify the exemption, the joint exploitation should relate to products, technologies or processes for which the use of the results of the research and development is decisive. Moreover, all the parties should agree in the research and development agreement that they will all have full access to the final results of the joint research and development, including any arising intellectual property rights and know-how, for the purposes of further research and development and exploitation, as soon as the final results become available. Access to the results should generally not be limited as regards the use of the results for the purposes of further research and development. However, where the parties, in accordance with this Regulation, limit their rights of exploitation, in particular where they specialise in the context of exploitation, access to the results for the purposes of exploitation may be limited accordingly. Moreover, where academic bodies, research institutes or undertakings which supply research and development as a commercial service without normally being active in the exploitation of results participate in research and development, they may agree to use the results of research and development solely for the purpose of further research. Depending on their capabilities and commercial needs, the parties may make unequal contributions to their research and development cooperation. Therefore, in order to reflect, and to make up for, the differences in the value or the nature of the parties' contributions, a research and development agreement benefiting from this Regulation may provide that one party is to compensate another for obtaining access to the results for the purposes of further research or exploitation. However, the compensation should not be so high as to effectively impede such access.

(12) Similarly, where the research and development agreement does not provide for any joint exploitation of the results, the parties should agree in the research and development agreement to grant each other access to their respective pre-existing know-how, as long as this know-how is indispensable for the purposes of the exploitation of the results by the other parties. The rates of any licence fee charged should not be so high as to effectively impede access to the know-how by the other parties.

(13) The exemption established by this Regulation should be limited to research and development agreements which do not afford the undertakings the possibility of eliminating competition in respect of a substantial part of the products, services or technologies in question. It is necessary to exclude from the block exemption agreements between

competitors whose combined share of the market for products, services or technologies capable of being improved or replaced by the results of the research and development exceeds a certain level at the time the agreement is entered into. However, there is no presumption that research and development agreements are either caught by Article 101(1) of the Treaty or that they fail to satisfy the conditions of Article 101(3) of the Treaty once the market share threshold set out in this Regulation is exceeded or other conditions of this Regulation are not met. In such cases, an individual assessment of the research and development agreement needs to be conducted under Article 101 of the Treaty.

(14) In order to ensure the maintenance of effective competition during joint exploitation of the results, provision should be made for the block exemption to cease to apply if the parties' combined share of the market for the products, services or technologies arising out of the joint research and development becomes too great. The exemption should continue to apply, irrespective of the parties' market shares, for a certain period after the commencement of joint exploitation, so as to await stabilisation of their market shares, particularly after the introduction of an entirely new product, and to guarantee a minimum period of return on the investments involved.

(15) This Regulation should not exempt agreements containing restrictions which are not indispensable to the attainment of the positive effects generated by a research and development agreement. In principle, agreements containing certain types of severe restrictions of competition such as limitations on the freedom of parties to carry out research and development in a field unconnected to the agreement, the fixing of prices charged to third parties, limitations on output or sales, and limitations on effecting passive sales for the contract products or contract technologies in territories or to customers reserved for other parties should be excluded from the benefit of the exemption established by this Regulation irrespective of the market share of the parties. In this context, field of use restrictions do not constitute limitations of output or sales, and also do not constitute territorial or customer restrictions.

(16) The market share limitation, the non-exemption of certain agreements and the conditions provided for in this Regulation normally ensure that the agreements to which the block exemption applies do not enable the parties to eliminate competition in respect of a substantial part of the products or services in question.

(17) The possibility cannot be ruled out that anti-competitive foreclosure effects may arise where one party finances several research and development projects carried out by competitors with regard to the same contract products or contract technologies, in particular where it obtains the exclusive right to exploit the results vis-à-vis third parties. Therefore the benefit of this Regulation should be conferred on such paid-for research and development agreements only if the combined market share of all the parties involved in the connected agreements, that is to say, the financing party and all the parties carrying out the research and development, does not exceed 25%.

(18) Agreements between undertakings which are not competing manufacturers of products, technologies or processes capable of being improved, substituted or replaced by the results of the research and development will only eliminate effective competition in research and development in exceptional circumstances. It is therefore appropriate to enable such agreements to benefit from the exemption established by this Regulation irrespective of market share and to address any exceptional cases by way of withdrawal of its benefit.

(19) The Commission may withdraw the benefit of this Regulation, pursuant to Article 29(1) of Council Regulation (EC) No 1/2003 of 16 December 2002 on the implementation of the rules on competition laid down in Articles 81 and 82 of the Treaty[3], where it finds in a particular case that an agreement to which the exemption provided for in this Regulation applies nevertheless has effects which are incompatible with Article 101(3) of the Treaty.

(20) The competition authority of a Member State may withdraw the benefit of this Regulation pursuant to Article 29(2) of Regulation (EC) No 1/2003 in respect of the territory of that Member State, or a part thereof where, in a particular case, an agreement to which the exemption established by this Regulation applies nevertheless has effects which are incompatible with Article 101(3) of the Treaty in the territory of that Member State, or in a part thereof, and where such territory has all the characteristics of a distinct geographic market.

(21) The benefit of this Regulation could be withdrawn pursuant to Article 29 of Regulation (EC) No 1/2003, for example, where the existence of a research and development agreement substantially restricts the scope for third parties to carry out research and development in the relevant field because of the limited research capacity available elsewhere, where because of the particular structure of supply, the existence of the research and development agreement substantially restricts the access of third parties to the market for the contract products or contract technologies, where without any objectively valid reason, the parties do not exploit the results of the joint research and development vis-à-vis third parties, where the contract products or contract technologies are not subject in the whole or a substantial part of the internal market to effective competition from products, technologies or processes considered by users as equivalent in view of their characteristics, price and intended use, or where the existence of the research and development agreement would restrict competition in innovation or eliminate effective competition in research and development on a particular market.

(22) As research and development agreements are often of a long-term nature, especially where the cooperation extends to the exploitation of the results, the period of validity of this Regulation should be fixed at 12 years,

NOTES

[1] OJ L285, 29.12.1971, p. 46.

* With effect from 1 December 2009, Article 81 of the EC Treaty has become Article 101 of the Treaty on the Functioning of the European Union (TFEU). The two articles are, in substance, identical. For the purposes of this Regulation, references to Article 101 of the TFEU should be understood as references to Article 81 of the EC Treaty where appropriate. The TFEU also introduced certain changes in terminology, such as the replacement of 'Community' by 'Union' and 'common market' by 'internal market'. The terminology of the TFEU will be used throughout this Regulation.

[2] OJ L304, 5.12.2000, p. 7.

[3] OJ L1, 4.1.2003, p. 1.

HAS ADOPTED THIS REGULATION:

[4.202]

Article 1 Definitions

1. For the purposes of this Regulation, the following definitions shall apply:

(a) 'research and development agreement' means an agreement entered into between two or more parties which relate to the conditions under which those parties pursue:

(i) joint research and development of contract products or contract technologies and joint exploitation of the results of that research and development;

(ii) joint exploitation of the results of research and development of contract products or contract technologies jointly carried out pursuant to a prior agreement between the same parties;

(iii) joint research and development of contract products or contract technologies excluding joint exploitation of the results;

(iv) paid-for research and development of contract products or contract technologies and joint exploitation of the results of that research and development;

(v) joint exploitation of the results of paid-for research and development of contract products or contract technologies pursuant to a prior agreement between the same parties; or

(vi) paid-for research and development of contract products or contract technologies excluding joint exploitation of the results;

(b) 'agreement' means an agreement, a decision by an association of undertakings or a concerted practice;

(c) 'research and development' means the acquisition of know-how relating to products, technologies or processes and the carrying out of theoretical analysis, systematic study or experimentation, including experimental production, technical testing of products or processes, the establishment of the necessary facilities and the obtaining of intellectual property rights for the results;

(d) 'product' means a good or a service, including both intermediary goods or services and final goods or services;

(e) 'contract technology' means a technology or process arising out of the joint research and development;

(f) 'contract product' means a product arising out of the joint research and development or manufactured or provided applying the contract technologies;

(g) 'exploitation of the results' means the production or distribution of the contract products or the application of the contract technologies or the assignment or licensing of intellectual property rights or the communication of know-how required for such manufacture or application;

(h) 'intellectual property rights' means intellectual property rights, including industrial property rights, copyright and neighbouring rights;

(i) 'know-how' means a package of non-patented practical information, resulting from experience and testing, which is secret, substantial and identified;

(j) 'secret', in the context of know-how, means that the know-how is not generally known or easily accessible;

(k) 'substantial', in the context of know-how, means that the know-how is significant and useful for the manufacture of the contract products or the application of the contract technologies;

(l) 'identified', in the context of know-how, means that the know-how is described in a sufficiently comprehensive manner so as to make it possible to verify that it fulfils the criteria of secrecy and substantiality;

(m) 'joint', in the context of activities carried out under a research and development agreement, means activities where the work involved is:

(i) carried out by a joint team, organisation or undertaking;

(ii) jointly entrusted to a third party; or

(iii) allocated between the parties by way of specialisation in the context of research and development or exploitation;

(n) 'specialisation in the context of research and development' means that each of the parties is involved in the research and development activities covered by the research and development agreement and they divide the research and development work between them in any way that they consider most appropriate; this does not include paid-for research and development;

(o) 'specialisation in the context of exploitation' means that the parties allocate between them individual tasks such as production or distribution, or impose restrictions upon each other regarding the exploitation of the results such as restrictions in relation to certain territories, customers or fields of use; this includes a scenario where only one party produces and distributes the contract products on the basis of an exclusive licence granted by the other parties;

(p) 'paid-for research and development' means research and development that is carried out by one party and financed by a financing party;

(q) 'financing party' means a party financing paid-for research and development while not carrying out any of the research and development activities itself;

(r) 'competing undertaking' means an actual or potential competitor;

(s) 'actual competitor' means an undertaking that is supplying a product, technology or process capable of being improved, substituted or replaced by the contract product or the contract technology on the relevant geographic market;

(t) 'potential competitor' means an undertaking that, in the absence of the research and development agreement, would, on realistic grounds and not just as a mere theoretical possibility, in case of a small but permanent increase in relative prices be likely to undertake, within not more than 3 years, the necessary additional investments or other necessary switching costs to supply a product, technology or process capable of being improved, substituted or replaced by the contract product or contract technology on the relevant geographic market;

(u) 'relevant product market' means the relevant market for the products capable of being improved, substituted or replaced by the contract products;

(v) 'relevant technology market' means the relevant market for the technologies or processes capable of being improved, substituted or replaced by the contract technologies.

2. For the purposes of this Regulation, the terms 'undertaking' and 'party' shall include their respective connected undertakings.

'Connected undertakings' means:

(a) undertakings in which a party to the research and development agreement, directly or indirectly:
   (i) has the power to exercise more than half the voting rights;
   (ii) has the power to appoint more than half the members of the supervisory board, board of management or bodies legally representing the undertaking; or
   (iii) has the right to manage the undertaking's affairs;
(b) undertakings which directly or indirectly have, over a party to the research and development agreement, the rights or powers listed in point (a);
(c) undertakings in which an undertaking referred to in point (b) has, directly or indirectly, the rights or powers listed in point (a);
(d) undertakings in which a party to the research and development agreement together with one or more of the undertakings referred to in points (a), (b) or (c), or in which two or more of the latter undertakings, jointly have the rights or powers listed in point (a);
(e) undertakings in which the rights or the powers listed in point (a) are jointly held by:
   (i) parties to the research and development agreement or their respective connected undertakings referred to in points (a) to (d); or
   (ii) one or more of the parties to the research and development agreement or one or more of their connected undertakings referred to in points (a) to (d) and one or more third parties.

NOTES

Application of this Article in relation to the UK: this Article is amended, in relation to the UK only, by the Competition (Amendment etc) (EU Exit) Regulations 2019, SI 2019/93, reg 63, Sch 3, Pt 2, para 7(2), as from IP completion day (as defined in the European Union (Withdrawal Agreement) Act 2020, s 39) (for transitional provisions and savings in relation to the operation of the 2019 Regulations, see Sch 4 to those Regulations at **[7.69]** et seq), as follows—

"(2) In Article 1(1), after point (q), insert—

"(ra) "the Chapter 1 prohibition" means the prohibition imposed by section 2(1) of the Competition Act 1998;".".

[4.203]
Article 2 Exemption

1. Pursuant to Article 101(3) of the Treaty and subject to the provisions of this Regulation, it is hereby declared that Article 101(1) of the Treaty shall not apply to research and development agreements.

This exemption shall apply to the extent that such agreements contain restrictions of competition falling within the scope of Article 101(1) of the Treaty.

2. The exemption provided for in paragraph 1 shall apply to research and development agreements containing provisions which relate to the assignment or licensing of intellectual property rights to one or more of the parties or to an entity the parties establish to carry out the joint research and development, paid-for research and development or joint exploitation, provided that those provisions do not constitute the primary object of such agreements, but are directly related to and necessary for their implementation.

NOTES

Application of this Article in relation to the UK: this Article is amended, in relation to the UK only, by the Competition (Amendment etc) (EU Exit) Regulations 2019, SI 2019/93, reg 63, Sch 3, Pt 2, para 7(3), as from IP completion day (as defined in the European Union (Withdrawal Agreement) Act 2020, s 39) (for transitional provisions and savings in relation to the operation of the 2019 Regulations, see Sch 4 to those Regulations at **[7.69]** et seq), as follows—

"(3) In Article 2(1)—

(a) for the first subparagraph substitute—

"Subject to the provisions of this Regulation, research and development agreements are exempt from the Chapter 1 prohibition.";

(b) in the second subparagraph, for "Article 101(1) of the Treaty" substitute "the Chapter 1 prohibition".".

[4.204]
Article 3 Conditions for exemption

1. The exemption provided for in Article 2 shall apply subject to the conditions set out in paragraphs 2 to 5.

2. The research and development agreement must stipulate that all the parties have full access to the final results of the joint research and development or paid-for research and development, including any resulting intellectual property rights and know-how, for the purposes of further research and development and exploitation, as soon as they become available. Where the parties limit their rights of exploitation in accordance with this Regulation, in particular where they specialise in the context of exploitation, access to the results for the purposes of exploitation may be limited accordingly. Moreover, research institutes, academic bodies, or undertakings which supply research and development as a commercial service without normally being active in the exploitation of results may agree to confine their use of the results for the purposes of further research. The research and development agreement may foresee that the parties compensate each other for giving access to the results for the purposes of further research or exploitation, but the compensation must not be so high as to effectively impede such access.

3. Without prejudice to paragraph 2, where the research and development agreement provides only for joint research and development or paid-for research and development, the research and development agreement must stipulate that each party must be granted access to any pre-existing know-how of the other parties, if this know-how is

indispensable for the purposes of its exploitation of the results. The research and development agreement may foresee that the parties compensate each other for giving access to their pre-existing know-how, but the compensation must not be so high as to effectively impede such access.

4. Any joint exploitation may only pertain to results which are protected by intellectual property rights or constitute know-how and which are indispensable for the manufacture of the contract products or the application of the contract technologies.

5. Parties charged with the manufacture of the contract products by way of specialisation in the context of exploitation must be required to fulfil orders for supplies of the contract products from the other parties, except where the research and development agreement also provides for joint distribution within the meaning of point (m)(i) or (ii) of Article 1(1) or where the parties have agreed that only the party manufacturing the contract products may distribute them.

[4.205]

Article 4 Market share threshold and duration of exemption

1. Where the parties are not competing undertakings, the exemption provided for in Article 2 shall apply for the duration of the research and development. Where the results are jointly exploited, the exemption shall continue to apply for 7 years from the time the contract products or contract technologies are first put on the market within the internal market.

2. Where two or more of the parties are competing undertakings, the exemption provided for in Article 2 shall apply for the period referred to in paragraph 1 of this Article only if, at the time the research and development agreement is entered into:

(a) in the case of research and development agreements referred to in point (a)(i), (ii) or (iii) of Article 1(1), the combined market share of the parties to a research and development agreement does not exceed 25% on the relevant product and technology markets; or

(b) in the case of research and agreements referred to in point (a)(iv), (v) or (vi) of Article 1(1), the combined market share of the financing party and all the parties with which the financing party has entered into research and development agreements with regard to the same contract products or contract technologies, does not exceed 25% on the relevant product and technology markets.

3. After the end of the period referred to in paragraph 1, the exemption shall continue to apply as long as the combined market share of the parties does not exceed 25% on the relevant product and technology markets.

NOTES

Application of this Article in relation to the UK: this Article is amended, in relation to the UK only, by the Competition (Amendment etc) (EU Exit) Regulations 2019, SI 2019/93, reg 63, Sch 3, Pt 2, para 7(4), as from IP completion day (as defined in the European Union (Withdrawal Agreement) Act 2020, s 39) (for transitional provisions and savings in relation to the operation of the 2019 Regulations, see Sch 4 to those Regulations at **[7.69]** et seq), as follows—

"(4) In Article 4(1), for "internal market" substitute "United Kingdom".".

[4.206]

Article 5 Hardcore restrictions

The exemption provided for in Article 2 shall not apply to research and development agreements which, directly or indirectly, in isolation or in combination with other factors under the control of the parties, have as their object any of the following:

(a) the restriction of the freedom of the parties to carry out research and development independently or in cooperation with third parties in a field unconnected with that to which the research and development agreement relates or, after the completion of the joint research and development or the paid-for research and development, in the field to which it relates or in a connected field;

(b) the limitation of output or sales, with the exception of:

(i) the setting of production targets where the joint exploitation of the results includes the joint production of the contract products;

(ii) the setting of sales targets where the joint exploitation of the results includes the joint distribution of the contract products or the joint licensing of the contract technologies within the meaning of point (m)(i) or (ii) of Article 1(1);

(iii) practices constituting specialisation in the context of exploitation; and

(iv) the restriction of the freedom of the parties to manufacture, sell, assign or license products, technologies or processes which compete with the contract products or contract technologies during the period for which the parties have agreed to jointly exploit the results;

(c) the fixing of prices when selling the contract product or licensing the contract technologies to third parties, with the exception of the fixing of prices charged to immediate customers or the fixing of licence fees charged to immediate licensees where the joint exploitation of the results includes the joint distribution of the contract products or the joint licensing of the contract technologies within the meaning of point (m)(i) or (ii) of Article 1(1);

(d) the restriction of the territory in which, or of the customers to whom, the parties may passively sell the contract products or license the contract technologies, with the exception of the requirement to exclusively license the results to another party;

(e) the requirement not to make any, or to limit, active sales of the contract products or contract technologies in territories or to customers which have not been exclusively allocated to one of the parties by way of specialisation in the context of exploitation;

(f) the requirement to refuse to meet demand from customers in the parties' respective territories, or from customers otherwise allocated between the parties by way of specialisation in the context of exploitation, who would market the contract products in other territories within the internal market;

(g) the requirement to make it difficult for users or resellers to obtain the contract products from other resellers within the internal market.

NOTES

Application of this Article in relation to the UK: this Article is amended, in relation to the UK only, by the Competition (Amendment etc) (EU Exit) Regulations 2019, SI 2019/93, reg 63, Sch 3, Pt 2, para 7(5), as from IP completion day (as defined in the European Union (Withdrawal Agreement) Act 2020, s 39) (for transitional provisions and savings in relation to the operation of the 2019 Regulations, see Sch 4 to those Regulations at **[7.69]** et seq), as follows—

"(5) In Article 5, in points (f) and (g), for "internal market" substitute "United Kingdom";".

[4.207]

Article 6 Excluded restrictions

The exemption provided for in Article 2 shall not apply to the following obligations contained in research and development agreements:

(a) the obligation not to challenge after completion of the research and development the validity of intellectual property rights which the parties hold in the internal market and which are relevant to the research and development or, after the expiry of the research and development agreement, the validity of intellectual property rights which the parties hold in the internal market and which protect the results of the research and development, without prejudice to the possibility to provide for termination of the research and development agreement in the event of one of the parties challenging the validity of such intellectual property rights;

(b) the obligation not to grant licences to third parties to manufacture the contract products or to apply the contract technologies unless the agreement provides for the exploitation of the results of the joint research and development or paid-for research and development by at least one of the parties and such exploitation takes place in the internal market vis-à-vis third parties.

NOTES

Application of this Article in relation to the UK: this Article is amended, in relation to the UK only, by the Competition (Amendment etc) (EU Exit) Regulations 2019, SI 2019/93, reg 63, Sch 3, Pt 2, para 7(6), as from IP completion day (as defined in the European Union (Withdrawal Agreement) Act 2020, s 39) (for transitional provisions and savings in relation to the operation of the 2019 Regulations, see Sch 4 to those Regulations at **[7.69]** et seq), as follows—

"(6) In Article 6—

(a) in point (a), for "which the parties hold in the internal market" (in both places it occurs) substitute "held by the parties which have effect in the United Kingdom";

(b) in point (b), for "internal market" substitute "United Kingdom".".

[4.208]

Article 7 Application of the market share threshold

For the purposes of applying the market share threshold provided for in Article 4 the following rules shall apply:

(a) the market share shall be calculated on the basis of the market sales value; if market sales value data are not available, estimates based on other reliable market information, including market sales volumes, may be used to establish the market share of the parties;

(b) the market share shall be calculated on the basis of data relating to the preceding calendar year;

(c) the market share held by the undertakings referred to in point (e) of the second subparagraph of Article 1(2) shall be apportioned equally to each undertaking having the rights or the powers listed in point (a) of that subparagraph;

(d) if the market share referred to in Article 4(3) is initially not more than 25% but subsequently rises above that level without exceeding 30%, the exemption provided for in Article 2 shall continue to apply for a period of two consecutive calendar years following the year in which the 25% threshold was first exceeded;

(e) if the market share referred to in Article 4(3) is initially not more than 25% but subsequently rises above 30%, the exemption provided for in Article 2 shall continue to apply for a period of one calendar year following the year in which the level of 30% was first exceeded;

(f) the benefit of points (d) and (e) may not be combined so as to exceed a period of two calendar years.

[4.209]

Article 8 Transitional period

The prohibition laid down in Article 101(1) of the Treaty shall not apply during the period from 1 January 2011 to 31 December 2012 in respect of agreements already in force on 31 December 2010 which do not satisfy the conditions for exemption provided for in this Regulation but which satisfy the conditions for exemption provided for in Regulation (EC) No 2659/2000.

NOTES

Repeal of this Article in relation to the UK: this Article is repealed, in relation to the UK only, by the Competition (Amendment etc) (EU Exit) Regulations 2019, SI 2019/93, reg 63, Sch 3, Pt 2, para 7(7), as from IP completion day (as defined in the European Union (Withdrawal Agreement) Act 2020, s 39) (for transitional provisions and savings in relation to the operation of the 2019 Regulations, see Sch 3, Pt 2, para 10 to those Regulations at **[7.68]**, and Sch 4 to those Regulations at **[7.69]** et seq).

[4.210]

Article 9 Period of validity

This Regulation shall enter into force on 1 January 2011.

It shall expire on 31 December 2022.

This Regulation shall be binding in its entirety and directly applicable in all Member States.

NOTES

Application of this Article in relation to the UK: this Article is amended, in relation to the UK only, by the Competition (Amendment etc) (EU Exit) Regulations 2019, SI 2019/93, reg 63, Sch 3, Pt 2, para 7(8), as from IP completion day (as defined in the European Union (Withdrawal Agreement) Act 2020, s 39) (for transitional provisions and savings in relation to the operation of the 2019 Regulations, see Sch 4 to those Regulations at **[7.69]** et seq), as follows—

"(8) In the words after Article 9, omit the words from "This Regulation shall be binding" to "Member States.".".

COMMISSION REGULATION

(1218/2010/EU)

of 14 December 2010

on the application of Article 101(3) of the Treaty on the Functioning of the European Union to certain categories of specialisation agreements

(Text with EEA relevance)

[4.211]

NOTES

Date of publication in OJ: OJ L335, 18.12.2010, p 43.

Application of this Regulation in relation to the UK: in accordance with the European Union (Withdrawal) Act 2018, s 3 at **[7.5]**, this Regulation became domestic law on IP completion day (as defined in the European Union (Withdrawal Agreement) Act 2020, s 39). In so far as applying to the UK, this Regulation is amended by the Competition (Amendment etc) (EU Exit) Regulations 2019, SI 2019/93, as from IP completion day. The amendments are set out below. With regard to these amendments, note that Articles that are repealed are reproduced in italics, and in the case of other amendments, the amending provision from SI 2019/93 is set out in full in the Notes to the amended Article, and the text of the amended Article has not been altered. For transitional provisions and savings in relation to the operation of the 2019 Regulations, see Sch 4 to those Regulations at **[7.69]** et seq.

Note also that Regulation 2821/71/EEC (under which this Regulation was made) is repealed, in relation to the UK, by the Competition (Amendment etc) (EU Exit) Regulations 2019, SI 2019/93, reg 63, Sch 3, para 1, as from IP completion day (as defined in the European Union (Withdrawal Agreement) Act 2020, s 39) (for transitional provisions and savings in relation to the operation of the 2019 Regulations, see Sch 4 to those Regulations at **[7.69]** et seq). However, see Sch 3, para 2 to those Regulations (at **[7.67]**) which provides for the continued application of this Regulation despite the repeal of Regulation 2821/71/EEC.

THE EUROPEAN COMMISSION,

Having regard to the Treaty on the Functioning of the European Union,

Having regard to Regulation (EEC) No 2821/71 of the Council of 20 December 1971 on application of Article 85(3) of the Treaty to categories of agreements, decisions and concerted practices[1],

Having published a draft of this Regulation,

After consulting the Advisory Committee on Restrictive Practices and Dominant Positions,

Whereas:

(1) Regulation (EEC) No 2821/71 empowers the Commission to apply Article 101(3) of the Treaty on the Functioning of the European Union[*] by regulation to certain categories of agreements, decisions and concerted practices falling within the scope of Article 101(1) of the Treaty which have as their object specialisation, including agreements necessary for achieving it.

(2) Commission Regulation (EC) No 2658/2000 of 29 November 2000 on the application of Article 81(3) of the Treaty to categories of specialisation agreements[2] defines categories of specialisation agreements which the Commission regarded as normally satisfying the conditions laid down in Article 101(3) of the Treaty. In view of the overall positive experience with the application of that Regulation, which expires on 31 December 2010, and taking into account further experience acquired since its adoption, it is appropriate to adopt a new block exemption regulation.

(3) This Regulation should meet the two requirements of ensuring effective protection of competition and providing adequate legal security for undertakings. The pursuit of those objectives should take account of the need to simplify administrative supervision and the legislative framework to as great an extent as possible. Below a certain level of market power it can in general be presumed, for the application of Article 101(3) of the Treaty, that the positive effects of specialisation agreements will outweigh any negative effects on competition.

(4) For the application of Article 101(3) of the Treaty by regulation, it is not necessary to define those agreements which are capable of falling within Article 101(1) of the Treaty. In the individual assessment of agreements under Article 101(1) of the Treaty, account has to be taken of several factors, and in particular the market structure on the relevant market.

(5) The benefit of the exemption established by this Regulation should be limited to those agreements for which it can be assumed with sufficient certainty that they satisfy the conditions of Article 101(3) of the Treaty.

(6) Agreements on specialisation in production are most likely to contribute to improving the production or distribution of goods if the parties have complementary skills, assets or activities, because they can concentrate on the manufacture of certain products and thus operate more efficiently and supply the products more cheaply. The same can generally be said about agreements on specialisation in the preparation of services. Given effective competition, it is likely that consumers will receive a fair share of the resulting benefits.

(7) Such advantages can arise from agreements whereby one party fully or partly gives up the manufacture of

certain products or preparation of certain services in favour of another party (unilateral specialisation), from agreements whereby each party fully or partly gives up the manufacture of certain products or preparation of certain services in favour of another party (reciprocal specialisation) and from agreements whereby the parties undertake to jointly manufacture certain products or prepare certain services (joint production). In the context of this Regulation, the concepts of unilateral and reciprocal specialisation do not require a party to reduce capacity, as it is sufficient if they reduce their production volumes. The concept of joint production, however, does not require the parties to reduce their individual production activities outside the scope of their envisaged joint production arrangement.

(8) The nature of unilateral and reciprocal specialisation agreements presupposes that the parties are active on the same product market. It is not necessary for the parties to be active on the same geographic market. Consequently, the application of this Regulation to unilateral and reciprocal specialisation agreements should be limited to scenarios where the parties are active on the same product market. Joint production agreements can be entered into by parties who are already active on the same product market but also by parties who wish to enter a product market by way of the agreement. Therefore, joint production agreements should fall within the scope of this Regulation irrespective of whether the parties are already active in the same product market.

(9) To ensure that the benefits of specialisation will materialise without one party leaving the market downstream of production entirely, unilateral and reciprocal specialisation agreements should only be covered by this Regulation where they provide for supply and purchase obligations or joint distribution. Supply and purchase obligations may, but do not have to, be of an exclusive nature.

(10) It can be presumed that, where the parties' share of the relevant market for the products which are the subject matter of a specialisation agreement does not exceed a certain level, the agreements will, as a general rule, give rise to economic benefits in the form of economies of scale or scope or better production technologies, while allowing consumers a fair share of the resulting benefits. However, where the products manufactured under a specialisation agreement are intermediary products which one or more of the parties fully or partly use as an input for their own production of certain downstream products which they subsequently sell on the market, the exemption conferred by this Regulation should also be conditional on the parties' share on the relevant market for these downstream products not exceeding a certain level. In such a case, merely looking at the parties' market share at the level of the intermediary product would ignore the potential risk of foreclosing or increasing the price of inputs for competitors at the level of the downstream products. However, there is no presumption that specialisation agreements are either caught by Article 101(1) of the Treaty or that they fail to satisfy the conditions of Article 101(3) of the Treaty once the market share threshold set out in this Regulation is exceeded or other conditions of this Regulation are not met. In such cases, an individual assessment of the specialisation agreement needs to be conducted under Article 101 of the Treaty.

(11) This Regulation should not exempt agreements containing restrictions which are not indispensable to the attainment of the positive effects generated by a specialisation agreement. In principle, agreements containing certain types of severe restrictions of competition relating to the fixing of prices charged to third parties, limitation of output or sales, and allocation of markets or customers should be excluded from the benefit of the exemption established by this Regulation irrespective of the market share of the parties.

(12) The market share limitation, the non-exemption of certain agreements and the conditions provided for in this Regulation normally ensure that the agreements to which the block exemption applies do not enable the parties to eliminate competition in respect of a substantial part of the products or services in question.

(13) The Commission may withdraw the benefit of this Regulation, pursuant to Article 29(1) of Council Regulation (EC) No 1/2003 of 16 December 2002 on the implementation of the rules on competition laid down in Articles 81 and 82 of the Treaty[3], where it finds in a particular case that an agreement to which the exemption provided for in this Regulation applies nevertheless has effects which are incompatible with Article 101(3) of the Treaty.

(14) The competition authority of a Member State may withdraw the benefit of this Regulation pursuant to Article 29(2) of Regulation (EC) No 1/2003 in respect of the territory of that Member State, or a part thereof where, in a particular case, an agreement to which the exemption established by this Regulation applies nevertheless has effects which are incompatible with Article 101(3) of the Treaty in the territory of that Member State, or in a part thereof, and where such territory has all the characteristics of a distinct geographic market.

(15) The benefit of this Regulation could be withdrawn pursuant to Article 29 of Regulation (EC) No 1/2003 where, for example, the relevant market is very concentrated and competition is already weak, in particular because of the individual market positions of other market participants or links between other market participants created by parallel specialisation agreements.

(16) In order to facilitate the conclusion of specialisation agreements, which can have a bearing on the structure of the parties, the period of validity of this Regulation should be fixed at 12 years,

NOTES

[1] OJ L285, 29.12.1971, p. 46.

[*] With effect from 1 December 2009, Article 81 of the EC Treaty has become Article 101 of the Treaty on the Functioning of the European Union (TFEU). The two Articles are, in substance, identical. For the purposes of this Regulation, references to Article 101 of the TFEU should be understood as references to Article 81 of the EC Treaty where appropriate. The TFEU also introduced certain changes in terminology, such as the replacement of 'Community' by 'Union' and 'common market' by 'internal market'. The terminology of the TFEU will be used throughout this Regulation.

[2] OJ L304, 5.12.2000, p. 3.

[3] OJ L1, 4.1.2003, p. 1.

HAS ADOPTED THIS REGULATION:

[4.212]

Article 1 Definitions

1. For the purposes of this Regulation, the following definitions shall apply:

(a) 'specialisation agreement' means a unilateral specialisation agreement, a reciprocal specialisation agreement or a joint production agreement;

(b) 'unilateral specialisation agreement' means an agreement between two parties which are active on the same product market by virtue of which one party agrees to fully or partly cease production of certain products or to refrain from producing those products and to purchase them from the other party, who agrees to produce and supply those products;

(c) 'reciprocal specialisation agreement' means an agreement between two or more parties which are active on the same product market, by virtue of which two or more parties on a reciprocal basis agree to fully or partly cease or refrain from producing certain but different products and to purchase these products from the other parties, who agree to produce and supply them;

(d) 'joint production agreement' means an agreement by virtue of which two or more parties agree to produce certain products jointly;

(e) 'agreement' means an agreement, a decision by an association of undertakings or a concerted practice;

(f) 'product' means a good or a service, including both intermediary goods or services and final goods or services, with the exception of distribution and rental services;

(g) 'production' means the manufacture of goods or the preparation of services and includes production by way of subcontracting;

(h) 'preparation of services' means activities upstream of the provision of services to customers;

(i) 'relevant market' means the relevant product and geographic market to which the specialisation products belong, and, in addition, where the specialisation products are intermediary products which one or more of the parties fully or partly use captively for the production of downstream products, the relevant product and geographic market to which the downstream products belong;

(j) 'specialisation product' means a product which is produced under a specialisation agreement;

(k) 'downstream product' means a product for which a specialisation product is used by one or more of the parties as an input and which is sold by those parties on the market;

(l) 'competing undertaking' means an actual or potential competitor;

(m) 'actual competitor' means an undertaking that is active on the same relevant market;

(n) 'potential competitor' means an undertaking that, in the absence of the specialisation agreement, would, on realistic grounds and not just as a mere theoretical possibility, in case of a small but permanent increase in relative prices be likely to undertake, within not more than 3 years, the necessary additional investments or other necessary switching costs to enter the relevant market;

(o) 'exclusive supply obligation' means an obligation not to supply a competing undertaking other than a party to the agreement with the specialisation product;

(p) 'exclusive purchase obligation' means an obligation to purchase the specialisation product only from a party to the agreement;

(q) 'joint', in the context of distribution, means that the parties:
   (i) carry out the distribution of the products by way of a joint team, organisation or undertaking; or
   (ii) appoint a third party distributor on an exclusive or non-exclusive basis, provided that the third party is not a competing undertaking;

(r) 'distribution' means distribution, including the sale of goods and the provision of services.

2. For the purposes of this Regulation, the terms 'undertaking' and 'party' shall include their respective connected undertakings.

'Connected undertakings' means:

(a) undertakings in which a party to the specialisation agreement, directly or indirectly:
   (i) has the power to exercise more than half the voting rights;
   (ii) has the power to appoint more than half the members of the supervisory board, board of management or bodies legally representing the undertaking; or
   (iii) has the right to manage the undertaking's affairs;

(b) undertakings which directly or indirectly have, over a party to the specialisation agreement, the rights or powers listed in point (a);

(c) undertakings in which an undertaking referred to in point (b) has, directly or indirectly, the rights or powers listed in point (a);

(d) undertakings in which a party to the specialisation agreement together with one or more of the undertakings referred to in points (a), (b) or (c), or in which two or more of the latter undertakings, jointly have the rights or powers listed in point (a);

(e) undertakings in which the rights or the powers listed in point (a) are jointly held by:
   (i) parties to the specialisation agreement or their respective connected undertakings referred to in points (a) to (d); or
   (ii) one or more of the parties to the specialisation agreement or one or more of their connected undertakings referred to in points (a) to (d) and one or more third parties.

NOTES

Application of this Article in relation to the UK: this Article is amended, in relation to the UK only, by the Competition (Amendment etc) (EU Exit) Regulations 2019, SI 2019/93, reg 63, Sch 3, Pt 2, para 8(2), as from IP completion day (as defined in the European Union (Withdrawal Agreement) Act 2020, s 39) (for transitional provisions and savings in relation to the operation of the 2019 Regulations, see Sch 4 to those Regulations at **[7.69]** et seq), as follows—

"(2) In Article 1(1), after point (h), insert—

"(ha) "the Chapter 1 prohibition" means the prohibition imposed by section 2(1) of the Competition Act 1998;".".

[4.213]

Article 2 Exemption

1. Pursuant to Article 101(3) of the Treaty and subject to the provisions of this Regulation, it is hereby declared that Article 101(1) of the Treaty shall not apply to specialisation agreements.

This exemption shall apply to the extent that such agreements contain restrictions of competition falling within the scope of Article 101(1) of the Treaty.

2. The exemption provided for in paragraph 1 shall apply to specialisation agreements containing provisions which relate to the assignment or licensing of intellectual property rights to one or more of the parties, provided that those provisions do not constitute the primary object of such agreements, but are directly related to and necessary for their implementation.

3. The exemption provided for in paragraph 1 shall apply to specialisation agreements whereby:

(a) the parties accept an exclusive purchase or exclusive supply obligation; or

(b) the parties do not independently sell the specialisation products but jointly distribute those products.

NOTES

Application of this Article in relation to the UK: this Article is amended, in relation to the UK only, by the Competition (Amendment etc) (EU Exit) Regulations 2019, SI 2019/93, reg 63, Sch 3, Pt 2, para 8(3), as from IP completion day (as defined in the European Union (Withdrawal Agreement) Act 2020, s 39) (for transitional provisions and savings in relation to the operation of the 2019 Regulations, see Sch 4 to those Regulations at **[7.69]** et seq), as follows—

"(3) In Article 2(1)—

(a) for the first subparagraph substitute—

"Subject to the provisions of this Regulation, specialisation agreements are exempt from the Chapter 1 prohibition.";

(b) in the second subparagraph, for "Article 101(1) of the Treaty" substitute "the Chapter 1 prohibition".".

[4.214]

Article 3 Market share threshold

The exemption provided for in Article 2 shall apply on condition that the combined market share of the parties does not exceed 20% on any relevant market.

[4.215]

Article 4 Hardcore restrictions

The exemption provided for in Article 2 shall not apply to specialisation agreements which, directly or indirectly, in isolation or in combination with other factors under the control of the parties, have as their object any of the following:

(a) the fixing of prices when selling the products to third parties with the exception of the fixing of prices charged to immediate customers in the context of joint distribution;

(b) the limitation of output or sales with the exception of:

(i) provisions on the agreed amount of products in the context of unilateral or reciprocal specialisation agreements or the setting of the capacity and production volume in the context of a joint production agreement; and

(ii) the setting of sales targets in the context of joint distribution;

(c) the allocation of markets or customers.

[4.216]

Article 5 Application of the market share threshold

For the purposes of applying the market share threshold provided for in Article 3 the following rules shall apply:

(a) the market share shall be calculated on the basis of the market sales value; if market sales value data are not available, estimates based on other reliable market information, including market sales volumes, may be used to establish the market share of the parties;

(b) the market share shall be calculated on the basis of data relating to the preceding calendar year;

(c) the market share held by the undertakings referred to in point (e) of the second subparagraph of Article 1(2) shall be apportioned equally to each undertaking having the rights or the powers listed in point (a) of that subparagraph;

(d) if the market share referred to in Article 3 is initially not more than 20% but subsequently rises above that level without exceeding 25%, the exemption provided for in Article 2 shall continue to apply for a period of 2 consecutive calendar years following the year in which the 20% threshold was first exceeded;

(e) if the market share referred to in Article 3 is initially not more than 20% but subsequently rises above 25%, the exemption provided for in Article 2 shall continue to apply for a period of 1 calendar year following the year in which the level of 25% was first exceeded;

(f) the benefit of points (d) and (e) may not be combined so as to exceed a period of 2 calendar years.

[4.217]

Article 6 Transitional period

The prohibition laid down in Article 101(1) of the Treaty shall not apply during the period from 1 January 2011 to 31 December 2012 in respect of agreements already in force on 31 December 2010 which do not satisfy the conditions for exemption provided for in this Regulation but which satisfy the conditions for exemption provided for in Regulation (EC) No 2658/2000.

NOTES

Repeal of this Article in relation to the UK: this Article is repealed, in relation to the UK only, by the Competition (Amendment etc) (EU Exit) Regulations 2019, SI 2019/93, reg 63, Sch 3, Pt 2, para 8(4), as from IP completion day (as defined in the European Union (Withdrawal Agreement) Act 2020, s 39) (for transitional provisions and savings in relation to the operation of the 2019 Regulations, see Sch 3, Pt 2, para 10 to those Regulations at **[7.68]**, and Sch 4 to those Regulations at **[7.69]** et seq).

[4.218]

Article 7 Period of validity

This Regulation shall enter into force on 1 January 2011.

It shall expire on 31 December 2022.

This Regulation shall be binding in its entirety and directly applicable in all Member States.

NOTES

Application of this Article in relation to the UK: this Article is amended, in relation to the UK only, by the Competition (Amendment etc) (EU Exit) Regulations 2019, SI 2019/93, reg 63, Sch 3, Pt 2, para 8(5), as from IP completion day (as defined in the European Union (Withdrawal Agreement) Act 2020, s 39) (for transitional provisions and savings in relation to the operation of the 2019 Regulations, see Sch 4 to those Regulations at **[7.69]** et seq), as follows—

"(5) In the words after Article 7, omit the words from "This Regulation shall be binding" to "Member States."."

COMMUNICATION FROM THE COMMISSION

(2011/C11/01)

Guidelines on the applicability of Article 101 of the Treaty on the Functioning of the European Union to horizontal co-operation agreements

(Text with EEA relevance)

[4.219]

NOTES

Date of publication in OJ: OJ C11, 14.1.2011, p 1. The text of this Communication incorporates the corrigendum published in OJ C33, 2.2.2011, p 20.

1. INTRODUCTION

1.1. Purpose and scope

[4.220]

1. These guidelines set out the principles for the assessment under Article 101 of the Treaty on the Functioning of the European Union* ('Article 101') of agreements between undertakings, decisions by associations of undertakings and concerted practices (collectively referred to as 'agreements') pertaining to horizontal co-operation. Co-operation is of a 'horizontal nature' if an agreement is entered into between actual or potential competitors. In addition, these guidelines also cover horizontal co-operation agreements between non-competitors, for example, between two companies active in the same product markets but in different geographic markets without being potential competitors.

2. Horizontal co-operation agreements can lead to substantial economic benefits, in particular if they combine complementary activities, skills or assets. Horizontal co-operation can be a means to share risk, save costs, increase investments, pool know-how, enhance product quality and variety, and launch innovation faster.

3. On the other hand, horizontal co-operation agreements may lead to competition problems. This is, for example, the case if the parties agree to fix prices or output or to share markets, or if the co-operation enables the parties to maintain, gain or increase market power and thereby is likely to give rise to negative market effects with respect to prices, output, product quality, product variety or innovation.

4. The Commission, while recognising the benefits that can be generated by horizontal co-operation agreements, has to ensure that effective competition is maintained. Article 101 provides the legal framework for a balanced assessment taking into account both adverse effects on competition and pro-competitive effects.

5. The purpose of these guidelines is to provide an analytical framework for the most common types of horizontal co-operation agreements; they deal with research and development agreements, production agreements including subcontracting and specialisation agreements, purchasing agreements, commercialisation agreements, standardisation agreements including standard contracts, and information exchange. This framework is primarily based on legal and economic criteria that help to analyse a horizontal co-operation agreement and the context in which it occurs. Economic criteria such as the market power of the parties and other factors relating to the market structure form a key element of the assessment of the market impact likely to be caused by a horizontal co-operation agreement and, therefore, for the assessment under Article 101.

6. These guidelines apply to the most common types of horizontal co-operation agreements irrespective of the level of integration they entail with the exception of operations constituting a concentration within the meaning of Article 3 of Council Regulation (EC) No 139/2004 of 20 January 2004 on the control of concentrations between undertakings[1] ('the Merger Regulation') as would be the case, for example, with joint ventures performing on a lasting basis all the functions of an autonomous economic entity ('full-function joint ventures').[2]

7. Given the potentially large number of types and combinations of horizontal co-operation and market circumstances in which they operate, it is difficult to provide specific answers for every possible scenario. These guidelines will nevertheless assist businesses in assessing the compatibility of an individual co-operation agreement with Article 101. Those criteria do not, however, constitute a 'checklist' which can be applied mechanically. Each case must be assessed on the basis of its own facts, which may require a flexible application of these guidelines.

8. The criteria set out in these guidelines apply to horizontal co-operation agreements concerning both goods and services (collectively referred to as 'products'). These guidelines complement Commission Regulation (EU) No 1217/2010 of 14 December 2010 on the application of Article 101(3) of the Treaty on the Functioning of the European Union to certain categories of research and development agreements[3] ('the R&D Block Exemption Regulation') and Commission Regulation (EU) No 1218/2010 of 14 December 2010 on the application of Article 101(3) of the Treaty on the Functioning of the European Union to certain categories of specialisation agreements[4] ('the Specialisation Block Exemption Regulation').

9. Although these guidelines contain certain references to cartels, they are not intended to give any guidance as to what does and does not constitute a cartel as defined by the decisional practice of the Commission and the case-law of the Court of Justice of the European Union.

10. The term 'competitors' as used in these guidelines includes both actual and potential competitors. Two companies are treated as actual competitors if they are active on the same relevant market. A company is treated as a potential competitor of another company if, in the absence of the agreement, in case of a small but permanent increase in relative prices it is likely that the former, within a short period of time,[5] would undertake the necessary additional investments or other necessary switching costs to enter the relevant market on which the latter is active. This assessment has to be based on realistic grounds, the mere theoretical possibility to enter a market is not sufficient (see Commission Notice on the definition of the relevant market for the purposes of Community competition law)[6] ('the Market Definition Notice').

11. Companies that form part of the same 'undertaking' within the meaning of Article 101(1) are not considered to be competitors for the purposes of these guidelines. Article 101 only applies to agreements between independent undertakings. When a company exercises decisive influence over another company they form a single economic entity and, hence, are part of the same undertaking.[7] The same is true for sister companies, that is to say, companies over which decisive influence is exercised by the same parent company. They are consequently not considered to be competitors even if they are both active on the same relevant product and geographic markets.

12. Agreements that are entered into between undertakings operating at a different level of the production or distribution chain, that is to say, vertical agreements, are in principle dealt with in Commission Regulation (EU) No 330/2010 of 20 April 2010 on the application of Article 101(3) of the Treaty on the Functioning of the European Union to categories of vertical agreements and concerted practices[8] ('the Block Exemption Regulation on Vertical Restraints') and the Guidelines on Vertical Restraints.[9] However, to the extent that vertical agreements, for example, distribution agreements, are concluded between competitors, the effects of the agreement on the market and the possible competition problems can be similar to horizontal agreements. Therefore, vertical agreements between competitors fall under these guidelines.[10] Should there be a need to also assess such agreements under the Block Exemption Regulation on Vertical Restraints and the Guidelines on Vertical Restraints, this will be specifically stated in the relevant chapter of these guidelines. In the absence of such a reference, only these guidelines will be applicable to vertical agreements between competitors.

13. Horizontal co-operation agreements may combine different stages of co-operation, for example research and development ('R&D') and the production and/or commercialisation of its results. Such agreements are generally also covered by these guidelines. When using these guidelines for the analysis of such integrated co-operation, as a general rule, all the chapters pertaining to the different parts of the co-operation will be relevant. However, where the relevant chapters of these guidelines contain graduated messages, for example with regard to safe harbours or whether certain conduct will normally be considered a restriction of competition by object or by effect, what is set out in the chapter pertaining to that part of an integrated co-operation which can be considered its 'centre of gravity' prevails for the entire co-operation.[11]

14. Two factors are in particular relevant for the determination of the centre of gravity of integrated cooperation: firstly, the starting point of the co-operation, and, secondly, the degree of integration of the different functions which are combined. For example, the centre of gravity of a horizontal co-operation agreement involving both joint R&D and joint production of the results would thus normally be the joint R&D, as the joint production will only take place if the joint R&D is successful. This implies that the results of the joint R&D are decisive for the subsequent joint production. The assessment of the centre of gravity would change if the parties would have engaged in the joint production in any event, that is to say, irrespective of the joint R&D, or if the agreement provided for a full integration in the area of production and only a partial integration of some R&D activities. In this case, the centre of gravity of the co-operation would be the joint production.

15. Article 101 only applies to those horizontal co-operation agreements which may affect trade between Member States. The principles on the applicability of Article 101 set out in these guidelines are therefore based on the assumption that a horizontal co-operation agreement is capable of affecting trade between Member States to an appreciable extent.

16. The assessment under Article 101 as described in these guidelines is without prejudice to the possible parallel application of Article 102 of the Treaty to horizontal co-operation agreements.[12]

17. These guidelines are without prejudice to the interpretation the Court of Justice of the European Union may give to the application of Article 101 to horizontal co-operation agreements.

18. These guidelines replace the Commission guidelines on the applicability of Article 81 of the EC Treaty to horizontal co-operation agreements[13] which were published by the Commission in 2001 and do not apply to the extent that sector specific rules apply as is the case for certain agreements with regard to agriculture,[14] transport[15] or

insurance.[16] The Commission will continue to monitor the operation of the R&D and Specialisation Block Exemption Regulations and these guidelines based on market information from stakeholders and national competition authorities and may revise these guidelines in the light of future developments and of evolving insight.

19. The Commission guidelines on the application of Article 81(3) of the Treaty[17] ('the General Guidelines') contain general guidance on the interpretation of Article 101. Consequently, these guidelines have to be read in conjunction with the General Guidelines.

1.2. Basic principles for the assessment under Article 101

20. The assessment under Article 101 consists of two steps. The first step, under Article 101(1), is to assess whether an agreement between undertakings, which is capable of affecting trade between Member States, has an anti-competitive object or actual or potential[18] restrictive effects on competition. The second step, under Article 101(3), which only becomes relevant when an agreement is found to be restrictive of competition within the meaning of Article 101(1), is to determine the pro-competitive benefits produced by that agreement and to assess whether those pro-competitive effects outweigh the restrictive effects on competition.[19] The balancing of restrictive and pro-competitive effects is conducted exclusively within the framework laid down by Article 101(3).[20] If the pro-competitive effects do not outweigh a restriction of competition, Article 101(2) stipulates that the agreement shall be automatically void.

21. The analysis of horizontal co-operation agreements has certain common elements with the analysis of horizontal mergers pertaining to the potential restrictive effects, in particular as regards joint ventures. There is often only a fine line between full-function joint ventures that fall under the Merger Regulation and non-full-function joint ventures that are assessed under Article 101. Hence, their effects can be quite similar.

22. In certain cases, companies are encouraged by public authorities to enter into horizontal co-operation agreements in order to attain a public policy objective by way of self-regulation. However, companies remain subject to Article 101 if a national law merely encourages or makes it easier for them to engage in autonomous anti-competitive conduct.[21] In other words, the fact that public authorities encourage a horizontal co-operation agreement does not mean that it is permissible under Article 101.[22] It is only if anti-competitive conduct is required of companies by national legislation, or if the latter creates a legal framework which precludes all scope for competitive activity on their part, that Article 101 does not apply.[23] In such a situation, the restriction of competition is not attributable, as Article 101 implicitly requires, to the autonomous conduct of the companies and they are shielded from all the consequences of an infringement of that article.[24] Each case must be assessed on its own facts according to the general principles set out in these guidelines.

1.2.1.
Article 101(1)

23. Article 101(1) prohibits agreements the object or effect of which is to restrict[25] competition.

(i)
Restrictions of competition by object

24. Restrictions of competition *by object* are those that by their very nature have the potential to restrict competition within the meaning of Article 101(1).[26] It is not necessary to examine the actual or potential effects of an agreement on the market once its anti-competitive object has been established.[27]

25. According to the settled case-law of the Court of Justice of the European Union, in order to assess whether an agreement has an anti-competitive object, regard must be had to the content of the agreement, the objectives it seeks to attain, and the economic and legal context of which it forms part. In addition, although the parties' intention is not a necessary factor in determining whether an agreement has an anti-competitive object, the Commission may nevertheless take this aspect into account in its analysis.[28] Further guidance with regard to the notion of restrictions of competition by object can be obtained in the General Guidelines.

(ii)
Restrictive effects on competition

26. If a horizontal co-operation agreement does not restrict competition by object, it must be examined whether it has appreciable restrictive effects on competition. Account must be taken of both actual and potential effects. In other words, the agreement must at least be likely to have anti-competitive effects.

27. For an agreement to have restrictive effects on competition within the meaning of Article 101(1) it must have, or be likely to have, an appreciable adverse impact on at least one of the parameters of competition on the market, such as price, output, product quality, product variety or innovation. Agreements can have such effects by appreciably reducing competition between the parties to the agreement or between any one of them and third parties. This means that the agreement must reduce the parties' decision-making independence,[29] either due to obligations contained in the agreement which regulate the market conduct of at least one of the parties or by influencing the market conduct of at least one of the parties by causing a change in its incentives.

28. Restrictive effects on competition within the relevant market are likely to occur where it can be expected with a reasonable degree of probability that, due to the agreement, the parties would be able to profitably raise prices or reduce output, product quality, product variety or innovation. This will depend on several factors such as the nature and content of the agreement, the extent to which the parties individually or jointly have or obtain some degree of market power, and the extent to which the agreement contributes to the creation, maintenance or strengthening of that market power or allows the parties to exploit such market power.

29. The assessment of whether a horizontal co-operation agreement has restrictive effects on competition within the meaning of Article 101(1) must be made in comparison to the actual legal and economic context in which competition would occur in the absence of the agreement with all of its alleged restrictions (that is to say, in the absence of the agreement as it stands (if already implemented) or as envisaged (if not yet implemented) at the time of assessment). Hence, in order to prove actual or potential restrictive effects on competition, it is necessary to take into account competition between the parties and competition from third parties, in particular actual or potential competition that would have existed in the absence of the agreement. This comparison does not take into account any potential efficiency gains generated by the agreement as these will only be assessed under Article 101(3).

30. Consequently, horizontal co-operation agreements between competitors that, on the basis of objective factors, would not be able to independently carry out the project or activity covered by the co-operation, for instance, due to the limited technical capabilities of the parties, will normally not give rise to restrictive effects on competition within the meaning of Article 101(1) unless the parties could have carried out the project with less stringent restrictions.[30]

31. General guidance with regard to the notion of restrictions of competition by effect can be obtained in the General Guidelines. These guidelines provide additional guidance specific to the competition assessment of horizontal co-operation agreements.

Nature and content of the agreement

32. The nature and content of an agreement relates to factors such as the area and objective of the co-operation, the competitive relationship between the parties and the extent to which they combine their activities. Those factors determine which kinds of possible competition concerns can arise from a horizontal co-operation agreement.

33. Horizontal co-operation agreements may limit competition in several ways. The agreement may:

— be exclusive in the sense that it limits the possibility of the parties to compete against each other or third parties as independent economic operators or as parties to other, competing agreements;

— require the parties to contribute such assets that their decision-making independence is appreciably reduced; or

— affect the parties' financial interests in such a way that their decision-making independence is appreciably reduced. Both financial interests in the agreement and also financial interests in other parties to the agreement are relevant for the assessment.

34. The potential effect of such agreements may be the loss of competition between the parties to the agreement. Competitors can also benefit from the reduction of competitive pressure that results from the agreement and may therefore find it profitable to increase their prices. The reduction in those competitive constraints may lead to price increases in the relevant market. Factors such as whether the parties to the agreement have high market shares, whether they are close competitors, whether the customers have limited possibilities of switching suppliers, whether competitors are unlikely to increase supply if prices increase, and whether one of the parties to the agreement is an important competitive force, are all relevant for the competitive assessment of the agreement.

35. A horizontal co-operation agreement may also:

— lead to the disclosure of strategic information thereby increasing the likelihood of coordination among the parties within or outside the field of the co-operation;

— achieve significant commonality of costs (that is to say, the proportion of variable costs which the parties have in common), so the parties may more easily coordinate market prices and output.

36. Significant commonality of costs achieved by a horizontal co-operation agreement can only allow the parties to more easily coordinate market prices and output where the parties have market power, the market characteristics are conducive to such coordination, the area of co-operation accounts for a high proportion of the parties' variable costs in a given market, and the parties combine their activities in the area of co-operation to a significant extent. This could, for instance, be the case, where they jointly manufacture or purchase an important intermediate product or jointly manufacture or distribute a high proportion of their total output of a final product.

37. A horizontal agreement may therefore decrease the parties' decision-making independence and as a result increase the likelihood that they will coordinate their behaviour in order to reach a collusive outcome but it may also make coordination easier, more stable or more effective for parties that were already coordinating before, either by making the coordination more robust or by permitting them to achieve even higher prices.

38. Some horizontal co-operation agreements, for example production and standardisation agreements, may also give rise to anti-competitive foreclosure concerns.

Market power and other market characteristics

39. Market power is the ability to profitably maintain prices above competitive levels for a period of time or to profitably maintain output in terms of product quantities, product quality and variety or innovation below competitive levels for a period of time.

40. In markets with fixed costs undertakings must price above their variable costs of production in order to ensure a competitive return on their investment. The fact that undertakings price above their variable costs is therefore not in itself a sign that competition in the market is not functioning well and that undertakings have market power that allows them to price above the competitive level. It is when competitive constraints are insufficient to maintain prices, output, product quality, product variety and innovation at competitive levels that undertakings have market power in the context of Article 101(1).

41. The creation, maintenance or strengthening of market power can result from superior skill, foresight or innovation. It can also result from reduced competition between the parties to the agreement or between any one of the parties and third parties, for example, because the agreement leads to anti-competitive foreclosure of competitors by raising competitors' costs and limiting their capacity to compete effectively with the contracting parties.

42. Market power is a question of degree. The degree of market power required for the finding of an infringement under Article 101(1) in the case of agreements that are restrictive of competition by effect is less than the degree of market power required for a finding of dominance under Article 102, where a substantial degree of market power is required.

43. The starting point for the analysis of market power is the position of the parties on the markets affected by the co-operation. To carry out this analysis the relevant market(s) have to be defined by using the methodology of the Commission's Market Definition Notice. Where specific types of markets, such as purchasing or technology markets, are concerned these guidelines will provide additional guidance.

44. If the parties have a low combined market share, the horizontal co-operation agreement is unlikely to give rise to restrictive effects on competition within the meaning of Article 101(1) and, normally, no further analysis will be required. What is considered to be a 'low combined market share' depends on the type of agreement in question and can be inferred from the 'safe harbour' thresholds set out in various chapters of these guidelines and, more generally, from the Commission Notice on agreements of minor importance which do not appreciably restrict competition under Article 81(1) of the Treaty establishing the European Community (*de minimis*)[31] ('the *De Minimis* Notice'). If one of just two parties has only an insignificant market share and if it does not possess important resources, even a high combined market share normally cannot be seen as indicating a likely restrictive effect on competition in the market.[32] Given the variety of horizontal co-operation agreements and the different effects they may cause in different market situations, it is not possible to give a general market share threshold above which sufficient market power for causing restrictive effects on competition can be assumed.

45. Depending on the market position of the parties and the concentration in the market, other factors such as the stability of market shares over time, entry barriers and the likelihood of market entry, and the countervailing power of buyers/suppliers also have to be considered.

46. Normally, the Commission uses current market shares in its competitive analysis.[33] However, reasonably certain future developments may also be taken into account, for instance in the light of exit, entry or expansion in the relevant market. Historic data may be used if market shares have been volatile, for instance when the market is characterised by large, lumpy orders. Changes in historic market shares may provide useful information about the competitive process and the likely future importance of the various competitors, for instance, by indicating whether undertakings have been gaining or losing market shares. In any event, the Commission interprets market shares in the light of likely market conditions, for instance, if the market is highly dynamic in character and if the market structure is unstable due to innovation or growth.

47. When entering a market is sufficiently easy, a horizontal co-operation agreement will normally not be expected to give rise to restrictive effects on competition. For entry to be considered a sufficient competitive constraint on the parties to a horizontal co-operation agreement, it must be shown to be likely, timely and sufficient to deter or defeat any potential restrictive effects of the agreement. The analysis of entry may be affected by the presence of horizontal co-operation agreements. The likely or possible termination of a horizontal co-operation agreement may influence the likelihood of entry.

1.2.2.
Article 101(3)

48. The assessment of restrictions of competition by object or effect under Article 101(1) is only one side of the analysis. The other side, which is reflected in Article 101(3), is the assessment of the pro-competitive effects of restrictive agreements. The general approach when applying Article 101(3) is presented in the General Guidelines. Where in an individual case a restriction of competition within the meaning of Article 101(1) has been proven, Article 101(3) can be invoked as a defence. According to Article 2 of Council Regulation (EC) No 1/2003 of 16 December 2002 on the implementation of the rules on competition laid down in Articles 81 and 82 of the Treaty,[34] the burden of proof under Article 101(3) rests on the undertaking(s) invoking the benefit of this provision. Therefore, the factual arguments and the evidence provided by the undertaking(s) must enable the Commission to arrive at the conviction that the agreement in question is sufficiently likely to give rise to pro-competitive effects or that it is not.[35]

49. The application of the exception rule of Article 101(3) is subject to four cumulative conditions, two positive and two negative:

— the agreement must contribute to improving the production or distribution of products or contribute to promoting technical or economic progress, that is to say, lead to efficiency gains;
— the restrictions must be indispensable to the attainment of those objectives, that is to say, the efficiency gains;
— consumers must receive a fair share of the resulting benefits, that is to say, the efficiency gains, including qualitative efficiency gains, attained by the indispensable restrictions must be sufficiently passed on to consumers so that they are at least compensated for the restrictive effects of the agreement; hence, efficiencies only accruing to the parties to the agreement will not suffice; for the purposes of these guidelines, the concept of 'consumers' encompasses the customers, potential and/or actual, of the parties to the agreement;[36] and
— the agreement must not afford the parties the possibility of eliminating competition in respect of a substantial part of the products in question.

50. In the area of horizontal co-operation agreements there are block exemption regulations based on Article 101(3) for research and development[37] and specialisation (including joint production)[38] agreements. Those Block Exemption Regulations are based on the premise that the combination of complementary skills or assets can be the source of substantial efficiencies in research and development and specialisation agreements. This may also be the case for other types of horizontal co-operation agreements. The analysis of the efficiencies of an individual agreement under Article 101(3) is therefore to a large extent a question of identifying the complementary skills and assets that each of the parties brings to the agreement and evaluating whether the resulting efficiencies are such that the conditions of Article 101(3) are fulfilled.

51. Complementarities may arise from horizontal co-operation agreements in various ways. A research and development agreement may bring together different research capabilities that allow the parties to produce better products more cheaply and shorten the time for those products to reach the market. A production agreement may allow the parties to achieve economies of scale or scope that they could not achieve individually.

52. Horizontal co-operation agreements that do not involve the combination of complementary skills or assets are less likely to lead to efficiency gains that benefit consumers. Such agreements may reduce duplication of certain costs, for instance because certain fixed costs can be eliminated. However, fixed cost savings are, in general, less likely to result in benefits to consumers than savings in, for instance, variable or marginal costs.

53. Further guidance regarding the Commission's application of the criteria of Article 101(3) can be obtained in the General Guidelines.

1.3. Structure of these guidelines

54. Chapter 2 will first set out some general principles for the assessment of the exchange of information, which are applicable to all types of horizontal co-operation agreements entailing the exchange of information. The subsequent chapters of these guidelines will each address one specific type of horizontal co-operation agreement. Each chapter will apply the analytical framework described in section 1.2 as well as the general principles on the exchange of information to the specific type of co-operation in question.

NOTES

* With effect from 1 December 2009, Article 81 of the EC Treaty has become Article 101 of the Treaty on the Functioning of the European Union ('TFEU'). The two Articles are, in substance, identical. For the purposes of these guidelines, references to Article 101 of the TFEU should be understood as references to Article 81 of the EC Treaty where appropriate. The TFEU also introduced certain changes in terminology, such as the replacement of 'Community' by 'Union' and 'common market' by 'internal market'. The terminology of the TFEU will be used throughout these guidelines.

1 OJ L 24, 29.1.2004, p 1.

2 See Article 3(4) of the Merger Regulation. However, in assessing whether there is a full-function joint venture, the Commission examines whether the joint venture is autonomous in an operational sense. This does not mean that it enjoys autonomy from its parent companies as regards the adoption of its strategic decisions (see Commission Consolidated Jurisdictional Notice under Council Regulation (EC) No 139/2004 on the control of concentrations between undertakings, OJ C95, 16.4.2008, p 1, paragraphs 91–109 ('Consolidated Jurisdictional Notice')). It also needs to be recalled that if the creation of a joint venture constituting a concentration under Article 3 of the Merger Regulation has as its object or effect the coordination of the competitive behaviour of undertakings that remain independent, then that coordination will be appraised under Article 101 of the Treaty (see Article 2(4) of the Merger Regulation).

3 OJ L355, 18.12.2010, p 36.

4 OJ L355, 18.12.2010, p 43.

5 What constitutes a 'short period of time' depends on the facts of the case at hand, its legal and economic context, and, in particular, on whether the company in question is a party to the agreement or a third party. In the first case, that is to say, where it is analysed whether a party to an agreement should be considered a potential competitor of the other party, the Commission would normally consider a longer period to be a 'short period of time' than in the second case, that is to say, where the capacity of a third party to act as a competitive constraint on the parties to an agreement is analysed. For a third party to be considered a potential competitor, market entry would need to take place sufficiently fast so that the threat of potential entry is a constraint on the parties' and other market participants' behaviour. For these reasons, both the R&D and the Specialisation Block Exemption Regulations consider a period of not more than three years a 'short period of time'.

6 OJ C372, 9.12.1997, p 5, paragraph 24; see also the Commission's Thirteenth Report on Competition Policy, point 55 and Commission Decision in Case IV/32.009, *Elopak/Metal Box-Odin*, OJ L 209, 8.8.1990, p 15.

7 See, for example, Case C-73/95, *Viho*, [1996] ECR I-5457, paragraph 51. The exercise of decisive influence by the parent company over the conduct of a subsidiary can be presumed in case of wholly-owned subsidiaries; see, for example, Case 107/82, *AEG*, [1983] ECR-3151, paragraph 50; Case C-286/98 P, *Stora*, [2000] ECR-I 9925, paragraph 29; or Case C-97/08 P, *Akzo*, [2009] ECR I-8237, paragraphs 60 *et seq*.

8 OJ L 102, 23.4.2010, p 1.

9 OJ C130, 19.5.2010, p 1.

10 This does not apply where competitors enter into a non-reciprocal vertical agreement and (i) the supplier is a manufacturer and a distributor of goods, while the buyer is a distributor and not a competing undertaking at the manufacturing level, or (ii) the supplier is a provider of services at several levels of trade, while the buyer provides its goods or services at the retail level and is not a competing undertaking at the level of trade where it purchases the contract services. Such agreements are exclusively assessed under the Block Exemption Regulation and the Guidelines on Vertical Restraints (see Article 2(4) of the Block Exemption Regulation on Vertical Restraints).

11 It should be noted that this test only applies to the relationship between the different chapters of these guidelines, not to the relationship between different block exemption regulations. The scope of a block exemption regulation is defined by its own provisions.

12 See Case T-51/89, *Tetra Pak I*, [1990] ECR-II 309, paragraphs 25 *et seq*. and Guidance on the Commission's enforcement priorities in applying Article 82 of the EC Treaty to abusive exclusionary conduct by dominant undertakings, OJ C45, 24.2.2009, p 7 ('Article 102 Guidance Paper').

13 OJ C3, 6.1.2001, p 2. These guidelines do not contain a separate chapter on 'environmental agreements' as was the case in the previous guidelines. Standard-setting in the environment sector, which was the main focus of the former chapter on environmental agreements, is more appropriately dealt with in the standardisation chapter of these guidelines. In general, depending on the competition issues 'environmental agreements' give rise to, they are to be assessed under the relevant chapter of these guidelines, be it the chapter on R&D, production, commercialisation or standardisation agreements.

14 Council Regulation (EC) No 1184/2006 of 24 July 2006 applying certain rules of competition to the production of, and trade in, agricultural products, OJ L 214, 4.8.2006, p 7.

15 Council Regulation (EC) No 169/2009 of 26 February 2009 applying rules of competition to transport by rail, road and inland waterway, OJ L 61, 5.3.2009, p 1; Council Regulation (EC) No 246/2009 of 26 February 2009 on the application of Article 81(3) of the Treaty to certain categories of agreements and concerted practices between liner shipping companies (consortia), OJ L 79, 25.3.2009, p 1; Commission Regulation (EC) No 823/2000 of 19 April 2000 on the application of Article 81(3) of the Treaty to certain categories of agreements, decisions and concerted practices between liner shipping companies (consortia), OJ L 100, 20.4.2000, p 24; Guidelines on the application of Article 81 of the EC

Treaty to maritime transport services, OJ C 245, 26.9.2008, p 2.

16 Commission Regulation (EU) No 267/2010 of 24 March 2010 on the application of Article 101(3) of the Treaty on the Functioning of the European Union to certain categories of agreements, decisions and concerted practices in the insurance sector, OJ L 83, 31.3.2010, p 1.

17 OJ C101, 27.4.2004, p 97.

18 Article 101(1) prohibits both actual and potential anti-competitive effects; see for example Case C-7/95 *P, John Deere*, [1998] ECR I-3111, paragraph 77; Case C-238/05, *Asnef-Equifax*, [2006] ECR I-11125, paragraph 50.

19 See Joined Cases C-501/06 P and others, *GlaxoSmithKline*, [2009] ECR I-9291, paragraph 95.

20 See Case T-65/98, *Van den Bergh Foods*, [2003] ECR II-4653, paragraph 107; Case T-112/99, *Métropole télévision (M6)* and others, [2001] ECR II-2459, paragraph 74; Case T-328/03, *O2*, [2006] ECR II-1231, paragraphs 69 *et seq.*, where the General Court held that it is only in the precise framework of Article 101(3) that the pro- and anti-competitive aspects of a restriction may be weighed.

21 See judgment of 14 October 2010 in Case C-280/08 P, *Deutsche Telekom*, ECR I not yet reported, paragraph 82 and the case-law cited therein.

22 See Case C-198/01, *CIF*, [2003] ECR I-8055, paragraphs 56–58; Joined Cases T-217/03 and T-245/03, *French Beef*, [2006] ECR II-4987, paragraph 92; Case T-7/92, *Asia Motor France II*, [1993] ECR II-669, paragraph 71; and Case T-148/89, *Tréfilunion*, [1995] ECR II-1063, paragraph 118.

23 See Case C-280/08 P, *Deutsche Telekom*, paragraph 80-81. This possibility has been narrowly interpreted; see, for example, Joined Cases 209/78 and others, *Van Landewyck*, [1980] ECR 3125, paragraphs 130–134; Joined Cases 240/82 and others, *Stichting Sigarettenindustrie*, [1985] ECR 3831, paragraphs 27–29; and Joined Cases C-359/95 P and C-379/95 P, *Ladbroke Racing*, [1997] ECR I-6265, paragraphs 33 *et seq.*

24 At least until a decision to disapply the national legislation has been adopted and that decision has become definitive; see Case C-198/01, *CIF*, paragraphs 54 *et seq.*

25 For the purpose of these guidelines, the term 'restriction of competition' includes the prevention and distortion of competition.

26 See, for example, Case C-209/07, *BIDS*, [2008] ECR I-8637, paragraph 17.

27 See, for example, Joined Cases C-501/06 P and others, *GlaxoSmithKline*, paragraph 55; Case C-209/07, *BIDS*, paragraph 16; Case C-8/08, *T-Mobile Netherlands*, ECR [2009] I-4529, paragraph 29 *et seq.*; Case C-7/95 P, *John Deere*, paragraph 77.

28 See, for example, Joined Cases C-501/06 P and others, *GlaxoSmithKline*, paragraph 58; Case C-209/07, *BIDS*, paragraphs 15 *et seq.*

29 See Case C-7/95 P, *John Deere*, paragraph 88; Case C-238/05, *Asnef-Equifax*, paragraph 51.

30 See also paragraph 18 of the General Guidelines.

31 OJ C368, 22.12.2001, p 13.

32 If there are more than two parties, then the collective share of all co-operating competitors has to be significantly greater than the share of the largest single participating competitor.

33 As to the calculation of market shares, see also Market Definition Notice, paragraphs 54–55.

34 OJ L 1, 4.1.2003, p 1.

35 See, for example, Joined Cases C-501/06 P and others, *GlaxoSmithKline*, paragraphs 93–95.

36 More detail on the concept of consumer is provided in paragraph 84 of the General Guidelines.

37 R&D Block Exemption Regulation.

38 Specialisation Block Exemption Regulation.

2. GENERAL PRINCIPLES ON THE COMPETITIVE ASSESSMENT OF INFORMATION EXCHANGE

2.1. Definition and scope

[4.221]

55. The purpose of this chapter is to guide the competitive assessment of information exchange. Information exchange can take various forms. Firstly, data can be directly shared between competitors. Secondly, data can be shared indirectly through a common agency (for example, a trade association) or a third party such as a market research organisation or through the companies' suppliers or retailers.

56. Information exchange takes place in different contexts. There are agreements, decisions by associations of undertakings, or concerted practices under which information is exchanged, where the main economic function lies in the exchange of information itself. Moreover, information exchange can be part of another type of horizontal co-operation agreement (for example, the parties to a production agreement share certain information on costs). The assessment of the latter type of information exchanges should be carried out in the context of the assessment of the horizontal co-operation agreement itself.

57. Information exchange is a common feature of many competitive markets and may generate various types of efficiency gains. It may solve problems of information asymmetries,[39] thereby making markets more efficient. Moreover, companies may improve their internal efficiency through benchmarking against each other's best practices. Sharing of information may also help companies to save costs by reducing their inventories, enabling quicker delivery of perishable products to consumers, or dealing with unstable demand etc. Furthermore, information exchanges may directly benefit consumers by reducing their search costs and improving choice.

58. However, the exchange of market information may also lead to restrictions of competition in particular in situations where it is liable to enable undertakings to be aware of market strategies of their competitors.[40] The competitive outcome of information exchange depends on the characteristics of the market in which it takes place (such as concentration, transparency, stability, symmetry, complexity etc) as well as on the type of information that is exchanged, which may modify the relevant market environment towards one liable to coordination.

59. Moreover, communication of information among competitors may constitute an agreement, a concerted practice, or a decision by an association of undertakings with the object of fixing, in particular, prices or quantities. Those types of information exchanges will normally be considered and fined as cartels. Information exchange may also facilitate the implementation of a cartel by enabling companies to monitor whether the participants comply with the agreed terms. Those types of exchanges of information will be assessed as part of the cartel.

Concerted practice

60. Information exchange can only be addressed under Article 101 if it establishes or is part of an agreement, a concerted practice or a decision by an association of undertakings. The existence of an agreement, a concerted practice or decision by an association of undertakings does not prejudge whether the agreement, concerted practice or decision by an association of undertakings gives rise to a restriction of competition within the meaning of Article 101(1). In line with the case-law of the Court of Justice of the European Union, the concept of a concerted practice refers to a form of coordination between undertakings by which, without it having reached the stage where an agreement properly so-called has been concluded, practical cooperation between them is knowingly substituted for the risks of competition.[41] The criteria of coordination and cooperation necessary for determining the existence of a concerted practice, far from requiring an actual plan to have been worked out, are to be understood in the light of the concept inherent in the provisions of the Treaty on competition, according to which each company must determine independently the policy which it intends to adopt on the internal market and the conditions which it intends to offer to its customers.[42]

61. This does not deprive companies of the right to adapt themselves intelligently to the existing or anticipated conduct of their competitors. It does, however, preclude any direct or indirect contact between competitors, the object or effect of which is to create conditions of competition which do not correspond to the normal competitive conditions of the market in question, regard being had to the nature of the products or services offered, the size and number of the undertakings, and the volume of the said market.[43] This precludes any direct or indirect contact between competitors, the object or effect of which is to influence conduct on the market of an actual or potential competitor, or to disclose to such competitor the course of conduct which they themselves have decided to adopt or contemplate adopting on the market, thereby facilitating a collusive outcome on the market.[44] Hence, information exchange can constitute a concerted practice if it reduces strategic uncertainty[45] in the market thereby facilitating collusion, that is to say, if the data exchanged is strategic. Consequently, sharing of strategic data between competitors amounts to concertation, because it reduces the independence of competitors' conduct on the market and diminishes their incentives to compete.

62. A situation where only one undertaking discloses strategic information to its competitor(s) who accept(s) it can also constitute a concerted practice.[46] Such disclosure could occur, for example, through contacts via mail, emails, phone calls, meetings etc. It is then irrelevant whether only one undertaking unilaterally informs its competitors of its intended market behaviour, or whether all participating undertakings inform each other of the respective deliberations and intentions. When one undertaking alone reveals to its competitors strategic information concerning its future commercial policy, that reduces strategic uncertainty as to the future operation of the market for all the competitors involved and increases the risk of limiting competition and of collusive behaviour.[47] For example, mere attendance at a meeting[48] where a company discloses its pricing plans to its competitors is likely to be caught by Article 101, even in the absence of an explicit agreement to raise prices.[49] When a company receives strategic data from a competitor (be it in a meeting, by mail or electronically), it will be presumed to have accepted the information and adapted its market conduct accordingly unless it responds with a clear statement that it does not wish to receive such data.[50]

63. Where a company makes a unilateral announcement that is also genuinely public, for example through a newspaper, this generally does not constitute a concerted practice within the meaning of Article 101(1).[51] However, depending on the facts underlying the case at hand, the possibility of finding a concerted practice cannot be excluded, for example in a situation where such an announcement was followed by public announcements by other competitors, not least because strategic responses of competitors to each other's public announcements (which, to take one instance, might involve readjustments of their own earlier announcements to announcements made by competitors) could prove to be a strategy for reaching a common understanding about the terms of coordination.

2.2. Assessment under Article 101(1)

2.2.1.
Main competition concerns[52]

64. Once it has been established that there is an agreement, concerted practice or decision by an association of undertakings, it is necessary to consider the main competition concerns pertaining to information exchanges.

Collusive outcome

65. By artificially increasing transparency in the market, the exchange of strategic information can facilitate coordination (that is to say, alignment) of companies' competitive behaviour and result in restrictive effects on competition. This can occur through different channels.

66. One way is that through information exchange companies may reach a common understanding on the terms of coordination, which can lead to a collusive outcome on the market. Information exchange can create mutually consistent expectations regarding the uncertainties present in the market. On that basis companies can then reach a common understanding on the terms of coordination of their competitive behaviour, even without an explicit agreement on coordination. Exchange of information about intentions concerning future conduct is the most likely means to enable companies to reach such a common understanding.

67. Another channel through which information exchange can lead to restrictive effects on competition is by increasing the internal stability of a collusive outcome on the market. In particular, it can do so by enabling the companies involved to monitor deviations. Namely, information exchange can make the market sufficiently transparent to allow the colluding companies to monitor to a sufficient degree whether other companies are deviating

from the collusive outcome, and thus to know when to retaliate. Both exchanges of present and past data can constitute such a monitoring mechanism. This can either enable companies to achieve a collusive outcome on markets where they would otherwise not have been able to do so, or it can increase the stability of a collusive outcome already present on the market (see Example 3, paragraph 107).

68. A third channel through which information exchange can lead to restrictive effects on competition is by increasing the external stability of a collusive outcome on the market. Information exchanges that make the market sufficiently transparent can allow colluding companies to monitor where and when other companies are attempting to enter the market, thus allowing the colluding companies to target the new entrant. This may also tie into the anti-competitive foreclosure concerns discussed in paragraphs 69 to 71. Both exchanges of present and past data can constitute such a monitoring mechanism.

Anti-competitive foreclosure

69. Apart from facilitating collusion, an exchange of information can also lead to anti-competitive foreclosure.[53]

70. An exclusive exchange of information can lead to anti-competitive foreclosure on the same market where the exchange takes place. This can occur when the exchange of commercially sensitive information places unaffiliated competitors at a significant competitive disadvantage as compared to the companies affiliated within the exchange system. This type of foreclosure is only possible if the information concerned is very strategic for competition and covers a significant part of the relevant market.

71. It cannot be excluded that information exchange may also lead to anti-competitive foreclosure of third parties in a related market. For instance, by gaining enough market power through an information exchange, parties exchanging information in an upstream market, for instance vertically integrated companies, may be able to raise the price of a key component for a market downstream. Thereby, they could raise the costs of their rivals downstream, which could result in anti-competitive foreclosure in the downstream market.

2.2.2.
Restriction of competition by object

72. Any information exchange with the objective of restricting competition on the market will be considered as a restriction of competition by object. In assessing whether an information exchange constitutes a restriction of competition by object, the Commission will pay particular attention to the legal and economic context in which the information exchange takes place.[54] To this end, the Commission will take into account whether the information exchange, by its very nature, may possibly lead to a restriction of competition.[55]

73. Exchanging information on companies' individualised intentions concerning future conduct regarding prices or quantities[56] is particularly likely to lead to a collusive outcome. Informing each other about such intentions may allow competitors to arrive at a common higher price level without incurring the risk of losing market share or triggering a price war during the period of adjustment to new prices (see Example 1, paragraph 105). Moreover, it is less likely that information exchanges concerning future intentions are made for pro-competitive reasons than exchanges of actual data.

74. Information exchanges between competitors of individualised data regarding intended future prices or quantities should therefore be considered a restriction of competition by object.[57] [58] In addition, private exchanges between competitors of their individualised intentions regarding future prices or quantities would normally be considered and fined as cartels because they generally have the object of fixing prices or quantities. Information exchanges that constitute cartels not only infringe Article 101(1), but, in addition, are very unlikely to fulfil the conditions of Article 101(3).

2.2.3.
Restrictive effects on competition

75. The likely effects of an information exchange on competition must be analysed on a case-by-case basis as the results of the assessment depend on a combination of various case specific factors. The assessment of restrictive effects on competition compares the likely effects of the information exchange with the competitive situation that would prevail in the absence of that specific information exchange.[59] For an information exchange to have restrictive effects on competition within the meaning of Article 101(1), it must be likely to have an appreciable adverse impact on one (or several) of the parameters of competition such as price, output, product quality, product variety or innovation. Whether or not an exchange of information will have restrictive effects on competition depends on both the economic conditions on the relevant markets and the characteristics of information exchanged.

76. Certain market conditions may make coordination easier to achieve, sustain internally, or sustain externally.[60] Exchanges of information in such markets may have more restrictive effects compared to markets with different conditions. However, even where market conditions are such that coordination may be difficult to sustain before the exchange, the exchange of information may change the market conditions in such a way that coordination becomes possible after the exchange – for example by increasing transparency in the market, reducing market complexity, buffering instability or compensating for asymmetry. For this reason it is important to assess the restrictive effects of the information exchange in the context of both the initial market conditions, and how the information exchange changes those conditions. This will include an assessment of the specific characteristics of the system concerned, including its purpose, conditions of access to the system and conditions of participation in the system. It will also be necessary to examine the frequency of the information exchanges, the type of information exchanged (for example, whether it is public or confidential, aggregated or detailed, and historical or current), and the importance of the information for the fixing of prices, volumes or conditions of service.[61] The following factors are relevant for this assessment.

(i)

Market characteristics

77. Companies are more likely to achieve a collusive outcome in markets which are sufficiently transparent, concentrated, non-complex, stable and symmetric. In those types of markets companies can reach a common understanding on the terms of coordination and successfully monitor and punish deviations. However, information exchange can also enable companies to achieve a collusive outcome in other market situations where they would not be able to do so in the absence of the information exchange. Information exchange can thereby facilitate a collusive outcome by increasing transparency in the market, reducing market complexity, buffering instability or compensating for asymmetry. In this context, the competitive outcome of an information exchange depends not only on the initial characteristics of the market in which it takes place (such as concentration, transparency, stability, complexity etc), but also on how the type of the information exchanged may change those characteristics.[62]

78. Collusive outcomes are more likely in transparent markets. Transparency can facilitate collusion by enabling companies to reach a common understanding on the terms of coordination, or/and by increasing internal and external stability of collusion. Information exchange can increase transparency and hence limit uncertainties about the strategic variables of competition (for example, prices, output, demand, costs etc). The lower the pre-existing level of transparency in the market, the more value an information exchange may have in achieving a collusive outcome. An information exchange that contributes little to the transparency in a market is less likely to have restrictive effects on competition than an information exchange that significantly increases transparency. Therefore it is the combination of both the pre-existing level of transparency and how the information exchange changes that level that will determine how likely it is that the information exchange will have restrictive effects on competition. The pre-existing degree of transparency, inter alia, depends on the number of market participants and the nature of transactions, which can range from public transactions to confidential bilateral negotiations between buyers and sellers. When evaluating the change in the level of transparency in the market, the key element is to identify to what extent the available information can be used by companies to determine the actions of their competitors.

79. Tight oligopolies can facilitate a collusive outcome on the market as it is easier for fewer companies to reach a common understanding on the terms of coordination and to monitor deviations. A collusive outcome is also more likely to be sustainable with fewer companies. With more companies coordinating, the gains from deviating are greater because a larger market share can be gained through undercutting. At the same time, gains from the collusive outcome are smaller because, when there are more companies, the share of the rents from the collusive outcome declines. Exchanges of information in tight oligopolies are more likely to cause restrictive effects on competition than in less tight oligopolies, and are not likely to cause such restrictive effects on competition in very fragmented markets. However, by increasing transparency, or modifying the market environment in another way towards one more liable to coordination, information exchanges may facilitate coordination and monitoring among more companies than would be possible in its absence.

80. Companies may find it difficult to achieve a collusive outcome in a complex market environment. However, to some extent, the use of information exchange may simplify such environments. In a complex market environment more information exchange is normally needed to reach a common understanding on the terms of coordination and to monitor deviations. For example, it is easier to achieve a collusive outcome on a price for a single, homogeneous product, than on numerous prices in a market with many differentiated products. It is nonetheless possible that to circumvent the difficulties involved in achieving a collusive outcome on a large number of prices, companies may exchange information to establish simple pricing rules (for example, pricing points).

81. Collusive outcomes are more likely where the demand and supply conditions are relatively stable.[63] In an unstable environment it may be difficult for a company to know whether its lost sales are due to an overall low level of demand or due to a competitor offering particularly low prices, and therefore it is difficult to sustain a collusive outcome. In this context, volatile demand, substantial internal growth by some companies in the market, or frequent entry by new companies, may indicate that the current situation is not sufficiently stable for coordination to be likely.[64] Information exchange in certain situations can serve the purpose of increasing stability in the market, and thereby may enable a collusive outcome in the market. Moreover, in markets where innovation is important, coordination may be more difficult since particularly significant innovations may allow one company to gain a major advantage over its rivals. For a collusive outcome to be sustainable, the reactions of outsiders, such as current and future competitors not participating in the coordination, as well as customers, should not be capable of jeopardising the results expected from the collusive outcome. In this context, the existence of barriers to entry makes it more likely that a collusive outcome on the market is feasible and sustainable.

82. A collusive outcome is more likely in symmetric market structures. When companies are homogenous in terms of their costs, demand, market shares, product range, capacities etc, they are more likely to reach a common understanding on the terms of coordination because their incentives are more aligned. However, information exchange may in some situations also allow a collusive outcome to occur in more heterogeneous market structures. Information exchange could make companies aware of their differences and help them to design means to accommodate for their heterogeneity in the context of coordination.

83. The stability of a collusive outcome also depends on the companies' discounting of future profits. The more companies value the current profits that they could gain from undercutting versus all the future ones that they could gain by the collusive outcome, the less likely it is that they will be able to achieve a collusive outcome.

84. By the same token, a collusive outcome is more likely among companies that will continue to operate in the same market for a long time, as in such a scenario they will be more committed to coordinate. If a company knows that it will interact with the others for a long time, it will have a greater incentive to achieve the collusive outcome because the stream of future profits from the collusive outcome will be worth more than the short term profit it could have if it deviated, that is to say, before the other companies detect the deviation and retaliate.

85. Overall, for a collusive outcome to be sustainable, the threat of a sufficiently credible and prompt retaliation must be likely. Collusive outcomes are not sustainable in markets in which the consequences of deviation are not sufficiently severe to convince coordinating companies that it is in their best interest to adhere to the terms of the collusive outcome. For example, in markets characterised by infrequent, lumpy orders, it may be difficult to establish a sufficiently severe deterrence mechanism, since the gain from deviating at the right time may be large, certain and immediate, whereas the losses from being punished small and uncertain, and only materialise after some time. The credibility of the deterrence mechanism also depends on whether the other coordinating companies have an incentive to retaliate, determined by their short-term losses from triggering a price war versus their potential long-term gain in case they induce a return to a collusive outcome. For example, companies' ability to retaliate may be reinforced if they are also interrelated by vertical commercial relationships which they can use as a threat of punishment for deviations.

(ii)

Characteristics of the information exchange

Strategic information

86. The exchange between competitors of strategic data, that is to say, data that reduces strategic uncertainty in the market, is more likely to be caught by Article 101 than exchanges of other types of information. Sharing of strategic data can give rise to restrictive effects on competition because it reduces the parties' decision-making independence by decreasing their incentives to compete. Strategic information can be related to prices (for example, actual prices, discounts, increases, reductions or rebates), customer lists, production costs, quantities, turnovers, sales, capacities, qualities, marketing plans, risks, investments, technologies and R&D programmes and their results. Generally, information related to prices and quantities is the most strategic, followed by information about costs and demand. However, if companies compete with regard to R&D it is the technology data that may be the most strategic for competition. The strategic usefulness of data also depends on its aggregation and age, as well as the market context and frequency of the exchange.

Market coverage

87. For an information exchange to be likely to have restrictive effects on competition, the companies involved in the exchange have to cover a sufficiently large part of the relevant market. Otherwise, the competitors that are not participating in the information exchange could constrain any anti-competitive behaviour of the companies involved. For example, by pricing below the coordinated price level companies unaffiliated within the information exchange system could threaten the external stability of a collusive outcome.

88. What constitutes 'a sufficiently large part of the market' cannot be defined in the abstract and will depend on the specific facts of each case and the type of information exchange in question. Where, however, an information exchange takes place in the context of another type of horizontal co-operation agreement and does not go beyond what is necessary for its implementation, market coverage below the market share thresholds set out in the relevant chapter of these guidelines, the relevant block exemption regulation[65] or the De Minimis Notice pertaining to the type of agreement in question will usually not be large enough for the information exchange to give rise to restrictive effects on competition.

Aggregated/individualised data

89. Exchanges of genuinely aggregated data, that is to say, where the recognition of individualised company level information is sufficiently difficult, are much less likely to lead to restrictive effects on competition than exchanges of company level data. Collection and publication of aggregated market data (such as sales data, data on capacities or data on costs of inputs and components) by a trade organisation or market intelligence firm may benefit suppliers and customers alike by allowing them to get a clearer picture of the economic situation of a sector. Such data collection and publication may allow market participants to make better-informed individual choices in order to adapt efficiently their strategy to the market conditions. More generally, unless it takes place in a tight oligopoly, the exchange of aggregated data is unlikely to give rise to restrictive effects on competition. Conversely, the exchange of individualised data facilitates a common understanding on the market and punishment strategies by allowing the coordinating companies to single out a deviator or entrant. Nevertheless, the possibility cannot be excluded that even the exchange of aggregated data may facilitate a collusive outcome in markets with specific characteristics. Namely, members of a very tight and stable oligopoly exchanging aggregated data who detect a market price below a certain level could automatically assume that someone has deviated from the collusive outcome and take market-wide retaliatory steps. In other words, in order to keep collusion stable, companies may not always need to know who deviated, it may be enough to learn that 'someone' deviated.

Age of data

90. The exchange of historic data is unlikely to lead to a collusive outcome as it is unlikely to be indicative of the competitors' future conduct or to provide a common understanding on the market.[66] Moreover, exchanging historic data is unlikely to facilitate monitoring of deviations because the older the data, the less useful it would be for timely detection of deviations and thus as a credible threat of prompt retaliation.[67] There is no predetermined threshold when data becomes historic, that is to say, old enough not to pose risks to competition. Whether data is genuinely historic depends on the specific characteristics of the relevant market and in particular the frequency of price re-negotiations in the industry. For example, data can be considered as historic if it is several times older than the average length of contracts in the industry if the latter are indicative of price re-negotiations. Moreover, the threshold when data becomes historic also depends on the data's nature, aggregation, frequency of the exchange, and the characteristics of the relevant market (for example, its stability and transparency).

Frequency of the information exchange

91. Frequent exchanges of information that facilitate both a better common understanding of the market and monitoring of deviations increase the risks of a collusive outcome. In more unstable markets, more frequent exchanges of information may be necessary to facilitate a collusive outcome than in stable markets. In markets with long-term contracts (which are indicative of infrequent price re-negotiations) a less frequent exchange of information

would normally be sufficient to achieve a collusive outcome. By contrast, infrequent exchanges would not tend to be sufficient to achieve a collusive outcome in markets with short-term contracts indicative of frequent price re-negotiations.[68] However, the frequency at which data needs to be exchanged to facilitate a collusive outcome also depends on the nature, age and aggregation of data.[69]

Public/non-public information

92. In general, exchanges of genuinely public information are unlikely to constitute an infringement of Article 101.[70] *Genuinely public information* is information that is generally equally accessible (in terms of costs of access) to all competitors and customers. For information to be genuinely public, obtaining it should not be more costly for customers and companies unaffiliated to the exchange system than for the companies exchanging the information. For this reason, competitors would normally not choose to exchange data that they can collect from the market at equal ease, and hence in practice exchanges of genuinely public data are unlikely. In contrast, even if the data exchanged between competitors is what is often referred to as being 'in the public domain', it is not genuinely public if the costs involved in collecting the data deter other companies and customers from doing so.[71] A possibility to gather the information in the market, for example to collect it from customers, does not necessarily mean that such information constitutes market data readily accessible to competitors.[72]

93. Even if there is public availability of data (for example, information published by regulators), the existence of an additional information exchange by competitors may give rise to restrictive effects on competition if it further reduces strategic uncertainty in the market. In that case, it is the incremental information that could be critical to tip the market balance towards a collusive outcome.

Public/non-public exchange of information

94. An *information exchange* is genuinely public if it makes the exchanged data equally accessible (in terms of costs of access) to all competitors and customers.[73] The fact that information is exchanged in public may decrease the likelihood of a collusive outcome on the market to the extent that non-coordinating companies, potential competitors, as well as customers may be able to constrain potential restrictive effect on competition.[74] However, the possibility cannot be entirely excluded that even genuinely public exchanges of information may facilitate a collusive outcome in the market.

2.3. Assessment under Article 101(3)

2.3.1.

Efficiency gains[75]

95. Information exchange may lead to efficiency gains. Information about competitors' costs can enable companies to become more efficient if they benchmark their performance against the best practices in the industry and design internal incentive schemes accordingly.

96. Moreover, in certain situations information exchange can help companies allocate production towards high-demand markets (for example, demand information) or low cost companies (for example, cost information). The likelihood of those types of efficiencies depends on market characteristics such as whether companies compete on prices or quantities and the nature of uncertainties on the market. Some forms of information exchanges in this context may allow substantial cost savings where, for example, they reduce unnecessary inventories or enable quicker delivery of perishable products to areas with high demand and their reduction in areas with low demand (see Example 6, paragraph 110).

97. Exchange of consumer data between companies in markets with asymmetric information about consumers can also give rise to efficiencies. For instance, keeping track of the past behaviour of customers in terms of accidents or credit default provides an incentive for consumers to limit their risk exposure. It also makes it possible to detect which consumers carry a lower risk and should benefit from lower prices. In this context, information exchange can also reduce consumer lock-in, thereby inducing stronger competition. This is because information is generally specific to a relationship and consumers would otherwise lose the benefit from that information when switching to another company. Examples of such efficiencies are found in the banking and insurance sectors, which are characterised by frequent exchanges of information about consumer defaults and risk characteristics.

98. Exchanging past and present data related to market shares may in some situations provide benefits to both companies and consumers by allowing companies to announce it as a signal of quality of their products to consumers. In situations of imperfect information about product quality, consumers often use indirect means to gain information on the relative qualities of products such as price and market shares (for example, consumers use best-selling lists in order to choose their next book).

99. Information exchange that is genuinely public can also benefit consumers by helping them to make a more informed choice (and reducing their search costs). Consumers are most likely to benefit in this way from public exchanges of current data, which are the most relevant for their purchasing decisions. Similarly, public information exchange about current input prices can lower search costs for companies, which would normally benefit consumers through lower final prices. Those types of direct consumer benefits are less likely to be generated by exchanges of future pricing intentions because companies which announce their pricing intentions are likely to revise them before consumers actually purchase based on that information. Consumers generally cannot rely on companies' future intentions when making their consumption plans. However, to some extent, companies may be disciplined not to change the announced future prices before implementation when, for example, they have repeated interactions with consumers and consumers rely on knowing the prices in advance or, for example, when consumers can make advance orders. In those situations, exchanging information related to the future may improve customers' planning of expenditure.

100. Exchanging present and past data is more likely to generate efficiency gains than exchanging information about future intentions. However, in specific circumstances announcing future intentions could also give rise to efficiency gains. For example, companies knowing early the winner of an R&D race could avoid duplicating costly efforts and wasting resources that cannot be recovered.[76]

2.3.2.
Indispensability

101. Restrictions that go beyond what is necessary to achieve the efficiency gains generated by an information exchange do not fulfil the conditions of Article 101(3). For fulfilling the condition of indispensability, the parties will need to prove that the data's subject matter, aggregation, age, confidentiality and frequency, as well as coverage, of the exchange are of the kind that carries the lowest risks indispensable for creating the claimed efficiency gains. Moreover, the exchange should not involve information beyond the variables that are relevant for the attainment of the efficiency gains. For instance, for the purpose of benchmarking, an exchange of individualised data would generally not be indispensable because information aggregated in for example some form of industry ranking could also generate the claimed efficiency gains while carrying a lower risk of leading to a collusive outcome (see Example 4, paragraph 108). Finally, it is generally unlikely that the sharing of individualised data on future intentions is indispensable, especially if it is related to prices and quantities.

102. Similarly, information exchanges that form part of horizontal co-operation agreements are also more likely to fulfil the conditions of Article 101(3) if they do not go beyond what is indispensable for the implementation of the economic purpose of the agreement (for example, sharing technology necessary for an R&D agreement or cost data in the context of a production agreement).

2.3.3.
Pass-on to consumers

103. Efficiency gains attained by indispensable restrictions must be passed on to consumers to an extent that outweighs the restrictive effects on competition caused by an information exchange. The lower is the market power of the parties involved in the information exchange, the more likely it is that the efficiency gains would be passed on to consumers to an extent that outweighs the restrictive effects on competition.

2.3.4.
No elimination of competition

104. The criteria of Article 101(3) cannot be met if the companies involved in the information exchange are afforded the possibility of eliminating competition in respect of a substantial part of the products concerned.

2.4. Examples

105. Exchange of intended future prices as a restriction of competition by object

Example 1

Situation: A trade association of coach companies in country X disseminates individualised information on intended future prices only to the member coach companies. The information contains several elements, such as the intended fare and the route to which the fare applies, the possible restrictions to this fare, such as which consumers can buy it, if advanced payment or minimum stay is required, the period during which tickets can be sold for the given fare (first and last ticket date), and the time during which the ticket with the given fare can be used for travel (first and last travel dates).

Analysis: This information exchange, which is triggered by a decision by an association of undertakings, concerns pricing intentions of competitors. This information exchange is a very efficient tool for reaching a collusive outcome and therefore restricts competition by object. This is because the companies are free to change their own intended prices as announced within the association at any time if they learn that their competitors intend to charge higher prices. This allows the companies to reach a common higher price level without incurring the cost of losing market share. For example, coach Company A can announce today a price increase on the route from city 1 to city 2 for travel as of the following month. Since this information is accessible to all other coach companies, Company A can then wait and see the reaction of its competitors to this price announcement. If a competitor on the same route, say, Company B, matched the price increase, then Company A's announcement would be left unchanged and later would likely become effective. However, if Company B did not match the price increase, then Company A could still revise its fare. The adjustment would continue until the companies converged to an increased anti-competitive price level. This information exchange is unlikely to fulfil the conditions of Article 101(3). The information exchange is only confined to competitors, that is to say, customers of the coach companies do not directly benefit from it.

106. Exchange of current prices with sufficient efficiency gains for consumers

Example 2

Situation: A national tourist office together with the coach companies in small country X agree to disseminate information on current prices of coach tickets through a freely accessible website (in contrast to Example 1, paragraph 105, consumers can already purchase tickets at the prices and conditions which are exchanged, thus they are not intended future prices but present prices of current and future services). The information contains several elements, such as the fare and the route to which the fare is applied, the possible restrictions to this fare, such as which consumers can buy it, if advanced payment or minimum stay is required, and the time during which the ticket with the given fare can be used for travel (first and last travel dates). Coach travel in country X is not in the same relevant market as train and air travel. It is presumed that the relevant market is concentrated, stable and relatively non-complex, and pricing becomes transparent with the information exchange.

Analysis: This information exchange does not constitute a restriction of competition by object. The companies are exchanging current prices rather than intended future prices because they are effectively already selling tickets at these prices (unlike in Example 1, paragraph 105). Therefore, this exchange of information is less likely to constitute an efficient mechanism for reaching a focal point for coordination. Nevertheless, given the market structure and strategic nature of the data, this information exchange is likely to constitute an efficient mechanism for monitoring deviations from a collusive outcome, which would be likely to occur in this type of market setting. Therefore, this information exchange could give rise to restrictive effects on competition within the meaning of Article 101(1). However, to the extent that some restrictive effects on competition could result from the possibility to monitor deviations, it is likely that the efficiency gains stemming from the information exchange would be passed on to consumers to an extent that outweighs the restrictive effects on competition in both their likelihood and magnitude. Unlike in Example 1, paragraph 105, the information exchange is public and consumers can actually purchase tickets at the prices and conditions that are exchanged. Therefore this information exchange is likely to directly benefit consumers by reducing their search costs and improving choice, and thereby also stimulating price competition. Hence, the conditions of Article 101(3) are likely to be met.

107. Current prices deduced from the information exchanged

Example 3

Situation: The luxury hotels in the capital of country A operate in a tight, non-complex and stable oligopoly, with largely homogenous cost structures, which constitute a separate relevant market from other hotels. They directly exchange individual information about current occupancy rates and revenues. In this case, from the information exchanged the parties can directly deduce their actual current prices.

Analysis: Unless it is a disguised means of exchanging information on future intentions, this exchange of information would not constitute a restriction of competition by object because the hotels exchange present data and not information on intended future prices or quantities. However, the information exchange would give rise to restrictive effects on competition within the meaning of Article 101(1) because knowing the competitors' actual current prices would be likely to facilitate coordination (that is to say, alignment) of companies' competitive behaviour. It would be most likely used to monitor deviations from the collusive outcome. The information exchange increases transparency in the market as even though the hotels normally publish their list prices, they also offer various discounts to the list price resulting from negotiations or for early or group bookings, etc. Therefore, the incremental information that is non-publicly exchanged between the hotels is commercially sensitive, that is to say, strategically useful. This exchange is likely to facilitate a collusive outcome on the market because the parties involved constitute a tight, non-complex and stable oligopoly involved in a long-term competitive relationship (repeated interactions). Moreover, the cost structures of the hotels are largely homogeneous. Finally, neither consumers nor market entry can constrain the incumbents' anti-competitive behaviour as consumers have little buyer power and barriers to entry are high. It is unlikely that in this case the parties would be able to demonstrate any efficiency gains stemming from the information exchange that would be passed on to consumers to an extent that would outweigh the restrictive effects on competition. Therefore it is unlikely that the conditions of Article 101(3) can be met.

108. Benchmarking benefits – criteria of Article 101(3) not fulfilled

Example 4

Situation: Three large companies with a combined market share of 80% in a stable, non-complex, concentrated market with high barriers to entry, non-publicly and frequently exchange information directly between themselves about a substantial fraction of their individual costs. The companies claim that they do this to benchmark their performance against their competitors and thereby intend to become more efficient.

Analysis: This information exchange does not in principle constitute a restriction of competition by object. Consequently, its effects on the market need to be assessed. Because of the market structure, the fact that the information exchanged relates to a large proportion of the companies' variable costs, the individualised form of presentation of the data, and its large coverage of the relevant market, the information exchange is likely to facilitate a collusive outcome and thereby gives rise to restrictive effects on competition within the meaning of Article 101(1). It is unlikely that the criteria of Article 101(3) are fulfilled because there are less restrictive means to achieve the claimed efficiency gains, for example by way of a third party collecting, anonymising and aggregating the data in some form of industry ranking. Finally, in this case, since the parties form a very tight, non-complex and stable oligopoly, even the exchange of aggregated data could facilitate a collusive outcome in the market. However, this would be very unlikely if this exchange of information happened in a non-transparent, fragmented, unstable, and complex market.

109. Genuinely public information

Example 5

Situation: The four companies owning all the petrol stations in a large country A exchange current gasoline prices over the telephone. They claim that this information exchange cannot have restrictive effects on competition because the information is public as it is displayed on large display panels at every petrol station.

Analysis: The pricing data exchanged over the telephone is not genuinely public, as in order to obtain the same information in a different way it would be necessary to incur substantial time and transport costs. One would have to travel frequently large distances to collect the prices displayed on the boards of petrol stations spread all over the country. The costs for this are potentially high, so that the information could in practice not be obtained but for the information exchange. Moreover, the exchange is systematic and covers the entire relevant market, which is a tight, non-complex, stable oligopoly. Therefore it is likely to create a climate of mutual certainty as to the competitors' pricing policy and thereby it is likely to facilitate a collusive outcome. Consequently, this information exchange is likely to give rise to restrictive effects on competition within the meaning of Article 101(1).

110. Improved meeting of demand as an efficiency gain

Example 6

Situation: There are five producers of fresh bottled carrot juice in the relevant market. Demand for this product is very unstable and vary from location to location in different points in time. The juice has to be sold and consumed within one day from the date of production. The producers agree to establish an independent market research company that on a daily basis collects current information about unsold juice in each point of sale, which it publishes on its website the following week in a form that is aggregated per point of sale. The published statistics allow producers and retailers to forecast demand and to better position the product. Before the information exchange was put in place, the retailers had reported large quantities of wasted juice and therefore had reduced the quantity of juice purchased from the producers; that is to say, the market was not working efficiently. Consequently, in some periods and areas there were frequent instances of unmet demand. The information exchange system, which allows better forecasting of oversupply and undersupply, has significantly reduced the instances of unmet consumer demand and increased the quantity sold in the market.

Analysis: Even though the market is quite concentrated and the data exchanged is recent and strategic, it is not very likely that this exchange would facilitate a collusive outcome because a collusive outcome would be unlikely to occur in such an unstable market. Even if the exchange creates some risk of giving rise to restrictive effects on competition, the efficiency gains stemming from increasing supply to places with high demand and decreasing supply in places with low demand is likely to offset potential restrictive effects. The information is exchanged in a public and aggregated form, which carries lower anti-competitive risks than if it were non-public and individualised. The information exchange therefore does not go beyond what is necessary to correct the market failure. Therefore, it is likely that this information exchange meets the criteria of Article 101(3).

NOTES

39 Economic theory on information asymmetries deals with the study of decisions in transactions where one party has more information than the other.

40 See Case C-7/95 P, *John Deere*, paragraph 88.

41 See for example Case C-8/08, *T-Mobile Netherlands*, paragraph 26; Joined Cases C-89/85 and others, *Wood Pulp*, [1993] ECR 1307, paragraph 63.

42 See Case C-7/95 P, *John Deere*, paragraph 86.

43 Case C-7/95 P, *John Deere*, paragraph 87.

44 See Cases 40/73 and others, *Suiker Unie*, [1975] ECR 1663, paragraph 173 *et seq.*

45 Strategic uncertainty in the market arises as there is a variety of possible collusive outcomes available and because companies cannot perfectly observe past and current actions of their competitors and entrants.

46 See for example Joined Cases T-25/95 and others, *Cimenteries*, [2000] ECR II-491, paragraph 1849: '[. . .] the concept of concerted practice does in fact imply the existence of reciprocal contacts [. . .]. That condition is met where one competitor discloses its future intentions or conduct on the market to another when the latter requests it or, at the very least, accepts it'.

47 See Opinion of Advocate General Kokott, Case C-8/08, *T-Mobile Netherlands*, [2009] ECR I-4529, paragraph 54.

48 See Case C-8/08, *T-Mobile Netherlands*, paragraph 59: 'Depending on the structure of the market, the possibility cannot be ruled out that a meeting on a single occasion between competitors, such as that in question in the main proceedings, may, in principle, constitute a sufficient basis for the participating undertakings to concert their market conduct and thus successfully substitute practical cooperation between them for competition and the risks that that entails.'

49 See Joined Cases T-202/98 and others, *Tate & Lyle* v *Commission*, [2001] ECR II-2035, paragraph 54.

50 See Case C-199/92 P, *Hüls*, [1999] ECR I-4287, paragraph 162; Case C-49/92 P, *Anic Partezipazioni*, [1999] ECR I-4125, paragraph 121.

51 This would not cover situations where such announcements involve invitations to collude.

52 The use of the term 'main competition concerns' means that the ensuing description of competition concerns is neither exclusive nor exhaustive.

53 With regard to foreclosure concerns that vertical agreements can give rise to, see paragraphs 100 *et seq.* of the Guidelines on Vertical Restraints.

54 See, for example, Joined Cases C-501/06 P and others, *GlaxoSmithKline*, paragraph 58; Case C-209/07, *BIDS*, paragraphs 15 *et seq.*

55 See also General Guidelines, paragraph 22.

56 Information regarding intended future quantities could for instance include intended future sales, market shares, territories, and sales to particular groups of consumers.

57 The notion of 'intended future prices' is illustrated in Example 1. In specific situations where companies are fully committed to sell in the future at the prices that they have previously announced to the public (that is to say, they can not revise them), such public announcements of future individualised prices or quantities would not be considered as intentions, and hence would normally not be found to restrict competition by object. This could occur, for example, because of the repeated interactions and the specific type of relationship companies may have with their customers, for instance since it is essential that the customers know future prices in advance or because they can already take advanced orders at these prices. This is because in these situations the information exchange would be a more costly means for reaching a collusive outcome in the market than exchanging information on future intentions, and would be more likely to be done for pro-competitive reasons. However, this does not imply that in general price commitment towards customers is necessarily pro-competitive. On the contrary, it could limit the possibility of deviating from a collusive outcome and hence render it more stable.

58 This is without prejudice to the fact that public announcements of intended individualised prices may give rise to efficiencies and that the parties to such exchange would have a possibility to rely on Article 101(3).

59 Case C-7/95 P, *John Deere* v *Commission*, paragraph 76.

60 Information exchange may restrict competition in a similar way to a merger if it leads to more effective, more stable or

more likely coordination in the market; see Case C-413/06 P, *Sony*, [2008] ECR I-4951, paragraph 123, where the Court of Justice endorsed the criteria established by the General Court in Case T-342/99, *Airtours*, [2002] ECR II-2585, paragraph 62.

61 Case C-238/05, *Asnef-Equifax*, paragraph 54.

62 It should be noted that the discussion in paragraphs 78 to 85 is not a complete list of relevant market characteristics. There may be other characteristics of the market which are important in the setting of certain information exchanges.

63 See Case T-35/92, *John Deere* v *Commission*, [1994] ECR II-957, paragraph 78.

64 See Commission Decision in Cases IV/31.370 and 31.446, *UK Agricultural Tractor Registration Exchange*, OJ L 68, 13.3.1992, p 19, paragraph 51 and Case T-35/92, *John Deere* v *Commission*, paragraph 78. It is not necessary that absolute stability be established or fierce competition excluded.

65 Exchanges of information in the context of an R&D agreement, if they do not exceed what is necessary for implementation of the agreement, can benefit from the safe harbour of 25% set out in the R&D Block Exemption Regulation. For the Specialisation Block Exemption Regulation, the relevant safe harbour is 20%.

66 The collection of historic data can also be used to convey a sector association's input to or analysis of a review of public policy.

67 For example, in past cases the Commission has considered the exchange of individual data which was more than one year old as historic and as not restrictive of competition within the meaning of Article 101(1), whereas information less than one year old has been considered as recent; Commission Decision in Case IV/31.370, *UK Agricultural Tractor Registration Exchange*, paragraph 50; Commission Decision in Case IV/36.069, *Wirtschaftsvereinigung Stahl*, OJ L 1, 3.1.1998, p 10, paragraph 17.

68 However, infrequent contracts could decrease the likelihood of a sufficiently prompt retaliation.

69 However, depending on the structure of the market and the overall context of the exchange, the possibility cannot be excluded that an isolated exchange may constitute a sufficient basis for the participating undertakings to concert their market conduct and thus successfully substitute practical co-operation between them for competition and the risks that that entails; see Case C-8/08, *T-Mobile Netherlands*, paragraph 59.

70 Joined Cases T-191/98 and others, *Atlantic Container Line (TACA)*, [2003] ECR II-3275, paragraph 1154. This may not be the case if the exchange underpins a cartel.

71 Moreover, the fact that the parties to the exchange have previously communicated the data to the public (for example through a daily newspaper or on their websites) does not imply that a subsequent non-public exchange would not infringe Article 101.

72 See Joined Cases T-202/98 and others, *Tate & Lyle* v *Commission*, paragraph 60.

73 This does not preclude that a database be offered at a lower price to customers which themselves have contributed data to it, as by doing so they normally would have also incurred costs.

74 Assessing barriers to entry and countervailing 'buyer power' in the market would be relevant for determining whether outsiders to the information exchange system would be able to jeopardise the outcomes expected from coordination. However, increased transparency to consumers may either decrease or increase scope for a collusive outcome because with increased transparency to consumers, as price elasticity of demand is higher, pay-offs from deviation are higher but retaliation is also harsher.

75 The discussion of potential efficiency gains from information exchange is neither exclusive nor exhaustive.

76 Such efficiencies need to be weighed against the potential negative effects of, for example, limiting competition for the market which stimulates innovation.

3. RESEARCH AND DEVELOPMENT AGREEMENTS

3.1. Definition

[4.222]

111. R&D agreements vary in form and scope. They range from outsourcing certain R&D activities to the joint improvement of existing technologies and co-operation concerning the research, development and marketing of completely new products. They may take the form of a co-operation agreement or of a jointly controlled company. This chapter applies to all forms of R&D agreements, including related agreements concerning the production or commercialisation of the R&D results.

3.2. Relevant markets

112. The key to defining the relevant market when assessing the effects of an R&D agreement is to identify those products, technologies or R&D efforts that will act as the main competitive constraints on the parties. At one end of the spectrum of possible situations, innovation may result in a product (or technology) which competes in an existing product (or technology) market. This is, for example, the case with R&D directed towards slight improvements or variations, such as new models of certain products. Here possible effects concern the market for existing products. At the other end of the spectrum, innovation may result in an entirely new product which creates its own new product market (for example, a new vaccine for a previously incurable disease). However, many cases concern situations in between those two extremes, that is to say, situations in which innovation efforts may create products (or technology) which, over time, replace existing ones (for example, CDs which have replaced records). A careful analysis of those situations may have to cover both existing markets and the impact of the agreement on innovation.

Existing product markets

113. Where the co-operation concerns R&D for the improvement of existing products, those existing products and their close substitutes form the relevant market concerned by the co-operation.[77]

114. If the R&D efforts aim at a significant change of existing products or even at a new product to replace existing ones, substitution with the existing products may be imperfect or long-term. It may be concluded that the old and the potentially emerging new products do not belong to the same relevant market.[78] The market for existing products may

nevertheless be concerned, if the pooling of R&D efforts is likely to result in the coordination of the parties' behaviour as suppliers of existing products, for instance because of the exchange of competitively sensitive information relating to the market for existing products.

115. If the R&D concerns an important component of a final product, not only the market for that component may be relevant for the assessment, but also the existing market for the final product. For instance, if car manufacturers co-operate in R&D related to a new type of engine, the car market may be affected by that R&D co-operation. The market for final products, however, is only relevant for the assessment if the component at which the R&D is aimed is technically or economically a key element of those final products and if the parties to the R&D agreement have market power with respect to the final products.

Existing technology markets

116. R&D co-operation may not only concern products but also technology. When intellectual property rights are marketed separately from the products to which they relate, the relevant technology market has to be defined as well. Technology markets consist of the intellectual property that is licensed and its close substitutes, that is to say, other technologies which customers could use as a substitute.

117. The methodology for defining technology markets follows the same principles as product market definition.[79] Starting from the technology which is marketed by the parties, those other technologies to which customers could switch in response to a small but non-transitory increase in relative prices need to be identified. Once those technologies are identified, market shares can be calculated by dividing the licensing income generated by the parties by the total licensing income of all licensors.

118. The parties' position in the market for existing technology is a relevant assessment criterion where the R&D co-operation concerns a significant improvement to an existing technology or a new technology that is likely to replace the existing technology. The parties' market shares can, however, only be taken as a starting point for this analysis. In technology markets, particular emphasis must be placed on potential competition. If companies which do not currently license their technology are potential entrants on the technology market they could constrain the ability of the parties to profitably raise the price for their technology. This aspect of the analysis may also be taken into account directly in the calculation of market shares by basing those on the sales of the products incorporating the licensed technology on downstream product markets (see paragraphs 123 to 126).

Competition in innovation (R&D efforts)

119. R&D co-operation may not only affect competition in existing markets, but also competition in innovation and new product markets. This is the case where R&D co-operation concerns the development of new products or technology which either may – if emerging – one day replace existing ones or which are being developed for a new intended use and will therefore not replace existing products but create a completely new demand. The effects on competition in innovation are important in these situations, but can in some cases not be sufficiently assessed by analysing actual or potential competition in existing product/technology markets. In this respect, two scenarios can be distinguished, depending on the nature of the innovative process in a given industry.

120. In the first scenario, which is, for instance, present in the pharmaceutical industry, the process of innovation is structured in such a way that it is possible at an early stage to identify competing R&D poles. Competing R&D poles are R&D efforts directed towards a certain new product or technology, and the substitutes for that R&D, that is to say, R&D aimed at developing substitutable products or technology for those developed by the co-operation and having similar timing. In this case, it can be analysed whether after the agreement there will be a sufficient number of remaining R&D poles. The starting point of the analysis is the R&D of the parties. Then credible competing R&D poles have to be identified. In order to assess the credibility of competing poles, the following aspects have to be taken into account: the nature, scope and size of any other R&D efforts, their access to financial and human resources, know-how/patents, or other specialised assets as well as their timing and their capability to exploit possible results. An R&D pole is not a credible competitor if it cannot be regarded as a close substitute for the parties' R&D effort from the viewpoint of, for instance, access to resources or timing.

121. Besides the direct effect on the innovation itself, the co-operation may also affect a new product market. It will often be difficult to analyse the effects on such a market directly as by its very nature it does not yet exist. The analysis of such markets will therefore often be implicitly incorporated in the analysis of competition in innovation. However, it may be necessary to consider directly the effects on such a market of aspects of the agreement that go beyond the R&D stage. An R&D agreement that includes joint production and commercialisation on the new product market may, for instance, be assessed differently than a pure R&D agreement.

122. In the second scenario, the innovative efforts in an industry are not clearly structured so as to allow the identification of R&D poles. In this situation, in the absence of exceptional circumstances, the Commission would not try to assess the impact of a given R&D co-operation on innovation, but would limit its assessment to existing product and/or technology markets which are related to the R&D co-operation in question.

Calculation of market shares

123. The calculation of market shares, both for the purposes of the R&D Block Exemption Regulation and of these guidelines, has to reflect the distinction between existing markets and competition in innovation. At the beginning of an R&D co-operation the reference point is the existing market for products capable of being improved, substituted or replaced by the products under development. If the R&D agreement only aims at improving or refining existing products, that market includes the products directly concerned by the R&D. Market shares can thus be calculated on the basis of the sales value of the existing products.

124. If the R&D aims at replacing an existing product, the new product will, if successful, become a substitute for the existing products. To assess the competitive position of the parties, it is again possible to calculate market shares on the basis of the sales value of the existing products. Consequently, the R&D Block Exemption Regulation bases its

exemption of those situations on the market share in the relevant market for the products capable of being improved, substituted or replaced by the contract products.[80] To fall under the R&D Block Exemption Regulation, that market share may not exceed 25%.[81]

125. For technology markets one way to proceed is to calculate market shares on the basis of each technology's share of total licensing income from royalties, representing a technology's share of the market where competing technologies are licensed. However, this may often be a mere theoretical and not very practical way to proceed because of lack of clear information on royalties, the use of royalty free cross-licensing, etc. An alternative approach is to calculate market shares on the technology market on the basis of sales of products or services incorporating the licensed technology on downstream product markets. Under that approach all sales on the relevant product market are taken into account, irrespective of whether the product incorporates a technology that is being licensed.[82] Also for that market the share may not exceed 25% (irrespective of the calculation method used) for the benefits of the R&D Block Exemption Regulation to apply.

126. If the R&D aims at developing a product which will create a completely new demand, market shares based on sales cannot be calculated. Only an analysis of the effects of the agreement on competition in innovation is possible. Consequently, the R&D Block Exemption Regulation treats those agreements as agreements between non-competitors and exempts them irrespective of market share for the duration of the joint R&D and an additional period of seven years after the product is first put on the market.[83] However, the benefit of the block exemption may be withdrawn if the agreement eliminated effective competition in innovation.[84] After the seven year period, market shares based on sales value can be calculated, and the market share threshold of 25% applies.[85]

3.3. Assessment under Article 101(1)

3.3.1. Main competition concerns

127. R&D co-operation can restrict competition in various ways. First, it may reduce or slow down innovation, leading to fewer or worse products coming to the market later than they otherwise would. Secondly, on product or technology markets the R&D co-operation may reduce significantly competition between the parties outside the scope of the agreement or it may make anti-competitive coordination on those markets likely, thereby leading to higher prices. A foreclosure problem may only arise in the context of co-operation involving at least one player with a significant degree of market power (which does not necessarily amount to dominance) for a key technology and the exclusive exploitation of the results.

3.3.2. Restrictions of competition by object

128. R&D agreements restrict competition by object if they do not truly concern joint R&D, but serve as a tool to engage in a disguised cartel, that is to say, otherwise prohibited price fixing, output limitation or market allocation. However, an R&D agreement which includes the joint exploitation of possible future results is not necessarily restrictive of competition.

3.3.3. Restrictive effects on competition

129. Most R&D agreements do not fall under Article 101(1). First, this can be said for many agreements relating to co-operation in R&D at a rather early stage, far removed from the exploitation of possible results.

130. Moreover, R&D co-operation between non-competitors does generally not give rise to restrictive effects on competition.[86] The competitive relationship between the parties has to be analysed in the context of affected existing markets and/or innovation. If, on the basis of objective factors, the parties are not able to carry out the necessary R&D independently, for instance, due to the limited technical capabilities of the parties, the R&D agreement will normally not have any restrictive effects on competition. This can apply, for example, to companies bringing together complementary skills, technologies and other resources. The issue of potential competition has to be assessed on a realistic basis. For instance, parties cannot be defined as potential competitors simply because the co-operation enables them to carry out the R&D activities. The decisive question is whether each party independently has the necessary means as regards assets, know-how and other resources.

131. Outsourcing of previously captive R&D is a specific form of R&D co-operation. In such a scenario, the R&D is often carried out by specialised companies, research institutes or academic bodies, which are not active in the exploitation of the results. Normally, such agreements are combined with a transfer of know-how and/or an exclusive supply clause concerning the possible results, which, due to the complementary nature of the co-operating parties in such a scenario, do not give rise to restrictive effects on competition within the meaning of Article 101(1).

132. R&D co-operation which does not include the joint exploitation of possible results by means of licensing, production and/or marketing rarely gives rise to restrictive effects on competition within the meaning of Article 101(1). Those pure R&D agreements can only cause a competition problem if competition with respect to innovation is appreciably reduced, leaving only a limited number of credible competing R&D poles.

133. R&D agreements are only likely to give rise to restrictive effects on competition where the parties to the co-operation have market power on the existing markets and/or competition with respect to innovation is appreciably reduced.

134. There is no absolute threshold above which it can be presumed that an R&D agreement creates or maintains market power and thus is likely to give rise to restrictive effects on competition within the meaning of Article 101(1). However, R&D agreements between competitors are covered by the R&D Block Exemption Regulation provided that their combined market share does not exceed 25% and that the other conditions for the application of the R&D Block Exemption Regulation are fulfilled.

135. Agreements falling outside the R&D Block Exemption Regulation because the combined market share of the parties exceeds 25% do not necessarily give rise to restrictive effects on competition. However, the stronger the combined position of the parties on existing markets and/or the more competition in innovation is restricted, the more likely it is that the R&D agreement can cause restrictive effects on competition.[87]

136. If the R&D is directed at the improvement or refinement of existing products or technologies, possible effects concern the relevant market(s) for those existing products or technologies. Effects on prices, output, product quality, product variety or innovation in existing markets are, however, only likely if the parties together have a strong position, entry is difficult and few other innovation activities are identifiable. Furthermore, if the R&D only concerns a relatively minor input of a final product, effects on competition in those final products are, if any, very limited.

137. In general, a distinction has to be made between pure R&D agreements and agreements providing for more comprehensive co-operation involving different stages of the exploitation of results (that is to say, licensing, production or marketing). As set out in paragraph 132, pure R&D agreements will only rarely give rise to restrictive effects on competition within the meaning of Article 101(1). This is in particular true for R&D directed towards a limited improvement of existing products or technologies. If, in such a scenario, the R&D co-operation includes joint exploitation only by means of licensing to third parties, restrictive effects such as foreclosure problems are unlikely. If, however, joint production and/or marketing of the slightly improved products or technologies are included, the effects on competition of the co-operation have to be examined more closely. Restrictive effects on competition in the form of increased prices or reduced output in existing markets are more likely if strong competitors are involved in such a situation.

138. If the R&D is directed at an entirely new product (or technology) which creates its own new market, price and output effects on existing markets are rather unlikely. The analysis has to focus on possible restrictions of innovation concerning, for instance, the quality and variety of possible future products or technologies or the speed of innovation. Those restrictive effects can arise where two or more of the few companies engaged in the development of such a new product start to co-operate at a stage where they are each independently rather near to the launch of the product. Such effects are typically the direct result of the agreement between the parties. Innovation may be restricted even by a pure R&D agreement. In general, however, R&D co-operation concerning entirely new products is unlikely to give rise to restrictive effects on competition unless only a limited number of credible alternative R&D poles exist. This principle does not change significantly if the joint exploitation of the results, even joint marketing, is involved. In those situations the issue of joint exploitation may only give rise to restrictive effects on competition where foreclosure from key technologies plays a role. Those problems would, however, not arise where the parties grant licences that allow third parties to compete effectively.

139. Many R&D agreements will lie somewhere in between the two situations described in paragraphs 137 and 138. They may therefore have effects on innovation as well as repercussions on existing markets. Consequently, both the existing market and the effect on innovation may be of relevance for the assessment with respect to the parties' combined positions, concentration ratios, number of players or innovators and entry conditions. In some cases there can be restrictive effects on competition in the form of increased prices or reduced output, product quality, product variety or innovation in existing markets and in the form of a negative impact on innovation by means of slowing down the development. For instance, if significant competitors on an existing technology market co-operate to develop a new technology which may one day replace existing products that co-operation may slow down the development of the new technology if the parties have market power on the existing market and also a strong position with respect to R&D. A similar effect can occur if the major player in an existing market co-operates with a much smaller or even potential competitor who is just about to emerge with a new product or technology which may endanger the incumbent's position.

140. Agreements may also fall outside the R&D Block Exemption Regulation irrespective of the parties' market power. This applies for instance to agreements which unduly restrict access of a party to the results of the R&D co-operation.[88] The R&D Block Exemption Regulation provides for a specific exception to this general rule in the case of academic bodies, research institutes or specialised companies which provide R&D as a service and which are not active in the industrial exploitation of the results of R&D.[89] Nevertheless, agreements falling outside the R&D Block Exemption Regulation and containing exclusive access rights for the purposes of exploitation may, where they fall under Article 101(1), fulfil the criteria of Article 101(3), particularly where exclusive access rights are economically indispensable in view of the market, risks and scale of the investment required to exploit the results of the research and development.

3.4. Assessment under Article 101(3)

3.4.1.
Efficiency gains

141. Many R&D agreements – with or without joint exploitation of possible results – bring about efficiency gains by combining complementary skills and assets, thus resulting in improved or new products and technologies being developed and marketed more rapidly than would otherwise be the case. R&D agreements may also lead to a wider dissemination of knowledge, which may trigger further innovation. R&D agreements may also give rise to cost reductions.

3.4.2.
Indispensability

142. Restrictions that go beyond what is necessary to achieve the efficiency gains generated by an R&D agreement do not fulfil the criteria of Article 101(3). In particular, the restrictions listed in Article 5 of the R&D Block Exemption Regulation may mean it is less likely that the criteria of Article 101(3) will be found to be met, following an individual assessment. It will therefore generally be necessary for the parties to an R&D agreement to show that such restrictions are indispensable to the co-operation.

3.4.3.
Pass-on to consumers

143. Efficiency gains attained by indispensable restrictions must be passed on to consumers to an extent that outweighs the restrictive effects on competition caused by the R&D agreement. For example, the introduction of new or improved products on the market must outweigh any price increases or other restrictive effects on competition. In general, it is more likely that an R&D agreement will bring about efficiency gains that benefit consumers if the R&D agreement results in the combination of complementary skills and assets. The parties to an agreement may, for instance, have different research capabilities. If, on the other hand, the parties' skills and assets are very similar, the most important effect of the R&D agreement may be the elimination of part or all of the R&D of one or more of the parties. This would eliminate (fixed) costs for the parties to the agreement but would be unlikely to lead to benefits which would be passed on to consumers. Moreover, the higher the market power of the parties the less likely they are to pass on the efficiency gains to consumers to an extent that would outweigh the restrictive effects on competition.

3.4.4.
No elimination of competition

144. The criteria of Article 101(3) cannot be met if the parties are afforded the possibility of eliminating competition in respect of a substantial part of the products (or technologies) in question.

3.4.5.
Time of the assessment

145. The assessment of restrictive agreements under Article 101(3) is made within the actual context in which they occur and on the basis of the facts existing at any given point in time. The assessment is sensitive to material changes in the facts. The exception rule of Article 101(3) applies as long as the four conditions of Article 101(3) are fulfilled and ceases to apply when that is no longer the case. When applying Article 101(3) in accordance with those principles it is necessary to take into account the initial sunk investments made by any of the parties and the time needed and the restraints required to making and recouping an efficiency enhancing investment. Article 101 cannot be applied without taking due account of such *ex ante* investment. The risk facing the parties and the sunk investment that must be made to implement the agreement can thus lead to the agreement falling outside Article 101(1) or fulfilling the conditions of Article 101(3), as the case may be, for the period of time needed to recoup the investment. Should the invention resulting from the investment benefit from any form of exclusivity granted to the parties under rules specific to the protection of intellectual property rights, the recoupment period for such an investment will generally be unlikely to exceed the exclusivity period established under those rules.

146. In some cases the restrictive agreement is an irreversible event. Once the restrictive agreement has been implemented the *ex ante* situation cannot be re-established. In such cases the assessment must be made exclusively on the basis of the facts pertaining at the time of implementation. For instance, in the case of an R&D agreement whereby each party agrees to abandon its respective research project and pool its capabilities with those of another party, it may from an objective point of view be technically and economically impossible to revive a project once it has been abandoned. The assessment of the anti-competitive and pro-competitive effects of the agreement to abandon the individual research projects must therefore be made as of the time of the completion of its implementation. If at that point in time the agreement is compatible with Article 101, for instance because a sufficient number of third parties have competing R&D projects, the parties' agreement to abandon their individual projects remains compatible with Article 101, even if at a later point in time the third party projects fail. However, the prohibition of Article 101 may apply to other parts of the agreement in respect of which the issue of irreversibility does not arise. If, for example, in addition to joint R&D, the agreement provides for joint exploitation, Article 101 may apply to that part of the agreement if, due to subsequent market developments, the agreement gives rise to restrictive effects on competition and does not (any longer) satisfy the conditions of Article 101(3) taking due account of *ex ante* sunk investments.

3.5. Examples

147. Impact of joint R&D on innovation markets/new product market

Example 1

Situation: A and B are the two major companies on the Union-wide market for the manufacture of existing electronic components. Both have a market share of 30%. They have each made significant investments in the R&D necessary to develop miniaturised electronic components and have developed early prototypes. They now agree to pool those R&D efforts by setting up a joint venture to complete the R&D and produce the components, which will be sold back to the parents, who will commercialise them separately. The remainder of the market consists of small companies without sufficient resources to undertake the necessary investments.

Analysis: Miniaturised electronic components, while likely to compete with the existing components in some areas, are essentially a new technology and an analysis must be made of the poles of research destined towards that future market. If the joint venture goes ahead then only one route to the necessary manufacturing technology will exist, whereas it would appear likely that A and B could reach the market individually with separate products. The agreement therefore reduces product variety. The joint production is also likely to directly limit competition between the parties to the agreement and lead them to agree on output levels, quality or other competitively important parameters. This would limit competition even though the parties will commercialise the products independently. The parties could, for instance, limit the output of the joint venture compared to what the parties would have brought to the market if they had decided their output on their own. The joint venture could also charge a high transfer price to the parties, thereby increasing the input costs for the parties which could lead to higher downstream prices. The parties have a large combined market share on the existing downstream market and the remainder of that market is fragmented. This situation is likely to become even more pronounced on the new downstream product market since the smaller competitors cannot invest in the new components. It is therefore quite likely that the joint production will restrict competition. Furthermore, the market for miniaturised electronic components is in the future likely to develop into a duopoly with a high degree of commonality of costs and possible exchange of commercially sensitive information between the parties. There may therefore also be a serious risk of anti-competitive coordination leading to a collusive outcome in the market. The R&D agreement is therefore likely to give rise to restrictive effects on competition within the meaning of Article 101(1). While the agreement could give rise to efficiency gains in the form of bringing a new technology forward quicker, the parties would face no competition at the R&D level, so their incentives to pursue the new technology at a high pace could be severely reduced. Although some of those concerns could be remedied if the parties committed to license key know-how for manufacturing miniature components to third parties on reasonable terms, it seems unlikely that this could remedy all concerns and fulfil the conditions of Article 101(3).

Example 2

Situation: A small research company (Company A) which does not have its own marketing organisation has discovered and patented a pharmaceutical substance based on new technology that will revolutionise the treatment of a certain disease. Company A enters into an R&D agreement with a large pharmaceutical producer Company B of products that have so far been used for treating the disease. Company B lacks any similar expertise and R&D programme and would not be able to build such expertise within a relevant timeframe. For the existing products Company B has a market share of around 75% in all Member States, but the patents will expire over the next five years. There exist two other poles of research with other companies at approximately the same stage of development using the same basic new technology. Company B will provide considerable funding and know-how for product development, as well as future access to the market. Company B is granted a licence for the exclusive production and distribution of the resulting product for the duration of the patent. It is expected that the product could be brought to market in five to seven years.

Analysis: The product is likely to belong to a new relevant market. The parties bring complementary resources and skills to the co-operation, and the probability of the product coming to market increases substantially. Although Company B is likely to have considerable market power on the existing market, that market power will be decreasing shortly. The agreement will not lead to a loss in R&D on the part of Company B, as it has no expertise in this area of research, and the existence of other poles of research are likely to eliminate any incentive to reduce R&D efforts. The exploitation rights during the remaining patent period are likely to be necessary for Company B to make the considerable investments needed and Company A has no marketing resources of its own. The agreement is therefore unlikely to give rise to restrictive effects on competition within the meaning of Article 101(1). Even if there were such effects, it is likely that the conditions of Article 101(3) would be fulfilled.

148. Risk of foreclosure

Example 3

Situation: A small research company (Company A) which does not have its own marketing organisation has discovered and patented a new technology that will revolutionise the market for a certain product for which there is a monopoly producer (Company B) worldwide as no competitors can compete with Company B's current technology. There exist two other poles of research with other companies at approximately the same stage of development using the same basic new technology. Company B will provide considerable funding and know-how for product development, as well as future access to the market. Company B is granted an exclusive licence for the use of the technology for the duration of the patent and commits to funding only the development of Company A's technology.

Analysis: The product is likely to belong to a new relevant market. The parties bring complementary resources and skills to the co-operation, and the probability of the product coming to market increases substantially. However, the fact that Company B commits to Company A's new technology may be likely to lead the two competing poles of research to abandon their projects as it could be difficult to receive continued funding once they have lost the most likely potential customer for their technology. In such a situation no potential competitors would be able to challenge Company B's monopoly position in the future. The foreclosure effect of the agreement would then be likely to be considered to give rise to restrictive effects on competition within the meaning of Article 101(1). In order to benefit from Article 101(3) the parties would have to show that the exclusivity granted would be indispensable to bring the new technology to the market.

Example 4

Situation: Company A has market power on the market of which its blockbuster medicine forms part. A small company (Company B) which is engaged in pharmaceutical R&D and active pharmaceutical ingredient ('API') production has discovered and filed a patent application for a new process that makes it possible to produce the API of Company A's blockbuster in a more economic fashion and continues to develop the process for industrial production. The compound (API) patent of the blockbuster expires in a little less than three years; thereafter there will remain a number of process patents relating to the medicine. Company B considers that the new process developed by it would not infringe the existing process patents of Company A and would allow the production of a generic version of the blockbuster once the API patent has expired. Company B could either produce the product itself or license the process to interested third parties, for example, generic producers or Company A. Before concluding its research and development in this area, Company B enters into an agreement with Company A, in which Company A makes a financial contribution to the R&D project being carried out by Company B on condition that it acquires an exclusive licence for any of Company B's patents related to the R&D project. There exist two other independent poles of research to develop a non-infringing process for the production of the blockbuster medicine, but it is not yet clear that they will reach industrial production.

Analysis: The process covered by Company B's patent application does not allow for the production of a new product. It merely improves an existing production process. Company A has market power on the existing market of which the blockbuster medicine forms part. Whilst that market power would decrease significantly with the actual market entry of generic competitors, the exclusive licence makes the process developed by Company B unavailable to third parties and is thus liable to delay generic entry (not least as the product is still protected by a number of process patents) and, consequently, restricts competition within the meaning of Article 101(1). As Company A and Company B are potential competitors, the R&D Block Exemption Regulation does not apply because Company A's market share on the market of which the blockbuster medicine forms part is above 25%. The cost savings based on the new production process for Company A are not sufficient to outweigh the restriction of competition. In any event, an exclusive licence is not indispensable to obtain the savings in the production process. Therefore, the agreement is unlikely to fulfil the conditions of Article 101(3).

149. Impact of R&D co-operation on dynamic product and technology markets and the environment

Example 5

Situation: Two engineering companies that produce vehicle components agree to set up a joint venture to combine their R&D efforts to improve the production and performance of an existing component. The production of that component would also have a positive effect on the environment. Vehicles would consume less fuel and therefore emit less CO_2. The companies pool their existing technology licensing businesses in the area, but will continue to manufacture and sell the components separately. The two companies have market shares in the Union of 15% and 20% on the Original Equipment Manufacturer ('OEM') product market. There are two other major competitors together with several in-house research programmes by large vehicle manufacturers. On the world-wide market for the licensing of technology for those products the parties have shares of 20% and 25%, measured in terms of revenue generated, and there are two other major technologies. The product life cycle for the component is typically two to three years. In each of the last five years one of the major companies has introduced a new version or upgrade.

Analysis: Since neither company's R&D effort is aimed at a completely new product, the markets to consider are those for the existing components and for the licensing of relevant technology. The parties' combined market share on both the OEM market (35%) and, in particular, on the technology market (45%) are quite high. However, the parties will continue to manufacture and sell the components separately. In addition, there are several competing technologies, which are regularly improved. Moreover, the vehicle manufacturers who do not currently license their technology are also potential entrants on the technology market and thus constrain the ability of the parties to profitably raise prices. To the extent that the joint venture has restrictive effects on competition within the meaning of Article 101(1), it is likely that it would fulfil the criteria of Article 101(3). For the assessment under Article 101(3) it would be necessary to take into account that consumers will benefit from a lower consumption of fuel.

NOTES

77 For market definition, see the Market Definition Notice.

78 See also Commission Guidelines on the application of Article 81 of the EC Treaty to technology transfer agreements, OJ C101, 27.4.2004, p 2 ('Technology Transfer Guidelines'), paragraph 33.

79 See Market Definition Notice; see also Technology Transfer Guidelines, paragraphs 19 *et seq.*

80 Point (u) of Article 1(1) of the R&D Block Exemption Regulation.

81 Article 4(2) of the R&D Block Exemption Regulation.

82 See also Technology Transfer Guidelines, paragraph 23.

83 Article 4(1) of the R&D Block Exemption Regulation.

84 See recitals 19, 20 and 21 in the preamble to the R&D Block Exemption Regulation.

85 Article 4(3) of the R&D Block Exemption Regulation.

86 R&D co-operation between non-competitors can, however, produce foreclosure effects under Article 101(1) if it relates to an exclusive exploitation of results and if it is concluded between companies, one of which has a significant degree of market power (which does not necessarily amount to dominance) with respect to a key technology.

87 This is without prejudice to the analysis of potential efficiency gains, including those that regularly exist in publicly co-funded R&D.

88 See Article 3(2) of the R&D Block Exemption Regulation.

89 See Article 3(2) of the R&D Block Exemption Regulation.

4. PRODUCTION AGREEMENTS

4.1. Definition and scope

[4.223]

150. Production agreements vary in form and scope. They can provide that production is carried out by only one party or by two or more parties. Companies can produce jointly by way of a joint venture, that is to say, a jointly controlled company operating one or several production facilities or by looser forms of co-operation in production such as subcontracting agreements where one party (the 'contractor') entrusts to another party (the 'subcontractor') the production of a good.

151. There are different types of subcontracting agreements. Horizontal subcontracting agreements are concluded between companies operating in the same product market irrespective of whether they are actual or potential competitors. Vertical subcontracting agreements are concluded between companies operating at different levels of the market.

152. Horizontal subcontracting agreements comprise unilateral and reciprocal specialisation agreements as well as subcontracting agreements with a view to expanding production. Unilateral specialisation agreements are agreements between two parties which are active on the same product market or markets, by virtue of which one party agrees to fully or partly cease production of certain products or to refrain from producing those products and to purchase them from the other party, which agrees to produce and supply the products. Reciprocal specialisation agreements are agreements between two or more parties which are active on the same products market or markets, by virtue of which two or more parties agree, on a reciprocal basis, to fully or partly cease or refrain from producing certain but different products and to purchase those products from the other parties, which agree to produce and supply them. In the case of subcontracting agreements with a view to expanding production the contractor entrusts the subcontractor with the production of a good, while the contractor does not at the same time cease or limit its own production of the good.

153. These guidelines apply to all forms of joint production agreements and horizontal subcontracting agreements. Subject to certain conditions, joint production agreements as well as unilateral and reciprocal specialisation agreements may benefit from the Specialisation Block Exemption Regulation.

154. Vertical subcontracting agreements are not covered by these guidelines. They fall within the scope of the Guidelines on Vertical Restraints and, subject to certain conditions, may benefit from the Block Exemption Regulation on Vertical Restraints. In addition, they may be covered by the Commission notice of 18 December 1978 concerning its assessment of certain subcontracting agreements in relation to Article 85(1) of the EEC Treaty[90] ('the Subcontracting Notice').

4.2. Relevant markets

155. In order to assess the competitive relationship between the co-operating parties, it is necessary first to define the relevant market or markets directly concerned by the co-operation in production, that is to say, the markets to which the products manufactured under the production agreement belong.

156. A production agreement can also have spill-over effects in markets neighbouring the market directly concerned by the co-operation, for instance upstream or downstream to the agreement (the so-called 'spill-over markets').[91] The spill-over markets are likely to be relevant if the markets are interdependent and the parties are in a strong position on the spill-over market.

4.3. Assessment under Article 101(1)

4.3.1. *Main competition concerns*

157. Production agreements can lead to a direct limitation of competition between the parties. Production agreements, and in particular production joint ventures, may lead the parties to directly align output levels and quality, the price at which the joint venture sells on its products, or other competitively important parameters. This may restrict competition even if the parties market the products independently.

158. Production agreements may also result in the coordination of the parties' competitive behaviour as suppliers leading to higher prices or reduced output, product quality, product variety or innovation, that is to say, a collusive outcome. This can happen, subject to the parties having market power and the existence of market characteristics conducive to such coordination, in particular when the production agreement increases the parties' commonality of costs (that is to say, the proportion of variable costs which the parties have in common) to a degree which enables them to achieve a collusive outcome, or if the agreement involves an exchange of commercially sensitive information that can lead to a collusive outcome.

159. Production agreements may furthermore lead to anti-competitive foreclosure of third parties in a related market (for example, the downstream market relying on inputs from the market in which the production agreement takes place). For instance, by gaining enough market power, parties engaging in joint production in an upstream market may be able to raise the price of a key component for a market downstream. Thereby, they could use the joint production to raise the costs of their rivals downstream and, ultimately, force them off the market. This would, in turn, increase the parties' market power downstream, which could enable them to sustain prices above the competitive level or otherwise harm consumers. Such competition concerns could materialise irrespective of whether the parties to the agreement are competitors on the market in which the co-operation takes place. However, for this kind of foreclosure to have anti-competitive effects, at least one of the parties must have a strong market position in the market where the risks of foreclosure are assessed.

4.3.2. *Restrictions of competition by object*

160. Generally, agreements which involve price-fixing, limiting output or sharing markets or customers restrict competition by object. However, in the context of production agreements, this does not apply where:

— the parties agree on the output directly concerned by the production agreement (for example, the capacity and production volume of a joint venture or the agreed amount of outsourced products), provided that the other parameters of competition are not eliminated; or

— a production agreement that also provides for the joint distribution of the jointly manufactured products envisages the joint setting of the sales prices for those products, and only those products, provided that that restriction is necessary for producing jointly, meaning that the parties would not otherwise have an incentive to enter into the production agreement in the first place.

161. In these two cases an assessment is required as to whether the agreement gives rise to likely restrictive effects on competition within the meaning of Article 101(1). In both scenarios the agreement on output or prices will not be assessed separately, but in the light of the overall effects of the entire production agreement on the market.

4.3.3.
Restrictive effects on competition

162. Whether the possible competition concerns that production agreements can give rise to are likely to materialise in a given case depends on the characteristics of the market in which the agreement takes place, as well as on the nature and market coverage of the co-operation and the product it concerns. These variables determine the likely effects of a production agreement on competition and thereby the applicability of Article 101(1).

163. Whether a production agreement is likely to give rise to restrictive effects on competition depends on the situation that would prevail in the absence of the agreement with all its alleged restrictions. Consequently, production agreements between companies which compete on markets on which the co-operation occurs are not likely to have restrictive effects on competition if the co-operation gives rise to a new market, that is to say, if the agreement enables the parties to launch a new product or service, which, on the basis of objective factors, the parties would otherwise not have been able to do, for instance, due to the technical capabilities of the parties.

164. In some industries where production is the main economic activity, even a pure production agreement can in itself eliminate key dimensions of competition, thereby directly limiting competition between the parties to the agreements.

165. Alternatively, a production agreement can lead to a collusive outcome or anti-competitive foreclosure by increasing the companies' market power or their commonality of costs or if it involves the exchange of commercially sensitive information. On the other hand, a direct limitation of competition between the parties, a collusive outcome or anti-competitive foreclosure is not likely to occur if the parties to the agreement do not have market power in the market in which the competition concerns are assessed. It is only market power that can enable them to profitably maintain prices above the competitive level, or profitably maintain output, product quality or variety below what would be dictated by competition.

166. In cases where a company with market power in one market co-operates with a potential entrant, for example, with a supplier of the same product in a neighbouring geographic or product market, the agreement can potentially increase the market power of the incumbent. This can lead to restrictive effects on competition if actual competition in the incumbent's market is already weak and the threat of entry is a major source of competitive constraint.

167. Production agreements which also involve commercialisation functions, such as joint distribution or marketing, carry a higher risk of restrictive effects on competition than pure joint production agreements. Joint commercialisation brings the co-operation closer to the consumer and usually involves the joint setting of prices and sales, that is to say, practices that carry the highest risks for competition. However, joint distribution agreements for products which have been jointly produced are generally less likely to restrict competition than stand-alone joint distribution agreements. Also, a joint distribution agreement that is necessary for the joint production agreement to take place in the first place is less likely to restrict competition than if it were not necessary for the joint production.

Market power

168. A production agreement is unlikely to lead to restrictive effects on competition if the parties to the agreement do not have market power in the market on which a restriction of competition is assessed. The starting point for the analysis of market power is the market share of the parties. This will normally be followed by the concentration ratio and the number of players in the market as well as by other dynamic factors such as potential entry, and changing market shares.

169. Companies are unlikely to have market power below a certain level of market share. Therefore, unilateral or reciprocal specialisation agreements as well as joint production agreements including certain integrated commercialisation functions such as joint distribution are covered by the Specialisation Block Exemption Regulation if they are concluded between parties with a combined market share not exceeding 20% in the relevant market or markets, provided that the other conditions for the application of the Specialisation Block Exemption Regulation are fulfilled. Moreover, as regards horizontal subcontracting agreements with a view to expanding production, in most cases it is unlikely that market power exists if the parties to the agreement have a combined market share not exceeding 20%. In any event, if the parties' combined market share does not exceed 20% it is likely that the conditions of Article 101(3) are fulfilled.

170. However, if the parties' combined market share exceeds 20%, the restrictive effects have to be analysed as the agreement does not fall within the scope of the Specialisation Block Exemption Regulation or the safe harbour for horizontal subcontracting agreements with a view to expanding production referred to in sentences 3 and 4 of paragraph 169. A moderately higher market share than allowed for in the Specialisation Block Exemption Regulation or the safe harbour referred to in sentences 3 and 4 of paragraph 169 does not necessarily imply a highly concentrated market, which is an important factor in the assessment. A combined market share of the parties of slightly more than 20% may occur in a market with a moderate concentration. Generally, a production agreement is more likely to lead to restrictive effects on competition in a concentrated market than in a market which is not concentrated. Similarly, a production agreement in a concentrated market may increase the risk of a collusive outcome even if the parties only have a moderate combined market share.

171. Even if the market shares of the parties to the agreement and the market concentration are high, the risks of restrictive effects on competition may still be low if the market is dynamic, that is to say, a market in which entry occurs and market positions change frequently.

172. In the analysis of whether the parties to a production agreement have market power, the number and intensity of links (for example, other co-operation agreements) between the competitors in the market are relevant to the assessment.

173. Factors such as whether the parties to the agreement have high market shares, whether they are close competitors, whether the customers have limited possibilities of switching suppliers, whether competitors are unlikely to increase supply if prices increase, and whether one of the parties to the agreement is an important competitive force, are all relevant for the competitive assessment of the agreement.

Direct limitation of competition between the parties

174. Competition between the parties to a production agreement can be directly limited in various ways. The parties to a production joint venture could, for instance, limit the output of the joint venture compared to what the parties would have brought to the market if each of them had decided their output on their own. If the main product characteristics are determined by the production agreement this could also eliminate the key dimensions of competition between the parties and, ultimately, lead to restrictive effects on competition. Another example would be a joint venture charging a high transfer price to the parties, thereby increasing the input costs for the parties which could lead to higher downstream prices. Competitors may find it profitable to increase their prices as a response, thereby contributing to price increases in the relevant market.

Collusive outcome

175. The likelihood of a collusive outcome depends on the parties' market power as well as the characteristics of the relevant market. A collusive outcome can result in particular (but not only) from commonality of costs or an exchange of information brought about by the production agreement.

176. A production agreement between parties with market power can have restrictive effects on competition if it increases their commonality of costs (that is to say, the proportion of variable costs which the parties have in common) to a level which enables them to collude. The relevant costs are the variable costs of the product with respect to which the parties to the production agreement compete.

177. A production agreement is more likely to lead to a collusive outcome if prior to the agreement the parties already have a high proportion of variable costs in common, as the additional increment (that is to say, the production costs of the product subject to the agreement) can tip the balance towards a collusive outcome. Conversely, if the increment is large, the risk of a collusive outcome may be high even if the initial level of commonality of costs is low.

178. Commonality of costs increases the risk of a collusive outcome only if production costs constitute a large proportion of the variable costs concerned. This is, for instance, not the case where the co-operation concerns products which require costly commercialisation. An example would be new or heterogeneous products requiring expensive marketing or high transport costs.

179. Another scenario where commonality of costs can lead to a collusive outcome could be where the parties agree on the joint production of an intermediate product which accounts for a large proportion of the variable costs of the final product with respect to which the parties compete downstream. The parties could use the production agreement to increase the price of that common important input for their products in the downstream market. This would weaken competition downstream and would be likely to lead to higher final prices. The profit would be shifted from downstream to upstream to be then shared between the parties through the joint venture.

180. Similarly, commonality of costs increases the anti-competitive risks of a horizontal subcontracting agreement where the input which the contractor purchases from the subcontractor accounts for a large proportion of the variable costs of the final product with which the parties compete.

181. Any negative effects arising from the exchange of information will not be assessed separately but in the light of the overall effects of the agreement. A production agreement can give rise to restrictive effects on competition if it involves an exchange of commercially strategic information that can lead to a collusive outcome or anti-competitive foreclosure. Whether the exchange of information in the context of a production agreement is likely to lead to restrictive effects on competition should be assessed according to the guidance given in Chapter 2.

182. If the information exchange does not exceed the sharing of data necessary for the joint production of the goods subject to the production agreement, then even if the information exchange had restrictive effects on competition within the meaning of Article 101(1), the agreement would be more likely to meet the criteria of Article 101(3) than if the exchange went beyond what was necessary for the joint production. In this case the efficiency gains stemming from producing jointly are likely to outweigh the restrictive effects of the coordination of the parties' conduct. Conversely, in the context of a production agreement the sharing of data which is not necessary for producing jointly, for example the exchange of information related to prices and sales, is less likely to fulfil the conditions of Article 101(3).

4.4. Assessment under Article 101(3)

4.4.1. *Efficiency gains*

183. Production agreements can be pro-competitive if they provide efficiency gains in the form of cost savings or better production technologies. By producing together companies can save costs that otherwise they would duplicate. They can also produce at lower costs if the co-operation enables them to increase production where marginal costs decline with output, that is to say, by economies of scale. Producing jointly can also help companies to improve product quality if they put together their complementary skills and know-how. Co-operation can also enable companies to increase product variety, which they could not have afforded, or would not have been able to achieve, otherwise. If joint production allows the parties to increase the number of different types of products, it can also provide cost savings by means of economies of scope.

4.4.2.

Indispensability

184. Restrictions that go beyond what is necessary to achieve the efficiency gains generated by a production agreement do not fulfil the criteria of Article 101(3). For instance, restrictions imposed in a production agreement on the parties' competitive conduct with regard to output outside the co-operation will normally not be considered to be indispensable. Similarly, setting prices jointly will not be considered indispensable if the production agreement does not also involve joint commercialisation.

4.4.3.

Pass-on to consumers

185. Efficiency gains attained by indispensable restrictions need to be passed on to consumers in the form of lower prices or better product quality or variety to an extent that outweighs the restrictive effects on competition. Efficiency gains that only benefit the parties or cost savings that are caused by output reduction or market allocation are not sufficient to meet the criteria of Article 101(3). If the parties to the production agreement achieve savings in their variable costs they are more likely to pass them on to consumers than if they reduce their fixed costs. Moreover, the higher the market power of the parties, the less likely they will pass on the efficiency gains to consumers to an extent that would outweigh the restrictive effects on competition.

4.4.4.

No elimination of competition

186. The criteria of Article 101(3) cannot be met if the parties are afforded the possibility of eliminating competition in respect of a substantial part of the products in question. This has to be analysed in the relevant market to which the products subject to the co-operation belong and in any possible spillover markets.

4.5. Examples

187. Commonality of costs and collusive outcomes

Example 1

Situation: Companies A and B, two suppliers of a product X decide to close their current old production plants and build a larger, modern and more efficient production plant run by a joint venture, which will have a higher capacity than the total capacity of the old plants of Companies A and B. No other such investments are planned by competitors, which are using their facilities at full capacity. Companies A and B have market shares of 20% and 25% respectively. Their products are the closest substitutes in a specific segment of the market, which is concentrated. The market is transparent and rather stagnant, there is no entry and the market shares have been stable over time. Production costs constitute a major part of Company A and Company B's variable costs for product X. Commercialisation is a minor economic activity in terms of costs and strategic importance compared to production: marketing costs are low as product X is homogenous and established and transport is not a key driver of competition.

Analysis: If Companies A and B share all or most of their variable costs, this production agreement could lead to a direct limitation of competition between them. It may lead the parties to limit the output of the joint venture compared to what they would have brought to the market if each of them had decided their output on their own. In the light of the capacity constraints of the competitors this reduction output could lead to higher prices.

Even if Companies A and B were not sharing most of their variable costs, but only a significant part thereof, this production agreement could lead to a collusive outcome between Companies A and B, thereby indirectly eliminating competition between the two parties. The likelihood of this depends not only on the issue of commonality of costs (which are high in this case) but also on the characteristics of the relevant market such as, for example, transparency, stability and level of concentration.

In either of the two situations mentioned above, it is likely, in the market configuration of this example, that the production joint venture of Companies A and B would give rise to restrictive effects on competition within the meaning of Article 101(1) on the market of X.

The replacement of two smaller old production plants by the larger, modern and more efficient one may lead the joint venture to increase output at lower prices to the benefits of consumers. However, the production agreement could only meet the criteria of Article 101(3) if the parties provided substantiated evidence that the efficiency gains would be passed on to consumers to such an extent that they would outweigh the restrictive effects on competition.

188. Links between competitors and collusive outcomes

Example 2

Situation: Two suppliers, Companies A and B, form a production joint venture with respect to product Y. Companies A and B each have a 15% market share on the market for Y. There are 3 other players on the market: Company C with a market share of 30%, Company D with 25% and Company E with 15%. Company B already has a joint production plant with Company D.

Analysis: The market is characterised by very few players and rather symmetric structures. Cooperation between Companies A and B would add an additional link in the market, *de facto* increasing the concentration in the market, as it would also link Company D to Companies A and B. This co-operation is likely to increase the risk of a collusive outcome and thereby likely to give rise to restrictive effects on competition within the meaning of Article 101(1). The criteria of Article 101(3) could only be fulfilled in the presence of significant efficiency gains which are passed on to consumers to such an extent that they would outweigh the restrictive effects on competition.

189. Anti-competitive foreclosure on a downstream market

Example 3

Situation: Companies A and B set up a production joint venture for the intermediate product X which covers their entire production of X. The production costs of X account for 70% of the variable costs of the final product Y with respect to which Companies A and B compete downstream. Companies A and B each have a share of 20% on the market for Y, there is limited entry and the market shares have been stable over time. In addition to covering their own demand for X, both Companies A and B each have a market share of 40% on the market for X. There are high barriers to entry on the market for X and existing producers are operating near full capacity. On the market for Y, there are two other significant suppliers, each with a 15% market share, and several smaller competitors. This agreement generates economies of scale.

Analysis: By virtue of the production joint venture, Companies A and B would be able to largely control supplies of the essential input X to their competitors in the market for Y. This would give Companies A and B the ability to raise their rivals' costs by artificially increasing the price of X, or by reducing the output. This could foreclose the competitors of Companies A and B in market for Y. Because of the likely anti-competitive foreclosure downstream, this agreement is likely to give rise to restrictive effects on competition within the meaning of Article 101(1). The economies of scale generated by the production joint venture are unlikely to outweigh the restrictive effects on competition and therefore this agreement would most likely not meet the criteria of Article 101(3).

190. Specialisation agreement as market allocation

Example 4

Situation: Companies A and B each manufacture both products X and Y. Company A's market share of X is 30% and of Y 10%. B's market share of X is 10% and of Y 30%. To obtain economies of scale they conclude a reciprocal specialisation agreement under which Company A will only produce X and Company B only Y. They do not cross-supply the products to each other so that Company A only sells X and Company B sells only Y. The parties claim that by specialising in this way they save costs due to the economies of scale and by focusing on only one product will improve their production technologies, which will lead to better quality products.

Analysis: With regard to its effects on competition in the market, this specialisation agreement is close to a hardcore cartel where parties allocate the market among themselves. Therefore, this agreement restricts competition by object. Because the claimed efficiencies in the form of economies of scale and improving production technology are only linked to the market allocation, they are unlikely to outweigh the restrictive effects, and therefore the agreement would not meet the criteria of Article 101(3). In any event, if Company A or B believes that it would be more efficient to focus on only one product, it can simply take the unilateral decision to only produce X or Y without at the same time agreeing that the other company will focus on producing the respective other product.

The analysis would be different if Companies A and B supplied each other with the product they focus on so that they both continue to sell X and Y. In such a case Companies A and B could still compete on price on both markets, especially if production costs (which become common through the production agreement) did not constitute a major share of the variable costs of their products. The relevant costs in this context are the commercialisation costs. Hence, the specialisation agreement would be unlikely to restrict competition if X and Y were largely heterogeneous products with a very high proportion of marketing and distribution costs (for example, 65–70% or more of total costs). In such a scenario the risks of a collusive outcome would not be high and the criteria of Article 101(3) may be fulfilled, provided that the efficiency gains would be passed on to consumers to such an extent that they would outweigh the restrictive effects on competition of the agreement.

191. Potential competitors

Example 5

Situation: Company A produces final product X and Company B produces final product Y. X and Y constitute two separate product markets, in which Companies A and B respectively have strong market power. Both companies use Z as an input for their production of X and Y and they both produce Z for captive use only. X is a low added value product for which Z is an essential input (X is quite a simple transformation of Z). Y is a high value added product, for which Z is one of many inputs (Z constitutes a small part of variable costs of Y). Companies A and B agree to jointly produce Z, which generates modest economies of scale.

Analysis: Companies A and B are not actual competitors with regard to X, Y or Z. However, since X is a simple transformation of input Z, it is likely that Company B could easily enter the market for X and thus challenge Company A's position on that market. The joint production agreement with regard to Z might reduce Company B's incentives to do so as the joint production might be used for side payments and limit the probability of Company B selling product X (as Company A is likely to have control over the quantity of Z purchased by Company B from the joint venture). However, the probability of Company B entering the market for X in the absence of the agreement depends on the expected profitability of the entry. As X is a low added value product, entry might not be profitable and thus entry by Company B could be unlikely in the absence of the agreement. Given that Companies A and B already have market power, the agreement is likely to give rise to restrictive effects on competition within the meaning of Article 101(1) if the agreement does indeed decrease the likelihood of entry of Company B into Company A's market, that is to say, the market for X. The efficiency gains in the form of economies of scale generated by the agreement are modest and therefore unlikely to outweigh the restrictive effects on competition.

192. Information exchange in a production agreement

Example 6

Situation: Companies A and B with high market power decide to produce together to become more efficient. In the context of this agreement they secretly exchange information about their future prices. The agreement does not cover joint distribution.

Analysis: This information exchange makes a collusive outcome likely and is therefore likely have as its object the restriction of competition within the meaning of Article 101(1). It would be unlikely to meet the criteria of Article 101(3) because the sharing of information about the parties' future prices is not indispensable for producing jointly and attaining the corresponding cost savings.

193. Swaps and information exchange

Example 7

Situation: Companies A and B both produce Z, a commodity chemical. Z is a homogenous product which is manufactured according to a European standard which does not allow for any product variations. Production costs are a significant cost factor regarding Z. Company A has a market share of 20% and Company B of 25% on the Union-wide market for Z. There are four other manufacturers on the market for Z, with respective market shares of 20%, 15%, 10% and 10%. The production plant of Company A is located in Member State X in northern Europe whereas the production plant of Company B is located in Member State Y in southern Europe. Even though the majority of Company A's customers are located in northern Europe, Company A also has a number of customers in southern Europe. The majority of Company B's customers are in southern Europe, although it also has a number of customers located in northern Europe. Currently, Company A provides its southern European customers with Z manufactured in its production plant in Member State X and transports it to southern Europe by truck. Similarly, Company B provides its northern European customers with Z manufactured in Member State Y and transports it to northern Europe by truck. Transport costs are quite high, but not so high as to make the deliveries by Company A to southern Europe and Company B to northern Europe unprofitable. Transport costs from Member State X to southern Europe are lower than from Member State Y to northern Europe.

Companies A and B decide that it would be more efficient if Company A stopped transporting Z from Member State X to southern Europe and if Company B stopped transporting the Z from Member State Y to northern Europe although, at the same time, they are keen on retaining their customers. To do so, Companies A and B intend to enter into a swap agreement which allows them to purchase an agreed annual quantity of Z from the other party's plant with a view to selling the purchased Z to those of their customers which are located closer to the other party's plant. In order to calculate a purchase price which does not favour one party over the other and which takes due account of the parties' different production costs and different savings on transport costs, and in order to ensure that both parties can achieve an appropriate margin, they agree to disclose to each other their main costs with regard to Z (that is to say, production costs and transport costs).

Analysis: The fact that Companies A and B – who are competitors – swap parts of their production does not in itself give rise to competition concerns. However, the envisaged swap agreement between Companies A and B provides for the exchange of both parties' production and transport costs with regard to Z. Moreover, Companies A and B have a strong combined market position in a fairly concentrated market for a homogenous commodity product. Therefore, due to the extensive information exchange on a key parameter of competition with regard to Z, it is likely that the swap agreement between Companies A and B will give rise to restrictive effects on competition within the meaning of Article 101(1) as it can lead to a collusive outcome. Even though the agreement will give rise to significant efficiency gains in the form of cost savings for the parties, the restrictions on competition generated by the agreement are not indispensable for their attainment. The parties could achieve similar cost savings by agreeing on a price formula which does not entail the disclosure of their production and transport costs. Consequently, in its current form the swap agreement does not fulfil the criteria of Article 101(3).

NOTES

[90] OJ C1, 3.1.1979, p 2.

[91] As also referred to in Article 2(4) of the Merger Regulation.

5. PURCHASING AGREEMENTS

5.1. Definition

[4.224]

194. This chapter focuses on agreements concerning the joint purchase of products. Joint purchasing can be carried out by a jointly controlled company, by a company in which many other companies hold non-controlling stakes, by a contractual arrangement or by even looser forms of co-operation (collectively referred to as 'joint purchasing arrangements'). Joint purchasing arrangements usually aim at the creation of buying power which can lead to lower prices or better quality products or services for consumers. However, buying power may, under certain circumstances, also give rise to competition concerns.

195. Joint purchasing arrangements may involve both horizontal and vertical agreements. In these cases a two-step analysis is necessary. First, the horizontal agreements between the companies engaging in joint purchasing have to be assessed according to the principles described in these guidelines. If that assessment leads to the conclusion that the joint purchasing arrangement does not give rise to competition concerns, a further assessment will be necessary to examine the relevant vertical agreements. The latter assessment will follow the rules of the Block Exemption Regulation on Vertical Restraints and the Guidelines on Vertical Restraints.

196. A common form of joint purchasing arrangement is an 'alliance', that is to say an association of undertakings formed by a group of retailers for the joint purchasing of products. Horizontal agreements concluded between the members of the alliance or decisions adopted by the alliance first have to be assessed as a horizontal co-operation agreement according to these guidelines. Only if that assessment does not reveal any competition concerns does it become relevant to assess the relevant vertical agreements between the alliance and an individual member thereof and between the alliance and suppliers. Those agreements are covered – subject to certain conditions – by the Block Exemption Regulation on Vertical Restraints. Vertical agreements not covered by that Block Exemption Regulation are not presumed to be illegal but require individual examination.

5.2. Relevant markets

197. There are two markets which may be affected by joint purchasing arrangements. First, the market or markets with which the joint purchasing arrangement is directly concerned, that is to say, the relevant purchasing market or markets. Secondly, the selling market or markets, that is to say, the market or markets downstream where the parties to the joint purchasing arrangement are active as sellers.

198. The definition of relevant purchasing markets follows the principles described in the Market Definition Notice and is based on the concept of substitutability to identify competitive constraints. The only difference from the definition of 'selling markets' is that substitutability has to be defined from the viewpoint of supply and not from the viewpoint of demand. In other words, the suppliers' alternatives are decisive in identifying the competitive constraints on purchasers. Those alternatives could be analysed, for instance, by examining the suppliers' reaction to a small but non-transitory price decrease. Once the market is defined, the market share can be calculated as the percentage of the purchases by the parties out of the total sales of the purchased product or products in the relevant market.

199. If the parties are, in addition, competitors on one or more selling markets, those markets are also relevant for the assessment. The selling markets have to be defined by applying the methodology described in the Market Definition Notice.

5.3. Assessment under Article 101(1)45

5.3.1.
Main competition concerns

200. Joint purchasing arrangements may lead to restrictive effects on competition on the purchasing and/or downstream selling market or markets, such as increased prices, reduced output, product quality or variety, or innovation, market allocation, or anti-competitive foreclosure of other possible purchasers.

201. If downstream competitors purchase a significant part of their products together, their incentives for price competition on the selling market or markets may be considerably reduced. If the parties have a significant degree of market power (which does not necessarily amount to dominance) on the selling market or markets, the lower purchase prices achieved by the joint purchasing arrangement are likely not to be passed on to consumers.

202. If the parties have a significant degree of market power on the purchasing market (buying power) there is a risk that they may force suppliers to reduce the range or quality of products they produce, which may bring about restrictive effects on competition such as quality reductions, lessening of innovation efforts, or ultimately sub-optimal supply.

203. Buying power of the parties to the joint purchasing arrangement could be used to foreclose competing purchasers by limiting their access to efficient suppliers. This is most likely if there are a limited number of suppliers and there are barriers to entry on the supply side of the upstream market.

204. In general, however, joint purchasing arrangements are less likely to give rise to competition concerns when the parties do not have market power on the selling market or markets.

5.3.2.
Restrictions of competition by object

205. Joint purchasing arrangements restrict competition by object if they do not truly concern joint purchasing, but serve as a tool to engage in a disguised cartel, that is to say, otherwise prohibited price fixing, output limitation or market allocation.

206. Agreements which involve the fixing of purchase prices can have the object of restricting competition within the meaning of Article 101(1).[92] However, this does not apply where the parties to a joint purchasing arrangement agree on the purchasing prices the joint purchasing arrangement may pay to its suppliers for the products subject to the supply contract. In that case an assessment is required as to whether the agreement is likely to give rise to restrictive effects on competition within the meaning of Article 101(1). In both scenarios the agreement on purchase prices will not be assessed separately, but in the light of the overall effects of the purchasing agreement on the market.

5.3.3.
Restrictive effects on competition

207. Joint purchasing arrangements which do not have as their object the restriction of competition must be analysed in their legal and economic context with regard to their actual and likely effects on competition. The analysis of the restrictive effects on competition generated by a joint purchasing arrangement must cover the negative effects on both the purchasing and the selling markets.

Market power

208. There is no absolute threshold above which it can be presumed that the parties to a joint purchasing arrangement have market power so that the joint purchasing arrangement is likely to give rise to restrictive effects on competition within the meaning of Article 101(1). However, in most cases it is unlikely that market power exists if the parties to the joint purchasing arrangement have a combined market share not exceeding 15% on the purchasing market or markets as well as a combined market share not exceeding 15% on the selling market or markets. In any event, if the parties' combined market shares do not exceed 15% on both the purchasing and the selling market or markets, it is likely that the conditions of Article 101(3) are fulfilled.

209. A market share above that threshold in one or both markets does not automatically indicate that the joint purchasing arrangement is likely to give rise to restrictive effects on competition. A joint purchasing arrangement which does not fall within that safe harbour requires a detailed assessment of its effects on the market involving, but not limited to, factors such as market concentration and possible countervailing power of strong suppliers.

210. Buying power may, under certain circumstances, cause restrictive effects on competition. Anti-competitive buying power is likely to arise if a joint purchasing arrangement accounts for a sufficiently large proportion of the total volume of a purchasing market so that access to the market may be foreclosed to competing purchasers. A high degree of buying power may indirectly affect the output, quality and variety of products on the selling market.

211. In the analysis of whether the parties to a joint purchasing arrangement have buying power, the number and intensity of links (for example, other purchasing agreements) between the competitors in the market are relevant.

212. If, however, competing purchasers co-operate who are not active on the same relevant selling market (for example, retailers which are active in different geographic markets and cannot be regarded as potential competitors), the joint purchasing arrangement is unlikely to have restrictive effects on competition unless the parties have a position in the purchasing markets that is likely to be used to harm the competitive position of other players in their respective selling markets.

Collusive outcome

213. Joint purchasing arrangements may lead to a collusive outcome if they facilitate the coordination of the parties' behaviour on the selling market. This can be the case if the parties achieve a high degree of commonality of costs through joint purchasing, provided the parties have market power and the market characteristics are conducive to coordination.

214. Restrictive effects on competition are more likely if the parties to the joint purchasing arrangement have a significant proportion of their variable costs in the relevant downstream market in common. This is, for instance, the case if retailers, which are active in the same relevant retail market or markets, jointly purchase a significant amount of the products they offer for resale. It may also be the case if competing manufacturers and sellers of a final product jointly purchase a high proportion of their input together.

215. The implementation of a joint purchasing arrangement may require the exchange of commercially sensitive information such as purchase prices and volumes. The exchange of such information may facilitate coordination with regard to sales prices and output and thus lead to a collusive outcome on the selling markets. Spill-over effects from the exchange of commercially sensitive information can, for example, be minimised where data is collated by a joint purchasing arrangement which does not pass on the information to the parties thereto.

216. Any negative effects arising from the exchange of information will not be assessed separately but in the light of the overall effects of the agreement. Whether the exchange of information in the context of a joint purchasing arrangement is likely to lead to restrictive effects on competition should be assessed according to the guidance given in Chapter 2. If the information exchange does not exceed the sharing of data necessary for the joint purchasing of the products by the parties to the joint purchasing arrangement, then even if the information exchange has restrictive effects on competition within the meaning of Article 101(1), the agreement is more likely to meet the criteria of Article 101(3) than if the exchange goes beyond what was necessary for the joint purchasing.

5.4. Assessment under Article 101(3)

5.4.1.
Efficiency gains

217. Joint purchasing arrangements can give rise to significant efficiency gains. In particular, they can lead to cost savings such as lower purchase prices or reduced transaction, transportation and storage costs, thereby facilitating economies of scale. Moreover, joint purchasing arrangements may give rise to qualitative efficiency gains by leading suppliers to innovate and introduce new or improved products on the markets.

5.4.2.
Indispensability

218. Restrictions that go beyond what is necessary to achieve the efficiency gains generated by a purchasing agreement do not meet the criteria of Article 101(3). An obligation to purchase exclusively through the co-operation may, in certain cases, be indispensable to achieve the necessary volume for the realisation of economies of scale. However, such an obligation has to be assessed in the context of the individual case.

5.4.3.
Pass-on to consumers

219. Efficiency gains, such as cost efficiencies or qualitative efficiencies in the form of the introduction of new or improved products on the market, attained by indispensable restrictions must be passed on to consumers to an extent that outweighs the restrictive effects of competition caused by the joint purchasing arrangement. Hence, cost savings or other efficiencies that only benefit the parties to the joint purchasing arrangement will not suffice. Cost savings need to be passed on to consumers, that is to say, the parties' customers. To take a notable example, this pass-on may occur through lower prices on the selling markets. Lower purchasing prices resulting from the mere exercise of buying power are not likely to be passed on to consumers if the purchasers together have market power on the selling markets, and thus do not meet the criteria of Article 101(3). Moreover, the higher the market power of the parties on the selling market or markets the less likely they will pass on the efficiency gains to consumers to an extent that would outweigh the restrictive effects on competition.

5.4.4.
No elimination of competition

220. The criteria of Article 101(3) cannot be fulfilled if the parties are afforded the possibility of eliminating competition in respect of a substantial part of the products in question. That assessment has to cover both purchasing and selling markets.

5.5. Examples

221. Joint purchasing by small companies with moderate combined market shares

Example 1

Situation: 150 small retailers conclude an agreement to form a joint purchasing organisation. They are obliged to purchase a minimum volume through the organisation, which accounts for roughly 50% of each retailer's total costs. The retailers can purchase more than the minimum volume through the organisation, and they may also purchase outside the co-operation. They have a combined market share of 23% on both the purchasing and the selling markets. Company A and Company B are their two large competitors. Company A has a 25% share on both the purchasing and selling markets, Company B 35%. There are no barriers which would prevent the remaining smaller competitors from also forming a purchasing group. The 150 retailers achieve substantial cost savings by virtue of purchasing jointly through the purchasing organisation.

Analysis: The retailers have a moderate market position on the purchasing and the selling markets. Furthermore, the co-operation brings about some economies of scale. Even though the retailers achieve a high degree of commonality of costs, they are unlikely to have market power on the selling market due to the market presence of Companies A and B, which are both individually larger than the joint purchasing organisation. Consequently, the retailers are unlikely to coordinate their behaviour and reach a collusive outcome. The formation of the joint purchasing organisation is therefore unlikely to give rise to restrictive effects on competition within the meaning of Article 101(1).

222. Commonality of costs and market power on the selling market

Example 2

Situation: Two supermarket chains conclude an agreement to jointly purchase products which account for roughly 80% of their variable costs. On the relevant purchasing markets for the different categories of products the parties have combined market shares between 25% and 40%. On the relevant selling market they have a combined market share of 60%. There are four other significant retailers each with a 10% market share. Market entry is not likely.

Analysis: It is likely that this purchasing agreement would give the parties the ability to coordinate their behaviour on the selling market, thereby leading to a collusive outcome. The parties have market power on the selling market and the purchasing agreement gives rise to a significant commonality of costs. Moreover, market entry is unlikely. The incentive for the parties to coordinate their behaviour would be reinforced if their cost structures were already similar prior to concluding the agreement. Moreover, similar margins of the parties would further increase the risk of a collusive outcome. This agreement also creates the risk that by the parties' withholding demand and, consequently, as a result of reduced quantity, downstream selling prices would increase. Hence, the purchasing agreement is likely to give rise to restrictive effects on competition within the meaning of Article 101(1). Even though the agreement is very likely to give rise to efficiency gains in the form of cost savings, due to the parties' significant market power on the selling market, these are unlikely to be passed on to consumers to an extent that would outweigh the restrictive effects on competition. Therefore, the purchasing agreement is unlikely to fulfil the criteria of Article 101(3).

223. Parties active in different geographic markets

Example 3

Situation: Six large retailers, which are each based in a different Member State, form a purchasing group to buy several branded durum wheat flour-based products jointly. The parties are allowed to purchase other similar branded products outside the co-operation. Moreover, five of them also offer similar private label products. The members of the purchasing group have a combined market share of approximately 22% on the relevant purchasing market, which is Union-wide. In the purchasing market there are three other large players of similar size. Each of the parties to the purchasing group has a market share between 20% and 30% on the national selling markets on which they are active. None of them is active in a Member State where another member of the group is active. The parties are not potential entrants to each other's markets.

Analysis: The purchasing group will be able to compete with the other existing major players on the purchasing market. The selling markets are much smaller (in turnover and geographic scope) than the Union-wide purchasing market and in those markets some of the members of the group may have market power. Even if the members of the purchasing group have a combined market share of more than 15% on the purchasing market, the parties are unlikely to coordinate their conduct and collude on the selling markets since they are neither actual nor potential competitors on the downstream markets. Consequently, the purchasing group is not likely to give rise to restrictive effects on competition within the meaning of Article 101(1).

224. Information exchange

Example 4

Situation: Three competing manufacturers A, B and C entrust an independent joint purchasing organisation with the purchase of product Z, which is an intermediary product used by the three parties for their production of the final product X. The costs of Z are not a significant cost factor for the production of X. The joint purchasing organisation does not compete with the parties on the selling market for X. All information necessary for the purchases (for example quality specifications, quantities, delivery dates, maximum purchase prices) is only disclosed to the joint purchasing organisation, not to the other parties. The joint purchasing organisation agrees the purchasing prices with the suppliers. A, B and C have a combined market share of 30% on each of the purchasing and selling markets. They have six competitors in the purchasing and selling markets, two of which have a market share of 20%.

Analysis: Since there is no direct information exchange between the parties, the transfer of the information necessary for the purchases to the joint purchasing organisation is unlikely to lead to a collusive outcome. Consequently, the exchange of information is unlikely to give rise to restrictive effects on competition within the meaning of Article 101(1).

NOTES

92 See Article 101(1)(a); Joined Cases T-217/03 and T-245/03, *French Beef*, paragraphs 83 et seq.; Case C-8/08, *T-Mobile Netherlands*, paragraph 37.

6. AGREEMENTS ON COMMERCIALISATION

6.1. Definition

[4.225]
225. Commercialisation agreements involve co-operation between competitors in the selling, distribution or promotion of their substitute products. This type of agreement can have widely varying scope, depending on the commercialisation functions which are covered by the co-operation. At one end of the spectrum, joint selling agreements may lead to a joint determination of all commercial aspects related to the sale of the product, including price. At the other end, there are more limited agreements that only address one specific commercialisation function, such as distribution, after-sales service, or advertising.

226. An important category of those more limited agreements is distribution agreements. The Block Exemption Regulation on Vertical Restraints and Guidelines on Vertical Restraints generally cover distribution agreements unless the parties to the agreement are actual or potential competitors. If the parties are competitors, the Block Exemption Regulation on Vertical Restraints only covers non-reciprocal vertical agreements between competitors, if (a) the supplier is a manufacturer and a distributor of goods, while the buyer is a distributor and not a competing undertaking at the manufacturing level or, (b) the supplier is a provider of services at several levels of trade, while the buyer provides its goods or services at the retail level and does not provide competing services at the level of trade where it purchases the contract services.[93]

227. If competitors agree to distribute their substitute products on a reciprocal basis (in particular if they do so on different geographic markets) there is a possibility in certain cases that the agreements have as their object or effect the partitioning of markets between the parties or that they lead to a collusive outcome. The same can be true for non-reciprocal agreements between competitors. Reciprocal agreements and non-reciprocal agreements between competitors thus have first to be assessed according to the principles set out in this Chapter. If that assessment leads to the conclusion that co-operation between competitors in the area of distribution would in principle be acceptable, a further assessment will be necessary to examine the vertical restraints included in such agreements. That second step of the assessment should be based on the principles set out in the Guidelines on Vertical Restraints.

228. A further distinction should be drawn between agreements where the parties agree only on joint commercialisation and agreements where the commercialisation is related to another type of co-operation upstream, such as joint production or joint purchasing. When analysing commercialisation agreements combining different stages of co-operation it is necessary to determine the centre of gravity of the co-operation in accordance with paragraphs 13 and 14.

6.2. Relevant markets

229. To assess the competitive relationship between the parties, the relevant product and geographic market or markets directly concerned by the co-operation (that is to say, the market or markets to which the products subject to the agreement belong) have to be defined. As a commercialisation agreement in one market may also affect the competitive behaviour of the parties in a neighbouring market which is closely related to the market directly concerned by the co-operation, any such neighbouring market also needs to be defined. The neighbouring market may be horizontally or vertically related to the market where the co-operation takes place.

6.3. Assessment under Article 101(1)

6.3.1.
Main competition concerns

230. Commercialisation agreements can lead to restrictions of competition in several ways. First, and most obviously, commercialisation agreements may lead to price fixing.

231. Secondly, commercialisation agreements may also facilitate output limitation, because the parties may decide on the volume of products to be put on the market, therefore restricting supply.

232. Thirdly, commercialisation agreements may become a means for the parties to divide the markets or to allocate orders or customers, for example in cases where the parties' production plants are located in different geographic markets or when the agreements are reciprocal.

233. Finally, commercialisation agreements may also lead to an exchange of strategic information relating to aspects within or outside the scope of the co-operation or to commonality of costs – in particular with regard to agreements not encompassing price fixing – which may result in a collusive outcome.

6.3.2.
Restrictions of competition by object

234. Price fixing is one of the major competition concerns arising from commercialisation agreements between competitors. Agreements limited to joint selling generally have the object of coordinating the pricing policy of competing manufacturers or service providers. Such agreements may not only eliminate price competition between the parties on substitute products but may also restrict the total volume of products to be delivered by the parties within the framework of a system for allocating orders. Such agreements are therefore likely to restrict competition by object.

235. That assessment does not change if the agreement is non-exclusive (that is to say, where the parties are free to sell individually outside the agreement), as long as it can be concluded that the agreement will lead to an overall coordination of the prices charged by the parties.

236. Another specific competition concern related to distribution arrangements between parties which are active in different geographic markets is that they can be an instrument of market partitioning. If the parties use a reciprocal distribution agreement to distribute each other's products in order to eliminate actual or potential competition between them by deliberately allocating markets or customers, the agreement is likely to have as its object a restriction of competition. If the agreement is not reciprocal, the risk of market partitioning is less pronounced. It is necessary, however, to assess whether the non-reciprocal agreement constitutes the basis for a mutual understanding to avoid entering each other's markets.

6.3.3.
Restrictive effects on competition

237. A commercialisation agreement is normally not likely to give rise to competition concerns if it is objectively necessary to allow one party to enter a market it could not have entered individually or with a more limited number of parties than are effectively taking part in the co-operation, for example, because of the costs involved. A specific application of this principle would be consortia arrangements that allow the companies involved to participate in projects that they would not be able to undertake individually. As the parties to the consortia arrangement are therefore not potential competitors for implementing the project, there is no restriction of competition within the meaning of Article 101(1).

238. Similarly, not all reciprocal distribution agreements have as their object a restriction of competition. Depending on the facts of the case at hand, some reciprocal distribution agreements may, nevertheless, have restrictive effects on competition. The key issue in assessing an agreement of this type is whether the agreement in question is objectively necessary for the parties to enter each other's markets. If it is, the agreement does not create competition problems of a horizontal nature. However, if the agreement reduces the decision-making independence of one of the parties with regard to entering the other parties' market or markets by limiting its incentives to do so, it is likely to give rise to restrictive effects on competition. The same reasoning applies to non-reciprocal agreements, where the risk of restrictive effects on competition is, however, less pronounced.

239. Moreover, a distribution agreement can have restrictive effects on competition if it contains vertical restraints, such as restrictions on passive sales, resale price maintenance, etc.

Market power

240. Commercialisation agreements between competitors can only have restrictive effects on competition if the parties have some degree of market power. In most cases, it is unlikely that market power exists if the parties to the agreement have a combined market share not exceeding 15%. In any event, if the parties' combined market share does not exceed 15% it is likely that the conditions of Article 101(3) are fulfilled.

241. If the parties' combined market share is greater than 15%, their agreement will fall outside the safe harbour of paragraph 240 and thus the likely impact of the joint commercialisation agreement on the market must be assessed.

Collusive outcome

242. A joint commercialisation agreement that does not involve price fixing is also likely to give rise to restrictive effects on competition if it increases the parties' commonality of variable costs to a level which is likely to lead to a collusive outcome. This is likely to be the case for a joint commercialisation agreement if prior to the agreement the parties already have a high proportion of their variable costs in common as the additional increment (that is to say, the commercialisation costs of the product subject to the agreement) can tip the balance towards a collusive outcome. Conversely, if the increment is large, the risk of a collusive outcome may be high even if the initial level of commonality of costs is low.

243. The likelihood of a collusive outcome depends on the parties' market power and the characteristics of the relevant market. Commonality of costs can only increase the risk of a collusive outcome if the parties have market power and if the commercialisation costs constitute a large proportion of the variable costs related to the products concerned. This is, for example, not the case for homogeneous products for which the highest cost factor is production. However, commonality of commercialisation costs increases the risk of a collusive outcome if the commercialisation agreement concerns products which entail costly commercialisation, for example, high distribution or marketing costs. Consequently, joint advertising or joint promotion agreements can also give rise to restrictive effects on competition if those costs constitute a significant cost factor.

244. Joint commercialisation generally involves the exchange of sensitive commercial information, particularly on marketing strategy and pricing. In most commercialisation agreements, some degree of information exchange is required in order to implement the agreement. It is therefore necessary to verify whether the information exchange can give rise to a collusive outcome with regard to the parties' activities within and outside the co-operation. Any negative effects arising from the exchange of information will not be assessed separately but in the light of the overall effects of the agreement.

245. For example, where the parties to a joint advertising agreement exchange pricing information, this may lead to a collusive outcome with regard to the sale of the jointly advertised products. In any event, the exchange of such information in the context of a joint advertising agreement goes beyond what would be necessary to implement that agreement. The likely restrictive effects on competition of information exchange in the context of commercialisation agreements will depend on the characteristics of the market and the data shared, and should be assessed in the light of the guidance given in Chapter 2.

6.4. Assessment under Article 101(3)

6.4.1. Efficiency gains

246. Commercialisation agreements can give rise to significant efficiency gains. The efficiencies to be taken into account when assessing whether a commercialisation agreement fulfils the criteria of Article 101(3) will depend on the nature of the activity and the parties to the co-operation. Price fixing can generally not be justified, unless it is indispensable for the integration of other marketing functions, and this integration will generate substantial efficiencies. Joint distribution can generate significant efficiencies, stemming from economies of scale or scope, especially for smaller producers.

247. In addition, the efficiency gains must not be savings which result only from the elimination of costs that are inherently part of competition, but must result from the integration of economic activities. A reduction of transport cost which is only a result of customer allocation without any integration of the logistical system can therefore not be regarded as an efficiency gain within the meaning of Article 101(3).

248. Efficiency gains must be demonstrated by the parties to the agreement. An important element in this respect would be the contribution by the parties of significant capital, technology, or other assets. Cost savings through reduced duplication of resources and facilities can also be accepted. However, if the joint commercialisation represents no more than a sales agency without any investment, it is likely to be a disguised cartel and as such unlikely to fulfil the conditions of Article 101(3).

6.4.2. Indispensability

249. Restrictions that go beyond what is necessary to achieve the efficiency gains generated by a commercialisation agreement do not fulfil the criteria of Article 101(3). The question of indispensability is especially important for those agreements involving price fixing or market allocation, which can only under exceptional circumstances be considered indispensable.

6.4.3. Pass-on to consumers

250. Efficiency gains attained by indispensable restrictions must be passed on to consumers to an extent that outweighs the restrictive effects on competition caused by the commercialisation agreement. This can happen in the form of lower prices or better product quality or variety. The higher the market power of the parties, however, the less likely it is that efficiency gains will be passed on to consumers to an extent that outweighs the restrictive effects on competition. Where the parties have a combined market share of below 15%, it is likely that any demonstrated efficiency gains generated by the agreement will be sufficiently passed on to consumers.

250. Efficiency gains attained by indispensable restrictions must be passed on to consumers to an extent that outweighs the restrictive effects on competition caused by the commercialisation agreement. This can happen in the form of lower prices or better product quality or variety. The higher the market power of the parties, however, the less likely it is that efficiency gains will be passed on to consumers to an extent that outweighs the restrictive effects on competition. Where the parties have a combined market share of below 15%, it is likely that any demonstrated efficiency gains generated by the agreement will be sufficiently passed on to consumers.

6.4.4. No elimination of competition

251. The criteria of Article 101(3) cannot be fulfilled if the parties are afforded the possibility of eliminating competition in respect of a substantial part of the products in question. This has to be analysed in the relevant market to which the products subject to the co-operation belong and in possible spill-over markets.

6.5. Examples

252. Joint commercialisation necessary to enter a market

Example 1

Situation: Four companies providing laundry services in a large city close to the border of another Member State, each with a 3% market share of the overall laundry market in that city, agree to create a joint marketing arm for the selling of laundry services to institutional customers (that is to say, hotels, hospitals and offices), whilst keeping their independence and freedom to compete for local, individual clients. In view of the new segment of demand (the institutional customers) they develop a common brand name, a common price and common standard terms including, inter alia, a maximum period of 24 hours before deliveries and schedules for delivery. They set up a common call centre where institutional clients can request their collection and/or delivery service. They hire a receptionist (for the call centre) and several drivers. They further invest in vans for dispatching, and in brand promotion, to increase their visibility. The agreement does not fully reduce their individual infrastructure costs (since they are keeping their own premises and still compete with each other for the individual local clients), but it increases their economies of scale and allows them to offer a more comprehensive service to other types of clients, which includes longer opening hours and dispatching to a wider geographic coverage. In order to ensure the viability of the project, it is indispensable that all four of them enter into the agreement. The market is very fragmented, with no individual competitor having more than 15% market share.

Analysis: Although the joint market share of the parties is below 15%, the fact that the agreement involves price fixing means that Article 101(1) could apply. However, the parties would not have been in a position to enter the market for providing laundry services to institutional customers, either individually or in co-operation with a fewer number of parties than the four currently taking part in the agreement. As such, the agreement would not create competition concerns, irrespective of the price-fixing restriction, which in this case can be considered as indispensable to the promotion of the common brand and the success of the project.

253. Commercialisation agreement by more parties than necessary to enter a market

Example 2

Situation: The same facts as in Example 1, paragraph 252, apply with one main difference: in order to ensure the viability of the project, the agreement could have been implemented by only three of the parties (instead of the four actually taking part in the co-operation).

Analysis: Although the joint market share of the parties is below 15%, the fact that the agreement involves price fixing and could have been carried out by fewer than the four parties means that Article 101(1) applies. The agreement thus needs to be assessed under Article 101(3). The agreement gives rise to efficiency gains as the parties are now able to offer improved services for a new category of customers on a larger scale (which they would not otherwise have been able to service individually). In the light of the parties' combined market share of below 15%, it is likely that they will sufficiently pass-on any efficiency gains to consumers. It is further necessary to consider whether the restrictions imposed by the agreement are indispensable to achieve the efficiencies and whether the agreement eliminates competition. Given that the aim of the agreement is to provide a more comprehensive service (including dispatch, which was not offered before) to an additional category of customers, under a single brand with common standard terms, the price fixing can be considered as indispensable to the promotion of the common brand and, consequently, the success of the project and the resulting efficiencies. Additionally, taking into account the market fragmentation, the agreement will not eliminate competition. The fact that there are four parties to the agreement (instead of the three that would have been strictly necessary) allows for increased capacity and contributes to simultaneously fulfilling the demand of several institutional customers in compliance with the standard terms (that is to say, meeting maximum delivery time terms). As such, the efficiency gains are likely to outweigh the restrictive effects arising from the reduction of competition between the parties and the agreement is likely to fulfil the conditions of Article 101(3).

254. Joint internet platform

Example 3

Situation: A number of small specialty shops throughout a Member State join an electronic web-based platform for the promotion, sale and delivery of gift fruit baskets. There are a number of competing web-based platforms. By means of a monthly fee, they share the running costs of the platform and jointly invest in brand promotion. Through the webpage, where a wide range of different types of gift baskets are offered, customers order (and pay for) the type of gift basket they want to be delivered. The order is then allocated to the specialty shop closest to the address of delivery. The shop individually bears the costs of composing the gift basket and delivering it to the client. It reaps 90% of the final price, which is set by the web-based platform and uniformly applies to all participating specialty shops, whilst the remaining 10% is used for the common promotion and the running costs of the web-based platform. Apart from the payment of the monthly fee, there are no further restrictions for specialty shops to join the platform, throughout the national territory. Moreover, specialty shops having their own company website are also able to (and in some cases do) sell gift fruit baskets on the internet under their own name and thus can still compete among themselves outside the co-operation. Customers purchasing over the web-based platform are guaranteed same day delivery of the fruit baskets and they can also choose a delivery time convenient to them.

Analysis: Although the agreement is of a limited nature, since it only covers the joint selling of a particular type of product through a specific marketing channel (the web-based platform), since it involves price-fixing, it is likely to restrict competition by object. The agreement therefore needs to be assessed under Article 101(3). The agreement gives rise to efficiency gains such as greater choice and higher quality service and the reduction of search costs, which benefit consumers and are likely to outweigh the restrictive effects on competition the agreement brings about. Given that the specialty stores taking part in the co-operation are still able to operate individually and to compete one with another, both through their shops and the internet, the price-fixing restriction could be considered as indispensable for the promotion of the product (since when buying through the web-based platform consumers do not know where they are buying the gift basket from and do not want to deal with a multitude of different prices) and the ensuing efficiency gains. In the absence of other restrictions, the agreement fulfils the criteria of Article 101(3). Moreover, as other competing web-based platforms exist and the parties continue to compete with each other, through their shops or over the internet, competition will not be eliminated.

255. Sales joint venture

Example 4

Situation: Companies A and B, located in two different Member States, produce bicycle tyres. They have a combined market share of 14% on the Union-wide market for bicycle tyres. They decide to set up a (non full-function) sales joint venture for marketing the tyres to bicycle producers and agree to sell all their production through the joint venture. The production and transport infrastructure remains separate within each party. The parties claim considerable efficiency gains stem from the agreement. Such gains mainly relate to increased economies of scale, being able to fulfil the demands of their existing and potential new customers and better competing with imported tyres produced in third countries. The joint venture negotiates the prices and allocates orders to the closest production plant, as a way to rationalise transport costs when further delivering to the customer.

Analysis: Even though the combined market share of the parties is below 15%, the agreement falls under Article 101(1). It restricts competition by object since it involves customer allocation and the setting of prices by the joint venture. The claimed efficiencies deriving from the agreement do not result from the integration of economic activities or from common investment. The joint venture would have a very limited scope and would only serve as an interface for allocating orders to the production plants. It is therefore unlikely that any efficiency gains would be passed on to consumers to such an extent that they would outweigh the restrictive effects on competition brought about by the agreement. Thus, the conditions of Article 101(3) would not be fulfilled.

256. Non-poaching clause in agreement on outsourcing of services

Example 5

Situation: Companies A and B are competing providers of cleaning services for commercial premises. Both have a market share of 15%. There are several other competitors with market shares between 10 and 15%. A has taken the (unilateral) decision to only focus on large customers in the future as servicing large and small customers has proved to require a somewhat different organisation of the work. Consequently, Company A has decided to no longer enter into contracts with new small customers. In addition, Companies A and B enter into an outsourcing agreement whereby Company B would directly provide cleaning services to Company A's existing small customers (which represent 1/3 of its customer base). At the same time, Company A is keen not to lose the customer relationship with those small customers. Hence, Company A will continue to keep its contractual relationships with the small customers but the direct provision of the cleaning services will be done by Company B. In order to implement the outsourcing agreement, Company A will necessarily need to provide Company B with the identities of Company A's small customers which are subject to the agreement. As Company A is afraid that Company B may try to poach those customers by offering cheaper direct services (thereby bypassing Company A), Company A insists that the outsourcing agreement contain a 'non-poaching clause'. According to that clause, Company B may not contact the small customers falling under the outsourcing agreements with a view to providing direct services to them. In addition, Companies A and B agree that Company B may not even provide direct services to those customers if Company B is approached by them. Without the 'non-poaching clause' Company A would not enter into an outsourcing agreement with Company B or any other company.

Analysis: The outsourcing agreement removes Company B as an independent supplier of cleaning services for Company A's small customers as they will no longer be able to enter into a direct contractual relationship with Company B. However, those customers only represent 1/3 of Company A's customer base, that is to say, 5% of the market. They will still be able to turn to Company A and Company B's competitors, which represent 70% of the market. Hence, the outsourcing agreement will not enable Company A to profitably raise the prices charged to the customers subject to the outsourcing agreement. In addition, the outsourcing agreement is not likely to give rise to a collusive outcome as Companies A and B only have a combined market share of 30% and they are faced with several competitors that have market shares similar to Company A's and Company B's individual market shares. Moreover, the fact that servicing large and small customers is somewhat different minimises the risk of spill-over effects from the outsourcing agreement to Company A's and Company B's behaviour when competing for large customers. Consequently, the outsourcing agreement is not likely to give rise to restrictive effects on competition within the meaning of Article 101(1).

NOTES

93 Article 2(4) of the Block Exemption Regulation on Vertical Restraints.

7. STANDARDISATION AGREEMENTS

7.1. Definition

Standardisation agreements

[4.226]

257. Standardisation agreements have as their primary objective the definition of technical or quality requirements with which current or future products, production processes, services or methods may comply.[94] Standardisation agreements can cover various issues, such as standardisation of different grades or sizes of a particular product or technical specifications in product or services markets where compatibility and interoperability with other products or systems is essential. The terms of access to a particular quality mark or for approval by a regulatory body can also be regarded as a standard. Agreements setting out standards on the environmental performance of products or production processes are also covered by this chapter.

258. The preparation and production of technical standards as part of the execution of public powers are not covered by these guidelines.[95] The European standardisation bodies recognised under Directive 98/34/EC of the European Parliament and of the Council of 22 June 1998 laying down a procedure for the provision of information in the field of technical standards and regulations and on rules on Information Society services[96] are subject to competition law to the extent that they can be considered to be an undertaking or an association of undertakings within the meaning of Articles 101 and 102.[97] Standards related to the provision of professional services, such as rules of admission to a liberal profession, are not covered by these guidelines.

Standard terms

259. In certain industries companies use standard terms and conditions of sale or purchase elaborated by a trade association or directly by the competing companies ('standard terms').[98] Such standard terms are covered by these guidelines to the extent that they establish standard conditions of sale or purchase of goods or services between

competitors and consumers (and not the conditions of sale or purchase between competitors) for substitute products. When such standard terms are widely used within an industry, the conditions of purchase or sale used in the industry may become *de facto* aligned.[99] Examples of industries in which standard terms play an important role are the banking (for example, bank account terms) and insurance sectors.

260. Standard terms elaborated individually by a company solely for its own use when contracting with its suppliers or customers are not horizontal agreements and are therefore not covered by these guidelines.

7.2. Relevant markets

261. Standardisation agreements may produce their effects on four possible markets, which will be defined according to the Market Definition Notice. First, standard-setting may have an impact on the product or service market or markets to which the standard or standards relates. Second, where the standard-setting involves the selection of technology and where the rights to intellectual property are marketed separately from the products to which they relate, the standard can have effects on the relevant technology market.[100] Third, the market for standard-setting may be affected if different standard-setting bodies or agreements exist. Fourth, where relevant, a distinct market for testing and certification may be affected by standard-setting.

262. As regards standard terms, the effects are, in general, felt on the downstream market where the companies using the standard terms compete by selling their product to their customers.

7.3. Assessment under Article 101(1)

7.3.1. *Main competition concerns*

Standardisation agreements

263. Standardisation agreements usually produce significant positive economic effects,[101] for example by promoting economic interpenetration on the internal market and encouraging the development of new and improved products or markets and improved supply conditions. Standards thus normally increase competition and lower output and sales costs, benefiting economies as a whole. Standards may maintain and enhance quality, provide information and ensure interoperability and compatibility (thus increasing value for consumers).

264. Standard-setting can, however, in specific circumstances, also give rise to restrictive effects on competition by potentially restricting price competition and limiting or controlling production, markets, innovation or technical development. This can occur through three main channels, namely reduction in price competition, foreclosure of innovative technologies and exclusion of, or discrimination against, certain companies by prevention of effective access to the standard.

265. First, if companies were to engage in anti-competitive discussions in the context of standard-setting, this could reduce or eliminate price competition in the markets concerned, thereby facilitating a collusive outcome on the market.[102]

266. Second, standards that set detailed technical specifications for a product or service may limit technical development and innovation. While a standard is being developed, alternative technologies can compete for inclusion in the standard. Once one technology has been chosen and the standard has been set, competing technologies and companies may face a barrier to entry and may potentially be excluded from the market. In addition, standards requiring that a particular technology is used exclusively for a standard or preventing the development of other technologies by obliging the members of the standard-setting organisation to exclusively use a particular standard, may lead to the same effect. The risk of limitation of innovation is increased if one or more companies are unjustifiably excluded from the standard-setting process.

267. In the context of standards involving intellectual property rights ('IPR'),[103] three main groups of companies with different interests in standard-setting can be distinguished in the abstract.[104] First, there are upstream-only companies that solely develop and market technologies. Their only source of income is licensing revenue and their incentive is to maximise their royalties. Secondly, there are downstream-only companies that solely manufacture products or offer services based on technologies developed by others and do not hold relevant IPR. Royalties represent a cost for them, and not a source of revenue, and their incentive is to reduce or avoid royalties. Finally, there are vertically integrated companies that both develop technology and sell products. They have mixed incentives. On the one hand, they can draw licensing revenue from their IPR. On the other hand, they may have to pay royalties to other companies holding IPR essential to the standard. They might therefore cross-license their own essential IPR in exchange for essential IPR held by other companies.

268. Third, standardisation may lead to anti-competitive results by preventing certain companies from obtaining effective access to the results of the standard-setting process (that is to say, the specification and/or the essential IPR for implementing the standard). If a company is either completely prevented from obtaining access to the result of the standard, or is only granted access on prohibitive or discriminatory terms, there is a risk of an anti-competitive effect. A system where potentially relevant IPR is disclosed up-front may increase the likelihood of effective access being granted to the standard since it allows the participants to identify which technologies are covered by IPR and which are not. This enables the participants to both factor in the potential effect on the final price of the result of the standard (for example choosing a technology without IPR is likely to have a positive effect on the final price) and to verify with the IPR holder whether they would be willing to license if their technology is included in the standard.

269. Intellectual property laws and competition laws share the same objectives[105] of promoting innovation and enhancing consumer welfare. IPR promote dynamic competition by encouraging undertakings to invest in developing new or improved products and processes. IPR are therefore in general pro-competitive. However, by virtue of its IPR, a participant holding IPR essential for implementing the standard, could, in the specific context of standard-setting, also acquire control over the use of a standard. When the standard constitutes a barrier to entry, the company could thereby control the product or service market to which the standard relates. This in turn could allow companies to behave in anti-competitive ways, for example by 'holding-up' users after the adoption of the standard either by

refusing to license the necessary IPR or by extracting excess rents by way of excessive[106] royalty fees thereby preventing effective access to the standard. However, even if the establishment of a standard can create or increase the market power of IPR holders possessing IPR essential to the standard, there is no presumption that holding or exercising IPR essential to a standard equates to the possession or exercise of market power. The question of market power can only be assessed on a case by case basis.

Standard terms

270. Standard terms can give rise to restrictive effects on competition by limiting product choice and innovation. If a large part of an industry adopts the standard terms and chooses not to deviate from them in individual cases (or only deviates from them in exceptional cases of strong buyer-power), customers might have no option other than to accept the conditions in the standard terms. However, the risk of limiting choice and innovation is only likely in cases where the standard terms define the scope of the end-product. As regards classical consumer goods, standard terms of sale generally do not limit innovation of the actual product or product quality and variety.

271. In addition, depending on their content, standard terms might risk affecting the commercial conditions of the final product. In particular, there is a serious risk that standard terms relating to price would restrict price competition.

272. Moreover, if the standard terms become industry practice, access to them might be vital for entry into the market. In such cases, refusing access to the standard terms could risk causing anti-competitive foreclosure. As long as the standard terms remain effectively open for use for anyone that wishes to have access to them, they are unlikely to give rise to anti-competitive foreclosure.

7.3.2.

Restrictions of competition by object

Standardisation agreements

273. Agreements that use a standard as part of a broader restrictive agreement aimed at excluding actual or potential competitors restrict competition by object. For instance, an agreement whereby a national association of manufacturers sets a standard and puts pressure on third parties not to market products that do not comply with the standard or where the producers of the incumbent product collude to exclude new technology from an already existing standard[107] would fall into this category.

274. Any agreements to reduce competition by using the disclosure of most restrictive licensing terms prior to the adoption of a standard as a cover to jointly fix prices either of downstream products or of substitute IPR or technology will constitute restrictions of competition by object.[108]

Standard terms

275. Agreements that use standard terms as part of a broader restrictive agreement aimed at excluding actual or potential competitors also restrict competition by object. An example would be where a trade association does not allow a new entrant access to its standards terms, the use of which is vital to ensure entry to the market.

276. Any standard terms containing provisions which directly influence the prices charged to customers (that is to say, recommended prices, rebates, etc) would constitute a restriction of competition by object.

7.3.3.

Restrictive effects on competition

Standardisation agreements

Agreements normally not restrictive of competition

277. Standardisation agreements which do not restrict competition by object must be analysed in their legal and economic context with regard to their actual and likely effect on competition. In the absence of market power,[109] a standardisation agreement is not capable of producing restrictive effects on competition. Therefore, restrictive effects are most unlikely in a situation where there is effective competition between a number of voluntary standards.

278. For those standard-setting agreements which risk creating market power, paragraphs 280 to 286 set out the conditions under which such agreements would normally fall outside the scope of Article 101(1).

279. The non-fulfilment of any or all of the principles set out in this section will not lead to any presumption of a restriction of competition within Article 101(1). However, it will necessitate a self-assessment to establish whether the agreement falls under Article 101(1) and, if so, if the conditions of Article 101(3) are fulfilled. In this context, it is recognised that there exist different models for standard-setting and that competition within and between those models is a positive aspect of a market economy. Therefore, standard-setting organisations remain entirely free to put in place rules and procedures that do not violate competition rules whilst being different to those described in paragraphs 280 to 286.

280. Where participation in standard-setting is **unrestricted** and the procedure for adopting the standard in question is **transparent**, standardisation agreements which contain **no obligation to comply**[110] with the standard and provide **access to the standard on fair, reasonable and non-discriminatory terms** will normally not restrict competition within the meaning of Article 101(1).

281. In particular, to ensure **unrestricted participation** the rules of the standard-setting organisation would need to guarantee that all competitors in the market or markets affected by the standard can participate in the process leading to the selection of the standard. The standard-setting organisations would also need to have objective and non-discriminatory procedures for allocating voting rights as well as, if relevant, objective criteria for selecting the technology to be included in the standard.

282. With respect to **transparency**, the relevant standard-setting organisation would need to have procedures which allow stakeholders to effectively inform themselves of upcoming, on-going and finalised standardisation work in good time at each stage of the development of the standard.

283. Furthermore, the standard-setting organisation's rules would need to ensure effective **access to the standard on fair, reasonable and non discriminatory terms.**[111]

284. In the case of a standard involving IPR, **a clear and balanced IPR policy**,[112] **adapted to the particular industry** and the needs of the standard-setting organisation in question, increases the likelihood that the implementers of the standard will be granted effective access to the standards elaborated by that standard-setting organisation.
285. In order to ensure effective access to the standard, the IPR policy would need to require participants wishing to have their IPR included in the standard to provide an irrevocable commitment in writing to offer to license their essential IPR to all third parties on fair, reasonable and non-discriminatory terms ('**FRAND commitment**').[113] That commitment should be given prior to the adoption of the standard. At the same time, the IPR policy should allow IPR holders to exclude specified technology from the standard-setting process and thereby from the commitment to offer to license, providing that exclusion takes place at an early stage in the development of the standard. To ensure the effectiveness of the FRAND commitment, there would also need to be a requirement on all participating IPR holders who provide such a commitment to ensure that any company to which the IPR owner transfers its IPR (including the right to license that IPR) is bound by that commitment, for example through a contractual clause between buyer and seller.
286. Moreover, the IPR policy would need to require **good faith disclosure**, by participants, of their IPR that might be essential for the implementation of the standard under development. This would enable the industry to make an informed choice of technology and thereby assist in achieving the goal of effective access to the standard. Such a disclosure obligation could be based on ongoing disclosure as the standard develops and on reasonable endeavours to identify IPR reading on the potential standard.[114] It is also sufficient if the participant declares that it is likely to have IPR claims over a particular technology (without identifying specific IPR claims or applications for IPR). Since the risks with regard to effective access are not the same in the case of a standard-setting organisation with a royalty-free standards policy, IPR disclosure would not be relevant in that context.

FRAND Commitments

287. FRAND commitments are designed to ensure that essential IPR protected technology incorporated in a standard is accessible to the users of that standard on fair, reasonable and non-discriminatory terms and conditions. In particular, FRAND commitments can prevent IPR holders from making the implementation of a standard difficult by refusing to license or by requesting unfair or unreasonable fees (in other words excessive fees) after the industry has been locked-in to the standard or by charging discriminatory royalty fees.
288. Compliance with Article 101 by the standard-setting organisation does not require the standard-setting organisation to verify whether licensing terms of participants fulfil the FRAND commitment. Participants will have to assess for themselves whether the licensing terms and in particular the fees they charge fulfil the FRAND commitment. Therefore, when deciding whether to commit to FRAND for a particular IPR, participants will need to anticipate the implications of the FRAND commitment, notably on their ability to freely set the level of their fees.
289. In case of a dispute, the assessment of whether fees charged for access to IPR in the standard-setting context are unfair or unreasonable should be based on whether the fees bear a reasonable relationship to the economic value of the IPR.[115] In general, there are various methods available to make this assessment. In principle, cost-based methods are not well adapted to this context because of the difficulty in assessing the costs attributable to the development of a particular patent or groups of patents. Instead, it may be possible to compare the licensing fees charged by the company in question for the relevant patents in a competitive environment before the industry has been locked into the standard (*ex ante*) with those charged after the industry has been locked in (*ex post*). This assumes that the comparison can be made in a consistent and reliable manner.[116]
290. Another method could be to obtain an independent expert assessment of the objective centrality and essentiality to the standard at issue of the relevant IPR portfolio. In an appropriate case, it may also be possible to refer to *ex ante* disclosures of licensing terms in the context of a specific standard-setting process. This also assumes that the comparison can be made in a consistent and reliable manner. The royalty rates charged for the same IPR in other comparable standards may also provide an indication for FRAND royalty rates. These guidelines do not seek to provide an exhaustive list of appropriate methods to assess whether the royalty fees are excessive.
291. However, it should be emphasised that nothing in these Guidelines prejudices the possibility for parties to resolve their disputes about the level of FRAND royalty rates by having recourse to the competent civil or commercial courts.

Effects based assessment for standardisation agreements

292. The assessment of each standardisation agreement must take into account the likely effects of the standard on the markets concerned. The following considerations apply to all standardisation agreements that depart from the principles as set out in paragraphs 280 to 286.
293. Whether standardisation agreements may give rise to restrictive effects on competition may depend on whether the members of a standard-setting organisation remain **free to develop alternative standards or products** that do not comply with the agreed standard.[117] For example, if the standard-setting agreement binds the members to only produce products in compliance with the standard, the risk of a likely negative effect on competition is significantly increased and could in certain circumstances give rise to a restriction of competition by object.[118] In the same vein, standards only covering minor aspects or parts of the end-product are less likely to lead to competition concerns than more comprehensive standards.
294. The assessment whether the agreement restricts competition will also focus on **access to the standard**. Where the result of a standard (that is to say, the specification of how to comply with the standard and, if relevant, the essential IPR for implementing the standard) is not at all accessible, or only accessible on discriminatory terms, for members or third parties (that is to say, non-members of the relevant standard-setting organisation) this may discriminate or foreclose or segment markets according to their geographic scope of application and thereby is likely to restrict competition. However, in the case of several competing standards or in the case of effective competition between the standardised solution and non-standardised solution, a limitation of access may not produce restrictive effects on competition.
295. If **participation in the standard-setting process** is open in the sense that it allows all competitors (and/or stakeholders) in the market affected by the standard to take part in choosing and elaborating the standard, this will lower the risks of a likely restrictive effect on competition by not excluding certain companies from the ability to

influence the choice and elaboration of the standard.[119] The greater the likely market impact of the standard and the wider its potential fields of application, the more important it is to allow equal access to the standard-setting process. However, if the facts at hand show that there is competition between several such standards and standard-setting organisations (and it is not necessary that the whole industry applies the same standards) there may be no restrictive effects on competition. Also, if in the absence of a limitation on the number of participants it would not have been possible to adopt the standard, the agreement would not be likely to lead to any restrictive effect on competition under Article 101(1).[120] In certain situations the potential negative effects of restricted participation may be removed or at least lessened by ensuring that stakeholders are **kept informed and consulted** on the work in progress.[121] The more transparent the procedure for adopting the standard, the more likely it is that the adopted standard will take into account the interests of all stakeholders.

296. To assess the effects of a standard-setting agreement, the **market shares of the goods or services based on the standard** should be taken into account. It might not always be possible to assess with any certainty at an early stage whether the standard will in practice be adopted by a large part of the industry or whether it will only be a standard used by a marginal part of the relevant industry. In many cases the relevant market shares of the companies having participated in developing the standard could be used as a proxy for estimating the likely market share of the standard (since the companies participating in setting the standard would in most cases have an interest in implementing the standard).[122] However, as the effectiveness of standardisation agreements is often proportional to the share of the industry involved in setting and/or applying the standard, high market shares held by the parties in the market or markets affected by the standard will not necessarily lead to the conclusion that the standard is likely to give rise to restrictive effects on competition.

297. Any standard-setting agreement which clearly **discriminates** against any of the participating or potential members could lead to a restriction of competition. For example, if a standard-setting organisation explicitly excludes upstream only companies (that is to say, companies not active on the downstream production market), this could lead to an exclusion of potentially better technologies.

298. As regards standard-setting agreements with **different types of IPR disclosure models** from the ones described in paragraph 286, it would have to be assessed on a case by case basis whether the disclosure model in question (for example a disclosure model not requiring but only encouraging IPR disclosure) guarantees effective access to the standard. In other words, it needs to be assessed whether, in the specific context, an informed choice between technologies and associated IPR is in practice not prevented by the IPR disclosure model.

299. Finally, standard-setting agreements providing for **ex ante disclosures of most restrictive licensing terms**, will not, in principle, restrict competition within the meaning of Article 101(1). In that regard, it is important that parties involved in the selection of a standard be fully informed not only as to the available technical options and the associated IPR, but also as to the likely cost of that IPR. Therefore, should a standard-setting organisation's IPR policy choose to provide for IPR holders to individually disclose their most restrictive licensing terms, including the maximum royalty rates they would charge, prior to the adoption of the standard, this will normally not lead to a restriction of competition within the meaning of Article 101(1).[123] Such unilateral ex ante disclosures of most restrictive licensing terms would be one way to enable the standard-setting organisation to take an informed decision based on the disadvantages and advantages of different alternative technologies, not only from a technical perspective but also from a pricing perspective.

Standard terms

300. The establishment and use of standard terms must be assessed in the appropriate economic context and in the light of the situation on the relevant market in order to determine whether the standard terms at issue are likely to give rise to restrictive effects on competition.

301. As long as participation in the actual establishment of standard terms is **unrestricted** for the competitors in the relevant market (either by participation in the trade association or directly), and the established standard terms are **non-binding** and **effectively accessible** for anyone, such agreements are not likely to give rise to restrictive effects on competition (subject to the caveats set out in paragraphs 303, 304, 305 and 307).

302. Effectively accessible and non-binding standard terms for the sale of consumer goods or services (on the presumption that they have no effect on price) thus generally do not have any restrictive effect on competition since they are unlikely to lead to any negative effect on product quality, product variety or innovation. There are, however, two general exceptions where a more in-depth assessment would be required.

303. Firstly, standard terms for the sale of consumer goods or services where the standard terms define the scope of the product sold to the customer, and where therefore the risk of limiting product choice is more significant, could give rise to restrictive effects on competition within the meaning of Article 101(1) where their common application is likely to result in a *de facto* alignment. This could be the case when the widespread use of the standard terms *de facto* leads to a limitation of innovation and product variety. For instance, this may arise where standard terms in insurance contracts limit the customer's practical choice of key elements of the contract, such as the standard risks covered. Even if the use of the standard terms is not compulsory, they might undermine the incentives of the competitors to compete on product diversification.

304. When assessing whether there is a risk that the standard terms are likely to have restrictive effects by way of a limitation of product choice, factors such as existing competition on the market should be taken into account. For example if there is a large number of smaller competitors, the risk of a limitation of product choice would seem to be less than if there are only a few bigger competitors.[124] The market shares of the companies participating in the establishment of the standard terms might also give a certain indication of the likelihood of uptake of the standard terms or of the likelihood that the standard terms will be used by a large part of the market. However, in this respect, it is not only relevant to analyse whether the standard terms elaborated are likely to be used by a large part of the market, but also whether the standard terms only cover part of the product or the whole product (the less extensive the standard terms, the less likely that they will lead, overall, to a limitation of product choice). Moreover, in cases where in the absence of the establishment of the standard terms it would not have been possible to offer a certain product, there would not be likely to be any restrictive effect on competition within the meaning of Article 101(1). In that scenario, product choice is increased rather than decreased by the establishment of the standard terms.

305. Secondly, even if the standard terms do not define the actual scope of the end-product they might be a decisive part of the transaction with the customer for other reasons. An example would be online shopping where customer confidence is essential (for example, in the use of safe payment systems, a proper description of the products, clear and transparent pricing rules, flexibility of the return policy, etc). As it is difficult for customers to make a clear assessment of all those elements, they tend to favour widespread practices and standard terms regarding those elements could therefore become a *de facto* standard with which companies would need to comply to sell in the market. Even though non-binding, those standard terms would become a *de facto* standard, the effects of which are very close to a binding standard and need to be analysed accordingly.

306. If the use of standard terms is binding, there is a need to assess their impact on product quality, product variety and innovation (in particular if the standard terms are binding on the entire market).

307. Moreover, should the standard terms (binding or non-binding) contain any terms which are likely to have a negative effect on competition relating to prices (for example terms defining the type of rebates to be given), they would be likely to give rise to restrictive effects on competition within the meaning of Article 101(1).

7.4. Assessment under Article 101(3)

7.4.1. Efficiency gains

Standardisation agreements

308. Standardisation agreements frequently give rise to significant efficiency gains. For example, Union wide standards may facilitate market integration and allow companies to market their goods and services in all Member States, leading to increased consumer choice and decreasing prices. Standards which establish technical interoperability and compatibility often encourage competition on the merits between technologies from different companies and help prevent lock-in to one particular supplier. Furthermore, standards may reduce transaction costs for sellers and buyers. Standards on, for instance, quality, safety and environmental aspects of a product may also facilitate consumer choice and can lead to increased product quality. Standards also play an important role for innovation. They can reduce the time it takes to bring a new technology to the market and facilitate innovation by allowing companies to build on top of agreed solutions.

309. To achieve those efficiency gains in the case of standardisation agreements, the information necessary to apply the standard must be effectively available to those wishing to enter the market.[125]

310. Dissemination of a standard can be enhanced by marks or logos certifying compliance thereby providing certainty to customers. Agreements for testing and certification go beyond the primary objective of defining the standard and would normally constitute a distinct agreement and market.

311. While the effects on innovation must be analysed on a case-by-case basis, standards creating compatibility on a horizontal level between different technology platforms are considered to be likely to give rise to efficiency gains.

Standard terms

312. The use of standard terms can entail economic benefits such as making it easier for customers to compare the conditions offered and thus facilitate switching between companies. Standard terms might also lead to efficiency gains in the form of savings in transaction costs and, in certain sectors (in particular where the contracts are of a complex legal structure), facilitate entry. Standard terms may also increase legal certainty for the contract parties.

313. The higher the number of competitors on the market, the greater the efficiency gain of facilitating the comparison of conditions offered.

7.4.2. Indispensability

314. Restrictions that go beyond what is necessary to achieve the efficiency gains that can be generated by a standardisation agreement or standard terms do not fulfil the criteria of Article 101(3).

Standardisation agreements

315. The assessment of each standardisation agreement must take into account its likely effect on the markets concerned, on the one hand, and the scope of restrictions that possibly go beyond the objective of achieving efficiencies, on the other.[126]

316. Participation in standard-setting should normally be open to all competitors in the market or markets affected by the standard unless the parties demonstrate significant inefficiencies of such participation or recognised procedures are foreseen for the collective representation of interests.[127]

317. As a general rule standardisation agreements should cover no more than what is necessary to ensure their aims, whether this is technical interoperability and compatibility or a certain level of quality. In cases where having only one technological solution would benefit consumers or the economy at large that standard should, be set on a non-discriminatory basis. Technology neutral standards can, in certain circumstances, lead to larger efficiency gains. Including substitute IPR[128] as essential parts of a standard while at the same time forcing the users of the standard to pay for more IPR than technically necessary would go beyond what is necessary to achieve any identified efficiency gains. In the same vein, including substitute IPR as essential parts of a standard and limiting the use of that technology to that particular standard (that is to say, exclusive use) could limit inter-technology competition and would not be necessary to achieve the efficiencies identified.

318. Restrictions in a standardisation agreement making a standard binding and obligatory for the industry are in principle not indispensable.

319. In a similar vein, standardisation agreements that entrust certain bodies with the exclusive right to test compliance with the standard go beyond the primary objective of defining the standard and may also restrict competition. The exclusivity can, however, be justified for a certain period of time, for example by the need to recoup

significant start-up costs.[129] The standardisation agreement should in that case include adequate safeguards to mitigate possible risks to competition resulting from exclusivity. This concerns, inter alia, the certification fee which needs to be reasonable and proportionate to the cost of the compliance testing.

Standard terms

320. It is generally not justified to make standard terms binding and obligatory for the industry or the members of the trade association that established them. The possibility cannot, however, be ruled out that making standard terms binding may, in a specific case, be indispensable to the attainment of the efficiency gains generated by them.

7.4.3.
Pass-on to consumers

Standardisation agreements

321. Efficiency gains attained by indispensable restrictions must be passed on to consumers to an extent that outweighs the restrictive effects on competition caused by a standardisation agreement or by standard terms. A relevant part of the analysis of likely pass-on to consumers is which procedures are used to guarantee that the interests of the users of standards and end consumers are protected. Where standards facilitate technical interoperability and compatibility or competition between new and already existing products, services and processes, it can be presumed that the standard will benefit consumers.

Standard terms

322. Both the risk of restrictive effects on competition and the likelihood of efficiency gains increase with the companies' market shares and the extent to which the standard terms are used. Hence, it is not possible to provide any general 'safe harbour' within which there is no risk of restrictive effects on competition or which would allow the presumption that efficiency gains will be passed on to consumers to an extent that outweighs the restrictive effects on competition.

323. However, certain efficiency gains generated by standard terms, such as increased comparability of the offers on the market, facilitated switching between providers, and legal certainty of the clauses set out in the standard terms, are necessarily beneficial for the consumers. As regards other possible efficiency gains, such as lower transaction costs, it is necessary to make an assessment on a case-by-case basis and in the relevant economic context whether these are likely to be passed on to consumers.

7.4.4.
No elimination of competition

324. Whether a standardisation agreement affords the parties the possibility of eliminating competition depends on the various sources of competition in the market, the level of competitive constraint that they impose on the parties and the impact of the agreement on that competitive constraint. While market shares are relevant for that analysis, the magnitude of remaining sources of actual competition cannot be assessed exclusively on the basis of market share except in cases where a standard becomes a *de facto* industry standard.[130] In the latter case competition may be eliminated if third parties are foreclosed from effective access to the standard. Standard terms used by a majority of the industry might create a *de facto* industry standard and thus raise the same concerns. However, if the standard or the standard terms only concern a limited part of the product or service, competition is not likely to be eliminated.

7.5. Examples

325. Setting standards competitors cannot satisfy

Example 1

Situation: A standard-setting organisation sets and publishes safety standards that are widely used by the relevant industry. Most competitors of the industry take part in the setting of the standard. Prior to the adoption of the standard, a new entrant has developed a product which is technically equivalent in terms of the performance and functional requirements and which is recognised by the technical committee of the standard-setting organisation. However, the technical specifications of the safety standard are, without any objective justification, drawn up in such a way as to not allow for this or other new products to comply with the standard.

Analysis: This standardisation agreement is likely to give rise to restrictive effects on competition within the meaning of Article 101(1) and is unlikely to meet the criteria of Article 101(3). The members of the standards development organisation have, without any objective justification, set the standard in such a way that products of their competitors which are based on other technological solutions cannot satisfy it, even though they have equivalent performance. Hence, this standard, which has not been set on a non-discriminatory basis, will reduce or prevent innovation and product variety. It is unlikely that the way the standard is drafted will lead to greater efficiency gains than a neutral one.

326. Non-binding and transparent standard covering a large part of the market

Example 2

Situation: A number of consumer electronics manufacturers with substantial market shares agree to develop a new standard for a product to follow up the DVD.

Analysis: Provided that (a) the manufacturers remain free to produce other new products which do not conform to the new standard, (b) participation in the standard-setting is unrestricted and transparent, and (c) the standardisation agreement does not otherwise restrict competition, Article 101(1) is not likely to be infringed. If the parties agreed to only manufacture products which conform to the new standard, the agreement would limit technical development, reduce innovation and prevent the parties from selling different products, thereby creating restrictive effects on competition within the meaning of Article 101(1).

327. Standardisation agreement without IPR disclosure

Example 3

Situation: A private standard-setting organisation active in standardisation in the ICT (information and communication technology) sector has an IPR policy which neither requires nor encourages disclosures of IPR which could be essential for the future standard. The standard-setting organisation took the conscious decision not to include such an obligation in particular considering that in general all technologies potentially relevant for the future standard are covered by many IPR. Therefore the standard-setting organisation considered that an IPR disclosure obligation would, on the one hand, not lead to the benefit of enabling the participants to choose a solution with no or little IPR and, on the other, would lead to additional costs in analysing whether the IPR would be potentially essential for the future standard. However, the IPR policy of the standard-setting organisation requires all participants to make a commitment to license any IPR that might read on the future standard on FRAND terms. The IPR policy allows for opt-outs if there is specific IPR that an IPR holder wishes to put outside the blanket licensing commitment. In this particular industry there are several competing private standard-setting organisations. Participation in the standard-setting organisation is open to anyone active in the industry.

Analysis: In many cases an IPR disclosure obligation would be pro-competitive by increasing competition between technologies ex ante. In general, such an obligation allows the members of a standard-setting organisation to factor in the amount of IPR reading on a particular technology when deciding between competing technologies (or even to, if possible, choose a technology which is not covered by IPR). The amount of IPR reading on a technology will often have a direct impact on the cost of access to the standard. However, in this particular context, all available technologies seem to be covered by IPR, and even many IPR. Therefore, any IPR disclosure would not have the positive effect of enabling the members to factor in the amount of IPR when choosing technology since regardless of what technology is chosen, it can be presumed that there is IPR reading on that technology. IPR disclosure would be unlikely to contribute to guaranteeing effective access to the standard which in this scenario is sufficiently guaranteed by the blanket commitment to license any IPR that might read on the future standard on FRAND terms. On the contrary, an IPR disclosure obligation might in this context lead to additional costs for the participants. The absence of IPR disclosure might also, in those circumstances, lead to a quicker adoption of the standard which might be important if there are several competing standard-setting organisations. It follows that the agreement is unlikely to give rise to any negative effects on competition within the meaning of Article 101(1).

328. Standards in the insurance sector

Example 4

Situation: A group of insurance companies comes together to agree non-binding standards for the installation of certain security devices (that is to say, components and equipment designed for loss prevention and reduction and systems formed from such elements). The non-binding standards set by the insurance companies (a) are agreed in order to address a specific need and to assist insurers to manage risk and offer risk-appropriate premiums; (b) are discussed with the installers (or their representatives) and their views are taken on board prior to finalisation of the standards; (c) are published by the relevant insurance association on a dedicated section of its website so that any installer or other interested party can access them easily.

Analysis: The process for setting these standards is transparent and allows for the participation of interested parties. In addition, the result is easily accessible on a reasonable and non-discriminatory basis for anyone that wishes to have access to it. Provided that the standard does not have negative effects on the downstream market (for example by excluding certain installers through very specific and unjustified requirements for installations) it is not likely to lead to restrictive effects on competition. However, even if the standards led to restrictive effects on competition, the conditions set out in Article 101(3) would seem to be fulfilled. The standards would assist insurers in analysing to what extent such installation systems reduce relevant risk and prevent losses so that they can manage risks and offer risk-appropriate premiums. Subject to the caveat regarding the downstream market, they would also be more efficient for installers, allowing them to comply with one set of standards for all insurance companies rather than be tested by every insurance company separately. They could also make it easier for consumers to switch between insurers. In addition, they could be beneficial for smaller insurers who may not have the capacity to test separately. As regards the other conditions of Article 101(3), it seems that the non-binding standards do not go beyond what is necessary to achieve the efficiencies in question, that benefits would be passed on to the consumers (some would even be directly beneficial for the consumers) and that the restrictions would not lead to an elimination of competition.

329. Environmental standards

Example 5

Situation: Almost all producers of washing machines agree, with the encouragement of a public body, to no longer manufacture products which do not comply with certain environmental criteria (for example, energy efficiency). Together, the parties hold 90% of the market. The products which will be thus phased out of the market account for a significant proportion of total sales. They will be replaced by more environmentally friendly, but also more expensive products. Furthermore, the agreement indirectly reduces the output of third parties (for example, electric utilities and suppliers of components incorporated in the products phased out). Without the agreement, the parties would not have shifted their production and marketing efforts to the more environmentally friendly products.

Analysis: The agreement grants the parties control of individual production and concerns an appreciable proportion of their sales and total output, whilst also reducing third parties' output. Product variety, which is partly focused on the environmental characteristics of the product, is reduced and prices will probably rise. Therefore, the agreement is likely to give rise to restrictive effects on competition within the meaning of Article 101(1). The involvement of the public authority is irrelevant for that assessment. However, newer, more environmentally friendly products are more technically advanced, offering qualitative efficiencies in the form of more washing machine programmes which can be used by consumers. Furthermore, there are cost efficiencies for the purchasers of the washing machines resulting from lower running costs in the form of reduced consumption of water, electricity and soap. Those cost efficiencies are realised on markets which are different from the relevant market of the agreement. Nevertheless, those efficiencies may be taken into account as the markets on which the restrictive effects on competition and the efficiency gains arise are related and the group of consumers affected by the restriction and the efficiency gains is substantially the same. The efficiency gains outweigh the restrictive effects on competition in the form of increased costs. Other alternatives to the agreement are shown to be less certain and less cost-effective in delivering the same net benefits. Various technical means are economically available to the parties in order to manufacture washing machines which do comply with the environmental characteristics agreed upon and competition will still take place for other product characteristics. Therefore, the criteria of Article 101(3) would appear to be fulfilled.

330. Government encouraged standardisation

Example 6

Situation: In response to the findings of research into the recommended levels of fat in certain processed food conducted by a government-funded think tank in one Member State, several major manufacturers of the processed foods in the same Member State agree, through formal discussions at an industry trade association, to set recommended fat levels for the products. Together, the parties represent 70% of sales of the products within the Member State. The parties' initiative will be supported by a national advertising campaign funded by the think tank highlighting the dangers of a high fat content in processed foods.

Analysis: Although the fat levels are recommendations and therefore voluntary, as a result of the wide publicity resulting from the national advertising campaign, the recommended fat levels are likely to be implemented by all manufacturers of the processed foods in the Member State. It is therefore likely to become a *de facto* maximum fat level in the processed foods. Consumer choice across the product markets could therefore be reduced. However, the parties will be able to continue to compete with regard to a number of other characteristics of the products, such as price, product size, quality, taste, other nutritional and salt content, balance of ingredients, and branding. Moreover, competition regarding the fat levels in the product offering may increase where parties seek to offer products with the lowest levels. The agreement is therefore unlikely to give rise to restrictive effects on competition within the meaning of Article 101(1).

331. Open standardisation of product packaging

Example 7

Situation: The major manufacturers of a fast-moving consumer product in a competitive market in a Member State – as well as manufacturers and distributors in other Member States who sell the product into the Member State ('importers') – agree with the major packaging suppliers to develop and implement a voluntary initiative to standardise the size and shape of the packaging of the product sold in that Member State. There is currently a wide variation in packaging sizes and materials within and across the Member States. This reflects the fact that the packaging does not represent a high proportion of total production costs and that switching costs for packaging producers are not significant. There is no actual or pending European standard for the packaging. The agreement has been entered into by the parties voluntarily in response to pressure from the Member State's government to meet environmental targets. Together, the manufacturers and importers represent 85% of sales of the product within the Member State. The voluntary initiative will give rise to a uniform-sized product for sale within the Member State that uses less packaging material, occupies less shelf space, has lower transport and packaging costs, and is more environmentally friendly through reduced packaging waste. It also reduces the recycling costs of producers. The standard does not specify that particular types of packaging materials must be used. The specifications of the standard have been agreed between manufacturers and importers in an open and transparent manner, with the draft specifications having been published for open consultation on an industry website in a timely manner prior to adoption. The final specifications adopted are also published on an industry trade association website that is freely accessible to any potential entrants, even if they are not members of the trade association.

Analysis: Although the agreement is voluntary, the standard is likely to become a *de facto* industry practice because the parties together represent a high proportion of the market for the product in the Member State and retailers are also being encouraged by the government to reduce packaging waste. As such, the agreement could in theory create barriers to entry and give rise to potential anti-competitive foreclosure effects in the Member State market. This would in particular be a risk for importers of the product in question who may need to repackage the product to meet the *de facto* standard in order to sell in the Member State if the pack size used in other Member States does not meet the standard. However, significant barriers to entry and foreclosure are unlikely to occur in practice because (a) the agreement is voluntary, (b) the standard has been agreed with major importers in an open and transparent manner, (c) switching costs are low, and (d) the technical details of the standard are accessible to new entrants, importers and all packaging suppliers. In particular, importers will have been aware of potential changes to packaging at an early stage of development and will have had the opportunity through the open consultation on the draft standards to put forward their views before the standard was eventually adopted. The agreement therefore may not give rise to restrictive effects on competition within the meaning of Article 101(1).

In any event, it is likely that the conditions of Article 101(3) will be fulfilled in this case: (i) the agreement will give rise to quantitative efficiencies through lower transport and packaging costs, (ii) the prevailing conditions of competition on the market are such that these costs reductions are likely to be passed on to consumers, (iii) the agreement includes only the minimum restrictions necessary to achieve the packaging standard and is unlikely to result in significant foreclosure effects and (iv) competition will not be eliminated in a substantial part of the products in question.

332. Closed standardisation of product packaging

Example 8

Situation: The situation is the same as in Example 7, paragraph 331, except the standard is agreed only between manufacturers of the fast-moving consumer product located within the Member State (who represent 65% of the sales of the product in the Member State), there was no open consultation on the specifications adopted (which include detailed standards on the type of packaging material that must be used) and the specifications of the voluntary standard are not published. This resulted in higher switching costs for producers in other Member States than for domestic producers.

Analysis: Similar to Example 7, paragraph 331, although the agreement is voluntary, it is very likely to become *de facto* standard industry practice since retailers are also being encouraged by the government to reduce packaging waste and the domestic manufacturers account for 65% of sales of the product within the Member State. The fact that relevant producers in other Member States were not consulted resulted in the adoption of a standard which imposes higher switching costs on them compared to domestic producers. The agreement may therefore create barriers to entry and give rise to potential anti-competitive foreclosure effects on packaging suppliers, new entrants and importers – all of whom were not involved in the standard-setting process – as they may need to repackage the product to meet the *de facto* standard in order to sell in the Member State if the pack size used in other Member States does not meet the standard.

Unlike in Example 7, paragraph 331, the standardisation process has not been carried out in an open and transparent manner. In particular, new entrants, importers and packaging suppliers have not been given the opportunity to comment on the proposed standard and may not even be aware of it until a late stage, creating the possibility that they may not be able to change their production methods or switch suppliers quickly and effectively. Moreover, new entrants, importers and packaging suppliers may not be able to compete if the standard is unknown or difficult to comply with. Of particular relevance here is the fact that the standard includes detailed specifications on the packaging materials to be used which, because of the closed nature of the consultation and the standard, importers and new entrants will struggle to comply with. The agreement may therefore restrict competition within the meaning of Article 101(1). This conclusion is not affected by the fact the agreement has been entered into in order to meet underlying environmental targets agreed with the Member State's government.

It is unlikely that the conditions of Article 101(3) will be fulfilled in this case. Although the agreement will give rise to similar quantitative efficiencies as arise under Example 7, paragraph 331, the closed and private nature of the standardisation agreement and the non-published detailed standard on the type of packaging material that must be used are unlikely to be indispensable to achieving the efficiencies under the agreement.

333. Non-binding and open standard terms used for contracts with end-users

Example 9

Situation: A trade association for electricity distributors establishes non-binding standard terms for the supply of electricity to end-users. The establishment of the standard terms is made in a transparent and non-discriminatory manner. The standard terms cover issues such as the specification of the point of consumption, the location of the connection point and the connection voltage, provisions on service reliability as well as the procedure for settling the accounts between the parties to the contract (for example, what happens if the customer does not provide the supplier with the readings of the measurement devices). The standard terms do not cover any issues relating to prices, that is to say, they contain no recommended prices or other clauses related to price. Any company active within the sector is free to use the standard terms as it sees fit. About 80% of the contracts concluded with end-users in the relevant market are based on these standard terms.

Analysis: These standard terms are not likely to give rise to restrictive effects on competition within the meaning of Article 101(1). Even if they have become industry practice, they do not seem to have any appreciable negative impact on prices, product quality or variety.

334. Standard terms used for contracts between companies

Example 10

Situation: Construction companies in a certain Member State come together to establish non-binding and open standard terms and conditions for use by a contractor when submitting a quotation for construction work to a client. A form of quotation is included together with terms and conditions suitable for building or construction. Together, the documents create the construction contract. Clauses cover such matters as contract formation, general obligations of the contractor and the client and non-price related payment conditions (for example, a provision specifying the contractor's right to give notice to suspend the work for non-payment), insurance, duration, handover and defects, limitation of liability, termination, etc. In contrast to Example 9, paragraph 333, these standard terms would often be used between companies, one active upstream and one active downstream.

Analysis: These standard terms are not likely to have restrictive effects on competition within the meaning of Article 101(1). There would normally not be any significant limitation in the customer's choice of the end-product, namely the construction work. Other restrictive effects on competition do not seem likely. Indeed, several of the clauses above (handover and defects, termination, etc) would often be regulated by law.

335. Standard terms facilitating the comparison of different companies' products

Example 11

Situation: A national association for the insurance sector distributes non-binding standard policy conditions for house insurance contracts. The conditions give no indication of the level of insurance premiums, the amount of the cover or the excesses payable by the insured. They do not impose comprehensive cover including risks to which a significant number of policyholders are not simultaneously exposed and do not require the policyholders to obtain cover from the same insurer for different risks. While the majority of insurance companies use standard policy conditions, not all their contracts contain the same conditions as they are adapted to each client's individual needs and therefore there is no *de facto* standardisation of insurance products offered to consumers. The standard policy conditions enable consumers and consumer organisations to compare the policies offered by the different insurers. A consumer association is involved in the process of laying down the standard policy conditions. They are also available for use by new entrants, on a non-discriminatory basis.

Analysis: These standard policy conditions relate to the composition of the final insurance product. If the market conditions and other factors would show that there might be a risk of limitation in product variety as a result of insurance companies using such standard policy conditions, it is likely that such possible limitation would be outweighed by efficiencies such as facilitation of comparison by consumers of conditions offered by insurance companies. Those comparisons in turn facilitate switching between insurance companies and thus enhance competition. Furthermore the switching of providers, as well as market entry by competitors, constitutes an advantage for consumers. The fact that the consumer association has participated in the process could, in certain instances, increase the likelihood of those efficiencies which do not automatically benefit the consumers being passed on. The standard policy conditions are also likely to reduce transaction costs and facilitate entry for insurers on a different geographic and/or product markets. Moreover, the restrictions do not seem to go beyond what is necessary to achieve the identified efficiencies and competition would not be eliminated. Consequently, the criteria of Article 101(3) are likely to be fulfilled.

NOTES

94 Standardisation can take different forms, ranging from the adoption of consensus based standards by the recognised European or national standards bodies, through consortia and fora, to agreements between independent companies.

95 See Case C-113/07, *SELEX*, [2009] ECR I-2207, paragraph 92.

96 OJ L 204, 21.7.1998, p 37.

97 See judgment of 12 May 2010 in Case T-432/05, *EMC Development AB* v. *Commission*, not yet reported.

98 Such standard terms might cover only a very small part of the clauses contained in the final contract or a large part thereof.

99 This refers to a situation where (legally non-binding) standard terms in practice are used by most of the industry and/or for most aspects of the product/service thus leading to a limitation or even lack of consumer choice.

100 See Chapter 3 on R&D agreements.

101 See also paragraph 308.

102 Depending on the circle of participants in the standard-setting process, restrictions can occur either on the supplier or on the purchaser side of the market for the standardised product.

103 In the context of this chapter IPR in particular refers to patent(s) (excluding non-published patent applications). However, in case any other type of IPR in practice gives the IPR holder control over the use of the standard the same principles should be applied.

104 In practice, many companies use a mix of these business models.

105 See Technology Transfer Guidelines, paragraph 7.

106 High royalty fees can only be qualified as excessive if the conditions for an abuse of a dominant position as set out in Article 102 of the Treaty and the case-law of the Court of Justice of the European Union are fulfilled. See for example Case 27/76, *United Brands*, [1978] ECR 207.

107 See for example Commission Decision in Case IV/35.691, *Pre-insulated pipes*, OJ L 24, 30.1.1999, p 1, where part of the infringement of Article 101 consisted in 'using norms and standards in order to prevent or delay the introduction of new technology which would result in price reductions' (paragraph 147).

108 This paragraph should not prevent unilateral ex ante disclosures of most restrictive licensing terms as described in paragraph 299. It also does not prevent patent pools created in accordance with the principles set out in the Technology Transfer Guidelines or the decision to license IPR essential to a standard on royalty-free terms as set out in this Chapter.

109 See by analogy paragraph 39 *et seq*. As regards market shares see also paragraph 296.

110 See also paragraph 293 in this regard.

111 For example effective access should be granted to the specification of the standard.

112 As specified in paragraphs 285 and 286.

113 It should be noted that FRAND can also cover royalty-free licensing.

114 To obtain the sought after result a good faith disclosure does not need to go as far as to require participants to compare their IPR against the potential standard and issue a statement positively concluding that they have no IPR reading on the potential standard.

115 See Case 27/76, *United Brands*, paragraph 250; see also Case C-385/07 P, *Der Grüne Punkt – Duales System Deutschland GmbH*, [2009] ECR I-6155, paragraph 142.

116 See Case 395/87, *Ministère public* v *Jean-Louis Tournier*, [1989] ECR 2521, paragraph 38; Joined Cases 110/88, 241/88 and 242/88, *Francois Lucazeau* v *SACEM*, [1989] ECR 2811, paragraph 33.

117 See Commission Decision in Case IV/29/151, *Philips/VCR*, OJ L 47, 18.2.1978, p 42, paragraph 23: 'As these standards were for the manufacture of VCR equipment, the parties were obliged to manufacture and distribute only cassettes and recorders conforming to the VCR system licensed by Philips. They were prohibited from changing to manufacturing and distributing other video cassette systems . . . This constituted a restriction of competition under Article 85(1)(b)'.

118 See Commission Decision in Case IV/29/151, *Philips/VCR*, paragraph 23.

119 In Commission Decision in Case IV/31.458, *X/Open Group*, OJ L 35, 6.2.1987, p 36, the Commission considered that even if the standards adopted were made public, the restricted membership policy had the effect of preventing non-members from influencing the results of the work of the group and from getting the know-how and technical understanding relating to the standards which the members were likely to acquire. In addition, non-members could not, in contrast to the members, implement the standard before it was adopted (see paragraph 32). The agreement was therefore in these circumstances seen to constitute a restriction under Article 101(1).

120 Or if the adoption of the standard would have been heavily delayed by an inefficient process, any initial restriction could be outweighed by efficiencies to be considered under Article 101(3).

121 See Commission Decision of 14 October 2009 in Case 39.416, *Ship Classification*. The Decision can be found at: ec.europa.eu/competition/antitrust/cases/index/by_nr_78.html#i39_416

122 See paragraph 261.

123 Any unilateral ex ante disclosures of most restrictive licensing terms should not serve as a cover to jointly fix prices either of downstream products or of substitute IPR/technologies which is, as outlined in paragraph 274, a restriction of competition by object.

124 If previous experience with standard terms on the relevant market shows that the standard terms did not lead to lessened

competition on product differentiation, this might also be an indication that the same type of standard terms elaborated for a neighbouring product will not lead to a restrictive effect on competition.

125 See Commission Decision in Case IV/31.458, *X/Open Group*, paragraph 42: 'The Commission considers that the willingness of the Group to make available the results as quickly as possible is an essential element in its decision to grant an exemption'.

126 In Case IV/29/151, *Philips/VCR*, compliance with the VCR standards led to the exclusion of other, perhaps better systems. Such exclusion was particularly serious in view of the pre-eminent market position enjoyed by Philips ' . . . [R]estrictions were imposed upon the parties which were not indispensable to the attainment of these improvements. The compatibility of VCR video cassettes with the machines made by other manufacturers would have been ensured even if the latter had to accept no more than an obligation to observe the VCR standards when manufacturing VCR equipment' (paragraph 31).

127 See Commission Decision in Case IV/31.458, *X/Open Group*, paragraph 45: '[T]he aims of the Group could not be achieved if any company willing to commit itself to the Group objectives had a right to become a member. This would create practical and logistical difficulties for the management of the work and possibly prevent appropriate proposals being passed.' See also Commission Decision of 14 October 2009 in Case 39.416, *Ship Classification*, paragraph 36: 'the Commitments strike an appropriate balance between maintaining demanding criteria for membership of IACS on the one hand, and removing unnecessary barriers to membership of IACS on the other hand. The new criteria will ensure that only technically competent CSs are eligible to become member of IACS, thus preventing that the efficiency and quality of IACS' work is unduly impaired by too lenient requirements for participation in IACS. At the same time, the new criteria will not hinder CSs, who are technically competent and willing to do so from joining IACS'.

128 Technology which is regarded by users or licensees as interchangeable with or substitutable for another technology, by reason of the characteristics and intended use of the technologies.

129 In this context see Commission Decision in Cases IV/34.179, 34.202, 216, *Dutch Cranes (SCK and FNK)*, OJ L 312, 23.12.1995, p 79, paragraph 23: 'The ban on calling on firms not certified by SCK as sub-contractors restricts the freedom of action of certified firms. Whether a ban can be regarded as preventing, restricting or distorting competition within the meaning of Article 85(1) must be judged in the legal and economic context. If such a ban is associated with a certification system which is completely open, independent and transparent and provides for the acceptance of equivalent guarantees from other systems, it may be argued that it has no restrictive effects on competition but is simply aimed at fully guaranteeing the quality of the certified goods or services'.

130 *De facto* standardisation refers to a situation where a (legally non-binding) standard, is, in practice, used by most of the industry.

C. VERTICAL AGREEMENTS

COUNCIL REGULATION

(19/65/EEC)

of 2 March 1965

on application of Article 85(3) of the Treaty to certain categories of agreements and concerted practices

[4.227]

NOTES

Date of publication in OJ: OJ L36, 6.3.1965, p 533 (S edn 1965–66, p 35).

Repeal of this Regulation in relation to the UK: this Regulation is repealed, in relation to the UK, by the Competition (Amendment etc) (EU Exit) Regulations 2019, SI 2019/93, reg 63, Sch 3, para 1, as from IP completion day (as defined in the European Union (Withdrawal Agreement) Act 2020, s 39) (for transitional provisions and savings in relation to the operation of the 2019 Regulations, see Sch 4 to those Regulations at **[7.69]** et seq). See also Sch 3, para 2 to the 2019 Regulations which provides that, despite the repeal of this Regulation, Level 2 Regulations made under it are not repealed.

Note: the reference to Article 85(3) of the Treaty in the title of this Regulation is a reference to Article 85(3) of the Treaty establishing the European Economic Community which, in due course, was replaced by Article 81(3) of the EC Treaty. With effect from 1 December 2009, the EC Treaty was replaced by the Treaty on the Functioning of the European Union. References in this document to provisions of the EEC Treaty should be construed accordingly. As to Article 81 of the EC Treaty, see now Article 101 of the Treaty on the Functioning of the European Union.

THE COUNCIL OF THE EUROPEAN ECONOMIC COMMUNITY,

Having regard to the Treaty establishing the European Economic Community, and in particular Article 87 thereof;

Having regard to the proposal from the Commission;[1] *Having regard to the Opinion of the European Parliament;*[2]

Having regard to the Opinion of the Economic and Social Committee;

Whereas Article 85(1) of the Treaty may in accordance with Article 85(3) be declared inapplicable to certain categories of agreements, decisions and concerted practices which fulfil the conditions contained in Article 85(3);

Whereas the provisions for implementation of Article 85(3) must be adopted by way of regulation pursuant to Article 87;

Whereas in view of the large number of notifications submitted in pursuance of Regulation No 17[3] *it is desirable that in order to facilitate the task of the Commission it should be enabled to declare by way of regulation that the provisions of Article 85(1) do not apply to certain categories of agreements and concerted practices;*

Whereas it should be laid down under what conditions the Commission, in close and constant liaison with the competent authorities of the Member States, may exercise such powers after sufficient experience has been gained in the light of individual decisions and it becomes possible to define categories of agreements and concerted practices in respect of which the conditions of Article 85(3) may be considered as being fulfilled;

Whereas the Commission has indicated by the action it has taken, in particular by Regulation No 153,[4] *that there can be no easing of the procedures prescribed by Regulation No 17 in respect of certain types of agreements and concerted practices that are particularly liable to distort competition in the common market;*

Whereas under Article 6 of Regulation No 17 the Commission may provide that a decision taken pursuant to Article 85(3) of the Treaty shall apply with retroactive effect; whereas it is desirable that the Commission be also empowered to adopt, by regulation, provisions to the like effect;

Whereas under Article 7 of Regulation No 17 agreements, decisions and concerted practices may, by decision of the Commission, be exempted from prohibition in particular if they are modified in such manner that they satisfy the requirements of Article 85(3); whereas it is desirable that the Commission be enabled to grant like exemption by regulation to such agreements and concerted practices if they are modified in such manner as to fall within a category defined in an exempting regulation;

Whereas, since there can be no exemption if the conditions set out in Article 85(3) are not satisfied, the Commission must have power to lay down by decision the conditions that must be satisfied by an agreement or concerted practice which owing to special circumstances has certain effects incompatible with Article 85(3);

NOTES

Repeal of this Regulation in relation to the UK: this Regulation is repealed in relation to the UK (as from IP completion day); see the introductory notes to this Regulation *ante*.

1. OJ 81, 27.5.64, p 1275/64.
2. OJ 197, 30.11.64, p 3320/64.
3. OJ 13, 21.12.62, p 204/62 (Regulation No 17 as amended by Regulation No 59 – OJ58, 10.7.62, p 1655/62 – and Regulation No 118/63/EEC –OJ 162, 7.11.63, p 2696/63).
4. OJ 139, 24.12.62, p 2918/62.

HAS ADOPTED THIS REGULATION—

[4.228]

Article 1

[1. Without prejudice to the application of Regulation No 17 and in accordance with Article 81(3) of the Treaty the Commission may by regulation declare that Article 81(1) shall not apply to—

(a) *categories of agreements which are entered into by two or more undertakings, each operating, for the purposes of the agreement, at a different level of the production or distribution chain, and which relate to the conditions under which the parties may purchase, sell or resell certain goods or services,*

(b) *categories of agreements to which only two undertakings are party and which include restrictions imposed in relation to the acquisition or use of industrial property rights, in particular of patents, utility models, designs or trade marks, or to the rights arising out of contracts for assignment of, or the right to use, a method of manufacture or knowledge relating to the use or to the application of industrial processes.]*

2. The regulation shall define the categories of agreements to which it applies and shall specify in particular—

(a) *the restrictions or clauses which must not be contained in the agreements;*

(b) *. . . the other conditions which must be satisfied.*

[3. Paragraphs 1 and 2 shall apply by analogy to categories of concerted practices.]

NOTES

Paras 1, 3 substituted, and words omitted from para 2 repealed, by Council Regulation 1215/99/EC, Art 1(1).

Repeal of this Regulation in relation to the UK: this Regulation is repealed in relation to the UK (as from IP completion day); see the introductory notes to this Regulation *ante*.

[4.229]

[Article 1a

A regulation pursuant to Article 1 may stipulate the conditions which may lead to the exclusion from its application of certain parallel networks of similar agreements or concerted practices operating on a particular market; when these circumstances are fulfilled the Commission may establish this by means of regulation and fix a period at the expiry of which the Regulation pursuant to Article 1 would no longer be applicable in respect of the relevant agreements or concerted practices on that market; such period must not be shorter than six months.]

NOTES

Inserted by Council Regulation 1215/99/EC, Art 1(2).

Repeal of this Regulation in relation to the UK: this Regulation is repealed in relation to the UK (as from IP completion day); see the introductory notes to this Regulation *ante*.

[4.230]

Article 2

1. A regulation pursuant to Article 1 shall be made for a specified period.

2. It may be repealed or amended where circumstances have changed with respect to any factor which was basic to its being made; in such case, a period shall be fixed for modification of the agreements and concerted practices to which the earlier regulation applies.

NOTES

Repeal of this Regulation in relation to the UK: this Regulation is repealed in relation to the UK (as from IP completion day); see the introductory notes to this Regulation *ante*.

[4.231]

Article 3

A regulation pursuant to Article 1 may stipulate that it shall apply with retroactive effect to agreements and concerted practices to which, at the date of entry into force of that regulation, a decision issued with retroactive effect in pursuance of Article 6 of Regulation No 17 would have applied.

NOTES

Repeal of this Regulation in relation to the UK: this Regulation is repealed in relation to the UK (as from IP completion day); see the introductory notes to this Regulation *ante*.

[4.232]

Article 4

1. A regulation pursuant to Article 1 may stipulate that the prohibition contained in Article 85(1) of the Treaty shall not apply, for such period as shall be fixed by that regulation, to agreements and concerted practices already in existence on 13 March 1962 which do not satisfy the conditions of Article 85(3), where—

[A regulation pursuant to Article 1 may stipulate that the prohibition contained in Article 85(1) of the Treaty shall not apply, for such period as shall be fixed by that regulation, to agreements and concerted practices already in existence at the date of accession to which Article 85 applies by virtue of accession and which do not satisfy the conditions of Article 85(3), where:]

— *within three months from the entry into force of the regulation, they are so modified as to satisfy the said conditions in accordance with the provisions of the regulation; and*

— *the modifications are brought to the notice of the Commission within the time limit fixed by the regulation.*

[The provisions of the preceding subparagraph shall apply in the same way in the case of the accession of the Hellenic Republic, the Kingdom of Spain and of the Portuguese Republic.]

[The provisions of the preceding subparagraphs shall apply in the same way in the case of the accession of Austria, Finland and Sweden.]

2. Paragraph 1 shall apply to agreements and concerted practices which had to be notified before 1 February 1963, in accordance with Article 5 of Regulation No 17, only where they have been so notified before that date.

[Paragraph 1 shall not apply to agreements and concerted practices to which Article 85(1) of the Treaty applies by virtue of accession and which must be notified before 1 July 1973, in accordance with Articles 5 and 25 of Regulation No 17, unless they have been so notified before that date.]

[Paragraph 1 shall not apply to agreements and concerted practices to which Article 85(1) of the Treaty applies by virtue of the accession of the Hellenic Republic and which must be notified before 1 July 1981, in accordance with Articles 5 and 25 of Regulation No 17, unless they have been so notified before that date.]

[Paragraph 2 shall not apply to agreements and concerted practices to which Article 85(1) of the Treaty applies by virtue of the accession of the Kingdom of Spain and of the Portuguese Republic and which must be notified before 1 July 1986, in accordance with Articles 5 and 25 of Regulation No 17, unless they have been so notified before that date.]

[Paragraph 1 shall not apply to agreements and concerted practices to which Article 85(1) of the Treaty applies by virtue of the accession of Austria, Finland and Sweden and which must be notified within six months of accession, in accordance with Articles 5 and 25 of Regulation No 17, unless they have been so notified within that period. The present paragraph shall not apply to agreements and concerted practices which at the date of accession already fall under Article 53(1) of the EEA agreement.]

3. The benefit of the provisions laid down pursuant to paragraph 1 may not be claimed in actions pending at the date of entry into force of a regulation adopted pursuant to Article 1; neither may it be relied on as grounds for claims for damages against third parties.

NOTES

Para 1: words in first pair of square brackets inserted by AA1; words in second pair of square brackets added by AA2, and substituted by AA3. Words in third pair of square brackets inserted by AA4, as adjusted by Council Decision 95/1/EC, Annex I(III)(A)(1).

Para 2: words in first pair of square brackets inserted by AA1. Words in second pair of square brackets inserted by AA2. Words in third pair of square brackets added by AA3. Words in fourth pair of square brackets inserted by AA4, as adjusted by Council Decision 95/1/EC, Annex I(III)(A)(1).

Repeal of this Regulation in relation to the UK: this Regulation is repealed in relation to the UK (as from IP completion day); see the introductory notes to this Regulation *ante*.

[4.233]

Article 5

Before adopting a regulation, the Commission shall publish a draft thereof and invite all persons concerned to submit their comments within such time limit, being not less than one month, as the Commission shall fix.

NOTES

Repeal of this Regulation in relation to the UK: this Regulation is repealed in relation to the UK (as from IP completion day); see the introductory notes to this Regulation *ante*.

[4.234]

Article 6

[1. The Commission shall consult the Advisory Committee on Restrictive Practices and Monopolies—

(a) with regard to a regulation pursuant to Article 1 before publishing a draft regulation and before adopting a regulation;

(b) with regard to a regulation pursuant to Article 1a before publishing a draft regulation if requested by a Member State, and before adopting a regulation.]

2. Article 10(5) and (6) of Regulation No 17, relating to consultation with the Advisory Committee, shall apply by analogy, it being understood that joint meetings with the Commission shall take place not earlier than one month after dispatch of the notice convening them.

NOTES

Para 1: substituted by Council Regulation 1215/99/EC, Art 1(3).

Repeal of this Regulation in relation to the UK: this Regulation is repealed in relation to the UK (as from IP completion day); see the introductory notes to this Regulation *ante*.

Article 7 *(Repealed by Council Regulation 1/2003/EC, Art 40.)*

[4.235]

Article 8

The Commission shall, before 1 January 1970, submit to the Council a proposal for a Regulation for such amendment of this Regulation as may prove necessary in the light of experience.

NOTES

Repeal of this Regulation in relation to the UK: this Regulation is repealed in relation to the UK (as from IP completion day); see the introductory notes to this Regulation *ante*.

COMMISSION NOTICE

of 18 December 1978

concerning its assessment of certain subcontracting agreements in relation to Article 85(1) of the EEC Treaty

[4.236]

NOTES

Date of publication in OJ: OJ C1, 3.1.1979, p 2.

Note: the reference to Article 85(1) of the EEC Treaty in the title of this Notice is a reference to Article 85(1) of the Treaty establishing the European Economic Community which, in due course, was replaced by Article 81(1) of the EC Treaty. With effect from 1 December 2009, the EC Treaty was replaced by the Treaty on the Functioning of the European Union. References in this document to provisions of the EEC Treaty should be construed accordingly. As to Article 81 of the EC Treaty, see now Article 101 of the Treaty on the Functioning of the European Union.

1. In this notice the Commission of the European Communities gives its view as to subcontracting agreements in relation to Article 85(1) of the Treaty establishing the European Economic Community. This class of agreement is at the present time a form of work distribution which concerns firms of all sizes, but which offers opportunities for development in particular to small and medium sized firms.

The Commission considers that agreements under which one firm, called "the contractor", whether or not in consequence of a prior order from a third party, entrusts to another, called "the subcontractor", the manufacture of goods, the supply of services or the performance of work under the contractor's instructions, to be provided to the contractor or performed on his behalf, are not of themselves caught by the prohibition in Article 85(1).

To carry out certain subcontracting agreements in accordance with the contractor's instructions, the subcontractor may have to make use of particular technology or equipment which the contractor will have to provide. In order to protect the economic value of such technology or equipment, the contractor may wish to restrict their use by the subcontractor to whatever is necessary for the purpose of the agreement. The question arises whether such restrictions are caught by Article 85(1). They are assessed in this notice with due regard to the purpose of such agreements, which distinguishes them from ordinary patent and know-how licensing agreements.

2. In the Commission's view, Article 85(1) does not apply to clauses whereby: – technology or equipment provided by the contractor may not be used except for the purposes of the subcontracting agreement,

– technology or equipment provided by the contractor may not be made available to third parties,
– the goods, services or work resulting from the use of such technology or equipment may be supplied only to the contractor or performed on his behalf,

provided that and in so far as this technology or equipment is necessary to enable the subcontractor under reasonable conditions to manufacture the goods, to supply the services or to carry out the work in accordance with the contractor's instructions. To that extent the subcontractor is providing goods, services or work in respect of which he is not an independent supplier in the market.

The above proviso is satisfied where performance of the subcontracting agreement makes necessary the use by the subcontractor of: – industrial property rights of the contractor or at his disposal, in the form of patents, utility models, designs protected by copyright, registered designs or other rights, or

– secret knowledge or manufacturing processes (know-how) of the contractor or at his disposal, or of
– studies, plans or documents accompanying the information given which have been prepared by or for the contractor, or
– dies, patterns or tools, and accessory equipment that are distinctively the contractor's,

which, even though not covered by industrial property rights nor containing any element of secrecy, permit the manufacture of goods which differ in form, function or composition from other goods manufactured or supplied on the market.

However, the restrictions mentioned above are not justifiable where the subcontractor has at his disposal or could under reasonable conditions obtain access to the technology and equipment needed to produce the goods, provide the services or carry out the work. Generally, this is the case when the contractor provides no more than general information which merely describes the work to be done. In such circumstances the restrictions could deprive the subcontractor of the possibility of developing his own business in the fields covered by the agreement.

3. The following restrictions in connection with the provision of technology by the contractor may in the Commission's view also be imposed by subcontracting agreements without giving grounds for objection under Article 85(1): – an undertaking by either of the parties not to reveal manufacturing processes or other know-how of a secret character, or confidential information given by the other party during the negotiation and performance of the agreement, as long as the know-how or information in question has not become public knowledge,

– an undertaking by the subcontractor not to make use, even after expiry of the agreement, of manufacturing processes or other know-how of a secret character received by him during the currency of the agreement, as long as they have not become public knowledge,
– an undertaking by the subcontractor to pass on to the contractor on a non-exclusive basis any technical improvements which he has made during the currency of the agreement, or, where a patentable invention has been discovered by the subcontractor, to grant non-exclusive licences in respect of inventions relating to improvements and new applications of the original invention to the contractor for the term of the patent held by the latter.

This undertaking by the subcontractor may be exclusive in favour of the contractor in so far as improvements and inventions made by the subcontractor during the currency of the agreement are incapable of being used independently of the contractor's secret know-how or patent, since this does not constitute an appreciable restriction of competition.

However, any undertaking by the subcontractor regarding the right to dispose of the results of his own research and development work may restrain competition, where such results are capable of being used independently. In such circumstances, the subcontracting relationship is not sufficient to displace the ordinary competition rules on the disposal of industrial property rights or secret know-how.

4. Where the subcontractor is authorized by a subcontracting agreement to use a specified trade mark, trade name or get up, the contractor may at the same time forbid such use by the subcontractor in the case of goods, services or work which are not to be supplied to the contractor.

5. Although this notice should in general obviate the need for firms to obtain a ruling on the legal position by an individual Commission Decision, it does not affect the right of the firms concerned to apply for negative clearance as defined by Article 2 of Regulation No 17 or to notify the agreement to the Commission under Article 4(1) of that Regulation.[1]

The 1968 notice on cooperation between enterprises[2], which lists a number of agreements that by their nature are not to be regarded as anti-competitive, is thus supplemented in the subcontracting field. The Commission also reminds firms that, in order to promote cooperation between small and medium sized businesses, it has published a notice concerning agreements of minor importance which do not fall under Article 85(1) of the Treaty establishing the European Economic Community[3].

This notice is without prejudice to the view that may be taken of subcontracting agreements by the Court of Justice of the European Communities.

NOTES

1 First Regulation implementing Articles 85 and 86 of the EEC Treaty (OJ No 13, 21.2.1962, p 204/62).

2 Notice concerning agreements, decisions and concerted practices relating to cooperation between enterprises (OJ No C75, 29.7.1968, p 3).

3 OJ No C313, 29.12.1977, p 3.

COMMISSION REGULATION

(330/2010/EU)

of 20 April 2010

on the application of Article 101(3) of the Treaty on the Functioning of the European Union to categories of vertical agreements and concerted practices

(Text with EEA relevance)

[4.237]

NOTES

Date of publication in OJ: OJ L102, 23.4.2010, p 1.

Expiry of this Regulation: note that this Regulation is due to expire on 31 May 2022 in so far as it applies in the European Union. See Article 10 *post*.

Application of this Regulation in relation to the UK: in accordance with the European Union (Withdrawal) Act 2018, s 3 at **[7.5]**, this Regulation became domestic law on IP completion day (as defined in the European Union (Withdrawal Agreement) Act 2020, s 39). In so far as applying to the UK, this Regulation is amended by the Competition (Amendment etc) (EU Exit) Regulations 2019, SI 2019/93, as from IP completion day. The amendments are set out below. With regard to these amendments, note that Articles that are repealed are reproduced in italics and, in the case of other amendments, the amending provision from SI 2019/93 is set out in full in the Notes to the amended Article, and the text of the amended Article has not been altered. For transitional provisions and savings in relation to the operation of the 2019 Regulations, see Sch 4 to those Regulations at **[7.69]** et seq.

Note also that Regulation 19/65/EEC (under which this Regulation was made) is repealed, in its application to the UK, by the Competition (Amendment etc) (EU Exit) Regulations 2019, SI 2019/93, reg 63, Sch 3, para 1, as from IP completion day (as defined in the European Union (Withdrawal Agreement) Act 2020, s 39) (for transitional provisions and savings in relation to the operation of the 2019 Regulations, see Sch 4 to those Regulations at **[7.69]** et seq). However, see Sch 3, para 2 to those Regulations (at **[7.67]**) which provides for the continued application of this Regulation despite the repeal of Regulation 19/65/EEC.

See also the list of consultations and draft documents in the Appendix at **[A1]**.

THE EUROPEAN COMMISSION,

Having regard to the Treaty on the Functioning of the European Union,

Having regard to Regulation No 19/65/EEC of the Council of 2 March 1965 on the application of Article 85(3) of the Treaty to certain categories of agreements and concerted practices,[1] and in particular Article 1 thereof,

Having published a draft of this Regulation,

After consulting the Advisory Committee on Restrictive Practices and Dominant Positions,

Whereas:

(1) Regulation No 19/65/EEC empowers the Commission to apply Article 101(3) of the Treaty on the Functioning of the European Union[2] by regulation to certain categories of vertical agreements and corresponding concerted practices falling within Article 101(1) of the Treaty.

(2) Commission Regulation (EC) No 2790/1999 of 22 December 1999 on the application of Article 81(3) of the Treaty to categories of vertical agreements and concerted practices[3] defines a category of vertical agreements which the Commission regarded as normally satisfying the conditions laid down in Article 101(3) of the Treaty. In view of the overall positive experience with the application of that Regulation, which expires on 31 May 2010, and taking into account further experience acquired since its adoption, it is appropriate to adopt a new block exemption regulation.

(3) The category of agreements which can be regarded as normally satisfying the conditions laid down in Article 101(3) of the Treaty includes vertical agreements for the purchase or sale of goods or services where those agreements are concluded between non-competing undertakings, between certain competitors or by certain associations of retailers of goods. It also includes vertical agreements containing ancillary provisions on the assignment or use of intellectual property rights. The term "vertical agreements" should include the corresponding concerted practices.

(4) For the application of Article 101(3) of the Treaty by regulation, it is not necessary to define those vertical agreements which are capable of falling within Article 101(1) of the Treaty. In the individual assessment of agreements under Article 101(1) of the Treaty, account has to be taken of several factors, and in particular the market structure on the supply and purchase side.

(5) The benefit of the block exemption established by this Regulation should be limited to vertical agreements for which it can be assumed with sufficient certainty that they satisfy the conditions of Article 101(3) of the Treaty.

(6) Certain types of vertical agreements can improve economic efficiency within a chain of production or distribution by facilitating better coordination between the participating undertakings. In particular, they can lead to a reduction in the transaction and distribution costs of the parties and to an optimisation of their sales and investment levels.

(7) The likelihood that such efficiency-enhancing effects will outweigh any anti-competitive effects due to restrictions contained in vertical agreements depends on the degree of market power of the parties to the agreement and, therefore, on the extent to which those undertakings face competition from other suppliers of goods or services regarded by their customers as interchangeable or substitutable for one another, by reason of the products' characteristics, their prices and their intended use.

(8) It can be presumed that, where the market share held by each of the undertakings party to the agreement on the relevant market does not exceed 30%, vertical agreements which do not contain certain types of severe restrictions of competition generally lead to an improvement in production or distribution and allow consumers a fair share of the resulting benefits.

(9) Above the market share threshold of 30%, there can be no presumption that vertical agreements falling within the scope of Article 101(1) of the Treaty will usually give rise to objective advantages of such a character and size as to compensate for the disadvantages which they create for competition. At the same time, there is no presumption that those vertical agreements are either caught by Article 101(1) of the Treaty or that they fail to satisfy the conditions of Article 101(3) of the Treaty.

(10) This Regulation should not exempt vertical agreements containing restrictions which are likely to restrict competition and harm consumers or which are not indispensable to the attainment of the efficiency-enhancing effects. In particular, vertical agreements containing certain types of severe restrictions of competition such as minimum and fixed resale-prices, as well as certain types of territorial protection, should be excluded from the benefit of the block exemption established by this Regulation irrespective of the market share of the undertakings concerned.

(11) n order to ensure access to or to prevent collusion on the relevant market, certain conditions should be attached to the block exemption. To this end, the exemption of non-compete obligations should be limited to obligations which do not exceed a defined duration. For the same reasons, any direct or indirect obligation causing the members of a selective distribution system not to sell the brands of particular competing suppliers should be excluded from the benefit of this Regulation.

(12) The market-share limitation, the non-exemption of certain vertical agreements and the conditions provided for in this Regulation normally ensure that the agreements to which the block exemption applies do not enable the participating undertakings to eliminate competition in respect of a substantial part of the products in question.

(13) The Commission may withdraw the benefit of this Regulation, pursuant to Article 29(1) of Council Regulation (EC) No 1/2003 of 16 December 2002 on the implementation of the rules on competition laid down in Articles 81 and 82 of the Treaty,[4] where it finds in a particular case that an agreement to which the exemption provided for in this Regulation applies nevertheless has effects which are incompatible with Article 101(3) of the Treaty.

(14) The competition authority of a Member State may withdraw the benefit of this Regulation pursuant to Article 29(2) of Regulation (EC) No 1/2003 in respect of the territory of that Member State, or a part thereof where, in a particular case, an agreement to which the exemption provided for in this Regulation applies nevertheless has effects which are incompatible with Article 101(3) of the Treaty in the territory of that Member State, or in a part thereof, and where such territory has all the characteristics of a distinct geographic market.

(15) In determining whether the benefit of this Regulation should be withdrawn pursuant to Article 29 of Regulation (EC) No 1/2003, the anti-competitive effects that may derive from the existence of parallel networks of vertical agreements that have similar effects which significantly restrict access to a relevant market or competition therein are of particular importance. Such cumulative effects may for example arise in the case of selective distribution or non-compete obligations.

(16) In order to strengthen supervision of parallel networks of vertical agreements which have similar anti-competitive effects and which cover more than 50% of a given market, the Commission may by regulation declare this Regulation inapplicable to vertical agreements containing specific restraints relating to the market concerned, thereby restoring the full application of Article 101 of the Treaty to such agreements,

NOTES

1 OJ 36, 6.3.1965, p 533.

2 With effect from 1 December 2009, Article 81 of the EC Treaty has become Article 101 of the Treaty on the Functioning of the European Union. The two Articles are, in substance, identical. For the purposes of this Regulation, references to Article 101 of the Treaty on the Functioning of the European Union should be understood as references to Article 81 of the EC Treaty where appropriate.

3 OJ L336, 29.12.1999, p 21.

4 OJ L1, 4.1.2003, p 1.

HAS ADOPTED THIS REGULATION—

[4.238]

Article 1 Definitions

1. For the purposes of this Regulation, the following definitions shall apply:

(a) "vertical agreement" means an agreement or concerted practice entered into between two or more undertakings each of which operates, for the purposes of the agreement or the concerted practice, at a different level of the production or distribution chain, and relating to the conditions under which the parties may purchase, sell or resell certain goods or services;

(b) "vertical restraint" means a restriction of competition in a vertical agreement falling within the scope of Article 101(1) of the Treaty;

(c) "competing undertaking" means an actual or potential competitor; "actual competitor" means an undertaking that is active on the same relevant market; "potential competitor" means an undertaking that, in the absence of the vertical agreement, would, on realistic grounds and not just as a mere theoretical possibility, in case of a small but permanent increase in relative prices be likely to undertake, within a short period of time, the necessary additional investments or other necessary switching costs to enter the relevant market;

(d) "non-compete obligation" means any direct or indirect obligation causing the buyer not to manufacture, purchase, sell or resell goods or services which compete with the contract goods or services, or any direct or indirect obligation on the buyer to purchase from the supplier or from another undertaking designated by the supplier more than 80% of the buyer's total purchases of the contract goods or services and their substitutes on the relevant market, calculated on the basis of the value or, where such is standard industry practice, the volume of its purchases in the preceding calendar year;

(e) "selective distribution system" means a distribution system where the supplier undertakes to sell the contract goods or services, either directly or indirectly, only to distributors selected on the basis of specified criteria and where these distributors undertake not to sell such goods or services to unauthorised distributors within the territory reserved by the supplier to operate that system;

(f) "intellectual property rights" includes industrial property rights, know how, copyright and neighbouring rights;

(g) "know-how" means a package of non-patented practical information, resulting from experience and testing by the supplier, which is secret, substantial and identified: in this context, "secret" means that the know-how is not generally known or easily accessible; "substantial" means that the know-how is significant and useful to the buyer for the use, sale or resale of the contract goods or services; "identified" means that the know-how is described in a sufficiently comprehensive manner so as to make it possible to verify that it fulfils the criteria of secrecy and substantiality;

(h) "buyer" includes an undertaking which, under an agreement falling within Article 101(1) of the Treaty, sells goods or services on behalf of another undertaking;

(i) "customer of the buyer" means an undertaking not party to the agreement which purchases the contract goods or services from a buyer which is party to the agreement.

2. For the purposes of this Regulation, the terms "undertaking", "supplier" and "buyer" shall include their respective connected undertakings.

"Connected undertakings" means:

(a) undertakings in which a party to the agreement, directly or indirectly:
   (i) has the power to exercise more than half the voting rights, or
   (ii) has the power to appoint more than half the members of the supervisory board, board of management or bodies legally representing the undertaking, or
   (iii) has the right to manage the undertaking's affairs;

(b) undertakings which directly or indirectly have, over a party to the agreement, the rights or powers listed in point (a);

(c) undertakings in which an undertaking referred to in point (b) has, directly or indirectly, the rights or powers listed in point (a);

(d) undertakings in which a party to the agreement together with one or more of the undertakings referred to in points (a), (b) or (c), or in which two or more of the latter undertakings, jointly have the rights or powers listed in point (a);

(e) undertakings in which the rights or the powers listed in point (a) are jointly held by:
   (i) parties to the agreement or their respective connected undertakings referred to in points (a) to (d), or
   (ii) one or more of the parties to the agreement or one or more of their connected undertakings referred to in points (a) to (d) and one or more third parties.

NOTES

Application of this Article in relation to the UK: this Article is amended, in relation to the UK only, by the Competition (Amendment etc) (EU Exit) Regulations 2019, SI 2019/93, reg 63, Sch 3, Pt 2, para 5(2), as from IP completion day (as defined in the European Union (Withdrawal Agreement) Act 2020, s 39) (for transitional provisions and savings in relation to the operation of the 2019 Regulations, see Sch 4 to those Regulations at **[7.69]** et seq), as follows—

"(2) In Article 1(1)—
(a) after point (a), insert—
"(aa) "the Chapter 1 prohibition" means the prohibition imposed by section 2(1) of the Competition Act 1998;";
(b) in point (b), for "Article 101(1) of the Treaty" substitute "the Chapter 1 prohibition";
(c) after point (c), insert—
"(ca) "retained block exemption regulation" has the meaning given in section 10(10) of the Competition Act 1998;
(cb) "block exemption order" has the meaning given in section 6 of the Competition Act 1998;";
(d) in point (h), for "Article 101(1) of the Treaty" substitute "the Chapter 1 prohibition".".

[4.239]

Article 2 Exemption

1. Pursuant to Article 101(3) of the Treaty and subject to the provisions of this Regulation, it is hereby declared that Article 101(1) of the Treaty shall not apply to vertical agreements.

This exemption shall apply to the extent that such agreements contain vertical restraints.

2. The exemption provided for in paragraph 1 shall apply to vertical agreements entered into between an association of undertakings and its members, or between such an association and its suppliers, only if all its members are retailers of goods and if no individual member of the association, together with its connected undertakings, has a total annual

turnover exceeding EUR 50 million. Vertical agreements entered into by such associations shall be covered by this Regulation without prejudice to the application of Article 101 of the Treaty to horizontal agreements concluded between the members of the association or decisions adopted by the association.

3. The exemption provided for in paragraph 1 shall apply to vertical agreements containing provisions which relate to the assignment to the buyer or use by the buyer of intellectual property rights, provided that those provisions do not constitute the primary object of such agreements and are directly related to the use, sale or resale of goods or services by the buyer or its customers. The exemption applies on condition that, in relation to the contract goods or services, those provisions do not contain restrictions of competition having the same object as vertical restraints which are not exempted under this Regulation.

4. The exemption provided for in paragraph 1 shall not apply to vertical agreements entered into between competing undertakings. However, it shall apply where competing undertakings enter into a non-reciprocal vertical agreement and:

(a) the supplier is a manufacturer and a distributor of goods, while the buyer is a distributor and not a competing undertaking at the manufacturing level; or

(b) the supplier is a provider of services at several levels of trade, while the buyer provides its goods or services at the retail level and is not a competing undertaking at the level of trade where it purchases the contract services.

5. This Regulation shall not apply to vertical agreements the subject matter of which falls within the scope of any other block exemption regulation, unless otherwise provided for in such a regulation.

NOTES

Application of this Article in relation to the UK: this Article is amended, in relation to the UK only, by the Competition (Amendment etc) (EU Exit) Regulations 2019, SI 2019/93, reg 63, Sch 3, Pt 2, para 5(3), as from IP completion day (as defined in the European Union (Withdrawal Agreement) Act 2020, s 39) (for transitional provisions and savings in relation to the operation of the 2019 Regulations, see Sch 4 to those Regulations at **[7.69]** et seq), as follows—

"(3) In Article 2—

(a) in paragraph 1, for the first subparagraph substitute—

"Subject to the provisions of this Regulation, vertical agreements are exempt from the Chapter 1 prohibition.";

(b) in paragraph 2—

(i) for "EUR 50 million" substitute "£44 million";

(ii) for "Article 101 of the Treaty" substitute "the Chapter 1 prohibition";

(c) in paragraph 5, for the words from "block exemption regulation" to the end substitute "retained block exemption regulation or of any block exemption order, unless otherwise provided for in such a regulation or order".".

[4.240]

Article 3 Market share threshold

1. The exemption provided for in Article 2 shall apply on condition that the market share held by the supplier does not exceed 30% of the relevant market on which it sells the contract goods or services and the market share held by the buyer does not exceed 30% of the relevant market on which it purchases the contract goods or services.

2. For the purposes of paragraph 1, where in a multi-party agreement an undertaking buys the contract goods or services from one undertaking party to the agreement and sells the contract goods or services to another undertaking party to the agreement, the market share of the first undertaking must respect the market share threshold provided for in that paragraph both as a buyer and a supplier in order for the exemption provided for in Article 2 to apply.

[4.241]

Article 4 Restrictions that remove the benefit of the block exemption — hardcore restrictions

The exemption provided for in Article 2 shall not apply to vertical agreements which, directly or indirectly, in isolation or in combination with other factors under the control of the parties, have as their object:

(a) the restriction of the buyer's ability to determine its sale price, without prejudice to the possibility of the supplier to impose a maximum sale price or recommend a sale price, provided that they do not amount to a fixed or minimum sale price as a result of pressure from, or incentives offered by, any of the parties;

(b) the restriction of the territory into which, or of the customers to whom, a buyer party to the agreement, without prejudice to a restriction on its place of establishment, may sell the contract goods or services, except:

(i) the restriction of active sales into the exclusive territory or to an exclusive customer group reserved to the supplier or allocated by the supplier to another buyer, where such a restriction does not limit sales by the customers of the buyer,

(ii) the restriction of sales to end users by a buyer operating at the wholesale level of trade,

(iii) the restriction of sales by the members of a selective distribution system to unauthorised distributors within the territory reserved by the supplier to operate that system, and

(iv) the restriction of the buyer's ability to sell components, supplied for the purposes of incorporation, to customers who would use them to manufacture the same type of goods as those produced by the supplier;

(c) the restriction of active or passive sales to end users by members of a selective distribution system operating at the retail level of trade, without prejudice to the possibility of prohibiting a member of the system from operating out of an unauthorised place of establishment;

(d) the restriction of cross-supplies between distributors within a selective distribution system, including between distributors operating at different level of trade;

(e) the restriction, agreed between a supplier of components and a buyer who incorporates those components, of the supplier's ability to sell the components as spare parts to end-users or to repairers or other service providers not entrusted by the buyer with the repair or servicing of its goods.

[4.242]

Article 5 Excluded restrictions

1. The exemption provided for in Article 2 shall not apply to the following obligations contained in vertical agreements:

(a) any direct or indirect non-compete obligation, the duration of which is indefinite or exceeds five years;

(b) any direct or indirect obligation causing the buyer, after termination of the agreement, not to manufacture, purchase, sell or resell goods or services;

(c) any direct or indirect obligation causing the members of a selective distribution system not to sell the brands of particular competing suppliers.

For the purposes of point (a) of the first subparagraph, a non-compete obligation which is tacitly renewable beyond a period of five years shall be deemed to have been concluded for an indefinite duration.

2. By way of derogation from paragraph 1(a), the time limitation of five years shall not apply where the contract goods or services are sold by the buyer from premises and land owned by the supplier or leased by the supplier from third parties not connected with the buyer, provided that the duration of the non-compete obligation does not exceed the period of occupancy of the premises and land by the buyer.

3. By way of derogation from paragraph 1(b), the exemption provided for in Article 2 shall apply to any direct or indirect obligation causing the buyer, after termination of the agreement, not to manufacture, purchase, sell or resell goods or services where the following conditions are fulfilled:

(a) the obligation relates to goods or services which compete with the contract goods or services;

(b) the obligation is limited to the premises and land from which the buyer has operated during the contract period;

(c) the obligation is indispensable to protect know-how transferred by the supplier to the buyer;

(d) the duration of the obligation is limited to a period of one year after termination of the agreement.

Paragraph 1(b) is without prejudice to the possibility of imposing a restriction which is unlimited in time on the use and disclosure of know-how which has not entered the public domain.

[4.243]

Article 6 Non-application of this Regulation

Pursuant to Article 1a of Regulation No 19/65/EEC, the Commission may by regulation declare that, where parallel networks of similar vertical restraints cover more than 50% of a relevant market, this Regulation shall not apply to vertical agreements containing specific restraints relating to that market.

NOTES

Repeal of this Article in relation to the UK: this Article is repealed, in relation to the UK only, by the Competition (Amendment etc) (EU Exit) Regulations 2019, SI 2019/93, reg 63, Sch 3, Pt 2, para 5(4), as from IP completion day (as defined in the European Union (Withdrawal Agreement) Act 2020, s 39) (for transitional provisions and savings in relation to the operation of the 2019 Regulations, see Sch 3, Pt 2, para 10 to those Regulations at **[7.68]**, and Sch 4 to those Regulations at **[7.69]** et seq).

[4.244]

Article 7 Application of the market share threshold

For the purposes of applying the market share thresholds provided for in Article 3 the following rules shall apply:

(a) the market share of the supplier shall be calculated on the basis of market sales value data and the market share of the buyer shall be calculated on the basis of market purchase value data. If market sales value or market purchase value data are not available, estimates based on other reliable market information, including market sales and purchase volumes, may be used to establish the market share of the undertaking concerned;

(b) the market shares shall be calculated on the basis of data relating to the preceding calendar year;

(c) the market share of the supplier shall include any goods or services supplied to vertically integrated distributors for the purposes of sale;

(d) if a market share is initially not more than 30% but subsequently rises above that level without exceeding 35%, the exemption provided for in Article 2 shall continue to apply for a period of two consecutive calendar years following the year in which the 30% market share threshold was first exceeded;

(e) if a market share is initially not more than 30% but subsequently rises above 35%, the exemption provided for in Article 2 shall continue to apply for one calendar year following the year in which the level of 35% was first exceeded;

(f) the benefit of points (d) and (e) may not be combined so as to exceed a period of two calendar years;

(g) the market share held by the undertakings referred to in point (e) of the second subparagraph of Article 1(2) shall be apportioned equally to each undertaking having the rights or the powers listed in point (a) of the second subparagraph of Article 1(2).

[4.245]

Article 8 Application of the turnover threshold

1. For the purpose of calculating total annual turnover within the meaning of Article 2(2), the turnover achieved during the previous financial year by the relevant party to the vertical agreement and the turnover achieved by its connected undertakings in respect of all goods and services, excluding all taxes and other duties, shall be added together. For this purpose, no account shall be taken of dealings between the party to the vertical agreement and its connected undertakings or between its connected undertakings.

2. The exemption provided for in Article 2 shall remain applicable where, for any period of two consecutive financial years, the total annual turnover threshold is exceeded by no more than 10%.

[4.246]

Article 9 Transitional period

The prohibition laid down in Article 101(1) of the Treaty shall not apply during the period from 1 June 2010 to 31 May 2011 in respect of agreements already in force on 31 May 2010 which do not satisfy the conditions for exemption provided for in this Regulation but which, on 31 May 2010, satisfied the conditions for exemption provided for in Regulation (EC) No 2790/1999.

NOTES

Repeal of this Article in relation to the UK: this Article is repealed, in relation to the UK only, by the Competition (Amendment etc) (EU Exit) Regulations 2019, SI 2019/93, reg 63, Sch 3, Pt 2, para 5(4), as from IP completion day (as defined in the European Union (Withdrawal Agreement) Act 2020, s 39) (for transitional provisions and savings in relation to the operation of the 2019 Regulations, see Sch 4 to those Regulations at **[7.69]** et seq).

[4.247]

Article 10 Period of validity

This Regulation shall enter into force on 1 June 2010.

It shall expire on 31 May 2022.

This Regulation shall be binding in its entirety and directly applicable in all Member States.

NOTES

Application of this Article in relation to the UK: this Article is amended, in relation to the UK only, by the Competition (Amendment etc) (EU Exit) Regulations 2019, SI 2019/93, reg 63, Sch 3, Pt 2, para 5(5), as from IP completion day (as defined in the European Union (Withdrawal Agreement) Act 2020, s 39) (for transitional provisions and savings in relation to the operation of the 2019 Regulations, see Sch 4 to those Regulations at **[7.69]** et seq), as follows—

"(5) In the words after Article 10, omit the words from "This Regulation shall be binding" to "Member States.".".

COMMISSION NOTICE

(2010/C130/01)

Guidelines on Vertical Restraints

(Text with EEA relevance)

[4.248]

NOTES

Date of publication in OJ: C130, 19.5.2010, p 1.

See also the list of consultations and draft documents in the Appendix at **[A1]**.

I. INTRODUCTION

1. PURPOSE OF THE GUIDELINES

[4.249]

(1) These Guidelines set out the principles for the assessment of vertical agreements under Article 101 of the Treaty on the Functioning of the European Union* (hereinafter "Article 101").[1] Article 1(1)(a) of Commission Regulation (EU) No 330/2010 of 20 April 2010 on the application of Article 101(3) of the Treaty on the Functioning of the European Union to categories of vertical agreements and concerted practices[2] (hereinafter referred to as the "Block Exemption Regulation") (see paragraphs (24) to (46)) defines the term "vertical agreement". These Guidelines are without prejudice to the possible parallel application of Article 102 of the Treaty on the Functioning of the European Union (hereinafter "Article 102") to vertical agreements. These Guidelines are structured in the following way:

— Section II (paragraphs (8) to (22)) describes vertical agreements which generally fall outside Article 101(1);
— Section III (paragraphs (23) to (73)) clarifies the conditions for the application of the Block Exemption Regulation;
— Section IV (paragraphs (74) to (85)) describes the principles concerning the withdrawal of the block exemption and the disapplication of the Block Exemption Regulation;
— Section V (paragraphs (86) to (95)) provides guidance on how to define the relevant market and calculate market shares;
— Section VI (paragraphs (96) to (229)) describes the general framework of analysis and the enforcement policy of the Commission in individual cases concerning vertical agreements.

(2) Throughout these Guidelines, the analysis applies to both goods and services, although certain vertical restraints are mainly used in the distribution of goods. Similarly, vertical agreements can be concluded for intermediate and final goods and services. Unless otherwise stated, the analysis and arguments in these Guidelines apply to all types of goods and services and to all levels of trade. Thus, the term "products" includes both goods and services. The terms "supplier" and "buyer" are used for all levels of trade. The Block Exemption Regulation and these Guidelines do not apply to agreements with final consumers where the latter are not undertakings, since Article 101 only applies to agreements between undertakings.

(3) By issuing these Guidelines, the Commission aims to help companies conduct their own assessment of vertical agreements under EU competition rules. The standards set forth in these Guidelines cannot be applied mechanically, but must be applied with due consideration for the specific circumstances of each case. Each case must be evaluated in the light of its own facts.

(4) These Guidelines are without prejudice to the case-law of the General Court and the Court of Justice of the European Union concerning the application of Article 101 to vertical agreements. The Commission will continue to monitor the operation of the Block Exemption Regulation and Guidelines based on market information from stakeholders and national competition authorities and may revise this notice in the light of future developments and of evolving insight.

2. APPLICABILITY OF ARTICLE 101 TO VERTICAL AGREEMENTS

(5) Article 101 applies to vertical agreements that may affect trade between Member States and that prevent, restrict or distort competition ("vertical restraints").[3] Article 101 provides a legal framework for the assessment of vertical restraints, which takes into consideration the distinction between anti-competitive and pro-competitive effects. Article 101(1) prohibits those agreements which appreciably restrict or distort competition, while Article 101(3) exempts those agreements which confer sufficient benefits to outweigh the anti-competitive effects.[4]

(6) For most vertical restraints, competition concerns can only arise if there is insufficient competition at one or more levels of trade, that is, if there is some degree of market power at the level of the supplier or the buyer or at both levels. Vertical restraints are generally less harmful than horizontal restraints and may provide substantial scope for efficiencies.

(7) The objective of Article 101 is to ensure that undertakings do not use agreements – in this context, vertical agreements – to restrict competition on the market to the detriment of consumers. Assessing vertical restraints is also important in the context of the wider objective of achieving an integrated internal market. Market integration enhances competition in the European Union. Companies should not be allowed to re-establish private barriers between Member States where State barriers have been successfully abolished.

NOTES

[*] With effect from 1 December 2009, Articles 81 and 82 of the EC Treaty have become Articles 101 and, 102, respectively, of the Treaty on the Functioning of the European Union ('TFEU'). The two sets of provisions are, in substance, identical. For the purposes of these Guidelines, references to Articles 101 and 102 of the TFEU should be understood as references to Articles 81 and 82, respectively, of the EC Treaty where appropriate. The TFEU also introduced certain changes in terminology, such as the replacement of 'Community' by 'Union' and 'common market' by 'internal market'. The terminology of the TFEU will be used throughout these Guidelines.

[1] These Guidelines replace the *Commission Notice – Guidelines on Vertical Restraints*, OJ C291, 13.10.2000, p 1.

[2] OJ L102, 23.4.2010, p 1.

[3] See *inter alia* judgments of the Court of Justice in Joined Cases 56/64 and 58/64 *Grundig-Consten v Commission* [1966] ECR 299; Case 56/65 *Technique Minière v Maschinenbau Ulm* [1966] ECR 235; and judgment of the Court of First Instance in Case T-77/92 *Parker Pen v Commission* [1994] ECR II-549.

[4] See Communication from the Commission – Notice – Guidelines on the application of Article 81(3) of the Treaty, OJ C101, 27.4.2004, p 97 for the Commission's general methodology and interpretation of the conditions for applying Article 101(1) and in particular Article 101(3).

II. VERTICAL AGREEMENTS WHICH GENERALLY FALL OUTSIDE THE SCOPE OF ARTICLE 101(1)

1. AGREEMENTS OF MINOR IMPORTANCE AND SMES

[4.250]

(8) Agreements that are not capable of appreciably affecting trade between Member States or of appreciably restricting competition by object or effect do not fall within the scope of Article 101(1). The Block Exemption Regulation applies only to agreements falling within the scope of application of Article 101(1). These Guidelines are without prejudice to the application of Commission Notice on agreements of minor importance which do not appreciably restrict competition under Article 81(1) of the Treaty establishing the European Community (*de minimis*)[5] or any future *de minimis* notice.

(9) Subject to the conditions set out in the *de minimis* notice concerning hardcore restrictions and cumulative effect issues, vertical agreements entered into by non-competing undertakings whose individual market share on the relevant market does not exceed 15% are generally considered to fall outside the scope of Article 101(1).[6] There is no presumption that vertical agreements concluded by undertakings having more than 15% market share automatically infringe Article 101(1). Agreements between undertakings whose market share exceeds the 15% threshold may still not have an appreciable effect on trade between Member States or may not constitute an appreciable restriction of competition.[7] Such agreements need to be assessed in their legal and economic context. The criteria for the assessment of individual agreements are set out in paragraphs (96) to (229).

(10) As regards hardcore restrictions referred to in the *de minimis* notice, Article 101(1) may apply below the 15% threshold, provided that there is an appreciable effect on trade between Member States and on competition. The applicable case-law of the Court of Justice and the General Court is relevant in this respect[8]. Reference is also made to the possible need to assess positive and negative effects of hardcore restrictions as described in particular in paragraph 947) of these Guidelines.

(11) In addition, the Commission considers that, subject to cumulative effect and hardcore restrictions, vertical agreements between small and medium-sized undertakings as defined in the Annex to Commission Recommendation of 6 May 2003 concerning the definition of micro, small and medium-sized enterprises[9] are rarely capable of appreciably affecting trade between Member States or of appreciably restricting competition within the meaning of Article 101(1), and therefore generally fall outside the scope of Article 101(1). In cases where such agreements

nonetheless meet the conditions for the application of Article 101(1), the Commission will normally refrain from opening proceedings for lack of sufficient interest for the European Union unless those undertakings collectively or individually hold a dominant position in a substantial part of the internal market.

2. AGENCY AGREEMENTS

2.1 Definition of agency agreements

(12) An agent is a legal or physical person vested with the power to negotiate and/or conclude contracts on behalf of another person (the principal), either in the agent's own name or in the name of the principal, for the:

— purchase of goods or services by the principal, or
— sale of goods or services supplied by the principal.

(13) The determining factor in defining an agency agreement for the application of Article 101(1) is the financial or commercial risk borne by the agent in relation to the activities for which it has been appointed as an agent by the principal.[10] In this respect it is not material for the assessment whether the agent acts for one or several principals. Neither is material for this assessment the qualification given to their agreement by the parties or national legislation.

(14) There are three types of financial or commercial risk that are material to the definition of an agency agreement for the application of Article 101(1). First, there are the contract-specific risks which are directly related to the contracts concluded and/or negotiated by the agent on behalf of the principal, such as financing of stocks. Secondly, there are the risks related to market-specific investments. These are investments specifically required for the type of activity for which the agent has been appointed by the principal, that is, which are required to enable the agent to conclude and/or negotiate this type of contract. Such investments are usually sunk, which means that upon leaving that particular field of activity the investment cannot be used for other activities or sold other than at a significant loss. Thirdly, there are the risks related to other activities undertaken on the same product market, to the extent that the principal requires the agent to undertake such activities, but not as an agent on behalf of the principal but for its own risk.

(15) For the purposes of applying Article 101(1), the agreement will be qualified as an agency agreement if the agent does not bear any, or bears only insignificant, risks in relation to the contracts concluded and/or negotiated on behalf of the principal, in relation to market-specific investments for that field of activity, and in relation to other activities required by the principal to be undertaken on the same product market. However, risks that are related to the activity of providing agency services in general, such as the risk of the agent's income being dependent upon its success as an agent or general investments in for instance premises or personnel, are not material to this assessment.

(16) For the purpose of applying Article 101(1), an agreement will thus generally be considered an agency agreement where property in the contract goods bought or sold does not vest in the agent, or the agent does not himself supply the contract services and where the agent:

(a) does not contribute to the costs relating to the supply/purchase of the contract goods or services, including the costs of transporting the goods. This does not preclude the agent from carrying out the transport service, provided that the costs are covered by the principal;
(b) does not maintain at its own cost or risk stocks of the contract goods, including the costs of financing the stocks and the costs of loss of stocks and can return unsold goods to the principal without charge, unless the agent is liable for fault (for example, by failing to comply with reasonable security measures to avoid loss of stocks);
(c) does not undertake responsibility towards third parties for damage caused by the product sold (product liability), unless, as agent, it is liable for fault in this respect;
(d) does not take responsibility for customers' non-performance of the contract, with the exception of the loss of the agent's commission, unless the agent is liable for fault (for example, by failing to comply with reasonable security or anti-theft measures or failing to comply with reasonable measures to report theft to the principal or police or to communicate to the principal all necessary information available to him on the customer's financial reliability);
(e) is not, directly or indirectly, obliged to invest in sales promotion, such as contributions to the advertising budgets of the principal;
(f) does not make market-specific investments in equipment, premises or training of personnel, such as for example the petrol storage tank in the case of petrol retailing or specific software to sell insurance policies in case of insurance agents, unless these costs are fully reimbursed by the principal;
(g) does not undertake other activities within the same product market required by the principal, unless these activities are fully reimbursed by the principal.

(17) This list is not exhaustive. However, where the agent incurs one or more of the risks or costs mentioned in paragraphs (14), (15) and (16), the agreement between agent and principal will not be qualified as an agency agreement. The question of risk must be assessed on a case-by-case basis, and with regard to the economic reality of the situation rather than the legal form. For practical reasons, the risk analysis may start with the assessment of the contract-specific risks. If contract-specific risks are incurred by the agent, it will be enough to conclude that the agent is an independent distributor. On the contrary, if the agent does not incur contract-specific risks, then it will be necessary to continue further the analysis by assessing the risks related to market-specific investments. Finally, if the agent does not incur any contract-specific risks and risks related to market-specific investments, the risks related to other required activities within the same product market may have to be considered.

2.2 The application of Article 101(1) to agency agreements

(18) In the case of agency agreements as defined in section 2.1, the selling or purchasing function of the agent forms part of the principal's activities. Since the principal bears the commercial and financial risks related to the selling and purchasing of the contract goods and services all obligations imposed on the agent in relation to the contracts concluded and/or negotiated on behalf of the principal fall outside Article 101(1). The following obligations on the

agent's part will be considered to form an inherent part of an agency agreement, as each of them relates to the ability of the principal to fix the scope of activity of the agent in relation to the contract goods or services, which is essential if the principal is to take the risks and therefore to be in a position to determine the commercial strategy:

(a) limitations on the territory in which the agent may sell these goods or services;
(b) limitations on the customers to whom the agent may sell these goods or services;
(c) the prices and conditions at which the agent must sell or purchase these goods or services.

(19) In addition to governing the conditions of sale or purchase of the contract goods or services by the agent on behalf of the principal, agency agreements often contain provisions which concern the relationship between the agent and the principal. In particular, they may contain a provision preventing the principal from appointing other agents in respect of a given type of transaction, customer or territory (exclusive agency provisions) and/or a provision preventing the agent from acting as an agent or distributor of undertakings which compete with the principal (single branding provisions). Since the agent is a separate undertaking from the principal, the provisions which concern the relationship between the agent and the principal may infringe Article 101(1). Exclusive agency provisions will in general not lead to anti-competitive effects. However, single branding provisions and post-term non-compete provisions, which concern inter-brand competition, may infringe Article 101(1) if they lead to or contribute to a (cumulative) foreclosure effect on the relevant market where the contract goods or services are sold or purchased (see in particular Section VI.2.1). Such provisions may benefit from the Block Exemption Regulation, in particular when the conditions provided in Article 5 of that Regulation are fulfilled. They can also be individually justified by efficiencies under Article 101(3) as for instance described in paragraphs (144) to (148).

(20) An agency agreement may also fall within the scope of Article 101(1), even if the principal bears all the relevant financial and commercial risks, where it facilitates collusion. That could, for instance, be the case when a number of principals use the same agents while collectively excluding others from using these agents, or when they use the agents to collude on marketing strategy or to exchange sensitive market information between the principals.

(21) Where the agent bears one or more of the relevant risks as described in paragraph (16), the agreement between agent and principal does not constitute an agency agreement for the purpose of applying Article 101(1). In that situation, the agent will be treated as an independent undertaking and the agreement between agent and principal will be subject to Article 101(1) as any other vertical agreement.

3. SUBCONTRACTING AGREEMENTS

(22) Subcontracting concerns a contractor providing technology or equipment to a subcontractor that undertakes to produce certain products on the basis thereof (exclusively) for the contractor. Subcontracting is covered by Commission notice of 18 December 1978 concerning the assessment of certain subcontracting agreements in relation to Article 85(1) of the EEC Treaty[11] (hereinafter "subcontracting notice"). According to that notice, which remains applicable, subcontracting agreements whereby the subcontractor undertakes to produce certain products exclusively for the contractor generally fall outside the scope of Article 101(1) provided that the technology or equipment is necessary to enable the subcontractor to produce the products. However, other restrictions imposed on the subcontractor such as the obligation not to conduct or exploit its own research and development or not to produce for third parties in general may fall within the scope of Article 101.[12]

NOTES

5 OJ C368, 22.12.2001, p 13.

6 For agreements between competing undertakings the *de minimis* market share threshold is 10% for their collective market share on each affected relevant market.

7 See judgment of the Court of First Instance in Case T-7/93 *Langnese-Iglo v Commission* [1995] ECR II-1533, paragraph 98.

8 See judgments of the Court of Justice in Case 5/69 *Völk v Vervaecke* [1969] ECR 295; Case 1/71 *Cadillon v Höss* [1971] ECR 351 and Case C-306/96 *Javico v Yves Saint Laurent* [1998] ECR I-1983, paragraphs 16 and 17.

9 OJ L124, 20.5.2003, p 36.

10 See judgment of the Court of First Instance in Case T-325/01 *Daimler Chrysler v Commission* [2005] ECR II-3319; judgments of the Court of Justice in Case C-217/05 *Confederación Espanola de Empresarios de Estaciones de Servicio v CEPSA* [2006] ECR I-11987; and Case C-279/06 *CEPSA Estaciones de Servicio SA v LV Tobar e Hijos SL* [2008] ECR I-6681.

11 OJ C1, 3.1.1979, p 2.

12 See paragraph 3 of the subcontracting notice.

III. APPLICATION OF THE BLOCK EXEMPTION REGULATION

1. SAFE HARBOUR CREATED BY THE BLOCK EXEMPTION REGULATION

[4.251]

(23) For most vertical restraints, competition concerns can only arise if there is insufficient competition at one or more levels of trade, that is, if there is some degree of market power at the level of the supplier or the buyer or at both levels. Provided that they do not contain hardcore restrictions of competition, which are restrictions of competition by object, the Block Exemption Regulation creates a presumption of legality for vertical agreements depending on the market share of the supplier and the buyer. Pursuant to Article 3 of the Block Exemption Regulation, it is the supplier's market share on the market where it sells the contract goods or services and the buyer's market share on the market where it purchases the contract goods or services which determine the applicability of the block exemption. In order for the block exemption to apply, the supplier's and the buyer's market share must each be 30% or less. Section V of these Guidelines provides guidance on how to define the relevant market and calculate the market shares. Above the market share threshold of 30%, there is no presumption that vertical agreements fall within the scope of Article 101(1) or fail to satisfy the conditions of Article 101(3) but there is also no presumption that vertical agreements falling within the scope of Article 101(1) will usually satisfy the conditions of Article 101(3).

2. SCOPE OF THE BLOCK EXEMPTION REGULATION

2.1 Definition of vertical agreements

(24) Article 1(1)(a) of the Block Exemption Regulation defines a "vertical agreement" as "an agreement or concerted practice entered into between two or more undertakings each of which operates, for the purposes of the agreement or the concerted practice, at a different level of the production or distribution chain, and relating to the conditions under which the parties may purchase, sell or resell certain goods or services".

(25) The definition of "vertical agreement" referred to in paragraph 924) has four main elements:

(a) The Block Exemption Regulation applies to agreements and concerted practices. The Block Exemption Regulation does not apply to unilateral conduct of the undertakings concerned. Such unilateral conduct can fall within the scope of Article 102 which prohibits abuses of a dominant position. For there to be an agreement within the meaning of Article 101 it is sufficient that the parties have expressed their joint intention to conduct themselves on the market in a specific way. The form in which that intention is expressed is irrelevant as long as it constitutes a faithful expression of the parties' intention. In case there is no explicit agreement expressing the concurrence of wills, the Commission will have to prove that the unilateral policy of one party receives the acquiescence of the other party. For vertical agreements, there are two ways in which acquiescence with a particular unilateral policy can be established. First, the acquiescence can be deduced from the powers conferred upon the parties in a general agreement drawn up in advance. If the clauses of the agreement drawn up in advance provide for or authorise a party to adopt subsequently a specific unilateral policy which will be binding on the other party, the acquiescence of that policy by the other party can be established on the basis thereof.[13] Secondly, in the absence of such an explicit acquiescence, the Commission can show the existence of tacit acquiescence. For that it is necessary to show first that one party requires explicitly or implicitly the cooperation of the other party for the implementation of its unilateral policy and second that the other party complied with that requirement by implementing that unilateral policy in practice.[14] For instance, if after a supplier's announcement of a unilateral reduction of supplies in order to prevent parallel trade, distributors reduce immediately their orders and stop engaging in parallel trade, then those distributors tacitly acquiesce to the supplier's unilateral policy. This can however not be concluded if the distributors continue to engage in parallel trade or try to find new ways to engage in parallel trade. Similarly, for vertical agreements, tacit acquiescence may be deduced from the level of coercion exerted by a party to impose its unilateral policy on the other party or parties to the agreement in combination with the number of distributors that are actually implementing in practice the unilateral policy of the supplier. For instance, a system of monitoring and penalties, set up by a supplier to penalise those distributors that do not comply with its unilateral policy, points to tacit acquiescence with the supplier's unilateral policy if this system allows the supplier to implement in practice its policy. The two ways of establishing acquiescence described in this paragraph can be used jointly;

(b) The agreement or concerted practice is between two or more undertakings. Vertical agreements with final consumers not operating as an undertaking are not covered by the Block Exemption Regulation. More generally, agreements with final consumers do not fall under Article 101(1), as that article applies only to agreements between undertakings, decisions by associations of undertakings and concerted practices of undertakings. This is without prejudice to the possible application of Article 102;

(c) The agreement or concerted practice is between undertakings each operating, for the purposes of the agreement, at a different level of the production or distribution chain. This means for instance that one undertaking produces a raw material which the other undertaking uses as an input, or that the first is a manufacturer, the second a wholesaler and the third a retailer. This does not preclude an undertaking from being active at more than one level of the production or distribution chain;

(d) The agreements or concerted practices relate to the conditions under which the parties to the agreement, the supplier and the buyer, "may purchase, sell or resell certain goods or services". This reflects the purpose of the Block Exemption Regulation to cover purchase and distribution agreements. These are agreements which concern the conditions for the purchase, sale or resale of the goods or services supplied by the supplier and/or which concern the conditions for the sale by the buyer of the goods or services which incorporate these goods or services. Both the goods or services supplied by the supplier and the resulting goods or services are considered to be contract goods or services under the Block Exemption Regulation. Vertical agreements relating to all final and intermediate goods and services are covered. The only exception is the automobile sector, as long as this sector remains covered by a specific block exemption such as that granted by Commission Regulation (EC) No 1400/2002 of 31 July 2002 on the application of Article 81(3) of the Treaty to categories of vertical agreements and concerted practices in the motor vehicle sector[15] or its successor. The goods or services provided by the supplier may be resold by the buyer or may be used as an input by the buyer to produce its own goods or services.

(26) The Block Exemption Regulation also applies to goods sold and purchased for renting to third parties. However, rent and lease agreements as such are not covered, as no good or service is sold by the supplier to the buyer. More generally, the Block Exemption Regulation does not cover restrictions or obligations that do not relate to the conditions of purchase, sale and resale, such as an obligation preventing parties from carrying out independent research and development which the parties may have included in an otherwise vertical agreement. In addition, Article 2(2) to (5) of the Block Exemption Regulation directly or indirectly excludes certain vertical agreements from the application of that Regulation.

2.2 Vertical agreements between competitors

(27) Article 2(4) of the Block Exemption Regulation explicitly excludes "vertical agreements entered into between competing undertakings" from its application. Vertical agreements between competitors are dealt with, as regards possible collusion effects, in the Commission Guidelines on the applicability of Article 81 of the EC Treaty to horizontal cooperation agreements[16]. However, the vertical aspects of such agreements need to be assessed under

these Guidelines. Article 1(1)(c) of the Block Exemption Regulation defines a competing undertaking as "an actual or potential competitor". Two companies are treated as actual competitors if they are active on the same relevant market. A company is treated as a potential competitor of another company if, absent the agreement, in case of a small but permanent increase in relative prices it is likely that this first company, within a short period of time normally not longer than one year, would undertake the necessary additional investments or other necessary switching costs to enter the relevant market on which the other company is active. That assessment must be based on realistic grounds; the mere theoretical possibility of entering a market is not sufficient.[17] A distributor that provides specifications to a manufacturer to produce particular goods under the distributor's brand name is not to be considered a manufacturer of such own-brand goods.

(28) Article 2(4) of the Block Exemption Regulation contains two exceptions to the general exclusion of vertical agreements between competitors. These exceptions concern non-reciprocal agreements. Non-reciprocal agreements between competitors are covered by the Block Exemption Regulation where (a) the supplier is a manufacturer and distributor of goods, while the buyer is only a distributor and not also a competing undertaking at the manufacturing level, or (b) the supplier is a provider of services operating at several levels of trade, while the buyer operates at the retail level and is not a competing undertaking at the level of trade where it purchases the contract services. The first exception covers situations of dual distribution, that is, the manufacturer of particular goods also acts as a distributor of the goods in competition with independent distributors of its goods. In case of dual distribution it is considered that in general any potential impact on the competitive relationship between the manufacturer and retailer at the retail level is of lesser importance than the potential impact of the vertical supply agreement on competition in general at the manufacturing or retail level. The second exception covers similar situations of dual distribution, but in this case for services, when the supplier is also a provider of products at the retail level where the buyer operates.

2.3 Associations of retailers

(29) Article 2(2) of the Block Exemption Regulation includes in its application vertical agreements entered into by an association of undertakings which fulfils certain conditions and thereby excludes from the Block Exemption Regulation vertical agreements entered into by all other associations. Vertical agreements entered into between an association and its members, or between an association and its suppliers, are covered by the Block Exemption Regulation only if all the members are retailers of goods (not services) and if each individual member of the association has a turnover not exceeding EUR 50 million. Retailers are distributors reselling goods to final consumers. Where only a limited number of the members of the association have a turnover exceeding the EUR 50 million threshold and where these members together represent less than 15% of the collective turnover of all the members combined, the assessment under Article 101 will normally not be affected.

(30) An association of undertakings may involve both horizontal and vertical agreements. The horizontal agreements must be assessed according to the principles set out in the Guidelines on the applicability of Article 81 of the EC Treaty to horizontal cooperation agreements.[18] If that assessment leads to the conclusion that a cooperation between undertakings in the area of purchasing or selling is acceptable, a further assessment will be necessary to examine the vertical agreements concluded by the association with its suppliers or its individual members. The latter assessment will follow the rules of the Block Exemption Regulation and these Guidelines. For instance, horizontal agreements concluded between the members of the association or decisions adopted by the association, such as the decision to require the members to purchase from the association or the decision to allocate exclusive territories to the members must first be assessed as a horizontal agreement. Once that assessment leads to the conclusion that the horizontal agreement is not anticompetitive, an assessment of the vertical agreements between the association and individual members or between the association and suppliers is necessary.

2.4 Vertical agreements containing provisions on intellectual property rights (IPRs)

(31) Article 2(3) of the Block Exemption Regulation includes vertical agreements containing certain provisions relating to the assignment of IPRs to or use of IPRs by the buyer in its application and thereby excludes all other vertical agreements containing IPR provisions from the Block Exemption Regulation. The Block Exemption Regulation applies to vertical agreements containing IPR provisions where five conditions are fulfilled:

(a) The IPR provisions must be part of a vertical agreement, that is, an agreement with conditions under which the parties may purchase, sell or resell certain goods or services;
(b) The IPRs must be assigned to, or licensed for use by, the buyer;
(c) The IPR provisions must not constitute the primary object of the agreement;
(d) The IPR provisions must be directly related to the use, sale or resale of goods or services by the buyer or its customers. In the case of franchising where marketing forms the object of the exploitation of the IPRs, the goods or services are distributed by the master franchisee or the franchisees;
(e) The IPR provisions, in relation to the contract goods or services, must not contain restrictions of competition having the same object as vertical restraints which are not exempted under the Block Exemption Regulation.

(32) Such conditions ensure that the Block Exemption Regulation applies to vertical agreements where the use, sale or resale of goods or services can be performed more effectively because IPRs are assigned to or licensed for use by the buyer. In other words, restrictions concerning the assignment or use of IPRs can be covered when the main object of the agreement is the purchase or distribution of goods or services.

(33) The first condition makes clear that the context in which the IPRs are provided is an agreement to purchase or distribute goods or an agreement to purchase or provide services and not an agreement concerning the assignment or licensing of IPRs for the manufacture of goods, nor a pure licensing agreement. The Block Exemption Regulation does not cover for instance:

(a) agreements where a party provides another party with a recipe and licenses the other party to produce a drink with this recipe;
(b) agreements under which one party provides another party with a mould or master copy and licenses the other party to produce and distribute copies;

(c) the pure licence of a trade mark or sign for the purposes of merchandising;
(d) sponsorship contracts concerning the right to advertise oneself as being an official sponsor of an event;
(e) copyright licensing such as broadcasting contracts concerning the right to record and/or broadcast an event.

(34) The second condition makes clear that the Block Exemption Regulation does not apply when the IPRs are provided by the buyer to the supplier, no matter whether the IPRs concern the manner of manufacture or of distribution. An agreement relating to the transfer of IPRs to the supplier and containing possible restrictions on the sales made by the supplier is not covered by the Block Exemption Regulation. That means, in particular, that subcontracting involving the transfer of know-how to a subcontractor[19] does not fall within the scope of application of the Block Exemption Regulation (see also paragraph 922)). However, vertical agreements under which the buyer provides only specifications to the supplier which describe the goods or services to be supplied fall within the scope of application of the Block Exemption Regulation.

(35) The third condition makes clear that in order to be covered by the Block Exemption Regulation, the primary object of the agreement must not be the assignment or licensing of IPRs. The primary object must be the purchase, sale or resale of goods or services and the IPR provisions must serve the implementation of the vertical agreement.

(36) The fourth condition requires that the IPR provisions facilitate the use, sale or resale of goods or services by the buyer or its customers. The goods or services for use or resale are usually supplied by the licensor but may also be purchased by the licensee from a third supplier. The IPR provisions will normally concern the marketing of goods or services. An example would be a franchise agreement where the franchisor sells goods for resale to the franchisee and licenses the franchisee to use its trade mark and know-how to market the goods or where the supplier of a concentrated extract licenses the buyer to dilute and bottle the extract before selling it as a drink.

(37) The fifth condition highlights the fact that the IPR provisions should not have the same object as any of the hardcore restrictions listed in Article 4 of the Block Exemption Regulation or any of the restrictions excluded from the coverage of the Block Exemption Regulation by Article 5 of that Regulation (see paragraphs (47) to (69) of these Guidelines).

(38) Intellectual property rights relevant to the implementation of vertical agreements within the meaning of Article 2(3) of the Block Exemption Regulation generally concern three main areas: trade marks, copyright and know-how.

Trade mark

(39) A trade mark licence to a distributor may be related to the distribution of the licensor's products in a particular territory. If it is an exclusive licence, the agreement amounts to exclusive distribution.

Copyright

(40) Resellers of goods covered by copyright (books, software, etc) may be obliged by the copyright holder only to resell under the condition that the buyer, whether another reseller or the end user, shall not infringe the copyright. Such obligations on the reseller, to the extent that they fall under Article 101(1) at all, are covered by the Block Exemption Regulation.

(41) Agreements, under which hard copies of software are supplied for resale and where the reseller does not acquire a licence to any rights over the software but only has the right to resell the hard copies, are to be regarded as agreements for the supply of goods for resale for the purpose of the Block Exemption Regulation. Under that form of distribution, licensing the software only occurs between the copyright owner and the user of the software. It may take the form of a "shrink wrap" licence, that is, a set of conditions included in the package of the hard copy which the end user is deemed to accept by opening the package.

(42) Buyers of hardware incorporating software protected by copyright may be obliged by the copyright holder not to infringe the copyright, and must therefore not make copies and resell the software or make copies and use the software in combination with other hardware. Such use-restrictions, to the extent that they fall within Article 101(1) at all, are covered by the Block Exemption Regulation.

Know-how

(43) Franchise agreements, with the exception of industrial franchise agreements, are the most obvious example of where know-how for marketing purposes is communicated to the buyer.[20] Franchise agreements contain licences of intellectual property rights relating to trade marks or signs and know-how for the use and distribution of goods or the provision of services. In addition to the licence of IPR, the franchisor usually provides the franchisee during the life of the agreement with commercial or technical assistance, such as procurement services, training, advice on real estate, financial planning etc The licence and the assistance are integral components of the business method being franchised.

(44) Licensing contained in franchise agreements is covered by the Block Exemption Regulation where all five conditions listed in paragraph (31) are fulfilled. Those conditions are usually fulfilled as under most franchise agreements, including master franchise agreements, the franchisor provides goods and/or services, in particular commercial or technical assistance services, to the franchisee. The IPRs help the franchisee to resell the products supplied by the franchisor or by a supplier designated by the franchisor or to use those products and sell the resulting goods or services. Where the franchise agreement only or primarily concerns licensing of IPRs, it is not covered by the Block Exemption Regulation, but the Commission will, as a general rule, apply the principles set out in the Block Exemption Regulation and these Guidelines to such an agreement.

(45) The following IPR-related obligations are generally considered necessary to protect the franchisor's intellectual property rights and are, where these obligations fall under Article 101(1), also covered by the Block Exemption Regulation:

(a) an obligation on the franchisee not to engage, directly or indirectly, in any similar business;

(b) an obligation on the franchisee not to acquire financial interests in the capital of a competing undertaking such as would give the franchisee the power to influence the economic conduct of such undertaking;

(c) an obligation on the franchisee not to disclose to third parties the know-how provided by the franchisor as long as this know-how is not in the public domain;

(d) an obligation on the franchisee to communicate to the franchisor any experience gained in exploiting the franchise and to grant the franchisor, and other franchisees, a non-exclusive licence for the know-how resulting from that experience;

(e) an obligation on the franchisee to inform the franchisor of infringements of licensed intellectual property rights, to take legal action against infringers or to assist the franchisor in any legal actions against infringers;

(f) an obligation on the franchisee not to use know-how licensed by the franchisor for purposes other than the exploitation of the franchise;

(g) an obligation on the franchisee not to assign the rights and obligations under the franchise agreement without the franchisor's consent.

2.5 Relationship to other block exemption regulations

(46) Article 2(5) states that the Block Exemption Regulation does "not apply to vertical agreements the subject matter of which falls within the scope of any other block exemption regulation, unless otherwise provided for in such a regulation". The Block Exemption Regulation does not therefore apply to vertical agreements covered by Commission Regulation (EC) No 772/2004 of 27 April 2004 on the application of Article 81(3) of the Treaty to categories of technology transfer agreements,[21] Regulation 1400/2002 on the application of Article 81(3) of the Treaty to categories of vertical agreements and concerted practices in the motor vehicle sector[22] or Commission Regulation (EC) No 2658/2000 of 29 November 2000 on the application of Article 81(3) of the Treaty to categories of specialisation agreements[23] and Commission Regulation (EC) No 2659/2000 of 29 November 2000 on the application of Article 81(3) of the Treaty to categories of research and development agreements[24] exempting vertical agreements concluded in connection with horizontal agreements, or any future regulations of that kind, unless otherwise provided for in such a regulation.

3. HARDCORE RESTRICTIONS UNDER THE BLOCK EXEMPTION REGULATION

(47) Article 4 of the Block Exemption Regulation contains a list of hardcore restrictions which lead to the exclusion of the whole vertical agreement from the scope of application of the Block Exemption Regulation.[25] Where such a hardcore restriction is included in an agreement, that agreement is presumed to fall within Article 101(1). It is also presumed that the agreement is unlikely to fulfil the conditions of Article 101(3), for which reason the block exemption does not apply. However, undertakings may demonstrate pro-competitive effects under Article 101(3) in an individual case.[26] Where the undertakings substantiate that likely efficiencies result from including the hardcore restriction in the agreement and demonstrate that in general all the conditions of Article 101(3) are fulfilled, the Commission will be required to effectively assess the likely negative impact on competition before making an ultimate assessment of whether the conditions of Article 101(3) are fulfilled.[27]

(48) The hardcore restriction set out in Article 4(a) of the Block Exemption Regulation concerns resale price maintenance (RPM), that is, agreements or concerted practices having as their direct or indirect object the establishment of a fixed or minimum resale price or a fixed or minimum price level to be observed by the buyer. In the case of contractual provisions or concerted practices that directly establish the resale price, the restriction is clear cut. However, RPM can also be achieved through indirect means. Examples of the latter are an agreement fixing the distribution margin, fixing the maximum level of discount the distributor can grant from a prescribed price level, making the grant of rebates or reimbursement of promotional costs by the supplier subject to the observance of a given price level, linking the prescribed resale price to the resale prices of competitors, threats, intimidation, warnings, penalties, delay or suspension of deliveries or contract terminations in relation to observance of a given price level. Direct or indirect means of achieving price fixing can be made more effective when combined with measures to identify price-cutting distributors, such as the implementation of a price monitoring system, or the obligation on retailers to report other members of the distribution network that deviate from the standard price level. Similarly, direct or indirect price fixing can be made more effective when combined with measures which may reduce the buyer's incentive to lower the resale price, such as the supplier printing a recommended resale price on the product or the supplier obliging the buyer to apply a most-favoured-customer clause. The same indirect means and the same "supportive" measures can be used to make maximum or recommended prices work as RPM. However, the use of a particular supportive measure or the provision of a list of recommended prices or maximum prices by the supplier to the buyer is not considered in itself as leading to RPM.

(49) In the case of agency agreements, the principal normally establishes the sales price, as the agent does not become the owner of the goods. However, where such an agreement cannot be qualified as an agency agreement for the purposes of applying Article 101(1) (see paragraphs (12) to (21)) an obligation preventing or restricting the agent from sharing its commission, fixed or variable, with the customer would be a hardcore restriction under Article 4(a) of the Block Exemption Regulation. In order to avoid including such a hardcore restriction in the agreement, the agent should thus be left free to lower the effective price paid by the customer without reducing the income for the principal.[28]

(50) The hardcore restriction set out in Article 4(b) of the Block Exemption Regulation concerns agreements or concerted practices that have as their direct or indirect object the restriction of sales by a buyer party to the agreement or its customers, in as far as those restrictions relate to the territory into which or the customers to whom the buyer or its customers may sell the contract goods or services. This hardcore restriction relates to market partitioning by territory or by customer group. That may be the result of direct obligations, such as the obligation not to sell to certain customers or to customers in certain territories or the obligation to refer orders from these customers to other distributors. It may also result from indirect measures aimed at inducing the distributor not to sell to such customers, such as refusal or reduction of bonuses or discounts, termination of supply, reduction of supplied volumes or limitation of supplied volumes to the demand within the allocated territory or customer group, threat of contract

termination, requiring a higher price for products to be exported, limiting the proportion of sales that can be exported or profit pass-over obligations. It may further result from the supplier not providing a Union-wide guarantee service under which normally all distributors are obliged to provide the guarantee service and are reimbursed for this service by the supplier, even in relation to products sold by other distributors into their territory.[29] Such practices are even more likely to be viewed as a restriction of the buyer's sales when used in conjunction with the implementation by the supplier of a monitoring system aimed at verifying the effective destination of the supplied goods, such as the use of differentiated labels or serial numbers. However, obligations on the reseller relating to the display of the supplier's brand name are not classified as hardcore. As Article 4(b) only concerns restrictions of sales by the buyer or its customers, this implies that restrictions of the supplier's sales are also not a hardcore restriction, subject to what is stated in paragraph 959) regarding sales of spare parts in the context of Article 4(e) of the Block Exemption Regulation. Article 4(b) applies without prejudice to a restriction on the buyer's place of establishment. Thus, the benefit of the Block Exemption Regulation is not lost if it is agreed that the buyer will restrict its distribution outlet(s) and warehouse(s) to a particular address, place or territory.

(51) There are four exceptions to the hardcore restriction in Article 4(b) of the Block Exemption Regulation. The first exception in Article 4(b)(i) allows a supplier to restrict active sales by a buyer party to the agreement to a territory or a customer group which has been allocated exclusively to another buyer or which the supplier has reserved to itself. A territory or customer group is exclusively allocated when the supplier agrees to sell its product only to one distributor for distribution in a particular territory or to a particular customer group and the exclusive distributor is protected against active selling into its territory or to its customer group by all the other buyers of the supplier within the Union, irrespective of sales by the supplier. The supplier is allowed to combine the allocation of an exclusive territory and an exclusive customer group by for instance appointing an exclusive distributor for a particular customer group in a certain territory. Such protection of exclusively allocated territories or customer groups must, however, permit passive sales to such territories or customer groups. For the application of Article 4(b) of the Block Exemption Regulation, the Commission interprets "active" and "passive" sales as follows:

— "Active" sales mean actively approaching individual customers by for instance direct mail, including the sending of unsolicited Emails, or visits; or actively approaching a specific customer group or customers in a specific territory through advertisement in media, on the internet or other promotions specifically targeted at that customer group or targeted at customers in that territory. Advertisement or promotion that is only attractive for the buyer if it (also) reaches a specific group of customers or customers in a specific territory, is considered active selling to that customer group or customers in that territory.
— "Passive" sales mean responding to unsolicited requests from individual customers including delivery of goods or services to such customers. General advertising or promotion that reaches customers in other distributors' (exclusive) territories or customer groups but which is a reasonable way to reach customers outside those territories or customer groups, for instance to reach customers in one's own territory, are considered passive selling. General advertising or promotion is considered a reasonable way to reach such customers if it would be attractive for the buyer to undertake these investments also if they would not reach customers in other distributors' (exclusive) territories or customer groups.

(52) The internet is a powerful tool to reach a greater number and variety of customers than by more traditional sales methods, which explains why certain restrictions on the use of the internet are dealt with as (re)sales restrictions. In principle, every distributor must be allowed to use the internet to sell products. In general, where a distributor uses a website to sell products that is considered a form of passive selling, since it is a reasonable way to allow customers to reach the distributor. The use of a website may have effects that extend beyond the distributor's own territory and customer group; however, such effects result from the technology allowing easy access from everywhere. If a customer visits the web site of a distributor and contacts the distributor and if such contact leads to a sale, including delivery, then that is considered passive selling. The same is true if a customer opts to be kept (automatically) informed by the distributor and it leads to a sale. Offering different language options on the website does not, of itself, change the passive character of such selling. The Commission thus regards the following as examples of hardcore restrictions of passive selling given the capability of these restrictions to limit the distributor's access to a greater number and variety of customers:

(a) an agreement that the (exclusive) distributor shall prevent customers located in another (exclusive) territory from viewing its website or shall automatically re-rout its customers to the manufacturer's or other (exclusive) distributors' websites. This does not exclude an agreement that the distributor's website shall also offer a number of links to websites of other distributors and/or the supplier;
(b) an agreement that the (exclusive) distributor shall terminate consumers' transactions over the internet once their credit card data reveal an address that is not within the distributor's (exclusive) territory;
(c) an agreement that the distributor shall limit its proportion of overall sales made over the internet. This does not exclude the supplier requiring, without limiting the online sales of the distributor, that the buyer sells at least a certain absolute amount (in value or volume) of the products offline to ensure an efficient operation of its brick and mortar shop (physical point of sales), nor does it preclude the supplier from making sure that the online activity of the distributor remains consistent with the supplier's distribution model (see paragraphs (54) and (56)). This absolute amount of required offline sales can be the same for all buyers, or determined individually for each buyer on the basis of objective criteria, such as the buyer's size in the network or its geographic location;
(d) an agreement that the distributor shall pay a higher price for products intended to be resold by the distributor online than for products intended to be resold offline. This does not exclude the supplier agreeing with the buyer a fixed fee (that is, not a variable fee where the sum increases with the realised offline turnover as this would amount indirectly to dual pricing) to support the latter's offline or online sales efforts.

(53) A restriction on the use of the internet by distributors that are party to the agreement is compatible with the Block Exemption Regulation to the extent that promotion on the internet or use of the internet would lead to active selling into, for instance, other distributors' exclusive territories or customer groups. The Commission considers online advertisement specifically addressed to certain customers as a form of active selling to those customers. For

instance, territory-based banners on third party websites are a form of active sales into the territory where these banners are shown. In general, efforts to be found specifically in a certain territory or by a certain customer group is active selling into that territory or to that customer group. For instance, paying a search engine or online advertisement provider to have advertisements displayed specifically to users in a particular territory is active selling into that territory.

(54) However, under the Block Exemption the supplier may require quality standards for the use of the internet site to resell its goods, just as the supplier may require quality standards for a shop or for selling by catalogue or for advertising and promotion in general. This may be relevant in particular for selective distribution. Under the Block Exemption, the supplier may, for example, require that its distributors have one or more brick and mortar shops or showrooms as a condition for becoming a member of its distribution system. Subsequent changes to such a condition are also possible under the Block Exemption, except where those changes have as their object to directly or indirectly limit the online sales by the distributors. Similarly, a supplier may require that its distributors use third party platforms to distribute the contract products only in accordance with the standards and conditions agreed between the supplier and its distributors for the distributors' use of the internet. For instance, where the distributor's website is hosted by a third party platform, the supplier may require that customers do not visit the distributor's website through a site carrying the name or logo of the third party platform.

(55) There are three further exceptions to the hardcore restriction set out in Article 4(b) of the Block Exemption Regulation. All three exceptions allow for the restriction of both active and passive sales. Under the first exception, it is permissible to restrict a wholesaler from selling to end users, which allows a supplier to keep the wholesale and retail level of trade separate. However, that exception does not exclude the possibility that the wholesaler can sell to certain end users, such as bigger end users, while not allowing sales to (all) other end users. The second exception allows a supplier to restrict an appointed distributor in a selective distribution system from selling, at any level of trade, to unauthorised distributors located in any territory where the system is currently operated or where the supplier does not yet sell the contract products (referred to as "the territory reserved by the supplier to operate that system" in Article 4(b)(iii)). The third exception allows a supplier to restrict a buyer of components, to whom the components are supplied for incorporation, from reselling them to competitors of the supplier. The term "component" includes any intermediate goods and the term "incorporation" refers to the use of any input to produce goods.

(56) The hardcore restriction set out in Article 4(c) of the Block Exemption Regulation excludes the restriction of active or passive sales to end users, whether professional end users or final consumers, by members of a selective distribution network, without prejudice to the possibility of prohibiting a member of the network from operating out of an unauthorised place of establishment. Accordingly, dealers in a selective distribution system, as defined in Article 1(1)(e) of the Block Exemption Regulation, cannot be restricted in the choice of users to whom they may sell, or purchasing agents acting on behalf of those users except to protect an exclusive distribution system operated elsewhere (see paragraph 951)). Within a selective distribution system the dealers should be free to sell, both actively and passively, to all end users, also with the help of the internet. Therefore, the Commission considers any obligations which dissuade appointed dealers from using the internet to reach a greater number and variety of customers by imposing criteria for online sales which are not overall equivalent to the criteria imposed for the sales from the brick and mortar shop as a hardcore restriction. This does not mean that the criteria imposed for online sales must be identical to those imposed for offline sales, but rather that they should pursue the same objectives and achieve comparable results and that the difference between the criteria must be justified by the different nature of these two distribution modes. For example, in order to prevent sales to unauthorised dealers, a supplier can restrict its selected dealers from selling more than a given quantity of contract products to an individual end user. Such a requirement may have to be stricter for online sales if it is easier for an unauthorised dealer to obtain those products by using the internet. Similarly, it may have to be stricter for offline sales if it is easier to obtain them from a brick and mortar shop. In order to ensure timely delivery of contract products, a supplier may impose that the products be delivered instantly in the case of offline sales. Whereas an identical requirement cannot be imposed for online sales, the supplier may specify certain practicable delivery times for such sales. Specific requirements may have to be formulated for an online after-sales help desk, so as to cover the costs of customers returning the product and for applying secure payment systems.

(57) Within the territory where the supplier operates selective distribution, this system may not be combined with exclusive distribution as that would lead to a hardcore restriction of active or passive selling by the dealers under Article 4(c) of the Block Exemption Regulation, with the exception that restrictions can be imposed on the dealer's ability to determine the location of its business premises. Selected dealers may be prevented from operating their business from different premises or from opening a new outlet in a different location. In that context, the use by a distributor of its own website cannot be considered to be the same thing as the opening of a new outlet in a different location. If the dealer's outlet is mobile, an area may be defined outside which the mobile outlet cannot be operated. In addition, the supplier may commit itself to supplying only one dealer or a limited number of dealers in a particular part of the territory where the selective distribution system is applied.

(58) The hardcore restriction set out in Article 4(d) of the Block Exemption Regulation concerns the restriction of cross-supplies between appointed distributors within a selective distribution system. Accordingly, an agreement or concerted practice may not have as its direct or indirect object to prevent or restrict the active or passive selling of the contract products between the selected distributors. Selected distributors must remain free to purchase the contract products from other appointed distributors within the network, operating either at the same or at a different level of trade. Consequently, selective distribution cannot be combined with vertical restraints aimed at forcing distributors to purchase the contract products exclusively from a given source. It also means that within a selective distribution network, no restrictions can be imposed on appointed wholesalers as regards their sales of the product to appointed retailers.

(59) The hardcore restriction set out in Article 4(e) of the Block Exemption Regulation concerns agreements that prevent or restrict end-users, independent repairers and service providers from obtaining spare parts directly from the manufacturer of those spare parts. An agreement between a manufacturer of spare parts and a buyer that incorporates

those parts into its own products (original equipment manufacturer (OEM)), may not, either directly or indirectly, prevent or restrict sales by the manufacturer of those spare parts to end users, independent repairers or service providers. Indirect restrictions may arise particularly when the supplier of the spare parts is restricted in supplying technical information and special equipment which are necessary for the use of spare parts by users, independent repairers or service providers. However, the agreement may place restrictions on the supply of the spare parts to the repairers or service providers entrusted by the original equipment manufacturer with the repair or servicing of its own goods. In other words, the original equipment manufacturer may require its own repair and service network to buy spare parts from it.

4. INDIVIDUAL CASES OF HARDCORE SALES RESTRICTIONS THAT MAY FALL OUTSIDE THE SCOPE OF ARTICLE 101(1) OR MAY FULFIL THE CONDITIONS OF ARTICLE 101(3)

(60) Hardcore restrictions may be objectively necessary in exceptional cases for an agreement of a particular type or nature[30] and therefore fall outside Article 101(1). For example, a hardcore restriction may be objectively necessary to ensure that a public ban on selling dangerous substances to certain customers for reasons of safety or health is respected. In addition, undertakings may plead an efficiency defence under Article 101(3) in an individual case. This section provides some examples for (re)sales restrictions, whereas for RPM this is dealt with in section VI.2.10.

(61) A distributor which will be the first to sell a new brand or the first to sell an existing brand on a new market, thereby ensuring a genuine entry on the relevant market, may have to commit substantial investments where there was previously no demand for that type of product in general or for that type of product from that producer. Such expenses may often be sunk and in such circumstances the distributor may not enter into the distribution agreement without protection for a certain period of time against (active and) passive sales into its territory or to its customer group by other distributors. For example such a situation may occur where a manufacturer established in a particular national market enters another national market and introduces its products with the help of an exclusive distributor and where this distributor needs to invest in launching and establishing the brand on this new market. Where substantial investments by the distributor to start up and/or develop the new market are necessary, restrictions of passive sales by other distributors into such a territory or to such a customer group which are necessary for the distributor to recoup those investments generally fall outside the scope of Article 101(1) during the first two years that the distributor is selling the contract goods or services in that territory or to that customer group, even though such hardcore restrictions are in general presumed to fall within the scope of Article 101(1).

(62) In the case of genuine testing of a new product in a limited territory or with a limited customer group and in the case of a staggered introduction of a new product, the distributors appointed to sell the new product on the test market or to participate in the first round(s) of the staggered introduction may be restricted in their active selling outside the test market or the market(s) where the product is first introduced without falling within the scope of Article 101(1) for the period necessary for the testing or introduction of the product.

(63) In the case of a selective distribution system, cross supplies between appointed distributors must normally remain free (see paragraph 958)). However, if appointed wholesalers located in different territories are obliged to invest in promotional activities in 'their' territories to support the sales by appointed retailers and it is not practical to specify in a contract the required promotional activities, restrictions on active sales by the wholesalers to appointed retailers in other wholesalers' territories to overcome possible free riding may, in an individual case, fulfil the conditions of Article 101(3).

(64) In general, an agreement that a distributor shall pay a higher price for products intended to be resold by the distributor online than for products intended to be resold offline ("dual pricing") is a hardcore restriction (see paragraph 952)). However, in some specific circumstances, such an agreement may fulfil the conditions of Article 101(3). Such circumstances may be present where a manufacturer agrees such dual pricing with its distributors, because selling online leads to substantially higher costs for the manufacturer than offline sales. For example, where offline sales include home installation by the distributor but online sales do not, the latter may lead to more customer complaints and warranty claims for the manufacturer. In that context, the Commission will also consider to what extent the restriction is likely to limit internet sales and hinder the distributor to reach more and different customers.

5. EXCLUDED RESTRICTIONS UNDER THE BLOCK EXEMPTION REGULATION

(65) Article 5 of the Block Exemption Regulation excludes certain obligations from the coverage of the Block Exemption Regulation even though the market share threshold is not exceeded. However, the Block Exemption Regulation continues to apply to the remaining part of the vertical agreement if that part is severable from the non-exempted obligations.

(66) The first exclusion is provided for in Article 5(1)(a) of the Block Exemption Regulation and concerns non-compete obligations. Non-compete obligations are arrangements that result in the buyer purchasing from the supplier or from another undertaking designated by the supplier more than 80% of the buyer's total purchases of the contract goods and services and their substitutes during the preceding calendar year (as defined by Article 1(1)(d) of the Block Exemption Regulation), thereby preventing the buyer from purchasing competing goods or services or limiting such purchases to less than 20% of total purchases. Where, in the first year after entering in the agreement, for the year preceding the conclusion of the contract no relevant purchasing data for the buyer are available, the buyer's best estimate of its annual total requirements may be used. Such non-compete obligations are not covered by the Block Exemption Regulation where the duration is indefinite or exceeds five years. Non-compete obligations that are tacitly renewable beyond a period of five years are also not covered by the Block Exemption Regulation (see the second subparagraph of Article 5(1)). In general, non-compete obligations are exempted under that Regulation where their duration is limited to five years or less and no obstacles exist that hinder the buyer from effectively terminating the non-compete obligation at the end of the five year period. If, for instance, the agreement provides for a five-year non-compete obligation and the supplier provides a loan to the buyer, the repayment of that loan should not hinder the

buyer from effectively terminating the non-compete obligation at the end of the five-year period. Similarly, when the supplier provides the buyer with equipment which is not relationship-specific, the buyer should have the possibility to take over the equipment at its market asset value once the non-compete obligation expires.

(67) The five-year duration limit does not apply when the goods or services are resold by the buyer "from premises and land owned by the supplier or leased by the supplier from third parties not connected with the buyer". In such cases the non-compete obligation may be of the same duration as the period of occupancy of the point of sale by the buyer (Article 5(2) of the Block Exemption Regulation). The reason for this exception is that it is normally unreasonable to expect a supplier to allow competing products to be sold from premises and land owned by the supplier without its permission. By analogy, the same principles apply where the buyer operates from a mobile outlet owned by the supplier or leased by the supplier from third parties not connected with the buyer. Artificial ownership constructions, such as a transfer by the distributor of its proprietary rights over the land and premises to the supplier for only a limited period, intended to avoid the five-year limit cannot benefit from this exception.

(68) The second exclusion from the block exemption is provided for in Article 5(1)(b) of the Block Exemption Regulation and concerns post term non-compete obligations on the buyer. Such obligations are normally not covered by the Block Exemption Regulation, unless the obligation is indispensable to protect know-how transferred by the supplier to the buyer, is limited to the point of sale from which the buyer has operated during the contract period, and is limited to a maximum period of one year (see Article 5(3) of the Block Exemption Regulation). According to the definition in Article 1(1)(g) of the Block Exemption Regulation the know-how needs to be "substantial", meaning that the know-how includes information which is significant and useful to the buyer for the use, sale or resale of the contract goods or services.

(69) The third exclusion from the block exemption is provided for in Article 5(1)(c) of the Block Exemption Regulation and concerns the sale of competing goods in a selective distribution system. The Block Exemption Regulation covers the combination of selective distribution with a non-compete obligation, obliging the dealers not to resell competing brands in general. However, if the supplier prevents its appointed dealers, either directly or indirectly, from buying products for resale from specific competing suppliers, such an obligation cannot enjoy the benefit of the Block Exemption Regulation. The objective of the exclusion of such an obligation is to avoid a situation whereby a number of suppliers using the same selective distribution outlets prevent one specific competitor or certain specific competitors from using these outlets to distribute their products (foreclosure of a competing supplier which would be a form of collective boycott).[31]

6. SEVERABILITY

(70) The Block Exemption Regulation exempts vertical agreements on condition that no hardcore restriction, as set out in Article 4 of that Regulation, is contained in or practised with the vertical agreement. If there are one or more hardcore restrictions, the benefit of the Block Exemption Regulation is lost for the entire vertical agreement. There is no severability for hardcore restrictions.

(71) The rule of severability does apply, however, to the excluded restrictions set out in Article 5 of the Block Exemption Regulation. Therefore, the benefit of the block exemption is only lost in relation to that part of the vertical agreement which does not comply with the conditions set out in Article 5.

7. PORTFOLIO OF PRODUCTS DISTRIBUTED THROUGH THE SAME DISTRIBUTION SYSTEM

(72) Where a supplier uses the same distribution agreement to distribute several goods/services some of these may, in view of the market share threshold, be covered by the Block Exemption Regulation while others may not. In that case, the Block Exemption Regulation applies to those goods and services for which the conditions of application are fulfilled.

(73) In respect of the goods or services which are not covered by the Block Exemption Regulation, the ordinary rules of competition apply, which means:

(a) there is no block exemption but also no presumption of illegality;

(b) if there is an infringement of Article 101(1) which is not exemptible, consideration may be given to whether there are appropriate remedies to solve the competition problem within the existing distribution system;

(c) if there are no such appropriate remedies, the supplier concerned will have to make other distribution arrangements.

Such a situation can also arise where Article 102 applies in respect of some products but not in respect of others.

NOTES

13 Judgment of the Court of Justice in Case C-74/04 P *Commission v Volkswagen AG* [2006] ECR I-6585.

14 Judgment of the Court of First Instance in Case T-41/96 *Bayer AG v Commission* [2000] ECR II-3383.

15 OJ L203, 1.8.2002, p 30.

16 OJ C3, 6.1.2001, p 2. A revision of those Guidelines is forthcoming.

17 See Commission Notice on the definition of the relevant market for the purposes of Community competition law, OJ C372, 9.12.1997, p 5, paragraphs 20 to 24, the Commission's Thirteenth Report on Competition Policy, point 55, and Commission Decision 90/410/EEC in Case No IV/32.009 — *Elopak/Metal Box-Odin*, OJ L209, 8.8.1990, p 15.

18 See paragraph 927).

19 See the subcontracting notice (referred to in paragraph 922)).

20 Paragraphs 43–45 apply by analogy to other types of distribution agreements which involve the transfer of substantial know-how from supplier to buyer.

21 OJ L123, 27.4.2004, p 11.

22 See paragraph 925).

23 OJ L304, 5.12.2000, p 3.

24 OJ L304, 5.12.2000, p 7.

25 This list of hardcore restrictions applies to vertical agreements concerning trade within the Union. In so far as vertical agreements concern exports outside the Union or imports/re-imports from outside the Union see judgment of the Court

of Justice in Case C-306/96 *Javico v Yves Saint Laurent* [1998] ECR I-1983. In that judgment the ECJ held in paragraph 20 that "an agreement in which the reseller gives to the producer an undertaking that it will sell the contractual products on a market outside the Community cannot be regarded as having the object of appreciably restricting competition within the common market or as being capable of affecting, as such, trade between Member States".

26 See in particular paragraphs 106 to 109 describing in general possible efficiencies related to vertical restraints and Section VI.2.10 on resale price restrictions. See for general guidance on this the Communication from the Commission – *Notice – Guidelines on the application of Article 81(3) of the Treaty*, OJ C101, 27.4.2004, p 97.

27 Although, in legal terms, these are two distinct steps, they may in practice be an iterative process where the parties and Commission in several steps enhance and improve their respective arguments.

28 See, for instance, Commission Decision 91/562/EEC in Case No IV/32.737 — *Eirpage*, OJ L306, 7.11.1991, p 22, in particular recital (6).

29 If the supplier decides not to reimburse its distributors for services rendered under the Union-wide guarantee, it may be agreed with these distributors that a distributor which makes a sale outside its allocated territory, will have to pay the distributor appointed in the territory of destination a fee based on the cost of the services (to be) carried out including a reasonable profit margin. This type of scheme may not be seen as a restriction of the distributors' sales outside their territory (see judgment of the Court of First Instance in Case T-67/01 *JCB Service v Commission* [2004] ECR II-49, paragraphs 136 to 145).

30 See paragraph 18 of Communication from the Commission – *Notice – Guidelines on the application of Article 81(3) of the Treaty*, OJ C101, 27.4.2004, p 97.

31 An example of indirect measures having such exclusionary effects can be found in Commission Decision 92/428/EEC in Case No IV/33.542 — *Parfum Givenchy*, OJ L236, 19.8.1992, p 11.

IV. WITHDRAWAL OF THE BLOCK EXEMPTION AND DISAPPLICATION OF THE BLOCK EXEMPTION REGULATION

1. WITHDRAWAL PROCEDURE

[4.252]

(74) The presumption of legality conferred by the Block Exemption Regulation may be withdrawn where a vertical agreement, considered either in isolation or in conjunction with similar agreements enforced by competing suppliers or buyers, comes within the scope of Article 101(1) and does not fulfil all the conditions of Article 101(3).

(75) The conditions of Article 101(3) may in particular not be fulfilled when access to the relevant market or competition therein is significantly restricted by the cumulative effect of parallel networks of similar vertical agreements practised by competing suppliers or buyers. Parallel networks of vertical agreements are to be regarded as similar if they contain restraints producing similar effects on the market. Such a situation may arise for example when, on a given market, certain suppliers practise purely qualitative selective distribution while other suppliers practise quantitative selective distribution. Such a situation may also arise when, on a given market, the cumulative use of qualitative criteria forecloses more efficient distributors. In such circumstances, the assessment must take account of the anti-competitive effects attributable to each individual network of agreements. Where appropriate, withdrawal may concern only a particular qualitative criterion or only the quantitative limitations imposed on the number of authorised distributors.

(76) Responsibility for an anti-competitive cumulative effect can only be attributed to those undertakings which make an appreciable contribution to it. Agreements entered into by undertakings whose contribution to the cumulative effect is insignificant do not fall under the prohibition provided for in Article 101(1)[32] and are therefore not subject to the withdrawal mechanism. The assessment of such a contribution will be made in accordance with the criteria set out in paragraphs (128) to (229).

(77) Where the withdrawal procedure is applied, the Commission bears the burden of proof that the agreement falls within the scope of Article 101(1) and that the agreement does not fulfil one or several of the conditions of Article 101(3). A withdrawal decision can only have *ex nunc* effect, which means that the exempted status of the agreements concerned will not be affected until the date at which the withdrawal becomes effective.

(78) As referred to in recital 14 of the Block Exemption Regulation, the competition authority of a Member State may withdraw the benefit of the Block Exemption Regulation in respect of vertical agreements whose anti-competitive effects are felt in the territory of the Member State concerned or a part thereof, which has all the characteristics of a distinct geographic market. The Commission has the exclusive power to withdraw the benefit of the Block Exemption Regulation in respect of vertical agreements restricting competition on a relevant geographic market which is wider than the territory of a single Member State. When the territory of a single Member State, or a part thereof, constitutes the relevant geographic market, the Commission and the Member State concerned have concurrent competence for withdrawal.

2. DISAPPLICATION OF THE BLOCK EXEMPTION REGULATION

(79) Article 6 of the Block Exemption Regulation enables the Commission to exclude from the scope of the Block Exemption Regulation, by means of regulation, parallel networks of similar vertical restraints where these cover more than 50% of a relevant market. Such a measure is not addressed to individual undertakings but concerns all undertakings whose agreements are defined in the regulation disapplying the Block Exemption Regulation.

(80) Whereas the withdrawal of the benefit of the Block Exemption Regulation implies the adoption of a decision establishing an infringement of Article 101 by an individual company, the effect of a regulation under Article 6 is merely to remove, in respect of the restraints and the markets concerned, the benefit of the application of the Block Exemption Regulation and to restore the full application of Article 101(1) and (3). Following the adoption of a regulation declaring the Block Exemption Regulation inapplicable in respect of certain vertical restraints on a particular market, the criteria developed by the relevant case-law of the Court of Justice and the General Court and by

notices and previous decisions adopted by the Commission will guide the application of Article 101 to individual agreements. Where appropriate, the Commission will take a decision in an individual case, which can provide guidance to all the undertakings operating on the market concerned.

(81) For the purpose of calculating the 50% market coverage ratio, account must be taken of each individual network of vertical agreements containing restraints, or combinations of restraints, producing similar effects on the market. Article 6 of the Block Exemption Regulation does not entail an obligation on the part of the Commission to act where the 50% market-coverage ratio is exceeded. In general, disapplication is appropriate when it is likely that access to the relevant market or competition therein is appreciably restricted. This may occur in particular when parallel networks of selective distribution covering more than 50% of a market are liable to foreclose the market by using selection criteria which are not required by the nature of the relevant goods or which discriminate against certain forms of distribution capable of selling such goods.

(82) In assessing the need to apply Article 6 of the Block Exemption Regulation, the Commission will consider whether individual withdrawal would be a more appropriate remedy. This may depend, in particular, on the number of competing undertakings contributing to a cumulative effect on a market or the number of affected geographic markets within the Union.

(83) Any regulation referred to in Article 6 of the Block Exemption Regulation must clearly set out its scope. Therefore, the Commission must first define the relevant product and geographic market(s) and, secondly, must identify the type of vertical restraint in respect of which the Block Exemption Regulation will no longer apply. As regards the latter aspect, the Commission may modulate the scope of its regulation according to the competition concern which it intends to address. For instance, while all parallel networks of single-branding type arrangements shall be taken into account in view of establishing the 50% market coverage ratio, the Commission may nevertheless restrict the scope of the disapplication regulation only to non-compete obligations exceeding a certain duration. Thus, agreements of a shorter duration or of a less restrictive nature might be left unaffected, in consideration of the lesser degree of foreclosure attributable to such restraints. Similarly, when on a particular market selective distribution is practised in combination with additional restraints such as non-compete or quantity-forcing on the buyer, the disapplication regulation may concern only such additional restraints. Where appropriate, the Commission may also provide guidance by specifying the market share level which, in the specific market context, may be regarded as insufficient to bring about a significant contribution by an individual undertaking to the cumulative effect.

(84) Pursuant to Regulation No 19/65/EEC of 2 March 1965 of the Council on the application of Article 85(3) of the Treaty to certain categories of agreements and concerted practices,[33] the Commission will have to set a transitional period of not less than six months before a regulation disapplying the Block Exemption Regulation becomes applicable. This should allow the undertakings concerned to adapt their agreements to take account of the regulation disapplying the Block Exemption Regulation.

(85) A regulation disapplying the Block Exemption Regulation will not affect the exempted status of the agreements concerned for the period preceding its date of application.

NOTES

[32] Judgment of the Court of Justice of 28 February 1991 in Case C-234/89, *Stergios Delimitis v Henninger Bräu AG* [1991] ECR I-935.

[33] OJ 36, 6.3.1965, p 533/65, English special edition: OJ Series I Chapter 1965–1966, p 35.

V. MARKET DEFINITION AND MARKET SHARE CALCULATION

1. COMMISSION NOTICE ON DEFINITION OF THE RELEVANT MARKET

[4.253]

(86) The Commission Notice on definition of the relevant market for the purposes of Community competition law[34] provides guidance on the rules, criteria and evidence which the Commission uses when considering market definition issues. That Notice will not be further explained in these Guidelines and should serve as the basis for market definition issues. These Guidelines will only deal with specific issues that arise in the context of vertical restraints and that are not dealt with in that notice.

2. THE RELEVANT MARKET FOR CALCULATING THE 30% MARKET SHARE THRESHOLD UNDER THE BLOCK EXEMPTION REGULATION

(87) Under Article 3 of the Block Exemption Regulation, the market share of both the supplier and the buyer are decisive to determine if the block exemption applies. In order for the block exemption to apply, the market share of the supplier on the market where it sells the contract products to the buyer, and the market share of the buyer on the market where it purchases the contract products, must each be 30% or less. For agreements between small and medium-sized undertakings it is in general not necessary to calculate market shares (see paragraph (11)).

(88) In order to calculate an undertaking's market share, it is necessary to determine the relevant market where that undertaking sells and purchases, respectively, the contract products. Accordingly, the relevant product market and the relevant geographic market must be defined. The relevant product market comprises any goods or services which are regarded by the buyers as interchangeable, by reason of their characteristics, prices and intended use. The relevant geographic market comprises the area in which the undertakings concerned are involved in the supply and demand of relevant goods or services, in which the conditions of competition are sufficiently homogeneous, and which can be distinguished from neighbouring geographic areas because, in particular, conditions of competition are appreciably different in those areas.

(89) The product market definition primarily depends on substitutability from the buyers' perspective. When the supplied product is used as an input to produce other products and is generally not recognisable in the final product, the product market is normally defined by the direct buyers' preferences. The customers of the buyers will normally not have a strong preference concerning the inputs used by the buyers. Usually, the vertical restraints agreed between

the supplier and buyer of the input only relate to the sale and purchase of the intermediate product and not to the sale of the resulting product. In the case of distribution of final goods, substitutes for the direct buyers will normally be influenced or determined by the preferences of the final consumers. A distributor, as reseller, cannot ignore the preferences of final consumers when it purchases final goods. In addition, at the distribution level the vertical restraints usually concern not only the sale of products between supplier and buyer, but also their resale. As different distribution formats usually compete, markets are in general not defined by the form of distribution that is applied. Where suppliers generally sell a portfolio of products, the entire portfolio may determine the product market when the portfolios and not the individual products are regarded as substitutes by the buyers. As distributors are professional buyers, the geographic wholesale market is usually wider than the retail market, where the product is resold to final consumers. Often, this will lead to the definition of national or wider wholesale markets. But retail markets may also be wider than the final consumers' search area where homogeneous market conditions and overlapping local or regional catchment areas exist.

(90) Where a vertical agreement involves three parties, each operating at a different level of trade, each party's market share must be 30% or less in order for the block exemption to apply. As specified in Article 3(2) of the Block Exemption Regulation, where in a multi-party agreement an undertaking buys the contract goods or services from one undertaking party to the agreement and sells the contract goods or services to another undertaking party to the agreement, the block exemption applies only if its market share does not exceed the 30% threshold both as a buyer and a supplier. If, for instance, in an agreement between a manufacturer, a wholesaler (or association of retailers) and a retailer, a non-compete obligation is agreed, then the market shares of the manufacturer and the wholesaler (or association of retailers) on their respective downstream markets must not exceed 30% and the market share of the wholesaler (or association of retailers) and the retailer must not exceed 30% on their respective purchase markets in order to benefit from the block exemption.

(91) Where a supplier produces both original equipment and the repair or replacement parts for that equipment, the supplier will often be the only or the major supplier on the after-market for the repair and replacement parts. This may also arise where the supplier (OEM supplier) subcontracts the manufacturing of the repair or replacement parts. The relevant market for application of the Block Exemption Regulation may be the original equipment market including the spare parts or a separate original equipment market and after-market depending on the circumstances of the case, such as the effects of the restrictions involved, the lifetime of the equipment and importance of the repair or replacement costs.[35] In practice, the issue is whether a significant proportion of buyers make their choice taking into account the lifetime costs of the product. If so, it indicates there is one market for the original equipment and spare parts combined.

(92) Where the vertical agreement, in addition to the supply of the contract goods, also contains IPR provisions — such as a provision concerning the use of the supplier's trademark — which help the buyer to market the contract goods, the supplier's market share on the market where it sells the contract goods is relevant for the application of the Block Exemption Regulation. Where a franchisor does not supply goods to be resold but provides a bundle of services and goods combined with IPR provisions which together form the business method being franchised, the franchisor needs to take account of its market share as a provider of a business method. For that purpose, the franchisor needs to calculate its market share on the market where the business method is exploited, which is the market where the franchisees exploit the business method to provide goods or services to end users. The franchisor must base its market share on the value of the goods or services supplied by its franchisees on this market. On such a market, the competitors may be providers of other franchised business methods but also suppliers of substitutable goods or services not applying franchising. For instance, without prejudice to the definition of such market, if there was a market for fast-food services, a franchisor operating on such a market would need to calculate its market share on the basis of the relevant sales figures of its franchisees on this market.

3. CALCULATION OF MARKET SHARES UNDER THE BLOCK EXEMPTION REGULATION

(93) The calculation of market shares needs to be based in principle on value figures. Where value figures are not available substantiated estimates can be made. Such estimates may be based on other reliable market information such as volume figures (see Article 7(a) of the Block Exemption Regulation).

(94) In-house production, that is, production of an intermediate product for own use, may be very important in a competition analysis as one of the competitive constraints or to accentuate the market position of a company. However, for the purpose of market definition and the calculation of market share for intermediate goods and services, in-house production will not be taken into account.

(95) However, in the case of dual distribution of final goods, that is, where a producer of final goods also acts as a distributor on the market, the market definition and market share calculation need to include sales of their own goods made by the producers through their vertically integrated distributors and agents (see Article 7(c) of the Block Exemption Regulation). "Integrated distributors" are connected undertakings within the meaning of Article 1(2) of the Block Exemption Regulation.[36]

NOTES

34 OJ C372, 9.12.1997, p 5.

35 See for example Commission Decision in *Pelikan/Kyocera* (1995), COM(96) 126 (not published), point 87, and Commission Decision 91/595/EEC in Case No IV/M.12 — *Varta/Bosch*, OJ L320, 22.11.1991, p 26, Commission Decision in Case No IV/M.1094 — *Caterpillar/Perkins Engines*, OJ C94, 28.3.1998, p 23, and Commission Decision in Case No IV/M.768 — *Lucas/Varity*, OJ C266, 13.9.1996, p 6. See also point 66 of the Notice on the definition of the relevant market for the purposes of Community competition law (see paragraph 86).

36 For these market definition and market share calculation purposes, it is not relevant whether the integrated distributor sells in addition products of competitors.

VI. ENFORCEMENT POLICY IN INDIVIDUAL CASES

1. THE FRAMEWORK OF ANALYSIS

[4.254]

(96) Outside the scope of the block exemption, it is relevant to examine whether in the individual case the agreement falls within the scope of Article 101(1) and if so whether the conditions of Article 101(3) are satisfied. Provided that they do not contain restrictions of competition by object and in particular hardcore restrictions of competition, there is no presumption that vertical agreements falling outside the block exemption because the market share threshold is exceeded fall within the scope of Article 101(1) or fail to satisfy the conditions of Article 101(3). Individual assessment of the likely effects of the agreement is required. Companies are encouraged to do their own assessment. Agreements that either do not restrict competition within the meaning of Article 101(1) or which fulfil the conditions of Article 101(3) are valid and enforceable. Pursuant to Article 1(2) of Council Regulation (EC) No 1/2003 of 16 December 2002 on the implementation of the rules on competition laid down in Articles 81 and 82 of the Treaty[37] no notification needs to be made to benefit from an individual exemption under Article 101(3). In the case of an individual examination by the Commission, the latter will bear the burden of proof that the agreement in question infringes Article 101(1). The undertakings claiming the benefit of Article 101(3) bear the burden of proving that the conditions of that paragraph are fulfilled. When likely anti-competitive effects are demonstrated, undertakings may substantiate efficiency claims and explain why a certain distribution system is indispensable to bring likely benefits to consumers without eliminating competition, before the Commission decides whether the agreement satisfies the conditions of Article 101(3).

(97) The assessment of whether a vertical agreement has the effect of restricting competition will be made by comparing the actual or likely future situation on the relevant market with the vertical restraints in place with the situation that would prevail in the absence of the vertical restraints in the agreement. In the assessment of individual cases, the Commission will take, as appropriate, both actual and likely effects into account. For vertical agreements to be restrictive of competition by effect they must affect actual or potential competition to such an extent that on the relevant market negative effects on prices, output, innovation, or the variety or quality of goods and services can be expected with a reasonable degree of probability. The likely negative effects on competition must be appreciable.[38] Appreciable anticompetitive effects are likely to occur when at least one of the parties has or obtains some degree of market power and the agreement contributes to the creation, maintenance or strengthening of that market power or allows the parties to exploit such market power. Market power is the ability to maintain prices above competitive levels or to maintain output in terms of product quantities, product quality and variety or innovation below competitive levels for a not insignificant period of time. The degree of market power normally required for a finding of an infringement under Article 101(1) is less than the degree of market power required for a finding of dominance under Article 102.

(98) Vertical restraints are generally less harmful than horizontal restraints. The main reason for the greater focus on horizontal restraints is that such restraints may concern an agreement between competitors producing identical or substitutable goods or services. In such horizontal relationships, the exercise of market power by one company (higher price of its product) may benefit its competitors. This may provide an incentive to competitors to induce each other to behave anti-competitively. In vertical relationships, the product of the one is the input for the other-, in other words, the activities of the parties to the agreement are complementary to each other. The exercise of market power by either the upstream or downstream company would therefore normally hurt the demand for the product of the other. The companies involved in the agreement therefore usually have an incentive to prevent the exercise of market power by the other.

(99) Such self-restraining character should not, however, be over-estimated. When a company has no market power, it can only try to increase its profits by optimising its manufacturing and distribution processes, with or without the help of vertical restraints. More generally, because of the complementary role of the parties to a vertical agreement in getting a product on the market, vertical restraints may provide substantial scope for efficiencies. However, when an undertaking does have market power it can also try to increase its profits at the expense of its direct competitors by raising their costs and at the expense of its buyers and ultimately consumers by trying to appropriate some of their surplus. This can happen when the upstream and downstream company share the extra profits or when one of the two uses vertical restraints to appropriate all the extra profits.

1.1 NEGATIVE EFFECTS OF VERTICAL RESTRAINTS

(100) The negative effects on the market that may result from vertical restraints which EU competition law aims at preventing are the following:

(a) anticompetitive foreclosure of other suppliers or other buyers by raising barriers to entry or expansion;

(b) softening of competition between the supplier and its competitors and/or facilitation of collusion amongst these suppliers, often referred to as reduction of inter-brand competition;[39]

(c) softening of competition between the buyer and its competitors and/or facilitation of collusion amongst these competitors, often referred to as reduction of intra-brand competition if it concerns distributors' competition on the basis of the brand or product of the same supplier;

(d) the creation of obstacles to market integration, including, above all, limitations on the possibilities for consumers to purchase goods or services in any Member State they may choose.

(101) Foreclosure, softening of competition and collusion at the manufacturers' level may harm consumers in particular by increasing the wholesale prices of the products, limiting the choice of products, lowering their quality or reducing the level of product innovation. Foreclosure, softening of competition and collusion at the distributors' level may harm consumers in particular by increasing the retail prices of the products, limiting the choice of price-service combinations and distribution formats, lowering the availability and quality of retail services and reducing the level of innovation of distribution.

(102) On a market where individual distributors distribute the brand(s) of only one supplier, a reduction of competition between the distributors of the same brand will lead to a reduction of intra-brand competition between these distributors, but may not have a negative effect on competition between distributors in general. In such a case, if inter-brand competition is fierce, it is unlikely that a reduction of intra-brand competition will have negative effects for consumers.

(103) Exclusive arrangements are generally more anti-competitive than non-exclusive arrangements. Exclusive arrangements, whether by means of express contractual language or their practical effects, result in one party sourcing all or practically all of its demand from another party. For instance, under a non-compete obligation the buyer purchases only one brand. Quantity forcing, on the other hand, leaves the buyer some scope to purchase competing goods. The degree of foreclosure may therefore be less with quantity forcing.

(104) Vertical restraints agreed for non-branded goods and services are in general less harmful than restraints affecting the distribution of branded goods and services. Branding tends to increase product differentiation and reduce substitutability of the product, leading to a reduced elasticity of demand and an increased possibility to raise price. The distinction between branded and non-branded goods or services will often coincide with the distinction between intermediate goods and services and final goods and services.

(105) In general, a combination of vertical restraints aggravates their individual negative effects. However, certain combinations of vertical restraints are less anti-competitive than their use in isolation. For instance, in an exclusive distribution system, the distributor may be tempted to increase the price of the products as intra-brand competition has been reduced. The use of quantity forcing or the setting of a maximum resale price may limit such price increases. Possible negative effects of vertical restraints are reinforced when several suppliers and their buyers organise their trade in a similar way, leading to so-called cumulative effects.

1.2. Positive effects of vertical restraints

(106) It is important to recognise that vertical restraints may have positive effects by, in particular, promoting non-price competition and improved quality of services. When a company has no market power, it can only try to increase its profits by optimising its manufacturing or distribution processes. In a number of situations vertical restraints may be helpful in this respect since the usual arm's length dealings between supplier and buyer, determining only price and quantity of a certain transaction, can lead to a sub-optimal level of investments and sales.

(107) While trying to give a fair overview of the various justifications for vertical restraints, these Guidelines do not claim to be complete or exhaustive. The following reasons may justify the application of certain vertical restraints:

(a) To solve a "free-rider" problem. One distributor may free-ride on the promotion efforts of another distributor. That type of problem is most common at the wholesale and retail level. Exclusive distribution or similar restrictions may be helpful in avoiding such free-riding. Free-riding can also occur between suppliers, for instance where one invests in promotion at the buyer's premises, in general at the retail level, that may also attract customers for its competitors. Non-compete type restraints can help to overcome free-riding.[40]

For there to be a problem, there needs to be a real free-rider issue. Free-riding between buyers can only occur on pre-sales services and other promotional activities, but not on after-sales services for which the distributor can charge its customers individually. The product will usually need to be relatively new or technically complex or the reputation of the product must be a major determinant of its demand, as the customer may otherwise very well know what it wants, based on past purchases. And the product must be of a reasonably high value as it is otherwise not attractive for a customer to go to one shop for information and to another to buy. Lastly, it must not be practical for the supplier to impose on all buyers, by contract, effective promotion or service requirements.

Free-riding between suppliers is also restricted to specific situations, namely to cases where the promotion takes place at the buyer's premises and is generic, not brand specific.

(b) To "open up or enter new markets". Where a manufacturer wants to enter a new geographic market, for instance by exporting to another country for the first time, this may involve special "first time investments" by the distributor to establish the brand on the market. In order to persuade a local distributor to make these investments, it may be necessary to provide territorial protection to the distributor so that it can recoup these investments by temporarily charging a higher price. Distributors based in other markets should then be restrained for a limited period from selling on the new market (see also paragraph 961) in Section III.4). This is a special case of the free-rider problem described under point (a).

(c) The "certification free-rider issue". In some sectors, certain retailers have a reputation for stocking only "quality" products. In such a case, selling through those retailers may be vital for the introduction of a new product. If the manufacturer cannot initially limit its sales to the premium stores, it runs the risk of being de-listed and the product introduction may fail. There may, therefore, be a reason for allowing for a limited duration a restriction such as exclusive distribution or selective distribution. It must be enough to guarantee introduction of the new product but not so long as to hinder large-scale dissemination. Such benefits are more likely with "experience" goods or complex goods that represent a relatively large purchase for the final consumer.

(d) The so-called "hold-up problem". Sometimes there are client-specific investments to be made by either the supplier or the buyer, such as in special equipment or training. For instance, a component manufacturer that has to build new machines and tools in order to satisfy a particular requirement of one of its customers. The investor may not commit the necessary investments before particular supply arrangements are fixed.

However, as in the other free-riding examples, there are a number of conditions that have to be met before the risk of under-investment is real or significant. Firstly, the investment must be relationship-specific. An investment made by the supplier is considered to be relationship-specific when, after termination of the contract, it cannot be used by the supplier to supply other customers and can only be sold at a significant loss. An investment made by the buyer is considered to be relationship-specific when, after termination of the contract, it cannot be used by the buyer to purchase and/or use products supplied by other suppliers and can only be sold at a significant loss. An investment is thus relationship-specific because it can only, for instance, be used to produce a brand-specific component or to store a particular brand and thus cannot be used profitably to produce or resell alternatives. Secondly, it must be a long-term investment that is not recouped in the short run. And thirdly, the investment must be asymmetric, that is, one party to the contract invests more than the other party. Where these conditions are met, there is usually a good reason to have a vertical restraint for the duration it takes to depreciate the investment. The appropriate vertical restraint will be of the non-compete type or quantity-forcing type when the investment is made by the supplier and of the exclusive distribution, exclusive customer allocation or exclusive supply type when the investment is made by the buyer.

(e) The "specific hold-up problem that may arise in the case of transfer of substantial know-how". The know-how, once provided, cannot be taken back and the provider of the know-how may not want it to be used for or by its competitors. In as far as the know-how was not readily available to the buyer, is substantial and indispensable for the operation of the agreement, such a transfer may justify a non-compete type of restriction, which would normally fall outside Article 101(1).

(f) The "vertical externality issue". A retailer may not gain all the benefits of its action taken to improve sales; some may go to the manufacturer. For every extra unit a retailer sells by lowering its resale price or by increasing its sales effort, the manufacturer benefits if its wholesale price exceeds its marginal production costs. Thus, there may be a positive externality bestowed on the manufacturer by such retailer's actions and from the manufacturer's perspective the retailer may be pricing too high and/or making too little sales efforts. The negative externality of too high pricing by the retailer is sometimes called the "double marginalisation problem" and it can be avoided by imposing a maximum resale price on the retailer. To increase the retailer's sales efforts selective distribution, exclusive distribution or similar restrictions may be helpful.[41]

(g) "Economies of scale in distribution". In order to have scale economies exploited and thereby see a lower retail price for its product, the manufacturer may want to concentrate the resale of its products on a limited number of distributors. To do so, it could use exclusive distribution, quantity forcing in the form of a minimum purchasing requirement, selective distribution containing such a requirement or exclusive sourcing.

(h) "Capital market imperfections". The usual providers of capital (banks, equity markets) may provide capital sub-optimally when they have imperfect information on the quality of the borrower or there is an inadequate basis to secure the loan. The buyer or supplier may have better information and be able, through an exclusive relationship, to obtain extra security for its investment. Where the supplier provides the loan to the buyer, this may lead to non-compete or quantity forcing on the buyer. Where the buyer provides the loan to the supplier, this may be the reason for having exclusive supply or quantity forcing on the supplier.

(i) "Uniformity and quality standardisation". A vertical restraint may help to create a brand image by imposing a certain measure of uniformity and quality standardisation on the distributors, thereby increasing the attractiveness of the product to the final consumer and increasing its sales. This can for instance be found in selective distribution and franchising.

(108) The nine situations listed in paragraph (107) make clear that under certain conditions, vertical agreements are likely to help realise efficiencies and the development of new markets and that this may offset possible negative effects. The case is in general strongest for vertical restraints of a limited duration which help the introduction of new complex products or protect relationship-specific investments. A vertical restraint is sometimes necessary for as long as the supplier sells its product to the buyer (see in particular the situations described in paragraph (107)(a), (e), (f), (g) and (i)).

(109) A large measure of substitutability exists between the different vertical restraints. As a result, the same inefficiency problem can be solved by different vertical restraints. For instance, economies of scale in distribution may possibly be achieved by using exclusive distribution, selective distribution, quantity forcing or exclusive sourcing. However, the negative effects on competition may differ between the various vertical restraints, which plays a role when indispensability is discussed under Article 101(3).

1.3. Methodology of Analysis

(110) The assessment of a vertical restraint generally involves the following four steps:[42]

(a) First, the undertakings involved need to establish the market shares of the supplier and the buyer on the market where they respectively sell and purchase the contract products.

(b) If the relevant market share of the supplier and the buyer each do not exceed the 30% threshold, the vertical agreement is covered by the Block Exemption Regulation, subject to the hardcore restrictions and excluded restrictions set out in that Regulation.

(c) If the relevant market share is above the 30% threshold for supplier and/or buyer, it is necessary to assess whether the vertical agreement falls within Article 101(1).

(d) If the vertical agreement falls within Article 101(1), it is necessary to examine whether it fulfils the conditions for exemption under Article 101(3).

1.3.1.
Relevant factors for the assessment under Article 101(1)

(111) In assessing cases above the market share threshold of 30%, the Commission will undertake a full competition analysis. The following factors are particularly relevant to establish whether a vertical agreement brings about an appreciable restriction of competition under Article 101(1):

(a) nature of the agreement;
(b) market position of the parties;
(c) market position of competitors;
(d) market position of buyers of the contract products;

(e) entry barriers;
(f) maturity of the market;
(g) level of trade;
(h) nature of the product;
(i) other factors.

(112) The importance of individual factors may vary from case to case and depends on all other factors. For instance, a high market share of the parties is usually a good indicator of market power, but in the case of low entry barriers it may not be indicative of market power. It is therefore not possible to provide firm rules on the importance of the individual factors.

(113) Vertical agreements can take many shapes and forms. It is therefore important to analyse the nature of the agreement in terms of the restraints that it contains, the duration of those restraints and the percentage of total sales on the market affected by those restraints. It may be necessary to go beyond the express terms of the agreement. The existence of implicit restraints may be derived from the way in which the agreement is implemented by the parties and the incentives that they face.

(114) The market position of the parties provides an indication of the degree of market power, if any, possessed by the supplier, the buyer or both. The higher their market share, the greater their market power is likely to be. This is particularly so where the market share reflects cost advantages or other competitive advantages vis-à-vis competitors. Such competitive advantages may, for instance, result from being a first mover on the market (having the best site, etc), from holding essential patents or having superior technology, from being the brand leader or having a superior portfolio.

(115) Such indicators, namely market share and possible competitive advantages, are used to assess the market position of competitors. The stronger the competitors are and the greater their number, the less risk there is that the parties will be able to individually exercise market power and foreclose the market or soften competition. It is also relevant to consider whether there are effective and timely counterstrategies that competitors would be likely to deploy. However, if the number of competitors becomes rather small and their market position (size, costs, R&D potential, etc) is rather similar, such a market structure may increase the risk of collusion. Fluctuating or rapidly changing market shares are in general an indication of intense competition.

(116) The market position of the parties' customers provides an indication of whether or not one or more of those customers possess buyer power. The first indicator of buyer power is the market share of the customer on the purchase market. That share reflects the importance of its demand for possible suppliers. Other indicators focus on the position of the customer on its resale market, including characteristics such as a wide geographic spread of its outlets, own brands including private labels and its brand image amongst final consumers. In some circumstances, buyer power may prevent the parties from exercising market power and thereby solve a competition problem that would otherwise have existed. This is particularly so when strong customers have the capacity and incentive to bring new sources of supply on to the market in the case of a small but permanent increase in relative prices. Where strong customers merely extract favourable terms for themselves or simply pass on any price increase to their customers, their position does not prevent the parties from exercising market power.

(117) Entry barriers are measured by the extent to which incumbent companies can increase their price above the competitive level without attracting new entry. In the absence of entry barriers, easy and quick entry would render price increases unprofitable. When effective entry, preventing or eroding the exercise of market power, is likely to occur within one or two years, entry barriers can, as a general rule, be said to be low. Entry barriers may result from a wide variety of factors such as economies of scale and scope, government regulations, especially where they establish exclusive rights, state aid, import tariffs, intellectual property rights, ownership of resources where the supply is limited due to for instance natural limitations,[43] essential facilities, a first mover advantage and brand loyalty of consumers created by strong advertising over a period of time. Vertical restraints and vertical integration may also work as an entry barrier by making access more difficult and foreclosing (potential) competitors. Entry barriers may be present at only the supplier or buyer level or at both levels. The question whether certain of those factors should be described as entry barriers depends particularly on whether they entail sunk costs. Sunk costs are those costs that have to be incurred to enter or be active on a market but that are lost when the market is exited. Advertising costs to build consumer loyalty are normally sunk costs, unless an exiting firm could either sell its brand name or use it somewhere else without a loss. The more costs are sunk, the more potential entrants have to weigh the risks of entering the market and the more credibly incumbents can threaten that they will match new competition, as sunk costs make it costly for incumbents to leave the market. If, for instance, distributors are tied to a manufacturer via a non-compete obligation, the foreclosing effect will be more significant if setting up its own distributors will impose sunk costs on the potential entrant. In general, entry requires sunk costs, sometimes minor and sometimes major. Therefore, actual competition is in general more effective and will weigh more heavily in the assessment of a case than potential competition.

(118) A mature market is a market that has existed for some time, where the technology used is well known and widespread and not changing very much, where there are no major brand innovations and in which demand is relatively stable or declining. In such a market, negative effects are more likely than in more dynamic markets.

(119) The level of trade is linked to the distinction between intermediate and final goods and services. Intermediate goods and services are sold to undertakings for use as an input to produce other goods or services and are generally not recognisable in the final goods or services. The buyers of intermediate products are usually well-informed customers, able to assess quality and therefore less reliant on brand and image. Final goods are, directly or indirectly, sold to final consumers that often rely more on brand and image. As distributors have to respond to the demand of final consumers, competition may suffer more when distributors are foreclosed from selling one or a number of brands than when buyers of intermediate products are prevented from buying competing products from certain sources of supply.

(120) The nature of the product plays a role in particular for final products in assessing both the likely negative and the likely positive effects. When assessing the likely negative effects, it is important whether the products on the market are more homogeneous or heterogeneous, whether the product is expensive, taking up a large part of the consumer's budget, or is inexpensive and whether the product is a one-off purchase or repeatedly purchased. In general, when the product is more heterogeneous, less expensive and resembles more a one-off purchase, vertical restraints are more likely to have negative effects.

(121) In the assessment of particular restraints other factors may have to be taken into account. Among these factors can be the cumulative effect, that is, the coverage of the market by similar agreements of others, whether the agreement is "imposed" (mainly one party is subject to the restrictions or obligations) or "agreed" (both parties accept restrictions or obligations), the regulatory environment and behaviour that may indicate or facilitate collusion like price leadership, pre-announced price changes and discussions on the "right" price, price rigidity in response to excess capacity, price discrimination and past collusive behaviour.

1.3.2. Relevant factors for the assessment under Article 101(3)

(122) Restrictive vertical agreements may also produce pro-competitive effects in the form of efficiencies, which may outweigh their anti-competitive effects. Such an assessment takes place within the framework of Article 101(3), which contains an exception from the prohibition rule of Article 101(1). For that exception to be applicable, the vertical agreement must produce objective economic benefits, the restrictions on competition must be indispensable to attain the efficiencies, consumers must receive a fair share of the efficiency gains, and the agreement must not afford the parties the possibility of eliminating competition in respect of a substantial part of the products concerned.[44]

(123) The assessment of restrictive agreements under Article 101(3) is made within the actual context in which they occur[45] and on the basis of the facts existing at any given point in time. The assessment is sensitive to material changes in the facts. The exception rule of Article 101(3) applies as long as the four conditions are fulfilled and ceases to apply when that is no longer the case.[46] When applying Article 101(3) in accordance with these principles it is necessary to take into account the investments made by any of the parties and the time needed and the restraints required to commit and recoup an efficiency enhancing investment.

(124) The first condition of Article 101(3) requires an assessment of what are the objective benefits in terms of efficiencies produced by the agreement. In this respect, vertical agreements often have the potential to help realise efficiencies, as explained in section 1.2, by improving the way in which the parties conduct their complementary activities.

(125) In the application of the indispensability test contained in Article 101(3), the Commission will in particular examine whether individual restrictions make it possible to perform the production, purchase and/or (re)sale of the contract products more efficiently than would have been the case in the absence of the restriction concerned. In making such an assessment, the market conditions and the realities facing the parties must be taken into account. Undertakings invoking the benefit of Article 101(3) are not required to consider hypothetical and theoretical alternatives. They must, however, explain and demonstrate why seemingly realistic and significantly less restrictive alternatives would be significantly less efficient. If the application of what appears to be a commercially realistic and less restrictive alternative would lead to a significant loss of efficiencies, the restriction in question is treated as indispensable.

(126) The condition that consumers must receive a fair share of the benefits implies that consumers of the products purchased and/or (re)sold under the vertical agreement must at least be compensated for the negative effects of the agreement.[47] In other words, the efficiency gains must fully off-set the likely negative impact on prices, output and other relevant factors caused by the agreement.

(127) The last condition of Article 101(3), according to which the agreement must not afford the parties the possibility of eliminating competition in respect of a substantial part of the products concerned, presupposes an analysis of remaining competitive pressures on the market and the impact of the agreement on such sources of competition. In the application of the last condition of Article 101(3), the relationship between Article 101(3) and Article 102 must be taken into account. According to settled case law, the application of Article 101(3) cannot prevent the application of Article 102.[48] Moreover, since Articles 101 and 102 both pursue the aim of maintaining effective competition on the market, consistency requires that Article 101(3) be interpreted as precluding any application of the exception rule to restrictive agreements that constitute an abuse of a dominant position.[49] The vertical agreement may not eliminate effective competition, by removing all or most existing sources of actual or potential competition. Rivalry between undertakings is an essential driver of economic efficiency, including dynamic efficiencies in the form of innovation. In its absence, the dominant undertaking will lack adequate incentives to continue to create and pass on efficiency gains. Where there is no residual competition and no foreseeable threat of entry, the protection of rivalry and the competitive process outweighs possible efficiency gains. A restrictive agreement which maintains, creates or strengthens a market position approaching that of a monopoly can normally not be justified on the grounds that it also creates efficiency gains.

2. ANALYSIS OF SPECIFIC VERTICAL RESTRAINTS

(128) The most common vertical restraints and combinations of vertical restraints are analysed in the remainder of these Guidelines following the framework of analysis developed in paragraphs (96) to (127). Other restraints and combinations exist for which no direct guidance is provided in these Guidelines. They will, however, be treated according to the same principles and with the same emphasis on the effect on the market.

2.1. Single branding

(129) Under the heading of "single branding" fall those agreements which have as their main element the fact that the buyer is obliged or induced to concentrate its orders for a particular type of product with one supplier. That component can be found amongst others in non-compete and quantity-forcing on the buyer. A non-compete arrangement is based

on an obligation or incentive scheme which makes the buyer purchase more than 80% of its requirements on a particular market from only one supplier. It does not mean that the buyer can only buy directly from the supplier, but that the buyer will not buy and resell or incorporate competing goods or services. Quantity-forcing on the buyer is a weaker form of non-compete, where incentives or obligations agreed between the supplier and the buyer make the latter concentrate its purchases to a large extent with one supplier. Quantity-forcing may for example take the form of minimum purchase requirements, stocking requirements or non-linear pricing, such as conditional rebate schemes or a two-part tariff (fixed fee plus a price per unit). A so-called "English clause", requiring the buyer to report any better offer and allowing him only to accept such an offer when the supplier does not match it, can be expected to have the same effect as a single branding obligation, especially when the buyer has to reveal who makes the better offer.

(130) The possible competition risks of single branding are foreclosure of the market to competing suppliers and potential suppliers, softening of competition and facilitation of collusion between suppliers in case of cumulative use and, where the buyer is a retailer selling to final consumers, a loss of in-store inter-brand competition. Such restrictive effects have a direct impact on inter-brand competition.

(131) Single branding is exempted by the Block Exemption Regulation where the supplier's and buyer's market share each do not exceed 30% and are subject to a limitation in time of five years for the non-compete obligation. The remainder of this section provides guidance for the assessment of individual cases above the market share threshold or beyond the time limit of five years.

(132) The capacity for single branding obligations of one specific supplier to result in anticompetitive foreclosure arises in particular where, without the obligations, an important competitive constraint is exercised by competitors that either are not yet present on the market at the time the obligations are concluded, or that are not in a position to compete for the full supply of the customers. Competitors may not be able to compete for an individual customer's entire demand because the supplier in question is an unavoidable trading partner at least for part of the demand on the market, for instance because its brand is a 'must stock item' preferred by many final consumers or because the capacity constraints on the other suppliers are such that a part of demand can only be provided for by the supplier in question.[50] The market position of the supplier is thus of main importance to assess possible anti-competitive effects of single branding obligations.

(133) If competitors can compete on equal terms for each individual customer's entire demand, single branding obligations of one specific supplier are generally unlikely to hamper effective competition unless the switching of supplier by customers is rendered difficult due to the duration and market coverage of the single branding obligations. The higher its tied market share, that is, the part of its market share sold under a single branding obligation, the more significant foreclosure is likely to be. Similarly, the longer the duration of the single branding obligations, the more significant foreclosure is likely to be. Single branding obligations shorter than one year entered into by non-dominant companies are generally not considered to give rise to appreciable anti-competitive effects or net negative effects. Single branding obligations between one and five years entered into by non-dominant companies usually require a proper balancing of pro- and anti-competitive effects, while single branding obligations exceeding five years are for most types of investments not considered necessary to achieve the claimed efficiencies or the efficiencies are not sufficient to outweigh their foreclosure effect. Single branding obligations are more likely to result in anti-competitive foreclosure when entered into by dominant companies.

(134) When assessing the supplier's market power, the market position of its competitors is important. As long as the competitors are sufficiently numerous and strong, no appreciable anti-competitive effects can be expected. Foreclosure of competitors is not very likely where they have similar market positions and can offer similarly attractive products. In such a case, foreclosure may, however, occur for potential entrants when a number of major suppliers enter into single branding contracts with a significant number of buyers on the relevant market (cumulative effect situation). This is also a situation where single branding agreements may facilitate collusion between competing suppliers. If, individually, those suppliers are covered by the Block Exemption Regulation, a withdrawal of the block exemption may be necessary to deal with such a negative cumulative effect. A tied market share of less than 5% is not considered in general to contribute significantly to a cumulative foreclosure effect.

(135) In cases where the market share of the largest supplier is below 30% and the market share of the five largest suppliers is below 50%, there is unlikely to be a single or a cumulative anti-competitive effect situation. Where a potential entrant cannot penetrate the market profitably, it is likely to be due to factors other than single branding obligations, such as consumer preferences.

(136) Entry barriers are important to establish whether there is anticompetitive foreclosure. Wherever it is relatively easy for competing suppliers to create new buyers or find alternative buyers for their product, foreclosure is unlikely to be a real problem. However, there are often entry barriers, both at the manufacturing and at the distribution level.

(137) Countervailing power is relevant, as powerful buyers will not easily allow themselves to be cut off from the supply of competing goods or services. More generally, in order to convince customers to accept single branding, the supplier may have to compensate them, in whole or in part, for the loss in competition resulting from the exclusivity. Where such compensation is given, it may be in the individual interest of a customer to enter into a single branding obligation with the supplier. But it would be wrong to conclude automatically from this that all single branding obligations, taken together, are overall beneficial for customers on that market and for the final consumers. It is in particular unlikely that consumers as a whole will benefit if there are many customers and the single branding obligations, taken together, have the effect of preventing the entry or expansion of competing undertakings.

(138) Lastly, "the level of trade" is relevant. Anticompetitive foreclosure is less likely in case of an intermediate product. When the supplier of an intermediate product is not dominant, the competing suppliers still have a substantial part of demand that is free. Below the level of dominance an anticompetitive foreclosure effect may however arise in a cumulative effect situation. A cumulative anticompetitive effect is unlikely to arise as long as less than 50% of the market is tied.

(139) Where the agreement concerns the supply of a final product at the wholesale level, the question whether a competition problem is likely to arise depends in large part on the type of wholesaling and the entry barriers at the wholesale level. There is no real risk of anticompetitive foreclosure if competing manufacturers can easily establish their own wholesaling operation. Whether entry barriers are low depends in part on the type of wholesaling, that is, whether or not wholesalers can operate efficiently with only the product concerned by the agreement (for example ice cream) or whether it is more efficient to trade in a whole range of products (for example frozen foodstuffs). In the latter case, it is not efficient for a manufacturer selling only one product to set up its own wholesaling operation. In that case, anti-competitive effects may arise. In addition, cumulative effect problems may arise if several suppliers tie most of the available wholesalers.

(140) For final products, foreclosure is in general more likely to occur at the retail level, given the significant entry barriers for most manufacturers to start retail outlets just for their own products. In addition, it is at the retail level that single branding agreements may lead to reduced in-store inter-brand competition. It is for these reasons that for final products at the retail level, significant anti-competitive effects may start to arise, taking into account all other relevant factors, if a non-dominant supplier ties 30% or more of the relevant market. For a dominant company, even a modest tied market share may already lead to significant anti-competitive effects.

(141) At the retail level, a cumulative foreclosure effect may also arise. Where all suppliers have market shares below 30%, a cumulative anticompetitive foreclosure effect is unlikely if the total tied market share is less than 40% and withdrawal of the block exemption is therefore unlikely. That figure may be higher when other factors like the number of competitors, entry barriers etc are taken into account. Where not all companies have market shares below the threshold of the Block Exemption Regulation but none is dominant, a cumulative anticompetitive foreclosure effect is unlikely if the total tied market share is below 30%.

(142) Where the buyer operates from premises and land owned by the supplier or leased by the supplier from a third party not connected with the buyer, the possibility of imposing effective remedies for a possible foreclosure effect will be limited. In that case, intervention by the Commission below the level of dominance is unlikely.

(143) In certain sectors, the selling of more than one brand from a single site may be difficult, in which case a foreclosure problem can better be remedied by limiting the effective duration of contracts.

(144) Where appreciable anti-competitive effects are established, the question of a possible exemption under Article 101(3) arises. For non-compete obligations, the efficiencies described in points (a) (free riding between suppliers), (d), (e) (hold-up problems) and (h) (capital market imperfections) of paragraph (107), may be particularly relevant.

(145) In the case of an efficiency as described in paragraph (107)(a), (107)(d) and (107)(h), quantity forcing on the buyer could possibly be a less restrictive alternative. A non-compete obligation may be the only viable way to achieve an efficiency as described in paragraph (107)(e), (hold-up problem related to the transfer of know-how).

(146) In the case of a relationship-specific investment made by the supplier (see paragraph (107)(d)), a non-compete or quantity forcing agreement for the period of depreciation of the investment will in general fulfil the conditions of Article 101(3). In the case of high relationship-specific investments, a non-compete obligation exceeding five years may be justified. A relationship-specific investment could, for instance, be the installation or adaptation of equipment by the supplier when this equipment can be used afterwards only to produce components for a particular buyer. General or market-specific investments in (extra) capacity are normally not relationship-specific investments. However, where a supplier creates new capacity specifically linked to the operations of a particular buyer, for instance a company producing metal cans which creates new capacity to produce cans on the premises of or next to the canning facility of a food producer, this new capacity may only be economically viable when producing for this particular customer, in which case the investment would be considered to be relationship-specific.

(147) Where the supplier provides the buyer with a loan or provides the buyer with equipment which is not relationship-specific, this in itself is normally not sufficient to justify the exemption of an anticompetitive foreclosure effect on the market. In case of capital market imperfection, it may be more efficient for the supplier of a product than for a bank to provide a loan (see paragraph (107)(h)). However, in such a case the loan should be provided in the least restrictive way and the buyer should thus in general not be prevented from terminating the obligation and repaying the outstanding part of the loan at any point in time and without payment of any penalty.

(148) The transfer of substantial know-how (paragraph (107)(e)) usually justifies a non-compete obligation for the whole duration of the supply agreement, as for example in the context of franchising.

(149) *Example of non-compete obligation*

The market leader in a national market for an impulse consumer product, with a market share of 40%, sells most of its products (90%) through tied retailers (tied market share 36%). The agreements oblige the retailers to purchase only from the market leader for at least four years. The market leader is especially strongly represented in the more densely populated areas like the capital. Its competitors, 10 in number, of which some are only locally available, all have much smaller market shares, the biggest having 12%. Those 10 competitors together supply another 10% of the market via tied outlets. There is strong brand and product differentiation in the market. The market leader has the strongest brands. It is the only one with regular national advertising campaigns. It provides its tied retailers with special stocking cabinets for its product.

The result on the market is that in total 46% (36% + 10%) of the market is foreclosed to potential entrants and to incumbents not having tied outlets. Potential entrants find entry even more difficult in the densely populated areas where foreclosure is even higher, although it is there that they would prefer to enter the market. In addition, owing to the strong brand and product differentiation and the high search costs relative to the price of the product, the absence of in-store inter-brand competition leads to an extra welfare loss for consumers. The possible efficiencies of the outlet exclusivity, which the market leader claims result from reduced transport costs and a possible hold-up problem concerning the stocking cabinets, are limited and do not outweigh the negative effects on competition. The efficiencies are limited, as the transport costs are linked to quantity and not exclusivity and the stocking cabinets do not contain special know-how and are not brand specific. Accordingly, it is unlikely that the conditions of Article 101(3) are fulfilled.

(150) *Example of quantity forcing*

A producer X with a 40% market share sells 80% of its products through contracts which specify that the reseller is required to purchase at least 75% of its requirements for that type of product from X. In return X is offering financing and equipment at favourable rates. The contracts have a duration of five years in which repayment of the loan is foreseen in equal instalments. However, after the first two years buyers have the possibility to terminate the contract with a six-month notice period if they repay the outstanding loan and take over the equipment at its market asset value. At the end of the five-year period the equipment becomes the property of the buyer. Most of the competing producers are small, twelve in total with the biggest having a market share of 20%, and engage in similar contracts with different durations. The producers with market shares below 10% often have contracts with longer durations and with less generous termination clauses. The contracts of producer X leave 25% of requirements free to be supplied by competitors. In the last three years, two new producers have entered the market and gained a combined market share of around 8%, partly by taking over the loans of a number of resellers in return for contracts with these resellers.

Producer X's tied market share is 24% (0,75 × 0,80 × 40%). The other producers' tied market share is around 25%. Therefore, in total around 49% of the market is foreclosed to potential entrants and to incumbents not having tied outlets for at least the first two years of the supply contracts. The market shows that the resellers often have difficulty in obtaining loans from banks and are too small in general to obtain capital through other means like the issuing of shares. In addition, producer X is able to demonstrate that concentrating its sales on a limited number of resellers allows him to plan its sales better and to save transport costs. In the light of the efficiencies on the one hand and the 25% non-tied part in the contracts of producer X, the real possibility for early termination of the contract, the recent entry of new producers and the fact that around half the resellers are not tied on the other hand, the quantity forcing of 75% applied by producer X is likely to fulfil the conditions of Article 101(3).

2.2 Exclusive distribution

(151) In an exclusive distribution agreement, the supplier agrees to sell its products to only one distributor for resale in a particular territory. At the same time, the distributor is usually limited in its active selling into other (exclusively allocated) territories. The possible competition risks are mainly reduced intra-brand competition and market partitioning, which may facilitate price discrimination in particular. When most or all of the suppliers apply exclusive distribution, it may soften competition and facilitate collusion, both at the suppliers' and distributors' level. Lastly, exclusive distribution may lead to foreclosure of other distributors and therewith reduce competition at that level.

(152) Exclusive distribution is exempted by the Block Exemption Regulation where both the supplier's and buyer's market share each do not exceed 30%, even if combined with other non-hardcore vertical restraints, such as a non-compete obligation limited to five years, quantity forcing or exclusive purchasing. A combination of exclusive distribution and selective distribution is only exempted by the Block Exemption Regulation if active selling in other territories is not restricted. The remainder of this section provides guidance for the assessment of exclusive distribution in individual cases above the 30% market share threshold.

(153) The market position of the supplier and its competitors is of major importance, as the loss of intra-brand competition can only be problematic if inter-brand competition is limited. The stronger the position of the supplier, the more serious is the loss of intra-brand competition. Above the 30% market share threshold, there may be a risk of a significant reduction of intra-brand competition. In order to fulfil the conditions of Article 101(3), the loss of intra-brand competition may need to be balanced with real efficiencies.

(154) The position of the competitors can have a dual significance. Strong competitors will generally mean that the reduction in intra-brand competition is outweighed by sufficient inter-brand competition. However, if the number of competitors becomes rather small and their market position is rather similar in terms of market share, capacity and distribution network, there is a risk of collusion and/or softening of competition. The loss of intra-brand competition can increase that risk, especially when several suppliers operate similar distribution systems. Multiple exclusive dealerships, that is, when different suppliers appoint the same exclusive distributor in a given territory, may further increase the risk of collusion and/or softening of competition. If a dealer is granted the exclusive right to distribute two or more important competing products in the same territory, inter-brand competition may be substantially restricted for those brands. The higher the cumulative market share of the brands distributed by the exclusive multiple brand dealers, the higher the risk of collusion and/or softening of competition and the more inter-brand competition will be reduced. If a retailer is the exclusive distributor for a number of brands this may have as result that if one producer cuts the wholesale price for its brand, the exclusive retailer will not be eager to transmit this price cut to the final consumer as it would reduce its sales and profits made with the other brands. Hence, compared to the situation without multiple exclusive dealerships, producers have a reduced interest in entering into price competition with one another. Such cumulative effect situations may be a reason to withdraw the benefit of the Block Exemption Regulation where the market shares of the suppliers and buyers are below the threshold of the Block Exemption Regulation.

(155) Entry barriers that may hinder suppliers from creating new distributors or finding alternative distributors are less important in assessing the possible anti-competitive effects of exclusive distribution. Foreclosure of other suppliers does not arise as long as exclusive distribution is not combined with single branding.

(156) Foreclosure of other distributors is not an issue where the supplier which operates the exclusive distribution system appoints a high number of exclusive distributors on the same market and those exclusive distributors are not restricted in selling to other non-appointed distributors. Foreclosure of other distributors may however become an issue where there is buying power and market power downstream, in particular in the case of very large territories where the exclusive distributor becomes the exclusive buyer for a whole market. An example would be a supermarket chain which becomes the only distributor of a leading brand on a national food retail market. The foreclosure of other distributors may be aggravated in the case of multiple exclusive dealership.

(157) Buying power may also increase the risk of collusion on the buyers' side when the exclusive distribution arrangements are imposed by important buyers, possibly located in different territories, on one or several suppliers.

(158) Maturity of the market is important, as loss of intra-brand competition and price discrimination may be a serious problem in a mature market but may be less relevant on a market with growing demand, changing technologies and changing market positions.

(159) The level of trade is important as the possible negative effects may differ between the wholesale and retail level. Exclusive distribution is mainly applied in the distribution of final goods and services. A loss of intra-brand competition is especially likely at the retail level if coupled with large territories, since final consumers may be confronted with little possibility of choosing between a high price/high service and a low price/low service distributor for an important brand.

(160) A manufacturer that chooses a wholesaler to be its exclusive distributor will normally do so for a larger territory, such as a whole Member State. As long as the wholesaler can sell the products without limitation to downstream retailers there are not likely to be appreciable anti-competitive effects. A possible loss of intra-brand competition at the wholesale level may be easily outweighed by efficiencies obtained in logistics, promotion etc, especially when the manufacturer is based in a different country. The possible risks for inter-brand competition of multiple exclusive dealerships are however higher at the wholesale than at the retail level. Where one wholesaler becomes the exclusive distributor for a significant number of suppliers, not only is there a risk that competition between these brands is reduced, but also that there is foreclosure at the wholesale level of trade.

(161) As stated in paragraph (155), foreclosure of other suppliers does not arise as long as exclusive distribution is not combined with single branding. But even when exclusive distribution is combined with single branding anticompetitive foreclosure of other suppliers is unlikely, except possibly when the single branding is applied to a dense network of exclusive distributors with small territories or in case of a cumulative effect. In such a case it may be necessary to apply the principles on single branding set out in section 2.1. However, when the combination does not lead to significant foreclosure, the combination of exclusive distribution and single branding may be pro-competitive by increasing the incentive for the exclusive distributor to focus its efforts on the particular brand. Therefore, in the absence of such a foreclosure effect, the combination of exclusive distribution with non-compete may very well fulfil the conditions of Article 101(3) for the whole duration of the agreement, particularly at the wholesale level.

(162) The combination of exclusive distribution with exclusive sourcing increases the possible competition risks of reduced intra-brand competition and market partitioning which may facilitate price discrimination in particular. Exclusive distribution already limits arbitrage by customers, as it limits the number of distributors and usually also restricts the distributors in their freedom of active selling. Exclusive sourcing, requiring the exclusive distributors to buy their supplies for the particular brand directly from the manufacturer, eliminates in addition possible arbitrage by the exclusive distributors, which are prevented from buying from other distributors in the system. As a result, the supplier's possibilities to limit intra-brand competition by applying dissimilar conditions of sale to the detriment of consumers are enhanced, unless the combination allows the creation of efficiencies leading to lower prices to all final consumers.

(163) The nature of the product is not particularly relevant to the assessment of possible anti-competitive effects of exclusive distribution. It is, however, relevant to an assessment of possible efficiencies, that is, after an appreciable anti-competitive effect is established.

(164) Exclusive distribution may lead to efficiencies, especially where investments by the distributors are required to protect or build up the brand image. In general, the case for efficiencies is strongest for new products, complex products, and products whose qualities are difficult to judge before consumption (so-called experience products) or whose qualities are difficult to judge even after consumption (so-called credence products). In addition, exclusive distribution may lead to savings in logistic costs due to economies of scale in transport and distribution.

(165) *Example of exclusive distribution at the wholesale level*

On the market for a consumer durable, A is the market leader. A sells its product through exclusive wholesalers. Territories for the wholesalers correspond to the entire Member State for small Member States, and to a region for larger Member States. Those exclusive distributors deal with sales to all the retailers in their territories. They do not sell to final consumers. The wholesalers are in charge of promotion in their markets, including sponsoring of local events, but also explaining and promoting the new products to the retailers in their territories. Technology and product innovation are evolving fairly quickly on this market, and pre-sale service to retailers and to final consumers plays an important role. The wholesalers are not required to purchase all their requirements of the brand of supplier A from the producer himself, and arbitrage by wholesalers or retailers is practicable because the transport costs are relatively low compared to the value of the product. The wholesalers are not under a non-compete obligation. Retailers also sell a number of brands of competing suppliers, and there are no exclusive or selective distribution agreements at the retail level. On the EU market of sales to wholesalers A has around 50% market share. Its market share on the various national retail markets varies between 40% and 60%. A has between 6 and 10 competitors on every national market. B, C and D are its biggest competitors and are also present on each national market, with market shares varying between 20% and 5%. The remaining producers are national producers, with smaller market shares. B, C and D have similar distribution networks, whereas the local producers tend to sell their products directly to retailers.

On the wholesale market described in this example, the risk of reduced intra-brand competition and price discrimination is low. Arbitrage is not hindered, and the absence of intra-brand competition is not very relevant at the wholesale level. At the retail level, neither intra- nor inter-brand competition are hindered. Moreover, inter-brand competition is largely unaffected by the exclusive arrangements at the wholesale level. Therefore it is likely, even if anti-competitive effects exist, that also the conditions of Article 101(3) are fulfilled.

(166) *Example of multiple exclusive dealerships in an oligopolistic market*

On a national market for a final product, there are four market leaders, which each have a market share of around 20%. Those four market leaders sell their product through exclusive distributors at the retail level. Retailers are given an exclusive territory which corresponds to the town in which they are located or a district of the town for large towns. In most territories, the four market leaders happen to appoint the same exclusive retailer ("multiple dealership"), often centrally located and rather specialised in the product. The remaining 20% of the national market is composed of small local producers, the largest of these producers having a market share of 5% on the national market. Those local producers sell their products in general through other retailers, in particular because the exclusive distributors of the four largest suppliers show in general little interest in selling less well-known and cheaper brands. There is strong brand and product differentiation on the market. The four market leaders have large national advertising campaigns and strong brand images, whereas the fringe producers do not advertise their products at the national level. The market is rather mature, with stable demand and no major product and technological innovation. The product is relatively simple.

In such an oligopolistic market, there is a risk of collusion between the four market leaders. That risk is increased through multiple dealerships. Intra-brand competition is limited by the territorial exclusivity. Competition between the four leading brands is reduced at the retail level, since one retailer fixes the price of all four brands in each territory. The multiple dealership implies that, if one producer cuts the price for its brand, the retailer will not be eager to transmit this price cut to the final consumer as it would reduce its sales and profits made with the other brands. Hence, producers have a reduced interest in entering into price competition with one another. Inter-brand price competition exists mainly with the low brand image goods of the fringe producers. The possible efficiency arguments for (joint) exclusive distributors are limited, as the product is relatively simple, the resale does not require any specific investments or training and advertising is mainly carried out at the level of the producers.

Even though each of the market leaders has a market share below the threshold, the conditions of Article 101(3) may not be fulfilled and withdrawal of the block exemption may be necessary for the agreements concluded with distributors whose market share is below 30% of the procurement market.

(167) *Example of exclusive distribution combined with exclusive sourcing*

Manufacturer A is the European market leader for a bulky consumer durable, with a market share of between 40% and 60% in most national retail markets. In Member States where it has a high market share, it has less competitors with much smaller market shares. The competitors are present on only one or two national markets. A's long time policy is to sell its product through its national subsidiaries to exclusive distributors at the retail level, which are not allowed to sell actively into each other's territories. Those distributors are thereby incentivised to promote the product and provide pre-sales services. Recently the retailers are in addition obliged to purchase manufacturer A's products exclusively from the national subsidiary of manufacturer A in their own country. The retailers selling the brand of manufacturer A are the main resellers of that type of product in their territory. They handle competing brands, but with varying degrees of success and enthusiasm. Since the introduction of exclusive sourcing, A applies price differences of 10% to 15% between markets with higher prices in the markets where it has less competition. The markets are relatively stable on the demand and the supply side, and there are no significant technological changes.

In the high price markets, the loss of intra-brand competition results not only from the territorial exclusivity at the retail level but is aggravated by the exclusive sourcing obligation imposed on the retailers. The exclusive sourcing obligation helps to keep markets and territories separate by making arbitrage between the exclusive retailers, the main resellers of that type of product, impossible. The exclusive retailers also cannot sell actively into each other's territory and in practice tend to avoid delivering outside their own territory. As a result, price discrimination is possible, without it leading to a significant increase in total sales. Arbitrage by consumers or independent traders is limited due to the bulkiness of the product.

While the possible efficiency arguments for appointing exclusive distributors may be convincing, in particular because of the incentivising of retailers, the possible efficiency arguments for the combination of exclusive distribution and exclusive sourcing, and in particular the possible efficiency arguments for exclusive sourcing, linked mainly to economies of scale in transport, are unlikely to outweigh the negative effect of price discrimination and reduced intra-brand competition. Consequently, it is unlikely that the conditions of Article 101(3) are fulfilled.

2.3. Exclusive customer allocation

(168) In an exclusive customer allocation agreement, the supplier agrees to sell its products to only one distributor for resale to a particular group of customers. At the same time, the distributor is usually limited in its active selling to other (exclusively allocated) groups of customers. The Block Exemption Regulation does not limit the way an exclusive customer group can be defined; it could for instance be a particular type of customers defined by their occupation but also a list of specific customers selected on the basis of one or more objective criteria. The possible competition risks are mainly reduced intra-brand competition and market partitioning, which may in particular facilitate price discrimination. Where most or all of the suppliers apply exclusive customer allocation, competition may be softened and collusion, both at the suppliers' and the distributors' level, may be facilitated. Lastly, exclusive customer allocation may lead to foreclosure of other distributors and therewith reduce competition at that level.

(169) Exclusive customer allocation is exempted by the Block Exemption Regulation when both the supplier's and buyer's market share does not exceed the 30% market share threshold, even if combined with other non-hardcore vertical restraints such as non-compete, quantity-forcing or exclusive sourcing. A combination of exclusive customer allocation and selective distribution is normally a hardcore restriction, as active selling to end-users by the appointed distributors is usually not left free. Above the 30% market share threshold, the guidance provided in paragraphs (151) to (167) applies also to the assessment of exclusive customer allocation, subject to the specific remarks in the remainder of this section.

(170) The allocation of customers normally makes arbitrage by the customers more difficult. In addition, as each appointed distributor has its own class of customers, non-appointed distributors not falling within such a class may find it difficult to obtain the product. Consequently, possible arbitrage by non-appointed distributors will be reduced.

(171) Exclusive customer allocation is mainly applied to intermediate products and at the wholesale level when it concerns final products, where customer groups with different specific requirements concerning the product can be distinguished.

(172) Exclusive customer allocation may lead to efficiencies, especially when the distributors are required to make investments in for instance specific equipment, skills or know-how to adapt to the requirements of their group of customers. The depreciation period of these investments indicates the justified duration of an exclusive customer allocation system. In general the case is strongest for new or complex products and for products requiring adaptation to the needs of the individual customer. Identifiable differentiated needs are more likely for intermediate products, that is, products sold to different types of professional buyers. Allocation of final consumers is unlikely to lead to efficiencies.

(173) *Example of exclusive customer allocation*

A company has developed a sophisticated sprinkler installation. The company has currently a market share of 40% on the market for sprinkler installations. When it started selling the sophisticated sprinkler it had a market share of 20% with an older product. The installation of the new type of sprinkler depends on the type of building that it is installed in and on the use of the building (office, chemical plant, hospital etc). The company has appointed a number of distributors to sell and install the sprinkler installation. Each distributor needed to train its employees for the general and specific requirements of installing the sprinkler installation for a particular class of customers. To ensure that distributors would specialise, the company assigned to each distributor an exclusive class of customers and prohibited active sales to each others' exclusive customer classes. After five years, all the exclusive distributors will be allowed to sell actively to all classes of customers, thereby ending the system of exclusive customer allocation. The supplier may then also start selling to new distributors. The market is quite dynamic, with two recent entries and a number of technological developments. Competitors, with market shares between 25% and 5%, are also upgrading their products.

As the exclusivity is of limited duration and helps to ensure that the distributors may recoup their investments and concentrate their sales efforts first on a certain class of customers in order to learn the trade, and as the possible anti-competitive effects seem limited in a dynamic market, the conditions of Article 101(3) are likely to be fulfilled.

2.4. SELECTIVE DISTRIBUTION

(174) Selective distribution agreements, like exclusive distribution agreements, restrict the number of authorised distributors on the one hand and the possibilities of resale on the other. The difference with exclusive distribution is that the restriction of the number of dealers does not depend on the number of territories but on selection criteria linked in the first place to the nature of the product. Another difference with exclusive distribution is that the restriction on resale is not a restriction on active selling to a territory but a restriction on any sales to non-authorised distributors, leaving only appointed dealers and final customers as possible buyers. Selective distribution is almost always used to distribute branded final products.

(175) The possible competition risks are a reduction in intra-brand competition and, especially in case of cumulative effect, foreclosure of certain type(s) of distributors and softening of competition and facilitation of collusion between suppliers or buyers. To assess the possible anti-competitive effects of selective distribution under Article 101(1), a distinction needs to be made between purely qualitative selective distribution and quantitative selective distribution. Purely qualitative selective distribution selects dealers only on the basis of objective criteria required by the nature of the product such as training of sales personnel, the service provided at the point of sale, a certain range of the products being sold etc[51] The application of such criteria does not put a direct limit on the number of dealers. Purely qualitative selective distribution is in general considered to fall outside Article 101(1) for lack of anti-competitive effects, provided that three conditions are satisfied. First, the nature of the product in question must necessitate a selective distribution system, in the sense that such a system must constitute a legitimate requirement, having regard to the nature of the product concerned, to preserve its quality and ensure its proper use. Secondly, resellers must be chosen on the basis of objective criteria of a qualitative nature which are laid down uniformly for all and made available to all potential resellers and are not applied in a discriminatory manner. Thirdly, the criteria laid down must not go beyond what is necessary.[52] Quantitative selective distribution adds further criteria for selection that more directly limit the potential number of dealers by, for instance, requiring minimum or maximum sales, by fixing the number of dealers, etc.

(176) Qualitative and quantitative selective distribution is exempted by the Block Exemption Regulation as long as the market share of both supplier and buyer each do not exceed 30%, even if combined with other non-hardcore vertical restraints, such as non-compete or exclusive distribution, provided active selling by the authorised distributors to each other and to end users is not restricted. The Block Exemption Regulation exempts selective distribution regardless of the nature of the product concerned and regardless of the nature of the selection criteria. However, where the characteristics of the product[53] do not require selective distribution or do not require the applied criteria, such as for instance the requirement for distributors to have one or more brick and mortar shops or to provide specific services, such a distribution system does not generally bring about sufficient efficiency enhancing effects to counterbalance a significant reduction in intra-brand competition. Where appreciable anti-competitive effects occur, the benefit of the Block Exemption Regulation is likely to be withdrawn. In addition, the remainder of this section provides guidance for the assessment of selective distribution in individual cases which are not covered by the Block Exemption Regulation or in the case of cumulative effects resulting from parallel networks of selective distribution.

(177) The market position of the supplier and its competitors is of central importance in assessing possible anti-competitive effects, as the loss of intra-brand competition can only be problematic if inter-brand competition is limited. The stronger the position of the supplier, the more problematic is the loss of intra-brand competition. Another important factor is the number of selective distribution networks present in the same market. Where selective distribution is applied by only one supplier on the market, quantitative selective distribution does not normally create

net negative effects provided that the contract goods, having regard to their nature, require the use of a selective distribution system and on condition that the selection criteria applied are necessary to ensure efficient distribution of the goods in question. The reality, however, seems to be that selective distribution is often applied by a number of the suppliers on a given market.

(178) The position of competitors can have a dual significance and plays in particular a role in case of a cumulative effect. Strong competitors will mean in general that the reduction in intra-brand competition is easily outweighed by sufficient inter-brand competition. However, when a majority of the main suppliers apply selective distribution, there will be a significant loss of intra-brand competition and possible foreclosure of certain types of distributors as well as an increased risk of collusion between those major suppliers. The risk of foreclosure of more efficient distributors has always been greater with selective distribution than with exclusive distribution, given the restriction on sales to non-authorised dealers in selective distribution. That restriction is designed to give selective distribution systems a closed character, making it impossible for non-authorised dealers to obtain supplies. Accordingly, selective distribution is particularly well suited to avoid pressure by price discounters (whether offline or online-only distributors) on the margins of the manufacturer, as well as on the margins of the authorised dealers. Foreclosure of such distribution formats, whether resulting from the cumulative application of selective distribution or from the application by a single supplier with a market share exceeding 30%, reduces the possibilities for consumers to take advantage of the specific benefits offered by these formats such as lower prices, more transparency and wider access.

(179) Where the Block Exemption Regulation applies to individual networks of selective distribution, withdrawal of the block exemption or disapplication of the Block Exemption Regulation may be considered in case of cumulative effects. However, a cumulative effect problem is unlikely to arise when the share of the market covered by selective distribution is below 50%. Also, no problem is likely to arise where the market coverage ratio exceeds 50%, but the aggregate market share of the five largest suppliers (CR5) is below 50%. Where both the CR5 and the share of the market covered by selective distribution exceed 50%, the assessment may vary depending on whether or not all five largest suppliers apply selective distribution. The stronger the position of the competitors which do not apply selective distribution, the less likely other distributors will be foreclosed. If all five largest suppliers apply selective distribution, competition concerns may arise with respect to those agreements in particular that apply quantitative selection criteria by directly limiting the number of authorised dealers or that apply qualitative criteria, such as a requirement to have one or more brick and mortar shops or to provide specific services, which forecloses certain distribution formats. The conditions of Article 101(3) are in general unlikely to be fulfilled if the selective distribution systems at issue prevent access to the market by new distributors capable of adequately selling the products in question, especially price discounters or online-only distributors offering lower prices to consumers, thereby limiting distribution to the advantage of certain existing channels and to the detriment of final consumers. More indirect forms of quantitative selective distribution, resulting for instance from the combination of purely qualitative selection criteria with the requirement imposed on the dealers to achieve a minimum amount of annual purchases, are less likely to produce net negative effects, if such an amount does not represent a significant proportion of the dealer's total turnover achieved with the type of products in question and it does not go beyond what is necessary for the supplier to recoup its relationship-specific investment and/or realise economies of scale in distribution. As regards individual contributions, a supplier with a market share of less than 5% is in general not considered to contribute significantly to a cumulative effect.

(180) Entry barriers are mainly of interest in the case of foreclosure of the market to non-authorised dealers. In general, entry barriers will be considerable as selective distribution is usually applied by manufacturers of branded products. It will in general take time and considerable investment for excluded retailers to launch their own brands or obtain competitive supplies elsewhere.

(181) Buying power may increase the risk of collusion between dealers and thus appreciably change the analysis of possible anti-competitive effects of selective distribution. Foreclosure of the market to more efficient retailers may especially result where a strong dealer organisation imposes selection criteria on the supplier aimed at limiting distribution to the advantage of its members.

(182) Article 5(1)(c) of the Block Exemption Regulation provides that the supplier may not impose an obligation causing the authorised dealers, either directly or indirectly, not to sell the brands of particular competing suppliers. Such a condition aims specifically at avoiding horizontal collusion to exclude particular brands through the creation of a selective club of brands by the leading suppliers. That kind of obligation is unlikely to be exemptible when the CR5 is equal to or above 50%, unless none of the suppliers imposing such an obligation belongs to the five largest suppliers on the market.

(183) Foreclosure of other suppliers is normally not a problem as long as other suppliers can use the same distributors, that is, as long as the selective distribution system is not combined with single branding. In the case of a dense network of authorised distributors or in the case of a cumulative effect, the combination of selective distribution and a non-compete obligation may pose a risk of foreclosure to other suppliers. In that case, the principles set out in section 2.1. on single branding apply. Where selective distribution is not combined with a non-compete obligation, foreclosure of the market to competing suppliers may still be a problem where the leading suppliers apply not only purely qualitative selection criteria, but impose on their dealers certain additional obligations such as the obligation to reserve a minimum shelf-space for their products or to ensure that the sales of their products by the dealer achieve a minimum percentage of the dealer's total turnover. Such a problem is unlikely to arise if the share of the market covered by selective distribution is below 50% or, where this coverage ratio is exceeded, if the market share of the five largest suppliers is below 50%.

(184) Maturity of the market is important, as loss of intra-brand competition and possible foreclosure of suppliers or dealers may be a serious problem on a mature market but is less relevant on a market with growing demand, changing technologies and changing market positions.

(185) Selective distribution may be efficient when it leads to savings in logistical costs due to economies of scale in transport and that may occur irrespective of the nature of the product (paragraph (107)(g)). However, such an efficiency is usually only marginal in selective distribution systems. To help solve a free-rider problem between the distributors (paragraph (107)(a)) or to help create a brand image (paragraph (107)(i)), the nature of the product is very relevant. In general, the case is strongest for new products, complex products, products whose qualities are difficult to judge before consumption (so-called experience products) or whose qualities are difficult to judge even after consumption (so-called credence products). The combination of selective distribution with a location clause, protecting an appointed dealer against other appointed dealers opening up a shop in its vicinity, may in particular fulfil the conditions of Article 101(3) if the combination is indispensable to protect substantial and relationship-specific investments made by the authorised dealer (paragraph (107)(d)).

(186) To ensure that the least anti-competitive restraint is chosen, it is relevant to see whether the same efficiencies can be obtained at a comparable cost by for instance service requirements alone.

(187) *Example of quantitative selective distribution*

On a market for consumer durables, the market leader (brand A) with a market share of 35%, sells its product to final consumers through a selective distribution network. There are several criteria for admission to the network: the shop must employ trained staff and provide pre-sales services, there must be a specialised area in the shop devoted to the sales of the product and similar hi-tech products, and the shop is required to sell a wide range of models of the supplier and to display them in an attractive manner. Moreover, the number of admissible retailers in the network is directly limited through the establishment of a maximum number of retailers per number of inhabitants in each province or urban area. Manufacturer A has 6 competitors in that market. Its largest competitors, B, C and D, have market shares of respectively 25, 15 and 10%, whilst the other producers have smaller market shares. A is the only manufacturer to use selective distribution. The selective distributors of brand A always handle a few competing brands. However, competing brands are also widely sold in shops which are not member of A's selective distribution network. Channels of distribution are various: for instance, brands B and C are sold in most of A's selected shops, but also in other shops providing a high quality service and in hypermarkets. Brand D is mainly sold in high service shops. Technology is evolving quite rapidly in this market, and the main suppliers maintain a strong quality image for their products through advertising.

On that market, the coverage ratio of selective distribution is 35%. Inter-brand competition is not directly affected by the selective distribution system of A. Intra-brand competition for brand A may be reduced, but consumers have access to low service/low price retailers for brands B and C, which have a comparable quality image to brand A. Moreover, access to high service retailers for other brands is not foreclosed, since there is no limitation on the capacity of selected distributors to sell competing brands, and the quantitative limitation on the number of retailers for brand A leaves other high service retailers free to distribute competing brands. In this case, in view of the service requirements and the efficiencies these are likely to provide and the limited effect on intra-brand competition the conditions of Article 101(3) are likely to be fulfilled.

(188) *Example of selective distribution with cumulative effects*

On a market for a particular sports article, there are seven manufacturers, whose respective market shares are: 25%, 20%, 15%, 15%, 10%, 8% and 7%. The five largest manufacturers distribute their products through quantitative selective distribution, whilst the two smallest use different types of distribution systems, which results in a coverage ratio of selective distribution of 85%. The criteria for access to the selective distribution networks are remarkably uniform amongst manufacturers: the distributors are required to have one or more brick and mortar shops, those shops are required to have trained personnel and to provide pre-sale services, there must be a specialised area in the shop devoted to the sales of the article and a minimum size for this area is specified. The shop is required to sell a wide range of the brand in question and to display the article in an attractive manner, the shop must be located in a commercial street, and that type of article must represent at least 30% of the total turnover of the shop. In general, the same dealer is appointed selective distributor for all five brands. The two brands which do not use selective distribution usually sell through less specialised retailers with lower service levels. The market is stable, both on the supply and on the demand side, and there is strong brand image and product differentiation. The five market leaders have strong brand images, acquired through advertising and sponsoring, whereas the two smaller manufacturers have a strategy of cheaper products, with no strong brand image.

On that market, access by general price discounters and online-only distributors to the five leading brands is denied. Indeed, the requirement that this type of article represents at least 30% of the activity of the dealers and the criteria on presentation and pre-sales services rule out most price discounters from the network of authorised dealers. The requirement to have one or more brick and mortar shops excludes online-only distributors from the network. As a consequence, consumers have no choice but to buy the five leading brands in high service/high price shops. This leads to reduced inter-brand competition between the five leading brands. The fact that the two smallest brands can be bought in low service/low price shops does not compensate for this, because the brand image of the five market leaders is much better. Inter-brand competition is also limited through multiple dealership. Even though there exists some degree of intra-brand competition and the number of retailers is not directly limited, the criteria for admission are strict enough to lead to a small number of retailers for the five leading brands in each territory.

The efficiencies associated with these quantitative selective distribution systems are low: the product is not very complex and does not justify a particularly high service. Unless the manufacturers can prove that there are clear efficiencies linked to their network of selective distribution, it is probable that the block exemption will have to be withdrawn because of its cumulative effects resulting in less choice and higher prices for consumers.

2.5. Franchising

(189) Franchise agreements contain licences of intellectual property rights relating in particular to trade marks or signs and know-how for the use and distribution of goods or services. In addition to the licence of IPRs, the franchisor usually provides the franchisee during the life of the agreement with commercial or technical assistance. The licence and the assistance are integral components of the business method being franchised. The franchisor is in general paid

a franchise fee by the franchisee for the use of the particular business method. Franchising may enable the franchisor to establish, with limited investments, a uniform network for the distribution of its products. In addition to the provision of the business method, franchise agreements usually contain a combination of different vertical restraints concerning the products being distributed, in particular selective distribution and/or non-compete and/or exclusive distribution or weaker forms thereof.

(190) The coverage by the Block Exemption Regulation of the licensing of IPRs contained in franchise agreements is dealt with in paragraphs (24) to (46). As for the vertical restraints on the purchase, sale and resale of goods and services within a franchising arrangement, such as selective distribution, non-compete obligations or exclusive distribution, the Block Exemption Regulation applies up to the 30% market share threshold.[54] The guidance provided in respect of those types of restraints applies also to franchising, subject to the following two specific remarks:

(a) The more important the transfer of know-how, the more likely it is that the restraints create efficiencies and/or are indispensable to protect the know-how and that the vertical restraints fulfil the conditions of Article 101(3);

(b) A non-compete obligation on the goods or services purchased by the franchisee falls outside the scope of Article 101(1) where the obligation is necessary to maintain the common identity and reputation of the franchised network. In such cases, the duration of the non-compete obligation is also irrelevant under Article 101(1), as long as it does not exceed the duration of the franchise agreement itself.

(191) *Example of franchising*

A manufacturer has developed a new format for selling sweets in so-called fun shops where the sweets can be coloured specially on demand from the consumer. The manufacturer of the sweets has also developed the machines to colour the sweets. The manufacturer also produces the colouring liquids. The quality and freshness of the liquid is of vital importance to producing good sweets. The manufacturer made a success of its sweets through a number of own retail outlets all operating under the same trade name and with the uniform fun image (style of lay-out of the shops, common advertising etc). In order to expand sales the manufacturer started a franchising system. The franchisees are obliged to buy the sweets, liquid and colouring machine from the manufacturer, to have the same image and operate under the trade name, pay a franchise fee, contribute to common advertising and ensure the confidentiality of the operating manual prepared by the franchisor. In addition, the franchisees are only allowed to sell from the agreed premises, to sell to end users or other franchisees and are not allowed to sell other sweets. The franchisor is obliged not to appoint another franchisee nor operate a retail outlet himself in a given contract territory. The franchisor is also under the obligation to update and further develop its products, the business outlook and the operating manual and make these improvements available to all retail franchisees. The franchise agreements are concluded for a duration of 10 years.

Sweet retailers buy their sweets on a national market from either national producers that cater for national tastes or from wholesalers which import sweets from foreign producers in addition to selling products from national producers. On that market the franchisor's products compete with other brands of sweets. The franchisor has a market share of 30% on the market for sweets sold to retailers. Competition comes from a number of national and international brands, sometimes produced by large diversified food companies. There are many potential points of sale of sweets in the form of tobacconists, general food retailers, cafeterias and specialised sweet shops. The franchisor's market share of the market for machines for colouring food is below 10%.

Most of the obligations contained in the franchise agreements can be deemed necessary to protect the intellectual property rights or maintain the common identity and reputation of the franchised network and fall outside Article 101(1). The restrictions on selling (contract territory and selective distribution) provide an incentive to the franchisees to invest in the colouring machine and the franchise concept and, if not necessary to, at least help maintain the common identity, thereby offsetting the loss of intra-brand competition. The non-compete clause excluding other brands of sweets from the shops for the full duration of the agreements does allow the franchisor to keep the outlets uniform and prevent competitors from benefiting from its trade name. It does not lead to any serious foreclosure in view of the great number of potential outlets available to other sweet producers. The franchise agreements of this franchisor are likely to fulfil the conditions for exemption under Article 101(3) in as far as the obligations contained therein fall under Article 101(1).

2.6 Exclusive supply

(192) Under the heading of exclusive supply fall those restrictions that have as their main element that the supplier is obliged or induced to sell the contract products only or mainly to one buyer, in general or for a particular use. Such restrictions may take the form of an exclusive supply obligation, restricting the supplier to sell to only one buyer for the purposes of resale or a particular use, but may for instance also take the form of quantity forcing on the supplier, where incentives are agreed between the supplier and buyer which make the former concentrate its sales mainly with one buyer. For intermediate goods or services, exclusive supply is often referred to as industrial supply.

(193) Exclusive supply is exempted by the Block Exemption Regulation where both the supplier's and buyer's market share does not exceed 30%, even if combined with other non-hardcore vertical restraints such as non-compete. The remainder of this section provides guidance for the assessment of exclusive supply in individual cases above the market share threshold.

(194) The main competition risk of exclusive supply is anticompetitive foreclosure of other buyers. There is a similarity with the possible effects of exclusive distribution, in particular when the exclusive distributor becomes the exclusive buyer for a whole market (see section 2.2, in particular paragraph (156)). The market share of the buyer on the upstream purchase market is obviously important for assessing the ability of the buyer to impose exclusive supply which forecloses other buyers from access to supplies. The importance of the buyer on the downstream market is however the factor which determines whether a competition problem may arise. If the buyer has no market power downstream, then no appreciable negative effects for consumers can be expected. Negative effects may arise when the market share of the buyer on the downstream supply market as well as the upstream purchase market exceeds 30%. Where the market share of the buyer on the upstream market does not exceed 30%, significant foreclosure effects may

still result, especially when the market share of the buyer on its downstream market exceeds 30% and the exclusive supply relates to a particular use of the contract products. Where a company is dominant on the downstream market, any obligation to supply the products only or mainly to the dominant buyer may easily have significant anti-competitive effects.

(195) It is not only the market position of the buyer on the upstream and downstream market that is important but also the extent to and the duration for which it applies an exclusive supply obligation. The higher the tied supply share, and the longer the duration of the exclusive supply, the more significant the foreclosure is likely to be. Exclusive supply agreements shorter than five years entered into by non-dominant companies usually require a balancing of pro- and anti-competitive effects, while agreements lasting longer than five years are for most types of investments not considered necessary to achieve the claimed efficiencies or the efficiencies are not sufficient to outweigh the foreclosure effect of such long-term exclusive supply agreements.

(196) The market position of the competing buyers on the upstream market is important as it is likely that competing buyers will be foreclosed for anti-competitive reasons, that is, to increase their costs, if they are significantly smaller than the foreclosing buyer. Foreclosure of competing buyers is not very likely where those competitors have similar buying power and can offer the suppliers similar sales possibilities. In such a case, foreclosure could only occur for potential entrants, which may not be able to secure supplies when a number of major buyers all enter into exclusive supply contracts with the majority of suppliers on the market. Such a cumulative effect may lead to withdrawal of the benefit of the Block Exemption Regulation.

(197) Entry barriers at the supplier level are relevant to establishing whether there is real foreclosure. In as far as it is efficient for competing buyers to provide the goods or services themselves via upstream vertical integration, foreclosure is unlikely to be a real problem. However, there are often significant entry barriers.

(198) Countervailing power of suppliers is relevant, as important suppliers will not easily allow themselves to be cut off from alternative buyers. Foreclosure is therefore mainly a risk in the case of weak suppliers and strong buyers. In the case of strong suppliers, the exclusive supply may be found in combination with non-compete obligations. The combination with non-compete obligations brings in the rules developed for single branding. Where there are relationship-specific investments involved on both sides (hold-up problem) the combination of exclusive supply and non-compete obligations that is, reciprocal exclusivity in industrial supply agreements may often be justified, in particular below the level of dominance.

(199) Lastly, the level of trade and the nature of the product are relevant for foreclosure. Anticompetitive foreclosure is less likely in the case of an intermediate product or where the product is homogeneous. Firstly, a foreclosed manufacturer that uses a certain input usually has more flexibility to respond to the demand of its customers than the wholesaler or retailer has in responding to the demand of the final consumer for whom brands may play an important role. Secondly, the loss of a possible source of supply matters less for the foreclosed buyers in the case of homogeneous products than in the case of a heterogeneous product with different grades and qualities. For final branded products or differentiated intermediate products where there are entry barriers, exclusive supply may have appreciable anti-competitive effects where the competing buyers are relatively small compared to the foreclosing buyer, even if the latter is not dominant on the downstream market.

(200) Efficiencies can be expected in the case of a hold-up problem (paragraph (107)(d) and (107)(e)), and such efficiencies are more likely for intermediate products than for final products. Other efficiencies are less likely. Possible economies of scale in distribution (paragraph (107)(g)) do not seem likely to justify exclusive supply.

(201) In the case of a hold-up problem and even more so in the case of economies of scale in distribution, quantity forcing on the supplier, such as minimum supply requirements, could well be a less restrictive alternative.

(202) *Example of exclusive supply*

On a market for a certain type of components (intermediate product market) supplier A agrees with buyer B to develop, with its own know-how and considerable investment in new machines and with the help of specifications supplied by buyer B, a different version of the component. B will have to make considerable investments to incorporate the new component. It is agreed that A will supply the new product only to buyer B for a period of five years from the date of first entry on the market. B is obliged to buy the new product only from A for the same period of five years. Both A and B can continue to sell and buy respectively other versions of the component elsewhere. The market share of buyer B on the upstream component market and on the downstream final goods market is 40%. The market share of the component supplier is 35%. There are two other component suppliers with around 20–25% market share and a number of small suppliers.

Given the considerable investments, the agreement is likely to fulfil the conditions of Article 101(3) in view of the efficiencies and the limited foreclosure effect. Other buyers are foreclosed from a particular version of a product of a supplier with 35% market share and there are other component suppliers that could develop similar new products. The foreclosure of part of buyer B's demand to other suppliers is limited to maximum 40% of the market.

2.7. UPFRONT ACCESS PAYMENTS

(203) Upfront access payments are fixed fees that suppliers pay to distributors in the framework of a vertical relationship at the beginning of a relevant period, in order to get access to their distribution network and remunerate services provided to the suppliers by the retailers. This category includes various practices such as slotting allowances,[55] the so called pay-to-stay fees,[56] payments to have access to a distributor's promotion campaigns etc Upfront access payments are exempted under the Block Exemption Regulation when both the supplier's and buyer's market share does not exceed 30%. The remainder of this section provides guidance for the assessment of upfront access payments in individual cases above the market share threshold.

(204) Upfront access payments may sometimes result in anticompetitive foreclosure of other distributors if such payments induce the supplier to channel its products through only one or a limited number of distributors. A high fee may make that a supplier wants to channel a substantial volume of its sales through this distributor in order to cover

the costs of the fee. In such a case, upfront access payments may have the same downstream foreclosure effect as an exclusive supply type of obligation. The assessment of that negative effect is made by analogy to the assessment of exclusive supply obligations (in particular paragraphs (194) to (199)).

(205) Exceptionally, upfront access payments may also result in anticompetitive foreclosure of other suppliers, where the widespread use of upfront access payments increases barriers to entry for small entrants. The assessment of that possible negative effect is made by analogy to the assessment of single branding obligations (in particular paragraphs (132) to (141)).

(206) In addition to possible foreclosure effects, upfront access payments may soften competition and facilitate collusion between distributors. Upfront access payments are likely to increase the price charged by the supplier for the contract products since the supplier must cover the expense of those payments. Higher supply prices may reduce the incentive of the retailers to compete on price on the downstream market, while the profits of distributors are increased as a result of the access payments. Such reduction of competition between distributors through the cumulative use of upfront access payments normally requires the distribution market to be highly concentrated.

(207) However, the use of upfront access payments may in many cases contribute to an efficient allocation of shelf space for new products. Distributors often have less information than suppliers on the potential for success of new products to be introduced on the market and, as a result, the amount of products to be stocked may be sub-optimal. Upfront access payments may be used to reduce this asymmetry in information between suppliers and distributors by explicitly allowing suppliers to compete for shelf space. The distributor may thus receive a signal of which products are most likely to be successful since a supplier would normally agree to pay an upfront access fee if it estimates a low probability of failure of the product introduction.

(208) Furthermore, due to the asymmetry in information mentioned in paragraph (207), suppliers may have incentives to free-ride on distributors' promotional efforts in order to introduce sub-optimal products. If a product is not successful, the distributors will pay part of the costs of the product failure. The use of upfront access fees may prevent such free riding by shifting the risk of product failure back to the suppliers, thereby contributing to an optimal rate of product introductions.

2.8. Category Management Agreements

(209) Category management agreements are agreements by which, within a distribution agreement, the distributor entrusts the supplier (the "category captain") with the marketing of a category of products including in general not only the supplier's products, but also the products of its competitors. The category captain may thus have an influence on for instance the product placement and product promotion in the shop and product selection for the shop. Category management agreements are exempted under the Block Exemption Regulation when both the supplier's and buyer's market share does not exceed 30%. The remainder of this section provides guidance for the assessment of category management agreements in individual cases above the market share threshold.

(210) While in most cases category management agreements will not be problematic, they may sometimes distort competition between suppliers, and finally result in anticompetitive foreclosure of other suppliers, where the category captain is able, due to its influence over the marketing decisions of the distributor, to limit or disadvantage the distribution of products of competing suppliers. While in most cases the distributor may not have an interest in limiting its choice of products, when the distributor also sells competing products under its own brand (private labels), the distributor may also have incentives to exclude certain suppliers, in particular intermediate range products. The assessment of such upstream foreclosure effect is made by analogy to the assessment of single branding obligations (in particular paragraphs (132) to (141)) by addressing issues like the market coverage of these agreements, the market position of competing suppliers and the possible cumulative use of such agreements.

(211) In addition, category management agreements may facilitate collusion between distributors when the same supplier serves as a category captain for all or most of the competing distributors on a market and provides these distributors with a common point of reference for their marketing decisions.

(212) Category management may also facilitate collusion between suppliers through increased opportunities to exchange via retailers sensitive market information, such as for instance information related to future pricing, promotional plans or advertising campaigns.[57]

(213) However, the use of category management agreements may also lead to efficiencies. Category management agreements may allow distributors to have access to the supplier's marketing expertise for a certain group of products and to achieve economies of scale as they ensure that the optimal quantity of products is presented timely and directly on the shelves. As category management is based on customers' habits, category management agreements may lead to higher customer satisfaction as they help to better meet demand expectations. In general, the higher the inter-brand competition and the lower consumers' switching costs, the greater the economic benefits achieved through category management.

2.9 Tying

(214) Tying refers to situations where customers that purchase one product (the tying product) are required also to purchase another distinct product (the tied product) from the same supplier or someone designated by the latter. Tying may constitute an abuse within the meaning of Article 102.[58] Tying may also constitute a vertical restraint falling under Article 101 where it results in a single branding type of obligation (see paragraphs (129) to (150)) for the tied product. Only the latter situation is dealt with in these Guidelines.

(215) Whether products will be considered as distinct depends on customer demand. Two products are distinct where, in the absence of the tying, a substantial number of customers would purchase or would have purchased the tying product without also buying the tied product from the same supplier, thereby allowing stand-alone production for both the tying and the tied product.[59] Evidence that two products are distinct could include direct evidence that, when given a choice, customers purchase the tying and the tied products separately from different sources of supply, or indirect evidence, such as the presence on the market of undertakings specialised in the manufacture or sale of the tied product

without the tying product,[60] or evidence indicating that undertakings with little market power, particularly on competitive markets, tend not to tie or not to bundle such products. For instance, since customers want to buy shoes with laces and it is not practicable for distributors to lace new shoes with the laces of their choice, it has become commercial usage for shoe manufacturers to supply shoes with laces. Therefore, the sale of shoes with laces is not a tying practice.

(216) Tying may lead to anticompetitive foreclosure effects on the tied market, the tying market, or both at the same time. The foreclosure effect depends on the tied percentage of total sales on the market of the tied product. On the question of what can be considered appreciable foreclosure under Article 101(1), the analysis for single branding can be applied. Tying means that there is at least a form of quantity-forcing on the buyer in respect of the tied product. Where in addition a non-compete obligation is agreed in respect of the tied product, this increases the possible foreclosure effect on the market of the tied product. The tying may lead to less competition for customers interested in buying the tied product, but not the tying product. If there is not a sufficient number of customers that will buy the tied product alone to sustain competitors of the supplier on the tied market, the tying can lead to those customers facing higher prices. If the tied product is an important complementary product for customers of the tying product, a reduction of alternative suppliers of the tied product and hence a reduced availability of that product can make entry onto the tying market alone more difficult.

(217) Tying may also directly lead to prices that are above the competitive level, especially in three situations. Firstly, if the tying and the tied product can be used in variable proportions as inputs to a production process, customers may react to an increase in price for the tying product by increasing their demand for the tied product while decreasing their demand for the tying product. By tying the two products the supplier may seek to avoid this substitution and as a result be able to raise its prices. Secondly, when the tying allows price discrimination according to the use the customer makes of the tying product, for example the tying of ink cartridges to the sale of photocopying machines (metering). Thirdly, when in the case of long-term contracts or in the case of after-markets with original equipment with a long replacement time, it becomes difficult for the customers to calculate the consequences of the tying.

(218) Tying is exempted under the Block Exemption Regulation when the market share of the supplier, on both the market of the tied product and the market of the tying product, and the market share of the buyer, on the relevant upstream markets, do not exceed 30%. It may be combined with other vertical restraints, which are not hardcore restrictions under that Regulation, such as non-compete obligations or quantity forcing in respect of the tying product, or exclusive sourcing. The remainder of this section provides guidance for the assessment of tying in individual cases above the market share threshold.

(219) The market position of the supplier on the market of the tying product is obviously of central importance to assess possible anti-competitive effects. In general, this type of agreement is imposed by the supplier. The importance of the supplier on the market of the tying product is the main reason why a buyer may find it difficult to refuse a tying obligation.

(220) The market position of the supplier's competitors on the market of the tying product is important in assessing the supplier's market power. As long as its competitors are sufficiently numerous and strong, no anti-competitive effects can be expected, as buyers have sufficient alternatives to purchase the tying product without the tied product, unless other suppliers are applying similar tying. In addition, entry barriers on the market of the tying product are relevant to establish the market position of the supplier. When tying is combined with a non-compete obligation in respect of the tying product, this considerably strengthens the position of the supplier.

(221) Buying power is relevant, as important buyers will not easily be forced to accept tying without obtaining at least part of the possible efficiencies. Tying not based on efficiency is therefore mainly a risk where buyers do not have significant buying power.

(222) Where appreciable anti-competitive effects are established, the question whether the conditions of Article 101(3) are fulfilled arises. Tying obligations may help to produce efficiencies arising from joint production or joint distribution. Where the tied product is not produced by the supplier, an efficiency may also arise from the supplier buying large quantities of the tied product. For tying to fulfil the conditions of Article 101(3), it must, however, be shown that at least part of these cost reductions are passed on to the consumer, which is normally not the case when the retailer is able to obtain, on a regular basis, supplies of the same or equivalent products on the same or better conditions than those offered by the supplier which applies the tying practice. Another efficiency may exist where tying helps to ensure a certain uniformity and quality standardisation (see paragraph (107)(i)). However, it needs to be demonstrated that the positive effects cannot be realised equally efficiently by requiring the buyer to use or resell products satisfying minimum quality standards, without requiring the buyer to purchase these from the supplier or someone designated by the latter. The requirements concerning minimum quality standards would not normally fall within the scope of Article 101(1). Where the supplier of the tying product imposes on the buyer the suppliers from which the buyer must purchase the tied product, for instance because the formulation of minimum quality standards is not possible, this may also fall outside the scope of Article 101(1), especially where the supplier of the tying product does not derive a direct (financial) benefit from designating the suppliers of the tied product.

2.10 Resale price restrictions

(223) As explained in section III.3, resale price maintenance (RPM), that is, agreements or concerted practices having as their direct or indirect object the establishment of a fixed or minimum resale price or a fixed or minimum price level to be observed by the buyer, are treated as a hardcore restriction. Where an agreement includes RPM, that agreement is presumed to restrict competition and thus to fall within Article 101(1). It also gives rise to the presumption that the agreement is unlikely to fulfil the conditions of Article 101(3), for which reason the block exemption does not apply. However, undertakings have the possibility to plead an efficiency defence under

Article 101(3) in an individual case. It is incumbent on the parties to substantiate that likely efficiencies result from including RPM in their agreement and demonstrate that all the conditions of Article 101(3) are fulfilled. It then falls to the Commission to effectively assess the likely negative effects on competition and consumers before deciding whether the conditions of Article 101(3) are fulfilled.

(224) RPM may restrict competition in a number of ways. Firstly, RPM may facilitate collusion between suppliers by enhancing price transparency on the market, thereby making it easier to detect whether a supplier deviates from the collusive equilibrium by cutting its price. RPM also undermines the incentive for the supplier to cut its price to its distributors, as the fixed resale price will prevent it from benefiting from expanded sales. Such a negative effect is particularly plausible where the market is prone to collusive outcomes, for instance if the manufacturers form a tight oligopoly, and a significant part of the market is covered by RPM agreements. Second, by eliminating intra-brand price competition, RPM may also facilitate collusion between the buyers, that is, at the distribution level. Strong or well organised distributors may be able to force or convince one or more suppliers to fix their resale price above the competitive level and thereby help them to reach or stabilise a collusive equilibrium. The resulting loss of price competition seems especially problematic when the RPM is inspired by the buyers, whose collective horizontal interests can be expected to work out negatively for consumers. Third, RPM may more generally soften competition between manufacturers and/or between retailers, in particular when manufacturers use the same distributors to distribute their products and RPM is applied by all or many of them. Fourth, the immediate effect of RPM will be that all or certain distributors are prevented from lowering their sales price for that particular brand. In other words, the direct effect of RPM is a price increase. Fifth, RPM may lower the pressure on the margin of the manufacturer, in particular where the manufacturer has a commitment problem, that is, where it has an interest in lowering the price charged to subsequent distributors. In such a situation, the manufacturer may prefer to agree to RPM, so as to help it to commit not to lower the price for subsequent distributors and to reduce the pressure on its own margin. Sixth, RPM may be implemented by a manufacturer with market power to foreclose smaller rivals. The increased margin that RPM may offer distributors, may entice the latter to favour the particular brand over rival brands when advising customers, even where such advice is not in the interest of these customers, or not to sell these rival brands at all. Lastly, RPM may reduce dynamism and innovation at the distribution level. By preventing price competition between different distributors, RPM may prevent more efficient retailers from entering the market or acquiring sufficient scale with low prices. It also may prevent or hinder the entry and expansion of distribution formats based on low prices, such as price discounters.

(225) However, RPM may not only restrict competition but may also, in particular where it is supplier driven, lead to efficiencies, which will be assessed under Article 101(3). Most notably, where a manufacturer introduces a new product, RPM may be helpful during the introductory period of expanding demand to induce distributors to better take into account the manufacturer's interest to promote the product. RPM may provide the distributors with the means to increase sales efforts and if the distributors on this market are under competitive pressure this may induce them to expand overall demand for the product and make the launch of the product a success, also for the benefit of consumers[61]. Similarly, fixed resale prices, and not just maximum resale prices, may be necessary to organise in a franchise system or similar distribution system applying a uniform distribution format a coordinated short term low price campaign (2 to 6 weeks in most cases) which will also benefit the consumers. In some situations, the extra margin provided by RPM may allow retailers to provide (additional) pre-sales services, in particular in case of experience or complex products. If enough customers take advantage from such services to make their choice but then purchase at a lower price with retailers that do not provide such services (and hence do not incur these costs), high-service retailers may reduce or eliminate these services that enhance the demand for the supplier's product. RPM may help to prevent such free-riding at the distribution level. The parties will have to convincingly demonstrate that the RPM agreement can be expected to not only provide the means but also the incentive to overcome possible free riding between retailers on these services and that the pre-sales services overall benefit consumers as part of the demonstration that all the conditions of Article 101(3) are fulfilled.

(226) The practice of recommending a resale price to a reseller or requiring the reseller to respect a maximum resale price is covered by the Block Exemption Regulation when the market share of each of the parties to the agreement does not exceed the 30% threshold, provided it does not amount to a minimum or fixed sale price as a result of pressure from, or incentives offered by, any of the parties. The remainder of this section provides guidance for the assessment of maximum or recommended prices above the market share threshold and for cases of withdrawal of the block exemption.

(227) The possible competition risk of maximum and recommended prices is that they will work as a focal point for the resellers and might be followed by most or all of them and/or that maximum or recommended prices may soften competition or facilitate collusion between suppliers.

(228) An important factor for assessing possible anti-competitive effects of maximum or recommended resale prices is the market position of the supplier. The stronger the market position of the supplier, the higher the risk that a maximum resale price or a recommended resale price leads to a more or less uniform application of that price level by the resellers, because they may use it as a focal point. They may find it difficult to deviate from what they perceive to be the preferred resale price proposed by such an important supplier on the market.

(229) Where appreciable anti-competitive effects are established for maximum or recommended resale prices, the question of a possible exemption under Article 101(3) arises. For maximum resale prices, the efficiency described in paragraph (107)(f) (avoiding double marginalisation), may be particularly relevant. A maximum resale price may also help to ensure that the brand in question competes more forcefully with other brands, including own label products, distributed by the same distributor.

NOTES

[37] OJ L1, 4.1.2003, p 1.

[38] See Section II.1.

[39] By collusion is meant both explicit collusion and tacit collusion (conscious parallel behaviour).

40 Whether consumers actually benefit overall from extra promotional efforts depends on whether the extra promotion informs and convinces and thus benefits many new customers or mainly reaches customers who already know what they want to buy and for whom the extra promotion only or mainly implies a price increase.

41 See however the previous footnote.

42 These steps are not intended to present a legal reasoning that the Commission should follow in this order to take a decision.

43 See Commission Decision 97/26/EC (Case No IV/M.619 — *Gencor/Lonrho*), OJ L11, 14.1.1997, p 30.

44 See Communication from the Commission – *Notice – Guidelines on the application of Article 81(3) of the Treaty*, OJ C101, 27.4.2004, p 97.

45 See Judgment of the Court of Justice in Joined Cases 25/84 and 26/84 *Ford* [1985] ECR 2725.

46 See in this respect for example Commission Decision 1999/242/EC (Case No IV/36.237 – *TPS*), OJ L90, 2.4.1999, p 6. Similarly, the prohibition of Article 101(1) also only applies as long as the agreement has a restrictive object or restrictive effects.

47 See paragraph 85 of Communication from the Commission – *Notice – Guidelines on the application of Article 81(3) of the Treaty*, OJ C101, 27.4.2004, p 97.

48 See Judgment of the Court of Justice in Joined Cases C-395/96 P and C-396/96 P *Compagnie Maritime Belge* [2000] ECR I-1365, paragraph 130. Similarly, the application of Article 101(3) does not prevent the application of the Treaty rules on the free movement of goods, services, persons and capital. These provisions are in certain circumstances applicable to agreements, decisions and concerted practices within the meaning of Article 101(1), see to that effect Judgment of the Court of Justice in Case C-309/99 *Wouters* [2002] ECR I-1577, paragraph 120.

49 See in this respect Judgment of the Court of First Instance in Case T-51/89 *Tetra Pak (I)* [1990] ECR II-309. See also paragraph 106 of Communication from the Commission – *Notice – Guidelines on the application of Article 81(3) of the Treaty*, OJ C101, 27.4.2004, p 97.

50 Judgment of the Court of First Instance in Case T-65/98 *Van den Bergh Foods v Commission* [2003] ECR II-4653, paragraphs 104 and 156.

51 See for example judgment of the Court of First Instance in Case T-88/92 *Groupement d'achat Édouard Leclerc v Commission* [1996] ECR II-1961.

52 See judgments of the Court of Justice in Case 31/80 *L'Oréal v PVBA* [1980] ECR 3775, paragraphs 15 and 16; Case 26/76 *Metro I* [1977] ECR 1875, paragraphs 20 and 21; Case 107/82 *AEG* [1983] ECR 3151, paragraph 35; and judgment of the Court of First Instance in Case T-19/91 *Vichy v Commission* [1992] ECR II-415, paragraph 65.

53 See for example judgments of the Court of First Instance in Case T-19/92, *Groupement d'achat Edouard Leclerc v Commission* [1996] ECR II-1851, paragraphs 112 to 123; Case T-88/92 *Groupement d'achat Edouard Leclerc v Commission* [1996] ECR II-1961, paragraphs 106 to 117, and the case law referred to in the preceding footnote.

54 See also paragraphs (86) to (95), in particular paragraph (92).

55 Fixed fees that manufacturers pay to retailers in order to get access to their shelf space.

56 Lump sum payments made to ensure the continued presence of an existing product on the shelf for some further period.

57 Direct information exchange between competitors is not covered by the Block Exemption Regulation, see Article 2(4) of that Regulation and paragraphs 27–28 of these Guidelines.

58 Judgment of the Court of Justice in Case C-333/94 P *Tetrapak v Commission* [1996] ECR I-5951, paragraph 37. See also Communication from the Commission – *Guidance on the Commission's enforcement priorities in applying Article 82 of the EC Treaty to abusive conduct by dominant undertakings*, OJ C45, 24.2.2009, p 7.

59 Judgment of the Court of First Instance in Case T-201/04 *Microsoft v Commission* [2007] ECR II-3601, paragraphs 917, 921 and 922.

60 Judgment of the Court of First Instance in Case T-30/89 *Hilti v Commission* [1991] ECR II-1439, paragraph 67.

61 This assumes that it is not practical for the supplier to impose on all buyers by contract effective promotion requirements, see also paragraph 107 point (a).

COMMISSION REGULATION

(461/2010/EU)

of 27 May 2010

on the application of Article 101(3) of the Treaty on the Functioning of the European Union to categories of vertical agreements and concerted practices in the motor vehicle sector

(Text with EEA relevance)

[4.255]

NOTES

Date of publication in OJ: OJ L129, 28.5.2010, p 52.

Application of this Regulation in relation to the UK: in accordance with the European Union (Withdrawal) Act 2018, s 3 at **[7.5]**, this Regulation became domestic law on IP completion day (as defined in the European Union (Withdrawal Agreement) Act 2020, s 39). In so far as applying to the UK, this Regulation is amended by the Competition (Amendment etc) (EU Exit) Regulations 2019, SI 2019/93, as from IP completion day. The amendments are set out below. With regard to these amendments, note that Articles that are repealed are reproduced in italics and, in the case of other amendments, the amending provision from SI 2019/93 is set out in full in the Notes to the amended Article, and the text of the amended Article has not been altered. For transitional provisions and savings in relation to the operation of the 2019 Regulations, see Sch 4 to those Regulations at **[7.69]** et seq.

Note also that Regulation 19/65/EEC (under which this Regulation was made) is repealed, in its application to the UK, by the Competition (Amendment etc) (EU Exit) Regulations 2019, SI 2019/93, reg 63, Sch 3, para 1, as from IP completion day (as defined in the European Union (Withdrawal Agreement) Act 2020, s 39) (for transitional provisions and savings in relation to the operation of the 2019 Regulations, see Sch 4 to those Regulations at **[7.69]** et seq). However, see Sch 3, para 2 to those Regulations (at **[7.67]**) which provides for the continued application of this Regulation despite the repeal of Regulation 19/65/EEC.

See also the list of consultations and draft documents in the Appendix at **[A1]**.

THE EUROPEAN COMMISSION,

Having regard to the Treaty on the Functioning of the European Union,

Having regard to Regulation No 19/65/EEC of the Council of 2 March 1965 on the application of Article 85(3) of the Treaty to certain categories of agreements and concerted practices,[1] and in particular Article 1 thereof,

Having published a draft of this Regulation,

After consulting the Advisory Committee on Restrictive Practices and Dominant Positions,

Whereas:

(1) Regulation No 19/65/EEC empowers the Commission to apply Article 101(3) of the Treaty on the Functioning of the European Union[1a] by regulation to certain categories of vertical agreements and corresponding concerted practices falling within Article 101(1) of the Treaty. Block exemption regulations apply to vertical agreements which fulfil certain conditions and may be general or sector-specific.

(2) The Commission has defined a category of vertical agreements which it regards as normally satisfying the conditions laid down in Article 101(3) of the Treaty and to this end has adopted Commission Regulation (EU) No 330/2010 of 20 April 2010 on the application of Article 101(3) of the Treaty on the Functioning of the European Union to categories of vertical agreements and concerted practices,[2] which replaces Commission Regulation (EC) No 2790/1999.[3]

(3) The motor vehicle sector, which includes both passenger cars and commercial vehicles, has been subject to specific block exemption regulations since 1985, the most recent being Commission Regulation (EC) No 1400/2002 of 31 July 2002 on the application of Article 81(3) of the Treaty to categories of vertical agreements and concerted practices in the motor vehicle sector.[4] Regulation (EC) No 2790/1999 expressly stated that it did not apply to vertical agreements the subject matter of which fell within the scope of any other block exemption regulation. The motor vehicle sector therefore fell outside the scope of that Regulation.

(4) Regulation (EC) No 1400/2002 expires on 31 May 2010. However, the motor vehicle sector should continue to benefit from a block exemption in order to simplify administration and reduce compliance costs for the undertakings concerned, while ensuring effective supervision of markets in accordance with Article 103(2)(b) of the Treaty.

(5) Experience acquired since 2002 regarding the distribution of new motor vehicles, the distribution of spare parts and the provision of repair and maintenance services for motor vehicles, makes it possible to define a category of vertical agreements in the motor vehicle sector which can be regarded as normally satisfying the conditions laid down in Article 101(3) of the Treaty.

(6) This category includes vertical agreements for the purchase, sale or resale of new motor vehicles, vertical agreements for the purchase, sale or resale of spare parts for motor vehicles and vertical agreements for the provision of repair and maintenance services for such vehicles, where those agreements are concluded between non-competing undertakings, between certain competitors, or by certain associations of retailers or repairers. It also includes vertical agreements containing ancillary provisions on the assignment or use of intellectual property rights. The term 'vertical agreements' should be defined accordingly to include both such agreements and the corresponding concerted practices.

(7) Certain types of vertical agreements can improve economic efficiency within a chain of production or distribution by facilitating better coordination between the participating undertakings. In particular, they can lead to a reduction in the transaction and distribution costs of the parties and to an optimisation of their sales and investment levels.

(8) The likelihood that such efficiency-enhancing effects will outweigh any anticompetitive effects due to restrictions contained in vertical agreements depends on the degree of market power of the parties to the agreement and, therefore, on the extent to which those undertakings face competition from other suppliers of goods or services regarded by their customers as interchangeable or substitutable for one another, by reason of the products' characteristics, their prices and their intended use. Vertical agreements containing restrictions which are likely to restrict competition and harm consumers, or which are not indispensable to the attainment of the efficiency-enhancing effects, should be excluded from the benefit of the block exemption.

(9) In order to define the appropriate scope of a block exemption regulation, the Commission must take into account the competitive conditions in the relevant sector. In this respect, the conclusions of the in-depth monitoring of the motor vehicle sector set out in the Evaluation Report on the operation of Commission Regulation (EC) No 1400/2002 of 28 May 2008[5] and in the Commission Communication on The Future Competition Law Framework applicable to the Motor Vehicle sector of 22 July 2009[6] have shown that a distinction should be drawn between agreements for the distribution of new motor vehicles and agreements for the provision of repair and maintenance services and distribution of spare parts.

(10) As regards the distribution of new motor vehicles, there do not appear to be any significant competition shortcomings which would distinguish this sector from other economic sectors and which could require the application of rules different from and stricter than those set out in Regulation (EU) No 330/2010. The market-share threshold, the non-exemption of certain vertical agreements and the other conditions laid down in that Regulation normally ensure that vertical agreements for the distribution of new motor vehicles comply with the requirements of Article 101(3) of the Treaty. Therefore, such agreements should benefit from the exemption granted by Regulation (EU) No 330/2010, subject to all the conditions laid down therein.

(11) As regards agreements for the distribution of spare parts and for the provision of repair and maintenance services, certain specific characteristics of the motor vehicle aftermarket should be taken into account. In particular, the experience acquired by the Commission in applying Regulation (EC) No 1400/2002 shows that price increases for individual repair jobs are only partially reflected in increased reliability of modern cars and lengthening of service

intervals. These latter trends are linked to technological evolution and to the increasing complexity and reliability of automotive components that the vehicle manufacturers purchase from original equipment suppliers. Such suppliers sell their products as spare parts in the aftermarket both through the vehicle manufacturers' authorised repair networks and through independent channels, thereby representing an important competitive force in the motor vehicle aftermarket. The costs borne on average by consumers in the Union for motor vehicle repair and maintenance services represent a very high proportion of total consumer expenditure on motor vehicles.

(12) Competitive conditions in the motor vehicle aftermarket also have a direct bearing on public safety, in that vehicles may be driven in an unsafe manner if they have been repaired incorrectly, as well as on public health and the environment, as emissions of carbon dioxide and other air pollutants may be higher from vehicles which have not undergone regular maintenance work.

(13) In so far as a separate aftermarket can be defined, effective competition on the markets for the purchase and sale of spare parts, as well as for the provision of repair and maintenance services for motor vehicles, depends on the degree of competitive interaction between authorised repairers, that is to say those operating within repair networks established directly or indirectly by vehicle manufacturers, as well as between authorised and independent operators, including independent spare parts suppliers and repairers. The latters' ability to compete depends on unrestricted access to essential inputs such as spare parts and technical information.

(14) Having regard to those specificities, the rules in Regulation (EU) No 330/2010, including the uniform market share threshold of 30%, are necessary but are not sufficient to ensure that the benefit of the block exemption is reserved only to those vertical agreements for the distribution of spare parts and for the provision of repair and maintenance services for which it can be assumed with sufficient certainty that the conditions of Article 101(3) of the Treaty are satisfied.

(15) Therefore, vertical agreements for the distribution of spare parts and for the provision of repair and maintenance services should benefit from the block exemption only if, in addition to the conditions for exemption set out in Regulation (EU) No 330/2010, they comply with stricter requirements concerning certain types of severe restrictions of competition that may limit the supply and use of spare parts in the motor vehicle aftermarket.

(16) In particular, the benefit of the block exemption should not be granted to agreements that restrict the sale of spare parts by members of the selective distribution system of a vehicle manufacturer to independent repairers, which use them for the provision of repair or maintenance services. Without access to such spare parts, independent repairers would not be able to compete effectively with authorised repairers, since they could not provide consumers with good quality services which contribute to the safe and reliable functioning of motor vehicles.

(17) Moreover, in order to ensure effective competition on the repair and maintenance markets and to allow repairers to offer end users competing spare parts, the block exemption should not cover vertical agreements which, although they comply with Regulation (EU) No 330/2010, nonetheless restrict the ability of a producer of spare parts to sell such parts to authorised repairers within the distribution system of a vehicle manufacturer, independent distributors of spare parts, independent repairers or end users. This does not affect the liability of producers of spare parts under civil law, or the ability of vehicle manufacturers to require the authorised repairers within their distribution system to only use spare parts that match the quality of the components used for the assembly of a certain motor vehicle. Moreover, in view of the vehicle manufacturers' direct contractual involvement in repairs under warranty, free servicing, and recall operations, agreements containing obligations on authorised repairers to use only spare parts supplied by the vehicle manufacturer for those repairs should be covered by the exemption.

(18) Finally, in order to allow authorised and independent repairers and end users to identify the manufacturer of motor vehicle components or of spare parts and to choose between alternative parts, the block exemption should not cover agreements by which a manufacturer of motor vehicles limits the ability of a manufacturer of components or original spare parts to place its trade mark or logo on those parts effectively and in a visible manner.

(19) In order to allow all operators time to adapt to this Regulation, it is appropriate to extend the period of application of the provisions of Regulation (EC) No 1400/2002 relating to vertical agreements for the purchase, sale and resale of new motor vehicles until 31 May 2013. As regards vertical agreements for the distribution of spare parts and for the provision of repair and maintenance services, this Regulation should apply from 1 June 2010 so as to continue to ensure adequate protection of competition on the motor vehicle aftermarkets.

(20) The Commission will, on a continuous basis, monitor developments in the motor vehicle sector and will take appropriate remedial action if competition shortcomings arise which may lead to consumer harm on the market for the distribution of new motor vehicles or the supply of spare parts or after-sales services for motor vehicles.

(21) The Commission may withdraw the benefit of this Regulation, pursuant to Article 29(1) of Council Regulation (EC) No 1/2003 of 16 December 2002 on the implementation of the rules on competition laid down in Articles 81 and 82 of the Treaty,[7] where it finds in a particular case that an agreement to which the exemption provided for in this Regulation applies nevertheless has effects which are incompatible with Article 101(3) of the Treaty.

(22) The competition authority of a Member State may withdraw the benefit of this Regulation pursuant to Article 29(2) of Regulation (EC) No 1/2003 in respect of the territory of that Member State, or a part thereof where, in a particular case, an agreement to which the exemption provided for in this Regulation applies nevertheless has effects which are incompatible with Article 101(3) of the Treaty in the territory of that Member State, or in a part thereof, and where such territory has all the characteristics of a distinct geographic market.

(23) In determining whether the benefit of this Regulation should be withdrawn pursuant to Article 29 of Regulation (EC) No 1/2003, the anti-competitive effects that may derive from the existence of parallel networks of vertical agreements that have similar effects which significantly restrict access to a relevant market or competition therein are of particular importance. Such cumulative effects may, for example, arise in the case of selective distribution or non-compete obligations.

(24) In order to strengthen supervision of parallel networks of vertical agreements which have similar anti-competitive effects and which cover more than 50% of a given market, the Commission may by regulation declare this Regulation inapplicable to vertical agreements containing specific restraints relating to the market concerned, thereby restoring the full application of Article 101 of the Treaty to such agreements.

(25) In order to assess the effects of this Regulation on competition in motor vehicle retailing, in the supply of spare parts and in after sales servicing for motor vehicles in the internal market, it is appropriate to draw up an evaluation report on the operation of this Regulation,

NOTES

[1] OJ 36, 6.3.1965, p 533/65.

[1a] With effect from 1 December 2009, Article 81 of the EC Treaty has become Article 101 of the Treaty on the Functioning of the European Union. The two Articles are, in substance, identical. For the purposes of this Regulation, references to Article 101 of the Treaty on the Functioning of the European Union should be understood as references to Article 81 of the EC Treaty where appropriate.

[2] OJ L102, 23.4.2010, p 1.

[3] OJ L336, 29.12.1999, p 21.

[4] OJ L203, 1.8.2002, p 30.

[5] SEC(2008) 1946.

[6] COM(2009) 388.

[7] OJ L1, 4.1.2003, p 1.

HAS ADOPTED THIS REGULATION—

CHAPTER I COMMON PROVISIONS

[4.256]

Article 1 Definitions

1. For the purposes of this Regulation, the following definitions shall apply:

(a) 'vertical agreement' means an agreement or concerted practice entered into between two or more undertakings each of which operates, for the purposes of the agreement or the concerted practice, at a different level of the production or distribution chain, and relating to the conditions under which the parties may purchase, sell or resell certain goods or services;

(b) 'vertical restraint' means a restriction of competition in a vertical agreement falling within the scope of Article 101(1) of the Treaty;

(c) 'authorised repairer' means a provider of repair and maintenance services for motor vehicles operating within the distribution system set up by a supplier of motor vehicles;

(d) 'authorised distributor' means a distributor of spare parts for motor vehicles operating within the distribution system set up by a supplier of motor vehicles;

(e) 'independent repairer' means:

  (i) a provider of repair and maintenance services for motor vehicles not operating within the distribution system set up by the supplier of the motor vehicles for which it provides repair or maintenance;

  (ii) an authorised repairer within the distribution system of a given supplier, to the extent that it provides repair or maintenance services for motor vehicles in respect of which it is not a member of the respective supplier's distribution system;

(f) 'independent distributor' means:

  (i) a distributor of spare parts for motor vehicles not operating within the distribution system set up by the supplier of the motor vehicles for which it distributes spare parts;

  (ii) an authorised distributor within the distribution system of a given supplier, to the extent that it distributes spare parts for motor vehicles in respect of which it is not a member of the respective supplier's distribution system;

(g) 'motor vehicle' means a self-propelled vehicle intended for use on public roads and having three or more road wheels;

(h) 'spare parts' means goods which are to be installed in or upon a motor vehicle so as to replace components of that vehicle, including goods such as lubricants which are necessary for the use of a motor vehicle, with the exception of fuel;

(i) 'selective distribution system' means a distribution system where the supplier undertakes to sell the contract goods or services, either directly or indirectly, only to distributors selected on the basis of specified criteria and where these distributors undertake not to sell such goods or services to unauthorised distributors within the territory reserved by the supplier to operate that system.

2. For the purposes of this Regulation, the terms 'undertaking', 'supplier', 'manufacturer' and 'buyer' shall include their respective connected undertakings.

'Connected undertakings' means:

(a) undertakings in which a party to the agreement, directly or indirectly:

  (i) has the power to exercise more than half the voting rights; or

  (ii) has the power to appoint more than half the members of the supervisory board, board of management or bodies legally representing the undertaking; or

  (iii) has the right to manage the undertaking's affairs;

(b) undertakings which directly or indirectly have, over a party to the agreement, the rights or powers listed in point (a);

(c) undertakings in which an undertaking referred to in point (b) has, directly or indirectly, the rights or powers listed in point (a);

(d) undertakings in which a party to the agreement together with one or more of the undertakings referred to in points (a), (b) or (c), or in which two or more of the latter undertakings, jointly have the rights or powers listed in point (a);

(e) undertakings in which the rights or the powers listed in point (a) are jointly held by:

  (i) parties to the agreement or their respective connected undertakings referred to in points (a) to (d); or

(ii) one or more of the parties to the agreement or one or more of their connected undertakings referred to in points (a) to (d) and one or more third parties.

NOTES

Application of this Article in relation to the UK: this Article is amended, in relation to the UK only, by the Competition (Amendment etc) (EU Exit) Regulations 2019, SI 2019/93, reg 63, Sch 3, Pt 2, para 6(2), as from IP completion day (as defined in the European Union (Withdrawal Agreement) Act 2020, s 39) (for transitional provisions and savings in relation to the operation of the 2019 Regulations, see Sch 4 to those Regulations at **[7.69]** et seq), as follows—

"(2) In Article 1(1)—

(a) after point (a), insert—

"(aa) "the Chapter 1 prohibition" means the prohibition imposed by section 2(1) of the Competition Act 1998;";

(b) in point (b), for "Article 101(1) of the Treaty" substitute "the Chapter 1 prohibition".".

CHAPTER II VERTICAL AGREEMENTS RELATING TO THE PURCHASE, SALE OR RESALE OF NEW MOTOR VEHICLES

[4.257]

Article 2 Application of Regulation (EC) No 1400/2002

Pursuant to Article 101(3) of the Treaty, from 1 June 2010 until 31 May 2013, Article 101(1) of the Treaty shall not apply to vertical agreements relating to the conditions under which the parties may purchase, sell or resell new motor vehicles, which fulfil the requirements for an exemption under Regulation (EC) No 1400/2002 that relate specifically to vertical agreements for the purchase, sale or resale of new motor vehicles.

NOTES

Repeal of this Article in relation to the UK: this Article is repealed, in relation to the UK only, by the Competition (Amendment etc) (EU Exit) Regulations 2019, SI 2019/93, reg 63, Sch 3, Pt 2, para 6(3), as from IP completion day (as defined in the European Union (Withdrawal Agreement) Act 2020, s 39) (for transitional provisions and savings in relation to the operation of the 2019 Regulations, see Sch 4 to those Regulations at **[7.69]** et seq).

[4.258]

Article 3 Application of Regulation (EU) No 330/2010

With effect from 1 June 2013, Regulation (EU) No 330/2010 shall apply to vertical agreements relating to the purchase, sale or resale of new motor vehicles.

CHAPTER III VERTICAL AGREEMENTS RELATING TO THE MOTOR VEHICLE AFTERMARKET

[4.259]

Article 4 Exemption

Pursuant to Article 101(3) of the Treaty and subject to the provisions of this Regulation Article 101(1) of the Treaty shall not apply to vertical agreements relating to the conditions under which the parties may purchase, sell or resell spare parts for motor vehicles or provide repair and maintenance services for motor vehicles, which fulfil the requirements for an exemption under Regulation (EU) No 330/2010 and do not contain any of the hardcore clauses listed in Article 5 of this Regulation.

This exemption shall apply to the extent that such agreements contain vertical restraints.

NOTES

Application of this Article in relation to the UK: this Article is amended, in relation to the UK only, by the Competition (Amendment etc) (EU Exit) Regulations 2019, SI 2019/93, reg 63, Sch 3, Pt 2, para 6(4), as from IP completion day (as defined in the European Union (Withdrawal Agreement) Act 2020, s 39) (for transitional provisions and savings in relation to the operation of the 2019 Regulations, see Sch 4 to those Regulations at **[7.69]** et seq), as follows—

"(4) For the first paragraph of Article 4 substitute—

"Subject to the provisions of this Regulation, a vertical agreement is exempt from the Chapter 1 prohibition if—

(a) it relates to the conditions under which the parties may purchase, sell or resell spare parts for motor vehicles or provide repair and maintenance services for motor vehicles;

(b) it fulfils the requirements for an exemption under Regulation (EU) No 330/2010; and

(c) it does not contain any of the hardcore clauses listed in Article 5 of this Regulation.".".

[4.260]

Article 5 Restrictions that remove the benefit of the block exemption — hardcore restrictions

The exemption provided for in Article 4 shall not apply to vertical agreements which, directly or indirectly, in isolation or in combination with other factors under the control of the parties, have as their object:

(a) the restriction of the sales of spare parts for motor vehicles by members of a selective distribution system to independent repairers which use those parts for the repair and maintenance of a motor vehicle;

(b) the restriction, agreed between a supplier of spare parts, repair tools or diagnostic or other equipment and a manufacturer of motor vehicles, of the supplier's ability to sell those goods to authorised or independent distributors or to authorised or independent repairers or end users;

(c) the restriction, agreed between a manufacturer of motor vehicles which uses components for the initial assembly of motor vehicles and the supplier of such components, of the supplier's ability to place its trade mark or logo effectively and in an easily visible manner on the components supplied or on spare parts.

CHAPTER IV FINAL PROVISIONS

[4.261]

Article 6 Non-application of this Regulation

Pursuant to Article 1a of Regulation No 19/65/EEC, the Commission may by regulation declare that, where parallel networks of similar vertical restraints cover more than 50% of a relevant market, this Regulation shall not apply to vertical agreements containing specific restraints relating to that market.

NOTES

Repeal of this Article in relation to the UK: this Article is repealed, in relation to the UK only, by the Competition (Amendment etc) (EU Exit) Regulations 2019, SI 2019/93, reg 63, Sch 3, Pt 2, para 6(5), as from IP completion day (as defined in the European Union (Withdrawal Agreement) Act 2020, s 39) (for transitional provisions and savings in relation to the operation of the 2019 Regulations, see Sch 3, Pt 2, para 10 to those Regulations at **[7.68]**, and Sch 4 to those Regulations at **[7.69]** et seq).

[4.262]

Article 7 Monitoring and evaluation report

The Commission will monitor the operation of this Regulation and draw up a report on its operation by 31 May 2021 at the latest, having regard in particular to the conditions set out in Article 101(3) of the Treaty.

NOTES

Repeal of this Article in relation to the UK: this Article is repealed, in relation to the UK only, by the Competition (Amendment etc) (EU Exit) Regulations 2019, SI 2019/93, reg 63, Sch 3, Pt 2, para 6(5), as from IP completion day (as defined in the European Union (Withdrawal Agreement) Act 2020, s 39) (for transitional provisions and savings in relation to the operation of the 2019 Regulations, see Sch 4 to those Regulations at **[7.69]** et seq).

[4.263]

Article 8 Period of validity

This Regulation shall enter into force on 1 June 2010.

It shall expire on 31 May 2023.

This Regulation shall be binding in its entirety and directly applicable in all Member States.

NOTES

Application of this Article in relation to the UK: this Article is amended, in relation to the UK only, by the Competition (Amendment etc) (EU Exit) Regulations 2019, SI 2019/93, reg 63, Sch 3, Pt 2, para 6(6), as from IP completion day (as defined in the European Union (Withdrawal Agreement) Act 2020, s 39) (for transitional provisions and savings in relation to the operation of the 2019 Regulations, see Sch 4 to those Regulations at **[7.69]** et seq), as follows—

"(6) In the words after Article 8, omit the words from "This Regulation shall be binding" to "Member States.".".

COMMISSION NOTICE

(2010/C138/05)

Supplementary guidelines on vertical restraints in agreements for the sale and repair of motor vehicles and for the distribution of spare parts for motor vehicles

(Text with EEA relevance)

[4.264]

NOTES

Date of publication in OJ: C138, 28.5.2010, p 16.

I. INTRODUCTION

1. PURPOSE OF THE GUIDELINES

[4.265]

(1) These Guidelines set out principles for assessing under Article 101 of the Treaty on the Functioning of the European Union[1] particular issues arising in the context of vertical restraints in agreements for the sale and repair of motor vehicles and for the distribution of spare parts. They accompany Commission Regulation (EU) No 461/2010 on the application of Article 101(3) of the Treaty on the Functioning of the European Union to categories of vertical agreements and concerted practices in the motor vehicle sector[2] (hereinafter 'the Motor Vehicle Block Exemption Regulation') and are aimed at helping companies to make their own assessment of such agreements.

(2) These Guidelines provide clarification on issues that are particularly relevant for the motor vehicle sector, including the interpretation of certain provisions of Commission Regulation (EU) No 330/2010 of 20 April 2010 on the application of Article 101(3) of the Treaty on the Functioning of the European Union to categories of vertical agreements and concerted practices[3] (hereinafter 'the General Vertical Block Exemption Regulation'). They are without prejudice to the applicability of the Guidelines on Vertical Restraints[4] (hereinafter 'the General Vertical Guidelines') and are therefore to be read in conjunction with and as a supplement to the General Vertical Guidelines.

(3) These Guidelines apply to both vertical agreements and concerted practices relating to the conditions under which the parties may purchase, sell or resell spare parts and/or provide repair and maintenance services for motor vehicles, and to vertical agreements and concerted practices relating to the conditions under which the parties may purchase, sell or resell new motor vehicles. As explained in Section II of these Guidelines, the latter category of agreements and concerted practices will remain subject to the relevant provisions of Commission Regulation (EC) No 1400/2002 of 31 July 2002 on the application of Article 81(3) of the Treaty to categories of vertical agreements and concerted practices in the motor vehicle sector[5] until 31 May 2013. Therefore, as regards vertical agreements and concerted practices for the purchase, sale or resale of new motor vehicles, these Guidelines will only apply as from 1 June 2013. These Guidelines do not apply to vertical agreements in sectors other than motor vehicles, and the principles set out herein may not necessarily be used to assess agreements in other sectors.

(4) These Guidelines are without prejudice to the possible parallel application of Article 102 of the Treaty to vertical agreements in the motor vehicle sector, or to the interpretation that the Court of Justice of the European Union may give in relation to the application of Article 101 of the Treaty to such vertical agreements.

(5) Unless otherwise stated, the analysis and arguments set out in these Guidelines apply to all levels of trade. The terms 'supplier' and 'distributor'[6] are used for all levels of trade. The General Vertical Block Exemption Regulation and the Motor Vehicle Block Exemption Regulation are collectively referred to as 'the Block Exemption Regulations'.

(6) The standards set forth in these Guidelines must be applied to each case having regard to the individual factual and legal circumstances. The Commission will apply[7] these Guidelines reasonably and flexibly, and having regard to the experience that it has acquired in the course of its enforcement and market monitoring activities.

(7) The history of competition enforcement in this sector shows that certain restraints can be arrived at either as a result of explicit direct contractual obligations or through indirect obligations or indirect means which nonetheless achieve the same anti-competitive result. Suppliers wishing to influence a distributor's competitive behaviour may, for instance, resort to threats or intimidation, warnings or penalties. They may also delay or suspend deliveries or threaten to terminate the contracts of distributors that sell to foreign consumers or fail to observe a price level. Transparent relationships between contracting parties would normally reduce the risk of manufacturers being held responsible for using such indirect forms of pressure aimed at achieving anticompetitive outcomes. Adhering to a Code of Conduct is one means of achieving greater transparency in commercial relationships between parties. Such codes may inter alia provide for notice periods for contract termination, which may be determined in function of the contract duration, for compensation to be given for outstanding relationship-specific investments made by the dealer in case of early termination without just cause, as well as for arbitration as an alternative mechanism for dispute resolution. If a supplier incorporates such a Code of Conduct into its agreements with distributors and repairers, makes it publicly available, and complies with its provisions, this will be regarded as a relevant factor for assessing the supplier's conduct in individual cases.

2. STRUCTURE OF THE GUIDELINES

(8) These Guidelines are structured as follows:

(a) Scope of the Motor Vehicle Block Exemption Regulation and relationship with the General Vertical Block Exemption Regulation (Section II)

(b) The application of the additional provisions in the Motor Vehicle Block Exemption Regulation (Section III)

(c) The assessment of specific restraints: single branding and selective distribution (Section IV)

NOTES

1 With effect from 1 December 2009, Articles 81 and 82 of the EC Treaty have become Articles 101 and 102, respectively, of the Treaty on the Functioning of the European Union ('TFEU'). The two sets of provisions are in substance identical. For the purposes of these Guidelines, references to Articles 101 and 102 of the TFEU should be understood as references to Articles 81 and 82, respectively, of the EC Treaty where appropriate. The TFEU also introduced certain changes in terminology, such as the replacement of 'Community' by 'Union' and 'common market' by 'internal market'. The terminology of the TFEU will be used throughout these Guidelines.

2 OJ L129, 28.5.2010, p 52.

3 OJ L102, 23.4.2010, p 1.

4 OJ C130, 19.5.2010, p 1.

5 OJ L203, 1.8.2002, p 30.

6 Retail level distributors are commonly referred to in the sector as 'dealers'.

7 Since the modernisation of the Union competition rules, the primary responsibility for such analysis lies with the parties to agreements. The Commission may however investigate the compatibility of agreements with Article 101 of the Treaty, on its own initiative or following a complaint.

II. SCOPE OF THE MOTOR VEHICLE BLOCK EXEMPTION REGULATION AND RELATIONSHIP WITH THE GENERAL VERTICAL BLOCK EXEMPTION REGULATION

[4.266]

(9) Pursuant to Article 4 thereof, the Motor Vehicle Block Exemption Regulation covers vertical agreements relating to the purchase, sale or resale of spare parts for motor vehicles and to the provision of repair and maintenance services for motor vehicles.

(10) Article 2 of the Motor Vehicle Block Exemption Regulation extends the application of the relevant provisions of Regulation (EC) No 1400/2002 until 31 May 2013 as far as they relate to vertical agreements for the purchase, sale or resale of new motor vehicles. Pursuant to Article 3 of the Motor Vehicle Block Exemption Regulation vertical agreements for the purchase, sale and resale of new motor vehicles will be covered by the General Vertical Block Exemption Regulation, from 1 June 2013.[1]

(11) The distinction that the new framework makes between the markets for the sale of new motor vehicles and the motor vehicle aftermarkets reflects the differing competitive conditions on these markets.

(12) On the basis of an in-depth market analysis set out in the Evaluation Report on the operation of Commission Regulation (EC) No 1400/2002 of 28 May 2008[2] and in the Commission Communication on The Future Competition Law Framework applicable to the Motor Vehicle Sector of 22 July 2009,[3] it appears that there are no significant competition shortcomings distinguishing the new motor vehicle distribution sector from other economic sectors and which could require the application of rules different from and stricter than those in the General Vertical Block Exemption Regulation. Consequently, the application of a market share threshold of 30%,[4] the non-exemption of certain vertical restraints and the conditions provided for in the General Vertical Block Exemption Regulation will normally ensure that vertical agreements for the distribution of new motor vehicles satisfy the conditions laid down in Article 101(3) of the Treaty without the need for any additional requirements over and above those applicable to other sectors.

(13) However, in order to allow all operators time to adapt to the general regime, in particular in view of relationship-specific investments which have been made in the long term, the period of application of Regulation (EC) No 1400/2002 is extended by three years until 31 May 2013 with regard to those requirements that relate specifically to vertical agreements for the purchase, sale or resale of new motor vehicles. From 1 June 2010 until 31 May 2013, those provisions of Regulation (EC) No 1400/2002 which relate to both agreements for the distribution of new motor vehicles and agreements for the purchase, sale and resale of spare parts for motor vehicles and/or the provision of repair and maintenance services, will apply only in respect of the former. During that period these Guidelines will not be used for interpreting the provisions of Regulation (EC) No 1400/2002. Instead, reference should be made to the Explanatory Brochure on that Regulation.[5]

(14) As regards vertical agreements relating to the conditions under which the parties may purchase, sell or resell spare parts for motor vehicles and/or provide repair and maintenance services for motor vehicles, the Motor Vehicle Block Exemption Regulation applies from 1 June 2010. This means that, in order to be exempted pursuant to Article 4 of that Regulation, those agreements not only need to fulfil the conditions for an exemption under the General Vertical Block Exemption Regulation, but must also not contain any serious restrictions of competition, commonly referred to as hardcore restrictions as listed in Article 5 of the Motor Vehicle Block Exemption Regulation.

(15) Because of the generally brand-specific nature of the markets for repair and maintenance services and for the distribution of spare parts, competition on those markets is inherently less intense compared to that on the market for the sale of new motor vehicles. While reliability has improved and service intervals have lengthened thanks to technological improvement, this evolution is outpaced by an upward price trend for individual repair and maintenance jobs. On the spare parts markets, parts bearing the motor vehicle manufacturer's brand face competition from those supplied by the original equipment suppliers (OES) and by other parties. This maintains price pressure on those markets, which in turn maintains pressure on prices on the repair and maintenance markets, since spare parts make up a large percentage of the cost of the average repair. Moreover, repair and maintenance as a whole represent a very high proportion of total consumer expenditure on motor vehicles, which itself accounts for a significant slice of the average consumer's budget.

(16) In order to address particular competition issues arising on the motor vehicle aftermarkets, the General Vertical Block Exemption Regulation is supplemented with three additional hardcore restrictions in the Motor Vehicle Block Exemption Regulation applying to agreements for the repair and maintenance of motor vehicles and for the supply of spare parts. Further guidance on those additional hardcore restrictions is given in Section III of these Guidelines.

NOTES

1 The expiry of Regulation (EC) No 1400/2002 and its replacement with the new legal framework explained in these Guidelines does not of itself require that existing contracts be terminated. See for example Case C-125/05 *Vulcan Silkeborg A/S v Skandinavisk Motor Co A/S* [2006] ECR I-7637.

2 SEC(2008) 1946.

3 COM(2009) 388.

4 Pursuant to Article 7 of the General Vertical Block Exemption Regulation, the calculation of this market share threshold is normally based on market sales value data or, if such data are not available, on other reliable market information, including market sales volumes. In this respect, the Commission takes note of the fact that, for the distribution of new motor vehicles, market shares are currently calculated by the industry on the basis of the volume of motor vehicles sold by the supplier on the relevant market, which includes all motor vehicles that are regarded by the buyer as interchangeable or substitutable, by reason of the products' characteristics, prices and intended use.

5 Explanatory brochure for Commission Regulation (EC) No 1400/2002 of 31 July 2002 — *Distribution and Servicing of Motor Vehicles in the European Union.*

III. THE APPLICATION OF THE ADDITIONAL PROVISIONS IN THE MOTOR VEHICLE BLOCK EXEMPTION REGULATION

[4.267]

(17) Agreements will not benefit from the block exemption if they contain hardcore restrictions. These restrictions are listed in Article 4 of the General Vertical Block Exemption Regulation and Article 5 of the Motor Vehicle Block Exemption Regulation. Including any such restrictions in an agreement gives rise to the presumption that the agreement falls within Article 101(1) of the Treaty. It also gives rise to the presumption that the agreement is unlikely to satisfy the conditions laid down in Article 101(3) of the Treaty, for which reason the block exemption does not apply. However, this is a rebuttable presumption which leaves open the possibility for undertakings to plead an efficiency defence under Article 101(3) of the Treaty in an individual case.

(18) One of the Commission's objectives as regards competition policy for the motor vehicle sector is to protect access by spare parts manufacturers to the motor vehicle aftermarkets, thereby ensuring that competing brands of spare parts continue to be available to both independent and authorised repairers, as well as to parts wholesalers. The availability of such parts brings considerable benefits to consumers, especially since there are often large differences

in price between parts sold or resold by a car manufacturer and alternative parts. Alternatives for parts bearing the trademark of the motor vehicle manufacturer (OEM parts) include original parts manufactured and distributed by original equipment suppliers (OES parts), while other parts matching the quality of the original components are supplied by 'matching quality' parts manufacturers.

(19) 'Original parts or equipment' means parts or equipment which are manufactured according to the specifications and production standards provided by the motor vehicle manufacturer for the production of parts or equipment for the assembly of the motor vehicle in question. This includes parts or equipment which are manufactured on the same production line as those parts or equipment. It is presumed unless the contrary is proven, that parts constitute original parts if the part manufacturer certifies that the parts match the quality of the components used for the assembly of the motor vehicle in question and have been manufactured according to the specifications and production standards of the motor vehicle (see Article 3(26) of Directive 2007/46/EC of the European Parliament and of the Council of 5 September 2007 establishing a framework for the approval of motor vehicles and their trailers, and of systems, components and separate technical units intended for such motor vehicles (Framework Directive)).[1]

(20) In order to be considered as 'matching quality', parts must be of a sufficiently high quality that their use does not endanger the reputation of the authorised network in question. As with any other selection standard, the motor vehicle manufacturer may bring evidence that a given spare part does not meet this requirement.

(21) Article 4(e) of the General Vertical Block Exemption Regulation describes it as a hardcore restriction for an agreement between a supplier of components and a buyer who incorporates those components, to prevent or restrict the supplier's ability to sell its components to end-users, independent repairers or other service providers not entrusted by the buyer with the repair or servicing of its goods. Article 5(a), (b) and (c) of the Motor Vehicle Block Exemption Regulation lay down three additional hardcore restrictions relating to agreements for the supply of spare parts.

(22) Article 5(a) of the Motor Vehicle Block Exemption Regulation concerns the restriction of the sale of spare parts for motor vehicles by members of a selective distribution system to independent repairers. This provision is most relevant for a particular category of parts, sometimes referred to as captive parts, which may only be obtained from the motor vehicle manufacturer or from members of its authorised networks. If a supplier and a distributor agree that such parts may not be supplied to independent repairers, this agreement would be likely to foreclose such repairers from the market for repair and maintenance services and fall foul of Article 101 of the Treaty.

(23) Article 5(b) of the Motor Vehicle Block Exemption Regulation concerns any direct or indirect restriction agreed between a supplier of spare parts, repair tools or diagnostic or other equipment and a manufacturer of motor vehicles, which limits the supplier's ability to sell these goods to authorised and/or independent distributors and repairers. So-called 'tooling arrangements' between component suppliers and motor vehicle manufacturers are one example of possible indirect restrictions of this type. Reference should be made in this respect to the Commission notice of 18 December 1978 concerning its assessment of certain subcontracting agreements in relation to Article 85(1) of the EEC Treaty[2] (the Sub-contracting Notice). Normally, Article 101(1) of the Treaty does not apply to an arrangement whereby a motor vehicle manufacturer provides a tool to a component manufacturer which is necessary for the production of certain components, shares in the product development costs, or contributes necessary[3] intellectual property rights, or know-how, and does not allow this contribution to be used for the production of parts to be sold directly in the aftermarket. On the other hand, if a motor vehicle manufacturer obliges a component supplier to transfer its ownership of such a tool, intellectual property rights, or know-how, bears only an insignificant part of the product development costs, or does not contribute any necessary tools, intellectual property rights, or know-how, the agreement at issue will not be considered to be a genuine sub-contracting arrangement. Therefore, it may be caught by Article 101(1) of the Treaty and be examined pursuant to the provisions of the Block Exemption Regulations.

(24) Article 5(c) of the Motor Vehicle Block Exemption Regulation relates to the restriction agreed between a manufacturer of motor vehicles which uses components for the initial assembly of motor vehicles and the supplier of such components, which limits the supplier's ability to place its trade mark or logo effectively and in an easily visible manner on the components supplied or on spare parts. In order to improve consumer choice, repairers and consumers should be able to identify which spare parts from alternative suppliers match a given motor vehicle, other than those bearing the car manufacturer's brand. Putting the trade mark or logo on the components and on spare parts facilitates the identification of compatible replacement parts which can be obtained from OES. By not allowing this, motor vehicle manufacturers can restrict the marketing of OES parts and limit consumers' choice in a manner that runs counter to the provisions of Article 101 of the Treaty.

NOTES

1 OJ L263, 9.10.2007, p 1.

2 OJ C1, 3.1.1979, p 2.

3 Where the motor vehicle manufacturer provides a tool, intellectual property rights (IPR) and/or know-how to a component supplier, this arrangement will not benefit from the Sub-contracting Notice if the component supplier already has this tool, IPR or know-how at its disposal, or could, under reasonable conditions obtain them, since under these circumstances the contribution would not be necessary.

IV. THE ASSESSMENT OF SPECIFIC RESTRAINTS

[4.268]

(25) Parties to vertical agreements in the motor vehicle sector should use these Guidelines as a supplement to and in conjunction with the General Vertical Guidelines in order to assess the compatibility of specific restraints with Article 101 of the Treaty. This section gives particular guidance as to single branding and selective distribution, which are two areas which may have particular relevance for assessing the category of agreements referred to in Section II of these Guidelines.

1. SINGLE BRANDING OBLIGATIONS

(I) Assessment of single-branding obligations under the Block Exemption Regulations

(26) Pursuant to Article 3 of the Motor Vehicle Block Exemption Regulation read in conjunction with Article 5(1)(a) of the General Vertical Block Exemption Regulation, a motor vehicle supplier and a distributor having a share of the relevant market that does not exceed 30% may agree on a single-branding obligation that obliges the distributor to purchase motor vehicles only from the supplier or from other firms designated by the supplier, on condition that the duration of such non-compete obligations is limited to five years or less. The same principles apply to agreements between suppliers and their authorised repairers and/or spare parts distributors. A renewal beyond five years requires explicit consent of both parties, and there should be no obstacles that hinder the distributor from effectively terminating the non-compete obligation at the end of the five-year period. Non-compete obligations are not covered by the Block Exemption Regulations when their duration is indefinite or exceeds five years, although in those circumstances the Block Exemption Regulations would continue to apply to the remaining part of the vertical agreement. The same applies to non-compete obligations that are tacitly renewable beyond a period of five years. Obstacles, threats of termination, or intimations that single-branding will be re-imposed before a sufficient period has elapsed to allow either the distributor or the new supplier to amortise their sunk investments would amount to a tacit renewal of the single-branding obligation in question.

(27) Pursuant to Article 5(1)(c) of the General Vertical Block Exemption Regulation, any direct or indirect obligation causing the members of a selective distribution system not to sell the brands of particular competing suppliers, are not covered by the exemption. Particular attention should be paid to the manner in which single branding obligations are applied to existing multi-brand distributors, in order to ensure that the obligations in question do not form part of an overall strategy aimed at eliminating competition from one or more specific suppliers, and in particular from newcomers or weaker competitors. This type of concern could arise in particular if the market share thresholds indicated in paragraph 34 of these Guidelines are exceeded and if the supplier applying this type of restraint has a position on the relevant market that enables it to contribute significantly to the overall foreclosure effect.[1]

(28) Non-compete obligations in vertical agreements do not constitute hardcore restrictions, but depending on the market circumstances, can nonetheless have negative effects which may cause the agreements to fall under Article 101(1) of the Treaty.[2] One such harmful effect may arise if barriers to entry or expansion are raised that foreclose competing suppliers, and harm consumers in particular by increasing the prices or limiting the choice of products, lowering their quality or reducing the level of product innovation.

(29) However, non-compete obligations may also have positive effects which may justify the application of Article 101(3) of the Treaty. They may in particular help to overcome a 'free-rider' problem, by which one supplier benefits from investments made by another. A supplier may, for instance, invest in a distributor's premises, but in doing so attract customers for a competing brand that is also sold from the same premises. The same applies to other types of investment made by the supplier which may be used by the distributor to sell motor vehicles of competing manufacturers, such as investments in training.

(30) Another positive effect of non-compete obligations in the motor vehicle sector relates to the enhancement of the brand image and reputation of the distribution network. Such restraints may help to create and maintain a brand image by imposing a certain measure of uniformity and quality standardisation on distributors, thereby increasing the attractiveness of that brand to the final consumer and increasing its sales.

(31) Article 1(d) of the General Vertical Block Exemption Regulation defines a non-compete obligation as:

"(a) any direct or indirect obligation causing the buyer not to manufacture, purchase, sell or resell goods or services which compete with the contract goods or services; or

(b) any direct or indirect obligation on the buyer to purchase from the supplier or from another undertaking designated by the supplier more than 80% of the buyer's total purchases of the contract goods or services and their substitutes on the relevant market."

(32) Apart from direct means to tie the distributor to its own brand(s), a supplier may also have recourse to indirect means having the same effect. In the motor vehicle sector, such indirect means may include qualitative standards specifically designed to discourage the distributors from selling products of competing brands,[3] bonuses made conditional on the distributor agreeing to sell exclusively one brand, target rebates or certain other requirements such as the requirement to set up a separate legal entity for the competing brand or the obligation to display the additional competing brand in a separate showroom in a geographic location where the fulfilment of such a requirement would not be economically viable (for example sparsely populated areas).

(33) The block exemption provided for in the General Vertical Block Exemption Regulation covers all forms of direct or indirect non-compete obligations provided that the market shares of both the supplier and the distributor do not exceed 30% and the duration of the non-compete obligation does not exceed five years. However, even in cases where individual agreements satisfy those conditions, the use of non-compete obligations may result in anti-competitive effects not outweighed by their positive effects. In the motor vehicle industry, such net anti-competitive effects could in particular result from cumulative effects leading to the foreclosure of competing brands.

(34) For the distribution of motor vehicles at the retail level, foreclosure of this type is unlikely to occur in markets where all suppliers have market shares below 30% and where the total percentage of all motor vehicle sales that are subject to single-branding obligations on the market in question (that is to say the total tied market share) is below 40%.[4] In a situation where there is one non-dominant supplier with a market share of more than 30% of the relevant market whereas all other suppliers' market shares are below 30%, cumulative anticompetitive effects are unlikely as long as the total tied market share does not exceed 30%.

(35) If access to the relevant market for the sale of new motor vehicles and competition therein is significantly restricted by the cumulative effect of parallel networks of similar vertical agreements containing single branding obligations, the benefit of the block exemption may be withdrawn by the Commission, pursuant to Article 29

of Council Regulation (EC) No 1/2003 of 16 December 2002 on the implementation of the rules on competition laid down in Articles 81 and 82 of the Treaty.[5] A withdrawal decision may be addressed in particular to those suppliers that contribute in a significant manner to a cumulative foreclosure effect on the relevant market. Where that effect occurs on a national market, the National Competition Authorities of that Member State may also withdraw the benefit of the block exemption in respect of that territory.

(36) In addition, if parallel networks of agreements containing similar vertical restraints cover more than 50% of a given market, the Commission may adopt a Regulation declaring the block exemption inapplicable to the market in question in respect of such restraints. In particular, such a situation may arise if cumulative effects resulting from the widespread use of single-branding obligations lead to consumer harm on that market.

(37) With regard to the assessment of minimum purchasing obligations calculated on the basis of the distributor's total annual requirements, it may be justified to withdraw the benefit of the block exemption if cumulative anticompetitive effects arise even if the supplier imposes a minimum purchasing obligation that is below the 80% limit established in Article 1(d) of the General Vertical Block Exemption Regulation. The parties need to consider whether, in the light of the relevant factual circumstances, an obligation on the distributor to ensure that a given percentage of its total purchases of motor vehicles bear the supplier's brand will prevent the distributor from taking on one or more additional competing brands. From that perspective, even a minimum purchasing requirement set at a level lower than 80% of total annual purchases will amount to a single-branding obligation if it obliges a distributor wishing to take up a new brand of its choice from a competing manufacturer to purchase so many motor vehicles of the brand that it currently sells that the distributor's business is made economically unsustainable.[6] Such a minimum purchasing obligation will also amount to a single branding obligation if it forces a competing supplier to split its envisaged sales volume in a given territory over several distributors, leading to duplication of investments and a fragmented sales presence.

(II) Assessment of single-branding obligations outside the scope of the Block Exemption Regulations

(38) Parties may also be called upon to assess the compatibility with the competition rules of single-branding obligations in respect of agreements that do not qualify for block exemption because the parties' market shares exceed 30% or the duration of the agreement exceeds five years. Such agreements will therefore be subject to individual scrutiny in order to ascertain whether they are caught by Article 101(1) of the Treaty and if so, whether efficiencies offsetting any possible anti-competitive effect can be demonstrated. If that is the case, they may be able to benefit from the exception laid down in Article 101(3) of the Treaty. For assessment in an individual case the general principles set out in Section VI.2.1 of the General Vertical Guidelines will apply.

(39) In particular, agreements entered into between a motor vehicle manufacturer or its importer, on the one hand, and spare parts distributors and/or authorised repairers, on the other, will fall outside the Block Exemption Regulations when the market shares held by the parties exceed the 30% threshold, which is likely to be the case for most such agreements. Single-branding obligations that will need to be assessed in such circumstances include all types of restriction that directly or indirectly limit authorised distributors' or repairers' ability to obtain original or matching quality spare parts from third parties. However, an obligation on an authorised repairer to use original spare parts supplied by the motor vehicle manufacturer for repairs carried out under warranty, free servicing and motor vehicle recall work would not be considered to be a single-branding obligation, but rather an objectively justified requirement.

(40) Single-branding obligations in agreements for the distribution of new motor vehicles will also need to be individually assessed where their duration exceeds five years or/and where the market share of the supplier exceeds 30%, which may be the case for certain suppliers in some Member States. In such circumstances, the parties should have regard not only to the supplier's and buyer's market share, but also to the total tied market share taking into account the thresholds indicated in paragraph 34. Above those thresholds, individual cases will be assessed in accordance with the general principles set out in Section VI.2.1 of the General Vertical Guidelines.

(41) Outside the scope of the Block Exemption Regulations, the assessment of minimum purchasing obligations calculated on the basis of the distributor's total annual requirements will take into account all the relevant factual circumstances. In particular, a minimum purchasing requirement set at a level lower than 80% of total annual purchases will amount to a single-branding obligation if it has the effect of preventing distributors from dealing in one or more additional competing brands.

2. SELECTIVE DISTRIBUTION

(42) Selective distribution is currently the predominant form of distribution in the motor vehicle sector. Its use is widespread in motor vehicle distribution, as well as for repair and maintenance and the distribution of spare parts.

(43) In purely qualitative selective distribution, distributors and repairers are only selected on the basis of objective criteria required by the nature of the product or service, such as the technical skills of sales personnel, the layout of sales facilities, sales techniques and the type of sales service to be provided by the distributor.[7] The application of such criteria does not put a direct limit on the number of distributors or repairers admitted to the supplier's network. Purely qualitative selective distribution is in general considered to fall outside Article 101(1) of the Treaty for lack of anti-competitive effects, provided that three conditions are satisfied. First, the nature of the product in question must necessitate the use of selective distribution, in the sense that such a system must constitute a legitimate requirement, having regard to the nature of the product concerned, to preserve its quality and ensure its proper use. Second, distributors or repairers must be chosen on the basis of objective criteria of a qualitative nature which are laid down uniformly for all potential resellers and are not applied in a discriminatory manner. Third, the criteria laid down must not go beyond what is necessary.

(44) Whereas qualitative selective distribution involves the selection of distributors or repairers only on the basis of objective criteria required by the nature of the product or service, quantitative selection adds further criteria for selection that more directly limit the potential number of distributors or repairers either by directly fixing their number, or for instance, requiring a minimum level of sales. Networks based on quantitative criteria are generally held to be more restrictive than those that rely on qualitative selection alone, and are accordingly more likely to be caught by Article 101(1) of the Treaty.

(45) If selective distribution agreements are caught by Article 101(1) of the Treaty, the parties will need to assess whether their agreements can benefit from the Block Exemption Regulations, or individually, from the exception in Article 101(3) of the Treaty.

(I) THE ASSESSMENT OF SELECTIVE DISTRIBUTION UNDER THE BLOCK EXEMPTION REGULATIONS

(46) The Block Exemption Regulations exempt selective distribution agreements, irrespective of whether quantitative or purely qualitative selection criteria are used, so long as the parties' market shares do not exceed 30%. However, that exemption is conditional on the agreements not containing any of the hardcore restrictions set out in Article 4 of the General Vertical Block Exemption Regulation and Article 5 of the Motor Vehicle Block Exemption Regulation, or any of the excluded restrictions described in Article 5 of the General Vertical Block Exemption Regulation.

(47) Three of the hardcore restrictions in the General Vertical Block Exemption Regulation relate specifically to selective distribution. Article 4(b) describes as hardcore the restriction of the territory into which, or of the customers to whom, a buyer party to the agreement may sell the contract goods or services, except the restriction of sales by the members of a selective distribution system to unauthorised distributors in markets where such a system is operated. Article 4(c) describes as hardcore agreements restricting active or passive sales to end users by members of a selective distribution system operating at the retail level of trade, without prejudice to the possibility of prohibiting a member of the system from operating out of an unauthorised place of establishment, while Article 4(d) relates to the restriction of cross-supplies between distributors within a selective distribution system, including between distributors operating at different levels of trade. Those three hardcore restrictions have special relevance for motor vehicle distribution.

(48) The internal market has enabled consumers to purchase motor vehicles in other Member States and take advantage of price differentials between them, and the Commission views the protection of parallel trade in this sector as an important competition objective. The consumer's ability to buy goods in other Member States is especially important as far as motor vehicles are concerned, given the high value of the goods and the direct benefits in the form of lower prices accruing to consumers buying motor vehicles elsewhere in the Union. The Commission is therefore concerned that distribution agreements should not restrict parallel trade, since this cannot be expected to satisfy the conditions laid down in Article 101(3) of the Treaty.[8]

(49) The Commission has brought several cases against motor vehicle manufacturers for impeding such trade, and its decisions have been largely confirmed by the European Courts.[9] This experience shows that restrictions on parallel trade may take a number of forms. A supplier may, for instance, put pressure on distributors, threaten them with contract termination, fail to pay bonuses, refuse to honour warranties on motor vehicles imported by a consumer or cross-supplied between distributors established in different Member States, or make a distributor wait significantly longer for delivery of an identical motor vehicle when the consumer in question is resident in another Member State.

(50) One particular example of indirect restrictions on parallel trade arises when a distributor is unable to obtain new motor vehicles with the appropriate specifications needed for cross-border sales. In those specific circumstances, the benefit of the block exemption may depend on whether a supplier provides its distributors with motor vehicles with specifications identical to those sold in other Member States for sale to consumers from those countries (the so-called 'availability clause').[10]

(51) For the purposes of the application of the Block Exemption Regulations, and in particular as regards the application of Article 4(c) of the General Vertical Block Exemption Regulation, the notion of 'end users' includes leasing companies. This means in particular that distributors in selective distribution systems may not be prevented from selling new motor vehicles to leasing companies of their choice. However, a supplier using selective distribution may prevent its distributors from selling new motor vehicles to leasing companies when there is a verifiable risk that those companies will resell them while still new. A supplier can therefore require a dealer to check, before selling to a particular company, the general leasing conditions applied so as to verify that the company in question is indeed a leasing company rather than an unauthorised reseller. However, an obligation on a dealer to provide its supplier with copies of each leasing agreement before the dealer sells a motor vehicle to a leasing company could amount to an indirect restriction on sales.

(52) The notion of 'end users' also encompasses consumers who purchase through an intermediary. An intermediary is a person or an undertaking which purchases a new motor vehicle on behalf of a named consumer without being a member of the distribution network. Those operators perform an important role in the motor vehicle sector, in particular by facilitating consumers' purchases of motor vehicles in other Member States. Evidence of intermediary status should as a rule be established by a valid mandate including the name and address of the consumer obtained prior to the transaction. The use of the Internet as a means to attract customers in relation to a given range of motor vehicles and collect electronic mandates from them does not affect intermediary status. Intermediaries are to be distinguished from independent resellers, which purchase motor vehicles for resale and do not operate on behalf of named consumers. Independent resellers are not to be considered as end users for the purposes of the Block Exemption Regulations.

(II) THE ASSESSMENT OF SELECTIVE DISTRIBUTION OUTSIDE THE SCOPE OF THE BLOCK EXEMPTION REGULATIONS

(53) As paragraph 175 of the General Vertical Guidelines explains, the possible competition risks brought about by selective distribution are a reduction in intra-brand competition and, especially in case of cumulative effect, foreclosure of certain type(s) of distributors and facilitation of collusion between suppliers or buyers.

(54) To assess the possible anti-competitive effects of selective distribution under Article 101(1) of the Treaty, a distinction needs to be made between purely qualitative selective distribution and quantitative selective distribution. As pointed out in paragraph 43, qualitative selective distribution is normally not caught by Article 101(1) of the Treaty.

(55) The fact that a network of agreements does not benefit from the block exemption because the market share of one or more of the parties is above the 30% threshold for exemption does not imply that such agreements are illegal. Instead, the parties to such agreements need to subject them to an individual analysis to check whether they fall under Article 101(1) of the Treaty and, if so, whether they may nonetheless benefit from the exception in Article 101(3) of the Treaty.

(56) As regards the specificities of new motor vehicle distribution, quantitative selective distribution will generally satisfy the conditions laid down in Article 101(3) of the Treaty if the parties' market shares do not exceed 40%. However, the parties to such agreements should bear in mind that the presence of particular selection standards could have an effect on whether their agreements satisfy the conditions laid down in Article 101(3) of the Treaty. For instance, although the use of location clauses in selective distribution agreements for new motor vehicles, that is to say agreements containing a prohibition on a member of a selective distribution system from operating out of an unauthorised place of establishment, will usually bring efficiency benefits in the form of more efficient logistics and predictable network coverage, those benefits may be outweighed by disadvantages if the market share of the supplier is very high, and in those circumstances such clauses might not be able to benefit from the exception in Article 101(3) of the Treaty.

(57) Individual assessment of selective distribution for authorised repairers also raises specific issues. Insofar as a market exists[11] for repair and maintenance services that is separate from that for the sale of new motor vehicles, this is considered to be brand-specific. On that market, the main source of competition results from the competitive interaction between independent repairers and authorised repairers of the brand in question.

(58) Independent repairers in particular provide vital competitive pressure, as their business models and their related operating costs are different from those in the authorised networks. Moreover, unlike authorised repairers, which to a large extent use car manufacturer-branded parts, independent garages generally have greater recourse to other brands, thereby allowing a motor vehicle owner to choose between competing parts. In addition, given that a large majority of repairs for newer motor vehicles are currently carried out in authorised repair shops, it is important that competition between authorised repairers remains effective, which may only be the case if access to the networks remains open for new entrants.

(59) The new legal framework makes it easier for the Commission and National Competition Authorities to protect competition between independent garages and authorised repairers, as well as between the members of each authorised repairer network. In particular, the reduction in the market share threshold for exemption of qualitative selective distribution from 100% to 30% broadens the scope for competition authorities to act.

(60) When assessing the competitive impact of vertical agreements on the motor vehicle aftermarkets, the parties should therefore be aware of the Commission's determination to preserve competition both between the members of authorised repair networks and between those members and independent repairers. To this end, particular attention should be paid to three specific types of conduct which may restrict such competition, namely preventing access of independent repairers to technical information, misusing the legal and/or extended warranties to exclude independent repairers, or making access to authorised repairer networks conditional upon non-qualitative criteria.

(61) Although the following three subsections refer specifically to selective distribution, the same anti-competitive foreclosure effects could stem from other types of vertical agreements that limit, directly or indirectly, the number of service partners contractually linked to a motor vehicle manufacturer.

Access to technical information by independent operators

(62) Although purely qualitative selective distribution is in general considered to fall outside Article 101(1) of the Treaty for lack of anti-competitive effects,[12] qualitative selective distribution agreements concluded with authorised repairers and/or parts distributors may be caught by Article 101(1) of the Treaty if, within the context of those agreements, one of the parties acts in a way that forecloses independent operators from the market, for instance by failing to release technical repair and maintenance information to them. In that context, the notion of independent operators includes independent repairers, spare parts manufacturers and distributors, manufacturers of repair equipment or tools, publishers of technical information, automobile clubs, roadside assistance operators, operators offering inspection and testing services and operators offering training for repairers.

(63) Suppliers provide their authorised repairers with the full scope of technical information needed to perform repair and maintenance work on motor vehicles of their brands and are often the only companies able to provide repairers with all of the technical information that they need on the brands in question. In such circumstances, if the supplier fails to provide independent operators with appropriate access to its brand-specific technical repair and maintenance information, possible negative effects stemming from its agreements with authorised repairers and/or parts distributors could be strengthened, and cause the agreements to fall within Article 101(1) of the Treaty.

(64) Moreover, a lack of access to necessary technical information could cause the market position of independent operators to decline, leading to consumer harm, in terms of a significant reduction in choice of spare parts, higher prices for repair and maintenance services, a reduction in choice of repair outlets and potential safety problems. In

those circumstances, the efficiencies that might normally be expected to result from the authorised repair and parts distribution agreements would not be such as to offset these anti-competitive effects, and the agreements in question would consequently fail to satisfy the conditions laid down in Article 101(3) of the Treaty.

(65) Regulation (EC) No 715/2007 of the European Parliament and of the Council of 20 June 2007 on type approval of motor vehicles with respect to emissions from light passenger and commercial vehicles (Euro 5 and Euro 6) and on access to vehicle repair and maintenance information[13] as well as Commission Regulation (EC) No 692/2008 of 18 July 2008 implementing and amending Regulation (EC) No 715/2007 of the European Parliament and of the Council on type-approval of motor vehicles with respect to emissions from light passenger and commercial vehicles (Euro 5 and Euro 6) and on access to vehicle repair and maintenance information[14] provide for a system for disseminating repair and maintenance information in respect of passenger cars put on the market from 1 September 2009. Regulation (EC) No 595/2009 of the European Parliament and of the Council of 18 June 2009 on type approval of motor vehicles and engines with respect to emissions from heavy duty vehicles (Euro 6) and on access to vehicle repair an maintenance information[15] and the ensuing implementing measures provide for such a system in respect of commercial vehicles put on the market from 1 January 2013. The Commission will take those Regulations into account when assessing cases of suspected withholding of technical repair and maintenance information concerning motor vehicles marketed before those dates. When considering whether withholding a particular item of information may lead the agreements at issue to be caught by Article 101(1) of the Treaty, a number of factors should be considered, including:

(a) whether the item in question is technical information, or information of another type, such as commercial information,[16] which may legitimately be withheld;

(b) whether withholding the technical information in question will have an appreciable impact on the ability of independent operators to carry out their tasks and exercise a competitive constraint on the market;

(c) whether the technical information in question is made available to members of the relevant authorised repair network; if it is made available to the authorised network in whatever form, it should also be made available to independent operators on a non-discriminatory basis;

(d) whether the technical information in question will ultimately[17] be used for the repair and maintenance of motor vehicles, or rather for another purpose,[18] such as for the manufacturing of spare parts or tools.

(66) Technological progress implies that the notion of technical information is fluid. Currently, particular examples of technical information include software, fault codes and other parameters, together with updates, which are required to work on electronic control units with a view to introducing or restoring settings recommended by the supplier, motor vehicle identification numbers or any other motor vehicle identification methods, parts catalogues, repair and maintenance procedures, working solutions resulting from practical experience and relating to problems typically affecting a given model or batch, and recall notices as well as other notices identifying repairs that may be carried out without charge within the authorised repair network. The part code and any other information necessary to identify the correct car manufacturer-branded spare part to fit a given individual motor vehicle (that is to say the part that the car manufacturer would generally supply to the members of its authorised repair networks to repair the motor vehicle in question) also constitute technical information.[19] The lists of items set out in Article 6(2) of Regulation (EC) No 715/2007 and Regulation (EC) No 595/2009 should also be used as a guide to what the Commission views as technical information for the purposes of applying Article 101 of the Treaty.

(67) The way in which technical information is supplied is also important for assessing the compatibility of authorised repair agreements with Article 101 of the Treaty. Access should be given upon request and without undue delay, the information should be provided in a usable form, and the price charged should not discourage access to it by failing to take into account the extent to which the independent operator uses the information. A supplier of motor vehicles should be required to give independent operators access to technical information on new motor vehicles at the same time as such access is given to its authorised repairers and should not oblige independent operators to purchase more than the information necessary to carry out the work in question. Article 101 of the Treaty does not, however, oblige a supplier to provide technical information in a standardised format or through a defined technical system, such as the CEN/ISO standard and the OASIS format as provided for by Regulation (EC) No 715/2007 and Commission Regulation (EC) No 295/2009 of 18 March 2009 concerning the classification of certain goods in the Combined Nomenclature.[20]

(68) The above considerations also apply to the availability of tools and training to independent operators. 'Tools' in this context includes electronic diagnostic and other repair tools, together with related software, including periodic updates thereof, and after-sales services for such tools.

Misuse of warranties

(69) Qualitative selective distribution agreements may also be caught by Article 101(1) of the Treaty if the supplier and the members of its authorised network explicitly or implicitly reserve repairs on certain categories of motor vehicles to the members of the authorised network. This might happen, for instance, if the manufacturer's warranty vis-à-vis the buyer, whether legal or extended, is made conditional on the end user having repair and maintenance work that is not covered by warranty carried out only within the authorised repair networks. The same applies to warranty conditions which require the use of the manufacturer's brand of spare parts in respect of replacements not covered by the warranty terms. It also seems doubtful that selective distribution agreements containing such practices could bring benefits to consumers in such a way as to allow the agreements in question to benefit from the exception in Article 101(3) of the Treaty. However, if a supplier legitimately refuses to honour a warranty claim on the grounds that the situation leading to the claim in question is causally linked to a failure on the part of a repairer to carry out a particular repair or maintenance operation in the correct manner or to the use of poor quality spare parts, this will have no bearing on the compatibility of the supplier's repair agreements with the competition rules.

Access to authorised repairer networks

(70) Competition between authorised and independent repairers is not the only form of competition that needs to be taken into account when analysing the compatibility of authorised repair agreements with Article 101 of the Treaty. Parties should also assess the degree to which authorised repairers within the relevant network are able to compete with one another. One of the main factors driving this competition relates to the conditions of access to the network established under the standard authorised repairer agreements. In view of the generally strong market position of networks of authorised repairers, their particular importance for owners of newer motor vehicles, and the fact that consumers are not prepared to travel long distances to have their cars repaired, the Commission considers it important that access to the authorised repair networks should generally remain open to all firms that meet defined quality criteria. Submitting applicants to quantitative selection is likely to cause the agreement to fall within Article 101(1) of the Treaty.

(71) A particular case arises when agreements oblige authorised repairers to also sell new motor vehicles. Such agreements are likely to be caught by Article 101(1) of the Treaty, since the obligation in question is not required by the nature of the contract services. Moreover, for an established brand, agreements containing such an obligation would not normally be able to benefit from the exception in Article 101(3) of the Treaty, since the impact would be to severely restrict access to the authorised repair network, thereby reducing competition without bringing corresponding benefits to consumers. However, in certain cases, a supplier wishing to launch a brand on a particular geographic market might initially find it difficult to attract distributors willing to make the necessary investment unless they could be sure that they would not face competition from 'stand-alone' authorised repairers that sought to free-ride on these initial investments. In those circumstances, contractually linking the two activities for a limited period of time would have a pro-competitive effect on the motor vehicle sales market by allowing a new brand to launch, and would have no effect on the potential brand-specific repair market, which would in any event not exist if the motor vehicles could not be sold. The agreements in question would therefore be unlikely to be caught by Article 101(1) of the Treaty.

NOTES

1 Commission notice on agreements of minor importance which do not appreciably restrict competition under Article 81(1) of the Treaty establishing the European Community (*de minimis*), OJ C368, 22.12.2001, p 13.

2 As regards the relevant factors to be taken into account to carry out the assessment of non-compete obligations under Article 101(1) of the Treaty, see the relevant section in the General Vertical Guidelines, in particular paragraphs 129 to 150.

3 See cases *BMW*, IP/06/302 – 13.3.2006 and *Opel 2006*, IP/06/303 – 13.3.2006.

4 See General Vertical Guidelines at paragraph 141.

5 OJ L1, 4.1.2003, p 1.

6 For instance, if a dealer purchases 100 cars of brand A in a year to meet demand, and wishes to buy 100 cars of brand B, an 80% minimum purchasing obligation as regards brand A would imply that the following year, the dealer would have to buy 160 brand A cars. Given that penetration rates are likely to be relatively stable, this would likely leave the dealer with a large unsold stock of brand A. It would therefore be forced to dramatically reduce its purchases of brand B in order to avoid such a situation. Depending on the specific circumstances of the case, such a practice can be viewed as a single-branding obligation.

7 It should be recalled however that, in accordance with the established case law of the European Courts, purely qualitative selective distribution systems may nevertheless restrict competition where the existence of a certain number of such systems does not leave any room for other forms of distribution based on a different way of competing. This situation will generally not arise on the markets for the sale of new motor vehicles, on which leasing and other similar arrangements are a valid alternative to outright purchase of a motor vehicle, nor in the markets for repair and maintenance, as long as independent repairers provide consumers with an alternative channel for the upkeep of their motor vehicles. See for example Case T-88/92 *Groupement d'achat Édouard Leclerc v Commission* [1996] ECR II-1961.

8 The notion that cross-border trade restrictions may harm consumers has been confirmed by the Court in Case C-551/03 P, *General Motors*, [2006] ECR I-3173, paragraphs 67 and 68; Case C-338/00 P, *Volkswagen/Commission*, [2003] ECR I-9189, paragraphs 44 and 49, and Case T-450/05, *Peugeot/Commission*, judgment of 9 July 2009, not yet reported, paragraphs 46–49.

9 Commission Decision 98/273/EC of 28 January 1998 in Case IV/35.733 — VW, Commission Decision 2001/146/EC of 20 September 2000 in Case COMP/36.653 — *Opel*, OJ L59, 28.2.2001, p 1, Commission Decision 2002/758/EC of 10 October 2001 in Case COMP/36.264 — *Mercedes-Benz*, OJ L257, 25.9.2002, p 1, Commission Decision 2006/431/EC of 5 October 2005 in Cases F-2/36.623/36.820/37.275 — *SEP et autres/Peugeot SA*.

10 Joined Cases 25 and 26/84 *Ford-Werke AG and Ford of Europe Inc. v Commission of the European Communities*, [1985] ECR 2725.

11 In some circumstances, a system market which includes motor vehicles and spare parts together may be defined, taking into account, inter alia, the life-time of the motor vehicle as well as the preferences and buying behaviour of the users. See Commission notice on the definition of the relevant market for the purposes of Community competition law, OJ C372, 9.12.1997, p 5, paragraph 56. One important factor is whether a significant proportion of buyers make their choice taking into account the lifetime costs of the motor vehicle or not. For instance, buying behaviour may significantly differ between buyers of trucks who purchase and operate a fleet, and who take into account maintenance costs at the moment of purchasing the motor vehicle and buyers of individual motor vehicles. Another relevant factor is the existence and relative position of part suppliers, repairers and/or parts distributors operating in the aftermarket independently from motor vehicle manufacturers. In most cases, there is likely to be a brand-specific aftermarket, in particular because the majority of buyers are private individuals or small and medium-size enterprises that purchase motor vehicles and aftermarket services separately and do not have systematic access to data permitting them to assess the overall costs of motor vehicle ownership in advance.

12 As pointed out in paragraph 54 above, this will generally be the case on the markets for repair and maintenance as long as independent repairers provide consumers with an alternative channel for the upkeep of their motor vehicles.

13 OJ L171, 29.6.2007, p 1.

14 OJ L199, 28.7.2008, p 1.

15 OJ L188, 18.7.2009, p 1.

16 Commercial information can be thought of as information that is used for carrying on a repair and maintenance business but is not needed to repair or maintain motor vehicles. Examples include billing software, or information on the hourly tariffs practiced within the authorised network.

17 Such as information supplied to publishers for resupply to motor vehicle repairers.

18 Information used for fitting a spare part to or using a tool on a motor vehicle should be considered as being used for repair and maintenance, while information on the design, production process or the materials used for manufacturing a spare part should not be considered to fall within this category, and may therefore be withheld.

19 The independent operator should not have to purchase the spare part in question to be able to obtain this information.

20 OJ L95, 9.4.2009, p 7.

FREQUENTLY ASKED QUESTIONS (FAQS) ON THE APPLICATION OF EU ANTITRUST RULES IN THE MOTOR VEHICLE SECTOR

(27 August 2012)

[4.269]

NOTES

These FAQs are available on the European Commission website at: ec.europa.eu/competition-policy/sectors/motor-vehicles/legislation_en.

[4.270]

Since the adoption of the new motor vehicle Block Exemption Regulation[1] and the Supplementary Guidelines,[2] the Commission's services have received a number of questions relating to the application of the new framework for motor vehicle distribution and repair and for the distribution of spare parts for motor vehicles. Where these questions have been frequently asked, or are otherwise likely to be of wider interest, they are reproduced below together with answers and explanations.

These Frequently Asked Questions ("FAQs") are intended to complement the Supplementary Guidelines and do not replace them. The FAQs aim, in particular, at helping firms and individuals operating in the sector and legal practitioners to understand how the Commission's Directorate General for Competition approaches particular issues regarding the motor vehicle markets.[3] The FAQs are not intended to constitute a statement of the law and are without prejudice to the interpretation of Articles 101 and 102 of the Treaty on the Functioning of the European Union ("TFEU") by the European Courts. Finally, the FAQs do not prejudge the application by the Commission of Articles 101 and 102 to the specific circumstances of an individual case.

The FAQs are organised into several general topics, namely the honouring of warranties, servicing in the context of leasing contracts, the supply of spare parts, the use/purchase of tools, access to technical information and access to authorised repairer networks.

NOTES

1 Commission Regulation (EU) No 461/2010 of 27 May 2010 on the application of Article 101(3) of the Treaty on the Functioning of the European Union to categories of vertical agreements and concerted practices in the motor vehicle sector. Official Journal L129 of 28.5.2010, p 52; see eur-lex.europa.eu/LexUriServ/LexUriServ.do?uri=OJ:L:2010:129:0052:0057:EN:PDF.

2 Supplementary guidelines on vertical restraints in agreements for the sale and repair of motor vehicles and for the distribution of spare parts for motor vehicles. Official Journal C138 of 28.5.2010, p 16; see eur-lex.europa.eu/LexUriServ/LexUriServ.do?uri=OJ:C:2010:138:0016:0027:EN:PDF.

3 These FAQs concern particular restrictions in the motor vehicle sector that, under certain circumstances, may cause the agreement between the vehicle manufacturer and its authorised dealers or repairers (or eventually with a supplier of spare parts, repair tools or diagnostic, components for the initial assembly of motor vehicles, or other equipment) to infringe EU competition rules. Generally, this will be the case because: (1) the restriction at stake is likely to cause or strengthen the anti-competitive effects of the agreements between the vehicle supplier and its dealers or authorised repairers and spare parts distributors and cause them to be caught by Article 101(1) TFEU; (2) the agreements in question are unlikely to benefit from the block exemption, because of the supplier's market share; and (3) these agreements are unlikely to benefit on an individual basis from the exception set out in Article 101(3) TFEU. In some other cases, particular conduct referred to in these FAQs may constitute a violation of the prohibition of the abuse by an undertaking of its dominant position, pursuant to Article 102 TFEU. Finally, the FAQs refer as well to conduct or agreements that are unlikely to be in breach of EU competition rules. In any event, the application of the said rules must ultimately be assessed in each particular case, having regard to its specific factual and legal circumstances.

WARRANTIES

[4.271]

The Supplementary Guidelines set out the general principle that, for qualitative selective distribution agreements to benefit from an exemption under the EU competition rules, the vehicle manufacturer's warranty must not be made conditional on the end user having repair and maintenance work that is not covered by the warranty carried out within the vehicle manufacturer's authorised repair networks.[4] Similarly, warranty conditions must not require the use of the vehicle manufacturer's brand of spare parts in respect of replacements not covered by the warranty terms. These two types of restriction, which are referred to respectively as servicing and parts restrictions in the remainder of the FAQs, are likely to cause the agreement between the vehicle manufacturer and its authorised dealers or repairers to infringe EU competition rules. The reasoning behind this general principle is that such behaviour may result in the foreclosure of independent repairers or the closing of alternative channels for the production and distribution of spare parts, which ultimately may have a bearing on the price that consumers pay for repair and maintenance services.

Questions have been asked about the scope of this general principle and as to whether it applies under particular circumstances. Questions have also been raised about whether a consumer can be prevented from benefitting from the warranty on a vehicle that (s)he has purchased from an authorised dealer in another EU Member State.

The answers given below are without prejudice to the application of national consumer protection laws, which may impose specific obligations and create specific rights. They also do not apply to so-called "generosity schemes", by which a vehicle supplier[5] instructs its dealers to repair certain defects free of charge beyond the warranty period.

1. Does the assessment of servicing or parts restrictions depend on whether they are set out in the purchase contract or rather in the servicing or warranty booklet? [6]

No. In practice, the servicing or parts restrictions may be contained not in the purchase contract, but rather in another document, such as the servicing or warranty booklet. The assessment of these restrictions is in principle the same irrespective of the document in which they appear.

> Irrespective of where the restriction is stipulated, it is likely to lead consumers to believe that the warranty will be invalidated if servicing work is carried out in independent garages or if alternative brands of spare parts are used. This, in turn, is likely to foreclose such operators or close alternative channels for spare parts' distribution.

2. Does the assessment of servicing or parts restrictions differ if they are set out in an extended warranty issued by the authorised network at the sale of the vehicle or shortly after?

No. The fact that the servicing or parts restrictions are not set out in the vehicle supplier's warranty but are instead found in an extended warranty issued by the authorised network at the moment of the sale of the vehicle (or shortly thereafter) will not generally alter the assessment of the said restrictions.

> Just like vehicle manufacturers or their importers, the dealers and authorised repairers within a selective distribution system are parties to a network of agreements. If these parties agree to offer a warranty scheme and the warranties in question contain a servicing or parts restriction, this is likely to foreclose independent repairers or shut off alternative spare parts' distribution channels. The warranty scheme is therefore likely to cause or strengthen the anti-competitive effects of the agreements between the vehicle supplier and its authorised repairers and spare parts distributors.

3. Does the assessment of servicing or parts restrictions differ if they are set out in an extended warranty arranged by the vehicle supplier (or by the authorised network at the sale of the vehicle or shortly after) through a third party such as an insurer?

No. The fact that warranties that contain a servicing or parts restriction are arranged through a third party (typically an insurer) by the vehicle supplier (or by the members of its authorised network at or shortly after the sale of the vehicle: see question 2 above) does not in principle alter the assessment of the said restrictions.

> The fact that the extended warranty containing the servicing or parts restriction is arranged through a third party does not change the analysis set out in the Supplementary Guidelines. The decisive element is whether the servicing or parts restriction is a factor within the control of one or more of the parties to the network of selective distribution agreements[7] and therefore whether its implementation is likely to foreclose independent repairers or shut off alternative channels for spare parts' distribution.

4. Does the assessment of servicing or parts restrictions differ if these restrictions are set out in an "extended" warranty bought by a consumer from an authorised repairer or from the vehicle supplier some years after the purchase of the vehicle?

Yes. Such a warranty is in general unlikely to result in a breach of EU competition rules.

> Years after the vehicle purchase, authorised dealers do not enjoy the same degree of privileged access to customers as they do in the period shortly after the purchase. As a consequence, alternative providers of extended warranties, such as chains of independent repairers and insurance firms are less likely to face significant barriers preventing them from offering their products to vehicle owners. In such circumstances, it seems unlikely that independent repairers could face a significant foreclosure effect even if car warranties issued by vehicle suppliers or their authorised networks contained servicing or parts restrictions.[8]

5. Should a consumer be able to benefit from the warranty on a vehicle that (s)he has purchased from an authorised dealer in another EU Member State?

Yes, although some limitations concerning the scope of the warranty may apply.

If vehicle suppliers fail either to honour warranties on vehicles purchased by consumers from authorised dealers in other Member States or to contractually oblige their authorised repairers to carry out warranty work on such vehicles, this would constitute a restriction on sales and the selective distribution agreements at stake are likely to be contrary to EU competition rules.[9]

The same reasoning applies to free servicing or work carried out as a result of a product recall.[10] The reasoning does not change if the consumer has bought the vehicle through a mandated intermediary. Warranties on vehicles bought from authorised dealers in other Member States should also not be subject to additional administrative procedures that lead to delays in the work being carried out.

However, it should be noted that warranty terms may vary from one Member State to another, and that vehicle suppliers typically take account of the cost of respecting a particular set of warranty terms when setting the recommended purchase price of the vehicle. If a vehicle is exported, the vehicle supplier may legitimately apply the terms of the original warranty applicable to the vehicle, and will thus be under no obligation to apply more beneficial warranty terms that may be included with vehicles sold in the Member State of import.

It should also be noted that if a consumer has paid separately for a mobility scheme, that scheme may be limited in scope to a particular Member State.

6. Does the assessment of a parts restriction differ if, for operations not covered by warranty, the vehicle manufacturer requires the use of a spare part (such as a lubricant) from a specific supplier (rather than stipulating that its own brand of spare parts be used)?

Generally, no. Such a restriction is likely to result in a breach of EU competition rules.

As with a parts restriction requiring the use of the vehicle manufacturer's brand of spare parts as condition for the warranty to apply, a parts restriction requiring (rather than merely recommending) the use of spare parts from a specific producer is likely to foreclose alternative channels for spare parts' distribution.

However, a vehicle manufacturer may legitimately refuse to honour warranties on the grounds that the situation leading to the claim in question is causally linked to a failure of a specific spare part provided by an alternative supplier.

NOTES

4 See Paragraph 69 of the Supplementary Guidelines, footnote number 2, above.

5 The term "vehicle supplier(s)" normally refers, in the context of this document, to the vehicle manufacturer(s), but may also include, when appropriate in the respective context, other categories of market players, such as importers or main dealers (with respect to sub-dealers).

6 Questions 1 to 3 are based on the understanding that the signing of the purchase contract or the handing over of the warranty booklet to the final consumer forms part of or relates to the agreement between the manufacturer and the dealer and thus can be addressed under Article 101 TFEU. These questions do not address the situation where the dealer is part of the manufacturer's group (e.g. it's a subsidiary of the manufacturer).

7 In general, such servicing or parts restrictions are unlikely to bring any benefit to the insurance company.

8 Such warranties are therefore unlikely to cause the selective distribution agreements in question to be caught by Article 101 TFEU.

9 These agreements will likely be caught by Article 101 TFEU. Moreover, they will not likely benefit from an exemption under Commission Regulation (EU) No 330/2010 on the application of Article 101(3) of the Treaty on the Functioning of the European Union to categories of vertical agreements and concerted practices (OJ L102 of 23.04.2010, p 1-7), because the clauses in question would constitute a restriction on sales within the meaning of Article 4(b) respectively 4(c) thereof, see eur-lex.europa.eu/LexUriServ/LexUriServ.do?uri=OJ:L:2010:102:0001:0007:EN:PDF. See also paragraph 50 and in particular footnote 4 of the Guidelines on Vertical Restraints. OJ C130 of 19.05.2010, to be found at eur-lex.europa.eu/LexUriServ/LexUriServ.do?uri=OJ:C:2010:130:0001:0046:EN:PDF. Finally, they will be unlikely to benefit from the exception set out in Article 101(3) TFEU. See also Judgment of the Court of Justice of 10 December 1985 in case 31/85, *ETA Fabriques d'Ebauches v. SA DK Investment and others*.

10 If vehicle manufacturers fail to carry out free servicing or work as a result of a product recall on vehicles purchased by consumers from authorised dealers in other Member States or to contractually oblige their authorised repairers to carry out product recall related services on these vehicles, this would likewise constitute a restriction on sales, and the selective distribution agreements at stake are likely to be contrary to EU competition rules.

LEASING

[4.272]

Leasing contracts between firms are not covered by the general EU rules on vertical agreements.[11] They also do not fall within the scope of the motor vehicle Block Exemption Regulation.[12] As to agreements between leasing firms and private motorists, these are not caught by Article 101 TFEU.

Nonetheless, the following question has frequently been asked.

7. If a vehicle is leased from a firm connected to the vehicle supplier, can that firm stipulate that servicing must be carried out within the vehicle supplier's authorised network and/or using exclusively branded parts from the vehicle supplier?

Yes, unless (or until) it is certain that a transfer of ownership over the vehicle to the lessee will take place at the expiry of the contract or the end of the leasing term.

In principle, for as long as there is no certainty that ownership of the vehicle will be transferred to the lessee, the leasing company will have an interest in maintaining the vehicle's residual value and may thus be entitled to place more value on the vehicle if it has always been maintained in the authorised repair network using exclusively vehicle-supplier branded parts.

By contrast, if a transfer of ownership is certain to occur (either because it is established as such in the contract or the applicable legislation or because the lessee has decided to execute an option to this effect), the leasing company cannot in principle claim a specific interest in the vehicle's residual value which would entitle it to place restrictions on the lessee concerning the use of independent repairers' services or the use of alternative spare parts. In this regard, the leasing company is in the same position as it would typically be under a regular purchase agreement.

NOTES

11 Guidelines on Vertical Restraints, paragraph 26, see footnote 9.

12 See Article 2 thereof.

SPARE PARTS

[4.273]

The supply of spare parts is the subject of three sector-specific hardcore clauses in the motor vehicle Block Exemption Regulation.[13] Certain questions have however been frequently asked relating to the supply of parts to both independent and authorised repairers.

8. May a vehicle supplier make bonuses or rebates for captive parts[14] conditional on the sourcing also of competitive parts?

This issue is not dealt with in the motor vehicle Block Exemption Regulation or the Supplementary Guidelines. Under certain circumstances, conditional rebates might constitute an abuse of a dominant position and thus lead to a breach of EU competition rules.

In most cases, bonus and rebate schemes are a legitimate and possibly pro-competitive means of motivating a repairer to sell more parts of the brand in question. However, care has to be taken as regards captive parts, in respect of which the vehicle supplier will have a dominant position. Making bonuses or rebates on these parts conditional on the repairer buying competitive parts of the vehicle supplier's brand could imply that the vehicle supplier is leveraging a dominant position on one market to abusively gain advantage on the other.[15]

9. May a vehicle supplier oblige its authorised repairers to store alternative brands of spare parts separately from parts of its own brand?

Generally, yes, for as long as this does not make it unduly difficult for the repairers in question to use alternative brands of parts.

A vehicle supplier may have a legitimate interest in ensuring that authorised repairers store spare parts in an orderly manner, since if the correct parts are readily at hand, this may have an impact on consumer perception of the brand. Vehicle suppliers may also have a legitimate interest in ensuring that alternative brands of parts are not mistakenly used for warranty repairs or servicing packages in respect of which they bear the costs.

However, requirements of this type should not unduly complicate stock control, increase required storage space, or impede access to such an extent that repairers are discouraged from using alternative brands of parts.[16] Examples of restrictions that might not be justified include obligations imposed by a vehicle supplier on its repairers to have a separate storeroom for such parts or not to store such parts in the work bays.

10. May an authorised repairer refuse to supply captive parts to independent garages?

Generally, yes. It is unlikely that EU competition rules would be infringed if an authorised repairer were merely to unilaterally refuse to supply spare parts to independent repairers.

In most cases, it is in the interest of authorised repairers to sell spare parts to independent repairers because they make a margin by so doing.

If for some reason an authorised repairer were to unilaterally decide not to sell captive spare parts to independent repairers, it is unlikely that this would breach EU competition rules.[17] Usually, the independent repairers are able to turn to another authorised repairer for the purchase of captive parts.

If, however, members of a selective distribution system were to agree with one another not to sell captive parts to independent repairers, the agreement in question would be likely to be anticompetitive.[18]

11. Under what circumstances would a vehicle supplier be obliged to supply spare parts directly to independent repairers?

If independent repairers encountered widespread difficulties in obtaining captive spare parts from authorised distributors of such parts, a failure on the part of the vehicle supplier to supply such parts directly might lead to a breach of EU competition rules.

Vehicle suppliers provide their authorised repairers with the full range of spare parts needed to perform repair and maintenance work on motor vehicles of their brands and are the only firms able to provide repairers and distributors with certain parts. If independent repairers are unable to source these captive parts from authorised distributors and the vehicle supplier refuses to supply independent repairers directly, possible negative effects stemming from its agreements with authorised repairers and/or parts distributors could be strengthened.[19] Specifically, a lack of access to captive parts could cause the market position of independent operators to decline, ultimately leading to consumer harm.

12. May a vehicle supplier prevent a member of its authorised parts distribution network from selling spare parts to independent repairers that use independent spare parts distributors as purchase agents?

Generally, no. If an authorised spare parts distributor were to unilaterally decide not to sell to independent repairers that use agents, this would not breach EU competition rules. However, if a vehicle supplier were to instruct its distributors not to sell through agents, its distribution agreements would be likely to infringe EU competition rules.

Most vehicle suppliers operate qualitative selective distribution systems for the sale of spare parts. Independent repairers are to be treated as end users of spare parts for the purposes of the motor vehicle Block Exemption Regulation.[20] If a vehicle supplier were to prevent its selective distributors from selling to such repairers when these use the services of agents, this would be an anticompetitive restriction on passive sales.

Agents are in principle to be treated as an extension of the contracting party. However, in order to be considered as an agent, the latter must have instructions to purchase a defined order and may not trade in parts that it has purchased from members of the selective distribution system. A vehicle supplier may legitimately instruct the members of such a system not to sell to firms that intend to resell the parts in question.

NOTES

13 See Article 5 thereof.

14 Captive spare parts are parts which may only be obtained from the motor vehicle manufacturer or from members of its authorised networks; see Supplementary Guidelines, paragraph 22. See footnote number 2, above.

15 This would amount to a breach of Article 102 TFEU. General guidance on the application of Article 102 TFEU can be found in the Communication from the Commission — Guidance on the Commission's enforcement priorities in applying Article 82 of the EC Treaty to abusive exclusionary conduct by dominant undertakings (OJ C45 of 24.2.2009, p 7-20), see eur-lex.europa.eu/LexUriServ/LexUriServ.do?uri=OJ:C:2009:045:0007:0020:EN:PDF. See in particular the section on tying and bundling.

16 Requirements that have such an effect might be considered to be indirect non-compete obligations, the impact of which should be assessed under the Guidelines on Vertical Restraints. See footnote number 9, above.

17 Article 101 TFEU would not be relevant, since the decision not to sell the spare parts would not result from any agreement. Article 102 TFEU would generally not be applicable, since it is unlikely that the authorised repairer in question could be considered to be in a dominant position.

18 Such an agreement would indeed be likely to be caught by Article 101 TFEU. It should also be noted that a supplier's restriction of spare parts sales by a member of its authorised network to independent repairers constitutes a hardcore restriction (see Art. 5 (a) of Regulation No 461/2010, see footnote 1, above) and is therefore also likely to be caught by Article 101 TFEU.

19 This would cause the agreements to fall within Article 101 TFEU. Under certain circumstances, if the parts in question were not available from authorised spare parts distributors, a failure to release such parts could amount to a breach of Article 102 TFEU.

20 Article 5(a) thereof. See footnote number 1, above.

ELECTRONIC TOOLS

[4.274]

There are two categories of electronic diagnostic and repair tools on the markets: the brand-specific tools manufactured by a third party but marketed by the vehicle supplier, and other tools which are designed to repair several brands of vehicles. Questions have been asked in respect of both.

13. May the agreements between the vehicle supplier and the members of its authorised repair network stipulate that the latter must use specified electronic diagnostic or repair tools or equipment for vehicle repair, servicing and maintenance, even when equivalent tools or equipment are available from other sources?

Generally, yes. Such a restriction is unlikely to lead to a breach of EU competition rules.[21]

Economies of scale are likely to result if a vehicle manufacturer agrees with a tool manufacturer that the whole of its authorised repair network should use a common tool or tools. Common solutions to technical problems are also likely to be more easily found if a common tool is used. Furthermore, training may be facilitated if a common tool is used by all technicians. In most circumstances, specifying that an authorised repairer must have access to a particular tool is therefore likely to be an acceptable qualitative criterion.[22]

14. Does the guidance on access to technical information set out in the Supplementary Guidelines also apply to tool manufacturers that wish to have access to such information in order to produce multi-brand repair tools?

No. When considering whether the withholding of technical information is likely to breach the EU competition rules, the Supplementary Guidelines make a distinction between technical information that will ultimately be used for the purpose of repair and maintenance of motor vehicles, as opposed to technical information used for another purpose, such as the manufacturing of tools.[23]

As regards access to technical information and tools for independent repairers, the Supplementary Guidelines aim to prevent vehicle manufacturers from discriminating between their authorised repairers and independent repairers as regards the provision of essential inputs that are entirely under the vehicle manufacturer's control and that are not available from other sources.[24] The objective of the Supplementary Guidelines is thus to ensure that independent repairers have access to the brand-specific repair tools on the same terms as members of the authorised networks.

The agreements between the vehicle manufacturer and the tool manufacturer fall under the general EU competition rules and should be assessed accordingly.[25]

NOTES

21 The Supplementary Guidelines (see footnote number 2, above) give clarifications on the relationship between tool manufacturers and vehicle suppliers. See, in particular, paragraphs 23 and 24.

22 Therefore, this restriction will not lead the agreements between manufacturer and repairer to be caught by Article 101(1) TFEU.

23 See paragraph 65, in particular 65 (d) of the Supplementary Guidelines; see footnote number 2, above.

24 In this case, the authorised repair agreements fall within the scope of Article 101 TFEU.

25 The vehicle supplier and the tool manufacturer should thus assess their agreements under Articles 101 and 102 TFEU and more in particular under Commission Regulation (EU) No 330/2010 on the application of Article 101(3) of the Treaty on the Functioning of the European Union to categories of vertical agreements and concerted practices and under the Guidelines on Vertical Restraints, see footnote 9 above.

ACCESS TO TECHNICAL INFORMATION

[4.275]
Despite the extensive clarifications given in the Supplementary Guidelines on this topic,[26] both the Commission and National Competition Authorities have been asked questions relating to safety and security, to pricing, and to the specific issue of vehicle service histories.

15. May a vehicle manufacturer refuse to grant access to technical information to independent operators for safety or security reasons?

Assuming that a vehicle manufacturer is likely to be the only source for the full range of technical information relating to vehicles of its brands (and its agreements concerning the supply of such information thus cannot benefit from the safe harbour created by the motor vehicle Block Exemption Regulation), the answer is generally, no. In such a case involving a (near) monopoly position, flat refusals to grant technical information for supposed reasons of security or safety will usually not be compatible with EU competition rules.

Vehicle manufacturers are in principle required to release technical information, for which they are the only source, to independent operators. Only exceptionally may a failure to provide such information be justified for safety or security reasons.[27] Factors to consider in individual cases include the following.

The scope of the information involved

Independent garages are generally familiar with systems with safety implications, including tyres, steering, brakes and shock absorbers, and indeed have historically worked on them without demonstrable negative consequences for safety. Imposing restrictions that affect the provision of parts for such systems on the grounds that they are safety-related would be unlikely to be deemed as justified.[28]

The availability of less-restrictive forms of protection

Safety: Where there is a need to restrict access to a safety-related part with which independent repairers are likely to be unfamiliar, such as a high-voltage electrical system that is specific to a particular model, or a technique for replacing carbon composite body panels, the vehicle manufacturer should adopt the least-restrictive means of achieving the desired result. One example might be to require independent repairers to attend training on the particular system or technique. Where the vehicle manufacturer or an undertaking acting on its behalf provides such training, the independent repairer should not be required to follow more training than it needs to work on the system or master the technique in respect of which the exception is invoked.

Security: As regards security-related information, a criminal records check can often be seen as an appropriate, less restrictive means of ensuring protection.

16. May a vehicle manufacturer grant discounts or refunds on technical information if an authorised repairer buys a certain volume of vehicle-manufacturer branded spare parts or tools?

This issue is not dealt with by the Block Exemption Regulation or the Supplementary Guidelines. Under certain circumstances, this conduct might constitute an abuse of a dominant position and thus lead to a breach of EU competition rules.

The vehicle manufacturer is likely to be the only source for the full range of technical information relating to vehicles of its brands. Granting discounts or refunds on technical information on condition that a repairer buys a certain volume of its own brand of parts or tools might imply that the vehicle manufacturer is leveraging a dominant position on one market to abusively gain advantage on the other.[29]

17. Can an independent repairer be prevented from accessing or updating a printed or electronic record of the vehicle's service history?

No, in so far as a vehicle supplier and/or its authorised repairers are likely to be the only source for a comprehensive record relating to vehicles of its brands. Any such refusal to grant access to the service record would be likely to cause the agreements between the vehicle supplier and its authorised repairers to breach EU competition rules.

Existing service and repair records, in whatever form, are to be treated as technical information for the purposes of applying the Supplementary Guidelines. Access to such records will generally be necessary to enable the repairer to tell what operations need to be carried out in order to bring the servicing schedule up to date.

An incomplete service and repair record would be likely to reduce the residual value of the vehicle and make it difficult to prove that warranty terms had been complied with. If independent repairers could not update such records, this would likely deter consumers from using independent repairers, and would foreclose such operators from a substantial part of the market.

NOTES

26 See, in particular, paragraphs 62ff. of the Supplementary Guidelines. See footnote number 2, above.

27 As the Supplementary Guidelines explain, in general failures to release technical information may cause the agreements between vehicle suppliers and their authorised repairers to be caught by Article 101 TFEU. See, in particular, paragraph 63 of the Supplementary Guidelines, see footnote number 2, above. However, in certain circumstances, vehicle suppliers may come to the conclusion that even if certain information is withheld, their agreements may benefit from the exception in Article 101(3) TFEU. However, this is unlikely in the situation of a (near) monopoly position.

28 These practices are therefore unlikely to benefit from the exception set out in Article 101(3) TFEU.

29 General guidance on the application of Article 102 TFEU can be found in the Commission Guidance on the Commission's enforcement priorities in applying Article 82 of the EC Treaty to abusive exclusionary conduct by dominant undertakings. See footnote number 15, above.

ACCESS TO AUTHORISED NETWORKS

[4.276]

The Supplementary Guidelines set out the principle that, outside the safe harbour created by the motor vehicle Block Exemption Regulation,[30] authorised repair networks should generally be open to all firms that meet the relevant qualitative criteria.[31] Nonetheless, a question has arisen as to whether certain access conditions are to be considered as not qualitative in nature (and thus would be deemed as constituting quantitative criteria).[32]

18. May a vehicle supplier refuse access to its authorised repair network on the grounds that the repairer in question is already authorised to repair vehicles of a brand of a competing vehicle supplier?

Where it concerns agreements outside the safe harbour created by the motor vehicle Block Exemption Regulation, the answer is generally, no. This would be likely to lead the agreements in question to breach EU competition rules.

In the vast majority of cases, vehicle suppliers use qualitative criteria in order to select their authorised repairers.[33] The question therefore arises as to whether a requirement not to be authorised to repair vehicles of another supplier's brands is a valid qualitative requirement. To determine this, one needs to examine whether or not this requirement is objective and required by the nature of the service. There is normally nothing in the nature of repair services for one brand that requires them to be carried out exclusively by firms that are not authorised to repair vehicles of other brands. Such an obligation therefore normally amounts to a non-qualitative criterion that may restrict competition on the relevant market, namely the market for repair and maintenance services of the concerned brand.

NOTES

[30] In most cases, authorised repair networks of car manufacturers are likely to exceed the 30% market share threshold in the relevant market(s).

[31] See, in particular, paragraph 70 and 71 of the Supplementary Guidelines. See footnote number 2, above.

[32] Selective distribution agreements are block exempted as long as the parties' market share is below 30%, subject to the conditions defined in the Regulation, see Paragraph 46 of the Supplementary Guidelines. See footnote number 2, above. Moreover, distribution agreements based on purely qualitative criteria are not caught by Article 101, irrespectively of the parties' market share. See Paragraph 43 of the Supplementary Guidelines (see footnote number 2, above).

[33] As explained in footnote number 32, above, qualitative selective distribution agreements are in principle not caught by Article 101 TFEU.

COMMISSION REGULATION

(316/2014/EU)

of 21 March 2014

on the application of Article 101(3) of the Treaty on the Functioning of the European Union to categories of technology transfer agreements

(Text with EEA relevance)

[4.277]

NOTES

Date of publication in OJ: OJ L93, 28.03.2014, p 17.

Application of this Regulation in relation to the UK: in accordance with the European Union (Withdrawal) Act 2018, s 3 at **[7.5]**, this Regulation became domestic law on IP completion day (as defined in the European Union (Withdrawal Agreement) Act 2020, s 39). In so far as applying to the UK, this Regulation is amended by the Competition (Amendment etc) (EU Exit) Regulations 2019, SI 2019/93, as from IP completion day. The amendments are set out below. With regard to these amendments, note that Articles that are repealed are reproduced in italics and, in the case of other amendments, the amending provision from SI 2019/93 is set out in full in the Notes to the amended Article, and the text of the amended Article has not been altered. For transitional provisions and savings in relation to the operation of the 2019 Regulations, see Sch 4 to those Regulations at **[7.69]** et seq.

Note also that Regulation 19/65/EEC (under which this Regulation was made) is repealed, in relation to the UK, by the Competition (Amendment etc) (EU Exit) Regulations 2019, SI 2019/93, reg 63, Sch 3, para 1, as from IP completion day (as defined in the European Union (Withdrawal Agreement) Act 2020, s 39) (for transitional provisions and savings in relation to the operation of the 2019 Regulations, see Sch 4 to those Regulations at **[7.69]** et seq). However, see Sch 3, para 2 to those Regulations (at **[7.67]**) which provides for the continued application of this Regulation despite the repeal of Regulation 19/65/EEC.

THE EUROPEAN COMMISSION,

Having regard to the Treaty on the Functioning of the European Union,

Having regard to Regulation No 19/65/EEC of the Council of 2 March 1965 on application of Article 85(3) of the Treaty to certain categories of agreements and concerted practices,[1] and in particular Article 1 thereof,

Having published a draft of this Regulation,

After consulting the Advisory Committee on Restrictive Practices and Dominant Positions,

Whereas:

(1) Regulation No 19/65/EEC empowers the Commission to apply Article 101(3) of the Treaty by regulation to certain categories of technology transfer agreements and corresponding concerted practices to which only two undertakings are party which fall within Article 101(1) of the Treaty.

(2) Pursuant to Regulation No 19/65/EEC, the Commission has, in particular, adopted Commission Regulation (EC) No 772/2004.[2] Regulation (EC) No 772/2004 defines categories of technology transfer agreements which the Commission regarded as normally satisfying the conditions laid down in Article 101(3) of the Treaty. In view of the overall positive experience with the application of that Regulation, which expires on 30 April 2014, and taking into account further experience acquired since its adoption, it is appropriate to adopt a new block exemption regulation.

(3) This Regulation should meet the two requirements of ensuring effective protection of competition and providing adequate legal security for undertakings. The pursuit of those objectives should take account of the need to simplify administrative supervision and the legislative framework to as great an extent as possible.

(4) Technology transfer agreements concern the licensing of technology rights. Such agreements will usually improve economic efficiency and be pro-competitive as they can reduce duplication of research and development, strengthen the incentive for the initial research and development, spur incremental innovation, facilitate diffusion and generate product market competition.

(5) The likelihood that such efficiency-enhancing and pro-competitive effects will outweigh any anti-competitive effects due to restrictions contained in technology transfer agreements depends on the degree of market power of the undertakings concerned and, therefore, on the extent to which those undertakings face competition from undertakings owning substitute technologies or undertakings producing substitute products.

(6) This Regulation should cover only technology transfer agreements between a licensor and a licensee. It should

cover such agreements even if the agreement contains conditions relating to more than one level of trade, for instance requiring the licensee to set up a particular distribution system and specifying the obligations the licensee must or may impose on resellers of the products produced under the licence. However, such conditions and obligations should comply with the competition rules applicable to supply and distribution agreements set out in Commission Regulation (EU) No 330/2010.[3] Supply and distribution agreements concluded between a licensee and buyers of its contract products should not be exempted by this Regulation.

(7) This Regulation should only apply to agreements where the licensor permits the licensee and/or one or more of its sub-contractors to exploit the licensed technology rights, possibly after further research and development by the licensee and/or its sub-contractors, for the purpose of producing goods or services. It should not apply to licensing in the context of research and development agreements which are covered by Commission Regulation (EU) No 1217/2010[4] or to licensing in the context of specialisation agreements which are covered by Commission Regulation (EU) No 1218/2010.[5] It should also not apply to agreements, the purpose of which is the mere reproduction and distribution of software copyright protected products as such agreements do not concern the licensing of a technology to produce but are more akin to distribution agreements. Nor should it apply to agreements to set up technology pools, that is to say, agreements for the pooling of technologies with the purpose of licensing them to third parties, or to agreements whereby the pooled technology is licensed out to those third parties.

(8) For the application of Article 101(3) of the Treaty by regulation, it is not necessary to define those technology transfer agreements that are capable of falling within Article 101(1) of the Treaty. In the individual assessment of agreements pursuant to Article 101(1), account has to be taken of several factors, and in particular the structure and the dynamics of the relevant technology and product markets.

(9) The benefit of the block exemption established by this Regulation should be limited to those agreements which can be assumed with sufficient certainty to satisfy the conditions of Article 101(3) of the Treaty. In order to attain the benefits and objectives of technology transfer, this Regulation should not only cover the transfer of technology as such but also other provisions contained in technology transfer agreements if, and to the extent that, those provisions are directly related to the production or sale of the contract products.

(10) For technology transfer agreements between competitors it can be presumed that, where the combined share of the relevant markets accounted for by the parties does not exceed 20% and the agreements do not contain certain severely anti-competitive restrictions, they generally lead to an improvement in production or distribution and allow consumers a fair share of the resulting benefits.

(11) For technology transfer agreements between non-competitors it can be presumed that, where the individual share of the relevant markets accounted for by each of the parties does not exceed 30% and the agreements do not contain certain severely anti-competitive restrictions, they generally lead to an improvement in production or distribution and allow consumers a fair share of the resulting benefits.

(12) If the applicable market-share threshold is exceeded on one or more product or technology markets, the block exemption should not apply to the agreement for the relevant markets concerned.

(13) There can be no presumption that, above those market-share thresholds, technology transfer agreements fall within the scope of Article 101(1) of the Treaty. For instance, exclusive licensing agreements between non-competing undertakings often fall outside the scope of Article 101(1). There can also be no presumption that, above those market-share thresholds, technology transfer agreements falling within the scope of Article 101(1) will not satisfy the conditions for exemption. However, it can also not be presumed that they will usually give rise to objective advantages of such a character and size as to compensate for the disadvantages which they create for competition.

(14) This Regulation should not exempt technology transfer agreements containing restrictions which are not indispensable to the improvement of production or distribution. In particular, technology transfer agreements containing certain severely anti-competitive restrictions, such as the fixing of prices charged to third parties, should be excluded from the benefit of the block exemption established by this Regulation irrespective of the market shares of the undertakings concerned. In the case of such hardcore restrictions the whole agreement should be excluded from the benefit of the block exemption.

(15) In order to protect incentives to innovate and the appropriate application of intellectual property rights, certain restrictions should be excluded from the benefit of the block exemption. In particular certain grant back obligations and non-challenge clauses should be excluded. Where such a restriction is included in a licence agreement only the restriction in question should be excluded from the benefit of the block exemption.

(16) The market-share thresholds and the non-exemption of technology transfer agreements containing the severely anti-competitive restrictions and the excluded restrictions provided for in this Regulation will normally ensure that the agreements to which the block exemption applies do not enable the participating undertakings to eliminate competition in respect of a substantial part of the products in question.

(17) The Commission may withdraw the benefit of this Regulation, pursuant to Article 29(1) of Council Regulation (EC) No 1/2003,[6] where it finds in a particular case that an agreement to which the exemption provided for in this Regulation applies nevertheless has effects which are incompatible with Article 101(3) of the Treaty. This may occur in particular where the incentives to innovate are reduced or where access to markets is hindered.

(18) The competition authority of a Member State may withdraw the benefit of this Regulation pursuant to Article 29(2) of Regulation (EC) No 1/2003 in respect of the territory of that Member State, or a part thereof where, in a particular case, an agreement to which the exemption provided for in this Regulation applies nevertheless has effects which are incompatible with Article 101(3) of the Treaty in the territory of that Member State, or in a part thereof, and where such territory has all the characteristics of a distinct geographic market.

(19) In order to strengthen supervision of parallel networks of technology transfer agreements which have similar restrictive effects and which cover more than 50% of a given market, the Commission may by regulation declare this Regulation inapplicable to technology transfer agreements containing specific restrictions relating to the market concerned, thereby restoring the full application of Article 101 of the Treaty to such agreements,

NOTES

[1] OJ 36, 6.3.1965, p 533/65.

[2] Commission Regulation (EC) No 772/2004 of 7 April 2004 on the application of Article 81(3) of the Treaty to categories of technology transfer agreements (OJ L123, 27.4.2004, p 11).

[3] Commission Regulation (EU) No 330/2010 of 20 April 2010 on the application of Article 101(3) of the Treaty on the Functioning of the European Union to categories of vertical agreements and concerted practices (OJ L102, 23.4.2010, p 1).

[4] Commission Regulation (EU) No 1217/2010 of 14 December 2010 on the application of Article 101(3) of the Treaty on the Functioning of the European Union to certain categories of research and development agreements (OJ L335, 18.12.2010, p 36).

[5] Commission Regulation (EU) No 1218/2010 of 14 December 2010 on the application of Article 101(3) of the Treaty on the Functioning of the European Union to certain categories of specialisation agreements (OJ L335, 18.12.2010, p 43).

[6] Council Regulation (EC) No 1/2003 of 16 December 2002 on the implementation of the rules on competition laid down in Articles 81 and 82 of the Treaty (OJ L1, 4.1.2003, p 1).

HAS ADOPTED THIS REGULATION:

[4.278]

Article 1 Definitions

1. For the purposes of this Regulation, the following definitions shall apply:
   (a) 'agreement' means an agreement, a decision of an association of undertakings or a concerted practice;
   (b) 'technology rights' means know-how and the following rights, or a combination thereof, including applications for or applications for registration of those rights:
      (i) patents,
      (ii) utility models,
      (iii) design rights,
      (iv) topographies of semiconductor products,
      (v) supplementary protection certificates for medicinal products or other products for which such supplementary protection certificates may be obtained,
      (vi) plant breeder's certificates and
      (vii) software copyrights;
   (c) 'technology transfer agreement' means:
      (i) a technology rights licensing agreement entered into between two undertakings for the purpose of the production of contract products by the licensee and/or its sub-contractor(s),
      (ii) an assignment of technology rights between two undertakings for the purpose of the production of contract products where part of the risk associated with the exploitation of the technology remains with the assignor;
   (d) 'reciprocal agreement' means a technology transfer agreement where two undertakings grant each other, in the same or separate contracts, a technology rights licence, and where those licences concern competing technologies or can be used for the production of competing products;
   (e) 'non-reciprocal agreement' means a technology transfer agreement where one undertaking grants another undertaking a technology rights licence, or where two undertakings grant each other such a licence but where those licences do not concern competing technologies and cannot be used for the production of competing products;
   (f) 'product' means goods or a service, including both intermediary goods and services and final goods and services;
   (g) 'contract product' means a product produced, directly or indirectly, on the basis of the licensed technology rights;
   (h) 'intellectual property rights' includes industrial property rights, in particular patents and trademarks, copyright and neighbouring rights;
   (i) 'know-how' means a package of practical information, resulting from experience and testing, which is:
      (i) secret, that is to say, not generally known or easily accessible,
      (ii) substantial, that is to say, significant and useful for the production of the contract products, and
      (iii) identified, that is to say, described in a sufficiently comprehensive manner so as to make it possible to verify that it fulfils the criteria of secrecy and substantiality;
   (j) 'relevant product market' means the market for the contract products and their substitutes, that is to say all those products which are regarded as interchangeable or substitutable by the buyer, by reason of the products' characteristics, their prices and their intended use;
   (k) 'relevant technology market' means the market for the licensed technology rights and their substitutes, that is to say all those technology rights which are regarded as interchangeable or substitutable by the licensee, by reason of the technology rights' characteristics, the royalties payable in respect of those rights and their intended use;
   (l) 'relevant geographic market' means the area in which the undertakings concerned are involved in the supply of and demand for products or the licensing of technology rights, in which the conditions of competition are sufficiently homogeneous and which can be distinguished from neighbouring areas because the conditions of competition are appreciably different in those areas;
   (m) 'relevant market' means the combination of the relevant product or technology market with the relevant geographic market;
   (n) 'competing undertakings' means undertakings which compete on the relevant market, that is to say:
      (i) competing undertakings on the relevant market where the technology rights are licensed, that is to say, undertakings which license out competing technology rights (actual competitors on the relevant market),

(ii) competing undertakings on the relevant market where the contract products are sold, that is to say, undertakings which, in the absence of the technology transfer agreement, would both be active on the relevant market(s) on which the contract products are sold (actual competitors on the relevant market) or which, in the absence of the technology transfer agreement, would, on realistic grounds and not just as a mere theoretical possibility, in response to a small and permanent increase in relative prices, be likely to undertake, within a short period of time, the necessary additional investments or other necessary switching costs to enter the relevant market(s) (potential competitors on the relevant market);

(o) 'selective distribution system' means a distribution system where the licensor undertakes to license the production of the contract products, either directly or indirectly, only to licensees selected on the basis of specified criteria and where those licensees undertake not to sell the contract products to unauthorised distributors within the territory reserved by the licensor to operate that system;

(p) 'exclusive licence' means a licence under which the licensor itself is not permitted to produce on the basis of the licensed technology rights and is not permitted to license the licensed technology rights to third parties, in general or for a particular use or in a particular territory;

(q) 'exclusive territory' means a given territory within which only one undertaking is allowed to produce the contract products, but where it is nevertheless possible to allow another licensee to produce the contract products within that territory only for a particular customer where the second licence was granted in order to create an alternative source of supply for that customer;

(r) 'exclusive customer group' means a group of customers to which only one party to the technology transfer agreement is allowed to actively sell the contract products produced with the licensed technology.

2. For the purposes of this Regulation, the terms 'undertaking', 'licensor' and 'licensee' shall include their respective connected undertakings.

'Connected undertakings' means:

(a) undertakings in which a party to the technology transfer agreement, directly or indirectly:
   (i) has the power to exercise more than half the voting rights, or
   (ii) has the power to appoint more than half the members of the supervisory board, board of management or bodies legally representing the undertaking, or
   (iii) has the right to manage the undertaking's affairs;

(b) undertakings which directly or indirectly have, over a party to the technology transfer agreement, the rights or powers listed in point (a);

(c) undertakings in which an undertaking referred to in point (b) has, directly or indirectly, the rights or powers listed in point (a);

(d) undertakings in which a party to the technology transfer agreement together with one or more of the undertakings referred to in points (a), (b) or (c), or in which two or more of the latter undertakings, jointly have the rights or powers listed in point (a);

(e) undertakings in which the rights or the powers listed in point (a) are jointly held by:
   (i) parties to the technology transfer agreement or their respective connected undertakings referred to in points (a) to (d), or
   (ii) one or more of the parties to the technology transfer agreement or one or more of their connected undertakings referred to in points (a) to (d) and one or more third parties.

NOTES

Application of this Article in relation to the UK: this Article is amended, in relation to the UK only, by the Competition (Amendment etc) (EU Exit) Regulations 2019, SI 2019/93, reg 63, Sch 3, Pt 2, para 9(2), as from IP completion day (as defined in the European Union (Withdrawal Agreement) Act 2020, s 39) (for transitional provisions and savings in relation to the operation of the 2019 Regulations, see Sch 4 to those Regulations at **[7.69]** et seq), as follows—

"(2) In Article 1(1), after point (c), insert—

"(ca) "the Chapter 1 prohibition" means the prohibition imposed by section 2(1) of the Competition Act 1998;".".

[4.279]

Article 2 Exemption

1. Pursuant to Article 101(3) of the Treaty and subject to the provisions of this Regulation, Article 101(1) of the Treaty shall not apply to technology transfer agreements.

2. The exemption provided for in paragraph 1 shall apply to the extent that technology transfer agreements contain restrictions of competition falling within the scope of Article 101(1) of the Treaty. The exemption shall apply for as long as the licensed technology rights have not expired, lapsed or been declared invalid or, in the case of know-how, for as long as the know-how remains secret. However, where know-how becomes publicly known as a result of action by the licensee, the exemption shall apply for the duration of the agreement.

3. The exemption provided for in paragraph 1 shall also apply to provisions, in technology transfer agreements, which relate to the purchase of products by the licensee or which relate to the licensing or assignment of other intellectual property rights or know-how to the licensee, if, and to the extent that, those provisions are directly related to the production or sale of the contract products.

NOTES

Application of this Article in relation to the UK: this Article is amended, in relation to the UK only, by the Competition (Amendment etc) (EU Exit) Regulations 2019, SI 2019/93, reg 63, Sch 3, Pt 2, para 9(3), as from IP completion day (as defined in the European Union (Withdrawal Agreement) Act 2020, s 39) (for transitional provisions and savings in relation to the operation of the 2019 Regulations, see Sch 4 to those Regulations at **[7.69]** et seq), as follows—

"(3) In Article 2—

(a) for paragraph 1 substitute—

"Subject to the provisions of this Regulation, technology transfer agreements are exempt from the Chapter 1 prohibition.";

(b) in paragraph 2, for "Article 101(1) of the Treaty" substitute "the Chapter 1 prohibition".".

[4.280]

Article 3 Market-share thresholds

1. Where the undertakings party to the agreement are competing undertakings, the exemption provided for in Article 2 shall apply on condition that the combined market share of the parties does not exceed 20% on the relevant market(s).

2. Where the undertakings party to the agreement are not competing undertakings, the exemption provided for in Article 2 shall apply on condition that the market share of each of the parties does not exceed 30% on the relevant market(s).

[4.281]

Article 4 Hardcore restrictions

1. Where the undertakings party to the agreement are competing undertakings, the exemption provided for in Article 2 shall not apply to agreements which, directly or indirectly, in isolation or in combination with other factors under the control of the parties, have as their object any of the following:

(a) the restriction of a party's ability to determine its prices when selling products to third parties;

(b) the limitation of output, except limitations on the output of contract products imposed on the licensee in a non-reciprocal agreement or imposed on only one of the licensees in a reciprocal agreement;

(c) the allocation of markets or customers except:

(i) the obligation on the licensor and/or the licensee, in a non-reciprocal agreement, not to produce with the licensed technology rights within the exclusive territory reserved for the other party and/or not to sell actively and/or passively into the exclusive territory or to the exclusive customer group reserved for the other party,

(ii) the restriction, in a non-reciprocal agreement, of active sales by the licensee into the exclusive territory or to the exclusive customer group allocated by the licensor to another licensee provided the latter was not a competing undertaking of the licensor at the time of the conclusion of its own licence,

(iii) the obligation on the licensee to produce the contract products only for its own use provided that the licensee is not restricted in selling the contract products actively and passively as spare parts for its own products,

(iv) the obligation on the licensee, in a non-reciprocal agreement, to produce the contract products only for a particular customer, where the licence was granted in order to create an alternative source of supply for that customer;

(d) the restriction of the licensee's ability to exploit its own technology rights or the restriction of the ability of any of the parties to the agreement to carry out research and development, unless such latter restriction is indispensable to prevent the disclosure of the licensed know-how to third parties.

2. Where the undertakings party to the agreement are not competing undertakings, the exemption provided for in Article 2 shall not apply to agreements which, directly or indirectly, in isolation or in combination with other factors under the control of the parties, have as their object any of the following:

(a) the restriction of a party's ability to determine its prices when selling products to third parties, without prejudice to the possibility of imposing a maximum sale price or recommending a sale price, provided that it does not amount to a fixed or minimum sale price as a result of pressure from, or incentives offered by, any of the parties;

(b) the restriction of the territory into which, or of the customers to whom, the licensee may passively sell the contract products, except:

(i) the restriction of passive sales into an exclusive territory or to an exclusive customer group reserved for the licensor,

(ii) the obligation to produce the contract products only for its own use provided that the licensee is not restricted in selling the contract products actively and passively as spare parts for its own products,

(iii) the obligation to produce the contract products only for a particular customer, where the licence was granted in order to create an alternative source of supply for that customer,

(iv) the restriction of sales to end-users by a licensee operating at the wholesale level of trade,

(v) the restriction of sales to unauthorised distributors by the members of a selective distribution system;

(c) the restriction of active or passive sales to end-users by a licensee which is a member of a selective distribution system and which operates at the retail level, without prejudice to the possibility of prohibiting a member of the system from operating out of an unauthorised place of establishment.

3. Where the undertakings party to the agreement are not competing undertakings at the time of the conclusion of the agreement but become competing undertakings afterwards, paragraph 2 and not paragraph 1 shall apply for the full life of the agreement unless the agreement is subsequently amended in any material respect. Such an amendment includes the conclusion of a new technology transfer agreement between the parties concerning competing technology rights.

[4.282]

Article 5 Excluded restrictions

1. The exemption provided for in Article 2 shall not apply to any of the following obligations contained in technology transfer agreements:

(a) any direct or indirect obligation on the licensee to grant an exclusive licence or to assign rights, in whole or in part, to the licensor or to a third party designated by the licensor in respect of its own improvements to, or its own new applications of, the licensed technology;

(b) any direct or indirect obligation on a party not to challenge the validity of intellectual property rights which the other party holds in the Union, without prejudice to the possibility, in the case of an exclusive licence, of providing for termination of the technology transfer agreement in the event that the licensee challenges the validity of any of the licensed technology rights.

2. Where the undertakings party to the agreement are not competing undertakings, the exemption provided for in Article 2 shall not apply to any direct or indirect obligation limiting the licensee's ability to exploit its own technology rights or limiting the ability of any of the parties to the agreement to carry out research and development, unless such latter restriction is indispensable to prevent the disclosure of the licensed know-how to third parties.

NOTES

Application of this Article in relation to the UK: this Article is amended, in relation to the UK only, by the Competition (Amendment etc) (EU Exit) Regulations 2019, SI 2019/93, reg 63, Sch 3, Pt 2, para 9(4), as from IP completion day (as defined in the European Union (Withdrawal Agreement) Act 2020, s 39) (for transitional provisions and savings in relation to the operation of the 2019 Regulations, see Sch 4 to those Regulations at **[7.69]** et seq), as follows—

"(4) In Article 5(1), in point (b), for "which the other party holds in the Union" substitute "held by the other party which have effect in the United Kingdom".".

[4.283]

Article 6 Withdrawal in individual cases

1. The Commission may withdraw the benefit of this Regulation, pursuant to Article 29(1) of Regulation (EC) No 1/2003, where it finds in any particular case that a technology transfer agreement to which the exemption provided for in Article 2 of this Regulation applies nevertheless has effects which are incompatible with Article 101(3) of the Treaty, and in particular where:

(a) access of third parties' technologies to the market is restricted, for instance by the cumulative effect of parallel networks of similar restrictive agreements prohibiting licensees from using third parties' technologies;

(b) access of potential licensees to the market is restricted, for instance by the cumulative effect of parallel networks of similar restrictive agreements prohibiting licensors from licensing to other licensees or because the only technology owner licensing out relevant technology rights concludes an exclusive license with a licensee who is already active on the product market on the basis of substitutable technology rights.

2. Where, in any particular case, a technology transfer agreement to which the exemption provided for in Article 2 of this Regulation applies has effects which are incompatible with Article 101(3) of the Treaty in the territory of a Member State, or in a part thereof, which has all the characteristics of a distinct geographic market, the competition authority of that Member State may withdraw the benefit of this Regulation, pursuant to Article 29(2) of Regulation (EC) No 1/2003, in respect of that territory, under the same circumstances as those set out in paragraph 1 of this Article.

NOTES

Repeal of this Article in relation to the UK: this Article is repealed, in relation to the UK only, by the Competition (Amendment etc) (EU Exit) Regulations 2019, SI 2019/93, reg 63, Sch 3, Pt 2, para 9(5), as from IP completion day (as defined in the European Union (Withdrawal Agreement) Act 2020, s 39) (for transitional provisions and savings in relation to the operation of the 2019 Regulations, see Sch 3, Pt 2, para 10 to those Regulations at **[7.68]**, and Sch 4 to those Regulations at **[7.69]** et seq).

[4.284]

Article 7 Non-application of this Regulation

1. Pursuant to Article 1a of Regulation (EC) No 19/65/EEC, the Commission may by regulation declare that, where parallel networks of similar technology transfer agreements cover more than 50% of a relevant market, this Regulation is not to apply to technology transfer agreements containing specific restrictions relating to that market.

2. A regulation pursuant to paragraph 1 shall not become applicable earlier than six months following its adoption.

NOTES

Repeal of this Article in relation to the UK: this Article is repealed, in relation to the UK only, by the Competition (Amendment etc) (EU Exit) Regulations 2019, SI 2019/93, reg 63, Sch 3, Pt 2, para 9(5), as from IP completion day (as defined in the European Union (Withdrawal Agreement) Act 2020, s 39) (for transitional provisions and savings in relation to the operation of the 2019 Regulations, see Sch 3, Pt 2, para 10 to those Regulations at **[7.68]**, and Sch 4 to those Regulations at **[7.69]** et seq).

[4.285]

Article 8 Application of the market-share thresholds

For the purposes of applying the market-share thresholds laid down in Article 3 the following rules shall apply:

(a) the market share shall be calculated on the basis of market sales value data; if market sales value data are not available, estimates based on other reliable market information, including market sales volumes, may be used to establish the market share of the undertaking concerned;

(b) the market share shall be calculated on the basis of data relating to the preceding calendar year;

(c) the market share held by the undertakings referred to in point (e) of the second subparagraph of Article 1(2) shall be apportioned equally to each undertaking having the rights or the powers listed in point (a) of the second subparagraph of Article 1(2);

(d) the market share of a licensor on a relevant market for the licensed technology rights shall be calculated on the basis of the presence of the licensed technology rights on the relevant market(s) (that is the product market(s) and the geographic market(s)) where the contract products are sold, that is on the basis of the sales data relating to the contract products produced by the licensor and its licensees combined;

(e) if the market share referred to in Article 3(1) or (2) is initially not more than 20% or 30% respectively, but subsequently rises above those levels, the exemption provided for in Article 2 shall continue to apply for a period of two consecutive calendar years following the year in which the 20% threshold or 30% threshold was first exceeded.

[4.286]
Article 9 Relationship with other block exemption regulations
This Regulation shall not apply to licensing arrangements in research and development agreements which fall within the scope of Regulation (EU) No 1217/2010 or in specialisation agreements which fall within the scope of Regulation (EU) No 1218/2010.

[4.287]
Article 10 Transitional period
The prohibition laid down in Article 101(1) of the Treaty shall not apply from 1 May 2014 until 30 April 2015 to agreements already in force on 30 April 2014 which do not satisfy the conditions for exemption provided for in this Regulation but which, on 30 April 2014, satisfied the conditions for exemption provided for in Regulation (EC) No 772/2004.

NOTES
Repeal of this Article in relation to the UK: this Article is repealed, in relation to the UK only, by the Competition (Amendment etc) (EU Exit) Regulations 2019, SI 2019/93, reg 63, Sch 3, Pt 2, para 9(5), as from IP completion day (as defined in the European Union (Withdrawal Agreement) Act 2020, s 39) (for transitional provisions and savings in relation to the operation of the 2019 Regulations, see Sch 4 to those Regulations at **[7.69]** et seq).

[4.288]
Article 11 Period of validity
This Regulation shall enter into force on 1 May 2014.
It shall expire on 30 April 2026.
This Regulation shall be binding in its entirety and directly applicable in all Member States.

NOTES
Application of this Article in relation to the UK: this Article is amended, in relation to the UK only, by the Competition (Amendment etc) (EU Exit) Regulations 2019, SI 2019/93, reg 63, Sch 3, Pt 2, para 9(6), as from IP completion day (as defined in the European Union (Withdrawal Agreement) Act 2020, s 39) (for transitional provisions and savings in relation to the operation of the 2019 Regulations, see Sch 4 to those Regulations at **[7.69]** et seq), as follows—

"(6) In the words after Article 11, omit the words from "This Regulation shall be binding" to "Member States."."

COMMUNICATION FROM THE COMMISSION

(2014/C89/03)

Guidelines on the application of Article 101 of the Treaty on the Functioning of the European Union to technology transfer agreements

[4.289]

NOTES
Date of publication in OJ: OJ C89, 28.3.2014, p 3.

1. INTRODUCTION

[4.290]
1. These guidelines set out the principles for the assessment of technology transfer agreements under Article 101 of the Treaty on the Functioning of the European Union[1] ('Article 101'). Technology transfer agreements concern the licensing of technology rights where the licensor permits the licensee to exploit the licensed technology rights for the production of goods or services, as defined in Article 1(1)(c) of Commission Regulation (EU) No 316/2014 of 21 March 2014 on the application of Article 101(3) of the Treaty on the Functioning of the European Union to categories of technology transfer agreements ('the TTBER').[2]

2. The purpose of these guidelines is to provide guidance on the application of the TTBER as well as on the application of Article 101 of the Treaty on the Functioning of the European Union ('the Treaty') to technology transfer agreements that fall outside the scope of the TTBER. The TTBER and the guidelines are without prejudice to the possible parallel application of Article 102 of the Treaty to technology transfer agreements.[3]

3. The standards set forth in these guidelines must be applied in the light of the circumstances specific to each case. This excludes a mechanical application. Each case must be assessed on its own facts and these guidelines must be applied reasonably and flexibly. Examples given serve as illustrations only and are not intended to be exhaustive.

4. These guidelines are without prejudice to the interpretation of Article 101 and the TTBER that may be given by the Court of Justice and the General Court.

NOTES
[1] With effect from 1 December 2009, Articles 81 and 82 of the EC Treaty have become Articles 101 and 102, respectively, of the Treaty on the Functioning of the European Union ('TFEU'). The two sets of provisions are, in substance, identical. For the purposes of these Guidelines, references to Articles 101 and 102 of the TFEU should be understood as references

to Articles 81 and 82, respectively, of the EC Treaty where appropriate. The TFEU also introduced certain changes in terminology, such as the replacement of 'Community' by 'Union' and 'common market' by 'internal market'. The terminology of the TFEU will be used throughout these Guidelines.

2 OJ L93, 28.3.2014. p 17. The TTBER replaces Commission Regulation (EC) No 772/2004 of 27 April 2004 on the application of Article 81(3) of the Treaty to categories of technology transfer agreements (OJ L123, 27.4.2004, p 11).

3 See by analogy Joined Cases C-395/96 P and C-396/96 P, *Compagnie Maritime Belge*, [2000] ECR I-1365, paragraph 130, and point 106 of the Commission Guidelines on the application of Article 81(3) of the Treaty, OJ C101, 27.4.2004, p 97.

2. GENERAL PRINCIPLES

2.1. ARTICLE 101 OF THE TREATY AND INTELLECTUAL PROPERTY RIGHTS

[4.291]

5. The aim of Article 101 of the Treaty as a whole is to protect competition on the market with a view to promoting consumer welfare and an efficient allocation of resources. Article 101(1) prohibits all agreements and concerted practices between undertakings and decisions by associations of undertakings[4] which may affect trade between Member States[5] and which have as their object or effect the prevention, restriction or distortion of competition.[6] As an exception to this rule Article 101(3) provides that the prohibition contained in Article 101(1) may be declared inapplicable in the case of agreements between undertakings which contribute to improving the production or distribution of products or to promoting technical or economic progress, while allowing consumers a fair share of the resulting benefits and which do not impose restrictions which are not indispensable to the attainment of these objectives and do not afford such undertakings the possibility of eliminating competition in respect of a substantial part of the products concerned.

6. Intellectual property laws confer exclusive rights on holders of patents, copyright, design rights, trademarks and other legally protected rights. The owner of intellectual property is entitled under intellectual property laws to prevent unauthorised use of its intellectual property and to exploit it, for example, by licensing it to third parties. Once a product incorporating an intellectual property right, with the exception of performance rights,[7] has been put on the market inside the European Economic Area (EEA) by the holder or with its consent, the intellectual property right is exhausted in the sense that the holder can no longer use it to control the sale of the product (principle of Union exhaustion).[8] The right holder has no right under intellectual property laws to prevent sales by licensees or buyers of such products incorporating the licensed technology. The principle of Union exhaustion is in line with the essential function of intellectual property rights, which is to grant the holder the right to exclude others from exploiting its intellectual property without its consent.

7. The fact that intellectual property laws grant exclusive rights of exploitation does not imply that intellectual property rights are immune from competition law intervention. Article 101 of the Treaty is in particular applicable to agreements whereby the holder licenses another undertaking to exploit its intellectual property rights.[9] Nor does it imply that there is an inherent conflict between intellectual property rights and the Union competition rules. Indeed, both bodies of law share the same basic objective of promoting consumer welfare and an efficient allocation of resources. Innovation constitutes an essential and dynamic component of an open and competitive market economy. Intellectual property rights promote dynamic competition by encouraging undertakings to invest in developing new or improved products and processes. So does competition by putting pressure on undertakings to innovate. Therefore, both intellectual property rights and competition are necessary to promote innovation and ensure a competitive exploitation thereof.

8. In the assessment of licence agreements under Article 101 of the Treaty it must be kept in mind that the creation of intellectual property rights often entails substantial investment and that this is often a risky endeavour. In order not to reduce dynamic competition and to maintain the incentive to innovate, the innovator must not be unduly restricted in the exploitation of intellectual property rights that turn out to be valuable. For these reasons the innovator should be free to seek appropriate remuneration for successful projects that is sufficient to maintain investment incentives, taking failed projects into account. Technology rights licensing may also require the licensee to make significant sunk investments (that is to say, that upon leaving that particular field of activity the investment cannot be used by the licensee for other activities or sold other than at a significant loss) in the licensed technology and production assets necessary to exploit it. Article 101 cannot be applied without considering such ex ante investments made by the parties and the risks relating thereto. The risk facing the parties and the sunk investment that must be committed may thus lead to the agreement falling outside Article 101(1) or fulfilling the conditions of Article 101(3), as the case may be, for the period of time required to recoup the investment.

9. In assessing licensing agreements under Article 101 of the Treaty, the existing analytical framework is sufficiently flexible to take due account of the dynamic aspects of technology rights licensing. There is no presumption that intellectual property rights and licence agreements as such give rise to competition concerns. Most licence agreements do not restrict competition and create pro-competitive efficiencies. Indeed, licensing as such is pro-competitive as it leads to dissemination of technology and promotes innovation by the licensor and licensee(s). In addition, even licence agreements that do restrict competition may often give rise to pro-competitive efficiencies, which must be considered under Article 101(3) and balanced against the negative effects on competition.[10] The great majority of licence agreements are therefore compatible with Article 101.

2.2. THE GENERAL FRAMEWORK FOR APPLYING ARTICLE 101

10. Article 101(1) of the Treaty prohibits agreements which have as their object or effect the restriction of competition. Article 101(1) applies both to restrictions of competition between the parties to an agreement and to restrictions of competition between any of the parties and third parties.

11. The assessment of whether a licence agreement restricts competition must be made within the actual context in which competition would occur in the absence of the agreement with its alleged restrictions.[11] In making this assessment it is necessary to take account of the likely impact of the agreement on inter-technology competition (that

is to say, competition between undertakings using competing technologies) and on intra-technology competition (that is to say, competition between undertakings using the same technology).[12] Article 101(1) prohibits restrictions of both inter-technology competition and intra-technology competition. It is therefore necessary to assess to what extent the agreement affects or is likely to affect these two aspects of competition on the market.

12. The following two questions provide a useful framework for making this assessment. The first question relates to the impact of the agreement on inter-technology competition while the second question relates to the impact of the agreement on intra-technology competition. As restrictions may be capable of affecting both inter-technology competition and intra-technology competition at the same time, it may be necessary to analyse a restriction in the light of the two questions in points (a) and (b) before it can be concluded whether or not competition within the meaning of Article 101(1) is restricted:

(a) Does the licence agreement restrict actual or potential competition that would have existed without the contemplated agreement? If so, the agreement may be caught by Article 101(1). In making this assessment it is necessary to take into account competition between the parties and competition from third parties. For instance, where two undertakings established in different Member States cross licence competing technologies and undertake not to sell products in each other's home markets, (potential) competition that existed prior to the agreement is restricted. Similarly, where a licensor imposes obligations on its licensees not to use competing technologies and these obligations foreclose third party technologies, actual or potential competition that would have existed in the absence of the agreement is restricted.

(b) Does the licence agreement restrict actual or potential competition that would have existed in the absence of the contractual restraint(s)? If so, the agreement may be caught by Article 101(1). For instance, where a licensor restricts its licensees, who were not actual or potential competitors before the agreement, from competing with each other, (potential) competition that could have existed between the licensees in the absence of the restraints is restricted. Such restrictions include vertical price fixing and territorial or customer sales restrictions between licensees. However, certain restraints may in certain cases not be caught by Article 101(1) when the restraint is objectively necessary for the existence of an agreement of that type or that nature.[13] Such exclusion of the application of Article 101(1) can only be made on the basis of objective factors external to the parties themselves and not the subjective views and characteristics of the parties. The question is not whether the parties in their particular situation would not have accepted to conclude a less restrictive agreement, but whether, given the nature of the agreement and the characteristics of the market, a less restrictive agreement would not have been concluded by undertakings in a similar setting.[14] Claims that in the absence of a restraint the supplier would have resorted to vertical integration are not sufficient. Decisions on whether or not to vertically integrate depend on a broad range of complex economic factors, a number of which are internal to the undertaking concerned.

13. The fact that Article 101(1) of the Treaty distinguishes between those agreements that have a restriction of competition as their object and those agreements that have a restriction of competition as their effect should be taken into account in the application of the analytical framework set out in point (12) of these guidelines. An agreement or contractual restraint is only prohibited by Article 101(1) if its object or effect is to restrict inter-technology competition and/or intra-technology competition.

14. Restrictions of competition by object are those that by their very nature restrict competition. These are restrictions which in the light of the objectives pursued by the Union competition rules have such a high potential for negative effects on competition that it is not necessary for the purposes of applying Article 101(1) to demonstrate any effects on the market.[15] Moreover, the conditions of Article 101(3) are unlikely to be fulfilled in the case of restrictions by object. The assessment of whether or not an agreement has as its object a restriction of competition is based on a number of factors. These factors include, in particular, the content of the agreement and the objective aims pursued by it. It may also be necessary to consider the context in which it is (to be) applied or the actual conduct and behaviour of the parties on the market.[16] In other words, an examination of the facts underlying the agreement and the specific circumstances in which it operates may be required before it can be concluded whether a particular restriction constitutes a restriction by object of competition. The way in which an agreement is actually implemented may reveal a restriction by object even where the formal agreement does not contain an express provision to that effect. Evidence of subjective intent on the part of the parties to restrict competition is a relevant factor but not a necessary condition. An agreement may be regarded as having a restrictive object even if it does not have the restriction of competition as its sole aim but also pursues other legitimate objectives.[17] For licence agreements, the Commission considers that the restrictions covered by the list of hardcore restrictions of competition set out in Article 4 of the TTBER are restrictive by their very object.[18]

15. If an agreement is not restrictive of competition by object it is necessary to examine whether it has restrictive effects on competition. Account must be taken of both actual and potential effects.[19] In other words the agreement must have likely anti-competitive effects. For licence agreements to be restrictive of competition by effect they must affect actual or potential competition to such an extent that on the relevant market negative effects on prices, output, innovation or the variety or quality of goods and services can be expected with a reasonable degree of probability. The likely negative effects on competition must be appreciable.[20] Appreciable anti-competitive effects are likely to occur when at least one of the parties has or obtains some degree of market power and the agreement contributes to the creation, maintenance or strengthening of that market power or allows the parties to exploit such market power. Market power is the ability to maintain prices above competitive levels or to maintain output in terms of product quantities, product quality and variety or innovation below competitive levels for a not insignificant period of time.[21] The degree of market power normally required for a finding of an infringement under Article 101(1) is less than the degree of market power required for a finding of dominance under Article 102.[22]

16. For the purposes of analysing restrictions of competition by effect it is normally necessary to define the relevant market and to examine and assess, in particular, the nature of the products and technologies concerned, the market position of the parties, the market position of competitors, the market position of buyers, the existence of potential

competitors and the level of entry barriers. In some cases, however, it may be possible to show anti-competitive effects directly by analysing the conduct of the parties to the agreement on the market. It may for example be possible to ascertain that an agreement has led to price increases.

17. However, licence agreements may also have substantial pro-competitive potential and the vast majority of those agreements are indeed pro-competitive. Licence agreements may promote innovation by allowing innovators to earn returns to cover at least part of their research and development costs. Licence agreements also lead to a dissemination of technologies, which may create value by reducing the production costs of the licensee or by enabling it to produce new or improved products. Efficiencies at the level of the licensee often stem from a combination of the licensor's technology with the assets and technologies of the licensee. Such integration of complementary assets and technologies may lead to a cost/output configuration that would not otherwise be possible. For instance, the combination of an improved technology of the licensor with more efficient production or distribution assets of the licensee may reduce production costs or lead to the production of a higher quality product. Licensing may also serve the pro-competitive purpose of removing obstacles to the development and exploitation of the licensee's own technology. In particular in sectors where large numbers of patents are prevalent licensing often occurs in order to create design freedom by removing the risk of infringement claims by the licensor. When the licensor agrees not to invoke its intellectual property rights to prevent the sale of the licensee's products, the agreement removes an obstacle to the sale of the licensee's product and thus generally promotes competition.

18. In cases where a licence agreement is caught by Article 101(1) of the Treaty the pro-competitive effects of the agreement must be balanced against its restrictive effects in the context of Article 101(3). When all four conditions of Article 101(3) are satisfied, the restrictive licence agreement in question is valid and enforceable, with no prior decision to that effect being required.[23] Hardcore restrictions are unlikely to fulfil the conditions of Article 101(3). Such agreements generally fail (at least) one of the first two conditions of Article 101(3). In general they do not create objective economic benefits or benefits for consumers. Moreover, these types of agreements generally fail the indispensability test (under the third condition). For example, if the parties fix the price at which the products produced under the licence must be sold, this will in principle lead to a lower output and a misallocation of resources and higher prices for consumers. The price restriction is also not indispensable to achieve the possible efficiencies resulting from the availability to both competitors of the two technologies.

2.3. MARKET DEFINITION

19. The Commission's approach to defining the relevant market is laid down in its Notice on the definition of the relevant market for the purposes of Community competition law.[24] These guidelines only address aspects of market definition that are of particular importance in the field of technology rights licensing.

20. Technology is an input, which is integrated either into a product or a production process. Technology right licensing can therefore affect competition both upstream in input markets and downstream in output markets. For instance, an agreement between two parties which sell competing products downstream and which also cross license technology rights relating to the production of these products upstream may restrict competition on the downstream goods or services market concerned. The cross licensing may also restrict competition on the upstream market for technology and possibly also on other upstream input markets. For the purposes of assessing the competitive effects of licence agreements it may therefore be necessary to define the relevant product market(s) as well as the relevant technology market(s).[25]

21. The relevant product market comprises the contract products (incorporating the licensed technology) and products which are regarded by the buyers as interchangeable with or substitutable for the contract products, by reason of the products' characteristics, their prices and their intended use. Contract products can be part of a final and/or an intermediate product market.

22. The relevant technology markets consist of the licensed technology rights and its substitutes, that is to say, other technologies which are regarded by the licensees as interchangeable with or substitutable for the licensed technology rights, by reason of the technologies' characteristics, their royalties and their intended use. Starting from the technology which is marketed by the licensor, it is necessary to identify those other technologies to which licensees could switch in response to a small but permanent increase in relative prices, that is to say, to the royalties. An alternative approach is to look at the market for products incorporating the licensed technology rights (cf. point (25) below).

23. The term 'relevant market' used in Article 3 of the TTBER and defined in Article 1(1)(m) refers to the relevant product market and the relevant technology market in both their product and geographic dimension.

24. The 'relevant geographic market' is defined in Article 1(1)(l) of the TTBER and comprises the area in which the undertakings concerned are involved in the supply of and demand for products or the licensing of technology, in which the conditions of competition are sufficiently homogeneous and which can be distinguished from neighbouring areas because the conditions of competition are appreciably different in those areas The geographic market of the relevant technology market(s) can differ from the geographic market of the relevant product market(s).

25. Once relevant markets have been defined, market shares can be assigned to the various sources of competition in the market and used as an indication of the relative strength of market players. In the case of technology markets, one way to proceed is to calculate market shares on the basis of each technology's share of total licensing income from royalties, representing a technology's share of the market where competing technologies are licensed. However, this may often be a merely theoretical and not a practical way to proceed because of lack of clear information on royalties. Another approach, which is the one used for calculating the safe harbour, as explained in Article 8(d) of the TTBER, is to calculate market shares on the technology market on the basis of sales of products incorporating the licensed technology on downstream product markets (see for more details point (86) ff.). In individual cases outside the safe

harbour of the TTBER it may be necessary, where practically possible, to apply both of the described approaches in order to assess the market strength of the licensor more accurately and to take into account other available factors which give a good indication of the relative strength of the available technologies (see for more factors points (157) and (159) ff.).[26]

26. Some licence agreements may affect competition in innovation. In analysing such effects, however, the Commission will normally confine itself to examining the impact of the agreement on competition within existing product and technology markets.[27] Competition on such markets may be affected by agreements that delay the introduction of improved products or new products that over time will replace existing products. In such cases innovation is a source of potential competition which must be taken into account when assessing the impact of the agreement on product markets and technology markets. In a limited number of cases, however, it may be useful and necessary to also analyse the effects on competition in innovation separately. This is particularly the case where the agreement affects innovation aiming at creating new products and where it is possible at an early stage to identify research and development poles.[28] In such cases it can be analysed whether after the agreement there will be a sufficient number of competing research and development poles left for effective competition in innovation to be maintained.

2.4. THE DISTINCTION BETWEEN COMPETITORS AND NON-COMPETITORS

27. In general, agreements between competitors pose a greater risk to competition than agreements between non-competitors. However, competition between undertakings that use the same technology (intra-technology competition between licensees) constitutes an important complement to competition between undertakings that use competing technologies (inter-technology competition). For instance, intra-technology competition may lead to lower prices for the products incorporating the technology in question, which may not only produce direct and immediate benefits for consumers of these products, but also spur further competition between undertakings that use competing technologies. In the context of licensing the fact that licensees are selling their own product must also be taken into account. They are not re-selling a product supplied by another undertaking. There may thus be greater scope for product differentiation and quality-based competition between licensees than in the case of vertical agreements for the resale of products.

28. In order to determine the competitive relationship between the parties it is necessary to examine whether the parties would have been actual or potential competitors in the absence of the agreement. If without the agreement the parties would not have been actual or potential competitors in any relevant market affected by the agreement they are deemed to be non-competitors.

29. In principle, the parties to an agreement are not considered competitors if they are in a one-way or two-way blocking position. A one-way blocking position exists where a technology right cannot be exploited without infringing upon another valid technology right, or where one party cannot be active in a commercially viable way on the relevant market without infringing the other party's valid technology right. This is, for instance, the case where one technology right covers an improvement of another technology right and the improvement cannot be legally used without a licence of the basic technology right. A two-way blocking position exists where neither technology right can be exploited without infringing upon the other valid technology right or where neither party can be active in a commercially viable way on the relevant market without infringing the other party's valid technology right and where the parties thus need to obtain a licence or a waiver from each other.[29] However, in practice there will be cases where there is no certainty whether a particular technology right is valid and infringed.

30. The parties are actual competitors on the product market if prior to the agreement both are already active on the same relevant product market. The fact that both parties are already active on the same relevant product market, without having entered into a licensing arrangement, is a strong indicator that the parties are not blocking each other. In such a scenario, the parties can be presumed to be actual competitors, unless and until a blocking position is proven (in particular by a final court judgment).

31. The licensee can be considered a potential competitor on the product market if it is likely that, in the absence of the agreement, it would undertake the necessary additional investments to enter the relevant market in response to a small but permanent increase in product prices. Likely entry should be assessed on realistic grounds, that is to say based on the facts of the case at hand. Entry is more likely if the licensee possesses assets that can easily be used to enter the market without incurring significant sunk costs or if it has already developed plans, or otherwise started to invest, to enter the market. There have to be real concrete possibilities for the licensee to enter the relevant market and compete with established undertakings.[30] Accordingly, the licensee cannot be described as a potential competitor if its entry into a market is not an economically viable strategy.[31]

32. In the specific context of intellectual property rights, an additional factor for assessing whether the parties are potential competitors on a particular market is the possibility that their intellectual property rights are in a blocking position, that is to say that the licensee cannot enter the respective market without infringing the intellectual property rights of the other party.

33. In the absence of certainty, for example in the form of a final court decision, that a blocking position exists, the parties, when addressing the question whether they are potential competitors, will have to base themselves on all the available evidence at the time, including the possibility that intellectual property rights are infringed and whether there are effective possibilities to work around existing intellectual property rights. Substantial investments already made or advanced plans to enter a particular market, can support the view that the parties are at least potential competitors, even if a blocking position cannot be excluded. Particularly convincing evidence of the existence of a blocking position may be required where the parties have a common interest in claiming the existence of a blocking position in order to be qualified as non-competitors, for instance where the alleged blocking position concerns technologies that are technological substitutes (see point (22)) or if there is a significant financial inducement from the licensor to the licensee.

34. In order to constitute a realistic competitive constraint entry has to be likely to occur within a short period.[32] Normally a period of one to two years is appropriate. However, in individual cases longer periods can be taken into account. The period of time needed for undertakings already on the market to adjust their capacities can be used as a yardstick to determine this period. For instance, the parties are likely to be considered potential competitors on the product market where the licensee produces on the basis of its own technology in one geographic market and starts producing in another geographic market on the basis of a licensed competing technology. In such circumstances, it is likely that the licensee would have been able to enter the second geographic market on the basis of its own technology, unless such entry is precluded by objective factors, including the existence of blocking intellectual property rights.

35. The parties are actual competitors on the technology market if they are either already both licensing out substitutable technology rights, or the licensee is already licensing out its technology rights and the licensor enters the technology market by granting a license for competing technology rights to the licensee.

36. The parties are considered to be potential competitors on the technology market if they own substitutable technologies and the licensee is not licensing-out its own technology, provided that it would be likely to do so in the event of a small but permanent increase in technology prices. In the case of technology markets, it is generally more difficult to assess whether the parties are potential competitors. This is why, for the application of the TTBER, potential competition on the technology market is not taken into account (see point (83)) and the parties are treated as non-competitors.

37. In some cases it may also be possible to conclude that while the licensor and the licensee produce competing products, they are non-competitors on the relevant product market and the relevant technology market because the licensed technology represents such a drastic innovation that the technology of the licensee has become obsolete or uncompetitive. In such cases the licensor's technology either creates a new market or excludes the licensee's technology from the existing market. It is, however, often not possible to come to this conclusion at the time the agreement is concluded. It is usually only when the technology or the products incorporating it have been available to consumers for some time that it becomes apparent that the older technology has become obsolete or uncompetitive. For instance, when CD technology was developed and players and discs were put on the market, it was not obvious that this new technology would replace LP technology. This only became apparent some years later. The parties will therefore be considered to be competitors if at the time of the conclusion of the agreement it is not obvious that the licensee's technology is obsolete or uncompetitive. However, given that both Articles 101(1) and Article 101(3) of the Treaty must be applied in the light of the actual context in which the agreement occurs, the assessment is sensitive to material changes in the facts. The classification of the relationship between the parties will therefore change into a relationship of non-competitors, if at a later point in time the licensee's technology becomes obsolete or uncompetitive on the market.

38. In some cases the parties may become competitors subsequent to the conclusion of the agreement because the licensee develops or acquires and starts exploiting a competing technology. In such cases the fact that the parties were non-competitors at the time of conclusion of the agreement and that the agreement was concluded in that context must be taken into account. The Commission will therefore mainly focus on the impact of the agreement on the licensee's ability to exploit its own (competing) technology. In particular, the list of hardcore restrictions applying to agreements between competitors will not be applied to such agreements unless the agreement is subsequently amended in any material respect after the parties have become competitors (see Article 4(3) of the TTBER).

39. The undertakings party to an agreement may also become competitors subsequent to the conclusion of the agreement where the licensee was already active on the relevant market where the contract product is sold prior to the licence and where the licensor subsequently enters the relevant market either on the basis of the licensed technology rights or a new technology. In this case also the hardcore list relevant for agreements between non-competitors will continue to apply to the agreement unless the agreement is subsequently amended in any material respect (see Article 4(3) of the TTBER). A material amendment includes the conclusion of a new technology transfer agreement between the parties concerning competing technology rights which can be used for the production of products competing with the contract products.

NOTES

[4] In the following the term 'agreement' includes concerted practices and decisions of associations of undertakings.

[5] See Commission Guidelines on the effect on trade concept contained in Articles 81 and 82 of the Treaty, OJ C101, 27.4.2004, p 81.

[6] In the following the term 'restriction' includes the prevention and distortion of competition.

[7] Which includes rental rights. See in this respect Case 158/86, *Warner Brothers and Metronome Video*, [1988] ECR 2605 and Case C-61/97, *Foreningen af danske videogramdistributører*, [1998] ECR I-5171.

[8] This principle of Union exhaustion is for example enshrined in Article 7(1) of Directive 2008/95/EC to approximate the laws of the Member States relating to trade marks (OJ L299, 8.11.2008, p 25), which provides that the trade mark shall not entitle the proprietor to prohibit its use in relation to goods which have been put on the market in the Union under that trade mark by the proprietor or with its consent, and Article 4(2) of Directive 2009/24/EC of the European Parliament and of the Council of 23 April 2009 on the legal protection of computer programs (OJ L111, 5.5.2009, p 16), which provides that the first sale in the Union of a copy of a program by the right holder or with its consent shall exhaust the distribution right within the Union of that copy, with the exception of the right to control further rental of the program or a copy thereof. See in this respect C-128/11, Used *Soft Gmbh* v. *Oracle International Corp.*, [2012] ECR not yet published.

[9] See e.g. Joined Cases 56/64 and 58/64, *Consten and Grundig*, [1966] ECR 429.

[10] The methodology for the application of Article 101(3) is set out in the Commission Guidelines on the application of Article 81(3) of the Treaty, cited in footnote 3.

[11] See Case 56/65, *Société Technique Minière*, [1966] ECR 337, and Case C-7/95 P, *John Deere*, [1998] ECR I-3111, paragraph 76.

[12] See in this respect e.g. judgment in *Consten and Grundig* cited in footnote 9.

13 See in this respect the judgment in *Société Technique Minière* cited in footnote 11 and Case 258/78, *Nungesser*, [1982] ECR 2015.

14 For examples see points (126) to (127).

15 See in this respect e.g. Case C-49/92 P, *Anic Partecipazioni*, [1999] ECR I-4125, paragraph 99.

16 See Joined Cases 29/83 and 30/83, *CRAM and Rheinzink*, [1984] ECR 1679, paragraph 26, and Joined Cases 96/82 and others, *ANSEAU-NAVEWA*, [1983] ECR 3369, paragraphs 23–25. Case T-491/07 *Groupement des cartes bancaires* v *Commission*, judgment of 29 November 2012, paragraph 146.

17 Case C-209/07 *Beef Industry Development Society and Barry Brothers* [2008] ECR I-8637, paragraph 21.

18 Further guidance with regard to the notion of restriction of competition by object can be obtained in the Commission Guidelines on the application of Article 81(3) of the Treaty, cited in footnote 3. See also Joined Cases C-501/06 P, C-513/06 P, C-515/06 P and C-519/06 P *GlaxoSmithKline Services and Others* v *Commission and Others* [2009] ECR I-9291, paragraphs 59 to 64; Case C-209/07 *Beef Industry Development Society and Barry Brothers* [2008] ECR I 8637, paragraphs 21 to 39; Case C-8/08 *T-Mobile Netherlands and Others* [2009] ECR I-4529, paragraphs 31 and 36 to 39 and Case C 32/11 *Allianz Hungária Biztosító and Others*, judgment of 14 March 2013, paragraphs 33 to 38.

19 See the judgment in *John Deere*, [1998] cited in footnote 11.

20 Guidance on the issue of appreciability can be found in the Commission Notice on agreements of minor importance which do not appreciably restrict competition under Article 81(1) of the Treaty establishing the European Community (OJ C368, 22.12.2001, p 13). This Notice defines appreciability in a negative way. Agreements, which fall outside the scope of the de minimis notice, do not necessarily have appreciable restrictive effects. An individual assessment is required.

21 Case T-321/05 *Astra Zeneca* v *Commission* [2010] ECR II-2805, paragraph 267.

22 Commission Guidelines on the application of Article 81(3) of the Treaty, point 26, cited in footnote 3.

23 See Article 1(2) of Council Regulation (EC) No 1/2003 of 16 December 2002 on the implementation of the rules on competition laid down in Articles 81 and 82 of the Treaty (OJ L1, 4.1.2003, p 1), last amended by Council Regulation (EC) No 1419/2006 of 25 September 2006 (OJ L269, 28.9.2006, p 1).

24 OJ C372, 9.12.1997, p 5.

25 See for example Commission Decision COMP/M.5675 *Syngenta/ Monsanto* where the Commission analysed the merger of two vertically integrated sunflower breeders by examining both (i) the upstream market for the trading (namely the exchange and licensing) of varieties (parental lines and hybrids) and (ii) the downstream market for the commercialisation of hybrids. In COMP/M.5406, *IPIC/MAN Ferrostaal AG*, the Commission defined besides a market for the production of high-grade melamine also an upstream technology market for the supply of melamine production technology. See also COMP/M.269, *Shell/Montecatini*.

26 See also Commission Decision COMP/M.5675 Syngenta/Monsanto and Decision COMP/M.5406 IPIC/MAN Ferrostaal AG.

27 See also points 119 to 122 of the Guidelines on the applicability of Article 101 of the Treaty on the Functioning of the European Union to horizontal cooperation agreements ('Horizontal Guidelines'), OJ C11, 14.1.2011, p 1.

28 See also point (157).

29 In a scenario where undertakings have given a general commitment to license certain intellectual property rights, for instance a License of Right or a FRAND commitment, the parties cannot be considered to be in a blocking position on the basis of these intellectual property rights.

30 Joined Cases T-374/94, T-375/94, T-384/94 and T-388/94, *European Night Services and Others* v *Commission* [1998] ECR II-3141, paragraph 137.

31 Case T-461/07, *Visa Europe Ltd and Visa International Service* v *European Commission* [2011] ECR II-1729, paragraph 167.

32 Case T-461/07, *Visa Europe Ltd and Visa International Service* v *European Commission* [2011] ECR II-1729, paragraph 189.

3. APPLICATION OF THE TTBER

3.1. THE EFFECTS OF THE TTBER

[4.292]

40. Categories of technology transfer agreements that fulfil the conditions set out in the TTBER are exempted from the prohibition rule contained in Article 101(1) of the Treaty. Block exempted agreements are legally valid and enforceable. Such agreements can only be prohibited for the future and only upon withdrawal of the block exemption by the Commission and the competition authorities of the Member States. Block exempted agreements cannot be prohibited under Article 101 by national courts in the context of private litigation.

41. Block exemption of categories of technology transfer agreements is based on the presumption that — to the extent that they are caught by Article 101(1) of the Treaty — those agreements fulfil the four conditions laid down in Article 101(3). It is thus presumed that the agreements give rise to economic efficiencies, that the restrictions contained in the agreements are indispensable to the attainment of these efficiencies, that consumers within the affected markets receive a fair share of the efficiency gains and that the agreements do not afford the undertakings concerned the possibility of eliminating competition in respect of a substantial part of the products in question. The market share thresholds (Article 3), the hardcore list (Article 4) and the excluded restrictions (Article 5) set out in the TTBER aim at ensuring that only restrictive agreements that can reasonably be presumed to fulfil the four conditions of Article 101(3) are block exempted.

42. As set out in section 4 of these guidelines, many licence agreements fall outside Article 101(1) of the Treaty, either because they do not restrict competition at all or because the restriction of competition is not appreciable.[33] To the extent that such agreements would anyhow fall within the scope of the TTBER, there is no need to determine whether they are caught by Article 101(1).[34]

43. Outside the scope of the block exemption it is relevant to examine whether in the individual case the agreement is caught by Article 101(1) of the Treaty and if so, whether the conditions of Article 101(3) are satisfied. There is no presumption that technology transfer agreements falling outside the block exemption are caught by Article 101(1) or fail to satisfy the conditions of Article 101(3). In particular, the mere fact that the market shares of the parties exceed the market share thresholds set out in Article 3 of the TTBER is not a sufficient basis for finding that the agreement is caught by Article 101(1).

Individual assessment of the likely effects of the agreement is required. It is only where agreements contain hardcore restrictions of competition, that it can normally be presumed that they are prohibited by Article 101.

3.2. SCOPE AND DURATION OF THE TTBER

3.2.1. THE CONCEPT OF TECHNOLOGY TRANSFER AGREEMENTS

44. The TTBER and these guidelines cover agreements for the transfer of technology. According to Article 1(1)(b) of the TTBER the concept of 'technology rights' covers know-how as well as patents, utility models, design rights, topographies of semiconductor products, supplementary protection certificates for medicinal products or other products for which such supplementary protection certificates may be obtained, plant breeder's certificates and software copyrights or a combination thereof as well as applications for these rights and for registration of these rights. The licensed technology rights should allow the licensee, with or without other input, to produce the contract products. The TTBER only applies in Member States where the licensor holds relevant technology rights. Otherwise, there are no technology rights to be transferred within the meaning of the TTBER.

45. Know-how is defined in Article 1(1)(i) of the TTBER as a package of practical information, resulting from experience and testing, which is secret, substantial and identified:

(a) 'Secret' means that the know-how is not generally known or easily accessible.

(b) 'Substantial' means that the know-how includes information which is significant and useful for the production of the products covered by the licence agreement or the application of the process covered by the licence agreement. In other words, the information must significantly contribute to or facilitate the production of the contract products. In cases where the licensed know-how relates to a product as opposed to a process, this condition implies that the know-how is useful for the production of the contract product. This condition is not satisfied where the contract product can be produced on the basis of freely available technology. However, the condition does not require that the contract product is of higher value than products produced with freely available technology. In the case of process technologies, this condition implies that the know-how is useful in the sense that it can reasonably be expected at the date of conclusion of the agreement to be capable of significantly improving the competitive position of the licensee, for instance by reducing its production costs.

(c) 'Identified' means that it is possible to verify that the licensed know-how fulfils the criteria of secrecy and substantiality. This condition is satisfied where the licensed know-how is described in manuals or other written form. However, in some cases this may not be reasonably possible. The licensed know-how may consist of practical knowledge possessed by the licensor's employees. For instance, the licensor's employees may possess secret and substantial knowledge about a certain production process which is passed on to the licensee in the form of training of the licensee's employees. In such cases it is sufficient to describe in the agreement the general nature of the know-how and to list the employees that will be or have been involved in passing it on to the licensee.

46. Provisions in technology transfer agreements relating to the purchase of products by the licensee are only covered by the TTBER if, and to the extent that, those provisions are directly related to the production or sale of the contract products. Therefore the TTBER does not apply to those parts of a technology transfer agreement relating to input and/or equipment that are used for other purposes than the production of the contract products. For instance, where milk is sold together with licensing of technology to produce cheese, only the milk used for the production of cheese with the licensed technology will be covered by the TTBER.

47. Provisions in technology transfer agreements relating to the licensing of other types of intellectual property such as trademarks and copyright, other than software copyright (on software copyright see points (44) and (62)), are only covered by the TTBER if, and to the extent that, they are directly related to the production or sale of the contract products. This condition ensures that provisions covering other types of intellectual property rights are block exempted to the extent that these other intellectual property rights serve to enable the licensee to better exploit the licensed technology rights. For instance, where a licensor authorises a licensee to use its trademark on the products incorporating the licensed technology, this trademark licence may allow the licensee to better exploit the licensed technology by allowing consumers to make an immediate link between the product and the characteristics imputed to it by the licensed technology rights. An obligation on the licensee to use the licensor's trademark may also promote the dissemination of technology by allowing the licensor to identify itself as the source of the underlying technology. The TTBER covers technology transfer agreements in this scenario even if the principal interest of the parties lies in the exploitation of the trademark rather than the technology.[35]

48. The TTBER does not cover licensing of copyright other than software copyright (except for the situation set out in point (47)). The Commission will, however, as a general rule apply the principles set out in the TTBER and these guidelines when assessing licensing of copyright for the production of contract products under Article 101 of the Treaty.

49. On the other hand, the licensing of rental rights and public performance rights protected by copyright, in particular for films or music, is considered to raise particular issues and it may not be warranted to assess such licensing on the basis of the principles developed in these guidelines. In the application of Article 101 the specificities of the work and the way in which it is exploited must be taken into account.[36] The Commission will therefore not apply the TTBER and the present guidelines by way of analogy to the licensing of these other rights.

50. The Commission will also not extend the principles developed in the TTBER and these guidelines to trademark licensing (except for the situation set out in point (47)). Trademark licensing often occurs in the context of distribution and resale of goods and services and is generally more akin to distribution agreements than technology licensing. Where a trademark licence is directly related to the use, sale or resale of goods and services and does not constitute the primary object of the agreement, the licence agreement is covered by Commission Regulation (EU) No 330/2010.[37]

3.2.2. The concept of 'transfer'

51. The concept of 'transfer' implies that technology must flow from one undertaking to another. Such transfers normally take the form of licensing whereby the licensor grants the licensee the right to use its technology rights against payment of royalties.

52. As set out in Article 1(1)(c) of the TTBER, assignments where part of the risk associated with the exploitation of the technology rights remains with the assignor are also deemed to be technology transfer agreements. In particular, this is the case where the sum payable in consideration of the assignment is dependent on the turnover obtained by the assignee in respect of products produced with the assigned technology, the quantity of such products produced or the number of operations carried out employing the technology.

53. An agreement whereby the licensor commits not to exercise its technology rights against the licensee can also be seen as a transfer of technology rights. Indeed, the essence of a pure patent licence is the right to operate inside the scope of the exclusive right of the patent. It follows that the TTBER also covers so-called non-assertion agreements and settlement agreements whereby the licensor permits the licensee to produce within the scope of the patent.[38]

3.2.3. Agreements between two parties

54. According to Article 1(1)(c) of the TTBER, the Regulation only covers technology transfer agreements 'between two undertakings'. Technology transfer agreements between more than two undertakings are not covered by the TTBER.[39] The decisive factor in terms of distinguishing between agreements between two undertakings and multiparty agreements is whether the agreement in question is concluded between more than two undertakings.

55. Agreements concluded by two undertakings fall within the scope of the TTBER even if the agreement stipulates conditions for more than one level of trade. For instance, the TTBER applies to a licence agreement concerning not only the production stage but also the distribution stage, stipulating the obligations that the licensee must or may impose on resellers of the products produced under the licence.[40]

56. Agreements establishing technology pools and licensing out from technology pools are generally multiparty agreements and are therefore not covered by the TTBER.[41] The notion of technology pools covers agreements whereby two or more parties agree to pool their respective technologies and license them as a package. The notion of technology pools also covers arrangements whereby two or more undertakings agree to license a third party and authorise it to license-on the package of technologies.

57. Licence agreements concluded between more than two undertakings often give rise to the same issues as licence agreements of the same nature concluded between two undertakings. In its individual assessment of licence agreements which are of the same nature as those covered by the block exemption but which are concluded between more than two undertakings, the Commission will apply by analogy the principles set out in the TTBER. However, technology pools and licensing out from technology pools are specifically dealt with in section 4.4.

3.2.4. Agreements for the production of contract products

58. It follows from Article 1(1)(c) of the TTBER that for licence agreements to be covered by it they must be entered into 'for the purpose of the production of contract products', that is to say, products incorporating or produced with the licensed technology rights. The licence must permit the licensee and/or its sub-contractor(s) to exploit the licensed technology for the purpose of producing goods or services (see also recital 7 in the preamble of the TTBER).

59. Where the purpose of the agreement is not the production of contract products but, for instance, merely to block the development of a competing technology, the licence agreement is not covered by the TTBER and these guidelines may also not be appropriate for the agreement's assessment. More generally, if the parties refrain from exploiting the licensed technology rights, no efficiency enhancing activity takes place, in which case the very rationale of the block exemption is absent. However, exploitation does not need to take the form of an integration of assets. Exploitation also occurs where the licence creates design freedom for the licensee by allowing it to exploit its own technology without facing the risk of infringement claims by the licensor. In the case of licensing between competitors, the fact that the parties do not exploit the licensed technology may be an indication that the arrangement is a disguised cartel. For these reasons the Commission will examine cases of non-exploitation very closely.

60. The TTBER applies to licence agreements for the purpose of the production of contract products by the licensee and/or its sub-contractor(s). Therefore, the TTBER does not apply to (those parts of) technology transfer agreements that allow for sublicensing. However, the Commission will apply by analogy the principles set out in the TTBER and these guidelines to 'master licensing' agreements between licensor and licensee (that is to say an agreement whereby the licensor allows the licensee to sublicense the technology). Agreements between the licensee and sub-licensees for the production of contract products are covered by the TTBER.

61. The term 'contract products' encompasses goods and services produced with the licensed technology rights. This is the case both where the licensed technology is used in the production process and where it is incorporated into the product itself. In these guidelines the term 'products incorporating the licensed technology' covers both situations. The TTBER applies in all cases where technology rights are licensed for the purposes of producing goods and services. The framework of the TTBER and these guidelines is based on the premise that there is a direct link between the licensed technology rights and a contract product. In cases where no such link exists, that is to say where the purpose of the agreement is not to enable the production of a contract product, the analytical framework of the TTBER and these guidelines may not be appropriate.

62. The licensing of software copyright for the purpose of mere reproduction and distribution of the protected work, that is to say, the production of copies for resale, is not considered to be 'production' within the meaning of the TTBER and thus is not covered by the TTBER and these guidelines. Such reproduction for distribution is instead covered by analogy by Commission Regulation (EU) No 330/2010[42] and the Guidelines on Vertical Restraints.[43] Reproduction for distribution exists where a licence is granted to reproduce the software on a carrier, regardless of the technical means by which the software is distributed. For instance, the TTBER and these guidelines do not cover the licensing of software copyright whereby the licensee is provided with a master copy of the software in order to reproduce and sell on the software to end users. Nor do they cover the licensing of software copyright and distribution of software by means of 'shrink wrap' licences, that is, a set of conditions included in the package of the hard copy which the end user is deemed to have accepted by opening the wrapping of the package, or the licensing of software copyright and distribution of software by means of online downloading.

63. However, where the licensed software is incorporated by the licensee in the contract product this is not considered as mere reproduction but production. For instance, the TTBER and these guidelines cover the licensing of software copyright where the licensee has the right to reproduce the software by incorporating it into a device with which the software interacts.

64. The TTBER covers 'subcontracting' whereby the licensor licenses technology rights to the licensee who undertakes to produce certain products on the basis thereof exclusively for the licensor. Subcontracting may also involve the supply of equipment by the licensor to be used in the production of the goods and services covered by the agreement. For the latter type of subcontracting to be covered by the TTBER as part of a technology transfer agreement, the supplied equipment must be directly related to the production of the contract products. Subcontracting is also covered by the Commission Notice on subcontracting agreements.[44] According to that notice, which remains applicable, subcontracting agreements whereby the subcontractor undertakes to produce certain products exclusively for the contractor generally fall outside Article 101(1) of the Treaty. Subcontracting agreements whereby the contractor determines the transfer price of the intermediate contract product between subcontractors in a value chain of subcontracting generally also fall outside Article 101(1) provided the contract products are exclusively produced for the contractor. However, other restrictions imposed on the subcontractor such as the obligation not to conduct or exploit its own research and development may be caught by Article 101.[45]

65. The TTBER also applies to agreements whereby the licensee must carry out development work before obtaining a product or a process that is ready for commercial exploitation, provided that a contract product has been identified. Even if such further work and investment is required, the object of the agreement is the production of an identified contract product, that is to say, products produced with the licensed technology rights.

66. The TTBER and these guidelines do not cover agreements whereby technology rights are licensed for the purpose of enabling the licensee to carry out further research and development in various fields, including further developing a product arising out of such research and development.[46] For instance, the TTBER and the guidelines do not cover the licensing of a technological research tool used in the process of further research activity. Nor do they cover research and development sub-contracting whereby the licensee undertakes to carry out research and development in the field of the licensed technology and to hand back the improved technology package to the licensor.[47] The main object of such agreements is the provision of research and development services aimed at improving the technology as opposed to the production of goods and services on the basis of the licensed technology.

3.2.5. DURATION

67. Subject to the duration of the TTBER, which expires on 30 April 2026, the block exemption applies for as long as the licensed property right has not lapsed, expired or been declared invalid. In the case of know-how the block exemption applies as long as the licensed know-how remains secret, except where the know-how becomes publicly known as a result of action by the licensee, in which case the exemption applies for the duration of the agreement (see Article 2 of the TTBER).

68. The block exemption applies to each licensed technology right covered by the agreement and ceases to apply on the date of expiry, invalidity or the coming into the public domain of the last technology right within the meaning of the TTBER.

3.2.6. RELATIONSHIP WITH OTHER BLOCK EXEMPTION REGULATIONS

69. The TTBER covers agreements between two undertakings concerning the licensing of technology rights for the purpose of the production of contract products. However, technology rights can also be an element of other types of agreements. In addition, the products incorporating the licensed technology are subsequently sold on the market. It is therefore necessary to address the interface between the TTBER and Commission Regulation (EU) No 1218/2010[48] on specialisation agreements, Commission Regulation (EU) No 1217/2010 on research and development agreements[49] and Commission Regulation (EU) No 330/2010[50] on vertical agreements.

3.2.6.1. The Block Exemption Regulations on specialisation and R&D agreements

70. The TTBER does not apply to licensing in the context of specialisation agreements which are covered by Regulation (EU) No 1218/2010 or to licensing in the context of research and development agreements which are covered by Regulation (EU) No 1217/2010 (see recital 7 and Article 9 of the TTBER).

71. According to Article 1(1)(d) of Regulation (EU) No 1218/2010 on specialisation agreements, that Regulation covers, in particular, joint production agreements by virtue of which two or more parties agree to produce certain products jointly. The Regulation extends to provisions concerning the assignment or use of intellectual property rights, provided that they do not constitute the primary object of the agreement, but are directly related to and necessary for its implementation.

72. Where undertakings establish a production joint venture and license the joint venture to exploit technology, which is used in the production of the products produced by the joint venture, such licensing is subject to Regulation (EU) No 1218/2010 on specialisation agreements and not to the TTBER. Accordingly, licensing in the context of a production joint venture normally falls to be considered under Regulation (EU) No 1218/2010. However, where the joint venture engages in licensing of the technology to third parties, the activity is not linked to production by the joint venture and therefore not covered by that Regulation. Such licensing arrangements, which bring together the technologies of the parties, constitute technology pools, which are dealt with in section 4.4 of these guidelines.

73. Regulation (EU) No 1217/2010 on research and development agreements covers agreements whereby two or more undertakings agree to jointly carry out research and development and to jointly exploit the results thereof. According to Article 1(1)(m) of that Regulation, research and development and the exploitation of the results are carried out jointly where the work involved is carried out by a joint team, organisation or undertakings, jointly entrusted to a third party or allocated between the parties by way of specialisation in research, development, production and distribution, including licensing. That Regulation also covers paid-for research and development agreements whereby two or more undertakings agree that the research and development is carried out by one party and financed by another party, with or without joint exploitation of the results thereof (see Article 1(1)(a) (vi) of Regulation (EU) No 1217/2010).

74. It follows that Regulation (EU) No 1217/2010 on research and development agreements covers licensing between the parties and by the parties to a joint entity in the context of a research and development agreement. Such licensing is subject only to Regulation (EU) No 1217/2010 and not to the TTBER. In the context of such agreements the parties can also determine the conditions for licensing the fruits of the research and development agreement to third parties. However, since third party licensees are not party to the research and development agreement, the individual licence agreement concluded with third parties is not covered by Regulation (EU) No 1217/2010. That licence agreement is covered by the block exemption in the TTBER if the conditions of it are fulfilled.

3.2.6.2.
The Block Exemption Regulation on vertical agreements

75. Commission Regulation (EU) No 330/2010 on vertical agreements covers agreements entered into between two or more undertakings each operating, for the purposes of the agreement, at different levels of the production or distribution chain, and relating to the conditions under which the parties may purchase, sell or resell certain goods or services. It thus covers supply and distribution agreements.[51]

76. Given that the TTBER only covers agreements between two parties and that a licensee, selling products incorporating the licensed technology, is a supplier for the purposes of Regulation (EU) No 330/2010, those two block exemption regulations are closely related. The agreement between licensor and licensee is subject to the TTBER whereas agreements concluded between a licensee and buyers of the contract products are subject to Regulation (EU) No 330/2010 and the Guidelines on Vertical Restraints.[52]

77. The TTBER also exempts agreements between the licensor and the licensee where the agreement imposes obligations on the licensee as to the way in which it must sell the products incorporating the licensed technology. In particular, the licensee can be obliged to establish a certain type of distribution system such as exclusive distribution or selective distribution. However, the distribution agreements concluded for the purposes of implementing such obligations must, in order to be covered by a block exemption, comply with Regulation (EU) No 330/2010. For instance, the licensor can oblige the licensee to establish a system based on exclusive distribution in accordance with specified rules. However, it follows from Article 4(b) of Regulation (EU) No 330/2010 that generally distributors must be free to make passive sales into the territories of other exclusive distributors of the licensee.

78. Furthermore, under Regulation (EU) No 330/2010 on vertical agreements distributors must in principle be free to sell both actively and passively into territories covered by the distribution systems of other suppliers, that is to say, other licensees producing their own products on the basis of the licensed technology rights. This is because for the purposes of Regulation (EU) No 330/2010 each licensee is a separate supplier. However, the reasons underlying the block exemption of active sales restrictions within a supplier's distribution system contained in that Regulation, may also apply where the products incorporating the licensed technology are sold by different licensees under a common brand belonging to the licensor. When the products incorporating the licensed technology are sold under a common brand identity there may be the same efficiency reasons for applying the same types of restraints between licensees' distribution systems as within a single vertical distribution system. In such cases the Commission would be unlikely to challenge restraints where by analogy the requirements of Regulation (EU) No 330/2010 are fulfilled. For a common brand identity to exist the products must be sold and marketed under a common brand, which is predominant in terms of conveying quality and other relevant information to the consumer. It does not suffice that in addition to the licensees' brands the product carries the licensor's brand, which identifies it as the source of the licensed technology.

3.3. THE MARKET SHARE THRESHOLDS OF THE SAFE HARBOUR

79. According to Article 3 of the TTBER, the block exemption of restrictive agreements, or in other words the safe harbour of the TTBER, is subject to market share thresholds, confining the scope of the block exemption to agreements that although they may be restrictive of competition can generally be presumed to fulfil the conditions of Article 101(3) of the Treaty. Outside the safe harbour created by the market share thresholds individual assessment is required. The fact that market shares exceed the thresholds does not give rise to any presumption either that the agreement is caught by Article 101(1) or that the agreement does not fulfil the conditions of Article 101(3). In the absence of hardcore restrictions as set out in Article 4 of the TTBER, market analysis is required.

RELEVANT MARKET SHARE THRESHOLDS

80. The market share threshold to be applied for the purpose of the safe harbour of the TTBER depends on whether the agreement is concluded between competitors or non-competitors.

81. The market share thresholds apply both to the relevant market(s) of the licensed technology rights and the relevant market(s) of the contract products. If the applicable market share threshold is exceeded on one or several product and technology market(s), the block exemption does not apply to the agreement for that relevant market(s). For instance, if the licence agreement concerns two separate product markets, the block exemption may apply to one of the markets and not to the other.

82. According to Article 3(1) TTBER the safe harbour provided for in Article 2 TTBER applies to agreements between competitors on condition that the combined market share of the parties does not exceed 20% on any relevant market. The market share threshold of Article 3(1) of the TTBER is applicable if the parties are actual competitors or potential competitors on the product market(s) and/or actual competitors on the technology market (for the distinction between competitors and non-competitors, see points (27) ff.).

83. Potential competition on the technology market is not taken into account for the application of the market share threshold or the hardcore list relating to agreements between competitors. Outside the safe harbour of the TTBER potential competition on the technology market is taken into account but does not lead to the application of the hardcore list relating to agreements between competitors.

84. Where the undertakings party to the licensing agreement are not competitors, the market share threshold of Article 3(2) of the TTBER applies. An agreement between non-competitors is covered if the market share of each party does not exceed 30% on the affected relevant technology and product markets.

85. Where the parties become competitors within the meaning of Article 3(1) TTBER at a later point in time, for instance where the licensee was already present, before the licensing, on the relevant market where the contract products are sold and the licensor subsequently becomes an actual or potential supplier on the same relevant market, the 20% market share threshold will apply from the point in time when they became competitors. However, in that case the hardcore list relevant for agreements between non-competitors will continue to apply to the agreement unless the agreement is subsequently amended in any material respect (see Article 4(3) of the TTBER and point (39) of these guidelines).

Calculating market shares for technology market(s) for the application of the safe harbour

86. The calculation of market shares on the relevant markets where the technology rights are licensed, under the TTBER, deviates from the usual practice for the reasons explained in point (87) of these guidelines. In the case of technology markets, it follows from Article 8(d) of the TTBER that, both for the product and the geographic dimension of the relevant market, the licensor's market share is to be calculated on the basis of the sales of the licensor and all its licensees of products incorporating the licensed technology. Under this approach the combined sales of the licensor and its licensees of contract products are calculated as part of all sales of competing products, irrespective of whether these competing products are produced with a technology that is being licensed.

87. This approach of calculating the market share of the licensor on the technology market as its 'footprint' at the product level, has been chosen because of the practical difficulties in calculating a licensor's market share based on royalty income (see point (25)). In addition to the general difficulty of obtaining reliable royalty income data, the actual royalty income may also seriously underestimate a technology's position on the market in the event that royalty payments are reduced as a result of cross licensing or of the supply of tied products. Basing the licensor's market share on the technology market on the products produced with that technology as compared with products produced with competing technologies would not carry that risk. Such a footprint at the product level will in general reflect the market position of the technology well.

88. Ideally that footprint would be calculated by excluding from the product market the products produced with in-house technologies that are not licensed out, as those in-house technologies are only an indirect constraint on the licensed technology. However, as it may be difficult in practice for licensor and licensees to know whether other products in the same product market are produced with licensed or in-house technologies, the calculation of the technology market share, for the purposes of the TTBER, is based on the products produced with the licensed technology as part of all products sold in that product market. This approach based on the technology's footprint on the overall product market(s) can be expected to reduce the calculated market share by including products produced with in-house technologies, but will nonetheless in general provide a good indicator of the strength of the technology. First, it captures any potential competition from undertakings that are producing with their own technology and that are likely to start licensing in the event of a small but permanent increase in the price for licenses. Secondly, even where it is unlikely that other technology owners would start licensing, the licensor does not necessarily have market power on the technology market even if it has a high share of licensing income. If the downstream product market is competitive, competition at this level may effectively constrain the licensor. An increase in royalties upstream affects the costs of the licensee, which makes it less competitive and thereby may cause it to lose sales. A technology's market share on the product market also captures this element and is thus normally a good indicator of licensor market power on the technology market.

89. To estimate the strength of the technology, the geographic dimension of the technology market has also to be taken into account. This might sometimes differ from the geographic dimension of the respective downstream product market. For the purpose of applying the TTBER, the geographic dimension of the relevant technology market is also determined by the product market(s). However, outside the TTBER safe harbour it may be appropriate to also consider a possibly wider geographic area, in which the licensor and licensees of competing technologies are involved in the licensing of these technologies, in which the conditions of competition are sufficiently homogeneous and which can be distinguished from neighbouring areas because the conditions of competition are appreciably different in those areas.

90. In the case of new technologies that did not generate any sales in the preceding calendar year, a zero market share is assigned. When sales commence the technology will start accumulating market share. If the market share rises subsequently above the relevant threshold of 20% or 30%, the safe harbour will continue to apply for a period of two consecutive calendar years following the year in which the threshold was exceeded (see Article 8(e) of the TTBER).

CALCULATING MARKET SHARES FOR PRODUCT MARKET(S) FOR THE APPLICATION OF THE SAFE HARBOUR

91. In the case of relevant markets where the contract products are sold, the licensee's market share is to be calculated on the basis of the licensee's sales of products incorporating the licensor's technology and competing products, that is to say, the total sales of the licensee on the product market in question. Where the licensor is also a supplier of products on the relevant market, the licensor's sales on the product market in question must also be taken into account. In the calculation of market shares for product markets, however, sales made by other licensees are not taken into account when calculating the licensee's and/or licensor's market share.

92. Market shares should be calculated on the basis of sales value data of the preceding year where such data are available. Such data normally provide a more accurate indication of the strength of a technology than volume data. However, where value based data are not available, estimates based on other reliable market information may be used, including market sales volume data.

93. The principles set out in section 3.3 of these guidelines can be illustrated by the following examples:

LICENSING BETWEEN NON-COMPETITORS

Example 1

Company A is specialised in developing bio-technological products and techniques and has developed a new product Xeran. It is not active as a producer of Xeran, for which it has neither the production nor the distribution facilities.

Company B is one of the producers of competing products, produced with freely available non-proprietary technologies. In year 1, B sold EUR 25 million worth of products produced with the freely available technologies. In year 2, A gives a licence to B to produce Xeran. In that year B sells EUR 15 million produced with the help of the freely available technologies and EUR 15 million of Xeran. In year 3 and the following years B produces and sells only Xeran worth EUR 40 million annually. In addition in year 2, A also licenses to C. C was not active on that product market before. C produces and sells only Xeran, EUR 10 million in year 2 and EUR 15 million in year 3 and thereafter. It is established that the total market of Xeran and its substitutes where B and C are active is worth EUR 200 million in each year.

In year 2, the year the licence agreements are concluded, A's market share on the technology market is 0% as its market share has to be calculated on the basis of the total sales of Xeran in the preceding year. In year 3 A's market share on the technology market is 12.5%, reflecting the value of Xeran produced by B and C in the preceding year 2. In year 4 and thereafter A's market share on the technology market is 27.5%, reflecting the value of Xeran produced by B and C in the preceding year.

In year 2 B's market share on the product market is 12.5%, reflecting B's EUR 25 million sales in year 1. In year 3 B's market share is 15% because its sales have increased to EUR 30 million in year 2. In year 4 and thereafter B's market share is 20% as its sales are EUR 40 million annually. C's market share on the product market is 0% in year 1 and 2, 5% in year 3 and 7.5% thereafter.

As the licence agreements between A and B, and between A and C, are between non-competitors and the individual market shares of A, B and C are below 30% each year, each agreement falls within the safe harbour of the TTBER.

Example 2

The situation is the same as in example 1, however now B and C are operating in different geographic markets. It is established that the total market of Xeran and its substitutes is worth EUR 100 million annually in each geographic market.

In this case, A's market share on the relevant technology markets has to be calculated on the basis of product sales data of each of the two geographic product markets separately. In the market where B is active A's market share depends on the sale of Xeran by B. As in this example the total market is assumed to be EUR 100 million, that is to say, half the size of the market in example 1, the market share of A is 0% in year 2, 15% in year 3 and 40% thereafter. B's market share is 25% in year 2, 30% in year 3 and 40% thereafter. In year 2 and 3 both A's and B's market share does not exceed the 30% threshold. The threshold is however exceeded from year 4 and this means that, in line with Article 8(e) of the TTBER, after year 6 the licence agreement between A and B can no longer benefit from the safe harbour but has to be assessed on an individual basis.

In the market where C is active A's market share depends on the sale of Xeran by C. A's market share on the technology market, based on C's sales in the previous year, is therefore 0% in year 2, 10% in year 3 and 15% thereafter. The market share of C on the product market is the same: 0% in year 2, 10% in year 3 and 15% thereafter. The licence agreement between A and C therefore falls within the safe harbour for the whole period.

LICENSING BETWEEN COMPETITORS

Example 3

Companies A and B are active on the same relevant product and geographic market for a certain chemical product. They also each own a patent on different technologies used to produce this product. In year 1 A and B sign a cross licence agreement licensing each other to use their respective technologies. In year 1 A and B produce only with their own technology and A sells EUR 15 million of the product and B sells EUR 20 million of the product. From year 2 they both use their own and the other's technology. From that year onward A sells EUR 10 million of the product produced with its own technology and EUR 10 million of the product produced with B's technology. From year 2 B sells EUR 15 million of the product produced with its own technology and EUR 10 million of the product produced with A's technology. It is established that the total market of the product and its substitutes is worth EUR 100 million in each year.

To assess the licence agreement under the TTBER, the market shares of A and B have to be calculated both on the technology market and the product market. The market share of A on the technology market depends on the amount of the product sold in the preceding year that was produced, by both A and B, with A's technology. In year 2 the market share of A on the technology market is therefore 15%, reflecting its own production and sales of EUR 15 million in year 1. From year 3 A's market share on the technology market is 20%, reflecting the EUR 20 million sale of the product produced with A's technology and produced and sold by A and B (EUR 10 million each). Similarly, in year 2 B's market share on the technology market is 20% and thereafter 25%.

The market shares of A and B on the product market depend on their respective sales of the product in the previous year, irrespective of the technology used. The market share of A on the product market is 15% in year 2 and 20% thereafter. The market share of B on the product market is 20% in year 2 and 25% thereafter.

As the agreement is between competitors, their combined market share, both on the technology and on the product market, has to be below the 20% market share threshold in order to benefit from the safe harbour. It is clear that this is not the case here. The combined market share on the technology market and on the product market is 35% in year 2 and 45% thereafter. This agreement between competitors will therefore have to be assessed on an individual basis.

3.4. HARDCORE RESTRICTIONS OF COMPETITION UNDER THE BLOCK EXEMPTION REGULATION

3.4.1. General principles

94. Article 4 of the TTBER contains a list of hardcore restrictions of competition. The classification of a restraint as a hardcore restriction of competition is based on the nature of the restriction and experience showing that such restrictions are almost always anti-competitive. In line with the case law of the Court of Justice and the General Court[53] such a restriction may result from the clear objective of the agreement or from the circumstances of the individual case (see point (14)). Hardcore restrictions may be objectively necessary in exceptional cases for an agreement of a particular type or nature[54] and therefore fall outside Article 101(1) of the Treaty. In addition, undertakings can always plead an efficiency defence under Article 101(3) in an individual case.[55]

95. It follows from Article 4(1) and 4(2) of the TTBER that, when a technology transfer agreement contains a hardcore restriction of competition, the agreement as a whole falls outside the scope of the block exemption. For the purposes of the TTBER hardcore restrictions cannot be severed from the rest of the agreement. Moreover, the Commission considers that in the context of individual assessment it is unlikely that hardcore restrictions of competition fulfil the four conditions of Article 101(3) (see point (18)).

96. Article 4 of the TTBER distinguishes between agreements between competitors and agreements between non-competitors.

3.4.2. Agreements between competitors

97. Article 4(1) TTBER lists the hardcore restrictions for licensing between competitors. According to Article 4(1), the TTBER does not cover agreements which, directly or indirectly, in isolation or in combination with other factors under the control of the parties, have as their object any of the following:

(a) the restriction of a party's ability to determine its prices when selling products to third parties;

(b) the limitation of output, except limitations on the output of contract products imposed on the licensee in a non-reciprocal agreement or imposed on only one of the licensees in a reciprocal agreement;

(c) the allocation of markets or customers except:

  (i) the obligation on the licensor and/or the licensee, in a non-reciprocal agreement, not to produce with the licensed technology rights within the exclusive territory reserved for the other party and/or not to sell, actively and/or passively, into the exclusive territory or to the exclusive customer group reserved for the other party;

  (ii) the restriction, in a non-reciprocal agreement, of active sales by the licensee into the exclusive territory or to the exclusive customer group allocated by the licensor to another licensee provided that the latter was not a competing undertaking of the licensor at the time of the conclusion of its own licence;

  (iii) the obligation on the licensee to produce the contract products only for its own use provided that the licensee is not restricted in selling the contract products actively and passively as spare parts for its own products;

  (iv) the obligation on the licensee, in a non-reciprocal agreement, to produce the contract products only for a particular customer, where the licence was granted in order to create an alternative source of supply for that customer;

(d) the restriction of the licensee's ability to exploit its own technology rights or the restriction of the ability of any of the parties to the agreement to carry out research and development, unless such latter restriction is indispensable to prevent the disclosure of the licensed know-how to third parties.

Distinction between reciprocal and non-reciprocal agreements between competitors

98. For a number of hardcore restrictions the TTBER makes a distinction between reciprocal and non-reciprocal agreements. The hardcore list is stricter for reciprocal agreements than for non-reciprocal agreements between competitors. Reciprocal agreements are cross licensing agreements where the licensed technologies are competing technologies or can be used for the production of competing products. A non-reciprocal agreement is an agreement where only one of the parties is licensing its technology rights to the other party or where, in the case of cross licensing, the licensed technologies rights are not competing technologies and the rights licensed cannot be used for the production of competing products. An agreement is not reciprocal for the purposes of the TTBER merely because the agreement contains a grant back obligation or because the licensee licenses back own improvements of the licensed technology. Where a non-reciprocal agreement subsequently becomes a reciprocal agreement due to the

conclusion of a second licence between the same parties, those parties may have to revise the first licence in order to avoid the agreement containing a hardcore restriction. In the assessment of the individual case the Commission will take into account the time lapsed between the conclusion of the first and the second licence.

Price restrictions between competitors

99. The hardcore restriction of competition contained in Article 4(1)(a) TTBER concerns agreements between competitors that have as their object the fixing of prices for products sold to third parties, including the products incorporating the licensed technology. Price fixing between competitors constitutes a restriction of competition by its very object. Price fixing can take the form of a direct agreement on the exact price to be charged or on a price list with certain allowed maximum rebates. It is immaterial whether the agreement concerns fixed, minimum, maximum or recommended prices. Price fixing can also be implemented indirectly by applying disincentives to deviate from an agreed price level, for example, by providing that the royalty rate will increase if product prices are reduced below a certain level. However, an obligation on the licensee to pay a certain minimum royalty does not in itself amount to price fixing.

100. When royalties are calculated on the basis of individual product sales, the amount of the royalty has a direct impact on the marginal cost of the product and thus a direct impact on product prices.[56] Competitors can therefore use cross licensing with reciprocal running royalties as a means of coordinating and/or increasing prices on downstream product markets.[57] However, the Commission will only treat cross licences with reciprocal running royalties as price fixing where the agreement is devoid of any pro-competitive purpose and therefore does not constitute a bona fide licensing arrangement. In such cases where the agreement does not create any value and therefore has no valid business justification, the arrangement is a sham and amounts to a cartel.

101. The hardcore restriction contained in Article 4(1)(a) TTBER also covers agreements whereby royalties are calculated on the basis of all product sales irrespective of whether the licensed technology is being used. Such agreements are also caught by Article 4(1)(d) according to which the licensee must not be restricted in its ability to use its own technology rights (see point (116) of these guidelines). In general such agreements restrict competition since the agreement raises the cost of using the licensee's own competing technology rights and restricts competition that existed in the absence of the agreement.[58] This is so both in the case of reciprocal and non-reciprocal arrangements.

102. Exceptionally, however, an agreement whereby royalties are calculated on the basis of all product sales may fulfil the conditions of Article 101(3) in an individual case where on the basis of objective factors it can be concluded that the restriction is indispensable for pro-competitive licensing to occur. This may be the case where in the absence of the restraint it would be impossible or unduly difficult to calculate and monitor the royalty payable by the licensee, for instance because the licensor's technology leaves no visible trace on the final product and practicable alternative monitoring methods are unavailable.

Output restrictions between competitors

103. The hardcore restriction of competition set out in Article 4(1)(b) TTBER concerns reciprocal output restrictions on the parties. An output restriction is a limitation on how much a party may produce and sell. Article 4(1)(b) does not apply to output limitations on the licensee in a non-reciprocal agreement or output limitations on one of the licensees in a reciprocal agreement provided that the output limitation only concerns products produced with the licensed technology. Article 4(1)(b) thus identifies as hardcore restrictions reciprocal output restrictions on the parties and output restrictions on the licensor in respect of its own technology. When competitors agree to impose reciprocal output limitations, the object and likely effect of the agreement is to reduce output in the market. The same is true of agreements that reduce the incentive of the parties to expand output, for example by applying reciprocal running royalties per unit which increase as output increases or by obliging each party to make payments if a certain level of output is exceeded.

104. The more favourable treatment of non-reciprocal quantity limitations is based on the consideration that a one-way restriction does not necessarily lead to a lower output on the market while the risk that the agreement is not a bona fide licensing arrangement is also lower when the restriction is non-reciprocal. When a licensee is willing to accept a one-way restriction, it is likely that the agreement leads to a real integration of complementary technologies or an efficiency enhancing integration of the licensor's superior technology with the licensee's productive assets. Similarly, in a reciprocal agreement an output restriction on only one of the licensees is likely to reflect the higher value of the technology licensed by one of the parties and may serve to promote pro-competitive licensing.

Market and customer allocation between competitors

105. The hardcore restriction of competition set out in Article 4(1)(c) TTBER concerns the allocation of markets and customers. Agreements whereby competitors share markets and customers have as their object the restriction of competition. An agreement whereby competitors agree, in a reciprocal agreement, not to produce in certain territories or not to sell actively and/or passively into certain territories or to certain customers reserved for the other party, is considered a hardcore restriction. Thus for instance reciprocal exclusive licensing between competitors is considered market sharing.

106. Article 4(1)(c) applies irrespective of whether the licensee remains free to use its own technology rights. Once the licensee has tooled up to use the licensor's technology to produce a given product, it may be costly to maintain a separate production line using another technology in order to serve customers covered by the restrictions. Moreover, given the anti-competitive potential of the restraints the licensee may have little incentive to produce under its own technology. Such restrictions are also highly unlikely to be indispensable for pro-competitive licensing to occur.

107. Under Article 4(1)(c)(i) it is not a hardcore restriction for the licensor in a non-reciprocal agreement to grant the licensee an exclusive licence to produce on the basis of the licensed technology in a particular territory and thus agree not to produce itself the contract products in or provide the contract products from that territory. Such exclusive licences are block exempted irrespective of the scope of the territory. If the licence is world-wide, the exclusivity

implies that the licensor will abstain from entering or remaining on the market. The block exemption also applies if in a non-reciprocal agreement the licensee is not allowed to produce in an exclusive territory reserved for the licensor. The purpose of such agreements may be to give the licensor and/or licensee an incentive to invest in and develop the licensed technology. The object of the agreement is therefore not necessarily to share markets.

108. According to Article 4(1)(c)(i) and for the same reason, the block exemption also applies to non-reciprocal agreements whereby the parties agree not to sell actively or passively into an exclusive territory or to an exclusive customer group reserved for the other party. For the application of the TTBER, the Commission interprets 'active' and 'passive' sales as defined in the Guidelines on Vertical Restraints.[59] Restrictions on licensee or licensor to sell actively and/or passively into the other party's territory or customer group are only block exempted if that territory or customer group has been exclusively reserved to that other party. However, in some specific circumstances, agreements containing such sales restrictions may, in an individual case, also fulfil the conditions of Article 101(3) if the exclusivity is shared on an ad hoc basis, for instance if necessary to alleviate a temporary shortage in the production of the licensor or licensee to which the territory or customer group is exclusively allocated. In such cases, the licensor or licensee is still likely to be sufficiently protected against active and/or passive sales to have the incentive to license its technology or invest to work with the licensed technology. Such restraints, even where restrictive of competition, would promote pro-competitive dissemination and integration of that technology into the production assets of the licensee.

109. By implication the fact that the licensor appoints the licensee as its sole licensee in a particular territory, implying that third parties will not be licensed to produce on the basis of the licensor's technology in the territory in question, does not constitute a hardcore restriction either. In the case of such sole licences the block exemption applies irrespective of whether the agreement is reciprocal or not given that the agreement does not affect the ability of the parties to fully exploit their own technology rights in their respective territories.

110. Article 4(1)(c)(ii) excludes from the hardcore list, and thus block exempts up to the market share threshold, restrictions in a non-reciprocal agreement on active sales by a licensee into the territory or to the customer group allocated by the licensor to another licensee. However, this presupposes that the protected licensee was not a competitor of the licensor when the agreement was concluded. It is not warranted to treat such restrictions in that situation as hardcore restrictions. By allowing the licensor to grant a licensee, who was not already on the market, protection against active sales by licensees which are competitors of the licensor and which for that reason were already established on the market, such restrictions are likely to induce the licensee to exploit the licensed technology more efficiently. On the other hand, if the licensees were to agree between themselves not to sell actively or passively into certain territories or to certain customer groups, the agreement would amount to a cartel amongst the licensees. Given that such an agreement does not involve any transfer of technology it would in addition fall outside the scope of the TTBER.

111. Article 4(1)(c)(iii) contains a further exception to the hardcore restriction of Article 4(1)(c), namely captive use restrictions, that is to say, requirements whereby the licensee may produce the products incorporating the licensed technology only for its own use. Where the contract product is a component the licensee can thus be obliged to produce that component only for incorporation into its own products and can be obliged not to sell the components to other producers. The licensee must be able, however, to sell the components as spare parts for its own products and must thus be able to supply third parties that perform after sale services on these products. Captive use restrictions may be necessary to encourage the dissemination of technology, particularly between competitors, and are covered by the block exemption. Such restrictions are also dealt with in section 4.2.5.

112. Finally, Article 4(1)(c)(iv) excludes from the hardcore list an obligation on the licensee in a non-reciprocal agreement to produce the contract products only for a particular customer with a view to creating an alternative source of supply for that customer. It is thus a condition for the application of Article 4(1)(c)(iv) that the licence is limited to creating an alternative source of supply for that particular customer. It is not a condition, however, that only one such licence is granted. Article 4(1)(c)(iv) also covers situations where more than one undertaking is licensed to supply the same specified customer.

Article 4(1)(c)(iv) applies regardless of the duration of the licence agreement. For instance, a one-off licence to fulfil the requirements of a project of a particular customer is covered by this exception. The potential of such agreements to share markets is limited where the licence is granted only for the purpose of supplying a particular customer. In such circumstances it can, in particular, not be assumed that the agreement will cause the licensee to cease exploiting its own technology.

113. Restrictions in agreements between competitors that limit the licence to one or more product markets or technical fields of use[60] are not hardcore restrictions. Such restrictions are block exempted up to the market share threshold of 20% irrespective of whether the agreement is reciprocal or not. Such restrictions are not considered to have as their object the allocation of markets or customers. It is a condition for the application of the block exemption, however, that the field of use restrictions do not go beyond the scope of the licensed technologies. For instance, where licensees are also limited in the technical fields in which they can use their own technology rights, the agreement amounts to market sharing.

114. The block exemption applies irrespective of whether the field of use restriction is symmetrical or asymmetrical. An asymmetrical field of use restriction in a reciprocal licence agreement implies that both parties are allowed to use the respective technologies that they license-in only within different fields of use. As long as the parties are unrestricted in the use of their own technologies, there is no assumption that the agreement leads the parties to abandon or refrain from entering the field(s) covered by the licence to the other party. Even if the licensees tool up to use the licensed technology within the licensed field of use, there may be no impact on assets used to produce outside the scope of the licence. It is important in this regard that the restriction relates to distinct product markets, industrial

sectors or fields of use and not to customers, allocated by territory or by group, who purchase products falling within the same product market or technical field of use. The risk of market sharing is considered substantially greater in the latter case (see point (106) above). In addition, field of use restrictions may be necessary to promote pro-competitive licensing (see point (212) below).

Restrictions on the parties' ability to carry out research and development

115. The hardcore restriction of competition set out in Article 4(1)(d) covers restrictions on any of the parties' ability to carry out research and development. Both parties must be free to carry out independent research and development. This rule applies irrespective of whether the restriction applies to a field covered by the licence or to other fields. However, the mere fact that the parties agree to provide each other with future improvements of their respective technologies does not amount to a restriction on independent research and development. The effect on competition of such agreements must be assessed in the light of the circumstances of the individual case. Article 4(1)(d) also does not extend to restrictions on a party to carry out research and development with third parties, where such restriction is necessary to protect the licensor's know-how against disclosure. In order to be covered by the exception, the restrictions imposed to protect the licensor's know-how against disclosure must be necessary and proportionate to ensure such protection. For instance, where the agreement designates particular employees of the licensee to be trained in and responsible for the use of the licensed know-how, it may be sufficient to oblige the licensee not to allow those employees to be involved in research and development with third parties. Other safeguards may be equally appropriate.

Restrictions on the use of the licensee's own technology

116. According to Article 4(1)(d) the licensee must also be unrestricted in the use of its own competing technology rights provided that in doing so it does not make use of the technology rights licensed from the licensor. In relation to its own technology rights the licensee must not be subject to limitations in terms of where it produces or sells, the technical fields of use or product markets within which it produces, how much it produces or sells and the price at which it sells. It must also not be obliged to pay royalties on products produced on the basis of its own technology rights (see point (101)). Moreover, the licensee must not be restricted in licensing its own technology rights to third parties. When restrictions are imposed on the licensee's use of its own technology rights or its right to carry out research and development, the competitiveness of the licensee's technology is reduced. The effect of this is to reduce competition on existing product and technology markets and to reduce the licensee's incentive to invest in the development and improvement of its technology. Article 4(1)(d) does not extend to restrictions on the licensee's use of third party technology which competes with the licensed technology. Although such non-compete obligations may have foreclosure effects on third party technologies (see section 4.2.7), they usually do not have the effect of reducing the incentive of licensees to invest in the development and improvement of their own technologies.

3.4.3. Agreements between non-competitors

117. Article 4(2) TTBER lists the hardcore restrictions for licensing between non-competitors. According to this provision, the TTBER does not cover agreements which, directly or indirectly, in isolation or in combination with other factors under the control of the parties, have as their object any of the following:

(a) the restriction of a party's ability to determine its prices when selling products to third parties, without prejudice to the possibility to impose a maximum sale price or recommend a sale price, provided that it does not amount to a fixed or minimum sale price as a result of pressure from, or incentives offered by, any of the parties;

(b) the restriction of the territory into which, or of the customers to whom, the licensee may passively sell the contract products, except:

  (i) the restriction of passive sales into an exclusive territory or to an exclusive customer group reserved for the licensor;

  (ii) the obligation to produce the contract products only for its own use provided that the licensee is not restricted in selling the contract products actively and passively as spare parts for its own products;

  (iii) the obligation to produce the contract products only for a particular customer, where the licence was granted in order to create an alternative source of supply for that customer;

  (iv) the restriction of sales to end users by a licensee operating at the wholesale level of trade;

  (v) the restriction of sales to unauthorised distributors by the members of a selective distribution system;

(c) the restriction of active or passive sales to end users by a licensee which is a member of a selective distribution system and which operates at the retail level, without prejudice to the possibility of prohibiting a member of the system from operating out of an unauthorised place of establishment.

Price fixing

118. The hardcore restriction of competition set out in Article 4(2)(a) concerns the fixing of prices charged when selling products to third parties. More specifically, that provision covers restrictions which have as their direct or indirect object the establishment of a fixed or a minimum selling price or a fixed or minimum price level to be observed by the licensor or the licensee when selling products to third parties. In the case of agreements that directly establish the selling price, the restriction is clear-cut. However, the fixing of selling prices can also be achieved through indirect means. Examples of the latter are agreements fixing margins, fixing the maximum level of discounts, linking the sales price to the sales prices of competitors, threats, intimidation, warnings, penalties, or contract terminations in relation to observance of a given price level. Direct or indirect means of achieving price fixing can be made more effective when combined with measures to identify price-cutting, such as the implementation of a price monitoring system, or the obligation on licensees to report price deviations. Similarly, direct or indirect price fixing can be made more effective when combined with measures that reduce the licensee's incentive to lower its selling price, such as the licensor obliging the licensee to apply a most-favoured-customer clause, that is to say, an obligation

to grant a customer any more favourable terms granted to any other customer. The same means can be used to make maximum or recommended prices work as fixed or minimum selling prices. However, the provision of a list of recommended prices to or the imposition of a maximum price on the licensee by the licensor is not considered in itself as leading to fixed or minimum selling prices.

Restrictions on passive sales by the licensee

119. Article 4(2)(b) identifies as hardcore restrictions of competition agreements or concerted practices that have as their direct or indirect object the restriction of passive sales[61] by licensees of products incorporating the licensed technology.[62] Passive sales restrictions on the licensee may be the result of direct obligations, such as the obligation not to sell to certain customers or to customers in certain territories or the obligation to refer orders from these customers to other licensees. It may also result from indirect measures aimed at inducing the licensee to refrain from making such sales, such as financial incentives and the implementation of a monitoring system aimed at verifying the effective destination of the licensed products. Quantity limitations may be an indirect means to restrict passive sales. The Commission will not assume that quantity limitations as such serve this purpose. However, it will assume otherwise where quantity limitations are used to implement an underlying market partitioning agreement. Indications thereof include the adjustment of quantities over time to cover only local demand, the combination of quantity limitations and an obligation to sell minimum quantities in the territory, as well as minimum royalty obligations linked to sales in the territory, differentiated royalty rates depending on the destination of the products and the monitoring of the destination of products sold by individual licensees. The general hardcore restriction covering passive sales by licensees is subject to a number of exceptions, which are dealt with in points (120) to (125).

120. Exception 1: Article 4(2)(b) does not cover sales restrictions (both active and passive) on the licensor. All sales restrictions on the licensor are block exempted up to the market share threshold of 30%. The same applies to all restrictions on active sales by the licensee, with the exception of what is said on active selling in point (125). The block exemption of restrictions on active selling is based on the assumption that such restrictions promote investments, non-price competition and improvements in the quality of services provided by the licensees by solving free rider problems and hold-up problems. In the case of restrictions of active sales between licensees' territories or customer groups, it is not necessary that the protected licensee has been granted an exclusive territory or an exclusive customer group. The block exemption also applies to active sales restrictions where more than one licensee has been appointed for a particular territory or customer group. Efficiency enhancing investment is likely to be promoted where a licensee can be sure that it will only face active sales competition from a limited number of licensees inside the territory and not also from licensees outside the territory.

121. Exception 2: Restrictions on active and passive sales by licensees into an exclusive territory or to an exclusive customer group reserved for the licensor do not constitute hardcore restrictions of competition (see Article 4(2)(b)(i)) and are block exempted. It is presumed that up to the market share threshold such restraints, where restrictive of competition, promote pro-competitive dissemination of technology and integration of such technology into the production assets of the licensee. For a territory or customer group to be reserved for the licensor, the licensor does not actually have to be producing with the licensed technology in the territory or for the customer group in question. A territory or customer group can also be reserved by the licensor for later exploitation.

122. Exception 3: Article 4(2)(b)(ii) brings under the block exemption a restriction whereby the licensee is obliged to produce products incorporating the licensed technology only for its own (captive) use. Where the contract product is a component the licensee can thus be obliged to use that product only for incorporation into its own products and can be obliged not to sell the product to other producers. The licensee must however be able to actively and passively sell the products as spare parts for its own products and must thus be able to supply third parties that perform after sale services on these products. Captive use restrictions are also dealt with in section 4.2.5.

123. Exception 4: As in the case of agreements between competitors (see point (112) above) the block exemption also applies to agreements whereby the licensee is obliged to produce the contract products only for a particular customer in order to provide that customer with an alternative source of supply, regardless of the duration of the licence agreement (cf. Article 4(2)(b)(iii)). In the case of agreements between non-competitors, such restrictions are unlikely to be caught by Article 101(1) of the Treaty.

124. Exception 5: Article 4(2)(b)(iv) brings under the block exemption an obligation on the licensee, if operating at the wholesale level of trade, not to sell to end users and thus only to sell to retailers. Such an obligation allows the licensor to assign the licensee to the wholesale distribution function and normally falls outside Article 101(1).[63]

125. Exception 6: Finally Article 4(2)(b)(v) brings under the block exemption a restriction on the licensee not to sell to unauthorised distributors. This exception allows the licensor to impose an obligation on the licensees to form part of a selective distribution system. In that case, however, the licensees must according to Article 4(2)(c) be permitted to sell both actively and passively to end users, without prejudice to the possibility to restrict the licensee to a wholesale function as provided for in Article 4(2)(b)(iv) (see point (124)). Within the territory where the licensor operates a selective distribution system, this system may not be combined with exclusive territories or exclusive customer groups where this would lead to a restriction of active or passive sales to end-users as that would lead to a hardcore restriction under Article 4(2)(c), without prejudice to the possibility of prohibiting a licensee from operating out of an unauthorised place of establishment.

126. Restrictions on passive sales by licensees into an exclusive territory or customer group allocated to another licensee, while normally a hardcore restriction, may fall outside Article 101(1) of the Treaty for a certain duration if the restraints are objectively necessary for the protected licensee to penetrate a new market. This may be the case where licensees have to commit substantial investments in production assets and promotional activities in order to start up and develop a new market. The risks facing a new licensee may therefore be substantial, in particular since promotional expenses and investment in assets required to produce on the basis of a particular technology are often sunk, that is to say, that upon leaving that particular field of activity the investment cannot be used by the licensee for other activities or sold other than at a significant loss. For instance, the licensee may be the first to produce and sell

a new type of product or the first to apply a new technology. In such circumstances, it is often the case that licensees would not enter into the licence agreement without protection for a certain period of time against (active and) passive sales into their territory or to their customer groups by other licensees. Where substantial investments by the licensee are necessary to start up and develop a new market, restrictions of passive sales by other licensees into such a territory or to such a customer group fall outside Article 101(1) for the period necessary for the licensee to recoup those investments. In most cases a period of up to two years from the date on which the contract product was first put on the market in the exclusive territory by the licensee in question or sold to its exclusive customer group would be considered sufficient for the licensee to recoup the investments made. However, in an individual case a longer period of protection for the licensee might be necessary in order for the licensee to recoup the costs incurred.

127. Similarly, a prohibition imposed on all licensees not to sell to certain categories of end users may not be restrictive of competition if such a restraint is objectively necessary for reasons of safety or health related to the dangerous nature of the product in question.

3.5. EXCLUDED RESTRICTIONS

128. Article 5 of the TTBER lists three types of restrictions that are not block exempted and which thus require individual assessment of their anti-competitive and pro-competitive effects. The purpose of Article 5 is to avoid block exemption of agreements that may reduce the incentive to innovate. It follows from Article 5 that the inclusion in a licence agreement of any of the restrictions contained in that Article does not prevent the application of the block exemption to the rest of the agreement, if the remainder is severable from the excluded restriction(s). It is only the individual restriction in question that is not covered by the block exemption, implying that individual assessment is required.

EXCLUSIVE GRANT BACKS

129. Article 5(1)(a) TTBER concerns exclusive grant backs (that is to say an exclusive licence back to the licensor of the licensee's improvement) or assignments to the licensor of improvements of the licensed technology. An obligation to grant the licensor an exclusive licence to improvements of the licensed technology or to assign such improvements to the licensor is likely to reduce the licensee's incentive to innovate since it hinders the licensee in exploiting the improvements, including by way of licensing to third parties. An exclusive grant back is defined as a grant back which prevents the licensee (which is the innovator and licensor of the improvement in this case) from exploiting the improvement (either for its own production or for licensing out to third parties). This is the case both where the improvement concerns the same application as the licensed technology and where the licensee develops new applications of the licensed technology. According to Article 5(1)(a) such obligations are not covered by the block exemption.

130. The application of Article 5(1)(a) does not depend on whether or not the licensor pays consideration in return for acquiring the improvement or for obtaining an exclusive licence. However, the existence and level of such consideration may be a relevant factor in the context of an individual assessment under Article 101. When grant backs are made against consideration it is less likely that the obligation creates a disincentive for the licensee to innovate. In the assessment of exclusive grant backs outside the scope of the block exemption the market position of the licensor on the technology market is also a relevant factor. The stronger the position of the licensor, the more likely it is that exclusive grant back obligations will have restrictive effects on competition in innovation. The stronger the position of the licensor's technology the more important it is that the licensee can become an important source of innovation and future competition. The negative impact of grant back obligations can also be increased in case of parallel networks of licence agreements containing such obligations. When available technologies are controlled by a limited number of licensors that impose exclusive grant back obligations on licensees, the risk of anti-competitive effects is greater than where there are a number of technologies only some of which are licensed on exclusive grant back terms.

131. Non-exclusive grant back obligations are covered by the safe harbour of the TTBER. This is the case even where they are non-reciprocal, that is to say, only imposed on the licensee, and where under the agreement the licensor is entitled to feed-on the improvements to other licensees. A non-reciprocal grant back obligation may promote the dissemination of new technology by permitting the licensor to freely determine whether and to what extent to pass on its own improvements to its licensees. A feed-on clause may also promote the dissemination of technology, in particular when each licensee knows at the time of contracting that it will be on an equal footing with other licensees in terms of the technology on the basis of which it is producing.

132. Non-exclusive grant back obligations may in particular have negative effects on innovation in the case of cross licensing between competitors where a grant back obligation on both parties is combined with an obligation on both parties to share improvements of its own technology with the other party. The sharing of all improvements between competitors may prevent each competitor from gaining a competitive lead over the other (see also point (241) below). However, the parties are unlikely to be prevented from gaining a competitive lead over each other where the purpose of the licence is to permit them to develop their respective technologies and where the licence does not lead them to use the same technological base in the design of their products. This is the case where the purpose of the licence is to create design freedom rather than to improve the technological base of the licensee.

NON-CHALLENGE AND TERMINATION CLAUSES

133. The excluded restriction set out in Article 5(1)(b) TTBER concerns non-challenge clauses, that is to say, direct or indirect obligations not to challenge the validity of the licensor's intellectual property, without prejudice to the possibility, in the case of an exclusive licence, for the licensor to terminate the technology transfer agreement in the event that the licensee challenges the validity of any of the licensed technology rights.

134. The reason for excluding non-challenge clauses from the scope of the block exemption is the fact that licensees are normally in the best position to determine whether or not an intellectual property right is invalid. In the interest of undistorted competition and in accordance with the principles underlying the protection of intellectual property,

invalid intellectual property rights should be eliminated. Invalid intellectual property stifles innovation rather than promoting it. Article 101(1) of the Treaty is likely to apply to non-challenge clauses where the licensed technology is valuable and therefore creates a competitive disadvantage for undertakings that are prevented from using it or are only able to use it against payment of royalties. In such cases the conditions of Article 101(3) are unlikely to be fulfilled. However, if the licensed technology is related to a technically outdated process which the licensee does not use, or if the licence is granted for free, no restriction of competition arises.[64] As to non-challenge clauses in the context of settlement agreements see points (242) and (243).

135. Generally a clause obliging the licensee not to challenge the ownership of the technology rights does not constitute a restriction of competition within the meaning of Article 101(1). Whether or not the licensor has the ownership of the technology rights, the use of the technology by the licensee and any other party is dependent on obtaining a licence in any event, and competition would thus generally not be affected.[65]

136. Article 5(1)(b) TTBER also excludes from the safe harbour of the block exemption the right, in the context of non-exclusive licences, for the licensor to terminate the agreement in the event that the licensee challenges the validity of any of the intellectual property rights that the licensor holds in the Union. Such a termination right can have the same effect as a non-challenge clause, in particular where switching away from the licensor's technology would result in a significant loss to the licensee (for example where the licensee has already invested in specific machines or tools which cannot be used for producing with another technology) or where the licensor's technology is a necessary input for the licensee's production. For example, in the context of standard essential patents the licensee producing a standard compliant product will necessarily have to use all patents reading on the standard. In such a case, challenging the validity of the relevant patents may result in a significant loss if the technology transfer agreement is terminated. Where the licensor's technology is not standard essential, but has a very significant market position, the disincentive to challenge may also be high considering the difficulty for the licensee in finding a viable alternative technology to license-in. The question whether the licensee's loss of profit would be significant, and therefore act as a strong disincentive to challenge, would need to be assessed on a case by case basis.

137. In the scenarios described in point (136), the licensee may be deterred from challenging the validity of the intellectual property right if it would risk the termination of the licensing agreement and thus face significant risks which go far beyond its royalty obligations. However, it should also be noted that, outside the context of these scenarios a termination clause will often not provide a significant disincentive to challenge and therefore not produce the same effect as a non-challenge clause.

138. The public interest of strengthening the incentive of the licensor to license out by not being forced to continue dealing with a licensee that challenges the very subject matter of the licence agreement has to be balanced against the public interest to eliminate any obstacle to economic activity which may arise where an intellectual property right was granted in error.[66] In balancing those interests it should be taken into account whether the licensee fulfils all the obligations under the agreement at the time of the challenge, in particular the obligation to pay the agreed royalties.

139. In the case of exclusive licensing, termination clauses are usually less likely on balance to have anti-competitive effects. Once the licence is granted, the licensor may find itself in a particular situation of dependency, as the licensee will be its only source of income as regards the licensed technology rights if royalties are dependent on production with the licensed technology rights, as may often be an efficient way to structure royalty payments. In this scenario, the incentives for innovation and for licensing out could be undermined if, for example, the licensor were to be locked into an agreement with an exclusive licensee which no longer makes significant efforts to develop, produce and market the product (to be) produced with the licensed technology rights.[67] This is why the TTBER block exempts termination clauses for exclusive licensing agreements as long as also the other conditions of the safe harbour, such as respecting the market share threshold, are fulfilled. Outside the safe harbour, a case by case assessment has to be carried out taking into account the different interests as described in point (138).

140. Moreover, the Commission takes a more favourable view of non-challenge and termination clauses relating to know-how where the recovery of the licensed know-how is likely to be impossible or very difficult once it is disclosed. In such cases, an obligation on the licensee not to challenge the licensed know-how promotes dissemination of new technology, in particular by allowing weaker licensors to license stronger licensees without fear of a challenge once the know-how has been absorbed by the licensee. Therefore, non-challenge and termination clauses solely concerning know-how are not excluded from the scope of the TTBER.

LIMITING THE LICENSEE'S USE OR DEVELOPMENT OF ITS OWN TECHNOLOGY (BETWEEN NON-COMPETITORS)

141. In the case of agreements between non-competitors, Article 5(2) excludes from the scope of the block exemption any direct or indirect obligation limiting the licensee's ability to exploit its own technology rights or limiting the ability of the parties to the agreement to carryout research and development, unless that restriction is indispensable to prevent the disclosure of licensed know-how to third parties. The content of this condition is the same as that of Article 4(1)(d) of the hardcore list concerning agreements between competitors, which is dealt with in points (115) and (116) of these guidelines. However, in the case of agreements between non-competitors it cannot be considered that such restrictions generally have negative effects on competition, or that the conditions of Article 101(3) of the Treaty are generally not satisfied.[68] Individual assessment is therefore required.

142. In the case of agreements between non-competitors, the licensee normally does not own a competing technology. However, there may be cases where for the purposes of the block exemption the parties are considered non-competitors despite the fact that the licensee does own a competing technology. This is the case where the licensee owns a technology but does not license it and the licensor is not an actual or potential supplier on the product market. For the purposes of the block exemption, in such circumstances, the parties are neither competitors on the technology market nor competitors on the downstream product market.[69] In such cases it is important to ensure that the licensee is not restricted in its ability to exploit its own technology and further develop it. This technology constitutes a competitive constraint in the market, which should be preserved. In such a situation restrictions on the licensee's use of its own technology rights or on research and development are normally considered to be restrictive

of competition and not to satisfy the conditions of Article 101(3) of the Treaty. For instance, an obligation on the licensee to pay royalties not only on the basis of products it produces with the licensed technology but also on the basis of products it produces only with its own technology will generally limit the ability of the licensee to exploit its own technology and thus be excluded from the scope of the block exemption.

143. In cases where the licensee does not own a competing technology or is not already developing such a technology, a restriction on the ability of the parties to carry out independent research and development may be restrictive of competition where only a few technologies are available. In that case the parties may be an important (potential) source of innovation in the market. This is particularly so where the parties possess the necessary assets and skills to carry out further research and development. In that case the conditions of Article 101(3) of the Treaty are unlikely to be fulfilled. In other cases where a number of technologies are available and where the parties do not possess special assets or skills, the restriction on research and development is likely either to fall outside Article 101(1) for lack of an appreciable restrictive effect or to satisfy the conditions of Article 101(3). The restraint may promote the dissemination of new technology by assuring the licensor that the licence does not create a new competitor and by inducing the licensee to focus on the exploitation and development of the licensed technology. Moreover, Article 101(1) only applies where the agreement reduces the licensee's incentive to improve and exploit its own technology. This is, for instance, not likely to be the case where the licensor is entitled to terminate the licence agreement once the licensee commences to produce on the basis of its own competing technology. Such a right does not reduce the licensee's incentive to innovate, since the agreement can only be terminated when a commercially viable technology has been developed and products produced on the basis thereof are ready to be put on the market.

3.6. WITHDRAWAL AND NON-APPLICATION OF THE BLOCK EXEMPTION REGULATION

3.6.1. WITHDRAWAL PROCEDURE

144. According to Article 6 of the TTBER, the Commission and the competition authorities of the Member States may withdraw the benefit of the block exemption in respect of individual agreements that are likely to have anticompetitive effects (account must be taken of both actual and potential effects) and do not fulfil the conditions of Article 101(3) of the Treaty. The power of the competition authorities of the Member States to withdraw the benefit of the block exemption is limited to cases where the relevant geographic market is no wider than the territory of the Member State in question.

145. The four conditions of Article 101(3) are cumulative and must all be fulfilled for the exception rule to be applicable.[70] The block exemption can therefore be withdrawn where a particular agreement fails to fulfil one or more of the four conditions.

146. Where the withdrawal procedure is applied, the withdrawing authority bears the burden of proving that the agreement falls within the scope of Article 101(1) and that the agreement does not satisfy all four conditions of Article 101(3). Given that withdrawal implies that the agreement in question restricts competition within the meaning of Article 101(1) and does not fulfil the conditions of Article 101(3), withdrawal is necessarily accompanied by a negative decision based on Articles 5, 7 or 9 of Regulation (EC) No 1/2003.

147. According to Article 6 of the TTBER, withdrawal may in particular be warranted in the following circumstances:

(a) access of third parties' technologies to the market is restricted, for instance by the cumulative effect of parallel networks of similar restrictive agreements prohibiting licensees from using third parties' technologies;

(b) access of potential licensees to the market is restricted, for instance by the cumulative effect of parallel networks of similar restrictive agreements preventing licensors from licensing to other licensees or because the only technology owner licensing out relevant technology rights concludes an exclusive license with a licensee who is already active on the product market on the basis of substitutable technology rights. In order to qualify as relevant, the technology rights need to be both technically and commercially substitutable in order for the licensee to be active on the relevant product market.

148. Articles 4 and 5 of the TTBER, containing the list of hardcore restrictions of competition and excluded restrictions, aim at ensuring that block exempted agreements do not reduce the incentive to innovate, do not delay the dissemination of technology, and do not unduly restrict competition between the licensor and licensee or between licensees. However, the list of hardcore restrictions and the list of excluded restrictions do not take into account all the possible impacts of licence agreements. In particular, the block exemption does not take account of any cumulative effect of similar restrictions contained in networks of licence agreements. Licence agreements may lead to foreclosure of third parties both at the level of the licensor and at the level of the licensee. Foreclosure of other licensors may stem from the cumulative effect of networks of licence agreements prohibiting the licensees from exploiting competing technologies, leading to the exclusion of other (potential) licensors. Foreclosure of licensors is likely to arise in cases where most of the undertakings on the market that could (efficiently) take a competing licence are prevented from doing so as a consequence of restrictive agreements and where potential licensees face relatively high barriers to entry. Foreclosure of other licensees may stem from the cumulative effect of licence agreements prohibiting licensors from licensing other licensees and thereby preventing potential licensees from gaining access to the necessary technology. The issue of foreclosure is examined in more detail in sections 4.2.2 and 4.2.7. In addition, the Commission is likely to withdraw the benefit of the block exemption where, in individual agreements, a significant number of licensors of competing technologies impose on their licensees to extend to them more favourable conditions agreed with other licensors.

3.6.2. NON-APPLICATION OF THE BLOCK EXEMPTION REGULATION

149. Article 7 of the TTBER enables the Commission to exclude from the scope of the TTBER, by means of regulation, parallel networks of similar agreements where these cover more than 50% of a relevant market. Such a measure is not addressed to individual undertakings but concerns all undertakings whose agreements are defined in the regulation declaring that the TTBER is not to apply.

150. Whereas withdrawal of the benefit of the TTBER by the Commission under Article 6 implies the adoption of a decision pursuant to Articles 7 or 9 of Regulation (EC) No 1/2003, the effect of a Commission regulation pursuant to Article 7 of the TTBER declaring that the TTBER is not to apply, is merely to remove the benefit of the TTBER and to restore the full application of Article 101(1) and (3) of the Treaty in respect of the restraints and the markets concerned. Following the adoption of a regulation declaring the TTBER not applicable for a particular market in respect of agreements containing certain restraints, the criteria developed by the relevant case law of the Union Courts and by notices and previous decisions adopted by the Commission will give guidance on the application of Article 101 to individual agreements. Where appropriate, the Commission will take a decision in an individual case, which can provide guidance to all the undertakings operating on the market concerned.

151. For the purpose of calculating the 50% market coverage ratio, account must be taken of each individual network of licence agreements containing restraints, or combinations of restraints, producing similar effects on the market.

152. Article 7 TTBER does not entail an obligation on the part of the Commission to act where the 50% market-coverage ratio is exceeded. In general, the adoption of a regulation pursuant to Article 7 is appropriate when it is likely that access to the relevant market or competition in that market is appreciably restricted. In assessing the need to apply Article 7, the Commission will consider whether individual withdrawal would be a more appropriate remedy. This may depend, in particular, on the number of competing undertakings contributing to a cumulative effect on a market or the number of affected geographic markets within the Union.

153. Any regulation adopted under Article 7 must clearly set out its scope. Therefore the Commission must first define the relevant product and geographic market(s) and, secondly, identify the type of licensing restraint in respect of which the TTBER will no longer apply. As regards the latter aspect, the Commission may modulate the scope of the regulation according to the competition concern which it intends to address. For instance, while all parallel networks of non-compete arrangements will be taken into account for the purpose of establishing the 50% market coverage ratio, the Commission may nevertheless restrict the scope of the regulation only to non-compete obligations exceeding a certain duration. Thus, agreements of a shorter duration or of a less restrictive nature might be left unaffected, due to the lesser degree of foreclosure attributable to such restraints. Where appropriate, the Commission may also provide guidance by specifying the market share level which, in the specific market context, may be regarded as insufficient to bring about a significant contribution by an individual undertaking to the cumulative effect. In general, when the market share of the products incorporating a technology licensed by an individual licensor does not exceed 5%, the agreement or network of agreements covering that technology is not considered to contribute significantly to a cumulative foreclosure effect.[71]

154. The transitional period of not less than six months that the Commission will have to set under Article 7(2) should allow the undertakings concerned to adapt their agreements to take account of the regulation declaring that the TTBER is not to apply.

155. A regulation declaring that the TTBER is not to apply will not affect the block exempted status of the agreements concerned for the period preceding its entry into force.

NOTES

33 See in this respect the Notice on agreements of minor importance cited in footnote 20.

34 According to Article 3(2) of Regulation (EC) No 1/2003, agreements which may affect trade between Member States but which are not prohibited by Article 101 can also not be prohibited by national competition law.

35 The TTBER could now cover the technology transfer agreement assessed in the Commission Decision in *Moosehead/Whitbread* (OJ L100, 20.4.1990, p 32), see in particular paragraph 16 of that decision.

36 See in this respect Case 262/81, *Coditel (II)*, [1982] ECR 3381.

37 OJ L102, 23.4.2010, p 1.

38 The terms 'licensing' and 'licensed' used in these Guidelines also include non-assertion and settlement arrangements as long as a transfer of technology rights takes place as described in this section. See further on settlement agreements points (234) ff.

39 Under Regulation (EEC) No 19/65 of the Council of 2 March 1965 on application of Article 85(3) of the Treaty to certain categories of agreements and concerted practices, OJ Special Edition Series I 1965–1966, p 35, the Commission is not empowered to block exempt technology transfer agreements concluded between more than two undertakings.

40 See recital 6 of the TTBER and further section 3.2.6.

41 See for more details point (247).

42 Commission Regulation (EU) No 330/2010 of 20 April 2010 on the application of Article 101(3) of the Treaty on the Functioning of the European Union to categories of vertical agreements and concerted practices, OJ L102, 23.4.2010, p 1.

43 OJ C130, 19.5.2010, p 1.

44 Commission Notice of 18 December 1978 concerning its assessment of certain subcontracting agreements in relation to Article 85(1) of the EEC Treaty, OJ C1, 3.1.1979, p 2.

45 See point 3 of Commission Notice on subcontracting agreements cited in footnote 44.

46 See also section 3.2.6.1.

47 However, this last example is covered by Regulation (EU) No 1217/2010 cited in footnote 49, see also section 3.2.6.1. below.

48 Commission Regulation (EU) No 1218/2010 of 14 December 2010 on the application of Article 101(3) of the Treaty on the Functioning of the European Union to certain categories of specialisation agreements, OJ L335, 18.12.2010, p 43.

49 Commission Regulation (EU) No 1217/2010 of 14 December 2010 on the application of Article 101(3) of the Treaty on the Functioning of the European Union to certain categories of research and development agreements, OJ L335, 18.12.2010, p 36.

50 Cited in footnote 42.

51 See also the brochure 'Competition policy in Europe — The competition rules for supply and distribution agreements', European Commission, Publications Office of the European Union 2012, Luxembourg.

52 Respectively OJ L102, 23.4.2010, p 1, and OJ C130, 19.5.2010, p 1.

53 See e.g. the case law cited in footnote 16.

54 See point 18 of the Commission Guidelines on the application of Article 81(3) of the Treaty, cited in footnote 3.

55 Case T-17/93 *Matra* [1994] ECR II-595, paragraph 85.

56 See in this respect point 98 of the Guidelines on the application of Article 81(3) of the Treaty cited in footnote 3.

57 This is also the case where one party grants a licence to the other party and accepts to buy a physical input from the licensee. The purchase price can serve the same function as the royalty.

58 See in this respect Case 193/83, *Windsurfing International*, [1986] ECR 611, paragraph 67.

59 OJ C130, 19.5.2010, p 1, point 51.

60 Field of use restrictions are further dealt with in points (208) ff.

61 For a definition of passive sales, see point (108) of these guidelines and the Guidelines on Vertical Restraints cited in footnote 52, point 51.

62 This hardcore restriction applies to technology transfer agreements concerning trade within the Union. In so far as technology transfer agreements concern exports outside the Union or imports/re-imports from outside the Union see judgment of the Court of Justice in Case C-306/96, *Javico* v *Yves Saint Laurent* [1998] ECR I-1983. In that judgment the ECJ held in paragraph 20 that 'an agreement in which the reseller gives to the producer an undertaking that it will sell the contractual products on a market outside the Community cannot be regarded as having the object of appreciably restricting competition within the common market or as being capable of affecting, as such, trade between Member States'.

63 See in this respect Case 26/76, *Metro (I)*, [1977] ECR 1875.

64 See in this respect Case 65/86, *Bayer* v *Süllhofer*, [1988] ECR 5249.

65 Cf. in respect of challenging the ownership of a trademark Commission Decision in *Moosehead/Whitbread* (OJ L100, 20.4.1990, p 32).

66 Case 193/83 *Windsurfing International* [1986] ECR 611, paragraph 92.

67 In the context of an agreement which is technically not an exclusive agreement, and where a termination clause is thus not covered by the safe harbour of the TTBER, the licensor may, in a specific case, be in a similar situation of dependency in relation to a licensee with considerable buyer power. Such dependency will be taken into account in the individual assessment.

68 See point (14) above.

69 See point (36) above.

70 See in this respect point 42 of the Guidelines on the application of Article 81(3) of the Treaty, cited in footnote 3.

71 See in this respect point 8 of the Commission Notice on agreements of minor importance, cited in footnote 20.

4. APPLICATION OF ARTICLE 101(1) AND 101(3) OF THE TREATY OUTSIDE THE SCOPE OF THE TTBER

4.1. THE GENERAL FRAMEWORK FOR ANALYSIS

[4.293]

156. Agreements that fall outside the block exemption, for example because the market share thresholds are exceeded or the agreement involves more than two parties, are subject to individual assessment. Agreements that either do not restrict competition within the meaning of Article 101(1) of the Treaty or which fulfil the conditions of Article 101(3) are valid and enforceable. It is recalled that there is no presumption of illegality of agreements that fall outside the scope of the block exemption provided that they do not contain hardcore restrictions of competition. In particular, there is no presumption that Article 101(1) applies merely because the market share thresholds are exceeded. Individual assessment based on the principles described in these guidelines is always required.

Safe harbour if there are sufficient independently controlled technologies

157. In order to promote predictability beyond the application of the TTBER and to confine detailed analysis to cases that are likely to present real competition concerns, the Commission takes the view that outside the area of hardcore restrictions Article 101 of the Treaty is unlikely to be infringed where there are four or more independently controlled technologies in addition to the technologies controlled by the parties to the agreement that may be substitutable for the licensed technology at a comparable cost to the user. In assessing whether the technologies are sufficiently substitutable the relative commercial strength of the technologies in question must be taken into account. The competitive constraint imposed by a technology is limited if it does not constitute a commercially viable alternative to the licensed technology. For instance, if due to network effects in the market consumers have a strong preference for products incorporating the licensed technology, other technologies already on the market or likely to come to the market within a reasonable period of time may not constitute a real alternative and may therefore impose only a limited competitive constraint.

158. The fact that an agreement falls outside the safe harbour described in point (157) does not imply that the agreement is caught by Article 101(1) of the Treaty and, if so, that the conditions of Article 101(3) are not satisfied. As for the market share safe harbour of the TTBER, this additional safe harbour merely creates a presumption that the agreement is not prohibited by Article 101. Outside the safe harbour individual assessment of the agreement based on the principles developed in these guidelines is required.

4.1.1. THE RELEVANT FACTORS

159. In the application of Article 101 of the Treaty to individual cases it is necessary to take due account of the way in which competition operates on the market in question. The following factors are particularly relevant in this respect:

(a) the nature of the agreement;
(b) the market position of the parties;
(c) the market position of competitors;
(d) the market position of buyers on the relevant markets;
(e) entry barriers and

(f) maturity of the market.

160. The importance of individual factors may vary from case to case and depends on all other factors. For instance, a high market share of the parties is usually a good indicator of market power, but in the case of low entry barriers it may not be indicative of market power. It is therefore not possible to provide firm rules on the importance of the individual factors.

161. Technology transfer agreements can take many shapes and forms. It is therefore important to analyse the nature of the agreement in terms of the competitive relationship between the parties and the restraints that it contains. In the latter regard it is necessary to go beyond the express terms of the agreement. The existence of implicit restraints may be derived from the way in which the agreement has been implemented by the parties and from the incentives that they face.

162. The market position of the parties, including any undertakings *de facto* or *de jure* controlled by the parties, provides an indication of the degree of market power, if any, possessed by the licensor, the licensee or both. The higher their market share the greater their market power is likely to be. This is particularly so where the market share reflects cost advantages or other competitive advantages vis-à-vis competitors. These competitive advantages may for instance result from being a first mover in the market, from holding essential patents or from having superior technology. However, market shares are always only one factor in assessing market positions. For instance, in particular in the case of technology markets, market shares may not always be a good indicator of the relative strength of the technology in question and the market share figures may differ considerably depending on the different calculation methods.

163. Market shares and possible competitive advantages and disadvantages are also used to assess the market position of competitors. The stronger the actual competitors and the greater their number the less risk there is that the parties will be able to exercise market power individually. However, if the number of competitors is rather small and their market position (size, costs, R&D potential, etc.) is rather similar, this market structure may increase the risk of collusion.

164. The market position of buyers provides an indication of whether or not one or more buyers possess buyer power. The first indicator of buyer power is the market share of the buyer on the purchase market. This share reflects the importance of its demand for possible suppliers. Other indicators focus on the position of the buyer on its resale market, including characteristics such as a wide geographic spread of its outlets, and its brand image amongst final consumers. In some circumstances buyer power may prevent the licensor and/or the licensee from exercising market power on the market and thereby solve a competition problem that would otherwise have existed. This is particularly so when strong buyers have the capacity and the incentive to bring new sources of supply on to the market in the case of a small but permanent increase in relative prices. Where the strong buyers merely extract favourable terms from the supplier or simply pass on any price increase to their customers, the position of the buyers is not such as to prevent the exercise of market power by the licensee on the product market and therefore not such as to solve the competition problem on that market.[72]

165. Entry barriers are measured by the extent to which incumbent companies can increase their price above the competitive level without attracting new entry. In the absence of entry barriers, easy and quick entry would render price increases unprofitable. When effective entry, preventing or eroding the exercise of market power, is likely to occur within one or two years, entry barriers can, as a general rule, be said to be low.

166. Entry barriers may result from a wide variety of factors such as economies of scale and scope, government regulations, especially where they establish exclusive rights, state aid, import tariffs, intellectual property rights, ownership of resources where the supply is limited due to for instance natural limitations, essential facilities, a first mover advantage or brand loyalty of consumers created by strong advertising over a period of time. Restrictive agreements entered into by undertakings may also work as an entry barrier by making access more difficult and foreclosing (potential) competitors. Entry barriers may be present at all stages of the research and development, production and distribution process. The question whether certain of these factors should be described as entry barriers depends particularly on whether they entail sunk costs. Sunk costs are those costs which have to be incurred to enter or be active on a market but which are lost when the market is exited. The more costs are sunk, the more potential entrants have to weigh the risks of entering the market and the more credibly incumbents can threaten that they will match new competition, as sunk costs make it costly for incumbents to leave the market. In general, entry requires sunk costs, sometimes minor and sometimes major. Therefore, actual competition is in general more effective and will weigh more heavily in the assessment of a case than potential competition.

167. In a mature market, that is to say a market that has existed for some time, where the technology used is well known and widespread and not changing very much and in which demand is relatively stable or declining, restrictions of competition are more likely to have negative effects than in more dynamic markets.

168. In the assessment of particular restraints other factors may have to be taken into account. Such factors include cumulative effects, that is to say, the coverage of the market by similar agreements, the duration of the agreements, the regulatory environment and behaviour that may indicate or facilitate collusion such as price leadership, pre-announced price changes and discussions on the 'right' price, price rigidity in response to excess capacity, price discrimination and past collusive behaviour.

4.1.2. Negative effects of restrictive licence agreements

169. The negative effects on competition on the market that may result from restrictive technology transfer agreements include the following:

(a) reduction of inter-technology competition between the companies operating on a technology market or on a market for products incorporating the technologies in question, including facilitation of collusion, both explicit and tacit;

(b) foreclosure of competitors by raising their costs, restricting their access to essential inputs or otherwise raising barriers to entry; and

(c) reduction of intra-technology competition between undertakings that produce products on the basis of the same technology.

170. Technology transfer agreements may reduce inter-technology competition, that is to say, competition between undertakings that license or produce on the basis of substitutable technologies. This is particularly the case where reciprocal obligations are imposed. For instance, where competitors transfer competing technologies to each other and impose a reciprocal obligation to provide each other with future improvements of their respective technologies and where this agreement prevents either competitor from gaining a technological lead over the other, competition in innovation between the parties is restricted (see also point (241)).

171. Licensing between competitors may also facilitate collusion. The risk of collusion is particularly high in concentrated markets. Collusion requires that the undertakings concerned have similar views on what is in their common interest and on how the co-ordination mechanisms function. For collusion to work the undertakings must also be able to monitor each other's market behaviour and there must be adequate deterrents to ensure that there is an incentive not to depart from the common policy on the market, while entry barriers must be high enough to limit entry or expansion by outsiders. Agreements can facilitate collusion by increasing transparency in the market, by controlling certain behaviour and by raising barriers to entry. Collusion can also exceptionally be facilitated by licensing agreements that lead to a high degree of commonality of costs, because undertakings that have similar costs are more likely to have similar views on the terms of coordination.[73]

172. Licence agreements may also affect inter-technology competition by creating barriers to entry for and expansion by competitors. Such foreclosure effects may stem from restraints that prevent licensees from licensing from third parties or create disincentives for them to do so. For instance, third parties may be foreclosed where incumbent licensors impose non-compete obligations on licensees to such an extent that an insufficient number of licensees are available to third parties and where entry at the level of licensees is difficult. Suppliers of substitutable technologies may also be foreclosed where a licensor with a sufficient degree of market power ties together various parts of a technology and licenses them together as a package while only part of the package is essential to produce a certain product.

173. Licence agreements may also reduce intra-technology competition, that is to say, competition between undertakings that produce on the basis of the same technology. An agreement imposing territorial restraints on licensees, preventing them from selling into each other's territory reduces competition between them. Licence agreements may also reduce intra-technology competition by facilitating collusion between licensees. Moreover, licence agreements that reduce intra-technology competition may facilitate collusion between owners of competing technologies or reduce inter-technology competition by raising barriers to entry.

4.1.3. Positive effects of restrictive licence agreements and the framework for analysing such effects

174. Even restrictive licence agreements often also produce pro-competitive effects in the form of efficiencies, which may outweigh their anti-competitive effects. The assessment of the possible pro-competitive effects takes place within the framework of Article 101(3), which contains an exception from the prohibition rule of Article 101(1) of the Treaty. For that exception to be applicable the licence agreement must produce objective economic benefits, the restrictions on competition must be indispensable to attain the efficiencies, consumers must receive a fair share of the efficiency gains, and the agreement must not afford the parties the possibility of eliminating competition in respect of a substantial part of the products concerned. An undertaking that relies on Article 101(3) must demonstrate, by means of convincing arguments and evidence, that the conditions for obtaining an exemption are satisfied.[74]

175. The assessment of restrictive agreements under Article 101(3) of the Treaty is made within the actual context in which they occur[75] and on the basis of the facts existing at any given point in time. The assessment is therefore sensitive to material changes in the facts. The exception rule of Article 101(3) applies as long as the four conditions are fulfilled and ceases to apply when that is no longer the case.[76] However, when applying Article 101(3) it is necessary to take into account the initial sunk investments made by any of the parties and the time needed and the restraints required to commit and recoup an efficiency enhancing investment. Article 101 cannot be applied without considering the *ex ante* investment and the risks relating thereto. The risk facing the parties and the sunk investment that must be committed to implement the agreement can thus lead to the agreement falling outside Article 101(1) or fulfilling the conditions of Article 101(3), as the case may be, for the period of time required to recoup the investment.

176. The first condition of Article 101(3) of the Treaty requires an assessment of the objective benefits in terms of efficiencies produced by the agreement. In this respect, licence agreements have the potential of bringing together complementary technologies and other assets allowing new or improved products to be put on the market or existing products to be produced at lower cost. Outside the context of hardcore cartels, licensing often occurs because it is more efficient for the licensor to licence the technology than to exploit it itself. This may particularly be the case where the licensee already has access to the necessary production assets. The agreement then allows the licensee to gain access to a technology that can be combined with those assets, allowing it to exploit new or improved technologies. Another example of potentially efficiency enhancing licensing is where the licensee already has a technology and the combination of this technology and the licensor's technology gives rise to synergies. When the two technologies are combined the licensee may be able to attain a cost/output configuration that would not otherwise be possible. Licence agreements may also give rise to efficiencies at the distribution stage in the same way as vertical distribution agreements. Such efficiencies can take the form of cost savings or the provision of valuable services to consumers. The positive effects of vertical agreements are described in the Guidelines on Vertical Restraints.[77] A further example of possible efficiency gains is to be found in agreements whereby technology owners assemble a technology package for licensing to third parties. Such pooling arrangements may in particular reduce transaction costs, as licensees do not have to conclude separate licence agreements with each licensor. Pro-competitive licensing may also occur to ensure design freedom. In sectors where large numbers of intellectual property rights exist and

where individual products may infringe upon a number of existing and future property rights, licence agreements whereby the parties agree not to assert their property rights against each other are often pro-competitive because they allow the parties to develop their respective technologies without the risk of subsequent infringement claims.

177. In the application of the indispensability test contained in Article 101(3) of the Treaty the Commission will in particular examine whether individual restrictions make it possible to perform the activity in question more efficiently than would have been the case in the absence of the restriction concerned. In making this assessment the market conditions and the realities facing the parties must be taken into account. Undertakings invoking the benefit of Article 101(3) are not required to consider hypothetical and theoretical alternatives. They must, however, explain and demonstrate why seemingly realistic and significantly less restrictive alternatives would be significantly less efficient. If the application of what appears to be a commercially realistic and less restrictive alternative would lead to a significant loss of efficiencies, the restriction in question is treated as indispensable. In some cases, it may also be necessary to examine whether the agreement as such is indispensable to achieve the efficiencies. This may for example be so in the case of technology pools that include complementary but non-essential technologies,[78] in which case it must be examined to what extent the inclusion of those technologies gives rise to particular efficiencies or whether, without a significant loss of efficiencies, the pool could be limited to technologies for which there are no substitutes. In the case of simple licensing between two parties it is generally not necessary to go beyond an examination of whether individual restraints are indispensable. Normally there is no less restrictive alternative to the licence agreement as such.

178. The condition that consumers must receive a fair share of the benefits implies that consumers of the products produced under the licence must at least be compensated for the negative effects of the agreement.[79] This means that the efficiency gains must fully off-set the likely negative impact on prices, output and other relevant factors caused by the agreement. They may do so by changing the cost structure of the undertakings concerned, giving them an incentive to reduce price, or by allowing consumers to gain access to new or improved products, compensating for any likely price increase.[80]

179. The last condition of Article 101(3) of the Treaty, according to which the agreement must not afford the parties the possibility of eliminating competition in respect of a substantial part of the products concerned, presupposes an analysis of remaining competitive pressures on the market and the impact of the agreement on such sources of competition. In the application of the last condition of Article 101(3) the relationship between Article 101(3) and Article 102 must be taken into account. According to settled case law, the application of Article 101(3) cannot prevent the application of Article 102 of the Treaty.[81] Moreover, since Articles 101 and 102 both pursue the aim of maintaining effective competition on the market, consistency requires that Article 101(3) be interpreted as precluding any application of the exception rule to restrictive agreements that constitute an abuse of a dominant position.[82]

180. The fact that the agreement substantially reduces one dimension of competition does not necessarily mean that competition is eliminated within the meaning of Article 101(3). A technology pool, for instance, can result in an industry standard, leading to a situation in which there is little competition in terms of the technological format. Once the main players in the market adopt a certain format, network effects may make it very difficult for alternative formats to survive. This does not imply, however, that the creation of a de facto industry standard always eliminates competition within the meaning of the last condition of Article 101(3). Within the standard, suppliers may compete on price, quality and product features. However, in order for the agreement to comply with Article 101(3), it must be ensured that the agreement does not unduly restrict competition and does not unduly restrict future innovation.

4.2. APPLICATION OF ARTICLE 101 TO VARIOUS TYPES OF LICENSING RESTRAINTS

181. This section deals with various types of restraints that are commonly included in licence agreements. Given their prevalence it is useful to provide guidance as to how they are assessed outside the safe harbour of the TTBER. Restraints that have already been dealt with in the other sections of these guidelines, in particular sections 3.4 and 3.5, are only dealt with briefly in this section.

182. This section covers both agreements between non-competitors and agreements between competitors. In respect of the latter a distinction is made — where appropriate — between reciprocal and non-reciprocal agreements. No such distinction is required in the case of agreements between non-competitors. Indeed, when undertakings are neither actual nor potential competitors on a relevant technology market or on a market for products incorporating the licensed technology, a reciprocal licence is for all practical purposes no different from two separate licences. The situation is different for arrangements whereby the parties assemble a technology package, which is then licensed to third parties. Such arrangements are technology pools, which are dealt with in section 4.

183. This section does not deal with obligations in licence agreements that are generally not restrictive of competition within the meaning of Article 101(1) of the Treaty. These obligations include but are not limited to:

(a) confidentiality obligations;
(b) obligations on licensees not to sub-license;
(c) obligations not to use the licensed technology rights after the expiry of the agreement, provided that the licensed technology rights remain valid and in force;
(d) obligations to assist the licensor in enforcing the licensed intellectual property rights;
(e) obligations to pay minimum royalties or to produce a minimum quantity of products incorporating the licensed technology; and
(f) obligations to use the licensor's trade mark or indicate the name of the licensor on the product.

4.2.1. ROYALTY OBLIGATIONS

184. The parties to a licence agreement are normally free to determine the royalty payable by the licensee and its mode of payment without being caught by Article 101(1) of the Treaty. This principle applies both to agreements between competitors and agreements between non-competitors. Royalty obligations may for instance take the form of lump sum payments, a percentage of the selling price or a fixed amount for each product incorporating the licensed technology. In cases where the licensed technology relates to an input which is incorporated into a final product it is

as a general rule not restrictive of competition that royalties are calculated on the basis of the price of the final product, provided that it incorporates the licensed technology.[83] In the case of software licensing royalties based on the number of users and royalties calculated on a per machine basis are generally compatible with Article 101(1).

185. In the case of licence agreements between competitors it should be borne in mind (see points (100) to (101) and (116) above) that in a limited number of circumstances royalty obligations may amount to price fixing, which is considered a hardcore restriction (see Article 4(1)(a)). It is a hardcore restriction under Article 4(1)(a) if competitors provide for reciprocal running royalties in circumstances where the licence is a sham, in that its purpose is not to allow an integration of complementary technologies or to achieve another pro-competitive aim. It is also a hardcore restriction under Article 4(1)(a) and 4(1)(d) if royalties extend to products produced solely with the licensee's own technology rights.

186. Other types of royalty arrangements between competitors are block exempted up to the market share threshold of 20% even if they restrict competition. Outside the safe harbour of the block exemption Article 101(1) of the Treaty may be applicable where competitors cross license and impose running royalties that are clearly disproportionate compared to the market value of the licence and where such royalties have a significant impact on market prices. In assessing whether the royalties are disproportionate it is necessary to examine the royalties paid by other licensees on the product market for the same or substitute technologies. In such cases it is unlikely that the conditions of Article 101(3) are satisfied.

187. Notwithstanding the fact that the block exemption only applies as long as the technology rights are valid and in force, the parties can normally agree to extend royalty obligations beyond the period of validity of the licensed intellectual property rights without falling foul of Article 101(1) of the Treaty. Once these rights expire, third parties can legally exploit the technology in question and compete with the parties to the agreement. Such actual and potential competition will normally be sufficient to ensure that the obligation in question does not have appreciable anti-competitive effects.

188. In the case of agreements between non-competitors the block exemption covers agreements whereby royalties are calculated on the basis of both products produced with the licensed technology and products produced with technologies licensed from third parties. Such arrangements may facilitate the metering of royalties. However, they may also lead to foreclosure by increasing the cost of using third party inputs and may thus have effects similar to those of a non-compete obligation. If royalties are paid not just on products produced with the licensed technology but also on products produced with third party technology, then the royalties will increase the cost of the latter products and reduce demand for third party technology. Outside the scope of the block exemption the question whether the restriction has foreclosure effects must therefore be considered. For that purpose it is appropriate to use the analytical framework set out in section 4.2.7 below. In the case of appreciable foreclosure effects such agreements are caught by Article 101(1) of the Treaty and unlikely to fulfil the conditions of Article 101(3), unless there is no other practical way of calculating and monitoring royalty payments.

4.2.2. Exclusive licensing and sales restrictions

189. For the purpose of these guidelines, it is useful to distinguish between restrictions as to production within a given territory (exclusive or sole licences) and restrictions on the sale of products incorporating the licensed technology into a given territory and to a given customer group (sales restrictions).

4.2.2.1.
Exclusive and sole licences

190. An 'exclusive licence' means that the licensor itself is not permitted to produce on the basis of the licensed technology rights, nor is it permitted to license the licensed technology rights to third parties, in general or for a particular use or in a particular territory. This means that, in general or for that particular use or in that particular territory, the licensee is the only one allowed to produce on the basis of the licensed technology rights.

191. Where the licensor undertakes not to produce itself or license others to produce within a given territory, this territory may cover the whole world or any part of it. Where the licensor undertakes only not to licence third parties to produce within a given territory, the licence is a sole licence. Exclusive or sole licensing is often accompanied by sales restrictions that limit the parties as to where they may sell products incorporating the licensed technology.

192. Reciprocal exclusive licensing between competitors falls under Article 4(1)(c) TTBER, which identifies market and customer sharing between competitors as a hardcore restriction. Reciprocal sole licensing between competitors is, however, block exempted up to the market share threshold of 20%. Under such an agreement the parties mutually commit not to license their competing technologies to third parties. In cases where the parties have a significant degree of market power such agreements may facilitate collusion by ensuring that the parties are the only sources of output in the market based on the licensed technologies.

193. Non-reciprocal exclusive licensing between competitors is block exempted up to the market share threshold of 20%. Above the market share threshold it is necessary to analyse the likely anti-competitive effects of such exclusive licensing. Where the exclusive licence is world-wide it implies that the licensor leaves the market. In cases where exclusivity is limited to a particular territory such as a Member State the agreement implies that the licensor abstains from producing goods and services inside the territory in question. In the context of Article 101(1) of the Treaty, the competitive significance of the licensor must, in particular, be assessed. If the licensor has a limited market position on the product market or lacks the capacity to effectively exploit the technology in the licensee's territory, the agreement is unlikely to be caught by Article 101(1). A special case exists where the licensor and the licensee only compete on the technology market and the licensor, for instance being a research institute or a small research based undertaking, lacks the production and distribution assets to effectively bring to market products incorporating the licensed technology. In such cases Article 101(1) is unlikely to be infringed.

194. Exclusive licensing between non-competitors — to the extent that it is caught by Article 101(1) of the Treaty[84] — is likely to fulfil the conditions of Article 101(3). The right to grant an exclusive licence is generally necessary in order to induce the licensee to invest in the licensed technology and to bring the products to market in a timely manner. This is in particular the case where the licensee must make large investments in further developing the licensed technology. To intervene against the exclusivity once the licensee has made a commercial success of the licensed technology would deprive the licensee of the fruits of its success and would be detrimental to competition, the dissemination of technology and innovation. The Commission will therefore only exceptionally intervene against exclusive licensing in agreements between non-competitors, irrespective of the territorial scope of the licence.

195. However, if the licensee already owns a substitutable technology used for in-house production, the exclusive license might not be necessary in order to give incentives to the licensee to bring a product to the market. In such a scenario, the exclusive licensing may instead be caught by Article 101(1) of the Treaty, in particular where the licensee has market power on the product market. The main situation in which intervention may be warranted is where a dominant licensee obtains an exclusive licence to one or more competing technologies. Such agreements are likely to be caught by Article 101(1) and unlikely to fulfil the conditions of Article 101(3). However, for Article 101(1) to apply entry into the technology market must be difficult and the licensed technology must constitute a real source of competition on the market. In such circumstances an exclusive licence may foreclose third party licensees, raise the barriers to entry and allow the licensee to preserve its market power.

196. Arrangements whereby two or more parties cross licence each other and undertake not to licence third parties give rise to particular concerns when the package of technologies resulting from the cross licences creates a de facto industry standard to which third parties must have access in order to compete effectively on the market. In such cases the agreement creates a closed standard reserved for the parties. The Commission will assess such arrangements according to the same principles as those applied to technology pools (see section 4.4). There will normally be a requirement that the technologies which support such a standard be licensed to third parties on fair, reasonable and non-discriminatory terms.[85] Where the parties to the arrangement compete with third parties on an existing product market and the arrangement relates to that product market, a closed standard is likely to have substantial exclusionary effects. This negative impact on competition can only be avoided by licensing also to third parties.

4.2.2.2.
Sales restrictions

197. Also as regards sales restrictions there is an important distinction to be made between licensing between competitors and between non-competitors.

198. Restrictions on active and passive sales by one or both parties in a reciprocal agreement between competitors are hardcore restrictions of competition under Article 4(1)(c) TTBER. Such sales restrictions are caught by Article 101(1) and are unlikely to fulfil the conditions of Article 101(3). Such restrictions are generally considered market sharing, since they prevent the affected party from selling actively and passively into territories and to customer groups which it actually served or could realistically have served in the absence of the agreement.

199. In the case of non-reciprocal agreements between competitors the block exemption applies to restrictions on active and/or passive sales by the licensee or the licensor into the exclusive territory or to the exclusive customer group reserved for the other party (see Article 4(1)(c)(i) TTBER). Above the market share threshold of 20% sales restrictions between licensor and licensee are caught by Article 101(1) of the Treaty when one or both of the parties have a significant degree of market power. Such restrictions may, however, be indispensable for the dissemination of valuable technologies and may therefore fulfil the conditions of Article 101(3). This may be the case where the licensor has a relatively weak market position in the territory where it exploits the technology itself. In such circumstances restrictions on active sales in particular may be indispensable to induce the licensor to grant the licence. In the absence of such restrictions the licensor would risk facing active competition in its main area of activity. Similarly, restrictions on active sales by the licensor may be indispensable, in particular, where the licensee has a relatively weak market position in the territory allocated to it and has to make significant investments in order to efficiently exploit the licensed technology.

200. The block exemption also covers restrictions on active sales into the territory or to the customer group allocated to another licensee, which was not a competitor of the licensor at the time when it concluded the licence agreement with the licensor. This is, however, only the case when the agreement between the parties in question is non-reciprocal (see Article 4(1)(c)(ii) TTBER). Above the market share threshold such active sales restrictions are likely to be caught by Article 101(1) of the Treaty when the parties have a significant degree of market power. The restraint is nevertheless likely to be indispensable within the meaning of Article 101(3) for the period of time required for the protected licensee to penetrate a new market and establish a market presence in the allocated territory or vis-à-vis the allocated customer group. This protection against active sales allows the licensee to overcome the asymmetry, which it faces due to the fact that some of the licensees are competing undertakings of the licensor and thus already established on the market. Restrictions on passive sales by licensees into a territory or to a customer group allocated to another licensee are hardcore restrictions under Article 4(1)(c) of the TTBER.

201. In the case of agreements between non-competitors sales restrictions between the licensor and a licensee are block exempted up to the market share threshold of 30%. Above the market share threshold restrictions on active and passive sales by licensees to territories or customer groups reserved exclusively for the licensor may be indispensable for the dissemination of valuable technologies and therefore fall outside Article 101(1) or fulfil the conditions of Article 101(3) of the Treaty. This may be the case where the licensor has a relatively weak market position in the territory where it exploits itself the technology. In such circumstances restrictions on active sales in particular may be indispensable to induce the licensor to grant the licence. In the absence of such restrictions the licensor would risk facing active competition in its main area of activity. In other cases sales restrictions on the licensee may be caught by Article 101(1) and may not fulfil the conditions of Article 101(3). This is likely to be the case where the licensor individually has a significant degree of market power and also where a series of similar agreements concluded by licensors which together hold a strong position on the market have a cumulative effect.

202. Sales restrictions on the licensor, when caught by Article 101(1) of the Treaty, are likely to fulfil the conditions of Article 101(3) unless there are no real alternatives to the licensor's technology on the market or such alternatives are licensed by the licensee from third parties. Such restrictions and in particular restrictions on active sales are likely to be indispensable within the meaning of Article 101(3) in order to induce the licensee to invest in the production, marketing and sale of the products incorporating the licensed technology. It is likely that the licensee's incentive to invest would be significantly reduced if it faced direct competition from the licensor whose production costs are not burdened by royalty payments, possibly leading to sub-optimal levels of investment.

203. As regards sales restrictions between licensees in agreements between non-competitors, the TTBER block exempts restrictions on active selling between territories or customer groups. Above the market share threshold of 30% restrictions on active sales between licensees' territories and customer groups limit intra-technology competition and are likely to be caught by Article 101(1) of the Treaty when the individual licensee has a significant degree of market power. However, such restrictions may fulfil the conditions of Article 101(3) where they are necessary to prevent free riding and to induce the licensee to make the investment necessary for efficient exploitation of the licensed technology inside its territory and to promote sales of the licensed product.

Restrictions on passive sales are covered by the hardcore list of Article 4(2)(b) of the TTBER (see points (119) to (127) above).

4.2.3. OUTPUT RESTRICTIONS

204. Reciprocal output restrictions in licence agreements between competitors constitute a hardcore restriction as set out in Article 4(1)(b) of the TTBER (see point (103) above). Article 4(1)(b) does not cover output restrictions on the licensor's technology imposed on the licensee in a non-reciprocal agreement or on one of the licensees in an reciprocal agreement. Such restrictions are block exempted up to the market share threshold of 20%. Above the market share threshold, output restrictions on the licensee may restrict competition where the parties have a significant degree of market power. However, Article 101(3) is likely to apply in cases where the licensor's technology is substantially better than the licensee's technology and the output limitation substantially exceeds the output of the licensee prior to the conclusion of the agreement. In that case the effect of the output limitation is limited even in markets where demand is growing. In the application of Article 101(3) of the Treaty it must also be taken into account that such restrictions may be necessary in order to induce the licensor to disseminate its technology as widely as possible. For instance, a licensor may be reluctant to license its competitors if it cannot limit the licence to a particular production site with a specific capacity (a site licence). Where the licence agreement leads to a real integration of complementary assets, output restrictions on the licensee may therefore fulfil the conditions of Article 101(3). However, this is unlikely to be the case where the parties have substantial market power.

205. Output restrictions in licence agreements between non-competitors are block exempted up to the market share threshold of 30%. The main anti-competitive risk flowing from output restrictions on licensees in agreements between non-competitors is reduced intra-technology competition between licensees. The significance of such anti-competitive effects depends on the market position of the licensor and the licensees and the extent to which the output limitation prevents the licensee from satisfying demand for the products incorporating the licensed technology.

206. When output restrictions are combined with exclusive territories or exclusive customer groups, the restrictive effects are increased. The combination of the two types of restraints makes it more likely that the agreement serves to partition markets.

207. Output limitations imposed on the licensee in agreements between non-competitors may also have pro-competitive effects by promoting the dissemination of technology. As a supplier of technology, the licensor should normally be free to determine the output produced with the licensed technology by the licensee. If the licensor were not free to determine the output of the licensee, a number of licence agreements might not come into existence in the first place, which would have a negative impact on the dissemination of new technology. This is particularly likely to be the case where the licensor is also a producer, since the licensee's output may find its way back into the licensor's main area of operation and thus have a direct impact on those activities. On the other hand, it is less likely that output restrictions are necessary in order to ensure dissemination of the licensor's technology when they are combined with sales restrictions on the licensee prohibiting it from selling into a territory or customer group reserved for the licensor.

4.2.4. FIELD OF USE RESTRICTIONS

208. Under a field of use restriction the licence is either limited to one or more technical fields of application or one or more product markets or industrial sectors. An industrial sector may encompass several product markets but not part of a product market. There are many cases in which the same technology can be used to make different products or can be incorporated into products belonging to different product markets. A new moulding technology may for instance be used to make plastic bottles and plastic glasses, each product belonging to a separate product market. However, a single product market may encompass several technical fields of use. For instance a new engine technology may be employed in four cylinder engines and six cylinder engines. Similarly, a technology to make chipsets may be used to produce chipsets with up to four CPUs and more than four CPUs. A licence limiting the use of the licensed technology to produce say four cylinder engines and chipsets with up to four CPUs constitutes a technical field of use restriction.

209. Given that field of use restrictions are covered by the block exemption and that certain customer restrictions are hardcore restrictions under Articles 4(1)(c) and 4(2)(b) of the TTBER, it is important to distinguish the two categories of restrictions. A customer restriction presupposes that specific customer groups are identified and that the parties are restricted in selling to such identified groups. The fact that a technical field of use restriction may correspond to certain groups of customers within a product market does not imply that the restraint is to be classified as a customer

restriction. For instance, the fact that certain customers buy predominantly or exclusively chipsets with more than four CPUs does not imply that a licence which is limited to chipsets with up to four CPUs constitutes a customer restriction. However, the field of use must be defined objectively by reference to identified and meaningful technical characteristics of the contract product.

210. Because certain output restrictions are hardcore restrictions under Article 4(1)(b) of the TTBER, it is important to note that field of use restrictions are not considered to be output restrictions because a field of use restriction does not limit the output the licensee may produce within the licensed field of use.

211. A field of use restriction limits the exploitation of the licensed technology by the licensee to one or more particular fields of use without limiting the licensor's ability to exploit the licensed technology. In addition, as with territories, these fields of use can be allocated to the licensee under an exclusive or sole licence. Field of use restrictions combined with an exclusive or sole licence also restrict the licensor's ability to exploit its own technology, by preventing it from exploiting it itself, including by way of licensing to others. In the case of a sole license only licensing to third parties is restricted. Field of use restrictions combined with exclusive and sole licences are treated in the same way as the exclusive and sole licenses dealt with in section 4.2.2 above. In particular, for licensing between competitors, this means that reciprocal exclusive licensing is hardcore under Article 4(1)(c).

212. Field of use restrictions may have pro-competitive effects by encouraging the licensor to license its technology for applications that fall outside its main area of focus. If the licensor could not prevent licensees from operating in fields where it exploits the technology itself or in fields where the value of the technology is not yet well established, it would be likely to create a disincentive for the licensor to license or would lead it to charge a higher royalty. The fact that in certain sectors licensing often occurs to ensure design freedom by preventing infringement claims must also be taken into account. Within the scope of the licence the licensee is able to develop its own technology without fearing infringement claims by the licensor.

213. Field of use restrictions on licensees in agreements between actual or potential competitors are block exempted up to the market share threshold of 20%. The main competitive concern in the case of such restrictions is the risk that the licensee ceases to be a competitive force outside the licensed field of use. This risk is greater in the case of cross licensing between competitors where the agreement provides for asymmetrical field of use restrictions. A field of use restriction is asymmetrical where one party is permitted to use the licensed technology within one industrial sector, product market or technical field of use and the other party is permitted to use the other licensed technology within another industrial sector, product market or technical field of use. Competition concerns may in particular arise where the licensee's production facility, which is tooled up to use the licensed technology, is also used to produce products outside the licensed field of use with its own technology. If the agreement is likely to lead the licensee to reduce output outside the licensed field of use, the agreement is likely to be caught by Article 101(1). Symmetrical field of use restrictions, that is to say, agreements whereby the parties are licensed to use each other's technologies within the same field(s) of use, are unlikely to be caught by Article 101(1) of the Treaty. Such agreements are unlikely to restrict competition that existed in the absence of the agreement. Article 101(1) is also unlikely to apply in the case of agreements that merely enable the licensee to develop and exploit its own technology within the scope of the licence without fearing infringement claims by the licensor. In such circumstances field of use restrictions do not in themselves restrict competition that existed in the absence of the agreement. In the absence of the agreement the licensee also risked infringement claims outside the scope of the licensed field of use. However, if the licensee terminates or scales back its activities in the area outside the licensed field of use without business justification, this may be an indication of an underlying market sharing arrangement amounting to a hardcore restriction under Article 4(1)(c) of the TTBER.

214. Field of use restrictions on licensee and licensor in agreements between non-competitors are block exempted up to the market share threshold of 30%. Field of use restrictions in agreements between non-competitors whereby the licensor reserves one or more product markets or technical fields of use for itself are generally either non-restrictive of competition or efficiency enhancing. They promote dissemination of new technology by giving the licensor an incentive to license for exploitation in fields in which it does not want to exploit the technology itself. If the licensor could not prevent licensees from operating in fields where the licensor exploits the technology itself, it would be likely to create a disincentive for the licensor to licence.

215. In agreements between non-competitors the licensor is normally also entitled to grant sole or exclusive licences to different licensees limited to one or more fields of use. Such restrictions limit intra-technology competition between licensees in the same way as exclusive licensing and are analysed in the same way (see section 4.2.2.1 above).

4.2.5. Captive use restrictions

216. A captive use restriction can be defined as an obligation on the licensee to limit its production of the licensed product to the quantities required for the production of its own products and for the maintenance and repair of its own products. In other words, this type of use restriction takes the form of an obligation on the licensee to use the products incorporating the licensed technology only as an input for incorporation into its own production; it does not cover the sale of the licensed product for incorporation into the products of other producers. Captive use restrictions are block exempted up to the respective market share thresholds of 20% and 30%. Outside the scope of the block exemption it is necessary to examine the pro-competitive and anti-competitive effects of the restraint. In this respect it is necessary to distinguish agreements between competitors from agreements between non-competitors.

217. In the case of licence agreements between competitors a restriction that imposes on the licensee to produce under the licence only for incorporation into its own products prevents it from supplying components to third party producers. If prior to the conclusion of the agreement, the licensee was not an actual or likely potential supplier of components to other producers, the captive use restriction does not change anything compared to the pre-existing situation. In those circumstances the restriction is assessed in the same way as in the case of agreements between non-competitors. If, on the other hand, the licensee is an actual or likely supplier of components, it is necessary to examine what is the impact of the agreement on that activity. If by tooling up to use the licensor's technology the licensee

ceases to use its own technology on a stand alone basis and thus to be a component supplier, the agreement restricts competition that existed prior to the agreement. It may result in serious negative market effects when the licensor has a significant degree of market power on the component market.

218. In the case of licence agreements between non-competitors there are two main competitive risks stemming from captive use restrictions: a restriction of intra-technology competition on the market for the supply of inputs and an exclusion of arbitrage between licensees enhancing the possibility for the licensor to impose discriminatory royalties on licensees.

219. Captive use restrictions, however, may also promote pro-competitive licensing. If the licensor is a supplier of components, the restraint may be necessary in order for the dissemination of technology between non-competitors to occur. In the absence of the restraint the licensor may not grant the licence or may do so only against higher royalties, because otherwise it would create direct competition with itself on the component market. In such cases a captive use restriction is normally either not restrictive of competition or covered by Article 101(3) of the Treaty. However, the licensee must not be restricted in selling the licensed product as replacement parts for its own products. The licensee must be able to serve the after-market for its own products, including independent service organisations that service and repair the products produced by him.

220. Where the licensor is not a component supplier on the relevant product market, the above reason for imposing captive use restrictions does not apply. In such cases a captive use restriction may in principle promote the dissemination of technology by ensuring that licensees do not sell to producers that compete with the licensor on other product markets. However, a restriction on the licensee not to sell into certain customer groups reserved for the licensor normally constitutes a less restrictive alternative. Consequently, in such cases a captive use restriction is normally not necessary for the dissemination of technology to take place.

4.2.6. Tying and bundling

221. In the context of technology licensing tying occurs when the licensor makes the licensing of one technology (the tying product) conditional upon the licensee taking a licence for another technology or purchasing a product from the licensor or someone designated by it (the tied product). Bundling occurs where two technologies or a technology and a product are only sold together as a bundle. In both cases, however, it is a condition that the products and technologies involved are distinct in the sense that there is distinct demand for each of the products and technologies forming part of the tie or the bundle. This is normally not the case where the technologies or products are by necessity linked in such a way that the licensed technology cannot be exploited without the tied product or both parts of the bundle cannot be exploited without the other. In the following the term 'tying' refers to both tying and bundling.

222. Article 3 of the TTBER, which limits the application of the block exemption by market share thresholds, ensures that tying and bundling are not block exempted above the market share thresholds of 20% in the case of agreements between competitors and 30% in the case of agreements between non-competitors. The market share thresholds apply to any relevant technology or product market affected by the licence agreement, including the market for the tied product. Above the market share thresholds it is necessary to balance the anti-competitive and pro-competitive effects of tying.

223. The main restrictive effect of tying is foreclosure of competing suppliers of the tied product. Tying may also allow the licensor to maintain market power in the market for the tying product by raising barriers to entry since it may force new entrants to enter several markets at the same time. Moreover, tying may allow the licensor to increase royalties, in particular when the tying product and the tied product are partly substitutable and the two products are not used in fixed proportion. Tying prevents the licensee from switching to substitute inputs in the face of increased royalties for the tying product. These competition concerns are independent of whether the parties to the agreement are competitors or not. For tying to produce likely anti-competitive effects the licensor must have a significant degree of market power in the tying product so as to restrict competition in the tied product. In the absence of market power in the tying product the licensor cannot use its technology for the anti-competitive purpose of foreclosing suppliers of the tied product. Furthermore, as in the case of non-compete obligations, the tie must cover a certain proportion of the market for the tied product for appreciable foreclosure effects to occur. In cases where the licensor has market power on the market for the tied product rather than on the market for the tying product, the restraint is analysed as a non-compete clause or quantity forcing, reflecting the fact that any competition problem has its origin on the market for the 'tied' product and not on the market for the 'tying' product.[86]

224. Tying can also give rise to efficiency gains. This is for instance the case where the tied product is necessary for a technically satisfactory exploitation of the licensed technology or for ensuring that production under the licence conforms to quality standards respected by the licensor and other licensees. In such cases tying is normally either not restrictive of competition or covered by Article 101(3) of the Treaty. Where the licensees use the licensor's trademark or brand name or where it is otherwise obvious to consumers that there is a link between the product incorporating the licensed technology and the licensor, the licensor has a legitimate interest in ensuring that the quality of the products is such that it does not undermine the value of its technology or its reputation as an economic operator. Moreover, where it is known to consumers that the licensees (and the licensor) produce on the basis of the same technology it is unlikely that licensees would be willing to take a licence unless the technology is exploited by all in a technically satisfactory way.

225. Tying is also likely to be pro-competitive where the tied product allows the licensee to exploit the licensed technology significantly more efficiently. For instance, where the licensor licenses a particular process technology the parties can also agree that the licensee buys a catalyst from the licensor which is developed for use with the licensed technology and which allows the technology to be exploited more efficiently than in the case of other catalysts. Where in such cases the restriction is caught by Article 101(1), the conditions of Article 101(3) are likely to be fulfilled even above the market share thresholds.

4.2.7. Non-compete obligations

226. Non-compete obligations in the context of technology licensing take the form of an obligation on the licensee not to use third party technologies which compete with the licensed technology. To the extent that a non-compete obligation covers a product or an additional technology supplied by the licensor the obligation is dealt with in section 4.2.6 on tying.

227. The TTBER exempts non-compete obligations both in the case of agreements between competitors and in the case of agreements between non-competitors up to the market share thresholds of 20% and 30% respectively.

228. The main competitive risk presented by non-compete obligations is foreclosure of third party technologies. Non-compete obligations may also facilitate collusion between licensors when several licensors use it in separate agreements (that is in the case of cumulative use). Foreclosure of competing technologies reduces competitive pressure on royalties charged by the licensor and reduces competition between the incumbent technologies by limiting the possibilities for licensees to substitute between competing technologies. As in both cases the main problem is foreclosure, the analysis can in general be the same in the case of agreements between competitors and agreements between non-competitors. However, in the case of cross licensing between competitors where both agree not to use third party technologies the agreement may facilitate collusion between them on the product market, thereby justifying the lower market share threshold of 20%.

229. Foreclosure may arise where a substantial proportion of potential licensees are already tied to one or, in the case of cumulative effects, more sources of technology and are prevented from exploiting competing technologies. Foreclosure effects may result from agreements concluded by a single licensor with a significant degree of market power or from the cumulative effect of agreements concluded by several licensors, even where each individual agreement or network of agreements is covered by the TTBER. In the latter case, however, a serious cumulative effect is unlikely to arise as long as less than 50% of the market is tied. Above that threshold significant foreclosure is likely to occur when there are relatively high barriers to entry for new licensees. If barriers to entry are low, new licensees are able to enter the market and exploit commercially attractive technologies held by third parties and thus represent a real alternative to incumbent licensees. In order to determine the real possibility for entry and expansion by third parties it is also necessary to take account of the extent to which distributors are tied to licensees by non-compete obligations. Third party technologies only have a real possibility of entry if they have access to the necessary production and distribution assets. In other words, the ease of entry depends not only on the availability of licensees but also the extent to which they have access to distribution. In assessing foreclosure effects at the distribution level the Commission will apply the analytical framework set out in section VI.2.1 of the Guidelines on Vertical Restraints.[87]

230. When the licensor has a significant degree of market power, obligations on licensees to obtain the technology only from the licensor can lead to significant foreclosure effects. The stronger the market position of the licensor the higher the risk of foreclosing competing technologies. For appreciable foreclosure effects to occur the non-compete obligations do not necessarily have to cover a substantial part of the market. Even in the absence thereof, appreciable foreclosure effects may occur where non-compete obligations are targeted at undertakings that are the most likely to license competing technologies. The risk of foreclosure is particularly high where there is only a limited number of potential licensees and the licence agreement concerns a technology which is used by the licensees to make an input for their own use. In such cases the entry barriers for a new licensor are likely to be high. Foreclosure may be less likely in cases where the technology is used to make a product that is sold to third parties. Although in this case the restriction also ties production capacity for the input in question, it does not tie demand downstream of the licensees. To enter the market in the latter case licensors only need access to one or more licensee(s) that have suitable production capacity. Unless only few undertakings possess or are able to obtain the assets required to take a licence, it is unlikely that by imposing non-compete obligations on its licensees the licensor is able to deny competitors access to efficient licensees.

231. Non-compete obligations may also produce pro-competitive effects. First, such obligations may promote dissemination of technology by reducing the risk of misappropriation of the licensed technology, in particular know-how. If a licensee is entitled to license competing technologies from third parties, there is a risk that particularly licensed know-how would be used in the exploitation of competing technologies and thus benefit competitors. When a licensee also exploits competing technologies, it normally also makes monitoring of royalty payments more difficult, which may act as a disincentive to licensing.

232. Second, non-compete obligations possibly in combination with an exclusive territory may be necessary to ensure that the licensee has an incentive to invest in and exploit the licensed technology effectively. In cases where the agreement is caught by Article 101(1) of the Treaty because of an appreciable foreclosure effect, it may be necessary in order to benefit from Article 101(3) to choose a less restrictive alternative, for instance to impose minimum output or royalty obligations, which normally have less potential to foreclose competing technologies.

233. Third, in cases where the licensor undertakes to make significant client specific investments for instance in training and tailoring of the licensed technology to the licensee's needs, non-compete obligations or alternatively minimum output or minimum royalty obligations may be necessary to induce the licensor to make the investment and to avoid hold-up problems. However, normally the licensor will be able to charge directly for such investments by way of a lump sum payment, implying that less restrictive alternatives are available.

4.3. SETTLEMENT AGREEMENTS

234. Licensing of technology rights in settlement agreements may serve as a means of settling disputes or avoiding that one party exercises its intellectual property rights to prevent the other party from exploiting its own technology rights.[88]

235. Settlement agreements in the context of technology disputes are, as in many other areas of commercial disputes, in principle a legitimate way to find a mutually acceptable compromise to a bona fide legal disagreement. The parties may prefer to discontinue the dispute or litigation because it proves to be too costly, time-consuming and/or uncertain

as regards its outcome. Settlements can also save courts and/or competent administrative bodies effort in deciding on the matter and can therefore give rise to welfare enhancing benefits. On the other hand, it is in the general public interest to remove invalid intellectual property rights as an unmerited barrier to innovation and economic activity.[89]

236. Licensing, including cross licensing, in the context of settlement agreements is generally not as such restrictive of competition since it allows the parties to exploit their technologies after the agreement is concluded. In cases where, in the absence of the licence, it is possible that the licensee could be excluded from the market, access to the technology at issue for the licensee by means of a settlement agreement is generally not caught by Article 101(1).

237. However, the individual terms and conditions of settlement agreements may be caught by Article 101(1). Licensing in the context of settlement agreements is treated in the same way as other licence agreements.[90] In these cases, it is particularly necessary to assess whether the parties are potential or actual competitors.

PAY-FOR-RESTRICTION IN SETTLEMENT AGREEMENTS

238. 'Pay-for-restriction' or 'pay-for-delay' type settlement agreements often do not involve the transfer of technology rights, but are based on a value transfer from one party in return for a limitation on the entry and/or expansion on the market of the other party and may be caught by Article 101(1).[91]

239. If, however, such a settlement agreement also includes a licensing of the technology rights concerned by the underlying dispute, and that agreement leads to a delayed or otherwise limited ability for the licensee to launch the product on any of the markets concerned, the agreement may be caught by Article 101(1) and would then need to be assessed in particular in the light of Articles 4(1)(c) and 4(1)(d) of the TTBER (see section 3.4.2 above). If the parties to such a settlement agreement are actual or potential competitors and there was a significant value transfer from the licensor to the licensee, the Commission will be particularly attentive to the risk of market allocation/market sharing.

CROSS LICENSING IN SETTLEMENT AGREEMENTS

240. Settlement agreements whereby the parties cross license each other and impose restrictions on the use of their technologies, including restrictions on the licensing to third parties, may be caught by Article 101(1) of the Treaty. Where the parties have a significant degree of market power and the agreement imposes restrictions that clearly go beyond what is required in order to unblock, the agreement is likely to be caught by Article 101(1) even if it is likely that a mutual blocking position exists. Article 101(1) is particularly likely to apply where the parties share markets or fix reciprocal running royalties that have a significant impact on market prices.

241. Where under the settlement agreement the parties are entitled to use each other's technology and the agreement extends to future developments, it is necessary to assess what is the impact of the agreement on the parties' incentive to innovate. In cases where the parties have a significant degree of market power the agreement is likely to be caught by Article 101(1) of the Treaty where the agreement prevents the parties from gaining a competitive lead over each other. Agreements that eliminate or substantially reduce the possibilities of one party to gain a competitive lead over the other reduce the incentive to innovate and thus adversely affect an essential part of the competitive process. Such agreements are also unlikely to satisfy the conditions of Article 101(3). It is particularly unlikely that the restriction can be considered indispensable within the meaning of the third condition of Article 101(3). The achievement of the objective of the agreement, namely to ensure that the parties can continue to exploit their own technology without being blocked by the other party, does not require that the parties agree to share future innovations. However, the parties are unlikely to be prevented from gaining a competitive lead over each other where the purpose of the licence is to allow the parties to develop their respective technologies and where the licence does not lead them to use the same technological solutions. Such agreements merely create design freedom by preventing future infringement claims by the other party.

NON-CHALLENGE CLAUSES IN SETTLEMENT AGREEMENTS

242. In the context of a settlement agreement, non-challenge clauses are generally considered to fall outside Article 101(1) of the Treaty. It is inherent in such agreements that the parties agree not to challenge *ex post* the intellectual property rights which were the centre of the dispute. Indeed, the very purpose of the agreement is to settle existing disputes and/or to avoid future disputes.

243. However, non-challenge clauses in settlement agreements can under specific circumstances be anti-competitive and may be caught by Article 101(1) of the Treaty. The restriction of the freedom to challenge an intellectual property right is not part of the specific subject-matter of an intellectual property right and may restrict competition. For instance, a non-challenge clause may infringe Article 101(1) where an intellectual property right was granted following the provision of incorrect or misleading information.[92] Scrutiny of such clauses may also be necessary if the licensor, besides licensing the technology rights, induces, financially or otherwise, the licensee to agree not to challenge the validity of the technology rights or if the technology rights are a necessary input for the licensee's production (see also point (136)).

4.4. TECHNOLOGY POOLS

244. Technology pools are defined as arrangements whereby two or more parties assemble a package of technology which is licensed not only to contributors to the pool but also to third parties. In terms of their structure technology pools can take the form of simple arrangements between a limited number of parties or of elaborate organisational arrangements whereby the organisation of the licensing of the pooled technologies is entrusted to a separate entity. In both cases the pool may allow licensees to operate on the market on the basis of a single licence.

245. There is no inherent link between technology pools and standards, but the technologies in the pool often support, in whole or in part, a *de facto* or *de jure* industry standard.[93] Different technology pools may support competing standards.[94] Technology pools can produce pro-competitive effects, in particular by reducing transaction costs and by setting a limit on cumulative royalties to avoid double marginalisation. The creation of a pool allows for one-stop licensing of the technologies covered by the pool. This is particularly important in sectors where intellectual

property rights are prevalent and licences need to be obtained from a significant number of licensors in order to operate on the market. In cases where licensees receive on-going services concerning the application of the licensed technology, joint licensing and servicing can lead to further cost reductions. Patent pools can also play a beneficial role in the implementation of pro-competitive standards.

246. Technology pools may also be restrictive of competition. The creation of a technology pool necessarily implies joint selling of the pooled technologies, which in the case of pools composed solely or predominantly of substitute technologies amounts to a price fixing cartel. Moreover, in addition to reducing competition between the parties, technology pools may also, in particular when they support an industry standard or establish a *de facto* industry standard, result in a reduction of innovation by foreclosing alternative technologies. The existence of the standard and a related technology pool may make it more difficult for new and improved technologies to enter the market.

247. Agreements establishing technology pools and setting out the terms and conditions for their operation are not — irrespective of the number of parties — covered by the block exemption, as the agreement to establish the pool does not permit a particular licensee to produce contract products (see section 3.2.4). Such agreements are addressed only by these guidelines. Pooling arrangements give rise to a number of particular issues regarding the selection of the included technologies and the operation of the pool, which do not arise in the context of other types of licensing. Licensing out from the pool is generally a multiparty agreement, taking into account that the contributors commonly determine the conditions for such licensing out, and is therefore also not covered by the block exemption. Licensing out from the pool is dealt with in point (261) and in section 4.4.2.

4.4.1. The Assessment of the Formation and Operation of Technology Pools

248. The way in which a technology pool is formed, organised and operated can reduce the risk of it having the object or effect of restricting competition and provide assurances to the effect that the arrangement is pro-competitive. In assessing the possible competitive risks and efficiencies, the Commission will, inter alia, take account of the transparency of the pool creation process; the selection and nature of the pooled technologies, including the extent to which independent experts are involved in the creation and operation of the pool and whether safeguards against exchange of sensitive information and independent dispute resolution mechanisms have been put in place.

Open participation

249. When participation in a standard and pool creation process is open to all interested parties it is more likely that technologies for inclusion into the pool are selected on the basis of price/quality considerations than when the pool is set up by a limited group of technology owners.

Selection and nature of the pooled technologies

250. The competitive risks and the efficiency enhancing potential of technology pools depend to a large extent on the relationship between the pooled technologies and their relationship with technologies outside the pool. Two basic distinctions must be made, namely (a) between technological complements and technological substitutes and (b) between essential and non-essential technologies.

251. Two technologies are complements as opposed to substitutes when they are both required to produce the product or carry out the process to which the technologies relate. Conversely, two technologies are substitutes when either technology allows the holder to produce the product or carry out the process to which the technologies relate.

252. A technology can be essential either (a) to produce a particular product or carry out a particular process to which the pooled technologies relate or (b) to produce such product or carry out such a process in accordance with a standard which includes the pooled technologies. In the first case, a technology is essential (as opposed to non-essential) if there are no viable substitutes (both from a commercial and technical point of view) for that technology inside or outside the pool and the technology in question constitutes a necessary part of the package of technologies for the purposes of producing the product(s) or carrying out the process(-es) to which the pool relates. In the second case, a technology is essential if it constitutes a necessary part (that is to say, there are no viable substitutes) of the pooled technologies needed to comply with the standard supported by the pool (standard essential technologies). Technologies that are essential are by necessity also complements. The fact that a technology holder merely declares that a technology is essential does not imply that such a technology is essential according to the criteria described in this point.

253. When technologies in a pool are substitutes, royalties are likely to be higher than they would otherwise be, because licensees do not benefit from rivalry between the technologies in question. When the technologies in the pool are complements the technology pool reduces transaction costs and may lead to lower overall royalties because the parties are in a position to fix a common royalty for the package as opposed to each party fixing a royalty for its own technology while not taking into account that a higher royalty for one technology will usually decrease the demand for complementary technologies. If royalties for complementary technologies are set individually, the total of these royalties may often exceed what would be collectively set by a pool for the package of the same complementary technologies. The assessment of the role of substitutes outside the pool is set out in point (262).

254. The distinction between complementary and substitute technologies is not clear-cut in all cases, since technologies may be substitutes in part and complements in part. When due to efficiencies stemming from the integration of two technologies licensees are likely to demand both technologies, the technologies are treated as complements, even if they are partly substitutable. In such cases it is likely that in the absence of the pool licensees would want to licence both technologies due to the additional economic benefit of using both technologies as opposed to using only one of them. Absent such demand based evidence on the complementarity of the pooled technologies, it is an indication that these technologies are complements if (i) the parties contributing technology to a pool remain free to license their technology individually and (ii) the pool is willing, besides licensing the package of technologies

of all parties, to license the technology of each party also separately and (iii) the total royalties charged when taking separate licences to all pooled technologies do not exceed the royalties charged by the pool for the whole package of technologies.

255. The inclusion of substitute technologies in the pool generally restricts inter-technology competition since it can amount to collective bundling and lead to price fixing between competitors. As a general rule the Commission considers that the inclusion of significant substitute technologies in the pool constitutes a violation of Article 101(1) of the Treaty. The Commission also considers that it is unlikely that the conditions of Article 101(3) will be fulfilled in the case of pools comprising to a significant extent substitute technologies. Given that the technologies in question are alternatives, no transaction cost savings accrue from including both technologies in the pool. In the absence of the pool licensees would not have demanded both technologies. To alleviate the competition concerns it is not sufficient that the parties remain free to license independently. This is because the parties are likely to have little incentive to license independently in order not to undermine the pool's licensing activity, which allows them to jointly exercise market power.

Selection and function of independent experts

256. Another relevant factor in assessing the competitive risks and the efficiencies of technology pools is the extent to which independent experts are involved in the creation and operation of the pool. For instance, the assessment of whether or not a technology is essential to a standard supported by a pool is often a complex matter that requires special expertise. The involvement in the selection process of independent experts can go a long way in ensuring that a commitment to include only essential technologies is implemented in practice. Where the selection of technologies to be included in the pool is carried out by an independent expert this may also further competition between available technological solutions.

257. The Commission will take into account how experts are selected and the functions that they are to perform. Experts should be independent from the undertakings that have formed the pool. If experts are connected to the licensors (or the licensing activity of the pool) or otherwise depend on them, the involvement of the expert will be given less weight. Experts must also have the necessary technical expertise to perform the various functions with which they have been entrusted. The functions of independent experts may include, in particular, an assessment of whether or not technologies put forward for inclusion into the pool are valid and whether or not they are essential.

258. Finally, any dispute resolution mechanisms foreseen in the instruments setting up the pool are relevant and should be taken into account. The more dispute resolution is entrusted to bodies or persons that are independent of the pool and its members, the more likely it is that the dispute resolution will operate in a neutral way.

Safeguards against exchange of sensitive information

259. It is also relevant to consider the arrangements for exchanging sensitive information between the parties.[95] In oligopolistic markets exchanges of sensitive information such as pricing and output data may facilitate collusion.[96] In such cases the Commission will take into account to what extent safeguards have been put in place, which ensure that sensitive information is not exchanged. An independent expert or licensing body may play an important role in this respect by ensuring that output and sales data, which may be necessary for the purposes of calculating and verifying royalties is not disclosed to undertakings that compete on affected markets.

260. Special care should be taken to put in place such safeguards when interested parties participate simultaneously in efforts to form pools of competing standards where this may lead to exchange of sensitive information between competing pools.

Safe harbour

261. The creation and operation of the pool, including the licensing out, generally falls outside Article 101(1) of the Treaty, irrespective of the market position of the parties, if all the following conditions are fulfilled:

(a) participation in the pool creation process is open to all interested technology rights owners;
(b) sufficient safeguards are adopted to ensure that only essential technologies (which therefore necessarily are also complements) are pooled;
(c) sufficient safeguards are adopted to ensure that exchange of sensitive information (such as pricing and output data) is restricted to what is necessary for the creation and operation of the pool;
(d) the pooled technologies are licensed into the pool on a non-exclusive basis;
(e) the pooled technologies are licensed out to all potential licensees on FRAND[97] terms;
(f) the parties contributing technology to the pool and the licensees are free to challenge the validity and the essentiality of the pooled technologies, and;
(g) the parties contributing technology to the pool and the licensee remain free to develop competing products and technology.

Outside the safe harbour

262. Where significant complementary but non-essential patents are included in the pool there is a risk of foreclosure of third party technologies. Once a technology is included in the pool and is licensed as part of the package, licensees are likely to have little incentive to license a competing technology when the royalty paid for the package already covers a substitute technology. Moreover, the inclusion of technologies which are not necessary for the purposes of producing the product(s) or carrying out the process(-es) to which the technology pool relates or to comply with the standard which includes the pooled technology also forces licensees to pay for technology that they may not need. The inclusion of such complementary technology thus amounts to collective bundling. Where a pool encompasses non-essential technologies, the agreement is likely to be caught by Article 101(1) where the pool has a significant position on any relevant market.

263. Given that substitute and complementary technologies may be developed after the creation of the pool, the need to assess essentiality does not necessarily end with the creation of the pool. A technology may become non-essential after the creation of the pool due to the emergence of new third party technologies. Where it is brought to the attention of the pool that such a new third party technology is offered to and demanded by licensees, foreclosure concerns may be avoided by offering to new and existing licensees a licence without the no-longer essential technology at a correspondingly reduced royalty rate. However, there may be other ways to ensure that third party technologies are not foreclosed.

264. In the assessment of technology pools comprising non-essential but complementary technologies, the Commission will in its overall assessment, *inter alia*, take account of the following factors:

(a) whether there are any pro-competitive reasons for including the non-essential technologies in the pool, for example due to the costs of assessing whether all the technologies are essential in view of the high number of technologies;

(b) whether the licensors remain free to license their respective technologies independently: where the pool is composed of a limited number of technologies and there are substitute technologies outside the pool, licensees may want to put together their own technological package composed partly of technology forming part of the pool and partly of technology owned by third parties;

(c) whether, in cases where the pooled technologies have different applications some of which do not require use of all of the pooled technologies, the pool offers the technologies only as a single package or whether it offers separate packages for distinct applications, each comprising only those technologies relevant to the application in question: in the latter case technologies which are not essential to a particular product or process are not tied to essential technologies;

(d) whether the pooled technologies are available only as a single package or whether licensees have the possibility of obtaining a licence for only part of the package with a corresponding reduction of royalties. The possibility to obtain a licence for only part of the package may reduce the risk of foreclosure of third party technologies outside the pool, in particular where the licensee obtains a corresponding reduction in royalties. This requires that a share of the overall royalty has been assigned to each technology in the pool. Where the licence agreements concluded between the pool and individual licensees are of relatively long duration and the pooled technology supports a de facto industry standard, the fact that the pool may foreclose access to the market of new substitute technologies must also be taken into account. In assessing the risk of foreclosure in such cases it is relevant to take into account whether or not licensees can terminate at reasonable notice part of the licence and obtain a corresponding reduction of royalties.

265. Even technology pool arrangements that restrict competition may give rise to pro-competitive efficiencies (see point (245)) which must be considered under Article 101(3) and balanced against the negative effects on competition. For example, if the technology pool includes non-essential patents but fulfils all the other criteria of the safe harbour listed in point (261), where there are pro-competitive reasons for including non-essential patents in the pool (see point (264)) and where licensees have the possibility of obtaining a licence for only part of the package with a corresponding reduction of royalties (see point (264)), the conditions of Article 101(3) are likely to be fulfilled.

4.4.2. ASSESSMENT OF INDIVIDUAL RESTRAINTS IN AGREEMENTS BETWEEN THE POOL AND ITS LICENSEES

266. Where the agreement to set up a technology pool does not infringe Article 101 of the Treaty, the next step is to assess the competitive impact of the licences agreed by the pool with its licensees. The conditions under which these licences are granted may be caught by Article 101(1). The purpose of this section is to address a certain number of restraints that in one form or another are commonly found in licensing agreements from technology pools and which need to be assessed in the overall context of the pool. Generally the TTBER does not apply to licence agreements concluded between the pool and third party licensees (see point (247)). This section therefore deals with the individual assessment of licensing issues that are particular to licensing in the context of technology pools.

267. In making its assessment of technology transfer agreements between the pool and its licensees the Commission will be guided by the following main principles:

(a) the stronger the market position of the pool the greater the risk of anti-competitive effects;

(b) the stronger the market position of the pool, the more likely that agreeing not to license to all potential licensees or to license on discriminatory terms will infringe Article 101;

(c) pools should not unduly foreclose third party technologies or limit the creation of alternative pools;

(d) the technology transfer agreements should not contain any of the hardcore restrictions listed in Article 4 of the TTBER (see section 3.4).

268. Undertakings setting up a technology pool that is compatible with Article 101 of the Treaty, are normally free to negotiate and fix royalties for the technology package (subject to any commitment given to license on fair, reasonable and non-discriminatory terms, FRAND) and each technology's share of the royalties either before or after the standard is set. Such agreement is inherent in the establishment of the pool and cannot in itself be considered restrictive of competition. In certain circumstances it may be more efficient if the royalties of the pool are agreed before the standard is chosen, to avoid that the choice of the standard increases the royalty rate by conferring a significant degree of market power on one or more essential technologies. However, licensees must remain free to determine the price of products produced under the licence.

269. Where the pool has a dominant position on the market, royalties and other licensing terms should be non-excessive and non-discriminatory and licences should be non-exclusive.[98] These requirements are necessary to ensure that the pool is open and does not lead to foreclosure and other anti-competitive effects on down-stream markets. These requirements, however, do not preclude different royalty rates for different uses. It is in general not considered restrictive of competition to apply different royalty rates to different product markets, whereas there should be no discrimination within product markets. In particular, the treatment of licensees of the pool should not depend on whether or not they are also licensors. The Commission will therefore take into account whether licensors and licensees are subject to the same royalty obligations.

270. Licensors and licensees should be free to develop competing products and standards. They should also be free to grant and obtain licences outside the pool. These requirements are necessary in order to limit the risk of foreclosure of third party technologies and ensure that the pool does not limit innovation and does not preclude the creation of competing technological solutions. Where pooled technology is included in a *(de facto)* industry standard and where the parties are subject to non-compete obligations, the pool creates a particular risk of preventing the development of new and improved technologies and standards.

271. Grant back obligations should be non-exclusive and limited to developments that are essential or important to the use of the pooled technology. This allows the pool to feed on and benefit from improvements to the pooled technology. It is legitimate for the parties to ensure by grant back obligations that the exploitation of the pooled technology cannot be held up by licensees, including subcontractors working under the licence of the licensee, that hold or obtain essential patents.

272. One of the problems identified with regard to technology pools is the risk that they may shield invalid patents. Pooling may raise the costs/risks for a successful challenge, because the challenge might fail if only one patent in the pool is valid. The shielding of invalid patents in the pool may oblige licensees to pay higher royalties and may also prevent innovation in the field covered by an invalid patent. In this context, non-challenge clauses, including termination clauses,[99] in a technology transfer agreement between the pool and third parties are likely to fall within Article 101(1) of the Treaty.

273. Pools often include both patents and patent applications. If patent applicants who submit their patent applications to pools, where available, use the patent application procedures that allow for a faster granting, this will achieve faster certainty on the validity and scope of these patents.

NOTES

72 See in this respect Case T-228/97, *Irish Sugar*, [1999] ECR II-2969, paragraph 101.

73 See in this respect point 36 of the Guidelines on horizontal cooperation agreements, cited in footnote 27.

74 Joined Cases C-501/06 P, C-513/06 P, C-515/06 P and C-519/06 P *GlaxoSmithKline Services and Others* v *Commission and Others* [2009] ECR I-9291, paragraph 82.

75 See Joined Cases 25/84 and 26/84, *Ford*, [1985] ECR 2725; Joined Cases C-501/06 P, C-513/06 P, C-515/06 P and C-519/06 P *GlaxoSmithKline Services and Others* v *Commission and Others* [2009] ECR I-9291, paragraph 103.

76 See in this respect for example Commission Decision of 3 March 1999, TPS (OJ L90, 2.4.1999, p 6). Similarly, the prohibition of Article 101(1) also only applies as long as the agreement has a restrictive object or restrictive effects.

77 Cited in footnote 52. See in particular paragraphs 106 et seq.

78 As to these concepts see section 4.4.1.

79 See point 85 of the Guidelines on the application of Article 81(3) of the Treaty, cited in footnote 3.

80 Idem, paragraphs 98 and 102.

81 See by analogy paragraph 130 of Joined Cases C-395/96 P and C-396/96 P, *Compagnie Maritime Belge*, cited in footnote 3. Similarly, the application of Article 101(3) does not prevent the application of the Treaty rules on the free movement of goods, services, persons and capital. These provisions are in certain circumstances applicable to agreements, decisions and concerted practices within the meaning of Article 101, see to that effect Case C-309/99, *Wouters*, [2002] ECR I-1577, paragraph 120.

82 See in this respect Case T-51/89, *Tetra Pak (I)*, [1990] ECR II-309. See also point 106 of the Guidelines on the application of Article 81(3) of the Treaty cited in footnote 3 above.

83 This is without prejudice to the possible application of Article 102 TFEU to the setting of royalties (see Case 27/76, United Brands, paragraph 250, see also Case C-385/07 P, Der Grüne Punkt — Duales System Deutschland GmbH [2009] ECR I-6155, paragraph 142).

84 See the judgment in *Nungesser* cited in footnote 13.

85 See in this respect the Commission's Notice in the Canon/Kodak Case (OJ C330, 1.11.1997, p 10) and the IGR Stereo Television Case mentioned in the XI Report on Competition Policy, paragraph 94.

86 For the applicable analytical framework see section 4.2.7 and points 129 *et seq.* of the Guidelines on Vertical Restraints cited in footnote 52.

87 See footnote 52.

88 The TTBER and its Guidelines are without prejudice to the application of Article 101 to settlement agreements which do not contain a licensing agreement.

89 Case 193/83 *Windsurfing v Commission* [1986] ECR 611, paragraph 92.

90 Cf. Case 65/86 *Bayer v. Sulhofer* [1988], ECR 5259, paragraph 15.

91 See, for instance, the Commission Decision in Lundbeck, not yet published.

92 Cf. Case C-457/10 P, *AstraZeneca v. Commission*, [2012] ECR not yet published.

93 See concerning the treatment of standards and the treatment of standardisation agreements the Horizontal Guidelines, point 257 ff., cited in footnote 27.

94 See in this respect the Commission's press release IP/02/1651 concerning the licensing of patents for third generation (3G) mobile services. This case involved five technology pools creating five different technologies, each of which could be used to produce 3G equipment.

95 For details on information sharing, see Horizontal Guidelines, point 55 pp., cited in footnote 27.

96 See in this respect the judgment in *John Deere* cited in footnote 11.

97 For details on FRAND see Horizontal Guidelines, point 287 pp., cited in footnote 27

98 However, if a technology pool has no market power, licensing out from the pool will normally not infringe Article 101(1) even if those conditions are not fulfilled.

99 See section 3.5.

D. TRANSPORT

COUNCIL REGULATION

(169/2009/EC)

of 26 February 2009

applying rules of competition to transport by rail, road and inland waterway

(Codified version)

(Text with EEA relevance)

[4.294]

NOTES

Date of publication in OJ: OJ L61, 5.3.2009, p 1.

Application of this Regulation in relation to the UK: in accordance with the European Union (Withdrawal) Act 2018, s 3 at **[7.5]**, this Regulation became domestic law on IP completion day (as defined in the European Union (Withdrawal Agreement) Act 2020, s 39). In so far as applying to the UK, this Regulation is amended by the Competition (Amendment etc) (EU Exit) Regulations 2019, SI 2019/93, as from IP completion day. The amendments are set out below. With regard to these amendments, note that the amending provision from SI 2019/93 is set out in full in the Notes to the amended Article, and the text of the amended Article has not been altered. For transitional provisions and savings in relation to the operation of the 2019 Regulations, see Sch 4 to those Regulations at **[7.69]** et seq.

Note: with effect from 1 December 2009, the Treaty establishing the European Community (the "EC Treaty") was replaced by the Treaty on the Functioning of the European Union. References in this document to provisions of the EC Treaty should be construed accordingly.

THE COUNCIL OF THE EUROPEAN UNION,

Having regard to the Treaty establishing the European Community, and in particular Article 83 thereof,

Having regard to the proposal from the Commission,

Having regard to the opinion of the European Parliament,[1]

Having regard to the opinion of the European Economic and Social Committee,[2]

Whereas:

(1) Regulation (EEC) No 1017/68 of the Council of 19 July 1968 applying rules of competition to transport by rail, road and inland waterway[3] has been substantially amended several times.[4] In the interests of clarity and rationality the said Regulation should be codified.

(2) Rules of competition for transport by rail, road and inland waterway are part of the common transport policy and of general economic policy.

(3) Rules of competition for those sectors should take account of the distinctive features of transport.

(4) Since the rules of competition for transport derogate from the general rules of competition, it should be made possible for undertakings to ascertain what rules apply in any particular case.

(5) The system of rules on competition for transport should apply equally to the joint financing or acquisition of transport equipment for the joint operation of services by certain groupings of undertakings, and also to certain operations in connection with transport by rail, road or inland waterway of providers of services ancillary to transport.

(6) In order to ensure that trade between Member States is not affected or competition within the internal market distorted, it is necessary to prohibit in principle for the three modes of transport specified above all agreements between undertakings, decisions of associations of undertakings and concerted practices between undertakings and all instances of abuse of a dominant position within the internal market which could have such effects.

(7) Certain types of agreement, decision and concerted practice in the transport sector the object and effect of which is merely to apply technical improvements or to achieve technical cooperation may be exempted from the prohibition on restrictive agreements since they contribute to improving productivity. In the light of experience following application of this Regulation, the Council may, on a proposal from the Commission, amend the list of such types of agreement.

(8) In order that an improvement may be fostered in the sometimes too dispersed structure of the industry in the road and inland waterway sectors, exemption from the prohibition on restrictive agreements should also be granted in the case of those agreements, decisions and concerted practices providing for the creation and operation of groupings of undertakings in these two transport sectors whose object is the carrying on of transport operations, including the joint financing or acquisition of transport equipment for the joint operation of services. Such overall exemption can be granted only on condition that the total carrying capacity of a grouping does not exceed a fixed maximum, and that the individual capacity of undertakings belonging to the grouping does not exceed certain limits so fixed as to ensure that no one undertaking can hold a dominant position within the grouping. The Commission should, however, have power to intervene if, in specific cases, such agreements should have effects incompatible with the conditions under which a restrictive agreement may be recognised as lawful, and should constitute an abuse of the exemption. Nevertheless, the fact that a grouping has a total carrying capacity greater than the fixed maximum, or cannot claim the overall exemption because of the individual capacity of the undertakings belonging to the grouping, does not in itself prevent such a grouping from constituting a lawful agreement, decision or concerted practice if it satisfies the relevant conditions laid down in this Regulation.

(9) It is for the undertakings themselves, in the first instance, to judge whether the predominant effects of their agreements, decisions or concerted practices are the restriction of competition or the economic benefits acceptable as justification for such restriction and to decide accordingly, on their own responsibility, as to the illegality or legality of such agreements, decisions or concerted practices.

(10) Therefore, undertakings should be allowed to conclude or operate agreements without declaring them. This exposes such agreements to the risk of being declared void with retroactive effect should they be examined following a complaint or on the Commission's own initiative, but does not prevent their being retroactively declared lawful in the event of such subsequent examination,

NOTES

1 OJ C219 E, 28.8.2008, p 67.
2 OJ C161, 13.7.2007, p 100.
3 OJ L175, 23.7.1968, p 1.
4 See Annex I.

HAS ADOPTED THIS REGULATION:

[4.295]

Article 1 Scope

The provisions of this Regulation shall, in the field of transport by rail, road and inland waterway, apply both to all agreements, decisions and concerted practices which have as their object or effect the fixing of transport rates and conditions, the limitation or control of the supply of transport, the sharing of transport markets, the application of technical improvements or technical cooperation, or the joint financing or acquisition of transport equipment or supplies where such operations are directly related to the provision of transport services and are necessary for the joint operation of services by a grouping within the meaning of Article 3 of road or inland waterway transport undertakings, and to the abuse of a dominant position on the transport market. These provisions shall apply also to operations of providers of services ancillary to transport which have any of those objects or effects.

[4.296]

Article 2 Exception for technical agreements

1. The prohibition in Article 81(1) of the Treaty shall not apply to agreements, decisions or concerted practices the object and effect of which is to apply technical improvements or to achieve technical cooperation by means of:
 (a) the standardisation of equipment, transport supplies, vehicles or fixed installations;
 (b) the exchange or pooling, for the purpose of operating transport services, of staff, equipment, vehicles or fixed installations;
 (c) the organisation and execution of successive, complementary, substitute or combined transport operations, and the fixing and application of inclusive rates and conditions for such operations, including special competitive rates;
 (d) the use, for journeys by a single mode of transport, of the routes which are most rational from the operational point of view;
 (e) the coordination of transport timetables for connecting routes;
 (f) the grouping of single consignments;
 (g) the establishment of uniform rules as to the structure of tariffs and their conditions of application, provided such rules do not lay down transport rates and conditions.

2. The Commission shall, where appropriate, submit proposals to the Council with a view to extending or reducing the list in paragraph 1.

NOTES

Application of this Article in relation to the UK: this Article is amended, in relation to the UK only, by the Competition (Amendment etc) (EU Exit) Regulations 2019, SI 2019/93, reg 63, Sch 3, Pt 2, para 3(2), as from IP completion day (as defined in the European Union (Withdrawal Agreement) Act 2020, s 39) (for transitional provisions and savings in relation to the operation of the 2019 Regulations, see Sch 4 to those Regulations at **[7.69]** et seq), as follows—

"(2) In Article 2—
 (a) in paragraph 1, for "in Article 81(1) of the Treaty" substitute "imposed by section 2(1) of the Competition Act 1998";
 (b) omit paragraph 2.".

[4.297]

Article 3 Exemption for groups of small and medium-sized undertakings

1. Agreements, decisions and concerted practices as referred to in Article 81(1) of the Treaty shall be exempt from the prohibition in that Article where their purpose is:
 (a) the constitution and operation of groupings of road or inland waterway transport undertakings with a view to carrying on transport activities;
 (b) the joint financing or acquisition of transport equipment or supplies, where these operations are directly related to the provision of transport services and are necessary for the joint operations of the aforesaid groupings;

always provided that the total carrying capacity of any grouping does not exceed:
 (i) 10,000 metric tons in the case of road transport;
 (ii) 500,000 metric tons in the case of transport by inland waterway.

The individual capacity of each undertaking belonging to a grouping shall not exceed 1,000 metric tons in the case of road transport or 50,000 metric tons in the case of transport by inland waterway.

2. If the implementation of any agreement, decision or concerted practice covered by paragraph 1 has, in a given case, effects which are incompatible with the requirements of Article 81(3) of the Treaty, undertakings or associations of undertakings may be required to make such effects cease.

NOTES

Application of this Article in relation to the UK: this Article is amended, in relation to the UK only, by the Competition (Amendment etc) (EU Exit) Regulations 2019, SI 2019/93, reg 63, Sch 3, Pt 2, para 3(3), as from IP completion day (as defined in the European Union (Withdrawal Agreement) Act 2020, s 39) (for transitional provisions and savings in relation to the operation of the 2019 Regulations, see Sch 4 to those Regulations at **[7.69]** et seq), as follows—

"(3) In Article 3—
(a) in paragraph 1, for the words from "Article 81(1)" to "that Article" substitute "section 2(1) of the Competition Act 1998 are exempt from the prohibition imposed by that provision";
(b) omit paragraph 2.".

[4.298]

Article 4 Repeal

Regulation (EEC) No 1017/68, as amended by the Regulation listed in Annex I, Part A, is repealed, with the exception of Article 13(3), which continues to apply to decisions adopted pursuant to Article 5 of Regulation (EEC) No 1017/68 prior to 1 May 2004 until the date of expiration of those decisions.

References to the repealed Regulation shall be construed as references to this Regulation and shall be read in accordance with the correlation table in Annex II.

[4.299]

Article 5 Entry into force, existing agreements

1. This Regulation shall enter into force on the 20th day following its publication in the *Official Journal of the European Union*.
2. The prohibition in Article 81(1) of the Treaty shall not apply to agreements, decisions and concerted practices which were in existence at the date of accession of Austria, Finland and Sweden or at the date of accession of the Czech Republic, Estonia, Cyprus, Latvia, Lithuania, Hungary, Malta, Poland, Slovenia and Slovakia and which, by reason of accession, fall within the scope of Article 81(1) of the Treaty if, within six months from the date of accession, they are so amended that they comply with the conditions laid down in Article 3 of this Regulation. This paragraph does not apply to agreements, decisions and concerted practices which at the date of accession already fall under Article 53(1) of the EEA Agreement.

This Regulation shall be binding in its entirety and directly applicable in all Member States.

NOTES

Application of this Article in relation to the UK: this Article is amended, in relation to the UK only, by the Competition (Amendment etc) (EU Exit) Regulations 2019, SI 2019/93, reg 63, Sch 3, Pt 2, para 3(4), (5), as from IP completion day (as defined in the European Union (Withdrawal Agreement) Act 2020, s 39) (for transitional provisions and savings in relation to the operation of the 2019 Regulations, see Sch 4 to those Regulations at **[7.69]** et seq), as follows—

"(4) Omit Article 5(2).
(5) In the words after Article 5, omit the words from "This Regulation shall be binding" to "Member States.".".

ANNEX I

PART A REPEALED REGULATION WITH ITS SUCCESSIVE AMENDMENT

(referred to in Article 4)

[4.300]

Regulation (EEC) No 1017/68 of the Council (OJ L175, 23.7.1968, p 1)	except Article 13(3)
Council Regulation (EC) No 1/2003 (OJ L1, 4.1.2003, p 1)	Article 36 only

PART B NON-REPEALED SUCCESSIVE AMENDMENTS

1972 Act of Accession
1979 Act of Accession
1994 Act of Accession
2003 Act of Accession

ANNEX II
CORRELATION TABLE

[4.301]

Regulation (EEC) No 1017/68	This Regulation
Article 1	Article 1
Article 3	Article 2
Article 4(1), first subparagraph, first introductory phrase, first indent	Article 3(1), first subparagraph, first introductory phrase, (a)
Article 4(1), first subparagraph, first introductory phrase, second indent	Article 3(1), first subparagraph, first introductory phrase, (b)
Article 4(1), first subparagraph, second introductory phrase, first indent	Article 3(1), first subparagraph, second introductory phrase, (i)

Regulation (EEC) No 1017/68	This Regulation
Article 4(1), first subparagraph, second introductory phrase, second indent	Article 3(1), first subparagraph, second introductory phrase, (ii)
Article 4(1), second subparagraph	Article 3(1), second subparagraph
Article 4(2)	Article 3(2)
—	Article 4
Article 30(1)	Article 5(1)
Article 30(3), second subparagraph	Article 5(2)
Article 31	—
—	Annex I
—	Annex II

COUNCIL REGULATION

(246/2009/EC)

of 26 February 2009

on the application of Article 81(3) of the Treaty to certain categories of agreements, decisions and concerted practices between liner shipping companies (consortia)

(Codified version)

(Text with EEA relevance)

[4.302]

NOTES

Date of publication in OJ: L79, 25.3.2009, p 1.

Repeal of this Regulation in relation to the UK: this Regulation is repealed, in relation to the UK, by the Competition (Amendment etc) (EU Exit) Regulations 2019, SI 2019/93, reg 63, Sch 3, para 1, as from IP completion day (as defined in the European Union (Withdrawal Agreement) Act 2020, s 39) (for transitional provisions and savings in relation to the operation of the 2019 Regulations, see Sch 4 to those Regulations at **[7.69]** et seq). See also Sch 3, para 2 to the 2019 Regulations which provides that, despite the repeal of this Regulation, Level 2 Regulations made under it are not repealed.

Note: with effect from 1 December 2009, the Treaty establishing the European Community (the "EC Treaty") was replaced by the Treaty on the Functioning of the European Union. References in this document to provisions of the EC Treaty should be construed accordingly. As to Article 81 of the EC Treaty, see now Article 101 of the Treaty on the Functioning of the European Union.

THE COUNCIL OF THE EUROPEAN UNION,

Having regard to the Treaty establishing the European Community, and in particular Article 83 thereof,

Having regard to the proposal from the Commission,

Having regard to the opinion of the European Parliament,[1]

Whereas:

(1) Council Regulation (EEC) No 479/92 of 25 February 1992 on the application of Article 85(3) of the Treaty to certain categories of agreements, decisions and concerted practices between liner shipping companies (consortia)[2] *has been substantially amended several times.*[3] *In the interests of clarity and rationality the said Regulation should be codified.*

(2) Article 81(1) of the Treaty may in accordance with Article 81(3) thereof be declared inapplicable to categories of agreements, decisions and concerted practices which fulfil the conditions contained in Article 81(3).

(3) Pursuant to Article 83 of the Treaty, the provisions for the application of Article 81(3) of the Treaty should be adopted by way of Regulation or Directive. According to Article 83(2)(b), these provisions must lay down detailed rules for the application of Article 81(3), taking into account the need to ensure effective supervision, on the one hand, and to simplify administration to the greatest possible extent on the other. According to Article 83(2)(d), these provisions are required to define the respective functions of the Commission and of the Court of Justice.

(4) Liner shipping is a capital intensive industry. Containerisation has increased pressures for cooperation and rationalisation. The Community shipping industry should attain the necessary economies of scale in order to compete successfully on the world liner shipping market.

(5) Joint-service agreements between liner shipping companies with the aim of rationalising their operations by means of technical, operational and/or commercial arrangements (described in shipping circles as consortia) can help to provide the necessary means for improving the productivity of liner shipping services and promoting technical and economic progress.

(6) Maritime transport is important for the development of the Community's trade and the consortia agreements may play a role in this respect, taking account of the special features of international liner shipping. The legalisation of these agreements is a measure which can make a positive contribution to improving the competitiveness of shipping in the Community;

(7) Users of the shipping services offered by consortia can obtain a share of the benefits resulting from the

improvements in productivity and service, by means of, inter alia, regularity, cost reductions derived from higher levels of capacity utilisation, and better service quality stemming from improved vessels and equipment.

(8) The Commission should be enabled to declare by way of Regulation that the provisions of Article 81(1) of the Treaty do not apply to certain categories of consortia agreements, decisions and concerted practices, in order to make it easier for undertakings to cooperate in ways which are economically desirable and without adverse effect from the point of view of competition policy. The Commission, in close and constant liaison with the competent authorities of the Member States, should be able to define precisely the scope of these exemptions and the conditions attached to them.

(9) Consortia in liner shipping are a specialised and complex type of joint venture. There is a great variety of different consortia agreements operating in different circumstances. The scope, parties, activities or terms of consortia are frequently altered. The Commission should therefore be given the responsibility of defining from time to time the consortia to which a group exemption should apply.

(10) In order to ensure that all the conditions of Article 81(3) of the Treaty are met, conditions should be attached to group exemptions to ensure in particular that a fair share of the benefits will be passed on to shippers and that competition is not eliminated,

NOTES

Repeal of this Regulation in relation to the UK: this Regulation is repealed in relation to the UK (as from IP completion day); see the introductory notes to this Regulation *ante*.

[1] Opinion of the European Parliament of 23 April 2008 (not yet published in the Official Journal).

[2] OJ L55, 29.2.1992, p 3.

[3] See Annex I.

HAS ADOPTED THIS REGULATION:

[4.303]

Article 1

1. The Commission may by Regulation and in accordance with Article 81(3) of the Treaty, declare that Article 81(1) of the Treaty shall not apply to certain categories of agreements between undertakings, decisions of associations of undertakings and concerted practices that have as an object to promote or establish cooperation in the joint operation of maritime transport services between liner shipping companies, for the purpose of rationalising their operations by means of technical, operational or commercial arrangements with the exception of price fixing (consortia).

2. Such Regulation adopted pursuant to paragraph 1 of this article shall define the categories of agreements, decisions and concerted practices to which it applies and shall specify the conditions and obligations under which, pursuant to Article 81(3) of the Treaty, they shall be considered exempted from the application of Article 81(1) of the Treaty.

NOTES

Repeal of this Regulation in relation to the UK: this Regulation is repealed in relation to the UK (as from IP completion day); see the introductory notes to this Regulation *ante*.

[4.304]

Article 2

1. The Regulation adopted pursuant to Article 1 shall apply for a period of five years, calculated as from the date of its entry into force.

2. The Regulation adopted pursuant to Article 1 may be repealed or amended where circumstances have changed with respect to any of the facts which were basic to its adoption.

NOTES

Repeal of this Regulation in relation to the UK: this Regulation is repealed in relation to the UK (as from IP completion day); see the introductory notes to this Regulation *ante*.

[4.305]

Article 3

The Regulation adopted pursuant to Article 1 may include a provision stating that it applies with retroactive effect to agreements, decisions and concerted practices which were in existence at the date of entry into force of such Regulation, provided they comply with the conditions established in that Regulation.

NOTES

Repeal of this Regulation in relation to the UK: this Regulation is repealed in relation to the UK (as from IP completion day); see the introductory notes to this Regulation *ante*.

[4.306]

Article 4

The Regulation adopted pursuant to Article 1 may stipulate that the prohibition contained in Article 81(1) of the Treaty shall not apply, for such a period as fixed by that Regulation, to agreements, decisions and concerted practices already in existence at 1 January 1995, to which Article 81(1) applies by virtue of the accession of Austria, Finland and Sweden and which do not satisfy the conditions of Article 81(3). However, this Article shall not apply to agreements, decisions and concerted practices which, as at 1 January 1995, already fell under Article 53(1) of the EEA Agreement.

NOTES

Repeal of this Regulation in relation to the UK: this Regulation is repealed in relation to the UK (as from IP completion day); see the introductory notes to this Regulation *ante*.

[4.307]

Article 5

Before adopting the Regulation referred to in Article 1, the Commission shall publish a draft thereof to enable all the persons and organisations concerned to submit their comments within such reasonable time limit as the Commission shall fix, but in no case less than one month.

NOTES

Repeal of this Regulation in relation to the UK: this Regulation is repealed in relation to the UK (as from IP completion day); see the introductory notes to this Regulation *ante*.

[4.308]

Article 6

Before publishing the draft Regulation and before adopting the Regulation pursuant to Article 1, the Commission shall consult the Advisory Committee on Restrictive Practices and Dominant Positions referred to in Article 14 of Council Regulation (EC) No 1/2003 of 16 December 2002 on the implementation of the rules on competition laid down in Articles 81 and 82 of the Treaty.[1]

NOTES

Repeal of this Regulation in relation to the UK: this Regulation is repealed in relation to the UK (as from IP completion day); see the introductory notes to this Regulation *ante*.

[1] OJ L1, 4.1.2003, p 1.

[4.309]

Article 7

Regulation (EEC) No 479/92, as amended by the acts listed in Annex I, is repealed.

References to the repealed Regulation shall be construed as references to this Regulation and shall be read in accordance with the correlation table in Annex II.

NOTES

Repeal of this Regulation in relation to the UK: this Regulation is repealed in relation to the UK (as from IP completion day); see the introductory notes to this Regulation *ante*.

[4.310]

Article 8

This Regulation shall enter into force on the 20th day following that of its publication in the Official Journal of the European Union.

NOTES

Repeal of this Regulation in relation to the UK: this Regulation is repealed in relation to the UK (as from IP completion day); see the introductory notes to this Regulation *ante*.

ANNEXES

ANNEX I
REPEALED REGULATION WITH LIST OF ITS SUCCESSIVE AMENDMENTS

(referred to in Article 7)

[4.311]

Council Regulation (EEC) No 479/92 (OJ L55, 29.2.1992, p 3)	
Council Regulation (EC) No 1/2003 (OJ L1, 4.1.2003, p 1)	*Article 42 only*
1994 Act of Accession, Article 29 and Annex I, point IIIA.4 (OJ C241, 29.8.1994, p 56)	

NOTES

Repeal of this Regulation in relation to the UK: this Regulation is repealed in relation to the UK (as from IP completion day); see the introductory notes to this Regulation *ante*.

ANNEX II
CORRELATION TABLE

[4.312]

Regulation (EEC) No 479/92	***This Regulation***
Articles 1, 2 and 3	*Articles 1, 2 and 3*
Article 3a	*Article 4*
Article 4	*Article 5*
Article 5	*Article 6*
—	*Article 7*
Article 7	*Article 8*
—	*Annex I*

Regulation (EEC) No 479/92	*This Regulation*
—	*Annex II*

NOTES

Repeal of this Regulation in relation to the UK: this Regulation is repealed in relation to the UK (as from IP completion day); see the introductory notes to this Regulation *ante*.

COUNCIL REGULATION

(487/2009/EC)

of 25 May 2009

on the application of Article 81(3) of the Treaty to certain categories of agreements and concerted practices in the air transport sector

(Codified version)

(Text with EEA relevance)

[4.313]

NOTES

Date of publication in OJ: OJ L148, 11.06.2009, p 1.

Repeal of this Regulation in relation to the UK: this Regulation is repealed, in relation to the UK, by the Competition (Amendment etc) (EU Exit) Regulations 2019, SI 2019/93, reg 63, Sch 3, para 1, as from IP completion day (as defined in the European Union (Withdrawal Agreement) Act 2020, s 39) (for transitional provisions and savings in relation to the operation of the 2019 Regulations, see Sch 4 to those Regulations at **[7.69]** et seq).

Note: with effect from 1 December 2009, the Treaty establishing the European Community (the "EC Treaty") was replaced by the Treaty on the Functioning of the European Union. References in this document to provisions of the EC Treaty should be construed accordingly. As to Article 81 of the EC Treaty, see now Article 101 of the Treaty on the Functioning of the European Union.

See also:

– Council Regulation 95/93/EEC on common rules for the allocation of slots at Community airports (OJ L14, 22.1.1993, p 1). Note that there is a consolidated version including all amendments on the EUR-Lex website at eur-lex.europa.eu/legal-content/EN/TXT/?uri=CELEX%3A01993R0095-20210220&qid=1635855082479.
– Commission Communication on the application of Regulation (EEC) No 95/93 on common rules for the allocation of slots at Community airports, as amended (30.4.2008, COM(2008) 227 final). See the EUR-Lex website at eur-lex.europa.eu/legal-content/EN/ALL/?uri=CELEX:52008DC0227.
– European Parliament and Council Regulation 1008/2008/EC on common rules for the operation of air services in the Community (Recast) (OJ L293, 31.10.2008, p 3). Note that there is a consolidated version including all amendments on the EUR-Lex website at eur-lex.europa.eu/legal-content/EN/TXT/?uri=CELEX%3A02008R1008-20201218&qid=1635855234612.
– European Parliament and Council Regulation 80/2009/EC on a code of conduct for computerised reservation systems and repealing Council Regulation (EEC) No 2299/89 (OJ L35, 4.2.2009, p 47). See the EUR-Lex website at eur-lex.europa.eu/legal-content/EN/TXT/?uri=CELEX:32009R0080.
– European Parliament and Council Regulation 2019/712/EU of the on safeguarding competition in air transport, and repealing Regulation (EC) No 868/2004. See the EUR-Lex website at eur-lex.europa.eu/legal-content/EN/TXT/?uri=CELEX:32019R0712.

THE COUNCIL OF THE EUROPEAN UNION,

Having regard to the Treaty establishing the European Community and in particular Article 83 thereof,

Having regard to the proposal from the Commission,

Having regard to the Opinion of the European Parliament,[1]

Whereas:

(1) Council Regulation (EEC) No 3976/87 of 14 December 1987 on the application of Article 85(3) of the Treaty to certain categories of agreements and concerted practices in the air transport sector[2] has been substantially amended several times.[3] In the interests of clarity and rationality the said Regulation should be codified.

(2) Common provisions for the application of Article 81(3) of the Treaty should be adopted by way of Regulation or Directive pursuant to Article 83 of the Treaty. The Commission should be enabled to declare by way of regulation that the provisions of Article 81(1) of the Treaty do not apply to certain categories of agreements between undertakings, decisions by associations of undertakings and concerted practices.

(3) The Commission should be empowered to grant block exemptions in the air transport sector in respect of traffic within the Community, as well as in respect of traffic between the Community and third countries.

(4) It should be laid down under what specific conditions and in what circumstances the Commission may exercise such powers in close and constant liaison with the competent authorities of the Member States.

(5) It is desirable, in particular, that block exemptions be granted for certain categories of agreements, decisions and concerted practices. Those exemptions should be granted for a limited period during which air carriers can adapt to a more competitive environment. The Commission, in close liaison with the Member States, should be able to define precisely the scope of those exemptions and the conditions attached to them.

(6) This Regulation is without prejudice to the application of Article 86 of the Treaty,

NOTES

Repeal of this Regulation in relation to the UK: this Regulation is repealed in relation to the UK (as from IP completion day); see the introductory notes to this Regulation *ante*.

[1] Opinion of 21 October 2008 (not yet published in the Official Journal).

[2] OJ L374, 31.12.1987, p 9.

[3] See Annex I.

HAS ADOPTED THIS REGULATION:

[4.314]

Article 1

This Regulation shall apply to air transport.

NOTES

Repeal of this Regulation in relation to the UK: this Regulation is repealed in relation to the UK (as from IP completion day); see the introductory notes to this Regulation *ante*.

[4.315]

Article 2

1. In accordance with Article 81(3) of the Treaty, the Commission may by Regulation declare that Article 81(1) of the Treaty shall not apply to certain categories of agreements between undertakings, decisions of associations of undertakings and concerted practices.

The Commission may, in particular, adopt such Regulations in respect of agreements, decisions or concerted practices which have as their object any of the following:

(a) joint planning and coordination of airline schedules;

(b) consultations on tariffs for the carriage of passengers and baggage and of freight on scheduled air services;

(c) joint operations on new less busy scheduled air services;

(d) slot allocation at airports and airport scheduling; the Commission shall take care to ensure consistency with Council Regulation (EEC) No 95/93 of 18 January 1993 on common rules for the allocation of slots at Community airports;[1]

(e) common purchase, development and operation of computer reservation systems relating to timetabling, reservations and ticketing by air transport undertakings; the Commission shall take care to ensure consistency with Council Regulation (EEC) No 2299/89 of 24 July 1989 on a code of conduct for computerised reservation systems.[2]

2. Without prejudice to the second subparagraph of paragraph 1, the Commission Regulations referred to therein shall define the categories of agreements, decisions or concerted practices to which they apply and shall specify in particular:

(a) the restrictions or clauses which may, or may not, appear in the agreements, decisions and concerted practices;

(b) the clauses which must be contained in the agreements, decisions and concerted practices, or any other conditions which must be satisfied.

NOTES

Repeal of this Regulation in relation to the UK: this Regulation is repealed in relation to the UK (as from IP completion day); see the introductory notes to this Regulation *ante*.

[1] OJ L14, 22.1.1993, p 1.

[2] OJ L220, 29.7.1989, p 1.

[4.316]

Article 3

Any Regulation adopted pursuant to Article 2 shall apply for a specified period.

It may be repealed or amended where circumstances have changed with respect to any of the factors which prompted its adoption; in such a case, a period shall be fixed for amendment of the agreements and concerted practices to which the earlier Regulation applied before repeal or amendment.

NOTES

Repeal of this Regulation in relation to the UK: this Regulation is repealed in relation to the UK (as from IP completion day); see the introductory notes to this Regulation *ante*.

[4.317]

Article 4

Regulations adopted pursuant to Article 2 shall include a provision stating that they apply with retroactive effect to agreements, decisions and concerted practices which were in existence at the date of the entry into force of such Regulations.

NOTES

Repeal of this Regulation in relation to the UK: this Regulation is repealed in relation to the UK (as from IP completion day); see the introductory notes to this Regulation *ante*.

[4.318]

Article 5

A Regulation adopted pursuant to Article 2 may stipulate that the prohibition contained in Article 81(1) of the Treaty shall not apply, for such a period as fixed by that Regulation, to agreements, decisions and concerted practices already in existence at the date of accession to which Article 81(1) applies by virtue of the accession of Austria, Finland and Sweden and which do not satisfy the conditions of Article 81(3) of the Treaty.

However, this Article shall not apply to agreements, decisions and concerted practices which at the date of accession already fall under Article 53(1) of the EEA Agreement.

NOTES

Repeal of this Regulation in relation to the UK: this Regulation is repealed in relation to the UK (as from IP completion day); see the introductory notes to this Regulation *ante*.

[4.319]

Article 6

Before adopting a Regulation pursuant to Article 2, the Commission shall publish a draft thereof and invite all persons and organisations concerned to submit their comments within a reasonable time-limit, being not less than one month, as the Commission shall fix.

NOTES

Repeal of this Regulation in relation to the UK: this Regulation is repealed in relation to the UK (as from IP completion day); see the introductory notes to this Regulation *ante*.

[4.320]

Article 7

The Commission shall consult the Advisory Committee on Restrictive Practices and Dominant Positions referred to in Article 14 of Council Regulation (EC) No 1/2003 of 16 December 2002 on the implementation of the rules on competition laid down in Articles 81 and 82 of the Treaty[1] *before publishing a draft Regulation and before adopting a Regulation pursuant to Article 2.*

NOTES

Repeal of this Regulation in relation to the UK: this Regulation is repealed in relation to the UK (as from IP completion day); see the introductory notes to this Regulation *ante*.

[1] OJ L1, 4.1.2003, p 1.

[4.321]

Article 8

Regulation (EEC) No 3976/87 is repealed.

References to the repealed Regulation shall be construed as references to this Regulation and be read in accordance with the correlation table set out in Annex II.

NOTES

Repeal of this Regulation in relation to the UK: this Regulation is repealed in relation to the UK (as from IP completion day); see the introductory notes to this Regulation *ante*.

[4.322]

Article 9

This Regulation shall enter into force on the 20th day following its publication in the Official Journal of the European Union.

NOTES

Repeal of this Regulation in relation to the UK: this Regulation is repealed in relation to the UK (as from IP completion day); see the introductory notes to this Regulation *ante*.

ANNEXES

ANNEX I
REPEALED REGULATION WITH LIST OF ITS SUCCESSIVE AMENDMENTS

[4.323]

Council Regulation (EEC) No 3976/87 (OJ L374, 31.12.1987, p 9).	
Council Regulation (EEC) No 2344/90 (OJ L217, 11.8.1990, p 15).	
Council Regulation (EEC) No 2411/92 (OJ L240, 24.8.1992, p 19).	
1994 Act of Accession, Annex I, Point III.A.3 (OJ C241, 29.8.1994, p 56).	
Council Regulation (EC) No 1/2003 (OJ L1, 4.1.2003, p 1).	*Only Article 41*
Council Regulation (EC) No 411/2004 (OJ L68, 6.3.2004, p 1).	*Only Article 2*

NOTES

Repeal of this Regulation in relation to the UK: this Regulation is repealed in relation to the UK (as from IP completion day); see the introductory notes to this Regulation *ante*.

ANNEX II
CORRELATION TABLE

[4.324]

Regulation (EEC) No 3976/87	***This Regulation***
Article 1	*Article 1*
Article 2(1)	*Article 2(1), first subparagraph*
Article 2(2), introductory wording	*Article 2(1), second subparagraph, introductory wording*
Article 2(2), first indent	*Article 2(1), second subparagraph, point (a)*
Article 2(2), second indent	*Article 2(1), second subparagraph, point (b)*
Article 2(2), third indent	*Article 2(1), second subparagraph, point (c)*
Article 2(2), fourth indent	*Article 2(1), second subparagraph, point (d)*
Article 2(2), fifth indent	*Article 2(1), second subparagraph, point (e)*
Article 2(3)	*Article 2(2)*
Articles 3 and 4	*Articles 3 and 4*
Article 4a, first sentence	*Article 5, first paragraph*
Article 4a, second sentence	*Article 5, second paragraph*
Article 5	*Article 6*
Article 6	*Article 7*
—	*Article 8*
Article 9	*Article 9*
—	*Annex I*
—	*Annex II*

NOTES

Repeal of this Regulation in relation to the UK: this Regulation is repealed in relation to the UK (as from IP completion day); see the introductory notes to this Regulation *ante*.

COMMISSION REGULATION

(906/2009/EC)

of 28 September 2009

on the application of Article 81(3) of the Treaty to certain categories of agreements, decisions and concerted practices between liner shipping companies (consortia)

(Text with EEA relevance)

[4.325]

NOTES

Date of publication in OJ: OJ L256, 29.9.2009, p 31.

Application of this Regulation in relation to the UK: in accordance with the European Union (Withdrawal) Act 2018, s 3 at **[7.5]**, this Regulation became domestic law on IP completion day (as defined in the European Union (Withdrawal Agreement) Act 2020, s 39). In so far as applying to the UK, this Regulation is amended by the Competition (Amendment etc) (EU Exit) Regulations 2019, SI 2019/93, as from IP completion day. The amendments are set out below. With regard to these amendments, note that the amending provision from SI 2019/93 is set out in full in the Notes to the amended Article, and the text of the amended Article has not been altered. For transitional provisions and savings in relation to the operation of the 2019 Regulations, see Sch 4 to those Regulations at **[7.69]** et seq.

Note also that Council Regulation (EC) No 246/2009 (under which this Regulation was made) is repealed, in relation to the UK, by the Competition (Amendment etc) (EU Exit) Regulations 2019, SI 2019/93, reg 63, Sch 3, para 1, as from IP completion day (as defined in the European Union (Withdrawal Agreement) Act 2020, s 39) (for transitional provisions and savings in relation to the operation of the 2019 Regulations, see Sch 4 to those Regulations at **[7.69]** et seq). However, see Sch 3, para 2 to those Regulations (at **[7.67]**) which provides for the continued application of this Regulation despite the repeal of Council Regulation (EC) No 246/2009.

Note: with effect from 1 December 2009, the Treaty establishing the European Community (the "EC Treaty") was replaced by the Treaty on the Functioning of the European Union. References in this document to provisions of the EC Treaty should be construed accordingly. As to Article 81 of the EC Treaty, see now Article 101 of the Treaty on the Functioning of the European Union.

THE COMMISSION OF THE EUROPEAN COMMUNITIES,

Having regard to the Treaty establishing the European Community,

Having regard to Council Regulation (EC) No 246/2009 of 26 February 2009 on the application of Article 81(3) of the Treaty to certain categories of agreements, decisions and concerted practices between liner shipping companies (consortia),[1] and in particular Article 1 thereof,

Having published a draft of this Regulation,[2]

After consulting the Advisory Committee on Restrictive Practices and Dominant Positions,

Whereas:

(1) Regulation (EC) No 246/2009 empowers the Commission to apply Article 81(3) of the Treaty by regulation to certain categories of agreements, decisions and concerted practices between shipping companies relating to the joint operation of liner shipping services (consortia), which, through the cooperation they bring about between the shipping companies that are parties thereto, are liable to restrict competition within the common market and to affect trade between Member States and may therefore be caught by the prohibition contained in Article 81(1) of the Treaty.

(2) The Commission has made use of its power by adopting Commission Regulation (EC) No 823/2000 of 19 April 2000 on the application of Article 81(3) of the Treaty to certain categories of agreements, decisions and concerted practices between liner shipping companies (consortia),[3] which will expire on 25 April 2010. On the basis of the Commission's experience to date it can be concluded that the justifications for a block exemption for liner consortia are still valid. However, certain changes are necessary in order to remove references to Council Regulation (EEC) No 4056/86 of 22 December 1986 laying down detailed rules for the application of Articles 85 and 86 of the Treaty to maritime transport[4] which allowed liner shipping lines to fix prices and capacity, but has now been repealed. Modifications are also necessary to ensure a greater convergence with other block exemption regulations for horizontal cooperation in force whilst taking into account current market practices in the liner industry.

(3) Consortium agreements vary significantly ranging from those that are highly integrated, requiring a high level of investment for example due to the purchase or charter by their members of vessels specifically for the purpose of setting up the consortium and the setting up of joint operations centres, to flexible slot exchange agreements. For the purposes of this Regulation a consortium agreement consists of one or a set of separate but interrelated agreements between liner shipping companies under which the parties operate the joint service. The legal form of the arrangements is less important than the underlying economic reality that the parties provide a joint service.

(4) The benefit of the block exemption should be limited to those agreements for which it can be assumed with a sufficient degree of certainty that they satisfy the conditions of Article 81(3) of the Treaty. However, there is no presumption that consortia which do not benefit from this Regulation fall within the scope of Article 81(1) of the Treaty or, if they do, that they do not satisfy the conditions of Article 81(3) of the Treaty. When conducting a self-assessment of the compatibility of their agreement with Article 81 of the Treaty, parties to such consortia may consider the specific features of markets with small volumes carried or situations where the market share threshold is exceeded as a result of the presence in the consortium of a small carrier without important resources and whose increment to the overall market share of the consortium is only insignificant.

(5) Consortia, as defined in this Regulation, generally help to improve the productivity and quality of available liner shipping services by reason of the rationalisation they bring to the activities of member companies and through the economies of scale they allow in the operation of vessels and utilisation of port facilities. They also help to promote technical and economic progress by facilitating and encouraging greater utilisation of containers and more efficient use of vessel capacity. For the purpose of establishing and running a joint service, an essential feature inherent in consortia is the ability to make capacity adjustments in response to fluctuations in supply and demand. By contrast, unjustified limitation of capacity and sales as well as the joint fixing of freight rates or market and customer allocation are unlikely to bring any efficiency. Therefore, the exemption provided for in this Regulation should not apply to consortium agreements that involve such activities, irrespective of the market power of the parties.

(6) A fair share of the benefits resulting from the efficiencies should be passed on to transport users. Users of the shipping services provided by consortia may benefit from the improvements in productivity which consortia can bring about. Those benefits may also take the form of an improvement in the frequency of sailings and port calls, or an improvement in scheduling as well as better quality and personalised services through the use of more modern vessels and other equipment, including port facilities.

(7) Users can benefit effectively from consortia only if there is sufficient competition in the relevant markets in which the consortia operate. This condition should be regarded as being met when a consortium remains below a given market share threshold and can therefore be presumed to be subject to effective actual or potential competition from carriers that are not members of that consortium. In order to assess the relevant market, account should be taken not only of direct trade between the ports served by a consortium but also of any competition from other liner services sailing from ports which may be substituted for those served by the consortium and, where appropriate, of other modes of transport.

(8) This Regulation should not exempt agreements containing restrictions of competition which are not indispensable to the attainment of the objectives justifying the grant of the exemption. To that end, severely anti-competitive restraints (hardcore restrictions) relating to the fixing of prices charged to third parties, the limitation of capacity or sales and the allocation of markets or customers should be excluded from the benefit of this Regulation. Other than the activities which are expressly exempted by this Regulation, only ancillary activities which are directly related to the operation of the consortium, necessary for its implementation and proportionate to it should be covered by this Regulation.

(9) The market share threshold and the other conditions set out in this Regulation, as well as the exclusion of certain conduct from its benefit, should normally ensure that the agreements to which the block exemption applies do not give the companies concerned the possibility of eliminating competition in a substantial part of the relevant market in question.

(10) For the assessment of whether a consortium fulfils the market share condition, the overall market shares of the consortium members should be added up. The market share of each member should take into account the overall volumes it carries within and outside the consortium. In the latter case account should be taken of all volumes carried

Part 4 EU & Retained EU Materials

by a member within another consortium or in relation to any service provided individually by the member, be it on its own vessels or on third party vessels pursuant to contractual arrangements such as slot charters.

(11) In addition, the benefit of the block exemption should be subject to the right of each consortium member to withdraw from the consortium provided that it gives reasonable notice. However, provision should be made for a longer notice period and a longer initial lock-in period in the case of highly integrated consortia in order to take account of the higher investments undertaken to set them up and the more extensive reorganisation entailed in the event of a member leaving.

(12) In particular cases in which the agreements falling under this Regulation nevertheless have effects incompatible with Article 81(3) of the Treaty, the Commission may withdraw the benefit of the block exemption, on the basis of Council Regulation (EC) No 1/2003 of 16 December 2002 on the implementation of the rules on competition laid down in Articles 81 and 82 of the Treaty.[5] In that respect, the negative effects that may derive from the existence of links between the consortium and/or its members and other consortia and/or liner carriers on the same relevant market are of particular importance.

(13) Furthermore, where agreements have effects which are incompatible with Article 81(3) of the Treaty in the territory of a Member State, or in a part thereof, which has all the characteristics of a distinct geographic market, the competition authority of that Member State may withdraw the benefit of the block exemption in respect of that territory pursuant to Regulation (EC) No 1/2003.

(14) This Regulation is without prejudice to the application of Article 82 of the Treaty.

(15) In view of the expiry of Regulation (EC) No 823/2000, it is appropriate to adopt a new Regulation renewing the block exemption,

NOTES

1 OJ L79, 25.3.2009, p 1.
2 OJ C266, 21.10.2008, p 1.
3 OJ L100, 20.4.2000, p 24.
4 OJ L378, 31.12.1986, p 4.
5 OJ L1, 4.1.2003, p 1.

HAS ADOPTED THIS REGULATION—

CHAPTER I SCOPE AND DEFINITIONS

[4.326]

Article 1 Scope

This Regulation shall apply to consortia only in so far as they provide international liner shipping services from or to one or more Community ports.

NOTES

Application of this Article in relation to the UK: this Article is amended, in relation to the UK only, by the Competition (Amendment etc) (EU Exit) Regulations 2019, SI 2019/93, reg 63, Sch 3, Pt 2, para 4(2), as from IP completion day (as defined in the European Union (Withdrawal Agreement) Act 2020, s 39) (for transitional provisions and savings in relation to the operation of the 2019 Regulations, see Sch 4 to those Regulations at **[7.69]** et seq), as follows—

"(2) In Article 1, for "Community ports" substitute "ports in the United Kingdom".".

[4.327]

Article 2 Definitions

For the purposes of this Regulation the following definitions shall apply:

1. "consortium" means an agreement or a set of interrelated agreements between two or more vessel-operating carriers which provide international liner shipping services exclusively for the carriage of cargo relating to one or more trades, the object of which is to bring about cooperation in the joint operation of a maritime transport service, and which improves the service that would be offered individually by each of its members in the absence of the consortium, in order to rationalise their operations by means of technical, operational and/or commercial arrangements;
2. "liner shipping" means the transport of goods on a regular basis on a particular route or routes between ports and in accordance with timetables and sailing dates advertised in advance and available, even on an occasional basis, to any transport user against payment;
3. "transport user" means any undertaking (such as shipper, consignee or forwarder) which has entered into, or intends to enter into, a contractual agreement with a consortium member for the shipment of goods;
4. "commencement of the service" means the date on which the first vessel sails on the service.

NOTES

Application of this Article in relation to the UK: this Article is amended, in relation to the UK only, by the Competition (Amendment etc) (EU Exit) Regulations 2019, SI 2019/93, reg 63, Sch 3, Pt 2, para 4(3), as from IP completion day (as defined in the European Union (Withdrawal Agreement) Act 2020, s 39) (for transitional provisions and savings in relation to the operation of the 2019 Regulations, see Sch 4 to those Regulations at **[7.69]** et seq), as follows—

(3) In Article 2, after paragraph 3 insert—

"3A. "the Chapter 1 prohibition" means the prohibition imposed by section 2(1) of the Competition Act 1998;".".

CHAPTER II EXEMPTIONS

[4.328]

Article 3 Exempted agreements

Pursuant to Article 81(3) of the Treaty and subject to the conditions laid down in this Regulation, it is hereby declared that Article 81(1) of the Treaty shall not apply to the following activities of a consortium:

1. the joint operation of liner shipping services including any of the following activities:
   (a) the coordination and/or joint fixing of sailing timetables and the determination of ports of call;
   (b) the exchange, sale or cross-chartering of space or slots on vessels;
   (c) the pooling of vessels and/or port installations;
   (d) the use of one or more joint operations offices;
   (e) the provision of containers, chassis and other equipment and/or the rental, leasing or purchase contracts for such equipment;
2. capacity adjustments in response to fluctuations in supply and demand;
3. the joint operation or use of port terminals and related services (such as lighterage or stevedoring services);
4. any other activity ancillary to those referred to in points 1, 2 and 3 which is necessary for their implementation, such as:
   (a) the use of a computerised data exchange system;
   (b) an obligation on members of a consortium to use in the relevant market or markets vessels allocated to the consortium and to refrain from chartering space on vessels belonging to third parties;
   (c) an obligation on members of a consortium not to assign or charter space to other vessel-operating carriers in the relevant market or markets except with the prior consent of the other members of the consortium.

NOTES

Application of this Article in relation to the UK: this Article is amended, in relation to the UK only, by the Competition (Amendment etc) (EU Exit) Regulations 2019, SI 2019/93, reg 63, Sch 3, Pt 2, para 4(4), as from IP completion day (as defined in the European Union (Withdrawal Agreement) Act 2020, s 39) (for transitional provisions and savings in relation to the operation of the 2019 Regulations, see Sch 4 to those Regulations at **[7.69]** et seq), as follows—

"(4) In Article 3, for the words before paragraph 1 substitute—

"Subject to the provisions of this Regulation, the following activities of a consortium are exempt from the Chapter 1 prohibition:".".

[4.329]

Article 4 Hardcore restrictions

The exemption provided for in Article 3 shall not apply to a consortium which, directly or indirectly, in isolation or in combination with other factors under the control of the parties, has as its object:

1. the fixing of prices when selling liner shipping services to third parties;
2. the limitation of capacity or sales except for the capacity adjustments referred to in Article 3(2);
3. the allocation of markets or customers.

CHAPTER III CONDITIONS FOR EXEMPTION

[4.330]

Article 5 Conditions relating to market share

1. In order for a consortium to qualify for the exemption provided for in Article 3, the combined market share of the consortium members in the relevant market upon which the consortium operates shall not exceed 30% calculated by reference to the total volume of goods carried in freight tonnes or 20-foot equivalent units.

2. For the purpose of establishing the market share of a consortium member the total volumes of goods carried by it in the relevant market shall be taken into account irrespective of whether those volumes are carried:
   (a) within the consortium in question;
   (b) within another consortium to which the member is a party; or
   (c) outside a consortium on the member's own or on third party vessels.

3. The exemption provided for in Article 3 shall continue to apply if the market share referred to in paragraph 1 of this Article is exceeded during any period of two consecutive calendar years by not more than one tenth.

4. Where one of the limits specified in paragraphs 1 and 3 of this Article is exceeded, the exemption provided for in Article 3 shall continue to apply for a period of six months following the end of the calendar year during which it was exceeded. That period shall be extended to 12 months if the excess is due to the withdrawal from the market of a carrier which is not a member of the consortium.

[4.331]

Article 6 Other conditions

In order to qualify for the exemption provided for in Article 3, the consortium must give members the right to withdraw without financial or other penalty such as, in particular, an obligation to cease all transport activity in the relevant market or markets in question, whether or not coupled with the condition that such activity may be resumed after a certain period has elapsed. That right shall be subject to a maximum period of notice of six months. The consortium may, however, stipulate that such notice can only be given after an initial period of a maximum of 24 months starting from the date of entry into force of the agreement or, if later, from the commencement of the service.

In the case of a highly integrated consortium the maximum period of notice may be extended to 12 months and the consortium may stipulate that such notice can only be given after an initial period of a maximum of 36 months starting from the date of entry into force of the agreement or, if later, from the commencement of the service.

CHAPTER IV FINAL PROVISIONS

[4.332]

Article 7 Entry into force

This Regulation shall enter into force on 26 April 2010.

It shall apply until [25 April 2024].

This Regulation shall be binding in its entirety and directly applicable in all Member States.

NOTES

Date in square brackets substituted by Commission Regulation 2020/436/EU, Art 1.

Application of this Article in relation to the UK: this Article is amended, in relation to the UK only, by the Competition (Amendment etc) (EU Exit) Regulations 2019, SI 2019/93, reg 63, Sch 3, Pt 2, para 4(5), as from IP completion day (as defined in the European Union (Withdrawal Agreement) Act 2020, s 39) (for transitional provisions and savings in relation to the operation of the 2019 Regulations, see Sch 4 to those Regulations at **[7.69]** et seq), as follows—

"(5) In the words after Article 7, omit the words from "This Regulation shall be binding" to "Member States."."

E. ENFORCEMENT

1. PROCEDURE

COMMISSION NOTICE

(2004/C101/05)

on the handling of complaints by the Commission under Articles 81 and 82 of the EC Treaty

(Text with EEA relevance)

[4.333]

NOTES

Date of publication in OJ: OJ C101, 27.4.2004, p 65.

Note: with effect from 1 December 2009, the EC Treaty was replaced by the Treaty on the Functioning of the European Union. References in this document to provisions of the EC Treaty should be construed accordingly. As to Articles 81 and 82 of the EC Treaty, see now Articles 101 and 102 of the Treaty on the Functioning of the European Union.

I. INTRODUCTION AND SUBJECT-MATTER OF THE NOTICE

[4.334]

1. Regulation 1/2003[1] establishes a system of parallel competence for the application of Articles 81 and 82 of the EC Treaty by the Commission and the Member States' competition authorities and courts. The Regulation recognises in particular the complementary functions of the Commission and Member States' competition authorities acting as public enforcers and the Member States' courts that rule on private lawsuits in order to safeguard the rights of individuals deriving from Articles 81 and 82.[2]

2. Under Regulation 1/2003, the public enforcers may focus their action on the investigation of serious infringements of Articles 81 and 82 which are often difficult to detect. For their enforcement activity, they benefit from information supplied by undertakings and by consumers in the market.

3. The Commission therefore wishes to encourage citizens and undertakings to address themselves to the public enforcers to inform them about suspected infringements of the competition rules. At the level of the Commission, there are two ways to do this, one is by lodging a complaint pursuant to Article 7(2) of Regulation 1/2003. Under Articles 5 to 9 of Regulation 773/2004,[3] such complaints must fulfil certain requirements.

4. The other way is the provision of market information that does not have to comply with the requirements for complaints pursuant to Article 7(2) of Regulation 1/2003. For this purpose, the Commission has created a special website to collect information from citizens and undertakings and their associations who wish to inform the Commission about suspected infringements of Articles 81 and 82. Such information can be the starting point for an investigation by the Commission.[4] Information about suspected infringements can be supplied to the following address:

europa.eu.int/dgcomp/info-on-anti-competitive-practices

or to:

Commission Européenne/Europese Commissie
Competition DG
B–1049 Bruxelles/Brussel

5. Without prejudice to the interpretation of Regulation 1/2003 and of Commission Regulation 773/2004 by the Community Courts, the present Notice intends to provide guidance to citizens and undertakings that are seeking relief from suspected infringements of the competition rules. The Notice contains two main parts:

— Part II gives indications about the choice between complaining to the Commission or bringing a lawsuit before a national court. Moreover, it recalls the principles related to the work-sharing between the Commission and the national competition authorities in the enforcement system established by Regulation 1/2003 that are explained in the Notice on cooperation within the network of competition authorities.[5]
— Part III explains the procedure for the treatment of complaints pursuant to Article 7(2) of Regulation 1/2003 by the Commission.

6. This Notice does not address the following situations:

— complaints lodged by Member States pursuant to Article 7(2) of Regulation 1/2003,
— complaints that ask the Commission to take action against a Member State pursuant to Article 86(3) in conjunction with Articles 81 or 82 of the Treaty,
— complaints relating to Article 87 of the Treaty on state aids,
— complaints relating to infringements by Member States that the Commission may pursue in the framework of Article 226 of the Treaty.[6]

NOTES

1 Council Regulation (EC) No 1/2003 of 16 December 2002 on the implementation of the rules on competition laid down in Articles 81 and 82 of the Treaty (OJ L1, 4.1.2003, p 1).

2 Cf. in particular Recitals 3–7 and 35 of Regulation 1/2003.

3 Commission Regulation (EC) No 773/2004 of 7 April 2004 relating to the conduct of proceedings by the Commission pursuant to Articles 81 and 82 of the EC Treaty (OJ 123, 27.4.2004).

4 The Commission handles correspondence from informants in accordance with its principles of good administrative practice.

5 Notice on cooperation within the Network of competition authorities (p 43).

6 For the handling of such complaints, cf. Commission communication of 10 October 2002, COM(2002) 141.

II. DIFFERENT POSSIBILITIES FOR LODGING COMPLAINTS ABOUT SUSPECTED INFRINGEMENTS OF ARTICLES 81 OR 82

A. COMPLAINTS IN THE NEW ENFORCEMENT SYSTEM ESTABLISHED BY REGULATION 1/2003

[4.335]

7. Depending on the nature of the complaint, a complainant may bring his complaint either to a national court or to a competition authority that acts as public enforcer. The present chapter of this Notice intends to help potential complainants to make an informed choice about whether to address themselves to the Commission, to one of the Member States' competition authorities or to a national court.

8. While national courts are called upon to safeguard the rights of individuals and are thus bound to rule on cases brought before them, public enforcers cannot investigate all complaints, but must set priorities in their treatment of cases. The Court of Justice has held that the Commission, entrusted by Article 85(1) of the EC Treaty with the task of ensuring application of the principles laid down in Articles 81 and 82 of the Treaty, is responsible for defining and implementing the orientation of Community competition policy and that, in order to perform that task effectively, it is entitled to give differing degrees of priority to the complaints brought before it.[7]

9. Regulation 1/2003 empowers Member States' courts and Member States' competition authorities to apply Articles 81 and 82 in their entirety alongside the Commission. Regulation 1/2003 pursues as one principal objective that Member States' courts and competition authorities should participate effectively in the enforcement of Articles 81 and 82.[8]

10. Moreover, Article 3 of Regulation 1/2003 provides that Member States' courts and competition authorities have to apply Articles 81 and 82 to all cases of agreements or conduct that are capable of affecting trade between Member States to which they apply their national competition laws. In addition, Articles 11 and 15 of the Regulation create a range of mechanisms by which Member States' courts and competition authorities cooperate with the Commission in the enforcement of Articles 81 and 82.

11. In this new legislative framework, the Commission intends to refocus its enforcement resources along the following lines:

— enforce the EC competition rules in cases for which it is well placed to act,[9] concentrating its resources on the most serious infringements;[10]

— handle cases in relation to which the Commission should act with a view to define Community competition policy and/or to ensure coherent application of Articles 81 or 82.

B. THE COMPLEMENTARY ROLES OF PRIVATE AND PUBLIC ENFORCEMENT

12. It has been consistently held by the Community Courts that national courts are called upon to safeguard the rights of individuals created by the direct effect of Articles 81(1) and 82.[11]

13. National courts can decide upon the nullity or validity of contracts and only national courts can grant damages to an individual in case of an infringement of Articles 81 and 82. Under the case law of the Court of Justice, any individual can claim damages for loss caused to him by a contract or by conduct which restricts or distorts competition, in order to ensure the full effectiveness of the Community competition rules. Such actions for damages before the national courts can make a significant contribution to the maintenance of effective competition in the Community as they discourage undertakings from concluding or applying restrictive agreements or practices.[12]

14. Regulation 1/2003 takes express account of the fact that national courts have an essential part to play in applying the EC competition rules.[13] By extending the power to apply Article 81(3) to national courts it removes the possibility for undertakings to delay national court proceedings by a notification to the Commission and thus eliminates an obstacle for private litigation that existed under Regulation No 17.[14]

15. Without prejudice to the right or obligation of national courts to address a preliminary question to the Court of Justice in accordance with Article 234 EC, Article 15(1) of Regulation 1/2003 provides expressly that national courts may ask for opinions or information from the Commission. This provision aims at facilitating the application of Articles 81 and 82 by national courts.[15]

16. Action before national courts has the following advantages for complainants:

— National courts may award damages for loss suffered as a result of an infringement of Article 81 or 82.

— National courts may rule on claims for payment or contractual obligations based on an agreement that they examine under Article 81.

— It is for the national courts to apply the civil sanction of nullity of Article 81(2) in contractual relationships between individuals.[16] They can in particular assess, in the light of the applicable national law, the scope and consequences of the nullity of certain contractual provisions under Article 81(2), with particular regard to all the other matters covered by the agreement.[17]

— National courts are usually better placed than the Commission to adopt interim measures.[18]

— Before national courts, it is possible to combine a claim under Community competition law with other claims under national law.

— Courts normally have the power to award legal costs to the successful applicant. This is never possible in an administrative procedure before the Commission.

17. The fact that a complainant can secure the protection of his rights by an action before a national court, is an important element that the Commission may take into account in its examination of the Community interest for investigating a complaint.[19]

18. The Commission holds the view that the new enforcement system established by Regulation 1/2003 strengthens the possibilities for complainants to seek and obtain effective relief before national courts.

C. WORK-SHARING BETWEEN THE PUBLIC ENFORCERS IN THE EUROPEAN COMMUNITY

19. Regulation 1/2003 creates a system of parallel competence for the application of Articles 81 and 82 by empowering Member States' competition authorities to apply Articles 81 and 82 in their entirety (Article 5). Decentralised enforcement by Member States' competition authorities is further encouraged by the possibility to exchange information (Article 12) and to provide each other assistance with investigations (Article 22).

20. The Regulation does not regulate the work-sharing between the Commission and the Member States' competition authorities but leaves the division of case work to the cooperation of the Commission and the Member States' competition authorities inside the European Competition Network (ECN). The Regulation pursues the objective of ensuring effective enforcement of Articles 81 and 82 through a flexible division of case work between the public enforcers in the Community.

21. Orientations for the work sharing between the Commission and the Member States' competition authorities are laid down in a separate Notice.[20] The guidance contained in that Notice, which concerns the relations between the public enforcers, will be of interest to complainants as it permits them to address a complaint to the authority most likely to be well placed to deal with their case.

22. The Notice on cooperation within the Network of Competition Authorities states in particular:[21]

"An authority can be considered to be well placed to deal with a case if the following three cumulative conditions are met:

— the agreement or practice has substantial direct actual or foreseeable effects on competition within its territory, is implemented within or originates from its territory;

— the authority is able effectively to bring to an end the entire infringement, ie it can adopt a cease-and desist order, the effect of which will be sufficient to bring an end to the infringement and it can, where appropriate, sanction the infringement adequately;

— it can gather, possibly with the assistance of other authorities, the evidence required to prove the infringement.

The above criteria indicate that a material link between the infringement and the territory of a Member State must exist in order for that Member State's competition authority to be considered well placed. It can be expected that in most cases the authorities of those Member States where competition is substantially affected by an infringement will be well placed provided they are capable of effectively bringing the infringement to an end through either single or parallel action unless the Commission is better placed to act (see below [. . .]).

It follows that a single NCA is usually well placed to deal with agreements or practices that substantially affect competition mainly within its territory [. . .].

Furthermore single action of an NCA might also be appropriate where, although more than one NCA can be regarded as well placed, the action of a single NCA is sufficient to bring the entire infringement to an end [. . .].

Parallel action by two or three NCAs may be appropriate where an agreement or practice has substantial effects on competition mainly in their respective territories and the action of only one NCA would not be sufficient to bring the entire infringement to an end and/or to sanction it adequately [. . .].

The authorities dealing with a case in parallel action will endeavour to coordinate their action to the extent possible. To that effect, they may find it useful to designate one of them as a lead authority and to delegate tasks to the lead authority such as for example the coordination of investigative measures, while each authority remains responsible for conducting its own proceedings.

The Commission is particularly well placed if one or several agreement(s) or practice(s), including networks of similar agreements or practices, have effects on competition in more than three Member States (cross-border markets covering more than three Member States or several national markets) [. . .].

Moreover, the Commission is particularly well placed to deal with a case if it is closely linked to other Community provisions which may be exclusively or more effectively applied by the Commission, if the Community interest requires the adoption of a Commission decision to develop Community competition policy when a new competition issue arises or to ensure effective enforcement."

23. Within the European Competition Network, information on cases that are being investigated following a complaint will be made available to the other members of the network before or without delay after commencing the first formal investigative measure.[22] Where the same complaint has been lodged with several authorities or where a case has not been lodged with an authority that is well placed, the members of the network will endeavour to determine within an indicative time-limit of two months which authority or authorities should be in charge of the case.

24. Complainants themselves have an important role to play in further reducing the potential need for reallocation of a case originating from their complaint by referring to the orientations on work sharing in the network set out in the present chapter when deciding on where to lodge their complaint. If nonetheless a case is reallocated within the network, the undertakings concerned and the complainant(s) are informed as soon as possible by the competition authorities involved.[23]

25. The Commission may reject a complaint in accordance with Article 13 of Regulation 1/2003, on the grounds that a Member State competition authority is dealing or has dealt with the case. When doing so, the Commission must, in accordance with Article 9 of Regulation 773/2004, inform the complainant without delay of the national competition authority which is dealing or has already dealt with the case.

NOTES

7 Case C-344/98, *Masterfoods v HB Ice Cream*, [2000] ECR I-11369, para 46; Case C-119/97P, Union *française de l'express (Ufex) and Others v Commission of the European Communities*, [1999] ECR I-1341, para 88; Case T-24/90, *Automec v Commission of the European Communities*, [1992] ECR II-2223, paras 73–77.

8 Cf. in particular Articles 5, 6, 11, 12, 15, 22, 29, 35 and Recitals 2 to 4 and 6 to 8 of Regulation 1/2003.

9 Cf. Notice on cooperation within the network of competition authorities . . . , points 5 ss.

10 Cf. Recital 3 of Regulation 1/2003.

11 Settled case law, cf. Case 127/73, *Belgische Radio en Televisie (BRT) v SABAM and Fonior*, [1974] ECR 51, para 16; Case C-282/95P, *Guérin automobiles v Commission of the European Communities*, [1997] ECR I-1503, para 39; Case C-453/99, *Courage v Bernhard Crehan*, [2001] ECR I-6297, para 23.

12 Case C-453/99, *Courage v Bernhard Crehan*, [2001] ECR I-6297, paras 26 and 27; the power of national courts to grant damages is also underlined in Recital 7 of Regulation 1/2003.

13 Cf. Articles 1, 6 and 15 as well as Recital 7 of Regulation 1/2003.

14 Regulation No 17: First Regulation implementing Articles 85 and 86 of the Treaty; OJ P13 of 21 February 1962, p 204; English special edition: Series I Chapter 1959–1962 p 87. Regulation No 17 is repealed by Article 43 of Regulation 1/2003 with effect from 1 May 2004.

15 For more detailed explanations of this mechanism, cf. Notice on the co-operation between the Commission and the courts of the EU Member States in the application of Articles 81 and 82 EC . . .

16 Case T-24/90, *Automec v Commission of the European Communities*, [1992] ECR II-2223, para 93.

17 Case C-230/96, *Cabour and Nord Distribution Automobile v Arnor "SOCO"*, [1998] ECR I-2055, para 51; Joined Cases T-185/96, T-189/96 and T-190/96, *Dalmasso and Others v Commission of the European Communities*, [1999] ECR II-93, para 50.

18 Cf. Article 8 of Regulation 1/2003 and para 80 below. Depending on the case, Member States' competition authorities may equally be well placed to adopt interim measures.

19 Cf. points 41 ss. below.

20 Notice on cooperation within the Network of competition authorities (p. 43).

21 Notice on cooperation within the Network of competition authorities . . . , points 8–15.

22 Article 11(2) and (3) of Regulation 1/2003; Notice on cooperation within the Network of Competition Authorities . . . , points 16/17.

23 Notice on cooperation within the Network of Competition Authorities, . . . , point 34.

III. THE COMMISSION'S HANDLING OF COMPLAINTS PURSUANT TO ARTICLE 7(2) OF REGULATION 1/2003

A. GENERAL

[4.336]

26. According to Article 7(2) of Regulation 1/2003 natural or legal persons that can show a legitimate interest[24] are entitled to lodge a complaint to ask the Commission to find an infringement of Articles 81 and 82 EC and to require that the infringement be brought to an end in accordance with Article 7(1) of Regulation 1/2003. The present part of this Notice explains the requirements applicable to complaints based on Article 7(2) of Regulation 1/2003, their assessment and the procedure followed by the Commission.

27. The Commission, unlike civil courts, whose task is to safeguard the individual rights of private persons, is an administrative authority that must act in the public interest. It is an inherent feature of the Commission's task as public enforcer that it has a margin of discretion to set priorities in its enforcement activity.[25]

28. The Commission is entitled to give different degrees of priority to complaints made to it and may refer to the Community interest presented by a case as a criterion of priority.[26] The Commission may reject a complaint when it considers that the case does not display a sufficient Community interest to justify further investigation. Where the Commission rejects a complaint, the complainant is entitled to a decision of the Commission[27] without prejudice to Article 7(3) of Regulation 773/2004.

B. MAKING A COMPLAINT PURSUANT TO ARTICLE 7(2) OF REGULATION 1/2003

(a) Complaint form

29. A complaint pursuant to Article 7(2) of Regulation 1/2003 can only be made about an alleged infringement of Articles 81 or 82 with a view to the Commission taking action under Article 7(1) of Regulation 1/2003. A complaint under Article 7(2) of Regulation 1/2003 has to comply with Form C mentioned in Article 5(1) of Regulation 773/2004 and annexed to that Regulation.

30. Form C is available at europa.eu.int/dgcomp/ complaints-form and is also annexed to this Notice. The complaint must be submitted in three paper copies as well as, if possible, an electronic copy. In addition, the complainant must provide a non-confidential version of the complaint (Article 5(2) of Regulation 773/2004). Electronic transmission to the Commission is possible via the website indicated, the paper copies should be sent to the following address:

Commission Européenne/Europese Commissie
Competition DG
B–1049 Bruxelles/Brussel

31. Form C requires complainants to submit comprehensive information in relation to their complaint. They should also provide copies of relevant supporting documentation reasonably available to them and, to the extent possible, provide indications as to where relevant information and documents that are unavailable to them could be obtained by the Commission. In particular cases, the Commission may dispense with the obligation to provide information in relation to part of the information required by Form C (Article 5(1) of Regulation 773/2004). The Commission holds the view that this possibility can in particular play a role to facilitate complaints by consumer associations where they, in the context of an otherwise substantiated complaint, do not have access to specific pieces of information from the sphere of the undertakings complained of.

32. Correspondence to the Commission that does not comply with the requirements of Article 5 of Regulation 773/2004 and therefore does not constitute a complaint within the meaning of Article 7(2) of Regulation 1/2003 will be considered by the Commission as general information that, where it is useful, may lead to an own-initiative investigation (cf. point 4 above).

(b) Legitimate interest

33. The status of formal complainant under Article 7(2) of Regulation 1/2003 is reserved to legal and natural persons who can show a legitimate interest.[28] Member States are deemed to have a legitimate interest for all complaints they choose to lodge.

34. In the past practice of the Commission, the condition of legitimate interest was not often a matter of doubt as most complainants were in a position of being directly and adversely affected by the alleged infringement. However, there are situations where the condition of a "legitimate interest" in Article 7(2) requires further analysis to conclude that it is fulfilled. Useful guidance can best be provided by a non-exhaustive set of examples.

35. The Court of First Instance has held that an association of undertakings may claim a legitimate interest in lodging a complaint regarding conduct concerning its members, even if it is not directly concerned, as an undertaking operating in the relevant market, by the conduct complained of, provided that, first, it is entitled to represent the interests of its members and secondly, the conduct complained of is liable to adversely affect the interests of its members.[29] Conversely, the Commission has been found to be entitled not to pursue the complaint of an association of undertakings whose members were not involved in the type of business transactions complained of.[30]

36. From this case law, it can be inferred that undertakings (themselves or through associations that are entitled to represent their interests) can claim a legitimate interest where they are operating in the relevant market or where the conduct complained of is liable to directly and adversely affect their interests. This confirms the established practice of the Commission which has accepted that a legitimate interest can, for instance, be claimed by the parties to the agreement or practice which is the subject of the complaint, by competitors whose interests have allegedly been damaged by the behaviour complained of or by undertakings excluded from a distribution system.

37. Consumer associations can equally lodge complaints with the Commission.[31] The Commission moreover holds the view that individual consumers whose economic interests are directly and adversely affected insofar as they are the buyers of goods or services that are the object of an infringement can be in a position to show a legitimate interest.[32]

38. However, the Commission does not consider as a legitimate interest within the meaning of Article 7(2) the interest of persons or organisations that wish to come forward on general interest considerations without showing that they or their members are liable to be directly and adversely affected by the infringement (pro bono publico).

39. Local or regional public authorities may be able to show a legitimate interest in their capacity as buyers or users of goods or services affected by the conduct complained of. Conversely, they cannot be considered as showing a legitimate interest within the meaning of Article 7(2) of Regulation 1/2003 to the extent that they bring to the attention of the Commission alleged infringements pro bono publico.

40. Complainants have to demonstrate their legitimate interest. Where a natural or legal person lodging a complaint is unable to demonstrate a legitimate interest, the Commission is entitled, without prejudice to its right to initiate proceedings of its own initiative, not to pursue the complaint. The Commission may ascertain whether this condition is met at any stage of the investigation.[33]

C. ASSESSMENT OF COMPLAINTS

(a) Community interest

41. Under the settled case law of the Community Courts, the Commission is not required to conduct an investigation in each case[34] or, a fortiori, to take a decision within the meaning of Article 249 EC on the existence or non-existence of an infringement of Articles 81 or 82,[35] but is entitled to give differing degrees of priority to the complaints brought before it and refer to the Community interest in order to determine the degree of priority to be applied to the various complaints it receives.[36] The position is different only if the complaint falls within the exclusive competence of the Commission.[37]

42. The Commission must however examine carefully the factual and legal elements brought to its attention by the complainant in order to assess the Community interest in further investigation of a case.[38]

43. The assessment of the Community interest raised by a complaint depends on the circumstances of each individual case. Accordingly, the number of criteria of assessment to which the Commission may refer is not limited, nor is the Commission required to have recourse exclusively to certain criteria. As the factual and legal circumstances may differ considerably from case to case, it is permissible to apply new criteria which had not before been considered.[39] Where appropriate, the Commission may give priority to a single criterion for assessing the Community interest.[40]

44. Among the criteria which have been held relevant in the case law for the assessment of the Community interest in the (further) investigation of a case are the following:

— The Commission can reject a complaint on the ground that the complainant can bring an action to assert its rights before national courts.[41]

— The Commission may not regard certain situations as excluded in principle from its purview under the task entrusted to it by the Treaty but is required to assess in each case how serious the alleged infringements are and how persistent their consequences are. This means in particular that it must take into account the duration and the extent of the infringements complained of and their effect on the competition situation in the Community.[42]

— The Commission may have to balance the significance of the alleged infringement as regards the functioning of the common market, the probability of establishing the existence of the infringement and the scope of the investigation required in order to fulfil its task of ensuring that Articles 81 and 82 of the Treaty are complied with.[43]

— While the Commission's discretion does not depend on how advanced the investigation of a case is, the stage of the investigation forms part of the circumstances of the case which the Commission may have to take into consideration.[44]

— The Commission may decide that it is not appropriate to investigate a complaint where the practices in question have ceased. However, for this purpose, the Commission will have to ascertain whether anti-competitive effects persist and if the seriousness of the infringements or the persistence of their effects does not give the complaint a Community interest.[45]

— The Commission may also decide that it is not appropriate to investigate a complaint where the undertakings concerned agree to change their conduct in such a way that it can consider that there is no longer a sufficient Community interest to intervene.[46]

45. Where it forms the view that a case does not display sufficient Community interest to justify (further) investigation, the Commission may reject the complaint on that ground. Such a decision can be taken either before commencing an investigation or after taking investigative measures.[47] However, the Commission is not obliged to set aside a complaint for lack of Community interest.[48]

(b) Assessment under Articles 81 and 82

46. The examination of a complaint under Articles 81 and 82 involves two aspects, one relating to the facts to be established to prove an infringement of Articles 81 or 82 and the other relating to the legal assessment of the conduct complained of.

47. Where the complaint, while complying with the requirements of Article 5 of Regulation 773/2004 and Form C, does not sufficiently substantiate the allegations put forward, it may be rejected on that ground.[49] In order to reject a complaint on the ground that the conduct complained of does not infringe the EC competition rules or does not fall within their scope of application, the Commission is not obliged to take into account circumstances that have not been brought to its attention by the complainant and that it could only have uncovered by the investigation of the case.[50]

48. The criteria for the legal assessment of agreements or practices under Articles 81 and 82 cannot be dealt with exhaustively in the present Notice. However, potential complainants should refer to the extensive guidance available from the Commission,[51] in addition to other sources and in particular the case law of the Community Courts and the case practice of the Commission. Four specific issues are mentioned in the following points with indications on where to find further guidance.

49. Agreements and practices fall within the scope of application of Articles 81 and 82 where they are capable of affecting trade between Member States. Where an agreement or practice does not fulfil this condition, national competition law may apply, but not EC competition law. Extensive guidance on this subject can be found in the Notice on the effect on trade concept.[52]

50. Agreements falling within the scope of Article 81 may be agreements of minor importance which are deemed not to restrict competition appreciably. Guidance on this issue can be found in the Commission's de minimis Notice.[53]

51. Agreements that fulfil the conditions of a block exemption regulation are deemed to satisfy the conditions of Article 81(3).[54] For the Commission to withdraw the benefit of the block exemption pursuant to Article 29 of Regulation 1/2003, it must find that upon individual assessment an agreement to which the exemption regulation applies has certain effects which are incompatible with Article 81(3).

52. Agreements that restrict competition within the meaning of Article 81(1) EC may fulfil the conditions of Article 81(3) EC. Pursuant to Article 1(2) of Regulation 1/2003 and without a prior administrative decision being required, such agreements are not prohibited. Guidance on the conditions to be fulfilled by an agreement pursuant to Article 81(3) can be found in the Notice on Article 81(3).[55]

D. THE COMMISSION'S PROCEDURES WHEN DEALING WITH COMPLAINTS

(a) Overview

53. As recalled above, the Commission is not obliged to carry out an investigation on the basis of every complaint submitted with a view to establishing whether an infringement has been committed. However, the Commission is under a duty to consider carefully the factual and legal issues brought to its attention by the complainant, in order to assess whether those issues indicate conduct which is liable to infringe Articles 81 and 82.[56]

54. In the Commission's procedure for dealing with complaints, different stages can be distinguished.[57]

55. During the first stage, following the submission of the complaint, the Commission examines the complaint and may collect further information in order to decide what action it will take on the complaint. That stage may include an informal exchange of views between the Commission and the complainant with a view to clarifying the factual and legal issues with which the complaint is concerned. In this stage, the Commission may give an initial reaction to the complainant allowing the complainant an opportunity to expand on his allegations in the light of that initial reaction.

56. In the second stage, the Commission may investigate the case further with a view to initiating proceedings pursuant to Article 7(1) of Regulation 1/2003 against the undertakings complained of. Where the Commission considers that there are insufficient grounds for acting on the complaint, it will inform the complainant of its reasons and offer the complainant the opportunity to submit any further comments within a time-limit which it fixes (Article 7(1) of Regulation 773/2004).

57. If the complainant fails to make known its views within the time-limit set by the Commission, the complaint is deemed to have been withdrawn (Article 7(3) of Regulation 773/2004). In all other cases, in the third stage of the procedure, the Commission takes cognisance of the observations submitted by the complainant and either initiates a procedure against the subject of the complaint or adopts a decision rejecting the complaint.[58]

58. Where the Commission rejects a complaint pursuant to Article 13 of Regulation 1/2003 on the grounds that another authority is dealing or has dealt with the case, the Commission proceeds in accordance with Article 9 of Regulation 773/2004.

59. Throughout the procedure, complainants benefit from a range of rights as provided in particular in Articles 6 to 8 of Regulation 773/2004. However, proceedings of the Commission in competition cases do not constitute adversarial proceedings between the complainant on the one hand and the companies which are the subject of the investigation on the other hand. Accordingly, the procedural rights of complainants are less far-reaching than the right to a fair hearing of the companies which are the subject of an infringement procedure.[59]

(b) Indicative time limit for informing the complainant of the Commission's proposed action

60. The Commission is under an obligation to decide on complaints within a reasonable time.[60] What is a reasonable duration depends on the circumstances of each case and in particular, its context, the various procedural steps followed by the Commission, the conduct of the parties in the course of the procedure, the complexity of the case and its importance for the various parties involved.[61]

61. The Commission will in principle endeavour to inform complainants of the action that it proposes to take on a complaint within an indicative time frame of four months from the reception of the complaint. Thus, subject to the circumstances of the individual case and in particular the possible need to request complementary information from the complainant or third parties, the Commission will in principle inform the complainant within four months whether or not it intends to investigate its case further. This time-limit does not constitute a binding statutory term.

62. Accordingly, within this four month period, the Commission may communicate its proposed course of action to the complainant as an initial reaction within the first phase of the procedure (see point 55 above). The Commission may also, where the examination of the complaint has progressed to the second stage (see point 56 above), directly proceed to informing the complainant about its provisional assessment by a letter pursuant to Article 7(1) of Regulation 773/2004.

63. To ensure the most expeditious treatment of their complaint, it is desirable that complainants cooperate diligently in the procedures,[62] for example by informing the Commission of new developments.

(c) Procedural rights of the complainant

64. Where the Commission addresses a statement of objections to the companies complained of pursuant to Article 10(1) of Regulation 773/2004, the complainant is entitled to receive a copy of this document from which business secrets and other confidential information of the companies concerned have been removed (non-confidential version of the statement of objections; cf. Article 6(1) of Regulation 773/2004). The complainant is invited to comment in writing on the statement of objections. A time-limit will be set for such written comments.

65. Furthermore, the Commission may, where appropriate, afford complainants the opportunity of expressing their views at the oral hearing of the parties to which a statement of objections has been addressed, if the complainants so request in their written comments.[63]

66. Complainants may submit, of their own initiative or following a request by the Commission, documents that contain business secrets or other confidential information. Confidential information will be protected by the Commission.[64] Under Article 16 of Regulation 773/2004, complainants are obliged to identify confidential information, give reasons why the information is considered confidential and submit a separate non-confidential version when they make their views known pursuant to Article 6(1) and 7(1) of Regulation 773/2004, as well as when they subsequently submit further information in the course of the same procedure. Moreover, the Commission may, in all other cases, request complainants which produce documents or statements to identify the documents or parts of the documents or statements which they consider to be confidential. It may in particular set a deadline for the complainant to specify why it considers a piece of information to be confidential and to provide a non-confidential version, including a concise description or non-confidential version of each piece of information deleted.

67. The qualification of information as confidential does not prevent the Commission from disclosing and using information where that is necessary to prove an infringement of Articles 81 or 82.[65] Where business secrets and confidential information are necessary to prove an infringement, the Commission must assess for each individual document whether the need to disclose is greater than the harm which might result from disclosure.

68. Where the Commission takes the view that a complaint should not be further examined, because there is no sufficient Community interest in pursuing the case further or on other grounds, it will inform the complainant in the form of a letter which indicates its legal basis (Article 7(1) of Regulation 773/2004), sets out the reasons that have led the Commission to provisionally conclude in the sense indicated and provides the complainant with the opportunity to submit supplementary information or observations within a time-limit set by the Commission. The Commission will also indicate the consequences of not replying pursuant to Article 7(3) of Regulation 773/2004, as explained below.

69. Pursuant to Article 8(1) of Regulation 773/2004, the complainant has the right to access the information on which the Commission bases its preliminary view. Such access is normally provided by annexing to the letter a copy of the relevant documents.

70. The time-limit for observations by the complainant on the letter pursuant to Article 7(1) of Regulation 773/2004 will be set in accordance with the circumstances of the case. It will not be shorter than four weeks (Article 17(2) of Regulation 773/2004). If the complainant does not respond within the time-limit set, the complaint is deemed to have been withdrawn pursuant to Article 7(3) of Regulation 773/2004. Complainants are also entitled to withdraw their complaint at any time if they so wish.

71. The complainant may request an extension of the time-limit for the provision of comments. Depending on the circumstances of the case, the Commission may grant such an extension.

72. In that case, where the complainant submits supplementary observations, the Commission takes cognisance of those observations. Where they are of such a nature as to make the Commission change its previous course of action, it may initiate a procedure against the companies complained of. In this procedure, the complainant has the procedural rights explained above.

73. Where the observations of the complainant do not alter the Commission's proposed course of action, it rejects the complaint by decision.[66]

(d) The Commission decision rejecting a complaint

74. Where the Commission rejects a complaint by decision pursuant to Article 7(2) of Regulation 773/2004, it must state the reasons in accordance with Article 253 EC, ie in a way that is appropriate to the act at issue and takes into account the circumstances of each case.

75. The statement of reasons must disclose in a clear and unequivocal fashion the reasoning followed by the Commission in such a way as to enable the complainant to ascertain the reasons for the decision and to enable the competent Community Court to exercise its power of review. However, the Commission is not obliged to adopt a position on all the arguments relied on by the complainant in support of its complaint. It only needs to set out the facts and legal considerations which are of decisive importance in the context of the decision.[67]

76. Where the Commission rejects a complaint in a case that also gives rise to a decision pursuant to Article 10 of Regulation 1/2003 (Finding of inapplicability of Articles 81 or 82) or Article 9 of Regulation 1/2003 (Commitments), the decision rejecting a complaint may refer to that other decision adopted on the basis of the provisions mentioned.

77. A decision to reject a complaint is subject to appeal before the Community Courts.[68]

78. A decision rejecting a complaint prevents complainants from requiring the reopening of the investigation unless they put forward significant new evidence. Accordingly, further correspondence on the same alleged infringement by former complainants cannot be regarded as a new complaint unless significant new evidence is brought to the attention of the Commission. However, the Commission may re-open a file under appropriate circumstances.

79. A decision to reject a complaint does not definitively rule on the question of whether or not there is an infringement of Articles 81 or 82, even where the Commission has assessed the facts on the basis of Articles 81 and 82. The assessments made by the Commission in a decision rejecting a complaint therefore do not prevent a Member State court or competition authority from applying Articles 81 and 82 to agreements and practices brought before it. The assessments made by the Commission in a decision rejecting a complaint constitute facts which Member States' courts or competition authorities may take into account in examining whether the agreements or conduct in question are in conformity with Articles 81 and 82.[69]

(e) Specific situations

80. According to Article 8 of Regulation 1/2003 the Commission may on its own initiative order interim measures where there is the risk of serious and irreparable damage to competition. Article 8 of Regulation 1/2003 makes it clear that interim measures cannot be applied for by complainants under Article 7(2) of Regulation 1/2003. Requests for interim measures by undertakings can be brought before Member States' courts which are well placed to decide on such measures.[70]

81. Some persons may wish to inform the Commission about suspected infringements of Articles 81 or 82 without having their identity revealed to the undertakings concerned by the allegations. These persons are welcome to contact the Commission. The Commission is bound to respect an informant's request for anonymity,[71] unless the request to remain anonymous is manifestly unjustified.

NOTES

24 For more extensive explanations on this notion in particular, cf. points 33 ss. below.

25 Case C-119/97P, *Union française de l'express (Ufex) and Others v Commission of the European Communities*, [1999] ECR I-1341, para 88; Case T-24/90, *Automec v Commission of the European Communities*, [1992] ECR II-2223, paras 73–77 and 85.

26 Settled case law since Case T-24/90, *Automec v Commission of the European Communities*, [1992] ECR II-2223, para 85.

27 Case C-282/95P, *Guérin automobiles v Commission of the European Communities*, [1997] ECR I-1503, para 36.

28 8 Cf. Article 5(1) of Regulation 773/2004.

29 Case T-114/92, *Bureau Européen des Médias et de l'Industrie Musicale (BEMIM) v Commission of the European Communities*, [1995] ECR II-147, para 28. Associations of undertakings were also the complainants in the cases underlying the judgments in Case 298/83, *Comité des industries cinématographiques des Communautés européennes (CICCE) v Commission of the European Communities*, [1985] ECR 1105 and Case T-319/99, *Federacion Nacional de Empresas (FENIN) v Commission of the European Communities*, not yet published in [2003] ECR.

30 Joined Cases T-133/95 and T-204/95, *International Express Carriers Conference (IECC) v Commission of the European Communities*, [1998] ECR II-3645, paras 79–83.

31 Case T-37/92, *Bureau Européen des Unions des Consommateurs (BEUC) v Commission of the European Communities*, [1994] ECR II-285, para 36.

32 This question is currently raised in a pending procedure before the Court of First Instance (Joined cases T-213 and 214/01). The Commission has also accepted as complainant an individual consumer in its Decision of 9 December 1998 in Case IV/D-2/34.466, *Greek Ferries*, OJ L109/24 of 27 April 1999, para 1.

33 Joined Cases T-133/95 and T-204/95, *International Express Carriers Conference (IECC) v Commission of the European Communities*, [1998] ECR II-3645, para 79.

34 Case T-24/90, *Automec v Commission of the European Communities*, [1992] ECR II-2223, para 76; Case C-91/95P, *Roger Tremblay and Others v Commission of the European Communities*, [1996] ECR I-5547, para 30.

35 Case 125/78, *GEMA v Commission of the European Communities*, [1979] ECR 3173, para 17; Case C-119/97/P, *Union française de l'express (Ufex) and Others v Commission of the European Communities*, [1999] ECR I-1341, para 87.

36 Settled case law since the Case T-24/90, *Automec v Commission of the European Communities*, [1992] ECR II-2223, paras 77 and 85; Recital 18 of Regulation 1/2003 expressly confirms this possibility.

37 Settled case law since Case T-24/90, *Automec v Commission of the European Communities*, [1992] ECR II-2223, para 75. Under Regulation 1/2003, this principle may only be relevant in the context of Article 29 of that Regulation.

38 Case 210/81, *Oswald Schmidt, trading as Demo-Studio Schmidt v Commission of the European Communities*, [1983] ECR 3045, para 19; Case C-119/97P, *Union française de l'express (Ufex) and Others v Commission of the European Communities*, [1999] ECR I-1341, para 86.

39 Case C-119/97P, *Union française de l'express (Ufex) and Others v Commission of the European Communities*, [1999] ECR I-1341, paras 79–80.

40 Case C-450/98P, *International Express Carriers Conference (IECC) v Commission of the European Communities*, [2001] ECR I-3947, paras 57–59.

41 Case T-24/90, *Automec v Commission of the European Communities*, [1992] ECR II-2223, paras 88ss.; Case T-5/93, *Roger Tremblay and Others v Commission of the European Communities*, [1995] ECR II-185, paras 65ss.; Case T-575/93, *Casper Koelman v Commission of the European Communities*, [1996] ECR II-1, paras 75–80; see also part II above where more detailed explanations concerning this situation are given.

42 Case C-119/97P, *Union française de l'express (Ufex) and Others v Commission of the European Communities*, [1999] ECR I-1341, paras 92/93.

43 Settled case law since Case T-24/90, *Automec v Commission of the European Communities*, [1992] ECR II-2223, para 86.

44 Case C-449/98P, *International Express Carriers Conference (IECC) v Commission of the European Communities* [2001] ECR I-3875, para 37.

45 Case T-77/95, *Syndicat français de l'Express International and Others v Commission of the European Communities* [1997] ECR II-1, para 57; Case C-119/97P, *Union française de l'express (Ufex) and Others v Commission of the European Communities*, [1999] ECR I-1341, para 95. Cf. also Case T-37/92, *Bureau Européen des Unions des Consommateurs (BEUC) v Commission of the European Communities*, [1994] ECR II-285, para 113, where an unwritten commitment between a Member State and a third county outside the common commercial policy was held not to suffice to establish that the conduct complained of had ceased.

46 Case T-110/95, *International Express Carriers (IECC) v Commission of the European Communities and Others*, [1998] ECR II-3605, para 57, upheld by Case 449/98P, *International Express Carriers (IECC) v Commission of the European Communities and Others*, [2001] ECR I-3875, paras 44–47.

47 Case C-449/98P, *International Express Carriers (IECC) v Commission of the European Communities* e.a. [2001] ECR I-3875, para 37.

48 Cf. Case T-77/92, *Parker Pen v Commission of the European Communities*, [1994] ECR II-549, paras 64/65.

49 Case 298/83, *Comité des industries cinématographiques des Communautés européennes (CICCE) v Commission of the European Communities*, [1985] ECR 1105, paras 21–24; Case T-198/98, *Micro Leader Business v Commission of the European Communities*, [1999] ECR II-3989, paras 32–39.

50 Case T-319/99, *Federación Nacional de Empresas (FENIN) v Commission of the European Communities*, not yet published in [2003] ECR, para 43.

51 Extensive guidance can be found on the Commission's website at europa.eu.int/comm/competition/index_en.html

52 Notice on the effect on trade concept contained in Articles 81 and 82 of the Treaty (p 81).

53 Commission Notice on agreements of minor importance which do not appreciably restrict competition under Article 81(1) of the Treaty establishing the European Community (de minimis), OJ C368 of 22 December 2002, p 13.

54 The texts of all block exemption regulations are available on the Commission's website at europa.eu.int/comm/competition/index_en.html

55 Commission Notice-Guidelines on the application of Article 81(3) of the Treaty (p 97).

56 Case 210/81, *Oswald Schmidt, trading as Demo-Studio Schmidt v Commission of the European Communities*, [1983] ECR 3045, para 19; Case T-24/90, *Automec v Commission of the European Communities*, [1992] ECR II-2223, para 79.

57 Cf. Case T-64/89, *Automec v Commission of the European Communities*, [1990] ECR II-367, paras 45–47; Case T-37/92, *Bureau Européen des Unions des Consommateurs (BEUC) v Commission of the European Communities*, [1994] ECR II-285, para 29.

58 Case C-282/95P, *Guérin automobiles v Commission of the European Communities*, [1997] ECR I-1503, para 36.

59 Joined Cases 142 and 156/84, British *American Tobacco Company and R. J. Reynolds Industries v Commission of the European Communities* [1987] ECR 249, paras 19/20.

60 Case C-282/95P, *Guérin automobiles v Commission of the European Communities*, [1997] ECR I-1503, para 37.

61 Joined Cases T-213/95 and T-18/96, *Stichting Certificatie Kraanverhuurbedrijf (SCK) and Federatie van Nederlandse Kraanbedrijven (FNK) v Commission of the European Communities*, [1997] ECR 1739, para 57.

62 The notion of "diligence" on the part of the complainant is used by the Court of First Instance in Case T-77/94, *Vereniging van Groothandelaren in Bloemkwekerijprodukten and Others v Commission of the European Communities*, [1997] ECR II-759, para 75.

63 Article 6(2) of Commission Regulation 773/2004.

64 Article 287 EC, Article 28 of Regulation 1/2003 and Articles 15 and 16 of Regulation 773/2004.

65 Article 27(2) of Regulation 1/2003.

66 Article 7(2) of Regulation 773/2004; Case C-282/95P, *Guérin automobiles v Commission of the European Communities*, [1997] ECR I-1503, para 36.

67 Settled case law, cf. i.a. Case T-114/92, *Bureau Européen des Médias et de l'Industrie Musicale (BEMIM) v Commission of the European Communities*, [1995] ECR II-147, para 41.

68 Settled case law since Case 210/81, *Oswald Schmidt, trading as Demo-Studio Schmidt v Commission of the European Communities*, [1983] ECR 3045.

69 Case T-575/93, *Casper Koelman v Commission of the European Communities*, [1996] ECR II-1, paras 41–43.

70 Depending on the case, Member States' competition authorities may equally be well placed to adopt interim measures.

71 Case 145/83, *Stanley George Adams v Commission of the European Communities*, [1985] ECR 3539.

[4.337]

ANNEX

FORM C COMPLAINT PURSUANT TO ARTICLE 7 OF REGULATION (EC) NO 1/2003

I. Information regarding the complainant and the undertaking(s) or association of undertakings giving rise to the complaint

1. Give full details on the identity of the legal or natural person submitting the complaint. Where the complainant is an undertaking, identify the corporate group to which it belongs and provide a concise overview of the nature and scope of its business activities. Provide a contact person (with telephone number, postal and Email address) from which supplementary explanations can be obtained.

2. Identify the undertakings(s) or association of undertakings whose conduct the complaint relates to, including, where applicable, all available information on the corporate group to which the undertaking(s) complained of belong and the nature and scope of the business activities pursued by them. Indicate the position of the complainant vis-à-vis the undertaking(s) or association of undertakings complained of (eg customer, competitor).

II. Details of the alleged infringement and evidence

3. Set out in detail the facts from which, in your opinion, it appears that there exists an infringement of Article 81 or 82 of the treaty and/or Article 53 or 54 of the EEA agreement. Indicate in particular the nature of the products (goods or services) affected by the alleged infringements and explain, where necessary, the commercial relationships concerning these products. Provide all available details on the agreements or practices of the undertakings or associations of undertakings to which this complaint relates. Indicate, to the extent possible, the relative market positions of the undertakings concerned by the complaint.

4. Submit all documentation in your possession relating to or directly connected with the facts set out in the complaint (for example, texts of agreements, minutes of negotiations or meetings, terms of transactions, business documents, circulars, correspondence, notes of telephone conversations . . .). State the names and address of the persons able to testify to the facts set out in the complaint, and in particular of persons affected by the alleged infringement. Submit statistics or other data in your possession which relate to the facts set out, in particular where they show developments in the marketplace (for example information relating to prices and price trends, barriers to entry to the market for new suppliers etc).

5. Set out your view about the geographical scope of the alleged infringement and explain, where that is not obvious, to what extent trade between Member States or between the Community and one or more EFTA States that are contracting parties of the EEA Agreement may be affected by the conduct complained of.

III. Finding sought from the Commission and legitimate interest

6. Explain what finding or action you are seeking as a result of proceedings brought by the Commission.

7. Set out the grounds on which you claim a legitimate interest as complainant pursuant to Article 7 of Regulation (EC) No 1/2003. State in particular how the conduct complained of affects you and explain how, in your view, intervention by the Commission would be liable to remedy the alleged grievance.

IV. Proceedings before national competition authorities or national courts

8. Provide full information about whether you have approached, concerning the same or closely related subject-matters, any other competition authority and/or whether a lawsuit has been brought before a national court. If so, provide full details about the administrative or judicial authority contacted and your submissions to such authority.

Declaration that the information given in this form and in the Annexes thereto is given entirely in good faith.

. . . .

Date and signature

COMMISSION NOTICE

(2004/C101/06)

on informal guidance relating to novel questions concerning Articles 81 and 82 of the EC Treaty that arise in individual cases (Guidance letters)

(Text with EEA relevance)

[4.338]

NOTES

Date of publication in OJ: OJ C101, 27.4.2004, p 78.

Note: with effect from 1 December 2009, the EC Treaty was replaced by the Treaty on the Functioning of the European Union. References in this document to provisions of the EC Treaty should be construed accordingly. As to Articles 81 and 82 of the EC Treaty, see now Articles 101 and 102 of the Treaty on the Functioning of the European Union.

I. REGULATION 1/2003

[4.339]

1. Regulation 1/2003[1] sets up a new enforcement system for Articles 81 and 82 of the Treaty. While designed to restore the focus on the primary task of effective enforcement of the competition rules, the Regulation also creates legal certainty inasmuch as it provides that agreements[2] which fall under Article 81(1) but fulfil the conditions in Article 81(3) are valid and fully enforceable ab initio without a prior decision by a competition authority (Article 1 of Regulation 1/2003).

2. The framework of Regulation 1/2003, while introducing parallel competence of the Commission, Member States' competition authorities and Member States' courts to apply Article 81 and 82 in their entirety, limits risks of inconsistent application by a range of measures, thereby ensuring the primary aspect of legal certainty for companies as reflected in the case law of the Court of Justice, ie that the competition rules are applied in a consistent way throughout the Community.

3. Undertakings are generally well placed to assess the legality of their actions in such a way as to enable them to take an informed decision on whether to go ahead with an agreement or practice and in what form. They are close to the facts and have at their disposal the framework of block exemption regulations, case law and case practice as well as extensive guidance in Commission guidelines and notices.[3]

4. Alongside the reform of the rules implementing Articles 81 and 82 brought about by Regulation 1/2003, the Commission has conducted a review of block exemption regulations, Commission notices and guidelines, with a view to further assist self-assessment by economic operators. The Commission has also produced guidelines on the application of Article 81(3).[4] This allows undertakings in the vast majority of cases to reliably assess their agreements with regard to Article 81. Furthermore, it is the practice of the Commission to impose more than symbolic fines[5] only in cases where it is established, either in horizontal instruments or in the case law and practice that a certain behaviour constitutes an infringement.

5. Where cases, despite the above elements, give rise to genuine uncertainty because they present novel or unresolved questions for the application of Articles 81 and 82, individual undertakings may wish to seek informal guidance from the Commission.[6] Where it considers it appropriate and subject to its enforcement priorities, the Commission may provide such guidance on novel questions concerning the interpretation of Articles 81 and/or 82 in a written statement (guidance letter). The present Notice sets out details of this instrument.

NOTES

1 Council Regulation (EC) No 1/2003 of 16 December 2002 on the implementation of the rules on competition laid down in Articles 81 and 82 of the Treaty (OJ L1, 4.1.2003, p 1).

2 In this Notice, the term "agreement" is used for agreements, decisions by associations of undertakings and concerted practices. The term "practices" refers to the conduct of dominant undertakings. The term "undertakings" equally covers "associations of undertakings".

3 All texts mentioned are available at: europa.eu.int/comm/competition/index_en.html

4 Commission Notice – Guidelines on the application of Article 81(3) of the Treaty (p 97).

5 Symbolic fines are normally set at 1000 EUR, cf. Commission Guidelines on the method of setting fines imposed pursuant to Article 15(2) of Regulation No 17 and Article 65(5) of the ECSC Treaty, (OJ C9, 14.1.1998).

6 Cf. Recital 38 of Regulation 1/2003.

II. FRAMEWORK FOR ASSESSING WHETHER TO ISSUE A GUIDANCE LETTER

[4.340]

6. Regulation 1/2003 confers powers on the Commission to effectively prosecute infringements of Articles 81 and 82 and to impose sanctions.[7] One major objective of the Regulation is to ensure efficient enforcement of the EC competition rules by removing the former notification system and thus allowing the Commission to focus its enforcement policy on the most serious infringements.[8]

7. While Regulation 1/2003 is without prejudice to the ability of the Commission to issue informal guidance to individual undertakings,[9] as set out in this Notice, this ability should not interfere with the primary objective of the Regulation, which is to ensure effective enforcement. The Commission may therefore only provide informal guidance to individual undertakings in so far as this is compatible with its enforcement priorities.

8. Subject to point 7, the Commission, seized of a request for a guidance letter, will consider whether it is appropriate to process it. Issuing a guidance letter may only be considered if the following cumulative conditions are fulfilled:

(a) The substantive assessment of an agreement or practice with regard to Articles 81 and/or 82 of the Treaty, poses a question of application of the law for which there is no clarification in the existing EC legal framework including the case law of the Community Courts, nor publicly available general guidance or precedent in decision-making practice or previous guidance letters.

(b) A prima facie evaluation of the specificities and background of the case suggests that the clarification of the novel question through a guidance letter is useful, taking into account the following elements:

— the economic importance from the point of view of the consumer of the goods or services concerned by the agreement or practice, and/or

— the extent to which the agreement or practice corresponds or is liable to correspond to more widely spread economic usage in the marketplace and/or

— the extent of the investments linked to the transaction in relation to the size of the companies concerned and the extent to which the transaction relates to a structural operation such as the creation of a non-full function joint venture.

(c) It is possible to issue a guidance letter on the basis of the information provided, ie no further fact-finding is required.

9. Furthermore, the Commission will not consider a request for a guidance letter in either of the following circumstances:

— the questions raised in the request are identical or similar to issues raised in a case pending before the European Court of First Instance or the European Court of Justice;

— the agreement or practice to which the request refers is subject to proceedings pending with the Commission, a Member State court or Member State competition authority.

10. The Commission will not consider hypothetical questions and will not issue guidance letters on agreements or practices that are no longer being implemented by the parties. Undertakings may however present a request for a guidance letter to the Commission in relation to questions raised by an agreement or practice that they envisage, ie before the implementation of that agreement or practice. In this case the transaction must have reached a sufficiently advanced stage for a request to be considered.

11. A request for a guidance letter is without prejudice to the power of the Commission to open proceedings in accordance with Regulation 1/2003 with regard to the facts presented in the request.

NOTES

[7] Cf. in particular Articles 7 to 9, 12, 17–24, 29 of Regulation 1/2003.

[8] Cf. in particular Recital 3 of Regulation 1/2003.

[9] Cf. Recital 38 of Regulation 1/2003.

III. INDICATIONS ON HOW TO REQUEST GUIDANCE

[4.341]

12. A request can be presented by an undertaking or undertakings which have entered into or intend to enter into an agreement or practice that could fall within the scope of Articles 81 and/or 82 of the Treaty with regard to questions of interpretation raised by such agreement or practice.

13. A request for a guidance letter should be addressed to the following address:

Commission Européenne/Europese Commissie
Competition DG
B–1049 Bruxelles/Brussel.

14. There is no form. A memorandum should be presented which clearly states:

— the identity of all undertakings concerned as well as a single address for contacts with the Commission;

— the specific questions on which guidance is sought;

— full and exhaustive information on all points relevant for an informed evaluation of the questions raised, including pertinent documentation;

— a detailed reasoning, having regard to point 8 a), why the request presents (a) novel question(s);

— all other information that permits an evaluation of the request in the light of the aspects explained in points 8–10 of this Notice, including in particular a declaration that the agreement or practice to which the request refers is not subject to proceedings pending before a Member State court or competition authority;

— where the request contains elements that are considered business secrets, a clear identification of these elements;

— any other information or documentation relevant to the individual case.

IV. PROCESSING OF THE REQUEST

[4.342]

15. The Commission will in principle evaluate the request on the basis of the information provided. Notwithstanding point 8 c), the Commission may use additional information at its disposal from public sources, former proceedings or any other source and may ask the applicant(s) to provide supplementary information. The normal rules on professional secrecy apply to the information supplied by the applicant(s).

16. The Commission may share the information submitted to it with the Member States' competition authorities and receive input from them. It may discuss the substance of the request with the Member States' competition authorities before issuing a guidance letter.

17. Where no guidance letter is issued, the Commission shall inform the applicant(s) accordingly.

18. An undertaking can withdraw its request at any point in time. In any case, information supplied in the context of a request for guidance remains with the Commission and can be used in subsequent procedures under Regulation 1/2003 (cf. point 11 above).

V. GUIDANCE LETTERS

[4.343]

19. A guidance letter sets out:
— a summary description of the facts on which it is based;
— the principal legal reasoning underlying the understanding of the Commission on novel questions relating to Articles 81 and/or 82 raised by the request.

20. A guidance letter may be limited to part of the questions raised in the request. It may also include additional aspects to those set out in the request.

21. Guidance letters will be posted on the Commission's web-site, having regard to the legitimate interest of undertakings in the protection of their business secrets. Before issuing a guidance letter, the Commission will agree with the applicants on a public version.

VI. THE EFFECTS OF GUIDANCE LETTERS

[4.344]

22. Guidance letters are in the first place intended to help undertakings carry out themselves an informed assessment of their agreements and practices.

23. A guidance letter cannot prejudge the assessment of the same question by the Community Courts.

24. Where an agreement or practice has formed the factual basis for a guidance letter, the Commission is not precluded from subsequently examining that same agreement or practice in a procedure under Regulation 1/2003, in particular following a complaint. In that case, the Commission will take the previous guidance letter into account, subject in particular to changes in the underlying facts, to any new aspects raised by a complaint, to developments in the case law of the European Courts or wider changes of the Commission's policy.

25. Guidance letters are not Commission decisions and do not bind Member States' competition authorities or courts that have the power to apply Articles 81 and 82. However, it is open to Member States' competition authorities and courts to take account of guidance letters issued by the Commission as they see fit in the context of a case.

DECISION OF THE PRESIDENT OF THE EUROPEAN COMMISSION

(2011/695/EU)

of 13 October 2011

on the function and terms of reference of the hearing officer in certain competition proceedings

(Text with EEA relevance)

[4.345]

NOTES

Date of publication in OJ: OJ L275, 20.10.2011, p 29.

This Decision repeals and replaces Commission Decision 2001/462/EC on the terms of reference of hearing officers in certain competition proceedings (OJ L162, 19.6.2001, p 21). By Article 18 of this Decision at **[4.363]**, procedural steps already taken under the 2001 Decision shall continue to have effect in relation to investigatory measures that were taken before 21 October 2011.

Application of this Decision to the United Kingdom: in accordance with the European Union (Withdrawal) Act 2018, s 3 at **[7.5]**, this Decision became domestic law on IP completion day (as defined in the European Union (Withdrawal Agreement) Act 2020, s 39).

THE PRESIDENT OF THE EUROPEAN COMMISSION,

Having regard to the Treaty on European Union,

Having regard to the Treaty on the Functioning of the European Union,

Having regard to the Agreement on the European Economic Area,

Having regard to the Rules of Procedure of the Commission,[1] and in particular Article 22 thereof,

Whereas:

(1) Under the system for competition law enforcement established under the Treaty on the Functioning of the European Union (hereinafter 'the Treaty'), the Commission investigates and decides on cases by administrative decision, subject to judicial review by the Court of Justice of the European Union (hereinafter 'the Court of Justice').

(2) The Commission has to conduct its competition proceedings fairly, impartially and objectively and must ensure respect of the procedural rights of the parties concerned as set out in Council Regulation (EC) No 1/2003 of 16 December 2002 on the implementation of the rules on competition laid down in Articles 81 and 82 of the Treaty,[2] Council Regulation (EC) No 139/2004 of 20 January 2004 on the control of concentrations between undertakings (the EC Merger Regulation),[3] Commission Regulation (EC) No 773/2004 of 7 April 2004 relating to the conduct of proceedings by the Commission pursuant to Articles 81 and 82 of the EC Treaty,[4] and Commission Regulation (EC) No 802/2004 of 7 April 2004 implementing Council Regulation (EC) No 139/2004 on the control of

concentrations between undertakings,[5] as well as in the relevant case-law of the Court of Justice. In particular, the right of the parties concerned to be heard before the adoption of any individual decision adversely affecting them is a fundamental right of European Union law recognised by the Charter of Fundamental Rights, and in particular Article 41 thereof.[6]

(3) In order to ensure the effective exercise of the procedural rights of the parties concerned, other involved parties within the meaning of Article 11(b) of Regulation (EC) No 802/2004 (hereinafter 'other involved parties'), complainants within the meaning of Article 7(2) of Regulation (EC) No 1/2003 (hereinafter 'complainants') and persons other than those referred to in Articles 5 and 11 of Regulation (EC) No 773/2004 and third persons within the meaning of Article 11 of Regulation (EC) No 802/2004 (hereinafter 'third persons') involved in competition proceedings, responsibility for safeguarding the observance of such rights should be entrusted to an independent person experienced in competition matters who has the integrity necessary to contribute to the objectivity, transparency and efficiency of those proceedings.

(4) The Commission created the function of hearing officer for these purposes in 1982, revised it in Commission Decision 94/810/ECSC, EC of 12 December 1994 on the terms of reference of hearing officers in competition procedures before the Commission[7] and in Commission Decision 2001/462/EC, ECSC of 23 May 2001 on the terms of reference of hearing officers in certain competition proceedings.[8] It is now necessary to clarify and further strengthen the role of the hearing officer and to adapt the terms of reference of the hearing officer in the light of developments in Union competition law.

(5) The function of the hearing officer has been generally perceived as an important contribution to the competition proceedings before the Commission due to the independence and expertise that hearing officers have brought to these proceedings. In order to ensure the continued independence of the hearing officer from the Directorate-General for Competition, he or she should be attached, for administrative purposes, to the member of the Commission with special responsibility for competition.

(6) The hearing officer should be appointed in accordance with the rules laid down in the Staff Regulations of Officials and the Conditions of Employment of Other Servants of the European Union. In accordance with those rules, consideration may also be given to candidates who are not officials of the Commission. Transparency as regards the appointment, termination of appointment and transfer of hearing officers should be ensured.

(7) The Commission may appoint one or more hearing officers and should provide for their supporting staff. Where the hearing officer perceives a conflict of interests in the performance of his or her functions, the hearing officer should cease from acting on a case. If the hearing officer is unable to act, his or her role should be carried out by another hearing officer.

(8) The hearing officer should operate as an independent arbiter who seeks to resolve issues affecting the effective exercise of the procedural rights of the parties concerned, other involved parties, complainants or interested third persons where such issues could not be resolved through prior contacts with the Commission services responsible for the conduct of competition proceedings, which must respect these procedural rights.

(9) The terms of reference of the hearing officer in competition proceedings should be framed in such a way as to safeguard the effective exercise of procedural rights throughout proceedings before the Commission pursuant to Articles 101 and 102 of the Treaty and Regulation (EC) No 139/2004, in particular the right to be heard.

(10) In order to strengthen this role, the hearing officer should be attributed with the function of safeguarding the effective exercise of procedural rights of undertakings and associations of undertakings in the context of the Commission's powers of investigation under Chapter V of Regulation (EC) No 1/2003, as well as pursuant to Article 14 of Regulation (EC) No 139/2004 which empowers the Commission to impose fines on undertakings and associations of undertakings. The hearing officer should also be attributed with specific functions during this investigative phase in relation to claims for legal professional privilege, the privilege against self-incrimination, deadlines for replying to decisions requesting information pursuant to Article 18(3) of Regulation (EC) No 1/2003, as well as with regard to the right of undertakings and associations of undertakings subject to an investigative measure by the Commission under Chapter V of Regulation (EC) No 1/2003 to be informed of their procedural status, namely whether they are subject to an investigation and, if so, the subject matter and purpose of that investigation. In assessing claims made in relation to privilege against self-incrimination, the hearing officer may consider whether undertakings make clearly unfounded claims for protection merely as a delaying tactic.

(11) The hearing officer should be able to facilitate the resolution of claims that a document is covered by legal professional privilege. To this end, if the undertaking or association of undertakings making the claim agrees, the hearing officer will be allowed to examine the document concerned and make an appropriate recommendation, referring to the applicable case-law of the Court of Justice.

(12) The hearing officer should be responsible for deciding whether a third person shows a sufficient interest to be heard. Consumer associations that apply to be heard should be generally regarded as having a sufficient interest, where the proceedings concern products or services used by end-consumers or products or services that constitute a direct input into such products or services.

(13) The hearing officer should decide whether to admit complainants and interested third persons to the oral hearing, taking into account the contribution they can make to the clarification of the relevant facts of the case.

(14) The right of the parties concerned to be heard before a final decision adversely affecting their interests is taken is guaranteed through their right to reply in writing to the preliminary position of the Commission, as set out in the statement of objections and their right to develop their arguments, if they so request, at the oral hearing. In order to exercise these rights effectively, parties to whom a statement of objections has been addressed have the right of access to the Commission's investigation file.

(15) In order to safeguard the effective exercise of the rights of defence of parties to whom a statement of objections has been addressed, the hearing officer should be responsible for ensuring that disputes about access to the file or about the protection of business secrets and other confidential information between those parties and the Commission's Directorate-General for Competition are resolved. In exceptional circumstances, the hearing officer may suspend the running of the time period in which an addressee of a statement of objections should reply to that

statement until a dispute about access to file has been resolved, if the addressee would not be in a position to reply within the deadline granted and an extension would not be an adequate solution at that point in time.

(16) In order to safeguard the effective exercise of procedural rights while respecting the legitimate interests of confidentiality, the hearing officer should, where appropriate, be able to order specific measures for access to the Commission's file. In particular, the hearing officer should have the power to decide that parts of the file are made accessible to the party requesting access in a restricted manner, for example by limiting the number or category of persons having access, and the use of the information being accessed.

(17) The hearing officer should be responsible for deciding on requests for the extension of time limits set for the reply to a statement of objections, a supplementary statement of objections or a letter of facts or time limits within which other involved parties, complainants or interested third persons may make comments, in case of disagreement between any such person and the Directorate-General for Competition.

(18) The hearing officer should promote the effectiveness of the oral hearing, by, inter alia, taking all appropriate preparatory measures, including the circulation, in due time before the hearing, of a provisional list of participants and a provisional agenda.

(19) The oral hearing allows the parties to whom the Commission has addressed a statement of objections and other involved parties to further exercise their right to be heard by developing their arguments orally before the Commission, which should be represented by the Directorate-General for Competition as well as other services that contribute to the further preparation of a decision to be taken by the Commission. It should provide an additional opportunity to ensure that all relevant facts – whether favourable or unfavourable to the parties concerned, including the factual elements relating to the gravity and duration of the alleged infringement – are clarified as much as possible. The oral hearing should also allow the parties to present their arguments as to the matters that may be of importance for the possible imposition of fines.

(20) To ensure the effectiveness of oral hearings, the hearing officer may allow the parties to whom a statement of objections has been addressed, other involved parties, complainants, other persons invited to the hearing, the Commission services and the authorities of the Member States to ask questions during the hearing. The oral hearing should not be public so as to guarantee that all participants can express themselves freely. Therefore, information disclosed during the oral hearing should not be used for a purpose other than judicial and/or administrative proceedings for the application of Articles 101 and 102 of the Treaty. Where justified to protect business secrets and other confidential information, the hearing officer should be able to hear persons in a closed session.

(21) Parties to the proceedings which offer commitments pursuant to Article 9 of Regulation (EC) No 1/2003, as well as parties which engage in settlement procedures in cartel cases pursuant to Article 10a of Regulation (EC) No 773/2004, should be able to call upon the hearing officer in relation to the effective exercise of their procedural rights.

(22) The hearing officer should report on the respect for the effective exercise of procedural rights throughout competition proceedings. Moreover, and separately from his or her reporting function, the hearing officer should also be able to make observations on the further progress and objectivity of the proceedings and thereby contribute to ensuring that competition proceedings are concluded on the basis of a sound assessment of all relevant facts.

(23) When disclosing information about natural persons, the hearing officer should have regard, in particular, to Regulation (EC) No 45/2001 of the European Parliament and of the Council of 18 December 2000 on the protection of individuals with regard to the processing of personal data by the Community institutions and bodies and on the free movement of such data.[9]

(24) Decision 2001/462/EC, ECSC should be repealed,

NOTES

[1] OJ L308, 8.12.2000, p 26.

[2] OJ L1, 4.1.2003, p 1.

[3] OJ L24, 29.1.2004, p 1.

[4] OJ L123, 27.4.2004, p 18.

[5] OJ L133, 30.4.2004, p 1.

[6] OJ C303, 14.12.2007, p 1.

[7] OJ L330, 21.12.1994, p 67.

[8] OJ L162, 19.6.2001, p 21.

[9] OJ L8, 12.1.2001, p 1.

HAS DECIDED AS FOLLOWS:

CHAPTER 1 ROLE, APPOINTMENT AND DUTIES OF THE HEARING OFFICER

[4.346]

Article 1

The Hearing Officer

1. There shall be one or more hearing officers for competition proceedings, whose powers and functions are laid down in the present decision.

2. The hearing officer shall safeguard the effective exercise of procedural rights throughout competition proceedings before the Commission for the implementation of Articles 101 and 102 of the Treaty, and under Regulation (EC) No 139/2004 (hereinafter 'competition proceedings').

[4.347]
Article 2
Appointment, Termination of Appointment and Deputising

1. The Commission shall appoint the hearing officer. The appointment shall be published in the *Official Journal of the European Union*. Any interruption, termination or transfer of the hearing officer shall be the subject of a reasoned decision of the Commission. That decision shall be published in the *Official Journal of the European Union*.
2. The hearing officer shall be attached, for administrative purposes, to the member of the Commission with special responsibility for competition (hereinafter 'the competent member of the Commission').
3. Where the hearing officer is unable to act, his or her role shall be carried out by another hearing officer. If no hearing officer is able to act, the competent member of the Commission, where appropriate after consultation of the hearing officer, shall designate another competent Commission official, who is not involved in the case in question, to carry out the hearing officer's duties.
4. In case of an actual or potential conflict of interests, the hearing officer shall refrain from acting on a case. Paragraph 3 shall apply.

[4.348]
Article 3
Method of Operation

1. In exercising his or her functions, the hearing officer shall act independently.
2. In exercising his or her functions, the hearing officer shall take account of the need for effective application of the competition rules in accordance with Union legislation in force and the principles laid down by the Court of Justice.
3. In exercising his or her functions, the hearing officer shall have access to any files relating to competition proceedings.
4. The hearing officer shall be kept informed by the director responsible for investigating the case in the Directorate-General for Competition (hereinafter 'the director responsible') about the development of the procedure.
5. The hearing officer may present observations on any matter arising out of any Commission competition proceeding to the competent member of the Commission.
6. If the hearing officer makes reasoned recommendations to the competent member of the Commission or takes decisions as foreseen in this decision, the hearing officer shall provide a copy of these documents to the director responsible and the Legal Service of the Commission.
7. Any issue regarding the effective exercise of the procedural rights of the parties concerned, other involved parties within the meaning of Article 11(b) of Regulation (EC) No 802/2004 (hereinafter 'the other involved parties'), complainants within the meaning of Article 7(2) of Regulation (EC) No 1/2003 (hereinafter 'complainants') and interested third persons within the meaning of Article 5 of this Decision involved in such proceedings shall first be raised by those persons with the Directorate-General for Competition. If the issue is not resolved, it may be referred to the hearing officer for independent review. Requests related to a measure for which a time limit applies must be made in due time, within the original time limit.

CHAPTER 2 INVESTIGATION

[4.349]
Article 4
Procedural rights in the investigation phase

1. The hearing officer shall safeguard the effective exercise of procedural rights which arise in the context of the exercise of the Commission's powers of investigation under Chapter V of Regulation (EC) No 1/2003 and in proceedings that can result in the imposition of fines pursuant to Article 14 of Regulation (EC) No 139/2004.
2. In particular, the hearing officer shall have the following functions, subject to Article 3(7):
   (a) The hearing officer may be asked by undertakings or associations of undertakings to examine claims that a document required by the Commission in the exercise of powers conferred on it pursuant to Article 18, 20 or 21 of Regulation (EC) No 1/2003, in inspections pursuant to Article 13 of Regulation (EC) No 139/2004 or in the context of investigatory measures in proceedings that can result in the imposition of fines pursuant to Article 14 of Regulation (EC) No 139/2004 and which was withheld from the Commission is covered by legal professional privilege, within the meaning of the case-law of the Court of Justice. The hearing officer may only review the matter if the undertaking or association of undertakings making the claim consent to the hearing officer viewing the information claimed to be covered by legal professional privilege as well as related documents that the hearing officer considers necessary for his or her review. Without revealing the potentially privileged content of the information, the hearing officer shall communicate to the director responsible and the undertaking or association of undertakings concerned his or her preliminary view, and may take appropriate steps to promote a mutually acceptable resolution. Where no resolution is reached, the hearing officer may formulate a reasoned recommendation to the competent member of the Commission, without revealing the potentially privileged content of the document. The party making the claim shall receive a copy of this recommendation.
   (b) Where the addressee of a request for information pursuant to Article 18(2) of Regulation (EC) No 1/2003 refuses to reply to a question in such a request invoking the privilege against self-incrimination, as determined by the case-law of the Court of Justice, it may refer the matter, in due time following the receipt of the request, to the hearing officer. In appropriate cases, and having regard to the need to avoid undue delay in proceedings, the hearing officer may make a reasoned recommendation as to whether the privilege against self-incrimination applies and inform the director responsible of the conclusions drawn, to be taken into account in case of any decision taken subsequently pursuant to Article 18(3) of Regulation (EC) No 1/2003. The addressee of the request shall receive a copy of the reasoned recommendation.
   (c) Where the addressee of a decision requesting information pursuant to Article 18(3) of Regulation (EC) No 1/2003 considers that the time limit imposed for its reply is too short, it may refer the matter to the hearing

officer, in due time before the expiry of the original time limit set. The hearing officer shall decide on whether an extension of the time limit should be granted, taking account of the length and complexity of the request for information and the requirements of the investigation.

(d) Undertakings or associations of undertakings subject to an investigative measure by the Commission under Chapter V of Regulation (EC) No 1/2003 shall have the right to be informed of their procedural status, namely whether they are subject to an investigation and, if so, the subject matter and purpose of that investigation. If such an undertaking or association of undertakings considers that it has not been properly informed by the Directorate-General for Competition of its procedural status, it may refer the matter to the hearing officer for resolution. The hearing officer shall take a decision that the Directorate-General for Competition will inform the undertaking or association of undertakings that made the request of their procedural status. This decision shall be communicated to the undertaking or association of undertakings that made the request.

CHAPTER 3 APPLICATIONS TO BE HEARD

[4.350]
Article 5
Interested third persons

1. Applications to be heard from persons other than those referred to in Articles 5 and 11 of Regulation (EC) No 773/2004 and third persons within the meaning of Article 11 of Regulation (EC) No 802/2004 (hereinafter 'third persons') shall be made in accordance with Article 13(1) of Regulation (EC) No 773/2004 and Article 16 of Regulation (EC) No 802/2004. Applications shall be submitted in writing and explain the applicant's interest in the outcome of the procedure.
2. The hearing officer shall decide as to whether third persons are to be heard after consulting the director responsible. In assessing whether a third person shows a sufficient interest, the hearing officer shall take into account whether and to what extent the applicant is sufficiently affected by the conduct which is the subject of the competition proceedings or whether the applicant fulfils the requirements of Article 18(4) of Regulation (EC) No 139/2004.
3. Where the hearing officer considers that an applicant has not shown a sufficient interest to be heard, he or she shall inform the applicant in writing of the reasons thereof. A time limit shall be fixed within which the applicant may make known its views in writing. If the applicant makes known its views in writing within the time limit set by the hearing officer and the written submission does not lead to a different assessment, that finding shall be stated in a reasoned decision which shall be notified to the applicant.
4. The hearing officer shall inform parties to competition proceedings as from the initiation of proceedings pursuant to Article 11(6) of Regulation (EC) No 1/2003 or Article 6(1)(c) of Regulation (EC) No 139/2004 of the identities of interested third persons to be heard, unless such disclosure would significantly harm a person or undertaking.

[4.351]
Article 6
Right to an oral hearing; participation of complainants and third persons in the oral hearing

1. At the request of parties to whom the Commission has addressed a statement of objections or other involved parties, the hearing officer shall conduct an oral hearing so that such parties can further develop their written submissions.
2. The hearing officer may, where appropriate and after consulting the director responsible, decide to afford complainants and interested third persons within the meaning of Article 5 the opportunity to express their views at the oral hearing of the parties to which a statement of objections has been issued, provided they so request in their written comments. The hearing officer may also invite representatives from competition authorities from third countries to attend the oral hearing as observers in accordance with agreements concluded between the Union and third countries.

CHAPTER 4 ACCESS TO FILE, CONFIDENTIALITY AND BUSINESS SECRETS

[4.352]
Article 7
Access to File and Access to Documents and Information

1. Where a party which has exercised its right of access to the file has reason to believe that the Commission has in its possession documents which have not been disclosed to it and that those documents are necessary for the proper exercise of the right to be heard, it may make a reasoned request for access to these documents to the hearing officer, subject to Article 3(7).
2. Subject to Article 3(7), other involved parties, complainants and interested third persons within the meaning of Article 5 may make a reasoned request to the hearing officer in the circumstances listed hereafter:
   (a) Other involved parties who have reason to believe that they have not been informed of the objections addressed to the notifying parties in accordance with Article 13(2) of Regulation (EC) No 802/2004.
   (b) A complainant who has been informed by the Commission of its intention to reject a complaint pursuant to Article 7(1) of Regulation (EC) No 773/2004 and has reason to believe that the Commission has in its possession documents which have not been disclosed to it and that those documents are necessary for the proper exercise of its rights in accordance with Article 8(1) of Regulation (EC) No 773/2004.
   (c) A complainant who considers that it has not received a copy of the non-confidential version of the statement of objections in accordance with Article 6(1) of Regulation (EC) No 773/2004 or that the non-confidential version of the statement of objections has not been established in a manner which enables it to exercise its rights effectively, with the exception of cases where the settlement procedure applies.
   (d) An interested third person within the meaning of Article 5 of this Decision who has reason to believe that it has not been informed of the nature and subject matter of a procedure in accordance with Article 13(1) of Regulation (EC) No 773/2004 and Article 16(1) of Regulation (EC) No 802/2004. The same applies to a complainant in a case to which the settlement procedure applies who has reason to believe that it has not been informed of the nature and subject matter of the procedure in accordance with Article 6(1) of Regulation (EC) No 773/2004.

3. The hearing officer shall take a reasoned decision on a request addressed to him or her under paragraph 1 or 2 and communicate such decision to the person that made the request and to any other person concerned by the procedure.

[4.353]
Article 8
Business secrets and other confidential information

1. Where the Commission intends to disclose information which may constitute a business secret or other confidential information of any undertaking or person, the latter shall be informed in writing of this intention and the reasons thereof by the Directorate-General for Competition. A time limit shall be fixed within which the undertaking or person concerned may submit any written comments.
2. Where the undertaking or person concerned objects to the disclosure of the information it may refer the matter to the hearing officer. If the hearing officer finds that the information may be disclosed because it does not constitute a business secret or other confidential information or because there is an overriding interest in its disclosure that finding shall be stated in a reasoned decision which shall be notified to the undertaking or person concerned. The decision shall specify the date after which the information will be disclosed. This date shall not be less than 1 week from the date of notification.
3. Paragraphs 1 and 2 shall apply *mutatis mutandis* to the disclosure of information by publication in the *Official Journal of the European Union*.
4. Where appropriate in order to balance the effective exercise of a party's rights of defence with legitimate interests of confidentiality, the hearing officer may decide that parts of the file which are indispensable for the exercise of the party's rights of defence will be made accessible to the party requesting access in a restricted manner, the details of which shall be determined by the hearing officer.

CHAPTER 5 EXTENSION OF TIME LIMITS

[4.354]
Article 9
Requests for extension of time limits

1. If an addressee of a statement of objections considers that the time limit imposed for its reply to the statement of objections is too short, it may seek an extension of that time limit by means of a reasoned request addressed to the director responsible. Such a request must be made in due time before the expiry of the original time limit in proceedings pursuant to Articles 101 and 102 of the Treaty and at least 5 working days before the expiry of the original time limit in proceedings under Regulation (EC) No 139/2004. If such a request is not granted or the addressee of the statement of objections making the request disagrees with the length of the extension granted, it may refer the matter to the hearing officer for review before the expiry of the original time limit. After hearing the director responsible, the hearing officer shall decide on whether an extension of the time limit is necessary to allow the addressee of a statement of objections to exercise its right to be heard effectively, while also having regard to the need to avoid undue delay in proceedings. In proceedings pursuant to Articles 101 and 102 of the Treaty, the hearing officer shall take into account, among others, the following elements:
   (a) the size and complexity of the file;
   (b) whether the addressee of the statement of objections making the request has had prior access to information;
   (c) any other objective obstacles which may be faced by the addressee of the statement of objections making the request in providing its observations.

For the purposes of assessing point (a) of the first subparagraph, the number of infringements, the alleged duration of the infringement(s), the size and number of documents and the size and complexity of expert studies may be taken into consideration.
2. If other involved parties, a complainant or an interested third person within the meaning of Article 5 considers that the time limit to make its views known is too short, it may seek an extension of that time limit by means of a reasoned request addressed to the director responsible in due time before the expiry of the original time limit. If such a request is not granted or the other involved party, complainant or interested third person disagrees with this decision, it may refer the matter to the hearing officer for review. After hearing the director responsible, the hearing officer shall decide on whether an extension of the time limit should be granted.

CHAPTER 6 THE ORAL HEARING

[4.355]
Article 10
Organisation and function

1. The hearing officer shall organise and conduct the hearings provided for in the provisions implementing Articles 101 and 102 of the Treaty and Regulation (EC) No 139/2004.
2. The oral hearing shall be conducted by the hearing officer in full independence.
3. The hearing officer shall ensure that the hearing is properly conducted and shall contribute to the objectivity of the hearing itself and of any decision taken subsequently.
4. The hearing officer shall ensure that the oral hearing provides addressees of the statement of objections, other involved parties, as well as complainants and interested third persons within the meaning of Article 5 which have been admitted to the oral hearing, with sufficient opportunity to develop their views as to the preliminary findings of the Commission.

[4.356]
Article 11
Preparation of the oral hearing

1. The hearing officer shall be responsible for the preparation of the oral hearing and shall take all appropriate measures in that regard. In order to ensure the proper preparation of the oral hearing, the hearing officer may, after consulting the director responsible, supply in advance to the persons invited to the hearing a list of questions on which

they are invited to make known their views. The hearing officer may also indicate to the persons invited to the hearing the focal areas for debate, having regard, in particular, to the facts and issues that the addressees of a statement of objections who have requested an oral hearing want to raise.

2. For this purpose, after consulting the director responsible, the hearing officer may hold a meeting with the persons invited to the hearing and, where appropriate, the Commission services, in order to prepare for the hearing itself.

3. The hearing officer may also ask for prior written notification of the essential contents of the intended statements of persons invited to the hearing.

4. The hearing officer may set a time limit for all persons invited to the oral hearing to provide a list of participants who will attend on their behalf. The hearing officer shall make this list available to all persons invited to the oral hearing in due time before the date of the hearing.

[4.357]
Article 12
Timing and conduct

1. After consulting the director responsible, the hearing officer shall determine the date, the duration and the place of the hearing. Where a postponement is requested, the hearing officer shall decide whether or not to allow it.

2. The hearing officer shall decide whether new documents should be admitted during the hearing and which persons should be heard on behalf of a party.

3. The hearing officer may allow the parties to whom a statement of objections has been addressed, other involved parties, complainants, other persons invited to the hearing, the Commission services and the authorities of the Member States to ask questions during the hearing. To the extent that, exceptionally, a question cannot be answered in whole or in part at the oral hearing, the hearing officer may allow the reply to be given in writing within a set time limit. Such written reply shall be distributed to all participants in the oral hearing, unless the hearing officer decides otherwise in order to protect the rights of defence of an addressee of a statement of objections or the business secrets or other confidential information of any person.

4. Where required by the need to ensure the right to be heard, the hearing officer may, after consulting the director responsible, afford the parties concerned, other involved parties, complainants or interested third persons within the meaning of Article 5 the opportunity to submit further written comments after the oral hearing. The hearing officer shall fix a date by which such submissions may be made. The Commission shall not be obliged to take into account written comments received after that date.

[4.358]
Article 13
Protection of business secrets and confidentiality at the oral hearing

Each person shall normally be heard in the presence of all other persons invited to attend the oral hearing. The hearing officer may also decide to hear persons separately in a closed session, having regard to their legitimate interest in the protection of their business secrets and other confidential information.

CHAPTER 7 INTERIM REPORT AND RIGHT TO MAKE OBSERVATIONS

[4.359]
Article 14
Interim report and observations

1. The hearing officer shall submit an interim report to the competent member of the Commission on the hearing and the conclusions he or she draws with regard to the respect for the effective exercise of procedural rights. The observations in this report shall concern procedural issues including the following:
   (a) disclosure of documents and access to the file;
   (b) time limits for replying to the statement of objections;
   (c) the observance of the right to be heard;
   (d) the proper conduct of the oral hearing.

A copy of the report shall be given to the Director-General for Competition, to the director responsible and to the other competent services of the Commission.

2. In addition to, and separately from, the report referred to in paragraph 1, the hearing officer may make observations on the further progress and impartiality of the proceedings. In so doing, the hearing officer shall seek to ensure in particular that, in the preparation of draft Commission decisions, due account is taken of all the relevant facts, whether favourable or unfavourable to the parties concerned, including the factual elements relevant to the gravity and duration of any infringement. Such observations may relate to, inter alia, the need for further information, the withdrawal of certain objections, the formulation of further objections or suggestions for further investigative measures pursuant to Chapter V of Regulation (EC) No 1/2003.

The Director-General for Competition, the director responsible and the Legal Service shall be informed of such observations.

CHAPTER 8 COMMITMENTS AND SETTLEMENTS

[4.360]
Article 15
Commitments and settlements

1. Parties to the proceedings which offer commitments to meet the concerns expressed to them by the Commission in its preliminary assessment pursuant to Article 9 of Regulation (EC) No 1/2003 may call upon the hearing officer at any stage in the procedure pursuant to Article 9, in order to ensure the effective exercise of their procedural rights.

2. Parties to proceedings in cartel cases which engage in settlement discussions pursuant to Article 10a of Regulation (EC) No 773/2004 may call upon the hearing officer at any stage during the settlement procedure in order to ensure the effective exercise of their procedural rights.

CHAPTER 9 FINAL REPORT

[4.361]
Article 16
Content and transmission prior to the adoption of a decision

1. The hearing officer shall, on the basis of the draft decision to be submitted to the Advisory Committee in the case in question, prepare a final report in writing on the respect for the effective exercise of procedural rights, as referred to in Article 14(1), at any stage of the proceedings. That report will also consider whether the draft decision deals only with objections in respect of which the parties have been afforded the opportunity of making known their views.
2. The final report shall be submitted to the competent member of the Commission, the Director-General for Competition, the director responsible and the other competent services of the Commission. It shall be communicated to the competent authorities of the Member States and, in accordance with the provisions on cooperation laid down in Protocols 23 and 24 of the EEA Agreement, to the EFTA Surveillance Authority.

[4.362]
Article 17
Submission to the Commission and publication

1. The hearing officer's final report shall be presented to the Commission together with the draft decision submitted to it, in order to ensure that, when it reaches a decision on an individual case, the Commission is fully apprised of all relevant information as to the course of the procedure and that the effective exercise of procedural rights has been respected throughout the proceedings.
2. The final report may be modified by the hearing officer in the light of any amendments to the draft decision prior to its adoption by the Commission.
3. The Commission shall communicate the hearing officer's final report, together with the decision, to the addressees of the decision. It shall publish the hearing officer's final report in the *Official Journal of the European Union*, together with the decision, having regard to the legitimate interest of undertakings in the protection of their business secrets.

CHAPTER 10 FINAL PROVISIONS

[4.363]
Article 18
Repeal and transitional provision

1. Decision 2001/462/EC, ECSC is repealed.
2. Procedural steps already taken under Decision 2001/462/EC, ECSC shall continue to have effect. In relation to investigatory measures that were taken before the entry into force of this Decision, the hearing officer may decline to exercise his or her powers pursuant to Article 4.
In cases where the initiation of proceedings pursuant to Article 11(6) of Regulation (EC) No 1/2003 or the initiation of proceedings pursuant to Article 6(1)(c) of Regulation (EC) No 139/2004 took place before the entry into force of the present Decision, the interim report pursuant to Article 14 of the present Decision and the final report pursuant to Article 16 shall not cover the investigation phase, unless the hearing officer decides otherwise.

[4.364]
Article 19
Entry into force

This Decision shall enter into force on the day following its publication in the *Official Journal of the European Union*.

COMMISSION NOTICE

(2011/C308/06)

on best practices for the conduct of proceedings concerning Articles 101 and 102 TFEU

(Text with EEA relevance)

[4.365]

NOTES

Date of publication in OJ: OJ C308, 20.10.2011, p 6.

1. SCOPE AND PURPOSE OF THE NOTICE

[4.366]

1. The principal purpose of this notice is to provide practical guidance on the conduct of proceedings before the European Commission (Commission) concerning Articles 101 and 102 of the Treaty on the Functioning of the European Union (TFEU)[1] in accordance with Regulation (EC) No 1/2003,[2] its Implementing Regulation[3] and the case law of the Court of Justice of the European Union. In this regard, the notice seeks to increase understanding of the Commission's investigation process[4] and thereby enhance the efficiency of investigations and ensure a high degree of transparency and predictability in the process. The notice covers the main proceedings[5] concerning alleged infringements of Articles 101 and 102 TFEU.

2. Infringement proceedings against Member States based notably on Article 106 TFEU in conjunction with Articles 101 and 102 TFEU fall outside the scope of this notice. Nor does it apply to proceedings under the Merger Regulation[6] or to State aid proceedings.[7]

3. Proceedings concerning the application of Articles 101 and 102 TFEU (hereafter generally referred to as 'proceedings') are in particular regulated by Regulation (EC) No 1/2003 and the Implementing Regulation. The Commission's notices on access to file[8] and handling of complaints,[9] as well as the terms of reference of the hearing officer[10] are also relevant for the conduct of proceedings. As regards submissions of reports of economic experts and submission of quantitative data, reference is made to the Best Practices on the submission of economic evidence.[11] This notice should therefore not be taken as an exhaustive account of all measures governing proceedings before the Commission. The notice should be read in conjunction with other such instruments and any relevant jurisprudence.

4. The investigation of cartels, as defined in the Leniency Notice,[12] may also be subject to the specific procedures on applications for leniency and on settlements.[13] These specific procedures are not covered by this notice. Moreover, the particular nature of cartel proceedings in some circumstances requires special provisions, in order not to interfere with possible leniency applications[14] or settlement discussions.[15] These special provisions are indicated where applicable.

5. This notice is structured in the following way. Section 2 sets out the procedure followed during the investigative phase. This part is relevant for any investigation regardless of whether it leads to a prohibition decision (Article 7 of Regulation (EC) No 1/2003), a commitment decision (Article 9 of Regulation (EC) No 1/2003) or a rejection of complaint decision (Article 7 of the Implementing Regulation). Section 3 describes the main procedural steps and rights of defence in the context of procedures leading to prohibition decisions. Section 4 describes the specific features of the commitment procedure. Section 5 covers rejection of complaints. The remaining sections are of general application: Section 6 describes the limits to use of information, Section 7 deals with the adoption, notification and publication of decisions and Section 8 with future revisions.

6. This notice is notably built upon the experience to date in the application of Regulation (EC) No 1/2003 and the Implementing Regulation. It reflects the views of the Commission at the time of publication and will be applied as from the date of publication for pending[16] and future cases. The specific features of an individual case may however require an adaptation of, or deviation from this notice, depending on the case at issue.

7. This notice does not create any new rights or obligations, nor alter, the rights or obligations which arise from the Treaty on the Functioning of the European Union (TFEU), Regulation (EC) No 1/2003, the Implementing Regulation and the case law of the Court of Justice of the European Union.

8. The Commission encourages the use of electronic information (e-mails or digital devices) for any case-related correspondence.

NOTES

1 With effect from 1 December 2009, Articles 81 and 82 of the EC Treaty have become Articles 101 and 102 respectively of the TFEU. The two sets of provisions are in substance identical. For the purposes of this document, references to Articles 101 and 102 TFEU should be understood as references to Articles 81 and 82 of the EC Treaty when appropriate.

2 Council Regulation (EC) No 1/2003 of 16 December 2002 on the implementation of the rules on competition laid down in Articles 81 and 82 of the Treaty (OJ L1, 4.1.2003, p 1), as amended by Council Regulation (EC) No 411/2004 of 26 February 2004 repealing Regulation (EEC) No 3975/87 and amending Regulations (EEC) No 3976/87 and (EC) No 1/2003, in connection with air transport between the Community and third countries (OJ L68, 6.3.2004, p 1) and Council Regulation (EC) No 1419/2006 of 25 September 2006 repealing Regulation (EEC) No 4056/86 laying down detailed rules for the application of Articles 85 and 86 of the Treaty to maritime transport, and amending Regulation (EC) No 1/2003 as regards the extension of its scope to include cabotage and international tramp services (OJ L269, 28.9.2006, p 1).

3 Commission Regulation (EC) No 773/2004 of 7 April 2004 relating to the conduct of proceedings by the Commission pursuant to Articles 81 and 82 of the EC Treaty (OJ L123, 27.4.2004, p 18), as amended by Commission Regulation (EC) No 622/2008 of 30 June 2008 amending Regulation (EC) No 773/2004, as regards the conduct of settlement procedures in cartel cases (OJ L171, 1.7.2008, p 3).

4 This notice applies exclusively to the Commission's procedures for the enforcement of Articles 101 and 102 TFEU and does not concern the national competition authorities when they apply these provisions.

5 This notice does not deal with specific procedures, for example for imposing fines on undertakings having provided misleading information, refused to submit to inspections or breached seals affixed by officials (see Article 23(1) of Regulation (EC) No 1/2003). It covers neither decisions on interim measures pursuant to Article 8 of Regulation (EC) No 1/2003 nor decisions on finding of inapplicability pursuant to Article 10 of Regulation (EC) No 1/2003.

6 See Council Regulation (EC) No 139/2004 of 20 January 2004 on the control of concentrations between undertakings (OJ L24, 29.1.2004, p 1). See in this respect the Directorate-General for Competition's Best Practices on the conduct of EC Merger Proceedings of 20 January 2004, published on the Directorate-General for Competition's website (ec.europa.eu/competition/mergers/legislation/proceedings.pdf).

7 See Council Regulation (EC) No 659/1999 of 22 March 1999 laying down detailed rules for the application of Article 93 (now Article 108 TFEU) of the EC Treaty (OJ L83, 27.3.1999, p 1). See in this respect the Commission notice on a Code of Best Practice for the conduct of State aid control procedures (OJ C136, 16.6.2009, p 13).

8 Commission notice on the rules for access to the Commission file in cases pursuant to Articles 81 and 82 of the EC Treaty, Articles 53, 54 and 57 of the EEA Agreement and Council Regulation (EC) No 139/2004 (OJ C325, 22.12.2005, p 7).

9 Commission notice on the handling of complaints by the Commission under Articles 81 and 82 of the EC Treaty (OJ C101, 27.4.2004, p 65).

10 Decision C(2011) 5742 of the President of the European Commission of 13 October 2011 on the function and terms of reference of the hearing officer in certain competition proceedings.

11 Staff working paper on Best Practices for the submission of economic evidence and data collection in cases concerning the application of Articles 101 and 102 TFEU and merger cases, ec.europa.eu/competition/index_en.html

12 Commission notice on immunity from fines and reduction of fines in cartel cases (OJ C298, 8.12.2006, p 17) (Leniency Notice), ie, secret 'agreements and/or concerted practices between two or more competitors aimed at coordinating their competitive behaviour on the market and/or influencing the relevant parameters of competition through practices such as the fixing of purchase or selling prices or other trading conditions, the allocation of production or sales quotas, the sharing of markets including bid-rigging, restrictions of imports or exports and/or anti-competitive actions against other

competitors. Such practices are among the most serious violations of (Article 101 TFEU)'.

13 Commission Regulation (EC) No 622/2008 of 30 June 2008 amending Regulation (EC) No 773/2004, as regards the conduct of settlement procedures in cartel cases (OJ L171, 1.7.2008, p 3); Commission notice on the conduct of settlement procedures in view of the adoption of Decisions pursuant to Article 7 and Article 23 of Council Regulation (EC) No 1/2003 in cartel cases OJ C167, 2.7.2008, p 1.

14 It should be noted that the Commission may disregard any application for immunity from fines on the ground that it has been submitted after the statement of objections has been issued (see paragraphs 14 and 29 of the Leniency Notice).

15 The Commission may disregard any application for immunity from fines or reductions of fines under the Leniency Notice on the ground that it has been submitted after the expiry of the time limit set for parties to declare in writing whether they envisage engaging in settlement discussions (see paragraph 13 of the Settlement Notice).

16 With regard to cases which are pending at the time of the publication of this document, the latter will apply to any procedural steps that remain to be taken after publication.

2. THE INVESTIGATIVE PHASE

2.1. ORIGIN OF CASES

[4.367]

9. A case concerning an alleged infringement of Article 101 or 102 TFEU may be based on a complaint by undertakings, other natural and legal persons and even Member States.

10. Information from citizens and undertakings is important in triggering investigations by the Commission. The Commission therefore encourages citizens and undertakings to inform it about suspected infringements of the competition rules.[17] This can be done either by lodging a formal complaint[18] or by simply providing market information to the Commission. Anyone who is able to show a legitimate interest as a complainant, and who submits a complaint in compliance with form C,[19] enjoys certain procedural rights. The details of the procedure to be followed are set out in the Implementing Regulation and in the notice on the handling of complaints. Natural and legal persons, other than complainants, which show a sufficient interest to be heard and which are admitted to the proceedings by the hearing officer also enjoy certain procedural rights in accordance with Article 13 of the Implementing Regulation.

11. The Commission may also open a case on its own initiative (*ex officio*). It may do so when certain facts have been brought to its attention, or further to information gathered in the context of sector enquiries, informal meetings with industry, monitoring of markets or on the basis of information exchanged within the European Competition Network (ECN) or with competition authorities of third countries. Cartel cases can also be initiated on the basis of an application for leniency by one of the cartel members.

2.2. INITIAL ASSESSMENT AND CASE ALLOCATION

12. All cases, irrespective of their origin, are subject to an initial assessment phase. During this phase the Commission examines whether the case merits further investigation[20] and, if so, provisionally defines its focus, in particular with regard to the parties, the markets and the conduct to be investigated. During this phase, the Commission may make use of investigative measures such as requests for information in accordance with Article 18(2) of Regulation (EC) No 1/2003.

13. In practice, the system of initial assessment means that some cases will be discarded at a very early stage because they are not deemed to merit further investigation. In this regard, the Commission focuses its enforcement resources on cases where it appears likely that an infringement may be found, in particular on cases with the most significant impact on the functioning of competition in the internal market and risk of consumer harm, as well as on cases which are likely to contribute to defining EU competition policy and/or to ensuring the coherent application of Articles 101 and/or 102 TFEU.[21]

14. This initial assessment phase also attempts to address, at an early stage, the allocation of cases within the ECN. Regulation (EC) No 1/2003 introduced the possibility of reallocating cases to other network members if they are well placed to deal with them. Accordingly, the Commission may reallocate a case to a national competition authority and vice versa.[22]

15. When the first investigative measure is addressed to them (normally a request for information[23] or an inspection), addressees are informed of the fact that they are subject to a preliminary investigation and about the subject matter and purpose of such investigation. In the context of requests for information, they will further be reminded that if the behaviour under investigation is confirmed to have taken place this might constitute an infringement of Articles 101 and/or 102 TFEU. After having received a request for information or being subject to an inspection, parties[24] may at any time inquire with the Directorate-General for Competition about the status of the investigation, including before the opening of proceedings. If such an undertaking considers that it has not been properly informed by the Directorate-General for Competition of its procedural status, it may refer the matter to the hearing officer for resolution, after having raised the matter with the Directorate-General for Competition.[25] The hearing officer shall take a decision that the Directorate-General for Competition will inform the undertaking or association of undertakings that made the request of their procedural status. This decision shall be communicated to the undertaking or association of undertakings that made the request. If at any stage during the initial assessment phase, the Commission decides not to investigate the case further (and thus not to open proceedings), the Commission will, at its own initiative, inform the party subject to the preliminary investigation thereof.

16. In cases based on a complaint, the Commission will endeavour to inform complainants within four months from the receipt of the complaint of the action that it proposes to take with regard to the complaint.[26] This time frame is indicative and will depend on the circumstances of the individual case and whether the Directorate-General for Competition has received sufficient information from the complainant or third parties, notably in response to its requests for information, in order for it to decide whether or not to investigate the case further.

2.3. OPENING OF PROCEEDINGS

17. The Commission will open proceedings[27] under Article 11(6) of Regulation (EC) No 1/2003 when the initial assessment leads to the conclusion that the case merits further investigation and where the scope of the investigation has been sufficiently defined.

18. The opening of proceedings determines the allocation of the case within the ECN[28] and in relation to the parties and the complainant, if applicable. It also signals a commitment on the part of the Commission to further investigate the case. The Commission will thus allocate resources to the case and will endeavour to deal with the case in a timely manner.

19. The decision to open proceedings identifies the parties subject to the proceedings and briefly describes the scope of the investigation. In particular, it sets out the behaviour constituting the alleged infringement of Articles 101 and/or 102 TFEU to be covered by the investigation and normally identifies the territory and sector(s) where that behaviour takes place.

20. Pursuant to Article 2 of the Implementing Regulation, the Commission may make the opening of proceedings public. The Commission's policy is to publish the opening of proceedings on the website of the Directorate-General for Competition and issue a press release, unless such publication may harm the investigation.

21. The parties subject to the investigation are informed orally or in writing of the opening of proceedings sufficiently in advance before the opening of proceedings is made public so as to enable them to prepare their own communication (in particular in relation to shareholders, the financial institutions and the press).

22. It should be emphasised that the opening of proceedings does not prejudge in any way the existence of an infringement. It merely indicates that the Commission will further pursue the case. This important clarification will be mentioned in the decision opening the proceedings (notified to the parties), as well as in all public communications concerning the opening of the case.

23. The opening of proceedings does not limit the right of the Commission to extend the scope and/or the addressees of the investigation at a later point in time. In case of such an extension of the scope of the investigation, the measures in paragraphs (20) to (21) apply.

24. In cartel cases, the opening of proceedings normally takes place simultaneously with the adoption of the Statement of Objections (see paragraph (4) above), though it may take place earlier.

2.4. LANGUAGES

25. Pursuant to Article 3 of Regulation No 1,[29] documents which the Commission sends to an undertaking based in the European Union will be drafted in the language of the Member State in which the undertaking is based.

26. Pursuant to Article 2 of that same Regulation, documents which an undertaking sends to the Commission may be drafted in any one of the official languages of the European Union selected by the sender. The reply and subsequent correspondence will be drafted in the same language.

27. In order to avoid delays due to translation, the addressees may waive their right to receive the text in the language resulting from the above rule and opt for another language. Duly authorised language waivers can be given for some specific documents and/or for the whole procedure.

28. As regards simple requests for information it is standard practice to send the cover letter in the language of the addressee's location or in English (including a reference to Article 3 of Regulation No 1) and to attach the questionnaire in English. The addressee is also clearly informed — in the language of the addressee's location — of its right to obtain a translation of the cover letter and/or questionnaire into the language of the addressee's location, as well as the right to reply in that language. This practice allows for more expeditious treatment of information requests, while preserving the rights of addressees.

29. The Statement of Objections, Preliminary Assessment and decisions pursuant to Articles 7, 9 and 23(2) of Regulation (EC) No 1/2003 are notified in the authentic language of the addressee unless it has signed the above mentioned language waiver.

30. Pursuant to Article 2 of Regulation No 1, the reply and the subsequent correspondence addressed to the complainant will be in the language of their complaint.

31. Participants in the oral hearing may request to be heard in an EU official language other than the language of proceedings. In that case, interpretation will be provided during the oral hearing, as long as sufficient advance notice of this requirement is given to the hearing officer.

2.5. INFORMATION REQUESTS

32. Pursuant to Article 18 of Regulation (EC) No 1/2003, the Commission is empowered to require undertakings and associations of undertakings to provide it with all necessary information. Information can be requested by letter ('simple request' (Article 18(2)) or by decision (Article 18(3)).[30] It should be underlined that requests for information are regularly sent not only to the undertakings under investigation, but also to other undertakings or associations of undertakings which may have information relevant for the case.

2.5.1. SCOPE OF REQUEST FOR INFORMATION

33. Pursuant to Article 18 of Regulation (EC) No 1/2003, the Commission may require undertakings and associations of undertakings to provide all necessary information. Information is necessary, in particular, if it may enable the Commission to verify the existence of the alleged infringement referred to in the request. The Commission enjoys a margin of appreciation in this respect.[31]

34. It is for the Commission to define the scope and the format of the request for information. Where appropriate, the Directorate-General for Competition might however discuss with the addressees the scope and the format of the request for information. This may be particularly useful in cases of requests concerning quantitative data.[32]

35. When, in a reply to a request for information, undertakings submit manifestly irrelevant information (in particular documents which are clearly not related to the subject matter of the investigation), the Directorate-General for Competition may, in order not to unnecessarily burden the often voluminous administrative file, return such information to the addressee of the request as early as possible after having received the reply. A short notice reporting this fact will be put in the file.

2.5.2. Self-incrimination

36. Where the addressee of a request for information pursuant to Article 18(2) of Regulation (EC) No 1/2003 refuses to reply to a question in such a request invoking the privilege against self-incrimination, as defined by the case law of the Court of Justice of the European Union,[33] it may refer the matter in due time following the receipt of the request to the hearing officer, after having raised the matter with the Directorate-General for Competition before the expiry of the original time limit set.[34] In appropriate cases, and having regard to the need to avoid undue delay in proceedings, the hearing officer may make a reasoned recommendation as to whether the privilege against self-incrimination applies and inform the director responsible of the conclusions drawn, to be taken into account in case of any decision taken subsequently pursuant to Article 18(3) of Regulation (EC) No 1/2003. The addressee of the request shall receive a copy of the reasoned recommendation. The addressee of an Article 18(3) decision will be reminded of the privilege against self-incrimination as defined by case law of the Court of Justice of the European Union.[35]

2.5.3. Time limits

37. The request for information specifies which information is required and fixes the time limit within which the information is to be provided.

38. Addressees are given a reasonable time limit to reply to the request, according to the length and complexity of the request taking into account the requirements of the investigation. In general, this time limit will be at least two weeks from the receipt of the request. If from the outset, it is considered that a longer period is required, the time limit to reply to the request will be set accordingly. When the scope of the request is limited, for example if it only covers a short clarification of information previously provided or information readily available to the addressee of the request, the time limit will normally be shorter (one week or less).

39. If they have difficulties responding within the time limit set, addressees may ask for it to be extended. A reasoned request should be made or confirmed in writing (letter or e-mail), sufficiently in advance of the expiry of the time limit. If the Commission considers the request to be justified, additional time (depending on the complexity of the information asked and other factors) will be granted. The Commission may also agree with the addressee of the request that certain parts of the requested information that are of particular importance or easily available for the addressee will be supplied within a shorter time limit, whereas additional time will be granted for supplying the remaining information.

40. Where the addressee of a decision requesting information pursuant to Article 18(3) Regulation (EC) No 1/2003 is unable to resolve its concerns about the time limit through the procedure outlined above, it may refer the matter to the hearing officer. Such a request should be made in due time before the expiry of the original time limit set.[36] The hearing officer shall decide on whether an extension of the time limit should be granted, taking account of the length and complexity of the request for information and the requirements of the investigation.

2.5.4. Confidentiality

41. The cover letter of the request for information also requires the addressee to indicate whether it considers that information provided in the reply is confidential. In that case, in accordance with Article 16(3) of the Implementing Regulation, the addressee must substantiate its claims individually with regard to each item of information and provide a non-confidential version of the information. Such a non-confidential version shall be provided in the same format as the confidential information, replacing deleted passages by summaries thereof. Unless otherwise agreed, a non-confidential version should be provided at the same time as the original submission. If undertakings fail to comply with these requirements, the Commission may assume that the documents or statements concerned do not contain confidential information pursuant to Article 16(4) of the Implementing Regulation.

2.5.5. Meetings and other contacts with the parties and third parties

42. During the investigative phase, the Directorate-General for Competition may hold meetings (or conduct phone calls) with the parties subject to the proceedings, complainants, or third parties. In particular, it will hold State of Play meetings or may hold triangular meetings as outlined in Sections 2.9 or 2.10 below.

43. When a meeting takes place at the request of the parties, complainants or third parties, they should as a general rule submit in advance a proposed agenda of topics to be discussed at the meeting, as well as a memorandum or a presentation which covers these issues in more detail. After meetings or phone calls on substantive issues, the parties, complainants or third parties may substantiate their statements or presentations in writing.

44. Any written documentation prepared by the undertakings which attended a meeting that is communicated to the Directorate-General for Competition will be put on the file. A non-confidential version of such documentation, together with a brief note prepared by the Directorate-General for Competition, will be made accessible to the parties subject to the investigation during their access to the file, if the case is further pursued. Subject to any anonymity requests[37] this note will mention the undertaking(s) attending the meeting (or participating in the phone call relating to substantive issues) and the timing and topic(s) covered by the meeting (or phone call).[38] Such a brief note will also be prepared when the meeting takes place on the Commission's initiative (eg, State of Play meetings).

45. The Commission may, after a meeting or other informal contact with the parties, complainants or third parties, request that they provide information in writing pursuant to Article 18 of Regulation (EC) No 1/2003 or invite them to make a statement pursuant to Article 19 of that Regulation.

2.5.6. POWER TO TAKE STATEMENTS (INTERVIEWS)

46. Regulation (EC) No 1/2003 and the Implementing Regulation establish a specific procedure for taking statements from natural or legal persons who may be in possession of useful information concerning an alleged infringement of Articles 101 and 102 TFEU (see Article 19 of Regulation (EC) No 1/2003 and Article 3 of the Implementing Regulation).[39]

47. The Commission may, under this procedure, interview by any means, such as by telephone or video-conference, any natural or legal person who consents to be interviewed for the purpose of collecting information relating to the subject matter of an investigation.

48. Before taking such statements, the Directorate-General for Competition will inform the interviewee of the legal basis of the interview, its voluntary nature and the right of the interviewee to consult a lawyer. The Directorate-General for Competition will further inform the interviewee of the purpose of the interview and of its intention to make a record of the interview. In practice this will be done by providing a document explaining the procedure to be signed by the interviewee. In order to enhance the accuracy of the statements, a copy of any recording will be made available shortly thereafter to the person interviewed for approval.

49. The procedure for taking statements pursuant to Article 19 of Regulation (EC) No 1/2003 and Article 3 of the Implementing Regulation applies only when it is expressly agreed between the interviewee and the Directorate-General for Competition that the conversation will be recorded as a formal interview under Article 19. It is within the discretion of the Commission to decide when to propose interviews. A party may however also make a request to the Directorate-General for Competition to have its statement recorded as an interview. Such a request will in principle be accepted, subject to the needs and requirements of the proper conduct of the investigation.

2.6. INSPECTIONS

50. In the context of an investigation the Commission has the power to conduct inspections at the premises of an undertaking and in certain circumstances at other premises, including private premises. The Commission's practice in relation to inspections at the premises of an undertaking is currently described in an explanatory note available on the website of the Directorate-General for Competition.[40]

2.7. LEGAL PROFESSIONAL PRIVILEGE

51. According to the case law of the Court of Justice of the European Union,[41] the main features of which are summarised below, certain communications between lawyer and client may, subject to strict conditions, be protected by legal professional privilege (also referred to as 'LPP') and thus be confidential as regards the Commission, as an exception to the latter's powers of investigation and examination of documents.[42] Communications between lawyer and client are protected by legal professional privilege provided that they are made for the purpose and interest of the exercise of the client's rights of defence in competition proceedings and that they emanate from independent lawyers.[43]

52. It is for the undertaking claiming the protection of legal professional privilege with regard to a given document to provide the Commission with appropriate justification and relevant material to substantiate its claim, while not being bound to disclose the contents of such document.[44] Redacted versions removing the parts covered by legal professional privilege should be submitted. Where the Commission considers that such evidence has not been provided, it may order production of the document in question and, if necessary, impose on the undertaking fines or periodic penalty payments for its refusal either to supply such additional necessary evidence or to produce the contested document.[45]

53. In many cases, a mere cursory look by Commission officials, normally during an inspection, at the general layout, heading, title or other superficial features of a document will enable them to confirm or not the accuracy of the reasons invoked by the undertaking. However, an undertaking is entitled to refuse to allow the Commission officials to take even a cursory look, provided that it gives appropriate reasons to justify why such a cursory look would be impossible without revealing the content of the document.[46]

54. Where, in the course of an inspection, the Commission officials consider that the undertaking has: (i) not substantiated its claim that the document concerned is covered by legal professional privilege; (ii) has only invoked reasons that, according to the case law, cannot justify such protection; or (iii) bases itself on factual assertions that are manifestly wrong, the Commission officials may immediately read the contents of the document and take a copy of it (without using the sealed envelope procedure). However, where, in the course of an inspection, the Commission officials consider that the material presented by the undertaking is not of such a nature as to prove that the document in question is protected by legal professional privilege as defined by the case law of the Court of Justice of the European Union, in particular where that undertaking refuses to give the Commission officials a cursory look at a document, but where it cannot be excluded that the document may be protected, the officials may place a copy of the contested document in a sealed envelope and bring it to the Commission's premises, with a view to a subsequent resolution of the dispute.

55. The hearing officer may be asked by undertakings or associations of undertakings to examine claims that a document required by the Commission in the exercise of Articles 18, 20 or 21 of Regulation (EC) No 1/2003 and which was withheld from the Commission is covered by legal professional privilege, within the meaning of the case law, if the undertaking has been unable to resolve the matter with the Directorate-General for Competition.[47] The undertaking making the claim may refer the matter to the hearing officer if they consent to the hearing officer viewing the information claimed to be covered by legal professional privilege and any other material necessary for the hearing officer's assessment. Without revealing the potentially privileged content of the information, the hearing officer shall communicate to the director responsible and the undertaking or association of undertakings concerned his or her preliminary view, and may take appropriate steps to promote a mutually acceptable resolution.

56. Where no resolution is reached, the hearing officer may formulate a reasoned recommendation to the competent member of the Commission, without revealing the potentially privileged content of the document. The party making the claim shall receive a copy of this recommendation. If the matter is not resolved on this basis, the Commission will examine the matter further. Where appropriate, it may adopt a decision rejecting the claim.

57. In cases where the undertaking has claimed the protection of legal professional privilege and has provided reasons substantiating its claims, the Commission (with the exception of the hearing officer if a claim has been referred to him or her on the basis of Article 4(2)(a) of the terms of reference of the hearing officer) will not read the contents of the document before it has adopted a decision rejecting this claim and allowed the undertaking concerned to refer the matter to the Court of Justice of the European Union. Thus, if the company brings an action for annulment and applies for interim relief within the specified time limit, the Commission will not open the sealed envelope and will not read the documents until the Court of Justice of the European Union has decided on this application for interim measures.[48]

58. Undertakings making clearly unfounded claims for protection under legal professional privilege merely as delaying tactics or opposing, without objective justification, any cursory look at the documents during an investigation may be subject to fines pursuant to Article 23(1) of Regulation (EC) No 1/2003, if the other conditions of this provision are met. Similarly, such actions may be taken into account as aggravating circumstances in any decision imposing a fine for infringement of Articles 101 and/or 102 TFEU.[49]

2.8. INFORMATION EXCHANGE BETWEEN COMPETITION AUTHORITIES

59. In the context of an investigation the Commission may also exchange information with national competition authorities pursuant to Article 12 of Regulation (EC) No 1/2003. The Commission's practice in relation to these exchanges is currently described in the Commission notice on cooperation within the Network of Competition Authorities.[50]

2.9. STATE OF PLAY MEETINGS

60. Throughout the procedure the Directorate-General for Competition endeavours to give, on its own initiative or upon request, parties subject to the proceedings ample opportunity for open and frank discussions — taking into account the stage of the investigation — and to make their points of view known.

61. In this respect the Commission will offer State of Play meetings at certain stages of the procedure. State of Play meetings, which are completely voluntary in nature for the parties, can contribute to the quality and efficiency of the decision making process and to ensure transparency and communication between the Directorate-General for Competition and the parties, notably to inform them of the status of the proceedings at key points in the procedure. State of Play meetings will only be offered to the parties being investigated and not to the complainant (except where the Commission has opened proceedings pursuant to Article 11(6) of Regulation (EC) No 1/2003 and intends to inform the complainant that it will reject its complaint by formal letter under Article 7(1) of the Implementing Regulation) nor to third parties. Where several parties are investigated, State of Play meetings will be offered to each party separately. In cartel proceedings, a State of Play meeting will be offered as provided for in paragraph (65).

2.9.1. FORMAT OF THE STATE OF PLAY MEETINGS

62. State of Play meetings are normally conducted at the Commission's premises, but if appropriate, they may also be held by telephone or video-conference. Senior management of the Directorate-General for Competition (Director or Deputy Director-General) will normally chair the meeting. However, in cases involving multiple parties, the meeting may be chaired by the responsible head of unit.

2.9.2. TIMING OF THE STATE OF PLAY MEETINGS

63. The Directorate-General for Competition will offer State of Play meetings at several key stages of the case. These correspond, in principle (although not normally in the context of cartel proceedings), to the following events:

1) Shortly after the opening of proceedings: the Directorate-General for Competition will inform the parties subject to the proceedings of the issues identified at this stage and of the anticipated scope of the investigation. This meeting provides the parties with an opportunity to react initially to the issues identified and may also serve to assist the Directorate-General for Competition in deciding on the appropriate framework for its further investigation. This meeting may also be used to discuss with the parties any relevant language waivers that may be appropriate for the conduct of the investigation. The Directorate-General for Competition will normally at this stage indicate a tentative timetable for the case. Such tentative timetable will, if appropriate, be updated at following State of Play meetings.
2) At a sufficiently advanced stage in the investigation: this meeting gives the parties subject to the proceedings an opportunity to understand the Commission's preliminary views on the status of the case following its investigation and on the competition concerns identified. The meeting may also be used by the Directorate-General for Competition and by the parties to clarify certain issues and facts relevant for the outcome of the case.

64. Where a Statement of Objections is issued, the parties will also be offered a State of Play meeting after their reply to the Statement of Objections or after the Oral Hearing, should one be held: the parties will at this meeting normally be informed of the Commission's preliminary view on how it intends to pursue the case further.

65. In the context of cartel proceedings one State of Play meeting will be offered after the oral hearing. Furthermore, two specific State of Play Meetings will be offered in the context of procedures leading to commitment decisions (see Section 4 below) and to complainants where the Commission has opened proceedings under Article 11(6) of Regulation (EC) No 1/2003 and intends to inform the complainant that it will reject its complaint by formal letter under Article 7(1) of the Implementing Regulation (see Section 5 below).

66. State of Play meetings do not in any way preclude discussions between the parties, complainants or third parties and the Directorate-General for Competition on substance or on timing issues on other occasions throughout the procedure as appropriate.

2.10. TRIANGULAR MEETINGS

67. In addition to bilateral meetings between the Directorate-General for Competition and each individual party such as the State of Play meetings, the Commission may exceptionally decide to invite the parties subject to the proceedings, and possibly also the complainant and/or third parties, to a so-called 'triangular' meeting. Such a meeting will be organised if the Directorate-General for Competition believes it to be in the interests of the investigation to hear the views on, or to verify the accuracy of, factual issues of all the parties in a single meeting. Such a meeting could be useful to the investigation, for example, where two or more opposing views or information have been put forward as to key data or evidence.

68. Any triangular meeting would normally take place at the initiative of the Commission and on a voluntary basis. Triangular meetings are normally chaired by senior management of the Directorate-General for Competition (Director or Deputy Director-General). A triangular meeting does not replace the formal Oral Hearing.

69. Where triangular meetings are held, this should be done as early as possible during the investigatory phase (after the opening of proceedings and before any issuing of Statement of Objections) in order to help the Commission reach a conclusion on substantive issues before the Commission decides whether to issue a Statement of Objections, although the holding of such meetings after the issue of the Statement of Objections in appropriate cases is not excluded. Triangular meetings should be prepared on the basis of an agenda established by the Directorate-General for Competition after consulting all parties that agree to attend the meeting. The preparation of the meeting may include a mutual exchange of non-confidential submissions between the attending parties sufficiently in advance of the meeting.

2.11. MEETINGS WITH THE COMMISSIONER OR THE DIRECTOR-GENERAL

70. If the parties so request, it is normal practice to offer senior officers of the parties subject to the proceedings and the complainant an opportunity to discuss the case either with the Director-General for competition, the Deputy Director-General for antitrust, or if appropriate, with the Commissioner responsible for Competition. The senior officers may be accompanied by their legal and/or economic advisors.

2.12. REVIEW OF KEY SUBMISSIONS

71. In the spirit of encouraging an open exchange of views the Commission will, in cases based on formal complaints, provide the parties subject to the proceedings, at an early stage (unless such is considered to likely prejudice the investigation) and at the latest shortly after the opening of proceedings, with the opportunity of commenting on a non-confidential version of the complaint.[51] However, this may not be the case where the complaint is rejected at an early stage without further in-depth investigation (eg, based on 'insufficient grounds for acting', also known as 'lack of European Union interest').

72. Early access to the complaint may allow the parties to provide useful information at an early stage of the procedure and facilitate the assessment of the case.

73. In the same spirit, the Commission's objective will be to provide the parties subject to the proceedings shortly after the opening of proceedings with the opportunity to review non-confidential versions of other 'key submissions' already submitted to the Commission. This would include significant submissions of the complainant or interested third parties, but not, for example, replies to requests for information. After this early stage, other such submissions will only be shared with the parties if this is in the interest of the investigation and would not risk unduly slowing down the investigative phase. The Commission will respect justified requests by the complainant or interested third parties for non-disclosure of their submissions prior to the issuing of a Statement of Objections where they have genuine concerns regarding confidentiality, including fears of retaliation and the protection of business secrets.

74. The review of key submissions will not be offered in the context of cartel proceedings (see paragraph (4) above).

2.13. POSSIBLE OUTCOMES OF THE INVESTIGATION PHASE

75. Once the Commission has reached a preliminary view of the main issues raised by a case, different procedural paths may be envisaged.

— The Commission may decide to proceed towards the adoption of a Statement of Objections with a view to adopting a prohibition decision relating to all or some of the issues identified at the opening of proceedings (see Section 3 below).

— The parties subject to the investigation may consider offering commitments which address the competition concerns arising from the investigation, or at least show their willingness to discuss such a possibility; in that case, the Commission may decide to engage in discussion with a view to a commitment decision (see Section 4 below).

— The Commission may decide that there are no grounds to continue the proceedings with regard to all or some of the parties and close the proceedings accordingly. If the case originated via a complaint, the Commission shall, before closing the case, give the complainant the possibility to express its views (see Section 5 on rejection of complaints).

76. When closing a case in relation to one or several parties in multi-party proceedings at an early stage after proceedings have been formally opened, the Commission will normally not only notify the decision to those parties but also in those cases where the opening of proceedings has been made public, note the closure on its website and/or issue a press release. The same applies in cases where proceedings have not been formally opened but the Commission has already made public its investigation (eg, by having confirmed that inspections have taken place).

NOTES

17 Or, when appropriate, the relevant national competition authority.

18 Pursuant to Article 7(2) of Regulation (EC) No 1/2003. Under Articles 5 to 9 of the Implementing Regulation, formal complaints have to fulfil certain requirements. Information contained in submissions that do not respect these requirements may nevertheless be taken into account as market information.

19 See Article 5(1) of the Implementing Regulation.

20 The Court of Justice of the European Union has recognised that the Commission is entitled to give differing degrees of priority to the complaints that it receives. This is settled case law since Case T-24/90, *Automec v Commission* (hereinafter '*Automec II*') (1992) ECR II-2223, para 85.

21 The Commission has made public a non-exhaustive list of criteria which it intends to use when examining whether or not complaints show a sufficient 'European Union interest'. The criteria were published in the Annual Report on Competition Policy 2005, adopted in June 2006. See as well paragraph 44 of the notice on handling of complaints.

22 See paragraphs 5 to 15 of the Commission notice on cooperation within the Network of Competition Authorities (OJ C101, 27.4.2004, p 43).

23 See Case T-99/04 *AC Treuhand v Commission* [2008] ECR II-1501, para. 56.

24 In this notice, 'parties' are defined as the parties subject to the investigation. If not explicitly mentioned, 'parties' does not include complainants and admitted third persons (also referred to as 'third parties' in this notice).

25 Article 4(2)(d) of the terms of reference of the hearing officer.

26 Notice on the handling of complaints, paragraph 61.

27 According to Article 2 of the Implementing Regulation, the Commission may decide to initiate proceedings with a view to adopting a decision (eg, a decision finding an infringement or a commitment decision) at any point in time, but no later than the date on which it issues a statement of objections, a preliminary assessment (as referred to in Article 9(1) of Regulation (EC) No 1/2003) or a notice pursuant to Article 27(4) of Regulation (EC) No 1/2003, whichever is the earlier.

28 The opening of proceedings relieves the national competition authorities of their competence to apply Articles 101 and 102 TFEU, see Article 11(6) of Regulation (EC) No 1/2003.

29 EEC Council: Regulation No 1 determining the languages to be used by the European Economic Community (OJ 17, 6.10.1958, p 385; Consolidated version of 1.1.2007).

30 Non-respect of an Article 18(3) decision requesting information (supplying incomplete information or not respecting the time limit set out) can lead to fines and periodic penalties, see Articles 23 and 24 of Regulation (EC) No 1/2003. Submitting incorrect or misleading information may lead to fines being imposed both in case of an Article 18(2) letter and an Article 18(3) decision (see Article 23 of Regulation (EC) No 1/2003).

31 As regards the Commission's discretion in shaping the enquiry, see Case T-141/94 *Thyssen Stahl v Commission* [1999] ECR II-347, paragraph 110; Case T-9/99 *HFB and Others v Commission* [2002] ECR II-1487, paragraph 384; Case T-48/00 *Corus UK v Commission* [2004] ECR II-2325, paragraph 212. In exercising its discretion, the Commission is bound by the principle of proportionality and, in relation to Article 18(3) decisions, must respect the privilege against self-incrimination.

32 See the Best Practices on the submission of economic evidence.

33 See for example Case C-301/04 P *Commission v SGL*, [2006] ECR I-5915, which specifies that addressees of an Article 18(3) decision may be required to provide pre-existing documents, such as minutes of cartel meetings, even if those documents may incriminate the party providing them.

34 Article 4(2)(b) of the terms of reference of the hearing officer.

35 See footnote 33.

36 Article 4(2)(c) of the terms of reference of the hearing officer.

37 See paragraph 143 below.

38 The provisions of this section also apply to State of Play meetings and triangular meetings (see Section 2.10 below).

39 This power to take statements pursuant to Article 19 of Regulation (EC) No 1/2003 should be distinguished from the power of the Commission, during an inspection, to ask any representative or member of staff of the undertaking or association of undertakings for explanations on facts or documents relating to the subject matter and purpose of the inspection and to record the answers, pursuant to Article 20(2)(e) of Regulation (EC) No 1/2003.

40 See: ec.europa.eu/competition/antitrust/legislation/legislation.html

41 The exclusion of certain communications between lawyers and clients from the Commission's powers of enquiry derives from the general principles of law common to the laws of the Member States as clarified by the Court of Justice of the European Union: Case 155/79 *AM&S Europe Limited v Commission* (hereinafter '*AM&S*') [1982] ECR 1575; Order in Case T-30/89 *Hilti v Commission* (hereinafter '*Hilti*') [1990] ECR II-163; Joined Cases T-125/03 and T-253/03 *Akzo Nobel Chemicals and Akcros Chemicals v Commission* (hereinafter '*Akzo*') [2007] ECR II-3523, as confirmed by Case C-550/07 P, *Akzo Nobel Chemicals and Akcros Chemicals v Commission*, judgment of 14 September 2010.

42 The Court of Justice of the European Union has considered that the protection of the confidentiality of communications between lawyer and client is an essential corollary to the full exercise of the rights of defence (*AM&S*, paragraphs 18 and 23). In any event, the principle of legal professional privilege does not prevent a lawyer's client from disclosing the written communications between them if the client considers that it is in his interest to do so (*AM&S*, paragraph 28).

43 *AM&S*, paragraphs 21, 22 and 27. According to the case law, the substantive scope of the protection of legal professional privilege covers also, further to written communications with an independent lawyer made for the purposes of the exercise of the client's rights of defence, (i) internal notes circulated within an undertaking which are confined to reporting the text or the content of communications with independent lawyers containing legal advice (*Hilti*, paragraphs 13, 16 to 18) and (ii) preparatory documents prepared by the client, even if not exchanged with a lawyer or not created for the purpose of being sent physically to a lawyer, provided that they were drawn up exclusively for the purpose of seeking legal advice from a lawyer in exercise of the rights of the defence (*Akzo*, paragraphs 120 to 123). As for the personal scope of the protection of legal professional privilege, it only applies to the extent that the lawyer is independent (ie, not bound to his client by a relationship of employment); in-house lawyers are explicitly excluded from legal professional privilege, irrespective of their membership of a Bar or Law Society or their subjection to professional discipline and ethics or protection under national law: *AM&S*, paragraphs 21, 22, 24 and 27; *Akzo*, paragraphs 166 to 168; confirmed by ECJ in its judgment of 14 September 2010, Case C-550/07 P, paragraphs 44 to 51. Moreover, according to the case law, protection

under legal professional privilege applies only to lawyers entitled to practise their profession in one of the EU Member States, regardless of the country in which the client lives (*AM&S*, paragraphs 25 and 26), and does not extend to other professional advisers such as patent attorneys, accountants, etc. Finally, it shall be observed that the protection of legal professional privilege covers, in principle, written communications exchanged after the initiation of the administrative procedure that may lead to a decision on the application of Articles 101 and/or 102 TFEU or to a decision imposing a pecuniary sanction on the undertaking; this protection can also extend to earlier written communications made for the purpose of exercising rights of the defence and which have a relationship to the subject matter of that procedure (*AM&S*, paragraph 23).

44 Hence, the mere fact that an undertaking claims that a document is protected by legal professional privilege is not sufficient to prevent the Commission from reading that document if the undertaking produces no relevant material of such a kind (*Akzo*, paragraph 80; see below). In order to substantiate its claim, the undertaking concerned may, in particular, inform the Directorate-General for Competition of the author of the document and for whom it was intended, explain the respective duties and responsibilities of each, and refer to the objective and the context in which the document was drawn up. Similarly, it may also mention the context in which the document was found, the way in which it was filed and any related documents (*Akzo*, paragraph 80).

45 *AM&S*, paragraphs 29 to 31. The undertaking may subsequently bring an action for the annulment of such a decision, where appropriate, coupled with a request for interim relief (*AM&S*, paragraphs 32; see below).

46 *Akzo*, paragraphs 81 and 82.

47 Article 4(2)(a) of the terms of reference of the hearing officer.

48 Thus, the Commission will wait until the time limit for bringing an action against the rejection decision has expired before reading the contents of the contested document. However, since such an action does not have suspensory effect, it is for the undertaking concerned to make a prompt application for interim relief seeking suspension of operation of the decision rejecting the request for legal professional privilege.

49 *Akzo*, paragraph 89.

50 OJ C101, 27.4.2004, p 43.

51 A non-confidential version of the reply of the party subject to the investigation to the complaint may thereafter be provided to the complainant.

3. PROCEDURES LEADING TO A PROHIBITION DECISION

[4.368]

77. An important procedural step in procedures which may lead to a prohibition decision is the adoption of a Statement of Objections. However, the adoption of a Statement of Objections does not prejudge the final outcome of the investigation. It may well lead to the closing of the case without the adoption of a prohibition decision or a commitment decision.

3.1. RIGHT TO BE HEARD

78. The right of the parties to the proceedings to be heard before a final decision adversely affecting their interests is taken is a fundamental principle of EU law. The Commission is committed to ensuring that the effective exercise of the right to be heard is respected in its proceedings.[52]

79. The hearing officers have the function of safeguarding the effective exercise of procedural rights, in particular the right to be heard, in competition proceedings.[53] The hearing officers carry out their tasks in full independence from the Directorate-General for Competition, and disputes arising between the latter and any party subject to the proceedings can be brought before the relevant hearing officer for resolution.

80. The hearing officer is directly involved throughout antitrust proceedings, including in particular the organisation and conduct of the oral hearing, if one is held. After the oral hearing, and taking into account the parties' written replies to the Statement of Objections, the hearing officer reports to the Commissioner responsible for Competition on the hearing and the conclusions to be drawn from it. Moreover, prior to a final decision being taken by the College of Commissioners, the hearing officer informs it whether the right to exercise procedural rights effectively has been respected throughout the administrative proceedings. The final report is sent to the parties subject to the proceedings, together with the Commission's final decision, and is published in the *Official Journal of the European Union*.

3.1.1. Statement of Objections

81. Before adopting a decision adversely affecting the interests of an addressee, in particular, a decision finding an infringement of Article 101 and 102 TFEU and ordering its termination (Article 7 of Regulation (EC) No 1/2003) and/or imposing fines (Article 23 of Regulation (EC) No 1/2003), the Commission will give the parties subject to the proceedings the opportunity to be heard on the matters to which the Commission has objected.[54] The Commission will do this by adopting a Statement of Objections, which is notified to each of the parties subject to the proceedings.

3.1.1.1. Purpose and content of the Statement of Objections

82. The Statement of Objections sets out the preliminary position of the Commission on the alleged infringement of Articles 101 and/or 102 TFEU, after an in-depth investigation. Its purpose is to inform the parties concerned of the objections raised against them with a view to enabling them to exercise their rights of defence in writing and orally (at the hearing). It thus constitutes an essential procedural safeguard which ensures that the right to be heard is observed. The parties concerned will be provided with all the information they need to defend themselves effectively and to comment on the allegations made against them.

3.1.1.2. Possible imposition of remedies and arguments of the parties

83. If the Commission intends to impose remedies on the parties, in accordance with Article 7(1) of Regulation (EC) No 1/2003, the Statement of Objections will indicate the remedies envisaged that may be necessary to bring the suspected infringement to an end. The information given should be sufficiently detailed to allow the parties to defend

themselves as to the necessity and proportionality of the remedies envisaged. If structural remedies are envisaged, in accordance with Article 7(1) of Regulation (EC) No 1/2003, the Statement of Objections will spell out why there is no equally effective behavioural remedy or why the Commission considers any equally effective behavioural remedy would be more burdensome for the undertaking concerned than the structural remedy.

3.1.1.3.
Possible imposition of fines and arguments of the parties

84. The Statement of Objections will clearly indicate whether the Commission intends to impose fines on the undertakings, should the objections be upheld (Article 23 of Regulation (EC) No 1/2003). In such cases, the Statement of Objections will refer to the relevant principles laid down in the Guidelines on setting fines.[55] In the Statement of Objections the Commission will indicate the essential facts and matters of law which may result in the imposition of a fine, such as the duration and gravity of the infringement and that the infringement was committed intentionally or by negligence. The Statement of Objections will also mention in a sufficiently precise manner that certain facts may give rise to aggravating circumstances and, to the extent possible, to attenuating circumstances.

85. Although under no legal obligation in this respect, in order to increase transparency, the Commission will endeavour to include in the Statement of Objections (using information available) further matters relevant to any subsequent calculation of fines, including the relevant sales figures to be taken into account and the year(s) that will be considered for the value of such sales. Such information may also be provided to the parties after the Statement of Objections. In both cases, the parties will be provided with an opportunity to comment.

86. Should the Commission intend to depart in its final decision from the elements of fact or of law set out in the Statement of Objections to the disadvantage of one or more parties or should the Commission intend to take account of additional inculpatory evidence, the party or parties concerned will always be given the opportunity to make their views known thereon in an appropriate manner.

87. In the Statement of Objections the Commission will also inform parties that in exceptional cases, it may, upon request, take account of the undertaking's inability to pay and reduce or cancel the fine that might otherwise be imposed if that fine would irretrievably jeopardise the economic viability of the undertaking, according to point 35 of the Guidelines on setting fines.[58]

88. The undertakings making such a request should be prepared to provide, detailed and up-to-date financial information to support their request. Usually, the Directorate-General for Competition will be in contact with the parties in order to collect additional information and/or clarify the information obtained, which will allow the parties to bring further relevant information to the attention of the Commission. When assessing an undertaking's claim that it is unable to pay, the Commission looks in particular at the financial statements for recent years and forecasts for the current and coming years; at ratios measuring the financial strength, profitability, solvency and liquidity; and the undertaking's relations with outside financial partners and with shareholders. The Commission also examines the specific social and economic context of each undertaking and assesses whether the fine would likely cause its assets to lose significantly their value.[57]

89. The assessment of the financial situation is carried out for all undertakings that have made an inability to pay request close to the adoption of the decision and on the basis of up-to-date information, irrespective of when the request was submitted.

90. The parties may also present their arguments as to the matters that may be of importance for the possible imposition of fines at the oral hearing.[58]

3.1.1.4.
Transparency

91. In order to enhance the transparency of the proceedings, the Commission will, as a general rule, publish a press release setting out the key issues in the Statement of Objections shortly after it is received by its addressees. This press release will explicitly state that the Statement of Objections does not predetermine the final outcome of the proceedings, once the parties have been heard.

3.1.2. Access to file

92. The addressees of the Statement of Objections are granted access to the Commission's file, in accordance with Article 27(2) of Regulation (EC) No 1/2003 and Articles 15 and 16 of the Implementing Regulation, so as to allow them to effectively express their views on the preliminary conclusions reached by the Commission in its Statement of Objections.

93. The practicalities of access to the file, as well as detailed indications on the type of documents that will be accessible and confidentiality issues, are covered by a separate notice on access to file.[59] Granting access to the Commission file is primarily the responsibility of the Directorate-General for Competition. The hearing officers will decide disputes between the parties, the information providers and the Directorate-General for Competition over access to information contained in the Commission's file in accordance with the notice on access to file, the applicable regulations and the principles laid down in the relevant case law. Lastly, special rules govern access to corporate statements in cartel cases and settlement procedures.[60]

94. Efficient access to file depends to a large extent on the cooperation of the parties and other undertakings having provided information included in the file. As noted in paragraph (41) above, information providers must, in accordance with Article 16(3) of the Implementing Regulation, substantiate their confidentiality claims and provide a non-confidential version of the information. Such a non-confidential version must be provided in the same format as the confidential information, replacing deleted passages with summaries thereof. Unless otherwise agreed, a non-confidential version should be provided at the same time as the original submission. In the case of a failure to provide a non-confidential version, it may be assumed that the documents do not contain confidential information.[61]

3.1.3. Procedures for facilitating the exchange of confidential information between parties to the proceedings

95. Further to the possibilities contemplated in the notice on access to the file, two additional procedures may be used for the purpose of alleviating the burden of drawing up non-confidential versions of submissions: the negotiated disclosure to a restricted circle of persons and the data room procedure.

96. First, the Directorate-General for Competition may accept in certain cases, especially those with a very voluminous file that the parties agree voluntarily to use a negotiated disclosure procedure. Under this procedure, the party entitled to access to file agrees bilaterally with the information providers claiming confidentiality to receive all or some of the information which the latter have provided to the Commission, including confidential information. The party being granted access to file limits access to the information to a restricted circle of persons (to be decided by the parties on a case-by-case basis, if requested, under the supervision of the Directorate-General for Competition). To the extent that such negotiated access to the file would amount to restricting a party's right to have access to the investigation file, that party must waive its right to access to the file vis-à-vis the Commission. Normally, the party would receive the information subject to the negotiated disclosure procedure directly from the information provider. However, if the information that is subject to such an agreement would, exceptionally, be provided to the restricted circle of persons by the Commission, the information providers must waive their rights to confidentiality vis-à-vis the Commission.

97. Second, the Directorate-General for Competition may organise the so-called data room procedure. This procedure is typically used for the disclosure of quantitative data relevant for econometric analysis. Under this procedure, part of the file, including confidential information, is gathered in a room, at the Commission's premises (the data room). Access to the data room is granted to a restricted group of persons, ie, the external legal counsel and/or the economic advisers of the party (collectively known as the 'advisers'), under the supervision of a Commission official. The advisers may make use of the information contained in the data room for the purpose of defending their client but may not disclose any confidential information to their client. The data room is equipped with several PC workstations and the necessary software (and if relevant the necessary data sets and a log of the regressions used to support the Commission's case). There is no network connection and no external communication is allowed. The advisers are permitted to remain in the data room during normal working hours and, if justified, access may be provided for several days. The advisers are strictly prohibited from taking copies, notes or summaries of the documents and may only remove a final report from the data room, which is to be verified by the case team in order to ensure that it does not contain any confidential information. Each adviser will sign a confidentiality agreement and will be presented with the conditions of special access to the data room before entering. To the extent that the use of such a data room procedure would restrict a party's right to have full access to the investigation file, the procedural guarantees provided for in Article 8 of the terms of reference of the hearing officer apply.

98. The hearing officer may decide pursuant to Article 8(4) of the terms of reference of the hearing officer that the data room procedure shall be used in those limited cases where access to certain confidential information is indispensable for a party's rights of defence and where the hearing officer considers that, on balance, the conflict between respect for confidentiality and the rights of defence is best solved in this way. The hearing officer will not take such decisions if he or she considers that the data room is not appropriate and that access to the information should be given in a different form (eg, a non-confidential version).

3.1.4. Written reply to the Statement of Objections

99. Pursuant to Article 27(1) of Regulation (EC) No 1/2003, the Commission shall give the addressees of a Statement of Objections the opportunity of being heard on matters to which the Commission has taken objection. The written reply gives the parties subject to the proceedings the opportunity to set out their views on the objections raised by the Commission.

100. The time limit for the reply to the Statement of Objections will take into account both the time required for the preparation of the submission and the urgency of the case.[62] The addressees of the Statement of Objections have the right to a minimum period of four weeks to reply in writing.[63] A longer period (normally, a period of two months, although this may be longer or shorter depending on the circumstances of the case) will be granted by the Directorate-General for Competition taking into account, inter alia, the following elements:

— the size and complexity of the file (eg, the number of infringements, the alleged duration of the infringement(s), the size and number of documents and/or the size and complexity of expert studies); and/or

— whether the addressee of the statement of objection making the request has had prior access to information (eg, key submissions, leniency applications); and/or

— any other objective obstacles which may be faced by the addressee of the Statement of Objections making the request in providing its observations.

101. An addressee of a Statement of Objections may, within the original time limit, seek an extension of the time limit to reply by means of a reasoned request to the Directorate-General for Competition at least 10 working days before the expiry of the original time limit. If such a request is not granted or the addressee of the Statement of Objections disagrees with the length of the extension granted, it may refer the matter to the hearing officer for review before the expiry of the original time limit.

102. The time limit will start to run from the date when access to the main documents of the file has been granted.[64] In particular, time limits will normally not start running before the addressee of the Statement of Objections has been offered access to documents which are only accessible on Commission premises, eg, corporate statements. The fact that access to the entire file has not been granted does not have the automatic consequence that a time limit has not started running.[65]

103. Where required by the rights of defence,[66] or where it may in the Commission's view help to further clarify factual and legal issues relevant for the case, the Commission may give parties a copy of the non-confidential version (or specific parts thereof) of other parties' written replies to the Statement of Objections. This would normally be done

prior to the oral hearing, so as to allow parties to comment on them at the oral hearing. The Commission may also decide to do so in appropriate cases with respect to complainants and admitted third parties. If access to other parties' replies is granted because it is required for the rights of the defence parties are also entitled to have sufficient additional time to comment on these replies.

3.1.5. Rights of complainants and interested third persons

104. Complainants are closely associated with the proceedings. Pursuant to Article 6(1) of the Implementing Regulation, they are entitled to receive a non-confidential version of the Statement of Objections, and the Commission shall set a time limit in which the complainant may make its views known in writing. A request for an extension of this time limit may be made by way of a reasoned request to the Commission in due time before the expiry of the original time limit. If such a request is not granted or the Directorate-General for Competition and the complainant disagree about a requested extension, the complainant may refer the matter to the hearing officer, by means of a reasoned request.[67]

105. Upon application, the Commission shall also hear other natural or legal persons which can demonstrate a sufficient interest in the outcome of the procedure in accordance with Article 13 of the Implementing Regulation. The hearing officer takes the decision on whether such third persons are admitted to the proceedings. Persons who have been admitted shall be informed in writing of the nature and subject matter of the procedure and a time limit shall be set by the Commission in which they may make their views known in writing. A request for an extension of this time limit may be made by way of a reasoned request to the Directorate-General for Competition in due time before the expiry of the original time limit. If such a request is not granted or the Directorate-General for Competition and the third person admitted to the proceedings disagree about a requested extension the third person may refer the matter to the hearing officer, by means of a reasoned request.[68]

3.1.6. Oral hearing

106. Every party to which a Statement of Objections has been addressed has the right to an oral hearing. An oral hearing may be requested within the time limit set for their written reply to the Statement of Objections.

107. The oral hearing allows the parties to develop orally the arguments that they submitted in writing and to supplement, where appropriate, the written evidence, or to inform the Commission of other matters that may be relevant. The oral hearing also allows the parties to present their arguments as to the matters that may be of importance for the possible imposition of fines. The fact that the hearing is not public guarantees that all attendees can express themselves freely. Any information disclosed during the hearing shall only be used for the purposes of judicial and/or administrative proceedings for the application of Articles 101 and 102 TFEU and shall not be disclosed or used for any other purpose by any participant in a hearing. This restriction also applies to the recording of the oral hearing, as well as any visual presentations. Should information disclosed during the oral hearing be used for a purpose other than judicial and/or administrative proceedings for the application of Articles 101 and 102 TFEU at any point in time with the involvement of outside counsel, the Commission may report the incident to the bar of that counsel, with a view to disciplinary action.

108. In view of the importance of the oral hearing, it is the practice of the Directorate-General for Competition to ensure the continuous presence of senior management of the Directorate-General for Competition (Director or Deputy Director-General), together with the case team of Commission officials responsible for the investigation. The competition authorities of the Member States, the Chief Economist's team, and associated Commission services,[69] including the Legal Service, are also invited to attend by the hearing officer.

3.1.7. Supplementary Statement of Objections and letter of facts

109. If, after the Statement of Objections has been issued, new evidence is identified which the Commission intends to rely upon or if the Commission intends to change its legal assessment to the disadvantage of the undertakings concerned, the undertakings in question shall be given an opportunity to present their observations on these new aspects.

110. If additional objections are issued or the intrinsic nature of the infringement with which an undertaking is charged is modified,[70] the Commission shall notify this to the parties in a Supplementary Statement of Objections. Before doing so, a State of Play meeting will normally be offered to the parties. The rules on setting the time limit for the reply to a Statement of Objections apply (see above), although a shorter time limit will typically be set in this context.

111. If, however, the objections already raised against the undertakings in the Statement of Objections are only corroborated by new evidence that the Commission intends to rely on, it will bring this to the attention of the parties concerned by a simple letter (letter of facts).[71] The letter of facts gives undertakings the opportunity to provide written comments on the new evidence within a fixed time limit. A request for an extension of this time limit may be made by way of a reasoned request to the Commission. If the Directorate-General for Competition and the addressee disagree about a requested extension, the addressee may refer the matter to the hearing officer, by means of a reasoned request.

112. The procedural rights which are triggered by the sending of the Statement of Objections apply *mutatis mutandis* where a Supplementary Statement of Objections is issued, including the right of the parties to request an oral hearing. Access to all evidence gathered between the initial Statement of Objections and the Supplementary Statement of Objections will also be provided. If a letter of facts is issued, access will in general be granted to evidence gathered after the Statement of Objections up to the date of the said letter of facts. However, in cases where the Commission only intends to rely upon specific evidence that concerns one or a limited number of parties and/or isolated issues (in particular those regarding the determination of the amount of the fine or issues of parental liability), access will be provided only to the parties directly concerned and to the evidence relating to the issue(s) in question.

3.2. POSSIBLE OUTCOMES OF THIS PHASE

113. If, having regard to the parties' replies given in writing and/or at the oral hearing and on the basis of a thorough assessment of all information obtained up to this stage the objections are substantiated, the Commission will proceed towards adopting a decision finding an infringement of the relevant competition rules. The Commission can also decide to withdraw certain objections and to continue towards a decision finding an infringement for the remaining part.

114. If, however, the objections at this stage are not substantiated, the Commission will close the case. In this case, the information measures described above in paragraph (76) would also apply.

NOTES

52 Article 27 of Regulation (EC) No 1/2003, mentioned above.

53 Article 1 of terms of reference of the hearing officer.

54 Article 27 of Regulation (EC) No 1/2003.

55 Guidelines on the method of setting fines imposed pursuant to Article 23(2)(a) of Regulation (EC) No 1/2003 (OJ C210, 1.9.2006, p 2).

56 See footnote 55.

57 See Note SEC(2010) 737/2 of 12 June 2010.

58 See paragraph 107 below.

59 Notice on the rules for access to the Commission file, mentioned above.

60 Commission Notice on Immunity from fines and reduction of fines in cartel cases (mentioned above), paragraphs 31 to 35 and Commission Notice on the conduct of settlement procedures (mentioned above), paragraphs 35 to 40.

61 See Article 16(4) of the Implementing Regulation.

62 See Case T-44/00 *Mannesmannröhren-Werke AG v Commission* [2004] ECR II-2223, para. 65.

63 See Article 17(2) of the Implementing Regulation. For the rule applicable to settlement procedures, see Article 10(a) of the Implementing Regulation.

64 In most cases, parties will be given access to the complete file by means of a CD-Rom containing all documents in the file.

65 See Case T-44/00, *Mannesmannröhren-Werke AG v Commission*, [2004] ECR II-2223, para 65. See also recital 15 of the terms of reference of the hearing officer which states 'In exceptional circumstances, the hearing officer may suspend the running of the time period in which an addressee of a statement of objections should reply to that statement until a dispute about access to file has been resolved, if the addressee would not be in a position to reply within the deadline granted and an extension would not be an adequate solution at that point in time.'

66 See Joined Cases T-191/98 and T-212/98 to T-214/98 *Atlantic Container Line and Others v Commission* [2003] ECR II-3275; Case T-54/03 *Lafarge v Commission* [2008] ECR II-120, paras 69–73; Case T-52/03 *Knauf v Commission* [2008] ECR II-115, paras 41–47, 67–79; Case C-407/08P *Knauf v Commission*, judgment of 1 July 2010 (not yet reported), paras 23–28.

67 Article 9(2) of the terms of reference of the hearing officer.

68 See footnote 67.

69 See further the document 'Key actors and checks and balances', available on the Directorate-General for Competition's website.

70 For example a supplementary Statement of Objections would be issued if the new evidence allows the Commission to extend the duration of the infringement, the geographic scope or the nature or scope of the infringement.

71 When the Commission merely communicates to a party a non-confidential version (or specific excerpts thereof) of the other parties' written replies to the Statement of Objections and gives it the opportunity to submit its comments (see paragraph 103 above), this does not constitute a letter of facts.

4. COMMITMENT PROCEDURES

[4.369]

115. Article 9 of Regulation (EC) No 1/2003 provides the possibility for undertakings to offer commitments that are intended to address the competition concerns identified by the Commission. If the Commission accepts these commitments, it may adopt a decision which makes them binding on the parties subject to the proceedings. It is at the discretion of the Commission whether or not to accept commitments. In light of the principle of proportionality, the Commission must verify that the commitments address the identified competition concerns and that the commitments offered do not manifestly go beyond what is necessary to address these concerns. When carrying out that assessment, the Commission will take into consideration the interests of third parties. However, it is not obliged to compare such voluntary commitments with measures it could impose under Article 7 of Regulation (EC) No 1/2003 and to regard as disproportionate any commitments which go beyond such measures.[72]

116. Commitment decisions are not appropriate in cases where the Commission considers that the nature of the infringement calls for the imposition of a fine.[73] Consequently, the Commission does not apply the Article 9 procedure to secret cartels that fall under the Notice on immunity from fines and reduction of fines in cartel cases.

117. The main difference between a prohibition decision pursuant to Article 7 and a commitment decision pursuant to Article 9 of Regulation (EC) No 1/2003 is that the former contains a finding of an infringement while the latter makes the commitments binding without concluding whether there was or still is an infringement. A commitment decision concludes that there are no longer grounds for action by the Commission. Moreover, commitments are offered by undertakings on a voluntary basis. Conversely, by an Article 7 decision, the Commission can impose remedies which are necessary to bring the infringement to an end (and/or fines) on undertakings.

4.1. INITIATION OF COMMITMENT DISCUSSIONS

118. Undertakings may contact the Directorate-General for Competition at any time to explore the Commission's readiness to pursue the case with the aim of reaching a commitment decision. The Commission encourages undertakings to signal at the earliest possible stage their interest in discussing commitments.

119. A State of Play meeting will be offered to the parties at that point. The Directorate-General for Competition will indicate to the undertaking the timeframe within which the discussions on potential commitments should be concluded and will present to them the preliminary competition concerns arising from the investigation.

120. In order to avoid delays due to translation, that meeting and the following steps of the procedure may be conducted in an agreed language on the basis of a duly provided 'language waiver' by which the parties accept to receive and submit documents in a language other than the language of the Member State in which they are located (see above Section 2.4).

4.2. PRELIMINARY ASSESSMENT

121. Once the Commission is convinced of the undertakings' genuine willingness to propose commitments which will effectively address the competition concerns, a Preliminary Assessment will be issued. Pursuant to Article 9 of Regulation (EC) No 1/2003 the Preliminary Assessment summarises the main facts of the case and identifies the competition concerns that would warrant a decision requiring that the infringement is brought to an end. Prior to issuing the Preliminary Assessment, the parties will also be offered a State of Play meeting.

122. The Preliminary Assessment will serve as a basis for the parties to formulate appropriate commitments addressing the competition concerns expressed by the Commission, or to better define previously discussed commitments.

123. If a Statement of Objections has already been sent to the parties, commitments may nevertheless still be accepted, in appropriate cases. In these circumstances, a Statement of Objections fulfils the requirements of a Preliminary Assessment, as it contains a summary of the main facts as well as an assessment of the competition concerns identified.

124. Parties to the proceedings which offer commitments to meet the concerns expressed to them by the Commission in its Preliminary Assessment may call upon the hearing officer at any time during which the procedure under Article 9 is followed in relation to the effective exercise of their procedural rights.[74]

125. The Commission or the undertaking(s) concerned may decide at any moment during the commitment procedure to discontinue their discussions. The Commission can then normally continue formal proceedings pursuant to Article 7 of Regulation (EC) No 1/2003.[75]

4.3. SUBMISSION OF THE COMMITMENTS

126. After receiving the Preliminary Assessment, the parties will normally have one month to formally submit their commitments. If the parties have received a Statement of Objections and subsequently decide to submit commitments, the time limit to reply to the Statement of Objections will generally not be extended. The submission of commitments does not necessarily imply that the parties agree with the Commission's Preliminary Assessment.

127. The parties can offer commitments of a behavioural or structural nature that address adequately the competition concerns identified. Commitments which do not adequately remedy these concerns will not be accepted by the Commission.

128. Commitments must be unambiguous and self-executing.[76] If need be, a trustee can be appointed to assist the Commission in their implementation (monitoring and/or divestiture trustee). Furthermore, when commitments cannot be implemented without the agreement of third parties (eg, where a third party that would not be a suitable buyer under the commitments holds a pre-emption right), the undertaking should submit evidence of the third party's agreement.

4.4. THE 'MARKET TEST' AND SUBSEQUENT DISCUSSIONS WITH THE PARTIES

129. In accordance with Article 27(4) of Regulation (EC) No 1/2003 the Commission must conduct a market test of the commitments before making them binding by decision. The Commission will only conduct a market test if it considers that the commitments offered prima facie address the competition concerns identified. The Commission must publish in the *Official Journal of the European Union* a notice (market test notice) containing a concise summary of the case and the main content of the commitments, whilst respecting the obligations of professional secrecy.[77] It will also publish on the Directorate-General for Competition's website the full text of the commitments[78] in the authentic language.[79] In order to enhance the transparency of the process, the Commission will also publish a press release setting out the key issues of the case and the proposed commitments. If the case is based on a complaint, the Commission will at this stage also inform the complainant about the market test and invite the complainant to submit comments. Similarly, third parties admitted to the procedure will be informed and invited to submit comments. At the Commission's discretion, triangular meetings with the parties and the complainant and/or admitted third parties may be held.

130. Interested third parties are invited to submit their observations within a fixed time limit of not less than one month in accordance with Article 27(4) of Regulation (EC) No 1/2003.

131. The Commission may send the market test document to other parties that may be potentially concerned by the outcome of the case (eg, consumer associations).

132. After receipt of the replies to the market test, a State of Play meeting will be organised with the parties. The Commission will inform the parties orally or in writing of the substance of the replies.

133. Where the Commission is of the view, on the basis of the results of the market test (and any other information available) that the competition concerns identified have not been addressed or that changes in the text of the commitments are necessary to make them effective, this will be brought to the attention of the undertakings offering the commitments. If the latter are willing to address the problems identified by the Commission, they should submit an amended version of the commitments. If the amended version of the commitments alters the very nature or scope of the commitments, a new market test will be conducted. If the undertakings are unwilling to submit an amended version of the commitments, where this is required by the Commission's assessment of the result of the market test, the Commission can revert to the Article 7 procedure.

NOTES

72 Case C-441/07 P *Commission v Alrosa*, judgment of 29 June 2010, paragraph 120.

73 See recital 13 of Regulation (EC) No 1/2003.

74 Article 15(1) of the terms of reference of the hearing officer.

75 See Section 3 of this notice.

76 That is, their implementation must not be dependant on the will of a third party which is not bound by the commitments.

77 Article 28 of Regulation (EC) No 1/2003.

78 Non-confidential version.

79 Without translation.

5. PROCEDURE FOR REJECTION OF COMPLAINTS

[4.370]

134. Formal complaints are an important tool in the implementation of the competition rules and are therefore carefully examined by the Commission. However, after appropriate assessment of the factual and legal circumstances of the individual case, the Commission may reject a complaint pursuant to the grounds and procedure set out below.[80]

5.1. GROUNDS FOR REJECTION

135. The rejection of complaints can be based on 'insufficient grounds for acting' (also known as 'lack of European Union interest'), lack of competence or lack of evidence to establish the existence of an infringement.

136. Rejections based on 'insufficient grounds for acting'[81] concern in particular complaints where, given the limited likelihood of establishing the proof of the alleged infringements and the substantial investigatory resources which the Commission would have to invest in order to verify their existence, allocating the resources necessary to further investigate the case would be disproportionate, in light of its expected limited impact on the functioning of the internal market and/or the possibility of the complainant to have recourse to other means.[82]

137. The Commission may also reject complaints for lack of substantiation (when the complainant fails to submit even a minimum of prima facie evidence necessary to substantiate an infringement of Articles 101 and/or 102 TFEU) or on substantive grounds (absence of an infringement).

138. If a national competition authority is dealing or has already dealt with the same case,[83] the Commission shall inform the complainant accordingly. In such a situation, the complainant may withdraw the complaint. If the complainant maintains the complaint, the Commission may reject it by decision pursuant to Article 13 of Regulation (EC) No 1/2003 and in accordance with Article 9 of the Implementing Regulation.[84] If a national court is dealing or has already dealt with the same case, the Commission may reject the complaint based on 'insufficient grounds for acting'.[85]

5.2. PROCEDURE

139. If the Commission, after careful examination of the case, comes to the preliminary conclusion that it should not pursue the case for any of the reasons mentioned above, it will first inform the complainant in a meeting or by phone that it has come to the preliminary view that the case may be rejected. Once informed, the complainant may decide to withdraw the complaint. Otherwise, the Commission will inform the complainant by a formal letter pursuant to Article 7(1) of the Implementing Regulation of its preliminary conclusion that there are insufficient grounds for acting and set a time limit for its written observations.[86] In this context, the complainant has the right to request access to the documents on which the Commission bases its provisional assessment.[87] If in the course of its examination of the complaint, the Commission has opened proceedings pursuant to Article 11(6) of Regulation (EC) No 1/2003 a State of Play meeting will be offered to the complainant prior to sending such a formal letter. The time limit set in the formal letter shall be at least four weeks.[88] The time limit will start to run from the date when access to the main documents on which the assessment was made has been granted. Where appropriate and upon reasoned request to the Directorate-General for Competition made before the expiry of the original time limit, the time limit may be extended.[89] If such a request is not granted or the Directorate-General for Competition and the complainant disagree about the extension requested, the addressee may refer the matter to the hearing officer, by means of a reasoned request.[90]

140. If the complainant does not react to the above mentioned letter of the Commission within the time limit, the complaint shall be deemed to have been withdrawn pursuant to Article 7(3) of the Implementing Regulation. The complainant will be informed accordingly about the administrative closure of the case.

141. If the submissions of the complainant in response to the above mentioned letter of the Commission, does not lead the Commission to a different assessment of the complaint, it will reject the complaint by formal decision pursuant to Article 7(2) of the Implementing Regulation. If the submissions of the complainant lead to a different assessment of the complaint, the Commission will continue its investigation.

NOTES

80 See also Commission notice on the handling of complaints (mentioned above).

81 Cf. in particular Case T-24/90, *Automec II*, [1992] ECR II-2223 and Case C-119/97 P, *Ufex*, [1999] ECR I-1341.

82 The Commission notice on the handling of complaints lists in paragraph 44 certain criteria that can be used in isolation or combination for rejections on the grounds of lack of 'European Union interest'. Moreover, the Commission identified in its Report on Competition Policy 2005 some criteria that it could use to decide whether or not there is 'European Union interest'. See also Case T-427/08, *Confédération européenne des associations d'horlogeurs-réparateurs (CEAHR) v Commission*, not yet reported.

83 The notion of same case essentially implies: infringement of the same nature, same product market, same geographic market, at least one of the same undertakings, same period of time.

84 Paragraph 25 of the Commission's notice on the handling of complaints.

85 See Annual Report on Competition Policy 2005, adopted in June 2006, p. 25 ff.

86 Article 7(1) of the Implementing Regulation; paragraph 68 of the Commission's notice on the handling of complaints.

87 Article 8 of Regulation of the Implementing Regulation; paragraph 69 of the Commission's notice on the handling of complaints.

88 Article 17(2) of the Implementing Regulation.

89 Article 17(4) of the Implementing Regulation.

90 See footnote 67.

6. LIMITS ON THE USE OF INFORMATION

[4.371]

142. Information exchanged in the course of these procedures, in particular in the context of access to file and review of key submissions, shall only be used for the purposes of judicial or administrative proceedings for the application of Articles 101 and 102 TFEU.[91]

143. At all stages of the proceedings, the Commission will respect genuine and justified requests from complainants or from information providers regarding the confidential nature of their submissions or contacts with the Commission, including, where appropriate, their identity, in order to protect their legitimate interests (in particular in case of possible retaliation) and to avoid discouraging them from coming forward to the Commission.[92]

144. Commission officials and the members of the Advisory Committee are bound by the obligation of professional secrecy set out in Article 28 of Regulation (EC) No 1/2003. They are therefore prohibited from disclosing any information of the kind covered by this obligation which they have acquired or exchanged in the context of the investigation and the preparation of, and the deliberations in, the Advisory Committee. As regards the Advisory Committee, its members also must not reveal the opinion of the Advisory Committee prior to its publication, if any, or any information concerning the deliberations which led to the formulation of the opinion.

NOTES

91 Cf. Article 15(4) of the Implementing Regulation.

92 See Article 16(1) of Regulation (EC) No 1/2003.

7. ADOPTION, NOTIFICATION AND PUBLICATION OF DECISIONS

[4.372]

145. All decisions pursuant to Articles 7, 9, 23 and 24 of Regulation (EC) No 1/2003 are adopted by the Commission, on a proposal of the Commissioner responsible for competition policy.

146. Immediately after the decision has been adopted, the addressees will be informed of the decision. The Directorate-General for Competition endeavours to send a courtesy copy to the parties. A certified copy of the full text of the decision as well as a copy of the final report of the hearing officer will then be notified to the addressees by express courier service.

147. A press release will be published after the adoption of the decision by the Commission. The press release describes the scope of the case and the nature of the infringement. It also indicates (where appropriate) the amount of fines for each undertaking concerned and/or the remedies imposed or, in decisions pursuant to Article 9 of Regulation (EC) No 1/2003, the commitments rendered binding.

148. The summary of the decision, the hearing officer's final report as well as the Opinion of the Advisory Committee will be published shortly after the adoption of the decision in the *Official Journal of the European Union* in all official languages.[93]

149. In addition to the requirements set out in Article 30(1) of Regulation (EC) No 1/2003, the Directorate-General for Competition will endeavour to publish as soon as possible on its website a non-confidential version of the decision in the authentic languages as well as in additional languages, if such versions are available. A non-confidential version of the decision will also be sent to the complainant. The addressees of the decision will normally be asked to provide the Commission within two weeks with a non-confidential version of the decision and to approve the summary. Should disputes arise regarding the deletion of business secrets, a provisional version of the decision excluding all information for which confidentiality has been requested will be made available on the website of the Directorate-General for Competition in any of the official languages in anticipation of a final version after resolution of the disputed parts.

150. In the interest of transparency, the Commission intends to make public on its website its decisions rejecting complaints (pursuant to Article 7 of the Implementing Regulation) or a summary thereof. If required for the protection of legitimate interests of the complainant, the published version of the decision will not identify the complainant. Decisions adopted pursuant to Article 7 of Regulation (EC) No 1/2003 or modifying commitments that have been made binding under Article 9 of that Regulation will also be made public on the website. Other types of decisions may also be published in appropriate cases.

NOTES

93 With the exception of Irish (see Article 2 of Council Regulation (EC) No 920/2005 of 13 June 2005).

8. FUTURE REVISION

[4.373]

151. This notice may be revised to reflect changes in the applicable legislation, significant developments in the case law of the Court of Justice of the European Union, or further experience gained in applying the competition rules. The Commission intends to engage in regular dialogue with the business and legal community and other interested parties on the experience gained through the application of this notice, of Regulation (EC) No 1/2003, the Implementing Regulation and its various notices and guidelines.

ANNEX 1

[4.374]

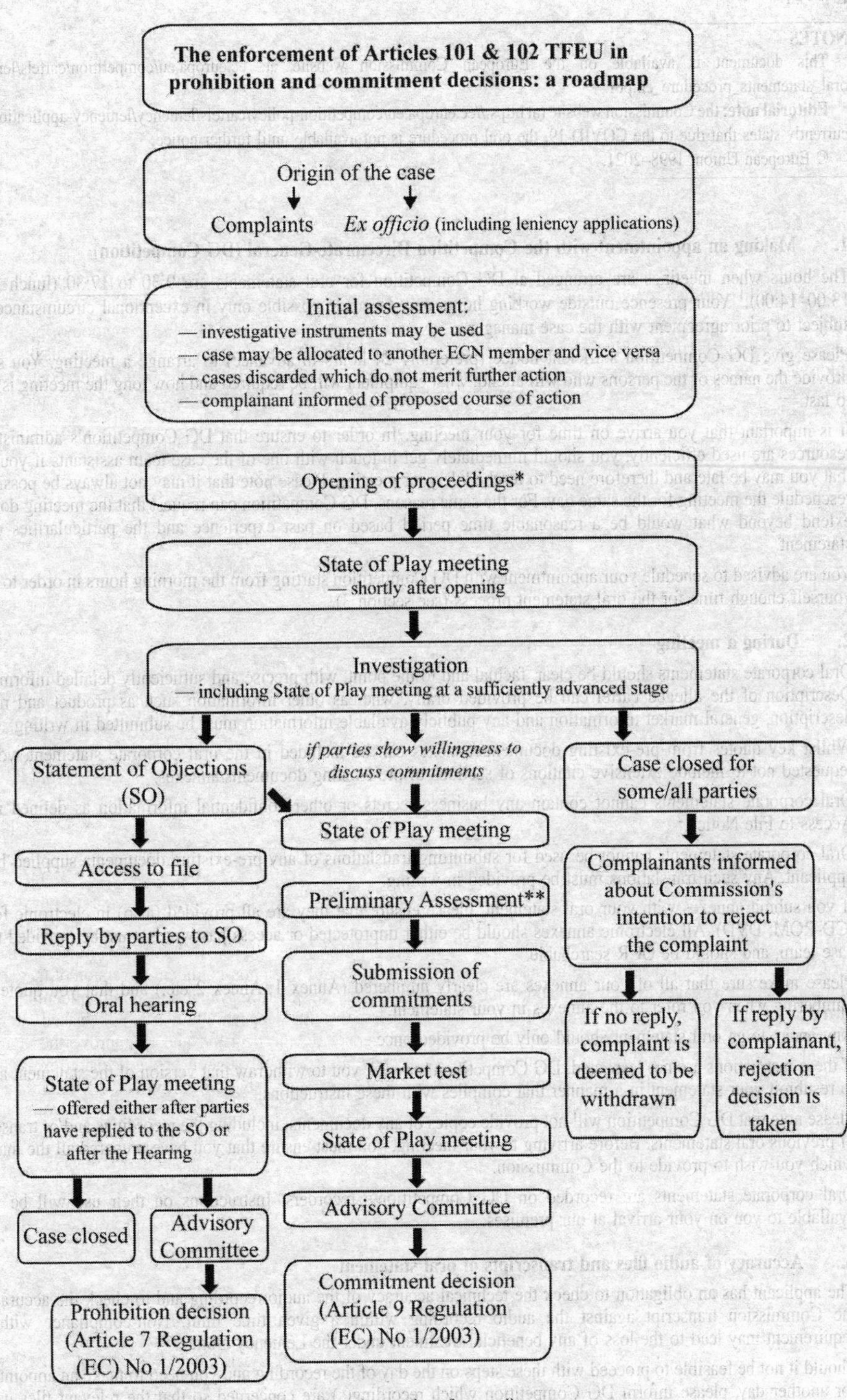
The enforcement of Articles 101 & 102 TFEU in prohibition and commitment decisions: a roadmap
Origin of the case
Complaints
Ex officio (including leniency applications)
Initial assessment:
— investigative instruments may be used
— case may be allocated to another ECN member and vice versa
— cases discarded which do not merit further action
— complainant informed of proposed course of action
Opening of proceedings*
State of Play meeting
— shortly after opening
Investigation
— including State of Play meeting at a sufficiently advanced stage
Statement of Objections (SO)
if parties show willingness to discuss commitments
Case closed for some/all parties
State of Play meeting
Access to file
Preliminary Assessment**
Complainants informed about Commission's intention to reject the complaint
Reply by parties to SO
Submission of commitments
If no reply, complaint is deemed to be withdrawn
If reply by complainant, rejection decision is taken
Oral hearing
Market test
State of Play meeting
— offered either after parties have replied to the SO or after the Hearing
State of Play meeting
Advisory Committee
Case closed
Advisory Committee
Commitment decision (Article 9 Regulation (EC) No 1/2003)
Prohibition decision (Article 7 Regulation (EC) No 1/2003)
* With the exception of cartel proceedings, where the opening of proceedings normally takes place simultaneously with the adoption of the Statement of Objections
** If an SO has already been issued, a Preliminary Assessment is not required

DELIVERING ORAL STATEMENTS AT DG COMPETITION

(8 October 2013)

[4.375]

NOTES

This document is available on the European Commission website at: ec.europa.eu/competition/cartels/leniency/oral_statements_procedure_en.pdf.

Editorial note: the Commission website (at https://ec.europa.eu/competition-policy/cartels/leniency/leniency-applications_en) currently states that due to the COVID-19, the oral procedure is not available until further notice.

1. Making an appointment with the Competition Directorate-General (DG Competition)

The hours when meetings are arranged at DG Competition for oral statements are 9:30 to 17:30 (lunch break: 13:00–14:00).[1] Your presence outside working hours may be made possible only in exceptional circumstances and subject to prior agreement with the case manager.

Please give DG Competition sufficient notice (preferably 24 hours in advance) to arrange a meeting. You should provide the names of the persons who will attend, what equipment will be required and how long the meeting is likely to last.

It is important that you arrive on time for your meeting. In order to ensure that DG Competition's administrative resources are used efficiently, you should immediately get in touch with one of the case team assistants if you think that you may be late and therefore need to reschedule your meeting. Please note that it may not always be possible to reschedule the meeting for the same day. For the same reasons, DG Competition can request that the meeting does not extend beyond what would be a reasonable time period based on past experience and the particularities of the statement.

You are advised to schedule your appointment with DG Competition starting from the morning hours in order to allow yourself enough time for the oral statement process (see section 3).

2. During a meeting

Oral corporate statements should be clear, factual and to the point, with precise and sufficiently detailed information. Description of the alleged cartel can be provided orally, whereas other information such as product and market description, general market information and any publicly available information must be submitted in writing.

Whilst key quotes from pre-existing documents/annexes can be included in the oral corporate statement, you are requested not to include extensive citations of sections of pre-existing documents/annexes.

Oral corporate statements cannot contain any business secrets or other confidential information as defined in the Access to File Notice.[2]

Oral corporate statements cannot be used for submitting translations of any pre-existing documents supplied by the applicant. Any such translations must be provided in writing.

If you submit annexes with your oral statement, please ensure that they are all provided (also) in electronic format (CD-ROM; DVD). All electronic annexes should be either unprotected or access passwords must be provided to the case team, and should be OCR searchable.

Please make sure that all of your annexes are clearly numbered (Annex 1, Annex 2 etc.) and that you quote such numbering when you refer to the annexes in your statement.

Any annex to an oral statement should only be provided once.

If these instructions are not respected, DG Competition may ask you to withdraw that version of the statement and/or to resubmit your statement in a manner that complies with these instructions.

Please note that DG Competition will not provide copies of any documents, including the recordings and/or transcripts of previous oral statements. Before arriving to your meeting, you must ensure that you have prepared all the material which you wish to provide to the Commission.

Oral corporate statements are recorded on DG Competition's recorders. Instructions on their use will be made available to you on your arrival at our premises.

3. Accuracy of audio files and transcripts of oral statement

The applicant has an obligation to check the technical accuracy of the audio recording and to check the accuracy of the Commission transcript against the audio recording within a given time limit. Non-compliance with this requirement may lead to the loss of any beneficial treatment under the Leniency Notice.

Should it not be feasible to proceed with these steps on the day of the recording and you need to make an appointment for another day, please inform DG Competition which recording(s) are concerned so that the relevant files can be retrieved from the case library ahead of the meeting and made available to you on the spot.

Any corrections to a Commission transcript (other than amendments to ensure accuracy with a recording) will need to be made as separate audio files which (along with the corresponding transcript) will also need to be checked by the applicant for accuracy.

Thank you for your cooperation!

NOTES

[1] DG Competition works Monday to Friday subject to the list of public holidays for the institutions of the European Union. Please check this list before contacting DG Competition at: ec.europa.eu/competition/mergers/information_en.html.
Our premises are located at Place Madou, Madouplein 1, 1210 Saint-Josse-ten-Noode /Sint-Joost-ten-Node Belgium

[2] Commission Notice on the rules for access to the Commission file in cases pursuant to Articles 81 and 82 of the EC Treaty [now Articles 101 and 102 TFEU], Articles 53, 54 and 57 of the EEA Agreement and Council Regulation (EC) No 139/2004, OJ C325, 22.12.2005, p 7 ('Access to File Notice'). See also Article 15(3) of Regulation (EC) No 773/2004 of 7 April 2004 relating to the conduct of proceedings by the Commission pursuant to Articles 81 and 82 of the EC Treaty [now Articles 101 and 102 TFEU], OJ L123, 27.4.2004, p 18.

GUIDANCE ON THE PREPARATION OF PUBLIC VERSIONS OF COMMISSION DECISIONS ADOPTED UNDER ARTICLES 7 TO 10, 23 AND 24 OF REGULATION 1/2003

(June 2015)

[4.376]

NOTES

Note that Council Regulation 1/2003/EC is repealed, in relation to the UK, by the Competition (Amendment etc) (EU Exit) Regulations 2019, SI 2019/93, reg 63, Sch 3, para 1, as from IP completion day (as defined in the European Union (Withdrawal Agreement) Act 2020, s 39) (for transitional provisions and savings in relation to the operation of the 2019 Regulations, see Sch 4 to those Regulations at **[7.69]** et seq).

This document is available on the European Commission website at: ec.europa.eu/competition-policy/antitrust/public-versions-commission-decisions_en.

1. Decisions are taken as openly as possible within the European Union, according to the second subparagraph of Article 1 of the Treaty on European Union. This principle is reflected in Article 15 of the Treaty on the Functioning of the European Union ("TFEU"), which requires the Union's institutions to conduct their work as openly as possible. The ability of the institutions to make acts which they adopt public is therefore the rule. EU law may provide for exceptions to this rule and prevent the disclosure of such acts or certain information contained therein.[1] Such exceptions include in particular the provisions ensuring compliance with the obligation of professional secrecy.[2]

2. In line with the general principles recalled above, the Commission makes as much information as possible available to the public, and only refrains from disclosing information to the extent that this is covered by its duty of professional secrecy or other public policy exceptions. According to the case law, three cumulative conditions must be met in order for information to fall, by its nature, within the ambit of the obligation of professional secrecy and thus to enjoy protection against disclosure to the public: (i) that it is known only to a limited number of persons, (ii) that its disclosure is liable to cause serious harm to the person who has provided it or to third parties and (iii) that the interests liable to be harmed by disclosure are, objectively, worthy of protection.[3]

3. Article 30 of Council Regulation (EC) No 1/2003[4] requires the Commission to publish the decisions which it takes pursuant to Articles 7 to 10, 23 and 24. The publication shall state the names of the parties and the main content of the decision, including any penalties imposed. It shall have regard to the legitimate interest of undertakings in the protection of their business secrets and other confidential information.

4. In compliance with Article 30 of Council Regulation (EC) No 1/2003, the Commission publishes a non-confidential summary of the decisions taken pursuant to Articles 7 to 10, 23 and 24, together with the final report of the Hearing Officer and the opinion of the Advisory Committee[5] in the Official Journal of the European Union (OJ).[6] In line with established practice, it also publishes a non-confidential text of the decision (public version) on the DG Competition website.[7] The documents published in the OJ are made available on the DG Competition website as well.[8]

5. The General Court has confirmed the right of the Commission to publish its decisions in the OJ and on the DG Competition website.[9] Addressees of decisions adopted under Articles 7 to 10, 23 and 24 of Council Regulation (EC) No 1/2003 cannot prevent the Commission from publishing such decisions. It is the Commission's practice to publish as much detail as possible in order to allow those interested to understand fully the reasoning behind such a decision.

6. This Guidance outlines:

a) what undertakings can claim for redaction as business secrets and confidential information and what is usually not considered to be confidential information;
b) how confidentiality for business secrets and other confidential information can be claimed;
c) what the Commission usually redacts on its own initiative in the public version of a decision; and
d) the procedure that should be followed to settle confidentiality claims in the context of publication of the Commission decision and related publications.

7. This Guidance only concerns the preparation of the public version of Commission decisions and related publications and does not cover the preparation of non-confidential submissions by undertakings in the context of the Commission's access to file procedure.

NOTES

1 See Judgment of the General Court of 28 January 2015, *Akzo Nobel NV and Eka v Commission*, T-345/12, ECLI:EU:T:2015:50, paragraph 60, Judgment of the General Court of 28 January 2015, *Evonik Degussa v Commission*, T-341/12, ECLI:EU:T:2015:51, paragraph 89 and Judgment of the Court of First Instance of 30 May 2006, *Bank Austria Creditanstalt v Commission*, T-198/03, ECLI:EU:T:2006:136, paragraph 69.

2 See Article 339 TFEU. The relevant provisions on professional secrecy in the context of antitrust proceedings are Article 28(2) of Council Regulation (EC) No 1/2003 of 16 December 2002 on the implementation of the rules on competition laid down in Articles 81 and 82 of the Treaty (OJ L1, 4.1.2003, p 1) and Article 16(1) of Commission Regulation (EC) No 773/2004 of 7 April 2004 relating to the conduct of proceedings by the Commission pursuant to Articles 81 and 82 of the EC Treaty, (OJ L123, 27.4.2004, p 18).

3 Judgment of the Court of First Instance of 30 May 2006, *Bank Austria Creditanstalt v Commission*, T-198/03, ECLI:EU:T:2006:136, paragraph 71, Judgment of the General Court of 28 January 2015, *Evonik Degussa v Commission*, T-341/12, ECLI:EU:T:2015:51, paragraph 94 and Judgment of the General Court of 28 January 2015, *Akzo Nobel NV and Eka v Commission* T-345/12, ECLI:EU:T:2015:50, paragraph 65.

4 Council Regulation (EC) No 1/2003 of 16 December 2002 on the implementation of the rules on competition laid down in Articles 81 and 82 of the Treaty (OJ L1, 4.1.2003, p 1).

5 If the Advisory Committee so recommends, see Article 14(6) of Council Regulation (EC) No 1/2003.

6 Article 17(3) of the Decision of the President of the European Commission of 13 October 2011 on the function and terms of reference of the hearing officer in certain competition proceedings, (OJ L275, 20.10.2011) p. 29 ("Hearing Officer Terms of Reference").

7 See paragraph 149 of the Commission notice on best practices for the conduct of proceedings concerning Articles 101 and 102 TFEU, OJ, C 308, p 6-32.

8 See the DG Competition website: ec.europa.eu/competition/index_en.html.

9 See Judgment of the Court of First Instance of 30 May 2006, *Bank Austria Creditanstalt v Commission*, T-198/03, ECLI-:EU:T:2006:136, paragraph 77, Judgment of the General Court of 28 January 2015, *Akzo Nobel NV and Eka v Commission*, T-345/12, ECLI:EU:T:2015:50, paragraph 90 and Judgment of the General Court of 28 January 2015, *Evonik Degussa v Commission*, T-341/12, ECLI:EU:T:2015:51, paragraph 120.

1 WHAT CAN AND CANNOT BE CLAIMED FOR REDACTION

[4.377]

8. Undertakings can claim confidentiality for business secrets and other confidential information that should not appear in the public version of the Commission decision and in the related publications.[10]

1.1 BUSINESS SECRETS

9. **Business secrets** are confidential information about an undertaking's business activity the disclosure of which could result in **serious harm** for the same undertaking.[11] The interests liable to be harmed by disclosure must, objectively, be worthy of protection.[12]

10. Examples of information that may qualify as business secrets in antitrust decisions include: technical and/or financial information relating to an undertaking's know-how; margins calculations and price structure; production secrets and processes; supply sources; quantities produced and sold; market shares; customers and distributors lists; marketing plans; cost and methods of assessing costs; and sales strategy.

1.2 OTHER CONFIDENTIAL INFORMATION

11. **Other confidential information**[13] is information other than business secrets, insofar as its disclosure would significantly harm a person or undertaking. The interests liable to be harmed by disclosure must, objectively, be worthy of protection.[14] Depending on the specific circumstances of each case, this may include information that would enable the parties to identify complainants or other third parties where those have a justified wish to remain anonymous.

1.3 INFORMATION NOT CONSIDERED CONFIDENTIAL

12. The assessment whether a piece of information constitutes a business secret or other confidential information is carried out by the Commission on a **case-by-case basis**. Generally, information that is not covered by the above definitions of "business secrets" and "other confidential information" will not be considered confidential.

13. By way of example, DG Competition considers that the following categories of information are normally **not** considered **confidential**:

a) the **Commission's own assessment**, as long as it does not explicitly refer to information falling into the category of "business secret" or "other confidential information". This covers for instance the Commission's analysis of evidence and of the results of its investigation;

b) information relating to an undertaking which is **publicly available** or made **known outside the undertaking** (in case of a group, outside the group), or outside the association to which it has been communicated by that undertaking (including information such as price targets, price increases, dates of implementation of such increases and customer names). For information to lose its confidential nature, it is sufficient for it to be available to specialist circles or capable of being inferred from publicly available information.[15]

c) information that has **lost its commercial importance**, for instance due to the passage of time. The General Court has considered a period of five years in itself to be sufficient for information to lose its qualification as a business secret or other confidential information. Confidential treatment of information may only exceptionally be granted to such data, if its provider can show that, notwithstanding its historical nature, it still constitutes an essential element of the commercial position of the undertaking concerned;[16]

d) data from or about **another undertaking** (such as price announcements, sales data etc). Exceptionally, data received pursuant to a contract with that undertaking which envisages confidentiality might be considered as confidential. General references to a non-disclosure agreement are insufficient to justify the confidentiality of such data; and

e) **statistical** or **aggregate information** (also in the form of graphs, for instance).

14. **Detailed reasons** must be given for any request to derogate from these principles in exceptional cases.

NOTES

10 Article 16(1) of Commission Regulation (EC) No 773/2004.

11 Point 18 of the Commission Notice on the rules for access to the Commission file in cases pursuant to Articles 81 and 82 of the EC Treaty, Articles 53, 54 and 57 of the EEA Agreement and Council Regulation (EC) No 139/2004 ("Notice on access to file") (OJ C325, 22.12.2005, p.7).

12 Judgment of the Court of First Instance of 30 May 2006, *Bank Austria Creditanstalt v Commission*, T-198/03, ECLI:EU:T:2006:136, paragraph 71.

13 Points 19-20 of the Notice on access to file.

14 Judgment of the Court of First Instance of 30 May 2006, *Bank Austria Creditanstalt v Commission*, T-198/03, ECLI:EU:T:2006:136, paragraph 71.

15 Order of the Court of First Instance of 29 May 1997, *British Steel v Commission*, T-89/96, ECLI:EU:T:1997:77, at paragraphs 26 and 27.

16 See, e.g., Judgment of the General Court of 28 January 2015, *Evonik Degussa v Commission*, T-341/12, ECLI:EU:T:2015:51, paragraphs 84-85.

2 HOW TO CLAIM CONFIDENTIALITY

[4.378]

15. An undertaking can claim confidentiality on the text of the decision or related publications within the deadline set by the Commission.

16. In general, an undertaking cannot claim confidentiality for an entire document or whole sections thereof as it is normally possible to protect confidential information with limited redactions.

17. If an undertaking wants to claim confidentiality for information that should not appear in the public version of the decision or related publications, it is required to:[17]

a) **identify any information** in the decision which is stemming from the undertaking and which it considers to fall within the ambit of professional secrecy as described in Sections 1.1 and 1.2 above;

b) **substantiate each claim** for confidentiality in writing, explaining in particular:

   i. why the information in question constitutes a business secret or other confidential information;

   ii. how the publication of this information would cause **serious harm** to the undertaking or a third party; and

   iii. which interests worthy of protection would be harmed by the disclosure;

Note: Generic and unsubstantiated claims (e.g. *"this is a business secret as its disclosure would harm my commercial interests"*) will not be taken into consideration.

c) **highlight** in the text of the decision, in a way that it remains legible, any text which contains information that it regards as business secrets or otherwise confidential; and

d) **provide** a concise but meaningful **non-confidential summary** of the redacted information, e.g.: "sales strategy: [add details about the redacted item such as the time period, the area concerned, etc.]". For figures (such as market shares or turnover figures) please indicate ranges. Please indicate the category into which the information falls, "[BUSINESS SECRETS]" or "[CONFIDENTIAL]".

18. The undertaking is required to provide the Commission with all relevant details in order to enable it to assess the confidentiality of a piece of information and to weigh up: (a) the public interest in ensuring that the activities of the EU institutions take place in the most transparent manner possible; and (b) the legitimate interests in protecting confidential information.

19. For the sake of efficient handling, confidentiality claims should be presented in a "tabular" format according to the following model:

Type of the document (decision, summary of the decision, final report of the hearing officer etc.) / page #, recital # (please indicate annex # if relevant)	Reasons for confidentiality request	Suggested non-confidential summary
Decision, page 28, recital 235, 2nd sentence	Business secret: Last year's production strategy. This is information not divulged outside the undertaking. Its disclosure would seriously harm (. . .)	[Last year's production strategy]

20. Further information on the administrative procedure for establishing a public version of the Commission decision, the summary of the decision, the final report of the Hearing Officer and the opinion of the Advisory Committee can be found on the DG Competition website.[18]

21. If the undertaking fails to identify the information which it considers to be confidential, **the Commission** may **assume** that the decision, and, where relevant, the summary of the decision, the final report of the Hearing Officer and the opinion of the Advisory Committee do not contain any business secrets or other confidential information and, consequently, that **the undertaking has no objections to the disclosure of the information in those documents**.[19]

NOTES

17 See Articles 16(2) and 16(3) of Commission Regulation (EC) No 773/2004.

18 ec.europa.eu/competition/antitrust/antitrust_manproc_3_2012_en.pdf

19 See Article 16(4) of Commission Regulation (EC) No 773/2004: "If undertakings or associations of undertakings fail to comply with paragraphs 2 and 3, the Commission may assume that the documents or statements concerned do not contain confidential information".

3 WHAT THE COMMISSION REDACTS IN THE PUBLIC VERSION OF A DECISION

[4.379]

22. Irrespective of claims for confidentiality, other information redacted by the Commission in the public version of the decision (and the related publications) may include:

a) personal data, in line with the requirements of Regulation (EC) No 45/2001[20] (for instance information relating to an identified or identifiable natural person);

b) information relating to undertakings participating in the infringement that are not mentioned in the operative part of the Decision. This information is covered by the presumption of innocence and the obligation of professional secrecy within the meaning of Article 339 TFEU;[21]

c) information which, if published, may jeopardise Commission investigations, including the leniency program. This includes:

   a. quotes from corporate statements submitted under the Leniency Notice;[22]

   b. information which could, directly or indirectly, allow for the identification of an applicant as the source of specific information submitted under the Commission Leniency program;

   c. voluntary admissions of the participation in an infringement made during the inspections, in replies to requests for information or the statement of objections and during the oral hearing.

d) depending on the specific circumstances of each case: information provided by third parties about undertakings which are able to place very considerable economic or commercial pressure on their competitors or on their trading partners, customers or suppliers;[23] and

e) military secrets.

NOTES

20 Regulation (EC) No 45/2001 of the European Parliament and of the Council of 18 December 2000 on the protection of individuals with regard to the processing of personal data by the Community institutions and bodies and on the free movement of such data (OJ L8, 12.1.2001, p 1).

21 Judgment of the Court of First instance of 12 October 2007, *Pergan Hilfsstoffe für industrielle Prozesse v Commission*, T-474/04, ECLI:EU:T:2007:306.

22 Commission Notice on Immunity from fines and reduction of fines in cartel cases (OJ C298, 8.12.2006, p 17).

23 Point 19 of the Notice on access to file.

4 PROCEDURAL ASPECTS

[4.380]

23. In cases with several addressees, if possible, the Commission deals with all confidentiality claims in parallel.

24. Once all confidentiality claims have been settled with all parties to the case, the Commission will send a consolidated public version of the decision to all addressees of the decision. In this text the confidential information will have been removed. Any confidential information will have been redacted and replaced by the corresponding non-confidential descriptions, summaries or square brackets. Absent a reply within the deadline set by the Commission, the Commission will be entitled to publish this redacted public version.[24]

25. If an undertaking considers that this public version of the decision still contains business secrets or other confidential information, it can refer the matter to the Hearing Officer within the deadline that will be set by the Commission.[25] If the undertaking fails to address the Hearing Officer within the given deadline the Commission will be entitled to publish this redacted public version.

26. The publication of a public version of the decision on the DG Competition website does not preclude the Commission from publishing a more complete version at a later stage,

provided that this publication does not contain confidential information.[26]

NOTES

24 See Article 16(4) of Commission Regulation (EC) No 773/2004: "If undertakings or associations of undertakings fail to comply with paragraphs 2 and 3, the Commission may assume that the documents or statements concerned do not contain confidential information".

25 Article 8 of the Hearing Officer Terms of Reference.

26 Judgment of the General Court of 28 January 2015, *Akzo Nobel NV and Eka v Commission*, T-345/12, ECLI-:EU:T:2015:50, paragraph 123.

EXPLANATORY NOTE ON COMMISSION INSPECTIONS PURSUANT TO ARTICLE 20(4) OF COUNCIL REGULATION NO 1/2003

Revised on 11 September 2015

[4.381]

NOTES

Editorial note: this online version of this document (at: ec.europa.eu/competition-policy/antitrust/procedures_en) has been updated the last official revision in September 2015. In particular, references to the "EU Data Protection rules (Regulation No 45/2001)" have been replaced with references to the new "EU Data Protection rules (Regulation No 2018/1725)".

Note that Council Regulation 1/2003/EC is repealed, in relation to the UK, by the Competition (Amendment etc) (EU Exit) Regulations 2019, SI 2019/93, reg 63, Sch 3, para 1, as from IP completion day (as defined in the European Union (Withdrawal Agreement) Act 2020, s 39) (for transitional provisions and savings in relation to the operation of the 2019 Regulations, see Sch 4 to those Regulations at **[7.69]** et seq).

This note is for information only and is without prejudice to any formal interpretation of the European Commission's powers of investigation.

1. Undertakings[1] are legally obliged to submit to an inspection ordered by decision of the Commission under Article 20(4) of Council Regulation No 1/2003. Written authorisations serve to name the officials and other accompanying persons authorised by the Commission to conduct the inspection ('the Inspectors'). The Inspectors will each provide a proof of identity.

2. The Inspectors cannot be required to expand upon the subject matter as set out in the decision or to justify the decision in any way. They may however explain procedural matters, particularly with regard to confidentiality, and the possible consequences of a refusal to submit to the inspection.

3. A certified copy of the decision is to be handed to the undertaking. The minute of notification of the decision serves only to certify delivery and its signature by the recipient does not imply submission to the inspection.

4. The Inspectors are empowered, pursuant to Article 20(2) of Regulation No 1/2003:
   a) to enter any premises, land and means of transport of undertakings and associations of undertakings;
   b) to examine the books and other records related to the business, irrespective of the medium on which they are stored;
   c) to take or obtain in any form copies of or extracts from such books or records;
   d) to seal any business premises, books or records for the period and to the extent necessary for the inspection;
   e) to ask any representative or member of staff of the undertaking, or association of undertakings, for explanations on facts or documents relating to the subject matter of the inspection and to record the answers.

5. The officials and other accompanying persons authorised or appointed by the competition authority of the Member State of the territory on which the inspection is conducted are entitled to actively assist the Inspectors in carrying out their duties. To this end, they enjoy the same powers under Article 20(2) of Council Regulation No 1/2003 as the Inspectors (see paragraph 4 above). They shall prove their identity in accordance with the relevant national rules.

6. The undertaking may consult an external legal counsel during the inspection. However, the presence of such a legal counsel is not a legal condition for the validity of the inspection. The Inspectors may enter the premises, notify the decision ordering the inspection and occupy the offices of their choice without waiting for the undertaking to consult its legal counsel. The Inspectors will, in any case, accept only a short delay pending consultation of the legal counsel before starting to examine the books and other records related to the business, taking copies or extracts of those documents, sealing business premises and books or records if need be or asking for oral explanations. Any such delay must be kept to the strict minimum.

7. Where any representative or member of staff of the undertaking gives, pursuant to Article 4(1) of the Commission Regulation No 773/2004, oral explanations on the spot on facts or documents relating to the subject matter of the inspection at the request of the Inspectors, the explanations may be recorded in any form. A copy of any such recording will be made available to the undertaking concerned after the inspection pursuant to Article 4(2) of the European Commission Regulation No 773/2004.

8. In cases where a member of staff of an undertaking who is not or was not authorised by the undertaking to provide explanations on behalf of the undertaking has been asked for explanations, the Commission sets a time-limit within which the undertaking may communicate to the Commission any rectification, amendment or supplement to the explanations given by such member of staff which then shall be added to the explanations as recorded during the inspection.

9. The Inspectors are entitled to examine any books and records related to the business, irrespective of the medium on which they are stored, and to take or obtain in any form copies of or extracts from such books or records. This includes the examination of electronic information and the taking of electronic or paper copies of such information.

10. The Inspectors may search the IT-environment (e.g. servers, desktop computers, laptops, tablets and other mobile devices) and all storage media (e.g. CD-ROMs, DVDs, USB-keys, external hard disks, backup tapes, cloud services) of the undertaking. This applies also to private devices and media that are used for professional reasons (Bring Your

Own Device - BYOD) when they are found on the premises. For this purpose, the Inspectors may not only use any built-in (keyword) search tool, but may also make use of their own dedicated software and/or hardware ("Forensic IT tools"). These Forensic IT tools allow the Commission to copy, search and recover data whilst respecting the integrity of the undertakings' systems and data.

11. The undertaking has the obligation to cooperate fully and actively with the inspection. This means that the undertaking may be required to provide appropriate representatives or members of staff to assist the Inspectors, not only for explanations on the organisation of the undertaking and its IT-environment, but also for specific tasks such as temporary blocking of individual email accounts, temporarily disconnecting running computers from the network, removing and re-installing hard drives from computers and providing 'administrator access rights'-support. When such actions are taken, the undertaking must not interfere in any way with these measures and it is the undertaking's responsibility to inform the employees affected accordingly. The Inspectors may ask to use hardware (e.g. hard disks, CD-ROMs, DVDs, USB-keys, connection cables, scanners, printers) provided by the undertaking, but cannot be obliged to use the undertaking's hardware.

12. Storage media selected for examination may be kept under the Inspectors' control until the end of the inspection on the spot. They may be returned earlier, for instance after a forensic copy of the data under investigation has been made. Such a forensic copy is an authentic duplicate of (part or all of) the data stored on the original medium. The examination of the authentic duplicate is equal to the examination of the original storage medium.

13. At the end of the inspection the Inspectors completely wipe[2] all Forensic IT tools on which company data have been stored. Hardware provided by the undertaking will not be wiped by the Inspectors, but returned to the undertaking.

14. If the selection of documents relevant for the investigation is not yet finished at the envisaged end of the on-site inspection at the undertaking's premises, the copy of the data set still to be searched may be collected to continue the inspection at a later time. This copy will be secured by placing it in a sealed envelope. The undertaking may request a duplicate. The Commission will invite the undertaking to be present when the sealed envelope is opened and during the continued inspection process at the Commission's premises. Alternatively, the Commission may decide to return the sealed envelope to the undertaking without opening it. The Commission may also ask the undertaking to keep the sealed envelope in a safe place to allow the Commission to continue the search process at the premises of the undertaking in the course of a further announced visit.

15. As regards the final data selected by the Inspectors during the inspection on the spot (or following a continued inspection) which are added to the Commission's case file, the undertaking will receive a data carrier (e.g. a DVD) on which all these data are stored. The undertaking will be requested to sign the printed list(s) of data items selected. Two identical copies of these data stored on data carriers will be taken along by the Inspectors.

16. Note that each evidence item selected during the course of the inspection may be collected and on-site listed in its technical entirety (if e.g. only one attachment to an email is selected, then the final export will consist of the cover email, along with all attachments that belong to that particular message). In the course of final processing into the case file at Commission premises each evidence item may be taken apart into its individual components (e.g. cover email, attachments and/or other embedded data items) and these may then be listed individually and accordingly receive individual reference numbers.

17. Where the undertaking makes available material for making copies at the request of the Inspectors, the Commission shall, at the request of the undertaking, reimburse the cost of the material used to produce copies for the Commission.

18. The documents / data copied during an inspection will be covered by the provisions of Article 28 of Council Regulation No 1/2003 concerning professional secrecy. If, at a later stage of the procedure, it becomes necessary to grant other parties access to those documents / data, the undertaking will be asked to identify any business secrets or other confidential information contained in the documents / data, to justify its claims and to provide nonconfidential copies for the purpose of granting access to the file.

19. Where the Inspectors decide to seal business premises, books or records, a minute will be made. The undertaking has to ensure that affixed seals are not broken until removed again by the Inspectors. A separate minute will be prepared at the time of the seals' removal which will record their state at that time.

20. The EU Data Protection rules (Regulation No 2018/1725) apply to all personal data collected by the Commission during anti-trust investigations. As EU antitrust rules apply only to undertakings, personal data of individuals as such are not the target of anti-trust investigations and inspections conducted by the Commission. Personal data of individual staff members of undertakings (such as their names, telephone numbers, email addresses) may, however, be contained in business documents / data related to such investigations and may therefore be copied or obtained during an inspection and may become part of the Commission file.

21. All personal data on Commission anti-trust files may only be used for the purpose for which they were collected (the enforcement of Articles 101 and/or 102 TFEU) and will be processed in compliance with Regulation 2018/1725.

NOTES

1 In this note the term "undertaking" includes both undertakings and associations of undertakings.

2 The technical term for this wiping is 'sanitize'. The goal of sanitising is to completely remove the data from a storage device in a way that the data cannot be reconstructed by any known technique.

CARTELS: ANONYMOUS WHISTLEBLOWER TOOL

(March 2017)

[4.382]

NOTES

This document is available on the European Commission website at: ec.europa.eu/competition/cartels/whistleblower/index.html.

[4.383]

Inside knowledge and assistance can be a powerful tool to help the European Commission uncover cartels and other anti-competitive practices more swiftly than might otherwise be possible. It can contribute to the success of our investigations

You as an individual can help in the fight against cartels and other anti-competitive practices, such as agreeing on prices or procurement bids, keeping products off the market or unfairly excluding rivals. These practices cause immense damage to Europe's economy. They can deny customers access to a wider choice of goods and services at reasonable prices, stifle innovation and put companies out of business.

If you are aware of business practices that you think are wrong, you can help us investigate such practices by voluntarily providing us with information. This information can be for example, facts concerning anti-competitive conduct, its circumstances and the individuals involved that are not publicly known but are known to you. They can concern past, ongoing or planned anti-competitive behaviour.

HOW TO BLOW THE WHISTLE

We are fully available to offer our assistance and to answer any questions you might have in case you decide to contact us.

You can help us best if you come forward openly (giving your name and position and naming the source of your information), since this will give your statement more credibility and is more likely to enable us to take action.

- **If you are willing to reveal your identity:**
  - you can send an e-mail to: comp-whistleblower@ec.europa.eu
  - or call: 0032-2-29 74800.
- **If you are not willing to reveal your identity:** you can send us an anonymous message (see: comp-eu.whistleblowernetwork.net/FrontPages/Default.aspx).

  We have taken detailed steps to **protect your anonymity** as far as possible.
  - We use an experienced and specialised external intermediary. The intermediary's state-of-the-art tool is designed to protect the anonymity of whistleblowers. Similar tools are used by competition authorities in Germany, Denmark and other Member States.
  - Once you enter your message into the intermediary's encryption tool, it will alert us.
  - If you want to, you can agree to two-way communication with us so that we can ask you for additional information or clarification, and so to increase the likelihood that we can take actions based on your information. In this case, the intermediary will give you a passcode that you can use to log into the intermediary's tool and see our response. The tool only delivers your message; it does not provide us with any additional information (such as your IP-address or password you have chosen to retrieve our messages).

If you already sent us a message and allowed for us to reply, click on the above hyperlink to check for a reply.

- **If you are empowered to represent a company involved in a cartel**: you can also apply for leniency (see: ec.europa.eu/competition-policy/cartels/leniency/leniency-applications_en) and thereby completely avoid or reduce fines for your company.
- How to file a Complaint (see: ec.europa.eu/competition-policy/antitrust/procedures/complaints_en).

Please note that the above mentioned telephone number, e-mail address and anonymous reporting tool are only to be used for whistleblowers. Given the importance of these communication channels, no other queries will be answered.

The telephone line is monitored from 09:00 to 17:00 on weekdays. Outside of these times, please use the e-mail address or the anonymous reporting tool.

ANNEX TO THE COMMUNICATION TO THE COMMISSION

Working Arrangements for the Functioning of the Advisory Committee on Restrictive Practices and Dominant Positions

Brussels, 29.3.2019

C(2019) 2310 final

[4.384]

NOTES

This document is available on the European Commission website at: ec.europa.eu/competition/antitrust/legislation/cooperation_nca.pdf.

I. INTRODUCTION

[4.385]

1. Pursuant to Article 14(1) of Council Regulation (EC) No 1/2003 of 16 December 2002 ("Regulation 1/2003"), the Commission is required to consult the Advisory Committee on Restrictive Practices and Dominant Positions (the "Advisory Committee") prior to the taking of a decision under Articles 7, 8, 9, 10, 23, 24(2) and 29(1) of the Regulation. According to Article 17(2), Article 14 applies *mutatis mutandis* where the Commission conducts a sector inquiry. The Advisory Committee is moreover consulted on draft Commission regulations as provided for in the relevant Council Regulations.[1] Section 4 of the Commission Notice on cooperation within the Network of Competition Authorities (2004/C101/03) ("Network Notice") further describes the role and functioning of the Advisory Committee under Regulation 1/2003.

2. Within this legal framework, the Advisory Committee's working practices have developed in the light of experience and are set out in this document. The present Working Arrangements relate only to consultations of the Advisory Committee concerning decisions, which are covered by Article 14(1) of Regulation 1/2003. It is their object to contribute to the optimal functioning of the Advisory Committee.

3. The Advisory Committee may be consulted in writing or through a meeting. Either way, the purpose of the consultation remains the same, namely to invite the Advisory Committee to give an opinion on a preliminary draft decision to be adopted by the Commission. This opinion is also an opportunity for the Advisory Committee to contribute to improving the quality of the decisions adopted by the Commission. To this end, members of the Advisory Committee should strive to give focused and substantiated advice.

4. It is possible to participate in some Advisory Committee meetings by video-conferencing. These Working Arrangements are therefore complemented by the *Modalities on the organization of and participation in Advisory Committee meetings by video-conferencing*, set out in the Annex. It should be noted that video-conferencing is not available for Advisory Committee meetings concerning fines.

5. The consultation of the Advisory Committee at a meeting or through a written procedure entails a degree of preparatory work on the part of the representatives of the Member States attending the Advisory Committee so that they have full knowledge of the main points of facts and law of the preliminary draft decision on which they are consulted. In particular, Article 14(3) of Commission Regulation (EC) No. 773/2004 ("Regulation 773/2004") provides that national competition authorities ("NCAs") are invited to oral hearings when they are requested to be held by the parties to the case. By participating in the oral hearing, NCAs can develop a better understanding of the case in the event the Commission later convenes an Advisory Committee meeting to consult on a preliminary draft decision.

6. The consultation of the Advisory Committee provides an opportunity for the Commission to discuss its draft decisions with experts from the competition authorities of the Member States in a confidential and dedicated forum, before these decisions are adopted. It is therefore in the common interest of the Commission and the NCAs to ensure that the consultation of the Advisory Committee can take place in the best possible circumstances. To this end, the members of the Advisory Committee shall receive, and have access to, the most important and other existing documents necessary for the assessment of a case, in accordance with Articles 11(2) and 14(3) of Regulation 1/2003.

7. The Commission and the members of the Advisory Committee must, in keeping with their obligation of professional secrecy set out in Article 28 of Regulation 1/2003, not disclose any information of the kind covered by this obligation which they have acquired or exchanged via the preparation of, and the deliberations in, the Advisory Committee. Nor should they reveal the opinion of the Advisory Committee prior to its publication, if any, or any information concerning the deliberations which led to the formulation of the opinion.

NOTES

[1] Cf. Article 33 of Regulation 1/2003, Council Regulation 19/65, Council Regulation 2821/71, Council Regulation 3976/87 and Council Regulation 479/92.

II. THE PREPARATORY FRAMEWORK

[4.386]

8. As required by Article 11(2) of Regulation 1/2003, the Commission will provide the NCAs with:

i. the statement of objections in all available languages following its notification to the parties concerned;
ii. the written submissions of the parties concerned in reply to the statement of objections received by the Commission pursuant to Article 10 of Regulation 773/2004;
iii. the preliminary assessment made pursuant to Article 9 of Regulation 1/2003;
iv. the observations made by interested third parties pursuant to a publication by the Commission under Article 27(4) of Regulation 1/2003; and
v. the other documents that fall within the scope of the "most important documents" referred to in Article 11(2).

Generally, these documents shall be sent in their confidential versions.

9. The above-mentioned documents should be delivered forthwith to the NCAs following the notification or receipt of the document, as the case may be.

10. In addition to the documents listed above in paragraph 8 and in accordance with Article 11(2) of Regulation 1/2003, each NCA can request the Commission to provide it with a copy of other existing documents necessary for the assessment of a case,[2] including in particular:

i. the written submissions of the complainant received by the Commission pursuant to Article 6 of Regulation 773/2004; and
ii. the written submissions of other persons received by the Commission pursuant to Article 13 of Regulation 773/2004.

11. The Commission's case team should be available for discussions with NCA representatives, as appropriate. The contact details of one or several members of the Commission's case team will be communicated to the NCAs following the appointment of the rapporteur[3] in a case. The Commission should maintain and, upon request, provide an up-to-date list of open Commission cases in which a statement of objections has been sent, together with the contact persons on the Commission's case team and the rapporteur acting on the case (if already nominated).

12. Where deemed useful, conference calls / video-conferences open to all members of the Advisory Committee can be used as a complementary discussion tool, provided that confidentiality is effectively guaranteed.

NOTES

2 The safeguards set out in point 35 of the Commission Notice on immunity from fines and reduction of fines in cartel cases (2006/C 298/11) and point 37 of the Commission Notice on the conduct of settlement procedures in view of the adoption of Decisions pursuant to Articles 7 and 23 of Council Regulation (EC) 1/2003 in cartel cases (2008/C 167/01) regarding corporate statements and settlement submissions shall be effectively respected.

3 See paragraph 39 et seq. on the rapporteur.

III. THE ORAL HEARING

[4.387]

13. Under Article 12 of Regulation 773/2004, the Commission shall hold an oral hearing if a party concerned so requests in its written submissions in response to the statement of objections.

14. The participation of the NCAs in the oral hearing of a case, if one is held, is useful for the efficient functioning of any subsequent meeting of the Advisory Committee convened to consider a preliminary draft decision on the case.

IV. THE ADVISORY COMMITTEE MEETING

1. CONVENING A MEETING

[4.388]

15. The Commission, as Chair of the Advisory Committee, invites NCAs to a meeting of the Advisory Committee. In accordance with Article 14(3) of Regulation 1/2003 this meeting is not held earlier than 14 days after dispatch of the notice convening it/invitation and the documents listed therein. An agenda should be sent with the invitation. In respect of decisions concerning interim measures, the meeting may be held seven days after the dispatch of the operative part of a draft decision. Where the Commission dispatches a notice convening the meeting which gives a shorter period of notice than those specified above, the meeting may take place on the proposed date in the absence of an objection by any Member State.

16. The Commission and the NCAs undertake to ensure that the timing of meetings of the Advisory Committee is effectively kept confidential, by using all appropriate practical means.

17. In setting the date for a meeting, the Commission should take into account the possible convenience or inconvenience of holding a meeting on a particular day, for example by grouping together similar or related issues in the same or adjacent meetings, or so as to facilitate the attendance of members at other meetings organized by the Commission in Brussels.

18. With the invitation to attend a meeting of the Advisory Committee, the Commission should transmit to the members of the Advisory Committee:

i. the summary of the case;
ii. an indication of the most important documents and copies thereof, if they have not already been transmitted;
iii. a copy of the preliminary draft decision in the authentic languages of the case and the Commission's working languages as they become available.

19. In accordance with Article 15(2) of Commission Decision 2001/462/EC, the Commission shall communicate the Hearing Officer's final report to the NCAs, as soon as it is available.

20. At the latest upon receipt of the invitation to the Advisory Committee meeting, each participating NCA should provide the Commission with the name and contact details of its representative for the purposes of this meeting. Any changes should be notified promptly to the Commission.

21. The Commission should maintain and, upon request, provide an up-to-date list containing the names and contact details of the NCA representatives participating in the Advisory Committee meeting (to the extent known). This list should also identify the rapporteur and the contact persons on the Commission's case team. This list shall be made

22. Where the Commission postpones a meeting upon request of an Advisory Committee member according to Article 14 (3), 2nd sentence of Regulation 1/2003, the Commission should inform the Advisory Committee about the reason for such postponement.

2. HOLDING OF THE MEETING(S)

23. Each NCA should make its best efforts to attend Advisory Committee meetings. If it is unable to attend, a NCA can submit any observations, comments or questions to the case-team and the rapporteur, as soon as is practicable before the meeting.

24. Only the observations and comments made by members present at the meeting shall be taken into account in the opinion of the Advisory Committee.

25. The Commission, as Chair, should determine the general structure of, and format for, the discussion to take place in the meeting. Having regard to the nature of the case, it may wish to strive for a balance between a formal "tour de table" format, which encourages active contribution from all NCAs, and a more informal format. The Commission may discuss with the rapporteur in advance of the meeting how it should best be conducted.

26. The Commission and the NCAs undertake to ensure that the confidentiality of their exchanges of views, in particular about the level of fines in the Advisory Committee is effectively preserved, by using all appropriate practical means.

27. With respect to a consultation on a decision on fixing the level of a fine, the Commission should distribute at the meeting a table outlining how the proposed fine was calculated, by precise references to the relevant provisions of the Commission's guidelines on fines. Upon request, the Chair may allow members of the Advisory Committee additional time within the meeting to consider the explanation given by the Commission. To preserve confidentiality, the table shall be collected at the end of the meeting and no photocopies or other copies which could allow the proposed fine to be disclosed should be made by those present at the meeting.

3. OPINION

28. The Committee will render a single Opinion.

29. The opinion is normally delivered in standard format by the Advisory Committee, assisted by the rapporteur. At the request of any of its members, the Advisory Committee may deliver a reasoned opinion.

30. The opinion of the Advisory Committee must be delivered before the conclusion of the meeting.

31. In the absence of unanimity on the Opinion or on a part of the opinion, the opinion is determined by a simple majority of the members of the Committee participating in the Advisory Committee meeting and voting on the opinion (not counting abstentions). This determination will be made by calling a vote.

32. In the absence of unanimity, the number of votes in favour and against the Opinion, as well as the number of abstentions will be recorded. The record should not identify the members of the Committee having voted in favour of the Opinion, against it or having abstained.

33. The Opinion may briefly record the reasons for views which diverge from, or go beyond, the analysis of the Commission in its draft decision, if a simple majority of the members of the Committee participating in the Advisory Committee meeting and voting on the opinion (not counting abstentions) agrees to the inclusion of such reasoning.

34. Each Member State, irrespective of the number of representatives which it sends to the meeting, has a single vote for the purposes of adopting an Opinion of the Committee.

35. Members of the Committee must participate in the Advisory Committee meeting in order to be able to contribute to content of the Opinion, or to vote on its adoption.

36. As required by Article 14 (6) of Regulation 1/2003, the Commission will append the written opinion of the Advisory Committee to the decision. If the Advisory Committee recommends publication of the opinion, the Commission will publish on DG COMP's website the Opinion together with the public version of the decision or a provisional version thereof within two months after the adoption of the decision, having regard to the need to protect legitimate business secrets. Should the public version or a provisional version thereof not be available within that timeframe, the Commission will nevertheless proceed to the publication of the Opinion on DG COMP's website.

37. The Commission will take the utmost account of the Opinion delivered by the Advisory Committee, and will inform the competent authorities of the Member States of the manner in which the Advisory Committee's Opinion has been taken into account. The Commission can do so for example by transmitting the final decision and highlighting any changes. The Commission will provide this information at the earliest feasible opportunity following the adoption of the relevant final decision.

38. In cases of a (partially) negative Opinion, the Commission shall explain in writing to the competent authorities of the Member States how it took the utmost account of the Opinion within 15 working days after the adoption of the Decision (if adopted) and offer a telephone conference to address possible questions in relation to its written explanations. This telephone conference shall take place within fifteen working days of receipt by the Commission of a Member State's request.

V THE RAPPORTEUR

1. ROLE

[4.389]

39. A representative of a NCA acts as a rapporteur for each case in which the Commission issues a statement of objections.

40. The rapporteur acts as a facilitator of the preparatory work and the discussions in the Advisory Committee and accordingly shall exercise his/her task in a strictly objective way at all times following his/her appointment. When informing NCAs about a case, the rapporteur should ensure that he/she is aware of all the relevant aspects of the case. To this end, the rapporteur and the Commission's case team should always closely cooperate, in particular when using the practices set out in paragraphs 55 and 56.

41. The identity of the rapporteur should not be disclosed beyond the members of the Advisory Committee and the Commission.

42. The rapporteur should seek to inform the NCAs of the essential issues raised by the case, without suggesting or advocating an opinion on the merits of the Commission's or the parties' arguments. Any notes prepared by the rapporteur shall contain a disclaimer displayed prominently to the effect that it is prepared solely as a means to facilitate debate on the case and that it does not reflect the position of the Commission, the Commission's services or any NCA. Any such note must be marked as confidential and shall only be circulated to the members of the Advisory Committee and the European Commission's case team, by secure means.

43. The work undertaken by the rapporteur does not replace or preclude any activity that NCAs may wish to undertake in a case, such as direct contacts with the Commission's services.

2. APPOINTMENT

44. In order to allow NCAs to plan their work, the Commission should appoint the NCA responsible for nominating the rapporteur as early as is reasonably feasible, and in any case not later than 45 days following the notification of the statement of objections to the parties concerned. The Commission shall ensure that the request to act as a rapporteur reaches the respective NCA without delay by using appropriate means of communication.

45. Appointments as rapporteur will be made in turn, following the list of European Presidencies, as follows:

1) Autorité de la Concurrence (FR)
2) Úřad pro ochranu hospodářské soutěže (CZ)
3) Konkurrensverket (SE)
4) Comision Nacional de los Mercados y la Competencia(ES)
5) Belgische Mededingingsautoriteit - Autorité belge de laConcurrence (BE)
6) Gazdasági Versenyhivatal (HU)
7) Urząd Ochrony Konkurencji i Konsumentów (PL)
8) Konkurrence-og Forbrugerstyrelsen (DK)
9) ΕπιτροπήΠροστασίας του Ανταγωνισμού - Commission for the protection of competition (CY)
10) Coimisiún um Iomaíocht agus Cosaint Tomhaltóiri (IE)
11) Lietuvos Respublikos konkurencijos taryba (LT)
12) Επιτροπή Ανταγωνισμού (EL)
13) Autorità Garante della Concorrenza e del Mercato (IT)
14) Konkurences padome (LV)
15) Conseil de la Concurrence (LU)
16) Autoriteit Consument en Markt (NL)
17) Protimonopolný úrad Slovenskeij republiky (SK)
18) Awtorita ta' Malta għall-Kompetizzjoni u għall-Affarijettal-Konsumatur - Malta Competition and Consumer Affairs Authority (MT)
19) Competition and Markets Authority (UK)
20) Konkurentsiamet (EE)
21) Комисия за защита на конкуренцията (BG)
22) Bundeswettbewerbsbehörde (AT)
23) Consiliul Concurenţei (RO)
24) Kilpailu- ja kuluttajaviraston (FI)
25) Bundeskartellamt (DE)
26) Autoridade da Concorrência (PT)
27) Javna Agencija Republike Slovenije za VarstvoKonkurence (SI)
28) Agencija za zaštitu tržišnog natjecanja (HR)

46. Exceptionally, the Commission, with the consent of the NCAs concerned, may decide to invert the order provided for in paragraph 45 ("swap" between two NCAs), for example, with a view to support the perception of the rapporteur's strict objectivity.

47. If a NCA refuses or fails to respond to the Commission within 10 days following notification of the request to act as rapporteur, the next NCA on the list provided for in paragraph 45 should be asked to nominate a representative from its authority, who will act as rapporteur, until a rapporteur is actually appointed.

48. Upon acceptance of the appointment, a NCA should advise the Commission of the name and contact details of the person acting as rapporteur within 14 days.

49. Where necessary, the rapporteur's NCA can replace its representative acting as rapporteur. Where this is done, the Commission should immediately be provided with the contact details of the new representative. To ensure continuity, the rapporteur should not be changed within 30 days prior to the meeting of the Advisory Committee, unless justified by objective reasons.

50. The Commission should promptly advise the nomination and any later changes of the rapporteur to the NCAs.

3. RELATIONSHIP WITH THE COMMISSION

51. The Commission and the rapporteur should agree on the modalities of their cooperation, such as the frequency and means by which the rapporteur is kept informed about the status of the case by the Commission's case team and the way in which the rapporteur informs the Commission's case team about how the rapporteur will strive to enhance the NCAs understanding of the case.

52. In addition to the documents transmitted to all NCAs, the Commission should make available to the rapporteur the existing list of documents prepared for access to file and provide the rapporteur with any further documents from the file the rapporteur may request in accordance with the second sentence of Article 11(2) of Regulation 1/2003.[4]

4. ENHANCING NCAS' UNDERSTANDING OF THE CASE

53. The rapporteur may wish to inform NCAs of significant procedural steps in the administrative proceedings and / or update NCAs about any procedural or substantive aspect of the case at any moment during the preparatory process. The nature, frequency and extent of this reporting will depend on the case.

54. Given the rapporteur's knowledge of the case at hand, the rapporteur may suggest the use of the written procedure to consult the Advisory Committee (see paragraph 57).

Recommended practices

55. It is recommended that the rapporteur, in order to facilitate the consultation of the Advisory Committee, employs the following practices:

i. Not later than 5 days prior to the Advisory Committee meeting, the rapporteur should circulate a list of key questions (to be answered with "yes", "no" or "abstention") in addition to asking:
• whether there is overall agreement with the preliminary draft decision;
• whether there are observations or any points which the Commission is asked to take into account; and
• whether the Committee should recommend the publication of the opinion.

In addition, a limited number of case-specific issues could be included, inviting the Advisory Committee to consider certain relevant aspects of the case in assessing the draft decision.

The above questions should be made available in a Commission working language.

ii. Following the opening of the (first) meeting the rapporteur should, as agreed with the chairperson, and in consultation with the Commission's case team:
• present an introduction to the case, with the assistance of the case-team where appropriate, as requested by the rapporteur;
• briefly describe the main issues in the case;
• present a list of key questions (see paragraph (i) above);
• present additional questions and comments, as he/she deems appropriate.

Optional practices

56. Without prejudice to paragraphs 53, 54 and 55, the rapporteur may furthermore choose to make use of the following practices. These practices are merely optional and their use is left to the rapporteur's discretion, taking into account the complexity of the case and the novelty of the issues raised. The rapporteur may also consider consulting with other NCAs when assessing the importance and implications of the case.

i. At any stage during the preparatory phase, the rapporteur may, in the appropriate case:
• prepare and circulate a short note to the members of the Advisory Committee and the Commission's case team highlighting crucial aspects raised by the case to help NCAs develop a better understanding of the case and to prepare for the oral hearing or the meeting of the Advisory Committee as the case may be;
• ask the Commission to convene a briefing session for the NCAs, in particular, if a suitable opportunity arises, e.g. adjacent to another meeting which is organised by the European Commission or by telephone conference or video-conference.

ii. Not later than 5 days prior to the meeting of the Advisory Committee, the rapporteur may:
• collect questions and written comments from NCAs and forward them to the Commission's case team and the NCAs;
• ask NCAs if they wish to issue a reasoned opinion and inform the Commission's case team and the members of the Advisory Committee of the results of that inquiry.

NOTES

4 The safeguards set out in point 35 of the Commission Notice on immunity from fines and reduction of fines in cartel cases (2006/C 298/11) and point 37 of the Commission Notice on the conduct of settlement procedures in view of the adoption of Decisions pursuant to Articles 7 and 23 of Council Regulation (EC) 1/2003 in cartel cases (2008/C 167/01) shall be effectively respected.

VI. THE WRITTEN PROCEDURE

1. DECIDING WHETHER TO PROPOSE THE WRITTEN PROCEDURE

[4.390]

57. The Commission shall assess whether or not to propose to NCAs a written procedure, taking account of the likely efficiency gains for both NCAs and the Commission, having regard to the nature of the case, the type of draft decision being considered and the likely nature of the comments if a meeting were held. The Commission should consult the rapporteur before making such a proposal to the Advisory Committee. Pursuant to Article 14(4) of Regulation 1/2003, if any Advisory Committee member so requests, the Commission shall convene a meeting.

2. LAUNCHING THE WRITTEN PROCEDURE

58. The launching of the consultation under a written procedure is done by a notice from the Commission to the Advisory Committee, accompanied by the documents set out in Article 14(3) of Regulation 1/2003. The timely transmission of the relevant documents is vital for the written procedure to be effective as means of consultation of the Advisory Committee.

59. In accordance with Article 14(4) of Regulation 1/2003, the Commission shall determine a time-limit of not less than 14 days within which the Member States are to put forward their observations for circulation to all other Member States. In case of decisions to be taken pursuant to Article 8, the time-limit is reduced to seven days.

60. Pursuant to Article 14(4) of Regulation 1/2003, the Commission may set shorter deadlines. This should be done only in exceptional circumstances. Members should endeavour to indicate to the Commission as early as possible and in principle within four working days following the dispatch of the notice if they object to the shorter deadline. In case of an objection, the deadlines foreseen in Article 14 (4) of Regulation 1/2003 would apply, counting from the dispatch of the documents.

61. If the rapporteur or any Advisory Committee member considers that a case where the Commission has proposed an oral procedure would be suitable for a written procedure, the rapporteur may communicate this opinion to the Commission. The Commission can follow up this suggestion by a notice to all Advisory Committee members, proposing that the consultation should take place by way of a written procedure.

62. The notice initiating the written procedure should contain the following:

i. the date by which members should indicate whether they request a meeting of the Advisory Committee ("procedural veto"); although this deadline is not preclusive, it is in the common interest to exercise procedural vetoes as early as possible, desirably within 7 days following the dispatch of the relevant documents as laid down in paragraph 58;

ii. the date by which members should submit their observations if the written procedure is maintained, observing the deadlines laid down in Article 14(4) of Regulation 1/2003;

iii. a proposed date for a meeting of the Advisory Committee in the event a member of the Advisory Committee requests a meeting pursuant to Article 14(4) of Regulation 1/2003.

3. THE WRITTEN CONSULTATION PROCESS

63. In a consultation conducted under the written procedure, the rapporteur shall submit to the Advisory Committee a list of key questions (that can be answered with ″yes″, ″no″ or ″abstention″) asking:

i. whether there is overall agreement with the preliminary draft decision,

ii. whether there are observations or any points which the Commission is asked to take into account, and

iii. whether the Committee should recommend the publication of the opinion.

64. In addition, a limited number of case-specific issues could be included, inviting the Advisory Committee to consider certain relevant aspects of the case in assessing the draft decision.

65. In addition to replying to the list of key questions, the Advisory Committee members may make any observations in writing. These observations, or at least a summary thereof, should be provided in a commonly understood and accepted language for the convenience of other Committee members. These observations should be sent to the Commission and the other Committee members in a secure way.

66. The fact that a member of the Advisory Committee has not replied to any of the questions asked should not be taken as tacit approval by the member of the draft decision. Members should use their best efforts to respond to the questions asked in order to ensure that the Commission is able to obtain meaningful conclusions from the consultation.

67. If the nature of the requests for explanations is such that an open-to-all discussion is warranted, the Commission would:

i. either organise a conference call/video-conference to deal with the questions and then restate the deadline for the written replies; or

ii. if the complexity of the issues justifies it or any member so requests, ″switch″ to the oral procedure by organising a meeting on the date specified in the original invitation. The consultation would then be concluded in this meeting (in which written replies already made would not be binding upon the members of the Committee).

In both cases, this will be considered the continuation of the same consultation launched according to paragraphs 58 et seq. The invitation to the conference call / video-conference or meeting would reiterate the date as set out under paragraph 62(iii), contain practical details and specify whether or not there exist any additional or modified documents.

68. At the end of the consultation process, the opinion would be drafted - normally in the standard format used for oral consultations - by the Commission's case team, in consultation with the rapporteur without delay. Members having participated in the consultation would be invited to confirm that the draft opinion correctly reflects the result of the consultation by e-mail as rapidly as possible and in any event by a specified date (which is normally not more than three working days after the conclusion of the consultation). This would be indicated in the request to confirm. In this context, the absence of a reply would be considered as a tacit approval of the draft opinion by the members having participated in the consultation.

69. Unless otherwise specified, paragraphs 28 to 38 apply accordingly.

VII. STATUS

[4.391]

70. Regulation 1/2003 does not require the adoption of any additional procedural rules for the Advisory Committee. The present Working Arrangements have been drawn up by DG Competition of the European Commission and the NCAs in close cooperation. The practices outlined in the present Working Arrangements should be applied in a spirit of cooperation and flexibility, taking account of the importance of the case under consideration and possible resource restraints of the competent authorities of the Member States. The practices set out in the Working Arrangements do not create any rights or obligations and do not alter or replace any rights or obligations set out in the Treaty on the Functioning of the European Union and Council Regulation 1/2003, and in particular Article 14 thereof, or the Commission implementing Regulation 773/2004 as interpreted by the case-law of the Community Courts. The Working Arrangements do not alter the Commission's interpretative notices and failure to comply with these arrangements in any respect is not intended to have any legal consequences for the application of Regulation 1/2003.

71. The present Working Arrangements shall apply to all Commission cases in which a statement of objections is issued after 01.04.2019.

72. The present Working Arrangements shall be regularly reviewed by the European Commission's DG Competition and the competent authorities of the Member States.

EUROPEAN COMMISSION: RECOMMENDATIONS FOR ELECTRONIC DOCUMENT SUBMISSION IN ANTITRUST AND CARTEL PROCEEDINGS[1]

(updated in August 2019)

[4.392]

NOTES

This document is available on the European Commission website at: ec.europa.eu/competition-policy/antitrust/contact_en.

TOOLS AND ADDRESSES

1. In antitrust and cartel proceedings, electronic communication with the Directorate-General for Competition (DG Competition) is possible via:

– e-mail to COMP-GREFFE-ANTITRUST@ec.europa.eu: for all case-related correspondence with the Antitrust Registry.

– eTrustEx: exchange platform for undertakings' submission of sensitive documents in a secure way.

2. Additional tools and e-mail addresses for specific purposes:

– eQuestionnaire: platform for undertakings replying to requests for information received via this electronic tool.

– eLeniency: platform for undertakings' submission of information in a secure way in Leniency, Settlement and non-cartel Cooperation cases. The electronic tool emulates the legal protections offered by an oral procedure. Applications for immunity and/or reduction of fines under the Commission's leniency policy can also be submitted via e-mail to COMP-LENIENCY@ec.europa.eu.

– Anonymous Whistleblower Tool: platform for individuals who wish to submit inside information on possible anti-competitive practices. The tool allows for anonymous two-way communication. Non-anonymous messages can be sent to COMP-WHISTLEBLOWER@ec.europa.eu.

NOTES

[1] These recommendations do not create any new legal rights or obligations, nor alter the legal rights and obligations which arise from the Treaty on Functioning of the European Union, secondary EU law and the case-law of the Court of Justice of the European Union. This note also does not alter the Commission's interpretative notices and established decisional practice.

FILE FORMAT AND NAMING OF ANNEXES AND EXHIBITS

3. Electronic submissions must be in a readable, non-corrupted, and non-restricted format.[2]

4. Newly created documents (referred to as 'Annexes') must be submitted in PDF machine searchable format. Spreadsheets must be submitted in MS-Excel or Open Office.

5. Pre-existing documents (referred to as 'Exhibits')[3] must be submitted in their native format, preserving and including the original metadata.[4] The Commission accepts all common office automation file formats: Acrobat Reader, MS Office and Open Office. The recommended e-mail formats are .msg and .eml[5]. Images (scanned documents or other images containing text) should be provided in PDF machine-searchable format.

6. Annexes and Exhibits must be clearly identified, preferably by means of the prefix ANNEX or EXHIBIT and by use of a continuous numbering throughout subsequent submissions (e.g.: "*Annex 023-Original filename.pdf*"; "*Exhibit 003-Original filename.msg*"). The numbering of Annexes should be independent from the numbering of the Exhibits.

7. It is recommended to submit translations in a language of the proceeding if the pre-existing documents (Exhibits) are in a non-EU language or in none of the procedural languages. Translations, if any, must be clearly separated from the document in the original language and identified by means of the prefix TR. (eg: "TR-Exhibit 003-Original filename.pdf/docx").

NOTES

[2] It should be possible to perform optical character recognition (OCR), to machine search, to print and to cut-and-paste. Non-restricted means that no special electronic security settings are activated.

[3] Documents that are not specially created for the purposes of the antitrust proceedings at hand.

[4] These pre-existing files submitted electronically must be an accurate copy of the original document and they must not be converted into PDF for the purposes of the submission. A declaration that a file submitted electronically is a true and complete copy of the original document and that shows the chain of custody of the document may always requested at any stage in the proceeding.

[5] Outlook .pst or Lotus Notes .nsf file formats must be avoided. They should be converted into single e-mail formats.

NON-CONFIDENTIAL VERSIONS

8. Non-confidential versions, if any, must be clearly separated from the original confidential version, identified by means of the prefix NC and provided in PDF format (e.g.: "*NC-Annex 023-Original filename.pdf*", "*NC-Exhibit003Original filename.pdf*").

9. It is entirely the submitting party's responsibility that non-confidential versions are structured clearly and that redacted information cannot be retrieved ex-post, for instance via forensic software.

RESTRICTIONS

10. E-mails sent to DG Competition should not exceed 15MB. In eTrustEx and eLeniency, individual files must not exceed 100MB and any submission must not exceed 1450 individual files in eTrustEx (respectively 1500 files in eLeniency) and the total maximum size of 4GB in eTrustEx (respectively 4.95 GB in eLeniency). In the Anonymous Whistleblower Tool, the size restriction is 25 MB with a maximum of 10 individual files.

11. Larger submissions can be split into several smaller subsequent submissions.[6]

12. Files must be virus-free (sanitised with an antivirus before submission to avoid any malware or other malicious software).

13. Do not submit any files that are encrypted, password-protected or restricted.[7] Do not submit executable files, archives (e.g. .zip files or other types of file container) or files containing macros. Avoid any form of embedded files.

14. Do not artificially join files together. For instance, do not combine multiple files in one single PDF or container. Where the pre-existing electronic files are in a container, only the relevant files in that container are to be submitted. If it is not possible to submit any form other than a container, the size of the container should not exceed 500MB.

NOTES

6 Alternatively, documents may also be put on external digital devices, such as USB sticks, CDs or DVDs, and sent to DG Competition via post. Floppy disks, magnetic tapes and FTP/cloud servers are not accepted.

7 Non-restricted = macro-free, without embedded files and without any special electronic security settings activated.

MODEL POWER OF ATTORNEY FOR ANTITRUST CASES

[4.393]

NOTES

This document is available on the European Commission website at: ec.europa.eu/competition-policy/antitrust/procedures/requests-information-rfi_en.

[COMPANY LETTERHEAD]

[Mr/Ms DIRECTOR] **[PLACE, DD/MM/YYYY]**

European Commission

Directorate General for Competition

Antitrust Registry

1049 Brussels

Belgium

e-mail: COMP-GREFFE-ANTITRUST@ec.europa.eu

SUBJECT: POWER OF ATTORNEY - CASE AT.[NUMBER - NAME]

Dear [Mr/Ms DIRECTOR],

[COMPANY NAME + COMPANY COMPLETE ADDRESS], hereafter "the Company" [including all its subsidiaries and affiliates[1] [in particular those mentioned in the attached list]], duly represented by [COMPANY RESPONSIBLE] hereby appoints [LAWYERS] of [LAW FIRM], [LAW FIRM COMPLETE ADDRESS] to represent the Company, in relation to European Commission's proceedings under Article [101/102] of the Treaty on the Functioning of the European Union for the case AT. [NUMBER – NAME] ("the Proceedings").

This representation includes authority to undertake, for and on behalf of the Company, all relevant actions regarding the Proceedings, including filings, receipt of documents, requests for information and representation of the Company in meetings with the European Commission.

Optional – if the Company wishes that a decision or other formal acts are notified to the Company via their legal representatives duly empowered by this power of attorney:

This representation includes also authority to receive for and on behalf of the Company notification of decisions and formal acts adopted by the European Commission regarding the Proceedings pursuant to Article 297 of the Treaty on the Functioning of the European Union.

Optional – if the Company wishes that their legal representatives are duly empowered by this power of attorney to grant a language waiver:

This representation further includes authority to waive on behalf of the Company, the right to receive all correspondence and any formal acts taken and notified by the European Commission during the course of the proceedings in the language(s) determined by Regulation no 1 of 1958 determining the languages to be used by the European Economic Community (OJ L17, 6.10.1958, p 385), in order to receive these in [LANGUAGE].

Signed,

[NAME AND FUNCTION OF PERSON OF THE COMPANY AUTHORIZED TO SIGN]

duly authorized to sign

on behalf of [**COMPANY**]

NOTES

[1] The power of attorney can be submitted by one company of the group in the name of all involved subsidiaries and affiliates, if all involved subsidiaries and affiliates state in writing to the Commission the explicit empowerment to this company for granting such power of attorney.

ANTITRUST MANUAL OF PROCEDURES INTERNAL DG COMPETITION WORKING DOCUMENTS ON PROCEDURES FOR THE APPLICATION OF ARTICLES 101 AND 102 TFEU (NOTE)

(November 2019)

[4.394]

NOTES

This document is not reproduced in this Handbook due to its size. It is available (as updated in November 2019) on the European Commission website at: ec.europa.eu/competition-policy/antitrust/procedures_en.

2. FINES

GUIDELINES ON THE METHOD OF SETTING FINES IMPOSED PURSUANT TO ARTICLE 23(2)(A) OF REGULATION NO 1/2003

(2006/C210/02)

(Text with EEA relevance)

[4.395]

NOTES

Date of publication in OJ: OJ C210, 1.9.2006, p 2.

Note that Council Regulation 1/2003/EC is repealed, in relation to the UK, by the Competition (Amendment etc) (EU Exit) Regulations 2019, SI 2019/93, reg 63, Sch 3, para 1, as from IP completion day (as defined in the European Union (Withdrawal Agreement) Act 2020, s 39) (for transitional provisions and savings in relation to the operation of the 2019 Regulations, see Sch 4 to those Regulations at **[7.69]** et seq).

Note also that with effect from 1 December 2009, the EC Treaty was replaced by the Treaty on the Functioning of the European Union. References in this document to provisions of the EC Treaty should be construed accordingly.

The Guidelines on the method of setting fines imposed pursuant to Article 15(2) of Regulation No 17 and Article 65(5) of the ECSC Treaty (1998/C9/03), published in OJ C9, 14.1.1998, p 3, continue to apply to decisions adopted prior to 1 May 2004.

INTRODUCTION

[4.396]

1. Pursuant to Article 23(2)(a) of Regulation No 1/2003,[1] the Commission may, by decision, impose fines on undertakings or associations of undertakings where, either intentionally or negligently, they infringe Article 81 or 82 of the Treaty.

2. In exercising its power to impose such fines, the Commission enjoys a wide margin of discretion[2] within the limits set by Regulation No 1/2003. First, the Commission must have regard both to the gravity and to the duration of the infringement. Second, the fine imposed may not exceed the limits specified in Article 23(2), second and third subparagraphs, of Regulation No 1/2003.

3. In order to ensure the transparency and impartiality of its decisions, the Commission published on 14 January 1998 guidelines on the method of setting fines.[3] After more than eight years of implementation, the Commission has acquired sufficient experience to develop further and refine its policy on fines.

4. The Commission's power to impose fines on undertakings or associations of undertakings which, intentionally or negligently, infringe Article 81 or 82 of the Treaty is one of the means conferred on it in order for it to carry out the task of supervision entrusted to it by the Treaty. That task not only includes the duty to investigate and sanction individual infringements, but it also encompasses the duty to pursue a general policy designed to apply, in competition matters, the principles laid down by the Treaty and to steer the conduct of undertakings in the light of those principles.[4] For this purpose, the Commission must ensure that its action has the necessary deterrent effect.[5] Accordingly, when the Commission discovers that Article 81 or 82 of the Treaty has been infringed, it may be necessary to impose a fine on those who have acted in breach of the law. Fines should have a sufficiently deterrent effect, not only in order to sanction the undertakings concerned (specific deterrence) but also in order to deter other undertakings from engaging in, or continuing, behaviour that is contrary to Articles 81 and 82 of the EC Treaty (general deterrence).

5. In order to achieve these objectives, it is appropriate for the Commission to refer to the value of the sales of goods or services to which the infringement relates as a basis for setting the fine. The duration of the infringement should also play a significant role in the setting of the appropriate amount of the fine. It necessarily has an impact on the potential consequences of the infringement on the market. It is therefore considered important that the fine should also reflect the number of years during which an undertaking participated in the infringement.

6. The combination of the value of sales to which the infringement relates and of the duration of the infringement is regarded as providing an appropriate proxy to reflect the economic importance of the infringement as well as the relative weight of each undertaking in the infringement. Reference to these factors provides a good indication of the order of magnitude of the fine and should not be regarded as the basis for an automatic and arithmetical calculation method.

7. It is also considered appropriate to include in the fine a specific amount irrespective of the duration of the infringement, in order to deter companies from even entering into illegal practices.

8. The sections below set out the principles which will guide the Commission when it sets fines imposed pursuant to Article 23(2)(a) of Regulation No 1/2003.

NOTES

1 Council Regulation (EC) No 1 of 16 December 2002 on the implementation of the rules on competition laid down in Articles 81 and 82 of the Treaty (OJ L1, 4.1.2003, p 1).

2 See, for example, Case C-189/02P, C-202/02P, C-205/02P to C-208/02P and C-213/02P, *Dansk Rørindustri A/S and others v Commission* [2005] ECR I-5425, paragraph 172.

3 Guidelines on the method of setting fines imposed pursuant to Article 15(2) of Regulation No 17 and Article 65(5) of the ECSC Treaty (OJ C9, 14.1.1998, p 3).

4 See, for example, *Dansk Rørindustri A/S and others v Commission*, cited above, paragraph 170.

5 See Joined Cases 100/80 to 103/80 *Musique Diffusion française and others v Commission* [1983] ECR 1825, paragraph 106.

METHOD FOR THE SETTING OF FINES

[4.397]

9. Without prejudice to point 37 below, the Commission will use the following two-step methodology when setting the fine to be imposed on undertakings or associations of undertakings.

10. First, the Commission will determine a basic amount for each undertaking or association of undertakings (see Section 1 below).

11. Second, it may adjust that basic amount upwards or downwards (see Section 2 below).

1. Basic amount of the fine

12. The basic amount will be set by reference to the value of sales and applying the following methodology.

A.

Calculation of the value of sales

13. In determining the basic amount of the fine to be imposed, the Commission will take the value of the undertaking's sales of goods or services to which the infringement directly or indirectly[1] relates in the relevant geographic area within the EEA. It will normally take the sales made by the undertaking during the last full business year of its participation in the infringement (hereafter "value of sales").

14. Where the infringement by an association of undertakings relates to the activities of its members, the value of sales will generally correspond to the sum of the value of sales by its members.

15. In determining the value of sales by an undertaking, the Commission will take that undertaking's best available figures.

16. Where the figures made available by an undertaking are incomplete or not reliable, the Commission may determine the value of its sales on the basis of the partial figures it has obtained and/or any other information which it regards as relevant and appropriate.

17. The value of sales will be determined before VAT and other taxes directly related to the sales.

18. Where the geographic scope of an infringement extends beyond the EEA (eg worldwide cartels), the relevant sales of the undertakings within the EEA may not properly reflect the weight of each undertaking in the infringement. This may be the case in particular with worldwide market-sharing arrangements.

In such circumstances, in order to reflect both the aggregate size of the relevant sales within the EEA and the relative weight of each undertaking in the infringement, the Commission may assess the total value of the sales of goods or services to which the infringement relates in the relevant geographic area (wider than the EEA), may determine the share of the sales of each undertaking party to the infringement on that market and may apply this share to the aggregate sales within the EEA of the undertakings concerned. The result will be taken as the value of sales for the purpose of setting the basic amount of the fine.

B.

Determination of the basic amount of the fine

19. The basic amount of the fine will be related to a proportion of the value of sales, depending on the degree of gravity of the infringement, multiplied by the number of years of infringement.

20. The assessment of gravity will be made on a case-by-case basis for all types of infringement, taking account of all the relevant circumstances of the case.

21. As a general rule, the proportion of the value of sales taken into account will be set at a level of up to 30% of the value of sales.

22. In order to decide whether the proportion of the value of sales to be considered in a given case should be at the lower end or at the higher end of that scale, the Commission will have regard to a number of factors, such as the nature of the infringement, the combined market share of all the undertakings concerned, the geographic scope of the infringement and whether or not the infringement has been implemented.

23. Horizontal price-fixing, market-sharing and output-limitation agreements,[2] which are usually secret, are, by their very nature, among the most harmful restrictions of competition. As a matter of policy, they will be heavily fined. Therefore, the proportion of the value of sales taken into account for such infringements will generally be set at the higher end of the scale.

24. In order to take fully into account the duration of the participation of each undertaking in the infringement, the amount determined on the basis of the value of sales (see points 20 to 23 above) will be multiplied by the number of years of participation in the infringement. Periods of less than six months will be counted as half a year; periods longer than six months but shorter than one year will be counted as a full year.

25. In addition, irrespective of the duration of the undertaking's participation in the infringement, the Commission will include in the basic amount a sum of between 15% and 25% of the value of sales as defined in Section A above in order to deter undertakings from even entering into horizontal price-fixing, market-sharing and output-limitation

agreements. The Commission may also apply such an additional amount in the case of other infringements. For the purpose of deciding the proportion of the value of sales to be considered in a given case, the Commission will have regard to a number of factors, in particular those referred in point 22.

26. Where the value of sales by undertakings participating in the infringement is similar but not identical, the Commission may set for each of them an identical basic amount. Moreover, in determining the basic amount of the fine, the Commission will use rounded figures.

2. Adjustments to the basic amount

27. In setting the fine, the Commission may take into account circumstances that result in an increase or decrease in the basic amount as determined in Section 1 above. It will do so on the basis of an overall assessment which takes account of all the relevant circumstances.

A.
Aggravating circumstances

28. The basic amount may be increased where the Commission finds that there are aggravating circumstances, such as:

- where an undertaking continues or repeats the same or a similar infringement after the Commission or a national competition authority has made a finding that the undertaking infringed Article 81 or 82: the basic amount will be increased by up to 100% for each such infringement established;
- refusal to cooperate with or obstruction of the Commission in carrying out its investigations;
- role of leader in, or instigator of, the infringement; the Commission will also pay particular attention to any steps taken to coerce other undertakings to participate in the infringement and/or any retaliatory measures taken against other undertakings with a view to enforcing the practices constituting the infringement.

B.
Mitigating circumstances

29. The basic amount may be reduced where the Commission finds that mitigating circumstances exist, such as:

- where the undertaking concerned provides evidence that it terminated the infringement as soon as the Commission intervened: this will not apply to secret agreements or practices (in particular, cartels);
- where the undertaking provides evidence that the infringement has been committed as a result of negligence;
- where the undertaking provides evidence that its involvement in the infringement is substantially limited and thus demonstrates that, during the period in which it was party to the offending agreement, it actually avoided applying it by adopting competitive conduct in the market: the mere fact that an undertaking participated in an infringement for a shorter duration than others will not be regarded as a mitigating circumstance since this will already be reflected in the basic amount;
- where the undertaking concerned has effectively cooperated with the Commission outside the scope of the Leniency Notice and beyond its legal obligation to do so;
- where the anti-competitive conduct of the undertaking has been authorized or encouraged by public authorities or by legislation.[3]

C.
Specific increase for deterrence

30. The Commission will pay particular attention to the need to ensure that fines have a sufficiently deterrent effect; to that end, it may increase the fine to be imposed on undertakings which have a particularly large turnover beyond the sales of goods or services to which the infringement relates.

31. The Commission will also take into account the need to increase the fine in order to exceed the amount of gains improperly made as a result of the infringement where it is possible to estimate that amount.

D.
Legal maximum

32. The final amount of the fine shall not, in any event, exceed 10% of the total turnover in the preceding business year of the undertaking or association of undertakings participating in the infringement, as laid down in Article 23(2) of Regulation No 1/2003.

33. Where an infringement by an association of undertakings relates to the activities of its members, the fine shall not exceed 10% of the sum of the total turnover of each member active on the market affected by that infringement.

E.
Leniency Notice

34. The Commission will apply the leniency rules in line with the conditions set out in the applicable notice.

F.
Ability to pay

35. In exceptional cases, the Commission may, upon request, take account of the undertaking's inability to pay in a specific social and economic context. It will not base any reduction granted for this reason in the fine on the mere finding of an adverse or loss-making financial situation. A reduction could be granted solely on the basis of objective evidence that imposition of the fine as provided for in these Guidelines would irretrievably jeopardise the economic viability of the undertaking concerned and cause its assets to lose all their value.

NOTES

1 Such will be the case for instance for horizontal price fixing arrangements on a given product, where the price of that product then serves as a basis for the price of lower or higher quality products.

2 This includes agreements, concerted practices and decisions by associations of undertakings within the meaning of Article 81 of the Treaty.

3 This is without prejudice to any action that may be taken against the Member State concerned.

FINAL CONSIDERATIONS

[4.398]

36. The Commission may, in certain cases, impose a symbolic fine. The justification for imposing such a fine should be given in its decision.

37. Although these Guidelines present the general methodology for the setting of fines, the particularities of a given case or the need to achieve deterrence in a particular case may justify departing from such methodology or from the limits specified in point 21.

38. These Guidelines will be applied in all cases where a statement of objections is notified after their date of publication in the Official Journal, regardless of whether the fine is imposed pursuant to Article 23(2) of Regulation No 1/2003 or Article 15(2) of Regulation 17/62.[1]

NOTES

1 Article 15(2) of Regulation 17/62 of 6 February 1962: First Regulation implementing Articles 85 and 86 [now 81 and 82] of the Treaty (OJ 13, 21.2.1962, p 204).

COMMISSION NOTICE

(2006/C298/11)

on immunity from fines and reduction of fines in cartel cases

(Text with EEA relevance)

[4.399]

NOTES

Date of publication in OJ: OJ C298, 8.12.2006, p 17.

Note: with effect from 1 December 2009, the EC Treaty was replaced by the Treaty on the Functioning of the European Union. References in this document to provisions of the EC Treaty should be construed accordingly.

1. INTRODUCTION

[4.400]

(1) This notice sets out the framework for rewarding cooperation in the Commission investigation by undertakings which are or have been party to secret cartels affecting the Community. Cartels are agreements and/or concerted practices between two or more competitors aimed at coordinating their competitive behaviour on the market and/or influencing the relevant parameters of competition through practices such as the fixing of purchase or selling prices or other trading conditions, the allocation of production or sales quotas, the sharing of markets including bid-rigging, restrictions of imports or exports and/or anti-competitive actions against other competitors. Such practices are among the most serious violations of Article 81 EC.[1]

(2) By artificially limiting the competition that would normally prevail between them, undertakings avoid exactly those pressures that lead them to innovate, both in terms of product development and the introduction of more efficient production methods. Such practices also lead to more expensive raw materials and components for the Community companies that purchase from such producers. They ultimately result in artificial prices and reduced choice for the consumer. In the long term, they lead to a loss of competitiveness and reduced employment opportunities.

(3) By their very nature, secret cartels are often difficult to detect and investigate without the cooperation of undertakings or individuals implicated in them. Therefore, the Commission considers that it is in the Community interest to reward undertakings involved in this type of illegal practices which are willing to put an end to their participation and co-operate in the Commission's investigation, independently of the rest of the undertakings involved in the cartel. The interests of consumers and citizens in ensuring that secret cartels are detected and punished outweigh the interest in fining those undertakings that enable the Commission to detect and prohibit such practices.

(4) The Commission considers that the collaboration of an undertaking in the detection of the existence of a cartel has an intrinsic value. A decisive contribution to the opening of an investigation or to the finding of an infringement may justify the granting of immunity from any fine to the undertaking in question, on condition that certain additional requirements are fulfilled.

(5) Moreover, co-operation by one or more undertakings may justify a reduction of a fine by the Commission. Any reduction of a fine must reflect an undertaking's actual contribution, in terms of quality and timing, to the Commission's establishment of the infringement. Reductions are to be limited to those undertakings that provide the Commission with evidence that adds significant value to that already in the Commission's possession.

(6) In addition to submitting pre-existing documents, undertakings may provide the Commission with voluntary presentations of their knowledge of a cartel and their role therein prepared specially to be submitted under this leniency programme. These initiatives have proved to be useful for the effective investigation and termination of cartel infringements and they should not be discouraged by discovery orders issued in civil litigation. Potential leniency applicants might be dissuaded from cooperating with the Commission under this Notice if this could impair their position in civil proceedings, as compared to companies who do not cooperate. Such undesirable effect would significantly harm the public interest in ensuring effective public enforcement of Article 81 EC in cartel cases and thus its subsequent or parallel effective private enforcement.

(7) The supervisory task conferred on the Commission by the Treaty in competition matters does not only include the duty to investigate and punish individual infringements, but also encompasses the duty to pursue a general policy. The protection of corporate statements in the public interest is not a bar to their disclosure to other addressees of the statement of objections in order to safeguard their rights of defence in the procedure before the Commission, to the extent that it is technically possible to combine both interests by rendering corporate statements accessible only at the Commission premises and normally on a single occasion following the formal notification of the objections. Moreover, the Commission will process personal data in the context of this notice in conformity with its obligations under Regulation (EC) No 45/2001.[2]

NOTES

[1] Reference in this text to Article 81 EC also covers Article 53 EEA when applied by the Commission according to the rules laid down in Article 56 of the EEA Agreement.

[2] OJ L8, 12.1.2001, p 1.

II. IMMUNITY FROM FINES

A. Requirements to qualify for immunity from fines

[4.401]

(8) The Commission will grant immunity from any fine which would otherwise have been imposed to an undertaking disclosing its participation in an alleged cartel affecting the Community if that undertaking is the first to submit information and evidence which in the Commission's view will enable it to:

(a) carry out a targeted inspection in connection with the alleged cartel;[3] or
(b) find an infringement of Article 81 EC in connection with the alleged cartel.

(9) For the Commission to be able to carry out a targeted inspection within the meaning of point (8)(a), the undertaking must provide the Commission with the information and evidence listed below, to the extent that this, in the Commission's view, would not jeopardize the inspections:

(a) A corporate statement[4] which includes, in so far as it is known to the applicant at the time of the submission:
  — A detailed description of the alleged cartel arrangement, including for instance its aims, activities and functioning; the product or service concerned, the geographic scope, the duration of and the estimated market volumes affected by the alleged cartel; the specific dates, locations, content of and participants in alleged cartel contacts, and all relevant explanations in connection with the pieces of evidence provided in support of the application.
  — The name and address of the legal entity submitting the immunity application as well as the names and addresses of all the other undertakings that participate(d) in the alleged cartel;
  — The names, positions, office locations and, where necessary, home addresses of all individuals who, to the applicant's knowledge, are or have been involved in the alleged cartel, including those individuals which have been involved on the applicant's behalf;
  — Information on which other competition authorities, inside or outside the EU, have been approached or are intended to be approached in relation to the alleged cartel; and
(b) Other evidence relating to the alleged cartel in possession of the applicant or available to it at the time of the submission, including in particular any evidence contemporaneous to the infringement.

(10) Immunity pursuant to point (8)(a) will not be granted if, at the time of the submission, the Commission had already sufficient evidence to adopt a decision to carry out an inspection in connection with the alleged cartel or had already carried out such an inspection.

(11) Immunity pursuant to point (8)(b) will only be granted on the cumulative conditions that the Commission did not have, at the time of the submission, sufficient evidence to find an infringement of Article 81 EC in connection with the alleged cartel and that no undertaking had been granted conditional immunity from fines under point (8)(a) in connection with the alleged cartel. In order to qualify, an undertaking must be the first to provide contemporaneous, incriminating evidence of the alleged cartel as well as a corporate statement containing the kind of information specified in point (9)(a), which would enable the Commission to find an infringement of Article 81 EC.

(12) In addition to the conditions set out in points (8)(a), (9) and (10) or in points (8)(b) and 11, all the following conditions must be met in any case to qualify for any immunity from a fine:

(a) The undertaking cooperates genuinely,[5] fully, on a continuous basis and expeditiously from the time it submits its application throughout the Commission's administrative procedure. This includes:
- providing the Commission promptly with all relevant information and evidence relating to the alleged cartel that comes into its possession or is available to it;
- remaining at the Commission's disposal to answer promptly to any request that may contribute to the establishment of the facts;
- making current (and, if possible, former) employees and directors available for interviews with the Commission;
- not destroying, falsifying or concealing relevant information or evidence relating to the alleged cartel; and
- not disclosing the fact or any of the content of its application before the Commission has issued a statement of objections in the case, unless otherwise agreed;

(b) The undertaking ended its involvement in the alleged cartel immediately following its application, except for what would, in the Commission's view, be reasonably necessary to preserve the integrity of the inspections;

(c) When contemplating making its application to the Commission, the undertaking must not have destroyed, falsified or concealed evidence of the alleged cartel nor disclosed the fact or any of the content of its contemplated application, except to other competition authorities.

(13) An undertaking which took steps to coerce other undertakings to join the cartel or to remain in it is not eligible for immunity from fines. It may still qualify for a reduction of fines if it fulfils the relevant requirements and meets all the conditions therefor.

B. Procedure

(14) An undertaking wishing to apply for immunity from fines should contact the Commission's Directorate General for Competition. The undertaking may either initially apply for a marker or immediately proceed to make a formal application to the Commission for immunity from fines in order to meet the conditions in points (8)(a) or (8)(b), as appropriate. The Commission may disregard any application for immunity from fines on the ground that it has been submitted after the statement of objections has been issued.

(15) The Commission services may grant a marker protecting an immunity applicant's place in the queue for a period to be specified on a case-by-case basis in order to allow for the gathering of the necessary information and evidence. To be eligible to secure a marker, the applicant must provide the Commission with information concerning its name and address, the parties to the alleged cartel, the affected product(s) and territory(-ies), the estimated duration of the alleged cartel and the nature of the alleged cartel conduct. The applicant should also inform the Commission on other past or possible future leniency applications to other authorities in relation to the alleged cartel and justify its request for a marker. Where a marker is granted, the Commission services determine the period within which the applicant has to perfect the marker by submitting the information and evidence required to meet the relevant threshold for immunity. Undertakings which have been granted a marker cannot perfect it by making a formal application in hypothetical terms. If the applicant perfects the marker within the period set by the Commission services, the information and evidence provided will be deemed to have been submitted on the date when the marker was granted.

(16) An undertaking making a formal immunity application to the Commission must:

(a) provide the Commission with all information and evidence relating to the alleged cartel available to it, as specified in points (8) and (9), including corporate statements; or

(b) initially present this information and evidence in hypothetical terms, in which case the undertaking must present a detailed descriptive list of the evidence it proposes to disclose at a later agreed date. This list should accurately reflect the nature and content of the evidence, whilst safeguarding the hypothetical nature of its disclosure. Copies of documents, from which sensitive parts have been removed, may be used to illustrate the nature and content of the evidence. The name of the applying undertaking and of other undertakings involved in the alleged cartel need not be disclosed until the evidence described in its application is submitted. However, the product or service concerned by the alleged cartel, the geographic scope of the alleged cartel and the estimated duration must be clearly identified.

(17) If requested, the Directorate General for Competition will provide an acknowledgement of receipt of the undertaking's application for immunity from fines, confirming the date and, where appropriate, time of the application.

(18) Once the Commission has received the information and evidence submitted by the undertaking under point (16)(a) and has verified that it meets the conditions set out in points (8)(a) or (8)(b), as appropriate, it will grant the undertaking conditional immunity from fines in writing.

(19) If the undertaking has presented information and evidence in hypothetical terms, the Commission will verify that the nature and content of the evidence described in the detailed list referred to in point (16)(b) will meet the conditions set out in points (8)(a) or (8)(b), as appropriate, and inform the undertaking accordingly. Following the disclosure of the evidence no later than on the date agreed and having verified that it corresponds to the description made in the list, the Commission will grant the undertaking conditional immunity from fines in writing.

(20) If it becomes apparent that immunity is not available or that the undertaking failed to meet the conditions set out in points (8)(a) or (8)(b), as appropriate, the Commission will inform the undertaking in writing. In such case, the undertaking may withdraw the evidence disclosed for the purposes of its immunity application or request the Commission to consider it under section III of this notice. This does not prevent the Commission from using its normal powers of investigation in order to obtain the information.

(21) The Commission will not consider other applications for immunity from fines before it has taken a position on an existing application in relation to the same alleged infringement, irrespective of whether the immunity application is presented formally or by requesting a marker.

(22) If at the end of the administrative procedure, the undertaking has met the conditions set out in point (12), the Commission will grant it immunity from fines in the relevant decision. If at the end of the administrative procedure, the undertaking has not met the conditions set out in point (12), the undertaking will not benefit from any favourable treatment under this Notice. If the Commission, after having granted conditional immunity ultimately finds that the immunity applicant has acted as a coercer, it will withhold immunity.

NOTES

[3] The assessment of the threshold will have to be carried out ex ante, ie without taking into account whether a given inspection has or has not been successful or whether or not an inspection has or has not been carried out. The assessment will be made exclusively on the basis of the type and the quality of the information submitted by the applicant.

[4] Corporate statements may take the form of written documents signed by or on behalf of the undertaking or be made orally.

[5] This requires in particular that the applicant provides accurate, not misleading, and complete information. Cfr judgement of the European Court of Justice of 29 June 2006 in case C-301/04P, *Commission v SGL Carbon AG a.o.*, at paragraphs 68–70, and judgement of the European Court of Justice of 28 June 2005 in cases C-189/02P, C-202/02P, C-205/02P, C-208/02P and C-213/02P, *Dansk Rørindustri A/S a.o. v Commission*, at paragraphs 395–399.

III. REDUCTION OF A FINE

A. Requirements to qualify for reduction of a fine

[4.402]

(23) Undertakings disclosing their participation in an alleged cartel affecting the Community that do not meet the conditions under section II above may be eligible to benefit from a reduction of any fine that would otherwise have been imposed.

(24) In order to qualify, an undertaking must provide the Commission with evidence of the alleged infringement which represents significant added value with respect to the evidence already in the Commission's possession and must meet the cumulative conditions set out in points (12)(a) to (12)(c) above.

(25) The concept of "added value" refers to the extent to which the evidence provided strengthens, by its very nature and/or its level of detail, the Commission's ability to prove the alleged cartel. In this assessment, the Commission will generally consider written evidence originating from the period of time to which the facts pertain to have a greater value than evidence subsequently established. Incriminating evidence directly relevant to the facts in question will generally be considered to have a greater value than that with only indirect relevance. Similarly, the degree of corroboration from other sources required for the evidence submitted to be relied upon against other undertakings involved in the case will have an impact on the value of that evidence, so that compelling evidence will be attributed a greater value than evidence such as statements which require corroboration if contested.

(26) The Commission will determine in any final decision adopted at the end of the administrative procedure the level of reduction an undertaking will benefit from, relative to the fine which would otherwise be imposed. For the:

— first undertaking to provide significant added value: a reduction of 30–50%,
— second undertaking to provide significant added value: a reduction of 20–30%,
— subsequent undertakings that provide significant added value: a reduction of up to 20%.

In order to determine the level of reduction within each of these bands, the Commission will take into account the time at which the evidence fulfilling the condition in point (24) was submitted and the extent to which it represents added value.

If the applicant for a reduction of a fine is the first to submit compelling evidence in the sense of point (25) which the Commission uses to establish additional facts increasing the gravity or the duration of the infringement, the Commission will not take such additional facts into account when setting any fine to be imposed on the undertaking which provided this evidence.

B. Procedure

(27) An undertaking wishing to benefit from a reduction of a fine must make a formal application to the Commission and it must present it with sufficient evidence of the alleged cartel to qualify for a reduction of a fine in accordance with point (24) of this Notice. Any voluntary submission of evidence to the Commission which the undertaking that submits it wishes to be considered for the beneficial treatment of section III of this Notice must be clearly identified at the time of its submission as being part of a formal application for a reduction of a fine.

(28) If requested, the Directorate General for Competition will provide an acknowledgement of receipt of the undertaking's application for a reduction of a fine and of any subsequent submissions of evidence, confirming the date and, where appropriate, time of each submission. The Commission will not take any position on an application for a reduction of a fine before it has taken a position on any existing applications for conditional immunity from fines in relation to the same alleged cartel.

(29) If the Commission comes to the preliminary conclusion that the evidence submitted by the undertaking constitutes significant added value within the meaning of points (24) and (25), and that the undertaking has met the conditions of points (12) and (27), it will inform the undertaking in writing, no later than the date on which a statement of objections is notified, of its intention to apply a reduction of a fine within a specified band as provided in point (26). The Commission will also, within the same time frame, inform the undertaking in writing if it comes to the preliminary conclusion that the undertaking does not qualify for a reduction of a fine. The Commission may disregard any application for a reduction of fines on the grounds that it has been submitted after the statement of objections has been issued.

(30) The Commission will evaluate the final position of each undertaking which filed an application for a reduction of a fine at the end of the administrative procedure in any decision adopted. The Commission will determine in any such final decision:

(a) whether the evidence provided by an undertaking represented significant added value with respect to the evidence in the Commission's possession at that same time;

(b) whether the conditions set out in points (12)(a) to (12)(c) above have been met;

(c) the exact level of reduction an undertaking will benefit from within the bands specified in point (26).

If the Commission finds that the undertaking has not met the conditions set out in point (12), the undertaking will not benefit from any favourable treatment under this Notice.

IV. CORPORATE STATEMENTS MADE TO QUALIFY UNDER THIS NOTICE

[4.403]

(31) A corporate statement is a voluntary presentation by or on behalf of an undertaking to the Commission of the undertaking's knowledge of a cartel and its role therein prepared specially to be submitted under this Notice. Any statement made vis-à-vis the Commission in relation to this notice, forms part of the Commission's file and can thus be used in evidence.

(32) Upon the applicant's request, the Commission may accept that corporate statements be provided orally unless the applicant has already disclosed the content of the corporate statement to third parties. Oral corporate statements will be recorded and transcribed at the Commission's premises. In accordance with Article 19 of Council Regulation (EC) No 1/2003[6] and Articles 3 and 17 of Commission Regulation (EC) No 773/2004,[7] undertakings making oral corporate statements will be granted the opportunity to check the technical accuracy of the recording, which will be available at the Commission's premises and to correct the substance of their oral statements within a given time limit. Undertakings may waive these rights within the said time-limit, in which case the recording will from that moment on be deemed to have been approved. Following the explicit or implicit approval of the oral statement or the submission of any corrections to it, the undertaking shall listen to the recordings at the Commission's premises and check the accuracy of the transcript within a given time limit. Non-compliance with the last requirement may lead to the loss of any beneficial treatment under this Notice.

(33) Access to corporate statements is only granted to the addressees of a statement of objections, provided that they commit – together with the legal counsels getting access on their behalf – not to make any copy by mechanical or electronic means of any information in the corporate statement to which access is being granted and to ensure that the information to be obtained from the corporate statement will solely be used for the purposes mentioned below. Other parties such as complainants will not be granted access to corporate statements. The Commission considers that this specific protection of a corporate statement is not justified as from the moment when the applicant discloses to third parties the content thereof.

[(34) In accordance with the Commission Notice on rules for access to the Commission file,[8] access to the file is only granted to the addressees of a statement of objections on the condition that the information thereby obtained may only be used for the purposes of judicial or administrative proceedings for the application of the Union competition rules. Any failure during the proceedings to comply with the provisions of Regulation (EC) No 773/2004[8A] on the use of information obtained through access to the file may be regarded as lack of cooperation within the meaning of points (12) and (27) of this Notice. Under certain circumstances it is subject to penalties to be laid down under national law.[8B] Moreover, if any such use is made after the Commission has already adopted a prohibition decision in the proceedings, the Commission may, in addition to applicable penalties under national law, in any legal proceedings before the Union Courts, ask the Court to increase the fine in respect of the responsible undertaking. Should any of the above limitations to the use of information be breached, at any point in time, with the involvement of an outside counsel, the Commission may report the incident to the bar of that counsel, with a view to disciplinary action.]

(35) Corporate statements made under the present Notice will only be transmitted to the competition authorities of the Member States pursuant to Article 12 of Regulation No 1/2003, provided that the conditions set out in the Network Notice[9] are met and provided that the level of protection against disclosure awarded by the receiving competition authority is equivalent to the one conferred by the Commission.

[(35a) In line with paragraph 26a of the Commission Notice on the co-operation between the Commission and the courts of the EU Member States in the application of Articles 101 and 102 of the Treaty, the Commission will not at any time transmit leniency corporate statements to national courts for use in actions for damages for breaches of those Treaty provisions.[9A] This paragraph is without prejudice to the situation referred to in Article 6(7) of Directive 2014/104/EU.]

NOTES

Point (34): substituted, together with associated footnotes, by Commission Communication 2015/C256/01, paras 1, 2.
Point (35a): inserted, together with associated footnote, by Commission Communication 2015/C256/01, paras 1, 3.

6 OJ L1, 4.1.2003, p 1.

7 OJ L123, 27.4.2004, p 18.

8 OJ C325, 22.12.2005, p 7.

8A Article 16a of Regulation (EC) No 773/2004, as amended by Commission Regulation (EU) 2015/1348 (OJ L208, 5.8.2015, p 3).

8B Articles 7 and 8 of Directive 2014/104/EU of the European Parliament and of the Council of 26 November 2014 on certain rules governing actions for damages under national law for infringements of the competition law provisions of the Member States and of the European Union (OJ L349, 5.12.2014, p 1).

9 Commission Notice on cooperation within the Network of Competition Authorities, OJ C101, 27.4.2004, p 43.

9A Commission Notice on the co-operation between the Commission and the courts of the EU Member States in the application of Articles 101 and 102 TFEU (OJ C101, 27.4.2004, p 54), as amended by the Communication from the Commission on Amendments to the Commission Notice on the cooperation between the Commission and courts of the EU Member States in the application of Articles 81 and 82 EC (OJ C256, 5.8.2015, p 5).

V. GENERAL CONSIDERATIONS

[4.404]

(36) The Commission will not take a position on whether or not to grant conditional immunity, or otherwise on whether or not to reward any application, if it becomes apparent that the application concerns infringements covered by the five years limitation period for the imposition of penalties stipulated in Article 25(1)(b) of Regulation 1/2003, as such applications would be devoid of purpose.

(37) From the date of its publication in the Official Journal, this notice replaces the 2002 Commission notice on immunity from fines and reduction of fines in cartel cases for all cases in which no undertaking has contacted the Commission in order to take advantage of the favourable treatment set out in that notice. However, points (31) to (35) of the current notice will be applied from the moment of its publication to all pending and new applications for immunity from fines or reduction of fines.

(38) The Commission is aware that this notice will create legitimate expectations on which undertakings may rely when disclosing the existence of a cartel to the Commission.

(39) In line with the Commission's practice, the fact that an undertaking cooperated with the Commission during its administrative procedure will be indicated in any decision, so as to explain the reason for the immunity or reduction of the fine. The fact that immunity or reduction in respect of fines is granted cannot protect an undertaking from the civil law consequences of its participation in an infringement of Article 81 EC.

(40) The Commission considers that normally public disclosure of documents and written or recorded statements received in the context of this notice would undermine certain public or private interests, for example the protection of the purpose of inspections and investigations, within the meaning of Article 4 of Regulation (EC) No 1049/2001,[10] even after the decision has been taken.

NOTES

[10] OJ L145, 31.5.2001, p 43.

COMMISSION REGULATION

(622/2008/EC)

of 30 June 2008

amending Regulation (EC) No 773/2004, as regards the conduct of settlement procedures in cartel cases

(Text with EEA relevance)

[4.405]

NOTES

Date of publication in OJ: OJ L171, 1.7.2008, p 3.

Repeal of this Regulation in relation to the UK: this Regulation is repealed, in relation to the UK, by the Competition (Amendment etc) (EU Exit) Regulations 2019, SI 2019/93, reg 63, Sch 3, para 2, as from IP completion day (as defined in the European Union (Withdrawal Agreement) Act 2020, s 39) (for transitional provisions and savings in relation to the operation of the 2019 Regulations, see Sch 4 to those Regulations at **[7.69]** et seq). Note also that Commission Regulation 773/2004/EC is also repealed by Sch 3, para 2 to the 2019 Regulations (as from the same date).

Note: with effect from 1 December 2009, the EC Treaty was replaced by the Treaty on the Functioning of the European Union. References in this document to provisions of the EC Treaty should be construed accordingly.

THE COMMISSION OF THE EUROPEAN COMMUNITIES,

Having regard to the Treaty establishing the European Community,

Having regard to the Agreement on the European Economic Area,

Having regard to Council Regulation (EC) No 1/2003 of 16 December 2002 on the implementation of the rules on competition laid down in Articles 81 and 82 of the Treaty,[1] and in particular Article 33 thereof,

Having published a draft of this Regulation,[2]

After consulting the Advisory Committee on Restrictive Practices and Dominant Positions,

Whereas:

(1) Commission Regulation (EC) No 773/2004 of 7 April 2004 relating to the conduct of proceedings by the Commission pursuant to Articles 81 and 82 of the EC Treaty[3] lays down rules concerning the participation of the parties concerned in such proceedings.

(2) Parties to the proceedings may be prepared to acknowledge their participation in a cartel violating Article 81 of the Treaty and their liability in respect of such participation, if they can reasonably anticipate the Commission's envisaged findings as regards their participation in the infringement and the level of potential fines and agree with those findings. It should be possible for the Commission to disclose to those parties, where appropriate, the objections which it intends to raise against them on the basis of the evidence in the file and the fines that they are likely to incur. Such early disclosure should enable the parties concerned to put forward their views on the objections which the Commission intends to raise against them as well as on their potential liability.

(3) When the Commission reflects the parties' settlement submissions in the statement of objections and the parties' replies confirm that the statement of objections corresponds to the contents of their settlement submissions, the Commission should be able to proceed to the adoption of a Decision pursuant to Article 7 and Article 23 of Regulation (EC) No 1/2003 after consultation of the Advisory Committee on Restrictive Practices and Dominant

Positions pursuant to Article 14 of Regulation (EC) No 1/2003.

(4) A settlement procedure should therefore be established in order to enable the Commission to handle faster and more efficiently cartel cases. The Commission retains a broad margin of discretion to determine which cases may be suitable to explore the parties' interest to engage in settlement discussions, as well as to decide to engage in them or discontinue them or to definitely settle. Therefore, the Commission may decide at any time during the procedure to discontinue settlement discussions altogether in a specific case or with respect to one or more of the parties. In this regard, account may be taken of the probability of reaching a common understanding regarding the scope of the potential objections with the parties involved within a reasonable timeframe, in view of factors such as number of parties involved, foreseeable conflicting positions on the attribution of liability, extent of contestation of the facts. The prospect of achieving procedural efficiencies in view of the progress made overall in the settlement procedure, including any unreasonable delays, such as delays associated with the resources required to provide access to non-confidential versions of documents from the file, will be considered. Other concerns such as the possibility of setting a precedent may also be considered.

(5) Complainants will be closely associated with settlement proceedings and be duly informed of the nature and subject matter of the procedure in writing to enable them to provide their views thereon and thereby cooperate with the Commission investigation. However, in the particular context of settlement proceedings, providing systematically a non-confidential version of the statement of objections to complainants would not always serve the purpose of enabling complainants to cooperate with the Commission's investigation and may occasionally discourage the parties to the proceedings from cooperating with the Commission. To this end, the Commission should not be obliged to provide a non-confidential version of the statement of objections to complainants.

(6) Regulation (EC) No 773/2004 should therefore be amended accordingly,

NOTES

Repeal of this Regulation in relation to the UK: this Regulation is repealed in relation to the UK (as from IP completion day); see the introductory notes to this Regulation *ante*.

[1] OJ L1, 4.1.2003, p 1. Regulation as last amended by Regulation (EC) No 1419/2006 (OJ L269, 28.9.2006, p 1).

[2] OJ C50, 27.10.2007, p 48.

[3] OJ L123, 27.4.2004, p 18. Regulation as amended by Regulation (EC) No 1792/2006 (OJ L362, 20.12.2006, p 1).

HAS ADOPTED THIS REGULATION—

Article 1 *(Amends Council Regulation 773/2004/EC at* **[4.83]** *et seq. Repealed as noted in the introductory notes to this Regulation ante.)*

[4.406]

Article 2

This Regulation shall enter into force on 1 July 2008.

This Regulation shall be binding in its entirety and directly applicable in all Member States.

NOTES

Repeal of this Regulation in relation to the UK: this Regulation is repealed in relation to the UK (as from IP completion day); see the introductory notes to this Regulation *ante*.

COMMISSION NOTICE

(2008/C167/01)

on the conduct of settlement procedures in view of the adoption of Decisions pursuant to Article 7 and Article 23 of Council Regulation (EC) No 1/2003 in cartel cases

(Text with EEA relevance)

[4.407]

NOTES

Date of publication in OJ: OJ C167, 2.7.2008, p 1.

Note that Council Regulation 1/2003/EC is repealed, in relation to the UK, by the Competition (Amendment etc) (EU Exit) Regulations 2019, SI 2019/93, reg 63, Sch 3, para 1, as from IP completion day (as defined in the European Union (Withdrawal Agreement) Act 2020, s 39) (for transitional provisions and savings in relation to the operation of the 2019 Regulations, see Sch 4 to those Regulations at **[7.69]** et seq).

Note: with effect from 1 December 2009, the EC Treaty was replaced by the Treaty on the Functioning of the European Union. References in this document to provisions of the EC Treaty should be construed accordingly.

1. INTRODUCTION

[4.408]

1. This Notice sets out the framework for rewarding cooperation in the conduct of proceedings commenced in view of the application of Article 81 of the EC Treaty[1] to cartel cases.[2] The settlement procedure may allow the Commission to handle more cases with the same resources, thereby fostering the public interest in the Commission's delivery of effective and timely punishment, while increasing overall deterrence. The cooperation covered by this Notice is different from the voluntary production of evidence to trigger or advance

the Commission's investigation, which is covered by the Commission Notice on Immunity from fines and reduction of fines in cartel cases[3] (the Leniency Notice). Provided that the cooperation offered by an undertaking qualifies under both Commission Notices, it can be cumulatively rewarded accordingly.[4]

2. When parties to the proceedings are prepared to acknowledge their participation in a cartel violating Article 81 of the Treaty and their liability therefore, they may also contribute to expediting the proceedings leading to the adoption of the corresponding decision pursuant to Article 7 and Article 23 of Council Regulation (EC) No 1/2003 of 16 December 2002 on the implementation of the rules on competition laid down in Articles 81 and 82 of the Treaty[5] in the way and with the safeguards specified in this Notice. Whilst the Commission, as the investigative authority and the guardian of the Treaty empowered to adopt enforcement decisions subject to judicial control by the Community Courts, does not negotiate the question of the existence of an infringement of Community law and the appropriate sanction, it can reward the cooperation described in this Notice.

3. Commission Regulation (EC) No 773/2004 of 7 April 2004 relating to the conduct of proceedings by the Commission pursuant to Articles 81 and 82 of the EC Treaty[6] lays down the core practical rules concerning the conduct of proceedings in antitrust cases including those applicable in the variant for settlement. In this regard, Regulation (EC) No 773/2004 bestows on the Commission the discretion whether to explore the settlement procedure or not in cartel cases, while ensuring that the choice of the settlement procedure cannot be imposed on the parties.

4. Effective enforcement of Community competition law is compatible with full respect of the parties' rights of defence, which constitutes a fundamental principle of Community law to be respected in all circumstances, and in particular in antitrust procedures which may give rise to penalties. It follows that the rules established to conduct the Commission proceedings to enforce Article 81 of the Treaty should ensure that the undertakings and associations of undertakings concerned are afforded the opportunity effectively to make known their views on the truth and relevance of the facts, objections and circumstances put forward by the Commission,[7] throughout the administrative procedure.

NOTES

1 References in this text to Article 81 also cover Article 53 EEA when applied by the Commission in accordance with the rules laid down in Article 56 of the EEA Agreement.

2 Cartels are agreements and/or concerted practices between two or more competitors aimed at coordinating their competitive behaviour on the market and/or influencing the relevant parameters of competition through practices such as the fixing of purchase or selling prices or other trading conditions, the allocation of production or sales quotas, the sharing of markets including bid-rigging, restrictions of imports or exports and/or anti-competitive actions against other competitors. Such practices are among the most serious violations of Article 81 EC.

3 OJ C298, 8.12.2006, p 17.

4 See point 33.

5 OJ L1, 4.1.2003, p 1. Regulation as last amended by Regulation (EC) No 1419/2006 (OJ L269, 28.9.2006, p 1).

6 OJ L123, 27.4.2004, p 18. Regulation as last amended by Regulation (EC) No 622/2008 (OJ L171, 1.7.2008, p 3).

7 Case 85/76, *Hoffmann-La Roche v Commission* [1979] ECR 461, at paragraphs 9 and 11.

2. PROCEDURE

[4.409]

5. The Commission retains a broad margin of discretion to determine which cases may be suitable to explore the parties' interest to engage in settlement discussions, as well as to decide to engage in them or discontinue them or to definitely settle. In this regard, account may be taken of the probability of reaching a common understanding regarding the scope of the potential objections with the parties involved within a reasonable timeframe, in view of factors such as number of parties involved, foreseeable conflicting positions on the attribution of liability, extent of contestation of the facts. The prospect of achieving procedural efficiencies in view of the progress made overall in the settlement procedure, including the scale of burden involved in providing access to non-confidential versions of documents from the file, will be considered. Other concerns such as the possibility of setting a precedent might apply. The Commission may also decide to discontinue settlement discussions if the parties to the proceedings coordinate to distort or destroy any evidence relevant to the establishment of the infringement or any part thereof or to the calculation of the applicable fine. Distortion or destruction of evidence relevant to the establishment of the infringement or any part thereof may also constitute an aggravating circumstance within the meaning of point 28 of the Commission Guidelines on the method of setting fines imposed pursuant to Article 23(2)(a) of Regulation (EC) No 1/2003[8] (the Guidelines on fines), and may be regarded as lack of cooperation within the meaning of points 12 and 27 of the Leniency Notice. The Commission may only engage in settlement discussions upon the written request of the parties concerned.

6. While parties to the proceedings do not have a right to settle, should the Commission consider that a case may, in principle, be suitable for settlement, it will explore the interest in settlement of all parties to the same proceedings.

7. The parties to the proceedings may not disclose to any third party in any jurisdiction the contents of the discussions or of the documents which they have had access to in view of settlement, unless they have a prior explicit authorization by the Commission. Any breach in this regard may lead the Commission to disregard the undertaking's request to follow the settlement procedure. Such disclosure may also constitute an aggravating circumstance, within the meaning of point 28 of the Guidelines on fines and may be regarded as lack of cooperation within the meaning of points 12 and 27 of the Leniency Notice.

2.1. Initiation of proceedings and exploratory steps regarding settlement

8. Where the Commission contemplates the adoption of a decision pursuant to Article 7 and/or Article 23 of Regulation (EC) No 1/2003, it is required in advance to identify and recognize as parties to the proceedings the legal persons on whom a penalty may be imposed for an infringement of Article 81 of the Treaty.

9. To this end, the initiation of proceedings pursuant to Article 11(6) of Regulation (EC) No 1/2003 in view of adopting such a decision can take place at any point in time, but no later than the date on which the Commission issues a statement of objections against the parties concerned. Article 2(1) of Regulation (EC) No 773/2004 further specifies that, should the Commission consider it suitable to explore the parties' interest in engaging in settlement discussions, it will initiate proceedings no later than the date on which it either issues a statement of objections or requests the parties to express in writing their interest to engage in settlement discussions, whichever is the earlier.

10. After the initiation of proceedings pursuant to Article 11(6) of Regulation (EC) No 1/2003, the Commission becomes the only competition authority competent to apply Article 81 of the Treaty to the case in point.

11. Should the Commission consider it suitable to explore the parties' interest to engage in settlement discussions, it will set a time-limit of no less than two weeks pursuant to Articles 10a(1) and 17(3) of Regulation (EC) No 773/2004 within which parties to the same proceedings should declare in writing whether they envisage engaging in settlement discussions in view of possibly introducing settlement submissions at a later stage. This written declaration does not imply an admission by the parties of having participated in an infringement or of being liable for it.

12. Whenever the Commission initiates proceedings against two or more parties within the same undertaking, the Commission will inform each of them of the other legal entities which it identifies within the same undertaking and which are also concerned by the proceedings. In such a case, should the concerned parties wish to engage in settlement discussions, they must appoint joint representatives duly empowered to act on their behalf by the end of the time-limit referred to in point 11. The appointment of joint representatives aims solely to facilitate the settlement discussions and it does not prejudge in any way the attribution of liability for the infringement amongst the different parties.

13. The Commission may disregard any application for immunity from fines or reduction of fines on the ground that it has been submitted after the expiry of the time-limit referred to in point 11.

2.2. Commencing the settlement procedure: settlement discussions

14. Should some of the parties to the proceedings request settlement discussions and comply with the requirements referred to in points 11 and 12, the Commission may decide to pursue the settlement procedure by means of bilateral contacts between the Commission Directorate-General for Competition and the settlement candidates.

15. The Commission retains discretion to determine the appropriateness and the pace of the bilateral settlement discussions with each undertaking. In line with Article 10a(2) of Regulation (EC) No 773/2004, this includes determining, in view of the progress made overall in the settlement procedure, the order and sequence of the bilateral settlement discussions as well as the timing of the disclosure of information, including the evidence in the Commission file used to establish the envisaged objections and the potential fine.[9] Information will be disclosed in a timely manner as settlement discussions progress.

16. Such an early disclosure in the context of settlement discussions pursuant to Article 10a(2) and Article 15(1a) of Regulation (EC) No 773/2004 will allow the parties to be informed of the essential elements taken into consideration so far, such as the facts alleged, the classification of those facts, the gravity and duration of the alleged cartel, the attribution of liability, an estimation of the range of likely fines, as well as the evidence used to establish the potential objections. This will enable the parties effectively to assert their views on the potential objections against them and will allow them to make an informed decision on whether or not to settle. Upon request by a party, the Commission services will also grant it access to non-confidential versions of any specified accessible document listed in the case file at that point in time, in so far as this is justified for the purpose of enabling the party to ascertain its position regarding a time period or any other aspect of the cartel.[10]

17. When the progress made during the settlement discussions leads to a common understanding regarding the scope of the potential objections and the estimation of the range of likely fines to be imposed by the Commission, and the Commission takes the preliminary view that procedural efficiencies are likely to be achieved in view of the progress made overall, the Commission may grant a final time-limit of at least 15 working days for an undertaking to introduce a final settlement submission pursuant to Articles 10a(2) and 17(3) of Regulation (EC) No 773/2004. The time-limit can be extended following a reasoned request. Before granting such time-limit, the parties will be entitled to have the information specified in point 16 disclosed to them upon request.

18. The parties may call upon the Hearing Officer at any time during the settlement procedure in relation to issues that might arise relating to due process. The Hearing Officer's duty is to ensure that the effective exercise of the rights of defence is respected.

19. Should the parties concerned fail to introduce a settlement submission, the procedure leading to the final decision in their regard will follow the general provisions, in particular Articles 10(2), 12(1) and 15(1) of Regulation (EC) No 773/2004, instead of those regulating the settlement procedure.

2.3. Settlement submissions

20. Parties opting for a settlement procedure must introduce a formal request to settle in the form of a settlement submission. The settlement submission provided for in Article 10a(2) of Regulation (EC) No 773/2004 should contain:

(a) an acknowledgement in clear and unequivocal terms of the parties' liability for the infringement summarily described as regards its object, its possible implementation, the main facts, their legal qualification, including the party's role and the duration of their participation in the infringement in accordance with the results of the settlement discussions;

(b) an indication[11] of the maximum amount of the fine the parties foresee to be imposed by the Commission and which the parties would accept in the framework of a settlement procedure;

(c) the parties' confirmation that, they have been sufficiently informed of the objections the Commission envisages raising against them and that they have been given sufficient opportunity to make their views known to the Commission;

(d) the parties' confirmation that, in view of the above, they do not envisage requesting access to the file or requesting to be heard again in an oral hearing, unless the Commission does not reflect their settlement submissions in the statement of objections and the decision;

(e) the parties' agreement to receive the statement of objections and the final decision pursuant to Articles 7 and 23 of Regulation (EC) No 1/2003 in an agreed official language of the European Community.

21. The acknowledgments and confirmations provided by the parties in view of settlement constitute the expression of their commitment to cooperate in the expeditious handling of the case following the settlement procedure. However, those acknowledgments and confirmations are conditional upon the Commission meeting their settlement request, including the anticipated maximum amount of the fine.

[22. Settlement submissions cannot be withdrawn unilaterally by the parties which have provided them. The statement of objections would be deemed to have endorsed the settlement submissions if it reflects their contents on the issues mentioned in point 20(a). Additionally, for a final decision to be deemed to have reflected the settlement submissions, it should not impose a fine which exceeds the maximum amount indicated therein.]

2.4. Statement of objections and reply

23. Pursuant to Article 10(1) of Regulation (EC) No 773/2004, the notification of a written statement of objections to each of the parties against whom objections are raised is a mandatory preparatory step before adopting any final decision. Therefore, the Commission will issue a statement of objections also in a settlement procedure.[12]

24. For the parties' rights of defence to be exercised effectively, the Commission should hear their views on the objections against them and supporting evidence before adopting a final decision and take them into account by amending its preliminary analysis, where appropriate.[13] The Commission must be able not only to accept or reject the parties' relevant arguments expressed during the administrative procedure, but also to make its own analysis of the matters put forward by them in order to either abandon such objections because they have been shown to be unfounded or to supplement and reassess its arguments both in fact and in law, in support of the objections which it maintains.

25. By introducing a formal settlement request in the form of a settlement submission prior to the notification of the statement of objections, the parties concerned enable the Commission to effectively take their views into account[14] already when drafting the statement of objections, rather than only before the consultation of the Advisory Committee on Restrictive Practices and Dominant Positions (hereinafter the "Advisory Committee") or before the adoption of the final decision.[15]

26. Should the statement of objections reflect the parties' settlement submissions, the parties concerned should within a time-limit of at least two weeks set by the Commission in accordance with Articles 10a(3) and 17(3) of Regulation (EC) No 773/2004, reply to it by simply confirming (in unequivocal terms) that the statement of objections corresponds to the contents of their settlement submissions and that they therefore remain committed to follow the settlement procedure. In the absence of such a reply, the Commission will take note of the party's breach of its commitment and may also disregard the party's request to follow the settlement procedure.

[27. The Commission retains the right to adopt a statement of objections which does not reflect the parties' settlement submission. If so, the general provisions in Articles 10(2), 12(1) and 15(1) of Regulation (EC) No 773/2004 will apply. The acknowledgements provided by the parties in the settlement submission will be disregarded by the Commission and cannot be used as evidence against any of the parties to the proceedings. Hence, the parties concerned will no longer be bound by their settlement submissions and will be granted a time-limit allowing them, upon request, to present their defence anew, including the possibility to access the file and to request an oral hearing.]

2.5. Commission decision and settlement reward

28. Upon the parties' replies to the statement of objections confirming their commitment to settle, Regulation (EC) No 773/2004 allows the Commission to proceed, without any other procedural step, to the adoption of the subsequent final decision pursuant to Articles 7 and/or 23 of Regulation (EC) No 1/2003, after consultation of the Advisory Committee pursuant to Article 14 of Regulation (EC) No 1/2003. In particular, this implies that no oral hearing or access to the file may be requested by those parties once their settlement submissions have been reflected by the statement of objections, in line with Articles 12(2) and 15(1a) of Regulation (EC) No 773/2004.

[29. The Commission retains the right to adopt a final position which departs from its preliminary position expressed in a statement of objections endorsing the parties' settlement submissions, either in view of the opinion provided by the Advisory Committee or for other appropriate considerations in view of the ultimate decisional autonomy of the Commission to this effect. However, should the Commission opt to follow that course, it will inform the parties and notify to them a new statement of objections in order to allow for the exercise of their rights of defence in accordance with the applicable general rules of procedure. It follows that the parties will then be entitled to have access to the file, to request an oral hearing and to reply to the statement of objections. The acknowledgments provided by the parties in the settlement submissions will be disregarded by the Commission and will not be used in evidence against any of the parties to the proceedings.]

30. The final amount of the fine in a particular case is determined in the decision finding an infringement pursuant to Article 7 and imposing a fine pursuant to Article 23 of Regulation (EC) No 1/2003.

31. In line with the Commission's practice, the fact that an undertaking cooperated with the Commission under this Notice during the administrative procedure will be indicated in the final decision, so as to explain the reason for the level of the fine.

32. Should the Commission decide to reward a party for settlement in the framework of this Notice, it will reduce by 10% the amount of the fine to be imposed after the 10% cap has been applied having regard to the Guidelines on the method of setting fines imposed pursuant to Article 23(2)(a) of Regulation (EC) No 1/2003.[16] Any specific increase for deterrence[17] used in their regard will not exceed a multiplication by two.

33. When settled cases involve also leniency applicants, the reduction of the fine granted to them for settlement will be added to their leniency reward.

NOTES

Points 22, 27, 29: substituted by Commission Communication 2015/C256/02, paras 1–4.

8 OJ C210, 1.9.2006, p 2.

9 Reference to the "potential fine" in Article 10a(2) of Regulation (EC) No 773/2004 affords the Commission services the possibility to inform the parties concerned by settlement discussions of an estimate of their potential fine in view of the guidance contained in the Guidelines on fines, the provisions of this Notice and the Leniency Notice, where applicable.

10 For that purpose, the parties will be provided with a list of all accessible documents in the case file at that point in time.

11 This would result from the discussions as set out in points 16 and 17.

12 In the context of settlement procedures, statements of objections should contain the information necessary to enable the parties to corroborate that it reflects their settlement submissions.

13 In line with settled case-law, the Commission shall base its decisions only on objections on which the parties concerned have been able to comment and, to this end, they shall be entitled to have access to the Commission's file, subject to the legitimate interest of undertakings in the protection of their business secrets.

14 In this regard, recital 2 of Regulation (EC) No 622/2008 states: "(. . .) Such early disclosure should enable the parties concerned to put forward their views on the objections which the Commission intends to raise against them as well as on their potential liability".

15 As required by Article 11(1) of Regulation (EC) No 773/2004 and Article 27(1) of Regulation (EC) No 1/2003, respectively.

16 OJ C210, 1.9.2006, p 2.

17 Point 30 of the Guidelines on fines.

3. GENERAL CONSIDERATIONS

[4.410]

34. This Notice applies to any case pending before the Commission at the time of or after its publication in the Official Journal of the European Union.

35. Access to settlement submissions is only granted to those addressees of a statement of objections who have not requested settlement, provided that they commit – together with the legal counsels getting access on their behalf – not to make any copy by mechanical or electronic means of any information in the settlement submissions to which access is being granted and to ensure that the information to be obtained from the settlement submission will solely be used for the purposes of judicial or administrative proceedings for the application of the Community competition rules at issue in the related proceedings. Other parties such as complainants will not be granted access to settlement submissions.

36. The use of such information for a different purpose during the proceeding may be regarded as lack of cooperation within the meaning of points 12 and 27 of the Leniency Notice. Moreover, if any such use is made after the Commission has already adopted a prohibition decision in the proceedings, the Commission may, in any legal proceedings before the Community Courts, ask the Court to increase the fine in respect of the responsible undertaking. Should the information be used for a different purpose, at any point in time, with the involvement of an outside counsel, the Commission may report the incident to the bar of that counsel, with a view to disciplinary action.

37. Settlement submissions made under this Notice will only be transmitted to the competition authorities of the Member States pursuant to Article 12 of Regulation (EC) No 1/2003, provided that the conditions set out in the Network Notice[18] are met and provided that the level of protection against disclosure awarded by the receiving competition authority is equivalent to the one conferred by the Commission.

38. Upon the applicant's request, the Commission may accept that settlement submissions be provided orally. Oral settlement submissions will be recorded and transcribed at the Commission's premises. In accordance with Article 19 of Regulation (EC) No 1/2003 and Articles 3(3) and 17(3) of Regulation (EC) No 773/2004 undertakings making oral settlement submissions will be granted the opportunity to check the technical accuracy of the recording, which will be available at the Commission's premises and to correct the substance of their oral settlement submissions and the accuracy of the transcript without delay.

[39. In line with paragraph 26a of the Commission Notice on the co-operation between the Commission and the courts of the EU Member States in the application of Articles 101 and 102 of the Treaty, the Commission will not at any time transmit settlement submissions to national courts for use in actions for damages for breaches of those Treaty provisions.[19] This paragraph is without prejudice to the situation referred to in Article 6(7) of Directive 2014/104/EU of the European Parliament and of the Council.[19A]]

40. The Commission considers that normally public disclosure of documents and written or recorded statements (including settlement submissions) received in the context of this Notice would undermine certain public or private interests, for example the protection of the purpose of inspections and investigations, within the meaning of Article 4 of Regulation (EC) No 1049/2001 of the European Parliament and of the Council of 30 May 2001 regarding public access to European Parliament, Council and Commission documents,[20] even after the decision has been taken.

41. Final decisions taken by the Commission under Regulation (EC) No 1/2003 are subject to judicial review in accordance with Article 230 of the Treaty. Moreover, as provided in Article 229 of the Treaty and Article 31 of Regulation (EC) No 1/2003, the Court of Justice has unlimited jurisdiction to review decisions on fines adopted pursuant to Article 23 of Regulation (EC) No 1/2003.

NOTES

Point 39: substituted, together with associated footnotes, by Commission Communication 2015/C256/02, paras 1, 5.

18 Commission Notice on cooperation within the Network of Competition Authorities (OJ C101, 27.4.2004, p 43).

19 Commission Notice on the co-operation between the Commission and the courts of the EU Member States in the application of Articles 101 and 102 TFEU (OJ C101, 27.4.2004, p 54), as amended by the Communication from the Commission on Amendments to the Commission Notice on the cooperation between the Commission and courts of the EU Member States in the application of Articles 81 and 82 EC (OJ C256, 5.8.2015, p 5).

19A Directive 2014/104/EU of the European Parliament and of the Council of 26 November 2014 on certain rules governing actions for damages under national law for infringements of the competition law provisions of the Member States and of the European Union (OJ L349, 5.12.2014, p 1).

20 OJ L145, 31.5.2001, p 43.

OVERVIEW OF THE PROCEDURE LEADING TO THE ADOPTION OF A (SETTLEMENT) DECISION PURSUANT TO ARTICLES 7 AND 23 OF REGULATION NO (EC) 1/2003

[4.411]

I. Investigation as usual

— Parties may express their interest in a hypothetical settlement.

II. Exploratory steps regarding settlement

— Letter to all companies (and MS) informing of the decision to initiate proceedings in view of settlement (Article 11(6)) and requesting them to express their interest in settlement.

III. Bilateral rounds of settlement discussions

— Disclosure and exchange of arguments on potential objections, liability, fines range.
— Disclosure of evidence used to establish potential objections, liability, fines.
— Disclosure of other non-confidential versions of documents in the file, when justified.

IV. Settlement

— Conditional settlement submissions by the companies, jointly represented where applicable.
— DG COMP sends acknowledgement of receipt.

V. "Settled" statement of objections

— Notification of streamlined SO endorsing company's settlement submissions, where appropriate.
— Company's reply to SO confirming clearly that it reflects its settlement submission.

VI. "Settlement" Decision pursuant to Articles 7 and 23 of Regulation No (EC) 1/2003

— Advisory Committee on a draft streamlined final decision.

If College of Commissioners agrees:

— Adoption of streamlined final decision.

EUROPEAN COMPETITION NETWORK: MODEL LENIENCY PROGRAMME

(As revised in November 2012)

[4.412]

NOTES

This document is available on the European Commission website at: ec.europa.eu/competition-policy/european-competition-network/documents_en. For further information see the following (all of which are available on the website mentioned above):

— Annex: Template for submission of a summary leniency application within the ECN
— About the 2012 revision (Memo)
— Frequently Asked Questions
— List of National Competition Authorities which operate a Leniency programme (Updated on 22 November 2012)
— List of National Competition Authorities accepting summary applications and applicable language regime for summary applications.

I. INTRODUCTION

[4.413]

1. In a system of parallel competences between the European Commission (hereinafter the Commission) and National Competition Authorities (hereinafter NCAs), an application for leniency[1] to one authority is not to be considered as an application for leniency to another authority. It is therefore in the interest of the applicant to apply for leniency to all Competition Authorities (hereinafter CAs) which have competence to apply Article 101 of the Treaty on the Functioning of the European Union (hereinafter TFEU) in the territory which is affected by the infringement and which may be considered well placed to act against the infringement in question.[2]

2. The purpose of the ECN Model Leniency Programme (hereinafter the ECN Model Programme) is to ensure that potential leniency applicants are not discouraged from applying as a result of the discrepancies between the existing leniency programmes within the ECN. The ECN Model Programme therefore sets out the treatment which an applicant can anticipate in any ECN jurisdiction once alignment of all programmes has taken place. In addition, the ECN Model Programme aims to alleviate the burden associated with multiple filings in cases for which the Commission is particularly well placed by introducing a model for a uniform summary application system.

3. The ECN Model Programme sets out a framework for rewarding the cooperation of undertakings which are party to agreements and practices falling within its scope. The ECN members commit to using their best efforts, within the limits of their competence, to align their respective programmes with the ECN Model Programme. The ECN Model Programme does not prevent a CA from adopting a more favourable approach towards applicants within its programme.

NOTES

1 The term "leniency" refers to immunity as well as a reduction of any fine which would otherwise have been imposed on a participant in a cartel, in exchange for the voluntary disclosure of information regarding the cartel which satisfies specific criteria prior to or during the investigative stage of the case (see paragraph 37 of the Commission Notice on cooperation within the Network of Competition Authorities (hereinafter the Network Notice)).

2 See paragraph 38 of the Network Notice.

II. SCOPE OF THE PROGRAMME

[4.414]

4. The ECN Model Programme concerns secret cartels, in particular agreements and/or concerted practices between two or more competitors aimed at restricting competition through, for example, the fixing of purchase or selling prices, the allocation of production or sales quotas or the sharing of markets including bid-rigging.

III. IMMUNITY FROM FINES

Type 1A

[4.415]

5. The CA will grant an undertaking immunity from any fine which would otherwise have been imposed provided:

a) The undertaking is the first to submit evidence which in the CA's view, at the time it evaluates the application, will enable the CA to carry out targeted inspections in connection with an alleged cartel;

b) The CA did not, at the time of the application, already have sufficient evidence to adopt an inspection decision/seek a court warrant for an inspection or had not already carried out an inspection in connection with the alleged cartel arrangement; and

c) The conditions attached to leniency are met.

6. With a view to enabling the CA to carry out targeted inspections, the undertaking should be in a position to provide the CA with the following:

- The name and address of the legal entity submitting the immunity application;
- The other parties to the alleged cartel;
- A detailed description of the alleged cartel, including:
  - The affected products;
  - The affected territory (-ies);
  - The duration; and
  - The nature of the alleged cartel conduct;
- Evidence of the alleged cartel in its possession or under its control (in particular any contemporaneous evidence);
- Information on any past or possible future leniency applications to any other CAs and competition authorities outside the EU in relation to the alleged cartel.

Type 1B

7. In cases where no undertaking had been granted conditional immunity from fines before the CA carried out an inspection or before it had sufficient evidence to adopt an inspection decision/seek a court warrant for an inspection, the CA will grant an undertaking immunity from any fine which would otherwise have been imposed if:

a) The undertaking is the first to submit evidence which in the CA's view, enables the finding of an infringement of Article 101 TFEU[3] in respect of an alleged cartel;

b) At the time of the submission, the CA did not have sufficient evidence to find an infringement of Article 101 TFEU in connection with the alleged cartel; and

c) The conditions attached to leniency are met.

Excluded immunity applicants

8. An undertaking which took steps to coerce another undertaking to participate in the cartel will not be eligible for immunity from fines under the programme.[4]

NOTES

3 For national programmes, the equivalent national legal basis should be added.

4 Germany and Greece note that the sole ringleader is not eligible for immunity from fines under their respective programmes.

IV. REDUCTION OF FINES: TYPE 2

[4.416]
9. Undertakings that do not qualify for immunity may benefit from a reduction of any fine that would otherwise have been imposed.

10. In order to qualify for a reduction of fines, an undertaking must provide the CA with evidence of the alleged cartel which, in the CA's view, represents significant added value relative to the evidence already in the CA's possession at the time of the application. The concept of 'significant added value' refers to the extent to which the evidence provided strengthens, by its very nature and/or its level of detail, the CA's ability to prove the alleged cartel.

11. In order to determine the appropriate level of reduction of the fine, the CA will take into account the time at which the evidence was submitted (including whether the applicant was the first, second or third, etc. undertaking to apply) and the CA's assessment of the overall value added to its case by that evidence. Reductions granted to an applicant following a Type 2 application shall not exceed 50% of the fine which would otherwise have been imposed.

12. If a Type 2 applicant submits compelling evidence which the CA uses to establish additional facts which have a direct bearing on the amount of the fine, this will be taken into account when setting any fine to be imposed on the undertaking which provided this evidence.

V. CONDITIONS ATTACHED TO LENIENCY

[4.417]
13. In order to qualify for leniency under this programme, the applicant must satisfy the following cumulative conditions:

(1) It ends its involvement in the alleged cartel immediately following its application[5] save to the extent that its continued involvement would, in the CA's view, be reasonably necessary to preserve the integrity of the CA's inspections;

(2) It cooperates genuinely, fully and on a continuous basis from the time of its application with the CA until the conclusion of the case; this includes in particular:
  - (a) providing the CA promptly with all relevant information and evidence that comes into the applicant's possession or under its control;
  - (b) remaining at the disposal of the CA to reply promptly to any requests that, in the CA's view, may contribute to the establishment of relevant facts;
  - (c) making current and, to the extent possible, former employees and directors available for interviews with the CA;
  - (d) not destroying, falsifying or concealing relevant information or evidence; and
  - (e) unless and to the extent otherwise explicitly authorised by the CA, not disclosing the fact or any of the content of the leniency application at least before the CA has notified its objections to the parties.[6]

(3) When contemplating making an application to the CA but prior to doing so, it must not have:
  - (a) destroyed evidence which falls within the scope of the application; or
  - (b) disclosed, directly or indirectly, the fact or any of the content of the application it is contemplating except to other CAs or any competition authority outside the EU.

NOTES

5 'Application' in this paragraph 13 refers to an application for a marker, a summary application or a full leniency application (as the case may be).

6 Due to the variety of procedures and investigative measures applied in the various jurisdictions, the ECN Model Programme has been drafted in a manner that takes into account both administrative and judicial proceedings. The terms "objections" and "statement of objections" should be read as covering all equivalent steps under the relevant procedures where the investigative stage has been completed and the parties are formally notified of the CA's objections.

VI. PROCEDURE

Approaching the CA

[4.418]
14. An undertaking wishing to benefit from leniency must apply to the CA and provide it with the information specified above. Before making a formal application, the applicant may on an anonymous basis approach the CA in order to seek informal guidance on the application of the leniency programme.

15. Once a formal application has been made, the CA will, upon request, provide an acknowledgement of receipt confirming the date and time of the application. The CA will assess applications in relation to the same alleged cartel in the order of receipt.

Procedure for immunity applications

Marker for immunity applicants

16. An undertaking wishing to make an application for immunity may initially apply for a 'marker'. A marker protects an applicant's place in the queue for a given period of time and allows it to gather the necessary information and evidence in order to meet the relevant evidential threshold for immunity.

17. The CA has discretion as to whether or not it grants a marker. Where a marker is granted, the CA determines the period within which the applicant has to 'perfect' the marker by submitting the information required to meet the relevant evidential threshold for immunity. If the applicant perfects the marker within the set period, the information and evidence provided will be deemed to have been submitted on the date when the marker was granted.

18. To be eligible to secure a marker, the applicant must provide the CA with its name and address as well as information concerning:

- The basis for the concern which led to the leniency approach;
- The parties to the alleged cartel;
- The affected product(s);
- The affected territory (-ies);
- The duration of the alleged cartel;
- The nature of the alleged cartel conduct; and
- Information on any past or possible future leniency applications to any other CAs and competition authorities outside the EU in relation to the alleged cartel.

Granting immunity

19. Once the CA has verified that the evidence submitted is sufficient to meet the relevant evidential threshold for immunity, it will grant the undertaking conditional immunity from fines in writing.

20. If the relevant evidential threshold is not met, the CA will inform the undertaking in writing that its application for immunity is rejected. The undertaking may in that case request the CA to consider its application for a reduction of the fine.

21. The CA will take its final position on the grant of immunity at the end of the procedure. If the CA, having granted conditional immunity, ultimately finds that the immunity applicant acted as a coercer or that the applicant has not fulfilled all of the conditions attached to leniency, the CA will inform the applicant of this promptly. If immunity is withheld because the CA finds at the end of the procedure that the conditions attached to leniency have not been fulfilled, the undertaking will not benefit from any other favourable treatment under this programme in respect of the same proceedings.

Procedure for reductions of fines applications

22. If the CA comes to the preliminary conclusion that the evidence submitted by an undertaking constitutes 'significant added value' within the meaning of the programme, it will inform the undertaking in writing of its intention to apply a reduction of fines. This confirmation will be given as early as possible and no later than the date the statement of objections is notified to the parties. The final amount of reduction will be determined at the latest by the end of the procedure.

23. If the CA finds that one or more of the conditions attached to leniency have not been fulfilled, the undertaking will not benefit from any favourable treatment under this programme in respect of the same proceedings.

Summary applications

24. In cases where the Commission is 'particularly well placed' to deal with a case in accordance with paragraph 14 of the Network Notice, the applicant that has or is in the process of filing a leniency application, either for immunity or for reduction of a fine, with the Commission may file summary applications with any NCAs which the applicant considers might be 'well placed' to act under the Network Notice. Summary applications should each have an identical substantive scope to the respective application with the Commission and should include a short description of the following:

- The name and address of the applicant;
- The other parties to the alleged cartel;
- The affected product(s);
- The affected territory(-ies);
- The duration;
- The nature of the alleged cartel conduct;
- The Member State(s) where the evidence is likely to be located; and
- Information on its other past or possible future leniency applications in relation to the alleged cartel.

25. Having received a summary application, the NCA will acknowledge receipt and grant the applicant a summary application marker based on the date and time when the information was provided to the NCA concerned. In addition, if the summary applicant is the first applicant in respect of the alleged cartel at the NCA concerned, the NCA will inform the summary applicant accordingly.

26. Should an NCA having received a summary application decide to request specific further information, the applicant should provide such information promptly. Should an NCA decide to act upon the case, it will determine a period of time within which the applicant must make a full submission of all relevant evidence and information required to meet the applicable threshold. If a Type 1A or Type 1B summary applicant submits such information within the set period to the NCA, the information provided will be deemed to have been submitted on the date when the summary application marker was granted. Type 2 summary applications will be assessed in the order created by summary application markers, subject to the threshold and other requirements applicable under the respective leniency programme. If an NCA requests the applicant to make a full submission, the applicant must submit to the NCA all information and evidence relating to the alleged cartel, subject to the requirements under the relevant leniency programme.

27. Summary applications are deemed to be applications within the meaning of paragraph 41(1) of the Network Notice.

Statements under the leniency programme and oral procedure

28. Upon the applicant's request, the CA may allow oral applications. In such cases the statements[7] may be provided orally and recorded in any form deemed appropriate by the CA. The applicant will still need to provide the CA with copies of all pre-existing documentary evidence of the cartel.

29. No access to any records of the statements (whether oral or written) will be granted before the CA has issued its statement of objections to the parties.

30. Statements (both oral and written) made under the present programme will only be exchanged between CAs pursuant to Article 12 of Regulation No 1/2003 if the conditions set out in the Network Notice are met and provided that the protection against disclosure granted by the receiving CA is equivalent to the one conferred by the transmitting CA.

NOTES

7 The term 'statement' refers both to corporate statements given by legal representatives on behalf of undertakings and witness statements made by employees and directors of the undertakings.

VII. REVIEW OF THE ECN MODEL PROGRAMME

[4.419]

31. The ECN Model Programme may be reviewed on the basis of the experience gathered by the ECN members. In any event, no later than at the end of the second year after the publication of the ECN Model Programme, the state of convergence of the leniency programmes of ECN members will be assessed.

ECN MODEL LENIENCY PROGRAMME
EXPLANATORY NOTES

I. INTRODUCTION

Importance of leniency programmes in the fight against cartels

[4.420]

1. Cartel activities are very serious violations of competition law. They injure consumers by raising prices and restricting supply. In the long term, they lead to a loss of competitiveness and reduced employment opportunities. Undertakings involved in these types of illegal activities that are willing to put an end to their participation and inform the European Commission and the National Competition Authorities (i.e. CAs) of the existence of such activities should not be dissuaded from doing so by the high fines to which they are potentially exposed. The CAs consider that it is in the public interest to grant favourable treatment to undertakings which co-operate with them.

2. The purpose of leniency programmes is to assist CAs in their efforts to detect and terminate cartels and to punish cartel participants. The CAs consider that the voluntary assistance with the above objectives has an intrinsic value for the economic well-being of individual Member States as well as the Common Market which may justify immunity in certain cases (Type 1A and 1B) and a reduction of a any fine in others (Type 2).

Safeguards for leniency information within the ECN

3. In order to prevent the mechanisms for cooperation between CAs established by Regulation No 1/2003[8] discouraging applicants from voluntarily reporting cartel activities, the Network Notice sets out special safeguards for leniency related information.[9] These safeguards enable the CAs to exchange and use in evidence leniency related information without jeopardising the effectiveness of their respective programmes.

4. According to paragraph 39 of the Network Notice, leniency related information submitted pursuant to Article 11 of Regulation 1/2003 cannot be used by other CAs to start an investigation.

5. According to paragraph 41, information submitted by a leniency applicant or collected on that basis, may only be exchanged between two CAs in the following circumstances:

- The applicant consents to the exchange; or
- The applicant has applied for leniency with both CAs in the same case; or
- The receiving CA provides a written commitment not to use the information transmitted or any information it may obtain after the date of the transmission to impose sanctions on the applicant, its subsidiaries or its employees. A copy of the written commitment is sent to the applicant.

Purpose of the ECN Model Programme

6. Making multiple parallel applications across the ECN is a complex exercise given the existing discrepancies between the different leniency regimes. Certain discrepancies may have adverse effects on the effectiveness of individual programmes. In addition, for cases involving a significant number of jurisdictions and for which the Commission is particularly well placed to act within the meaning of the Network Notice, the multiple filing of complete applications to all other possibly well placed CAs can be a cumbersome process which could discourage certain applicants from applying for leniency under any programme.

7. The purpose of the ECN Model Programme is to address the issue of multiple parallel applications and to provide a greater degree of predictability for potential applicants. The ECN Model Programme is based on the common experience of the CAs having operated a leniency programme for a number of years and has two principal objectives. Firstly, the ECN Model Programme is meant to trigger soft harmonisation of the existing leniency programmes and to facilitate the adoption of such programmes by the few CAs who do not currently operate one. Secondly, it sets out the features of a uniform type of short form applications (so-called summary applications) designed to alleviate the burden on both undertakings and CAs associated with multiple filing in large, cross-border cartel cases.

8. While it is highly desirable to ensure that all CAs operate a leniency programme, the variety of legislative frameworks, procedures and sanctions across the EU makes it difficult to adopt one uniform system. The ECN Model Programme therefore sets out the principal elements which, after the soft harmonisation process has occurred, should

Part 4 EU & Retained EU Materials

be common to all leniency programmes across the ECN. This would be without prejudice to the possibility for a CA to add further detailed provisions which suit its own enforcement system or to provide for a more favourable treatment of its applicants if it considers it to be necessary in order to ensure effective enforcement.

9. The Commission and the NCAs are committed to seeking the alignment of the programmes in their jurisdictions within the framework specified by the ECN Model Programme. It is recognised that some ECN members do not have the power to implement changes in their national leniency programmes as this power is held by other bodies. However, the existence of the ECN Model Programme should assist all relevant bodies (ECN members as well as other decision-making bodies) in implementing an efficient policy and making sure that cooperation within the ECN works as efficiently and effectively as possible.

NOTES

[8] OJ L1, 4.1.2003, page 1.

[9] See paragraphs 39–42 of the Network Notice. Leniency related information covers not only information contained in the leniency application itself, but all information that has been collected following any fact-finding measures that could not have been carried out but for the leniency application.

II. THE ECN MODEL PROGRAMME

[4.421]

10. The ECN Model Programme sets out a framework for rewarding the cooperation of undertakings which are party to agreements and practices falling within its scope. The ECN Model Programme does not give rise to any legal or other legitimate expectations on the part of any undertaking.

A. Scope of the programme

11. The ECN Model Programme concerns secret cartels. Secrecy does not imply that all aspects of the conduct should be secret, while in particular such elements that make the full extent of the conduct and the fact that it constitutes a cartel more difficult to detect are not known to the public or the customers/suppliers.

12. Cartels constitute very serious violations of competition rules which are often extremely difficult to detect and investigate without the cooperation of at least one of the participants. The interests of consumers and citizens in ensuring that such cartels are detected, terminated and punished outweighs the interest in fining those undertakings that enable a CA to detect, terminate and punish such illegal practices.

13. For the purpose of the ECN Model Programme cartels are agreements and/or concerted practices between competitors aimed at restricting competition by co-ordinating their competitive behaviour or influencing the relevant parameters of competition within the EEA. Cartel participants would typically collude to fix their purchase or selling prices, and/or to allocate production or sales quotas and/or to share markets. These cartel practices include arrangements which either directly or indirectly affect prices, volumes, market shares and other relevant parameters of competition. By way of example, collusive practices such as restrictions on imports or exports, bid-rigging or joint boycotts fall within the scope of the ECN Model Programme.[10]

14. Other types of restriction such as vertical agreements and horizontal restrictions other than cartels are normally less difficult to detect and/or investigate and therefore do not justify being dealt with under a leniency programme. In addition, including agreements other than cartels within the scope of a leniency programme may risk re-introducing a kind of de facto notification system which would be undesirable. It is not excluded, however, that a cartel which includes vertical elements may be covered by the leniency programme.

15. The ECN Model Programme only concerns corporate leniency. It does not cover sanctions on natural persons which are not undertakings. In order to ensure that corporate leniency programmes work efficiently, it is however important to protect to the greatest extent possible employees and directors of the undertakings applying for immunity. It may also be appropriate to offer protection from individual sanctions to employees and directors of applicants for a reduction of any fine. A number of CAs have leniency programmes that allow both individuals and undertakings involved in a cartel to individually apply for leniency. This is not in any way impeded by the ECN Model Programme's alignment of the corporate leniency programmes.

B. Immunity from fines: Type 1A and 1B

Evidential thresholds for immunity

16. The ECN Model Programme contains two different evidential thresholds for granting immunity:

- one for the first undertaking that provides the CA with sufficient evidence to enable it to carry out targeted inspections in connection with an alleged cartel (Type 1A); and
- one for the first undertaking that submits evidence which in the CA's view may enable the finding of an infringement of Article 101 TFEU in connection with an alleged cartel (Type 1B).

17. Immunity is no longer available under Type 1B if it has already been granted under Type 1A.

18. Immunity is available under a lower threshold in Type 1A compared to Type 1B in order to create an incentive for cartel participants to leave the cartel and to report infringements which are not yet known to the CAs.

19. The threshold in a Type 1A situation is that the applicant must provide the CA with sufficient information to allow it to carry out targeted inspections. The assessment of the threshold will have to be carried out ex ante, i.e. without taking into account whether a given inspection has or has not been successful or whether or not an inspection has or has not been carried out. The assessment will be made exclusively on the basis of the type and the quality of the information submitted by the applicant. The list contained in the ECN Model Programme and described in more detail below should serve as guidance for the applicant to anticipate what is usually required by a CA.

20. In order to meet the evidential threshold in Type 1A cases, undertakings should generally be in a position to provide the CA with the following information and evidence:

- The name and address of the legal entity submitting the immunity application, as well as the names of individuals who are or have been involved in the alleged cartel on its behalf;
- The identity of all the other undertakings which participate(d) in the alleged cartel as well as of the individuals who, to the applicant's knowledge, are or have been involved in the alleged cartel;
- A detailed description of the alleged cartel conduct, including for instance its aims, activities and functioning; the product(s) or service(s) concerned, the geographic coverage, the duration and the estimated market volumes affected by the alleged cartel; the dates, locations, content and participants of alleged cartel contacts; all relevant explanations in connection with evidence provided in support of the application;
- Evidence relating to the alleged cartel in the possession of the applicant or available to it at the time of the submission, in particular contemporaneous evidence; and
- Information on which other CAs, inside or outside the EU, have been approached or are intended to be approached by the applicant in relation to the alleged cartel.

21. If a CA has carried out an inspection or already has in its possession sufficient evidence to carry out an inspection, immunity under Type 1A will no longer be available.

Excluded applicants

22. An undertaking which has taken steps to coerce one or more undertakings to join or remain in the cartel should, as a matter of principle, be excluded from the benefit of immunity. Considerations of natural justice prevent an undertaking that has played such a role from escaping sanction altogether. The scope of the exclusion is narrow, however, so as to avoid creating uncertainty for potential applicants.

C. Reduction of fines: Type 2

23. It is in the interest of CAs to obtain the cooperation in the proceedings of those undertakings which do not qualify for immunity, either because they failed to meet the relevant evidential threshold or because of the role they played in the cartel. Such cooperation ensures that cartel activities are more efficiently investigated and penalised.

24. The value of the cooperation depends on the timing (including whether the applicant was the first, second or third, etc. to apply) and the quality and nature of the evidence submitted. There are various ways of combining these parameters to reward the contribution of the applicant. However, all systems should ensure that there is a significant difference between immunity from fines and reductions of fines in order to make applications for immunity significantly more attractive. Significant added value for type 2 applications should therefore not be rewarded with a reduction of any fine of more than 50%.

25. Applicants are required to adduce evidence which constitutes in the CA's view significant added value with respect to the evidence already in its possession at the time the application was submitted. The CA will generally consider written evidence originating from the period to which the facts pertain to have a greater value than evidence subsequently created, and incriminating evidence directly relevant to the facts in question will generally be considered to have a greater value than that with only indirect relevance. Similarly, the degree of corroboration from other sources required to rely on the evidence submitted will have an impact on the value of that evidence.

26. The ECN Model Programme contains a provision to counter any potentially adverse consequences for Type 2 applicants when they submit compelling evidence relating to additional facts which have a direct bearing on the amount of the fines.

D. Conditions attached to leniency

27. Qualifying for conditional immunity or bringing significant added value to an investigation will entitle an applicant to immunity or a reduction of fines provided that three cumulative conditions are met.

28. The final assessment of full compliance with the conditions attached to leniency is made at the end of the procedure.

29. The first condition relates to the termination of the alleged cartel conduct. Undertakings should terminate all cartel activities as soon as possible. However, experience shows that immediate termination, e.g. sudden unexplained absences from regular cartel meetings, after the application and before the CA has undertaken inspections can seriously undermine the effectiveness of subsequent inspections by alerting other cartel participants and allowing them to conceal or destroy evidence. It is therefore in the public interest to delay the complete termination of all cartel activities until the point in time necessary to safeguard the integrity of the inspection. This derogation to the general rule should be agreed to only when it is necessary and should strike the appropriate balance between bringing an end to the illegal activities of the applicant as soon as possible and protecting the effectiveness of the CA's investigation. This is also necessary to allow coordination between the various CAs in the event of parallel proceedings and to avoid applicants from being exposed to conflicting demands. The need to continue with certain cartel conduct should be discussed between the applicant and the CA at a very early stage.

30. The second condition is the obligation to cooperate with the CA throughout the procedure. This obligation is an essential feature of the leniency programme. It starts from the date of application to the CA and lasts throughout the procedure. In this respect, there is no reason to distinguish between applicants for immunity and those for a reduction of fines. In all cases, the cooperation has to be genuine, i.e., the assistance of the applicant, in addition to being comprehensive and immediate, should reveal a sincere spirit of cooperation.[11] It has various facets and therefore the list of duties that can be drawn is necessarily non-exhaustive. It involves among others:

- providing without delay any pre-existing evidence and information which is available to the applicant or comes into its possession or under its control during the investigation;
- answering without delay any question from the CA and making current and, where possible former, individual employees and directors available for interviews with the CA. This encompasses, inter alia, gathering all relevant information and material relevant to substantiate the leniency application that may be in possession of an employee or a director prior to their dismissal[12] or their voluntary departure;

- not destroying, falsifying or concealing evidence which falls within the scope of the application after having applied for leniency;
- not revealing (directly or indirectly) the fact or any of the content of its leniency application before the CA has notified its objections to the parties.

31. The obligation of non-disclosure of the application shall not be considered breached if the applicant informs another competition authority of the existence or the content of the leniency application, in the context of multiple applications by the same leniency applicant. Similarly, the obligation of nondisclosure shall not be considered breached if the applicant involves external counsel for the purpose of obtaining legal advice, provided the applicant ensures that the external counsel does not disclose any such information to any third party. Leniency applicants are encouraged to take necessary internal measures that would allow them to show to the CA, upon request, who has been informed by the applicant, at what date and time, about the fact or any of the content of the (contemplated or submitted) leniency application.

32. Unless otherwise explicitly authorised by the CA, an applicant's obligation of non-disclosure lasts at least until the CA has notified its objections to the parties. CAs may apply the obligation for a longer period, beyond the notification of objections to the parties, for example throughout their entire procedure. Leniency applicants who have submitted multiple applications with several CAs are encouraged to carefully verify throughout the duration of the procedures at the different CAs until when the obligation of non-disclosure is applicable to them under each leniency regime, in order to comply with all of them.

33. The third condition requires that the applicant should not, when contemplating making a leniency application to the CA but before doing so, have:

a) destroyed evidence which falls within the scope of the application; or
b) disclosed, directly or indirectly, the fact or any of the content of its contemplated application except to other CAs.

34. Failure to comply fully with any of these conditions will disqualify the applicant from the leniency programme in the relevant proceedings.

E. Procedure

Approaching the CA

35. All CAs accept anonymous approaches by potential applicants wishing to obtain guidance on their respective programmes. Some CAs have more formalised systems for such approaches, such as hypothetical applications.

Marker for immunity applicants

36. A marker protects an applicant's place in the queue for a given period of time. It allows the applicant to complete its internal investigation to gather the required information and evidence in order to meet the threshold.

37. In the ECN Model Programme, markers are available at the discretion of the CA. Some CAs may choose only to grant markers when it is clear that immunity is available or in certain type of situations, whereas certain others may grant markers in every case. Taking account of the specificities of each individual case the CA may decide the duration of the marker. In the event of parallel action by a number of CAs, the CAs will endeavour to use their discretion in a manner that allows their respective investigations to be coordinated smoothly.

38. The ECN Model Programme specifies the information required to secure a marker within the meaning of this programme. It is broadly equivalent to what is required to file a summary application. Some CAs however may decide to protect the applicant's place in the queue on the basis of more limited information, depending on the case at hand. In any event, an applicant would as a minimum have to provide its name and address and to satisfy a CA that it has a concrete basis for a reasonable concern that it has participated in cartel conduct.

Procedure for immunity and reduction of fines applications

39. CAs should deal with an application in a manner which ensures a high degree of legal certainty for the applicant. This implies that the applicant is informed as early as possible of the status of its application and that it will receive an acknowledgement of receipt of its submission(s).

40. If a CA has granted conditional immunity, no fines will be imposed on the applicant in relation to the cartel which is the subject of the application, provided that the conditions attached to leniency are fulfilled during the procedure and that it is not found that the applicant has acted as a coercer. Similarly, any position taken on an application for reduction of fines is subject to the conditions set out in the programme.

Summary applications

41. Experience has shown that applicants often choose to apply to several CAs simultaneously in cases for which the Commission is particularly well placed to act under paragraph 14 of the Network Notice. Such precautionary multiple applications are time-consuming both for the NCAs and the applicants. They are however useful to allow network members to have an informed view on whether or not they want to act on a case and to protect the position of the applicant in the event of a case being reallocated, given that an application to one CA does not count as an application to all CAs.

42. In order to alleviate the burden associated with multiple parallel applications on both undertakings and NCAs, the ECN Model Programme contains a model for a uniform system of summary applications. By filing a summary application, the applicant protects its position under the leniency programme of the NCA concerned for the alleged cartel on which it has submitted, or is in the process of submitting, a leniency application to the Commission. Summary applications will be possible irrespective of the applicant's position(s) in the leniency queue at the Commission and the NCA, i.e. in Type 1A, Type 1B and Type 2 applications.

43. If the applicant files a summary application before 'well placed' NCAs, in accordance with paragraph 24 of the ECN Model Programme, each NCA concerned will grant the applicant a summary application marker. The summary application marker aims at protecting the applicant's position under the leniency programme before the concerned NCAs, in particular during the phase of case allocation. As concerns Type 1A or Type 1B summary applicants, the summary application marker will mean that, if it is perfected at a later point in time, in particular after a reallocation of the case to the NCAs concerned, all information then provided to the NCAs concerned will be deemed to have been submitted by the applicant to the respective NCAs at the time of the summary application marker. Type 2 summary applications will be assessed in the order created by summary application markers, insofar as relevant under the applicable leniency programme.

44. A summary application is an application for leniency and CAs having received such an application are entitled to exchange information without the consent of the applicant, in accordance with paragraph 41(1) of the Network Notice.

45. The NCAs will not process summary applications, i.e. they will not grant or deny conditional immunity or leniency. They will only (a) acknowledge receipt to the applicant, (b) grant the applicant a summary application marker and (c) confirm that the applicant would have a given period of time in which to complete the application, should the NCA at any point later request the applicant to make a full application. In addition, if the summary applicant is the first applicant in respect of the alleged cartel at the NCA concerned (i.e. in Type 1A or Type 1B cases), the NCA will inform the summary applicant accordingly.

46. As long as the CA has not decided to take action in the case, the applicant's duty to provide further information and generally assist with the investigation only exists towards the Commission. However, since the scope of a summary application marker is essentially determined by the content of the leniency application, applicants should consider the following. From a substantive point of view, a summary application should be a proper summary of the leniency application submitted at the Commission. Therefore, if a leniency applicant has received a summary application marker from an NCA, and it subsequently provides information and evidence to the Commission which indicates that the alleged cartel is significantly different in scope than reported to the NCAs in its summary applications (for example, it covers an additional product), the applicant should consider updating the NCAs where it has filed summary applications in order to keep the scope of its protection at the NCAs identical to the scope of protection at the Commission. The duties specified under paragraphs 13(2)(d) (no destruction, falsification or concealment) and 13(2)(e) (no disclosure of contents or existence of the application) of the ECN Model Programme will also be owed to the NCA which has received the summary application.

47. In addition, the applicant must comply with any specific additional information requests of an NCA which has received a summary application in particular for the NCA to reach an informed view on the issue of case allocation. Failure to comply with such requests by an NCA fully and expeditiously would result in loss of the summary application marker. If the applicant is requested by an NCA to perfect the summary application into a full application, the applicant must submit to the NCA all information and evidence that relates to the alleged cartel. Normally, this would require the applicant to provide NCAs with all information and evidence that it has also supplied to the Commission. In this context, applicants are encouraged to verify the requirements applicable under the relevant leniency programmes with the NCAs concerned. Moreover, the applicant shall provide the NCA with any additional information that may be required under the relevant leniency programme.

48. The timing of the termination by the applicant of its participation in the cartel in summary application cases is for the Commission to determine.

49. The ECN Model Programme lists the information which must be contained in a summary application. Firstly, the information and the level of detail must be sufficient to enable the CA to decide whether it wants to act in the case. Secondly, it must allow the CA to determine whether the applicant should be granted a summary application marker. NCAs agree to show flexibility (to the extent legally permissible) as to the language(s) in which summary applications can be made. **Annex 1** to the explanatory notes contains a template in English that applicants may use when preparing a summary application. Applicants should duly consider the applicable language requirements when submitting a summary application.

Statements under the leniency programme and oral procedure

50. The ECN members are strong proponents of effective civil proceedings for damages against cartel participants. However, they consider it inappropriate that undertakings which cooperate with them in revealing cartels should be placed in a worse position in respect of civil damage claims than cartel members that refuse to cooperate. The discovery in civil damage proceedings of statements which have been made specifically to a CA in the context of its leniency programme risks creating this very result and, by dissuading cooperation in the CAs' leniency programmes, could undermine the effectiveness of the CAs' fight against cartels. Such a result could also have a negative impact on the fight against cartels in other jurisdictions. The risk that an applicant becomes subject to a discovery order depends to some extent on the affected territories and the nature of the cartel in which it has participated. Experience has so far shown that it is more likely that discovery orders will be made in cases which the Commission is particularly well placed to deal with than in cartels that are limited to a certain region or a certain Member State.

51. In order to limit any such negative consequences for the CAs' leniency programmes, the ECN Model Programme allows for oral applications (summary, marker or full applications) in all cases where this would appear to be justified and proportionate. Oral applications are always justified and proportionate in cases where the Commission is particularly well placed to act under paragraph 14 of the Network Notice. Some CAs will accept oral applications without requiring the applicant to demonstrate that its request is justified and proportionate.

52. The ECN Model Programme also stipulates that no access will be granted to any records of any statements (oral and written) before the statement of objections has been issued. In addition, given the differences in the rules concerning access to the file and/or public access to documents in the various jurisdictions, the ECN Model

Programme stipulates that the exchange of records of statements (oral or written) between CAs is limited to cases where the protections afforded to such records by the receiving CA are equivalent to those afforded by the transmitting CA.

NOTES

10 This is a non-exhaustive list of examples. See also paragraph 59 of the Guidelines on the applicability of Article 101 of the Treaty on the Functioning of the European Union to horizontal co-operation agreements, OJ C011, 14/01/2011, p 1–72.

11 See, for example, the judgment of the Court of Justice of 29 June 2006 in Case C-301/04 P, *Commission v. SGL Carbon AG, a.o.*, at paragraphs 66 to 80; the judgment of the Court of Justice of 28 June 2005 in Cases C-189/02 P, C-202/02 P, C-205/02 P, C-208/02 P and C-213 /02 P, *Dansk Rørindustri A/S a.o. v. Commission*, at paragraphs 395 and 399; and the judgment of the General Court of 9 September 2011 in Case T-12/06, *Deltafina SpA v Commission*, at paragraphs 124 to 134.

12 The applicant is encouraged to inform the CA beforehand of any contemplated dismissal of an employee or director who may be in possession of information and material relevant to the leniency application.

EUROPEAN COMPETITION NETWORK: PROTECTION OF LENIENCY MATERIAL IN THE CONTEXT OF CIVIL DAMAGES ACTIONS

Resolution of the Meeting of Heads of the European Competition Authorities of 23 May 2012

[4.422]

NOTES

This Resolution is available on the European Commission website at: ec.europa.eu/competition-policy/european-competition-network/documents_en.

The purpose of this Resolution is to explain the joint position of all ECN Competition Authorities (CAs) on the importance of appropriate protection of leniency material[1] in the context of civil damages actions. Such protection is fundamental for the effectiveness of anti-cartel enforcement. The CAs consider that it is necessary to reiterate the pertinence of such protection following the *Pfleiderer* judgment.[2]

The application of leniency programmes[3] by the CAs has successfully uncovered numerous secret cartels throughout the European Union. These programmes are among the most effective tools for the detection, investigation and punishment of cartels as well as for providing effective deterrence against cartelisation. Anti-cartel enforcement constitutes one of the core competences and obligations of CAs in the general – European and national – interest. The CAs also welcome the developing private enforcement of competition rules, in particular through damages actions, as a complementary tool to enforce competition rules.

Secret cartels are difficult to detect and investigate. Therefore, cooperation by cartel participants is often crucial to uncover and punish these highly detrimental illegal practices. Leniency programmes destabilise cartels as cartelists face the risk that any cartel member may report the cartel to CAs in the light of incentives offered. Through leniency programmes, cartels are uncovered and put to an end, preventing further damage being inflicted on businesses and consumers and helping cartel victims to bring forward their claims for damages. At the same time, the possibility that any cartel member may apply for leniency makes it more risky to form new cartels.

The CAs are determined to defend the effectiveness of leniency programmes in order to ensure a high level of anti-cartel enforcement. This effectiveness heavily depends on the incentives which the leniency programmes offer to potential leniency applicants to come forward and cooperate with CAs. The most important of these incentives is the immunity from penalties (or the reduction of penalties) which would otherwise have been imposed. The experience of the CAs shows that when deciding whether or not to cooperate with CAs under a leniency programme, potential leniency applicants consider as an important factor the impact of such cooperation on their position in civil proceedings as compared with the situation where they decide not to cooperate with CAs.

The CAs recognise the importance of effective recovery of damages caused by cartels. The existence of such a right also strengthens the working of the EU competition rules and discourages illegal practices.[4] From that point of view, civil damage actions can make a very significant contribution to the maintenance of effective competition in the European Union.

Civil damage claims and leniency programmes are complementary tools to enforce competition law and deter further infringements. However, at present, civil damage claims in cartel cases in the European Union mostly rely on public enforcement (follow-on actions) and public anti-cartel enforcement is nourished by leniency programmes. Thus, appropriate protection of leniency material is necessary to ensure the effectiveness of leniency programmes and to enable the authorities to uncover and terminate cartels as well as to document and establish their existence and the participation therein of the companies up to the requisite legal standard. It is often this action by the authorities that in turn constitutes the basis for civil damages claims for harm caused by cartels. Therefore, if the incentives to cooperate under the leniency programmes are not preserved, the victims of currently hidden and future cartels are unlikely to learn about those cartels in the first place and would be deprived of exercising their rights to an effective remedy. It is thus through the public enforcement of competition law, complemented by the emerging private enforcement, that fierce competition, strong innovation, economic growth and consumer welfare can be fostered in the European Union.

Moreover, an equivalent standard of appropriate protection of leniency material across the European Union facilitates opportunities for constructive cooperation among CAs, as well as the effective allocation of cases and resources and contributes to the effectiveness of their enforcement tools. Competition enforcement is closely interlinked across Europe and even world-wide.

In conclusion, as far as possible under the applicable laws in their respective jurisdictions and without unduly restricting the right to civil damages, CAs take the joint position that leniency materials should be protected against disclosure to the extent necessary to ensure the effectiveness of leniency programmes.

NOTES

1 The term "leniency material" refers to statements by leniency applicants submitted under the leniency programme and witness statements made by employees and directors of undertakings cooperating under the leniency programme (whether oral or written). Depending on the protection in the relevant jurisdictions, other information submitted to the CA by a leniency applicant (including pre-existing documents) will also qualify for protection as leniency material.

2 Judgment of the European Court of Justice in Case C-360/09, *Pfleiderer AG v Bundeskartellamt*.

3 The term "leniency" refers to immunity as well as a reduction of any penalty which would otherwise have been imposed on a participant in a cartel, in exchange for the voluntary disclosure of information regarding the cartel which satisfies specific criteria prior to or during the investigative stage of the case. A "leniency programme" sets out the framework for leniency in a particular jurisdiction.

4 See Case C-360/09, *Pfleiderer AG v Bundeskartellamt*.

APPLICATION FOR INABILITY TO PAY (2014)

[4.423]

NOTES

This document is available on the European Commission website at: ec.europa.eu/competition-policy/antitrust/procedures/fines/inability-pay_en.

To: European Commission

Directorate-General for Competition

For the attention of the Antitrust Registry
By email: comp-greffe-antitrust@ec.europa.eu

CC: COMP-ITP@ec.europa.eu

Date:

Case – Application for inability to pay

<insert company name(s)> hereby submit(s)[1] a request for inability to pay pursuant to point 35 of the Guidelines on the method of setting fines imposed pursuant to Article 23(2)(a) of Regulation 1/2003.

Company representative:

NOTES

1 This application is sent in English, without prejudice to the company's right to send DG Competition documents in another official language, according to EEC Regulation No 1 determining the languages to be used by the European Economic Community.

QUESTIONNAIRE REGARDING INABILITY TO PAY

(7 October 2015)

[4.424]

NOTES

This document is available on the European Commission website at: ec.europa.eu/competition-policy/antitrust/procedures/fines/inability-pay_en.

Case [Number] – [Name]
Deadline for Reply: [Date]

Please provide any updates/changes to the information requested below pertaining to new developments after the due date for the replies to this questionnaire as well as any new information relevant for the analysis of your ITP request.

With a view to examining the claim of inability to pay presented by your undertaking in the sense of point 35 of the Fines Guidelines 2006, please provide the following information:

1. Please provide the **financial statements** (consisting in (a) a balance sheet, (b) an income statement, (c) a statement of changes in equity, (d) a cash-flow statement and (e) notes[1]) of each of the ITP applicant(s) for the following business years:
   a) for business Years N-5 until N-1: audited financial statements. If the financial statements for business Year N-1 have not yet been audited, please provide them in a non-audited form and indicate when you expect to be able to provide the audited version. The latter indication should emanate from or be confirmed by the auditor.
   b) for business Year N: *interim* financial statements up to the latest closed quarter, along with comparable figures for the corresponding part of the preceding business Year N-1.
   c) for business Years N until N+3: the latest *forecasted* financial statements (consisting in (a) a balance sheet, (b) an income statement and (c) a cash-flow statement) and specify when they were established.

NOTES

[1] *Cf.* Commission Regulation 1126/2008 of 3 November 2008 adopting certain international accounting standards in accordance with Regulation 1606/2002 of the European Parliament and the Council, OJ 2008, L320/1 at pp 5-6, point 8; for the cash flow statement, see p 27. The cash flow statement should preferably use the direct method to report cash flows from operating activities (OJ 2008, L320, p 30, point 19).

2. If (one of) the ITP applicant(s) has shareholdings in subsidiaries, please provide the **consolidated financial statements** (consisting in (a) a balance sheet, (b) an income statement, (c) a statement of changes in equity, (d) a cash-flow statement and (e) notes[1]) of the group consolidated under the ITP applicant for the following business years:
   a) for business Years N-5 until N-1: audited financial statements. If the financial statements for business Year N-1 have not yet been audited, please provide them in a non-audited form and indicate when you expect to be able to provide the audited version. The latter indication should emanate from or be confirmed by the auditor.
   b) for business Year N: *interim* financial statements up to the latest closed quarter, along with comparable figures for the corresponding part of the preceding business Year N-1.
   c) for business Years N until N+3: the latest *forecasted* financial statements (consisting in (a) a balance sheet, (b) an income statement and (c) a cash-flow statement) and specify when they were established.

NOTES

[1] See footnote 1 *ante*.

3. Please provide the **consolidated financial statements** (consisting in (a) a balance sheet, (b) an income statement, (c) a statement of changes in equity, (d) a cash-flow statement and (e) notes[1]) of the group to which the ITP applicant(s) belong(s) for the following business years:
   a) for business Years N-5 until N-1: audited financial statements. If the financial statements for business Year N-1 have not yet been audited, please provide them in a non-audited form and indicate when you expect to be able to provide the audited version. The latter indication should emanate from or be confirmed by the auditor.
   b) for business Year N: *interim* financial statements up to the latest closed quarter, along with comparable figures for the corresponding part of the preceding business Year N-1.
   c) for business Years N until N+3: the latest *forecasted* financial statements (consisting in (a) a balance sheet, (b) an income statement, (c) a cash-flow statement), and specify when they were established.

Replies to point c) of the preceding three questions should take into account that the provided forecasts should (a) be approved by the Management and (b) be accompanied by a document (such as the business plan) identifying the main assumptions underlying the preparation of these forecasts namely in respect to the future evolution shown for those key financial indicators/accounts represented in Table 1 (See question 4 below).

NOTES

[1] See footnote 1 *ante*.

4. Please fill in **Table 1 on the key financial figures** for each of the ITP applicant(s) and for the consolidated group to which the applicant(s) belong(s), for the period [business Years N-5 until N+3]:
   a) for business Years N-5 until N-1: If the financial statements for business Year N-1 have not yet been audited, please provide the non-audited figures for that year.
   b) for business Year N: provide *interim* figures up to the latest closed quarter, along with comparable figures for the corresponding part of the preceding business Year N-1.
   c) for business Years N until N+3: provide the latest *forecasted* figures.

   Please note that an external auditor should certify the key figures in the table relating to the past business Years N-5 to N-1.
5. Please provide:
   a) a description of the internal cash and bank account management within the group to which the ITP applicant(s) belong(s);
   b) a description of the external cash and bank account management (i.e. relations with banks and other financing institutions) of the group to which the ITP applicant(s) belong(s) indicating also which of the group's companies are parties to the respective agreements;
   c) a description of the ITP applicant's (group's) current relationship with their banks and the outlook for the future (*standstill etc.*);
   d) a summary of any financing arrangements that each company of the group to which the ITP applicant(s) belong(s) has(ve) with their banks by filling in **Table 2**;
   e) the copies of the above financing arrangements;

f) a list of any other invoice-based financing instruments (e.g. factoring, securitisation, letters of credit arrangements, etc.).

Please make sure that the copies of the financing agreements are cross-referenced to **Tables 2 and 3** (both on the first page of each agreement and through the name of the electronic file).

6. Please fill in **Table 3 on the utilisation of current-account bank facilities** for each company of the group to which the ITP applicant(s) belong(s).
7. Please fill in **Table 4 on fixed assets** with detailed information of the **fixed assets** (such as type, location, date of acquisition, acquisition price, book value, market value, mortgage, etc.) owned by each company of the group to which the ITP applicant(s) belong(s). Table 4 should identify all fixed assets such as land, buildings and plants and all other fixed assets' items with acquisition price equal or above 50,000€.
8. Please also indicate the following **ratio** and specify each of its components for the last day of business Years N-4, N-3 and N-2 for each of the ITP applicants and for the consolidated group to which they belong. For business Year N-1 and any past quarter of business Year N, provide the ratio for the last day of each quarter. For the remaining part of business Year N and for business Years N+1 and N+2, provide projections for the last day of each quarter:
   Cash + Cash equivalent + expected incoming payments in the upcoming 3 weeks/Payments due immediately + payments due in the upcoming 3 weeks
9. Please quantify (a) any **provisions** made for payment of an anticipated EU antitrust/cartel fine, (b) any provisions made for payment of any other antitrust/cartel fine and (c) the other provisions made. For the provisions mentioned under (a) and (b), please indicate also (d) when and by which company(ies) they were made originally, and (e) when and by how much they were subsequently modified.
10. Please quantify for the last closed business year and for the current business year any **loans, current accounts, advances or any similar financial links** other than shareholding (a) from: or (b) to: shareholders and/or undertakings with which there are any other shareholding links and indicate (c) under which headings of the balance sheet(s) they appear and (d) when these financial links were originated.
11. Please indicate whether there have been in the last closed business year and/or in the current business year **transactions other than payment of dividends** between the ITP applicant(s) or any of their subsidiaries on the one hand, and any of their shareholders and/or undertakings with which there are any other shareholding links on the other hand. If yes, please describe these transactions in detail.
12. Please provide **investor reports** of rating agencies or any other reports assessing the undertaking's/group's financial situation.
13. Please indicate the elements which make it likely that the imposition of a fine would irretrievably jeopardise the **economic viability** of the ITP applicant(s) and of the group to which the ITP applicant(s) belong(s) and **cause its/their assets to lose all their value** (cf. point 35 of the Fines Guidelines 2006).
14. Please indicate the elements which in your perception constitute a **specific economic context** in which the ITP applicant(s) and the group to which the ITP applicant(s) belong(s) find(s) itself/themselves (cf. point 35 of the Fines Guidelines 2006).
15. Please indicate the elements which in your perception constitute a **specific social context** in which the ITP applicant(s) and the group to which the ITP applicant(s) belong(s) find(s) itself/themselves (cf. point 35 of the Fines Guidelines 2006).

Replies to the preceding three questions should include information on (a) the evolution of employment for the period covered by this questionnaire (Years N-5 to N+3), (b) all subsidies received in the same period and (c) all major investments and divestments (including plant closures) that occurred or are planned for this period.

16. Please provide information on the stock exchange listing the ITP applicant or of the group to which the ITP applicant(s) belong(s). Where is it listed and since when?
17. Please provide an organisational chart showing the current structure (up to the ultimate shareholders) of the group to which the ITP applicant(s) belong(s), including the percentages for each shareholding link.
18. Please indicate:
    a) the exact denomination of any natural or legal person holding at least **10% of shares** in the ITP applicant(s), directly or indirectly; and
    b) the percentage of participation of each such owner.

GUIDANCE

The terms used in the Table 1 are consistent with the International Financial Reporting Standards (IFRS) as adopted by the European Union[2]. Please indicate and explain clearly any deviations from or refinements of these definitions. Additional guidance is provided below with the sole purpose of helping filling in the table. In no way does such guidance alter the substance of the applicable legal framework.

Total Assets is the sum of all assets – current and non-current – composing the balance-sheet, and should therefore also be equal to the sum of Total Equity and Total Liabilities.

Current Assets[3] excludes current portion of deferred tax assets[4].

Inventories are assets held for sale in the ordinary course of business, in the process of production for such sale, or in the form of materials or supplies to be consumed in the production process or in the rendering of services.

Total Liabilities includes provisions, deferred tax liabilities and minorities, and corresponds to the difference between the balance sheet total and equity.

Current Liabilities[5] are those liabilities that must be paid within one year after the balance sheet date. This includes short-term notes payable, accounts payable, current maturities of long-term debt, current portion of capital leases, accrued expenses, income taxes, and other current liabilities.

Total Debt is the total financial liabilities, both current and long-term. It therefore excludes trade payables or provisions.

Subordinated debt is debt which ranks after other debts should a company fall into receivership or be closed.

Equity (book value) represents the shareholders' ownership interest in the company. It includes preferred stock, net common stock, capital surplus, retained earnings minus treasury stock and other liabilities. Minority interests should be excluded.

Equity (market value): In the case of a publicly traded company, please also indicate the market value of the equity (stock value multiplied by number of stock outstanding) on the last day of the period concerned.

Retained Earnings are accounting earnings that are not paid out as dividends but are retained by the firm for reinvestment in its operations. It excludes legal reserves. The figures indicated in the table should be the retained earnings accumulated during the lifetime of the company. Any adjustment for currency translation should be included.

EBITDA is earnings before interest, taxes, depreciation and amortization on tangible and intangible fixed assets. It excludes any extraordinary items.

EBIT is earnings before interest and taxes. It excludes any extraordinary items.

Net income is the profit/loss after income taxes.

Please provide any updates/changes to the information requested above pertaining to new developments after the due date for the replies to this questionnaire as well as any new information relevant for the analysis of your ITP request.

THANK YOU FOR YOUR COOPERATION

EXCEL TABLES:

Table 1: Excel table on key financial figures

Table 2: Excel table on loans/credit lines

Table 3: Excel table on current account bank facilities

Table 4: Excel table on fixed assets overview

NOTES

[2] *Cf.* Commission Regulation 1126/2008 of 3 November 2008 adopting certain international accounting standards in accordance with Regulation 1606/2002 of the European Parliament and the Council, OJ 2008, L320/1

[3] *Cf.* OJ 2008, L320, p 11, point 57 and OJ 2008, L320, p 22, point 6

[4] *Cf.* OJ 2008, L320, p 13, point 70

[5] *Cf.* OJ 2008, L320, p 12, point 60

E-LENIENCY

(March 2019)

[4.425]

NOTES

This document is available on the European Commission website at: ec.europa.eu/competition-policy/cartels/leniency/eleniency_en.

eLeniency is a new online IT tool designed to make it easy and less burdensome to submit statements and documents to DG COMP.

eLeniency is available at: eleniency.ec.europa.eu.

WHO CAN USE ELENIENCY

eLeniency is open to companies and to the lawyers representing them as part of antitrust and cartel proceedings run by DG COMP.

eLeniency is available in English but statements can be made in all 24 official EU languages.

WHAT BENEFITS DOES ELENIENCY PROVIDE

Companies and their lawyers can use eLeniency to file statements and submissions in the context of leniency applications (immunity from fines or reduction of a fine). eLeniency can also be used for providing replies to requests for information made under point 12(a) of the Leniency Notice. The system enables companies and their lawyers to type-in corporate statements directly online on DG COMP's secure server and to upload supporting documents. All submissions are to be made in writing, with no recording of the statements.

eLeniency avoids the need for companies or their lawyers to travel to DG COMP's premises to dictate oral corporate statements. eLeniency is available online 24 hours a day, 7 days a week.

eLeniency can be used as part of cartel settlement procedures for submitting documents, providing comments or making formal settlement submissions to the Commission.

eLeniency can also be used to submit corporate statements, provide comments or make formal settlement submissions to the Commission in non-cartel proceedings under Articles 101 and 102 TFEU, where an undertaking cooperates with a view to acknowledging an infringement of competition rules.

CONFIDENTIALITY AND LEGAL PROTECTION

The eLeniency system provides the same guarantees in terms of confidentiality and legal protection as the traditional procedure. All data is transferred securely and can't be copied or printed. Corporate statements under the Leniency Notice that are made via eLeniency are protected from disclosure.

In practice:

- Statements or submissions can't be saved. They must be typed in one go. Once a user starts making a statement or submission, the session remains open for 24 hours. For long statements that can take longer than 24 hours to type-in, fragmented statements with proper referencing are also accepted.
- Before a user formally submits and uploads a statement or submission to the eLeniency server, he or she can preview it and make corrections.
- The Commission can't retrieve any statement or submission, or any supporting documents, until they've been formally submitted in eLeniency.
- Once a statement or submission has been uploaded to the eLeniency server, only the Commission can access it and no trace of it remains on the user's computer.
- The user receives a timestamp confirming the recorded date and time of submission to the Commission.

HOW TO ACCESS ELENIENCY

1. To access eLeniency the first time, users must first create an EU Login account (or use an existing EU Login account). An EU Login can be created for a law firm or individually (by lawyer or by partner).

2. Users must then send an email to comp-leniency@ec.europa.eu **indicating the email address linked to their EU Login account** asking to have their EU Login registered with the eLeniency system. This ensures only authorised users have access. The registration of user requests will be done from 09.00 to 17.00 on weekdays.

3. Registered users can then login to eLeniency at: eleniency.ec.europa.eu

NB: As the registration process may require some time, companies and their lawyers are advised to register in advance before using eLeniency.

NB: Before a change in position (eg: no longer working in the same law firm or company), an information email from the user to comp-leniency@ec.europa.eu will be appreciated.

GUIDANCE FOR SUBMITTING SUPPORTING DOCUMENTS

Users are advised to follow the guidance for submitting supporting documents in eLeniency.

BACKGROUND

eLeniency is part of a family of online digital solutions supported by the ISA2 programme[1] that will be gradually set up in 2019 and 2020 to facilitate the sending of confidential documents (eTrustEx exchange platform), the processing of confidentiality claims (eConfidentiality) and of requests for information (eRFI).

Use of the eLeniency system is voluntary. Companies and their lawyers can continue to make statements and submissions using the current oral procedure.

NOTES

1 The ISA2 Programme supports the development of digital solutions for the modernisation of public administrations. The solutions developed enable public administrations, businesses and citizens in Europe to communicate digitally saving time and costs for all parties involved.

3. DAMAGES

COMMUNICATION FROM THE COMMISSION

(2013/C167/07)

on quantifying harm in actions for damages based on breaches of Article 101 or 102 of the Treaty on the Functioning of the European Union

(Text with EEA relevance)

[4.426]

NOTES

Date of publication in OJ: OJ C167, 13.6.2013, p 19.

1. COMPENSATION FOR VICTIMS OF COMPETITION LAW INFRINGEMENTS: THE CHALLENGE OF QUANTIFYING THE HARM SUFFERED

[4.427]

1. Infringements of Article 101 or 102 of the Treaty on the Functioning of the European Union ('TFEU'), hereafter the 'EU competition rules', cause great harm to the economy as a whole and hamper the proper functioning of the internal market. In order to prevent such harm, the Commission has the power to impose fines on undertakings and associations of undertakings for infringing EU competition rules.[1] The objective of the fines imposed by the Commission is deterrence, i.e. sanctioning the undertakings concerned (specific deterrence) and deterring other undertakings from engaging in, or continuing, behaviour that is contrary to Articles 101 and 102 TFEU (general deterrence).[2]

2. Moreover, infringements of Article 101 or 102 TFEU cause great harm to consumers and undertakings. Anyone who has suffered harm through an infringement of EU competition rules has a right to compensation. This is guaranteed by EU law, as the Court of Justice has repeatedly emphasised.[3] While the objective of the fines is deterrence, the point of damages claims is to repair the harm suffered because of an infringement. More effective remedies for consumers and undertakings to obtain damages would, inherently, also produce beneficial effects in terms of deterring future infringements and ensuring greater compliance with those rules.[4]

3. A major difficulty encountered by courts, tribunals and parties in damages actions is how to quantify the harm suffered. Quantification is based on comparing the actual position of claimants with the position they would find themselves in had the infringement not occurred. In any hypothetical assessment of how market conditions and the interactions of market participants would have evolved without the infringement, complex and specific economic and competition law issues often arise. Courts and parties are increasingly confronted with these matters and with considering the methods and techniques available to address them.

NOTES

1 See Article 23(2) of Council Regulation (EC) No 1/2003 on the implementation of the rules on competition laid down in Articles 81 and 82 of the Treaty, OJ L1, 4.1.2003, p 1. With effect from 1 December 2009, Articles 81 and 82 of the EC Treaty have become Articles 101 and 102 TFEU. Their substance has not been changed.

2 Commission Guidelines on the method of setting fines imposed pursuant to Article 23(2) of Regulation (EC) No 1/2003, OJ C210, 1.9.2006, p 2, at paragraph 4.

3 Case C-453/99, *Courage and Crehan* [2001] ECR I-6297; Joined Cases C-295–298/04, *Manfredi* [2006] ECR I-6619; Case C-360/09, *Pfleiderer* [2011] ECR I-5161 and Case C-199/11, *European Community* v *Otis NV and others* [2012], not yet reported.

4 Case C-453/99, *Courage and Crehan* [2001] ECR I-6297, 27; Joined Cases C-295–298/04, *Manfredi* [2006] ECR I-6619, 91.

2. INTERPLAY OF RULES AND PRINCIPLES OF EU LAW AND NATIONAL LAW

2.1. *ACQUIS COMMUNAUTAIRE*

[4.428]

4. Articles 101 and 102 TFEU are a matter of public policy[5] and are central to the functioning of the internal market, which includes a system to ensure that competition is not distorted.[6] These Treaty provisions create rights and obligations for individuals, be they undertakings or consumers. Such rights become part of the legal assets of these individuals[7] and are protected under the Charter of Fundamental Rights of the European Union.[8] National courts have a duty under EU law to enforce such rights and obligations fully and effectively in any proceedings brought before them.

5. Amongst the rights guaranteed by EU law is the right to compensation for harm suffered because of an infringement of Article 101 or 102 TFEU: the full effectiveness of EU competition rules would be put at risk if injured parties were not able to claim damages for losses caused to them by an infringement of these rules. Anyone can claim compensation for the harm suffered where there is a causal relationship between that harm and an agreement or practice prohibited by the EU competition rules.[9]

6. Compensation for harm suffered means placing the injured parties in the position they would have been in had there been no infringement of Article 101 or 102 TFEU. Parties injured by an infringement of directly effective EU rules should therefore have the full real value of their losses restored: the entitlement to full compensation covers the actual loss (*damnum emergens*), as well as compensation for loss of profit (*lucrum cessans*) suffered as a result of the infringement;[10] and entitlement to interest from the time the damage occurred.[11]

7. In so far as there are no EU rules governing damages actions for breaches of Article 101 or 102 TFEU, it is for the domestic legal system of each Member State to lay down the detailed rules governing the exercise of the right to compensation guaranteed by EU law. Such rules must not, however, render the exercise of rights conferred by EU law excessively difficult or practically impossible (principle of effectiveness). Nor may they be less favourable than those governing damages actions for breaches of similar rights conferred by domestic law (principle of equivalence).[12]

2.2. NATIONAL LAW AND ITS INTERACTION WITH THE PRINCIPLES OF EU LAW

8. On the question of quantifying harm, to the extent that such exercise is not governed by EU law, the legal rules of the Member States determine the appropriate standard of proof and the required degree of precision in showing the amount of harm suffered. National rules will also assign the burden of proof and of the respective responsibilities of the parties to make factual submissions to the court. National law may provide for the burden of proof to shift once the claimant has proved a certain set of factors, and may provide for simplified rules of calculation and presumptions of a rebuttable or irrefutable nature. National law further determines to what extent and how courts are empowered to quantify the harm suffered on the basis of approximate best estimates or to make use of equitable considerations. All these national rules and procedures governing the quantification of harm should be laid down and applied in individual cases in a way that allows parties injured by EU competition law infringements to obtain full compensation for the harm suffered without any disproportionate difficulties; in no circumstances may they be less effective than in similar actions based on domestic law.

9. One consequence of the principle of effectiveness is that applicable national legal rules and their interpretation should reflect the difficulties and limits inherent to quantifying harm in competition cases. The quantification of such harm requires comparing the actual position of the injured party with the position this party would have been in without the infringement. This is something that cannot be observed in reality; it is impossible to know with certainty how market conditions and the interactions between market participants would have evolved in the absence of the infringement. All that is possible is an estimate of the scenario likely to have existed without the infringement. Quantification of harm in competition cases has always, by its very nature, been characterised by considerable limits to the degree of certainty and precision that can be expected. Sometimes only approximate estimates are possible.[13]

NOTES

5 Joined Cases C-295–298/04, *Manfredi* [2006] ECR I-6619, 31.

6 Protocol (No 27) to the Treaty on European Union, on the internal market and competition.

7 Case C-453/99, *Courage and Crehan* [2001] ECR I-6297, 19 and 23; Joined Cases C-295–298/04, *Manfredi* [2006] ECR I-6619, 39.

8 See Article 17 of the Charter for the protection of an individual's assets; the right to an effective remedy for breaches of rights guaranteed by the law of the Union is set out in Article 47 of the Charter.

9 Case C-360/09, *Pfleiderer* [2011] ECR I-5161, 28; Case C-199/11, *European Community* v *Otis NV and others* [2012], not yet reported, 43.

10 Joined Cases C-295–298/04, *Manfredi* [2006] ECR I-6619, 95–96 and Joined Cases C-46/93 and C-48/93, *Brasserie du Pêcheur and Factortame* [1996] ECR I-1029, 87.

11 Joined Cases C-295–298/04, *Manfredi* [2006] ECR I-6619, 97, referring to Case C-271/91, *Marshall* [1993] ECR I-4367, 31.

12 Case C-453/99, *Courage and Crehan* [2001] ECR I-6297, 29; Joined Cases C-295–298/04, *Manfredi* [2006] ECR I-6619, 62.

13 The limits of such assessments of a hypothetical situation have been recognised by the Court of Justice in the context of quantifying the loss of earnings in an action for damages against the European Community, see Joined Cases C-104/89 and C-37/90, *Mulder and others* v *Council* [2000] ECR I-203, 79.

3. GUIDANCE ON THE QUANTIFICATION OF HARM

[4.429]

10. Against this background, the Commission's services have drawn up a practical guide on the quantification of harm in actions for damages based on breaches of Article 101 or 102 TFEU (the 'practical guide').

11. The aim of the practical guide is to offer assistance to national courts and parties involved in actions for damages by making information on quantifying harm caused by infringements of the EU competition rules more widely available. It therefore provides insights into various forms of harm typically caused by anticompetitive practices and, in particular, sets out information on the methods and techniques available to quantify such harm. Giving such information wider circulation will enhance the effectiveness of actions for damages. It should also make such actions more foreseeable, thereby increasing legal certainty for all parties involved. The practical guide can also help parties find a consensual resolution of their disputes, be it within or outside the context of judicial or alternative dispute resolution proceedings.

12. This practical guide is purely informative and does not bind national courts or parties. It does not therefore alter the legal rules of the Member States governing actions for damages and does not affect the rights and obligations of Member States or of natural or legal persons under EU law.

13. In particular, the practical guide should not be seen as raising or lowering the standard of proof or the level of detail of the factual submissions required from the parties in the legal systems of the Member States. Nor should it be seen as affecting the rules and practices in the Member States regarding the burden of proof. National courts have often adopted, within their legal systems, pragmatic approaches to determining the amount of damages to be awarded,

including the use of presumptions, shifts in the burden of proof, or the power of courts to make approximate best estimate assessments. The practical guide is intended to provide information that can be used within the framework of national legal rules and practices, not instead of them. Depending on the legal rules applicable and on the specific features of each case, it may therefore well be sufficient for the parties to provide facts and evidence on the damages quantum which are less detailed than those required by some of the methods and techniques mentioned in the practical guide.

14. The practical guide explains the particular features, including the strengths and weaknesses, of various methods and techniques available to quantify antitrust harm. It is up to the applicable law to determine which approach to quantification can be considered appropriate in the specific circumstances of a given case. Relevant considerations include — alongside the standard and burden of proof under applicable law — the availability of data, the costs and time involved and their proportionality in relation to the value of the damages claim.

15. The practical guide also presents and discusses a range of practical examples. These illustrate the typical effects that infringements of EU competition rules tend to have, and how the abovementioned methods and techniques for quantifying harm can be applied in practice.

16. Economic insights into the harm caused by antitrust infringements and methods and techniques for quantifying it can evolve over time in line with the theoretical and empirical economic research and judicial practice in this area. The practical guide should therefore not be seen as a comprehensive or definitive account of the insights, methods and techniques available.

COMMISSION STAFF WORKING DOCUMENT PRACTICAL GUIDE QUANTIFYING HARM IN ACTIONS FOR DAMAGES BASED ON BREACHES OF ARTICLE 101 OR 102 OF THE TREATY ON THE FUNCTIONING OF THE EUROPEAN UNION

***Accompanying the* Communication from the commission on quantifying harm in actions for damages based on breaches of Article 101 or 102 of the Treaty on the Functioning of the European Union**

Strasbourg, 11.6.2013

SWD(2013) 205

{C(2013) 3440}

[4.430]

NOTES

This document is available on the European Commission website at: ec.europa.eu/competition/antitrust/actionsdamages/quantification_en.html.

PART 1 — CONTEXT AND GENERAL APPROACH TO QUANTIFYING HARM IN COMPETITION CASES

I. LEGAL CONTEXT

A. The right to compensation

[4.431]

1. Everyone who has suffered harm because of an infringement of Article 101 or 102 of the Treaty on the Functioning of the European Union (TFEU) has a right to be compensated for that harm. The Court of Justice of the EU held that this right is guaranteed by primary EU law.[1] Compensation means placing the injured party in the position it would have been in had there been no infringement. Therefore, compensation includes reparation not only for actual loss suffered (*damnum emergens*), but also for loss of profit (*lucrum cessans*) and the payment of interest.[2] Actual loss means a reduction in a person's assets; loss of profit means that an increase in those assets, which would have occurred without the infringement, did not happen.[3]

2. Civil actions for compensation are generally adjudicated by national courts.[4] In so far as there are no EU rules governing the matter, it is for the domestic legal system of each Member State to lay down detailed rules on the exercise of the right to compensation guaranteed by EU law. Such rules, however, must not render excessively difficult or practically impossible the exercise of rights conferred on individuals by EU law (principle of effectiveness), and must not be less favourable than those governing damages actions for breaches of similar rights conferred by domestic law (principle of equivalence).[5]

B. National rules on quantification and this Practical Guide

3. In an action for compensation of harm suffered because of an infringement of Article 101 or 102 TFEU, national courts have to determine whether the claimant suffered a harm because of the infringement, and, if that is the case, the amount to be awarded to the claimant as compensation for that harm.[6] This determination – assessing and proving the

quantum of damages – is often difficult.[7] Normally, this determination is only necessary once the national court has made a finding concerning the other legal requirements for a damages claim, in particular a finding of an infringement and the causal link between this infringement and the harm suffered by the claimant.[8]

4. The legal framework in which courts deal with the quantification of harm is defined by EU and national law, including rules on:

- the heads of damages to be compensated and general rules of liability governing claims for compensation;
- requirements such as causality or proximity that link the illegal act and the harm. The Court of Justice has clarified in this respect that in so far as there are no rules at EU level on this matter, it is for national law to prescribe the rules on the application of the concept of 'causal relationship', provided that the principles of equivalence and effectiveness are observed;[9]
- the procedural framework in which claims for damages are adjudicated. National rules typically provide for an allocation of the burden of proof and of the respective responsibilities of the parties to make factual submissions to the court;[10]
- the appropriate standard of proof, which may vary between different stages of the proceedings, and may also be different for questions of liability for damages and those of the quantum of damages;
- to what extent and how courts are empowered to quantify the harm suffered on the basis of approximate best estimates or equitable considerations; and
- the admissibility and the role of evidence in civil litigation and its evaluation (and in particular of expert evidence).

5. Within their respective legal frameworks, legislators and courts have often adopted pragmatic approaches in determining the amount of damages to be awarded, for instance, by establishing presumptions. The burden of proof may shift, for example once a party has provided a certain amount of facts and evidence. Also, the law of the Member States may provide that the illicit profit made by the infringing undertaking(s) plays a role — either directly or indirectly — in estimating the harm suffered by injured parties.[11]

6. The purpose of this Practical Guide is to place at the disposal of courts and parties to damages actions economic and practical insights that may be of use when national rules and practices are applied. To this end, the Practical Guide gives insights into the harm caused by anticompetitive practices prohibited by the Treaty and information on the main methods and techniques available to quantify such harm.[12] Such guidance may help the claimant make factual submissions to the court concerning the amount of damages claimed and may assist the defendant in pleading his position vis-à-vis these submissions by the claimant. The guidance may also help parties in finding a consensual resolution of their disputes, be it within or outside the context of judicial proceedings or alternative dispute resolution mechanisms.

7. This Practical Guide is purely informative, does not bind national courts and does not alter the legal rules applicable in the Member States to damages actions based on infringements of Article 101 or 102 TFEU.[13]

8. In particular, whether the use of any and, if so, which of the methods and techniques described in this Practical Guide are considered appropriate in a given case depends on national law applied in accordance with the above-mentioned EU law principles of effectiveness and equivalence. Relevant considerations in this respect are likely to include

- whether a certain method or technique meets the standard required under national law;
- whether sufficient data are available to the party charged with the burden of proof to apply the method or technique; and
- whether the burden and costs involved are proportionate to the value of the damages claim at stake.

Excessive difficulties in exercising the right to damages guaranteed by EU law and therefore concerns in view of the principle of effectiveness could arise, for instance, through disproportionate costs or through overly demanding requirements regarding the degree of certainty and precision of a quantification of the harm suffered.[14]

9. Nothing in this Practical Guide should be understood as arguing against the use of more pragmatic approaches, or as raising or lowering the standard of proof or the level of detail of the factual submissions required from the parties in the legal systems of the Member States. Indeed, it may well be sufficient for the parties to provide facts and evidence on the quantum of damages that are less detailed than the methods and techniques discussed in this Practical Guide.

10. It should also be noted that the economic insights into the harm caused by antitrust infringements and methods and techniques to quantify such harm can evolve over time along with theoretical and empirical research and the judicial practice in this area. The present paper should therefore not be seen as exhaustive.

II. GENERAL APPROACH TO QUANTIFYING HARM IN COMPETITION CASES

11. Compensation for harm suffered aims to place the injured party in the position in which it would have been had the infringement of Article 101 or 102 TFEU not occurred: the actual position of the injured party has to be compared with the position in which this party would have been but for the infringement. This assessment is sometimes called 'but-for analysis'.

12. The central question in antitrust damages quantification is hence to determine what is likely to have happened without the infringement. This hypothetical situation cannot be observed directly and some form of estimation is necessary to construct a reference scenario with which the actual situation can be compared. This reference scenario is referred to as the 'non-infringement scenario' or the 'counterfactual scenario'.

13. In a specific case, the starting point for determining if the infringement has in fact harmed the claimant and, if so, the quantum of that harm, are the specificities of the case at hand and the evidence at the disposal of the court (including decisions by competition authorities). The concrete (alleged) infringement in question and how it could affect a particular market stand at the beginning of any determination of the quantum of harm caused by that infringement.

14. National courts can, in a particular case, use pieces of direct evidence relevant for the quantification of harm, such as documents produced by an infringing undertaking regarding agreed price increases and their implementation or assessing the development of its market position. Oral evidence given by witnesses can be used as well. The availability of such evidence may play an important role when a court decides whether any, and if so which, of the methods and techniques set out below can be used by a party to meet the required standard of proof under applicable law.

15. The type of harm for which the claimant seeks compensation determines which kind of economic variables (such as prices, sales volumes, profits, costs or market shares) need to be considered. For example, in a cartel leading to higher prices for customers of the cartelists, a non-infringement price will need to be estimated in order to establish a reference point for comparing it with the price actually paid by these customers. In an abuse of dominance case leading to the market foreclosure of competitors, the profits lost by these competitors may be measured by comparing their actual turnover and profit margins with the turnover and profit margins they were likely to have generated without the infringement.

16. It is impossible to know with certainty how a market would have exactly evolved in the absence of the infringement of Article 101 or 102 TFEU. Prices, sales volumes, and profit margins depend on a range of factors and complex, often strategic interactions between market participants that are not easily estimated. Estimation of the hypothetical non-infringement scenario will thus by definition rely on a number of assumptions.[15] In practice, the unavailability or inaccessibility of data will often add to this intrinsic limitation.

17. For these reasons, quantification of harm in competition cases is, by its very nature, subject to considerable limits as to the degree of certainty and precision that can be expected. There cannot be a single 'true' value of the harm suffered that could be determined, but only best estimates relying on assumptions and approximations.[16] Applicable national legal rules and their interpretation should reflect these inherent limits in the quantification of harm in damages actions for breaches of Articles 101 and 102 TFEU in accordance with the EU law principle of effectiveness so that the exercise of the right to damages guaranteed by the Treaty is not made practically impossible or excessively difficult.

18. This Practical Guide outlines a number of methods and techniques that have been developed in economics and legal practice to establish a suitable reference scenario and to estimate the value of the economic variable of interest (for example, in a price cartel the likely price that would have been charged for the product had the infringement not occurred).[17] The methods and techniques are based on different approaches and vary in terms of the underlying assumptions and the variety and detail of data needed. They also differ in the extent to which they control for factors other than the infringement that may have affected the situation of the claimant. As a result, these methods and techniques may be more or less difficult, time-consuming and cost-intensive to apply.

19. Once a value for the relevant economic variable (such as prices, profit margins, or sales volumes) in the hypothetical non-infringement scenario has been estimated, a comparison with the actual circumstances (e.g. the price actually paid by the injured party) is necessary to quantify the harm caused by the infringement of Article 101 or 102 TFEU.

20. Addition of interest will also need to be considered. The award of interest is an essential component of compensation. As the Court of Justice has emphasised, full compensation for the harm suffered must include the reparation of the adverse effects resulting from the lapse of time since the occurrence of the harm caused by the infringement.[18] These effects are monetary devaluation[19] and the lost opportunity for the injured party to have the capital at its disposal.[20] National law may account for these effects in the form of statutory interest or other forms of interest, as long as they are in accordance with the above-mentioned principles of effectiveness and equivalence.

III. STRUCTURE OF THE PRACTICAL GUIDE

21. The basis of a claim for damages is the submission that an infringement of Article 101 or 102 TFEU adversely affected the situation of the claimant. Broadly speaking, two principal categories of harmful effects of such infringements can be distinguished:

(a) Infringements can result in a raise in the prices paid by customers of infringing undertakings.[21] Among the infringements having such effect are cartel infringements of Article 101 TFEU, such as price fixing, market sharing or output limitation cartels. Also, exploitative abuses within the meaning of Article 102 TFEU can have the same effect.

Increased prices mean that the customers who purchase the affected product or service[22] pay an overcharge. Moreover, a rise in prices may also lead to less demand and may entail a loss of profits for customers who use the product for their own commercial activities.[23]

(b) Undertakings can also infringe Articles 101 and 102 TFEU by illegal practices which exclude competitors from a market or reduce their market share.[24] Typical examples are abuses of a dominant position through margin squeeze, predatory pricing or tying, or certain vertical exclusivity agreements between suppliers and distributors that infringe competition law.[25] Such practices have a significant effect on competitors, who suffer harm as they forego business opportunities and profit in this market. Where foreclosure of competitors is successful and competitive pressure in a market diminishes, customers will be harmed too, typically by a rise in prices.

22. Infringements of Articles 101 and 102 TFEU can also have further harmful effects, for example adverse impacts on product quality and innovation. The Practical Guide focuses on the two principal categories of harm and the categories of injured parties[26] described in paragraph 21. The methods and techniques described in the Practical Guide may, nonetheless, also be relevant in damages actions concerning other types of harm and other injured parties.

23. Part 3 of the Practical Guide addresses specifically the quantification of the kind of harm referred to in paragraph 21(a). This part includes a description of the basic effects on the market of price increases resulting from an infringement and illustrates how these types of harm (in particular the harm resulting from the payment of an overcharge and the harm associated with a reduction in demand) can be quantified.

24. Part 4 of the Practical Guide addresses specifically the quantification of the kind of harm referred to in paragraph 21(b). This part includes a description of the possible effects of the exclusion of competitors from a market and illustrates through examples how these types of harm (namely the loss of profit of the excluded competitor and the harm to customers) can be quantified.

25. The main methods and techniques available to quantify the harm resulting from infringements of Article 101 or 102 TFEU are common to all kinds of harm caused by such infringements. Part 2 of the Practical Guide therefore provides a general overview of these methods and techniques, and it gives more information on the basic assumptions on which these methods rely and explains their application in practice.

NOTES

1 Case C-453/99 *Courage* [2001] ECR I-6297, 26; joined cases C-295/04 to C-298/04 *Manfredi* [2006] ECR I-6619, 60; case C-360/09 *Pfleiderer*, [2011] ECR I-5161, 36 and case C-199/11, *European Community v. Otis NV and others*, [2012], not yet reported. These cases concern Article 101 TFEU (ex Article 81 EC Treaty); the same principles apply however also to Article 102 TFEU (ex Article 82 EC Treaty) – case C-360/09 *Pfleiderer*, [2011] ECR I-5161, 36.

2 Joined cases C-295/04 to C-298/04 *Manfredi* [2006] ECR I-6619, 95.

3 Opinion of Advocate General Capotorti in case 238/78 *Ireks-Arkady GmbH v Council and Commission* [1979] ECR 2955, 9.

4 The international jurisdiction of the national court is often determined by Council Regulation (EC) No 44/2001 of 22 December 2000 on jurisdiction and the recognition and enforcement of judgments in civil and commercial matters, OJ L12, 16.1.2001, p 1. This Regulation has been recently replaced by Regulation (EU) No 1215/2012 of 12 December 2012 on jurisdiction and the recognition and enforcement of judgments in civil and commercial matters, OJ L351, 20.12.2012, p 1, which for the most part will enter into force on 10 January 2015. The substantive law applicable in a given individual case will often be determined by EU Regulations, in particular Article 6 of Regulation 864/2007 on the law applicable to non-contractual obligations, OJ L199, 31.7.2007, p 40. The applicable procedural rules will usually be those in force in the country of the court hearing the action (*lex fori*). Actions for damages can also be decided by arbitration tribunals and by courts of non-EU states.

5 Case C-453/99 *Courage* [2001] ECR I-6297, 29; joined cases C-295/04 to C-298/04 *Manfredi* [2006] ECR I-6619, 62.

6 This Practical Guide is only concerned with the assessment of harm in the context of claims for financial (monetary) compensation. While the present paper does not specifically cover the determination of the award in other civil law remedies, its insights may also be used in making such determination, in particular with regard to actions for restitution.

7 See in more detail paragraphs 11 *ff.* in Section II below.

8 Art. 16 of Reg. 1/2003. This paper does not specifically deal with the question whether a certain practice infringes Articles 101 or 102 TFEU.

9 Joined cases C-295/04 to C-298/04 *Manfredi* [2006] ECR I-6619, 61, 64; case C-453/99 *Courage* [2001] ECR I-6297, 29.

10 See, for an example of distribution of this burden in competition cases, *Kammergericht Berlin* (Higher Regional Court, Berlin), decision of 1 October 2009, case No 2 U 10/03 Kart *(Vitaminpreise)*.

11 See paragraph 146 in Part 3 below.

12 The Commission has found useful assistance in preparing this Practical Guide in various studies it commissioned as well as in the comments received from external experts; see ec.europa.eu/competition/antitrust/actionsdamages/index.html.

13 Neither does it affect the rights and obligations of Member States and natural or legal persons under EU law.

14 See also paragraphs 16 and 17 below.

15 The limits and implications of such assessment of a hypothetical situation have been recognised by the Court of Justice (in the context of quantifying loss of earnings in an action for damages against the European Community in the agricultural sector): 'the loss of earnings is the result not of a simple mathematical calculation but of an evaluation and assessment of complex economic data. The Court is thus called upon to evaluate economic activities which are of a largely hypothetical nature. Like a national court, it therefore has a broad discretion as to both the figures and the statistical data to be chosen and also, above all, as to the way in which they are to be used to calculate and evaluate the damage', see joined cases C-104/89 and C-37/90 *Mulder and others v Council and Commission* [2000] ECR I-203, 79.

16 For an example of the reconstruction of a counterfactual by a national court and the issues arising from the underlying assumptions see for instance *Competition Appeal Tribunal*, decision of 28 March 2013, case No 1166/5/7/10 (*Albion Water Limited v Dŵr Cymru Cyfyngedig*).

17 See Part 2 below.

18 Case C-271/91 *Marshall* [1993] ECR I-4367, 31; joined cases C-295/04 to C-298/04 *Manfredi* [2006] ECR I-6619, 97; European Commission, White Paper on damages actions for breach of the EC antitrust rules (COM(2008) 165), section 2.5 and the accompanying Commission Staff Working Paper (SEC(2008) 404), paragraph 187.

19 Case C-308/87 *Grifoni II* [1994] ECR I-341, 40; Opinion of Advocate General Tesauro in Case C-308/87 *Grifoni II* [1994] ECR I-341, 25; joined cases C-104/89 and C-37/90 *Mulder and others v Council and Commission* [2000] ECR I-203, 51. In the context of loss of purchasing power, see joined cases T-17/89, T-21/89 and T-25/89 *Brazzelli Lualdi* [1992] ECR II-293, 40.

20 Opinion of Advocate General Saggio in joined cases C-104/89 and C-37/90 *Mulder and others v Council and Commission* [2000] ECR I-203, 105.

21 Where the infringement affects the buying activity of the infringing undertakings, the corresponding effect will be the decrease in the purchase prices that these undertakings have to pay to their suppliers. See paragraph 134 in Part 3, Section 1 for more details.

22 For ease of presentation, in the following reference will only be made to 'products' affected by an infringement, which should however be understood as also referring to the 'services' affected.

23 See paragraphs 128 *ff.* in Part 3, Section I for more details.

24 Case C-209/10 *Post Danmark*, not yet reported, 22, 23 and 24.

25 Vertical agreements are those concluded between undertakings from different levels of the supply chain.

26 The Practical Guide does not specifically address the situation of persons other than those mentioned in points (a) and (b) of paragraph 21, although other persons (such as suppliers of the infringers or customers of law-abiding competitors

of the infringers) may also be harmed by infringements leading to price overcharges or the exclusion of competitors; see also footnote 107.

PART 2 — METHODS AND TECHNIQUES

I. OVERVIEW

[4.432]

26. Various methods are available to construct a non-infringement scenario for the purposes of quantifying the harm in damages actions in competition cases.

27. The methods most widely used by parties and courts estimate what would have happened without the infringement by looking at the time periods before or after the infringement or at other markets that have not been affected by the infringement. Such comparator-based methods take the data (prices, sales volumes, profit margins or other economic variables) observed in the unaffected period or on the unaffected markets as an indication of the hypothetical scenario without the infringement. The implementation of these methods is sometimes refined by the use of econometric techniques, which combine economic theory with statistical or quantitative methods to identify and measure economic relationships between variables. Various comparator-based methods and techniques to implement these methods are described in Section II below (paras. 32 to 95).

28. Methods other than comparator-based are addressed in Section III below (paras 96 to 121). One of these methods uses economic models fitted to the actual market to simulate the likely market outcome that would have occurred without the infringement. These models draw on economic theory to explain the likely functioning of a market in view of its main features (e.g. the number of competitors, the way they compete with each other, the degree of product differentiation, entry barriers). Further methods include the cost-based method, which uses production costs for the affected product and a mark-up for a 'reasonable' profit margin to estimate the hypothetical non-infringement scenario or finance-based approaches that take the financial performance of the claimant or the defendant as a starting point.

29. Each of these methods and techniques has particular features, strengths and weaknesses that may make them more or less suitable to estimate the harm suffered in a given set of circumstances. In particular, they differ in the degree to which they rely on data that are the outcome of actual market interactions or on assumptions based on economic theory and in the extent to which they control for factors other than the infringement that may have affected the claimant for damages. Moreover, the methods and techniques differ in the degree to which they are simple to use and in the kind and amount of data required.

30. While these methods seek to construct how the market in question would have evolved absent the infringement, more direct evidence available to the parties and to the court (for instance, internal documents of the infringing undertakings on agreed price increases) may also provide, under applicable national legal rules, useful information for assessing quantum of damages in a given case.[27]

31. Section IV below sets out considerations on the choice of method, which will usually depend on the specific features of that case and on the requirements under applicable law.

II. COMPARATOR-BASED METHODS

32. In order to appreciate how comparator-based methods work in practice, it is useful to consider a (entirely fictitious) example of a damages action based on a hypothetical cartel infringing Article 101 TFEU.[28]

The flour cartel

Assume that all of the milling companies in a particular Member State have been found, by the national competition authority, to have fixed among themselves the prices for the grinding of cereals and the production of flour.

A bakery that regularly purchased flour in recent years brings a damages claim against one of the milling companies. The bakery submits that the infringement has led to an illegal rise in prices for the flour it purchased from that milling company. The bakery asks for compensation for this price overcharge it paid over the past years.

33. The key question regarding the quantification of harm in the aforementioned example is to find out what price the claimant bakery would have paid for flour had there been no infringement. If a comparator-based method is used to do so, these methods compare the price in the infringement scenario with a non-infringement scenario that is established on the basis of price data observed either:

- on the same market at a time before and/or after the infringement (1); or
- on a different but similar geographic market (2); or
- on a different but similar product market (3).

It is also possible to combine a comparison over time with a comparison across different geographic or product markets (4).

34. In the example of the flour cartel, the application of the methods focuses on prices. It is, however, likewise possible to use these methods to estimate other economic variables such as market shares, profit margins, rate of return on capital, value of assets, or the level of costs of an undertaking. Which economic variable can be usefully considered for the purposes of damages quantification depends on the circumstances of the case at hand.

35. The data used in such a comparison across markets or over time can be data that relate to the entire market (i.e. the average of the price for flour charged to all bakeries operating in a neighbouring geographic market) or data that relate to certain specific market participants only (i.e. the price charged for flour to certain customer groups such as wholesale purchasers operating in a neighbouring market).

36. It could also be appropriate, in particular in cases concerning exclusionary practices, to compare data relating to only one market participant. An example for such a comparison between individual companies, i.e. the injured party and a sufficiently similar comparator firm, may be the comparison between the profits achieved by a company trying

to enter a new market where it faced exclusionary practices in breach of the EU competition rules and the profits that a comparable new entrant achieved on a different but similar geographic market without being affected by anticompetitive practices. Sections A.1 to 4 below cover the comparison with aggregated market data and firm-level data alike.[29]

37. The strength of all comparator-based methods lies in the fact that they use real-life data that are observed on the same or a similar market.[30] The comparator-based methods rely on the premise that the comparator scenario can be considered representative of the likely non-infringement scenario and that the difference between the infringement data and the data chosen as a comparator is due to the infringement. Important market characteristics which can play a role in considering whether two markets are sufficiently similar are the degrees of competition and concentration on those markets, cost and demand characteristics and barriers to entry. Whether the level of similarity between infringement and comparator markets or time periods is considered sufficient in order for the results of such comparison to be used in quantifying harm depends on national legal systems.[31] Where significant differences exist between the time periods or markets considered, various techniques are available to account for such differences.[32]

A. Methods for establishing a non-infringement scenario

(1) Comparison over time on the same market

38. One frequently used method consists in comparing the actual situation during the period when the infringement produced effects with the situation on the same market before the infringement produced effects or after they ceased.[33] For instance, where an undertaking abused its dominant position by foreclosing a competitor from the market during 2004 and 2005, the method could look at e.g. the competitor's profits during the infringement period and its profits in 2002 and 2003 when there was not yet an infringement.[34] Another example would be a price fixing cartel (such as the flour cartel example mentioned above) that lasted from 2005 to 2007 where the method could compare the price paid by the cartel customers during the infringement period with the price paid by customers in a period after the infringement, e.g. in 2008 and 2009.[35]

39. There are, in principle, three different points of reference that can be used for the comparison over time:[36]

- an unaffected *pre*-infringement period (comparison 'before and during' — in the flour cartel example: comparison of the prices paid for flour in the same market *before* the infringement had effects with those affected by the infringement);
- unaffected *post*-infringement period (comparison 'during and after' — in the flour cartel example: comparison of the prices affected by the infringement with prices paid in the same market *after* the infringement ended); and
- both an unaffected *pre- and post*-infringement period (comparison 'before, during and after').

40. Making an informed choice of reference period and type of data will usually require good knowledge of the industry in question and will have to take the specific case at hand as a starting point. The choice will also be influenced by the availability of data and the requirements of applicable rules regarding the standard and burden of proof.

41. An advantage of all methods comparing, over time, data from the *same* geographic and product market is that market characteristics such as the degree of competition, market structure, costs and demand characteristics may be more comparable than in a comparison with different product or geographic markets.

42. However, also in comparisons over time it happens that some differences between the two data sets are not only due to the infringement. In such cases, it may be appropriate to make adjustments to the data observed in the comparator period to account for differences with the infringement period[37] or to choose a different comparator period or market. For instance, in the case of a long-lasting infringement, the assumption that e.g. prices of 10 years ago would have remained unchanged over time absent the infringement is probably overly strong and may lead to opting e.g. for a comparison with the pre-infringement period *and* the post-infringement period. In cases of long infringement periods, it may also be appropriate to address practical issues of comparability of data that result from changes in the way that data have been recorded by companies (e.g. changes in accounting practices or changes in the data organisation software).

43. Where data are available, the choice between a comparison 'before and during', 'during and after' or 'before, during and after' can be determined by a range of factors. It is highly unlikely to find any reference period where market circumstances exactly represent what would have happened in the infringement period had the infringement not occurred. It is only possible to identify a sufficiently similar time period that allows a likely non-infringement scenario to be reasonably approximated. Factors to be considered in this context may include uncertainties as to which time periods were actually not affected by the infringement. Some infringements start, or cease, gradually; and often doubts exist regarding the exact beginning of an infringement and, in particular, the effects it produces. Indeed, decisions of competition authorities regularly mention evidence suggesting that the infringement may have started earlier than the period established as the infringement period for the purposes of the decision.[38] Econometric analysis of observed data can be a way to identify when the infringement's effects started or ceased.

44. The ending of an infringement and its effects may be more easily established than its beginning, but here too uncertainties could arise as to whether the period immediately after the infringement's end is unaffected by the anticompetitive behaviour.[39] For example, when there is some delay until market conditions return to a non-infringement level, using data from the period immediately after the infringement could lead to an underestimation of the effect of the infringement. It may also occur that prices are, for a short period after the end of a cartel, particularly low as companies might temporarily engage in aggressive pricing strategies until the 'normal', i.e. non-infringement, equilibrium on the market is reached.

45. Specifically in oligopolistic markets another issue may arise, namely that the participants in a cartel can use the knowledge gained through the operation of the cartel to coordinate their behaviour afterwards without infringing Article 101. In such a situation, post-infringement prices are likely to be higher than without the infringement and can only serve to make a lower-bound estimate of the harm suffered. The pre-infringement period may be a more suitable reference point where central market characteristics changed radically towards the end of the infringement period due to exogenous factors (e.g. a steep increase in raw material costs or an increase in demand for the product).[40]

46. Nonetheless, even when there are doubts as to whether or not a certain period before or after the infringement was affected by the infringement, this period could, in principle, still serve as a reference period in order to obtain a safe estimate of the harm that will at least have been suffered ("lower-bound" estimate or "minimum damage").[41]

47. In certain circumstances, the non-infringement scenario may be appropriately estimated on the basis of two reference periods (before and after the infringement), for example, by using the average from these periods or by using other techniques to reflect a trend in the development of market circumstances during the infringement.[42] Pre-infringement data could also be used as the reference period up to a certain point during the infringement when a significant change in market circumstances occurred, and post-infringement data as the reference period for the time thereafter.

48. Also the choice of data can contribute to building a sufficiently similar basis for the comparison: there can be situations where aggregated data such as industry price averages (or averages for certain groups of firms) are sufficiently representative,[43] whilst in other situations it would be more appropriate to use only data from pre- or post-infringement transactions by the injured company or average data that relate to similar companies. For example, where the injured party belongs to a specific group of market players such as wholesale customers (as opposed to end customers), pre- or post-infringement prices charged to wholesale customers may be an appropriate reference point.

(2)

Comparison with data from other geographic markets

49. Another comparator-based method consists in looking at data observed in a different geographic market[44] for the purpose of estimating a non-infringement scenario.[45] These may be data observed across the entire geographic comparator market or data observed in relation to certain market participants only. For instance, in the example of a flour cartel mentioned above at paragraph 32, the prices paid by the claimant bakery during the infringement period could be compared with the prices paid on average by similar bakeries, in a different geographic market untouched by the infringement. The same type of comparison can be undertaken with regard to any other economic variable, e.g. the market shares, profit margins, rate of return on capital, value of assets, or level of costs of an undertaking. A comparison with the commercial performance of firms active on another geographic market that is unaffected by the infringement[46] will be particularly relevant in cases of exclusionary behaviour.

50. The more a geographic market is similar (except for the infringement effects) to the market affected by the infringement, the more it is likely to be suitable as a comparator market. This means that the products traded in the two geographic markets compared should be the same or, at least, sufficiently similar. Also the competitive characteristics of the geographic comparator market should be similar to the characteristics of the affected market except for the infringement. This may well be a market that is not perfectly competitive.

51. The method of using geographic comparator markets for deriving a non-infringement scenario is, in practice, mainly used when the infringement concerns geographic markets that are local, regional or national in scope.[47] Where the infringement market and the geographic comparator market are neighbouring areas, possibly within one country, there may be an increased likelihood that they are sufficiently similar for the purpose of a comparison.[48]

52. The comparator market does not always need to be sufficiently similar in its entirety. Where, for instance, the prices paid by one customer group (e.g. wholesalers) or the profits earned by one competitor company (e.g. a new entrant) in the comparator market are used as a reference, it is important that the market position of this customer group or this competitor is sufficiently similar to that of the injured party on the infringement market.

53. The choice of a geographic comparator market may also be influenced by uncertainties about the geographic scope of an infringement. Geographic markets on which the same or a similar infringement occurred are, in principle, not good candidates for being used as comparator markets. Also neighbouring markets on which no similar infringement occurred may still have been influenced by the anticompetitive practices on the infringement market (e.g. because prices on the neighbouring market were raised in view of the increased prices on the infringement market and lesser competitive pressure emanating from this market). A comparison with such markets will not show the full extent of the harm suffered, but they may, nonetheless, constitute a useful basis to establish a lower-bound estimate of the harm caused on the infringement market. This means that a party to an action for damages could, in principle, safely choose to rely on the comparison with a geographic market that was influenced by the same or a similar infringement, in particular where such influence is likely to have been rather small.

(3)

Comparison with data from other product markets

54. Similar to the comparison across geographic markets is the approach to look at a different product market[49] with similar market characteristics.[50] For example, in a case of exclusionary behaviour partially foreclosing a company selling one product, the profit margin earned by that company in the infringement market could be compared with the profit margin for another product that is traded (by a similar or the same company) in a distinct but similar product market.

55. The considerations discussed in the context of geographic comparator markets are, *mutatis mutandis*, also likely to be relevant for the choice of a suitable comparator product market. They will often relate to the degree of similarity between the two product markets. In particular, the comparator product should be carefully chosen with a view to the

nature of the products compared, the way they are traded and the characteristics of the market e.g. in terms of number of competitors, their cost structure and the buying power of customers.[51] Uncertainties as to whether a potential comparator product market was affected by the infringement or a similar infringement of Article 101 or 102 TFEU can also play a role.

(4)
Combining comparisons over time and across markets

56. Where sufficient data are available, it may be possible to combine comparisons over time and comparisons across markets. This approach is sometimes called the 'difference in differences' method because it looks at the development of the relevant economic variable (e.g. the price for flour) in the infringement market during a certain period (difference over time on the infringement market) and compares it to the development of the same variable during the same time period on an unaffected comparator market (difference over time on the non-infringement market).[52] The comparison shows the difference between these two differences over time. This gives an estimate of the change in the variable produced by the infringement and excludes all those factors that affected both the infringement and the comparator market in the same way. The method is thus a way to isolate the effects of the infringement from other influences on the relevant variable common to both markets.

57. A simple example derived from the flour cartel mentioned above may illustrate the method: assume that a before, during and after comparison reveals an increase in price of € 40 per 100 kg bag of flour in the Member State where the cartel occurred between 2005 and 2008. Looking at an unaffected geographic market over the same period may show that prices for flour rose by € 10 per 100 kg bag due to increased costs for an input product (cereals). Assuming that the increased input costs also concerned the infringement market, a comparison of the different development of prices on the infringement and the comparator market would indicate the price difference caused by the flour cartel. In the example, this would be € 30 per unit.

58. The strength of the 'difference in differences' method is therefore that it can subtract out changes unrelated to the infringement that occurred during the same time period as the infringement.[53] It rests, however, to a large extent on the assumption that these other changes affected both markets similarly.[54] The considerations regarding the application of the comparison over time and across market methods, in particular the need for sufficient similarity of the markets in question, are also relevant for the difference in differences method. From a practical point of view, this method usually requires a range of data from different markets and periods of time that may not always be easy to obtain; lesser amounts of data may, however, still allow lower-bound or approximate estimates to be derived.[55]

B. Implementing the method in practice: techniques for estimating the price or other economic variable in the non-infringement scenario

59. Once a suitable comparator-based method for establishing a non-infringement scenario has been chosen, various techniques are available to implement this method in practice. These techniques differ mainly in the degree to which they rely on individual or average data (e.g. price observations), and in the degree to which the data observed in the comparator market[56] or period are subject to further adjustment. As a consequence, these techniques differ in the amount of data they require in order to be carried out.

60. One possibility in implementing comparator-based methods is to use comparator data directly in the form they are observed and to estimate on this basis a value for the economic variable under consideration in the non-infringement scenario (e.g., in the above example, the price of flour). Where more than one data observation is available (e.g. the price of flour in a range of transactions on a geographic comparator market), they can be combined through a calculation of averages into one or more values for the non-infringement scenario. Such average value(s) for the non-infringement scenarios could then be compared to the average value(s) actually observed during the infringement, e.g. the prices really paid for flour (see in more detail in Section (1) below).

61. Where certain factors (such as an increase in raw material prices) have influenced only the comparator or only the infringement market or period, it should be considered, depending on the standard of proof required and depending on applicable rules regarding causality, whether adjustments need to be made to the observed data in order to account for such influences. These could be simple adjustments to the data in cases where the influencing factor and the magnitude of its effects can be relatively easily ascertained and accounted for (see Section (1) below). More sophisticated adjustments of observed comparator data can be obtained on the basis of econometric techniques, in particular through the use of regression analysis, which is described in Section (2) below. Whether it is for the defendant or the claimant to plead, substantiate and prove such adjustments is a matter of applicable law.[57]

62. In a given case, the choice between these different techniques depends on the specific circumstances of the case and applicable legal rules, taking account of the different advantages and disadvantages of these techniques, for instance with regard to their accuracy and precision and the data requirements they entail (see Section (3) below).

(1)
Simple techniques: individual data observations, averages, interpolation and simple adjustments

63. Depending on the requirements under applicable national law and on the circumstances of the case, especially the degree of similarity between the infringement market and the comparator market or period, the data observed may be compared directly, i.e. without further adjustments, with the data observed in the infringement market.[58]

64. The amount of data observed for the variable of interest (e.g., in the flour cartel example, the price for flour) in the comparator markets or comparator time periods may range from only one or very few data observations (i.e. the price observed in a small number of transactions) to a large number of data observations. In bidding markets, for example, auctions may occur very infrequently and at the time of the damages estimation only the price observed in the one tender after the infringement may be available. A similar situation could occur in industries where long-term contracts are common. It may be appropriate to use damages estimations based on single data observations where these are sufficiently representative for the period of interest.

65. Where looking at comparator markets or time periods produces a greater number of data observations, e.g. the prices paid by the injured party in a series of post-infringement transactions, or the prices paid by a number of customers in another geographic market, these data observations can be used either individually or in the form of averages.[59]

66. The use of various forms of averages or other forms of data aggregation can be appropriate, provided that like with like is compared. For example, where a wholesaler claims damages for having purchased a product in January, May, July and October 2009 from the participants in a price cartel and where the chosen method is comparison with another geographic market, the monthly average prices paid in that market by the *same type of customer* (wholesaler) during the *same months* may be the appropriate reference point (i.e. comparing January data with January data, May data with May data, and so forth). Comparing data from the same months will, for instance, account for seasonal differences over a year and thus make the comparison more reliable. If, however, little monthly price variation exists, the average price on the comparator market for the entire year of 2009 may be considered an appropriate indicator. It may also be the case that yearly data or other average data (e.g. aggregated industry data) are simply the only information available. Legal systems in the Member States may generally allow parties to rely on average data whilst granting the defendant the opportunity to show that significant differences exist, and they may require the use of more disaggregated data where available.

67. Another simple technique for deriving a comparator value from a range of data observations is linear interpolation. Where a comparison over time has produced price series from before and after the infringement, the 'non-infringement' or 'counterfactual' price during the infringement period can be estimated by drawing a line between the pre-infringement price and the post-infringement price, as shown in the illustration below. From this line, a comparator value can be read for each relevant point in time during the infringement period. Compared with the calculation of a single average value for price during the entire infringement period, interpolation therefore allows to some degree to account for trends in price developments over time that are not due to the infringement. Reading comparator data from the interpolated line will, therefore, produce more accurate results than using an average value for the period, e.g. in cases where damages are claimed that result from transactions (or other events) which occurred only towards the beginning or the end of the infringement period.[60] The following illustration gives a simple example of linear interpolation (the dotted line shows the interpolated non-infringement price, the full line the actually observed prices):

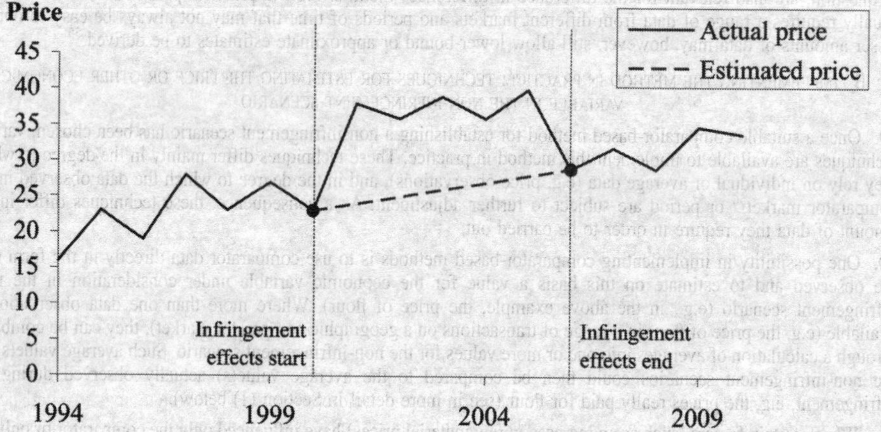

Linear extrapolation works similarly to interpolation except that the line is continued from either only pre- or only post-infringement data.[61]

68. There may be situations where it is quite straightforward to identify a differentiating factor between an infringement market (or period) and a comparator market (or period) and to make the corresponding adjustment to the value of the observed comparator data. For example, certain seasonal effects occurring on a market or effects stemming from changes in input prices or exchange rates may have a pattern and a magnitude that can in some cases be rather easily understood from internal business records of a party or from other sources, such as expert statements. In these cases, for example, the straight line obtained in a simple linear interpolation should be adjusted to reflect such patterns.[62]

(2)
Regression analysis

a.
Concept and purpose of regression analysis

69. Regression analysis is a statistical techniques which helps to investigate patterns in the relationship between economic variables and to measure to what extent a certain variable of interest[63] (e.g., in the flour cartel example, the price for flour)[64] is influenced by the infringement as well as by other variables that are not affected by the infringement[65] (e.g. raw material costs, variations in customer demand, product characteristics, the level of market concentration).[66] Regression analysis therefore makes it possible to assess whether, and by how much, observable factors other than the infringement have contributed to the difference between the value of the variable of interest observed on the infringement market during the infringement period and the value observed in a comparator market

or during a comparator time period. Regression analysis is thus a way to account for alternative causes for the difference between the compared data sets. All comparator-based methods are, in principle, capable of being implemented through regression analysis provided that sufficient data observations are available.[67]

70. In a regression analysis, a number of data observations for the variable of interest and the likely influencing variables are examined by means of statistical techniques. The relationship identified is usually described in the form of an equation (referred to as a 'regression equation' or 'regression model'). This equation makes it possible to estimate the effects of influencing variables on the variable of interest and to isolate them from the effects of the infringement. Regression analysis estimates how closely the relevant variables are correlated[68] with each other, which may in some instances be suggestive of a causal influence of one variable on the other.[69]

71. There are two main approaches to carrying out a regression analysis for damages estimation, depending on whether only data from non-infringement periods (markets) are used to build the regression equation or whether, in addition to non-infringement data, also data from within the infringement period (market) are used. If only data from non-infringement periods are used to estimate the regression, the regression equation would be used to 'forecast' the effect on the variable of interest during the infringement period on the basis of the pattern identified outside this period ('forecasting approach').[70] Where, in addition, also data from the infringement period (market) are used to estimate the regression, the effect of the infringement would be accounted for in the regression equation through a separate indicator variable (called 'dummy variable').[71]

72. Whether it is more appropriate to apply the forecasting or the dummy variable approach will depend on the circumstances of the case: In particular, while the forecasting method has the advantage of allowing the choice of a regression model that is only based on data observations from the non-infringement period (and hence, untainted by the effects of the infringement), using data from both periods/markets may allow a more precise and accurate estimation of the parameters of interest, in particular if the available non-infringement data are limited or do not allow the dynamics of the industry at hand to be fully captured. In practice, both methods can often be combined, e.g. by selecting the model on the basis of the pre-infringement period and estimating a dummy-variable regression using data from both periods (and allowing, if appropriate, the effects of the other influencing variables to vary in the infringement and non-infringement periods).

b.
Examples and illustrations

73. A simple example that, for illustrative purposes, looks only at one potential influencing variable may show the basic steps in regression analysis. Assume that, in the above-mentioned example of a flour cartel, the prices paid by bakeries during the cartel period to the milling companies are compared with the prices paid by bakeries to the milling companies in the pre-infringement period, and that this comparison shows a price increase during the infringement period of 20%. Assume further that there are indications that this increase is not exclusively due to the cartel but that during the infringement period costs for an important input material (e.g. cereals) also increased significantly. It is therefore not clear how much of the increase in price for flour is due to the infringement and how much is due to the increased input costs (the rise in cereals prices).

74. One option to address this uncertainty could be to use data from another period or market where input costs (price for cereals) were more similar and no infringement existed, but there may be situations where this is not possible.[72] Regression analysis can offer a tool to account for the variation in input costs, by showing the statistical relationship between input costs and price for flour. To this end, a range of data observations on input costs (cereal prices) and on prices for flour during the period not affected by the infringement could be examined.[73] Through applying statistical techniques to these data observations, it is possible to establish a pattern of how the prices for cereals influenced the price for flour in a period where the flour prices were not influenced by the infringement. It is then possible to deduce a statistical relationship between the price for flour and the price for cereals from this period. By applying the insight on this relationship to the prices for flour from the infringement period, it is possible to eliminate the part of the increase of prices for flour not imputable to the infringement, but to the change in input costs. This allows to 'forecast' prices for flour without the cartel overcharge but including the price increase caused by higher input costs.

75. The following graph gives a simple illustration of how such a statistical relationship is deduced. The chart shows several data observations of the input costs (cereals prices) and the corresponding price for flour at the same point in time during a non-infringement period. For instance, when at one particular moment the price for cereals was 60, the price for flour was 128. It is possible to calculate the coordinates of the line that best fits all data observations in order to represent the statistical relationship (correlation) between the price for cereals and the price for flour. This relationship is expressed in the graph below as a line and can be, and usually is, also expressed as an equation.[74] The steepness of this line shows what increase in the price for flour is associated with a certain increase in the price for cereals. In the example shown in the graph, the identified relationship indicates that e.g. a rise in the price for cereals from 50 to 60 relates to a rise in price for flour from 120 to 130. As an increase in input costs (cereals) by € 10 is associated with a flour price increase of € 10, the statistical relationship thus shows that an increase in this input cost is fully passed on.

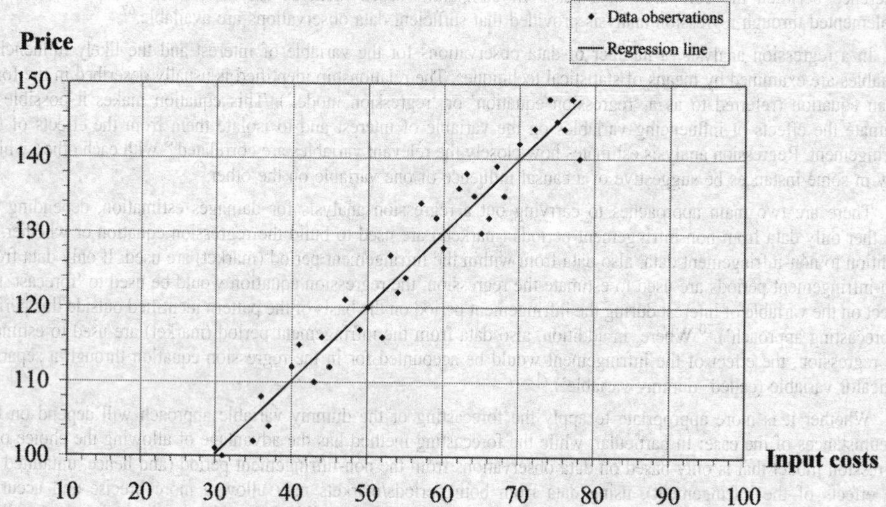

76. Knowing the pattern of how the input cost (cereals prices) influenced prices for flour outside the infringement period makes it possible to estimate ('forecast') how much the observed higher values of these costs (cereals prices) during the infringement period influenced prices for flour. Excluding these effects from the price comparison allows the price overcharge caused by the infringement to be estimated on a more reliable basis than without the regression analysis. In the above example, if during the infringement period the price for flour was 140 instead of 120 during the non-infringement period, but the input cost (cereals prices) increased from 50 to 60, the likely price for flour without the cartel would not be 120 but 130.

77. Whilst the example described so far concerned only the influence of a *single* other variable (cereals price as input cost) on the variable of interest (flour price), regression analysis in competition practice usually has to account for *several* other factors influencing the variable of interest (*multiple* regression analysis).[75] In this situation, data need to be observed for all additional relevant influencing variables and a regression equation needs to be deduced from these data that reflects their relationship to the variable of interest. For instance, in the above-mentioned flour cartel example, it may be the case that during the infringement period the milling companies not only had to pay higher prices for cereals, but were also subject to an increase in energy and labour costs and introduced a more efficient milling and packaging technology, all of which may have had an impact on the price of the flour they sold to bakeries during the cartel period. To identify the statistical pattern of how these factors influenced the flour price, series of data observations for each of these influencing variables need to be analysed.

78. When undertaking a regression analysis, it is important to consider all variables that are relevant in the specific case. Suppose that either the defendant or the claimant uses, in a comparison of the flour prices charged by a mill before and during an infringement, a multiple regression analysis to control for the potential influence on the flour price of the above-mentioned factors (i.e. the cereal prices, energy and labour costs and milling and packaging technology). If, however, a significant demand change took place during the cartel (e.g. higher demand by bakeries for flour due to an increased demand by end customers for bread and cake) and if the influence of this event on the price for flour is not accounted for in the regression equation, the estimate of the infringement effect is likely to be biased, despite the otherwise comprehensive regression analysis.[76] It is for the applicable national law to determine, in accordance with the principle of effectiveness, the party on which the burden falls to invoke and prove facts, such as the above-mentioned change in demand or the completeness of the variables considered in a regression analysis.

79. The basis of each damages quantification using regression analysis is thus the statistical relationship between the variable of interest (e.g. price) and the relevant explanatory variable(s) expressed in a regression equation. When the forecasting approach is used,[77] the estimation of a regression equation using data from the non-infringement period constitutes the first step. In a second step, using this regression equation and the observed values of these relevant variables during the infringement period, the price injured parties are likely to have paid without the infringement can then be estimated. In a third step, the difference between this likely non-infringement price and the price actually paid by the injured parties gives an estimate of the overcharge resulting from the infringement. The graph below illustrates the second and the third step. When the dummy variable approach is used, the regression analysis combines the three steps described above.[78]

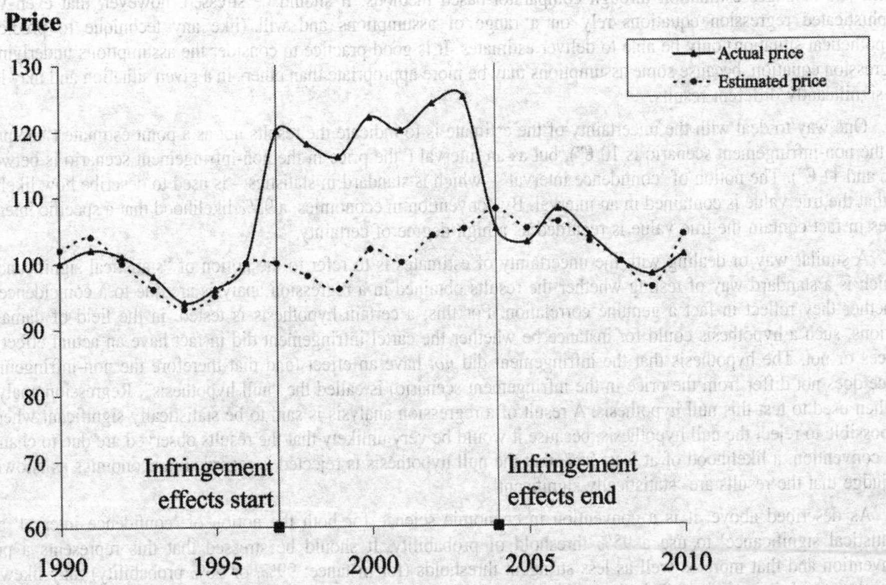

80. The regression analysis illustrated in this graph is based on the forecasting approach, in which a regression is carried out on pre- and post-infringement data to establish in an equation the statistical relationship between price and various relevant explanatory variables (input costs and other relevant factors). Using this equation and the observed values of the relevant explanatory variables, an estimated price can be derived that is likely to have prevailed absent the infringement (dotted line). The continuous line is the actually observed price. The difference between the continuous and the dotted line during the infringement period is the estimated overcharge. The dotted line outside the infringement period is also derived from the regression equation and can serve, through comparison with the actually observed non-infringement prices (continuous line), to assess the predictive power of the regression model.

c.
Requirements for applying regression analysis

81. Carrying out a regression analysis requires knowledge of various statistical techniques to measure the relationship between variables, to construct an appropriate regression equation and to calculate the precision of the parameters in this equation. In addition, it is necessary to have a good understanding of the industry concerned, in the first place, to formulate the right hypotheses when constructing the regression equation and to make the right choice as to the factors that are likely to have significantly influenced the variable of interest (and which should therefore be included in the analysis). Industry understanding is furthermore necessary to make informed choices about which statistical techniques to use in a given situation, for instance, to account for unusual observations (outliers) or other specific features in data sets. In particular, where the influencing variables were themselves affected by the infringement, biased results may occur if this aspect is not taken into account, e.g. through applying specific statistical techniques[79] or through using data observations that lie outside the infringement period or market.[80]

82. Without a sufficient number of data observations, statistical analysis cannot identify relationships between economic variables. To identify the effect of influencing variables on the variable of interest therefore requires that a sufficient range of data observations is available for all variables considered. Regression analysis therefore typically requires extensive data. However, statistical techniques may help to overcome some gaps in data or biases in their interpretation[81] and there can be situations where also the analysis of a smaller number of data observations is meaningful.

83. Data observations can, in principle, be gathered at different levels of aggregation. For example, where the relationship between price and input cost is to be analysed, data series either for the prices charged in individual transactions, for annual industry average prices or — in between — monthly data at firm level could be examined next to data series either for individual input costs per unit or for industry cost averages respectively. Using disaggregated data makes it possible to analyse a greater number of observations and therefore to obtain more precise estimates. Where such disaggregated data do not exist or are not accessible to the party carrying out the regression analysis, the analysis of aggregated data may still produce informative results, in particular if the aggregated data have a high frequency.

84. Having a sufficient range of data observations and the level of data aggregation are examples of the importance of data reliability and data relevance for economic analysis. However, most datasets are incomplete, and not all relevant facts may be observed or measured with high accuracy. It is therefore proper to explicitly acknowledge those imperfections. Deficiencies in the data should not prevent an economic analysis from being given proper weight, though conclusions should be drawn with caution.[82]

85. Where used appropriately and on the basis of sufficient data observations, regression analysis can considerably refine the damages estimation through comparator-based methods. It should be stressed, however, that even very sophisticated regression equations rely on a range of assumptions and will (like any technique to predict a hypothetical situation) only be able to deliver estimates. It is good practice to consider the assumptions underlying a regression equation, because some assumptions may be more appropriate than others in a given situation and may lead to significantly different results.

86. One way to deal with the uncertainty of the estimate is to indicate the results not as a point estimate ("the price in the non-infringement scenario is 10 €"), but as an interval ("the price in the non-infringement scenario is between 9 € and 11 €"). The notion of 'confidence interval' – which is standard in statistics – is used to describe how likely it is that the true value is contained in an interval. By convention in economics, a 95% likelihood that a specific interval does in fact contain the true value is regarded as a high degree of certainty.

87. A similar way of dealing with the uncertainty of estimates is to refer to the notion of "statistical significance", which is a standard way of testing whether the results obtained in a regression analysis are due to a coincidence or whether they reflect in fact a genuine correlation. For this, a certain hypothesis is tested: in the field of damages actions, such a hypothesis could for instance be whether the cartel infringement did in fact have an actual effect on prices or not. The hypothesis that the infringement did *not* have an effect (and that therefore the non-infringement price does not differ from the price in the infringement scenario) is called the "null hypothesis". Regression analysis is then used to test this null hypothesis. A result of a regression analysis is said to be statistically significant when it is possible to reject the null hypothesis, because it would be very unlikely that the results observed are due to chance. By convention, a likelihood of at least 95% that the null hypothesis is rejected is regarded in economics as allowing to judge that the results are 'statistically significant'.

88. As described above, it is a convention in economic science for both the notion of 'confidence interval' and 'statistical significance' to use a 95% threshold of probability. It should be stressed that this represents a pure convention and that more as well as less stringent thresholds (for instance: 99%, or 90% probability) may likewise provide useful information. This is because statistical significance is determined, in part, by the number of observations in the data set: other things being equal, the statistical significance increases as the sample size increases. It is good practice to indicate the probability threshold chosen. In a damages action, it is then for the court, under applicable law to decide, the probative value of such regression analysis and the procedural consequences (in particular with regard to the burden of fact-pleading and proof) which such analysis may entail.

89. Whether, by which party and at which stage of the proceedings a regression analysis is carried out in a court case will *inter alia* depend on the existence or accessibility of data and the rules under applicable law regarding fact pleading requirements, disclosure of evidence, the standard of proof and the allocation of the burden of proof between the claimant and the defendant.

90. The different forms of regression analysis mentioned above (paragraphs 71 *ff.*) are sometimes referred to as 'reduced form' approaches, as they directly estimate parameters of an equation that are themselves derived from other economic relationships (e.g. the interaction of supply and demand), without modelling these explicitly. Alternatively, econometric models can be built to estimate these underlying economic relationships. Although such econometric models, which are usually referred to as 'structural', often rely on particularly strong assumptions, they may bring a deeper understanding of the market concerned and form an integral part of simulation exercises to estimate damages (as further detailed in section III.A).

(3)
Choice of techniques

91. Sections 1 and 2 above have described different techniques whereby comparator-based methods can be implemented in practice. In a given case, the choice of technique will usually depend on a range of aspects, in particular the legal requirements and the factual circumstances of the case. Considerations relating to the standard and burden of proof are likely to be very relevant in practice.

92. Econometric techniques can increase the degree of accuracy of a damages estimate and may thus help in meeting a higher standard of proof if required under applicable rules. Whether regression analysis is required (possibly in addition to other evidence available) to meet such a standard, and on which party the burden of proof falls in this respect are questions of applicable law, including the EU law principle of effectiveness. It should be considered that carrying out an econometric analysis usually requires a significant number of data observations, which may not always be accessible. Moreover, it may also be that in a given procedural situation the applicable standard of proof does not require the party charged with the burden of proof to go further than the techniques mentioned in Section 1 above. This could be because the national legal system concerned considers the markets or periods compared as sufficiently similar and the estimate of damages resulting from the simple comparison as sufficiently accurate for what the party has to show in the given procedural situation. It may also be that the legal system, in view of the damages estimation presented by a claimant and the data that are reasonably accessible to him, provides for a shift of the burden of proof from the claimant to the defendant. In such a situation, the defendant may consider carrying out a regression analysis to rebut the submission of the claimant.

93. Considerations of proportionality may also play an important role, as the gathering of data and their econometric analysis can entail considerable costs (including those of third parties) that may be disproportionate to or even exceed the value of the damages claim at hand. Such considerations may also become relevant with a view to the principle of effectiveness.[83]

94. Courts in the EU have mainly used straightforward implementations of comparator-based methods without regression analysis, often on the basis of averages.[84] They have also accepted simple adjustments to the value of observed data when it is quite straightforward to identify a differentiating factor between an infringement market (or

period) and a comparator market (or period). To date, little experience exists with econometric analysis in actions for antitrust damages before courts in the EU,[85] although such techniques can, as described above, provide valuable help in quantifying the harm suffered through infringements of Article 101 or 102 TFEU.

95. Courts in the EU sometimes also apply a 'safety discount', i.e. they deduct from the observed data values an amount sufficient, under the standards of applicable law, to take account of uncertainties in a damages estimate.[86] Regression analysis can also be considered to account for these other possible influencing factors, and to obtain a "lower bound estimate" of the damages incurred.[87]

III. SIMULATION MODELS, COST-BASED AND FINANCE-BASED ANALYSIS AND OTHER METHODS

96. Alongside comparator-based methods, other methods exist to establish an estimate for the hypothetical non-infringement situation. Such other methods include, in particular, the simulation of market outcomes on the basis of economic models (A), and the approach to estimate a likely non-infringement scenario on the basis of costs of production and a reasonable profit margin (B).

A. Simulation models

97. Simulation methods draw on economic models of market behaviour. Economic studies on how markets function and how firms compete with each other have shown that markets with certain characteristics may allow the likely outcomes of market interaction to be predicted, for instance the likely price or production levels or profit margins. The branch of economics known as industrial organisation has developed models of competition for various types of markets that can simulate such outcomes. These models range from monopoly models to, at the other end of the spectrum, perfect competition models.

98. Intermediate models designed to reflect firm behaviour in oligopolistic markets are, in particular, those designed originally in the 19th century by the economists Augustin Cournot and Joseph Bertrand. The Bertrand oligopoly model of competition describes a market with a relatively small number of firms (and high barriers to entry) that compete on price, not output quantity. Firms set their price simultaneously, based on their beliefs about the prices their competitors will charge. In this model, prices increase with the degree of product differentiation. The Cournot oligopoly model of competition describes a market with a relatively small number of firms (and high barriers to entry) that compete on the amount of output they will produce. Before they choose prices, they set their quantity (or capacity) simultaneously on the basis of how much they each believe the other firms will produce. Numerous extensions and variations of the Cournot and Bertrand models exist. These include, in particular, dynamic oligopoly models based on game theory[88] that take into account the repeated interaction between firms in the market.[89]

99. Prices are likely to be highest (and sales volumes lowest) in a monopoly and prices are likely to be lowest (and sales volumes highest) in a situation of perfect competition. Bertrand oligopolies in markets with differentiated goods[90] and Cournot oligopolies will normally lead to prices and volumes somewhere between perfect competition and monopoly levels; the exact outcome depends inter alia on the number of firms in the market and barriers to entry, on the degree of differentiation between them and their products and on other characteristics of the market at hand, such as demand characteristics (especially, how sensitive customers are to changes in price), and the capacities and cost structure of producers.

100. Based on such theoretical insights that link the market outcome e.g. in terms of prices to a given set of market characteristics, simulation models can be built to estimate the prices (or other variables) that are likely to have prevailed in the market had an infringement of Article 101 or 102 TFEU not occurred. The simulation model should be constructed in such a way that it replicates (a) the most significant factors influencing supply (in particular, the way competition takes place between firms ('competitive interactions')[91] and the cost structure of firms) and (b) demand conditions (in particular, the extent to which customers respond to price changes). These factors would be expressed as a set of equations in which a number of parameter values need to be included. These values may be known, estimated econometrically or assumed so that the output of the model matches some observed variables. When using simulation models to generate a non-infringement scenario, the relevant market structure and other characteristics must be those that would have existed without the infringement; these may correspond to the structure and other characteristics of the market observed in the infringement scenario, but they may also differ to some extent.[92]

101. An example may illustrate the use of simulation modelling to estimate damages. In the example of a cartel on a differentiated product market (e.g. confectionary chocolates), non-infringement prices could be estimated as follows, using data from the non-infringement period. First, one would estimate how the demand for each chocolate product varies with its own price (own-price elasticity) and with the price of competing products (cross-price elasticity).[93] Second, one would decide which model appropriately reflects the competitive interaction between firms in the non-infringement period (e.g. the Bertrand model of competition in the confectionary chocolates example). On this basis, it can be calculated at which prices the profits of the firms are maximised in view of the cost parameters (e.g. marginal costs) and demand parameters (e.g. the level of demand).[94] The value of some of these parameters can then be adapted to reflect the relevant conditions during the infringement period (e.g. supposing the cost of cocoa increases by 10%). With all this information expressed in equations, it can be simulated (under the assumption that firms strive for maximised profits) what prices these firms are likely to have charged during the infringement period. The cartel overcharge can then be estimated by taking the difference between the observed prices and the simulated non-infringement prices.

102. This example is particularly demanding in terms of data requirements and assumptions. Simpler simulation models may be envisaged to estimate damages but they rely even more heavily on crucial assumptions that are difficult to verify. For example, damages following a cartel infringement could be calculated by comparing monopoly prices (aimed at reflecting prices during the cartel) with prices expected under a Cournot model (aimed at reflecting prices in the non-infringement scenario), using data such as market shares, costs, and market price elasticity. However,

such a method crucially depends on the assumed competitive interactions in the infringement and non-infringement scenarios and entails the risk that these do not mirror sufficiently closely the way in which the cartel operates during the infringement period and the way in which competition on the market would have operated absent the infringement.

103. Simulation models can be used to estimate market outcomes not only in cartel cases (or other price raising infringements), but also in cases of exclusionary behaviour. For example, an oligopoly model could be used to simulate the sales volume and the market share a foreclosed competitor would have attained had the infringement not taken place.

104. Each model simulating market outcomes is an approximation of reality and relies on theoretical and often also factual assumptions regarding market characteristics and the likely behaviour of producers and customers. Although, by their very nature, models rely on simplification of reality, even simple models may in certain cases provide useful insights regarding the likely damages. Therefore, pointing out that a model relies on seemingly simplifying assumptions should therefore on its own not be sufficient to dismiss it; rather, one should consider how some of the simplifying assumptions are likely to affect its results. Building a comprehensive model that replicates a range of specific features of the market in question, if it can be properly solved and evaluated, can increase the likelihood that the result of the simulation is a reasonable estimate for the hypothetical non-infringement scenario. Even very comprehensive models, though, still depend very much on the right assumptions being made, in particular regarding the central questions of what is the likely mode of competition and the likely customer demand in the non-infringement scenario. Moreover, the development of complex simulation models can be technically demanding and may require significant amounts of data that may not always be accessible to the party concerned or possible to be estimated with sufficient reliability.

105. Nonetheless, both simple and more complex simulation models could provide useful insights when estimating the outcomes that a market would have produced absent an infringement of Article 101 or 102 TFEU. Whether and in which procedural situation legal systems will consider that the use of an economic simulation is appropriate and its results are sufficiently reliable will depend on the specific circumstances of the case in point and the requirements under applicable legal rules.

B. Cost-based and finance-based methods

106. Other approaches to estimating the likely prices that would have emerged absent the infringement is provided by the cost-based method[95] or by methods based on the financial performance of claimant or defendant undertakings (finance-based methods).

107. The cost-based method consists in using some measure of production costs per unit, and adding a mark-up for a profit that would have been 'reasonable' in the non-infringement scenario. The resulting estimate for a per unit non-infringement price can be compared to the per unit price actually charged by the infringing undertaking(s) to obtain an estimate of the overcharge.[96]

108. Different types of production costs may be suitable for implementing the cost-based method, depending on the characteristics of the industry concerned. It is, however, essential to ensure that the treatment of costs and margins is consistent. For example, if variable costs (i.e. costs that vary with the level of production) are considered as the basis of this exercise, a gross margin (i.e. the margin earned once variable costs have been deducted) should be added to calculate the price. It should also be noted that the relevant cost for determining prices may be not only the cost of the infringer, but also the cost of one of its competitors (e.g. if the price in the market is determined by the least efficient producer).

109. The first step of the cost-based method is to determine the production cost per unit. Per unit costs can be estimated by dividing the actual relevant production costs incurred by the infringer(s) for the relevant business activity by the total number of products produced. This approach can be rather straightforward where companies or separate business divisions of companies produce only one main product. Such companies or business divisions sometimes publish their major cost data or file this information as part of their audited accounts with public registries. In other situations, the access to data and the allocation of costs to the product affected by the infringement is more difficult. Where accounting data are available, adjustments may be necessary given that the notions of costs in accounting terms can differ from the notions of costs in economic terms.

110. It may occur that the observed production costs during the infringement are not representative of the production costs that would have been likely without the infringement. This could mainly be for two reasons: first, in the event of infringements of Article 101, companies which due to their collusive behaviour are not subject to the competitive pressure that would exist in the non-infringement scenario may operate less efficiently and therefore generate higher production costs than under competitive pressure. Second, infringers may restrict output and may therefore, during the infringement, forego economies of scale that would have led to lower production costs. Where indications for such situations exist, adjustments to the observed costs data of the infringer(s) may be appropriate. Where such adjustments are not made, the observed costs may still contribute, under the cost-based method, to a lower-bound estimate of the possible price overcharge.

111. The second step of the cost-based method requires a 'reasonable' profit margin to be estimated and added to the per unit production costs. Various approaches exist to estimate a 'reasonable' profit margin. They are based either on a comparison over time or across markets, or on economic models, and thus have commonalities with the methods described in the preceding Sections. For instance, an estimate for the profit margin that could reasonably be expected in a non-infringement scenario may be derived from the profit margins made by similar undertakings in a comparable geographic market not affected by the infringement or in comparable product markets.[97] Similarly, the profit margins of the infringing (or a similar) undertaking during the pre- or post infringement periods could be used as a basis for the estimate. Both these comparator-based methods rest on the assumption that the reference period, market or firm are sufficiently similar,[98] in particular with respect to market characteristics that are relevant for profit margins such

as the level of competition in the market,[99] the cost structure of producers (including costs of innovation), capacity utilisation and capacity constraints. These assumptions are not always easily verified, as a large number of factors and strategic decisions are likely to determine a firm's price and margin setting.

112. Another approach to estimating a 'reasonable' profit margin is to consider the nature of competition and the characteristics of the market absent the infringement and to derive a likely profit margin from the insights from industrial organisation models.[100] For instance, absent the infringement, prices may be likely to tend towards costs due to relative homogeneity of goods and overcapacities in the market; in such cases, the likely profit margin of producers would be relatively low.[101]

113. It is clear from the above that both the estimation of likely non-infringement costs and the estimation of a 'reasonable' profit margin can, in practice, require a range of difficult issues to be considered. In addition, the cost-based method supposes access to data that may be in the possession of the opposing party or a third party. Nonetheless, depending on the circumstances of the particular case and on the requirements under applicable legal rules, it may provide useful insights to support an estimation of the harm suffered through an antitrust infringement.

114. Methods based on financial analysis take the financial performance of the claimant or the defendant undertaking as the starting point for estimating whether the claimant has suffered harm and the amount of that harm.

115. Where the claimant in an action for damages is an undertaking and the infringement has caused harm to that undertaking, it is possible that an analysis of the financial situation of that undertaking (and in particular its profitability) may give useful insights into that harm. This may be particularly useful in instances where loss of profits is claimed, for example in the case of a competitor illegally foreclosed from a market.

116. On this basis, standard methods to assess the profitability of an undertaking (such as for instance the 'net present value' method, which calculates the present value of future cash flows of an undertaking) may be used to give insights into the amount of harm. Likewise, methods of business valuations, including accounting methods, may yield useful insights.

117. For all of these methods, the appropriate counterfactual scenario has to be determined: once the actual profitability of the claimant undertaking has been calculated, it must be assessed how that profitability would have been had there been no infringement. It is possible to build this counterfactual by using profitability data from a comparator market – this approach is then similar to the comparator-based methods discussed above.[102] For instance, the profitability of the claimant before and after the infringement could be used to construct a non-infringement scenario. It is also possible to use an alternative standard to construct the counterfactual. One possibility in this regard is to use the cost of capital as a benchmark: this measure describes the minimal profit margin necessary in a particular industry to attract capital and it can therefore be appropriate to presume that the undertaking in question would at least have obtained that minimum profit in the non-infringement scenario.

118. One advantage of financial methods is that in some case, the information necessary to apply them may be held by undertakings because of accounting requirements, or may even be publicly available, as may be the case of publicly traded companies.

C. Other methods

119. The methods described in this Practical Guide are those that have received most consideration so far in legal practice and academic scholarship. They should, however, not be seen as an exhaustive list, firstly, as the methods described could further evolve or others could be developed in practice.

120. Secondly, there are methods *not* discussed in this Practical Guide could nonetheless prove useful, in particular, in order to establish an upper- or lower-bound[103] or approximate estimate[104] for the harm suffered. Especially where the legal systems provide for the possibility of an approximate estimation, national courts have opted for pragmatic techniques rather than a sophisticated implementation of the methods set out in Sections A and B above to establish the amount of damages to be awarded to injured parties. For instance, in cases where a new entrant has been foreclosed in breach of Article 101 or 102 TFEU, business plans have sometimes been used[105] as a source of information on the likely profits of a business, albeit in some instances adjusted depending on the market circumstances or through the use of data from a comparator market or undertaking.

121. It is for national courts to establish whether, under the applicable rules, a method can be accepted for the quantification of harm in a given case, provided that the principles of effectiveness and equivalence of EU law are observed.

IV. Choice of methods

122. Each of the methods described in Sections II and III above can, in principle, provide useful insights in relation to all infringements of Article 101 or 102 TFEU and the different types of harm such infringements tend to produce. In particular, they make it possible to estimate not only the amount of illegal price overcharge in a price fixing cartel but also, for example, the sales volume or the profit lost by a company suffering harm through an exclusionary abuse by a dominant competitor.

123. It should be stressed that it is only possible to estimate, not to measure with certainty and precision, what the hypothetical non-infringement scenario is likely to have looked like. There is no method that could be singled out as the one that would in all cases be more appropriate than others. Each of the methods described above has particular features, strengths and weaknesses that may make it more or less suitable to estimate the harm suffered in a given set of circumstances. In particular, the methods differ in the degree to which they are simple to apply, in the degree to which they rely on data that are the outcome of actual market interactions or on assumptions based on economic theory and in the extent to which they take into account factors other than the infringement that may have affected the situation of the parties.

124. In the specific circumstances of any given case, the appropriate approach to quantification must be determined under the applicable rules of law. Relevant considerations may include, alongside the standard and burden of proof under applicable legal rules, the availability of data, the costs and time involved and their proportionality in relation to the value of the damages claim at stake. The costs to be considered in this context may not only be those incurred when the party bearing the burden of proof applies the method, but also include the costs for the other party to rebut its submissions and the costs to the judicial system when the court assesses the results produced by the method, possibly with the help of a court-appointed expert. The costs and burden for an injured party and their proportionality may become particularly relevant with a view to the principle of effectiveness.[106] Moreover, the decision under applicable law as to whether and, if so, which of the methods and techniques described in this Practical Guide should be used may also depend on the availability of other evidence, for instance documentary evidence produced by the undertakings on the course of business showing that an illegally agreed price increase was actually implemented at a certain amount.

125. It may be that in a given case the application of *several* methods (e.g. comparison over time and comparison across geographic markets) is envisaged, either alternatively or cumulatively. Where two different methods yield results that are similar, such findings may lead a legal system to attribute stronger evidentiary value to the damages estimate, possibly a lower bound, based on these methods. Where, however, the application of two methods produces apparently contradictory results (especially when two opposing parties each rely on a different method), it is normally not appropriate to simply take the average of the two results, nor would it be appropriate to consider that the contradictory results cancel each other out in the sense that both methods should be disregarded. In such a scenario it would rather be appropriate to examine the reasons for the diverging results and to carefully consider the strengths and weaknesses of each method and its implementation in the case at hand.

NOTES

27 See for an example of such an approach *Oberlandesgericht Karlsruhe* (Higher Regional Court, Karlsruhe), decision of 11 June 2010, case No 6 U 118/05, where specifically agreed price increases of the infringing undertakings of a cartel were used, under applicable legal rules on the distribution of fact pleading and the establishment of *prima facie* evidence, to determine the damages award. This part of the decision was confirmed on appeal by the *Bundesgerichtshof* (Federal Court of Justice), decision of 28 June 2011, case no KZR 75/10.

28 This example is further developed at paragraph 147.

29 The comparison with firm-level data of another company could, theoretically, be made not only for companies that operate in another geographic or product market as discussed in Sections 2–4 below, but also for data of companies operating in the same product and geographic market as the injured party. In practice, such intra-market comparisons do not play a significant role, possibly because within the same market it can be difficult to find a sufficiently comparable other company that was not affected by the infringement. The following sections therefore do not further discuss such comparisons within a market.

30 This aspect is emphasised, for instance, by the *Bundesgerichtshof* (Federal Court of Justice, Germany), decision of 19 June 2007, case No KRB 12/07 (*Paper Wholesale Cartel*).

31 See for more detail paragraph 94. For an example of issues that may arise when assessing comparability of data see for instance *Tribunal Administratif de Paris* (Administrative Court of Paris), decision of 27 Mars 2009, (*SNCF v Bouygues*).

32 See for more detail paragraphs 59–95 in Section B below.

33 See, for example, *Corte d'Appello di Milano* (Court of Appeal, Milan), decision of 11 July 2003, (*Bluvacanze*) and *Corte d'Appello di Milano* (Court of Appeal, Milan), decision of 3 February 2000, case No I, 308 (*Inaz Paghe* v *Associazione Nazionale Consulenti del Lavoro*) (in both cases, comparison before, during and after); *Landgericht Dortmund* (Regional Court, Dortmund), decision of 1 April 2004, case No 13 O 55/02 Kart (*Vitaminpreise*) (during and after comparison); *Landesgericht für Zivilrechtssachen Graz* (Regional Civil Court of Graz), decision of 17 August 2007, case No 17 R 91/07 p (*Driving school*) (accepting a comparison during and after).

34 For more detailed examples of the method's application in cases of exclusionary practices, see Part 4 below.

35 For more detailed examples of the method's application in cases of infringements that lead to a price overcharge, see Part 3 below.

36 The comparison over time method is also referred to as the 'before-after method' or 'benchmark method'.

37 On such adjustments and, in particular, the possibility to use regression analysis, see paragraphs 59–95 in Section B below.

38 It is possible that a competition authority limits the finding of an infringement to a certain period, while in fact the infringement may have had a longer duration.

39 See the decision of the *Oberlandesgericht Karlsruhe* (Higher Regional Court, Karlsruhe) of 11 June 2010 in case No 6 U 118/05, for an example where a national court ruled that the prices charged in the five months after the infringement ended were still influenced by the cartel.

40 For the short period of the infringement after such a change, post-infringement data can be the more appropriate comparator as they may better reflect the market characteristics after the change. However, where the change in market characteristics was caused by the infringement itself (e.g. where due to anticompetitive foreclosure several competitors exited the market), the post-infringement period is obviously not a suitable comparator to estimate the situation that would have existed without the infringement.

41 If during the infringement exogenous factors lead to a decrease in prices (e.g. a sharp fall in input costs of the infringer), the inference of a lower bound could be rebutted.

42 For example, interpolation or regression analysis. For these different techniques to implement comparator-based methods, see paragraphs 59–95 in Section B below.

43 For further detail on the use of averages in implementing comparator-based approaches, see paragraph 70 in Part 2, Section II below.

44 For the concepts of relevant (geographic and product) market, see Commission Notice on the definition of the relevant market for the purposes of Community competition law, OJ C372, 9.12.1997, p 5.

45 This method is also referred to as 'yardstick method' or 'cross-sectional method'. These terms are also used to refer to the comparator-based method that looks at data observed in different but similar product markets, see paragraphs 54–55 in Section 3 below.

For examples of the use of the comparator-based method looking at different geographic markets see, for instance, *Cour d'Appel de Paris* (Court of Appeal, Paris), decision of 23 June 2003 (*Lescarcelle-De Memoris v OGF*); *Juzgado Mercantil numero 5 de Madrid* (Commercial Court, Madrid), decision of 11 November 2005, case No 85/2005 (*Conduit-Europe, S.A. v Telefónica de España S.A.*), confirmed by *Audiencia Provincial de Madrid* (Court of Appeal, Madrid), decision of 25 May 2006, case No 73/2006; *Bundesgerichtshof* (Federal Court of Justice, Germany), decision of 19 June 2007, case No KBR 12/07 (*Paper Wholesale Cartel*) (in the context of assessing the illicit gain by cartelists for the purpose of calculating a fine).

46 The comparator firm might, in principle, also be a firm active on the infringement market provided that its performance was not significantly influenced by the exclusionary behaviour. Even if the comparator firm was not directly affected by the infringement, it may still have been indirectly affected, e.g. by gaining market shares from a foreclosed competitor. The risk of being directly or indirectly influenced by the infringement is lower if the comparison is carried out in relation to a similar firm active on another geographic market. Characteristics that could be relevant when considering the sufficient similarity of firms include their size, cost structure, customers and features of the product they sell.

47 It might, however, also be used when the relevant market is wider than national provided that a sufficiently similar comparator market can be identified.

48 See, however, paragraph 53 below.

49 For the concepts of the relevant (geographic and product) market, see Commission Notice on the definition of the relevant market for the purposes of Community competition law, OJ C372, 9.12.1997, p 5.

50 This method is sometimes also referred to as 'yardstick method' or 'cross-sectional method' (as is the comparator-based method looking at different geographic markets).

51 Similarity of market characteristics may be more likely if the two products compared are traded in the same geographic market. However, the circumstances may also be sufficiently similar where the same or similar products from different geographic markets are compared.

52 This can be a geographic or a product comparator market.

53 Compared to a simple comparison across markets, the 'difference in differences' method also has the advantage of filtering out fixed differences between markets (such as differences due to constantly lower input costs in one of the markets).

54 If, for example, price increases unrelated to the infringement were higher in the affected market than in the comparator market during the infringement period, application of the difference in differences method using simple averages would overestimate the amount of damages. An econometric implementation of the difference in differences technique may help control for such factors.

55 See, for an example of a national court establishing a lower bound in the course of estimating the quantum of damages (although not using the difference-in-differences method, but the comparison over time method), *Kammergericht Berlin* (Higher Regional Court, Berlin), decision of 1 October 2009, case No 2 U 10/03 Kart.

56 As mentioned in paragraph 35 above, the data used in such comparison across markets or over time can be data that relate to the entire market or data that relate to certain specific market participants only.

57 See, for instance, *Kammergericht Berlin* (Higher Regional Court, Berlin), decision of 1 October 2009, case No 2 U 10/03 Kart., as an example of the distribution of fact pleading obligations in the quantification of harm.

58 For instance, time-based comparison could be based on the simple observation of prices before and during the infringement. For an example of the legal implications of such method see *Corte Suprema di Cassazione* (Supreme Court of Cassation, Italy), decision of 2 February 2007, case No 2305 (*Fondiaria SAI SpA v Nigriello*).

59 For the purposes of this Practical Guide, the term 'average' is used as referring to the mean, i.e. the average calculated by dividing the sum of observations by the number of observations. There may, however, be situations where it may be more appropriate to use other descriptive statistics (i.e. the median or the mode). For example, where in a market of 25 companies, 21 charge a price of € 50 and four a price of €75, the modal price of € 50 (the price most observed in the sample) may be the more meaningful representation of the market price than the mean of €54 (in this example, the modal price equals the median price, which is the price charged by the middle-ranked company).

60 Interpolation likewise has advantages over using averages where the number of transactions (or other events) is unevenly distributed during the infringement period.

61 Extrapolation thus extends a trend existing in a time series either before or after the infringement. For example, if in the three years before a cartel prices were €12, €13.20, and €14.52 respectively (reflecting a 10% increase each year), a simple technique would be to estimate that prices during the two-year duration of a cartel were €15.97 and € 17.57 respectively; a more accurate estimation of the underlying trend could be obtained through using regression analysis.

62 Such adjustment, could, data permitting, be done in a more sophisticated way by using regression analysis as explained in the following section.

63 Also referred to as an 'explained variable' or 'dependent variable'.

64 Possible other variables of interest for which regression analysis may be applied include, for instance, sales volumes, market shares or profit margins (e.g. those of an excluded competitor who claims damages for loss of profits through a reduction of sales or a decrease in its margins), costs of production (which may also be relevant in the context of a loss of profits estimation).

65 Also referred to as 'explanatory variable(s)' or 'influencing variable(s)'.

66 Other factors influencing the variable of interest may, for example, include customer and order sizes, the technology used for production, the size and cost structure of the firms offering the product, or advertising expenditure.

67 A sufficient number of data observations is, however, required to apply statistical methods in a meaningful manner. Such sets of data observations could be obtained (in comparisons over time) from time series of observations, or (in comparisons at one point in time) from a range of comparator markets or from a range of firms or a range of transactions, or a combination of both (observations over time from a range of markets, firms or transactions).

68 In multivariate regression analysis (see in more detail below), the correlation established is a conditional correlation, i.e. one where the effect of other variables is controlled for.

69 Provided this is consistent with a coherent economic framework and with other pieces of qualitative and quantitative evidence.

70 This 'forecasting approach' is sometimes also referred to as a 'residual model approach'. This approach is illustrated in the graph in paragraph 79 below.

71 Such a 'dummy variable' measures whether there has been an upward shift in the variable of interest during the infringement period.

72 For instance, because reliable data from other periods (or markets) are not available or because in such other periods (or markets) market characteristics differed significantly.

73 On the possibility of whether or not to also consider data from the infringement period (market), see paragraph 82 below.

74 Estimating a regression of price (as the variable of interest) over input costs (as the influencing variable) provides the coordinates of this line. In this example, the ordinary least squares (OLS) technique is used to calculate the coordinates of a straight line that is located at a minimal distance ('least squares') from the set of data points on the graph. The OLS technique is a common statistical method to estimate the parameters of a linear regression model.

75 Also referred to as 'multivariate regression analysis' as opposed to 'single variable ('univariate') regression analysis' as used in the above example.

76 It is, however, important not only to include all relevant factors in the regression model, but also to refrain from including variables that appear clearly irrelevant (on the basis of industry knowledge). In fact, damages estimates could be wrongly lowered (even down to zero) if irrelevant variables are included in order to explain the price variation in the model.

77 The alternative approach is the dummy variable approach; see paragraph 71 above. Unlike the forecasting approach, the dummy variable approach estimates the effect of the infringement in a single step, by carrying out a regression analysis using data from both the infringement and non-infringement periods. In the case of the example above, this approach would estimate the effect of the cartel as the upward shift in price that is observed during the cartel period (i.e. the coefficient of the dummy variable in the regression equation) and is not explained by changes in other influencing variables, such as raw material costs.

78 In this case, the regression equation is estimated using data from both the infringement and non-infringement periods and directly indicates how much the variable of interest changed during the infringement period after accounting for the effect of other explanatory variables.

79 For example, the use of instrumental variables, an econometric technique that may be applied to correct such bias.

80 In particular, by using the forecasting approach described above, where the value of the influencing variables included in the model to predict the counterfactual are corrected for the infringement effect on these variables.

81 E.g. where a sample of data observations is not fully representative.

82 See for a further explanation on the importance of data reliability and data relevance: DG COMP Best Practices for the submission of economic evidence and data collection in cases concerning the application of Articles 101 and 102 TFEU and in merger cases, at ec.europa.eu/competition/antitrust/legislation/best_practices_submission_en.pdf.

83 See above paragraph 2 in Part 1, Section 1.

84 The use of averages was accepted in e.g. *Landgericht Dortmund* (Regional Court, Dortmund), decision of 1 April 2004, Case No 13 O 55/02 Kart (*Vitaminpreise*); WuW/DE-R 1352.

85 For a recent example concerning lost profits in an exclusionary case see *Juzgado Mercantil numero 2 de Barcelona* (Commercial Court, Barcelona), decision of 20 January 2011, case No 45/2010 (*Céntrica Energìa S.L.U./Endesa Distribuciòn Eléctrica S.A.*)

86 For instance, to exclude the effects on the variable of interest of possible other factors. See e.g. *Kammergericht Berlin* (Higher Regional Court, Berlin), decision of 1 October 2009, case No 2 U 10/03 Kart.; *Oberlandesgericht Karlsruhe* (Higher Regional Court, Karlsruhe) of 11 June 2010 in case No 6 U 118/05.

87 Indeed, in addition to providing damages estimates that already control for the influence of other factors, regression analysis also measures the precision of these estimates (in the form of 'standard errors'), from which lower (and upper) bounds on the estimated damages can be obtained.

88 Game theory is the study of how people and firms behave in strategic situations in which they must consider how others respond to their action.

89 Taking into account the repeated interaction between firms in the market can be useful to explain, for instance, coordinated behaviour between firms or market entry of a new competitor.

90 In a market with homogeneous goods with no capacity constraints, Bertrand price competition will, in contrast, lead to very competitive outcomes. Homogenous goods are goods that have little differences in terms of quality or features.

91 The term 'competitive interactions' is used to indicate how competition between firms takes place, e.g. (but not limited to) Bertrand or Cournot competition, or how firms refrain from competing between each other (in the case of collusive behaviour infringing competition rules). Markets on which price formation occurs through auctions or other bidding processes may also be conducive to modelling as interaction between competitors often follows fixed rules (prices or output quantities likely to result from an auction or other bidding process not affected by the infringement could, in particular, be estimated by oligopoly models that incorporate game theory to simulate the likely bidding behaviour of competitors in a non-infringement scenario).

92 As the infringement may have led to a change in the market structure or may have prevented changes in the market that would otherwise have occurred (e.g. the exit of an inefficient competitor), the (hypothetical) market characteristics in the non-infringement scenario are not necessarily the same as those that could be observed in the infringement scenario. In addition, market shares observed during an infringement may significantly differ from those that would have prevailed in the absence of the infringement as cartel members may allocate markets between themselves.

93 Technically, this would involve estimating a demand system, which is an example of the structural econometric analysis mentioned in paragraph 90.

94 The value of these parameters (e.g. the value for marginal costs used in the calculation) in the non-infringement period can be determined so that the derived prices and volumes match the observed data.

95 This method is also referred to as the 'cost plus method' or 'bottom-up costing method'. It is mentioned, as a subsidiary approach in cases where comparator-based methods are not appropriate, by the *Bundesgerichtshof* (Federal Court of Justice, Germany), decision of 19 June 2007, case No KBR 12/07 (*Paper Wholesale Cartel*).

96 Usually, the cost-based method is considered for quantifying price overcharges. The method, or elements of it, may, however, also be used for quantifying other forms of harm such as the profits lost by foreclosed competitors. For instance, the *Oberlandesgericht Düsseldorf* (Higher Regional Court, Düsseldorf), decision of 16 April 2008, case No VI-2 U (kart) 8/06, 2 U 8/06 (*Stadtwerke Düsseldorf*), estimated the lost profits of a foreclosed competitor by considering the costs of the competitor and the likely profit margin expressed as a proportion of these costs.

97 *Bundesgerichtshof* (Federal Court of Justice, Germany), decision of 19 June 2007, case No KBR 12/07 (*Paper Wholesale Cartel*), referring to the profit margins generated in 'comparable industries'.

98 For relevant considerations regarding sufficient similarity see above paragraphs 38–58 in Part 2, Section II.

99 E.g. whether competition would have been so strong as to drive the price downwards towards marginal costs (as assumed in the model of perfect competition) or whether profit margins, due to an oligopolistic structure, would have been higher even without the infringement.

100 See above paragraphs 97 *ff.* in Part 2, Section III.

101 The cost of capital (i.e. the cost at which a firm can obtain capital on the market) is sometimes considered as an approximation of a 'reasonable' profit margin in such cases. However, margins in the absence of an infringement may significantly differ from the cost of capital, for example in the absence of perfect competition or in the presence of firm-specific cost advantages for certain firms, or demand and supply shocks.

102 See in more detail at paragraph 32 *ff.*

103 For example, an upper-bound estimation could be obtained through critical loss analysis. This technique assesses for a price increase what loss in quantities would make that price increase unprofitable.

104 For instance, counterfactual profits could be *prima facie* identified by taking as a benchmark the cost of capital, on the assumption that, absent the infringement, the undertaking would have earned the cost of capital, which represents the minimum return required by providers of capital to an undertaking. On the limitations of this approach, see footnote 101.

105 See for instance *Højesteret* (Danish Supreme Court), judgment of 20 April 2005, case UFR 2005.217H *(GT Linien A/S v De Danske Statsbaner DSB and Scandlines A/S).*

106 See above paragraph 2 in Part 1, Section 1.

PART 3 — QUANTIFYING HARM CAUSED BY A RISE IN PRICES

I. EFFECTS OF INFRINGEMENTS LEADING TO A RISE IN PRICES

[4.433]

126. Anticompetitive practices can have the effect of raising the prices that direct and often also indirect customers[107] of the infringing undertakings pay for the product concerned. The direct customers of the infringing undertakings are those who purchase a product directly from one of the infringing undertakings; indirect customers are those who purchase a product affected by the infringement from such direct customers or from other indirect customers.

127. Typical examples of infringements leading to such increases are price cartels, or excessive pricing by a dominant undertaking. Customers can also be affected by practices that limit output or allocate customers or markets — distortions of competition which in turn normally lead to a rise in prices. A different type of harm is caused where infringements adversely affect the market position of competitors; the quantification of such harm and its consequences for customers is discussed in Part 4 below.

128. In so far as infringements lead to a rise in prices for the products concerned, two main kinds[108] of harm caused by such infringement can be distinguished:

(a) the harm resulting from the fact that direct and indirect customers of the infringing undertakings have to pay more for each product they purchase than without the infringement (the 'overcharge'). This type of harm is further discussed in Section II; and

(b) the harm resulting from the so-called 'volume effect', which is caused by the fact that fewer of the products in question are bought due to the rise in prices. This type of harm is further discussed in Section III.

The following figure represents in a stylised way these two main effects:

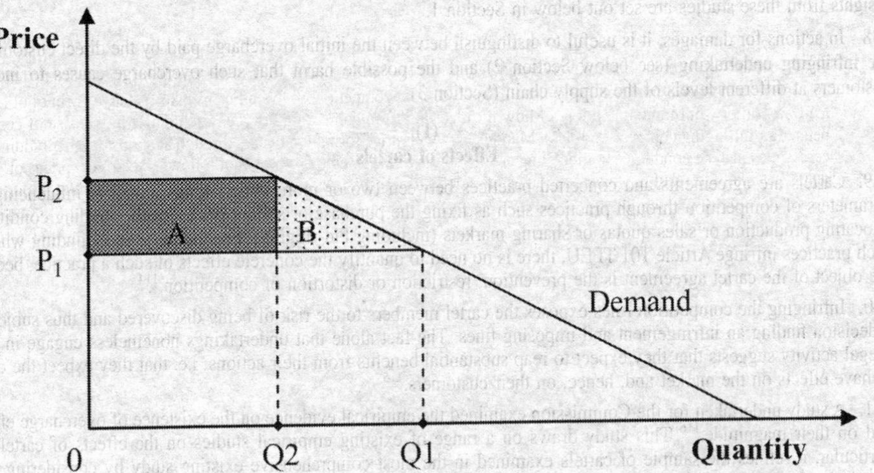

129. P_1 is the price charged if no infringement of Article 101 or 102 TFEU affects the market. In a perfectly competitive market, this price will equal the supplier's cost of producing one more unit ('the marginal cost'). Many markets are in fact not perfectly competitive and non-infringement prices on these markets will be above the level of marginal costs. At price P_1, Q_1 is the quantity of the product bought by customers.

130. P_2 is the higher price resulting from an infringement having an effect on price. This in turn leads to lower demand (Q_2) because some customers will consider that the higher price they have to pay exceeds the value of owning the product or of benefiting from the service. This effect is referred to as the 'volume effect' or the 'quantity effect'.

The degree to which a rise in prices affects demand depends on demand elasticity: Demand elasticity measures by what percentage the quantity sold of a product in a given market varies in response to a one percent price change for a particular demand level, and provides a useful indication of the magnitude of the volume effect for small price changes.

131. Rectangle A represents the value transferred from the customers to the infringers due to the infringement: the customers who buy at the higher price P_2 have to transfer more money to the infringing undertaking(s) in order to obtain the product. They can demand compensation for having had to pay more and Section II below will explain how to quantify this harm.

132. Triangle B represents the volume effect and thus the value foregone by those who would have bought the product for price P_1, but refrain from doing so when the price rises to P_2.[109]

133. Some customers use the product in question for their own commercial activities — for example to sell it on or to manufacture other goods. When they do not buy at price P_2 (or buy less), they forego the profit they would have made had they been able to purchase at price P_1. They can claim reparation for this loss of profit and Section III below will illustrate how to quantify this harm. Other customers are end-consumers. If these do not purchase at price P_2 this means that they fail to enjoy the utility of these products or services, for which they would have been prepared to pay price P_1.[110] Applicable legal rules may provide that some or all of such harm should be compensated for such failure to enjoy the usefulness of the product. At a minimum, end-consumers who have to bear higher costs (for example for the purchase of a substitute good) and who therefore have suffered an actual loss[111] must be able to obtain compensation.

134. The foregoing summarises the basic effects on the market of infringements that lead to a *higher* selling price. Infringements of Article 101 or 102 TFEU can also affect the demand side and lead to lower purchasing prices paid by infringers in their own supply with products, for example in the case of a buyers' cartel or in the abuse of market power exercised by a dominant buyer vis-à-vis its suppliers. In such a case, the price effects would consist in an 'undercharge' for the supplier of the infringer, and often also an overcharge on the downstream markets, i.e. for the direct and indirect customers of the infringer.[112] The same methods used to quantify an overcharge can, in principle, also be used to quantify the undercharge, e.g. the lower prices paid by the members of a buyers' cartel vis-à-vis their suppliers.

135. The same methods can, in principle, also be used[113] where at first sight no overcharge is visible, because the infringement served to artificially stabilise prices over a certain period of time in which prices would under normal market circumstances (i.e. without infringement) have declined. In the following, the term "overcharge" designates also these situations.

II. QUANTIFYING THE OVERCHARGE

136. Different types of infringements lead directly or indirectly to overcharges. Antitrust damages actions often deal with overcharges caused by cartels, which will be addressed in Section A below. The quantification of overcharges caused by other types of infringements will be addressed in Section B below.

A. QUANTIFYING OVERCHARGES CAUSED BY CARTELS

137. In an action for compensation, it will be necessary — within the framework of applicable legal rules — to quantify the overcharge paid by the claimant(s). Economic and legal studies have analysed the effects of cartels; some insights from these studies are set out below in Section 1.

138. In actions for damages, it is useful to distinguish between the initial overcharge paid by the direct customer of the infringing undertaking (see below Section 2) and the possible harm that such overcharge causes to indirect customers at different levels of the supply chain (Section 3).

(1)
Effects of cartels

139. Cartels are agreements and concerted practices between two or more undertakings aimed at influencing the parameters of competition through practices such as fixing the purchase or selling price or other trading conditions, allocating production or sales quotas or sharing markets (including bid-rigging). For the purpose of finding whether such practices infringe Article 101 TFEU, there is no need to quantify the concrete effects of such a practice, because the object of the cartel agreement is the prevention, restriction or distortion of competition.[114]

140. Infringing the competition rules exposes the cartel members to the risk of being discovered and thus subject to a decision finding an infringement and imposing fines. The fact alone that undertakings nonetheless engage in such illegal activity suggests that they expect to reap substantial benefits from their actions, i.e. that they expect the cartel to have effects on the market and, hence, on their customers.[115]

141. A study undertaken for the Commission examined the empirical evidence on the existence of overcharge effects and on their magnitude.[116] This study draws on a range of existing empirical studies on the effects of cartels. In particular, it refines the sample of cartels examined in the most comprehensive existing study by considering only cartels (a) that started after 1960 (thus taking into account only more recent cartels), (b) for which an estimate of the average overcharge was available (rather than only an estimate of the highest or lowest overcharge), (c) for which the relevant background study explicitly explained the method for calculating the average overcharge estimate, and (d) which were discussed in peer-reviewed academic articles or chapters in books.[117] While some care is required in interpreting the results of this exercise,[118] the study undertaken for the Commission contains some useful information as to the effects of cartels.

142. On the basis of the data observed, this study found that in 93% of all cartel cases considered, cartels do lead to an overcharge. As to the magnitude of the cartel overcharge, this study made the following findings:[119]

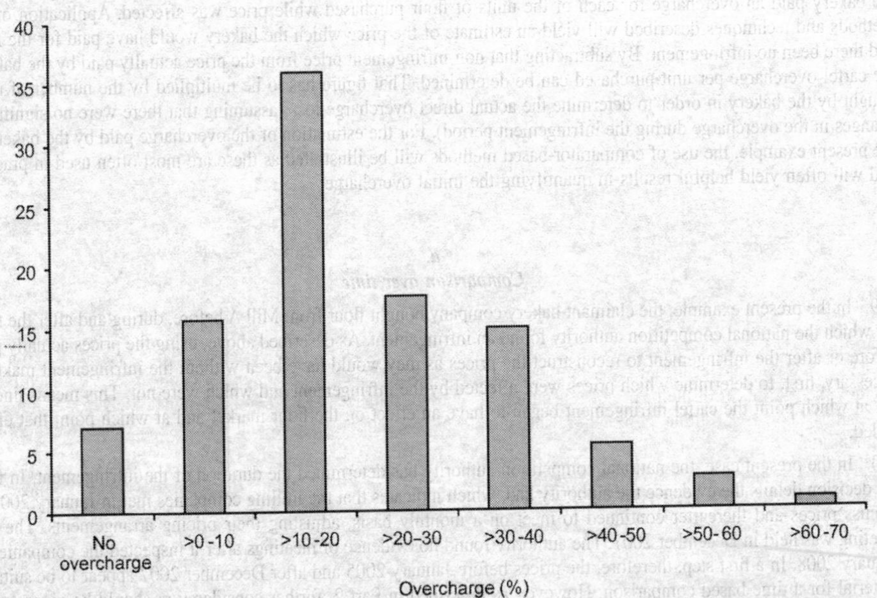

143. According to this study, there is thus a considerable spread of the overcharges observed (with some cartels even having an overcharge of more than 50%). About 70% of all cartels considered in this study have an overcharge of between 10% and 40%. The average overcharge observed in these cartels is around 20%.

144. The insights of this study concord with those of other available empirical studies, namely that (a) the vast majority of cartels do in fact lead to an overcharge, and (b) there is considerable variance in the overcharges observed. Also, all of these other empirical studies come largely to a similar estimate of the magnitude of the average overcharges as described above.[120]

145. These insights into the effects of cartels do not replace the quantification of the specific harm suffered by claimants in a particular case. However, national courts have, on the basis of such empirical knowledge, asserted that it is likely that cartels normally do lead to an overcharge and that the longer and more sustainable a cartel was, the more difficult it would be for a defendant to argue that no adverse impact on price did take place in a concrete case.[121] Such inferences, however, are a matter for the applicable legal rules.

(2)
The initial overcharge paid by the direct customer

146. All of the methods and techniques described above in Part 2 can, in principle, be used to quantify the initial overcharge paid by the direct customers of the infringing undertakings. Other types of evidence (such as, for instance, a specific agreement on the rise in prices as shown by internal documents) may also provide valuable insights into the scope of the overcharge. As the initial overcharge is a transfer of money from the direct customer to the infringing undertaking(s), any information that may exist on the illicit profits made by infringers can also serve to quantify this overcharge, although this will likely underestimate the amount of overcharge paid.[122]

147. In order to illustrate how methods and techniques can be used to estimate prices in a non-infringement scenario and, based on this estimate, to determine the overcharge paid by the customers of infringing undertakings, it is useful to consider the stylised example of a flour cartel already mentioned in Part 2.[123]

The flour cartel

In this example, all the flour in a certain Member State is produced by four milling companies (Mill A, Mill B, Mill C and Mill D). These mills purchase cereals from various farmers, grind the cereals and apply the appropriate treatments, package the flour and sell it on to bakers. These bakers use the flour to bake bread, which they sell on to consumers as well as to supermarkets.

The national competition authority investigates the market on suspicion of price-fixing and in January 2008 carries out unannounced inspections on the premises of the milling companies.

In July 2010 the competition authority adopts a decision in which it establishes that all four milling companies infringed Article 101 TFEU by participating, during the period from 1 January 2005 till 31 December 2007, in a single and continuous infringement regarding the production of flour, covering the whole Member State, which consisted of fixing prices.

A bakery company having purchased flour from one of the milling companies (Mill A) sues this company for compensation of the harm suffered because of the infringement of Article 101 TFEU.[124] The bakery claims that the infringement has led to a rise in prices for the flour and demands compensation for the payment of this overcharge for all purchases made in 2005, 2006 and 2007.

148. The bakery is a direct customer of one of the infringing undertakings. If the infringement caused higher prices, the bakery paid an overcharge for each of the units of flour purchased while price was affected. Application of the methods and techniques described will yield an estimate of the price which the bakery would have paid for the flour had there been no infringement. By subtracting that non-infringement price from the price actually paid by the bakery, the cartel overcharge per unit purchased can be determined. That figure has to be multiplied by the number of units bought by the bakery in order to determine the actual direct overcharge loss (assuming that there were no significant changes in the overcharge during the infringement period). For the estimation of the overcharge paid by the bakery in the present example, the use of comparator-based methods will be illustrated as these are most often used in practice and will often yield helpful results in quantifying the initial overcharge.

a.
Comparison over time

149. In the present example, the claimant bakery company bought flour from Mill A before, during and after the time for which the national competition authority found an infringement. As described above, using the prices actually paid before or after the infringement to reconstruct the prices as they would have been without the infringement makes it necessary, first, to determine which prices were affected by the infringement and which were not. This means finding out at which point the cartel infringement began to have an effect on the flour market and at which point that effect ended.

150. In the present case, the national competition authority has determined the duration of the infringement. In fact, the decision details the evidence the authority had, which indicates that the milling companies met in January 2005 to discuss prices and thereafter continued to meet on a monthly basis, adjusting their pricing arrangements. The last meeting was held in December 2007. The authority found no evidence of meetings after it inspected the companies in January 2008. In a first step, therefore, the prices before January 2005 and after December 2007 appear to be suitable material for a time-based comparison. However, as described in Part 2, further consideration should be given to the extent to which these figures are useful to serve as comparators.

151. As mentioned above, the decision by a competition authority might limit the finding of an infringement to a certain period for which solid evidence is available to the authority, while indicating that the infringement might have had a longer duration.[125]

It may then be appropriate not to use the relevant price data for the period that might have been affected by the infringement (and thus include an overcharge), although such data may nonetheless be used to determine a lower bound for the damages estimation, i.e. a safe estimate of what the harm suffered has been at least.

152. Also, the timing of the cartel infringement may be different from the timing of the effects of the infringement: the milling companies infringed Article 101 TFEU by entering into an anticompetitive agreement. For the purpose of determining which prices observed could be regarded as unaffected by the infringement, it is necessary to look at the timing of the effects of that agreement, not its conclusion. If it can be shown that the companies met in January 2005 for the first time, but that their agreement was implemented from March 2005 onwards, prices before March 2005 would not be tainted by the infringement.

153. As regards the suitability of using post-infringement price observations, it is possible that the cartel produced effects on the market even after the cartel members had ceased to engage in the kind of cooperation forbidden by Article 101 TFEU.[126] This may, in particular, be the case in oligopoly markets, where the information gathered because of the cartel might allow cartel members to adopt on a sustainable basis — after the cartel infringement has ended — a course of action aimed at selling at a price higher than the price likely associated with absence of the cartel infringement, without engaging in the sort of practices forbidden by Article 101 TFEU.[127] It is also possible that, after the end of the cartel, former cartel members resort to another type of infringement of the competition rules that raises prices for their customers. In these cases any time comparison based on the prices observed after the infringement ceased might lead to an underestimation of the overcharge paid by the customers of the infringers, as the post-infringement prices might still be influenced by an infringement. Where in the present example, the claimant bakery has reasons to believe that this might be the case for the prices paid in 2008 and thereafter, it could only use these prices in its submission to the court to estimate a lower bound of the overcharge harm suffered.

154. In the present example, the claimant bakery finds that the prices paid before the infringement are well suited to estimate the likely hypothetical price. If the bakery compares infringement and non-infringement prices as they are observed, it implicitly assumes that the entire difference between the prices paid in the non-infringement years 2003 and 2004 and the prices paid in the infringement years 2005, 2006 and 2007 is due to the infringement. It is possible, however, that causes other than the infringement had a significant influence on the development of prices during the infringement period. Changes in grain prices, for instance, might be an alternative cause that influenced price developments, and they may be accounted for by using the techniques set out in Part 2, Section II B above. In so far as significant other influences can be identified and the price data are adjusted for their effects, the submission that the remaining difference between the prices in the non-infringement and the infringement periods is due to the infringement gains additional strength.[128]

The circumstances in which such adjustments would be required from claimants or defendants will depend on the rules of applicable law.

b.
Other comparator-based methods

155. Besides comparisons over time, other comparator-based methods as described above in Part 2 may also be useful in quantifying the amount of the initial overcharge paid by the direct customer. In the example of the flour cartel, the claimant bakery could alternatively use a comparison with prices from another geographic market or another product market to show what the prices in its own market are likely to have been without the infringement.

156. One possibility would be the comparison with price data observed on a different geographic market for flour. On the assumption that the flour cartel as described above covered a national market, price data from another Member State could be used to construct the non-infringement price. In the case of markets with a sub-national regional scope, sales prices for flour from a different regional market could be a suitable reference point.

157. In order to be a suitable indicator for the prices as they would have been absent the infringement, the comparator prices should themselves not be influenced by the same or a similar infringement of the competition rules. If in the example of the flour cartel price data from a neighbouring geographic market are used and there is evidence that the anticompetitive agreement also covered that neighbouring market, prices from that market would lead to an underestimation of the overcharge. Also, in the case of neighbouring markets, the infringement in one market may have had an influence on that neighbouring market (for example through a rise in demand in the market without infringement), which might therefore not reflect non-infringement prices either.

158. Where the comparator market has different market characteristics, price data from that market might likewise not be sufficiently indicative of the prices as they would have been had there been no infringement. In the present example, the market concerned by the infringement is supplied by four milling companies. For instance, if it can be shown that prior to entering into the infringing practices, vigorous competition existed, price data from a neighbouring market characterised by the presence of a dominant milling company might not adequately reflect the prices as they would have been had there been no cartel and may only serve as a basis for a lower-bound estimate.

159. If the claimant bakery uses price data from a different geographic market in the form in which they are observed, it makes the implicit assumption that the remaining differences between the prices actually paid to the infringers and the prices prevailing on that comparator market are due to the infringement. Depending on the circumstances of the case and requirements under applicable law, the techniques described in Part 2 Section II B above may be used to identify and account for possible alternative influences on prices.

160. A further possibility to estimate the non-infringement price is comparison with price data observed on other product markets. In the case of flour, it may, however, be difficult to find a sufficiently similar product market not affected by the same or a similar infringement.

(3)
The pass-on of overcharges

161. Direct customers of the infringing undertakings who pay an overcharge caused by the cartel may themselves sell on the affected products (or use them as input for their own production of other goods or services). In the example of the flour cartel discussed above, the bakeries are the direct customers of the infringing undertakings and they use the purchased flour to bake bread, which they then sell on either directly to final customers or to supermarkets. These direct customers (bakeries), in reaction to the price increase they face, may raise the prices for their own goods or services (the bread they sell on), thereby passing on some or the entire initial overcharge to their own customers (the consumers or supermarkets). The same effect exists where it is *indirect* customers (such as the supermarkets in the present example) who themselves raise their own selling prices in their business deals with their customers, thereby passing on an overcharge which was first passed on to them.

162. Such pass-on of overcharges normally entails a volume effect: as described above in paragraphs 128 *ff.*, a rise in prices normally leads to a decrease in demand. In the example of the flour cartel, in so far as the bakery passes on the overcharge by raising the prices it charges for the bread to the supermarkets and end customers, it may reduce the adverse financial impact of the overcharge on itself, but it will suffer decreased demand.[129] This decrease in demand means, for the bakery, less sales and a loss of profit — harm that is also caused by the infringement and should be compensated (see Section III below).

163. The price increase through pass-on and the reduction in sales are thus intrinsically connected. In fact, both pass-on and volume effects are determined by the same factors, in particular, the elasticity of demand from downstream customers. This is because the market conditions regarding downstream demand affect both the sales price and the corresponding sales volumes at which the bakery would maximise its profits.

164. In the context of a claim for compensation of overcharges in an antitrust damages action, the pass-on of overcharges can become relevant in two different types of situations:

(a) In an action brought by the direct customer claiming reparation for the initial overcharge paid by him (in the present example: the claim by the bakery against Mill A), the defendant cartel infringer might argue that the direct customer should not, in fact, be compensated for the overcharge harm to the extent that he raised his own prices and thus passed on the overcharge. This is commonly referred to as the 'passing-on defence'. Pass-on by the purchaser may, as mentioned above, lead to a loss of sales and therefore a loss of profit for him.

(b) An action brought by an indirect customer against the infringer (for example, a supermarket or a consumer who purchased bread from the bakery and who brings a claim against the milling companies) will also depend on a pass-on argument. Indeed, the indirect purchaser can claim compensation for an overcharge only where the initial overcharge paid by the direct customer has been passed on partially or entirely to him. This can be of relevance for claimants situated at different levels of the supply chain, including end customers.

165. Different legal rules exist concerning the availability of the passing-on defence and the burden of proof in this context.[130] The economic insights into the quantification of pass-on set out in paragraphs 168 *ff.* below can be of use no matter how these rules are designed.

166. In both situations considered above, claimants and defendants could rely on two different approaches to substantiate their claim that the overcharge was passed on to the indirect customer: they could either

(a) quantify the initial overcharge and determine the pass-on rate to the indirect customer, possibly at several levels of the supply chain and using the econometric techniques outlined above, or

(b) use the methods and techniques outlined above to determine whether the indirect customer concerned paid an overcharge. This second approach will often be easier to implement.

167. For instance, where an indirect customer brings a claim for compensation of an overcharge caused by a cartel, that indirect customer can either show that there was an initial overcharge and that this overcharge was passed on to him[131] or he may quantify the overcharge passed on to his level in the same manner as a direct customer would quantify an initial overcharge, namely by comparing the actual price he paid with the likely price in a non-infringement scenario: comparator-based methods can provide useful insights into the amount of overcharge paid by indirect customers, without it being necessary to identify the degree of pass-on. By using a time comparison, for instance, for the prices paid by the indirect customer before and during the infringement, it can be possible to ascertain how much those prices rose because of the infringement, without having to make a finding concerning the pass-on rate.

168. It is not possible to establish a typical pass-on rate that would apply in most situations. Rather, careful examination of all the characteristics of the market in question will be necessary to assess pass-on rates. In a specific case, the existence and degree of pass-on is determined by a range of different criteria and can therefore only be assessed having regard to the conditions of the market in question.

169. Where the direct customer of the infringing undertakings uses the cartelised goods to compete in a downstream market, it is likely that the direct customer will normally not be able to pass on this increase in cost (or only to a very limited degree) if his own competitors in that downstream market are not subject to the same or a similar overcharge (for example, where they receive their input from a market that is not subject to the cartel). In the example of the flour cartel, the claimant bakery is in competition with other bakeries for the production and supply of bread. In so far as these other bakeries do not obtain their flour from the cartel members, but are able to buy it at a lower price elsewhere, the bakery having to buy from the cartel is placed at a competitive disadvantage vis-à-vis its own competitors that prevents it from passing on the extra cost of the overcharge.

170. Where all the undertakings in that downstream market are hit by the cartel and are thus similarly exposed to the payment of the direct overcharge, it is likely that the direct customer will be able to pass on at least part of that overcharge. The degree of such pass-on is influenced by the intensity of competition in the downstream market: if the downstream market is perfectly competitive, the pass-on rate in this case will be virtually 100%. This reflects the fact that in perfectly competitive markets, price equals marginal costs and a rise in prices for the input will therefore directly lead to an equal rise in cost/output price. For less than perfectly competitive markets, it is likely that affected firms will pass on at least part of the overcharge, though not necessarily 100%. For example, if the direct customer is a monopolist on the downstream market, he will choose a pass-on rate that reflects — for him — a profit-maximising price in view of the decrease in demand that the pass-on of the overcharge is likely to generate.[132]

171. The other characteristics that may also have an influence on the degree of pass-on in such situations (everything else being constant) include:

- The price elasticity of demand and the question whether customers become more or less sensitive to price as prices rise. In particular, pass-on is generally more likely if customers do not easily switch to other products following a price increase (inelastic demand) and if customers become less sensitive to price increases when prices are higher.
- The variation of marginal cost with output changes. For instance, a substantial pass-on is less likely if marginal cost significantly decreases following a reduction in output, because the lower output would become less costly to produce (e.g. in the presence of capacity constraints). Conversely, a substantial pass-on is more likely if marginal cost does not significantly decrease following a reduction in output (e.g. due to the absence of capacity constraints).
- The impact of the infringement on different types of costs. Where the infringement impacts on variable costs, this renders pass-on more likely than if the impact is on fixed costs.
- The duration of the infringement and the frequency of business exchanges. Where infringements last for a long time, it is more likely that some level of pass-on occurs; the same applies to sectors where business exchanges and price adjustments are frequent.

B. Quantifying overcharges caused by other types of infringements leading to overcharge harm

172. Cartels are but one of the infringements leading to a rise in prices for customers of the infringing undertakings and thus to overcharge harm (or, in the case of infringements pertaining to the supply to the infringing undertakings, to an 'undercharge'). Other examples of behaviour that can lead to overcharge harm include infringements of Article 101 TFEU by way of certain anti-competitive joint ventures and the abusive charging of excessive prices by a dominant undertaking within the meaning of Article 102 TFEU.

173. A common feature of these infringements is the fact that they may directly or indirectly allow the infringing undertaking(s) to raise the prices for their customers.[133] The payment of such overcharge in turn leads to a decrease in demand and thus to a volume effect as described above.

174. The methods and techniques whose application to the case of cartel overcharge has been described above[134] can in principle be used to quantify the overcharge harm caused by other infringements. The starting point is the question how the position of the claimant would have been had the specific infringement in question not taken place.

III. QUANTIFYING THE HARM CAUSED BY THE VOLUME EFFECT

175. A rise in prices for a particular product leads to less demand. The degrees to which both prices rise and quantities decrease following an infringement depend on the same cost and demand parameters, and are determined jointly. Hence, the overcharge and volume effects are intrinsically linked.

176. For an overcharge to an intermediate customer (as discussed above in paragraphs 161 *ff.*), the volume effect is also closely linked to the pass-on of overcharges along the supply chain to the final customer: where a customer of the infringing undertakings does not pass on the overcharge and thus absorbs it entirely, his own sales will not decrease because of the infringement as his customers will not experience a rise in prices due to the infringement. Where, however, the overcharge is passed on partly or entirely to the final customer, that customer will be subject to the rise in prices described in paragraph 128 and will reduce his demand. This in turn will reduce demand upstream in the supply chain.

177. As explained above, for those direct or indirect customers of the infringing undertakings who use the product in question for their own commercial activities, this decrease in demand ('volume effect') means that they sell less because of the infringement and therefore forego the profit they would have made on the units they failed to sell because of this effect. This loss of profit is harm for which compensation may be awarded[135] and, in principle, the methods and techniques described above in Part 2 could be used to quantify it.[136]

178. In particular, the comparator-based methods and techniques, whose application to the quantification of the initial overcharge paid by the direct customer is discussed above, can provide the claimant with useful insights in determining the decrease in his turnover and profits. For instance, a comparison over time or across markets can be used to reconstruct the sales volume in the non-infringement scenario, i.e. how many units the claimant would have been able to sell had there been no infringement. Likewise, the application of these methods and techniques can be used to arrive at the hypothetical profit margin in a non-infringement scenario. In some instances, a court may also agree to these methods being used in a simplified fashion, for instance by determining an average profit margin per transaction and then multiplying it by the units that were not sold because of the infringement.[137]

179. Loss of profit is a form of harm often associated with infringements that have the effect of excluding competitors from the market. Part 4 of the Practical Guide discusses the quantification of such harm in more detail. The insights presented in that part can also be relevant when it comes to quantifying the loss of profit caused by a rise in prices.

NOTES

107 In some instances, undertakings that do not infringe the competition rules themselves can raise their prices, as market prices are higher because of the infringement. Customers who purchase from these undertakings are sometimes referred to as 'umbrella customers'. To what extent such customers can claim compensation for the harm from the infringing undertakings depends on the applicable legal rules.

108 For other kinds of harm, see above paragraph 22 in Part 1, Section III.

109 For the economy as a whole, this triangle therefore represents the loss in value for customers due to a reduction in output: while the overcharge affects the distribution of assets within the economy, triangle B means welfare not created because of the infringement. This is referred to in economics as 'deadweight loss'.

110 It is also possible that customers would have been prepared to pay a price higher than P_1, but lower than P_2.

111 See, for this legal term, joined cases C-295/04 to C-298/04 *Manfredi* [2006] ECR I-6619, 95.

112 In order to drive down input prices, the cartel members/dominant buyers with downstream market power are likely to restrict their input purchases, hence also reducing output sales and increasing downstream prices.

113 Only the method based on comparison between time periods in the variant of 'before and during' comparison (i.e. comparing the infringement prices with pre-infringement prices) would obviously be unsuitable, unless regression analysis or simple adjustments are applied to account for the factors that would lead to a price decrease under normal market circumstances (e.g. decreased raw material costs).

114 Judgments of the General Court in joined cases T-25/95 etc. *Cimenteries CBR SA v Commission* [2000] ECR II-491, 837, 1531, 2589; case T-202/98 *Tate & Lyle v Commission* [2001] ECR II-2035, 72–74; Communication from the Commission: Guidelines on the application of Article 81(3) of the Treaty, OJ C101, 27.4.2004, p 97, 20–23.

115 See also the decision of the *Kammergericht Berlin* (Higher Regional Court, Berlin) of 1 October 2009 in case No 2 U 10/03, where the court referred to a similar argument.

116 External study prepared for the Commission 'Quantifying antitrust damages' (2009), pages 88 *ff.*, available at ec.europa.eu/competition/antitrust/actionsdamages/index.html.

117 In all, the study considers 114 cartels based on different types of collusion, including bid-rigging. The sample includes international and national cartels that affected a wide range of different industries. The geographic spread of the sample extends to the US and Canada as well as cartels from Europe and other regions.

118 In particular, it seems possible that cartels that do have an effect on the market receive more attention in empirical studies than those that have no effects, which may lead to a certain bias in the findings; see the study 'Quantifying antitrust damages', page 89 (ref. in footnote 116), for further details about the interpretation of the data used in the study.

119 Study 'Quantifying antitrust damages', page 91 (ref. in footnote 116). That magnitude is expressed as a percentage of the actual price. This means that if the actual price (meaning the price paid as influenced by the infringement) is € 100 and the overcharge is said to be 10%, the price absent the infringement is deemed to be €90.

120 For details and further references see the study 'Quantifying antitrust damages', pages 89 *ff.* (ref. in footnote 116).

121 See for example *Bundesgerichtshof* (Federal Court of Justice, Germany), decision of 28 June 2005, case No KRB 2/05 (*Transportable concrete*) (in the context of assessing the illicit gain by cartelists for the purpose of calculating a fine).

122 See also Section 33(3)(3) of the German Act against restraints on competition (*Gesetz gegen Wettbewerbsbeschränkungen*), which states that the proportion of the profit which the infringing undertaking made from the infringement may be taken into account when estimating damages.

123 Any resemblance of this fictitious example to real events would be purely coincidental; the example cannot be seen as reflecting the Commission's views regarding any specific undertaking or sector or the market definition in such a sector.

124 National law might well provide that all members of a cartel are jointly and severally liable for the entire harm caused by the cartel. The present example has no implications for these rules.

125 See paragraph 43 in Part 2, Section II.

126 See also paragraph 44 in Part 2, Section II.

127 For further insights into the workings of such 'coordinated effects', see Commission, Guidelines on the assessment of

horizontal mergers under the Council Regulation on the control of concentrations between undertakings, OJ C31, 5.2.2004, p 5, paragraph 39.

128 This is without implications for the application of national rules allowing the claimant to use the basic, unadjusted comparisons between prices charged in infringement and non-infringement periods to make an initial pleading, or to fulfil the duties incumbent upon him under national legal rules with regard to fact-pleading (in particular where national law allows a court to determine the damages award by way of approximate estimation or determination on an *ex-aequo-et-bono* basis). Also, rules on the standard and the burden of proof remain unaffected.

129 This connection between a company passing on an overcharge and its own sales volume has, in a different context, also been emphasised by the Court of Justice in case C-147/01 *Weber's Wine World* [2003] ECR I-11365, 98-99: "even where it is established that the (. . .) charge (. . .) has been passed on in whole or in part to third parties (. . .) the person may suffer as a result of a fall in the volume of his sales".

130 See Commission White Paper on damages actions for breach of the EC antitrust rules (COM(2008) 165 final, 2.4.2008) for policy proposals concerning the treatment of pass-on in antitrust damages actions.

131 Where the indirect customer substantiates his claim with reference to a pass-on rate and the infringement concerns a cost factor which is small compared to the entire cost of the product, the pass-on rates of other, more important cost factors that may be more easily estimated might serve as a useful indicator.

132 The exact extent of this pass-on will depend on the demand the direct customer faces and his cost structure. For example, in the simple case of a monopolist facing linear demand (meaning that the relationship between the quantity and price can be represented by a straight line) and constant marginal costs, the pass-on will be 50% of the direct overcharge.

133 Or, if the infringement relates to the supply to the infringing undertakings, to lower the price these suppliers obtain from their customers.

134 See paragraphs 149 and following, and 155 and following.

135 Joined cases C-295/04 to C-298/04 *Manfredi* [2006] ECR I-6619, 95.

136 Except for the cost-based method.

137 See also below, paragraph 191.

PART 4 — QUANTIFYING HARM FROM EXCLUSIONARY PRACTICES

I. EFFECTS OF EXCLUSIONARY PRACTICES

[4.434]

180. Infringements of Article 101 or 102 TFEU can have the effect of completely excluding competitors from a market or of reducing their market shares. Such effects of infringements on competitors are commonly referred to as 'foreclosure'. Examples of these practices are abuses of a dominant position prohibited by Article 102 TFEU through, for instance, predation, exclusive dealing, refusal to supply, tying, bundling, or margin squeeze.[138] Such abuses are called 'exclusionary abuses'. Foreclosure of a competitor can also be the object or effect of a practice prohibited by Article 101 TFEU. It is therefore possible to refer to 'exclusionary practices', covering both infringements of Article 101 and of Article 102 TFEU.

181. Through exclusionary practices prohibited by the Treaty's competition rules, infringers distort competition in order to improve or artificially maintain their position on the market. This immediately affects their competitors by deteriorating their position in a market, driving them out of a market or preventing them from entering a market. Exclusionary practices can affect the costs borne by a competitor, the price it is able to charge for its products, or the quantities it is capable of producing and selling. They typically lead to a loss of profit for the competitors concerned.

182. Moreover, by illegally affecting the market position of competitors and thereby the level of competition in the market, such practices lead to harm to customers in the form of higher prices or reduced choice, quality or innovation. However, the detrimental effects of exclusionary practices on customers may not always manifest themselves immediately, as these practices target competitors in the first place, thereby reducing the competitive constraints exerted by them on the infringer(s). Whereas infringements of the kind described in Part 3 normally produce an immediate illegal profit for the infringers and immediate harm for their customers, exclusionary practices could result in an initial disadvantage for the infringers and in better prices for customers in the short run, as typically occurs in predatory pricing. The following sections will separately approach the issues of quantifying harm suffered by competitors (Section II) and harm suffered by customers (Section III).

183. The Treaty guarantees consumers and undertakings that have suffered harm caused by an exclusionary practice a right to compensation regardless of whether they are customers or competitors of the infringers. As already stated, the Court of Justice has specified that such compensation encompasses the actual loss suffered *(damnum emergens)*, compensation for the profit they have lost due to the infringement *(lucrum cessans)*, and the payment of interest.[139] For the purposes of quantifying harm from exclusionary practices, the following Sections will primarily refer to the concept of 'loss of profit', in line with the case-law of the Court of Justice. The concept of 'loss of profit' will be used in a broad sense, as meaning any difference between the actual profits generated by an undertaking and the profits it would have generated in the absence of the infringement. The approaches to quantifying such loss of profit described in the following are without prejudice to the possibility of injured parties to claim compensation under other heads of damage under national law. Indeed, some elements of lost profits in a broad sense may be classified under different legal concepts under the law of Member States (such as loss of chance[140] or loss of reputation) and there may also be heads of damage caused by exclusionary behaviour that go beyond the notion of lost profits.

II. QUANTIFYING HARM TO COMPETITORS

184. Loss of profit to competitors can be caused by reduced revenues (e.g. through the reduction in the quantity that such competitors can sell) or increased costs (e.g. when the infringement affects the price of an input). The overall situation can be reflected in a decrease in the competitor's market share. In the following Sections, after a short

description of how exclusionary practices affect competitors over time (A), and an outline of the general approach to the quantification of lost profits (B), some typical situations in the quantification of exclusionary practices will be addressed, namely in cases where they affect existing competitors (C) and new entrants (D) and when the harm they produce extends also to the future (E).

A. The time dimension of exclusionary practices

185. Depending on the period considered, exclusionary practices can affect competitors in different ways. When an exclusionary practice starts, competitors typically face difficulties in selling their products or (where the practice concerns the upstream market) obtaining supplies. This translates into a deterioration of their profit through higher costs or reduced revenues. Competitors may typically suffer a drop in their market shares, or a lower market share than they could have expected absent the infringement (for instance where their expansion is prevented). This phase may coincide with an increase in profits for infringers. This is, however, not necessarily so, since infringers may have to bear costs due to the implementation of the exclusionary practice (e.g. by lowering their price, by not supplying a competitor and thus reducing their own sales, or by offering rebates or other advantages to customers that could lower profits in the short term). Competitors may eventually be forced out of the market.

186. Once competitors have been successfully prevented from entering a market, or once their market presence has been reduced or eliminated, infringers usually recoup and benefit from increased profits to the detriment of customers and foreclosed competitors. When this occurs (either very soon after the infringement started or after a certain period of time), customers may have to pay a higher price and suffer a loss of quality or choice. The full exclusion of a competitor from a market is not a prerequisite for these effects on customers. Such effects may occur also from the very beginning of the exclusionary practice, and even if competitors are still on the market, provided the competitive pressure they exercise is weakened.

187. When the exclusionary practice is detected by public enforcers or brought to an end as a result of private actions, competitive conditions could be progressively restored. It is important to stress that the restoration of market conditions as if the infringement had not occurred is factually impossible in many cases. This depends mainly on structural effects of the infringement that may be difficult and lengthy to undo (existing contractual obligations, network effects, or other barriers to the re-entry of a foreclosed competitor). Therefore, in some instances full convergence between the non-infringement scenario and the actual market development cannot take place.

B. General approach to the quantification of lost profits

188. In order to determine whether and to what extent competitors have suffered a loss of profits, it is necessary to compare the profit obtained by competitors during the infringement in the market affected by it with the profit they would have obtained from those products in a non-infringement scenario (i.e. the counterfactual scenario).[141] Whenever it can be shown that the foreclosed competitor would have earned higher profits in a non-infringement scenario, and that the difference is caused by the infringement, the competitor has suffered harm, even if its market share is unchanged or profits increased due to other factors.[142]

189. The actual profits earned by the undertaking in question are normally determined by deducting the actual costs incurred from the actual revenues earned. Similarly, profits that would have been obtained in a non-infringement scenario (counterfactual profits) can be determined by deducting the estimated costs in a non-infringement scenario (counterfactual costs)[143] from the revenues expected in the absence of the infringement (counterfactual revenues).[144] The amount of profits lost is the difference between counterfactual and actual profits. In the case of prevented entry, the actual profits are normally zero, or can even be a negative number if the foreclosed competitor incurred costs (e.g. investment to enter the market) that did not return any revenue.

190. This basic approach to calculating lost profits can be put into practice in different ways. For instance, it is possible to compare the revenues of the foreclosed competitor in the non-infringement scenario with actual revenues from the market as affected by the infringement. Once the lost revenues have been established, it is possible to deduct the costs that the undertaking has avoided due to the lower volumes produced, in order to obtain a value of lost profits. This approach to assessing lost profits does not make it necessary to quantify the entire costs that would have been incurred by the company, but only an estimate of those costs that have not been incurred because of the infringement.

191. There are also some further pragmatic approaches to assessing lost profits that may be suitable in certain specific cases. For instance, an average profit margin per unit of the product traded in the non-infringement scenario could be estimated and then multiplied by the number of units that have not been sold due to the infringement.[145]

Such an estimate of the average per unit profit may be based on one or more transactions that can be considered as sufficiently representative of the claimant's business for the product concerned. It is worth noting that in this calculation the avoided costs would implicitly be included.[146]

192. Practice of antitrust damages actions shows that foreclosed competitors sometimes choose to claim damages only for part of the harm, for instance the costs incurred in order to respond to an exclusionary practice,[147] the non-recoverable costs ('sunk costs') incurred with a view to entering a market from which they have been foreclosed[148] or the amount judged excessive in cases of margin squeeze or of discriminatory pricing[149] that infringe EU competition law. This choice is sometimes prompted by the consideration that quantifying such heads of damage is more straightforward or may require less data, and that evidence is more easily available. Also when claimants seek compensation for loss of profits, quantification of harm on the basis of additional costs incurred (sunk and non-sunk) will generally constitute a lower bound when estimating the full loss of profit.

193. Whichever the method or technique chosen, quantifying lost profits may entail evaluating complex data referring to a hypothetical non-infringement situation against which the actual position of the foreclosed competitor needs to be assessed, often with a view at likely future developments. Assessing the profits that a company would

have made, including future profits, may depend on such a number of factors that it could be appropriate to provide for less demanding requirements when it comes to quantification. Therefore, legal systems may allow courts to exercise some discretion as to the figures and statistical method to be chosen, and the way in which they are to be used to evaluate the damage.[150]

C. Existing competitors

194. In order to quantify the harm they suffered because of an exclusionary practice, competitors may choose to rely on the methods or techniques described in Part 2. The non-infringement scenario could be reconstructed by comparison with the performance of the same undertaking in a time period that was not affected by an infringement, a similar undertaking on the same market, aggregated industry profits[151] or the performance of the same or a similar undertaking in a market other than the one in which the exclusionary practice occurred. Alternatively, methods based on simulations may provide an estimate of the non-infringement scenario, i.e. simulating on the basis of a number of assumptions (regarding e.g. the type of competitive interactions among firms) what the likely situation would have been if the excluded competitor could have been active on the market and unaffected by the exclusionary practice. The use of other methods is also possible, e.g. financial data from the undertakings involved could provide useful insights on the likely returns of companies had they not been affected by an infringement.

Refusal to supply an essential input for commercial solvents

Worldco is a leading international producer of raw materials that are an essential input in the manufacturing of commercial solvents. Eusolv is a company that has been active on the market for commercial solvents since 1995, and most of its turnover is made from sales of Betanol. In order to produce Betanol, Eusolv purchases Rawbeta from Worldco. Worldco is dominant in the production of Rawbeta, which is the only raw material suitable for producing Betanol on an industrial scale and at prices that enable Betanol to be marketed. Worldco also supplies Rawbeta to its subsidiary Subco, which since 2004 has been producing Betanol and competes with Eusolv.

In 2006, Worldco decides to stop supplying Rawbeta to companies selling Betanol in the European Union, with the exception of its own subsidiary Subco. Eusolv initially tries to acquire sufficient Rawbeta from alternative suppliers or to replace its Rawbeta input with other raw materials produced through experimental processes, which are significantly more costly and produce sharp rises in the sales price of Betanol, together with a decrease in its quality and suitability for commercial purposes. As a consequence, Eusolv suffers a progressive decline in its sales and finally discontinues the production of Betanol in 2010. In the same year, Eusolv brings a damages action against Worldco and its subsidiary Subco in order to recover the profits it lost due to the refusal to supply. The court holds that Worldco's practice amounted to an abuse of a dominant position prohibited by Article 102 TFEU.

(1)
Comparison over time

195. When an exclusionary practice affects existing competitors, it is likely that data from the same undertaking in an unaffected period are available. In such cases, the profits lost by the harmed competitor could be estimated by means of a comparison over time. The non-infringement scenario could, for example, be constructed by reference to data on revenues and costs of the harmed undertaking before the exclusionary infringement produced effects.[152] In many exclusionary practices cases, data from after the infringement may not be available or would not be equally suitable, particularly if the infringement produced effects that may alter the structure of a market and are unlikely to disappear in the short term, for instance when the competitor is excluded from the market and there are barriers to re-entry in the short term, or when the competitor has lost market shares that could be difficult to regain because of network effects.[153]

In the Betanol example, reliable data from after the infringement are not available, since Eusolv, the harmed undertaking, is no longer active on the market, and its effective re-entry into the market may not occur promptly after the termination of the infringement. Eusolv thus decides to construct a likely non-infringement scenario by using data from before 2006, when the exclusionary practice was initiated.

196. Under some circumstances, the pre-infringement revenue and cost data used for the comparison could be refined. For instance, and depending on applicable national rules on evidence and on the burden of proof, a defendant may challenge the amount estimated by the claimant by indicating other elements that may have adversely influenced the performance of an undertaking and are not related to the infringement, such as a drop in marketing investment, a loss of competitiveness of the product, or an increase in the cost of inputs that is specific to the competitor claiming damages. Conversely, it could be shown that the harmed competitor's situation in the non-infringement scenario would have been better than it was before the infringement, for instance because it had a potential for growth. Generally, the reference to an earlier unaffected time period on the same market is likely to be more reliable the longer the competitor has been on that market and the more stable its market position has been. In other words, the reference to a pre-infringement scenario could benefit more from adjustments[154] if the harmed competitor was a recent entrant on the market, since its market share could have been more likely subject to fluctuations.

In the example, Eusolv provides data on its overall actual revenues and costs from the production and sale of Betanol, as set out in the following chart:

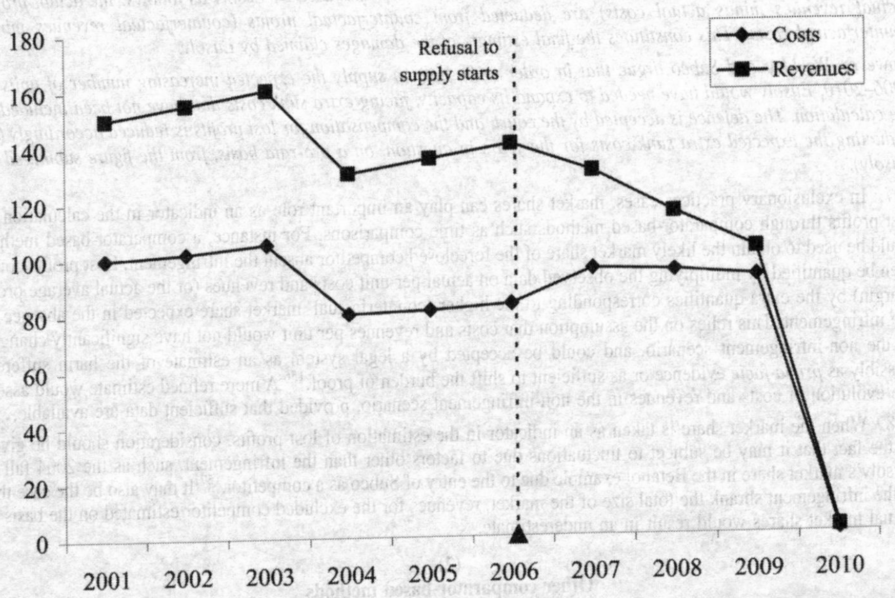

In order to establish a reliable non-infringement scenario, data from before 2004 are not taken into account because Subco, the most significant competitor of Eusolv, was not yet active on the market, whereas after 2004 and until 2006 Eusolv held a stable share of the market.

Eusolv, in accordance with national rules on the burden and the standard of proof, provides figures on the 'counterfactual' quantities, revenues and costs that would have occurred in the absence of the infringement.

Due to increasing industrial applications of Betanol, it is observed that the total demand for this product (thus, the size of the market) has grown steadily. The stability of Eusolv's market share after Subco's entry into the Betanol market is used by Eusolv to rely on the assumption that, absent the infringement, it would have maintained a similar market share. On this assumption Eusolv provides figures on its 'counterfactual' revenues for the years 2006–2010, calculated on the basis of the total value of the market and Eusolv's share of it. From its internal accounts, Eusolv provides figures on its unit costs for the years 2004 to 2006.[155] *It is shown that costs closely followed the prices of the inputs for the production of Betanol, i.e. that, for instance, a rise in the input prices directly leads to a corresponding increase in costs. Using available industry data on input prices, Eusolv's experts estimate 'counterfactual' unit costs and, e.g. through regression analysis, account for the evolution in input prices and efficiencies related to the production of higher volumes. The figure for overall 'counterfactual' costs in the years 2006–2010 is then obtained by multiplying the estimated 'counterfactual' unit cost by the number of units it would have sold in the absence of the infringement.*

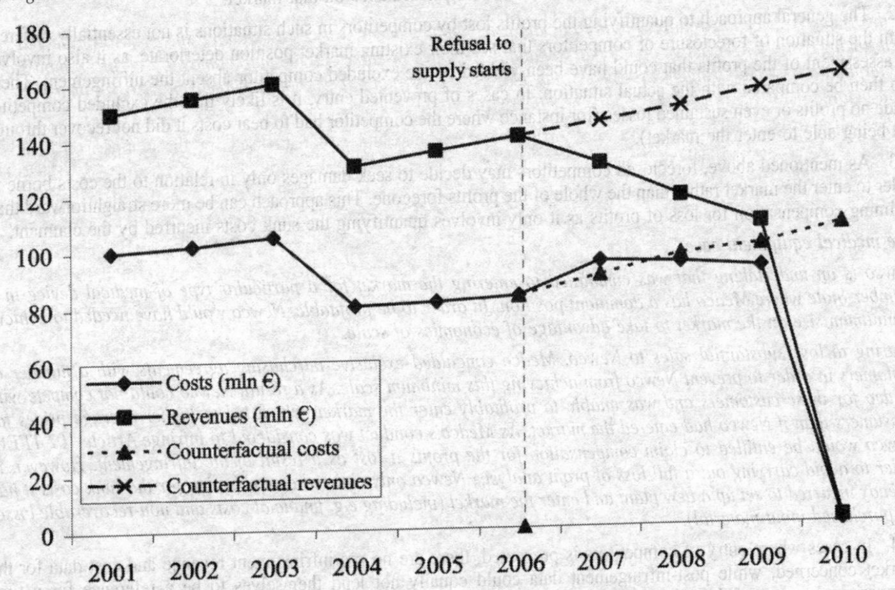

Part 4 EU & Retained EU Materials

The figures obtained are compared with the actual revenues and costs faced by Eusolv as follows: the actual profits (actual revenues minus actual costs) are deducted from counterfactual profits (counterfactual revenues minus counterfactual costs). This constitutes the final estimate of the damages claimed by Eusolv.

However, Worldco and Subco argue that in order to be able to supply the expected increasing number of units in 2006–2010, Eusolv would have needed to expand its capacity, facing extra sunk costs that have not been included in the calculation. The defence is accepted by the court, and the compensation for lost profits is reduced accordingly (by deducting the expected extra sunk costs for the years in question, on a pro-rata basis, from the figure submitted by Eusolv).

197. In exclusionary practices cases, market shares can play an important role as an indicator in the calculation of lost profits through comparator-based methods such as time comparisons. For instance, a comparator-based method could be used to obtain the likely market share of the foreclosed competitor absent the infringement. Lost profits could then be quantified by multiplying the observed data on actual per-unit costs and revenues (or the actual average profit margin) by the extra quantities corresponding to the higher 'counterfactual' market share expected in the absence of the infringement. This relies on the assumption that costs and revenues per unit would not have significantly changed in the non-infringement scenario, and could be accepted by a legal system as an estimate of the harm suffered, possibly as *prima facie* evidence or as sufficient to shift the burden of proof.[156] A more refined estimate would assess the evolution of costs and revenues in the non-infringement scenario, provided that sufficient data are available.

198. When the market share is taken as an indicator in the estimation of lost profits, consideration should be given to the fact that it may be subject to fluctuations due to factors other than the infringement, such as the 2004 fall in Eusolv's market share in the Betanol example due to the entry of Subco as a competitor.[157] It may also be the case that if the infringement shrank the total size of the market, revenues for the excluded competitor estimated on the basis of actual market shares would result in an underestimate.

(2)
Other comparator-based methods

199. Other geographic or product markets may also be used as a comparator in order to construct the non-infringement scenario.[158] Thus, costs and revenues of the same or a similar undertaking on a different market could be taken as a reference to estimate the costs and revenues that would have been yielded by the harmed competitor had the infringement not occurred. These methods can also be used as a means to assess the reliability of an estimation obtained by a comparison over time or other methods. For instance, if the pre-infringement performance of the sole competitor of a historically monopolistic undertaking indicates that it would have held a certain market share absent the infringement, the estimation could be comforted by the finding that the same or a similar undertaking which competes with the formerly monopolistic incumbent on a comparable geographic market actually holds a similar market share, taking into account possible differences between the undertakings or the markets concerned.

D. PREVENTED ENTRY OF COMPETITORS

200. Exclusionary practices can not only lead to the deterioration of the market position of an existing competitor, but also prevent the entry of a potential competitor that was not already active on the market. The foreclosure of new entrants can cause them a very significant harm for which they are entitled to compensation. Legal systems should take account of the inherent difficulties of quantifying such harm and should ensure that damages actions by prevented market entrants are not made practically impossible or excessively difficult.[159]

201. The situation of prevented entry presents some peculiar circumstances that can be taken into account when quantifying the harm. In particular, if the harmed undertaking was willing to enter a market where it was not active before, there is an inherent lack of observable data on its performance on that market.

202. The general approach to quantifying the profits lost by competitors in such situations is not essentially different from the situation of foreclosure of competitors that see their existing market position deteriorate, as it also involves an assessment of the profits that could have been yielded by the excluded competitor absent the infringement. These can then be compared with the actual situation. In cases of prevented entry, it is likely that the excluded competitor made no profits or even sustained losses (for instance where the competitor had to bear costs it did not recover through not being able to enter the market).

203. As mentioned above, foreclosed competitors may decide to seek damages only in relation to the costs borne in order to enter the market rather than the whole of the profits foregone. This approach can be more straightforward than claiming compensation for loss of profits as it only involves quantifying the sunk costs incurred by the claimant.

The medical equipment case

Newco is an undertaking that was committed to entering the market for a particular type of medical device in a Member State where Medco has a dominant position. In order to be profitable, Newco would have needed to achieve a minimum size on the market to take advantage of economies of scale.

Fearing to lose substantial sales to Newco, Medco concluded exclusive purchasing agreements with a number of customers in order to prevent Newco from achieving this minimum scale. As a result, Newco could not compete with Medco for these customers and was unable to profitably enter the market, which led to higher average prices for consumers than if Newco had entered the market. As Medco's conduct was considered to infringe Article 102 TFEU, Newco would be entitled to claim compensation for the profits it lost as a result of the infringement. However, in order to avoid carrying out a full loss of profit analysis, Newco only claimed compensation for the sunk costs it had already incurred to set up a new plant and enter the market (including e.g. financial costs and non-recoverable losses on purchased input material).

204. In cases where entry of competitors is prevented, there are no pre-infringement revenue and cost data for the market concerned, while post-infringement data could equally not lend themselves to be a reference for a time comparison because of the effects of the infringement. In such instances, reference to a comparable geographic or

product market where the same or a comparable undertaking is active could prove a better means to construct a non-infringement scenario. Product or geographic markets concerned should offer a sufficient degree of similarity, although it may be possible to adjust for some differences between the markets.[160]

205. In some cases, assessment of the competitor's financial performance may suffice to find data in order to estimate the profits in the non-infringement scenario.[161]

In the situation referred in the example above, assume that Newco is willing to supply the three biggest private health centres in a Member State with an innovative type of films for X-ray machines. Assume that normally the market for this type of medical equipment for private health centres is a bidding market. Thanks to a technological improvement, Newco is capable of offering its products at a lower price than Medco. However, Medco, which holds a dominant position in the market for X-ray machines, ties the products by applying a higher price for X-ray machines to centres that do not purchase films from it. As a result, Newco does not obtain any contract. In such circumstances, Newco showed that it was actually capable of supplying the quantities demanded by the centres for the price offered, and provided detailed data on its own costs. On the basis of these data, and on the assumption that Newco would have been chosen as a contractor in those instances where it offered the lowest price, expected profit margins could be estimated without resorting to a comparison in time or with other geographic or product markets.

E. Compensation for future loss

206. When foreclosed competitors claim compensation, they may seek compensation not only for the profits lost during the infringement period, but also for the profits foregone after its termination.[162] This is relevant, in particular, where they could not re-enter the market or fully recover their market share because of lasting effects of the terminated infringement. Compensation would then be asked for future profits, i.e. profits that are likely to be lost after the claim for compensation is brought and adjudicated.

207. The challenges for quantifying such loss not only lie in the techniques to be deployed, but also have to do with the time frame during which a lost profit can still be identified and compensated. National law plays an important role in this context, for instance by determining under which circumstances a future loss can be recovered, or by establishing pragmatic rules to address this issue on a case-by-case basis.[163]

208. Factors likely to affect the choice of the relevant limit in time for claiming loss of future profit may encompass, for instance, the likely time needed to re-enter the market in question. In other cases, this assessment could be easier because of the circumstances of the case. For instance, in the X-ray machine example above, the duration of the contracts Newco was bidding for could constitute a reasonable lapse of time over which loss of future profits should be compensated under applicable national rules. In other cases, the time over which the undertaking could reasonably have continued producing goods or providing services in the absence of new investments could also be considered.

In the Betanol example, Eusolv may claim compensation also for the profits it could have obtained after 2010, when it was driven out of the market and brought an action for damages. In such a case, it would be possible to use the same techniques employed to reconstruct the non-infringement scenario in the years 2006–2010 and project it further into the future. Of course, lost profits for the future cannot be claimed for an indefinite duration. Eusolv decided to take as a benchmark the likely lapse of time that would be needed for Eusolv to re-enter the market once the infringement was brought to an end.

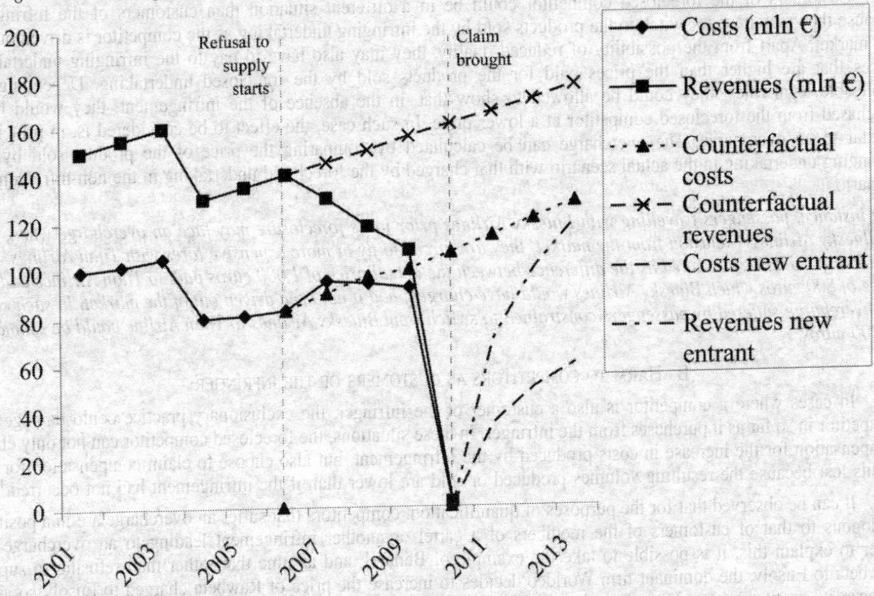

III. QUANTIFYING HARM TO CUSTOMERS

209. Undertakings that collude or abuse their dominant position in order to foreclose a competitor might face costs or a temporary reduction in their profits in order to implement the infringement. This sacrifice is borne in order to achieve a distortion of the competitive process that will eventually place the infringers in a position where they gain higher profits thanks to the distorted market conditions achieved, thus allowing them to recoup, at the expense of their

Part 4 EU & Retained EU Materials

customers, the temporary loss or reduction in profits borne in order to attain that position. The following sections will address two typical situations of harm to customers caused by exclusionary practices. For the purposes of quantification, the harm caused to customers by exclusionary practices can be analogous to that caused by infringements leading to a rise in prices, which is discussed in more detail in Part 3 of the Practical Guide.

A. Recoupment

210. The most straightforward example of the harm caused to customers in the recoupment phase of exclusionary practices is price predation, where an undertaking abuses its dominant position by setting its prices at an artificially low level that cannot be matched by its competitors, who will eventually leave the market or suffer a reduction in their market share. Once the competitors have been excluded from the market, or once a higher market share has been achieved, infringers can enjoy higher profits due to the weaker competitive constraints.

211. Recoupment can be seen as a complementary phase of the infringement that can result in overcharge effects for the customers of the infringers. These overcharge effects constitute harm caused by the exclusionary practice, and compensation for them can be sought by customers.

Recoupment in a predatory pricing case

Consider, for example, the market for flights on a particular route between two cities. Operating on this market in a dominant position is Titan Airlines, an established undertaking which offers high quality in-flight service for a standard fare of 1,000 euros. Another player on this specific market is the smaller Bluesky Airlines, which recently started operating on the same route with prices of 800 euros.

Titan Airlines engages in predatory pricing by strategically lowering its fares to a standard price of 500 euros. Bluesky Airlines experiences difficulties in meeting these predatory fares, as a result of which it fails to remain profitable, and is eventually driven out of the market. The dominant Titan Airlines will in that case take advantage of the reduction of competition and increase its profits by raising fares to a level beyond pre-predation fares, i.e. exceeding its initial standard price of 1,000 euros. If Titan Airlines, until re-entry of a competitor, were to charge a price of 1,100 euros, its customers would, due to the infringement, pay an overcharge of 100 euros.

212. When overcharges resulting from recoupment are to be quantified, the conceptual framework that applies is in principle not different from that discussed in Part 3, namely regarding infringements leading more directly to a rise in prices. Since the harm caused by an exclusionary practice is not confined to competitors of the infringer but extends to all customers in a specific market, the issues discussed in the framework of overcharge harm are thus relevant also in this scenario.

213. The position achieved by an undertaking on the market due to an exclusionary infringement does not lead in all cases to a rise in price for customers of the infringing undertaking. However, also in such cases customers may still be harmed by the infringement, for instance if it results in reduced quality. In the example, it could happen that the dominant undertaking Titan Airlines reinstates the same standard price of 1,000 euros, not exceeding the fares it charged prior to the exclusion of Bluesky Airlines. Passengers travelling on this particular route are nevertheless adversely affected, for instance, if Titan Airlines seizes the opportunity of less competitive constraints to lower the standard of its in-flight service.

214. Customers of the foreclosed competitor could be in a different situation than customers of the infringers, because they may have to switch to the products sold by the infringing undertaking as the competitor is driven out of the market. Apart from the possibility of reduced quality, they may also have to pay to the infringing undertaking prices that are higher than the prices paid for the products sold by the foreclosed undertaking. Depending on applicable legal rules, they could be allowed to show that, in the absence of the infringement, they would have purchased from the foreclosed competitor at a lower price. In such case, the effect to be considered is, in principle, similar to an overcharge. The overcharge can be calculated by comparing the price of the product sold by the infringing undertaking in the actual scenario with that charged by the foreclosed undertaking in the non-infringement scenario.

For instance, passengers travelling with Bluesky Airlines prior to its foreclosure may face an overcharge when, due to Bluesky Airlines' exclusion from the market, they are forced to fly at more expensive fares with Titan Airlines. The overcharge could be estimated as the difference between the actual price of 1,000 euros paid to Titan Airlines and the price of 800 euros which Bluesky Airlines would have charged, had it not been driven out of the market. In such case, the overcharge suffered by passengers constrained to switch from Bluesky Airlines to Titan Airline could be estimated at 200 euros.

B. Harm to competitors as customers of the infringers

215. In cases where a competitor is also a customer of the infringer, the exclusionary practice could damage the competitor in so far as it purchases from the infringer. In these situations, the foreclosed competitor can not only claim compensation for the increase in costs produced by the infringement, but also choose to claim compensation for the profits lost because the resulting volumes produced or sold are lower than if the infringement had not occurred.[164]

216. It can be observed that for the purposes of quantification, competitors that suffer an overcharge are in a position analogous to that of customers of the members of a cartel or another infringement leading to an overcharge. In order to explain this, it is possible to take the example of Betanol, and assume that rather than refusing to supply Rawbeta to Eusolv, the dominant firm Worldco decides to increase the price of Rawbeta charged to Eusolv so as to squeeze its profit margins. In such a situation, similar considerations arise as in the case of an increase in price generated by other types of infringements. In the example Eusolv would claim compensation for the overcharge represented by the difference between the price it paid as a result of the exclusionary practice and the price it would have paid in the absence of the infringement. If the overcharge has been passed on, claims for damages could be also brought by Eusolv's own customers, and Eusolv itself could claim compensation for the volumes lost because of the price increase.

NOTES

138 For a description of these practices see also Communication from the Commission — Guidance on the Commission's enforcement priorities in applying Article 82 of the EC Treaty to abusive exclusionary conduct by dominant undertakings, OJ C45, 24.2.2009, p 7.

139 Joined cases C-295/04 to 298/04 *Manfredi* [2006] ECR I-6619, 95.

140 Loss of a chance identifies the business opportunities forgone by an undertaking due to the illegal exclusionary practice.

141 This does not concern claims aimed at recovering only part of that loss, e.g. only the additional costs incurred. Such claims arise in practice also because of the availability of more straightforward approaches to quantifying the harm suffered. See below, paragraph 192.

142 For instance, a new entrant with high potential for growth may maintain its profit levels but would have increased them absent the infringement.

143 When estimating the profit lost by the undertaking in question, it is necessary to take into account the additional costs it would have naturally faced to increase production. In this respect, the cost per unit incurred by the undertaking does not necessarily correspond to its cost per unit in the counterfactual scenario. For instance, in the case of increasing returns to scale, the cost per unit in the counterfactual scenario would be lower than the observed cost as the undertaking's production would be higher in the counterfactual scenario (i.e. had it not been affected by the infringement).

144 E.g. *Stockholms tingsrätt* (Stockholm District Court), judgment of 20 November 2008, joined cases T 32799-05 and T 34227-05 (*Europe Investor Direct AB and others v VPC Aktiebolag)*, appeal pending.

145 For an example of a pragmatic approach based on real data on costs and revenues implemented through regression techniques, see *Juzgado Mercantil numero 2 de Barcelona* (Commercial Court, Barcelona), decision of 20 January 2011, case No 45/2010 (Céntrica Energìa S.L.U./Endesa Distribuciòn Eléctrica S.A.)

146 In order to estimate the average profit margin, it could be still appropriate to consider how costs and revenues in the counterfactual scenario would have evolved without the infringement. For example, profit margins observed in a pre-infringement period could have been reduced during the infringement period for reasons unrelated to the infringement, due to a reduction in demand or an increase in input costs that are caused by other factors. In addition, the reduction in the output of the excluded competitor could affect its unit cost, hence also affecting the margin on the units it continues to sell.

147 E.g. additional marketing expenses necessary to retain the market position.

148 E.g. the costs of building a new factory on that market.

149 See for instance *Lietuvos apeliacinis teismas* (Lithuanian Court of Appeal), decision of 26 May 2006, case No 2A-41/2006 (*Stumbras*); *Højesteret* (Supreme Court, Denmark), decision of 20 April 2005, case No 387/2002 (*GT Linien A/S v DSB*).

150 See for instance Joined cases C-104/89 and C-37/90 *Mulder and others v Council and Commission* [2000] ECR I-203, 79.

151 See above at paragraphs 35, 48 and 66.

152 For an example of the application of a before and during comparison to estimate the harm from an exclusionary practice prohibited by Article 101 TFEU see *Corte d'Appello di Milano* (Court of Appeal, Milan), decision of 3 February 2000, case No I, 308 (*Inaz Paghe v Associazione Nazionale Consulenti del Lavoro*).

153 A product is subject to network effects if its value for each user increases as the number of users increases.

154 Such adjustments could be performed through the techniques described above at paragraphs 59 *ff.*

155 These include sunk costs, distributed over time.

156 For an example of a court estimation based on multiplying the total number of contracts concluded by the infringer by the market share held by claimants before the exclusionary practice started, see *Corte d'Appello di Roma* (Court of Appeal, Rome), decision of 20 January 2003, case No I, 2474 (*Albacom S.p.A. v Telecom Italia S.p.A.*).

157 For this reason, in the example the market share considered for the quantification is the stable market share held by Eusolv after 2004.

158 *Juzgado Mercantil numero 5 de Madrid* (Commercial Court, Madrid), decision of 11 November 2005, case No 85/2005 (*Conduit-Europe, S.A. v Telefónica de España S.A.*), confirmed by *Audiencia Provincial de Madrid* (Court of Appeal, Madrid), decision of 25 May 2006, case No 73/2006.

159 In some cases it is possible under applicable legal rules to quantify this harm through pragmatic approaches, such as calculation of the total value of the lost market in terms of profits, multiplied by a percentage expressing the share of the market that the foreclosed undertaking would have been likely to acquire. For instance if the total profits generated by undertakings active on the relevant market after the infringement amount to 200 million euros, and it is estimated that, in the absence of the infringement, the foreclosed competitor would have held a market share of 30 per cent, the lost profit could be estimated, under this approach, at 60 million euros.

160 This could be done, for instance, through regression analysis, provided that sufficient data are available. See above, paragraph 69*ff*. For an example of an exclusionary practice where the use of a different geographic market was, in principle, accepted as a comparator see *Juzgado Mercantil numero 5 de Madrid* (Commercial Court, Madrid), decision of 11 November 2005, case No 85/2005 (*Conduit-Europe, S.A. v Telefónica de España S.A.*), confirmed by *Audiencia Provincial de Madrid* (Court of Appeal, Madrid), decision of 25 May 2006, case No 73/2006.

161 For an illustration of the quantification of harm to a foreclosed new entrant in a bidding market see *Oberlandesgericht Düsseldorf* (Higher Regional Court, Düsseldorf), decision of 16 April 2008, case No VI-2 U (kart) 8/06, 2 U 8/06 (*Stadtwerke Düsseldorf*).

162 For an example of a damages award also for the period subsequent to the end of an infringement see *Østre landsrets* (Eastern High Court, Denmark), decision of 20 May 2009, case No B-3355-06 (*Forbruger-Kontakt a-s v Post Danmark A/S*).

163 When future profits are estimated, it is normally appropriate to discount their value in order to reflect the loss in the value of money over time.

164 For an example of the estimation of damages in a discriminatory pricing affecting a competitor as a customer of the infringer, see *Højesteret* (Supreme Court, Denmark), decision of 20 April 2005, case No 387/2002 (*GT Linien A/S v DSB*).

TABLE OF CASES CITED

COURT OF JUSTICE OF THE EU

[4.435]

Case 238/78 *Ireks-Arkady GmbH v Council and Commission* [1979] ECR 2955.

Case C-271/91 *Marshall* [1993] ECR I-4367.

Case C-308/87 *Grifoni II* [1994] ECR I-341.

Joined Cases C-104/89 and C-37/90 *Mulder and others v Council and Commission* [2000] ECR I-203.

Case C-453/99 *Courage* [2001] ECR I- 6297.

Case C-147/01 *Weber's Wine World* [2003] ECR I-11365.

Joined Cases C-295/04 to 298/04 *Manfredi* [2006] ECR I-6619.

Case C-360/09 *Pfleiderer*, [2011] ECR I-5161.

Case C-199/11, *European Community v. Otis NV and others*, [2012], not yet reported.

GENERAL COURT

Case T-202/98 *Tate & Lyle v Commission* [2001] ECR II-2035

Joined Cases T-25/95 etc. *Cimenteries CBR SA v Commission* [2000] ECR II-491

COURTS OF THE MEMBER STATES

Corte d'Appello di Milano (Court of Appeal, Milan), decision of 3 February 2000, case No I, 308 (*Inaz Paghe v Associazione Nazionale Consulenti del Lavoro*).

Corte d'Appello di Roma (Court of Appeal, Rome), decision of 20 January 2003, case No I, 2474 (*Albacom S.p.A. v Telecom Italia S.p.A.*).

Corte d'Appello di Milano (Court of Appeal, Milan), decision of 11 July 2003, (*Bluvacanze*)

Cour d'Appel de Paris (Court of Appeal, Paris), decision of 23 June 2003 (*Lescarcelle-De Memoris v OGF*)

Landgericht Dortmund (Regional Court, Dortmund), decision of 1 April 2004, Case No 13 O 55/02 Kart (*Vitaminpreise*).

Højesteret (Supreme Court, Denmark), decision of 20 April 2005, case No 387/2002 (*GT Linien A/S v DSB*).

Bundesgerichtshof (Federal Court of Justice, Germany), decision of 28 June 2005, case No KRB 2/05 (*Transportable concrete*)

Juzgado Mercantil numero 5 de Madrid (Commercial Court, Madrid), decision of 11 November 2005, case No 85/2005 (*Conduit-Europe, S.A. v Telefónica de España S.A.*),

Audiencia Provincial de Madrid (Court of Appeal, Madrid), decision of 25 May 2006, case No 73/2006.

Lietuvos apeliacinis teismas (Lithuanian Court of Appeal), decision of 26 May 2006, case No 2A-41/2006 (*Stumbras*)

Corte Suprema di Cassazione (Supreme Court of Cassation, Italy), decision of 2 February 2007, case No 2305 (*Fondiaria SAI SpA v Nigriello*).

Bundesgerichtshof (Federal Court of Justice, Germany), decision of 19 June 2007, case No KBR 12/07 (*Paper Wholesale Cartel*)

Landesgericht für Zivilrechtssachen Graz (Regional Civil Court of Graz), decision of 17 August 2007, case No 17 R 91/07 p (*Driving school*).

Oberlandesgericht Düsseldorf (Higher Regional Court, Düsseldorf), decision of 16 April 2008, case No VI-2 U (kart) 8/06, 2 U 8/06 (*Stadtwerke Düsseldorf*).

Stockholms tingsrätt (Stockholm District Court), judgment of 20 November 2008, joined cases T 32799-05 and T 34227-05 (*Europe Investor Direct AB and others v VPC Aktiebolag*), appeal pending.

Tribunal Administratif de Paris (Administrative Court of Paris), decision of 27 Mars 2009, *(SNCF v Bouygues)*.

Østre landsrets (Eastern High Court, Denmark), decision of 20 May 2009, case No B-3355-06 (*Forbruger-Kontakt a-s v Post Danmark A/S*).

Kammergericht Berlin (Higher Regional Court, Berlin), decision of 1 October 2009, case No 2 U 10/03 Kart.

Oberlandesgericht Karlsruhe (Higher Regional Court, Karlsruhe), decision of 11 June 2010, case No 6 U 118/05; appealed to the Federal Court of Justice (see below).

Juzgado Mercantil numero 2 de Barcelona (Commercial Court, Barcelona), decision of 20 January 2011, case No 45/2010 (*Céntrica Energìa S.L.U./Endesa Distribuciòn Eléctrica S.A.*).

Bundesgerichtshof (Federal Court of Justice), decision of 28 June 2011, case KZR 75/10.

Competition Appeal Tribunal, decision of 28 March 2013, case No 1166/5/7/10 (*Albion Water Limited v Dwr Cymru Cyfyngedig*).

COMMISSION RECOMMENDATION

(2013/396/EU)

of 11 June 2013

on common principles for injunctive and compensatory collective redress mechanisms in the Member States concerning violations of rights granted under Union Law

[4.436]

NOTES

Date of publication in OJ: OJ L201, 26.7.2013, p 60.

THE EUROPEAN COMMISSION,

Having regard to the Treaty on the Functioning of the European Union, and in particular Article 292 thereof,

Whereas:

(1) The Union has set itself the objective of maintaining and developing an area of freedom, security and justice, inter alia, by facilitating access to justice, as well as the objective of ensuring a high level of consumer protection.

(2) The modern economy sometimes creates situations in which a large number of persons can be harmed by the same illegal practices relating to the violation of rights granted under Union law by one or more traders or other persons ('mass harm situation'). They may therefore have cause to seek the cessation of such practices or to claim damages.

(3) The Commission adopted a Green Paper on antitrust damages actions in 2005[1] and a White Paper in 2008, which included policy suggestions on antitrust-specific collective redress.[2] In 2008 the Commission published a Green Paper on consumer collective redress.[3] In 2011 the Commission carried out a public consultation 'Towards a more coherent European approach to collective redress'.[4]

(4) On 2 February 2012 the European Parliament adopted the resolution 'Towards a Coherent European Approach to Collective Redress', in which it called for any proposal in the field of collective redress to take the form of a horizontal framework including a common set of principles providing uniform access to justice via collective redress within the Union and specifically but not exclusively dealing with the infringement of consumer rights. The Parliament also stressed the need to take due account of the legal traditions and legal orders of the individual Member States and enhance the coordination of good practices between Member States.[5]

(5) On 11 June 2013 the Commission issued a Communication 'Towards a European Horizontal Framework for Collective Redress',[6] which took stock of the actions to date and the opinions of stakeholders and of the European Parliament, and presented the Commission's position on some central issues regarding collective redress.

(6) It is a core task of public enforcement to prevent and punish the violations of rights granted under Union law. The possibility for private persons to pursue claims based on violations of such rights supplements public enforcement. Where this Recommendation refers to the violation of rights granted under Union Law, it covers all the situations where the breach of rules established at Union level has caused or is likely to cause prejudice to natural and legal persons.

(7) Amongst those areas where the supplementary private enforcement of rights granted under Union law in the form of collective redress is of value, are consumer protection, competition, environment protection, protection of personal data, financial services legislation and investor protection. The principles set out in this Recommendation should be applied horizontally and equally in those areas but also in any other areas where collective claims for injunctions or damages in respect of violations of the rights granted under Union law would be relevant.

(8) Individual actions, such as the small claims procedure for consumer cases, are the usual tools to address disputes to prevent harm and also to claim for compensation.

(9) In addition to individual redress, different types of collective redress mechanisms have been introduced by all Member States. These measures are intended to prevent and stop unlawful practices as well as to ensure that compensation can be obtained for the detriment caused in mass harm situations. The possibility of joining claims and pursuing them collectively may constitute a better means of access to justice, in particular when the cost of individual actions would deter the harmed individuals from going to court.

(10) The aim of this Recommendation is to facilitate access to justice in relation to violations of rights under Union law and to that end to recommend that all Member States should have collective redress systems at national level that follow the same basic principles throughout the Union, taking into account the legal traditions of the Member States and safeguarding against abuse.

(11) In the area of injunctive relief, the European Parliament and the Council have already adopted Directive 2009/22/EC on injunctions for the protection of consumers' interests.[7] The injunction procedure introduced by the Directive does not, however, enable those who claim to have suffered detriment as a result of an illicit practice to obtain compensation.

(12) Procedures to bring collective claims for compensatory relief have been introduced in some Member States, and to differing extents. However, the existing procedures for bringing claims for collective redress vary widely between the Member States.

(13) This Recommendation puts forward a set of principles relating both to judicial and out-of-court collective redress that should be common across the Union, while respecting the different legal traditions of the Member States. These principles should ensure that fundamental procedural rights of the parties are preserved and should prevent abuse through appropriate safeguards.

(14) This Recommendation addresses both compensatory and – as far as appropriate and pertinent to the particular principles – injunctive collective redress. It is without prejudice to the existing sectorial mechanisms of injunctive relief provided for by Union law.

(15) Collective redress mechanisms should preserve procedural safeguards and guarantees of parties to civil

actions. In order to avoid the development of an abusive litigation culture in mass harm situations, the national collective redress mechanisms should contain the fundamental safeguards identified in this Recommendation. Elements such as punitive damages, intrusive pre-trial discovery procedures and jury awards, most of which are foreign to the legal traditions of most Member States, should be avoided as a general rule.

(16) Alternative dispute resolution procedures can be an efficient way of obtaining redress in mass harm situations. They should always be available alongside, or as a voluntary element of, judicial collective redress.

(17) Legal standing to bring a collective action in the Member States depends on the type of collective redress mechanism. In certain types of collective actions, such as group actions where the action can be brought jointly by those who claim to have suffered harm, the issue of standing is more straightforward than in the context of representative actions, where accordingly the issue of legal standing should be clarified.

(18) In the case of a representative action, the legal standing to bring the representative action should be limited to ad hoc certified entities, designated representative entities that fulfil certain criteria set by law or to public authorities. The representative entity should be required to prove the administrative and financial capacity to be able to represent the interest of claimants in an appropriate manner.

(19) The availability of funding for collective redress litigation should be arranged in such a way that it cannot lead to an abuse of the system or a conflict of interest.

(20) In order to avoid an abuse of the system and in the interest of the sound administration of justice, no judicial collective redress action should be permitted to proceed unless admissibility conditions set out by law are met.

(21) A key role should be given to courts in protecting the rights and interests of all the parties involved in collective redress actions as well as in managing the collective redress actions effectively.

(22) In fields of law where a public authority is empowered to adopt a decision finding that there has been a violation of Union law, it is important to ensure consistency between the final decision concerning that violation and the outcome of the collective redress action. Moreover, in the case of collective actions following a decision by a public authority (follow-on actions), the public interest and the need to avoid abuse can be presumed to have been taken into account already by the public authority as regards the finding of a violation of Union law.

(23) With regard to environmental law, this Recommendation takes account of the provisions of Article 9(3), (4) and (5) of the UN/ECE Convention on Access to Information, Public Participation in Decision-Making and Access to Justice in Environmental Matters ('the Aarhus Convention') which, respectively, encourage wide access to justice in environmental matters, set out criteria that procedures should respect, including criteria that they be timely and not prohibitively expensive, and address information to the public and the consideration of assistance mechanisms.

(24) The Member States should take the necessary measures to implement the principles set out in this Recommendation at the latest two years after its publication.

(25) The Member States should report to the Commission on the implementation of this Recommendation. Based on this reporting, the Commission should monitor and assess the measures taken by Member States.

(26) Within four years after publication of this Recommendation, the Commission should assess if any further action, including legislative measures, is needed, in order to ensure that the objectives of this Recommendation are fully met. The Commission should in particular assess the implementation of this Recommendation and its impact on access to justice, on the right to obtain compensation, on the need prevent abusive litigation and on the functioning of the single market, the economy of the European Union and consumer trust,

NOTES

1 COM(2005) 672, 19.12.2005.

2 COM(2008) 165, 2.4.2008.

3 COM(2008) 794, 27.11.2008.

4 COM(2010) 135 final, 31.3.2010.

5 2011/2089(INI).

6 COM(2013) 401 final.

7 OJ L110, 1.5.2009, p 30.

HAS ADOPTED THIS RECOMMENDATION:

I. PURPOSE AND SUBJECT MATTER

[4.437]

1. The purpose of this Recommendation is to facilitate access to justice, stop illegal practices and enable injured parties to obtain compensation in mass harm situations caused by violations of rights granted under Union law, while ensuring appropriate procedural safeguards to avoid abusive litigation.

2. All Member States should have collective redress mechanisms at national level for both injunctive and compensatory relief, which respect the basic principles set out in this Recommendation. These principles should be common across the Union, while respecting the different legal traditions of the Member States. Member States should ensure that the collective redress procedures are fair, equitable, timely and not prohibitively expensive.

II. DEFINITIONS AND SCOPE

[4.438]

3. For the purposes of this Recommendation:

(a) 'collective redress' means: (i) a legal mechanism that ensures a possibility to claim cessation of illegal behaviour collectively by two or more natural or legal persons or by an entity entitled to bring a representative action (injunctive collective redress); (ii) a legal mechanism that ensures a possibility to claim compensation collectively by two or more natural or legal persons claiming to have been harmed in a mass harm situation or by an entity entitled to bring a representative action (compensatory collective redress);

(b) 'mass harm situation' means a situation where two or more natural or legal persons claim to have suffered harm causing damage resulting from the same illegal activity of one or more natural or legal persons;

(c) 'action for damages' means an action by which a claim for damages is brought before a national court;

(d) 'representative action' means an action which is brought by a representative entity, an ad hoc certified entity or a public authority on behalf and in the name of two or more natural or legal persons who claim to be exposed to the risk of suffering harm or to have been harmed in a mass harm situation whereas those persons are not parties to the proceedings;

(e) 'collective follow-on action' means a collective redress action that is brought after a public authority has adopted a final decision finding that there has been a violation of Union law.

This Recommendation identifies common principles which should apply in all instances of collective redress, and also those specific either to injunctive or to compensatory collective redress.

III. PRINCIPLES COMMON TO INJUNCTIVE AND COMPENSATORY COLLECTIVE REDRESS

STANDING TO BRING A REPRESENTATIVE ACTION

[4.439]

4. The Member States should designate representative entities to bring representative actions on the basis of clearly defined conditions of eligibility. These conditions should include at least the following requirements:

(a) the entity should have a non-profit making character;

(b) there should be a direct relationship between the main objectives of the entity and the rights granted under Union law that are claimed to have been violated in respect of which the action is brought; and

(c) the entity should have sufficient capacity in terms of financial resources, human resources, and legal expertise, to represent multiple claimants acting in their best interest.

5. The Member States should ensure that the designated entity will lose its status if one or more of the conditions are no longer met.

6. The Member States should ensure that representative actions can only be brought by entities which have been officially designated in advance as recommended in point 4 or by entities which have been certified on an ad hoc basis by a Member State's national authorities or courts for a particular representative action.

7. In addition, or as an alternative, the Member States should empower public authorities to bring representative actions.

ADMISSIBILITY

8. The Member States should provide for verification at the earliest possible stage of litigation that cases in which conditions for collective actions are not met, and manifestly unfounded cases, are not continued.

9. To this end, the courts should carry out the necessary examination of their own motion.

INFORMATION ON A COLLECTIVE REDRESS ACTION

10. The Member States should ensure that it is possible for the representative entity or for the group of claimants to disseminate information about a claimed violation of rights granted under Union law and their intention to seek an injunction to stop it as well as about a mass harm situation and their intention to pursue an action for damages in the form of collective redress. The same possibilities for the representative entity, ad hoc certified entity, a public authority or for the group of claimants should be ensured as regards the information on the ongoing compensatory actions.

11. The dissemination methods should take into account the particular circumstances of the mass harm situation concerned, the freedom of expression, the right to information, and the right to protection of the reputation or the company value of a defendant before its responsibility for the alleged violation or harm is established by the final judgement of the court.

12. The dissemination methods are without prejudice to the Union rules on insider dealing and market manipulation.

REIMBURSEMENT OF LEGAL COSTS OF THE WINNING PARTY

13. The Member States should ensure that the party that loses a collective redress action reimburses necessary legal costs borne by the winning party ('loser pays principle'), subject to the conditions provided for in the relevant national law.

FUNDING

14. The claimant party should be required to declare to the court at the outset of the proceedings the origin of the funds that it is going to use to support the legal action.

15. The court should be allowed to stay the proceedings if in the case of use of financial resources provided by a third party:

(a) there is a conflict of interest between the third party and the claimant party and its members;

(b) the third party has insufficient resources in order to meet its financial commitments to the claimant party initiating the collective redress procedure;

(c) the claimant party has insufficient resources to meet any adverse costs should the collective redress procedure fail.

16. The Member States should ensure, that in cases where an action for collective redress is funded by a private third party, it is prohibited for the private third party:

(a) to seek to influence procedural decisions of the claimant party, including on settlements;

(b) to provide financing for a collective action against a defendant who is a competitor of the fund provider or against a defendant on whom the fund provider is dependant;

(c) to charge excessive interest on the funds provided.

CROSS-BORDER CASES

17. The Member States should ensure that where a dispute concerns natural or legal persons from several Member States, a single collective action in a single forum is not prevented by national rules on admissibility or standing of the foreign groups of claimants or the representative entities originating from other national legal systems.

18. Any representative entity that has been officially designated in advance by a Member State to have standing to bring representative actions should be permitted to seize the court in the Member State having jurisdiction to consider the mass harm situation.

IV. SPECIFIC PRINCIPLES RELATING TO INJUNCTIVE COLLECTIVE REDRESS

EXPEDIENT PROCEDURES FOR CLAIMS FOR INJUNCTIVE ORDERS

[4.440]

19. The courts and the competent public authorities should treat claims for injunctive orders requiring cessation of or prohibiting a violation of rights granted under Union law with all due expediency, where appropriate by way of summary proceedings, in order to prevent any or further harm causing damage because of such violation.

EFFICIENT ENFORCEMENT OF INJUNCTIVE ORDERS

20. The Member States should establish appropriate sanctions against the losing defendant with a view to ensuring the effective compliance with the injunctive order, including the payments of a fixed amount for each day's delay or any other amount provided for in national legislation.

V. SPECIFIC PRINCIPLES RELATING TO COMPENSATORY COLLECTIVE REDRESS

CONSTITUTION OF THE CLAIMANT PARTY BY 'OPT-IN' PRINCIPLE

[4.441]

21. The claimant party should be formed on the basis of express consent of the natural or legal persons claiming to have been harmed ('opt-in' principle). Any exception to this principle, by law or by court order, should be duly justified by reasons of sound administration of justice.

22. A member of the claimant party should be free to leave the claimant party at any time before the final judgement is given or the case is otherwise validly settled, subject to the same conditions that apply to withdrawal in individual actions, without being deprived of the possibility to pursue its claims in another form, if this does not undermine the sound administration of justice.

23. Natural or legal persons claiming to have been harmed in the same mass harm situation should be able to join the claimant party at any time before the judgement is given or the case is otherwise validly settled, if this does not undermine the sound administration of justice.

24. The defendant should be informed about the composition of the claimant party and about any changes therein.

COLLECTIVE ALTERNATIVE DISPUTE RESOLUTION AND SETTLEMENTS

25. The Member States should ensure that the parties to a dispute in a mass harm situation are encouraged to settle the dispute about compensation consensually or out-of-court, both at the pre-trial stage and during civil trial, taking also into account the requirements of Directive 2008/52/EC of the European Parliament and of the Council of 21 May 2008 on certain aspects of mediation in civil and commercial matters.[1]

26. The Member States should ensure that judicial collective redress mechanisms are accompanied by appropriate means of collective alternative dispute resolution available to the parties before and throughout the litigation. Use of such means should depend on the consent of the parties involved in the case.

27. Any limitation period applicable to the claims should be suspended during the period from the moment the parties agree to attempt to resolve the dispute by means of an alternative dispute resolution procedure until at least the moment at which one or both parties expressly withdraw from that alternative dispute resolution procedure.

28. The legality of the binding outcome of a collective settlement should be verified by the courts taking into consideration the appropriate protection of interests and rights of all parties involved.

LEGAL REPRESENTATION AND LAWYERS' FEES

29. The Member States should ensure that the lawyers' remuneration and the method by which it is calculated do not create any incentive to litigation that is unnecessary from the point of view of the interest of any of the parties.

30. The Member States should not permit contingency fees which risk creating such an incentive. The Member States that exceptionally allow for contingency fees should provide for appropriate national regulation of those fees in collective redress cases, taking into account in particular the right to full compensation of the members of the claimant party.

PROHIBITION OF PUNITIVE DAMAGES

31. The compensation awarded to natural or legal persons harmed in a mass harm situation should not exceed the compensation that would have been awarded, if the claim had been pursued by means of individual actions. In particular, punitive damages, leading to overcompensation in favour of the claimant party of the damage suffered, should be prohibited.

FUNDING OF COMPENSATORY COLLECTIVE REDRESS

32. The Member States should ensure, that, in addition to the general principles of funding, for cases of private third party funding of compensatory collective redress, it is prohibited to base remuneration given to or interest charged by the fund provider on the amount of the settlement reached or the compensation awarded unless that funding arrangement is regulated by a public authority to ensure the interests of the parties.

COLLECTIVE FOLLOW-ON ACTIONS

33. The Member States should ensure that in fields of law where a public authority is empowered to adopt a decision finding that there has been a violation of Union law, collective redress actions should, as a general rule, only start after any proceedings of the public authority, which were launched before commencement of the private action, have been concluded definitively. If the proceedings of the public authority are launched after the commencement of the collective redress action, the court should avoid giving a decision which would conflict with a decision contemplated by the public authority. To that end, the court may stay the collective redress action until the proceedings of the public authority have been concluded.

34. The Member States should ensure that in the case of follow-on actions, the persons who claim to have been harmed are not prevented from seeking compensation due to the expiry of limitation or prescription periods before the definitive conclusion of the proceedings by the public authority.

NOTES

[1] OJ L136, 24.5.2008, p 3.

VI. GENERAL INFORMATION

REGISTRY OF COLLECTIVE REDRESS ACTIONS

[4.442]

35. The Member States should establish a national registry of collective redress actions.

36. The national registry should be available free of charge to any interested person through electronic means and otherwise. Websites publishing the registries should provide access to comprehensive and objective information on the available methods of obtaining compensation, including out of court methods.

37. The Member States, assisted by the Commission should endeavour to ensure coherence of the information gathered in the registries and their interoperability.

VII. SUPERVISION AND REPORTING

[4.443]

38. The Member States should implement the principles set out in this Recommendation in national collective redress systems by 26 July 2015 at the latest.

39. The Member States should collect reliable annual statistics on the number of out-of-court and judicial collective redress procedures and information about the parties, the subject matter and outcome of the cases.

40. The Member States should communicate the information collected in accordance with point 39 to the Commission on an annual basis and for the first time by 26 July 2016 at the latest.

41. The Commission should assess the implementation of the Recommendation on the basis of practical experience by 26 July 2017 at the latest. In this context, the Commission should in particular evaluate its impact on access to justice, on the right to obtain compensation, on the need to prevent abusive litigation and on the functioning of the single market, on SMEs, the competitiveness of the economy of the European Union and consumer trust. The Commission should assess also whether further measures to consolidate and strengthen the horizontal approach reflected in the Recommendation should be proposed.

FINAL PROVISIONS

42. The Recommendation should be published in the *Official Journal of the European Union.*

EUROPEAN PARLIAMENT AND COUNCIL DIRECTIVE

(2014/104/EU)

of 26 November 2014

on certain rules governing actions for damages under national law for infringements of the competition law provisions of the Member States and of the European Union

(Text with EEA relevance)

[4.444]

NOTES

Date of publication in OJ: OJ L349, 5.12.2014, p 1.

Application of EU Directives in the UK post IP completion day: the European Union (Withdrawal) Act 2018, s 3 provides for the incorporation of "direct EU legislation" into domestic law. "Direct EU legislation" is generally defined as EU Regulations, EU Decisions and EU tertiary legislation (for the full definition, see s 3 of the 2018 Act at **[7.5]**). EU Directives, therefore, are not "direct EU legislation" and, as such, do not form part of UK law post IP completion day. Note that "EU-derived domestic legislation" (UK legislation made under the powers conferred by s 2(2) of, or Sch 2, para 1A to, the European Communities Act 1972) is saved despite the repeal of the 1972 Act both during, and after, the implementation period (see ss 1B and 2 of the 2018 Act respectively at **[7.3]** and **[7.4]**). This Directive was implemented in the UK by the Claims in respect of Loss or Damage arising from Competition Infringement (Competition Act 1998 and Other Enactments (Amendment)) Regulations 2017, SI 2017/385, which amended the Competition Act 1998 and made other consequential amendments.

THE EUROPEAN PARLIAMENT AND THE COUNCIL OF THE EUROPEAN UNION,

Having regard to the Treaty on the Functioning of the European Union, and in particular Articles 103 and 114 thereof, Having regard to the proposal from the European Commission,

After transmission of the draft legislative act to the national parliaments,

Having regard to the opinion of the European Economic and Social Committee,[1] Acting in accordance with the ordinary legislative procedure,[2]

Whereas:

(1) Articles 101 and 102 of the Treaty on the Functioning of the European Union (TFEU) are a matter of public policy and should be applied effectively throughout the Union in order to ensure that competition in the internal market is not distorted.

(2) The public enforcement of Articles 101 and 102 TFEU is carried out by the Commission using the powers provided by Council Regulation (EC) No 1/2003.[3] Upon the entry into force of the Treaty of Lisbon on 1 December 2009, Articles 81 and 82 of the Treaty establishing the European Community became Articles 101 and 102 TFEU, and they remain identical in substance. Public enforcement is also carried out by national competition authorities, which may take the decisions listed in Article 5 of Regulation (EC) No 1/2003. In accordance with that Regulation, Member States should be able to designate administrative as well as judicial authorities to apply Articles 101 and 102 TFEU as public enforcers and to carry out the various functions conferred upon competition authorities by that Regulation.

(3) Articles 101 and 102 TFEU produce direct effects in relations between individuals and create, for the individuals concerned, rights and obligations which national courts must enforce. National courts thus have an equally essential part to play in applying the competition rules (private enforcement). When ruling on disputes between private individuals, they protect subjective rights under Union law, for example by awarding damages to the victims of infringements. The full effectiveness of Articles 101 and 102 TFEU, and in particular the practical effect of the prohibitions laid down therein, requires that anyone — be they an individual, including consumers and undertakings, or a public authority — can claim compensation before national courts for the harm caused to them by an infringement of those provisions. The right to compensation in Union law applies equally to infringements of Articles 101 and 102 TFEU by public undertakings and by undertakings entrusted with special or exclusive rights by Member States within the meaning of Article 106 TFEU.

(4) The right in Union law to compensation for harm resulting from infringements of Union and national competition law requires each Member State to have procedural rules ensuring the effective exercise of that right. The need for effective procedural remedies also follows from the right to effective judicial protection as laid down in the second subparagraph of Article 19(1) of the Treaty on European Union (TEU) and in the first paragraph of Article 47 of the Charter of Fundamental Rights of the European Union. Member States should ensure effective legal protection in the fields covered by Union law.

(5) Actions for damages are only one element of an effective system of private enforcement of infringements of competition law and are complemented by alternative avenues of redress, such as consensual dispute resolution and public enforcement decisions that give parties an incentive to provide compensation.

(6) To ensure effective private enforcement actions under civil law and effective public enforcement by competition authorities, both tools are required to interact to ensure maximum effectiveness of the competition rules. It is necessary to regulate the coordination of those two forms of enforcement in a coherent manner, for instance in relation to the arrangements for access to documents held by competition authorities. Such coordination at Union level will also avoid the divergence of applicable rules, which could jeopardise the proper functioning of the internal market.

(7) In accordance with Article 26(2) TFEU, the internal market comprises an area without internal frontiers in which the free movement of goods, persons, services and capital is ensured. There are marked differences between the rules in the Member States governing actions for damages for infringements of Union or national competition law. Those differences lead to uncertainty concerning the conditions under which injured parties can exercise the right to compensation they derive from the TFEU and affect the substantive effectiveness of such right. As injured parties often choose their Member State of establishment as the forum in which to claim damages, the discrepancies between the national rules lead to an uneven playing field as regards actions for damages and may thus affect competition on the markets on which those injured parties, as well as the infringing undertakings, operate.

(8) Undertakings established and operating in various Member States are subject to differing procedural rules that significantly affect the extent to which they can be held liable for infringements of competition law. This uneven enforcement of the right to compensation in Union law may result not only in a competitive advantage for some undertakings which have infringed Article 101 or 102 TFEU but also in a disincentive to the exercise of the rights of establishment and provision of goods or services in those

Member States where the right to compensation is enforced more effectively. As the differences in the liability regimes applicable in the Member States may negatively affect both competition and the proper functioning of the internal market, it is appropriate to base this Directive on the dual legal bases of Articles 103 and 114 TFEU.

(9) It is necessary, bearing in mind that large-scale infringements of competition law often have a cross-border element, to ensure a more level playing field for undertakings operating in the internal market and to improve the conditions for consumers to exercise the rights that they derive from the internal market. It is appropriate to increase legal certainty and to reduce the differences between the Member States as to the national rules governing actions for damages for infringements of both Union competition law and national competition law where that is applied in parallel with Union competition law. An approximation of those rules will help to prevent the increase of differences between the Member States' rules governing actions for damages in competition cases.

(10) Article 3(1) of Regulation (EC) No 1/2003 provides that '[w]here the competition authorities of the Member States or national courts apply national competition law to agreements, decisions by associations of undertakings or concerted practices within the meaning of Article [101(1) TFEU] which may affect trade between Member States within the meaning of that provision, they shall also apply Article [101 TFEU] to such agreements, decisions or concerted practices. Where the competition authorities of the Member States or national courts apply national competition law to any abuse prohibited by Article [102 TFEU], they shall also apply Article [102 TFEU].' In the interests of the proper functioning of the internal market and with a view to greater legal certainty and a more level playing field for undertakings and consumers, it is appropriate that the scope of this Directive extend to actions for damages based on the infringement of national competition law where it is applied pursuant to Article 3(1) of Regulation (EC) No 1/2003. Applying differing rules on civil liability in respect of infringements of Article 101 or 102 TFEU and in respect of infringements of rules of national competition law which must be applied in the same cases in parallel to Union competition law would otherwise adversely affect the position of claimants in the same case and the scope of their claims, and would constitute an obstacle to the proper functioning of the internal market. This Directive should not affect actions for damages in respect of infringements of national competition law which do not affect trade between Member States within the meaning of Article 101 or 102 TFEU.

(11) In the absence of Union law, actions for damages are governed by the national rules and procedures of the Member States. According to the case-law of the Court of Justice of the European Union (Court of Justice), any person can claim compensation for harm suffered where there is a causal relationship between that harm and an infringement of competition law. All national rules governing the exercise of the right to compensation for harm resulting from an infringement of Article 101 or 102 TFEU, including those concerning aspects not dealt with in this Directive such as the notion of causal relationship between the infringement and the harm, must observe the principles of effectiveness and equivalence. This means that they should not be formulated or applied in a way that makes it excessively difficult or practically impossible to exercise the right to compensation guaranteed by the TFEU or less favourably than those applicable to similar domestic actions. Where Member States provide other conditions for compensation under national law, such as imputability, adequacy or culpability, they should be able to maintain such conditions in so far as they comply with the case-law of the Court of Justice, the principles of effectiveness and equivalence, and this Directive.

(12) This Directive reaffirms the *acquis communautaire* on the right to compensation for harm caused by infringements of Union competition law, particularly regarding standing and the definition of damage, as stated in the case-law of the Court of Justice, and does not pre-empt any further development thereof. Anyone who has suffered harm caused by such an infringement can claim compensation for actual loss (*damnum emergens*), for gain of which that person has been deprived (loss of profit or *lucrum cessans*), plus interest, irrespective of whether those categories are established separately or in combination in national law. The payment of interest is an essential component of compensation to make good the damage sustained by taking into account the effluxion of time and should be due from the time when the harm occurred until the time when compensation is paid, without prejudice to the qualification of such interest as compensatory or default interest under national law and to whether effluxion of time is taken into account as a separate category (interest) or as a constituent part of actual loss or loss of profit. It is incumbent on the Member States to lay down the rules to be applied for that purpose.

(13) The right to compensation is recognised for any natural or legal person — consumers, undertakings and public authorities alike — irrespective of the existence of a direct contractual relationship with the infringing undertaking, and regardless of whether or not there has been a prior finding of an infringement by a competition authority. This Directive should not require Member States to introduce collective redress mechanisms for the enforcement of Articles 101 and 102 TFEU. Without prejudice to compensation for loss of opportunity, full compensation under this Directive should not lead to overcompensation, whether by means of punitive, multiple or other damages.

(14) Actions for damages for infringements of Union or national competition law typically require a complex factual and economic analysis. The evidence necessary to prove a claim for damages is often held exclusively by the opposing party or by third parties, and is not sufficiently known by, or accessible to, the claimant. In such circumstances, strict legal requirements for claimants to assert in detail all the facts of their case at the beginning of an action and to proffer precisely specified items of supporting evidence can unduly impede the effective exercise of the right to compensation guaranteed by the TFEU.

(15) Evidence is an important element for bringing actions for damages for infringement of Union or national competition law. However, as competition law litigation is characterised by an information asymmetry, it is appropriate to ensure that claimants are afforded the right to obtain the disclosure of

evidence relevant to their claim, without it being necessary for them to specify individual items of evidence. In order to ensure equality of arms, those means should also be available to defendants in actions for damages, so that they can request the disclosure of evidence by those claimants. National courts should also be able to order that evidence be disclosed by third parties, including public authorities. Where a national court wishes to order disclosure of evidence by the Commission, the principle in Article 4(3) TEU of sincere cooperation between the Union and the Member States and Article 15(1) of Regulation (EC) No 1/2003 as regards requests for information apply. Where national courts order public authorities to disclose evidence, the principles of legal and administrative cooperation under Union or national law apply.

(16) National courts should be able, under their strict control, especially as regards the necessity and proportionality of disclosure measures, to order the disclosure of specified items of evidence or categories of evidence upon request of a party. It follows from the requirement of proportionality that disclosure can be ordered only where a claimant has made a plausible assertion, on the basis of facts which are reasonably available to that claimant, that the claimant has suffered harm that was caused by the defendant. Where a request for disclosure aims to obtain a category of evidence, that category should be identified by reference to common features of its constitutive elements such as the nature, object or content of the documents the disclosure of which is requested, the time during which they were drawn up, or other criteria, provided that the evidence falling within the category is relevant within the meaning of this Directive. Such categories should be defined as precisely and narrowly as possible on the basis of reasonably available facts.

(17) Where a court in one Member State requests a competent court in another Member State to take evidence or requests that evidence be taken directly in another Member State, the provisions of Council Regulation (EC) No 1206/2001[4] apply.

(18) While relevant evidence containing business secrets or otherwise confidential information should, in principle, be available in actions for damages, such confidential information needs to be protected appropriately. National courts should therefore have at their disposal a range of measures to protect such confidential information from being disclosed during the proceedings. Those measures could include the possibility of redacting sensitive passages in documents, conducting hearings in camera, restricting the persons allowed to see the evidence, and instructing experts to produce summaries of the information in an aggregated or otherwise non-confidential form. Measures protecting business secrets and other confidential information should, nevertheless, not impede the exercise of the right to compensation.

(19) This Directive affects neither the possibility under the laws of the Member States to appeal disclosure orders, nor the conditions for bringing such appeals.

(20) Regulation (EC) No 1049/2001 of the European Parliament and of the Council[5] governs public access to European Parliament, Council and Commission documents, and is designed to confer on the public as wide a right of access as possible to documents of those institutions. That right is nonetheless subject to certain limits based on reasons of public or private interest. It follows that the system of exceptions laid down in Article 4 of that Regulation is based on a balancing of the opposing interests in a given situation, namely, the interests which would be favoured by the disclosure of the documents in question and those which would be jeopardised by such disclosure. This Directive should be without prejudice to such rules and practices under Regulation (EC) No 1049/2001.

(21) The effectiveness and consistency of the application of Articles 101 and 102 TFEU by the Commission and the national competition authorities require a common approach across the Union on the disclosure of evidence that is included in the file of a competition authority. Disclosure of evidence should not unduly detract from the effectiveness of the enforcement of competition law by a competition authority. This Directive does not cover the disclosure of internal documents of, or correspondence between, competition authorities.

(22) In order to ensure the effective protection of the right to compensation, it is not necessary that every document relating to proceedings under Article 101 or 102 TFEU be disclosed to a claimant merely on the grounds of the claimant's intended action for damages since it is highly unlikely that the action for damages will need to be based on all the evidence in the file relating to those proceedings.

(23) The requirement of proportionality should be carefully assessed when disclosure risks unravelling the investigation strategy of a competition authority by revealing which documents are part of the file or risks having a negative effect on the way in which undertakings cooperate with the competition authorities. Particular attention should be paid to preventing 'fishing expeditions', i.e. non-specific or overly broad searches for information that is unlikely to be of relevance for the parties to the proceedings. Disclosure requests should therefore not be deemed to be proportionate where they refer to the generic disclosure of documents in the file of a competition authority relating to a certain case, or the generic disclosure of documents submitted by a party in the context of a particular case. Such wide disclosure requests would not be compatible with the requesting party's duty to specify the items of evidence or the categories of evidence as precisely and narrowly as possible.

(24) This Directive does not affect the right of courts to consider, under Union or national law, the interests of the effective public enforcement of competition law when ordering the disclosure of any type of evidence with the exception of leniency statements and settlement submissions.

(25) An exemption should apply in respect of any disclosure that, if granted, would unduly interfere with an ongoing investigation by a competition authority concerning an infringement of Union or national competition law. Information that was prepared by a competition authority in the course of its proceedings for the enforcement of Union or national competition law and sent to the parties to those proceedings (such as a 'Statement of Objections') or prepared by a party thereto (such as replies to

requests for information of the competition authority or witness statements) should therefore be disclosable in actions for damages only after the competition authority has closed its proceedings, for instance by adopting a decision under Article 5 or under Chapter III of Regulation (EC) No 1/2003, with the exception of decisions on interim measures.

(26) Leniency programmes and settlement procedures are important tools for the public enforcement of Union competition law as they contribute to the detection and efficient prosecution of, and the imposition of penalties for, the most serious infringements of competition law. Furthermore, as many decisions of competition authorities in cartel cases are based on a leniency application, and damages actions in cartel cases generally follow on from those decisions, leniency programmes are also important for the effectiveness of actions for damages in cartel cases. Undertakings might be deterred from cooperating with competition authorities under leniency programmes and settlement procedures if self-incriminating statements such as leniency statements and settlement submissions, which are produced for the sole purpose of cooperating with the competition authorities, were to be disclosed. Such disclosure would pose a risk of exposing cooperating undertakings or their managing staff to civil or criminal liability under conditions worse than those of co-infringers not cooperating with the competition authorities. To ensure undertakings' continued willingness to approach competition authorities voluntarily with leniency statements or settlement submissions, such documents should be exempted from the disclosure of evidence. That exemption should also apply to verbatim quotations from leniency statements or settlement submissions included in other documents. Those limitations on the disclosure of evidence should not prevent competition authorities from publishing their decisions in accordance with the applicable Union or national law. In order to ensure that that exemption does not unduly interfere with injured parties' rights to compensation, it should be limited to those voluntary and self-incriminating leniency statements and settlement submissions.

(27) The rules in this Directive on the disclosure of documents other than leniency statements and settlement submissions ensure that injured parties retain sufficient alternative means by which to obtain access to the relevant evidence that they need in order to prepare their actions for damages. National courts should themselves be able, upon request by a claimant, to access documents in respect of which the exemption is invoked in order to verify whether the contents thereof fall outside the definitions of leniency statements and settlement submissions laid down in this Directive. Any content falling outside those definitions should be disclosable under the relevant conditions.

(28) National courts should be able, at any time, to order, in the context of an action for damages, the disclosure of evidence that exists independently of the proceedings of a competition authority ('pre-existing information').

(29) The disclosure of evidence should be ordered from a competition authority only when that evidence cannot reasonably be obtained from another party or from a third party.

(30) Pursuant to Article 15(3) of Regulation (EC) No 1/2003, competition authorities, acting upon their own initiative, can submit written observations to national courts on issues relating to the application of Article 101 or 102 TFEU. In order to preserve the contribution made by public enforcement to the application of those Articles, competition authorities should likewise be able, acting upon their own initiative, to submit their observations to a national court for the purpose of assessing the proportionality of a disclosure of evidence included in the authorities' files, in light of the impact that such disclosure would have on the effectiveness of the public enforcement of competition law. Member States should be able to set up a system whereby a competition authority is informed of requests for disclosure of information when the person requesting disclosure or the person from whom disclosure is sought is involved in that competition authority's investigation into the alleged infringement, without prejudice to national law providing for ex parte proceedings.

(31) Any natural or legal person that obtains evidence through access to the file of a competition authority should be able to use that evidence for the purposes of an action for damages to which it is a party. Such use should also be allowed on the part of any natural or legal person that succeeded in its rights and obligations, including through the acquisition of its claim. Where the evidence was obtained by a legal person forming part of a corporate group constituting one undertaking for the application of Articles 101 and 102 TFEU, other legal persons belonging to the same undertaking should also be able to use that evidence.

(32) However, the use of evidence obtained through access to the file of a competition authority should not unduly detract from the effective enforcement of competition law by a competition authority. In order to ensure that the limitations on disclosure laid down in this Directive are not undermined, the use of evidence of the types referred to in recitals 24 and 25 which is obtained solely through access to the file of a competition authority should be limited under the same circumstances. The limitation should take the form of inadmissibility in actions for damages or the form of any other protection under applicable national rules capable of ensuring the full effect of the limits on the disclosure of those types of evidence. Moreover, evidence obtained from a competition authority should not become an object of trade. The possibility of using evidence that was obtained solely through access to the file of a competition authority should therefore be limited to the natural or legal person that was originally granted access and to its legal successors. That limitation to avoid trading of evidence does not, however, prevent a national court from ordering the disclosure of that evidence under the conditions provided for in this Directive.

(33) The fact that a claim for damages is initiated, or that an investigation by a competition authority is started, entails a risk that persons concerned may destroy or hide evidence that would be useful in substantiating an injured party's claim for damages. To prevent the destruction of relevant evidence and to ensure that court orders as to disclosure are complied with, national courts should be able to impose sufficiently deterrent penalties. In so far as parties to the proceedings are concerned, the risk of adverse

inferences being drawn in the proceedings for damages can be a particularly effective penalty, and can help avoid delays. Penalties should also be available for non-compliance with obligations to protect confidential information and for the abusive use of information obtained through disclosure. Similarly, penalties should be available if information obtained through access to the file of a competition authority is used abusively in actions for damages.

(34) Ensuring the effective and consistent application of Articles 101 and 102 TFEU by the Commission and the national competition authorities necessitates a common approach across the Union on the effect of national competition authorities' final infringement decisions on subsequent actions for damages. Such decisions are adopted only after the Commission has been informed of the decision envisaged or, in the absence thereof, of any other document indicating the proposed course of action pursuant to Article 11(4) of Regulation (EC) No 1/2003, and if the Commission has not relieved the national competition authority of its competence by initiating proceedings pursuant to Article 11(6) of that Regulation. The Commission should ensure the consistent application of Union competition law by providing, bilaterally and within the framework of the European Competition Network, guidance to the national competition authorities. To enhance legal certainty, to avoid inconsistency in the application of Articles 101 and 102 TFEU, to increase the effectiveness and procedural efficiency of actions for damages and to foster the functioning of the internal market for undertakings and consumers, the finding of an infringement of Article 101 or 102 TFEU in a final decision by a national competition authority or a review court should not be relitigated in subsequent actions for damages. Therefore, such a finding should be deemed to be irrefutably established in actions for damages brought in the Member State of the national competition authority or review court relating to that infringement. The effect of the finding should, however, cover only the nature of the infringement and its material, personal, temporal and territorial scope as determined by the competition authority or review court in the exercise of its jurisdiction. Where a decision has found that provisions of national competition law are infringed in cases where Union and national competition law are applied in the same case and in parallel, that infringement should also be deemed to be irrefutably established.

(35) Where an action for damages is brought in a Member State other than the Member State of a national competition authority or a review court that found the infringement of Article 101 or 102 TFEU to which the action relates, it should be possible to present that finding in a final decision by the national competition authority or the review court to a national court as at least prima facie evidence of the fact that an infringement of competition law has occurred. The finding can be assessed as appropriate, along with any other evidence adduced by the parties. The effects of decisions by national competition authorities and review courts finding an infringement of the competition rules are without prejudice to the rights and obligations of national courts under Article 267 TFEU.

(36) National rules on the beginning, duration, suspension or interruption of limitation periods should not unduly hamper the bringing of actions for damages. This is particularly important in respect of actions that build upon a finding by a competition authority or a review court of an infringement. To that end, it should be possible to bring an action for damages after proceedings by a competition authority, with a view to enforcing national and Union competition law. The limitation period should not begin to run before the infringement ceases and before a claimant knows, or can reasonably be expected to know, the behaviour constituting the infringement, the fact that the infringement caused the claimant harm and the identity of the infringer. Member States should be able to maintain or introduce absolute limitation periods that are of general application, provided that the duration of such absolute limitation periods does not render practically impossible or excessively difficult the exercise of the right to full compensation.

(37) Where several undertakings infringe the competition rules jointly, as in the case of a cartel, it is appropriate to make provision for those co-infringers to be held jointly and severally liable for the entire harm caused by the infringement. A co-infringer should have the right to obtain a contribution from other co-infringers if it has paid more compensation than its share. The determination of that share as the relative responsibility of a given infringer, and the relevant criteria such as turnover, market share, or role in the cartel, is a matter for the applicable national law, while respecting the principles of effectiveness and equivalence.

(38) Undertakings which cooperate with competition authorities under a leniency programme play a key role in exposing secret cartel infringements and in bringing them to an end, thereby often mitigating the harm which could have been caused had the infringement continued. It is therefore appropriate to make provision for undertakings which have received immunity from fines from a competition authority under a leniency programme to be protected from undue exposure to damages claims, bearing in mind that the decision of the competition authority finding the infringement may become final for the immunity recipient before it becomes final for other undertakings which have not received immunity, thus potentially making the immunity recipient the preferential target of litigation. It is therefore appropriate that the immunity recipient be relieved in principle from joint and several liability for the entire harm and that any contribution it must make vis-à-vis co-infringers not exceed the amount of harm caused to its own direct or indirect purchasers or, in the case of a buying cartel, its direct or indirect providers. To the extent that a cartel has caused harm to those other than the customers or providers of the infringers, the contribution of the immunity recipient should not exceed its relative responsibility for the harm caused by the cartel. That share should be determined in accordance with the same rules used to determine the contributions between infringers. The immunity recipient should remain fully liable to the injured parties other than its direct or indirect purchasers or providers only where they are unable to obtain full compensation from the other infringers.

(39) Harm in the form of actual loss can result from the price difference between what was actually paid and what would otherwise have been paid in the absence of the infringement. When an injured party has reduced its actual loss by passing it on, entirely or in part, to its own purchasers, the loss which has been passed on no longer constitutes harm for which the party that passed it on needs to be compensated. It is therefore in principle appropriate to allow an infringer to invoke the passing-on of actual loss as a defence against a claim for damages. It is appropriate to provide that the infringer, in so far as it invokes the passing-on defence, must prove the existence and extent of pass-on of the overcharge. This burden of proof should not affect the possibility for the infringer to use evidence other than that in its possession, such as evidence already acquired in the proceedings or evidence held by other parties or third parties.

(40) In situations where the passing-on resulted in reduced sales and thus harm in the form of a loss of profit, the right to claim compensation for such loss of profit should remain unaffected.

(41) Depending on the conditions under which undertakings are operating, it may be commercial practice to pass on price increases down the supply chain. Consumers or undertakings to whom actual loss has thus been passed on have suffered harm caused by an infringement of Union or national competition law. While such harm should be compensated for by the infringer, it may be particularly difficult for consumers or undertakings that did not themselves make any purchase from the infringer to prove the extent of that harm. It is therefore appropriate to provide that, where the existence of a claim for damages or the amount of damages to be awarded depends on whether or to what degree an overcharge paid by a direct purchaser from the infringer has been passed on to an indirect purchaser, the latter is regarded as having proven that an overcharge paid by that direct purchaser has been passed on to its level where it is able to show prima facie that such passing-on has occurred. This rebuttable presumption applies unless the infringer can credibly demonstrate to the satisfaction of the court that the actual loss has not or not entirely been passed on to the indirect purchaser. It is furthermore appropriate to define under what conditions the indirect purchaser is to be regarded as having established such prima facie proof. As regards the quantification of passing-on, national courts should have the power to estimate which share of the overcharge has been passed on to the level of indirect purchasers in disputes pending before them.

(42) The Commission should issue clear, simple and comprehensive guidelines for national courts on how to estimate the share of the overcharge passed on to indirect purchasers.

(43) Infringements of competition law often concern the conditions and the price under which goods or services are sold, and lead to an overcharge and other harm for the customers of the infringers. The infringement may also concern supplies to the infringer (for example in the case of a buyers' cartel). In such cases, the actual loss could result from a lower price paid by infringers to their suppliers. This Directive and in particular the rules on passing-on should apply accordingly to those cases.

(44) Actions for damages can be brought both by those who purchased goods or services from the infringer and by purchasers further down the supply chain. In the interest of consistency between judgments resulting from related proceedings and hence to avoid the harm caused by the infringement of Union or national competition law not being fully compensated or the infringer being required to pay damages to compensate for harm that has not been suffered, national courts should have the power to estimate the proportion of any overcharge which was suffered by the direct or indirect purchasers in disputes pending before them. In this context, national courts should be able to take due account, by procedural or substantive means available under Union and national law, of any related action and of the resulting judgment, particularly where it finds that passing-on has been proven. National courts should have at their disposal appropriate procedural means, such as joinder of claims, to ensure that compensation for actual loss paid at any level of the supply chain does not exceed the overcharge harm caused at that level. Such means should also be available in cross-border cases. This possibility to take due account of judgments should be without prejudice to the fundamental rights of the defence and the rights to an effective remedy and a fair trial of those who were not parties to the judicial proceedings, and without prejudice to the rules on the evidenciary value of judgments rendered in that context. It is possible for actions pending before the courts of different Member States to be considered as related within the meaning of Article 30 of Regulation (EU) No 1215/2012 of the European Parliament and of the Council.[6] Under that Article, national courts other than that first seized may stay proceedings or, under certain circumstances, may decline jurisdiction. This Directive is without prejudice to the rights and obligations of national courts under that Regulation.

(45) An injured party who has proven having suffered harm as a result of a competition law infringement still needs to prove the extent of the harm in order to obtain damages. Quantifying harm in competition law cases is a very fact-intensive process and may require the application of complex economic models. This is often very costly, and claimants have difficulties in obtaining the data necessary to substantiate their claims. The quantification of harm in competition law cases can thus constitute a substantial barrier preventing effective claims for compensation.

(46) In the absence of Union rules on the quantification of harm caused by a competition law infringement, it is for the domestic legal system of each Member State to determine its own rules on quantifying harm, and for the Member States and for the national courts to determine what requirements the claimant has to meet when proving the amount of the harm suffered, the methods that can be used in quantifying the amount, and the consequences of not being able to fully meet those requirements. However, the requirements of national law regarding the quantification of harm in competition law cases should not be less favourable than those governing similar domestic actions (principle of equivalence), nor should they render the exercise of the Union right to damages practically impossible or excessively difficult (principle of effectiveness). Regard should be had to any information asymmetries between the parties and to the fact that quantifying the harm means assessing how the market in question would have

evolved had there been no infringement. This assessment implies a comparison with a situation which is by definition hypothetical and can thus never be made with complete accuracy. It is therefore appropriate to ensure that national courts have the power to estimate the amount of the harm caused by the competition law infringement. Member States should ensure that, where requested, national competition authorities may provide guidance on quantum. In order to ensure coherence and predictability, the Commission should provide general guidance at Union level.

(47) To remedy the information asymmetry and some of the difficulties associated with quantifying harm in competition law cases, and to ensure the effectiveness of claims for damages, it is appropriate to presume that cartel infringements result in harm, in particular via an effect on prices. Depending on the facts of the case, cartels result in a rise in prices, or prevent a lowering of prices which would otherwise have occurred but for the cartel. This presumption should not cover the concrete amount of harm. Infringers should be allowed to rebut the presumption. It is appropriate to limit this rebuttable presumption to cartels, given their secret nature, which increases the information asymmetry and makes it more difficult for claimants to obtain the evidence necessary to prove the harm.

(48) Achieving a 'once-and-for-all' settlement for defendants is desirable in order to reduce uncertainty for infringers and injured parties. Therefore, infringers and injured parties should be encouraged to agree on compensating for the harm caused by a competition law infringement through consensual dispute resolution mechanisms, such as out-of-court settlements (including those where a judge can declare a settlement binding), arbitration, mediation or conciliation. Such consensual dispute resolution should cover as many injured parties and infringers as legally possible. The provisions in this Directive on consensual dispute resolution are therefore meant to facilitate the use of such mechanisms and increase their effectiveness.

(49) Limitation periods for bringing an action for damages could be such that they prevent injured parties and infringers from having sufficient time to come to an agreement on the compensation to be paid. In order to provide both sides with a genuine opportunity to engage in consensual dispute resolution before bringing proceedings before national courts, limitation periods need to be suspended for the duration of the consensual dispute resolution process.

(50) Furthermore, when parties decide to engage in consensual dispute resolution after an action for damages for the same claim has been brought before a national court, that court should be able to suspend the proceedings before it for the duration of the consensual dispute resolution process. When considering whether to suspend the proceedings, the national court should take into account the advantages of an expeditious procedure.

(51) To encourage consensual settlements, an infringer that pays damages through consensual dispute resolution should not be placed in a worse position vis-à-vis its co-infringers than it would otherwise be without the consensual settlement. That might happen if a settling infringer, even after a consensual settlement, continued to be fully jointly and severally liable for the harm caused by the infringement. A settling infringer should in principle therefore not contribute to its non-settling co-infringers when the latter have paid damages to an injured party with whom the first infringer had previously settled. The corollary to this non-contribution rule is that the claim of the injured party should be reduced by the settling infringer's share of the harm caused to it, regardless of whether the amount of the settlement equals or is different from the relative share of the harm that the settling co-infringer inflicted upon the settling injured party. That relative share should be determined in accordance with the rules otherwise used to determine the contributions among infringers. Without such a reduction, non-settling infringers would be unduly affected by settlements to which they were not a party. However, in order to ensure the right to full compensation, settling co-infringers should still have to pay damages where that is the only possibility for the settling injured party to obtain compensation for the remaining claim. The remaining claim refers to the claim of the settling injured party reduced by the settling co-infringer's share of the harm that the infringement inflicted upon the settling injured party. The latter possibility to claim damages from the settling co-infringer exists unless it is expressly excluded under the terms of the consensual settlement.

(52) Situations should be avoided in which settling co-infringers, by paying contribution to non-settling co-infringers for damages they paid to non-settling injured parties, pay a total amount of compensation exceeding their relative responsibility for the harm caused by the infringement. Therefore, when settling co-infringers are asked to contribute to damages subsequently paid by non-settling co-infringers to non-settling injured parties, national courts should take account of the damages already paid under the consensual settlement, bearing in mind that not all co-infringers are necessarily equally involved in the full substantive, temporal and geographical scope of the infringement.

(53) This Directive respects the fundamental rights and observes the principles recognised in the Charter of Fundamental Rights of the European Union.

(54) Since the objectives of this Directive, namely to establish rules concerning actions for damages for infringements of Union competition law in order to ensure the full effect of Articles 101 and 102 TFEU, and the proper functioning of the internal market for undertakings and consumers, cannot be sufficiently achieved by the Member States, but can rather, by reason of the requisite effectiveness and consistency in the application of Articles 101 and 102 TFEU, be better achieved at Union level, the Union may adopt measures, in accordance with the principle of subsidiarity as set out in Article 5 TEU. In accordance with the principle of proportionality, as set out in that Article, this Directive does not go beyond what is necessary in order to achieve those objectives.

(55) In accordance with the Joint Political Declaration of 28 September 2011 of Member States and the Commission on explanatory documents,[7] Member States have undertaken to accompany, in justified cases, the notification of their transposition measures with one or more documents explaining the

relationship between the components of a directive and the corresponding parts of national transposition instruments. With regard to this Directive, the legislator considers the transmission of such documents to be justified.

(56) It is appropriate to provide rules for the temporal application of this Directive,

NOTES

1 OJ C67, 6.3.2014, p 83.

2 Position of the European Parliament of 17 April 2014 (not yet published in the Official Journal) and decision of the Council of 10 November 2014.

3 Council Regulation (EC) No 1/2003 of 16 December 2002 on the implementation of the rules of competition laid down in Articles 81 and 82 of the Treaty (OJ L1, 4.1.2003, p 1).

4 Council Regulation (EC) No 1206/2001 of 28 May 2001 on cooperation between the courts of the Member States in the taking of evidence in civil or commercial matters (OJ L174, 27.6.2001, p 1).

5 Regulation (EC) No 1049/2001 of the European Parliament and of the Council of 30 May 2001 regarding public access to European Parliament, Council and Commission documents (OJ L145, 31.5.2001, p 43).

6 Regulation (EU) No 1215/2012 of the European Parliament and of the Council of 12 December 2012 on jurisdiction and the recognition and enforcement of judgments in civil and commercial matters (OJ L351, 20.12.2012, p 1).

7 OJ C369, 17.12.2011, p 14.

HAVE ADOPTED THIS DIRECTIVE:

CHAPTER I SUBJECT MATTER, SCOPE AND DEFINITIONS

[4.445]

Article 1 Subject matter and scope

1. This Directive sets out certain rules necessary to ensure that anyone who has suffered harm caused by an infringement of competition law by an undertaking or by an association of undertakings can effectively exercise the right to claim full compensation for that harm from that undertaking or association. It sets out rules fostering undistorted competition in the internal market and removing obstacles to its proper functioning, by ensuring equivalent protection throughout the Union for anyone who has suffered such harm.

2. This Directive sets out rules coordinating the enforcement of the competition rules by competition authorities and the enforcement of those rules in damages actions before national courts.

[4.446]

Article 2 Definitions

For the purposes of this Directive, the following definitions apply:

(1) 'infringement of competition law' means an infringement of Article 101 or 102 TFEU, or of national competition law;

(2) 'infringer' means an undertaking or association of undertakings which has committed an infringement of competition law;

(3) 'national competition law' means provisions of national law that predominantly pursue the same objective as Articles 101 and 102 TFEU and that are applied to the same case and in parallel to Union competition law pursuant to Article 3(1) of Regulation (EC) No 1/2003, excluding provisions of national law which impose criminal penalties on natural persons, except to the extent that such criminal penalties are the means whereby competition rules applying to undertakings are enforced;

(4) 'action for damages' means an action under national law by which a claim for damages is brought before a national court by an alleged injured party, or by someone acting on behalf of one or more alleged injured parties where Union or national law provides for that possibility, or by a natural or legal person that succeeded in the right of the alleged injured party, including the person that acquired the claim;

(5) 'claim for damages' means a claim for compensation for harm caused by an infringement of competition law;

(6) injured party' means a person that has suffered harm caused by an infringement of competition law;

(7) 'national competition authority' means an authority designated by a Member State pursuant to Article 35 of Regulation (EC) No 1/2003, as being responsible for the application of Articles 101 and 102 TFEU;

(8) 'competition authority' means the Commission or a national competition authority or both, as the context may require;

(9) 'national court' means a court or tribunal of a Member State within the meaning of Article 267 TFEU;

(10) 'review court' means a national court that is empowered by ordinary means of appeal to review decisions of a national competition authority or to review judgments pronouncing on those decisions, irrespective of whether that court itself has the power to find an infringement of competition law;

(11) 'infringement decision' means a decision of a competition authority or review court that finds an infringement of competition law;

(12) 'final infringement decision' means an infringement decision that cannot be, or that can no longer be, appealed by ordinary means;

(13) 'evidence' means all types of means of proof admissible before the national court seized, in particular documents and all other objects containing information, irrespective of the medium on which the information is stored;

(14) 'cartel' means an agreement or concerted practice between two or more competitors aimed at coordinating their competitive behaviour on the market or influencing the relevant parameters of competition through practices such as, but not limited to, the fixing or coordination of purchase or selling prices or other trading conditions, including in relation to intellectual property rights, the allocation of production or sales quotas, the sharing of markets and customers, including bid-rigging, restrictions of imports or exports or anti-competitive actions against other competitors;

(15) 'leniency programme' means a programme concerning the application of Article 101 TFEU or a corresponding provision under national law on the basis of which a participant in a secret cartel, independently of the other

undertakings involved in the cartel, cooperates with an investigation of the competition authority, by voluntarily providing presentations regarding that participant's knowledge of, and role in, the cartel in return for which that participant receives, by decision or by a discontinuation of proceedings, immunity from, or a reduction in, fines for its involvement in the cartel;

(16) 'leniency statement' means an oral or written presentation voluntarily provided by, or on behalf of, an undertaking or a natural person to a competition authority or a record thereof, describing the knowledge of that undertaking or natural person of a cartel and describing its role therein, which presentation was drawn up specifically for submission to the competition authority with a view to obtaining immunity or a reduction of fines under a leniency programme, not including pre-existing information;

(17) 'pre-existing information' means evidence that exists irrespective of the proceedings of a competition authority, whether or not such information is in the file of a competition authority;

(18) 'settlement submission' means a voluntary presentation by, or on behalf of, an undertaking to a competition authority describing the undertaking's acknowledgement of, or its renunciation to dispute, its participation in an infringement of competition law and its responsibility for that infringement of competition law, which was drawn up specifically to enable the competition authority to apply a simplified or expedited procedure;

(19) 'immunity recipient' means an undertaking which, or a natural person who, has been granted immunity from fines by a competition authority under a leniency programme;

(20) 'overcharge' means the difference between the price actually paid and the price that would otherwise have prevailed in the absence of an infringement of competition law;

(21) 'consensual dispute resolution' means any mechanism enabling parties to reach the out-of-court resolution of a dispute concerning a claim for damages;

(22) 'consensual settlement' means an agreement reached through consensual dispute resolution.

(23) 'direct purchaser' means a natural or legal person who acquired, directly from an infringer, products or services that were the object of an infringement of competition law;

(24) 'indirect purchaser' means a natural or legal person who acquired, not directly from an infringer, but from a direct purchaser or a subsequent purchaser, products or services that were the object of an infringement of competition law, or products or services containing them or derived therefrom.

[4.447]
Article 3 Right to full compensation

1. Member States shall ensure that any natural or legal person who has suffered harm caused by an infringement of competition law is able to claim and to obtain full compensation for that harm.

2. Full compensation shall place a person who has suffered harm in the position in which that person would have been had the infringement of competition law not been committed. It shall therefore cover the right to compensation for actual loss and for loss of profit, plus the payment of interest.

3. Full compensation under this Directive shall not lead to overcompensation, whether by means of punitive, multiple or other types of damages.

[4.448]
Article 4 Principles of effectiveness and equivalence

In accordance with the principle of effectiveness, Member States shall ensure that all national rules and procedures relating to the exercise of claims for damages are designed and applied in such a way that they do not render practically impossible or excessively difficult the exercise of the Union right to full compensation for harm caused by an infringement of competition law. In accordance with the principle of equivalence, national rules and procedures relating to actions for damages resulting from infringements of Article 101 or 102 TFEU shall not be less favourable to the alleged injured parties than those governing similar actions for damages resulting from infringements of national law.

CHAPTER II DISCLOSURE OF EVIDENCE

[4.449]
Article 5 Disclosure of evidence

1. Member States shall ensure that in proceedings relating to an action for damages in the Union, upon request of a claimant who has presented a reasoned justification containing reasonably available facts and evidence sufficient to support the plausibility of its claim for damages, national courts are able to order the defendant or a third party to disclose relevant evidence which lies in their control, subject to the conditions set out in this Chapter. Member States shall ensure that national courts are able, upon request of the defendant, to order the claimant or a third party to disclose relevant evidence.

This paragraph is without prejudice to the rights and obligations of national courts under Regulation (EC) No 1206/2001.

2. Member States shall ensure that national courts are able to order the disclosure of specified items of evidence or relevant categories of evidence circumscribed as precisely and as narrowly as possible on the basis of reasonably available facts in the reasoned justification.

3. Member States shall ensure that national courts limit the disclosure of evidence to that which is proportionate. In determining whether any disclosure requested by a party is proportionate, national courts shall consider the legitimate interests of all parties and third parties concerned. They shall, in particular, consider:

(a) the extent to which the claim or defence is supported by available facts and evidence justifying the request to disclose evidence;

(b) the scope and cost of disclosure, especially for any third parties concerned, including preventing non-specific searches for information which is unlikely to be of relevance for the parties in the procedure;

(c) whether the evidence the disclosure of which is sought contains confidential information, especially concerning any third parties, and what arrangements are in place for protecting such confidential information.

4. Member States shall ensure that national courts have the power to order the disclosure of evidence containing confidential information where they consider it relevant to the action for damages. Member States shall ensure that, when ordering the disclosure of such information, national courts have at their disposal effective measures to protect such information.
5. The interest of undertakings to avoid actions for damages following an infringement of competition law shall not constitute an interest that warrants protection.
6. Member States shall ensure that national courts give full effect to applicable legal professional privilege under Union or national law when ordering the disclosure of evidence.
7. Member States shall ensure that those from whom disclosure is sought are provided with an opportunity to be heard before a national court orders disclosure under this Article.
8. Without prejudice to paragraphs 4 and 7 and to Article 6, this Article shall not prevent Member States from maintaining or introducing rules which would lead to wider disclosure of evidence.

[4.450]

Article 6 Disclosure of evidence included in the file of a competition authority

1. Member States shall ensure that, for the purpose of actions for damages, where national courts order the disclosure of evidence included in the file of a competition authority, this Article applies in addition to Article 5.
2. This Article is without prejudice to the rules and practices on public access to documents under Regulation (EC) No 1049/2001.
3. This Article is without prejudice to the rules and practices under Union or national law on the protection of internal documents of competition authorities and of correspondence between competition authorities.
4. When assessing, in accordance with Article 5(3), the proportionality of an order to disclose information, national courts shall, in addition, consider the following:
 (a) whether the request has been formulated specifically with regard to the nature, subject matter or contents of documents submitted to a competition authority or held in the file thereof, rather than by a non-specific application concerning documents submitted to a competition authority;
 (b) whether the party requesting disclosure is doing so in relation to an action for damages before a national court; and
 (c) in relation to paragraphs 5 and 10, or upon request of a competition authority pursuant to paragraph 11, the need to safeguard the effectiveness of the public enforcement of competition law.
5. National courts may order the disclosure of the following categories of evidence only after a competition authority, by adopting a decision or otherwise, has closed its proceedings:
 (a) information that was prepared by a natural or legal person specifically for the proceedings of a competition authority;
 (b) information that the competition authority has drawn up and sent to the parties in the course of its proceedings; and
 (c) settlement submissions that have been withdrawn.
6. Member States shall ensure that, for the purpose of actions for damages, national courts cannot at any time order a party or a third party to disclose any of the following categories of evidence:
 (a) leniency statements; and
 (b) settlement submissions.
7. A claimant may present a reasoned request that a national court access the evidence referred to in point (a) or (b) of paragraph 6 for the sole purpose of ensuring that their contents correspond to the definitions in points (16) and (18) of Article 2. In that assessment, national courts may request assistance only from the competent competition authority. The authors of the evidence in question may also have the possibility to be heard. In no case shall the national court permit other parties or third parties access to that evidence.
8. If only parts of the evidence requested are covered by paragraph 6, the remaining parts thereof shall, depending on the category under which they fall, be released in accordance with the relevant paragraphs of this Article.
9. The disclosure of evidence in the file of a competition authority that does not fall into any of the categories listed in this Article may be ordered in actions for damages at any time, without prejudice to this Article.
10. Member States shall ensure that national courts request the disclosure from a competition authority of evidence included in its file only where no party or third party is reasonably able to provide that evidence.
11. To the extent that a competition authority is willing to state its views on the proportionality of disclosure requests, it may, acting on its own initiative, submit observations to the national court before which a disclosure order is sought.

[4.451]

Article 7 Limits on the use of evidence obtained solely through access to the file of a competition authority

1. Member States shall ensure that evidence in the categories listed in Article 6(6) which is obtained by a natural or legal person solely through access to the file of a competition authority is either deemed to be inadmissible in actions for damages or is otherwise protected under the applicable national rules to ensure the full effect of the limits on the disclosure of evidence set out in Article 6.
2. Member States shall ensure that, until a competition authority has closed its proceedings by adopting a decision or otherwise, evidence in the categories listed in Article 6(5) which is obtained by a natural or legal person solely through access to the file of that competition authority is either deemed to be inadmissible in actions for damages or is otherwise protected under the applicable national rules to ensure the full effect of the limits on the disclosure of evidence set out in Article 6.
3. Member States shall ensure that evidence which is obtained by a natural or legal person solely through access to the file of a competition authority and which does not fall under paragraph 1 or 2, can be used in an action for damages only by that person or by a natural or legal person that succeeded to that person's rights, including a person that acquired that person's claim.

[4.452]
Article 8 Penalties

1. Member States shall ensure that national courts are able effectively to impose penalties on parties, third parties and their legal representatives in the event of any of the following:

(a) their failure or refusal to comply with the disclosure order of any national court; (b)their destruction of relevant evidence;

(c) their failure or refusal to comply with the obligations imposed by a national court order protecting confidential information;

(d) their breach of the limits on the use of evidence provided for in this Chapter.

2. Member States shall ensure that the penalties that can be imposed by national courts are effective, proportionate and dissuasive. The penalties available to national courts shall include, with regard to the behaviour of a party to proceedings for an action for damages, the possibility to draw adverse inferences, such as presuming the relevant issue to be proven or dismissing claims and defences in whole or in part, and the possibility to order the payment of costs.

CHAPTER III EFFECT OF NATIONAL DECISIONS, LIMITATION PERIODS, JOINT AND SEVERAL LIABILITY

[4.453]
Article 9 Effect of national decisions

1. Member States shall ensure that an infringement of competition law found by a final decision of a national competition authority or by a review court is deemed to be irrefutably established for the purposes of an action for damages brought before their national courts under Article 101 or 102 TFEU or under national competition law.

2. Member States shall ensure that where a final decision referred to in paragraph 1 is taken in another Member State, that final decision may, in accordance with national law, be presented before their national courts as at least prima facie evidence that an infringement of competition law has occurred and, as appropriate, may be assessed along with any other evidence adduced by the parties.

3. This Article is without prejudice to the rights and obligations of national courts under Article 267 TFEU.

[4.454]
Article 10 Limitation periods

1. Member States shall, in accordance with this Article, lay down rules applicable to limitation periods for bringing actions for damages. Those rules shall determine when the limitation period begins to run, the duration thereof and the circumstances under which it is interrupted or suspended.

2. Limitation periods shall not begin to run before the infringement of competition law has ceased and the claimant knows, or can reasonably be expected to know:

(a) of the behaviour and the fact that it constitutes an infringement of competition law;

(b) of the fact that the infringement of competition law caused harm to it; and

(c) the identity of the infringer.

3. Member States shall ensure that the limitation periods for bringing actions for damages are at least five years.

4. Member States shall ensure that a limitation period is suspended or, depending on national law, interrupted, if a competition authority takes action for the purpose of the investigation or its proceedings in respect of an infringement of competition law to which the action for damages relates. The suspension shall end at the earliest one year after the infringement decision has become final or after the proceedings are otherwise terminated.

[4.455]
Article 11 Joint and several liability

1. Member States shall ensure that undertakings which have infringed competition law through joint behaviour are jointly and severally liable for the harm caused by the infringement of competition law; with the effect that each of those undertakings is bound to compensate for the harm in full, and the injured party has the right to require full compensation from any of them until he has been fully compensated.

2. By way of derogation from paragraph 1, Member States shall ensure that, without prejudice to the right of full compensation as laid down in Article 3, where the infringer is a small or medium-sized enterprise (SME) as defined in Commission Recommendation 2003/361/EC,[1] the infringer is liable only to its own direct and indirect purchasers where:

(a) its market share in the relevant market was below 5% at any time during the infringement of competition law; and

(b) the application of the normal rules of joint and several liability would irretrievably jeopardise its economic viability and cause its assets to lose all their value.

3. The derogation laid down in paragraph 2 shall not apply where:

(a) the SME has led the infringement of competition law or has coerced other undertakings to participate therein; or

(b) the SME has previously been found to have infringed competition law.

4. By way of derogation from paragraph 1, Member States shall ensure that an immunity recipient is jointly and severally liable as follows:

(a) to its direct or indirect purchasers or providers; and

(b) to other injured parties only where full compensation cannot be obtained from the other undertakings that were involved in the same infringement of competition law.

Member States shall ensure that any limitation period applicable to cases under this paragraph is reasonable and sufficient to allow injured parties to bring such actions.

5. Member States shall ensure that an infringer may recover a contribution from any other infringer, the amount of which shall be determined in the light of their relative responsibility for the harm caused by the infringement of competition law. The amount of contribution of an infringer which has been granted immunity from fines under a leniency programme shall not exceed the amount of the harm it caused to its own direct or indirect purchasers or providers.

6. Member States shall ensure that, to the extent the infringement of competition law caused harm to injured parties other than the direct or indirect purchasers or providers of the infringers, the amount of any contribution from an immunity recipient to other infringers shall be determined in the light of its relative responsibility for that harm.

NOTES

[1] Commission Recommendation 2003/361/EC of 6 May 2003 concerning the definition of micro, small and medium-sized enterprises (OJ L124, 20.5.2003, p 36).

CHAPTER IV THE PASSING-ON OF OVERCHARGES

[4.456]

Article 12 Passing-on of overcharges and the right to full compensation

1. To ensure the full effectiveness of the right to full compensation as laid down in Article 3, Member States shall ensure that, in accordance with the rules laid down in this Chapter, compensation of harm can be claimed by anyone who suffered it, irrespective of whether they are direct or indirect purchasers from an infringer, and that compensation of harm exceeding that caused by the infringement of competition law to the claimant, as well as the absence of liability of the infringer, are avoided.
2. In order to avoid overcompensation, Member States shall lay down procedural rules appropriate to ensure that compensation for actual loss at any level of the supply chain does not exceed the overcharge harm suffered at that level.
3. This Chapter shall be without prejudice to the right of an injured party to claim and obtain compensation for loss of profits due to a full or partial passing-on of the overcharge.
4. Member States shall ensure that the rules laid down in this Chapter apply accordingly where the infringement of competition law relates to a supply to the infringer.
5. Member States shall ensure that the national courts have the power to estimate, in accordance with national procedures, the share of any overcharge that was passed on.

[4.457]

Article 13 Passing-on defence

Member States shall ensure that the defendant in an action for damages can invoke as a defence against a claim for damages the fact that the claimant passed on the whole or part of the overcharge resulting from the infringement of competition law. The burden of proving that the overcharge was passed on shall be on the defendant, who may reasonably require disclosure from the claimant or from third parties.

[4.458]

Article 14 Indirect purchasers

1. Member States shall ensure that, where in an action for damages the existence of a claim for damages or the amount of compensation to be awarded depends on whether, or to what degree, an overcharge was passed on to the claimant, taking into account the commercial practice that price increases are passed on down the supply chain, the burden of proving the existence and scope of such a passing-on shall rest with the claimant, who may reasonably require disclosure from the defendant or from third parties.
2. In the situation referred to in paragraph 1, the indirect purchaser shall be deemed to have proven that a passing-on to that indirect purchaser occurred where that indirect purchaser has shown that:
   (a) the defendant has committed an infringement of competition law;
   (b) the infringement of competition law has resulted in an overcharge for the direct purchaser of the defendant; and
   (c) the indirect purchaser has purchased the goods or services that were the object of the infringement of competition law, or has purchased goods or services derived from or containing them.

This paragraph shall not apply where the defendant can demonstrate credibly to the satisfaction of the court that the overcharge was not, or was not entirely, passed on to the indirect purchaser.

[4.459]

Article 15 Actions for damages by claimants from different levels in the supply chain

1. To avoid that actions for damages by claimants from different levels in the supply chain lead to a multiple liability or to an absence of liability of the infringer, Member States shall ensure that in assessing whether the burden of proof resulting from the application of Articles 13 and 14 is satisfied, national courts seized of an action for damages are able, by means available under Union or national law, to take due account of any of the following:
   (a) actions for damages that are related to the same infringement of competition law, but that are brought by claimants from other levels in the supply chain;
   (b) judgments resulting from actions for damages as referred to in point (a);
   (c) relevant information in the public domain resulting from the public enforcement of competition law.
2. This Article shall be without prejudice to the rights and obligations of national courts under Article 30 of Regulation (EU) No 1215/2012.

[4.460]

Article 16 Guidelines for national courts

The Commission shall issue guidelines for national courts on how to estimate the share of the overcharge which was passed on to the indirect purchaser.

CHAPTER V QUANTIFICATION OF HARM

[4.461]

Article 17 Quantification of harm

1. Member States shall ensure that neither the burden nor the standard of proof required for the quantification of harm renders the exercise of the right to damages practically impossible or excessively difficult. Member States shall ensure that the national courts are empowered, in accordance with national procedures, to estimate the amount of harm if it is established that a claimant suffered harm but it is practically impossible or excessively difficult precisely to quantify the harm suffered on the basis of the evidence available.
2. It shall be presumed that cartel infringements cause harm. The infringer shall have the right to rebut that presumption.
3. Member States shall ensure that, in proceedings relating to an action for damages, a national competition authority may, upon request of a national court, assist that national court with respect to the determination of the quantum of damages where that national competition authority considers such assistance to be appropriate.

CHAPTER VI CONSENSUAL DISPUTE RESOLUTION

[4.462]

Article 18 Suspensive and other effects of consensual dispute resolution

1. Member States shall ensure that the limitation period for bringing an action for damages is suspended for the duration of any consensual dispute resolution process. The suspension of the limitation period shall apply only with regard to those parties that are or that were involved or represented in the consensual dispute resolution.
2. Without prejudice to provisions of national law in matters of arbitration, Member States shall ensure that national courts seized of an action for damages may suspend their proceedings for up to two years where the parties thereto are involved in consensual dispute resolution concerning the claim covered by that action for damages.
3. A competition authority may consider compensation paid as a result of a consensual settlement and prior to its decision imposing a fine to be a mitigating factor.

[4.463]

Article 19 Effect of consensual settlements on subsequent actions for damages

1. Member States shall ensure that, following a consensual settlement, the claim of the settling injured party is reduced by the settling co-infringer's share of the harm that the infringement of competition law inflicted upon the injured party.
2. Any remaining claim of the settling injured party shall be exercised only against non-settling co-infringers. Non-settling co-infringers shall not be permitted to recover contribution for the remaining claim from the settling co-infringer.
3. By way of derogation from paragraph 2, Member States shall ensure that where the non-settling co-infringers cannot pay the damages that correspond to the remaining claim of the settling injured party, the settling injured party may exercise the remaining claim against the settling co-infringer.
The derogation referred to in the first subparagraph may be expressly excluded under the terms of the consensual settlement.
4. When determining the amount of contribution that a co-infringer may recover from any other co-infringer in accordance with their relative responsibility for the harm caused by the infringement of competition law, national courts shall take due account of any damages paid pursuant to a prior consensual settlement involving the relevant co-infringer.

CHAPTER VII FINAL PROVISIONS

[4.464]

Article 20 Review

1. The Commission shall review this Directive and shall submit a report thereon to the European Parliament and the Council by 27 December 2020.
2. The report referred to in paragraph 1 shall, inter alia, include information on all of the following:
   (a) the possible impact of financial constraints flowing from the payment of fines imposed by a competition authority for an infringement of competition law on the possibility for injured parties to obtain full compensation for the harm caused by that infringement of competition law;
   (b) the extent to which claimants for damages caused by an infringement of competition law established in an infringement decision adopted by a competition authority of a Member State are able to prove before the national court of another Member State that such an infringement of competition law has occurred;
   (c) the extent to which compensation for actual loss exceeds the overcharge harm caused by the infringement of competition law or suffered at any level of the supply chain.
3. If appropriate, the report referred to in paragraph 1 shall be accompanied by a legislative proposal.

[4.465]

Article 21 Transposition

1. Member States shall bring into force the laws, regulations and administrative provisions necessary to comply with this Directive by 27 December 2016. They shall forthwith communicate to the Commission the text thereof.
When Member States adopt those measures, they shall contain a reference to this Directive or be accompanied by such a reference on the occasion of their official publication. Member States shall determine how such reference is to be made.
2. Member States shall communicate to the Commission the text of the main provisions of national law which they adopt in the field covered by this Directive.

[4.466]

Article 22 Temporal application

1. Member States shall ensure that the national measures adopted pursuant to Article 21 in order to comply with substantive provisions of this Directive do not apply retroactively.

2. Member States shall ensure that any national measures adopted pursuant to Article 21, other than those referred to in paragraph 1, do not apply to actions for damages of which a national court was seized prior to 26 December 2014.

[4.467]

Article 23 Entry into force

This Directive shall enter into force on the twentieth day following that of its publication in the *Official Journal of the European Union*.

[4.468]

Article 24 Addressees

This Directive is addressed to the Member States.

COMMUNICATION FROM THE COMMISSION

Guidelines for national courts on how to estimate the share of overcharge which was passed on to the indirect purchaser

(July 2019)

[4.469]

NOTES

Date of publication in OJ: OJ L267, 9.8.2019, p 4.

TABLE OF CONTENTS

TABLE OF BOXES

1. INTRODUCTION

1.1 PURPOSE, SCOPE AND STRUCTURE OF THESE GUIDELINES

[4.470]

(1) These guidelines intend to provide national courts, judges and other stakeholders in damages actions for infringements of Articles 101 and 102 of the Treaty on the Functioning of the European Union ('TFEU') with practical guidance on how to estimate the passing-on of overcharges. In particular, they set out the economic principles, methods and terminology concerning passing-on *inter alia* by reference to a number of examples. Further, these guidelines are designed to help determine the sources of relevant evidence, whether a disclosure request is proportionate, and assessing the statements of the parties on passing-on and any economic expert opinion that may be presented to the court.

(2) The legal basis for the guidelines is Article 16 of the Damages Directive.[1] They are non-binding and do not alter existing rules under EU law or the laws of the Member States. Accordingly, there is no obligation on a national court to follow them. The guidelines are also without prejudice to the jurisprudence of the Court of Justice of the European Union ('CJEU'). They refer to the harmonized rules set out in the Damages Directive noting that in practice national courts will apply national rules, including those transposing the Damages Directive.

(3) As a reference source for good practices, the guidelines give indications on the relevant parameters that can be taken into account when dealing with economic evidence relevant for assessing the passing-on of overcharges. They build upon relevant economic studies gathered by the Commission and complement the Practical Guide on quantifying harm in actions for damages based on breaches of Article 101 or 102 TFEU ('Practical Guide')[2] accompanying the Communication from the Commission on quantifying antitrust harm in a damages action.[3] While the Practical Guide focuses on the overcharge, these guidelines specifically address in more detail the passing-on of such overcharges.[4] The Practical Guide and these guidelines should be read together.[5]

(4) As explained in paragraphs (17)–(19) below, these guidelines may be useful when an infringer invokes passing-on in its defence against a damages claim ('shield') or when an indirect purchaser claims damages from the infringer alleging passing-on of an overcharge ('sword'). However, as in any damages action, the degree to which the court has to consider the facts of a case will depend on the way the action is brought by the claimant and the nature of the defence raised by the defendant. For example, in some cases a claimant may not claim for loss of profit as a result of the volume effect because of the additional complexity this may involve.[6] However, a claim by an indirect purchaser against an infringer will typically involve consideration of passing-on, since that is essential to the claim.

(5) Similarly, the manner in which a national court would wish to approach the assessment and estimation of passing-on is likely to be influenced by the nature and size of the claim, the merits of the submission and the availability of data. When assessing the proportionality of an order to disclose information, such a court could take into account the choice of economic method and approach from among the different options explained in the guidelines. What may be appropriate in terms of the scope of data required and cost of expert analysis for a claim of 20 million Euro may not be proportionate for a claim of 200,000 Euro.

(6) By reference to legal principles, established jurisprudence and the provisions in the Damages Directive, these guidelines set out the legal context of passing-on. A short legal section summarises the procedural rules and instruments according to which national courts may take into account the passing-on of overcharges in damages actions. The legal context relates to EU law, national law and the respective practice. In this context, judges need to pay particular attention to the principles of effectiveness and equivalence.[7] Firstly, this means that they must apply national rules in such a way that the application does not render practically impossible or excessively difficult the exercise of the right to full compensation for harm caused by an infringement of EU competition law (principle of effectiveness).[8] Secondly, judges must bear in mind that national rules and procedures relating to actions for damages resulting from infringements of Article 101 or 102 TFEU must not be less favourable to the alleged injured parties than those governing similar actions for damages resulting from infringements of national competition law (principle of equivalence).

(7) The main section of these guidelines deals with the economics of passing-on, namely the economic theory and quantification methods relevant for the purpose of estimating passing-on. The part on the economic theory focuses on the theoretical concepts underlying passing-on and sets out factors that can have an impact on it. In the part on economic quantification, different approaches and methods to quantify the passing-on effects are presented.

1.2. WHAT IS PASSING-ON OF OVERCHARGES?

(8) The passing-on of overcharges may occur at different levels of the supply chain. It is illustrated in Box 1 below by reference to a hypothetical example. For illustration purposes, and as a starting point for variations to further explain passing-on, the example in Box 1 sets out a relatively simple case of fixed prices for copper and the passing-on of the respective price increase in the automotive industry. In practice, passing-on can occur in even more complex supply chains, the cartelised product or service may constitute an even smaller input and the end product could be affected by more than one anti-competitive practice.

Box 1: Passing-on of a price increase for copper (hypothetical example)

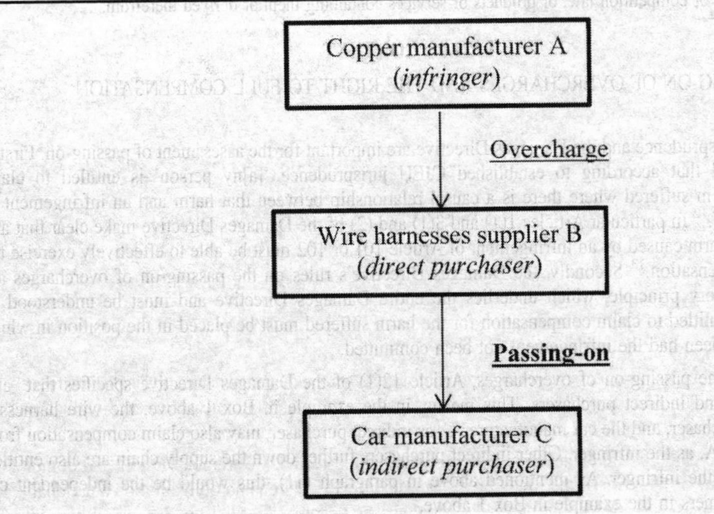

Undertaking A is a manufacturer of copper and formed a cartel by agreeing with its competitors to fix sales prices for copper in violation of Article 101 TFEU. The agreement allowed A to charge its customers, including undertaking B, higher prices for copper.

The price difference between the price actually paid and the price that would otherwise have prevailed in the absence of the infringement of EU competition law is referred to as the overcharge.[9]

Undertaking B is a supplier of automotive parts and used the copper it purchased from A to produce wire harnesses which it sold to car manufacturer C. After the cartel-related price increase for copper, B also increased its sales price for the wire harnesses it supplied to C. This behaviour constitutes passing-on of overcharges, in this case from B to C. Based on the definitions in the Damages Directive, A can be referred to as *infringer*, B as *direct purchaser* and C as *indirect purchaser*.[10]

(9) Again, there are more complicated examples of passing-on. Some of them are referred to in additional boxes below. The purpose of these boxes is to highlight certain aspects of passing-on and how national courts have previously approached estimating the share of overcharge which was passed on to the indirect purchaser.

(10) When the direct purchaser, fully or partially, passes on the overcharge to the indirect purchaser, the latter will not only face a price effect but in many cases also reduce its demand, so that the direct purchaser sells less. The value of the sale that is lost can be referred to as the volume effect of passing-on. Its legal and economic implications are discussed in more detail below.

(11) An overcharge may be passed on down an entire supply chain and can concern products or services. For example, following the example in Box 1 above, the car manufacturer C may have similarly increased the prices it charged its customer, the independent car retailer D. Subsequently, D may have also increased its end consumer price for the car in which the cartelised copper can be found. C, D and the end consumers are all indirect purchasers within the meaning of the definition of the Damages Directive.[11]

NOTES

1 Directive 2014/104/EU of the European Parliament and of the Council of 26 November 2014 on certain rules governing actions for damages under national law for infringements of the competition law provisions of the Member States and of the European Union, OJ L349/1, 05.12.2014.

2 Commission, Staff Working Document – Practical Guide on Quantifying Harm in Actions for damages based on breaches of Article 101 or 102 of the Treaty on the Functioning of the European Union, 11.6.2013, SWD(2013) 205.

3 Communication from the Commission on quantifying harm in actions for damages based on breaches of Article 101 or 102 of the Treaty on the Functioning of the European Union, OJ C167/19, 13.06.2013.

4 The Practical Guide only briefly deals with passing-on, namely in its paragraphs 161-171.

5 These guidelines focus on passing-on of overcharges in the context of infringements of Article 101 TFEU, in particular cartels within the meaning of Article 2(14) Damages Directive and other horizontal restraints. However, they may also be a reference source for good practices in damages actions before national courts for vertical restraints, e.g. resale price maintenance, and infringements of Article 102 TFEU, i.e. an abuse of dominance, such as excessive pricing, provided the specificities of the applicable EU rules are sufficiently taken into account.

6 The volume effect is briefly explained in paragraph (10) below. Chapter 6 describes methods for the quantification and estimation of this effect.

7 See Article 4 Damages Directive.

8 For the right to full compensation see paragraphs (12) et seq. below.

9 See Article 2(20) Damages Directive.

10 See Article 2(2), (23) and (24) Damages Directive.

11 According to Article 2(24) Damages Directive "'indirect" purchaser means a natural or legal person who acquired, not directly from an infringer, but from a direct purchaser or a subsequent purchaser, products or services that were the object

of an infringement of competition law, or products or services containing them or derived therefrom.'

2. THE LEGAL CONTEXT

2.1. PASSING-ON OF OVERCHARGES AND THE RIGHT TO FULL COMPENSATION

[4.471]

(12) Both the CJEU jurisprudence and the Damages Directive are important for the assessment of passing-on. Firstly, it is important to recall that according to established CJEU jurisprudence '[a]ny person' is entitled to claim compensation for the harm suffered where there is a causal relationship between that harm and an infringement of Article 101 or 102 TFEU.[12] In particular Articles 1(1) and 3(1) and (2) of the Damages Directive make clear that any person having suffered harm caused by an infringement of Article 101 or 102 must be able to effectively exercise the right to claim full compensation.[13] Secondly, the Damages Directive's rules on the passing-on of overcharges are rooted in the compensatory principle, which underlies the entire Damages Directive and must be understood as requiring that a person entitled to claim compensation for the harm suffered must be placed in the position in which that person would have been had the infringement not been committed.

(13) In the context of the passing-on of overcharges, Article 12(1) of the Damages Directive specifies that 'any person' includes direct and indirect purchasers. This means, in the example in Box 1 above, the wire harnesses producer B, as direct purchaser, and the car manufacturer C, as indirect purchaser, may also claim compensation from the copper manufacturer A, as the infringer. Other indirect purchasers further down the supply chain are also entitled to obtain damages from the infringer. As mentioned above in paragraph (11), this would be the independent car retailer D and end consumers in the example in Box 1 above.

(14) It should be noted that the elements of the compensatory principle, i.e. a person's right to claim full compensation for harm causally linked to an infringement of EU competition law, apply also to direct and indirect *suppliers* of an infringer. The Damages Directive refers to the situation of a buyer's cartel as an example in which harm could result from a lower price paid by infringers to their suppliers.[14]

(15) Full compensation covers compensation for actual loss (*damnum emergens*) and for loss of profit (*lucrum cessans*), plus the payment of interest.[15] Generally, actual loss refers to a reduction in a person's assets and loss of profit refers to an increase in those assets which would have occurred if the harmful act had not taken place.[16] In the context of passing-on, the distinction plays a particular role with regard to the characteristic economic effects and their legal classification. The general rule is set out below.

— The price effect relates to the overcharge as an increase in the price that a direct or an indirect purchaser had to pay for a product or services due to the infringement of EU competition law.[17] It includes umbrella pricing.[18] The price effect may be reflected in a direct or indirect purchaser's claim for compensation of actual loss. It is the part of the harm which is referred to as overcharge harm in the Damages Directive.[19] However, the direct or indirect purchaser may be able to pass on the overcharge further down the supply chain, either partially or fully. Thus, when national courts estimate the partial or full passing-on of an overcharge in a damages action, they will need to identify the overcharge harm which remains at a given level of the supply chain. Depending on the legal system, the national court may consider such passing-on as a reduction of the actual loss or by reference to other rules or principles, such as *compensatio lucri cum damno*.[20]

— The volume effect can be described, more generally, as the harm that is caused by the fact that fewer of the products or services are purchased as a result of the overcharge.[21] However, the focus of these guidelines is on the volume effect understood as the profit loss due to reduced sales resulting from passing-on. As mentioned in the Damages Directive, it can be recoverable as loss of profit.[22]

(16) While, on the basis of the Damages Directive, one may distinguish between actual loss because of the overcharge, on the one hand, and loss of profit due to reduced sales, on the other hand, there is an inherent link between the underlying price effect and volume effect.[23] Therefore, if passing-on becomes relevant, both effects and their interaction should be taken into account. The economic methods to do so are set out further below.

2.2. SCENARIOS IN WHICH NATIONAL COURTS MAY FACE PASSING-ON ISSUES

(17) In actions for damages based on EU competition law infringements national courts typically deal with the passing-on of overcharges in two scenarios.

(18) Firstly, an infringer may invoke the passing-on of overcharges in its defence against damages claims, i.e. arguing that the direct or indirect purchaser has passed on the overcharge, entirely or in part, to its own purchasers.[24] This situation, in which passing-on can be described as a shield, is illustrated in Box 2 below by reference to a direct purchaser's claim. It has to be noted that the passing-on defence may also be invoked against claims of indirect purchasers further down the supply chain.

(19) Secondly, indirect purchasers may base their damages actions on the argument that the direct purchasers of the infringers have passed on (parts of) the overcharge to them and that they have therefore suffered harm. In such a scenario passing-on can be described as a sword. This scenario is also illustrated in Box 2 below.

Box 2: The two typical scenarios of passing-on

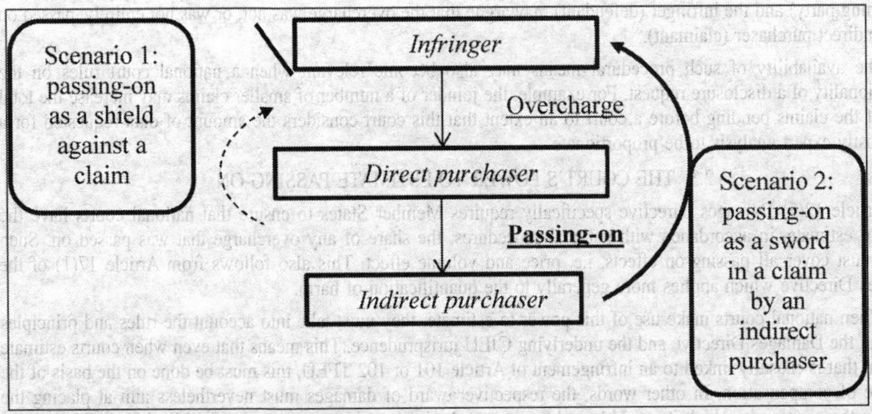

(20) At the outset, it should be noted that Article 17(2) of the Damages Directive establishes the general presumption that cartel infringements cause harm. In addition, Articles 13 and 14 of the Damages Directive include specific rules on the burden of proof in the context of passing-on.

(21) In the first scenario, i.e. when the passing-on of overcharges is used as a defence against an action based on an infringement of EU competition law, the defendant needs to prove that the claimant has passed on the overcharge.[25] This burden of proof relates to the existence and extent of the passing-on of the overcharge. If the passing-on defence is fully or partially successful, Article 12(3) of the Damages Directive requires that, according to national procedural law, taking into account the principle of effectiveness and equivalence, the claimant may still claim compensation for loss of profit.[26] In this case, the burden of proving such passing-on related volume effect is on the claimant.

(22) The Damages Directive also includes rules applicable in the second scenario, i.e. when an indirect purchaser claims that it suffered harm due to the passing-on of overcharges. In this scenario, the burden of proving the existence and scope of such passing-on rests with the indirect purchaser seeking damages from the infringer.

(23) However, the Damages Directive specifically addresses the difficulties that indirect purchasers face when they seek compensation for the harm resulting from the passing-on of an overcharge.[27] Firstly, Article 14(1) of the Damages Directive and Recital 41 of the Damages Directive refer to the fact that it can be a commercial practice to pass on price increases down the supply chain. If such a commercial practice has been identified, national courts may rely on prima facie proof of passing-on. Building upon this reference, Article 14(2) of the Damages Directive stipulates a rebuttable presumption pursuant to which a claimant (i.e. the indirect purchaser) is deemed to have proved that a passing-on from the direct purchaser to the indirect purchaser occurred, provided that the claimant can show that the following conditions are fulfilled:

(a) the defendant has committed an infringement of EU competition law;[28]
(b) the infringement of EU competition law has resulted in an overcharge for the direct purchaser of the defendant; and
(c) the indirect purchaser has purchased the goods or services that were the object of the infringement of EU competition law, or has purchased goods or services derived from or containing them.

(24) This presumption does not apply if the infringer can credibly demonstrate to the satisfaction of the court that the overcharge was not, or was not entirely, passed on to the indirect purchaser.[29]

(25) As a result of (i) the compensatory principle, (ii) the practice of passing-on of overcharges and (iii) the presumptions, mentioned above, it is possible that there are parallel claims from purchasers at different levels in the supply chain. In such situations, national courts should seek to avoid both over-compensation and under compensation.[30] This can be achieved *inter alia* by taking due account, as far as this is possible, of any actions for damages that are related to the same infringement of EU competition law, judgments resulting from such damages actions and relevant information in the public domain resulting from the public enforcement of EU competition law in the case at hand.[31] It is in the interest of the parties to a damages action to make the national court aware of such actions, judgments or information and explain why they are relevant in the case at hand.

(26) Further, where related actions are pending in the courts of different Member States, national courts may apply Article 30 of Regulation (EU) No 1215/2012[32] to which the Damages Directive makes reference.[33] This article stipulates that national courts other than that first seized may stay proceedings or, under certain circumstances, may decline jurisdiction. The court of a Member State may also use national rules on stays, if they are available under national law.

(27) In the interest of consistency between judgments resulting from related proceedings, national courts should also consider and allow for the use of appropriate procedural means that are at their disposal under national law. By way of example, the Damages Directive refers to the joinder of claims.[34] It also refers to the possibility that a person may acquire the claim of another person.[35] The goal of such acquisition may be to bring a joint action which may contribute to ensuring consistency between damages actions that are related to the same competition law infringement.[36]

(28) Depending on the national legal system, other instruments may be applied, such as collective redress mechanisms, third-party notices or interventions and rules on stays. For example, a direct purchaser may intervene in the damages action of an indirect purchaser against the infringer. In such a case, both the direct purchaser (the intervening party) and the infringer (defendant) may argue that the overcharge was not, or was not entirely, passed on to the indirect purchaser (claimant).

(29) The availability of such procedural means may also become relevant when a national court rules on the proportionality of a disclosure request. For example, the joinder of a number of smaller claims may increase the total value of the claims pending before a court to an extent that this court considers the amount of data requested for a more costly expert analysis to be proportionate.

2.3. THE COURT'S POWER TO ESTIMATE PASSING-ON

(30) Article 12(5) Damages Directive specifically requires Member States to ensure that national courts have the power to estimate, in accordance with national procedures, the share of any overcharge that was passed on. Such power must cover all passing-on effects, i.e. price and volume effect. This also follows from Article 17(1) of the Damages Directive which applies more generally to the quantification of harm.

(31) When national courts make use of this power to estimate, they must take into account the rules and principles set out in the Damages Directive and the underlying CJEU jurisprudence. This means that even when courts estimate the harm that is causally linked to an infringement of Article 101 or 102 TFEU, this must be done on the basis of the principle of compensation. In other words, the respective award of damages must nevertheless aim at placing the victim in the position in which it would have been absent the infringement (see paragraph (12) above). To this end, national courts must also use their procedural instruments accordingly. In particular, they must apply the applicable rules on the burden and standard of proof so that the full effectiveness of Article 101 TFEU is not put at risk.

(32) For example, the CJEU held in Kone that the victims of umbrella pricing may obtain compensation for the loss caused by an infringement of EU competition law, stating that the full effectiveness of Article 101 TFEU would be put at risk if national law categorically and regardless of the particular circumstances of the case excluded their right to claim compensation for harm suffered. Further, Kone highlights that in damages actions for infringements of EU competition law factual and legal questions of causation may arise. Such questions also arise in the context of passing-on.[37]

(33) Similarly, when national courts estimate, in accordance with national procedures, the amount of harm and share of any overcharge that was passed on, as foreseen in the Damages Directive, they must observe the abovementioned principles of equivalence and effectiveness. As regards the power to estimate, this means that national courts cannot reject submissions on passing-on merely because a party is unable to precisely quantify the passing-on effects.

(34) Furthermore, the power to estimate, as stipulated in Article 12(5) of the Damages Directive and Article 17(1) of the Damages Directive, requires national courts to, firstly, base their assessment on the information reasonably available and, secondly, strive for an approximation of the amount or share of passing-on which is plausible. This follows from the Damages Directive which stresses the existence of information asymmetries and acknowledges that harm can hardly be quantified with perfect accuracy.[38] The exercise of estimation is subject to national law. In fact, a number of Member States already had rules in place which correspond to the power to estimate, as foreseen in the Damages Directive.[39]

(35) In practice, national courts will often have to rely on assumptions, e.g. in relation to hypothetical prices, sales volumes or profit. They may have broad discretion as to both the figures and the statistical data to be chosen and, above all, as to the way in which they are to be used for the calculation and the assessment of damages.[40] Moreover, assumptions are typically important when building a counter-factual for the purpose of quantifying passing-on and volume effects, as described in section 4 below. Due to this importance, it may be advisable to ask that in any type of submission to the court the assumptions are carefully laid out and the sensitivity of predictions to changes to the assumptions are made explicit, as the Directorate- General for Competition of the Commission requires in its 'Best practices for the submission of economic evidence and data collection in cases concerning the application of Article 101 and 102 TFEU and in merger cases' ('Best Practices').[41]

2.4. THE ROLE OF EVIDENCE

(36) The legal assessment of passing-on typically requires a complex factual and economic analysis. While the taking of necessary evidence generally forms an important element in every action for damages resulting from infringements of Article 101 or 102 TFEU, the role of evidence on passing-on varies depending on the two scenarios mentioned above and the extent to which a presumption applies.[42] In any case, the facts that are actually relevant and available may determine the taking of evidence and ultimately the assessment of passing-on.

(37) The type of evidence necessary to show and quantify passing-on will depend on which of the economic methods, described in sections 5 and 6 below, is used. Evidence may be categorized in different ways but it is typically divided into qualitative and quantitative evidence. The Damages Directive itself makes clear that 'evidence' means all types of means of proof admissible before the national court.[43] This could include the following:

— qualitative evidence to understand a firm's business behaviour or pricing strategies comprising e.g. (i) contracts, (ii) internal documents, (iii) financial and accounting reports, (iv) witness statements, (v) expert opinions as well as (vi) industry reports and market studies; or

— quantitative evidence relating particularly to data for the use of econometric techniques,[44] such as (i) sales prices, retail and end consumer prices of the product or service in question, and of comparable products or services, (ii) financial reports, (iii) expert opinions (iv) prices set by regulation, (v) volume sales, (vi) rebates as well as (vii) other input costs and cost elements.

As can be drawn from the non-exhaustive lists immediately above, certain types of evidence may qualify as both qualitative and quantitative evidence, e.g. financial reports and expert opinions.

(38) As explained more generally in the Practical Guide, normally, the specificities of the case at hand and the evidence provided are the starting point for establishing if the infringement has in fact harmed the claimant, and, if this is the case, for determining the quantum of that harm.[45] The relevant evidence may include direct evidence which, at least in the context of passing-on, can be understood as covering documents produced by the direct or indirect purchaser as well as witness statements on whether the overcharge has been passed on. The availability of such evidence may play an important role when a court decides whether any, and if so which, of the methods described below can be used by a party to meet the required standard of proof under the applicable law.

(39) Further, when it comes to the assessment of passing-on, national courts often face economic expert opinions. Depending on the means available under national law, these opinions may be submitted by party-appointed experts, by an expert that the court itself has appointed for the purpose of assistance, or by both party and court-appointed experts. To the extent possible, the national court may wish to guide any of these economic experts, potentially at an early stage of the proceedings when parties request the disclosure of evidence, and ask more concrete questions in relation to the quantification method to be used and the data needed. Such guidance and questions can be relevant for case management purposes but also for the substantive assessment. In particular, as mentioned above, when national courts estimate passing-on effects they may consider whether an economic expert opinion complies with best practices, e.g. whether it carefully lays out the relevant assumptions and the sensitivity of predictions to changes to these assumptions. In the same vein and again subject to national law, national courts may ask economic experts to address alternative explanations for their findings, ensure replicability and let the parties comment.

(40) The Damages Directive aims to ensure the effective exercise of rights and equality of arms by stipulating rules to request the disclosure of evidence. Such rules apply in both passing-on scenarios mentioned above. As regards the scenario in which passing-on is used as a defence, Article 13 of the Damages Directive specifically mentions that the defendant may reasonably require disclosure from the claimant or from third parties. In a scenario in which an indirect purchaser seeks compensation, Article 14(1) of the Damages Directive stipulates that this indirect purchaser may reasonably require disclosure from the defendant or third parties.

(41) These rules of the Damages Directive limit disclosure of evidence in the sense that the party bearing the burden of proving the existence and scope of passing-on may only reasonably require disclosure. In line with the general rules on disclosure stipulated in Article 5 Damages Directive, the national court may require that the requesting party has made a plausible assertion that the overcharge harm has been passed on by the direct purchaser onto the indirect purchaser. The requesting party must also use the facts which are already reasonably available to it. In the context of passing-on, this may include information gathered during the course of business with the other party or information reasonably available from third parties, such as market intelligence providers.

(42) The first sentence of Article 5(3) of the Damages Directive establishes a general principle of proportionality in the sense that it requires national courts to 'limit the disclosure of evidence to that which is proportionate'. This principle is important for case management in damages actions resulting from infringements of Article 101 or 102 TFEU. As mentioned above, judges apply national procedural rules and must pay particular attention to the principles of effectiveness and equivalence. However, within the scope of these legal rules, national courts may take into account the costs and benefits of ordering the requested disclosure. For example, this means that national courts may come to the conclusion that the evidence presented by the parties already allows them to estimate the share of the overcharge that was passed on instead of gathering further data.

(43) Evidence may be requested from the other party or third parties through and under the strict control of the national court. The request must concern specific items or categories of evidence.[46] Provided that the national court considers the general principles of proportionality and the protection of legitimate interests, it may even order the disclosure of evidence containing confidential information to the party bearing the burden of proving passing-on effects. For example, this information may include documents or data on revenues, prices or margins. However, when ordering the disclosure of such evidence, it is crucial for the national court to have measures in place to protect the confidential information.[47] By way of example, the Damages Directive refers to a few measures, such as the possibility of redacting sensitive passages in documents, conducting hearings in camera, restricting the persons allowed to see the evidence, and instructing experts to produce summaries of the information in an aggregated or otherwise non-confidential form.[48] In accordance with national law, national courts may also consider the measures referred to in the Best Practices, such as a data room procedure,[49] and in Article 9(2) of the Trade Secrets Directive.[50]

(44) Disclosure of evidence included in the file of a competition authority could potentially be relevant for the quantification of the overcharge but is generally less relevant in the context of passing-on (in particular because the passing-on of overcharges deals with the pricing behaviour of the purchasers on which the file of a competition authority typically does not include any information). Further, the public version of the infringement decision may include more general information that can be relevant, such as information on which products or services were subject to the anti-competitive conduct. As Article 6(10) of the Damages Directive provides, disclosure of evidence from a competition authority is only a measure of last resort.

(45) Finally, as indicated in Article 15(1) of the Damages Directive, actions for damages related to the same infringement of EU competition law and related judgments may also form a source of information relevant for the quantification of passing-on.

NOTES

12 CJEU, judgment of 14 March 2019, case C-724/17 (*Skanska*) ECLI:EU:C:2019:204, paragraph 26 and CJEU, judgment of 28 March 2019, case C-637/17 (*Cogeco*) ECLI:EU:C:2019:263, paragraph 40, both with references to CJEU, judgment of 05 June 2014, case C-557/12 (*Kone*) ECLI:EU:C:2014:1317, paragraph 22 and the jurisprudence mentioned therein, namely CJEU, judgment of 13 July 2006, case C-295/04 (*Manfredi*) ECLI:EU:C:2006:461, paragraph 61 and CJEU, judgment of 06 November 2012, case C 199/11 (*Otis and Others*) ECLI: EU:C:2012:684, paragraph 43.

13 In the absence of EU rules governing the matter, it is for the domestic legal system of each Member State to lay down the detailed rules governing the exercise of the right to claim compensation for the harm resulting from an agreement or practice prohibited under Article 101 TFEU, including those on the application of the concept of 'causal relationship',

provided that the principles of equivalence and effectiveness are observed (CJEU, judgment of 05 June 2014, case C-557/12 (*Kone*) ECLI:EU:C:2014:1317, paragraph 24; CJEU, judgment of 13 July 2006, case C-295/04 (*Manfredi*) ECLI:EU:C:2006:461, paragraph 64).

14 See Recital 43 Damages Directive. In the situation of a *buyers' cartel*, the lower price paid by the infringers can be referred to as 'undercharge' and there could also be related upstream volume effects. However, it should be noted that suppliers can also be adversely affected in the situation of a *seller's cartel*. This can be the case if they supply less to the infringers because of the volume effect, i.e. a loss of profit due to the reduction in demand at the direct or even indirect purchaser level down the supply chain. The reduction in demand in relation to the cartelised input may also cause a reduction in demand of other inputs. The suppliers of such other inputs may also claim damages, provided they can show a causal link between their harm and the infringement of EU competition law.

15 See the second sentence of Article 3(2) Damages Directive.

16 Opinion of Advocate General Capotorti delivered on 12 September 1979 in case 238/78 (*Ireks-Arkady v Council and Commission*) ECLI:EU:C:1979:203, paragraph 9.

17 Recital 39 Damages Directive.

18 Umbrella pricing refers to a situation in which 'undertakings that are not themselves party to a cartel, benefiting from the protection of the cartel's practices (operating 'under the cartel's umbrella', so to speak), knowingly or unknowingly set their own prices higher than they would otherwise have been able to under competitive conditions', Opinion of Advocate General Kokott delivered on 30 January 2014 in case C-557/12 (*Kone*) ECLI:EU:C:2014:45, paragraph 2.

19 Article 12(2) Damages Directive.

20 In other words, these guidelines are without prejudice to the consideration of passing-on under national law, provided such law complies with the principle of equivalence and effectiveness, see paragraph (6) above. When they refer to passing-on as a reduction of the actual loss, this includes a consideration of passing-on by reference to other rules and principles, such as *compensatio lucri cum damno*.

21 Practical Guide, paragraph 128.

22 See Article 12(3) Damages Directive.

23 The intuitive link between the price effect and the volume effect is explained in further detail in Annex 1.

24 See Recital 39 Damages Directive.

25 See the second sentence of Article 13 Damages Directive.

26 Article 12(3) Damages Directive stipulates that the rules on passing-on shall be without prejudice to the right of an injured party to claim and obtain compensation for loss of profits due to a full or partial passing-on of the overcharge.

27 Recital 41 Damages Directive.

28 In particular, the indirect purchaser may show that this first condition is fulfilled by reference to the binding effects that a decision of the Commission or a national competition authority has. As regards decisions of the Commission, Article 16(1) of Council Regulation (EC) No 1/2003 of 16 December 2002 on the implementation of the rules of competition laid down in Articles 81 and 82 of the Treaty (OJ L1, 04.01.2003, page 1) stipulates that national courts, when they rule on agreements, decisions or practices under Article 101 TFEU which are already the subject of a Commission decision, cannot take decisions running counter to the decision adopted by the Commission. As regards final infringement decisions of national competition authorities, purchasers may benefit from Article 9 Damages Directive. This Article differentiates according to which national competition authority has issued the relevant infringement decision. According to Article 9(1) Damages Directive a final decision of the national competition authority of a Member State is deemed to establish irrefutably an infringement of competition law before the courts of that particular Member State whereas Article 9(2) Damages Directive stipulates that national courts are required to consider a final decision of another Member State's national competition authority at least as *prima facie* evidence of the existence of an infringement.

29 See last sentence of Article 14(2) Damages Directive.

30 See Articles 12(1), 12(2) and 15 Damages Directive.

31 See Article 15(1) Damages Directive.

32 Regulation (EU) No 1215/2012 of the European Parliament and of the Council of 12 December 2012 on jurisdiction and the recognition and enforcement of judgments in civil and commercial matters (OJ L351, 20.12.2012, page 1).

33 See Recital 44 and Article 15(2) Damages Directive.

34 Recital 44 Damages Directive.

35 See Article 2(4) Damages Directive at the end.

36 See COMMISSION STAFF WORKING PAPER accompanying the WHITE PAPER on Damages actions for breach of the EC antitrust rules, COM(2008) 165 final, paragraphs 223-224.

37 The potential tension between economic and legal causation in the context of passing-on has become apparent in judgments of national courts limiting the use of passing-on as a shield by reference to national law, in particular in the UK (see Competition Appeal Tribunal, judgment of 14 July 2016, [2016] CAT 23 (*Sainsbury's Supermarkets Ltd v MasterCard Inc*), in particular paragraph 484, and the Court of Appeal, judgment of 04 July 2018, [2018] EWCA 1536 (Civ) (*Sainsbury's Supermarkets Ltd v Mastercard Inc*), in particular at paragraphs 332 and 340) and in the Netherlands (*Hoge Raad* (Supreme Court, Netherlands), judgment of 08 July 2016, case 15/00167 (*TenneT v ABB*), paragraphs 4.4.1-4.4.5).

38 See Recital 46 Damages Directive. To address such issues the Damages Directive includes *inter alia* rules on disclosure (see paragraphs (40) et seq. below), the possibility to request assistance from national competition authorities in accordance with Article 17(3) Damages Directive and the obligation to take into account other proceedings relating to the same infringement (see paragraph (25) above).

39 E.g., in the UK national courts may quantify harm 'by the exercise of a sound imagination and the practice of the broad axe' (established in *Watson Laidlaw & Co Ltd v Pott Cassels & Williamson* [1914] S.C. (H.L.) 18 at paragraphs 29-30 and later applied also in the context of damages actions for competition law infringements, see e.g. Court of Appeal, judgment of 14 October 2008, [2008] EWCA Civ 1086 (*Devenish Nutrition Ltd v Sanofi-Aventis SA*) at paragraph 110), in the Netherlands the national court awarding damages may quantify the amount of the harm to the extent that this is possible (see Article 612 Wetboek van Burgerlijke Rechtsvordering) and estimate it in the manner that is the best fit for the characteristics of the harm (see Article 6:97 Burgerlijk Wetboek).

40 Practical Guide, paragraph 16 and footnote 15 with reference to CJEU, judgment of 27 January 2000, joined cases C-104/89 and C-37/90 (*Mulder and others v Council and Commission*) ECLI:EU:C:2000:38, paragraph 79. The general

approach to quantifying harm in competition cases is also set out in paragraphs 11-20 of the Practical Guide.

41 Available at http://ec.europa.eu/competition/antitrust/legislation/best_practices_submission_en.pdf.

42 See paragraphs (17) et seq. above.

43 See Article 2(13) Damages Directive which explicitly clarifies that 'evidence' includes documents and all other objects containing information, irrespective of the medium on which the information is stored.

44 Econometric techniques are explained in section 5 below and in Annex 2.

45 See also paragraphs 13 et seq. of the Practical Guide.

46 Recital 16 Damages Directive clarifies that a category of evidence should be identified by reference to common features of its constitutive elements such as the nature, object or content of the documents the disclosure of which is requested, the time during which they were drawn up, or other criteria.

47 See Article 5(4) Damages Directive.

48 Recital 18 Damages Directive.

49 See Best Practices, paragraph 45.

50 Directive (EU) 2016/943 of the European Parliament and of the Council of 8 June 2016 on the protection of undisclosed know how and business information (trade secrets) against their acquisition, use and disclosure, OJ L157, 15.06.2016, pages 1-18.

3. THE ECONOMIC THEORY OF PASSING-ON

3.1. OVERVIEW

[4.472]

(46) The passing-on of overcharges and the associated price and volume effects arise because of a firm's incentives to respond to increases in its costs by raising prices.[51] The initial overcharge may be understood as an increase in the input costs for the direct purchaser. To estimate the passing-on effects, the court would typically need to consider how such a cost increase would affect 1) prices set by the direct purchaser in the downstream market and 2) the value of the lost sales supplied by the direct purchaser.

(47) National courts estimate passing-on based on the circumstances of the specific case. However, a general understanding of the economic theory of passing-on and the associated effects may be important for the court for several reasons. Firstly, predictions from economic theory may serve as one of several factors relevant for assessing whether the required standard of proof is met in a specific case. For instance, economic theory provides the court with a framework within which quantitative and qualitative evidence could be evaluated.[52] Secondly, particularly at an early stage of the litigation, economic theory may assist judges when making decisions in relation to the disclosure of data or information by assessing its relevance. Finally, theoretical or conceptual considerations can also form a basis for discerning the credibility and reliability of different economic explanations underpinning the link between overcharge and passing-on put forward by the parties.

(48) The Damages Directive does not distinguish between harm resulting from 1) increased prices (price effects) and the passing-on of overcharges including the volume effect and 2) other effects, such as reduced quality of products or hampered innovation (non-price effects) which may arise. These guidelines focus on the passing-on of price increases and the related volume effects.[53]

(49) According to economic theory, the existence and the magnitude of the passing-on effects, i.e. the associated price and volume effects, are determined by a range of factors.[54] These factors affect the outcome of a passing-on scenario simultaneously, and their interdependency should be taken into account.

(50) Further, the relative importance of each factor might vary from case to case. Thus, it may be relevant for the judge to understand which factors are likely to affect the degree of passing-on in a particular case. For this, depending on national law, the judge may refer to explanations from the parties' economic experts or its own court-appointed economic expert. Moreover, in practice, a firm may not always take pricing decisions that are entirely consistent with the predictions on the basis of economic theory. It is therefore important to also assess the insights from economic theory in the light of the factual evidence available in the case at hand. Such evidence may be of both qualitative and quantitative nature, such as internal documents describing the degree of passing-on and the quantitative methods explained in section 4 below.

(51) As set out in further detail in Annex 1, according to economic theory, the most important factors affecting the existence and magnitude of the passing-on effects include:

- (i) the nature of input costs[55] subject to an overcharge (whether these costs are fixed or variable, whether the infringement leads to increases of these costs only to one customer or to all or the vast majority of customers on a given market)
- (ii) the nature of the product demand that the direct or indirect customers face (in particular, the link between the demand and price level);
- (iii) the strength and intensity of competition in the markets where the direct or indirect customers are active; and
- (iv) other elements, such as price adjustment costs, the proportion of a firm's costs affected by the overcharge, buyer power, vertical integration of direct and indirect customers, price regulation or the timing of the pricing decisions undertaken at the various levels of the supply chain.

(52) Firstly, the nature of the input costs subject to an overcharge affects whether and to what extent this overcharge can be passed on. When the overcharge impacts the direct purchaser's costs which do not vary according to the input quantity (i.e. fixed costs), it is less likely to be passed on because such costs typically do not affect the direct purchaser's price setting, at least not in the short run. However, in the long run, fixed costs may affect a firm's strategic decision analysis, too, e.g. the production capacity, which, in turn, might impact the subsequent (short run) price formation mechanism. In such a scenario, fixed costs may also be passed on. By contrast, when the overcharge impacts the direct purchaser's costs which actually vary according to the input quantity (i.e. variable

costs), it will generally be more likely to be passed on, at least to some extent. This is because marginal costs (a subcategory of variable costs that can be defined as the cost increment incurred when purchasing one additional input)[56] typically affect the direct purchaser's price-setting decisions.[57]

(53) Secondly, the product demand that the direct customer faces affects the level of passing-on. A standard price formation mechanism builds on the fact that the demand a firm faces (i.e. the quantity it sells) decreases when it raises its price. The extent to which a direct purchaser raises its own price when facing an overcharge depends on whether the demand reacts strongly to such a price change or not. For instance, if the direct purchaser is a monopolist and the demand that it faces is equally sensitive to a change in prices for all price levels and the direct purchaser is facing constant marginal costs, economic theory suggests that half of the overcharge will be passed on. If the demand the monopolist faces drops 'more and more' (i.e. at an increasing rate) when price increases, it is less likely that the overcharge will be passed on as compared to a situation in which the demand that such a monopolist faces drops 'less and less' (i.e. at a decreasing rate) as the price increases, all else being equal.[58]

(54) Thirdly, the nature and intensity of the competitive interaction between the firms on the market on which the direct purchasers are active also affects the level of passing-on. It is important to keep in mind that the effect that increased competition can have on the degree of passing-on depends on whether the initial overcharge affects only the direct customer (i.e. firm-specific overcharge) or also the competitors of the direct customer (i.e. industry-wide overcharge). If the overcharge affects only one direct purchaser, fiercely competing with other direct purchasers, passing-on is less likely compared to a situation where the only affected direct purchaser faces weak competition. However, if there is an industry-wide overcharge, a large number of fiercely competing direct purchasers will generally favour a higher passing-on of that overcharge compared to a situation where there is weaker competition among these direct purchasers.[59]

(55) A number of judgments from national courts in damages actions have underlined the importance of considering how demand reacts to changes in prices, the intensity of competition and whether or not the direct purchaser's competitors are affected by the overcharge.[60]

(56) Fourthly, as mentioned in paragraph (51) and in Annex 1, other elements may, under certain circumstances, play a crucial role in the direct purchaser's price formation mechanism, and, hence, for passing-on of the overcharge by the direct purchaser. For instance, one element which might be important in order to quantify passing-on is whether the input affected by the overcharge represents a large or small share of the direct purchaser's variable costs. A direct purchaser may face costs when changing its prices, so-called 'price adjustment costs'. If the overcharge only represents a small share of the variable costs, the direct purchaser may not find it profitable to pass on such overcharge due to the price adjustment costs. Further, other aspects that may also affect the degree of passing-on are the degree of buyer power or the timing of the pricing decisions undertaken at the various levels of the supply chain, for instance. Some of the factors mentioned in paragraph (51) have also been considered by national courts in cases involving passing-on.[61]

(57) The existence and extent of passing-on are linked to the loss of sales that generally will accompany any increase in prices. As described above, this loss of sales may be characterised as the volume effect, which a purchaser may claim for as loss of profit. The volume effect arises because the purchaser usually faces a downward sloping demand curve. If the initial overcharge is passed on down the supply chain, a volume effect will arise at all levels of the vertical chain. Hence, when the claim includes damages for volume effects, courts may have to estimate such an effect as well.

(58) As mentioned above, any victim of an infringement of EU competition law has the right to seek full compensation for the harm suffered causally linked to the infringement. When passing-on is invoked, an assessment of the volume effect may become important to quantify the overcharge harm in a damages action. In such a case, however, it should be noted that an estimation of the total harm by simply subtracting the passing-on related price effect from the overcharge effect would lead to an underestimation of the harm suffered by the direct or indirect customer if the volume effect is not taken into account.

(59) The lost volume stemming from an overcharge is influenced by the sensitivity of demand that the purchaser faces and how the purchaser's competitors react to the overcharge. For example, if the purchaser faces an inelastic demand, i.e. its customers are only to a small extent sensitive to increases in price, the price increase leads to a relatively small decrease in the volume sold. This will, everything else being equal, lead to a smaller volume effect than in the case of a more elastic demand. At the same time, if the purchaser's competitors also increase their prices after an overcharge, this might also reduce the impact of the purchaser's own price increase on its sales.[62]

3.2. EXAMPLES

(60) The hypothetical examples below intend to illustrate the relevance of the insights from economic theory explained in this section and in Annex 1.

(61) Example 1 describes firm-specific overcharges in a market with strong competition.

Example 1

Situation: There are 10 producers of apple juice in the same relevant market. One of the producers sources apples from a supplier involved in a price fixing cartel. This apple juice producer claims damages as compensation for an overcharge. However, the defendant (the supplier of apples) raises the passing-on defence and argues that the apple juice producer has passed on the entire overcharge to the indirect purchasers.

Analysis: The apple juice producer facing the overcharge is in strong competition with nine other companies for the production and supply of apple juice. All products sold by the ten companies are rather homogeneous to consumers. In so far as the other producers do not obtain apples from the cartel members, but are able to buy them at a lower price elsewhere, the producer having to buy from the cartel is placed at a competitive disadvantage vis-à-vis its competitors. The apple juice producer's ability to pass on the cost increase would hence be constrained due to the fact that it would lose sale (and profit) to its competitors to a very large extent if it passed on the overcharge, even only partially. The stronger the competition between the 10 apple juice producers, the greater the constraint on the ability to pass on the cost increase. Hence, in this scenario, the direct customer will normally not be able to pass on the increase in cost (the overcharge).

(62) Example 2 sets out a situation of industry-wide overcharges and the intensity of competition.

Example 2

Situation: All of the 10 producers of apple juice in Example 1 source apples from suppliers involved in a price fixing cartel. The members of the cartel claim that any overcharge is passed on to the indirect purchasers.

Analysis: The producers of apple juice are similarly exposed to the overcharge and the market is characterised as competitive. Since all of the producers are faced with the overcharge, one firm will not have a competitive disadvantage compared to the other firms. It is therefore more likely that each apple juice producer to a large extent will pass on the overcharge, in contrast to the case detailed in Example 1 (where the overcharge is firm-specific). As an illustration, in a perfectly competitive market, the price equals marginal costs and a rise in the cost of an input will therefore directly lead to an equal rise in the price.

(63) Example 3 describes the issue of the passing-on rate of monopolists facing different demand.

Example 3

Situation: Apple juice producer A is a monopolist in the market for the production of apple juice in Member State 1, while apple juice producer B is a monopolist in the same product market in Member State 2. The cost of producing one additional batch of apple juice is constant and similar for A and B.

The two apple juice producers sourced apples from C, a supplier involved in a price fixing cartel. As a consequence, both A and B faced an overcharge of 6 Euro per box of apples because they bought apples from C.

A and B faced different demands from the grocery retail chains in each Member State. In Member State 1, demand was equally sensitive to a change in prices for all price levels (the demand was linear, see Box 15). In Member State 2, this was not the case. There, demand dropped 'less and less' (at a decreasing rate) when price increased (the demand was convex, see also Box 15).

A and B claim compensation from C (the member of the cartel) for the harm resulting from the overcharge. C raises the passing-on defence, claiming that A and B have passed on half of the overcharge.

Analysis: The monopolists in Member State 1 and Member State 2 faced different demand from the retail grocery chains in each Member State. Their costs when producing one additional batch of apple juice were constant. The overcharge of 6 Euro per box of apples was considered as an increase in the marginal costs for each of them. Following such a cost increase, the scope to adjust the prices upwards would have depended on how much output each would have had to sacrifice to pass on a certain amount of the cost change, i.e. to have increased prices.

This is because, if the volume lost when increasing prices is relatively low, the price increase will be more attractive compared to the situation where the loss of volume is high. The loss of volume when increasing prices is related to the curvature of the demand that a monopolist faces, i.e. whether the demand is linear, convex or concave. This is also further explained in Box 15 below.

Regarding the monopolist A in Member State 1, on the basis of economic theory it may be possible to argue that the monopolist has passed on half of the overcharge, i.e. 3 Euro. However, as the monopolist B faced a convex demand, the remaining demand would have become less price sensitive as the price went up. Compared to A, who faces a linear demand, B would have lost less volume when increasing prices by 3 Euro. This implies that B has had an incentive to pass on more than 3 Euro.

(64) Example 4 describes the issue of price adjustment costs and variable vs. fixed costs in the short and long run.

Example 4

Situation: Firms A and B are the only firms owning and leasing out tower cranes in Member State 1. From 2005 to 2015 firms A and B participated in a cartel, agreeing to increase the leasing-price of tower cranes by 80 percent. Firm C is a construction firm operating in cities throughout Member State 1. The company designs, constructs and sells residential apartments in skyscrapers to final customers. The prices of the apartments are advertised in a range of different media and locations, including on the internet, in newspapers and on street-posters. The national competition authority in Member State 1 has found the agreement on prices in the construction sector to be a violation of competition law, and their decision imposing fines on the cartel members was not appealed by firm A or B.

Firm C is a direct customer of the cartel. It claims damages from the cartel members A and B. However, firms A and B have raised the passing-on defence, claiming that firm C has passed on the entire overcharge to the indirect purchasers, i.e. the final customers buying apartments in skyscrapers.

Analysis: Leasing of tower cranes is one of many input costs that firm C faces when designing and constructing skyscrapers. Examples of other input costs are raw materials such as steel and concrete, labour and financial costs. Hence, it is likely that the leasing of tower cranes only constitutes a small portion of the total costs. Since the prices of the apartments are advertised broadly, firm C may incur significant price adjustment costs. However, since the cartel had a duration of 10 years, the price adjustment costs may be negligible compared to the overcharge after a certain period, eventually giving firm C the incentive to take into account the overcharge when setting prices on apartments. Hence, it may be the case that, due to the price adjustment costs, firm C may not have the incentive to pass on the overcharge in the short run. However, the incentive to pass on the overcharge may change during the infringement period. In order to assess the actual passing-on during the relevant period, the court should therefore estimate the passing-on effect based on the evidence available, for instance by using one of the methods set out in section 4.

NOTES

51 These incentives are explained in more detail in Annex 1.

52 Such evidence is further explained in section 4.1.

53 It cannot be excluded, however, that the methods and techniques described in these guidelines may be applied in damages actions concerning other types of harm, i.e. non-price effects.

54 The reasons why the factors listed in paragraph (51) might be important in determining the existence and the degree of the passing-on related price effect and the passing-on related volume effect are explained in this section. A more detailed explanation of the impact of each factor is provided in Annex 1, together with an explanation of the standard price formation mechanism.

55 This is further explained in Annex 1.

56 See paragraph (159) below.

57 See also Guidelines on the assessment of horizontal mergers under the Council Regulation on the control of concentrations between undertakings, OJ C31, 05.02.2004, paragraph 80. However, it is possible that in certain cases, fixed costs may also be taken into account by an undertaking when determining its prices. If this is the case, it should be demonstrated by the party that supports such a view, for instance by using the methods for estimation explained in section 4.

58 The importance of the shape of the product demand is further explained in Example 3 in chapter 3.2 and in Annex 1.

59 These predictions from economic theory are further illustrated and explained in Example 2 in chapter 3.2.

60 For examples of judgments dealing with the importance of market dynamics and how demand reacts to changes in prices, see for instance the German judgments *Bundesgerichtshof* (Federal Court of Justice, Germany), judgment of 28 June 2011, case KZR 75/10 (ORWI) paragraphs 59 and 69 and *Landgericht Düsseldorf* (Regional Court, Düsseldorf), judgment of 19 November 2015, case 14d O 4/14 (*German Car Glass*), paragraph 221. The importance of the degree of competition and whether the initial overcharge is firm-specific or industry-wide is also dealt within a number of judgments from national courts, see for example a Danish judgment, *Sø-og Handelsretten* (Maritime and Commercial High Court, Denmark) judgment of 03 October 2002, case V 15/01 (UfR2004.2600S) (*EKKO v Brandt Group Norden et al*), and a Spanish judgment, *Tribunal Supremo de España* (Supreme Court, Spain), judgment of 07 November 2013, case 5819/2013 (*Nestle et al v Ebro Puleva*).

61 For an example of a case considering whether passing-on is likely when the input affected by the overcharge represents a small share of the direct purchaser's variable costs, see for instance a French judgment, *Cour d'Appel de Paris* (Court of Appeal, Paris), judgment of 27 February 2014, case 10/18285 (*SNC Doux Aliments Bretagne et al v Société Ajinomoto Eurolysine*), this judgment is also further explained in Box 10 below.

62 If only the purchaser increases its price, its customers might switch to buying from the competitors. If, however, the competitors also raise their prices to some extent, the switch might be less attractive for the customers, so the overall sales of the first purchaser might be reduced less. It should be noted though that if some or all customers respond to a market wide price increase by stopping to buy the product altogether, the volume effect might even be larger than in the single purchaser price increase case.

4. THE QUANTIFICATION OF PASSING-ON AND VOLUME EFFECTS – GENERAL ASPECTS

[4.473]

(65) Compensation for harm suffered aims at placing the injured party in the position in which it would have been had the infringement not occurred. In order to be able to assess this position, one needs to compare the observed situation, i.e. the situation in which the infringement took place, with a hypothetical situation, i.e. the situation in which the infringement did not take place. This hypothetical situation is referred to as the 'counterfactual scenario'.

(66) The purpose of building a counterfactual scenario is to isolate the effect of the infringement from other factors affecting the price of a product or service, which would have affected such a price even if the infringement had not taken place.[63] For instance, an increase in demand would typically lead to a price increase even absent a cartel. Direct or indirect purchasers should not be compensated for that effect. Hence, when constructing a counterfactual scenario, it is necessary to control for factors that are not related to the infringement.[64]

(67) As the counterfactual scenario is hypothetical, it cannot be directly observed. As described below, different methods and techniques have been developed in economics and legal practice to establish the counterfactual. These vary in terms of the underlying assumptions and the variety of data needed.

(68) While these methods seek to construct how the market would have evolved absent the infringement, direct evidence available to the parties and the court (e.g. internal documents describing how the direct purchaser has passed on the initial overcharge in a specific situation) may also provide, under applicable national legal rules, important information for assessing damages in a specific case.[65]

(69) When dealing with passing-on in a damages action for an infringement of competition law, national courts may have to consider three components that relate to the harm for which a direct or indirect purchaser may claim compensation, namely the overcharge, the passing-on related price effect and the passing-on related volume effect.[66] National courts and economic experts may choose to estimate these three components sequentially, i.e. in a three-step procedure set out below.

(70) In a first step, the overcharge may be quantified or estimated. A number of different methods can be employed to do this. However, the methods most widely used by parties and courts to estimate the initial overcharge are the so-called comparator-based methods. The different methods for estimating the overcharge are considered in detail in the Practical Guide.

(71) A second step involves estimating the magnitude of the passing-on related price effect. The extent of this effect may be estimated directly by employing the comparator-based methods, i.e. similar methods as when quantifying the overcharge. If certain assumptions are fulfilled, the extent of this effect may also be estimated indirectly by obtaining

an estimate of the rate at which the increase in the affected input cost should have been passed on and combining this estimate with information on the overcharge and sales. Sections 5.1 to 5.2 provide an overview of different approaches for the quantification of these effects.

(72) In a third step the passing-on related volume effect is estimated. Similar to the estimation of the passing-on related price effect, the volume effect may be estimated directly or indirectly. Different approaches for quantifying these effects are considered in Sections 6.2 and 6.3.

(73) Other approaches, such as a simulation approach, accounting simultaneously for passing-on related price and volume effects, may also be used to quantify the harm in damages actions before national courts for the infringement of EU competition law. The simulation approach is briefly explained in section 5.2.

4.1 DATA AND INFORMATION NEEDED WHEN QUANTIFYING THE PASSING-ON EFFECTS

(74) As explained in section 2.2, the Damages Directive includes rules governing the disclosure of evidence. Data and information in the hands of the parties or third parties are important factors in order to carry out a sound economic analysis of the passing-on effects. Hence, a useful first step when quantifying the passing-on related price effect may be to identify the need for and the availability of data for building the counterfactual.

(75) When deciding which type of data and information is relevant in a specific case, it may be helpful for the judge to take into account the general insights from economic theory explained in section 3. These insights may also be relevant if the judge needs to assess conflicting views of economic experts.[67] Furthermore, the type of data needed for estimating the passing-on will usually require good knowledge of the industry in question and the prevailing market characteristics in the case at hand. Therefore, it may be useful to initially consider documents which indicate the plausibility of passing-on in the first place, such as existing court decisions, parallel civil proceedings at the same or a different level of the supply chain in the same market, market studies or decisions from competition authorities describing the relevant market dynamics.[68]

(76) The court may have to consider evidence of both qualitative and quantitative nature.[69] Qualitative evidence, such as internal documents on pricing, strategy, contracts and financial reporting, may be analysed in the context of economic theory. They may also give information on whether there is evidence of a link between the downstream pricing and the upstream overcharge that results from the infringement.

(77) However, in order to construct a counterfactual and control for different factors affecting passing-on, quantitative evidence may also be useful in many cases. Such evidence may include data on actual prices, costs or margins as well as external indicators which would influence pricing decisions of firms, e.g. aggregated measures of economic activity (such as GDP growth, inflation and employment rates). In some cases, regional variables of economic activity might be useful to control for different regional tendencies which are not related to the infringement.

(78) The court may also take into account more industry or firm-specific factors influencing the price formation. For instance, in the example in Box 1 above, if plastic had also been an essential input for the production of wire harness during the infringement period when copper manufacturer A had agreed with its competitors to fix prices for copper as the other essential input for the wire harness supplier B, it is likely that B would have passed on to its customer also an increase in prices for plastic which was not subject to an infringement of EU competition law. In this case, an estimation of passing-on which fails to take into account the effects related to the increase in prices for plastic could materially overestimate the passing-on of the overcharge by wrongly attributing the entire price increase to the infringement. Similar reasoning applies to potential decreases in other input costs which, if not accounted for and passed on down the supply chain, would artificially decrease the estimated passing-on of the cartel overcharge.

(79) In the examples that follow, the application of the methods focuses on the price. Depending on the availability of data and the circumstances of a given case, the court may also consider the same methods to estimate other economic variables, such as profit margins or the level of costs of an undertaking. The data used to compare the affected market with the counterfactual may relate to the entire market (e.g. the average of the price of wire harnesses for all customers in other product markets or geographic markets) or to certain customers or customer groups.

4.2. THE USE OF ECONOMIC EXPERTS

(80) In many cases where passing-on of overcharges is assessed, economic experts may be involved in damages actions before national courts. The rules on expert evidence vary significantly between the Member States.[70] In any case, national courts may find it helpful to have guidance on general principles and tools relevant for the involvement of economic experts.

(81) Early in the proceedings, the court may, if the national legislation allows it, facilitate a discussion between experts representing the parties involved. Such discussions may aim at narrowing down areas of agreement and disagreement on issues relevant to the case, including issues related to disclosure requirements. An example of such an approach is provided in Box 3 below.

Box 3: Example of a case involving evidence provided by economic experts[71]

In a case before a UK court, economic experts representing each side (the infringer and the claimant) had proposed their own distinct method for estimating passing-on. The judge expressed concerns about the potential complexity of the expert evidence and requested the parties' experts' to reach an agreement on the proposed approach to economic evidence on passing-on before any disclosure was ordered. If the experts failed to reach an agreement on the approach, the judge would hear submissions on the respective approaches, including an explanation of what each expert proposed, the information required and the cost of the exercise, and then decide which method should be applied.

(82) In some jurisdictions national courts may appoint economic experts who assist the judge when estimating passing-on and they have traditionally taken this approach to estimate the initial overcharge. The court may employ a similar approach when estimating passing-on, e.g. by using the so-called comparator-based methods. The experience from using court-appointed experts when estimating the overcharge may, therefore, also be relevant for the estimation of passing-on. An example of an approach where the court has appointed an economic expert is provided in Box 4 below.

Box 4: Example of a case in which the court appoints an economic expert[72]

In a case before a German court, an economic expert was appointed by the court. The expert's task was to propose a methodology and subsequently quantify the overcharge. As a first step, the expert proposed an empirical method for estimation of the overcharges. The approach suggested by the expert was discussed in written format and in oral hearings before the court decided on which approach to take.

In the next step, the chosen method was applied and overcharges were calculated. The underlying data used for the calculations was submitted to the court and to the parties.

The third step was a robustness check according to which the parties were given the opportunity to give comments and ask questions. These comments were taken into account in a final assessment delivered to the court. The final assessment also considered the plausibility of the estimated results, the robustness of the estimated effects and the quality of the underlying data.

(83) In a case in which the economic experts representing the parties have conflicting views on which approach to employ in order to estimate passing-on, the national court may also seek advice from the national competition authority on which method to employ.[73] Moreover, to assess the degree of passing-on, a national court may in principle also rely on information included in a decision issued by a competition authority, e.g. regarding the initial overcharge.[74]

NOTES

63 It should be noted that the need to construct a counterfactual when assessing passing-on is in line with the jurisprudence of the CJEU on passing-on in the context of reimbursement of unlawful levies and custom duties charged by Member States, see CJEU, judgment of 04 October 1979, case C-238/78 (*Ireks-Arkady v Council and Commission*) ECLI:EU:C:1979:226, paragraph 14; CJEU, judgment of 21 December 2000, case C-441/98 (*Michailidis*) ECLI:EU:C:2000:479, paragraphs 33 et seq.; CJEU, judgment of 06 September 2011, case C-398/09 (*Lady & Kid and Others*) ECLI:EU:C:2011:540. Further, in the Opinion of Advocate General Geelhoed delivered 03 June 2003 in case C-129/00 (*Commission v Italian Republic*) ECLI:EU:C:2003:319, paragraph 78, the Advocate General pointed to the fact that a counterfactual would be required to show what would have occurred to prices in the downstream market in the absence of the initial overcharge.

64 See the related discussion in paragraph (77).

65 See also the Practical Guide, paragraphs 14 and 30.

66 See Box 16 in Annex 1.

67 See paragraph (39) above.

68 See paragraph (25) above.

69 See paragraph (37) above and the examples in Box 9 and Box 10 below.

70 For instance, courts in France, the Netherlands and the United Kingdom to a large extent deal directly with economic experts appointed by the parties. In other Member States, such as Belgium, Denmark, Germany, Hungary and Italy, courts have in many cases sought to seek advice from court-appointed experts. There are also variations in national legislation with regard to whom the expert owes a duty. In some Member States, such as the United Kingdom and Ireland, the expert owes a duty to the court, even if their fees are paid by the parties. In Spain, experts appointed by the parties have a duty of objectiveness and independence, while in some Member States, such as Germany and Italy, there is no such explicit requirement.

71 *High Court of Justice of England and Wales*, judgment of 04 October 2017, [2017] EWHC 2420 (Ch) (*Emerald Supplies v British Airways Plc*).

72 *Oberlandesgericht Düsseldorf* (Higher Regional Court, Düsseldorf), judgment of 26 June 2009, case VI-2a Kart 2 – 06/08 (*Zement*).

73 It follows from Article 17(3) Damages Directive that a national competition authority may, upon request of a national court, assist that national court with respect to the determination of the quantum of damages where that national competition authority considers such assistance to be appropriate.

74 See e.g. *Oberlandesgericht Düsseldorf* (Higher Regional Court, Düsseldorf), judgment of 15 April 2013, case VI-4 Kart 2 – 6/10 (*OWi*), and subsequently the *Bundesgerichtshof* (Federal Court of Justice, Germany), judgment of 09 October 2018, case KRB 51/16 (*Flüssiggas I*) on *Bundeskartellamt* (German national competition authority) decisions of 14.12.2007, 26.2.2008, 12.02.2009 and 09.04.2009, case B11-20/50 (*Flüssiggas*) in which the *Bundeskartellamt* took into account the additional revenues gained through the infringement (*kartellbedingter Mehrerlös*) and the discussions on different methods to calculate the overcharge.

5. THE QUANTIFICATION AND ESTIMATION OF PASSING-ON RELATED PRICE EFFECTS

[4.474]

(84) When estimating the passing-on related price effect national courts may rely on different types of economic approaches to quantification, particularly the comparator-based approaches, but also the passing-on rate approach[75] or the simulation approach. These approaches, as described in this chapter, build on quantitative data to estimate the passing-on effect. In many cases, the court may find it useful to also assess qualitative evidence, such as internal documents or oral evidence from witnesses, when estimating the passing-on effect. The availability of such qualitative evidence may play an important role when deciding whether any, and if so which, of the techniques can be used by a party to meet the required standard of proof under the applicable law.[76]

5.1. COMPARATOR-BASED METHODS

(85) The passing-on related price effect at various stages in the supply chain may be computed by estimating directly the increase in prices or change in margins that has resulted from the impact of the initial overcharge. When assessing whether an overcharge is passed on from the direct purchaser, this method compares the price set by the direct purchaser during the infringement period with the price set in the comparator market(s).

(86) When estimating the passing-on related price effect, the court may estimate the differences between the observed and the counterfactual prices or margins[77] using the same comparator-based methods as used to compute the initial overcharge. While the underlying concept of these methods are described in detail in the Practical Guide, further guidance on the implementation of such methods in the context of passing-on is provided in the sections below.

(87) Comparator-based methods have the advantage that they use real-life data observed on the same or a similar market.[78] They rely on the fact that the comparator scenario can be considered representative of the non-infringement scenario. These methods have also been recognised and employed by competition authorities in Europe in order to undertake analyses of similar character as the estimation of passing-on, e.g. when performing ex-post evaluation of competition policy.[79]

(88) When employing the comparator-based method, one would ideally compare the price or margin during the infringement period with the exact same market absent the infringement. However, it is naturally not possible to know exactly how a market would have evolved in the absence of an infringement. For instance, it may be the case that important factors affecting the prices set by the direct purchaser, such as changes in demand or prices of other inputs, will not have a similar impact on prices during the infringement period and in the counterfactual scenario.

(89) These factors are crucial to have in mind when considering whether a given comparator market is suitable as the counterfactual scenario. As further explained in section 5.1.1, various techniques are available to account for differences between the market affected by the infringement and the comparator markets. Whether the level of similarity between the market on which the infringement took place and the comparator markets is considered to be sufficient in order for the results of such comparison to be used to estimate passing-on depends on the national legal systems.[80]

5.1.1. *APPROACHES*

(90) When the comparator-based method is used to estimate the passing-on effect, the price set by the direct or indirect purchaser during the infringement period is compared to the non-infringement, or counterfactual, scenario. The counterfactual scenario can be established on the basis of:[81]

— price or margin data concerning this market before and/or after the infringement, usually referred to as the before-during-after approach;

— data concerning the same (product) market but in a different geographical area, or another product market that is considered to evolve in a similar manner to the market where the direct or indirect purchaser operates, usually referred to as the cross-sectional approach; or

— a combination of comparisons over time and comparisons across markets, usually referred to as the difference-in-differences approach

5.1.1.1.
The before-during-after approach

(91) An approach frequently used when estimating initial overcharges is to compare prices over time on the same market, i.e. before-during-after comparison (illustrated in Box 5 below).[82] When applying this approach to estimate passing-on, the comparator market is the exact same product market as the market on which the direct or indirect purchaser was active when the infringement took place, but analysed at different points in time. Hence, the underlying assumption is that the product market in question in the non-infringement period provides a good approximation of the counterfactual, i.e. the situation that would have prevailed on the product market if no infringement had happened during the period of infringement. This assumption may be wrong because, in a practical sense, there is no comparator market irrespective of geography or product to account for an additional element of isolation in relation to the effect stemming from the infringement.

Box 5: Illustrated example of a before-during-after approach[83]

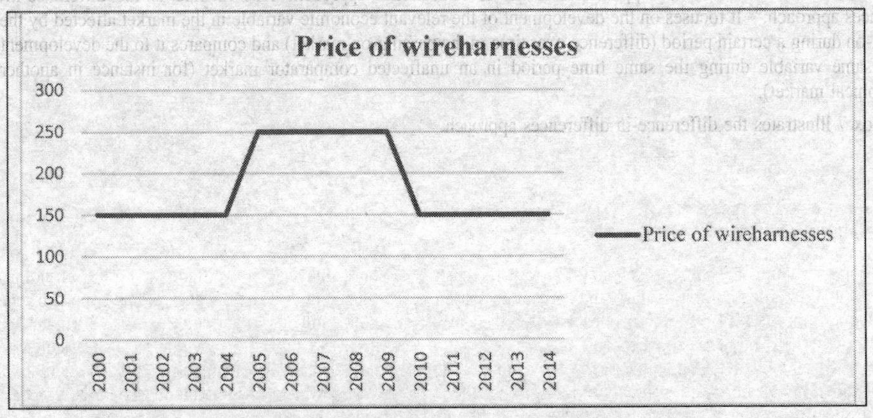

(92) In the example illustrated in Box 5 above, it is assumed that the illegal price fixing in the copper-industry had a duration of five years from 2005 to 2010. In this period[84] the initial overcharge was passed on to the car manufacturer C. When applying this method the price paid by the car manufacturer during the infringement period is compared to the price paid by the car manufacturer in a period not affected by the infringement and the passing-on, e.g. in 2003 and 2004. An example of a case where a claimant applied this approach is given in Box 8 below.

5.1.1.2.
The cross-sectional approach

(93) In some cases, it may be challenging to observe price developments over time in the comparator or infringement markets. If this is the case, another comparator-based method could be employed, namely a method which compares different geographical markets. The underlying assumption of this approach is that the other geographical market is similar to the infringement market in all aspects but for the infringement event. Again, this assumption may go too far.

(94) Box 6For example, as shown in Box 6 below, a national court may consider the comparison of prices paid by the car manufacturer C_1 during the infringement period in Member State 1 (*p1*), with the average price paid by similar car manufacturers in Member State 2, i.e. on a separate geographical market which is unaffected by the infringement (*p2*). This method is referred to as cross-market comparison.[85]

Box 6: Illustrated example of a cross-sectional approach

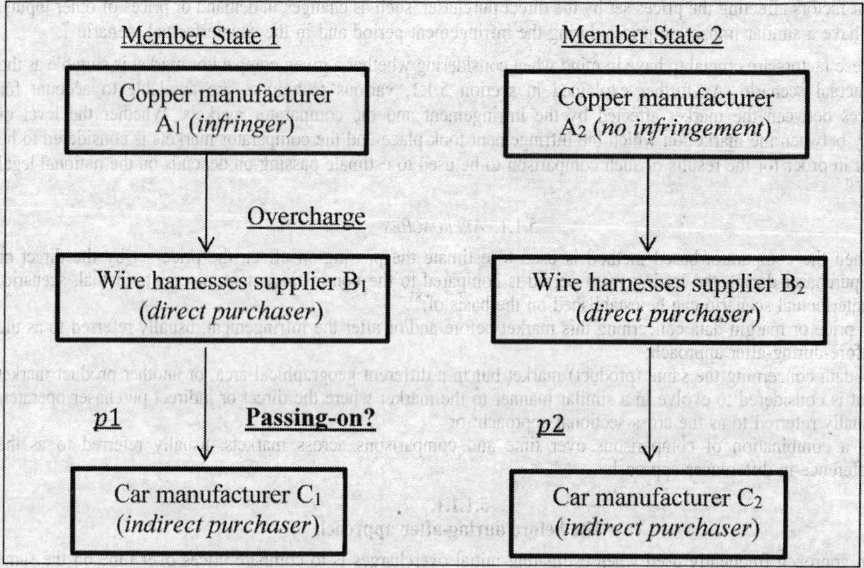

If *p*1 is found to be higher than *p*p2, this finding indicates a passing-on related price effect from wire harnesses supplier B1 to car Manufacturer C_1 in Member State 1. The same type of comparison can be undertaken with regard to any other economic variable, e.g. margins or volumes sold.

5.1.1.3.
The difference-in-differences approach

(95) From an economic point of view, the most accurate method of the comparator-based methods is the one that combines the before-during-after approach and the cross-sectional approach. This method is the difference-in-differences approach.[86] It focuses on the development of the relevant economic variable in the market affected by the passing-on during a certain period (difference over time in the passing-on market) and compares it to the development of the same variable during the same time period in an unaffected comparator market (for instance in another geographical market).

(96) Box 7 illustrates the difference-in differences approach.

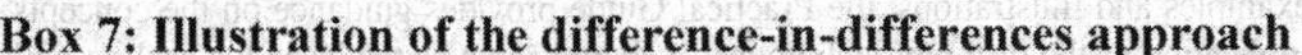

Box 7: Illustration of the difference-in-differences approach

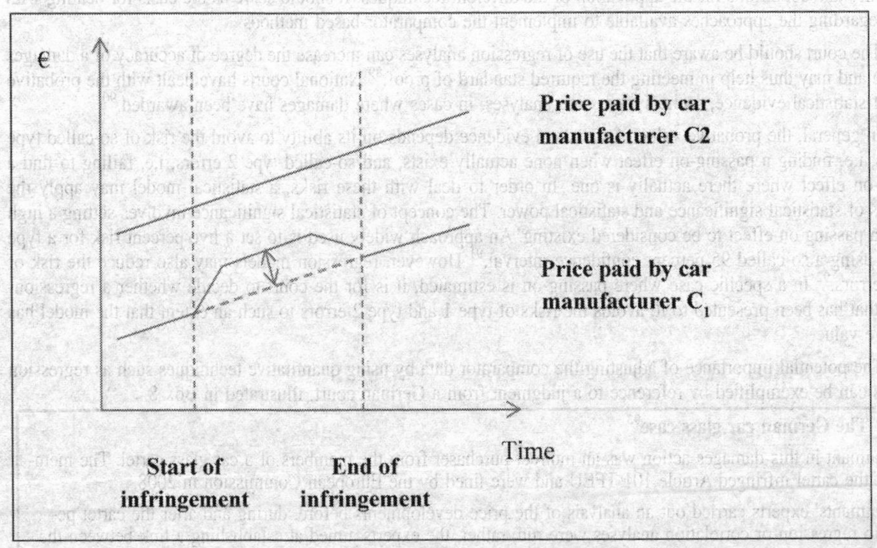

(97) Assuming, in a case on which Box 5 and Box 6 are based, car manufacturer C1 in Member State 1 (the indirect purchaser) claims damages from the copper manufacturer A1 (the infringer). As explained in paragraph (8), any harm that C1 suffers stems from the passing-on of overcharges from the wire harnesses supplier B1. Using a difference-in-differences approach would involve an assessment of the development of the price paid by the car manufacturer C1 in Member State 1 (the market with a passing-on related price effect) during a certain period, and comparing it to the development of the price paid by the car manufacturer C2 in Member State 2 (unaffected by the infringement and hence with no passing-on related price effects) in the same time period. The comparison shows the difference between these two differences over time. This provides an estimate of the change in the price paid by the car manufacturer, excluding all those factors that affected the markets both in Member State 1 and Member State 2 in the same way. Hence, the method isolates the passing-on related price effect from other influences on the price of wire harnesses common to both markets.

(98) Another variation of the case, which Box 6 and Box 7 are based on, may illustrate the method. Assuming that a before-during-after comparison reveals an increase in the unit price of wire harnesses of 100 Euro in the Member State 1 (where the infringement and passing-on occurred) between 2005 and 2010. An analysis of the unaffected market in Member State 2 over the same period may show that the unit price of wire harnesses has increased by only 10 Euro, due to an increase in another input cost, e.g. plastic. Assuming that the higher input cost (of plastic) also concerned Member State 1, and provided that all other conditions are the same, a comparison of the different development of prices on wire harnesses in Member States 1 and 2 would indicate the price increase caused by the passing-on effect. In the example, this would be 90 Euro.

(99) Therefore, a significant strength of the difference-in-differences approach is that it can filter out changes unrelated to the passing-on related price effect that occurred during the same period as the passing-on. However, it rests on the assumption that other factors, in the example above the price of plastic, affect the markets similarly. If this is not the case, an econometric implementation of the difference-indifferences technique may be necessary. Implementations of such techniques are described in more detail in section 5.1.2 below.

5.1.2. Implementing comparator-based approaches in practice

(100) Various techniques are available for estimating passing-on related price effects based on the comparator-approach. Certain factors, such as an increase in the raw material costs in the example above, may influence only the comparator market or only the market affected by the passing-on. As explained above, adjustments should be made to the observed data in order to account for such influences. These could be simple adjustments to the data in cases where the influencing factor and the magnitude of its effects can relatively easily be accounted for.

(101) In certain cases, when the availability and quality of the data permit, adjustments of comparator data can be made on the basis of econometric techniques, in particular through the use of regression analysis. Regression analysis is a statistical technique which helps to analyse patterns in the relationship between economic variables.

(102) In a regression analysis, a number of data observations for the variable under consideration and the likely influencing variables are examined. The relationship identified is usually expressed in the form of an equation. This equation makes it possible to estimate the effects of influencing variables on the variable under consideration and to isolate them from the effects of the infringement. Based on a regression analysis, it is possible to estimate how closely the relevant variables are correlated with each other, which may in some instances be suggestive of a causal influence of one variable on the other.[87]

(103) The different techniques available for adjustments of comparator data are described in more detail in the Practical Guide.[88] By reference to examples and illustrations, the Practical Guide provides guidance on the concepts, approaches and conditions for the application of the different techniques. It should serve as the basis for dealing with issues regarding the approaches available to implement the comparator-based methods.

(104) The court should be aware that the use of regression analyses can increase the degree of accuracy of a damages estimate and may thus help in meeting the required standard of proof.[89] National courts have dealt with the probative value of statistical evidence, such as regression analyses, in cases where damages have been awarded.[90]

(105) In general, the probative value of statistical evidence depends on its ability to avoid the risk of so-called type 1 errors, i.e. finding a passing-on effect when none actually exists, and so-called type 2 errors, i.e. failing to find a passing-on effect where there actually is one. In order to deal with these risks, a statistical model may apply the concepts of statistical significance and statistical power. The concept of statistical significance involves setting a high bar for a passing-on effect to be considered existing. An approach widely used is to set a five percent risk for a type 1 error, using a so-called 95 percent confidence interval.[91] However, regression models may also reduce the risk of type 2 errors.[92] In a specific case where passing-on is estimated, it is for the court to decide whether a regression-model, that has been presented to it, avoids the risks of type 1 and type 2 errors to such an extent that the model has probative value.

(106) The potential importance of adjusting the comparator data by using quantitative techniques such as regression analyses can be exemplified by reference to a judgment from a German court, illustrated in Box 8.

Box 8: The German car glass case[93]

The claimant in this damages action was an indirect purchaser from the members of a car glass cartel. The members of the cartel infringed Article 101 TFEU and were fined by the European Commission in 2008.

The claimants' experts carried out an analysis of the price developments before, during and after the cartel period. No regression or correlation analyses were run, rather, the experts aimed at establishing a link between the price of car glass (the cartelised product) and replacement car glass purely by observing the price patterns.

The court however considered that this analysis failed to show any sufficiently direct causal link between the pricing of the two products mentioned above. This was particularly because of the data used in the claimants' expert analysis and the fact that it did not take due account of other effects on prices as well as market trends. The court also took into account the market conditions in the case at hand to dismiss the passing-on arguments.

(107) However, techniques based on econometric analyses may in certain cases entail considerable costs. In such cases, the court may find it sufficient to estimate the passing-on by simultaneously assessing quantitative data without the use of regression analysis and by taking into consideration qualitative evidence. Moreover, the court may in most cases also find it useful to assess qualitative evidence, such as direct evidence on passing-on, also when employing the quantitative methods described in this section.

(108) When estimating passing-on based on qualitative evidence, internal documents describing a firm's pricing policy may be of particular relevance. When assessing internal documents, the court should be aware of the fact that firms in different industries, or even within the same industry, may adopt different pricing policies. In some cases, a firm may have a clear policy or established practice which identifies the price adjustments that will result from specific changes in cost. For example, in some cases purchasers may link price adjustments to changes in certain indices which may not be affected by the infringers' anti-competitive conduct, e.g. consumer price indices. In other cases, purchasers may seek to achieve certain performance objectives, e.g. apply a specific margin to the pricing of the products they supply. In principle, the former policy may speak against the finding of passing-on whereas the later suggests that the purchaser would pass on cost changes.

(109) Moreover, when assessing pricing policies, the court should also take into account whether the pricing policy of the relevant firm has actually been implemented, e.g. by considering price data to determine whether these correspond to the pricing policy in question.

(110) Examples of cases in which national courts have taken into consideration qualitative evidence are given below.

Box 9: Estimating passing-on based on qualitative evidence – *Cheminova* (2015)[94]

In this judgment, the court found that a producer of pesticide had passed on 50 percent of the initial overcharge to the indirect customers. This finding was based on economic theory. In this case, the court could rely on publicly available market studies characterising the market on which the direct customer was active as a monopoly market. In a report provided by the direct customer, it was argued that the market should in fact be characterised as competitive rather than a monopoly. The direct customer *inter alia* submitted that a large number of products were competing on the market and that moderate market shares indicated a competitive market. However, due to the facts of the specific case, the court disagreed with this approach.

Box 10: Estimating passing-on based on qualitative evidence – *DOUX Aliments* (2014)[95]

In this judgment, the court found that the claimant had demonstrated the absence of passing-on. The overcharge in this case concerned lysine, an input into the production of chickens. The court found that lysine only represented one percent of the costs of chicken production. Such a small increase in costs was not sufficient evidence to convince the court that it would also lead to an increase in prices of chicken. The court found that the prices responded to other factors, such as competition with other meat products and buyer power. When concluding that the overcharge was not passed on to the indirect retailers, the court referred to the fact that chickens were sold on an international and competitive market and that grocery retail chains had strong buyer power.

(111) When applying comparator-based methods for the estimation of overcharges, courts have also sometimes applied a so-called safety discount. This means they adjusted an amount that would sufficiently take account of uncertainties in the estimate from the observed data.[96] If the implementation of econometric analysis is not feasible, such an approach may also be applied for the estimation of passing-on. The objective of such an approach would be to exclude the effects of other possible factors on the variable under consideration, for instance the price offered by the indirect customer.

5.1.3. CHALLENGES

(112) When estimating the passing-on related price effect, the court may particularly consider techniques which, to the largest extent possible, control for factors other than the one stemming from the infringement. The difference-in-differences method is such a technique. It requires information or data from a comparator market (for instance another geographical market) and time-series data from the market affected by the passing-on. However, the court should be aware that there are potential challenges that may affect how valid the comparator-based methods may be.

(113) Ideally, the comparator market is similar to the infringement market, but itself not affected by the infringement. However, the purchasers on each of the markets often use the same input. In such a case, it might be difficult to find an unaffected comparator. In particular, if the scope of the infringement covers a broad geographic area, it is likely that products, similar to the product in question and incorporating the same input, have potentially been affected, as well. This can make it difficult to find a suitable comparator market.

(114) In other circumstances, the comparator market may be indirectly affected by the initial overcharge. In the stylised example of the copper cartel in Box 6, the wire harnesses supplier B1 purchases copper from the infringer A1. Even though the wire harnesses supplier B2 in the comparator market does not purchase from the infringer A1, the wire harnesses suppliers B2 and B1 may be competitors on the same geographic downstream markets. This implies that, if the wire harnesses supplier B1 increases its prices in response to the initial infringement, its competitors may raise their prices, as well. In this case, the price that the wire harnesses supplier B2 offers may have been indirectly affected by the infringement, and as a result may not provide a suitable comparator.[97]

(115) As regards comparison over time, it may be challenging to identify with sufficient precision the period when the market was affected by a certain infringement. The parties may present a decision issued by a competition authority which mentions an infringement period, i.e. sets out dates at which the infringement started and ended. However, this period may not correspond to the period in which a market was actually affected by the infringement. It is also important to note that determining the dates of either the infringement period or the period in which the market was affected, can have a strong impact on the outcome of the analysis. In reality, the effect of the infringement may not be limited to the period provided in such decision.[98] On the one hand, the start date identified by the competition authority may post-date the actual start of the infringement, for instance due to lack of reliable evidence.[99] On the other hand, the end date provided in an infringement decision may pre-date the end of the actual infringement.

(116) The effects of an infringement may also not be limited to the duration of the infringement. It is possible that the infringement will affect the market concerned even after the conduct prohibited under EU competition law has ceased. In particular, this may be the case in oligopolistic markets, if the information gathered during the infringement allows the suppliers of a certain product to adopt, on a sustainable basis after the infringement has ended, a course of action aimed at selling at a higher price than the competitive price, i.e. that would have been charged in the absence of the infringement, without engaging in practices prohibited by EU competition law.[100]

(117) The possibility that purchasers at different levels of the supply chain may delay the passing-on of an overcharge can also affect the comparison significantly.[101] The example in Box 1 above may illustrate this. Suppose the car manufacturer C negotiates prices with the wire harnesses supplier B on an annual basis. The wire harnesses supplier B only adjusts prices once a year after the negotiations with the car manufacturer C have been finalised. If a price fixing cartel in the copper market is established just after the negotiations between the wire harness supplier and the car manufacturer have ended, it is only when the next year's annual negotiations take place that the wire harnesses supplier may have had an opportunity to pass on the copper-price increase in their own price.

(118) Hence, the delay of passing-on down the supply chain may result in difficulties when deciding on the relevant period for comparing prices during and before or during and after the infringement (or both). The court may adjust the analysis by considering the nature of each case, for instance by analysing the pricing policy of the parties and, based on that, introducing a certain time lag when analysing the pricing patterns at different levels of the supply chain.

(119) The use of regression analyses when employing the comparator-based approach may increase the accuracy of the estimated passing-on effect. A judge should be aware that, while these types of regression models offer a direct estimate of the passing-on effect, they do not quantify the extent to which each of the theoretical factors affecting the passing-on, discussed in section 3 above (e.g. nature of input costs and nature of the product demand), contributed to the effect. A strength of using regression analyses is that it is less likely to make assumptions related to economic theory that are wrong. While such a factor-by-factor quantitative breakdown of the estimated passing-on effects is usually not necessary for the estimation of the passing-on effect, it can be noted that the techniques described in section 5.2.3 below might provide a quantitative breakdown of the factors.

5.2. OTHER METHODS

5.2.1 THE PASSING-ON RATE APPROACH

(120) The section above describes methods and techniques for comparator-based approaches to estimate the passing-on related price effect. In general, the comparator-based approach is preferable when it is feasible and proportionate to implement. This is due to the method's clear advantage of allowing for an estimation of passing-on based on the actual prices set by a direct or indirect purchaser during the infringement period. However, it relies inter alia on the availability of data on these prices, in addition to prices in one or several comparator market(s). Such information may

be available in many cases. However, if information on actual prices in the infringement market and the comparator market(s) cannot be presented before the court, for instance if the court finds that disclosure of such information is disproportionate to the value of the claim in the case at hand, passing-on may be estimated on the basis of other methods, such as the passing-on rate approach.

(121) This passing-on rate approach can be implemented by analysing how previous changes in a firm's costs have affected its prices before or after the infringement period. For instance, in the example in Box 1 above, the passing-on rate may be estimated by analysing how historical changes in the cost of copper have affected the price of wire harnesses. Put simply, if an increase in the cost of copper by 10 Euro is followed by a price increase of wire harnesses by 5 Euro, the passing-on rate is estimated to be 50 percent. To estimate the passing-on during the infringement period, the court could then combine this estimated passing-on rate with information on the overcharge and sales.

(122) However, the passing-on rate approach is not without risks and can even deliver misleading results in some cases. This is because when using this approach to estimate passing-on, the court can neither establish if the overcharge is actually passed on nor can it observe whether changes in the cost of the affected input are reflected in prices in the downstream markets. It is therefore crucial for the court to be aware that the passing-on rate approach relies on the assumption that, during the infringement period, changes in input costs are reflected in prices downstream. If this assumption is incorrect, this approach may produce estimates which are misleading in that they find a passing-on of overcharges where none has actually happened.

(123) When using the passing-on rate approach, the court would typically endeavour to estimate the passing-on based on how changes in the cost of the affected input have previously been reflected in prices downstream. However, if such information is not available, the court may look at the development of other components of the purchaser's marginal cost and analyse how such cost changes affect downstream prices. In the hypothetical case set out in paragraph (8) and further modified and explained in paragraph (78) and (98) above, this means that a court could consider an analysis of the relationship between the price of wire harnesses and the cost of plastic (not affected by the infringement), and estimate a passing-on rate based on the latter relationship.

(124) In most cases the infringement at issue concerns the cost of an input which constitutes just one component of the purchaser's marginal cost. If the input affected by the infringement constitutes only a very small fraction of the marginal cost, even a significant increase in the cost of that input may hardly be detected in the purchaser's price data, even if it is passed on in full. Although an alternative approach may be to estimate the passing-on rate based on changes in costs of more significant inputs and not just the cost of the affected less significant input, such an approach comes at the price of an assumption that may go too far, namely that the marginal cost increases are being passed on at an identical rate irrespective of the source for the cost increase. Moreover, if a comparator-based method, i.e. actual price based estimation, finds no statistically significant passing-on this can be considered as evidence supporting the hypothesis that no passing-on actually happened. In other words, the finding that there was no passing-on on the basis of the comparator-based method is neither a valid nor a sufficient argument, as such, to adopt a passing-on rate method.

(125) As explained in Annex 1, there are also good reasons why firms may not always pass on small changes in their marginal costs, at least not in the short run, even if they would pass on larger cost changes. Hence, it may not be legitimate to assume that the passing-on rate will be similar for different changes in the input cost. One explanation may be that the firm may incur so-called price adjustment costs, and thus prefer waiting until marginal cost increases accumulate beyond a certain threshold before changing its prices.

(126) When assessing the indirect evidence of passing-on based developments of cost components that are not affected by the overcharge, it is advisable to also take into account qualitative evidence that may show that the passing-on of small cost increases is in the specific case in line with the commercial practice of the direct or indirect purchaser.

(127) In certain cases, information on prices set by the direct purchaser during the infringement period, and only for this period, may be available. The passing-on rate approach may deliver misleading results also in such scenarios. This is because it would identify passing-on related price effects on the basis of changes in the costs of the input that has been subject to a competition law infringement. In many cases, it is not unlikely that, during the infringement period, the changes in the costs of the input that has been subject to a competition law infringement are substantially smaller than the cost increase resulting from the infringement. As explained above, small cost increases may not be passed on to the same extent as larger cost increases, and hence looking at relatively small cost and price changes during the infringement period could lead to an imprecise estimate of the passing-on effect.

5.2.2. Implementing the passing-on rate approach in practice

(128) The passing-on rate approach requires information on the initial overcharge and the relevant passing-on rate. If no prior estimation of the overcharge is available, the court may consider the techniques mentioned in the Practical Guide.[102]

(129) An advantage of the comparator-based method is that it allows for the construction of a counterfactual. As mentioned in paragraph (66) above, the purpose of this exercise is to isolate the effect of the infringement from other factors also affecting prices. While the passing-on rate method does not allow for such an approach, it is still important to control for factors that are not related to the infringement. One approach may be to use quantitative techniques, for instance regression analysis.[103] For instance, in the example in Box 1 above, a court may take into account an analysis of the relationship between the prices charged by the wire harnesses supplier and changes in the input costs of wire harnesses. However, other factors may have also affected the price at the downstream level, e.g. fluctuations in the demand of car manufacturers. If the court fails to take into account such additional factors, the estimated passing-on rate will most likely be biased.

(130) A regression analysis typically requires a large amount of data on costs and prices. Thus, for the purpose of estimating the passing-on rate, the court may alternatively consider whether estimates from other sources could provide a reasonable estimate for the passing-on rate. Examples of such other sources may include passing-on rates

found in other cases concerning the same industry or in other industries, academic studies relevant for the industry in the case at hand or evidence provided in witness statements. This is a particularly viable alternative when the necessary data is not available or quantitative methods fail to include relevant control factors.

(131) However, it is crucial to be aware that estimates based on other sources bear the risk of not taking into account factors relevant for the passing-on rate in the case at hand. In particular, it may be important to consider the methodology underlying the estimate found in other sources and the sensitivity of any result to potential differences between such an estimate and the passing-on rate. To do this, the court may take into account the relevant insights from economic theory, as explained in section 2.3 above and in Annex 1, such as the degree of competition. If there is only limited information, e.g. on the different market conditions or how the passing-on rate was determined, the passing-on rate approach may not be suitable.

5.2.3. The simulation approach

(132) The Practical Guide also introduces a so-called simulation approach as another way of quantifying harm of a competition law infringement.[104] This approach can also be used to estimate the passing-on related price and volume effect. It simultaneously accounts for the passing-on related price and volume effects. In order to employ this method, an economic expert will need to develop a model of competition at the stage of the distribution chain where the claimant is active, and simulate the effect of the relevant overcharge on the claimant's profit during the infringement period. For instance, the economic expert may test how different curvatures of the demand curve may affect the degree of passing-on. Based on the specifications of the demand side and the supply side, the equilibrium prices in the relevant market can be calculated. Furthermore, in a next step, it is possible to evaluate how these prices are affected by an overcharge.

(133) It is important for a judge to be aware that this approach requires extensive data on prices and quantity in the market concerned. Furthermore, it rests on assumptions about firms' and consumers' behaviour, which may go too far and might be difficult to validate. Hence, it may in many cases be difficult to meet the required standard of proof under applicable law when applying this method.

NOTES

75 The passing-on rate approach relies *inter alia* on the assumption that changes in input costs are passed on at an identical rate irrespective of the relevance of the input costs and the extent of the change in such input costs. This assumption may go too far. As further explained below in paragraphs (120) et seq., the passing-on rate approach should normally only be considered if the assumption is plausible based on the facts of the case.

76 See also the Practical Guide, paragraph 14.

77 The approach using margin data is explained in more detail in the section 6.3 on the estimation of the volume effect below.

78 This fact is emphasised in the Practical Guide, paragraph 37 and the jurisprudence on the estimation of overcharges cited there. A German court, also in the context of the estimation of overcharges, holds the view that comparable methods can be preferable compared to other approaches, see *Oberlandesgericht Düsseldorf* (Higher Regional Court, Düsseldorf), judgment of 26 June 2009, case VI-2a Kart 2 – 06/08 (*Zement*), paragraphs 469 et seq.

79 See for instance 'Reference guide on ex-post evaluation of competition agencies' enforcement decisions', OECD 2016.

80 The Practical Guide deals with this issue in the context of assessment of overcharges, see for example paragraphs 37 and 59- 95.

81 If for a counterfactual scenario comparator markets in foreign countries are taken into consideration, the national court should also keep in mind possible differences in legislation. This is particularly important when dealing with regulated markets, e.g. pharmaceuticals or energy.

82 See Practical Guide, paragraphs 38-48.

83 For the sake of simplicity, this graph only illustrates the effect on price stemming from the infringement. In a real-world scenario prices will also be affected by other factors than the passing-on rate, such as inflation and other cost shocks.

84 Note however that the issue of delayed passing-on, mentioned in Annex 1, may be of importance when comparing prices during the infringement with price before and after.

85 This method has been employed frequently to assess the initial overcharge in actions for damages, see for instance the cases cited in footnote 45 of the Practical Guide.

86 See also paragraph (112) below.

87 Regression analyses are explained in detail in the Practical Guide, paragraphs 69 et seq.

88 Ibid, chapter II B.

89 See also the Practical Guide, paragraph 92.

90 See for instance a case from the UK: High Court of Justice of England and Wales, judgment of 09 October 2018, [2018] EWHC 2616 (Ch) (*Britned v ABB*), permission to appeal given.

91 The use of confidence intervals when estimating damages is also explained in the Practical Guide, paragraphs 86 et seq.

92 There is a certain trade-off between the two error types in the following sense; for a given data sample size, further reducing the risk of type 1 errors (e.g., using a tighter, 99 percent confidence interval instead of the 95 percent interval) generally increases the risk of type 2 errors. In general, limiting both types of errors is only possible through increasing the sample size. Hence, in practice, it is important to assess whether the methods are applied on a sufficiently large dataset.

93 *Landgericht Düsseldorf* (Regional Court, Düsseldorf), judgment of 19 November 2015, case 14d O 4/14 (*German Car Glass*).

94 *Sø-og Handelsretten* (Maritime and Commercial High Court, Denmark), judgment of 15 January 2015, case SH2015.U-0004-07 (*Cheminova A/S v Akzo Nobel Functional Chemicals BV et al*).

95 *Cour d'Appel de Paris* (Court of Appeal, Paris), judgment of 27 February 2014, case 10/18285 (*SNC Doux Aliments Bretagne et al v Société Ajinomoto Eurolysine*).

96 See also the Practical Guide, paragraph 95.

97 This effect is similar to the effects of umbrella pricing mentioned in paragraph (32) above.

98 See also Practical Guide, paragraph 43.

[99] National courts may wish to consider that the relatively high burden of proof that competition authorities have to meet in their infringement proceedings is not *de facto* used to the detriment of the victim of a competition law infringement when these courts estimate the harm in a damages action of such victim.

[100] See also the Practical Guide, paragraph 153. For example, a case in which a national court ruled that the prices charged in the five months after the infringement ended were still influenced by the cartel, see *Oberlandesgericht Karlsruhe* (Higher Regional Court, Karlsruhe), judgment of 11 June 2010, case 6 U 118/05, also cited in the Practical Guide, paragraph 44.

[101] Moreover, undertakings may be aware that there is a risk of facing claims for damages, and that the scope of such a claim may be estimated based on post-infringement prices. Thus, they may have the incentives to maintain the price level after the infringement has come to an end.

[102] See Practical Guide, paragraphs 26 et seq.

[103] See paragraphs (101) et seq. above. The concept of regression analysis is explained in detail in the Practical Guide, chapter II (2).

[104] Practical Guide, paragraphs 96 et seq.

6. THE QUANTIFICATION AND ESTIMATION OF VOLUME EFFECTS

SECTION 6.1 INTRODUCTION

[4.475]

(134) When there is a passing-on related price effect, this necessarily implies, at least in theory, a volume effect.[105] Therefore, if the price effect is taken into account without the volume effect, this can underestimate the true harm. Hence, in order to avoid over- or under-compensation, the estimation of the volume effect is as essential as the estimation of the passing-on related price effect, provided the purchaser claims damages for loss of profit due to the volume effect.[106]

(135) As illustrated in Box 11 below, the volume effect refers to the loss of profit due to reduced sales that result from passing-on, i.e. less volume sold because of increased prices. In the sequential approach, mentioned above in paragraph (69), the third step of quantifying damages as a result of an overcharge is to estimate the magnitude of the volume effect.

Box 11: The volume effect

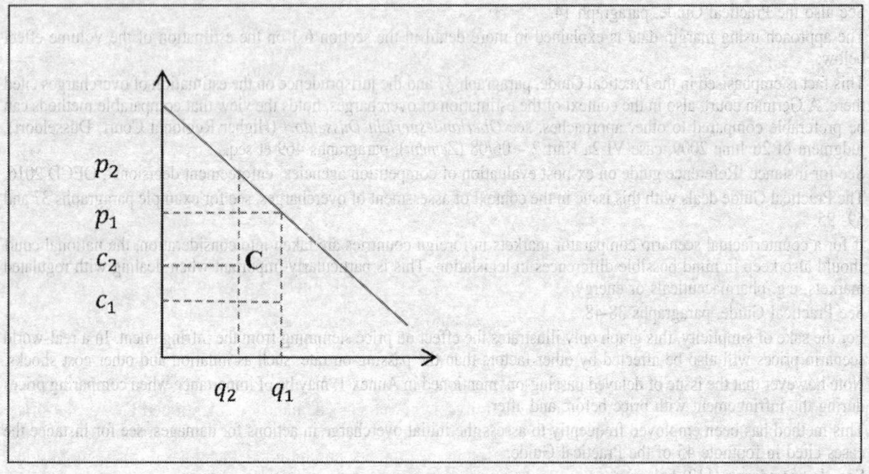

(136) The volume effect corresponds to the difference between q_1 and q_2. Area C represents the lost profit stemming from the loss in sales. It can be quantified by multiplying the lost volume with the profit margin (p_1-c_1) that the purchaser would have achieved in the absence of the infringement without any passing-on.

(137) The estimation of the volume effect requires an assessment of two factors, namely (i) the change in quantity due to increased prices and (ii) the counterfactual margin. To estimate these factors it is necessary to have data on parameters other than the ones necessary for the estimation of the passing-on related price effect. Depending on the data available, different methods may be employed. As for the estimation of the passing-on related price effect, the court may take into account qualitative evidence of direct nature when estimating the volume effect.[107] The existence of such evidence may play an important role when a court decides which, if any, of the different methods described in more detail below are to be used in a specific case.

(138) The volume effect has, so far, only been estimated by national courts in a limited number of cases. One example is given in Box 12 below. In this case, an economic expert appointed by the court used both qualitative and quantitative data to estimate the volume effect.

Box 12: Estimation of volume effects – *Cheminova* (2015)[108]

As explained in Box 9 above, this case concerns the sales of pesticides in Denmark. The court concluded that half of the initial overcharge was passed on by the direct purchaser. Based on the assessment of a court-appointed expert, the volume effect was estimated, as well. The expert estimated the volume effect as the counterfactual margin multiplied by the number of sales that had not been made due to the passing-on.

In order to estimate the number of sales that had not been made during the infringement period, the expert used an amended version of the elasticity approach which is further explained in section 6.3 below. Since quantitative data on prices and volume was not available, the expert derived a measure of elasticity by averaging the elasticities found in 23 market studies for pesticides. Further, the expert estimated the counterfactual margin by adjusting the realised margin during the infringement period. Based on this, the court concluded that damages resulting from the volume effect were equal to 20 percent of the overcharge amount.

SECTION 6.2. COMPARATOR-BASED APPROACH

6.2.1. Information needed

(139) The comparator-based approach for the purpose of estimating the volume effect requires information on (i) the observed quantity sold by the firm affected by the overcharge, (ii) the counterfactual volume sold and (iii) the price-cost margin that would have been achieved by the purchaser in the absence of the infringement. However, it is important to note that the observed price-cost margin is not the relevant margin required to estimate the volume effect. For instance, if the purchaser passes on half of the overcharge, this will reduce its margin, implying that the observed margin will be smaller than in the counterfactual. In this case, using the observed margin would understate the size of the volume effect.

(140) Moreover, the court should be aware that the relevant margin to estimate the volume effect does not necessarily correspond to standard measures of a firm's accounting margin, such as 'earnings before interest and taxes' (EBIT) or the net income of the firm.

(141) The relevant margins for the assessment of the volume effects are defined by the prices of the relevant products subtracted by the avoided costs, i.e. costs that have been saved as a result of the output reduction. Hence, in addition to an assessment of which costs are considered to be avoidable, the court may order disclosure of prices of the relevant products. In this context, it may also order disclosure of internal documents providing information on the contribution margins the purchaser uses for its own pricing decisions.

6.2.2. Methods and challenges

(142) The lost profit associated with the volume effect can be estimated comparator-based by multiplying the counterfactual margin by the reduction in sales volumes stemming from the passing-on of overcharges.

(143) Using the relevant data from the purchaser, the court may consider the comparator-based techniques described above to estimate the counterfactual margin and the counterfactual quantity. Since the observed profit margin and quantity may be affected by other factors unrelated to the infringement, it will in many cases be necessary to control for such additional factors. Hence, it would normally be necessary to employ one of the approaches described above in order to control for factors unrelated to the infringement, for instance a regression analysis.

(144) If the data needed to perform the difference-in-differences approach is not available, other techniques of the ones described above may be considered, namely cross-market comparison or comparison over time. However, if such techniques are employed, it is also important to construct a sound counterfactual taking into account factors varying between the different markets or time periods.

(145) The comparator-based methods rest on the assumption that the reference period or market is sufficiently similar, in particular with respect to market characteristics that are relevant for profit margins, such as the level of competition in the market or the cost structure of the suppliers. This assumption is not easily verified, as a large number of factors and strategic decisions are likely to determine a firm's margins.

6.3. ELASTICITY APPROACH

(146) The volume effect may also be estimated by combining the price increase observed as a result of the passing-on related price effect with an estimate of the price sensitivity of the relevant demand. As mentioned above, the price sensitivity of demand determines the strength of the relationship between price and demand. For example, if a price increase of 1 Euro is associated with a significant reduction in the quantity purchased, demand is said to be more price sensitive than if the purchase quantity reduction is less important for the same price increase of 1 Euro. The so-called price elasticity of demand shows the percentage change in demanded quantity associated with a one percent price increase.[109]

6.3.1. Methods and information needed

(147) In general, the decrease in volume, illustrated by the decrease in sales from q_1 to q_2 in Box 11 above, will be affected by a firm's own price increase as well as changes in the prices of the competitors, given that firms compete on prices. Hence, the magnitude of the loss in volume will require an assessment of how the passing-on has affected prices of all competitors in the market, as well as the sensitivity of demand to those price changes. When assessing this method, the volume effect[110] is estimated by multiplying the volume loss by the counterfactual margin.

(148) The data requirements when estimating the volume effect by reference to the elasticity approach will depend on whether the relevant firms are equally affected by the overcharge, i.e. whether it is an industry-wide overcharge. The volume effects of both the own-price and the cross-price elasticity could be captured by the market price elasticity. Under such circumstances the volume effect may be estimated based on the counterfactual margin, the market elasticity of demand and observed prices (p_1) and quantities (q_2).

(149) The counterfactual margin may be estimated by employing the comparator-based approach as well. A quantitative estimation of the market elasticity of demand may require a vast amount of data on prices and quantities, which may not be available or proportionate in a specific case. Under such circumstances, the court may find it sufficient to use other sources of evidence, for instance information in previous market studies of the relevant market or internal documents providing information on the relevant elasticity.[111]

(150) Another simplified approach may be to use insights from economic theory to estimate the volume effect. Such an approach may be based on the price set by the direct purchaser during the infringement period (the passing-on related price effect) and the counterfactual volume. Since a firm's ability to raise prices depends on how price sensitive the demand for its product is, an inverse relationship is normally predicted between a firm's margin and the own-price elasticity of demand. Drawing on this, the own-price elasticity and the counterfactual margin can be 'cancelled out'. Since information on the price set by the direct purchaser (the passing-on related price effect) will already be available at this stage of a case, the only additional input required in order to estimate the volume effect is the counterfactual volume.

6.3.2. Challenges

(151) When employing the elasticity approach the court may estimate the relevant elasticity parameters. One way to do this is to develop a demand model and use econometrics. However, as mentioned above, such an approach is demanding in terms of data requirements and assumptions. If data is not available and other sources are used, e.g. market studies or information from previous cases, it is important to note that such sources may not be appropriate if the market in the case at hand is different from the market described in the studies in terms of market structure. Under such circumstances, the elasticity approach might not provide an accurate estimate of the volume effect.

(152) As mentioned in the introduction of this section on quantification, the three potential components of the harm in a damages case derive from the initial overcharge, the passing-on related price effect and the volume effect.[112] The court may choose to estimate the three components sequentially, where quantification of the overcharge would constitute the first step, estimation of the passing-on related price effect the second step and the estimation of the passing-on related volume effect the third step.

NOTES

105 Given the fact that the purchaser usually faces a downward sloping demand curve. The economic intuition behind this is further explained in Annex 1.

106 National courts in the EU Member States have in several cases confirmed the importance of estimating the volume effect. For instance, a German court, *Oberlandesgericht Karlsruhe* (Higher Regional Court, Karlsruhe), judgment of 09 November 2016, case 6 U 214/15 Kart (2) (*Grauzementkartell*), found that the passing-on of an overcharge may subsequently lead to a reduction in the quantity sold by the direct purchaser.

107 For instance internal documents from the direct or indirect customer explaining how a price increase on the infringement product during the infringement has affected the volume supplied.

108 *Sø-og Handelsretten* (Maritime and Commercial High Court, Denmark), judgment of 15 January 2015, case SH2015.U-0004- 07 (*Cheminova A/S v Akzo Nobel Functional Chemicals BV et al*).

109 See also Annex 1, paragraph (167).

110 The volume effect is illustrated by area C in Box 11 above and Box 14 below.

111 See for example *Sø-og Handelsretten* (Maritime and Commercial High Court, Denmark), judgment of 15 January 2015, case SH2015.U-0004-07 (*Cheminova A/S v Akzo Nobel Functional Chemicals BV et al*).

112 See paragraph (69).

7. CHOICE OF METHOD

[4.476]

(153) The choice of a method to estimate the passing-on related price and volume effects will usually depend on a range of aspects. For instance, if the claimant and the defendant rely on different methods and the application of these methods leads to contradictory results, it is normally not appropriate to consider the estimated passing-on to be the average of the two results, nor would it be appropriate to consider that the contradictory results cancel each other out in the sense that both methods should be disregarded. As mentioned in the Practical Guide, in such a scenario it would rather be appropriate to examine the reasons for the diverging results and to consider the strengths and weaknesses of each method and its implementation.[113]

(154) The different techniques for the estimation of passing-on related price and volume effects provided in sections 5 and 6 vary in complexity and data requirements, from analyses based on qualitative evidence on the one hand to econometric techniques[114] based on quantitative data on the other. Different techniques also imply different accuracies in estimating the various effects.

(155) In this context, there is no technique that could be singled out as the one that would in all cases be more appropriate than others. The use of econometric techniques is an example of this. In most cases, the implementation of such techniques may increase the degree of accuracy of an estimate. However, such techniques usually require a significant amount of data which may not always be available. Hence, the gathering of data and their economic analyses may entail considerable costs for the parties, third parties and the court. These costs may be disproportionate to the amount of damages in question.

(156) When estimating the passing-on effects, national courts may use pieces of direct evidence relevant for the case. For instance, internal documents or other documents of a qualitative nature produced by the direct or indirect purchaser regarding the relationship between the overcharge and changes in its own prices. If this type of evidence is available, the court may find it sufficient to estimate the passing-on related effects (price and volume effects) by taking into consideration qualitative evidence or making adjustments to the quantitative data without the use of a regression analysis. Hence, the availability of qualitative evidence may play an important role when a court decides whether any or which of the quantitative techniques set out in the sections above can be used by a party to meet the required standard of proof under the applicable law.[115]

NOTES

113 See also the Practical guide, paragraph 125.

114 The concept of econometric techniques is further explained in section 5 above and in Annex 2.

115 This is also pointed out in the Practical Guide, paragraph 14.

8. ANNEX 1 – ECONOMIC THEORY

8.1. INTRODUCTION

[4.477]

(157) This annex explains in more detail the insights from economic theory relevant in the context of estimating the passing-on. As described in paragraph (49) et seq. above, different factors may affect the degree of passing-on, such as the nature of input costs subject to an overcharge, the nature of the product demand faced by the direct or indirect customer, the nature and intensity of competitive interaction between the firms in the market where the direct or indirect customers are active and other elements such as the share of a firm's various inputs affected by the overcharge or the time horizon of the infringement.

SECTION 8.2. INPUT COSTS AND THEIR EFFECT ON PRICING DECISIONS

(158) As explained in paragraph (46) above, the initial overcharge results in an input cost increase for purchasers of the overcharged products or services. Whether these purchasers are able and willing to pass on the overcharge to their own customers – and, if so, to what extent – depends, among other factors, on the cost structure of the purchasers.

(159) To identify passing-on effects, it is important to determine whether the input cost incurred by a purchaser facing an overcharge varies with the input quantity it orders (i.e. variable input cost) or not (i.e. fixed input cost). Indeed, economic theory indicates that the relevant cost category for short run price formation is variable costs or more precisely, marginal cost, i.e. the cost increment incurred when purchasing one additional input (see Box 13 below). The opposite of such costs are fixed costs which, in turn, typically affect the long run strategic decisions of firms, such as market participation, product introduction and level of investment.

Box 13: Examples of marginal and fixed costs

In order to explain the concepts of marginal (variable) and fixed costs it is useful to consider the example in Box 1 above.

There, the variable costs of the wire harnesses supplier would be the costs associated with producing one additional wire harness. Such costs may include inputs needed to produce the additional wire harness, including copper and plastic, electricity and labour-costs associated with the additional production.

However, the wire harnesses supplier also incurs fixed costs in its production, such as marketing of its products and investment in new machinery. These costs are not affected by the production of one additional wire harness, and are hence considered to be fixed.

(160) Typically, the relevant starting point for the assessment of passing-on effects would be the impact of the overcharge on the purchaser's marginal or variable costs.

(161) Contracts between firms at different levels of the supply chain, which set out the conditions at which firms would supply their products or services to purchasers, may concern components considered either as variable or fixed costs. For instance, often some components of the price paid by a purchaser are not dependent on the volume purchased, whereas some other components are. It follows that in a damages action involving any passing-on argument it is important to determine whether the price components affected by the infringement are fixed costs or not from the point of view of the purchaser.

(162) The time frame over which pricing is considered will affect whether costs are categorized as variable or fixed. Generally, economic theory suggests that the longer the relevant time frame, the greater the proportion of total costs that should be considered as variable. In other words, a certain cost category which is viewed as fixed in the short run might be regarded as variable by the firm when considering a longer time frame. When assessing the relevant time frame in a specific case, the court may wish to consider information from the party's internal documents, e.g. information on the costs that the firms take into account in their own pricing decisions.

(163) The considerations of fixed and variable costs are of particular importance when the volume effect is estimated, as the estimation of this effect requires an assessment of the margin of the firms involved in the case at hand.

SECTION 8.3 CHARACTERISTICS OF DEMAND AND LINKS TO PRICES

(164) Another factor crucial for estimating passing-on effects is the nature of demand that the direct purchasers face on the market where they are active. In economics, the relationship between demand and the price level is an important factor when describing how markets function. In any market, demand is referred to as the quantity of the good or service in question that purchasers on this market would buy at a given price level.

(165) Most typically, the higher the price level the lower the aggregate quantity of the products that the purchasers on the market are willing to buy. The price sensitivity of demand determines the strength of the relationship between price and demand. If, for example, an increase in price of 1 Euro is associated with a significant reduction in the quantity purchased demand is said to be more price-sensitive than if the purchase quantity reduction is less important for the same 1 Euro price increase.

(166) The standard downward sloping inverse demand curve is illustrated in Box 14 below.[116] In this Box, area A corresponds to the overcharge from the infringement. The price increase that harms the direct purchaser is taken into account as an increase of this purchasers' input costs. It is determined by c_2-c_1. The passing-on related price effect is illustrated by area B, while its volume effect is illustrated by area C. As illustrated, a relatively high price level (p_2) correspond to a relatively low quantity supplied (q_2).

Box 14: The standard demand curve – price and volume effects

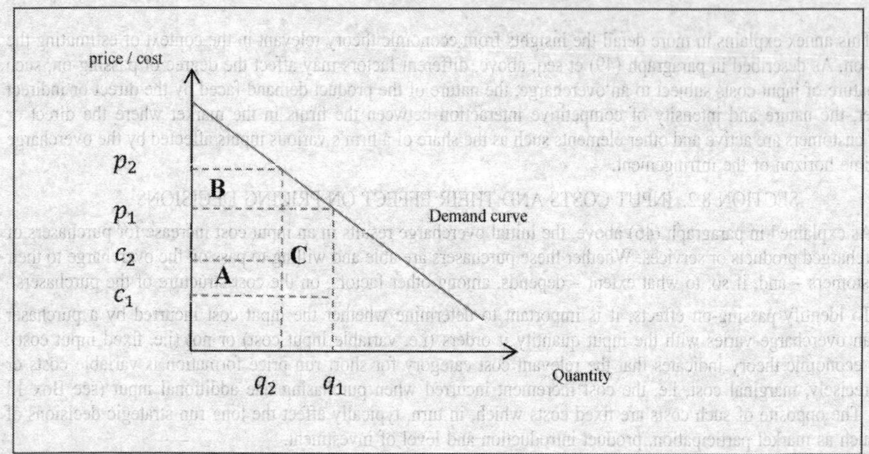

(167) A commonly used summary of this price sensitivity is the so-called price elasticity of demand. It shows the percent change in demand quantity associated with a one percent price increase. For example, a firm's own price demand elasticity of -0.5 means that a one percent price increase is associated with a 0.5 percent reduction in demand. An elasticity of -0.2, on the other hand, implies only a 0.2 percent reduction in demand for a one percent price increase. In the latter case, demand is said to be less elastic than in the former case, that is, less price sensitive as the purchase quantity reacts less strongly to the price increase.

(168) When assessing the passing-on of an overcharge from a direct purchaser to an indirect purchaser, the demand that the direct purchaser faces is the one of interest. The indirect purchaser might reduce its demand as a response to a price increase by the direct purchaser.

(169) The extent of the volume effect is directly affected by the price sensitivity of the demand. This is because the price sensitivity determines the reduction of demand following a price increase. For a given price increase, the reduction of output is larger, the more price sensitive the demand is. Therefore, the volume effect, i.e. the profit lost by the infringer's customer due to the reduction of output (demand), is closely linked to the price sensitivity of demand.

(170) The extent of the passing-on, and hence the size of the passing-on effects, is also related to the relationship between the demand and the price level. In this case, however, it is not the demand price sensitivity that is directly relevant, it is rather the change of the demand price sensitivity as the price level changes. This change of the price sensitivity with respect to the price level is referred to as the curvature of demand.

(171) The curvature of demand is the rate at which the responsiveness of demand to price-changes varies as price or output changes. When the demand curve is linear, it has no curvature and the slope is constant. In the case of convex demand, the demand becomes less sensitive to price changes as the price increases. This may be the case if the products or services affected by the overcharge are characterised as essential goods. A hypothetical example may be the demand for drinking water in the desert, because an average customer may be decreasingly sensitive to a price increase as the quantity available is reduced. Conversely, such a customer may be increasingly sensitive to a price increase as the quantity available is increased.

(172) If the demand curve is concave, as shown in the centre of Box 15, the demand becomes more sensitive to price changes as the price increases. This could for instance be the case if a substitute of the product affected by the overcharge is available to the customer. An example may be the demand for gasoline. At a certain price level, the customers may switch their consumption away from cars using gasoline to electrical cars. This would imply that the demand for gasoline will become more sensitive to price changes, as more customers switch their supply if the price on gasoline increases.

(173) The curvature of the demand curve may have a significant impact on the passing-on of overcharges. For a given level of competition the passing-on of an industry-wide overcharge will increase the more convex the demand curve is. If demand is sufficiently convex, the passing-on rate may exceed 100 percent.

Box 15: Other curvatures of demand

Depending on the characteristics of the market, the demand curve may be linear, convex or concave as illustrated below. The downward shape of a demand curve indicates that, as price decreases, customers will demand more of a product. The slope of the demand curve illustrates how the quantity of demand changes with the price. A steeper demand curve implies that demand is less sensitive to price increases.

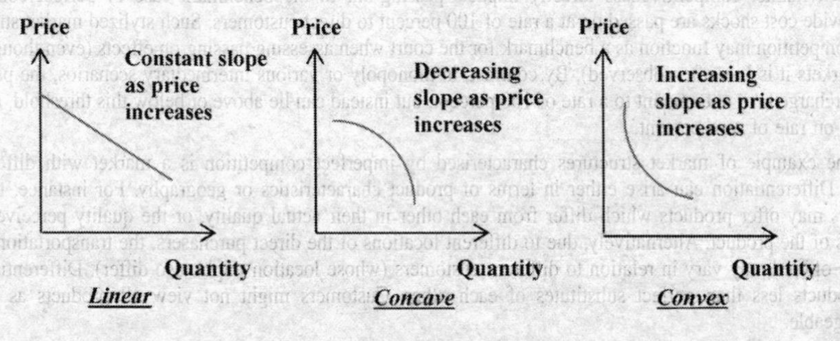

8.4. A FIRM'S PRICING DECISION

(174) As explained above in paragraphs (52) and (53), a firm's incentive to pass on an overcharge to its purchasers is determined by the type of demand and costs concerned.[117] According to economic theory, a firm will adjust prices only where this will increase profits. However, in order to receive a higher price, a firm will usually have to accept reduced sales. The assessment of the trade-off between increased profit from higher prices and decreased profit from reduced sales is important to understand the extent of the passing-on effects in damages actions.

(175) This trade-off is illustrated in Box 16 below. If a firm, for instance a direct customer of a producer of raw materials, increases prices, the effect on profit from higher prices may be illustrated by the area A in the left section of Box 16. The corresponding lost profit stemming from decreased sales is equal to the area B. When the effect of another small increase in the price is such that area A is equal to area B, there is no scope to earn additional profit through further price adjustments. If prices are increased beyond this point, the profit margin lost through the resulting reduction in sales volumes will outweigh the increased margins earned on the remaining sales.

(176) If the direct purchaser faces higher costs of raw materials, for instance if the suppliers of raw materials increase prices in violation of Article 101 TFEU, this may alter the terms of the trade-off described in paragraph (175) above. An increase in the direct purchaser's costs will reduce the margins earned on the sales at the prevailing price. In profit terms, this makes it less costly to increase the price at the expense of losing some sales. The lost profit due to lower sales when costs have increased is represented by area D in the right section of Box 16 below. As area D is smaller than area B, the direct customer has an incentive to increase its price in response to the cost increase, i.e. to pass on the cost change, at least to some extent.

Box 16: Trade-off between price increase and lost sales

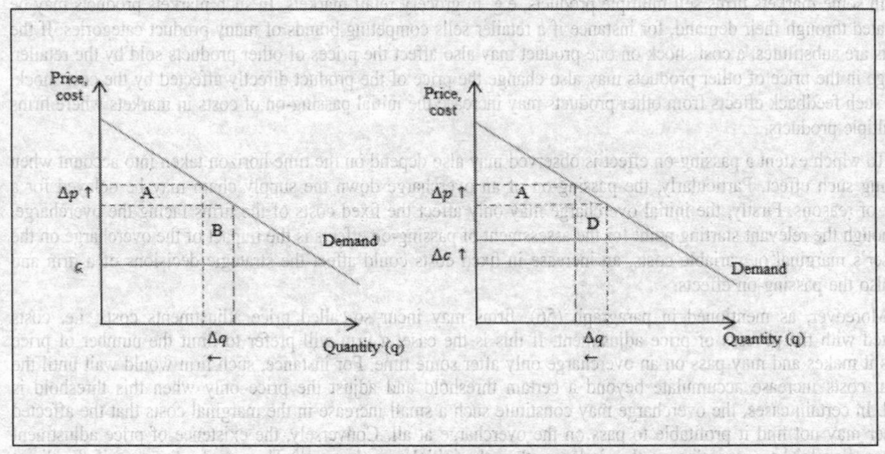

SECTION 8.5. INTENSITY OF COMPETITION AND LINKS TO PASSING-ON

8.5.1. CONTINUUM OF COMPETITIVENESS OF MARKETS

(177) At a given level of the supply chain, competition between firms can be more or less intense. At one extreme, when a firm is a monopolist at its level of the supply chain, there is no competition. At the other extreme, competition between firms can be very intense (e.g. when many firms sell rather homogeneous products in a market with low barriers to entry), such that each firm acts as a price-taker and does not influence market prices which will be at or very close to the marginal costs of production. This latter case is referred to as perfect competition. In between these two extreme cases lies a broad range of intermediary scenarios, where competition could be more or less intense, depending e.g. on the number of firms in the industry or whether products sold by different firms are close substitutes or not.

(178) Such market competitiveness directly impacts passing-on. In the benchmark case of perfect competition, industry-wide cost shocks are passed on at a rate of 100 percent to direct customers. Such stylized market structure of perfect competition may function as a benchmark for the court when assessing passing-on effects (even though in real world markets it is less often observed). By contrast, in monopoly or various intermediary scenarios, the passing-on of an overcharge may not amount to a rate of 100 percent, but instead can lie above or below this threshold, including a passing-on rate of zero percent.

(179) One example of market structures characterised by imperfect competition is a market with differentiated products. Differentiation can arise either in terms of product characteristics or geography. For instance, the direct purchasers may offer products which differ from each other in their actual quality, or the quality perceived by the customers of the product. Alternatively, due to different locations of the direct purchasers, the transportation costs of the goods offered may vary in relation to different customers (whose location might also differ). Differentiation can make products less than perfect substitutes of each other. Customers might not view all products as perfectly interchangeable.

(180) This less than perfect substitutability might result in reduced competitive pressure on suppliers who may not face competitors offering closely interchangeable products. In other words, according to economic theory, the intensity of competition will be reduced when product differentiation increases. As explained in paragraphs (177) et seq. above, weaker competition will decrease the passing-on rate of an industry-wide overcharge, i.e. as the differentiation of the direct purchasers' products increases, and the passing-on rate of the industry-wide overcharge they were subject to will approach the rate where each direct purchaser is a monopolist. Conversely, when the product differentiation is limited, the passing-on rate of an industry-wide overcharge will be larger.

8.5.2. INDUSTRY-WIDE VS. FIRM-SPECIFIC OVERCHARGE AND PASSING-ON

(181) The passing-on of overcharges by a given purchaser vis-à-vis its own customers typically differs depending on whether the purchaser's competitors are also affected by the overcharge or not. When a single purchaser is impacted by the overcharge the passing-on will necessarily be firm-specific. By contrast, if all purchasers at a given level of the supply chain are impacted by the overcharge one may consider passing-on rates for each firm but also the industry-wide passing-on.

(182) If only one purchaser is affected, i.e. the overcharge is firm-specific, the passing-on effects could be rather limited, in particular when this purchaser is not able to affect selling prices in its market due to intense pressure from its competitors.

(183) Conversely, where all the undertakings in a market are affected by an overcharge, i.e. the overcharge is industry-wide, all of the undertakings will face higher input costs, implying that they may be able to pass on at least part of the overcharge to their own customers. However, an industry-wide overcharge may still affect competitors differently.

SECTION 8.6. SOME FURTHER FACTORS IMPACTING PASSING-ON

(184) In some markets firms sell multiple products, e.g. in grocery retail markets. In such markets products may be interrelated through their demand, for instance if a retailer sells competing brands of many product categories. If the products are substitutes, a cost shock on one product may also affect the prices of other products sold by the retailer. A change in the price of other products may also change the price of the product directly affected by the cost shock. Hence, such feedback effects from other products may increase the initial passing-on of costs in markets where firms sell multiple products.

(185) To which extent a passing-on effect is observed may also depend on the time horizon taken into account when estimating such effect. Particularly, the passing-on of an overcharge down the supply chain may be delayed for a number of reasons. Firstly, the initial overcharge may only affect the fixed costs of the firms facing the overcharge. Even though the relevant starting point for the assessment of passing-on effects is the impact of the overcharge on the purchaser's marginal or variable costs, an increase in fixed costs could affect the strategic decisions of a firm and hence also the passing-on effects.

(186) Moreover, as mentioned in paragraph (56), firms may incur so-called price adjustments costs, i.e. costs associated with the process of price adjustment. If this is the case, a firm will prefer to limit the number of price changes it makes and may pass on an overcharge only after some time. For instance, such firm would wait until the marginal costs increase accumulate beyond a certain threshold and adjust the price only when this threshold is reached. In certain cases, the overcharge may constitute such a small increase in the marginal costs that the affected purchaser may not find it profitable to pass on the overcharge at all. Conversely, the existence of price adjustment costs may also lead to a passing-on that is larger than the initial overcharge.[118] This can be the case if the direct purchaser would be on the verge of changing its prices in the absence of any overcharges. Hence, a small overcharge

itself may trigger a large price increase that reflects not only the overcharge but all other cost increases accumulated after the last price adjustment. Whereas such other cost increases may not be attributable to the infringer, a national court may wish to be aware of the fact that, in such a scenario, even a relatively small overcharge may lead to a significant price increase.

(187) Another example of how price adjustment costs may affect the degree of passing-on is related to the existence of so-called 'psychological pricing'. In many markets, typically retail markets, prices a little less than a round number are common, e.g. 99 Euro or 19.900 Euro. The consumers may perceive such prices lower than they actually are. The use of such a pricing strategy may make it more likely that a direct purchaser chooses not to pass on an overcharge, as the change in price, for instance from 19.900 Euro to 20.000 Euro, would lead to a significant drop in the direct purchaser's demand. The possible impact on the estimation of passing-on effects from the existence of price adjustment costs is further discussed in section 5.2.1.

(188) Further in some circumstances, an indirect purchaser may be able to use its negotiating strength to limit the ability of a direct purchaser to pass on an overcharge. The indirect purchaser's negotiating strength may be referred to as countervailing buyer power.[119] Buyer power is not only limited to the ability to switch to other suppliers, but also e.g. to integrate upstream.

(189) In general, buyer power will not prevent passing-on if there is an industry-wide overcharge but it will affect the degree of passing-on. On the one hand, one can think of a scenario where strong buyer power forces the direct purchasers to accept the overcharge and thus limit passing-on. On the other hand, one could also think of a scenario where the strong bargaining power of the indirect purchaser forces direct purchasers to make a zero mark-up and to sell at a price only covering their marginal costs, thus resulting in a passing-on rate of 100 percent in case of an overcharge.

(190) As the degree of buyer power and its implications for the passing-on effects will depend on the nature of the individual negotiations and the specific context in which they take place, the court may assess this topic on a case-by-case basis.

(191) Further, if the direct purchaser facing an overcharge is vertically integrated into a downstream retail market, i.e. also active on the market where the indirect purchasers operate, this may affect the direct purchaser's incentive to pass on the initial overcharge. Moreover, in such a scenario, the direct purchaser facing an overcharge may have an incentive to pass on the entire overcharge within its integrated firm. However, the passing-on rate to non-integrated indirect purchasers would generally differ from this, e.g. depending on the level of costs or profit margins of the different indirect purchasers.

(192) In certain industries, the price offered by the direct or indirect purchaser may be subject to regulation, e.g. price regulation by governmental agencies. Price regulation may affect the extent of passing-on. For instance, if the regulated price is set independently of the specific costs of the product subject to an overcharge when setting the price, the passing-on related price effect may be limited or zero. However, as also mentioned in paragraph (48), harm stemming from a violation of EU competition law may also affect non-price factors. Conversely, if the regulator fully takes into account the cost of the product subject to an overcharge when setting the regulated price, the degree of passing-on may be substantial also in regulated markets.

NOTES

[116] The figure illustrates prices (vertical axis) as a function of quantity demanded (horizontal axis). This demand curve is often referred to as the 'inverse demand curve', while a curve depicting demand on the vertical axis as a function of prices on the horizontal axis is simply referred to as 'demand curve'. In the subsequent graphical examples, inverse demand curves are shown. However, for ease of language they are referred to as 'demand curves'.

[117] See also 'Guidelines on the application of Article 81 (3) of the Treaty' (2004/C 101/08), paragraph 98.

[118] Note that economic theory also shows that even in the absence of any price adjustments costs a passing-on could be larger than the initial overcharge. This is the case, e.g., when the demand curve is sufficiently convex (see discussion in section 8.3 above).

[119] The assessment of countervailing buyer power is an important factor in the area of EU merger control. In the Commission's guidelines for horizontal mergers, paragraph 64, countervailing buyer power is defined as the bargaining strength that the buyer has vis-à-vis the seller in commercial negotiations due to its size, its commercial significance to the seller and its ability to switch to alternative suppliers.

9. ANNEX 2 – GLOSSARY

[4.478]

(193) This annex gives an overview of economic terms used throughout the guidelines.

— Curvature of the demand: The change of the elasticity of demand as the price level changes.
— Demand: The quantity of a good or service that purchasers on a market would buy at a given price level.
— Demand curve: An illustration of the relationship between the quantity demanded and the price of a product.
— Econometric technique: Also referred to as regression analysis, this technique is statistical in its nature and helps to analyse patterns in the relationship between economic variables, for instance how the development of costs affects the development of prices in a given market.
— Elasticity of demand: Percentage change in quantity demanded in response to a one percent price increase.
— Firm-specific overcharge: Only one single purchaser is impacted by the overcharge.
— Fixed costs: Costs that do not vary with the quantity of output produced.
— Industry-wide overcharge: All purchasers at a given level of the supply chain are impacted by the overcharge.
— Marginal costs: The increase in total costs that arises from an extra unit of production.
— Regression analysis: See econometric technique.
— Slope of the demand: Ratio of a change in quantity to the change in prices between two points of the demand curve chosen arbitrarily close to one another.
— Variable costs: Costs that vary with the quantity of output produced.

COMMUNICATION FROM THE COMMISSION

(2020/C242/01)

Communication on the protection of confidential information by national courts in proceedings for the private enforcement of EU competition law

[4.479]

NOTES

Date of publication in OJ: OJ C242, 22.7.2020, p 1.

I. SCOPE AND PURPOSE OF THIS COMMUNICATION

[4.480]

1. This Communication concerns the protection of confidential information in civil proceedings before national courts concerning the application of Articles 101 or 102 of the Treaty on the Functioning of the European Union ('TFEU')

2. Depending on the applicable national rules, private enforcement actions before national courts in the EU may take different forms, for example, damages actions, declaratory actions or actions for injunctions. During the last few years, the number of so-called follow-on damages actions, by which a victim of a competition law infringement claims damages following the decision of a competition authority or a final ruling by a review court, is rapidly growing.[1]

3. Access to evidence is an important element for enforcing the rights that individuals, including consumers and undertakings, or public authorities derive from Articles 101 or 102 TFEU in private enforcement actions before national courts.

4. National courts may thus receive requests for disclosure of evidence in proceedings for the private enforcement of EU competition law. National courts will need to ensure effective private enforcement actions by granting access to the relevant information for substantiating the respective claim or defence if the conditions for its disclosure are met. At the same time, national courts need to protect the interests of the party or third party whose confidential information is subject to disclosure.

5. To this end, national courts should have at their disposal measures to protect confidential information in a way that does not impede the parties' effective access to justice or the exercise of the right to full compensation.[2]

6. In particular, in damages actions, the Damages Directive[3] requires Member States to ensure that national courts have the power to order disclosure of evidence containing confidential information, if a number of criteria are fulfilled. Member States shall also ensure that national courts have at their disposal effective measures to protect such confidential information, while ensuring the exercise of the right to full compensation.[4] This is important because national courts may have limited resources to handle disclosure requests.

7. In this context, this Communication identifies measures that may be considered by national courts when dealing with disclosure of confidential information in private enforcement actions.

8. This Communication aims to be a source of inspiration and guidance for national courts, and is not binding on them. It does not modify or bring about changes to existing EU[5] or Member State laws nor to the national procedural rules applicable to civil proceedings or to legal professional privilege.[6] In particular, the measures to protect confidential information set out in Section III of this Communication may be used if they are available under and compatible with national rules, as well as with the rights of the parties in judicial proceedings as recognised under EU and national law.

NOTES

1 Jean-François Laborde, *Cartel damages actions in Europe: How courts have assessed cartel overcharges* (2019 ed), Concurrences Review No 4-2019, Art. No 92227, November 2019, available at www.concurrences.com.

2 In relation to the right to compensation, see judgment of the Court of Justice of 5 June 2014, *Kone AG and Others* v *ÖBB-Infrastruktur AG*, Case C-557/12, EU:C:2014:1317, paragraphs 21 and 22.

3 Directive 2014/104/EU of the European Parliament and of the Council of 26 November 2014 on certain rules governing actions for damages under national law for infringements of the competition law provisions of the Member States and of the European Union (OJ L349, 5.12.2014, p1) ('Damages Directive').

4 See Article 5 of the Damages Directive. See also recital 18 of the Damages Directive.

5 This Communication is, for instance, without prejudice to the provisions of: Council Regulation (EC) No 1206/2001 of 28 May 2001 on cooperation between the courts of the Member States in the taking of evidence in civil or commercial matters (OJ L174, 27.6.2001, p1); Regulation (EU) 2018/1725 of the European Parliament and of the Council of 23 October 2018 on the protection of natural persons with regard to the processing of personal data by the Union institutions, bodies, offices and agencies and on the free movement of such data (OJ L295, 21.11.2018, p39); or Regulation (EU) 2016/679 of the European Parliament and of the Council of 27 April 2016 on the protection of natural persons with regard to the processing of personal data and on the free movement of such data, and repealing Directive 95/46/EC (OJ L119, 4.5.2016, p1).

This Communication is also without prejudice to Regulation (EC) No 1049/2001 of the European Parliament and of the Council of 30 May 2001 regarding public access to European Parliament, Council and Commission documents (OJ L145, 31.5.2001, p43), which concerns transparency and is intended for disclosure of information to the wider public; see judgment of the General Court of 12 May 2015, *Unión de Almacenistas de Hierros de España* v *Commission*, Case T-623/13, EU:T:2015:268, paragraph 86, and judgment of the Court of Justice of 27 February 2014, *Commission* v *EnBW Energie Baden-Württemberg AG*, Case C-365/12 P, EU:C:2014:112, paragraphs 100-109. Following the transposition of the Damages Directive, claimants can fully rely on the national rules transposing Articles 5 and 6 of it for the disclosure of relevant information.

6 For damages actions, see Article 5(6) of the Damages Directive.

II. REQUESTS FOR THE DISCLOSURE OF EVIDENCE CONTAINING CONFIDENTIAL INFORMATION BEFORE NATIONAL COURTS

A. RELEVANT CONSIDERATIONS FOR DISCLOSURE REQUESTS OF EVIDENCE

[4.481]

9. In the context of private enforcement of EU competition law, the ability of the parties to civil proceedings (claimant(s) and defendant(s)) to exercise effectively their rights may depend on the possibility to access relevant evidence. However, such evidence may not always be in the possession of or readily accessible to the party that bears the burden of proof.

10. Therefore, upon request of a party, national courts may decide to order the disclosure of evidence. Disclosure will be subject to national procedural rules as well as to administrative and procedural economy considerations.

11. In particular, for damages actions, the Damages Directive requires Member States to provide for the right for claimants and defendants to obtain disclosure of evidence relevant to their claim or defence under the following conditions.[7]

12. First, national courts shall determine whether the claim for damages is plausible and whether the disclosure request concerns relevant evidence and is proportionate.[8] The Damages Directive stipulates that the assessment of proportionality should consider the scope and cost of disclosure, including preventing non-specific searches for information that is unlikely to be of relevance for the parties in the procedure. Very broad or generalised disclosure requests will likely fail to meet such requirements.[9]

13. Second, disclosure requests shall identify specified items of evidence or relevant categories of evidence '*as precisely and as narrowly as possible*' based on reasonably available facts.[10] Categories of evidence might be identified by the reference to common features of its constitutive elements such as the nature, object or content of the documents sought to disclose, the time during which they were drawn up or other criteria. For example, a request for categories of evidence could refer to sales data of company A to company B of product Y between years N and N + 5.

14. Third, regarding the disclosure of information included in the file of the Commission or of a national competition authority, the Damages Directive specifies that, when assessing the proportionality of a disclosure order, a national court must, among others, consider whether '*the request has been formulated specifically with regard to the nature, subject matter or contents of documents submitted to a competition authority or held in the file thereof, rather than by a non-specific application concerning documents submitted to a competition authority*'.[11]

15. It must be recalled that the Damages Directive provides that leniency statements and settlements submissions can never be disclosed (also known as 'black list documents').[12] Moreover, if the Commission or a national competition authority has not yet closed its proceedings, the national court cannot order the disclosure of information that was prepared by a natural or legal person specifically for the proceedings of a competition authority; of information that the competition authority has drawn up and sent to the parties in the course of its proceedings; or of settlement submissions that have been withdrawn (also known as 'grey list documents').[13]

16. National courts may order any of the parties (defendant and/or claimant) or third parties to disclose information that lies in their control.[14] In most cases, one of the parties or a third party to the proceedings will hold the evidence required. In some instances, the defendant(s) will possess evidence relevant for finding an infringement or defining its temporal scope, obtained through access to a competition authority's file (e.g. pre-existing documents, responses to requests for information, etc.). In other cases, for instance, in a damages action, the defendant or claimant might possess additional evidence that was not included in a competition authority's file but that is relevant to a damages claim or defence (e.g. concerning the causal link between the infringement and the harm, quantifying the harm,[15] estimating a possible 'passing-on' of an overcharge by the defendants,[16] etc.). This may be particularly the case for information concerning customer-specific prices, revenues or other data such as the pricing behaviour of the purchasers, etc.

17. If the parties or any other third party could not produce the evidence sought and the request for disclosure concerns a document in the file of the Commission or a national competition authority, the national court may address an order for disclosure to them.[17]

B. CONFIDENTIAL INFORMATION

18. The protection of business secrets and other confidential information is enshrined in Article 339 TFEU and also a general principle of EU law.[18] However, the fact that information is of a confidential nature is no absolute bar to its disclosure in national proceedings.[19] National courts will decide what may constitute confidential information for the private enforcement of EU competition law on a case-by-case basis pursuant to national and EU rules and relevant jurisprudence.

19. For that reason, this Communication does not seek to provide a definition of confidential information. Nevertheless, inspiration might be drawn from the jurisprudence of the EU courts and the Commission's practice.[20]

20. The EU courts qualify as confidential information that meets the following cumulative conditions:[21]

(i) it is known only to a limited number of persons; and

(ii) its disclosure is liable to cause serious harm to the person who provided it or to third parties; and

(iii) the interests liable to be harmed by the disclosure of confidential information are, objectively, worthy of protection.

21. In relation to the first condition, information may lose its confidential nature as soon as it becomes '*available to specialist circles or capable of being inferred from publicly available information*'.[22]

22. In relation to the second condition, it is worth noting that to assess the potential for causing harm it is relevant to consider first the nature of the information. Disclosure of information that has commercial, financial or strategic value is usually considered capable of causing serious harm.[23] Second, it is necessary to consider how recent the information is. Commercially sensitive information concerning an ongoing or future business relationship, internal business plans and other forward looking commercial information could often qualify (at least partially) as confidential information. However, such information may lose its confidential nature when it has 'lost its commercial importance due to the passage of time'.[24]

23. In relation to the third condition, the interest of a party to protect itself or its reputation against any order for damages made by a national court because of its participation in an infringement of competition law is not an interest worthy of protection[25].

24. Finally, trade secrets as defined in the Trade Secrets Directive are to be considered confidential information.[26]

C. COOPERATION BETWEEN THE COMMISSION AND NATIONAL COURTS IN THE CONTEXT OF DISCLOSURE OF EVIDENCE

25. In civil proceedings for the application of Articles 101 and 102 TFEU, a national court may request the Commission under Article 15(1) of Council Regulation (EC) No 1/2003[27] for an opinion on questions concerning the application of EU competition law, or to transmit any legal, economic or procedural information in its possession in line with the principle of loyal cooperation of Article 4(3) of the Treaty on European Union.[28]

26. Under the Damages Directive, the national court may order, for example, the disclosure of documents from the Commission's file, if no other (third) party can reasonably provide them.[29] In this regard, it is important to recall that, as set out above, the Commission will not transmit black listed documents or, if its proceedings are not closed, grey listed documents (see paragraph 15 above).[30]

27. Moreover, the Commission's assistance to national courts must not undermine the guarantees that natural and legal persons have following the principle of professional secrecy pursuant to Article 339 TFEU and Article 28 of Regulation (EC) No 1/2003.[31]

28. When the Commission considers that information requested by the national court may be confidential in the case pending before it, it will ask the national court whether it can and will guarantee the protection of confidential information before transmitting it.[32] The national court should then effectively guarantee the appropriate protection of confidential information that belongs to legal or natural persons from whom the Commission had obtained the information.[33]

29. If the national court offers a guarantee that it will protect the confidential information, the Commission will transmit the information requested. The national court may then disclose the information in national proceedings by applying the measures to protect the confidentiality of information communicated to the Commission and taking into account any observations provided on this matter by the Commission.

NOTES

7 See recital 15 and Article 5(1) of the Damages Directive.

8 See Article 5(1) and (3) of the Damages Directive; See, also, observations of the Commission to the UK High Court of Justice of 27 January 2017 pursuant to Article 15(3) of Regulation (EC) No 1/2003, in the EURIBOR case, paragraph 24, available at http://ec.europa.eu/competition/court/antitrust_amicus_curiae.html.

9 See recital 23 of the Damages Directive regarding the principle of proportionality and the prevention of fishing expeditions, i.e. non-specific or overly broad searches of information that is unlikely to be of relevance for the parties to the proceedings.

10 See recital 16 and Article 5(2) of the Damages Directive.

11 Article 6(4)(a) of the Damages Directive.

12 Article 6(6) of the Damages Directive.

13 Article 6(5) of the Damages Directive.

14 Article 5(1) of the Damages Directive.

15 Communication from the Commission on quantifying harm in antitrust damages actions (OJ C167, 13.6.2013, p 19), and Practical Guide, quantifying harm in actions for damages based on breaches of Article 101 or 102 of the Treaty on the Functioning of the European Union (11.6.2013).

16 For example, where a defendant argues that the claimant has passed on to its own customers the overcharge from the infringement (so called passing-on defence), the defendant might require access to evidence that is in possession of the claimant or third parties. See, Guidelines for national courts on how to estimate the share of overcharge which was passed on to the indirect purchaser (OJ C267, 9.8.2019, p 4).

17 See Article 4(3) TEU on the principle of sincere cooperation between the Union and the Member States and Article 15(1) of Regulation (EC) No 1/2003 as regards requests for information to the Commission. In damages actions, Article 6(10) of the Damages Directive specifically provides that disclosure from a competition authority is only a measure of last resort ('*Member States shall ensure that national courts request the disclosure from a competition authority of evidence included in its file only where no party or third party is reasonably able to provide that evidence*').

18 See judgment of the Court of Justice of 14 February 2008, *Varec* v *Belgian State*, Case C-450/06, EU:C:2008:91, paragraph 49. See, also, judgment of the Court of Justice of 24 June 1986, *Akzo Chemie* v *Commission*, Case C-53/85, EU:C:1986:256, paragraph 28; judgment of the Court of Justice of 19 May 1994, *SEP* v *Commission*, Case C-36/92 P, EU:C:1994:205, paragraph 37, and judgment of the Court of Justice of 19 June 2018, *Baumeister*, Case C-15/16, EU:C:2018:464, paragraph 53. The protection of confidential information is also a corollary of everyone's right to respect for his or her private and family life laid down in Article 7 of the Charter of Fundamental Rights of the European Union (OJ C326, 26.10.2012, p 391) (see also judgment in *Varec* v *Belgian State*, cited above, paragraph 48).

19 Judgment of the General Court of 18 September 1996, *Postbank*, Case T-353/94, EU:T:1996:119, paragraphs 66 and 89; see also, for inspiration, Commission Notice on the cooperation between the Commission and the courts of the EU Member States in the application of Articles 81 and 82 EC, OJ C101, 27.4.2004, p 54 ('Notice on Cooperation with Na-

tional Courts'), paragraph 24; and Commission Notice on the rules for access to the Commission file in cases pursuant to Articles 81 and 82 of the EC Treaty, Articles 53, 54 and 57 of the EEA Agreement and Council Regulation (EC) No 139/2004 (OJ C325, 22.12.2005, p 7) ('Access to File Notice'), paragraph 24. See, also, Articles 3 and 9 of Directive (EU) 2016/943 of the European Parliament and of the Council of 8 June 2016 on the protection of undisclosed know-how and business information (trade secrets) against their unlawful acquisition, use and disclosure (OJ L157, 15.6.2016, p 1) ('Trade Secrets Directive').

20 See, for example, Access to File Notice, paragraphs 17-19, Chapter 11 of DG Competition's Manual of Procedure for the application of Articles 101 and 102 TFEU (available at https://ec.europa.eu/competition/antitrust/antitrust_manproc_11_2019_en.pdf), and Guidance on confidentiality claims during Commission antitrust procedures, paragraphs 8-17 (available at https://ec.europa.eu/competition/antitrust/business_secrets_en.pdf).

However, depending on the circumstances, national courts may need to assess the confidentiality of information anew in the context of private enforcement actions, even if it had been established in the context of the public enforcement of EU competition law. For instance, parties to administrative proceedings may have made confidentiality claims vis-à-vis other parties to the administrative proceedings, but may need to make different claims vis-à-vis the parties requesting disclosure before the national court in civil proceedings. This would also apply to third parties from whom the Commission or a national competition authority might have obtained information during the administrative proceedings. Due to the passage of time between different proceedings, it may be also relevant that information is assessed anew as to whether or not it has lost its confidential nature (see, also, paragraph 22 below).

21 Judgment of the General Court of 30 May 2006, *Bank Austria* v *Commission*, Case T-198/03, EU:T:2006:136, paragraph 71; judgment of the General Court of 8 November 2011, *Idromacchine* v *Commission*, Case T-88/09, EU:T:2011:641, paragraph 45; judgment of the General Court of 28 January 2015, *Akzo Nobel and Others* v *Commission*, Case T-345/12, EU:T:2015:50, paragraph 65; and judgment of the Court of Justice of 14 March 2017, *Evonik Degussa* v *Commission*, Case C-162/15 P, EU:C:2017:205, paragraph 107.

22 See, for instance, Order of the General Court of 19 June 1996, *NMH Stahlwerke* v *Commission*, Joined Cases T-134/94, etc., EU: T:1996:85, paragraph 40; Order of the General Court of 29 May 1997, *British Steel* v *Commission*, Case T-89/96, EU:T:1997:77, paragraph 29; Order of the General Court of 15 June 2006, *Deutsche Telekom* v *Commission*, Case T-271/03, EU:T:2006:163, paragraphs 64 and 65; and Order of the General Court of 2 March 2010, *Telefónica* v *Commission*, Case T-336/07, EU:T:2008:299, paragraphs 39, 63 and 64; See also, Access to File Notice, paragraph 23.

23 This is also relevant concerning the protection of third parties from the risk of retaliation by a competitor or trading partner that can exercise significant commercial or economic pressure on them. See, for example, judgment of the Court of Justice of 6 April 1995, *BPB Industries and British Gypsum* v *Commission*, Case C-310/93, EU:C:1995:101, paragraphs 26 and 27.

24 Information that was confidential but dates from five years or more ago, must be considered historical, unless exceptionally the applicant shows that it still constitutes an essential element of its commercial position or that of a third party; see in this respect *Evonik Degussa* v *Commission*, cited above, paragraph 64; *Baumeister*, cited above, paragraph 54; and judgment of the General Court of 15 July 2015, *Pilkington Group Ltd* v *Commission*, Case T-462/12, EU:T:2015:508, paragraph 58. See also, Access to File Notice, paragraph 23.

25 Judgment of the General Court of 15 December 2011, *CDC Hydrogene Peroxide* v *Commission*, Case T-437/08, EU:T:2011:752, paragraph 49 (*'[. . .] the interest of a company which took part in a cartel in avoiding such actions [. . .] does not constitute an interest deserving of protection, having regard, in particular, to the fact that any individual has the right to claim damages for loss caused to him by conduct which is liable to restrict or distort competition (Case C-453/99 Courage and Crehan [2001] ECR I-6297, paragraphs 24 and 26, and Joined Cases C-295/04 to C-298/04 Manfredi and Others [2006] ECR I-6619, paragraphs 59 and 61)'*). Similarly, Article 5(5) of the Damages Directive states that the interest of undertakings to avoid actions for damages following an infringement of competition law shall not constitute an interest that warrants protection.

26 See Article 2(1) of the Trade Secrets Directive for the definition of trade secret that must be read in conjunction with Article 3(2) of the same directive.

27 OJ L1, 4.1.2003, p 1.

28 Article 15(1) of Regulation (EC) No 1/2003; Notice on Cooperation with National Courts, paragraphs 21, 27 and 29; *Postbank*, cited above, paragraph 65; see, also, Order of the Court of Justice of 13 July 1990, *Imm Zwartveld*, Case C-2/88, EU:C:1990:315, paragraphs 21-22. It should be noted that where the coherent application of Article 101 or Article 102 TFEU so requires, the Commission, acting on its own initiative, may submit written observations to courts of the Member States, and for that purpose it may request the relevant court of the Member State to transmit or ensure the transmission to it of any documents necessary for the assessment of the case, see Article 15(3) of Regulation (EC) No 1/2003.

29 See Article 6(10) of the Damages Directive.

30 See Article 16a(2) of Commission Regulation (EC) No 773/2004 of 7 April 2004 relating to the conduct of proceedings by the Commission pursuant to Articles 81 and 82 of the EC Treaty as amended (OJ L123, 27.4.2004, p 18). See, also, Notice on Cooperation with National Courts, paragraph 26, for refusal to transmit information due to overriding reasons relating to the need to safeguard the interests of the Union or to avoid any interference with its functioning and independence.

31 *Postbank*, cited above, paragraph 90. See, also, Article 7 of the Charter of Fundamental Rights of the European Union, cited above.

32 Notice on Cooperation with National Courts, paragraph 25.

33 See paragraph 12 of Commission Opinion of 22 December 2014 following a request under Article 15(1) of Council Regulation (EC) No 1/2003 of 16 December 2002 on the implementation of the rules on competition laid down in Articles 81 and 82 of the Treaty, *The Secretary of State for Health and others* v *Servier Laboratories Limited and others*, C(2014) 10264 final, available at http://ec.europa.eu/competition/court/confidentiality_rings_final_opinion_en.pdf.

III. MEASURES FOR PROTECTION OF CONFIDENTIAL INFORMATION

A. INTRODUCTION

[4.482]

30. When evidence that contains confidential information is disclosed, measures should be introduced to protect such information. By way of example, the Damages Directive refers to a few measures such as the possibility of redacting documents, conducting hearings *in camera*, restricting the persons allowed to see the evidence and instructing experts to produce summaries of the information in an aggregated form or otherwise non-confidential form.[34]

31. Naturally, the choice of measure used to protect confidential information when ordering disclosure will depend on the specific national procedural rules including to what extent certain measures are at all available. National courts may also request that the parties seek an agreement on the measures to protect confidential information.

32. National courts shall decide upon the most effective measure or a combination of measures to protect confidentiality on a case-by-case basis. The choice may depend on several factors, such as, inter alia:

(i) the nature and commercial/financial/strategic value of the information subject to disclosure (e.g. customer names, prices, structure of costs, margins, etc.) and whether for the purpose of the exercise of the rights of the party requesting disclosure, access to such information can be given in an aggregated or anonymised form or not;

(ii) the extent of the requested disclosure (i.e. volume or number of documents to be disclosed);

(iii) the number of parties concerned by the litigation and disclosure. Certain measures for the protection of confidentiality might be more effective than others, depending on whether there is more than one party requesting disclosure and/or disclosing party;

(iv) the relationship between the parties (for example, whether the disclosing party is a direct competitor of the party seeking disclosure,[35] whether the parties have an ongoing supply relationship, etc.);

(v) whether the information to be disclosed originates from third parties. The rights of third parties to the civil proceedings in the protection of their confidential information must also be considered.[36] The disclosing party may have in its possession third party documents that are confidential towards the party requesting disclosure or towards other parties to the proceedings.[37]

(vi) the circle of individuals allowed to access the information (i.e. whether disclosure should be granted only to external representatives or whether the party requesting disclosure (i.e. company representatives) would also be allowed to access the information);

(vii) the risk of inadvertent disclosure;

(viii) the ability of the court to protect confidential information throughout the civil proceedings and even after the proceedings are closed; national courts may conclude that, in order to effectively protect confidential information, a single measure will not suffice and other measures may need to be adopted throughout the proceedings; and

(ix) any other constraints or administrative burdens[38] associated with the disclosure such as increased costs or additional administrative steps for the national judicial system,[39] costs for the parties, potential delays to the proceedings, etc.

33. In order to avoid that parties use confidential documents outside the proceedings in which they have been disclosed, it is important that national courts are able to impose deterrent penalties for non-compliance with obligations to protect confidential information.[40] The choice of the most effective measure(s) to protect confidential information may depend on the existence of and ability to impose and enforce sanctions for failure or refusal to comply with such measure(s). For damages actions, under Article 8 of the Damages Directive, national courts must be able to impose penalties effectively on parties, third parties and their legal counsel in the event of their failure or refusal to comply with the obligations imposed by a national court order protecting confidential information.[41]

34. The precise nature and scope of the sanctions will depend on the national rules. Pursuant to the Damages Directive, sanctions for, inter alia, the failure to comply with a disclosure order or with the obligations imposed by a national court order protecting confidential information shall include the possibility to draw adverse inferences, and the possibility to order the payment of costs.[42] External legal counsels or experts may also be subject to disciplinary sanctions by their professional associations (e.g. suspension, fines, etc.).

35. In conclusion, the choice of measure(s) to protect confidential information may require a comprehensive evaluation of multiple factors. To assist national courts in this assessment, this Communication provides an overview of the most common measures that – subject to their availability under Member States' procedural rules – may be used to protect confidential information, and of relevant considerations as regards their effectiveness.

B. REDACTION

36. National courts may consider ordering the disclosing party to edit copies of documents by removing the confidential information. This procedure is known as redaction.

37. Redaction may involve the replacement of each piece of confidential information with anonymised data or aggregate figures, the substitution of deleted paragraphs by informative or meaningful non-confidential summaries or even the entire blacking-out of parts of the documents containing the confidential information.

38. Disclosing parties shall be required to limit redaction to what is strictly necessary to protect the interests of those from whom the information originates (e.g. third parties). Limited redaction of certain confidential information may suffice to protect all confidential information in one or a number of documents. For example, depending on the circumstances of the case, redacting customers' names while leaving un-redacted the respective quantities of product supplied to them may be sufficient to protect confidentiality.[43]

39. Redaction of confidential information without replacing the information by a non-confidential text may not strike the right balance between the right of a party to protect its confidential information and the right of the party requesting access to the evidence to substantiate its claim or defence. Redactions applied to entire pages or sections of documents or entire annexes may be considered excessive and may not be acceptable for the purpose of the proceedings.

B.1. REDACTION AS AN EFFECTIVE MEANS FOR PROTECTING CONFIDENTIALITY

40. Redaction may be an effective measure to protect confidential information when, despite the replacement of the confidential information with non-confidential text, the documents and information disclosed remain meaningful and suitable for the exercise of the rights of the party requesting disclosure.

41. Hence, the measure of redaction may be especially effective where the confidential information concerns market data or figures (e.g. turnover, profits, market shares, etc.) which can be substituted with representative ranges, or where qualitative data can be meaningfully summarised.

42. Redaction may also be an effective measure to protect confidential information when the volume of confidential information subject to disclosure is limited. If a very large number of documents needs to be redacted, other measures to protect confidential information (e.g. confidentiality ring, etc.), may, depending on the circumstances of the case, be considered to be more appropriate, taking into account the time, cost and resources necessary to prepare non-confidential versions.

43. Finally, redaction of third party confidential information may also be a useful measure where the disclosing party has in its possession information from third parties that may not be confidential to this party, but that may be confidential vis-à-vis the party requesting disclosure.[44] For example, this could be the case if the requesting party who would receive access to the information and the third party are competitors. In such cases, the disclosing party may need to seek the view of the third party on what information is confidential or otherwise obtain the third party's agreement to a proposal for redaction.

44. However, national courts may find that redaction is a less efficient measure in those cases where the request includes a large number of third party documents because the process of liaising with third parties in this respect might add complexity to the task.

B.2. REDACTING CONFIDENTIAL INFORMATION

45. Depending on the different procedural rules, national courts may be more or less actively involved in the process of redaction. National courts may oversee and control the redaction process and be the interlocutor for the parties and third parties. Alternatively, parties may be primarily responsible for producing non-confidential versions and/or obtaining third parties' agreement to the proposals for redaction where applicable.

46. In any case, to steer the process of preparing non-confidential versions, national courts may find it useful to issue general guidance to parties and/or case-specific guidance for the proceedings pending before it, if this is possible under national procedural rules. Such guidance may be valuable to set out the procedure that courts may expect parties to follow when preparing non-confidential versions.

47. For an efficient handling of the applications for redaction, national courts may request parties:[45]

(i) to mark all the confidential information in the original confidential documents in square brackets and highlighted in a way that remains legible before taking a decision on what should be redacted;[46]

(ii) to draft a list of all the information proposed to be redacted (each word, data, paragraph and/or section to be redacted);

(iii) for each proposed redaction, to submit the specific reasons why the information should be treated confidentially;

(iv) to substitute the redacted information with an informative and meaningful non-confidential summary of the redacted information.[47] Simple indications such as 'business secret', 'confidential' or 'confidential information' are generally insufficient. When redacting quantitative data (e.g. sales, turnover, profits, market shares, prices, etc.) meaningful ranges or aggregate figures may be used. For example, for sales and/or turnover data, ranges wider than 20% of the precise figure may not be meaningful; in the same vein, depending on the circumstances of the case pending before the court, for market shares, ranges wider than 5% may not be meaningful;[48]

(v) to submit non-confidential versions of the documents concerned which mirror the structure and format of the confidential versions. In particular, the information in the original document such as titles or headings, page numbers and paragraph listings shall remain unmodified so that the person reading the document is able to understand the extent of the redactions and the impact of the redactions on the ability to understand the information once disclosed;

(vi) to ensure that the non-confidential versions submitted are technically reliable and that the information redacted cannot be retrieved by any means including the use of forensic tools.

48. Once the parties submit their respective applications for redaction or agree on a proposal for redaction, it will be for the national court to decide whether the proposed redactions are acceptable.

49. Once redacted, the non-confidential versions of the original documents may be used throughout the civil proceedings and no further protection may be required.

C. CONFIDENTIALITY RINGS

50. A confidentiality ring is a disclosure measure whereby the disclosing party makes specified categories of information, including confidential information, available only to defined categories of individuals.[49]

C.1. Confidentiality rings as an effective means for protecting confidentiality

51. Confidentiality rings can be an effective measure for national courts to protect confidentiality in a variety of circumstances.

52. First, confidentiality rings can be effective to ensure disclosure of quantitative data (e.g. revenues, prices, margins, etc.)[50] or very strategic commercial information that, while relevant for the claim of the party, are very difficult to summarise in a meaningful way[51] or cannot be disclosed without risking being excessively redacted,[52] and thus without losing evidentiary value.

53. Second, confidentiality rings may allow for procedural economies and cost efficiencies, in particular when the number of documents requested is voluminous and all the documents are placed entirely in the ring (i.e. in their original version without redaction). In practice, parties may not agree to disclose unredacted versions of certain documents in the confidentiality ring and may still be required to prepare confidential and non-confidential versions of some documents. Nevertheless, even in such cases, confidentiality rings may reduce the need for confidentiality discussions between parties and thereby potential delays.

54. Third, confidentiality rings can be organised electronically (e.g. e-disclosure). Therefore, confidentiality rings do not necessarily require the physical handing out of the information or the physical presence of the members of the ring in a particular location.

55. Confidentiality rings may help to strike a balance between the need for disclosure and the obligation to protect confidential information.[53] By disclosing documents in a confidentiality ring, relevant confidential information is effectively disclosed but the potential harm caused by the disclosure is controlled or minimised by allowing access to a limited circle of individuals depending on the different circumstances of the case (e.g. nature of the documents, relationship of the parties, composition of the ring, third party documents, etc.).

56. However, in considering whether and to what extent evidence should be placed in a confidentiality ring, national courts may attach importance to the fact that information placed in a confidentiality ring may limit the extent to which it may be accessible and/or used in subsequent stages of the procedure (e.g. hearings, publication, etc.). National courts may also consider relevant whether non-confidential versions of documents would still be required and, if so, the amount of documents that would in any event need to be redacted.

C.2. Organising a confidentiality ring

57. If a national court considers that a confidentiality ring is an effective measure of disclosure in a given case, it may, by way of a court order, decide on a number of relevant aspects, such as (a) the information that is to be placed in the confidentiality ring; (b) the composition of the confidentiality ring; (c) the confidentiality undertakings that are to be made by the parties; and (d) the logistical organisation of the confidentiality ring. Some aspects may already be established by national procedural rules or general guidance issued by the national court.[54]

a.
Identifying the information accessible in the confidentiality ring

58. Any confidentiality ring ordered by a national court will typically identify the categories of information or specific items of evidence that should be included in the confidentiality ring. In practice, parties may agree or be invited by the court to agree on the documents or information that should be included in the confidentiality ring before the court issues its order.

b.
Composition of the confidentiality ring

59. After considering the submissions of the parties, either in writing or at an oral hearing, or upon agreement of the parties, the court may order who will be members of the confidentiality ring as well as the members' access rights.[55]

60. The members of the confidentiality ring may be those individuals who will have the right to review documents in the confidentiality ring. The decision on the composition of the confidentiality ring will depend on the circumstances of the case, in particular the nature of the information concerned by the disclosure request.

61. The members of the confidentiality ring may range from external advisers of the parties (e.g. external legal counsel or other advisers) to in-house legal counsel and/or other company representatives. Depending on the national rules and the specific circumstances of the case, confidentiality rings may be composed of external advisers only or of a combination of external and internal advisers.

External advisers

62. External advisers may include legal counsel and other advisers or experts such as accountants, economists, financial advisors or auditors, depending on the needs of the case at hand.

63. Subject to the relationship between the requesting and the disclosing parties, and the information to be disclosed, the court may consider necessary to limit access to the confidentiality ring to advisers that are not involved in the decision-making processes of the companies they represent.[56] This is often the case for external advisers.

64. As opposed to external advisers, in-house legal counsel or company representatives may serve the company in a variety of corporate functions and may often be involved, directly or indirectly, in the strategic decision-making of the company. Therefore, in certain circumstances, there may be a risk that the in-house legal counsel's commercial or strategic advice to the company management is influenced by access to certain confidential information in the confidentiality ring. This might be the case, for example, where the parties to the civil proceedings are actual or potential competitors and access to commercially sensitive or strategic information may give them an unwarranted competitive advantage; where the parties are in a supply relationship; or where the information to be disclosed includes agreements that are still in force.

65. In deciding whether to limit access to external advisers only, national courts may deem the nature of the information relevant, as well as whether such restricted access allows the parties to effectively exercise their rights in judicial proceedings as recognised under EU[57] and national law.

In-house legal counsel and/or other company representatives

66. There may be circumstances where the national court may deem it appropriate for in-house legal counsel and/or company representatives (e.g. managers or other staff)[58] to access confidentiality rings. Access by in-house legal counsel and/or company representatives may be assessed on a case-by-case basis and may depend on the closeness of the individuals suggested by the parties to the business, area of activity or operational business concerned by the request, or other factual circumstances.

67. Such access may be granted when (all or part of) the confidential information in question is regarded as less commercially sensitive or where disclosure to company employees may not be liable to cause harm due to, for example, the relationship between the parties.

68. Access to certain information by in-house legal counsel and/or other company representatives may also be granted upon a reasoned request by the parties,[59] typically when the external legal counsel that had access to the information consider that they cannot adequately represent their client's interests without certain information being disclosed to their client. This is the case, for instance, where the external legal counsel is unable to judge the accuracy or the relevance of the information for the party's claim or where the information is very technical or product-/service-specific and requires sector or industry knowledge to make a relevance assessment.[60]

69. Furthermore, in the legal orders of some Member States, it may be possible in specific situations to seek the national court's consent to share specific items of information with in-house legal counsel or with company representatives without allowing the individuals to become members of the confidentiality ring.

Access rights

70. Where the confidentiality ring is composed of a combination of external advisers and in-house legal counsel and/or company representatives, it is possible that all members of the ring have access to all the information disclosed in the ring or that different access rights are granted.

71. It is also possible that confidentiality rings are organised with two access levels: an inner ring level composed by external legal counsel and/or other external advisers who have the right to access the most sensitive information; and an outer ring level composed of in-house legal counsel and/or company representatives who have the right to access the remaining confidential information.

72. Upon a justified request of the disclosing party, the court may – depending on national procedures – impose also specific restrictions in relation to the access of certain members of the confidentiality ring to specific documents.

73. It may be possible that access to the confidentiality rings is also given to administrative and/or support personnel (including, for example, external electronic disclosure or litigation support providers of electronic technical services) under the supervision of the other persons identified in the ring and under the same confidentiality obligations.

74. Finally, once the court has taken a decision on the composition of the confidentiality ring, it may be appropriate to identify each individual member by name, role or function and relation to the parties.[61] The court may also identify the personnel of the court that shall be present or can access the ring alongside the parties or at any other time in case of confidentiality rings at a physical location.

c.
Written undertakings of the members of the confidentiality ring

75. The court may request that the members of the confidentiality ring submit written undertakings to the court. Those undertakings would concern their obligations regarding accessing the confidentiality ring and in particular, the confidential treatment of certain information included in the confidentiality ring.[62]

76. Such undertakings may concern, inter alia, the duty not to disclose the confidential information to any person different from those listed by the court as confidentiality ring members, without the express consent of the court; the obligation to use the confidential information only for the purpose of the civil proceedings in which the disclosure order was issued; the obligation to ensure adequate custody of the information; the obligation to adopt any measure necessary in the circumstances to prevent unauthorised access; the obligation not to copy, print, download, otherwise replicate, transmit or communicate the documents accessed; the obligation to return or destroy any copies of documents containing confidential information; the obligation to make the documents unavailable to the identified persons from any computer or devices after a specific date, etc.

77. In cases where the court allows access to the confidentiality ring by external advisers only, it may impose on them the obligation not to disclose the confidential information to their clients. This may be of significant relevance in those jurisdictions in which external legal counsel are bound, pursuant to deontological bar rules or other rules, to share the information with their clients.[63] For this purpose, should the parties agree to such restrictions for the purpose of the confidentiality ring, they may need to expressly release the external legal counsel that are members of the confidentiality ring (and possibly their law firm) from the obligation to disclose to them information included in the confidentiality ring.[64]

78. In addition, where in-house legal counsel or company representatives participate in a confidentiality ring, they may be subject to additional requirements. For example, the national court may deem it appropriate to prescribe that, for a limited period, the employee in question does not work in the line of business concerned by the claim.

d.
Logistical organisation of a confidentiality ring

79. Confidentiality rings may require national courts to decide on various organisational, infrastructure and logistical measures.

80. First, confidentiality rings may involve the physical or the electronic disclosure of confidential information. Physical disclosure may be organised at the court premises with court personnel in control of the disclosure or by the parties at their premises with no involvement of the court. Physical disclosure may involve handing over paper copies of documents but also the disclosure of evidence by means of a CD, DVD or a USB key in a physical location, in court premises or at parties' premises.

81. If the disclosure of the information into the confidentiality ring occurs at the court's premises, the court may need to ensure that the facilities for accessing the information are adequate, unless the persons accessing the confidentiality ring are allowed to bring their own equipment.

82. Disclosure of information in a confidentiality ring may occur also by electronic means. In such case, the information is uploaded and stored in an electronic location (e.g. cloud), and access to the information is protected by adequate encryption.

83. Second, the court may determine the duration of the accessibility to the confidentiality ring.

84. Third, the court may furthermore decide on the hours of availability of the disclosure rooms (e.g. during business hours only), whether court personnel must be present in the disclosure rooms, whether notes or files can be brought into the rooms, etc.

85. Finally, to ensure that confidential information disclosed in a confidentiality ring is protected throughout the proceedings, national courts may request that parties submit both a confidential and a non-confidential version of their pleadings (the latter, for instance, only including quantitative data in an aggregated or anonymised form), that confidential information is only referred to in a confidential annex, or that other measures are taken to protect the confidential nature of the information. For more detail in this respect, please refer to Section IV below.

D. APPOINTMENT OF EXPERTS

86. In some jurisdictions, national courts may decide to appoint a third party individual with expertise in a specific field (e.g. accounting, finance, competition law, audit, etc.) to access certain confidential information concerned by a disclosure request. The role of such court appointed expert may be different from party appointed experts, who are frequently used in some jurisdictions to support a party's claim or defence.

87. If national procedural rules allow it, the expert's assignment may for example be to draft a meaningful non-confidential summary of the information to be made available to the party requesting disclosure. Alternatively, and depending on the national procedural rules applicable, the expert may be asked to draft a confidential report that may be made available only to the external legal counsel and/or other external advisers of the party requesting disclosure, while a non-confidential version of the report may be made available to the requesting party itself.

D.1. Appointing experts as an effective means for protecting confidentiality

88. First, the appointment of experts may prove to be an effective measure where the information to be disclosed is commercially very sensitive, and quantitative or technical in nature (e.g. information included in commercial or accounting books, customer data, manufacturing processes, etc.). In such cases, the experts may summarise and/or aggregate confidential information with a view to making it accessible to the party requesting disclosure.

89. Second, the appointment of experts may also be effective where one party requests further access to confidential documents containing underlying data, for example, to evaluate the robustness of methodologies used to assess the extent of damages, overcharges passed on, etc.

90. Third, in cases where a large number of the documents to be disclosed concerns third party confidential information, courts may consider it more effective to appoint an expert to access the information and give his or her opinion as to the confidential nature of the information, than to engage in discussions with parties about the scope of redaction or to set up a confidentiality ring.

D.2. Instructing experts

91. The national court may appoint and instruct the appointed experts. Depending on the different procedural rules, national courts may be able to appoint third party independent experts from a list of 'court approved' experts, from a list of experts proposed by the parties, etc. Pursuant to national procedural rules, when appointing an expert, the national court may also need to decide who will bear the expert costs.

92. Once the expert is appointed, national courts may request the expert to submit written undertakings regarding the confidential treatment of any information accessed.

93. As in the case of the members of a confidentiality ring, experts may be required to agree not to disclose confidential information to any person other than those listed by the court or without the express consent of the court; to use the confidential information only for the purpose of the civil proceedings in which the disclosure order was issued; to ensure adequate custody of the information; to adopt any measure necessary in the circumstances to prevent unauthorised access and to return or destroy any copies of documents containing confidential information, etc. These undertakings may also provide for penalties in case of breach of the duty of confidentiality.

94. Experts may be required to declare any conflicts of interests that may prevent them from carrying out their task.

95. Furthermore, the court may instruct the expert on the type of report to be produced and on whether both a confidential and a non-confidential version of the report may be needed.

96. Whenever a confidential version of the expert report is produced, the court may decide that the report is shared only with the external advisers of the parties, while the parties may receive access only to a non-confidential version of the report. If the national court restricts access to the confidential version of the report prepared by an expert only to a party's external adviser, the external adviser will not be allowed to share the confidential information contained therein with his or her client.[65] If the court decides that the underlying data used by the independent expert may also be disclosed to the external adviser, separate confidentiality arrangements may be necessary.

97. If in-house legal counsel and/or company representatives are allowed to access a confidential version of the expert's report, the court may request that they also submit written undertakings regarding the confidential treatment of the information to which they have access.

NOTES

[34] See recital 18 of the Damages Directive.

[35] For example, if the parties are direct competitors, the measure chosen must ensure that the way in which the information is disclosed will not enable the parties to collude or give a competitive advantage to the party requesting disclosure.

[36] See, in particular, Article 5(7) of the Damages Directive ('*Member States shall ensure that those from whom disclosure is sought are provided with an opportunity to be heard before a national court orders disclosure* [. . .]').

[37] The disclosing party may not necessarily be the party from which the information originates. For example, a party may have accessed information from third parties during the administrative proceedings before the Commission or a national competition authority. Having had access to the information does not entitle this party to disclose further the confidential information of a third party. For example, in relation to non-confidential versions of documents regarding a data collection process that was prepared specifically for access to the file purposes, see Commission Opinion of 29 October 2015, in application of Article 15(1) of Council Regulation (EC) No 1/2003 of 16 December 2002 on the implementation of the rules on competition laid down in Articles 81 and 82 of the Treaty, *Sainsbury's Supermarkets Ltd* v *Mastercard Incorporated and Others*, (C(2015) 7682 final), paragraph 23, where the Commission stated that, for the purposes of the Commission's investigation, it had been unnecessary to take a position as to whether the information was confidential vis-à-vis other parties, but that third parties who provided the information might object to sharing the information with the claimant. The opinion concluded that '[. . .], *the fact that Mastercard might be satisfied with particular arrangements made, such as a confidentiality ring, would not necessarily satisfy third parties who submitted the information.*' The Opinion is available at http://ec.europa.eu/competition/court/sainsbury_opinion_en.pdf.

[38] See paragraphs 6 and 10 above.

[39] The protection of confidential information in the context of disclosure requests may require changes to the usual functioning of the court's logistic or even telematics procedures, or putting in place *ad hoc* procedures on a case-by-case basis within the boundaries of the applicable national procedural laws.

[40] See, for example, Article 16 of the Trade Secrets Directive that provides for the possibility of imposing sanctions on any person who fails or refuses to comply with measures ordered to preserve the confidentiality of trade secrets in the course of legal proceedings.

[41] See, also, recital 33 of the Damages Directive. The recourse to sanctions is of the essence considering that in most cases national courts might be unable to exercise real time supervision of the parties' compliance with the rules of the disclosure order, notably in the case of a confidentiality ring.

[42] Article 8(2) of the Damages Directive.

[43] Accessibility to information on volumes supplied may be essential to quantify the harm suffered on the lower level of the supply chain (i.e. by indirect customers).

[44] This can occur because the third party documents do not include confidential information *vis-à-vis* the disclosing party or because the disclosing party already had access to a non-confidential version of the documents, in which information regarded as confidential *vis-à-vis* the disclosing party had been previously redacted.

[45] For inspiration, see Access to File Notice, paragraphs 35-38; Guidance on confidentiality claims during Commission antitrust procedures, paragraphs 18 to 26, available at https://ec.europa.eu/competition/antitrust/business_secrets_en.pdf, and DG Competition informal guidance paper on confidentiality claims, available at https://ec.europa.eu/competition/antitrust/guidance_en.pdf.

[46] For example, a colour coding system could be used to indicate to which party the confidential information belongs or whether it relates to third party information.

[47] See, for example, Article 103(3) of the Rules of Procedure of the General Court.

[48] For ranges on sales, turnover data and market shares, see paragraph 22 of the Guidance on confidentiality claims during Commission antitrust procedures, available at https://ec.europa.eu/competition/antitrust/business_secrets_en.pdf.

[49] Depending on the jurisdiction, this disclosure measure is also referred to as confidentiality clubs or data rooms. This type of measure can also be used in administrative proceedings. For Commission procedures, see Commission Notice on Best Practices for the conduct of proceedings concerning Articles 101 and 102 TFEU (OJ C308, 20.10.2011, p 6), paragraphs 96 and 97; for data rooms, see Best Practices on the disclosure of information in data rooms in proceedings under Articles 101 and 102 TFEU and under the EU Merger Regulation, paragraph 9, available at http://ec.europa.eu/competition/mergers/legislation/disclosure_information_data_rooms_en.pdf For confidentiality rings, see Guidance on the use of confidentiality rings in Commission proceedings, available at http://ec.europa.eu/competition/antitrust/conf_rings.pdf

[50] See, Passing-on Guidelines, cited above, paragraph 43.

[51] See, for example, OECD report of 5 October 2011 on Procedural fairness: transparency issues in civil and administrative enforcement proceedings, p. 12, available at www.oecd.org/competition/mergers/48825133.pdf; see also, Scoping note on Transparency and Procedural Fairness as a long-term theme for 2019-2020, 6-8 June 2018, OECD Conference Centre, pp. 4-5, available at www.oecd.org/officialdocuments/publicdisplaydocumentpdf/?cote=DAF/COMP/WD(2018)6&docLanguage=En.

[52] For example, in relation to data collected by external contractors from the participants in a Commission's survey, in its Opinion in *Sainsbury's Supermarkets Ltd* v *MasterCard Incorporated and Others*, cited above, paragraph 21, the Commission concluded that the information could not be anonymised in a way that fully respected the data providers' legitimate interest in the protection of their confidential information.

[53] See in this respect the disclosure into a confidentiality ring ordered by the General Court in its judgment of 14 March 2014, *Cementos Portland Valderrivas, SA* v *Commission*, Case T-296/11, EU:T:2014:121 paragraph 24: '[. . .] *with*

a view to reconciling the adversarial principle and the characteristics of the preliminary investigation stage of the procedure, when the undertaking concerned has neither the right to be informed of the essential evidence on which the Commission relies, nor a right of access to the file, the order of 14 May 2013 limited inspection of the information supplied by the Commission to the applicant's lawyers and made such inspection conditional upon them giving an undertaking of confidentiality.'

54 For an example of measures of organisation of procedure, see the Practice Rules for the Implementation of the Rules of Procedure of the General Court adopted by the General Court, and in particular Section VI dealing with confidentiality (OJ L152, 18.6.2015, p 1). For example, for the confidentiality ring rules and data room rules used for the purpose of Commission administrative procedures, see Section 4.3 of the Best Practices on the disclosure of information in data room proceedings under Articles 101 and 102 TFEU and under the EU Merger Regulation, cited above; Annex A to the Best Practices, the Standard data room rules (for the disclosure of confidential information on external advisor only basis), available at https://ec.europa.eu/competition/antitrust/data_room_rules_en.pdf; and the Guidance on the use of confidentiality rings and in particular, Section 5, on the negotiated disclosure agreement, cited above.

55 The decision of the composition of the confidentiality ring may also define the maximum number of members per party.

56 See recital 18 of the Damages Directive (*'restricting the persons allowed to see the evidence'*).

57 See, for example, Article 9(2) of the Trade Secrets Directive..

58 E.g. individuals employed by the requesting party through labour contracts or other type of service or contractual agreements.

59 See, for inspiration, Access to File Notice, cited above, paragraph 47.

60 In litigation regarding the disclosure of trade secrets, Article 9(2) of the Trade Secrets Directive prescribes that the restricted circle of persons entitled to access the evidence shall be composed of at least one natural person from each of the parties. This requirement is limited to (alleged) trade secrets.

61 See Commission Opinion in Servier, cited above, paragraph. 22.

62 For example, in its administrative procedures, the Commission uses a standard non-disclosure agreement, which is available at https://ec.europa.eu/competition/antitrust/nda_en.pdf.

63 This is a departure from the usual practice in which a party's external legal counsel discloses to his/her client information and pleadings received from other parties in the proceeding and discusses them freely with his/her client.

64 In its administrative practice, the Commission may also seek a waiver of the lawyer-client disclosure duty; see, for instance the Guidance on the use of confidentiality rings, cited above, paragraph 13 and Best Practices on the disclosure of information in data rooms, cited above, paragraph 23.

65 As in the case of confidentiality rings for external legal counsel, clients may need to release the external advisers from any obligation to disclose to them the confidential information included in the report. See paragraph 77 above.

IV. PROTECTION OF THE CONFIDENTIAL INFORMATION THROUGHOUT AND FOLLOWING THE PROCEEDINGS

[4.483]

98. When disclosure of confidential information has taken place, national courts may consider how that information can be used throughout and after the proceedings.[66] For example, if the parties' external or internal advisers use information accessed in a confidentiality ring or included in a confidential expert report in their pleadings, national courts may ask them to refer only to such information in confidential annexes to be submitted alongside the main pleadings.[67]

99. If parties' external legal counsel or witnesses wish to refer to confidential information during the court's hearing or when an expert is heard on such evidence, national courts may organise *in camera* (i.e. closed) hearings, if possible under the applicable procedural rules. Alternatively, it may be possible for the parties' advisers to direct the judge orally to such information without disclosing it in open court.

100. The need to protect confidential information may also arise later, for example, at the time of the adoption, notification or publication of the judgment, during appeal proceedings or in the case of requests for access to court's records.

A. IN CAMERA HEARINGS

101. Pursuant to the principle of open justice, civil proceedings are generally public in nature[68] and national courts may weigh the interest to the protection of confidential information against the need to limit the interference with the principle of open justice.

102. Subject to national rules, courts may decide to exclude references to confidential information at public hearings, or to hold *in camera* those parts of the hearings where confidential information might be discussed. In the second case, national courts would have to decide who would be allowed to attend the closed session. This decision may depend on how and to whom the confidential information was disclosed (e.g. to the parties' external advisers, to an expert, to the parties' company representatives, etc.).

103. During *in camera* (parts of) hearings, generally only those external advisers and/or internal legal counsel or other company representatives who were granted access to the confidential documents in the confidentiality ring and (if applicable) the expert who accessed the information would be permitted to participate.

104. Hearings *in camera* may be an effective means to cross-examine parties or witnesses on confidential evidence disclosed through a confidentiality ring or to hear an expert on the confidential evidence included in his or her report.

B. NOTIFICATION TO THE PARTIES AND PUBLICATION

105. The court may have to consider how to protect the confidential information in the version of the judgment to be notified to the parties, without prejudice to the right of appeal of the parties.

106. In addition, if decisions or judgments are published, national courts may have to protect confidential information. To protect confidential information of the parties or third parties, when rendering the judgment and ordering its publication, national courts may consider to anonymise any information that could identify the source of

the information/or to redact from the publicly available version of the ruling those parts referring to confidential information.[69] In this process, the court may ask the parties' assistance in identifying information that should not be disclosed to the wider public (e.g. by requesting a mark-up version).[70]

C. ACCESS TO COURT RECORDS

107. National courts may need to protect confidential information in relation to requests for access to the court's records (either the confidential version of the judgment or the entire file), if such requests can be made under national procedural rules.

108. Depending on the national rules, courts may decide to restrict access to the court's records either with regard to part of the file (e.g. to refuse access to documents disclosed in a confidentiality ring, expert reports, minutes of *in camera* hearings, confidential version of pleadings, etc.) or with regard to the entirety of the file.

109. In that respect, national courts may consider, inter alia, asking parties to indicate which documents are confidential so that they are not accessible to non-parties to the proceedings, or requesting non-confidential versions of the documents concerned for the court's records. For example, if a significant number of confidential documents were disclosed in the proceedings and measures such as confidentiality rings were used to protect confidentiality, the court may also consider registering into the court's records only non-confidential versions of pleadings, minutes of *in camera* hearings[71] or expert reports. The court may also consider sealing the court's file from access, partially or entirely, for a specific period.

110. When deciding whether to restrict, partially or entirely, access, the courts may need to evaluate, inter alia, who is requesting access to the court's file. For example, courts may need to take into account that persons requesting access may operate in the same market or business activity as the parties involved in the civil proceedings (e.g. competitors of the parties, business partners, etc.) and may have a special interest in getting access to the court's file after the proceedings are closed.

NOTES

66 The protection of confidential information is a general principle of EU law. See footnote 18 above.

67 The non-confidential versions of the pleadings must allow the other parties to understand the arguments and the evidence being referred to so that they can discuss the case with their legal representatives and instruct them accordingly.

68 See Article 6 of the European Convention of Human Rights and Article 47 of the Charter of Fundamental Rights of the European Union, cited above. Exceptions to this principle may relate in some Member States to the maintenance of public order, the protection of fundamental rights or other overarching objectives.

69 See, also, Article 9.2(c) of the Trade Secrets Directive.

70 As a source of inspiration on how to carry out this process, see Guidance on the preparation of public versions of Commission Decisions, available at https://ec.europa.eu/competition/antitrust/guidance_on_preparation_of_public_versions_antitrust_04062015.pdf.

71 If confidential information was referred to during the in camera hearing and read into the record, this measure may be necessary. However, if possible under applicable national rules, the court may decide that some information is referred to in camera without reading it on the record. In that situation, it may be unnecessary to prepare non-confidential versions of the minutes of in camera hearings.

4. COOPERATION / NATIONAL COMPETITION AUTHORITIES

JOINT STATEMENT OF THE COUNCIL AND THE COMMISSION ON THE FUNCTIONING OF THE NETWORK OF COMPETITION AUTHORITIES (2002)

[4.484]

NOTES

This document is taken from the European Commission website at: ec.europa.eu/competition-policy/european-competition-network/documents_en.

Note: with effect from 1 December 2009, the EC Treaty was replaced by the Treaty on the Functioning of the European Union. References in this document to provisions of the EC Treaty should be construed accordingly.

[4.485]

"1. The today adopted Regulation on the implementation of the rules on competition laid down in Articles 81 and 82 of the Treaty establishes a directly applicable exception system in which the competition authorities and courts of the Member States, along with the Commission, have the power to apply not only Articles 81(1) and 82 of the Treaty, which have direct applicability by virtue of the case-law of the Court of Justice of the European Communities, but also Article 81(3) of the Treaty.

2. In order to ensure that the Community competition rules are applied effectively and consistently, the Commission and the national competition authorities designated by the Member States (hereafter NCAs) form together a network of competition authorities (hereafter the Network) for the application in close cooperation of Articles 81 and 82 of the Treaty.

3. This Joint Statement is political in nature and does therefore not create any legal rights or obligations. It is limited to setting out common political understanding shared by all Member States and the Commission on the principles of the functioning of the Network.

4. Details will be set out in a Commission notice which will be drafted and updated as necessary in close cooperation with Member States.

General principles

5. The cooperation within the Network is dedicated to the effective enforcement of EC competition rules throughout the Community.

6. Decentralization of the implementation of Community competition rules strengthens the position of the NCAs. These will be fully competent to apply Article 81 and 82 of the Treaty, actively contributing to the development of competition policy, law and practice.

7. All competition authorities within the Network are independent from one another. Cooperation between NCAs and with the Commission takes place on the basis of equality, respect and solidarity.

8. Member States accept that their enforcement systems differ but nonetheless mutually recognize the standards of each other's system as a basis for cooperation.

9. The Commission, as the guardian of the Treaty, has the ultimate but not the sole responsibility for developing policy and safeguarding efficiency and consistency. Therefore, the instruments of the Commission on the one hand and of the NCAs on the other hand are not identical. The additional powers the Commission has been granted to fulfil its responsibilities will be exercised with the utmost regard for the cooperative nature of the Network.

10. Cooperation within the Network and the management of information will be as efficient as possible. All members of the Network will minimize the administrative burden of participating in the Network on the understanding that any information exchanged under Article 11 of the Regulation will be made available and easily accessible to all Network members.

Division of work

11. Without prejudice to Article 11(6) of the Regulation, all Network members have full parallel competence to apply Articles 81 and 82 of the Treaty.

12. Case allocation will be completed as quickly as possible. An indicative time limit (up to 3 months) will be used within the Network. Normally, this allocation will remain definitive to the end of the proceedings provided that the facts known about the case remain substantially the same. If so, this implies that the competition authority which has notified the case to the Network, will normally remain the responsible competition authority if it is well placed to deal with the case and no other competition authority raises objections during the indicative time period.

13. All members of the Network will endeavour to make allocation a predictable process with business and other interested parties receiving guidance as to where to direct complaints.

14. Members of the Network will ensure that those cases which merit a detailed investigation by a competition authority are adequately allocated and assessed. This principle does not prejudice the discretion of all Network members to decide whether or not to investigate a case.

Authority (-ies) well placed to act

15. Members of the Network will ensure an effective enforcement of Articles 81 and 82 of the Treaty. Cases will be dealt with by an authority, or by authorities, able to restore or maintain competition in the market. To that effect, the members of the Network will take into account all relevant factors in particular in which markets the main anti-competitive effects are felt and which authority is most able to deal with a case successfully depending on the ability of the authority to gather evidence, to bring the infringement to an end and to apply sanctions effectively.

16. Cases will be dealt with by a single competition authority as often as possible. A single NCA will be usually well placed to act if only one Member State is substantially affected by an agreement or practice, particularly when the main anti-competitive effects appear in the same Member State and all participating companies to an agreement or an abusive behaviour have their seat in that Member State.

17. Where an agreement or practice substantially affects competition in more than one Member State, the Network members will seek to agree between them who is best placed to deal with the case successfully.

18. In cases where single action is not possible (when competition in several Member States is affected and no NCA can deal with the case alone successfully), the Network members should coordinate their action and seek to designate one competition authority as the lead institution.

19. The Commission will be particularly well placed to deal with a case if more than three Member States are substantially affected by an agreement or practice, if it is closely linked to other Community provisions which may be exclusively or more effectively applied by the Commission, if Community interest requires the adoption of a Commission decision to develop Community competition policy particularly when a new competition issue arises or to ensure effective enforcement.

Consistent application of Community competition rules

20. After the initial allocation period, when the same case (same market, same parties, same conduct/agreement) is being dealt with by more than one NCA well placed to do so, one national competition authority will take a formal decision, whilst others stay their proceedings or, if this is not possible, the NCAs will deal with the case in close cooperation.

21. After the initial allocation period, when a case is being dealt with by one or several competition authority (-ies) which is (are) well placed to do so, the Commission will normally not open proceedings with the effects of relieving them of their competence pursuant to Article 11(6) of the Regulation unless one of the following situations arises:

- (a) Network members envisage conflicting decisions in the same case;
- (b) Network members envisage a decision which is obviously in conflict with consolidated case law; the standards defined in the judgements of the Community courts and in previous decisions and regulations of the Commission should serve as a yardstick; concerning facts, only a significant divergence will trigger an intervention of the Commission;
- (c) Network member(s) is (are) unduly drawing out proceedings;
- (d) There is a need to adopt a Commission decision to develop Community competition policy in particular when a similar competition issue arises in several Member States;
- (e) The national competition authority does not object.

Should the Commission decide to open proceedings with the effects of Article 11(6) of the Regulation, it will do so as soon as possible.

22. If an NCA is already acting on a case, the Commission will explain the reasons for the application of Article 11(6) of the Regulation in writing to the NCA concerned and to the other members of the Network.

23. The Commission will normally not – and to the extent that Community interest is not at stake – adopt a decision which is in conflict with a decision of an NCA after proper information pursuant to both Article 11(3) and (4) of the Regulation has been provided and the Commission has made no use of Article 11(6) of the Regulation.

24. Network members will inform the other members of the Network about rejections of complaints and the termination of investigations on all cases which have been notified within the Network pursuant to Article 11(2) and 11(3) of the Regulation."

COMMISSION NOTICE

(2004/C101/03)

on cooperation within the network of competition authorities

(Text with EEA relevance)

[4.486]

NOTES

Date of publication in OJ: OJ C101, 27.4.2004, p 43.

Note that the following authorities in EU Member States operate a leniency programme; see the European Commission website at: ec.europa.eu/competition-policy/european-competition-network/documents_en:

— Austria (Federal Competition Authority)
— Belgium (Competition Council)
— Bulgaria (Commission on Protection of Competition)
— Cyprus (Commission for the Protection of Competition – CPC)
— Czech Republic (Office for the Protection of Competition)
— Estonia (Estonian Competition Board)

— Finland (Finnish Competition Authority)
— France (Competition Council)
— Germany (Federal Cartel Office)
— Greece (Hellenic Competition Commission)
— Hungary (GVH – Hungarian Office of Economic Competition)
— Ireland (The Competition Authority)
— Italy (Autorità garante della Concorrenza e del Mercato)
— Latvia (Competition Council Republic of Latvia)
— Lithuania (Competition Council of the Republic of Lithuania)
— Luxembourg (Conseil de la Concurrence: Inspection de la Concurrence)
— Netherlands – (Nederlandse Mededingingsautoriteit (NMa))
— Poland (Office for Competition and Consumer Protection)
— Portugal (Autoridade da Concorrência)
— Romania (Competition Council)
— Slovakia (AMO – Antimonopoly Office of the Slovak Republic)
— Sweden (Swedish Competition Authority)
— *United Kingdom (Office of Fair Trading (OFT) (now the Competition and Markets Authority). Note that the UK left the EU at 11pm on 31 January 2020 (subject to the transitional or implementation period provided for in Article 126 of the EU-UK Withdrawal Agreement).*

Note: with effect from 1 December 2009, the EC Treaty was replaced by the Treaty on the Functioning of the European Union. References in this document to provisions of the EC Treaty should be construed accordingly.

1. INTRODUCTION

[4.487]

1. Council Regulation (EC) No 1/2003 of 16 December 2002 on the implementation of the rules on competition laid down in Articles 81 and 82 of the Treaty[1] (hereafter the "Council Regulation") creates a system of parallel competences in which the Commission and the Member States' competition authorities (hereafter the "NCAs")[2] can apply Article 81 and Article 82 of the EC Treaty (hereafter the "Treaty"). Together the NCAs and the Commission form a network of public authorities: they act in the public interest and cooperate closely in order to protect competition. The network is a forum for discussion and cooperation in the application and enforcement of EC competition policy. It provides a framework for the cooperation of European competition authorities in cases where Articles 81 and 82 of the Treaty are applied and is the basis for the creation and maintenance of a common competition culture in Europe. The network is called "European Competition Network" (ECN).

2. The structure of the NCAs varies between Member States. In some Member States, one body investigates cases and takes all types of decisions. In other Member States, the functions are divided between two bodies, one which is in charge of the investigation of the case and another, often a college, which is responsible for deciding the case. Finally, in certain Member States, prohibition decisions and/or decisions imposing a fine can only be taken by a court: another competition authority acts as a prosecutor bringing the case before that court. Subject to the general principle of effectiveness, Article 35 of the Council Regulation allows Member States to choose the body or bodies which will be designated as national competition authorities and to allocate functions between them. Under general principles of Community law, Member States are under an obligation to set up a sanctioning system providing for sanctions which are effective, proportionate and dissuasive for infringements of EC law.[3] The enforcement systems of the Member States differ but they have recognised the standards of each other's systems as a basis for cooperation.[4]

3. The network formed by the competition authorities should ensure both an efficient division of work and an effective and consistent application of EC competition rules. The Council Regulation together with the joint statement of the Council and the Commission on the functioning of the European Competition Network sets out the main principles of the functioning of the network. This notice presents the details of the system.

4. Consultations and exchanges within the network are matters between public enforcers and do not alter any rights or obligations arising from Community or national law for companies. Each competition authority remains fully responsible for ensuring due process in the cases it deals with.

NOTES

1 OJ L1, 4.1.2003, p 1.

2 In this notice, the European Commission and the NCAs are collectively referred to as "the competition authorities".

3 Cf. ECJ case 68/88 – *Commission v. Greece* [1989] ECR 2965 (recitals 23 to 25).

4 See paragraph 8 of the Joint Statement of the Council and the Commission on the functioning of the network available from the Council register at
ec.europa.eu/competition/ecn/joint_statement_en.pdf (document No 15435/02 ADD 1).

2. DIVISION OF WORK

2.1. PRINCIPLES OF ALLOCATION

[4.488]

5. The Council Regulation is based on a system of parallel competences in which all competition authorities have the power to apply Articles 81 or 82 of the Treaty and are responsible for an efficient division of work with respect to those cases where an investigation is deemed to be necessary. At the same time each network member retains full discretion in deciding whether or not to investigate a case. Under this system of parallel competences, cases will be dealt with by:

— a single NCA, possibly with the assistance of NCAs of other Member States; or
— several NCAs acting in parallel; or
— the Commission.

6. In most instances the authority that receives a complaint or starts an ex-officio procedure[5] will remain in charge of the case. Re-allocation of a case would only be envisaged at the outset of a procedure (see paragraph 18 below) where either that authority considered that it was not well placed to act or where other authorities also considered themselves well placed to act (see paragraphs 8 to 15 below).

7. Where re-allocation is found to be necessary for an effective protection of competition and of the Community interest, network members will endeavour to re-allocate cases to a single well placed competition authority as often as possible.[6] In any event, re-allocation should be a quick and efficient process and not hold up ongoing investigations.

8. An authority can be considered to be well placed to deal with a case if the following three cumulative conditions are met:

1. the agreement or practice has substantial direct actual or foreseeable effects on competition within its territory, is implemented within or originates from its territory;
2. the authority is able to effectively bring to an end the entire infringement, ie it can adopt a cease-and-desist order the effect of which will be sufficient to bring an end to the infringement and it can, where appropriate, sanction the infringement adequately;
3. it can gather, possibly with the assistance of other authorities, the evidence required to prove the infringement.

9. The above criteria indicate that a material link between the infringement and the territory of a Member State must exist in order for that Member State's competition authority to be considered well placed. It can be expected that in most cases the authorities of those Member States where competition is substantially affected by an infringement will be well placed provided they are capable of effectively bringing the infringement to an end through either single or parallel action unless the Commission is better placed to act (see below paragraphs 14 and 15).

10. It follows that a single NCA is usually well placed to deal with agreements or practices that substantially affect competition mainly within its territory.

Example 1: Undertakings situated in Member State A are involved in a price fixing cartel on products that are mainly sold in Member State A.

The NCA in A is well placed to deal with the case.

11. Furthermore single action of an NCA might also be appropriate where, although more than one NCA can be regarded as well placed, the action of a single NCA is sufficient to bring the entire infringement to an end.

Example 2: Two undertakings have set up a joint venture in Member State A. The joint venture provides services in Member States A and B and gives rise to a competition problem. A cease-and-desist order is considered to be sufficient to deal with the case effectively because it can bring an end to the entire infringement. Evidence is located mainly at the offices of the joint venture in Member State A.

The NCAs in A and B are both well placed to deal with the case but single action by the NCA in A would be sufficient and more efficient than single action by NCA in B or parallel action by both NCAs.

12. Parallel action by two or three NCAs may be appropriate where an agreement or practice has substantial effects on competition mainly in their respective territories and the action of only one NCA would not be sufficient to bring the entire infringement to an end and/or to sanction it adequately.

Example 3: Two undertakings agree on a market sharing agreement, restricting the activity of the company located in Member State A to Member State A and the activity of the company located in Member State B to Member State B.

The NCAs in A and B are well placed to deal with the case in parallel, each one for its respective territory.

13. The authorities dealing with a case in parallel action will endeavour to coordinate their action to the extent possible. To that effect, they may find it useful to designate one of them as a lead authority and to delegate tasks to the lead authority such as for example the coordination of investigative measures, while each authority remains responsible for conducting its own proceedings.

14. The Commission is particularly well placed if one or several agreement(s) or practice(s), including networks of similar agreements or practices, have effects on competition in more than three Member States (cross-border markets covering more than three Member States or several national markets).

Example 4: Two undertakings agree to share markets or fix prices for the whole territory of the Community. The Commission is well placed to deal with the case.

Example 5: An undertaking, dominant in four different national markets, abuses its position by imposing fidelity rebates on its distributors in all these markets. The Commission is well placed to deal with the case. It could also deal with one national market so as to create a "leading" case and other national markets could be dealt with by NCAs, particularly if each national market requires a separate assessment.

15. Moreover, the Commission is particularly well placed to deal with a case if it is closely linked to other Community provisions which may be exclusively or more effectively applied by the Commission, if the Community interest requires the adoption of a Commission decision to develop Community competition policy when a new competition issue arises or to ensure effective enforcement.

2.2. MECHANISMS OF COOPERATION FOR THE PURPOSE OF CASE ALLOCATION AND ASSISTANCE

2.2.1. INFORMATION AT THE BEGINNING OF THE PROCEDURE (ARTICLE 11 OF THE COUNCIL REGULATION)

16. In order to detect multiple procedures and to ensure that cases are dealt with by a well placed competition authority, the members of the network have to be informed at an early stage of the cases pending before the various competition authorities.[7] If a case is to be re-allocated, it is indeed in the best interest both of the network and of the undertakings concerned that the re-allocation takes place quickly.

17. The Council Regulation creates a mechanism for the competition authorities to inform each other in order to ensure an efficient and quick re-allocation of cases. Article 11(3) of the Council Regulation lays down an obligation for NCAs to inform the Commission when acting under Article 81 or 82 of the Treaty before or without delay after commencing the first formal investigative measure. It also states that the information may be made available to other NCAs.[8] The rationale of Article 11(3) of the Council Regulation is to allow the network to detect multiple procedures and address possible case re-allocation issues as soon as an authority starts investigating a case. Information should therefore be provided to NCAs and the Commission before or just after any step similar to the measures of investigation that can be undertaken by the Commission under Articles 18 to 21 of the Council Regulation. The Commission has accepted an equivalent obligation to inform NCAs under Article 11(2) of the Council Regulation. Network members will inform each other of pending cases by means of a standard form containing limited details of the case, such as the authority dealing with the case, the product, territories and parties concerned, the alleged infringement, the suspected duration of the infringement and the origin of the case. They will also provide each other with updates when a relevant change occurs.

18. Where case re-allocation issues arise, they should be resolved swiftly, normally within a period of two months, starting from the date of the first information sent to the network pursuant to Article 11 of the Council Regulation. During this period, competition authorities will endeavour to reach an agreement on a possible re-allocation and, where relevant, on the modalities for parallel action.

19. In general, the competition authority or authorities that is/are dealing with a case at the end of the re-allocation period should continue to deal with the case until the completion of the proceedings. Re-allocation of a case after the initial allocation period of two months should only occur where the facts known about the case change materially during the course of the proceedings.

2.2.2. SUSPENSION OR TERMINATION OF PROCEEDINGS (ARTICLE 13 OF THE COUNCIL REGULATION)

20. If the same agreement or practice is brought before several competition authorities, be it because they have received a complaint or have opened a procedure on their own initiative, Article 13 of the Council Regulation provides a legal basis for suspending proceedings or rejecting a complaint on the grounds that another authority is dealing with the case or has dealt with the case. In Article 13 of the Council Regulation, "dealing with the case" does not merely mean that a complaint has been lodged with another authority. It means that the other authority is investigating or has investigated the case on its own behalf.

21. Article 13 of the Council Regulation applies when another authority has dealt or is dealing with the competition issue raised by the complainant, even if the authority in question has acted or acts on the basis of a complaint lodged by a different complainant or as a result of an ex-officio procedure. This implies that Article 13 of the Council Regulation can be invoked when the agreement or practice involves the same infringement(s) on the same relevant geographic and product markets.

22. An NCA may suspend or close its proceedings but it has no obligation to do so. Article 13 of the Council Regulation leaves scope for appreciation of the peculiarities of each individual case. This flexibility is important: if a complaint was rejected by an authority following an investigation of the substance of the case, another authority may not want to re-examine the case. On the other hand, if a complaint was rejected for other reasons (eg the authority was unable to collect the evidence necessary to prove the infringement), another authority may wish to carry out its own investigation and deal with the case. This flexibility is also reflected, for pending cases, in the choice open to each NCA as to whether it closes or suspends its proceedings. An authority may be unwilling to close a case before the outcome of another authority's proceedings is clear. The ability to suspend its proceedings allows the authority to retain its ability to decide at a later point whether or not to terminate its proceedings. Such flexibility also facilitates consistent application of the rules.

23. Where an authority closes or suspends proceedings because another authority is dealing with the case, it may transfer – in accordance with Article 12 of the Council Regulation – the information provided by the complainant to the authority which is to deal with the case.

24. Article 13 of the Council Regulation can also be applied to part of a complaint or to part of the proceedings in a case. It may be that only part of a complaint or of an ex-officio procedure overlaps with a case already dealt or being dealt with by another competition authority. In that case, the competition authority to which the complaint is brought is entitled to reject part of the complaint on the basis of Article 13 of the Council Regulation and to deal with the rest of the complaint in an appropriate manner. The same principle applies to the termination of proceedings.

25. Article 13 of the Council Regulation is not the only legal basis for suspending or closing ex-officio proceedings or rejecting complaints. NCAs may also be able to do so according to their national procedural law. The Commission may also reject a complaint for lack of Community interest or other reasons pertaining to the nature of the complaint.[9]

2.2.3. EXCHANGE AND USE OF CONFIDENTIAL INFORMATION (ARTICLE 12 OF THE COUNCIL REGULATION)

26. A key element of the functioning of the network is the power of all the competition authorities to exchange and use information (including documents, statements and digital information) which has been collected by them for the purpose of applying Article 81 or Article 82 of the Treaty. This power is a precondition for efficient and effective allocation and handling of cases.

27. Article 12 of the Council Regulation states that for the purpose of applying Articles 81 and 82 of the Treaty, the Commission and the competition authorities of the Member States shall have the power to provide one another with and use in evidence any matter of fact or of law, including confidential information. This means that exchanges of information may not only take place between an NCA and the Commission but also between and amongst NCAs. Article 12 of the Council Regulation takes precedence over any contrary law of a Member State. The question whether information was gathered in a legal manner by the transmitting authority is governed on the basis of the law applicable to this authority. When transmitting information the transmitting authority may inform the receiving authority whether the gathering of the information was contested or could still be contested.

28. The exchange and use of information contains in particular the following safeguards for undertakings and individuals.

(a) First, Article 28 of the Council Regulation states that "the Commission and the competition authorities of the Member States, their officials, servants and other persons working under the supervision of these authorities (. . .) shall not disclose information acquired or exchanged by them pursuant to the" Council Regulation which is "of the kind covered by the obligation of professional secrecy". However, the legitimate interest of undertakings in the protection of their business secrets may not prejudice the disclosure of information necessary to prove an infringement of Articles 81 and 82 of the Treaty. The term "professional secrecy" used in Article 28 of the Council Regulation is a Community law concept and includes in particular business secrets and other confidential information. This will create a common minimum level of protection throughout the Community.

(b) The second safeguard given to undertakings relates to the use of information which has been exchanged within the network. Under Article 12(2) of the Council Regulation, information so exchanged can only be used in evidence for the application of Articles 81 and 82 of the Treaty and for the subject matter for which it was collected.[10] According to Article 12(2) of the Council Regulation, the information exchanged may also be used for the purpose of applying national competition law in parallel in the same case. This is, however, only possible if the application of national law does not lead to an outcome as regards the finding of an infringement different from that under Articles 81 and 82 of the Treaty.

(c) The third safeguard given by the Council Regulation relates to sanctions on individuals on the basis of information exchanged pursuant to Article 12(1). The Council Regulation only provides for sanctions on undertakings for violations of Articles 81 and 82 of the Treaty. Some national laws also provide for sanctions on individuals in connection with violations of Articles 81 and 82 of the Treaty. Individuals normally enjoy more extensive rights of defence (eg a right to remain silent compared to undertakings which may only refuse to answer questions which would lead them to admit that they have committed an infringement[11]). Article 12(3) of the Council Regulation ensures that information collected from undertakings cannot be used in a way which would circumvent the higher protection of individuals. This provision precludes sanctions being imposed on individuals on the basis of information exchanged pursuant to the Council Regulation if the laws of the transmitting and the receiving authorities do not provide for sanctions of a similar kind in respect of individuals, unless the rights of the individual concerned as regards the collection of evidence have been respected by the transmitting authority to the same standard as they are guaranteed by the receiving authority. The qualification of the sanctions by national law ("administrative" or "criminal") is not relevant for the purpose of applying Article 12(3) of the Council Regulation. The Council Regulation intends to create a distinction between sanctions which result in custody and other types of sanctions such as fines on individuals and other personal sanctions. If both the legal system of the transmitting and that of the receiving authority provide for sanctions of a similar kind (eg in both Member States, fines can be imposed on a member of the staff of an undertaking who has been involved in the violation of Article 81 or 82 of the Treaty), information exchanged pursuant to Article 12 of the Council Regulation can be used by the receiving authority. In that case, procedural safeguards in both systems are considered to be equivalent. If on the other hand, both legal systems do not provide for sanctions of a similar kind, the information can only be used if the same level of protection of the rights of the individual has been respected in the case at hand (see Article 12(3) of the Council Regulation). In that latter case however, custodial sanctions can only be imposed where both the transmitting and the receiving authority have the power to impose such a sanction.

2.2.4. INVESTIGATIONS (ARTICLE 22 OF THE COUNCIL REGULATION)

29. The Council Regulation provides that an NCA may ask another NCA for assistance in order to collect information on its behalf. An NCA can ask another NCA to carry out fact-finding measures on its behalf. Article 12 of the Council Regulation empowers the assisting NCA to transmit the information it has collected to the requesting NCA. Any exchange between or amongst NCAs and use in evidence by the requesting NCA of such information shall be carried out in accordance with Article 12 of the Council Regulation. Where an NCA acts on behalf of another NCA, it acts pursuant to its own rules of procedure, and under its own powers of investigation.

30. Under Article 22(2) of the Council Regulation, the Commission can ask an NCA to carry out an inspection on its behalf. The Commission can either adopt a decision pursuant to Article 20(4) of the Council Regulation or simply issue a request to the NCA. The NCA officials will exercise their powers in accordance with their national law. The agents of the Commission may assist the NCA during the inspection.

2.3. POSITION OF UNDERTAKINGS

2.3.1. General

31. All network members will endeavour to make the allocation of cases a quick and efficient process. Given the fact that the Council Regulation has created a system of parallel competences, the allocation of cases between members of the network constitutes a mere division of labour where some authorities abstain from acting. The allocation of cases therefore does not create individual rights for the companies involved in or affected by an infringement to have the case dealt with by a particular authority.

32. If a case is re-allocated to a given competition authority, it is because the application of the allocation criteria set out above led to the conclusion that this authority is well placed to deal with the case by single or parallel action. The competition authority to which the case is re-allocated would have been in a position, in any event, to commence an ex-officio procedure against the infringement.

33. Furthermore, all competition authorities apply Community competition law and the Council Regulation sets out mechanisms to ensure that the rules are applied in a consistent way.

34. If a case is re-allocated within the network, the undertakings concerned and the complainant(s) are informed as soon as possible by the competition authorities involved.

2.3.2. Position of complainants

35. If a complaint is lodged with the Commission pursuant to Article 7 of the Council Regulation and if the Commission does not investigate the complaint or prohibit the agreement or practice complained of, the complainant has a right to obtain a decision rejecting his complaint. This is without prejudice to Article 7(3) of the Commission implementing regulation.[12] The rights of complainants who lodge a complaint with an NCA are governed by the applicable national law.

36. In addition, Article 13 of the Council Regulation gives all NCAs the possibility of suspending or rejecting a complaint on the ground that another competition authority is dealing or has dealt with the same case. That provision also allows the Commission to reject a complaint on the ground that a competition authority of a Member State is dealing or has dealt with the case. Article 12 of the Council Regulation allows the transfer of information between competition authorities within the network subject to the safeguards provided in that Article (see paragraph 28 above).

2.3.3. Position of applicants claiming the benefit of a leniency programme

37. The Commission considers[13] that it is in the Community interest to grant favourable treatment to undertakings which co-operate with it in the investigation of cartel infringements. A number of Member States have also adopted leniency programmes[14] relating to cartel investigations. The aim of these leniency programmes is to facilitate the detection by competition authorities of cartel activity and also thereby to act as a deterrent to participation in unlawful cartels.

38. In the absence of a European Union-wide system of fully harmonised leniency programmes, an application for leniency to a given authority is not to be considered as an application for leniency to any other authority. It is therefore in the interest of the applicant to apply for leniency to all competition authorities which have competence to apply Article 81 of the Treaty in the territory which is affected by the infringement and which may be considered well placed to act against the infringement in question.[15] In view of the importance of timing in most existing leniency programmes, applicants will also need to consider whether it would be appropriate to file leniency applications with the relevant authorities simultaneously. It is for the applicant to take the steps which it considers appropriate to protect its position with respect to possible proceedings by these authorities.

39. As for all cases where Articles 81 and 82 of the Treaty are applied, where an NCA deals with a case which has been initiated as a result of a leniency application, it must inform the Commission and may make the information available to other members of the network pursuant to Article 11(3) of the Council Regulation (cf. paragraphs 16 et subseq). The Commission has accepted an equivalent obligation to inform NCAs under Article 11(2) of the Council Regulation. In such cases, however, information submitted to the network pursuant to Article 11 will not be used by other members of the network as the basis for starting an investigation on their own behalf whether under the competition rules of the Treaty or, in the case of NCAs, under their national competition law or other laws.[16] This is without prejudice to any power of the authority to open an investigation on the basis of information received from other sources or, subject to paragraphs 40 and 41 below, to request, be provided with and use information pursuant to Article 12 from any member of the network, including the network member to whom the leniency application was submitted.

40. Save as provided under paragraph 41, information voluntarily submitted by a leniency applicant will only be transmitted to another member of the network pursuant to Article 12 of the Council Regulation with the consent of the applicant. Similarly other information that has been obtained during or following an inspection or by means of or following any other fact-finding measures which, in each case, could not have been carried out except as a result of the leniency application will only be transmitted to another authority pursuant to Article 12 of the Council Regulation if the applicant has consented to the transmission to that authority of information it has voluntarily submitted in its application for leniency. The network members will encourage leniency applicants to give such consent, in particular as regards disclosure to authorities in respect of which it would be open to the applicant to obtain lenient treatment. Once the leniency applicant has given consent to the transmission of information to another authority, that consent may not be withdrawn. This paragraph is without prejudice, however, to the responsibility of each applicant to file leniency applications to whichever authorities it may consider appropriate.

41. Notwithstanding the above, the consent of the applicant for the transmission of information to another authority pursuant to Article 12 of the Council Regulation is not required in any of the following circumstances:

1. No consent is required where the receiving authority has also received a leniency application relating to the same infringement from the same applicant as the transmitting authority, provided that at the time the information is transmitted it is not open to the applicant to withdraw the information which it has submitted to that receiving authority.
2. No consent is required where the receiving authority has provided a written commitment that neither the information transmitted to it nor any other information it may obtain following the date and time of transmission as noted by the transmitting authority, will be used by it or by any other authority to which the information is subsequently transmitted to impose sanctions:
   (a) on the leniency applicant;
   (b) on any other legal or natural person covered by the favourable treatment offered by the transmitting authority as a result of the application made by the applicant under its leniency programme;
   (c) on any employee or former employee of any of the persons covered by (a) or (b).

   A copy of the receiving authority's written commitment will be provided to the applicant.
3. In the case of information collected by a network member under Article 22(1) of the Council Regulation on behalf of and for the account of the network member to whom the leniency application was made, no consent is required for the transmission of such information to, and its use by, the network member to whom the application was made.

42. Information relating to cases initiated as a result of a leniency application and which has been submitted to the Commission under Article 11(3) of the Council Regulation[17] will only be made available to those NCAs that have committed themselves to respecting the principles set out above (see paragraph 72). The same principle applies where a case has been initiated by the Commission as a result of a leniency application made to the Commission. This does not affect the power of any authority to be provided with information under Article 12 of the Council Regulation, provided however that the provisions of paragraphs 40 and 41 are respected.

NOTES

5 In this Notice the term "procedure" is used for investigations and/or formal proceedings for the adoption of a decision pursuant to the Council Regulation conducted by an NCA or the Commission, as the case may be.

6 See Recital 18 of the Council Regulation.

7 For cases initiated following a leniency application see paragraphs 37 et subseq.

8 The intention of making any information exchanged pursuant to Article 11 available and easily accessible to all network members is however expressed in the Joint Statement on the functioning of the network mentioned above in footnote 4.

9 See Commission notice on complaints.

10 See ECJ case 85/87 – *Dow Benelux*, [1989] ECR 3137 (recitals 17–20).

11 See ECJ case 374/87 – *Orkem* [1989] ECR 3283 and CFI, case T-112/98 – *Mannesmannröhren-Werke AG*, [2001] ECR II-729.

12 Commission Regulation (EC) No 773/2004, OJ L123, 27.4.2004.

13 OJ C45, 19.2.2002, p 3 at paragraph 3.

14 In this Notice, the term "leniency programme" is used to describe all programmes (including the Commission's programme) which offer either full immunity or a significant reduction in the penalties which would otherwise have been imposed on a participant in a cartel, in exchange for the freely volunteered disclosure of information on the cartel which satisfies specific criteria prior to or during the investigative stage of the case. The term does not cover reductions in the penalty granted for other reasons. The Commission will publish on its website a list of those authorities that operate a leniency programme.

15 See paragraphs 8 to 15 above.

16 Similarly, information transmitted with a view to obtaining assistance from the receiving authority under Articles 20 or 21 of the Council Regulation or of carrying out an investigation or other fact-finding measure under Article 22 of the Council Regulation may only be used for the purpose of the application of the said Articles.

17 See paragraph 17.

3. CONSISTENT APPLICATION OF EC COMPETITION RULES[18]

3.1. MECHANISM OF COOPERATION (ARTICLE 11(4) AND 11(5) OF THE COUNCIL REGULATION)

[4.489]

43. The Council Regulation pursues the objective that Articles 81 and 82 of the Treaty are applied in a consistent manner throughout the Community. In this respect NCAs will respect the convergence rule contained in Article 3(2) of the Council Regulation. In line with Article 16(2) they cannot – when ruling on agreements, decisions and practices under Article 81 or Article 82 of the Treaty which are already the subject of a Commission decision – take decisions, which would run counter to the decisions adopted by the Commission. Within the network of competition authorities the Commission, as the guardian of the Treaty, has the ultimate but not the sole responsibility for developing policy and safeguarding consistency when it comes to the application of EC competition law.

44. According to Article 11(4) of the Council Regulation, no later than 30 days before the adoption of a decision applying Articles 81 or 82 of the Treaty and requiring that an infringement be brought to an end, accepting commitments or withdrawing the benefit of a block-exemption regulation, NCAs shall inform the Commission. They have to send to the Commission, at the latest 30 days before the adoption of the decision, a summary of the case, the envisaged decision or, in the absence thereof, any other document indicating the proposed course of action.

45. As under Article 11(3) of the Council Regulation, the obligation is to inform the Commission, but the information may be shared by the NCA informing the Commission with the other members of the network.

46. Where an NCA has informed the Commission pursuant to Article 11(4) of the Council Regulation and the 30 days deadline has expired, the decision can be adopted as long as the Commission has not initiated proceedings. The Commission may make written observations on the case before the adoption of the decision by the NCA. The NCA and the Commission will make the appropriate efforts to ensure the consistent application of Community law (cf. paragraph 3 above).

47. If special circumstances require that a national decision is taken in less than 30 days following the transmission of information pursuant to Article 11(4) of the Council Regulation, the NCA concerned may ask the Commission for a swifter reaction. The Commission will endeavour to react as quickly as possible.

48. Other types of decisions, ie decisions rejecting complaints, decisions closing an ex-officio procedure or decisions ordering interim measures, can also be important from a competition policy point of view, and the network members may have an interest in informing each other about them and possibly discussing them. NCAs can therefore on the basis of Article 11(5) of the Council Regulation inform the Commission and thereby inform the network of any other case in which EC competition law is applied.

49. All members of the network should inform each other about the closure of their procedures which have been notified to the network pursuant to Article 11(2) and (3) of the Council Regulation.[19]

3.2. THE INITIATION OF PROCEEDINGS BY THE COMMISSION UNDER ARTICLE 11(6) OF THE COUNCIL REGULATION

50. According to the case law of the Court of Justice, the Commission, entrusted by Article 85(1) of the Treaty with the task of ensuring the application of the principles laid down in Articles 81 and 82 of the Treaty, is responsible for defining and implementing the orientation of Community competition policy.[20] It can adopt individual decisions under Articles 81 and 82 of the Treaty at any time.

51. Article 11(6) of the Council Regulation states that the initiation by the Commission of proceedings for the adoption of a decision under the Council Regulation shall relieve all NCAs of their competence to apply Articles 81 and 82 of the Treaty. This means that once the Commission has opened proceedings, NCAs cannot act under the same legal basis against the same agreement(s) or practice(s) by the same undertaking(s) on the same relevant geographic and product market.

52. The initiation of proceedings by the Commission is a formal act[21] by which the Commission indicates its intention to adopt a decision under Chapter III of the Council Regulation. It can occur at any stage of the investigation of the case by the Commission. The mere fact that the Commission has received a complaint is not in itself sufficient to relieve NCAs of their competence.

53. Two situations can arise. First, where the Commission is the first competition authority to initiate proceedings in a case for the adoption of a decision under the Council Regulation, national competition authorities may no longer deal with the case. Article 11(6) of the Council Regulation provides that once the Commission has initiated proceedings, the NCAs can no longer start their own procedure with a view to applying Articles 81 and 82 of the Treaty to the same agreement(s) or practice(s) by the same undertaking(s) on the same relevant geographic and product market.

54. The second situation is where one or more NCAs have informed the network pursuant to Article 11(3) of the Council Regulation that they are acting on a given case. During the initial allocation period (indicative time period of two months, see paragraph 18 above), the Commission can initiate proceedings with the effects of Article 11(6) of the Council Regulation after having consulted the authorities concerned. After the allocation phase, the Commission will in principle only apply Article 11(6) of the Council Regulation if one of the following situations arises:

(a) Network members envisage conflicting decisions in the same case.
(b) Network members envisage a decision which is obviously in conflict with consolidated case law; the standards defined in the judgements of the Community courts and in previous decisions and regulations of the Commission should serve as a yardstick; concerning the assessment of the facts (eg market definition), only a significant divergence will trigger an intervention of the Commission;
(c) Network member(s) is (are) unduly drawing out proceedings in the case;
(d) There is a need to adopt a Commission decision to develop Community competition policy in particular when a similar competition issue arises in several Member States or to ensure effective enforcement;
(e) The NCA(s) concerned do not object.

55. If an NCA is already acting on a case, the Commission will explain the reasons for the application of Article 11(6) of the Council Regulation in writing to the NCA concerned and to the other members of the Network.[22]

56. The Commission will announce to the network its intention of applying Article 11(6) of the Council Regulation in due time, so that Network members will have the possibility of asking for a meeting of the Advisory Committee on the matter before the Commission initiates proceedings.

57. The Commission will normally not – and to the extent that Community interest is not at stake – adopt a decision which is in conflict with a decision of an NCA after proper information pursuant to both Article 11(3) and (4) of the Council Regulation has taken place and the Commission has not made use of Article 11(6) of the Council Regulation.

NOTES

[18] Article 15 of the Council Regulation empowers NCAs and the Commission to submit written and, with the permission of the Court, oral submissions in court proceedings for the application of Articles 81 and 82 of the Treaty. This is a very important tool for ensuring consistent application of Community rules. In exercising this power NCAs and the Commission will cooperate closely.

[19] See paragraph 24 of the Joint Statement on the functioning of the network mentioned above in footnote 4.

[20] See ECJ case C-344/98 – *Masterfoods Ltd*, [2000] ECR I-11369.

[21] The ECJ has defined that concept in the case 48/72 – *SA Brasserie de Haecht*, [1973] ECR 77: "the initiation of a

procedure within the meaning of Article 9 of Regulation No 17 implies an authoritative act of the Commission, evidencing its intention of taking a decision."

[22] See paragraph 22 of the Joint Statement mentioned above in footnote 4.

4. THE ROLE AND THE FUNCTIONING OF THE ADVISORY COMMITTEE IN THE NEW SYSTEM

[4.490]

58. The Advisory Committee is the forum where experts from the various competition authorities discuss individual cases and general issues of Community competition law.[23]

4.1. SCOPE OF THE CONSULTATION

4.1.1. DECISIONS OF THE COMMISSION

59. The Advisory Committee is consulted prior to the Commission taking any decision pursuant to Articles 7, 8, 9, 10, 23, 24(2) or 29(1) of the Council Regulation. The Commission must take the utmost account of the opinion of the Advisory Committee and inform the Committee of the manner in which its opinion has been taken into account.

60. For decisions adopting interim measures, the Advisory Committee is consulted following a swifter and lighter procedure, on the basis of a short explanatory note and the operative part of the decision.

4.1.2. DECISIONS OF NCAS

61. It is in the interest of the network that important cases dealt with by NCAs under Articles 81 and 82 of the Treaty can be discussed in the Advisory Committee. The Council Regulation enables the Commission to put a given case being dealt with by an NCA on the agenda of the Advisory Committee. Discussion can be requested by the Commission or by any Member State. In either case, the Commission will put the case on the agenda after having informed the NCA(s) concerned. This discussion in the Advisory Committee will not lead to a formal opinion.

62. In important cases, the Advisory Committee could also serve as a forum for the discussion of case allocation. In particular, where the Commission intends to apply Article 11(6) of the Council Regulation after the initial allocation period, the case can be discussed in the Advisory Committee before the Commission initiates proceedings. The Advisory Committee may issue an informal statement on the matter.

4.1.3. IMPLEMENTING MEASURES, BLOCK-EXEMPTION REGULATIONS, GUIDELINES AND OTHER NOTICES (ARTICLE 33 OF THE COUNCIL REGULATION)

63. The Advisory Committee will be consulted on draft Commission regulations as provided for in the relevant Council Regulations.

64. Beside regulations, the Commission may also adopt notices and guidelines. These more flexible tools are very useful for explaining and announcing the Commission's policy, and for explaining its interpretation of the competition rules. The Advisory Committee will also be consulted on these notices and guidelines.

4.2. PROCEDURE

4.2.1. NORMAL PROCEDURE

65. For consultation on Commission draft decisions, the meeting of the Advisory Committee takes place at the earliest 14 days after the invitation to the meeting is sent by the Commission. The Commission attaches to the invitation a summary of the case, a list of the most important documents, ie the documents needed to assess the case, and a draft decision. The Advisory Committee gives an opinion on the Commission draft decision. At the request of one or several members, the opinion shall be reasoned.

66. The Council Regulation allows for the possibility of the Member States agreeing upon a shorter period of time between the sending of the invitation and the meeting.

4.2.2. WRITTEN PROCEDURE

67. The Council Regulation provides for the possibility of a written consultation procedure. If no Member State objects, the Commission can consult the Member States by sending the documents to them and setting a deadline within which they can comment on the draft. This deadline would not normally be shorter than 14 days, except for decisions on interim measures pursuant to Article 8 of the Council Regulation. Where a Member State requests that a meeting takes place, the Commission will arrange for such a meeting.

4.3. PUBLICATION OF THE OPINION OF THE ADVISORY COMMITTEE

68. The Advisory Committee can recommend the publication of its opinion. In that event, the Commission will carry out such publication simultaneously with the decision, taking into account the legitimate interest of undertakings in the protection of their business secrets.

NOTES

[23] In accordance with Article 14(2) of the Council Regulation, where horizontal issues such as block-exemption regulations and guidelines are being discussed, Member States can appoint an additional representative competent in competition matters and who does not necessarily belong to the competition authority.

5. FINAL REMARKS

[4.491]

69. This Notice is without prejudice to any interpretation of the applicable Treaty and regulatory provisions by the Court of First Instance and the Court of Justice.

70. This Notice will be the subject of periodic review carried out jointly by the NCAs and the Commission. On the basis of the experience acquired, it will be reviewed no later than at the end of the third year after its adoption.

71. This notice replaces the Commission notice on cooperation between national competition authorities and the Commission in handling cases falling within the scope of Articles 81 and 82 of the Treaty published in 1997.[24]

NOTES

[24] OJ C313, 15.10.1997, p 3.

6. STATEMENT BY OTHER NETWORK MEMBERS

[4.492]

72. The principles set out in this notice will also be abided by those Member States' competition authorities which have signed a statement in the form of the Annex to this Notice. In this statement they acknowledge the principles of this notice, including the principles relating to the protection of applicants claiming the benefit of a leniency programme[25] and declare that they will abide by them. A list of these authorities is published on the website of the European Commission. It will be updated if appropriate.

NOTES

[25] See paragraphs 37 et seq.

ANNEX
STATEMENT REGARDING THE COMMISSION NOTICE ON COOPERATION WITHIN THE NETWORK OF COMPETITION AUTHORITIES

[4.493]

In order to cooperate closely with a view to protecting competition within the European Union in the interest of consumers, the undersigned competition authority:

1. Acknowledges the principles set out in the Commission Notice on Cooperation within the Network of Competition Authorities; and

2. Declares that it will abide by those principles, which include principles relation to the protection of applicants claiming the benefit of a leniency programme, in any case in which it is acting or may act and to which those principles apply.

. . . .

(place) (date)

COMMISSION NOTICE

(2004/C101/04)

on the co-operation between the Commission and the courts of the EU Member States in the application of Articles 81 and 82 EC

(Text with EEA relevance)

[4.494]

NOTES

Date of publication in OJ: OJ C101, 27.4.2004, p 54.

This Notice is reproduced as amended by Commission Communication 2015/C256/04 (OJ C256, 5.8.2015, p 5) and as corrected by the corrigendum published in OJ C230, 15.7.2017, p 56.

Note: with effect from 1 December 2009, the EC Treaty was replaced by the Treaty on the Functioning of the European Union. References in this document to provisions of the EC Treaty should be construed accordingly. As to Articles 81 and 82 of the EC Treaty, see now Articles 101 and 102 of the Treaty on the Functioning of the European Union.

I. THE SCOPE OF THE NOTICE

[4.495]

1. The present notice addresses the co-operation between the Commission and the courts of the EU Member States, when the latter apply Articles 81 and 82 EC. For the purpose of this notice, the "courts of the EU Member States" (hereinafter "national courts") are those courts and tribunals within an EU Member State that can apply Articles 81 and 82 EC and that are authorised to ask a preliminary question to the Court of Justice of the European Communities pursuant to Article 234 EC.[1]

2. The national courts may be called upon to apply Articles 81 or 82 EC in lawsuits between private parties, such as actions relating to contracts or actions for damages. They may also act as public enforcer or as review court. A national court may indeed be designated as a competition authority of a Member State (hereinafter "the national competition authority") pursuant to Article 35(1) of Regulation (EC) No 1/2003 (hereinafter "the regulation").[2] In that case, the co-operation between the national courts and the Commission is not only covered by the present notice, but also by the notice on the co-operation within the network of competition authorities.[3]

NOTES

[1] For the criteria to determine which entities can be regarded as courts or tribunals within the meaning of Article 234 EC, see eg case C-516/99 *Schmid* [2002] ECR I-4573, 34: "The Court takes account of a number of factors, such as whether the body is established by law, whether it is permanent, whether its jurisdiction is compulsory, whether its

procedure is inter partes, whether it applies rules of law and whether it is independent".

[2] Council Regulation (EC) No 1/2003 of 16 December 2002 on the implementation of the rules on competition laid down in Articles 81 and 82 of the Treaty (OJ L1, 4.1.2003, p 1).

[3] Notice on the co-operation within the network of competition authorities (OJ C101, 27.4.2004, p 43). For the purpose of this notice, a "national competition authority" is the authority designated by a Member State in accordance with Article 35(1) of the regulation.

II. THE APPLICATION OF EC COMPETITION RULES BY NATIONAL COURTS

A. THE COMPETENCE OF NATIONAL COURTS TO APPLY EC COMPETITION RULES

[4.496]

3. To the extent that national courts have jurisdiction to deal with a case,[4] they have the power to apply Articles 81 and 82 EC.[5] Moreover, it should be remembered that Articles 81 and 82 EC are a matter of public policy and are essential to the accomplishment of the tasks entrusted to the Community, and, in particular, for the functioning of the internal market.[6] According to the Court of Justice, where, by virtue of domestic law, national courts must raise of their own motion points of law based on binding domestic rules which have not been raised by the parties, such an obligation also exists where binding Community rules, such as the EC competition rules, are concerned. The position is the same if domestic law confers on national courts a discretion to apply of their own motion binding rules of law: national courts must apply the EC competition rules, even when the party with an interest in application of those provisions has not relied on them, where domestic law allows such application by the national court. However, Community law does not require national courts to raise of their own motion an issue concerning the breach of provisions of Community law where examination of that issue would oblige them to abandon the passive role assigned to them by going beyond the ambit of the dispute defined by the parties themselves and relying on facts and circumstances other than those on which the party with an interest in application of those provisions bases his claim.[7]

4. Depending on the functions attributed to them under national law, national courts may be called upon to apply Articles 81 and 82 EC in administrative, civil or criminal proceedings.[8] In particular, where a natural or legal person asks the national court to safeguard his individual rights, national courts play a specific role in the enforcement of Articles 81 and 82 EC, which is different from the enforcement in the public interest by the Commission or by national competition authorities.[9] Indeed, national courts can give effect to Articles 81 and 82 EC by finding contracts to be void or by awards of damages.

5. National courts can apply Articles 81 and 82 EC, without it being necessary to apply national competition law in parallel. However, where a national court applies national competition law to agreements, decisions by associations of undertakings or concerted practices which may affect trade between Member States within the meaning of Article 81(1) EC[10] or to any abuse prohibited by Article 82 EC, they also have to apply EC competition rules to those agreements, decisions or practices.[11]

6. The regulation does not only empower the national courts to apply EC competition law. The parallel application of national competition law to agreements, decisions of associations of undertakings and concerted practices which affect trade between Member States may not lead to a different outcome from that of EC competition law. Article 3(2) of the regulation provides that agreements, decisions or concerted practices which do not infringe Article 81(1) EC or which fulfil the conditions of Article 81(3) EC cannot be prohibited either under national competition law.[12] On the other hand, the Court of Justice has ruled that agreements, decisions or concerted practices that violate Article 81(1) and do not fulfil the conditions of Article 81(3) EC cannot be upheld under national law.[13] As to the parallel application of national competition law and Article 82 EC in the case of unilateral conduct, Article 3 of the regulation does not provide for a similar convergence obligation. However, in case of conflicting provisions, the general principle of primacy of Community law requires national courts to disapply any provision of national law which contravenes a Community rule, regardless of whether that national law provision was adopted before or after the Community rule.[14]

7. Apart from the application of Articles 81 and 82 EC, national courts are also competent to apply acts adopted by EU institutions in accordance with the EC Treaty or in accordance with the measures adopted to give the Treaty effect, to the extent that these acts have direct effect. National courts may thus have to enforce Commission decisions[15] or regulations applying Article 81(3) EC to certain categories of agreements, decisions or concerted practices. When applying these EC competition rules, national courts act within the framework of Community law and are consequently bound to observe the general principles of Community law.[16]

8. The application of Articles 81 and 82 EC by national courts often depends on complex economic and legal assessments.[17] When applying EC competition rules, national courts are bound by the case law of the Community courts as well as by Commission regulations applying Article 81(3) EC to certain categories of agreements, decisions or concerted practices.[18] Furthermore, the application of Articles 81 and 82 EC by the Commission in a specific case binds the national courts when they apply EC competition rules in the same case in parallel with or subsequent to the Commission.[19] Finally, and without prejudice to the ultimate interpretation of the EC Treaty by the Court of Justice, national courts may find guidance in Commission regulations and decisions which present elements of analogy with the case they are dealing with, as well as in Commission notices and guidelines relating to the application of Articles 81 and 82 EC[20] and in the annual report on competition policy.[21]

B. PROCEDURAL ASPECTS OF THE APPLICATION OF EC COMPETITION RULES BY NATIONAL COURTS

9. The procedural conditions for the enforcement of EC competition rules by national courts and the sanctions they can impose in case of an infringement of those rules, are largely covered by national law. However, to some extent, Community law also determines the conditions in which EC competition rules are enforced. Those Community law provisions may provide for the faculty of national courts to avail themselves of certain instruments, eg to ask for

the Commission's opinion on questions concerning the application of EC competition rules[22] or they may create rules that have an obligatory impact on proceedings before them, eg allowing the Commission and national competition authorities to submit written observations.[23] These Community law provisions prevail over national rules. Therefore, national courts have to set aside national rules which, if applied, would conflict with these Community law provisions. Where such Community law provisions are directly applicable, they are a direct source of rights and duties for all those affected, and must be fully and uniformly applied in all the Member States from the date of their entry into force.[24]

10. In the absence of Community law provisions on procedures and sanctions related to the enforcement of EC competition rules by national courts, the latter apply national procedural law and – to the extent that they are competent to do so – impose sanctions provided for under national law. However, the application of these national provisions must be compatible with the general principles of Community law. In this regard, it is useful to recall the case law of the Court of Justice, according to which:

(a) where there is an infringement of Community law, national law must provide for sanctions which are effective, proportionate and dissuasive;[25]

(b) where the infringement of Community law causes harm to an individual, the latter should under certain conditions be able to ask the national court for damages;[26]

(c) the rules on procedures and sanctions which national courts apply to enforce Community law

— must not make such enforcement excessively difficult or practically impossible (the principle of effectiveness)[27] and they

— must not be less favourable than the rules applicable to the enforcement of equivalent national law (the principle of equivalence).[28]

On the basis of the principle of primacy of Community law, a national court may not apply national rules that are incompatible with these principles.

C. PARALLEL OR CONSECUTIVE APPLICATION OF EC COMPETITION RULES BY THE COMMISSION AND BY NATIONAL COURTS

11. A national court may be applying EC competition law to an agreement, decision, concerted practice or unilateral behaviour affecting trade between Member States at the same time as the Commission or subsequent to the Commission.[29] The following points outline some of the obligations national courts have to respect in those circumstances.

12. Where a national court comes to a decision before the Commission does, it must avoid adopting a decision that would conflict with a decision contemplated by the Commission.[30] To that effect, the national court may ask the Commission whether it has initiated proceedings regarding the same agreements, decisions or practices[31] and if so, about the progress of proceedings and the likelihood of a decision in that case.[32] The national court may, for reasons of legal certainty, also consider staying its proceedings until the Commission has reached a decision.[33] The Commission, for its part, will endeavour to give priority to cases for which it has decided to initiate proceedings within the meaning of Article 2(1) of Commission Regulation (EC) No 773/2004 and that are the subject of national proceedings stayed in this way, in particular when the outcome of a civil dispute depends on them. However, where the national court cannot reasonably doubt the Commission's contemplated decision or where the Commission has already decided on a similar case, the national court may decide on the case pending before it in accordance with that contemplated or earlier decision without it being necessary to ask the Commission for the information mentioned above or to await the Commission's decision.

13. Where the Commission reaches a decision in a particular case before the national court, the latter cannot take a decision running counter to that of the Commission. The binding effect of the Commission's decision is of course without prejudice to the interpretation of Community law by the Court of Justice. Therefore, if the national court doubts the legality of the Commission's decision, it cannot avoid the binding effects of that decision without a ruling to the contrary by the Court of Justice.[34] Consequently, if a national court intends to take a decision that runs counter to that of the Commission, it must refer a question to the Court of Justice for a preliminary ruling (Article 234 EC). The latter will then decide on the compatibility of the Commission's decision with Community law. However, if the Commission's decision is challenged before the Community courts pursuant to Article 230 EC and the outcome of the dispute before the national court depends on the validity of the Commission's decision, the national court should stay its proceedings pending final judgment in the action for annulment by the Community courts unless it considers that, in the circumstances of the case, a reference to the Court of Justice for a preliminary ruling on the validity of the Commission decision is warranted.[35]

14. When a national court stays proceedings, eg awaiting the Commission's decision (situation described in point 12 of this notice) or pending final judgement by the Community courts in an action for annulment or in a preliminary ruling procedure (situation described in point 13), it is incumbent on it to examine whether it is necessary to order interim measures in order to safeguard the interests of the parties.[36]

NOTES

[4] The jurisdiction of a national court depends on national, European and international rules of jurisdiction. In this context, it may be recalled that Council Regulation (EC) No 44/2001 of 22 December 2000 on jurisdiction and the recognition and enforcement of judgements in civil and commercial matters (OJ L12, 16.1.2001, p 1) is applicable to all competition cases of a civil or commercial nature.

[5] See Article 6 of the regulation.

[6] See Articles 2 and 3 EC, case C-126/97 *Eco Swiss* [1999] ECR I-3055, 36; case T-34/92 *Fiatagri UK and New Holland Ford* [1994] ECR II-905, 39 and case T-128/98 *Aéroports de Paris* [2000] ECR II-3929, 241.

[7] Joined cases C-430/93 and C-431/93 *van Schijndel* [1995] ECR I-4705, 13 to 15 and 22.

[8] According to the last sentence of recital 8 of Regulation (EC) No 1/2003, the regulation does not apply to national laws which impose criminal sanctions on natural persons except to the extent that such sanctions are the means whereby competition rules applying to undertakings are enforced.

9 Case T-24/90 *Automec* [1992] ECR II-2223, 85.

10 For further clarification of the effect on trade concept, see the notice on this issue (OJ L101, 27.4.2004, p 81).

11 Article 3(1) of the regulation.

12 See also the notice on the application of Article 81(3) EC (OJ L101, 27.4.2004, p 2).

13 Case 14/68 *Walt Wilhelm* [1969] ECR 1 and joined cases 253/78 and 1 to 3/79 *Giry and Guerlain* [1980] ECR 2327, 15 to 17.

14 Case 106/77 *Simmenthal* [1978] ECR 629, 21 and case C-198/01, *Consorzio Industrie Fiammiferi* (CIF) [2003] 49.

15 Eg a national court may be asked to enforce a Commission decision taken pursuant to Articles 7 to 10, 23 and 24 of the regulation.

16 See eg case 5/88 *Wachauf* [1989] ECR 2609, 19.

17 Joined cases C-215/96 and C-216/96 *Bagnasco* [1999] ECR I-135, 50.

18 Case 63/75 *Fonderies Roubaix* [1976] ECR 111, 9 to 11 and case C-234/89 *Delimitis* [1991] ECR I-935, 46.

19 On the parallel or consecutive application of EC competition rules by national courts and the Commission, see also points 11 to 14.

20 Case 66/86 *Ahmed Saeed Flugreisen* [1989] ECR 803, 27 and case C-234/89 *Delimitis* [1991] ECR I-935, 50. A list of Commission guidelines, notices and regulations in the field of competition policy, in particular the regulations applying Article 81(3) EC to certain categories of agreements, decisions or concerted practices, are annexed to this notice. For the decisions of the Commission applying Articles 81 and 82 EC (since 1964), see ec.europa.eu/competition/antitrust/cases/.

21 Joined cases C-319/93, C-40/94 and C-224/94 *Dijkstra* [1995] ECR I-4471, 32.

22 On the possibility for national courts to ask the Commission for an opinion, see further in points 27 to 30.

23 On the submission of observations, see further in points 31 to 35.

24 Case 106/77 *Simmenthal* [1978] ECR 629, 14 and 15.

25 Case 68/88 *Commission v Greece* [1989] ECR 2965, 23 to 25.

26 On damages in case of an infringement by an undertaking, see case C-453/99 *Courage and Crehan* [2001] ECR 6297, 26 and 27. On damages in case of an infringement by a Member State or by an authority which is an emanation of the State and on the conditions of such state liability, see eg joined cases C-6/90 and C-9/90 *Francovich* [1991] ECR I-5357, 33 to 36; case C-271/91 *Marshall v Southampton and South West Hampshire Area Health Authority* [1993] ECR I-4367, 30 and 34 to 35; joined cases C-46/93 and C-48/93 *Brasserie du Pêcheur and Factortame* [1996] ECR I-1029; case C-392/93 *British Telecommunications* [1996] ECR I-1631, 39 to 46 and joined cases C-178/94, C-179/94 and C-188/94 to 190/94 *Dillenkofer* [1996] ECR I-4845, 22 to 26 and 72.

27 See eg case 33/76 *Rewe* [1976] ECR 1989, 5; case 45/76 *Comet* [1976] ECR 2043, 12 and case 79/83 *Harz* [1984] ECR 1921, 18 and 23.

28 See eg case 33/76 *Rewe* [1976] ECR 1989, 5; case 158/80 *Rewe* [1981] ECR 1805, 44; case 199/82 *San Giorgio* [1983] ECR 3595, 12 and case C-231/96 *Edis* [1998] ECR I-4951, 36 and 37.

29 Article 11(6), juncto Article 35(3) and (4) of the regulation prevents a parallel application of Articles 81 or 82 EC by the Commission and a national court only when the latter has been designated as a national competition authority.

30 Article 16(1) of the regulation.

31 The Commission makes the initiation of its proceedings with a view to adopting a decision pursuant to Article 7 to 10 of the regulation public (see Article 2(2) of Commission Regulation (EC) No 773/2004 of 7 April relating to proceedings pursuant to Articles 81 and 82 of the EC Treaty (OJ C 101, 27.4.2004). According to the Court of Justice, the initiation of proceedings implies an authoritative act of the Commission, evidencing its intention of taking a decision (case 48/72 *Brasserie de Haecht* [1973] ECR 77, 16).

32 Case C-234/89 *Delimitis* [1991] ECR I-935, 53, and joined cases C-319/93, C-40/94 and C-224/94 *Dijkstra* [1995] ECR I-4471, 34. See further on this issue point 21 of this notice.

33 See Article 16(1) of the regulation and case C-234/89 *Delimitis* [1991] ECR I-935, 47 and case C-344/98 *Masterfoods* [2000] ECR I-11369, 51.

34 Case 314/85 *Foto-Frost* [1987] ECR 4199, 12 to 20.

35 See Article 16(1) of the regulation and case C-344/98 *Masterfoods* [2000] ECR I-11369, 52 to 59.

36 Case C-344/98 *Masterfoods* [2000] ECR, I-11369, 58.

III. THE CO-OPERATION BETWEEN THE COMMISSION AND NATIONAL COURTS

[4.497]

15. Other than the co-operation mechanism between the national courts and the Court of Justice under Article 234 EC, the EC Treaty does not explicitly provide for co-operation between the national courts and the Commission. However, in its interpretation of Article 10 EC, which obliges the Member States to facilitate the achievement of the Community's tasks, the Community courts found that this Treaty provision imposes on the European institutions and the Member States mutual duties of loyal co-operation with a view to attaining the objectives of the EC Treaty. Article 10 EC thus implies that the Commission must assist national courts when they apply Community law.[37] Equally, national courts may be obliged to assist the Commission in the fulfilment of its tasks.[38]

16. It is also appropriate to recall the co-operation between national courts and national authorities, in particular national competition authorities, for the application of Articles 81 and 82 EC. While the co-operation between these national authorities is primarily governed by national rules, Article 15(3) of the regulation provides for the possibility for national competition authorities to submit observations before the national courts of their Member State. Points 31 and 33 to 35 of this notice are *mutatis mutandis* applicable to those submissions.

A. THE COMMISSION AS *AMICUS CURIAE*

17. In order to assist national courts in the application of EC competition rules, the Commission is committed to help national courts where the latter find such help necessary to be able to decide on a case. Article 15 of the regulation refers to the most frequent types of such assistance: the transmission of information (points 21 to 26) and

the Commission's opinions (points 27 to 30), both at the request of a national court and the possibility for the Commission to submit observations (points 31 to 35). Since the regulation provides for these types of assistance, it cannot be limited by any Member States' rule. However, in the absence of Community procedural rules to this effect and to the extent that they are necessary to facilitate these forms of assistance, Member States must adopt the appropriate procedural rules to allow both the national courts and the Commission to make full use of the possibilities the regulation offers.[39]

18. The national court may send its request for assistance in writing to

European Commission
Directorate General for Competition
B–1049 Brussels
Belgium

or send it electronically to comp-amicus@ec.europa.eu

19. It should be recalled that whatever form the co-operation with national courts takes, the Commission will respect the independence of national courts. As a consequence, the assistance offered by the Commission does not bind the national court. The Commission has also to make sure that it respects its duty of professional secrecy and that it safeguards its own functioning and independence.[40] In fulfilling its duty under Article 10 EC, of assisting national courts in the application of EC competition rules, the Commission is committed to remaining neutral and objective in its assistance. Indeed, the Commission's assistance to national courts is part of its duty to defend the public interest. It has therefore no intention to serve the private interests of the parties involved in the case pending before the national court. As a consequence, the Commission will not hear any of the parties about its assistance to the national court. In case the Commission has been contacted by any of the parties in the case pending before the court on issues which are raised before the national court, it will inform the national court thereof, independent of whether these contacts took place before or after the national court's request for co-operation.

20. The Commission will publish a summary concerning its co-operation with national courts pursuant to this notice in its annual Report on Competition Policy. It may also make its opinions and observations available on its website.

1.
The Commission's duty to transmit information to national courts

21. The duty for the Commission to assist national courts in the application of EC competition law is mainly reflected in the obligation for the Commission to transmit information it holds to national courts. A national court may, eg, ask the Commission for documents in its possession or for information of a procedural nature to enable it to discover whether a certain case is pending before the Commission, whether the Commission has initiated a procedure or whether it has already taken a position. A national court may also ask the Commission when a decision is likely to be taken, so as to be able to determine the conditions for any decision to stay proceedings or whether interim measures need to be adopted.[41]

22. In order to ensure the efficiency of the co-operation with national courts, the Commission will endeavour to provide the national court with the requested information within one month from the date it receives the request. Where the Commission has to ask the national court for further clarification of its request or where the Commission has to consult those who are directly affected by the transmission of the information, that period starts to run from the moment that it receives the required information.

23. In transmitting information to national courts, the Commission has to uphold the guarantees given to natural and legal persons by Article 287 EC.[42] Article 287 EC prevents members, officials and other servants of the Commission from disclosing information covered by the obligation of professional secrecy. The information covered by professional secrecy may be both confidential information and business secrets. Business secrets are information of which not only disclosure to the public but also mere transmission to a person other than the one that provided the information might seriously harm the latter's interests.[43]

24. The combined reading of Articles 10 and 287 EC does not lead to an absolute prohibition for the Commission to transmit information which is covered by the obligation of professional secrecy to national courts. The case law of the Community courts confirms that the duty of loyal co-operation requires the Commission to provide the national court with whatever information the latter asks for, even information covered by professional secrecy. However, in offering its co-operation to the national courts, the Commission may not in any circumstances undermine the guarantees laid down in Article 287 EC.

25. Consequently, before transmitting information covered by professional secrecy to a national court, the Commission will remind the court of its obligation under Community law to uphold the rights which Article 287 EC confers on natural and legal persons and it will ask the court whether it can and will guarantee protection of confidential information and business secrets. If the national court cannot offer such guarantee, the Commission shall not transmit the information covered by professional secrecy to the national court.[44] Only when the national court has offered a guarantee that it will protect the confidential information and business secrets, will the Commission transmit the information requested, indicating those parts which are covered by professional secrecy and which parts are not and can therefore be disclosed.

[26. There are further exceptions to the disclosure of information by the Commission to national courts. Particularly, the Commission may refuse to transmit information to national courts for overriding reasons relating to the need to safeguard the interests of the European Union or to avoid any interference with its functioning and independence, in particular by jeopardising the accomplishment of the tasks entrusted to it.[45] Disclosure of information to national courts should not unduly affect the effectiveness of enforcement of the competition rules by the Commission, in particular so as not to interfere with pending investigations nor with the functioning of leniency programmes and settlement procedures.]

[26a. For that purpose, the Commission will not at any time transmit the following information to national courts for use in actions for damages for breaches of Article 101 or 102 of the Treaty:

— leniency corporate statements, within the meaning of Article 4a(2) of Regulation (EC) No 773/2004,[45A] and

— settlement submissions, within the meaning of Article 10a(2) of Regulation (EC) No 773/2004.

This paragraph is without prejudice to the situation referred to in Article 6(7) of Directive 2014/104/EU of the European Parliament and of the Council.[45B]]

[26b. As regards other types of information, the Commission will not transmit the following to the national courts for use in actions for damages for breaches of Article 101 or 102 of the Treaty, before it has closed its proceedings against all investigated parties by adopting a decision referred to in Article 7, 9 or 10 of Regulation (EC) No 1/2003 or before it has otherwise terminated its administrative procedure:

— information that was prepared by a natural or legal person specifically for the proceedings of the Commission, and

— information that the Commission has drawn up and sent to the parties in the course of its proceedings.

When it is asked to transmit the said information to national courts for other purposes than the use in actions for damages for breaches of Article 101 or 102 of the Treaty, the Commission will in principle apply the limitation in time mentioned in the first subparagraph, in order to protect its pending investigations.]

2.

Request for an opinion on questions concerning the application of EC competition rules

27. When called upon to apply EC competition rules to a case pending before it, a national court may first seek guidance in the case law of the Community courts or in Commission regulations, decisions, notices and guidelines applying Articles 81 and 82 EC.[46] Where these tools do not offer sufficient guidance, the national court may ask the Commission for its opinion on questions concerning the application of EC competition rules. The national court may ask the Commission for its opinion on economic, factual and legal matters.[47] The latter is of course without prejudice to the possibility or the obligation for the national court to ask the Court of Justice for a preliminary ruling regarding the interpretation or the validity of Community law in accordance with Article 234 EC.

28. In order to enable the Commission to provide the national court with a useful opinion, it may request the national court for further information.[48] In order to ensure the efficiency of the co-operation with national courts, the Commission will endeavour to provide the national court with the requested opinion within four months from the date it receives the request. Where the Commission has requested the national court for further information in order to enable it to formulate its opinion, that period starts to run from the moment that it receives the additional information.

29. When giving its opinion, the Commission will limit itself to providing the national court with the factual information or the economic or legal clarification asked for, without considering the merits of the case pending before the national court. Moreover, unlike the authoritative interpretation of Community law by the Community courts, the opinion of the Commission does not legally bind the national court.

30. In line with what has been said in point 19 of this notice, the Commission will not hear the parties before formulating its opinion to the national court. The latter will have to deal with the Commission's opinion in accordance with the relevant national procedural rules, which have to respect the general principles of Community law.

3.

The Commission's submission of observations to the national court

31. According to Article 15(3) of the regulation, the national competition authorities and the Commission may submit observations on issues relating to the application of Articles 81 or 82 EC to a national court which is called upon to apply those provisions. The regulation distinguishes between written observations, which the national competition authorities and the Commission may submit on their own initiative, and oral observations, which can only be submitted with the permission of the national court.[49]

32. The regulation specifies that the Commission will only submit observations when the coherent application of Articles 81 or 82 EC so requires. That being the objective of its submission, the Commission will limit its observations to an economic and legal analysis of the facts underlying the case pending before the national court.

33. In order to enable the Commission to submit useful observations, national courts may be asked to transmit or ensure the transmission to the Commission of a copy of all documents that are necessary for the assessment of the case. In line with Article 15(3), second subparagraph, of the regulation, the Commission will only use those documents for the preparation of its observations.[50]

34. Since the regulation does not provide for a procedural framework within which the observations are to be submitted, Member States' procedural rules and practices determine the relevant procedural framework. Where a Member State has not yet established the relevant procedural framework, the national court has to determine which procedural rules are appropriate for the submission of observations in the case pending before it.

35. The procedural framework should respect the principles set out in point 10 of this notice. That implies amongst others that the procedural framework for the submission of observations on issues relating to the application of Articles 81 or 82 EC

(a) has to be compatible with the general principles of Community law, in particular the fundamental rights of the parties involved in the case;

(b) cannot make the submission of such observations excessively difficult or practically impossible (the principle of effectiveness);[51] and

(c) cannot make the submission of such observations more difficult than the submission of observations in court proceedings where equivalent national law is applied (the principle of equivalence).

B. THE NATIONAL COURTS FACILITATING THE ROLE OF THE COMMISSION IN THE ENFORCEMENT OF EC COMPETITION RULES

36. Since the duty of loyal co-operation also implies that Member States' authorities assist the European institutions with a view to attaining the objectives of the EC Treaty,[52] the regulation provides for three examples of such assistance: (1) the transmission of documents necessary for the assessment of a case in which the Commission would like to submit observations (see point 33), (2) the transmission of judgements applying Articles 81 or 82 EC); and (3) the role of national courts in the context of a Commission inspection.

1.
The transmission of judgements of national courts applying Articles 81 or 82 EC

37. According to Article 15(2) of the regulation, Member States shall send to the Commission a copy of any written judgement of national courts applying Articles 81 or 82 EC without delay after the full written judgement is notified to the parties. The transmission of national judgements on the application of Articles 81 or 82 EC and the resulting information on proceedings before national courts primarily enable the Commission to become aware in a timely fashion of cases for which it might be appropriate to submit observations where one of the parties lodges an appeal against the judgement.

2.
The role of national courts in the context of a Commission inspection

38. Finally, national courts may play a role in the context of a Commission inspection of undertakings and associations of undertakings. The role of the national courts depends on whether the inspections are conducted in business premises or in non-business premises.

39. With regard to the inspection of business premises, national legislation may require authorisation from a national court to allow a national enforcement authority to assist the Commission in case of opposition of the undertaking concerned. Such authorisation may also be sought as a precautionary measure. When dealing with the request, the national court has the power to control that the Commission's inspection decision is authentic and that the coercive measures envisaged are neither arbitrary nor excessive having regard to the subject matter of the inspection. In its control of the proportionality of the coercive measures, the national court may ask the Commission, directly or through the national competition authority, for detailed explanations in particular on the grounds the Commission has for suspecting infringement of Articles 81 and 82 EC, as well as on the seriousness of the suspected infringement and on the nature of the involvement of the undertaking concerned.[53]

40. With regard to the inspection of non-business premises, the regulation requires the authorisation from a national court before a Commission decision ordering such an inspection can be executed. In that case, the national court may control that the Commission's inspection decision is authentic and that the coercive measures envisaged are neither arbitrary nor excessive having regard in particular to the seriousness of the suspected infringement, to the importance of the evidence sought, to the involvement of the undertaking concerned and to the reasonable likelihood that business books and records relating to the subject matter of the inspection are kept in the premises for which the authorisation is requested. The national court may ask the Commission, directly or through the national competition authority, for detailed explanations on those elements that are necessary to allow its control of the proportionality of the coercive measures envisaged.[54]

41. In both cases referred to in points 39 and 40, the national court may not call into question the lawfulness of the Commission's decision or the necessity for the inspection nor can it demand that it be provided with information in the Commission's file.[55] Furthermore, the duty of loyal co-operation requires the national court to take its decision within an appropriate timeframe that allows the Commission to effectively conduct its inspection.[56]

NOTES

Para 26: substituted, together with associated footnote, by Commission Communication 2015/C256/04, paras 1, 2.

Para 26a: inserted, together with associated footnotes, by Commission Communication 2015/C256/04, paras 1, 3.

Para 26b: inserted by Commission Communication 2015/C256/04, paras 1, 3.

37 Case C-2/88 *Imm Zwartveld* [1990] ECR I-3365, 16 to 22 and case C-234/89 *Delimitis* [1991] I-935, 53.

38 C-94/00 *Roquette Frères* [2002] ECR 9011, 31.

39 On the compatibility of such national procedural rules with the general principles of Community law, see points 9 and 10 of this notice.

40 On these duties, see eg points 23 to 26 of this notice.

41 Case C-234/89 *Delimitis* [1991] ECR I-935, 53, and joined cases C-319/93, C-40/94 and C-224/94 *Dijkstra* [1995] ECR I-4471, 34.

42 Case C-234/89 *Delimitis* [1991] I-935, 53.

43 Case T-353/94 *Postbank* [1996] ECR II-921, 86 and 87 and case 145/83 *Adams* [1985] ECR 3539, 34.

44 Case C-2/88 *Zwartveld* [1990] ECR I-4405, 10 and 11 and case T-353/94 *Postbank* [1996] ECR II-921, 93.

45 Order in *Zwartveld*, C-2/88, EU:C:1990:440, paragraphs 10 and 11; Judgment in *First and Franex*, C-275/00, EU:C:2002:711, paragraph 49 and Judgment of 18 September 1996, *Postbank*, T-353/94, ECR, EU:T:1996:119, paragraph 93.

45A Regulation (EC) No 773/2004, as amended by Commission Regulation (EU) 2015/1348 (OJ L208, 5.8.2015, p 3).

45B Directive 2014/104/EU of the European Parliament and of the Council of 26 November 2014 on certain rules governing actions for damages under national law for infringements of the competition law provisions of the Member States and of the European Union (OJ L349, 5.12.2014, p 1).

46 See point 8 of this notice.

47 Case C-234/89 *Delimitis* [1991] ECR I-935, 53, and joined cases C-319/93, C-40/94 and C-224/94 *Dijkstra* [1995] ECR I-4471, 34.

48 Compare with case 96/81 *Commission v the Netherlands* [1982] ECR 1791, 7 and case 272/86 *Commission v Greece* [1988] ECR 4875, 30.

49 According to Article 15(4) of the regulation, this is without prejudice to wider powers to make observations before courts conferred on national competition authorities under national law.

50 See also Article 28(2) of the regulation, which prevents the Commission from disclosing the information it has acquired and which is covered by the obligation of professional secrecy.

51 Joined cases 46/87 and 227/88 *Hoechst* [1989] ECR, 2859, 33. See also Article 15(3) of the regulation.

52 Case C-69/90 *Commission v Italy* [1991] ECR 6011, 15.

53 Article 20(6) to (8) of the regulation and case C-94/00 *Roquette Frères* [2002] ECR 9011.

54 Article 21(3) of the regulation.

55 Case C-94/00 *Roquette Frères* [2002] ECR 9011, 39 and 62 to 66.

56 See also ibidem, 91 and 92.

IV. FINAL PROVISIONS

[4.498]

42. This notice is issued in order to assist national courts in the application of Articles 81 and 82 EC. It does not bind the national courts, nor does it affect the rights and obligations of the EU Member States and natural or legal persons under Community law.

43. This notice replaces the 1993 notice on co-operation between national courts and the Commission in applying Articles 85 and 86 of the EEC Treaty.[57]

NOTES

57 OJ C39, 13.2.93, p 6.

ANNEX
COMMISSION BLOCK EXEMPTION REGULATIONS, NOTICES AND GUIDELINES

[4.499]

This list is also available and updated on the website of the Directorate General for Competition of the European Commission:

ec.europa.eu/competition/antitrust/legislation/legislation.html

A. NON-SECTOR SPECIFIC RULES

1. Notices of a general nature

— Notice on the definition of the relevant market for the purposes of Community competition law (OJ C372, 9.12.1997, p 5)
— Notice on agreements of minor importance which do not appreciably restrict competition under Article 81(1) of the Treaty establishing the European Community (de minimis) (OJ C368, 22.12.2001, p 13)
— Notice on the effect on trade concept contained in Articles 81 and 82 of the Treaty (OJ C101, 27.4.2004, p 81)
— Guidelines on the application of Article 81(3) of the Treaty (OJ C101, 27.4.2004, p 2)

2. Vertical agreements

— Regulation (EC) No 2790/1999 of 22 December 1999 on the application of Article 81(3) of the Treaty to categories of vertical agreements and concerted practices (OJ L336, 29.12.1999, p 21)
— Guidelines on Vertical Restraints (OJ C291, 13.10.2000, p 1)

3. Horizontal co-operation agreements

— Regulation (EC) No 2658/2000 of 29 November 2000 on the application of Article 81(3) of the Treaty to categories of specialisation agreements (OJ L304, 5.12.2000, p 3)
— Regulation (EC) No 2659/2000 of 29 November 2000 on the application of Article 81(3) of the Treaty to categories of research and development agreements (OJ L304, 5.12.2000, p 7)
— Guidelines on the applicability of Article 81 to horizontal co-operation agreements (OJ C 3, 6.1.2001, p 2)

4. Licensing agreements for the transfer of technology

— Regulation (EC) No 773/2004 of 27 April 2004 on the application of Article 81(3) of the Treaty to categories of technology transfer agreements (OJ L123, 27.4.2004)
— Guidelines on the application of Article 81 of the EC Treaty to technology transfer agreements (OJ C 101, 27.4.2004, p 2)

B. SECTOR SPECIFIC RULES

1. Insurance

— Regulation (EC) No 358/2003 of 27 February 2003 on the application of Article 81(3) of the Treaty to certain categories of agreements, decisions and concerted practices in the insurance sector (OJ L53, 28.2.2003, p 8)

2. Motor vehicles

— Regulation (EC) No 1400/2002 of 31 July 2002 on the application of Article 81(3) of the Treaty to categories of vertical agreements and concerted practices in the motor vehicle sector (OJ L203, 1.8.2002, p 30)

3. Telecommunications and postal services

- Guidelines on the application of EEC competition rules in the telecommunications sector (OJ C233, 6.9.1991, p 2)
- Notice on the application of the competition rules to the postal sector and on the assessment of certain State measures relating to postal services (OJ C39, 6.2.1998, p 2)
- Notice on the application of the competition rules to access agreements in the telecommunications sector-Framework, relevant markets and principles (OJ C265, 22.8.1998, p 2)
- Guidelines on market analysis and the assessment of significant market power under the Community regulatory framework for electronic communications networks and services (OJ C165, 11.7.2002, p 6)

4. Transport

- Regulation (EEC) No 1617/93 on the application of Article 81(3) of the Treaty to certain categories of agreements and concerted practices concerning joint planning and co-ordination of schedules, joint operations, consultations on passenger and cargo tariffs on scheduled air services and slot allocation at airports (OJ L155, 26.6.1993, p 18)
- Communication on clarification of the Commission recommendations on the application of the competition rules to new transport infrastructure projects (OJ C298, 30.9.1997, p 5)
- Regulation (EC) No 823/2000 of 19 April 2000 on the application of Article 81(3) of the Treaty to certain categories of agreements, decisions and concerted practices between liner shipping companies (consortia) (OJ L100, 20.4.2000, p 24)

DIRECTIVE OF THE EUROPEAN PARLIAMENT AND OF THE COUNCIL

(2019/1/EU)

of 11 December 2018

to empower the competition authorities of the Member States to be more effective enforcers and to ensure the proper functioning of the internal market

(Text with EEA relevance)

[4.500]

NOTES

Application of EU Directives in the UK post IP completion day: the European Union (Withdrawal) Act 2018, s 3 provides for the incorporation of "direct EU legislation" into domestic law. "Direct EU legislation" is generally defined as EU Regulations, EU Decisions and EU tertiary legislation (for the full definition, see s 3 of the 2018 Act at **[7.5]**). EU Directives, therefore, are not "direct EU legislation" and, as such, do not form part of UK law post IP completion day. Note that "EU-derived domestic legislation" (UK legislation made under the powers conferred by s 2(2) of, or Sch 2, para 1A to, the European Communities Act 1972) is saved despite the repeal of the 1972 Act both during, and after, the implementation period (see ss 1B and 2 of the 2018 Act respectively at **[7.3]** and **[7.4]**). Note, however, that this Directive was not implemented in the UK prior to the UK leaving the European Union.

Date of publication in OJ: OJ L11, 14.1.2019, p 3.

THE EUROPEAN PARLIAMENT AND THE COUNCIL OF THE EUROPEAN UNION,

Having regard to the Treaty on the Functioning of the European Union, and in particular Articles 103 and 114 thereof,

Having regard to the proposal from the European Commission,

After transmission of the draft legislative act to the national parliaments,

Having regard to the opinion of the European Economic and Social Committee,[1]

Acting in accordance with the ordinary legislative procedure,[2]

Whereas:

(1) Articles 101 and 102 of the Treaty on the Functioning of the European Union (TFEU) are a matter of public policy and should be applied effectively throughout the Union to ensure that competition in the internal market is not distorted. Effective enforcement of Articles 101 and 102 TFEU is necessary to ensure fairer and more open competitive markets in the Union, in which undertakings compete more on their merits and without company- erected barriers to market entry, enabling them to generate wealth and create jobs. It protects consumers and undertakings active on the internal market from business practices that keep the prices of goods and services artificially high and enhances their choice of innovative goods and services.

(2) The public enforcement of Articles 101 and 102 TFEU is carried out by the national competition authorities (NCAs) of the Member States in parallel to the Commission pursuant to Council Regulation (EC) No 1/2003.[3] Together, the NCAs and the Commission form a network of public authorities that apply the Union competition rules in close cooperation (the 'European Competition Network').

(3) Article 3(1) of Regulation (EC) No 1/2003 obliges NCAs and national courts to apply Articles 101 and 102 TFEU to agreements, to decisions by associations of undertakings, to concerted practices or to the abuse of a dominant position which are capable of affecting trade between Member States. In practice, most NCAs apply national competition law in parallel to Articles 101 and 102 TFEU. Therefore, this Directive, the objective of which is to ensure that NCAs have the guarantees of independence, resources, and enforcement and fining powers necessary to apply Articles 101 and 102 TFEU effectively, inevitably has an impact on national competition law when it is applied

in parallel by NCAs. Furthermore, the application by the NCAs of national competition law to agreements, to decisions by associations of undertakings or to concerted practices, which may affect trade between Member States, should not lead to a different outcome to the one reached by the NCAs under Union law pursuant to Article 3(2) of Regulation (EC) No 1/2003. Therefore, in such cases of parallel application of national competition law and Union law, it is essential that the NCAs have the same guarantees of independence, resources, and enforcement and fining powers necessary to ensure that a different outcome is not reached.

(4) Moreover, providing NCAs with the power to obtain all information related to the undertaking subject to the investigation, including in digital form, irrespective of the medium on which it is stored, would also affect the scope of the NCAs' powers when, at the early stages of their proceedings, they take the relevant investigative measure on the basis of national competition law applied in parallel to Articles 101 and 102 TFEU. Providing NCAs with inspection powers of a different scope, depending on whether they will ultimately apply only national competition law or also apply Articles 101 and 102 TFEU in parallel, would hamper the effectiveness of competition law enforcement in the internal market. Accordingly, the scope of the Directive should cover both the application of Articles 101 and 102 TFEU on a stand-alone basis and the parallel application of national competition law to the same case. As regards the protection of leniency statements and settlement submissions, this Directive should also cover the application of national competition law on a stand-alone basis.

(5) National law prevents many NCAs from having the necessary guarantees of independence, resources, and enforcement and fining powers to be able to enforce Union competition rules effectively. This undermines their ability to effectively apply Articles 101 and 102 TFEU and to apply national competition law in parallel to Articles 101 and 102 TFEU. For example, under national law many NCAs do not have effective tools to find evidence of infringements of Articles 101 and 102 TFEU or to fine undertakings which break the law, or do not have adequate human and financial resources and operational independence to apply Articles 101 and 102 TFEU effectively. This is capable of preventing NCAs from taking any action at all or limiting their enforcement actions. The lack of guarantees of independence, resources, and enforcement and fining powers for many NCAs to be able to apply Articles 101 and 102 TFEU effectively means that undertakings engaging in anti-competitive practices might face very different outcomes in proceedings, depending on the Member State in which they are active. They might be subject to no enforcement under Article 101 or 102 TFEU or they might only be subject to ineffective enforcement. For example, in some Member States, undertakings can escape liability for fines simply by restructuring.

(6) Uneven enforcement of Articles 101 and 102 TFEU, whether applied on a stand-alone basis or in parallel with national competition law, results in missed opportunities to remove barriers to market entry and to create fairer competitive markets throughout the Union where undertakings compete on their merits. Undertakings and consumers particularly suffer in those Member States where NCAs are less equipped to be effective enforcers. Undertakings cannot compete on the merits if there are safe havens for anti-competitive practices, for example, because evidence of anti-competitive practices cannot be collected or because undertakings are able to escape liability for fines. Undertakings therefore have a disincentive to enter such markets, to exercise their rights of establishment, and to provide goods and services there. Consumers based in Member States where there is less enforcement miss out on the benefits of effective competition enforcement. Uneven enforcement of Articles 101 and 102 TFEU, whether applied on a stand-alone basis or in parallel with national competition law, throughout the Union thus distorts competition in the internal market and undermines its proper functioning.

(7) Gaps and limitations in the tools and guarantees of NCAs undermine the system of parallel powers for the enforcement of Articles 101 and 102 TFEU, which is designed to work as a cohesive whole based on close cooperation within the European Competition Network. This system depends on authorities being able to rely on each other to carry out fact-finding measures on each other's behalf in order to foster cooperation and mutual assistance among the Member States. However, it does not work well when there are still NCAs that do not have adequate fact-finding tools. In other key respects, NCAs are not able to provide each other with mutual assistance. For example, in the majority of Member States, undertakings that operate across borders are able to evade paying fines simply by not having a legal presence in some of the territories of Member States in which they are active. This reduces incentives to comply with Articles 101 and 102 TFEU. The resulting ineffective enforcement distorts competition for law-abiding undertakings and undermines consumer confidence in the internal market, particularly in the digital environment.

(8) In order to ensure a truly common competition enforcement area in the Union that provides a more even level playing field for undertakings operating in the internal market and reduces unequal conditions for consumers, there is a need to put in place fundamental guarantees of independence, adequate financial, human, technical and technological resources and minimum enforcement and fining powers for applying Articles 101 and 102 TFEU and for applying national competition law in parallel to those Articles so that national administrative competition authorities can be fully effective.

(9) It is appropriate to base this Directive on the dual legal basis of Articles 103 and 114 TFEU. This is because this Directive covers not only the application of Articles 101 and 102 TFEU and the application of national competition law in parallel to those Articles, but also covers the gaps and limitations in the tools and guarantees of NCAs needed to apply Articles 101 and 102 TFEU, because such gaps and limitations negatively affect both competition and the proper functioning of the internal market.

(10) Putting in place fundamental guarantees to ensure that NCAs apply Articles 101 and 102 TFEU uniformly and effectively should be without prejudice to the ability of Member States to maintain or introduce more extensive guarantees of independence and resources for national administrative competition authorities and more detailed rules on the enforcement and fining powers of NCAs. In particular, Member States should be able to endow NCAs with additional powers beyond the core set provided for in this Directive to further enhance their effectiveness, such as powers to impose fines on natural persons or, by way of exception, the power to carry out inspections with the consent of those subject to inspection.

(11) Conversely, detailed rules are necessary in the area of conditions for granting leniency for secret cartels. Undertakings will only disclose secret cartels in which they have participated if they have sufficient legal certainty that they will benefit from immunity from fines. The marked differences between the leniency programmes in the Member States lead to legal uncertainty for potential leniency applicants. This may weaken their incentives to apply

for leniency. If Member States were able to implement or apply clearer and harmonised rules for leniency in the area covered by this Directive, this would not only contribute to the objective of maintaining incentives for applicants to disclose secret cartels, in order to render competition enforcement in the Union as effective as possible, but would also guarantee a level playing field for undertakings operating in the internal market. This should not prevent Member States from applying leniency programmes that cover not only secret cartels, but also other infringements of Article 101 TFEU and equivalent provisions of national competition law, or from accepting leniency applications from natural persons acting in their own name. This Directive should also be without prejudice to leniency programmes that exclusively provide for immunity from sanctions in criminal judicial proceedings for the enforcement of Article 101 TFEU.

(12) This Directive should not apply to national laws insofar as they provide for the imposition of criminal sanctions on natural persons, with the exception of the rules governing the interplay of leniency programmes with the imposition of sanctions on natural persons. It also should not apply to national laws that provide for the imposition of administrative sanctions on natural persons that do not operate as an independent economic actor on a market.

(13) Pursuant to Article 35 of Regulation (EC) No 1/2003, Member States can entrust the enforcement of Articles 101 and 102 TFEU exclusively to an administrative authority, as is the case in most jurisdictions, or they can entrust this to both judicial and administrative authorities. In the latter case, the administrative authority is at least primarily responsible for conducting the investigation, while the judicial authority is typically entrusted with the power to take decisions imposing fines and can have the power to take other decisions, such as finding an infringement of Articles 101 and 102 TFEU.

(14) The exercise of the powers, conferred by this Directive on NCAs, including the investigative powers, should be subject to appropriate safeguards which at least comply with the general principles of Union law and the Charter of Fundamental Rights of the European Union, in accordance with the case law of the Court of Justice of the European Union, in particular in the context of proceedings which could give rise to the imposition of penalties. These safeguards include the right to good administration and the respect of undertakings' rights of defence, an essential component of which is the right to be heard. In particular, NCAs should inform the parties under investigation of the preliminary objections raised against them under Article 101 or Article 102 TFEU in the form of a statement of objections or a similar measure prior to taking a decision finding an infringement, and those parties should have an opportunity to make their views on those objections known effectively before such a decision is taken. Parties to whom preliminary objections about an alleged infringement of Article 101 or Article 102 TFEU have been notified should have the right to access the relevant case file of NCAs, to be able to exercise their rights of defence effectively. The right to access the file should be subject to the legitimate interest of undertakings in the protection of their business secrets and should not extend to confidential information and internal documents of, and correspondence between, the NCAs and the Commission. Moreover, for decisions of NCAs, in particular those decisions finding an infringement of Article 101 or Article 102 TFEU, and imposing remedies or fines, the addressees should have the right to an effective remedy before a tribunal, in accordance with Article 47 of the Charter of Fundamental Rights of the European Union. Such decisions should be reasoned so as to allow addressees of such decisions to ascertain the reasons for the decision and to exercise their right to an effective remedy. Moreover, in accordance with the right to good administration, Member States should ensure that, when applying Articles 101 and 102 TFEU, NCAs conduct proceedings within a reasonable timeframe, taking into account the specificities of each case. The design of those safeguards should strike a balance between the respect of the fundamental rights of undertakings and the duty to ensure that Articles 101 and 102 TFEU are effectively enforced.

(15) The exchange of information between NCAs, and the use of such information in evidence for the application of Article 101 or Article 102 TFEU, should be carried out pursuant to Article 12 of Regulation (EC) No 1/2003.

(16) Empowering national administrative competition authorities to apply Articles 101 and 102 TFEU impartially and in the common interest of the effective enforcement of the Union competition rules is an essential component of the effective and uniform application of those rules.

(17) The operational independence of national administrative competition authorities should be strengthened in order to ensure the effective and uniform application of Articles 101 and 102 TFEU. To this end, express provision should be made in national law to ensure that when applying Articles 101 and 102 TFEU, national administrative competition authorities are protected against external intervention or political pressure that is liable to jeopardise their independent assessment of the matters before them. For that purpose, the grounds regarding the dismissal from the national administrative competition authority of those persons who take decisions exercising the powers referred to in Articles 10, 11, 12, 13 and 16 of this Directive should be laid down in advance in national law in order to remove any reasonable doubt as to their impartiality and their imperviousness to external factors. Similarly, clear and transparent rules and procedures for the selection, recruitment or appointment of those persons should be laid down in advance in national law. Moreover, to ensure the impartiality of national administrative competition authorities, the fines that they impose for infringements of Articles 101 and 102 TFEU should not be used to finance these authorities directly.

(18) To ensure the operational independence of national administrative competition authorities, their heads, staff and those who take decisions should act with integrity and refrain from any action which is incompatible with the performance of their duties. To prevent the independent assessment by heads, staff and those who take decisions from being jeopardised, they should refrain from any incompatible actions, whether gainful or not, both during their employment or term of office and for a reasonable period thereafter.

(19) This means that during their employment or their term of office, the staff and those who take decisions should not be able to deal with proceedings for the application of Article 101 or 102 TFEU in which they have been involved or which directly concern undertakings or associations of undertakings by which they have been employed or otherwise professionally engaged, if this has the potential to compromise their impartiality in a specific case. Similarly, the staff and those who take decisions, as well as their close relatives, should not have any interest in any businesses or organisations which are subject to proceedings for the application of Article 101 or 102 TFEU in which they take part, if this has the potential to compromise their impartiality in a specific case. The assessment of whether their impartiality might be impaired in a specific case should take into account the nature and the magnitude of the interest and the level of involvement or engagement of the individual concerned. Where it is necessary to ensure the impartiality of the

investigation and the decision-making process, the individual concerned should be required to recuse herself or himself from the specific case.

(20) This also means that, for a reasonable period after leaving the national administrative competition authority, whenever former staff or those who took decisions engage in an occupation which is related to the proceedings for the application of Article 101 or 102 TFEU with which they were dealing during their employment or term of office, they should not be involved in the same case in their new occupation.

The length of that period might be determined by taking into account the nature of the new occupation of the individuals concerned as well as the level of their involvement and responsibility in the same proceedings during their employment or term in office in the national administrative competition authority.

(21) Every national administrative competition authority should publish a code of conduct that, without prejudice to the application of stricter national rules, covers rules on conflicts of interest.

(22) The operational independence of national administrative competition authorities should not preclude either judicial review or parliamentary supervision in accordance with national law. Accountability requirements should also contribute to ensuring the credibility and the legitimacy of the actions of national administrative competition authorities. Proportionate accountability requirements include the publication by national administrative competition authorities of periodic reports on their activities to a governmental or parliamentary body. National administrative competition authorities might also be subject to control or monitoring of their financial expenditure, provided this does not affect their independence.

(23) National administrative competition authorities should be able to prioritise their proceedings for the enforcement of Articles 101 and 102 TFEU to make effective use of their resources, and to allow them to focus on preventing and bringing anti-competitive behaviour that distorts competition in the internal market to an end. For this purpose, they should be able to reject complaints on the grounds that they are not a priority, with the exception of complaints lodged by public authorities which share competence with a national administrative competition authority for enforcing Articles 101 and 102 TFEU and national competition law, where applicable. This should be without prejudice to the power of national administrative competition authorities to reject complaints on other grounds, such as a lack of competence, or to decide that there are no grounds for action on their part. In cases of formally filed complaints, such rejections should be subject to effective remedies in accordance with national law. The power of national administrative competition authorities to prioritise their enforcement proceedings is without prejudice to the right of a government of a Member State to issue to national administrative competition authorities general policy rules or priority guidelines that are not related to sector inquiries or specific proceedings for the enforcement of Articles 101 and 102 TFEU.

(24) NCAs should have sufficient resources, in terms of qualified staff able to conduct proficient legal and economic assessments, financial means, technical and technological expertise and equipment including adequate information technology tools, to ensure they are able to perform their tasks effectively when applying Articles 101 and 102 TFEU. In the event that the duties and powers of NCAs under national law are extended, Member States should ensure that NCAs have sufficient resources to perform those tasks effectively.

(25) The independence of NCAs should be enhanced by enabling them to decide independently on the spending of the budget allocations for the purpose of carrying out their duties, without prejudice to national budgetary rules and procedures.

(26) To ensure that national administrative competition authorities have the necessary resources to perform their tasks, different means of financing might be considered, such as financing from alternative sources other than the state budget.

(27) In order to ensure effective monitoring of the implementation of this Directive, Member States should ensure that national administrative competition authorities submit periodic reports on their activities and resources to a governmental or parliamentary body. Those reports should include information about the appointments and dismissals of members of the decision-making body, the amount of resources that were allocated in the relevant year and any changes in that amount compared to previous years. Such reports should be made publicly available.

(28) NCAs require a minimum set of common investigative and decision-making powers to be able to effectively enforce Articles 101 and 102 TFEU.

(29) National administrative competition authorities should have effective powers of investigation to detect any agreement, decision or concerted practice prohibited by Article 101 TFEU or any abuse of a dominant position prohibited by Article 102 TFEU at any stage of the proceedings before them. The national administrative competition authorities should be able to apply those powers to undertakings and associations of undertakings which are the subject of proceedings for the application of Articles 101 and 102 TFEU, as well as to other market players which may be in possession of information which is of relevance to such proceedings. Granting such effective investigative powers to all national administrative competition authorities should ensure that they are in a position to assist each other effectively when requested to carry out an inspection or any other fact-finding measure on their own territory on behalf of and for the account of another NCA pursuant to Article 22 of Regulation (EC) No 1/2003.

(30) The investigative powers of national administrative competition authorities should be adequate to meet the enforcement challenges of the digital environment, and should enable NCAs to obtain all information related to the undertaking or association of undertakings which is subject to the investigative measure in digital form, including data obtained forensically, irrespective of the medium on which the information is stored, such as on laptops, mobile phones, other mobile devices or cloud storage.

(31) National administrative competition authorities should be able to carry out all necessary inspections of premises of undertakings and associations of undertakings where, in line with the case law of the Court of Justice of the European Union, they can show that there are reasonable grounds for suspecting an infringement of Article 101 or 102 TFEU. This Directive should not prevent Member States from requiring prior authorisation by a national judicial authority for such inspections.

(32) To be effective, the power of national administrative competition authorities to carry out inspections should enable them to access information that is accessible to the undertaking or association of undertakings or person subject

to the inspection and which is related to the undertaking or the association of undertakings under investigation. This should necessarily include the power to search for documents, files or data on devices which are not precisely identified in advance. Without such power, it would be impossible to obtain the information necessary for the investigation where undertakings or associations of undertakings adopt an obstructive attitude or refuse to cooperate. The power to examine books or records should cover all forms of correspondence, including electronic messages, irrespective of whether they appear to be unread or have been deleted.

(33) To minimise the unnecessary prolongation of inspections, national administrative competition authorities should have the power to continue making searches and to select copies or extracts of books and records related to the business of the undertaking or association of undertakings being inspected at the authority's premises or at other designated premises. Such searches should ensure the continued due respect of undertakings' rights of defence.

(34) Experience shows that business records may be kept in the homes of directors, managers and other members of staff of undertakings or of associations of undertakings, in particular because of the increased use of more flexible working arrangements. In order to ensure that inspections are effective, national administrative competition authorities should have the power to enter any premises, including private homes, if they can show that there is a reasonable suspicion that business records which may be relevant to prove an infringement of Article 101 or 102 TFEU are being kept in those premises. The exercise of that power should be subject to the national administrative competition authority having obtained prior authorisation from a national judicial authority, which may include a public prosecutor in certain national legal systems. This should not prevent Member States in cases of extreme urgency from entrusting the tasks of a national judicial authority to a national administrative competition authority acting as a judicial authority or, by way of exception, allowing for such inspections to be carried out with the consent of those subject to inspection. The conduct of such inspections might be entrusted by a national administrative competition authority to the police or an equivalent enforcement authority, provided that the inspection is carried out in the presence of the national administrative competition authority. This should be without prejudice to the right of the national administrative competition authority to conduct the inspection itself and to obtain the necessary assistance of the police or an equivalent enforcement authority, including assistance, as a precautionary measure, to overcome possible opposition on the part of those subject to the inspection.

(35) NCAs should have effective powers to require undertakings or associations of undertakings to provide information necessary to detect infringements of Articles 101 and 102 TFEU. To that end, NCAs should be able to require the disclosure of information that may enable them to investigate putative infringements. This should include the right to require information in any digital form, including emails and instant messaging system messages, irrespective of where it is stored, including in clouds and on servers, provided it is accessible to the undertaking or association of undertakings which is the addressee of the request for information. That right should not result in an obligation on the part of the undertaking or association of undertakings which is disproportionate to the requirements of the investigation. For example, it should not result in excessive costs or efforts being incurred by the undertaking or association of undertakings. While the right to require information is crucial for the detection of infringements, such requests should be appropriate in scope. Such requests should not compel an undertaking or association of undertakings to admit that it has committed an infringement, which is incumbent upon the NCAs to prove. This should be without prejudice to the obligations of undertakings or associations of undertakings to answer factual questions and to provide documents. Similarly, NCAs should have effective tools to require any other natural or legal person to provide information that may be relevant for the application of Articles 101 and 102 TFEU. Member States should be free to provide for procedural rules on such requests for information, such as the legal form they take, provided that those rules allow for the effective use of this tool. Experience also shows that information provided on a voluntary basis in response to non-compulsory requests for information can be a valuable source of information for informed and robust enforcement. Similarly, the provision of information by third parties, such as competitors, customers and consumers in the market, on their own initiative can contribute to effective enforcement and NCAs should encourage this.

(36) Experience shows that the power to conduct interviews is a useful tool to collect evidence and to help competition authorities assess the value of already-collected evidence. NCAs should have effective means to summon for an interview any representative of an undertaking or association of undertakings, any representative of other legal persons and any natural person who may possess information relevant for the application of Articles 101 and 102 TFEU. Member States should be free to provide for rules governing the conduct of such interviews, provided that such rules allow for the effective use of this tool.

(37) It is indispensable for NCAs to be able to require undertakings and associations of undertakings to bring infringements of Article 101 or 102 TFEU to an end, including where the infringement continues after the NCAs have formally initiated proceedings. Moreover, NCAs should have effective means to restore competition in the market by imposing structural and behavioural remedies which are proportionate to the infringement committed and which are necessary to bring the infringement to an end. The principle of proportionality requires that, when choosing between two equally effective remedies, NCAs should choose the remedy that is least burdensome for the undertaking. Structural remedies, such as obligations to dispose of a shareholding in a competitor or to divest a business unit, affect the assets of an undertaking and can be presumed to be more burdensome for the undertaking than behavioural remedies. However, this should not preclude NCAs from finding that the circumstances of a particular infringement justify the imposition of a structural remedy because it would be more effective in bringing the infringement to an end than a behavioural remedy.

(38) Interim measures can be an important tool to ensure that, while an investigation is ongoing, the infringement being investigated does not seriously and irreparably harm competition. This tool is important to avoid market developments that could be very difficult to reverse by a decision taken by an NCA at the end of the proceedings. NCAs should therefore have the power to impose interim measures by decision. As a minimum, this power should apply in cases where an NCA has made a prima facie finding of infringement of Article 101 or 102 TFEU and where there is a risk of serious and irreparable harm to competition. Member States are free to provide NCAs with more extensive powers to impose interim measures. A decision imposing interim measures should only be valid for a specified period, either until the conclusion of the proceedings by an NCA, or for a fixed time period which can be renewed insofar as it is necessary and appropriate. Member States should ensure that the legality, including the proportionality, of such

measures can be reviewed in expedited appeal procedures or other procedures which also provide for expedited judicial control. Furthermore, Member States should create the conditions necessary to ensure that NCAs can make use of interim measures in practice. There is a particular need to enable all competition authorities to deal with developments in fast-moving markets and therefore to reflect within the European Competition Network on the use of interim measures and to take this experience into account in any relevant soft measure or future review of this Directive.

(39) Where, in the course of proceedings which might lead to an agreement or a practice being prohibited, undertakings or associations of undertakings offer NCAs commitments which meet their concerns, these NCAs should be able to adopt decisions which make these commitments binding on, and enforceable against, the undertakings or associations of undertakings concerned. In principle, such commitment decisions are not appropriate in the case of secret cartels, in respect of which NCAs should impose fines. Commitment decisions should find that there are no longer grounds for action by the NCAs, without reaching a conclusion as to whether there has been an infringement of Article 101 or 102 TFEU. It should be at the discretion of NCAs whether to accept commitments. Commitment decisions are without prejudice to the powers of competition authorities and national courts to make such a finding of an infringement and decide upon a case. Moreover, effective means of monitoring compliance by undertakings or associations of undertakings with commitments and effective means of imposing sanctions in cases of non-compliance have proven to be effective tools for competition authorities. NCAs should have effective means for the reopening of proceedings in cases where there have been material changes to any of the facts on which a commitment decision was based, where the undertaking or association of undertakings acted contrary to their commitments, or where a commitment decision was based on incomplete, incorrect or misleading information provided by the parties.

(40) To ensure the effective and uniform enforcement of Articles 101 and 102 TFEU, national administrative competition authorities should have the power to impose effective, proportionate and dissuasive fines on undertakings and associations of undertakings for infringements of Article 101 or 102 TFEU, either directly themselves in their own proceedings, in particular in administrative proceedings, provided that such proceedings enable the direct imposition of effective, proportionate and dissuasive fines, or by seeking the imposition of fines in non-criminal judicial proceedings. This is without prejudice to national laws which provide for the imposition of sanctions on undertakings and associations of undertakings by courts in criminal proceedings for the infringement of Articles 101 and 102 TFEU where the infringement is a criminal offence under national law and provided that it does not affect the effective and uniform enforcement of Articles 101 and 102 TFEU.

(41) To ensure that undertakings and associations of undertakings have incentives to comply with the investigative measures and decisions of the NCAs, national administrative competition authorities should be able either to impose effective fines for non-compliance with the measures and decisions referred to in Articles 6, 8, 9, 10, 11 and 12 directly themselves in their own proceedings or to seek the imposition of fines in non-criminal judicial proceedings. This is without prejudice to national law which provide for the imposition of such fines on undertakings and associations of undertakings by courts in criminal judicial proceedings.

(42) In accordance with the Charter of Fundamental Rights of the European Union, in proceedings before national administrative competition authorities or, as the case may be, in non-criminal judicial proceedings, fines should be imposed where the infringement has been committed intentionally or negligently. The notions of intent and negligence should be interpreted in line with the case law of the Court of Justice of the European Union on the application of Articles 101 and 102 TFEU and not in line with the notions of intent and negligence in proceedings conducted by criminal authorities relating to criminal matters. This is without prejudice to national laws under which the finding of an infringement is based on the criterion of objective liability, provided that it is compatible with the case law of the Court of Justice of the European Union. This Directive does not affect national rules on the standard of proof or the obligations of NCAs to ascertain the facts of the relevant case, provided that such rules and obligations are compatible with general principles of Union law.

(43) Fines should be determined in proportion to the total worldwide turnover of the undertakings and associations of undertakings concerned.

(44) Periodic penalty payments are a key tool to ensure that NCAs have effective means to tackle continuing and future non-compliance by undertakings and associations of undertakings with their measures and decisions as referred to in Articles 6, 8, 9, 10, 11 and 12. They should not apply to findings of infringements that have been committed in the past. The power to impose periodic penalty payments is without prejudice to the power of NCAs to punish non-compliance with the measures referred to in Article 13(2). Such periodic penalty payments should be determined in proportion to the average daily total worldwide turnover of the undertakings and associations of undertakings concerned.

(45) For the purpose of imposing fines and periodic penalty payments, the term 'decision' should include any measure which produces binding legal effects capable of affecting the interests of the addressee by bringing about a distinct change in his or her legal position.

(46) To ensure the effective and uniform application of Articles 101 and 102 TFEU, the notion of 'undertaking', as contained in Articles 101 and 102 TFEU, which should be applied in accordance with the case law of the Court of Justice of the European Union, designates an economic unit, even if it consists of several legal or natural persons. Accordingly, NCAs should be able to apply the notion of undertaking to find a parent company liable, and impose fines on it, for the conduct of one of its subsidiaries, where the parent company and its subsidiary form a single economic unit. To prevent undertakings escaping liability for fines for infringements of Articles 101 and 102 TFEU through legal or organisational changes, NCAs should be able to find legal or economic successors of the undertaking liable, and to impose fines on them, for infringements of Articles 101 and 102 TFEU, in accordance with the case law of the Court of Justice of the European Union.

(47) To ensure that the fines imposed for infringements of Articles 101 and 102 TFEU reflect the economic significance of the infringement, NCAs should take into account the gravity of the infringement. NCAs should also be able to set fines that are proportionate to the duration of the infringement. These factors should be assessed in accordance with the relevant case law of the Court of Justice of the European Union and in a way that ensures deterrence. The assessment of gravity should be made on a case-by-case basis for all types of infringements, taking into account all circumstances of the case. Factors that might be taken into consideration include the nature of the

infringement, the combined market share of all undertakings concerned, the geographic scope of the infringement, whether the infringement has been implemented, the value of the undertaking's sales of goods and services to which the infringement directly or indirectly relates and the size and market power of the undertaking concerned. The existence of repeated infringements by the same perpetrator shows its propensity to commit such infringements and is therefore a very significant indication that the level of the penalty needs to be increased to achieve effective deterrence. Accordingly, NCAs should have the possibility to increase the fine to be imposed on an undertaking or association of undertakings where the Commission or an NCA has previously taken a decision finding that that undertaking or association of undertakings has infringed Article 101 or 102 TFEU and that undertaking or association of undertakings continues to commit the same infringement or commits a similar infringement. In accordance with Directive 2014/104/EU of the European Parliament and of the Council,[4] NCAs should be able to take into account any compensation paid as a result of a consensual settlement. In addition, in exceptional circumstances, NCAs should be able to take into account the economic viability of the undertaking concerned.

(48) Experience has shown that associations of undertakings regularly play a role in competition infringements and NCAs should therefore be able to fine such associations effectively. When assessing the gravity of the infringement, in order to determine the amount of the fine in proceedings brought against associations of undertakings, where the infringement relates to the activities of its members, it should be possible to consider the sum of the sales of goods and services to which the infringement directly or indirectly relates by the undertakings that are members of the association. When a fine is imposed not only on the association but also on its members, the turnover of the members on which a fine is imposed should not be taken into account when calculating the fine of the association. In order to ensure effective recovery of fines imposed on associations of undertakings for infringements that they have committed, it is necessary to lay down the conditions in which it is at NCAs' discretion to require payment of the fine from the members of the association where the association is not solvent. In doing so, NCAs should have regard to the relative size of the undertakings that belong to the association and, in particular, to the situation of small and medium-sized enterprises. Payment of the fine by one or several members of an association is without prejudice to rules of national law that provide for recovery of the amount paid from other members of the association.

(49) The deterrent effect of fines differs widely across the Union, and in some Member States the maximum amount of the fine that can be imposed is very low. To ensure NCAs can impose dissuasive fines, the maximum amount of the fine that is possible to be imposed for each infringement of Article 101 or 102 TFEU should be set at a level of not less than 10% of the total worldwide turnover of the undertaking concerned. This should not prevent Member States from maintaining or introducing a higher maximum fine that can be imposed.

(50) Leniency programmes are a key tool for the detection of secret cartels, and thus contribute to the efficient prosecution of, and the imposition of penalties for, the most serious infringements of competition law. However, there are currently marked differences between the leniency programmes applicable in the Member States. Those differences lead to legal uncertainty on the part of infringing undertakings concerning the conditions under which they are able to apply for leniency, as well as uncertainty about their immunity status under the respective leniency programmes. Such uncertainty might weaken incentives for potential leniency applicants to apply for leniency. This in turn can lead to less effective competition enforcement in the Union, as fewer secret cartels are uncovered.

(51) The differences between leniency programmes at Member State level also jeopardise the level playing field for undertakings operating in the internal market. It is therefore appropriate to increase legal certainty for undertakings in the internal market and to boost the attractiveness of leniency programmes across the Union by reducing these differences by enabling all NCAs to grant immunity and reduction from fines and accept summary applications under the same conditions. Further efforts by the European Competition Network to align leniency programmes could be needed in the future.

(52) NCAs should be able to grant undertakings immunity from fines and reductions of fines, if certain conditions are met. Associations of undertakings which perform an economic activity on their own behalf should be eligible for immunity from fines or reductions of fines in cases where they participate in an alleged cartel on their own behalf and not on behalf of their members.

(53) For a cartel to be considered a secret cartel, not all aspects of the conduct need to be secret. In particular, a cartel can be considered a secret cartel when elements of the cartel which make the full extent of the conduct more difficult to detect are not known to the public or the customers or suppliers.

(54) In order to qualify for leniency, the applicant should end its involvement in the alleged secret cartel, except in cases where an NCA considers that its continued involvement is reasonably necessary to preserve the integrity of the investigation, for example, in order to ensure that other alleged participants in the cartel do not discover that the NCA was made aware of the alleged cartel before it carries out investigative measures such as unannounced inspections.

(55) In order to qualify for leniency, the applicant should cooperate genuinely, fully, on a continuous basis and expeditiously with the NCA. This means, inter alia, that when contemplating the making of an application to the NCA the applicant should not destroy, falsify or conceal evidence of the alleged secret cartel. When an undertaking is contemplating the making of an application, there is a risk that its directors, managers and other staff might destroy evidence in order to conceal their involvement in a cartel, but the destruction of evidence could also occur for other reasons. Therefore, NCAs should take into account the specific circumstances under which evidence was destroyed and the significance of such destruction when considering whether the destruction of evidence calls into question the genuine cooperation of the applicant.

(56) In order to fulfil the condition of genuine, full, continuous and expeditious cooperation, when contemplating the making of an application to the NCA, the applicant should not have disclosed the fact or any of the content of its contemplated application, except to other NCAs, the Commission or competition authorities of third countries. This does not preclude an applicant from reporting its behaviour to other public authorities as required by relevant laws, but only prevents it from disclosing the fact that it is contemplating an application for leniency and from handing over leniency statements to those authorities. However, when fulfilling its obligations under those relevant laws, the applicant should also consider the importance of not adversely impacting the potential investigation by the NCA.

(57) Applicants should have the possibility of submitting leniency statements, in relation to full or summary

applications, in writing, and NCAs should also have a system in place that enables them to accept such statements either in oral form or by other means that permit applicants not to take possession, custody, or control of such submitted statements. NCAs should be able to choose the means by which they accept leniency statements.

(58) Undertakings that wish to make an application for immunity should be able to initially request NCAs for a marker for a place in the queue for leniency before they formally submit the application for immunity, in order to give the applicant time to gather the necessary information and evidence to meet the relevant evidential threshold. This is without prejudice to the ability of Member States to allow undertakings to apply for a marker in the case of applications for a reduction of fines.

(59) Moreover, in order to reduce the administrative and other considerable burdens in terms of time, it should be possible for applicants to submit leniency statements in relation to full or summary applications, as well as in relation to requests for markers, either in an official language of the Member State of the NCA concerned, or, where bilaterally agreed between the NCA and the applicant, in another official language of the Union. Such agreement would be deemed to exist where the NCAs generally accept such submissions in that language.

(60) In view of the shared competences between the Commission and the NCAs for the enforcement of Articles 101 and 102 TFEU, it is key to have a smoothly functioning system of summary applications in place. Applicants which have applied for leniency to the Commission in relation to an alleged secret cartel should be able to submit summary applications to NCAs in relation to the same cartel, provided that the application to the Commission covers more than three Member States as affected territories. This is without prejudice to the possibility for the Commission to deal with cases if they are closely linked to other Union provisions which may be exclusively or more effectively applied by the Commission, where the Union interest requires the adoption of a Commission decision to develop Union competition policy when a new competition issue arises, or to ensure effective enforcement.

(61) The summary application system should allow undertakings to submit a leniency application to NCAs containing a limited set of information where a full application has been submitted to the Commission in relation to such an alleged cartel. NCAs should therefore accept summary applications that contain a minimum set of information in relation to the alleged cartel for each of the items set out in Article 22(2). This is without prejudice to the possibility for the applicant to provide more detailed information at a later time. At the request of the leniency applicant, NCAs should provide it with an acknowledgement of receipt stating the date and time of receipt. If an NCA has not yet received such a prior leniency application from another leniency applicant about the same alleged secret cartel, and considers that the summary application fulfils the requirements of Article 22(2), the NCA should inform the applicant accordingly.

(62) The aim of the system of summary applications is to reduce the administrative burden on applicants which submit a leniency application to the Commission in relation to an alleged secret cartel that covers more than three Member States as affected territories. Given that in such cases the Commission receives a full application, it should be the main interlocutor of the leniency applicant in the period before clarity has been gained as to whether the Commission will pursue the case in full or in part, in particular with respect to providing instructions on the conduct of any further internal investigation by the applicant. The Commission is to endeavour to decide on this matter within a reasonable period of time and inform the NCAs accordingly, without prejudice to Article 11(6) of Regulation (EC) No 1/2003. In exceptional circumstances, when strictly necessary for case delineation or case allocation, an NCA should be able to request the applicant to submit a full application before such clarity has been gained. This possibility should be used very rarely. In other cases, the applicant should only be asked to submit a full application to an NCA which has received a summary application once it is clear that the Commission does not intend to pursue the case in whole or in part.

(63) Applicants should be given the opportunity to submit full leniency applications to the NCAs to which they have submitted summary applications. If the applicants submit such full applications within the period specified by the NCA, the information contained in those applications should be deemed to have been submitted at the time at which the summary application was submitted, provided that the summary application covers the same affected products and territories and the same duration of the alleged cartel as the leniency application filed with the Commission, which might have been updated. The onus should be on applicants to inform the NCAs to which they have submitted summary applications if the scope of their leniency application with the Commission has changed and to update their summary applications accordingly. NCAs should be able to check whether the scope of the summary application corresponds to the scope of the leniency application filed with the Commission, through cooperation within the European Competition Network.

(64) Legal uncertainty as to whether current and former directors, managers and other members of staff of applicants for immunity are shielded from individual sanctions such as fines, disqualification or imprisonment, could prevent potential applicants from applying for leniency. In light of their contribution to the detection and investigation of secret cartels, those individuals should thus, in principle, be protected from sanctions in relation to their involvement in the secret cartel covered by the application imposed by public authorities in criminal, administrative and non-criminal judicial proceedings pursuant to national laws that predominantly pursue the same objectives to those pursued by Article 101 TFEU, such as national laws on bid-rigging, where the conditions set out in this Directive are fulfilled. One of these conditions is that the application for immunity should predate the time when those individuals were made aware by the competent national authorities of the proceedings that could lead to the imposition of sanctions. Such proceedings include the moment those individuals become suspected of violating such national laws. Member States are free to provide under national law for modalities as to how those individuals should cooperate with the relevant authorities to ensure the effective functioning of this protection. Protection from criminal sanctions includes cases in which the competent national authorities refrain from prosecution under certain conditions or subject to instructions as to the future behaviour of the individual.

(65) By way of derogation, in order to ensure that the protection from sanctions to be imposed on individuals in criminal proceedings is in conformity with the existing basic principles of their legal system, Member States might provide that the competent authorities are able to choose between protecting the individual from sanctions or only mitigating those sanctions, depending on the outcome of weighing the interest in prosecuting and/or sanctioning the individual against the individual's contribution to the detection and investigation of the cartel. When assessing the

interest in prosecuting and/or sanctioning those individuals, their personal responsibility or contribution to the infringement, among other factors, may be taken into account.

(66) Member States are not precluded from also protecting the current or former directors, managers and other members of staff of the applicants for reduction of fines from sanctions, or from mitigating such sanctions.

(67) In order to allow the protection to function in situations where more than one jurisdiction is involved, Member States should provide that in cases where the competent sanctioning or prosecuting authority is not in the same jurisdiction as the competition authority that is pursuing the case, the necessary contacts between those authorities should be ensured by the NCA of the jurisdiction of the competent sanctioning or prosecuting authority.

(68) In a system in which the Commission and NCAs have parallel powers to apply Articles 101 and 102 TFEU, close cooperation is required among NCAs and between NCAs and the Commission. In particular when an NCA carries out an inspection or an interview under its national law on behalf of another NCA pursuant to Article 22(1) of Regulation (EC) No 1/2003, the presence and assistance of the officials from the applicant authority should be enabled to enhance the effectiveness of such inspections and interviews by providing additional resources, knowledge and technical expertise. NCAs should also be empowered to ask other NCAs to assist in establishing whether undertakings or associations of undertakings have failed to comply with investigative measures and decisions taken by the applicant NCAs.

(69) Arrangements should be put in place to allow NCAs to request mutual assistance for the notification of documents related to the application of Article 101 or 102 TFEU on a cross-border basis to parties to the proceedings or other undertakings, associations of undertakings or natural persons which may be the addressees of such notifications. Similarly, NCAs should be able to request the enforcement of decisions imposing fines or periodic penalty payments by authorities in other Member States where the applicant authority has made reasonable efforts to ascertain that the undertaking against which the fine or periodic penalty payment is to be enforced does not have sufficient assets in the Member State of the applicant authority. Member States should also provide, in particular, that where the undertaking against which the fine or periodic penalty payment is enforceable is not established in the Member State of the applicant authority, the requested authority may enforce decisions adopted by the applicant authority, at the request of the applicant authority. This would ensure the effective enforcement of Articles 101 and 102 TFEU and would contribute to the proper functioning of the internal market. In order to ensure that NCAs devote sufficient resources to the requests for mutual assistance, and in order to incentivise such assistance, the requested authorities should be able to recover the costs they incur in providing that assistance. Such mutual assistance is without prejudice to the application of Council Framework Decision 2005/214/JHA.[5]

(70) To ensure the effective enforcement of Articles 101 and 102 TFEU by NCAs there is a need to provide for workable rules on limitation periods. In particular, in a system of parallel powers, national limitation periods should be suspended or interrupted for the duration of proceedings before NCAs of another Member State or the Commission. Such suspension or interruption should not prevent Member States from maintaining or introducing absolute limitation periods, provided that the duration of such absolute limitation periods does not render the effective enforcement of Articles 101 and 102 TFEU practically impossible or excessively difficult.

(71) To ensure that cases are dealt with efficiently and effectively within the European Competition Network, in those Member States where both a national administrative competition authority and a national judicial competition authority are designated as NCAs for the purpose of enforcing Articles 101 and 102 TFEU as referred to in Articles 6, 7, 8, 9, 10, 11, 12, 13 and 16 of this Directive, national administrative competition authorities should be able to bring the action directly before the national judicial competition authority. In addition, to the extent that national courts act in proceedings brought against decisions taken by NCAs applying Article 101 or 102 TFEU, national administrative competition authorities should be fully entitled to participate in their own right as a prosecutor, defendant or respondent in those proceedings, and should enjoy the same rights of such a public party to those proceedings.

(72) The risk of self-incriminating material being disclosed outside the context of the investigation for the purposes of which it was provided could weaken the incentives for potential leniency applicants to cooperate with competition authorities. As a consequence, regardless of the form in which leniency statements are submitted, information in leniency statements that has been obtained through access to the file should be used only where necessary for the exercise of rights of defence in proceedings before national courts in certain very limited cases which are directly related to the case for which access has been granted. This should not prevent competition authorities from publishing their decisions in accordance with applicable Union or national law.

(73) Evidence is an important element in the enforcement of Articles 101 and 102 TFEU. NCAs should be able to consider relevant evidence, irrespective of whether it is written, oral, or in an electronic or recorded form. This should include the ability to consider covert recordings made by natural or legal persons which are not public authorities, provided those recordings are not the sole source of evidence. This should be without prejudice to the right to be heard and without prejudice to the admissibility of any recordings made or obtained by public authorities. Similarly, NCAs should be able to consider electronic messages as relevant evidence, irrespective of whether those messages appear to be unread or have been deleted.

(74) Ensuring that NCAs have the powers they need in order to be more effective enforcers reinforces the need for close cooperation and effective multilateral and bilateral communication in the European Competition Network. This should include the development of soft measures to facilitate and support the implementation of this Directive.

(75) To support close cooperation in the European Competition Network, the Commission should maintain, develop, host, operate and support a central information system (European Competition Network System) in compliance with the relevant confidentiality, data protection and data security standards. The European Competition Network relies on interoperability in order to function effectively and efficiently. The general budget of the Union should bear the costs of maintenance, development, hosting, user support and operation of the European Competition Network System, as well as other administrative costs incurred in connection with the functioning of the European Competition Network, in particular the costs related to the organisation of meetings. Until 2020, provision has been made for the costs for the European Competition Network System to be covered by the Programme on interoperability solutions and common frameworks for European public administrations, businesses and citizens (ISA^2 programme) established by Decision (EU) 2015/2240 of the European Parliament and of the Council,[6] subject to the

programme's available resources, eligibility and prioritisation criteria.

(76) Since the objectives of this Directive, namely ensuring that NCAs have the necessary guarantees of independence, resources, and enforcement and fining powers to be able to effectively apply Articles 101 and 102 TFEU and national competition law in parallel to Articles 101 and 102 TFEU, and ensuring the effective functioning of the internal market and the European Competition Network, cannot be sufficiently achieved by the Member States, but can rather by reason of the requisite effectiveness and uniformity in the application of Articles 101 and 102 TFEU be better achieved at Union level in particular in view of the territorial scope of the Directive, the Union may adopt measures in accordance with the principle of subsidiarity as set out on Article 5 of the Treaty on European Union. In accordance with the principle of proportionality, as set out in that Article, this Directive does not go beyond what is necessary to achieve those objectives.

(77) In accordance with the Joint Political Declaration of 28 September 2011 of Member States and the Commission on explanatory documents,[7] Member States have undertaken to accompany, in justified cases, the notification of their transposition measures with one or more documents explaining the relationship between the components of a directive and the corresponding parts of national transposition instruments. With regard to this Directive, the transmission of such documents is considered to be justified,

NOTES

[1] OJ C345, 13.10.2017, p 70.

[2] Position of the European Parliament of 14 November 2018 (not yet published in the Official Journal) and decision of the Council of 4 December 2018.

[3] Council Regulation (EC) No 1/2003 of 16 December 2002 on the implementation of the rules on competition laid down in Articles 81 and 82 of the Treaty (OJ L1, 4.1.2003, p 1).

[4] Directive 2014/104/EU of the European Parliament and of the Council of 26 November 2014 on certain rules governing actions for damages under national law for infringements of the competition law provisions of the Member States and of the European Union (OJ L349, 5.12.2014, p 1).

[5] Council Framework Decision 2005/214/JHA of 24 February 2005 on the application of the principle of mutual recognition to financial penalties (OJ L76, 22.3.2005, p 16).

[6] Decision (EU) 2015/2240 of the European Parliament and of the Council of 25 November 2015 establishing a programme on interoperability solutions and common frameworks for European public administrations, businesses and citizens (ISA[2] programme) as a means for modernising the public sector (OJ L318, 4.12.2015, p 1).

[7] OJ C369, 17.12.2011, p 14.

HAVE ADOPTED THIS DIRECTIVE:

CHAPTER I SUBJECT MATTER, SCOPE AND DEFINITIONS

[4.501]

Article 1 Subject matter and scope

1. This Directive sets out certain rules to ensure that national competition authorities have the necessary guarantees of independence, resources, and enforcement and fining powers to be able to effectively apply Articles 101 and 102 TFEU so that competition in the internal market is not distorted and that consumers and undertakings are not put at a disadvantage by national laws and measures which prevent national competition authorities from being effective enforcers.

2. This Directive covers the application of Articles 101 and 102 TFEU and the parallel application of national competition law to the same case. As regards Article 31(3) and (4) of this Directive, this Directive also covers the application of national competition law on a stand-alone basis.

3. This Directive sets out certain rules on mutual assistance to safeguard the smooth functioning of the internal market and the smooth functioning of the system of close cooperation within the European Competition Network.

[4.502]

Article 2 Definitions

1. For the purposes of this Directive, the following definitions apply:

(1) 'national competition authority' means an authority designated by a Member State pursuant to Article 35 of Regulation (EC) No 1/2003 as being responsible for the application of Articles 101 and 102 TFEU; Member States may designate one or more administrative competition authorities (national administrative competition authorities), as well as judicial authorities (national judicial competition authorities);

(2) 'national administrative competition authority' means an administrative authority designated by a Member State to carry out all or some of the functions of a national competition authority;

(3) 'national judicial competition authority' means a judicial authority designated by a Member State to carry out some of the functions of a national competition authority;

(4) 'competition authority' means a national competition authority, the Commission or both, as the context may require;

(5) 'European Competition Network' means the network of public authorities formed by the national competition authorities and the Commission to provide a forum for discussion and cooperation as regards the application and enforcement of Articles 101 and 102 TFEU;

(6) 'national competition law' means provisions of national law that predominantly pursue the same objective as Articles 101 and 102 TFEU and that are applied to the same case and in parallel to Union competition law pursuant to Article 3(1) of Regulation (EC) No 1/2003, as well as provisions of national law that predominantly pursue the same objective as Articles 101 and 102 TFEU and that are applied on a stand-alone basis as regards Article 31(3) and (4) of this Directive, excluding provisions of national law which impose criminal penalties on natural persons;

(7) 'national court' means a court or tribunal of a Member State within the meaning of Article 267 TFEU;

(8) 'review court' means a national court that is empowered by ordinary means of appeal to review decisions of a national competition authority or to review judgments pronouncing on those decisions, irrespective of whether that court itself has the power to find an infringement of competition law;

(9) 'enforcement proceedings' means the proceedings before a competition authority for the application of Article 101 or 102 TFEU, until that competition authority has closed such proceedings by taking a decision referred to in Article 10, 12 or 13 of this Directive in the case of a national competition authority, or by taking a decision referred to in Article 7, 9 or 10 of Regulation (EC) No 1/2003 in the case of the Commission, or as long as the competition authority has not concluded that there are no grounds for further action on its part;

(10) 'undertaking' as referred to in Articles 101 and 102 TFEU, means any entity engaged in an economic activity, regardless of its legal status and the way in which it is financed;

(11) 'cartel' means an agreement or concerted practice between two or more competitors aimed at coordinating their competitive behaviour on the market or influencing the relevant parameters of competition through practices such as, but not limited to, the fixing or coordination of purchase or selling prices or other trading conditions, including in relation to intellectual property rights, the allocation of production or sales quotas, the sharing of markets and customers, including bid-rigging, restrictions of imports or exports or anti-competitive actions against other competitors;

(12) 'secret cartel' means a cartel, the existence of which is partially or wholly concealed;

(13) 'immunity from fines' means an exemption from fines that would otherwise be imposed on an undertaking for its participation in a secret cartel, in order to reward it for its cooperation with a competition authority in the framework of a leniency programme;

(14) 'reduction of fines' means a reduction in the amount of the fine that would otherwise be imposed on an undertaking for its participation in a secret cartel, in order to reward it for its cooperation with a competition authority in the framework of a leniency programme;

(15) 'leniency' means both immunity from fines and reduction of fines;

(16) 'leniency programme' means a programme concerning the application of Article 101 TFEU or a corresponding provision under national competition law on the basis of which a participant in a secret cartel, independently of the other undertakings involved in the cartel, cooperates with an investigation of the competition authority, by voluntarily providing presentations regarding that participant's knowledge of, and role in, the cartel in return for which that participant receives, by decision or by a discontinuation of proceedings, immunity from, or a reduction of, fines for its involvement in the cartel;

(17) 'leniency statement' means an oral or written presentation voluntarily provided by, or on behalf of, an undertaking or a natural person to a competition authority or a record thereof, describing the knowledge of that undertaking or natural person of a cartel and describing its role therein, which presentation was drawn up specifically for submission to the competition authority with a view to obtaining immunity or a reduction of fines under a leniency programme, not including evidence that exists irrespective of the enforcement proceedings, whether or not such information is in the file of a competition authority, namely pre-existing information;

(18) 'settlement submission' means a voluntary presentation by, or on behalf of, an undertaking to a competition authority, describing the undertaking's acknowledgement of, or its renunciation to dispute, its participation in an infringement of Article 101 or 102 TFEU or national competition law and its responsibility for that infringement, which was drawn up specifically to enable the competition authority to apply a simplified or expedited procedure;

(19) 'applicant' means an undertaking that applies for immunity from, or a reduction of, fines under a leniency programme;

(20) 'applicant authority' means a national competition authority which makes a request for mutual assistance as referred to in Article 24, 25, 26, 27 or 28;

(21) 'requested authority' means a national competition authority which receives a request for mutual assistance and in the case of a request for assistance as referred to in Article 25, 26, 27 or 28 means the competent public body which has principal responsibility for the enforcement of such decisions under national laws, regulations and administrative practice;

(22) 'final decision' means a decision that cannot be, or that can no longer be, appealed by ordinary means.

2. All references to the application or infringement of Articles 101 and 102 TFEU in this Directive shall be understood as including the parallel application of national competition law to the same case.

CHAPTER II FUNDAMENTAL RIGHTS

[4.503]

Article 3 Safeguards

1. Proceedings concerning infringements of Article 101 or 102 TFEU, including the exercise of the powers referred to in this Directive by national competition authorities, shall comply with general principles of Union law and the Charter of Fundamental Rights of the European Union.

2. Member States shall ensure that the exercise of the powers referred to in paragraph 1 is subject to appropriate safeguards in respect of the undertakings' rights of defence, including the right to be heard and the right to an effective remedy before a tribunal.

3. Member States shall ensure that enforcement proceedings of national competition authorities are conducted within a reasonable timeframe. Member States shall ensure that, prior to taking a decision pursuant to Article 10 of this Directive, national competition authorities adopt a statement of objections.

CHAPTER III INDEPENDENCE AND RESOURCES

[4.504]

Article 4 Independence

1. To guarantee the independence of national administrative competition authorities when applying Articles 101 and 102 TFEU, Member States shall ensure that such authorities perform their duties and exercise their powers impartially and in the interests of the effective and uniform application of those provisions, subject to proportionate accountability requirements and without prejudice to close cooperation between competition authorities in the European Competition Network.

2. In particular, Member States shall at a minimum ensure that the staff and persons who take decisions exercising the powers in Articles 10 to 13 and Article 16 of this Directive in national administrative competition authorities:

(a) are able to perform their duties and to exercise their powers for the application of Articles 101 and 102 TFEU independently from political and other external influence;

(b) neither seek nor take any instructions from government or any other public or private entity when carrying out their duties and exercising their powers for the application of Articles 101 and 102 TFEU, without prejudice to the right of a government of a Member State, where applicable, to issue general policy rules that are not related to sector inquiries or specific enforcement proceedings; and

(c) refrain from taking any action which is incompatible with the performance of their duties and/or with the exercise of their powers for the application of Articles 101 and 102 TFEU and are subject to procedures that ensure that, for a reasonable period after leaving office, they refrain from dealing with enforcement proceedings that could give rise to conflicts of interest.

3. The persons who take decisions exercising the powers in Articles 10 to 13 and Article 16 of this Directive in national administrative competition authorities shall not be dismissed from such authorities for reasons related to the proper performance of their duties or to the proper exercise of their powers for the application of Articles 101 and 102 TFEU, as referred to in Article 5(2) of this Directive. They may be dismissed only if they no longer fulfil the conditions required for the performance of their duties or if they have been found guilty of serious misconduct under national law. The conditions required for the performance of their duties, and what constitutes serious misconduct, shall be laid down in advance in national law, taking into account the need to ensure effective enforcement.

4. Member States shall ensure that the members of the decision-making body of national administrative competition authorities are selected, recruited or appointed according to clear and transparent procedures laid down in advance in national law.

5. National administrative competition authorities shall have the power to set their priorities for carrying out the tasks for the application of Articles 101 and 102 TFEU as referred to in Article 5(2) of this Directive. To the extent that national administrative competition authorities are obliged to consider formal complaints, those authorities shall have the power to reject such complaints on the grounds that they do not consider such complaints to be an enforcement priority. This is without prejudice to the power of national administrative competition authorities to reject complaints on other grounds defined by national law.

[4.505]

Article 5 Resources

1. Member States shall ensure at a minimum that national competition authorities have a sufficient number of qualified staff and sufficient financial, technical and technological resources that are necessary for the effective performance of their duties, and for the effective exercise of their powers for the application of Articles 101 and 102 TFEU as set out in paragraph 2 of this Article.

2. For the purposes of paragraph 1 national competition authorities shall be able, at a minimum, to conduct investigations with a view to applying Articles 101 and 102 TFEU, to adopt decisions applying those provisions on the basis of Article 5 of Regulation (EC) No 1/2003; and to cooperate closely in the European Competition Network with a view to ensuring the effective and uniform application of Articles 101 and 102 TFEU. To the extent provided for under national law, national competition authorities shall also be able to advise public institutions and bodies, where appropriate, on legislative, regulatory and administrative measures which may have an impact on competition in the internal market as well as promote public awareness of Articles 101 and 102 TFEU.

3. Without prejudice to national budgetary rules and procedures, Member States shall ensure that national competition authorities are granted independence in the spending of the allocated budget for the purpose of carrying out their duties as set out in paragraph 2.

4. Member States shall ensure that national administrative competition authorities submit periodic reports on their activities and their resources to a governmental or parliamentary body. Member States shall ensure that such reports include information about the appointments and dismissals of members of the decision-making body, the amount of resources that were allocated in the relevant year, and any changes in that amount compared to previous years. Such reports shall be made publicly available.

CHAPTER IV POWERS

[4.506]

Article 6 Power to inspect business premises

1. Member States shall ensure that national administrative competition authorities are able to conduct all necessary unannounced inspections of undertakings and associations of undertakings for the application of Articles 101 and 102 TFEU. Member States shall ensure that the officials and other accompanying persons authorised or appointed by national competition authorities to conduct such inspections are, at a minimum, empowered:

(a) to enter any premises, land, and means of transport of undertakings and associations of undertakings;

(b) to examine the books and other records related to the business irrespective of the medium on which they are stored, and to have the right to access any information which is accessible to the entity subject to the inspection;

(c) to take or obtain, in any form, copies of or extracts from such books or records and, where they consider it appropriate, to continue making such searches for information and the selection of copies or extracts at the premises of the national competition authorities or at any other designated premises;

(d) to seal any business premises and books or records for the period and to the extent necessary for the inspection;

(e) to ask any representative or member of staff of the undertaking or association of undertakings for explanations on facts or documents relating to the subject matter and purpose of the inspection and to record the answers.

2. Member States shall ensure that undertakings and associations of undertakings are required to submit to the inspections referred to in paragraph 1. Member States shall also ensure that, where an undertaking or association of undertakings opposes an inspection that has been ordered by a national administrative competition authority and/or that has been authorised by a national judicial authority, national competition authorities are able to obtain the necessary assistance of the police or of an equivalent enforcement authority so as to enable them to conduct the inspection. Such assistance may also be obtained as a precautionary measure.

3. This Article is without prejudice to requirements under national law for the prior authorisation of such inspections by a national judicial authority.

[4.507]

Article 7 Power to inspect other premises

1. Member States shall ensure that if a reasonable suspicion exists that books or other records related to the business and to the subject matter of the inspection, which may be relevant to prove an infringement of Article 101 or Article 102 TFEU, are being kept in any premises, land or means of transport other than those referred to in point (a) of Article 6(1) of this Directive, including the homes of directors, managers, and other members of staff of undertakings or associations of undertakings, national administrative competition authorities are able to conduct unannounced inspections in such premises, land and means of transport.

2. Such inspections shall not be carried out without the prior authorisation of a national judicial authority.

3. Member States shall ensure that the officials and other accompanying persons authorised or appointed by national competition authorities to conduct an inspection in accordance with paragraph 1 of this Article at a minimum have the powers set out in points (a), (b) and (c) of Article 6(1) and Article 6(2).

[4.508]

Article 8 Requests for information

Member States shall ensure that national administrative competition authorities may require undertakings and associations of undertakings to provide all necessary information for the application of Articles 101 and 102 TFEU within a specified and reasonable time limit. Such requests for information shall be proportionate and not compel the addressees of the requests to admit an infringement of Articles 101 and 102 TFEU. The obligation to provide all necessary information covers information which is accessible to such undertakings or associations of undertakings. National competition authorities shall also be empowered to require any other natural or legal persons to provide information that may be relevant for the application of Articles 101 and 102 TFEU within a specified and reasonable time limit.

[4.509]

Article 9 Interviews

Member States shall ensure that national administrative competition authorities at a minimum are empowered to summon any representative of an undertaking or association of undertakings, any representative of other legal persons, and any natural person, where such representative or person may possess information relevant for the application of Articles 101 and 102 TFEU, to appear for an interview.

[4.510]

Article 10 Finding and termination of infringement

1. Member States shall ensure that where national competition authorities find an infringement of Article 101 or 102 TFEU, they may by decision require the undertakings and associations of undertakings concerned to bring that infringement to an end. For that purpose, they may impose any behavioural or structural remedies which are proportionate to the infringement committed and necessary to bring the infringement effectively to an end. When choosing between two equally effective remedies, national competition authorities shall choose the remedy that is least burdensome for the undertaking, in line with the principle of proportionality.

Member States shall ensure that national competition authorities are empowered to find that an infringement of Article 101 or 102 TFEU has been committed in the past.

2. Where, having informed the Commission in accordance with Article 11(3) of Regulation (EC) No 1/2003, national competition authorities decide that there are no grounds to continue enforcement proceedings and as a result close those enforcement proceedings, Member States shall ensure that those national competition authorities inform the Commission accordingly.

[4.511]

Article 11 Interim measures

1. Member States shall ensure that national competition authorities are empowered to act on their own initiative to order by decision the imposition of interim measures on undertakings and associations of undertakings, at least in cases where there is urgency due to the risk of serious and irreparable harm to competition, on the basis of a prima facie finding of an infringement of Article 101 or Article 102 TFEU. Such a decision shall be proportionate and shall apply either for a specified time period, which may be renewed in so far that is necessary and appropriate, or until the final decision is taken. The national competition authorities shall inform the European Competition Network of the imposition of those interim measures.

2. Member States shall ensure that the legality, including the proportionality, of the interim measures referred to in paragraph 1 can be reviewed in expedited appeal procedures.

[4.512]

Article 12 Commitments

1. Member States shall ensure that, in enforcement proceedings initiated with a view to adopting a decision requiring that an infringement of Article 101 or Article 102 TFEU be brought to an end, national competition authorities may, after formally or informally seeking the views of market participants, by decision make commitments offered by undertakings or associations of undertakings binding, where those commitments meet the concerns expressed by the national competition authorities. Such a decision may be adopted for a specified period, and shall conclude that there are no longer grounds for action by the national competition authority concerned.
2. Member States shall ensure that national competition authorities have effective powers to monitor the implementation of the commitments referred to in paragraph 1.
3. Member States shall ensure that national competition authorities are able to reopen enforcement proceedings where there have been material changes to any of the facts on which a decision referred to in paragraph 1 was based, where undertakings or associations of undertakings act contrary to their commitments, or where a decision referred to in paragraph 1 was based on incomplete, incorrect or misleading information provided by the parties.

CHAPTER V FINES AND PERIODIC PENALTY PAYMENTS

[4.513]

Article 13 Fines on undertakings and associations of undertakings

1. Member States shall ensure that national administrative competition authorities may either impose by decision in their own enforcement proceedings, or request in non-criminal judicial proceedings, the imposition of effective, proportionate and dissuasive fines on undertakings and associations of undertakings where, intentionally or negligently, they infringe Article 101 or 102 TFEU.
2. Member States shall ensure at a minimum that national administrative competition authorities may either impose by decision in their own enforcement proceedings, or, request in non-criminal judicial proceedings, the imposition of effective, proportionate and dissuasive fines on undertakings and associations of undertakings. Such fines shall be determined in proportion to their total worldwide turnover, where intentionally or negligently:
   (a) they fail to comply with an inspection as referred to in Article 6(2);
   (b) seals affixed by the officials or other accompanying persons authorised or appointed by the national competition authorities as referred to in point (d) of Article 6(1)) have been broken;
   (c) in response to a question referred to in point (e) of Article 6(1), they give an incorrect, misleading answer, fail or refuse to provide a complete answer;
   (d) they supply incorrect, incomplete or misleading information in response to a request referred to in Article 8 or do not supply information within the specified time limit;
   (e) they fail to appear at an interview referred to in Article 9;
   (f) they fail to comply with a decision referred to in Articles 10, 11 and 12.
3. Member States shall ensure that the proceedings referred to in paragraphs 1 and 2 allow for the imposition of effective, proportionate and dissuasive fines.
4. This Article is without prejudice to national laws allowing for the imposition of sanctions in criminal judicial proceedings provided that the application of such laws does not affect the effective and uniform enforcement of Articles 101 and 102 TFEU.
5. Member States shall ensure that for the purpose of imposing fines on parent companies and legal and economic successors of undertakings, the notion of undertaking applies.

[4.514]

Article 14 Calculation of fines

1. Member States shall ensure that national competition authorities have regard both to the gravity and to the duration of the infringement when determining the amount of the fine to be imposed for an infringement of Article 101 or 102 TFEU.
2. Member States shall ensure that national competition authorities may consider compensation paid as a result of a consensual settlement when determining the amount of the fine to be imposed for an infringement of Article 101 or 102 TFEU, in accordance with Article 18(3) of Directive 2014/104/EU.
3. Member States shall ensure that, where a fine for an infringement of Article 101 or 102 TFEU is imposed on an association of undertakings taking account of the turnover of its members and the association is not solvent, the association is obliged to call for contributions from its members to cover the amount of the fine.
4. Member States shall ensure that, where contributions referred to in paragraph 3 have not been made in full to the association of undertakings within the time limit fixed by national competition authorities, national competition authorities may require the payment of the fine directly by any of the undertakings whose representatives were members of the decision-making bodies of that association. Where necessary to ensure full payment of the fine, after the national competition authorities have required payment from such undertakings, they may also require the payment of the outstanding amount of the fine by any of the members of the association which were active on the market on which the infringement occurred. However, payment under this paragraph shall not be required from undertakings which show that they did not implement the infringing decision of the association and either were not aware of its existence or have actively distanced themselves from it before the investigation started.

[4.515]

Article 15 Maximum amount of the fine

1. Member States shall ensure that the maximum amount of the fine that national competition authorities may impose on each undertaking or association of undertakings participating in an infringement of Article 101 or 102 TFEU is not less than 10% of the total worldwide turnover of the undertaking or association of undertakings in the business year preceding the decision referred to in Article 13(1).

2. Where an infringement by an association of undertakings relates to the activities of its members, the maximum amount of the fine shall be not less than 10% of the sum of the total worldwide turnover of each member active on the market affected by the infringement of the association. However, the financial liability of each undertaking in respect of the payment of the fine shall not exceed the maximum amount set in accordance with paragraph 1.

[4.516]
Article 16 Periodic penalty payments
1. Member States shall ensure that national administrative competition authorities may by decision impose effective, proportionate and dissuasive periodic penalty payments on undertakings and associations of undertakings. Such periodic penalty payments shall be determined in proportion to the average daily total worldwide turnover of such undertakings or associations of undertakings in the preceding business year per day and calculated from the date appointed by that decision in order to compel those undertakings or associations of undertakings at least:
(a) to supply complete and correct information in response to a request referred to in Article 8,
(b) to appear at an interview referred to in Article 9.
2. Member States shall ensure that national competition authorities may by decision impose effective, proportionate and dissuasive periodic penalty payments on undertakings and associations of undertakings. Such periodic penalty payments shall be determined in proportion to the average daily total worldwide turnover of such undertakings or associations of undertakings in the preceding business year per day and calculated from the date appointed by that decision in order to compel them at least:
(a) to submit to an inspection as referred to in Article 6(2);
(b) to comply with a decision referred to in Articles 10, 11 and 12.

CHAPTER VI LENIENCY PROGRAMMES FOR SECRET CARTELS

[4.517]
Article 17 Immunity from fines
1. Member States shall ensure that national competition authorities have in place leniency programmes that enable them to grant immunity from fines to undertakings for disclosing their participation in secret cartels. This is without prejudice to national competition authorities having in place leniency programmes for infringements other than secret cartels or leniency programmes that enable them to grant immunity from fines to natural persons.
2. Member States shall ensure that immunity from fines is granted only where the applicant:
(a) fulfils the conditions laid down in Article 19;
(b) discloses its participation in a secret cartel; and
(c) is the first to submit evidence which:
(i) at the time the national competition authority receives the application, enables the national competition authority to carry out a targeted inspection in connection with the secret cartel, provided that the national competition authority did not yet have in its possession sufficient evidence to carry out such an inspection or had not already carried out such an inspection; or
(ii) in the national competition authority's view, is sufficient for it to find an infringement covered by the leniency programme, provided that the authority did not yet have in its possession sufficient evidence to find such an infringement and that no other undertaking previously qualified for immunity from fines under point (i) in relation to that secret cartel.
3. Member States shall ensure that all undertakings are eligible for immunity from fines, with the exception of undertakings that have taken steps to coerce other undertakings to join a secret cartel or to remain in it.
4. Member States shall ensure that national competition authorities inform the applicant of whether or not it has been granted conditional immunity from fines. The applicant may request that it be informed by the national competition authority of the result of its application in writing. In cases where the national competition authority rejects an application for immunity from fines, the applicant concerned may request that national competition authority to consider its application as an application for reduction of fines.

[4.518]
Article 18 Reduction of fines
1. Member States shall ensure that national competition authorities have in place leniency programmes that enable them to grant a reduction of fines to undertakings which do not qualify for immunity from fines. This is without prejudice to national competition authorities having in place leniency programmes for infringements other than secret cartels or leniency programmes that enable them to grant a reduction of fines to natural persons.
2. Member States shall ensure that a reduction of fines is granted only if the applicant:
(a) fulfils the conditions laid down in Article 19;
(b) discloses its participation in a secret cartel; and
(c) submits evidence of the alleged secret cartel which represents significant added value for the purpose of proving an infringement covered by the leniency programme, relative to the evidence already in the national competition authority's possession at the time of the application.
3. Member States shall ensure that if the applicant submits compelling evidence which the national competition authority uses to prove additional facts which lead to an increase in fines as compared to the fines that would otherwise have been imposed on the participants in the secret cartel, the national competition authority shall not take such additional facts into account when setting any fine to be imposed on the applicant for reduction of fines which provided this evidence.

[4.519]
Article 19 General conditions for leniency
Member States shall ensure that, in order to qualify for leniency for participation in secret cartels, the applicant is required to satisfy the following conditions:

(a) it ended its involvement in the alleged secret cartel at the latest immediately following its leniency application, except for what would, in the competent national competition authority's view, be reasonably necessary to preserve the integrity of its investigation;

(b) it cooperates genuinely, fully, on a continuous basis and expeditiously with the national competition authority from the time of its application until the authority has closed its enforcement proceedings against all parties under investigation by adopting a decision or has otherwise terminated its enforcement proceedings; such cooperation includes:

 (i) providing the national competition authority promptly with all relevant information and evidence relating to the alleged secret cartel that comes into the applicant's possession or is accessible to it, in particular:

 — the name and address of the applicant,
 — the names of all other undertakings that participate or participated in the alleged secret cartel,
 — a detailed description of the alleged secret cartel, including the affected products, the affected territories, the duration, and the nature of the alleged secret cartel conduct,
 — information on any past or possible future leniency applications made to any other competition authorities or competition authorities of third countries in relation to the alleged secret cartel;

 (ii) remaining at the national competition authority's disposal to answer any request that may contribute to the establishment of facts;

 (iii) making directors, managers and other members of staff available for interviews with the national competition authority and making reasonable efforts to make former directors, managers and other members of staff available for interviews with the national competition authority;

 (iv) not destroying, falsifying or concealing relevant information or evidence; and

 (v) not disclosing the fact of, or any of the content of, its leniency application before the national competition authority has issued objections in the enforcement proceedings before it, unless otherwise agreed; and

(c) during the contemplation of making a leniency application to the national competition authority it must not have:

 (i) destroyed, falsified or concealed evidence of the alleged secret cartel; or

 (ii) disclosed the fact of, or any of the content of, its contemplated application, other than to any other competition authorities or competition authorities of third countries.

[4.520]

Article 20 Form of leniency statements

1. Member States shall ensure that applicants are able to submit leniency statements, in relation to full or summary applications, in writing, and shall ensure that national competition authorities also have a system in place that enables them to accept such statements either in oral form or by other means that permit applicants not to take possession, custody, or control of such submitted statements.

2. If requested by the applicant, the national competition authority shall acknowledge the receipt of the full or summary application in writing, stating the date and time of receipt.

3. Applicants shall be able to submit leniency statements in relation to full or summary applications in the official language, or one of the official languages, of the Member State of the national competition authority concerned, or in another official language of the Union bilaterally agreed between the national competition authority and the applicant.

[4.521]

Article 21 Markers for applications for immunity from fines

1. Member States shall ensure that undertakings wishing to apply for immunity from fines may be initially granted a place in the queue for leniency, where they so request, for a period specified on a case-by-case basis by the national competition authority, in order for the applicant to gather the necessary information and evidence in order to meet the relevant evidential threshold for immunity from fines.

2. Member States shall ensure that national competition authorities have discretion whether or not to grant the request pursuant to paragraph 1.

An undertaking submitting such a request shall provide information, where available, to the national competition authority, such as:

 (a) the name and address of the applicant;
 (b) the basis for the concern which led to the request;
 (c) the names of all other undertakings that participate or participated in the alleged secret cartel;
 (d) the affected products and territories;
 (e) the duration and the nature of the alleged secret cartel conduct;
 (f) information on any past or possible future leniency applications made to any other competition authorities or competition authorities of third countries in relation to the alleged secret cartel.

3. Member States shall ensure that any information and evidence provided by the applicant within the period specified in accordance with paragraph 1 is deemed to have been submitted at the time of the initial request.

4. The applicant shall be able to submit a request pursuant to paragraph 1 in the official language or one of the official languages of the Member State of the national competition authority concerned or in another official language of the Union bilaterally agreed between the national competition authority and the applicant.

5. Member States may also provide for the possibility for undertakings wishing to make an application for the reduction of fines to request initially a place in the queue for leniency.

[4.522]

Article 22 Summary applications

1. Member States shall ensure that national competition authorities accept summary applications from applicants that have applied to the Commission for leniency, either by applying for a marker or by submitting a full application in relation to the same alleged secret cartel, provided that those applications cover more than three Member States as affected territories.

2. Summary applications shall consist of a short description of each of the following:

(a) the name and address of the applicant;
(b) the names of other parties to the alleged secret cartel;
(c) the affected products and territories;
(d) the duration and the nature of the alleged secret cartel conduct;
(e) the Member State(s) where the evidence of the alleged secret cartel is likely to be located; and
(f) information on any past or possible future leniency applications made to any other competition authorities or competition authorities of third countries in relation to the alleged secret cartel.

3. Where the Commission receives a full application and national competition authorities receive summary applications in relation to the same alleged cartel, the Commission shall be the main interlocutor of the applicant, in the period before clarity has been gained as to whether the Commission intends to pursue the case in whole or in part, in particular in providing instructions to the applicant on the conduct of any further internal investigations. In this period, the Commission shall inform the national competition authorities concerned about the state of play at their request.

Member States shall ensure that national competition authorities may request the applicant to provide specific clarifications only regarding the items set out in paragraph 2 before they require the submission of a full application pursuant to paragraph 5.

4. Member States shall ensure that national competition authorities which receive summary applications verify whether they have already received a summary or full application from another applicant in relation to the same alleged secret cartel at the time of receipt of such applications. If a national competition authority has not received such an application from another applicant and considers the summary application to fulfil the requirements of paragraph 2, it shall inform the applicant accordingly.

5. Member States shall ensure that, once the Commission has informed the national competition authorities concerned that it does not intend to pursue the case in whole or in part, applicants are given the opportunity to submit full applications to the national competition authorities concerned. Only in exceptional circumstances, when strictly necessary for case delineation or case allocation, may a national competition authority request the applicant to submit the full application before the Commission has informed the national competition authorities concerned that it does not intend to pursue the case in whole or in part. The national competition authorities shall have the power to specify a reasonable period within which the applicant is to submit the full application together with the corresponding evidence and information. This is without prejudice to the right of the applicant to voluntarily submit a full application at an earlier stage.

6. Member States shall ensure that if the applicant submits the full application in accordance with paragraph 5, within the period specified by the national competition authority, the full application is deemed to have been submitted at the time of the summary application, provided that the summary application covers the same affected product(s) and territory(ies), as well as the same duration of the alleged secret cartel, as the leniency application filed with the Commission, which may have been updated.

[4.523]

Article 23 Interplay between applications for immunity from fines and sanctions on natural persons

1. Member States shall ensure that current and former directors, managers and other members of staff of applicants for immunity from fines to competition authorities are fully protected from sanctions imposed in administrative and non-criminal judicial proceedings, in relation to their involvement in the secret cartel covered by the application for immunity from fines, for violations of national laws that pursue predominantly the same objectives to those pursued by Article 101 TFEU, if:

(a) the application for immunity from fines of the undertaking to the competition authority pursuing the case fulfils the requirements set out in points (b) and (c) of Article 17(2);
(b) those current and former directors, managers and other members of staff actively cooperate in this respect with the competition authority pursuing the case; and
(c) the application for immunity from fines of the undertaking predates the time when those current or former directors, managers and other members of staff concerned were made aware by the competent authorities of the Member States of the proceedings leading to the imposition of sanctions referred to in this paragraph.

2. Member States shall ensure that current and former directors, managers and other members of staff of applicants for immunity from fines to competition authorities are protected from sanctions imposed in criminal proceedings, in relation to their involvement in the secret cartel covered by the application for immunity from fines, for violations of national laws that pursue predominantly the same objectives to those pursued by Article 101 TFEU, if they meet the conditions set out in paragraph 1 and actively cooperate with the competent prosecuting authority. If the condition of cooperation with the competent prosecuting authority is not fulfilled, that competent prosecuting authority may proceed with the investigation.

3. In order to ensure conformity with the existing basic principles of their legal system, by way of derogation from paragraph 2, Member States may provide that the competent authorities are able not to impose a sanction or only to mitigate the sanction to be imposed in criminal proceedings to the extent that the contribution of the individuals, referred to in paragraph 2, to the detection and investigation of the secret cartel outweighs the interest in prosecuting and/or sanctioning those individuals.

4. In order to allow the protection referred to in paragraphs 1, 2 and 3 to function in situations where more than one jurisdiction is involved, Member States shall provide that in cases where the competent sanctioning or prosecuting authority is in a different jurisdiction than that of the jurisdiction of the competition authority pursuing the case, the necessary contacts between them shall be ensured by the national competition authority of the jurisdiction of the competent sanctioning or prosecuting authority.

5. This Article is without prejudice to the right of victims who have suffered harm caused by an infringement of competition law to claim full compensation for that harm, in accordance with Directive 2014/104/EU.

CHAPTER VII MUTUAL ASSISTANCE

[4.524]

Article 24 Cooperation between national competition authorities

1. Member States shall ensure that where national administrative competition authorities carry out an inspection or interview on behalf of and for the account of other national competition authorities pursuant to Article 22 of Regulation (EC) No 1/2003, officials and other accompanying persons authorised or appointed by the applicant national competition authority shall be permitted to attend and actively assist the requested national competition authority, under the supervision of the officials of the requested national competition authority, in the inspection or interview when the requested national competition authority exercises the powers referred to in Articles 6, 7 and 9 of this Directive.

2. Member States shall ensure that national administrative competition authorities are empowered in their own territory to exercise the powers referred to in Articles 6 to 9 of this Directive, in accordance with their national law on behalf of and for the account of other national competition authorities in order to establish whether there has been a failure by undertakings or associations of undertakings to comply with the investigative measures and decisions of the applicant national competition authority, as referred to in Articles 6 and 8 to 12 of this Directive. The applicant national competition authority and the requested national competition authority shall have the power to exchange and to use information in evidence for this purpose, subject to the safeguards set out in Article 12 of Regulation (EC) No 1/2003.

[4.525]

Article 25 Requests for the notification of preliminary objections and other documents

Without prejudice to any other form of notification made by an applicant authority in accordance with the rules in force in its Member State, Member States shall ensure that at the request of the applicant authority, the requested authority shall notify to the addressee on behalf of the applicant authority:

(a) any preliminary objections to the alleged infringement of Article 101 or 102 TFEU and any decisions applying those Articles;

(b) any other procedural act adopted in the context of enforcement proceedings which should be notified in accordance with national law; and

(c) any other relevant documents related to the application of Article 101 or 102 TFEU, including documents which relate to the enforcement of decisions imposing fines or periodic penalty payments.

[4.526]

Article 26 Requests for the enforcement of decisions imposing fines or periodic penalty payments

1. Member States shall ensure that at the request of the applicant authority, the requested authority shall enforce decisions imposing fines or periodic penalty payments adopted in accordance with Articles 13 and 16 by the applicant authority. This shall apply only to the extent that, after having made reasonable efforts in its own territory, the applicant authority has ascertained that the undertaking or association of undertakings against which the fine or periodic penalty payment is enforceable does not have sufficient assets in the Member State of the applicant authority to enable recovery of such fine or periodic penalty.

2. For cases not covered by paragraph 1 of this Article, in particular cases where the undertaking or association of undertakings against which the fine or periodic penalty payment is enforceable is not established in the Member State of the applicant authority, Member States shall provide that the requested authority may enforce decisions imposing fines or periodic penalty payments adopted in accordance with Articles 13 and 16 by the applicant authority, where the applicant authority so requests.

Point (d) of Article 27(3) shall not apply for the purposes of this paragraph.

3. The applicant authority may only request the enforcement of a final decision.

4. Questions regarding limitation periods for the enforcement of fines or periodic penalty payments shall be governed by the national law of the Member State of the applicant authority.

[4.527]

Article 27 General principles of cooperation

1. Member States shall ensure that the requests as referred to in Articles 25 and 26 are executed by the requested authority in accordance with the national law of the Member State of the requested authority.

2. Requests referred to in Articles 25 and 26 shall be executed without undue delay by means of a uniform instrument which shall be accompanied by a copy of the act to be notified or enforced. Such uniform instrument shall indicate:

(a) the name, known address of the addressee, and any other relevant information for the identification of the addressee;

(b) a summary of the relevant facts and circumstances;

(c) a summary of the attached copy of the act to be notified or enforced;

(d) the name, address and other contact details of the requested authority; and

(e) the period within which notification or enforcement should be effected, such as statutory deadlines or limitation periods.

3. For requests referred to in Article 26, in addition to the requirements set out in paragraph 2 of this Article, the uniform instrument shall provide the following:

(a) information about the decision permitting enforcement in the Member State of the applicant authority;

Part 4 EU & Retained EU Materials

(b) the date when the decision became final;
(c) the amount of the fine or periodic penalty payment; and
(d) information showing the reasonable efforts made by the applicant authority to enforce the decision in its own territory.

4. The uniform instrument permitting enforcement by the requested authority shall constitute the sole basis for the enforcement measures taken by the requested authority, subject to the requirements of paragraph 2. It shall not be subject to any act of recognition, supplementing or replacement in the Member State of the requested authority. The requested authority shall take all necessary measures for the execution of this request, unless the requested authority invokes paragraph 6.

5. The applicant authority shall ensure that the uniform instrument is sent to the requested authority in the official language, or in one of the official languages, of the Member State of the requested authority, unless the requested authority and the applicant authority bilaterally agree on a case-by-case basis that the uniform instrument may be sent in another language. Where required under the national law of the Member State of the requested authority, the applicant authority shall provide a translation of the act to be notified or the decision permitting enforcement of the fine or periodic penalty payment into the official language, or into one of the official languages, of the Member State of the requested authority. This shall be without prejudice to the right of the requested authority and applicant authority to bilaterally agree, on a case-by-case basis, that such translation may be provided in a different language.

6. The requested authority shall not be obliged to execute a request referred to in Article 25 or 26 if:
(a) the request does not comply with the requirements of this Article; or
(b) the requested authority is able to demonstrate reasonable grounds showing how the execution of the request would be manifestly contrary to public policy in the Member State in which enforcement is sought.

If the requested authority intends to refuse a request for assistance referred to in Article 25 or 26 or requires additional information, it shall contact the applicant authority.

7. Member States shall ensure that, where requested by the requested authority, the applicant authority bears all reasonable additional costs in full, including translation, labour and administrative costs, in relation to actions taken as referred to in Article 24 or 25.

8. The requested authority may recover the full costs incurred in relation to actions taken as referred to in Article 26 from the fines or periodic penalty payments it has collected on behalf of the applicant authority, including translation, labour and administrative costs. If the requested authority is unsuccessful in collecting the fines or periodic penalty payments, it may request the applicant authority to bear the costs incurred.

Member States are free to provide that the requested authority may also recover the costs incurred in relation to the enforcement of such decisions from the undertaking against which the fine or periodic penalty payment is enforceable.

The requested authority shall recover the amounts due in the currency of its Member State, in accordance with the laws, regulations and administrative procedures or practices in that Member State.

The requested authority shall, if necessary, in accordance with its national law and practice, convert the fines or periodic penalty payments into the currency of the Member State of the requested authority at the rate of exchange applying on the date on which the fines or periodic penalty payments were imposed.

[4.528]

Article 28 Disputes concerning requests for notification or enforcement of decisions imposing fines or periodic penalty payments

1. Disputes shall fall within the competence of the competent bodies of the Member State of the applicant authority, and shall be governed by the law of that Member State, where they concern:
(a) the lawfulness of an act to be notified in accordance with Article 25 or a decision to be enforced in accordance with Article 26; and
(b) the lawfulness of the uniform instrument permitting enforcement in the Member State of the requested authority.

2. Disputes concerning the enforcement measures taken in the Member State of the requested authority or concerning the validity of a notification made by the requested authority shall fall within the competence of the competent bodies of the Member State of the requested authority and shall be governed by the law of that Member State.

CHAPTER VIII LIMITATION PERIODS

[4.529]

Article 29 Rules on limitation periods for the imposition of fines and periodic penalty payments

1. Member States shall ensure that the limitation periods for the imposition of fines or periodic penalty payments by the national competition authorities pursuant to Articles 13 and 16 shall be suspended or interrupted for the duration of enforcement proceedings before national competition authorities of other Member States or the Commission in respect of an infringement concerning the same agreement, decision of an association, concerted practice or other conduct prohibited by Article 101 or 102 TFEU.

The suspension of the limitation period shall start, or the interruption of the limitation period shall take place, from the notification of the first formal investigative measure to at least one undertaking subject to the enforcement proceedings. It shall apply to all undertakings or associations of undertakings which have participated in the infringement.

The suspension or interruption shall end on the day the competition authority concerned closes its enforcement proceedings by taking a decision referred to in Article 10, 12 or 13 of this Directive or pursuant to Article 7, 9 or 10 of Regulation (EC) No 1/2003, or has concluded that there are no grounds for further action on its part. The duration of such suspension or interruption is without prejudice to absolute limitation periods provided for under national law.

2. The limitation period for the imposition of fines or periodic penalty payments by a national competition authority shall be suspended or interrupted for as long as the decision of that national competition authority is the subject of proceedings pending before a review court.

3. The Commission shall ensure that the notification of the first formal investigative measure received from a national competition authority under Article 11(3) of Regulation (EC) No 1/2003 is made available to the other national competition authorities within the European Competition Network.

CHAPTER IX GENERAL PROVISIONS

[4.530]

Article 30 Role of national administrative competition authorities before national courts

1. Member States which designate both a national administrative competition authority and a national judicial competition authority as being responsible for the application of Articles 101 and 102 TFEU shall ensure that actions before the national judicial competition authority can be brought directly by the national administrative competition authority.

2. To the extent that national courts act in proceedings brought against decisions taken by national competition authorities exercising the powers referred to in Chapter IV and Articles 13 and 16 of this Directive for the application of Article 101 or 102 TFEU, including the enforcement of fines and periodic penalty payments imposed in that respect, Member States shall ensure that the national administrative competition authority is of its own right fully entitled to participate as appropriate as a prosecutor, defendant or respondent in those proceedings and to enjoy the same rights as such public parties to these proceedings.

3. The national administrative competition authority shall be empowered with the same rights as set out in paragraph 2 to appeal against:

(a) decisions of national courts pronouncing on decisions taken by national competition authorities as referred to in Chapter IV and Articles 13 and 16 of this Directive, concerning the application of Article 101 or 102 TFEU, including the enforcement of fines and periodic penalty payments imposed in that respect; and

(b) the refusal of a national judicial authority to grant prior authorisation of an inspection referred to in Articles 6 and 7 of this Directive, to the extent that such an authorisation is required.

[4.531]

Article 31 Access to file by parties and limitations on the use of information

1. Member States may provide that where a national competition authority requires a natural person to provide information on the basis of measures referred to in point (e) of Article 6(1), Article 8 or Article 9, that information shall not be used in evidence to impose sanctions on that natural person or on her or his close relatives.

2. Member States shall ensure that national competition authorities, their officials, staff and other persons working under the supervision of those authorities, do not disclose information that was acquired on the basis of the powers referred to in this Directive and that is of the kind covered by the obligation of professional secrecy, except where such disclosure is allowed under national law.

3. Member States shall ensure that access to leniency statements or settlement submissions is only granted to parties subject to the relevant proceedings and only for the purposes of exercising their rights of defence.

4. Member States shall ensure that the party having obtained access to the file of the enforcement proceedings of the national competition authorities may only use information taken from leniency statements and settlement submissions where necessary to exercise its rights of defence in proceedings before national courts in cases that are directly related to the case for which access has been granted, and only where such proceedings concern:

(a) the allocation between cartel participants of a fine imposed jointly and severally on them by a national competition authority; or

(b) the review of a decision by which a national competition authority found an infringement of Article 101 or 102 TFEU or national competition law provisions.

5. Member States shall ensure that the following categories of information obtained by a party during enforcement proceedings before a national competition authority shall not be used by that party in proceedings before national courts before the national competition authority has closed its enforcement proceedings with respect to all parties under investigation by adopting a decision referred to in Article 10 or Article 12 or otherwise has terminated its proceedings:

(a) information that was prepared by other natural or legal persons specifically for the enforcement proceedings of the national competition authority;

(b) information that the national competition authority has drawn up and sent to the parties in the course of its enforcement proceedings; and

(c) settlement submissions that have been withdrawn.

6. Member States shall ensure that leniency statements shall only be exchanged between national competition authorities pursuant to Article 12 of Regulation (EC) No 1/2003 either:

(a) with the consent of the applicant; or

(b) where the national competition authority receiving the leniency statement has also received a leniency application relating to the same infringement from the same applicant as the national competition authority transmitting the leniency statement, provided that, at the time the leniency statement is transmitted, it is not open to the applicant to withdraw the information which it has submitted to the national competition authority receiving the leniency statement.

7. The form in which leniency statements are submitted pursuant to Article 20 shall not affect the application of paragraphs 3 to 6 of this Article.

[4.532]

Article 32 Admissibility of evidence before national competition authorities

Member States shall ensure that the types of proof that are admissible as evidence before a national competition authority include documents, oral statements, electronic messages, recordings and all other objects containing information, irrespective of the form it takes and the medium on which information is stored.

[4.533]
Article 33 The operation of European Competition Network
1. The costs incurred by the Commission in connection with the maintenance and the development of the central information system of the European Competition Network (European Competition Network System) and in connection with cooperation within the European Competition Network shall be borne by the general budget of the Union within the limit of the available appropriations.
2. The European Competition Network shall be able to develop and, where appropriate, publish best practices and recommendations on matters such as independence, resources, powers, fines and mutual assistance.

[4.534]
Article 34 Transposition
1. Member States shall bring into force the laws, regulations and administrative provisions necessary to comply with this Directive by 4 February 2021. They shall immediately inform the Commission thereof.
When Member States adopt those measures, they shall contain a reference to this Directive or shall be accompanied by such reference on the occasion of their official publication. The methods of making such reference shall be laid down by Member States.
2. Member States shall communicate to the Commission the text of the main measures of national law which they adopt in the field covered by this Directive.

[4.535]
Article 35 Review
By 12 December 2024, the Commission shall present a report to the European Parliament and to the Council on the transposition and implementation of this Directive. When appropriate, the Commission may review this Directive and, if necessary, present a legislative proposal.

[4.536]
Article 36 Entry into force
This Directive shall enter into force on the twentieth day following that of its publication in the *Official Journal of the European Union*.

[4.537]
Article 37 Addressees
This Directive is addressed to the Member States.

DECLARATION OF THE COMMISSION

[4.538]
The Commission takes note of the text of Article 11 agreed by the European Parliament and the Council on interim measures.

Interim measures can be a key tool for competition authorities to ensure that competition is not harmed while an investigation is on-going.

With a view to enabling competition authorities to deal more effectively with developments in fast-moving markets, the Commission commits that it will undertake an analysis of whether there are means to simplify the adoption of interim measures within the European Competition Network within two years from the date of transposition of this Directive. The results of this will be presented to the European Parliament and the Council.

F. CONCENTRATIONS

1. GENERAL

COUNCIL REGULATION

(139/2004/EC)

of 20 January 2004

on the control of concentrations between undertakings

(The EC Merger Regulation)

[4.539]

NOTES

Date of publication in OJ: OJ L24, 29.1.2004, p 1.

Repeal of this Regulation in relation to the UK: this Regulation is repealed, in relation to the UK, by the Competition (Amendment etc) (EU Exit) Regulations 2019, SI 2019/93, reg 63, Sch 3, para 1, as from IP completion day (as defined in the European Union (Withdrawal Agreement) Act 2020, s 39) (for transitional provisions and savings in relation to the operation of the 2019 Regulations, see Sch 4 to those Regulations at **[7.69]** et seq).

Note: with effect from 1 December 2009, the Treaty establishing the European Community (the "EC Treaty") was replaced by the Treaty on the Functioning of the European Union. References in this document to provisions of the EC Treaty should be construed accordingly.

THE COUNCIL OF THE EUROPEAN UNION,

Having regard to the Treaty establishing the European Community, and in particular Articles 83 and 308 thereof,

Having regard to the proposal from the Commission,[1]

Having regard to the opinion of the European Parliament,[2]

Having regard to the opinion of the European Economic and Social Committee,[3]

Whereas:

(1) Council Regulation (EEC) No 4064/89 of 21 December 1989 on the control of concentrations between undertakings[4] *has been substantially amended. Since further amendments are to be made, it should be recast in the interest of clarity.*

(2) For the achievement of the aims of the Treaty, Article 3(1)(g) gives the Community the objective of instituting a system ensuring that competition in the internal market is not distorted. Article 4(1) of the Treaty provides that the activities of the Member States and the Community are to be conducted in accordance with the principle of an open market economy with free competition. These principles are essential for the further development of the internal market.

(3) The completion of the internal market and of economic and monetary union, the enlargement of the European Union and the lowering of international barriers to trade and investment will continue to result in major corporate reorganisations, particularly in the form of concentrations.

(4) Such reorganisations are to be welcomed to the extent that they are in line with the requirements of dynamic competition and capable of increasing the competitiveness of European industry, improving the conditions of growth and raising the standard of living in the Community.

(5) However, it should be ensured that the process of reorganisation does not result in lasting damage to competition; Community law must therefore include provisions governing those concentrations which may significantly impede effective competition in the common market or in a substantial part of it.

(6) A specific legal instrument is therefore necessary to permit effective control of all concentrations in terms of their effect on the structure of competition in the Community and to be the only instrument applicable to such concentrations. Regulation (EEC) No 4064/89 has allowed a Community policy to develop in this field. In the light of experience, however, that Regulation should now be recast into legislation designed to meet the challenges of a more integrated market and the future enlargement of the European Union. In accordance with the principles of subsidiarity and of proportionality as set out in Article 5 of the Treaty, this Regulation does not go beyond what is necessary in order to achieve the objective of ensuring that competition in the common market is not distorted, in accordance with the principle of an open market economy with free competition.

(7) Articles 81 and 82, while applicable, according to the case-law of the Court of Justice, to certain concentrations, are not sufficient to control all operations which may prove to be incompatible with the system of undistorted competition envisaged in the Treaty. This Regulation should therefore be based not only on Article 83 but, principally, on Article 308 of the Treaty, under which the Community may give itself the additional powers of action necessary for the attainment of its objectives, and also powers of action with regard to concentrations on the markets for agricultural products listed in Annex I to the Treaty.

(8) The provisions to be adopted in this Regulation should apply to significant structural changes, the impact of which on the market goes beyond the national borders of any one Member State. Such concentrations should, as a general rule, be reviewed exclusively at Community level, in application of a "one-stop shop" system and in

compliance with the principle of subsidiarity. Concentrations not covered by this Regulation come, in principle, within the jurisdiction of the Member States.

(9) The scope of application of this Regulation should be defined according to the geographical area of activity of the undertakings concerned and be limited by quantitative thresholds in order to cover those concentrations which have a Community dimension. The Commission should report to the Council on the implementation of the applicable thresholds and criteria so that the Council, acting in accordance with Article 202 of the Treaty, is in a position to review them regularly, as well as the rules regarding pre-notification referral, in the light of the experience gained; this requires statistical data to be provided by the Member States to the Commission to enable it to prepare such reports and possible proposals for amendments. The Commission's reports and proposals should be based on relevant information regularly provided by the Member States.

(10) A concentration with a Community dimension should be deemed to exist where the aggregate turnover of the undertakings concerned exceeds given thresholds; that is the case irrespective of whether or not the undertakings effecting the concentration have their seat or their principal fields of activity in the Community, provided they have substantial operations there.

(11) The rules governing the referral of concentrations from the Commission to Member States and from Member States to the Commission should operate as an effective corrective mechanism in the light of the principle of subsidiarity; these rules protect the competition interests of the Member States in an adequate manner and take due account of legal certainty and the "one-stop shop" principle.

(12) Concentrations may qualify for examination under a number of national merger control systems if they fall below the turnover thresholds referred to in this Regulation. Multiple notification of the same transaction increases legal uncertainty, effort and cost for undertakings and may lead to conflicting assessments. The system whereby concentrations may be referred to the Commission by the Member States concerned should therefore be further developed.

(13) The Commission should act in close and constant liaison with the competent authorities of the Member States from which it obtains comments and information.

(14) The Commission and the competent authorities of the Member States should together form a network of public authorities, applying their respective competences in close cooperation, using efficient arrangements for information-sharing and consultation, with a view to ensuring that a case is dealt with by the most appropriate authority, in the light of the principle of subsidiarity and with a view to ensuring that multiple notifications of a given concentration are avoided to the greatest extent possible. Referrals of concentrations from the Commission to Member States and from Member States to the Commission should be made in an efficient manner avoiding, to the greatest extent possible, situations where a concentration is subject to a referral both before and after its notification.

(15) The Commission should be able to refer to a Member State notified concentrations with a Community dimension which threaten significantly to affect competition in a market within that Member State presenting all the characteristics of a distinct market. Where the concentration affects competition on such a market, which does not constitute a substantial part of the common market, the Commission should be obliged, upon request, to refer the whole or part of the case to the Member State concerned. A Member State should be able to refer to the Commission a concentration which does not have a Community dimension but which affects trade between Member States and threatens to significantly affect competition within its territory. Other Member States which are also competent to review the concentration should be able to join the request. In such a situation, in order to ensure the efficiency and predictability of the system, national time limits should be suspended until a decision has been reached as to the referral of the case. The Commission should have the power to examine and deal with a concentration on behalf of a requesting Member State or requesting Member States.

(16) The undertakings concerned should be granted the possibility of requesting referrals to or from the Commission before a concentration is notified so as to further improve the efficiency of the system for the control of concentrations within the Community. In such situations, the Commission and national competition authorities should decide within short, clearly defined time limits whether a referral to or from the Commission ought to be made, thereby ensuring the efficiency of the system. Upon request by the undertakings concerned, the Commission should be able to refer to a Member State a concentration with a Community dimension which may significantly affect competition in a market within that Member State presenting all the characteristics of a distinct market; the undertakings concerned should not, however, be required to demonstrate that the effects of the concentration would be detrimental to competition. A concentration should not be referred from the Commission to a Member State which has expressed its disagreement to such a referral. Before notification to national authorities, the undertakings concerned should also be able to request that a concentration without a Community dimension which is capable of being reviewed under the national competition laws of at least three Member States be referred to the Commission. Such requests for pre-notification referrals to the Commission would be particularly pertinent in situations where the concentration would affect competition beyond the territory of one Member State. Where a concentration capable of being reviewed under the competition laws of three or more Member States is referred to the Commission prior to any national notification, and no Member State competent to review the case expresses its disagreement, the Commission should acquire exclusive competence to review the concentration and such a concentration should be deemed to have a Community dimension. Such pre-notification referrals from Member States to the Commission should not, however, be made where at least one Member State competent to review the case has expressed its disagreement with such a referral.

(17) The Commission should be given exclusive competence to apply this Regulation, subject to review by the Court of Justice.

(18) The Member States should not be permitted to apply their national legislation on competition to concentrations with a Community dimension, unless this Regulation makes provision therefor. The relevant powers of national authorities should be limited to cases where, failing intervention by the Commission, effective competition is likely to be significantly impeded within the territory of a Member State and where the competition interests of that Member State cannot be sufficiently protected otherwise by this Regulation. The Member States concerned must act

promptly in such cases; this Regulation cannot, because of the diversity of national law, fix a single time limit for the adoption of final decisions under national law.

(19) Furthermore, the exclusive application of this Regulation to concentrations with a Community dimension is without prejudice to Article 296 of the Treaty, and does not prevent the Member States from taking appropriate measures to protect legitimate interests other than those pursued by this Regulation, provided that such measures are compatible with the general principles and other provisions of Community law.

(20) It is expedient to define the concept of concentration in such a manner as to cover operations bringing about a lasting change in the control of the undertakings concerned and therefore in the structure of the market. It is therefore appropriate to include, within the scope of this Regulation, all joint ventures performing on a lasting basis all the functions of an autonomous economic entity. It is moreover appropriate to treat as a single concentration transactions that are closely connected in that they are linked by condition or take the form of a series of transactions in securities taking place within a reasonably short period of time.

(21) This Regulation should also apply where the undertakings concerned accept restrictions directly related to, and necessary for, the implementation of the concentration. Commission decisions declaring concentrations compatible with the common market in application of this Regulation should automatically cover such restrictions, without the Commission having to assess such restrictions in individual cases. At the request of the undertakings concerned, however, the Commission should, in cases presenting novel or unresolved questions giving rise to genuine uncertainty, expressly assess whether or not any restriction is directly related to, and necessary for, the implementation of the concentration. A case presents a novel or unresolved question giving rise to genuine uncertainty if the question is not covered by the relevant Commission notice in force or a published Commission decision.

(22) The arrangements to be introduced for the control of concentrations should, without prejudice to Article 86(2) of the Treaty, respect the principle of non-discrimination between the public and the private sectors. In the public sector, calculation of the turnover of an undertaking concerned in a concentration needs, therefore, to take account of undertakings making up an economic unit with an independent power of decision, irrespective of the way in which their capital is held or of the rules of administrative supervision applicable to them.

(23) It is necessary to establish whether or not concentrations with a Community dimension are compatible with the common market in terms of the need to maintain and develop effective competition in the common market. In so doing, the Commission must place its appraisal within the general framework of the achievement of the fundamental objectives referred to in Article 2 of the Treaty establishing the European Community and Article 2 of the Treaty on European Union.

(24) In order to ensure a system of undistorted competition in the common market, in furtherance of a policy conducted in accordance with the principle of an open market economy with free competition, this Regulation must permit effective control of all concentrations from the point of view of their effect on competition in the Community. Accordingly, Regulation (EEC) No 4064/89 established the principle that a concentration with a Community dimension which creates or strengthens a dominant position as a result of which effective competition in the common market or in a substantial part of it would be significantly impeded should be declared incompatible with the common market.

(25) In view of the consequences that concentrations in oligopolistic market structures may have, it is all the more necessary to maintain effective competition in such markets. Many oligopolistic markets exhibit a healthy degree of competition. However, under certain circumstances, concentrations involving the elimination of important competitive constraints that the merging parties had exerted upon each other, as well as a reduction of competitive pressure on the remaining competitors, may, even in the absence of a likelihood of coordination between the members of the oligopoly, result in a significant impediment to effective competition. The Community courts have, however, not to date expressly interpreted Regulation (EEC) No 4064/89 as requiring concentrations giving rise to such non-coordinated effects to be declared incompatible with the common market. Therefore, in the interests of legal certainty, it should be made clear that this Regulation permits effective control of all such concentrations by providing that any concentration which would significantly impede effective competition, in the common market or in a substantial part of it, should be declared incompatible with the common market. The notion of significant impediment to effective competition in Article 2(2) and (3) should be interpreted as extending, beyond the concept of dominance, only to the anti-competitive effects of a concentration resulting from the non-coordinated behaviour of undertakings which would not have a dominant position on the market concerned.

(26) A significant impediment to effective competition generally results from the creation or strengthening of a dominant position. With a view to preserving the guidance that may be drawn from past judgments of the European courts and Commission decisions pursuant to Regulation (EEC) No 4064/89, while at the same time maintaining consistency with the standards of competitive harm which have been applied by the Commission and the Community courts regarding the compatibility of a concentration with the common market, this Regulation should accordingly establish the principle that a concentration with a Community dimension which would significantly impede effective competition, in the common market or in a substantial part thereof, in particular as a result of the creation or strengthening of a dominant position, is to be declared incompatible with the common market.

(27) In addition, the criteria of Article 81(1) and (3) of the Treaty should be applied to joint ventures performing, on a lasting basis, all the functions of autonomous economic entities, to the extent that their creation has as its consequence an appreciable restriction of competition between undertakings that remain independent.

(28) In order to clarify and explain the Commission's appraisal of concentrations under this Regulation, it is appropriate for the Commission to publish guidance which should provide a sound economic framework for the assessment of concentrations with a view to determining whether or not they may be declared compatible with the common market.

(29) In order to determine the impact of a concentration on competition in the common market, it is appropriate to take account of any substantiated and likely efficiencies put forward by the undertakings concerned. It is possible that the efficiencies brought about by the concentration counteract the effects on competition, and in particular the potential harm to consumers, that it might otherwise have and that, as a consequence, the concentration would not significantly impede effective competition, in the common market or in a substantial part of it, in particular as a result

of the creation or strengthening of a dominant position. The Commission should publish guidance on the conditions under which it may take efficiencies into account in the assessment of a concentration.

(30) Where the undertakings concerned modify a notified concentration, in particular by offering commitments with a view to rendering the concentration compatible with the common market, the Commission should be able to declare the concentration, as modified, compatible with the common market. Such commitments should be proportionate to the competition problem and entirely eliminate it. It is also appropriate to accept commitments before the initiation of proceedings where the competition problem is readily identifiable and can easily be remedied. It should be expressly provided that the Commission may attach to its decision conditions and obligations in order to ensure that the undertakings concerned comply with their commitments in a timely and effective manner so as to render the concentration compatible with the common market. Transparency and effective consultation of Member States as well as of interested third parties should be ensured throughout the procedure.

(31) The Commission should have at its disposal appropriate instruments to ensure the enforcement of commitments and to deal with situations where they are not fulfilled. In cases of failure to fulfil a condition attached to the decision declaring a concentration compatible with the common market, the situation rendering the concentration compatible with the common market does not materialise and the concentration, as implemented, is therefore not authorised by the Commission. As a consequence, if the concentration is implemented, it should be treated in the same way as a non-notified concentration implemented without authorisation. Furthermore, where the Commission has already found that, in the absence of the condition, the concentration would be incompatible with the common market, it should have the power to directly order the dissolution of the concentration, so as to restore the situation prevailing prior to the implementation of the concentration. Where an obligation attached to a decision declaring the concentration compatible with the common market is not fulfilled, the Commission should be able to revoke its decision. Moreover, the Commission should be able to impose appropriate financial sanctions where conditions or obligations are not fulfilled.

(32) Concentrations which, by reason of the limited market share of the undertakings concerned, are not liable to impede effective competition may be presumed to be compatible with the common market. Without prejudice to Articles 81 and 82 of the Treaty, an indication to this effect exists, in particular, where the market share of the undertakings concerned does not exceed 25% either in the common market or in a substantial part of it.

(33) The Commission should have the task of taking all the decisions necessary to establish whether or not concentrations with a Community dimension are compatible with the common market, as well as decisions designed to restore the situation prevailing prior to the implementation of a concentration which has been declared incompatible with the common market.

(34) To ensure effective control, undertakings should be obliged to give prior notification of concentrations with a Community dimension following the conclusion of the agreement, the announcement of the public bid or the acquisition of a controlling interest. Notification should also be possible where the undertakings concerned satisfy the Commission of their intention to enter into an agreement for a proposed concentration and demonstrate to the Commission that their plan for that proposed concentration is sufficiently concrete, for example on the basis of an agreement in principle, a memorandum of understanding, or a letter of intent signed by all undertakings concerned, or, in the case of a public bid, where they have publicly announced an intention to make such a bid, provided that the intended agreement or bid would result in a concentration with a Community dimension. The implementation of concentrations should be suspended until a final decision of the Commission has been taken. However, it should be possible to derogate from this suspension at the request of the undertakings concerned, where appropriate. In deciding whether or not to grant a derogation, the Commission should take account of all pertinent factors, such as the nature and gravity of damage to the undertakings concerned or to third parties, and the threat to competition posed by the concentration. In the interest of legal certainty, the validity of transactions must nevertheless be protected as much as necessary.

(35) A period within which the Commission must initiate proceedings in respect of a notified concentration and a period within which it must take a final decision on the compatibility or incompatibility with the common market of that concentration should be laid down. These periods should be extended whenever the undertakings concerned offer commitments with a view to rendering the concentration compatible with the common market, in order to allow for sufficient time for the analysis and market testing of such commitment offers and for the consultation of Member States as well as interested third parties. A limited extension of the period within which the Commission must take a final decision should also be possible in order to allow sufficient time for the investigation of the case and the verification of the facts and arguments submitted to the Commission.

(36) The Community respects the fundamental rights and observes the principles recognised in particular by the Charter of Fundamental Rights of the European Union.[5] *Accordingly, this Regulation should be interpreted and applied with respect to those rights and principles.*

(37) The undertakings concerned must be afforded the right to be heard by the Commission when proceedings have been initiated; the members of the management and supervisory bodies and the recognised representatives of the employees of the undertakings concerned, and interested third parties, must also be given the opportunity to be heard.

(38) In order properly to appraise concentrations, the Commission should have the right to request all necessary information and to conduct all necessary inspections throughout the Community. To that end, and with a view to protecting competition effectively, the Commission's powers of investigation need to be expanded. The Commission should, in particular, have the right to interview any persons who may be in possession of useful information and to record the statements made.

(39) In the course of an inspection, officials authorised by the Commission should have the right to ask for any information relevant to the subject matter and purpose of the inspection; they should also have the right to affix seals during inspections, particularly in circumstances where there are reasonable grounds to suspect that a concentration has been implemented without being notified; that incorrect, incomplete or misleading information has been supplied to the Commission; or that the undertakings or persons concerned have failed to comply with a condition or obligation imposed by decision of the Commission. In any event, seals should only be used in exceptional circumstances, for the period of time strictly necessary for the inspection, normally not for more than 48 hours.

(40) Without prejudice to the case-law of the Court of Justice, it is also useful to set out the scope of the control that the national judicial authority may exercise when it authorises, as provided by national law and as a precautionary measure, assistance from law enforcement authorities in order to overcome possible opposition on the part of the undertaking against an inspection, including the affixing of seals, ordered by Commission decision. It results from the case-law that the national judicial authority may in particular ask of the Commission further information which it needs to carry out its control and in the absence of which it could refuse the authorisation. The case-law also confirms the competence of the national courts to control the application of national rules governing the implementation of coercive measures. The competent authorities of the Member States should cooperate actively in the exercise of the Commission's investigative powers.

(41) When complying with decisions of the Commission, the undertakings and persons concerned cannot be forced to admit that they have committed infringements, but they are in any event obliged to answer factual questions and to provide documents, even if this information may be used to establish against themselves or against others the existence of such infringements.

(42) For the sake of transparency, all decisions of the Commission which are not of a merely procedural nature should be widely publicised. While ensuring preservation of the rights of defence of the undertakings concerned, in particular the right of access to the file, it is essential that business secrets be protected. The confidentiality of information exchanged in the network and with the competent authorities of third countries should likewise be safeguarded.

(43) Compliance with this Regulation should be enforceable, as appropriate, by means of fines and periodic penalty payments. The Court of Justice should be given unlimited jurisdiction in that regard pursuant to Article 229 of the Treaty.

(44) The conditions in which concentrations, involving undertakings having their seat or their principal fields of activity in the Community, are carried out in third countries should be observed, and provision should be made for the possibility of the Council giving the Commission an appropriate mandate for negotiation with a view to obtaining non-discriminatory treatment for such undertakings.

(45) This Regulation in no way detracts from the collective rights of employees, as recognised in the undertakings concerned, notably with regard to any obligation to inform or consult their recognised representatives under Community and national law.

(46) The Commission should be able to lay down detailed rules concerning the implementation of this Regulation in accordance with the procedures for the exercise of implementing powers conferred on the Commission. For the adoption of such implementing provisions, the Commission should be assisted by an Advisory Committee composed of the representatives of the Member States as specified in Article 23,

NOTES

Repeal of this Regulation in relation to the UK: this Regulation is repealed in relation to the UK (as from IP completion day); see the introductory notes to this Regulation *ante*.

[1] OJ C20, 28.1.2003, p 4.

[2] Opinion delivered on 9.10.2003 (not yet published in the Official Journal).

[3] Opinion delivered on 24.10.2003 (not yet published in the Official Journal).

[4] OJ L395, 30.12.1989, p 1. Corrected version in OJ L257, 21.9.1990, p 13. Regulation as last amended by Regulation (EC) No 1310/97 (OJ L180, 9.7.1997, p 1). Corrigendum in OJ L40,13.2.1998, p 17.

[5] OJ C364, 18.12.2000, p 1.

HAS ADOPTED THIS REGULATION—

[4.540]

Article 1 Scope

1. Without prejudice to Article 4(5) and Article 22, this Regulation shall apply to all concentrations with a Community dimension as defined in this Article.

2. A concentration has a Community dimension where:

(a) the combined aggregate worldwide turnover of all the undertakings concerned is more than EUR 5,000 million; and

(b) the aggregate Community-wide turnover of each of at least two of the undertakings concerned is more than EUR 250 million,

unless each of the undertakings concerned achieves more than two-thirds of its aggregate Community-wide turnover within one and the same Member State.

3. A concentration that does not meet the thresholds laid down in paragraph 2 has a Community dimension where:

(a) the combined aggregate worldwide turnover of all the undertakings concerned is more than EUR 2,500 million;

(b) in each of at least three Member States, the combined aggregate turnover of all the undertakings concerned is more than EUR 100 million;

(c) in each of at least three Member States included for the purpose of point (b), the aggregate turnover of each of at least two of the undertakings concerned is more than EUR 25 million; and

(d) the aggregate Community-wide turnover of each of at least two of the undertakings concerned is more than EUR 100 million,

unless each of the undertakings concerned achieves more than two-thirds of its aggregate Community-wide turnover within one and the same Member State.

4. On the basis of statistical data that may be regularly provided by the Member States, the Commission shall report to the Council on the operation of the thresholds and criteria set out in paragraphs 2 and 3 by 1 July 2009 and may present proposals pursuant to paragraph 5.

5. Following the report referred to in paragraph 4 and on a proposal from the Commission, the Council, acting by a qualified majority, may revise the thresholds and criteria mentioned in paragraph 3.

NOTES

Repeal of this Regulation in relation to the UK: this Regulation is repealed in relation to the UK (as from IP completion day); see the introductory notes to this Regulation *ante*.

[4.541]

Article 2 Appraisal of concentrations

1. Concentrations within the scope of this Regulation shall be appraised in accordance with the objectives of this Regulation and the following provisions with a view to establishing whether or not they are compatible with the common market.

In making this appraisal, the Commission shall take into account:

(a) the need to maintain and develop effective competition within the common market in view of, among other things, the structure of all the markets concerned and the actual or potential competition from undertakings located either within or outwith the Community;

(b) the market position of the undertakings concerned and their economic and financial power, the alternatives available to suppliers and users, their access to supplies or markets, any legal or other barriers to entry, supply and demand trends for the relevant goods and services, the interests of the intermediate and ultimate consumers, and the development of technical and economic progress provided that it is to consumers' advantage and does not form an obstacle to competition.

2. A concentration which would not significantly impede effective competition in the common market or in a substantial part of it, in particular as a result of the creation or strengthening of a dominant position, shall be declared compatible with the common market.

3. A concentration which would significantly impede effective competition, in the common market or in a substantial part of it, in particular as a result of the creation or strengthening of a dominant position, shall be declared incompatible with the common market.

4. To the extent that the creation of a joint venture constituting a concentration pursuant to Article 3 has as its object or effect the coordination of the competitive behaviour of undertakings that remain independent, such coordination shall be appraised in accordance with the criteria of Article 81(1) and (3) of the Treaty, with a view to establishing whether or not the operation is compatible with the common market.

5. In making this appraisal, the Commission shall take into account in particular:

— whether two or more parent companies retain, to a significant extent, activities in the same market as the joint venture or in a market which is downstream or upstream from that of the joint venture or in a neighbouring market closely related to this market,

— whether the coordination which is the direct consequence of the creation of the joint venture affords the undertakings concerned the possibility of eliminating competition in respect of a substantial part of the products or services in question.

NOTES

Repeal of this Regulation in relation to the UK: this Regulation is repealed in relation to the UK (as from IP completion day); see the introductory notes to this Regulation *ante*.

[4.542]

Article 3 Definition of concentration

1. A concentration shall be deemed to arise where a change of control on a lasting basis results from:

(a) the merger of two or more previously independent undertakings or parts of undertakings, or

(b) the acquisition, by one or more persons already controlling at least one undertaking, or by one or more undertakings, whether by purchase of securities or assets, by contract or by any other means, of direct or indirect control of the whole or parts of one or more other undertakings.

2. Control shall be constituted by rights, contracts or any other means which, either separately or in combination and having regard to the considerations of fact or law involved, confer the possibility of exercising decisive influence on an undertaking, in particular by:

(a) ownership or the right to use all or part of the assets of an undertaking;

(b) rights or contracts which confer decisive influence on the composition, voting or decisions of the organs of an undertaking.

3. Control is acquired by persons or undertakings which:

(a) are holders of the rights or entitled to rights under the contracts concerned; or

(b) while not being holders of such rights or entitled to rights under such contracts, have the power to exercise the rights deriving therefrom.

4. The creation of a joint venture performing on a lasting basis all the functions of an autonomous economic entity shall constitute a concentration within the meaning of paragraph 1(b).

5. A concentration shall not be deemed to arise where:

(a) credit institutions or other financial institutions or insurance companies, the normal activities of which include transactions and dealing in securities for their own account or for the account of others, hold on a temporary basis securities which they have acquired in an undertaking with a view to reselling them, provided that they do not exercise voting rights in respect of those securities with a view to determining the competitive behaviour of that undertaking or provided that they exercise such voting rights only with a view to preparing the disposal of all or part of that undertaking or of its assets or the disposal of those securities and that any such disposal takes place within one year of the date of acquisition; that period may be extended by the Commission on request where such institutions or companies can show that the disposal was not reasonably possible within the period set;

(b) control is acquired by an office-holder according to the law of a Member State relating to liquidation, winding up, insolvency, cessation of payments, compositions or analogous proceedings;

(c) *the operations referred to in paragraph 1(b) are carried out by the financial holding companies referred to in Article 5(3) of Fourth Council Directive 78/660/EEC of 25 July 1978 based on Article 54(3)(g) of the Treaty on the annual accounts of certain types of companies*[1] *provided however that the voting rights in respect of the holding are exercised, in particular in relation to the appointment of members of the management and supervisory bodies of the undertakings in which they have holdings, only to maintain the full value of those investments and not to determine directly or indirectly the competitive conduct of those undertakings.*

NOTES

Repeal of this Regulation in relation to the UK: this Regulation is repealed in relation to the UK (as from IP completion day); see the introductory notes to this Regulation *ante*.

[1] OJ L222, 14.8.1978, p 11. Directive as last amended by Directive 2003/51/EC of the European Parliament and of the Council (OJ L178, 17.7.2003, p 16).

[4.543]

Article 4 Prior notification of concentrations and pre-notification referral at the request of the notifying parties

1. Concentrations with a Community dimension defined in this Regulation shall be notified to the Commission prior to their implementation and following the conclusion of the agreement, the announcement of the public bid, or the acquisition of a controlling interest.

Notification may also be made where the undertakings concerned demonstrate to the Commission a good faith intention to conclude an agreement or, in the case of a public bid, where they have publicly announced an intention to make such a bid, provided that the intended agreement or bid would result in a concentration with a Community dimension.

For the purposes of this Regulation, the term "notified concentration" shall also cover intended concentrations notified pursuant to the second subparagraph. For the purposes of paragraphs 4 and 5 of this Article, the term "concentration" includes intended concentrations within the meaning of the second sub-paragraph.

2. A concentration which consists of a merger within the meaning of Article 3(1)(a) or in the acquisition of joint control within the meaning of Article 3(1)(b) shall be notified jointly by the parties to the merger or by those acquiring joint control as the case may be. In all other cases, the notification shall be effected by the person or undertaking acquiring control of the whole or parts of one or more undertakings.

3. Where the Commission finds that a notified concentration falls within the scope of this Regulation, it shall publish the fact of the notification, at the same time indicating the names of the undertakings concerned, their country of origin, the nature of the concentration and the economic sectors involved. The Commission shall take account of the legitimate interest of undertakings in the protection of their business secrets.

4. Prior to the notification of a concentration within the meaning of paragraph 1, the persons or undertakings referred to in paragraph 2 may inform the Commission, by means of a reasoned submission, that the concentration may significantly affect competition in a market within a Member State which presents all the characteristics of a distinct market and should therefore be examined, in whole or in part, by that Member State.

The Commission shall transmit this submission to all Member States without delay. The Member State referred to in the reasoned submission shall, within 15 working days of receiving the submission, express its agreement or disagreement as regards the request to refer the case. Where that Member State takes no such decision within this period, it shall be deemed to have agreed.

Unless that Member State disagrees, the Commission, where it considers that such a distinct market exists, and that competition in that market may be significantly affected by the concentration, may decide to refer the whole or part of the case to the competent authorities of that Member State with a view to the application of that State's national competition law.

The decision whether or not to refer the case in accordance with the third subparagraph shall be taken within 25 working days starting from the receipt of the reasoned submission by the Commission. The Commission shall inform the other Member States and the persons or undertakings concerned of its decision. If the Commission does not take a decision within this period, it shall be deemed to have adopted a decision to refer the case in accordance with the submission made by the persons or undertakings concerned.

If the Commission decides, or is deemed to have decided, pursuant to the third and fourth subparagraphs, to refer the whole of the case, no notification shall be made pursuant to paragraph 1 and national competition law shall apply. Article 9(6) to (9) shall apply mutatis mutandis.

5. With regard to a concentration as defined in Article 3 which does not have a Community dimension within the meaning of Article 1 and which is capable of being reviewed under the national competition laws of at least three Member States, the persons or undertakings referred to in paragraph 2 may, before any notification to the competent authorities, inform the Commission by means of a reasoned submission that the concentration should be examined by the Commission.

The Commission shall transmit this submission to all Member States without delay.

Any Member State competent to examine the concentration under its national competition law may, within 15 working days of receiving the reasoned submission, express its disagreement as regards the request to refer the case.

Where at least one such Member State has expressed its disagreement in accordance with the third subparagraph within the period of 15 working days, the case shall not be referred. The Commission shall, without delay, inform all Member States and the persons or undertakings concerned of any such expression of disagreement.

Where no Member State has expressed its disagreement in accordance with the third subparagraph within the period of 15 working days, the concentration shall be deemed to have a Community dimension and shall be notified to the Commission in accordance with paragraphs 1 and 2. In such situations, no Member State shall apply its national competition law to the concentration.

6. The Commission shall report to the Council on the operation of paragraphs 4 and 5 by 1 July 2009. Following this report and on a proposal from the Commission, the Council, acting by a qualified majority, may revise paragraphs 4 and 5.

NOTES

Repeal of this Regulation in relation to the UK: this Regulation is repealed in relation to the UK (as from IP completion day); see the introductory notes to this Regulation *ante*.

[4.544]

Article 5 Calculation of turnover

1. Aggregate turnover within the meaning of this Regulation shall comprise the amounts derived by the undertakings concerned in the preceding financial year from the sale of products and the provision of services falling within the undertakings' ordinary activities after deduction of sales rebates and of value added tax and other taxes directly related to turnover. The aggregate turnover of an undertaking concerned shall not include the sale of products or the provision of services between any of the undertakings referred to in paragraph 4.

Turnover, in the Community or in a Member State, shall comprise products sold and services provided to undertakings or consumers, in the Community or in that Member State as the case may be.

2. By way of derogation from paragraph 1, where the concentration consists of the acquisition of parts, whether or not constituted as legal entities, of one or more undertakings, only the turnover relating to the parts which are the subject of the concentration shall be taken into account with regard to the seller or sellers.

However, two or more transactions within the meaning of the first subparagraph which take place within a two-year period between the same persons or undertakings shall be treated as one and the same concentration arising on the date of the last transaction.

3. In place of turnover the following shall be used:

(a) for credit institutions and other financial institutions, the sum of the following income items as defined in Council Directive 86/635/EEC,[1] after deduction of value added tax and other taxes directly related to those items, where appropriate:

(i) interest income and similar income;

(ii) income from securities:

— income from shares and other variable yield securities,

— income from participating interests,

— income from shares in affiliated undertakings;

(iii) commissions receivable;

(iv) net profit on financial operations;

(v) other operating income.

The turnover of a credit or financial institution in the Community or in a Member State shall comprise the income items, as defined above, which are received by the branch or division of that institution established in the Community or in the Member State in question, as the case may be;

(b) for insurance undertakings, the value of gross premiums written which shall comprise all amounts received and receivable in respect of insurance contracts issued by or on behalf of the insurance undertakings, including also outgoing reinsurance premiums, and after deduction of taxes and parafiscal contributions or levies charged by reference to the amounts of individual premiums or the total volume of premiums; as regards Article 1(2)(b) and (3)(b), (c) and (d) and the final part of Article 1(2) and (3), gross premiums received from Community residents and from residents of one Member State respectively shall be taken into account.

4. Without prejudice to paragraph 2, the aggregate turnover of an undertaking concerned within the meaning of this Regulation shall be calculated by adding together the respective turnovers of the following:

(a) the undertaking concerned;

(b) those undertakings in which the undertaking concerned, directly or indirectly:

(i) owns more than half the capital or business assets, or

(ii) has the power to exercise more than half the voting rights, or

(iii) has the power to appoint more than half the members of the supervisory board, the administrative board or bodies legally representing the undertakings, or

(iv) has the right to manage the undertakings' affairs;

(c) those undertakings which have in the undertaking concerned the rights or powers listed in (b);

(d) those undertakings in which an undertaking as referred to in (c) has the rights or powers listed in (b);

(e) those undertakings in which two or more undertakings as referred to in (a) to (d) jointly have the rights or powers listed in (b).

5. Where undertakings concerned by the concentration jointly have the rights or powers listed in paragraph 4(b), in calculating the aggregate turnover of the undertakings concerned for the purposes of this Regulation:

(a) no account shall be taken of the turnover resulting from the sale of products or the provision of services between the joint undertaking and each of the undertakings concerned or any other undertaking connected with any one of them, as set out in paragraph 4(b) to (e);

(b) account shall be taken of the turnover resulting from the sale of products and the provision of services between the joint undertaking and any third undertakings. This turnover shall be apportioned equally amongst the undertakings concerned.

NOTES

Repeal of this Regulation in relation to the UK: this Regulation is repealed in relation to the UK (as from IP completion day); see the introductory notes to this Regulation *ante*.

1 OJ L372, 31.12.1986, p 1. Directive as last amended by Directive 2003/51/EC of the European Parliament and of the Council.

[4.545]

Article 6 Examination of the notification and initiation of proceedings

1. The Commission shall examine the notification as soon as it is received.

(a) *Where it concludes that the concentration notified does not fall within the scope of this Regulation, it shall record that finding by means of a decision.*

(b) *Where it finds that the concentration notified, although falling within the scope of this Regulation, does not raise serious doubts as to its compatibility with the common market, it shall decide not to oppose it and shall declare that it is compatible with the common market.*

A decision declaring a concentration compatible shall be deemed to cover restrictions directly related and necessary to the implementation of the concentration.

(c) *Without prejudice to paragraph 2, where the Commission finds that the concentration notified falls within the scope of this Regulation and raises serious doubts as to its compatibility with the common market, it shall decide to initiate proceedings. Without prejudice to Article 9, such proceedings shall be closed by means of a decision as provided for in Article 8(1) to (4), unless the undertakings concerned have demonstrated to the satisfaction of the Commission that they have abandoned the concentration.*

2. Where the Commission finds that, following modification by the undertakings concerned, a notified concentration no longer raises serious doubts within the meaning of paragraph 1(c), it shall declare the concentration compatible with the common market pursuant to paragraph 1(b).

The Commission may attach to its decision under paragraph 1(b) conditions and obligations intended to ensure that the undertakings concerned comply with the commitments they have entered into vis-à-vis the Commission with a view to rendering the concentration compatible with the common market.

3. The Commission may revoke the decision it took pursuant to paragraph 1(a) or (b) where:

(a) *the decision is based on incorrect information for which one of the undertakings is responsible or where it has been obtained by deceit,*

or

(b) *the undertakings concerned commit a breach of an obligation attached to the decision.*

4. In the cases referred to in paragraph 3, the Commission may take a decision under paragraph 1, without being bound by the time limits referred to in Article 10(1).

5. The Commission shall notify its decision to the undertakings concerned and the competent authorities of the Member States without delay.

NOTES

Repeal of this Regulation in relation to the UK: this Regulation is repealed in relation to the UK (as from IP completion day); see the introductory notes to this Regulation *ante*.

[4.546]

Article 7 Suspension of concentrations

1. A concentration with a Community dimension as defined in Article 1, or which is to be examined by the Commission pursuant to Article 4(5), shall not be implemented either before its notification or until it has been declared compatible with the common market pursuant to a decision under Articles 6(1)(b), 8(1) or 8(2), or on the basis of a presumption according to Article 10(6).

2. Paragraph 1 shall not prevent the implementation of a public bid or of a series of transactions in securities including those convertible into other securities admitted to trading on a market such as a stock exchange, by which control within the meaning of Article 3 is acquired from various sellers, provided that:

(a) *the concentration is notified to the Commission pursuant to Article 4 without delay; and*

(b) *the acquirer does not exercise the voting rights attached to the securities in question or does so only to maintain the full value of its investments based on a derogation granted by the Commission under paragraph 3.*

3. The Commission may, on request, grant a derogation from the obligations imposed in paragraphs 1 or 2. The request to grant a derogation must be reasoned. In deciding on the request, the Commission shall take into account inter alia the effects of the suspension on one or more undertakings concerned by the concentration or on a third party and the threat to competition posed by the concentration. Such a derogation may be made subject to conditions and obligations in order to ensure conditions of effective competition. A derogation may be applied for and granted at any time, be it before notification or after the transaction.

4. The validity of any transaction carried out in contravention of paragraph 1 shall be dependent on a decision pursuant to Article 6(1)(b) or Article 8(1), (2) or (3) or on a presumption pursuant to Article 10(6).

This Article shall, however, have no effect on the validity of transactions in securities including those convertible into other securities admitted to trading on a market such as a stock exchange, unless the buyer and seller knew or ought to have known that the transaction was carried out in contravention of paragraph 1.

NOTES

Repeal of this Regulation in relation to the UK: this Regulation is repealed in relation to the UK (as from IP completion day); see the introductory notes to this Regulation *ante*.

[4.547]

Article 8 Powers of decision of the Commission

1. Where the Commission finds that a notified concentration fulfils the criterion laid down in Article 2(2) and, in the cases referred to in Article 2(4), the criteria laid down in Article 81(3) of the Treaty, it shall issue a decision declaring the concentration compatible with the common market.

A decision declaring a concentration compatible shall be deemed to cover restrictions directly related and necessary to the implementation of the concentration.

2. Where the Commission finds that, following modification by the undertakings concerned, a notified concentration fulfils the criterion laid down in Article 2(2) and, in the cases referred to in Article 2(4), the criteria laid down in Article 81(3) of the Treaty, it shall issue a decision declaring the concentration compatible with the common market.

The Commission may attach to its decision conditions and obligations intended to ensure that the undertakings concerned comply with the commitments they have entered into vis-à-vis the Commission with a view to rendering the concentration compatible with the common market.

A decision declaring a concentration compatible shall be deemed to cover restrictions directly related and necessary to the implementation of the concentration.

3. Where the Commission finds that a concentration fulfils the criterion defined in Article 2(3) or, in the cases referred to in Article 2(4), does not fulfil the criteria laid down in Article 81(3) of the Treaty, it shall issue a decision declaring that the concentration is incompatible with the common market.

4. Where the Commission finds that a concentration:

(a) has already been implemented and that concentration has been declared incompatible with the common market, or

(b) has been implemented in contravention of a condition attached to a decision taken under paragraph 2, which has found that, in the absence of the condition, the concentration would fulfil the criterion laid down in Article 2(3) or, in the cases referred to in Article 2(4), would not fulfil the criteria laid down in Article 81(3) of the Treaty,

the Commission may:

— require the undertakings concerned to dissolve the concentration, in particular through the dissolution of the merger or the disposal of all the shares or assets acquired, so as to restore the situation prevailing prior to the implementation of the concentration; in circumstances where restoration of the situation prevailing before the implementation of the concentration is not possible through dissolution of the concentration, the Commission may take any other measure appropriate to achieve such restoration as far as possible,

— order any other appropriate measure to ensure that the undertakings concerned dissolve the concentration or take other restorative measures as required in its decision.

In cases falling within point (a) of the first subparagraph, the measures referred to in that subparagraph may be imposed either in a decision pursuant to paragraph 3 or by separate decision.

5. The Commission may take interim measures appropriate to restore or maintain conditions of effective competition where a concentration:

(a) has been implemented in contravention of Article 7, and a decision as to the compatibility of the concentration with the common market has not yet been taken;

(b) has been implemented in contravention of a condition attached to a decision under Article 6(1)(b) or paragraph 2 of this Article;

(c) has already been implemented and is declared incompatible with the common market.

6. The Commission may revoke the decision it has taken pursuant to paragraphs 1 or 2 where:

(a) the declaration of compatibility is based on incorrect information for which one of the undertakings is responsible or where it has been obtained by deceit; or

(b) the undertakings concerned commit a breach of an obligation attached to the decision.

7. The Commission may take a decision pursuant to paragraphs 1 to 3 without being bound by the time limits referred to in Article 10(3), in cases where:

(a) it finds that a concentration has been implemented

(i) in contravention of a condition attached to a decision under Article 6(1)(b), or

(ii) in contravention of a condition attached to a decision taken under paragraph 2 and in accordance with Article 10(2), which has found that, in the absence of the condition, the concentration would raise serious doubts as to its compatibility with the common market; or

(b) a decision has been revoked pursuant to paragraph 6.

8. The Commission shall notify its decision to the undertakings concerned and the competent authorities of the Member States without delay.

NOTES

Repeal of this Regulation in relation to the UK: this Regulation is repealed in relation to the UK (as from IP completion day); see the introductory notes to this Regulation *ante*.

[4.548]

Article 9 Referral to the competent authorities of the Member States

1. The Commission may, by means of a decision notified without delay to the undertakings concerned and the competent authorities of the other Member States, refer a notified concentration to the competent authorities of the Member State concerned in the following circumstances.

2. Within 15 working days of the date of receipt of the copy of the notification, a Member State, on its own initiative or upon the invitation of the Commission, may inform the Commission, which shall inform the undertakings concerned, that:

(a) a concentration threatens to affect significantly competition in a market within that Member State, which presents all the characteristics of a distinct market, or

(b) a concentration affects competition in a market within that Member State, which presents all the characteristics of a distinct market and which does not constitute a substantial part of the common market.

3. If the Commission considers that, having regard to the market for the products or services in question and the geographical reference market within the meaning of paragraph 7, there is such a distinct market and that such a threat exists, either:

(a) it shall itself deal with the case in accordance with this Regulation; or

(b) it shall refer the whole or part of the case to the competent authorities of the Member State concerned with a view to the application of that State's national competition law.

If, however, the Commission considers that such a distinct market or threat does not exist, it shall adopt a decision to that effect which it shall address to the Member State concerned, and shall itself deal with the case in accordance with this Regulation.

In cases where a Member State informs the Commission pursuant to paragraph 2(b) that a concentration affects competition in a distinct market within its territory that does not form a substantial part of the common market, the Commission shall refer the whole or part of the case relating to the distinct market concerned, if it considers that such a distinct market is affected.

4. A decision to refer or not to refer pursuant to paragraph 3 shall be taken:

(a) as a general rule within the period provided for in Article 10(1), second subparagraph, where the Commission, pursuant to Article 6(1)(b), has not initiated proceedings; or

(b) within 65 working days at most of the notification of the concentration concerned where the Commission has initiated proceedings under Article 6(1)(c), without taking the preparatory steps in order to adopt the necessary measures under Article 8(2), (3) or (4) to maintain or restore effective competition on the market concerned.

5. If within the 65 working days referred to in paragraph 4(b) the Commission, despite a reminder from the Member State concerned, has not taken a decision on referral in accordance with paragraph 3 nor has taken the preparatory steps referred to in paragraph 4(b), it shall be deemed to have taken a decision to refer the case to the Member State concerned in accordance with paragraph 3(b).

6. The competent authority of the Member State concerned shall decide upon the case without undue delay.

Within 45 working days after the Commission's referral, the competent authority of the Member State concerned shall inform the undertakings concerned of the result of the preliminary competition assessment and what further action, if any, it proposes to take. The Member State concerned may exceptionally suspend this time limit where necessary information has not been provided to it by the undertakings concerned as provided for by its national competition law.

Where a notification is requested under national law, the period of 45 working days shall begin on the working day following that of the receipt of a complete notification by the competent authority of that Member State.

7. The geographical reference market shall consist of the area in which the undertakings concerned are involved in the supply and demand of products or services, in which the conditions of competition are sufficiently homogeneous and which can be distinguished from neighbouring areas because, in particular, conditions of competition are appreciably different in those areas. This assessment should take account in particular of the nature and characteristics of the products or services concerned, of the existence of entry barriers or of consumer preferences, of appreciable differences of the undertakings' market shares between the area concerned and neighbouring areas or of substantial price differences.

8. In applying the provisions of this Article, the Member State concerned may take only the measures strictly necessary to safeguard or restore effective competition on the market concerned.

9. In accordance with the relevant provisions of the Treaty, any Member State may appeal to the Court of Justice, and in particular request the application of Article 243 of the Treaty, for the purpose of applying its national competition law.

NOTES

Repeal of this Regulation in relation to the UK: this Regulation is repealed in relation to the UK (as from IP completion day); see the introductory notes to this Regulation *ante*.

[4.549]

Article 10 Time limits for initiating proceedings and for decisions

1. Without prejudice to Article 6(4), the decisions referred to in Article 6(1) shall be taken within 25 working days at most. That period shall begin on the working day following that of the receipt of a notification or, if the information to be supplied with the notification is incomplete, on the working day following that of the receipt of the complete information.

That period shall be increased to 35 working days where the Commission receives a request from a Member State in accordance with Article 9(2) or where, the undertakings concerned offer commitments pursuant to Article 6(2) with a view to rendering the concentration compatible with the common market.

2. Decisions pursuant to Article 8(1) or (2) concerning notified concentrations shall be taken as soon as it appears that the serious doubts referred to in Article 6(1)(c) have been removed, particularly as a result of modifications made by the undertakings concerned, and at the latest by the time limit laid down in paragraph 3.

3. Without prejudice to Article 8(7), decisions pursuant to Article 8(1) to (3) concerning notified concentrations shall be taken within not more than 90 working days of the date on which the proceedings are initiated. That period shall be increased to 105 working days where the undertakings concerned offer commitments pursuant to Article 8(2), second subparagraph, with a view to rendering the concentration compatible with the common market, unless these commitments have been offered less than 55 working days after the initiation of proceedings.

The periods set by the first subparagraph shall likewise be extended if the notifying parties make a request to that effect not later than 15 working days after the initiation of proceedings pursuant to Article 6(1)(c). The notifying parties may make only one such request. Likewise, at any time following the initiation of proceedings, the periods set by the first sub-paragraph may be extended by the Commission with the agreement of the notifying parties. The total duration of any extension or extensions effected pursuant to this subparagraph shall not exceed 20 working days.

4. The periods set by paragraphs 1 and 3 shall exceptionally be suspended where, owing to circumstances for which one of the undertakings involved in the concentration is responsible, the Commission has had to request information by decision pursuant to Article 11 or to order an inspection by decision pursuant to Article 13.

The first subparagraph shall also apply to the period referred to in Article 9(4)(b).

5. Where the Court of Justice gives a judgment which annuls the whole or part of a Commission decision which is subject to a time limit set by this Article, the concentration shall be re-examined by the Commission with a view to adopting a decision pursuant to Article 6(1).

The concentration shall be re-examined in the light of current market conditions.

The notifying parties shall submit a new notification or supplement the original notification, without delay, where the original notification becomes incomplete by reason of intervening changes in market conditions or in the information provided. Where there are no such changes, the parties shall certify this fact without delay.

The periods laid down in paragraph 1 shall start on the working day following that of the receipt of complete information in a new notification, a supplemented notification, or a certification within the meaning of the third subparagraph.

The second and third subparagraphs shall also apply in the cases referred to in Article 6(4) and Article 8(7).

6. Where the Commission has not taken a decision in accordance with Article 6(1)(b), (c), 8(1), (2) or (3) within the time limits set in paragraphs 1 and 3 respectively, the concentration shall be deemed to have been declared compatible with the common market, without prejudice to Article 9.

NOTES

Repeal of this Regulation in relation to the UK: this Regulation is repealed in relation to the UK (as from IP completion day); see the introductory notes to this Regulation *ante*.

[4.550]

Article 11 Requests for information

1. In order to carry out the duties assigned to it by this Regulation, the Commission may, by simple request or by decision, require the persons referred to in Article 3(1)(b), as well as undertakings and associations of undertakings, to provide all necessary information.

2. When sending a simple request for information to a person, an undertaking or an association of undertakings, the Commission shall state the legal basis and the purpose of the request, specify what information is required and fix the time limit within which the information is to be provided, as well as the penalties provided for in Article 14 for supplying incorrect or misleading information.

3. Where the Commission requires a person, an undertaking or an association of undertakings to supply information by decision, it shall state the legal basis and the purpose of the request, specify what information is required and fix the time limit within which it is to be provided. It shall also indicate the penalties provided for in Article 14 and indicate or impose the penalties provided for in Article 15. It shall further indicate the right to have the decision reviewed by the Court of Justice.

4. The owners of the undertakings or their representatives and, in the case of legal persons, companies or firms, or associations having no legal personality, the persons authorised to represent them by law or by their constitution, shall supply the information requested on behalf of the undertaking concerned. Persons duly authorised to act may supply the information on behalf of their clients. The latter shall remain fully responsible if the information supplied is incomplete, incorrect or misleading.

5. The Commission shall without delay forward a copy of any decision taken pursuant to paragraph 3 to the competent authorities of the Member State in whose territory the residence of the person or the seat of the undertaking or association of undertakings is situated, and to the competent authority of the Member State whose territory is affected. At the specific request of the competent authority of a Member State, the Commission shall also forward to that authority copies of simple requests for information relating to a notified concentration.

6. At the request of the Commission, the governments and competent authorities of the Member States shall provide the Commission with all necessary information to carry out the duties assigned to it by this Regulation.

7. In order to carry out the duties assigned to it by this Regulation, the Commission may interview any natural or legal person who consents to be interviewed for the purpose of collecting information relating to the subject matter of an investigation. At the beginning of the interview, which may be conducted by telephone or other electronic means, the Commission shall state the legal basis and the purpose of the interview.

Where an interview is not conducted on the premises of the Commission or by telephone or other electronic means, the Commission shall inform in advance the competent authority of the Member State in whose territory the interview takes place. If the competent authority of that Member State so requests, officials of that authority may assist the officials and other persons authorised by the Commission to conduct the interview.

NOTES

Repeal of this Regulation in relation to the UK: this Regulation is repealed in relation to the UK (as from IP completion day); see the introductory notes to this Regulation *ante*.

[4.551]

Article 12 Inspections by the authorities of the Member States

1. At the request of the Commission, the competent authorities of the Member States shall undertake the inspections which the Commission considers to be necessary under Article 13(1), or which it has ordered by decision pursuant to Article 13(4). The officials of the competent authorities of the Member States who are responsible for conducting these inspections as well as those authorised or appointed by them shall exercise their powers in accordance with their national law.

2. If so requested by the Commission or by the competent authority of the Member State within whose territory the inspection is to be conducted, officials and other accompanying persons authorised by the Commission may assist the officials of the authority concerned.

NOTES

Repeal of this Regulation in relation to the UK: this Regulation is repealed in relation to the UK (as from IP completion day); see the introductory notes to this Regulation *ante*.

[4.552]

Article 13 The Commission's powers of inspection

1. In order to carry out the duties assigned to it by this Regulation, the Commission may conduct all necessary inspections of undertakings and associations of undertakings.

2. The officials and other accompanying persons authorised by the Commission to conduct an inspection shall have the power:

- *(a) to enter any premises, land and means of transport of undertakings and associations of undertakings;*
- *(b) to examine the books and other records related to the business, irrespective of the medium on which they are stored;*
- *(c) to take or obtain in any form copies of or extracts from such books or records;*
- *(d) to seal any business premises and books or records for the period and to the extent necessary for the inspection;*
- *(e) to ask any representative or member of staff of the undertaking or association of undertakings for explanations on facts or documents relating to the subject matter and purpose of the inspection and to record the answers.*

3. Officials and other accompanying persons authorised by the Commission to conduct an inspection shall exercise their powers upon production of a written authorisation specifying the subject matter and purpose of the inspection and the penalties provided for in Article 14, in the production of the required books or other records related to the business which is incomplete or where answers to questions asked under paragraph 2 of this Article are incorrect or misleading. In good time before the inspection, the Commission shall give notice of the inspection to the competent authority of the Member State in whose territory the inspection is to be conducted.

4. Undertakings and associations of undertakings are required to submit to inspections ordered by decision of the Commission. The decision shall specify the subject matter and purpose of the inspection, appoint the date on which it is to begin and indicate the penalties provided for in Articles 14 and 15 and the right to have the decision reviewed by the Court of Justice. The Commission shall take such decisions after consulting the competent authority of the Member State in whose territory the inspection is to be conducted.

5. Officials of, and those authorised or appointed by, the competent authority of the Member State in whose territory the inspection is to be conducted shall, at the request of that authority or of the Commission, actively assist the officials and other accompanying persons authorised by the Commission. To this end, they shall enjoy the powers specified in paragraph 2.

6. Where the officials and other accompanying persons authorised by the Commission find that an undertaking opposes an inspection, including the sealing of business premises, books or records, ordered pursuant to this Article, the Member State concerned shall afford them the necessary assistance, requesting where appropriate the assistance of the police or of an equivalent enforcement authority, so as to enable them to conduct their inspection.

7. If the assistance provided for in paragraph 6 requires authorisation from a judicial authority according to national rules, such authorisation shall be applied for. Such authorisation may also be applied for as a precautionary measure.

8. Where authorisation as referred to in paragraph 7 is applied for, the national judicial authority shall ensure that the Commission decision is authentic and that the coercive measures envisaged are neither arbitrary nor excessive having regard to the subject matter of the inspection. In its control of proportionality of the coercive measures, the national judicial authority may ask the Commission, directly or through the competent authority of that Member State, for detailed explanations relating to the subject matter of the inspection. However, the national judicial authority may not call into question the necessity for the inspection nor demand that it be provided with the information in the Commission's file. The lawfulness of the Commission's decision shall be subject to review only by the Court of Justice.

NOTES

Repeal of this Regulation in relation to the UK: this Regulation is repealed in relation to the UK (as from IP completion day); see the introductory notes to this Regulation *ante*.

[4.553]

Article 14 Fines

1. The Commission may by decision impose on the persons referred to in Article 3(1)b, undertakings or associations of undertakings, fines not exceeding 1% of the aggregate turnover of the undertaking or association of undertakings concerned within the meaning of Article 5 where, intentionally or negligently:

- *(a) they supply incorrect or misleading information in a submission, certification, notification or supplement thereto, pursuant to Article 4, Article 10(5) or Article 22(3);*
- *(b) they supply incorrect or misleading information in response to a request made pursuant to Article 11(2);*
- *(c) in response to a request made by decision adopted pursuant to Article 11(3), they supply incorrect, incomplete or misleading information or do not supply information within the required time limit;*
- *(d) they produce the required books or other records related to the business in incomplete form during inspections under Article 13, or refuse to submit to an inspection ordered by decision taken pursuant to Article 13(4);*
- *(e) in response to a question asked in accordance with Article 13(2)(e),*
  - *— they give an incorrect or misleading answer,*
  - *— they fail to rectify within a time limit set by the Commission an incorrect, incomplete or misleading answer given by a member of staff, or*
  - *— they fail or refuse to provide a complete answer on facts relating to the subject matter and purpose of an inspection ordered by a decision adopted pursuant to Article 13(4);*
- *(f) seals affixed by officials or other accompanying persons authorised by the Commission in accordance with Article 13(2)(d) have been broken.*

2. The Commission may by decision impose fines not exceeding 10% of the aggregate turnover of the undertaking concerned within the meaning of Article 5 on the persons referred to in Article 3(1)b or the undertakings concerned where, either intentionally or negligently, they:

- *(a) fail to notify a concentration in accordance with Articles 4 or 22(3) prior to its implementation, unless they are expressly authorised to do so by Article 7(2) or by a decision taken pursuant to Article 7(3);*
- *(b) implement a concentration in breach of Article 7;*

(c) *implement a concentration declared incompatible with the common market by decision pursuant to Article 8(3) or do not comply with any measure ordered by decision pursuant to Article 8(4) or (5);*
(d) *fail to comply with a condition or an obligation imposed by decision pursuant to Articles 6(1)(b), Article 7(3) or Article 8(2), second subparagraph.*

3. In fixing the amount of the fine, regard shall be had to the nature, gravity and duration of the infringement.

4. Decisions taken pursuant to paragraphs 1, 2 and 3 shall not be of a criminal law nature.

NOTES

Repeal of this Regulation in relation to the UK: this Regulation is repealed in relation to the UK (as from IP completion day); see the introductory notes to this Regulation *ante*.

[4.554]

Article 15 Periodic penalty payments

1. The Commission may by decision impose on the persons referred to in Article 3(1)b, undertakings or associations of undertakings, periodic penalty payments not exceeding 5% of the average daily aggregate turnover of the undertaking or association of undertakings concerned within the meaning of Article 5 for each working day of delay, calculated from the date set in the decision, in order to compel them:
(a) *to supply complete and correct information which it has requested by decision taken pursuant to Article 11(3);*
(b) *to submit to an inspection which it has ordered by decision taken pursuant to Article 13(4);*
(c) *to comply with an obligation imposed by decision pursuant to Article 6(1)(b), Article 7(3) or Article 8(2), second sub-paragraph; or;*
(d) *to comply with any measures ordered by decision pursuant to Article 8(4) or (5).*

2. Where the persons referred to in Article 3(1)(b), undertakings or associations of undertakings have satisfied the obligation which the periodic penalty payment was intended to enforce, the Commission may fix the definitive amount of the periodic penalty payments at a figure lower than that which would arise under the original decision.

NOTES

Repeal of this Regulation in relation to the UK: this Regulation is repealed in relation to the UK (as from IP completion day); see the introductory notes to this Regulation *ante*.

[4.555]

Article 16 Review by the Court of Justice

The Court of Justice shall have unlimited jurisdiction within the meaning of Article 229 of the Treaty to review decisions whereby the Commission has fixed a fine or periodic penalty payments; it may cancel, reduce or increase the fine or periodic penalty payment imposed.

NOTES

Repeal of this Regulation in relation to the UK: this Regulation is repealed in relation to the UK (as from IP completion day); see the introductory notes to this Regulation *ante*.

[4.556]

Article 17 Professional secrecy

1. Information acquired as a result of the application of this Regulation shall be used only for the purposes of the relevant request, investigation or hearing.

2. Without prejudice to Article 4(3), Articles 18 and 20, the Commission and the competent authorities of the Member States, their officials and other servants and other persons working under the supervision of these authorities as well as officials and civil servants of other authorities of the Member States shall not disclose information they have acquired through the application of this Regulation of the kind covered by the obligation of professional secrecy.

3. Paragraphs 1 and 2 shall not prevent publication of general information or of surveys which do not contain information relating to particular undertakings or associations of undertakings.

NOTES

Repeal of this Regulation in relation to the UK: this Regulation is repealed in relation to the UK (as from IP completion day); see the introductory notes to this Regulation *ante*.

[4.557]

Article 18 Hearing of the parties and of third persons

1. Before taking any decision provided for in Article 6(3), Article 7(3), Article 8(2) to (6), and Articles 14 and 15, the Commission shall give the persons, undertakings and associations of undertakings concerned the opportunity, at every stage of the procedure up to the consultation of the Advisory Committee, of making known their views on the objections against them.

2. By way of derogation from paragraph 1, a decision pursuant to Articles 7(3) and 8(5) may be taken provisionally, without the persons, undertakings or associations of undertakings concerned being given the opportunity to make known their views beforehand, provided that the Commission gives them that opportunity as soon as possible after having taken its decision.

3. The Commission shall base its decision only on objections on which the parties have been able to submit their observations. The rights of the defence shall be fully respected in the proceedings. Access to the file shall be open at least to the parties directly involved, subject to the legitimate interest of undertakings in the protection of their business secrets.

4. In so far as the Commission or the competent authorities of the Member States deem it necessary, they may also hear other natural or legal persons. Natural or legal persons showing a sufficient interest and especially members of the administrative or management bodies of the undertakings concerned or the recognised representatives of their employees shall be entitled, upon application, to be heard.

NOTES

Repeal of this Regulation in relation to the UK: this Regulation is repealed in relation to the UK (as from IP completion day); see the introductory notes to this Regulation *ante*.

[4.558]

Article 19 Liaison with the authorities of the Member States

1. The Commission shall transmit to the competent authorities of the Member States copies of notifications within three working days and, as soon as possible, copies of the most important documents lodged with or issued by the Commission pursuant to this Regulation. Such documents shall include commitments offered by the undertakings concerned vis-à-vis the Commission with a view to rendering the concentration compatible with the common market pursuant to Article 6(2) or Article 8(2), second subparagraph.

2. The Commission shall carry out the procedures set out in this Regulation in close and constant liaison with the competent authorities of the Member States, which may express their views upon those procedures. For the purposes of Article 9 it shall obtain information from the competent authority of the Member State as referred to in paragraph 2 of that Article and give it the opportunity to make known its views at every stage of the procedure up to the adoption of a decision pursuant to paragraph 3 of that Article; to that end it shall give it access to the file.

3. An Advisory Committee on concentrations shall be consulted before any decision is taken pursuant to Article 8(1) to (6), Articles 14 or 15 with the exception of provisional decisions taken in accordance with Article 18(2).

4. The Advisory Committee shall consist of representatives of the competent authorities of the Member States. Each Member State shall appoint one or two representatives; if unable to attend, they may be replaced by other representatives. At least one of the representatives of a Member State shall be competent in matters of restrictive practices and dominant positions.

5. Consultation shall take place at a joint meeting convened at the invitation of and chaired by the Commission. A summary of the case, together with an indication of the most important documents and a preliminary draft of the decision to be taken for each case considered, shall be sent with the invitation. The meeting shall take place not less than 10 working days after the invitation has been sent. The Commission may in exceptional cases shorten that period as appropriate in order to avoid serious harm to one or more of the undertakings concerned by a concentration.

6. The Advisory Committee shall deliver an opinion on the Commission's draft decision, if necessary by taking a vote. The Advisory Committee may deliver an opinion even if some members are absent and unrepresented. The opinion shall be delivered in writing and appended to the draft decision. The Commission shall take the utmost account of the opinion delivered by the Committee. It shall inform the Committee of the manner in which its opinion has been taken into account.

7. The Commission shall communicate the opinion of the Advisory Committee, together with the decision, to the addressees of the decision. It shall make the opinion public together with the decision, having regard to the legitimate interest of undertakings in the protection of their business secrets.

NOTES

Repeal of this Regulation in relation to the UK: this Regulation is repealed in relation to the UK (as from IP completion day); see the introductory notes to this Regulation *ante*.

[4.559]

Article 20 Publication of decisions

1. The Commission shall publish the decisions which it takes pursuant to Article 8(1) to (6), Articles 14 and 15 with the exception of provisional decisions taken in accordance with Article 18(2) together with the opinion of the Advisory Committee in the Official Journal of the European Union.

2. The publication shall state the names of the parties and the main content of the decision; it shall have regard to the legitimate interest of undertakings in the protection of their business secrets.

NOTES

Repeal of this Regulation in relation to the UK: this Regulation is repealed in relation to the UK (as from IP completion day); see the introductory notes to this Regulation *ante*.

[4.560]

Article 21 Application of the Regulation and jurisdiction

1. This Regulation alone shall apply to concentrations as defined in Article 3, and Council Regulations (EC) No 1/2003,[1] (EEC) No 1017/68,[2] (EEC) No 4056/86[3] and (EEC) No 3975/87[4] shall not apply, except in relation to joint ventures that do not have a Community dimension and which have as their object or effect the coordination of the competitive behaviour of undertakings that remain independent.

2. Subject to review by the Court of Justice, the Commission shall have sole jurisdiction to take the decisions provided for in this Regulation.

3. No Member State shall apply its national legislation on competition to any concentration that has a Community dimension.

The first subparagraph shall be without prejudice to any Member State's power to carry out any enquiries necessary for the application of Articles 4(4), 9(2) or after referral, pursuant to Article 9(3), first subparagraph, indent (b), or Article 9(5), to take the measures strictly necessary for the application of Article 9(8).

4. Notwithstanding paragraphs 2 and 3, Member States may take appropriate measures to protect legitimate interests other than those taken into consideration by this Regulation and compatible with the general principles and other provisions of Community law.

Public security, plurality of the media and prudential rules shall be regarded as legitimate interests within the meaning of the first subparagraph.

Any other public interest must be communicated to the Commission by the Member State concerned and shall be recognised by the Commission after an assessment of its compatibility with the general principles and other provisions of Community law before the measures referred to above may be taken. The Commission shall inform the Member State concerned of its decision within 25 working days of that communication.

NOTES

Repeal of this Regulation in relation to the UK: this Regulation is repealed in relation to the UK (as from IP completion day); see the introductory notes to this Regulation *ante*.

[1] OJ L1, 4.1.2003, p 1.

[2] OJ L175, 23.7.1968, p 1. Regulation as last amended by Regulation (EC) No 1/2003 (OJ L1, 4.1.2003, p 1).

[3] OJ L378, 31.12.1986, p 4. Regulation as last amended by Regulation (EC) No 1/2003.

[4] OJ L374, 31.12.1987, p 1. Regulation as last amended by Regulation (EC) No 1/2003.

[4.561]

Article 22 Referral to the Commission

1. One or more Member States may request the Commission to examine any concentration as defined in Article 3 that does not have a Community dimension within the meaning of Article 1 but affects trade between Member States and threatens to significantly affect competition within the territory of the Member State or States making the request.

Such a request shall be made at most within 15 working days of the date on which the concentration was notified, or if no notification is required, otherwise made known to the Member State concerned.

2. The Commission shall inform the competent authorities of the Member States and the undertakings concerned of any request received pursuant to paragraph 1 without delay.

Any other Member State shall have the right to join the initial request within a period of 15 working days of being informed by the Commission of the initial request.

All national time limits relating to the concentration shall be suspended until, in accordance with the procedure set out in this Article, it has been decided where the concentration shall be examined. As soon as a Member State has informed the Commission and the undertakings concerned that it does not wish to join the request, the suspension of its national time limits shall end.

3. The Commission may, at the latest 10 working days after the expiry of the period set in paragraph 2, decide to examine, the concentration where it considers that it affects trade between Member States and threatens to significantly affect competition within the territory of the Member State or States making the request. If the Commission does not take a decision within this period, it shall be deemed to have adopted a decision to examine the concentration in accordance with the request.

The Commission shall inform all Member States and the undertakings concerned of its decision. It may request the submission of a notification pursuant to Article 4.

The Member State or States having made the request shall no longer apply their national legislation on competition to the concentration.

4. Article 2, Article 4(2) to (3), Articles 5, 6, and 8 to 21 shall apply where the Commission examines a concentration pursuant to paragraph 3. Article 7 shall apply to the extent that the concentration has not been implemented on the date on which the Commission informs the undertakings concerned that a request has been made.

Where a notification pursuant to Article 4 is not required, the period set in Article 10(1) within which proceedings may be initiated shall begin on the working day following that on which the Commission informs the undertakings concerned that it has decided to examine the concentration pursuant to paragraph 3.

5. The Commission may inform one or several Member States that it considers a concentration fulfils the criteria in paragraph 1. In such cases, the Commission may invite that Member State or those Member States to make a request pursuant to paragraph 1.

NOTES

Repeal of this Regulation in relation to the UK: this Regulation is repealed in relation to the UK (as from IP completion day); see the introductory notes to this Regulation *ante*.

[4.562]

Article 23 Implementing provisions

1. The Commission shall have the power to lay down in accordance with the procedure referred to in paragraph 2:

- *(a) implementing provisions concerning the form, content and other details of notifications and submissions pursuant to Article 4;*
- *(b) implementing provisions concerning time limits pursuant to Article 4(4), (5) Articles 7, 9, 10 and 22;*
- *(c) the procedure and time limits for the submission and implementation of commitments pursuant to Article 6(2) and Article 8(2);*
- *(d) implementing provisions concerning hearings pursuant to Article 18.*

2. The Commission shall be assisted by an Advisory Committee, composed of representatives of the Member States.

- *(a) Before publishing draft implementing provisions and before adopting such provisions, the Commission shall consult the Advisory Committee.*
- *(b) Consultation shall take place at a meeting convened at the invitation of and chaired by the Commission. A draft of the implementing provisions to be taken shall be sent with the invitation. The meeting shall take place not less than 10 working days after the invitation has been sent.*
- *(c) The Advisory Committee shall deliver an opinion on the draft implementing provisions, if necessary by taking a vote. The Commission shall take the utmost account of the opinion delivered by the Committee.*

NOTES

Repeal of this Regulation in relation to the UK: this Regulation is repealed in relation to the UK (as from IP completion day); see the introductory notes to this Regulation *ante*.

[4.563]

Article 24 Relations with third countries

1. The Member States shall inform the Commission of any general difficulties encountered by their undertakings with concentrations as defined in Article 3 in a third country.

2. Initially not more than one year after the entry into force of this Regulation and, thereafter periodically, the Commission shall draw up a report examining the treatment accorded to undertakings having their seat or their principal fields of activity in the Community, in the terms referred to in paragraphs 3 and 4, as regards concentrations in third countries. The Commission shall submit those reports to the Council, together with any recommendations.

3. Whenever it appears to the Commission, either on the basis of the reports referred to in paragraph 2 or on the basis of other information, that a third country does not grant undertakings having their seat or their principal fields of activity in the Community, treatment comparable to that granted by the Community to undertakings from that country, the Commission may submit proposals to the Council for an appropriate mandate for negotiation with a view to obtaining comparable treatment for undertakings having their seat or their principal fields of activity in the Community.

4. Measures taken under this Article shall comply with the obligations of the Community or of the Member States, without prejudice to Article 307 of the Treaty, under international agreements, whether bilateral or multilateral.

NOTES

Repeal of this Regulation in relation to the UK: this Regulation is repealed in relation to the UK (as from IP completion day); see the introductory notes to this Regulation *ante*.

[4.564]

Article 25 Repeal

1. Without prejudice to Article 26(2), Regulations (EEC) No 4064/89 and (EC) No 1310/97 shall be repealed with effect from 1 May 2004.

2. References to the repealed Regulations shall be construed as references to this Regulation and shall be read in accordance with the correlation table in the Annex.

NOTES

Repeal of this Regulation in relation to the UK: this Regulation is repealed in relation to the UK (as from IP completion day); see the introductory notes to this Regulation *ante*.

[4.565]

Article 26 Entry into force and transitional provisions

1. This Regulation shall enter into force on the 20th day following that of its publication in the Official Journal of the European Union.

It shall apply from 1 May 2004.

2. Regulation (EEC) No 4064/89 shall continue to apply to any concentration which was the subject of an agreement or announcement or where control was acquired within the meaning of Article 4(1) of that Regulation before the date of application of this Regulation, subject, in particular, to the provisions governing applicability set out in Article 25(2) and (3) of Regulation (EEC) No 4064/89 and Article 2 of Regulation (EEC) No 1310/97.

3. As regards concentrations to which this Regulation applies by virtue of accession, the date of accession shall be substituted for the date of application of this Regulation.

NOTES

Repeal of this Regulation in relation to the UK: this Regulation is repealed in relation to the UK (as from IP completion day); see the introductory notes to this Regulation *ante*.

ANNEX

CORRELATION TABLE

[4.566]

Regulation (EEC) No 4064/89	***This Regulation***
Article 1(1), (2) and (3)	*Article 1(1), (2) and (3)*
Article 1(4)	*Article 1(4)*
Article 1(5)	*Article 1(5)*
Article 2(1)	*Article 2(1)*
—	*Article 2(2)*
Article 2(2)	*Article 2(3)*
Article 2(3)	*Article 2(4)*
Article 2(4)	*Article 2(5)*
Article 3(1)	*Article 3(1)*
Article 3(2)	*Article 3(4)*
Article 3(3)	*Article 3(2)*
Article 3(4)	*Article 3(3)*
—	*Article 3(4)*
Article 3(5)	*Article 3(5)*
Article 4(1) first sentence	*Article 4(1) first subparagraph*

Regulation (EEC) No 4064/89	This Regulation
Article 4(1) second sentence	—
—	Article 4(1) second and third subparagraphs
Article 4(2) and (3)	Article 4(2) and (3)
—	Article 4(4) to (6)
Article 5(1) to (3)	Article 5(1) to (3)
Article 5(4), introductory words	Article 5(4), introductory words
Article 5(4) point (a)	Article 5(4) point (a)
Article 5(4) point (b), introductory words	Article 5(4) point (b), introductory words
Article 5(4) point (b), first indent	Article 5(4) point (b)(i)
Article 5(4) point (b), second indent	Article 5(4) point (b)(ii)
Article 5(4) point (b), third indent	Article 5(4) point (b)(iii)
Article 5(4) point (b), fourth indent	Article 5(4) point (b)(iv)
Article 5(4) points (c), (d) and (e)	Article 5(4) points (c), (d) and (e)
Article 5(5)	Article 5(5)
Article 6(1), introductory words	Article 6(1), introductory words
Article 6(1) points (a) and (b)	Article 6(1) points (a) and (b)
Article 6(1) point (c)	Article 6(1) point (c), first sentence
Article 6(2) to (5)	Article 6(2) to (5)
Article 7(1)	Article 7(1)
Article 7(3)	Article 7(2)
Article 7(4)	Article 7(3)
Article 7(5)	Article 7(4)
Article 8(1)	Article 6(1) point (c), second sentence
Article 8(2)	Article 8(1) and (2)
Article 8(3)	Article 8(3)
Article 8(4)	Article 8(4)
—	Article 8(5)
Article 8(5)	Article 8(6)
Article 8(6)	Article 8(7)
—	Article 8(8)
Article 9(1) to (9)	Article 9(1) to (9)
Article 9(10)	—
Article 10(1) and (2)	Article 10(1) and (2)
Article 10(3)	Article 10(3) first subparagraph, first sentence
—	Article 10(3) first subparagraph, second sentence
—	Article 10(3) second subparagraph
Article 10(4)	Article 10(4) first subparagraph
—	Article 10(4), second subparagraph
Article 10(5)	Article 10(5), first and fourth subparagraphs
—	Article 10(5), second, third and fifth subparagraphs
Article 10(6)	Article 10(6)
Article 11(1)	Article 11(1)
Article 11(2)	—
Article 11(3)	Article 11(2)
Article 11(4)	Article 11(4) first sentence
—	Article 11(4) second and third sentences
Article 11(5) first sentence	—
Article 11(5) second sentence	Article 11(3)
Article 11(6)	Article 11(5)
—	Article 11(6) and (7)
Article 12	Article 12
Article 13(1) first subparagraph	Article 13(1)

Regulation (EEC) No 4064/89	*This Regulation*
Article 13(1) second subparagraph, introductory words	*Article 13(2) introductory words*
Article 13(1) second subparagraph, point (a)	*Article 13(2) point (b)*
Article 13(1) second subparagraph, point (b)	*Article 13(2) point (c)*
Article 13(1) second subparagraph, point (c)	*Article 13(2) point (e)*
Article 13(1) second subparagraph, point (d)	*Article 13(2) point (a)*
—	*Article 13(2) point (d)*
Article 13(2)	*Article 13(3)*
Article 13(3)	*Article 13(4) first and second sentences*
Article 13(4)	*Article 13(4) third sentence*
Article 13(5)	*Article 13(5), first sentence*
—	*Article 13(5), second sentence*
Article 13(6) first sentence	*Article 13(6)*
Article 13(6) second sentence	—
—	*Article 13(7) and (8)*
Article 14(1) introductory words	*Article 14(1) introductory words*
Article 14(1) point (a)	*Article 14(2) point (a)*
Article 14(1) point (b)	*Article 14(1) point (a)*
Article 14(1) point (c)	*Article 14(1) points (b) and (c)*
Article 14(1) point (d)	*Article 14(1) point (d)*
—	*Article 14(1) points (e) and (f)*
Article 14(2) introductory words	*Article 14(2) introductory words*
Article 14(2) point (a)	*Article 14(2) point (d)*
Article 14(2) points (b) and (c)	*Article 14(2) points (b) and (c)*
Article 14(3)	*Article 14(3)*
Article 14(4)	*Article 14(4)*
Article 15(1) introductory words	*Article 15(1) introductory words*
Article 15(1) points (a) and (b)	*Article 15(1) points (a) and (b)*
Article 15(2) introductory words	*Article 15(1) introductory words*
Article 15(2) point (a)	*Article 15(1) point (c)*
Article 15(2) point (b)	*Article 15(1) point (d)*
Article 15(3)	*Article 15(2)*
Articles 16 to 20	*Articles 16 to 20*
Article 21(1)	*Article 21(2)*
Article 21(2)	*Article 21(3)*
Article 21(3)	*Article 21(4)*
Article 22(1)	*Article 21(1)*
Article 22(3)	—
—	*Article 22(1) to (3)*
Article 22(4)	*Article 22(4)*
Article 22(5)	—
—	*Article 22(5)*
Article 23	*Article 23(1)*
—	*Article 23(2)*
Article 24	*Article 24*
—	*Article 25*
Article 25(1)	*Article 26(1), first subparagraph*
—	*Article 26(1), second subparagraph*
Article 25(2)	*Article 26(2)*
Article 25(3)	*Article 26(3)*
—	*Annex*

NOTES

Repeal of this Regulation in relation to the UK: this Regulation is repealed in relation to the UK (as from IP completion day); see the introductory notes to this Regulation *ante*.

COMMISSION REGULATION

(802/2004/EC)

of 21 April 2004

implementing Council Regulation (EC) No 139/2004 on the control of concentrations between undertakings

[4.567]

NOTES

Date of publication in OJ: OJ L133, 30.4.2004, p 1. The text of this Regulation incorporates the corrigendum published in OJ L172, 6.5.2004, p 9.

Repeal of this Regulation in relation to the UK: this Regulation is repealed, in relation to the UK, by the Competition (Amendment etc) (EU Exit) Regulations 2019, SI 2019/93, reg 63, Sch 3, para 2, as from IP completion day (as defined in the European Union (Withdrawal Agreement) Act 2020, s 39) (for transitional provisions and savings in relation to the operation of the 2019 Regulations, see Sch 4 to those Regulations at **[7.69]** et seq). Note also that Council Regulation 139/2004/EC is also repealed by Sch 3, para 1 to the 2019 Regulations (as from the same date).

Note: with effect from 1 December 2009, the Treaty establishing the European Community (the "EC Treaty") was replaced by the Treaty on the Functioning of the European Union. References in this document to provisions of the EC Treaty should be construed accordingly.

THE COMMISSION OF THE EUROPEAN COMMUNITIES,

Having regard to the Treaty establishing the European Community,

Having regard to the Agreement on the European Economic Area,

Having regard to Council Regulation (EC) No 139/2004 of 20 January 2004 on the control of concentrations between undertakings (EC Merger Regulation),[1] *and in particular Article 23(1) thereof,*

Having regard to Council Regulation (EEC) No 4064/89 of 21 December 1989 on the control of concentrations between undertakings,[2] *as last amended by Regulation (EC) No 1310/97,*[3] *and in particular Article 23 thereof,*

Having consulted the Advisory Committee,

Whereas:

(1) Council Regulation (EEC) No 4064/89 of 21 December 1989 on the control of concentrations between undertakings has been recast, with substantial amendments to various provisions of that Regulation.

(2) Commission Regulation (EC) No 447/98[4] *of 1 March 1998 on the notifications, time-limits and hearings provided for in Council Regulation (EEC) No 4064/89 must be modified in order to take account of those amendments. For the sake of clarity it should therefore be repealed and replaced by a new regulation.*

(3) The Commission has adopted measures concerning the terms of reference of hearing officers in certain competition proceedings.

(4) Regulation (EC) No 139/2004 is based on the principle of compulsory notification of concentrations before they are put into effect. On the one hand, a notification has important legal consequences which are favourable to the parties to the proposed concentration, while, on the other hand, failure to comply with the obligation to notify renders the parties liable to fines and may also entail civil law disadvantages for them. It is therefore necessary in the interests of legal certainty to define precisely the subject matter and content of the information to be provided in the notification.

(5) It is for the notifying parties to make a full and honest disclosure to the Commission of the facts and circumstances which are relevant for taking a decision on the notified concentration.

(6) Regulation (EC) No 139/2004 also allows the undertakings concerned to request, in a reasoned submission, prior to notification, that a concentration fulfilling the requirements of that Regulation be referred to the Commission by one or more Member States, or referred by the Commission to one or more Member States, as the case may be. It is important to provide the Commission and the competent authorities of the Member States concerned with sufficient information, in order to enable them to assess, within a short period of time, whether or not a referral ought to be made. To that end, the reasoned submission requesting the referral should contain certain specific information.

(7) In order to simplify and expedite examination of notifications and of reasoned submissions, it is desirable to prescribe that forms be used.

(8) Since notification sets in motion legal time-limits pursuant to Regulation (EC) No 139/2004, the conditions governing such time-limits and the time when they become effective should also be determined.

(9) Rules must be laid down in the interests of legal certainty for calculating the time-limits provided for in Regulation (EC) No 139/2004. In particular, the beginning and end of time periods and the circumstances suspending the running of such periods must be determined, with due regard to the requirements resulting from the exceptionally tight legal timeframe available for the proceedings.

(10) The provisions relating to the Commission's procedure must be framed in such a way as to safeguard fully the right to be heard and the rights of defence. For these purposes, the Commission should distinguish between the parties who notify the concentration, other parties involved in the proposed concentration, third parties and parties regarding whom the Commission intends to take a decision imposing a fine or periodic penalty payments.

(11) The Commission should give the notifying parties and other parties involved in the proposed concentration, if they so request, an opportunity before notification to discuss the intended concentration informally and in strict

confidence. In addition, the Commission should, after notification, maintain close contact with those parties, to the extent necessary to discuss with them any practical or legal problems which it discovers on a first examination of the case, with a view, if possible, to resolving such problems by mutual agreement.

(12) In accordance with the principle of respect for the rights of defence, the notifying parties must be given the opportunity to submit their comments on all the objections which the Commission proposes to take into account in its decisions. The other parties involved in the proposed concentration should also be informed of the Commission's objections and should be granted the opportunity to express their views.

(13) Third parties demonstrating a sufficient interest must also be given the opportunity of expressing their views, if they make a written application to that effect.

(14) The various persons entitled to submit comments should do so in writing, both in their own interests and in the interests of sound administration, without prejudice to their right to request a formal oral hearing, where appropriate, to supplement the written procedure. In urgent cases, however, the Commission must be enabled to proceed immediately to formal oral hearings of the notifying parties, of other parties involved or of third parties.

(15) It is necessary to define the rights of persons who are to be heard, to what extent they should be granted access to the Commission's file and on what conditions they may be represented or assisted.

(16) When granting access to the file, the Commission should ensure the protection of business secrets and other confidential information. The Commission should be able to ask undertakings that have submitted documents or statements to identify confidential information.

(17) In order to enable the Commission to carry out a proper assessment of commitments offered by the notifying parties with a view to rendering the concentration compatible with the common market, and to ensure due consultation with other parties involved, with third parties and with the authorities of the Member States as provided for in Regulation (EC) No 139/2004, in particular Article 18(1), 18(4), Article 19(1), 19(2), 19(3) and 19(5) thereof, the procedure and time-limits for submitting the commitments referred to in Article 6(2) and Article 8(2) of that Regulation should be laid down.

(18) It is also necessary to define the rules applicable to certain time limits set by the Commission.

(19) The Advisory Committee on Concentrations must deliver its opinion on the basis of a preliminary draft decision. It must therefore be consulted on a case after the inquiry in to that case has been completed. Such consultation does not, however, prevent the Commission from reopening an inquiry if need be.

NOTES

Repeal of this Regulation in relation to the UK: this Regulation is repealed in relation to the UK (as from IP completion day); see the introductory notes to this Regulation *ante*.

[1] OJ L24, 29.1.2004, p 1.

[2] OJ L395, 30.12.1989, p 1.

[3] OJ L180, 9.7.1997, p 1.

[4] OJ L61, 2.3.1998, p 1. Regulation as amended by the 2003 Act of Accession.

HAS ADOPTED THIS REGULATION:

CHAPTER I SCOPE

[4.568]

Article 1 Scope

This Regulation shall apply to the control of concentrations conducted pursuant to Regulation (EC) No 139/2004.

NOTES

Repeal of this Regulation in relation to the UK: this Regulation is repealed in relation to the UK (as from IP completion day); see the introductory notes to this Regulation *ante*.

CHAPTER II NOTIFICATIONS AND OTHER SUBMISSIONS

[4.569]

Article 2 Persons entitled to submit notifications

1. Notifications shall be submitted by the persons or undertakings referred to in Article 4(2) of Regulation (EC) No 139/2004.

[2. Where notifications are signed by authorised external representatives of persons or of undertakings, such representatives shall produce written proof that they are authorised to act.]

3. Joint notifications shall be submitted by a joint representative who is authorised to transmit and to receive documents on behalf of all notifying parties.

NOTES

Para 2: substituted by Commission Regulation 1269/2013/EU, Art 1(1).

Repeal of this Regulation in relation to the UK: this Regulation is repealed in relation to the UK (as from IP completion day); see the introductory notes to this Regulation *ante*.

[4.570]

Article 3 Submission of notifications

1. Notifications shall be submitted in the manner prescribed by Form CO as set out in Annex I. Under the conditions set out in Annex II, notifications may be submitted in Short Form as defined therein. Joint notifications shall be submitted on a single form.

[2. The Form CO and the supporting documents shall be submitted to the Commission in the format and with the number of copies specified by the Commission from time to time in the Official Journal of the European Union. The notification shall be delivered to the address referred to in Article 23(1).]

3. The supporting documents shall be either originals or copies of the originals; in the latter case the notifying parties shall confirm that they are true and complete.

4. Notifications shall be in one of the official languages of the Community. For the notifying parties, this language shall also be the language of the proceeding, as well as that of any subsequent proceedings relating to the same concentration. Supporting documents shall be submitted in their original language. Where the original language is not one of the official languages of the Community, a translation into the language of the proceeding shall be attached.

5. Where notifications are made pursuant to Article 57 of the Agreement on the European Economic Area, they may also be submitted in one of the official languages of the EFTA States or the working language of the EFTA Surveillance Authority. If the language chosen for the notifications is not an official language of the Community, the notifying parties shall simultaneously supplement all documentation with a translation into an official language of the Community. The language which is chosen for the translation shall determine the language used by the Commission as the language of the proceeding for the notifying parties.

NOTES

Para 2: substituted by Commission Regulation 1269/2013/EU, Art 1(2).

Repeal of this Regulation in relation to the UK: this Regulation is repealed in relation to the UK (as from IP completion day); see the introductory notes to this Regulation *ante*.

[4.571]

Article 4 Information and documents to be provided

[1. Notifications shall contain the information, including documents, requested in the applicable forms set out in Annexes I and II. The information shall be correct and complete.]

2. The Commission may dispense with the obligation to provide any particular information in the notification, including documents, or with any other requirement specified in Annexes I and II where the Commission considers that compliance with those obligations or requirements is not necessary for the examination of the case.

3. The Commission shall without delay acknowledge in writing to the notifying parties or their representatives receipt of the notification and of any reply to a letter sent by the Commission pursuant to Article 5(2) and 5(3).

NOTES

Para 1: substituted by Commission Regulation 1269/2013/EU, Art 1(3).

Repeal of this Regulation in relation to the UK: this Regulation is repealed in relation to the UK (as from IP completion day); see the introductory notes to this Regulation *ante*.

[4.572]

Article 5 Effective date of notification

1. Subject to paragraphs 2, 3 and 4, notifications shall become effective on the date on which they are received by the Commission.

2. Where the information, including documents, contained in the notification is incomplete in any material respect, the Commission shall inform the notifying parties or their representatives in writing without delay. In such cases, the notification shall become effective on the date on which the complete information is received by the Commission.

3. Material changes in the facts contained in the notification coming to light subsequent to the notification which the notifying parties know or ought to know, or any new information coming to light subsequent to the notification which the parties know or ought to know and which would have had to be notified if known at the time of notification, shall be communicated to the Commission without delay. In such cases, when these material changes or new information could have a significant effect on the appraisal of the concentration, the notification may be considered by the Commission as becoming effective on the date on which the relevant information is received by the Commission; the Commission shall inform the notifying parties or their representatives of this in writing and without delay.

4. Incorrect or misleading information shall be considered to be incomplete information.

5. When the Commission publishes the fact of the notification pursuant to Article 4(3) of Regulation (EC) No 139/2004, it shall specify the date upon which the notification has been received. Where, further to the application of paragraphs 2, 3 and 4 of this Article, the effective date of notification is later than the date specified in that publication, the Commission shall issue a further publication in which it shall state the later date.

NOTES

Repeal of this Regulation in relation to the UK: this Regulation is repealed in relation to the UK (as from IP completion day); see the introductory notes to this Regulation *ante*.

[4.573]

Article 6 Specific provisions relating to reasoned submissions, supplements and certifications

1. Reasoned submissions within the meaning of Article 4(4) and 4(5) of Regulation (EC) No 139/2004 shall contain the information, including documents, requested in accordance with Annex III to this Regulation.

[2. Article 2, Article 3(1), third sentence, Article 3(2) to (5), Article 4, Article 5(1) to (4), Article 21 and Article 23 of this Regulation shall apply mutatis mutandis to reasoned submissions within the meaning of Article 4(4) 4(5) of Regulation (EC) No 139/2004.]

Article 2, Article 3(1), third sentence, 3(2) to (5), Article 4, Article 5(1) to (4), Article 21 and Article 23 of this Regulation shall apply mutatis mutandis to supplements to notifications and certifications within the meaning of Article 10(5) of Regulation (EC) No 139/2004.

NOTES

Para 2: first sub-paragraph substituted by Commission Regulation 1269/2013/EU, Art 1(4).

Repeal of this Regulation in relation to the UK: this Regulation is repealed in relation to the UK (as from IP completion day); see the introductory notes to this Regulation *ante*.

CHAPTER III TIME-LIMITS

[4.574]

Article 7 Beginning of time periods

Time periods shall begin on the working day, as defined in Article 24 of this Regulation, following the event to which the relevant provision of Regulation (EC) No 139/2004 refers.

NOTES

Repeal of this Regulation in relation to the UK: this Regulation is repealed in relation to the UK (as from IP completion day); see the introductory notes to this Regulation *ante*.

[4.575]

Article 8 Expiry of time periods

A time period calculated in working days shall expire at the end of its last working day.

A time period set by the Commission in terms of a calendar date shall expire at the end of that day.

NOTES

Repeal of this Regulation in relation to the UK: this Regulation is repealed in relation to the UK (as from IP completion day); see the introductory notes to this Regulation *ante*.

[4.576]

Article 9 Suspension of time limit

1. The time limits referred to in Articles 9(4), Article 10(1) and 10(3) of Regulation (EC) No 139/2004 shall be suspended where the Commission has to take a decision pursuant to Article 11(3) or Article 13(4) of that Regulation, on any of the following grounds:

- *(a) information which the Commission has requested pursuant to Article 11(2) of Regulation (EC) No 139/2004 from one of the notifying parties or another involved party, as defined in Article 11 of this Regulation, is not provided or not provided in full within the time limit fixed by the Commission;*
- *(b) information which the Commission has requested pursuant to Article 11(2) of Regulation (EC) No 139/2004 from a third party, as defined in Article 11 of this Regulation, is not provided or not provided in full within the time limit fixed by the Commission owing to circumstances for which one of the notifying parties or another involved party, as defined in Article 11 of this Regulation, is responsible;*
- *(c) one of the notifying parties or another involved party, as defined in Article 11 of this Regulation, has refused to submit to an inspection deemed necessary by the Commission on the basis of Article 13(1) of Regulation (EC) No 139/2004 or to cooperate in the carrying out of such an inspection in accordance with Article 13(2) of that Regulation;*
- *(d) the notifying parties have failed to inform the Commission of material changes in the facts contained in the notification, or of any new information of the kind referred to in Article 5(3) of this Regulation.*

2. The time limits referred to in Articles 9(4), Article 10(1) and 10(3) of Regulation (EC) No 139/2004 shall be suspended where the Commission has to take a decision pursuant to Article 11(3) of that Regulation, without proceeding first by way of simple request for information, owing to circumstances for which one of the undertakings involved in the concentration is responsible.

3. The time limits referred to in Articles 9(4), Article 10(1) and (3) of Regulation (EC) No 139/2004 shall be suspended:

- *(a) in the cases referred to in points (a) and (b) of paragraph 1, for the period between the expiry of the time limit set in the simple request for information, and the receipt of the complete and correct information required by decision;*
- *(b) in the cases referred to in point (c) of paragraph 1, for the period between the unsuccessful attempt to carry out the inspection and the completion of the inspection ordered by decision;*
- *(c) in the cases referred to in point (d) of paragraph 1, for the period between the occurrence of the change in the facts referred to therein and the receipt of the complete and correct information;*
- *(d) in the cases referred to in paragraph 2 for the period between the expiry of the time limit set in the decision and the receipt of the complete and correct information required by decision.*

4. The suspension of the time limit shall begin on the working day following the date on which the event causing the suspension occurred. It shall expire with the end of the day on which the reason for suspension is removed. Where such a day is not a working day, the suspension of the time-limit shall expire with the end of the following working day.

NOTES

Repeal of this Regulation in relation to the UK: this Regulation is repealed in relation to the UK (as from IP completion day); see the introductory notes to this Regulation *ante*.

[4.577]

Article 10 Compliance with the time-limits

1. The time limits referred to in Article 4(4), fourth subparagraph, Article 9(4), Article 10(1) and (3), and Article 22(3) of Regulation (EC) No 139/2004 shall be met where the Commission has taken the relevant decision before the end of the period.

2. The time limits referred to in Article 4(4), second subparagraph, Article 4(5), third subparagraph, Article 9(2), Article 22(1), second subparagraph, and 22(2), second subparagraph, of Regulation (EC) No 139/2004 shall be met by a Member State concerned where that Member State, before the end of the period, informs the Commission in writing or makes or joins the request in writing, as the case may be.

3. The time limit referred to in Article 9(6) of Regulation (EC) No 139/2004 shall be met where the competent authority of a Member State concerned informs the undertakings concerned in the manner set out in that provision before the end of the period.

NOTES

Repeal of this Regulation in relation to the UK: this Regulation is repealed in relation to the UK (as from IP completion day); see the introductory notes to this Regulation *ante*.

CHAPTER IV EXERCISE OF THE RIGHT TO BE HEARD; HEARINGS

[4.578]

Article 11 Parties to be heard

For the purposes of the rights to be heard pursuant to Article 18 of Regulation (EC) No 139/2004, the following parties are distinguished:

(a) notifying parties, that is, persons or undertakings submitting a notification pursuant to Article 4(2) of Regulation (EC) No 139/2004;

(b) other involved parties, that is, parties to the proposed concentration other than the notifying parties, such as the seller and the undertaking which is the target of the concentration;

(c) third persons, that is natural or legal persons, including customers, suppliers and competitors, provided they demonstrate a sufficient interest within the meaning of Article 18(4), second sentence, of Regulation (EC) No 139/2004, which is the case in particular

- *for members of the administrative or management bodies of the undertakings concerned or the recognised representatives of their employees;*
- *for consumer associations, where the proposed concentration concerns products or services used by final consumers.*

(d) parties regarding whom the Commission intends to take a decision pursuant to Article 14 or Article 15 of Regulation (EC) No 139/2004.

NOTES

Repeal of this Regulation in relation to the UK: this Regulation is repealed in relation to the UK (as from IP completion day); see the introductory notes to this Regulation *ante*.

[4.579]

Article 12 Decisions on the suspension of concentrations

1. Where the Commission intends to take a decision pursuant to Article 7(3) of Regulation (EC) No 139/2004 which adversely affects one or more of the parties, it shall, pursuant to Article 18(1) of that Regulation, inform the notifying parties and other involved parties in writing of its objections and shall set a time limit within which they may make known their views in writing.

2. Where the Commission, pursuant to Article 18(2) of Regulation (EC) No 139/2004, has taken a decision referred to in paragraph 1 of this Article provisionally without having given the notifying parties and other involved parties the opportunity to make known their views, it shall without delay send them the text of the provisional decision and shall set a time limit within which they may make known their views in writing.

[Once the notifying parties and other involved parties have made known their views, the Commission shall take a final decision repealing, amending or confirming the provisional decision.] Where they have not made known their views in writing within the time limit set, the Commission's provisional decision shall become final with the expiry of that period.

NOTES

Para 2: words in square brackets substituted by Commission Regulation 1269/2013/EU, Art 1(5).

Repeal of this Regulation in relation to the UK: this Regulation is repealed in relation to the UK (as from IP completion day); see the introductory notes to this Regulation *ante*.

[4.580]

Article 13 Decisions on the substance of the case

1. Where the Commission intends to take a decision pursuant to Article 6(3) or Article 8(2) to (6) of Regulation (EC) No 139/2004, it shall, before consulting the Advisory Committee on Concentrations, hear the parties pursuant to Article 18(1) and (3) of that Regulation.

Article 12(2) of this Regulation shall apply mutatis mutandis where, in application of Article 18(2) of Regulation (EC) No 139/2004, the Commission has taken a decision pursuant to Article 8(5) of that Regulation provisionally.

2. The Commission shall address its objections in writing to the notifying parties.

The Commission shall, when giving notice of objections, set a time limit within which the notifying parties may inform the Commission of their comments in writing.

The Commission shall inform other involved parties in writing of these objections.

The Commission shall also set a time limit within which those other involved parties may inform the Commission of their comments in writing.

The Commission shall not be obliged to take into account comments received after the expiry of a time limit which it has set.

[3. The parties to whom the Commission's objections have been addressed or who have been informed of those objections may submit their comments on the objections. Any comments shall be submitted in writing within the time limit set. In their written comments, they may set out all facts and matters known to them which are relevant to their defence, and shall attach any relevant documents as proof of the facts set out. They may also propose that the Commission hear persons who may corroborate those facts. They shall submit their comments to the Commission at the address referred to in Article 23(1). The format in which the comments are to be submitted and the number of copies required shall be specified by the Commission from time to time in the Official Journal of the European Union. The Commission shall forward copies of such written comments without delay to the competent authorities of the Member States.]

4. Where the Commission intends to take a decision pursuant to Article 14 or Article 15 of Regulation (EC) No 139/2004, it shall, before consulting the Advisory Committee on Concentrations, hear pursuant to Article 18(1) and (3) of that Regulation the parties regarding whom the Commission intends to take such a decision.

The procedure provided for in paragraph 2, first and second subparagraphs, and paragraph 3 shall apply, mutatis mutandis.

NOTES

Para 3: substituted by Commission Regulation 1269/2013/EU, Art 1(6).

Repeal of this Regulation in relation to the UK: this Regulation is repealed in relation to the UK (as from IP completion day); see the introductory notes to this Regulation *ante*.

[4.581]

Article 14 Oral hearings

1. Where the Commission intends to take a decision pursuant to Article 6(3) or Article 8(2) to (6) of Regulation (EC) No 139/2004, it shall afford the notifying parties who have so requested in their written comments the opportunity to develop their arguments in a formal oral hearing. It may also, at other stages in the proceedings, afford the notifying parties the opportunity of expressing their views orally.

2. Where the Commission intends to take a decision pursuant to Article 6(3) or Article 8(2) to (6) of Regulation (EC) No 139/2004, it shall also afford other involved parties who have so requested in their written comments the opportunity to develop their arguments in a formal oral hearing. It may also, at other stages in the proceedings, afford other involved parties the opportunity of expressing their views orally.

3. Where the Commission intends to take a decision pursuant to Article 14 or Article 15 of Regulation (EC) No 139/2004, it shall afford parties on whom it proposes to impose a fine or periodic penalty payment the opportunity to develop their arguments in a formal oral hearing, if so requested in their written comments. It may also, at other stages in the proceedings, afford such parties the opportunity of expressing their views orally.

NOTES

Repeal of this Regulation in relation to the UK: this Regulation is repealed in relation to the UK (as from IP completion day); see the introductory notes to this Regulation *ante*.

[4.582]

Article 15 Conduct of formal oral hearings

1. Formal oral hearings shall be conducted by the Hearing Officer in full independence.

2. The Commission shall invite the persons to be heard to attend the formal oral hearing on such date as it shall determine.

3. The Commission shall invite the competent authorities of the Member States to take part in any formal oral hearing.

4. Persons invited to attend shall either appear in person or be represented by legal representatives or by representatives authorised by their constitution as appropriate. Undertakings and associations of undertakings may also be represented by a duly authorised agent appointed from among their permanent staff.

5. Persons heard by the Commission may be assisted by their lawyers or other qualified and duly authorised persons admitted by the Hearing Officer.

6. Formal oral hearings shall not be public. Each person may be heard separately or in the presence of other persons invited to attend, having regard to the legitimate interest of the undertakings in the protection of their business secrets and other confidential information.

7. The Hearing Officer may allow all parties within the meaning of Article 11, the Commission services and the competent authorities of the Member States to ask questions during the formal oral hearing.

The Hearing Officer may hold a preparatory meeting with the parties and the Commission services, so as to facilitate the efficient organisation of the formal oral hearing.

8. The statements made by each person heard shall be recorded. Upon request, the recording of the formal oral hearing shall be made available to the persons who attended that hearing. Regard shall be had to the legitimate interest of the undertakings in the protection of their business secrets and other confidential information.

NOTES

Repeal of this Regulation in relation to the UK: this Regulation is repealed in relation to the UK (as from IP completion day); see the introductory notes to this Regulation *ante*.

[4.583]

Article 16 Hearing of third persons

1. If third persons apply in writing to be heard pursuant to Article 18(4), second sentence, of Regulation (EC) No 139/2004, the Commission shall inform them in writing of the nature and subject matter of the procedure and shall set a time limit within which they may make known their views.

2. The third persons referred to in paragraph 1 shall make known their views in writing within the time limit set. The Commission may, where appropriate, afford such third parties who have so requested in their written comments the opportunity to participate in a formal hearing. It may also in other cases afford such third parties the opportunity of expressing their views orally.

3. The Commission may likewise invite any other natural or legal person to express its views, in writing as well as orally, including at a formal oral hearing.

NOTES

Repeal of this Regulation in relation to the UK: this Regulation is repealed in relation to the UK (as from IP completion day); see the introductory notes to this Regulation *ante*.

CHAPTER V ACCESS TO THE FILE AND TREATMENT OF CONFIDENTIAL INFORMATION

[4.584]

Article 17 Access to the file and use of documents

1. If so requested, the Commission shall grant access to the file to the parties to whom it has addressed a statement of objections, for the purpose of enabling them to exercise their rights of defence. Access shall be granted after the notification of the statement of objections.

2. The Commission shall, upon request, also give the other involved parties who have been informed of the objections access to the file in so far as this is necessary for the purposes of preparing their comments.

[3. The right of access to the file shall not extend to confidential information, or to internal documents of the Commission or of the competent authorities of the Member States. The right of access to the file shall equally not extend to correspondence between the Commission and the competent authorities of the Member States, between the competent authorities of the Member States and between the Commission and other competition authorities.]

4. Documents obtained through access to the file pursuant to this Article may only be used for the purposes of the relevant proceeding pursuant to Regulation (EC) No 139/2004.

NOTES

Para 3: substituted by Commission Regulation 1269/2013/EU, Art 1(7).

Repeal of this Regulation in relation to the UK: this Regulation is repealed in relation to the UK (as from IP completion day); see the introductory notes to this Regulation *ante*.

[4.585]

Article 18 Confidential information

1. Information, including documents, shall not be communicated or made accessible by the Commission in so far as it contains business secrets or other confidential information the disclosure of which is not considered necessary by the Commission for the purpose of the procedure.

2. Any person which makes known its views or comments pursuant to Articles 12, Article 13 and Article 16 of this Regulation, or supplies information pursuant to Article 11 of Regulation (EC) No 139/2004, or subsequently submits further information to the Commission in the course of the same procedure, shall clearly identify any material which it considers to be confidential, giving reasons, and provide a separate non-confidential version by the date set by the Commission.

3. Without prejudice to paragraph 2, the Commission may require persons referred to in Article 3 of Regulation (EC) No 139/2004, undertakings and associations of undertakings in all cases where they produce or have produced documents or statements pursuant to Regulation (EC) No 139/2004 to identify the documents or parts of documents which they consider to contain business secrets or other confidential information belonging to them and to identify the undertakings with regard to which such documents are to be considered confidential.

The Commission may also require persons referred to in Article 3 of Regulation (EC) No 139/2004, undertakings or associations of undertakings to identify any part of a statement of objections, case summary or a decision adopted by the Commission which in their view contains business secrets.

Where business secrets or other confidential information are identified, the persons, undertakings and associations of undertakings shall give reasons and provide a separate non-confidential version by the date set by the Commission.

[4. If persons, undertakings or associations of undertakings fail to comply with paragraphs 2 or 3, the Commission may assume that the documents or statements concerned do not contain confidential information.]

NOTES

Para 4: added by Commission Regulation 1033/2008/EC, Art 1(1).

Repeal of this Regulation in relation to the UK: this Regulation is repealed in relation to the UK (as from IP completion day); see the introductory notes to this Regulation *ante*.

CHAPTER VI COMMITMENTS OFFERED BY THE UNDERTAKINGS CONCERNED

[4.586]

Article 19 Time limits for submission of commitments

1. Commitments offered by the undertakings concerned pursuant to Article 6(2) of Regulation (EC) No 139/2004 shall be submitted to the Commission within not more than 20 working days from the date of receipt of the notification.

[2. Commitments offered by the undertakings concerned pursuant to Article 8(2) of Regulation (EC) No 139/2004 shall be submitted to the Commission within not more than 65 working days from the date on which proceedings were initiated.

Where the undertakings concerned first offer commitments within less than 55 working days from the date on which proceedings were initiated but submit a modified version of the commitments 55 or more working days from that date, the modified commitments shall be deemed to be new commitments for the purpose of applying the second sentence of Article 10(3) of Regulation (EC) No 139/2004.]

Where pursuant to Article 10(3), second subparagraph, of Regulation (EC) No 139/2004 the period for the adoption of a decision pursuant to Article 8(1), (2) and (3) is extended, the period of 65 working days for the submission of commitments shall automatically be extended by the same number of working days.

In exceptional circumstances, the Commission may accept commitments offered after the expiry of the time limit for their submission within the meaning of this paragraph provided that the procedure provided for in Article 19(5) of Regulation (EC) No 139/2004 is complied with.

3. Articles 7, 8 and 9 shall apply mutatis mutandis.

NOTES

Para 2: words in square brackets substituted by Commission Regulation 1269/2013/EU, Art 1(8).

Repeal of this Regulation in relation to the UK: this Regulation is repealed in relation to the UK (as from IP completion day); see the introductory notes to this Regulation *ante*.

[4.587]

Article 20 Procedure for the submission of commitments

[1. The commitments offered by the undertakings concerned pursuant to Article 6(2) or Article 8(2) of Regulation (EC) No 139/2004 shall be submitted to the Commission at the address referred to in Article 23(1) in the format and with the number of copies specified by the Commission from time to time in the Official Journal of the European Union. The Commission shall forward copies of such commitments without delay to the competent authorities of the Member States.]

[1a. In addition to the requirements set out in paragraph 1, the undertakings concerned shall, at the same time as offering commitments pursuant to Article 6(2) or Article 8(2) of Regulation (EC) No 139/2004, submit one original of the information and documents prescribed by the Form RM relating to remedies (Form RM) as set out in Annex IV to this Regulation as well as the number of copies specified by the Commission from time to time in the Official Journal of the European Union. The information submitted shall be correct and complete.]

2. When offering commitments pursuant to Articles 6(2) or Article 8(2) of Regulation (EC) No 139/2004, the undertakings concerned shall at the same time clearly identify any information which they consider to be confidential, giving reasons, and shall provide a separate non-confidential version.

NOTES

Para 1: substituted by Commission Regulation 1269/2013/EU, Art 1(9).

Para 1a: inserted by Commission Regulation 1033/2008/EC, Art 1(2). Subsequently substituted by Commission Regulation 1269/2013/EU, Art 1(9).

Repeal of this Regulation in relation to the UK: this Regulation is repealed in relation to the UK (as from IP completion day); see the introductory notes to this Regulation *ante*.

[4.588]

[Article 20a Trustees

1. The commitments offered by the undertakings concerned pursuant to Article 6(2) or Article 8(2) of Regulation (EC) No 139/2004 may include, at the own expense of the undertakings concerned, the appointment of an independent trustee (or trustees) assisting the Commission in overseeing the parties' compliance with the commitments or having a mandate to implement the commitments. The trustee may be appointed by the parties, after the Commission has approved its identity, or by the Commission. The trustee shall carry out its tasks under the supervision of the Commission.

2. The Commission may attach such trustee-related provisions of the commitments as conditions and obligations pursuant to Article 6(2) or Article 8(2) of Regulation (EC) No 139/2004.]

NOTES

Inserted by Commission Regulation 1033/2008/EC, Art 1(3).

Repeal of this Regulation in relation to the UK: this Regulation is repealed in relation to the UK (as from IP completion day); see the introductory notes to this Regulation *ante*.

CHAPTER VII MISCELLANEOUS PROVISIONS

[4.589]

Article 21 Transmission of documents

[1. The Commission may transmit documents and invitations to the addressees in any of the following ways:

- *(a) delivery by hand against receipt;*
- *(b) registered letter with acknowledgement of receipt;*
- *(c) fax with a request for acknowledgement of receipt;*
- *(d) electronic mail with a request for acknowledgement of receipt.]*

2. Unless otherwise provided in this Regulation, paragraph 1 also applies to the transmission of documents from the notifying parties, from other involved parties or from third parties to the Commission.

[3. Where a document is sent by fax or by electronic mail, it shall be presumed that it has been received by the addressee on the day on which it was sent.]

NOTES

Paras 1, 3: substituted by Commission Regulation 1269/2013/EU, Art 1(10).

Repeal of this Regulation in relation to the UK: this Regulation is repealed in relation to the UK (as from IP completion day); see the introductory notes to this Regulation *ante*.

[4.590]

Article 22 Setting of time limits

In setting the time limits provided for pursuant to Article 12(1) and (2), Article 13(2) and Article 16(1), the Commission shall have regard to the time required for the preparation of statements and to the urgency of the case. It shall also take account of working days as well as public holidays in the country of receipt of the Commission's communication.

Time limits shall be set in terms of a precise calendar date.

NOTES

Repeal of this Regulation in relation to the UK: this Regulation is repealed in relation to the UK (as from IP completion day); see the introductory notes to this Regulation *ante*.

[4.591]

Article 23 Receipt of documents by the Commission

1. In accordance with the provisions of Article 5(1) of this Regulation, notifications shall be delivered to the Commission at the address of the Commission's Directorate General for Competition as published by the Commission in the Official Journal of the European Union.

2. Additional information requested to complete notifications must reach the Commission at the address referred to in paragraph 1.

3. Written comments on Commission communications pursuant to Article 12(1) and (2), Article 13(2) and Article 16(1) of this Regulation must have reached the Commission at the address referred to in paragraph 1 before the expiry of the time limit set in each case.

[4. Where the Commission specifies that documents submitted to it or any additional copies thereof are to be submitted electronically, it shall specify the format from time to time in the Official Journal of the European Union. Submissions sent by electronic mail shall be sent to the electronic mail address as published by the Commission from time to time in the Official Journal of the European Union.]

NOTES

Para 4: added by Commission Regulation 1269/2013/EU, Art 1(11).

Repeal of this Regulation in relation to the UK: this Regulation is repealed in relation to the UK (as from IP completion day); see the introductory notes to this Regulation *ante*.

[4.592]

Article 24 Definition of working days

The expression working days in Regulation (EC) No 139/2004 and in this Regulation means all days other than Saturdays, Sundays, and Commission holidays as published in the Official Journal of the European Union before the beginning of each year.

NOTES

Repeal of this Regulation in relation to the UK: this Regulation is repealed in relation to the UK (as from IP completion day); see the introductory notes to this Regulation *ante*.

[4.593]

Article 25 Repeal and transitional provision

1. Without prejudice to paragraphs 2 and 3, Regulation (EC) No 447/98 is repealed with effect from 1 May 2004. References to the repealed Regulation shall be construed as references to this Regulation.

2. Regulation (EC) No 447/98 shall continue to apply to any concentration falling within the scope of Regulation (EEC) No 4064/89.

3. For the purposes of paragraph 2, Sections 1 to 12 of the Annex to Regulation (EC) No 447/98 shall be replaced by Sections 1 to 11 of Annex I to this Regulation. In such cases references in those sections to the "EC Merger Regulation" and to the "Implementing Regulation" shall be read as referring to the corresponding provisions of Regulation (EEC) No 4064/89 and Regulation (EC) No 447/98, respectively.

NOTES

Repeal of this Regulation in relation to the UK: this Regulation is repealed in relation to the UK (as from IP completion day); see the introductory notes to this Regulation *ante*.

[4.594]

Article 26 Entry into force

This Regulation shall enter into force on 1 May 2004.

NOTES

Repeal of this Regulation in relation to the UK: this Regulation is repealed in relation to the UK (as from IP completion day); see the introductory notes to this Regulation *ante*.

ANNEXES

[ANNEX I

FORM CO RELATING TO THE NOTIFICATION OF A CONCENTRATION PURSUANT TO REGULATION (EC) NO 139/2004

INTRODUCTION

[4.595]

1.1. ***The purpose of this Form CO***

This Form CO specifies the information that must be provided by notifying parties when submitting a notification to the European Commission of a proposed merger, acquisition or other concentration. The merger control system of the European Union is laid down in Council Regulation (EC) No 139/2004 of 20 January 2004 on the control of concentrations between undertakings[1] (hereinafter referred to as 'the Merger Regulation') and in Commission Regulation (EC) No 802/2004[2] (hereinafter referred to as 'the Implementing Regulation'), to which this Form CO is annexed. The text of these regulations, as well as other relevant documents, can be found on the Competition page of the Commission's Europa website. Your attention is drawn to the corresponding provisions of the Agreement on the European Economic Area[3] (hereinafter referred to as 'the EEA Agreement').

In order to limit the time and expense involved in complying with various merger control procedures in several individual countries, the European Union has put in place a system of merger control by which concentrations having a Union dimension[4] (normally, where the parties to the concentration fulfil certain turnover thresholds)[5] are assessed by the European Commission in a single procedure (the 'one stop shop' principle). Concentrations which do not meet the turnover thresholds may fall within the competence of the Member States' and/or the EFTA States' authorities in charge of merger control.

The Merger Regulation requires the Commission to reach a decision within a legal deadline. In an initial phase the Commission normally has 25 working days to decide whether to clear the concentration or to 'initiate proceedings', that is to say to undertake an in-depth investigation.[6] If the Commission decides to initiate proceedings, it normally has to take a final decision on the operation within no more than 90 working days of the date when proceedings are initiated.[7]

In view of these deadlines, and for the 'one stop shop' principle to work, it is essential that the Commission is provided, in a timely fashion, with the information required to carry out the necessary investigation and to assess the impact of the concentration on the markets concerned. This requires that a certain amount of information be provided at the time of notification.

1.2. ***Pre-notification contacts***

It is recognised that the information requested in this Form CO is substantial. However, experience has shown that, depending on the specific characteristics of the case, not all information is always necessary for an adequate examination of the proposed concentration. Accordingly, if you consider that any particular information requested by this Form CO may not be necessary for the Commission's examination of the case, you are encouraged to ask the Commission to dispense with the obligation to provide certain information (see point 1.4(g) of this Introductory Part for more details).

The possibility to engage in pre-notification contacts is a service offered by the Commission to notifying parties on a voluntary basis in order to prepare the formal merger review procedure. As such, while not mandatory, pre-notification contacts can be extremely valuable to both the notifying parties and the Commission in determining, amongst other things, the precise amount of information required in a notification and, in the majority of cases, will result in a significant reduction of the information required.

Accordingly, whilst the parties are solely responsible for deciding whether to engage in pre-notification contacts and when exactly to notify, parties are encouraged to consult the Commission on a voluntary basis regarding the adequacy of the scope and type of information on which they intend to base their notification.

In addition, it should be noted that certain concentrations, which are unlikely to pose any competition concerns, can be notified using a Short Form CO, which is attached to the Implementing Regulation, as Annex II.

Notifying parties may refer to the 'Best Practices on the conduct of EC merger control proceedings' of the Commission's Directorate-General for Competition ('DG Competition'), as published on DG Competition's website and updated from time to time, which provide guidance on pre-notification contacts and the preparation of notifications.

1.3. ***Who must notify***

In the case of a merger within the meaning of Article 3(1)(a) of the Merger Regulation or the acquisition of joint control of an undertaking within the meaning of Article 3(1)(b) of the Merger Regulation, the notification must be completed jointly by the parties to the merger or by those acquiring joint control, as the case may be.[8]

In case of the acquisition of a controlling interest in one undertaking by another, the acquirer must complete the notification.

In the case of a public bid to acquire an undertaking, the bidder must complete the notification.

Each party completing the notification is responsible for the accuracy of the information which it provides.

1.4. ***The requirement for a correct and complete notification***

All information required by this Form CO must be correct and complete. The information required must be supplied in the appropriate Section of this Form CO.

In particular you should note that:

- *(a) In accordance with Article 10(1) of the Merger Regulation and Article 5(2) and (4) of the Implementing Regulation, the time-limits of the Merger Regulation linked to the notification will not begin to run until all the information that has to be supplied with the notification has been received by the Commission. This requirement is to ensure that the Commission is able to assess the notified concentration within the strict time-limits provided by the Merger Regulation.*
- *(b) The notifying party or parties must verify, in the course of preparing their notification, that contact names and numbers, and in particular fax numbers and e-mail addresses, provided to the Commission are accurate, relevant and up-to-date.[9]*
- *(c) Incorrect or misleading information in the notification will be considered to be incomplete information (Article 5(4) of the Implementing Regulation).*
- *(d) If a notification is incomplete, the Commission will inform the notifying parties or their representatives in writing and without delay. The notification will only become effective on the date on which the complete and accurate information is received by the Commission (Article 10(1) of the Merger Regulation, Articles 5(2) and (4) of the Implementing Regulation).*
- *(e) Under Article 14(1)(a) of the Merger Regulation, notifying parties who, either intentionally or negligently, supply incorrect or misleading information, may be liable to fines of up to 1% of the aggregate turnover of the undertaking concerned. In addition, pursuant to Article 6(3)(a) and Article 8(6)(a) of the Merger Regulation the Commission may revoke its decision on the compatibility of a notified concentration where it is based on incorrect information for which one of the undertakings is responsible.*
- *(f) You may request in writing that the Commission accept that the notification is complete notwithstanding the failure to provide information required by this Form CO, if such information is not reasonably available to you in part or in whole (for example, because of the unavailability of information on a target company during a contested bid).*

  The Commission will consider such a request, provided that you give reasons for the unavailability of that information, and provide your best estimates for missing data together with the sources for the estimates. Where possible, indications as to where any of the requested information that is unavailable to you could be obtained by the Commission should also be provided.

(g) *In accordance with Article 4(2) of the Implementing Regulation, the Commission may dispense with the obligation to provide any particular information in the notification, including documents, or with any other requirement specified in this Form CO where the Commission considers that compliance with those obligations or requirements is not necessary for the examination of the case. Accordingly, you may, in pre-notification, submit a written request for a waiver, asking the Commission to dispense with the obligation to provide such information if you consider that that information is not necessary for the Commission's examination of the case.*

The Commission's experience shows that particular categories of information required by this Form CO, although necessary for the Commission's examination of certain cases, may not be necessary for the Commission's examination of a significant number of other cases. These categories of information are specifically indicated in this Form CO (see footnotes 15, 16, 18, 20, 23, 27, 28, 30 and 31). You are particularly invited to consider whether to request a waiver for any of these categories of information.

Waiver requests should be submitted together with a draft Form CO in order to allow the Commission to determine whether or not the information in relation to which a waiver is being requested is necessary for the examination of the case. Waiver requests should be made either within the text of the draft Form CO itself or as an e-mail or letter addressed to the responsible case manager and/or head of unit.

The Commission will consider waiver requests, provided that you give adequate reasons why the information in question is not necessary for the examination of the case. Waiver requests will be dealt with in the context of the review of a draft Form CO. Therefore, in accordance with DG Competition's Best Practices on the conduct of EC merger control proceedings, DG Competition would normally require five working days before responding to waiver requests.

For the avoidance of doubt, it should be noted that the fact that the Commission may have accepted that any particular information requested by this Form CO was not necessary for the complete notification of a concentration (using the Form CO) does not in any way prevent the Commission from requesting that information at any time, in particular by way of request for information pursuant to Article 11 of the Merger Regulation.

1.5. ***How to notify***

The notification must be completed in one of the official languages of the European Union. This language will thereafter be the language of the proceedings for all notifying parties. Where notifications are made in accordance with Article 12 of Protocol 24 to the EEA Agreement in an official language of an EFTA State which is not an official language of the Union, the notification must simultaneously be supplemented with a translation into an official language of the Union.

The information requested by this Form CO is to be set out using the sections and paragraph numbers of the Form CO, signing a declaration as provided in Section 11, and annexing supporting documentation. The original of the Form CO must be signed by persons authorised by law to act on behalf of each notifying party or by one or more authorised external representatives of the notifying party or parties. In completing Sections 7 to 9 of this Form CO, the notifying parties are invited to consider whether, for purposes of clarity, these sections are best presented in numerical order, or whether they can be grouped together for each individual affected market (or group of affected markets).

For the sake of clarity, certain information may be put in annexes. However, it is essential that all key substantive pieces of information, and in particular market share information for the parties and their largest competitors, are presented in the body of Form CO. Annexes to this Form CO must only be used to supplement the information supplied in the Form CO itself.

Contact details must be provided in a format provided by DG Competition on its website. For a proper investigatory process, it is essential that the contact details are accurate. Multiple instances of incorrect contact details may be a ground for declaring a notification incomplete.

Supporting documents are to be submitted in their original language; where this is not an official language of the Union, they must be translated into the language of the proceeding (Article 3(4) of the Implementing Regulation).

Supporting documents may be originals or copies of the originals. In the latter case, the notifying party must confirm that they are true and complete.

One original and the required number of copies of the Form CO and the supporting documents must be submitted to DG Competition. The required number and format (paper and/or electronic) of copies will be published from time to time in the Official Journal of the European Union as well as on DG Competition's website.

The notification must be delivered to the address referred to in Article 23(1) of the Implementing Regulation. This address is published in the Official Journal of the European Union and available on DG Competition's website. The notification must be delivered to the Commission on working days as defined by Article 24 of the Implementing Regulation during the opening hours indicated on DG Competition's website. The security instructions given on DG Competition's website must be adhered to.

All electronic copies of the Form CO and supporting documents must be provided in a usable and searchable format as specified on DG Competition's website.

1.6. ***Confidentiality***

Article 17(2) of the Merger Regulation as well as the corresponding provisions of the EEA Agreement[10] *require the Commission, the Member States, the EFTA Surveillance Authority and the EFTA States, their officials and other servants not to disclose information they have acquired through the application of the Regulation of the kind covered by the obligation of professional secrecy. The same principle must also apply to protect confidentiality between notifying parties.*

If you believe that your interests would be harmed if any of the information you are asked to supply were to be published or otherwise divulged to other parties, submit this information separately with each page clearly marked 'Business Secrets'. You should also give reasons why this information should not be divulged or published.

In the case of mergers or joint acquisitions, or in other cases where the notification is completed by more than one of the parties, business secrets may be submitted under separate cover, and referred to in the notification as an annex. All such annexes must be included in the submission in order for a notification to be considered complete.

1.7. ***Definitions and instructions for purposes of this Form CO***

Notifying party or parties: in cases where a notification is submitted by only one of the undertakings who is a party to an operation, 'notifying parties' is used to refer only to the undertaking actually submitting the notification.

Party(ies) to the concentration or parties: these terms relate to both the acquiring and acquired parties, or to the merging parties, including all undertakings in which a controlling interest is being acquired or which is the subject of a public bid.

Except where otherwise specified, the terms notifying party(ies) and party(ies) to the concentration include all the undertakings which belong to the same groups as those parties.

Affected markets: Section 6 of this Form CO requires the notifying parties to define the relevant product markets, and further to identify which of those relevant markets are likely to be affected by the notified operation. This definition of affected market is used as the basis for requiring information for a number of other questions contained in this Form CO. This term can refer to a relevant market made up either of products or of services.

Year: all references to the word year in this Form CO must be read as meaning calendar year, unless otherwise stated. All information requested in this Form CO must, unless otherwise specified, relate to the year preceding that of the notification.

The financial data requested in Section 4 must be provided in euro at the average exchange rates prevailing for the years or other periods in question.

All references to provisions of law contained in this Form CO are to the relevant articles and paragraphs of the Merger Regulation, unless otherwise stated.

1.8. ***Description of quantitative economic data collected by the undertakings concerned***

In cases in which quantitative economic analysis for the affected markets is likely to be useful, briefly describe the data that each of the undertakings concerned collects and stores in the ordinary course of its business operations and which could be useful for such analysis.

The following are three examples of cases where and the data could be useful for quantitative economic analysis in those cases: a concentration between two providers of services that business customers purchase on the basis of structured procurement processes where candidate suppliers bid against each other and where suppliers or customers collect bidding data, that is to say data about the participants, offers and outcomes of past procurement processes; a concentration between producers of retail products that are sold to final consumers and where 'scanning data' about consumers' purchases in shops are collected over a significant period of time; a concentration amongst providers of mobile telephony services to end customers and where regulatory authorities for telecommunication collect data on customer switching between the providers of mobile telephony services.

The data description should include, in particular, information about the type of such data (information on sales or bids, profit margins, procurement process details, etc.), the level of disaggregation (per country, per product, per customer, per contract, etc.), the time period for which the data are available and the format.

The information requested under this introductory part point 1.8 is not required for the Form CO to be considered as complete. However, given the statutory deadlines for Union merger control, notifying parties are encouraged to provide such descriptions as early as possible in cases and for the markets for which quantitative analysis is likely to be useful.

For further orientation, the undertakings concerned may refer to DG Competition's 'Best Practices for the submission of economic evidence and data collection in cases concerning the application of articles 101 and 102 TFEU and in merger cases' as published on DG Competition's website and updated from time to time.

1.9. ***International cooperation between the Commission and other competition authorities***

The Commission encourages the undertakings concerned to facilitate the international cooperation between the Commission and other competition authorities reviewing the same concentration. In the Commission's experience, good cooperation between the Commission and competition authorities in jurisdictions outside the EEA entails substantial benefits for the undertakings concerned. To this end, the Commission encourages notifying parties to submit together with this Form CO a list of those jurisdictions outside the EEA where the concentration is subject to regulatory clearance under merger control rules before or after closing.

Furthermore, the Commission encourages the undertakings concerned to submit waivers of confidentiality that would enable the Commission to share information with other competition authorities outside the EEA reviewing the same concentration. Each waiver facilitates joint discussion and analysis of a concentration as it allows the Commission to share relevant information with another competition authority reviewing the same concentration, including confidential business information obtained from the undertakings concerned. To this end, the Commission encourages the undertakings concerned to use the Commission's model waiver, which is published on DG Competition's website and updated from time to time.

1.10. ***Provision of information to employees and their representatives***

The Commission would like to draw attention to the obligations to which the parties to a concentration may be subject under Union and/or national rules on information and consultation regarding transactions of a concentrative nature vis-à-vis employees and/or their representatives.

SECTION 1 DESCRIPTION OF THE CONCENTRATION

1.1. Provide an executive summary of the concentration, specifying the parties to the concentration, the nature of the concentration (for example, merger, acquisition, or joint venture), the areas of activity of the parties to the concentration, the markets on which the concentration will have an impact (including the main affected markets),[11] and the strategic and economic rationale for the concentration.

1.2. Provide a summary (up to 500 words) of the information provided under Section 1.1. It is intended that this summary will be published on DG Competition's website upon notification. The summary must be drafted so that it contains no confidential information or business secrets.

SECTION 2 INFORMATION ABOUT THE PARTIES

*2.1. **Information on notifying party (or parties) and other parties to the concentration**[12]*

For each notifying party as well as for each other party to the concentration provide:

2.1.1. name of undertaking;

2.1.2. name, address, telephone number, fax number and e-mail address of, and position held by, the appropriate contact person; the address given must be an address for service to which documents and, in particular, Commission decisions and other procedural documents may be notified, and the contact person given must be deemed to be authorised to accept service;

2.1.3. if one or more authorised external representatives of the undertaking are appointed, the representative or representatives to which documents and, in particular, Commission decisions and other procedural documents may be notified:

2.1.3.1. name, address, telephone number, fax number and e-mail address of, and position held by, each representative; and

2.1.3.2. the original written proof that each representative is authorised to act (based on the model Power of Attorney available on DG Competition's website).

*2.2. **Nature of the parties' business***

For each of the notifying parties and the other parties to the concentration, describe the nature of the undertaking's business.

SECTION 3 DETAILS OF THE CONCENTRATION, OWNERSHIP AND CONTROL[13]

The information sought in this section may be illustrated by the use of organisation charts or diagrams to show the structure of ownership and control of the undertakings before and after completion of the concentration.

3.1. Describe the nature of the concentration being notified. By reference to the relevant criteria of the Merger Regulation and the Commission Consolidated Jurisdictional Notice:[14]

3.1.1. identify the undertakings or persons solely or jointly controlling each of the undertakings concerned, directly or indirectly, and describe the structure of ownership and control of each of the undertakings concerned before the completion of the concentration;

3.1.2. explain whether the proposed concentration is:

(i) a full merger,

(ii) an acquisition of sole or joint control, or

(iii) a contract or other means of conferring direct or indirect control within the meaning of Article 3(2) of the Merger Regulation;

(iv) the acquisition of joint control in a full-function joint venture within the meaning of Article 3(4) of the Merger Regulation, and, if so, the reasons why the joint venture is considered to be full-function.[15]

3.1.3. explain how the concentration will be implemented (for example by conclusion of an agreement, by the launch of a public bid, etc.);

3.1.4. by reference to Article 4(1) of the Merger Regulation explain which of the following have taken place at the time of notification:

(i) an agreement has been concluded,

(ii) a controlling interest has been acquired,

(iii) (the intention to launch) a public bid has been announced, or

(iv) the undertakings concerned have demonstrated a good faith intention to conclude an agreement.

3.1.5. indicate the expected date of any major events designed to bring about the completion of the concentration;

3.1.6. explain the structure of ownership and control of each of the undertakings concerned after the completion of the concentration.

3.2. Describe the economic rationale of the concentration.

3.3. State the value of the transaction (the purchase price (or the value of all the assets involved, as the case may be); specify whether this is in the form of equity, cash, or other assets).

3.4. Describe any financial or other support received from public authorities by any of the parties and the nature and amount of this support.

3.5. For the parties to the concentration (other than the seller) provide a list of all other undertakings which are active in affected markets in which the undertakings, or persons, of the group hold individually or collectively 10% or more of the voting rights, issued share capital or other securities, identifying the holder and stating the percentage held;[16] *and*

3.6. Provide details of acquisitions made during the last three years by the groups identified in Section 2.1 of undertakings active in affected markets.[17]

SECTION 4 TURNOVER

For each of the undertakings concerned provide the following data for the last financial year:[18]

4.1. Worldwide turnover;

4.2. EU-wide turnover;

4.3. EEA-wide turnover (EU and EFTA);

4.4. turnover in each Member State (indicate the Member State, if any, in which more than two-thirds of EU-wide turnover is achieved);

4.5. EFTA-wide turnover;

4.6. turnover in each EFTA State (indicate the EFTA State, if any, in which more than two-thirds of EFTA-wide turnover is achieved; also indicate whether the combined turnover of the undertakings concerned in the territory of the EFTA States equals 25% or more of their total turnover in the EEA territory).

Turnover data must be provided by filling in the Commission's template table available on DG Competition's website.

SECTION 5 SUPPORTING DOCUMENTATION

The notifying party or parties must provide the following:

5.1. copies of the final or most recent versions of all documents bringing about the concentration, whether by agreement between the parties to the concentration, acquisition of a controlling interest or a public bid;

5.2. in a public bid, a copy of the offer document; if it is unavailable at the time of notification, a copy of the most recent document demonstrating the intention to launch a public bid must be provided and a copy of the offer document must be submitted as soon as possible and not later than when it is posted to shareholders;

5.3. an indication of the internet address, if any, at which the most recent annual reports and accounts of the parties to the concentration are available, or if no such internet address exists, copies of the most recent annual reports and accounts of the parties to the concentration; and

5.4. copies of the following documents prepared by or for or received by any member(s) of the board of management, the board of directors, or the supervisory board, as applicable in the light of the corporate governance structure, or the other person(s) exercising similar functions (or to whom such functions have been delegated or entrusted), or the shareholders' meeting:

- *(i) minutes of the meetings of the board of management, board of directors, supervisory board and shareholders' meeting at which the transaction has been discussed, or excerpts of those minutes relating to the discussion of the transaction;*
- *(ii) analyses, reports, studies, surveys, presentations and any comparable documents for the purpose of assessing or analysing the concentration with respect to its rationale (including documents where the transaction is discussed in relation to potential alternative acquisitions), market shares, competitive conditions, competitors (actual and potential), potential for sales growth or expansion into other product or geographic markets, and/or general market conditions;*[19]
- *(iii) analyses, reports, studies, surveys and any comparable documents from the last two years for the purpose of assessing any of the affected markets*[20] *with respect to market shares, competitive conditions, competitors (actual and potential) and/or potential for sales growth or expansion into other product or geographic markets.*[21]

Provide a list of the documents mentioned in this section 5.4, indicating for each document the date of preparation and the name and title of the addressee(s).

SECTION 6 MARKET DEFINITIONS

The relevant product and geographic markets serve to identify the scope within which the market power of the new entity resulting from the concentration must be assessed.[22] *When presenting relevant product and geographic markets, the notifying party or parties must submit, in addition to any product and geographic market definitions they consider relevant, all plausible alternative product and geographic market definitions. Plausible alternative product and geographic market definitions can be identified on the basis of previous Commission decisions and judgments of the Union Courts and (in particular where there are no Commission or Court precedents) by reference to industry reports, market studies and the notifying parties' internal documents.*

The notifying party or parties must provide the information requested in this Form CO having regard to the following definitions:

6.1. ***Relevant product markets:***

A relevant product market comprises all those products and/or services which are regarded as interchangeable or substitutable by the consumer, by reason of the products' characteristics, their prices and their intended use. A relevant product market may in some cases be composed of a number of individual products and/or services which present largely identical physical or technical characteristics and are interchangeable.

Factors relevant to the assessment of the relevant product market include the analysis of why the products or services in these markets are included and why others are excluded by using the above definition, and having regard to, for example, substitutability of products and services, prices, cross-price elasticity of demand or other relevant factors (such as supply-side substitutability in appropriate cases).

6.2. ***Relevant geographic markets:***

The relevant geographic market comprises the area in which the undertakings concerned are involved in the supply and demand of relevant products or services, in which the conditions of competition are sufficiently homogeneous and which can be distinguished from neighbouring geographic areas because, in particular, conditions of competition are appreciably different in those areas.

Factors relevant to the assessment of the relevant geographic market include, inter alia, the nature and characteristics of the products or services concerned, the existence of entry barriers, consumer preferences, appreciable differences in the undertakings' market shares between neighbouring geographic areas or substantial price differences.

6.3. ***Affected markets:***

For purposes of information required in this Form CO, affected markets consist of all relevant product and geographic markets, as well as plausible alternative relevant product and geographic markets, on the basis of which in the EEA territory:

(a) *two or more of the parties to the concentration are engaged in business activities in the same relevant market and where the concentration will lead to a combined market share of 20% or more. These are horizontal relationships;*

(b) *one or more of the parties to the concentration are engaged in business activities in a relevant market, which is upstream or downstream of a relevant market in which any other party to the concentration is engaged, and any of their individual or combined market shares at either level is 30% or more, regardless of whether there is or is not any existing supplier/customer relationship between the parties to the concentration.*[23] *These are vertical relationships.*

On the basis of the definitions and market share thresholds set out in Section 6, identify each affected market.[24]

6.4. ***Other markets in which the notified operation may have a significant impact***

On the basis of the definitions in Section 6, describe the product and geographic scope under all plausible alternative market definitions of markets (where such markets include the whole or a part of the EEA) other than affected markets identified in Section 6.1. in which the notified operation may have a significant impact, for example, where:

(a) *any of the parties to the concentration has a market share larger than 30% and any other party to the concentration is a potential competitor into that market. A party may be considered a potential competitor, in particular, where it has plans to enter a market, or has developed or pursued such plans in the past three years;*

(b) *any of the parties to the concentration has a market share larger than 30% and any other party to the concentration holds important intellectual property rights for that market;*

(c) *any of the parties to the concentration is present in a product market, which is a neighbouring market closely related to a product market in which any other party to the concentration is engaged, and the individual or combined market shares of the parties in any one of these markets is 30% or more. Product markets are closely related neighbouring markets when the products are complementary to each other*[25] *or when they belong to a range of products that is generally purchased by the same set of customers for the same end use.*[26]

In order to enable the Commission to consider, from the outset, the competitive impact of the proposed concentration in the markets identified under Section 6.4, notifying parties are invited to submit the information under Sections 7 and 8 of this Form CO also in relation to those markets.

SECTION 7 INFORMATION ON AFFECTED MARKETS

For each horizontally affected market, for each vertically affected market and for each of the other markets where the notified operation may have a significant impact, and for each of the last three years,[27] *provide the following:*

7.1. for each of the parties to the concentration, the nature of the undertaking's business, the main subsidiaries active and/or brands, product names and/or trademarks used in each of these markets;

7.2. an estimate of the total size of the market in terms of sales value (in euro) and volume (units).[28] *Indicate the basis and sources for the calculations and provide documents where available to confirm these calculations;*

7.3. the sales in value and volume, as well as an estimate of the market shares, of each of the parties to the concentration;

7.4. an estimate of the market share in value (and where appropriate, volume) of all competitors (including importers) having at least 5% of the relevant market under consideration. Identify the sources used to calculate these market shares and provide documents where available to confirm the calculation.

7.5. an estimate of the total Union-wide and EEA-wide capacity. Over the last three years what proportion of this capacity has been accounted for by each of the parties to the concentration, and what have their respective rates of capacity utilisation been? If applicable, identify the location and capacity of the manufacturing facilities of each of the parties to the concentration in affected markets.[29]

SECTION 8 STRUCTURE OF SUPPLY IN AFFECTED MARKETS

8.1. Provide a brief explanation of the structure of supply in each of the affected markets. Specify in particular:

(a) *the manner in which the parties to the concentration produce, price and sell the products and/or services; for example, whether they manufacture, sell and price locally;*

(b) *the nature and extent of vertical integration of each of the parties to the concentration compared with their largest competitors;*

(c) *the distribution systems prevailing in the market and their importance, and to what extent distribution is performed by third parties and/or undertakings belonging to the same group as the parties, as well as the importance of exclusive distribution contracts and other types of long-term contracts; and*

(d) *the service networks (for example, maintenance and repair) prevailing and their importance in these markets. To what extent are such services performed by third parties and/or undertakings belonging to the same group as the parties?*

If you consider any other supply-side considerations to be relevant, they should be specified.

STRUCTURE OF DEMAND IN AFFECTED MARKETS

8.2. Provide a brief explanation of the structure of demand in each affected market, specifying, in particular:

(a) *the phases of the markets in terms of, for example, take-off, expansion, maturity and decline, and a forecast of the growth rate of demand;*

(b) *the importance of customer preferences, for example in terms of brand loyalty, the provision of pre- and after-sales services, the provision of a full range of products, or network effects;*

(c) *the role of switching costs (in terms of time and expense) for customers when changing from one supplier to another,*

 (i) *for existing products and*

 (ii) *for new products replacing existing products (including the normal time horizon of customer contracts);*

(d) *the degree of concentration or dispersion of customers;*

(e) *the way customers purchase the products or services in question, in particular whether they use procurement techniques such as requests for proposal and bidding procedures.*

PRODUCT DIFFERENTIATION AND CLOSENESS OF COMPETITION

8.3. Provide a brief explanation of the degree of product differentiation in each affected market, specifying, in particular:

(a) *the role and importance of product differentiation in terms of quality ('vertical differentiation') and other product characteristics ('horizontal' and 'spatial differentiation');*

(b) *any segmentation of customers into different groups with a description of the 'typical customer' for each group; and*

(c) *the rivalry between the parties to the concentration in general, as well as the closeness of substitution between the products of the parties to the concentration, including for each of the customer groups and 'typical customers' identified in response to the question in point (b).*

MARKET ENTRY AND EXIT

8.4. Over the last five years, has there been any significant entry into any affected market?

If so, identify such entrants and provide an estimate of the current market share of each such entrant.

8.5. In the opinion of the notifying parties, are there undertakings (including those at present operating only outside the EU or the EEA) that are likely to enter any affected market?

If so, explain why such entry is likely and provide an estimate of the time within which such entry is likely to occur.

8.6. Provide a brief description of the main factors influencing entry into each of the affected markets, examining entry from both a geographical and product viewpoint. In so doing, take account of the following where appropriate:

(a) *the total costs of entry (R & D, production, establishing distribution systems, promotion, advertising, servicing, and so forth) on a scale equivalent to a significant viable competitor, indicating the market share of such a competitor;*

(b) *any legal or regulatory barriers to entry, such as government authorisation or standard setting in any form;*

(c) *any barriers to access to customers, such as those resulting from product certification procedures, or the importance of reputation and a proven track record;*

(d) *any need and possibility to obtain access to patents, know-how and other intellectual property rights in these markets;*

(e) *the extent to which each of the parties to the concentration are holders, licensees or licensors of patents, know-how and other rights in the relevant markets;*

(f) *the importance of economies of scale and scope and of network effects for the production or distribution of products and/or services in the affected markets; and*

(g) *access to sources of supply, such as availability of raw materials and necessary infrastructure.*

8.7. Explain whether any of the parties to the concentration, or any of the competitors, have products likely to be brought to market in the short or medium term ('pipeline products'), or plans to expand production or sales capacity in any of the affected markets. If so, provide an estimate of the projected sales and market shares of the parties to the concentration over the next three to five years.

8.8. Over the last five years, has there been any exit from any affected market?

If so, identify the firm having exited the market and provide an estimate of its market share in the year prior to the exit.

RESEARCH AND DEVELOPMENT

8.9. Give an account for the affected markets of the importance of research and development in firms' ability to compete in the long term. Explain the nature of the research and development in affected markets carried out by the parties to the concentration.

In so doing, take account of the following, where appropriate:

(a) *trends and intensities of research and development*[30] *in these markets and for the parties to the concentration;*

(b) *the course of technological development for these markets over an appropriate time period (including the frequency of introduction of new products and/or services, developments in products and/or services, production processes, distribution systems, and so on); and*

(c) the parties' own research planning and priorities over the next three years.

COOPERATIVE AGREEMENTS

8.10. To what extent do cooperative agreements (horizontal, vertical, or other) exist in the affected markets?

8.11. If relevant, give details of the most important cooperative agreements engaged in by the parties to the concentration in the affected markets, such as research and development, licensing, joint production, specialization, distribution, long term supply and exchange of information agreements and, where deemed useful, provide a copy of these agreements.[31]

TRADE BETWEEN MEMBER STATES AND IMPORTS FROM OUTSIDE THE EEA

8.12. Explain the extent to which trade within the territory of the EEA in the products at stake is affected by transportation and other costs.

8.13. For the affected markets, provide an estimate of the total value and volume and source of imports from outside the EEA territory and identify:

(a) the proportion of such imports that are derived from the groups to which the parties to the concentration belong;
(b) an estimate of the extent to which any quotas, tariffs or non-tariff barriers to trade, affect these imports; and
(c) an estimate of the extent to which transportation and other costs affect these imports.

TRADE ASSOCIATIONS

8.14. With respect to the trade associations in the affected markets:

(a) identify those of which the parties to the concentration are members;
(b) identify the most important trade associations to which the customers of the parties to the concentration belong; and
(c) provide the name, address, telephone number, fax number and e-mail address of the appropriate contact person for all trade associations listed in this section.[31]

CONTACT DETAILS

8.15. Provide the name, address, telephone number, fax number and e-mail address of the head of the legal department (or other person exercising similar functions; and in cases where there is no such person, the chief executive) for:[32]

(a) the competitors identified under section 7.4;
(b) each of the parties' top five customers in each of the affected markets;
(c) the recent entrants identified under section 8.4; and
(d) the potential entrants identified under section 8.5.

Contact details must be provided using the Commission's template available on DG Competition's website.

SECTION 9 EFFICIENCIES

Should you wish the Commission specifically to consider from the outset[33] whether efficiency gains generated by the concentration are likely to enhance the ability and incentive of the new entity to act pro-competitively for the benefit of consumers, provide a description of, and supporting documents relating to, each efficiency (including cost savings, new product introductions, and service or product improvements) that the parties anticipate will result from the proposed concentration relating to any relevant product.[34]

For each claimed efficiency, provide:

(i) a detailed explanation of how the proposed concentration would allow the new entity to achieve the efficiency. Specify the steps that the parties anticipate taking to achieve the efficiency, the risks involved in achieving the efficiency, and the time and costs required to achieve it;
(ii) where reasonably possible, a quantification of the efficiency and a detailed explanation of how the quantification was calculated. Where relevant, also provide an estimate of the significance of efficiencies related to new product introductions or quality improvements. For efficiencies that involve cost savings, state separately the one-time fixed cost savings, recurring fixed cost savings, and variable cost savings (in EUR per unit and EUR per year);
(iii) the extent to which customers are likely to benefit from the efficiency and a detailed explanation of how this conclusion is arrived at; and
(iv) the reason why the party or parties could not achieve the efficiency to a similar extent by means other than through the concentration proposed, and in a manner that is not likely to raise competition concerns.

SECTION 10 COOPERATIVE EFFECTS OF A JOINT VENTURE

10. In the case of a joint venture, for the purpose of Article 2(4) of the Merger Regulation, answer the following questions:

(a) Do two or more parents retain to a significant extent activities in the same market as the joint venture or in a market which is upstream or downstream from that of the joint venture or in a neighbouring market closely related to this market?[35]

If the answer is affirmative, indicate for each of the markets referred to here:

— the turnover of each parent company in the preceding financial year;
— the economic significance of the activities of the joint venture in relation to this turnover;
— the market share of each parent.

(b) If the answer to (a) is affirmative and in your view the creation of the joint venture does not lead to coordination between independent undertakings that restricts competition within the meaning of Article 101(1) of the Treaty on the Functioning of the European Union ('TFEU'), and, where applicable, the corresponding provisions of the EEA Agreement,[36] give your reasons.

(c) Without prejudice to the answers to (a) and (b) and in order to ensure that a complete assessment of the case can be made by the Commission, if you consider that the criteria of Article 101(3) TFEU and, where applicable, the corresponding provisions of the EEA Agreement[37] apply, explain why this is the case. Under Article 101(3) TFEU, the provisions of Article 101(1) TFEU may be declared inapplicable if the operation:

(i) contributes to improving the production or distribution of goods, or to promoting technical or economic progress;

(ii) allows consumers a fair share of the resulting benefit;

(iii) does not impose on the undertakings concerned restrictions which are not indispensable to the attainment of these objectives; and

(iv) does not afford such undertakings the possibility of eliminating competition in respect of a substantial part of the products in question.

SECTION 11 DECLARATION

The notification must conclude with the following declaration which is to be signed by or on behalf of all the notifying parties:

'The notifying party or parties declare that, to the best of their knowledge and belief, the information given in this notification is true, correct, and complete, that true and complete copies of documents required by Form CO have been supplied, that all estimates are identified as such and are their best estimates of the underlying facts, and that all the opinions expressed are sincere.

They are aware of the provisions of Article 14(1)(a) of the Merger Regulation.']

NOTES

Annex I substituted by Commission Regulation 1269/2013, Art 1(12), Annex.

Repeal of this Regulation in relation to the UK: this Regulation is repealed in relation to the UK (as from IP completion day); see the introductory notes to this Regulation *ante*.

1 OJ L24, 29.1.2004, p 1.

2 OJ L133, 30.4.2004, p 1.

3 See in particular Article 57 of the EEA Agreement, point 1 of Annex XIV to the EEA Agreement, Protocols 21 and 24 to the EEA Agreement, as well as Protocol 4 to the Agreement between the EFTA States on the establishment of a Surveillance Authority and a Court of Justice (hereinafter referred to as the 'Surveillance and Court Agreement'). Any reference to EFTA States must be understood to mean those EFTA States which are Contracting Parties to the EEA Agreement. As of 1 May 2004, these States are Iceland, Liechtenstein and Norway.

4 With effect from 1 December 2009, the Treaty on the Functioning of the European Union ('TFEU') has introduced certain changes, such as the replacement of 'Community' by 'Union' and 'common market' by 'internal market'. The terminology of the TFEU will be used throughout this Form CO.

5 The term 'concentration' is defined in Article 3 of the Merger Regulation and the term 'Union dimension' in Article 1 thereof. Furthermore, Article 4(5) provides that in certain circumstances where the Union turnover thresholds are not met, notifying parties may request that the Commission treat their proposed concentration as having a Union dimension.

6 See Article 10(1) of the Merger Regulation.

7 See Article 10(3) of the Merger Regulation.

8 See Article 4(2) of the Merger Regulation.

9 Any personal data submitted in this Form CO will be processed in compliance with Regulation (EC) No 45/2001 of the European Parliament and of the Council of 18 December 2000 on the protection of individuals with regard to the processing of personal data by the Community institutions and bodies and on the free movement of such data (OJ L8, 12.1.2001, p 1).

10 See, in particular, Article 122 of the EEA Agreement, Article 9 of Protocol 24 to the EEA Agreement and Article 17(2) of Chapter XIII of Protocol 4 to the Agreement between the EFTA States on the establishment of a Surveillance Authority and a Court of Justice (ESA Agreement).

11 See Section 6.3 for the definition of affected markets.

12 This includes the target company in the case of a contested bid, in which case the details should be completed as far as is possible.

13 See Articles 3(3), 3(4) and 3(5) and Article 5(4) of the Merger Regulation.

14 See Commission Consolidated Jurisdictional Notice under Council Regulation (EC) No 139/2004 on the control of concentrations between undertakings (OJ C95, 16.4.2008, p 1).

15 See Section B IV of the Consolidated Jurisdictional Notice.

16 As set out in points 1.2 and 1.4(g) in the introductory part, before notification, the notifying party or parties may want to discuss with the Commission to what extent dispensation (waivers) to provide some of the requested information (in this context, data on participations in other undertakings) would be appropriate. On the other hand, the Commission may for specific concentrations require the following for a complete notification based on this Form CO: with respect to the parties to the concentration and each undertaking or person identified in response to sections 3.1.1 or 3.1.6, provide a list for each undertaking of the members of their boards of management who are also members of the boards of management or of the supervisory boards of any other undertaking which is active in affected markets; and where applicable for each undertaking a list of the members of their supervisory boards who are also members of the boards of management of any other undertaking which is active in affected markets. In each case, identify the name of the other undertaking and the positions held by the management or supervisory board member.

17 As set out in points 1.2 and 1.4(g) in the introductory part, before notification, the notifying party or parties may want to discuss with the Commission to what extent dispensation (waivers) to provide some of the requested information (in this context, past acquisitions of undertakings) would be appropriate.

18 On the concepts of 'undertaking concerned' and the calculation of turnover see Commission Consolidated Jurisdictional

Notice under Council Regulation (EC) No 139/2004 on the control of concentrations between undertakings (OJ C95, 16.4.2008, p 1).

19 As set out in points 1.2 and 1.4(g) in the introductory part, before notification, the notifying party or parties may want to discuss with the Commission to what extent dispensation (waivers) to provide some of the requested information (in this context, documents) would be appropriate.

20 See Section 6.3 for the definition of affected markets.

21 As set out in points 1.2 and 1.4(g) in the introductory part, before notification, the notifying party or parties may want to discuss with the Commission to what extent dispensation (waivers) to provide some of the requested information (in this context, documents) would be appropriate.

22 See Commission Notice on the definition of the relevant market for the purposes of Community competition law (OJ C372, 9.12.1997, p 5).

23 For example, if a party to the concentration holds a market share larger than 30% in a market that is upstream to a market in which the other party is active, then both the upstream and the downstream markets are affected markets. Similarly, if a vertically integrated company merges with another party, which is active at the downstream level, and the concentration leads to a combined market share downstream of 30% or more, then both the upstream and the downstream markets are affected markets.

24 As indicated in DG Competition's Best Practices on the conduct of EC merger control proceedings, notifying parties are advised, in pre-notification, to disclose information relating to all potentially affected markets even if they ultimately consider that they are not affected and notwithstanding that they may take a particular view in relation to the issue of market definition. In this regard, as set out in introductory Parts 1.2 and 1.4(g), before notification, the notifying party or parties may want to discuss with the Commission to what extent dispensation (waivers) to provide some of the requested information (in this context, for certain affected markets, or for certain other markets as described under Section 6.4 would be appropriate.

25 Products (or services) are called complementary when, for example, the use (or consumption) of one product essentially implies the use (or consumption) of the other product, such as for staple machines and staples, and printers and printer cartridges.

26 Examples of products belonging to such a range would be whisky and gin sold to bars and restaurants, and different materials for packaging a certain category of goods sold to producers of such goods.

27 Without prejudice to Article 4(2) of the Implementing Regulation.

28 The value and volume of a market must reflect output less exports plus imports for the geographic areas under consideration. As set out in points 1.2 and 1.4(g) in the introductory part, before notification, the notifying party or parties may want to discuss with the Commission to what extent dispensation (waivers) to provide some of the requested information (in this context, value- or volume-based data for market size and shares) would be appropriate.

29 As set out in points 1.2 and 1.4(g) in the introductory part, before notification, the notifying party or parties may want to discuss with the Commission to what extent dispensation (waivers) to provide some of the requested information (in this context, capacity data) would be appropriate. A reason for a waiver could be that capacity does not appear relevant for competition in the market in question.

30 Research and development intensity can for instance be illustrated by research and development expenditure as a proportion of turnover.

31 As set out in points 1.2 and 1.4(g) in the introductory part, before notification, the notifying party or parties may want to discuss with the Commission to what extent dispensation (waivers) to provide some of the requested information would be appropriate.

32 The Commission may at any time, including for a complete notification of a concentration based on this Form CO, request a higher number of contact details for each of the categories of market participants identified in this Form CO and request contact details for other categories of market participants, for example suppliers.

33 It should be noted that submitting information in response to Section 9 is not required for a complete notification and is therefore voluntary. The notifying party or parties are not required to offer any justification for not completing this section. Failure to provide information on efficiencies will not be taken to imply that the proposed concentration does not create efficiencies or that the rationale for the concentration is to increase market power. Not providing the requested information on efficiencies at the notification stage does not preclude providing the information at a later stage. However, the earlier the information is provided, the better the Commission can verify the efficiency claims.

34 For further guidance on the assessment of efficiencies, see the Commission Guidelines on the assessment of horizontal mergers under the Council Regulation on the control of concentrations between undertakings (OJ C31, 5.2.2004, p 5).

35 For market definitions refer to Section 6.

36 See Article 53(1) of the EEA Agreement.

37 See Article 53(3) of the EEA Agreement.

[ANNEX II
SHORT FORM CO FOR THE NOTIFICATION OF A CONCENTRATION PURSUANT TO REGULATION (EC) NO 139/2004

INTRODUCTION

[4.596]

*1.1. **The purpose of the Short Form CO***

The Short Form CO specifies the information that must be provided by the notifying parties when submitting a notification to the European Commission of certain proposed mergers, acquisitions or other concentrations that are unlikely to raise competition concerns.

In completing this Short Form CO, your attention is drawn to Council Regulation (EC) No 139/2004 of 20 January 2004 on the control of concentrations between undertakings[1] (hereinafter referred to as 'the Merger Regulation'), and Commission Regulation (EC) No 802/2004[2] (hereinafter referred to as 'the Implementing Regulation'), to which this Short Form CO is annexed. The text of those Regulations, as well as other relevant documents, can be found on the Competition page of the Commission's Europa website. Your attention is also drawn to the corresponding provisions of the Agreement on the European Economic Area[3] *(hereinafter referred to as 'the EEA Agreement'). In completing this Short Form CO, your attention is also drawn to the Commission's Notice on a simplified procedure for treatment of certain concentrations.*[4]

As a general rule, the Short Form CO may be used for the purpose of notifying concentrations, where one of the following conditions is met:

1. *in the case of a joint venture, the joint venture has no, or negligible, actual or foreseen activities within the territory of the European Economic Area (EEA). Such cases occur where:*
   (a) *the turnover of the joint venture and/or the turnover of the contributed activities is less than EUR 100 million in the EEA territory at the time of notification; and*
   (b) *the total value of the assets transferred to the joint venture is less than EUR 100 million in the EEA territory at the time of notification;*
2. *two or more undertakings merge, or one or more undertakings acquire sole or joint control of another undertaking, provided that none of the parties to the concentration are engaged in business activities in the same product and geographic market,*[5] *or in a product market which is upstream or downstream from a product market in which any other party to the concentration is engaged;*[6 7]
3. *two or more undertakings merge, or one or more undertakings acquire sole or joint control of another undertaking and:*
   (a) *the combined market share of all the parties to the concentration that are engaged in business activities in the same product and geographic market (horizontal relationships) is less than 20%;*[8] *and*
   (b) *none of the individual or combined market shares of all the parties to the concentration that are engaged in business activities in a product market which is upstream or downstream from a product market in which any other party to the concentration is engaged (vertical relationships) is at either level 30% or more;*[9]

   as regards the conditions in point 3(a) and (b), in the case of an acquisition of joint control, relationships that occur only between the undertakings acquiring joint control are not considered horizontal or vertical relationships for the purpose of this Short Form CO but may be dealt with as concentrations where an issue of coordination arises;
4. *a party is to acquire sole control of an undertaking over which it already has joint control.*

The Commission may also accept a Short Form CO where two or more of the parties to the concentration are in a horizontal relationship,[10] *provided that the increment ('delta') of the Herfindahl-Hirschman Index ('HHI') resulting from the concentration is below 150*[11] *and the parties' combined market share is below 50%.*[12] *The Commission will decide on a case-by-case basis whether, under the particular circumstances of the case at hand, the increase in market concentration level indicated by the HHI delta is such that a Short Form CO can be accepted. The Commission is less likely to accept a Short Form CO if any of the special circumstances mentioned in the Commission's guidelines on the assessment of horizontal mergers are present,*[13] *for instance – but not limited to – where the market is already concentrated, in the case of a concentration that eliminates an important competitive force, in the case of a concentration between two important innovators, or in the case of a concentration involving a firm that has promising pipeline products.*

The Commission may always require a Form CO where it appears that the conditions for using the Short Form CO are not met, or, exceptionally where they are met, but the Commission determines, nonetheless, that a notification under Form CO is necessary for an adequate investigation of possible competition concerns.

Examples of cases where a notification under Form CO may be necessary are concentrations where it is difficult to define the relevant markets (for example, in emerging markets or where there is no established case practice); where a party is a new or potential entrant, or an important patent holder; where it is not possible to adequately determine the parties' market shares; in markets with high entry barriers, with a high degree of concentration or known competition problems; where at least two parties to the concentration are present in closely related neighbouring markets;[14] *and in concentrations where an issue of coordination arises, as referred to in Article 2(4) of the Merger Regulation. Similarly, a Form CO may be required in the case of a party acquiring sole control of a joint venture in which it currently holds joint control, where the acquiring party and the joint venture, together, have a strong market position, or the joint venture and the acquiring party have strong positions in vertically related markets.*[15]

1.2. ***Reversion to the normal procedure and notification under Form CO***

In assessing whether a concentration may be notified under the Short Form CO, the Commission will ensure that all relevant circumstances are established with sufficient clarity. In this respect, the responsibility to provide correct and complete information rests with the notifying parties.

If, after the concentration has been notified, the Commission considers that the case is not appropriate for notification under the Short Form CO, the Commission may require full, or where appropriate partial, notification under Form CO. This may be the case where:

(a) *it appears that the conditions for using the Short Form CO are not met;*
(b) *although the conditions for using the Short Form CO are met, a full or partial notification under Form CO appears to be necessary for an adequate investigation of possible competition concerns or to establish that the transaction is a concentration within the meaning of Article 3 of the Merger Regulation;*
(c) *the Short Form CO contains incorrect or misleading information;*
(d) *a Member State or an EFTA State expresses substantiated competition concerns about the notified concentration within 15 working days of receipt of the copy of the notification; or*
(e) *a third party expresses substantiated competition concerns within the time-limit laid down by the Commission for such comments.*

In such cases, the notification may be treated as being incomplete in a material respect pursuant to Article 5(2) of the Implementing Regulation. The Commission will inform the notifying parties or their representatives of this in writing and without delay. The notification will only become effective on the date on which all information required is received.

1.3. ***Pre-notification contacts***

It is recognised that the information requested in this Short Form CO can be substantial. However, experience has shown that, depending on the specific characteristics of the case, not all information is always necessary for an adequate examination of the proposed concentration. Accordingly, if you consider that any particular information requested by this Short Form CO may not be necessary for the Commission's examination of the case, you are encouraged to ask the Commission to dispense with the obligation to provide certain information ('waiver') (see point 1.6(g) of this introductory part for more details).

Under the Merger Regulation, notifying parties are entitled to notify a concentration at any time, provided the notification is complete. The possibility to engage in pre-notification contacts is a service offered by the Commission to notifying parties on a voluntary basis in order to prepare the formal merger review procedure. As such, while not mandatory, pre-notification contacts can be extremely valuable to both the notifying parties and the Commission in determining the precise amount of information required in a notification and, in the majority of cases, will result in a significant reduction of the information required.

Accordingly, whilst the parties are solely responsible to decide whether to engage in pre-notification contacts and when exactly to notify, parties are encouraged to consult the Commission regarding the adequacy of the scope and type of information on which they intend to base their notification. Similarly, in cases where the parties wish to submit a Short Form CO, they are encouraged to engage in pre-notification contacts with the Commission to discuss whether the case is one for which it is appropriate to use a Short Form CO.

Notifying parties are also encouraged to engage in pre-notification contacts where they wish to submit a Short Form CO in situations where two or more of the parties to the concentration are in a horizontal relationship with an HHI delta resulting from the concentration of below 150.

Nonetheless, pre-notification contacts, in particular the submission of a draft notification, may be less useful in cases falling under point 5(b) of the Commission's Notice on a simplified procedure for treatment of certain concentrations. This concerns cases where the parties are not engaged in business activities in the same product and geographic market, or in a product market which is upstream or downstream from a product market in which any other party to the concentration is engaged. In such circumstances, notifying parties may prefer to notify immediately without submitting a draft notification before-hand.[16]

Notifying parties may refer to the 'Best Practices on the conduct of EC merger control proceedings' of the Commission's Directorate-General for Competition ('DG Competition') as published on DG Competition's website and updated from time to time. These Best Practices provide guidance on pre-notification contacts and the preparation of notifications.

1.4. ***Who must notify***

In the case of a merger within the meaning of Article 3(1)(a) of the Merger Regulation or the acquisition of joint control of an undertaking within the meaning of Article 3(1)(b) of the Merger Regulation, the notification must be completed jointly by the parties to the merger or by those acquiring joint control, as the case may be.[17]

In the case of the acquisition of a controlling interest in one undertaking by another, the acquirer must complete the notification.

In the case of a public bid to acquire an undertaking, the bidder must complete the notification.

Each party completing the notification is responsible for the accuracy of the information which it provides.

1.5. ***The information to be provided***

Different Sections of this Short Form CO must be filled in, depending on the reasons[18] *why the concentration qualifies for simplified treatment and notification under the Short Form CO:*

(a) *Sections 1, 2, 3, 4, 5 and 10 must be completed for all cases. Section 9 must be completed in the case of a joint venture.*
(b) *If the concentration gives rise to one or more reportable markets,*[19] *sections 6 and 7 must be completed.*
(c) *If the concentration does not give rise to one or more reportable markets,*[20] *section 8 must be completed; sections 6 and 7 do not need to be completed.*

1.6. ***The requirement for a correct and complete notification***

All information required by this Short Form CO must be correct and complete. The information required must be supplied in the appropriate Section of this Short Form CO.

In particular you should note that:

(a) *In accordance with Article 10(1) of the Merger Regulation and Article 5(2) and (4) of the Implementing Regulation, the time-limits of the Merger Regulation linked to the notification will not begin to run until all the information that must be supplied with the notification has been received by the Commission. This requirement is to ensure that the Commission is able to assess the notified concentration within the strict time-limits provided by the Merger Regulation.*
(b) *The notifying party or parties must verify, in the course of preparing their notification, that contact names and numbers, and in particular fax numbers and e-mail addresses, provided to the Commission are accurate, relevant and up-to-date.*[21]
(c) *Incorrect or misleading information in the notification will be considered to be incomplete information (Article 5(4) of the Implementing Regulation).*

(d) *If a notification is incomplete, the Commission will inform the notifying parties or their representatives in writing and without delay. The notification will only become effective on the date on which the complete and accurate information is received by the Commission (Article 10(1) of the Merger Regulation, Article 5(2) and (4) of the Implementing Regulation).*

(e) *Under Article 14(1)(a) of the Merger Regulation, notifying parties who, either intentionally or negligently, supply incorrect or misleading information, may be liable to fines of up to 1% of the aggregate turnover of the undertaking concerned. In addition, pursuant to Article 6(3)(a) and Article 8(6)(a) of the Merger Regulation the Commission may revoke its decision on the compatibility of a notified concentration where it is based on incorrect information for which one of the undertakings is responsible.*

(f) *You may request in writing that the Commission accept that the notification is complete notwithstanding the failure to provide information required by this Short Form CO, if such information is not reasonably available to you in part or in whole (for example, because of the unavailability of information on a target company during a contested bid).*

The Commission will consider such a request, provided that you give reasons for the unavailability of that information, and provide your best estimates for missing data together with the sources for the estimates. Where possible, indications as to where any of the requested information that is unavailable to you could be obtained by the Commission should also be provided.

(g) *In accordance with Article 4(2) of the Implementing Regulation, the Commission may dispense with the obligation to provide any particular information in the notification, including documents, or with any other requirement specified in this Short Form CO where the Commission considers that compliance with those obligations or requirements is not necessary for the examination of the case. Accordingly, you may, in pre-notification, submit a written request for a waiver, asking the Commission to dispense with the obligation to provide such information if you consider that that information is not necessary for the Commission's examination of the case.*

Waiver requests should be at the same time as the draft Short Form CO in order to allow the Commission to determine whether or not the information in relation to which a waiver is being requested is necessary for the examination of the case. Waiver requests should be made either within the text of a draft Short Form CO itself or as an e-mail or letter addressed to the responsible case manager and/or head of unit.

The Commission will consider waiver requests, provided that you give adequate reasons why the information in question is not necessary for the examination of the case. Waiver requests will be dealt with in the context of the review of a draft Short Form CO. Therefore, in accordance with DG Competition's Best Practices on the conduct of EC merger control proceedings, DG Competition would normally require five working days before responding to waiver requests.

For the avoidance of doubt, it should be noted that the fact that a section is not mentioned in point 1.5. of this introductory part nor the fact that the Commission may have accepted, pursuant to point 1.6, that any particular information requested by this Short Form CO was not necessary for the complete notification of a concentration (using the Short Form CO), does not in any way prevent the Commission from requesting this particular information at any time, in particular by way of request for information pursuant to Article 11 of the Merger Regulation.

1.7. ***How to notify***

The notification must be completed in one of the official languages of the European Union. This language will thereafter be the language of the proceedings for all notifying parties. Where notifications are made in accordance with Article 12 of Protocol 24 to the EEA Agreement in an official language of an EFTA State which is not an official language of the Union, the notification must simultaneously be supplemented with a translation into an official language of the Union.

The information requested by this Short Form CO is to be set out using the sections and paragraph numbers of the Short Form CO, signing a declaration as provided in Section 10, and annexing supporting documentation. The original of the Short Form CO must be signed by persons authorised by law to act on behalf of each notifying party or by one or more authorised external representatives of the notifying party or parties. In completing Section 7 of this Short Form CO, the notifying parties are invited to consider whether, for purposes of clarity, this section is best presented in numerical order, or whether information can be grouped together for each individual reportable market (or group of reportable markets).

For the sake of clarity, certain information may be put in annexes. However, it is essential that all key substantive pieces of information, in particular, market share information for the parties and their largest competitors, are presented in the body of this Short Form CO. Annexes to this Short Form CO must only be used to supplement the information supplied in the Short Form CO itself.

Contact details must be provided in a format provided by the DG Competition on its website. For a proper investigatory process, it is essential that the contact details are accurate. Multiple instances of incorrect contact details may be a ground for declaring a notification incomplete.

Supporting documents are to be submitted in their original language; where this is not an official language of the Union, they must be translated into the language of the proceeding (Article 3(4) of the Implementing Regulation).

Supporting documents may be originals or copies of the originals. In the latter case, the notifying party must confirm that they are true and complete.

One original and the required number of copies of the Short Form CO and the supporting documents must be submitted to the Commission's DG Competition. The Commission has published the required number and format (paper or electronic) of copies in the Official Journal of the European Union as well as on DG Competition's website.

The notification must be delivered to the address referred to in Article 23(1) of the Implementing Regulation. This address is published in the Official Journal of the European Union and available on DG Competition's website. The notification must be delivered to the Commission on working days as defined by Article 24 of the Implementing Regulation during the opening hours indicated on DG Competition's website. The security instructions given on DG Competition's website must be adhered to.

All electronic copies of the Short Form CO and supporting documents must be provided in a usable and searchable format as further specified on DG Competition's website.

1.8. ***Confidentiality***

Article 339 of the Treaty on the Functioning of the European Union ('TFEU') and Article 17(2) of the Merger Regulation as well as the corresponding provisions of the EEA Agreement[22] *require the Commission, the Member States, the EFTA Surveillance Authority and the EFTA States, their officials and other servants not to disclose information they have acquired through the application of the Regulation of the kind covered by the obligation of professional secrecy. The same principle must also apply to protect confidentiality between notifying parties.*

If you believe that your interests would be harmed if any of the information you are asked to supply were to be published or otherwise divulged to other parties, submit this information separately with each page clearly marked 'Business Secrets'. You should also give reasons why this information should not be divulged or published.

In the case of mergers or joint acquisitions, or in other cases where the notification is completed by more than one of the parties, business secrets may be submitted under separate cover, and referred to in the notification as an annex. All such annexes must be included in the submission in order for a notification to be considered complete.

1.9. ***Definitions and instructions for purposes of this Short Form CO***

Notifying party or parties: in cases where a notification is submitted by only one of the undertakings who is a party to an operation, 'notifying parties' is used to refer only to the undertaking actually submitting the notification.

Party(ies) to the concentration or parties: these terms relate to both the acquiring and acquired parties, or to the merging parties, including all undertakings in which a controlling interest is being acquired or which is the subject of a public bid.

Except where otherwise specified, the terms notifying party(ies) and party(ies) to the concentration include all the undertakings which belong to the same groups as those parties.

Year: all references to the word year in this Short Form CO must be read as meaning calendar year, unless otherwise stated. All information requested in this Short Form CO must, unless otherwise specified, relate to the year preceding that of the notification.

The financial data requested in Section 4 must be provided in euro at the average exchange rates prevailing for the years or other periods in question.

All references to provisions of law contained in this Short Form CO are to the relevant articles and paragraphs of the Merger Regulation, unless otherwise stated.

1.10. ***International cooperation between the Commission and other competition authorities***

The Commission encourages the undertakings concerned to facilitate the international cooperation between the Commission and other competition authorities reviewing the same concentration. In the Commission's experience, good cooperation between the Commission and competition authorities in jurisdictions outside the EEA entails substantial benefits for the undertakings concerned. To this end, the Commission encourages notifying parties to submit together with this Short Form CO a list of those jurisdictions outside the EEA where the concentration is subject to regulatory clearance under merger control rules before or after closing.

1.11. ***Provision of information to employees and their representatives***

The Commission would like to draw attention to the obligations to which the parties to a concentration may be subject under Union and/or national rules on information and consultation regarding transactions of a concentrative nature vis-à-vis employees and/or their representatives.

SECTION 1 DESCRIPTION OF THE CONCENTRATION

1.1. Provide an executive summary of the concentration, specifying the parties to the concentration, the nature of the concentration (for example, merger, acquisition, or joint venture), the areas of activity of the parties to the concentration, the markets on which the concentration will have an impact (including the main reportable markets),[23] *and the strategic and economic rationale for the concentration.*

1.2. Provide a non-confidential summary (up to 500 words) of the information provided under Section 1.1. It is intended that this summary will be published on DG Competition's website at the date of notification. The summary must be drafted so that it contains no confidential information or business secrets.

1.3. Provide an explanation of the reasons why the concentration qualifies for simplified treatment by reference to the relevant provisions of the Commission Notice on a simplified procedure for treatment of certain concentrations under Council Regulation (EC) No 139/2004.

SECTION 2 INFORMATION ABOUT THE PARTIES

For each notifying party as well as for each other party to the concentration[24] *provide:*

2.1.1. name of undertaking;

2.1.2. name, address, telephone number, fax number and e-mail address of, and position held by, the appropriate contact person; the address given must be an address for service to which documents and, in particular, Commission decisions and other procedural documents may be notified, and the contact person given shall be deemed to be authorised to accept service;

2.1.3. if one or more authorised external representatives of the undertaking are appointed, the representative or representatives to which documents and, in particular, Commission decisions and other procedural documents may be notified:

2.1.3.1. name, an address for service, telephone number, fax number and e-mail address of, and position held by, each representative; and

2.1.3.2. the original of written proof that each authorised external representative is authorised to act (based on the model Power of Attorney available on DG Competition's website).

SECTION 3 DETAILS OF THE CONCENTRATION, OWNERSHIP AND CONTROL[25]

The information sought in this section may be illustrated by the use of organisation charts or diagrams to show the structure of ownership and control of the undertakings before and after completion of the concentration.

3.1. Describe the nature of the concentration being notified. By reference to the relevant criteria of the Merger Regulation and the Commission Consolidated Jurisdictional Notice:[26]

3.1.1. identify the undertakings or persons solely or jointly controlling each of the undertakings concerned, directly or indirectly, and describe the structure of ownership and control of each of the undertakings concerned before the completion of the concentration;

3.1.2. explain whether the proposed concentration is:

(i) a full merger,

(ii) an acquisition of sole or joint control, or

(iii) a contract or other means of conferring direct or indirect control within the meaning of Article 3(2) of the Merger Regulation; or

(iv) the acquisition of joint control in a full-function joint venture within the meaning of Article 3(4) of the Merger Regulation, and if so, the reasons why the joint venture is considered to be full-function;[27]

3.1.3. explain how the concentration will be implemented (for example by conclusion of an agreement, by the launch of a public bid, etc.);

3.1.4. by reference to Article 4(1) of the Merger Regulation explain which of the following have taken place at the time of notification:

(i) an agreement has been concluded,

(ii) a controlling interest has been acquired,

(iii) (the intention to launch) a public bid has been announced, or

(iv) the undertakings concerned have demonstrated a good faith intention to conclude an agreement;

3.1.5. indicate the expected date of any major events designed to bring about the completion of the concentration;

3.1.6. explain the structure of ownership and control of each of the undertakings concerned after the completion of the concentration.

3.2. Describe the economic rationale of the concentration.

3.3. State the value of the transaction (the purchase price (or the value of all the assets involved as the case may be); specify whether this is in the form of equity, cash, or other assets).

3.4. Describe any financial or other support received from public authorities by any of the parties and the nature and amount of this support.

SECTION 4 TURNOVER

For each of the undertakings concerned provide the following data for the last financial year:[28]

4.1. Worldwide turnover;

4.2. EU-wide turnover;

4.3. EEA-wide turnover (EU and EFTA);

4.4. turnover in each Member State (indicate the Member State, if any, in which more than two-thirds of EU-wide turnover is achieved);

4.5. EFTA-wide turnover;

4.6. turnover in each EFTA State (indicate the EFTA State, if any, in which more than two-thirds of EFTA-wide turnover is achieved; also indicate whether the combined turnover of the undertakings concerned in the territory of the EFTA States equals 25% or more of their total turnover in the EEA territory).

Turnover data must be provided by filling in the Commission's template table available on DG Competition's website.

SECTION 5 SUPPORTING DOCUMENTATION

Notifying parties must provide the following:

5.1. Copies of the final or most recent versions of all documents bringing about the concentration, whether by agreement between the parties to the concentration, acquisition of a controlling interest or a public bid; and

5.2. An indication of the internet address, if any, at which the most recent annual reports and accounts of all the parties to the concentration are available, or if no such internet address exists, copies of the most recent annual reports and accounts of the parties to the concentration.

5.3. The following information needs to be provided only in cases where the concentration gives rise to one or more reportable markets in the EEA: copies of all presentations prepared by or for or received by any members of the board of management, or the board of directors, or the supervisory board, as applicable in the light of the corporate governance structure, or the other person(s) exercising similar functions (or to whom such functions have been delegated or entrusted), or the shareholders' meeting analysing the notified concentration.

Provide a list of the documents mentioned in this section 5.3 indicating for each document the date of preparation and the name and title of the addressee(s).

SECTION 6 MARKET DEFINITIONS

This section needs to be completed for concentrations that give rise to one or more reportable markets.[29]

6.1. ***Market definitions***

The relevant product and geographic markets serve to identify the scope within which the market power of the new entity resulting from the concentration must be assessed.[30]

The notifying party or parties must provide the information requested in this Short Form CO having regard to the following definitions:

6.1.1. Relevant product markets

A relevant product market comprises all those products and/or services which are regarded as interchangeable or substitutable by the consumer, by reason of the products' characteristics, their prices and their intended use. A relevant product market may in some cases be composed of a number of individual products and/or services which present largely identical physical or technical characteristics and are interchangeable.

Factors relevant to the assessment of the relevant product market include the analysis of why the products or services in these markets are included and why others are excluded by using the definition, and having regard to, for example, substitutability, prices, cross-price elasticity of demand or other relevant factors (such as supply-side substitutability in appropriate cases).

6.1.2. Relevant geographic markets

The relevant geographic market comprises the area in which the undertakings concerned are involved in the supply and demand of relevant products or services, in which the conditions of competition are sufficiently homogeneous and which can be distinguished from neighbouring geographic areas because, in particular, conditions of competition are appreciably different in those areas.

Factors relevant to the assessment of the relevant geographic market include, inter alia, the nature and characteristics of the products or services concerned, the existence of entry barriers, consumer preferences, appreciable differences in the undertakings' market shares between neighbouring geographic areas, or substantial price differences.

6.2. ***Reportable markets***

For purposes of information required in this Short Form CO, reportable markets consist of all relevant product and geographic markets, as well as plausible alternative relevant product and geographic markets,[31] *on the basis of which in the EEA territory:*

(a) two or more of the parties to the concentration (in case of acquisition of joint control in a joint venture, the joint venture and at least one of the acquiring parties) are engaged in business activities in the same relevant market (horizontal relationships);

(b) one or more of the parties to the concentration (in case of acquisition of joint control in a joint venture, the joint venture and at least one of the acquiring parties) are engaged in business activities in a product market, which is upstream or downstream of a market in which any other party to the concentration is engaged, regardless of whether there is or is not any existing supplier/customer relationship between the parties to the concentration (vertical relationships).

On the basis of the definitions set out in Section 6, identify all reportable markets.

If the concentration falls within the scope of point 5(c) of the Commission Notice on a simplified procedure for treatment of certain concentrations under Council Regulation (EC) No 139/2004, you must confirm that there is no affected market as defined in Form CO Section 6.3 under any plausible product and geographic market definition.

SECTION 7 INFORMATION ON MARKETS

This section needs to be completed for concentrations that give rise to one or more reportable markets.

7.1. For each reportable market described in Section 6, for the year preceding the operation, provide the following:

7.1.1. for each of the parties to the concentration, the nature of the undertaking's business, the main subsidiaries active and/or brands, product names and/or trademarks used in each of these markets.

7.1.2. an estimate of the total size of the market in terms of sales value (in euro) and volume (units).[32] *Indicate the basis and sources for the calculations and provide documents where available to confirm these calculations;*

7.1.3. the sales in value and volume, as well as an estimate of the market shares, of each of the parties to the concentration. Indicate if there have been significant changes to the sales and market shares for the last three financial years; and

7.1.4. for horizontal and vertical relationships, an estimate of the market share in value (and where appropriate, volume) of the three largest competitors (indicating the basis for the estimates). Provide the name, address, telephone number, fax number and e-mail address of the head of the legal department (or other person exercising similar functions; and in cases where there is no such person, then the chief executive) for these competitors.)

7.2. If the concentration falls within the scope of point 6 of the Commission Notice on a simplified procedure for treatment of certain concentrations under Council Regulation (EC) No 139/2004, explain the following for each reportable market where the parties have a combined horizontal market share of 20% or more:

7.2.1. Explain whether any of the special circumstances mentioned in point 20 of the Commission's Guidelines on the assessment of horizontal mergers[33] *are present; in particular discuss the degree of market concentration, whether the proposed concentration would combine important innovators, whether the proposed concentration would eliminate an important competitive force and whether the proposed concentration involves a firm that has promising pipeline products.*

7.2.2. Provide the sales in value and volume, as well as an estimate of the market shares, of each of the parties to the concentration for each of the last 3 years.

7.2.3. In respect of each party to the concentration provide a brief description of:

7.2.3.1. the intensity of research and development;[34]

7.2.3.2. the main innovations in products and/or services brought to market during the last 3 years, pipeline products to be brought to the market within the next 3 years, as well as important intellectual property rights owned or controlled.

SECTION 8 ACTIVITIES OF THE TARGET IF NO REPORTABLE MARKETS

This section needs to be completed for concentrations that do not give rise to any reportable markets.

8.1. ***Business activities of the party or parties acquiring control***

For each of the party or parties acquiring control describe the nature of the undertaking's business.

8.2. ***Business activities of the target***

8.2.1. Explain the existing and future business activities of the undertaking(s) over which control is acquired.

8.2.2. In the case of a joint venture with no actual or foreseen activities within the territory of the EEA within the meaning of paragraph 5(a) of the Commission Notice on a simplified procedure for treatment of certain concentrations under Council Regulation (EC) No 139/2004, it is sufficient to explain:

8.2.2.1. the products or services provided by the joint venture currently and in the future; and

8.2.2.2. why the joint venture would not have any effect, directly or indirectly, on markets within the EEA.

8.3. ***Absence of reportable markets***

Please explain why you consider that the proposed concentration does not give rise to any reportable market in the EEA.

SECTION 9 COOPERATIVE EFFECTS OF A JOINT VENTURE

In the case of a joint venture, for the purpose of Article 2(4) of the Merger Regulation, answer the following questions:

(a) Do two or more parents retain to a significant extent activities in the same market as the joint venture or in a market which is upstream or downstream from that of the joint venture or in a neighbouring market closely related to this market?[35]

If the answer is affirmative, indicate for each of the markets referred to here:

(i) the turnover of each parent company in the preceding financial year;

(ii) the economic significance of the activities of the joint venture in relation to this turnover;

(iii) the market share of each parent.

(b) If the answer to (a) is affirmative and in your view the criteria of Article 101(1) TFEU, and, where applicable, the corresponding provisions of the EEA Agreement[36] *are not met, give your reasons.*

(c) Without prejudice to the answers to (a) and (b) and in order to ensure that a complete assessment of the case can be made by the Commission, if you consider that the criteria of Article 101(3) TFEU and, where applicable, the corresponding provisions of the EEA Agreement[37] *apply, explain why this is the case. Under Article 101(3) TFEU, the provisions of Article 101(1) may be declared inapplicable if the operation:*

(i) contributes to improving the production or distribution of goods, or to promoting technical or economic progress;

(ii) allows consumers a fair share of the resulting benefit;

(iii) does not impose on the undertakings concerned restrictions which are not indispensable to the attainment of these objectives; and

(iv) does not afford such undertakings the possibility of eliminating competition in respect of a substantial part of the products in question.

SECTION 10 DECLARATION

The notification must conclude with the following declaration which is to be signed by or on behalf of all the notifying parties:

'The notifying party or parties declare that, to the best of their knowledge and belief, the information given in this notification is true, correct, and complete, that true and complete copies of documents required by Short Form CO have been supplied, that all estimates are identified as such and are their best estimates of the underlying facts, and that all the opinions expressed are sincere.

They are aware of the provisions of Article 14(1)(a) of the Merger Regulation.']

NOTES

Annex II substituted by Commission Regulation 1269/2013, Art 1(12), Annex.

Repeal of this Regulation in relation to the UK: this Regulation is repealed in relation to the UK (as from IP completion day); see the introductory notes to this Regulation *ante*.

1 OJ L24, 29.1.2004, p 1.

2 OJ L133, 30.4.2004, p 1.

3 See in particular Article 57 of the EEA Agreement, point 1 of Annex XIV to the EEA Agreement, Protocols 21 and 24 to the EEA Agreement, as well as Protocol 4 to the Agreement between the EFTA States on the establishment of a Surveillance Authority and a Court of Justice (hereinafter referred to as the 'Surveillance and Court Agreement'). Any reference to EFTA States shall be understood to mean those EFTA States which are Contracting Parties to the EEA Agreement. As of 1 May 2004, these States are Iceland, Liechtenstein and Norway.

4 The Commission Notice on a simplified procedure for treatment of certain concentrations under Council Regulation (EC) No 139/2004 (OJ C366, 14.12.2013, p 1).

5 Any reference in this Short Form CO to undertakings' activities in markets should be understood as activities in markets within the EEA territory or markets which include the EEA territory, but may be wider than the EEA territory.

6 A vertical relationship normally presupposes that the product or service of the undertaking active in the upstream market in question constitutes an important input to the product or service of the undertaking active in the downstream market: for more details see Commission Guidelines on the assessment of non-horizontal mergers under the Council Regulation on the control of concentrations between undertakings (OJ C265, 18.10.2008, p 6), point 34.

7 In the case of an acquisition of joint control, relationships that occur only between the undertakings acquiring joint control are not considered horizontal or vertical relationships for the purpose of this Short Form CO but may be dealt with as concentrations where an issue of coordination arises.

8 The thresholds for horizontal and vertical relationships apply to any plausible alternative product and geographic market definition that may have to be considered in a given case. It is important that the underlying market definitions set out in the notification are precise enough to justify the assessment that these thresholds are not met, and that all plausible alternative market definitions that may have to be considered are mentioned (including geographic markets narrower than national).

9 See footnotes 5 and 7.

10 In the case of an acquisition of joint control, relationships that occur only between the undertakings acquiring joint control outside the field of activity of the joint venture, are not considered horizontal or vertical relationships for the purpose of this Short Form CO but may be dealt with as concentrations where an issue of coordination arises.

11 The HHI is calculated by summing the squares of the individual market shares of all the firms in the market; the change in the HHI stemming from a concentration can be calculated independently of the overall market concentration, on the basis of the market shares of the parties to the concentration only. See Commission Guidelines on the assessment of horizontal mergers under the Council Regulation on the control of concentrations between undertakings (OJ C31, 5.2.2004, page 5), point 16 and footnote 19. However, in order to calculate the HHI delta resulting from the concentration, it is sufficient to subtract from the square of the sum of the market shares of the parties to the concentration (in other words, the square of the merged entity's market share post-concentration) the sum of the squares of the parties' individual market shares (since the market shares of all other competitors in the market remain unchanged and thus do not influence the result of the equation). In other words, the HHI delta can be calculated on the basis of only the market shares of the parties to the concentration, without a need to know the market shares of any other competitors in the market.

12 See footnote 7.

13 See Commission Guidelines on the assessment of horizontal mergers under the Council Regulation on the control of concentrations between undertakings, in particular point 20.

14 Product markets are closely related neighbouring markets when the products are complementary to each other or when they belong to a range of products that is generally purchased by the same set of customers for the same end use; see Commission Guidelines on the assessment of non-horizontal mergers under the Council Regulation on the control of concentrations between undertakings (OJ C265, 18.10.2008, p 6), point 91.

15 See Commission Notice on a simplified procedure for treatment of certain concentrations under Council Regulation (EC) No 139/2004, points 8 to 19.

16 In light of the DG Competition *Best Practices on the conduct of EC merger control proceedings*, the Commission would nevertheless encourage parties to submit in advance a request for the allocation of a DG Competition case-team.

17 See Article 4(2) of the Merger Regulation.

18 See the conditions in points 5 and 6 of the Commission Notice on a simplified procedure for treatment of certain concentrations under Council Regulation (EC) No 139/2004 (OJ C366, 14.12.2013, p 1).

19 Reportable markets within the meaning of section 6.

20 Reportable markets within the meaning of section 6.

21 Any personal data submitted in this Short Form CO will be processed in compliance with Regulation (EC) No 45/2001 of the European Parliament and of the Council of 18 December 2000 on the protection of individuals with regard to the processing of personal data by the Community institutions and bodies and on the free movement of such data (OJ L8, 12.1.2001, p 1).

22 See, in particular, Article 122 of the EEA Agreement, Article 9 of Protocol 24 to the EEA Agreement and Article 17(2) of Chapter XIII of Protocol 4 to the Agreement between the EFTA States on the establishment of a Surveillance Authority and a Court of Justice (ESA Agreement).

23 Reportable markets within the meaning of section 6.

24 This includes the target company in the case of a contested bid, in which case the details should be completed as far as is possible.

25 See Articles 3(3), 3(4) and 3(5) and Article 5(4) of the Merger Regulation.

26 See Commission Consolidated Jurisdictional Notice under Council Regulation (EC) No 139/2004 on the control of concentrations between undertakings (OJ C95, 16.4.2008, p 1).

27 See section B IV of the Consolidated Jurisdictional Notice.

28 On the concepts of 'undertaking concerned' and the calculation of turnover see Commission Consolidated Jurisdictional Notice under Council Regulation (EC) No 139/2004 on the control of concentrations between undertakings (OJ C95, 16.4.2008, p 1).

29 Reportable markets within the meaning of section 6.

30 ee Commission Notice on the definition of the relevant market for the purposes of Union competition law (OJ C372, 9.12.1997, p 5).

31 Plausible alternative product and geographic market definitions can be identified on the basis of previous Commission decisions and judgments of the Union Courts and (in particular where there are no Commission or Court precedents) by reference to industry reports, market studies and the notifying parties' internal documents.

32 The value and volume of a market must reflect output less exports plus imports for the geographic areas under consideration.

33 See Commission Guidelines on the assessment of horizontal mergers under the Council Regulation on the control of

concentrations between undertakings (OJ C31, 5.2.2004, p 5).

34 Research and development intensity can for instance be illustrated by research and development expenditure as a proportion of turnover.

35 For market definitions refer to Section 6.

36 See Article 53(1) of the EEA Agreement.

37 See Article 53(3) of the EEA Agreement.

[ANNEX III
FORM RS
(RS = REASONED SUBMISSION PURSUANT TO ARTICLE 4(4) AND (5) OF COUNCIL REGULATION (EC) NO 139/2004)
FORM RS RELATING TO REASONED SUBMISSIONS PURSUANT TO ARTICLES 4(4) AND 4(5) OF REGULATION (EC) NO 139/2004

INTRODUCTION

[4.597]

1.1. ***The purpose of this Form RS***

This Form RS specifies the information that submitting parties must provide when making a reasoned submission for a pre-notification referral under Article 4(4) or (5) of Council Regulation (EC) No 139/2004 of 20 January 2004 on the control of concentrations between undertakings[1] (hereinafter referred to as 'the Merger Regulation').

Your attention is drawn to the Merger Regulation and to Commission Regulation (EC) No 802/2004[2] (hereinafter referred to as 'the Implementing Regulation'), to which this Form RS is annexed. The text of those regulations, as well as other relevant documents, can be found on the Competition page of the Commission's Europa website. Your attention is also drawn to the corresponding provisions of the Agreement on the European Economic Area[3] (hereinafter referred to as 'the EEA Agreement').

It is recognised that the information requested in this Form RS can be substantial. However, experience has shown that, depending on the specific characteristics of the case, not all information is always necessary for an adequate reasoned submission. Accordingly, if you consider that any particular information requested by this Form RS may not be necessary for the reasoned submission in your case, you are encouraged to ask the Commission to dispense with the obligation to provide certain information. See point 1.3(e) of this introductory part for more details.

The possibility to engage in prior contacts is a service offered by the Commission to submitting parties on a voluntary basis in order to prepare the formal submission of this Form RS. Prior contacts are extremely valuable to both the submitting parties and the Commission in determining the precise amount of information required in a reasoned submission and, in the majority of cases, will result in a significant reduction of the information required. Accordingly, parties are encouraged to consult the Commission and the relevant Member State/s or EFTA State/s on a voluntary basis regarding the adequacy of the scope and type of information on which they intend to base their reasoned submission.

The parties may refer to the 'Best Practices on the conduct of EC merger control proceedings' of the Commission's Directorate-General for Competition ('DG Competition') as published on DG Competition's website and updated from time to time, which provide guidance on prior contacts and the preparation of notifications and reasoned submissions.

1.2. ***Persons entitled to submit a reasoned submission***

In the case of a merger within the meaning of Article 3(1)(a) of the Merger Regulation or the acquisition of joint control of an undertaking within the meaning of Article 3(1)(b) of the Merger Regulation, the reasoned submission must be completed jointly by the parties to the merger or by those acquiring joint control as the case may be.

In the case of the acquisition of a controlling interest in one undertaking by another, the acquirer must complete the reasoned submission.

In the case of a public bid to acquire an undertaking, the bidder must complete the reasoned submission.

Each party completing a reasoned submission is responsible for the accuracy of the information which it provides.

1.3. ***The requirement for a reasoned submission to be correct and complete***

All information required by this Form RS must be correct and complete. The information required must be supplied in the appropriate section of this Form RS.

Incorrect or misleading information in the reasoned submission will be considered to be incomplete information (Article 5(4) of the Implementing Regulation).

In particular you should note that:

- *(a) In accordance with Articles 4(4) and (5) of the Merger Regulation, the Commission is obliged to transmit reasoned submissions to the Member States and the EFTA States without delay. The time limits for considering a reasoned submission will begin upon receipt of the submission by the relevant Member State/s or EFTA State/s. The decision whether or not to accede to a reasoned submission will normally be taken on the basis of the information contained therein, without further investigation efforts being undertaken by the authorities involved.*
- *(b) The submitting parties must therefore verify, in the course of preparing their reasoned submission, that all information and arguments relied upon are sufficiently supported by independent sources.*
- *(c) Under Article 14(1)(a) of the Merger Regulation, parties making a reasoned submission who, either intentionally or negligently, provide incorrect or misleading information, may be liable to fines of up to 1% of the aggregate turnover of the undertaking concerned.*

(d) In accordance with the Implementing Regulation, the Commission may dispense with the obligation to provide any particular information in the reasoned submission or with any other requirement specified in this Form RS. Accordingly, you may submit a written request for a waiver, asking the Commission to dispense with the obligation to provide such information, if such information is not reasonably available to you in part or in whole (for example, because of the unavailability of information on a target company during a contested bid).

Waiver requests should be submitted at the same time as the draft Form RS. Waiver requests should be made either within the text of the draft Form RS itself or as an e-mail or letter addressed to the responsible case manager and/or head of unit.

The Commission will consider such waiver requests, provided that you give reasons for the non-availability of that information and provide your best estimates for missing data together with the sources for the estimates. Where possible, indications as to where any of the requested information that is unavailable to you could be obtained by the Commission or the relevant Member State/s and EFTA State/s should also be provided.

Requests for waivers will be dealt with in accordance with DG Competition's Best Practices on the conduct of EC merger control proceedings and DG Competition would normally require five working days before responding to a waiver request.

(e) In accordance with the Implementing Regulation, the Commission may dispense with the obligation to provide any particular information in the reasoned submission or with any other requirement specified in this Form RS where the Commission considers that compliance with those obligations or requirements are not necessary for the examination of the pre-notification referral request. Accordingly, you may submit a written request for a waiver, asking the Commission to dispense with the obligation to provide such information, if you consider that any particular information required by this Form RS may not be necessary for the Commission's or the relevant Member State/s' or EFTA State/s' examination of the pre-notification referral request.

Waiver requests should be made simultaneously with the submission of the draft Form RS in order to allow the Commission to determine whether or not the information in relation to which a waiver is being requested is necessary for the examination of the pre-notification referral request. Waiver requests should be made either within the text of the draft Form RS itself or as an e-mail or letter addressed to the responsible case manager and/or head of unit.

The Commission will consider such waiver requests, provided that you give adequate reasons why the information in question is not necessary for dealing with your request for a pre-notification referral. The Commission may consult with the relevant Member State or EFTA State authority or authorities before deciding whether to accede to such a request.

Requests for waivers will be dealt with in accordance with DG Competition's Best Practices on the conduct of EC merger control proceedings and DG Competition would normally require five working days before responding to a waiver request.

For the avoidance of doubt, it should be noted that the fact that the Commission may have accepted that any particular information requested by this Form RS was not necessary for the complete reasoned submission for a concentration, does not in any way prevent the Commission from requesting this particular information at any time, in particular by way of request for information pursuant to Article 11 of the Merger Regulation.

*1.4. **How to make a reasoned submission***

The reasoned submission must be completed in one of the official languages of the European Union. This language will thereafter be the language of the proceedings for all submitting parties.

In order to facilitate treatment of Form RS by Member State and EFTA State authorities, parties are strongly encouraged to provide the Commission with a translation of their reasoned submission in a language or languages which will be understood by all addressees of the information. As regards requests for referral to (a) Member State/s or (an) EFTA State/s, the requesting parties are strongly encouraged to include a copy of the request in the language/s of the Member State/s and EFTA State/s to which referral is being requested.

The information requested by this Form RS is to be set out using the sections and paragraph numbers of the Form RS, signing the declaration at the end, and annexing supporting documentation. The original of the Form RS must be signed by persons authorised by law to act on behalf of each of the submitting party or parties or by one or more authorised external representatives of the submitting party or parties.

For the sake of clarity, certain information may be put in annexes. However, it is essential that all key substantive pieces of information are presented in the body of Form RS. Annexes to this Form RS must only be used to supplement the information supplied in the Form RS itself.

Supporting documents are to be submitted in their original language; where this is not an official language of the European Union, they must be translated into the language of the proceeding.

Supporting documents may be originals or copies of the originals. In the latter case, the submitting party must confirm that they are true and complete.

One original and the required number of copies of the Form RS and of the supporting documents must be submitted to the Commission. The required number and format (paper or electronic) of copies will be published from time to time in the Official Journal of the European Union as well as on DG Competition's website.

The submission must be delivered to the address referred to in Article 23(1) of the Implementing Regulation. This address is published in the Official Journal of the European Union and available on DG Competition's website. The submission must be delivered to the Commission on working days as defined by Article 24 of the Merger Implementing

Regulation during the opening hours indicated on DG Competition's website. The security instructions given on DG Competition's website must be adhered to.

All electronic copies of the Form RS and supporting documents must be provided in a usable and searchable format as specified on DG Competition's website.

1.5. ***Confidentiality***

Article 287 of the Treaty and Article 17(2) of the Merger Regulation, as well as the corresponding provisions of the EEA Agreement[4] require the Commission, the Member States, the EFTA Surveillance Authority and the EFTA States, their officials and other servants not to disclose information they have acquired through the application of the Regulation of the kind covered by the obligation of professional secrecy. The same principle must also apply to protect confidentiality between submitting parties.

If you believe that your interests would be harmed if any of the information supplied were to be published or otherwise divulged to other parties, submit this information separately with each page clearly marked 'Business Secrets'. You should also give reasons why this information should not be divulged or published.

In the case of mergers or joint acquisitions, or in other cases where the reasoned submission is completed by more than one of the parties, business secrets may be submitted in separate annexes, and referred to in the submission as an annex. All such annexes must be included in the reasoned submission.

1.6. ***Definitions and instructions for purposes of this Form RS***

Submitting party or parties: in cases where a reasoned submission is made by only one of the undertakings who is a party to an operation, 'submitting parties' is used to refer only to the undertaking actually making the submission.

Party(ies) to the concentration or parties: these terms relate to both the acquiring and acquired parties, or to the merging parties, including all undertakings in which a controlling interest is being acquired or which is the subject of a public bid.

Except where otherwise specified, the terms 'submitting party(ies)' and 'party(ies) to the concentration' include all the undertakings which belong to the same groups as those 'parties'.

Affected markets: Section 4 of this Form RS requires the submitting parties to define the relevant product markets, and further to identify which of those relevant markets are likely to be affected by the operation. This definition of affected market is used as the basis for requiring information for a number of other questions contained in this Form RS. The definitions thus submitted by the submitting parties are referred to in this Form RS as the affected market(s). This term can refer to a relevant market made up either of products or of services.

Year: all references to the word 'year' in this Form RS must be read as meaning calendar year, unless otherwise stated. All information requested in this Form RS relates, unless otherwise specified, to the year preceding that of the reasoned submission.

The financial data requested in this Form RS must be provided in euro at the average exchange rates prevailing for the years or other periods in question.

All references to provisions of law contained in this Form RS are to the relevant Articles and paragraphs of the Merger Regulation, unless otherwise stated.

1.7. ***International cooperation between the Commission and other competition authorities***

The Commission encourages the undertakings concerned to facilitate the international cooperation between the Commission and other competition authorities reviewing the same concentration. In the Commission's experience, good cooperation between the Commission and competition authorities in jurisdictions outside the EEA entails substantial benefits for the undertakings concerned. To this end, the Commission encourages submitting parties to submit together with this Form RS a list of those jurisdictions outside the EEA where the concentration is subject to regulatory clearance under merger control rules before or after completion.

SECTION 1

1.1. ***Background information***

1.1.1. Provide an executive summary of the concentration, specifying the parties to the concentration, the nature of the concentration (for example, merger, acquisition, or joint venture), the areas of activity of the parties to the concentration, the markets on which the concentration will have an impact (including the main affected markets), and the strategic and economic rationale for the concentration.

1.1.2. Indicate whether the reasoned submission is made under Article 4(4) or (5) of the Merger Regulation and/or pursuant to the provisions of the EEA Agreement:

- *Article 4(4) referral to Member State(s) and/or referral to EFTA State(s);*
- *Article 4(5) referral to the Commission.*

1.2. ***Information on submitting party (or parties) and other parties to the concentration***[5]

For each party making the reasoned submission as well as for each other party to the concentration provide:

1.2.1. name of undertaking;

1.2.2. name, address, telephone number, fax number and e-mail address of, and position held by, the appropriate contact person; the address given must be an address for service to which documents and, in particular, Commission decisions and other procedural documents may be notified, and the contact person given shall be deemed to be authorised to accept service;

1.2.3. if one or more authorised external representatives of the undertaking are appointed, to which documents and, in particular, Commission decisions and other procedural documents may be notified:

1.2.3.1. name, address, telephone number, fax number and e-mail address of, and position held by, each representative; and

1.2.3.2. the original of written proof that each representative is authorised to act (based on the model Power of Attorney available on DG Competition's website).

SECTION 2 GENERAL BACKGROUND AND DETAILS OF THE CONCENTRATION

The information sought in this section may be illustrated by the use of organization charts or diagrams to show the structure of ownership and control of the undertakings.

2.1. Describe the nature of the concentration being notified. By reference to the relevant criteria of the Merger Regulation and the Commission Consolidated Jurisdictional Notice:[6]

2.1.1. identify the undertakings or persons solely or jointly controlling each of the undertakings concerned, directly or indirectly, and describe the structure of ownership and control of each of the undertakings concerned before the completion of the concentration;

2.1.2. explain whether the proposed concentration is:

(i) a full merger,

(ii) an acquisition of sole or joint control, or

(iii) a contract or other means of conferring direct or indirect control within the meaning of Article 3(2) of the Merger Regulation;

(iv) the acquisition of joint control in a full-function joint venture within the meaning of Article 3(4) of the Merger Regulation, and if so, the reasons why the joint venture is considered to be full-function;[7]

2.1.3. explain how the concentration will be implemented (for example by conclusion of an agreement, by the launch of a public bid, etc.);

2.1.4. by reference to Article 4(1) of the Merger Regulation explain whether to bring about the concentration at the time of notification:

(i) an agreement has been concluded,

(ii) a controlling interest has been acquired,

(iii) (the intention to launch) a public bid has been announced, or

(iv) the undertakings concerned have demonstrated a good faith intention to conclude an agreement;

2.1.5. indicate the expected date of any major events designed to bring about the completion of the concentration;

2.1.6. explain the structure of ownership and control of each of the undertakings concerned after the completion of the concentration.

2.2. Describe the economic rationale of the concentration.

2.3. State the value of the concentration (the purchase price (or the value of all the assets involved as the case may be); specify whether this is in the form of equity, cash, or other assets).

2.4. Describe any financial or other support received from public authorities by any of the parties and the nature and amount of this support.

2.5. Provide sufficient financial or other data to show that the concentration meets OR does not meet the jurisdictional thresholds under Article 1 of the Merger Regulation by providing the following information for each of the undertakings concerned by the concentration for the last financial year:[8]

2.5.1. Worldwide turnover;

2.5.2. EU-wide turnover;

2.5.3. EEA-wide turnover (EU and EFTA);

2.5.4. turnover in each Member State (indicate the Member State, if any, in which more than two-thirds of EU-wide turnover is achieved);

2.5.5. EFTA-wide turnover;

2.5.6. turnover in each EFTA State (indicate the EFTA State, if any, in which more than two-thirds of EFTA-wide turnover is achieved; also indicate whether the combined turnover of the undertakings concerned in the territory of the EFTA States equals 25% or more of their total turnover in the EEA territory).

Turnover data must be provided by filling in the Commission's template table available on DG Competition's website.

SECTION 3 MARKET DEFINITIONS

The relevant product and geographic markets serve to identify the scope within which the market power of the new entity resulting from the concentration must be assessed.[9] *When presenting relevant product and geographic markets, the submitting party or parties must submit, in addition to any product and geographic market definitions they consider relevant, all plausible alternative product and geographic market definitions. Plausible alternative product and geographic market definitions can be identified on the basis of previous Commission decisions and judgments of the Union Courts and (in particular where no Commission or Court precedents exist) by reference to industry reports, market studies and the submitting parties' internal documents.*

The submitting party or parties must provide the information requested in this Form RS having regard to the following definitions:

3.1. ***Relevant product markets:***

A relevant product market comprises all those products and/or services which are regarded as interchangeable or substitutable by the consumer, by reason of the products' characteristics, their prices and their intended use. A relevant product market may in some cases be composed of a number of individual products and/or services which present largely identical physical or technical characteristics and are interchangeable.

Factors relevant to the assessment of the relevant product market include the analysis of why the products or services in these markets are included and why others are excluded by using the definition, and having regard to, for example, substitutability of products and services, prices, cross-price elasticity of demand or other relevant factors (such as supply-side substitutability in appropriate cases).

3.2. ***Relevant geographic markets:***

The relevant geographic market comprises the area in which the undertakings concerned are involved in the supply and demand of relevant products or services, in which the conditions of competition are sufficiently homogeneous and which can be distinguished from neighbouring geographic areas because, in particular, conditions of competition are appreciably different in those areas.

Factors relevant to the assessment of the relevant geographic market include, inter alia, the nature and characteristics of the products or services concerned, the existence of entry barriers, consumer preferences, appreciable differences in the undertakings' market shares between neighbouring geographic areas or substantial price differences.

*3.3. **Affected markets:***

For purposes of information required in this Form RS, affected markets consist of all relevant product and geographic markets, as well as plausible alternative relevant product and geographic markets, on the basis of which in the EEA territory:

(a) two or more of the parties to the concentration are engaged in business activities in the same relevant market and where the concentration will lead to a combined market share of 20% or more. These are horizontal relationships;

(b) one or more of the parties to the concentration are engaged in business activities in a relevant market, which is upstream or downstream of a relevant market in which any other party to the concentration is engaged, and any of their individual or combined market shares at either level is 30% or more, regardless of whether there is or is not any existing supplier/customer relationship between the parties to the concentration.[10] *These are vertical relationships.*

On the basis of the definitions set out in Section 3 (including all plausible alternative market definitions) and market share thresholds, identify each affected market.[11]

SECTION 4 INFORMATION ON AFFECTED MARKETS

For each affected market, for the last financial year, provide the following information:

4.1. For each of the parties to the concentration, the nature of the undertaking's business, the main subsidiaries active and/or brands, product names and/or trademarks used in each of these markets.

4.2. An estimate of the total size of the market in terms of sales value (in euro) and volume (units).[12] *Indicate the basis and sources for the calculations and provide documents where available to confirm these calculations.*

4.3. The sales in value and volume, as well as an estimate of the market shares, of each of the parties to the concentration; if in response to this question you do not provide market shares at the level of Member States, for each of the parties to the concentration indicate the geographic location of the five largest customers.

4.4. An estimate of the market share in value (and where appropriate volume) of the three largest competitors (indicating the basis for the estimates).

4.5. If the concentration is a joint venture, do two or more parents retain to a significant extent activities in the same market as the joint venture or in a market which is downstream or upstream from that of the joint venture?[13]

4.6. Describe the likely impact of the proposed concentration on competition in the affected markets and how the proposed concentration is likely to affect the interests of intermediate and ultimate consumers.

SECTION 5 DETAILS OF THE REFERRAL REQUEST AND REASONS WHY THE CASE SHOULD BE REFERRED

5.1. Indicate whether the reasoned submission is made pursuant to Article 4(4) or 4(5) of the Merger Regulation and/or pursuant to the provisions of the EEA Agreement, and fill in only the relevant sub-section:

— *Article 4(4) referral to Member State(s) and/or referral to EFTA State(s);*

— *Article 4(5) referral to the Commission.*

5.2. (for Article 4(4) referrals and/or referrals pursuant to the provisions of the EEA Agreement)

5.2.1. Identify the Member State/s and EFTA State/s which, pursuant to Article 4(4) of the Merger Regulation, you submit should examine the concentration, indicating whether or not you have made informal contact with this Member State/s and/or EFTA State/s.

5.2.2. Specify whether you are requesting referral of the whole or part of the case.

If you are requesting referral of part of the case, specify clearly the part or parts of the case for which you request the referral.

If you are requesting referral of the whole of the case, you must confirm that there are no affected markets outside the territory of the Member State/s and EFTA State/s to which you request the referral to be made.

5.2.3. Explain in what way each of the affected markets in the Member State/s and EFTA State/s to which referral is requested presents all the characteristics of a distinct market within the meaning of Article 4(4) of the Merger Regulation.

5.2.4. Explain in what way competition may be significantly affected in each of the above-mentioned distinct markets within the meaning of Article 4(4) of the Merger Regulation.[14]

5.2.5. In the event of a Member State/s and/or EFTA State/s becoming competent to review the whole or part of the case following a referral pursuant to Article 4(4) of the Merger Regulation, do you consent to the information contained in this Form RS being relied upon by the Member State/s and/or EFTA State/s in question for the purpose of its/their national proceedings relating to that case or part thereof? YES or NO.

5.3. (for Article 4(5) referrals and/or referrals pursuant to the provisions of the EEA Agreement)

5.3.1. For each Member State and/or EFTA State, specify whether the concentration is or is not capable of being reviewed under its national competition law. This information must be provided by filling in the Commission's template table available on DG Competition's website. You must tick one box for each and every Member State and/or EFTA State.[15]

5.3.2. For each Member State and/or EFTA State, provide sufficient financial or other data to show that the concentration meets or does not meet the relevant jurisdictional criteria under the applicable national law.

5.3.3. Explain why the case should be examined by the Commission. Explain in particular whether the concentration might affect competition beyond the territory of one Member State and/or EFTA State.[16]

SECTION 6 DECLARATION

The reasoned submission must conclude with the following declaration which is to be signed by or on behalf of all the submitting parties:

> *'The submitting party or parties declare that, following careful verification, the information given in this reasoned submission is to the best of their knowledge and belief true, correct, and complete, that true and complete copies of documents required by Form RS have been supplied, that all estimates are identified as such and are their best estimates of the underlying facts, and that all the opinions expressed are sincere.*
> *They are aware of the provisions of Article 14(1)(a) of the Merger Regulation.']*

NOTES

Annex III substituted by Commission Regulation 1269/2013, Art 1(12), Annex.

Repeal of this Regulation in relation to the UK: this Regulation is repealed in relation to the UK (as from IP completion day); see the introductory notes to this Regulation *ante*.

1 OJ L24, 29.1.2004, p 1.

2 OJ L133, 30.4.2004, p 1.

3 See in particular Article 57 of the EEA Agreement, point 1 of Annex XIV to the EEA Agreement, Protocols 21 and 24 to the EEA Agreement, as well as Protocol 4 to the Agreement between the EFTA States on the establishment of a Surveillance Authority and a Court of Justice (hereinafter referred to as the 'Surveillance and Court Agreement'). Any reference to EFTA States must be understood to mean those EFTA States which are Contracting Parties to the EEA Agreement. As of 1 May 2004, these States are Iceland, Liechtenstein and Norway.

4 See, in particular, Article 122 of the EEA Agreement, Article 9 of Protocol 24 to the EEA Agreement and Article 17(2) of Chapter XIII of Protocol 4 to the Surveillance and Court Agreement.

5 This includes the target company in the case of a contested bid, in which case the details should be completed as far as is possible.

6 See Commission Consolidated Jurisdictional Notice under Council Regulation (EC) No 139/2004 on the control of concentrations between undertakings (OJ C95, 16.4.2008, p 1).

7 See section B IV of the Consolidated Jurisdictional Notice.

8 On the concepts of 'undertaking concerned' and the calculation of turnover see Commission Consolidated Jurisdictional Notice under Council Regulation (EC) No 139/2004 on the control of concentrations between undertakings (OJ C95, 16.4.2008, p 1).

9 See Commission Notice on the definition of the relevant market for the purposes of Community competition law (OJ C372, 9.12.1997, p 5).

10 For example, if a party to the concentration holds a market share larger than 30% in a market that is upstream to a market in which the other party is active, then both the upstream and the downstream markets are affected markets. Similarly, if a vertically integrated company merges with another party, which is active at the downstream level, and the concentration leads to a combined market share downstream of 30% or more, then both the upstream and the downstream markets are affected markets.

11 As indicated in DG Competition's Best Practices on the conduct of EC merger control proceedings, submitting parties are advised to disclose information relating to all potentially affected markets even if they ultimately consider that they are not affected and notwithstanding that they may take a particular view in relation to the issue of market definition.

12 The value and volume of a market must reflect output less exports plus imports for the geographic areas under consideration. As set out in points 1.1 and 1.3(e) in the Introductory Part, before notification, the submitting party or parties may want to discuss with the Commission to what extent dispensation (waivers) to provide some of the requested information (in this context value- or volume-based data for market size and shares) would be appropriate.

13 For market definitions refer to Section 3.

14 For guiding principles of case referrals see Commission Notice on case referral in respect of concentrations ('Referral Notice') (OJ C56, 5.3.2005, p 2). In practice, the existence of 'affected markets' within the meaning of Form RS would generally be considered sufficient to meet the requirements of Article 4(4) in this regard. However, the existence of 'affected markets' within the meaning of Form RS is not a necessary condition for meeting those requirements. See recital 17 and footnote 21 of the Referral Notice.

15 Failure to indicate YES or NO for any Member State and/or EFTA State shall be deemed to constitute an indication of YES for that Member State and/or EFTA State.

16 For guiding principles of case referrals see Commission Notice on case referral in respect of concentrations ('Referral Notice') (OJ C56, 5.3.2005, p 2). Cases where the market(s) in which there may be a potential impact on competition is/are wider than national in geographic scope, or where some of the potentially affected markets are wider than national and the main economic impact of the concentration is connected to such markets, are the most appropriate candidate cases for referral to the Commission. See recital 28 of the Referral Notice.

[ANNEX IV

FORM RM RELATING TO THE INFORMATION CONCERNING COMMITMENTS SUBMITTED PURSUANT TO ARTICLE 6(2) AND ARTICLE 8(2) OF REGULATION (EC) NO 139/2004

FORM RM RELATING TO REMEDIES

INTRODUCTION

[4.598]

This form specifies the information and documents to be submitted by the undertakings concerned at the same time as offering commitments pursuant to Article 6(2) or Article 8(2) of Regulation (EC) No 139/2004. The information requested is necessary to allow the Commission to examine whether the commitments are capable of rendering the concentration compatible with the common market in that they will prevent a significant impediment to effective competition. The Commission may dispense with the obligation to provide any particular information in respect of the commitments offered, including documents, or with any other requirement laid down in this form where it considers that compliance with those obligations or requirements is not necessary for the examination of the commitments offered. The level of information required will vary according to the type and structure of the remedy proposed. For example, carve-out remedies will typically require more detailed information than divestitures of stand-alone businesses. The Commission is available to discuss the scope of the information required with the parties upfront. If you consider that any particular information requested by this Form may not be necessary for the Commission's assessment, you may approach the Commission asking to dispense with certain requirements, giving adequate reasons why that information is not relevant.

SECTION 1 DESCRIPTION OF THE COMMITMENT

1.1. Provide detailed information on

(i) the object of the commitments offered, and

(ii) the conditions for their implementation.

1.2. Where the commitments offered consist in the divestiture of a business, Section 5 provides for the specific information required.

SECTION 2 SUITABILITY TO REMOVE COMPETITION CONCERNS

2. Provide information showing the suitability of the commitments offered to remove the significant impediment of effective competition identified by the Commission.

SECTION 3 DEVIATION FROM MODEL TEXTS

3. Identify any deviations of the commitments offered from the pertinent Model Commitments texts published by the Commission's services, as revised from time-to-time, and explain the reasons for the deviations.

SECTION 4 SUMMARY OF THE COMMITMENTS

4. Provide a non-confidential summary of the nature and scope of the commitments offered and why, in your view, they are suitable to remove any significant impediment to effective competition. The Commission may use this summary for the market test of the commitments offered with third parties.

SECTION 5 INFORMATION ON A BUSINESS TO BE DIVESTED

5. Where the commitments offered consist in the divestiture of a business, provide the following information and documents.

General information on the business to be divested

The following information should be provided as to the current operation of the business to be divested and changes already planned for the future:

5.1. Describe the business to be divested generally, including the entities belonging to it, their registered place of business and place of management, other locations for production or provisions of services, the general organisational structure and any other relevant information relating to the administrative structure of the business to be divested.

5.2. State whether there are and describe any legal obstacles for the transfer of the business to be divested or the assets, including third party rights and administrative approvals required.

5.3. List and describe the products manufactured or services provided, in particular their technical and other characteristics, the brands involved, the turnover generated with each of these products or services, and any innovations or new products or services planned.

5.4. Describe the level on which the essential functions of the business to be divested are operated if they are not operated on the level of the business to be divested itself, including such functions as research and development, production, marketing and sales, logistics, relations with customers, relations with suppliers, IT systems, etc. The description should contain the role performed by those other levels, the relations with the business to be divested and the resources (personnel, assets, financial resources, etc) involved in the function.

5.5. Describe in detail the links between the business to be divested and other undertakings controlled by the notifying parties (irrespective of the direction of the link), such as:

— supply, production, distribution, service or other contracts,
— shared tangible or intangible assets,
— shared or seconded personnel,
— shared IT systems or other systems, and
— shared customers.

5.6. Describe in general terms all relevant tangible and intangible assets used and/or owned by the business to be divested, including, in any case, IP rights and brands.

5.7. Submit an organisational chart identifying the number of personnel currently working in each of the functions of the business to be divested and a list of those employees who are indispensable for the operation of the business to be divested, describing their functions.

5.8. Describe the customers of the business to be divested, including a list of customers, a description of the corresponding records available, and provide the total turnover generated by the business to be divested with each of these customers (in EUR and as percentage of the total turnover of business to be divested).

5.9. Provide financial data for the business to be divested, including the turnover and the EBITDA achieved in the last two years, and the forecast for the next two years.

5.10. Identify and describe any changes that have occurred in the last two years, in the organisation of the business to be divested or in the links with other undertakings controlled by the notifying parties.

5.11. Identify and describe any changes, planned for the next two years, in the organisation of the business to be divested or in the links with other undertakings controlled by the notifying parties.

General information on the business to be divested as described in the commitments

5.12. Describe any areas where the business to be divested as set out in the commitments offered differs from the nature and scope of the business as currently operated.

Acquisition by a suitable purchaser

5.13. Explain the reasons why, in your view, the business will be acquired by a suitable purchaser in the time-frame proposed in the commitments offered.]

NOTES

Added by Commission Regulation 1033/2008/EC, Art 1(4) Annex, para 1(4).

Repeal of this Regulation in relation to the UK: this Regulation is repealed in relation to the UK (as from IP completion day); see the introductory notes to this Regulation *ante*.

DECISION OF THE EEA JOINT COMMITTEE

(78/2004)

of 8 June 2004

amending Annex XIV (competition), Protocol 21 (on the implementation of competition rules applicable to undertakings), Protocol 22 (concerning the definition of "undertaking" and "turnover" (Article 56)) and Protocol 24 (on cooperation in the field of control of concentrations) to the EEA Agreement

[4.599]

NOTES

Date of publication in OJ: OJ L219, 19.6.2004, p 13. The text of this Decision incorporates the corrigendum published in OJ L349, 25.11.2004, p 70.

Repeal of Annex XIV to the EEA Agreement: note that Annex XIV to the EEA Agreement, insofar as it forms part of domestic law on and after IP completion day by virtue of s 3(1) of the European Union (Withdrawal) Act 2018, is repealed in relation to the UK, by the Competition (Amendment etc) (EU Exit) Regulations 2019, SI 2019/93, reg 63, Sch 3, para 1, as from IP completion day (as defined in the European Union (Withdrawal Agreement) Act 2020, s 39) (for transitional provisions and savings in relation to the operation of the 2019 Regulations, see Sch 4 to those Regulations at **[7.69]** et seq).

Note: with effect from 1 December 2009, the EC Treaty was replaced by the Treaty on the Functioning of the European Union. References in this document to provisions of the EC Treaty should be construed accordingly.

THE EEA JOINT COMMITTEE,

Having regard to the Agreement on the European Economic Area, as amended by the Protocol adjusting the Agreement on the European Economic Area, hereinafter referred to as "the Agreement', and in particular Article 98 thereof,

Whereas:

(1) Annex XIV to the Agreement was amended by the Agreement on the participation of the Czech Republic, the Republic of Estonia, the Republic of Cyprus, the Republic of Latvia, the Republic of Lithuania, the Republic of Hungary, the Republic of Malta, the Republic of Poland, the Republic of Slovenia and the Slovak Republic in the European Economic Area signed on 14 October 2003 in Luxemburg.[1]

(2) Protocol 21 to the Agreement was amended by the Agreement on the participation of the Czech Republic, the Republic of Estonia, the Republic of Cyprus, the Republic of Latvia, the Republic of Lithuania, the Republic of Hungary, the Republic of Malta, the Republic of Poland, the Republic of Slovenia and the Slovak Republic in the European Economic Area signed on 14 October 2003 in Luxemburg.

(3) Protocol 22 to the Agreement has not previously been amended by the EEA Joint Committee.

(4) Protocol 24 to the Agreement has not previously been amended by the EEA Joint Committee,

(5) Article 57 of the Agreement provides the legal basis for the control of concentrations within the European Economic Area.

(6) Article 57 must be applied in accordance with Protocols 21 and 24 and Annex XIV, laying down the applicable rules on the control of concentrations.

(7) Council Regulation (EEC) No 4064/89 of 21 December 1989 on the control of concentrations between undertakings is incorporated into Annex XIV and Protocol 21, and referred to in Protocol 24 to the Agreement.

(8) Annex XIV and Protocol 21 were amended by Decision of the EEA Joint Committee No 27/1998 of 27 March 1998,[2] incorporating Council Regulation (EC) No 1310/97 of 30 June 1997, amending Regulation (EEC) No 4064/89,[3] into the Agreement in line with the objective of maintaining a dynamic and homogenous EEA based on common rules and equal conditions on competition.

(9) Regulation (EC) No 1310/97 amending Regulation (EEC) No 4064/89 amends Article 5(3) of that Regulation. It is appropriate to amend Protocol 22 to the Agreement correspondingly.

(10) Council Regulation (EC) No 139/2004 of 20 January 2004 on the control of concentrations between

undertakings (the EC Merger Regulation)[4] repeals and replaces Regulation (EC) No 4064/89.

(11) Regulation (EC) No 139/2004 should be incorporated into Annex XIV and Protocol 21, and referred to in Protocol 24 to the Agreement in order to maintain equal conditions of competition within the EEA.

NOTES

[1] OJ L130, 29.4.2004, p 3.

[2] OJ L310, 19.11.1998, p 9 and EEA Supplement No 48, 19.11.1998, p 190.

[3] OJ L189, 7.9.1997, p 1.

[4] OJ L24, 29.1.2004, p 1.

HAS DECIDED AS FOLLOWS:

[4.600]
Article 1
Annex XIV to the Agreement shall be amended as specified in Annex I to this Decision.

[4.601]
Article 2
Protocol 21 to the Agreement shall be amended as specified in Annex II to this Decision.

[4.602]
Article 3
Protocol 22 to the Agreement shall be amended as specified in Annex III to this Decision.

[4.603]
Article 4
Protocol 24 to the Agreement shall be replaced as specified in Annex IV to this Decision.

[4.604]
Article 5
The texts of Regulation (EC) No 139/2004 in the Icelandic and Norwegian languages, to be published in the EEA Supplement to the *Official Journal of the European Union*, shall be authentic.

[4.605]
Article 6
This Decision shall enter into force on 9 June 2004, provided that all the notifications under Article 103(1) of the Agreement have been made to the EEA Joint Committee*.

NOTES

* No constitutional requirements indicated.

[4.606]
Article 7
This Decision shall be published in the EEA Section of, and in the EEA Supplement to, the *Official Journal of the European Union*.

ANNEX I
TO DECISION OF THE EEA JOINT COMMITTEE NO 78/2004

[4.607]
The text of point 1 (Council Regulation (EEC) No 4064/89) in Annex XIV to the Agreement shall be replaced by the following:

'**32004 R 0139**: Council Regulation (EC) No 139/2004 of 20 January 2004 on the control of concentrations between undertakings (the EC Merger Regulation) (OJ L24, 29.1.2004, p 1).

The provisions of the Regulation shall, for the purposes of the Agreement, be read with the following adaptations:

(a) In Article 1(1), the phrase "or the corresponding provisions in Protocol 21 and Protocol 24 to the EEA Agreement" shall be inserted after the words "Without prejudice to Article 4(5)";

furthermore, the term "Community dimension" shall read "Community or EFTA dimension";

(b) In Article 1(2), the term "Community dimension" shall read "Community or EFTA dimension respectively";

furthermore, the term "Community-wide turnover" shall read "Community-wide turnover or EFTA wide turnover";

in the last subparagraph, the term "Member State" shall read "EC Member State or EFTA State";

(c) In Article 1(3), the "Community dimension" shall read "Community or EFTA dimension respectively";

furthermore, the term "Community-wide turnover" shall read "Community-wide turnover or EFTA-wide turnover";

in Article 1(3)(b) and (c), the term "Member States" shall read "EC Member States or in each of at least three EFTA States";

in the last subparagraph, the term "Member State" shall read "EC Member State or EFTA State";

(d) Article 1(4) and (5) shall not apply;

(e) In Article 2(1), first subparagraph, the term "common market" shall read "functioning of the EEA Agreement";

(f) In Article 2(2), at the end, the term "common market" shall read "functioning of the EEA Agreement";

(g) In Article 2(3), at the end, the term "common market" shall read "functioning of the EEA Agreement";

(h) In Article 2(4), at the end, the term "common market" shall read "functioning of the EEA Agreement";

(i) In Article 3(5)(b), the term "Member State" shall read "EC Member State or EFTA State";

(j) In Article 4(1), first subparagraph, the term "Community dimension" shall read "Community or EFTA dimension";

furthermore, in the first sentence, the phrase "in accordance with Article 57 of the EEA Agreement" shall be inserted after the words "shall be notified to the Commission";

in Article 4(1), second subparagraph, the term "Community dimension" shall read "Community or EFTA dimension";

(k) In Article 5(1), the last subparagraph shall read:

"Turnover, in the Community or in an EC Member State, shall comprise products sold and services provided to undertakings or consumers, in the Community or in that EC Member State as the case may be. The same shall apply as regards turnover in the territory of the EFTA States as a whole or in an EFTA State.";

(l) In Article 5(3)(a), the last subparagraph shall read:

"The turnover of a credit or financial institution in the Community or in an EC Member State shall comprise the income items, as defined above, which are received by the branch or division of that institution established in the Community or the EC Member State in question as the case may be. The same shall apply as regards turnover of a credit or financial institution in the territory of the EFTA States as a whole or in an EFTA State.";

(m) In Article 5(3)(b), the last phrase ", . . . gross premiums received from Community residents and from residents of one Member State respectively shall be taken into account." shall read:

", . . . gross premiums received from Community residents and from residents of one EC Member State respectively shall be taken into account. The same shall apply as regards gross premiums received from residents in the territory of the EFTA States as a whole and from residents in one EFTA State, respectively.'"

ANNEX II
TO DECISION OF THE EEA JOINT COMMITTEE NO 78/2004

[4.608]

The text of point 1(1) (Council Regulation (EEC) No 4064/89) in Article 3 of Protocol 21 to the Agreement shall be replaced by the following:

"**32004 R 0139**: Article 4(4) and (5), Articles 6 to 12, Articles 14 to 21 and Articles 23 to 26 of Council Regulation (EC) No 139/2004 of 20 January 2004 on the control of concentrations between undertakings (the EC Merger Regulation) (OJ L24, 29.1.2004, p 1)."

ANNEX III
TO DECISION OF THE EEA JOINT COMMITTEE NO 78/2004

[4.609]

The text of Article 3 in Protocol 22 to the Agreement shall be replaced by the following:

"In place of turnover the following shall be used:

(a) for credit institutions and other financial institutions, the sum of the following income items as defined in Council Directive 86/635/EEC, after deduction of value added tax and other taxes directly related to those items, where appropriate:

(i) interest income and similar income;

(ii) income from securities:

— income from shares and other variable yield securities,

— income from participating interests,

— income from shares in affiliated undertakings;

(iii) commissions receivable;

(iv) net profit on financial operations;

(v) other operating income.

The turnover of a credit or financial institution in the territory covered by the Agreement shall comprise the income items, as defined above, which are received by the branch or division of that institution established in the territory covered by the Agreement;

(b) for insurance undertakings, the value of gross premiums written which shall comprise all amounts received and receivable in respect of insurance contracts issued by or on behalf of the insurance undertakings, including also outgoing reinsurance premiums, and after deduction of taxes and parafiscal contributions or levies charged by reference to the amounts of individual premiums or the total volume of premiums; as regards Article 1(2)(b) and (3)(b), (c) and (d) and the final part of Article 1(2) and (3) of Council Regulation (EC) No 139/2004, gross premiums received from residents in the territory covered by the Agreement shall be taken into account."

ANNEX IV
TO DECISION OF THE EEA JOINT COMMITTEE NO 78/2004

[4.610]

Protocol 24 to the Agreement shall be replaced by the following:

"PROTOCOL 24

ON COOPERATION IN THE FIELD OF CONTROL OF CONCENTRATIONS

GENERAL PRINCIPLES

Article 1

1. The EFTA Surveillance Authority and the EC Commission shall exchange information and consult each other on general policy issues at the request of either of the surveillance authorities.

2. In cases falling under Article 57(2)(a) of the Agreement, the EC Commission and the EFTA Surveillance Authority shall cooperate in the handling of concentrations as provided for in the provisions set out below.

3. For the purposes of this Protocol, the term "territory of a surveillance authority' shall mean for the EC Commission the territory of the EC Member States to which the Treaty establishing the European Community applies, upon the terms laid down in that Treaty, and for the EFTA Surveillance Authority the territories of the EFTA States to which the Agreement applies.

Article 2

1. Cooperation shall take place, in accordance with the provisions set out in this Protocol, where:
   (a) the combined turnover of the undertakings concerned in the territory of the EFTA States equals 25 per cent or more of their total turnover within the territory covered by the Agreement, or
   (b) each of at least two of the undertakings concerned has a turnover exceeding EUR 250 million in the territory of the EFTA States, or
   (c) the concentration is liable to significantly impede effective competition, in the territories of the EFTA States or a substantial part thereof, in particular as a result of the creation or strengthening of a dominant position.

2. Cooperation shall also take place where:
   (a) the concentration fulfils the criteria for referral pursuant to Article 6.
   (b) an EFTA State wishes to adopt measures to protect legitimate interests as set out in Article 7.

INITIAL PHASE OF THE PROCEEDINGS

Article 3

1. The EC Commission shall transmit to the EFTA Surveillance Authority copies of notifications of the cases referred to in Article 2(1) and (2)(a) within three working days and, as soon as possible, copies of the most important documents lodged with or issued by the EC Commission.

2. The EC Commission shall carry out the procedures set out for the implementation of Article 57 of the Agreement in close and constant liaison with the EFTA Surveillance Authority. The EFTA Surveillance Authority and EFTA States may express their views upon those procedures. For the purposes of Article 6(1) of this Protocol, the EC Commission shall obtain information from the competent authority of the EFTA State concerned and give it the opportunity to make known its views at every stage of the procedures up to the adoption of a decision pursuant to that Article. To that end, the EC Commission shall give it access to the file.

Documents to be transmitted from the Commission to an EFTA State and from an EFTA State to the Commission pursuant to this Protocol shall be submitted via the EFTA Surveillance Authority.

HEARINGS

Article 4

In cases referred to in Article 2(1) and (2)(a), the EC Commission shall invite the EFTA Surveillance Authority to be represented at the hearings of the undertakings concerned. The EFTA States may likewise be represented at those hearings.

THE EC ADVISORY COMMITTEE ON CONCENTRATIONS

Article 5

1. In cases referred to in Article 2(1) and (2)(a), the EC Commission shall in due time inform the EFTA Surveillance Authority of the date of the meeting of the EC Advisory Committee on Concentrations and transmit the relevant documentation.

2. All documents forwarded for that purpose from the EFTA Surveillance Authority, including documents emanating from EFTA States, shall be presented to the EC Advisory Committee on Concentrations together with the other relevant documentation sent out by the EC Commission.

3. The EFTA Surveillance Authority and the EFTA States shall be entitled to be present in the EC Advisory Committee on Concentrations and to express their views therein; they shall not have, however, the right to vote.

RIGHTS OF INDIVIDUAL STATES

Article 6

1. The EC Commission may, by means of a decision notified without delay to the undertakings concerned, to the competent authorities of the EC Member States and to the EFTA Surveillance Authority, refer a notified concentration, in whole or in part, to an EFTA State where:

(a) a concentration threatens to affect significantly competition in a market within that EFTA State, which presents all the characteristics of a distinct market, or

(b) a concentration affects competition in a market within that EFTA State, which presents all the characteristics of a distinct market and which does not constitute a substantial part of the territory covered by the Agreement.

2. In cases referred to in paragraph 1, any EFTA State may appeal to the European Court of Justice, on the same grounds and conditions as an EC Member State under Articles 230 and 243 of the Treaty establishing the European Community, and in particular request the application of interim measures, for the purpose of applying its national competition law.

3. (No text)

4. Prior to the notification of a concentration within the meaning of Article 4(1) of Regulation (EC) No 139/2004 the persons or undertakings referred to in Article 4(2) of Regulation (EC) No 139/2004 may inform the EC Commission, by means of a reasoned submission, that the concentration may significantly affect competition in a market within an EFTA State which presents all the characteristics of a distinct market and should therefore be examined, in whole or in part, by that EFTA State.

The EC Commission shall transmit all submissions pursuant to Article 4(4) of Regulation (EC) No 139/2004 and this paragraph to the EFTA Surveillance Authority without delay.

5. With regard to a concentration as defined in Article 3 of Regulation (EC) No 139/2004 which does not have a Community dimension within the meaning of Article 1 of that Regulation and which is capable of being reviewed under the national competition laws of at least three EC Member States and at least one EFTA State, the persons or undertakings referred to in Article 4(2) of that Regulation may, before any notification to the competent authorities, inform the EC Commission by means of a reasoned submission that the concentration should be examined by the Commission.

The EC Commission shall transmit all submissions pursuant to Article 4(5) of Regulation (EC) No 139/2004 to the EFTA Surveillance Authority without delay.

Where at least one such EFTA State has expressed its disagreement as regards the request to refer the case, the competent EFTA State(s) shall retain their competence, and the case shall not be referred from the EFTA States pursuant to this paragraph.

Article 7

1. Notwithstanding the sole competence of the EC Commission to deal with concentrations of a Community dimension as set out in Council Regulation (EC) No 139/2004, EFTA States may take appropriate measures to protect legitimate interests other than those taken into consideration according to the above Regulation and compatible with the general principles and other provisions as provided for, directly or indirectly, under the Agreement.

2. Public security, plurality of media and prudential rules shall be regarded as legitimate interests within the meaning of paragraph 1.

3. Any other public interest must be communicated to the EC Commission and shall be recognized by the EC Commission after an assessment of its compatibility with the general principles and other provisions as provided for, directly or indirectly, under the Agreement before the measures referred to above may be taken. The EC Commission shall inform the EFTA Surveillance Authority and the EFTA State concerned of its decision within 25 working days of that communication.

ADMINISTRATIVE ASSISTANCE

Article 8

1. When the EC Commission requires by decision a person, an undertaking or an association of undertakings located within the territory of the EFTA Surveillance Authority to supply information, it shall without delay forward a copy of the decision to the EFTA Surveillance Authority. At the specific request of the EFTA Surveillance Authority, the EC Commission shall also forward to the EFTA Surveillance Authority copies of simple requests for information relating to a notified concentration.

2. At the request of the EC Commission, the EFTA Surveillance Authority and the EFTA States shall provide the EC Commission with all necessary information to carry out the duties assigned to it by Article 57 of the Agreement.

3. When the EC Commission interviews a consenting natural or legal person in the territory of the EFTA Surveillance Authority, the EFTA Surveillance Authority shall be informed in advance thereof. The EFTA Surveillance Authority may be present during the interview, as well as officials from the competition authority on whose territory the interviews are conducted.

4. (No text)

5. (No text)

6. (No text)

7. Where the EC Commission carries out inspections within the territory of the Community, it shall, as regards cases falling under Article 2(1) and (2)(a), inform the EFTA Surveillance Authority of the fact that such investigations have taken place and on request transmit in an appropriate way the relevant results of the investigations.

NOTES

Note: point 7 above is set out including the corrigendum published in OJ L349, 25.11.2004, p 70, which provides that for the words "7. Where the EC Commission caries out investigations . . . ", there shall be read "7. Where the EC Commission carries out inspections . . . ". It does not provide that the word "investigations" should be changed elsewhere in the paragraph.

PROFESSIONAL SECRECY

Article 9

1. Information acquired as a result of the application of this Protocol shall be used only for the purpose of procedures under Article 57 of the Agreement.

2. The EC Commission, the EFTA Surveillance Authority, the competent authorities of the EC Member States and of the EFTA States, their officials and other servants and other persons working under the supervision of these authorities as well as officials and civil servants of other authorities of the Member States and of the EFTA States shall not disclose information acquired by them as a result of the application of this Protocol and of the kind covered by the obligation of professional secrecy.

3. Rules on professional secrecy and restricted use of information provided for in the Agreement or the legislation of the Contracting Parties shall not prevent the exchange and use of information as set out in this Protocol.

NOTIFICATIONS

Article 10

1. Undertakings shall address their notifications to the competent surveillance authority in accordance with Article 57(2) of the Agreement.

2. Notifications or complaints addressed to the authority which, pursuant to Article 57 of the Agreement, is not competent to take decisions on a given case shall be transferred without delay to the competent surveillance authority.

Article 11

The date of submission of a notification shall be the date on which it is received by the competent surveillance authority.

LANGUAGES

Article 12

1. Undertakings shall be entitled to address and be addressed by the EFTA Surveillance Authority and the EC Commission in an official language of an EFTA State or the Community which they choose as regards notifications. This shall also cover all instances of a proceeding.

2. If undertakings choose to address a surveillance authority in a language which is not one of the official languages of the States falling within the competence of that authority, or a working language of that authority, they shall simultaneously supplement all documentation with a translation into an official language of that authority.

3. As far as undertakings are concerned which are not parties to the notification, they shall likewise be entitled to be addressed by the EFTA Surveillance Authority and the EC Commission in an appropriate official language of an EFTA State or of the Community or in a working language of one of those authorities. If they choose to address a surveillance authority in a language which is not one of the official languages of the States falling within the competence of that authority, or a working language of that authority, paragraph 2 shall apply.

4. The language which is chosen for the translation shall determine the language in which the undertakings may be addressed by the competent authority.

TIME LIMITS AND OTHER PROCEDURAL QUESTIONS

Article 13

As regards time limits and other procedural provisions, including the procedures for referral of a concentration between the EC Commission and one or more EFTA States, the rules implementing Article 57 of the Agreement shall apply also for the purpose of the cooperation between the EC Commission and the EFTA Surveillance Authority and EFTA States, unless otherwise provided for in this Protocol.

The calculation of the time limits referred to in Article 4(4) and (5) and Article 9(2) and (6) of Regulation (EC) No 139/2004 shall start, for the EFTA Surveillance Authority and the EFTA States, upon receipt of the relevant documents by the EFTA Surveillance Authority.

TRANSITION RULE

Article 14

Article 57 of the Agreement shall not apply to any concentration which was the subject of an agreement or announcement or where control was acquired before the date of entry into force of the Agreement. It shall not in any circumstances apply to a concentration in respect of which proceedings were initiated before that date by a national authority with responsibility for competition."

DECISION OF THE EEA JOINT COMMITTEE

(79/2004)

of 8 June 2004

amending Annex XIV (competition), Protocol 21 (on the implementation of competition rules applicable to undertakings), and Protocol 24 (on cooperation in the field of control of concentrations) to the EEA Agreement

[4.611]

NOTES

Date of publication in OJ: OJ L219, 19.6.2004, p 24.

Repeal of Annex XIV to the EEA Agreement: note that Annex XIV to the EEA Agreement, insofar as it forms part of domestic law on and after IP completion day by virtue of s 3(1) of the European Union (Withdrawal) Act 2018, is repealed in relation to the UK, by the Competition (Amendment etc) (EU Exit) Regulations 2019, SI 2019/93, reg 63, Sch 3, para 1, as from IP completion day (as defined in the European Union (Withdrawal Agreement) Act 2020, s 39) (for transitional provisions and savings in relation to the operation of the 2019 Regulations, see Sch 4 to those Regulations at **[7.69]** et seq).

THE EEA JOINT COMMITTEE,

Having regard to the Agreement on the European Economic Area, as amended by the Protocol adjusting the Agreement on the European Economic Area, hereinafter referred to as "the Agreement", and in particular Article 98 thereof,

Whereas:

(1) Annex XIV to the Agreement was amended by the Agreement on the participation of the Czech Republic, the Republic of Estonia, the Republic of Cyprus, the Republic of Latvia, the Republic of Lithuania, the Republic of Hungary, the Republic of Malta, the Republic of Poland, the Republic of Slovenia and the Slovak Republic in the European Economic Area signed on 14 October 2003 in Luxemburg.[1]

(2) Protocol 21 to the Agreement was amended by the Agreement on the participation of the Czech Republic, the Republic of Estonia, the Republic of Cyprus, the Republic of Latvia, the Republic of Lithuania, the Republic of Hungary, the Republic of Malta, the Republic of Poland, the Republic of Slovenia and the Slovak Republic in the European Economic Area signed on 14 October 2003 in Luxemburg.[1]

(3) Protocol 24 to the Agreement has not previously been amended by the EEA Joint Committee.

(4) Council Regulation (EC) No 139/2004 of 20 January 2004 on the control of concentrations between undertakings (the EC Merger Regulation)[2] was incorporated into the Agreement by Decision of the EEA Joint Committee No 78/2004 of 8 June 2004.[3]

(5) Articles 13 and 22 of Regulation (EC) No 139/2004 were not incorporated by Decision of the EEA Joint Committee No 78/2004 of 8 June 2004.

(6) Articles 13 and 22 of Regulation (EC) No 139/2004 should be incorporated into the Agreement,

NOTES

[1] OJ L130, 29.4.2004, p 3.
[2] OJ L24, 29.1.2004, p 1.
[3] OJ L219, 19.6.2004, p 13.

HAS DECIDED AS FOLLOWS:

[4.612]
Article 1

In point 1 (Council Regulation (EC) No 139/2004) of Annex XIV to the Agreement, the text of adaptation (a) shall be replaced by the following:

'In Article 1(1), the phrase "or the corresponding provisions in Protocol 21 and Protocol 24 to the EEA Agreement" shall be inserted after the words "Without prejudice to Article 4(5) and Article 22";

furthermore, the term "Community dimension" shall read "Community or EFTA dimension";'

[4.613]
Article 2

The text of point 1(1) (Council Regulation (EC) No 139/2004) in Article 3 of Protocol 21 to the Agreement shall be replaced by the following:

"**32004 R 0139**: Article 4(4) and (5) and Articles 6 to 26 of Council Regulation (EC) No 139/2004 of 20 January 2004 on the control of concentrations between undertakings (the EC Merger Regulation) (OJ L24, 29.1.2004, p 1)."

[4.614]

Article 3

Protocol 24 to the Agreement shall be amended as follows:

1. The following new paragraph 3 shall be inserted in Article 6:

"3. Where the concentration may affect trade between one or more EC Member States and one or more EFTA States, the EC Commission shall inform the EFTA Surveillance Authority of any request received from an EC Member State pursuant to Article 22 of Regulation (EC) No 139/2004 without delay.

One or more EFTA States may join a request as referred to in subparagraph 1 where the concentration affects trade between one or more EC Member States and one or more EFTA States and threatens to significantly affect competition within the territory of the EFTA State or States joining the request.

Upon receipt of a copy of a request as referred to in subparagraph 1, all national time limits relating to the concentration shall be suspended in the EFTA States until it has been decided where the concentration shall be examined. As soon as an EFTA State has informed the Commission and the undertakings concerned that it does not wish to join the request, the suspension of its national time limits shall end.

Where the Commission decides to examine the concentration, the EFTA State or States having joined the request shall no longer apply their national legislation on competition to the concentration."

2. The following new paragraphs 4, 5 and 6 shall be inserted in Article 8:

"4. At the request of the EC Commission, the EFTA Surveillance Authority shall undertake inspections within its territory.

5. The EC Commission is entitled to be represented and take an active part in inspections carried out pursuant to paragraph 4.

6. All information obtained during such inspections on request shall be transmitted to the EC Commission immediately after their finalization."

3. In Article 13, second subparagraph, the words "Article 4(4) and (5) and Article 9(2) and (6)" shall be replaced by the words "Article 4(4) and (5), Article 9(2) and (6) and Article 22(2)".

[4.615]

Article 4

This Decision shall enter into force on 9 June 2004, provided that all the notifications under Article 103(1) of the Agreement have been made to the EEA Joint Committee.*

NOTES

* Constitutional requirements indicated.

[4.616]

Article 5

This Decision shall be published in the EEA Section of, and in the EEA Supplement to, the *Official Journal of the European Union*.

DG COMPETITION INFORMATION NOTE ON ART 6(1)C 2ND SENTENCE OF REGULATION 139/2004 (ABANDONMENT OF CONCENTRATIONS)

[4.617]

NOTES

The text of this note is available on the European Commission website at ec.europa.eu/competition-policy/mergers/legislation/notices-and-guidelines_en.

Note that Regulation 139/2004/EC is repealed, in relation to the UK, by the Competition (Amendment etc) (EU Exit) Regulations 2019, SI 2019/93, reg 63, Sch 3, para 1, as from IP completion day (as defined in the European Union (Withdrawal Agreement) Act 2020, s 39) (for transitional provisions and savings in relation to the operation of the 2019 Regulations, see Sch 4 to those Regulations at **[7.69]** et seq).

The revised EC Merger Regulation[1] introduced a new provision related to the closure of merger control procedures without a final decision after the Commission has initiated proceedings under Art 6(1)c 1st sentence. That sentence reads as follows: "Without prejudice to Article 9, such proceedings shall be closed by means of a decision as provided for in Article 8(1) to (4), unless the undertakings concerned have demonstrated to the satisfaction of the Commission that they have abandoned the concentration". Prior to the initiation of proceedings, such requirements do not apply.

This note sets out the requirements for this satisfaction to be achieved.

As a general principle, the requirements for the proof of the abandonment must correspond in terms of legal form, format, intensity etc to the initial act that was considered sufficient to make the concentration notifiable. In case the parties proceed from that initial act to a strengthening of their contractual links during the procedure, for example by concluding a binding agreement after the transaction was notified on the basis of a good faith intention, the requirements for the proof of the abandonment must correspond also to the latest act.

In line with this principle, in case of implementation of the concentration prior to a Commission decision, the re-establishment of the *status quo ante* has to be shown.

In other cases, the mere withdrawal of the notification is not considered as sufficient proof that the concentration has been abandoned in the sense of Article 6(1)c. Likewise, minor modifications of a concentration, for example as regards the agreed time of implementation or minor changes in the shareholding percentages which do not affect the change in control or the quality of that change, cannot be considered as an abandonment of the original concentration.[2]

- Binding agreement: proof of the legally binding cancellation of the agreement in the form envisaged by the initial agreement (ie usually a document signed by all the parties) will be required. Expressions of intention to cancel the agreement or not to implement the notified concentration, as well as unilateral declarations by the parties will not be considered sufficient.
- Good faith intention to conclude an agreement: In case of a letter of intent or memorandum of understanding reflecting such good faith intention, documents proving that this basis for the good faith intention has been cancelled will be required. As for possible other forms that indicated the good faith intention, the abandonment must reverse this good faith intention and correspond in terms of form and intensity to the initial expression of intent.
- Public announcement of a public bid or of the intention to make a public bid: a public announcement terminating the bidding procedure will be required. The format and public reach of this announcement must be comparable to the initial announcement.
- Implemented concentrations: In case the concentration has been implemented prior to a Commission decision, the parties will be required to show that the situation prevailing before the implementation of the concentration has been re-established.

It is for the parties to submit the necessary documentation to meet these requirements.

This information is without prejudice to the interpretation of Community law which may be given by the Court of Justice or the Court of First Instance of the European Communities.

NOTES

1 Council Regulation No 139/2004 of 20 January 2004 on the control of concentrations between undertakings; OJ L24/1, 29.1.2004.

2 The qualification of a modification as "minor" in the sense of this paragraph does not prejudge the assessment whether the modification requires to submit additional information to the Commission under Art 5(3) Reg 802/2004.

2. PROCEDURE

BEST PRACTICES ON THE CONDUCT OF EC MERGER CONTROL PROCEEDINGS (2004)

[4.618]

NOTES

The text of this note is available on the European Commission website at ec.europa.eu/competition-policy/mergers/legislation/best-practices_en.

Note that the Merger Regulation (Council Regulation 4064/89/EEC) was replaced by a recast Merger Regulation (Council Regulation 139/2004/EC on the control of concentrations between undertakings at **[4.539]**). This guidance also applies to the recast Merger Regulation (see footnote 2 below). The recast Merger Regulation is repealed, in relation to the UK, by the Competition (Amendment etc) (EU Exit) Regulations 2019, SI 2019/93, reg 63, Sch 3, para 1, as from IP completion day (as defined in the European Union (Withdrawal Agreement) Act 2020, s 39) (for transitional provisions and savings in relation to the operation of the 2019 Regulations, see Sch 4 to those Regulations at **[7.69]** et seq).

Note: with effect from 1 December 2009, the Treaty establishing the European Community (the "EC Treaty") was replaced by the Treaty on the Functioning of the European Union. References in this document to provisions of the EC Treaty should be construed accordingly.

1. SCOPE AND PURPOSE OF THE BEST PRACTICES

[4.619]

1. The principal aim of these Best Practices is to provide guidance for interested parties on the day-to-day conduct of EC merger control proceedings. They are intended to foster and build upon a spirit of co-operation and better understanding between DG Competition and the legal and business community. In this regard, the Best Practices seek to increase understanding of the investigation process and thereby to further enhance the efficiency of investigations and to ensure a high degree of transparency and predictability of the review process. In particular, they aim at making the short time available in EC merger procedures as productive and efficient as possible for all parties concerned.

2. The Best Practices are built on the experience to date of DG Competition in the application of Council Regulation (EEC) No 4064/89[1] (the Merger Regulation) and replace the current Best Practices of 1999. They reflect the views and practice of DG Competition at the time of publication.[2]

The specificity of an individual case may require an adaptation of, or deviation from these Best Practices depending on the case at hand.

NOTES

[1] Council Regulation No 4064/89, OJ L395, 30.12.1989, p 1; corrigendum OJ L257 of 21.9.1990, p 13; Regulation as last amended by Regulation (EC) No 1310/97 (OJ L180, 9. 7. 1997, p 1, corrigendum OJ L40, 13.2.1998, p 17).

[2] It is to be noted that a recast Merger Regulation replacing Regulation 4064/89 will apply from 1 May 2004. The Best Practices are equally applicable under Regulation 4064/89 and will continue to be applicable, possibly with further amendments, under the recast Merger Regulation. Appropriate references to the recast Merger Regulation are made throughout the Best Practices by means of footnotes. Those references will only become applicable from 1 May 2004.

2. RELATIONSHIP TO COMMUNITY LAW

[4.620]

3. These Best Practices should not be taken as a full or comprehensive account of the relevant legislative, interpretative and administrative measures which govern Community merger control. They should be read in conjunction with such measures.

4. The Best Practices do not create or alter any rights or obligations as set out in the Treaty establishing the European Community, the Merger Regulation, its Implementing Regulation[3] as amended from time to time and as interpreted by the case-law of the Community Courts. Nor do they alter the Commission's interpretative notices. The Best Practices do not apply to proceedings under Council Regulation No 17,[4] to be replaced by Council Regulation No 1/2003[5] as of 1 May 2004, implementing Articles 81 and 82 of the Treaty.

NOTES

[3] Commission Regulation (EC) No 447/98 of 1 March 1998 on the notifications, time limits and hearings provided for in the Merger Regulation, OJ L61, 2.3.1998, p 1.

[4] OJ P013, 21.02.1962, p 204.

[5] Council Regulation (EC) No 1/2003 of 16 December 2002 on the implementation of the rules on competition laid down in Articles 81 and 82 of the Treaty, OJ L1, 04.01.2003, p 1.

3. PRE-NOTIFICATION

Purpose of pre-notification contacts

[4.621]

5. In DG Competition's experience the pre-notification phase of the procedure is an important part of the whole review process. As a general rule, DG Competition finds it useful to have pre-notification contacts with notifying parties even in seemingly non-problematic cases. DG Competition will therefore always give notifying parties and other involved parties the opportunity, if they so request, to discuss an intended concentration informally and in confidence prior to notification (cf. also Recital 10 Implementing Regulation).

6. Pre-notification contacts provide DG Competition and the notifying parties with the possibility, prior to notification, to discuss jurisdictional and other legal issues. They also serve to discuss issues such as the scope of the information to be submitted and to prepare for the upcoming investigation by identifying key issues and possible competition concerns (theories of harm) at an early stage.

7. Further, it is in the interests of DG Competition and the business and legal community to ensure that notification forms are complete from the outset so that declarations of incompleteness are avoided as far as possible. It is DG Competition's experience that in cases in which notifications have been declared incomplete, usually there were no or very limited pre-notification contacts. Accordingly, for this reason it is recommended that notifying parties contact DG Competition prior to notification.

8. Pre-notification discussions are held in strict confidence. The discussions are a voluntary part of the process and remain without prejudice to the handling and investigation of the case following formal notification. However, the mutual benefits for DG Competition and the parties of a fruitful pre-notification phase can only materialise if discussions are held in an open and co-operative atmosphere, where all potential issues are addressed in a constructive way.

9. In DG Competition's experience it is generally preferable that both legal advisers and business representatives, who have a good understanding of the relevant markets, are available for pre-notification discussions with the case-team. This normally results in more informed discussions on the business rationale for the transaction and the functioning of the markets in question.

Timing and extent of pre-notification contacts

10. Pre-notification contacts should preferably be initiated at least two weeks before the expected date of notification. The extent and format of the pre-notification contacts required is, however, linked to the complexity of the individual case in question. In more complex cases a more extended pre-notification period may be appropriate and in the interest of the notifying parties. In all cases it is advisable to make contact with DG Competition as soon as possible as this will facilitate planning of the case.

11. Pre-notification contacts should be launched with a submission that allows the selection of an appropriate DG Competition case-team.[6] This memorandum should provide a brief background to the transaction, a brief description of the relevant sector(s) and market(s) involved and the likely impact of the transaction on competition in general terms. It should also indicate the case language. In straightforward cases, the parties may chose to submit a draft Form CO as a basis for further discussions with DG Competition.

12. After initial contacts have been made between the case-team and the notifying parties, it will be decided, whether it will suffice for DG Competition to make comments orally or in writing on the submissions made. This would typically be considered in straightforward cases. In more complex cases and cases that raise jurisdictional or other procedural issues, one or more pre-notification meetings are normally considered appropriate.

13. The first pre-notification meeting is normally held on the basis of a more substantial submission or a first draft Form CO. This allows for a more fruitful discussion about the proposed transaction in question or potential issue in point. Subsequent meetings may cover additional information submitted or outstanding issues.

14. Any submission sent to DG Competition should be provided sufficiently ahead of meetings or other contacts in order to allow for well prepared and fruitful discussions. In this regard, preparatory briefing memoranda/ draft Form COs sent in preparation of meetings should be filed in good time before the meeting (at least three working days) unless agreed otherwise with the case team. In case of voluminous submissions and in less straightforward cases, this time may need to be extended to allow DG Competition to properly prepare for the meeting.

15. Irrespective of whether pre-notification meetings have taken place or not, it is advisable that the notifying parties systematically provide a substantially complete draft Form CO before filing a formal notification. DG Competition would thereafter normally require five working days to review the draft before being asked to comment, at a meeting or on the telephone, on the adequacy of the draft. In case of voluminous submissions, this time will normally be extended.

Information to be provided/preparation of the Form CO

16. The format and the timing of all prenotification submissions should be decided together with the case-team. Notifying parties are advised to fully and frankly disclose information relating to all potentially affected markets and possible competition concerns, even if they may ultimately consider that they are not affected and notwithstanding that they may take a particular view in relation to, for example, the issue of market definition. This will allow for an early market testing of alternative market definitions and/or the notifying parties' position on the market/s in question. In DG Competition's experience this approach minimises surprise submissions from third parties, and may avoid requests for additional information from the notifying parties at a late stage in the procedure and possible declarations of incompleteness under Article 4(2) of the Implementing Regulation or a decision under Article 11(5) of the Merger Regulation.

17. In addition, DG Competition recommends that notifying parties should, as early as possible in pre-notification, submit internal documents such as board presentations, surveys, analyses, reports and studies discussing the proposed concentration, the economic rationale for the concentration and competitive significance or the market context in which it takes place. Such documents provide DG Competition with an early and informed view of the transaction and its potential competitive impact and can thus allow for a productive discussion and finalisation of the Form CO.

18. Where appropriate, it is also recommended that notifying parties put forward, already at the pre-notification stage, any elements demonstrating that the merger leads to efficiency gains that they would like the Commission to take into account for the purposes of its competitive assessment of the proposed transaction. Such claims are likely to require extensive analysis. It is thus in the interests of the notifying parties to present these claims as early as possible to allow sufficient time for DG Competition to appropriately consider these elements in its assessment of a proposed transaction.

19. Pre-notification discussions provide the opportunity for the Commission and the notifying parties to discuss the amount of information to be provided in a notification. The notifying parties may in pre-notification request the Commission to waive the obligation to provide certain information that is not necessary for the examination of the case. All requests to omit any part of the information specified should be discussed in detail and any waiver has to be agreed with DG Competition prior to notification.[7]

Completeness of the notification

20. Given that a notification is not considered effective until the information to be submitted in Form CO is complete in all material respects, the notifying parties and their advisers should ensure that the information contained in Form CO has been carefully prepared and verified: incorrect and misleading information is considered incomplete information.[8] In this regard, the notifying parties should take special care that the appropriate contact details are provided for customers, suppliers and competitors. If such information is not correct or provided in full it will significantly delay the investigation and therefore may lead to a declaration of incompleteness.

21. Further, to facilitate the effective and expeditious handling of their notification, notifying parties should also endeavour to provide the contact details required in Form CO electronically, at the latest on the day of notification, using the appropriate electronic form which can be provided by the case team.

22. Provided that the notifying parties follow the above described guidance, DG Competition will in principle, be prepared to confirm informally the adequacy of a draft notification at the pre-notification stage or, if appropriate, to identify in what material respects the draft Form CO is incomplete. However it has to be recognised that it will not be possible for DG Competition to exclude the fact that it may have to declare a notification incomplete in appropriate cases after notification.

23. In the event that DG Competition discovers omissions in the Form CO after formal notification, the notifying parties may be given an opportunity to urgently put right such omissions before a declaration of incompleteness is adopted. Due to the time constraints in merger procedures, the time allowed for such rectification is normally limited to 1 or 2 days. This opportunity will not be granted, however, in cases where DG Competition finds that the omissions immediately hinder the proper investigation of the proposed transaction.

Procedural questions and inter-agency co-operation

24. In addition to substantive issues, the notifying parties may in the pre-notification phase seek DG Competition's opinion on procedural matters such as jurisdictional questions.

25. Informal guidance may be provided if they are directly related to an actual, planned transaction and if sufficiently detailed background information is submitted by the notifying parties to properly assess the issue in question.[9] Further matters for prenotification discussions include the possibility of referrals to or from national EU jurisdictions,[10] parallel proceedings in other non-EU jurisdictions and the issue of waivers on information sharing with other jurisdictions. As regards transactions likely to be reviewed in more than one jurisdiction, DG Competition invites the notifying parties to discuss the timing of the case with a view to enhance efficiency of the respective investigations, to reduce burdens on the merging parties and third parties, and to increase overall transparency of the merger review process. In this regard, notifying parties should also have regard to the EU-US Best Practices on cooperation in merger investigations.[11]

NOTES

6 Case teams for new cases are normally set up in weekly DG Competition's Merger Management Meetings.

7 See Article 3(2) Implementing Regulation. See also Commission Notice on a simplified procedure for treatment of certain concentrations under Council Regulation (EEC) No 4064/89, OJ C217, 29.07.2000, p 32.

8 In addition, the Commission may impose fines on the notifying parties where they supply incorrect or misleading information in a notification under Article 14(1)(b) Merger Regulation.

9 Such informal guidance cannot be regarded as creating legitimate expectations regarding the proper interpretation of applicable jurisdictional or other rules.

10 Such jurisdictional discussions will become particularly pertinent under the recast Merger Regulation, which becomes applicable from 1 May 2004. Pursuant to Articles 4(4) and 4(5) of the recast Merger Regulation, notifying parties may, before notification, request on the basis of a reasoned submission, referral of a case to or from the Commission. DG Competition will be ready to discuss with notifying parties informally the possibility of such pre-notification referrals and to guide them through the pre-notification referral process.

11 ec.europa.eu/competition/mergers/legislation/international_cooperation.html

4. FACT FINDING/REQUESTS FOR INFORMATION

[4.622]

26. In carrying out its duties the Commission may obtain all necessary information from relevant persons, undertakings, associations of undertakings and competent authorities of Member States (see Article 11(1) Merger Regulation). That investigation normally starts after the notification of a proposed concentration. However, DG Competition may exceptionally decide that, in the interest of its investigation, market contacts could be initiated informally prior to notification. Such pre-notification contacts/enquiries would only take place if the existence of the transaction is in the public domain and once the notifying parties have had the opportunity to express their views on such measures.

27. The Commission's investigation is mainly conducted in the form of written Requests for Information (requests pursuant to Article 11 of the Merger Regulation) to customers, suppliers, competitors and other relevant parties. Such requests may also be addressed to the notifying parties. In addition to such Article 11 requests, the views of the notifying parties, other involved parties and third parties are also sought orally.

28. In the interest of an efficient investigation, DG Competition may consult the notifying parties, other involved parties or third parties on methodological issues regarding data and information gathering in the relevant economic sector. It may also seek external economic and/or industrial expertise and launch its own economic studies.

5. COMMUNICATION AND MEETINGS WITH THE NOTIFYING PARTIES, OTHER INVOLVED PARTIES AND 3RD PARTIES

[4.623]

29. One of the aims of these Best Practices is to enhance transparency in the day to day handling of merger cases and in particular, to ensure good communication between DG Competition, the merging parties and third parties. In this regard, DG Competition endeavours to give all parties involved in the proceeding ample opportunity for open and frank discussions and to make their points of view known throughout the procedure.

5.1. State of Play meetings with notifying parties

Aim and format of the State of Play meetings

30. The objective of the State of Play meetings is to contribute to the quality and efficiency of the decision-making process and to ensure transparency and communication between DG Competition and the notifying parties. As such these meetings should provide a forum for the mutual exchange of information between DG Competition and the notifying parties at key points in the procedure. They are entirely voluntary in nature.

31. State of Play meetings may be conducted in the form of meetings at the Commission's premises, or alternatively, if appropriate, by telephone or video-conference. In order for the meetings to operate properly they should be carefully prepared on the basis of an agenda agreed in advance. Further, senior DG Competition management will normally chair the meetings.

32. The State of Play meetings will not exclude discussions and exchanges of information between the notifying parties and DG Competition at other occasions throughout the procedure as appropriate. In this regard, notifying parties are advised to inform DG Competition, as soon as possible, about any important procedural or substantive developments that may be of relevance for the assessment of the proposed transaction. Such developments may include any remedy proposals the notifying parties are offering or are considering to offer in other jurisdictions, so as to facilitate co-ordination of the timing and substance of such remedy proposals. This also concerns matters already discussed at a State of Play meeting, in respect of which the parties consider it necessary to provide additional comments.

Timing of the State of Play meetings

33. Notifying parties will normally be offered the opportunity of attending a State of Play meeting at the following five different points in the Phase I and Phase II procedure:

a) where it appears that "serious doubts" within the meaning of Article 6(1)(c) of the Merger Regulation are likely to be present a meeting will be offered before the expiry of 3 weeks[12] into Phase I. In addition to informing the notifying parties of the preliminary result of the initial investigation, this meeting provides an opportunity for the notifying parties to prepare the formulation of a possible remedy proposal in Phase I before expiry of the deadline provided in Article 18 of the Implementing Regulation.

b) normally within 2 weeks following the adoption of the Article 6(1)(c) decision. In order to prepare for this meeting, the notifying parties should provide DG Competition with their comments on the Article 6(1)(c) decision and on any documents in the Commission's file, which they may have had the opportunity to review (see below section 7.2) by way of a written memorandum in advance of the meeting. The notifying parties should contact the case team to discuss an appropriate schedule for the filing of this memorandum.

   The main purpose of the post Article 6(1)(c) meeting is to facilitate the notifying parties' understanding of the Commission's concerns at an early stage of the Phase II proceedings. The meeting also serves to assist DG Competition in deciding the appropriate framework for its further investigation by discussing with the notifying parties matters such as the market definition and competition concerns outlined in the Article 6(1)(c) decision. The meeting is also intended to serve as a forum for mutually informing each other of any planned economic or other studies. The approximate timetable of the Phase II procedure may also be discussed.[13]

c) before the issuing of a Statement of Objections (SO). This pre-SO meeting gives the notifying parties an opportunity to understand DG Competition's preliminary view on the outcome of the Phase II investigation and to be informed of the type of objections DG Competition may set out in the SO. The meeting may also be used by DG Competition to clarify certain issues and facts before it finalises its proposal on the issuing of a SO.

d) following the reply to the SO and the Oral Hearing. This post-SO State of Play meeting provides the notifying parties with an opportunity to understand DG Competition's position after it has considered their reply and heard them at an Oral Hearing. If DG Competition indicates that it is minded to maintain some or all of its objections, the meeting may also serve as an opportunity to discuss the scope and timing of possible remedy proposals.[14]

e) before the Advisory Committee meets. The primary purpose of this meeting is to enable the notifying parties to discuss with DG Competition its views on any proposed remedies and where relevant, the results of the market testing of such remedies. It also provides the notifying parties where necessary, with the opportunity to formulate improvements to their remedies proposal.[15]

5.2. Involvement of third parties

34. According to Community merger control law, third parties considered as having a "sufficient interest" in the Commission's procedure include customers, suppliers, competitors, members of the administration or management organs of the undertakings concerned or recognised workers' representatives of those undertakings.[16] Their important role in the Commission's procedure is stressed in particular in Article 18(4) of the Merger Regulation and Articles 16(1) and (2) of the Implementing Regulation. In addition, the Commission also welcomes the views of any other interested third parties including consumer organisations.[17]

35. The primary way for third parties to contribute to the Commission's investigation is by means of replies to requests for information (Article 11 Merger Regulation).[18] However, DG Competition also welcomes any individual submission apart from direct replies to questionnaires, where third parties provide information and comments they consider relevant for the assessment of a given transaction. DG Competition may also invite third parties for meetings to discuss and clarify specific issues raised.

36. In addition, DG Competition may in the interest of the investigation in appropriate cases provide third parties that have shown a sufficient interest in the procedure with an edited version of the SO from which business secrets have been removed, in order to allow them to make their views known on the Commission's preliminary assessment. In such cases, the SO is provided under strict confidentiality obligations and restrictions of use, which the third parties have to accept prior to receipt.

37. If third parties wish to express competition concerns as regards the transaction in question or to put forward views on key market data or characteristics that deviate from the notifying parties' position, it is essential that they are communicated as early as possible to DG Competition, so that they can be considered, verified and taken into account properly. Any point raised should be substantiated and supported by examples, documents and other factual evidence. Furthermore, in accordance with Article 17(2) of the Implementing Regulation, third parties should always provide the DG Competition with a non-confidential version of their submissions at the time of filing or shortly thereafter to facilitate access to the file and other measures intended to ensure transparency for the benefit of the decision making process (see further below section 7).

5.3. "Triangular" and other meetings

38. In addition to bilateral meetings between DG Competition and the notifying parties, other involved parties or third parties, DG Competition may decide to invite third parties and the notifying parties to a "triangular" meeting where DG Competition believes it is desirable, in the interests of the fact-finding investigation, to hear the views of the notifying parties and such third parties in a single forum. Such triangular meetings, which will be on a voluntary basis and which are not intended to replace the formal oral hearing, would take place in situations where two or more opposing views have been put forward as to key market data and characteristics and the effects of the concentration on competition in the markets concerned.

39. Triangular meetings should ideally be held as early in the investigation as possible in order to enable DG Competition to reach a more informed conclusion as to the relevant market characteristics and to clarify issues of substance before deciding on the issuing of an SO. Triangular meetings are normally chaired by senior DG Competition management. They are prepared in advance on the basis of an agenda established by DG Competition after consultation of all parties that agreed to attend the meeting. The preparation will normally include a mutual exchange of non-confidential submissions between the notifying parties and the third party in question sufficiently in advance of the meeting. The meeting will not require the disclosure of confidential information or business secrets, unless otherwise agreed by the parties.

NOTES

12 Fifteen working days under the recast Merger Regulation.

13 Once the recast Merger Regulation becomes applicable, this post Article 6(1)(c) State of Play meeting will also serve to discuss the possibility of any extensions to the Phase II deadline pursuant to Article 10(3) of the recast Merger Regulation.

14 It is to be noted that, under the recast Merger Regulation (Article 10(3)), the submission of remedies could lead to an automatic extension of the Phase II deadline.

15 Modifications to remedies are only possible under those conditions set out in Article 18 of the Implementing Regulation and point 43 of the Commission's Notice on Remedies.

16 See Article 11 of the Implementing Regulation.

17 Article 16(3) Implementing Regulation. To this effect, DG Competition has appointed a Consumer Liaison Officer responsible for contacts with consumer organisations.

18 Article 11(7) of the recast Merger Regulation expressly provides for the Commission's competence to interview any natural or legal person who consents to be interviewed for the purpose of collecting information relating to the subject-matter of an investigation.

6. REMEDIES DISCUSSIONS

[4.624]

40. As stated above, the State of Play meetings in both Phase I and Phase II, in addition to providing a forum for discussing issues related to the investigation, also serve to discuss possible remedy proposals. Detailed guidance on the requirements for such proposals is set out in the Commission Notice on remedies acceptable under Council Regulation (EEC) No 4064/89 and under Commission Regulation (EC) No 447/98[19] (the Remedies Notice). In particular, the Remedies Notice sets out the general principles applicable to remedies, the main types of commitments that have previously been accepted by the Commission, the specific requirements which proposals of remedies need to fulfil in both phases of the procedure, and guidance on the implementation of remedies. As regards the design of divestiture commitment proposals, the notifying parties are advised to take due account of the Commission's "Best Practice Guidelines on Divestiture Commitments".[20]

41. Although it is for the notifying parties to formulate suitable remedies proposals, DG Competition will provide guidance to the parties as to the general appropriateness of their draft proposal in advance of submission. In order to allow for such discussions, a notifying party should contact DG Competition in good time before the relevant deadline in Phase I or Phase II, in order to be able to address comments DG Competition may have on the draft proposal.[21]

NOTES

19 OJ C68, 02.03.2001, p 3.

20 Available under

ec.europa.eu/competition/mergers/legislation/note.pdf.

[21] It is to be noted that under the recast Merger Regulation (Articles 10(1) and (3)), the submission of remedies could lead to an automatic extension of the Phase I and II deadlines.

7. PROVISION OF DOCUMENTS IN THE COMMISSION'S FILE/CONFIDENTIALITY

7.1. Access to the file

[4.625]
42. According to Community law, the notifying parties have upon request a right to access the Commission's file after the Commission has issued an SO (see Article 18(3) of the Merger Regulation and Article 13(3) of the Implementing Regulation).

43. Further, the notifying parties will be given the opportunity to have access to documents received after the issuing of the SO up until the consultation of the Advisory Committee.

44. Access to the file will be provided subject to the legitimate interest of the protection of third parties' business secrets and other confidential information.

7.2. Review of key documents

45. DG Competition believes in the merits of an open exchange of views with ample opportunities for the notifying parties and third parties to make their points of view known throughout the procedure. This enables DG Competition to assess the main issues arising during the investigation with as much information at its disposal as possible. In this spirit, DG Competition's objective will be to provide the notifying parties with the opportunity of reviewing and commenting on "key documents" obtained by the Commission. Such documents would comprise substantiated submissions of third parties running counter to the notifying parties' own contentions received during Phase I and thereafter,[22] including key submissions to which specific reference is made in the Article 6(1)(c) decision and market studies.

46. DG Competition will use its best endeavours to provide notifying parties in a timely fashion, with the opportunity to review such documents following the initiation of proceedings and thereafter on an *ad hoc* basis. DG Competition will respect justified requests by third parties for non-disclosure of their submissions prior to the issuing of the SO relating to genuine concerns regarding confidentiality, including fears of retaliation and the protection of business secrets.

7.3. Confidentiality Rules

47. In accordance with Article 287 of the EC Treaty and Article 17(1) of the Implementing Regulation, the Commission will, throughout its investigation, protect confidential information and business secrets contained in submissions provided by all parties involved in EC merger proceedings. Given the short legal deadlines of EC merger procedures, parties are encouraged to clarify as soon as possible any queries related to confidentiality claims with members of the case team. Guidance on what is considered to be business secrets or other confidential information is provided in the Commission's Notice on Access to file.[23]

NOTES

[22] This would in particular include substantiated "complaints" contending that the notified transaction may give rise to competition concerns. The word "complaint" is to be understood in the non-technical sense of the term as no formal complaints procedure exists in merger cases.

[23] OJ C23, 23/01/97, p 3.

8. RIGHT TO BE HEARD AND OTHER PROCEDURAL RIGHTS

[4.626]
48. The right of the parties concerned to be heard before a final decision affecting their interests is taken is a fundamental principle of Community law. That right is also set out in the Merger Regulation (Article 18) and the Implementing Regulation (Articles 14–16). These Best Practices do not alter any such rights under Community law.

49. Any issues related to the right to be heard and other procedural issues, including access to the file, time limits for replying to the SO and the objectivity of any enquiry conducted in order to assess the competition impact of commitments proposed in EC merger proceedings can be raised with the Hearing Officer, in accordance with Commission Decision of 23 May 2001 on the terms of reference of hearing officers in certain competition proceedings.[24]

NOTES

[24] Official Journal L162, 19.06.2001, p 21. The text can also be found at: ec.europa.eu/competition/hearing_officers/legislation.html.

9. FUTURE REVIEW

[4.627]
50. These Best Practices may be revised to reflect changes to legislative, interpretative and administrative measures or due to case law of the European Courts, which govern EC merger control or any experience gained in applying such framework. DG Competition further intends to engage, on a regular basis, in a dialogue with the business and legal community on the experience gained through the application of the Merger Regulation in general, and these Best Practices in particular.

COMMISSION NOTICE

(2005/C56/02)

on case referral in respect of concentrations

(Text with EEA relevance)

[4.628]

NOTES

Date of publication in OJ: OJ C56, 5.3.2005, p 2.

Editorial note: see also the Communication from the Commission: Guidance on the application of the referral mechanism set out in Article 22 of the Merger Regulation to certain categories of cases (2021) at **[4.688]**.

Note: with effect from 1 December 2009, the EC Treaty was replaced by the Treaty on the Functioning of the European Union. References in this document to provisions of the EC Treaty should be construed accordingly.

[4.629]

1. The purpose of this Notice is to describe in a general way the rationale underlying the case referral system in Article 4(4) and (5), Article 9 and Article 22 of Council Regulation (EC) No 139/2004 of 20 January 2004 on the control of concentrations between undertakings (the EC Merger Regulation)[1] (hereinafter "the Merger Regulation"), including the recent changes made to the system, to catalogue the legal criteria that must be fulfilled in order for referrals to be possible, and to set out the factors which may be taken into consideration when referrals are decided upon. The Notice also provides practical guidance regarding the mechanics of the referral system, in particular regarding the pre-notification referral mechanism provided for in Article 4(4) and (5) of the Merger Regulation. The guidance provided in this notice applies, *mutatis mutandis*, to the referral rules contained in the EEA Agreement.[2]

NOTES

1 OJ L24, 29.1.2004, p 1. This Regulation has recast Council Regulation (EEC) No 4064/89 of 21 December 1989 on the control of concentrations between undertakings (OJ L395, 30.12.1989, p 1. Corrected version in OJ L257, 21.9.1990, p 13).

2 See EEA Joint Committee Decision No 78/2004 of 8 June 2004 (OJ L219, 8.6.2004, p 13).

I. INTRODUCTION

2. Community jurisdiction in the field of merger control is defined by the application of the turnover-related criteria contained in Articles 1(2) and 1(3) of the Merger Regulation. When dealing with concentrations, the Commission and Member States do not have concurrent jurisdiction. Rather, the Merger Regulation establishes a clear division of competence. Concentrations with a "Community dimension", ie those above the turnover thresholds in Article 1 of the Merger Regulation, fall within the exclusive jurisdiction of the Commission; Member States are precluded from applying national competition law to such concentrations by virtue of Article 21 of the Merger Regulation. Concentrations falling below the thresholds remain within the competence of the Member States; the Commission has no jurisdiction to deal with them under the Merger Regulation.

3. Determining jurisdiction exclusively by reference to fixed turnover-related criteria provides legal certainty for merging companies. While the financial criteria generally serve as effective proxies for the category of transactions for which the Commission is the more appropriate authority, Regulation (EEC) No 4064/89 complemented this "bright-line" jurisdictional scheme with a possibility for cases to be re-attributed by the Commission to Member States and vice versa, upon request and provided certain criteria were fulfilled.

4. When Regulation (EEC) No 4064/89 was first introduced, it was envisaged by the Council and Commission that case referrals would only be resorted to in "exceptional circumstances" and where "the interests in respect of competition of the Member State concerned could not be adequately protected in any other way".[3] There have, however, been a number of developments since the adoption of Regulation (EEC) No 4064/89. First, merger control laws have been introduced in almost all Member States. Second, the Commission has exercised its discretion to refer a number of cases to Member States pursuant to Article 9 in circumstances where it was felt that the Member State in question was in a better position to carry out the investigation than the Commission.[4] Likewise, in a number of cases,[5] several Member States decided to make a joint referral of a case pursuant to Article 22 in circumstances where it was felt that the Commission was the authority in a better position to carry out the investigation.[6] Third, there has been an increase in the number of transactions not meeting the thresholds in Article 1 of the Merger Regulation which must be filed in multiple Member State jurisdictions, a trend which is likely to continue in line with the Community's growing membership. Many of these transactions affect competition beyond the territories of individual Member States.[7]

5. The revisions made to the referral system in the Merger Regulation are designed to facilitate the re-attribution of cases between the Commission and Member States, consistent with the principle of subsidiarity, so that the more appropriate authority or authorities for carrying out a particular merger investigation should in principle deal with the case. At the same time, the revisions are intended to preserve the basic features of the Community merger control system introduced in 1989, in particular the provision of a "one-stop-shop" for the competition scrutiny of mergers with a cross-border impact and an alternative to multiple merger control notifications within the Community.[8] Such multiple filings often entail considerable cost for competition authorities and businesses alike.

6. The case re-attribution system now provides that a referral may also be triggered before a formal filing has been made in any Member State jurisdiction, thereby affording merging companies the possibility of ascertaining, at as early as possible a stage, where jurisdiction for scrutiny of their transaction will ultimately lie. Such pre-notification referrals have the advantage of alleviating the additional cost, notably in terms of time delay, associated with post-filing referral.

7. The revisions made to the referral system in Regulation (EC) No 139/2004 were motivated by a desire that it should operate as a jurisdictional mechanism which is flexible[9] but which at the same time ensures effective protection of competition and limits the scope for "forum shopping" to the greatest extent possible. However, having regard in particular to the importance of legal certainty, it should be stressed that referrals remain a derogation from the general rules which determine jurisdiction based upon objectively determinable turnover thresholds. Moreover, the Commission and Member States retain a considerable margin of discretion in deciding whether to refer cases falling within their "original jurisdiction", or whether to accept to deal with cases not falling within their "original jurisdiction", pursuant to Article 4(4) and (5), Article 9(2)(a) and Article 22.[10] To that extent, the current Notice is intended to provide no more than general guidance regarding the appropriateness of particular cases or categories of cases for referral.

NOTES

[3] See the Notes on Council Regulation (EEC) No 4064/89 ["Merger Control in the European union", European Commission, Brussels-Luxembourg, 1998, at p 54]. See also Case T-119/02 *Philips v Commission* [2003] ECR II-1433 (Case M.2621 *SEB/Moulinex*) at paragraph 354.

[4] It is a fact that some concentrations of Community dimension affect competition in national or sub-national markets within one or more Member States.

[5] M.2698 *Promatech/Sulzer*; M.2738 *GE/Unison*; M.3136 *GE/AGFA*.

[6] In the same vein, Member States' competition authorities, in the context of the European Competition Authorities' association, have issued a recommendation designed to provide guidance as to the principles upon which national competition authorities should deal with cases eligible for joint referrals under Article 22 of the Merger Regulation – *Principles on the application, by National Competition Authorities within the ECA network, of Article 22 of the EC Merger Regulation.*

[7] While the introduction of Article 1(3) in 1997 has brought some such cases under the jurisdiction of the Merger Regulation, many are unaffected. See paragraph 21 et seq of the Commission's Green Paper of 11 December 2001 (COM(2001) 745 final).

[8] See Recitals 11, 12 and 14 to the Merger Regulation.

[9] See Recital 11 to the Merger Regulation.

[10] See, however, *infra*, footnote 14. It should moreover be noted that, pursuant to Article 4(5), the Commission has no discretion as to whether or not to accept a case not falling within its original jurisdiction.

II. REFERRAL OF CASES

Guiding principles

[4.630]

8. The system of merger control established by the Merger Regulation, including the mechanism for re-attributing cases between the Commission and Member States contained therein, is consistent with the principle of subsidiarity enshrined in the EC Treaty.[11] Decisions taken with regard to the referral of cases should accordingly take due account of all aspects of the application of the principle of subsidiarity in this context, in particular which is the authority more appropriate for carrying out the investigation, the benefits inherent in a "one-stop-shop" system, and the importance of legal certainty with regard to jurisdiction.[12] These factors are inter-linked and the respective weight placed upon each of them will depend upon the specificities of a particular case. Above all, in considering whether or not to exercise their discretion to make or accede to a referral, the Commission and Member States should bear in mind the need to ensure effective protection of competition in all markets affected by the transaction.[13]

More appropriate authority

9. In principle, jurisdiction should only be re-attributed to another competition authority in circumstances where the latter is the more appropriate for dealing with a merger, having regard to the specific characteristics of the case as well as the tools and expertise available to the authority. Particular regard should be had to the likely locus of any impact on competition resulting from the merger. Regard may also be had to the implications, in terms of administrative effort, of any contemplated referral.[14]

10. The case for re-attributing jurisdiction is likely to be more compelling where it appears that a particular transaction may have a significant impact on competition and thus may deserve careful scrutiny.

One-stop-shop

11. Decisions on the referral of cases should also have regard to the benefits inherent in a "one-stop-shop", which is at the core of the Merger Regulation.[15] The provision of a one-stop-shop is beneficial to competition authorities and businesses alike. The handling of a merger by a single competition authority normally increases administrative efficiency, avoiding duplication and fragmentation of enforcement effort as well as potentially incoherent treatment (regarding investigation, assessment and possible remedies) by multiple authorities. It normally also brings advantages to businesses, in particular to merging firms, by reducing the costs and burdens arising from multiple filing obligations and by eliminating the risk of conflicting decisions resulting from the concurrent assessment of the same transaction by a number of competition authorities under diverse legal regimes.

12. Fragmentation of cases through referral should therefore be avoided where possible,[16] unless it appears that multiple authorities would be in a better position to ensure that competition in all markets affected by the transaction is effectively protected. Accordingly, while partial referrals are possible under Article 4(4) and Article 9, it would normally be appropriate for the whole of a case (or at least all connected parts thereof) to be dealt with by a single authority.[17]

Legal certainty

13. Due account should also be taken of the importance of legal certainty regarding jurisdiction over a particular concentration, from the perspective of all concerned.[18] Accordingly, referral should normally only be made when there is a compelling reason for departing from "original jurisdiction" over the case in question, particularly at the post-notification stage. Similarly, if a referral has been made prior to notification, a post-notification referral in the same case should be avoided to the greatest extent possible.[19]

14. The importance of legal certainty should also be borne in mind with regard to the legal criteria for referral, and particularly – given the tight deadlines – at the pre-notification stage. Accordingly, pre-filing referrals should in principle be confined to those cases where it is relatively straightforward to establish, from the outset, the scope of the geographic market and/or the existence of a possible competitive impact, so as to be able to promptly decide upon such requests

CASE REFERRALS: LEGAL REQUIREMENTS AND OTHER FACTORS TO BE CONSIDERED

Pre-notification referrals

15. The system of pre-notification referrals is triggered by a reasoned submission lodged by the parties to the concentration. When contemplating such a request, the parties to the concentration are required, first, to verify whether the relevant legal requirements set out in the Merger Regulation are fulfilled, and second, whether a pre-notification referral would be consistent with the guiding principles outlined above.

Referral of cases by the Commission to Member States under Article 4(4)

Legal requirements

16. In order for a referral to be made by the Commission to one or more Member States pursuant to Articles 4(4), two legal requirements must be fulfilled:

(i) there must be indications *that the concentration may significantly affect competition* in a market or markets;

(ii) the market(s) in question must be within a Member State and *present all the characteristics of a distinct market*.

17. As regards the *first criterion*, the requesting parties are in essence required to demonstrate that the transaction is liable to have a potential impact on competition on a distinct market in a Member State, which may prove to be significant, thus deserving close scrutiny. Such indications may be no more than preliminary in nature, and would be without prejudice to the outcome of the investigation. While the parties are not required to demonstrate that the effect on competition is likely to be an adverse one,[20] they should point to indicators which are generally suggestive of the existence of some competitive effects stemming from the transaction.[21]

18. As regards the *second criterion*, the requesting parties are required to show that a geographic market in which competition is affected by the transaction in the manner just described (paragraph 17) is national, or narrower than national in scope.[22]

Other factors to be considered

19. Other than verification of the legal requirements, in order to anticipate to the greatest extent possible the likely outcome of a referral request, merging parties contemplating a request should also consider whether referral of the case is likely to be considered appropriate. This will involve an examination of the application of the guiding principles referred to above (paragraphs 8 to 14), and in particular whether the competition authority or authorities to which they are contemplating requesting the referral of the case is the most appropriate authority for dealing with the case. To this end, consideration should be given in turn both to the likely locus of the competitive effects of the transaction and to how appropriate the national competition authority (NCA) would be for scrutinising the operation.

20. Concentrations with a Community dimension which are likely to affect competition in markets that have a national or narrower than national scope, and the effects of which are likely to be confined to, or have their main economic impact in, a single Member State,[23] are the most appropriate candidate cases for referral to that Member State. This applies in particular to cases where the impact would occur on a distinct market which does not constitute a substantial part of the common market. To the extent that referral is made to one Member State only, the benefit of a "one-stop-shop" is also preserved.

21. The extent to which a concentration with a Community dimension which, despite having a potentially significant impact on competition in a nation-wide market, nonetheless potentially engenders substantial cross-border effects (eg because the effects of the concentration in one geographic market may have significant repercussions in geographic markets in other Member States, or because it may involve potential foreclosure effects and consequent fragmentation of the common market[24]), may be an appropriate candidate for referral will depend on the specific circumstances of the case. As both the Commission and Member States may be equally well equipped or be in an equally good position to deal with such cases, a considerable margin of discretion should be retained in deciding whether or not to refer such cases.

22. The extent to which concentrations with a Community dimension, and potentially affecting competition in a series of national or narrower than national markets in more than one Member State, may be appropriate candidates for referral to Member States will depend on factors specific to each individual case, such as the number of national markets likely to be significantly affected, the prospect of addressing any possible concerns by way of proportionate, non-conflicting remedies, and the investigative efforts that the case may require. To the extent that a case may

engender competition concerns in a number of Member States, and require coordinated investigations and remedial action, this may militate in favour of the Commission retaining jurisdiction over the entirety of the case in question.[25] On the other hand, to the extent that the case gives rise to competition concerns which, despite involving national markets in more than one Member State, do not appear to require coordinated investigation and/or remedial action, a referral may be appropriate. In a limited number of cases,[26] the Commission has even found it appropriate to refer a concentration to more than one Member State, in view of the significant differences in competitive conditions that characterised the affected markets in the Member States concerned. While fragmentation of the treatment of a case deprives the merging parties of the benefit of a one-stop-shop in such cases, this consideration is less pertinent at the pre-notification stage, given that the referral is triggered by a voluntary request from the merging parties.

23. Consideration should also, to the extent possible, be given to whether the NCA(s) to which referral of the case is contemplated may possess specific expertise concerning local markets,[27] or be examining, or about to examine, another transaction in the sector concerned.[28]

Referral of cases from Member States to the Commission under Article 4(5)

Legal requirements

24. Under Article 4(5), only two legal requirements must be met in order for the parties to the transaction to request the referral of the case to the Commission: the transaction must be a concentration within the meaning of Article 3 of the Merger Regulation, and the concentration must be *capable of being reviewed under the national competition laws for the control of mergers of at least three Member States* (see also paragraphs 65 et seq and 70 et seq).

Other factors to be considered

25. Other than verification of the legal requirements, in order to anticipate to the greatest extent possible the likely outcome of a referral request, merging parties contemplating a request should also consider whether referral of the case is likely to be considered appropriate. This will involve an examination of the application of the guiding principles referred to above, and in particular whether the Commission is the more appropriate authority for dealing with the case.

26. In this regard, Recital 16 to the Merger Regulation states that "requests for pre-notification referrals to the Commission would be particularly pertinent in situations where the concentration would affect competition beyond the territory of one Member State." Particular consideration should therefore be given to the likely locus of any competitive effects resulting from the transaction, and to how appropriate it would be for the Commission to scrutinise the operation.

27. It should in particular be assessed whether the case is genuinely cross-border in nature, having regard to elements such as its likely effects on competition and the investigative and enforcement powers likely to be required to address any such effects. In this regard, particular consideration should be given to whether the case is liable to have a potential impact on competition in one or more markets affected by the concentration. In any case, indications of possible competitive impact may be no more than preliminary in nature,[29] and would be without prejudice to the outcome of the investigation. Nor would it be necessary for the parties to demonstrate that the effect on competition is likely to be an adverse one.

28. Cases where the market(s) in which there may be a potential impact on competition is/are wider than national in geographic scope,[30] or where some of the potentially affected markets are wider than national and the main economic impact of the concentration is connected to such markets, are the most appropriate candidate cases for referral to the Commission. In such cases, as the competitive dynamics extend over territories reaching beyond national boundaries, and may consequently require investigative efforts in several countries as well as appropriate enforcement powers, the Commission is likely to be in the best position to carry out the investigation.

29. The Commission may be more appropriately placed to treat cases (including investigation, assessment and possible remedial action) that give rise to potential competition concerns in a series of national or narrower than national markets located in a number of different Member States.[31] The Commission is likely to be in the best position to carry out the investigation in such cases, given the desirability of ensuring consistent and efficient scrutiny across the different countries, of employing appropriate investigative powers, and of addressing any competition concerns by way of coherent remedies.

30. Similarly to what has been said above in relation to Article 4(4), the appropriateness of referring concentrations which, despite having a potentially significant impact on competition in a nation-wide market, nonetheless potentially engender substantial cross-border effects, will depend on the specific circumstances of the case. As both the Commission and Member States may be in an equally good position to deal with such cases, a considerable margin of discretion should be retained in deciding whether or not to refer such cases.

31. Consideration should also, to the extent possible, be given to whether the Commission is particularly well equipped to properly scrutinise the case, in particular having regard to factors such as specific expertise, or past experience in the sector concerned. The greater a merger's potential to affect competition beyond the territory of one Member State, the more likely it is that the Commission will be better equipped to conduct the investigation, particularly in terms of fact finding and enforcement powers.

32. Finally, the parties to the concentration might submit that, despite the apparent absence of an effect on competition, there is a compelling case for having the operation treated by the Commission, having regard in particular to factors such as the cost and time delay involved in submitting multiple Member State filings.[32]

Post-notification referrals

Referrals from the Commission to Member States pursuant to Article 9

33. Under Article 9 there are two options for a Member State wishing to request referral of a case following its notification to the Commission: Articles 9(2)(a) and 9(2)(b) respectively.

Article 9(2)(a)

Legal requirements

34. In order for a referral to be made to a Member State or States pursuant to Article 9(2)(a), the following legal requirements must be fulfilled:

(i) the concentration must *threaten to affect significantly competition in a market*; and
(ii) the market in question must be *within the requesting Member State, and present all the characteristics of a distinct market.*

35. As regards the *first criterion*, in essence a requesting Member State is required to demonstrate that, based on a preliminary analysis, there is a real risk that the transaction may have a significant adverse impact on competition, and thus that it deserves close scrutiny. Such preliminary indications may be in the nature of *prima facie* evidence of such a possible significant adverse impact, but would be without prejudice to the outcome of a full investigation.

36. As regards the second criterion, the Member State is required to show that a geographic market(s) in which competition is affected by the transaction in the manner just described (paragraph 35) is/are national, or narrower than national in scope.[33]

Other factors to be considered

37. Other than verification of the legal requirements, other factors should also be considered in assessing whether referral of a case is likely to be considered appropriate. This will involve an examination of the application of the guiding principles referred to above, and in particular whether the competition authority or authorities requesting the referral of the case is/are in the best position to deal with the case. To this end, consideration should be given in turn both to the likely locus of the competitive effects of the transaction and to how well equipped the NCA would be to scrutinise the operation (see above at paragraphs 19–23).

Article 9(2)(b)

Legal requirements

38. In order for a referral to be made to a Member State or States pursuant to Article 9(2)(b), the following legal requirements must be fulfilled:

(i) the concentration must *affect competition in a market*; and
(ii) the market in question must *be within the requesting Member State, present all the characteristics of a distinct market, and must not constitute a substantial part of the common market.*

39. As regards the *first criterion*, a requesting Member State is required to show, based on a preliminary analysis, that the concentration is liable to have an impact on competition in a market. Such preliminary indications may be in the nature of *prima facie* evidence of a possible adverse impact, but would be without prejudice to the outcome of a full investigation.

40. As to the *second criterion*, a requesting Member State is required to show not only that the market in which competition is affected by the operation in the manner just described (paragraph 38) constitutes a distinct market within a Member State, but also that the market in question does not constitute a substantial part of the common market. In this respect, based on the past practice and case-law,[34] it appears that such situations are generally limited to markets with a narrow geographic scope, within a Member State.

41. If these conditions are met, the Commission has an obligation to refer the case.

Referrals from Member States to the Commission pursuant to Article 22

Legal requirements

42. In order for a referral to be made by one or more Member States to the Commission pursuant to Article 22, two legal requirements must be fulfilled:

(i) the concentration must *affect trade between Member States*; and
(ii) it must *threaten to significantly affect competition within the territory of the Member State or States making the request*.

43. As to the *first criterion*, a concentration fulfils this requirement to the extent that it is liable to have some discernible influence on the pattern of trade between Member States.[35]

44. As to the *second criterion*, as under Article 9(2)(a), a referring Member State or States is/are required in essence to demonstrate that, based on a preliminary analysis, there is a real risk that the transaction may have a significant adverse impact on competition, and thus that it deserves close scrutiny. Such preliminary indications may be in the nature of *prima facie* evidence of such a possible significant adverse impact, but would be without prejudice to the outcome of a full investigation.

Other factors to be considered

45. As post-notification referrals to the Commission may entail additional cost and time delay for the merging parties, they should normally be limited to those cases which appear to present a real risk of negative effects on competition and trade between Member States, and where it appears that these would be best addressed at the Community level.[36] The categories of cases normally most appropriate for referral to the Commission pursuant to Article 22 are accordingly the following:

— cases which give rise to serious competition concerns in one or more markets which are wider than national in geographic scope, or where some of the potentially affected markets are wider than national, and where the main economic impact of the concentration is connected to such markets,

— cases which give rise to serious competition concerns in a series of national or narrower than national markets located in a number of Member States, in circumstances where coherent treatment of the case (regarding possible remedies, but also, in appropriate cases, the investigative efforts as such) is considered desirable, and where the main economic impact of the concentration is connected to such markets.

NOTES

11 See Article 5 of the EC Treaty.

12 See Recitals 11 and 14 to the Merger Regulation.

13 See Article 9(8) of the Merger Regulation; see also *Philips v Commission* (paragraph 343) where the Court of First Instance of the European Communities states that " . . . although the first subparagraph of Article 9(3) of Regulation (EEC) No 4064/89 confers on the Commission broad discretion as to whether or not to refer a concentration, it cannot decide to make such a referral if, when the Member State's request for referral is examined, it is clear, on the basis of a body of precise and coherent evidence, that such a referral cannot safeguard effective competition on the relevant market"; see also T-346/02 and T-347/02 *Cableuropa SA v Commission* of 30 September 2003, case not yet reported (paragraph 215). Circumstances relevant for the purpose of the Commission assessment include, *inter alia*, the fact that a Member State: (i) has specific laws for the control of concentrations on competition grounds and specialised bodies to ensure that these laws are implemented under the supervision of the national courts; (ii) has accurately identified the competition concerns raised by the concentration on the relevant markets in that Member State (see paragraphs 346–347 of *Philips v Commission*, cited above).

14 This may involve consideration of the relative cost, time delay, legal uncertainty and the risk of conflicting assessment which may be associated with the investigation, or a part of the investigation, being carried out by multiple authorities.

15 See Recital 11 of the Merger Regulation.

16 The Court of First Instance in *Philips v Commission* took the view, *obiter dictum*, that "fragmentation" of cases, while possible as a result of the application of Article 9, is "undesirable in view of the "one-stop-shop" principle on which Regulation (EEC) No 4064/89 is based". Moreover, the Court, while recognising that the risk of "inconsistent, or even irreconcilable" decisions by the Commission and Member States" is inherent in the referral system established by Article 9", made it clear that this is not, in its view, desirable. (See paragraphs 350 and 380).

17 This is consistent with the Commission's decision in cases M.2389 *Shell/DEA* and M.2533 *BP/E.ON* to refer to Germany all of the markets for downstream oil products. The Commission retained the parts of the cases involving upstream markets. Likewise, in M.2706 *P&O Princess/Carnival*, the Commission exercised its discretion not to refer a part of the case to the United Kingdom, because it wished to avoid a fragmentation of the case (See Commission press release of 11.4.2002, IP/02/552).

18 See Recital 11 of the Merger Regulation.

19 See Recital 14 to the Merger Regulation. This is of course subject to the parties having made a full and honest disclosure of all relevant facts in their request for a pre-filing referral.

20 See Recital 16, which states that "the undertakings concerned should not . . . be required to demonstrate that the effects of the concentration would be detrimental to competition".

21 The existence of "affected markets" within the meaning of Form RS would generally be considered sufficient to meet the requirements of Article 4(4). However, the parties can point to any factors which may be relevant for the competitive analysis of the case (market overlap, vertical integration, etc).

22 To this end, the requesting parties should consider those factors which are typically suggestive of national or narrower than national markets, such as, primarily, the product characteristics (eg low value of the product as opposed to significant costs of transport), specific characteristics of demand (eg end consumers sourcing in proximity to their centre of activity) and supply, significant variation of prices and market shares across countries, national consumer habits, different regulatory frameworks, taxation or other legislation. Further guidance can be found in the Commission Notice on the definition of the relevant market for the purposes of Community competition law (OJ C372, 9.12.1997, p 5).

23 See, for example, the Commission's referral of certain distinct oil storage markets for assessment by the French authorities in Cases M.1021 *Compagnie Nationale de Navigation-SOGELF*, M.1464 *Total/Petrofina*, and Case M.1628 *Totalfina/Elf Aquitaine*, Case M.1030 *Lafarge/Redland*, Case M.1220 *Alliance Unichem/Unifarma*, Case M.2760 *Nehlsen/Rethmann/SWB/Bremerhavener Energiewirtschaft*, and Case M.2154 *C3D/Rhone/Go-ahead*; Case M.2845 *Sogecable/Canal Satelite Digital/Vias Digital*.

24 See Case M.580 *ABB/Daimler Benz*, where the Commission did not accede to Germany's request for referral of a case under Article 9 in circumstances where, while the competition concerns were confined to German markets, the operation (which would create the largest supplier of railway equipment in the world) would have significant repercussions throughout Europe. See also Case M.*2434 Hidroelectrica del Cantabrico/EnBW/Grupo Vilar Mir*, where, despite a request by Spain to have the case referred under Article 9, the Commission pursued the investigation and adopted a decision pursuant to Article 8(2).

25 For some examples, see M.1383 *Exxon/Mobil*, where the Commission, despite the United Kingdom request to have the part of the concentration relating to the market for motor fuel retailing in North west of Scotland referred to it, pursued the investigation as the case required a single and coherent remedy package designed to address all the problematic issues in the sector concerned; see also M.2706 *P&O Princess/Carnival*, where, despite the fact that the UK authorities were assessing a rival bid by Royal Caribbean, the Commission did not accede to a request for a partial referral, so as to avoid a fragmentation of the case and secure a single investigation of the various national markets affected by the operation.

26 See M. 2898, *Le Roy Merlin/Brico*, M.1030, *Redland/Lafarge*, M. 1684, *Carrefour/Promodes*.

27 In Case M.330 *MacCormick/CPC/Rabobank/Ostmann*, the Commission referred a case to Germany, because it was better placed to investigate local conditions in 85,000 sales points in Germany; a referral to the Netherlands was made in Case M.1060 *Vendex/KBB*, because it was better placed to assess local consumer tastes and habits; See also Case M.1555 *Heineken/Cruzcampo*, Case M.2621 *SEB/Moulinex* (where consumer preferences and commercial and marketing practices were specific to the French market); Case M.2639 *Compass/Restorama/Rail Gourmet/Gourmet*, and Case M.2662 *Danish-Crown/Steff-Houlberg*.

28 In Case M.716 *Gehe/Lloyds Chemists*, for example, the Commission referred a case because Lloyds was also subject to another bid not falling under ECMR thresholds but being scrutinised by the UK authorities: the referral allowed both bids to be scrutinised by the same authority; in M.1001/M.1019 *Preussag/Hapag-Lloyd/TUI*, a referral was made to Germany of two transactions, which together with a third one notified in Germany, would present competition concerns: the referral ensured that all three operations were dealt with in like manner; in case M.2044 *Interbrew/Bass*, the Commission

referred the case to the UK authorities, because they were at the same time assessing Interbrew's acquisition of another brewer, Whitbread, and because of their experience in recent investigations in the same markets; similarly, see also Cases M.2760 *Nehlsen/Rethmann/SWB/Bremerhavener Energiewirtschaft*, M.2234 *Metsalilitto Osuuskunta/Vapo Oy/JV*, M.2495 *Haniel/Fels*, M.2881 *Koninklijke BAM NBM/HBG*, and M.2857/M.3075–3080 *ECS/IEH* and six other acquisitions by Electrabel of local distributors. In M.2706 *P&O Princess/Carnival*, however, despite the fact that the UK authorities were already assessing a rival bid by Royal Caribbean, the Commission did not accede to a request for a partial referral. The Commission had identified preliminary competition concerns in other national markets affected by the merger and thus wished to avoid a fragmentation of the case (See Commission press release of 11.4.2002, IP/02/552).

[29] The existence of "affected markets" within the meaning of Form RS would generally be considered sufficient. However, the parties can point to any factors which may be relevant for the competitive analysis of the case (market overlap, vertical integration, etc).

[30] See the joint referral by seven Member States to the Commission of a transaction affecting worldwide markets in M.2738 *GE/Unison*, and the joint referral by seven Member States to the Commission of a transaction affecting a Western European market in M.2698 *Promatech/Sulzer*; See also Principles on the application, by National Competition Authorities within the ECA network, of Article 22 of the EC Merger Regulation, a paper published by the European Competition Authorities (ECA), at paragraph 11.

[31] This may, for example, be the case in relation to operations where the affected markets, while national (or even narrower than national in scope for the purposes of a competition assessment), are nonetheless characterised by common Europe-wide or world-wide brands, by common Europe-wide or world-wide intellectual property rights, or by centralised manufacture or distribution – at least to the extent that such centralised manufacture or distribution would be likely to impact upon any remedial measures.

[32] See Recitals 12 and 16 of the Merger Regulation.

[33] See Commission notice on the definition of relevant market for the purposes of Community competition law (OJ C372, 9.12.1997, p 5).

[34] See Commission referrals granted under Article 9(2)(b) in: M.2446, *Govia/Connex South Central*, where the operation affected competition on specific railway routes in the London/Gatwick-Brighton area in the United Kingdom; in M.2730, *Connex/DNVBVG*, where the transaction affected competition in local public transport services in the Riesa area (Saxony, Germany); and in M. 3130, *Arla Foods/Express Diaries*, where the transaction affected competition in the market for the supply of bottled milk to doorstep deliverers in the London, Yorkshire and Lancashire regions of the United Kingdom. For the purpose of defining the notion of a non-substantial part of the common market, some guidance can also be found in the case-law relating to the application of Article 82 of EC Treaty. In that context, the Court of Justice has articulated quite a broad notion of what may constitute a substantial part of the common market, resorting *inter alia* to empirical evidence. In the case-law there can be found, for instance, indications essentially based on practical criteria such as "the pattern and volume of the production and consumption of the said product as well as the habits and economic opportunities of vendors and purchasers", see Case 40/73, *Suiker Unie v Commission*, [1975] ECR 1663. See also Case C-179/90, *Porto di Genova* [1991] ECR 5889, where the Port of Genova was considered as constituting a substantial part of the common market. In its case-law the Court has also stated that a series of separate markets may be regarded as together constituting a substantial part of the common market. See, for example, Case C-323/93, *Centre d'insémination de la Crespelle* [1994] ECR I-5077, paragraph. 17, where the Court stated "In this case, by making the operation of the insemination centres subject to authorization and providing that each centre should have the exclusive right to serve a defined area, the national legislation granted those centres exclusive rights. By thus establishing, in favour of those undertakings, a contiguous series of monopolies territorially limited but together covering the entire territory of a Member State, those national provisions create a dominant position, within the meaning of Article 86 of the Treaty, in a substantial part of the common market".

[35] See also, by analogy, the Commission Notice – Guidelines on the effect on trade concept contained in Articles 81 and 82 of the Treaty (OJ C101, 27.4.2004, p 81).

[36] See the joint referral by seven Member States to the Commission of a transaction affecting worldwide markets in M.2738 *GE/Unison*, and the joint referral by seven Member States to the Commission of a transaction affecting a Western European market in M.2698 *Promatech/Sulzer*; See also *Principles on the application, by National Competition Authorities within the ECA network, of Article 22 of the EC Merger Regulation*, a paper published by the European Competition Authorities (ECA), at paragraph 11.

III. MECHANICS OF THE REFERRAL SYSTEM

A. OVERVIEW OF THE REFERRAL SYSTEM

[4.631]

46. The Merger Regulation sets out the relevant legal rules for the functioning of the referral system. The rules contained in Article 4(4) and (5), Article 9 and Article 22 set out in detail the various steps required for a case to be referred from the Commission to Member States and vice versa.

47. Each of the four relevant referral provisions establishes a self-contained mechanism for the referral of a given category of concentration. The provisions can be categorised in the following way:

(a) Pre-notification referrals:
   (i) From the Commission to Member States (Article 4(4))
   (ii) From Member States to the Commission (Article 4(5))
(b) Post-notification referrals:
   (i) From the Commission to Member States (Article 9)
   (ii) From Member States to the Commission (Article 22).

48. The flowcharts in Annex I to this Notice describe in graphical form the various procedural steps to be followed in the referral mechanisms set out in Articles 4(4) and (5), Article 9 and Article 22.

Pre-notification referrals

49. Pre-notification referrals can only be requested by the undertakings concerned.[37] It is for the undertakings concerned to verify whether the concentration meets the criteria specified in Article 4(4) (that the concentration has a Community dimension but may significantly affect competition in a distinct market within a Member State) or Article 4(5) (that the concentration does not have a Community dimension but is capable of being reviewed under the national competition laws of at least three Member States). The undertakings concerned may then decide to request a referral to or from the Commission by submitting a reasoned request on Form RS. The request is transmitted without delay by the Commission to all Member States. The remainder of the process differs under Article 4(4) and Article 4(5).

- Under Article 4(4), the Member State or States concerned[38] have 15 working days from the date they receive the submission to express agreement or disagreement with the request. Silence on the part of a Member State is deemed to constitute agreement.[39] If the Member State or States concerned agree to the referral, the Commission has an additional period of approximately 10 working days (25 working days from the date the Commission received Form RS) in which it may decide to refer the case. Silence on the part of the Commission is deemed to constitute assent. If the Commission assents, the case (or one or more parts thereof) is referred to the Member States or States as requested by the undertakings concerned. If the referral is made, the Member State or States concerned apply their national law to the referred part of the case.[40] Articles 9(6) to 9(9) apply.
- Under Article 4(5), the Member States concerned[41] have 15 working days from the date they receive the submission to express agreement or disagreement with the request. At the end of that period, the Commission checks whether any Member State competent to examine the concentration under its national competition law has expressed disagreement. If there is no expression of disagreement by any such competent Member State, the case is deemed to acquire a Community dimension and is thus referred to the Commission which has exclusive jurisdiction over it. It is then for the parties to notify the case to the Commission, using Form CO. On the other hand, if one or more competent Member States have expressed their disagreement, the Commission informs all Member States and the undertakings concerned without delay of any such expression of disagreement and the referral process ends. It is then for the parties to comply with any applicable national notification rules.

Post-notification referrals

50. Pursuant to Article 9(2) and Article 22(1), post-notification referrals are triggered by Member States either on their own initiative or following an invitation by the Commission pursuant to Article 9(2) and Article 22(5) respectively. The procedures differ according to whether the referral is from or to the Commission.

- Under Article 9, a Member State may request that the Commission refer to it a concentration with Community dimension, or a part thereof, which has been notified to the Commission and which threatens to significantly affect competition within a distinct market within that Member State (Article 9(2)(a)), or which affects such a distinct market not constituting a substantial part of the common market (Article 9(2)(b)). The request must be made within 15 working days from the date the Member State received a copy of Form CO. The Commission must first verify whether those legal criteria are met. It may then decide to refer the case, or a part thereof, exercising its administrative discretion. In the case of a referral request made pursuant to Article 9(2)(b), the Commission must (ie has no discretion) make the referral if the legal criteria are met. The decision must be taken within 35 working days from notification or, where the Commission has initiated proceedings, within 65 working days.[42] If the referral is made, the Member State concerned applies its own national competition law, subject only to Article 9(6) and (8).
- Under Article 22, a Member State may request that the Commission examine a concentration which has no Community dimension but which affects trade between Member States and threatens to significantly affect competition within its territory. The request must be made within 15 working days from the date of national notification or, where no notification is required, the date when the concentration was "made known"[43] to the Member State concerned. The Commission transmits the request to all Member States. Any other Member States can decide to join the request[44] within a period of 15 working days from the date they receive a copy of the initial request. All national time limits relating to the concentration are suspended a decision has been taken as to where it will be examined; a Member State can re-start the national time limits before the expiry of the 15 working day period by informing the Commission and the merging parties that it does not wish to join the request. At the latest 10 working days following the expiry of the 15 working day period, the Commission must decide whether to accept the case from the requesting Member State(s). If the Commission accepts jurisdiction, national proceedings in the referring Member State(s) are terminated and the Commission examines the case pursuant to Article 22(4) of the Merger Regulation on behalf of the requesting State(s).[45] Non-requesting States can continue to apply national law.

51. The following section of the Notice focuses on a number of detailed elements of the system with the aim in particular of providing further guidance to undertakings contemplating making requests at the pre-notification stage, or who may be party to transactions subject to the possibility of post-notification referral.

B. DETAILS OF THE REFERRAL MECHANISM

52. This section of this Notice provides guidance regarding certain aspects of the functioning of the referral system set out in Article 4(4) and(5), Article 9 and Article 22 of the Merger Regulation.

1. The network of competition authorities

53. Article 19(2) of the Merger Regulation provides that the Commission is to carry out the procedures set out in that Regulation in close and constant liaison with the competent authorities of the Member States (the NCAs). Cooperation and dialogue between the Commission and the NCAs, and between the NCAs themselves, is particularly important in the case of concentrations which are subject to the referral system set out in the Merger Regulation.

54. According to Recital 14 to the Merger Regulation, "the Commission and the NCAs should form together a network of public authorities, applying their respective competences in close cooperation using efficient arrangements for information sharing and consultation with a view to ensuring that a case is dealt with by the most appropriate authority, in the light of the principle of subsidiarity, and with a view to ensuring that multiple notifications of a given concentration are avoided to the greatest extent possible".

55. The network should ensure the efficient re-attribution of concentrations according to the principles described in section II above. This involves facilitating the smooth operation of the pre-notification referral mechanism, as well as providing, to the extent foreseeable, a system whereby potential post-notification referral requests are identified as soon as possible.[46]

56. Pursuant to Article 4(4) and (5), the Commission must transmit reasoned requests made by the undertakings concerned "without delay".[47] The Commission will endeavour to transmit such documents on the working day following that on which they are received or issued. Information within the network will be exchanged by various means, depending on the circumstances: Email, surface mail, courier, fax, telephone. It should be noted that for sensitive information or confidential information exchanges will be carried out by secure Email or by any other protected means of communication between these contact points.

57. All members of the network, including the Commission and all NCAs, their officials and other servants, and other persons working under the supervision of those authorities as well as officials and civil servants of other authorities of the Member States, will be bound by the professional secrecy obligations set out in Article 17 of the Merger Regulation. They must not disclose non-public information they have acquired through the application of the Merger Regulation, unless the natural or legal person who provided that information has consented to its disclosure.

58. Consultations and exchanges within the network is a matter between public enforcement agencies and do not alter any rights or obligations arising from Community or national law for companies. Each competition authority remains fully responsible for ensuring that due process is observed in the cases it deals with.

2. Triggering the pre-notification referral system; information to be provided by the requesting parties

59. For the referral system to work swiftly and smoothly, it is crucial that the requesting parties, provide complete and accurate information, whenever required, in a timely fashion and in the most efficient way possible. Legal requirements concerning the information to be provided and the consequences of providing incorrect, incomplete or misleading information are set out in the Merger Regulation, Regulation (EC) No 802/2004 (hereinafter "the Merger Implementing Regulation") and Form RS.[48]

60. Form RS states that all information submitted in a reasoned submission must be correct and complete. If parties submit incorrect or incomplete information, the Commission has the power to either adopt a decision pursuant to Article 6(1)(a) of the Merger Regulation (where failure to fulfil the conditions of Article 4(5) comes to its attention during the course of the investigation), or to revoke any decision it adopts pursuant to Article 6 or Article 8, following an Article 4(5) referral, pursuant to Article 6(3)(a) or 8(6)(a) of the Merger Regulation. Following the adoption of a decision pursuant to Article 6(1)(a) or following revocation, national competition laws would once again be applicable to the transaction. In the case of referrals under Article 4(4) made on the basis of incorrect or incomplete information, the Commission may require a notification pursuant to Article 4(1). In addition, the Commission has the power to impose fines under Article 14(1)(a) of the Merger Regulation. Finally, parties should also be aware that, if a referral is made on the basis of incorrect or incomplete information included in Form RS, the Commission and/or the Member States may consider making a post-notification referral reversing a pre-notification referral based on such incorrect or incomplete information.[49]

61. When providing information on Form RS or generally in making a request for a pre-notification referral, it is not envisaged or necessary for the undertakings concerned to show that their concentration will lead to detrimental effects on competition.[50] They should, however, provide as much information as possible showing clearly in what way the concentration meets the relevant legal criteria set out in Article 4(4) and (5) and why the concentration would be most appropriately dealt with by the competition authority or authorities specified in the request. The Merger Regulation does not require publication of the fact that a Form RS has been lodged, and it is not intended to do so. A non-public transaction can consequently be the subject of a pre-notification referral request.

62. Even though, according to the Merger Implementing Regulation, the Commission will accept Form RS in any official Community language, undertakings concerned providing information which is to be distributed to the network are strongly encouraged to use a language which will be understood by all addressees of the information. This will facilitate Member State treatment of such requests. Moreover, as regards requests for referral to a Member State or States, the requesting parties are strongly encouraged to include a copy of the request in the language(s) of the Member State(s) to which the referral is being requested.

63. Beyond the legal requirements specified in Form RS, the undertakings concerned should be prepared to provide additional information, if required, and to discuss the matter with the Commission and the NCAs in a frank and open manner in order to enable the Commission and the NCAs to assess whether the concentration in question should be the subject of referral.

64. Informal contacts between merging parties contemplating lodging a pre-filing referral request, on the one hand, and the Commission and/or Member State authorities, on the other, are actively encouraged, even following the submission of Form RS. The Commission is committed to providing informal, early guidance to firms wishing to use the pre-notification referrals system set out in Article 4(4) and (5) of the Merger Regulation.[51]

3. Concentrations eligible for referral

65. Only concentrations within the meaning of Article 3 of the Merger Regulation are eligible for referral pursuant to Article 4(5) and Article 22. Only concentrations falling within the ambit of the relevant national competition laws for the control of mergers are eligible for referral pursuant to Article 4(4) and Article 9.[52]

66. Pre-filing referral requests pursuant to Article 4(4) and (5) of the Merger Regulation must concern concentrations the plans for which are sufficiently concrete. In that regard, there must at least exist a good faith intention to merge on the part of the undertakings concerned, or, in the case of a public bid, at least a public announcement of an intention to make such a bid.[53]

4. The concept of "prior to notification" under Article 4(4) and (5)

67. Article 4(4) and (5) only apply at the pre-notification stage.

68. Article 4(4) specifies that the undertakings concerned may make a referral request by means of reasoned submission (Form RS), "prior to the notification of a concentration within the meaning of paragraph 1". This means that the request can only be made where no Form CO has been submitted pursuant to Article 4(1).

69. Likewise, Article 4(5) specifies that the request may be made "before any notification to the competent national authorities". This means that the concentration in question must not have been formally notified in any Member State jurisdiction for that provision to apply. Even one notification anywhere in the Community will preclude the undertakings concerned from triggering the mechanism of Article 4(5). In the Commission's view, no penalty should be imposed for non-notification of a transaction at the national level while a request pursuant to Article 4(5) is pending.

5. The concept of a "concentration capable of being reviewed under national competition law" and the concept of "competent Member State" in Article 4(5)

70. Article 4(5) enables the undertakings concerned to request a pre-notification referral of a concentration which does not have a Community dimension and which is "capable of being reviewed under the national competition laws of at least three Member States".

71. "Capable of being reviewed" or reviewable should be interpreted as meaning a concentration which falls within the jurisdiction of a Member State under its national competition law for the control of mergers. There is no need for a mandatory notification requirement, ie it is not necessary for the concentration to be required to be notified under national law.[54]

72. Pursuant to the third and fourth subparagraphs of Article 4(5), where at least one Member State "competent to examine the concentration under its national competition law" has expressed its disagreement with the referral, the case must not be referred. A "competent" Member State is one where the concentration is reviewable and which therefore has the power to examine the concentration under its national competition law.

73. All Member States, and not only those "competent" to review the case, receive a copy of the Form RS. However, only Member States "competent" to review the case are counted for the purposes of the third and fourth subparagraphs of Article 4(5). Pursuant to the third subparagraph of Article 4(5), "competent" Member States have 15 working days from the date they receive the Form RS to express their agreement or disagreement with the referral. If they all agree, the case will be deemed to acquire a Community dimension pursuant to the fifth subparagraph of Article 4(5). According to the fourth subparagraph of Article 4(5), by contrast, if even only one "competent" Member State disagrees, no referral will take place from any Member State.

74. Given the above mechanism, it is crucial to the smooth operation of Article 4(5) that all Member States where the case is reviewable under national competition law, and which are hence "competent" to examine the case under national competition law, are identified correctly. Form RS therefore requires the undertakings concerned to provide sufficient information to enable each and every Member State to identify whether or not it is competent to review the concentration pursuant to its own national competition law.

75. In situations where Form RS has been filled in correctly, no complications should arise. The undertakings concerned will have identified correctly all Member States which are competent to review the case. In situations, however, where the undertakings concerned have not filled in Form RS correctly, or where there is a genuine disagreement as to which Member States are "competent" to review the case, complications may arise.

- Within the period of 15 working days provided for in the third subparagraph of Article 4(5), a Member State which is not identified in Form RS as being competent may inform the Commission that it is competent and may, like any other competent Member State, express its agreement or disagreement with the referral.
- Likewise, within the period of 15 working days provided for in the third subparagraph of Article 4(5), a Member State which has been identified as competent in Form RS may inform the Commission that it is not "competent". That Member State would then be disregarded for the purposes of Article 4(5).

76. Once the period of 15 working days has expired without any disagreement having been expressed, the referral, will be considered valid. This ensures the validity of Commission decisions taken under Articles 6 or 8 of the Merger Regulation following an Article 4(5) referral.

77. This is not to say, however, that undertakings concerned can abuse the system by negligently or intentionally providing incorrect information, including as regards the reviewability of the concentration in the Member States, on Form RS. As noted at paragraph 60 above, the Commission may take measures to rectify the situation and to deter such violations. The undertakings concerned should also be aware that, in such circumstances, where a referral has been made on the basis of incorrect or incomplete information, a Member State which believes it was competent to deal with the case but did not have the opportunity to veto the referral due to incorrect information being supplied, may request a post-notification referral.

6. Notification and Publication of Decisions

78. According to the fourth subparagraph of Article 4(4), the fourth subparagraph of Article 4(5), Article 9(1) and the second subparagraph of Article 22(3), the Commission is obliged to inform the undertakings or persons concerned and all Member States of any decision taken pursuant to those provisions as to the referral of a concentration.

79. The information will be provided by means of a letter addressed to the undertakings concerned (or for decisions adopted pursuant to Article 9(1) or Article 22(3), a letter addressed to the Member State concerned). All Member States will receive a copy thereof.

80. There is no requirement that such decisions be published in the Official Journal of the European Union.[55] The Commission will, however, give adequate publicity to such decisions on DG Competition's website, subject to confidentiality requirements.

7. Article 9(6)

81. Article 9(6) provides that, when the Commission refers a notified concentration to a Member State in accordance with Article 4(4) or Article 9(3), the NCA concerned must deal with the case "without undue delay". Accordingly, the competent authority concerned should deal as expeditiously as possible with the case under national law.

82. In addition, Article 9(6) provides that the competent national authority must, within 45 working days after the Commission's referral or following receipt of a notification at the national level if requested inform the undertakings concerned of the result of the "preliminary competition assessment" and what "further action", if any, it proposes to take. Accordingly, within 45 working days after the referral or notification, as appropriate, the merging parties should be provided with sufficient information to enable them to understand the nature of any preliminary competition concerns the authority may have and be informed of the likely extent and duration of the investigation. The Member State concerned may only exceptionally suspend this time limit, where necessary information has not been provided to it by the undertakings concerned as required under its national competition law.

NOTES

37 The term "undertakings concerned" includes "persons" within the meaning of Article 3(1)(b).

38 The Member State or States concerned are the ones identified in Form RS to which the case will be referred if the request is granted.

39 This mechanism is an essential feature of all referral procedures set out in the Merger Regulation. The mechanism may be termed "positive silence" or non-opposition: that is to say that failure to take a decision on the part of the Commission or a Member State will be deemed to constitute the taking of a positive decision. This mechanism was already a feature of Regulation (EEC) No 4064/89, in Article 9(5). It is now included in Article 4(4) (second and fourth sub-paragraphs), Article 4(5) (fourth sub-paragraph), Article 9(5) and Article 22(3) (first sub-paragraph, last sentence) of the Merger Regulation. The positive silence mechanism is, however, not applicable with regard to decisions by Member States to join a request under Article 22(2).

40 Article 4(4) allows merging parties to request partial or full referrals. The Commission and Member States must either accede to or refuse the request, and may not vary its scope by, for example, referring only a part of case when a referral of the whole of the case had been requested. In the case of a partial referral, the Member State concerned will apply its national competition law to the referred part of the case. For the remainder of the case, the Merger Regulation will continue to apply in the normal way, that is the undertakings concerned will be obliged to make a notification of the non-referred part of the concentration on Form CO pursuant to Article 4(1) of the Merger Regulation. By contrast, if the whole of the case is referred to a Member State, Article 4(4) final subparagraph specifies that there will be no obligation to notify the case also to the Commission. The case will thus not be examined by the Commission. The Member State concerned will apply its national law to the whole of the case; no other Member State can apply national competition law to the concentration in question.

41 That is, those that would be competent to review the case under their national competition law in the absence of a referral. For the concept of "competent to review the case", see section B5 below.

42 As regards cases where the Commission takes preparatory steps within 65 working days, see Article 9(4)(b) and (5).

43 The notion of "made known", derived from the wording of Article 22, should in this context be interpreted as implying sufficient information to make a preliminary assessment as to the existence of the criteria for the making of a referral request pursuant to Article 22.

44 It should be noted that Article 22 enables a Member State to join the initial request even if the concentration has not yet been notified to it. However, Member States may be unable to do so if they have not yet received the necessary information from the merging parties at the time of being informed by the Commission that a referral request has been lodged by another Member State. Notwithstanding the Member State's ability to contact the merging parties in order to verify whether they are competent to review any particular transaction, the notifying parties are therefore strongly encouraged to file, where feasible, their notification to all competent Member States simultaneously.

45 Where the Commission examines a concentration on behalf of one or more Member States pursuant to Article 22, it can adopt all the substantive decisions provided for in Articles 6 and 8 of the Merger Regulation. This is established in Article 22(4) of that Regulation. It is to be noted that the Commission examines the concentration upon the request of and on behalf of the requesting Member States. This provision should therefore be interpreted as requiring the Commission to examine the impact of the concentration within the territory of those Member States. The Commission will not examine the effects of the concentration in the territory of Member States which have not joined the request unless this examination is necessary for the assessment of the effects of the concentration within the territory of the requesting Member States (for example, where the geographic market extends beyond the territory/or territories of the requesting Member State(s).

46 Advance knowledge of the possibility of a referral request might, for example, be taken into account by the Commission in deciding not to accede to a request for derogation from the suspensive effect pursuant to Article 7(3) of the Merger Regulation.

47 It should be noted that, as provided for in Article 19(1) of the Merger Regulation, the Commission is also under an obligation to transmit to the NCAs copies of notifications and of the most important documents lodged with or issued by the Commission.

48 Form RS is annexed to Commission Regulation (EC) No 802/2004 of 7 April 2004 implementing Council Regulation (EC) No 139/2004 on the control of concentrations between undertakings (OJ L133, 30.4.2004, p 1).

49 This would be the appropriate "remedy" where the requesting parties have submitted incorrect or incomplete information not affecting fulfilment of the conditions of Article 4(5), which comes to the Commission's attention during the course of the investigation.

50 See Recital 16 to the Merger Regulation.

51 A request for derogation from the suspensive effect pursuant to Article 7(3) of the Merger Regulation would normally be inconsistent with an intention to make a pre-notification referral request pursuant to Article 4(4).

52 By contrast, the reference to "national legislation on competition" in Article 21(3) and Article 22(3) should be understood as referring to all aspects of national competition law.

53 See Recital 34 to, and Article 4(1) of, the Merger Regulation.

54 Even in circumstances where a notification is voluntary *de jure*, the parties may in practice wish or be expected to file a notification.

55 Pursuant to Article 20 of the Merger Regulation this is only required for decisions taken under Article 8(1)–(6) and Articles 14 and 15.

IV. FINAL REMARKS

[4.632]

83. This Notice will be the subject of periodic review, in particular following any revision of the referral provisions in the Merger Regulation. In that regard, it should be noted that, according to Article 4(6) of the Merger Regulation, the Commission must report to the Council on the operation of the pre-notification referral provisions in Article 4(4) and (5), by 1 July 2009.

84. This Notice is without prejudice to any interpretation of the applicable Treaty and regulatory provisions by the Court of First Instance and the Court of Justice of the European Communities.

ANNEXES: REFERRAL CHARTS

ARTICLE 4(4) CONCENTRATION WITH COMMUNITY DIMENSION

[4.633]

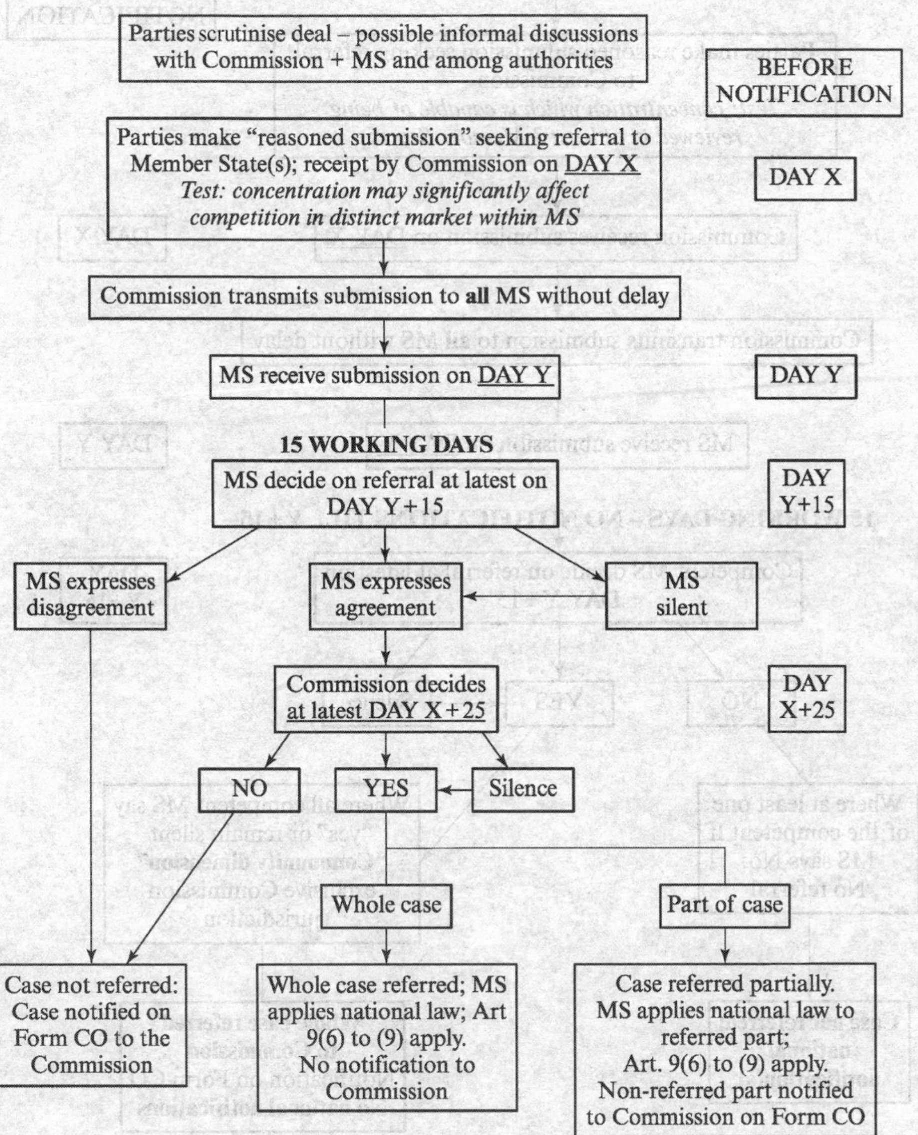

ARTICLE 4(5) CONCENTRATION WITHOUT COMMUNITY DIMENSION REVIEWABLE IN AT LEAST THREE MS UNDER NATIONAL LAW

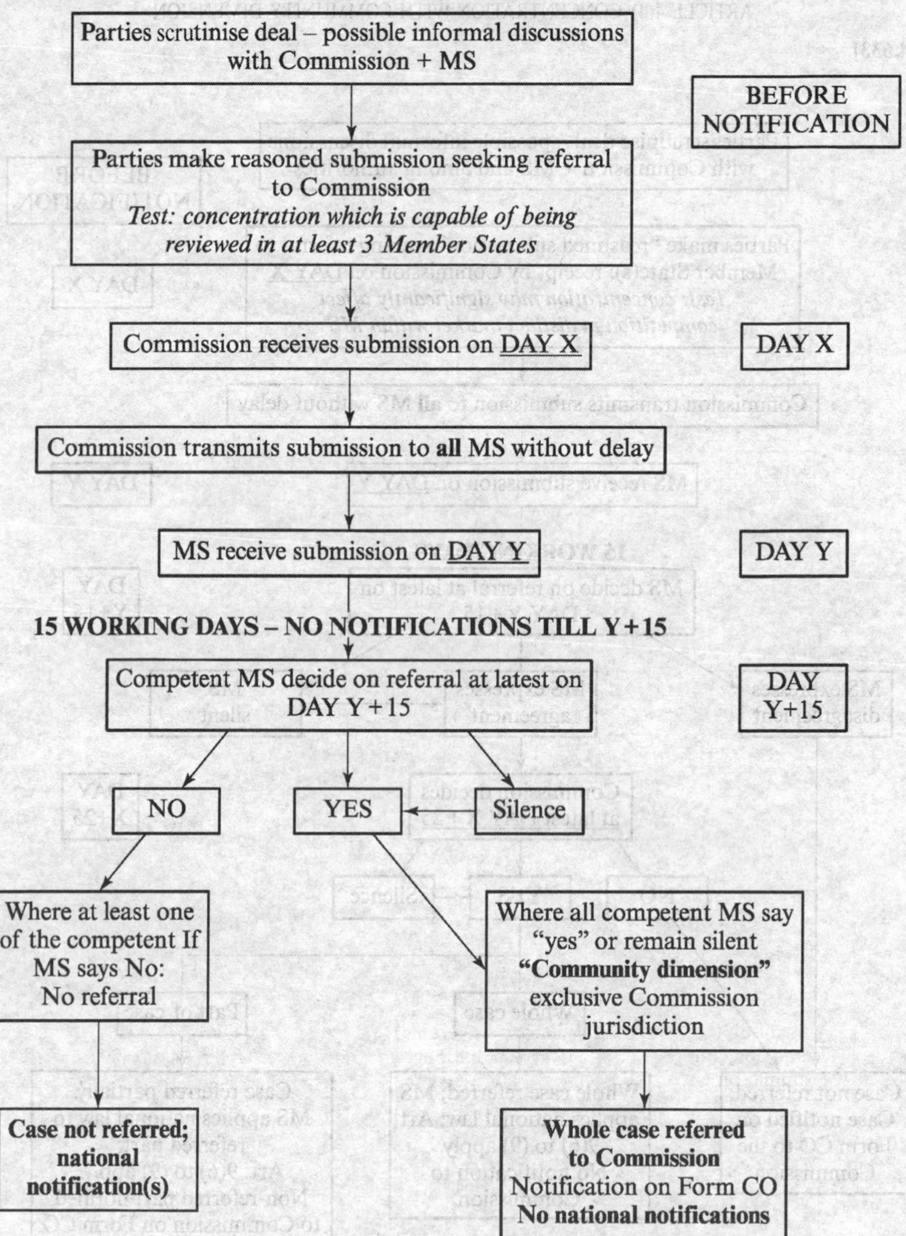

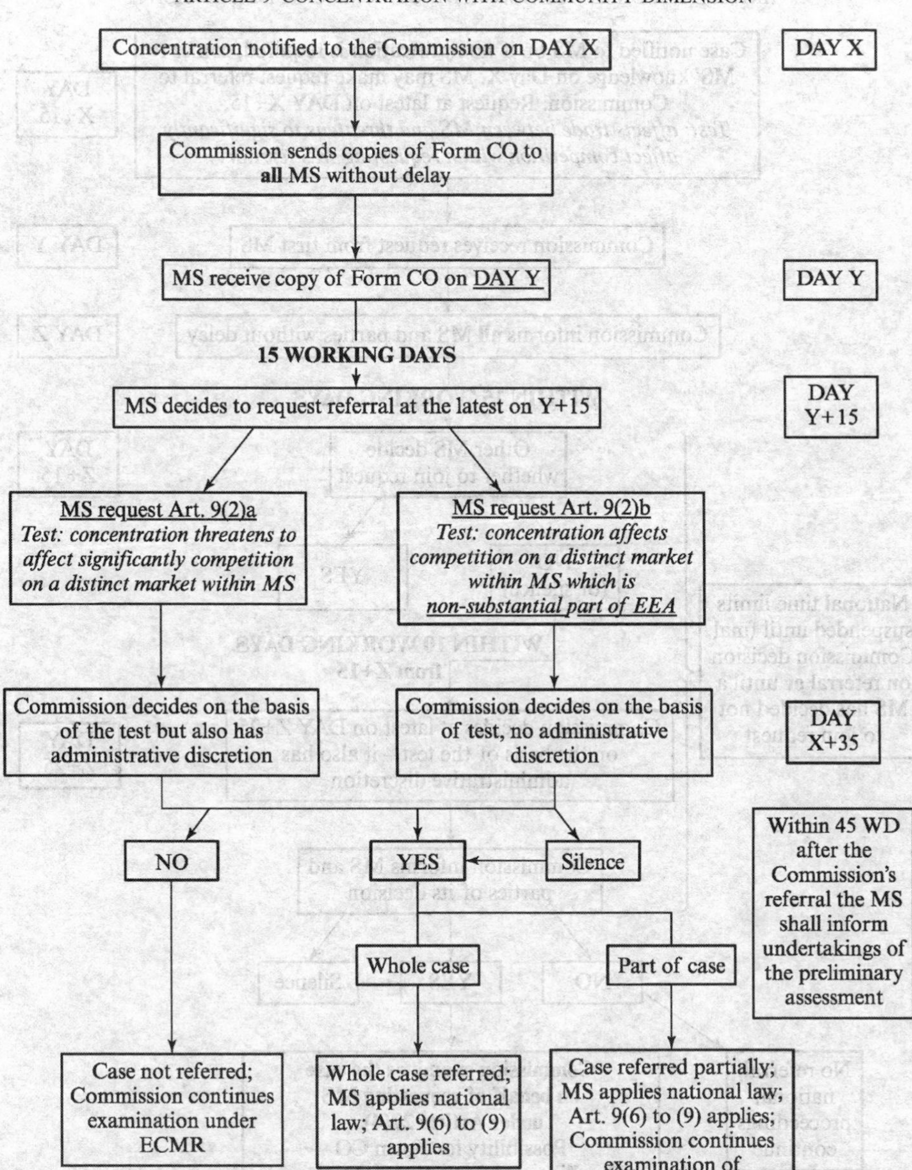
ARTICLE 9 CONCENTRATION WITH COMMUNITY DIMENSION
Concentration notified to the Commission on DAY X
DAY X
Commission sends copies of Form CO to all MS without delay
MS receive copy of Form CO on DAY Y
DAY Y
15 WORKING DAYS
MS decides to request referral at the latest on Y+15
DAY Y+15
MS request Art. 9(2)a
Test: concentration threatens to affect significantly competition on a distinct market within MS
MS request Art. 9(2)b
Test: concentration affects competition on a distinct market within MS which is non-substantial part of EEA
Commission decides on the basis of the test but also has administrative discretion
Commission decides on the basis of test, no administrative discretion
DAY X+35
NO
YES
Silence
Within 45 WD after the Commission's referral the MS shall inform undertakings of the preliminary assessment
Whole case
Part of case
Case not referred; Commission continues examination under ECMR
Whole case referred; MS applies national law; Art. 9(6) to (9) applies
Case referred partially; MS applies national law; Art. 9(6) to (9) applies; Commission continues examination of non-referred part

ARTICLE 22 CONCENTRATION WITHOUT COMMUNITY DIMENSION

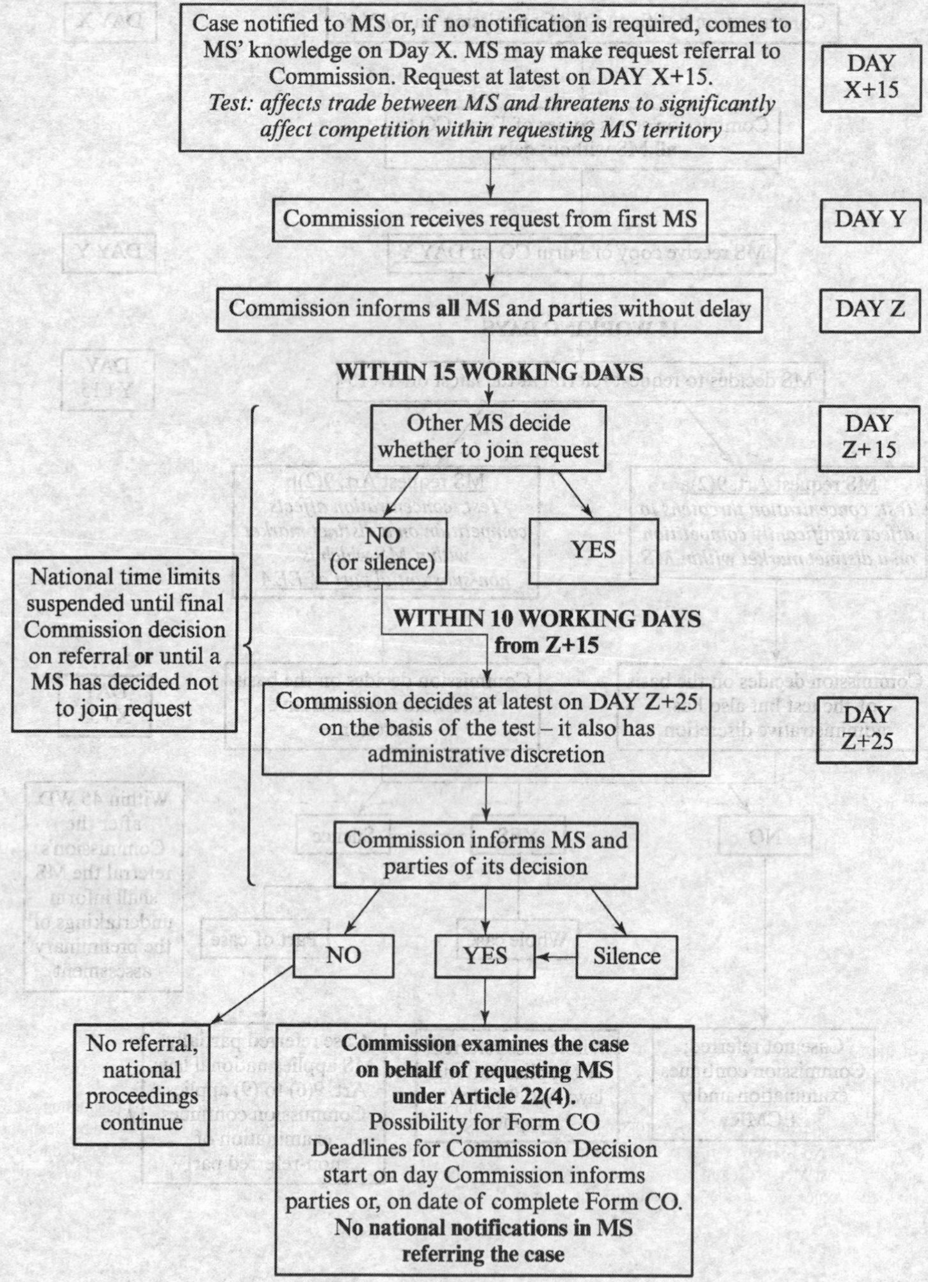

COMMISSION NOTICE

(2008/C95/01)

Commission Consolidated Jurisdictional Notice under Council Regulation (EC) No 139/2004 on the control of concentrations between undertakings

[4.634]

NOTES

Date of publication in OJ: OJ C95, 16.4.2008, p 1.

Note that Council Regulation (EC) No 139/2004 is repealed, in relation to the UK, by the Competition (Amendment etc) (EU Exit) Regulations 2019, SI 2019/93, reg 63, Sch 3, para 1, as from IP completion day (as defined in the European Union (Withdrawal Agreement) Act 2020, s 39) (for transitional provisions and savings in relation to the operation of the 2019 Regulations, see Sch 4 to those Regulations at **[7.69]** et seq).

Note: with effect from 1 December 2009, the EC Treaty was replaced by the Treaty on the Functioning of the European Union. References in this document to provisions of the EC Treaty should be construed accordingly.

A. INTRODUCTION

[4.635]

1. The purpose of this Notice is to provide guidance as to jurisdictional issues under Council Regulation (EC) No 139/2004, OJ L24, 29.1.2003, page 1 (the Merger Regulation).[1] This formal guidance should enable firms to establish more quickly, in advance of any contact with the Commission, whether and to what extent their operations may be covered by Community control of concentrations.

2. This Notice replaces the Notice on the concept of concentration,[2] the Notice on the concept of full-function joint ventures,[3] the Notice on the concept of undertakings concerned[4] and the Notice on calculation of turnover.[5]

3. This Notice deals with the concepts of a concentration and of a full-function joint venture, undertakings concerned and the calculation of turnover as set out in Articles 1, 3 and 5 of the Merger Regulation. Issues concerning referrals are dealt with in the Notice on referrals.[6] The Commission's interpretation of Articles 1, 3 and 5 in the present Notice is without prejudice to the interpretation which may be given by the Court of Justice or by the Court of First Instance of the European Communities.

4. The guidance set out in this Notice reflects the Commission's experience in applying the recast Merger Regulation and the former Merger Regulation since the latter entered into force on 21 September 1990. The general principles governing the issues dealt with in this Notice have not been changed by the entry into force of Regulation (EC) No 139/2004, but where changes have occurred, the Notice deals with them explicitly. The principles contained in the Notice will be applied and further developed by the Commission in individual cases.

5. According to Article 1, the Merger Regulation only applies to operations that satisfy two conditions. First, there must be a concentration of two or more undertakings within the meaning of Article 3 of the Merger Regulation. Secondly, the turnover of the undertakings concerned, calculated in accordance with Article 5, must satisfy the thresholds set out in Article 1 of the Regulation. The notion of a concentration (including the particular requirements for joint ventures), as the first condition, is dealt with under Part B; the identification of undertakings concerned and the calculation of their turnover as relevant for the second condition are dealt with under Part C.

6. The Commission addresses the question of its jurisdiction over a concentration in decisions according to Article 6 of the Merger Regulation.[7]

NOTES

1 Where it is necessary in this Notice to distinguish between Regulation 139/2004 and Council Regulation (EEC) No 4064/89 (OJ L395, 30.12.1989, corrected version in OJ L257, 21.9.1990, p 13, Regulation last amended by Regulation (EC) No 1310/97, OJ L180, 9.7.1997, p 1, corrigendum in OJ L40, 13.2.1998, p 17), the former will be referred to as the "recast Merger Regulation" whereas the latter will be referred to as the "former Merger Regulation". Articles without reference refer to the recast Merger Regulation.

2 OJ C66, 2.3.1998, p 5.

3 OJ C66, 2.3.1998, p 1.

4 OJ C66, 2.3.1998, p 14.

5 OJ C66, 2.3.1998, p 25.

6 OJ C56, 5.3.2005, p 2.

7 See also opinion of AG Kokott in Case C-202/06 *Cementbouw v Commission* of 26 April 2007, paragraph 56 (not yet reported).

B. THE CONCEPT OF CONCENTRATION

[4.636]

7. According to Article 3(1) of the Merger Regulation, a concentration only covers operations where a change of control in the undertakings concerned occurs on a lasting basis. Recital 20 in the preamble to the Merger Regulation further explains that the concept of concentration is intended to relate to operations which bring about a lasting change in the structure of the market. Because the test in Article 3 is centred on the concept of control, the existence of a concentration is to a great extent determined by qualitative rather than quantitative criteria.

8. Article 3(1) of the Merger Regulation defines two categories of concentrations:

— those arising from a merger between previously independent undertakings (point (a));

— those arising from an acquisition of control (point (b)).

These are treated respectively in Sections I and II below.

I. MERGERS BETWEEN PREVIOUSLY INDEPENDENT UNDERTAKINGS

[4.637]

9. A merger within the meaning of Article 3(1)(a) of the Merger Regulation occurs when two or more independent undertakings amalgamate into a new undertaking and cease to exist as separate legal entities. A merger may also occur when an undertaking is absorbed by another, the latter retaining its legal identity while the former ceases to exist as a legal entity.[8]

10. A merger within the meaning of Article 3(1)(a) may also occur where, in the absence of a legal merger, the combining of the activities of previously independent undertakings results in the creation of a single economic unit.[9] This may arise in particular where two or more undertakings, while retaining their individual legal personalities, establish contractually a common economic management[10] or the structure of a dual listed company.[11] If this leads to a *de facto* amalgamation of the undertakings concerned into a single economic unit, the operation is considered to be a merger. A prerequisite for the determination of such a *de facto* merger is the existence of a permanent, single economic management. Other relevant factors may include internal profit and loss compensation or a revenue distribution as between the various entities within the group, and their joint liability or external risk sharing. The *de facto* amalgamation may be solely based on contractual arrangements,[12] but it can also be reinforced by cross-shareholdings between the undertakings forming the economic unit.

II. ACQUISITION OF CONTROL

1. Concept of control

1.1. Person or undertaking acquiring control

[4.638]

11. Article 3(1)(b) provides that a concentration occurs in the case of an acquisition of control. Such control may be acquired by one undertaking acting alone or by several undertakings acting jointly.

Person controlling another undertaking

12. Control may also be acquired by a person in circumstances where that person already controls (whether solely or jointly) at least one other undertaking or, alternatively, by a combination of persons (which control another undertaking) and undertakings. The term "person" in this context extends to public bodies[13] and private entities, as well as natural persons. Acquisitions of control by natural persons are only considered to bring about a lasting change in the structure of the undertakings concerned if those natural persons carry out further economic activities on their own account or if they control at least one other undertaking.[14]

Acquirer of control

13. Control is normally acquired by persons or undertakings which are the holders of the rights or are entitled to rights conferring control under the contracts concerned (Article 3(3)(a)). However, there are also situations where the formal holder of a controlling interest differs from the person or undertaking having in fact the real power to exercise the rights resulting from this interest. This may be the case, for example, where an undertaking uses another person or undertaking for the acquisition of a controlling interest and has the power to exercise the rights conferring control through this person or undertaking, ie the latter is formally the holder of the rights, but acts only as a vehicle. In such a situation, control is acquired by the undertaking which in reality is behind the operation and in fact enjoys the power to control the target undertaking (Article 3(3)(b)). The Court of First Instance concluded from this provision that control held by commercial companies can be attributed to their exclusive shareholder, their majority shareholders or to those jointly controlling the companies since these companies comply in any event with the decisions of those shareholders.[15] A controlling shareholding which is held by different entities in a group is normally attributed to the undertaking exercising control over the different formal holders of the rights. In other cases, the evidence needed to establish this type of indirect control may include, either separately or in combination and to be assessed on a case-by-case basis, factors such as shareholdings, contractual relations, source of financing or family links.[16]

Acquisition of control by investment funds

14. Specific issues may arise in the case of acquisitions of control by investment funds. The Commission will analyse structures involving investment funds on a case-by-case basis, but some general features of such structures can be set out on the basis of the Commission's past experience.

15. Investment funds are often set up in the legal form of limited partnerships, in which the investors participate as limited partners and normally do not exercise control, either individually or collectively. The investment funds usually acquire the shares and voting rights which confer control over the portfolio companies. Depending on the circumstances, control is normally exercised by the investment company which has set up the fund as the fund itself is typically a mere investment vehicle; in more exceptional circumstances, control may be exercised by the fund itself. The investment company usually exercises control by means of the organisational structure, eg by controlling the general partner of fund partnerships, or by contractual arrangements, such as advisory agreements, or by a combination of both. This may be the case even if the investment company itself does not own the company acting as a general partner, but their shares are held by natural persons (who may be linked to the investment company) or by a trust. Contractual arrangements with the investment company, in particular advisory agreements, will become even more important if the general partner does not have any own resources and personnel for the management of the portfolio companies, but only constitutes a company structure whose acts are performed by persons linked to the

investment company. In these circumstances, the investment company normally acquires indirect control within the meaning of Article 3(1)(b) and 3(3)(b) of the Merger Regulation, and has the power to exercise the rights which are directly held by the investment fund.[17]

1.2. Means of control

16. Control is defined by Article 3(2) of the Merger Regulation as the possibility of exercising decisive influence on an undertaking. It is therefore not necessary to show that the decisive influence is or will be actually exercised. However, the possibility of exercising that influence must be effective.[18] Article 3(2) further provides that the possibility of exercising decisive influence on an undertaking can exist on the basis of rights, contracts or any other means, either separately or in combination, and having regard to the considerations of fact and law involved. A concentration therefore may occur on a legal or a *de facto* basis, may take the form of sole or joint control, and extend to the whole or parts of one or more undertakings (cf. Article 3(1)(b)).

Control by the acquisition of shares or assets

17. Whether an operation gives rise to an acquisition of control therefore depends on a number of legal and/or factual elements. The most common means for the acquisition of control is the acquisition of shares, possibly combined with a shareholders' agreement in cases of joint control, or the acquisition of assets.

Control on a contractual basis

18. Control can also be acquired on a contractual basis. In order to confer control, the contract must lead to a similar control of the management and the resources of the other undertaking as in the case of acquisition of shares or assets. In addition to transferring control over the management and the resources, such contracts must be characterised by a very long duration (ordinarily without a possibility of early termination for the party granting the contractual rights). Only such contracts can result in a structural change in the market.[19] Examples of such contracts are organisational contracts under national company law[20] or other types of contracts, eg in the form of agreements for the lease of the business, giving the acquirer control over the management and the resources despite the fact that property rights or shares are not transferred. In this respect, Article 3(2)(a) specifies that control may also be constituted by a right to use the assets of an undertaking.[21] Such contracts may also lead to a situation of joint control if both the owner of the assets as well as the undertaking controlling the management enjoy veto rights over strategic business decisions.[22]

Control by other means

19. In line with these considerations, franchising agreements as such do not normally confer control over the franchisee's business on the franchisor. The franchisee usually exploits the entrepreneurial resources on its own account even if essential parts of the assets may belong to the franchisor.[23] Furthermore, purely financial agreements, such as sale-and-lease-back transactions with arrangements for a buyback of the assets at the end of the term, do not normally constitute a concentration as they do not change control over the management and the resources.

20. Furthermore, control can also be established by any other means. Purely economic relationships may play a decisive role for the acquisition of control. In exceptional circumstances, a situation of economic dependence may lead to control on a *de facto* basis where, for example, very important long-term supply agreements or credits provided by suppliers or customers, coupled with structural links, confer decisive influence.[24] In such a situation, the Commission will carefully analyse whether such economic links, combined with other links, are sufficient to lead to a change of control on a lasting basis.[25]

21. There may be an acquisition of control even if it is not the declared intention of the parties or if the acquirer is only passive and the acquisition of control is triggered by action of third parties. Examples are situations where the change of control results from the inheritance of a shareholder or where the exit of a shareholder triggers a change of control, in particular a change from joint to sole control.[26] Article 3(1)(b) covers such scenarios in specifying that control may also be acquired "by any other means".

Control and national company law

22. National legislation within a Member State may provide specific rules on the structure of bodies representing the organization of decision-making within an undertaking. While such legislation may confer some power of control upon persons other than the shareholders, in particular on representatives of employees, the concept of control under the Merger Regulation is not related to such a means of influence as the Merger Regulation focuses on decisive influence enjoyed on the basis of rights, assets or contracts or equivalent *de facto* means. Restrictions in the articles of association or in general law concerning the persons eligible to sit on the board, such as a provisions requiring the appointment of independent members or excluding persons holding office or employment in the parent companies, do not exclude the existence of control as long as the shareholders decide the composition of the decision-making bodies.[27] Similarly, despite provisions of national law foreseeing that decisions of a company must be taken by its company organs in its interests, those persons holding the voting rights have the power to adopt those decisions and therefore have the possibility to exercise decisive influence on the company.[28]

Control in other areas of legislation

23. The concept of control under the Merger Regulation may be different from that applied in specific areas of Community and national legislation concerning, for example, prudential rules, taxation, air transport or the media. The interpretation of "control" in other areas is therefore not necessarily decisive for the concept of control under the Merger Regulation

1.3.
Object of control

24. The Merger Regulation provides in Article 3(1)(b), (2) that the object of control can be one or more, or also parts of, undertakings which constitute legal entities, or the assets of such entities, or only some of these assets. The acquisition of control over assets can only be considered a concentration if those assets constitute the whole or a part of an undertaking, ie a business with a market presence, to which a market turnover can be clearly attributed.[29] The transfer of the client base of a business can fulfil these criteria if this is sufficient to transfer a business with a market turnover.[30] A transaction confined to intangible assets such as brands, patents or copyrights may also be considered to be a concentration if those assets constitute a business with a market turnover. In any case, the transfer of licences for brands, patents or copyrights, without additional assets, can only fulfil these criteria if the licences are exclusive at least in a certain territory and the transfer of such licences will transfer the turnover-generating activity.[31] For non-exclusive licences it can be excluded that they may constitute on their own a business to which a market turnover is attached.

25. Specific issues arise in cases where an undertaking outsources in-house activities, such as the provision of services or the manufacturing of products, to a service provider. Typical cases are the outsourcing of IT services to specialised IT companies. Outsourcing contracts can take several forms; their common characteristic is that the outsourcing service supplier shall provide those services to the customer which the latter has performed in-house before. Cases of simple outsourcing do not involve any transfer of assets or employees to the outsourcing service suppliers, but it is usually the case that any assets or employees are retained by the customer. Such an outsourcing contract is akin to a normal service contract and even if the outsourcing service supplier acquires a right to direct those assets and employees of the customer, no concentration arises if the assets and employees will be used exclusively to service the customer.

26. The situation may be different if the outsourcing service supplier, in addition to taking over a certain activity which was previously provided internally, is transferred the associated assets and/or personnel. A concentration only arises in these circumstances if the assets constitute the whole or part of an undertaking, ie a business with access to the market. This requires that the assets previously dedicated to in-house activities of the seller will enable the outsourcing service supplier to provide services not only to the outsourcing customer but also to third parties, either immediately or within a short period after the transfer. This will be the case if the transfer relates to an internal business unit or a subsidiary already engaged in the provision of services to third parties. If third parties are not yet supplied, the assets transferred in the case of manufacturing should contain production facilities, the product know-how (it is sufficient if the assets transferred allow the build-up of such capabilities in the near future) and, if there is no existing market access, the means for the purchaser to develop a market access within a short period of time (eg including existing contracts or brands).[32] As regards the provision of services, the assets transferred should include the required know-how (eg the relevant personnel and intellectual property) and those facilities which allow market access (such as, eg, marketing facilities).[33] The assets transferred therefore have to include at least those core elements that would allow an acquirer to build up a market presence in a time-frame similar to the start-up period for joint ventures as set out below under paragraphs 97, 100. As in the case of joint ventures, the Commission will take account of substantiated business plans and general market features for assessing this.

27. If the assets transferred do not allow the purchaser to at least develop a market presence, it is likely that they will be used only for providing services to the outsourcing customer. In such circumstances, the transaction will not result in a lasting change in the market structure and the outsourcing contract is again similar to a service contract. The transaction will not constitute a concentration. The specific requirements under which a joint venture for the provision of outsourcing services is qualified as a concentration are assessed in the present Notice in the section on full-function joint ventures.

1.4.
Change of control on a lasting basis

28. Article 3(1) of the Merger Regulation defines the concept of a concentration in such a manner as to cover operations only if they bring about a lasting change in the control of the undertakings concerned and, as recital 20 adds, in the structure of the market. The Merger Regulation therefore does not deal with transactions resulting only in a temporary change of control. However, a change of control on a lasting basis is not excluded by the fact that the underlying agreements are entered into for a definite period of time, provided those agreements are renewable. A concentration may arise even in cases in which agreements envisage a definite end-date, if the period envisaged is sufficiently long to lead to a lasting change in the control of the undertakings concerned.[34]

29. The question whether an operation results in a lasting change in the market structure is also relevant for the assessment of several operations occurring in succession, where the first transaction is only transitory in nature. Several scenarios can be distinguished in this respect.

30. In one scenario, several undertakings come together solely for the purpose of acquiring another company on the basis of an agreement to divide up the acquired assets according to a pre-existing plan immediately upon completion of the transaction. In such circumstances, in a first step, the acquisition of the entire target company is carried out by one or several undertakings. In a second step, the acquired assets are divided among several undertakings. The question is then whether the first transaction is to be considered as a separate concentration, involving an acquisition of sole control (in the case of a single purchaser) or of joint control (in the case of a joint purchase) of the entire target undertaking, or whether only the acquisitions in the second step constitute concentrations, whereby each of the acquiring undertakings acquires its relevant part of the target undertaking.

31. The Commission considers that the first transaction does not constitute a concentration, and examines the acquisitions of control by the ultimate acquirers, provided a number of conditions are met: First, the subsequent break-up must be agreed between the different purchasers in a legally binding way. Second, there must not be any

uncertainty that the second step, the division of the acquired assets, will take place within a short time period after the first acquisition. The Commission considers that normally the maximum time-frame for the division of the assets should be one year.[35]

32. If both conditions are met, the first acquisition does not result in a structural change on a lasting basis. There is no effective concentration of economic power between the acquirer(s) and the target company as a whole since the acquired assets are not held in an undivided way on a lasting basis, but only for the time necessary to carry out the immediate split-up of the acquired assets. In those circumstances, only the acquisitions of the different parts of the undertaking in the second step will constitute concentrations, whereby each of these acquisitions by different purchasers will constitute a separate concentration. This is irrespective of whether the first acquisition is carried out by only one undertaking[36] or jointly by the undertakings which are also involved in the second step.[37] In any case, it must be noted that the scope of a clearance decision will only allow for a takeover of the entire target if the break-up can proceed within a short time-frame afterwards and the different parts of the target undertaking are directly sold on to the respective ultimate buyer.

33. However, if these conditions are not fulfilled, in particular if it is not certain that the second step will proceed within a short time-frame after the first acquisition, the Commission will consider the first transaction as a separate concentration, involving the entire target undertaking. This, eg, is the case if the first transaction may also proceed independently of the second transaction[38] or if a longer transitory period is needed to divide up the target undertaking.[39]

34. A second scenario is an operation leading to joint control for a starting-up period but, according to legally binding agreements, this joint control will be converted to sole control by one of the shareholders. As the joint control situation may not constitute a lasting change of control, the whole operation may be considered to be an acquisition of sole control. In the past, the Commission accepted that such a start-up period could last up to three years.[40] Such a period seems to be too long to exclude that the joint control scenario has an impact on the structure of the market. The period therefore should, in general, not exceed one year and the joint control period should be only transitory in nature.[41] Only such a relatively short period will make it unlikely that the joint control period will have a distinct impact on the market structure and can therefore be considered as not leading to a change in control on a lasting basis.

35. In a third scenario, an undertaking is "parked" with an interim buyer, often a bank, on the basis of an agreement on the future onward sale of the business to an ultimate acquirer. The interim buyer generally acquires shares "on behalf" of the ultimate acquirer, which often bears the major part of the economic risks and may also be granted specific rights. In such circumstances, the first transaction is only undertaken to facilitate the second transaction and the first buyer is directly linked to the ultimate acquirer. Contrary to the situation described in the first scenario in paragraphs 30–33, no other ultimate acquirer is involved, the target business remains unchanged, and the sequence of transactions is initiated alone by the sole ultimate acquirer. From the date of the adoption of this Notice, the Commission will examine the acquisition of control by the ultimate acquirer, as provided for in the agreements entered into by the parties. The Commission will consider the transaction by which the interim buyer acquires control in such circumstances as the first step of a single concentration comprising the lasting acquisition of control by the ultimate buyer.

1.5. Interrelated transactions

1.5.1. Relation between Article 3 and Article 5(2) second subparagraph

36. Several transactions can be treated as a single concentration under the Merger Regulation either according to the general rule of Article 3 – as the transactions are interdependent – or according to the specific provision of Article 5(2) second subparagraph.

37. Article 5(2) second subparagraph governs a different question from that referred to by Article 3 of the Merger Regulation. Article 3 defines the existence of a "concentration" in general and material terms, but does not directly determine the question of the Commission's competence in respect of concentrations. Article 5 intends to specify the scope of the Merger Regulation, in particular by defining the turnover to be taken into account for the purpose of determining whether a concentration has Community dimension, and Article 5(2) second subparagraph allows the Commission in this respect to consider two or more concentrative transactions to constitute a single concentration for the purposes of calculating the turnover of the undertakings concerned. The assessment whether, in application of Article 3, a number of transactions give rise to a single concentration or whether those transactions must be regarded as giving rise to a number of concentrations, is thereby logically precedent to the question addressed in Article 5(2) second subparagraph.[42]

1.5.2. Interdependent transactions under Article 3

38. The general and teleological definition of a concentration set out in Article 3(1) – the result being control of one or more undertakings – implies that it makes no difference whether control was acquired by one or several legal transactions, provided that the end result constitutes a single concentration. Two or more transactions constitute a single concentration for the purposes of Article 3 if they are unitary in nature. It should therefore be determined whether the result leads to conferring one or more undertakings direct or indirect economic control over the activities of one or more other undertakings. For the assessment, the economic reality underlying the transactions is to be

identified and thus the economic aim pursued by the parties. In other words, in order to determine the unitary nature of the transactions in question, it is necessary, in each individual case, to ascertain whether those transactions are interdependent, in such a way that one transaction would not have been carried out without the other.[43]

39. Recital 20 to the Merger Regulation explains in this respect that it is appropriate to treat as a single concentration transactions that are closely connected in that they are linked by condition. The requirement that the transactions are interdependent as set out by the Court of First Instance in the Cementbouw judgment[44] thereby corresponds to the explanation set out in recital 20 that the transactions are linked by condition.

40. This general approach reflects, on the one hand, that under the Merger Regulation transactions which stand or fall together according to the economic objectives pursued by the parties should also be analysed in one procedure. In these circumstances, the change of the market structure is brought about by these transactions together. On the other hand, if different transactions are not interdependent and if the parties would proceed with one of the transactions if the other ones would not succeed, it seems appropriate to assess these transactions individually under the Merger Regulation.

41. However, several transactions, even if linked by condition upon each other, can only be treated as a single concentration, if control is acquired ultimately by the same undertaking(s). Only in these circumstances two or more transactions can be considered to be unitary in nature and therefore to constitute a single concentration for the purposes of Article 3.[45] This excludes de-mergers of joint ventures by which different parts of an undertaking are split between its former parent companies. The Commission will consider those transactions as separate concentrations.[46] The same applies to transactions where two (or more) companies exchange assets in transactions involving de-mergers of joint ventures or assets swaps. Although the parties will normally consider those transactions as interdependent, the purpose of the Merger Regulation requires a separate assessment of the results of each of the transactions: Several undertakings acquire control of different assets; a separate combination of resources takes place for each of the acquiring undertakings; and the impact on the market of each of those acquisitions of control needs to be analysed separately under the Merger Regulation.

42. The acquisition of different degrees of control (for example joint control of one business and sole control of another business) raises specific questions. An operation involving the acquisition of joint control of one part of an undertaking and sole control of another part is in principle regarded as two separate concentrations under the Merger Regulation.[47] Those transactions constitute only one concentration if they are interdependent and if the undertaking acquiring sole control is also acquiring joint control. In any case, such a scenario is considered to constitute one concentration where a corporate entity is acquired to which both the solely controlled and the jointly controlled undertaking belong. On the basis of the interpretation in recital 20, the situation where the same undertaking acquires sole and joint control of other undertakings based on interdependent agreements is not to be treated differently. These transactions, if they are interdependent, therefore constitute a single concentration.

Requirement of conditionality of transactions

43. The required conditionality implies that none of the transactions would take place without the others and they therefore constitute a single operation.[48] Such conditionality is normally demonstrated if the transactions are linked *de jure*, ie the agreements themselves are linked by mutual conditionality. If *de facto* conditionality can be satisfactorily demonstrated, it may also suffice for treating the transactions as a single concentration. This requires an economic assessment of whether each of the transactions necessarily depends on the conclusion of the others.[49] Further indications of the interdependence of several transactions may be the statements of the parties themselves or the simultaneous conclusion of the relevant agreements. A conclusion of *de facto* interconditionality of several transactions will be difficult to reach in the absence of their simultaneity. A pronounced lack of simultaneity of legally interconditional transactions may likewise put into doubt their true interdependence.

44. The principle that several transactions can be treated as a single concentration under the mentioned conditions only applies if the result is that control of one or more undertakings is acquired by the same person(s) or undertaking(s). First, this may be the case if a single business or undertaking is acquired via several legal transactions. Second, also the acquisition of control of several undertakings – which could constitute concentrations in themselves – can be linked in such a way that it constitutes a single concentration. However, it is not possible under the Merger Regulation to link different legal transactions which only partly concern the acquisition of control of undertakings, but partly also the acquisition of other assets, such as non-controlling minority stakes in other companies. It would not be in line with the general framework and the purpose of the Merger Regulation if different transactions, linked by conditionality, were assessed as a whole under the Merger Regulations if only some of these transactions lead to a change in control of a given target.

Acquisition of a single business

45. A single concentration may therefore exist if the same purchaser(s) acquire control of a single business, ie a single economic entity, via several legal transactions if those are inter-conditional. This is the case irrespective of whether the business is acquired in a corporate structure, consisting of one or several companies, or whether various assets are acquired which form a single business, ie a single economic entity managed for a common commercial purpose to which all the assets contribute. Such a business may comprise majority and minority stakes in companies as well as tangible and intangible assets. If several legal transactions which are interdependent are required to transfer such a business, these transactions constitute one concentration.[50]

Parallel and serial acquisitions of control

46. For the treatment of several acquisitions of control as a single concentration, several scenarios have arisen in the Commission's past decisional practice. One such scenario is a parallel acquisition of control, ie undertaking A acquires control of undertaking B and C in parallel from separate sellers on condition that A is not obliged to buy

either and neither seller is obliged to sell, unless both transactions proceed.[51] Another scenario is a serial acquisition of control, ie undertaking A acquires control of undertaking B conditional on B's prior or simultaneous acquisition of undertaking C, as illustrated by the Kingfisher case.[52]

Serial acquisition of sole/joint control

47. In the same way as the Kingfisher scenario, the Commission approaches cases where, in a serial transaction, an undertaking agrees to acquire first sole control of a target undertaking, with a view to directly selling on parts of the acquired stake in the target to another undertaking, finally resulting in joint control of both acquirers over the target company. If both acquisitions are inter-conditional, the two transactions constitute a single concentration and only the acquisition of joint control, as the final result of the transactions, will be considered by the Commission.[53]

1.5.3. Series of transactions in securities

48. Recital 20 of the Merger Regulation further explains that a single concentration will also arise in cases where control over one undertaking is acquired by a series of transactions in securities from one or several sellers taking place within a reasonably short period of time. The concentration in these scenarios is not limited to the acquisition of the "one and decisive" share, but will cover all the acquisitions of securities which take place in the reasonably short period of time.

1.5.4. Article 5(2) subparagraph 2

49. Article 5(2) subparagraph 2 provides a specific rule which allows the Commission to consider successive transactions occurring in a fixed period of time a single concentration for the purposes of calculating the turnover of the undertakings concerned. The purpose of this provision is to ensure that the same persons do not break a transaction down into series of sales of assets over a period of time, with the aim of avoiding the competence conferred on the Commission by the Merger Regulation.[54]

50. If two or more transactions (each of them bringing about an acquisition of control) take place within a two-year period between the same persons or undertakings, they shall be qualified as a single concentration,[55] irrespective of whether or not those transactions relate to parts of the same business or concern the same sector. This does not apply where the same persons or undertakings are joined by other persons or undertakings for only some of the transactions involved. It is sufficient if the transactions, although not carried out between the same companies, are carried out between companies belonging to the same respective groups. The provision also applies to two or more transactions between the same persons or undertakings if they are carried out simultaneously. Whenever they lead to acquisitions of control by the same undertaking, such simultaneous transactions between the same parties form a single concentration even if they are not conditional upon each other.[56] However, Article 5(2) subparagraph 2 would not appear to apply to different transactions at least one of which involves an undertaking concerned which is distinct from the common seller(s) and buyer(s). In situations involving two transactions where one transaction results in sole control and the other in joint control, Article 5(2) subparagraph 2 therefore does not apply unless the other jointly controlling parent(s) in the latter transaction are the seller(s) of the solely controlling stake in the former transaction.

1.6. Internal restructuring

51. A concentration within the meaning of the Merger Regulation is limited to changes in control. An internal restructuring within a group of companies does not constitute a concentration. This applies, eg, to increases in shareholdings not accompanied by changes of control or to restructuring operations such as a merger of a dual listed company into a single legal entity or a merger of subsidiaries. A concentration could only arise if the operation leads to a change in the quality of control of one undertaking and therefore is no longer purely internal.

1.7. Concentrations involving State-owned undertakings

52. An exceptional situation exists where both the acquiring and acquired undertakings are companies owned by the same State (or by the same public body or municipality). In this case, whether the operation is to be regarded as an internal restructuring depends in turn on the question whether both undertakings were formerly part of the same economic unit. Where the undertakings were formerly part of different economic units having an independent power of decision, the operation will be deemed to constitute a concentration and not an internal restructuring.[57] However, where the different economic units will continue to have an independent power of decision also after the operation, the operation is only to be regarded as an internal restructuring, even if the shares of the undertakings, constituting different economic units, should be held by a single entity, such as a pure holding company.[58]

53. However, the prerogatives exercised by a State acting as a public authority rather than as a shareholder, in so far as they are limited to the protection of the public interest, do not constitute control within the meaning of the Merger Regulation to the extent that they have neither the aim nor the effect of enabling the State to exercise a decisive influence over the activity of the undertaking.[59]

2. Sole Control

54. Sole control is acquired if one undertaking alone can exercise decisive influence on an undertaking. Two general situations in which an undertaking has sole control can be distinguished. First, the solely controlling undertaking enjoys the power to determine the strategic commercial decisions of the other undertaking. This power is typically achieved by the acquisition of a majority of voting rights in a company. Second, a situation also conferring sole

control exists where only one shareholder is able to veto strategic decisions in an undertaking, but this shareholder does not have the power, on his own, to impose such decisions (the so-called negative sole control). In these circumstances, a single shareholder possesses the same level of influence as that usually enjoyed by an individual shareholder which jointly controls a company, ie the power to block the adoption of strategic decisions. In contrast to the situation in a jointly controlled company, there are no other shareholders enjoying the same level of influence and the shareholder enjoying negative sole control does not necessarily have to cooperate with specific other shareholders in determining the strategic behaviour of the controlled undertaking. Since this shareholder can produce a deadlock situation, the shareholder acquires decisive influence within the meaning of Article 3(2) and therefore control within the meaning of the Merger Regulation.[60]

55. Sole control can be acquired on a *de jure* and/or *de facto* basis.

De jure sole control

56. Sole control is normally acquired on a legal basis where an undertaking acquires a majority of the voting rights of a company. In the absence of other elements, an acquisition which does not include a majority of the voting rights does not normally confer control even if it involves the acquisition of a majority of the share capital. Where the company statutes require a supermajority for strategic decisions, the acquisition of a simple majority of the voting rights may not confer the power to determine strategic decisions, but may be sufficient to confer a blocking right on the acquirer and therefore negative control.

57. Even in the case of a minority shareholding, sole control may occur on a legal basis in situations where specific rights are attached to this shareholding. These may be preferential shares to which special rights are attached enabling the minority shareholder to determine the strategic commercial behaviour of the target company, such as the power to appoint more than half of the members of the supervisory board or the administrative board. Sole control can also be exercised by a minority shareholder who has the right to manage the activities of the company and to determine its business policy on the basis of the organisational structure (eg as a general partner in a limited partnership which often does not even have a shareholding).

58. A typical situation of negative sole control occurs where one shareholder holds 50% in an undertaking whilst the remaining 50% is held by several other shareholders (assuming this does not lead to positive sole control on a *de facto* basis), or where there is a supermajority required for strategic decisions which in fact confers a veto right upon only one shareholder, irrespective of whether it is a majority or a minority shareholder.[61]

De facto sole control

59. A minority shareholder may also be deemed to have sole control on a *de facto* basis. This is in particular the case where the shareholder is highly likely to achieve a majority at the shareholders' meetings, given the level of its shareholding and the evidence resulting from the presence of shareholders in the shareholders' meetings in previous years.[62] Based on the past voting pattern, the Commission will carry out a prospective analysis and take into account foreseeable changes of the shareholders' presence which might arise in future following the operation.[63] The Commission will further analyse the position of other shareholders and assess their role. Criteria for such an assessment are in particular whether the remaining shares are widely dispersed, whether other important shareholders have structural, economic or family links with the large minority shareholder or whether other shareholders have a strategic or a purely financial interest in the target company; these criteria will be assessed on a case-by-case basis.[64] Where, on the basis of its shareholding, the historic voting pattern at the shareholders' meeting and the position of other shareholders, a minority shareholder is likely to have a stable majority of the votes at the shareholders' meeting, then that large minority shareholder is taken to have sole control.[65]

60. An option to purchase or convert shares cannot in itself confer sole control unless the option will be exercised in the near future according to legally binding agreements.[66] However, in exceptional circumstances an option, together with other elements, may lead to the conclusion that there is *de facto* sole control.[67]

Sole control acquired by other means than voting rights

61. Apart from the acquisition of sole control on the basis of voting rights, the considerations outlined in section 1.2 concerning the acquisition of sole control by purchase of assets, by contract, or by any other means also apply.

3. JOINT CONTROL

62. Joint control exists where two or more undertakings or persons have the possibility of exercising decisive influence over another undertaking. Decisive influence in this sense normally means the power to block actions which determine the strategic commercial behaviour of an undertaking. Unlike sole control, which confers upon a specific shareholder the power to determine the strategic decisions in an undertaking, joint control is characterized by the possibility of a deadlock situation resulting from the power of two or more parent companies to reject proposed strategic decisions. It follows, therefore, that these shareholders must reach a common understanding in determining the commercial policy of the joint venture and that they are required to cooperate.[68]

63. As in the case of sole control, the acquisition of joint control can also be established on a *de jure* or *de facto* basis. There is joint control if the shareholders (the parent companies) must reach agreement on major decisions concerning the controlled undertaking (the joint venture).

3.1.
Equality in voting rights or appointment to decision-making bodies

64. The clearest form of joint control exists where there are only two parent companies which share equally the voting rights in the joint venture. In this case, it is not necessary for a formal agreement to exist between them. However, where there is a formal agreement, it must be consistent with the principle of equality between the parent

companies, by laying down, for example, that each is entitled to the same number of representatives in the management bodies and that none of the members has a casting vote.[69] Equality may also be achieved where both parent companies have the right to appoint an equal number of members to the decision-making bodies of the joint venture.

3.2.
Veto rights

65. Joint control may exist even where there is no equality between the two parent companies in votes or in representation in decision-making bodies or where there are more than two parent companies. This is the case where minority shareholders have additional rights which allow them to veto decisions which are essential for the strategic commercial behaviour of the joint venture.[70] These veto rights may be set out in the statute of the joint venture or conferred by agreement between its parent companies. The veto rights themselves may operate by means of a specific quorum required for decisions taken at the shareholders' meeting or by the board of directors to the extent that the parent companies are represented on this board. It is also possible that strategic decisions are subject to approval by a body, eg supervisory board, where the minority shareholders are represented and form part of the quorum needed for such decisions.

66. These veto rights must be related to strategic decisions on the business policy of the joint venture. They must go beyond the veto rights normally accorded to minority shareholders in order to protect their financial interests as investors in the joint venture. This normal protection of the rights of minority shareholders is related to decisions on the essence of the joint venture, such as changes in the statute, an increase or decrease in the capital or liquidation. A veto right, for example, which prevents the sale or winding-up of the joint venture does not confer joint control on the minority shareholder concerned.[71]

67. In contrast, veto rights which confer joint control typically include decisions on issues such as the budget, the business plan, major investments or the appointment of senior management. The acquisition of joint control, however, does not require that the acquirer has the power to exercise decisive influence on the day-to-day running of an undertaking. The crucial element is that the veto rights are sufficient to enable the parent companies to exercise such influence in relation to the strategic business behaviour of the joint venture. Moreover, it is not necessary to establish that an acquirer of joint control of the joint venture will actually make use of its decisive influence. The possibility of exercising such influence and, hence, the mere existence of the veto rights, is sufficient.

68. In order to acquire joint control, it is not necessary for a minority shareholder to have all the veto rights mentioned above. It may be sufficient that only some, or even one such right, exists. Whether or not this is the case depends upon the precise content of the veto right itself and also the importance of this right in the context of the specific business of the joint venture.

Appointment of senior management and determination of budget

69. Very important are the veto rights concerning decisions on the appointment and dismissal of the senior management and the approval of the budget. The power to co-determine the structure of the senior management, such as the members of the board, usually confers upon the holder the power to exercise decisive influence on the commercial policy of an undertaking. The same is true with respect to decisions on the budget since the budget determines the precise framework of the activities of the joint venture and, in particular, the investments it may make.

Business plan

70. The business plan normally provides details of the aims of a company together with the measures to be taken in order to achieve those aims. A veto right over this type of business plan may be sufficient to confer joint control even in the absence of any other veto right. In contrast, where the business plan contains merely general declarations concerning the business aims of the joint venture, the existence of a veto right will be only one element in the general assessment of joint control but will not, on its own, be sufficient to confer joint control.

Investments

71. In the case of a veto right on investments, the importance of this right depends, first, on the level of investments which are subject to the approval of the parent companies and, secondly, on the extent to which investments constitute an essential feature of the market in which the joint venture is active. In relation to the first criterion, where the level of investments necessitating approval of the parent companies is extremely high, this veto right may be closer to the normal protection of the interests of a minority shareholder than to a right conferring a power of co-determination over the commercial policy of the joint venture. With regard to the second, the investment policy of an undertaking is normally an important element in assessing whether or not there is joint control. However, there may be some markets where investment does not play a significant role in the market behaviour of an undertaking.

Market-specific rights

72. Apart from the typical veto rights mentioned above, there exist a number of other possible veto rights related to specific decisions which are important in the context of the particular market of the joint venture. One example is the decision on the technology to be used by the joint venture where technology is a key feature of the joint venture's activities. Another example relates to markets characterized by product differentiation and a significant degree of innovation. In such markets, a veto right over decisions relating to new product lines to be developed by the joint venture may also be an important element in establishing the existence of joint control.

Overall context

73. In assessing the relative importance of veto rights, where there are a number of them, these rights should not be evaluated in isolation. On the contrary, the determination of whether or not joint control exists is based upon an assessment of these rights as a whole. However, a veto right which does not relate either to strategic commercial policy, to the appointment of senior management or to the budget or business plan cannot be regarded as giving joint control to its owner.[72]

3.3.
Joint exercise of voting rights

74. Even in the absence of specific veto rights, two or more undertakings acquiring minority shareholdings in another undertaking may obtain joint control. This may be the case where the minority shareholdings together provide the means for controlling the target undertaking. This means that the minority shareholders, together, will have a majority of the voting rights; and they will act together in exercising these voting rights. This can result from a legally binding agreement to this effect, or it may be established on a *de facto* basis.

75. The legal means to ensure the joint exercise of voting rights can be in the form of a (jointly controlled) holding company to which the minority shareholders transfer their rights, or an agreement by which they undertake to act in the same way (pooling agreement).

76. Very exceptionally, collective action can occur on a *de facto* basis where strong common interests exist between the minority shareholders to the effect that they would not act against each other in exercising their rights in relation to the joint venture. The greater the number of parent companies involved in such a joint venture, however, the more remote is the likelihood of this situation occurring.

77. Indicative for such a commonality of interests is a high degree of mutual dependency as between the parent companies to reach the strategic objectives of the joint venture. This is in particular the case when each parent company provides a contribution to the joint venture which is vital for its operation (eg specific technologies, local know-how or supply agreements).[73] In these circumstances, the parent companies may be able to block the strategic decisions of the joint venture and, thus, they can operate the joint venture successfully only with each other's agreement on the strategic decisions even if there is no express provision for any veto rights. The parent companies will therefore be required to cooperate.[74] Further factors are decision making procedures which are tailored in such a way as to allow the parent companies to exercise joint control even in the absence of explicit agreements granting veto rights or other links between the minority shareholders related to the joint venture.[75]

78. Such a scenario may not only occur in a situation where two or more minority shareholders jointly control an undertaking on a *de facto* basis, but also where there is high degree of dependency of a majority shareholder on a minority shareholder. This may be the case where the joint venture economically and financially depends on the minority shareholder or where only the minority shareholder has the required know-how for, and will play a major role in, the operation of the joint undertaking whereas the majority shareholder is a mere financial investor.[76] In such circumstances, the majority shareholder will not be able to enforce its position, but the joint venture partner may be able to block strategic decisions so that both parent undertakings will be required to cooperate permanently. This leads to a situation of *de facto* joint control which prevails over a pure *de jure* assessment according to which the majority shareholder could have been considered to have sole control.

79. These criteria apply to the formation of a new joint venture as well as to acquisitions of minority shareholdings, together conferring joint control. In case of acquisitions of shareholdings, there is a higher probability of a commonality of interests if the shareholdings are acquired by means of concerted action. However, an acquisition by way of a concerted action is not alone sufficient for the purposes of establishing *de facto* joint control. In general, a common interest as financial investors (or creditors) of a company in a return on investment does not constitute a commonality of interests leading to the exercise of *de facto* joint control.

80. In the absence of strong common interests such as those outlined above, the possibility of changing coalitions between minority shareholders will normally exclude the assumption of joint control. Where there is no stable majority in the decision-making procedure and the majority can on each occasion be any of the various combinations possible amongst the minority shareholders, it cannot be assumed that the minority shareholders (or a certain group thereof) will jointly control the undertaking.[77] In this context, it is not sufficient that there are agreements between two or more parties having an equal shareholding in the capital of an undertaking which establish identical rights and powers between the parties, where these fall short of strategic veto rights. For example, in the case of an undertaking where three shareholders each own one-third of the share capital and each elect one-third of the members of the Board of Directors, the shareholders do not have joint control since decisions are required to be taken on the basis of a simple majority.

3.4.
Other considerations related to joint control

Unequal role of the parent companies

81. Joint control is not incompatible with the fact that one of the parent companies enjoys specific knowledge of and experience in the business of the joint venture. In such a case, the other parent company can play a modest or even non-existent role in the daily management of the joint venture where its presence is motivated by considerations of a financial, long-term-strategy, brand image or general policy nature. Nevertheless, it must always retain the real possibility of contesting the decisions taken by the other parent company on the basis of equality in voting rights or rights of appointment to decision making bodies or of veto rights related to strategic issues. Without this, there would be sole control.

Casting vote

82. For joint control to exist, there should not be a casting vote for one parent company only as this would lead to sole control of the company enjoying the casting vote. However, there can be joint control when this casting vote is in practice of limited relevance and effectiveness. This may be the case when the casting vote can be exercised only after a series of stages of arbitration and attempts at reconciliation or in a very limited field or if the exercise of the casting vote triggers a put option implying a serious financial burden or if the mutual interdependence of the parent companies would make the exercise of the casting vote unlikely.[78]

III. CHANGES IN THE QUALITY OF CONTROL

[4.639]

83. The Merger Regulation covers operations resulting in the acquisition of sole or joint control, including operations leading to changes in the quality of control. First, such a change in the quality of control, resulting in a concentration, occurs if there is a change between sole and joint control. Second, a change in the quality of control occurs between joint control scenarios before and after the transaction if there is an increase in the number or a change in the identity of controlling shareholders. However, there is no change in the quality of control if a change from negative to positive sole control occurs. Such a change affects neither the incentives of the negatively controlling shareholder nor the nature of the control structure, as the controlling shareholder did not necessarily have to cooperate with specific shareholders at the time when it enjoyed negative control. In any case, mere changes in the level of shareholdings of the same controlling shareholders, without changes of the powers they hold in a company and of the composition of the control structure of the company, do not constitute a change in the quality of control and therefore are not a notifiable concentration.

84. These changes in the quality of control will be discussed in two categories: first, an entrance of one or more new controlling shareholders irrespective of whether or not they replace existing controlling shareholders and, second, a reduction of the number of controlling shareholders.

1. Entry of controlling shareholders

85. An entry of new controlling shareholders leading to a joint control scenario can either result from a change from sole to joint control, or from the entry of an additional shareholder or a replacement of an existing shareholder in an already jointly controlled undertaking.

86. A move from sole control to joint control is considered a notifiable operation as this changes the quality of control of the joint venture. First, there is a new acquisition of control for the shareholder entering the controlled undertaking. Second, only the new acquisition of control makes the controlled undertaking to a joint venture which changes decisively also the situation for the remaining controlling undertaking under the Merger Regulation: In the future, it has to take into account the interests of one or more other controlling shareholder(s) and it is required to cooperate permanently with the new shareholder(s). Before, it could either determine the strategic behaviour of the controlled undertaking alone (in the case of sole control) or was not forced to take into account the interests of specific other shareholders and was not forced to cooperate with those shareholders permanently.

87. The entry of a new shareholder in a jointly controlled undertaking – either in addition to the already controlling shareholders or in replacement of one of them – also constitutes a notifiable concentration, although the undertaking is jointly controlled before and after the operation.[79] First, also in this scenario there is a shareholder newly acquiring control of the joint venture. Second, the quality of control of the joint venture is determined by the identity of all controlling shareholders. It lies in the nature of joint control that, since each shareholder alone has a blocking right concerning strategic decisions, the jointly controlling shareholders have to take into account each others interests and are required to cooperate for the determination of the strategic behaviour of the joint venture.[80] The nature of joint control therefore does not exhaust itself in a pure mathematical addition of the blocking rights exercised by several shareholders, but is determined by the composition of the jointly controlling shareholders. One of the most obvious scenarios leading to a decisive change in the nature of the control structure of a jointly controlled undertaking is a situation where in a joint venture, jointly controlled by a competitor of the joint venture and a financial investor, the financial investor is replaced by another competitor. In these circumstances, the control structure and the incentives of the joint venture may entirely change, not only because of the entry of the new controlling shareholder, but also due to the change in the behaviour of the remaining shareholder. The replacement of a controlling shareholder or the entry of a new shareholder in a jointly controlled undertaking therefore constitutes a change in the quality of control.[81]

88. However, the entry of new shareholders only results in a notifiable concentration if one or several shareholders acquire sole or joint control by virtue of the operation. The entry of new shareholders may lead to a situation where joint control can neither be established on a *de jure* basis nor on a *de facto* basis as the entry of the new shareholder leads to the consequence that changing coalitions between minority shareholders are possible.[82]

2. Reduction in the number of shareholders

89. A reduction in the number of controlling shareholders constitutes a change in the quality of control and is thus to be considered as a concentration if the exit of one or more controlling shareholders results in a change from joint to sole control. Decisive influence exercised alone is substantially different from decisive influence exercised jointly, since in the latter case the jointly controlling shareholders have to take into account the potentially different interests of the other party or parties involved.[83]

90. Where the operation involves a reduction in the number of jointly controlling shareholders, without leading to a change from joint to sole control, the transaction will normally not lead to a notifiable concentration.

IV. JOINT VENTURES – THE CONCEPT OF FULL-FUNCTIONALITY

[4.640]

91. Article 3(1)(b) provides that a concentration shall be deemed to arise where control is acquired by *one or more* undertakings of the whole or parts of another undertaking. The new acquisition of another undertaking by several jointly controlling undertakings therefore constitutes a concentration under the Merger Regulation. As in the case of the acquisition of sole control of an undertaking, such an acquisition of joint control will lead to a structural change in the market even if, according to the plans of the acquiring undertakings, the acquired undertaking would no longer be considered full-function after the transaction (eg because it will sell exclusively to the parent undertakings in future). Thus, a transaction involving several undertakings acquiring joint control of another undertaking or parts of another undertaking, fulfilling the criteria set out in paragraph 24, from third parties will constitute a concentration according to Article 3(1) without it being necessary to consider the full-functionality criterion.[84]

92. Article 3(4) provides in addition that the creation of a joint venture performing on a lasting basis all the functions of an autonomous economic entity (so called full-function joint ventures) shall constitute a concentration within the meaning of the Merger Regulation. The full-functionality criterion therefore delineates the application of the Merger Regulation for the creation of joint ventures by the parties, irrespective of whether such a joint venture is created as a "greenfield operation" or whether the parties contribute assets to the joint venture which they previously owned individually. In these circumstances, the joint venture must fulfil the full-functionality criterion in order to constitute a concentration.

93. The fact that a joint venture may be a full-function undertaking and therefore economically autonomous from an operational viewpoint does not mean that it enjoys autonomy as regards the adoption of its strategic decisions. Otherwise, a jointly controlled undertaking could never be considered a full-function joint venture and therefore the condition laid down in Article 3(4) would never be complied with.[85] It is therefore sufficient for the criterion of full-functionality if the joint venture is autonomous in operational respect.

1. Sufficient resources to operate independently on a market

94. Full function character essentially means that a joint venture must operate on a market, performing the functions normally carried out by undertakings operating on the same market. In order to do so the joint venture must have a management dedicated to its day-to-day operations and access to sufficient resources including finance, staff, and assets (tangible and intangible) in order to conduct on a lasting basis its business activities within the area provided for in the joint-venture agreement.[86] The personnel do not necessarily need to be employed by the joint venture itself. If it is standard practice in the industry where the joint venture is operating, it may be sufficient if third parties envisage the staffing under an operational agreement or if staff is assigned by an interim employment agency. The secondment of personnel by the parent companies may also be sufficient if this is done either only for a start-up period or if the joint venture deals with the parent companies in the same way as with third parties. The latter case requires that the joint venture deals with the parents at arm's length on the basis of normal commercial conditions and that the joint venture is also free to recruit its own employees or to obtain staff via third parties.

2. Activities beyond one specific function for the parents

95. A joint venture is not full-function if it only takes over one specific function within the parent companies' business activities without its own access to or presence on the market. This is the case, for example, for joint ventures limited to R&D or production. Such joint ventures are auxiliary to their parent companies' business activities. This is also the case where a joint venture is essentially limited to the distribution or sales of its parent companies' products and, therefore, acts principally as a sales agency. However, the fact that a joint venture makes use of the distribution network or outlet of one or more of its parent companies normally will not disqualify it as "full-function" as long as the parent companies are acting only as agents of the joint venture.[87]

96. A frequent example where this question arises are joint ventures involved in the holding of real estate property, which are typically set up for tax and other financial reasons. As long as the purpose of the joint venture is limited to the acquisition and/or holding of certain real estate for the parents and based on financial resources provided by the parents, it will not usually be considered to be full-function, as it lacks an autonomous, long term business activity on the market and will typically also lack the necessary resources to operate independently. This has to be distinguished from joint ventures that are actively managing a real estate portfolio and who act on their own behalf on the market, which typically indicates full-functionality.[88]

3. Sale/purchase relations with the parents

97. The strong presence of the parent companies in upstream or downstream markets is a factor to be taken into consideration in assessing the full-function character of a joint venture where this presence results in substantial sales or purchases between the parent companies and the joint venture. The fact that, for an initial start-up period only, the joint venture relies almost entirely on sales to or purchases from its parent companies does not normally affect its full-function character. Such a start-up period may be necessary in order to establish the joint venture on a market. But the period will normally not exceed a period of three years, depending on the specific conditions of the market in question.[89]

Sales to the parents

98. Where sales from the joint venture to the parent companies are intended to be made on a lasting basis, the essential question is whether, regardless of these sales, the joint venture is geared to play an active role on the market and can be considered economically autonomous from an operational viewpoint. In this respect the relative proportion of sales made to its parents compared with the total production of the joint venture is an important factor. Due to the particularities of each individual case, it is impossible to define a specific turnover ratio which distinguishes full-function from other joint ventures. If the joint venture achieves more than 50% of its turnover with third parties, this will typically be an indication of full-functionality. Below this indicative threshold, a case-by-case analysis is

required, whereby, for the finding of operational autonomy, the relationship between the joint venture and its parents must be truly commercial in character. For this purpose, it is to be demonstrated that the joint venture will supply its goods or services to the purchaser who values them most and will pay most and that the joint venture will also deal with its parents' companies at arm's length on the basis of normal commercial conditions.[90] Under these circumstances, ie if the joint venture will treat its parent companies in the same commercial way as third parties, it may be sufficient that at least 20% of the joint venture's predicted sales will go to third parties. However, the greater the proportion of sales likely to be made to the parents, the greater will be the need for clear evidence of the commercial character of the relationship.

99. For the determination of the proportion between sales to the parents and to third parties, the Commission will take past accounts and substantiated business plans into account. However, especially where substantial third-party sales cannot be readily foreseen, the Commission will base its finding also on the general market structure. This may be a relevant factor as well for the assessment whether the joint venture will deal with its parents on an arm's length basis.

100. These issues frequently arise with regard to outsourcing agreements, where an undertaking creates a joint venture with a service provider[91] which will carry out functions that were previously dealt with by the undertaking in-house. The JV typically cannot be considered to be full-function in these scenarios: it provides its services exclusively to the client undertaking, and it is dependent for its services on input from the service provider. The fact that the joint venture's business plan often at least does not exclude that the joint venture can provide its services to third parties does not alter this assessment, as in the typical outsourcing setup any third party revenues are likely to remain ancillary to the joint venture's main activities for the client undertaking. However, this general rule does not exclude that there are outsourcing situations where the joint venture partners, for example for reasons of economies of scale, set up a joint venture with the perspective of significant market access. This could qualify the joint venture as full function if significant third-party sales are foreseen and if the relationship between the joint venture and its parent will be truly commercial in character and if the joint venture deals with its parents on the basis of normal commercial conditions.

Purchases from the parents

101. In relation to purchases made by the joint venture from its parent companies, the full-function character of the joint venture is questionable in particular where little value is added to the products or services concerned at the level of the joint venture itself. In such a situation, the joint venture may be closer to a joint sales agency.

Trade markets

102. However, in contrast to this situation where a joint venture is active in a trade market and performs the normal functions of a trading company in such a market, it normally will not be an auxiliary sales agency but a full-function joint venture. A trade market is characterised by the existence of companies which specialise in the selling and distribution of products without being vertically integrated in addition to those which are integrated, and where different sources of supply are available for the products in question. In addition, many trade markets may require operators to invest in specific facilities such as outlets, stockholding, warehouses, depots, transport fleets and sales and service personnel. In order to constitute a full-function joint venture in a trade market, an undertaking must have the necessary facilities and be likely to obtain a substantial proportion of its supplies not only from its parent companies but also from other competing sources.[92]

4. OPERATION ON A LASTING BASIS

103. Furthermore, the joint venture must be intended to operate on a lasting basis. The fact that the parent companies commit to the joint venture the resources described above normally demonstrates that this is the case. In addition, agreements setting up a joint venture often provide for certain contingencies, for example, the failure of the joint venture or fundamental disagreement as between the parent companies.[93] This may be achieved by the incorporation of provisions for the eventual dissolution of the joint venture itself or the possibility for one or more parent companies to withdraw from the joint venture. This kind of provision does not prevent the joint venture from being considered as operating on a lasting basis. The same is normally true where the agreement specifies a period for the duration of the joint venture where this period is sufficiently long in order to bring about a lasting change in the structure of the undertakings concerned,[94] or where the agreement provides for the possible continuation of the joint venture beyond this period.

104. By contrast, the joint venture will not be considered to operate on a lasting basis where it is established for a short finite duration. This would be the case, for example, where a joint venture is established in order to construct a specific project such as a power plant, but it will not be involved in the operation of the plant once its construction has been completed.

105. A joint venture also lacks the sufficient operations on a lasting basis at a stage where there are decisions of third parties outstanding that are of an essential core importance for starting the joint venture's business activity. Only decisions that go beyond mere formalities and the award of which is typically uncertain qualify for these scenarios. Examples are the award of a contract (eg, in public tenders), licences (eg, in the telecoms sector) or access rights to property (eg, exploration rights for oil and gas). Pending the decision on such factors, it is unclear whether the joint venture will become operational at all. Thus, at that stage the joint venture cannot be considered to perform economic functions on a lasting basis and consequently does not qualify as full function. However, once a decision has been taken in favour of the joint venture in question, this criterion is fulfilled and a concentration arises.[95]

5. CHANGES IN THE ACTIVITIES OF THE JOINT VENTURE

106. The parents may decide to enlarge the scope of the activities of the joint venture in the course of its lifetime. This will be considered as a new concentration that may trigger a notification requirement if this enlargement entails the acquisition of the whole or part of another undertaking from the parents that would, considered in isolation, qualify as a concentration as explained in paragraph 24 of this Notice.[96]

107. A concentration may also arise if the parent companies transfer significant additional assets, contracts, know-how or other rights to the joint venture and these assets and rights constitute the basis or nucleus of an extension of the activities of the joint venture into other product or geographic markets which were not the object of the original joint venture, and if the joint venture performs such activities on a full-function basis. As the transfer of the assets or rights shows that the parents are the real players behind the extension of the joint venture's scope, the enlargement of the activities of the joint venture can be considered in the same way as the creation of a new joint venture within the meaning of Article 3(4).[97]

108. If the scope of a joint venture is enlarged without additional assets, contracts, know-how or rights being transferred, no concentration will be deemed to arise.

109. A concentration arises if a change in the activity of an existing non-full-function joint venture occurs so that a full-function joint venture within the meaning of Article 3(4) is created. The following examples may be given: a change of the organisational structure of a joint venture so that it fulfils the full functionality criterion;[98] a joint venture that used to supply only the parent companies, which subsequently starts a significant activity on the market; or scenarios, as described in paragraph 105 above, where a joint venture can only start its activity on the market once it has essential input (such as a licence for a joint venture in the telecoms sector). Such a change in the activity of the joint venture will frequently require a decision by its shareholders or its management. Once the decision is taken that leads to the joint venture meeting the full functionality criterion, a concentration arises.

V. EXCEPTIONS

[4.641]

110. Article 3(5) sets out three exceptional situations where the acquisition of a controlling interest does not constitute a concentration under the Merger Regulation.

111. First, the acquisition of securities by companies whose normal activities include transactions and dealing in securities for their own account or for the account of others is not deemed to constitute a concentration if such an acquisition is made in the framework of these businesses and if the securities are held on only a temporary basis (Article 3(5)(a)). In order to fall within this exception, the following requirements must be fulfilled:

— the acquiring undertaking must be a credit or other financial institution or insurance company the normal activities of which are described above;
— the securities must be acquired with a view to their resale;
— the acquiring undertaking must not exercise the voting rights with a view to determining the strategic commercial behaviour of the target company or must exercise these rights only with a view to preparing the total or partial disposal of the undertaking, its assets or the securities;
— the acquiring undertaking must dispose of its controlling interest within one year of the date of the acquisition, that is, it must reduce its shareholding within this one-year period at least to a level which no longer confers control. This period, however, may be extended by the Commission where the acquiring undertaking can show that the disposal was not reasonably possible within the one-year period.

112. Second, there is no change of control, and hence no concentration within the meaning of the Merger Regulation, where control is acquired by an office-holder according to the law of a Member State relating to liquidation, winding-up, insolvency, cessation of payments, compositions or analogous proceedings (Article 3(5)(b));

113. Third, a concentration does not arise where a financial holding company within the meaning of Article 5(3) of the Council Directive 78/660/EEC[99] acquires control. The notion of "financial holding company" is thus limited to companies whose sole purpose it is to acquire holdings in other undertakings without involving themselves directly or indirectly in the management of those undertakings, the foregoing without prejudice to their rights as shareholders. Such investment companies must be further structured in a way that compliance with these limitations can be supervised by an administrative or judicial authority. The Merger Regulation provides for an additional condition for this exception to apply: such companies may exercise the voting rights in the other undertakings only to maintain the full value of those investments and not to determine directly or indirectly the strategic commercial conduct of the controlled undertaking.

114. The exceptions under Article 3(5) of the Merger Regulation only apply to a very limited field. First, these exceptions only apply if the operation would otherwise be a concentration in its own right, but not if the transaction is part of a broader, single concentration, in circumstances in which the ultimate acquirer of control would not fall within the terms of Article 3(5) (see eg paragraph 35 above). Second, the exceptions under Article 3(5)(a) and (c) only apply to acquisitions of control by way of purchase of securities, not to acquisitions of assets.

115. The exceptions do not apply to typical investment fund structures. According to their objectives, these funds usually do not limit themselves in the exercise of the voting rights, but adopt decisions to appoint the members of the management and the supervisory bodies of the undertakings or to even restructure those undertakings. This would not be compatible with the requirement under both Article 3(5)(a) and (c) that the acquiring companies do not exercise the voting rights with a view to determine the competitive conduct of the other undertaking.[100]

116. The question may arise whether an operation to rescue an undertaking before or from insolvency proceedings constitutes a concentration under the Merger Regulation. Such a rescue operation typically involves the conversion of existing debt into a new company, through which a syndicate of banks may acquire joint control of the company concerned. Where such an operation meets the criteria for joint control, as outlined above, it will normally be considered to be a concentration.[101] Although the primary intention of the banks is to restructure the financing of the

undertaking concerned for its subsequent resale, the exception set out in Article 3(5)(a) is normally not applicable to such an operation. In a similar way as set out for investment funds, the restructuring programme normally requires the controlling banks to determine the strategic commercial behaviour of the rescued undertaking. Furthermore, it is not normally a realistic proposition to transform a rescued company into a commercially viable entity and to resell it within the permitted one-year period. Moreover, the length of time needed to achieve this aim may be so uncertain that it would be difficult to grant an extension of the disposal period.

VI. ABANDONMENT OF CONCENTRATIONS

[4.642]

117. A concentration ceases to exist and the Merger Regulation ceases to be applicable if the undertakings concerned abandon the concentration.

118. In this respect, the revised Merger Regulation 139/2004 introduced a new provision related to the closure of procedures concerning the control of concentrations without a final decision after the Commission has initiated proceedings under Article 6(1)(c), first sentence. That sentence reads as follows: "Without prejudice to Article 9, such proceedings shall be closed by means of a decision as provided for in Article 8(1) to (4), unless the undertakings concerned have demonstrated to the satisfaction of the Commission that they have abandoned the concentration". Prior to the initiation of proceedings, such requirements do not apply.

119. As a general principle, the requirements for the proof of the abandonment must correspond in terms of legal form, intensity etc to the initial act that was considered sufficient to make the concentration notifiable. In case the parties proceed from that initial act to a strengthening of their contractual links during the procedure, for example by concluding a binding agreement after the transaction was notified on the basis of a good faith intention, the requirements for the proof of the abandonment must correspond also to the nature of the latest act.

120. In line with this principle, in case of implementation of the concentration prior to a Commission decision, the re-establishment of the status quo ante has to be shown. The mere withdrawal of the notification is not considered as sufficient proof that the concentration has been abandoned in the sense of Article 6(1)(c). Likewise, minor modifications of a concentration which do not affect the change in control or the quality of that change, cannot be considered as an abandonment of the original concentration.[102]

— Binding agreement: proof of the legally binding cancellation of the agreement in the form envisaged by the initial agreement (ie usually a document signed by all the parties) will be required. Expressions of intention to cancel the agreement or not to implement the notified concentration, as well as unilateral declarations by (one of) the parties will not be considered sufficient.[103]

— Good faith intention to conclude an agreement: In case of a letter of intent or memorandum of understanding reflecting such good faith intention, documents proving that this basis for the good faith intention has been cancelled will be required. As for possible other forms that indicated the good faith intention, the abandonment must reverse this good faith intention and correspond in terms of form and intensity to the initial expression of intent.

— Public announcement of a public bid or of the intention to make a public bid: a public announcement terminating the bidding procedure or renouncing to the intention to make a public bid will be required. The format and public reach of this announcement must be comparable to the initial announcement.

— Implemented concentrations: In case the concentration has been implemented prior to a Commission decision, the parties will be required to show that the situation prevailing before the implementation of the concentration has been re-established.

121. It is for the parties to submit the necessary documentation to meet these requirements in due time.

VII. CHANGES OF TRANSACTIONS AFTER A COMMISSION AUTHORISATION DECISION

[4.643]

122. In some cases, parties may wish not to implement the concentration in the form foreseen after authorisation of the concentration by the Commission. The question arises whether the Commission's authorisation decision still covers the changed structure of the transaction.

123. Broadly speaking, if, before implementation of the authorised concentration, the transactional structure is changed from an acquisition of control, falling under Article 3(1)(b), to a merger according to Article 3(1)(a), or vice versa, then the change in the transactional structure is considered a different concentration under the Merger Regulation and a new notification is required.[104] However, less significant modifications of the transaction, for example minor changes in the shareholding percentages which do not affect the change in control or the quality of that change, changes in the offer price in the case of public bids or changes in the corporate structure by which the transaction is implemented without effects on the relevant control situation under the Merger Regulation, are considered as being covered by the Commission's authorisation decision.

NOTES

[8] See, for example, Case COMP/M. 1673 – *Veba/VIAG* of 13 June 2000; Case COMP/M.1806 – *AstraZeneca/Novartis* of 26 July 2000; Case COMP/M.2208 – *Chevron/Texaco* of 26 January 2001; and Case IV/M.1383 – *Exxon/Mobil* of 29 September 1999. A merger in the meaning of Article 3(1)(a) is not deemed to occur if a target company is merged with a subsidiary of the acquiring company to the effect that the parent company acquires control of the target undertaking under Article 3(1)(b), see Case COMP/M.2510 – *Cendant/Galileo* of 24 September 2001.

[9] In determining the previous independence of undertakings, the issue of control may be relevant as the merger might otherwise only be an internal restructuring within the group. In this specific context, the assessment of control also follows the general concept set out below and includes *de jure* as well as *de facto* control.

[10] This could apply for example in the case of a "*Gleichordnungskonzern*" in German law, certain "*Groupements d'Intérêt Economique*" in French law, and the amalgamation of partnerships, as in Case IV/M.1016 – *Price Waterhouse/Coopers&Lybrand* of 20 May 1998.

11 Case IV/M.660 – RTZ/CRA of 7 December 1995; Case COMP/M.3071 – *Carnival Corporation/P&O Princess II* of 24 July 2002.

12 See Case IV/M.1016 – *Price Waterhouse/Coopers&Lybrand* of 20 May 1998; Case COMP/M.2824 – *Ernst & Young/Andersen Germany* of 27 August 2002.

13 Including the State itself, eg Case IV/M.157 – *Air France/Sabena*, of 5 October 1992 in relation to the Belgian State, or other public bodies such as the Treuhandanstalt in Case IV/M.308 – *Kali und Salz/MDK/Treuhand*, of 14 December 1993. See, however, recital 22 of the Merger Regulation.

14 Case IV/M.82 – *Asko/Jakobs/Adia* of 16 May 1991 including a private individual as undertaking concerned.; Case COMP/M3762 – *Apax/Travelex* of 16 June 2005 in which a private individual acquiring joint control was not considered an undertaking concerned.

15 Judgment in Case T-282/02 *Cementbouw v Commission*, paragraph 72, [2006] ECR II-319.

16 See Case M.754 – *Anglo American Corporation/Lonrho* of 23 April 1997.

17 This structure also has an effect on how the turnover is calculated in situations involving investment funds, see paragraphs 189ff.

18 Judgment in Case T-282/02 *Cementbouw v Commission*, paragraph 58, [2006] ECR II-319

19 In Case COMP/M.3858 – *Lehman Brothers/SCG/Starwood/Le Meridien* of 20 July 2005 the management agreements had a duration of 10-15 years; in Case COMP/M.2632 – *Deutsche Bahn/ECT International/United Depots/JV* of 11 February 2002 the contract had a duration of 8 years.

20 Examples of such specific contracts under national company law are the "Beherrschungsvertrag" in German law or the "Contrato de subordinação" in Portuguese law; such contracts do not exist in all Member States.

21 See Case COMP/M.2060 – *Bosch/Rexroth* of 12 January 2001 concerning a control contract (Beherrschungsvertrag) in combination with a business lease; Case COMP/M.3136 – *GE/Agfa NDT* of 5 December 2003 concerning a specific contract to transfer control over entrepreneurial resources, management and risks; Case COMP/M.2632 – *Deutsche Bahn/ECT International/United Depots/JV* of 11 February 2002 concerning a business lease.

22 Case COMP/M.3858 – *Lehman Brothers/SCG/Starwood/Le Meridien* of 20 July 2005; see also case IV/M.126 – *Accor/Wagon-Lits* of 28 April 1992 in the context of Article 5(4)(b) of the Merger Regulation.

23 Case M.940 – *UBS/Mister Minit*, in the context of Article 5(4)(b) of the Merger Regulation. For the treatment of franchising relationships in the competitive assessment, see Case COMP/M.4220 – *Food Service Project/Tele Pizza* of 6 June 2006. The situation in Case IV/M.126 – *Accor/Wagon-Lits* of 28 April 1992 has to be distinguished from franchising agreements. In this case, again in the context of Article 5(4)(b), the hotel company had a right to manage also hotels in which it only owned a minority stake as it had entered into long-term hotel management agreements giving it decisive influence over the day-to-day operations of these hotels, including decisions on budgetary matters.

24 See Case IV/M.794 – *Coca-Cola/Amalgamated Beverages GB* of 22 January 1997; Case IV/ECSC.1031 – *US/Sollac/Bamesa* of 28 July 1993; Case IV/M.625 – *Nordic Capital/Transpool* of 23 August 1995; for the criteria see also Case IV/M.697 – *Lockheed Martin Corporation/Loral Corporation*, of 27 March 1996.

25 See Case IV/M.258 – *CCIE/GTE*, of 25 September 1992 where the Commission did not find control due to the temporary nature of the commercial agreements involved.

26 See Case COMP/M.3330 – *RTL/M6* of 12 March 2004; Case COMP/M.452 – *Avesta (II)* of 9 June 1994.

27 Judgment in Case T-282/02 *Cementbouw v Commission*, paragraphs 70, 73, 74 [2006] ECR II-319.

28 Judgment in Case T-282/02 *Cementbouw v Commission*, paragraphs 79 [2006] ECR II-319.

29 See, eg, Case COMP/M. 3867 – *Vattenfall/Elsam* and E2 Assets of 22 December 2005.

30 Case COMP/M.2857 – *ECS/IEH* of 23 December 2002.

31 In addition, the granting of licences and the transfer of patent licences will only constitute a concentration if this is done on a lasting basis. In this respect, similar considerations as set out above in paragraph 18 for the acquisition of control by (long-term) agreements apply.

32 See Case COMP/M.1841 – *Celestica/IBM* of 25 February 2000; Case COMP/M.1849 – *Solectron/Ericsson* of 29 February 2000; Case COMP/M.2479 – *Flextronics/Alcatel* – of 29 June 2001; Case COMP/M.2629 – *Flextronics/Xerox* of 12 November 2001.

33 See, in the context of joint ventures, Case IV/M.560 – *EDS/Lufthansa* of 11 May 1995; Case COMP/M.2478 – *IBM Italia/Business Solutions/JV* of 29 June 2001.

34 See, in cases of joint ventures, Case COMP/M.2903 – *DaimlerChrysler/Deutsche Telekom/JV* of 30 April 2003 where a period of 12 years was considered sufficient; Case COMP/M.2632 – *Deutsche Bahn/ECT International/United Depots/JV* of 11 February 2002 with a contract duration of 8 years. In Case COMP/M.3858 *Lehman Brothers/Starwood/Le Meridien* of 20 July 2005, the Commission considered a minimum period of 10-15 years sufficient, but not a period of three years. The acquisition of control by the acquisition of shares or assets is not normally confined to a definite period of time and is therefore assumed to lead to a change of control on a lasting basis. Only in the scenarios set out in paragraphs 29 ff., will an acquisition of control by shares or assets be exceptionally considered to be transitory in nature and thus not to lead to a lasting change in the control of the undertakings concerned.

35 See, eg, Cases COMP/M. Case No COMP/M.3779 – *Pernod Ricard/Allied Domecq* of 24 June 2005 and COMP/M.3813 – *Fortune Brands/Allied Domecq* of 10 June 2005, where the split-up of the assets was foreseen to become effective within 6 months after the acquisition.

36 For a first acquisition by only one undertaking see Case COMP/M.3779 – *Pernod Ricard/Allied Domecq* of 24 June 2005 and Case COMP/M.3813 – *Fortune Brands/Allied Domecq/Pernod Ricard* of 10 June 2005; Case COMP/M.2060 – *Bosch/Rexroth* of 12 January 2001.

37 For a joint acquisition see Case COMP/M.1630 – *Air Liquide/BOC* of 18 January 2000; Case COMP/M.1922 – *Siemens/Bosch/Atecs* of 11 August 2000; Case COMP/M.2059 – *Siemens/Dematic/VDO Sachs* of 29 August 2000.

38 See Case COMP/M.2498 – *UPM-Kymmene/Haindl* of 21 November 2001 and Case COMP/M.2499 – *Norske Skog/Parenco/Walsum* of 21 November 2001.

39 Case COMP/M.3372 – *Carlsberg/Holsten* of 16 March 2004.

40 Case IV/M.425 – *British Telecom/Santander* of 28 March 1994.

41 See Case M.2389 – *Shell/DEA* of 20 December 2001 where the ultimate acquirer of sole control had a strong influence in the operational management during the joint control period; Case M.2854 – *RAG/Degussa* of 18 November 2002 where the transitional period was designed to facilitate internal post-merger restructuring.

42 Judgment in Case T-282/02 *Cementbouw v Commission*, paragraphs 113-119 [2006] ECR II-319.

43 Judgment in Case T-282/02 *Cementbouw v Commission*, paragraphs 104-109 [2006] ECR II-319.

44 Judgment in Case T-282/02 *Cementbouw v Commission*, paragraphs 106-109 [2006] ECR II-319.

45 This also covers situations where an undertaking sells a business to a purchaser and then acquirers the seller including the business sold, see Case COMP/M.4521 – *LGI/Telenet* of 26 February 2007.

46 See parallel cases COMP/M.3293 – *Shell/BEB* and COMP/M.3294 – *ExxonMobil/BEB* of 20 November 2003; case IV/M.197 – *Solvay/Laporte* of 30 April 1992.

47 See Case IV/M.409 *ABB/Renault Automation* of 9 March 1994.

48 Judgment in Case T-282/02 *Cementbouw v Commission*, paragraphs 127 et seq [2006] ECR II-319.

49 Judgment in Case T-282/02 *Cementbouw v Commission*, paragraphs 131 et seq [2006] ECR II-319. See Case COMP/M.4521 – *LGI/Telenet* of 26 February 2007, where the interdependence was based on the fact that two transactions were decided and carried out simultaneously and that, according to the economic aims of the parties, each of the transactions would not have been carried out without the other.

50 See Case IV/M.470 – *Gencor/Shell* of 29 August 1994; COMP/M.3410 – *Total/Gaz de France* of 8 October 2004; Case IV/M.957 – *L'Oreal/Procasa/Cosmetique Iberica/Albesa* of 19 September 1997; Case IV/M.861 – *Textron/Kautex* of 18 December 1996 where all the assets were also used in the same product market. The same considerations apply if a joint venture is created by several companies, forming a single business, see Case M.4048 —*Sonae Industria/Tarkett* of 12 June 2006 where the interdependence of transactions establishing, respectively, a production and a distribution joint venture was necessary in order to demonstrate that there was a single concentration that would create a full-function joint venture.

51 Case COMP/M.2926 – *EQT/H&R/Dragoco* – of 16 September 2002; the same considerations apply to the question when several mergers constitute one concentration in the meaning of Article 3(1)(a), Case COMP/M. 2824 – *Ernst & Young/Andersen Germany* of 27 August 2002.

52 Case IV/M.1188 – *Kingfisher/Wegert/ProMarkt* of 18 June 1998; case COMP/M.2650 – *Haniel/Cementbouw/JV (CVK)* of 26 June 2002.

53 Case COMP/M.2420 – *Mitsui/CVRD/Caemi* of 30 October 2001.

54 Judgment in Case T-282/02 *Cementbouw v Commission*, paragraph 118 [2006] ECR II-319.

55 See Case COMP/M.3173 – *E.ON/Fortum Burghausen/Smaland/Endenderry* of 13 June 2003. This also applies to situations where sole control is acquired whereby only parts of the undertaking were previously jointly controlled by the acquiring undertaking, case COMP/M. 2679 – *EdF/TXU/Europe/24 Seven* of 20 December 2001.

56 Case IV/M.1283 – *Volkswagen/RollsRoyce/Cosworth* of 24 August 1998.

57 Case IV/M.097 – *Péchiney/Usinor*, of 24 June 1991; Case IV/M.216 – *CEA Industrie/France Telecom/SGS-Thomson*, of 22 February 1993; Case IV/M.931 – *Neste/IVO* of 2 June 1998. See also recital 22 of the Merger Regulation.

58 Specific issues concerning the calculation of turnover for state-owned companies are dealt with in paragraphs 192-194.

59 Case IV/M.493 – *Tractebel/Distrigaz II*, of 1 September 1994.

60 Since this shareholder is the only undertaking acquiring a controlling influence, only this shareholder is obliged to submit a notification under the Merger Regulation.

61 See consecutive Cases COMP/M.3537 – *BBVA/BNL* of 20 August 2004 and M.3768 – *BBVA/BNL* of 27 April 2005; Case M.3198 – *VW-Audi/VW-Audi Vertriebszentren* of 29 July 2003; Case COMP/M.2777 – *Cinven Limited/Angel Street Holdings* of 8 May 2002; Case IV/M.258 – *CCIE/GTE*, of 25 September 1992. In Case COMP/M.3876 – *Diester Industrie/Bunge/JV* of 30 September 2005, there was the specific situation that a joint venture held a stake in a company by which it had negative sole control over this company.

62 Case IV/M.343 – *Société Générale de Belgique/Générale de Banque*, of 3 August 1993; Case COMP/M.3330 – *RTL/M6* of 12 March 2004; Case IV/M.159 – *Mediobanca/Generali* of 19 December 1991.

63 See Case COMP/M.4336 – *MAN/Scania* of 20 December 2006 as regards the question whether Volkswagen had acquired control of MAN.

64 Case IV/M.754 – *Anglo American/Lonrho* of 23 April 1997; Case IV/M.025 – *Arjomari/Wiggins Teape*, of 10 February 1990.

65 See also Case COMP/M.2574 – *Pirelli/Edizione/Olivetti/Telecom Italia* of 20 September 2001; Case IV/M.1519 – *Renault/Nissan* of 12 May 1999.

66 Judgment in Case T 2/93, Air France v Commission [1994] ECR II-323. Even though an option does normally not in itself lead to a concentration, it can be taken into account for the substantive assessment in a related concentration, see Case COMP/M.3696 – E.ON/MOL of 21 December 2005, at paragraphs 12-14, 480, 762 et subseq.

67 Case IV/M.397 – Ford/Hertz of 7 March 1994.

68 See also Judgment in Case T-282/02 *Cementbouw v Commission*, paragraphs 42, 52, 67 [2006] ECR II-319.

69 Case COMP/M.3097 – *Maersk Data/Eurogate IT; Global Transport Solutions JV* of 12 March 2003; Case IV/M.272 – *Matra/CAP Gemini Sogeti*, of 17 March 1993.

70 Case T 2/93, *Air France v Commission* [1994] ECR II-323; Case IV/M.010 – *Conagra/Idea*, of 3 May 1991.

71 Case IV/M.062 – *Eridania/ISI*, of 30 July 1991.

72 Case IV/M.295 – *SITA-RPC/SCORI*, of 19 March 1993.

73 Case COMP/JV.55 *Hutchison/RCPM/ECT* of 3 July 2001; see also Case IV/M.553 – *RTL/Veronica/Endemol* of 20 September 1995.

74 Judgment in Case T-282/02 *Cementbouw v Commission*, paragraphs 42, 52, 67 [2006] ECR II-319.

75 Case COMP/JV.55 *Hutchison/RCPM/ECT* of 3 July 2001. See also Case IV/M.553 – *RTL/Veronica/Endemol* of 20 September 1995.

76 Case IV/M. 967 – *KLM/Air UK* of 22 September 1997; Case COMP/M.4085 – *Arcelor/Oyak/Erdemir* of 13 February 2006.

77 Case IV/JV.12 – *Ericsson/Nokia/Psion/Motorola* of 22 December 1998.

78 Case COMP/M.2574 – *Pirelli/Edizione/Olivetti/Telecom Italia* of 20 September 2001; Case IV/M.553 – *RTL/Veronica/Endemol* of 20 September 1995; Case IV/M.425 – *British Telecom/Banco Santander*, of 28 March 1994.

79 See, eg, Case COMP/M.3440 – *ENI/EDP/GdP* of 9 December 2004.

80 Judgment in Case T-282/02 *Cementbouw v Commission*, paragraph 67 [2006] ECR II-319.

81 Generally, it should be noted that the Commission will not assess as a separate concentration the indirect replacement of a controlling shareholder in a joint control scenario which takes place via an acquisition of control of one of its parent undertakings. The Commission will assess any changes occurring in the competitive situation of the joint venture in the framework of the overall acquisition of control of its parent undertaking. In those circumstances, the other controlling shareholders in the joint venture will therefore not be undertakings concerned by the concentration which relates to its parent undertaking.

82 Case IV/JV.12 – *Ericsson/Nokia/Psion/Motorola* of 22 December 1998.

83 See Case IV/M023 – *ICI/Tioxide*, of 28 November 1990; see also paragraph 5 (d) of the Commission Notice on a simplified procedure for treatment of certain concentrations under Council Regulation (EC) No 139/2004.

84 These considerations do not apply to Article 2(4) in the same way. Whereas the interpretation of Article 3, paragraphs (1) and (4) relates to the applicability of the Merger Regulation to joint ventures, Article 2(4) relates to the substantive analysis of joint ventures. The "creation of a joint venture constituting a concentration pursuant to Article 3", as provided for in Article 2(4), comprises the acquisition of joint control according to Article 3, paragraphs (1) and (4).

85 Judgment in Case T-282/02 *Cementbouw v Commission*, paragraph 62 [2006] ECR II-319.

86 Case IV/M.527 – *Thomson CSF/Deutsche Aerospace*, of 2 December 1994 – intellectual rights, Case IV/M.560 *EDS/Lufthansa* of 11 May 1995 – outsourcing, Case IV/M.585 – *Voest Alpine Industrieanlagenbau GmbH/Davy International Ltd*, of 7 September 1995 – joint venture's right to demand additional expertise and staff from its parent companies, Case IV/M.686 – *Nokia/Autoliv*, of 5 February 1996, joint venture able to terminate "service agreements" with parent company and to move from site retained by parent company, Case IV/M.791 – *British Gas Trading Ltd/Group 4 Utility Services Ltd*, of 7 October 1996, joint venture's intended assets will be transferred to leasing company and leased by joint venture.

87 Case IV/M.102 – *TNT/Canada Post etc* of 2 December 1991.

88 See Case IV/M.929 – *DIA/Veba Immobilien/Deutschbau* of 23 June 1997; Case COMP/M. 3325 – *Morgan Stanley/Glick/Canary Wharf* of 23 January 2004.

89 Case IV/M.560 – *EDS/Lufthansa* of 11 May 1995; Case IV/M.686 *Nokia/Autoliv* of 5 February 1996; to be contrasted with Case IV/M.904 – *RSB/Tenex/Fuel Logistics* of 2 April 1997 and Case IV/M.979 – *Preussag/Voest-Alpine* of 1 October 1997. A special case exists where sales by the joint venture to its parent are caused by a legal monopoly downstream of the joint venture, see Case IV/M.468 – *Siemens/Italtel* of 17 February 1995, or where the sales to a parent company consist of by-products, which are of minor importance to the joint venture, see Case IV/M.550 – *Union Carbide/Enichem* of 13 March 1995.

90 Case IV/M.556 – *Zeneca/Vanderhave* of 9 April 1996; Case IV/M.751 – *Bayer/Hüls* of 3 July 1996.

91 The question under which circumstances an outsourcing arrangement qualifies as a concentration is dealt with in paragraphs 25ff. of this Notice.

92 Case IV/M.788 – *AgrEVO/Marubeni* of 3 September 1996.

93 Case IV/M.891 – *Deutsche Bank/Commerzbank/J.M. Voith* of 23 April 1997.

94 See Case COMP/M.2903 – *DaimlerChrysler/Deutsche Telekom/JV* of 30 April 2003 where a period of 12 years was considered sufficient; Case COMP/M.2632 – *Deutsche Bahn/ECT International/United Depots/JV* of 11 February 2002 with a contract duration of 8 years. In Case COMP/M.3858 *Lehman Brothers/Starwood/Le Meridien* of 20 July 2005, the Commission considered a minimum period of 10-15 years sufficient, but not a period of three years.

95 Subject to the other criteria mentioned in this chapter of the Notice.

96 See Case COMP/M.3039 – *Soprol/Céréol/Lesieur* of 30 January 2003.

97 The triggering event for the notification in such a case will be the agreement or other legal act underlying the transfer of the assets, contracts, know-how or other rights.

98 Case COMP/M.2276 – *The Coca-Cola Company/Nestlé/JV* of 27 September 2001.

99 Fourth Council Directive 78/660/EEC of 25 July 1978 based on Article 54 (3) (g) of the Treaty on the annual accounts of certain types of companies, OJ L222, 14.8.1978, p 11, as last amended by Directive 2003/51/EC of 18 June 2003, OJ L178, 17.7.2003, p 16. Article 5(3) of this Directive defines financial holding companies as "those companies the sole objective of which is to acquire holdings in other undertakings, and to manage such holdings and turn them to profit, without involving themselves directly or indirectly in the management of those undertakings, the foregoing without prejudice to their rights as shareholders. The limitations imposed on the activities of these companies must be such that compliance with them can be supervised by an administrative or judicial authority".

100 Case IV/M.669 – *Charterhouse/Porterbrook*, of 11 December 1995.

101 Case IV/M.116 – *Kelt/American Express*, of 28 August 1991.

102 This paragraph does not prejudge the assessment whether the modification requires submitting additional information to the Commission under Article 5(3) of Regulation (EC) No 802/2004.

103 See Case COMP/M.4381 – *JCI/VB/FIAMM* of 10 May 2007, paragraph 15, where only one party did no longer wished to implement an agreement, whereas the other party still considered the agreement to be binding and enforceable.

104 See cases COMP/M.2706 – *Carnival Corporation/P&O Princess* of 11 April 2002 and COMP/M.3071 – *Carnival Corporation/P&O Princess* of 10 February 2003. In such circumstances, the identity of the notifying parties changes, as both parties to a merger must notify, whereas only the party acquiring control must do so. However, if the parties implement an acquisition of control over a target company and only subsequently decide to merge with the newly acquired subsidiary, this would be regarded as an internal restructuring that does not give rise to a change in control and would thus not fall within the terms of Article 3 of the Merger Regulation.

C. COMMUNITY DIMENSION

I. THRESHOLDS

[4.644]

124. A two fold test defines the operations to which the Merger Regulation applies. The first test is that the operation must be a concentration within the meaning of Article 3. The second comprises the turnover thresholds contained in Article 1, designed to identify those operations which have an impact upon the Community and can be deemed to be of "Community dimension". Turnover is used as a proxy for the economic resources being combined in a concentration, and is allocated geographically in order to reflect the geographic distribution of those resources.

125. Two sets of thresholds are set out in Article 1 to establish whether the operation has a Community dimension. Article 1(2) establishes three different criteria: The worldwide turnover threshold is intended to measure the overall dimension of the undertakings concerned; the Community turnover threshold seek to determine whether the concentration involves a minimum level of activities in the Community; and the two-thirds rule aims to exclude purely domestic transactions from Community jurisdiction.

126. This second set of thresholds, contained in Article 1(3), is designed to tackle those concentrations which fall short of achieving Community dimension under Article 1(2), but would have a substantial impact in at least three Member States leading to multiple notifications under national competition rules of those Member States. For this purpose, Article 1(3) provides for lower turnover thresholds, both worldwide and Community-wide, and for a minimum level of activities of the undertakings concerned, jointly and individually, in at least three Member States. Similarly to Article 1(2), Article 1(3) also contains a two-thirds rule excluding predominantly domestic concentrations.[105]

127. The thresholds as such are designed to govern jurisdiction and not to assess the market position of the parties to the concentration nor the impact of the operation. In so doing they include turnover derived from, and thus the resources devoted to, all areas of activity of the parties, and not just those directly involved in the concentration. The thresholds are purely quantitative, since they are only based on turnover calculation instead of market share or other criteria. They pursue the objective to provide a simple and objective mechanism that can be easily handled by the companies involved in a merger in order to determine if their transaction has a Community dimension and is therefore notifiable.

128. Whereas Article 1 sets out the numerical thresholds to establish jurisdiction, the purpose of Article 5 is to explain how turnover should be calculated to ensure that the resulting figures are a true representation of economic reality.

II. NOTION OF UNDERTAKING CONCERNED

1. General

[4.645]

129. From the point of view of determining jurisdiction, the undertakings concerned are those participating in a concentration, ie a merger or an acquisition of control as foreseen in Article 3(1). The individual and aggregate turnover of those undertakings will be decisive in determining whether the thresholds are met.

130. Once the undertakings concerned have been identified in a given transaction, their turnover for the purposes of determining jurisdiction is to be calculated according to the rules set out in Article 5. Article 5(4) sets out detailed criteria to identify undertakings whose turnover may be attributed to the undertaking concerned because of certain direct or indirect links with the latter. The legislator's intention was to lay down concrete rules which, seen together, can be taken to establish the notion of a "group" for the purposes of the turnover thresholds in the Merger Regulation. The term "group" will be used in the following sections exclusively to refer to the collection of undertakings whose relations with an undertaking concerned come within the terms of one or more of the sub-paragraphs of Article 5(4) of the Merger Regulation.

131. It is important, when referring to the various undertakings which may be involved in a procedure, not to confuse the concept of "undertakings concerned" under Articles 1 and 5 with the terminology used elsewhere in the Merger Regulation and in Commission Regulation (EC) No 802/2004 of 7 April 2004 implementing Council Regulation (EC) No 139/2004 on the control of concentrations between undertakings (hereinafter referred to as the "Implementing Regulation")[106] referring to the various undertakings which may be involved in a procedure. This terminology refers to the notifying parties, other involved parties, third parties and parties who may be subject to fines or periodic penalty payments, and they are defined in Chapter IV of the Implementing Regulation, along with their respective rights and duties.

2. Mergers

132. In a merger the undertakings concerned are each of the merging entities.

3. Acquisition of control

133. In the remaining cases, it is the concept of "acquiring control" that will determine which are the undertakings concerned. On the acquiring side, there can be one or more undertakings acquiring sole or joint control. On the acquired side, there can be one or more undertakings as a whole or parts thereof. As a general rule, each of these undertakings will be an undertaking concerned within the meaning of the Merger Regulation.

Acquisition of sole control

134. Acquisition of sole control of the whole undertaking is the most straightforward case of acquisition of control. The undertakings concerned will be the acquiring undertaking and the target undertaking.

135. Where the target undertaking is acquired by a group through one of its subsidiaries, the undertakings concerned are the target undertaking and the acquiring subsidiary if this is not a mere acquisition vehicle. However, even though the subsidiary is normally the undertaking concerned for the purpose of calculating turnover, the turnover of all undertakings with which the undertaking concerned has the links as specified in Article 5(4) shall be included in the threshold calculations. In this respect, the group is considered to be a single economic unit and the different companies belonging to the same group cannot be considered as different undertakings concerned for jurisdictional purposes under the Merger Regulation. The actual notification can be made by the subsidiary concerned or by its parent company.

Acquisition of parts of an undertaking and staggered operations – Article 5(2)

136. The first subparagraph of Article 5(2) of the Merger Regulation provides that when the operation concerns the acquisition of parts of one or more undertakings, only those parts which are the subject of the transaction shall be taken into account with regard to the seller. The possible impact of the transaction on the market will depend only on the combination of the economic and financial resources that are the subject of the transaction with those of the acquirer and not on the remaining business of the seller. In this case, the undertakings concerned will be the acquirer(s) and the acquired part(s) of the target undertaking, but the remaining businesses of the seller will be ignored.

137. The second subparagraph of Article 5(2) includes a special provision on staggered operations or follow-up deals. The previous concentrations (within two years) involving the same parties become (re)notifiable with the most recent transaction, provided this constitutes a concentration, if the thresholds are met whether for one or more of the transactions taken in isolation or cumulatively. In this case, the undertakings concerned are the acquirer(s) and the different acquired part(s) of the target company taken as a whole.

Change from joint to sole control

138. If the acquisition of control occurs by way of a change from joint control to sole control, one shareholder normally acquires the stake previously held by the other shareholder(s). In this situation, the undertakings concerned are the acquiring shareholder and the joint venture. As is the case for any other seller, the "exiting" shareholder is not an undertaking concerned.[107]

Acquisition of joint control

139. In the case of acquisition of joint control of a newly-created undertaking, the undertakings concerned are each of the companies acquiring control of the newly set-up joint venture (which, as it does not yet exist, cannot be considered to be an undertaking concerned and moreover, as yet, has no turnover of its own). The same rule applies where one undertaking contributes a pre-existing subsidiary or a business (over which it previously exercised sole control) to a newly created joint venture. In these circumstances, each of the jointly-controlling undertakings is considered an undertaking concerned whereas any company or business contributed to the joint venture is not an undertaking concerned, and its turnover is part of the turnover of the initial parent company.

140. The situation is different if undertakings newly acquire joint control of a pre-existing undertaking or business. The undertakings concerned are each of the undertakings acquiring joint control on the one hand, and the pre-existing acquired undertaking or business on the other.

141. The acquisition of a company with a view to immediately split up the assets is, as explained above in paragraph 32, mostly not considered as an acquisition of joint control of the entire target company, but as the acquisition of sole control by each of the ultimate acquirers of the respective parts of the target company. In line with the considerations for the acquisition of sole control, undertakings concerned are the acquiring undertakings and the acquired parts in each of the transactions.

Changes of controlling shareholders in cases of joint control of an existing joint venture

142. A notifiable concentration may arise, as explained above, where a change in the quality of control occurs in a joint control structure due to the entrance of new controlling shareholders, irrespective of whether or not they replace existing controlling shareholders.

143. In the case where one or more shareholders acquire control, either by entry or by substitution of one or more shareholders, in a situation of joint control both before and after the operation, the undertakings concerned are the shareholders (both existing and new) who exercise joint control and the joint venture itself.[108] On the one hand, similar to the acquisition of joint control of an existing company, the joint venture itself can be considered as an undertaking concerned as it is an already pre-existing undertaking. On the other hand, as set out above, the entry of a new shareholder is not only in itself a new acquisition of control, but also leads to a change in the quality of control for the remaining controlling shareholders as the quality of control of the joint venture is determined by the identity and composition of the controlling shareholders and therefore also by the relationship between them. Furthermore, the Merger Regulation considers a joint venture as a combination of the economic resources of the parent companies, together with the joint venture if it already generates turnover on the market. For these reasons, the newly entering controlling shareholders are undertakings concerned alongside with the remaining controlling shareholders. Due to the change of the quality in control, all of them are considered to undertake an acquisition of control.

144. As Article 4(2) first sentence of the Merger Regulation foresees that all acquisitions of joint control shall be notified jointly by the undertakings acquiring joint control, existing and new shareholders in principle have to notify concentrations arising from such changes in joint control scenarios jointly.

Acquisition of control by a joint venture

145. In transactions where a joint venture acquires control of another company, the question arises whether or not the joint venture should be regarded as the undertaking concerned (the turnover of which would include the turnover of its parent companies), or whether each of its parent companies should individually be regarded as undertakings concerned. This question may be decisive for jurisdictional purposes.[109] Whereas, in principle, the undertaking concerned is the joint venture as the direct participant in the acquisition of control, there may be circumstances where companies set up "shell" companies and the parent companies will individually be considered as undertakings concerned. In this type of situation, the Commission will look at the economic reality of the operation to determine which are the undertakings concerned.

146. Where the acquisition is carried out by a full-function joint venture, with the features set out above, and already operates on the same market, the Commission will normally consider the joint venture itself and the target undertaking to be the undertakings concerned (and not the joint venture's parent companies).

147. Conversely, where the joint venture can be regarded as a mere vehicle for an acquisition by the parent companies, the Commission will consider each of the parent companies themselves to be the undertakings concerned, rather than the joint venture, together with the target company. This is the case in particular where the joint venture is set up especially for the purpose of acquiring the target company or has not yet started to operate, where an existing joint venture has no full-function character as referred to above or where the joint venture is an association of undertakings. The same applies where there are elements which demonstrate that the parent companies are in fact the real players behind the operation. These elements may include a significant involvement by the parent companies themselves in the initiation, organisation and financing of the operation. In those cases, the parent companies are regarded as undertakings concerned.

Break-up of joint ventures and exchange of assets

148. When two (or more) undertakings break up a joint venture and split the assets (constituting businesses) between them, this will normally be considered as more than one acquisition of control, as explained above in paragraph 41. For example, undertakings A and B form a joint venture and subsequently split it up, in particular with a new asset configuration. The break-up of the joint venture involves a change from joint control over the joint venture's entire assets to sole control over the divided assets by each of the acquiring undertakings.[110]

149. For each break-up operation, and in line with the consideration to the acquisition of sole control, the undertakings concerned will be, on the one hand, the acquiring party and, on the other, the assets that this undertaking will acquire.

150. Similar to the break-up scenario is the situation where two (or more) companies exchange assets constituting a business on each side. In this case, each acquisition of control is considered an independent acquisition of sole control. The undertakings concerned will be, for each transaction, the acquiring companies and the acquired undertaking or assets.

Acquisitions of control by natural persons

151. Control may also be acquired by natural persons, within the meaning of Article 3 of the Merger Regulation, if those persons themselves carry out further economic activities (and are therefore classified as economic undertakings in their own right) or if they control one or more other economic undertakings. In such a situation, the undertakings concerned are the target undertaking and the individual acquirer (with the turnover of the undertaking(s) controlled by that natural person being included in the calculation of the natural person's turnover to the extent that the terms of Article 5(4) are satisfied).[111]

152. An acquisition of control of an undertaking by its managers is also an acquisition by natural persons, and paragraph 151 above is also relevant. However, the managers may pool their interests through a "vehicle company", so that it acts with a single voice and also to facilitate decision-making. Such a vehicle company may be, but is not necessarily, an undertaking concerned. The general guidance given above in paragraphs 145-147 on acquisitions of control by a joint venture also applies here.

Acquisition of control by a State-owned undertaking

153. As described above, a merger or an acquisition of control arising between two undertakings owned by the same State (or the same public body) may constitute a concentration if the undertakings were formerly part of different economic units having an independent power of decision. If this is the case, both of them will qualify as undertakings concerned although both are owned by the same State.[112]

III. RELEVANT DATE FOR ESTABLISHING JURISDICTION

[4.646]

154. The legal situation for establishing the Commission's jurisdiction has been changed under the recast Merger Regulation. Under the former Merger Regulation, the relevant date was the triggering event for a notification according to Article 4(1) of this Regulation – the conclusion of a final agreement or the announcement of a public bid or the acquisition of a controlling interest – or, at the latest, the time when the parties were obliged to notify (ie one week after a triggering event for a notification).[113]

155. Under the recast Merger Regulation, there is no longer an obligation for the parties to notify within a certain time-frame (provided the parties do not implement the planned concentration before notification). Moreover, according to Article 4(1) second subparagraph, the undertakings concerned can already notify the transaction on the basis of a good faith intention to conclude an agreement or, in the case of a public bid, where they have publicly announced an intention to make such a bid. At the time of the notification at the latest, the Commission – as well as national competition authorities – must be able to determine their jurisdiction. Article 4(1) subparagraph 1 of the Merger Regulation provides, generally, that concentrations shall be notified following the conclusion of the agreement, the announcement of the public bid, or the acquisition of a controlling interest. The dates of these events are therefore still decisive under the recast Merger Regulation in order to determine the relevant date for establishing jurisdiction, if a notification does not occur before such events on the basis of a good faith intention or an announced intention.[114]

156. The relevant date for establishing Community jurisdiction over a concentration is therefore the date of the conclusion of the binding legal agreement, the announcement of a public bid or the acquisition of a controlling interest or the date of the first notification, whichever date is earlier.[115] Regarding the date of notification, a notification to either the Commission or to a Member State authority is relevant. The relevant date needs in particular to be considered for the question whether acquisitions or divestitures which occur after the period covered by the relevant account, but before the relevant date, require adaptations to those accounts according to the principles set out in paragraphs 172 and 173.

IV. TURNOVER

1. THE CONCEPT OF TURNOVER

[4.647]

157. The concept of turnover as used in Article 5 of the Merger Regulation comprises "the amounts derived [. . .] from the sale of products and the provision of services". Those amounts generally appear in company accounts under the heading "sales". In the case of products, turnover can be determined without difficulty, namely by identifying each commercial act involving a transfer of ownership.

158. In the case of services, the method of calculating turnover in general does not differ from that used in the case of products: the Commission takes into consideration the total amount of sales. However, the calculation of the amounts derived from the provision of services may be more complex as this depends on the exact service provided and the underlying legal and economic arrangements in the sector in question. Where one undertaking provides the entire service directly to the customer, the turnover of the undertaking concerned consists of the total amount of sales for the provision of services in the last financial year.

159. In other areas, this general principle may have to be adapted to the specific conditions of the service provided. In certain sectors of activity (such as package holidays and advertising), the service may be sold through intermediaries.[116] Even if the intermediary invoices the entire amount to the final customer, the turnover of the undertaking acting as an intermediary consists solely of the amount of its commission. For package holidays, the entire amount paid by the final customer is then allocated to the tour operator which uses the travel agency as distribution network. In the case of advertising, only the amounts received (without the commission) are considered to constitute the turnover of the TV channel or the magazine since media agencies, as intermediaries, do not constitute the distribution channel for the sellers of advertising space, but are chosen by the customers, ie those undertakings wishing to place advertising.

160. The examples mentioned show that, due to the diversity of services, many different situations may arise and the underlying legal and economic relations have to be carefully analysed. Similarly, specific situations for the calculation of turnover may arise in the areas of credit, financial services and insurance. These issues will be dealt with in Section VI.

2. ORDINARY ACTIVITIES

161. Article 5(1) provides that the amounts to be included in the calculation of turnover should correspond to the "ordinary activities" of the undertakings concerned. This is the turnover achieved from the sale of products or the provision of services in the normal course of its business. It generally excludes those items which are listed under the headers "financial income" or "extraordinary income" in the company's accounts. Such extraordinary income may be derived from the sale of businesses or of fixed assets. However, company accounts do not necessarily delineate the revenues derived from ordinary activities in the way required for the purposes of turnover calculation under the Merger Regulation. In some cases, the qualification of the items in the accounts may have to be adapted to the requirements of the Merger Regulation.[117]

162. The revenues do not necessarily have to be derived from the customer of the products or services. With regard to aid granted to undertakings by public bodies, any aid has to be included in the calculation of turnover if the undertaking is itself the recipient of the aid and if the aid is directly linked to the sale of products and the provision of services by the undertaking. The aid is therefore an income of the undertaking from the sale of products or provision of services in addition to the price paid by the consumer.[118]

163. Specific issues have arisen for the calculation of turnover of a business unit which only had internal revenues in the past. This may in particular apply for transactions involving the outsourcing of services by transfer of a business unit. If such a transaction constitutes a concentration on the basis of the considerations outlined in paragraphs 25 ff. of this Notice, the Commission's practice is that the turnover should normally be calculated on the basis of the previously internal turnover or of publicly quoted prices where such prices exist (eg in the oil industry). Where the previously internal turnover does not appear to correspond to a market valuation of the activities in question (and, thus, to the expected future turnover on the market), the forecast revenues to be received on the basis of an agreement with the former parent may be a suitable proxy.

3. "NET" TURNOVER

164. The turnover to be taken into account is "net" turnover, after deduction of a number of components specified in the Regulation. The aim is to adjust turnover in such a way as to enable it to reflect the real economic strength of the undertaking.

3.1. Deduction of rebates and taxes

165. Article 5(1) provides for the "deduction of sales rebates and of value added tax and other taxes directly related to turnover". "Sales rebates" mean all rebates or discounts which are granted by the undertakings to their customers and which have a direct influence on the amounts of sales.

166. As regards the deduction of taxes, the Merger Regulation refers to VAT and "other taxes directly related to turnover". The concept of "taxes directly related to turnover" refers to indirect taxation linked to turnover, such as, for example, taxes on alcoholic beverages or cigarettes.

3.2. The treatment of "internal" turnover

167. The first subparagraph of Article 5(1) states that "the aggregate turnover of an undertaking concerned shall not include the sale of products or the provision of services between any of the undertakings referred to in paragraph 4", ie the group to which the undertaking concerned belongs. The aim is to exclude the proceeds of

business dealings within a group so as to take account of the real economic weight of each entity in the form of market turnover. Thus, the "amounts" taken into account by the Merger Regulation reflect only the transactions which take place between the group of undertakings on the one hand and third parties on the other.

168. Article 5(5)(a) of the Merger Regulation applies the principle that double counting is to be avoided specifically to the situation where two or more undertakings concerned in a concentration jointly have the rights or powers listed in Article 5(4)(b) in another company. According to this provision, the turnover resulting from the sale of products or the provision of services between the joint venture and each of the undertakings concerned (or any other undertaking connected with any one of them in the sense of Article 5(4)) should be excluded. As regards joint ventures between undertakings concerned and third parties, insofar as their turnover is taken into account according to Article 5(4)(b) as set out in paragraph 181 below, the turnover generated by sales between the joint venture and the undertaking concerned (as well as undertakings linked to the undertaking concerned in accordance with the criteria set out in Article 5(4)) is not taken into account according to Article 5(1).

4. TURNOVER CALCULATION AND FINANCIAL ACCOUNTS

4.1. The general rule

169. The Commission seeks to base itself upon the most accurate and reliable figures available. Generally, the Commission will refer to accounts which relate to the closest financial year to the date of the transaction and which are audited under the standard applicable to the undertaking in question and compulsory for the relevant financial year.[119] An adjustment of the audited figures should only take place if this is required by the provisions of the Merger Regulation, including the cases explained in more detail in paragraph 172.

170. The Commission is reluctant to rely on management or any other form of provisional accounts in any but exceptional circumstances.[120] Where a concentration takes place within the first months of the year and audited accounts are not yet available for the most recent financial year, the figures to be taken into account are those relating to the previous year. Where there is a major divergence between the two sets of accounts, due to significant and permanent changes in the undertaking concerned, and, in particular, when the final draft figures for the most recent year have been approved by the board of management, the Commission may decide to take those figures into account.

171. Despite the general rule, in cases where major differences between the Community's accounting standards and those of a non-member country are observed, the Commission may consider it necessary to restate these accounts in accordance with Community standards in respect of turnover.

4.2. Adjustments after the date of the last audited accounts

172. Notwithstanding the foregoing paragraphs, an adjustment must always be made to account for permanent changes in the economic reality of the undertakings concerned, such as acquisitions or divestments which are not or not fully reflected in the audited accounts. Such changes have to be taken into account in order to identify the true resources being concentrated and to better reflect the economic situation of the undertakings concerned. Those adjustments are only selective in nature and do not endanger the principle that there should be a simple and objective mechanism to determine the Commission's jurisdiction as they do not require a complete revision of the audited accounts.[121] First, this applies to acquisitions, divestments or closure of part of its business subsequent to the date of the audited accounts. This is relevant if a company closes a transaction concerning the divestment and closure of part of its business at any time before the relevant date for establishing jurisdiction (see paragraph 154) or where such a divestment or closure of a business is a pre-condition for the operation.[122] In this case, the turnover to be attributed to that part of the business must be subtracted from the turnover of the notifying party as shown in its last audited accounts. If an agreement for the sale of part of its business is signed, but the closing of the sale (in other words, its legal implementation and the transfer of the legal title to the shares or assets acquired) has not yet occurred, such a change is not taken into account,[123] unless the sale is a pre-condition for the notified operation. Conversely, the turnover of those businesses whose acquisition has been closed subsequent to the preparation of the most recent audited accounts, but before the relevant date for establishing jurisdiction, must be added to a company's turnover for notification purposes.

173. Second, an adjustment may also be necessary for acquisitions, divestments or closure of part of the business which have taken place during the financial year for which the audited accounts are drawn up. If acquisitions, divestments or closure of part of the business within this period are made, the changes in the economic resources may only partly be reflected in the audited accounts of the undertaking concerned. As the turnover of the businesses acquired may be included in the accounts only from the time of their acquisition, this may not reflect the full annual turnover of the acquired business. Conversely, the turnover of the businesses divested or closed may still be included in the audited accounts up to the point in time of their actual divestment or closure. In these cases, adjustments have to be made to remove the turnover generated by the divested or closed businesses from the audited accounts until the time of de-consolidation and to add the turnover which the acquired businesses have generated in the year until the time they have been consolidated in the accounts. As a result, the turnover of the businesses divested or closed must be excluded in full and the full annual turnover of the businesses acquired must be included.

174. Other factors that may affect turnover on a temporary basis such as a decrease in orders for the product or a slow-down in the production process within the period prior to the transaction will be ignored for the purposes of calculating turnover. No adjustment to the definitive accounts will be made to incorporate them.

5. Attribution of turnover under Article 5(4)

5.1. Identification of undertakings whose turnover is taken into account

175. When an undertaking concerned by a concentration belongs to a group, not only the turnover of the undertaking concerned is considered, but the Merger Regulation requires to also take into account the turnover of those undertakings with which the undertaking concerned has links consisting in the rights or powers listed in Article 5(4) in order to determine whether the thresholds contained in Article 1 of the Merger Regulation are met. The aim is again to capture the total volume of the economic resources that are being combined through the operation irrespective of whether the economic activities are carried out directly by the undertaking concerned or whether they are undertaken indirectly via undertakings with which the undertaking concerned possesses the links described in Article 5(4).

176. The Merger Regulation does not delineate the concept of a group in a single abstract definition, but sets out in Article 5(4)(b) certain rights or powers. If an undertaking concerned directly or indirectly has such links with other companies, those are to be regarded as part of its group for purposes of turnover calculation under the Merger Regulation.

177. Article 5(4) of the Merger Regulation provides the following: "Without prejudice to paragraph 2 [acquisitions of parts], the aggregate turnover of an undertaking concerned within the meaning of Article 1(2) and (3) shall be calculated by adding together the respective turnovers of the following:

(a) the undertaking concerned;
(b) those undertakings in which the undertaking concerned directly or indirectly:
   (i) owns more than half the capital or business assets, or
   (ii) has the power to exercise more than half the voting rights, or
   (iii) has the power to appoint more than half the members of the supervisory board, the administrative board or bodies legally representing the undertakings, or
   (iv) has the right to manage the undertaking's affairs;
(c) those undertakings which have in an undertaking concerned the rights or powers listed in (b);
(d) those undertakings in which an undertaking as referred to in (c) has the rights or powers listed in (b);
(e) those undertakings in which two or more undertakings as referred to in (a) to (d) jointly have the rights or powers listed in (b)."

An undertaking which has in another undertaking the rights and powers mentioned in Article 5(4)(b) will be referred to as the "parent" of the latter in the present section of this Notice dealing with the calculation of turnover, whereas the latter is referred to as "subsidiary" of the former. In short, Article 5(4) therefore provides that the turnover of the undertaking concerned by the concentration (point (a)) should include its subsidiaries (point (b)), its parent companies (point (c)), the other subsidiaries of its parent undertakings (point (d)) and any other subsidiary jointly held by two or more of the undertakings identified under (a)–(d) (point (e)).

178. A graphic example is as follows:
The undertaking concerned and its group:

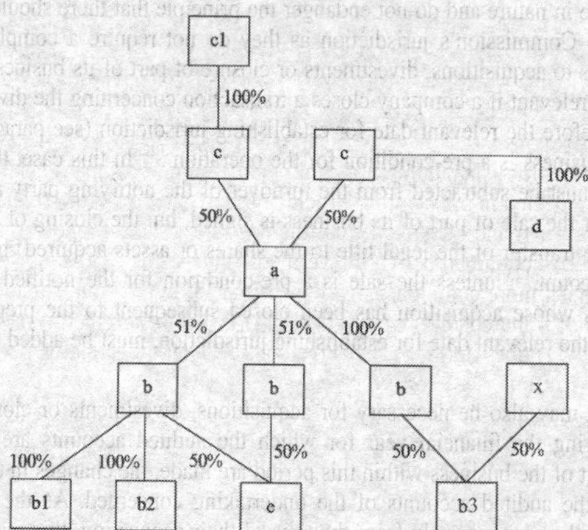

a: The undertaking concerned[124]
b: Its subsidiaries, jointly held companies together with third parties (b3) and their own subsidiaries (b1 and b2)
c: Its parent companies and their own parent companies (c1)
d: Other subsidiaries of the parent companies of the undertaking concerned
e: Companies jointly held by two (or more) companies of the group
x: Third party

Note: the letters a–e correspond to the relevant points of Article 5(4). Percentages set out in the graph relate to the percentage of voting rights held by the respective parent company.

179. The rights or powers listed in Article 5(4)(b)(i)–(iii) can be identified in a rather straightforward way as they refer to quantitative thresholds. These thresholds are fulfilled if the undertaking concerned owns more than half of the capital or business assets of other undertakings, has more than half of the voting rights or has legally the power to

appoint more than half of the board members in other undertakings. However, the thresholds are also met if the undertaking concerned *de facto* has the power to exercise more than half of the voting rights in the shareholders' assembly or the power to appoint more than half of the board members in other undertakings.[125]

180. The provision contained in Article 5(4)(b)(iv) refers to the right to manage the undertaking's affairs. Such a right to manage exists under company law in particular on the basis of organisational contracts such as a "*Beherrschungsvertrag*" under German law, on the basis of business lease agreements or on the basis of the organisation structure for the general partner in a limited partnership.[126] However, the "right to manage" may also result from the holding of voting rights (alone or in combination with contractual arrangements, such as a shareholders' agreement) which enable, on a stable, *de jure* basis, to determine the strategic behaviour of an undertaking.

181. The right to manage also covers situations in which the undertaking concerned jointly has the right to manage an undertaking's affairs together with third parties.[127] The underlying consideration is that the undertakings exercising joint control have jointly the right to manage the controlled undertakings' affairs even if each of them individually may have those rights only in a negative sense, ie in the form of veto rights. In the example, the undertaking (b3) which is jointly controlled by the undertaking concerned (a) and a third party (x) is taken into account as both (a) and (x) have veto rights in (b3) on the basis of their equal shareholding in (b3).[128] Under Article 5(4)(b)(iv) the Commission only takes into account those joint ventures in which the undertaking concerned and third parties have *de jure* rights that give rise to a clear-cut right to manage. The inclusion of joint ventures is therefore limited to situations where the undertaking concerned and third parties have a joint *right* to manage on the basis of an agreement, eg a shareholders' agreement, or where the undertaking concerned and a third party have an equality of voting rights to the effect that they have the right to appoint an equal number of members to the decision-making bodies of the joint venture.

182. In the same way, where two or more companies jointly control the undertaking concerned in the sense that the agreement of each and all of them is needed in order to manage the undertaking affairs, the turnover of all of them is included. In the example, the two parent companies (c) of the undertaking concerned (a) would be taken into account as well as their own parent companies (c1 in the example). This interpretation results from the referral from Article 5(4)(c), dealing with this case, to Article 5(4)(b), which is applicable to jointly controlled companies as set out in the preceding paragraph.

183. When any of the companies identified on the basis of Article 5(4) also has links as defined in Article 5(4) with other undertakings, these should also be brought into the calculation. In the example, one of the subsidiaries of the undertaking concerned a (called b) has in turn its own subsidiaries b1 and b2 and one of the parent companies (called c) has its own subsidiary (d).

184. Article 5(4) sets out specific criteria for identifying undertakings whose turnover can be attributed to the undertaking concerned. These criteria, including the "right to manage the undertaking's affairs", are not coextensive with the notion of "control" under Article 3(2). There are significant differences between Articles 3 and 5, as those provisions fulfil different roles. The differences are most apparent in the field of *de facto* control. Whereas under Article 3(2) even a situation of economic dependence may lead to control on a *de facto* basis (see in detail above), a solely controlled subsidiary is only taken into account on a *de facto* basis under Article 5(4)(b) if it is clearly demonstrated that the undertaking concerned has the power to exercise more than half of the voting rights or to appoint more than half of the board members. Concerning joint control scenarios, Article 5(4)(b)(iv) covers those scenarios where the controlling undertakings jointly have a right to manage on the basis of individual veto rights. However, Article 5(4) would not cover situations where joint control occurs on a *de facto* basis due to strong common interests between different minority shareholders of the joint venture company on the basis of shareholders' attendance. The difference is reflected in the fact that Article 5(4)(b)(iv) refers to the *right* to manage, and not a power (as in subparagraph (b)(ii) and (iii)) and is explained by the need for precision and certainty in the criteria used for calculating turnover so that jurisdiction can be readily verified. Under Article 3(3), however, the question whether a concentration arises can be much more comprehensively investigated. In addition, situations of negative sole control are only exceptionally covered (if the conditions of Article 5(4)(b)(i)–(iii) are met in the specific case); the "right to manage" under Article 5(4)(b)(iv) does not cover negative control scenarios. Finally, Article 5(4)(b)(i), for example, covers situations where "control" under Article 3(2) may not exist.

5.2.
Allocation of turnover of the undertakings identified

185. In general, as long as the test under Article 5(4)(b) is fulfilled, the whole turnover of the subsidiary in question will be taken into account regardless of the actual shareholding which the undertaking concerned holds in the subsidiary. In the chart, the whole turnover of the subsidiaries called b of the undertaking concerned a will be taken into account.

186. However, the Merger Regulation includes specific rules for joint ventures. Article 5(5)(b) provides that for joint ventures between two or more undertakings concerned, the turnover of the joint venture (as far as the turnover is generated from activities with third parties as set out above in paragraph 168) should be apportioned equally amongst the undertakings concerned, irrespective of their share of the capital or the voting rights.

187. The principle contained in Article 5(5)(b) is followed by analogy for the allocation of turnover for joint ventures between undertakings concerned and third parties if their turnover is taken into account according to Article 5(4)(b) as set out above in paragraph 181. The Commission's practice has been to allocate to the undertaking concerned the turnover of the joint venture on a per capita basis according to the number of undertakings exercising joint control. In the example, half of the turnover of b3 is taken into account.

188. The rules of Article 5(4) also have to be adapted in situations involving a change from joint to sole control in order to avoid double counting of the turnover of the joint venture. Even if the acquiring undertaking has rights or powers in the joint venture which satisfy the requirements of Article 5(4), the turnover of the acquiring shareholder has to be calculated without the turnover of the joint venture, and the turnover of the joint venture has to be taken without the turnover of the acquiring shareholder.

5.3. Allocation of turnover in case of investment funds

189. The investment company, as set out above in paragraph 15, normally acquires indirect control over portfolio companies held by an investment fund. In the same way, the investment company may be considered to indirectly have the powers and rights which are set out in Article 5(4)(b), in particular to indirectly have the power to exercise the voting rights held by the investment fund in the portfolio companies.

190. The same considerations, as set out above in the framework of Article 3 (paragraph 15), may also apply if an investment company sets up several investment funds with possibly different investors. Typically, on the basis of the organisational structure, in particular links between the investment company and the general partner(s) of the different funds organised as limited partnerships, or contractual arrangements, especially advisory agreements between the general partner or the investment fund and the investment company, the investment company will indirectly have the power to exercise the voting rights held by the investment fund in the portfolio companies or indirectly have one of the other powers or rights set out in Article 5(4)(b). In these circumstances, the investment company may exercise a common control structure over the different funds which it has set up and the common operation of the different funds by the investment company is often indicated by a common brand for the funds.

191. Consequently, such an organisation of the different funds by the investment company may lead to the result that the turnover of all portfolio companies held by different funds is taken into account for the purpose of assessing whether the turnover thresholds in Article 1 are met if the investment company acquires indirect control of a portfolio company via one of the funds.

5.4. Allocation of turnover for State-owned undertakings

192. As regards the calculation of turnover of State-owned undertakings, Article 5(4) should be read in conjunction with recital 22 of the Merger Regulation. This recital declares that, in order to avoid discrimination between the public and private sectors, "in the public sector, calculation of the turnover of an undertaking concerned in a concentration needs, therefore, to take account of undertakings making up an economic unit with an independent power of decision, irrespective of the way in which their capital is held or of the rules of administrative supervision applicable to them".[129]

193. This recital clarifies that Member States (or other public bodies) are not considered as "undertakings" under Article 5(4) simply because they have interests in other undertakings which satisfy the conditions of Article 5(4). Therefore, for the purposes of calculating turnover of State-owned undertakings, account is only taken of those undertakings which belong to the same economic unit, having the same independent power of decision.

194. Thus, where a State-owned company is not subject to any coordination with other State-controlled holdings, it should be treated as independent for the purposes of Article 5, and the turnover of other companies owned by that State should not be taken into account. Where, however, several State-owned companies are under the same independent centre of commercial decision-making, then the turnover of those businesses should be considered part of the group of the undertaking concerned for the purposes of Article 5.

V. GEOGRAPHIC ALLOCATION OF TURNOVER

[4.648]

195. The thresholds concerning Community-wide and Member State turnover in Article 1(2) and (3) aim to identify cases which have sufficient turnover within the Community in order to be of Community interest and which are primarily cross-border in nature. They require turnover to be allocated geographically to the Community and to individual Member States. Since audited accounts often do not provide a geographical breakdown as required by the Merger Regulation, the Commission will rely on the best figures available provided by the undertakings. The second subparagraph of Article 5(1) provides that the location of turnover is determined by the location of the customer at the time of the transaction: "Turnover, in the Community or in a Member State, shall comprise products sold and services provided to undertakings or consumers, in the Community or in that Member State as the case may be."

General rule

196. The Merger Regulation does not discriminate between "products sold" and "services provided" for the geographic allocation of turnover. In both cases, the general rule is that turnover should be attributed to the place where the customer is located. The underlying principle is that turnover should be allocated to the location where competition with alternative suppliers takes place. This location is normally also the place where the characteristic action under the contract in question is to be performed, ie where the service is actually provided and the product is actually delivered. In the case of Internet transactions, it may be difficult for the undertakings to determine the location of the customer at the time when the contract is concluded via the Internet. If the product or the service itself is not supplied via the Internet, focusing on the place where the characteristic action under the contract is performed may avoid those difficulties. In the following, the sale of goods and the provision of services are dealt with separately as they exhibit certain different features in terms of allocation of turnover.

Sale of goods

197. For the sale of goods, particular situations may arise in situations in which the place where the customer was located at the time of concluding the purchase agreement is different from the billing address and/or the place of delivery. In these situations, the place where the purchase agreement was entered into and the place of delivery are more important than the billing address. As the delivery is in general the characteristic action for the sale of goods, the place of delivery may even be prevailing over the place where the customer was located at the time when the purchase agreement was concluded. This will depend on whether the place of delivery is to be considered the place where competition takes place for the sale of goods or whether competition rather takes place at the residence of the customer. In the case of a sale of mobile goods, such as a motor car, to a final consumer, the place where the car is delivered to the customer is decisive even if the agreement was concluded via the phone or the Internet before.

198. A specific situation arises in cases where a multinational corporation has a Community buying strategy and sources all its requirements for a good from one location. As a central purchasing organisation can take different forms, it is necessary to consider its concrete form since this may determine how to allocate the turnover. Where goods are purchased by and delivered to the central purchasing organisation and are subsequently re-distributed internally to different plants in a variety of Member States, turnover is allocated only to the Member State where the central purchasing organisation is located. In this case, competition takes place at the location of the central purchasing organisation and this is also the place where the characteristic action under the sales contract is performed. The situation is different in case of direct links between the seller and the different subsidiaries. This comprises the case where the central purchasing organisation concludes a mere framework agreement, but the individual orders are placed by and the products are directly delivered to the subsidiaries in different Member States as well as the case where the individual orders are placed via the central purchasing organisation, but the products are directly delivered to the subsidiaries. In both cases, turnover is to be allocated to the different Member States in which the subsidiaries are located, irrespective of whether the central purchasing organisation or the subsidiaries receive the bills and effect the payment. The reason is that in both cases competition with alternative suppliers takes place for the delivery of products to the different subsidiaries even though the contract is concluded centrally. In the first case, in addition, the subsidiaries actually decide upon the quantities to be delivered and on an element essential for competition on their own.

Provision of services

199. For services, the Merger Regulation foresees that the place of their provision to the customer is relevant. Services containing cross-border elements can be considered to fall into three general categories. The first category comprises cases where the service provider travels, the second category cases where the customer travels. The third category comprises those cases where a service is provided without either the service provider or the customer having to travel. In the first two categories, the turnover generated is to be allocated to the place of destination of the traveller, ie the place where the service is actually provided to the customer. In the third category, the turnover is generally to be allocated to the location of the customer. For the central sourcing of services the above outlined principles for the central purchasing of goods apply in an analogous way.

200. An example of the first category would be a situation where a non-European company provides special airplane maintenance services to a carrier in a Member State. In this case, the service provider travels to the Community where the service is actually provided and where also competition for this service takes place. If a European tourist hires a car or books a hotel directly in the United States, this falls into the second category as the service is provided outside the Community and also competition takes place between hotels and rental car companies at the location chosen. However, the case is different for package holidays. For this kind of holiday, the service starts with the sale of the package through a travel agent at the customer's location and competition for the sale of holidays through travel agents takes place locally, as with retail shopping, even though parts of the service may be provided in a number of distant locations. The case therefore falls into the third category and the turnover generated is to be allocated to the customer's location. The third category also comprises cases like the supply of software or the distribution of films which are made outside the Community, but are supplied to a customer in a Member State so that the service is actually provided to the customer within the Community.

201. Cases concerning the transport of goods are different as the customer, to whom those services are provided, does not travel, but the transport service is provided to the customer at its location. Those cases fall into the third category and the location of the customer is the relevant criterion for the allocation of the turnover.

202. In telecom cases, the qualification of call termination services may raise problems. Although call termination would appear to fall into the third category, there are reasons to treat it differently. Call termination services are provided, eg, in situations where a call, originating from a European operator, is being terminated in the United States. Although neither the European nor the US operator travels, the signal travels and the service is provided by the US network to the European operator in the United States. This is also the place where competition takes place (if any). The turnover is therefore to be considered as non-Community turnover.[130]

Specific sectors

203. Certain sectors do, however, pose very particular problems with regard to the geographical allocation of turnover. These will be dealt with in Section VI below.

VI. CONVERSION OF TURNOVER INTO EURO

[4.649]

204. When converting turnover figures into euro great care should be taken with the exchange rate used. The annual turnover of a company should be converted at the average rate for the twelve months concerned. This average can be obtained via DG Competition's website.[131] The audited annual turnover figures should be converted as such and not be broken down into quarterly or monthly figures which would then be converted individually.

205. When a company has sales in a range of currencies, the procedure is no different. The total turnover given in the consolidated audited accounts and in that company's reporting currency is converted into euros at the yearly average rate. Local currency sales should not be converted directly into euros since these figures are not from the consolidated audited accounts of the company.

VII. PROVISIONS FOR CREDIT AND OTHER FINANCIAL INSTITUTIONS AND INSURANCE UNDERTAKINGS

1. Scope of application

[4.650]

206. Due to the specific nature of the sector, Article 5(3) contains specific rules for the calculation of turnover of credit and other financial institutions as well as insurance undertakings.

207. In order to define the terms "credit institutions and other financial institutions" under the Merger Regulation, the Commission in its practice has consistently adopted the definitions provided in the applicable European regulation in the banking sector. The Directive on the taking up and pursuit of the business of credit institutions foresees that:[132]

— "Credit institution shall mean an undertaking whose business is to receive deposits or other repayable funds from the public and to grant credits for its own account."

— "Financial institution shall mean an undertaking other than a credit institution, the principal activity of which is to acquire holdings or to carry on one or more of the activities listed in points 2 to 12 of Annex I."

208. Financial institutions within the meaning of Article 5(3) of the Merger Regulation are, accordingly, on the one hand holding companies and, on the other hand, undertakings which perform on a regular basis as a principal activity one or more activities expressly mentioned in points 2 to 12 of the Annex of the banking Directive. These activities include:

— lending (comprising activities such as consumer credit, mortgage credit, factoring);
— financial leasing;
— money transmission services;
— issuing and administering means of payment (eg credit cards, travellers' cheques and bankers' drafts);
— guarantees and commitments;
— trading for own account or for account of customers in money market instruments, (cheques, bills, certificates of deposit, etc), foreign exchange, financial futures and options, exchange and interest rate instruments, transferable securities;
— participation in securities issues and the provision of services related to such issues;
— money broking;
— portfolio management and advice; and
— safekeeping and administration of securities.

2. Calculation of turnover

209. Article 5(3) of the Merger Regulation sets out the methods of calculation of turnover for credit and other financial institutions and for insurance undertakings. In the following Section, some supplementary questions related to turnover calculation for the abovementioned types of undertakings are addressed.

2.1.
Calculation of turnover of credit and financial institutions (other than financial holding companies)

2.1.1.
General

210. There are normally no particular difficulties in applying the banking income criterion for the definition of the worldwide turnover to credit institutions and other kinds of financial institutions. For the geographic allocation of turnover to the Community and to individual Member States, the specific provision of Article 5 (3)(a) second subparagraph applies. It specifies that the turnover is to be allocated to the branch or division established in the Community or in the Member State which receives this income.

2.1.2.
Turnover of leasing companies

211. There is a fundamental distinction to be made between financial leases and operating leases. Basically, financial leases are made for longer periods than operating leases and ownership is generally transferred to the lessee at the end of the lease term by means of a purchase option included in the lease contract. Under an operating lease, on the contrary, ownership is not transferred to the lessee at the end of the lease term and the costs of maintenance, repair and insurance of the leased equipment are included in the lease payments. A financial lease therefore functions as a loan by the lessor to enable the lessee to purchase a given asset.

212. As already mentioned above, a company performing as its principal activity financial leasing is a financial institution within the meaning of Article 5(3)(a) and its turnover is to be calculated according to the specific rules set out in this provision. All payments on financial leasing contracts, except for the redemption part, are to be taken into account; a sale of future leasing payments at the beginning of the contract for re-financing purposes is not relevant.

213. Operational leasing activities are, however, not considered to be carried out by financial institutions, and therefore the general turnover calculation rules of Article 5(1) apply.[133]

2.2.
Insurance undertakings

214. In order to measure the turnover of insurance undertakings, Article 5(3)(b) of the Merger Regulation provides that gross premiums written are taken into account. The gross premiums written are the sum of received premiums, including any received reinsurance premiums if the undertaking concerned has activities in the field of reinsurance. Outgoing or outward reinsurance premiums, ie all amounts paid and payable by the undertaking concerned to get reinsurance cover, are only costs related to the provision of insurance coverage and are not to be deducted from the gross premiums written.

215. The premiums to be taken into account are not only related to new insurance contracts made during the accounting year being considered but also to all premiums related to contracts made in previous years which remain in force during the period taken into consideration.

216. In order to constitute appropriate reserves allowing for the payment of claims, insurance undertakings, usually hold a portfolio of investments in shares, interest-bearing securities, land and property and other assets providing annual revenues. The annual revenues coming from those sources are not considered as turnover for insurance undertakings under Article 5(3)(b). However, a distinction has to be made between pure financial investments, which do not confer the rights and powers specified in Article 5(4) to the insurance undertaking in the undertakings in which the investment has been made, and those investments leading to the acquisition of an interest which meets the criteria specified in Article 5(4)(b). In the latter case, Article 5(4) of the Merger Regulation applies, and the turnover of this undertaking has to be added to the turnover of the insurance undertaking, as calculated according to Article 5(3)(b), for the determination of the thresholds laid down in the Merger Regulation.[134]

2.3.
Financial holding companies

217. As an "other financial institution" within the meaning of Article 5(3)(a) of the Merger Regulation, the turnover of a financial holding company has to be calculated according to the specific rules set out in this provision. However, in the same way as mentioned above for insurance undertakings, Article 5(4) applies to those participations which meet the criteria specified in Article 5(4)(b). Thus, the turnover of a financial holding is to be basically calculated according to Article 5(3), but it may be necessary to add turnover of undertakings falling within the categories set out in Article 5(4) ("Art 5(4) companies").[135]

218. In practice, the turnover of the financial holding company (non-consolidated) must first be taken into account. Then the turnover of the Art. 5(4) companies must be added, whilst taking care to deduct dividends and other income distributed by those companies to the financial holdings. The following provides an example for this kind of calculation:

		(EUR million)
1.	Turnover related to financial activities (from non-consolidated P&L)	3,000
2.	Turnover related to insurance Art. 5(4) companies (gross premiums written)	300
3.	Turnover of industrial Article 5(4) companies	2,000
4.	Deduct dividends and other income derived from Art. 5(4) companies 2 and 3	<200>
Total turnover financial holding and its group		5,100

219. In such calculations different accounting rules may need to be taken into consideration. Whilst this consideration applies to any type of undertaking concerned by the Merger Regulation, it is particularly important in the case of financial holding companies[136] where the number and the diversity of enterprises controlled and the degree of control the holding holds on its subsidiaries, affiliated companies and other companies in which it has shareholding requires careful examination.

220. Turnover calculation for financial holding companies as described above may in practice prove onerous. Therefore a strict and detailed application of this method will be necessary only in cases where it seems that the turnover of a financial holding company is likely to be close to the Merger Regulation thresholds; in other cases it may well be obvious that the turnover is far from the thresholds of the Merger Regulation, and therefore the published accounts are adequate for the establishment of jurisdiction.

NOTES

105 A concentration is further deemed to have a Community dimension if it is referred to the Commission under Article 4(5) of the Merger Regulation. These cases are dealt with in the Commission Notice on Case Referral in respect of concentrations, OJ C56, 5.3.2005, p 2.

106 OJ L133, 30.4.2004, p 1.

107 Case IV/M.023 – *ICI/Tioxide*, of 28 November 1990.

108 See Case IV/M.376 – *Synthomer/Yule Catto*, of 22 October 1993.

109 Assume the following scenario: The target company has an aggregate Community turnover of less than EUR 250 million, and the acquiring parties are two (or more) undertakings, each with a Community turnover exceeding EUR 250 million. If the target is acquired by a "shell" company set up between the acquiring undertakings, there would only be one undertaking (the "shell" company) with a Community turnover exceeding EUR 250 million, and thus one of the cumulative threshold conditions for Community jurisdiction, namely, the existence of at least two undertakings with a Community turnover exceeding EUR 250 million, would not be fulfilled. Conversely, if instead of acting through a "shell" company, the acquiring undertakings acquire the target undertaking themselves, then the turnover threshold would be met and the Merger Regulation would apply to this transaction. The same considerations apply to the national turnover thresholds referred to in Article 1(3).

110 See parallel cases COMP/M.3293 – *Shell/BEB* and COMP/M.3294 – *ExxonMobil/BEB* of 20 November 2003; Case IV/M.197 – *Solvay/Laporte* of 30 April 1992.

111 See Case IV/M.082 – *Asko/Jacobs/Adia*, of 16 May 1991 where a private individual with other economic activities acquired joint control of an undertaking and was considered an undertaking concerned.

112 See recital 22 of the Merger Regulation, directly related to the calculation of turnover of a state-owned undertaking concerned in the context of Article 5(4).

113 See Case COMP/M.1741 – *MCI Worldcom/Sprint* of 28 June 2000.

114 The alternative possibility that turnover should be defined on the latest date when the relevant parties are obliged to notify (seven days after the "triggering event" under the former Merger Regulation) cannot be retained under the recast merger Regulation, because there is no deadline for notification.

115 See also opinion of AG Kokott in Case C-202/06 *Cementbouw v Commission* of 26 April 2007, paragraph 46 (not yet reported). Only the recast merger Regulation has provided for the possibility to take into account the first notification if this is earlier than the date of the conclusion of the binding legal agreement, the announcement of a public bid or the acquisition of a controlling interest, see fn. 35 of the opinion.

116 An undertaking will normally not act as an intermediary if it sells products via a commercial act which involves a transfer of ownership, Judgment in Case T-417/05, *Endesa v Commission*, paragraph 213, [2006] ECR II-2533.

117 In Case IV/M.126 – *Accor/Wagons-Lits*, of 28 April 1992, the Commission decided to consider certain income from car-hire activities as revenues from ordinary activities although they were included as "other operating proceeds" in *Wagons-Lits*' profit and loss account.

118 See Case IV/M.156 – *Cereol/Continentale Italiana* of 27 November 1991. In this case, the Commission excluded Community aid from the calculation of turnover because the aid was not intended to support the sale of products manufactured by one of the undertakings involved in the merger, but the producers of the raw materials (grain) used by the undertaking, which specialised in the crushing of grain.

119 See Case COMP/M.3986 – *Gas Natural/Endesa* of 15 November 2005; confirmed by Judgment in Case T-417/05, *Endesa v Commission*, paragraphs 128, 131, [2006] ECR II-2533.

120 See Case COMP/M.3986 – *Gas Natural/Endesa* of 15 November 2005; confirmed by Judgment in Case T-417/05, *Endesa v Commission*, paragraphs 176, 179, [2006] ECR II-2533.

121 Judgment in Case T-417/05, *Endesa v Commission*, paragraph 209, [2006] ECR II-2533.

122 See Judgment in Case T-3/93, *Air France v Commission*, [1994] ECR II-121 paragraphs 100 et seq in relation to Case IV/M.278 – *British Airways/Dan Air*; Case IV/M.588 – *Ingersoll-Rand/Clark Equipment*.

123 Case IV/M.632 – *Rhône Poulenc Rorer/Fisons* of 21 September 1995; Case COMP/M.1741 – *MCI Worldcom/Sprint* of 28 June 2000.

124 For the graph it is assumed that the joint venture itself is the undertaking concerned according to the criteria set out in paragraph 146 (acquisition by a full-function JV operating on the same market).

125 Case IV/M.187 – *Ifint/Exor* of 2 March 1992; Case IV/M.062 – *Eridania/ISI* of 30 July 1991.

126 Case IV/M.126 – *Accor/WagonLits* of 28 April 1992.

127 Case COMP/M.1741 – *MCI Worldcom/Sprint*; Case IV/M. 187 – *Ifint/Exor*; Case IV/M.1046 – *Ameritech/Tele Danmark*.

128 However, only half of the turnover generated by b3 is taken into account, see paragraph 187.

129 See also Case IV/M.216 – *CEA Industrie/France Telecom/Finmeccanica/SGS-Thomson*, of 22 February 1993.

130 This does not affect the turnover which the European telephony operator generates vis-à-vis its own customer with this call.

131 See europa.eu.int/comm/competition/mergers/others/exchange_rates.html#footnote_1. The website makes reference to the European Central Bank's Monthly Bulletin.

132 The definitions are to be found in Article 1 (1) and (5) of Directive 2000/12/EC of the European Parliament and of the Council of 20 March 2000 relating to the taking up and pursuit of the business of credit institutions (OJ L126, 26. 5.2000, p 1).

133 See Case IV/M.234 – *GECC/Avis Lease*, 15 July 1992.

134 See Case IV/M.018 – *AG/AMEV*, of 21 November 1990.

135 The principles for financial holding companies may to a certain extent be applied to fund management companies.

136 See for example Case IV/M.166 – *Torras/Sarrió*, of 24 February 1992.

CASE TEAM ALLOCATION REQUEST – MERGERS

[4.651]

NOTES

This document was first published on 16 October 2008, but has been updated since then. The text is taken from the European Commission website at: ec.europa.eu/competition/contacts/mergers_mail.html.

To be sent	**by email to comp-merger-registry@ec.europa.eu**
	or by fax to +32-2-296.43.01

Please indicate the information below:

1) Your contact details:

Name:

Company/law firm:

Telephone number:

Email:

2) Dossier type Pre-notification

[ ] Form CO

[ ] Form CO simplified

[ ] Form RS Art. 4(4)

[ ] Form RS Art. 4(5)

[ ] Consultation on Art. 22

3) Extended level of confidentiality in the pre-notification phase

Information submitted in pre-notification is protected by Article 17 of the Merger Regulation and pre-notification contacts are kept confidential. Nevertheless, some highly market sensitive transactions may require additional protection. If this is the case, please indicate this below providing a justification for the need for additional protection.

Only where requests for an extended level of confidentiality are considered justified, the Commission will use a code name for the transaction. Please indicate below the code name to be used.

An extended level of confidentiality is requested because:

[ ] a) the transaction involves publicly traded companies, is not yet known to the market and is highly market sensitive

[ ] b) other reason (please explain)

Suggested code name (only if one of the boxes above is ticked):

4) Companies involved country of origin, role and turnover:[1]

Companies	Country	Role[2]	Turnover (million EUR)		Year of turnover[3]
			World	EU	
–					
–					
–					

5) Name the main product(s) / Economic activities

Name of product(s)/activities	NACE code

6) Brief description of the parties, the transaction, the markets involved and complexity of the case

7) Is case linked with or related to any other current or previous case?

[ ] Yes, case number

[ ] No

8) Expected date of first draft:

9) Expected date of notification:

10) Proposed case language

BG - CS – DA - DE – EL - EN – ES - ET – FI - FR – HR – HU - IT – LT – LV - MT - NL – PL - PT – RO - SK – SL - SV *(please choose)*

11) Any other information you want to submit at this stage:
Date:

NOTES

[1] For pre-notification, complete turnover if available.

[2] A/P = Acquirer/Parent(s)
A = Acquirer
T = Target
NC = Newly created company constituting a JV
MP = Merging Party

[3] If fiscal year does not fall together with calendar year, indicate end of fiscal year in full date format (dd/mm/yyyy)

PROVISION OF ADDRESS DETAILS IN ELECTRONIC FORMAT FOR COMMISSION MARKET INVESTIGATIONS

(10 March 2010)

[4.652]

NOTES

This document was published on 10 March 2010. The text is taken from the European Commission website at: ec.europa.eu/competition-policy/mergers/procedures/equestionnaire_en. The Excel template it refers to is available on the same webpage.

INSTRUCTIONS TO FILL IN THE EXCEL TEMPLATE

This Excel template[1] has been created for the purpose of providing customer, competitor, etc contact details in an electronic format as required by the Form CO. Once the notification of the merger transaction is filed and a market investigation is initiated, questionnaires will be sent out electronically – via the eQuestionnaire application – on the basis of the contact information inserted into this template.

eQuestionnaire has been progressively introduced by the Commission since December 2009. It is a new email- and web-based market investigation tool, replacing the previous fax-based system. The eQuestionnaire application sends the first letter (providing information to access the application) to addressees via email only. Therefore it is particularly important that personalized and correct email addresses are submitted as part of the contact details during notification.

NOTES

[1] The template is available on: ec.europa.eu/competition/mergers/equestionnaire_en.html

1. WHEN TO SUBMIT THE CONTACT DETAILS

You are strongly recommended to liaise with the respective case team at an early Prenotification stage with respect to providing contact details in order to clarify:

- whether you should provide the contact details of the companies which are the parties' direct customers or rather the address of their ultimate parent companies. The same applies for competitors and suppliers.
- the number of contact details to be provided.

Please always submit the contact details in advance together with the draft Form CO to avoid any delay in the market investigation.

2. INPUT OF DATA

GENERAL PRINCIPLES:

1. It is essential that you do not deviate from the template. Please do not:
   (i) change the order of the columns;
   (ii) delete any of the existing columns;
   (iii) change the title of the columns or
   (iv) merge any cells.
2. Please fill-in the contact details of each company/association by:
   (i) entering only one entity per row.
   (ii) filling in all columns for each row
   (iii) using wherever possible the same contact details for the same company. If, for example, both parties have the same customer or the same customer buys from the parties several products belonging to different markets, please provide if possible the same contact details for this customer in all these instances.

3. Due to technical limitations of our IT tool, special Polish and Czech Characters are not recognized. Please use wherever possible plain characters such as "s" instead of "š", "r" instead of "ř" and so on.

4. Please also be mindful to avoid adding extra "invisible" characters (such as blank spaces or tabs after the text) to the tables that may cause problems when importing the data.

5. In the spreadsheet, you will find two worksheets called "Country codes" and "Language codes". These worksheets contain reference tables with all codes that appear in the drop-down menu of the main table. Please do not modify those tables.

HOW TO FILL IN THE CELLS IN THE EXCEL TEMPLATE:

COMPANY, CONTACT, STREET, ZIP-POSTAL CODE and CITY

- Insert the details in plain text (please note the remarks 2, 3 and 4 above)

COUNTRY

- Select the country from the drop-down list available on the spreadsheet.
- If the drop-down list does not appear, this means that the cell properties have been overwritten. In this case, copy the cell from a working row.

PHONE and FAX columns

- Please provide only 1 record per cell.
- Please make sure you insert personal phone numbers of the contact persons, not general switchboard numbers.
- Please use this format:
  - insert the full international dialling code preceded by "00" or "+", followed by the phone or fax number without special characters
  - please do not add:
    - — a "0" between the international dialling code and the domestic number (except for Italy)
    - — any alphabetical characters or any other formatting characters

Examples:

003223012345 (for Belgium)

0039**0**6123456 (for Italy)

EMAIL

- Be sure to enter only one email address per cell.
- Please equally make sure that you indicate personal Email addresses of the contact persons listed and not general company mailbox which may only rarely be checked.

LANGUAGE

- Select the language from the drop-down list in the spreadsheet. If the drop-down list does not appear, this means that the cell properties have been overwritten. In this case, copy the cell from a working row.
- For the countries outside EU using other than one of the community languages, insert EN.

CATEGORY

- It is crucial to provide in timely manner complete data for each category of addressee (competitors, customers, suppliers, trade associations) in each relevant market.
- There are two ways to provide information on more than one market, either in one single Excel file or in several files (you may want to discuss the best option with the case team):

A. **One single file:** All data for all third parties can be submitted in one Excel sheet with the specific category or market indicated clearly under the "Category" column. Please do not distinguish these markets by subtitles inserted as additional lines.

B. **As several files:** You can fill in one file by category or by market. Files should be given names that allow them to be easily identified.

Example: if the Form CO entails the assessment of two affected markets for which address details of competitors, customers, suppliers and trade associations have to be provided according to section 7 and 8 and the affected product markets are "supply of electricity" and "electricity trading", the following input data files would be created in Excel format:

- *SupplyElectricityComp.xls* (List of competitors for "supply of electricity")
- *SupplyElectricityCust.xls* (List of customers for "supply of electricity")
- *SupplyElectricitySupp.xls* (List of suppliers for "supply of electricity")
- *ElectricityTradingComp.xls* (List of competitors for "electricity trading")
- *ElectricityTradingCust.xls* (List of customers for "electricity trading")
- *ElectricityTradingSupp.xls* (List of suppliers for "electricity trading")
- *ElectricityAsso.xls* (List of trade associations for "supply of electricity" and "electricity trading")

EXAMPLE of COMPANY INFORMATION:

To enter the address below into the spreadsheet:

Electricity Lights Company
Mr Firstname Lastname
Rue de Lumière 70
B-1000 Brussels
(Belgium)
Phone: +32-2-299.11.11 or 0032-2-299.11.11
Fax: +32-2-296.43.01 or 0032-2-296.43.01
Email: Firstname.Lastname@electricity.com

Fill in the template as follows:

Company	Contact	Street	Zip/ Postal Code	City	Country	Phone	Fax	EMail	Language	Category
Electricity Lights Company	Mr Firstname Lastname	Rue de Lumière 70	B-1000	Brussels	BEL-Belgium	+3222991111	+3222964301	Firstname. Lastname @electricity.com	FR	Supply Electri-city Comp

PROCEDURE FOR CONTROLLING MERGER OPERATIONS BETWEEN ENTERPRISES (DECEMBER 2014)

[4.653]

NOTES

The following flowchart is taken from Section A (Overview) of the 2014 document entitled "EU Competition Law: Rules Applicable to Merger Control" which is available on the European Commission website at: ec.europa.eu/competition/mergers/legislation/Merger2015.pdf.

Legal base: Council Regulation (EC) No 139/2004

When to notify?

Either following
- conclusion of the agreement
- announcement of a public bid
- acquisition of control

Or

after manifestation of good faith intent to do so

Notification

- Mandatory for all concentrations with a Community dimension [1]
- Such concentrations shall not be implemented either before its notification or until it has been declared compatible with the common market pursuant to a Commission decision, or on the basis of a presumption (certain exemptions for public bids).

Phase I deadline commences

- On the date when the complete notification is received by the Commission

Phase I: Initial Examination

- Detailed appraisal via: request for information, interviews, inspections carried out by the competent Authorities of the Member States and the Commission
- Member States can request referral within 15 working days of notification.

Phase I deadlines

Article 6 decision to be taken
- within 25 working days after receipt of the complete notification
- unless increased to 35 working days if a Member State makes a 9(2) request, or
- unless increased to 35 working days if the undertakings concerned offer commitments

Article 6: decision

- 6(1)a : the concentration does not fall within the scope of the Merger Regulation
- 6(1)b : the concentration does not raise serious doubts as to its compatibility with the common market: approval
- 6(1)c : the concentration raises serious doubts: phase 2 of procedure

Phase II deadline commences

- On the date of the Article 6(1)c decision

Phase II: Initiation of proceedings

- Detailed appraisal via: request for information, interviews, inspections carried out by the competent Authorities of the Member States and the Commission
- Declaration of incompatibility is preceded by the issuing of a statement of objections, with a right for the parties to access the file and to request a formal oral hearing
- Advisory Committee of Member States: meeting and delivery of opinion

Phase II deadlines

Article 8 decision to be taken

- within **90** working days of initiation of proceedings, **or**
- within **105** working days if the notifying parties offer commitments later than 55 working days from initiation of proceedings.

Extension of up to 20 working days upon request by, or with the agreement of, the notifying parties: maximum duration of phase II = **125** working days

Article 8: final decision

- 8(1): approval in case of compatibility with the common market
- 8(2): approval with conditions and obligations rendering the concentration compatible with the common market
- 8 (3):prohibition in case of incompatibility with the common market
- 8(4): dissolution of the merger in case of premature implementation or implementation in breach of a condition for clearance
- 8(5): interim measures
- 8(6): revocation of a clearance decision in case of incorrect information or breach of obligation.

Two months from the date of the decision to lodge an appeal

***Possibility:* Review by the European Court of First Instance and ultimately by the European Court of Justice**

[1] **A concentration has a Community dimension, if**

- the combined aggregate worldwide turnover (from ordinary activities and after turnover taxes) of all the undertakings concerned (in the case of the acquisition of parts of undertakings, only the turnover relating to the parts which are the subject of the concentration shall be taken into account with regard to the seller(s)) is more than EUR 5 000 million (special rules apply to banks), **and**
- the aggregate Community-wide turnover of each of at least two of the undertakings concerned is more than EUR 250 million,

  unless
- each of the undertakings concerned achieves more than two-thirds of its aggregate Community-wide turnover within one and the same Member State.

In case these thresholds are not met a concentration has nevertheless Community dimension, if

- the combined aggregate world-wide turnover of all the undertakings concerned is more than EUR 2 500 million, **and**
- in each of at least three Member States, the combined aggregate turnover of all the undertakings concerned is more than EUR 100 million, **and**
- in each of at least three Member States included for the purpose of the second point above, the aggregate turnover of each of at least two of the undertakings concerned is more than EUR 25 million, **and**
- the aggregate Community-wide turnover of each of at least two of the undertakings concerned is more than EUR 100 million,

  unless
- each of the undertakings concerned achieves more than two-thirds of its aggregate Community-wide turnover within one and the same Member State.

COMMUNICATION FROM THE COMMISSION

(2013/C64/01)

Communication Pursuant to Article 23(1) of Commission Regulation (EC) No 802/2004 implementing Council Regulation (EC) No 139/2004 on the control of concentrations between undertakings (Address for Delivery)

(Text with EEA relevance)

[4.654]

NOTES

Date of publication in OJ: OJ C64, 5.3.2013, p 1.

Note that Commission Regulation 802/2004/EC and Council Regulation 139/2004/EC are repealed, in their application to the UK, by the Competition (Amendment etc) (EU Exit) Regulations 2019, SI 2019/93, reg 63, Sch 3, paras 1, 2, as from IP completion day (as defined in the European Union (Withdrawal Agreement) Act 2020, s 39) (for transitional provisions and savings in relation to the operation of the 2019 Regulations, see Sch 4 to those Regulations at **[7.69]** et seq).

Address of the Commission's Directorate General for Competition

European Commission
Directorate General for Competition
Merger Registry
Place Madou/Madouplein 1
1210 Saint-Josse-ten-Noode/Sint-Joost-ten-Noode
BELGIQUE/BELGIË

CONTACT FOR MERGERS

[4.655]

NOTES

The following is taken from the European Commission website at: ec.europa.eu/competition-policy/mergers/contact_en.

In all your correspondence, please specify the name of the case and the case number

It is essential that the correspondents use only the contact information below for any official communication relating to merger cases. This will facilitate and accelerate the treatment of your correspondence. Communications sent to other numbers/addresses may be treated with delay.

How to contact the Merger Registry	
Email:	comp-merger-registry@ec.europa.eu
Postal address:	European Commission Directorate-General for Competition Merger Registry 1049 Bruxelles/Brussel BELGIQUE/BELGIË
Delivery by hand:	European Commission DG Competition Merger Registry Place Madou / Madouplein 1 1210 Saint-Josse-ten-Noode / Sint-Joost-ten-Node Belgique / België 09:00 to 12:00 and 14:00 to 17:00 on Mondays to Thursdays 09:00 to 12:00 and 14:00 to 16:00 on Fridays and days preceding Commission holidays
Tel:	+32 2 296.55.77
Fax:	+32 2 296.43.01

Delivery of merger-related documents

- Please note that the delivery at the above mentioned address is a legal obligation pursuant to Article 23(1) of Commission Regulation No. (EC) 802/2004 implementing Council Regulation (EC) No 139/2004 on the control of concentrations between undertakings.
- Hand deliveries must be made on working days during the above-mentioned opening hours. Working days are all days other than Saturdays, Sundays and Commission holidays as published in the Official Journal of the European Union.
- *Security procedures:*

1. Prior to delivery, at Place Madou / Madouplein 1, the law firm or the legal representative of the notifying company must call the Merger Registry (phone numbers: +32 2 296.55.77, fax number: +32 2 296.43.01)
2. An estimated delivery time and the name of the individual from the firm or company who will be making the delivery must be provided along with a description of the item to be delivered (number of envelopes, packages or boxes
3. Packages and envelopes to be submitted must clearly indicate the name of the office delivering the filing
4. The Registry will confirm the receipt of the items being delivered

Allocation of cases

Please send this case allocation request[1] (.docx format) to the Merger Registry by email or by fax no later than 12.00 noon on a Friday, so that DG Competition can allocate staff the following week.

General Queries

For general queries on merger issues, please contact: COMP-Mergers@ec.europa.eu

EDITORIAL NOTE

[1] See case team allocation request form at **[4.651]**.

COMMISSION NOTICE ON A SIMPLIFIED PROCEDURE FOR TREATMENT OF CERTAIN CONCENTRATIONS UNDER COUNCIL REGULATION (EC) NO 139/2004

(2013/C366/04)

[4.656]

NOTES

Date of publication in OJ: OJ C366, 14.12.2013, p 5. The text of this Notice is reproduced as corrected by the corrigendum published in OJ C11, 15.1.2014, p 6.

Note that Council Regulation (EC) No 139/2004 is repealed, in relation to the UK, by the Competition (Amendment etc) (EU Exit) Regulations 2019, SI 2019/93, reg 63, Sch 3, para 1, as from IP completion day (as defined in the European Union (Withdrawal Agreement) Act 2020, s 39) (for transitional provisions and savings in relation to the operation of the 2019 Regulations, see Sch 4 to those Regulations at **[7.69]** et seq).

See also the list of consultations and draft documents in the Appendix at **[A1]**.

I. INTRODUCTION

[4.657]

1. This Notice sets out a simplified procedure under which the Commission intends to treat certain concentrations pursuant to Council Regulation (EC) No 139/2004[1] (the 'Merger Regulation') on the basis that they do not raise competition concerns. This Notice replaces the Notice on a simplified procedure for treatment of certain concentrations under Council Regulation (EC) No 139/2004 published in 2005.[2] The Commission's experience gained in applying the Merger Regulation, including Council Regulation (EEC) No 4064/89,[3] which preceded the current Merger Regulation, has shown that certain categories of notified concentrations are normally cleared without having raised any substantive doubts, provided that there were no special circumstances.

2. The purpose of this Notice is to set out the conditions under which the Commission usually adopts a short-form decision declaring a concentration compatible with the internal market pursuant to the simplified procedure and to provide guidance in respect of the procedure itself. When the necessary conditions set forth at point 5 or 6 of this Notice are met and provided there are no special circumstances, the Commission adopts a short-form clearance decision within 25 working days from the date of notification, pursuant to Article 6(1)(b) of the Merger Regulation.[4]

3. However, the Commission may launch an investigation and/or adopt a full decision under the Merger Regulation in respect of any proposed concentration, in particular if the safeguards or exclusions set forth at points 8 to 19 of this Notice are applicable.

4. By following the procedure outlined in the following sections, the Commission aims to make Union merger control more focused and effective.

NOTES

[1] Council Regulation (EC) No 139/2004 of 20 January 2004 on the control of concentrations between undertakings (OJ L24, 29.1.2004, p 1).

[2] OJ C56, 5.3.2005, p 32.

[3] Council Regulation (EEC) No 4064/89 of 21 December 1989 on the control of concentrations between undertakings (OJ L395, 30.12.1989 p 1); corrected version OJ L257, 21.9.1990, p 13.

[4] The notification requirements are set out in Annex I and II to Council Regulation (EC) No 802/2004 implementing Council Regulation (EC) No 139/2004 on the control of concentrations between undertakings (the 'Implementing Regulation').

II. CATEGORIES OF CONCENTRATIONS SUITABLE FOR TREATMENT UNDER THE SIMPLIFIED PROCEDURE

Eligible concentrations

[4.658]

5. The Commission will in principle apply the simplified procedure to each of the following categories of concentrations:[5]

(a) two or more undertakings acquire joint control of a joint venture, provided that the joint venture has no, or negligible, actual or foreseen activities within the territory of the European Economic Area (EEA); such cases occur where:

(i) the turnover of the joint venture and/or the turnover of the contributed activities[6] is less than EUR 100 million in the EEA territory at the time of notification;[7] and

(ii) the total value of assets transferred to the joint venture is less than EUR 100 million in the EEA territory at the time of notification;[8]

(b) two or more undertakings merge, or one or more undertakings acquire sole or joint control of another undertaking, provided that none of the parties to the concentration are engaged in business activities in the same product and geographic market,[9] or in a product market which is upstream or downstream from a product market in which any other party to the concentration is engaged;[10]

(c) two or more undertakings merge, or one or more undertakings acquire sole or joint control of another undertaking and both of the following conditions are fulfilled:

(i) the combined market share of all the parties to the concentration that are engaged in business activities in the same product and geographic market[11] (horizontal relationships) is less than 20%;[12]

(ii) the individual or combined market shares of all the parties to the concentration that are engaged in business activities in a product market which is upstream or downstream from a product market in which any other party to the concentration is engaged (vertical relationships)[13] are less than 30%;[14]

(d) a party is to acquire sole control of an undertaking over which it already has joint control.

6. The Commission may also apply the simplified procedure where two or more undertakings merge, or one or more undertakings acquire sole or joint control of another undertaking, and both of the following conditions are fulfilled:

(i) the combined market share of all the parties to the concentration that are in a horizontal relationship is less than 50%; and

(ii) the increment (delta) of the Herfindahl-Hirschman Index (HHI) resulting from the concentration is below 150.[15][16]

7. For the purpose of the application of points 5(b), 5(c) and 6 in the case of an acquisition of joint control, relationships that exist only between the undertakings acquiring joint control outside the field of activity of the joint venture are not considered horizontal or vertical relationships for the purpose of this Notice. Those relationships may however give rise to coordination as referred to in Article 2(4) of the Merger Regulation; such situations are dealt with in point 15 of this Notice.

Safeguards and exclusions

8. In assessing whether a concentration falls into one of the categories referred to in points 5 and 6, the Commission will ensure that all relevant circumstances are established with sufficient clarity. Given that market definitions are likely to be a key element in this assessment, the parties should provide information on all plausible alternative market definitions, generally during the pre-notification phase (see point 22). Notifying parties are responsible for describing all alternative relevant product and geographic markets on which the notified concentration could have an impact and for providing data and information relating to the definition of such markets.[17] The Commission retains the discretion to take the ultimate decision on market definition, basing its decision on an analysis of the facts of the case. Where it is difficult to define the relevant markets or to determine the parties' market shares, the Commission will not apply the simplified procedure. In addition, to the extent that concentrations involve novel legal issues of a general interest, the Commission would normally abstain from adopting short-form decisions, and would normally revert to a normal first phase merger procedure.

9. While it can normally be assumed that concentrations falling into the categories referred to in points 5 and 6 will not raise serious doubts as to their compatibility with the internal market, there may nonetheless be certain situations which exceptionally require a closer investigation and/or a full decision. In such cases, the Commission may revert to a normal first phase merger procedure.

10. The following are indicative examples of types of cases which may be excluded from the simplified procedure.

11. The Commission is less likely to accept a proposed concentration under the simplified procedure if any of the special circumstances mentioned in the Commission's Guidelines on the assessment of horizontal mergers[18] are present. This includes instances where the market is already concentrated, where the proposed concentration would eliminate an important competitive force, where the proposed concentration would combine two important innovators, where the proposed concentration involves a firm that has promising pipeline products or where there are indications that the proposed concentration would allow the merging parties to hinder the expansion of their competitors.

12. The same may also apply where it is not possible to determine the parties' precise market shares. This is often the case when the parties operate in new or little developed markets.

13. Certain types of concentrations may increase the parties' market power by combining technological, financial or other resources, even if the parties to the concentration do not operate in the same market. Concentrations where at least two parties to the concentration are present in closely related neighbouring markets[19] may also be unsuitable for the simplified procedure, in particular, where one or more of the parties to the concentration holds individually a market share of 30% or more in any product market in which there is no horizontal or vertical relationship between the parties but which is a neighbouring market to a market where another party is active.[20]

14. The Commission may consider it appropriate to carry out a full assessment under the normal merger procedure of certain joint ventures with a turnover below the threshold specified in point 5(a) in the EEA at the time of notification, but which can be expected to significantly surpass that threshold in the EEA within the following 3 years. In cases falling under point 5(a) a normal procedure may also be considered appropriate if there are horizontal or vertical relationships between the parties to the concentration on the basis of which it cannot be excluded that the concentration will raise serious doubts as to its compatibility with the internal market or if any of the special circumstances set out in point 11 are present.

15. Furthermore, the Commission may revert to a full assessment under the normal merger procedure where an issue of coordination as referred to in Article 2(4) of the Merger Regulation arises.

16. The Commission's experience to date has shown that a change from joint to sole control may exceptionally require closer investigation and/or a full decision. A particular competition concern could arise in circumstances where a former joint venture is integrated into the group or network of its remaining single controlling shareholder, whereby the disciplining constraints exercised by the potentially diverging incentives of the different controlling shareholders are removed and its strategic market position could be strengthened. For example, in a scenario in which undertaking A and undertaking B jointly control a joint venture C, a concentration pursuant to which A acquires sole control of C may give rise to competition concerns in circumstances in which C is a direct competitor of A, where C and A will hold a substantial combined market position and where this removes a degree of independence previously held by C.[21] In cases where such scenarios require a closer analysis, the Commission may revert to a normal first phase merger procedure.[22]

17. The Commission may also revert to a normal first phase merger procedure where neither the Commission nor the competent authorities of Member States have reviewed the prior acquisition of joint control of the joint venture in question.

18. In the case of concentrations described in point 6, the Commission will decide on a case-by-case basis whether, under the particular circumstances of the case at hand, the increase in market concentration level indicated by the HHI delta is such that the case should be examined under the normal first phase merger procedure.

19. If a Member State expresses substantiated concerns about the notified concentration within 15 working days of receipt of the copy of the notification, or if a third party expresses substantiated concerns within the time limit laid down for such comments, the Commission will revert to a normal first phase merger procedure.

Referral requests

20. The simplified procedure will not be applied if a Member State requests the referral of a notified concentration pursuant to Article 9 of the Merger Regulation or if the Commission accepts a request from one or more Member States for referral of a notified concentration pursuant to Article 22 of the Merger Regulation.

Pre-notification referrals at the request of the notifying parties

21. Subject to the safeguards and exclusions set out in this Notice, the Commission may apply the simplified procedure to concentrations where:

(a) following a reasoned submission pursuant to Article 4(4) of the Merger Regulation, the Commission decides not to refer the case to a Member State; or

(b) following a reasoned submission pursuant to Article 4(5) of the Merger Regulation the case is referred to the Commission.

NOTES

5 The following categories apply alternatively, not cumulatively, i.e. fulfilling all the criteria of any of the categories mentioned in point 5 (a), (b), (c) or (d) or point 6 will in principle make a notified concentration eligible for the simplified procedure. A transaction may fulfil the criteria of more than one of the categories described in this Notice. Accordingly, notifying parties may submit a notification of a transaction on the basis of more than one of the categories described in this Notice.

6 The expression 'and/or' refers to the variety of situations covered; for example:

— in the case of a joint acquisition of a target company, the turnover to be taken into account is the turnover of this target (the joint venture),

— in the case of the creation of a joint venture to which the parent companies contribute their activities, the turnover to be taken into account is that of the contributed activities,

— in the case of entry of a new controlling party into an existing joint venture, the turnover of the joint venture and the turnover of the activities contributed by the new parent company (if any) must be taken into account.

7 The turnover of the joint venture can be determined according to the most recent audited accounts of the parent companies, or the joint venture itself, depending upon the availability of separate accounts for the resources combined in the joint venture.

8 The total value of assets of the joint venture can be determined according to the last prepared and approved balance sheet of each parent company. The term 'assets' includes: (i) all tangible and intangible assets that will be transferred to the joint venture (examples of tangible assets include production plants, wholesale or retail outlets, and inventory of goods; examples of intangible assets include intellectual property, goodwill, etc.), and (ii) any amount of credit or any obligations of the joint venture which any parent company of the joint venture has agreed to extend or guarantee. Where the assets transferred generate turnover at the time of notification, then neither the value of the assets nor that of the annual turnover may exceed EUR 100 million.

9 See Commission Notice on the definition of relevant market for the purposes of Community competition law (OJ C372, 9.12.1997, p 5). Any reference in this Notice to undertakings' activities in markets should be understood as activities in markets within the EEA territory or markets which include the EEA territory, but may be wider than the EEA territory.

10 A vertical relationship normally presupposes that the product or service of the undertaking active in the upstream market in question constitutes an important input to the product or service of the undertaking active in the downstream market: see the Commission's Guidelines on the assessment of non-horizontal mergers under the Council Regulation on the control of concentrations between undertakings (OJ C265, 18.10.2008, p 6), paragraph 34.

11 See footnote 9.

12 The thresholds for horizontal and vertical relationships apply to any plausible alternative product and geographic market definition that may have to be considered in a given case. It is important that the underlying market definitions set out in the notification are precise enough to justify the assessment that these thresholds are not met, and that all plausible alternative market definitions that may have to be considered are mentioned (including geographic markets narrower than national).

13 See footnote 10.

14 See footnote 12.

15 The HHI is calculated by summing the squares of the individual market shares of all the firms in the market: see Commission Guidelines on the assessment of horizontal mergers under the Council Regulation on the control of concentrations between undertakings (OJ C31, 5.2.2004, p 5), point 16. However, in order to calculate the HHI delta resulting from the concentration, it is sufficient to subtract from the square of the sum of the market shares of the parties to the concentration (in other words, the square of the merged entity's market share post-concentration) the sum of the squares of the parties' individual market shares (since the market shares of all other competitors in the market remain unchanged and thus do not influence the result of the equation). In other words, the HHI delta can be calculated on the basis of only the market shares of the parties to the concentration, without a need to know the market shares of any other competitors in the market.

16 See footnote 12.

17 As with all other notifications, the Commission may revoke the short-form decision if it is based on incorrect information for which one of the undertakings concerned is responsible (Article 6(3)(a) of the Merger Regulation).

18 See Commission Guidelines on the assessment of horizontal mergers under the Council Regulation on the control of concentrations between undertakings (OJ C31, 5.2.2004, p 5), in particular paragraph 20.

19 Product markets are closely related neighbouring markets when the products are complementary to each other or when they belong to a range of products that is generally purchased by the same set of customers for the same end use.

20 See the Commission's Guidelines on the assessment of non-horizontal mergers under the Council Regulation on the control of concentrations between undertakings (OJ C265, 18.10.2008, p 6), in particular paragraph 25 and Section V.

21 Case COMP/M.5141 *KLM/Martinair*, 17.12.2008, recitals 14?22.

22 Case COMP/M.2908 *Deutsche Post/DHL (II)*, 18.9.2002.

III. PROCEDURAL PROVISIONS

Pre-notification contacts

[4.659]

22. The Commission has found pre-notification contacts between notifying parties and the Commission on a voluntary basis beneficial even in seemingly unproblematic cases.[23] The Commission's experience of the simplified procedure has shown that candidate cases for the simplified procedure may raise complex issues, for instance of market definition (see point 8), which should preferably be resolved prior to notification. Such contacts allow the Commission and the notifying parties to determine the precise amount of information to be provided in a notification. Pre-notification contacts should be initiated at least 2 weeks prior to the expected date of notification. Notifying parties are particularly encouraged to engage in pre-notification contacts where they wish to request the Commission to apply the simplified procedure in the situation described in point 6. Under the Merger Regulation, notifying parties are entitled to notify a concentration at any time, provided the notification is complete. The possibility to engage in pre-notification contacts is a service offered by the Commission to notifying parties on a voluntary basis in order to prepare the formal merger review procedure. As such, while not mandatory, pre-notification contacts can be extremely valuable to both the notifying parties and the Commission in determining the precise amount of information required in a notification and, in the majority of cases, will result in a significant reduction of the information required.

23. Nonetheless, pre-notification contacts, in particular the submission of a draft notification, may be less useful in cases falling under point 5(b), that is in cases where there are no reportable markets[24] since the parties are not engaged in business activities in the same product and geographic market, or in a product market which is upstream or downstream from a product market in which any other party to the concentration is engaged. In such circumstances, notifying parties may prefer to notify immediately without submitting a draft notification before-hand.[25]

24. The determination of the absence of reportable markets needs to be undertaken in accordance with point 8 of this Notice. It therefore remains the responsibility of the notifying parties to submit all the information necessary for the Commission to conclude that the proposed concentration does not give rise to any reportable market in the EEA. The Commission will not apply the simplified procedure on the basis of point 5(b) if it is difficult to conclude that the proposed concentration does not give rise to any reportable markets. In such cases, the Commission may revert to the normal procedure and consider the notification as being incomplete in a material respect as set out under point 26 of this Notice.

Publication of the fact of notification

25. The information to be published in the *Official Journal of the European Union* upon receipt of a notification[26] will include: the names of the parties to the concentration, their country of origin, the nature of the concentration and the economic sectors involved, as well as an indication that, on the basis of the information provided by the notifying party, the concentration may qualify for a simplified procedure. Interested parties will then have the opportunity to submit observations, in particular on circumstances which might require an investigation.

Short-form decision

26. If the Commission is satisfied that the concentration fulfils the criteria for the simplified procedure (see points 5 and 6), it will normally issue a short-form decision. This includes appropriate cases not giving rise to any competition concerns where it receives a full form notification. The concentration will thus be declared compatible with the internal market, within 25 working days from the date of notification, pursuant to Article 10(1) and (6) of the Merger Regulation. The Commission will endeavour to issue a short-form decision as soon as practicable following expiry of

the 15 working day period during which Member States may request referral of a notified concentration pursuant to Article 9 of the Merger Regulation. However, in the period leading up to the 25 working day deadline, the option of reverting to a normal first phase merger procedure and thus launching investigations and/or adopting a full decision remains open to the Commission, should it judge such action appropriate in the case in question. In such cases, the Commission may also consider the notification as being incomplete in a material respect pursuant to Article 5(2) of the Implementing Regulation if it has not received a full form notification.

Publication of the short-form decision

27. The Commission will publish a notice of the fact of the decision in the *Official Journal of the European Union* as it does for full clearance decisions. The public version of the decision will be made available on the website of the Directorate-General for Competition. The short-form decision will contain the information about the notified concentration published in the *Official Journal of the European Union* at the time of notification (names of the parties, their country of origin, nature of the concentration and economic sectors concerned) and a statement that the concentration is declared compatible with the internal market because it falls within one or more of the categories described in this Notice, with the applicable category(ies) being explicitly identified.

NOTES

23 See the Directorate-Gerneral for Competition's Best Practices on the conduct of EC merger control proceedings (the 'Best Practices') e online (ec.europa.eu/competition/mergers/legislation/proceedings.pdf).

24 For the definition of reportable markets, see Section 6.2 of the Short Form CO (Annex II to the Implementing Regulation).

25 In light of the Best Practices, the Commission would nevertheless encourage parties to submit in advance a request for the allocation of a Directorate-General for Competition case team.

26 Article 4(3) of the Merger Regulation.

IV. ANCILLARY RESTRICTIONS

[4.660]

28. The simplified procedure is not suited to cases in which the undertakings concerned request an express assessment of restrictions which are directly related to, and necessary for, the implementation of the concentration.

MODEL POWER OF ATTORNEY FOR NOTIFICATIONS

[4.661]

NOTES

This document is available on the European Commission website at: ec.europa.eu/competition-policy/mergers/practical-information_en. It has been updated since its original publication.

Model Power of Attorney ('PoA')

This model PoA contains the basic information which should be included for notification purposes. It may be adapted to the specific circumstances of the case.

The company name and address should exactly match that indicated in Section 2 on the Form CO.

[COMPANY LETTERHEAD]

POWER OF ATTORNEY - CASE M. [XXXX] - [CASE NAME]

[COMPANY NAME], [COMPANY ADDRESS] duly represented by **[NAME AND FUNCTION OF PERSON OF THE COMPANY AUTHORISED TO SIGN THE PoA]** hereby confers full power of attorney on **[LAWYER'S NAME]**, established at **[LAWYER'S ADDRESS]** for the purpose of acting in the name of **[COMPANY NAME]**, and on its behalf for the purpose of carrying out all acts related to the notification, in accordance with Council Regulation (EC) 139/2004 on the control of concentrations between undertakings, of the proposed **[DESCRIPTION OF THE PROPOSED TRANSACTION]** (the "Proposed Transaction"). This power of attorney shall comprise the authority to make all necessary or useful submissions to the European Commission in order for the Proposed Transaction to be declared compatible with the internal market, including but not limited to replying to requests for information, submitting comments to objections raised by the European Commission, and offering commitments with a view to rendering the Proposed Transaction compatible with the internal market. ***[please modify/delete as appropriate in case the Notifying Party does not wish the power of attorney to extend to any particular procedural act].***

[The Notifying Party should also include the following wording to ensure that the Commission's Decisions and any Statement of Objections regarding the notified transaction may be directly notified to the authorised external representative of the Notifying Party:

[COMPANY NAME]*, hereby also confers full power to* ***[LAWYER'S NAME]****, established at* ***[LAWYER'S ADDRESS]****, to receive on its behalf notification of the confidential version of the European Commission's decisions and any statement of objections under Council Regulation (EC) 139/2004 in the case* **M. [XXXX] - [CASE NAME]**, *pursuant to Article 297 of the Treaty on the Functioning of the European Union and to provide a copy of such decisions and statement of objections redacted as appropriate to* ***[COMPANY NAME]****, thus having waived its right to receive such notification.]*

Signed the **[DATE]** in **[PLACE]**

[NAME AND FUNCTION OF PERSON OF THE COMPANY AUTHORISED TO SIGN]

duly authorised to sign on behalf of **[COMPANY NAME]**

MODEL POWER OF ATTORNEY FOR REASONED SUBMISSIONS

[4.662]

NOTES

This document is available on the European Commission website at: ec.europa.eu/competition-policy/mergers/practical-information_en.

Model Power of Attorney ('PoA')

This model PoA contains the basic information which should be included for purposes of making a reasoned submission pursuant to Article 4(4) or 4(5) of Council Regulation (EC) No 139/2004. It may be adapted to the specific circumstances of the case.

[COMPANY LETTERHEAD]

POWER OF ATTORNEY - CASE M.[CASE NUMBER] - [CASE NAME]

[COMPANY NAME], [COMPANY ADDRESS] duly represented by **[NAME AND FUNCTION OF PERSON OF THE COMPANY AUTHORISED TO SIGN THE PoA]** hereby confers full power of attorney on **[LAWYER'S NAME]**, established at **[LAWYER'S ADDRESS]** for the purpose of acting in the name of **[COMPANY NAME]**, and on its behalf for the purpose of carrying out all acts related to the reasoned submission, in accordance with Council Regulation (EC) No 139/2004 on the control of concentrations between undertakings, regarding the referral of the proposed **[DESCRIPTION OF THE PROPOSED TRANSACTION]**.

[In case the reasoned submission is made pursuant to Article 4(4) of Council Regulation (EC) No 139/2004, the Submitting Party should also include the following wording to ensure that the Commission's Decisions regarding the reasoned submission may be directly notified to the legal representative of the Submitting Party:

[COMPANY NAME]*, hereby also confers full power to* ***[LAWYER'S NAME]****, established at* ***[LAWYER'S ADDRESS]*** *to receive on its behalf notification of the confidential version of the European Commission's decisions regarding its reasoned submission under Council Regulation (EC) 139/2004 in the case* ***M.[CASE NUMBER] - [CASE NAME]****, pursuant to Article 297 of the Treaty on the Functioning of the European Union and to provide a copy of such decisions redacted as appropriate to* ***[COMPANY NAME]****, thus having waived its right to receive such notification.]*

Signed the **[DATE]** in **[PLACE]**

[NAME AND FUNCTION OF PERSON OF THE COMPANY AUTHORISED TO SIGN]

duly authorised to sign on behalf of **[COMPANY NAME]**

TEMPLATE: TABLE FOR TURNOVER DATA FOR NOTIFICATIONS

[4.663]

NOTES

This document is available on the European Commission website at: ec.europa.eu/competition-policy/mergers/practical-information_en. The template has not been updated since the UK left the EU.

Section 4 of Form CO, section 4 of Short Form CO and section 2.5 of Form RS [Annex I, Annex II and Annex III of Regulation (EC) No 802/2004]

	Undertaking 1	**Undertaking 2**[1]	**Aggregate**
World-wide turnover:			
EU-wide turnover:			
EEA-wide turnover (EU and EFTA)			
Turnover in each EU Member State (indicate the Member State, if any, in which more than two-thirds of EU-wide turnover is achieved):			
Belgium			
Bulgaria			
Czech Republic			
Denmark			
Germany			

Estonia			
Ireland			
Greece			
Spain			
France			
Croatia			
Italy			
Cyprus			
Latvia			
Lithuania			
Luxembourg			
Hungary			
Malta			
Netherlands			
Austria			
Poland			
Portugal			
Romania			
Slovenia			
Slovakia			
Finland			
Sweden			
United Kingdom			
EFTA-wide turnover:			
Turnover in each EFTA State:			
(Indicate the EFTA State, if any, in which more than two-thirds of EFTA-wide turnover is achieved Also indicate whether the combined turnover of the undertakings concerned in the territory of the EFTA States equals 25% or more of their total turnover in the EEA territory.)			
Iceland			
Norway			
Liechtenstein			

NOTES

[1] If there are more than two parties to the concentration, please add a column for each additional undertaking.

INFORMATION ON NATIONAL FILING OBLIGATIONS FOR REASONED SUBMISSIONS FORM RS, SECTION 5.3, TEMPLATE TABLE

[4.664]

NOTES

This document is available on the European Commission website at: ec.europa.eu/competition-policy/mergers/practical-information_en. The template has not been updated since the UK left the EU.

Note that Form RS is in Annex III to the EU Merger Implementing Regulation (Commission Regulation 802/2004/EC) and that the 2004 Regulation is repealed, in relation to the UK, by the Competition (Amendment etc) (EU Exit) Regulations 2019, SI 2019/93, reg 63, Sch 3, para 2, as from IP completion day (as defined in the European Union (Withdrawal Agreement) Act 2020, s 39) (for transitional provisions and savings in relation to the operation of the 2019 Regulations, see Sch 4 to those Regulations at **[7.69]** et seq).

Form RS, Section 5.3

Template Table

For each Member State and/or EFTA State, specify whether the concentration is or is not capable of being reviewed under its national competition law.

You must tick one box ('Yes' or 'No') for each and every Member State and/or EFTA State. Failure to indicate 'Yes' or 'No' for any Member State and/or EFTA State shall be deemed to constitute an indication of 'Yes' for that Member State and/or EFTA State.

Belgium:	YES	NO
Bulgaria:	YES	NO
Czech Republic:	YES	NO
Denmark:	YES	NO
Germany:	YES	NO
Estonia:	YES	NO
Ireland:	YES	NO
Greece:	YES	NO
Spain:	YES	NO
France:	YES	NO
Croatia	YES	NO
Italy:	YES	NO
Cyprus:	YES	NO
Latvia:	YES	NO
Lithuania:	YES	NO
Luxembourg:	YES	NO
Hungary:	YES	NO
Malta:	YES	NO
Netherlands:	YES	NO
Austria:	YES	NO
Poland:	YES	NO
Portugal:	YES	NO
Romania:	YES	NO
Slovenia:	YES	NO
Slovakia:	YES	NO
Finland:	YES	NO
Sweden:	YES	NO
United Kingdom:	YES	NO
Iceland:	YES	NO
Norway:	YES	NO
Liechtenstein:	YES	NO

EUROPEAN COMMISSION CONFIDENTIALITY WAIVER

[4.665]

NOTES

This document is taken from the European Commission website at: ec.europa.eu/competition-policy/system/files/2021-06/confidentiality_waiver_merger_investigations.pdf.

WAIVER

1. On behalf of Company X and Company Y we confirm that each of X and Y agree to waive the confidentiality restrictions which govern the European Commission under EC Council Regulation 139/04 and other applicable laws (hereinafter referred to as "the confidentiality rules") to the extent necessary to permit the European Commission to disclose, for the purpose of its enquiries and analysis into the proposed merger/acquisition between X and Y (hereinafter referred to as the "proposed transaction"), to [*competition authority B*] any information obtained from Company X and/or Y during the course of its enquiry into the proposed transaction.

2. A corresponding waiver has or will be submitted to [*competition authority B*], enabling that authority to share information, obtained from Company X or Y during the course of its enquiry into the proposed transaction and which would otherwise be subject to the confidentiality rules of that jurisdiction, with the European Commission.

3. Specifically Company X and Y agree that the staff of the European Commission may share with [*competition authority B*] any documents, statements, data and information, supplied by Company X and /or Y, as well as the Commission's own internal analysis that contain or refer to X and Y's materials that would otherwise be prevented by the confidentiality rules.

CAVEAT

4. This letter does not constitute a waiver by X or Y of their rights under the confidentiality rules with respect to the protection afforded to X or Y against the direct or indirect disclosure of information to any third party other than [*competition authority B*]. This waiver is limited to information obtained by the Commission in relation to its review of the proposed transaction and does not apply to information obtained in the course of any other review of any case either now or in the future.

CONDITIONS

– Use of Information by Receiving Jurisdiction ("Competition Authority B")

5. For the avoidance of doubt information transmitted pursuant to this waiver may be used by [*competition authority B*] only for the purposes of conducting its enquiry into the proposed transaction and for no other purpose. Disclosure is made openly on the basis and subject to the express condition that such information remains confidential to [*competition authority B*] and may not be disclosed to any third party. It is understood and agreed that failure by [*competition authority B*] to comply with the foregoing does not engender any liability on the part of the European Commission

– Use of Information by Sending Jurisdiction ("Competition Authority A")

6. The waiver referred to in the first paragraph of this letter is subject to the following conditions:

(1) that the European Commission shall itself maintain the confidentiality of the information and/or documentation provided to [*competition authority B*] by X and/or Y and which is subsequently obtained from [*competition authority B*] and shall treat such information as if it had been obtained directly from X and /or Y;

(2) that the European Commission shall consider all information and/or documentation obtained from [*competition authority B*] pursuant to this waiver as confidential information or business secrets unless it is clearly identified as having been obtained from a publicly accessible source;

(3) that the European Commission shall not make any information and/or documentation obtained from [*competition authority B*] available to any third party including competitors, customers and suppliers of X and Y;

(4) that the information and/or documentation obtained from [*competition authority B*] shall be used only for the purposes of the European Commission's review of the proposed transaction under Council Regulation 139/04 and for no other purpose; and

(5) that the European Commission shall not disclose to [*competition authority B*] any information or documentation obtained from X and /or Y in relation to which either X or Y has asserted a claim of legal privilege in [*the jurisdiction in competition authority B*] and that is clearly identified as being subject to such client/attorney privilege. It is understood and agreed that Company X or Y is responsible for informing the Commission of the existence of such privileged information.

Each of Company X or Y has obtained the consent of its affiliates to the sharing of their documents and information produced by each of Company X or Y respectively on the same conditions as outlined above.

If you wish to discuss any matter arising form this waiver, please contact [name of responsible representative(s)]. A copy of this letter has been sent to the [competition authority B].

(Signed by the duly authorised representative of)

(Signatures)

Company X Company Y

COMMUNICATION PURSUANT TO ARTICLES 3(2), 6(2), 13(3), 20(1), 20(1A) AND 23(4) OF COMMISSION REGULATION (EC) NO 802/2004[1] IMPLEMENTING COUNCIL REGULATION (EC) NO 139/2004[2] ON THE CONTROL OF CONCENTRATIONS BETWEEN UNDERTAKINGS, LAST AMENDED BY COMMISSION IMPLEMENTING REGULATION (EU) NO 1269/2013 (FORMAT AND NUMBER OF COPIES OF NOTIFICATIONS)[3]

(2014/C25/04)

(Text with EEA relevance)

[4.666]

NOTES

Date of publication in OJ: OJ C25, 28.1.2014, p 4. This Communication is reproduced as corrected by the corrigendum published in OJ C270, 19.8.2014, p 9.

Note that Commission Regulation 802/2004/EC and Council Regulation 139/2004/EC are repealed, in their application to the UK, by the Competition (Amendment etc) (EU Exit) Regulations 2019, SI 2019/93, reg 63, Sch 3, paras 1,2, as from IP completion day (as defined in the European Union (Withdrawal Agreement) Act 2020, s 39) (for transitional provisions and savings in relation to the operation of the 2019 Regulations, see Sch 4 to those Regulations at **[7.69]** et seq).

See also the list of consultations and draft documents in the Appendix at **[A1]**.

[1] OJ L133, 30.4.2004, p 1.

[2] OJ L24, 29.1.2004, p 1.

[3] OJ L336, 14.12.2013, p 1.

INTRODUCTION

Articles 3(2), 6(2), 13(3), 20(1) and 20(1a) of Regulation (EC) No 802/2004 require notifications, reasoned submissions, comments on the Commission's objections, commitments offered by the undertakings concerned and the Form RM to be submitted to the Commission in the format and with the number of copies specified by the Commission in the *Official Journal of the European Union*.

The Commission hereby specifies, pursuant to Articles 3(2), 6(2), 13(3), 20(1) and 20(1a) of Commission Regulation (EC) No 802/2004, the number and format in which notifications, reasoned submissions, comments on the Commission's objections, commitments offered by the undertakings concerned and the Form RM should be delivered.

Article 23(4) of Regulation (EC) No 802/2004 requires that documents or any additional copies of documents submitted to the Commission electronically should be submitted in the format specified by the Commission in the *Official Journal of the European* Union and that submissions sent by electronic mail should be sent to the electronic mail address published by the Commission in the *Official Journal of the European Union*.

The Commission hereby specifies, pursuant to Article 23(4) of Regulation (EC) No 802/2004, the format in which electronic submissions should be sent and the e-mail address to which submissions sent by e-mail should be sent.

Notifications: Form CO and Short Form CO (Annexes I, II to Commission Regulation (EC) No 802/2004)

Reasoned submissions:[4] Form RS (Annex III to Commission Regulation (EC) No 802/2004)

Commitments offered by the undertakings concerned and Form RM (Annex IV to Commission Regulation (EC) No 802/2004)

Comments on the Commission's objections

(1) One signed original on paper.

(2) Three paper copies of the entire submission. Paper copies may be waived or extra copies may be requested by the case team.

(3) Two copies of the submission in CD- or DVD-ROM format (the 'medium'). The following specifications shall be adhered to:

(a) The files in this medium shall be in non-protected, searchable Portable Document Format (PDF) or in non-protected spreadsheet format and should preferably not exceed 40 MB (megabytes) each in size. The copy of the submission may be contained on several CD- or DVD-ROMs.

(b) Files should be named in a way which allows easy identification of the section in the Form CO, Short Form CO, Form RS or Form RM they refer to.

(c) Each file shall bear the number of the proceeding for which the submission is made.

(d) A list of all files in the medium shall be delivered as a separate file in the medium.

Format of electronic submissions

Any submissions other than the ones mentioned above should adhere to the following rules:

— Containers (zip, rar, 7zip, etc.) should be avoided.

— If possible, .pst files should be avoided. If not possible, size should not exceed 500 MB.

— The size of non-searchable Adobe Portable Document Format (PDF) should be limited to 30 MB. Multiple files should not be packed into a single PDF.

— Lotus Notes files should be avoided.

— Individual files should not be password protected. If protection is needed, TrueCrypt should be used for encryption.

E-mail address for e-mail correspondence

Correspondence sent by e-mail should be sent to comp-merger-registry@ec.europa.eu

Date of applicability of this communication

The instructions contained in this communication shall be applicable as of the day following its publication.

NOTES

[4] Reasoned submissions within the meaning of Article 4(4) and 4(5) of Council Regulation (EC) No 139/2004.

GUIDANCE ON THE PREPARATION OF PUBLIC VERSIONS OF COMMISSION DECISIONS ADOPTED UNDER THE MERGER REGULATION (JUNE 2015)

[4.667]

NOTES

This document is available on the European Commission website at: ec.europa.eu/competition-policy/mergers/procedures_en.

Note that Council Regulation (EC) No 139/2004 (the Merger Regulation) is repealed, in relation to the UK, by the Competition (Amendment etc) (EU Exit) Regulations 2019, SI 2019/93, reg 63, Sch 3, para 1, as from IP completion day (as defined in the European Union (Withdrawal Agreement) Act 2020, s 39) (for transitional provisions and savings in relation to the operation of the 2019 Regulations, see Sch 4 to those Regulations at **[7.69]** et seq).

---

1. Decisions are taken as openly as possible within the European Union, according to the second subparagraph of Article 1 of the Treaty on European Union. This principle is reflected in Article 15 of the Treaty on the Functioning of the European Union ("TFEU"), which requires the Union's institutions to conduct their work as openly as possible. The ability of the institutions to make acts which they adopt public is therefore the rule. EU law may provide for exceptions to this rule and prevent the disclosure of such acts or certain information contained therein.[1] Such exceptions include in particular the provisions ensuring compliance with the obligation of professional secrecy.[2]

2. In line with the general principles recalled above, the Commission makes as much information as possible available to the public, and only refrains from disclosing information to the extent that this is covered by its duty of professional secrecy or other public policy exceptions. According to the case law, three cumulative conditions must be met in order for information to fall, by its nature, within the ambit of the obligation of professional secrecy and thus to enjoy protection against disclosure to the public: (i) that it is known only to a limited number of persons, (ii) that its disclosure is liable to cause serious harm to the person who has provided it or to third parties and (iii) that the interests liable to be harmed by disclosure are, objectively, worthy of protection.[3]

3. Article 20 of Council Regulation (EC) No 139/2004[4] ("Merger Regulation") requires the Commission to publish the decisions which it takes pursuant to Articles 8(1) to (6), 14 and 15, together with the opinion of the Advisory Committee. The publication shall state the names of the parties and the main content of the decision. It shall have regard to the legitimate interest of undertakings in the protection of their business secrets and other confidential information.

4. In compliance with Article 20 of the Merger Regulation, the Commission publishes a non-confidential summary of the decisions taken pursuant to Articles 8(1) to 8(6), 14 and 15, together with the final report of the Hearing Officer and the opinion of the Advisory Committee,[5] in the Official Journal of the European Union (OJ).[6] In line with established practice, it also publishes a non-confidential text of the decision (public version) on the DG Competition website.[7] The documents published in the OJ are made available on the DG Competition website as well.

5. In application of the transparency principle mentioned above, and as an established practice,[8] the Commission also publishes on its website the non-confidential versions of decisions adopted pursuant to Article 6(1)(b) and to Article 6(1)(b) in conjunction with Article 6(2) of the Merger Regulation.

6. This Guidance outlines:

a) what undertakings can claim for redaction as business secrets and confidential information and what is not usually considered to be confidential information;
b) how confidentiality for business secrets and other confidential information can be claimed;
c) what the Commission usually redacts on its own initiative in the public version of a decision; and
d) the procedure that should be followed to settle confidentiality claims in the context of publication of the Commission decision and the related publications.

7. This Guidance only concerns the preparation of the public version of Commission decisions and related publications and does not cover the preparation of non-confidential submissions by undertakings in the context of the Commission's access to file procedure.

NOTES

1 See Judgment of the General Court of 28 January 2015, *Akzo Nobel NV and Eka v Commission*, T-345/12, ECLI:EU:T:2015:50, paragraph 60, Judgment of the General Court of 28 January 2015, *Evonik Degussa v Commission*, T-341/12, ECLI:EU:T:2015:51, paragraph 89 and Judgment of the Court of First Instance of 30 May 2006, *Bank Austria Creditanstalt v Commission*, T-198/03, ECLI:EU:T:2006:136, paragraph 69.

2 See Article 339 of the TFEU. The relevant provision on professional secrecy in the context of merger control is Article 17(2) of Council Regulation (EC) No 139/2004.

3 Judgment of the Court of First Instance of 30 May 2006, *Bank Austria Creditanstalt v Commission*, T 198/03, ECLI:EU:T:2006:136, paragraph 71, Judgment of the General Court of 28 January 2015, *Evonik Degussa v Commission*, T-341/12, ECLI:EU:T:2015:51, paragraph 94 and Judgment of the General Court of 28 January 2015, *Akzo Nobel NV and Eka v Commission*, T-345/12, ECLI:EU:T:2015:50, paragraph 65.

4 Council Regulation (EC) No 139/2004 of 20 January 2004 on the control of concentrations between undertakings, OJ L24,29.1.2004, p 1-22

5 Article 19(7) of the Merger Regulation.

6 Article 17(3) of the Decision of the President of the European Commission of 13 October 2011 on the function and terms of reference of the hearing officer in certain competition proceedings, (OJ L275, 20.10.2011 p. 29) ("Hearing Officer Terms of Reference").

7 See the DG Competition website: ec.europa.eu/competition/index_en.html.

8 See Judgment of the Court of First Instance of 30 May 2006, *Bank Austria Creditanstalt v Commission*, T-198/03, ECLI-:EU:T:2006:136, paragraph 77, Judgment of the General Court of 28 January 2015, *Akzo Nobel NV and Eka v Commission*, T-345/12, ECLI:EU:T:2015:50, paragraph 90 and Judgment of the General Court of 28 January 2015, *Evonik Degussa v Commission*, T-341/12, ECLI:EU:T:2015:51, paragraph 120.

1 WHAT CAN AND CANNOT BE CLAIMED FOR REDACTION

[4.668]

8. Undertakings can claim confidentiality for business secrets and other confidential information that should not appear in the public version of the Commission decision and in the related publications. Claims can be put forward by the addressee/s of the decision or by any other undertaking[9] which submitted information to the Commission during the investigation of the merger.

1.1 BUSINESS SECRETS

9. **Business secrets** are confidential information about an undertaking's business activity, the disclosure of which could result in **serious harm** for the same undertaking.[10] The interests liable to be harmed by disclosure must, objectively, be worthy of protection.[11]

10. Typical examples of information that may qualify as business secrets in merger decisions are:

a) cost structure and methods of assessing manufacturing and distribution costs;
b) margins calculations and price structure;
c) production secrets[12] and processes, as well as information relating to an undertaking's know-how;
d) supply sources;
e) quantities produced and sold;
f) market shares;[13]
g) customers and distributors lists;
h) business and marketing plans, sales policy and strategy, strategic decisions; and
i) information about the financial situation of a company, including financing agreements.

1.2 OTHER CONFIDENTIAL INFORMATION

11. **Other confidential information**[14] is information other than business secrets, insofar as its disclosure would significantly harm a person or undertaking. The interests liable to be harmed by disclosure must, objectively, be worthy of protection.[15] Depending on the specific circumstances of each case, this may include information that would enable the parties to identify complainants or other third parties where those have a justified wish to remain anonymous.

1.3 INFORMATION NOT CONSIDERED CONFIDENTIAL

12. The assessment whether a piece of information constitutes a business secret or other confidential information is carried out by the Commission on a **case-by-case basis**. Generally information that is not covered by the above definitions of "business secrets" and "other confidential information" will not be considered confidential.

13. By way of example, DG Competition considers that the following categories of information are normally **not** considered **confidential**:

a) the **Commission's own assessment**, as long as it does not explicitly refer to information falling into the category of ″business secret″ or ″other confidential information″. This covers for instance the Commission's analysis of the content of internal documents and the Commission's analysis of the results of its market investigation, including quotes from participants in the market investigation;
b) the Commission's general description of the **functioning of markets** object of the investigation;
c) information which is **publicly available**, including information available only upon payment through specialised information services (however, copyright limitations must be respected in the latter example);
d) Information that has **lost its commercial importance**, for instance due to the passage of time. The General Court has considered a period of five years in itself to be sufficient for information to lose its qualification as a business secret or other confidential information. Confidential treatment of information may only exceptionally be granted to such data, if its provider can show that, notwithstanding its historical nature, it still constitutes an essential element of the commercial position of the undertaking concerned;[16]
e) information which is **common knowledge among specialists** in the field (for example common knowledge among engineers or medical doctors);
f) **statistical or aggregate information** (also in the form of graphs, for instance);
g) **a market share is above or below a certain level** and/or that **an undertaking is larger than its competitors**; and
h) **arguments put forward by the notifying party(ies)**, for example relating to market share data, so long as they do not explicitly refer to information falling under the category of ″business secret″ or ″other confidential information″.

14. A non-exhaustive list of examples of the information which shall not be considered confidential alongside the categories indicated above is provided in Annex II to this document.

15. **Detailed reasons** must be given for any request to derogate from these principles in exceptional cases.

Generally information that is not covered by the above definitions of "business secrets" and "other confidential information" will not be considered confidential.

NOTES

9 Namely, parties to the concentration which are not notifying parties (within the meaning of paragraph 1.7 of Annex 1 of Commission Regulation (EC) No 802/2004 of 21 April 2004 implementing Council regulation (EC) No 139/2004 on the control of concentrations between undertakings, OJ L133, 30.04.2004, p 1-39) or third parties which submitted information which could be disclosed to the parties / to the notifying party but not to the general public.

10 Point 18 of the Commission Notice on the rules for access to the Commission file in cases pursuant to Articles 81 and 82 of the EC Treaty, Articles 53, 54 and 57 of the EEA Agreement and Council Regulation (EC) No 139/2004 (″Notice on access to file″) (OJ C325, 22.12.2005, p.7).

11 Judgment of the Court of First Instance of 30 May 2006, *Bank Austria Creditanstalt v Commission*, T-198/03, ECLI:EU:T:2006:136, paragraph 71.

12 A secret, commercially valuable plan, formula, process or device that is used for the making, preparing, compounding, or processing of a product and that can be said to be the end product of either innovation or substantial effort.

13 Market shares must be replaced by ranges as indicated in Annex I to this document.

14 Points 19-20 of the Notice on access to file.

15 Judgment of the Court of First Instance of 30 May 2006, *Bank Austria Creditanstalt v Commission*, T-198/03, ECLI:EU:T:2006:136, paragraph 71.

16 See, e.g., Judgment of the General Court of 28 January 2015, *Evonik Degussa v Commission*, T-341/12, ECLI-:EU:T:2015:51, paragraphs 84-85.

2. HOW TO CLAIM CONFIDENTIALITY

[4.669]

16. An undertaking can claim confidentiality on the text of the decision or related publications within the deadline set by the Commission.

17. In general, an undertaking cannot claim confidentiality for an entire document or whole sections thereof as it is normally possible to protect confidential information with limited redactions.

18. If an undertaking wants to claim confidentiality for information that should not appear in the public version of the decision or the related publications, it is required to:[17]

a) **identify any information** in the decision which is stemming from the undertaking and which it considers as falling within the ambit of professional secrecy as described in Sections 1.1 and 1.2 above;

b) **substantiate each claim** for confidentiality in writing, explaining, in particular:
   i. why the information in question constitutes a business secret or other confidential information; and
   ii. how the publication of this information would cause **serious harm** to your undertaking or would significantly harm a person or undertaking; and
   iii. which interests worthy of protection would be harmed by the disclosure;

c) **highlight** in the text of the decision, in a way that it remains legible, any text which contains information that it regards as business secrets or otherwise confidential; and

d) **provide** a concise but meaningful **non-confidential summary** of the redacted information, e.g.: ″sales strategy: [add details about the redacted item such as the time period, the area concerned, etc.]″. For figures (such as market shares or turnover figures) please indicate ranges (See Annex I ″MARKET SHARE RANGES IN NON-CONFIDENTIAL VERSIONS OF MERGER DECISIONS″). Please indicate the category into which the information falls, ″[BUSINESS SECRETS]″ or ″[CONFIDENTIAL]″.

19. The undertaking is required to provide the Commission with all relevant details in order to enable it to assess the confidentiality of a piece of information and to weigh up: (a) the public interest in ensuring that the activities of the EU institutions take place in the most transparent manner possible; and (b) the legitimate interests in protecting confidential information.

20. For the sake of efficient handling, confidentiality claims should be presented in a ″tabular″ format according to the following model:

Recital number of original decision	Information subject to the redaction request	Reasons for redaction request	Suggested non-confidential summary
Recital 30, 2nd sentence)		This is information not divulged outside the company. Its disclosure would . . .	[Last yeaŕs production strategy]
Recital 31, 1st sentence)			

21. If the undertaking fails to identify the information which it considers to be confidential, **the Commission** may **assume** that the decision, and, where relevant, the summary of the decision, the final report of the Hearing Officer and the opinion of the Advisory Committee do not contain any business secrets or other confidential information and, consequently, that **the undertaking has no objections to the disclosure of the information in those documents**.[18]

NOTES

17 See Articles 18(2) and 18(3) of the Merger Implementing Regulation: ″[. . .] (2) Any person which makes known its views or comments pursuant to Articles 12, Article 13 and Article 16 of this Regulation, or supplies information pursuant to Article 11 of Regulation (EC) No 139/2004, or subsequently submits further information to the Commission in the course of the same procedure, shall clearly identify any material which it considers to be confidential, giving reasons, and provide a separate non-confidential version by the date set by the Commission. (3) The Commission may also require persons referred to in Article 3 of Regulation (EC) No 139/2004, undertakings or associations of undertakings to identify any part of a [statement of objections,] case summary or a decision adopted by the Commission which in their view contains business secrets. Where business secrets or other confidential information are identified, the persons, undertakings and associations of undertakings shall give reasons and provide a separate non-confidential version by the date set by the Commission.[. . .]″, Commission Regulation (EC) No 802/2004 of 21 April 2004 implementing Council Regulation (EC) No 139/2004 on the control of concentrations between undertakings, OJ L133, 30.4.2004, p.1.

18 See Article 18(4) of the Merger Implementing Regulation ″If persons, undertakings or associations of undertakings fail to comply with paragraphs 2 or 3, the Commission may assume that the documents or statements concerned do not contain confidential information.″ See footnote 7 above.

3 WHAT THE COMMISSION REDACTS IN THE PUBLIC VERSION OF A DECISION

[4.670]

22. Irrespective of claims for confidentiality, other information redacted by the Commission in the public version of the decision (and the related publications) may include:

a) personal data, in line with the requirements of Regulation (EC) No 45/2001 (for instance information relating to an identified or identifiable natural person);[19]

b) depending on the specific circumstances of each case: information provided by third parties about undertakings which are able to place very considerable economic or commercial pressure on their competitors or on their trading partners, customers or suppliers;[20] and

c) military secrets.

NOTES

[19] Regulation (EC) No 45/2001 of the European Parliament and of the Council of 18 December 2000 on the protection of individuals with regard to the processing of personal data by the Community institutions and bodies and on the free movement of such data, OJ L8, 12.1.2001, p 1–22.

[20] Point 19 of the Notice on access to file.

4. PROCEDURAL ASPECTS

[4.671]

23. Once all confidentiality claims have been settled, the Commission will send a consolidated public version of the decision in which the text of the confidential information will have been removed for approval for publication. Any confidential information will have been redacted and replaced by the corresponding non-confidential descriptions, summaries or square brackets. Absent a reply within the deadline set by the Commission, the Commission will be entitled to publish this redacted public version.[21]

24. If the undertaking considers that this public version of the decision still contains business secrets or other confidential information, it can refer the matter to the Hearing Officer within the deadline that will be set by the Commission.[22] If the undertaking fails to address the Hearing Officer within the given deadline the Commission will be entitled to publish this redacted public version.

25. The publication of a public version of the decision on the DG Competition website does not preclude the Commission from publishing a more complete version at a later stage, provided that this publication does not contain confidential information.[23]

NOTES

[21] See Article 18(4) of the Merger Implementing Regulation: *"If persons, undertakings or associations of undertakings fail to comply with paragraphs 2 or 3, the Commission may assume that the documents or statements concerned do not contain confidential information"*..

[22] Article 8 of the Hearing Officer Terms of Reference.

[23] Judgment of the General Court of 28 January 2015, *Akzo Nobel NV and Eka v Commission*, T-345/12, ECLI-:EU:T:2015:50, paragraph 123.

ANNEXES

ANNEX I
MARKET SHARE RANGES IN NON-CONFIDENTIAL VERSIONS OF MERGER DECISIONS

[4.672]

In order to prepare non-confidential versions of final decisions in merger cases the notifying party(ies) has/have to provide the Commission within seven days with a proposal for a non-confidential version of the decision by replacing all business secrets by [. . .] and replacing market shares by ranges.

Save exceptional circumstances, DG Competition considers that the following market share ranges are suitable for protecting business secrets contained in a decision.

Ranges to be used in non-confidential version: Between 0 and 4.99% [0–5]%

Between 5.0 and 9.99% [5–10]%

Between 10.0 and 19.99% [10–20]%

Between 20.0 and 29.99% [20–30]%

Between 30.0 and 39.99% [30–40]%

Between 40.0 and 49.99% [40–50]%

Between 50.0 and 59.99% [50–60]%

Between 60.0 and 69.99% [60–70]%

Between 70.0 and 79.99% [70–80]%

Between 80.0 and 89.99% [80–90]%

Between 90.0 and 100% [90–100]%

ANNEX II
EXAMPLES OF INFORMATION NOT CONSIDERED CONFIDENTIAL

[4.673]

By way of example, DG Competition considers that the following information is **not normally considered confidential**:

a) the **Commission's own assessment**, so long as it does not explicitly refer to information falling under the category of "business secret" or "other confidential information": this covers for instance the Commission's analysis of the content of internal documents and the Commission's analysis of the results of its market investigation, including quotes from participants in the market investigation;

Example	Confidentiality assessment
"Company A will not enjoy any veto rights over strategic decisions at Company B post-Transaction."	This information is based on the Commission's own analysis and cannot be redacted. Moreover, if Company A did enjoy a strategic veto right, it would have to be a notifying party whose identity would have to be published in the Official Journal of the EU and on DG COMP's website.
"In light of the above considerations and taking into account Company A's most recent business plans, the Commission concludes that Company A is most likely not able to continue financing Company B."	
"Regarding the results of the study provided by the notifying party, the Commission considers that these are weakened by many elements, such as the reservations to representativeness of the samples and the precise circumstances of the surveys. The results of the surveys are weakened by the lack of information on the type of dolls that are used for playing or for decoration and the fact that some stores offer a wide range of items, such as dolls and other types of toys. The conclusion that there is a robust link between the time spent in a store and buying dolls for playing or for decoration cannot therefore be established."	This type of information cannot be redacted because it is based on the Commission's own reasoning and not referring to any explicit business secret.
"Given that the target Company's offering is currently distributed by a third party in several countries, its market share is probably understated. After the merger, the acquiring Company would most likely distribute the target Company's offering with its own offering and would terminate the target Company's distribution agreements."	
"The notifying party argues that undertaking A's high EBITDA level is not an indication for a good business performance. There is a discrepancy in the notifying party's statements, because low EBITDA levels were claimed as an indication of a poor business performance in the past, whereas currently high EBITDA levels are not an indication of a good business performance."	
"The analysis invalidates the notifying party's claim that the terms of the agreements that Company A and Company B obtain from [accepted redaction] and [accepted redaction]* are equal. In addition, the Commission concludes that regarding all customers, Company A obtains better terms of the agreements on many important negotiation aspects. Finally, the terms of the agreements that Company A obtains from smaller customers are [accepted redaction]* than the terms of the agreements that Company A obtains from bigger customers."*	
'Suppliers established in Country A actively target customers across the border into the North-Eastern region of Country B. Imports thus play an important role as a competitive constraint on the Notifying parties, as confirmed by internal documents. See for instance Board presentation of 1 April 2002, 'Country B and Country A: Strategic outlook for the second quarter of 2002', page 208."	In a case such as this one, the title of the internal document cannot be redacted because it does not itself refer to any explicit business secret.

b) the Commission's **general description of the functioning of markets** object of the investigation;

Example	**Confidentiality assessment**
"As a result of the economic downturn, demand for this commodity has been constantly decreasing over the last three years. As a result, plants in the area are operating at reduced capacity utilisation levels. Spare capacities at plants owned by the parties and competitors in this Member State are on average 50% and in some cases as high as 60%. This sets in motion a downward pressure on prices, and lower margins for suppliers. Competitors and customers broadly confirmed this within the market investigation".	This type of information cannot be redacted because it generally describes the competitive dynamic in a given market and is not referring to any explicit business secret.
"Finally, the notifying party and its main competitors typically use market share estimations provided by the industry representative, when they negotiate with customers."	

c) information which is **publicly available**, including information available only upon payment through specialised information services (however, copyright limitations must be verified in the latter example);

Example	**Confidentiality assessment**
"1908 was a year of high financial losses for Company A plc. According to the company's financial annual report for 1908. Company A's net loss increased from EUR 999 million in 1907 to EUR 9,999 million in 1908. Company A attributes the bulk of the losses to the complete write-off of its investment in Company B Inc. (EUR 8,888 million) and other impairments, asset revaluations and losses from discontinued operations."	If the information included in this example were to be available from public annual account statements, it could not be redacted.
"Even the biggest customers that buy dolls, namely Company A and Company B, [accepted redaction], are not currently active in all EEA countries. This is also confirmed by customers and competitors."*	If the information included in this example were to be available to the market, it could not be redacted.
"The undertakings concerned have a combined worldwide turnover of more than EUR 5,000 million (A: EUR 1,234 million; B: [accepted redaction])."*	The turnover of the undertakings concerned is in most cases publicly available and therefore cannot be redacted. However, even if the turnover of an undertaking concerned is publicly available, the turnover of the group to which it belongs might be treated as confidential, if it is not publicly available. Also, sometimes the worldwide turnover is publicly available but the EEA-wide or national turnovers are not. As a consequence, in such cases the Commission would agree to redact but the EEA-wide or national turnovers.

d) Information which is **common knowledge among specialists in the field** (for example common knowledge among engineers or medical doctors);

Example	**Confidentiality assessment**
"In the context of the market investigation, prescribers and medical specialists stated that drug A is usually prescribed as the first line of treatment for X type of disorders, while drug B is more suitable for Z type of disorders, thus not responding to the same medical needs. Drug A and B are therefore not substitutable from a medical perspective".	This information is common knowledge for experts in the medical field and therefore cannot be redacted.

e) **Statistical or aggregate** information (even in the form of graphs, for instance).

Example				**Confidentiality assessment**
Table X: Overall Country A pumpkin consumption (Q1 of 1315 and 1316)				This information would not be considered confidential because it would have been compiled from all the data submitted by competitors without specifying the individual shares.
Pumpkins production Q1	Q1 1315	Q1 1316	Diff. %	
Domestic consumption	4270	3448	-19.25%	
Export	1010	607	-39.90%	
Total	5280	4055	-23.20%	

f) **a market share is above or below a certain level** and/or that **an undertaking is larger than its competitors**;

Example	Confidentiality assessment
"In many countries the combined undertakings' biggest competitor will be half the size of, or even four or more times smaller than the combined undertaking."	This information is not confidential because it only reports a general threshold without specifying a precise figure.

g) **arguments put forward by the notifying party(ies)**, for example relating to market share data, so long as they do not explicitly refer to information falling under the category of "business secret" or "other confidential information";

Example	Confidentiality assessment
"The notifying party challenges the reliability of the market share data collected by the industry representative. The notifying party states that, in some instances, the market share data understates the market position of the smaller stores and exaggerates the combined market share of the big stores. The notifying party points to limitations of the data. For example, the notifying party argues that since the market share estimations provided by the industry representative cannot cover the whole market (and the sales excluded from the scope of the surveys are probable sales made by smaller stores), the element used for estimation of the entire size of the market is merely a speculation of some staff members of the industry representative."	This information is not confidential because it relates to arguments of the notifying party(ies) in relation to data available to market participants.
"The notifying party declares that, according to the general view in the toys industry, the dancing dolls are the most important developing business model, and it will continue to develop and will be very significant in the future."	
*"The notifying party submits that: (a) It cannot otherwise fight the decline of the market and therefore it has an incentive to develop new stores that sell dolls and entice customers away from making their own dolls; (b) Stores selling certain types of dolls are generating significant revenues; and (c) The concern that the notifying party has any incentive to block the growth of stores selling certain types of dolls is inconsistent with the Commission's acknowledgement that the notifying party policy is to conclude agreements [*accepted redaction*]*."*	

WORKING ARRANGEMENTS FOR THE FUNCTIONING OF THE ADVISORY COMMITTEE ON CONCENTRATIONS[1]

(November 2016)

[4.674]

NOTES

This document, and the accompanying Annex, are available on the European Commission website at: ec.europa.eu/competition-policy/mergers/procedures_en.

[1] These Working Arrangements have been drawn up by the European Commission's DG Competition and the competent authorities of the Member States. The Arrangements have been drawn up bearing in mind the joint declaration on the Advisory Committee on concentrations adopted by the Council and the Commission on 20 January 2004, on the occasion of the adoption by the Council for Economic and Financial Affairs of Council Regulation (EC) No 139/2004 on the control of concentration between undertakings (the EC Merger Regulation), and on the basis of preparatory work undertaken by the competent authorities of the Member States in the context of the ECA working group on merger control and by DG Competition. The current version of the Working Arrangements reflects the agreement reached between the European Commission's DG Competition and the competent authorities of the Member States on 28 June 2016.

PURPOSE

[4.675]

The purpose of these Working Arrangements is to contribute to the proper functioning of the Advisory Committee on concentrations established by Article 19 of Council Regulation (EC) No. 139/2004 (hereafter "the Merger Regulation"),[2] and thereby to strengthen the close and constant liaison between the Commission and the competent authorities of the Member States which is envisaged by that Article.

1. These Working Arrangements are complemented by the modalities on the organisation of and participation in Advisory Committee meetings by video-link, provided in the Annex.

NOTES

[2] Council Regulation (EC) No. 139/2004 of 20 January 2004 on the control of concentrations between undertakings (OJ L24, 29.01.2004) [the "Merger Regulation"].

CONVENING A MEETING

[4.676]

2. The Commission, as Chair of the Advisory Committee on concentrations, will convene a meeting on its own initiative by sending invitations to the "competent authorities of the Member States",[3] as set out in Article 19 (5) of the Merger Regulation.

3. In setting the date for a meeting, the Commission should take into account the possible convenience or inconvenience of holding a meeting on a particular day, for example by grouping together similar or related issues in the same or adjacent meetings, or so as to facilitate the attendance of members at other meetings in Brussels.

4. Where appropriate, the Commission as Chair can allow representatives of the competent authorities to attend remotely by video-link a meeting held in person. Such meetings are organised in accordance with the modalities on the organisation of and participation in Advisory Committee meetings by video-link, provided in the Annex. A meeting may, on the initiative of the Commission as Chair and in the absence of disagreement by any of the competent authorities of the Member States, also take place by telephone conference. Normally speaking, it is considered that holding a meeting by telephone conference should only be contemplated in cases where the issues involved are not generally regarded as substantively or procedurally contentious, or where particular urgency justifies resorting to this format for discussion.

NOTES

[3] This is the term used in Article 19.

REPRESENTATION

[4.677]

5. Each of the competent authorities of the Member States should make its best efforts to attend Advisory Committee meetings and, if it does, will be represented by one or two representatives in the manner set out in Article 19(4) of the Merger Regulation.

THE "RAPPORTEUR"

[4.678]

6. It has for many years been the practice for a rapporteur to be appointed from among the representatives of the competent authorities of the Member States in the Advisory Committee so as to facilitate discussion in the Committee meeting.

APPOINTMENT OF THE RAPPORTEUR

7. Shortly after the adoption of a decision pursuant to Article 6(1)(c) of the Merger Regulation initiating a second phase investigation, the Commission, as Chair of the Advisory Committee, should appoint one Member State whose representative will serve as rapporteur at the Advisory Committee meeting on the case in question. The nomination of a rapporteur should normally be made in accordance with an order derived from the list of Presidencies of the Council.

8. Once the selection of a Member State has been made, the Commission should normally then notify the competent authorities of that Member State, and ask them to confirm that the Member State has no objection to its representative being appointed as rapporteur. The rapporteur should be the representative of the competent authorities of that Member State on the Advisory Committee in question, or one of its two representatives.

9. If the competent authorities of the Member State accept the appointment, an individual should be designated as the rapporteur, which individual may in turn request that he or she be supported in his/her functions by a "co-rapporteur". The nomination of such a co-rapporteur should likewise normally be made in accordance with an order derived from the list of Presidencies of the Council.

10. Once appointed, the rapporteur and co-rapporteur should normally determine between themselves how they wish to share the tasks of rapporteur.

11. If the competent authorities of the Member State decline the appointment of its representative or one of its representatives as rapporteur or co-rapporteur, a reason should be given for doing so and the Commission should proceed to choose an alternative nominee from the rotating list of Presidencies of the Council.

12. Once an individual has been appointed as rapporteur or co-rapporteur, the Commission should without delay inform the competent authorities of the Member States accordingly.

ROLE OF THE RAPPORTEUR BEFORE THE MEETING

13. The rapporteur may wish to prepare for the discussion within the Advisory Committee meeting by familiarising him/her-self with the case during the period of time between being appointed and the meeting taking place. The Commission should facilitate this preparation by ensuring that the appropriate staff are made available to meet with the rapporteur upon his/her request, or by ensuring that the appropriate staff are made available to show documents in the case file to the rapporteur upon his/her request. The latter documents may, in particular, consist of significant third party comments submitted during the course of the Commission's investigation.

14. The rapporteur should generally, in advance of the meeting, send to the competent authorities of the Member States and the Commission a list of questions to be raised, or a summary of issues to be discussed, at the meeting. A summary of issues to be discussed may include a summary of the main issues raised by third parties during the course of the investigation. A Member State representative may wish to suggest to the rapporteur and the Commission, in advance of the meeting, any further questions which he/she believes ought to be raised, or any further issues which he/she believes ought to be discussed, at the meeting.

ROLE OF THE RAPPORTEUR DURING THE MEETING

15. The rapporteur has the function of stimulating a probing discussion of the Commission's draft decision at the meeting of the Advisory Committee. To this end, the rapporteur may propose to the Chair the format for discussion which he/she feels would be most appropriate for the case in question.

DOCUMENTATION TO BE SENT TO MEMBERS OF THE COMMITTEE

DOCUMENTATION TO BE SENT DURING THE COURSE OF THE INVESTIGATION

[4.679]

16. As set out in Article 19(1) of the Merger Regulation, the Commission will send to the competent authorities of the Member States copies of notifications (Form CO)[4] within 3 working days of receiving them.

17. The Commission will, moreover, in keeping with what is set out in Article 19(1) of the Merger Regulation concerning "copies of the most important documents lodged with or issued by the Commission", send copies of, in particular, the following documents to the competent authorities of the Member States, as soon as possible following their promulgation or receipt:

— Copies of Form RS,[5] together with a note to Member States setting out the preliminary views of the Commission's services concerning the referral request;
— Copies of all decisions adopted under the Merger Regulation, including in particular those taken pursuant to Articles 6(1)(a), 6(1)(b), 6(1)(c), 4(4), 8, 9, 14, 15, 21 and 22;
— Copies of "statements of objections";[6]
— Copies of legal and economic replies to statements of objections;[7]
— The report of the Hearing Officer;
— Copies of commitments offered by the notifying parties.[8]

Generally, those copies shall be sent in their confidential versions, with the exception of copies of commitments, in which the divestiture deadline will be redacted.

18. As set out in Article 11(5) of the Merger Regulation, copies of decisions taken pursuant to Art. 11(3) will be sent to the competent authorities of the Member State/s in whose territory the undertaking in question is located and to the competent authorities of the Member State/s whose territory is "affected", as soon as possible following their promulgation. Upon a "specific request" of a competent national authority, that authority will also be sent copies of "simple requests for information".

19. Beyond this, as set out above, the Commission should facilitate the preparation of the Advisory Committee meeting by ensuring that documents in its case file - in particular significant legal and economic submissions by the parties (other than those mentioned in paragraph 18) and significant third party comments submitted during the course of the Commission's investigation - can be made accessible to the rapporteur upon his or her request. In addition, a representative of a competent authority of a Member State may wish to prepare for the discussion at the Advisory Committee meeting by familiarising him/her-self with documentation not normally transmitted to the competent authorities of the Member States. In the context of the close and constant liaison between the Commission and the competent authorities of the Member States as envisaged by Article 19 of the Merger Regulation, the Commission should facilitate such preparation by ensuring that documents in the case file can be made accessible to a representative of the competent authority of a Member State upon his or her request in their confidential version. Those documents may, in particular, consist of

— legal and economic submissions by the parties (other than those mentioned in paragraph 18), including copies of legal and economic replies to decisions pursuant to Article 6(1)(c) of the Merger Regulation;
— and significant third party comments submitted during the course of the Commission's investigation, including responses to the Commission's requests for information from selected third parties.

DOCUMENTATION TO BE SENT IN ADVANCE OF THE ADVISORY COMMITTEE MEETING

20. As set out in Article 19(5) of the Merger Regulation, the Commission will send a preliminary draft of the decision to be taken in the case, as well as a summary of the case and an indication of the most important documents, to the competent authorities of the Member States not less than 10 working days in advance of the Advisory Committee meeting.

21. In exceptional cases, the Commission may send this documentation to Member States less than 10 working days before the Advisory Committee meeting, as appropriate in order to avoid serious harm to one or more of the undertakings concerned by a concentration. However the period of time allowed should nevertheless be sufficient in order to allow adequate consultation of Member States.

MEANS OF TRANSMISSION

22. Transmission of documentation to Member States should, to the extent possible, be carried out by electronic means or in electronic format.

[4] Annex I to Commission Regulation (EC) No 802/2004 of 7 April 2004 implementing Council Regulation (EC) No. 139/2004, OJ L133/1, 30 April 2004 ("Implementing Regulation").

[5] Annex III to Commission Regulation (EC) No 802/2004.

[6] See Article 18(1) & (3) of the Merger Regulation, and Article 13(1)-(3) of the Implementing Regulation.

[7] See Article 18(1) & (3) of the Merger Regulation, and Article 13(1)-(3) of the Implementing Regulation.

[8] See Article 19(1), second sentence, of the Merger Regulation.

CONDUCT OF THE MEETING

[4.680]

23. The Advisory Committee meeting is chaired by the Commission.

24. The Commission, as Chair of the meeting, should draw up an agenda for the meeting. This agenda should be sent to the competent authorities of the Member States, together with the invitation.

25. The Commission as Chair should determine the general structure of, and format for, the discussion taking place in the meeting; in doing so and, according to what is most appropriate for the case in question, it may wish to strive for a balance between a formal "tour de table" format, which encourages active contribution by all Member States, and a more informal format. The Commission should at the same time accord a prominent role to the rapporteur in that discussion, in the manner described above, and may discuss with the rapporteur in advance of the meeting how it should best be conducted.

OPINION OF THE COMMITTEE

[4.681]

26. The Committee will render a single Opinion.

27. In the absence of unanimity on the Opinion or on a part of the opinion, the opinion is determined by a simple majority of the members of the Committee participating in the Advisory Committee meeting and voting on the opinion (not counting abstentions). This determination will be made by calling a vote, as provided for in Article 19(6) of the Merger Regulation.

28. In the absence of unanimity, the number of votes in favour and against the Opinion, as well as the number of abstentions will be recorded. The record should not identify the members of the Committee having voted in favour of the Opinion, against it or having abstained.

29. The Opinion may briefly record the reasons for views which diverge from, or go beyond, the analysis of the Commission in its draft decision, if a simple majority of the members of the Committee participating in the Advisory Committee meeting and voting on the opinion (not counting abstentions) agrees to the inclusion of such reasoning.

30. Each Member State, irrespective of the number of representatives which it sends to the meeting, is considered as having a single vote for the purposes of adopting an Opinion of the Committee.

31. Members of the Committee must participate in the Advisory Committee meeting in order to be able to contribute to content of the Opinion, or to vote on its adoption. The Opinion should be delivered by the Advisory Committee before the conclusion of the Advisory Committee meeting.

32. As set out in Article 19(7) of the Merger Regulation, the Commission will communicate the Opinion of the Advisory Committee to the notifying parties together with the decision. Moreover, the Commission will publish on DG COMP's website the Opinion together with the public version of the decision or a provisional version thereof within two months after the adoption of the decision, having regard to the need to protect legitimate business secrets. Should the public version or a provisional version thereof not be available within that timeframe, the Commission will nevertheless proceed to the publication of the Opinion on DG COMP's website.

33. The Commission will take the utmost account of the Opinion delivered by the Advisory Committee, and will inform the competent authorities of the Member States of the manner in which the Advisory Committee's Opinion has been taken into account. The Commission will do so at the earliest feasible opportunity following the adoption of the final decision in relation to which the Opinion was rendered. Generally, this could be done on the occasion of the first meeting of an Advisory Committee following the adoption of the decision, or by some other appropriate means. In cases of a (partially) negative Opinion, the Commission shall explain in writing to the competent authorities of the Member States how it took the utmost account of the Opinion within 15 working days after the adoption of the Decision and offer a telephone conference to address possible questions in relation to its written explanations. This telephone conference shall take place within fifteen working days upon receipt by the Commission of a request by a Member State.

SECRETARIAL SUPPORT

[4.682]

34. The Commission, as Chair of the meeting, should provide secretarial support for the Committee.

ATTENDANCE LIST

[4.683]

35. The Commission, as Chair of the meeting, should draw up and distribute an attendance list specifying the authorities to which the persons designated by the competent authorities of the Member States to represent them belong.

CONFIDENTIALITY

[4.684]

36. The Commission and the members of the Advisory Committee on concentrations will, in keeping with their obligation of professional secrecy set out in Article 17 of the Merger Regulation, not disclose any information of the kind covered by this obligation which they have acquired via the deliberations of the Advisory Committee. Nor should they reveal the Opinion of the Committee before it is made public or any information concerning the deliberations which led to the formulation of that Opinion.

STATUS

[4.685]

37. The European Commission's DG Competition and the competent authorities of the Member States intend to make their best efforts to fully adhere to these Working Arrangements. However, these arrangements do not create any rights or obligations going beyond those set out in the Treaties, the Merger Regulation, and in particular Article 19 thereof, or its Implementing Regulation, as amended from time to time, and as interpreted by the case law of the Court of Justice of the European Union. These arrangements do not alter the Commission's interpretative notices, and failure to abide by them in any respect is not intended to have any legal consequences for the application of the Merger Regulation.

38. The European Commission's DG Competition and the competent authorities of the Member States may from time to time decide to amend these arrangements. It is intended that the operation of these arrangements should be reviewed two years following their adoption.

ANNEX
ORGANISATION OF AND PARTICIPATION IN ADVISORY COMMITTEE MEETINGS BY VIDEO-LINK — MODALITIES

PURPOSE

[4.686]

1. The purpose of these Modalities is to complement the Working Arrangements for the optimal functioning of Advisory Committee meetings established by Article 19 of Council Regulation (EC) No. 139/2004 (Working Arrangements for the Advisory Committee on Concentrations) and by Article 14 of Council Regulation (EC) No. 1/2003 (Working Arrangements for the functioning of the Advisory Committee on Restrictive Practices and Dominant Positions), and to define the conditions for participation in the case of attendance of the competent authorities of the Member States by video-link. In particular, the Modalities replace paragraph 4 and complement paragraph 31 of the Working Arrangements for the Advisory Committee on Concentrations and complement paragraphs 13-27 of the Working Arrangements for the functioning of the Advisory Committee on Restrictive Practices and Dominant Positions.

CONVENING A MEETING

2. As established in the respective Working Arrangements for Advisory Committee meetings, the European Commission, as Chair of the Advisory Committee meetings, will convene a meeting on its own initiative by sending invitations to the 'competent authorities of the Member States' (CAs). Where appropriate, the European Commission can convene the meeting as a video-link meeting, allowing for the attendance of CA representatives remotely by video-link.

CONFIRMATION OF PARTICIPATION

3. The CAs will inform the Commission beforehand of the names of their representatives as well as whether these representatives will participate in the meeting in person or remotely by video-link.

4. If the meeting concerns a case for which a rapporteur has been appointed, the rapporteur attends the meeting in person.

PARTICIPATION BY VIDEO-LINK

5. CAs whose representatives participate remotely by video-link commit themselves that the participation via video-link takes place from secure premises with restricted access. They ensure that access for unauthorised (i.e. unannounced to the Commission pursuant to paragraph 3 above) persons to the premises during the video-conferencing meeting is prohibited.

6. CAs whose representatives participate remotely by video-link further commit themselves to ensuring that the video-link established from their premises to the Commission premises is secure and compatible with the video-conferencing system of the Commission.

7. They also ensure that a computer with secure email connection is available on their premises for the purposes of signing the Opinion before the end of the meeting (see paragraph 18 below).

8. If the video-link connection with one or several remote participant(s) is interrupted during the meeting, the CA(s) concerned is/are deemed to be absent and not represented. This does not affect the Advisory Committee's capacity to deliver an Opinion pursuant to Article 19(6) of Regulation (EC) No. 139/2004 and Article 14(3) of Regulation (EC) 1/2003.

9. Recording of the video-conferencing meeting by CAs is not permitted.

LANGUAGES SPOKEN AND INTERPRETATION

10. Due to current technical restrictions, it is not possible to interpret interventions made by remote participants into any other language for the benefit of the other participants, which participate remotely by video-link or are present in the meeting room. The same restrictions limit the interpretation of interventions made by participants present in the meeting room for the benefit of remote participants. The interpretation arrangements for the participants present in the meeting room remain as in current practice.

11. At the beginning of each meeting, CAs whose representatives participate remotely by video-link shall agree that their representatives intervene in the meeting in one commonly understood language.

12. They further agree that interpretation for the representatives participating remotely is done in that commonly understood language.

13. A CA or CA representative who cannot agree to this modality has to attend the meeting in person.

ORGANISATION OF THE DISCUSSIONS

14. CAs agree that the chair of the Advisory Committee steers the discussion and gives the floor to representatives participating remotely by video-link in the same way as to participants attending in person.

ADOPTION OF THE ADVISORY COMMITTEE OPINION

15. The chair of the Advisory Committee takes note of the positions taken by the CAs participating remotely by video-link or present in person in the meeting room.

16. At the end of the meeting, the Opinion is transcribed into a document. In line with Article 14(3) in fine of Regulation 1/2003, this Opinion shall be reasoned if so requested by one or several representatives.

17. The text of the Opinion is read out in the meeting to ascertain that all representatives, whether attending in person or remotely by video-link, have the opportunity to verify that the text is correct and to point out any errors.

18. As regards the signature of the Opinion, representatives present in the meeting room sign the transcript in person in line with current practice. Once signed by the participants present in the meeting room, the Opinion is sent to the remote participants for signature via secure email. The remote participants shall immediately sign the Opinion to confirm their agreement and return it forthwith by secure email. The meeting will be closed once all participants, present and remote, have signed the Opinion.

AGREEMENT WITH THESE MODALITIES

19. The CAs agree to the aforementioned modalities and commit their representatives to abide by them.

DOCUMENT EXCHANGE PLATFORM IN DG COMPETITION (E-TRUSTEX)

(February 2019)

[4.687]

NOTES

This document is available on the European Commission website at: ec.europa.eu/competition-policy/index/etrustex_en. Note that this webpage has been updated since its original publication. Note also that the footnotes included below are not part of the original webpage, but have been included in place of hypertext links contained in that webpage.

eTrustEx (Trusted Document Exchange) is a web based exchange platform that ensures secure transmission of documents between DG Competition and external stakeholders.

eTrustEx serves as a secure communication channel to send documents to DG Competition. eTrustEx supports message encryption, message integrity through the use of checksum algorithms, authentication via EU Login and traceability. For more information see **eTrustEx User Manual**[1].

The current limits for document transmission via eTrustEx are the following:

- Maximum size of transmission: 4GB;
- Maximum size of each file uploaded in the same transmission: 100MB;
- Maximum number of files uploaded in the same transmission: 500;

For Merger cases you can use eTrustEx to submit to the Commission, for example:

- Draft Form CO
- Responses to Requests For Information
- Responses to requests for internal documents, if smaller than 4 GB
- Response to a Statement of Objections
- Submission of draft remedies
- Any other submission to the Commission

For Antitrust cases you can use eTrustEx to submit to the Commission, for example:

- Complaints
- Comments on complaints
- Responses to Requests For Information
- Response to a Statement of Objections, a Preliminary Assessment or comments on the Article 7(1) letter
- Any other submission to the Commission

For submissions larger than 4GB, please either split into more sendings or use a physical external carrier (DVD, USB, external hard drive).

For registration to eTrustEx, please click **here**[2].

For further information, please contact COMP-ETRUSTEX@ec.europa.eu

NOTES

[1] The eTrustEx User Manual is at ec.europa.eu/competition/contacts/etrustex_user_guide.pdf.

[2] For creation of an EU login account (you will need an EU login to access eTrustEx): webgate.ec.europa.eu/cas.

COMMUNICATION FROM THE COMMISSION GUIDANCE ON THE APPLICATION OF THE REFERRAL MECHANISM SET OUT IN ARTICLE 22 OF THE MERGER REGULATION TO CERTAIN CATEGORIES OF CASES

(2021/C113/01)

[4.688]

NOTES

Date of publication in OJ: OJ 113, 31.3.2021, p 1.

Note that the Merger Regulation (Council Regulation 139/2004/EC) was repealed by the Competition (Amendment etc) (EU Exit) Regulations 2019, SI 2019/93, reg 63, Sch 3, para 1, as from IP completion day (as defined in the European Union (Withdrawal Agreement) Act 2020, s 39).

1. The purpose of this document is to provide practical guidance regarding the Commission's approach to the use of the referral mechanism set out in Article 22 of Council Regulation (EC) No 139/2004 of 20 January 2004 on the control of concentrations between undertakings ('the Merger Regulation').[1] The aim is to facilitate and clarify its application in certain categories of appropriate cases.

2. This document complements, for such cases, the guidance provided in the Commission Notice on Case Referral,[2] which provides general guidance on the overall case referral system established in Article 4(4) and (5), Article 9 and Article 22 of the Merger Regulation.

3. The document aims to provide only general guidance on the appropriateness of particular categories of cases for referral under Article 22 of the Merger Regulation: the Member States and the Commission retain a considerable margin of discretion in deciding whether to refer cases or accept referrals, respectively.[3] The Commission may revise this Guidance at any time in light of future developments. It may also decide to consolidate the content of this Guidance in the Notice on Case Referral, in the light of experience gathered in applying the revised approach to referrals under Article 22.

4. This Guidance applies, *mutatis mutandis*, to the referral rules contained in the EEA Agreement.[4]

1. Introduction

5. The Merger Regulation grants the Commission exclusive jurisdiction to review concentrations with an EU dimension, defined by the application of combined turnover-based thresholds. Such thresholds delineate the transactions whose impact on the market is deemed to go beyond the national borders of any one Member State and which, as such, are in principle best dealt with at the EU level.[5] The Merger Regulation contains a corrective mechanism to the application of these quantitative jurisdictional thresholds, allowing, under specific circumstances, a referral of individual cases between the Commission and one or several Member States.[6] This system of referrals aims to ensure that the more appropriate authority or authorities for carrying out a particular merger investigation review(s) the case despite not being initially competent.

6. Article 22 of the Merger Regulation allows for one or more Member States to request the Commission to examine, for those Member States, any concentration that does not have an EU dimension but affects trade between Member States and threatens to significantly affect competition within the territory of the Member State or States making the request. It is clear from the wording, the legislative history and the purpose of Article 22 of the Merger Regulation, as well as from the Commission's enforcement practice, that Article 22 is applicable to all concentrations,[7] not only those that meet the respective jurisdictional criteria of the referring Member States.[8]

7. The mechanism set out in Article 22 of the Merger Regulation has allowed the Commission to review a significant number of transactions in a wide array of economic sectors, such as industrial, manufacturing, pharmaceutical and digital. These have included cases eventually subject to an in-depth investigation and/or authorised only following modification by the remedies offered by the parties.[9]

8. With the progressive implementation of national regimes for merger control in almost all Member States, the Commission, in exercising the discretion granted to it by the Merger Regulation,[10] developed a practice of discouraging referral requests under Article 22 from Member States that did not have original jurisdiction over the transaction at stake. This practice was notably based on the experience that such transactions were not generally likely to have a significant impact on the internal market.

9. In recent years, however, market developments have resulted in a gradual increase of concentrations involving firms that play or may develop into playing a significant competitive role on the market(s) at stake despite generating little or no turnover at the moment of the concentration. These developments appear particularly significant in the digital economy, where services regularly launch with the aim of building up a significant user base and/or commercially valuable data inventories, before seeking to monetise the business. Similarly, in sectors such as pharmaceuticals and others where innovation is an important parameter of competition, there have been transactions involving innovative companies conducting research & development projects and with strong competitive potential, even if these companies have not yet finalised, let alone exploited commercially, the results of their innovation activities. Similar considerations apply to companies with access to or impact on competitively valuable assets, such as raw materials, intellectual property rights, data or infrastructure.

10. Against this background, the Commission has examined the effectiveness of the turnover-based jurisdictional thresholds of the EU Merger Regulation in its Evaluation of procedural and jurisdictional aspects of the EU Merger control.[11] It has concluded that, while these thresholds, complemented by the referral mechanisms set out in the Merger Regulation, have generally been effective in capturing transactions with a significant impact on competition in the EU internal market, a number of cross-border transactions which could potentially also have such an impact have escaped review by both the Commission and the Member States. This includes in particular transactions in the digital and pharma sectors.

11. The Commission considers that a reappraisal of the application of Article 22 of the Merger Regulation can contribute to addressing this issue. In the light of the above considerations, the Commission intends, in certain circumstances, to encourage and accept referrals in cases where the referring Member State does not have initial jurisdiction over the case (but where the criteria of Article 22 are met). This change in approach will permit Member States and the Commission to ensure that additional transactions that merit review under the Merger Regulation are examined by the Commission,[12] without imposing a notification obligation on transactions that would not warrant such review. This change in the current practice does not require a modification of the relevant provisions of the Merger Regulation.

12. This Guidance provides indications about the categories of cases that may constitute suitable candidates for a referral in situations where the transaction is not notifiable under the laws of the referring Member State(s), and thus on the criteria that the Commission may take into account in such situations when encouraging or accepting such a referral. It also provides guidance on certain procedural aspects. Therefore, the Guidance aims to increase transparency, predictability and legal certainty as regards a wider application of Article 22 of the Merger Regulation.

2. Guiding principles for the referral of cases which are not notifiable under the laws of the referring Member State(s)

2.1. Legal requirements

13. Article 22 of the Merger Regulation states that, in order for a referral to be made by one or more Member States to the Commission, two legal requirements must be fulfilled. The concentration must:

(i) affect trade between Member States; and

(ii) threaten to significantly affect competition within the territory of the Member State or States making the request.

14. For the first criterion, the Notice on Case Referral explains that a concentration fulfils the requirement if it is liable to have some discernible influence on the pattern of trade between Member States.[13] The concept of 'trade' covers all cross-border economic activity and encompasses cases where the transaction affects the competitive structure of the market. The Commission will in particular assess whether the transaction may have an influence, direct or indirect, actual or potential, on the pattern of trade between Member States. Specific factors which could be relevant may include the location of (potential) customers, the availability and offering of the products or services at stake, the collection of data in several Member States, or the development and implementation of R&D projects whose results, including intellectual property rights, if successful, may be commercialised in more than one Member State.

15. For the second criterion, the Notice on Case Referral states that a referring Member State is required, in essence, to demonstrate that, based on a preliminary analysis, there is a real risk that the transaction may have a significant adverse impact on competition, and thus it deserves close scrutiny. Such preliminary analysis may be based on prima facie evidence of a possible significant adverse impact on competition, but would be without prejudice to the outcome of a full investigation.[14] The Commission Horizontal[15] and Non-Horizontal Merger Guidelines[16]) contain guidance as to how the Commission assesses concentrations when the undertakings concerned are actual or potential competitors on the same relevant market and when the undertakings concerned are active on different relevant markets, respectively. For the purposes of assessing cases covered by this Guidance, relevant considerations for deciding whether the transaction threatens to significantly affect competition may include the creation or strengthening of a dominant position of one of the undertakings concerned; the elimination of an important competitive force, including the elimination of a recent or future entrant or the merger between two important innovators; the reduction of competitors' ability and/or incentive to compete, including by making their entry or expansion more difficult or by hampering their access to supplies or markets; or the ability and incentive to leverage a strong market position from one market to another by means of tying or bundling or other exclusionary practices.

16. When examining both criteria, the Commission will particularly take into account the prospective nature of the merger control assessment.

17. The application of these two criteria ensures that the transaction has a sufficient nexus with the EU and the referring Member State(s).

2.2. Other factors which may be considered

18. As indicated in the Notice on Case Referral, when considering whether or not to exercise their discretion to make or accede to a referral request, the Member States and the Commission should above all bear in mind the need to ensure effective protection of competition in all markets affected by the transaction.[17]

19. Besides the principles set out in the Notice on Case Referral,[18], the categories of cases that will normally be appropriate for a referral under Article 22 of the Merger Regulation where the merger is not notifiable in the referring Member State(s) consist of transactions where the turnover of at least one of the undertakings concerned does not reflect its actual or future competitive potential. This would include, for example, cases where the undertaking: (1) is a start-up or recent entrant with significant competitive potential that has yet to develop or implement a business model generating significant revenues (or is still in the initial phase of implementing such business model); (2) is an important innovator or is conducting potentially important research; (3) is an actual or potential important competitive force;[19] (4) has access to competitively significant assets (such as for instance raw materials, infrastructure, data or intellectual property rights); and/or (5) provides products or services that are key inputs/components for other industries. In its assessment, the Commission may also take into account whether the value of the consideration received by the seller is particularly high compared to the current turnover of the target.

20. The list above is provided for purely illustrative purposes. It is not limited to any specific economic sector or sectors and cannot be deemed in any way comprehensive.

21. While the referral is subject to the deadlines set out in Article 22, the fact that a transaction has already been closed does not preclude a Member State from requesting a referral.[20] However, the time elapsed since the closing is a factor that the Commission may consider when exercising its discretion to accept or reject a referral request. Although assessments are carried out on a case-by-case basis, the Commission would generally not consider a referral appropriate where more than six months has passed after the implementation of the concentration. If the implementation of the concentration was not in the public domain, this period of six months would run from the moment when material facts about the concentration have been made public in the EU. In exceptional situations, however, a later referral may also be appropriate, based on, for example, the magnitude of the potential competition concerns and of the potential detrimental effect on consumers.

22. Finally, a circumstance where the transaction has already been notified in one or several Member States that did not request a referral or join such a referral request may constitute a factor against accepting the referral. However, the Commission will make its decision based on all relevant circumstances, including, as mentioned in the paragraph above, the extent of the potential harm, and also the geographic scope of the relevant markets.

3. Procedural aspects

23. The Commission will cooperate closely with the competent authorities of the Member States to identify concentrations that may constitute potential candidates for a referral under Article 22 of the Merger Regulation but do not meet the jurisdictional criteria relevant under the respective national laws. It may exchange information to that effect with national competition authorities.[21] In such exchanges, confidential information will be protected in accordance with the applicable laws.[22]

24. Merging parties may voluntarily come forward with information about their intended transactions. Where appropriate, the Commission may in such cases give them an early indication that it does not consider that their concentration would constitute a good candidate for a referral under Article 22 of the Merger Regulation, if sufficient information to make such a preliminary assessment has been submitted.

25. Third parties may contact the Commission or the competent authorities of the Member States and inform them of a concentration that, in their opinion, could be a candidate for a referral under Article 22 of the Merger Regulation. To enable the Commission and the competent authorities of the Member States to assess whether or not the transaction may be a candidate for referral, such contact should include sufficient information to make a preliminary assessment as to whether the criteria for referral are met, to the extent such information is available to the third party. Article 22 of the Merger Regulation does not impose any obligation on the competent authorities of the Member States or on the Commission to take any action following a contact by a third party.

26. Where the Commission becomes aware of a concentration that it considers as meeting the relevant criteria for a referral, it may inform the Member State(s) potentially concerned and invite that Member State or those Member States to make a referral request.[23] It is up to the competent authorities of a Member State to decide whether they wish to make the request.

27. If a referral request is being considered, the Commission will inform the parties to the transaction as soon as possible.[24] While being made aware of such consideration does not oblige the undertakings concerned to take or refrain from taking any action in relation to the implementation of the transaction,[25] they may decide to take measures they consider appropriate, such as delaying the transaction's implementation until it has been decided whether a referral request will be made.

28. If no notification is required, a referral request must be made at most within 15 working days of the date on which the concentration is otherwise made known to the Member State concerned.[26] The notion of 'made known' should be interpreted as implying sufficient information to make a preliminary assessment as to the existence of the criteria relevant for the assessment of the referral.[27]

29. Once a referral request has been made, the Commission will inform the competent authorities of the Member States and the undertakings concerned without delay. Other Member States may join the initial request within a period of 15 working days of being informed by the Commission of the initial request.[28] The Commission encourages the Member States to inform each other and the Commission as soon as possible whether or not they intend to join the referral request.[29]

30. At the latest 10 working days after the expiry of the 15-working-day period for Member States to join the referral request, the Commission may decide to examine the concentration if it considers that it affects trade between Member States and threatens to significantly affect competition within the territory of the Member State or States making the request. If the Commission does not take a decision within this period, it will be deemed to have adopted a decision to examine the concentration in accordance with the request.[30]

31. The suspension obligation set out in Article 7 of the Merger Regulation applies to the extent the concentration has not been implemented on the date on which the Commission informs the undertakings concerned that a referral request has been made.[31] The suspension obligation ceases if the Commission subsequently decides not to examine the concentration.

NOTES

1 OJ L24, 29.1.2004, p 1..

2 Commission Notice on Case Referral in respect of concentrations. OJ C56, 5.3.2005, p 2. This Guidance should thus be read in conjunction with the Notice on Case Referral. Additional guidance can be found in the European Competition Authorities ('ECA') *Principles on the application, by National Competition Authorities within the ECA, of Articles 4(5) and 22 of the EC Merger Regulation (2005)*..

3 Cf. point 7 of the Notice on Case Referral..

4 According to Article 6(3) of Protocol 24 of the EEA Agreement, one or more EFTA countries may join a request for referral made by a Member State under Article 22 of the Merger Regulation if the concentration affects trade between one or more Member countries and one or more EFTA countries and threatens to significantly affect competition within the territory of the ETFA country or countries joining the request..

5 Cf. Article 1 of the Merger Regulation. Concentrations with an EU dimension, i.e. those above these turnover thresholds, fall within the exclusive jurisdiction of the Commission. Concentrations falling below these thresholds may fall within the competence of the Member States, according to the jurisdictional rules of their respective national regimes..

6 Cf. Article 4(4) and (5), Article 9 and Article 22 of the Merger Regulation..

7 As defined in Article 3 of the Merger Regulation..

8 Article 22 of the Merger Regulation is also applicable when the referring Member State has not established a dedicated national merger control regime..

9 Under, respectively, Article 6(1)(c) and Articles 6(1)(b) with 6(2) and Article 8(2) of the Merger Regulation..

10 Cf. Article 22(3) of the Merger Regulation. See also point 7 of the Notice on Case Referral..

11 See Commission Staff Working Document of 26 March 2021..

12 As explained in the Notice on Case Referral (cf. footnote 45), the Commission examines the concentration upon the request of and on behalf of the requesting Member States. Article 22 of the Merger Regulation should therefore be interpreted as requiring the Commission to examine the impact of the concentration within the territory of those Member States. The Commission will not examine the effects of the concentration in the territory of Member States which have not joined the request unless this examination is necessary for the assessment of the effects of the concentration within the territory of the requesting Member States (for example, where the geographic market extends beyond the territory/or territories of the requesting Member State(s))..

13 Notice on Case Referral, point 43..

14 Cf. point 44..

15 Guidelines on the assessment of horizontal mergers under the Council Regulation on the control of concentrations between undertakings (OJ C31, 5.2.2004, p 5) ('Horizontal Merger Guidelines')..

16 Guidelines on the assessment of non-horizontal mergers under the Council Regulation on the control of concentrations between undertakings (OJ C265, 18.10.2008, p 6)..

17 Notice on Case Referral, point 8..

18 Cf. point 45..

19 In the sense of paragraphs 37 and 38 of the Horizontal Merger Guidelines..

20 The Merger Regulation acknowledges this possibility in Article 22(4)..

21 Notice on Case Referral, points 53 et seq. See also ECA Principles, paragraphs 3, 20 and 23 and 26–29..

22 Notice on Case Referral, points 57 and 58. See also ECA Principles, paragraph 34..

23 Article 22(5) of the Merger Regulation. See also ECA Principles, paragraph 22..

24 According to the ECA Principles, if a joint referral request is being considered, the national competition authorities should inform the parties to the transaction as soon as possible (cf. paragraph 25)..

25 The suspension obligation set out in Article 7 of the Merger Regulation only applies as of the date on which the Commission informs the undertakings concerned that a request has been made, to the extent that the concentration has not been implemented on that date. See Article 22(4) of the Merger Regulation, first sub-paragraph..

26 Article 22(1) of the Merger Regulation, second sub-paragraph. See also Notice on Case Referral, point 50..

27 Cf. Notice on Case Referral, footnote 43. See also ECA Principles, paragraph 31..

28 Article 22(2) of the Merger Regulation. See also Notice on Case Referral, point 50 and ECA Principles, paragraph 24..

29 ECA Principles, paragraph 24..

30 Article 22(3) of the Merger Regulation, first sub-paragraph..

31 Article 22(4) of the Merger Regulation, first sub-paragraph..

COMMISSION HOLIDAYS (2021, 2022)

[4.689]

NOTES

This is an amalgamation of two separate documents, ie, the Schedule for public holidays for 2021 and 2022. See, respectively, OJ C69, 3.3.2020, p 8 and OJ CI24, 22.1.2021, p 1.

THE PUBLIC HOLIDAYS IN 2021 FOR STAFF IN BRUSSELS AND LUXEMBOURG ARE AS FOLLOWS:

1 January: Friday, New Year's Day

1 April: Maundy Thursday

2 April: Good Friday

5 April: Easter Monday

13 May: Thursday, Ascension Day

14 May: Friday, the day following Ascension Day

24 May: Whit Monday

23 June: Wednesday, Luxembourg National Holiday *(for staff in Luxembourg)*

21 July: Wednesday, Belgian National Holiday *(for staff in Brussels)*

1 November: Monday, All Saints' Day

2 November: Tuesday, All Souls' Day

23 December to 31 December: Thursday to Friday (7 end-of-year days)

TOTAL: 17 days

Work will resume as normal on Monday 3 January 2022.

THE PUBLIC HOLIDAYS IN 2022 FOR STAFF IN BRUSSELS AND LUXEMBOURG ARE AS FOLLOWS:

14 April: Maundy Thursday

15 April: Good Friday

18 April: Easter Monday

9 May: Anniversary of the Declaration by President Schuman in 1950

26 May: Thursday, Ascension Day

27 May: Day after Ascension Day

6 June: Whit Monday

23 June: Luxembourg National Holiday *(for staff in Luxembourg)*

21 July: Belgian National Holiday *(for staff in Brussels)*

15 August: Assumption

1 November: All Saints' Day

2 November: All Souls' Day

23 December to 30 December: 6 end-of-year days

TOTAL 2022: 17 days

3. SUBSTANTIVE ASSESSMENT AND REMEDIES

COMMISSION NOTICE

(2004/C31/03)

Guidelines on the assessment of horizontal mergers under the Council Regulation on the control of concentrations between undertakings

[4.690]

NOTES

Date of publication in OJ: OJ C31, 5.2.2004, p 5.

Note that Council Regulation (EC) No 139/2004 on the control of concentrations between undertakings is repealed, in relation to the UK, by the Competition (Amendment etc) (EU Exit) Regulations 2019, SI 2019/93, reg 63, Sch 3, para 1, as from IP completion day (as defined in the European Union (Withdrawal Agreement) Act 2020, s 39) (for transitional provisions and savings in relation to the operation of the 2019 Regulations, see Sch 4 to those Regulations at **[7.69]** et seq).

Note: with effect from 1 December 2009, the EC Treaty was replaced by the Treaty on the Functioning of the European Union. References in this document to provisions of the EC Treaty should be construed accordingly.

I. INTRODUCTION

[4.691]

1. Article 2 of Council Regulation (EC) No 139/2004 of 20 January 2004 on the control of concentrations between undertakings[1] (hereinafter: the "Merger Regulation") provides that the Commission has to appraise concentrations within the scope of the Merger Regulation with a view to establishing whether or not they are compatible with the common market. For that purpose, the Commission must assess, pursuant to Article 2(2) and (3), whether or not a concentration would significantly impede effective competition, in particular as a result of the creation or strengthening of a dominant position, in the common market or a substantial part of it.

2. Accordingly, the Commission must take into account any significant impediment to effective competition likely to be caused by a concentration. The creation or the strengthening of a dominant position is a primary form of such competitive harm. The concept of dominance was defined in the context of Council Regulation (EEC) No 4064/89 of 21 December 1989 on the control of concentrations between undertakings (hereinafter "Regulation No 4064/89") as:

> "a situation where one or more undertakings wield economic power which would enable them to prevent effective competition from being maintained in the relevant market by giving them the opportunity to act to a considerable extent independently of their competitors, their customers and, ultimately, of consumers".[2]

3. For the purpose of interpreting the concept of dominance in the context of Regulation No 4064/89, the Court of Justice referred to the fact that it "is intended to apply to all concentrations with a Community dimension insofar as they are likely, because of their effect on the structure of competition within the Community, to prove incompatible with the system of undistorted competition envisaged by the Treaty".[3]

4. The creation or strengthening of a dominant position held by a single firm as a result of a merger has been the most common basis for finding that a concentration would result in a significant impediment to effective competition. Furthermore, the concept of dominance has also been applied in an oligopolistic setting to cases of collective dominance. As a consequence, it is expected that most cases of incompatibility of a concentration with the common market will continue to be based upon a finding of dominance. That concept therefore provides an important indication as to the standard of competitive harm that is applicable when determining whether a concentration is likely to impede effective competition to a significant degree, and hence, as to the likelihood of intervention.[4] To that effect, the present notice is intended to preserve the guidance that can be drawn from past decisional practice and to take full account of past case-law of the Community Courts.

5. The purpose of this notice is to provide guidance as to how the Commission assesses concentrations[5] when the undertakings concerned are actual or potential competitors on the same relevant market.[6] In this notice such mergers will be denoted "horizontal mergers". While the notice presents the analytical approach used by the Commission in its appraisal of horizontal mergers it cannot provide details of all possible applications of this approach. The Commission applies the approach described in the notice to the particular facts and circumstances of each case.

6. The guidance set out in this notice draws and elaborates on the Commission's evolving experience with the appraisal of horizontal mergers under Regulation No 4064/89 since its entry into force on 21 September 1990 as well as on the case-law of the Court of Justice and the Court of First Instance of the European Communities. The principles contained here will be applied and further developed and refined by the Commission in individual cases. The Commission may revise this notice from time to time in the light of future developments.

7. The Commission's interpretation of the Merger Regulation as regards the appraisal of horizontal mergers is without prejudice to the interpretation which may be given by the Court of Justice or the Court of First Instance of the European Communities.

NOTES

1 Council Regulation (EC) No 139/2004 of 20 January 2004 (OJ L24, 29.1.2004, p 1).

2 Case T-102/96, *Gencor v Commission*, [1999] ECR II-753, paragraph 200. See Joined Cases C-68/94 and C-30/95, *France and others v Commission* (hereinafter "*Kali and Salz*"), [1998] ECR I-1375, paragraph 221. In exceptional circumstances, a merger may give rise to the creation or the strengthening of a dominant position on the part of an undertaking which is not a party to the notified transaction (see Case IV/M.1383—*Exxon/Mobil*, points 225–229; Case

Part 4 EU & Retained EU Materials

COMP/M.2434—*Grupo Villar MIR/EnBW/Hidroelectrica del Cantabrico*, points 67–71).

3 See also Joined Cases C-68/94 and C-30/95, *Kali and Salz*, paragraph 170.

4 See Recitals 25 and 26 of the Merger Regulation.

5 The term "concentration" used in the Merger Regulation covers various types of transactions such as mergers, acquisitions, takeovers, and certain types of joint ventures. In the remainder of this notice, unless otherwise specified, the term "merger" will be used as a synonym for concentration and therefore cover all the above types of transactions.

6 The notice does not cover the assessment of the effects of competition that a merger has in other markets, including vertical and conglomerate effects. Nor does it cover the assessment of the effects of a joint venture as referred to in Article 2(4) of the Merger Regulation.

II. OVERVIEW

[4.692]

8. Effective competition brings benefits to consumers, such as low prices, high quality products, a wide selection of goods and services, and innovation. Through its control of mergers, the Commission prevents mergers that would be likely to deprive customers of these benefits by significantly increasing the market power of firms. By "increased market power" is meant the ability of one or more firms to profitably increase prices, reduce output, choice or quality of goods and services, diminish innovation, or otherwise influence parameters of competition. In this notice, the expression "increased prices" is often used as shorthand for these various ways in which a merger may result in competitive harm.[7] Both suppliers and buyers can have market power. However, for clarity, market power will usually refer here to a supplier's market power. Where a buyer's market power is the issue, the term "buyer power" is employed.

9. In assessing the competitive effects of a merger, the Commission compares the competitive conditions that would result from the notified merger with the conditions that would have prevailed without the merger.[8] In most cases the competitive conditions existing at the time of the merger constitute the relevant comparison for evaluating the effects of a merger. However, in some circumstances, the Commission may take into account future changes to the market that can reasonably be predicted.[9] It may, in particular, take account of the likely entry or exit of firms if the merger did not take place when considering what constitutes the relevant comparison.[10]

10. The Commission's assessment of mergers normally entails:

(a) definition of the relevant product and geographic markets;
(b) competitive assessment of the merger.

The main purpose of market definition is to identify in a systematic way the immediate competitive constraints facing the merged entity. Guidance on this issue can be found in the Commission's Notice on the definition of the relevant market for the purposes of Community competition law.[11] Various considerations leading to the delineation of the relevant markets may also be of importance for the competitive assessment of the merger.

11. This notice is structured around the following elements:

(a) The approach of the Commission to market shares and concentration thresholds (Section III).
(b) The likelihood that a merger would have anti-competitive effects in the relevant markets, in the absence of countervailing factors (Section IV).
(c) The likelihood that buyer power would act as a countervailing factor to an increase in market power resulting from the merger (Section V).
(d) The likelihood that entry would maintain effective competition in the relevant markets (Section VI).
(e) The likelihood that efficiencies would act as a factor counteracting the harmful effects on competition which might otherwise result from the merger (Section VII).
(f) The conditions for a failing firm defence (Section VIII).

12. In order to assess the foreseeable impact[12] of a merger on the relevant markets, the Commission analyses its possible anti-competitive effects and the relevant countervailing factors such as buyer power, the extent of entry barriers and possible efficiencies put forward by the parties. In exceptional circumstances, the Commission considers whether the conditions for a failing firm defence are met.

13. In the light of these elements, the Commission determines, pursuant to Article 2 of the Merger Regulation, whether the merger would significantly impede effective competition, in particular through the creation or the strengthening of a dominant position, and should therefore be declared incompatible with the common market. It should be stressed that these factors are not a "checklist" to be mechanically applied in each and every case. Rather, the competitive analysis in a particular case will be based on an overall assessment of the foreseeable impact of the merger in the light of the relevant factors and conditions. Not all the elements will always be relevant to each and every horizontal merger, and it may not be necessary to analyse all the elements of a case in the same detail.

NOTES

7 The expression should be understood to also cover situations where, for instance, prices are decreased less, or are less likely to decrease, than they otherwise would have without the merger and where prices are increased more, or are more likely to increase, than they otherwise would have without the merger.

8 By analogy, in the case of a merger that has been implemented without having been notified, the Commission would assess the merger in the light of the competitive conditions that would have prevailed without the implemented merger.

9 See, eg Commission Decision 98/526/EC in Case IV/M.950—*Hoffmann La Roche/Boehringer Mannheim*, OJ L234, 21.8.1998, p 14, point 13; Case IV/M.1846—*Glaxo Wellcome/SmithKline Beecham*, points 70–72; Case COMP/M.2547—*Bayer/Aventis Crop Science*, points 324 et seq.

10 See, eg Case T-102/96, *Gencor v Commission*, [1999] ECR II-753, paragraphs 247–263.

11 OJ C372, 9.12.1997, p 5.

12 See Case T-102/96, *Gencor v Commission*, [1999] ECR II-753, paragraph 262, and Case T-342/99, *Airtours v Commission*, [2002] ECR II-2585, paragraph 280.

III. MARKET SHARE AND CONCENTRATION LEVELS

[4.693]

14. Market shares and concentration levels provide useful first indications of the market structure and of the competitive importance of both the merging parties and their competitors.

15. Normally, the Commission uses current market shares in its competitive analysis.[13] However, current market shares may be adjusted to reflect reasonably certain future changes, for instance in the light of exit, entry or expansion.[14] Post-merger market shares are calculated on the assumption that the post-merger combined market share of the merging parties is the sum of their pre-merger market shares.[15] Historic data may be used if market shares have been volatile, for instance when the market is characterised by large, lumpy orders. Changes in historic market shares may provide useful information about the competitive process and the likely future importance of the various competitors, for instance, by indicating whether firms have been gaining or losing market shares. In any event, the Commission interprets market shares in the light of likely market conditions, for instance, if the market is highly dynamic in character and if the market structure is unstable due to innovation or growth.[16]

16. The overall concentration level in a market may also provide useful information about the competitive situation. In order to measure concentration levels, the Commission often applies the Herfindahl-Hirschman Index (HHI).[17] The HHI is calculated by summing the squares of the individual market shares of all the firms in the market.[18] The HHI gives proportionately greater weight to the market shares of the larger firms. Although it is best to include all firms in the calculation, lack of information about very small firms may not be important because such firms do not affect the HHI significantly. While the absolute level of the HHI can give an initial indication of the competitive pressure in the market post-merger, the change in the HHI (known as the "delta") is a useful proxy for the change in concentration directly brought about by the merger.[19]

Market share levels

17. According to well-established case law, very large market shares—50% or more—may in themselves be evidence of the existence of a dominant market position.[20] However, smaller competitors may act as a sufficient constraining influence if, for example, they have the ability and incentive to increase their supplies. A merger involving a firm whose market share will remain below 50% after the merger may also raise competition concerns in view of other factors such as the strength and number of competitors, the presence of capacity constraints or the extent to which the products of the merging parties are close substitutes. The Commission has thus in several cases considered mergers resulting in firms holding market shares between 40% and 50%,[21] and in some cases below 40%,[22] to lead to the creation or the strengthening of a dominant position.

18. Concentrations which, by reason of the limited market share of the undertakings concerned, are not liable to impede effective competition may be presumed to be compatible with the common market. Without prejudice to Articles 81 and 82 of the Treaty, an indication to this effect exists, in particular, where the market share of the undertakings concerned does not exceed 25%[23] either in the common market or in a substantial part of it.[24]

HHI levels

19. The Commission is unlikely to identify horizontal competition concerns in a market with a post-merger HHI below 1,000. Such markets normally do not require extensive analysis.

20. The Commission is also unlikely to identify horizontal competition concerns in a merger with a post-merger HHI between 1,000 and 2,000 and a delta below 250, or a merger with a post-merger HHI above 2,000 and a delta below 150, except where special circumstances such as, for instance, one or more of the following factors are present:

(a) a merger involves a potential entrant or a recent entrant with a small market share;
(b) one or more merging parties are important innovators in ways not reflected in market shares;
(c) there are significant cross-shareholdings among the market participants;[25]
(d) one of the merging firms is a maverick firm with a high likelihood of disrupting coordinated conduct;
(e) indications of past or ongoing coordination, or facilitating practices, are present;
(f) one of the merging parties has a pre-merger market share of 50% of more.[26]

21. Each of these HHI levels, in combination with the relevant deltas, may be used as an initial indicator of the absence of competition concerns. However, they do not give rise to a presumption of either the existence or the absence of such concerns.

NOTES

13 As to the calculation of market shares, see also Commission Notice on the definition of the relevant market for the purposes of Community competition law, OJ C372, 9.12.1997, p 3, paragraphs 54–55.

14 See, eg Case COMP/M.1806—*Astra Zeneca/Novartis*, points 150 and 415.

15 When relevant, market shares may be adjusted, in particular, to account for controlling interests in other firms (See, eg Case IV/M.1383—*Exxon/Mobil*, points 446–458; Case COMP/M.1879—*Boeing/Hughes*, points 60–79; Case COMP/JV 55—*Hutchison/RCPM/ECT*, points 66–75), or for other arrangements with third parties (See, for instance, as regards sub-contractors, Commission Decision 2001/769/EC in Case COMP/M.1940—*Framatome/Siemens/Cogema*, OJ L289, 6.11.2001, p 8, point 142).

16 See, eg Case COMP/M.2256—*Philips/Agilent Health Care Technologies*, points 31–32, and Case COMP/M.2609—*HP/Compaq*, point 39.

17 See, eg Case IV/M.1365—*FCC/Vivendi*, point 40; Case COMP/JV 55—*Hutchison/RCPM/ECT*, point 50. If appropriate, the Commission may also use other concentration measures such as, for instance, concentration ratios, which measure the aggregate market share of a small number (usually three or four) of the leading firms in a market.

18 For example, a market containing five firms with market shares of 40%, 20%, 15%, 15%, and 10%, respectively, has an HHI of 2,550 ($40^2 + 20^2 + 15^2 + 15^2 + 10^2 = 2,550$). The HHI ranges from close to zero (in an atomistic market) to 10,000 (in the case of a pure monopoly).

19 The increase in concentration as measured by the HHI can be calculated independently of the overall market concentration by doubling the product of the market shares of the merging firms. For example, a merger of two firms

with market shares of 30% and 15% respectively would increase the HHI by 900 (30 × 15 × 2 = 900). The explanation for this technique is as follows: Before the merger, the market shares of the merging firms contribute to the HHI by their squares individually: $(a)^2 + (b)^2$. After the merger, the contribution is the square of their sum: $(a + b)^2$, which equals $(a)^2 + (b)^2 + 2ab$. The increase in the HHI is therefore represented by 2ab.

20 Case T-221/95, *Endemol v Commission*, [1999] ECR II-1299, paragraph 134, and Case T-102/96, *Gencor v Commission*, [1999] ECR II-753, paragraph 205. It is a distinct question whether a dominant position is created or strengthened as a result of the merger.

21 See, eg Case COMP/M.2337—*Nestlé/Ralston Purina*, points 48–50.

22 See, eg Commission Decision 1999/674/EC in Case IV/M.1221—*Rewe/Meinl*, OJ L274, 23.10.1999, p 1, points 98–114; Case COMP/M.2337—*Nestlé/Ralston Purina*, points 44–47.

23 The calculation of market shares depends critically on market definition. It must be emphasised that the Commission does not necessarily accept the parties' proposed market definition.

24 Recital 32 of the Merger Regulation. However, such an indication does not apply to cases where the proposed merger creates or strengthens a collective dominant position involving the "undertakings concerned" and other third parties (see Joined Cases C-68/94 and C-30/95, *Kali and Salz*, [1998] ECR I-1375, paragraphs 171 et seq; and Case T-102/96, *Gencor v Commission*, [1999] ECR II-753, paragraphs 134 et seq).

25 In markets with cross-shareholdings or joint ventures the Commission may use a modified HHI, which takes into account such share-holdings (see, eg Case IV/M.1383—*Exxon/Mobil*, point 256).

26 See paragraph 17.

IV. POSSIBLE ANTI-COMPETITIVE EFFECTS OF HORIZONTAL MERGERS

[4.694]

22. There are two main ways in which horizontal mergers may significantly impede effective competition, in particular by creating or strengthening a dominant position:

(a) by eliminating important competitive constraints on one or more firms, which consequently would have increased market power, without resorting to coordinated behaviour (non-coordinated effects);

(b) by changing the nature of competition in such a way that firms that previously were not coordinating their behaviour, are now significantly more likely to coordinate and raise prices or otherwise harm effective competition. A merger may also make coordination easier, more stable or more effective for firms which were coordinating prior to the merger (coordinated effects).

23. The Commission assesses whether the changes brought about by the merger would result in any of these effects. Both instances mentioned above may be relevant when assessing a particular transaction.

Non-coordinated effects[27]

24. A merger may significantly impede effective competition in a market by removing important competitive constraints on one or more sellers, who consequently have increased market power. The most direct effect of the merger will be the loss of competition between the merging firms. For example, if prior to the merger one of the merging firms had raised its price, it would have lost some sales to the other merging firm. The merger removes this particular constraint. Non-merging firms in the same market can also benefit from the reduction of competitive pressure that results from the merger, since the merging firms' price increase may switch some demand to the rival firms, which, in turn, may find it profitable to increase their prices.[28] The reduction in these competitive constraints could lead to significant price increases in the relevant market.

25. Generally, a merger giving rise to such non-coordinated effects would significantly impede effective competition by creating or strengthening the dominant position of a single firm, one which, typically, would have an appreciably larger market share than the next competitor post-merger. Furthermore, mergers in oligopolistic markets[29] involving the elimination of important competitive constraints that the merging parties previously exerted upon each other together with a reduction of competitive pressure on the remaining competitors may, even where there is little likelihood of coordination between the members of the oligopoly, also result in a significant impediment to competition. The Merger Regulation clarifies that all mergers giving rise to such non-coordinated effects shall also be declared incompatible with the common market.[30]

26. A number of factors, which taken separately are not necessarily decisive, may influence whether significant non-coordinated effects are likely to result from a merger. Not all of these factors need to be present for such effects to be likely. Nor should this be considered an exhaustive list.

Merging firms have large market shares

27. The larger the market share, the more likely a firm is to possess market power. And the larger the addition of market share, the more likely it is that a merger will lead to a significant increase in market power. The larger the increase in the sales base on which to enjoy higher margins after a price increase, the more likely it is that the merging firms will find such a price increase profitable despite the accompanying reduction in output. Although market shares and additions of market shares only provide first indications of market power and increases in market power, they are normally important factors in the assessment.[31]

Merging firms are close competitors

28. Products may be differentiated[32] within a relevant market such that some products are closer substitutes than others.[33] The higher the degree of substitutability between the merging firms' products, the more likely it is that the merging firms will raise prices significantly.[34] For example, a merger between two producers offering products which a substantial number of customers regard as their first and second choices could generate a significant price increase. Thus, the fact that rivalry between the parties has been an important source of competition on the market may be a central factor in the analysis.[35] High pre-merger margins[36] may also make significant price increases more likely. The merging firms' incentive to raise prices is more likely to be constrained when rival firms produce close substitutes to

the products of the merging firms than when they offer less close substitutes.[37] It is therefore less likely that a merger will significantly impede effective competition, in particular through the creation or strengthening of a dominant position, when there is a high degree of substitutability between the products of the merging firms and those supplied by rival producers.

29. When data are available, the degree of substitutability may be evaluated through customer preference surveys, analysis of purchasing patterns, estimation of the cross-price elasticities of the products involved,[38] or diversion ratios.[39] In bidding markets it may be possible to measure whether historically the submitted bids by one of the merging parties have been constrained by the presence of the other merging party.[40]

30. In some markets it may be relatively easy and not too costly for the active firms to reposition their products or extend their product portfolio. In particular, the Commission examines whether the possibility of repositioning or product line extension by competitors or the merging parties may influence the incentive of the merged entity to raise prices. However, product repositioning or product line extension often entails risks and large sunk costs[41] and may be less profitable than the current line.

Customers have limited possibilities of switching supplier

31. Customers of the merging parties may have difficulties switching to other suppliers because there are few alternative suppliers[42] or because they face substantial switching costs.[43] Such customers are particularly vulnerable to price increases. The merger may affect these customers' ability to protect themselves against price increases. In particular, this may be the case for customers that have used dual sourcing from the two merging firms as a means of obtaining competitive prices. Evidence of past customer switching patterns and reactions to price changes may provide important information in this respect.

Competitors are unlikely to increase supply if prices increase

32. When market conditions are such that the competitors of the merging parties are unlikely to increase their supply substantially if prices increase, the merging firms may have an incentive to reduce output below the combined pre-merger levels, thereby raising market prices.[44] The merger increases the incentive to reduce output by giving the merged firm a larger base of sales on which to enjoy the higher margins resulting from an increase in prices induced by the output reduction.

33. Conversely, when market conditions are such that rival firms have enough capacity and find it profitable to expand output sufficiently, the Commission is unlikely to find that the merger will create or strengthen a dominant position or otherwise significantly impede effective competition.

34. Such output expansion is, in particular, unlikely when competitors face binding capacity constraints and the expansion of capacity is costly[45] or if existing excess capacity is significantly more costly to operate than capacity currently in use.

35. Although capacity constraints are more likely to be important when goods are relatively homogeneous, they may also be important where firms offer differentiated products.

Merged entity able to hinder expansion by competitors

36. Some proposed mergers would, if allowed to proceed, significantly impede effective competition by leaving the merged firm in a position where it would have the ability and incentive to make the expansion of smaller firms and potential competitors more difficult or otherwise restrict the ability of rival firms to compete. In such a case, competitors may not, either individually or in the aggregate, be in a position to constrain the merged entity to such a degree that it would not increase prices or take other actions detrimental to competition. For instance, the merged entity may have such a degree of control, or influence over, the supply of inputs[46] or distribution possibilities[47] that expansion or entry by rival firms may be more costly. Similarly, the merged entity's control over patents[48] or other types of intellectual property (eg brands[49] may make expansion or entry by rivals more difficult. In markets where interoperability between different infrastructures or platforms is important,[50] a merger may give the merged entity the ability and incentive to raise the costs or decrease the quality of service of its rivals.[51] In making this assessment the Commission may take into account, *inter alia*, the financial strength of the merged entity relative to its rivals.[52]

Merger eliminates an important competitive force

37. Some firms have more of an influence on the competitive process than their market shares or similar measures would suggest. A merger involving such a firm may change the competitive dynamics in a significant, anti-competitive way, in particular when the market is already concentrated.[53] For instance, a firm may be a recent entrant that is expected to exert significant competitive pressure in the future on the other firms in the market.

38. In markets where innovation is an important competitive force, a merger may increase the firms' ability and incentive to bring new innovations to the market and, thereby, the competitive pressure on rivals to innovate in that market. Alternatively, effective competition may be significantly impeded by a merger between two important innovators, for instance between two companies with "pipeline" products related to a specific product market. Similarly, a firm with a relatively small market share may nevertheless be an important competitive force if it has promising pipeline products.[54]

Coordinated effects

39. In some markets the structure may be such that firms would consider it possible, economically rational, and hence preferable, to adopt on a sustainable basis a course of action on the market aimed at selling at increased prices. A merger in a concentrated market may significantly impede effective competition, through the creation or the strengthening of a collective dominant position, because it increases the likelihood that firms are able to coordinate their behaviour in this way and raise prices, even without entering into an agreement or resorting to a concerted practice within the meaning of Article 81 of the Treaty.[55] A merger may also make coordination easier, more stable or more effective for firms, that were already coordinating before the merger, either by making the coordination more robust or by permitting firms to coordinate on even higher prices.

40. Coordination may take various forms. In some markets, the most likely coordination may involve keeping prices above the competitive level. In other markets, coordination may aim at limiting production or the amount of new capacity brought to the market. Firms may also coordinate by dividing the market, for instance by geographic area[56] or other customer characteristics, or by allocating contracts in bidding markets.

41. Coordination is more likely to emerge in markets where it is relatively simple to reach a common understanding on the terms of coordination. In addition, three conditions are necessary for coordination to be sustainable. First, the coordinating firms must be able to monitor to a sufficient degree whether the terms of coordination are being adhered to. Second, discipline requires that there is some form of credible deterrent mechanism that can be activated if deviation is detected. Third, the reactions of outsiders, such as current and future competitors not participating in the coordination, as well as customers, should not be able to jeopardise the results expected from the coordination.[57]

42. The Commission examines whether it would be possible to reach terms of coordination and whether the coordination is likely to be sustainable. In this respect, the Commission considers the changes that the merger brings about. The reduction in the number of firms in a market may, in itself, be a factor that facilitates coordination. However, a merger may also increase the likelihood or significance of coordinated effects in other ways. For instance, a merger may involve a "maverick" firm that has a history of preventing or disrupting coordination, for example by failing to follow price increases by its competitors, or has characteristics that gives it an incentive to favour different strategic choices than its coordinating competitors would prefer. If the merged firm were to adopt strategies similar to those of other competitors, the remaining firms would find it easier to coordinate, and the merger would increase the likelihood, stability or effectiveness of coordination.

43. In assessing the likelihood of coordinated effects, the Commission takes into account all available relevant information on the characteristics of the markets concerned, including both structural features and the past behaviour of firms.[58] Evidence of past coordination is important if the relevant market characteristics have not changed appreciably or are not likely to do so in the near future.[59] Likewise, evidence of coordination in similar markets may be useful information.

Reaching terms of coordination

44. Coordination is more likely to emerge if competitors can easily arrive at a common perception as to how the coordination should work. Coordinating firms should have similar views regarding which actions would be considered to be in accordance with the aligned behaviour and which actions would not.

45. Generally, the less complex and the more stable the economic environment, the easier it is for the firms to reach a common understanding on the terms of coordination. For instance, it is easier to coordinate among a few players than among many. It is also easier to coordinate on a price for a single, homogeneous product, than on hundreds of prices in a market with many differentiated products. Similarly, it is easier to coordinate on a price when demand and supply conditions are relatively stable than when they are continuously changing.[60] In this context volatile demand, substantial internal growth by some firms in the market or frequent entry by new firms may indicate that the current situation is not sufficiently stable to make coordination likely.[61] In markets where innovation is important, coordination may be more difficult since innovations, particularly significant ones, may allow one firm to gain a major advantage over its rivals.

46. Coordination by way of market division will be easier if customers have simple characteristics that allow the coordinating firms to readily allocate them. Such characteristics may be based on geography; on customer type or simply on the existence of customers who typically buy from one specific firm. Coordination by way of market division may be relatively straightforward if it is easy to identify each customer's supplier and the coordination device is the allocation of existing customers to their incumbent supplier.

47. Coordinating firms may, however, find other ways to overcome problems stemming from complex economic environments short of market division. They may, for instance, establish simple pricing rules that reduce the complexity of coordinating on a large number of prices. One example of such a rule is establishing a small number of pricing points, thus reducing the coordination problem. Another example is having a fixed relationship between certain base prices and a number of other prices, such that prices basically move in parallel. Publicly available key information, exchange of information through trade associations, or information received through cross-shareholdings or participation in joint ventures may also help firms reach terms of coordination. The more complex the market situation is, the more transparency or communication is likely to be needed to reach a common under-standing on the terms of coordination.

48. Firms may find it easier to reach a common understanding on the terms of coordination if they are relatively symmetric,[62] especially in terms of cost structures, market shares, capacity levels and levels of vertical integration.[63] Structural links such as cross-shareholding or participation in joint ventures may also help in aligning incentives among the coordinating firms.[64]

Monitoring deviations

49. Coordinating firms are often tempted to increase their share of the market by deviating from the terms of coordination, for instance by lowering prices, offering secret discounts, increasing product quality or capacity or trying to win new customers. Only the credible threat of timely and sufficient retaliation keeps firms from deviating. Markets therefore need to be sufficiently transparent to allow the coordinating firms to monitor to a sufficient degree whether other firms are deviating, and thus know when to retaliate.[65]

50. Transparency in the market is often higher, the lower the number of active participants in the market. Further, the degree of transparency often depends on how market transactions take place in a particular market. For example, transparency is likely to be high in a market where transactions take place on a public exchange or in an open outcry auction.[66] Conversely, transparency may be low in a market where transactions are confidentially negotiated between buyers and sellers on a bilateral basis.[67] When evaluating the level of transparency in the market, the key element is to identify what firms can infer about the actions of other firms from the available information.[68] Coordinating firms should be able to interpret with some certainty whether unexpected behaviour is the result of deviation from the terms of coordination. For instance, in unstable environments it may be difficult for a firm to know whether its lost sales are

due to an overall low level of demand or due to a competitor offering particularly low prices. Similarly, when overall demand or cost conditions fluctuate, it may be difficult to interpret whether a competitor is lowering its price because it expects the coordinated prices to fall or because it is deviating.

51. In some markets where the general conditions may seem to make monitoring of deviations difficult, firms may nevertheless engage in practices which have the effect of easing the monitoring task, even when these practices are not necessarily entered into for such purposes. These practices, such as meeting-competition or most-favoured-customer clauses, voluntary publication of information, announcements, or exchange of information through trade associations, may increase transparency or help competitors interpret the choices made. Cross-directorships, participation in joint ventures and similar arrangements may also make monitoring easier.

Deterrent mechanisms

52. Coordination is not sustainable unless the consequences of deviation are sufficiently severe to convince coordinating firms that it is in their best interest to adhere to the terms of coordination. It is thus the threat of future retaliation that keeps the coordination sustainable.[69] However the threat is only credible if, where deviation by one of the firms is detected, there is sufficient certainty that some deterrent mechanism will be activated.[70]

53. Retaliation that manifests itself after some significant time lag, or is not certain to be activated, is less likely to be sufficient to offset the benefits from deviating. For example, if a market is characterised by infrequent, large-volume orders, it may be difficult to establish a sufficiently severe deterrent mechanism, since the gain from deviating at the right time may be large, certain and immediate, whereas the losses from being punished may be small and uncertain and only materialise after some time. The speed with which deterrent mechanisms can be implemented is related to the issue of transparency. If firms are only able to observe their competitors' actions after a substantial delay, then retaliation will be similarly delayed and this may influence whether it is sufficient to deter deviation.

54. The credibility of the deterrence mechanism depends on whether the other coordinating firms have an incentive to retaliate. Some deterrent mechanisms, such as punishing the deviator by temporarily engaging in a price war or increasing output significantly, may entail a short-term economic loss for the firms carrying out the retaliation. This does not necessarily remove the incentive to retaliate since the short-term loss may be smaller than the long-term benefit of retaliating resulting from the return to the regime of coordination.

55. Retaliation need not necessarily take place in the same market as the deviation.[71] If the coordinating firms have commercial interaction in other markets, these may offer various methods of retaliation.[72] The retaliation could take many forms, including cancellation of joint ventures or other forms of cooperation or selling of shares in jointly owned companies.

Reactions of outsiders

56. For coordination to be successful, the actions of non-coordinating firms and potential competitors, as well as customers, should not be able to jeopardise the outcome expected from coordination. For example, if coordination aims at reducing overall capacity in the market, this will only hurt consumers if non-coordinating firms are unable or have no incentive to respond to this decrease by increasing their own capacity sufficiently to prevent a net decrease in capacity, or at least to render the coordinated capacity decrease unprofitable.[73]

57. The effects of entry and countervailing buyer power of customers are analysed in later sections. However, special consideration is given to the possible impact of these elements on the stability of coordination. For instance, by concentrating a large amount of its requirements with one supplier or by offering long-term contracts, a large buyer may make coordination unstable by successfully tempting one of the coordinating firms to deviate in order to gain substantial new business.

Merger with a potential competitor

58. Concentrations where an undertaking already active on a relevant market merges with a potential competitor in this market can have similar anti-competitive effects to mergers between two undertakings already active on the same relevant market and, thus, significantly impede effective competition, in particular through the creation or the strengthening of a dominant position.

59. A merger with a potential competitor can generate horizontal anti-competitive effects, whether coordinated or non-coordinated, if the potential competitor significantly constrains the behaviour of the firms active in the market. This is the case if the potential competitor possesses assets that could easily be used to enter the market without incurring significant sunk costs. Anti-competitive effects may also occur where the merging partner is very likely to incur the necessary sunk costs to enter the market in a relatively short period of time after which this company would constrain the behaviour of the firms currently active in the market.[74]

60. For a merger with a potential competitor to have significant anti-competitive effects, two basic conditions must be fulfilled. First, the potential competitor must already exert a significant constraining influence or there must be a significant likelihood that it would grow into an effective competitive force. Evidence that a potential competitor has plans to enter a market in a significant way could help the Commission to reach such a conclusion.[75] Second, there must not be a sufficient number of other potential competitors, which could maintain sufficient competitive pressure after the merger.[76]

Mergers creating or strengthening buyer power in upstream markets

61. The Commission may also analyse to what extent a merged entity will increase its buyer power in upstream markets. On the one hand, a merger that creates or strengthens the market power of a buyer may significantly impede effective competition, in particular by creating or strengthening a dominant position. The merged firm may be in a position to obtain lower prices by reducing its purchase of inputs. This may, in turn, lead it also to lower its level of output in the final product market, and thus harm consumer welfare.[77] Such effects may in particular arise when upstream sellers are relatively fragmented. Competition in the downstream markets could also be adversely affected if, in particular, the merged entity were likely to use its buyer power vis-à-vis its suppliers to foreclose its rivals.[78]

62. On the other hand, increased buyer power may be beneficial for competition. If increased buyer power lowers input costs without restricting downstream competition or total output, then a proportion of these cost reductions are likely to be passed onto consumers in the form of lower prices.

63. In order to assess whether a merger would significantly impede effective competition by creating or strengthening buyer power, an analysis of the competitive conditions in upstream markets and an evaluation of the possible positive and negative effects described above are therefore required.

NOTES

27 Also often called "unilateral" effects.

28 Such expected reactions by competitors may be a relevant factor influencing the merged entity's incentives to increase prices.

29 An oligopolistic market refers to a market structure with a limited number of sizeable firms. Because the behaviour of one firm has an appreciable impact on the overall market conditions, and thus indirectly on the situation of each of the other firms, oligopolistic firms are interdependent.

30 Recital 25 of the Merger Regulation.

31 See, in particular, paragraphs 17 and 18.

32 Products may be differentiated in various ways. There may, for example, be differentiation in terms of geographic location, based on branch or stores location; location matters for retail distribution, banks, travel agencies, or petrol stations. Likewise, differentiation may be based on brand image, technical specifications, quality or level of service. The level of advertising in a market may be an indicator of the firms' effort to differentiate their products. For other products, buyers may have to incur switching costs to use a competitor's product.

33 For the definition of the relevant market, see the Commission's Notice on the definition of the relevant market for the purposes of Community competition law, cited above.

34 See for example Case COMP/M.2817—*Barilla/BPS/Kamps*, point 34; Commission Decision 2001/403/EC in Case COMP/M.1672—*Volvo/Scania*, OJ L143, 29.5.2001, p 74, points 107–148.

35 See, eg Commission Decision 94/893/EC in Case IV/M.430—*Procter & Gamble/VP Schickedanz (II)*, OJ L354, 21.6.1994, p 32, Case T-290/94, *Kaysersberg v Commission*, [1997] II-2137, paragraph 153; Commission Decision 97/610/EC in Case IV/M.774—*Saint-Gobain/Wacker-Chemie/NOM*, OJ L247, 10.9.1997, p 1, point 179; Commission Decision 2002/156/EC in Case COMP/M.2097—*SCA/Metsä Tissue*, OJ L57, 27.2.2002, p 1, points 94–108; Case T-310/01, *Schneider v Commission*, [2002] II-4071, paragraph 418.

36 Typically, the relevant margin (m) is the difference between price (p) and the incremental cost (c) of supplying one more unit of output expressed as a percentage of price ($m = (p - c)p$)).

37 See, eg Case IV/M.1980—*Volvo/Renault VI*, point 34; Case COMP/M.2256—*Philips Agilent/Health Care Solutions*, points 33–35; Case COMP/M.2537—*Philips/Marconi Medical Systems*, points 31–34.

38 The cross-price elasticity of demand measures the extent to which the quantity of a product demanded changes in response to a change in the price of some other product, all other things remaining equal. The own-price elasticity measures the extent to which demand for a product changes in response to the change in the price of the product itself.

39 The diversion ratio from product A to product B measures the proportion of the sales of product A lost due to a price increase of A that are captured by product B.

40 Commission Decision 97/816/EC in Case IV/M.877—*Boeing/McDonnell Douglas*, OJ L336, 8.12.1997, p 16, points 58 et seq; Case COMP/M.3083—*GE/Instrumentarium*, points 125 et seq.

41 Sunk costs are costs which are unrecoverable upon exit from the market.

42 See eg Commission Decision 2002/156/EC in Case IV/M.877—*Boeing/McDonnell Douglas*, OJ L336, 8.12.1997, p 16, point 70.

43 See, eg Case IV/M. 986 *Agfa Gevaert/DuPont*, OJ L211, 29.7.1998, p 22, points 63–71.

44 See, eg Case COMP/M.2187—*CVC/Lenzing*, points 162–170.

45 When analysing the possible expansion of capacity by rivals, the Commission considers factors similar to those described in Section VI on entry. See, eg Case COMP/M.2187—*CVC/Lenzing*, points 162–173.

46 See, eg Case T-221/95, *Endemol v Commission*, [1999] ECR II-1299, paragraph 167.

47 See, eg Case T-22/97, *Kesko v Commission*, [1999], ECR II-3775, paragraphs 141 et seq.

48 See, eg Commission Decision 2001/684/EC in Case M.1671—*Dow Chemical/Union Carbide* OJ L245, 14.9.2001, p 1, points 107–114.

49 See, eg Commission Decision 96/435/EC in Case IV/M.623—*Kimberly-Clark/Scott*, OJ L183, 23.7.1996, p 1; Case T-114/02, *Babyliss SA v Commission* (*"Seb/Moulinex"*), [2003] ECR II-000, paragraphs 343 et seq.

50 This is, for example, the case in network industries such as energy, telecommunications and other communication industries.

51 Commission Decision 99/287/EC in Case IV/M.1069—*Worldcom/MCI*, OJ L116, 4.5.1999, p 1, points 117 et seq; Case IV/M.1741—*MCI Worldcom/Sprint*, points 145 et seq; Case IV/M.1795—*Vodafone Airtouch/Mannesmann*, points 44 et seq.

52 Case T-156/98 *RJB Mining v Commission* [2001] ECR II-337.

53 Commission Decision 2002/156/EC in Case IV/M.877—*Boeing/McDonnell Douglas*, OJ L336, 8.12.1997, p 16, point 58; Case COMP/M.2568—*Haniel/Ytong*, point 126.

54 For an example of pipeline products of one merging party likely to compete with the other party's pipeline or existing products, see, eg Case IV/M.1846—*Glaxo Wellcome/SmithKline Beecham*, point 188.

55 Case T-102/96, *Gencor v Commission*, [1999] ECR II-753, paragraph 277; Case T-342/99, *Airtours v Commission*, [2002] ECR II-2585, paragraph 61.

56 This may be the case if the oligopolists have tended to concentrate their sales in different areas for historic reasons.

57 Case T-342/99, *Airtours v Commission*, [2002] ECR II-2585, paragraph 62.

58 See Commission Decision 92/553/EC in Case IV/M.190—*Nestlé/Perrier*, OJ L356, 5.12.1992, p 1, points 117–118.

59 See, eg Case IV/M.580—*ABB/Daimler-Benz*, point 95.

60 See, eg Commission Decision 2002/156/EC in Case COMP/M.2097—*SCA/Metsä Tissue*, OJ L57, 27.2.2002, p 1, point 148.

61 See, eg Case IV/M.1298—*Kodak/Imation*, point 60.

62 Case T-102/96, *Gencor v Commission*, [1999] ECR II-753, paragraph 222; Commission Decision 92/553/EC in Case IV/M.190 *Nestlé/Perrier*, OJ L356, 5.12.1992, p 1, points 63–123.

63 In assessing whether or not a merger may increase the symmetry of the various firms present on the market, efficiency gains may provide important indications (see also paragraph 82 of the notice).

64 See, eg Commission Decision 2001/519/EC in Case COMP/M.1673—*VEBA/VIAG*, OJ L188, 10.7.2001, p 1, point 226; Case COMP/M.2567—*Nordbanken/Postgirot*, point 54.

65 See, eg Case COMP/M.2389—*Shell/DEA*, points 112 et seq; and Case COMP/M.2533—*BP/E.ON*, points 102 et seq.

66 See also Commission Decision 2000/42/EC in Case IV/M.1313—*Danish Crown/Vestjyske Slagterier*, OJ L20, 25.1.2000, p 1, points 176–179.

67 See, eg Case COMP/M.2640—*Nestlé/Schöller*, point 37; Commission Decision 1999/641/EC in Case COMP/M.1225—*Enso/Stora*, OJ L254, 29.9.1999, p 9, points 67–68.

68 See, eg Case IV/M.1939—*Rexam (PLM)/American National Can*, point 24.

69 See Case COMP/M.2389—*Shell/DEA*, point 121, and Case COMP/M.2533—*BP/E.ON*, point 111.

70 Although deterrent mechanisms are sometimes called "punishment" mechanisms, this should not be understood in the strict sense that such a mechanism necessarily punishes individually a firm that has deviated. The expectation that coordination may break down for a certain period of time, if a deviation is identified as such, may in itself constitute a sufficient deterrent mechanism.

71 See, eg Commission Decision 2000/42/EC in Case IV/M.1313—*Danish Crown/Vestjyske Slagterier*, OJ L20, 25.1.2000, p 1, point 177.

72 See Case T-102/96, *Gencor v Commission*, [1999] ECR II-753, paragraph 281.

73 These elements are analysed in a similar way to non-coordinated effects.

74 See, eg Case IV/M.1630—*Air Liquide/BOC*, points 201 et seq. For an example of a case where entry by the other merging firm was not sufficiently likely in the short to medium term (Case T-158/00, *ARD v Commission*, [2003] ECR II-000, paragraphs 115–127).

75 Commission Decision 2001/98/EC in Case IV/M.1439—*Telia/Telenor*, OJ L40, 9.2.2001, p 1, points 330–331, and Case IV/M.1681—*Akzo Nobel/Hoechst Roussel Vet*, point 64.

76 Case IV/M.1630—*Air Liquide/BOC*, point 219; Commission Decision 2002/164/EC in Case COMP/M.1853—*EDF/EnBW*, OJ L59, 28.2.2002, p 1, points 54–64.

77 See Commission Decision 1999/674/EC in Case M.1221—*Rewe/Meinl*, OJ L274, 23.10.1999, p 1, points 71–74.

78 Case T-22/97, *Kesko v Commission*, [1999] ECR II-3775, paragraph 157; Commission Decision 2002/156/EC in Case M.877—*Boeing/McDonnell Douglas*, OJ L336, 8.12.1997, p 16, points 105–108.

V. COUNTERVAILING BUYER POWER

[4.695]

64. The competitive pressure on a supplier is not only exercised by competitors but can also come from its customers. Even firms with very high market shares may not be in a position, post-merger, to significantly impede effective competition, in particular by acting to an appreciable extent independently of their customers, if the latter possess countervailing buyer power.[79] Countervailing buyer power in this context should be understood as the bargaining strength that the buyer has vis-à-vis the seller in commercial negotiations due to its size, its commercial significance to the seller and its ability to switch to alternative suppliers.

65. The Commission considers, when relevant, to what extent customers will be in a position to counter the increase in market power that a merger would otherwise be likely to create. One source of countervailing buyer power would be if a customer could credibly threaten to resort, within a reasonable timeframe, to alternative sources of supply should the supplier decide to increase prices[80] or to otherwise deteriorate quality or the conditions of delivery. This would be the case if the buyer could immediately switch to other suppliers,[81] credibly threaten to vertically integrate into the upstream market or to sponsor upstream expansion or entry[82] for instance by persuading a potential entrant to enter by committing to placing large orders with this company. It is more likely that large and sophisticated customers will possess this kind of countervailing buyer power than smaller firms in a fragmented industry.[83] A buyer may also exercise countervailing buying power by refusing to buy other products produced by the supplier or, particularly in the case of durable goods, delaying purchases.

66. In some cases, it may be important to pay particular attention to the incentives of buyers to utilise their buyer power.[84] For example, a downstream firm may not wish to make an investment in sponsoring new entry if the benefits of such entry in terms of lower input costs could also be reaped by its competitors.

67. Countervailing buyer power cannot be found to sufficiently off-set potential adverse effects of a merger if it only ensures that a particular segment of customers,[85] with particular bargaining strength, is shielded from significantly higher prices or deteriorated conditions after the merger.[86] Furthermore, it is not sufficient that buyer power exists prior to the merger, it must also exist and remain effective following the merger. This is because a merger of two suppliers may reduce buyer power if it thereby removes a credible alternative.

NOTES

79 See, eg Case IV/M.1882—*Pirelli/BICC*, points 73–80.

80 See, eg Case IV/M.1245—*Valeo/ITT Industries*, point 26.

81 Even a small number of customers may not have sufficient buyer power if they are to a large extent "locked in" because of high switching costs (see Case COMP/M.2187—*CVC/Lenzing*, point 223).

82 Commission Decision 1999/641/EC in Case COMP/M.1225—*Enso/Stora*, OJ L254, 29.9.1999, p 9, points 89–91.

83 It may also be appropriate to compare the concentration existing on the customer side with the concentration on the supply side (Case COMP/JV 55—*Hutchison/RCPM/ECT*, point 119, and Commission Decision 1999/641/EC in Case COMP/M.1225—*Enso/Stora*, OJ L254, 29.9.1999, p 9, point 97).

84 Case COMP/JV 55—*Hutchison/RCPM/ECT*, points 129–130.

85 Commission Decision 2002/156/EC in Case COMP/M.2097—*SCA/Metsä Tissue*, OJ L57, 27.2.2002, point 88. Price discrimination between different categories of customers may be relevant in some cases in the context of market

definition (See the Commission's notice on the definition of the relevant market, cited above, at paragraph 43).

86 Accordingly, the Commission may assess whether the various purchasers will hold countervailing buyer power, see, eg Commission Decision 1999/641/EC in Case COMP/M.1225—*Enso/Stora*, OJ L254, 29.9.1999, p 9, points 84–97.

VI. ENTRY

[4.696]

68. When entering a market is sufficiently easy, a merger is unlikely to pose any significant anti-competitive risk. Therefore, entry analysis constitutes an important element of the overall competitive assessment. For entry to be considered a sufficient competitive constraint on the merging parties, it must be shown to be likely, timely and sufficient to deter or defeat any potential anti-competitive effects of the merger.

Likelihood of entry

69. The Commission examines whether entry is likely or whether potential entry is likely to constrain the behaviour of incumbents post-merger. For entry to be likely, it must be sufficiently profitable taking into account the price effects of injecting additional output into the market and the potential responses of the incumbents. Entry is thus less likely if it would only be economically viable on a large scale, thereby resulting in significantly depressed price levels. And entry is likely to be more difficult if the incumbents are able to protect their market shares by offering long-term contracts or giving targeted pre-emptive price reductions to those customers that the entrant is trying to acquire. Furthermore, high risk and costs of failed entry may make entry less likely. The costs of failed entry will be higher, the higher is the level of sunk cost associated with entry.[87]

70. Potential entrants may encounter barriers to entry which determine entry risks and costs and thus have an impact on the profitability of entry. Barriers to entry are specific features of the market, which give incumbent firms advantages over potential competitors. When entry barriers are low, the merging parties are more likely to be constrained by entry. Conversely, when entry barriers are high, price increases by the merging firms would not be significantly constrained by entry. Historical examples of entry and exit in the industry may provide useful information about the size of entry barriers.

71. Barriers to entry can take various forms:

(a) Legal advantages encompass situations where regulatory barriers limit the number of market participants by, for example, restricting the number of licences.[88] They also cover tariff and non-tariff trade barriers.[89]

(b) The incumbents may also enjoy technical advantages, such as preferential access to essential facilities, natural resources,[90] innovation and R&D,[91] or intellectual property rights,[92] which make it difficult for any firm to compete successfully. For instance, in certain industries, it might be difficult to obtain essential input materials, or patents might protect products or processes. Other factors such as economies of scale and scope, distribution and sales networks,[93] access to important technologies, may also constitute barriers to entry.

(c) Furthermore, barriers to entry may also exist because of the established position of the incumbent firms on the market. In particular, it may be difficult to enter a particular industry because experience or reputation is necessary to compete effectively, both of which may be difficult to obtain as an entrant. Factors such as consumer loyalty to a particular brand,[94] the closeness of relationships between suppliers and customers, the importance of promotion or advertising, or other advantages relating to reputation[95] will be taken into account in this context. Barriers to entry also encompass situations where the incumbents have already committed to building large excess capacity,[96] or where the costs faced by customers in switching to a new supplier may inhibit entry.

72. The expected evolution of the market should be taken into account when assessing whether or not entry would be profitable. Entry is more likely to be profitable in a market that is expected to experience high growth in the future[97] than in a market that is mature or expected to decline.[98] Scale economies or network effects may make entry unprofitable unless the entrant can obtain a sufficiently large market share.[99]

73. Entry is particularly likely if suppliers in other markets already possess production facilities that could be used to enter the market in question, thus reducing the sunk costs of entry. The smaller the difference in profitability between entry and non-entry prior to the merger, the more likely such a reallocation of production facilities.

Timeliness

74. The Commission examines whether entry would be sufficiently swift and sustained to deter or defeat the exercise of market power. What constitutes an appropriate time period depends on the characteristics and dynamics of the market, as well as on the specific capabilities of potential entrants.[100] However, entry is normally only considered timely if it occurs within two years.

Sufficiency

75. Entry must be of sufficient scope and magnitude to deter or defeat the anti-competitive effects of the merger.[101] Small-scale entry, for instance into some market "niche", may not be considered sufficient.

NOTES

87 Commission Decision 97/610/EC in Case IV/M.774—*Saint-Gobain/Wacker-Chemie/NOM*, OJ L247, 10.9.1997, p 1, point 184.

88 Case IV/M.1430—*Vodafone/Airtouch*, point 27; Case IV/M.2016—*France Télécom/Orange*, point 33.

89 Commission Decision 2002/174/EC in Case COMP/M.1693—*Alcoa/Reynolds*, OJ L58, 28.2.2002, point 87.

90 Commission Decision 95/335/EC in Case IV/M.754—*Anglo American Corp./Lonrho*, OJ L149, 20.5.1998, p 21, points 118–119.

91 Commission Decision 97/610/EC in Case IV/M.774—*Saint-Gobain/Wacker-Chemie/NOM*, OJ L247, 10.9.1997, p 1, points 184–187.

92 Commission Decision 94/811/EC in Case IV/M.269—*Shell/Montecatini*, OJ L332, 22.12.1994, p 48, point 32.

93 Commission Decision 98/327/EC in Case IV/M.833—*The Coca-Cola Company/Carlsberg A/S*, OJ L145, 15.5.1998, p 41, point 74.

94 Commission Decision 98/327/EC in Case IV/M.833—*The Coca-Cola Company/Carlsberg A/S*, OJ L145, 15.5.1998, p 41, points 72–73.

95 Commission Decision 2002/156/EC in Case COMP/M—2097 *SCA/Metsä Tissue*, OJ L57, 27.2.2002, p 1, points 83–84.

96 Commission Decision 2001/432/EC in Case IV/M.1813—*Industri Kapital Nordkem/Dyno*, OJ L154, 9.6.2001, p 41, point 100.

97 See, eg Commission Decision 98/475/EC in Case IV/M.986—*Agfa-Gevaert/Dupont*, OJ L211, 29.7.1998, p 22, points 84–85.

98 Case T-102/96, *Gencor v Commission*, [1999] ECR II-753, paragraph 237.

99 See, eg Commission Decision 2000/718/EC in Case IV/M.1578—*Sanitec/Sphinx*, OJ L294, 22.11.2000, p 1, point 114.

100 See, eg Commission Decision 2002/174/EC in Case COMP/M.1693—*Alcoa/Reynolds*, L58, 28.2.2002, points 31–32, 38.

101 Commission Decision 91/535/EEC in Case IV/M.68—*Tetra Pak/Alfa Laval*, OJ L290, 22.10.1991, p 35, point 3.4.

VII. EFFICIENCIES

[4.697]

76. Corporate reorganisations in the form of mergers may be in line with the requirements of dynamic competition and are capable of increasing the competitiveness of industry, thereby improving the conditions of growth and raising the standard of living in the Community.[102] It is possible that efficiencies brought about by a merger counteract the effects on competition and in particular the potential harm to consumers that it might otherwise have.[103] In order to assess whether a merger would significantly impede effective competition, in particular through the creation or the strengthening of a dominant position, within the meaning of Article 2(2) and (3) of the Merger Regulation, the Commission performs an overall competitive appraisal of the merger. In making this appraisal, the Commission takes into account the factors mentioned in Article 2(1), including the development of technical and economic progress provided that it is to the consumers' advantage and does not form an obstacle to competition.[104]

77. The Commission considers any substantiated efficiency claim in the overall assessment of the merger. It may decide that, as a consequence of the efficiencies that the merger brings about, there are no grounds for declaring the merger incompatible with the common market pursuant to Article 2(3) of the Merger Regulation. This will be the case when the Commission is in a position to conclude on the basis of sufficient evidence that the efficiencies generated by the merger are likely to enhance the ability and incentive of the merged entity to act pro-competitively for the benefit of consumers, thereby counteracting the adverse effects on competition which the merger might otherwise have.

78. For the Commission to take account of efficiency claims in its assessment of the merger and be in a position to reach the conclusion that as a consequence of efficiencies, there are no grounds for declaring the merger to be incompatible with the common market, the efficiencies have to benefit consumers, be merger-specific and be verifiable. These conditions are cumulative.

Benefit to consumers

79. The relevant benchmark in assessing efficiency claims is that consumers[105] will not be worse off as a result of the merger. For that purpose, efficiencies should be substantial and timely, and should, in principle, benefit consumers in those relevant markets where it is otherwise likely that competition concerns would occur.

80. Mergers may bring about various types of efficiency gains that can lead to lower prices or other benefits to consumers. For example, cost savings in production or distribution may give the merged entity the ability and incentive to charge lower prices following the merger. In line with the need to ascertain whether efficiencies will lead to a net benefit to consumers, cost efficiencies that lead to reductions in variable or marginal costs[106] are more likely to be relevant to the assessment of efficiencies than reductions in fixed costs; the former are, in principle, more likely to result in lower prices for consumers.[107] Cost reductions, which merely result from anti-competitive reductions in output, cannot be considered as efficiencies benefiting consumers.

81. Consumers may also benefit from new or improved products or services, for instance resulting from efficiency gains in the sphere of R&D and innovation. A joint venture company set up in order to develop a new product may bring about the type of efficiencies that the Commission can take into account.

82. In the context of coordinated effects, efficiencies may increase the merged entity's incentive to increase production and reduce prices, and thereby reduce its incentive to coordinate its market behaviour with other firms in the market. Efficiencies may therefore lead to a lower risk of coordinated effects in the relevant market.

83. In general, the later the efficiencies are expected to materialise in the future, the less weight the Commission can assign to them. This implies that, in order to be considered as a counteracting factor, the efficiencies must be timely.

84. The incentive on the part of the merged entity to pass efficiency gains on to consumers is often related to the existence of competitive pressure from the remaining firms in the market and from potential entry. The greater the possible negative effects on competition, the more the Commission has to be sure that the claimed efficiencies are substantial, likely to be realised, and to be passed on, to a sufficient degree, to the consumer. It is highly unlikely that a merger leading to a market position approaching that of a monopoly, or leading to a similar level of market power, can be declared compatible with the common market on the ground that efficiency gains would be sufficient to counteract its potential anti-competitive effects.

Merger specificity

85. Efficiencies are relevant to the competitive assessment when they are a direct consequence of the notified merger and cannot be achieved to a similar extent by less anticompetitive alternatives. In these circumstances, the efficiencies are deemed to be caused by the merger and thus, merger-specific.[108] It is for the merging parties to provide in due time all the relevant information necessary to demonstrate that there are no less anti-competitive, realistic and attainable

alternatives of a non-concentrative nature (eg a licensing agreement, or a cooperative joint venture) or of a concentrative nature (eg a concentrative joint venture, or a differently structured merger) than the notified merger which preserve the claimed efficiencies. The Commission only considers alternatives that are reasonably practical in the business situation faced by the merging parties having regard to established business practices in the industry concerned.

Verifiability

86. Efficiencies have to be verifiable such that the Commission can be reasonably certain that the efficiencies are likely to materialise, and be substantial enough to counteract a merger's potential harm to consumers. The more precise and convincing the efficiency claims are, the better the Commission can evaluate the claims. Where reasonably possible, efficiencies and the resulting benefit to consumers should therefore be quantified. When the necessary data are not available to allow for a precise quantitative analysis, it must be possible to foresee a clearly identifiable positive impact on consumers, not a marginal one. In general, the longer the start of the efficiencies is projected into the future, the less probability the Commission may be able to assign to the efficiencies actually being brought about.

87. Most of the information, allowing the Commission to assess whether the merger will bring about the sort of efficiencies that would enable it to clear a merger, is solely in the possession of the merging parties. It is, therefore, incumbent upon the notifying parties to provide in due time all the relevant information necessary to demonstrate that the claimed efficiencies are merger-specific and likely to be realised. Similarly, it is for the notifying parties to show to what extent the efficiencies are likely to counteract any adverse effects on competition that might otherwise result from the merger, and therefore benefit consumers.

88. Evidence relevant to the assessment of efficiency claims includes, in particular, internal documents that were used by the management to decide on the merger, statements from the management to the owners and financial markets about the expected efficiencies, historical examples of efficiencies and consumer benefit, and pre-merger external experts' studies on the type and size of efficiency gains, and on the extent to which consumers are likely to benefit.

NOTES

102 See Recital 4 of the Merger Regulation.

103 See Recital 29 of the Merger Regulation.

104 Cf Article 2(1)(b) of the Merger Regulation.

105 Pursuant to Article 2(1)(b), the concept of "consumers" encompasses intermediate and ultimate consumers, ie users of the products covered by the merger. In other words, consumers within the meaning of this provision include the customers, potential and/or actual, of the parties to the merger.

106 Variable costs should be viewed as those costs that vary with the level of production or sales over the relevant time period. Marginal costs are those costs associated with expanding production or sales at the margin.

107 Generally, fixed cost savings are not given such weight as the relationship between fixed costs and consumer prices is normally less direct, at least in the short run.

108 In line with the general principle set out in paragraph 9 of this notice.

VIII. FAILING FIRM

[4.698]

89. The Commission may decide that an otherwise problematic merger is nevertheless compatible with the common market if one of the merging parties is a failing firm. The basic requirement is that the deterioration of the competitive structure that follows the merger cannot be said to be caused by the merger.[109] This will arise where the competitive structure of the market would deteriorate to at least the same extent in the absence of the merger.[110]

90. The Commission considers the following three criteria to be especially relevant for the application of a "failing firm defence". First, the allegedly failing firm would in the near future be forced out of the market because of financial difficulties if not taken over by another undertaking. Second, there is no less anti-competitive alternative purchase than the notified merger. Third, in the absence of a merger, the assets of the failing firm would inevitably exit the market.[111]

91. It is for the notifying parties to provide in due time all the relevant information necessary to demonstrate that the deterioration of the competitive structure that follows the merger is not caused by the merger.

NOTES

109 Joined Cases C-68/94 and C-30/95, *Kali and Salz*, paragraph 110.

110 Joined Cases C-68/94 and C-30/95, *Kali and Salz*, paragraph 114. See also Commission Decision 2002/365/EC in Case COMP/M.2314—*BASF/Pantochim/Eurodiol*, OJ L132, 17.5.2002, p 45, points 157–160. This requirement is linked to the general principle set out in paragraph 9 of this notice.

111 The inevitability of the assets of the failing firm leaving the market in question may, in particular in a case of merger to monopoly, underlie a finding that the market share of the failing firm would in any event accrue to the other merging party. See Joined Cases C-68/94 and C-30/95, *Kali and Salz*, paragraphs 115–116.

COMMISSION NOTICE

(2005/C56/03)

on restrictions directly related and necessary to concentrations

(Text with EEA relevance)

[4.699]

NOTES

Date of publication in OJ: OJ C56, 5.3.2005, p 24.

Note: with effect from 1 December 2009, the EC Treaty was replaced by the Treaty on the Functioning of the European Union. References in this document to provisions of the EC Treaty should be construed accordingly.

I. INTRODUCTION

[4.700]

1. Council Regulation (EC) No 139/2004 of 20 January 2004 on the control of concentrations between undertakings (the EC Merger Regulation)[1] provides in Article 6(1)(b), second subparagraph, in Article 8(1), second subparagraph and in Article 8(2), third subparagraph that a decision declaring a concentration compatible with the common market "*shall be deemed to cover restrictions directly related and necessary to the implementation of the concentration*".

2. The amendment of the rules governing the assessment of restrictions directly related and necessary to the implementation of the concentration (hereinafter also referred to as "ancillary restraints") introduces a principle of self-assessment of such restrictions. This reflects the intention of the legislature not to oblige the Commission to assess and individually address ancillary restraints. The treatment of ancillary restraints under the EC Merger Regulation is further explained in recital 21 in the preamble to the EC Merger Regulation, which states that "*Commission decisions declaring concentrations compatible with the common market in application of this Regulation should automatically cover such restrictions, without the Commission having to assess such restrictions in individual cases*". While the Recital envisages that the Commission will exercise a residual function with regard to specific novel or unresolved issues giving rise to genuine uncertainty, it is in all other scenarios the task of the undertakings concerned to assess for themselves whether and to what extent their agreements can be regarded as ancillary to a transaction. Disputes as to whether restrictions are directly related and necessary to the implementation of the concentration, and thus automatically covered by the Commission's clearance decision, may be resolved before national courts.

3. The Commission's residual function is addressed in recital 21 of the Merger Regulation, where it is stated that the Commission should, at the request of the undertakings concerned, expressly assess the ancillary character of restrictions if a case presents "*novel and unresolved questions giving rise to genuine uncertainty*". The Recital subsequently defines a "novel or unresolved question giving rise to genuine uncertainty" as a question that is "*not covered by the relevant Commission notice in force or a published Commission decision.*"

4. In order to provide legal certainty to the undertakings concerned, this Notice provides guidance on the interpretation of the notion of ancillary restraints. The guidance given in the following sections reflects the essence of the Commission's practice, and sets out principles for assessing whether and to what extent the most common types of agreements are deemed to be ancillary restraints.

5. However, cases involving exceptional circumstances that are not covered by this Notice may justify departing from these principles. Parties may find further guidance in published Commission decisions[2] as to whether their agreements can be regarded as ancillary restraints or not. To the extent that cases involving exceptional circumstances have been previously addressed by the Commission in its published decisions,[3] they do not constitute "novel or unresolved questions" within the meaning of recital 21) of the Merger Regulation.

6. Accordingly, a case presents a "novel and unresolved question giving rise to genuine uncertainty" if those restrictions are not covered by this Notice and have not been previously addressed by the Commission in its published decisions. As envisaged in recital 21 of the Merger Regulation, the Commission will, at the request of the parties, expressly assess such restrictions in these cases. Subject to confidentiality requirements, the Commission will provide adequate publicity as regards such assessments that further develop the principles set out in this Notice.

7. To the extent that restrictions are directly related and necessary to the implementation of the concentration, Article 21(1) of the Merger Regulation provides that this Regulation alone applies, to the exclusion of Council Regulations (EC) No 1/2003,[4] (EEC) No 1017/68[5] and (EEC) No 4056/86.[6] By contrast, for restrictions that cannot be regarded as directly related and necessary to the implementation of the concentration, Articles 81 and 82 of the EC Treaty remain potentially applicable. However, the mere fact that an agreement or arrangement is not deemed to be ancillary to a concentration is not, as such, prejudicial to the legal status thereof. Such agreements or arrangements are to be assessed in accordance with Article 81 and 82 of the EC Treaty and the related regulatory texts and notices.[7] They may also be subject to any applicable national competition rules. Hence, agreements which contain a restriction on competition, but are not considered directly related and necessary to the implementation of the concentration pursuant to this notice, may nevertheless be covered by those provisions.

8. The Commission's interpretation of Article 6(1)(b), second subparagraph, and Article 8(1), second subparagraph, and (2), third subparagraph, of the Merger Regulation is without prejudice to the interpretation which may be given by the Court of Justice or the Court of First Instance of the European Communities.

9. This Notice replaces the Commission's previous Notice regarding restrictions directly related and necessary to concentrations.[8]

NOTES

1 OJ L24, 29.1.2004, p 1.

2 For the purpose of this Notice, a decision is considered to be published when it is published in the *Official Journal of the European Union* or when it is made available to the public on the Commission's web site.

3 See for example Commission Decision of 1 September 2000 (COMP/M.1980 – *Volvo/Renault V.I.*, paragraph 56) – *high degree of customer loyalty*; Commission Decision of 23 October 1998 (IV/M.1298 – *Kodak/Imation*, paragraph 73) – *long product life cycle*; Commission Decision of 13 March 1995 (IV/M.550 – *Union Carbide/Enichem*, paragraph 99) – *limited number of alternative producers*; Commission Decision of 30 April 1992 (IV/M.197 – *Solvay-Laporte/Interox*, paragraph 50) – *longer protection of know-how required.*

4 Council Regulation (EC) No 1/2003 of 16 December 2002 on the implementation of the rules on competition laid down

in Articles 81 and 82 of the Treaty, OJ L1, 4.1.2003, p 1; Regulation as last amended by Regulation (EC) No 411/2004 (OJ L68, 6.3.2004, p 1).

5 Council Regulation (EEC) No 1017/68 of 19 July 1968 applying rules of competition to transport by rail, road and inland waterway, OJ L175, 23.7.1968, p 1; Regulation as last amended by Regulation (EC) No 1/2003.

6 Council Regulation (EEC) No 4056/86 of 22 December 1986 laying down detailed rules for the application of Articles 81 and 82 of the Treaty to maritime transport, OJ L378, 31.12.1986, p 4; Regulation as last amended by Regulation (EC) No 1/2003.

7 See, for example, for licence agreements Regulation (EC) No 772/2004 of 27 April 2004 on the application of Article 81(3) of the Treaty to categories of technology transfer agreements, OJ L123, 27.4.2004, p 11; see for supply and purchase agreements eg Commission Regulation (EC) No 2790/1999 of 22 December 1999 on the application of Article 81(3) of the Treaty to categories of vertical agreements and concerted practices, OJ L336, 29.12.1999, p 21.

8 OJ C188, 4.7.2001, p 5.

II. GENERAL PRINCIPLES

[4.701]

10. A concentration consists of contractual arrangements and agreements establishing control within the meaning of Article 3(2) of the Merger Regulation. All agreements which carry out the main object of the concentration,[9] such as those relating to the sale of shares or assets of an undertaking, are integral parts of the concentration. In addition to these arrangements and agreements, the parties to the concentration may enter into other agreements which do not form an integral part of the concentration but can restrict the parties' freedom of action in the market. If such agreements contain ancillary restraints, these are automatically covered by the decision declaring the concentration compatible with the Common Market.

11. The criteria of direct relation and necessity are objective in nature. Restrictions are not directly related and necessary to the implementation of a concentration simply because the parties regard them as such.

12. For restrictions to be considered "directly related to the implementation of the concentration", they must be closely linked to the concentration itself. It is not sufficient that an agreement has been entered into in the same context or at the same time as the concentration.[10] Restrictions which are directly related to the concentration are economically related to the main transaction and intended to allow a smooth transition to the changed company structure after the concentration.

13. Agreements must be "necessary to the implementation of the concentration",[11] which means that, in the absence of those agreements, the concentration could not be implemented or could only be implemented under considerably more uncertain conditions, at substantially higher cost, over an appreciably longer period or with considerably greater difficulty.[12] Agreements necessary to the implementation of a concentration are typically aimed at protecting the value transferred,[13] maintaining the continuity of supply after the break-up of a former economic entity,[14] or enabling the start-up of a new entity.[15] In determining whether a restriction is necessary, it is appropriate not only to take account of its nature, but also to ensure that its duration, subject matter and geographical field of application does not exceed what the implementation of the concentration reasonably requires. If equally effective alternatives are available for attaining the legitimate aim pursued, the undertakings must choose the one which is objectively the least restrictive of competition.

14. For concentrations which are carried out in stages, the contractual arrangements relating to the stages before the establishment of control within the meaning of Article 3(1) and (2) of the Merger Regulation cannot normally be considered directly related and necessary to the implementation of the concentration. However, an agreement to abstain from material changes in the target's business until completion is considered directly related and necessary to the implementation of the joint bid.[16] The same applies, in the context of a joint bid, to an agreement by the joint purchasers of an undertaking to abstain from making separate competing offers for the same undertaking, or otherwise acquiring control.

15. Agreements which serve to facilitate the joint acquisition of control are to be considered directly related and necessary to the implementation of the concentration. This will apply to arrangements between the parties for the joint acquisition of control aimed at implementing the division of assets in order to divide the production facilities or distribution networks among themselves, together with the existing trademarks of the undertaking acquired jointly.

16. To the extent that such a division involves the break-up of a pre-existing economic entity, arrangements that make the break-up possible under reasonable conditions are to be considered directly related and necessary to the implementation of the concentration, under the principles set out below.

NOTES

9 See eg Commission Decision of 10 August 1992 (IV/M.206 – *Rhône-Poulenc/SNIA*, paragraph 8.3); Commission Decision of 19 December 1991 (IV/M.113 – *Courtaulds/SNIA*, paragraph 35); Commission Decision of 2 December 1991 (IV/M.102 – *TNT/Canada Post/DBP Postdienst/La Poste/PTT Poste & Sweden Post*, paragraph 46).

10 Likewise, a restriction could, if all other requirements are fulfilled, be "directly related" even if it has not been entered into at the same time as the agreement carrying out the main object of the concentration.

11 See European Court of Justice, Case 42/84 (*Remia*), [1985] ECR 2545, paragraph 20; Court of First Instance, Case T–112/99 (*Métropole Télévision – M6*), [2001] ECR II–2459, paragraph 106.

12 Commission Decision of 18 December 2000 (COMP/M.1863 – *Vodafone/BT/Airtel JV*, paragraph 20).

13 Commission Decision of 30 July 1998 (IV/M.1245 – *VALEO/ITT Industries*, paragraph 59); Commission Decision of 3 March 1999 (IV/M.1442 – *MMP/AFP*, paragraph 17); Commission Decision of 9 March 2001 (COMP/M.2330 – *Cargill/Banks*, paragraph 30); Commission Decision of 20 March 2001 (COMP/M.2227 – *Goldman Sachs/Messer Griesheim*, paragraph 11).

14 Commission Decision of 25 February 2000 (COMP/M.1841 – *Celestica/IBM*, paragraph 21).

15 Commission Decision of 30 March 1999 (IV/JV.15 – *BT/AT&T*, paragraphs 207–214); Commission Decision of 22 December 2000 (COMP/M.2243 – *Stora Enso/Assidoman/JV*, paragraphs 49, 56 and 57).

[16] Commission Decision of 27 July 1998 (IV/M.1226 – *GEC/GPTH*, paragraph 22); Commission Decision of 2 October 1997 (IV/M.984 – *Dupont/ICI*, paragraph 55); Commission Decision of 19 December 1997 (IV/M.1057 – *Terra Industries/ICI*, paragraph 16); Commission Decision of 18 December 1996 (IV/M.861 – *Textron/Kautex*, paragraphs 19 and 22); Commission Decision of 7 August 1996 (IV/M.727 – *BP/Mobil*, paragraph 50).

III. PRINCIPLES APPLICABLE TO COMMONLY ENCOUNTERED RESTRICTIONS IN CASES OF ACQUISITION OF AN UNDERTAKING

[4.702]

17. Restrictions agreed between the parties in the context of a transfer of an undertaking may be to the benefit of the purchaser or of the vendor. In general terms, the need for the purchaser to benefit from certain protection is more compelling than the corresponding need for the vendor. It is the purchaser who needs to be assured that she/he will be able to acquire the full value of the acquired business. Thus, as a general rule, restrictions which benefit the vendor are either not directly related and necessary to the implementation of the concentration at all,[17] or their scope and/or duration need to be more limited than that of clauses which benefit the purchaser.[18]

A.
Non-competition clauses

18. Non-competition obligations which are imposed on the vendor in the context of the transfer of an undertaking or of part of it can be directly related and necessary to the implementation of the concentration. In order to obtain the full value of the assets transferred, the purchaser must be able to benefit from some protection against competition from the vendor in order to gain the loyalty of customers and to assimilate and exploit the know-how. Such non-competition clauses guarantee the transfer to the purchaser of the full value of the assets transferred, which in general include both physical assets and intangible assets, such as the goodwill accumulated or the know-how[19] developed by the vendor. These are not only directly related to the concentration but are also necessary to its implementation because, without them, there would be reasonable grounds to expect that the sale of the undertaking or of part of it could not be accomplished.

19. However, such non-competition clauses are only justified by the legitimate objective of implementing the concentration when their duration, their geographical field of application, their subject matter and the persons subject to them do not exceed what is reasonably necessary to achieve that end.[20]

20. Non-competition clauses are justified for periods of up to three years,[21] when the transfer of the undertaking includes the transfer of customer loyalty in the form of both goodwill and know-how.[22] When only goodwill is included, they are justified for periods of up to two years.[23]

21. By contrast, non-competition clauses cannot be considered necessary when the transfer is in fact limited to physical assets (such as land, buildings or machinery) or to exclusive industrial and commercial property rights (the holders of which could immediately take action against infringements by the transferor of such rights).

22. The geographical scope of a non-competition clause must be limited to the area in which the vendor has offered the relevant products or services before the transfer, since the purchaser does not need to be protected against competition from the vendor in territories not previously penetrated by the vendor.[24] That geographical scope can be extended to territories which the vendor was planning to enter at the time of the transaction, provided that he had already invested in preparing this move.

23. Similarly, non-competition clauses must remain limited to products (including improved versions or updates of products as well as successor models) and services forming the economic activity of the undertaking transferred. This can include products and services at an advanced stage of development at the time of the transaction, or products which are fully developed but not yet marketed. Protection against competition from the vendor in product or service markets in which the transferred undertaking was not active before the transfer is not considered necessary.[25]

24. The vendor may bind herself/himself, her/his subsidiaries and commercial agents. However, an obligation to impose similar restrictions on others would not be regarded as directly related and necessary to the implementation of the concentration. This applies, in particular, to clauses which would restrict the freedom of resellers or users to import or export.

25. Clauses which limit the vendor's right to purchase or hold shares in a company competing with the business transferred shall be considered directly related and necessary to the implementation of the concentration under the same conditions as outlined above for non-competition clauses, unless they prevent the vendor from purchasing or holding shares purely for financial investment purposes, without granting him/her, directly or indirectly, management functions or any material influence in the competing company.[26]

26. Non-solicitation and confidentiality clauses have a comparable effect and are therefore evaluated in a similar way to non-competition clauses.[27]

B.
Licence agreements

27. The transfer of an undertaking or of part of it can include the transfer to the purchaser, with a view to the full exploitation of the assets transferred, of intellectual property rights or know-how. However, the vendor may remain the owner of the rights in order to exploit them for activities other than those transferred. In these cases, the usual means for ensuring that the purchaser will have the full use of the assets transferred is to conclude licensing agreements in his/her favour. Likewise, where the vendor has transferred intellectual property rights with the business, she/he may still want to continue using some or all of these rights for activities other than those transferred; in such a case the purchaser will grant a licence to the vendor.

28. Licences of patents,[28] of similar rights, or of know-how,[29] can be considered necessary to the implementation of the concentration. They may equally be considered an integral part of the concentration and, in any event, need not be limited in time. These licences can be simple or exclusive and may be limited to certain fields of use, to the extent that they correspond to the activities of the undertaking transferred.

29. However, territorial limitations on manufacture reflecting the territory of the transferred activity are not necessary to the implementation of the operation. As regards licences granted by the seller of a business to the buyer, the seller can be made subject to territorial restrictions in the licence agreement under the same conditions as laid down for non-competition clauses in the context of the sale of a business.

30. Restrictions in licence agreements going beyond the above provisions, such as those which protect the licensor rather than the licensee, are not necessary to the implementation of the concentration.[30]

31. Similarly, in the case of licences of trademarks, business names, design rights, copyrights or similar rights, there may be situations in which the vendor wishes to remain the owner of such rights in relation to activities retained, but the purchaser needs those rights in order to market the goods or services produced by the undertaking or part of the undertaking transferred. Here, the same considerations as above apply.[31]

C.

Purchase and supply obligations

32. In many cases, the transfer of an undertaking or of part of it can entail the disruption of traditional lines of purchase and supply which have existed as a result of the previous integration of activities within the economic unity of the vendor. In order to enable the break-up of the economic unity of the vendor and the partial transfer of the assets to the purchaser under reasonable conditions, it is often necessary to maintain, for a transitional period, the existing or similar links between the vendor and the purchaser. This objective is normally attained by purchase and supply obligations for the vendor and/or the purchaser of the undertaking or of part of it. Taking into account the particular situation resulting from the break-up of the economic unity of the vendor, such obligations can be recognised as directly related and necessary to the implementation of the concentration. They may be in favour of the vendor as well as the purchaser, depending on the particular circumstances of the case.

33. The aim of such obligations may be to ensure the continuity of supply to either of the parties of products necessary for carrying out the activities retained by the vendor or taken over by the purchaser. However, the duration of purchase and supply obligations must be limited to a period necessary for the replacement of the relationship of dependency by autonomy in the market. Thus, purchase or supply obligations aimed at guaranteeing the quantities previously supplied can be justified for a transitional period of up to five years.[32]

34. Both supply and purchase obligations providing for fixed quantities, possibly with a variation clause, are recognised as directly related and necessary to the implementation of the concentration. However, obligations providing for unlimited quantities,[33] exclusivity or conferring preferred-supplier or preferred-purchaser status,[34] are not necessary to the implementation of the concentration.

35. Service and distribution agreements are equivalent in their effect to supply arrangements; consequently the same considerations as above shall apply.

NOTES

17 Commission Decision of 27 July 1998 (IV/M.1226 – *GEC/GPTH*, paragraph 24).

18 See, for example, for a clause aiming at the protection of a part of the business remaining with the vendor: Commission Decision of 30 August 1993 (IV/M.319 – *BHF/CCF/Charterhouse*, paragraph 16).

19 As defined in Article 1(1)(i) of Regulation (EC) No 772/2004.

20 See European Court of Justice, Case 42/84 (*Remia*), [1985] ECR 2545, paragraph 20; Court of First Instance, Case T–112/99 (*Métropole Télévision – M6*), [2001] ECR II–2459, paragraph 106.

21 See for exceptional cases in which longer periods may be justified eg Commission Decision of 1 September 2000 (COMP/M.1980 – *Volvo/Renault V.I.*, paragraph 56); Commission Decision of 27 July 1995 (IV/M.612 – *RWE-DEA/Enichem Augusta*, paragraph 37); Commission decision of 23 October 1998 (IV/M.1298 – *Kodak/Imation*, paragraph 74).

22 Commission Decision of 2 April 1998 (IV/M.1127 – *Nestlé/Dalgety*, paragraph 33); Commission Decision of 1 September 2000 (COMP/M.2077 – *Clayton Dubilier & Rice/Iteltel*, paragraph 15); Commission Decision of 2 March 2001 (COMP/M.2305 – *Vodafone Group PLC/EIRCELL*, paragraphs 21 and 22).

23 Commission Decision of 12 April 1999 (IV/M.1482 – *KingFisher/Grosslabor*, paragraph 26); Commission Decision of 14 December 1997 (IV/M.884 – *KNP BT/Bunzl/Wilhelm Seiler*, paragraph 17).

24 Commission Decision of 14 December 1997 (IV/M.884 – *KNP BT/Bunzl/Wilhelm Seiler*, paragraph 17); Commission Decision of 12 April 1999 (IV/M.1482 – *KingFisher/Grosslabor*, paragraph 27); Commission Decision of 6 April 2001 (COMP/M.2355 – *Dow/Enichem Polyurethane*, paragraph 28); Commission Decision of 4 August 2000 (COMP/M.1979 – *CDC/Banco Urquijo/JV*, paragraph 18).

25 Commission Decision of 14 December 1997 (IV/M.884 – *KNP BT/Bunzl/Wilhelm Seiler*, paragraph 17); Commission Decision of 2 March 2001 (COMP/M.2305 – *Vodafone Group PLC/EIRCELL*, paragraph 22); Commission Decision of 6 April 2001 (COMP/M.2355 – *Dow/Enichem Polyurethane*, paragraph 28); Commission Decision of 4 August 2000 (COMP/M.1979 – *CDC/Banco Urquijo/JV*, paragraph 18).

26 Commission Decision of 4 February 1993 (IV/M.301 – *Tesco/Catteau*, paragraph 14); Commission Decision of 14 December 1997 (IV/M.884 – *KNP BT/Bunzl/Wilhelm Seiler*, paragraph 19); Commission Decision of 12 April 1999 (IV/M.1482 – *Kingfisher/Grosslabor*, paragraph 27); Commission Decision of 6 April 2000 (COMP/M.1832 – *Ahold/ICA Förbundet/Canica*, paragraph 26).

27 Accordingly, confidentiality clauses on customer details, prices and quantities cannot be extended. By contrast, confidentiality clauses concerning technical know-how may exceptionally be justified for longer periods, see Commission Decision of 29 April 1998 (IV/M.1167 – *ICI/Williams*, paragraph 22); Commission Decision of 30 April 1992 (IV/M.197 – *Solvay-Laporte/Interox*, paragraph 50).

28 Including patent applications, utility models, applications for registration of utility models, designs, topographies of semiconductor products, supplementary protection certificates for medicinal products or other products for which such supplementary protection certificates may be obtained and plant breeder's certificates (as referred to in Article 1(1)(h) of Regulation (EC) No 772/2004.

29 As defined in Article 1(1)(i) of Regulation (EC) No 772/2004.

30 To the extent that they fall within Article 81(1) of the EC Treaty, such agreements may nevertheless fall under Regulation (EC) No 772/2004, or other Community legislation.

31 Commission Decision of 1 September 2000 (COMP/M.1980 – *Volvo/Renault V.I.*, paragraph 54).

32 Commission Decision of 5 February 1996 (IV/M.651 – *AT&T/Philips*, VII.); Commission Decision of 30 March 1999 (IV/JV.15 – *BT/AT&T*, paragraph 209; see for exceptional cases Commission Decision of 13 March 1995 (IV/M.550 – *Union Carbide/Enichem*, paragraph 99); Commission Decision of 27 July 1995 (IV/M.612 – *RWE-DEA/Enichem Augusta*, paragraph 45).

33 In line with the principle of proportionality, obligations providing for fixed quantities with a variation clause are, in these cases, less restrictive on competition, see eg Commission Decision of 18 September 1998 (IV/M.1292 – *Continental/ITT*, paragraph 19).

34 Commission Decision of 30 July 1998 (IV/M.1245 – *VALEO/ITT Industries*, paragraph 64); see for exceptional cases (eg absence of a market) Commission Decision of 13 March 1995 (IV/M.550 – *Union Carbide/Enichem*, paragraphs 92 to 96); Commission Decision of 27 July 1995 (IV/M.612 – *RWE-DEA/Enichem Augusta*, paragraphs 38 et seq).

IV. PRINCIPLES APPLICABLE TO COMMONLY ENCOUNTERED RESTRICTIONS IN CASES OF JOINT VENTURES WITHIN THE MEANING OF ARTICLE 3(4) OF THE MERGER REGULATION

A.
Non-competition obligations

[4.703]

36. A non-competition obligation between the parent undertakings and a joint venture may be considered directly related and necessary to the implementation of the concentration where such obligations correspond to the products, services and territories covered by the joint venture agreement or its by-laws. Such non-competition clauses reflect, *inter alia*, the need to ensure good faith during negotiations; they may also reflect the need to fully utilise the joint venture's assets or to enable the joint venture to assimilate know-how and goodwill provided by its parents; or the need to protect the parents' interests in the joint venture against competitive acts facilitated, *inter alia*, by the parents' privileged access to the know-how and goodwill transferred to or developed by the joint venture. Such non-competition obligations between the parent undertakings and a joint venture can be regarded as directly related and necessary to the implementation of the concentration for the lifetime of the joint venture.[35]

37. The geographical scope of a non-competition clause must be limited to the area in which the parents offered the relevant products or services before establishing the joint venture.[36] That geographical scope can be extended to territories which the parent companies were planning to enter at the time of the transaction, provided that they had already invested in preparing this move.

38. Similarly, non-competition clauses must be limited to products and services constituting the economic activity of the joint venture. This may include products and services at an advanced stage of development at the time of the transaction, as well as products and services which are fully developed but not yet marketed.

39. If the joint venture is set up to enter a new market, reference will be made to the products, services and territories in which it is to operate under the joint venture agreement or by-laws. However, the presumption is that one parent's interest in the joint venture does not need to be protected against competition from the other parent in markets other than those in which the joint venture will be active from the outset.

40. Additionally, non-competition obligations between non-controlling parents and a joint venture are not directly related and necessary to the implementation of the concentration.

41. The same principles as for non-competition clauses apply to non-solicitation and confidentiality clauses.

B.
Licence agreements

42. A licence granted by the parent undertakings to the joint venture may be considered directly related and necessary to the implementation of the concentration. This applies regardless of whether or not the licence is an exclusive one and whether or not it is limited in time. The licence may be restricted to a particular field of use which corresponds to the activities of the joint venture.

43. Licences granted by the joint venture to one of its parents, or cross-licence agreements, can be regarded as directly related and necessary to the implementation of the concentration under the same conditions as in the case of the acquisition of an undertaking. Licence agreements between the parents are not considered directly related and necessary to the implementation of a joint venture.

C.
Purchase and supply obligations

44. If the parent undertakings remain present in a market upstream or downstream of that of the joint venture, any purchase and supply agreements, including service and distribution agreements are subject to the principles applicable in the case of the transfer of an undertaking.

NOTES

[35] Commission Decision of 15 January 1998 (IV/M.1042 – *Eastman Kodak/Sun Chemical*, paragraph 40); Commission Decision of 7 August 1996 (IV/M.727 – *BP/Mobil*, paragraph 51); Commission Decision of 3 July 1996 (IV/M.751 – *Bayer/Hüls*, paragraph 31); Commission Decision of 6 April 2000 (COMP/M.1832 – *Ahold/ICA Förbundet/Canica*, paragraph 26).

[36] Commission Decision of 29 August 2000 (COMP/M.1913 – *Lufthansa/Menzies/LGS/JV*; paragraph 18); Commission Decision of 22 December 2000 (COMP/M.2243 – *Stora Enso/Assidoman/JV*, paragraph 49, last sentence).

COMMISSION NOTICE

Guidelines on the assessment of non-horizontal mergers under the Council Regulation on the control of concentrations between undertakings

[4.704]

NOTES

Date of publication in OJ: OJ C265, 18.10.2008, p 6.

Note that Council Regulation (EC) No 139/2004 on the control of concentrations between undertakings is repealed, in relation to the UK, by the Competition (Amendment etc) (EU Exit) Regulations 2019, SI 2019/93, reg 63, Sch 3, para 1, as from IP completion day (as defined in the European Union (Withdrawal Agreement) Act 2020, s 39) (for transitional provisions and savings in relation to the operation of the 2019 Regulations, see Sch 4 to those Regulations at **[7.69]** et seq).

Note: with effect from 1 December 2009, the EC Treaty was replaced by the Treaty on the Functioning of the European Union. References in this document to provisions of the EC Treaty should be construed accordingly.

I. INTRODUCTION

[4.705]

1. Article 2 of Council Regulation (EC) No 139/2004 of 20 January 2004 on the control of concentrations between undertakings[1] (hereinafter: the "Merger Regulation") provides that the Commission has to appraise concentrations within the scope of the Merger Regulation with a view to establishing whether or not they are compatible with the common market. For that purpose, the Commission must assess, pursuant to Article 2(2) and (3), whether or not a concentration would significantly impede effective competition, in particular as a result of the creation or strengthening of a dominant position in the common market or a substantial part of it.

2. This document develops guidance as to how the Commission assesses concentrations[2] where the undertakings concerned are active on different relevant markets.[3] In this document, these concentrations will be called "non-horizontal mergers".

3. Two broad types of non-horizontal mergers can be distinguished: vertical mergers and conglomerate mergers.

4. Vertical mergers involve companies operating at different levels of the supply chain. For example, when a manufacturer of a certain product (the "upstream firm") merges with one of its distributors (the "downstream firm"), this is called a vertical merger.[4]

5 Conglomerate mergers are mergers between firms that are in a relationship which is neither horizontal (as competitors in the same relevant market) nor vertical (as suppliers or customers).[5] In practice, the focus of the present guidelines is on mergers between companies that are active in closely related markets (eg mergers involving suppliers of complementary products or products that belong to the same product range).

6. The general guidance already given in the Notice on horizontal mergers is also relevant in the context of non-horizontal mergers. The purpose of the present document is to concentrate on the competition aspects that are relevant to the specific context of non-horizontal mergers. In addition, it will set out the Commission's approach to market shares and concentration thresholds in this context.

7. In practice, mergers may entail both horizontal and non-horizontal effects. This may for instance be the case where the merging firms are not only in a vertical or conglomerate relationship, but are also actual or potential competitors of each other in one or more of the relevant markets concerned.[6] In such a case, the Commission will appraise horizontal, vertical and/or conglomerate effects in accordance with the guidance set out in the relevant notices.[7]

8. The guidance set out in this document draws and elaborates on the Commission's evolving experience with the appraisal of non-horizontal mergers under Regulation No 4064/89 since its entry into force on 21 September 1990, the Merger Regulation presently in force as well as on the case-law of the Court of Justice and the Court of First Instance of the European Communities. The principles contained here will be applied and further developed and refined by the Commission in individual cases. The Commission may revise the notice on non-horizontal mergers from time to time in the light of future developments and of evolving insight.

9. The Commission's interpretation of the Merger Regulation as regards the appraisal of non-horizontal mergers is without prejudice to the interpretation which may be given by the Court of Justice or the Court of First Instance of the European Communities.

NOTES

[1] Council Regulation (EC) No 139/2004 of 20 January 2004, Official Journal L24, 29.01.2004, p 1.

[2] The term *concentration* used in the Merger Regulation covers various types of transactions such as mergers, acquisitions, takeovers, and certain types of joint ventures. In the remainder of this Document, unless otherwise specified, the term "merger" will be used as a synonym for concentration and therefore cover all the above types of transactions.

[3] Guidance on the assessment of mergers involving undertakings which are actual or potential competitors on the same

relevant market ("horizontal mergers") is given in the Commission Notice: Guidelines on the assessment of horizontal mergers under the Council Regulation on the control of concentrations between undertakings. OJ C31, 05.02.2004, pages 5–18 ("Notice on Horizontal Mergers").

4 In the present Document, the terms "downstream" and "upstream" are used to describe the (potential) commercial relationship that the merging entities have with each other. Generally the commercial relationship is one where the "downstream" firm purchases the output from the "upstream" firm and uses it as an input in its own production, which it then sells on to its customers. The market where the former transactions take place is referred to as the intermediate market (upstream market). The latter market is referred to as the downstream market.

5 The distinction between conglomerate mergers and horizontal mergers may be subtle, eg when a conglomerate merger involves products that are weak substitutes for each other. The same holds true for the distinction between conglomerate mergers and vertical mergers. For instance, products may be supplied by some companies with the inputs already integrated (vertical relationship), whereas other producers leave it to the customers to select and assemble the inputs themselves (conglomerate relationship).

6 For instance, in certain markets upstream or downstream firms are often well-placed potential entrants. See, eg, in the electricity and gas sector, Case COMP/M.3440 – *EDP/ENI/GDP* (2004). The same may hold for producers of complementary products. See, eg, in the liquid packaging sector, Case COMP/M.2416 – *TetraLaval/Sidel* (2001).

7 Guidance on the assessment of mergers with a potential competitor is given in the Notice on horizontal mergers, in particular at paragraphs 58 to 60 thereof.

II. OVERVIEW

[4.706]

10. Effective competition brings benefits to consumers, such as low prices, high quality products, a wide selection of goods and services, and innovation. Through its control of mergers, the Commission prevents mergers that would be likely to deprive customers of these benefits by significantly increasing the market power of firms. An "increase in market power" in this context refers to the ability of one or more firms to profitably increase prices, reduce output, choice or quality of goods and services, diminish innovation, or otherwise negatively influence parameters of competition.[8]

11. Non-horizontal mergers are generally less likely to significantly impede effective competition than horizontal mergers.

12. First, unlike horizontal mergers, vertical or conglomerate mergers do not entail the loss of direct competition between the merging firms in the same relevant market.[9] As a result, the main source of anti-competitive effect in horizontal mergers is absent from vertical and conglomerate mergers.

13. Second, vertical and conglomerate mergers provide substantial scope for efficiencies. A characteristic of vertical mergers and certain conglomerate mergers is that the activities and/or the products of the companies involved are complementary to each other.[10] The integration of complementary activities or products within a single firm may produce significant efficiencies and be pro-competitive. In vertical relationships for instance, as a result of the complementarity, a decrease in mark-ups downstream will lead to higher demand also upstream. A part of the benefit of this increase in demand will accrue to the upstream suppliers. An integrated firm will take this benefit into account. Vertical integration may thus provide an increased incentive to seek to decrease prices and increase output because the integrated firm can capture a larger fraction of the benefits. This is often referred to as the "internalisation of double mark-ups". Similarly, other efforts to increase sales at one level (eg improve service or stepping up innovation) may provide a greater reward for an integrated firm that will take into account the benefits accruing at other levels.

14. Integration may also decrease transaction costs and allow for a better co-ordination in terms of product design, the organisation of the production process, and the way in which the products are sold. Similarly, mergers which involve products belonging to a range or portfolio of products that are generally sold to the same set of customers (be they complementary products or not) may give rise to customer benefits such as one-stop-shopping.

15. However, there are circumstances in which non-horizontal mergers may significantly impede effective competition, in particular as a result of the creation or strengthening of a dominant position. This is essentially because a non-horizontal merger may change the ability and incentive to compete on the part of the merging companies and their competitors in ways that cause harm to consumers.

16. In the context of competition law, the concept of "consumers" encompasses intermediate and ultimate consumers.[11] When intermediate customers are actual or potential competitors of the parties to the merger, the Commission focuses on the effects of the merger on the customers to which the merged entity and those competitors are selling. Consequently, the fact that a merger affects competitors is not in itself a problem. It is the impact on effective competition that matters, not the mere impact on competitors at some level of the supply chain.[12] In particular, the fact that rivals may be harmed because a merger creates efficiencies cannot in itself give rise to competition concerns.

17. There are two main ways in which non-horizontal mergers may significantly impede effective competition: non-coordinated effects and coordinated effects.[13]

18. Non-coordinated effects may principally arise when non-horizontal mergers give rise to foreclosure. In this document, the term "foreclosure" will be used to describe any instance where actual or potential rivals' access to supplies or markets is hampered or eliminated as a result of the merger, thereby reducing these companies' ability and/or incentive to compete. As a result of such foreclosure, the merging companies – and, possibly, some of its competitors as well – may be able to profitably increase the price[14] charged to consumers. These instances give rise to a significant impediment to effective competition and are therefore referred to hereafter as "anticompetitive foreclosure".

Part 4 EU & Retained EU Materials

19. Coordinated effects arise where the merger changes the nature of competition in such a way that firms that previously were not coordinating their behaviour, are now significantly more likely to coordinate to raise prices or otherwise harm effective competition. A merger may also make coordination easier, more stable or more effective for firms which were coordinating prior to the merger.

20. In assessing the competitive effects of a merger, the Commission compares the competitive conditions that would result from the notified merger with the conditions that would have prevailed without the merger.[15] In most cases the competitive conditions existing at the time of the merger constitute the relevant comparison for evaluating the effects of a merger. However, in some circumstances, the Commission will take into account future changes to the market that can reasonably be predicted. It may, in particular, take account of the likely entry or exit of firms if the merger did not take place when considering what constitutes the relevant comparison. The Commission may take into account future market developments that result from impending regulatory changes.[16]

21. In its assessment, the Commission will consider both the possible anti-competitive effects arising from the merger and the possible pro-competitive effects stemming from substantiated efficiencies benefiting consumers.[17] The Commission examines the various chains of cause and effect with a view to ascertaining which of them is the most likely. The more immediate and direct the perceived anti-competitive effects of a merger, the more likely the Commission is to raise competition concerns. Likewise, the more immediate and direct the pro-competitive effects of a merger, the more likely the Commission is to find that they counteract any anti-competitive effects.

22. This document describes the main scenarios of competitive harm and sources of efficiencies in the context of vertical mergers and, subsequently, in the context of conglomerate mergers.

NOTES

8 In this Document, the expression "increased prices" is often used as shorthand for these various ways in which a merger may result in competitive harm. The expression should also be understood to cover situations where, for instance, prices are decreased less, or are less likely to decrease, than they otherwise would have without the merger and where prices are increased more, or are more likely to increase, than they otherwise would have without the merger.

9 Such a loss of direct competition can, nevertheless, arise where one of the merging firms is a potential competitor in the relevant market where the other merging firm operates. See paragraph 7 above.

10 In this document, products or services are called "complementary" (or "economic complements") when they are worth more to a customer when used or consumed together than when used or consumed separately. Also a merger between upstream and downstream activities can be seen as a combination of complements which go into the final product. For instance, both production and distribution fulfil a complementary role in getting a product to the market.

11 See Article 2(1)(b) of the Merger Regulation and paragraph 84 of the Communication from the Commission – Notice – Guidelines on the application of Article 81(3) of the Treaty, Official Journal C101, 27.04.2004, p 97.

12 One example of this approach can be found in the case COMP/M.3653 *Siemens/VA Tech* (2005), in which the Commission assessed the effect of the transaction on the two complementary markets for electrical rail vehicles and electrical traction systems for rail vehicles, which combine into a full rail vehicle. While the merger allegedly reduced the independent supply of electrical traction systems, there would still be several integrated suppliers which could deliver the rail vehicle. The Commission thus concluded that even if the merger had negative consequences for independent suppliers of electrical rail vehicles "sufficient competition would remain in the relevant downstream market for rail vehicles"

13 See Section II of the Notice on Horizontal Mergers.

14 For the meaning of the expression "increased prices" see footnote 8.

15 By analogy, in the case of a merger that has been implemented without having been notified, the Commission would assess the merger in the light of the competitive conditions that would have prevailed without the implemented merger.

16 This may be particularly relevant in cases where effective competition is expected to arise in the future as a result of market opening. See eg Case COMP/M.3696 – *E.ON/MOL* (2005), at points 457 to 463.

17 See Section VII on efficiencies in the Notice on Horizontal Mergers.

III. MARKET SHARE AND CONCENTRATION LEVELS

[4.707]

23. Non-horizontal mergers pose no threat to effective competition unless the merged entity has a significant degree of market power (which does not necessarily amount to dominance) in at least one of the markets concerned. The Commission will examine this issue before proceeding to assess the impact of the merger on competition.

24. Market shares and concentration levels provide useful first indications of the market power and the competitive importance of both the merging parties and their competitors.[18]

25. The Commission is unlikely to find concern in non-horizontal mergers, be it of a coordinated or of a non-coordinated nature, where the market share post-merger of the new entity in each of the markets concerned is below 30%[19] and the post-merger HHI is below 2000.

26. In practice, the Commission will not extensively investigate such mergers, except where special circumstances such as, for instance, one or more of the following factors are present:

(a) a merger involves a company that is likely to expand significantly in the near future, eg because of a recent innovation;

(b) there are significant cross-shareholdings or cross-directorships among the market participants;

(c) one of the merging firms is a firm with a high likelihood of disrupting coordinated conduct;

(d) indications of past or ongoing coordination, or facilitating practices, are present.

27. The Commission will use the above market share and HHI thresholds as an initial indicator of the absence of competition concerns. However, these thresholds do not give rise to a legal presumption. The Commission is of the opinion that it is less appropriate in this context to present market share and concentration levels above which competition concerns would be deemed to be likely, as the existence of a significant degree of market power in at least one of the markets concerned is a necessary condition for competitive harm, but is not a sufficient condition.[20]

NOTES

[18] See also Section III of the Notice on Horizontal Mergers. The calculation of market shares depends critically on market definition (see Commission notice on the definition of the relevant market for the purposes of Community competition law, OJ C372/5, 9 December 1997). Special care must be taken in contexts where vertically integrated companies supply products internally.

[19] In analogy to the indications given in Commission Regulation (EC) No 2790/1999 of 22 December 1999 on the application of Article 81(3) of the Treaty to categories of vertical agreements and concerted practices, Official Journal L336, 29.12.1999, pages 21–25. Where a merged entity would have a market share just above the 30% threshold on one market but substantially below on other, related, markets competition concerns will be less likely.

[20] See Sections IV and V.

IV. VERTICAL MERGERS

[4.708]

28. This section sets out the Commission's framework of analysis in the context of vertical mergers. In its assessment, the Commission will consider both the possible anti-competitive effects arising from vertical mergers and the possible pro-competitive effects stemming from efficiencies substantiated by the parties.

A. NON-COORDINATED EFFECTS: FORECLOSURE

29. A merger is said to result in foreclosure where actual or potential rivals' access to supplies or markets is hampered or eliminated as a result of the merger, thereby reducing these companies' ability and/or incentive to compete. Such foreclosure may discourage entry or expansion of rivals or encourage their exit. Foreclosure thus can be found even if the foreclosed rivals are not forced to exit the market: It is sufficient that the rivals are disadvantaged and consequently led to compete less effectively. Such foreclosure is regarded as anti-competitive where the merging companies – and, possibly, some of its competitors as well – are as a result able to profitably increase the price charged to consumers.[21]

30. Two forms of foreclosure can be distinguished. The first is where the merger is likely to raise the costs of downstream rivals by restricting their access to an important input (input foreclosure). The second is where the merger is likely to foreclose upstream rivals by restricting their access to a sufficient customer base (customer foreclosure).[22]

1. INPUT FORECLOSURE

31. Input foreclosure arises where, post-merger, the new entity would be likely to restrict access to the products or services that it would have otherwise supplied absent the merger, thereby raising its downstream rivals' costs by making it harder for them to obtain supplies of the input under similar prices and conditions as absent the merger. This may lead the merged entity to profitably increase the price charged to consumers, resulting in a significant impediment to effective competition. As indicated above, for input foreclosure to lead to consumer harm, it is not necessary that the merged firm's rivals are forced to exit the market. The relevant benchmark is whether the increased input costs would lead to higher prices for consumers. Any efficiencies resulting from the merger may, however, lead the merged entity to reduce price, so that the overall likely impact on consumers is neutral or positive. A graphical presentation of this mechanism is provided in Figure 1.

Figure 1 – Input foreclosure

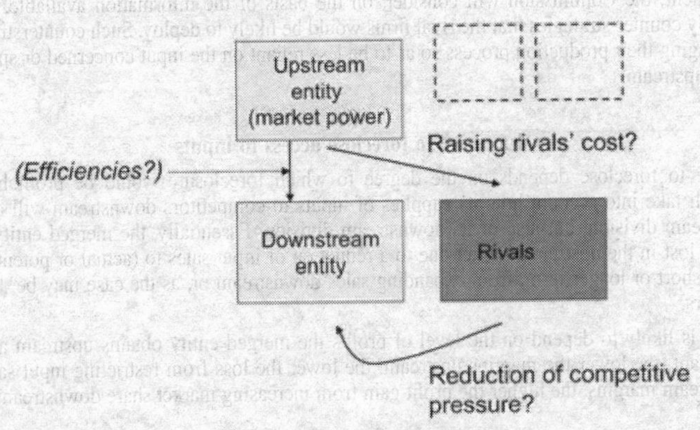

32. In assessing the likelihood of an anticompetitive input foreclosure scenario, the Commission examines, first, whether the merged entity would have, post-merger, the ability to substantially foreclose access to inputs, second, whether it would have the incentive to do so, and third, whether a foreclosure strategy would have a significant detrimental effect on competition downstream.[23] In practice, these factors are often examined together since they are closely intertwined.

A.
Ability to foreclose access to inputs[24]

33. Input foreclosure may occur in various forms. The merged entity may decide not to deal with its actual or potential competitors in the vertically related market. Alternatively, the merged firm may decide to restrict supplies and/or to raise the price it charges when supplying competitors and/or to otherwise make the conditions of supply less favourable than they would have been absent the merger.[25] Further, the merged entity may opt for a specific choice of technology within the new firm which is not compatible with the technologies chosen by rival firms.[26] Foreclosure may also take more subtle forms, such as the degradation of the quality of input supplied.[27] In its assessment, the Commission may consider a series of alternative or complementary possible strategies.

34. Input foreclosure may raise competition problems only if it concerns an important input for the downstream product.[28] This is the case, for example, when the input concerned represents a significant cost factor relative to the price of the downstream product. Irrespective of its cost, an input may also be sufficiently important for other reasons. For instance, the input may be a critical component without which the downstream product could not be manufactured or effectively sold on the market,[29] or it may represent a significant source of product differentiation for the downstream product.[30] It may also be that the cost of switching to alternative inputs is relatively high.

35. For input foreclosure to be a concern, the vertically integrated firm resulting from the merger must have a significant degree of market power in the upstream market. It is only in these circumstances that the merged firm can be expected to have a significant influence on the conditions of competition in the upstream market and thus, possibly, on prices and supply conditions in the downstream market.

36. The merged entity would only have the ability to foreclose downstream competitors if, by reducing access to its own upstream products or services, it could negatively affect the overall availability of inputs for the downstream market in terms of price or quality. This may be the case where the remaining upstream suppliers are less efficient, offer less preferred alternatives, or lack the ability to expand output in response to the supply restriction, for example because they face capacity constraints or, more generally, face decreasing returns to scale.[31] Also, the presence of exclusive contracts between the merged entity and independent input providers may limit the ability of downstream rivals to have adequate access to inputs.

37. When determining the extent to which input foreclosure may occur, it must be taken into account that the decision of the merged entity to rely on its upstream division's supply of inputs may also free up capacity on the part of the remaining input suppliers from which the downstream division used to purchase before. In fact, the merger may merely realign purchase patterns among competing firms.

38. When competition in the input market is oligopolistic, a decision of the merged entity to restrict access to its inputs reduces the competitive pressure exercised on remaining input suppliers, which may allow them to raise the input price they charge to non-integrated downstream competitors. In essence, input foreclosure by the merged entity may expose its downstream rivals to non-vertically integrated suppliers with increased market power.[32] This increase in third-party market power will be greater the lower the degree of product differentiation between the merged entity and other upstream suppliers and the higher the degree of upstream concentration. However, the attempt to raise the input price may fail when independent input suppliers, faced with a reduction in the demand for their products (from the downstream division of the merged entity or from independent downstream firms), respond by pricing more aggressively.[33]

39. In its assessment, the Commission will consider, on the basis of the information available, whether there are effective and timely counter-strategies that the rival firms would be likely to deploy. Such counterstrategies include the possibility of changing their production process so as to be less reliant on the input concerned or sponsoring the entry of new suppliers upstream.

B.
Incentive to foreclose access to inputs

40. The incentive to foreclose depends on the degree to which foreclosure would be profitable. The vertically integrated firm will take into account how its supplies of inputs to competitors downstream will affect not only the profits of its upstream division, but also of its downstream division. Essentially, the merged entity faces a trade-off between the profit lost in the upstream market due to a reduction of input sales to (actual or potential) rivals and the profit gain, in the short or longer term, from expanding sales downstream or, as the case may be, being able to raise prices to consumers.

41. The trade-off is likely to depend on the level of profits the merged entity obtains upstream and downstream.[34] Other things constant, the lower the margins upstream, the lower the loss from restricting input sales. Similarly, the higher the downstream margins, the higher the profit gain from increasing market share downstream at the expense of foreclosed rivals.[35]

42. The incentive for the integrated firm to raise rivals' costs further depends on the extent to which downstream demand is likely to be diverted away from foreclosed rivals and the share of that diverted demand that the downstream division of the integrated firm can capture.[36] This share will normally be higher the less capacity constrained the merged entity will be relative to non-foreclosed downstream rivals and the more the products of the merged entity and foreclosed competitors are close substitutes. The effect on downstream demand will also be higher if the affected input represents a significant proportion of downstream rivals' costs or if the affected input represents a critical component of the downstream product.[37]

43. The incentive to foreclose actual or potential rivals may also depend on the extent to which the downstream division of the integrated firm can be expected to benefit from higher price levels downstream as a result of a strategy to raise rivals' costs.[38] The greater the market shares of the merged entity downstream, the greater the base of sales on which to enjoy increased margins.[39]

44. An upstream monopolist that is already able to fully extract all available profits in vertically related markets may not have any incentive to foreclose rivals following a vertical merger. The ability to extract available profits from the consumers does not follow immediately from a very high market share.[40] Such a finding would require a more thorough analysis of the actual and future constraints under which the monopolist operates. When all available profits cannot be extracted, a vertical merger – even if it involves an upstream monopolist – may give the merged entity the incentive to raise the costs of downstream rivals, thereby reducing the competitive constraint they exert on the merged entity in the downstream market.

45. In its assessment of the likely incentives of the merged firm, the Commission may take into account various considerations such as the ownership structure of the merged entity,[41] the type of strategies adopted on the market in the past[42] or the content of internal strategic documents such as business plans.

46. In addition, when the adoption of a specific course of conduct by the merged entity is an essential step in foreclosure, the Commission examines both the incentives to adopt such conduct and the factors liable to reduce, or even eliminate, those incentives, including the possibility that the conduct is unlawful. Conduct may be unlawful inter alia because of competition rules or sector-specific rules at the EU or national levels. This appraisal, however, does not require an exhaustive and detailed examination of the rules of the various legal orders which might be applicable and of the enforcement policy practised within them.[43] Moreover, the illegality of a conduct may be likely to provide significant disincentives for the merged entity to engage in such conduct only in certain circumstances. In particular, the Commission will consider, on the basis of a summary analysis: (i) the likelihood that this conduct would be clearly, or highly probably, unlawful under Community law,[44] (ii) the likelihood that this illegal conduct could be detected,[45] and (iii) the penalties which could be imposed.

C.
Overall likely impact on effective competition

47. In general, a merger will raise competition concerns because of input foreclosure when it would lead to increased prices in the downstream market thereby significantly impeding effective competition.

48. First, anticompetitive foreclosure may occur when a vertical merger allows the merging parties to increase the costs of downstream rivals in the market thereby leading to an upward pressure on their sales prices. Significant harm to effective competition normally requires that the foreclosed firms play a sufficiently important role in the competitive process on the downstream market. The higher the proportion of rivals which would be foreclosed on the downstream market, the more likely the merger can be expected to result in a significant price increase in the downstream market and, therefore, to significantly impede effective competition therein.[46] Despite a relatively small market share compared to other players, a specific firm may play a significant competitive role compared to other players,[47] for instance because it is a close competitor of the vertically integrated firm or because it is a particularly aggressive competitor.

49. Second, effective competition may be significantly impeded by raising barriers to entry to potential competitors.[48] A vertical merger may foreclose potential competition on the downstream market when the merged entity would be likely not to supply potential downstream entrants, or only on less favourable terms than absent the merger. The mere likelihood that the merged entity would carry out a foreclosure strategy post-merger may already create a strong deterrent effect on potential entrants.[49] Effective competition on the downstream market may be significantly impeded by raising barriers to entry, in particular if input foreclosure would entail for such potential competitors the need to enter at both the downstream and the upstream level in order to compete effectively on either market. The concern of raising entry barriers is particularly relevant in those industries that are opening up to competition or are expected to do so in the foreseeable future.[50]

50. If there remain sufficient credible downstream competitors whose costs are not likely to be raised, for example because they are themselves vertically integrated[51] or they are capable of switching to adequate alternative inputs, competition from those firms may constitute a sufficient constraint on the merged entity and therefore prevent output prices from rising above pre-merger levels.

51. The effect on competition on the downstream market must also be assessed in light of countervailing factors such as the presence of buyer power[52] or the likelihood that entry upstream would maintain effective competition.[53]

52. Further, the effect on competition needs to be assessed in light of efficiencies substantiated by the merging parties.[54] The Commission may decide that, as a consequence of the efficiencies that the merger brings about, there are no grounds for declaring the merger incompatible with the common market pursuant to Article 2(3) of the Merger Regulation. This will be the case when the Commission is in a position to conclude on the basis of sufficient evidence that the efficiencies generated by the merger are likely to enhance the ability and incentive of the merged entity to act pro-competitively for the benefit of consumers, thereby counteracting the adverse effects on competition which the merger might otherwise have.

53. When assessing efficiencies in the context of non-horizontal mergers, the Commission applies the principles already set out in Section VII of the Notice on Horizontal Mergers In particular, for the Commission to take account of efficiency claims in its assessment of the merger, the efficiencies have to benefit consumers, be merger-specific and be verifiable. These conditions are cumulative.[55]

54. Vertical mergers may entail some specific sources of efficiencies, the list of which is not exhaustive.

55. In particular, a vertical merger allows the merged entity to internalise any pre-existing double mark-ups resulting from both parties setting their prices independently premerger.[56] Depending on the market conditions, reducing the combined mark-up (relative to a situation where pricing decisions at both levels are not aligned) may allow the vertically integrated firm to profitably expand output on the downstream market.[57]

56. A vertical merger may further allow the parties to better coordinate the production and distribution process, and therefore to save on inventories costs.

57. More generally, a vertical merger may align the incentives of the parties with regard to investments in new products, new production processes and in the marketing of products. For instance, whereas before the merger, a downstream distributor entity might have been reluctant to invest in advertising and informing customers about the qualities of products of the upstream entity when such investment would also have benefited the sale of other downstream firms, the merged entity may reduce such incentive problems.

2. CUSTOMER FORECLOSURE

58. Customer foreclosure may occur when a supplier integrates with an important customer in the downstream market.[58] Because of this downstream presence, the merged entity may foreclose access to a sufficient customer base to its actual or potential rivals in the upstream market (the input market) and reduce their ability or incentive to compete. In turn, this may raise downstream rivals' costs by making it harder for them to obtain supplies of the input under similar prices and conditions as absent the merger. This may allow the merged entity profitably to establish higher prices on the downstream market. Any efficiencies resulting from the merger, however, may lead the merged entity to reduce price, so that there is overall not a negative impact on consumers. For customer foreclosure to lead to consumer harm, it is thus not necessary that the merged firm's rivals are forced to exit the market. The relevant benchmark is whether the increased input costs would lead to higher prices for consumers. A graphical presentation of this mechanism is provided in Figure 2.

Figure 2 – Customer foreclosure

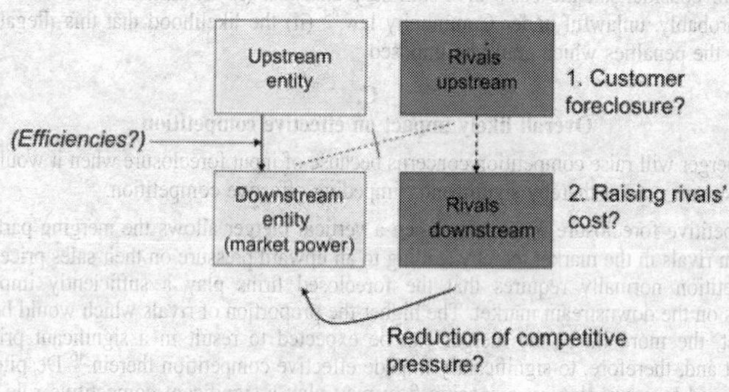

59. In assessing the likelihood of an anticompetitive customer foreclosure scenario, the Commission examines, first, whether the merged entity would have the ability to foreclose access to downstream markets by reducing its purchases from its upstream rivals, second, whether it would have the incentive to reduce its purchases upstream, and third, whether a foreclosure strategy would have a significant detrimental effect on consumers in the downstream market.[59]

A.

Ability to foreclose access to downstream markets

60. A vertical merger may affect upstream competitors by increasing their cost to access downstream customers or by restricting access to a significant customer base. Customer foreclosure may take various forms. For instance, the merged entity may decide to source all of its required goods or services from its upstream division and, as a result, may stop purchasing from its upstream competitors. It may also reduce its purchases from upstream rivals, or purchase from those rivals on less favourable terms than it would have done absent the merger.[60]

61. When considering whether the merged entity would have the ability to foreclose access to downstream markets, the Commission examines whether there are sufficient economic alternatives in the downstream market for the upstream rivals (actual or potential) to sell their output.[61] For customer foreclosure to be a concern, it must be the case that the vertical merger involves a company which is an important customer with a significant degree of market power in the downstream market.[62] If, on the contrary, there is a sufficiently large customer base, at present or in the future, that is likely to turn to independent suppliers, the Commission is unlikely to raise competition concerns on that ground.[63]

62. Customer foreclosure can lead to higher input prices in particular if there are significant economies of scale or scope in the input market or when demand is characterised by network effects.[64] It is mainly in such circumstances that the ability to compete of upstream rivals, be they actual or potential, can be impaired.

63. For instance, customer foreclosure can lead to higher input prices when existing upstream rivals operate at or close to their minimum efficient scale. To the extent that customer foreclosure and the corresponding loss of output for the upstream rivals increases their variable costs of production, this may result in an upward pressure on the prices they charge to their customers operating in the downstream market.

64. In the presence of economies of scale or scope, customer foreclosure may also render entry upstream by potential entrants unattractive by significantly reducing the revenue prospects of potential entrants. When customer foreclosure effectively results in entry deterrence, input prices may remain at a higher level than otherwise would have been the case, thereby raising the cost of input supply to downstream competitors of the merged firm.

65. Further, when customer foreclosure primarily impacts upon the revenue streams of upstream rivals, it may significantly reduce their ability and incentive to invest in cost reduction, R&D and product quality.[65] This may reduce their ability to compete in the long run and possibly even cause their exit from the market.

66. In its assessment, the Commission may take into account the existence of different markets corresponding to different uses for the input. If a substantial part of the downstream market is foreclosed, an upstream supplier may fail to reach efficient scale and may also operate at higher costs in the other market(s). Conversely, an upstream supplier may continue to operate efficiently if it finds other uses or secondary markets for its input without incurring significantly higher costs.

67. In its assessment, the Commission will consider, on the basis of the information available, whether there are effective and timely counter-strategies, sustainable over time, that the rival firms would be likely to deploy. Such counterstrategies include the possibility that upstream rivals decide to price more aggressively to maintain sales levels in the downstream market, so as to mitigate the effect of foreclosure.[66]

B.
Incentive to foreclose access to downstream markets

68. The incentive to foreclose depends on the degree to which it is profitable. The merged entity faces a trade-off between the possible costs associated with not procuring products from upstream rivals and the possible gains from doing so, for instance, because it allows the merged entity to raise price in the upstream or downstream markets.

69. The costs associated with reducing purchases from rival upstream suppliers are higher, when the upstream division of the integrated firm is less efficient than the foreclosed suppliers. Such costs are also higher if the upstream division of the merged firm is capacity constrained or rivals' products are more attractive due to product differentiation.

70. The incentive to engage in customer foreclosure further depends on the extent to which the upstream division of the merged entity can benefit from possibly higher price levels in the upstream market arising as a result of upstream rivals being foreclosed. The incentive to engage in customer foreclosure also becomes higher, the more the downstream division of the integrated firm can be expected to enjoy the benefits of higher price levels downstream resulting from the foreclosure strategy. In this context, the greater the market shares of the merged entity's downstream operations, the greater the base of sales on which to enjoy increased margins.[67]

71. When the adoption of a specific conduct by the merged entity is an essential step in foreclosure, the Commission examines both the incentives to adopt such conduct and the factors liable to reduce, or even eliminate, those incentives, including the possibility that the conduct is unlawful.[68]

C.
Overall likely impact on effective competition

72. Foreclosing rivals in the upstream market may have an adverse impact in the downstream market and harm consumers. By denying competitive access to a significant customer base for the foreclosed rivals' (upstream) products, the merger may reduce their ability to compete in the foreseeable future. As a result, rivals downstream are likely to be put at a competitive disadvantage, for example in the form of raised input costs. In turn, this may allow the merged entity to profitably raise prices or reduce the overall output on the downstream market.

73. The negative impact on consumers may take some time to materialise when the primary impact of customer foreclosure is on the revenue streams of upstream rivals, reducing their incentives to make investments in cost reduction, product quality or in other competitive dimensions so as to remain competitive.

74. It is only when a sufficiently large fraction of upstream output is affected by the revenue decreases resulting from the vertical merger that the merger may significantly impede effective competition on the upstream market. If there remain a number of upstream competitors that are not affected, competition from those firms may be sufficient to prevent prices from rising in the upstream market and, consequently, in the downstream market. Sufficient competition from these non-foreclosed upstream firms requires that they do not face barriers to expansion eg through capacity constraints or product differentiation.[69] When the reduction of competition upstream affects a significant fraction of output downstream, the merger is likely, as with input foreclosure, to result in a significant increase of the price level in the downstream market and, therefore, to significantly impede effective competition.[70]

75. Effective competition on the upstream market may also be significantly impeded by raising barriers to entry to potential competitors. This may be so in particular if customer foreclosure would entail for such potential competitors the need to enter at both the downstream and the upstream level in order to compete effectively on either market. In such a context, customer foreclosure and input foreclosure may thus be part of the same strategy. The concern of raising entry barriers is particularly relevant in those industries that are opening up to competition or are expected to do so in the foreseeable future.[71]

76. The effect on competition must be assessed in light of countervailing factors such as the presence of countervailing buyer power[72] or the likelihood that entry would maintain effective competition in the upstream or downstream markets.[73]

77. Further, the effect on competition needs to be assessed in light of efficiencies substantiated by the merging parties.[74]

B. OTHER NON-COORDINATED EFFECTS

78. The merged entity may, by vertically integrating, gain access to commercially sensitive information regarding the upstream or downstream activities of rivals.[75] For instance, by becoming the supplier of a downstream competitor, a company may obtain critical information, which allows it to price less aggressively in the downstream market to the detriment of consumers.[76] It may also put competitors at a competitive disadvantage, thereby dissuading them to enter or expand in the market.

C. COORDINATED EFFECTS

79. As set out in Section IV of the Notice on Horizontal Mergers, a merger may change the nature of competition in such a way that firms that previously were not coordinating their behaviour, are now significantly more likely to coordinate and raise prices or otherwise harm effective competition. A merger may also make coordination easier, more stable or more effective for firms which were coordinating prior to the merger.[77]

80. Market coordination may arise where competitors are able, without entering into an agreement or resorting to a concerted practice within the meaning of Article 81 of the Treaty, to identify and pursue common objectives, avoiding the normal mutual competitive pressure by a coherent system of implicit threats. In a normal competitive setting, each firm constantly has an incentive to compete. This incentive is ultimately what keeps prices low, and what prevents firms from jointly maximising their profits. Coordination involves a departure from normal competitive conditions in that firms are able to sustain prices in excess of what independent short term profit maximisation would yield. Firms will refrain from undercutting the high prices charged by their competitors in a coordinated way because they anticipate that such behaviour would jeopardise coordination in the future. For coordinated effects to arise, the profit that firms could make by competing aggressively in the short term ("deviating") has to be less than the expected reduction in revenues that this behaviour would entail in the longer term, as it would be expected to trigger an aggressive response by competitors ("a punishment").

81. Coordination is more likely to emerge in markets where it is relatively simple to reach a common understanding on the terms of coordination. In addition, three conditions are necessary for coordination to be sustainable. First, the coordinating firms must be able to monitor to a sufficient degree whether the terms of coordination are being adhered to. Second, discipline requires that there is some form of deterrent mechanism that can be activated if deviation is detected. Third, the reactions of outsiders, such as current and future competitors not participating in the coordination, as well as customers, should not be able to jeopardise the results expected from the coordination.[78]

Reaching terms of coordination

82. A vertical merger may make it easier for the firms in the upstream or downstream market to reach a common understanding on the terms of coordination.[79]

83. For instance, when a vertical merger leads to foreclosure,[80] it results in a reduction in the number of effective competitors in the market. Generally speaking, a reduction in the number of players makes it easier to coordinate among the remaining market players.

84. Vertical mergers may also increase the degree of symmetry between firms active in the market.[81] This may increase the likelihood of coordination by making it easier to reach a common understanding on the terms of coordination. Likewise, vertical integration may increase the level of market transparency, making it easier to coordinate among the remaining market players.

85. Further, a merger may involve the elimination of a maverick in a market. A maverick is a supplier that for its own reasons is unwilling to accept the co-ordinated outcome and thus maintains aggressive competition. The vertical integration of the maverick may alter its incentives to such an extent that co-ordination will no longer be prevented.

Monitoring deviations

86. Vertical integration may facilitate coordination by increasing the level of market transparency between firms through access to sensitive information on rivals or by making it easier to monitor pricing. Such concerns may arise, for example, if the level of price transparency is higher downstream than upstream. This could be the case when prices to final consumers are public, while transactions at the intermediate market are confidential. Vertical integration may give upstream producers control over final prices and thus monitor deviations more effectively.

87. When it leads to foreclosure, a vertical merger may also induce a reduction in the number of effective competitors in a market. A reduction in the number of players may make it easier to monitor each other's actions in the market.

Deterrent mechanisms

88. Vertical mergers may affect coordinating firms' incentives to adhere to the terms of coordination. For instance, a vertically integrated company may be in a position to more effectively punish rival companies when they choose to deviate from the terms of coordination, because it is either a crucial customer or supplier to them.[82]

Reactions of outsiders

89. Vertical mergers may reduce the scope for outsiders to destabilise the coordination by increasing barriers to enter the market or otherwise limiting the ability to compete on the part of outsiders to the coordination.

90. A vertical merger may also involve the elimination of a disruptive buyer in a market. If upstream firms view sales to a particular buyer as sufficiently important, they may be tempted to deviate from the terms of co-ordination in an effort to secure their business. Similarly, a large buyer may be able to tempt the co-ordinating firms to deviate from these terms by concentrating a large amount of its requirements on one supplier or by offering long term contracts. The acquisition of such a buyer may increase the risk of co-ordination in a market.

NOTES

21 For the meaning of the expression "increased prices" see footnote 8. For the meaning of "consumers", see paragraph 16.

22 See Merger Regulation, Article 2(1)(b), referring to "*access to supplies*" and "*access to [. . .] markets*", respectively.

23 See eg Case COMP/M.4300 – *Philips/Intermagnetics*, COMP/ M.4314 – *Johnson & Johnson/Pfizer Consumer Healthcare*, COMP/M.4389 – WLR/BST, COMP/ M.4403 – *Thales/Finmeccanica/Alcatel Alenia Space and Telespazio*, COMP/ M.4494 – *Evraz/Highveld*, and COMP/M.4561 – *GE/ Smiths Aerospace*.

24 The term "inputs" is used here as a generic term and may also cover services, access to infrastructure and access to intellectual property rights.

25 See eg Case COMP/M.1693 – *Alcoa/Reynolds* (2000), Case COMP/M.4403 – *Thales/ Finmeccanica/ Alcatel Alenia Space/ Telespazio*, points 257–260.

26 See, eg, Case COMP/M.2861 – *Siemens/Drägerwerk*/JV (2003), Case COMP/M.3998 *Axalto*, point 75.

27 See, eg, Case COMP/M.4314 – *Johnson & Johnson/ Pfizer Consumer Healthcare*, points 127–130

28 See, eg, Case COMP/M.3868 *Dong/Elsam/Energi E2*, Case COMP/M.4094 *Ineos/ BP Dormagen*, points 183–184, Case COMP/M.4561, *GE/Smiths Aerospace*, points 48–50.

29 For instance, an engine starter can be considered a critical component to an engine (Case T-210/01, *General Electric v. Commission* [2005], ECR II-000); see also, eg, Case COMP/M.3410 – *Total/GDF*, points 53–54 and 60–61.

30 For instance, personal computers are often sold with specific reference to the type of microprocessor they contain.

31 See, eg, Case COMP/M.4494 *Evraz/ Highveld*, point 92 and points 97–112.

32 The analysis of the likely effect of the removal of a competitive constraint is similar to the analysis of non-coordinated effects with horizontal mergers (See Section IV of the Notice on Horizontal Mergers)

33 Also the nature of the supply contracts between upstream suppliers and the downstream independent firms may be important in this respect. For instance, when these contracts use a price system combining a fixed fee and a per-unit supply price, the effect on downstream competitors' marginal costs may be affected less than when these contracts involve only per-unit supply prices.

34 See, eg, Case COMP/M.4300 – *Philips/ Intermagnetics*, points 56–62, Case COMP/M.4576 – *AVR/ Van Gansewinkel*, points 33–38.

35 It has to be considered that upstream and downstream margins may change as a result of the merger. This may impact upon the merged entity's incentive to engage in foreclosure.

36 See, eg Case COMP/M.3943 – *Saint-Gobain/BPB* (2005), point 78. The Commission noted that it would be very unlikely that BPB, the main supplier of plaster board in the UK, would cut back on supplies to rival distributors of Saint-Gobain, in part because expansion of Saint-Gobain's distribution capacity was difficult.

37 Conversely, if the input accounts only for a small share of the downstream product and is not a critical component, even a high market share upstream may not give the merged entity the incentive to foreclose downstream rivals because few, if any, sales would be diverted to the integrated firm's downstream unit. See, eg Case COMP/M.2738 *GEES/ Unison*; Case COMP M.4561, *GE/Smiths Aerospace*, points 60–62.

38 See, eg, Case COMP/M.4314 – *Johnson & Johnson/ Pfizer Consumer Healthcare*, points 131–132

39 It must be noted that the less the merged firm can target a specific downstream market, the less it is likely to raise its prices for the input it supplies, as it would have to incur opportunity costs in other downstream markets. In this respect, the extent to which the merged entity can price discriminate when the merged entity supplies several downstream markets and/or ancillary markets may be taken into account (eg for spare parts).

40 One situation in which this may not be the case would be when the monopolist has a so-called commitment problem which it is unable to solve. For example, a downstream buyer may be willing to pay a high price to an upstream monopolist if the latter does not subsequently sell additional quantities to a competitor. But once the terms of supply are fixed with one downstream firm, the upstream supplier may have an incentive to increase its supplies to other downstream firms, thereby making the first purchase unprofitable. Since downstream firms will anticipate this kind of opportunistic behaviour, the upstream supplier will be unable to fully exploit its market power. Vertical integration may restore the upstream supplier's ability to commit not to expand input sales as this would harm its own downstream division. Another case in which the monopolist cannot obtain all available monopoly profits may arise when the company cannot differentiate its prices among customers.

41 For instance, in cases where two companies have joint control over a firm active in the upstream market, and only one of them is active downstream, the company without downstream activities may have little interest in foregoing input sales. In such cases, the incentive to foreclose is smaller than when the upstream company is fully controlled by a company with downstream activities. See eg Case COMP/M.3440 – *EDP/ENI/GDP* (2004), Case COMP/M.4403 – *Thales/ Finmeccanica/ Alcatel Alenia Space/ Telespazio*, points 121 and 268.

42 The fact that, in the past, a competitor with a similar market position as the merged entity has stopped supplying inputs may demonstrate that it is commercially rational to adopt such a strategy (See eg *Alcan/Pechiney*, M. 3225 (2004), at point 40).

43 Case C-12/03 P, *Commission v. Tetra Laval BV*, ECR I-000, paragraphs 74–76. Case T-210/01, *General Electric v. Commission* [2005], ECR II-000, at paragraph 73.

44 Case T-210/01, *General Electric v. Commission* [2005], ECR II-000, specifically at points 74–75 and 311–312.

45 For instance, in Case M.3696 *E.ON/MOL* (2005), points 433 and 443–446, the Commission attached importance to the fact that the national Hungarian regulator for the gas sector indicated that in a number of settings, although it has the right to control and to force market players to act without discrimination, it would not be able to obtain adequate information on the commercial behaviour of the operators. See also Case COMP/M.3440 – *EDP/ENI/GDP* (2004), point 424.

46 See, eg, Case COMP/M.4494 *Evraz/ Highveld*, points 97–112.

47 See eg Case COMP/M.3440 – *EDP/ENI/GDP* (2004).

48 See, eg, Case COMP/M.4180 *Gaz de France/ Suez*, points 876–931, Case COMP/M.4576 – *AVR/ Van Gansewinkel*, points 33–38.

49 See Case COMP/M.3696 – *E.ON/MOL* (2005), at point 662 et seq.

50 See paragraph 20. It is important that regulatory measures aimed at opening a market are not rendered ineffective through vertically-related incumbent companies merging and thereby closing off the market, or eliminating each other as potential entrants.

51 See eg Case COMP/M.3653 – *Siemens/VA Tech* (2005), at point 164.

52 See Section V on countervailing buyer power in the Notice on Horizontal Mergers.

53 See Section VI on entry in the Notice on Horizontal Mergers.

54 See Section VII on efficiencies in the Notice on Horizontal Mergers.

55 See, more specifically, paragraphs 79 to 88 of the Notice on Horizontal Mergers.

56 See also paragraph 13 above.

57 It is important to recognise, however, that the problem of double mark-ups is not always present or significant pre-merger, for instance because the merging parties had already concluded a supply agreement with a price mechanism providing for volume discounts eliminating the mark-up. The efficiencies associated with the elimination of double

mark-ups may thus not always be merger specific because vertical cooperation or vertical agreements may, short of a merger, achieve similar benefits with less anti-competitive effects. In addition, a merger may not fully eliminate the double mark-up when the supply of the input is limited by capacity constraints and there is an equally profitable alternative use for the input. In such circumstances, the internal use of the input entails an opportunity cost for the vertically integrated company: using more of the input internally to increase output downstream means selling less in the alternative market. As a result, the incentive to use the input internally and increase output downstream is less than when there is no opportunity cost.

58 See footnote 4 for the definition of "downstream" and "upstream".

59 See eg Case COMP/M.4389 – *WLR/ BST*.

60 For instance, in cases involving distribution, the merged entity may be less likely to grant access to its outlets under the same conditions as absent the merger.

61 The loss of the integrated firm as a customer is normally less significant if that firm's pre-merger purchases from non-integrated firms are a small share of the available sales base for those firms. In that case, sufficient alternative customers are more likely to be available. The presence of exclusive contracts between the merged entity and other downstream firms may limit the ability of upstream rivals to reach a sufficient sales volume.

62 See eg Case COMP/M.2822 – *ENBW/ENI/GVS* (2002) at points 54–57.

63 See eg Case COMP/M.81 – *VIAG/Continental Can* (1991), point 51, See, eg, Case COMP/M.4389 – WLR/ BST, points 33–35.

64 Economies of scale or scope exist when an increase in scale or scope of production leads to a reduction in average unit cost. Network effects occur when the value of a product for a customer increases when the number of other customers also using it increases. Examples include communication devices, specific software programmes, products requiring standardisation, and platforms bringing together buyers and sellers.

65 An input supplier foreclosed from an important customer may prefer to stay out of the market if it fails to reach some minimum viable scale following the investment. Such minimum viable scale may be achieved, however, if a potential entrant has access to a broader customer base including customers in other relevant markets. See Case No COMP/M. 1879 – *Boeing/Hughes* (2000); Case No COMP/M.2978 – *Lagardère/Natexis/VU*P (2003);

66 For instance, in Case COMP/M.1879 – *Boeing/Hughes* (2000), point 100, it was considered, among several other factors, that in view of the high fixed costs involved, if competing satellite launch vehicle providers were to become less cost-competitive relative to the merged entity, they would try to cut prices in order to salvage volume and recoup at least part of their fixed costs rather than accept losing a contract and incur a higher loss. The most likely impact would therefore be greater price competition rather than market monopolisation.

67 If the vertically integrated firm partially supplies inputs to downstream competitors it may benefit from the ability to expand sales, or as the case may be, to increase input prices.

68 The analysis of these incentives will be conducted as set out in paragraph 46 above.

69 The analysis of such non-coordinated effects bears similarities with the analysis of non-coordinated effects in horizontal mergers (See Section IV of the Notice on Horizontal Mergers).

70 See paragraph 47–50 of the present Notice.

71 It is important that regulatory measures aimed at opening a market are not rendered ineffective through vertically-related incumbent companies merging and thereby closing off the market, or eliminating each other as potential entrants.

72 See Section V on countervailing buyer power in the Notice on Horizontal Mergers.

73 See Section VI on entry in the Notice on Horizontal Mergers.

74 For the assessment of efficiencies in a vertical context, see Section V.A.1 above.

75 See Case COMP/M.1879 – *Boeing/Hughes* (2000); Case COMP/M.2510 – *Cendant/Galileo*, point 37; Case COMP/M.2738 – *Gees/Unison*, point 21; Case COMP/M.2925 – *Charterhouse/CDC/Telediffusion de France*, point 37–38; Case COMP/M.3440 – *EDP/ENL/GDP* (2004).

76 See eg Case COMP/M.2822 – *ENBW/ENI/GVS* (2002), at point 56; Case COMP/M.3440 – *EDP/ENI/GDP* (2004), points 368–379; Case COMP/M.3653 – *Siemens/VA Tech* (2005) points 159–164.

77 See Case COMP/M.3101 – *Accor/Hilton/Six Continents*, points 23–28.

78 See Case T-342/99, *Airtours v Commission*, [2002] ECR II-2585, paragraph 62.

79 See, eg, Case COMP/M.3314 – *Air Liquide/ Messer Targets*, points 91–100

80 Foreclosure would have to be shown by the Commission along the lines of Part A of this section.

81 See Case COMP/M.2389 – *Shell/DEA*; Case COMP/M.2533 – *BP/EON*. Alternatively, vertical integration may also decrease the degree of symmetry between firms active in the market, rendering coordination more difficult.

82 For instance, in a case that was subsequently withdrawn (Case COMP/M.2322 – *CRH/Addtek* (2001)) the merger involved an upstream dominant supplier of cement and a downstream producer or pre-cast concrete products, both active in Finland. The Commission provisionally took the view in the administrative procedure that the new entity would be able to discipline the downstream rivals by using the fact that they would be highly dependent on cement supplies of the merged entity. As a result, the downstream entity would be able to increase the price of its pre-cast concrete products while making sure that the competitors would follow these price increases and avoiding that they turn to cement imports from the Baltic states and Russia.

V. CONGLOMERATE MERGERS

[4.709]

91. Conglomerate mergers are mergers between firms that are in a relationship which is neither purely horizontal (as competitors in the same relevant market) nor vertical (as supplier and customer). In practice, the focus is on mergers between companies that are active in closely related markets[83] (eg mergers involving suppliers of complementary products or of products which belong to a range of products that is generally purchased by the same set of customers for the same end use).

92. Whereas it is acknowledged that conglomerate mergers in the majority of circumstances will not lead to any competition problems, in certain specific cases there may be harm to competition. In its assessment, the Commission will consider both the possible anti-competitive effects arising from conglomerate mergers and the possible pro-competitive effects stemming from efficiencies substantiated by the parties.

A. NON-COORDINATED EFFECTS: FORECLOSURE

93. The main concern in the context of conglomerate mergers is that of foreclosure. The combination of products in related markets may confer on the merged entity the ability and incentive to leverage[84] a strong market position from one market to another by means of tying or bundling or other exclusionary practices.[85] Tying and bundling as such are common practices that often have no anticompetitive consequences. Companies engage in tying and bundling in order to provide their customers with better products or offerings in cost-effective ways. Nevertheless, in certain circumstances, these practices may lead to a reduction in actual or potential rivals' ability or incentive to compete. This may reduce the competitive pressure on the merged entity allowing it to increase prices.

94. In assessing the likelihood of such a scenario, the Commission examines, first, whether the merged firm would have the ability to foreclose its rivals, second, whether it would have the economic incentive to do so and, third, whether a foreclosure strategy would have a significant detrimental effect on competition, thus causing harm to consumers.[86] In practice, these factors are often examined together as they are closely intertwined.

A.
Ability to foreclose

95. The most immediate way in which the merged entity may be able to use its market power in one market to foreclose competitors in another is by conditioning sales in a way that links the products in the separate markets together. This is done most directly either by tying or bundling.

96. "Bundling" usually refers to the way products are offered and priced by the merged entity. One can distinguish in this respect between pure bundling and mixed bundling. In the case of pure bundling the products are only sold jointly in fixed proportions. With mixed bundling the products are also available separately, but the sum of the stand-alone prices is higher than the bundled price.[87] Rebates, when made dependent on the purchase of other goods, may be considered a form of mixed bundling.

97. "Tying" usually refers to situations where customers that purchase one good (the tying good) are required to also purchase another good from the producer (the tied good). Tying can take place on a technical or contractual basis. For instance, technical tying occurs when the tying product is designed in such a way that it only works with the tied product (and not with the alternatives offered by competitors). Contractual tying entails that the customer when purchasing the tying good undertakes only to purchase the tied product (and not the alternatives offered by competitors).

98. The specific characteristics of the products may be relevant for determining whether any of these means of linking sales between separate markets are available to the merged entity. For instance, pure bundling is very unlikely to be possible if products are not bought simultaneously or by the same customers.[88] Similarly, technical tying is only an option in certain industries.

99. In order to be able to foreclose competitors, the new entity must have a significant degree of market power, which does not necessarily amount to dominance, in one of the markets concerned. The effects of bundling or tying can only be expected to be substantial when at least one of the merging parties' products is viewed by many customers as particularly important and there are few relevant alternatives for that product, eg because of product differentiation[89] or capacity constraints on the part of rivals.

100. Further, for foreclosure to be a potential concern it must be the case that there is a large common pool of customers for the individual products concerned. The more customers tend to buy both products (instead of only one of the products), the more demand for the individual products may be affected through bundling or tying. Such a correspondence in purchasing behaviour is more likely to be significant when the products in question are complementary.

101. Generally speaking, the foreclosure effects of bundling and tying are likely to be more pronounced in industries where there are economies of scale and the demand pattern at any given point in time has dynamic implications for the conditions of supply in the market in the future. Notably, where a supplier of complementary goods has market power in one of the products (product A), the decision to bundle or tie may result in reduced sales by the non-integrated suppliers of the complementary good (product B). If further there are network externalities at play[90] this will significantly reduce these rivals' scope for expanding sales of product B in the future. Alternatively, where entry into the market for the complementary product is contemplated by potential entrants, the decision to bundle by the merged entity may have the effect of deterring such entry. The limited availability of complementary products with which to combine may, in turn, discourage potential entrants to enter market A.

102. It can also be noted that the scope for foreclosure tends to be smaller where the merging parties cannot commit to making their tying or bundling strategy a lasting one, for example through technical tying or bundling which is costly to reverse.

103. In its assessment, the Commission considers, on the basis of the information available, whether there are effective and timely counter-strategies that the rival firms may deploy. One such example is when a strategy of bundling would be defeated by single product companies combining their offers so as to make them more attractive to customers.[91] Bundling is further less likely to lead to foreclosure if a company in the market would purchase the bundled products and profitably resell them unbundled. In addition, rivals may decide to price more aggressively to maintain market share, mitigating the effect of foreclosure.[92]

104. Customers may have a strong incentive to buy the range of products concerned from a single source (one-stop-shopping) rather than from many suppliers, eg because it saves on transaction costs. The fact that the merged entity will have a broad range or portfolio of products does not, as such, raise competition concerns.[93]

B.
Incentive to foreclose

105. The incentive to foreclose rivals through bundling or tying depends on the degree to which this strategy is profitable. The merged entity faces a trade-off between the possible costs associated with bundling or tying its products and the possible gains from expanding market shares in the market(s) concerned or, as the case may be, being able to raise price in those market(s) due to its market power.

106. Pure bundling and tying may entail losses for the merged company itself. For instance, if a significant number of customers are not interested in buying the bundle, but instead prefers to buy only one product (eg the product used to leverage), sales of that product (as contained in the bundle) may significantly fall. Furthermore, losses on the leveraging product may arise where customers who, before the merger, used to "mix and match" the leveraging product of a merging party with the product of another company, decide to purchase the bundle offered by rivals or no longer to purchase at all.[94]

107. In this context it may thus be relevant to assess the relative value of the different products. By way of example, it is unlikely that the merged entity would be willing to forego sales on one highly profitable market in order to gain market shares on another market where turnover is relatively small and profits are modest.

108. However, the decision to bundle and tie may also increase profits by gaining market power in the tied goods market, protecting market power in the tying goods market, or a combination of the two (See Section C below).

109. In its assessment of the likely incentives of the merged firm, the Commission may take into account other factors such as the ownership structure of the merged entity,[95] the type of strategies adopted on the market in the past or the content of internal strategic documents such as business plans.

110. When the adoption of a specific conduct by the merged entity is an essential step in foreclosure, the Commission examines both the incentives to adopt such conduct and the factors liable to reduce, or even eliminate, those incentives, including the possibility that the conduct is unlawful.[96]

C.
Overall likely impact on prices and choice

111. Bundling or tying may result in a significant reduction of sales prospects faced by single-component rivals in the market. The reduction in sales by competitors is not in and of itself a problem. Yet, in particular industries, if this reduction is significant enough, it may lead to a reduction in rivals' ability or incentive to compete. This may allow the merged entity to subsequently acquire market power (in the market for the tied or bundled good) and/or to maintain market power (in the market for the tying or leveraging good).

112. In particular, foreclosure practices may deter entry by potential competitors. They may do so for a specific market by reducing sales prospects for potential rivals in that market to a level below minimum viable scale. In the case of complementary products, deterring entry in one market through bundling or tying may also allow the merged entity to deter entry in another market if the bundling or tying forces potential competitors to enter both product markets at the same time rather than entering only one of them or entering them sequentially. The latter may have a significant impact in particular in those industries where the demand pattern at any given point in time has dynamic implications for the conditions of supply in the market in the future.

113. It is only when a sufficiently large fraction of market output is affected by foreclosure resulting from the merger that the merger may significantly impede effective competition. If there remain effective single-product players in either market, competition is unlikely to deteriorate following a conglomerate merger. The same holds when few single-product rivals remain, but these have the ability and incentive to expand output.

114. The effect on competition needs to be assessed in light of countervailing factors such as the presence of countervailing buyer power[97] or the likelihood that entry would maintain effective competition in the upstream or downstream markets.[98]

115. Further, the effect on competition needs to be assessed in light of the efficiencies substantiated by the merging parties.[99]

116. Many of the efficiencies identified in the context of vertical mergers may, mutatis mutandis, also apply to conglomerate mergers involving complementary products.

117. Notably, when producers of complementary goods are pricing independently, they will not take into account the positive effect of a drop in the price of their product on the sales of the other product. Depending on the market conditions, a merged firm may internalise this effect and may have a certain incentive to lower margins if this leads to higher overall profits (this incentive is often referred to as the "Cournot effect"). In most cases, the merged firm will make the most out of this effect by means of mixed bundling, ie by making the price drop conditional upon whether or not the customer buys both products from the merged entity.[100]

118. Specific to conglomerate mergers is that they may produce cost savings in the form of economies of scope (either on the production or the consumption side), yielding an inherent advantage to supplying the goods together rather than apart.[101] For instance, it may be more efficient that certain components are marketed together as a bundle rather than separately. Value enhancements for the customer can result from better compatibility and quality assurance of complementary components. Such economies of scope however are necessary but not sufficient to provide an efficiency justification for bundling or tying. Indeed, benefits from economies of scope frequently can be realised without any need for technical or contractual bundling.

B. CO-ORDINATED EFFECTS

119. Conglomerate mergers may in certain circumstances facilitate anticompetitive coordination in markets, even in the absence of an agreement or a concerted practice within the meaning of Article 81 of the Treaty. The framework set out in Section IV of the Notice on Horizontal Mergers also applies in this context. In particular, coordination is more likely to emerge in markets where it is fairly easy to identify the terms of co-ordination and where such co-ordination is sustainable.

120. One way in which a conglomerate merger may influence the likelihood of a coordinated outcome in a given market is by reducing the number of effective competitors to such an extent that tacit coordination becomes a real possibility. Also when rivals are not excluded from the market, they may find themselves in a more vulnerable situation. As a result, foreclosed rivals may choose not to contest the situation of co-ordination, but may prefer instead to live under the shelter of the increased price level.

121. Further, a conglomerate merger may increase the extent and importance of multi-market competition. Competitive interaction on several markets may increase the scope and effectiveness of disciplining mechanisms in ensuring that the terms of coordination are being adhered to.

NOTES

83 See also Form CO, Section IV, 6.3 (c).

84 There is no received definition of "leveraging" but, in a neutral sense, it implies being able to increase sales of a product in one market (the "tied market" or "bundled market"), by virtue of the strong market position of the product to which it is tied or bundled (the "tying market" or "leveraging market").

85 These concepts are defined further below.

86 See Case T-210/01, *General Electric v Commission*, [2005], ECR II-000, paragraphs 327, 362–363, 405; Case COMP/M.3304 – *GE/Amersham* (2004), point 37, and Case COMP/M.4561 – *GE/Smiths Aerospace*, points 116–126.

87 The distinction between mixed bundling and pure bundling is not necessarily clear-cut. Mixed bundling may come close to pure bundling when the prices charged for the individual offerings are high.

88 See, eg, Case COMP.M.3304 – *GE/Amersham* (2004), point 35.

89 For instance, in the context of branded products, particularly important products are sometimes referred to as "must stock" products. See, eg, Case COMP/M.3732 – *Procter&Gamble/Gillette* (2005), point 110.

90 When a product features network externalities, this means that customers or producers derive benefit from the fact that other customers or producers are using the same products as well. Examples include communication devices, specific software programmes, products requiring standardisation, and platforms bringing together buyers and sellers.

91 See, eg, Case COMP/M.3304 – *GE/Amersham* (2004), point 39.

92 See, eg, Case COMP/M.1879 – *Boeing/Hughes* (2000), point 100; Case COMP/M.3304 – *GE/Amersham* (2004), point 39. The resulting loss of revenues may, however, in certain circumstances, have an impact on the ability of rivals to compete. See Section C.

93 See, eg, Case COMP/M.2608 – *INA/ FAG*, point 34

94 See, eg, Case COMP/M.3304 – *GE/Amersham* (2004), point 59.

95 For instance, in cases where two companies have joint control over a firm active in one market, and only one of them is active on the neighbouring market, the company without activities on the latter market may have little interest in foregoing sales in the former market. See eg Case T-210/01, *General Electric v Commission*, [2005], ECR II-000, paragraph 385 and Case COMP M.4561, *GE/Smiths Aerospace*, point 119.

96 The analysis of these incentives will be conducted as set out in paragraph 46 above.

97 See Section V on countervailing buyer power in the Notice on Horizontal Mergers.

98 See, eg, Case COMP/M.3732 – *Procter&Gamble/Gillette* (2005), point 131. See also Section VI on entry in the Notice on Horizontal Mergers.

99 See Section VII on efficiencies in the Notice on Horizontal Mergers.

100 It is important to recognise however that the problem of double mark-ups is not always present or significant pre-merger. In the context of mixed bundling, it must further be noted that while the merged entity may have an incentive to reduce the price for the bundle, the effect on the prices of the individual products is less clear cut. The incentive for the merged entity to raise its single product prices may come from the fact that it counts on selling more bundled products instead. The merged entity's bundle price and prices of the individually sold products (if any) will further depend on the price reactions of rivals in the market.

101 See, eg, Case COMP/M.3732 – *Procter&Gamble/Gillette* (2005), point 131.

COMMISSION NOTICE

(2008/C267/01)

on remedies acceptable under Council Regulation (EC) No 139/2004 and under Commission Regulation (EC) No 802/2004

(Text with EEA relevance)

[4.710]

NOTES

Date of publication in OJ: OJ C267, 22.10.2008, p 1.

Note that Council Regulation 139/2004/EC and Commission Regulation 802/2004/EC are repealed, in their application to the UK, by the Competition (Amendment etc) (EU Exit) Regulations 2019, SI 2019/93, reg 63, Sch 3, paras 1,2, as from IP completion day (as defined in the European Union (Withdrawal Agreement) Act 2020, s 39) (for transitional provisions and savings in relation to the operation of the 2019 Regulations, see Sch 4 to those Regulations at **[7.69]** et seq).

I. INTRODUCTION

[4.711]

1. Council Regulation (EC) No 139/2004 of 20 January 2004 on the control of concentrations between undertakings[1] (hereinafter referred to as "the Merger Regulation") in Articles 6(2) and 8(2) expressly provides that the Commission may decide to declare a concentration compatible with the common market following modification by the parties,[2] both before and after the initiation of proceedings. To that end, the Commission may attach to its decision conditions and obligations intended to ensure that the undertakings concerned comply with the commitments they have entered into vis-à-vis the Commission with a view to rendering the concentration compatible with the common market.[3]

2. The purpose of this Notice is to provide guidance on modifications to concentrations, in particular commitments by the undertakings concerned to modify a concentration. Such modifications are more commonly described as "remedies" since their object is to eliminate the competition concerns[4] identified by the Commission. The guidance set out in this Notice reflects the Commission's evolving experience with the assessment, acceptance and implementation of remedies under the Merger Regulation since its entry into force on 21 September 1990. The revision of the Commission's 2001 Notice on remedies[5] is entailed by the entry into force of the recast Merger Regulation (EC) No 139/2004[6] and of Commission Regulation (EC) No 802/2004 (the "Implementing Regulation")[7] on 1 May 2004, case-law of the Court of Justice and the Court of First Instance, the conclusions drawn from the systematic ex post review of the Commission of past remedies case,[8] and decisional practice of the Commission in cases involving remedies in recent years. The principles contained herein will be applied and further developed and refined by the Commission in individual cases. The guidance provided in this Notice is without prejudice to the interpretation which may be given by the Court of Justice or by the Court of First Instance of the European Communities.

3. This Notice sets out the general principles applicable to remedies acceptable to the Commission, the main types of commitments that may be accepted by the Commission in cases under the Merger Regulation, the specific requirements which proposals of commitments need to fulfil in both phases of the procedure, and the main requirements for the implementation of commitments. In any case, the Commission will take due account of the particular circumstances of the individual case.

NOTES

1 OJ L24, 29.1.2004, p 1-22.

2 The references to "parties" and "merging parties" also cover situations with one notifying party.

3 Articles 6(2) and 8(2), second subparagraphs respectively. See also Recital 30 of the Merger Regulation which states that "where the undertakings concerned modify a notified concentration, in particular by offering commitments with a view to rendering the concentration compatible with the common market, the Commission should be able to declare the concentration, as modified, compatible with the common market. Such commitments should be proportionate to the competition problem and entirely eliminate it". Recital 30 further explains that "it is also appropriate to accept commitments before the initiation of proceedings where the competition problem is readily identifiable and can easily be remedied".

4 Save where the contrary is indicated, in the following, the term "competition concerns" corresponds, according to the stage of the procedure, to serious doubts or preliminary findings that the concentration is likely to significantly impede effective competition in the common market or in a substantial part of it, in particular as a result of the creation or strengthening of a dominant position.

5 Commission Notice on remedies acceptable under Council Regulation (EEC) No 4064/89 and under Commission Regulation (EC) No 447/98 (OJ C68, 2.3.2001, p 3).

6 Regulation replacing Council Regulation (EEC) No 4064/89 (OJ L395, 30.12.1989, corrected version in OJ L257, 21.9.1990, p 13.

7 Commission Regulation (EC) No 802/2004 of 7 April 2004 implementing Council Regulation (EC) No 139/2004 on the control of concentrations between undertakings (OJ L133, 30.4.2004, p 1). This Regulation replaces Commission Regulation (EC) No 447/98 implementing Council Regulation (EEC) No 4064/89 on the control of concentrations between undertakings (OJ L61, 2.3.1998, p 1).

8 DG COMP, Merger Remedies Study, October 2005.

II. GENERAL PRINCIPLES

[4.712]

4. Under the Merger Regulation, the Commission assesses the compatibility of a notified concentration with the common market on the basis of its effect on the structure of competition in the Community.[9] The test for compatibility under Article 2(2) and (3) of the Merger Regulation is whether or not a concentration would significantly impede effective competition in the common market or a substantial part of it, in particular as a result of the creation or strengthening of a dominant position. A concentration that significantly impedes effective competition as described above is incompatible with the common market and the Commission is required to prohibit it. For the creation of a joint venture, the Commission will also examine the concentration under Article 2(4) of the Merger Regulation. The principles set out in this Notice will generally also apply to remedies submitted to eliminate competition concerns identified under Article 2(4).

5. Where a concentration raises competition concerns in that it could significantly impede effective competition, in particular as a result of the creation or strengthening of a dominant position, the parties may seek to modify the concentration in order to resolve the competition concerns and thereby gain clearance of their merger. Such modifications may be fully implemented in advance of a clearance decision. However, it is more common that the parties submit commitments with a view to rendering the concentration compatible with the common market and that those commitments are implemented following clearance.

6. Under the structure of the Merger Regulation, it is the responsibility of the Commission to show that a concentration would significantly impede competition.[10] The Commission communicates its competition concerns to the parties to allow them to formulate appropriate and corresponding remedies proposals.[11] It is then for the parties to

the concentration to put forward commitments; the Commission is not in a position to impose unilaterally any conditions to an authorisation decision, but only on the basis of the parties' commitments.[12] The Commission will inform the parties about its preliminary assessment of remedies proposals. If, however, the parties do not validly propose remedies adequate to eliminate the competition concerns, the only option for the Commission will be to adopt a prohibition decision.[13]

7. The Commission has to assess whether the proposed remedies, once implemented, would eliminate the competition concerns identified. Only the parties have all the relevant information necessary for such an assessment, in particular as to the feasibility of the commitments proposed and the viability and competitiveness of the assets proposed for divestiture. It is therefore the responsibility of the parties to provide all such information available that is necessary for the Commission's assessment of the remedies proposal. To this end, the Implementing Regulation obliges the notifying parties to provide, with the commitments, detailed information on the content of the commitments offered, the conditions for their implementation and showing their suitability to remove any significant impediment of effective competition, as set out in the annex to the Implementing Regulation ("Form RM"). For commitments consisting in the divestiture of a business, parties have to describe in detail in particular how the business to be divested is currently operated. This information will enable the Commission to assess the viability, competitiveness and marketability of the business by comparing its current operation to its proposed scope under the commitments. The Commission can adapt the precise requirements to the information necessary in the individual case at hand and will be available to discuss the scope of the information required with the parties in advance of submission of Form RM.

8. Whereas the parties have to propose commitments sufficient to remove the competition concerns and submit the necessary information to assess them, it is for the Commission to establish whether or not a concentration, as modified by commitments validly submitted, must be declared incompatible with the common market because it leads, despite the commitments, to a significant impediment of effective competition. The burden of proof for a prohibition or authorisation of a concentration modified by commitments is therefore subject to the same criteria as an unmodified concentration.[14]

Basic conditions for acceptable commitments

9. Under the Merger Regulation, the Commission only has power to accept commitments that are deemed capable of rendering the concentration compatible with the common market so that they will prevent a significant impediment of effective competition. The commitments have to eliminate the competition concerns entirely[15] and have to be comprehensive and effective from all points of view.[16] Furthermore, commitments must be capable of being implemented effectively within a short period of time as the conditions of competition on the market will not be maintained until the commitments have been fulfilled.

10. Structural commitments, in particular divestitures, proposed by the parties will meet these conditions only in so far as the Commission is able to conclude with the requisite degree of certainty that it will be possible to implement them and that it will be likely that the new commercial structures resulting from them will be sufficiently workable and lasting to ensure that the significant impediment to effective competition will not materialise.[17]

11. The requisite degree of certainty concerning the implementation of the proposed commitments may in particular be affected by risks in relation to the transfer of a business to be divested, such as conditions attached by the parties to the divestiture, third party rights in relation to the business or the risks of finding a suitable purchaser, as well as risks in relation to the degradation of the assets until the divestiture has taken place. It is incumbent on the parties to remove such uncertainties as to the implementation of the remedy when submitting it to the Commission.[18]

12. In assessing the second condition, whether the proposed commitment will likely eliminate the competition concerns identified, the Commission will consider all relevant factors relating to the proposed remedy itself, including, inter alia, the type, scale and scope of the remedy proposed, judged by reference to the structure and particular characteristics of the market in which the competition concerns arise, including the position of the parties and other players on the market.

13. In order for the commitments to comply with these principles, there has to be an effective implementation and ability to monitor the commitments.[19] Whereas divestitures, once implemented, do not require any further monitoring measures, other types of commitments require effective monitoring mechanisms in order to ensure that their effect is not reduced or even eliminated by the parties. Otherwise, such commitments would have to be considered as mere declarations of intention by the parties and would not amount to binding obligations, as, due to the lack of effective monitoring mechanisms, any breach of them could not result in the revocation of the decision according to the provisions of the Merger Regulation.[20]

14. Where, however, the parties submit remedies proposals that are so extensive and complex that it is not possible for the Commission to determine with the requisite degree of certainty, at the time of its decision, that they will be fully implemented and that they are likely to maintain effective competition in the market, an authorisation decision cannot be granted.[21] The Commission may reject such remedies in particular on the grounds that the implementation of the remedies cannot be effectively monitored and that the lack of effective monitoring diminishes, or even eliminates, the effect of the commitments proposed.

Appropriateness of different types of remedies

15. According to the case law of the Court, the basic aim of commitments is to ensure competitive market structures.[22] Accordingly, commitments which are structural in nature, such as the commitment to sell a business unit, are, as a rule, preferable from the point of view of the Merger Regulation's objective, inasmuch as such commitments prevent, durably, the competition concerns which would be raised by the merger as notified, and do not, moreover, require medium or long-term monitoring measures. Nevertheless, the possibility cannot automatically be ruled out that other types of commitments may also be capable of preventing the significant impediment of effective competition.[23]

16. The Commission stresses that the question of whether a remedy and, more specifically, which type of remedy is suitable to eliminate the competition concerns identified, has to be examined on a case-by-case basis.

17. Nevertheless, a general distinction can be made between divestitures, other structural remedies, such as granting access to key infrastructure or inputs on non-discriminatory terms, and commitments relating to the future behaviour of the merged entity. Divestiture commitments are the best way to eliminate competition concerns resulting from horizontal overlaps, and may also be the best means of resolving problems resulting from vertical or conglomerate concerns.[24] Other structural commitments may be suitable to resolve all types of concerns if those remedies are equivalent to divestitures in their effects, as explained in more detail below in paragraphs 61 *et seq*. Commitments relating to the future behaviour of the merged entity may be acceptable only exceptionally in very specific circumstances.[25] In particular, commitments in the form of undertakings not to raise prices, to reduce product ranges or to remove brands, etc, will generally not eliminate competition concerns resulting from horizontal overlaps. In any case, those types of remedies can only exceptionally be accepted if their workability is fully ensured by effective implementation and monitoring in line with the considerations set out in paragraphs 13-14, 66, 69, and if they do not risk leading to distorting effects on competition.[26]

Procedure

18. The Commission may accept commitments in either phase of the procedure.[27] However, given the fact that an in-depth market investigation is only carried out in phase II, commitments submitted to the Commission in phase I must be sufficient to clearly rule out "serious doubts" within the meaning of Article 6(1)(c) of the Merger Regulation.[28] Pursuant to Article 10(2) of the Merger Regulation, the Commission has to take a clearance decision as soon as the serious doubts referred to in Article 6(1)(c) of the Merger Regulation are removed as a result of commitments submitted by the parties. This rule applies to commitments proposed in phase II proceedings before the Commission issues a Statement of Objections.[29] If the Commission reaches the preliminary view that the merger leads to a significant impediment to effective competition and issues a Statement of Objections, the commitments must be sufficient to eliminate such a significant impediment to effective competition.

19. Whilst commitments have to be offered by the parties, the Commission will ensure the enforceability of commitments by making the authorisation of the merger subject to compliance with the commitments. A distinction must be made between conditions and obligations. The requirement for achievement of the structural change of the market is a condition — for example, that a business is to be divested. The implementing steps which are necessary to achieve this result are generally obligations on the parties, eg such as the appointment of a trustee with an irrevocable mandate to sell the business.

20. Where the undertakings concerned commit a breach of an obligation, the Commission may revoke clearance decisions issued either under Article 6(2) or Article 8(2) of the Merger Regulation, acting pursuant to Article 6(3) or Article 8(6), respectively. In case of a breach of an obligation, the parties may also be subject to fines and periodic penalty payments as provided in Article 14(2)(d) and 15(1)(c) respectively of the Merger Regulation. Where, however, a condition is breached, eg a business is not divested in the time-frame foreseen in the commitments or afterwards re-acquired, the compatibility decision is no longer applicable. In such circumstances, the Commission may, first, take interim measures appropriate to maintain conditions of effective competition pursuant to Article 8(5)(b) of the Merger Regulation. Second, it may, if the conditions of Article 8(4)(b) are met, order any appropriate measure to ensure that the undertakings concerned dissolve the concentration or take other restorative measures or, according to Article 8(7), take a decision pursuant to Article 8(1)-(3). In addition, the parties may also be subject to fines as provided in Article 14(2)(d).

Model Texts for divestiture commitments

21. The Commission services have issued Best Practice Guidelines for divestiture commitments, consisting of a Model Text for Divestiture Commitments and a Model Text for Trustee Mandates.[30] These model texts are neither intended to provide an exhaustive coverage of all issues that may become relevant in all cases, nor are they legally binding upon parties in a merger procedure. They complement the present Notice as they outline the typical arrangements for divestiture commitments in a format which can be used by the parties. At the same time, the model texts leave the flexibility to adapt them to the requirements of the specific case.

NOTES

9 Recital 6 of the Merger Regulation.

10 In phase I and before the issuance of a Statement of Objections, this corresponds to *serious doubts* as to the significant impediment to effective competition.

11 The Merger Regulation provides for formal steps where the parties are informed of the competition concerns identified by the Commission (Article 6(1)(c) decision, Statement of Objections). In addition, the DG COMPETITION Best Practices on the conduct of EC merger control proceedings foresee that "state of play" meetings will normally be offered at key stages of the procedure where the Commission will explain its concerns to the parties in order to allow them to respond with remedies proposals.

12 Judgment of the CFI in Case T-210/01 *General Electric v Commission* [2005] ECR II-5575, paragraph 52; see judgment of the CFI in Case T-87/05 *EDP v Commission* [2005] ECR II-3745, paragraph 105.

13 See Case COMP/M.2220 — *GE/Honeywell* of 3 July 2001, confirmed by judgment of the CFI in Case T-210/01 *General Electric v Commission* [2005] ECR II-5575, paragraph 555 *et seq*, 612 *et seq*; Case COMP/M.3440 — *EDP/ENI/GDP* of 9 December 2004, confirmed by judgment of the CFI in Case T-87/05 *EDP v Commission* [2005] ECR II-3745, paragraphs 63 *et seq*, 75 *et seq*; Case IV/M.469 — *MSG Media Service* of 9 November 1994; Case IV/M.490 — *Nordic Satellite Distribution* of 19 July 1995; Case IV/M.553 — *RTL/Veronica/Endemol* of 20 September 1995; Case IV/M.993 — *Bertelsmann/Kirch/Prèmiere* of 27 May 1998; Case IV/M.1027 — *Deutsche Telekom BetaResearch* of 27 May 1998; Case IV/M.774 — *St Gobain/Wacker Chemie* of 4 December 1996; Case IV/M.53 — *Aerospatiale/Alenia/De Havilland* of 2 October 1991; Case IV/M.619 — *Gencor/Lonrho* of 24 April 1996, confirmed by judgment of the CFI in Case T-102/96 *Gencor v Commission* [1999] ECR II-753.

14 See judgment of the CFI in Case T-87/05 *EDP v Commission* [2005] ECR II-3745, paragraphs 62 ff.

15 See recital 30 of the Merger Regulation and judgment of the CFI in Case T-282/02 *Cementbouw v Commission* [2006] ECR II-319, paragraph 307.

16 CFI, Case T-210/01 *General Electrics v Commission* [2005] ECR II-5575, paragraph 52; Case T-87/05 *EDP v Commission* [2005] ECR II-3745, paragraph 105.

17 CFI, Case T-210/01 *General Electric v Commission* [2005] ECR II-5575, paragraphs 555, 612.

18 Depending on the nature of the risks, specific safeguards may aim at compensating for them. For example, the risk arising from third party rights in relation to the assets to be divested may be compensated by the proposal of an alternative divestiture. Such safeguards will be discussed in more detail below.

19 CFI, Case T-177/04 *easyJet v Commission* [2006] ECR II-1931, paragraph 188.

20 CFI, Case T-177/04 *easyJet v Commission* [2006] ECR II-1931, paragraph 186 *et seq*; CFI, judgment in Case T-87/05 *EDP v Commission* [2005] ECR II-3745, paragraph 72.

21 See, as an example for such a complex and inappropriate remedy, Case COMP/M.3440 — *ENI/EDP/GDP* of 9 December 2004; confirmed by CFI, judgment in Case T-87/05 *EDP v Commission* [2005] ECR II-3745, paragraph 102; Case COMP/M.1672 — *Volvo/Scania* of 15 March 2000.

22 See recital 8 of the Merger Regulation; judgment of CFI in Case T-102/96 *Gencor v Commission* [1999] ECR II-753, at paragraph 316; ECJ in Case C-12/03 P *Commission v Tetra Laval* [2005] ECR I-987, paragraph 86; judgment of CFI in Case T-158/00 *ARD v Commission* [2003] ECR II-3825, at paragraphs 192 *et seq.*

23 ECJ, judgment in Case C-12/03 P *Commission v Tetra Laval* [2005] ECR I-987, paragraph 86; CFI, judgment of 25 March 1999 in Case T-102/96 *Gencor v Commission* [1999] ECR II-753, paragraphs 319 *et seq*; CFI, judgment of 30 September 2003 in Case T-158/00 *ARD v Commission* [2003] ECR II-3825, paragraph 193; CFI in Case T-177/04 *easyJet v Commission* [2006] ECR II-1931, paragraph 182; CFI, judgment in Case T-87/05 *EDP v Commission* [2005] ECR II-3745, paragraph 101.

24 See divestiture of storage facilities in Case COMP/M.3868 — *DONG/Elsam/Energi E2* of 14 March 2006, paragraphs 170 *et seq*; Case COMP/M.3696 — *E.ON/MOL* of 21 December 2005, paragraphs 735 *et seq*, for an example of "ownership unbundling" to eliminate structural links between the parties in the gas storage sector; further Case COMP/M.4314 — *Johnson&Johnson/Pfizer* of 11 December 2006, Case COMP/M.4494 — *Evraz/Highveld* of 20 February 2007.

25 See, in relation to conglomerate effects of a concentration, ECJ, judgment of 15 February 2005 in Case C-12/03 P *Commission v Tetra Laval* [2005] ECR I-987, paragraphs 85, 89.

26 For example, commitments regarding a certain pricing behaviour such as price caps which contain the risk to lead to an anticompetitive alignment of prices among competitors.

27 As foreseen in recital 30 of the Merger Regulation, the Commission will ensure transparency and effective consultation of Member States in both phases of the procedure.

28 Commitments in phase I can only be accepted in certain types of situations; see below in paragraph 81.

29 See, inter alia, Case COMP/M.2972 — *DSM/Roche Vitamins* of 23 July 2003; Case COMP/M.2861 — *Siemens/Drägerwerk/JV* of 30 April 2003; Case IV/JV.15 — *BT/AT & T* of 30 March 1999; Case IV/M.1532 — *BP Amoco/Arco* of 29 September 1999.

30 See website of DG COMP, released in May 2003, available at:ec.europa.eu/comm/competition/mergers/legislation/legislation.html. The model texts may be continuously up-dated and, if there should be a need, further best practice guidelines in the field of remedies may be issued.

III. DIFFERENT TYPES OF REMEDIES

1. DIVESTITURE OF A BUSINESS TO A SUITABLE PURCHASER

[4.713]

22. Where a proposed concentration threatens to significantly impede effective competition the most effective way to maintain effective competition, apart from prohibition, is to create the conditions for the emergence of a new competitive entity or for the strengthening of existing competitors via divestiture by the merging parties.

1.1. Divestiture of a viable and competitive business

23. The divested activities must consist of a viable business that, if operated by a suitable purchaser, can compete effectively with the merged entity on a lasting basis and that is divested as a going concern.[31] For the business to be viable, it may also be necessary to include activities which are related to markets where the Commission did not identify competition concerns if this is required to create an effective competitor in the affected markets.[32]

24. In proposing a viable business for divestiture, it is necessary to take into account the uncertainties and risks related to the transfer of a business to a new owner. These risks may limit the competitive impact of the divested business, and, therefore, may lead to a market situation where the competition concerns at stake will not necessarily be eliminated.

Scope of the business to be divested

25. The business has to include all the assets which contribute to its current operation or which are necessary to ensure its viability and competitiveness and all personnel which is currently employed or which is necessary to ensure the business' viability and competitiveness.[33]

26. Personnel and assets which are currently shared between the business to be divested and other businesses of the parties, but which contribute to the operation of the business or which are necessary to ensure its viability and competitiveness, also have to be included. Otherwise, the viability and competitiveness of the business to be divested would be endangered. Therefore, the divested business has to contain the personnel providing essential functions for the business such as, for instance, group R&D and information technology staff even where such personnel is currently employed by another business unit of the parties — at least in a sufficient proportion to meet the on-going needs of the divested business. In the same way shared assets have to be included even if those assets are owned by or allocated to another business unit.

27. In order for the Commission to be able to identify the scope of the business to be divested, the parties have to include a precise definition of the scope of the divested business in the commitments (the "description of the business"). The description of the business has to be adapted to the individual case at hand and should contain all the elements that are part of the business to be divested: tangible (eg R&D, production, distribution, sales and marketing activities) and intangible assets (such as intellectual property rights, know-how and goodwill); licences, permits and authorisations by governmental organisations granted to the business; contracts, leases and commitments (eg arrangements with suppliers and customers) for the benefit of the business to be divested; and customer, credit and other records. In the description of the business, the parties have to include the personnel to be transferred in general terms, including staff seconded and temporary employees, and to insert a list of the key personnel, ie the personnel essential for the viability and competitiveness of the business. The transfer of those employees is without prejudice to the application of the Council Directives on collective redundancies;[34] on safeguarding employees' rights in the event of transfers of undertakings;[35] and on informing and consulting employees[36] as well as national provisions implementing those Directives and other national laws. The remedy has to include a non-solicitation commitment by the parties with regard to the key personnel.

28. In the description of the business, the parties also have to set out the arrangements for the supply of products and services by them to the divested business or by the divested business to them. Such on-going relationships of the divested business may be necessary to maintain the full economic viability and competitiveness of the divested business for a transitional basis. The Commission will only accept such arrangements if they do not affect the independence of the divested business from the parties.

29. In order to avoid any misunderstanding about the business to be divested, assets or personnel that are used within or employed by the business but that should not, according to the parties, be transferred with the divestiture, have to be expressly excluded by the parties in the commitments text. The Commission will only be able to accept such exclusion of assets or personnel if the parties can clearly show that this does not affect the viability and competitiveness of the business.

30. The business to be divested has to be viable as such. Therefore, the resources of a possible or even presumed future purchaser are not taken into account by the Commission at the stage of assessing the remedy. The situation is different if already during the procedure a sale and purchase agreement with a specific purchaser is concluded whose resources can be taken into account at the time of the assessment of the commitment. This situation will be dealt with in more detail below in paragraphs 56 ff.

31. Once a purchaser is identified after adoption of an authorisation decision, some of the assets or personnel included in the divested business may not be needed by the proposed purchaser. In the purchaser approval process, the Commission may, upon request by the parties, approve the divestiture of the business to the proposed purchaser without one or more assets or parts of the personnel if this does not affect the viability and competitiveness of the business to be divested after the sale, taking account of the resources of the proposed purchaser.

1.2. STAND-ALONE BUSINESS AND CONDITIONS FOR ACCEPTABILITY OF ALTERNATIVES

32. Normally, a viable business is a business that can operate on a stand-alone-basis, which means independently of the merging parties as regards the supply of input materials or other forms of cooperation other than during a transitory period.

33. The Commission has a clear preference for an existing stand-alone business. This may take the form of a pre-existing company or group of companies, or of a business division which was not previously legally incorporated as such.

34. Where the competition concern results from a horizontal overlap, the parties may be able to choose between two businesses. In cases involving a hostile bid, a commitment to divest activities of the target company may, in such circumstances of limited information available to the notifying parties about the business to be divested, increase the risk that this business might not, after a divestiture, result in a viable competitor which could effectively compete in the market on a lasting basis. It may therefore be more appropriate for the parties to propose to divest activities of the acquiring company in such scenarios.

Carve-outs

35. Even though normally the divestiture of an existing viable stand-alone business is required, the Commission, taking into account the principle of proportionality, may also consider the divestiture of businesses which have existing strong links or are partially integrated with businesses retained by the parties and therefore need to be "carved out" in those respects. In order to reduce the risks for the viability and competitiveness to a minimum in such circumstances, an option for the parties is to submit commitments proposing to carve out those parts of an existing business which do not necessarily have to be divested. In effect, an existing, stand-alone business is being divested in those circumstances although, by way of a "reverse carve-out", the parties may carve-out the limited parts which they may keep.

36. In any case, the Commission will only be able to accept commitments which require the carve-out of a business if it can be certain that, at least at the time when the business is transferred to the purchaser, a viable business on a stand-alone basis will be divested and the risks for the viability and competitiveness caused by the carve-out will thereby be reduced to a minimum. The parties therefore have to ensure, as set out in detail below in paragraph 113, that the carve-out is started in the interim period, ie the period between the adoption of the Commission decision up to the completion of the divestiture (meaning the legal and factual transfer of the business to the purchaser). Consequently, at the end of this period, a viable business on a stand-alone basis will be divested. If this should not be possible or if the carve-out should be particularly difficult, parties may provide the requisite degree of certainty for the Commission by proposing an up-front buyer solution, as further detailed below in paragraph 55.

Divestiture of assets, in particular of brands and licences

37. A divestiture consisting of a combination of certain assets which did not form a uniform and viable business in the past creates risks as to the viability and competitiveness of the resulting business. This is in particular the case if assets from more than one party are involved. Such an approach may be accepted by the Commission only if the viability of the business is ensured notwithstanding the fact that the assets did not form a uniform business in the past. This may be the case if the individual assets can already be considered a viable and competitive business.[37] Similarly, only in exceptional cases a divestiture package including only brands and supporting production and/or distribution assets may be sufficient to create the conditions for effective competition.[38] In such circumstances, the package consisting of brands and assets must be sufficient to allow the Commission to conclude that the resulting business will be immediately viable in the hands of a suitable purchaser.

38. Divestitures of a business generally appear preferable to the granting of licenses to IP rights, as the granting of a license involve more uncertainties, will not enable the licensee to compete immediately in the market, requires an on-going relationship with the parties which may allow the licensor to influence the licensee in its competitive behaviour and may give rise to disputes between the licensor and the licensee over the scope and the terms and conditions of the license. The granting of a license will therefore generally not be considered appropriate where a divestiture of a business seems feasible. Where the competition concerns arise from the market position held for such a technology or such IP rights, a divestiture of the technology or the IP rights is the preferable remedy as it eliminates a lasting relationship between the merged entity and its competitors.[39] However, the Commission may accept licensing arrangements as an alternative to divestiture where, for instance, a divestiture would impede efficient, on-going research or where a divestiture would be impossible due to the nature of the business.[40] Such licences will have to enable the licensee to compete effectively with the parties in a similar way as if a divestiture had taken place. They will normally be exclusive licences and have to be without any field-of-use and any geographical restrictions on the licensee. Where there might be any uncertainty as regards the scope of the licence or its terms and conditions, the parties will have to divest the underlying IP right, but may obtain a licence back. If there is uncertainty that the license will actually be granted to a suitable licensee, the parties may consider to propose an up-front licensee or a fix-it-first solution according to the considerations set out below in paragraphs 56, in order to enable the Commission to conclude with the requisite degree of certainty that the remedy will be implemented.[41]

Re-branding

39. In exceptional cases, the Commission has accepted commitments to grant an exclusive, time-limited licence for a brand with the purpose of allowing the licensee to re-brand the product in the period foreseen. After the first licence phase of these so-called re-branding commitments, the parties commit in a second phase to abstain from any use of the brand (blackout phase). The goal of such commitments is to allow the licensee to transfer the customers from the licensed brand to its own brand in order to create a viable competitor, without the licensed brand being permanently divested.

40. A re-branding remedy carries substantially higher risks for restoring effective competition than a divestiture, including the divestiture of a brand as there is considerable uncertainty whether the licensee will succeed in establishing itself as an active competitor in the market on the basis of the re-branded product. A re-branding remedy may be acceptable in circumstances where the brand at stake is widely used and a high proportion of its turnover is generated in markets outside those in which competition concerns have been identified.[42] In those circumstances, a re-branding remedy has to be defined in such a way as to ensure that the granting of the licence will effectively maintain competition in the market on a lasting basis and that the licensee will be an effective competitor after re-branding the products.

41. As the success of re-branding commitments is substantially linked to the viability of the licensed brand a number of preconditions have to be met for the design of such commitments. Firstly, the brand to be transferred must be well-known and one of considerable strength to guarantee both immediate viability of the licensed brand and its economic survival in the re-branding period. Secondly, part of the assets related to the production or the distribution of the products marketed under the licensed brand or the transfer of know-how may be necessary to ensure the viability of the remedy.[43] Thirdly, the licence has to be exclusive and normally comprehensive, ie not limited to a certain range of products within a specific market, and has to include the intellectual property rights to ensure that customers will acknowledge the familiarity of the re-branded product. The parties will not be allowed to use similar words or signs as this could undermine the effect of the re-branding exercise.[44] Fourthly, both the licence and the black-out period have to be sufficiently long, account being taken of the particularities of the case, so that the re-branding remedy is in its effects similar to a divestiture.[45]

42. The identity of the potential licensee will be a key factor for the success of the commitment. If there is uncertainty that a number of suitable licensees are available, being able and having strong incentives to carry out the re-branding exercise, the parties may consider proposing an up-front or fix-it-first solution, in line with the considerations set out in paragraph 53 below.

1.3. Non-reacquisition clause

43. In order to maintain the structural effect of a remedy, the commitments have to foresee that the merged entity cannot subsequently acquire influence[46] over the whole or parts of the divested business. The commitments will normally have to foresee that no re-acquisition of material influence is possible for a significant period, generally of 10 years. However, the commitments can also provide for a waiver allowing the Commission to relieve the parties from this obligation if it subsequently finds that the structure of the market has changed to such an extent that the absence of influence over the divested business is no longer necessary to render the concentration compatible with the common market. Even in the absence of an explicit clause, a re-acquisition of the business would violate an implicit obligation on the parties under the commitments as this would affect the effectiveness of the remedies.

1.4. Alternative divestiture commitments: Crown Jewels

44. In certain cases, the implementation of the parties' preferred divestiture option (of a viable business solving the competition concerns) might be uncertain in view, for example, of third parties' pre-emption rights or uncertainty as to the transferability of key contracts, intellectual property rights, or the uncertainty of finding a suitable purchaser. Nevertheless, the parties may consider that they would be able to divest this business to a suitable purchaser within a very short time period.

45. In such circumstances, the Commission cannot take the risk that, in the end, effective competition will not be maintained. Accordingly, the Commission will only accept such divestiture commitments under the following conditions: (a) absent the uncertainty, the first divestiture proposed in the commitments would consist of a viable business, and (b) the parties will have to propose a second alternative divestiture which the parties will be obliged to implement if they are not able to implement the first commitment within the given time frame for the first divestiture.[47] Such an alternative commitment normally has to be a "crown jewel",[48] ie it should be as least as good as the first proposed divestiture in terms of creating a viable competitor once implemented, it should not involve any uncertainties as to its implementation and it should be capable of being implemented quickly in order to avoid that the overall implementation period exceeds what would normally be regarded as acceptable in the conditions of the market in question. In order to limit the risks in the interim period, it is indispensable that interim preservation and holding separate measures apply to all assets included in both divestiture alternatives. Furthermore, the commitment has to establish clear criteria and a strict timetable as to how and when the alternative divestiture obligation will become effective and the Commission will require shorter periods for its implementation.

46. If there is uncertainty as to the implementation of the divestiture due to third party rights or as to finding a suitable purchaser crown jewel commitments and up-front buyers as discussed below in paragraphs 54 address the same concerns, and the parties may therefore choose between both structures.

1.5. Transfer to a suitable purchaser

47. The intended effect of the divestiture will only be achieved if and once the business is transferred to a suitable purchaser in whose hands it will become an active competitive force in the market. The potential of a business to attract a suitable purchaser is an important element already of the Commission's assessment of the appropriateness of the proposed commitment.[49] In order to ensure that the business is divested to a suitable purchaser, the commitments have to include criteria to define its suitability which will allow the Commission to conclude that the divestiture of the business to such a purchaser will likely remove the competition concerns identified.

(a)
Suitability of a purchaser

48. The standard purchaser requirements are the following:

— the purchaser is required to be independent of and unconnected to the parties,

— the purchaser must possess the financial resources, proven relevant expertise and have the incentive and ability to maintain and develop the divested business as a viable and active competitive force in competition with the parties and other competitors, and

— the acquisition of the business by a proposed purchaser must neither be likely to create new competition problems nor give rise to a risk that the implementation of the commitments will be delayed. Therefore, the proposed purchaser must reasonably be expected to obtain all necessary approvals from the relevant regulatory authorities for the acquisition of the business to be divested.

49. The standard purchaser requirements may have to be supplemented on a case-by-case basis. An example is the requirement, where appropriate, that the purchaser should be an industrial, rather than a financial purchaser.[50] The commitments will normally contain such a clause where, due to the specific circumstances of the case, a financial buyer might not be able or might not have the incentives to develop the business as a viable and competitive force in the market even considering that it could obtain the necessary management expertise (eg by recruiting managers experienced in the sector at stake) and therefore the acquisition by a financial buyer would not remove the competition concerns with sufficient certainty.

(b)
Identification of a suitable purchaser

50. In general, there are three ways to ensure that the business is transferred to a suitable purchaser. First, the business is transferred within a fixed time-limit after adoption of the decision to a purchaser which is approved by the Commission on the basis of the purchaser requirements. Second, in addition to the conditions set out for the first category, the commitments foresee that the parties may not complete the notified operation before having entered into a binding agreement with a purchaser for the business, approved by the Commission (so-called "up-front-buyer"). Third, the parties identify a purchaser for the business and enter into a binding agreement already during the Commission's procedure[51] (so-called "fix-it-first"[52] remedy). The main difference between the two latter options is that in the case of an up-front buyer, the identity of the purchaser is not known to the Commission prior to the authorisation decision.

51. The choice of the category depends on the risks involved in the case and therefore on the measures which enable the Commission to conclude with the requisite degree of certainty that the commitment will be implemented. This will depend on the nature and the scope of the business to be divested, the risks of degradation of the business in the interim period up to divestiture and any uncertainties inherent in the transfer and implementation, in particular the risks of finding a suitable purchaser.

1.
Sale of the divested business within a fixed time-limit after the decision

52. In the first category, the parties may proceed with the sale of the divested business on the basis of the purchaser requirements within a fixed time-limit after the adoption of the decision. This procedure is likely to be appropriate in the majority of cases, provided that a number of purchasers can be envisaged for a viable business and that no specific issues complicate or stand in the way of the divestiture. Where the purchaser needs to have special qualifications, this procedure may be appropriate if there are sufficient interested potential purchasers available which fulfil the specific purchaser requirements to be included in the commitments in such cases. In these circumstances the Commission may be able to conclude that the divestiture will be implemented and that there are no reasons for the implementation of the notified concentration to be suspended after the Commission decision.

2.
Up-front buyer

53. There are cases where only the proposal of an up-front buyer will allow the Commission to conclude with the requisite degree of certainty that the business will be effectively divested to a suitable purchaser. The parties therefore have to undertake in the commitments that they are not going to complete the notified operation before having entered into a binding agreement with a purchaser for the divested business, approved by the Commission.[53]

54. First, this concerns cases where there are considerable obstacles for a divestiture, such as third party rights, or uncertainties as to finding a suitable purchaser[54] In such cases, an up-front buyer will allow the Commission to conclude with the requisite degree of certainty that the commitments will be implemented, as such a commitment creates greater incentives for the parties to close the divestiture in order to be able to complete their own concentration. In these circumstances, parties may choose between proposing an up-front buyer and an alternative divestiture commitment, as set out above in paragraph 46.

55. Second, an up-front buyer may be necessary in cases which cause considerable risks of preserving the competitiveness and saleability of the divestment business in the interim period until divestiture. This category comprises cases where the risks of a degradation of the divestment business appear to be high, in particular due to a risk of losing employees being key for the business, or where the interim risks are increased as the parties are not able to undertake the carve-out process in the interim period, but the carve-out process can only take place once a sales and purchase agreement with a purchaser is entered into. The up-front buyer provision may accelerate the transfer of the business to be divested — given the increased incentives for the parties to close the divestiture in order to be able to complete their own concentration — to such an extent that the commitments may allow the Commission to conclude with the requisite degree of certainty that those risks are limited and the divestiture will be effectively implemented.[55]

3.
Fix-it-first remedies

56. The third category involves cases where the parties identify and enter into a legally binding agreement with a buyer outlining the essentials of the purchase during the Commission procedure.[56] The Commission will be able to decide in the final decision whether the transfer of the divested business to the identified purchaser will remove the competition concerns. If the Commission authorises the notified concentration, no additional Commission decision for the purchaser approval will be needed and the closing of the sale of the divested business may take place shortly afterwards.

57. The Commission welcomes fix-it-first remedies in particular in cases where the identity of the purchaser is crucial for the effectiveness of the proposed remedy. This concerns cases where, given the circumstances, only very few potential purchasers can be considered suitable, in particular as the divested business is not a viable business in itself, but its viability will only be ensured by specific assets of the purchaser, or where the purchaser needs to have specific characteristics in order for the remedy to solve the competition concerns.[57] If the parties choose to enter into a binding agreement with a suitable purchaser during the procedure by way of a fix-it-first solution, the Commission can in those circumstances conclude with the requisite degree of certainty that the commitments will be implemented with a sale to a suitable purchaser. In these situations, an "upfront buyer" solution containing specific requirements as to the suitability of a buyer will generally be considered equivalent and acceptable.

2. REMOVAL OF LINKS WITH COMPETITORS

58. Divestiture commitments may also be used for removing links between the parties and competitors in cases where these links contribute to the competition concerns raised by the merger. The divestiture of a minority shareholding in a joint venture may be necessary in order to sever a structural link with a major competitor,[58] or, similarly, the divestiture of a minority shareholding in a competitor.[59]

59. Although the divestiture of such stakes is the preferable solution, the Commission may exceptionally accept the waiving of rights linked to minority stakes in a competitor where it can be excluded, given the specific circumstances of the case, that the financial gains derived from a minority shareholding in a competitor would in themselves raise competition concerns.[60] In such circumstances, the parties have to waive all the rights linked to such a shareholding which were relevant for behaviour in terms of competition, such as representations on the board, veto rights and also information rights.[61] The Commission may only be able to accept such a severing of the link with a competitor if those rights are waived comprehensively and in a permanent way.[62]

60. Where competition concerns result from agreements with companies supplying the same products or providing the same services, a suitable remedy may be the termination of the respective agreement, such as distribution agreements with competitors[63] or agreements resulting in the coordination of certain commercial behaviour.[64]

However, the termination of a distribution agreement alone will only remove the competition concerns if it is ensured that the product of a competitor will also be distributed in the future and exercise effective competitive pressure on the parties.

3. OTHER REMEDIES

61. Whilst being the preferred remedy, divestitures or the removal of links with competitors are not the only remedy possible to eliminate certain competition concerns. However, divestitures are the benchmark for other remedies in terms of effectiveness and efficiency. The Commission therefore may accept other types of commitments, but only in circumstances where the other remedy proposed is at least equivalent in its effects to a divestiture.[65]

Access remedies

62. In a number of cases, the Commission has accepted remedies foreseeing the granting of access to key infrastructure, networks, key technology, including patents, know-how or other intellectual property rights, and essential inputs. Normally, the parties grant such access to third parties on a non-discriminatory and transparent basis.

63. Commitments granting access to infrastructure and networks may be submitted in order to facilitate market entry by competitors. They may be acceptable to the Commission in circumstances where it is sufficiently clear that there will be actual entry of new competitors that would eliminate any significant impediment to effective competition.[66] Other examples of access commitments are commitments granting access to pay-TV platforms[67] and to energy via gas release programs.[68] Often, a sufficient reduction of entry barriers is not achieved by individual measures, but by a package comprising a combination of divestiture remedies and access commitments or a commitments package aimed at overall facilitating entry of competitors by a whole range of different measures. If those commitments actually make the entry of sufficient new competitors timely and likely, they can be considered to have a similar effect on competition in the market as a divestiture. If it cannot be concluded that the lowering of the entry barriers by the proposed commitments will likely lead to the entry of new competitors in the market, the Commission will reject such a remedies package.[69]

64. Commitments granting non-discriminatory access to infrastructure or networks of the merging parties may also be submitted in order to ensure that competition is not significantly impeded as a result of foreclosure. In past Commission decisions, commitments have foreseen the granting of access to pipelines[70] and to telecom or similar networks.[71] The Commission will only accept such commitments if it can be concluded that these commitments will be effective and competitors will likely use them so that foreclosure concerns will be eliminated. In specific cases, it may be appropriate to link such a commitment with an up-front or fix-it-first provision in order to allow the Commission to conclude with the requisite degree of certainty that the commitment will be implemented.[72]

65. Similarly, the control of key technology or IP rights may lead to concerns of foreclosure of competitors which depend on the technology or IP rights as essential input for the activities in a downstream market. This, for example, concerns cases where competition problems arise as the parties may withhold information necessary for the interoperability of different equipment. In such circumstances, commitments to grant competitors access to the necessary information may eliminate the competition concerns.[73] Similarly, in sectors where players commonly have to cooperate by licensing patents to each other, concerns that the merged entity would no longer have the incentive to provide licences to the same extent and under the same conditions as before may be eliminated by commitments to grant licenses on the same basis also in the future.[74] In those cases, commitments should foresee non-exclusive licences or the disclosure of information on a non-exclusive basis to all third parties which depend on the IP rights or information for their activities. It has to be further ensured that the terms and conditions under which the licenses are granted do not impede the effective implementation of such a license remedy. If no clearly determined terms and conditions for the granting of licenses exist in the market at stake, the terms and conditions, including the pricing, should be clearly apparent from the commitments (eg by way of pricing formulas). An alternative solution may be to rely on royalty-free licences. Furthermore, depending on the case, the granting of licenses may also transmit sensitive information to the licensor on the competitive behaviour of the licensees which are active as competitors in the downstream market, eg by transmitting the number of licenses used in the downstream market. In such cases, in order for the remedy to be suitable, the commitments will have to exclude such confidentiality problems. Generally, as set out in the preceding paragraph, the Commission will only accept such commitments if it can be concluded that they will be effective and competitors will likely use them.

66. Access commitments are often complex in nature and necessarily include general terms for determining the terms and conditions under which access is granted. In order to render them effective, those commitments have to contain the procedural requirements necessary for monitoring them, such as the requirement of separate accounts for the infrastructure in order to allow a review of the costs involved,[75] and suitable monitoring devices. Normally, such monitoring has to be done by the market participants themselves, eg by those undertakings wishing to benefit from the commitments. Measures allowing third parties themselves to enforce the commitments are in particular access to a fast dispute resolution mechanism via arbitration proceedings (together with trustees)[76] or via arbitration proceedings involving national regulatory authorities if existing for the markets concerned.[77] If the Commission can conclude that the mechanisms foreseen in the commitments will allow the market participants themselves to effectively enforce them in a timely manner, no permanent monitoring of the commitments by the Commission is required. In those cases, an intervention by the Commission would only be necessary in cases where the parties do not comply with the solutions found by those dispute resolution mechanisms.[78] However, the Commission will only be able to accept such commitments where the complexity does not lead to a risk of their effectiveness from the outset and where the monitoring devices proposed ensure that those commitments will be effectively implemented and the enforcement mechanism will lead to timely results.[79]

Change of long-term exclusive contracts

67. The change in the market structure resulting from a proposed concentration can cause existing contractual arrangements to be inimical to effective competition. This is in particular true for exclusive long-term supply agreements if such agreements foreclose either, up-stream, the input for competitors or, down-stream, their access to customers. Where the merged entity will have the ability and the incentives to foreclose competitors in this way, the foreclosure effects resulting from existing exclusive agreements may contribute to significantly impeding effective competition.[80]

68. In such circumstances, the termination or change of existing exclusive agreements may be considered appropriate to eliminate the competition concerns.[81] However, the available evidence must allow the Commission to clearly determine that no de facto exclusivity will be maintained. Furthermore, such change of long-term agreements will normally only be sufficient as part of a remedies package to remove the competition concerns identified.

Other non-divestiture remedies

69. As indicated above in paragraph 17, non-structural types of remedies, such as promises by the parties to abstain from certain commercial behaviour (eg bundling products), will generally not eliminate the competition concerns resulting from horizontal overlaps. In any case, it may be difficult to achieve the required degree of effectiveness of such a remedy due to the absence of effective monitoring of its implementation, as already set out above in paragraph 13(f).[82] Indeed, it may be impossible for the Commission to verify whether or not the commitment is complied with and even other market participants, such as competitors, may not be able to establish at all or with the requisite degree of certainty whether the parties meet the conditions of the commitment in practice. In addition, competitors may also not have an incentive to alert the Commission as they do not directly benefit from the commitments. Therefore, the Commission may examine other types of non-divestiture remedies, such as behavioural promises, only exceptionally in specific circumstances, such as in respect of competition concerns arising in conglomerate structures.[83]

Time limit for non-divestiture remedies

70. The Commission may accept that non-divestiture remedies are limited in their duration. The acceptability of a time limit and the duration will depend on the individual circumstances of the case and cannot be pre-defined in a general manner in the present Notice.

4. REVIEW CLAUSE

71. Irrespective of the type of remedy, commitments will usually include a review clause.[84] This may allow the Commission, upon request by the parties showing good cause, to grant an extension of deadlines or, in exceptional circumstances, to waive, modify or substitute the commitments.

72. Modifying commitments by extending the deadlines is in particular relevant for divestiture commitments. Parties have to submit a request for an extension within the deadline. Where parties apply for an extension for the first divestiture period, the Commission will only accept that they have shown good cause if the parties were not able to meet the deadline for reasons outside their responsibility and if it can be expected that the parties subsequently will succeed in divesting the business within a short time-frame. Otherwise, the divestiture trustee may be better placed to undertake the divestiture and to fulfil the commitments for the parties.

73. The Commission may grant waivers or accept modifications or substitutions of the commitments only in exceptional circumstances. This will very rarely be relevant for divestiture commitments. As divestiture commitments have to be implemented within a short time-frame after the decision, it is very unlikely that changes of market circumstances will have occurred in such a short time-frame and the Commission will normally not accept any modifications under the general review clause. For specific situations the commitments normally foresee more targeted review clauses.[85]

74. A waiver, modification or substitution of commitments may be more relevant for non-divestiture commitments, such as access commitments, which may be on-going for a number of years and for which not all contingencies can be predicted at the time of the adoption of the Commission decision. Exceptional circumstances justifying a waiver, modification or substitution may, first, be accepted for such commitments if parties show that market circumstances have changed significantly and on a permanent basis. For showing this, a sufficient long time-span, normally at least several years, between the Commission decision and a request by the parties is required. Second, exceptional circumstances may also be present if the parties can show that the experience gained in the application of the remedy demonstrates that the objective pursued with the remedy will be better achieved if modalities of the commitment are changed. For any waiver, modification or substitution of commitments, the Commission will also take into account the view of third parties and the impact a modification may have on the position of third parties and thereby on the overall effectiveness of the remedy. In this regard, the Commission will also consider whether modifications affect the right already acquired by third parties after implementation of the remedy.[86]

75. If at the time of the adoption of the decision the Commission for particular reasons cannot anticipate all contingencies in relation to the implementation of such commitments, it may also be appropriate for the parties to include a clause in the commitments, allowing the Commission to trigger a limited modification to the commitments. Such modifications may be necessary if the original commitments do not achieve the envisaged results set out in those commitments, and therefore do not effectively remove the competition concerns. Procedurally, the parties may be obliged in such cases to propose a change to the commitments in order to achieve the result defined in those commitments, or the Commission may itself, after hearing the parties, modify the conditions and obligations to this end. This type of clause will typically be limited to cases where specific modalities risk to jeopardise effective implementation of the commitments. Such clauses have been used, for example, in relation to the modalities of gas release programs.[87]

76. The Commission may, upon request, adopt a formal decision for any waiver, modification or substitution of commitments or simply take note of satisfactory amendments of the remedy by the parties, where such amendments improve the effectiveness of the remedy and result in legally binding obligations of the parties, eg by contractual arrangements. A change of the commitments will normally only be effective *ex nunc*. Consequently, a modification of the commitments will not heal retroactively any breach of the commitments which has been committed before the time of the modification. The Commission may therefore, where appropriate, further pursue a breach under Articles 14, 15 of the Merger Regulation.

NOTES

31 This includes, under certain conditions, businesses that have to be carved out from a party's business or individual assets; see below paragraphs 35 ff.

32 Case IV/M.913 — *Siemens/Elektrowatt* of 18 November 1997; Case IV/M.1578 — *Sanitec/Sphinx* of 1 December 1999, at paragraph 255; Case COMP/M.1802 — *Unilever/Amora-Maille* of 8 March 2000; Case COMP/M.1990 — *Unilever/Bestfoods* of 28 September 2000.

33 Notifying parties will have to undertake in the commitments that the business to be divested includes all those assets and personnel. Where the detailed description of the business, to be provided by the parties as set out in paragraph 27, will at a later point in time appear to be incomplete in that respect and the parties do not complement the business with the necessary additional assets or personnel, the Commission may consider revoking the conditional clearance decision.

34 Council Directive 98/59/EC of 20 July 1998 on the approximation of the laws of the Member States relating to collective redundancies (OJ L225, 12.8.1998, p 16).

35 Council Directive 2001/23/EC of 12 March 2001 on the approximation of the laws of the Member States relating to the safeguarding of employees' rights in the event of transfers of undertakings, businesses or parts of undertakings or businesses (OJ L82, 22.3.2001, p 16).

36 Council Directive 94/45/EC of 22 September 1994 on the establishment of a European Works Council or a procedure in Community-scale undertakings and Community-scale groups of undertakings for the purposes of informing and consulting employees (OJ L254, 30.9.1994, p 64); Directive 2002/14/EC of the European Parliament and of the Council of 11 March 2002 establishing a general framework for informing and consulting employees in the European Community (OJ L80, 23.3.2002, p 29).

37 Case COMP/M.1806 — *AstraZeneca/Novartis* of 26 July 2000; COMP/M.1628 — *TotalFina/Elf* of 9 February 2000; Case IV/M.603 — *Crown Cork & Seal/CarnaudMetalbox* of 14 November 1995.

38 Case COMP/M.2544 — *Masterfoods/Royal Canin* of 15 February 2002; Case COMP/M.2337 — *Nestlé/Ralston Purina* of 27 July 2001; Case IV/M.623 — *Kimberly-Clark/Scott Paper* of 16 January 1996; Case COMP/M.3779 — *Pernod Ricard/Allied Domecq* of 24 June 2005.

39 See Case COMP/M.2972 — *DSM/Roche Vitamins* of 23 July 2003; Case IV/M.1378 — *Hoechst/Rhône-Poulenc* of 9 August 1999; Case COMP/M.1601 — *Allied Signal/Honeywell* of 1 December 1999; Case COMP/M.1671 — *Dow/UCC* of 3 May 2000.

40 Case COMP/M.2949 — *Finmeccanica/Alenia Telespazio* of 30 October 2002; Case COMP/M.3593 — *Apollo/Bakelite* of 11 April 2005, commitment on carbon bond refractory licence; for cases from the pharmaceutical industry see Case COMP/M.2972 — *DSM/Roche Vitamins* of 23 July 2003; Case IV/M.555 — *Glaxo/Wellcome* of 28 February 1995.

41 Case COMP/M.2972 — *DSM/Roche Vitamins* of 23 July 2003.

42 However, even in these conditions a divestiture of the brand may be more appropriate, especially if the resulting split in the ownership of the brand corresponds to common practice in the industry, see for the pharmaceutical industry Case COMP/M.3544 — *Bayer Healthcare/Roche (OTC)* of 19 November 2004, paragraph 59 concerning the divestiture of the Desenex brand.

43 COMP/M.3149 — *Procter&Gamble/Wella* paragraph 60; IV/M.623 — *Kimberly-Clark/Scott Paper* of 16 January 1996, paragraph 236(i). This is particularly important during the licence phase in which the licensee has to prepare for the launch of a new competitive brand. Such a launch of a new brand appears to not be feasible if the purchaser had to spend considerable resources on the production process, marketing and distribution of the licensed brand; COMP/M.2337 — *Nestlé/Ralston Purina* of 27 July 2001, paragraphs 67 *et seq*; COMP/M.2621 — *SEB/Moulinex* of 8 January 2002, paragraph 140.

44 COMP/M.3149 — *Procter&Gamble/Wella* of 30 July 2003, paragraph 61; COMP/M.2337 — *Nestlé/Ralstone Purina* of 27 July 2001, paragraph 68; COMP/M.2621 — *SEB/Moulinex* of 8 January 2002, paragraph 141; IV/M.623 — *Kimberly-Clark/Scott Paper* of 16 January 1996, paragraph 236(ii).

45 For example taking into account the life cycle of products, c.f. COMP/M.2621 — *SEB/Moulinex* of 8 January 2002, paragraph 141, where effectively the duration of the commitments covered a period equal to about three product life cycles; confirmed by judgment of CFI in Case T-119/02 *Royal Philips Electronics NV v Commission* [2003] ECR II-1433, paragraphs 112 *et seq.*

46 An influence by the previous owner of the business in the competitive behaviour of the divested business risking to frustrate the objective of the remedy.

47 See judgment of the CFI in Case T-210/01 *General Electric v Commission* [2005] ECR II-5575, paragraph 617; COMP/M.1453 — *AXA/GRE* of 8 April 1999.

48 The alternative may consist of an entirely different business or, in case of uncertainty as to finding a suitable buyer, of additional businesses and assets that are added to the initial package.

49 Case IV/M.913 — *Siemens/Elektrowatt* of 18 November 1997.

50 See commitments in Case COMP/M.2621 — *SEB/Moulinex* of 8 January 2002, which foresee that the licensee needs to have its own trademark used in the sector concerned. Certain markets may require a sufficient degree of recognition by customers for a purchaser to be able to translate the business to be divested into a competitive force on the market.

51 The transfer of the business may be implemented after the Commission decision.

52 This terminology might be used differently in other jurisdictions.

53 Case COMP/M.3796 — *Omya/Huber PCC* of 19 July 2006; Case COMP/M.2972 — *DSM/Roche Vitamins* of 23 July 2003; Case COMP/M.2060 — *Bosch/Rexroth* of 13 December 2000; Case COMP/M.2337 — *Nestlé/Ralston Purina* of 27 July 2001; Case COMP/M.2544 — *Masterfoods/Royal Canin* of 15 February 2002; Case COMP/M.2947 — *Verbund/Energie Allianz* of 11 June 2003.

54 See Case COMP/M.2060 — *Bosch/Rexroth* of 13 December 2000, paragraph 92.

55 See Case COMP/M.2060 — *Bosch/Rexroth* of 13 December 2000, paragraph 95.

56 Such agreements are normally conditional to the final Commission decision accepting the remedy in question.

57 See Case COMP/M.3916 — *T-Mobile Austria/tele.ring* of April 2006, the divestiture of certain mobile telephony sites and frequencies, not constituting a viable business, could only take place to a competitor which was likely to play a similar role in the market as tele.ring; Case COMP/M.4000 — *Inco/Falconbridge* of 4 July 2006, the divestiture of a nickel processing business could only take place to a competitor vertically integrated into the supply of nickel; Case COMP/M.4187 — *Metso/Aker Kvaerner* of 12 December 2006, only one purchaser was suitable for acquiring the businesses to be divested as it was the only one with the necessary know-how and the necessary presence in neighbouring markets; Case COMP/M.3436 — *Continental/Phoenix* of 26 October 2004, only the partner in the distribution joint venture was able to render the divested business viable; Case COMP/M.3136 — *GE/Agfa* of 5 December 2003.

58 Case IV/M.942 — *VEBA/Degussa* of 3 December 1997.

59 Case COMP/M.3653 — *Siemens/VA Tech* of 13 July 2005, paragraphs 491, 493 ff.

60 See Case COMP/M.3653 — *Siemens/VA Tech* of 13 July 2005, paragraphs 327 ff., where effects from the minority stake in financial respect could be excluded as a put option for the sale of this stake had already been exercised.

61 Case COMP/M.4153 — *Toshiba/Westinghouse* of 19 September 2006.

62 See Case COMP/M.3440 — *ENI/EDP/GDP* of 9 December 2004, paragraphs 648–672.

63 See for the termination of distribution agreements Case COMP/M.3779 — *Pernod Ricard/Allied Domecq* of 24 June 2005; Case COMP/M.3658 — *Orkla/Chips* of 3 March 2005.

64 See particularly the sea transport sector, Case COMP/M.3829 — *Maersk/PONL* of 29 July 2005 and Case COMP/M.3863 — *TUI/CP Ships* of 12 October 2005. In those cases, the parties committed to withdraw from certain liner conferences and consortia.

65 Case COMP/M.3680 — *Alcatel/Finmeccanica/Alcatel Alenia Space & Telespazio* of 28 April 2005, where a divestiture was impossible.

66 See judgment of the CFI in Case T-177/04 *easyJet v Commission* [2006] ECR II-1931, at paragraphs 197 *et seq.*

67 See Case COMP/M.2876 — *Newscorp/Telepiù* of 2 April 2003, paragraphs 225 *et seq*, where the commitments package included access of competitors to all essential elements of a pay-TV network, such as 1. access to the necessary content; 2. access to the technical platform as well as 3. access to the necessary technical services. Similarly, in Case COMP/JV.37 — *BskyB/Kirch Pay TV* of 21 March 2000, confirmed by judgment of CFI in Case T-158/00 *ARD v Commission* [2003] ECR II-3825, the Commission accepted a commitments package which allowed other operators comprehensive access to the pay-TV market.

68 See Case COMP/M.3696 — *E.ON/MOL* of 21 December 2005; Case COMP/M.3868 — *DONG/Elsam/Energi E2* of 14 March 2006.

69 In air transport mergers, a mere reduction of barriers to entry by a commitment of the parties to offer slots on specific airports may not always be sufficient to ensure the entry of new competitors on those routes where competition problems arise and to render the remedy equivalent in its effects to a divestiture.

70 Case COMP/M.2533 — *BP/E.ON* of 20 December 2001, access to pipelines in addition to divestiture of shares in a pipeline company; Case COMP/M.2389 — *Shell/DEA* of 20 December 2001, access to an ethylene import terminal.

71 For access to telecom networks, see Case COMP/M.2803 — *Telia/Sonera* of 10 July 2002; Case IV/M.1439 — *Telia/Telenor* of 13 October 1999; Case COMP/M.1795 — *Vodafone/Mannesmann* of 12 April 2000. See also Case COMP/M.2903 — *DaimlerChrysler/Deutsche Telekom/JV* of 30 April 2003, where the Commission accepted a commitments package to grant third parties access to a telematics network and to reduce the entry barriers by allowing them to use parts of a telematics device, designed for toll collection, provided by the parties.

72 See the "qualitative moratorium" in Case COMP/M.2903 — *DaimlerChrysler/Deutsche Telekom/JV* of 30 April 2003, paragraph 76.

73 Case COMP/M.3083 — *GE/Instrumentarium* of 2 September 2003; Case COMP/M.2861 — *Siemens/Draegerwerk* of 30 April 2003.

74 See Case COMP/M.3998 — *Axalto/Gemplus* of 19 May 2006.

75 See eg Case COMP/M.2803 — *Telia/Sonera* of 10 July 2002; Case COMP/M.2903 — *DaimlerChrysler/Deutsche Telekom/JV* of 30 April 2003.

76 As to the effects of arbitration clauses, see judgment of CFI in Case T-158/00 *ARD v Commission* [2003] ECR II-3825, paragraphs 212, 295, 352; CFI judgment in Case T-177/04 *easyJet v Commission* [2006] ECR II-1931, paragraph 186.

77 See Case COMP/M.2876 — *Newscorp/Telepiù*; Case COMP/M.3916 — *T-Mobile Austria/tele.ring*.

78 CFI, judgment in Case T-158/00 *ARD v Commission* [2003] ECR II-3825, paragraphs 212, 295, 352.

79 See judgments of the CFI in Case T-87/05 *EDP v Commission* [2005] ECR II-3745, at paragraphs 102 *et seq*; and Case T-177/04 *easyJet v Commission* [2006] ECR II-1931, at paragraph 188.

80 See Commission Notice on non-horizontal mergers [. . .]; Case IV/M.986 — *AGFA Gevaert/DuPont* of 11 February 1998.

81 Case COMP/M.2876 — *Newscorp/Telepiù* of 2 April 2003, paragraphs 225 *et seq*, granting unilateral termination rights to suppliers of TV content, limiting the scope of the exclusivity clauses and limiting the duration of future exclusive agreements relating to supply of content; Case COMP/M.2822 — *ENI/EnBW/GVS* of 17 December 2002, granting of early termination rights to all local gas distributors concerning long-term gas supply agreements; Case IV/M.1571 — *New Holland* of 28 October 1999; Case IV/M.1467 — *Rohm and Haas/Morton* of 19 April 1999.

82 See, as an example for such remedies, Case COMP/M.3440 — *ENI/EDP/GDP* of 9 December 2004, paragraphs 663, 719.

83 See, in relation to conglomerate effects of a concentration, ECJ, judgment of 15 February 2005 in Case C-12/03 P *Commission v Tetra Laval* [2005] ECR I-987, paragraphs 85, 89.

84 However, the review clause is of particular relevance for access remedies, which systematically should include such a clause; see below paragraph 74.

85 As mentioned in paragraph 30, the Commission may approve a purchaser without some of the assets or personnel foreseen if this does not affect the competitiveness and viability of the divested business. Similarly, the non-requisition clause, as explained in paragraph 43, prohibits the re-acquisition of control over the assets divested only if

the Commission has not previously found that the market structure has changed to such an extent that the divestiture is no longer necessary.

86 See examples in judgment of CFI in Case T-119/02 *Royal Philips Electronics NV v Commission* [2003] ECR II-1433, paragraph 184.

87 See Case COMP/M.3868 — *DONG/Elsam/Energi E2* of 14 March 2006, paragraph 24 of the Annex.

IV. ASPECTS OF PROCEDURE FOR SUBMISSION OF COMMITMENTS

1. Phase I

[4.714]

77. Pursuant to Article 6(2) of the Merger Regulation the Commission may declare a concentration compatible with the common market also before the initiation of proceedings, where it is confident that following modification a notified concentration no longer raises serious doubts within the meaning of paragraph 1(c).

78. Parties can submit proposals for commitments to the Commission on an informal basis, even before notification. Parties have to submit commitments within not more than 20 working days from the date of the receipt of the notification.[88] The Commission informs the parties about its serious doubts in due time before that deadline.[89] Where the parties submit commitments, the deadline for the Commission's decision pursuant to Article 6(1) of the Merger Regulation is extended from 25 to 35 working days.[90]

79. In order to form the basis of a decision pursuant to Article 6(2), proposals for commitments must meet the following requirements:

(a) they shall fully specify the substantive and implementing commitments entered into by the parties;
(b) they shall be signed by a person duly authorised to do so;
(c) they shall be accompanied by the information on the commitments offered as provided for in the Implementing Regulation (as explained above in paragraph 7); and
(d) they shall be accompanied by a non-confidential version of the commitments[91] for the purposes of market testing them with third parties. The non-confidential version of the commitments must allow third parties to fully assess the workability and the effectiveness of the proposed remedies to remove the competition concerns.

80. Proposals submitted by the parties in accordance with these requirements will be assessed by the Commission. The Commission will consult the authorities of the Member States on the proposed commitments and, when considered appropriate, also third parties in the form of a market test, including in particular those third parties and the recognised representatives[92] of those employees whose positions are directly affected by the proposed remedies. In markets with national regulatory authorities the Commission may also, if appropriate, consult the competent national regulatory authorities.[93] In addition, in cases involving a geographic market that is wider than the European Economic Area ("EEA") or where, for reasons related to the viability of the business, the scope of the business to be divested is wider than the EEA territory, the non-confidential version of the proposed remedies may also be discussed with non-EEA competition authorities in the framework of the Community's bilateral cooperation agreements with these countries.

81. Commitments in phase I can only be accepted where the competition problem is readily identifiable and can easily be remedied.[94] The competition problem therefore needs to be so straightforward and the remedies so clear-cut that it is not necessary to enter into an in-depth investigation and that the commitments are sufficient to clearly rule out "serious doubts" within the meaning of Article 6(1)(c) of the Merger Regulation.[95] Where the assessment confirms that the proposed commitments remove the grounds for serious doubts on this basis, the Commission clears the merger in phase I.

82. Due to the time-constraints in phase I, it is particularly important for the parties to submit in a timely manner to the Commission the information required in the Implementing Regulation to properly assess the content and workability of the commitments and their suitability to maintain conditions of effective competition in the common market on a permanent basis. If the parties do not comply with the obligation in the Implementing Regulation, the Commission may not be able to conclude that the proposed commitments will remove the grounds for serious doubts.

83. Where the assessment shows that the commitments offered are not sufficient to remove the competition concerns raised by the concentration, the parties will be informed accordingly. Given that phase I remedies are designed to provide a clear-cut answer to a readily identifiable competition concern, only limited modifications can be accepted to the proposed commitments. Such modifications, presented as an immediate response to the result of the consultations, may include clarifications, refinements and/or other improvements designed to ensure that the commitments are workable and effective. However, such modifications may only be accepted in circumstances where it is ensured that the Commission can carry out a proper assessment of those commitments.[96]

84. If the Commission's final assessment of a case shows that there are no competition concerns in one or more markets, the parties will be informed accordingly and may withdraw the unnecessary commitments for such markets. If the parties do not withdraw them, the Commission will normally ignore them in the decision. In any event, such commitment proposals do not constitute a condition for clearance.

85. Where the parties are informed that the Commission intends to maintain in its final decision that the transaction raises competition concerns for a specific market, it is for the parties to propose commitments. The Commission is not in a position to impose unilaterally any conditions to an authorisation decision, but only on the basis of the parties' commitments.[97] However, the Commission will review whether the commitments submitted by the parties are proportionate to the competition problem when assessing whether to attach them as conditions or obligations to its

final decision.[98] Nevertheless, it has to be stressed that, in a commitments proposal, all those elements which are required to fulfil the basic conditions for acceptable commitments as set out above in paragraphs 9 *et seq* will be considered necessary. This paragraph as well as the previous one also applies to commitments in phase II.

86. If the Commission concludes that the commitments offered by the parties do not remove the serious doubts, it will issue an Article 6(1)(c) decision and open proceedings.

2.
Phase II

87. Pursuant to Article 8(2) of the Merger Regulation, the Commission must declare a concentration compatible with the common market, where following modification a notified concentration does no longer significantly impede effective competition within the meaning of Article 2(3) of the Merger Regulation.

88. Commitments proposed to the Commission pursuant to Article 8(2) must be submitted to the Commission within not more than 65 working days from the day on which proceedings were initiated. Where the deadlines for the final decision have been extended according to Article 10(3) of the Merger Regulation, also the deadline for remedies is automatically extended by the same number of days.[99] Only in exceptional circumstances, the Commission may accept that commitments are submitted for the first time after the expiry of this period. The request by the parties for an extension of the deadline must be received within the period and has to set forth the exceptional circumstances which, according to the parties, justify it. In addition to the existence of exceptional circumstances, an extension is only possible where there is sufficient time to make a proper assessment of the proposal by the Commission and to allow adequate consultation with Member States and third parties.[100]

89. The question whether or not submitting remedies will extend the deadline for the Commission to take a final decision depends on the time in the procedure when the commitments are submitted. Where the parties submit commitments within less than 55 working days after the initiation of proceedings, the Commission has to take a final decision within not more than 90 working days of the date of initiation of proceedings.[101] Where the parties submit commitments on working day 55 or afterwards (even after working day 65, if those commitments should be acceptable due to exceptional circumstances as described above in paragraph 88), the period for the Commission to take a final decision is increased to 105 working days according to Article 10(3), subparagraph 2. Where the parties submit commitments within less than 55 working days, but submit a modified version on day 55 or thereafter, the period to take a final decision will also be extended to 105 working days.

90. The Commission is available to discuss suitable commitments well in advance of the end of the 65 working day period. The parties are encouraged to submit draft proposals dealing with both substantive and implementation aspects which are necessary to ensure that the commitments are fully workable. If the parties are of the opinion that more time is needed for the investigation of the competition concerns and for the corresponding design of appropriate commitments, they may also suggest to the Commission to extend the final deadline under Article 10(3), subparagraph 1. Such a request will have to be made before the end of the 65 working day period. Indeed, the Commission will normally not extend the period for adopting a final decision according to Article 10(3), subparagraph 1 where the request for extension is presented after the deadline for submitting remedies foreseen in the Implementing Regulation, ie after working day 65.[102]

91. In order to meet the requirements for a decision pursuant to Article 8(2), commitments must meet the following requirements:

(a) they shall address all competition concerns raised by the concentration and shall fully specify the substantive and implementing commitments entered into by the parties;
(b) they shall be signed by a person duly authorised to do so;
(c) they shall by accompanied by the information on the commitments offered as provided for in the Implementing Regulation (as explained above in paragraph 7); and
(d) they shall be accompanied by a non-confidential version of the commitments[103] for the purposes of market testing them with third parties, fulfilling the requirements set out above in paragraph 79.

92. Proposals submitted by the parties in accordance with these requirements will be assessed by the Commission. If the assessment confirms that the proposed commitments remove the serious doubts (if no Statement of Objection has been issued yet by the Commission) or the competition concerns raised in the Statement of Objections, following the consultations as set out in paragraph 80 above, the Commission will adopt a conditional clearance decision.

93. Conversely, where the assessment leads to the conclusion that the proposed commitments appear not to be sufficient to resolve the competition concerns raised by the concentration, the parties will be informed accordingly.[104]

94. The Merger Regulation does not impose any obligation on the Commission to accept commitments after the legal deadline for remedies, unless the Commission voluntarily undertakes to assess commitments in specific circumstances.[105] In view of this, where parties subsequently modify the proposed commitments after the deadline of 65 working days, the Commission will only accept these modified commitments where it can clearly determine — on the basis of its assessment of information already received in the course of the investigation, including the results of prior market testing, and without the need for any other market test — that such commitments, once implemented, fully and unambiguously resolve the competition concerns identified and where there is sufficient time to allow for an adequate assessment by the Commission and for proper consultation with Member States.[106, 107] The Commission will normally reject modified commitments which do not fulfil those conditions.[108]

NOTES

88 Article 19(1) of the Implementing Regulation.

89 The notifying parties will normally be offered the opportunity of attending a state of play meeting in such circumstances, see point 33 of the DG COMPETITION Best Practices on the conduct of EC merger control proceedings.

90 Article 10(1), subparagraph 2 of the Merger Regulation.

[91] Article 20(2) of the Implementing Regulation.

[92] Cf. Article 2(1)(c) of Council Directive 2001/23/EC of 12 March 2001 on the approximation of the laws of the Member States relating to the safeguarding of employees' rights in the event of transfers of undertakings, businesses or parts of undertakings or businesses (OJ L82, 22.3.2001, p 16). See also Article 2(1)(g) of Council Directive 94/45/EC of 22 September 1994 on the establishment of a European Works Council or a procedure in Community-scale undertakings and Community-scale groups of undertakings for the purposes of informing and consulting employees (OJ L254, 30.9.1994, p 64).

[93] For the role of national regulatory authorities in a dispute resolution mechanism, see paragraph 66.

[94] See recital 30 of the Merger Regulation.

[95] See judgment of CFI in Case T-119/02 *Royal Philips Electronics NV v Commission* [2003] ECR II-1433, paragraphs 79 *et seq.*

[96] See recital 17 of the Implementing Regulation and judgment of the CFI, Case T-119/02 *Royal Philips Electronics NV v Commission* [2003] ECR II-1433, paragraphs 237 *et seq.*

[97] See above paragraph 6.

[98] See judgment of ECJ of 18 December 2007 in Case C-202/06 P *Cementbouw v Commission* [2007], paragraph 54.

[99] Article 19(2), subparagraph 2 of the Implementing Regulation.

[100] Article 19(2), subparagraph 3 of the Implementing Regulation. See Case COMP/M.1439 — *Telia/Telenor* of 13 October 1999; Case IV/M.754 — *Anglo American Corporation/Lonrho* of 23 April 1997.

[101] Where the deadlines for the final decision have been extended according to Article 10(3) subparagraph 2 of the Merger Regulation before working day 55, this period is also extended.

[102] The Court of First Instance confirmed that the Merger Regulation and the Implementing Regulation do not impose any obligations on the Commission to accept commitments which are submitted after the legal deadline, as set out below in paragraph 94, see Case T-87/05 *EDP v Commission* [2005] ECR II-3745, at paragraph 161. Therefore, the Commission is not bound to consider any remedies which are submitted by the parties after the deadline for remedies, even if the parties were to agree to extend the final deadline. Moreover, this would not correspond to the purpose, as explained in recital 35 of the Merger Regulation, of the extensions foreseen in Article 10(3). The extension foreseen in Article 10(3), subparagraph 1 is to allow for sufficient time for the investigation of the competitive concerns, whereas it is the purpose of the extension laid down in Article 10(3), subparagraph 2 to allow for sufficient time for the analysis and market testing of commitments.

[103] Article 20(2) of the Implementing Regulation.

[104] See paragraphs 30 ff. of the DG Competition Best Practices on the conduct of EC merger proceedings which provide for several state of play meetings between the Commission and the parties throughout the procedure.

[105] See judgment of CFI in Case T-87/05 *EDP v Commission* [2005] ECR II-3745, at paragraphs 161 *et seq*. See also judgement of CFI in case T-290/94 *Kaysersberg SA v Commission* [1997] ECR II-2137.

[106] Case COMP/M.3440 — *ENI/EDP/GDP* of 9 December 2004, paragraphs 855 *et seq*; confirmed by Judgment of CFI in Case T-87/05 *EDP v Commission* [2005] ECR II-3745, at paragraphs 162 *et seq*; Case COMP/M.1628 — *TotalFina/Elf* of 9 March 2000, at paragraph 345.

[107] This consultation normally requires that the Commission has to be able to send a draft of the final decision, including an assessment of the modified commitments, to the Member States not less than 10 working days before the Advisory Committee with Member States. This period may only be shortened in exceptional circumstances (Article 19(5) of the Merger Regulation).

[108] See Case COMP/M.3440 — *ENI/EDP/GDP* of 9 December 2004, paragraph 913.

V. REQUIREMENTS FOR IMPLEMENTATION OF COMMITMENTS

[4.715]

95. Commitments are offered as a means of securing a clearance, with the implementation normally taking place after the decision. Commitments therefore require safeguards to ensure their effective and timely implementation. These implementing provisions will normally form part of the commitments entered into by the parties vis-à-vis the Commission.

96. In the following, detailed guidance is given on the implementation of divestiture commitments, as the most typical commitment. Afterwards, some aspects of the implementation of other types of commitments are discussed.

1. DIVESTITURE PROCESS

97. The divestiture has to be completed within a fixed time period agreed between the parties and the Commission. In the Commission's practice, the total time period is divided into a period for entering into a final agreement and a further period for the closing, the transfer of legal title, of the transaction. The period for entering into a binding agreement is further normally divided into a first period in which the parties can look for a suitable purchaser (the "first divestiture period") and, if the parties do not succeed to divest the business, a second period in which a divestiture trustee obtains the mandate to divest the business at no minimum price (the "trustee divestiture period").

98. The Commission's experience has shown that short divestiture periods contribute largely to the success of the divestiture as, otherwise, the business to be divested will be exposed to an extended period of uncertainty. The time periods should therefore be as short as feasible. The Commission will normally consider a period of around six months for the first divestiture period and an additional period of three months for the trustee divestiture period as appropriate. A period of further three months is normally foreseen for closing the transaction. These periods may be modified on a case-by-case basis. In particular, they may have to be shortened if there is a high risk of degradation of the business' viability in the interim period.

99. The deadline for the divestiture shall normally start on the day of the adoption of the Commission decision. An exception might be justified for a transaction via public bid where the parties commit to divest a business belonging to the target. Where in such circumstances the parties cannot prepare for the divestiture of the target's business before closing of the notified concentration, the Commission might accept that the periods for such a divestiture only start

with the date of closing the notified transaction. Similarly, such a solution may be considered if the date of closing of the concentration is not under the control of the parties as it, eg requires state approval.[109] In return, it may be appropriate to shorten the deadlines in order to reduce the time of uncertainty for the business to be divested.

100. Whereas for up-front buyer solutions the above-described procedure applies, the procedure will be different for fix-it-first solutions. In general, a binding agreement with a purchaser will already be entered into during the procedure so that after the decision only a further period for the closing of the transaction has to be foreseen. If before the decision only a framework agreement has been concluded with the purchaser, the periods to be foreseen for entering into a full agreement and the closing afterwards will have to be decided on a case-by-case basis.[110]

2. APPROVAL OF THE PURCHASER AND OF THE SALE AND PURCHASE AGREEMENT

101. In order to ensure the effectiveness of the commitment, the sale to a proposed purchaser is subject to prior approval by the Commission. When the parties (or the divestiture trustee) have reached a final agreement with a purchaser, they have to submit a reasoned and documented proposal to the Commission. The parties or the divestiture trustee, as the case may be, will be required to demonstrate to the satisfaction of the Commission that the proposed purchaser meets the purchaser requirements, and that the business is divested in a manner consistent with the Commission's decision and the commitments. Where the commitments allow that different purchasers are being proposed for different parts of the package, the Commission will assess whether each individual proposed purchaser is acceptable and that the total package solves the competition concern.

102. In assessing any proposed purchaser, the Commission will interpret the purchaser requirements in the light of the purpose of the commitments, to immediately maintain effective competition in the market where competition concerns had been found, and of the market circumstances as set out in the decision.[111] Generally, the basis for the Commission's assessment of the purchaser requirements will be the submission of the parties, the assessment of the monitoring trustee and, in particular, discussions with the proposed purchaser and its business plan. The Commission will further analyse whether the underlying assumptions of the purchaser appear plausible according to the market circumstances.

103. The requirement that the purchaser has to have the necessary financial resources extends in particular to the way the acquisition is financed by the proposed purchaser. The Commission will normally not accept any financing of the divestiture by the seller, and, in particular, any seller financing if this were to give the seller a share in the profits of the divested business in the future.

104. In assessing whether the proposed purchaser threatens to create competition problems, the Commission will undertake a prima facie assessment in the light of the information available to the Commission in the purchaser approval process. Where the purchase results in a concentration that has a Community dimension, this new operation will have to be notified under the Merger Regulation and cleared under normal procedures.[112] Where this is not the case, the Commission's approval of a proposed purchaser is without prejudice to the merger control jurisdiction of national authorities. In addition, the proposed purchaser must be expected to obtain all other necessary approvals from the relevant regulatory authorities. Where it can be foreseen, in the light of the information available to the Commission, that difficulties in obtaining merger control clearance or other approvals may unduly delay the timely implementation of the commitment, it will be considered that the proposed purchaser does not meet the purchaser requirements. Otherwise, the competition concerns identified by the Commission would not be removed in the appropriate time-frame.

105. The requirement for an approval by the Commission does usually not only extend to the identity of the purchaser, but also to the sale and purchase agreement and any other agreement entered into between the parties and the proposed purchaser, including transitory agreements. The Commission will verify whether the divestiture according to the agreements is in line with the commitments.[113]

106. The Commission will communicate its view as to the suitability of the proposed purchaser to the parties. If the Commission concludes that the proposed purchaser does not meet the purchaser requirements, it will adopt a decision that the proposed purchaser is not a purchaser under the commitments.[114] If the Commission concludes that the sale and purchase agreement (or any ancillary agreements) does not foresee a divestiture in line with the commitments, the Commission will communicate this to the parties without necessarily rejecting the purchaser as such. If the Commission concludes that the purchaser is suitable under the commitments and that the contracts agree a divestiture in line with the commitments, the Commission will approve the divestiture to the proposed purchaser.[115] The Commission will issue the necessary approvals as expeditiously as possible.

3. OBLIGATIONS OF THE PARTIES IN THE INTERIM PERIOD

107. Parties have to fulfil certain obligations in the interim period (as defined above in paragraph 36). The following should normally be included in the commitments in this respect: (i) safeguards for the interim preservation of the viability to the business; (ii) the necessary steps for a carve-out process, if relevant; and (iii) the necessary steps to prepare the divestiture of the business.

Interim preservation of the divested business

108. It is the parties' responsibility to reduce to the minimum any possible risk of loss of competitive potential of the business to be divested resulting from the uncertainties inherent in the transfer of a business. Up to the transfer of the business to the purchaser, the Commission will require the parties to offer commitments to maintain the independence, economic viability, marketability and competitiveness of the business. Only such commitments will allow the Commission to conclude with the requisite degree of certainty that the divestiture of the business will be implemented in the way as proposed by the parties in the commitments.

109. Generally, these commitments should be designed to keep the business separate from the business retained by the parties, and to ensure that it is managed as a distinct and saleable business in its best interest, with a view to ensuring its continued economic viability, marketability and competitiveness and its independence from the businesses retained by the parties.

110. The parties will be required to ensure that all assets of the business are maintained, pursuant to good business practice and in the ordinary course of business, and that no acts which might have a significant adverse impact on the business are carried out. This relates in particular to the maintenance of fixed assets, know-how or commercial information of a confidential or proprietary nature, the customer base and the technical and commercial competence of the employees. Furthermore, the parties must maintain the business in the same conditions as before the concentration, in particular provide sufficient resources, such as capital or a line of credit, on the basis and continuation of existing business plans, the same administrative and management functions, or other factors relevant for maintaining competition in the specific sector. The commitments also have to foresee that the parties should take all reasonable steps, including appropriate incentive schemes, to encourage all key personnel to remain with the business, and that the parties may not solicit or move any personnel to their remaining businesses.

111. The parties should further hold the business separate from its retained business and ensure that the key personnel of the business to be divested do not have any involvement into the retained businesses and vice versa. If the business to be divested is in corporate form and a strict separation of the corporate structure appears necessary, the parties' rights as shareholders, in particular the voting rights, should be exercised by the monitoring trustee which should also have the power to replace the board members appointed on behalf of the parties. In relation to information, the parties must ring-fence the business to be divested and take all necessary measures to ensure that the parties do not obtain any business secrets or other confidential information. Any documents or information confidential to the business obtained by the parties before adoption of the decision have to be returned to the business or destroyed.

112. The parties are further generally required to appoint a hold-separate manager with the necessary expertise, who will be responsible for the management of the business and the implementation of the hold-separate and ring-fencing obligations. The hold-separate manager should act under the supervision of the monitoring trustee who may issue instructions to the hold-separate manager. The commitments have to provide that the appointment should take place immediately after the adoption of the decision and even before the parties may close the notified concentration. Whereas the parties can appoint the hold-separate manager on their own, the commitments have to foresee that the monitoring trustee is able to remove the hold-separate manager if s/he does not act in line with the commitments or endangers their timely and proper implementation. A new appointment of a hold-separate manager afterwards will be subject to the approval of the monitoring trustee.

Steps for a carve-out

113. As outlined above in paragraph 35, the Commission may accept in appropriate circumstances that the divestiture of a business which needs to be carved out from the remaining businesses of the parties can be considered a suitable remedy. Nevertheless, also in such circumstances only the transfer of a viable business to a purchaser which can maintain and develop this business as an active competitive force in the market will remove the Commission's competition concerns. Therefore, the parties have to commit to a result-oriented obligation to carry out, in the interim period, a carve-out of the assets that contribute to the divested business. The result has to be that a viable and competitive business, which is stand-alone and separate from the other businesses of the parties, can be transferred to a suitable purchaser at the end of the interim period. The parties will have to bear the costs and risks of such a carve-out in the interim period.

114. The carve-out will need to be carried out by the parties under the supervision of the trustee and in cooperation with the hold-separate manager. First, those assets and parts of the personnel which are shared between the business to be divested and remaining businesses of the parties have to be allocated to the business to the extent that this is not excluded in the commitments.[116] The allocation of the assets and the personnel will be monitored and has to be approved by the monitoring trustee. Second, the carve-out process may also require a replication for the business of assets held or functions performed by other parts of the parties' businesses if this is necessary to ensure the viability and competitiveness of the business to be divested. An example is the termination of the business' participation in a central information technology network and an installation of a separate IT system for the business. In general, the major steps of such a carve-out process and the functions to be replicated should be decided on a case-by-case basis and described in the commitments.

115. At the same time, it has to be ensured that the viability of the business to be divested is not affected by such measures. In the interim period, the parties therefore have to maintain the use of shared assets by and to continue to provide services to the business to the same extent as in the past as long as the business is not yet viable on a stand-alone basis.

Specific obligations of the parties concerning the divestiture process

116. For the divestiture process, the commitments should foresee that potential purchasers can carry out a due diligence exercise and obtain, dependent on the stage of the procedure, sufficient information concerning the divested business to allow the purchaser to fully assess the value, scope and commercial potential of the business, and have direct access to its personnel. The parties further have to submit periodic reports on potential purchasers and developments in the negotiations. The divestiture will only be implemented once the transaction is closed, that is the legal title has passed to the approved purchaser, and the assets have been actually transferred. At the end of the process, the parties will have to send a final report, confirming the closing and the transfer of the assets.

4. THE MONITORING AND THE DIVESTITURE TRUSTEE

Role of the monitoring trustee

117. As the Commission cannot, on a daily basis, be directly involved in overseeing the implementation of the commitments, the parties have to propose the appointment of a trustee to oversee the parties' compliance with the commitments, in particular with their obligations in the interim period and the divestiture process (the so-called

"monitoring trustee"). Thereby, the parties guarantee the effectiveness of the commitments submitted by them and allow the Commission to ensure that the modification of the notified concentration, as proposed by the parties, will be carried out with the requisite degree of certainty.

118. The monitoring trustee will carry out its tasks under the supervision of the Commission and is to be considered the Commission's "eyes and ears". It shall be the guardian that the business is managed and kept properly on a stand-alone basis in the interim period. The Commission may therefore give any orders and instructions to the monitoring trustee in order to ensure compliance with the commitments, and the trustee may propose to the parties any measures it considers necessary for carrying out its tasks. The parties, however, may not issue any instructions to the trustee without approval by the Commission.

119. The Commitments will generally set out the tasks of the monitoring trustee. Its duties and obligations will be specified in detail in the trustee mandate, to be concluded between the parties and the trustee, and its tasks shall be further detailed in a work-plan. The tasks of the monitoring trustee will normally start immediately after the adoption of the Commission decision and last until the legal and actual transfer of the business to the approved purchaser. Five main, non-exhaustive tasks can be distinguished which the monitoring trustee should carry out under the supervision of the Commission:

— first, the monitoring trustee will be called upon to oversee the safeguards for the business to be divested in the interim period,
— second, in carve-out cases, the monitoring trustee has to monitor the splitting of assets and the allocation of the personnel between the divested business and retained businesses by the parties as well as the replication of assets and functions in the business previously provided by the parties,
— third, the monitoring trustee shall be responsible for overseeing the parties' efforts to find a potential purchaser and to transfer the business. In general, it shall review the progress of the divestiture process and the potential purchasers included in the process. It shall verify that potential purchasers receive sufficient information relating to the business — in particular by reviewing the information memorandum (if available), the data room or the due diligence process. Once a purchaser is proposed, the monitoring trustee shall submit to the Commission a reasoned opinion as to whether the proposed purchaser fulfils the purchaser requirements in the commitments and whether the business is sold in a manner consistent with the commitments. At the end of the process, the monitoring trustee has to oversee the legal and actual transfer of the business to the purchaser and make a final report, confirming the transfer,
— fourth, the monitoring trustee shall act as a contact point for any requests by third parties, in particular potential purchasers, in relation to the commitments. The parties shall inform interested third parties of the identity and the tasks of the monitoring trustee, including any potential purchasers. In case of disagreement between the parties and third parties in relation to matters dealt with by the commitments, the monitoring trustee shall discuss those matters with both sides and report to the Commission. In order to be able to carry out its role, the monitoring trustee will keep confidential any business secrets of the parties and third parties,
— fifth, the monitoring trustee shall report on these issues to the Commission in periodic compliance reports and shall also submit additional reports upon request by the Commission.

120. The commitments will also comprehensively set out the monitoring trustee's needs for support by and cooperation with the parties; the Commission will supervise the relationship between the parties and the trustee also in this respect. In order to fulfil its tasks, the trustee shall have access to books and records of the parties and of the divested business, insofar and as long as this is relevant for the implementation of the commitments, may ask for managerial and administrative support by the parties, shall be informed of potential purchasers and all developments in the divestiture process, and shall be provided with the information submitted to potential purchasers. In addition, the parties shall indemnify the trustee and allow the trustee to appoint advisors, if appropriate for the fulfilment of its tasks under the commitments. The commitments will also enable the Commission to share the parties' information with the monitoring trustee in order to allow the monitoring trustee to fulfil its tasks. The monitoring trustee will be bound to keep this information confidential.

Role of the divestiture trustee

121. As for the monitoring trustee, the parties have to propose to appoint a divestiture trustee in order to make the commitments submitted by them effective and allow the Commission to ensure that the modification of the notified concentration, as proposed by them, will be carried out. If the parties do not succeed in finding a suitable purchaser within the first divestiture period, then in the trustee divestiture period, the divestiture trustee will be given an irrevocable and exclusive mandate to dispose of the business, under the supervision of the Commission, within a specific deadline at no minimum price to a suitable purchaser. The commitments shall allow the divestiture trustee to include in the sale and purchase agreement such terms and conditions as it considers appropriate for an expedient sale, in particular customary representations, warranties and indemnities. The sale of the business by the divestiture trustee is in the same way subject to the prior approval of the Commission as the sale by the parties.

122. The commitments will set out that the parties shall support and inform the divestiture trustee and cooperate with the trustee in the same way as this is foreseen for the monitoring trustee. For the divestiture, the parties have to grant to the divestiture trustee comprehensive powers of attorney, covering all stages of the divestiture.

Approval of the trustee and the trustee mandate

123. Depending on the commitment, the monitoring trustee may or may not be the same person or institution as the divestiture trustee. The parties shall propose one or several potential trustees to the Commission, including the full terms of the mandate and an outline of a work-plan. It is of the essence that the monitoring trustee is in place immediately after the Commission decision. Therefore, the parties should propose a suitable trustee immediately after the Commission decision[117] and the commitments normally have to foresee that the notified concentration can only be

implemented once the monitoring trustee is appointed, after being approved by the Commission.[118] The situation is different for the divestiture trustee who should be appointed well ahead of the end of the first divestiture period[119] so that its mandate can take effect with the beginning of the trustee divestiture period.

124. Both types of trustees will be appointed by the parties on the basis of a trustee mandate, entered into by the parties and the trustee. The appointment and the mandate will be subject to the approval by the Commission which will have discretion in the selection of the trustee and will assess whether the proposed candidate is suitable for the tasks in the specific case. The trustee shall be independent of the parties, possess the necessary qualifications to carry out its mandate and shall not be, or become, exposed to a conflict of interests.

125. The Commission will assess the necessary qualifications in the light of the requirements of the specific case, including the geographic area and the sector concerned. According to the Commission's experience, auditing firms and other consulting firms may be particularly well placed to fulfil the tasks of a monitoring trustee. Individuals who have worked in the specific industry may also be suitable candidates for performing such a role if they have the necessary resources available to deal with the tasks at stake. Investment banks seem to be particularly suitable for the role of a divestiture trustee. The independence of the trustee is crucial in order to enable the trustee to properly fulfil its role of monitoring the parties' compliance for the Commission and to ensure its credibility vis-à-vis third parties. In particular, the Commission will not accept persons or institutions as trustees which are at the same time the parties' auditors or their investment advisors in the divestiture. However, no conflicts of interests will arise by relations of the trustee with the parties if those relations will not impair the Trustee's objectivity and independence in discharging its tasks. It is the parties' responsibility to supply the Commission with adequate information for it to verify that the trustee fulfils the requirements. The appointment of the trustee after approval by the parties is irrevocable unless the trustee is replaced with the approval of or upon request by the Commission.

126. The trustee mandate shall define the tasks as specified in the commitments further and shall include all provisions necessary to enable the trustee to fulfil its tasks under the commitments accepted by the Commission. The parties are responsible for remuneration of the trustee under the mandate, and the remuneration structure must be such as to not impede the trustee's independence and effectiveness in fulfilling the mandate. The Commission will approve a trustee only together with a suitable mandate. In appropriate cases, it may publish the identity of the trustee and a summary of its tasks.

127. When the specific commitments with which the trustee has been entrusted have been implemented – that is to say, when legal title for the business to be divested has passed, the assets have been actually transferred to the purchaser and specific arrangements which may continue post-divestiture have been fulfilled – the mandate will provide for the trustee to request the Commission for a discharge from further responsibilities. Even after the discharge has been given, it may be necessary for the Commission to require the reappointment of the trustee on the basis of the commitments, if it appears subsequently to the Commission that the relevant commitments might not have been fully and properly implemented.

5. OBLIGATIONS OF THE PARTIES FOLLOWING IMPLEMENTATION OF THE DIVESTITURE

128. The Commitments also have to foresee that for a period of 10 years after the adoption of the decision accepting the commitments the Commission may request information from the parties. This will allow the Commission to monitor the effective implementation of the remedy.

6. IMPLEMENTATION OF OTHER COMMITMENTS

129. Many of the principles discussed above for the implementation of divestiture commitments can equally be applied to other types of commitments if those commitments need to be implemented subsequent to the Commission decision. For example, if it is foreseen that the beneficiary of a licence needs to be approved by the Commission, the considerations regarding the purchaser approval can be applied. Given the wide range of non-divestiture commitments, no general and comprehensive requirements for the implementation of non-divestiture commitments can be set out.

130. However, given the long duration of non-divestiture commitments and their frequent complexity, they often require a very high monitoring effort and specific monitoring tools in order to allow the Commission to conclude that they will effectively be implemented. Therefore, the Commission will often require the involvement of a trustee to oversee the implementation of such commitments and the establishment of a fast-track arbitration procedure in order to provide for a dispute resolution mechanism and to render the commitments enforceable by the market participants themselves. In past cases, the Commission has often required both the appointment of a trustee and an arbitration clause.[120] In those circumstances, the trustee will oversee the implementation of the commitments, but will also be able to assist in arbitral proceedings to the effect that they may be finalised in a short period of time.

NOTES

109 However, also in those circumstances, other provisions in the commitments, in particular the provisions establishing the safeguards in the interim period, should start running on the date of the adoption of the decision.

110 See Case COMP/M.3916 — *T-Mobile Austria/tele.ring* of 20 April 2006.

111 See judgment of the CFI in Case T-342/00 *Petrolessence v Commission* [2003] ECR II-1161.

112 Case IV/M.1383 — *Exxon/Mobil* of 29 September 1999 and the follow-up Cases COMP/M.1820 — *BP/JV Dissolution* of 2 February 2000 and COMP/M.1822 — *Mobil/JV Dissolution* of 2 February 2000.

113 As discussed above, the parties may apply to the Commission to approve the divestiture of the business to the proposed purchaser without one or more assets or parts of the personnel if this does not affect the viability and competitiveness of the Divestment Business after the sale, taking account of the resources of the proposed purchaser.

114 COMP/M.1628 — *TotalFina/Elf* of 9 February 2000, motorway service stations; confirmed by judgment of the CFI in Case T-342/00 *Petrolessence v Commission* [2003] ECR II-1161.

115 Depending on the circumstances of the divestiture, the parties may also have to ensure, for example through appropriate provisions in the purchase agreement, that the purchaser will maintain the divested business as a competitive force in the market and will not sell on the business within a short time-span.

116 See paragraph 26 above for the question how shared assets have to be dealt with in commitments.

117 Normally, the commitments should foresee that a monitoring trustee is proposed within two weeks of the date of the decision.

118 See Case COMP/M.4180 — *GdF/Suez* of 14 November 2006; Case COMP/M.4187 — *Metso/Aker Kvaerner* of 12 December 2006; Case COMP/M.3916 — *T-Mobile/tele.ring* of 20 April 2006.

119 The Commission will normally require an appointment at least one month ahead of the end of the first divestiture period.

120 Such an approach of combined monitoring by arbitration and a monitoring trustee was, eg used in Case COMP/M.2803 — *Telia/Sonera* of 10 July 2002; Case COMP/M.3083 — *GE/Instrumentarium* of 2 September 2003; and Case COMP/M.3225 — *Alcan/Pechiney II* of 29 September 2003.

BEST PRACTICE GUIDELINES: THE COMMISSION'S MODEL TEXTS FOR DIVESTITURE COMMITMENTS AND THE TRUSTEE MANDATE UNDER THE EC MERGER REGULATION (EXPLANATORY NOTE)

(5 December 2013)

[4.716]

NOTES

This document is available on the European Commission website at: ec.europa.eu/competition-policy/mergers/legislation/best-practices_en.

Note that Council Regulation (EC) No 139/2004 (the EC Merger Regulation) is repealed, in relation to the UK, by the Competition (Amendment etc) (EU Exit) Regulations 2019, SI 2019/93, reg 63, Sch 3, para 1, as from IP completion day (as defined in the European Union (Withdrawal Agreement) Act 2020, s 39) (for transitional provisions and savings in relation to the operation of the 2019 Regulations, see Sch 4 to those Regulations at **[7.69]** et seq).

1. The European Commission's model texts for divestiture commitments and trustee mandates are designed to serve as best practice guidelines for notifying parties submitting commitments under the Merger Regulation.[1] These texts are (1) the model to be used for divestiture commitments (the "***Standard Model for Divestiture Commitments****" or the* "***Standard Commitments***"); and (2) the model for the mandate of the two types of trustees referred to in the Standard Commitments, that is, the mandate appointing monitoring and divestiture trustees (the "***Standard Trustee Mandate***").

2. The model texts (the "***Standard Models***") are based upon the experience the Commission has gained to date from merger cases involving remedies and are drafted in line with the remedies policy set out in the Commission's Notice on Remedies[2] (the "**Remedies *Notice***"). The Standard Models are neither intended to provide an exhaustive coverage of all issues that may become relevant in all cases, nor are they legally binding upon parties in a merger procedure. Rather, they contain the elements for all standard provisions that should be included in commitments and trustee mandates relating to divestitures. In providing a framework for commitments and trustee mandates to be submitted in concrete cases, the Standard Models leave the flexibility to adapt the texts to the specific requirements of the case in question.

3. The Standard Models are designed to apply to all remedy proceedings in both Phase I and Phase II, therefore to all Commission decisions according to Articles 6(2) and 8(2) of the Merger Regulation. The Standard Models deal specifically with divestiture commitments inasmuch as the Commission's Remedies Notice stipulates that divestiture commitments are normally the preferred form of merger remedies; they are also the most common. However, it should be underlined that the Commission will consider the acceptability of other types of commitments in appropriate circumstances, as set out in the Remedies Notice. Individual provisions contained in the Standard Models can be used in cases involving such other types of commitments.

4. Since the Standard Models were first published in 2003, they have been updated in 2013 in order to take into account the experience gained since. It is expected that the text of these models will further evolve, based on ongoing practice, and will continue to be regularly up-dated by the Commission, taking into consideration both the developments of the Commission's remedies policy and the experience gained from working with the merging parties and trustees in future matters.

THE PURPOSE OF THE STANDARD MODELS

5. The Commission recognises that timing is crucial when merging parties reach the remedies stage in merger review procedures, where they offer commitments in order to resolve the Commission's competition concerns in a given case. Through the use of standardised models, the merging parties and the Commission will be relieved of the heavy demands – both in terms of time and resources – that would otherwise be required to negotiate the standard terms and provisions for commitments and trustee mandates under tight time constraints. The use of standardised models will expedite the proceedings and allow the merging parties to concentrate more on the actual substance and implementation of the commitments.

6. The use of the standard models will ensure consistency across cases and will thereby contribute to increasing the level of transparency and legal certainty for the merging parties offering commitments to the Commission.

OVERVIEW OF THE CONTENTS OF THE STANDARD MODELS

7. The Standard Model for Divestiture Commitments sets out all requirements for achieving full and effective compliance with divestiture commitments offered by the merging parties (the "**Parties**") to obtain a clearance decision. More specifically, this Model is designed (i) to describe clearly the business to be divested (the "**Divestment Business**"), the divestiture procedure and the obligations of the parties in relation to the Divestment Business for the interim period until divestiture has been completed, (ii) to set out the various responsibilities that the merging parties will thereby have, respectively, to the Commission, the Trustee, and the Divestment Business; and (iii) to enshrine the importance which the Commission places upon requiring an acceptable purchaser for the Divestment Business in order to ensure the viability and competitiveness of the new entity in the market where the divestiture takes place.

8. The Standard Model for Trustee Mandates sets out the role and functions of the Trustee, as provided in the Standard Commitments, in a contractual relationship between the Parties responsible for the divestiture and the Trustee. As the Commitments set out the basis for the responsibilities of the Trustee, the Standard Trustee Mandate has been prepared in conformity with the requirements laid down for the Trustee in the Standard Model for Divestiture Commitments.

9. Although the Standard Trustee Mandate is a bilateral contract between the Parties responsible for the divestiture and the Trustee, this document forms the basis for a tri-partite relationship among the Commission, the Trustee, and the Parties. The relationship between the Parties and the Trustee is not a traditional trusteeship. The Trustee rather benefits from a status which makes it independent from the Parties and which is characterised by the role of the Trustee to monitor (Monitoring Trustee) or even to effectuate (Divestiture Trustee) the Parties' compliance with the commitments. Accordingly, the Parties are not entitled to give instructions to the Trustee, whereas the Commission is allowed to do so. This specific relationship is also confirmed by the fact that the Trustee Mandate requires the Commission's approval.

10. The Standard Trustee Mandate is designed (i) to facilitate the smooth and timely appointment of the Trustee and the approval of the Trustee Mandate; (ii) to clarify the relationship among the Commission, the Trustee, and the Parties; and (iii) to set out the tasks of the Trustee in the process in order to enable the Trustee to expedite compliance with the commitments. Whereas the Standard Trustee Mandate defines the role of a Monitoring and a Divestiture Trustee in one text, they can be assigned to different Trustees in practice.

11. In providing guidance for the interpretation of the Standard Texts, a certain hierarchy is established. The Standard Trustee Mandate should be interpreted in the light of the Standard Commitments, as they lay the foundation for the application of the Trustee Mandate. To the extent that they are attached as conditions and obligations, the commitments are to be interpreted in the light of the respective Commission decision. Moreover, both Standard Texts should be interpreted in the general framework of European Union law, in particular in the light of the Merger Regulation, and by reference to the Commission's Remedies Notice setting out the Commission's remedies policy.

DESCRIPTION OF THE PROVISIONS OF THE STANDARD MODELS

12. The most important provisions contained in both Standard Models are briefly set out below.

STANDARD MODEL FOR DIVESTITURE COMMITMENTS

13. The Standard Model for Commitments consists of the following main elements:

14. Section A contains a definitions section.

15. Section B contains the commitment to divest and the definition of the Divestment Business. After spelling out the general obligation to divest the Divestment Business as a going concern, paragraph 2 describes the divestiture procedure, which may take two phases. The Commitments provide that in the first phase (that is, the First Divestiture Period), the Parties have the sole responsibility for finding a suitable purchaser for the Divestment Business. If the Parties do not succeed in divesting the business on their own in the Divestiture Period, then a Divestiture Trustee will be appointed with an exclusive mandate to dispose of the Divestment Business at no minimum price, in the Trustee Divestiture Period. The individual deadlines are determined in the definitions section. The experience of the Commission has shown that short divestiture periods contribute largely to the success of the divestiture as, otherwise, the Divestment Business will be exposed to an extended period of uncertainty. The Commission will normally consider a period of around 6 months for the Divestiture Period and an additional period of 3 to 6 months for the Extended Divestiture Period as appropriate. These periods may be modified according to the particular requirements of the case in question.

16. The divestiture commitment will take a special form in those cases where the Parties propose an up-front buyer. The Parties commit not to implement the proposed concentration unless and until they have entered into a binding agreement with a purchaser for the Divestment Business, approved by the Commission. The qualification of the buyer are the same as in other divestiture commitments. The up-front buyer concept has been applied in several cases[3] and will be used in the specific circumstances as described in the Notice.[4] The structure of the divestiture commitment also needs to be adapted in cases of alternative divestitures, in particular "Crown Jewels" structures, i.e. structures in which the Parties commit to divest a very attractive business if they have not divested the originally proposed business until the end of a period fixed in the commitments. The circumstances in which the Commission will accept alternative divestiture commitments are also set out in the Remedies Notice.[5]

17. The divestiture commitment includes the commitment not to re-acquire direct or indirect influence over the Divestment Business (paragraph 5). This re-acquisition prohibition is limited to ten years after the date of the decision and serves to maintain the structural effects of the Commitments. The Commission may grant a waiver if the structure of the market has changed to such an extent that the absence of influence over the Divestment Business is no longer necessary to render the concentration compatible with the internal market.

18. Section B, together with the Schedule to the Commitments, defines what is included in the Divestment Business. The clear identification of the Divestment Business is of great importance as thereby the scope of the divestiture and of the hold-separate obligations are defined. As set out in the Notice, the divested activities must consist of a viable business that, if operated by a suitable purchaser, can compete effectively with the merged entity on a lasting basis and that is divested as a going concern. Normally, a viable business is a business that can operate on a stand-alone-basis, which means independently of the merging parties as regards the supply of input materials or other forms of cooperation other than during a transitory period. The Divestment Business is the minimum which is to be divested by the Parties in order to comply with the Commitments. In order to make the package more attractive to buyers, the Parties may add, on their own initiative, other assets. The Divestment Business must include all the assets which contribute to its current operation or which are necessary to ensure its viability and competitiveness and all personnel which is currently employed or which is necessary to ensure the business' viability and competitiveness.[6] Whereas this principle is set out as an undertaking of the Parties in paragraph 6 of the Standard Commitments, the Parties have to give a detailed factual description of the Divestment Business in the Schedule to the Standard Commitments.

19. The Divestment Business must comprise the Personnel and the Key Personnel retained by the Divestment Business as well as the personnel providing essential functions for the Divestment Business, such as the central R&D staff. The personnel (according to groups and functions performed) is to be listed in the Schedule to the Commitments, the Key Personnel is to be listed separately. The principle, indicated in paragraph 6 (d), is that the personnel should be transferred with the Divestment Business. If the Divestment Business takes the form of a company or if the transfer of undertakings legislation applies, the personnel will normally be transferred by operation of law. In other cases, the acquirer of the business can retain and select the personnel and can make offers of employment. The transfer – whichever form it takes – is without prejudice to the application of Council Directives, where applicable, on collective redundancies;[7] on safeguarding employees rights in the event of transfers of undertakings;[8] and on informing and consulting employees,[9] as well as relevant national law on these matters.

20. Furthermore, the Standard Commitments foresee that the Divestment Business shall be entitled to benefit from products or services provided by the Parties for a transitional period, determined on a case-by-case basis, if this is necessary to maintain the full economic viability and competitiveness of the Divestment Business (paragraph 7 of the Standard Commitments referring to the products or services detailed in the Schedule).

21. Section C contains a number of related commitments, which are designed to maintain, pending divestiture, the viability, marketability and competitiveness of the Divestment Business. These provisions deal with the preservation of the divested entity's viability and independence, as well as the hold-separate and ring-fencing obligations. The Hold Separate Manager, to be appointed by the Parties and normally the manager of the Divestment Business, is responsible for the management of the Divestment Business as a distinct entity separate from the businesses retained by the Parties, and is supervised by the Monitoring Trustee.

22. In certain cases it may also be necessary for the hold-separate obligation to apply to the corporate structure itself. That is, in cases where the Divestment Business takes the form of a company and a strict separation of the corporate structure is necessary, the Monitoring Trustee must be given the authority to (i) exercise the Parties' rights as shareholders in the Divestment Business and (ii) to replace members of the supervisory board or non-executive directors on the board of directors who have been appointed on behalf of the Parties (cf. paragraph 11 of the Standard Commitments and paragraph 7 (d) of the Standard Trustee Mandate).

23. Of particular importance is the ring-fencing of competitively sensitive information of the Divestment Business. The parties are obliged to implement all necessary measures to ensure that they do not obtain such information of the Divestment Business and, in particular, to sever its participation in a central information technology network. The Monitoring Trustee may allow the disclosure of information to the divesting party if this is reasonably necessary for the divestiture of the Divestment Business or required by law (e.g. information necessary for group accounts).

24. The related commitments further contain a non-solicitation clause for Key Personnel of the Divestment Business. According to the experience of the Commission, the non-solicitation period, dependent on the circumstances of the case, should normally be two years. Where exceptionally, Key Personnel needs to be replaced, the procedure prescribed in the commitments must be followed. In addition, the Commission may request the inclusion of a non-compete clause in the commitments protecting the customers of the Divestment Business for a start-up period. This may be required to enable the Divestment Business to be active as a viable competitor in the market. The period for such customer protection clause will depend on the market in question.

25. During the Divestiture Period, the divestiture lies in the hands of the divesting party. The Commission does not have a preference as to the method the parties use to select an acceptable purchaser as long as they meet the objective of the divestiture, to maintain or restore competition. However, as part of the due diligence procedure, it is foreseen that the divesting party shall provide to potential purchasers sufficient information as regards the Divestment Business and allow them access to its personnel (paragraph 14 of the Standard Commitments) in order to enable them to determine whether it will be possible to maintain and to develop the Divestment Business as active and viable competitive force in the market after the divestiture.

26. The divesting party shall further submit regular reports on potential purchasers and developments in the divestiture process to the Commission and the Monitoring Trustee (paragraph 15 of the Standard Commitments). This reporting mechanism gives the Monitoring Trustee the basis on which to assess the progress of the divestiture process as well as potential purchasers (for the Trustee's report, see paragraph 28 (vi) of the Standard Commitments) and keeps the Commission informed.

27. Section D sets out the requirements to be met by the Purchaser. The aim of this section is to ensure that the Divestment Business will be sold to a suitable purchaser who is independent of and unconnected to the Notifying Parties and their Affiliated Undertakings, and who possesses the financial resources, proven expertise and incentive to maintain and develop the Divestment Business as a viable and active competitive force in the marketplace. These Purchaser Requirements can generally be met by either industrial or financial investors. The latter must demonstrate

the necessary management capabilities and "proven expertise" which can in particular be met by financing a management buy-out. The acquisition of the Divestment Business by the Purchaser must neither be likely to create, in light of the information available to the Commission, prima facie competition concerns nor give rise to a risk that the implementation of the Commitments will be delayed.

28. Section D also deals with the approval process. After finalising the agreement(s), the divesting party shall submit a fully documented and reasoned proposal to the Commission. The Commission will verify that the purchaser will fulfil the requirements and that the Divestment Business is being sold in a manner consistent with the Commission Decision and the Commitments. One element for its assessment will be the report of the Monitoring Trustee according to paragraph 28 (viii). The Commission may approve the sale of the Divestment Business without parts of the assets or personnel of the Divestment Business if this does not affect the viability and competitiveness of the Divestment Business, in particular if the Purchaser provides for such assets or personnel itself.

29. Section E deals with both the Monitoring and Divestiture Trustees. It identifies the terms for their appointment, as well as the content of the Trustee Mandates, and conditions for replacement of the Trustee during the divestiture periods if that becomes necessary. A Monitoring Trustee must be proposed by the Parties within two weeks after the adoption of the decision, whereas a Divestiture Trustee must be proposed no later than one month before the end of the Divestiture Period, (paragraph 23 of the Standard Commitments). The Commission wishes to emphasise the importance it attaches to compliance with these deadlines in practise, as otherwise the Parties are in breach of the commitments and the divestiture procedure is endangered.

30. Section E also sets out the duties and obligations of both types of Trustees. The Monitoring Trustee's responsibilities (mainly set out in paragraph 28 of the Standard Commitments) relate to both the management of the Divestment Business during the hold-separate period and the monitoring of the divestiture process itself. The supervision of the management shall in particular ensure the viability, marketability and competitiveness of the Divestment Business and the compliance with the hold-separate and ring-fencing obligations. The Standard Commitments further assign certain monitoring tasks concerning the divestiture process to the Monitoring Trustee in the Divestiture Period. Once the Parties have proposed a purchaser for the Divestment Business, the Monitoring Trustee assesses the independence and suitability of the proposed purchaser and the viability of the Divestment Business after the sale to the purchaser, in order to assist the Commission in assessing the suitability of the proposed purchaser.

31. In the Extended Divestiture Period, the Divestiture Trustee will have an exclusive mandate to sell the Divestment Business at no minimum price and is empowered to include in the sale and purchase agreement such terms and conditions as it considers appropriate for an expedient sale. However, it is foreseen that the Trustee has to protect the legitimate financial interests of the divesting parties, subject to its unconditional obligation to divest at no minimum price. The Divestiture Trustee must report regularly on the progress of the divestiture process.

32. Also in Section E (paragraphs 32–39), the duties and obligations of the Parties are defined. Beside the provision of information, the Parties are in particular obliged to provide the Monitoring Trustee with all managerial and administrative support necessary for the Divestment Business and to grant to the Divestiture Trustee comprehensive powers of attorney covering all steps of the sale of the Divestment Business. An indemnification clause is included in order to reinforce the independent status of the Trustee from the Parties. Such a clause is common practice in the trustee mandates submitted to the Commission for approval. The Trustee may further, at the expense of the Parties, retain advisors with specialised skills, in particular for corporate finance or legal advice.

33. Section E further foresees that trustees may only be removed in exceptional circumstances and with the approval of the Commission before the complete implementation of the Commitments.

34. Section F contains a review clause, which allows the Commission to extend the periods specified in the Commitments and to waive or modify the undertakings in the Commitments. The Parties must show good cause in order to be able to benefit from the exercise of the review clause. Requests for the extension of time periods shall, normally, be submitted no later than one month before the expiry of the time period in question. The divesting party is entitled to request an extension within the last month of any period only in exceptional circumstances.

STANDARD MODEL FOR TRUSTEE MANDATES

35. The Standard Model for Trustee Mandates sets out the duties and responsibilities of both Monitoring and Divestiture Trustee in a single text. However, the language makes clear that the Commission does not have a preference for the appointment of a single person to serve in the dual role of both Monitoring and Divestiture Trustee. Rather, the decision as to whether one or more trustees are appointed should be determined on a case-by-case basis by the Parties. If more than one trustee shall serve in these roles, only the provisions relevant for the Monitoring or Divestiture Trustee, respectively, have to be included in the individual mandate.

36. The Standard Trustee Mandate consists of the following main elements:

37. Section A contains some definitions and references the definitions included in the Standard Commitments.

38. Sections B to G contain provisions regarding the appointment of the Trustee (Section B), its general duties (Section C), the specific duties and obligations of the Monitoring and Divestiture Trustees (Sections D and E), reporting obligations identifying certain important subjects that should be discussed in each report (Section F), and duties and obligations of the Parties vis-à-vis the Trustee (Section G). These arrangements are based on the provisions established in the Standard Commitments in relation to the Trustee and described above

39. Sections H to J cover additional trustee-related provisions, including provisions regarding the remuneration of the Trustee(s), procedures concerning the termination of the Mandate, and certain additional provisions, such as determination of applicable national law.

40. In particular, the independence of the trustee and the absence of conflicts of interests of the trustee are of great importance for the Commission in deciding on the approval of the Trustee and the respective mandate. The provisions in the Standard Trustee Mandate (paragraphs 24 to 27) ensuring the independence of the Trustee from the parties and the absence of conflicts of interest foresee the following procedure: (1) The Trustee must disclose current relationships with the Notifying Parties and Affiliated undertakings (paragraph 24) at the time at which the Trustee Mandate is entered into; (2) During the term of the mandate, the Trustee undertakes not to create a conflict of interest by having or accepting employment or appointment as a Member of the Board of the Parties or Affiliated Undertakings or by having or accepting any assignments or other business relationships with, or financial interests in, the Parties or Affiliated Undertakings that might lead to a Conflict of Interest or by having or accepting appointments, assignments or other business relationships that may be regarded as impairing the Trustee's objectivity and independence in discharging its duties. (3) As legal consequences it is foreseen that, if the Trustee becomes aware of a conflict of interest during the Mandate, the Trustee must notify the Commission and resolve the problem immediately and, if the conflict of interest cannot subsequently be resolved, the Commission may require the termination of the trustee mandate. These rules concerning conflicts of interests apply to the Trustee itself, members of the Trustee Team and the Trustee Partner Firms as members of the same organisation. (4) For a period of one year[10] following termination of the Mandate, the members of the Trustee Team shall not provide services to the Parties or Affiliated Undertakings without the Commission's prior approval and must establish measures to ensure the independence and integrity of the members of the Trustee Team.

41. In addition to the rules laid down in the Standard Trustee Mandate, it is up to the Parties and the Trustee to include provisions dealing with other potential conflicts of interests, such as conflicts of interests of the Trustee with potential purchasers.

NOTES

1 Council Regulation (EC) No 139/2004 of 20 January 2004 on the control of concentrations between undertakings (OJ L24, 29.1.2004 p 1).

2 Commission Notice on remedies acceptable under Council Regulation (EC) No 139/2004 and under Commission Regulation (EC) No 802/2004 (OJ C267, 22.10.2008, p 1)

3 See for example cases COMP/M.6203 – *Western Digital Ireland/Viviti Technologies*, Commission Decision dated 23 November 2011; COMP/M.5611 – *Agilent/Varian*, Commission Decision dated 20 January 2010; COMP/M.2544 - *Masterfood/Royal Canin*, Commission Decision dated 15 February 2002; COMP/M.1915 - *The Post Office/TPG/SPPL*, Commission Decision dated 13 March 2001; and COMP/M.2060 - *Bosch/Rexroth*, Commission Decision dated 4 December 2000.

4 See in particular paragraphs 53–55 of the Remedies Notice.

5 See in particular paragraphs 44–46 of the Remedies Notice.

6 See in particular part III of the Remedies Notice.

7 Council Directive 98/59/EC of 20 July 1998 on the approximation of the laws of the Member States relating to collective redundancies (OJ L225, 12.8.1998, p16).

8 Council Directive 77/187/EEC on the approximation of the laws of the Member States relating to the safeguarding of employees rights in the event of transfers of undertakings, businesses or parts of a business (OJ L61, 5.3.1977, p 26) as amended.

9 Directive 2009/38/EC of the European Parliament and of the Council of 6 May 2009 on the establishment of a European Works Council or a procedure in Community-scale undertakings and Community-scale groups of undertakings for the purposes of informing and consulting employees (OJ L122, 16.5.2009, p 28).

10 This period can in particular circumstances, e.g. in cases of behavioural commitments extending over several years or sale of the Divestiture Business occurring in the Trustee Divestiture Period, be extended to three years.

MODEL TEXT FOR DIVESTITURE COMMITMENTS

(5 December 2013)

[4.717]

NOTES

This document is available on the European Commission website at: ec.europa.eu/competition-policy/mergers/legislation/best-practices_en.

CASE M. [NO . . .] – [TITLE . . .]
COMMITMENTS TO THE EUROPEAN COMMISSION

XX/XX/XXXX

Pursuant to [Article 6(2), *if Phase I Commitments*] [Article 8(2), *if Phase II Commitments*] [Articles 8(2) and 10(2), *if in Phase II Commitments prior to the sending out of the Statement of Objections*] of Council Regulation (EC) No 139/2004 (the "***Merger Regulation***"), [*Indicate the name of the undertaking or undertakings offering the Commitments*] (the "***Notifying Party/Notifying Parties***") hereby enter into the following Commitments (the "***Commitments***") vis-à-vis the European Commission (the "***Commission***") with a view to rendering [*Description of the operation: e.g. the acquisition of . . . ; the creation of a full-function joint venture between . . .*] (the "***Concentration***") compatible with the internal market and the functioning of the EEA Agreement.

This text shall be interpreted in light of the Commission's decision pursuant to [Article 6(1)(b) of the Merger Regulation, *if Phase I Commitments*] [Article 8(2), *if Phase II Commitments*] of the Merger Regulation to declare the Concentration compatible with the internal market and the functioning of the EEA Agreement (the "***Decision***"), in the general framework of European Union law, in particular in light of the Merger Regulation, and by reference to the Commission Notice on remedies acceptable under Council Regulation (EC) No 139/2004 and under Commission Regulation (EC) No 802/2004 (the "*Remedies Notice*").

SECTION A. DEFINITIONS

1. For the purpose of the Commitments, the following terms shall have the following meaning:

Affiliated Undertakings: undertakings controlled by the Parties and/or by the ultimate parents of the Parties, including the joint venture [*Only in the case when the proposed operation is a creation of a joint venture*], whereby the notion of control shall be interpreted pursuant to Article 3 of the Merger Regulation and in light of the Commission Consolidated Jurisdictional Notice under Council Regulation (EC) No 139/2004 on the control of concentrations between undertakings (the "*Consolidated Jurisdictional Notice*").

Assets: the assets that contribute to the current operation or are necessary to ensure the viability and competitiveness of the Divestment Business as indicated in Section B, paragraph 6 (a), (b) and (c) and described more in detail in the Schedule.

Closing: the transfer of the legal title to the Divestment Business to the Purchaser.

Closing Period: the period of 3 months from the approval of the Purchaser and the terms of sale by the Commission.

Confidential Information: any business secrets, know-how, commercial information, or any other information of a proprietary nature that is not in the public domain.

Conflict of Interest: any conflict of interest that impairs the Trustee's objectivity and independence in discharging its duties under the Commitments.

Divestment Business: the business or businesses as defined in Section B and in the Schedule which the Notifying Party/Notifying Parties commit to divest.

Divestiture Trustee: one or more natural or legal person(s) who is/are approved by the Commission and appointed by [*X*] and who has/have received from [*X*] the exclusive Trustee Mandate to sell the Divestment Business to a Purchaser at no minimum price.

Effective Date: the date of adoption of the Decision.

First Divestiture Period: the period of [•] months from the Effective Date.

Hold Separate Manager: the person appointed by [*X*] for the Divestment Business to manage the day-to-day business under the supervision of the Monitoring Trustee.

Key Personnel: all personnel necessary to maintain the viability and competitiveness of the Divestment Business, as listed in the Schedule, including the Hold Separate Manager.

Monitoring Trustee: one or more natural or legal person(s) who is/are approved by the Commission and appointed by [*X*], and who has/have the duty to monitor [*X's*] compliance with the conditions and obligations attached to the Decision.

Parties: the Notifying Party/Notifying Parties and the undertaking that is the target of the concentration.

Personnel: all staff currently employed by the Divestment Business, including staff seconded to the Divestment Business, shared personnel as well as the additional personnel listed in the Schedule.

Purchaser: the entity approved by the Commission as acquirer of the Divestment Business in accordance with the criteria set out in Section D.

Purchaser Criteria: the criteria laid down in paragraph 17 of these Commitments that the Purchaser must fulfil in order to be approved by the Commission.

Schedule: the schedule to these Commitments describing more in detail the Divestment Business.

Trustee(s): the Monitoring Trustee and/or the Divestiture Trustee as the case may be.

Trustee Divestiture Period: the period of [•] months from the end of the First Divestiture Period.

[*X*]: [*Indicate the name of the undertaking that will divest its business/es*], incorporated under the laws of [•], with its registered office at [•] and registered with the Commercial/Company Register at [•] under number [•].

SECTION B. THE COMMITMENT TO DIVEST AND THE DIVESTMENT BUSINESS

COMMITMENT TO DIVEST

2. In order to maintain effective competition, [*X*] commits to divest, or procure the divestiture of the Divestment Business by the end of the Trustee Divestiture Period as a going concern to a purchaser and on terms of sale approved by the Commission in accordance with the procedure described in paragraph 18 of these Commitments. To carry out the divestiture, [X] commits to find a purchaser and to enter into a final binding sale and purchase agreement for the sale of the Divestment Business within the First Divestiture Period. If [*X*] has not entered into such an agreement at the end of the First Divestiture Period, [*X*] shall grant the Divestiture Trustee an exclusive mandate to sell the Divestment Business in accordance with the procedure described in paragraph 30 in the Trustee Divestiture Period.

3. [*The following sentence should be inserted in case of an "up-front buyer"*: The proposed concentration shall not be implemented before [*X*] or the Divestiture Trustee has entered into a final binding sale and purchase agreement for the sale of the Divestment Business and the Commission has approved the purchaser and the terms of sale in accordance with paragraph 18].

4. [*X*] shall be deemed to have complied with this commitment if:

(a) by the end of the Trustee Divestiture Period, [*X*] or the Divestiture Trustee has entered into a final binding sale and purchase agreement and the Commission approves the proposed purchaser and the terms of sale as being consistent with the Commitments in accordance with the procedure described in paragraph 18; and
(b) the Closing of the sale of the Divestment Business to the Purchaser takes place within the Closing Period.

5. In order to maintain the structural effect of the Commitments, the Notifying Party/Notifying Parties shall, for a period of 10 years after Closing, not acquire, whether directly or indirectly, the possibility of exercising influence (as defined in paragraph 43 of the Remedies Notice, footnote 3) over the whole or part of the Divestment Business, unless, following the submission of a reasoned request from the Notifying Party showing good cause and accompanied by a report from the Monitoring Trustee (as provided in paragraph 44 of these Commitments), the Commission finds that the structure of the market has changed to such an extent that the absence of influence over the Divestment Business is no longer necessary to render the proposed concentration compatible with the internal market.

STRUCTURE AND DEFINITION OF THE DIVESTMENT BUSINESS

6. The Divestment Business consists of [*Provide a summary description of the Divestment Business*]. The legal and functional structure of the Divestment Business as operated to date is described in the Schedule. The Divestment Business, described in more detail in the Schedule, includes all assets and staff that contribute to the current operation or are necessary to ensure the viability and competitiveness of the Divestment Business, in particular:
(a) all tangible and intangible assets (including intellectual property rights);
(b) all licences, permits and authorisations issued by any governmental organisation for the benefit of the Divestment Business;
(c) all contracts, leases, commitments and customer orders of the Divestment Business; all customer, credit and other records of the Divestment Business; and
(d) the Personnel.

7. [*To be included in* cases *in which the Divestment Business needs an on-going relationship with the Parties in order to be fully competitive and viable*: In addition, the Divestment Business includes the benefit, for a transitional period of up to [*insert*] years after Closing and on terms and conditions equivalent to those at present afforded to the Divestment Business, of all current arrangements under which [*X*] or its Affiliated Undertakings supply products or services to the Divestment Business, as detailed in the Schedule, unless otherwise agreed with the Purchaser. Strict firewall procedures will be adopted so as to ensure that any competitively sensitive information related to, or arising from such supply arrangements (for example, product roadmaps) will not be shared with, or passed on to, anyone outside the [*insert the relevant business unit/division providing the product/service*] operations.]

SECTION C. RELATED COMMITMENTS

PRESERVATION OF VIABILITY, MARKETABILITY AND COMPETITIVENESS

8. From the Effective Date until Closing, the Notifying Party/Notifying Parties shall preserve or procure the preservation of the economic viability, marketability and competitiveness of the Divestment Business, in accordance with good business practice, and shall minimise as far as possible any risk of loss of competitive potential of the Divestment Business. In particular [*X*] undertakes:
(a) not to carry out any action that might have a significant adverse impact on the value, management or competitiveness of the Divestment Business or that might alter the nature and scope of activity, or the industrial or commercial strategy or the investment policy of the Divestment Business;
(b) to make available, or procure to make available, sufficient resources for the development of the Divestment Business, on the basis and continuation of the existing business plans;
(c) to take all reasonable steps, or procure that all reasonable steps are being taken, including appropriate incentive schemes (based on industry practice), to encourage all Key Personnel to remain with the Divestment Business, and not to solicit or move any Personnel to [*X's*] remaining business. Where, nevertheless, individual members of the Key Personnel exceptionally leave the Divestment Business, [*X*] shall provide a reasoned proposal to replace the person or persons concerned to the Commission and the Monitoring Trustee. [*X*] must be able to demonstrate to the Commission that the replacement is well suited to carry out the functions exercised by those individual members of the Key Personnel. The replacement shall take place under the supervision of the Monitoring Trustee, who shall report to the Commission.

HOLD-SEPARATE OBLIGATIONS

9. The Notifying Party/Notifying Parties commit(s), from the Effective Date until Closing, to keep the Divestment Business separate from the business(es) it is retaining [*In an Upfront Buyer situation replace by:* to procure that the Divestment Business is kept separate from the business(es) that the Notifying Party /Notifying Parties will be retaining and, after closing of the notified transaction to keep the Divestment Business Separate from the business that the Notifying Party /Notifying Parties is retaining] and to ensure that unless explicitly permitted under these Commitments: (i) management and staff of the business(es) retained by [*X*] have no involvement in the Divestment Business; (ii) the Key Personnel and Personnel of the Divestment Business have no involvement in any business retained by [*X*] and do not report to any individual outside the Divestment Business.

10. Until Closing, [*X*] shall assist the Monitoring Trustee in ensuring that the Divestment Business is managed as a distinct and saleable entity separate from the business(es) which [X] is retaining. Immediately after the adoption of the Decision, [*X*] shall appoint a Hold Separate Manager. The Hold Separate Manager, who shall be part of the Key Personnel, shall manage the Divestment Business independently and in the best interest of the business with a view to ensuring its continued economic viability, marketability and competitiveness and its independence from the

businesses retained by *[X]*. The Hold Separate Manager shall closely cooperate with and report to the Monitoring Trustee and, if applicable, the Divestiture Trustee. Any replacement of the Hold Separate Manager shall be subject to the procedure laid down in paragraph 8(c) of these Commitments. The Commission may, after having heard [*X*], require [*X*] to replace the Hold Separate Manager.

11. [*The following is to be inserted in cases in which a company or a share in a company is to be divested and a strict separation of the corporate structure is necessary*: To ensure that the Divestment Business is held and managed as a separate entity the Monitoring Trustee shall exercise [*X*'s] rights as shareholder in the legal entity or entities that constitute the Divestment Business (except for its rights in respect of dividends that are due before Closing), with the aim of acting in the best interest of the business, which shall be determined on a stand-alone basis, as an independent financial investor, and with a view to fulfilling [*X's*] obligations under the Commitments. Furthermore, the Monitoring Trustee shall have the power to replace members of the supervisory board or non-executive directors of the board of directors, who have been appointed on behalf of [*X*]. Upon request of the Monitoring Trustee, [*X*] shall resign as a member of the boards or shall cause such members of the boards to resign.]

RING-FENCING

12. [*X*] shall implement, or procure to implement, all necessary measures to ensure that it does not, after the Effective Date, obtain any Confidential Information relating to the Divestment Business and that any such Confidential Information obtained by [*X*] before the Effective Date will be eliminated and not be used by [*X*]. This includes measures vis-à-vis [*X's*] appointees on the supervisory board and/or board of directors of the Divestment Business. In particular, the participation of the Divestment Business in any central information technology network shall be severed to the extent possible, without compromising the viability of the Divestment Business. [*X*] may obtain or keep information relating to the Divestment Business which is reasonably necessary for the divestiture of the Divestment Business or the disclosure of which to [*X*] is required by law.

NON-SOLICITATION CLAUSE

13. The Parties undertake, subject to customary limitations, not to solicit, and to procure that Affiliated Undertakings do not solicit, the Key Personnel transferred with the Divestment Business for a period of [•] after Closing.

DUE DILIGENCE

14. In order to enable potential purchasers to carry out a reasonable due diligence of the Divestment Business, [*X*] shall, subject to customary confidentiality assurances and dependent on the stage of the divestiture process:
- (a) provide to potential purchasers sufficient information as regards the Divestment Business;
- (b) provide to potential purchasers sufficient information relating to the Personnel and allow them reasonable access to the Personnel.

REPORTING

15. [*X*] shall submit written reports in [*Indicate the language of the procedure or another language agreed with the Commission*] on potential purchasers of the Divestment Business and developments in the negotiations with such potential purchasers to the Commission and the Monitoring Trustee no later than 10 days after the end of every month following the Effective Date (or otherwise at the Commission's request). [*X*] shall submit a list of all potential purchasers having expressed interest in acquiring the Divestment Business to the Commission at each and every stage of the divestiture process, as well as a copy of all the offers made by potential purchasers within five days of their receipt.

16. [*X*] shall inform the Commission and the Monitoring Trustee on the preparation of the data room documentation and the due diligence procedure and shall submit a copy of any information memorandum to the Commission and the Monitoring Trustee before sending the memorandum out to potential purchasers.

SECTION D. THE PURCHASER

17. In order to be approved by the Commission, the Purchaser must fulfil the following criteria:
- (a) The Purchaser shall be independent of and unconnected to the Notifying Party/Notifying Parties and its/their Affiliated Undertakings (this being assessed having regard to the situation following the divestiture).
- (b) The Purchaser shall have the financial resources, proven expertise and incentive to maintain and develop the Divestment Business as a viable and active competitive force in competition with the Parties and other competitors;
- (c) The acquisition of the Divestment Business by the Purchaser must neither be likely to create, in light of the information available to the Commission, *prima facie* competition concerns nor give rise to a risk that the implementation of the Commitments will be delayed. In particular, the Purchaser must reasonably be expected to obtain all necessary approvals from the relevant regulatory authorities for the acquisition of the Divestment Business.

18. The final binding sale and purchase agreement (as well as ancillary agreements) relating to the divestment of the Divestment Business shall be conditional on the Commission's approval. When [*X*] has reached an agreement with a purchaser, it shall submit a fully documented and reasoned proposal, including a copy of the final agreement(s), within one week to the Commission and the Monitoring Trustee. [*X*] must be able to demonstrate to the Commission that the purchaser fulfils the Purchaser Criteria and that the Divestment Business is being sold in a manner consistent with the Commission's Decision and the Commitments. For the approval, the Commission shall verify that the purchaser fulfils the Purchaser Criteria and that the Divestment Business is being sold in a manner consistent with the Commitments including their objective to bring about a lasting structural change in the market. The Commission may approve the sale of the Divestment Business without one or more Assets or parts of the Personnel, or by

substituting one or more Assets or parts of the Personnel with one or more different assets or different personnel, if this does not affect the viability and competitiveness of the Divestment Business after the sale, taking account of the proposed purchaser.

SECTION E. TRUSTEE

I. APPOINTMENT PROCEDURE

19. [*X*] shall appoint a Monitoring Trustee to carry out the functions specified in these Commitments for a Monitoring Trustee. The Notifying Party/Notifying Parties commit(s) not to close the Concentration before the appointment of a Monitoring Trustee.

20. If [*X*] has not entered into a binding sale and purchase agreement regarding the Divestment Business one month before the end of the First Divestiture Period or if the Commission has rejected a purchaser proposed by [*X*] at that time or thereafter, [*X*] shall appoint a Divestiture Trustee. The appointment of the Divestiture Trustee shall take effect upon the commencement of the Trustee Divestiture Period.

21. The Trustee shall:

(i) at the time of appointment, be independent of the Notifying Party/Notifying Parties and its/their Affiliated Undertakings;

(ii) possess the necessary qualifications to carry out its mandate, for example have sufficient relevant experience as an investment banker or consultant or auditor; and

(iii) neither have nor become exposed to a Conflict of Interest.

22. The Trustee shall be remunerated by the Notifying Parties in a way that does not impede the independent and effective fulfilment of its mandate. In particular, where the remuneration package of a Divestiture Trustee includes a success premium linked to the final sale value of the Divestment Business, such success premium may only be earned if the divestiture takes place within the Trustee Divestiture Period.

PROPOSAL BY [X]

23. No later than two weeks after the Effective Date, [*X*] shall submit the name or names of one or more natural or legal persons whom [*X*] proposes to appoint as the Monitoring Trustee to the Commission for approval. No later than one month before the end of the First Divestiture Period or on request by the Commission, [*X*] shall submit a list of one or more persons whom [X] proposes to appoint as Divestiture Trustee to the Commission for approval. The proposal shall contain sufficient information for the Commission to verify that the person or persons proposed as Trustee fulfil the requirements set out in paragraph 21 and shall include:

(a) the full terms of the proposed mandate, which shall include all provisions necessary to enable the Trustee to fulfil its duties under these Commitments;

(b) the outline of a work plan which describes how the Trustee intends to carry out its assigned tasks;

(c) an indication whether the proposed Trustee is to act as both Monitoring Trustee and Divestiture Trustee or whether different trustees are proposed for the two functions.

APPROVAL OR REJECTION BY THE COMMISSION

24. The Commission shall have the discretion to approve or reject the proposed Trustee(s) and to approve the proposed mandate subject to any modifications it deems necessary for the Trustee to fulfil its obligations. If only one name is approved, [*X*] shall appoint or cause to be appointed the person or persons concerned as Trustee, in accordance with the mandate approved by the Commission. If more than one name is approved, [*X*] shall be free to choose the Trustee to be appointed from among the names approved. The Trustee shall be appointed within one week of the Commission's approval, in accordance with the mandate approved by the Commission.

NEW PROPOSAL BY THE [X]

25. If all the proposed Trustees are rejected, [*X*] shall submit the names of at least two more natural or legal persons within one week of being informed of the rejection, in accordance with paragraphs 19 and 24 of these Commitments.

TRUSTEE NOMINATED BY THE COMMISSION

26. If all further proposed Trustees are rejected by the Commission, the Commission shall nominate a Trustee, whom [*X*] shall appoint, or cause to be appointed, in accordance with a trustee mandate approved by the Commission.

II. FUNCTIONS OF THE TRUSTEE

27. The Trustee shall assume its specified duties and obligations in order to ensure compliance with the Commitments. The Commission may, on its own initiative or at the request of the Trustee or [*X*], give any orders or instructions to the Trustee in order to ensure compliance with the conditions and obligations attached to the Decision.

DUTIES AND OBLIGATIONS OF THE MONITORING TRUSTEE

28. The Monitoring Trustee shall:

(i) propose in its first report to the Commission a detailed work plan describing how it intends to monitor compliance with the obligations and conditions attached to the Decision.

(ii) oversee, in close co-operation with the Hold Separate Manager, the on-going management of the Divestment Business with a view to ensuring its continued economic viability, marketability and competitiveness and monitor compliance by [*X*] with the conditions and obligations attached to the Decision. To that end the Monitoring Trustee shall:

(a) monitor the preservation of the economic viability, marketability and competitiveness of the Divestment Business, and the keeping separate of the Divestment Business from the business retained by the Parties, in accordance with paragraphs 8 and 9 of these Commitments;

(b) supervise the management of the Divestment Business as a distinct and saleable entity, in accordance with paragraph 10 of these Commitments;

(c) with respect to Confidential Information:

– determine all necessary measures to ensure that [X] does not after the Effective Date obtain any Confidential Information relating to the Divestment Business,

– in particular strive for the severing of the Divestment Business' participation in a central information technology network to the extent possible, without compromising the viability of the Divestment Business,

– make sure that any Confidential Information relating to the Divestment Business obtained by [X] before the Effective Date is eliminated and will not be used by [X] and

– decide whether such information may be disclosed to or kept by [X] as the disclosure is reasonably necessary to allow [X] to carry out the divestiture or as the disclosure is required by law;

(d) monitor the splitting of assets and the allocation of Personnel between the Divestment Business and [*X*] or Affiliated Undertakings;

(iii) propose to [*X*] such measures as the Monitoring Trustee considers necessary to ensure [*X*]'s compliance with the conditions and obligations attached to the Decision, in particular the maintenance of the full economic viability, marketability or competitiveness of the Divestment Business, the holding separate of the Divestment Business and the non-disclosure of competitively sensitive information;

(iv) review and assess potential purchasers as well as the progress of the divestiture process and verify that, dependent on the stage of the divestiture process:

(a) potential purchasers receive sufficient and correct information relating to the Divestment Business and the Personnel in particular by reviewing, if available, the data room documentation, the information memorandum and the due diligence process, and

(b) potential purchasers are granted reasonable access to the Personnel;

(v) act as a contact point for any requests by third parties, in particular potential purchasers, in relation to the Commitments;

(vi) provide to the Commission, sending [*X*] a non-confidential copy at the same time, a written report within 15 days after the end of every month that shall cover the operation and management of the Divestment Business as well as the splitting of assets and the allocation of Personnel so that the Commission can assess whether the business is held in a manner consistent with the Commitments and the progress of the divestiture process as well as potential purchasers;

(vii) promptly report in writing to the Commission, sending [*X*] a non-confidential copy at the same time, if it concludes on reasonable grounds that [*X*] is failing to comply with these Commitments;

(viii) within one week after receipt of the documented proposal referred to in paragraph 18 of these Commitments, submit to the Commission, sending [X] a non-confidential copy at the same time, a reasoned opinion as to the suitability and independence of the proposed purchaser and the viability of the Divestment Business after the Sale and as to whether the Divestment Business is sold in a manner consistent with the conditions and obligations attached to the Decision, in particular, if relevant, whether the Sale of the Divestment Business without one or more Assets or not all of the Personnel affects the viability of the Divestment Business after the sale, taking account of the proposed purchaser;

(ix) assume the other functions assigned to the Monitoring Trustee under the conditions and obligations attached to the Decision.

29. If the Monitoring and Divestiture Trustee are not the same [legal or natural] persons, the Monitoring Trustee and the Divestiture Trustee shall cooperate closely with each other during and for the purpose of the preparation of the Trustee Divestiture Period in order to facilitate each other's tasks.

Duties and obligations of the Divestiture Trustee

30. Within the Trustee Divestiture Period, the Divestiture Trustee shall sell at no minimum price the Divestment Business to a purchaser, provided that the Commission has approved both the purchaser and the final binding sale and purchase agreement (and ancillary agreements) as in line with the Commission's Decision and the Commitments in accordance with paragraphs 17 and 18 of these Commitments. The Divestiture Trustee shall include in the sale and purchase agreement (as well as in any ancillary agreements) such terms and conditions as it considers appropriate for an expedient sale in the Trustee Divestiture Period. In particular, the Divestiture Trustee may include in the sale and purchase agreement such customary representations and warranties and indemnities as are reasonably required to effect the sale. The Divestiture Trustee shall protect the legitimate financial interests of [*X*], subject to the Notifying Party/Notifying Parties' unconditional obligation to divest at no minimum price in the Trustee Divestiture Period.

31. In the Trustee Divestiture Period (or otherwise at the Commission's request), the Divestiture Trustee shall provide the Commission with a comprehensive monthly report written in [*Please indicate the language of the procedure or a different language agreed with the Commission*] on the progress of the divestiture process. Such reports shall be submitted within 15 days after the end of every month with a simultaneous copy to the Monitoring Trustee and a non-confidential copy to the Notifying Party/Notifying Parties.

III. DUTIES AND OBLIGATIONS OF THE PARTIES

32. [*X*] shall provide and shall cause its advisors to provide the Trustee with all such co-operation, assistance and information as the Trustee may reasonably require to perform its tasks. The Trustee shall have full and complete access to any of [*X's*] or the Divestment Business' books, records, documents, management or other personnel, facilities, sites and technical information necessary for fulfilling its duties under the Commitments and [*X*] and the Divestment Business shall provide the Trustee upon request with copies of any document. [*X*] and the Divestment Business shall make available to the Trustee one or more offices on their premises and shall be available for meetings in order to provide the Trustee with all information necessary for the performance of its tasks.

33. *[X]* shall provide the Monitoring Trustee with all managerial and administrative support that it may reasonably request on behalf of the management of the Divestment Business. This shall include all administrative support functions relating to the Divestment Business which are currently carried out at headquarters level. *[X]* shall provide and shall cause its advisors to provide the Monitoring Trustee, on request, with the information submitted to potential purchasers, in particular give the Monitoring Trustee access to the data room documentation and all other information granted to potential purchasers in the due diligence procedure. *[X]* shall inform the Monitoring Trustee on possible purchasers, submit lists of potential purchasers at each stage of the selection process, including the offers made by potential purchasers at those stages, and keep the Monitoring Trustee informed of all developments in the divestiture process.

34. *[X]* shall grant or procure Affiliated Undertakings to grant comprehensive powers of attorney, duly executed, to the Divestiture Trustee to effect the sale (including ancillary agreements), the Closing and all actions and declarations which the Divestiture Trustee considers necessary or appropriate to achieve the sale and the Closing, including the appointment of advisors to assist with the sale process. Upon request of the Divestiture Trustee, *[X]* shall cause the documents required for effecting the sale and the Closing to be duly executed.

35. *[X]* shall indemnify the Trustee and its employees and agents (each an "***Indemnified Party***") and hold each Indemnified Party harmless against, and hereby agrees that an Indemnified Party shall have no liability to *[X]* for, any liabilities arising out of the performance of the Trustee's duties under the Commitments, except to the extent that such liabilities result from the wilful default, recklessness, gross negligence or bad faith of the Trustee, its employees, agents or advisors.

36. At the expense of *[X]*, the Trustee may appoint advisors (in particular for corporate finance or legal advice), subject to *[X's]* approval (this approval not to be unreasonably withheld or delayed) if the Trustee considers the appointment of such advisors necessary or appropriate for the performance of its duties and obligations under the Mandate, provided that any fees and other expenses incurred by the Trustee are reasonable. Should *[X]* refuse to approve the advisors proposed by the Trustee the Commission may approve the appointment of such advisors instead, after having heard *[X]*. Only the Trustee shall be entitled to issue instructions to the advisors. Paragraph 35 of these Commitments shall apply *mutatis mutandis*. In the Trustee Divestiture Period, the Divestiture Trustee may use advisors who served *[X]* during the Divestiture Period if the Divestiture Trustee considers this in the best interest of an expedient sale.

37. *[X]* agrees that the Commission may share Confidential Information proprietary to *[X]* with the Trustee. The Trustee shall not disclose such information and the principles contained in Article 17 (1) and (2) of the Merger Regulation apply *mutatis mutandis*.

38. The Notifying Party/Notifying Parties agree that the contact details of the Monitoring Trustee are published on the website of the Commission's Directorate-General for Competition and they shall inform interested third parties, in particular any potential purchasers, of the identity and the tasks of the Monitoring Trustee.

39. For a period of 10 years from the Effective Date the Commission may request all information from the Parties that is reasonably necessary to monitor the effective implementation of these Commitments.

IV. REPLACEMENT, DISCHARGE AND REAPPOINTMENT OF THE TRUSTEE

40. If the Trustee ceases to perform its functions under the Commitments or for any other good cause, including the exposure of the Trustee to a Conflict of Interest:

(a) the Commission may, after hearing the Trustee and *[X]*, require *[X]* to replace the Trustee; or

(b) [X] may, with the prior approval of the Commission, replace the Trustee.

41. If the Trustee is removed according to paragraph 40 of these Commitments, the Trustee may be required to continue in its function until a new Trustee is in place to whom the Trustee has effected a full hand over of all relevant information. The new Trustee shall be appointed in accordance with the procedure referred to in paragraphs 19-26 of these Commitments.

42. Unless removed according to paragraph 40 of these Commitments, the Trustee shall cease to act as Trustee only after the Commission has discharged it from its duties after all the Commitments with which the Trustee has been entrusted have been implemented. However, the Commission may at any time require the reappointment of the Monitoring Trustee if it subsequently appears that the relevant remedies might not have been fully and properly implemented.

SECTION F. THE REVIEW CLAUSE

43. The Commission may extend the time periods foreseen in the Commitments in response to a request from *[X]* or, in appropriate cases, on its own initiative. Where *[X]* requests an extension of a time period, it shall submit a reasoned request to the Commission no later than one month before the expiry of that period, showing good cause. This request shall be accompanied by a report from the Monitoring Trustee, who shall, at the same time send a non-confidential copy of the report to the Notifying Party. Only in exceptional circumstances shall *[X]* be entitled to request an extension within the last month of any period.

44. The Commission may further, in response to a reasoned request from the Notifying Parties showing good cause waive, modify or substitute, in exceptional circumstances, one or more of the undertakings in these Commitments. This request shall be accompanied by a report from the Monitoring Trustee, who shall, at the same time send a non-confidential copy of the report to the Notifying Party. The request shall not have the effect of suspending the application of the undertaking and, in particular, of suspending the expiry of any time period in which the undertaking has to be complied with.

SECTION G. ENTRY INTO FORCE

45. The Commitments shall take effect upon the date of adoption of the Decision.

. . . .

duly authorised for and on behalf of

[*Indicate the name of each of the Notifying Parties*]

SCHEDULE

1. The Divestment Business as operated to date has the following legal and functional structure: [*Describe the legal and functional structure of the Divestment Business, including the organisational chart*].

2. In accordance with paragraph [6] of these Commitments, the Divestment Business includes, but is not limited to:

(a) the following main tangible assets: [*Indicate the essential tangible assets, e.g. xyz factory/warehouse/pipelines located at abc and the real estate/property on which the factory/warehouse is located; the R&D facilities*];

(b) the following main intangible assets: [*Indicate the main intangible assets. This should in particular include (i) the brand names and (ii) all other Intellectual Property Rights used in conducting the Divestment Business.*];

(c) the following main licences, permits and authorisations: [*Indicate the main licences, permits and authorisations*];

(d) the following main contracts, agreements, leases, commitments and understandings [*Indicate the main contracts, etc.*];

(e) the following customer, credit and other records: [*Indicate the main customer, credit and other records, according to further sector specific indications, where appropriate*];

(f) the following Personnel: [*Indicate the personnel to be transferred in general, including personnel providing essential functions for the Divestment Business, such as central R&D staff*];

(g) the following Key Personnel: [*Indicate the names and functions of the Key Personnel, including the Hold Separate Manager, where appropriate*]; and

(h) the arrangements for the supply with the following products or services by [X] or Affiliated Undertakings for a transitional period of up to [•] after Closing: [*Indicate the products or services to be provided for a transitional period in order to maintain the economic viability and competitiveness of the Divestment Business*].

3. The Divestment Business shall not include:

(a) . . . ;

(b) [*It is the responsibility of the Parties to indicate clearly what the Divestment Business will not encompass*].

4. If there is any asset or personnel which is not be covered by paragraph 2 of this Schedule but which is both used (exclusively or not) in the Divestment Business and necessary for the continued viability and competitiveness of the Divestment Business, that asset or adequate substitute will be offered to potential purchasers.

MODEL TEXT FOR THE TRUSTEE MANDATE

(5 December 2013)

[4.718]

NOTES

This document is available on the European Commission website at:ec.europa.eu/competition-policy/mergers/legislation/best-practices_en.

TRUSTEE MANDATE

DD/MM/YYYY

BETWEEN:

1. [X] [*Indicate the name(s) of the undertaking(s) that will divest its/their businesses*] (hereafter [*X*]), a company organised under the laws of [*Indicate law of origin*], which has its registered seat at [*Indicate complete address*], represented by [*Indicate name and title of individual representing X for the Mandate*],

AND

2. [*Insert name, address, and, as the case may be, company details of the Trustee*], (the "**Trustee**").

[*X*] and the Trustee are hereafter referred to as the "***Mandate Parties***".

WHEREAS

In [*Indicate full case name and number*] and pursuant to [*Article 6(2)/Article 8(2)*] of Council Regulation (EC) No 139/2004 (the "***Merger Regulation***"), [*X*] entered into commitments (the "***Commitments***"), attached hereto as Annex 1, vis-à-vis the European Commission (the "***Commission***") with a view to rendering [*Description of the operation: e.g. the acquisition of . . . ; the creation of a full-function joint venture between . . .*] compatible with the internal market and the functioning of the EEA Agreement. The Commission approved the operation by its decision pursuant to [*Article 6(1)(b)/Article 8(2)*] of the Merger Regulation (the "***Decision***"), subject to full compliance with the Commitments, which are attached to the Decision as conditions and obligations.

According to the Commitments, [*X*] undertakes to divest the [*Indicate the business to be divested*] and, in the meantime, to preserve the economic viability, marketability and competitiveness of that business. Therefore, [*X*] undertakes to appoint a Monitoring Trustee for the monitoring of the hold separate obligations and of the divestiture procedure, and to appoint a Divestiture Trustee for the divestiture of the said business if [*X*] has not succeeded in divesting it during the First Divestiture Period. In accordance with the Commitments, [*X*] hereby engages the Trustee and this agreement forms the mandate referred to in the Commitments (hereafter the "***Mandate***").

The appointment of the Trustee and the terms of this Mandate were approved by the Commission on [*Indicate date of approval letter*].

In case of doubt or conflict, this Mandate shall be interpreted in the light of (1) the Commitments and the Decision, (2) the general framework of European Union law, in particular in the light of the Merger Regulation, and (3) the Commission Notice on remedies acceptable under Council Regulation (EC) No 139/2004 and under Commission Regulation (EC) No 802/2004.

IT HAS BEEN AGREED AS FOLLOWS:

SECTION A. DEFINITIONS

1. Terms used in this Mandate shall have the meaning set out in Section A of the Commitments. In addition, for the purpose of this Mandate, the following terms shall have the following meanings:

Sale: the entering into a binding sale and purchase agreement for the selling of the Divestment Business to the Purchaser.

Trustee Partner Firms: the other firms belonging to the same organisation of individual partnerships and companies as the Trustee.

Trustee Team: The key persons responsible for carrying out the tasks assigned by this Mandate and identified in paragraph [4].

Work-Plan: the outline of the work-plan submitted to the Commission by the Trustee before the approval of the Trustee and attached hereto as Annex [·], a more detailed version of which will be prepared by the Trustee and submitted to the Commission in its first report.

SECTION B. APPOINTMENT OF TRUSTEE

2. [*X*] hereby appoints the Trustee to act as exclusive trustee to carry out the functions specified in the Commitments for a [Monitoring Trustee and/or Divestiture Trustee] according to the Commitments and the Trustee hereby accepts the said appointment in accordance with the terms of this Mandate.

3. The appointment and this Mandate shall become effective on the date hereof except for the provisions specifically addressing the duties and obligations of the Divestiture Trustee which shall become effective with the beginning of the Trustee Divestiture Period.

4. The Trustee Team shall consist of the following key persons: [*Indicate name and title of each of the key persons (partners/leading persons)*]. The Trustee shall not replace the members of the Trustee Team without prior approval of the Commission and [*X*].

SECTION C. GENERAL DUTIES AND OBLIGATIONS OF THE TRUSTEE

5. The Trustee shall act on behalf of the Commission to ensure [*X*'s] compliance with the Commitments and assume the duties specified in the Commitments for a [*Monitoring and/or Divestiture Trustee*]. The Trustee shall carry out the duties under this Mandate in accordance with the Work-Plan as well as revisions of the Work-Plan, approved by the Commission. The Commission may, on its own initiative or at the request of the Trustee or [*X*], give any orders or instructions to the Trustee in order to ensure compliance with the Commitments. [*X*] may not give instructions to the Trustee.

6. The Trustee shall propose to [*X*] such measures as the Trustee considers necessary to ensure [*X*'s] compliance with the Commitments and/or the Mandate, and the Trustee shall propose necessary measures to the Commission in the event that [*X*] does not comply with the Trustee's proposals within the timeframe set by the Trustee.

SECTION D. DUTIES AND OBLIGATIONS OF THE MONITORING TRUSTEE

MONITORING AND MANAGEMENT OF THE DIVESTMENT BUSINESS

7. The Monitoring Trustee shall, in conformity with the Commitments, oversee, in close cooperation with the Hold Separate Manager, the on-going management of the Divestment Business with a view to ensuring its continued economic viability, marketability and competitiveness and monitor the compliance by [*X*] with the Commitments. To that end, the Monitoring Trustee shall until Closing in particular:

(a) monitor
- (i) the preservation of the economic viability, marketability and competitiveness of the Divestment Business in accordance with good business practice,
- (ii) the minimisation, as far as possible, of any risk of loss of competitive potential of the Divestment Business;
- (iii) that [*X*] or Affiliated Undertakings do not carry out any action that might have a significant adverse impact on the value, management or competitiveness of the Divestment Business or that might alter the nature and scope of activity, or the industrial or commercial strategy or the investment policy of the Divestment Business;
- (iv) that [*X*] makes available sufficient resources for the Divestment Business to develop, based on the existing business plans and their continuation, and
- (v) that [*X*] takes all reasonable steps, including appropriate incentive schemes (based on business practice), to encourage all Key Personnel to remain with the Divestment Business;

(b) monitor
- (i) the holding separate of the Divestment Business from the businesses [*X*] is retaining and Affiliated Undertakings,
- (ii) the absence of involvement of Key Employees of the Divestment Business – including the Hold Separate Manager – in any business retained and vice versa, and
- (iii) the absence of reporting of the Personnel of the Divestment Business to any individual outside the Divestment Business, except where permitted in the Commitments;

(c) seek to ensure that the Divestment Business is managed as a distinct and saleable entity separate from [*X*'s] or Affiliated Undertakings' businesses and that the Hold Separate Manager manages the Divestment Business independently and in the best interest of the business and ensuring its continued economic viability, marketability and competitiveness as well as its independence from the businesses retained by the Parties;

[(d) *the following paragraph is to be inserted in cases in which the Commitments foresee the voting of shares by the Monitoring Trustee and/or the replacement of member of the supervisory board/board of directors*: exercise [*X*'s] rights as shareholder in the legal entity or entities that constitute the Divestment Business (except for its rights in respect of dividends that are due before Closing), with the aim of acting in the best interest of the business, which shall be determined on a stand-alone basis, as an independent financial investor, and with a view to fulfilling [*X's*] obligations under the Commitments. Consequently, [*X*] grants a comprehensive and duly executed proxy to the Monitoring Trustee in Annex [·] for the exercise of the voting rights attached to [*X*'s] shares in the Divestment Business. The Monitoring Trustee shall have the power to replace members of the supervisory board or non-executive directors of the board of directors of the Divestment Business, who have been appointed on behalf of [*X*]. Upon request of the Monitoring Trustee, [*X*] shall resign as a member of the boards or shall cause such members of the boards to resign. The representatives of the Monitoring Trustee to be appointed to the board shall be one or more persons from the Trustee Team. The consent of the Commission shall be required to appoint members to the board(s) who are not members of the Trustee Team;]

(e) monitor the splitting of assets and the allocation of Personnel between the Divestment Business and [*X*] or Affiliated Undertakings;

(f) determine all necessary measures to ensure that [*X*] does not, after the Effective Date, obtain Confidential Information relating to the Divestment Business, in particular:

   (i) strive for the severing of the Divestment Business' participation in any central information technology network to the extent possible, without compromising the viability of the Divestment Business,

   (ii) make sure that any Confidential Information relating to the Divestment Business obtained by [*X*] before the Effective Date is eliminated and will not be used by [*X*] and

   (iii) decide whether such information may be disclosed to or kept by [*X*] as the disclosure is reasonably necessary to allow [*X*] to carry out the divestiture or is required by law.

MONITORING OF DIVESTITURE

8. Until the end of the First Divestiture Period, the Monitoring Trustee shall assist the Commission in reviewing the divestiture process and assessing proposed purchasers. Therefore the Monitoring Trustee shall, during the First Divestiture Period:

(a) review and assess the progress of the divestiture process and potential purchasers;

(b) verify that, dependent on the stage of the divestiture process, (i) potential purchasers receive sufficient and correct information relating to the Divestment Business and the Personnel, in particular by reviewing, if available, the data room documentation, the information memorandum and the due diligence process, and (ii) potential purchasers are granted reasonable access to the Personnel;

(c) act as a contact point for any requests by third parties, in particular potential purchasers, in relation to the Commitments and agree to have its contact details published on the website of the Commission's Directorate-General for Competition.

9. Once [*X*] has submitted a proposal for a purchaser to the Commission, the Trustee shall, within one week after receipt of the documented proposal by the Parties, submit to the Commission a reasoned opinion as to the suitability and independence of the proposed purchaser and the viability of the Divestment Business after the Sale and as to whether the Divestment Business is sold in a manner consistent with the Commission's Decision and the Commitments, in particular whether it ensures the lasting structural change in the market intended by the Commitments and, if relevant, whether the Sale of the Divestment Business without one or more Assets or members of the Personnel affects the viability of the Divestment Business after the Sale, taking account of the proposed purchaser.

10. If the Monitoring and Divestiture Trustee are not the same natural or legal person, the Monitoring Trustee and the Divestiture Trustee shall cooperate closely with each other during and for the purpose of the preparation of the Trustee Divestiture Period in order to facilitate each other's tasks.

SECTION E. DUTIES AND OBLIGATIONS OF THE DIVESTITURE TRUSTEE

11. With effect from the commencement of the Trustee Divestiture Period, [*X*] hereby gives the Trustee an exclusive mandate to sell the Divestment Business to a purchaser in accordance with this section and the Commitments.

12. The purchaser shall fulfil the Purchaser Requirements and both the purchaser and the final sale and purchase agreement shall be approved by the Commission in accordance with the procedure laid down in paragraph [18] of the Commitments.

13. The Divestiture Trustee shall sell the Divestment Business at no minimum price and on such terms and conditions as it considers appropriate for an expedient sale in the Trustee Divestiture Period. In particular, the Divestiture Trustee may include in the sale and purchase agreement (as well as in ancillary agreements) such customary representations and warranties and indemnities as are reasonably required to effect the Sale. At the same time, the Divestiture Trustee shall protect the legitimate financial interests of [*X*], subject to the Notifying Parties' unconditional obligation to divest at no minimum price in the Trustee Divestiture Period.

14. [*X*] hereby grants a comprehensive and duly executed power of attorney to the Divestiture Trustee, set out in Annex [·], to effect the Sale of the Divestment Business, the Closing and all actions and declarations which the Trustee considers necessary or appropriate for achieving the Sale of the Divestment Business or the Closing, including the power to appoint advisors to assist with the sale process. The power of attorney shall include the authority to grant

sub-powers of attorney to members of the Trustee Team. If necessary to accomplish the Sale, *[X]* shall grant the Divestiture Trustee further powers of attorney, duly executed, or cause the documents required for the effecting of the Sale and the Closing to be duly executed. Any power of attorney granted by *[X]*, including any sub-powers of attorney granted pursuant to them, shall expire on the earlier of the termination of this Mandate or the discharge of the Trustee.

15. The Trustee shall comply with the Commission's instructions as regards any aspects of the conduct or conclusion of the sale, in particular in ending negotiations with any prospective purchaser, if the Commission notifies the Trustee and *[X]* of the Commission's determination that the negotiations are being conducted with an unacceptable purchaser.

SECTION F. REPORTING OBLIGATIONS

16. Within 15 days of the end of each month or as otherwise agreed with the Commission, the Monitoring Trustee shall submit a written report to the Commission, sending *[X]* a non-confidential copy at the same time. The report shall cover the Monitoring Trustee's fulfilment of its obligations under the Mandate and the compliance of the Parties with the Commitments. The report shall furthermore cover the operation and management of the Divestment Business and the splitting of assets and the allocation of Personnel so that the Commission can assess whether the business is held in a manner consistent with the Commitments, as well as the progress of the divestiture process as well as potential purchasers.

17. The reports shall cover in particular the following topics:

(a) Operational and financial performance of the Divestment Business in the relevant period;

(b) Any issues or problems which have arisen in the execution of the obligations as Monitoring Trustee, in particular any issues of non-compliance by [X] or the Divestment Business with the Conditions and Obligations;

(c) Monitoring of the preservation of the economic viability, marketability and competitiveness of the Divestment Business and of [X's] compliance with the hold separate and ring-fencing obligations as well as monitoring of the splitting of assets and of the allocation of Personnel between the Divestment Business and the businesses retained by [X] or Affiliated Undertakings;

(d) Review and assessment of the progress of the divestiture process, including reporting on potential purchasers and all other information received from [X] regarding the divestiture;

(e) Any particular issues as set out in the Work-Plan;

(f) Estimated future timetable, including the date of next anticipated reporting;

(g) A proposal for a detailed Work-Plan in the first report as well as revisions in subsequent reports.

18. During the Trustee Divestiture Period, within 15 days after the end of every month, the Divestiture Trustee shall provide to the Commission, with a simultaneous copy to the Monitoring Trustee and a non-confidential copy to *[X]*, a comprehensive report written in *[Indicate the language]* on the discharge of its obligations under this Mandate and the progress of the divestiture process, covering in particular the following information:

(a) List of potential purchasers and a preliminary assessment of each of them;

(b) State of negotiations with potential purchasers;

(c) Any issues or problems regarding the sale of the Divestment Business, including any issues and problems regarding the negotiation of the necessary agreement(s);

(d) Need for advisers for the sale of the Divestment Business and a list of advisers selected by the Trustee for that purpose;

(e) Any particular issues as set out in the Work-Plan;

(f) A proposal for a detailed Work-Plan in the first report as well as revisions in subsequent reports.

19. At any time, the Trustee will provide to the Commission, at its request (or on the Trustee's own initiative), a written or oral report on matters falling within the Trustee's Mandate. The Trustee shall send *[X]* simultaneously a non-confidential copy of such additional written reports and shall inform *[X]* promptly of the non-confidential content of any oral reports.

20. The Trustee shall send *[X]* non-confidential copies of the written Trustee reports provided for in the Commitments and the Trustee Mandate at the same time as such reports are sent to the Commission.

SECTION G. DUTIES AND OBLIGATIONS OF [X]

21. *[X]* shall provide and shall cause its advisors to provide the Trustee with all such co-operation, assistance and information as the Trustee may reasonably require to perform its tasks. The Trustee shall have full and complete access to any of *[X's]* or the Divestment Business' books, records, documents, management or other personnel, facilities, sites and technical information necessary for fulfilling its duties under the Mandate. *[X]* and the Divestment Business shall provide the Trustee upon request with copies of any document. *[X]* and the Divestment Business shall make available to the Trustee one or more offices on their premises. They shall be available for meetings in order to provide the Trustee with all information necessary for the performance of its tasks.

22. *[X]* shall provide the Monitoring Trustee with all managerial and administrative support that it may reasonably request on behalf of the management of the Divestment Business. This shall include all administrative support functions relating to the Divestment Business which are currently carried out at headquarters level. *[X]* shall provide and shall cause its advisors to provide the Monitoring Trustee, on request, with access to the information submitted to potential purchasers, in particular to the data room documentation and all other information granted to potential purchasers in the due diligence procedure. *[X]* shall inform the Monitoring Trustee on possible purchasers, submit lists of potential purchasers at each stage of the selection process, including the offers made by potential purchasers at those stages, and keep the Monitoring Trustee informed of all developments in the divestiture process. Once a purchaser has been chosen, *[X]* shall submit a fully documented and reasoned proposal, including a copy of the final agreement(s), to the Monitoring Trustee and allow the Monitoring Trustee to have confidential contacts with the proposed purchaser in order for the Monitoring Trustee to determine whether or not, in its opinion, the proposed purchaser meets the Purchaser Criteria.

23. At the expense of [*X*], the Trustee may appoint advisors (in particular for corporate finance or legal advice), subject to [*X*'s] approval (this approval not to be unreasonably withheld or delayed) if the Trustee considers the appointment of such advisors necessary or appropriate for the performance of its duties and obligations under the Mandate, provided that any fees and other expenses incurred by the Trustee are reasonable. Should [*X*] refuse to approve the advisors proposed by the Trustee, the Commission may, after having heard [*X*], approve the appointment of such advisors. Only the Trustee shall be entitled to issue instructions to the advisors. Paragraph 31 [of this Mandate] shall apply to the advisors *mutatis mutandis*. In the Trustee Divestiture Period, the Divestiture Trustee may use advisors who served [*X*] during the First Divestiture Period if the Divestiture Trustee considers this to be in the best interest of an expedient sale.

SECTION H. TRUSTEE RELATED PROVISIONS

CONFLICTS OF INTEREST

24. The Trustee's, the Trustee Team's and the Trustee Partner Firms' current relationships with the Notifying Parties and Affiliated Undertakings are disclosed in Annex [·]. On this basis, the Trustee confirms that, as of the date of this Mandate, the Trustee and each member of the Trustee Team is independent of [*X*] and Affiliated Undertakings and has no Conflict of Interest.

25. The Trustee undertakes not to create a Conflict of Interest during the term of the Mandate. The Trustee, the members of the Trustee Team and the Trustee Partner Firms may therefore not during the term of this Mandate:

(a) have or accept any employment by or be or accept any appointment as Member of the Board or member of other management bodies of the Parties or Affiliated Undertakings other than appointments pertaining to the establishment and performance of the Mandate;

(b) have or accept any assignments or other business relationships with or financial interests in the Parties or Affiliated Undertakings that might lead to a Conflict of Interest;

(c) have or accept any other appointments, assignments or other business relationships that may, in view of the circumstances of the particular case, be regarded as impairing the Trustee's objectivity and independence in discharging its duties under the Mandate.

26. The provision laid down in paragraph 25(b) of this Mandate shall affect neither assignments or other business relationships between the Trustee or Trustee Partner Firms and the Parties or Affiliated Undertakings nor investments by the Trustee or Trustee Partner Firms in the stock or securities of the Parties or Affiliated Undertakings if such assignments, business relationships or investments are in the normal course of business and are material neither to the Trustee or the Trustee Partner Firms nor to the Parties or Affiliated Undertakings.

27. Should the Trustee, the Trustee Partner Firms or members of the Trustee Team wish to undertake an assignment, business relationship or investment, such a person shall seek the prior approval of the Commission. Should the Trustee become aware of a Conflict of Interest, the Trustee shall promptly inform [*X*] and the Commission, of such Conflict of Interest. In the event that [*X*] becomes aware that the Trustee or the Trustee Partner Firms have or may have a Conflict of Interest, [*X*] shall promptly notify the Trustee and the Commission, of such Conflict of Interest. Where a Conflict of Interest occurs during the term of the Mandate the Trustee undertakes to resolve it immediately. Where the Conflict of Interest cannot be resolved or is not resolved by the Trustee in a timely manner, the Mandate may be terminated in accordance with paragraph 33 below.

28. *[It is up to the Mandate Parties to insert suitable provisions regarding conflicts of interest of the Trustee and the Trustee Partner Firms with (potential) purchasers.]*

29. Should a member of the Trustee Team wish, during the term of this Mandate and for a period of one year following termination of the Mandate, to provide services to the Parties or Affiliated Undertakings, such a person shall seek the prior approval of the Commission. This period can in particular circumstances, e.g. in cases of behavioural commitments extending over several years or sale of the Divestiture Business occurring in the Trustee Divestiture Period, be extended to three years. Moreover, the Trustee undertakes to establish measures to ensure the independence and integrity of the Trustee Team and the Trustee's employees and agents directly assigned to the Trustee Team ("***Assigned Persons***") during the term of this Mandate and for a period of one year or longer as appropriate following termination of the Mandate, from any undue influence that might interfere with or in any way compromise the Trustee Team in the performance of its duties under this Mandate. In particular:

(a) access to confidential information shall be limited to the Trustee Team and Assigned Persons; and

(b) the Trustee Team and Assigned Persons shall be prohibited from communicating any information relating to this Mandate to any other of the Trustee's personnel, except for information of a general nature (e.g. Trustee's appointment, fees, etc.), and except for information whose disclosure is required by law.

REMUNERATION

30. [*It is up to the Mandate Parties to agree on a suitable fee structure. As set out in the Standard Commitments Text, the Trustee shall be remunerated in such a way that it does not impede its independence and effectiveness in fulfilling the Mandate. Regarding the Divestiture Trustee, the Commission is in favour of fee structures that, at least to a significant part, are contingent on the Divestiture Trustee's accomplishing a timely divestiture. In particular, if the remuneration package includes a success premium linked to the final sale value of the Divestment Business, the fee should also be linked to a divestiture within the Trustee Divestiture Period as specified in the Commitments. It should be noted that the fee structure – as well as the entire Mandate – is subject to the Commission's approval.*]

INDEMNITY

31. [*X*] shall indemnify the Trustee and its employees and agents (each an "***Indemnified Party***") and hold each Indemnified Party harmless against, and hereby agrees that an Indemnified Party shall have no liability to [*X*] for any liabilities arising out of the performance of the Mandate, except to the extent that such liabilities result from the wilful default, recklessness, gross negligence or bad faith of the Trustee, its employees, agents or advisors.

CONFIDENTIALITY

32. [*It is up to the Mandate Parties to agree a suitable confidentiality provision prohibiting the use, or disclosure to anyone other than the Commission of any sensitive or proprietary information gained as a result of performing the Trustee role. As a matter of course, the Mandate cannot limit the disclosure of information by the Trustee vis-à-vis the Commission and by the Commission to the Trustee. However, the Trustee must not disclose certain information gained as a result of the Trustee role to the Parties. This in particular applies to information gained on the Divestment Business to which the ring-fencing provisions apply and to information received from (potential) purchasers of the Divestment Business.*]

SECTION I. TERMINATION OF THE MANDATE

33. This Mandate may only be terminated under the conditions set out in paragraphs 34–37.

REGULAR TERMINATION OF THE MANDATE

34. This Mandate shall automatically terminate if the Commission approves the discharge in writing of the Trustee from its obligations under this Mandate. The approval of the discharge of the Trustee may be requested after the Trustee has completed the performance of its obligations under the Mandate.

35. The Mandate Parties acknowledge that the Commission may at any time request the reappointment of the Trustee by [*X*] if it subsequently appears that the Commitments might not have been fully and properly implemented. The Trustee hereby accepts such a reappointment in accordance with the terms and conditions of this Mandate.

TERMINATION OF THE MANDATE BEFORE THE DISCHARGE

36. [*X*] may only terminate the Mandate before the discharge of the Trustee in accordance with paragraph 40 of the Commitments. The Trustee may only terminate the Mandate for good cause, by giving written notice to [*X*], with a copy to the Commission. The Trustee shall continue to carry out its functions under this Mandate until it has effected a full handover of all relevant information to a new trustee appointed by [*X*] pursuant to the procedure laid down in the Commitments.

SURVIVING PROVISIONS

37. Paragraphs [29] – [32] shall survive the termination of the Mandate.

SECTION J. ADDITIONAL PROVISIONS

AMENDMENTS TO THIS MANDATE

38. This Mandate may only be amended in writing and with the Commission's prior approval. The Mandate Parties agree to amend this Mandate if required by the Commission, after consultation with the Mandate Parties, in order to secure compliance with the Commitments, in particular if the amendment is necessary in order to adapt this Mandate to amendments of the Commitments under the Review Clause.

GOVERNING LAW AND DISPUTE RESOLUTION

39. This Mandate shall be governed by, and construed in accordance with, the laws of [*Indicate the state by whose laws the Mandate shall be governed*].

40. In the event that a dispute arises concerning the Mandate Parties' obligations under this Mandate, such dispute shall be submitted to the non-exclusive jurisdiction of the [*Indicate the state whose courts shall have jurisdiction for disputes regarding the Mandate*] courts. *[Mandate Parties may agree instead to resolve such issues via arbitration. Details on such alternative dispute resolution mechanism are to be provided in this paragraph 40]*

SEVERABILITY

41. [*It is up to the Mandate Parties to agree on a suitable provision on severability, taking into account the rules under the governing law.*]

NOTICES

42. All notices sent under this Mandate shall be made in writing and be deemed to have been duly given if served by personal delivery upon the party for whom it is intended or the Commission or delivered by registered or certified mail, with request of return receipt, or if sent by fax, upon receipt of oral confirmation that such transmission has been received, to the person at the address set forth below:

If to [*X*], addressed as follows:
[·]

If to the Trustee, addressed as follows:
[·]

If to the Commission, addressed as follows:
To the attention of the Director
Directorate [*Indicate directorate name in charge of the case*]
European Commission
Directorate General for Competition
Place Madou / Madouplein 1
1210 Saint-Josse-ten-Noode /
Sint-Joost-ten-Node
Belgium
Ref: Case No COMP/M[·]

Fax: + 32 2 296 43 01

Or to any such other address or person as the relevant party may from time to time advise by notice in writing given pursuant to this section. The date of receipt of any such notice, request, consent, agreement or approval shall be deemed to be the date of delivery thereof.

[*Indicate place and date*]

By:

Title:

By:

Title:

ANNEX [·]

Power of Attorney, duly executed, for the exercise of [*X's*] rights as shareholder (pursuant to paragraph 7 (d) of the Mandate)

ANNEX [·]

Power of Attorney, duly executed, for the Divestiture Trustee (pursuant to paragraph 14 of the Mandate)

ANNEX [·]

Disclosure of current relationships between the Trustee, the Trustee Team and the Trustees Partner Firm and *[X]* and Affiliated Undertakings.

4. COOPERATION

EUROPEAN COMPETITION AUTHORITIES: PRINCIPLES ON THE APPLICATION, BY NATIONAL COMPETITION AUTHORITIES WITHIN THE ECA, OF ARTICLES 4(5) AND 22 OF THE EC MERGER REGULATION (JANUARY 2005)

[4.719]

NOTES

This document is available on the European Commission website at: ec.europa.eu/competition-policy/mergers/national-competition-authorities/eu-merger-working-group_en.

Note that Council Regulation (EC) No 139/2004 on the control of concentrations between undertakings (the EC Merger Regulation) is repealed, in relation to the UK, by the Competition (Amendment etc) (EU Exit) Regulations 2019, SI 2019/93, reg 63, Sch 3, para 1, as from IP completion day (as defined in the European Union (Withdrawal Agreement) Act 2020, s 39) (for transitional provisions and savings in relation to the operation of the 2019 Regulations, see Sch 4 to those Regulations at **[7.69]** et seq).

I. INTRODUCTION

[4.720]

1. These Principles were agreed by the National Competition Authorities (NCAs)[1] within the European Competition Authorities Association ('ECA') in 2005 and relate to Articles 4(5) and 22 EC Merger Regulation ('ECMR') as set out in Council Regulation (EC) No 139/04 of 20 January 2004 on the control of concentrations between undertakings.[2] They replace the version of 2002[3] and may be reviewed by the NCAs from time to time to reflect legislative developments (European or national) or decisional practice.[4]

The Principles should be read in conjunction with and as complementary to the EU Commission's Notice on Case Referrals in respect of concentrations[5] (the EU Commission Notice) and the relevant parts of Commission Regulation (EC) No 802/2004 implementing the ECMR including its annexes (Form CO, Short Form CO and Form RS).[6]

2. In the area of merger control there is a clear separation of competencies between the European Commission (the 'EU Commission') and the Member States. The EU Commission has exclusive competence to review concentrations as defined in Art. 3(1) ECMR when the turnover of the parties to the concentration meet the thresholds pursuant to Art. 1(2) or 1(3) ECMR Concentrations falling below these turnover thresholds remain within the competence of the Member States as provided for by their respective national merger control provisions. However, a referral system makes it possible in certain circumstances for concentrations falling below ECMR thresholds to be dealt with by the EU Commission, and vice versa.

3. The Council negotiations leading to Council Regulation (EC) No 139/04, focused on making the referral system more flexible and effective in order to ensure that a concentration would be dealt with by the authority best placed to analyse its competitive effects and, where appropriate, to restore effective competition, whilst taking account of the principles of subsidiarity and the 'one stop shop' as well as maintaining legal certainty to the utmost extent possible. Articles 4(5) and 22 ECMR, to which these Principles refer, provide for referrals of cases from the Member States to the EU Commission.

According to recital (14) ECMR, referrals of concentrations should be made in an efficient manner avoiding, to the greatest extent possible, situations where a concentration is subject to both pre- and post-filing referrals. This entails close cooperation with efficient information-sharing and consultation between the EU Commission and the NCAs in applying their respective competencies.

4. NCAs have in the past debated multiple filing issues within the framework of the ECA Working Group on Multi-jurisdictional Mergers. Cooperation and coordination among competition authorities on mergers of common concern can enhance the efficiency and effectiveness of the review process, help achieve consistent, coordinated and non-conflicting outcomes, and reduce transaction costs. In order to achieve this, in 2001 the ECA established a system that provides for a prompt exchange of information as well as closer cooperation in the assessment of multi-jurisdictional concentrations.[7]

In the light of the experience gained and with a view to enhancing transparency in the application of Article 22 of Regulation 4064/89, NCAs published in 2002 a document on joint referrals entitled 'Principles on the Application, by National Competition Authorities within the ECA Network, of Article 22 of the EC Merger Regulation' (the 'ECA Principles') which explained the factors taken into consideration when dealing with a case that may be a candidate for a joint referral to the EU Commission.

Council Regulation 139/2004, by reviewing the former Article 22 ECMR and introducing through Article 4(5) ECMR the possibility of pre-filing referrals to the EU Commission, established a new framework for referrals that requires amendment to the ECA Principles.

5. NCAs will have regard to these non-binding Principles when considering possible referrals to the EU Commission. However, given that each concentration is unique, each case will be considered in the light of its particular circumstances, the available information and the particular time constraints. NCAs will therefore apply these Principles flexibly on a case by case basis.

NOTES

[1] These are the National Competition Authorities of the EU and the EEA EFTA States. For the sake of clarity, the term 'NCA' in the following refers to these authorities.

2 Published in OJ L24, 29.1.2004;

3 These Principles were based on the European Merger Control Regulation No 4064/89.

4 After the current discussions regarding the new EEA Agreement are finished, changes in this Agreement may need to be reflected in these Principles.

5 available at: ec.europa.eu/competition/mergers/legislation/case_referrals.html.

6 available at: ec.europa.eu/competition/mergers/legislation/regulations.html#impl_reg; OJ L133, 30.4.2004, pages 1-39.

7 see the ECA Procedures Guide 'The Exchange of Information between Members on Multi-jurisdictional Mergers', which is published at the websites of some of the NCAs.

II. PRINCIPLES

[4.721]

6. Only concentrations within the meaning of Article 3 ECMR are eligible for referrals under Articles 4(5) and 22 ECMR from Member States to the EU Commission.

Cooperation on pre-filing referrals from Member States to the EU Commission pursuant to Article 4(5) ECMR

(i) *Legal Provisions and Substantive Criteria*

7. According to Article 4(5) ECMR, notifying parties ('the parties') may request that a concentration which does not have a Community dimension within the meaning of Article 1 ECMR and is capable of being reviewed under the national competition law for the control of mergers of at least three Member States be referred to the EU Commission.[8]

Article 4(5) ECMR does not permit partial referrals by only some of the Member States capable of reviewing a concentration. If any Member State capable of reviewing the concentration expresses its disagreement, the concentration remains subject to the applicable national competition law for the control of mergers. If no Member State capable of reviewing the concentration expresses its disagreement, the Commission has no discretion but has to accept that referred concentration.

8. Taking into account the specific characteristics of the concentration, a concentration where a potentially significant competitive impact extends beyond national boundaries will generally deserve careful scrutiny as a possible candidate for a pre-notification referral.

In general, NCAs, when considering whether a transaction is suitable for referral to the Commission under Article 4(5) ECMR, will take account of the following factors:

- whether the market(s) in which there may be a potentially significant impact on competition is/are wider than national in scope[9] and whether the main competitive impact of the concentration is linked to such market/s;[10]
- whether NCAs expect to encounter difficulties in information-gathering as the parties or the main third party(ies) from whom information is likely to be sought is/are not based in their Member State, or
- whether there are potentially significant competition concerns in a number of national or sub-national markets located in the EEA, and whether NCAs expect problems in identifying and/or enforcing appropriate and proportionate remedies ('suitable remedies'), should these prove necessary, in particular where suitable remedies could not be secured by the NCAs under national law or through cooperation among NCAs.

9. Some examples of circumstances in which a NCA might be less inclined to agree to a referral request could include the following:

- where the NCA is already examining a concentration which involves the same parties and/or the same product markets;
- where the concentration has its main competitive impact in that NCA's national or sub-national market(s);
- where it would avoid a risk of a subsequent referral back from the EU Commission under Article 9 ECMR.

(ii) *Procedure*

Pre-referral contacts by parties with NCAs

10. Pre-Form RS filing contacts with NCAs and with the EU Commission may be helpful in order to confirm that the criteria of Article 4(5) ECMR are met. However, NCAs cannot decide whether they agree to refer a concentration before they have received and studied the Form RS.

Pre-referral contacts with NCAs will be particularly useful whenever parties identify any need for clarification, in particular when they have questions related to:

- whether a concentration is capable of being reviewed by a particular Member State. Form RS needs to include sufficient information for each Member State to be able to verify whether the concentration qualifies for review under the applicable national competition law for the control of mergers.
- whether additional information regarding the geographic or product market definition may be needed or advisable,
- what language to use in the request for referral.

Parties are welcome to contact NCAs concerning any other relevant issue they wish to discuss before they file Form RS with the EU Commission.

Since it may be useful for NCAs to have informal contacts with each other at the pre-referral stage on common issues, it might be helpful to provide details about which other NCAs are likely to be capable of reviewing the concentration. Parties should also state whether the proposed concentration has been or is about to be made public or whether it remains confidential.

11. If parties wish to benefit from short pre-referral consultations between NCAs capable of reviewing the concentration, they should be prepared to provide confidentiality waivers to the NCAs.

The Reasoned Submission and its information requirements

12. Form RS sets out in general terms the information parties should provide if they wish to have their concentration referred from Member States to the EU Commission prior to notification.[11] Upon its receipt, NCAs will first check whether the proposed concentration meets the legal criteria, in particular whether the concentration is capable of review under their national competition law for the control of mergers. They will also consider other substantive criteria such as those set out in the EU Commission Notice and in paragraph 8 and 9 above and, using their discretion, decide on the request within 15 working days.

13. NCAs will normally assess the referral request based on information provided in the Form RS, without undertaking further investigation. It is in the parties' interest to ensure that the Reasoned Submission is correct and complete as any doubts may result in the request being vetoed by a Member State.[12]

14. When filling in Form RS, parties should take careful note of the following issues which are particularly important for Member States' ability to properly assess whether they agree to refer the concentration:

- the scope and type of information on which they intend to base their Reasoned Submission;[13]
- in order to verify which Member State is capable of reviewing the concentration, the relevant data has to be checked by all NCAs. It follows, therefore, that Reasoned Submissions should be made in a language that all NCAs understand; and
- if parties wish to submit supporting documents, they are encouraged to contact NCAs capable of reviewing the concentration to verify whether a translation of all or part of a document is advisable or whether an executive summary would suffice. If a NCA asks for an executive summary, the submitting party should confirm that it is correct and complete.

Contacts among NCAs

16. If questions of mutual interest concerning the data submitted in the Reasoned Submission arise, NCAs may wish to contact each other to exchange views on the relevant issue. Apart from informal discussions among NCAs on general issues such as market definition or precedents, informal debate with the EU Commission might also be constructive for clarifying issues.

If a NCA considers that it is unlikely to agree to the request, it will try to inform the other NCAs and the EU Commission as soon as possible.

Communication between the EU Commission and NCAs and between NCAs concerning Article 4(5) ECMR cases are confidential. All written exchanges of information will take place using secure means such as the Merger-Referrals Mailbox operated by the EU Commission. NCAs will not exchange confidential information unless they are either entitled to do so under national law or have been given waivers by the parties. Likewise, they will keep any information they receive from other NCAs concerning another NCA's decision under Article 4(5) ECMR confidential unless that NCA itself has made its decision public.

Cooperation on post-filing referrals from Member States to the EU Commission pursuant to Article 22 ECMR

(i)

Legal Provisions and Substantive Criteria

17. While the following principles concentrate on *joint* referrals from several Member States to the EU Commission, NCAs might also wish to apply all or part of the criteria described below when a concentration is referred to the EU Commission by only one Member State.

18. According to Article 22(1) ECMR, one or more Member State(s) may request the EU Commission to examine a concentration that does not have a Community dimension within the meaning of Article 1 ECMR but affects trade between Member States and threatens to significantly affect competition within the territory of the Member State(s) making the request.

Any other Member State shall have the right to join the initial request within a period of 15 working days of being informed by the EU Commission of the initial request, according to Article 22(2) ECMR.

In contrast to the situation under Article 4(5), Article 22 ECMR permits referral by one or some of the Member States examining the concentration (partial referrals). If there is a partial referral, the NCAs examining the concentration will, insofar as timing permits, co-operate with each other and with the EU Commission in order to avoid, to the greatest extent possible, conflicting results.

19. In addition to the legal criteria referred to in Article 22(1) ECMR, when trying to establish whether a concentration might be a suitable candidate for a joint referral, NCAs will take account of the following factors:

— whether the relevant geographic market(s) affected by the concentration is/are wider than national in scope and whether the main competitive impact of the concentration is linked to such market/s;

— whether NCAs expect to encounter difficulties in information gathering as the parties or the main third party(ies) from whom information is likely to be sought is/are not based in their Member State; or

— whether there are potentially significant competition concerns in a number of national or sub-national markets located in the EEA, and whether NCAs expect problems in identifying and/or enforcing suitable remedies, should they prove necessary, in particular where suitable remedies could not be secured by the NCAs under national law or through cooperation among NCAs.

(ii)
Procedure

Informing the NCAs about a multijurisdictional merger

20. Whenever a NCA receives a notification or learns about a concentration which might be a possible candidate for a referral to the EU Commission, it will ask the parties concerned:

— whether the concentration is capable of being reviewed by any other NCA within the ECA and,
— which NCA will or has received a notification.

When the parties to a concentration inform a NCA that the concentration is subject to review by another NCA within the ECA, the information procedure as described in the ECA Procedures Guide will be put into effect. In particular, all NCAs within the ECA network should be informed of the concentration and which NCAs, according to the parties, are capable of reviewing the concentration. Thus, the process of identifying a concentration as a possible candidate for a joint referral does not depend on it having been notified to all NCAs which are capable of reviewing it under their applicable national competition law for the control of mergers.

The assessment of the concentration

21. NCAs assessing whether the concentration might be suitable for a joint referral to the EU Commission under Article 22(1) ECMR should try to evaluate as quickly as possible whether the concentration is expected to fulfil the above mentioned legal and substantive criteria. This can only be done on a *prima facie* basis.

Launching the referral

22. If a NCA involved in the assessment of a concentration considers that it might be a suitable candidate for a referral, it will inform all other NCAs.

Alternatively, according to Article 22(5) ECMR, the EU Commission may inform one or several Member State(s) that it considers a concentration to be suitable for a referral and invite that or those Member State(s) to make a request pursuant to Article 22(1) ECMR NCAs that have received such an invitation will inform all other NCAs of this fact.

Notifying parties may also informally indicate to one or several NCAs that they would favour a concentration to be referred.

The consultation process

Contacts between NCAs

23. After the first NCA has informed the others that it considers a concentration is a suitable candidate for a joint referral, consultations will be conducted without delay in view of tight deadlines, in order to verify as soon as possible, whether there is support for a joint referral.

Since under Article 22(2) ECMR all national time limits relating to the concentration are suspended when a referral request is made by an NCA, any NCA seriously considering triggering the referral by making a request should inform the other NCAs without delay.

24. Once a request for referral to the EU Commission has been made under Article 22(1) ECMR by one or more Member States, the EU Commission forwards it to all the NCAs and national time limits relating to the concentration are suspended. Under Article 22(2) ECMR, other NCAs can join the request within 15 working days of being informed by the Commission of the request made.

Every NCA should inform the other NCAs and the Commission as soon as possible of its decision whether or not to join the request.

As soon as a NCA informs the EU Commission that it is *not* joining the request but examining the concentration itself, the suspension of that NCA's national time limits ends. That NCA should also inform the other NCAs of the fact and should continue to co-operate with the other NCAs and the EU Commission during the parallel examination of the concentration. It should also inform the other NCAs and the Commission about the results of its examination.

Whilst NCAs will try to avoid as far as possible diverging decisions on whether or not to jointly refer a concentration to the EU Commission, national conditions for competition may lead a NCA to conclude that its participation in the joint request would not be appropriate. No NCA is bound by another NCA's decision.

Contacts with the parties

25. NCAs should inform the parties as soon as possible that a joint referral of the concentration is being considered.

If a NCA learns about a concentration which has not been notified to it but that is being considered by other NCAs as a possible candidate for a referral, the NCA might wish to contact the parties to ask for details concerning the concentration with a view to starting national merger control proceedings.

Consultations with the EU Commission

26. The NCAs should contact the EU Commission as soon as possible in order to verify its position regarding a possible (joint) referral. The Commission's informal agreement to a referral should be sought and the other NCAs accordingly kept informed.

The Coordinator of the procedure

27. The NCAs participating in a joint referral will try to identify amongst themselves an informal Coordinator to act as an informal liaison contact among NCAs, the EU Commission and the parties.

The Coordinator will act as a focal point for information. He/she maintains contact with the NCAs and the EU Commission informing them about the state of affairs and also exploring their views on the initiative.

28. The Coordinator should consult NCAs verifying their position regarding initiating the referral or later joining it. Moreover, he/she should secure coordination on procedural and substantive issues relating to any joint referral, as far as national confidentiality rules permit. Both the intention and the execution of any initial request for referral should be communicated to all NCAs concerned without delay as this affects all other national procedures. The Coordinator should keep NCAs informed about which Member State has joined the initial request for referral.

29. The role of the Coordinator is meant to facilitate cooperation among NCAs. It does not prevent NCAs from undertaking their own consultations with the EU Commission and/or the parties. It will also not influence any NCA's independent assessment of whether it considers a case suitable for a referral under Article 22(1) ECMR or whether it will join any initial request according to Article 22(2) ECMR.

Timing

30. According to Article 22(1) ECMR, a referral request must be made within 15 working days of the date on which the concentration was notified or, if no notification is required, otherwise made known to the Member State concerned. As far as possible, NCAs will endeavour to reach informal consensus among themselves as regards the joint referral before the expiry of the deadline.

31. With regard to Member States which do not have a mandatory notification system, 'made known', which triggers the 15 working day period as laid down in Article 22(1) ECMR, should be interpreted as implying sufficient information to make a preliminary assessment as to the existence of the criteria for the making of a referral request pursuant to Article 22 ECMR.[14]

The request for referral

32. In either initiating a request under Article 22(1) ECMR or in joining the request under Article 22(2) ECMR, the NCAs agree generally to address, where appropriate, the following issues:

i) that the merger is a concentration as defined in Article 3 ECMR;
ii) that the concentration has no community dimension within the meaning of Article 1 ECMR;
iii) whether a relevant geographic market is wider than national;
iv) the jurisdictions under which it is subject to review;
v) the potential of the concentration, on a prima facie assessment, to significantly affect competition within the territory of the Member State making the request
vi) potential problems in identifying and/or enforcing suitable remedies should these prove necessary;
vii) the possible effect of the concentration on trade between Member States;
viii) the fact that the deadline imposed by Article 22(1) or (2) ECMR is met;
ix) whether consensus has been reached between several NCAs to refer jointly the concentration to the EU Commission; and
x) whether, if known, the parties are favourable (or not) to the referral.

NCAs may address any other point they might find important.

The transmission of the request to the EU Commission

33. Each NCA is responsible for transmitting its own referral request to the EU Commission.

The conclusion of the proceedings

34. According to Article 22(3) ECMR, the EU Commission has discretion whether to accept the referral. Should the EU Commission inform the NCAs that it has decided to examine the concentration, the referring NCAs will transmit to the EU Commission as quickly as possible the documents received in the context of the national proceeding, to the extent that this is possible under national confidentiality rules. Where national confidentiality rules do not permit this, a waiver from the parties will be necessary before transmitting the documents to the EU Commission. In such circumstances, NCAs will, in anticipation of the referral, ask the parties as well as third parties where appropriate, to give a waiver concerning the documents they provided to the NCAs during its national investigation.

NOTES

8 Note, however, that Article 4(5) ECMR is applicable only if no notification has been made within the EU.

9 As the EU Commission and the Court of First Instance have explained, NCAs are deemed to be at least as well placed as the EU Commission to examine mergers that affect national markets due to the prior experience and direct knowledge in dealing with the relevant markets, the parties to the merger and third parties within their respective Member States. See judgment of the Court of First Instance, T-346/02 and T-347/02 (*Cableuropa et al against Commission*), para. 178.

10 Note, however, that the mere fact that an undertaking is active in more than one Member State is not in itself an indication that markets are greater than national (see judgment of Court of First Instance, T-346/02 and T-347/02, *Cableuropa et al. against Commission*; para. 126.

11 Form RS is ANNEX III to Commission Regulation (EC) No 802/2004 of 7 April 2004 implementing Council Regulation (EC) No 139/2004 on the control of concentrations between undertakings; see Footnote 6.

12 Furthermore, the provision of incorrect or misleading information in the Reasoned Submission could lead to the Commission revoking the decision it had taken under Article 6 or 8 ECMR and/or imposing fines. The provision of incorrect or misleading information could also lead to a post-notification referral of a case from the EU Commission to the Member States, rectifying any referral made at the pre-notification stage.

13 This is particularly pertinent in situations where the EU Commission has given waivers for information normally required in Form RS.

[14] See footnote 44 of EU Commission Notice.

US-EU MERGER WORKING GROUP BEST PRACTICES ON COOPERATION IN MERGER INVESTIGATIONS

(14 October 2011)

[4.722]

NOTES

This document is taken from the European Commission website at: ec.europa.eu/competition-policy/mergers/legislation/international-cooperation_en.

[4.723]

Recognizing the 20th anniversary of the Agreement between the European Communities and the Government of the United States of America Regarding the Application of their Competition Laws, and

Celebrating two decades of cooperation between the Competition Directorate-General of the European Commission and the United States federal antitrust agencies, the Federal Trade Commission and the Antitrust Division of the Department of Justice, that continues to benefit consumers and firms in both jurisdictions,

The three agencies reaffirm their strong commitment to this mutually beneficial cooperative relationship. In order to enhance their relationship, the three agencies have today adopted the following revised Best Practices on Merger Cooperation in cases where a US agency and the Competition Directorate-General of the European Commission are reviewing the same merger.

This document provides an advisory framework for interagency cooperation by setting forth best practices that the United States federal antitrust agencies (the US Department of Justice ("DOJ") and the US Federal Trade Commission ("FTC"), hereinafter the "US agencies") and the Competition Directorate-General of the European Commission (hereinafter "DG Competition") will seek to apply, to the extent consistent with their respective laws and enforcement responsibilities, when they review the same merger.[1] This document also acknowledges the substantial contribution that merging parties can make in facilitating cooperation among reviewing agencies in the merger review process.

Cooperation between the US agencies and DG Competition is based primarily upon the 1991 US-EU Agreement on the application of their competition laws. The purpose of that Agreement is "to promote cooperation and coordination and lessen the possibility or impact of differences between the Parties in the application of their competition laws."[2]

This document revises the best practices agreed between DG Competition and the US agencies in 2002[3] and builds on the experience gained in a significant number of cases since 2002. This restatement of best practices sets out the conditions under which trans-Atlantic inter-agency cooperation in merger investigations should be conducted, while at the same time confirming and building upon current practice. The US agencies and DG Competition reserve their full discretion in the implementation of these best practices and nothing in this document is intended to modify or create any enforceable rights.

NOTES

[1] These Best Practices apply to mergers that are subject to the EU Merger Regulation, Council Regulation (EC) No 139/2004 of 20 January 2004 on the control of concentrations between undertakings, OJ L24/1 (29 January 2004), and to § 7 of the Clayton Act, 15 U.S.C. § 18, regardless of whether the merger is subject to the Hart Scott Rodino Act, 15 U.S.C. § 18a.

[2] Agreement between the European Communities and the Government of the United States of America regarding the application of their competition laws, 23 Sept. 1991, *reprinted in* 4 Trade Reg. Rpt. (CCH) 13, 504, and OJ L95 (27 Apr. 1995) *corrected at* OJ L131/38 (15 June 1995), art. I.1, *available at:* www.ftc.gov/bc/international/docs/agree_eurocomm.pdf; www.justice.gov/atr/public/international/docs/0525.htm; and ec.europa.eu/competition/international/legislation/usa01.pdf.

[3] US-EU Merger Working Group, Best Practices on Cooperation in Merger Investigations, *available at* ec.europa.eu/competition/international/bilateral/eu_us.pdf; www.justice.gov/atr/public/international/docs/200405.htm; and www.ftc.gov/opa/2002/10/mergerbestpractices.shtm.

I. OBJECTIVES

[4.724]

1. In today's global economy, many mergers involving international businesses are likely to be subject to review in both the European Union ("EU") and the United States ("US"), as well as in other jurisdictions. When the US agencies[4] and DG Competition are reviewing the same merger, both have an interest in reaching, insofar as possible, consistent, or at least non-conflicting, outcomes.

2. Cooperation between DG Competition and the US agencies is beneficial not only for the agencies, but also for merging parties and third parties, as it increases the efficiency of the respective investigations, reduces the burden on merging parties and third parties, and increases the overall transparency of the merger review process.

3. Given legal constraints in both jurisdictions, effective coordination between the US agencies and DG Competition depends to a considerable extent on the cooperation and goodwill of the merging parties and of third parties. Agency cooperation is most effective when the merging parties and third parties allow the agencies to share information, the

disclosure of which is subject to confidentiality restrictions. In addition, cooperation is more effective when the investigation timetables of DG Competition and the US agencies allow the investigative staffs of each agency to engage with one another and with the merging parties and third parties on substantive issues at key stages of their respective investigations. The reviewing agencies, working together and with the merging parties, can seek to align their timetables accordingly. At the same time, the US agencies and DG Competition recognize that whether to facilitate such cooperation is within the discretion of the merging parties. Accordingly, while a party's choice not to follow some or all of these best practices may complicate cooperation between the agencies, that decision will not of itself prejudice the conduct or outcome of the agencies' investigations.

4. An increasing number of mergers reviewed by DG Competition and the US agencies also are subject to review by other competition authorities around the world. The merging parties are encouraged to inform the US agencies and DG Competition of the competition authorities in other jurisdictions that are reviewing or are expected to review the same merger, and DG Competition and the US agencies seek to cooperate with those other authorities pursuant to the relevant OECD Recommendation,[5] bilateral cooperation arrangement,[6] and/or the principles developed by the International Competition Network for interagency cooperation.[7]

NOTES

4 Pursuant to Rule 803.20(b)(1) of the Code of Federal Regulations (16 C.F.R. § 803.20(b)(1)), only one US agency – either the DOJ or the FTC – reviews each pertinent transaction and, accordingly, coordinates with DG Competition regarding that transaction.

5 OECD Revised Recommendation of the Council concerning cooperation between member countries on anticompetitive practices affecting international trade, C(95)130/FINAL, July 27–28, 1995, *available at:* www.oecd.org/daf/competition/21570317.pdf.

6 Bilateral arrangements to which the United States is a party are collected at: www.ftc.gov/oia/agreements.shtm and www.justice.gov/atr/public/international/int-arrangements.html; bilateral agreements to which the European Commission is a party are collected at: ec.europa.eu/competition/international/bilateral/.

7 *See*, in particular, principles of interagency coordination in Section X of the ICN Recommended Practices for Merger Notification Procedures available at www.internationalcompetitionnetwork.org/uploads/library/doc588.pdf.

II. COMMUNICATION BETWEEN REVIEWING AGENCIES

[4.725]

5. The reviewing agencies, via liaison officers or otherwise, are to contact one another promptly upon learning of a merger that appears to require review in both the US and EU.[8] The nature and frequency of communication between DG Competition and the US agencies may differ depending on the characteristics of the particular case under review.

6. For example, at the start of any investigation in which it appears that substantial cooperation between the US agencies and DG Competition may be beneficial, the relevant DOJ Section Chief or FTC Assistant Director and DG Competition Unit Head (or their designees) should seek to agree on a tentative timetable for regular inter-agency consultations, which takes into account the nature and timing of the merger. While it will normally be beneficial to keep each other informed on a continuous basis and discussions may take place at any time between the reviewing agencies, consultations are likely to be particularly useful at key stages of the investigation, including: (a) before the relevant US agency either closes an investigation without taking action or issues a second request; (b) no later than three weeks after the European Commission initiates a Phase I investigation; (c) before the European Commission opens a Phase II investigation or clears the merger without initiating a Phase II investigation; (d) before the European Commission closes a Phase II investigation without issuing a Statement of Objections or before DG Competition anticipates issuing a Statement of Objections; (e) before the relevant DOJ section/FTC division makes its case recommendation to senior leadership; (f) at the commencement of remedies negotiations with the merging parties; and (g) prior to a reviewing agency's final decision to seek to prohibit a merger.[9] Consultations between the senior leadership of DG Competition and their counterparts in the US agencies may also be appropriate at any time. The senior leadership of the reviewing agencies should be kept informed of key milestones throughout the investigation. Consultations also may take place between the reviewing agencies' economic counterparts at appropriate points in the investigation.

7. To facilitate the communication envisaged in paragraph 6, at the start of any investigation in which it appears that substantial cooperation between DG Competition and the US agencies may be beneficial, each agency should designate a contact person responsible for, *inter alia*: setting up a schedule for communications between the relevant investigative staffs of each agency; discussing with the merging parties the possibility of coordinating timing of the respective investigations (see Section III below); and coordinating information gathering or discovery efforts, including seeking waivers from the merging parties and from third parties.

NOTES

8 Subject to the normal conditions for cooperation in the pre-notification phase, DG Competition may discuss with the US agencies preparatory steps in cases that are in the process of being referred to the Commission by the Member States under Article 4(5) of the Merger Regulation, in particular if the parties have granted a waiver at that stage.

9 Pursuant to the terms of the Administrative Arrangements on Attendance of 1999, officials of the relevant US agency and DG Competition, as appropriate, may attend certain key events in the other's investigative process.

III. COORDINATION ON TIMING

[4.726]

8. Cooperation between the US agencies and DG Competition with respect to mergers subject to review by both jurisdictions is most effective when the reviewing agencies' respective investigation timetables allow for meaningful communication throughout the merger review processes, including at key decision-making stages, recognizing that

there are differences between the US and EU merger review investigation timetables. To facilitate coordination, DG Competition and the US agencies should endeavour to keep one another informed of important developments related to timing throughout the course of their respective merger investigations.

9. In appropriate cases, the reviewing agencies should endeavour to coordinate the phases of their investigations, including by holding joint calls or meetings with the merging parties and the relevant US agency and DG Competition staffs to discuss timing of the respective investigations. The success of this effort depends on the active participation and cooperation of the merging parties and will be facilitated if the parties discuss timing with the reviewing agencies as soon as feasible after the parties inform the reviewing agencies of a merger that requires review by the US agencies and DG Competition. To inform these discussions, the merging parties are encouraged to provide basic information about the merger to the reviewing agencies, including:

- The names and activities of the merging parties;
- The geographic areas in which they conduct business;
- The sector or sectors involved (short description for both the US and EU);
- The names of other jurisdictions in which they have made or intend to make a filing;
- The actual or anticipated date for the filing in each jurisdiction; and
- Any issues relevant to the timing of the merger.

The reviewing agencies and the merging parties should be prepared to discuss ways to coordinate the timing of the US and EU investigations, to the extent possible under US and EU law respectively. Topics addressed may include the appropriate times to file and suggested timeframes for the submission of documents or other information and interviews, including in DG Competition's pre-notification phase, so as to allow cooperation before formal notification in the EU.

10. The parties' timing of their filings should allow the reviewing agencies to communicate and cooperate meaningfully at key decision-making stages of their respective investigations. In considering the timing of their filings, the parties should take into account the stages of the respective reviewing agencies' processes, and in particular, the initial phases. One option to facilitate coordination of the timing of the investigations between the reviewing agencies is parallel filings in the US and the EU; if filings in the EU and US are not made in parallel, meaningful cooperation can still be achieved if the timing of the filings allows for cooperation of the agencies at key decision-making stages of their respective investigations.

11. Merging parties also can facilitate coordination of investigations throughout the process, including when DG Competition is conducting pre-notification consultations or a Phase I investigation with or without remedies, and the US agency has already opened an investigation. Such facilitation of coordination, including the timing of filings, is particularly important in cases in which the merging parties anticipate that the US agency will issue a second request and will seek remedies, and the merging parties are seeking a Phase I clearance decision with commitments from the European Commission. After the issuance of a second request in the US and the opening of a Phase II investigation in the EU, the parties can further facilitate coordination of the investigation timetables by using the timing flexibility provided for in the respective procedures at this stage. For example, the parties can negotiate a timing agreement with the reviewing US agency based on the date on which the parties will certify compliance with the second request. In the EU, parties can request to extend the review period by up to 20 working days.

12. In any event, if the timing of the filings in the US and the EU is such that a final decision in one jurisdiction is reached before filing has taken place in the other, any possibility for meaningful cooperation between the agencies will have been excluded. As a result, the respective investigations are likely to be less efficient and effective for the reviewing agencies, the merging parties, and third parties.

IV. COLLECTION AND EVALUATION OF EVIDENCE

[4.727]

13. In matters under review that raise issues of concern in both jurisdictions, the reviewing agencies should seek to coordinate with one another throughout the course of their investigations and to keep one another informed of their progress; such coordination may well start in DG Competition's pre-notification phase. This coordination may include sharing publicly available information and, consistent with the agencies' confidentiality obligations, discussing their respective analyses at various stages of an investigation, including market definitions, assessments of competitive effects and efficiencies, theories of competitive harm, economic theories, and empirical evidence needed to test those theories. Views on necessary remedial measures and relevant past investigations and cases also may be discussed. In addition, the reviewing agencies may discuss and coordinate information or discovery requests to the merging parties and third parties, including exchanging draft questionnaires to the extent permitted by the respective jurisdictions' laws and regulations. Efficient investigatory coordination will benefit the merging parties, third parties, and the reviewing agencies. For example, in appropriate cases, the reviewing agencies might encourage and provide opportunities for parties to organize presentations or interviews jointly with both agencies, and to allow for the concurrent submission of documents.

14. Waivers of confidentiality executed by merging parties enable more complete communication between the reviewing agencies and with the merging parties regarding evidence that is relevant to the investigation. Such confidentiality waivers have become routine practice in cases involving cooperation between DG Competition and the US agencies. This results in more informed decision-making and more effective coordination between the reviewing agencies, thereby helping to avoid inconsistent or conflicting analyses and outcomes as well as expediting merger review. Accordingly, as soon as feasible after the parties inform the reviewing agencies of a merger that requires review by the US agencies and DG Competition, the staff of the reviewing agencies should, in appropriate cases, enter into discussion with the merging parties with a view to receiving confidentiality waivers from the merging parties, normally at DG Competition's pre-notification stage.[10]

15. Similarly, waivers of confidentiality executed by third parties enable more complete communication between the reviewing agencies and with third parties and can reduce the investigative burden imposed on third parties. Where appropriate, the reviewing agencies may, therefore, request that third parties waive confidentiality, or request that third parties provide the same information to both reviewing agencies concurrently.

NOTES

10 *See,* for a sample confidentiality waiver letter, International Competition Network, Waivers of Confidentiality in Merger Investigations, *available at*: www.internationalcompetitionnetwork.org/uploads/library/doc330.pdf. For examples of the US agencies' model waivers, *see* www.ftc.gov/oia/waivers/index.shtm and www.justice.gov/atr/public/international. As the rules governing legal professional privilege are different in the EU and the US, in particular with regard to in-house lawyers, the agencies will accept a stipulation in parties' waivers given to DG Competition that excludes from the scope of the waiver evidence that is properly identified by the parties as and qualifies for the in-house counsel privilege under US law.

V. REMEDIES/SETTLEMENTS

[4.728]

16. Cooperation will be especially valuable for both the reviewing agencies and the merging parties in mergers for which remedies need to be considered in both jurisdictions, or for which remedies offered to one agency may have effects in the other jurisdiction. For example, when a case involves markets that are global in scope or at least affect both the EU and the US, the remedies offered to the reviewing agencies may be similar or identical. Even if the geographic market is limited to only one jurisdiction, or the product markets or competitive effects of the merger are not identical in both jurisdictions, the remedies offered in one jurisdiction may be linked to, dependent on, or have an effect on, those offered in the other jurisdiction.

17. To the extent consistent with their respective law enforcement responsibilities, the reviewing agencies should strive to ensure that the remedies they accept do not impose inconsistent or conflicting obligations on the merging parties. It is clearly in the interest of the merging parties to coordinate the timing and substance of remedy proposals being made to the US agencies and DG Competition, so as to minimize the risk of inconsistent or conflicting results or subsequent difficulties in implementation. This will normally also require coordination on the overall timing of the investigations so as to allow for meaningful cooperation between the reviewing agencies on the substantive assessment of the merger before the remedial stage. If the timing of the respective filings and therefore of the investigations does not allow for such cooperation, the reviewing agencies may ultimately not be able to agree on consistent and non-conflicting remedies in relation to their respective investigations.

18. Consistent with their confidentiality and/or non-disclosure obligations and their common objective of ensuring efficient outcomes, implementation, and monitoring of remedies, the reviewing agencies should seek to keep one another informed of remedy discussions with the parties and of other relevant developments with respect to remedies, to the extent the remedies may impact the other reviewing agency's review. Where appropriate, and consistent with confidentiality and/or non-disclosure obligations, the reviewing agencies should share draft remedy proposals and participate in joint discussions with the merging parties, prospective buyers, and trustees. Practice has shown that it is particularly important for both the merging parties and reviewing agencies to communicate and coordinate early and frequently when the remedies under consideration include an up-front buyer and when DG Competition is considering a remedy in its Phase I investigation.

19. Cooperation is beneficial throughout the remedial process. Cooperating on the design of possible remedies may result in a single proposal for a remedial package to address concerns of both reviewing agencies. The remedy proposals may, for example, be similar or even identical in relation to the scope of a business to be divested, interim supply relations with the parties, or other interim safeguards. Cooperation on the implementation of the remedies may allow, in appropriate cases, the appointment of common trustees or monitors, or agreement on the same purchasers for assets to be divested in both jurisdictions. As effective cooperation at both stages will depend significantly on the timing and the content of the merging parties' proposals, the merging parties have an important role in enabling meaningful cooperation between the reviewing agencies.

20. Specific issues necessitating cooperation may arise in cases in which the European Commission and the relevant US agency agree with the merging parties on similar remedies to address common competitive concerns, but conclude that different implementation procedures are warranted. For example, the US agency may conclude that an upfront buyer of the assets to be divested is necessary, but the European Commission may conclude that the parties should be allowed to propose a purchaser after a clearance decision. In that circumstance, the US agency and DG Competition would benefit from close cooperation to seek to achieve a compatible outcome. Depending on the circumstances of the case, an identical purchaser may be desirable or even necessary, and the reviewing agencies intend to cooperate in making their determination in such a situation. It will be in the interests of the merging parties to coordinate their proposal for a purchaser with both reviewing agencies, taking into account the reviewing agencies' respective procedures and timing requirements to allow for meaningful cooperation between the reviewing agencies before either agency makes a decision, so that the risk of inconsistent or conflicting implementation is minimized.

EU MERGER WORKING GROUP BEST PRACTICES ON CO-OPERATION BETWEEN EU NATIONAL COMPETITION AUTHORITIES IN MERGER REVIEW

(8 November 2011)

[4.729]

NOTES

This document is available on the European Commission website at: ec.europa.eu/competition-policy/mergers/national-competition-authorities/eu-merger-working-group_en.

1 INTRODUCTION

[4.730]

1.1 The national competition authorities of the EU who have responsibility for merger review ("NCAs") operate in compliance with different national legal systems. They believe, however, that it is desirable to cooperate in the review of some mergers which meet the requirements for notification or investigation in more than one Member State ("multi-jurisdictional mergers"), and have therefore decided jointly to publish an agreed set of Best Practices on Co-operation in Merger Review.

1.2 This document, which has been drawn up by the EU Merger Working Group,[1] sets out the Best Practices which the NCAs, to the extent consistent with their respective laws and enforcement priorities, aim to follow when they review the same merger transaction. It also sets out the steps that merging parties and third parties are encouraged to take in order to facilitate cooperation between NCAs. Cooperation extending beyond the existing ECA Notice system[2] is limited to NCAs who are reviewing the same merger transaction ("the NCAs concerned"). It is not intended that cooperation should provide a forum whereby NCAs not concerned will be involved in the review of a specific case.[3]

1.3 This document is intended to provide a non-binding reference for cooperation between NCAs. NCAs reserve their full discretion in the implementation of these Best Practices and nothing in this document is intended to create new rights or obligations which may fetter that discretion.

NOTES

[1] The EU Merger Working Group ("the Working Group") was established in Brussels in January 2010. It consists of representatives of the European Commission and the national competition authorities ("NCAs") of the European Union ("EU") together with observers from the NCAs of the European Economic Area ("EEA"). The objective of the Working Group is to foster increased convergence and cooperation between the EU merger jurisdictions in order to ensure effective administration and enforcement of merger control laws.

[2] The European Competition Authorities ("ECA") Notice system is an information system among the NCAs of the EU and EEA EFTA States ("ECAs"). An ECA Notice is a notice which is distributed to all other ECAs by the first NCA to be notified of a multi-jurisdictional merger. It sets out the names of the merging parties, the sector/industry concerned and/or products concerned, the date of the notification, the name of the case handler, and the other member states concerned. See *ECA procedures guide on the exchange of information between members on multi-jurisdictional mergers* (2001); Available for example on ec.europa.eu/competition/ecn/eca_information_exchange_procedures_en.pdf.

[3] Some cooperation may, however, be necessary in order to determine the NCAs concerned. NCAs may also wish to consult non-involved NCAs about past experiences with similar mergers both as regards the substantive assessment and remedies, and these Best Practices do not preclude such discussions. For example, it may be helpful to exchange non-confidential information when assessing the effectiveness of a remedy, eg, if the remedy concerns facilities or assets located in another Member State that is not reviewing the merger.

2 OBJECTIVES OF COOPERATION

[4.731]

2.1 Cooperation is beneficial for the NCAs concerned, for the merging parties themselves and for third parties. The Best Practices are intended to provide clarity on how cooperation among NCAs will operate in multi-jurisdictional merger cases. Where the merging parties provide full and consistent information to NCAs concerned, cooperation can reduce burdens on merging parties and third parties by facilitating, where possible, the alignment of timing and the overall efficiency, transparency, effectiveness and timeliness of the merger review processes.

2.2 In cases where serious concerns or difficult analytical issues arise, cooperation can be invaluable in helping to reach informed and consistent or at least non-conflicting outcomes. In such cases, cooperation will ensure that NCAs are in a better position to exchange views on, for example, possible conceptual frameworks for the assessment of the transaction and theories of competitive harm, types of empirical evidence and so on.

2.3 Cooperation is also beneficial both for the NCAs concerned and for the merging parties in relation to any remedial action which may be necessary. Remedies in a merger that is reviewable in more than one jurisdiction may differ across jurisdictions depending on the competition concern identified in each one; indeed, remedies may not be necessary in every jurisdiction. Nevertheless, where the merger affects a market or markets in more than one jurisdiction, a remedy accepted in one jurisdiction may have an impact in another jurisdiction (see section 3.2(iii)). Cooperation can therefore contribute to avoiding inconsistent remedies and obtaining those that are more coherent.

2.4 These Best Practices are intended to promote the achievement of all these ends.

3 SCOPE OF APPLICATION OF BEST PRACTICES

[4.732]

3.1 These Best Practices address cooperation in multi-jurisdictional merger cases. While it is always useful for NCAs to provide basic case information[4] to each other in merger cases which are notifiable in more than one Member State, further cooperation will not be necessary, or even efficient, in the case of every multi-jurisdictional merger. This is particularly the case where it is clear during the early stages of an investigation that the merger does not raise any significant competition or procedural issues in any Member State or that it does so only in one Member State, or where such issues are not decisive for the outcome of any of the different merger reviews. Close cooperation is not an end in itself: its benefits depend on the specific circumstances of each case.

3.2 Where multi-jurisdictional mergers raise similar or comparable issues in relation to jurisdictional or substantive questions, the NCAs concerned will decide on a case-by-case basis whether cooperation may be necessary or appropriate.[5] For example:

(i) Cooperation may assist the NCAs in forming a view as to whether a transaction qualifies for notification or investigation under merger control laws in their respective jurisdictions. It is noted that although jurisdictional rules and practices may differ across jurisdictions, cooperation may assist the NCAs in reaching an informed view.

(ii) Cooperation may assist the NCAs in relation to mergers which may have an impact on competition in more than one Member State, when markets affected by the transaction cover more than one Member State or when a merger affects national or sub-national markets in more than one Member State, if such national or sub-national markets are the same or similar from the product standpoint.

(iii) Cooperation may also be of value in relation to mergers where remedies need to be designed or examined in more than one Member State, such as in situations where the same remedy is designed to address competition issues in different Member States or where one remedy affects the effectiveness of a different remedy in another Member State.

3.3 These Best Practices are without prejudice to the existing guidance on the system of reattribution of cases between the Member States and the Commission (see the Commission's referral notice and ECA's Principles on the application of Art. 4(5) and 22 of Regulation 139/2004).[6] Nevertheless, the enhanced cooperation recommended in these Best Practices may also facilitate the smooth functioning of the reattribution mechanisms set out in Regulation (EC) 139/2004. In particular, where NCAs are contemplating an Article 22 referral request, contacts between them can facilitate the referral, and, if done before notification, can also assist merging parties in forming a view whether it is appropriate for them to speed up the referral process by themselves making an Art. 4(5) referral request (see further the description of pre-notification contacts in section 5.5).

NOTES

4 See model ECA notice (cf. Fn 2 above) as agreed in the *ECA procedures guide on the exchange of information between members on multijurisdictional mergers* (2001); available for example on ec.europa.eu/competition/ecn/eca_information_exchange_procedures_en.pdf.

5 Although the NCAs concerned will keep under review throughout the merger control process the need for cooperation, it will sometimes be possible for them to form a view in this regard at an early stage of the process, ie, during pre-notification contacts (where such contacts take place) or following notification.

6 Article 4(5) provides for referral of cases from the Member States to the Commission **prior** to notification with the purpose of providing a "one-stop-shop" review. Article 22 provides for referral from the Member States to the Commission **after** notification where it is considered that the Commission is better positioned to investigate a merger. See also Commission Notice on Case Referral in respect of concentrations (OJ C 56, 05.03.2005, p 2–23). See ECA principles on the application, by National Competition Authorities within the ECA, of Articles 4 (5) and 22 of the Merger Regulation (2005). Available for example on ec.europa.eu/competition/ecn/eca_referral_principles_en.pdf

4 ROLE OF NATIONAL COMPETITION AUTHORITIES

[4.733]

4.1 In all cases that relate to a merger transaction that is reviewable in more than one EU Member State, the NCAs concerned will inform the other NCAs by means of the existing ECA Notice system, which involves the exchange of basic non-confidential case information after a notification in such a multi-jurisdictional merger case has been received.[7]

4.2 To facilitate cooperation, the NCAs concerned will aim to update the information contained in the ECA notice by informing the other NCAs about any decision to commence second phase proceedings/in-depth investigations, and any final decision, including a decision with remedies.

4.3 In cases where closer cooperation is necessary or appropriate (see paragraph 3.2 above), the NCAs, having due regard to confidentiality issues (see section 6 below), will aim to cooperate in particular in the following ways:

(i) The NCAs concerned will liaise with one another and keep one another appraised of their progress at key stages of their respective investigations. The key stages will vary depending on the procedural framework of each NCA concerned. The NCAs concerned will keep each other informed of the outcome of the first phase investigation, including, where relevant, the intention to open an in-depth investigation, and the outcome of the in-depth investigation. The NCAs concerned will also keep each other appraised of the launch and progress of any remedies discussions, if not conducted jointly.

(ii) Where it is helpful to do so, the NCAs concerned may discuss their respective jurisdictional and/or substantive analyses. Where necessary, having regard to the possible effects of the transaction on the national territories of the NCAs concerned, such discussions may relate to issues such as market definition, assessment of competitive effects, efficiencies, theories of competitive harm, and the empirical evidence needed to test those theories. NCAs concerned will also, where it is helpful to do so, exchange views on necessary remedial measures or submitted remedies.

NOTES

7 See model ECA notice as agreed in the *ECA procedures guide on the exchange of information between members on multijurisdictional mergers* (2001); Available for example on ec.europa.eu/competition/ecn/eca_information_exchange_procedures_en.pdf.

5 ROLE OF MERGING PARTIES

[4.734]

5.1 Effective cooperation between NCAs requires the active assistance of the merging parties at all stages of the review process, both as regards the jurisdictional and/or substantive review and, where required, the assessment of remedies.

5.2 Parties to merger investigations play an important role with regard to cooperation between the NCAs concerned. They can contribute significantly to the alignment of the review proceedings in different Member States, taking into account, among other things, procedural requirements and review periods. Such alignment will be of benefit both to merging parties and to NCAs.

5.3 Therefore, where a transaction is expected to fulfil the requirements for notification or investigation in more than one jurisdiction, the merging parties are encouraged, unless it is clear and obvious from the outset that paragraph 3.2 above does not apply, to contact each of the NCAs concerned as soon as practicable and provide them with the following basic information:

(i) The name of each jurisdiction in which they intend to make a filing;
(ii) The date of the proposed filing in each jurisdiction;
(iii) The names and activities of the merging parties;
(iv) The geographic areas in which they carry on business;[8]
(v) The sector or sectors involved (short description and/or NACE code).

5.4 It is important to note that the provision of this information by the parties will not of itself be a trigger for cooperation among the NCAs concerned. That will depend rather upon whether the case is one where cooperation is necessary or appropriate, as set out in paragraph 3.2 of these Best Practices. However, it will assist the NCAs concerned to decide at an early stage whether there might be a need for cooperation in the particular case.

5.5 Depending on the circumstances of the case it may be possible to provide much of this information at the pre-notification stage. For this purpose, and where it is permitted by law, it may be helpful for merging parties and the NCAs concerned to organize pre-notification contacts as early as possible. Such contacts can assist the parties and the NCAs concerned to align as far as possible the timing of parallel proceedings and can, ultimately, contribute to the reduction of the overall burden that falls on merging parties in the course of a multijurisdictional merger. It may at times, where circumstances permit, be useful for the merging parties and the NCAs concerned to engage in joint pre-notification contacts.

5.6 Merging parties have a crucial role in helping NCAs to ensure that remedies in different Member States do not lead to inconsistent or untenable results. As already stated above, remedies in a merger that is reviewable in more than one Member State may differ across Member States depending on the competition concern identified in each one; indeed, remedies may not be necessary in every Member State. Nevertheless, a remedy accepted in one Member State may have an impact on the effectiveness of remedies targeted at competition problems in another Member State. It is therefore clearly in the interest of the merging parties to coordinate the timing and substance of remedy proposals to the NCAs concerned, so as to ensure coherent remedies and to avoid inconsistent remedies. In certain cases, where circumstances permit, it might be appropriate for merging parties and the reviewing NCAs to engage in joint discussions on proposed remedies.

NOTES

8 The phrase "carry on business" does not include a situation where an undertaking is merely registered in a particular place.

6 CONFIDENTIAL INFORMATION

[4.735]

6.1 It will often be helpful for the NCAs concerned to be able to exchange and discuss confidential information when reviewing the same merger. Therefore, while a certain degree of cooperation is feasible through the exchange of non-confidential information, waivers of confidentiality executed by merging parties can enable more effective communication between the NCAs concerned regarding evidence that is relevant to the investigation.

6.2 For that reason, the merging parties are encouraged to be proactive and to provide waivers of confidentiality to all NCAs concerned, including, where appropriate, at the pre-notification phase. The merging parties are encouraged to use the ICN model waiver provided in the Annex to these Best Practices.

6.3 For the same reasons, where appropriate, third parties are also encouraged to provide waivers of confidentiality to all NCAs concerned. Third parties are also encouraged to use the ICN model waiver provided in the Annex to these Best Practices.

6.4 NCAs are fully aware that it lies within the discretion of the merging or third parties whether to provide a waiver. The scope of the waiver to be provided may be adapted to the specific circumstances of the case, but is essential that the waiver should fulfil the purpose of allowing for an effective information exchange between the NCAs concerned.

6.5 Where a waiver has been provided the NCAs concerned will share the information covered by the waiver without further notice to the parties. NCAs will discuss with each other, prior to any exchange of confidential information as provided for in Sections 4 and 5, how it may best be protected. Confidential information and business secrets are protected under national law in all Member States.

6.6 Confidential information exchanged on the basis of a waiver will not be used for any purpose other than the review of the relevant merger, unless the national law provides otherwise (see paragraph 6.5).

ANNEX

[4.736]
[CONTACT NAME AT AGENCY A]

[ADDRESS]

Re: [CASE REFERENCE]

Dear :

On behalf of COMPANY A, I confirm that COMPANY A, subject to the conditions and limitations set forth herein, agrees to waive the confidentiality restrictions under [RELEVANT STATUTORY OR REGULATORY AUTHORITY] and other applicable laws and rules (collectively the "Confidentiality Obligations") that prevent AGENCY X from disclosing to FOREIGN AGENCY Y confidential information obtained from COMPANY A in connection with its proposed transaction with COMPANY B. Specifically, COMPANY A agrees that AGENCY X staff may share with FOREIGN AGENCY Y [any of COMPANY A's documents, statements, data and information, as well as AGENCY A's own internal analyses that contain or refer to COMPANY A's materials that would otherwise be foreclosed by the confidentiality Obligations].[1]

This waiver is granted only with respect to disclosures to FOREIGN AGENCY Y and only on the condition that FOREIGN AGENCY Y will treat as confidential information it obtains from AGENCY X in accordance with the terms of the attached letter from [CONTACT NAME] of FOREIGN AGENCY Y.[2] This agreement does not constitute a waiver by COMPANY A of its rights under the Confidentiality Obligations with respect to the protection afforded to COMPANY A against the direct or indirect disclosures of information to any third-party other than FOREIGN AGENCY Y.

COMPANY A submits this waiver under the condition and understanding that, with respect to information that AGENCY X obtains from COMPANY A and provides to the FOREIGN AGENCY Y pursuant to this waiver, AGENCY X should continue to protect the confidentiality of such information with respect to other outside parties in accordance with the Confidentiality Obligations.

A copy of this letter is being sent to [CONTACT PERSON AT FOREIGN AGENCY Y].

Sincerely,

[ATTORNEY FOR COMPANY A]

cc: [CONTACT FOR FOREIGN AGENCY Y]

NOTES

1 NOTE: This model language is intended for those situations where a waiver with respect to any and all documents and information provided to Agency X is contemplated. There may be instances where such a broad waiver is not desired. In those cases, the parties may opt for a waiver limited in scope, such as to allow the agencies to discuss potential remedies that each is considering and the reasons for such remedies, or to discuss specific limited issues such as product market definition or barriers to entry. Parties and agency staff should consider the scope of the waiver that is desired to assist them in their investigation so as to not unnecessarily burden parties or other competition agencies.

2 NOTE: "Foreign Agency Y" should provide a letter describing the confidentiality protections provided by that country. (In some cases, the parties and Agency X staff may be satisfied if that letter is directed to that contact person by representatives of the parties, with a written confirmation that Foreign Agency Y agrees to the terms of that letter.) Attached to this model form at Appendix [D] are sample confidentiality letters.

PART 5
STATE AID

A. GENERAL

COMMISSION NOTICE

(2002/C119/12)

on the determination of the applicable rules for the assessment of unlawful State aid

(notified under document number C(2002) 458)

(Text with EEA relevance)

[5.1]

NOTES

Date of publication in OJ: OJ C119, 22.5.2002, p 22.

Note: with effect from 1 December 2009, the Treaty establishing the European Community (the "EC Treaty") was replaced by the Treaty on the Functioning of the European Union. References in this document to provisions of the EC Treaty should be construed accordingly.

A number of instruments approved by the Commission over the years contain a provision to the effect that unlawful State aid, ie, aid put into effect in contravention of Article 88(3) of the EC Treaty, shall be assessed in accordance with the texts in force at the time when the aid was granted. This is for example the case for the Community guidelines on State aid for environmental protection[1] and the multisectoral framework on regional aid for large investment projects.[2]

For the purpose of transparency and legal certainty, the Commission informs Member States and third parties that it has decided to apply the same rule in respect of all instruments indicating how the Commission will exercise its discretion in order to assess the compatibility of State aid with the common market (frameworks, guidelines, communications, notices). Therefore, the Commission shall always assess the compatibility of unlawful State aid with the common market in accordance with the substantive criteria set out in any instrument in force at the time when the aid was granted.

The present notice is without prejudice to the more specific rules contained in the Community guidelines on State aid for rescuing and restructuring firms in difficulty.[3]

The present notice is without prejudice to the interpretation of Council and Commission regulations in the field of State aid.

NOTES

[1] OJ C37, 3.2.2001, p 3.

[2] OJ C70, 19.3.2002, p 8.

[3] OJ C288, 9.10.1999, p 2.

COMMUNICATION FROM THE COMMISSION

(2003/C297/03)

No C(2003) 4582 of 1 December 2003

on professional secrecy in State aid decisions

[5.2]

NOTES

Date of publication in OJ: OJ C297, 9.12.2003, p 6.

Note: with effect from 1 December 2009, the Treaty establishing the European Community (the "EC Treaty") was replaced by the Treaty on the Functioning of the European Union. References in this document to provisions of the EC Treaty should be construed accordingly.

1. INTRODUCTION

[5.3]

(1) This Communication sets out how the Commission intends to deal with requests by Member States, as addressees of State aid decisions, to consider parts of such decisions as covered by the obligation of professional secrecy and thus not to be disclosed when the decision is published.

(2) This involves two aspects, namely:

(a) the identification of the information which might be covered by the obligation of professional secrecy; and

(b) the procedure to be followed for dealing with such requests.

2. LEGAL FRAMEWORK

[5.4]

(3) Article 287 of the Treaty states that: 'The members of the institutions of the Community, the members of committees, and the officials and other servants of the Community shall be required, even after their duties have ceased, not to disclose information of the kind covered by the obligation of professional secrecy, in particular information about undertakings, their business relations or their cost components'.

(4) This is also reflected in Articles 24 and 25 of Council Regulation (EC) No 659/1999 of 22 March 1999 laying down detailed rules for the application of Article 93 of the EC Treaty.[1]

(5) Article 253 of the Treaty states: 'Regulations, directives and decisions adopted jointly by the European Parliament and the Council, and such acts adopted by the Council or the Commission, shall state the reasons on which they are based and shall refer to any proposals or opinions which were required to be obtained pursuant to this Treaty'.

(6) Article 6(1), first sentence of Regulation (EC) No 659/1999 further stipulates with regard to decisions to initiate the formal investigation procedures: 'The decision to initiate the formal investigation procedure shall summarise the relevant issues of fact and law, shall include a preliminary assessment of the Commission as to the aid character of the proposed measure and shall set out the doubts as to its compatibility with the common market [. . .]'.

NOTES

[1] OJ L83, 27.3.1999, p 1.

3. IDENTIFICATION OF INFORMATION WHICH CAN BE COVERED BY PROFESSIONAL SECRECY

[5.5]

(7) The Court of Justice has established that although Article 287 of the Treaty primarily refers to information gathered from undertakings, the expression 'in particular' shows that the principle in question is a general one which applies also to other confidential information.[2]

(8) It follows that professional secrecy covers both business secrets and other confidential information.

(9) There is no reason why the notions of business secret and other confidential information should be interpreted differently from the meaning given to these terms in the context of antitrust and merger procedures. The fact that in antitrust and merger procedures the addressees of the Commission decision are undertakings, while in State aid procedures the addressees are Member States, does not constitute an obstacle to a uniform approach as to the identification of what can constitute business secrets or other confidential information.

3.1. BUSINESS SECRETS

(10) Business secrets can only concern information relating to a business which has actual or potential economic value, the disclosure or use of which could result in economic benefits for other companies. Typical examples are methods of assessing manufacturing and distribution costs, production secrets (that is to say, a secret, commercially valuable plan, formula, process or device that is used for the making, preparing, compounding, or processing of trade commodities and that can be said to be the end product of either innovation or substantial effort) and processes, supply sources, quantities produced and sold, market shares, customer and distributor lists, marketing plans, cost price structure, sales policy, and information on the internal organisation of the undertaking.

(11) It would appear that in principle business secrets can only relate to the beneficiary of the aid (or other third party) and can only concern information submitted by the Member State (or third party). Hence, statements from the Commission itself (for example, expressing doubts about feasibility of a restructuring plan) cannot be covered by the obligation of professional secrecy.

(12) The simple fact that disclosure of information might cause harm to the company is not of itself sufficient grounds to consider that such information should be considered as business secret. For example, a Commission decision to initiate the formal investigation procedure in the case of a restructuring aid may cast doubt on certain aspects of the restructuring plan in the light of information the Commission has received. Such a decision could (further) affect the credit-position of that company. However, that would not necessarily lead to the conclusion that the information on which that decision was based must be considered as business secrets.

(13) In general, the Commission will apply the following non-exhaustive list of criteria to determine whether information can be deemed to constitute business secrets:

(a) the extent to which the information is known outside the company;
(b) the extent to which measures have been taken to protect the information within the company, for example, through non-compete clauses or non-disclosure agreements imposed on employees or agents, etc;
(c) the value of the information for the company and its competitors;
(d) the effort or investment which the undertaking had to undertake to acquire the information;
(e) the effort which others would need to undertake to acquire or copy the information;
(f) the degree of protection offered to such information under the legislation of the Member State concerned.

(14) In principle, the Commission considers that the following information would not normally be covered by the obligation of professional secrecy:

(a) information which is publicly available, including information available only upon payment through specialised information services or information which is common knowledge among specialists in the field (for example common knowledge among engineers or medical doctors). Likewise, turnover is not normally considered as a business secret, as it is a figure published in the annual accounts or otherwise known to the market. Reasons must be given for requests for confidentiality concerning turnover figures which are not in the public domain and the requests must be evaluated on a case-by-case basis. The fact that information is not publicly available does not necessarily mean that the information can be regarded as a business secret;

(b) historical information, in particular information at least five years old;
(c) statistical or aggregate information;
(d) names of aid recipients, sector of activity, purpose and amount of the aid, etc.

(15) Detailed reasons must be given for any request to derogate from these principles in exceptional cases.

3.2. OTHER CONFIDENTIAL INFORMATION

(16) In antitrust and merger cases, confidential information includes certain types of information communicated to the Commission on condition that confidentiality is observed (for example a market study commissioned by an undertaking which is party to the procedure and forming part of its property). It seems that a similar approach could be retained for State aid decisions.

(17) In the field of State aid, there may, however, be some forms of confidential information, which would not necessarily be present in antitrust and merger procedures, referring specifically to secrets of the State or other confidential information relating to its organisational activity. Generally, in view of the Commission's obligation to state the reasons for its decisions and the transparency requirement, such information can only in very exceptional circumstances be covered by the obligation of professional secrecy. For example, information regarding the organisation and costs of public services will not normally be considered 'other confidential information' (although it may constitute a business secret, if the criteria laid down in section 3.1 are met).

NOTES

[2] Case 145/83 *Adams v Commission* [1985] ECR 3539, paragraph 34, and Case T-353/94 *Postbank v Commission* [1996] ECR II-921, paragraph 86.

4. APPLICABLE PROCEDURE

4.1. GENERAL PRINCIPLES

[5.6]

(18) The Commission's main task is to reconcile two opposing obligations, namely the requirement to state the reasons for its decisions under Article 253 of the Treaty and therefore ensure that its decisions contain all the essential elements on which they are based, and that of safeguarding the obligation of professional secrecy.

(19) Besides the basic obligation to state the reasons for its decisions, the Commission has to take into account the need for effective application of the State aid rules (*inter alia*, by giving Member States, beneficiaries and interested parties the possibility to comment on or challenge its decisions) and for transparency of its policy. There is therefore an overriding interest in making public the full substance of its decisions. As a general principle, requests for confidential treatment can only be granted where strictly necessary to protect business secrets or other confidential information meriting similar protection.

(20) Business secrets and other confidential information do not enjoy an absolute protection: this means for example that they could be divulged when they are essential for the Commission's statement of the reasons for its decisions. This means that information necessary for the identification of an aid measure and its beneficiary cannot normally be covered by the obligation of professional secrecy. Similarly, information necessary to demonstrate that the conditions of Article 87(1) of the Treaty are met, cannot normally be covered by the obligation of professional secrecy. However, the Commission will have to consider carefully whether the need for publication is more important, given the specific circumstances of a case, than the prejudice that might be generated for that Member State or undertaking involved.

(21) The public version of a Commission decision can only feature deletions from the adopted version for reasons of professional secrecy. Paragraphs cannot be moved, and no sentence can be added or altered. Where the Commission considers that certain information cannot be disclosed, a footnote may be added, paraphrasing the non-disclosed information or indicating a range of magnitude or size, if useful to assure the comprehensibility and coherence of the decision.

(22) Requests not to disclose the full text of a decision or substantial parts of it which would undermine the understanding of the Commission's statement of reasons cannot be accepted.

(23) If there is a complainant involved, the Commission will take into account the complainant's interest in ascertaining the reasons why the Commission adopted a certain decision, without the need to have recourse to Court proceedings.[3] Hence, requests by Member States for parts of the decision which address concerns of complainants to be covered by the obligation of professional secrecy will need to be particularly well reasoned and persuasive. On the other hand, the Commission will not normally be inclined to disclose information alleged to be of the kind covered by the obligation of professional secrecy where there is a suspicion that the complaint has been lodged primarily to obtain access to the information.

(24) Member States cannot invoke professional secrecy to refuse to provide information to the Commission which the Commission considers necessary for the examination of aid measures. In this respect, reference is made to the procedure set out in Regulation (EC) No 659/1999 (in particular Articles 2(2), 5, 10 and 16).

4.2. PROCEDURE

(25) The Commission currently notifies its decisions to the Member State concerned without delay and gives the latter the opportunity to indicate, normally within a time period of 15 working days, which information it considers to be covered by the obligation of professional secrecy. This time period may be extended by agreement between the Commission and the Member State concerned.

(26) Where the Member State concerned does not indicate which information it considers to be covered by the obligation of professional secrecy within the period prescribed by the Commission, the decision will normally be disclosed in full.

(27) Where the Member State concerned wishes certain information to be covered by the obligation of professional secrecy, it must indicate the parts it considers to be covered and provide a justification in respect of each part for which non-disclosure is requested.

(28) The Commission will then examine the request from the Member State without delay. If the Commission does not accept that certain parts of the decision are covered by the obligation of professional secrecy, it will state the reasons why in its view those parts cannot be left out of the public version of the decision. In the absence of an acceptable justification by the Member State for its request (ie, reasoning which is not manifestly irrelevant or manifestly wrong), the Commission need not further specify the reasons why those parts cannot be left out of the public version of the decision other than by referring to the absence of justification.

(29) If the Commission decides to accept that certain parts are covered by the obligation of professional secrecy without agreeing in full with the Member State's request, it will notify its decision with a new draft to the Member State indicating the parts which have been omitted. If the Commission accepts that the parts indicated by the Member State are covered by the obligation of professional secrecy, the text of the decision will be published pursuant to Article 26 of Regulation (EC) No 659/1999, with the omission of the parts covered by the obligation of professional secrecy. Such omissions will be indicated in the text.[4]

(30) The Member State will have 15 working days following receipt of the Commission's decision stating the reasons for its refusal to accept the non-disclosure of certain parts, to react and provide additional elements to justify its request.

(31) If the Member State concerned does not react further within the period prescribed by the Commission, the Commission will normally publish the decision as indicated in its reply to the original request made by the Member State.

(32) If the Member State concerned does submit any additional elements within the prescribed period, those elements will be examined by the Commission without delay. If the Commission accepts that the parts indicated by the Member State are covered by the obligation of professional secrecy, the text of the decision will be published as set out in paragraph (29).

(33) In the event that it is not possible to reach agreement, the Commission will proceed with the publication of its decision to initiate the formal investigation procedure forthwith. Such decisions must summarise the relevant issues of fact and law, include a preliminary assessment of the aid character of the proposed measure and set out the doubts as to its compatibility with the common market. Clearly certain essential information must be included in order to enable third parties and the other Member States to comment usefully. The duty of the Commission to provide such essential information will normally prevail over any claim to the protection of business secrets or other confidential information. Furthermore, it is in the interest of the beneficiary as well as interested parties to have access to such a decision as quickly as possible. Permitting any delay in this respect would jeopardise the process of State aid control.

(34) In the event that it is not possible to reach agreement on requests for certain information in decisions not to raise objections and decisions to close the formal investigation procedure to be covered by the obligation of professional secrecy, the Commission will notify its final decision to the Member State together with the text it intends to publish, giving the Member State another 15 working days to react. In the absence of an answer which the Commission considers pertinent, the Commission will normally proceed with the publication of the text.

(35) The Commission is currently reviewing its State aid notification forms. In order to avoid unnecessary correspondence with Member States and delay in the publication of decisions, it intends, in the future, to include in the form a question asking whether the notification contains information which should not be published, and the reasons for non-publication. Only if that question is answered in the affirmative will the Commission enter into correspondence with the Member State in respect of specific cases. Similarly, if additional information is required by the Commission, the Member State will have to indicate at the moment it provides the information requested whether such information should not be published, and the reasons for non-publication. If the Commission uses the information thus identified by the Member State in its decision, it will communicate the adopted decision to the Member State, stating the reasons why in its view these parts cannot be left out from the public version of the decision as laid down in paragraph (28).

(36) Once the Commission has decided what text it will publish and notified the Member State of its final decision, it is for the Member State to decide whether or not to make use of any judicial procedures available to it, including any interim measures, within the time limits provided for in Article 230 of the EC Treaty.

4.3. THIRD PARTIES

(37) Where third parties other than the Member State concerned (for example, complainants, other Member States or the beneficiary) submit information in the context of State aid procedures, these guidelines will be applied *mutatis mutandis*.

4.4. APPLICATION IN TIME

(38) These guidelines cannot establish binding legal rules and do not purport to do so. They merely set out in advance, in the interests of sound administration, the manner in which the Commission intends to address the issue of confidentiality in State aid procedures. As a rule, if agreement cannot be reached, the Commission's decision to publish may be the subject of specific judicial review proceedings. As these guidelines merely pertain to procedural matters (and to a large extent set out existing practice), they will be applied with immediate effect, including for decisions not to raise objections[5] adopted before the entry into force of Regulation (EC) No 659/1999 to which third parties seek access.

NOTES

[3] Case C-367/95 P *Commission v Sytraval* [ECR] 1998 I-1719, paragraph 64.

[4] Using square brackets [. . .] and indicating in a footnote 'covered by the obligation of professional secrecy'.

5 Decisions to initiate the formal investigation procedure and final decisions adopted before that date were already published in full in the *Official Journal of the European Communities*. Prior to publication, Member States could indicate whether any information was covered by the obligation of professional secrecy.

COMMUNICATION FROM THE COMMISSION

(2004/C115/01)

concerning the obsolescence of certain State aid policy documents

(Text with EEA relevance)

[5.7]

NOTES

Date of publication in OJ: OJ C115, 30.4.2004, p 1.

Note: with effect from 1 December 2009, the Treaty establishing the European Community (the "EC Treaty") was replaced by the Treaty on the Functioning of the European Union. References in this document to provisions of the EC Treaty should be construed accordingly.

Over the years, the Commission has adopted a number of texts concerning procedural issues in the field of State aid. Some of these texts have taken the form of Commission Communications to the Member States and have been published in the *Official Journal of the European Union*. Other texts have been published in volume IIA of the Competition Law in the European Communities series, Rules applicable to State aid, situation at 30 June 1998 (ISBN 92-828-4008-5).

Following the adoption by the Commission of Commission Regulation (EC) No 794/2004[1] implementing Council Regulation (EC) No 659/1999 of 22 March 1999 laying down detailed rules for the application of Article 93 of the EC Treaty,[2] a number of these texts have become obsolete. These texts concern the notification obligation, notification procedures, including accelerated notifications, annual reporting, timelimits and recovery of unlawful aid.

Accordingly the Commission wishes to inform Member States and interested parties that from the date of publication of this communication in the *Official Journal of the European Union*, the Commission no longer intends to apply, in relation to any matter, the following documents, irrespective of their legal status:

1. Commission communication on the notification of State aid to the Commission pursuant to Article 93(3) of the EEC Treaty: the failure of Member States to respect their obligations;[3]
2. Commission communication (on the notification obligation);[4]
3. Commission communication on the cumulation of aids for different purposes;[5]
4. Commission letter to Member States SG(89) D/5521 of 27 April 1989 (on the definition of putting an aid into effect);[6]
5. Commission letter to Member States SG(91) D/4577 of 4 March 1991 (Communication to Member States concerning the procedures for the notification of aid plans and procedures applicable when aid is provided in breach of the rules of Article 93(3) of the EEC Treaty);[7]
6. Guidance note on use of the de minimis facility provided for in the SME guidelines (letter of 23 March 1993, IV/D/ 6878 from DG IV to the Member States);[8]
7. Commission letter to Member States of 22 February 1995 (interest rates to be applied when aid granted unlawfully is being recovered);[9]
8. Commission communication to the Member States (on the recovery of aid granted unlawfully);[10]
9. Commission letter to Member States of 22 February 1994 (concerning notifications);[11]
10. Section A of the joint procedure for reporting and notification under the EC Treaty and under the WTO Agreement as identified in Commission letter to Member States of 2 August 1995;[12]
11. Commission letter to Member States SG(81) 12740 of 2 October 1981 (time limits for decisions);[13]
12. Commission letter to Member States of 30 April 1987 (Procedure pursuant to Article 93(2) of the EEC Treaty – time-limits);[14]
13. Commission communication to the Member States on the accelerated clearance of aid schemes for SMEs and of amendments of existing schemes;[15]
14. Accelerated procedure for processing notifications of employment aid Standard notification form;[16]
15. Commission letter to Member States of 27 June 1989 (Procedure pursuant to Article 93(2) of the EEC Treaty – Notice to Member States and other parties concerned to submit their comments);[17]
16. Commission Letter to Member States of 11 October 1990 (Notice to Member States and other parties about aid cases not objected to by the Commission);[18]
17. 'Guide to procedures in State aid cases'.[19]

However, the Commission also wishes to inform Member States and interested parties that in so far as the provisions of Chapter V of Regulation (EC) 794/2004 only apply to decisions ordering the recovery of unlawful aid notified to Member States after the date of entry into force of the Regulation, the Commission communication of 8 May 2003 on the interest rates to be applied when aid granted unlawfully is being recovered[20] remains in effect as regards the execution by Member States of recovery orders notified before that date.

NOTES

1 OJ L140, 30.4.2004.

2 OJ L83, 27.3.1999, p 1.

3 OJ C252, 30.9.1980, p 2.

[4] OJ C318, 24.11.1983, p 3.
[5] OJ C3, 05.01.1985, p 2.
[6] Competition Law in the European Communities, Volume IIA, Rules applicable to State aid, Brussels-Luxembourg 1999, ISBN 92-828- 4008-5, English Version p 58.
[7] Competition Law in the European Communities, Volume IIA, Rules applicable to State aid, Brussels-Luxembourg 1999, ISBN 92-828- 4008-5, English Version p 59.
[8] Competition Law in the European Communities, Volume IIA, Rules applicable to State aid, Brussels-Luxembourg 1999, ISBN 92-828- 4008-5, English Version p 64.
[9] Competition Law in the European Communities, Volume IIA, Rules applicable to State aid, Brussels-Luxembourg 1999, ISBN 92-828- 4008-5, English Version p 68.
[10] OJ C156, 22.6.1995, p 5.
[11] Competition Law in the European Communities, Volume IIA, Rules applicable to State aid, Brussels-Luxembourg 1999, ISBN 92-828- 4008-5, English Version p 70.
[12] Competition Law in the European Communities, Volume IIA, Rules applicable to State aid, Brussels-Luxembourg 1999, ISBN 92-828- 4008-5, English Version p 72. Section B of this letter, which covers reporting to the WTO under Article 25 of the Agreement on Subsidies and Countervailing Measures, remains applicable.
[13] Competition Law in the European Communities, Volume IIA, Rules applicable to State aid, Brussels-Luxembourg 1999, ISBN 92-828- 4008-5, English Version p 89.
[14] Competition Law in the European Communities, Volume IIA, Rules applicable to State aid, Brussels-Luxembourg 1999, ISBN 92-828- 4008-5, English Version p 90.
[15] OJ C213, 19.08.1992, p 10.
[16] OJ C218, 27.07.1996, p 4.
[17] Competition Law in the European Communities, Volume IIA, Rules applicable to State aid, Brussels-Luxembourg 1999, ISBN 92-828- 4008-5, English Version p 99.
[18] Competition Law in the European Communities, Volume IIA, Rules applicable to State aid, Brussels-Luxembourg 1999, ISBN 92-828- 4008-5, English Version p 100.
[19] Competition Law in the European Communities, Volume IIA, Rules applicable to State aid, Brussels-Luxembourg 1999, ISBN 92-828- 4008-5, English Version p 23.
[20] OJ C110, 8.5.2003, p 21.

COMMISSION REGULATION

(794/2004/EC)

[implementing Council Regulation (EU) 2015/1589 laying down detailed rules for the application of Article 108 of the Treaty on the Functioning of the European Union] (Implementing Regulation)

of 21 April 2004

[5.8]

NOTES

Date of publication in OJ: OJ L140, 30.4.2004, p 1.

Repeal of this Regulation in relation to the UK: this Regulation is repealed, in relation to the UK, by the State Aid (Revocations and Amendments) (EU Exit) Regulations 2020, SI 2020/1470, reg 5, as from IP completion day (as defined in the European Union (Withdrawal Agreement) Act 2020, s 39) (for transitional provisions and savings in relation to claims before a court or tribunal relating to State aid infringement before IP completion day, see Sch 3 to those Regulations at **[7.89]**).

The title of this Regulation was substituted by Commission Regulation 2015/2282/EU, Art 1(1).

The text of this Regulation incorporates the corrigenda published in OJ L25, 28.1.2005, p 74 and OJ L131, 25.5.2005, p 45. Note that Annex I (Standard form for notification of state aids pursuant to Article 88(3) EC Treaty and for the provision of information on unlawful aid), Annex II (Simplified notification form), Annex IIIA (Standardised reporting format for existing state aid (all sectors except agriculture)), Annex IIIB (Standardised reporting format for existing state aid (agriculture)), Annex IIIC (Information to be Contained in the Annual Report to be Provided to the Commission), and Annex IV (Form for the submission of complaints concerning alleged unlawful state aid or misuse of state aid) of this Regulation have been omitted from this edition due to space considerations. The consolidated version of this Regulation (including the Annexes) is available on the Europa website at: eur-lex.europa.eu/legal-content/EN/TXT/?uri=CELEX:02004R0794-20161222.

THE COMMISSION OF THE EUROPEAN COMMUNITIES,

Having regard to the Treaty establishing the European Community,

Having regard to Council Regulation (EC) No 659/1999 of 22 March 1999 laying down detailed rules for the application of Article 93 of the EC Treaty,[1] and in particular Article 27 thereof,

After consulting the Advisory Committee on State Aid,

Whereas:

(1) In order to facilitate the preparation of State aid notifications by Member States, and their assessment by the Commission, it is desirable to establish a compulsory notification form. That form should be as comprehensive as possible.

(2) The standard notification form as well as the summary information sheet and the supplementary information sheets should cover all existing guidelines and frameworks in the state aid field. They should be subject to modification or replacement in accordance with the further development of those texts.

(3) Provision should be made for a simplified system of notification for certain alterations to existing aid. Such

simplified arrangements should only be accepted if the Commission has been regularly informed on the implementation of the existing aid concerned.

(4) In the interests of legal certainty it is appropriate to make it clear that small increases of up to 20% of the original budget of an aid scheme, in particular to take account of the effects of inflation, should not need to be notified to the Commission as they are unlikely to affect the Commission's original assessment of the compatibility of the scheme, provided that the other conditions of the aid scheme remain unchanged.

(5) Article 21 of Regulation (EC) No 659/1999 requires Member States to submit annual reports to the Commission on all existing aid schemes or individual aid granted outside an approved aid scheme in respect of which no specific reporting obligations have been imposed in a conditional decision.

(6) For the Commission to be able to discharge its responsibilities for the monitoring of aid, it needs to receive accurate information from Member States about the types and amounts of aid being granted by them under existing aid schemes. It is possible to simplify and improve the arrangements for the reporting of State aid to the Commission which are currently described in the joint procedure for reporting and notification under the EC Treaty and under the World Trade Organisation (WTO) Agreement set out in the Commission's letter to Member States of 2 August 1995. The part of that joint procedure relating to Member States reporting obligations for subsidy notifications under Article 25 of the WTO Agreement on Subsidies and Countervailing measures and under Article XVI of GATT 1994, adopted on 21 July 1995 is not covered by this Regulation.

(7) The information required in the annual reports is intended to enable the Commission to monitor overall aid levels and to form a general view of the effects of different types of aid on competition. To this end, the Commission may also request Member States to provide, on an ad hoc basis, additional data for selected topics. The choice of subject matter should be discussed in advance with Member States.

(8) The annual reporting exercise does not cover the information, which may be necessary in order to verify that particular aid measures respect Community law. The Commission should therefore retain the right to seek undertakings from Member States, or to attach to decisions conditions requiring the provision of additional information.

(9) It should be specified that time-limits for the purposes of Regulation (EC) No 659/1999 should be calculated in accordance with Regulation (EEC, Euratom) No 1182/71 of the Council of 3 June 1971 determining the rules applicable to periods, dates and time limits,[2] *as supplemented by the specific rules set out in this Regulation. In particular, it is necessary to identify the events, which determine the starting point for time-limits applicable in State aid procedures. The rules set out in this Regulation should apply to pre-existing time-limits which will continue to run after the entry into force of this Regulation.*

(10) The purpose of recovery is to re-establish the situation existing before aid was unlawfully granted. To ensure equal treatment, the advantage should be measured objectively from the moment when the aid is available to the beneficiary undertaking, independently of the outcome of any commercial decisions subsequently made by that undertaking.

(11) In accordance with general financial practice it is appropriate to fix the recovery interest rate as an annual percentage rate.

(12) The volume and frequency of transactions between banks results in an interest rate that is consistently measurable and statistically significant, and should therefore form the basis of the recovery interest rate. The inter-bank swap rate should, however, be adjusted in order to reflect general levels of increased commercial risk outside the banking sector. On the basis of the information on inter-bank swap rates the Commission should establish a single recovery interest rate for each Member State. In the interest of legal certainty and equal treatment, it is appropriate to fix the precise method by which the interest rate should be calculated, and to provide for the publication of the recovery interest rate applicable at any given moment, as well as relevant previously applicable rates.

(13) A State aid grant may be deemed to reduce a beneficiary undertaking's medium-term financing requirements. For these purposes, and in line with general financial practice, the medium-term may be defined as five years. The recovery interest rate should therefore correspond to an annual percentage rate fixed for five years.

(14) Given the objective of restoring the situation existing before the aid was unlawfully granted, and in accordance with general financial practice, the recovery interest rate to be fixed by the Commission should be annually compounded. For the same reasons, the recovery interest rate applicable in the first year of the recovery period should be applied for the first five years of the recovery period, and the recovery interest rate applicable in the sixth year of the recovery period for the following five years.

(15) This Regulation should apply to recovery decisions notified after the date of entry into force of this Regulation,

NOTES

Repeal of this Regulation in relation to the UK: this Regulation is repealed in relation to the UK (as from IP completion day); see the introductory notes to this Regulation *ante*.

[1] OJ L83, 27.3.1999, p 1. Regulation as amended by the 2003 Act of Accession.

[2] OJ L124, 8.6.1971, p 1.

HAS ADOPTED THIS REGULATION—

CHAPTER I SUBJECT MATTER AND SCOPE

[5.9]

Article 1 **Subject matter and scope**

1. This Regulation sets out detailed provisions concerning the form, content and other details of notifications and annual reports referred to in Regulation (EC) No 659/1999. It also sets out provisions for the calculation of time limits in all procedures concerning State aid and of the interest rate for the recovery of unlawful aid.

2. This Regulation shall apply to aid in all sectors.

NOTES

Repeal of this Regulation in relation to the UK: this Regulation is repealed in relation to the UK (as from IP completion day); see the introductory notes to this Regulation *ante*.

CHAPTER II NOTIFICATIONS

[5.10]

Article 2 Notification forms

Without prejudice to Member States' obligations to notify state aids in the coal sector under Commission Decision 2002/871/CE,[1] *notifications of new aid pursuant to Article 2(1) of Regulation (EC) No 659/1999, other than those referred to in Article 4(2), shall be made on the notification form set out in Part I of Annex I to this Regulation.*

Supplementary information needed for the assessment of the measure in accordance with regulations, guidelines, frameworks and other texts applicable to State aid shall be provided on the supplementary information sheets set out in Part III of Annex I.

Whenever the relevant guidelines or frameworks are modified or replaced, the Commission shall adapt the corresponding forms and information sheets.

NOTES

Repeal of this Regulation in relation to the UK: this Regulation is repealed in relation to the UK (as from IP completion day), as noted in the introductory notes to this Regulation *ante*.

[1] OJ L300, 5.11.2002, p 42.

[5.11]

[Article 3 Transmission of notifications

1. The notification shall be transmitted to the Commission by means of the electronic validation carried out by the person designated by the Member State. Such validated notification shall be considered as sent by the Permanent Representative.

2. The Commission shall address its correspondence to the Permanent Representative of the Member State concerned, or to any other address designated by that Member State.

3. As from 1 July 2008, notifications shall be transmitted electronically via the web application State Aid Notification Interactive (SANI).

All correspondence in connection with a notification shall be transmitted electronically via the secured Email system Public Key Infrastructure (PKI).

4. In exceptional circumstances and upon the agreement of the Commission and the Member State concerned, an agreed communication channel other than those referred to in paragraph 3 may be used for submission of a notification or any correspondence in connection with a notification.

In the absence of such an agreement, any notification or correspondence in connection with a notification sent to the Commission by a Member State through a communication channel other than those referred to in paragraph 3 shall not be considered as submitted to the Commission.

5. Where the notification or correspondence in connection with a notification contains confidential information, the Member State concerned shall clearly identify such information and give reasons for its classification as confidential.

6. The Member States shall refer to the State aid identification number allocated to an aid scheme by the Commission in each grant of aid to a final beneficiary.

The first subparagraph shall not apply to aid granted through fiscal measures.]

NOTES

Substituted by Commission Regulation 271/2008/EC, Art 1(1).

Repeal of this Regulation in relation to the UK: this Regulation is repealed in relation to the UK (as from IP completion day); see the introductory notes to this Regulation *ante*.

[5.12]

Article 4 Simplified notification procedure for certain alterations to existing aid

1. For the purposes of Article 1(c) of Regulation (EC) No 659/1999, an alteration to existing aid shall mean any change, other than modifications of a purely formal or administrative nature which cannot affect the evaluation of the compatibility of the aid measure with the common market. However an increase in the original budget of an existing aid scheme by up to 20% shall not be considered an alteration to existing aid.

2. The following alterations to existing aid shall be notified on the simplified notification form set out in Annex II:

(a) increases in the budget of an authorised aid scheme exceeding 20%;

(b) prolongation of an existing authorised aid scheme by up to six years, with or without an increase in the budget;

(c) tightening of the criteria for the application of an authorised aid scheme, a reduction of aid intensity or a reduction of eligible expenses;

The Commission shall use its best endeavours to take a decision on any aid notified on the simplified notification form within a period of one month.

3. The simplified notification procedure shall not be used to notify alterations to aid schemes in respect of which Member States have not submitted annual reports in accordance with Article 5, 6, and 7, unless the annual reports for the years in which the aid has been granted are submitted at the same time as the notification.

NOTES

Repeal of this Regulation in relation to the UK: this Regulation is repealed in relation to the UK (as from IP completion day); see the introductory notes to this Regulation *ante*.

CHAPTER III ANNUAL REPORTS

[5.13]

Article 5 Form and content of annual reports

1. Without prejudice to the second and third subparagraphs of this Article and to any additional specific reporting requirements laid down in a conditional decision adopted pursuant to Article 7(4) of Regulation (EC) No 659/1999, or to the observance of any undertakings provided by the Member State concerned in connection with a decision to approve aid, Member States shall compile the annual reports on existing aid schemes referred to in Article 21(1) of Regulation (EC) No 659/1999 in respect of each whole or part calendar year during which the scheme applies in accordance with the standardised reporting format set out in Annex IIIA.

Annex IIIB sets out the format for annual reports on existing aid schemes relating to the production, processing and marketing of agricultural products listed in Annex I of the Treaty.

Annex IIIC sets out the format for annual reports on existing aid schemes for state aid relating to the production, processing or marketing of fisheries products listed in Annex I of the Treaty.

2. The Commission may ask Member States to provide additional data for selected topics, to be discussed in advance with Member States.

NOTES

Repeal of this Regulation in relation to the UK: this Regulation is repealed in relation to the UK (as from IP completion day); see the introductory notes to this Regulation *ante*.

[5.14]

Article 6 Transmission and publication of annual reports

1. Each Member State shall transmit its annual reports to the Commission in electronic form no later than 30 June of the year following the year to which the report relates.

In justified cases Member States may submit estimates, provided that the actual figures are transmitted at the very latest with the following year's data.

2. Each year the Commission shall publish a State aid synopsis containing a synthesis of the information contained in the annual reports submitted during the previous year.

NOTES

Repeal of this Regulation in relation to the UK: this Regulation is repealed in relation to the UK (as from IP completion day); see the introductory notes to this Regulation *ante*.

[5.15]

Article 7 Status of annual reports

The transmission of annual reports shall not be considered to constitute compliance with the obligation to notify aid measures before they are put into effect pursuant to Article 88(3) of the Treaty, nor shall such transmission in any way prejudice the outcome of an investigation into allegedly unlawful aid in accordance with the procedure laid down in Chapter III of Regulation (EC) No 659/1999.

NOTES

Repeal of this Regulation in relation to the UK: this Regulation is repealed in relation to the UK (as from IP completion day); see the introductory notes to this Regulation *ante*.

CHAPTER IV TIME-LIMITS

[5.16]

Article 8 Calculation of time-limits

[1. Time-limits provided for in Regulation (EC) No 659/1999 and in this Regulation or fixed by the Commission pursuant to Article 108 of the Treaty shall be calculated in accordance with Regulation (EEC, Euratom) No 1182/71, and the specific rules set out in paragraphs 2 to 5b of this Article. In case of conflict, the provisions of this Regulation shall prevail.]

2. Time limits shall be specified in months or in working days.

[3. With regard to time-limits for action by the Commission, the receipt of the notification or subsequent correspondence in accordance with Article 3(1) and Article 3(3) of this Regulation shall be the relevant event for the purpose of Article 3(1) of Regulation (EEC, Euratom) No 1182/71.

4. With regard to time-limits for action by Member States, the receipt of the relevant notification or correspondence from the Commission in accordance with Article 3(2) of this Regulation shall be the relevant event for the purposes of Article 3(1) of Regulation (EEC, Euratom) No 1182/71.]

5. With regard to the time-limit for the submission of comments following initiation of the formal investigation procedure referred to in Art. 6(1) of Regulation (EC) No 659/1999 by third parties and those Member States which are not directly concerned by the procedure, the publication of the notice of initiation in the Official Journal of the European Union shall be the relevant event for the purposes of Article 3(1) of Regulation (EEC, Euratom) No 1182/71.

[5a. With regard to the time-limit for the submission of the information requested from third parties pursuant to Article 6a(6) of Regulation (EC) No 659/1999, the receipt of the request for information shall be the relevant event for the purposes of Article 3(1) of Regulation (EEC, Euratom) No 1182/71.

5b. With regard to the time-limit for the submission of the information requested from third parties pursuant to Article 6a(7) of Regulation (EC) No 659/1999, the notification of the decision shall be the relevant event for the purposes of Article 3(1) of Regulation (EEC, Euratom) No 1182/71.]

6. Any request for the extension of a time-limit shall be duly substantiated, and shall be submitted in writing to the address designated by the party fixing the time-limit at least two working days before expiry.

NOTES

Para 1: substituted by Commission Regulation 372/2014/EU, Art 1(1)(a).

Paras 3, 4: substituted by Commission Regulation 271/2008/EC, Art 1(2).

Paras 5a, 5b: inserted by Commission Regulation 372/2014/EU, Art 1(1)(b).

Repeal of this Regulation in relation to the UK: this Regulation is repealed in relation to the UK (as from IP completion day); see the introductory notes to this Regulation *ante*.

CHAPTER V INTEREST RATE FOR THE RECOVERY OF UNLAWFUL AID

[5.17]

[Article 9 Method for fixing the interest rate

1. Unless otherwise provided for in a specific decision, the interest rate to be used for recovering State aid granted in breach of Article 88(3) of the Treaty shall be an annual percentage rate which is fixed by the Commission in advance of each calendar year.

2. The interest rate shall be calculated by adding 100 basis points to the one-year money market rate. Where those rates are not available, the three-month money market rate will be used, or in the absence thereof, the yield on State bonds will be used.

3. In the absence of reliable money market or yield on stock bonds or equivalent data or in exceptional circumstances the Commission may, in close co-operation with the Member State(s) concerned, fix a recovery rate on the basis of a different method and on the basis of the information available to it.

4. The recovery rate will be revised once a year. The base rate will be calculated on the basis of the one-year money market recorded in September, October and November of the year in question. The rate thus calculated will apply throughout the following year.

5. In addition, to take account of significant and sudden variations, an update will be made each time the average rate, calculated over the three previous months, deviates more than 15% from the rate in force. This new rate will enter into force on the first day of the second month following the months used for the calculation.]

NOTES

Substituted by Commission Regulation 271/2008/EC, Art 1(3).

Repeal of this Regulation in relation to the UK: this Regulation is repealed in relation to the UK (as from IP completion day); see the introductory notes to this Regulation *ante*.

[5.18]

Article 10 Publication

The Commission shall publish current and relevant historical State aid recovery interest rates in the Official Journal of the European Union and for information on the Internet.

NOTES

Repeal of this Regulation in relation to the UK: this Regulation is repealed in relation to the UK (as from IP completion day); see the introductory notes to this Regulation *ante*.

[5.19]

Article 11 Method for applying interest

1. The interest rate to be applied shall be the rate applicable on the date on which unlawful aid was first put at the disposal of the beneficiary.

2. The interest rate shall be applied on a compound basis until the date of the recovery of the aid. The interest accruing in the previous year shall be subject to interest in each subsequent year.

[3. The interest rate referred to in paragraph 1 shall be applied throughout the whole period until the date of recovery. However, if more than one year has elapsed between the date on which the unlawful aid was first put at the disposal of the beneficiary and the date of the recovery of the aid, the interest rate shall be recalculated at yearly intervals, taking as a basis the rate in force at the time of recalculation.]

NOTES

Para 3: substituted by Commission Regulation 271/2008/EC, Art 1(4).

Repeal of this Regulation in relation to the UK: this Regulation is repealed in relation to the UK (as from IP completion day); see the introductory notes to this Regulation *ante*.

[CHAPTER VA HANDLING OF COMPLAINTS

[5.20]

Article 11a Admissibility of complaints

1. Any person submitting a complaint pursuant to Articles 10(1) and 20(2) of Regulation (EC) No 659/1999 shall demonstrate that it is an interested party within the meaning of Article 1(h) of that Regulation.

2. Interested parties shall duly complete the form set out in Annex IV and provide all the mandatory information requested therein. On a reasoned request by an interested party, the Commission may dispense with the obligation to provide some of the information required by the form.

3. Complaints shall be submitted in one of the official languages of the Union.]

NOTES

Inserted by Commission Regulation 372/2014/EU, Art 1(2).

Repeal of this Regulation in relation to the UK: this Regulation is repealed in relation to the UK (as from IP completion day); see the introductory notes to this Regulation *ante*.

[CHAPTER VB IDENTIFICATION AND PROTECTION OF CONFIDENTIAL INFORMATION

[5.21]

Article 11b Protection of business secrets and other confidential information

Any person submitting information pursuant to Regulation (EC) No 659/1999 shall clearly indicate which information it considers to be confidential, stating the reasons for such confidentiality, and provide the Commission with a separate non-confidential version of the submission. When information must be provided by a certain deadline, the same deadline shall apply for providing the non-confidential version.]

NOTES

Inserted by Commission Regulation 372/2014/EU, Art 1(2).

Repeal of this Regulation in relation to the UK: this Regulation is repealed in relation to the UK (as from IP completion day); see the introductory notes to this Regulation *ante*.

CHAPTER VI FINAL PROVISIONS

[5.22]

Article 12 Review

The Commission shall in consultation with the Member States, review the application of this Regulation within four years after its entry into force.

NOTES

Repeal of this Regulation in relation to the UK: this Regulation is repealed in relation to the UK (as from IP completion day); see the introductory notes to this Regulation *ante*.

[5.23]

Article 13 Entry into force

This Regulation shall enter into force on the twentieth day following that of its publication in the Official Journal of the European Union.

Chapter II shall apply only to those notifications transmitted to the Commission more than five months after the entry into force of this Regulation.

Chapter III shall apply to annual reports covering aid granted from 1 January 2003 onwards.

Chapter IV shall apply to any time limit, which has been fixed but which has not yet expired on the date of entry into force of this Regulation.

Articles 9 and 11 shall apply in relation to any recovery decision notified after the date of entry into force of this Regulation.

NOTES

Repeal of this Regulation in relation to the UK: this Regulation is repealed in relation to the UK (as from IP completion day); see the introductory notes to this Regulation *ante*.

ANNEXES I–IV

(Omitted for reasons of space; see further the introductory notes to this Regulation at **[5.8]**. *Note that this Regulation is repealed in relation to the UK (as from IP completion day); see the introductory notes to this Regulation ante.)*

COMMISSION NOTICE

(2005/C237/03)

Details of arrangement for the electronic transmission of State aid notifications including addresses together with the arrangements for the protection of confidential information

Article 3(6) of Commission Regulation (EC) No 794/2004 of 21 April 2004 implementing Council Regulation (EC) No 659/1999 laying down detailed rules for the application of Article 93 of the EC Treaty

(Text with EEA relevance)

[5.24]

NOTES

Date of publication in OJ: OJ C237, 27.9.2005, p 3.

As to the substitution of the title of Commission Regulation 794/2004/EC see **[5.8]** *ante*. Note that Council Regulation 659/1999/EC was repealed Council Regulation 2015/1589/EU. Note also that the reference to Article 93 of the Treaty in the subtitle of this Regulation is a reference to the original Article 93 of the EC Treaty which, following its amendment and renumbering by the Treaty of Amsterdam, became Article 88. With effect from 1 December 2009, the EC Treaty was replaced by the Treaty on the Functioning of the European Union. References in this document to Article 93 (now Article 108 TFEU) should be construed accordingly.

1. The present notice sets out the detailed arrangements for the transmission of the electronic notification forms, which will be compulsory as of 1 January 2006. It is based on Article 3(6) of Commission Regulation (EC) No 794/2004 of 21 April 2004 implementing Council Regulation (EC) No 659/1999 laying down detailed rules for the application of Article 93 of the Treaty. Article 3(6) requests the Commission to publish these arrangements before 30 September 2005. The advisory Committee for State aids has been consulted.

2. The notifications forms of Annexe I Part 1 and 2 of Regulation (EC) No 794/2004 will be made available in a Web-application, the different supplementary information sheets (Part III of Annexe I) will be annexed as a word document. The address of the web application will be the following:

webgate.cec.eu.int/competition/sani

3. Member States are requested to nominate a Local Administrator as well as the person authorised to validate notifications as well as a replacement. The Commission will grant them a login and password for the web-application which will make sure that the incoming notifications are authorised.

Member States will have the possibility to sub-delegate certain access rights to other persons depending on the internal organisation of the Member States administration for the State aid notifications. The sub-delegation shall not modify the authorisation to validate the notification.

4. Subsequent correspondence between the Member States and the Commission relating to the same notification will be sent electronically via a PKI (Public Key Infrastructure) encrypted Email system.

The address for this Email system will be a functional mailbox established within each DG responsible for the treatment of State aid notifications. Each DG will introduce a certification system which will make the Email correspondence secure and confidential.

5. Upon validation of the notification form and the corresponding Supplementary Information Sheet (SIS), the system will dispatch the notification to the Sec. Gen. and transfer the core data into the ISIS (Integrated State Aid Information System) database. Following that a notification of receipt will automatically be send to the notifying Member State indicating the delay within which the Commission intends to assess the case preliminary as well as the DG which the case has been attributed to by the system.

The delay will depend upon whether the Member State avails himself of the simplified procedure of Article 4 of Regulation (EC) No 794/2004.

6. In the case of the simplified procedures, the Commission will use its best endeavours to preliminarily assess the case within a month's period.

In all other cases, the delay will be fixed at two months.

Subsequent correspondence relating to the particular notification will be exchanged between the Member State and the DG responsible via a PKI (Public Key Infrastructure) secured system. Member States will inform the Commission of their representative authorised to receive the key and to manage the security system. Two keys will be available per Member State. Member States are responsible for the security guarantee of their own Emailing system between the sending point and the Authorised Disclosure Officer (ADO)

7. Withdrawal of notifications should be done via the same secured Email system. Decisions that a notification is deemed to be withdrawn are decisions of the Commission; they will be communicated to the Member State through the secured Email system.

8. Pre-notifications shall not be submitted via the web-based system, but shall be sent by Email. Upon finalisation of the informal contacts Member States will be requested to fill in the formal notification through the web-application.

9. The Commission will establish a functional mailbox where all suggestions for improvements of the functioning of the system and the Web based application shall/could be sent to by Member States.

COMMISSION DIRECTIVE

(2006/111/EC)

of 16 November 2006

on the transparency of financial relations between Member States and public undertakings as well as on financial transparency within certain undertakings

(Text with EEA relevance)

(Codified version)

[5.25]

NOTES

Date of publication in OJ: OJ L318, 17.11.2006, p 17.

Application of EU Directives in the UK post IP completion day: the European Union (Withdrawal) Act 2018, s 3 provides for the incorporation of "direct EU legislation" into domestic law. "Direct EU legislation" is generally defined as EU Regulations, EU Decisions and EU tertiary legislation (for the full definition, see s 3 of the 2018 Act at **[7.5]**). EU Directives, therefore, are not "direct EU legislation" and, as such, do not form part of UK law post IP completion day. Note that "EU-derived domestic legislation" (UK legislation made under the powers conferred by s 2(2) of, or Sch 2, para 1A to, the European Communities Act 1972) is saved despite the repeal of the 1972 Act both during, and after, the implementation period (see ss 1B and 2 of the 2018 Act respectively at **[7.3]** and **[7.4]**). Note that this Directive was implemented in the UK by the Financial Transparency (EC Directive) Regulations 2009, SI 2009/2331 at **[2.188]**.

Note: with effect from 1 December 2009, the EC Treaty was replaced by the Treaty on the Functioning of the European Union. References in this document to provisions of the EC Treaty should be construed accordingly.

THE COMMISSION OF THE EUROPEAN COMMUNITIES,

Having regard to the Treaty establishing the European Community, and in particular Article 86(3) thereof,

Whereas:

(1) Commission Directive 80/723/EEC of 25 June 1980 on the transparency of financial relations between Member States and public undertakings as well as on financial transparency within certain undertakings[1] has been substantially amended several times.[2] In the interests of clarity and rationality the said Directive should be codified.

(2) Public undertakings play a substantial role in the national economy of the Member States.

(3) Member States sometimes grant special or exclusive rights to particular undertakings, or make payments or give some other kind of compensation to particular undertakings entrusted with the operation of services of general economic interest. These undertakings are often also in competition with other undertakings.

(4) Article 295 of the Treaty provides that the Treaty is in no way to prejudice the rules in Member States governing the system of property ownership. There should be no unjustified discrimination between public and private undertakings in the application of the rules on competition. This Directive should apply to both public and private undertakings.

(5) The Treaty requires the Commission to ensure that Member States do not grant undertakings, public or private, aids incompatible with the common market.

(6) However, the complexity of the financial relations between national public authorities and public undertakings tends to hinder the performance of this duty.

(7) A fair and effective application of the aid rules in the Treaty to both public and private undertakings will be possible only if these financial relations are made transparent.

(8) Such transparency applied to public undertakings should enable a clear distinction to be made between the role of the State as public authority and its role as proprietor.

(9) Article 86(1) of the Treaty imposes obligations on Member States in the case of public undertakings and undertakings to which Member States grant special or exclusive rights. Article 86(2) of the Treaty applies to undertakings entrusted with the operation of services of general economic interest. Article 86(3) of the Treaty requires the Commission to ensure the application of the provisions of that Article and provides it with the requisite means to this end. In order to ensure the application of the provisions of Article 86 of the Treaty the Commission must have the necessary information. This entails defining the conditions for ensuring such transparency.

(10) It should be made clear what is to be understood by the terms "public authorities" and "public undertakings".

(11) The Member States have differing administrative territorial structures. This Directive should cover public authorities at all levels in each Member State.

(12) Public authorities may exercise a dominant influence on the behaviour of public undertakings not only where they are the proprietor or have a majority participation but also by virtue of powers they hold in management or supervisory bodies as a result either of the rules governing the undertaking or of the manner in which the shareholdings are distributed.

(13) The provision of public funds to public undertakings may take place either directly or indirectly. Transparency must be achieved irrespective of the manner in which such provision of public funds is made. It may also be necessary to ensure that adequate information is made available as regards the reasons for such provision of public funds and their actual use.

(14) Complex situations linked to the diverse forms of public and private undertakings granted special or exclusive rights or entrusted with the operation of services of general economic interest as well as the range of activities that might be carried on by a single undertaking and the different degrees of market liberalisation in the various Member States could complicate application of the competition rules, and particularly Article 86 of the Treaty. It is therefore necessary for Member States and the Commission to have detailed data about the internal and financial and organisational structure of such undertakings, in particular separate and reliable accounts relating to different activities carried on by the same undertaking.

(15) The accounts should show the distinction between different activities, the costs and revenues associated with each activity and the methods of cost and revenue assignment and allocation. Such separate accounts should be available in relation to, on the one hand, products and services in respect of which the Member State has granted a special or exclusive right or entrusted the undertaking with the operation of a service of general economic interest, as well as, on the other hand, for each other product or service in respect of which the undertaking is active. The obligation of separation of accounts should not apply to undertakings whose activities are limited to the provision of services of general economic interest and which do not operate activities outside the scope of these services of general economic interest. It does not seem necessary to require separation of accounts within the area of services of general economic interest or within the area of the special or exclusive rights, as far as this is not necessary for the cost and revenue allocation between these services and products and those outside the services of general economic interest or the special or exclusive rights.

(16) Requiring Member States to ensure that the relevant undertakings maintain such separate accounts is the most efficient means by which fair and effective application of the rules of competition to such undertakings can be assured. In 1996 the Commission adopted a Communication on services of general interest in Europe,[3] which was supplemented by another Communication in 2001,[4] in which it emphasised the importance of such services. It is necessary to take account of the importance of the sectors concerned, which may involve services of general interest, the strong market position that the relevant undertakings may have and the vulnerability of emerging competition in the sectors being liberalised. In accordance with the principle of proportionality it is necessary and appropriate for the achievement of the basic objective of transparency to lay down rules on such separate accounts. This Directive does

not go beyond what is necessary in order to achieve the objectives pursued, in accordance with the provisions of the third paragraph of Article 5 of the Treaty.

(17) In certain sectors provisions adopted by the Community require Member States and certain undertakings to maintain separate accounts. It is necessary to ensure an equal treatment for all economic activities throughout the Community and to extend the requirement to maintain separate accounts to all comparable situations. This Directive should not amend specific rules established for the same purpose in other Community provisions and should not apply to activities of undertakings covered by those provisions.

(18) Certain undertakings should be excluded from the application of this Directive by virtue of the size of their turnover. This applies to those public undertakings whose business is not conducted on such a scale as to justify the administrative burden of ensuring transparency. In view of the limited potential for an effect on trade between Member States, it is not necessary, at this time, to require separate accounts in relation to the supply of certain categories of services.

(19) This Directive is without prejudice to other provisions of the Treaty, notably Articles 86(2), 88 and 296, and to any other rules concerning the provision of information by Member States to the Commission.

(20) In cases where the compensation for the fulfilment of services of general economic interest has been fixed for an appropriate period following an open, transparent and non-discriminatory procedure it does not seem necessary to require such undertakings to maintain separate accounts.

(21) The undertakings in question being in competition with other undertakings, information acquired should be covered by the obligation of professional secrecy.

(22) A reporting system based on ex post facto checks of the financial flows between public authorities and public undertakings operating in the manufacturing sector will enable the Commission to fulfil its obligations. That system of control must cover specific financial information.

(23) In order to limit the administrative burden on Member States, the reporting system should make use of both publicly available data and information available to majority shareholders. The presentation of consolidated reports is to be permitted. Incompatible aid to major undertakings operating in the manufacturing sector will have the greatest distortive effect on competition in the common market. Therefore, such a reporting system may at present be limited to undertakings with a yearly turnover of more than EUR 250 million.

(24) This Directive should be without prejudice to the obligations of the Member States relating to the time-limits for transposition into national law of the Directives set out in Annex I, Part B,

NOTES

1 OJ L195, 29.7.1980, p 35. Directive as last amended by Directive 2005/81/EC (OJ L312, 29.11.2005, p 47).

2 See Annex I, Part A.

3 OJ C281, 26.9.1996, p 3.

4 OJ C17, 19.1.2001, p 4.

HAS ADOPTED THIS DIRECTIVE:

[5.26]
Article 1

1. The Member States shall ensure that financial relations between public authorities and public undertakings are transparent as provided in this Directive, so that the following emerge clearly:

(a) public funds made available directly by public authorities to the public undertakings concerned;
(b) public funds made available by public authorities through the intermediary of public undertakings or financial institutions;
(c) the use to which these public funds are actually put.

2. Without prejudice to specific provisions laid down by the Community the Member States shall ensure that the financial and organisational structure of any undertaking required to maintain separate accounts is correctly reflected in the separate accounts, so that the following emerge clearly:

(a) the costs and revenues associated with different activities;
(b) full details of the methods by which costs and revenues are assigned or allocated to different activities.

[5.27]
Article 2

For the purpose of this Directive:

(a) "public authorities" means all public authorities, including the State and regional, local and all other territorial authorities;

(b) "public undertakings" means any undertaking over which the public authorities may exercise directly or indirectly a dominant influence by virtue of their ownership of it, their financial participation therein, or the rules which govern it.

A dominant influence on the part of the public authorities shall be presumed when these authorities, directly or indirectly in relation to an undertaking:

(i) hold the major part of the undertaking's subscribed capital; or
(ii) control the majority of the votes attaching to shares issued by the undertakings; or
(iii) can appoint more than half of the members of the undertaking's administrative, managerial or supervisory body;

(c) "public undertakings operating in the manufacturing sector" means all undertakings whose principal area of activity, defined as being at least 50% of total annual turnover, is in manufacturing. These undertakings are those whose operations fall under Section D – Manufacturing being subsection DA up to and including subsection DN of the NACE (Rev.1) classification;[1]

(d) "undertaking required to maintain separate accounts" means any undertaking that enjoys a special or exclusive right granted by a Member State pursuant to Article 86(1) of the Treaty or is entrusted with the operation of a service of general economic interest pursuant to Article 86(2) of the Treaty, that receives public service compensation in any form whatsoever in relation to such service and that carries on other activities;
(e) "different activities" means, on the one hand, all products or services in respect of which a special or exclusive right is granted to an undertaking or all services of general economic interest with which an undertaking is entrusted and, on the other hand, each other separate product or service in respect of which the undertaking is active;
(f) "exclusive rights" means rights that are granted by a Member State to one undertaking through any legislative, regulatory or administrative instrument, reserving it the right to provide a service or undertake an activity within a given geographical area;
(g) "special rights" means rights that are granted by a Member State to a limited number of undertakings, through any legislative, regulatory or administrative instrument, which, within a given geographical area:

- (i) limits to two or more the number of such undertakings, authorised to provide a service or undertake an activity, otherwise than according to objective, proportional and non-discriminatory criteria; or
- (ii) designates, otherwise than according to such criteria, several competing undertakings, as being authorised to provide a service or undertake an activity; or
- (iii) confers on any undertaking or undertakings, otherwise than according to such criteria, any legal or regulatory advantages which substantially affect the ability of any other undertaking to provide the same service or to operate the same activity in the same geographical area under substantially equivalent conditions.

NOTES

[1] OJ L83, 3.4.1993, p 1.

[5.28]
Article 3

The transparency referred to in Article 1(1) shall apply in particular to the following aspects of financial relations between public authorities and public undertakings:

- (a) the setting-off of operating losses;
- (b) the provision of capital;
- (c) non-refundable grants, or loans on privileged terms;
- (d) the granting of financial advantages by forgoing profits or the recovery of sums due;
- (e) the forgoing of a normal return on public funds used;
- (f) compensation for financial burdens imposed by the public authorities.

[5.29]
Article 4

1. To ensure the transparency referred to in Article 1(2), the Member States shall take the measures necessary to ensure that for any undertaking required to maintain separate accounts:

- (a) the internal accounts corresponding to different activities are separate;
- (b) all costs and revenues are correctly assigned or allocated on the basis of consistently applied and objectively justifiable cost accounting principles;
- (c) the cost accounting principles according to which separate accounts are maintained are clearly established.

2. Paragraph 1 shall only apply to activities which are not covered by specific provisions laid down by the Community and shall not affect any obligations of Member States or undertakings arising from the Treaty or from such specific provisions.

[5.30]
Article 5

1. As far as the transparency referred to in Article 1(1) is concerned, this Directive shall not apply to financial relations between the public authorities and:

- (a) public undertakings, as regards services the supply of which is not liable to affect trade between Member States to an appreciable extent;
- (b) central banks;
- (c) public credit institutions, as regards deposits of public funds placed with them by public authorities on normal commercial terms;
- (d) public undertakings whose total annual net turnover over the period of the two financial years preceding that in which the funds referred to in Article 1(1) are made available or used has been less than EUR 40 million. However, for public credit institutions the corresponding threshold shall be a balance sheet total of EUR 800 million.

2. As far as the transparency referred to in Article 1(2) is concerned, this Directive shall not apply:

- (a) to undertakings, as regards services the supply of which is not liable to affect trade between Member States to an appreciable extent;
- (b) to undertakings whose total annual net turnover over the period of the two financial years preceding any given year in which it enjoys a special or exclusive right granted by a Member State pursuant to Article 86(1) of the Treaty, or in which it is entrusted with the operation of a service of general economic interest pursuant to Article 86(2) of the Treaty is less than EUR 40 million; however, for public credit institutions the corresponding threshold shall be a balance sheet total of EUR 800 million;
- (c) to undertakings which have been entrusted with the operation of services of general economic interest pursuant to Article 86(2) of the Treaty if the compensation they receive, in any form whatsoever, was fixed for an appropriate period following an open, transparent and non-discriminating procedure.

[5.31]
Article 6

1. Member States shall ensure that information concerning the financial relations referred to in Article 1(1) be kept at the disposal of the Commission for five years from the end of the financial year in which the public funds were made available to the public undertakings concerned. However, where the same funds are used during a later financial year, the five-year time limit shall run from the end of that financial year.
2. Member States shall ensure that information concerning the financial and organisational structure of undertakings referred to in Article 1(2) be kept at the disposal of the Commission for five years from the end of the financial year to which the information refers.
3. Member States shall, where the Commission considers it necessary so to request, supply to it the information referred to in paragraphs 1 and 2, together with any necessary background information, notably the objectives pursued.

[5.32]
Article 7

The Commission shall not disclose such information supplied to it pursuant to Article 6(3) as is of a kind covered by the obligation of professional secrecy.

The first paragraph shall not prevent publication of general information or surveys which do not contain information relating to particular public undertakings to which this Directive applies.

[5.33]
Article 8

1. Member States whose public undertakings operate in the manufacturing sector shall supply the financial information as set out in paragraphs 2 and 3 to the Commission on an annual basis within the timetable contained in paragraph 5.
2. The financial information required for each public undertaking operating in the manufacturing sector and in accordance with paragraph 4 shall be the annual report and annual accounts, in accordance with the definition of Council Directive 78/660/EEC.[1] The annual accounts and annual report include the balance sheet and profit/loss account, explanatory notes, together with accounting policies, statements by directors, segmental and activity reports. Moreover, notices of shareholders' meetings and any other pertinent information shall be provided.

The reports required shall be provided for each individual public undertaking separately, as well as for the holding or subholding company which consolidates several public undertakings in so far as the consolidated sales of the holding or subholding company lead to its being classified as "manufacturing".

3. The following details, in so far as not disclosed in the annual report and annual accounts of each public undertaking, shall be provided in addition to the information referred to in paragraph 2:
   - (a) the provision of any share capital or quasi-capital funds similar in nature to equity, specifying the terms of its or their provision (whether ordinary, preference, deferred or convertible shares and interest rates; the dividend or conversion rights attaching thereto);
   - (b) non-refundable grants, or grants which are only refundable in certain circumstances;
   - (c) the award to the enterprise of any loans, including overdrafts and advances on capital injections, with a specification of interest rates and the terms of the loan and its security, if any, given to the lender by the enterprise receiving the loan;
   - (d) guarantees given to the enterprise by public authorities in respect of loan finance (specifying terms and any charges paid by enterprises for these guarantees);
   - (e) dividends paid out and profits retained;
   - (f) any other forms of State intervention, in particular, the forgoing of sums due to the State by a public undertaking, including *inter alia* the repayment of loans, grants, payment of corporate or social taxes or any similar charges.

The share capital referred to in (a) shall include share capital contributed by the State directly and any share capital received contributed by a public holding company or other public undertaking, including financial institutions, whether inside or outside the same group, to a given public undertaking. The relationship between the provider of the finance and the recipient shall always be specified.

4. The information required by paragraphs 2 and 3 shall be provided for all public undertakings whose turnover for the most recent financial year was more than EUR 250 million.

The information required above shall be supplied separately for each public undertaking including those located in other Member States, and shall include, where appropriate, details of all intra- and inter-group transactions between different public undertakings, as well as transactions conducted directly between public undertakings and the State.

Certain public enterprises split their activities into several legally distinct undertakings. For such enterprises the Commission is willing to accept one consolidated report. The consolidation should reflect the economic reality of a group of enterprises operating in the same or closely related sectors. Consolidated reports from diverse, and purely financial, holdings shall not be sufficient.

5. The information required under paragraphs 2 and 3 shall be supplied to the Commission on an annual basis.

The information shall be provided within 15 working days of the date of publication of the annual report of the public undertaking concerned. In any case, and specifically for undertakings which do not publish an annual report, the required information shall be submitted not later than nine months following the end of the undertaking's financial year.

6. In order to assess the number of companies covered by this reporting system, Member States shall supply to the Commission a list of the companies covered by this Article and their turnover. The list is to be updated by 31 March of each year.
7. Member States will furnish the Commission with any additional information that it deems necessary in order to complete a thorough appraisal of the data submitted.

NOTES

[1] OJ L222, 14.8.1978, p 11.

[5.34]

Article 9

The Commission shall regularly inform the Member States of the results of the operation of this Directive.

[5.35]

Article 10

Directive 80/723/EEC, as amended by the Directives listed in Annex I, Part A, is repealed, without prejudice to the obligations of the Member States relating to the time-limits for transposition into national law of the Directives set out in Annex I, Part B.

References to the repealed Directive shall be construed as references to this Directive and shall be read in accordance with the correlation table in Annex II.

[5.36]

Article 11

This Directive shall enter into force on 20 December 2006.

[5.37]

Article 12

This Directive is addressed to the Member States.

ANNEX I

PART A REPEALED DIRECTIVE WITH ITS SUCCESSIVE AMENDMENTS

(referred to in Article 10)

[5.38]

Commission Directive 80/723/EEC	(OJ L195, 29.7.1980, p 35)
Commission Directive 85/413/EEC	(OJ L229, 28.8.1985, p 20)
Commission Directive 93/84/EEC	(OJ L254, 12.10.1993, p 16)
Commission Directive 2000/52/EC	(OJ L193, 29.7.2000, p 75)
Commission Directive 2005/81/EC	(OJ L312, 29.11.2005, p 47)

PART B LIST OF TIME LIMITS FOR TRANSPOSITION INTO NATIONAL LAW

(referred to in Article 10)

Directive	Time limit for transposition
80/723/EEC	31 December 1981
85/413/EEC	1 January 1986
93/84/EEC	1 November 1993
2000/52/EC	31 July 2001
2005/81/EC	19 December 2006

ANNEX II

CORRELATION TABLE

[5.39]

Directive 80/723/EEC	This Directive
Article 1	Article 1
Article 2(1), introductory sentence	Article 2, introductory sentence
Article 2(1), point (a)	Article 2, point (a)
Article 2(1), point (b)	Article 2, point (b), first subparagraph
Article 2(1), points (c) to (f)	Article 2, points (c) to (f)
Article 2(1), point (g), introductory words	Article 2, point (g), introductory words
Article 2(1), point (g), first indent	Article 2, point (g)(i)
Article 2(1), point (g), second indent	Article 2, point (g)(ii)
Article 2(1), point (g), third indent	Article 2, point (g)(iii)
Article 2(2), introductory sentence	Article 2, point (b), second subparagraph, introductory sentence
Article 2(2), point (a)	Article 2, point (b), second subparagraph, point (i)
Article 2(2), point (b)	Article 2, point (b), second subparagraph, point (ii)
Article 2(2), point (c)	Article 2, point (b), second subparagraph, point (iii)
Article 3	Article 3

Directive 80/723/EEC	This Directive
Article 3a	Article 4
Article 4	Article 5
Article 5	Article 6
Article 5a(1)	Article 8(1)
Article 5a(2), first subparagraph, introductory sentence	Article 8(2), first subparagraph
Article 5a(2), first subparagraph, point (i)	Article 8(2), first subparagraph
Article 5a(2), second subparagraph, introductory sentence	Article 8(3), first subparagraph, introductory sentence
Article 5a(2), second subparagraph, point (ii)	Article 8(3), first subparagraph, point (a)
Article 5a(2), second subparagraph, point (iii)	Article 8(3), first subparagraph, point (b)
Article 5a(2), second subparagraph, point (iv)	Article 8(3), first subparagraph, point (c)
Article 5a(2), second subparagraph, point (v)	Article 8(3), first subparagraph, point (d)
Article 5a(2), second subparagraph, point (vi)	Article 8(3), first subparagraph, point (e)
Article 5a(2), second subparagraph, point (vii)	Article 8(3), first subparagraph, point (f)
Article 5a(3), first subparagraph	Article 8(4), first subparagraph
Article 5a(3), second subparagraph, first sentence	Article 8(4), second subparagraph
Article 5a(3), second subparagraph, second sentence	Article 8(3), second subparagraph, first sentence
Article 5a(3), second subparagraph, third sentence	Article 8(3), second subparagraph, second sentence
Article 5a(3), second subparagraph, last sentence	Article 8(2), second subparagraph
Article 5a(3), third subparagraph	Article 8(4), third subparagraph
Article 5a(4), first subparagraph	Article 8(5), first subparagraph
Article 5a(4), second subparagraph	Article 8(5), second subparagraph
Article 5a(4), third subparagraph	Article 8(6)
Article 5a(5)	—
Article 5a(6)	Article 8(7)
Article 6(1)	Article 7, first paragraph
Article 6(2)	Article 7, second paragraph
Article 7	Article 9
Article 8	—
—	Article 10
—	Article 11
Article 9	Article 12
—	Annex I
—	Annex II

COMMUNICATION FROM THE COMMISSION

(2008/C14/02)

on the revision of the method for setting the reference and discount rates

(This communication replaces the previous notices on the method for setting the reference and discount rates.)

[5.40]

NOTES

Date of publication in OJ: OJ C14, 19.1.2008, p 6.

REFERENCE AND DISCOUNT RATES

Within the framework of the Community control of State aid, the Commission makes use of reference and discount rates. The reference and discount rates are applied as a proxy for the market rate and to measure the grant equivalent of aid, in particular when it is disbursed in several instalments and to calculate the aid element resulting from interest subsidy schemes. They are also used to check compliance with the de minimis rule and block exemption regulations.

BACKGROUND TO THE REFORM

The main reason for re-examining the methodology for setting reference and discount rates is that the required financial parameters are not always available in all Member States, especially in the new ones.[1] In addition, the current method could be improved in order to take account of the debtor's creditworthiness and collaterals.

Therefore, this Communication presents a revised method for setting reference and discount rates. The proposed approach builds on the current arrangement, which is accepted by all Member States and practical to apply, to develop a new method that mitigates some of the current shortcomings, is compatible with the various financial systems in the EU (in particular in the new Member States) and remains simple to implement.

NOTES

[1] The current reference rates for these Member States are those communicated by the Member States as reflecting a suitable market rate. The methodology for arriving at these rates diverges from one Member State to another.

STUDY

A study by Deloitte & Touche,[2] commissioned by DG Competition, proposes a system based on two pillars: a "standard" approach and an "advanced" approach.

Standard approach

In this approach, the Commission publishes, each quarter, a base rate calculated on several maturities – 3 months, 1 year, 5 years and 10 years – and for various currencies. IBOR rates[3] and ask swap rates are used or, in the absence of these parameters, government bond rates. The premium applied to obtain the reference rate for a loan is calculated according to the borrower's creditworthiness and collaterals. According to the rating category of the company ("rating" provided by rating agencies in the case of major companies or by banks in the case of SMEs), the margin applicable to the default case (normal rating and normal collateralisation[4]) represents 220 basis points. The increase could be up to 1 650 in the case of "low" creditworthiness and low collateralisation.

Advanced approach

This approach would allow Member States to appoint an independent calculation agent – a central bank for instance – in charge of publishing regularly a fair reference interest rate, for a higher number of maturities and on a more frequent basis than the standard approach. This approach would be justified by the knowledge and proximity of the financial and banking data available to this institution in comparison with the Commission. In that case, the Commission and an external auditor would validate calculation methods. In this approach, opting out, in certain cases, could be considered.

Weaknesses

Despite the economic relevance of the two methods, certain difficulties can be underlined.

Standard approach:

— it does not solve the problem of the lack of financial data in the new Member States and adds new, not readily accessible parameters,

— this standard method could favour large companies to the detriment of SMEs for which either no rating is available, or a less advantageous one exists (in particular because of information asymmetry with respect to the lender). It could give rise to multiple disputes on the subject of calculation methods for the premium to be applied according to creditworthiness and the level of collaterals,

— it does not simplify the task of Member States, in particular regarding calculations to check compliance with the de minimis rule and the block exemption regulations.

Advanced method:

— the advanced method could prove problematic when applied to aid schemes: the volatility of market rates might make the difference between the underlying rate of a loan scheme and the then valid reference rate so advantageous to the borrower that some measures would become incompatible with the State aid rules,

— a quarterly adjustment of the rates would complicate the handling of cases as the calculated aid amounts may vary considerably between the beginning of the assessment phase and the date of the final decision taken by the Commission,

— these arrangements seem overly complicated and may fail to ensure consistently fair treatment across Member States.

NOTES

[2] Available on the website of DG Competition: ec.europa.eu/comm/competition/state_aid/others/

[3] Inter-bank offered rate on the money market.

[4] Cases where the recipient shows a satisfactory rating (BB) and a loss given default rate between 31% and 59%.

NEW METHODOLOGY

To avoid these difficulties, the Commission proposes a method that:

— is easy to apply (in particular for the Member States when dealing with measures falling under the *de minimis* or block exemption regulations),

— ensures equal treatment across Member States with minimum deviations from current practice and facilitating the application of reference rates for the new Member States,

— uses simplified criteria taking into account firms' creditworthiness instead of the mere size of undertakings, which seems a too simplistic criterion.

Moreover, this method makes it possible to avoid adding uncertainty and complexity to calculation methods in a changing banking and financial environment due to the implementation of the Basel II framework, which could have a significant impact on the allocation of capital as well as on banks' behaviour. The Commission will continue to monitor this changing environment and, if necessary, provide further guidance.

COMMISSION NOTICE

The main reason for re-examining the methodology for setting reference and discount rates is that the required financial parameters are not always available in all Member States. In addition, the current method can be improved in order to take account of the debtor's creditworthiness and collaterals.

The Commission therefore adopts the following methodology for setting the reference rates:

— Calculation basis: 1-year IBOR

The base rate is based on 1-year money market rates, available in almost all Member States, the Commission reserving the right to use shorter or longer maturities adapted to certain cases.

Where those rates are not available, the 3-month money market rate will be used.

In the absence of reliable or equivalent data or in exceptional circumstances the Commission may, in close cooperation with the Member State(s) concerned and in principle based on data from that Member State's Central Bank, determine another calculation basis.

— Margins[5]

The following margins are to be applied in principle depending on the rating of the undertaking concerned and the collateral[6] offered.

Loan margins in basis points			
Rating Category	**Collateralisation**		
	High	**Normal**	**Low**
Strong (AAA-A)	67	75	100
Good (BBB)	75	100	220
Satisfactory (BB)	100	220	400
Weak (B)	220	400	650
Bad/Financial difficulties (CCC and below)	400	650	1000[1]

[1] Subject to the application of the specific provisions for rescue and restructuring aid, as currently laid down in the Community guidelines on State aid for rescuing and restructuring firms in difficulty (OJ C244, 1.10.2004, p 2) and in particular point 25(a), which refers to "a rate at least comparable with the rates observed for loans to healthy companies, and in particular at the reference rates adopted by the Commission". Hence, for rescue aid cases, the 1-year IBOR increased with at least 100 basis points shall be applied.

Normally, 100 basis points are added to the base rate. This assumes (i) loans to undertakings with satisfactory rating and high collateral; or (ii) loans to undertakings with good rating and normal collateral.

For borrowers that do not have a credit history or a rating based on a balance sheet approach, such as certain special-purpose companies or start-up companies, the base rate should be increased by at least 400 basis points (depending on the available collaterals) and the margin can never be lower than the one which would be applicable to the parent company.

Ratings do not need to be obtained from specific rating agencies – national rating systems or rating systems used by banks to reflect default rates are equally acceptable.[7]

The above margins may be revised from time to time to take account of the market situation.

— Update

An update of the reference rate will be carried out every year. The base rate will thus be calculated on the basis of the 1-year IBOR recorded in September, October and November of the previous year. The then fixed base rate will be in force as from the first of January. For the period from 1 July 2008 until 31 December 2008, the reference rate will exceptionally be calculated on the basis of the 1-year IBOR recorded in February, March and April 2008, subject to the application of the next paragraph.

In addition, to take account of significant and sudden variations, an update will be made each time the average rate, calculated over the previous three months, deviates by more than 15% from the rate in force. This new rate will enter into force on the first day of the second month following the months used for the calculation.

— Discount rate: Calculation of net present value

The reference rate is also to be used as a discount rate, for calculating present values. To that end, in principle, the base rate increased by a fixed margin of 100 basis points will be used.

— The present methodology will enter into force as of 1 July 2008.

NOTES

5 As follows from the study, the margin is largely independent of the maturity of the loan.

6 Normal collateral should be understood as the level of collateral normally required by financial institutions as a guarantee for their loan. The level of collaterals can be measured as the Loss Given Default (LGD), which is the expected loss in percentage of the debtor's exposure taking into account recoverable amounts from collateral and the bankruptcy assets; as a consequence the LGD is inversely proportional to the validity of collaterals. For the present communication it is assumed that "High" collateralisation implies an LGD below or equal to 30%, "Normal" collateralisation an LGD between 31% and 59%, and "Low" collateralisation an LGD above or equal to 60%. For more details, on the notion LGD, see Basel II: International Convergence of Capital Measurement and Capital Standards: A Revised Framework – Comprehensive Version, available on: www.bis.org/publ/bcbs128.pdf

7 For a comparison between the most commonly used credit rating mechanisms, see eg Table 1 in Working Paper No 207 of the Bank for International settlements: www.bis.org/publ/work207.pdf

FORM FOR THE SUBMISSION OF COMPLAINTS CONCERNING ALLEGED UNLAWFUL STATE AID OR MISUSE OF AID

[5.41]

NOTES

This Form is available on the European Commission's website at: https://ec.europa.eu/competition-policy/state-aid/complaints_en. See that webpage for details as to where to send the complaint.

The mandatory fields are marked with a star (*).

1. Information regarding the complainant

First Name:*
Surname:*
Address line 1:*
Address line 2:
Town/City:*
County/State/Province:
Postcode:*
Country:*
Telephone:
Mobile Telephone:
E-mail address:*
Fax:

2. I am submitting the complaint on behalf of somebody (a person or a firm)

Yes* No*

If yes, please also provide the following information
Name of the person/firm you represent*:
Registration nr. of the entity:
Address line 1:*
Address line 2:
Town/City:*
County/State/Province:
Postcode:*
Country:*
Telephone 1:
Telephone 2:
E-mail address:*
Fax:
Please attach proof that the representative is authorized to act on behalf of this person/firm.*

3. Please select one of the following options, describing your identity*

a) Competitor of the beneficiary or beneficiaries
b) Trade association representing the interests of competitors
c) Non-governmental organisation
d) Trade union
e) EU citizen
f) Other, please specify

....

Please explain why and to what extent the alleged State aid affects your competitive position / the competitive position of the person/firm you represent. Provide as much concrete evidence as possible.

Please be aware that, by virtue of Article 20(2) of Council Regulation (EC) No 659/1999 of 22 March 1999 laying down detailed rules for the application of Article 108 of the Treaty on the Functioning of the European Union, only interested parties within the meaning of Article 1(h) of that Regulation may submit formal complaints. Therefore, in the absence of a demonstration that you are an interested party, the present form will not be registered as a complaint, and the information provided therein will be kept as general market information.

....

....

4. Please select one of the following two options*

☐ Yes, you may reveal my identity
☐ No, you may not reveal my identity

If not, please specify the reasons:

....

....

Confidentiality: If you do not wish your identity or certain documents or information to be disclosed, please indicate this clearly, identify the confidential parts of any documents and give your reasons. In the absence of any indication about confidentiality of your identity or certain documents or information, those elements will be treated as non-confidential and may be shared with the Member State allegedly granting the State aid. The information contained in points **5 and 6** cannot be designated as confidential.

5. Information regarding the Member State granting the aid*

Please be aware: the information provided under this point is regarded as non-confidential.

a) Country:

b) If known, specify which institution or body granted the alleged unlawful State aid:
Central government:
Region (please specify):
Other (please specify):

6. Information regarding the alleged aid measure

Please be aware: the information provided under this point is regarded as non-confidential.

a) Please provide a description of the alleged aid, and indicate in what form it was granted (loans, grants, guarantees, tax incentives or exemptions etc.).

....

b) For what purpose was the alleged aid given (if known)?

....

....

c) What is the amount of the alleged aid (if known)? If you do not have the exact figure, please provide an estimate and as much justifying evidence as possible.

....

d) Who is the beneficiary? Please give as much information as possible, including a description of the main activities of the beneficiary/firm(s) concerned.

....

....

e) To your knowledge, when was the alleged aid granted?

....

f) Please select one of the following options:

☐ According to my knowledge, the State aid was not notified to the Commission.

☐ According to my knowledge, the State aid was notified, but it was granted before the decision of the Commission. If known, please indicate the notification reference number or indicate when the aid was notified.

....

☐ According to my knowledge, the State aid was notified and approved by the Commission, but its implementation did not respect the applicable conditions. If known, please indicate the notification reference number or indicate when the aid was notified and approved.

....

☐ According to my knowledge, the State aid was granted under a block exemption regulation, but its implementation did not respect the applicable conditions.

7. **Grounds of complaint***

Please note that, for a measure to qualify as State aid under Article 107(1) TFEU, the alleged aid has to be granted by a Member State or through State resources, it has to distort or threaten to distort competition by favouring certain undertakings or the production of certain goods, and affect trade between Member States.

a) Please explain to what extent public resources are involved (if known) and, if the measure was not adopted by a public authority (but for instance by a public undertaking), please explain why, in your view, it is imputable to public authorities of a Member State.

....

....

b) Please explain why, in your opinion, the alleged State aid is selective (i.e. favours certain commercial undertakings or the production of certain goods).

....

....

c) Please explain how, in your opinion, the alleged State aid provides an economic advantage for the beneficiary or beneficiaries.

....

....

d) Please explain why, in your view, the alleged State aid distorts or threatens to distort competition.

....

....

e) Please explain why, in your view, the alleged aid affects trade between Member States.

....

....

8. Compatibility of the aid

Please indicate the reasons why in your view the alleged aid is not compatible with the internal market.

....

....

9. Information on alleged infringement of other rules of European Union law and on other procedures

a) If known, please indicate what other rules of European Union law you think have been infringed by the granting of the alleged aid. Please be aware that this does not imply necessarily that those potential infringements will be dealt with within the State aid investigation.

....

....

b) Have you already approached the Commission's services or any other European institution concerning the same issue? *

Yes No

If yes, please attach copies of correspondence.

c) Have you already approached national authorities or national courts concerning the same issue? *

Yes No

If yes, please indicate which authorities or courts; also, if there has already been a decision or judgement, please attach a copy (if available); if, on the contrary, the case is still pending, please indicate its reference (if available).

....

d) Please provide any other information that may be relevant for the assessment of this case.

....

10. Supporting documents

Please list any documents and evidence which are submitted in support of the complaint and add annexes if necessary

- Whenever possible, a copy of the national law or other measure which provides the legal basis for the payment of the alleged aid should be provided.
- Whenever possible, please attach any available evidence that the State aid was granted (e.g. press release, published accounts).
- If the complaint is submitted on behalf of someone else (a natural person or a firm) please attach proof that you as a representative are authorised to act.
- Where applicable, please attach copies of all previous correspondence with the European Commission or any other European or national institution concerning the same issue.
- If the issue has already been dealt with by a national court/authority, please attach a copy of the judgement/decision, if available.

....

I hereby declare that all the information in this form and annexes is provided in good faith.

Place, date and signature of complainant"

COMMUNICATION FROM THE COMMISSION

(2014/C198/02)

amending the Communications from the Commission on EU Guidelines for the application of State aid rules in relation to the rapid deployment of broadband networks, on Guidelines on regional State aid for 2014–2020, on State aid for films and other audiovisual works, on Guidelines on State aid to promote risk finance investments and on Guidelines on State aid to airports and airlines

[5.42]

NOTES

Date of publication in OJ: OJ C198, 27.06.2014, p 30.

See also the list of consultations and draft documents in the Appendix at **[A1]**.

I. INTRODUCTION

[5.43]

One of the main objectives of the State aid modernisation[1] is to enable the Commission to focus on the most distortive cases while leaving more flexibility to Member States to put in place less distortive aid. In this context, the new General Block-Exemption Regulation,[2] which has a broader scope, makes it possible for Member States to grant aid on the basis of pre-defined criteria with no need to notify to the Commission, thereby saving time, reducing the administrative burden and promoting models of aid which is well-designed, targeted at identified market failures and objectives of common interest, and least distortive ('good aid'). Transparency in relation to aid awards is a key component of the modernisation.

Transparency promotes accountability and enables citizens to be better informed about public policies. A better informed constituency helps create a better dialogue between citizens and government officials and results in better policy decisions. In recent decades, civil society and governments around the world have made great advances in increasing transparency at both the local and national levels. Yet there is still a need for greater and more meaningful participation and accountability, particularly when it comes to how public resources are allocated.

In the area of State aid, transparency is even more important. Transparency promotes compliance, reduces uncertainties and enables companies to check whether aid granted to competitors is legal. It promotes a level playing field across Member States and companies in the internal market, which is even more important in the present economic context. It facilitates enforcement for national and regional authorities by increasing awareness of aid granted at various levels, hence ensuring better control and follow-up at national and local levels. Finally, better transparency makes it possible to reduce reporting obligations and the administrative burden linked to reporting.

While the Commission already publishes the names of beneficiaries of notified individual aid and the amount of aid in its decisions,[3] there is no requirement for public information on beneficiaries of aid awarded under notified schemes or schemes covered by a block-exemption (which represent almost 90% of the total State aid expenditures in the Union),[4] with the exception of large grants of regional aid and aid for research and development.[5]

Some Member States have recently put in place websites disclosing information on aid awards[6] or are required to provide information to the public, such as information on all types of public spending, or to give access to information on public spending upon citizens' requests. Member States also disclose full information on expenditures under European Structural and Investment Funds[7] and their beneficiaries. For aid granted under European Structural and Investment Funds, and in order to avoid duplication in the collection of information, the State aid websites referred to in this Communication could extract the relevant information from the same systems used for Structural funds reporting.

Member States already collect information on all State aid expenditures in the context of the annual reporting exercise pursuant to Commission Regulation (EC) No 794/2004.[8] That information[9] is then transmitted to the Commission for publication through the annual State aid Scoreboard[10] and on the Eurostat website.[11]

To ensure transparency, Member States shall, as a condition for granting aid in line with the relevant guidelines, establish comprehensive State aid websites, at regional or national level, for the publication of information on aid measures and their beneficiaries. Following standard practice regarding publication of information,[12] a standard format shall be used which allows the information to be easily published on the internet, searched and downloaded. The transparency requirement applies in general to all State aid, except for smaller aid awards of less than EUR 500,000.

Moreover, with a view to ensuring tax confidentiality and the protection of business secrets, it is not requested to disclose information on the companies' tax base or the exact amount of their tax relief. However, since fiscal aid constitutes selective derogations, confers an advantage to undertakings and thus constitutes State aid, accountability on the use of public resources and State aid control also have to be preserved. Accordingly for aid granted under fiscal schemes or under risk finance schemes, information on aid amounts can be provided in ranges.

A transitional period of two years is set out in order to ensure that those Member States which do not have transparency mechanisms have sufficient time to put them in place. For that purpose, existing information systems already deployed at national, regional and local level for state aid reporting (SARI)[13] will be further developed so as to put Member States in a position to facilitate the collection and processing of information for subsequent publication on the Member States' websites. In addition, technical assistance under European Structural and Investment Funds can be used by Member States under the conditions referred to in Article 59 of Regulation (EU) No 1303/2013.

Greater transparency makes it possible to simplify reporting obligations. As a first step, the Commission proposes removing most of the current reporting obligations set out in the State aid Guidelines revised in the context of the State aid Modernisation initiative. Once the websites are put in place by Member States, the reporting obligations set out in Regulation (EC) No 794/2004 will be further simplified, while guaranteeing that an equivalent level of information is obtained from transparency: this means in practice that, if Member States opt for greater transparency (e.g. through a lower threshold of aid in respect of which information must be published), the remaining reporting obligations will become unnecessary; in addition, less systematic monitoring actions could be envisaged.

In the framework of the State aid modernisation, and in order to further ensure that distortions of competition and trade are limited, the Commission may require that certain schemes are subject to an evaluation. This condition may apply in particular to some aid schemes with a large budget as defined by Article 1(2)(a) of new General Block Exemption Regulation. Such schemes will be exempted under the Regulation for an initial period of six months, which the Commission may extend upon approval of the evaluation plan to be notified by the Member State. Upon notification of the evaluation plan, the Commission will assess the compatibility of such schemes solely on the basis of the evaluation plan.

NOTES

1 Communication from the Commission to the European Parliament, the Council, the European Economic and Social Committee and the Committee of the Regions on EU State aid Modernisation, COM/2012/209, 8.5.2012.

2 Commission Regulation (EU) No 651/2014 of 17 June 2014 declaring certain categories of aid compatible with the internal market in application of Articles 107 and 108 of the Treaty (OJ L187, 26.6.2014, p 1).

3 Commission communication on professional secrecy in State aid decisions (OJ C297, 9.12.2003, p 6).

4 See ec.europa.eu/competition/state_aid/scoreboard/index_en.html

5 See ec.europa.eu/competition/state_aid/register/

6 See for instance in Estonia www.fin.ee/riigiabi or in the Czech Republic (for R&D) www.isvav.cz/index.jsp

7 Regulation (EU) No 1303/2013 of the European Parliament and of the Council of 17 December 2013 laying down common provisions the European Regional Development Fund, the European Social Fund, the Cohesion Fund, the European Agricultural Fund for Rural Development and the European Maritime and Fisheries Fund and laying down general provisions on the European Regional Development Fund, the European Social Fund, the Cohesion Fund and the European Maritime and Fisheries Fund and repealing Council Regulation (EC) No 1083/2006 (OJ L347, 20.12.2013, p 320).

8 Commission Regulation (EC) No 794/2004 of 21 April 2004 implementing Council Regulation (EC) No 659/1999 laying down detailed rules for the application of Article 93 of the EC Treaty (OJ L140, 30.4.2004, p 1).

9 This information is transmitted in aggregated manner for schemes, and per individual beneficiaries for individual aid.

10 See https://ec.europa.eu/competition-policy/state-aid/scoreboard_en

11 See for instance
https://ec.europa.eu/eurostat/

12 See for instance Directive 2003/98/EC of the European Parliament and of the Council of 17 November 2003 on the re-use of public sector information (OJ L345, 31.12.2003, p 90), and Directive 2013/37/EU of the European Parliament and of the Council of 26 June2013 amending Directive 2003/98/EC on the re-use of public sector information (OJ L175 27.6. 2013, p 1).

13 State Aid Reporting Interactive tool (SARI).

II. AMENDMENTS TO THE COMMUNICATIONS

II.1. JUSTIFICATION OF THE AMENDMENTS

[5.44]
The principle of transparency is already set out in the Commission Guidelines related to State aid rules for the rapid deployment of broadband networks,[1] regional State aid for 2014–2020,[2] State aid for films and other audiovisual works,[3] State aid to promote risk finance investments[4] and State aid to airports and airlines.[5]

Following public consultations on guidelines[6] [7] and on the General Block-Exemption Regulation,[8] the transparency requirement should be adapted through this Communication in order to align the transparency provisions across the revised State aid guidelines, ensuring proportionality, preventing the disclosure of information not related to State aid and providing Member States with a transitional implementation phase.

In addition, and as a consequence of the introduction of transparency, the requirement in the Guidelines on regional State aid for 2014–2020 to transmit information to the Commission on each individual aid exceeding EUR 3 million can also be simplified through this Communication.

The principle of evaluation is already set out in the Commission Guidelines related to State aid rules for the rapid deployment of broadband networks, regional State aid for 2014–2020, State aid to promote risk finance investments and State aid to airports and airlines.

Following adoption of the new General Block-Exemption Regulation, the evaluation provision should be amended through this Communication in order to specify that in the case of an aid scheme excluded from the Regulation exclusively on the grounds of its large budget (as defined in Article 1(2)(a) of the Regulation) and fulfilling the other conditions for exemption laid down in the Regulation, the Commission will assess its compatibility solely on the basis of the evaluation plan notified by the Member State. This would not apply to alterations of such schemes, as referred to Article 1(2)(b) of the Regulation, since these alterations must take into account the results of the evaluation.

NOTES

1 Communication from the Commission, EU Guidelines for the application of State aid rules in relation to the rapid deployment of broadband networks (OJ C25, 26.1.2013, p 1).

2 Communication from the Commission, Guidelines on regional State aid for 2014–2020 (OJ C209, 23.7.2013, p 1).

3 Communication from the Commission, State aid for films and other audiovisual works (OJ C332, 15.11.2013, p 1).

4 Communication from the Commission, Guidelines on State aid to promote risk finance investments (OJ C19, 22.1.2014, p 4).
5 Communication from the Commission, Guidelines on State aid to airports and airlines (OJ C99, 4.4.2014, p 3).
6 ec.europa.eu/competition/consultations/2013_state_aid_rdi/index_en.html
7 ec.europa.eu/competition/consultations/2013_state_aid_environment/index_en.html
8 ec.europa.eu/competition/consultations/2013_consolidated_gber/index_en.html

II.2

(*Amends the EU Guidelines for the application of State aid rules in relation to the rapid deployment of broadband networks at* **[5.346]**, *the Guidelines on regional State aid for 2014–2020 at* **[5.274]**, *the Commission Communication on State aid for films and other audiovisual works at* **[5.337]**, *the Guidelines on State aid to airports and airlines at* **[5.416]** *and the Guidelines on State aid to promote risk finance investment at* **[5.322]**; *these amendments have been incorporated at the appropriate place.*)

COMMISSION STAFF WORKING DOCUMENT COMMON METHODOLOGY FOR STATE AID EVALUATION

Brussels, 28.5.2014

SWD(2014) 179 final

[5.45]

NOTES

This document is available on the European Commission website at: ec.europa.eu/competition-policy/state-aid/legislation/modernisation/transparency-and-evaluation_en.

1 INTRODUCTION

[5.46]

Member States provide State aid to help achieve a wide variety of policy objectives, for example, to reduce regional disparities within a country, to promote research and development and innovation activities, or to promote a high level of environmental protection.

In determining which types of aid are compatible with the common market, EU State aid rules are based on a system of ex-ante scrutiny: aid schemes[1] are approved on the basis of predefined assessment criteria on the assumption that, if they comply with these assessment criteria, their positive effects will outweigh any negative effects. Typically, this assessment of schemes is performed without sufficient evaluation of their actual impact on markets over time.

To date, when applying EU State aid rules, relatively limited importance has been attached to ex-post evidence on what has actually been achieved with public funds or on the impact of State aid on competition. It is however essential for decision makers both at the Member State and EU level to consider the measurable results of State aid granted in the past, and the lessons learnt. This will help to ensure that schemes financed by State aid are more effective and create less distortion in markets, and will also improve the efficiency of future schemes and, possibly, of future rules for granting State aid.

A number of countries already evaluate their subsidy measures, even if not always on a regular basis.[2] Similarly, EU spending (including financing from the EU Structural and Investment Funds such as the ERDF, the ESF and the EAFRD) is subject to ex-ante, ongoing and ex-post evaluation in accordance with the applicable regulations and with the guidance documents published by the Commission.[3] In order to avoid duplication in the evaluations carried out by Member States, the "Concepts and Recommendations" guidance document on monitoring and evaluation clarifies that the evaluation requirements of the European Structural and Investment Funds can be fulfilled by carrying out the evaluations required by the rules for State aid.

The State aid modernisation initiative[4] aims to focus the Commission's enforcement efforts on larger aid schemes that are likely to have the most significant impact on the common market. At the same time, the analysis of cases of a more local nature with minor or more limited effects on trade will be simplified, including by providing more flexibility for Member States in terms of implementing such aid measures by increasing the scope of the new General Block Exemption Regulation.[5] In order to ensure that, overall, the positive effects of State aid (in fulfilling its original objective) continue to outweigh the potential negative effects on competition and trade, and to prevent undue distortion to the market, greater simplification should be combined with greater transparency, enhanced control of compliance with State aid rules at national and European level and effective evaluation.[6]

This paper sets out a common methodology for evaluating State aid schemes. It is designed to provide guidance to public authorities involved in planning and conducting evaluations.

NOTES

1 Aid schemes account for the majority of all granted aid: according to the 2013 Scoreboard data, approved aid schemes represent 23% of all aid measures and 55% of aid amounts, and a further set of block-exempted schemes represent 63% of all aid measures and around 32% of aid amounts. Council Regulation No 659/1999 defines 'aid scheme' as "any act on the basis of which, without further implementing measures being required, individual aid awards may be made to undertakings defined within the act in a general and abstract manner and any act on the basis of which aid which is not

linked to a specific project may be awarded to one or several undertakings for an indefinite period of time and/or for an indefinite amount".

2 For example, in several Member States, State aid evaluation reports are regularly prepared for the Court of Auditors or the Parliament.

3 The Commission guidance documents on evaluation for the 2014–20 funding period (available here: https://ec.europa.eu/regional_policy/en/policy/evaluations/guidance/) set out in detail the relevant concepts and recommendations.

4 Communication from the Commission to the European Parliament, the Council, the European Economic and Social Committee and the Committee of the Regions, EU State Aid Modernisation (SAM), 8.5.2012, COM(2012) 209 final.

5 Commission Regulation (EU) No . . . /2014 of XXX declaring certain categories of aid compatible with the internal market in application of Articles 107 and 108 of the Treaty

6 See also the Council conclusions on Reform of state aid control of 13 November 2012.

2 THE OBJECTIVES OF STATE AID EVALUATION

[5.47]

The overall objective of State aid evaluation is to assess the relative positive and negative effects of a scheme, i.e. the public objective of the aid relative to its impact on competition and trade between Member States. State aid evaluation can explain whether and to what extent the original objectives of an aid scheme have been fulfilled (i.e. assessing the positive effects) and determine the impact of the scheme on markets and competition (i.e. possible negative effects). Evaluation therefore differs in its purpose from the two ex-post exercises currently carried out by the Commission with regard to State aid schemes – monitoring[7] and reporting.[8]

State aid evaluation should in particular allow the direct incentive effect of the aid on the beneficiary to be assessed (i.e. whether the aid has caused the beneficiary to take a different course of action, and how significant the impact of the aid has been). It should also provide an indication of the general positive and negative effects of the aid scheme on the attainment of the desired policy objective and on competition and trade, and could examine the proportionality and appropriateness of the chosen aid instrument.

Based on this assessment, the evaluation can confirm whether the assumptions underlying the ex-ante approval of the aid scheme are still valid and can help to improve the design of future aid schemes and rules governing State aid. It could provide the basis for adjusting future State interventions so as to improve the effectiveness and efficiency of the aid to the extent necessary to guarantee that the positive effects are sufficient to justify accepting the distortion to the market caused by the intervention. Such improvements on future schemes could range from adjustments to the design, including changes to the selection criteria and a more extensive assessment of the incentive effect, to more significant changes such as promoting the use of an alternative form of aid, redefining objectives or target beneficiaries or considering non-aid options to achieve the same policy objectives.

It is important to set an appropriate timeline for the evaluation, allowing enough time to collect sufficient evidence whilst also providing results to policy-makers as soon as possible, so that potential improvements can be introduced in due time.[9] In view of this, State aid evaluations should normally be considered as ongoing evaluations, to be conducted while the aid scheme is still in operation, rather than as purely ex-post ones, conducted only after the implementation of the scheme is completed. Account should be taken of particular cases where the full effects of an intervention might be perceivable in a longer timeline and where the evaluation will only be able to capture and measure initial effects.

State aid evaluation should ultimately be a learning exercise for both the Commission and Member States. For this to be possible, the evaluation should meet a certain minimum standard of quality. The Commission should therefore ensure that appropriate quality control of evaluations takes place. In particular, the Commission will analyse in detail the overall reliability of the evaluation and will highlight potential shortcomings at the two crucial stages, namely the evaluation plan and the final report. Where appropriate, the Commission could seek the support of external independent experts to assist in the quality control of the evaluation.

The Commission could also organise training sessions and workshops for national administrations on methods and techniques of evaluation. Furthermore, successful experiences and best practices from Member States could be shared and used to help design more effective aid schemes in the future.

The benefits of conducting evaluations will become evident within a few years, when the first evaluation reports are ready and their findings and recommendations are made available. These will then be able to be used to improve the design of subsequent aid schemes and, possibly, rules governing State aid. In the medium to long term, evaluation could gradually lead to more fundamental changes in the general approach taken to State aid.

NOTES

7 The Commission's monitoring exercise is a periodic review of the legality of a sample of State aid measures implemented by Member States. It is designed to ensure that Member States are implementing Commission decisions correctly and are complying with the relevant legal provisions (i.e. those embodied in the General Block Exemption Regulation). The Commission also assesses compliance with the ex-ante rules and conditions among a representative sample of cases.

8 The primary objective of the annual reporting by Member States is to increase the transparency of State aid granted by Member States. It also provides a source of reliable statistics for policy-making and monitoring purposes. The data in annual reports provide information primarily in quantitative terms (for example, to show the objectives towards which State aid was directed and with what level of budget. The Commission uses Member States' reports to prepare the State aid Scoreboard.

9 Some State aid guidelines refer to a normal duration of four years for evaluated aid schemes.

3 THE EVALUATION PLAN

[5.48]

It is essential that a comprehensive plan for evaluating a State aid scheme be drafted at an early stage, in parallel with the design the scheme. Approval by the Commission of the evaluation plan is crucial to ensure equal treatment. This plan must then be rigorously implemented.

Indeed, it is generally recognised that evaluations are more effective when properly planned and prepared for in advance, in particular as this makes it easier to collect the appropriate data. Early planning is also likely to significantly reduce the resources required for the evaluation, and ultimately to improve its quality.

The evaluation plan to be notified by the Member State, according to the relevant rules, to the Commission should contain at least the following minimum elements.

3.1 OBJECTIVES OF THE AID SCHEME TO BE EVALUATED

The first stage in evaluating a scheme is to set out clearly the underlying 'intervention logic' of the aid scheme, describing the needs and problems the scheme intends to address, the target beneficiaries and investments, its general and specific objectives, and the expected impact. The main assumptions relating to external factors that might affect the scheme should also be mentioned.

3.2 THE EVALUATION QUESTIONS

The evaluation plan should define the scope of the evaluation, i.e. it should include precise questions that can be answered quantitatively and with the necessary supporting evidence. These evaluation questions should focus on the impact of the State aid scheme and can be classified according to the following three levels:

1. Direct impact of the aid on beneficiaries, e.g.:
   - Has the aid had a significant effect on the course of action taken by the aid beneficiaries? (incentive effect)
   - Has the aid had an effect on the situation of the beneficiaries? (For example, has its competitive position or default risk changed?)
   - To what extent has the aid had the effects expected?
   - Have beneficiaries been affected differently by the aid? (For example, according to their size, location or sector)
2. Indirect impact of the aid scheme, e.g.:
   - Has the scheme had spill-over effects on the activity of other firms or on other geographical regions? Did the aid crowd out investment from other competitors or attract activity away from neighbouring locations?
   - Has the scheme contributed to the relevant policy objective?
   - Can the scheme's aggregated effects on competition and trade be measured?
3. Proportionality and appropriateness of the aid scheme, e.g.:
   - Was the aid scheme proportionate to the problem being addressed? Could the same effects have been obtained with less aid or a different form of aid? (for example, loans instead of grants)
   - Was the most effective aid instrument chosen? Would other aid instruments or types of intervention have been more appropriate for achieving the objective in question?

The evaluation should, as far as is possible, assess the impact of the aid scheme at all three levels, addressing the relevant questions in respect of the scheme's objectives. However, the direct impact of aid on the beneficiaries is typically the type of impact that can most robustly be measured. In practice, the majority of evaluation methods that have been developed are designed for assessing this type of impact. Furthermore, evaluation of the direct effects of the aid, including the incentive effect, is of paramount importance as it can provide valuable insight into the types of indirect effects and distortions to be expected. In particular, where the aid provides no incentive effect, it can be assumed that the aid is distortive, in the sense that it provides the beneficiaries in question with windfall gains.

3.3 RESULT INDICATORS

The evaluation questions should lead to the choice of specific result indicators that capture quantified information about results achieved by the State aid scheme. Annex II provides an indicative and non-exhaustive list of result indicators covering both the direct and indirect impact of a scheme, including the possible effects on competition and trade. The result indicators will depend on the objective of the aid being evaluated. The evaluation plan should explain why the chosen indicators are the most relevant for measuring the impact of this aid scheme.

3.4 METHODS: FINDING AN APPROPRIATE BASIS FOR COMPARISON

State aid evaluations should be able to identify the causal impact of the scheme itself, undistorted by other variables that may have had an effect on the observed outcome, e.g. general macroeconomic conditions or firm heterogeneity (e.g. differences in firm size, firm location, financial means or management capabilities). The evaluation plan should set out the main methods that will be used in order to identify the effect of the aid, and discuss why these methods are likely to be appropriate for the scheme in question.

This causal impact is the difference between the outcome with the aid and the outcome in the absence of the aid. While the outcome with the aid is observed for firms who receive the aid, the outcome in the absence of the aid is only measured for firms who do not receive aid. By definition, we do not observe what the outcome would have been without the aid for the firms who received the aid. To estimate the effect of the aid on aid beneficiaries, it is therefore necessary to construct this counterfactual, based on the most comparable firm(s) or control group.

The quality of this control group is crucial for the validity of the evaluation.

Firms who receive aid may well be in a different situation from firms who do not receive aid. They might, for example, face different local supply and demand conditions, have less easy access to credit or be more or less efficient. These factors may all have an impact on the performance or activity level of the firms, both when they receive aid and when they do not. Comparing the performance of beneficiaries with that of non-beneficiaries is likely to reflect this reality more than the effect of the aid itself. An evaluation of the aid scheme cannot therefore rely on a simple comparison between beneficiaries and non-beneficiaries, but must take into account the different characteristics of the two groups of firms, both those which can be observed and those which cannot.

In the case of regional aid for example, aid beneficiaries in regions where market conditions are unfavourable (i.e. where the local product, labour or capital markets are weak) typically perform worse than non-beneficiaries in more prosperous regions. This by no means reflects the effect of the aid itself, however. The relevant question is whether they performed better than they would have without the aid, not whether they performed better than non-beneficiaries in other regions.

Similarly, general industry trends must also be taken into account when identifying the effect of the aid. Even if beneficiaries of regional aid reduce their staff numbers, the aid may still have been effective. For example, when conditions within a particular industry as a whole are deteriorating and all firms are cutting jobs, aid beneficiaries might reduce employment to a lesser extent than they would have otherwise. This is illustrated in the graph below, which shows a negative trend in the amount of employment provided by firms receiving aid, both before and after the aid was granted. Nevertheless, the trend becomes less negative after the firm has received the aid. The difference in the extended trend line without aid and the line showing employment actually offered by the firm after receiving the aid isolates the positive influence of the aid.

Figure 1 — positive influence of the aid where the current trend is negative

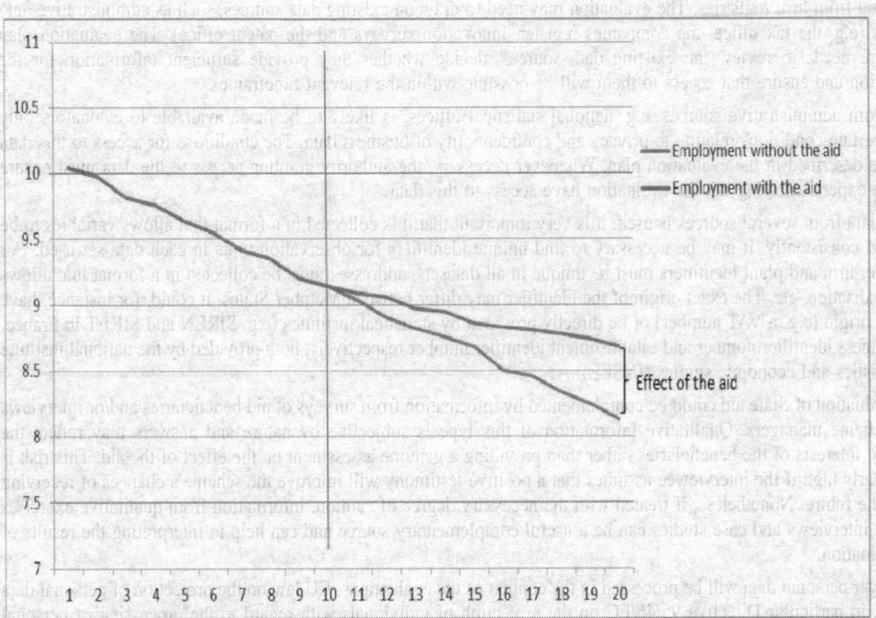

A specific problem emerges in terms of identifying a control group when non-beneficiaries have decided themselves to apply or not to apply for aid. For instance, if all firms are eligible (i.e. all firms who propose a project and apply for aid do receive some aid), then the firms who do not apply are likely to be those without projects. The firms' results may show that firms that did not receive aid performed worse in absolute and relative terms than those who did receive aid. This finding may however be entirely explained by the mere fact that the former group had no project to begin with, whereas the latter did, i.e. the management of the former group are lacking interest or creativity. It is therefore crucial that firms in the control group (firms who did not benefit from aid) are part of that group for reasons that have no influence on the measured outcomes. In particular, where firms have self-selected and voluntarily decided not to apply for aid, this condition may not be fulfilled.

Any systematic difference between State aid beneficiaries and non-beneficiaries should be properly accounted for in the design of the evaluation, in order to avoid a bias in the results (selection bias). In recent decades, several reliable methods have been developed to address this issue. The choice of method depends on the design of a particular State aid scheme and on the data available. The methods each have their limitations and are only valid when certain assumptions hold. Recognising and discussing these limitations and assumptions openly is crucial for the credibility of a study.

Randomising the process used for selecting beneficiaries is one way of making sure that the evaluation is unbiased. If aid beneficiaries are selected entirely at random, any systematic difference observed in the performance of the firms can be attributed to the aid. This method may however be difficult to implement in practice, in particular for large existing schemes. Other methods aim to use existing sources of exogenous variation in the environment in which firms operate (i.e. variation not determined by parameters and variables in the model) to identify causality.[10] Annex I to this guidance paper presents in more detail the most relevant methods, focusing on the practical aspects of their use. It discusses the way in which each method identifies causality, this being of particular importance in the context of State aid evaluations where the ex-ante design of the evaluation serves to ensure that a proper evaluation of the effects of the aid is possible.

Finally, the impact of multiple aid, either from one scheme, from several schemes or ad-hoc aid, should be controlled for. If non-beneficiaries in the given programme receive aid from other programmes, or if beneficiaries of the given programme receive additional aid from other programmes, the evaluation of the effects of the given aid scheme are likely to be distorted.

3.5 DATA COLLECTION: USING THE BEST POSSIBLE SOURCES

Consistent and sufficient data must be collected on both the aid beneficiaries and the control group Identifying the data required and obtaining access to the sources of the data forms are part of the planning of the evaluation.

Effective monitoring of the intervention and accurate collection and processing of data are crucial for ensuring the quality of the evaluation. As soon as the aid scheme is approved, a mechanism should therefore be put in place to monitor the intervention and to collect and process the appropriate data. This is likely to significantly reduce the costs of the evaluation.

Making sure that the necessary data on aid applicants and beneficiaries is collected is a crucial step in designing the evaluation plan, if the availability of this data can be made part of the eligibility conditions for aid.

With the exception of data on aid applications (including rejected applicants, when available), the data sources for aid beneficiaries and for the control group must be identical, for the data to be comparable. It is very likely that data will have to be taken from multiple sources, e.g. combining data from databases containing information about aid receipts with data from firm registries. The evaluation may need to draw on existing data sources, such as administrative data sources (e.g. the tax office, the companies register, innovation surveys and the patent office). The evaluation plan therefore needs to review the existing data sources, decide whether they provide sufficient information for the evaluation and ensure that access to them will be possible within the relevant timeframes.

Data from administrative sources, e.g. national statistical offices, is likely to be made available to evaluators only under certain conditions relating to privacy and confidentiality of business data. The conditions for access to this data must be described in the evaluation plan. Whenever necessary, the authority granting access to the data must ensure that the experts carrying out the evaluation have access to this data.

When data from several sources is used, it is very important that it is collected in a format that allows variables to be matched consistently. It may be necessary to find unique identifiers for observation units in each data set used. For example, firm and plant identifiers must be unique in all datasets, addresses must be collected in a format that allows geo-localisation, etc. The exact origin of the identifier may differ between Member States. It could, for instance, have a fiscal origin (e.g. a VAT number) or be directly provided by statistical institutes (e.g. SIREN and SIRET in France, the business identifier number and establishment identifier number respectively, both provided by the national institute for statistics and economic studies (INSEE)).

The evaluation of State aid could be complemented by information from surveys of aid beneficiaries and/or interviews with scheme managers. Qualitative information of this type is subjective by nature and answers may reflect the strategic interests of the beneficiaries rather than providing a genuine assessment on the effect of the aid. This risk is particularly high if the interviewee assumes that a positive testimony will improve the scheme's chances of receiving aid in the future. Nonetheless, if treated with the necessary degree of caution, information from qualitative exercises such as interviews and case studies can be a useful complementary source and can help in interpreting the results of the evaluation.

Whenever personal data will be processed in the context of the evaluations, EU law on the protection of personal data applies, in particular Directive 95/46/EC on the protection of individuals with regard to the processing of personal data and on the free movement of such data and the national legislation implementing it as well as Regulation (EC) No 45/2001 on the protection of individuals with regard to the processing of personal data by the Community institutions and bodies and on the free movement of such data.

3.6 TIMELINE OF THE EVALUATION

An evaluation plan should provide information on the precise timeline of the evaluation, which will be set in accordance with the approved duration of the scheme, and should include milestones, i.e. for collecting the data, carrying out the evaluation and submitting the final report. The timeline could vary according to the scheme and should therefore be discussed and agreed with the Commission on a case-by-case basis. Those involved in the management of schemes are advised to facilitate informal discussion on the content of the plan before submitting their official notification to the Commission.

In order to allow a proposed extension to an aid scheme to be assessed, the final evaluation report should be submitted to the Commission in sufficient time (e.g. six months before the scheme is scheduled to end). If no extension is envisaged the report can be submitted once the scheme has come to an end.

Figure 2 — overview of the evaluation process in the case of a notified scheme

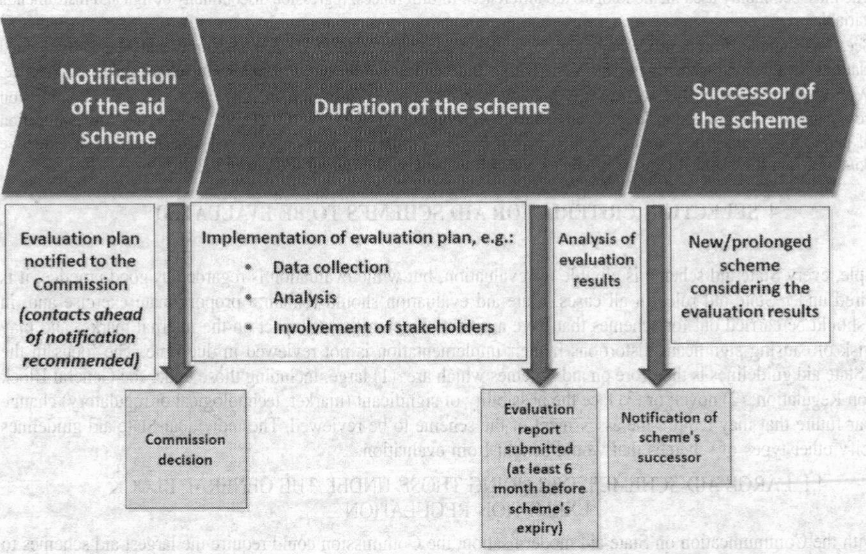

3.7 THE BODY CONDUCTING THE EVALUATION: ENSURING INDEPENDENCE AND EXPERTISE

Evaluation of the impact of State aid schemes should be objective, rigorous, impartial and transparent.[11] Each evaluation should be conducted on the basis of sound methodologies, by experts who have the adequate and proven experience and the methodological knowledge to carry out the exercise.

Evaluations should be carried out by a body that is at least functionally independent from the authority granting the aid, and that has the necessary and proven skills and appropriately qualified personnel to carry out such evaluations. The functional independence of the evaluator from the authority granting the aid is critical for ensuring the quality and credibility of the evaluation. This does not necessarily mean that a new body needs to be set up, nor that the evaluation needs to be outsourced to commercial evaluators. Depending on the specific organisations present in each Member State, it could be possible, for example, to make use of the independence and skills of organisations such as statistical offices, central banks, courts of auditors, public or private universities or research centres. This can be decided on a case-by-case basis for each scheme.

Early involvement of the body conducting the evaluation, for instance at the point of designing the scheme, is important for the success of an evaluation. It ensures that the State aid scheme will be able to be evaluated in the way proposed and guarantees that the necessary data will be collected. Whenever possible therefore, the evaluation plan should be drafted by, or at least in very close collaboration with, the designated evaluator. It should also include information, even if only of an indicative nature, on the necessary human and financial resources that will be made available for carrying out the evaluation. Information on the identity and role of each key expert involved in the evaluation and an estimate of their level of involvement are of particular relevance.

The evaluation plan should describe precisely the body conducting the evaluation or, if not yet chosen, the detailed criteria that will be used for its selection, in particular regarding independence, experience and skills. It should include existing alternatives whenever possible. Where the evaluator has not yet been selected, or has been selected but has not participated actively in the drafting of the evaluation plan, the reasons for this must be clearly stated. Even in this situation, the evaluation plan must be sufficiently detailed to allow a proper assessment of the validity of the evaluation to be made.

3.8 PUBLICITY: FACILITATING THE INVOLVEMENT OF STAKEHOLDERS

The evaluation should be made public. This implies that both the evaluation plan and the final evaluation report, once approved, should be given adequate publicity by being made available in the places described in the evaluation plan, for example, on a website. The Commission could also make these documents public.[12]

If data used for the evaluation is personal and/or confidential, confidentiality needs to be guaranteed throughout the process of the evaluation, namely in accordance with Articles 8, 16 and 17 of the EU Charter of Fundamental Rights. Nevertheless, confidentiality does not extend to the results of the evaluation. In particular, no confidentiality clause can be included in the contract for the evaluation, apart from: 1. non-disclosure obligations applying to personal and/or confidential data; and 2. obligations to comply with general provisions of national statistical law and statistical secrecy, such as related to the presentation of the results.

The data collected during the evaluation should be made accessible for the purpose of replicating results or for further studies under conditions not more restrictive than those imposed on the body conducting the initial evaluation.

The authority granting the aid could ensure appropriate involvement of relevant stakeholders, who should be consulted at least once during the implementation of the evaluation plan. For example, stakeholders could be invited to discuss initial evaluation findings on the basis of an interim report. Such arrangements should be included in the evaluation plan.

NOTES

10 The most commonly used methodologies are differences-in-differences, regression discontinuity design and instrumental variables.

11 See, for example, European Commission's Evaluation Standards, OECD Evaluation Norms and Standards, United Nations' Evaluation Standards and the World Bank's Independent Evaluation: Principles, Guidelines and Good Practice.

12 With the exception of business secrets and other confidential information in duly justified cases (Commission communication on professional secrecy in State aid decisions, C(2003) 4582, OJ C297, 9.12.2003, p 6). Any publication of personal data must be done in compliance with EU law on the protection of personal data, in particular Directive 95/46/EC and the national legislation implementing it as well as Regulation (EC) No 45/2001.

4 SELECTION CRITERIA FOR AID SCHEMES TO BE EVALUATED

[5.49]

In principle, every State aid scheme is eligible for evaluation, but while evaluation is regarded as good practice, it is not required under State aid rules in all cases. State aid evaluation should remain a proportionate exercise and, in general, should be carried out for schemes that have a potentially significant impact on the internal market and may carry a risk of causing significant distortions if their implementation is not reviewed in due time. The focus in the relevant State aid guidelines is therefore on aid schemes which are: (1) large, including those under the General Block Exemption Regulation; (2) novel; or (3) face the possibility of significant (market, technological or regulatory) change in the near future that may require the assessment of the scheme to be reviewed. The individual State aid guidelines also specify other types of schemes that would benefit from evaluation.

4.1 LARGE AID SCHEMES, INCLUDING THOSE UNDER THE GENERAL BLOCK EXEMPTION REGULATION

In line with the Communication on State aid modernisation, the Commission could require the largest aid schemes to be subject to evaluation, since: (1) such schemes can impact the single market most severely if not well designed; (2) the largest efficiency gains can be made due to their high budgets; and (3) large schemes with many different types of beneficiaries can provide sufficient data for evaluation.

Certain aid schemes may still not be subject to evaluation if, despite their size, they do not entail any specific problematic aspect (e.g. routine cases, cases where a high number of beneficiaries is each receiving small amounts of aid, and cases where there is no risk of significant changes or when no serious distortions could arise).

Furthermore, the new General Block Exemption Regulation (GBER) defines large aid schemes on the basis of their budget (average annual budget exceeding EUR 150 million) and, for some categories of aid[13] provides for their evaluation.

In order not to delay the entry into force of these large schemes, but also to ensure that they will be subject to an effective evaluation, the GBER provides for an exemption from notification for a maximum period of six months, which can be extended by the Commission upon approval of the evaluation plan.[14] The evaluation plan should be notified as soon as possible and at the latest within 20 working days following the scheme's entry into force.

The new GBER also foresees the case of modifications or successors of these large schemes subject to evaluation, which should be notified unless the modifications are of a purely formal and administrative nature or are carried out within the framework of the EU co-financed measures.

4.2 NOVEL AID SCHEMES

The definition of 'novelty' could vary across aid instruments and across Member States. Novelty will in principle be considered in terms of the nature of the aid scheme or the markets it is targeting, e.g. emerging markets where market developments are at a very early stage. These schemes have the potential to shape industries in a lasting and fundamental way. The scope for both benefits and distortions is therefore particularly large. Such novelty could include, for example, the introduction of a new capacity mechanism in the energy sector, aid to new types of technologies, or a novel type of support for renewable energy sources in the context of environmental aid. Evaluation of novel schemes also helps those currently designing new schemes as it allows them to take into account the latest developments on the market.

4.3 AID SCHEMES AFFECTED BY SIGNIFICANT FORESEEN CHANGES

The possibility of significant (market, technological or regulatory) changes in the near future will be assessed on a case-by-case basis. Such significant changes could include, for example, the anticipated revision of an applicable regulation or aid to fast-moving industries where the market environment and the available technologies are developing at a rapid pace. If schemes are not adapted to the effects of these significant changes, there is a risk that public funding will not be used effectively (for example, funding may be given to a potential 'market failure' which will cease to exist) or that significant distortions will arise affecting new market entrants differently to incumbent companies, or creating unequal conditions for new technologies and legacy technologies. As illustrative examples, the revision of an existing regulatory framework (for example, in the electronic communication sector), the high fluctuation of input or output prices (for example, in the case of solar panels) or the launch of a new technology on the market (for example, the availability of the fourth generation mobile network for broadband services) are all cases where evaluation could be justified, in order that future schemes can take new market developments into account.

4.4 OTHER AID SCHEMES

The guidelines for the different State aid fields also identify certain aid schemes where an evaluation would be particularly relevant.

Figure 3 — selection of aid schemes for evaluation purposes

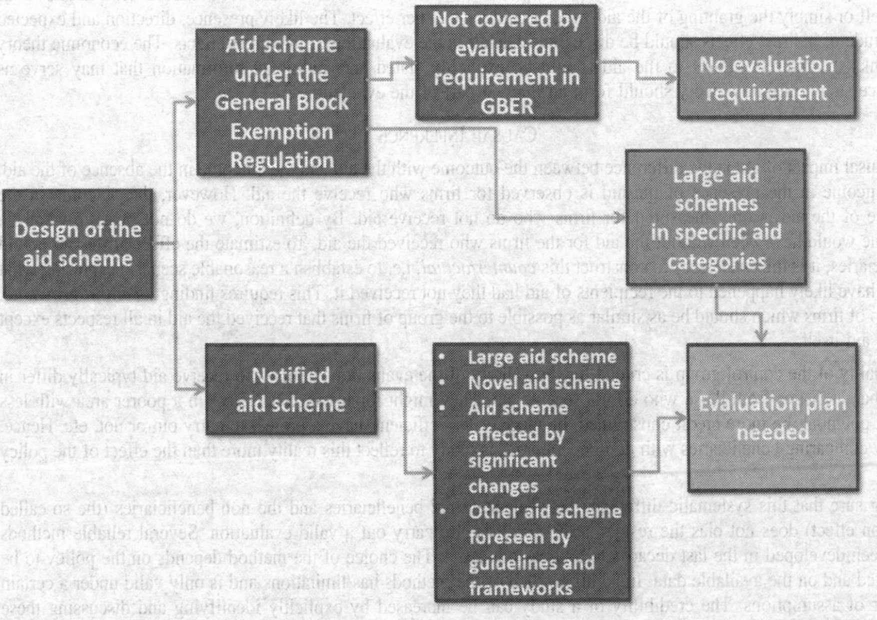

NOTES

13 Regional aid (except regional operating aid), aid for SMEs, aid for access to finance for SMEs, aid for R&D&I, aid for environmental protection (except aid in the form of reductions in environmental taxes under Directive 2003/96/EC) and aid for broadband infrastructures.

14 The Commission could also exceptionally decide that an evaluation is not necessary given the specificities of the case.

ANNEX I:
TECHNICAL APPENDIX ON RELEVANT METHODS TO IDENTIFY THE CAUSAL IMPACT

[5.50]

A State aid scheme can have impact at very different levels. It is normally expected to have a direct effect at the level of the beneficiary. Understanding the magnitude of this effect is crucial to assess the level of efficiency and effectiveness of a public measure. However, since aid is directed towards firms who interact in markets or regions which compete to attract economic activity, State aid also normally has indirect effects. These effects could for instance be spill-over effects on other firms (e.g. positive spill-overs from R&D or the crowding out of investment by other competing firms) or displacement effects (e.g. shifts in economic activity from one region to another). These indirect effects are the basis for both the potential harm and the benefits stemming from State intervention in the economy. Therefore, evaluating public measures requires assessing the magnitude of these indirect effects as well.

Measuring the direct and indirect effects of a policy normally requires the use of different tools. The last decades have seen an important development of methodologies and techniques intended at assessing the direct effect of policies on its beneficiaries. These techniques are presented in greater detail later in this section. Unfortunately, it is only in rare circumstances that these techniques will also allow assessing the indirect effects of the aid scheme on firms or regions. The evaluation of the indirect effects of the State aid scheme usually requires other types of evidence than what is used for assessing the direct effects on the recipients and interpretation normally relies more on economic theory and modelling. It is more difficult to provide precise guidance on this type of exercise as it has to be tailor made to the possible and expected positive and negative effects of the policy. Therefore, this evaluation has to be carried out after a careful and rigorous analysis of the most credible possible indirect effects of the policy. Based on this analysis, evaluators can derive measures based on micro data from non-aid beneficiaries, in particular in the same region, cluster or industry, as well as in neighbouring regions. This should form the core of the assessment of the indirect effects of the State aid scheme. If necessary, this can be complemented by more macroeconomic data and, most importantly, carefully chosen case studies.

The evaluation of direct effects is a necessary and crucial first step However, a rigorously performed assessment of the indirect effects of the aid serves as an important piece of evidence in the assessment of the broader effects of the scheme. If the absence of additional investment by aid beneficiaries is, broadly, indicative of failure of the policy, even a positive effect is not sufficient to conclude a policy has fulfilled its objectives. In particular, if it turns out that the direct impact of the aid on the beneficiaries is very small or even non-existent, the scheme is very likely to be considered as not fulfilling its goal, unless very convincing arguments can be made about the existence of large and beneficial indirect effects. The contrary is also true: even if the evaluation finds that positive direct effects for the aid, the question remains whether there may be negative indirect effects that offset or even outweigh these.

Moreover, it is not always easy to clearly separate direct and indirect effects. A firm might have invested more (alleged direct effect) because its own investment has crowed out investment by competing firms (interacting indirect effect). A firm might also invest more because it expects spill-overs and investments by other firms. Moreover, it might be the aid itself or simply the granting of the aid which could have either effect. The likely presence, direction and expected magnitude of indirect effects should be discussed in detail in the evaluation of the direct effects. The economic theory that links the indirect effects to the aid should be explicitly stated and additional information that may serve as evidence supporting this theory should form an integral part of the evaluation.[15]

CAUSAL INFERENCE

The causal impact of aid is the difference between the outcome with the aid and the outcome in the absence of the aid. The outcome in the presence of the aid is observed for firms who receive the aid. However, the outcome in the absence of the aid is only measured for firms who do not receive aid. By definition, we do not observe what the outcome would have been without the aid for the firms who received the aid. To estimate the effect of the aid on aid beneficiaries, it is thus necessary to construct this *counterfactual*, i.e. to establish a reasonable scenario capturing what would have likely happened to the recipients of aid had they not received it. This requires finding a *control group*, i.e. a group of firms which should be as similar as possible to the group of firms that received the aid in all respects except for the aid itself.

The quality of the control group is crucial for the validity of the evaluation. Firms who receive aid typically differ in their characteristics from those who do not receive aid. They might for instance be active in a poorer area with less market potential, be more credit constrained, be more or less efficient, have a project to carry out or not, etc. Hence, naively comparing beneficiaries with non-beneficiaries is likely to reflect this reality more than the effect of the policy itself.

Making sure that this systematic difference between State aid beneficiaries and the non-beneficiaries (the so-called selection effect) does not bias the results is the core issue to carry out a valid evaluation. Several reliable methods have been developed in the last decades to address this issue. The choice of the method depends on the policy to be evaluated and on the available data. In addition, each of the methods has limitations and is only valid under a certain number of assumptions. The credibility of a study can be increased by explicitly identifying and discussing these limitations. This technical annex presents the most relevant methods, focusing on the most practical aspects and stressing the importance of a good identification strategy.[16]

A. RANDOMISED EXPERIMENTS

The identification of a proper control group is key to obtaining good (i.e. unbiased) estimates of the effect of the policy. The most favourable case is when there is no selection effect because beneficiaries were selected randomly.[17] Then, there is no systematic difference between beneficiaries and non-beneficiaries apart from the aid and the difference in the outcomes can be attributed to the policy.

However, random selection of aid beneficiaries is sometimes criticised for being at odds with the aim of many schemes to select the best possible aid beneficiaries on the basis of objective criteria. Still, in certain circumstances it might be possible to introduce elements of randomness in the eligibility or in the incentives to participate of beneficiaries. One example is setting a fixed budget for the given scheme. If the applicants' demand for support exceeds the budget and they are fairly equal in their characteristics, then one may try to establish randomness in treatment. Another example is randomly exposing potential recipients of aid to different levels of information about the scheme.

Pilot projects provide further opportunities for random allocation of aid. In case of innovative policies it might be advisable to evaluate a smaller scale pilot first. This pilot could have a smaller size and beneficiaries may more easily be chosen randomly. Another alternative would be to ramp-up a scheme, for instance to make eligible 25% of randomly selected firms the first year to respectively 50, 75 and 100% the second, third and fourth year (or alternatively, to advertise the scheme to a larger and larger audience). For a new policy, a period of ramp-up is in many cases an administrative necessity.

These ideas may be better suited for the implementation of totally new schemes or a large variation of existing schemes. It is probably fairly difficult to randomise eligibility (directly or indirectly) for the continuation of an existing scheme. However, this does not mean that random experiments cannot be used for parts of their evaluation. In particular, it is still possible to randomly select beneficiaries for potentially more efficient, more targeted and/or less distortive variants of the scheme. For instance, in the case of a grant scheme, it may be possible to randomly propose a newly introduced loan scheme instead.

B. QUASI-EXPERIMENTAL METHODS

Even though random experiments are the best possible way to evaluate the effect of policies, it is not always possible to implement them. Other methods have been developed to evaluate the effects of a policy from an ex-post perspective. They share the aim to use exogenous variations of the environment in which firms operate, to create situations very close to experiments (so-called natural or quasi-experiments).

It is generally a challenge for ex-post assessment to identify natural or quasi-experiments. However, a careful analysis of the design of the policy can entail an analysis of the existence of sufficient exogenous variation. If necessary, the initial setup can be adjusted to introduce more elements to allow identification of the effects of the policy.

CONTROLLING FOR OBSERVABLE DIFFERENCES

As explained above, there normally exist significant differences between aid beneficiaries and non-aid beneficiaries. It is then necessary to account for these differences when comparing the outcomes between the two groups of aid and non-aid beneficiaries.

Many of the differences in characteristics are typically observable. The most common way to take these differences into account is to use linear regression. Linear regression seeks to control for the influence of observed characteristics on the outcomes. It assumes a linear relationship between the outcome, for instance the investment in R&D, and other characteristics of the firm, for instance the sector, age, size etc., including the granting of the aid. It is possible to see linear regression as a linear approximation of more complicated relationships.[18] Linear regressions can be seen as general purpose techniques and are used in many different evaluation contexts.

An alternative to linear regression is to use matching techniques. Matching techniques aim at pairing each beneficiary with another firm that 'looks' very similar but did not receive aid. The observables used for matching can be firm characteristics or the estimated probability to receive aid (propensity score matching). Matching can be a useful way to control for observables in the context of a valid empirical strategy.

However, both simple linear regression and matching have some intrinsic limitations. Both are only valid under the so-called conditional independence assumption. This condition requires that, once the impact of the observable characteristics has been taken into account, the outcome is independent of the observable characteristics. In practice, this normally requires that every variable that impacts both the outcome and the selection is observable (and is taken into account with the proper functional form). If this is not the case, the mere fact that a firm participates reflects certain (unobserved) characteristics of the firm that also drive its performance. Both linear regression and matching will fail to provide a valid evaluation. For instance, if a firm has a 'promising project', this both affects the likelihood that it will apply for aid (and get aid) and the likelihood that the firm is successful in growing a business. Not taking this into account will bias the results.

In particular, in the case of matching, comparing the outcomes between a beneficiary and its matched 'twin' without aid, allows avoiding the selection effect only if the granting of the aid is unrelated to unobserved variables that also influence the outcome. In reality, this assumption will rarely be fulfilled. Measuring all the variables that have an impact on the fact of applying or getting aid is rarely possible. Implementing matching techniques moreover requires that firms who get aid are very similar in their observable characteristics to those not getting it. If the matched firms are truly similar in every observable aspect, the reason why some firms received aid and some others did not are, by definition, unobserved. The justification to the validity of a matching-based evaluation or a simpler classical linear regression can thus not be the mere existence of a very complete dataset with many observed characteristics.

On the contrary, the potential justification for the use of matching or simpler linear regression in evaluation relies on the fact that these unobserved reasons that explain eligibility or attribution of aid have no direct or indirect influence on the outcomes (once controlled for the observables). For an evaluation based on simple matching or linear regression to be valid, one would need to be confident that the set of firms who did not receive aid has been exogenously determined. This requires that once the observables are controlled for, there remains no unobserved factor explaining eligibility or attribution of aid that would also directly or indirectly influence the outcomes. In general, matching firms that are equally eligible for aid will not fulfil this latter criterion. For instance, if all firms are eligible, firms who get investment aid are much more likely to have a project than firms who did not get aid (as they would also have applied and been granted aid otherwise). Overall, firms with a project are more likely to grow in terms of sales or employment, but this is not related to aid and matching on observables is not able to disentangle the two (unless we measure the existence of a comparable investment project).

In many situations, the conditional independence assumption is bound to fail. It may therefore be necessary to implement different techniques than mere linear regression or matching to account for the existence of unobserved selection into the treatment.

The remainder of this section presents the most common methodologies used to assess policy impact in this context in more detail, i.e. Differences-in-Differences, Regression Discontinuity Design (RDD), Instrumental Variables (IV). These methodologies derive their validity from different assumptions and the best choice is normally driven by the context of the policy and the availability of data. This presentation sets out the merits and weaknesses of each particular technique. With the noticeable exception of randomised controlled treatments ('RCT') presented above, there exists no technique superior to all the other ones in every aspect. The choice of a particular technique has to be guided by a careful analysis of the context of the measure and the available data.

It is worth stressing here that it is not the use of a specific econometric technique that allows identifying the effects of a policy; it is the exogeneity of the control group and hence the quality of the counterfactual. The quality of the evaluation study will therefore crucially depend on how convincingly the researcher can establish the exogeneity of the control group In cases where residual biases might remain, it is essential to discuss these biases in detail, including their sources and the directions and likely magnitude of their effects on the results.

A.
Difference in Difference

Rationale and identification

As explained earlier, a simple comparison between beneficiaries and even a well-chosen group of non-beneficiaries is unlikely to lead to a valid evaluation. The reason for this is that it is not possible to exclude the existence of unobserved differences between the two groups, leading to a persistent difference in outcomes even in the absence of the aid. Moreover, simply comparing the outcomes before and after the aid for beneficiaries is also likely to lead to a spurious evaluation. It does not allow disentangling the effects of the aid from the effects of other factors that also affect the outcome of the two groups, for instance the general economic trend, changes in the regulatory environment or increasing labour cost.

However, combining the two approaches might allow assessing the causal effect of the aid: this is the Difference-in-Difference approach. The general idea is to consider the difference in outcome between firms over time. Pre-existing differences would be attributed to other factors than the State aid. Only the change in these differences (the 'Difference-in-Difference') would be attributed to the aid. In other words, the method compares the difference in the performance between beneficiaries and control group *before* the aid as well as *after* the aid and then attributes the change in the difference to the aid. The method works if, over time, both the beneficiaries and the control group are affected by the other factors that also affect performance in the same way. It can then be concluded that the aid is the only relevant factor that explains the observed change in performance of beneficiaries relative to the control group.

The crucial assumption is that the differences between beneficiaries and control group are stable over time and that both groups are affected identically by common shocks (deviations from the mean) during the period. This assumption can fail in practice. For instance, if beneficiaries are the more vulnerable firms, they are likely to be more affected by economic downturns and general business climate. Therefore, the control group has equally to be made of vulnerable firms. Overall, the choice of the control group is the key for the validity of the method. Identification does not lie in the use of differences-in-differences, which is the mere technical implementation, but in the proper choice of control group.

Special care in the construction of the control group is needed if non-beneficiaries decided themselves not to apply for aid. Applying or not for aid can be expected to be related to the returns of getting the aid. Therefore, there are reasons to believe that the anticipated outcomes of firms who do not apply for aid (in terms of employment, productivity, sales, etc.) differ from the expected outcomes for beneficiaries. For instance, if all firms who apply for aid get some aid, the only eligible firms who do not apply are those without a project (assuming the cost to apply is low). These firms are not only likely to perform worse in absolute terms but also comparatively worse as time passes, while better firms implement projects and grow. Employment, productivity or sales cannot be expected to remain parallel and double differentiation does not, in general, solve the problem.

Therefore, firms in the control group who did not benefit from aid need to have been selected for reasons that have no influence on the measured outcomes. They cannot have self-selected and voluntarily decided not to participate. The most convincing setup is when nonparticipation is related to non-eligibility that is the consequence of a natural experiment. In this case, non-eligibility is unlikely to be due to unobserved factors that also have an influence on the outcomes. Control groups could for instance be firms located in regions no longer eligible for aid (if this eligibility is not related to their own performance but rather to an exogenous event).

Implementation

From a technical point of view, difference-in-difference methods can be implemented either within a linear regression model or with matching. In the former case, the control group is chosen independently of the observable characteristics and therefore overall comparable to the whole group of the aid beneficiaries. Then, observable differences are taken into account in a classical linear regression. In the second case, the control group is made of firms that are individually comparable to each aided-firm in the sample based on observable factors. The outcome for each firm is compared to the outcome of its most comparable firm(s) and the results are aggregated. The two methods are two different ways to take observable differences into consideration but there is no a fundamental difference in terms of identification of the causal effect of the policy.

Depending on the circumstances, it may be worthwhile to compare the variations of outcomes of the beneficiaries and the control group before the aid. If the outcomes systematically start diverging already before the aid has actually been granted, it is likely that the control group and the group of the beneficiaries are diverging for reasons unrelated to the aid and the method does not give a valid estimate of the causal effect of the aid. This does not constitute a rigorous test of the validity of the assumption: such a test does not exist. However, this is at least a useful first sanity check.

Additional methods and robustness tests can be used when there several potential control groups exist which are a priori valid. The first and most natural robustness check is to implement several difference-in-difference estimators and to compare the results. In addition, it is also possible to use these different control groups to build a more reliable estimate. Imagine a scheme targeted at SMEs in a particular region. Two potential control groups are the non-SME firms in this region or SMEs is an adjacent region. None of these firms voluntarily decided not to apply for aid, they were simply not eligible. Nevertheless, neither of these control groups is perfect: larger firms in the same region are likely to be affected differently by general economic trends while SMEs in an adjacent region might be subject to different regional shocks. Instead of choosing between these two possible difference-indifference estimators, it is possible to combine them and implement a triple difference estimator (DDD): starting from the 'classical' difference-in-difference between SMEs and non-SMEs in the concerned region, one can subtract the same difference-in-difference from the adjacent region to cancel the variation in outcomes between SMEs and non-SMEs in the region with aid.[19] Alternatively, one could systematically try to build a synthetic control group, made of SMEs from several adjacent regions and non-SMEs from the same region in order better replicate the pattern of the outcome for the beneficiaries before the aid (see Abadie, Diamond and Hainmuller, 2010 for details).

Inference

In addition to a careful design and choice of control group, the issue of inference has to be specifically addressed. The notion of inference in this context refers to the question of whether the effects that have been estimated are really significant. Statistical significance is a different issue from economic significance. The second one refers to the magnitude of the estimated effects compared to the other relevant parameters from an economic theory point of view. As explained earlier, economic significance is crucial. However, this discussion is in principle only relevant when, from a statistical point of view, the effects are estimated precisely enough, i.e. one can exclude that there is no effect at all.

There are reasons to believe that a straightforward inference under standard assumptions (such as the homoscedasticity assumption and the assumption of no autocorrelation) is likely to overestimate the statistical significance of the effects.[20]

The first problem is related to clustering of data. If the control group as well as the group of the beneficiaries are each very homogenous (even if distinct from each other), all firms in each group are likely to be affected by similar deviations from the mean (shocks). In statistical terms, this means that the error term has a common component. If the variance of this common component is large compared to variation in outcomes observed for individual firms, the inference will be biased. With two periods and two groups, the problem can be particularly severe and borderline to an identification issue: it is impossible to separate the effect of the shocks shared within each group from the effect of the policy. The problem does not need to be as severe if the groups are not so homogeneous. However, it is always necessary to reflect on the presence of common shocks for homogeneous subsets of the groups. For instance if demand is local, it will normally be necessary to correct for the clustered structure of the error term at the level of localities. The same could apply to industries or sectors.

The second problem emerges when panel data are used. Error terms of most firm level data like employment, productivity and investment are normally auto-correlated. This means that deviations from the mean in one period are likely to persist in the next period. Ignoring this issue leads to overestimating the precision of the estimation of the effects and to rejecting, more often than one should, the hypothesis that the policy has had no effect. This problem can be severe, as shown in Bertrand, Duflo, and Mullainathan (2004).

B.
Instrumental Variables

Rationale and identification

Instrumental variables ('IV') is a classical method to deal with endogeneity of explanatory variables. Since benefiting from aid can be seen as an endogenous explanatory variable of the performance of a firm in a linear regression context, it is natural to use instrumental variables to evaluate the effect of aid.

A variable is endogenous when it is correlated with an unobserved element, which also determines the outcome. For example, imagine that one tries to identify the effect of State grant on firms' employment by regressing employment on programme participation and other observables. Let us imagine that the aid programme targets underperforming firms who are likely to face difficult local market conditions. Market conditions are not observable by the evaluator and hence cannot be controlled for directly. However, when this variable is left unaccounted for, the effect of the grant is likely to be underestimated by the evaluator due to the endogeneity of programme participation. Whether the firm faces favourable or difficult market conditions has an impact on both programme participation and on employment, i.e. programme participation is correlated with the error term explaining employment. The impact of market conditions on programme participation means that it is impossible to attribute the entire correlation between programme participation and employment to the causal impact of aid.

However, there also exist other factors explaining programme participation but not employment. For instance, as in Criscuolo et al (2012), geographical location may determine the total amount of money available for the programme in the region. Moreover the list of regions covered by the programme changes over time. If the programme budget for a given region changed over time for external reasons (e.g. average EU's GDP per capita dropped), this has an effect on the programme participation but not on firm's local market conditions. The change in employment that is related to the exogenous change in the programme coverage is not related to local market conditions. By focusing on this 'part' of programme participation variable it is possible to isolate the true impact of the participation on firm's employment without interference of local market conditions. This is the logic of instrumental variables.

For the evaluation of State aid, an instrumental variable is a variable that can explain the fact of receiving the aid but has no direct impact on the other unobserved determinants of the outcome that has to be measured. Instrumental variables then allow focusing on the participation in the scheme without interference from the selection effects. For illustrative purposes, one can see the logic of instrumental variable as follows.[21] In a first step, programme participation is regressed on all the exogenous variables, including the instrumental variables. In a second step, the participation variable (the variable indicating whether the aid was received) is replaced with the participation as predicted in the first step: this expected participation is not correlated with the unobserved element that also determines the outcome.

Issues with weak instruments

An instrumental variable is a variable that can explain the fact of receiving the aid but has no direct impact on the other unobserved determinants of the outcome that has to be measured. This simple and classical definition, however hides a number of practical difficulties. There exist tests aimed at checking for the consistency of instruments when more instruments are used than what is strictly necessary to identify a model. However, there exists no test of the validity of instruments. The main focus of a study using instrumental variables generally is to explain why each individual instrument can be assumed to be uncorrelated with the unobserved determinants of the performance of the firms, would it be employment, productivity, sales, investment, etc. Such explanations, based both on economic arguments and factual elements, are necessary to assess the validity of the evaluation. However, they are not sufficient, especially when several instruments are used.

The discussion of the quality of instrumental variables should include the issue of weak instruments, i.e. instruments weakly correlated with the outcome variable. When instrumental variables are poorly correlated with the endogenous variable, estimates are likely to be imprecise. One might be tempted to add more instrumental variables in that situation. It is well known that by instrumenting with a large enough number of variables, it is possible to recover enough of the initial variable to get statistically significant results. At the same time, the two stage least squares naturally gets closer and closer to the biased ordinary least squares estimate.[22] The potential for such bias should be explicitly addressed in any evaluation using the IV method. In particular, the issue of the credibility, not only of their individual, but also of their joined exogeneity has to be addressed.

A special case arises when the endogenous variable is assumed to be auto-correlated. If the source of endogeneity is assumed to be solely contemporaneous, it is then possible to use past values as instrumental variables. However, one would then have to reflect on the exact validity of this approach. For instance, if explanatory variables are auto-correlated, this could also be the case of the measured outcome. Then, the lagged variables are also endogenous. More generally, if the autocorrelation of the explanatory variables is very large, exogeneity assumptions might fail. If it is small, one could resort to using many lags (and potentially future values) and would risk falling in the pitfall of using many weak instruments described before. Overall, instrumenting by past values could be a valid strategy but it should be used with caution.

Generally speaking, to avoid the problems described earlier, it is highly advisable to only use a small number of convincing instruments. It is then, however also necessary to show that the instruments are good predictors of the endogenous explanatory variable.[23]

Variations of two step estimations: Heckman (1979) selection model

When the endogeneous variable is a treatment variable (participation dummy), the first regression of the two stage least squares can be seen as a linear probability model of the probability to be treated. This linear probability model is a linear approximation. However, in some cases, the probability to be treated, even restricting to eligible firms, might be low. Then, linear approximations might be too coarse to effectively approximate this probability to be treated and to focus on the tails of the distribution, which are precisely the matter of interest. There are several ways to deal with this issue. They all rely on replacing the linear probability model of the probability to be treated by a non-linear function.[24]

A classical approach is to treat the evaluation problem in the context of a selection model (Heckman, 1979). This approach treats the selection effect as an omitted variable problem in the linear regression of the outcome on the observables and the participation.[25] Several variants of this methodology exist, for example estimating the whole model by maximum likelihood, or instrumenting the granting of aid by the predicted value of the selection equation.[26]

However, it is crucial to reflect on the identification and in particular on the choice of variables. It is not satisfactory to use the same variables in both steps of the estimation, even if the results are sufficiently precise.[27]

It is only reliable to estimate a selection model with a so-called exclusion variable. An excluded variable is a variable that explains selection of the aid beneficiary but not the outcome. It is not sufficient to remove one variable from the main equation to add it to the list of explanatory variables of the selection equation. On the contrary, this exclusion variable has to explain the selection but have no impact on the outcome one is trying to explain. It is in substance very close to a valid instrumental variable. The choice of such a variable cannot be driven by convenience; it has to come from economic theory, institutional structure and/or experience.

C.
Regression Discontinuity Design

Regression discontinuity design (RDD) is the latest addition to the evaluation toolbox.[28] It has known a large success in the academic community in the last decade, mostly due to its simplicity. This method exploits the existence of a variable which has a discontinuous impact on the probability to be affected by a policy. In the context of State aid schemes, several types of discontinuities can be useful. The first one is geographical borders: the eligibility of schemes can be linked to precise administrative borders, like localities, NUTS regions, etc. The second one comes from conditions imposed on the firms which benefit from a scheme, in particular in terms of age and size.

Let us consider an example. Imagine that projects presented by firms are rated by points (out of 100) and firms who get at least 70 points get aid while the others get no aid. A firm who scores 71 has a marginally better project than a firm who scores 69. However, the consequence of this marginal difference is dramatic: one gets some aid, while the second gets no aid at all. Comparing the outcomes for these two firms is thus very indicative of the causal effect of the aid.

Formally, the RDD requires that the probability to receive aid is discontinuous, while all the other variables are continuous.[29] The technical implementation can be very close to this of instrumental variable, using a threshold crossing dummy as instrument. However, there are two main differences. The first one is that RDD relies on weaker assumptions. In particular, we do not a priori require the independence of the instrument. For instance, in the case of scoring, firms with better project might apply more than firms with bad projects. The only requirement is that around the threshold the probability to apply should not be discontinuous. The second difference is that the estimates are built only on firms very close to both sides of the threshold. Weaker assumptions thus come at a cost: RDD estimates are even more local than estimates by instrumental variables generally are. If the effects of the aid differ for firms further away from the threshold, the RDD estimates are not a correct estimate of the effect on all aid beneficiaries.

The locality of these estimates can be of concern if one would expect large discrepancies of effects away from the threshold. Moreover, individual companies on the other side of the border could be very significantly affected by the policy. This could for instance be the case if displacement effects are important. Then, the use of RDD at the geographical border is not a good empirical strategy. Last, the strength of the RDD is to focus on a narrow bandwidth around the discontinuity. If the bandwidth is large, the impact of the other characteristics cannot be assumed to be constant. This issue is normally not solved by controlling for the observables, which assumes a particular functional form.

Graphical inspection of the data can provide comfort as regards the reliability of the assumption underlying RDD. In particular, it is very important to control for three things. The first one is that there indeed is a discontinuity on the granting of aid at the threshold. The second one is that the outcomes to be measured have a discontinuity at the same moment and no other discontinuity of the same kind anywhere else. Third, it is also necessary to check that there exists no discontinuity in the other parameters correlated with the outcome, including the propensity to apply for aid. At last, discontinuities might be created deliberately in order to allow an evaluation of the scheme. In particular, ramp-up of policies could be used to create discontinuities and help the identification of the effects of a policy.

C. STRUCTURAL ESTIMATION

In some instances, it is possible to go a step further and confront a theoretical model, for instance of firms' investments, with the data in order to recover the key parameters of interest. This approach is qualitatively different from those presented before. Structural estimation uses a completely specified theoretical model of firm behaviour.

Estimation then allows recovering parameters determining firm's behaviour. This allows an evaluation at the closest of the determinants of the individual behaviour of firms and enables to carry out simulations about the efficiency of other tools. However, structural estimation is generally more demanding in terms of resources and data as well as in terms of assumptions.

It is impossible to provide precise guidance on structural estimation as the identification, estimation and inference has to be derived on a case by case basis. Nevertheless, the general guidance provided before still applies. First, it is necessary that the theoretical model matches the key stylised facts of the market. Second, the issues of unobserved characteristics and selection have to be explicitly and properly addressed.

D. ADDITIONAL METHODOLOGICAL REMARKS

Heterogeneity of treatment effects

The previous sections focused on the estimation of the average treatment effect on the treated. The very name suggests that the effect of the aid varies between beneficiaries. This heterogeneity may have many roots and many consequences. The first consequence might be that, if aid is very effective for some firms but much less for others, the average effect might be statistically insignificant. This absence of statistically significant effect does not mean that the aid has no effect for any firms. From a policy perspective, the average performance of a scheme is a very interesting first indicator. However, trying to understand the determinants of this heterogeneity is as important for the design of better schemes. It allows focusing directly on firms where the aid is the most effective and least distortive.

Thereby, whenever possible, the effect of the aid should be estimated for different types of firms, such as small firms vs large firms, young firms vs old firms, innovative firms, credit constrained firms, etc.[30]

Distortions on the non-aided firms

Evaluating the impact of the scheme on non-participants, either directly or indirectly, is very informative for the evaluation of State aid. State aid may be distorting markets via effects on the non-beneficiaries, for example by knowledge spill overs from beneficiaries or by the reduction in relative competitiveness vis-à-vis beneficiaries, etc.

Moreover, the effects on the non-aided firms or locations can have an effect on the validity of the evaluation. For example, a part of the effect of regional aid could materialise by opportunities at the border: firms historically located on the 'wrong' side of the border moving their location just on the other side. Then, an RDD at the border would mostly capture this displacement effect and would risk overestimating the real aggregate effect of the policy. In such a situation, another empirical strategy has to be used (for example it may be useful to check the robustness of the evaluation on wider regions).

E. DATA

Having access to appropriate microeconomic data that enables conducting impact evaluation is crucial. These data have to be consistent between beneficiaries and non-beneficiaries. Therefore, they need to have the same source, with the natural exception of information on the aid itself. The data should be from accessible at the most refined level although in some cases some form of aggregation at a later stage may be necessary.

Data capturing the result indicators of both the treatment as well as the control group are necessary, including the time at which the outcome is measured. Furthermore, as much data as possible on factors potentially influencing outcomes and the entities' decision to participate in the aid programme are necessary. This data is used to 'control for' differences between the treatment and control groups. For example, on the firm level such data may include location, size and demographics, as well as production inputs used.

The most natural source of data is of administrative origin, such as fiscal balance sheet data, or national surveys. These sources provide information on the location and activity of firms, and sometimes of individual plants. They normally allow to track investment and sales by activity as well as to compute financial ratios. Large national or community surveys, such as Community Innovation Surveys are also of interest. They cover a large and representative sample and provide very complementary information on specific topics. Last, merged employer-employees datasets are also a relevant source of information. They normally allow relating labour characteristics to each plant location. This can be crucial when the geographical dimension of labour is a matter of interest.

Apart from indicators on results and recipient characteristics, data about the aid and the aid granting process is necessary. This information would usually come from the aid granting authority itself. This includes data on the amount and timing of granting of the aid to beneficiaries. However, general data on the process of attribution of the aid is also particularly helpful. Data on rejected applicants is important, especially if the granting of the aid is made using a scoring mechanism.[31]

Access to such confidential data is normally regulated. Securing timely access to these data for the whole of the scientific team performing the evaluation is therefore crucial. Moreover, these administrative sources are normally accessible at a delay. It is important to take into account data availability when designing the evaluation plan.

F. EXAMPLES

Example 1 (Regional aid): Criscuolo et al. (2012)[32] have evaluated the Regional Selective Assistance ('RSA') scheme in the UK between 1986 and 2004. In this period, RSA provided discretional grants to firms in disadvantaged areas. It was the main business support scheme in the UK. The scope for aid given under the RSA was governed by the Regional Aid Guidelines, in particular the maps of eligible regions ('regional aid maps'). These maps have evolved over time. By and large, the criterion for eligibility for a region is the relative position of the region in terms of GDP per capita or unemployment. Thereby, the status of a region can change either because it had developed over time or because the average EU per capita GDP changed (for instance when new member states joined the EU in 1995). Moreover, the indicators used to determine eligibility also change over time. Therefore, part of the change of eligibility of the firms does not depend on the situation of the firms themselves, but rather on events occurring outside of the UK or on changes in administrative rules. By focusing on this part of the changes in eligibility and assessing how these changes resulted in changes in investment activity, employment and productivity, Criscuolo et al. (2012) are able to convincingly identify the impact of the aid.[33]

Example 2 (Enterprise support): Martini and Bondonio (2012)[34] have examined two cases of enterprise support — an investment grant available throughout Italy (Law 488) and various SME schemes in the region of Piemonte. The first evaluation is particularly interesting. It compares the firms who saw their aid application approved (i.e. the aid-beneficiaries) with comparable firms who saw their aid application rejected as the budget that was available for the aid had reached its limit. The use of rejected applicants in the evaluation is particularly useful to avoid the selection bias which typically arises if one were to just compare applicants with non-applicants. This group of firms had passed the first quality check, which means that they had a credible investment project. Therefore, they shared with the aid beneficiaries the same ambition to invest in a credible project. However, because of budgetary limits (rationing), they did not receive aid. The difference in performance between (just) successful applicants and (closely) rejected applicants provided a reliable estimate of the effect of aid.

Example 3 (Loan guarantees): Lelarge, Sraer and Thesmar (2010) evaluate the effects of a loan guarantee programme in France. The 'SOFARIS' programme provides insurance to lenders against borrowers' risk of default through guarantees. Borrowers pay an insurance premium, but this premium is subsidised. Lelarge, Sraer and Thesmar (2010) explicitly describe the nature of the selection effects. First, firms with more profitable projects are more likely to accept to pay the fee associated to the guarantee. Second, programme managers are likely to select socially desirable projects which might not otherwise get access to private funding. Overall, firms self-select into the programme and selection also occurs at the granting phase. This is likely to affect the results of naïve evaluations, based for instance on classical linear regressions or comparisons with the most comparable firm.[35] However, the factual and institutional context of the programme provides a source of identification of the effects of the policy. The programme was set up in the late 1980s and was initially restricted to firms active in the manufacturing and business services industries. In 1995, the public endowment of the programme was increased and new industries (construction, retail and wholesale trade, transportation, hotels and restaurants and personal services) became eligible. Lelarge, Sraer and Thesmar (2010) compare the newly eligible firms to the previously eligible firms to assess the effect of the programme on various indicators, like debt, employment, capital growth, financial expenses and probability of bankruptcy. Firms in these two groups are likely to differ. However, firms should be affected by similar macroeconomic shocks and therefore, their differences should not change over time, except for the expected effects of the policy itself.[36]

Example 4 (Creative Credit): Bakhshi et al.,[37] use a randomised control trial experiment to assess the effect of an innovative business support scheme. The pilot study, which began in Manchester in 2009, was structured so that vouchers, or 'Creative Credits', would be randomly allocated to small and medium-sized businesses applying to invest in creative projects such as developing websites, video production and creative marketing campaigns, to see if they had a real effect on innovation. Creative Credits created genuinely new relationships between SMEs and creative businesses, with the award of a Creative Credit increasing the likelihood that firms would undertake an innovation project with a creative business they had not previously worked with by at least 84 per cent. The research found that the firms who were awarded Creative Credits enjoyed a short-term boost in their innovation and sales growth in the six months following completion of their creative projects. However, the positive effects were not sustained, and after 12 months there was no longer a statistically significant difference between the groups that received the credits and those that didn't. The report argues that these results would have remained hidden using the normal evaluation methods used by government, and calls for RCTs to be used more widely when evaluating policies to support business growth.

Example 5 (R&D&I support): Einiö (2013) has studied the impacts of Tekes's R&D subsidies on R&D investment, employment, and productivity in the period 2000–2006. Tekes is a national innovation agency responsible for the major part of R&D support in Finland. The study exploits regional variation in potentially awardable Tekes R&D support budget that arises from the higher ERDF funding in parts of the Northern and Eastern Finland (Objective 1 areas). These areas were initially determined in the accession negotiations of Finland in 1995 and were based on the no more than 8 persons per square kilometre population density rule. As a result of the relatively larger R&D support budget, the likelihood of receiving the support was higher in Objective 1 areas as compared to other parts of the country. This induced regional variation in treatment with a substantially larger fraction of companies being supported in the Objective 1 region. Because the regional allocation was based on the predetermined population density rule based on the 1993 densities (and not on expected future levels of R&D investment or economic performance, for example), the study controls for the 1993 population density which effectively addresses concerns about regional selection. In practice, the treatment effects are estimated with an instrumental variables approach where an indicator for Objective 1 region is used as an instrument for programme entry. This approach identifies the impact of the support among those companies that entered the support scheme as a result of higher funding in the Objective 1 area. Validity of the setup is confirmed by showing that pre-programme trends between companies that entered the programme and the control group were not different. Einiö (2013) find positive impacts on R&D investment, employment and sales among the participants who were granted an R&D subsidy as a result of additional aggregate R&D-support funding in their region. While there are no instantaneous impacts on productivity, the study provides evidence of long-term productivity gains.

NOTES

15 Although this document focuses on the direct effects of aid, the fact that the aid may have indirect effects does impose some analytical challenges on the assessment of direct effects, and special care has to be taken to the effects of market interactions.

16 This annex offers a quick and non-technical presentation of the econometric methods for policy evaluation. This presentation takes many elements from Givord (2010), other very good presentations can be found in Imbens and Wooldridge (2009) and Angrist and Pischke (2008).

17 Randomised experiments have for instance been the only acceptable methodology for the assessment of the effects of drugs and medical treatments for decades.

18 Moreover, it is possible to interact characteristics (for instance sales and sector) and to introduce functions of these characteristics (for instance squares of variables).

19 Consider the example of a regional SME scheme to create new employment. Imagine that at the end of the scheme it appears that SMEs in the region have performed 20% better than large enterprises in that region in terms of job creation. If in a comparable adjacent region (where no aid was given) SMEs also performed better than large enterprises (say 15% better), the impact of the aid may be estimated at roughly 5%.

20 This issue has been emphasised largely in the context of difference-in-difference technique, but the same problems can emerge with the other techniques covered by this paper.

21 In practice, two stage least squares are implemented in one step for well-known inference reasons.

22 A very interesting practical discussion about the biases created by weak instruments can be found in Bound, Jeager and Baker's (1995) discussion of the statistical biases in Angrist and Krueger (1991). Moreover, instrumental variable estimates are biased at finite distance. Therefore, even with sufficiently large datasets to ensure apparent statistical significance, non-asymptotic biases can still be important.

23 This can take the form of computing the Fisher statistics of the first step regression. The higher this Fisher, the less likely it is that instruments are weak. Stock, Wright and Yogo (2002) propose a formal test. For one instrument, it is for instance necessary that the Fisher statistics of the first step regression is larger than 10.

24 This section provides a very brief description of the selection models in this section. For a more complete presentation, the reader is referred to the seminal paper of Heckman (1979) and, mainly, Wooldridge (2002), chapter 17.

25 This omitted variable is the difference in conditional expectation of the outcome for the selected sample (here the aid-beneficiaries). Under certain assumptions on the selection process of the aid beneficiaries (for instance a probit or logit model), this difference can be formally derived (the inverse Mills ratio) and is a function of the selection parameters. Then, the effect of the policy can be identified by adding the omitted variable to the regression. The selection parameters are unknown, but consistent parameters can be recovered in a first step estimation of the selection process. This leads to the estimation procedure sometimes referred to as 'Heckit'. It first requires recovering the parameters of interest for the selection of the aid beneficiaries, for instance a probit or logit specification. Then, a consistent estimator of the effect of the policy can be recovered by adding the estimated inverse Mills ratio to the linear regression. Statistical software packages normally have a feature to perform this Heckman estimation.

26 For the presentation of all these methods, readers can for instance refer to, Wooldridge (2002), chapter 17.

27 When the selection equation is non-linear, the inverse Mills ratio is not collinear to the other explanatory variables, even when the first equation includes only a subset of these explanatory variables. Then, in theory, the model is already identified. In this case, the inverse Mills ratio very often does not show enough variation, which leads to very imprecise estimates. However, especially with large samples, the estimation could still lead to significant results. Nevertheless, when all the variables of the selection model are also in the main equation, the model is solely identified due to the non-linearities of a particular parametric form.

28 A formal and complete description of RDD can be found in Imbens et Lemieux (2008).

29 Formally, there are two different regression discontinuity designs: the sharp and the fuzzy design. In the sharp design, which is implicitly the one described here, all firms, and only them, are treated above a certain threshold. In the fuzzy design, the discontinuity is less drastic: there is a discontinuity of the probability to be treated, but this does not change from 0 to 1. In absolute term, as far as state aid schemes based on eligibility conditions are concerned, it is only if one considers the treatment to be the eligibility that the design is sharp Otherwise, if the treatment is to receive aid, we are in a fuzzy design. On the contrary, when the allocation is based on a scoring, we only consider firms who apply and the design is sharp.

30 Another approach would be to systematically estimate different treatment effects for firms in different points of the conditional distribution. There is a growing body of literature estimating such quantile treatment effects, starting from Abadie, Angrist and Imbens (2002). This is a very useful tool to understand the intrinsic nature of the heterogeneity of treatment. However, it is less useful from a strict policy point of view, unless it is possible to directly target different firms depending on their position in the conditional distribution.

31 Having data on rejected applications is particularly valuable for studies pursuing a regression discontinuity approach..

32 Criscuolo, C., R. Martin, H. Overman and J. Van Reenen, 2012.'The causal effects of an industrial policy,' CEPR Discussion Papers 8818, C.E.P.R. Discussion Papers.

33 Technically, Criscuolo et al. (2012) are using an instrumental variable approach, as presented before in this technical appendix.

34 Report for DG REGIO. A. Martini, D. Bondonio: 'Counterfactual impact evaluation of cohesion policy: impact and cost effectiveness of investment subsidies in Italy' (2012).

35 This is an instance where matching techniques, here one-to-one nearer neighbour matching, is not a better way to solve selection problems than ordinary least squares. As explained earlier in this technical appendix, matching techniques are not, in general, a way to solve the issue of selection effects in the absence of natural experiments.

36 In practice, the authors implement a Heckman selection model with an exclusion variable at firm level and a classical IV strategy at sector level. See before in this technical annex for more details on these methodologies.

37 Report for Nesta, Creative Credits, a randomised controlled industrial policy experiment, Bakhshi, H., J. Edwards, S. Roper, J. Scully, D. Shaw, L. Morley and N. Rathbone, June 2013, available at ec.europa.eu/growth/content/creative-credits-randomized-controlled-industrial-policy-experiment-0_en.

ANNEX II: LIST OF POSSIBLE RESULT INDICATORS

[5.51]
It should be noted that below is an indicative list for illustration purposes only. The actual result indicators should be set in accordance with the objective of the aid scheme and that of the evaluation.

DIRECT IMPACT OF THE AID AT THE LEVEL OF BENEFICIARIES

	RESULT DIMENSION	RESULT INDICATORS
Regional aid	Positive impacts	Private investment matching public support Employment increase in the supported enterprises
Research, development and innovation aid	Additional RDI activity	Private investment matching public support Additional RDI expenditure undertaken by supported companies Number of new researchers employed in supported companies Number of new patents registered Number of enterprises supported to introduce new to the markets
Environmental aid	Positive environmental impacts	Reduced CO2 emissions of the beneficiary firms Additional capacity of renewable energy production Reduction of the share of waste landfilled or incinerated, Number of contaminated sites cleaned
	Early adoption of environmental standards	Percentage of companies reaching new environmental standards at least X months/years before they come into force [as minimum 1year has been required and higher aid intensities have been allowed if earlier than 3 years]
Energy (infrastructure) aid	Reduced energy consumption	Number of households with improved energy consumption classification Decrease of annual primary energy consumption of public buildings Number of additional energy users connected to smart grids
	Renewable energy support	Production share of energy from RES
Risk finance	Positive impacts	Returns achieved in the fund; Leverage of private investments Number of firms receiving risk capital
	Picking losers:	Poor average performance of investee firms due to deficient commercial management/insufficient private participation
	Lack of sufficient degree of diversification	Too small/regionally constrained funds with limited return prospects that remain unattractive for private investors
Broadband aid	Increased broadband coverage	Additional household coverage with at least 30 Mbps broadband connection Additional household coverage or take up with at least 100 Mbps broadband connection
	Efficiency	Investments costs/aid per connecting a household (homes passed) Number of households signing up to new services
Rescue and restructuring	Positive impacts	Maintenance of employment and activity at firm-specific and regional level Changes in market share and productivity of aided firms
Aviation	Positive impacts	Number of air carriers using the airport; Private investment matching public support; Increase in regional productivity and/or gross value added (GVA))

	RESULT DIMENSION	RESULT INDICATORS
	Negative effects	Duplication of lossmaking infrastructure or air routes; Deterioration of traffic of existing infrastructure (eg. other airports in the catchment area or other means of transport

INDIRECT IMPACT OF THE AID SCHEME

	RESULT DIMENSION	RESULT INDICATORS
Possible positive effects	Macro-economic gains	Employment increase Increase in productivity and/or gross value added (GVA)
	Diversification of the regional economy	Number of industries under different NACE codes
	Increased cooperation between private and public	Number of enterprises cooperating with research institutions
	Positive externality / spill-over effects	Number of indirect beneficiaries (e.g. number of third parties accessing the facility) Changes in employment or activity in other firms and regions (aviation) Number of inhabitants with improved transportation means in the catchment area;
Possible negative effects on competition and trade	Sectoral bias	Aid was predominantly granted to one industry in a multi-sectoral scheme
	Bias towards loss-making firms or firms with low productivity (prevention of exit)	Proportion of high vs low productivity firms
	Bias towards incumbents	Proportion of old vs young firms
	Reinforce the market power	Change in market power of a dominant player
	Location effect	Relocation from a poorer region to a more developed one
	For security of supply	Locking-in in high-carbon energy sources, Assess whether the concerns in terms of black-outs are real and continue to exist; Foreclosure of national electricity markets
	For energy infrastructure:	Foreclosure of national electricity markets, reinforce the market power of an incumbent
	Rescue and restructuring	Changes in employment or activity in other firms and regions Changes in market share and productivity of aided firms
	Aviation	Duplication of lossmaking infrastructure or air routes; Deterioration of traffic of existing infrastructure (e. g. other airports in the catchment area or other means of transport

ANNEX III:
GLOSSARY

[5.52]

Baseline	The value of the indicator before the policy intervention at stake is undertaken.
Control group	Counterfactual analysis requires finding the most comparable firm(s) or control group, i.e. a group of firms which should be as similar as possible to the group of firms that received the aid — except that they have not benefitted from that aid.
Counterfactual	To estimate the effect of the aid on aid beneficiaries, it is necessary to construct a 'counterfactual', i.e. to establish a reasonable scenario capturing what would have likely happened to the aid beneficiaries if they had not received it.

Evaluation	The systematic collection and analysis of information about programmes and projects, their purpose and delivery; it derives knowledge on their impact as a basis for judgments. Evaluations are used to improve effectiveness and inform decisions about current and future programming.
Impact	The change that can be credibly attributed to an intervention. Same as 'effect' of intervention or 'contribution to change'.
Indicator	A variable that provides quantitative or qualitative information on a phenomenon. It normally includes a value and a measurement unit.
Method	Methods are families of evaluation techniques and tools that fulfil different purposes. They usually consist of procedures and protocols that ensure systemisation and consistency in the way evaluations are undertaken. Methods may focus on the collection or analysis of information and data; may be quantitative or qualitative; and may attempt to describe, explain, predict or inform action. The choice of methods follows from the nature of the intervention, the evaluation questions being asked and the mode of enquiry — causal, exploratory, normative etc.
Result	The specific dimension of the well-being of people that motivates policy action, i.e. that is expected to be modified by the interventions designed and implemented by a policy. Examples are: the mobility in an area; the competence in a given sector of activity.
Result indicator	An indicator describing a specific aspect of a result, a feature which can be measured. Examples are: the time needed to travel from W to Y at an average speed, as an aspect of mobility; the results of tests in a given topic, as an aspect of competence; the share of firms denied credit at any interest rate, as an aspect of banks' rationing.

ANNEX IV: REFERENCES

[5.53]

Abadie, A., J. Angrist and G. W. Imbens (2002), 'Instrumental Variables Estimates of the Effect of Subsidised Training on the Quantiles of Trainee Earnings,' Econometrica, 70(1), 91–117.

Abadie, A., A. Diamond and J. Hainmueller (2007), 'Synthetic Control Methods for Comparative Case Studies: Estimating the Effect of California's Tobacco Control Programme,' Journal of the American Statistical Association, June 2010, Vol. 105, No 490,

Angrist, J. and A. Krueger (1991), 'Does Compulsory School Attendance Affect Schooling and Earnings,' Quarterly Journal of Economics, 106.

Angrist, J. and J. Pischke (2008), "Mostly Harmless Econometrics: An Empiricist's Companion", Princeton University Press.

Angrist, J. D., and J. Pischke (2010), 'The Credibility Revolution in Empirical Economics: How Better Research Design Is Taking the Con out of Econometrics.' Journal of Economic Perspectives, 24(2): 3–30.

Bakhshi, H., J. Edwards, S. Roper, J. Scully, D. Shaw, L. Morley and N. Rathbone (2013), "Creative credits, a randomized controlled industrial policy experiment", Report for Nesta, available at ec.europa.eu/growth/content/creative-credits-randomized-controlled-industrial-policy-experiment-0_en.

Bertrand, M., E. Duflo and S. Mullainathan (2004), 'How much should we trust differences-in-differences estimates?,' The Quarterly Journal of Economics, 119, 249–275.

Bound, J., D. Jeager and R. Baker (1995), 'Problems with Instrumental Variable Estimation When the Correlation Between the Instruments and the Endogenous is weak,' Journal of the American Statistical Association, 90(430), 443–450.

Criscuolo, C, R. Martin, H. Overman and J. Van Reenen (2012), 'The causal effects of an industrial policy,' CEPR Discussion Papers 8818, C.E.P.R. Discussion Papers.

Duflo, E., R. Glennerster & M. Kremer (2007), 'Using Randomisation in Development Economics Research: A Toolkit,' CEPR Discussion Papers 6059, C.E.P.R. Discussion Papers.

Duflo, E., and M. Kremer (2005), Use of Randomisation in the Evaluation of Development Effectiveness,' in Evaluating Development Effectiveness, ed. by O. Feinstein, G. K. Ingram, and G. K. Pitman. New Brunswick, New Jersey and London, UK: Transaction Publishers, vol. 7, pp 205{232}.

Einiö, Elias (2013), 'R&D Subsidies and Company Performance: Evidence from Geographic Variation in Government Funding Based on the ERDF Population-Density Rule', *The Review of Economics and Statistics* (forthcoming).

European Commission's Evaluation Standards. Available at: ec.europa.eu/dgs/secretariat_general/evaluation/docs/standards_c_2002_5267_final_en.pdf.

Garicano, L. C. Lelarge and J. Van Reenen, (2012), 'Firm Size Distortions and the Productivity Distribution: Evidence from France,' CEP Discussion Papers dp1128, Centre for Economic Performance, LSE.

Givord, P. (2010), « Méthodes économétriques pour l'évaluation de politiques publiques », WPD3E n° G2010-08.

Givord, P., Rathelot, R. and P. Sillard (2013), 'Place-based tax exemptions and displacement effects: An evaluation of the Zones Franches Urbaines programme", Regional Science and Urban Economics', Volume 43, Issue 1, January 2013, Pages 151–163

Heckman, J. J. (1979), 'Sample Selection Bias as a Specification Error,' Econometrica 47, 153–161.

Imbens, G. and J. Wooldridge (2009), *Recent Developments in the Econometrics of Programme Evaluation*, Journal of Economic Literature, 47:1, 5–86

Imbens, G. W., et T. Lemieux (2008), 'Regression discontinuity designs: A guide to practice,' Journal of Econometrics, 142(2), 615–635.

C. Lelarge, D. Sraer and D. Thesmar (2010), 'Entrepreneurship and Credit Constraints: Evidence from a French Loan Guarantee Programme,' NBER Chapters, in: International Differences in Entrepreneurship, pages 243–273, National Bureau of Economic Research, Inc.

Keane, M. P. (2010), 'A Structural Perspective on the Experimentalist School.' Journal of Economic Perspectives, 24(2): 47–58.

Martini, A. and D. Bondonio (2012), 'Counterfactual impact evaluation of cohesion policy: impact and cost effectiveness of investment subsidies in Italy', Report for European Commission, DG Regio.

Nederlandse Rijksoverheid (2012), 'Durf te meten', Eindrapport Expertwerkgroep Effectmeting, available at www.rijksoverheid.nl/documenten-enpublicaties/rapporten/2012/11/23/durf-te-meten-eindrapport-expertwerkgroepeffectmeting.html

Nevo, A. and M. D. Whinston, (2010), 'Taking the Dogma out of Econometrics: Structural Modelling and Credible Inference.' Journal of Economic Perspectives, 24(2): 69–82.

OECD Evaluation Norms and Standards. Available at: www.oecd.org/dac/evaluation/dcdndep/41612905.pdf.

Sims, C. A. (2010), 'But Economics Is Not an Experimental Science.' Journal of Economic Perspectives, 24(2): 59–68.

Stock, J., J. Wrightand and M. Yogo (2002): 'A Survey of Weak Instruments and Weak Identification in Generalised Method of Moments,' Journal of Business and Economic Statistics, 20(4), 518–29.

United Nations Evaluation Group (2005),' "Standards for Evaluation in the UN System" Available at: www.uneval.org/papersandpubs/documentdetail.jsp?doc_id=22.

Wooldridge, J. (2002), "Econometric Analysis of Cross Section and Panel Data", Cambridge: MIT Press.

World Bank (2003), "Independent Evaluation: Principles, Guidelines and Good Practice".

Available at: siteresources.worldbank.org/INTDGF/Resources/Evaluation&LearningNote.pdf.

COMMISSION REGULATION

(1407/2013/EU)

of 18 December 2013

on the application of Articles 107 and 108 of the Treaty on the Functioning of the European Union to *de minimis* aid

(Text with EEA relevance)

[5.54]

NOTES

Date of publication in OJ: OJ L352, 24.12.2013, p 1.

Repeal of this Regulation in relation to the UK: this Regulation is repealed, in relation to the UK, by the State Aid (Revocations and Amendments) (EU Exit) Regulations 2020, SI 2020/1470, reg 5, as from IP completion day (as defined in the European Union (Withdrawal Agreement) Act 2020, s 39) (for transitional provisions and savings in relation to claims before a court or tribunal relating to State aid infringement before IP completion day, see Sch 3 to those Regulations at **[7.89]**).

THE EUROPEAN COMMISSION,

Having regard to the Treaty on the Functioning of the European Union, and in particular Article 108(4) thereof,

Having regard to Council Regulation (EC) No 994/98 of 7 May 1998 on the application of Articles 107 and 108 of the Treaty on the Functioning of the European Union to certain categories of horizontal State aid,[1]

Having published a draft of this Regulation,[2]

After consulting the Advisory Committee on State Aid,

Whereas:

(1) State funding meeting the criteria in Article 107(1) of the Treaty constitutes State aid and requires notification to the Commission by virtue of Article 108(3) of the Treaty. However, under Article 109 of the Treaty, the Council may determine categories of aid that are exempted from this notification requirement. In accordance with Article 108(4) of the Treaty the Commission may adopt regulations relating to those categories of State aid. By virtue of Regulation (EC) No 994/98 the Council decided, in accordance with Article 109 of the Treaty, that de minimis aid could constitute one such category. On that basis, de minimis aid, being aid granted to a single undertaking over a given period of time that does not exceed a certain fixed amount, is deemed not to meet all the criteria laid down in Article 107(1) of the Treaty and is therefore not subject to the notification procedure.

(2) The Commission has, in numerous decisions, clarified the notion of aid within the meaning of Article 107(1) of the Treaty. The Commission has also stated its policy with regard to a de minimis ceiling below which Article 107(1) of the Treaty can be considered not to apply, initially in its notice on the de minimis rule for State aid[3] *and subsequently in Commission Regulations (EC) No 69/2001*[4] *and (EC) No 1998/2006.*[5] *In the light of the experience gained in*

applying Regulation (EC) No 1998/2006, it is appropriate to revise some of the conditions laid down in that Regulation and to replace it.

(3) It is appropriate to maintain the ceiling of EUR 200,000 as the amount of de minimis aid that a single undertaking may receive per Member State over any period of three years. That ceiling remains necessary to ensure that any measure falling under this Regulation can be deemed not to have any effect on trade between Member States and not to distort or threaten to distort competition.

(4) For the purposes of the rules on competition laid down in the Treaty an undertaking is any entity engaged in an economic activity, regardless of its legal status and the way in which it is financed.[6] The Court of Justice of the European Union has ruled that all entities which are controlled (on a legal or on a de facto basis) by the same entity should be considered as a single undertaking.[7] For the sake of legal certainty and to reduce the administrative burden, this Regulation should provide an exhaustive list of clear criteria for determining when two or more enterprises within the same Member State are to be considered as a single undertaking. The Commission has selected from the well-established criteria for defining 'linked enterprises' in the definition of small or medium-sized enterprises (SMEs) in Commission Recommendation 2003/361/EC[8] and in Annex I to Commission Regulation (EC) No 800/2008[9] those criteria that are appropriate for the purposes of this Regulation. The criteria are already familiar to public authorities and should be applicable, given the scope of this Regulation, to both SMEs and large undertakings. Those criteria should ensure that a group of linked enterprises is considered as one single undertaking for the application of the de minimis rule, but that enterprises which have no relationship with each other except for the fact that each of them has a direct link to the same public body or bodies are not treated as being linked to each other. The specific situation of enterprises controlled by the same public body or bodies, which may have an independent power of decision, is therefore taken into account.

(5) In order to take account of the small average size of undertakings active in the road freight transport sector, it is appropriate to maintain the ceiling of EUR 100,000 for undertakings performing road freight transport for hire or reward. The provision of an integrated service where the actual transportation is only one element, such as removal services, postal or courier services or waste collection or processing services, should not be considered a transport service. In view of the overcapacity in the road freight transport sector and the objectives of transport policy as regards road congestion and freight transport, aid for the acquisition of road freight transport vehicles by undertakings performing road freight transport for hire or reward should be excluded from the scope of application of this Regulation. In view of the development of the road passenger transport sector, it is no longer appropriate to apply a lower ceiling to this sector.

(6) In view of the special rules which apply in the sectors of primary production of agricultural products, fishery and aquaculture and of the risk that amounts of aid below the ceiling laid down in this Regulation could nonetheless fulfil the criteria in Article 107(1) of the Treaty, this Regulation should not apply to those sectors.

(7) Considering the similarities between the processing and marketing of agricultural products and of non-agricultural products, this Regulation should apply to the processing and marketing of agricultural products, provided that certain conditions are met. Neither on-farm activities necessary for preparing a product for the first sale, such as harvesting, cutting and threshing of cereals, or packing of eggs, nor the first sale to resellers or processors should be considered as processing or marketing in this respect.

(8) The Court of Justice of the European Union has established that, once the Union has legislated for the establishment of a common organisation of the market in a given sector of agriculture, Member States are under an obligation to refrain from taking any measure which might undermine or create exceptions to it.[10] For that reason, this Regulation should not apply to aid the amount of which is fixed on the basis of the price or quantity of products purchased or put on the market. Nor should it apply to support which is linked to an obligation to share the aid with primary producers.

(9) This Regulation should not apply to export aid or aid contingent upon the use of domestic over imported products. In particular, it should not apply to aid financing the establishment and operation of a distribution network in other Member States or in third countries. Aid towards the costs of participating in trade fairs, or of studies or consultancy services needed for the launch of a new or existing product on a new market in another Member State or a third country does not normally constitute export aid.

(10) The period of three years to be taken into account for the purposes of this Regulation should be assessed on a rolling basis so that, for each new grant of de minimis aid, the total amount of de minimis aid granted in the fiscal year concerned and during the previous two fiscal years needs to be taken into account.

(11) Where an undertaking is active in sectors excluded from the scope of this Regulation and is also active in other sectors or has other activities, this Regulation should apply to those other sectors or activities provided that the Member State concerned ensures, by appropriate means such as separation of activities or distinction of costs, that the activities in the excluded sectors do not benefit from the de minimis aid. The same principle should apply where an undertaking is active in sectors to which lower de minimis ceilings apply. If it cannot be ensured that the activities in sectors to which lower de minimis ceilings apply benefit from de minimis aid only up to those lower ceilings, the lowest ceiling should apply to all activities of the undertaking.

(12) This Regulation should lay down rules to ensure that it is not possible to circumvent maximum aid intensities laid down in specific regulations or Commission decisions. It should also provide for clear rules on cumulation that are easy to apply.

(13) This Regulation does not exclude the possibility that a measure might be considered not to be State aid within the meaning of Article 107(1) of the Treaty on grounds other than those set out in this Regulation, for instance because the measure complies with the market economy operator principle or because the measure does not involve a transfer of State resources. In particular, Union funding centrally managed by the Commission which is not directly or indirectly under the control of the Member State does not constitute State aid and should not be taken into account in determining whether the relevant ceiling is complied with.

(14) For the purposes of transparency, equal treatment and effective monitoring, this Regulation should apply only to de minimis aid for which it is possible to calculate precisely the gross grant equivalent ex ante without any need

to undertake a risk assessment ('transparent aid'). Such a precise calculation can, for instance, be made for grants, interest rate subsidies, capped tax exemptions or other instruments that provide for a cap ensuring that the relevant ceiling is not exceeded. Providing for a cap means that as long as the precise amount of aid is not or not yet known, the Member State has to assume that the amount equals the cap in order to ensure that several aid measures together do not exceed the ceiling set out in this Regulation and to apply the rules on cumulation.

(15) For the purposes of transparency, equal treatment and the correct application of the de minimis ceiling, all Member States should apply the same method of calculation. In order to facilitate such calculation, aid amounts not taking the form of a cash grant should be converted into their gross grant equivalent. Calculation of the gross grant equivalent of transparent types of aid other than grants and of aid payable in several instalments requires the use of market interest rates prevailing at the time such aid is granted. With a view to uniform, transparent and simple application of the State aid rules, the market rates applicable for the purposes of this Regulation should be the reference rates, as set out in the Communication from the Commission on the revision of the method for setting the reference and discount rates.[11]

(16) Aid comprised in loans, including de minimis risk finance aid taking the form of loans, should be considered transparent de minimis aid if the gross grant equivalent has been calculated on the basis of market interest rates prevailing at the time the aid is granted. In order to simplify the treatment of small loans of short duration, this Regulation should provide for a clear rule that is easy to apply and takes into account both the amount of the loan and its duration. Based on the Commission's experience, loans that are secured by collateral covering at least 50% of the loan and that do not exceed either EUR 1,000,000 and a duration of five years or EUR 500,000 and a duration of 10 years can be considered as having a gross grant equivalent not exceeding the de minimis ceiling. Given the difficulties linked to determining the gross grant equivalent of aid granted to undertakings that may not be able to repay the loan, this rule should not apply to such undertakings.

(17) Aid comprised in capital injections should not be considered as transparent de minimis aid, unless the total amount of the public injection does not exceed the de minimis ceiling. Aid comprised in risk finance measures taking the form of equity or quasi-equity investments, as referred to in the risk finance guidelines,[12] *should not be considered as transparent de minimis aid unless the measure concerned provides capital not exceeding the de minimis ceiling.*

(18) Aid comprised in guarantees, including de minimis risk finance aid taking the form of guarantees, should be considered as transparent if the gross grant equivalent has been calculated on the basis of safe-harbour premiums laid down in a Commission notice for the type of undertaking concerned.[13] *In order to simplify the treatment of guarantees of short duration securing up to 80% of a relatively small loan, this Regulation should provide for a clear rule that is easy to apply and takes into account both the amount of the underlying loan and the duration of the guarantee. This rule should not apply to guarantees on underlying transactions not constituting a loan, such as guarantees on equity transactions. Where the guarantee does not exceed 80% of the underlying loan, the amount guaranteed does not exceed EUR 1,500,000 and the duration of the guarantee does not exceed five years the guarantee can be considered as having a gross grant equivalent not exceeding the de minimis ceiling. The same applies where the guarantee does not exceed 80% of the underlying loan, the amount guaranteed does not exceed EUR 750,000 and the duration of the guarantee does not exceed 10 years. In addition, Member States can use a methodology to calculate the gross grant equivalent of guarantees which has been notified to the Commission under another Commission Regulation in the State aid area applicable at that time and which has been accepted by the Commission as being in line with the Guarantee Notice, or any successor notice, provided that the accepted methodology explicitly addresses the type of guarantee and the type of underlying transaction at stake in the context of the application of this Regulation. Given the difficulties linked to determining the gross grant equivalent of aid granted to undertakings that may not be able to repay the loan, this rule should not apply to such undertakings.*

(19) Where a de minimis aid scheme is implemented through financial intermediaries, it should be ensured that the latter do not receive any State aid. This can be done, for example, by requiring financial intermediaries that benefit from a State guarantee to pay a market-conform premium or to fully pass on any advantage to the final beneficiaries, or by respecting the de minimis ceiling and other conditions of this Regulation also at the level of the intermediaries.

(20) Upon notification by a Member State, the Commission may examine whether a measure which does not consist of a grant, loan, guarantee, capital injection or risk finance measure taking the form of an equity or quasi-equity investment leads to a gross grant equivalent that does not exceed the de minimis ceiling and could therefore fall within the scope of this Regulation.

(21) The Commission has a duty to ensure that State aid rules are complied with and in accordance with the cooperation principle laid down in Article 4(3) of the Treaty on European Union, Member States should facilitate the fulfilment of this task by establishing the necessary tools in order to ensure that the total amount of de minimis aid granted to a single undertaking under the de minimis rule does not exceed the overall permissible ceiling. To that end, when granting de minimis aid, Member States should inform the undertaking concerned of the amount of de minimis aid granted and of its de minimis character and should make express reference to this Regulation. Member States should be required to monitor aid granted to ensure the relevant ceilings are not exceeded and the cumulation rules are complied with. To comply with that obligation, before granting such aid, the Member State concerned should obtain from the undertaking a declaration about other de minimis aid covered by this Regulation or by other de minimis regulations received during the fiscal year concerned and the previous two fiscal years. Alternatively it should be possible for Member States to set up a central register with complete information on de minimis aid granted and check that any new grant of aid does not exceed the relevant ceiling.

(22) Before granting any new de minimis aid each Member State should verify that the de minimis ceiling will not be exceeded in that Member State by the new de minimis aid and that the other conditions of this Regulation are complied with.

(23) Having regard to the Commission's experience and in particular the frequency with which it is generally necessary to revise State aid policy, the period of application of this Regulation should be limited. If this Regulation expires without being extended, Member States should have an adjustment period of six months with regard to de minimis aid covered by this Regulation,

NOTES

Repeal of this Regulation in relation to the UK: this Regulation is repealed in relation to the UK (as from IP completion day); see the introductory notes to this Regulation *ante*.

[1] OJ L142, 14.5.1998, p 1.

[2] OJ C229, 8.8.2013, p 1.

[3] Commission notice on the *de minimis* rule for State aid (OJ C68, 6.3.1996, p 9).

[4] Commission Regulation (EC) No 69/2001 of 12 January 2001 on the application of Articles 87 and 88 of the EC Treaty to *de minimis* aid (OJ L10, 13.1.2001, p 30).

[5] Commission Regulation (EC) No 1998/2006 of 15 December 2006 on the application of Articles 87 and 88 of the Treaty to *de minimis* aid (OJ L379, 28.12.2006, p 5).

[6] Case C-222/04 *Ministero dell'Economia e delle Finanze v Cassa di Risparmio di Firenze SpA et al.* [2006] ECR I-289.

[7] Case C-382/99 *Netherlands v Commission* [2002] ECR I-5163.

[8] Commission Recommendation 2003/361/EC of 6 May 2003 concerning the definition of micro, small and medium-sized enterprises (OJ L124, 20.5.2003, p 36).

[9] Commission Regulation (EC) No 800/2008 of 6 August 2008 declaring certain categories of aid compatible with the common market in application of Articles 87 and 88 of the Treaty (OJ L214, 9.8.2008, p 3).

[10] Case C-456/00 *France v Commission* [2002] ECR I-11949.

[11] Communication from the Commission on the revision of the method for setting the reference and discount rates (OJ C14, 19.1.2008, p 6).

[12] Community guidelines on state aid to promote risk capital investments in small and medium-sized enterprises (OJ C194, 18.8.2006, p 2).

[13] For instance, Commission Notice on the application of Articles 87 and 88 of the EC Treaty to State aid in the form of guarantees (OJ C155, 20.6.2008, p 10).

HAS ADOPTED THIS REGULATION:

[5.55]

Article 1 Scope

1. This Regulation applies to aid granted to undertakings in all sectors, with the exception of:

(a) aid granted to undertakings active in the fishery and aquaculture sector, as covered by Council Regulation (EC) No 104/2000;[1]

(b) aid granted to undertakings active in the primary production of agricultural products;

(c) aid granted to undertakings active in the sector of processing and marketing of agricultural products, in the following cases:

(i) where the amount of the aid is fixed on the basis of the price or quantity of such products purchased from primary producers or put on the market by the undertakings concerned;

(ii) where the aid is conditional on being partly or entirely passed on to primary producers;

(d) aid to export-related activities towards third countries or Member States, namely aid directly linked to the quantities exported, to the establishment and operation of a distribution network or to other current expenditure linked to the export activity;

(e) aid contingent upon the use of domestic over imported goods.

2. Where an undertaking is active in the sectors referred to in points (a), (b) or (c) of paragraph 1 and is also active in one or more of the sectors or has other activities falling within the scope of this Regulation, this Regulation shall apply to aid granted in respect of the latter sectors or activities, provided that the Member State concerned ensures, by appropriate means such as separation of activities or distinction of costs, that the activities in the sectors excluded from the scope of this Regulation do not benefit from the de minimis aid granted in accordance with this Regulation.

NOTES

Repeal of this Regulation in relation to the UK: this Regulation is repealed in relation to the UK (as from IP completion day); see the introductory notes to this Regulation *ante*.

[1] Council Regulation (EC) No 104/2000 of 17 December 1999 on the common organisation of the markets in fishery and aquaculture products (OJ L17, 21.1.2000, p 22).

[5.56]

Article 2 Definitions

1. For the purposes of this Regulation the following definitions shall apply:

(a) 'agricultural products' means products listed in Annex 1 to the Treaty, with the exception of fishery and aquaculture products covered by Regulation (EC) No 104/2000;

(b) 'processing of agricultural products' means any operation on an agricultural product resulting in a product which is also an agricultural product, except on-farm activities necessary for preparing an animal or plant product for the first sale;

(c) 'marketing of agricultural products' means holding or display with a view to sale, offering for sale, delivery or any other manner of placing on the market, except the first sale by a primary producer to resellers or processors and any activity preparing a product for such first sale; a sale by a primary producer to final consumers shall be considered as marketing if it takes place in separate premises reserved for that purpose.

2. 'Single undertaking' includes, for the purposes of this Regulation, all enterprises having at least one of the following relationships with each other:

(a) one enterprise has a majority of the shareholders' or members' voting rights in another enterprise;

(b) one enterprise has the right to appoint or remove a majority of the members of the administrative, management or supervisory body of another enterprise;

(c) one enterprise has the right to exercise a dominant influence over another enterprise pursuant to a contract entered into with that enterprise or to a provision in its memorandum or articles of association;

(d) one enterprise, which is a shareholder in or member of another enterprise, controls alone, pursuant to an agreement with other shareholders in or members of that enterprise, a majority of shareholders' or members' voting rights in that enterprise.

Enterprises having any of the relationships referred to in points (a) to (d) of the first subparagraph through one or more other enterprises shall also be considered to be a single undertaking.

NOTES

Repeal of this Regulation in relation to the UK: this Regulation is repealed in relation to the UK (as from IP completion day); see the introductory notes to this Regulation *ante*.

[5.57]

Article 3 De minimis aid

1. Aid measures shall be deemed not to meet all the criteria in Article 107(1) of the Treaty, and shall therefore be exempt from the notification requirement in Article 108(3) of the Treaty, if they fulfil the conditions laid down in this Regulation.

2. The total amount of de minimis aid granted per Member State to a single undertaking shall not exceed EUR 200,000 over any period of three fiscal years.

The total amount of de minimis aid granted per Member State to a single undertaking performing road freight transport for hire or reward shall not exceed EUR 100,000 over any period of three fiscal years. This de minimis aid shall not be used for the acquisition of road freight transport vehicles.

3. If an undertaking performs road freight transport for hire or reward and also carries out other activities to which the ceiling of EUR 200,000 applies, the ceiling of EUR 200,000 shall apply to the undertaking, provided that the Member State concerned ensures, by appropriate means such as separation of activities or distinction of costs, that the benefit to the road freight transport activity does not exceed EUR 100,000 and that no de minimis aid is used for the acquisition of road freight transport vehicles.

4. De minimis aid shall be deemed granted at the moment the legal right to receive the aid is conferred on the undertaking under the applicable national legal regime irrespective of the date of payment of the de minimis aid to the undertaking.

5. The ceilings laid down in paragraph 2 shall apply irrespective of the form of the de minimis aid or the objective pursued and regardless of whether the aid granted by the Member State is financed entirely or partly by resources of Union origin. The period of three fiscal years shall be determined by reference to the fiscal years used by the undertaking in the Member State concerned.

6. For the purposes of the ceilings laid down in paragraph 2, aid shall be expressed as a cash grant. All figures used shall be gross, that is, before any deduction of tax or other charge. Where aid is granted in a form other than a grant, the aid amount shall be the gross grant equivalent of the aid.

Aid payable in several instalments shall be discounted to its value at the moment it is granted. The interest rate to be used for discounting purposes shall be the discount rate applicable at the time the aid is granted.

7. Where the relevant ceiling laid down in paragraph 2 would be exceeded by the grant of new de minimis aid, none of that new aid may benefit from this Regulation.

8. In the case of mergers or acquisitions, all prior de minimis aid granted to any of the merging undertakings shall be taken into account in determining whether any new de minimis aid to the new or the acquiring undertaking exceeds the relevant ceiling. De minimis aid lawfully granted before the merger or acquisition shall remain lawful.

9. If one undertaking splits into two or more separate undertakings, de minimis aid granted prior to the split shall be allocated to the undertaking that benefited from it, which is in principle the undertaking taking over the activities for which the de minimis aid was used. If such an allocation is not possible, the de minimis aid shall be allocated proportionately on the basis of the book value of the equity capital of the new undertakings at the effective date of the split.

NOTES

Repeal of this Regulation in relation to the UK: this Regulation is repealed in relation to the UK (as from IP completion day); see the introductory notes to this Regulation *ante*.

[5.58]

Article 4 Calculation of gross grant equivalent

1. This Regulation shall apply only to aid in respect of which it is possible to calculate precisely the gross grant equivalent of the aid ex ante without any need to undertake a risk assessment ('transparent aid').

2. Aid comprised in grants or interest rate subsidies shall be considered as transparent de minimis aid.

3. Aid comprised in loans shall be considered as transparent de minimis aid if:

(a) the beneficiary is not subject to collective insolvency proceedings nor fulfils the criteria under its domestic law for being placed in collective insolvency proceedings at the request of its creditors. In case of large undertakings, the beneficiary shall be in a situation comparable to a credit rating of at least B-; and

(b) the loan is secured by collateral covering at least 50% of the loan and the loan amounts to either EUR 1,000,000 (or EUR 500,000 for undertakings performing road freight transport) over five years or EUR 500,000 (or EUR 250,000 for undertakings performing road freight transport) over 10 years; if a loan is for less than those amounts and/or is granted for a period of less than five or 10 years respectively, the gross grant equivalent of that loan shall be calculated as a corresponding proportion of the relevant ceiling laid down in Article 3(2); or

(c) the gross grant equivalent has been calculated on the basis of the reference rate applicable at the time of the grant.

4. Aid comprised in capital injections shall only be considered as transparent de minimis aid if the total amount of the public injection does not exceed the de minimis ceiling.

5. Aid comprised in risk finance measures taking the form of equity or quasi-equity investments shall only be considered as transparent de minimis aid if the capital provided to a single undertaking does not exceed the de minimis ceiling.

6. Aid comprised in guarantees shall be treated as transparent de minimis aid if:

(a) the beneficiary is not subject to collective insolvency proceedings nor fulfils the criteria under its domestic law for being placed in collective insolvency proceedings at the request of its creditors. In case of large undertakings, the beneficiary shall be in a situation comparable to a credit rating of at least B-; and

(b) the guarantee does not exceed 80% of the underlying loan and either the amount guaranteed is EUR 1,500,000 (or EUR 750,000 for undertakings performing road freight transport) and the duration of the guarantee is five years or the amount guaranteed is EUR 750,000 (or EUR 375,000 for undertakings performing road freight transport) and the duration of the guarantee is 10 years; if the amount guaranteed is lower than these amounts and/or the guarantee is for a period of less than five or 10 years respectively, the gross grant equivalent of that guarantee shall be calculated as a corresponding proportion of the relevant ceiling laid down in Article 3(2); or

(c) the gross grant equivalent has been calculated on the basis of safe-harbour premiums laid down in a Commission notice; or

(d) before implementation,

(i) the methodology used to calculate the gross grant equivalent of the guarantee has been notified to the Commission under another Commission Regulation in the State aid area applicable at that time and accepted by the Commission as being in line with the Guarantee Notice, or any successor Notice; and

(ii) that methodology explicitly addresses the type of guarantee and the type of underlying transaction at stake in the context of the application of this Regulation.

7. Aid comprised in other instruments shall be considered as transparent de minimis aid if the instrument provides for a cap ensuring that the relevant ceiling is not exceeded.

NOTES

Repeal of this Regulation in relation to the UK: this Regulation is repealed in relation to the UK (as from IP completion day); see the introductory notes to this Regulation *ante*.

[5.59]

Article 5 Cumulation

1. De minimis aid granted in accordance with this Regulation may be cumulated with de minimis aid granted in accordance with Commission Regulation (EU) No 360/2012[1] *up to the ceiling laid down in that Regulation. It may be cumulated with de minimis aid granted in accordance with other de minimis regulations up to the relevant ceiling laid down in Article 3(2) of this Regulation.*

2. De minimis aid shall not be cumulated with State aid in relation to the same eligible costs or with State aid for the same risk finance measure, if such cumulation would exceed the highest relevant aid intensity or aid amount fixed in the specific circumstances of each case by a block exemption regulation or a decision adopted by the Commission. De minimis aid which is not granted for or attributable to specific eligible costs may be cumulated with other State aid granted under a block exemption regulation or a decision adopted by the Commission.

NOTES

Repeal of this Regulation in relation to the UK: this Regulation is repealed in relation to the UK (as from IP completion day); see the introductory notes to this Regulation *ante*.

[5.60]

Article 6 Monitoring

1. Where a Member State intends to grant de minimis aid in accordance with this Regulation to an undertaking, it shall inform that undertaking in writing of the prospective amount of the aid expressed as a gross grant equivalent and of its de minimis character, making express reference to this Regulation and citing its title and publication reference in the Official Journal of the European Union. Where de minimis aid is granted in accordance with this Regulation to different undertakings on the basis of a scheme and different amounts of individual aid are granted to those undertakings under that scheme, the Member State concerned may choose to fulfil that obligation by informing the undertakings of a fixed sum corresponding to the maximum aid amount to be granted under that scheme. In such case, the fixed sum shall be used for determining whether the relevant ceiling laid down in Article 3(2) is reached. Before granting the aid, the Member State shall obtain a declaration from the undertaking concerned, in written or electronic form, about any other de minimis aid received to which this Regulation or other de minimis regulations apply during the previous two fiscal years and the current fiscal year.

2. Where a Member State has set up a central register of de minimis aid containing complete information on all de minimis aid granted by any authority within that Member State, paragraph 1 shall cease to apply from the moment the register covers a period of three fiscal years.

3. A Member State shall grant new de minimis aid in accordance with this Regulation only after having checked that this will not raise the total amount of de minimis aid granted to the undertaking concerned to a level above the relevant ceiling laid down in Article 3(2) and that all the conditions laid down in this Regulation are complied with.

4. Member States shall record and compile all the information regarding the application of this Regulation. Such records shall contain all information necessary to demonstrate that the conditions of this Regulation have been complied with. Records regarding individual de minimis aid shall be maintained for 10 fiscal years from the date on which the aid was granted. Records regarding a de minimis aid scheme shall be maintained for 10 fiscal years from the date on which the last individual aid was granted under such a scheme.

5. On written request, the Member State concerned shall provide the Commission, within a period of 20 working days or such longer period as may be fixed in the request, with all the information that the Commission considers necessary for assessing whether the conditions of this Regulation have been complied with, and in particular the total amount of de minimis aid within the meaning of this Regulation and of other de minimis regulations received by any undertaking.

NOTES

Repeal of this Regulation in relation to the UK: this Regulation is repealed in relation to the UK (as from IP completion day); see the introductory notes to this Regulation *ante*.

1 Commission Regulation (EU) No 360/2012 of 25 April 2012 on the application of Articles 107 and 108 of the Treaty on the Functioning of the European Union to *de minimis* aid granted to undertakings providing services of general economic interest (OJ L114, 26.4.2012, p 8).

[5.61]

Article 7 Transitional provisions

1. This Regulation shall apply to aid granted before its entry into force if the aid fulfils all the conditions laid down in this Regulation. Any aid which does not fulfil those conditions will be assessed by the Commission in accordance with the relevant frameworks, guidelines, communications and notices.

2. Any individual de minimis aid which was granted between 2 February 2001 and 30 June 2007 and fulfils the conditions of Regulation (EC) No 69/2001 shall be deemed not to meet all the criteria in Article 107(1) of the Treaty and shall therefore be exempt from the notification requirement in Article 108(3) of the Treaty.

3. Any individual de minimis aid granted between 1 January 2007 and 30 June 2014 and which fulfils the conditions of Regulation (EC) No 1998/2006 shall be deemed not to meet all the criteria in Article 107(1) of the Treaty and shall therefore be exempt from the notification requirement in Article 108(3) of the Treaty.

4. At the end of the period of validity of this Regulation, any de minimis aid scheme which fulfils the conditions of this Regulation shall remain covered by this Regulation for a further period of six months.

NOTES

Repeal of this Regulation in relation to the UK: this Regulation is repealed in relation to the UK (as from IP completion day); see the introductory notes to this Regulation *ante*.

[5.62]

Article 8 Entry into force and period of application

This Regulation shall enter into force on 1 January 2014.

[It shall apply until 31 December 2023.]

This Regulation shall be binding in its entirety and directly applicable in all Member States.

NOTES

Words in square brackets substituted by Commission Regulation 2020/972/EU, Art 1.

Repeal of this Regulation in relation to the UK: this Regulation is repealed in relation to the UK (as from IP completion day); see the introductory notes to this Regulation *ante*.

COMMISSION REGULATION

(651/2014/EU)

of 17 June 2014

declaring certain categories of aid compatible with the internal market in application of Articles 107 and 108 of the Treaty (General Block Exemption Regulation)

(Text with EEA relevance)

[5.63]

NOTES

Date of publication in OJ: OJ L187, 26.06.2014, p 1

Repeal of this Regulation in relation to the UK: this Regulation is repealed, in relation to the UK, by the State Aid (Revocations and Amendments) (EU Exit) Regulations 2020, SI 2020/1470, reg 5, as from IP completion day (as defined in the European Union (Withdrawal Agreement) Act 2020, s 39) (for transitional provisions and savings in relation to claims before a court or tribunal relating to State aid infringement before IP completion day, see Sch 3 to those Regulations at **[7.89]**).

See also the list of consultations and draft documents in the Appendix at **[A1]**.

THE EUROPEAN COMMISSION,

Having regard to the Treaty on the Functioning of the European Union, and in particular Article 108(4) thereof,

Having regard to Council Regulation (EC) No 994/98 of 7 May 1998 on the application of Articles 92 and 93 of the Treaty establishing the European Community to certain categories of horizontal State aid,[1] *and in particular Article 1(1)(a) and (b) thereof,*

After consulting the Advisory Committee on State Aid,

Whereas:

(1) State funding meeting the criteria in Article 107(1) of the Treaty constitutes State aid and requires notification to the Commission by virtue of Article 108(3) of the Treaty. However, according to Article 109 of the Treaty, the Council may determine categories of aid that are exempted from this notification requirement. In accordance with Article 108(4)

of the Treaty the Commission may adopt regulations relating to those categories of State aid. Council Regulation (EC) No 994/98 empowers the Commission to declare, in accordance with Article 109 of the Treaty, that the following categories may, under certain conditions, be exempted from the notification requirement: aid to small and medium-sized enterprises (SMEs), aid in favour of research and development, aid in favour of environmental protection, employment and training aid and aid that complies with the map approved by the Commission for each Member State for the grant of regional aid. On that basis, the Commission adopted Commission Regulation (EC) No 800/2008.[2] Regulation (EC) No 800/2008 originally applied until 31 December 2013 but was subsequently prolonged by Commission Regulation (EU) No 1224/2013 of 29 November 2013 amending Regulation (EC) No 800/2008 as regards its period of application[3] and now expires on 30 June 2014. On 22 July 2013 Regulation (EC) No 994/98 was amended by Council Regulation (EU) No 733/2013 of 22 July 2013 amending Regulation (EC) No 994/98 on the application of Articles 92 and 93 of the Treaty establishing the European Community to certain categories of horizontal State aid[4] to empower the Commission to extend the block exemption to new categories of aid, in respect of which clear compatibility conditions can be defined. Such new categories of block exempted aid include: aid to make good the damage caused by certain natural disasters, social aid for transport for residents of remote regions, aid for broadband infrastructures, aid for innovation, aid for culture and heritage conservation, aid for sport and multifunctional recreational infrastructures. Provided that sufficient case experience is further developed allowing the design of operational exemption criteria ensuring the ex-ante compatibility of other categories of aid, the Commission intends to review the scope of this Regulation with a view to including certain types of aid in those areas. In particular, the Commission envisages developing criteria for port and airport infrastructure by December 2015.

(2) With its Communication on EU State Aid Modernisation (SAM),[5] the Commission launched a wider review of the State aid rules. The main objectives of this modernisation are (i) to achieve sustainable, smart and inclusive growth in a competitive internal market, while contributing to Member State efforts towards a more efficient use of public finances, (ii) to focus Commission ex ante scrutiny of aid measures on cases with the biggest impact on the internal market, while strengthening Member State cooperation in State aid enforcement, and (iii) to streamline the rules and provide for faster, better informed and more robust decisions based on a clear economic rationale, a common approach and clear obligations. The review of Regulation (EC) No 800/2008 constitutes a central element of SAM.

(3) This Regulation should allow for better prioritisation of State aid enforcement activities, greater simplification and should enhance transparency, effective evaluation and the control of compliance with the State aid rules at national and Union levels, while preserving the institutional competences of the Commission and the Member States. In accordance with the principle of proportionality this Regulation does not go beyond what is necessary in order to achieve those objectives.

(4) The Commission's experience in applying Regulation (EC) No 800/2008 has allowed it to better define the conditions under which certain categories of aid can be considered compatible with the internal market and to extend the scope of block exemptions. It also revealed the necessity to strengthen transparency, monitoring and proper evaluation of very large schemes in light of their effect on competition in the internal market.

(5) The general conditions for the application of this Regulation should be defined on the basis of a set of common principles that ensure the aid serves a purpose of common interest, has a clear incentive effect, is appropriate and proportionate, is granted in full transparency and subject to a control mechanism and regular evaluation, and does not adversely affect trading conditions to an extent that is contrary to the common interest.

(6) Aid that fulfils all the conditions laid down in this Regulation both general and specific to the relevant categories of aid should be exempted from the notification obligation laid down in Article 108(3) of the Treaty.

(7) State aid within the meaning of Article 107(1) of the Treaty not covered by this Regulation remains subject to the notification requirement of Article 108(3) of the Treaty. This Regulation is without prejudice to the possibility for Member States to notify aid the objectives of which correspond to objectives covered by this Regulation.

(8) In view of the greater potential impact of large schemes on trade and competition, aid schemes with an average annual State aid budget exceeding a threshold based on an absolute value should in principle be subject to State aid evaluation. The evaluation should aim at verifying whether the assumptions and conditions underlying the compatibility of the scheme have been achieved, as well as the effectiveness of the aid measure in the light of its general and specific objectives and should provide indications on the impact of the scheme on competition and trade. In order to ensure equal treatment, State aid evaluation should be carried out on the basis of an evaluation plan approved by the Commission. While such plan should normally be drawn up at the moment of the design of the scheme and approved in time for the scheme to enter into force, this may not be possible in all cases. Therefore, in order not to delay their entry into force, this Regulation will apply to such schemes for a maximum period of six months. The Commission may decide to extend this period, upon approval of the evaluation plan. To this end, the evaluation plan should be notified to the Commission within 20 working days following the entry into force of the scheme. The Commission can also exceptionally decide that an evaluation is not necessary given the specificities of the case. The Commission should receive from the Member State the necessary information to be able to carry out the assessment of the evaluation plan and request additional information without undue delay allowing the Member State to complete the missing elements for the Commission to take a decision. In view of the novelty of this process, the Commission will provide, in a separate document, a detailed guidance on the procedure applicable during the 6 months period for the approval of the evaluation plan and the relevant templates through which the evaluation plans will have to be submitted. Alterations of schemes subject to evaluation, other than modifications which cannot affect the compatibility of the aid scheme under this Regulation or cannot significantly affect the content of the approved evaluation plan, should be assessed taking account of the outcome of such evaluation and should be excluded from the scope of this Regulation. The alterations such as purely formal modifications, administrative modifications or alterations carried out within the framework of the EU co-financed measures should not, in principle, be considered as significantly affecting the content of the approved evaluation plan.

(9) This Regulation should not apply to aid contingent upon the use of domestic over imported products or aid to export-related activities. In particular, it should not apply to aid financing the establishment and operation of a distribution network in other countries. Aid towards the cost of participating in trade fairs or of studies or consultancy

services needed for the launch of a new or existing product on a new market in another Member State or third country does not normally constitute aid to export-related activities.

(10) This Regulation should apply in principle across most sectors of the economy. However, in some sectors, such as the fisheries and aquaculture sector and primary agricultural production, the scope should be limited in the light of the special rules applicable.

(11) This Regulation should apply to the processing and marketing of agricultural products, provided that certain conditions are met. For the purposes of this Regulation neither on-farm activities necessary for preparing a product for the first sale, nor the first sale by a primary producer to resellers or processors or any activity preparing a product for a first sale should be considered processing or marketing.

(12) This Regulation should not apply to aid to facilitate the closure of uncompetitive coal mines, which is dealt with by the Council Decision of 10 December 2010 on State aid to facilitate the closure of uncompetitive coal mines.[6] *This Regulation should apply to other types of aid in the coal sector, with the exception of regional aid.*

(13) The Commission should ensure that authorised aid does not adversely affect trading conditions to an extent that is contrary to the common interest. Therefore, aid in favour of a beneficiary which is subject to an outstanding recovery order following a previous Commission decision declaring an aid illegal and incompatible with the internal market should be excluded from the scope of this Regulation, with the exception of aid schemes to make good the damage caused by certain natural disasters.

(14) Aid granted to undertakings in difficulty should be excluded from the scope of this Regulation, since such aid should be assessed under the Community guidelines on State aid for rescuing and restructuring firms in difficulty of 1 October 2004[7] *as prolonged by Commission communication concerning the prolongation of the application of the Community guidelines on State aid for rescuing and restructuring firms in difficulty of 1 October 2004*[8] *or their successor Guidelines, in order to avoid their circumvention, with the exception of aid schemes to make good the damage caused by certain natural disasters. In order to provide legal certainty, it is appropriate to establish clear criteria that do not require an assessment of all the particularities of the situation of an undertaking to determine whether an undertaking is considered to be in difficulty for the purposes of this Regulation.*

(15) State aid enforcement is highly dependent on the cooperation of Member States. Therefore, Member States should take all necessary measures to ensure compliance with this Regulation, including compliance of individual aid granted under block-exempted schemes.

(16) Due to the high risk of adversely affecting trading conditions, large amounts of aid granted either individually or cumulatively should be assessed by the Commission upon notification. Thresholds should therefore be set for each category of aid falling within the scope of this Regulation at a level which takes into account the category of aid concerned and its likely effect on trading conditions. Any aid granted above those thresholds should remain subject to the notification requirement of Article 108(3) of the Treaty. The thresholds set out in this Regulation should not be circumvented by artificially splitting up aid schemes or aid projects into several aid schemes or projects with similar characteristics, objectives or beneficiaries.

(17) For the purpose of transparency, equal treatment and effective monitoring, this Regulation should apply only to aid in respect of which it is possible to calculate precisely the gross grant equivalent ex ante without the need to undertake a risk assessment ('transparent aid'). For certain specific aid instruments, such as loans, guarantees, tax measures, risk finance measures and, in particular, repayable advances, this Regulation should define the conditions under which they can be considered transparent. Capital injections should not be considered transparent aid, without prejudice to specific conditions concerning risk finance and start-up aid. Aid comprised in guarantees should be considered as transparent if the gross grant equivalent has been calculated on the basis of safeharbour premiums laid down for the respective type of undertaking. In the case of small and medium-sized enterprises (SMEs), the Commission Notice on the application of Articles 87 and 88 of the EC Treaty to State aid in the form of guarantees[9] *indicates levels of annual premium above which a State guarantee would be deemed not to constitute aid.*

(18) In order to ensure that the aid is necessary and acts as an incentive to further develop activities or projects, this Regulation should not apply to aid for activities in which the beneficiary would in any case engage even in the absence of the aid. Aid should only be exempted from notification under this Regulation if the work on the aided project or activity starts after the beneficiary has submitted a written application for the aid.

(19) As regards any ad hoc aid covered by this Regulation granted to a beneficiary who is a large enterprise, the Member State should ensure that, in addition to complying with the conditions relating to incentive effect which apply to beneficiaries who are SMEs, the beneficiary has analysed, in an internal document, the viability of the aided project or activity with aid and without aid. The Member State should verify that this internal document confirms a material increase in the scope of the project/activity, a material increase in the total amount spent by the beneficiary on the subsidised project or activity or a material increase in the speed of completion of the project/activity concerned. Regional aid should be considered to have an incentive effect if the investment project would not have been carried out in the assisted region concerned in the absence of the aid.

(20) Automatic aid schemes in the form of tax advantages should continue to be subject to a specific condition concerning the incentive effect, due to the fact that this kind of aid is granted under different procedures than other categories of aid. Such schemes should already have been adopted before work on the aided project or activity started. However, this condition should not apply in the case of fiscal successor schemes provided the activity was already covered by the previous fiscal schemes in the form of tax advantages. For the assessment of the incentive effect of such schemes, the crucial moment is the moment when the tax measure was set out for the first time in the original scheme, which is then replaced by the successor scheme.

(21) As regards regional operating aid, regional urban development aid, aid for access to finance for SMEs, aid for the recruitment of disadvantaged workers, aid for employment of workers with disabilities and aid compensating for the additional costs of employing workers with disabilities, aid in the form of reductions in environmental taxes, aid to make good the damage caused by certain natural disasters, social aid for transport for residents of remote regions and aid for culture and heritage conservation, the requirement regarding the existence of an incentive effect

does not apply or should be presumed as having been complied with, if the specific conditions set out for those categories of aid in this Regulation are fulfilled.

(22) With a view to ensuring that aid is proportionate and limited to the amount necessary, maximum aid amounts should, whenever possible, be defined in terms of aid intensities in relation to a set of eligible costs. Where the maximum aid intensity cannot be set, because eligible costs cannot be identified or in order to provide simpler instruments for small amounts, maximum aid amounts defined in nominal terms should be set out in order to ensure proportionality of aid measures. The aid intensity and the maximum aid amounts should be fixed, in the light of the Commission's experience, at a level that minimises distortions of competition in the aided sector while appropriately addressing the market failure or cohesion issue. For regional investment aid, the aid intensity should comply with the allowable aid intensities under the regional aid maps.

(23) For the calculation of aid intensity, only eligible costs should be included. The Regulation shall not exempt aid which exceeds the relevant aid intensity as a result of including ineligible costs. The identification of eligible costs should be supported by clear, specific and up-to date documentary evidence. All figures used should be taken before any deduction of tax or other charges. Aid payable in several instalments should be discounted to its value at the moment it is granted. The eligible costs should also be discounted to their value at the moment of granting. The interest rate to be used for discounting purposes and for calculating the amount of aid in the case of aid which does not take the form of a grant should be respectively the discount rate and the reference rate applicable at the time of the grant, as laid down in the Commission Communication on the revision of the method for setting the reference and discount rates.[10] Where aid is granted by means of tax advantages, aid tranches should be discounted on the basis of the discount rates applicable on the various dates when the tax advantages become effective. The use of aid in the form of repayable advances should be promoted, since such risk-sharing instruments are conducive to strengthened incentive effect of aid. It is therefore appropriate to establish that where aid is granted in the form of repayable advances the applicable aid intensities laid down in this Regulation may be increased, with the exception of regional aid since the latter may only be exempted if it complies with approved maps.

(24) In the case of tax advantages on future taxes, the applicable discount rate and the exact amount of the aid tranches may not be known in advance. In such cases, Member States should set in advance a cap on the discounted value of the aid respecting the applicable aid intensity. Subsequently, when the amount of the aid tranche at a given date becomes known, discounting can take place on the basis of the discount rate applicable at that time. The discounted value of each aid tranche should be deducted from the overall amount of the cap (capped amount).

(25) To determine whether the notification thresholds and the maximum aid intensities laid down in this Regulation are respected, the total amount of State aid measures for the aided activity or project should be taken into account. Moreover, this Regulation should specify the circumstances under which different categories of aid may be cumulated. Aid exempted by this Regulation and any other compatible aid exempted under other Regulation or approved by the Commission may be cumulated as long as those measures concern different identifiable eligible costs. Where different sources of aid are related to the same — partly or fully overlapping — identifiable eligible costs, cumulation should be allowed up to the highest aid intensity or aid amount applicable to that aid under this Regulation. This Regulation should also set out special rules for cumulation of aid measures with and without identifiable eligible costs, for cumulation with de minimis aid and for cumulation with aid in favour of workers with disabilities. De minimis aid is often not granted for or attributable to specific identifiable eligible costs. In such a case it should be possible to freely cumulate de minimis aid with State aid exempted under this Regulation. Where, however, de minimis aid is granted for the same identifiable eligible costs as State aid exempted under this Regulation, cumulation should only be allowed up to the maximum aid intensity as set out in Chapter III of this Regulation.

(26) Union funding centrally managed by the institutions, agencies, joint undertakings or other bodies of the Union, that is not directly or indirectly under the control of Member States, does not constitute State aid. Where such Union funding is combined with State aid, only the latter should be considered for determining whether notification thresholds and maximum aid intensities are respected, provided the total amount of public funding granted in relation to the same eligible costs does not exceed the most favourable funding rate laid down in the applicable rules of Union law.

(27) Given that State aid within the meaning of Article 107(1) of the Treaty is, in principle, prohibited, it is important for all parties to be able to check whether an aid is granted in compliance with the applicable rules. Transparency of State aid is, therefore, essential for the correct application of Treaty rules and leads to better compliance, greater accountability, peer review and ultimately more effective public spending. To ensure transparency, Member States should be required to establish comprehensive State aid websites, at regional or national level, setting out summary information about each aid measure exempted under this Regulation. That obligation should be a condition for the compatibility of the individual aid with the internal market. Following the standard practice regarding the publication of information in Directive 2013/37/EU of the European Parliament and of the Council of 26 June 2013 amending Directive 2003/98/EC on the re-use of public sector information,[11] a standard format should be used which allows the information to be searched, downloaded and easily published on the internet. The links to the State aid websites of all the Member States should be published on the Commission's website. In accordance with Article 3 of Regulation (EC) No 994/98, as amended by Regulation (EU) No 733/2013, summary information on each aid measure exempted under this Regulation should be published on the website of the Commission.

(28) To ensure effective monitoring of aid measures in accordance with Regulation (EC) No 994/98, as amended by Regulation (EU) No 733/2013, it is appropriate to establish requirements regarding the reporting by the Member States of aid measures which have been exempted pursuant to this Regulation and the application of this Regulation. Moreover, it is appropriate to establish rules concerning the records that Member States should keep regarding the aid exempted by this Regulation, in light of the limitation period established in Article 15 of Council Regulation (EC) No 659/1999 of 22 March 1999 laying down detailed rules for the application of Article 93 of the EC Treaty.[12]

(29) To reinforce the effectiveness of compatibility conditions set out in this Regulation, it should be possible for the Commission to withdraw the benefit of the block exemption for the future aid measures in the event of failure to comply with these requirements. The Commission should be able to restrict the withdrawal of the benefit of the block

exemption to certain types of aid, certain beneficiaries or aid measures adopted by certain authorities, where non-compliance with this Regulation affects only a limited group of measures or certain authorities. Such a targeted withdrawal should provide a proportionate remedy directly linked to the identified non-compliance with this Regulation. In case of failure to meet compatibility conditions set out in Chapters I and III, aid granted is not covered by this Regulation and, as a consequence, constitutes unlawful aid, which the Commission will examine in the framework of the relevant procedure as set out in Regulation No (EC) No 659/1999. In case of failure to fulfil the requirements of Chapter II, the withdrawal of the benefit of the block exemption in respect of the future aid measures does not affect the fact that the past measures complying with this Regulation were block exempted.

(30) To eliminate differences that might give rise to distortions of competition and to facilitate coordination between different Union and national initiatives concerning SMEs, as well as for reasons of administrative clarity and legal certainty, the definition of SME used for the purpose of this Regulation should be based on the definition in Commission Recommendation 2003/361/EC of 6 May 2003 concerning the definition of micro, small and medium sized enterprises.[13]

(31) By addressing the handicaps of disadvantaged regions, regional aid promotes the economic, social and territorial cohesion of Member States and the Union as a whole. Regional aid is designed to assist the development of the most disadvantaged areas by supporting investment and job creation in a sustainable context. In areas fulfilling the conditions of Article 107(3)(a) of the Treaty, regional aid may be granted to promote the setting-up of new establishments, the extension of the capacity of an existing establishment, the diversification of the output of an establishment or a fundamental change in the overall production process of an existing establishment. Considering that large enterprises are less affected by regional handicaps than SMEs when investing in an area fulfilling the conditions of Article 107(3)(c) of the Treaty, regional aid to large enterprises should be exempted from the notification requirement only for initial investments in favour of new economic activity in those areas.

(32) Where a regional aid scheme is targeted at a limited number of sectors of the economy, the objective and likely effects of the scheme may be sectorial rather than horizontal. Therefore, sectorial schemes cannot be exempted from the notification requirement. However, the Commission, upon notification, can assess their possible positive effects under the applicable guidelines or frameworks or decisions. In particular, this is the case for aid schemes covering economic activities in the coal sector, the shipbuilding sector, the transport sector. Furthermore, due to particular characteristics of the steel and synthetic fibres sectors, it is considered that the negative effects of regional aid in those sectors cannot be outweighed by the positive cohesion effects; for those reasons, regional aid cannot be granted in these sectors. Finally, the tourism and broadband sectors play an important role in national economies and, in general, have a particularly positive effect on regional development. Regional aid schemes aimed at tourism activities and broadband should therefore be exempted from the notification requirement. Processing and marketing of agricultural products are also strongly linked with local and regional economies and should benefit from the block exemption.

(33) Energy generation, distribution and infrastructure are subject to sector-specific internal market legislation, which is reflected in the criteria for ensuring that aid in these areas is compatible with the internal market and consistent with the Union's environmental and energy policies. Regional aid granted under Section 1 of this Regulation pursues economic development and cohesion objectives, and is therefore subject to very different compatibility conditions. The provisions of this Regulation on regional aid should therefore not apply to measures concerning energy generation, distribution and infrastructure.

(34) Investments enabling undertakings to go beyond Union standards or increase the level of environmental protection in the absence of Union standards, investments for early adaptation to future Union standards, investments for energy efficiency measures, including energy efficiency projects in buildings, investments for remediation of contaminated sites and aid for environmental studies do not directly influence the functioning of energy markets. At the same time, such investments may contribute to both regional policy objectives and to the energy and environmental objectives of the European Union. In such cases, the provisions of this Regulation relating to both regional aid and aid for environmental protection may be applicable, depending on the main objective pursued by the measure concerned.

(35) In order not to favour capital investment over investment in labour costs, it should be possible to measure regional investment aid on the basis of either the costs of the investment or the wage costs of employment directly created by an investment project.

(36) Regional investment aid should not be exempted from notification when it is granted to a beneficiary that has closed down the same or a similar activity in the European Economic Area in the two years preceding its application for regional investment aid or, at the time of the aid application, has concrete plans to close down such an activity within a period of up to two years after the initial investment for which aid is requested is completed in the area concerned.

(37) The Commission has gained sufficient experience in the application of Article 107(3)(a) and (c) of the Treaty as regards regional operating aid to compensate for the additional transport costs of goods produced in the outermost regions or in sparsely populated areas, and of goods further processed in those areas, as well as the additional production and operating costs (other than additional transport costs) incurred by beneficiaries established in the outermost regions. Since there is a risk of over-compensation for transport costs resulting from additional support under the POSEI programmes in the agriculture sector and since it cannot be excluded that some agricultural products are not produced in an alternative location, the agriculture sector should be excluded from regional operating aid to compensate the additional transport costs of goods produced in the outermost regions or in sparsely populated areas under this Regulation. Regional operating aid to compensate for additional costs in the outermost regions, other than additional transport costs, should only be considered compatible with the internal market and exempted from the notification requirement of Article 108(3) of the Treaty in so far as the level of that aid is limited to either 15% of the gross value added annually created by the beneficiary in the outermost region concerned or 25% of the annual labour costs incurred by the beneficiary in the outermost region concerned, or 10% of the annual turnover of the beneficiary in the outermost region concerned. Where the aid does not exceed the amount resulting from one of those alternative methods to determine the additional operating costs (other than transport costs), it can be considered as justified in

terms of contributing to regional development and proportionate to the handicaps that undertakings face in the outermost regions.

(38) By addressing the high concentration of economic, environmental and social problems of urban areas located in assisted areas identified in a regional aid map, urban development aid contributes to the economic, social and territorial cohesion of the Member States and the Union as a whole. The market failures to be addressed by urban development aid refer to the urban development funding environment, the lack of an integrated urban development approach, a funding deficit necessitating greater leverage of scarce public resources and the need for a more commercial approach to the regeneration of urban areas. Urban development aid to support the development of participative, integrated and sustainable strategies to tackle the additional problems identified in the assisted areas should therefore be covered by the block exemption.

(39) Investments corresponding to the Europe 2020[14] priorities in green technologies and the shift towards a low carbon economy, undertaken in assisted areas as identified in the relevant regional aid map, should be eligible for higher aid amounts by means of a regional bonus.

(40) SMEs play a decisive role in job creation and, more generally, act as a factor of social stability and economic development. However, their development may be hampered by market failures, leading to these SMEs suffering from the following typical handicaps. SMEs often have difficulties in obtaining capital or loans, given the risk averse nature of certain financial markets and the limited collateral that they may be able to offer. Their limited resources may also restrict their access to information, notably regarding new technology and potential markets. To facilitate the development of the economic activities of SMEs, this Regulation should therefore exempt certain categories of aid when they are granted in favour of SMEs. Those categories should include, in particular SME investment aid and SME participation in fairs.

(41) SMEs participating in the European Territorial Cooperation (ETC) projects covered by Regulation (EU) No 1299/2013 of the European Parliament and of the Council of 17 December 2013 on specific provisions for the support from the European Regional Development Fund to the European territorial cooperation goal[15] often find difficulties in financing additional costs stemming from the cooperation between partners located in different regions and in different Member States or third countries. Given the importance of the ETC for the cohesion policy providing a framework for the implementation of joint actions and policy exchanges between national, regional and local actors from different Member States or third countries, this Regulation should address certain difficulties faced by ETC projects in order to facilitate their compliance with State aid rules. The ETC-specific issues that this Regulation should address relate to the applicable regional aid intensity for ETC projects, SMEs' cooperation costs linked to ETC projects and to obligations concerning publication and information, reporting and keeping records for monitoring purposes.

(42) Having regard to the specific handicaps and differences between SMEs, different basic aid intensities and different bonuses may apply.

(43) On the basis of the experience gained in applying the Community guidelines on State aid to promote risk capital investments in SMEs,[16] there are a number of specific risk capital market failures in the Union in respect of certain types of investments at the different stages of the undertakings' development. Those market failures result from an imperfect matching of supply and demand for risk capital. As a result, the level of risk capital provided in the market may be too restricted and undertakings do not obtain funding despite having a valuable business model and growth prospects. The main source of market failure relevant to risk capital markets, which particularly affects access to capital by SMEs and which may justify public intervention, relates to imperfect or asymmetric information. It not only affects the provision of risk capital, but also hampers access to debt finance for certain SMEs. Consequently, risk finance measures which seek to attract private capital for risk finance provision to unlisted SMEs affected by the funding gap and which ensure profit-driven financing decisions and commercial management of financial intermediaries should be exempted from the notification requirement under certain conditions.

(44) Start-up aid for small enterprises, aid to alternative trading platforms specialised in SMEs and aid for costs related to the scouting of SMEs should also be exempted from the notification requirement under certain conditions.

(45) Aid for research and development and innovation aid can contribute to sustainable economic growth, strengthen competitiveness and boost employment. Experience with the application of Regulation (EC) No 800/2008 and the Community framework for State aid for research and development and innovation[17] shows that market failures may prevent the market from reaching optimal output and lead to inefficiencies related to externalities, public goods/knowledge spill-overs, imperfect and asymmetric information, and coordination and network failures.

(46) SMEs, may experience difficulties in gaining access to new technological developments, knowledge transfer or highly qualified personnel. Aid for research and development projects, aid for feasibility studies and innovation aid for SMEs, including aid to cover the costs of industrial property rights, may remedy those problems and should therefore be exempted from the notification requirement under certain conditions.

(47) As regards project aid for research and development, the aided part of the research project should completely fall within the categories of fundamental research, industrial research or experimental development. When a project encompasses different tasks, each task should be qualified as falling under one of those categories or as not falling under any of those categories. That qualification need not necessarily be chronological, moving sequentially over time from fundamental research to activities closer to the market. Accordingly, a task which is carried out at a late project stage may be qualified as industrial research. Similarly, an activity carried out at an earlier stage may constitute experimental development. The aided part of the project may also include feasibility studies preparatory to research activities.

(48) High-quality research infrastructures are increasingly necessary for ground-breaking research and innovation because they attract global talent and are essential in supporting new information and communication technologies and key enabling technologies. Public research infrastructures should continue to partner with industry research. Access to publicly funded research infrastructures should be granted on a transparent and nondiscriminatory basis and on market terms. If those conditions are not respected, the aid measure should not be exempted from the notification requirement. Multiple parties may own, operate and use a given research infrastructure, and public entities and undertakings may use the infrastructure collaboratively.

(49) Research infrastructures may perform both economic and non-economic activities. In order to avoid granting State aid to economic activities through public funding of non-economic activities, the costs and financing of economic and non-economic activities should be clearly separated. Where an infrastructure is used for both economic and non-economic activities, the funding through State resources of the costs linked to the noneconomic activities of the infrastructure does not constitute State aid. Public funding falls under State aid rules only insofar as it covers costs linked to the economic activities. Only the latter should be taken into account with a view to ensuring compliance with the notification thresholds and maximum aid intensities. If the infrastructure is used almost exclusively for a non-economic activity, its funding may fall outside State aid rules in its entirety, provided that the economic use remains purely ancillary, that is to say, an activity which is directly related to and necessary for the operation of the infrastructure or intrinsically linked to its main non-economic use, and is limited in scope. This should be considered to be the case when the economic activities consume the same inputs (such as material, equipment, labour and fixed capital) as the non-economic activities and the capacity allocated each year to such economic activity does not exceed 20% of the research infrastructure's overall annual capacity.

(50) Aid for innovation clusters aims at tackling market failures linked with coordination problems hampering the development of clusters, or limiting the interactions and knowledge flows within clusters. State aid can either support investment in open and shared infrastructures for innovation clusters, or support the operation of clusters, so that collaboration, networking and learning is enhanced. Operating aid for innovation clusters should, however, only be allowed on a temporary basis for a limited period not exceeding 10 years. The ratio of the total amount of aid granted to the total eligible costs should not exceed 50% during the period over which the aid is granted,

(51) Process and organisational innovation may suffer from market failures in the form of imperfect information and positive externalities, which should be addressed by specific measures. Aid for this type of innovation is mainly relevant for SMEs, as they face constraints that may hamper their capability to improve their production or delivery methods or to significantly enhance their business practices, workplace organisation and external relations. In order to stimulate large enterprises to collaborate with SMEs in process and organisational innovation activities, aid measures which support the costs of large enterprises for such activities should also benefit from the block exemption regulation under certain conditions.

(52) The promotion of training and the recruitment/employment of disadvantaged workers and of workers with disabilities constitutes a central objective of the economic and social policies of the Union and its Member States.

(53) Training usually generates positive externalities for society as a whole, since it increases the pool of skilled workers from which other firms may draw, improves the competitiveness of the Union industry and plays an important role in the Union employment strategy. Aid to promote training should therefore be exempted from the notification requirement under certain conditions. In the light of the particular handicaps which SMEs face and the higher relative costs that they must bear when they invest in training, the intensities of aid exempted by this Regulation should be increased for SMEs. Furthermore, the intensities of aid exempted by this Regulation should be increased if the training is given to disadvantaged workers or to workers with disabilities. The characteristics of training in the maritime transport sector justify a specific approach for that sector.

(54) Certain categories of disadvantaged workers and workers with disabilities still experience particular difficulties in entering and remaining in the labour market. For this reason, public authorities may apply measures providing incentives to undertakings to increase the levels of employment of these categories of workers, in particular of young people. As employment costs form part of the normal operating costs of any undertaking aid for the employment of disadvantaged workers and of workers with disabilities should have a positive effect on employment levels of those categories of workers and should not merely enable undertakings to reduce costs which they would otherwise have to bear. Consequently, such aid should be exempted from the notification requirement when it is likely to assist those categories of workers in entering or re-entering and remaining in the job market. As set out in the Communication from the Commission to The European Parliament, the Council, the European Economic And Social Committee and the Committee Of The Regions — European Disability Strategy 2010–2020: A Renewed Commitment to a Barrier-Free Europe[18] the core elements of the EU disability strategy, combine anti-discrimination, equal opportunities and active inclusion measures and reflect the United Nations Convention on the Rights of Persons with Disabilities to which the EU and the majority of the Member States are a party. This Regulation should refer to aid for workers with disabilities in the sense of Article 1 of the Convention.

(55) As stated in the Communication from the Commission — Europe 2020: A strategy for smart, sustainable and inclusive growth,[19] Sustainable growth for a resource efficient, greener and more competitive economy is one of the main pillars of the Europe 2020 objective of the smart, sustainable and inclusive growth strategy. Sustainable development is based, amongst other things, on a high level of protection and improvement of the quality of the environment. The area of environmental protection is confronted with market failures so that, under normal market conditions, undertakings may not necessarily have an incentive to reduce the pollution caused by them since any such reduction may increase their costs without corresponding benefits. When undertakings are not obliged to internalise the costs of pollution, society as a whole bears these costs.

(56) Introducing mandatory environmental standards can address such market failure. A higher level of environmental protection can be achieved by investments that go beyond mandatory Union standards. In order to incentivise undertakings to improve the level of environmental protection beyond these mandatory Union standards, State aid in this area should be covered by the block exemption. In order not to dissuade Member States from setting mandatory national standards which are more stringent than the corresponding Union standards, such State aid should be exempt, irrespective of the presence of mandatory national standards that are more stringent than the Union standard.

(57) In principle aid should not be granted where investments bring undertakings into compliance with Union standards already adopted and not yet in force. However, State aid may result in undertakings improving their environmental behaviour if such State aid incentivises undertakings to adapt early to future Union standards before such standards enter into force and as long as such standards do not apply retroactively. Aid to undertakings to adapt to future Union standards, may result in a high level of environmental protection being achieved sooner and such aid should therefore be exempted.

(58) As part of the Europe 2020 strategy, the Union has set itself the objective of achieving a 20% increase in energy efficiency by 2020 and has, in particular, adopted Directive 2012/27/EU of the European Parliament and of the Council of 25 October 2012 on energy efficiency, amending Directives 2009/125/EC and 2010/30/EU and repealing Directives 2004/8/EC and 2006/32/EC[20] which establishes a common framework to promote energy efficiency within the Union pursuing the overall objective of saving at least 20% of the Union's primary energy consumption. In order to facilitate the achievement of those targets, measures supporting energy efficiency, high efficiency cogeneration as well as energy efficient district heating and cooling should be covered by the block exemption.

(59) Measures increasing the energy efficiency of buildings correspond to Europe 2020 priorities concerning a shift towards a low carbon economy. Due to the lack of an integrated approach for energy efficiency in buildings, such investments may often face a funding deficit necessitating greater leverage of scarce public resources. Therefore the Member States should have the possibility to support energy efficiency investments in buildings by granting aid in the form of direct grants to the building owners or tenants in line with the general provisions on energy efficiency measures but also in the form of loans and guarantees via financial intermediaries chosen under a transparent selection mechanism under the specific provisions for energy efficiency projects in buildings.

(60) To achieve the Union's renewable energy targets set out in Directive 2009/28/EC of the European Parliament and of the Council of 23 April 2009 on the promotion of the use of energy from renewable sources and amending and subsequently repealing Directives 2001/77/EC and 2003/30/EC[21] and to the extent that additional support is needed on top of a regulatory framework such as the Union emission trading scheme in Directive 2003/87/EC of the European Parliament and of the Council of 13 October 2003 establishing a scheme for greenhouse gas emission allowance trading within the Community and amending Council Directive 96/61/EC,[22] aid granted to investments supporting energy from renewable sources should be covered by the block exemption.

(61) In view of the limited distortions of trade and competition, the block exemption should also cover operating aid for small scale installations producing renewable energy, subject to well-defined conditions. Operating aid to larger scale installations should be covered by the block exemption where distortions of competition are limited. Therefore, such operating aid can be block exempted when granted to new and innovative technologies if the aid is granted on the basis of a competitive bidding process open to at least one such technology using a mechanism which exposes renewable energy producers to market prices. The total aid granted on this basis cannot be granted for more than 5% of the planned new electricity capacity from renewable energy sources. Aid granted through bidding processes open to all renewable energy technologies should be fully covered by the block exemption. Operating aid schemes should in principle be opened to other EEA countries and contracting parties of the Energy Community to limit the overall distortive effects. Member States are encouraged to consider having a cooperation mechanism in place before allowing cross border support. In the absence of a cooperation mechanism, production from installations in other countries will not count towards their national renewable energy target. In view of these constraints, Member States should be allowed sufficient lead time in order to design appropriate support schemes that are open to other countries. Therefore, such opening is not a condition for exemption from notification, to the extent it is not required under the Treaty.

(62) With regard to aid for the production of hydropower, its impact can be twofold. On the one hand, it has a positive impact in terms of low greenhouse gas emissions and on the other hand it might also have a negative impact on water systems and biodiversity. Therefore, when granting aid to hydropower Member States should comply with Directive 2000/60/EC of the European Parliament and of the Council of 23 October 2000 establishing a framework for Community action in the field of water policy[23] and in particular Article 4(7) which lays down criteria in relation to allowing new modifications of bodies of water.

(63) Aid should only be granted to sustainable forms of renewable energy. Aid to biofuels should only be covered by this Regulation in so far as it is granted for sustainable biofuels in accordance with the Directive 2009/28/EC of the European Parliament and the Council. However, aid for food based biofuels should be excluded from aid under this Regulation to incentivise the shift towards the production of more advanced forms of biofuels. Aid to biofuels that are subject to a supply or blending obligation should be excluded from the scope of the block exemption as the above legal obligation may provide sufficient incentive for investments in these types of renewable energy.

(64) Aid in the form of tax reductions pursuant to Council Directive 2003/96/EC of 27 October 2003 restructuring the Community framework for the taxation of energy products and electricity[24] favouring environmental protection covered by this Regulation can indirectly benefit the environment. However, environmental taxes should reflect the social cost of emissions while reductions from taxes may adversely impact on this objective. It therefore seems appropriate to limit their duration to the period of application of this Regulation. After this period, Member States should re-evaluate the appropriateness of the tax reductions concerned. In order to minimise the distortion of competition, the aid should be granted in the same way for all competitors found to be in a similar factual situation. To better preserve the price signal for undertakings which the environmental tax aims to give, Member States should have the option to design the tax reduction scheme based on a fixed annual compensation amount (tax refund) disbursement mechanism.

(65) In the light of the 'polluter pays principle', the costs of measures to deal with pollution should be borne by the polluter who causes the pollution. Aid for the remediation of contaminated sites is justified in cases where the person liable under the applicable law for the contamination cannot be identified. However, the conditions on environmental liability with regard to the prevention and remediation of environmental damage as defined in the Directive 2004/35/EC of the European Parliament and of the Council of 21 April 2004 on environmental liability with regard to the prevention and remedying of environmental damage[25] as amended by Directive 2006/21/EC of the European Parliament and of the Council of 15 March 2006 on the management of waste from extractive industries and amending Directive 2004/35/EC[26] and Directive 2009/31/EC of the European Parliament and of the Council of 23 April 2009 on the geological storage of carbon dioxide and amending Council Directive 85/337/EEC, European Parliament and Council Directives 2000/60/EC, 2001/80/EC, 2004/35/EC, 2006/12/EC, 2008/1/EC and Regulation (EC) No 1013/2006[27] should apply. Therefore, to facilitate the correction of existing environmental damage, this type of aid should be covered by the block exemption under certain conditions.

(66) In line with the waste hierarchy established in the European Union's Waste Framework Directive, the

Seventh Environment Action Programme identifies waste re-use and recycling as key priorities of the European Union environmental policy. State aid for these activities can contribute to environmental protection provided that Article 4(1) of Directive 2008/98/EC of the European Parliament and of the Council of 19 November 2008 on waste and repealing certain Directives (Waste Framework Directive)[28] are respected. Moreover, such aid should not indirectly relieve the polluters of a burden they should bear under Union law, or of a burden that should be considered a normal company cost. Therefore, aid benefitting such activities should be covered by the block exemption including when it concerns waste of other undertakings and where the materials treated would otherwise be disposed of, or be treated in a less environmentally friendly manner.

(67) A modern energy infrastructure is crucial both for an integrated energy market and to enable the Union to meet its climate and energy goals. In particular, infrastructure construction and upgrade in assisted regions contribute to the economic, social and territorial cohesion of Member States and the Union as a whole by supporting investment and job creation and the functioning of energy markets in the most disadvantaged areas. In order to limit any undue distortive effects of such aid, only aid to infrastructures subject to and in accordance with the internal energy market legislation should be block exempted.

(68) Environmental studies can help to identify the investments necessary to achieve a higher level of environmental protection. State aid to support the carrying out of environmental studies which aim to support investments in environmental protection as covered by this Regulation should therefore be covered by the block exemption. As energy audits are mandatory for large enterprises, they should not benefit from State aid.

(69) In accordance with Article 107(2)(b) of the Treaty, aid to make good the damage caused by natural disasters is compatible with the internal market. In order to provide legal certainty it is necessary to define the type of events that may constitute a natural disaster exempted by this Regulation. For the purposes of this Regulation, earthquakes, landslides, floods, in particular floods brought about by waters overflowing river banks or lake shores, avalanches, tornadoes, hurricanes, volcanic eruptions and wildfires of natural origin should be considered events constituting a natural disaster. Damage caused by adverse weather conditions such as frost, hail, ice, rain or drought, which occur on a more regular basis, should not be considered a natural disaster within the meaning of Article 107(2)(b) of the Treaty. In order to ensure that aid granted to make good the damage caused by natural disasters is indeed covered by the exemption, this Regulation should lay down conditions following established practice the fulfilment of which will ensure that aid schemes to make good the damage caused by natural disasters can benefit from block exemption. Those conditions should relate, in particular, to the formal recognition by the competent Member States' authorities of the character of the event as a natural disaster and to a direct causal link between the natural disaster and the damages suffered by the beneficiary undertaking, which may include undertakings in difficulty, and should ensure that overcompensation is avoided. The compensation should not exceed what is necessary to enable the beneficiary to return to the situation prevailing before the disaster occurred.

(70) Aid has a social character for air and maritime passenger transport where it addresses the problem of steady connectivity for residents of remote regions by reducing certain transport ticket costs for them. This may be the case for outermost regions, Malta, Cyprus, Ceuta and Melilla, other islands which are part of the territory of a Member State and sparsely populated areas. Where a remote region is linked to the European Economic Area by several transport routes, including indirect routes, aid should be possible for all those routes and for transport by all carriers operating on these routes. Aid should be granted without discrimination as to the identity of the carrier or type of service and may include regular, charter and low-cost services.

(71) Broadband connectivity is of strategic importance for the achievement of the Europe 2020 objective of smart, sustainable and inclusive growth and innovation and for social and territorial cohesion.[29] Investment aid for broadband infrastructure aims at fostering the deployment of such infrastructure and related civil engineering works in areas where no comparable infrastructure exists nor is likely to be deployed by market operators in the near future. In the light of the Commission's experience, such investment aid does not give rise to undue distortions of trade and competition, provided that certain conditions are met. Such conditions should aim, in particular, at limiting distortions of competition by subjecting aid to technology-neutral competitive selection and by ensuring wholesale access to the subsidised networks, taking into account the aid received by the network operator. Although under certain conditions virtual unbundling may be considered equivalent to physical unbundling, until more experience is acquired, there is a need to assess on a case by case basis whether a particular non-physical or virtual wholesale access product should be considered equivalent to local loop unbundling of a copper or fibre network. For this reason, and until such experience in individual State aid cases or in the ex ante regulatory context can be taken into account in a future review, physical unbundling should be required for the purposes of benefiting from the present block exemption regulation. Where future costs and revenue developments are uncertain and there is a strong asymmetry of information, Member States should also adopt financing models that include monitoring and claw-back elements to allow a balanced sharing of unanticipated gains. To avoid a disproportionate burden on small, local projects, such models should be put in place only for projects exceeding a minimum threshold.

(72) In the culture and heritage conservation sector, a number of measures taken by Member States may not constitute aid because they do not fulfil all the criteria of Article 107(1) of the Treaty, for example because the activity is not economic or because trade between Member States is not affected. To the extent that such measures are covered by Article 107(1) of the Treaty, cultural institutions and projects do not typically give rise to any significant distortion of competition, and case practice has shown that such aid has limited effects on trade. Article 167 of the Treaty recognises the importance of promoting culture for the Union and its Member States and provides that the Union should take cultural aspects into account in its action under other provisions of the Treaty, in particular in order to respect and to promote the diversity of its cultures. As natural heritage is often crucial to shaping of artistic and cultural heritage, heritage conservation in the sense of this Regulation should be understood to cover also natural heritage linked to cultural heritage or formally recognised by the competent public authorities of a Member State. Because of the dual nature of culture, being on the one hand an economic good that offers important opportunities for the creation of wealth and employment, and, on the other, a vehicle of identities, values and meanings that mirror and shape our societies, State aid rules should acknowledge the specificities of culture and the economic activities related to it. A list of eligible cultural purposes and activities should be established and eligible costs should be specified. The

block exemption should cover both investment and operating aid below determined thresholds provided that overcompensation is excluded. In general, activities which, although they may present a cultural aspect, have a predominantly commercial character because of the higher potential for competition distortions, such as press and magazines (written or electronic), should not be covered. Furthermore, the list of eligible cultural purposes and activities should not include commercial activities such as fashion, design or video games.

(73) Audiovisual works play an important role in shaping European identities and reflect the different traditions of Member States and regions. While there is strong competition between films produced outside the Union, there is limited circulation of European films outside their country of origin due to the fragmentation into national or regional markets. The sector is characterised by high investment costs, a perceived lack of profitability due to limited audiences and difficulties to generate additional private funding. Due to these factors the Commission has developed specific criteria to assess the necessity, proportionality and adequacy of aid to script-writing, development, production, distribution and promotion of audiovisual works. New criteria were determined in the Communication from the Commission on State aid for films and other audiovisual works[30] *and should be reflected in block exemption rules for aid schemes for audiovisual works. Higher aid intensities are justified for cross-border productions and co-productions which are more likely to be distributed in several Member States.*

(74) Investment aid measures for sport infrastructures should be covered by the block exemption if they fulfil the conditions laid down in this Regulation, to the extent they constitute State aid. In the sport sector a number of measures taken by Member States may not constitute State aid because the beneficiary does not carry out an economic activity or because there is no effect on trade between Member States. This could be, under certain circumstances, the case for aid measures which have a purely local character or which are taken in the field of amateur sport. Article 165 of the Treaty recognises the importance of promoting European sporting issues, while taking account of the specific nature of sport, its structures based on voluntary activity and its social and educational function. Aid to infrastructures which serve more than one purpose of recreation and are thus multifunctional should also be covered by the block exemption. However, aid to multifunctional tourism infrastructures such as leisure parks and hotel facilities should only be exempted if it is part of a regional aid scheme aimed at tourism activities in an assisted region which have a particular positive effect on regional development. The compatibility conditions regarding aid for sport or multifunctional infrastructures should ensure, in particular, open and non-discriminatory access to the infrastructures and a fair process of assignment of concessions to a third party in accordance with the relevant provisions of Union law and the case law of the Union to construct, upgrade and/or operate the infrastructure. If sport infrastructure is used by professional sport clubs, pricing conditions for the use of the infrastructure by those clubs should be made publicly available to ensure transparency and equal treatment of users. The exclusion of overcompensation should be ensured.

(75) As emphasized by the conclusions of the European Council of the 17 June 2010 endorsing the Europe 2020 Strategy,[31] *efforts should seek to address the main bottlenecks constraining growth at EU level, including those related to the functioning of the internal market and infrastructure. The availability of local infrastructures is an important prerequisite for development of business and consumer environment and for modernising and developing the industrial base in order to ensure the full functioning of the internal market as referred to in the Council Recommendation on broad guidelines for economic policies of the Member States and of the Union,*[32] *which form part of the Europe 2020 integrated guidelines. Such infrastructures, made available to interested parties on an open, transparent and non-discriminatory basis, enable the creation of an environment conducive to private investment and growth, thus contributing positively to objectives of common interest, and in particular to the Europe 2020 priorities and objectives,*[33] *while the risks of distortions remain limited. A number of measures taken by Member States with regard to local infrastructures do not constitute aid because they do not fulfil all the criteria of Article 107(1) of the Treaty, for example because the beneficiary does not carry out an economic activity, because there is no effect on trade between Member States, or because the measure consists of compensation for a service of general economic interest which fulfils all the criteria of the Altmark case-law.*[34] *However, where the financing of such local infrastructures does constitute State aid within the meaning of Article 107(1) of the Treaty, such aid should be exempted from the notification requirement when only small amounts of aid are granted.*

(76) Since aid for other types of infrastructures may be subject to specific and well-designed criteria which ensure its compatibility with the internal market, the provisions of this Regulation regarding aid for local infrastructures should not apply to aid to the following types of infrastructures: research infrastructures, innovation clusters, energy efficient district heating and cooling, energy infrastructures, waste recycling and re-use, broadband infrastructures, culture and heritage conservation, sport and multifunctional recreational infrastructures, airports and ports.

(77) In the light of the Commission's experience in this area, State aid policy should periodically be revised. The period of application of this Regulation should therefore be limited. It is appropriate to lay down transitional provisions, including the rules applicable to exempted aid schemes at the end of the period of application of this Regulation. Such rules should give Member States time to adapt to any future regime. The adjustment period should not, however, apply to regional aid schemes, including regional urban development aid schemes, the exemption of which must expire on the date on which the approved regional aid maps expire, and to certain risk finance aid schemes,

NOTES

Repeal of this Regulation in relation to the UK: this Regulation is repealed in relation to the UK (as from IP completion day); see the introductory notes to this Regulation *ante*.

1 OJ L142, 14.5.1998, p 1.
2 OJ L241, 9.8.2008, p 3.
3 OJ L320, 30.11.2013, p 22.
4 OJ L204, 31.7.2013, p 11.
5 COM(2012) 209, 8.5.2012.
6 OJ L336, 21.12.2010, p 24.
7 OJ C244, 1.10.2004, p 2.
8 OJ C296, 2.10.2012, p 3.
9 OJ C155, 20.6.2008, p 10.

10 OJ C14, 19.1.2008, p 6.
11 OJ L175 27.6.2013, p 1.
12 OJ L83, 27.3.1999, p 1.
13 OJ L124, 20.5.2003, p 36.
14 EUCO 13/10 REV 1.
15 OJ L347, 20.12.2013, p 259.
16 OJ C194, 18.8.2006, p 2.
17 OJ C323, 30.12.2006, p 1.
18 Com(2010)636, 15.11.2010.
19 Com(2010) 2020, 3.3.2010.
20 OJ L315, 14.11.2012, p 1.
21 OJ L140, 5.6.2009, p 16.
22 OJ L275, 25.10.2003, p 32.
23 OJ L327, 22.12.2000, p 1.
24 OJ L283, 31.10.2003, p 51.
25 OJ L143, 30.4.2004, p 56.
26 OJ L102, 11.4.2006, p 15.
27 OJ L140, 5.6.2009, p 114.
28 OJ L312, 22.11.2008, p 3.
29 COM(2010) 245, 19.5.2010.
30 OJ C332, 15.11.2013, p 1.
31 EUCO 13/10 REV 1.
32 OJ L191, 23.7.2010, p 28.
33 Com(2010)2020, 3.3.2010.
34 Judgment of the Court of Justice of 24 July 2003 in Case C-280/00, *Altmark Trans GmbH and Regierungspräsidium Magdeburg v Nahverkehrsgesellschaft Altmark GmbH and Oberbundesanwalt beim Bundesverwaltungsgericht* ([2003] ECR I-7747).

HAS ADOPTED THIS REGULATION:

CHAPTER I COMMON PROVISIONS

[5.64]

Article 1 Scope

1. This Regulation shall apply to the following categories of aid:

(a) regional aid;
(b) aid to SMEs in the form of investment aid, operating aid and SMEs' access to finance;
(c) aid for environmental protection;
(d) aid for research and development and innovation;
(e) training aid;
(f) recruitment and employment aid for disadvantaged workers and workers with disabilities;
(g) aid to make good the damage caused by certain natural disasters;
(h) social aid for transport for residents of remote regions;
(i) aid for broadband infrastructures;
(j) aid for culture and heritage conservation;
[(k) aid for sport and multifunctional recreational infrastructure;
(l) aid for local infrastructures;]
[(m) aid for regional airports;
(n) aid for ports;]
[(o) aid for European Territorial Cooperation projects; and
(p) aid involved in financial products supported by the InvestEU Fund.]

2. This Regulation shall not apply to:

[(a) schemes under Sections 1 (with the exception of Article 15), 2, 3, 4, 7 (with the exception of Article 44) and 10 of Chapter III of this Regulation and aid implemented in the form of financial products under Section 16 of that Chapter, if the average annual State aid budget per Member State exceeds EUR 150 million, from six months after their entry into force. For aid under Section 16 of Chapter III of this Regulation, only contributions by a Member State to the Member State compartment of the EU guarantee, referred to in Article 9(1), point (b), of Regulation (EU) 2021/523 of the European Parliament and the Council,[1] which are earmarked for a specific financial product shall be taken into account for assessing whether the average annual State aid budget of that Member State related to the financial product exceeds EUR 150 million. The Commission may decide that this Regulation shall continue to apply for a longer period to any of these aid schemes after having assessed the relevant evaluation plan notified by the Member State to the Commission, within 20 working days from the scheme's entry into force. Where the Commission has already extended the application of this Regulation beyond the initial six months as regards such schemes, Member States may decide to extend those schemes until the end of the period of application of this Regulation, provided that the Member State concerned has submitted an evaluation report in line with the evaluation plan approved by the Commission. However, regional aid granted under this Regulation may be extended, by derogation, until the end of the period of validity of the relevant regional aid maps;]

(b) any alterations of schemes referred to in Article 1(2)(a), other than modifications which cannot affect the compatibility of the aid scheme under this Regulation or cannot significantly affect the content of the approved evaluation plan;

(c) *aid to export-related activities towards third countries or Member States, namely aid directly linked to the quantities exported, to the establishment and operation of a distribution network or to other current costs linked to the export activity;*

(d) *aid contingent upon the use of domestic over imported goods.*

3. *[This Regulation shall not apply to:*

[(a) aid granted in the fishery and aquaculture sector, as covered by Regulation (EU) No 1379/2013 of the European Parliament and of the Council[2]*. with the exception of training aid, aid for SMEs' access to finance, aid in the field of research and development, innovation aid for SMEs, aid for disadvantaged workers and workers with disabilities, regional investment aid in outermost regions, regional operating aid schemes, aid for European Innovation Partnership for agricultural productivity and sustainability ("EIP") Operational Group projects, aid for community-led local development ("CLLD") projects, aid to European Territorial Cooperation projects, and aid involved in financial products supported by the InvestEU Fund, except for operations listed in Article 1(1) of Commission Regulation (EU) No 717/2014;*[3]

(b) aid granted in the primary agricultural production sector, with the exception of regional investment aid in outermost regions, regional operating aid schemes, aid for consultancy in favour of SMEs, risk finance aid, aid for research and development, innovation aid for SMEs, environmental aid, training aid, aid for disadvantaged workers and workers with disabilities, aid to European Innovation Partnership for agricultural productivity and sustainability (EIP) Operational Group projects, aid to community-led local development (CLLD) projects, aid to European Territorial Cooperation projects and aid involved in financial products supported by the InvestEU Fund;]

(c) aid granted in the sector of processing and marketing of agricultural products, in the following cases:

(i) where the amount of the aid is fixed on the basis of the price or quantity of such products purchased from primary producers or put on the market by the undertakings concerned;

(ii) where the aid is conditional on being partly or entirely passed on to primary producers;

(d) aid to facilitate the closure of uncompetitive coal mines, as covered by Council Decision 2010/787/EU;[2]

(e) the categories of regional aid referred to in Article 13.]

Where an undertaking is active in the excluded sectors as referred to in points (a), (b) or (c) of the first subparagraph and in sectors which fall within the scope of this Regulation, this Regulation applies to aid granted in respect of the latter sectors or activities, provided that Member States ensure by appropriate means, such as separation of activities or distinction of costs, that the activities in the excluded sectors do not benefit from the aid granted in accordance with this Regulation.

[4. This Regulation shall not apply to:

(a) aid schemes which do not explicitly exclude the payment of individual aid in favour of an undertaking which is subject to an outstanding recovery order following a previous Commission decision declaring an aid granted by the same Member State illegal and incompatible with the internal market, with the exception of aid schemes to make good the damage caused by certain natural disasters and aid schemes covered by Article 19b, Section 2a as well as Section 16 of Chapter III;

(b) ad hoc aid in favour of an undertaking as referred to in point (a);

(c) aid to undertakings in difficulty, with the exception of aid schemes to make good the damage caused by certain natural disasters, start-up aid schemes, regional operating aid schemes, aid schemes covered by Article 19b, aid to SMEs under Article 56f and aid to financial intermediaries under Articles 16, 21, 22 and 39 as well as Section 16 of Chapter III, provided undertakings in difficulty are not treated more favourably than other undertakings. However, this Regulation shall apply, by derogation, to undertakings which were not in difficulty on 31 December 2019but became undertakings in difficulty during the period from 1 January 2020to 31 December 2021.]

5. This Regulation shall not apply to State aid measures, which entail, by themselves, by the conditions attached to them or by their financing method a non-severable violation of Union law, in particular:

(a) aid measures where the grant of aid is subject to the obligation for the beneficiary to have its headquarters in the relevant Member State or to be predominantly established in that Member State; However, the requirement to have an establishment or branch in the aid granting Member State at the moment of payment of the aid is allowed.

(b) aid measures where the grant of aid is subject to the obligation for the beneficiary to use nationally produced goods or national services;

(c) aid measures restricting the possibility for the beneficiaries to exploit the research, development and innovation results in other Member States.

NOTES

Para 1: points (k), (l) substituted and points (m), (n) added by Commission Regulation 2017/1084/EU, Art 1(1)(a). Points (m), (n) subsequently substituted, and points (o), (p) added, by Commission Regulation 2021/1237/EU, Art 1(1)(a), as from 1 August 2021.

Para 2: point (a) substituted by Commission Regulation 2021/1237/EU, Art 1(1)(b), as from 1 August 2021.

Para 3: words in square brackets from the beginning to the end of point (e) substituted by Commission Regulation 2017/1084/EU, Art 1(1)(b). Points (a), (b) substituted by Commission Regulation 2021/1237/EU, Art 1(1)(c), as from 1 August 2021.

Para 4: substituted by Commission Regulation 2021/1237/EU, Art 1(1)(d), as from 1 August 2021.

Repeal of this Regulation in relation to the UK: this Regulation is repealed in relation to the UK (as from IP completion day); see the introductory notes to this Regulation *ante*.

1 Regulation (EU) 2021/523 of the European Parliament and the Council of 24 March 2021 establishing the InvestEU Programme and amending Regulation (EU) 2015/1017 (OJ L107, 26.3.2021, p 30).

2 Regulation (EU) No 1379/2013 of the European Parliament and of the Council of 11 December 2013 on the common organisation of the markets in fishery and aquaculture products, amending Council Regulations (EC) No 1184/2006 and (EC) No 1224/2009 and repealing Council Regulation (EC) No 104/2000 (OJ L354, 28.12.2013, p 1).

3 Commission Regulation (EU) No 717/2014 of 27 June 2014 on the application of Articles 107 and 108 of the Treaty on

the Functioning of the European Union to de minimis aid in the fishery and aquaculture sector (OJ L190, 28.6.2014, p 45.

[5.65]

Article 2 Definitions

For the purposes of this Regulation the following definitions shall apply:

(1) 'aid' means any measure fulfilling all the criteria laid down in Article 107(1) of the Treaty;

(2) 'small and medium-sized enterprises' or 'SMEs' means undertakings fulfilling the criteria laid down in Annex I;

(3) 'worker with disabilities' means any person who:

(a) is recognised as worker with disabilities under national law; or

(b) has long-term physical, mental, intellectual or sensory impairment(s) which, in interaction with various barriers, may hinder their full and effective participation in a work environment on an equal basis with other workers;

(4) 'disadvantaged worker' means any person who:

(a) has not been in regular paid employment for the previous 6 months; or

(b) is between 15 and 24 years of age; or

(c) has not attained an upper secondary educational or vocational qualification (International Standard Classification of Education 3) or is within two years after completing full-time education and who has not previously obtained his or her first regular paid employment; or

(d) is over the age of 50 years; or

(e) lives as a single adult with one or more dependents; or

(f) works in a sector or profession in a Member State where the gender imbalance is at least 25% higher than the average gender imbalance across all economic sectors in that Member State, and belongs to that underrepresented gender group; or

(g) is a member of an ethnic minority within a Member State and who requires development of his or her linguistic, vocational training or work experience profile to enhance prospects of gaining access to stable employment;

(5) 'transport' means transport of passengers by aircraft, maritime transport, road, rail, or by inland waterway or freight transport services for hire or reward;

(6) 'transport costs' means the costs of transport for hire or reward actually paid by the beneficiaries per journey, comprising:

(a) freight charges, handling costs and temporary stocking costs, in so far as these costs relate to the journey;

(b) insurance costs applied to the cargo;

(c) taxes, duties or levies applied to the cargo and, if applicable, to the deadweight, both at point of origin and point of destination; and

(d) safety and security control costs, surcharges for increased fuel costs;

(7) 'remote regions' means outermost regions, Malta, Cyprus, Ceuta and Melilla, islands which are part of the territory of a Member State and sparsely populated areas;

(8) 'marketing of agricultural products' means holding or display with a view to sale, offering for sale, delivery or any other manner of placing on the market, except the first sale by a primary producer to resellers or processors and any activity preparing a product for such first sale; a sale by a primary producer to final consumers shall be considered to be marketing if it takes place in separate premises reserved for that purpose;

(9) 'primary agricultural production' means production of products of the soil and of stock farming, listed in Annex I to the Treaty, without performing any further operation changing the nature of such products;

(10) 'processing of agricultural products' means any operation on an agricultural product resulting in a product which is also an agricultural product, except on-farm activities necessary for preparing an animal or plant product for the first sale;

(11) 'agricultural product' means the products listed in Annex I to the Treaty, except fishery and aquaculture products listed in Annex I to Regulation (EU) No 1379/2013 of the European Parliament and of the Council of 11 December 2013;

(12) 'outermost regions' means regions as defined in Article 349 of the Treaty. In accordance with European Council Decision 2010/718/EU, from 1 January 2012, Saint-Barthélemy ceased to be an outermost region. In accordance with European Council Decision 2012/419/EU on 1 January 2014, Mayotte became an outermost region;

(13) 'coal' means high-grade, medium-grade and low-grade category A and B coal within the meaning of the international codification system for coal established by the United Nations Economic Commission for Europe and clarified in the Council decision of 10 December 2010 on State aid to facilitate the closure of uncompetitive coal mines;[1]

(14) 'individual aid' means:

(i) ad hoc aid; and

(ii) awards of aid to individual beneficiaries on the basis of an aid scheme;

(15) 'aid scheme' means any act on the basis of which, without further implementing measures being required, individual aid awards may be made to undertakings defined within the act in a general and abstract manner and any act on the basis of which aid which is not linked to a specific project may be granted to one or several undertakings for an indefinite period of time and/or for an indefinite amount;

(16) 'evaluation plan' means a document containing at least the following minimum elements: the objectives of the aid scheme to be evaluated, the evaluation questions, the result indicators, the envisaged methodology to conduct the evaluation, the data collection requirements, the proposed timing of the evaluation including the date of submission of the final evaluation report, the description of the independent body conducting the evaluation or the criteria that will be used for its selection and the modalities for ensuring the publicity of the evaluation;

(17) 'ad hoc aid' means aid not granted on the basis of an aid scheme;

(18) 'undertaking in difficulty' means an undertaking in respect of which at least one of the following circumstances occurs:

(a) In the case of a limited liability company (other than an SME that has been in existence for less than three years or, for the purposes of eligibility for risk finance aid, an SME within 7 years from its first commercial sale that qualifies for risk finance investments following due diligence by the selected financial intermediary), where more than half of its subscribed share capital has disappeared as a result of accumulated losses. This is the case when deduction of accumulated losses from reserves (and all other elements generally considered as part of the own funds of the company) leads to a negative cumulative amount that exceeds half of the subscribed share capital. For the purposes of this provision, 'limited liability company' refers in particular to the types of company mentioned in Annex I of Directive 2013/34/EU[2] and 'share capital' includes, where relevant, any share premium.

(b) In the case of a company where at least some members have unlimited liability for the debt of the company (other than an SME that has been in existence for less than three years or, for the purposes of eligibility for risk finance aid, an SME within 7 years from its first commercial sale that qualifies for risk finance investments following due diligence by the selected financial intermediary), where more than half of its capital as shown in the company accounts has disappeared as a result of accumulated losses. For the purposes of this provision, 'a company where at least some members have unlimited liability for the debt of the company' refers in particular to the types of company mentioned in Annex II of Directive 2013/34/EU.

(c) Where the undertaking is subject to collective insolvency proceedings or fulfils the criteria under its domestic law for being placed in collective insolvency proceedings at the request of its creditors.

(d) Where the undertaking has received rescue aid and has not yet reimbursed the loan or terminated the guarantee, or has received restructuring aid and is still subject to a restructuring plan.

(e) In the case of an undertaking that is not an SME, where, for the past two years:

(1) the undertaking's book debt to equity ratio has been greater than 7.5 and

(2) the undertaking's EBITDA interest coverage ratio has been below 1,0.

(19) 'territorial spending obligations': mean the obligations imposed by the authority granting the aid on beneficiaries to spend a minimum amount and/or conduct a minimum level of production activity in a particular territory;

(20) 'adjusted aid amount' means the maximum permissible aid amount for a large investment project, calculated according to the following formula:

$$\text{maximum aid amount} = R \times (A + 0,50 \times B + 0 \times C)$$

where: R is the maximum aid intensity applicable in the area concerned established in an approved regional map and which is in force on the date of granting the aid, excluding the increased aid intensity for SMEs; A is the initial EUR 50 million of eligible costs, B is the part of eligible costs between EUR 50 million and EUR 100 million and C is the part of eligible costs above EUR 100 million;

(21) 'repayable advance' means a loan for a project which is paid in one or more instalments and the conditions for the reimbursement of which depend on the outcome of the project;

(22) 'gross grant equivalent' means the amount of the aid if it had been provided in the form of a grant to the beneficiary, before any deduction of tax or other charge;

(23) 'start of works' means the earlier of either the start of construction works relating to the investment, or the first legally binding commitment to order equipment or any other commitment that makes the investment irreversible. Buying land and preparatory works such as obtaining permits and conducting feasibility studies are not considered start of works. For take-overs, 'start of works' means the moment of acquiring the assets directly linked to the acquired establishment;

(24) 'large enterprises' means undertakings not fulfilling the criteria laid down in Annex I;

(25) 'fiscal successor scheme' means a scheme in the form of tax advantages which constitutes an amended version of a previously existing scheme in the form of tax advantages and which replaces it.

(26) 'aid intensity' means the gross aid amount expressed as a percentage of the eligible costs, before any deduction of tax or other charge;

[(27) 'assisted areas' means areas designated in an approved regional aid map approved in application of Articles2020-2021, 107(3)(a) and (c) of the Treaty for the period from 1 July 2014 to 31 December 2021 for regional aid granted until 31 December 2021 and areas designated in an approved regional aid map approved in application of Articles 107(3)(a) and (c) of the Treaty for the period from 1 January 2022 to 31 December 2027 for regional aid granted after 31 December 2021;]

(28) 'date of granting of the aid' means the date when the legal right to receive the aid is conferred on the beneficiary under the applicable national legal regime;

(29) 'tangible assets' means assets consisting of land, buildings and plant, machinery and equipment;

(30) 'intangible assets' means assets that do not have a physical or financial embodiment such as patents, licences, know-how or other intellectual property;

(31) 'wage cost' means the total amount actually payable by the beneficiary of the aid in respect of the employment concerned, comprising over a defined period of time the gross wage before tax and compulsory contributions such as social security, child care and parent care costs;

(32) 'net increase in the number of employees' means a net increase in the number of employees in the establishment concerned compared with the average over a given period in time, and that any posts lost during that period must therefore be deducted and that the number of persons employed full-time, part-time and seasonal has to be considered with their annual labour unit fractions;

(33) 'dedicated infrastructure' means infrastructure that is built for ex-ante identifiable undertaking(s) and tailored to their needs;

(34) 'financial intermediary' means any financial institution regardless of its form and ownership, including fund-of-funds, private equity investment funds, public investment funds, banks, micro-finance institutions and guarantee societies;

(35) 'journey' means the movement of goods from the point of origin to the point of destination, including any intermediary sections or stages within or outside the Member State concerned, made using one or more means of transport;

(36) 'fair rate of return (FRR)' means the expected rate of return equivalent to a risk-adjusted discount rate which reflects the level of risk of a project and the nature and level of capital the private investors plan to invest;

(37) 'total financing' means the overall investment amount made into an eligible undertaking or project under Section 3 or under Articles 16 or 39 of this Regulation to the exclusion of entirely private investments provided on market terms and outside the scope of the relevant State aid measure;

(38) 'competitive bidding process' means a non-discriminatory bidding process that provides for the participation of a sufficient number of undertakings and where the aid is granted on the basis of either the initial bid submitted by the bidder or a clearing price. In addition, the budget or volume related to the bidding process is a binding constraint leading to a situation where not all bidders can receive aid;

[(39) 'operating profit' means the difference between the discounted revenues and the discounted operating costs over the economic lifetime of the investment, where this difference is positive. The operating costs include costs such as personnel costs, materials, contracted services, communications, energy, maintenance, rent, administration, but exclude depreciation charges and the costs of financing if these have been covered by investment aid. Discounting revenues and operating costs using an appropriate discount rate allows a reasonable profit to be made;]

Definitions applying to regional aid

(40) Definitions applying to aid for broadband infrastructures (Section 10) are applicable to the relevant regional aid provisions.

(41) 'regional investment aid' means regional aid granted for an initial investment or an initial investment in favour of a new economic activity;

[(42) 'regional operating aid' means aid to reduce an undertaking's current expenditure. This includes cost categories such as personnel costs, materials, contracted services, communications, energy, maintenance, rent, administration, but excludes depreciation charges and the costs of financing if these have been included in the eligible costs when granting investment aid;]

(43) 'steel sector' means all activities related to the production of one or more of the following products:

- *(a) pig iron and ferro-alloys:*
  pig iron for steelmaking, foundry and other pig iron, spiegeleisen and high-carbon ferro-manganese, not including other ferro-alloys;
- *(b) crude and semi-finished products of iron, ordinary steel or special steel:*
  liquid steel whether or not cast into ingots, including ingots for forging semi-finished products: blooms, billets and slabs; sheet bars and tinplate bars; hot-rolled wide coils, with the exception of production of liquid steel for castings from small and medium-sized foundries;
- *(c) hot finished products of iron, ordinary steel or special steel:*
  rails, sleepers, fishplates, soleplates, joists, heavy sections of 80 mm and over, sheet piling, bars and sections of less than 80 mm and flats of less than 150 mm, wire rod, tube rounds and squares, hot-rolled hoop and strip (including tube strip), hot-rolled sheet (coated or uncoated), plates and sheets of 3 mm thickness and over, universal plates of 150 mm and over, with the exception of wire and wire products, bright bars and iron castings;
- *(d) cold finished products:*
  tinplate, terneplate, blackplate, galvanised sheets, other coated sheets, cold-rolled sheets, electrical sheets and strip for tinplate, cold-rolled plate, in coil and in strip;
- *(e) tubes:*
  all seamless steel tubes, welded steel tubes with a diameter of over 406.4 mm;

(44) 'synthetic fibres sector' means:

- *(a) extrusion/texturisation of all generic types of fibre and yarn based on polyester, polyamide, acrylic or polypropylene, irrespective of their end-uses; or*
- *(b) polymerisation (including polycondensation) where it is integrated with extrusion in terms of the machinery used; or*
- *(c) any ancillary process linked to the contemporaneous installation of extrusion/texturisation capacity by the prospective beneficiary or by another company in the group to which it belongs and which, in the specific business activity concerned, is normally integrated with such capacity in terms of the machinery used;*

(45) 'transport sector' means the transport of passengers by aircraft, maritime transport, road or rail and by inland waterway or freight transport services for hire or reward; more specifically, the 'transport sector' means the following activities in terms of NACE Rev. 2:

- *(a) NACE 49: Land transport and transport via pipelines, excluding NACE 49.32 Taxi operation, 49.42 Removal services, 49.5 Transport via pipeline;*
- *(b) NACE 50: Water transport;*
- *(c) NACE 51: Air transport, excluding NACE 51.22 Space transport.*

(46) 'scheme targeted at a limited number of specific sectors of economic activity' means a scheme which covers activities falling within the scope of less than five classes (four-digit numerical code) of the NACE Rev. 2 statistical classification.

(47) 'tourism activity' means the following activities in terms of NACE Rev. 2:

- *(a) NACE 55:Accommodation;*

(b) NACE 56: Food and beverage service activities;
(c) NACE 79: Travel agency, tour operator reservation service and related activities;
(d) NACE 90: Creative, arts and entertainment activities;
(e) NACE 91: Libraries, archives, museums and other cultural activities;
(f) NACE 93: Sports activities and amusement and recreation activities;

[(48) 'sparsely populated areas' means NUTS 2 regions with less than 8 inhabitants per km2 or NUTS 3 regions with less than 12,5 inhabitants per km2 or areas which are recognized by the Commission as such in an individual decision on a regional aid map in force at the time the aid is granted;]

[(48a) 'very sparsely populated areas' means NUTS 2 regions with less than 8 inhabitants per km2 or areas which are recognized by the Commission as such in an individual decision on a regional aid map in force at the time the aid is granted;]

(49) 'initial investment' means:

(a) an investment in tangible and intangible assets related to the setting-up of a new establishment, extension of the capacity of an existing establishment, diversification of the output of an establishment into products not previously produced in the establishment or a fundamental change in the overall production process of an existing establishment; or

(b) an acquisition of assets belonging to an establishment that has closed or would have closed had it not been purchased, and is bought by an investor unrelated to the seller and excludes sole acquisition of the shares of an undertaking;

(50) 'the same or a similar activity' means an activity falling under the same class (four-digit numerical code) of the NACE Rev. 2 statistical classification of economic activities as laid down in Regulation (EC) No 1893/2006 of the European Parliament and of the Council of 20 December 2006 establishing the statistical classification of economic activities NACE Revision 2 and amending Council Regulation (EEC) No 3037/90 as well as certain EC Regulations on specific statistical domains;[3]

(51) 'initial investment in favour of new economic activity' means:

(a) an investment in tangible and intangible assets related to the setting up of a new establishment, or to the diversification of the activity of an establishment, under the condition that the new activity is not the same or a similar activity to the activity previously performed in the establishment;

(b) the acquisition of the assets belonging to an establishment that has closed or would have closed had it not been purchased, and is bought by an investor unrelated to the seller, under the condition that the new activity to be performed using the acquired assets is not the same or a similar activity to the activity performed in the establishment prior to the acquisition;

(52) 'large investment project' means an initial investment with eligible costs exceeding EUR 50 million, calculated at prices and exchange rates on the date of granting the aid;

(53) 'point of destination' means the place where the goods are unloaded;

(54) 'point of origin' means the place where the goods are loaded for transport;

[(55) 'areas eligible for operating aid' means an outermost region referred to in Article 349 of the Treaty, a sparsely populated area or a very sparsely populated area;]

(56) 'means of transport' means rail transport, road freight transport, inland waterway transport, maritime transport, air transport, and intermodal transport;

(57) 'urban development fund' ('UDF') means a specialised investment vehicle set up for the purpose of investing in urban development projects under an urban development aid measure. UDFs are managed by an urban development fund manager;

(58) 'urban development fund manager' means a professional management company with legal personality, selecting and making investments in eligible urban development projects;

(59) 'urban development project' ('UDP') means an investment project that has the potential to support the implementation of interventions envisaged by an integrated approach to sustainable urban development and contribute to achieving of the objectives defined therein, including projects with an internal rate of return which may not be sufficient to attract financing on a purely commercial basis. An urban development project may be organised as a separate block of finance within the legal structures of the beneficiary private investor or as a separate legal entity, e.g. a special purpose vehicle;

(60) 'integrated sustainable urban development strategy' means a strategy officially proposed and certified by a relevant local authority or public sector agency, defined for a specific urban geographic area and period, that set out integrated actions to tackle the economic, environmental, climate, demographic and social challenges affecting urban areas;

(61) 'in-kind contribution' means the contribution of land or real estate where the land or real estate forms part of the urban development project;

[(61a) 'relocation' means a transfer of the same or similar activity or part thereof from an establishment in one contracting party to the EEA Agreement (initial establishment) to the establishment in which the aided investment takes place in another contracting party to the EEA Agreement (aided establishment). There is a transfer if the product or service in the initial and in the aided establishments serves at least partly the same purposes and meets the demands or needs of the same type of customers and jobs are lost in the same or similar activity in one of the initial establishments of the beneficiary in the EEA;]

Definitions for Aid to SMEs

(62) 'employment directly created by an investment project' means employment concerning the activity to which the investment relates, including employment created following an increase in the utilisation rate of the capacity created by the investment;

(63)–(65) . . .

Definitions for Aid for access to finance for SMEs

(66) 'quasi-equity investment' means a type of financing that ranks between equity and debt, having a higher risk than senior debt and a lower risk than common equity and whose return for the holder is predominantly based

on the profits or losses of the underlying target undertaking and which are unsecured in the event of default. Quasi-equity investments can be structured as debt, unsecured and subordinated, including mezzanine debt, and in some cases convertible into equity, or as preferred equity;

(67) *'guarantee' in the context of sections 1, 3 and 7 of the Regulation means a written commitment to assume responsibility for all or part of a third party's newly originated loan transactions such as debt or lease instruments, as well as quasi-equity instruments.;*

(68) *'guarantee rate' means the percentage of loss coverage by a public investor of each and every transaction eligible under the relevant State aid measure;*

(69) *'exit' means the liquidation of holdings by a financial intermediary or investor, including trade sale, write-offs, repayment of shares/loans, sale to another financial intermediary or another investor, sale to a financial institution and sale by public offering, including an initial public offering (IPO);*

(70) *'financial endowment' means a repayable public investment made to a financial intermediary for the purposes of making investments under a risk finance measure, and where all the proceeds shall be returned to the public investor;*

(71) *'risk finance investment' means equity and quasi-equity investments, loans including leases, guarantees, or a mix thereof to eligible undertakings for the purposes of making new investments;*

(72) *'independent private investor' means a private investor who is not a shareholder of the eligible undertaking in which it invests, including business angels and financial institutions, irrespective of their ownership, to the extent that they bear the full risk in respect of their investment. Upon the creation of a new company, private investors, including the founders, are considered to be independent from that company;*

(73) *'natural person' for the purpose of Articles 21 and 23 means a person other than a legal entity who is not an undertaking for the purposes of Article 107(1) of the Treaty;*

(74) *'equity investment' means the provision of capital to an undertaking, invested directly or indirectly in return for the ownership of a corresponding share of that undertaking;*

(75) *'first commercial sale' means the first sale by a company on a product or service market, excluding limited sales to test the market;*

(76) *'unlisted SME' means an SME which is not listed on the official list of a stock exchange, except for alternative trading platforms.*

(77) *'follow-on investment' means additional risk finance investment in a company subsequent to one or more previous risk finance investment rounds;*

(78) *'replacement capital' means the purchase of existing shares in a company from an earlier investor or shareholder;*

(79) *'entrusted entity' means the European Investment Bank and the European Investment Fund, an international financial institution in which a Member State is a shareholder, or a financial institution established in a Member State aiming at the achievement of public interest under the control of a public authority, a public law body, or a private law body with a public service mission: the entrusted entity can be selected or directly appointed in accordance with the provisions of Directive 2004/18/EC on the coordination of procedures for the award of public works contracts, public supply contracts and public service contracts,[4] or any subsequent legislation replacing that Directive in full or in part;*

(80) *'innovative enterprise' means an enterprise:*

   (a) *that can demonstrate, by means of an evaluation carried out by an external expert that it will in the foreseeable future develop products, services or processes which are new or substantially improved compared to the state of the art in its industry, and which carry a risk of technological or industrial failure, or*

   (b) *the research and development costs of which represent at least 10% of its total operating costs in at least one of the three years preceding the granting of the aid or, in the case of a start-up enterprise without any financial history, in the audit of its current fiscal period, as certified by an external auditor;*

(81) *'alternative trading platform' means a multilateral trading facility as defined in Article 4(1)(15) of Directive 2004/39/EC where the majority of the financial instruments admitted to trading are issued by SMEs;*

(82) *'loan' means an agreement which obliges the lender to make available to the borrower an agreed amount of money for an agreed period of time and under which the borrower is obliged to repay the amount within the agreed period. It may take the form of a loan, or another funding instrument, including a lease, which provides the lender with a predominant component of minimum yield. The refinancing of existing loans shall not be an eligible loan.*

Definitions for Aid for research and development and innovation

(83) *'research and knowledge-dissemination organisation' means an entity (such as universities or research institutes, technology transfer agencies, innovation intermediaries, research-oriented physical or virtual collaborative entities), irrespective of its legal status (organised under public or private law) or way of financing, whose primary goal is to independently conduct fundamental research, industrial research or experimental development or to widely disseminate the results of such activities by way of teaching, publication or knowledge transfer. Where such entity also pursues economic activities the financing, the costs and the revenues of those economic activities must be accounted for separately. Undertakings that can exert a decisive influence upon such an entity, in the quality of, for example, shareholders or members, may not enjoy preferential access to the results generated by it;*

(84) *'fundamental research' means experimental or theoretical work undertaken primarily to acquire new knowledge of the underlying foundations of phenomena and observable facts, without any direct commercial application or use in view;*

(85) *'industrial research' means the planned research or critical investigation aimed at the acquisition of new knowledge and skills for developing new products, processes or services or for bringing about a significant improvement in existing products, processes or services. It comprises the creation of components parts of*

complex systems, and may include the construction of prototypes in a laboratory environment or in an environment with simulated interfaces to existing systems as well as of pilot lines, when necessary for the industrial research and notably for generic technology validation;

(86) *'experimental development' means acquiring, combining, shaping and using existing scientific, technological, business and other relevant knowledge and skills with the aim of developing new or improved products, processes or services. This may also include, for example, activities aiming at the conceptual definition, planning and documentation of new products, processes or services;*

Experimental development may comprise prototyping, demonstrating, piloting, testing and validation of new or improved products, processes or services in environments representative of real life operating conditions where the primary objective is to make further technical improvements on products, processes or services that are not substantially set. This may include the development of a commercially usable prototype or pilot which is necessarily the final commercial product and which is too expensive to produce for it to be used only for demonstration and validation purposes.

Experimental development does not include routine or periodic changes made to existing products, production lines, manufacturing processes, services and other operations in progress, even if those changes may represent improvements;

(87) *'feasibility study' means the evaluation and analysis of the potential of a project, which aims at supporting the process of decision-making by objectively and rationally uncovering its strengths and weaknesses, opportunities and threats, as well as identifying the resources required to carry it through and ultimately its prospects for success;*

(88) *'personnel costs' means the costs of researchers, technicians and other supporting staff to the extent employed on the relevant project or activity;*

(89) *'arm's length' means that the conditions of the transaction between the contracting parties do not differ from those which would be stipulated between independent enterprises and contain no element of collusion. Any transaction that results from an open, transparent and non-discriminatory procedure is considered as meeting the arm's length principle;*

(90) *'effective collaboration' means collaboration between at least two independent parties to exchange knowledge or technology, or to achieve a common objective based on the division of labour where the parties jointly define the scope of the collaborative project, contribute to its implementation and share its risks, as well as its results. One or several parties may bear the full costs of the project and thus relieve other parties of its financial risks. Contract research and provision of research services are not considered forms of collaboration.*

(91) *'research infrastructure' means facilities, resources and related services that are used by the scientific community to conduct research in their respective fields and covers scientific equipment or sets of instruments, knowledge-based resources such as collections, archives or structured scientific information, enabling information and communication technology-based infrastructures such as grid, computing, software and communication, or any other entity of a unique nature essential to conduct research. Such infrastructures may be 'single-sited' or 'distributed' (an organised network of resources) in accordance with Article 2(a) of Council Regulation (EC) No 723/2009 of 25 June 2009 on the Community legal framework for a European Research Infrastructure Consortium (ERIC);*[5]

(92) *'innovation clusters' means structures or organised groups of independent parties (such as innovative start-ups, small, medium and large enterprises, as well as research and knowledge dissemination organisations, non-for-profit organisations and other related economic actors) designed to stimulate innovative activity through promotion, sharing of facilities and exchange of knowledge and expertise and by contributing effectively to knowledge transfer, networking, information dissemination and collaboration among the undertakings and other organisations in the cluster;*

(93) *'highly qualified personnel' means staff having a tertiary education degree and at least 5 years of relevant professional experience which may also include doctoral training;*

(94) *'innovation advisory services' means consultancy, assistance and training in the fields of knowledge transfer, acquisition, protection and exploitation of intangible assets, use of standards and regulations embedding them;*

(95) *'innovation support services' means the provision of office space, data banks, libraries, market research, laboratories, quality labelling, testing and certification for the purpose of developing more effective products, processes or services;*

(96) *'organisational innovation' means the implementation of a new organisational method in an undertaking's business practices, workplace organisation or external relations, excluding changes that are based on organisational methods already in use in the undertaking, changes in management strategy, mergers and acquisitions, ceasing to use a process, simple capital replacement or extension, changes resulting purely from changes in factor prices, customisation, localisation, regular, seasonal and other cyclical changes and trading of new or significantly improved products;*

(97) *'process innovation' means the implementation of a new or significantly improved production or delivery method (including significant changes in techniques, equipment or software), excluding minor changes or improvements, increases in production or service capabilities through the addition of manufacturing or logistical systems which are very similar to those already in use, ceasing to use a process, simple capital replacement or extension, changes resulting purely from changes in factor prices, customisation, localisation, regular, seasonal and other cyclical changes and trading of new or significantly improved products;*

(98) *'secondment' means temporary employment of staff by a beneficiary with the right for the staff to return to the previous employer;*

Definitions for aid for disadvantaged workers and for workers with disabilities

(99) *'severely disadvantaged worker' means any person who:*

(a) *has not been in regular paid employment for at least 24 months; or*

(b) has not been in regular paid employment for at least 12 months and belongs to one of the categories (b) to (g) mentioned under the definition of 'disadvantaged worker'.

(100) 'sheltered employment' means employment in an undertaking where at least 30% of workers are workers with disabilities;

Definitions applying to aid for environmental protection

(101) 'environmental protection' means any action designed to remedy or prevent damage to physical surroundings or natural resources by a beneficiary's own activities, to reduce risk of such damage or to lead to a more efficient use of natural resources, including energy-saving measures and the use of renewable sources of energy;

(102) 'Union standard' means:

(a) a mandatory Union standard setting the levels to be attained in environmental terms by individual undertakings; or

(b) the obligation under Directive 2010/75/EU of the European Parliament and of the Council[6] to use the best available techniques (BAT) and ensure that emission levels of pollutants are not higher than they would be when applying BAT; for the cases where emission levels associated with the BAT have been defined in implementing acts adopted under Directive 2010/75/EU, those levels will be applicable for the purpose of this Regulation; where those levels are expressed as a range, the limit where the BAT is first achieved will be applicable;

[(102a) "recharging infrastructure" means a fixed or mobile infrastructure supplying road vehicles with electricity;

(102b) "refuelling infrastructure" means a fixed or mobile infrastructure supplying road vehicles with hydrogen;

(102c) "renewable hydrogen" means hydrogen produced through the electrolysis of water (in an electrolyser, powered by electricity stemming from renewable sources), or through the reforming of biogas or biochemical conversion of biomass, if in compliance with sustainability criteria set out in Article 29 of Directive (EU) 2018/2001 of the European Parliament and of the Council.[*]]

(103) 'energy efficiency' means an amount of saved energy determined by measuring and/or estimating consumption before and after implementation of an energy-efficiency improvement measure, whilst ensuring normalisation for external conditions that affect energy consumption;

[(103a) "residential building" means a building constituted exclusively of single-family or multi-family dwellings;

(103b) "social services" means clearly identified services, meeting social needs, in particular as regards health and long-term care, childcare, access to and reintegration into the labour market, social housing (which means housing for disadvantaged citizens or socially less advantaged groups who due to solvency constraints are unable to obtain housing at market conditions) and the care and social inclusion of vulnerable groups (as explained in recital 11 of Commission Decision 2012/21/EU);[**]

(103c) "digitalisation" means the adoption of technologies carried out by electronic devices and/or systems which make it possible to increase product functionality, develop online services, modernise processes, or migrate to business models based on the disintermediation of goods production and service delivery, eventually producing a transformative impact;

(103d) "smart readiness" means the capability of buildings (or building units) to adapt their operation to the needs of the occupant, including optimising energy efficiency and overall performance, and to adapt their operation in reaction to signals from the grid;

(103e) "small mid-cap" means an undertaking that is not an SME and whose number of employees does not exceed 499, calculated in accordance with Articles 3 to 6 of Annex I, the annual turnover of which does not exceed EUR 100 million or the annual balance sheet of which does not exceed EUR 86 million; several entities shall be considered as one undertaking if any of the conditions listed in Article 3(3) of Annex I is fulfilled;]

(104) 'energy efficiency project' means an investment project that increases the energy efficiency of a building;

(105) 'energy efficiency fund (EEF)' means a specialised investment vehicle set up for the purpose of investing in energy efficiency projects aimed at improving the energy efficiency of buildings in both the domestic and non-domestic sectors. EEFs are managed by an energy efficiency fund manager;

(106) 'energy efficiency fund manager' means a professional management company with a legal personality, selecting and making investments in eligible energy efficiency projects;

(107) 'high-efficiency cogeneration' means cogeneration which satisfies the definition of high efficiency cogeneration as set out in Article 2(34) of Directive 2012/27/EU of the European Parliament and of the Council of 25 October 2012 on energy efficiency, amending Directives 2009/125/EC and 2010/30/EU and repealing Directives 2004/8/EC and 2006/32/EC;[7]

(108) 'cogeneration' or combined heat and power (CHP) means the simultaneous generation in one process of thermal energy and electrical and/or mechanical energy;

(109) 'energy from renewable energy sources' means energy produced by plants using only renewable energy sources, as well as the share in terms of calorific value of energy produced from renewable energy sources in hybrid plants which also use conventional energy sources. It includes renewable electricity used for filling storage systems, but excludes electricity produced as a result of storage systems;

(110) 'renewable energy sources' means the following renewable non-fossil energy sources: wind, solar, aerothermal, geothermal, hydrothermal and ocean energy, hydropower, biomass, landfill gas, sewage treatment plant gas and biogases;

(111) 'biofuel' means liquid or gaseous fuel for transport produced from biomass;

(112) 'sustainable biofuel' means a biofuel fulfilling the sustainability criteria set out in Article 17 of Directive 2009/28/EC;

(113) 'food based biofuel' means a biofuel produced from cereal and other starch rich crops, sugars and oil crops as defined in the Commission's Proposal for a Directive of the European Parliament and of the Council amending Directive 98/70/EC relating to the quality of petrol and diesel fuels and amending Directive 2009/28/EC on the promotion of the use of energy from renewable sources;[8]

(114) 'new and innovative technology' means a new and unproven technology compared to the state of the art in the industry, which carries a risk of technological or industrial failure and is not an optimisation or scaling up of an existing technology;

(115) 'balancing responsibilities' means responsibility for imbalances (deviations between generation, consumption and commercial transactions) of a market participant or its chosen representative, referred to as the 'Balance Responsible Party', within a given period of time, referred to as the 'Imbalance Settlement Period';

(116) 'standard balancing responsibilities' means non-discriminatory balancing responsibilities across technologies which do not exempt any generator from those responsibilities;

(117) 'biomass' means the biodegradable fraction of products, waste and residues from agriculture (including vegetal and animal substances), forestry and related industries including fisheries and aquaculture, as well as biogases and the biodegradable fraction of industrial and municipal waste;

(118) 'total levelized costs of producing energy' is a calculation of the cost of generating electricity at the point of connection to a load or electricity grid. It includes the initial capital, discount rate, as well as the costs of continuous operation, fuel, and maintenance;

(119) 'environmental tax' means a tax with a specific tax base that has a clear negative effect on the environment or which seeks to tax certain activities, goods or services so that the environmental costs may be included in their price and/or so that producers and consumers are oriented towards activities which better respect the environment;

(120) 'Union minimum tax level' means the minimum level of taxation provided for in the Union legislation; for energy products and electricity it means the minimum level of taxation laid down in Annex I to Council Directive 2003/96/EC of 27 October 2003 restructuring the Community framework for the taxation of energy products and electricity;[9]

(121) 'contaminated site' means a site where there is a confirmed presence, caused by man, of hazardous substances of such a level that they pose a significant risk to human health or the environment taking into account current and approved future use of the land;

(122) 'polluter pays principle' or 'PPP' means that the costs of measures to deal with pollution should be borne by the polluter who causes the pollution;

(123) 'pollution' means the damage caused by a polluter directly or indirectly damaging the environment, or by creating conditions leading to such damage to physical surroundings or natural resources;

(124) 'energy efficient district heating and cooling' means a district heating and cooling system which satisfies the definition of efficient district heating and cooling system set out in Article 2(41) and (42) of Directive 2012/27/EU. The definition includes the heating/cooling production plants and the network (including related facilities) necessary to distribute the heat/cooling from the production units to the customer premises;

(125) 'polluter' means someone who directly or indirectly damages the environment or who creates conditions leading to such damage.

(126) 're-use' means any operation by which products or components that are not waste are used again for the same purpose for which they were conceived;

(127) 'preparing for re-use' means checking, cleaning or repairing recovery operations, by which products or components of products that have become waste are prepared so that they can be re-used without any other pre-processing;

(128) 'recycling' means any recovery operation by which waste materials are reprocessed into products, materials or substances whether for the original or other purposes. It includes the reprocessing of organic material but does not include energy recovery and the reprocessing into materials that are to be used as fuels or for backfilling operations;

(129) 'state of the art' means a process in which the re-use of a waste product to manufacture an end product is economically profitable normal practice. Where appropriate, the concept of state of the art must be interpreted from a Union technological and internal market perspective;

(130) 'energy infrastructure' means any physical equipment or facility which is located within the Union or linking the Union to one or more third countries and falling under the following categories:

(a) concerning electricity:

(i) infrastructure for transmission, as defined in Article 2(3) by Directive 2009/72/EC of 13 July 2009 concerning common rules for internal market in electricity;[10]

(ii) infrastructure for distribution, as defined in Article 2(5) by Directive 2009/72/EC;

(iii) electricity storage, defined as facilities used for storing electricity on a permanent or temporary basis in above-ground or underground infrastructure or geological sites, provided they are directly connected to high-voltage transmission lines designed for a voltage of 110 kV or more;

(iv) any equipment or installation essential for the systems defined in points (i) to (iii) to operate safely, securely and efficiently, including protection, monitoring and control systems at all voltage levels and substations; and

(v) smart grids, defined as any equipment, line, cable or installation, both at transmission and low and medium voltage distribution level, aiming at two-way digital communication, real-time or close to realtime, interactive and intelligent monitoring and management of electricity generation, transmission, distribution and consumption within an electricity network in view of developing a network efficiently integrating the behaviour and actions of all users connected to it — generators, consumers and those that do both — in order to ensure an economically efficient, sustainable electricity system with low losses and high quality and security of supply and safety;

(b) concerning gas:

(i) *transmission and distribution pipelines for the transport of natural gas and biogas that form part of a network, excluding high-pressure pipelines used for upstream distribution of natural gas;*

(ii) *underground storage facilities connected to the high-pressure gas pipelines mentioned in point (i);*

(iii) *reception, storage and regasification or decompression facilities for liquefied natural gas ('LNG') or compressed natural gas ('CNG'); and*

(iv) *any equipment or installation essential for the system to operate safely, securely and efficiently or to enable bi-directional capacity, including compressor stations;*

(c) *concerning oil:*

(i) *pipelines used to transport crude oil;*

(ii) *pumping stations and storage facilities necessary for the operation of crude oil pipelines; and*

(iii) *any equipment or installation essential for the system in question to operate properly, securely and efficiently, including protection, monitoring and control systems and reverse-flow devices;*

(d) *concerning CO_2: networks of pipelines, including associated booster stations, for the transport of CO_2 to storage sites, with the aim to inject the CO_2 in suitable underground geological formations for permanent storage;*

(131) *'internal energy market legislation' includes Directive 2009/72/EC of the European Parliament and of the Council of 13 July 2009 concerning common rules for the internal market in electricity, Directive 2009/73/EC of the European Parliament and of the Council of 13 July 2009 concerning common rules for the internal market in natural gas,[11] Regulation (EC) No 713/2009 of the European Parliament and of the Council of 13 July 2009 establishing an Agency for the Cooperation of Energy Regulators;[12] Regulation (EC) No 714/2009 of the European Parliament and of the Council of 13 July 2009 on conditions for access to the network for cross-border exchanges[13] and Regulation (EC) No 715/2009 of the European Parliament and of the Council of 13 July 2009 on conditions for access to the natural gas transmission networks[14] or any subsequent legislation replacing these acts in full or in part;*

Definitions applying to social aid for transport for residents of remote regions

(132) *'normal residence' means the place where a natural person lives for at least 185 days, in each calendar year, because of personal and occupational ties; in the case of a person whose occupational ties are in a different place from his/her personal ties and who lives in two or more Member States, the place of normal residence is regarded as the place of his/her personal ties provided that he/she returns there regularly; where a person is living in a Member State in order to carry out a task of a set duration, the place of residence is still regarded as being the place of his/her personal ties, irrespective of whether he/she returns there during the course of this activity; attendance at a university or school in another Member State does not constitute a transfer of normal residence; alternatively, 'normal residence' shall have the meaning attributed to it in Member States' national law.*

Definitions for aid for broadband infrastructures

(133) . . .

(134) *'broadband-related civil engineering works' means the civil engineering works which are necessary for the deployment of a broadband network, such as digging up a road in order to enable the placement of (broadband) ducts.*

(135) *'ducts' means underground pipes or conduits used to house (fibre, copper or coax) cables of a broadband network.*

(136) *'physical unbundling' grants access to the end-consumer access line and allows competitors' own transmission systems to directly transmit over it.*

[(137) *"passive network" means a network without any active element, such as: civil engineering infrastructure, pipes, ducts, inspection chambers, manholes, dark fibre, cabinets, power supply, antenna installations, passive antennas, masts, poles and towers;*]

(138) . . .

(139) *'wholesale access' means access which enables an operator to utilise the facilities of another operator. The widest possible access to be provided over the relevant network shall include, on the basis of the current technological developments, at least the following access products. For FTTH/FTTB networks: ducts access, access to dark fibre, unbundled access to the local loop, and bitstream access. For cable networks: duct access and bit-stream access. For FTTC networks: duct access, sub-loop unbundling and bit-stream access. For passive network infrastructure: duct access, access to dark fibre and/or unbundled access to the local loop. For ADSL-based broadband networks: unbundled access to the local loop, bit-stream access. For mobile or wireless networks: bit-stream, sharing of physical masts and access to the backhaul networks. For satellite platforms: bit-stream access.*

[(139a) *"premises passed" means premises which can be connected within a short period of time at the normal activation fee for the end-user, regardless of whether those premises are connected to the network. An operator shall report premises as passed only if, following a request from an end-user, it commits to connect the premises for normal activation fees, meaning without any additional or exceptional cost and, in any case, not exceeding the average activation fee in the Member State concerned. The provider of electronic communications networks and services shall be able to connect and activate the service at the specific premises within four weeks from the date of the request;*

(139b) *"socioeconomic drivers" means entities which by their mission, nature or location can directly or indirectly generate important socioeconomic benefits to citizens, business and local communities located in their surrounding territory or in their area of influence, including among others public authorities, public or private entities entrusted with the operation of services of general interest or of services of general economic interest as set out in Article 106(2) of the Treaty and digitally intensive enterprises;*

(139c) "5G corridor" means a transport path, road, railway or inland waterway, fully covered with digital connectivity infrastructure, in particular 5G systems, and enabling the uninterrupted provision of synergy digital services as defined in Regulation (EU) 2021/1153 of the European Parliament and of the Council,[***] *such as connected and automated mobility, similar smart mobility services for railways or digital connectivity on inland waterways;*

Definitions for aid for culture and heritage conservation

(140) 'difficult audiovisual works': means the works identified as such by Member States on the basis of pre-defined criteria when setting up schemes or granting the aid and may include films whose sole original version is in a language of a Member State with a limited territory, population or language area, short films, films by first-time and second-time directors, documentaries, or low budget or otherwise commercially difficult works.

(141) Development Assistance Committee (DAC) List of the OECD: means all countries and territories that are eligible to receive official development assistance and included in the list compiled by the Organisation for Economic Cooperation and Development (OECD);

(142) 'reasonable profit' shall be determined with respect to the typical profit for the sector concerned. In any event, a rate of return on capital that does not exceed the relevant swap rate plus a premium of 100 basis points will be considered to be reasonable.

Definitions for aid for sport and multifunctional recreational infrastructures

(143) 'professional sport' means the practice of sport in the nature of gainful employment or remunerated service, irrespective of whether or not a formal labour contract has been established between the professional sports-person and the relevant sport organisation, where the compensation exceeds the cost of participation and constitutes a significant part of the income for the sports-person. Travel and accommodation expenses to participate to the sport event shall not be considered as compensation for the purposes of this Regulation.

[Definitions for Aid for regional airports

(144) 'airport infrastructure' means infrastructure and equipment for the provision of airport services by the airport to airlines and the various service providers, including runways, terminals, aprons, taxiways, centralised ground handling infrastructure and any other facilities that directly support the airport services, excluding infrastructure and equipment which is primarily necessary for pursuing non-aeronautical activities;

(145) 'airline' means any airline with a valid operating licence issued by a Member State or a Member of the Common European Aviation Area pursuant to Regulation (EC) No 1008/2008 of the European Parliament and of the Council;[15]

(146) 'airport' means an entity or group of entities performing the economic activity of providing airport services to airlines;

(147) 'airport services' means services provided to airlines by an airport or any of its subsidiaries, to ensure the handling of aircraft, from landing to take-off, and of passengers and freight, so as to enable airlines to provide air transport services, including the provision of ground handling services and the provision of centralised ground handling infrastructure;

(148) 'average annual passenger traffic' means a figure determined on the basis of the inbound and outbound passenger traffic during the two financial years preceding that in which the aid is granted;

(149) 'centralised ground handling infrastructure' means infrastructure which is normally operated by the airport manager and put at the disposal of the various providers of ground handling services active at the airport in exchange for remuneration, excluding equipment owned or operated by the providers of ground handling services;

(150) 'high-speed train' means a train capable of reaching speeds of over 200 km/h;

(151) 'ground handling services' means services provided to airport users at airports as described in the Annex to Council Directive 96/67/EC;[16]

(152) 'non-aeronautical activities' means commercial services to airlines or other users of the airport, including ancillary services to passengers, freight forwarders or other service providers, renting out of offices and shops, car parking and hotels;

(153) 'regional airport' means an airport with average annual passenger traffic of up to 3 million passengers;

Definitions for Aid for ports

(154) 'port' means an area of land and water made up of such infrastructure and equipment, so as to permit the reception of waterborne vessels, their loading and unloading, the storage of goods, the receipt and delivery of those goods and the embarkation and disembarkation of passengers, crew and other persons and any other infrastructure necessary for transport operators in the port;

(155) 'maritime port' means a port for, principally, the reception of sea-going vessels;

(156) 'inland port' means a port other than a maritime port, for the reception of inland waterway vessels;

(157) 'port infrastructure' means infrastructure and facilities for the provision of transport related port services, for example berths used for the mooring of ships, quay walls, jetties and floating pontoon ramps in tidal areas, internal basins, backfills and land reclamation, alternative fuel infrastructure and infrastructure for the collection of ship-generated waste and cargo residues;

(158) 'port superstructure' means surface arrangements (such as for storage), fixed equipment (such as warehouses and terminal buildings) as well as mobile equipment (such as cranes) located in a port for the provision of transport related port services;

(159) 'access infrastructure' means any type of infrastructure necessary to ensure access and entry from land or sea and river by users to a port, or in a port, such as roads, rail tracks, channels and locks;

(160) 'dredging' means the removal of sediments from the bottom of the waterway access to a port, or in a port;

(161) 'alternative fuel infrastructure' means a fixed, mobile or offshore port infrastructure allowing a port to supply vessels with energy sources such as electricity, hydrogen, biofuels as defined in point (i) of Article 2 of

Directive 2009/28/EC, synthetic and paraffinic fuels, natural gas, including biomethane, in gaseous form (compressed natural gas (CNG)) and liquefied form (liquefied natural gas (LNG)), and liquefied petroleum gas (LPG) which serve, at least partly, as a substitute for fossil oil sources in the energy supply to transport and which have the potential to contribute to its decarbonisation and enhance the environmental performance of the transport sector;

(162) 'vessels' mean floating structures, whether self-propelled or not, with one or more surface displacement hulls;

(163) 'sea-going vessels' mean vessels other than those which navigate solely or mainly in inland waterways or in waters within, or closely adjacent to, sheltered waters;

(164) 'inland waterway vessels' mean vessels intended solely or mainly for navigation on inland waterways or in waters within, or closely adjacent to, sheltered waters;

(165) 'infrastructure for the collection of ship-generated waste and cargo residues' means fixed, floating or mobile port facilities capable of receiving ship-generated waste or cargo residues as defined in Directive 2000/59/EC of the European Parliament and of the Council.[17]]

[Definitions for aid involved in financial products supported by the InvestEU Fund (terms defined under other headings of this Article shall have the same meaning as laid down therein also for aid involved in financial products supported by the InvestEU Fund)

(166) "InvestEU Fund", "EU guarantee", "financial product", "national promotional banks or institutions" and "implementing partner" have the meaning set out in Article 2 of Regulation (EU) 2021/523;

(167) "financial intermediary" for the purposes of Section 16 means a financial intermediary within the meaning of point (34), with the exception of implementing partners;

(168) "commercial financial intermediary" means a financial intermediary which operates on a for profit basis and at full own risk, without a public guarantee, national promotional banks or institutions are not considered to be commercial financial intermediaries;

(169) "TEN-T urban node" has the meaning set out in Article 3, point (p), of Regulation (EU) No 1315/2013 of the European Parliament and of the Council;[18]

(170) "new entrant" means a railway undertaking within the meaning of Article 3(1) of Directive 2012/34/EU of the European Parliament and of the Council,[19], which fulfils the following conditions:

(a) it received a licence pursuant to Article 17(3) of Directive 2012/34/EU for the relevant market segment less than 20 years before the aid is granted;

(a) it is not linked within the meaning of Article 3(3) of Annex I to this Regulation to a railway undertaking that received a license within the meaning of Article 3(14) of Directive 2012/34/EU prior to 1 January 2010;

(171) "urban transport" means transport within a city or an agglomeration and its commuting zones;

(172) "ecosystem", "biodiversity" and "the good condition of an ecosystem" have the meaning set out in Article 2 of Regulation (EU) 2020/852 of the European Parliament and of the Council.[20]].

NOTES

Point (27) substituted by Commission Regulation 2020/972/EU, Art 2(2).

Points (39), (42), (48), (55) substituted, points (48a), (61a) inserted and points (144)–(165) added (and the preceding heading), by Commission Regulation 2017/1084/EU, Art 1(2).

Points (63)–(65), (137), (138) repealed, points (102a)–(102c), (103a)–(103e), (139a)–(139c) and (162)–(167) (and the preceding heading) inserted, and point (137) substituted, by Commission Regulation 2021/1237/EU, Art 1(2), as from 1 August 2021.

Repeal of this Regulation in relation to the UK: this Regulation is repealed in relation to the UK (as from IP completion day); see the introductory notes to this Regulation *ante*.

[1] OJ L336, 21.12.2010, p 24.

[2] Directive 2013/34/EU of the European Parliament and of the Council of 26 June 2013 on the annual financial statements, consolidated financial statements and related reports of certain types of undertakings, amending Directive 2006/43/EC of the European Parliament and of the Council and repealing Council Directives 78/660/EEC and 83/349/EEC.

[3] OJ L393, 30.12.2006, p 1.

[4] OJ L134, 30.4.2004, p 114.

[5] OJ L206, 8.8.2009, p 1.

[6] OJ L24, 29.1.2008, p 8.

[*] Directive (EU) 2018/2001 of the European Parliament and of the Council of 11 December 2018 on the promotion of the use of energy from renewable sources (OJ L328, 21.12.2018, p 82).

[**] Commission Decision 2012/21/EU of 20 December 2011 on the application of Article 106(2) of the Treaty on the Functioning of the European Union to State aid in the form of public service compensation granted to certain undertakings entrusted with the operation of services of general economic interest (OJ L7, 11.1.2012, p 3)).

[7] OJ L315, 14.11.2012, p 1.

[8] COM (2012) 595, 17.10.2012.

[9] OJ L283, 31.10.2003, p 51.

[10] OJ L211, 14.8.2009, p 55.

[11] OJ L211, 14.8.2009, p 94.

[12] OJ L211, 14.8.2009, p 1.

[13] OJ L211, 14.8.2009, p 15.

[14] OJ L211, 14.8.2009, p 36.

[***] Regulation (EU) 2021/1153 of the European Parliament and of the Council of 7 July 2021 establishing the Connecting Europe Facility and repealing Regulations (EU) No 1316/2013 and (EU) No 283/2014 (OJ L249, 14.7.2021, p 38).

[15] Regulation (EC) No 1008/2008 of the European Parliament and of the Council of 24 September 2008 on common rules for the operation of air services in the Community (OJ L293, 31.10.2008, p 3).

[16] Council Directive 96/67/EC of 15 October 1996 on access to the groundhandling market at Community airports (OJ L272, 25.10.1996, p 36).

[17] Directive 2000/59/EC of the European Parliament and of the Council of 27 November 2000 on port reception facilities for ship-generated waste and cargo residues (OJ L332, 28.12.2000, p 81).

[18] Regulation (EU) No 1315/2013 of the European Parliament and of the Council of 11 December 2013 on Union guidelines for the development of the trans-European transport network and repealing Decision No 661/2010/EU (OJ L348, 20.12.2013, p 1).

[19] Directive 2012/34/EU of the European Parliament and of the Council of 21 November 2012 establishing a single European railway area (OJ L343, 14.12.2012, p 32).

[20] Regulation (EU) 2020/852 of the European Parliament and of the Council of 18 June 2020 on the establishment of a framework to facilitate sustainable investment, and amending Regulation (EU) 2019/2088 (OJ L198, 22.6.2020, p 13).

[5.66]
Article 3 Conditions for exemption

Aid schemes, individual aid granted under aid schemes and ad hoc aid shall be compatible with the internal market within the meaning of Article 107(2) or (3) of the Treaty and shall be exempted from the notification requirement of Article 108(3) of the Treaty provided that such aid fulfils all the conditions laid down in Chapter I of this Regulation, as well as the specific conditions for the relevant category of aid laid down in Chapter III of this Regulation.

NOTES

Repeal of this Regulation in relation to the UK: this Regulation is repealed in relation to the UK (as from IP completion day); see the introductory notes to this Regulation *ante*.

[5.67]
Article 4 Notification thresholds

1. This Regulation shall not apply to aid which exceeds the following thresholds:

(a) for regional investment aid: the 'adjusted aid amount' of aid, as calculated in accordance with the mechanism defined in Article 2, point 20 for an investment with eligible costs of EUR 100 million;
(b) for regional urban development aid, EUR 20 million as laid down in Article 16(3);
(c) for investment aid to SMEs: EUR 7.5 million per undertaking per investment project;
(d) for aid for consultancy in favour of SMEs: EUR 2 million per undertaking, per project;
(e) for aid to SMEs for participation in fairs: EUR 2 million per undertaking, per year;
[(f) for aid for undertakings participating in European Territorial Cooperation projects: for aid under Article 20, EUR 2 million per undertaking, per project; for aid under Article 20a, the amounts laid down in Article 20a(2) per undertaking, per project;]
(g) for risk finance aid: EUR 15 million per eligible undertaking as laid down in Article 21(9);
(h) for aid for start-ups: the amounts laid down per undertaking in Article 22(3), (4) and (5);
(i) for aid for research and development:
  (i) if the project is predominantly fundamental research: EUR 40 million per undertaking, per project; that is the case where more than half of the eligible costs of the project are incurred through activities which fall within the category of fundamental research;
  (ii) if the project is predominantly industrial research: EUR 20 million per undertaking, per project; that is the case where more than half of the eligible costs of the project are incurred through activities which fall within the category of industrial research or within the categories of industrial research and fundamental research taken together;
  (iii) if the project is predominantly experimental development: EUR 15 million per undertaking, per project; that is the case where more than half of the eligible costs of the project are incurred through activities which fall within the category of experimental development;
  (iv) if the project is a Eureka project or is implemented by a Joint Undertaking established on the basis of Article 185 or of Article 187 of the Treaty, the amounts referred to in points (i) to (iii) are doubled.
  (v) if the aid for research and development projects is granted in the form of repayable advances which, in the absence of an accepted methodology to calculate their gross grant equivalent, are expressed as a percentage of the eligible costs and the measure provides that in case of a successful outcome of the project, as defined on the basis of a reasonable and prudent hypothesis, the advances will be repaid with an interest rate at least equal to the discount rate applicable at the time of grant, the amounts referred to in points (i) to (iv) are increased by 50%;
  (vi) aid for feasibility studies in preparation for research activities: EUR 7.5 million per study;
  [(vii) for aid for SMEs for research and development projects awarded a Seal of Excellence quality label and implemented under Article 25a, the amount referred to in Article 25a;
  (viii) for aid Marie Skłodowska-Curie actions and ERC Proof of Concept actions implemented under Article 25b, the amounts referred to in Article 25b;
  (ix) for aid involved in co-funded research and development projects implemented under Article 25c, the amounts referred to in Article 25c;
  (x) for aid for Teaming actions, the amounts referred to in Article 25d;]
(j) for investment aid for research infrastructures: EUR 20 million per infrastructure;
(k) for aid for innovation clusters: EUR 7.5 million per cluster;
(l) innovation aid for SMEs: EUR 5 million per undertaking, per project;
(m) for aid for process and organisational innovation: EUR 7.5 million per undertaking, per project;
(n) for training aid: EUR 2 million per training project;
(o) for aid for the recruitment of disadvantaged workers: EUR 5 million per undertaking, per year;
(p) for aid for the employment of workers with disabilities in the form of wage subsidies: EUR 10 million per undertaking, per year;

(q) *for aid for compensating the additional costs of employing workers with disabilities: EUR 10 million per undertaking, per year;*

(r) *for aid for compensating the costs of assistance provided to disadvantaged workers: EUR 5 million per undertaking, per year;*

[(s) *for investment aid for environmental protection, excluding investment aid for publicly accessible recharging or refuelling infrastructure for zero or low emission vehicles, investment aid for the remediation of contaminated sites and aid for the distribution network part of the energy efficient district heating and cooling installation: EUR 15 million per undertaking per investment project; EUR 30 million for aid for energy efficiency investments in certain buildings falling within the scope of Article 38(3a); and EUR 30 million of total nominal outstanding financing for aid for energy efficiency investments in certain buildings falling within the scope of Article 38(7);]*

[(sa) *for investment aid for publicly accessible recharging or refuelling infrastructure for zero or low emission vehicles: EUR 15 million per undertaking per project and, in the case of schemes, an average annual budget of up to EUR 150 million;]*

[(t) *for investment aid for energy efficiency projects, the amounts set out in Article 39(5);]*

(u) *for investment aid for remediation of contaminated sites: EUR 20 million per undertaking per investment project;*

(v) *for operating aid for the production of electricity from renewable sources and operating aid for the promotion of energy from renewable sources in small scale installations: EUR 15 million per undertaking per project. When the aid is granted on the basis of a competitive bidding process under Article 42: EUR 150 million per year taking into account the combined budget of all schemes falling under Article 42;*

(w) *for investment aid for the district heating or cooling distribution network: EUR 20 million per undertaking per investment project;*

(x) *for investment aid for energy infrastructure: EUR 50 million per undertaking, per investment project;*

[(y) *for aid for the deployment of fixed broadband networks awarded in the form of a grant: EUR 100 million total costs per project; for aid for fixed broadband infrastructures awarded in the form of a financial instrument the nominal amount of total financing provided to any final beneficiary per project must not exceed EUR 150 million;]*

[(ya) *for aid for the deployment of 4G or 5G mobile networks awarded in the form of a grant: EUR 100 million total costs per project; for aid for 4G or 5G mobile networks awarded in the form of a financial instrument the nominal amount of total financing provided to any final beneficiary per project must not exceed EUR 150 million;*

(yb) *for aid for certain projects of common interest in the area of trans-European digital connectivity infrastructures financed under Regulation (EU) 2021/1153 or awarded a Seal of Excellence quality label under that Regulation awarded in the form of a grant: EUR 100 million total costs per project; for aid for certain projects of common interest in the area of trans-European digital connectivity infrastructures awarded in the form of a financial instrument the nominal amount of total financing provided to any final beneficiary per project must not exceed EUR 150 million;*

(yc) *for aid in the form of connectivity vouchers schemes: the total State aid budget over 24 months for all connectivity voucher schemes in a Member State must not exceed EUR 50 million (total amount including national and regional or local voucher schemes);]*

[(z) *for investment aid for culture and heritage conservation: EUR 150 million per project; operating aid for culture and heritage conservation: EUR 75 million per undertaking per year;]*

(aa) *for aid schemes for audiovisual works: EUR 50 million per scheme per year;*

[(bb) *for investment aid for sport and multifunctional recreational infrastructures: EUR 30 million or the total costs exceeding EUR 100 million per project; operating aid for sport infrastructure: EUR 2 million per infrastructure per year;]*

(cc) *for investment aid for local infrastructures: EUR 10 million or the total costs exceeding EUR 20 million for the same infrastructure;*

[(dd) *for aid for regional airports: the aid intensities and aid amounts laid down in Article 56a;*

(ee) *for aid for maritime ports: eligible costs of EUR 130 million per project (or EUR 150 million per project in a maritime port included in the work plan of a Core Network Corridor as referred to in Article 47 of Regulation (EU) No 1315/2013 of the European Parliament and of the Council*[1]*); as regards dredging a project is defined as all dredging carried out within one calendar year;*

(ff) *for aid for inland ports: eligible costs of EUR 40 million per project (or EUR 50 million per project in an inland port included in the work plan of a Core Network Corridor as referred to in Article 47 of Regulation (EU) No 1315/2013); as regards dredging a project is defined as all dredging carried out within one calendar year;]*

[(gg) *for aid involved in financial products supported by the InvestEU Fund: the amounts laid down in Section 16 of Chapter III;*

(hh) *for aid to SMEs for costs incurred by participating in community-led local development ("CLLD") projects and European Innovation Partnership for agricultural productivity and sustainability ("EIP") Operational Group projects: for aid under Article 19a, EUR 2 million per undertaking, per project; for aid under Article 19b, the amounts laid down in Article 19b(2) per project].*

2. *The thresholds set out or referred to in paragraph 1 shall not be circumvented by artificially splitting up the aid schemes or aid projects.*

NOTES

Para 1 is amended as follows:

Points (z), (bb) substituted, and points (dd)–(ff) inserted, by Commission Regulation 2017/1084/EU, Art 1(3).

All other words in square brackets were substituted or inserted by Commission Regulation 2021/1237/EU, Art 1(3), as from 1 August 2021.

Repeal of this Regulation in relation to the UK: this Regulation is repealed in relation to the UK (as from IP completion day); see the introductory notes to this Regulation *ante*.

[1] Regulation (EU) No 1315/2013 of the European Parliament and of the Council of 11 December 2013 on Union guidelines for the development of the trans-European transport network and repealing Decision No 661/2010/EU (OJ L348, 20.12.2013, p 1).

[5.68]

Article 5 Transparency of aid

1. This Regulation shall apply only to aid in respect of which it is possible to calculate precisely the gross grant equivalent of the aid ex ante without any need to undertake a risk assessment ('transparent aid').

2. The following categories of aid shall be considered to be transparent:

(a) aid comprised in grants and interest rate subsidies;

(b) aid comprised in loans, where the gross grant equivalent has been calculated on the basis of the reference rate prevailing at the time of the grant;

(c) aid comprised in guarantees:

(i) where the gross grant equivalent has been calculated on the basis of safe-harbour premiums laid down in a Commission notice; or

(ii) where before the implementation of the measure, the methodology to calculate the gross grant equivalent of the guarantee has been accepted on the basis of the Commission Notice on the application of Articles 87 and 88 of the EC Treaty to State aid in the form of guarantees,[1] or any successor notice, following notification of that methodology to the Commission under any regulation adopted by the Commission in the State aid area applicable at the time, and the approved methodology explicitly addresses the type of guarantee and the type of underlying transaction at stake in the context of the application of this Regulation;

(d) aid in the form of tax advantages, where the measure provides for a cap ensuring that the applicable threshold is not exceeded;

(e) aid for regional urban development if the conditions laid down in Article 16 are fulfilled;

[(ea) aid to undertakings for their participation in European Territorial Cooperation projects under Article 20a, where it provides for a cap ensuring that the applicable threshold laid down in Article 20a is not exceeded;]

(f) aid comprised in risk finance measures if the conditions laid down in Article 21 are fulfilled;

(g) aid for start-ups if the conditions laid down in Article 22 are fulfilled;

(h) aid for energy efficiency projects if the conditions laid down in Article 39 are fulfilled;

(i) aid in the form of premiums in addition to the market price if the conditions laid down in Article 42 are fulfilled;

(j) aid in the form of repayable advances, if the total nominal amount of the repayable advance does not exceed the thresholds applicable under this Regulation or if, before implementation of the measure, the methodology to calculate the gross grant equivalent of the repayable advance has been accepted following its notification to the Commission;

[(k) aid in the form of the sale or the lease of tangible assets below market rates where the value is established either by an independent expert evaluation prior to the transaction or by reference to a publicly available, regularly updated and generally accepted benchmark;]

[(l) aid involved in financial products supported by the InvestEU Fund, if the conditions laid down in Section 16 of Chapter III are fulfilled].

NOTES

Para 2: point (k) added by Commission Regulation 2017/1084/EU, Art 1(4). Point (ea) inserted, and point (l) added, by Commission Regulation 2021/1237/EU, Art 1(4), as from 1 August 2021.

Repeal of this Regulation in relation to the UK: this Regulation is repealed in relation to the UK (as from IP completion day); see the introductory notes to this Regulation *ante*.

[1] OJ C155, 20.6.2008, p 10.

[5.69]

Article 6 Incentive effect

1. This Regulation shall apply only to aid which has an incentive effect.

2. Aid shall be considered to have an incentive effect if the beneficiary has submitted a written application for the aid to the Member State concerned before work on the project or activity starts. The application for the aid shall contain at least the following information:

(a) undertaking's name and size;

(b) description of the project, including its start and end dates;

(c) location of the project;

(d) list of project costs;

(e) type of aid (grant, loan, guarantee, repayable advance, equity injection or other) and amount of public funding needed for the project;

3. Ad hoc aid granted to large enterprises shall be considered to have an incentive effect if, in addition to ensuring that the condition laid down in paragraph 2 is fulfilled, the Member State has verified, before granting the aid concerned, that documentation prepared by the beneficiary establishes that the aid will result in one or more of the following:

(a) in the case of regional investment aid: that a project is carried out, which would not have been carried out in the area concerned or would not have been sufficiently profitable for the beneficiary in the area concerned in the absence of the aid.

(b) in all other cases, that there is:

— a material increase in the scope of the project/activity due to the aid, or

— *a material increase in the total amount spent by the beneficiary on the project/activity due to the aid, or*

— *a material increase in the speed of completion of the project/activity concerned;*

4. By way of derogation from paragraphs 2 and 3, measures in the form of tax advantages shall be deemed to have an incentive effect if the following conditions are fulfilled:

(a) the measure establishes a right to aid in accordance with objective criteria and without further exercise of discretion by the Member State; and

(b) the measure has been adopted and is in force before work on the aided project or activity has started, except in the case of fiscal successor schemes, where the activity was already covered by the previous schemes in the form of tax advantages.

5. By way of derogation from paragraphs 2, 3 and 4, the following categories of aid are not required to have or shall be deemed to have an incentive effect:

[(a) regional operating aid and regional urban development aid, where the relevant conditions laid down in Articles 15 and 16 are fulfilled;]

(b) aid for access to finance for SMEs, if the relevant conditions laid down in Articles 21 and 22 are fulfilled,

(c) aid for the recruitment of disadvantaged workers in the form of wage subsidies and aid for the employment of workers with disabilities in the form of wage subsidies, if the relevant conditions laid down in Articles 32 and 33 respectively are fulfilled,

[(d) aid compensating for the additional costs of employing workers with disabilities and aid for compensating the costs of assistance provided to disadvantaged workers, where the relevant conditions laid down in Articles 34 and 35 are fulfilled;]

(e) aid in the form of reductions in environmental taxes under Directive 2003/96/EC, if the conditions laid down in Article 44 of this Regulation are fulfilled;

(f) aid to make good the damage caused by certain natural disasters, if the conditions laid down in Article 50 are fulfilled;

(g) social aid for transport for residents of remote regions, if the conditions laid down in Article 51 are fulfilled;

(h) aid for culture and heritage conservation, if the conditions laid down in Article 53 are fulfilled;

[(i) aid for undertakings participating in European Territorial Cooperation projects, if the relevant conditions in Article 20 or Article 20a are fulfilled;

(j) aid for research and development projects awarded a Seal of Excellence quality label, Marie Skłodowska-Curie actions and ERC Proof of Concept actions awarded a Seal of Excellence quality label, aid involved in co-funded projects and in co-funded Teaming actions, if the relevant conditions laid down in Article 25a, Article 25b, Article 25c or Article 25d are fulfilled;

(k) aid involved in financial products supported by the InvestEU Fund, if the conditions laid down in Section 16 of Chapter III are fulfilled;

(l) aid for SMEs participating in or benefitting from community-led local development ("CLLD") projects and European Innovation Partnership for agricultural productivity and sustainability ("EIP") Operational Group projects, if the relevant conditions in Article 19a or Article 19b are fulfilled].

NOTES

Para 5: points (a), (d) substituted by Commission Regulation 2017/1084/EU, Art 1(5). Points (i)–(l) added by Commission Regulation 2021/1237/EU, Art 1(5), as from 1 August 2021.

Repeal of this Regulation in relation to the UK: this Regulation is repealed in relation to the UK (as from IP completion day); see the introductory notes to this Regulation *ante*.

[5.70]

Article 7 Aid intensity and eligible costs

1. For the purposes of calculating aid intensity and eligible costs, all figures used shall be taken before any deduction of tax or other charge. [The amounts of eligible costs may be calculated in accordance with the simplified cost options set out in Regulation (EU) No 1303/2013 of the European Parliament and of the Council, or Regulation (EU) 2021/1060 of the European Parliament and of the Council,** whichever is applicable provided that the operation is at least partly financed through a Union fund that allows the use of those simplified cost options and that the category of costs is eligible according to the relevant exemption provision.]*

[The amounts of eligible costs may be calculated in accordance with the simplified cost options set out in Regulation (EU) No 1303/2013 of the European Parliament and of the Council,[1] provided that the operation is at least partly financed through a Union fund that allows the use of those simplified cost options and that the category of costs is eligible according to the relevant exemption provision.]

2. Where aid is granted in a form other than a grant, the aid amount shall be the gross grant equivalent of the aid.

3. [Aid payable in the future, including aid payable in several instalments, shall be discounted to its value at the moment it is granted.] The eligible costs shall be discounted to their value at the moment the aid is granted. The interest rate to be used for discounting purposes shall be the discount rate applicable at the moment the aid is granted.

4. . . .

5. Where aid is granted in the form of repayable advances which, in the absence of an accepted methodology to calculate their gross grant equivalent, are expressed as a percentage of the eligible costs and the measure provides that in case of a successful outcome of the project, as defined on the basis of a reasonable and prudent hypothesis, the advances will be repaid with an interest rate at least equal to the discount rate applicable at the moment the aid is granted, the maximum aid intensities laid down in Chapter III may be increased by 10 percentage points.

6. Where regional aid is granted in the form of repayable advances, the maximum aid intensities established in a regional aid map in force at the moment the aid is granted may not be increased.

NOTES

Para 1: words in first pair of square brackets substituted by Commission Regulation 2021/1237/EU, Art 1(6), as from 1 August 2021. The second sub-paragraph was added by Commission Regulation 2017/1084/EU, Art 1(6)(a).

Para 3: words in square brackets substituted by Commission Regulation 2017/1084/EU, Art 1(6)(b).

Para 4: repealed by Commission Regulation 2017/1084/EU, Art 1(6)(c).

Repeal of this Regulation in relation to the UK: this Regulation is repealed in relation to the UK (as from IP completion day); see the introductory notes to this Regulation *ante*.

* Regulation (EU) No 1303/2013 of the European Parliament and of the Council of 17 December 2013 laying down common provisions on the European Regional Development Fund, the European Social Fund, the Cohesion Fund, the European Agricultural Fund for Rural Development and the European Maritime and Fisheries Fund and laying down general provisions on the European Regional Development Fund, the European Social Fund, the Cohesion Fund and the European Maritime and Fisheries Fund and repealing Council Regulation (EC) No 1083/2006 (OJ L347, 20.12.2013, p 320).

** Regulation (EU) 2021/1060 of the European Parliament and of the Council of 24 June 2021 laying down common provisions on the European Regional Development Fund, the European Social Fund Plus, the Cohesion Fund, the Just Transition Fund and the European Maritime, Fisheries and Aquaculture Fund and financial rules for those and for the Asylum, Migration and Integration Fund, the Internal Security Fund and the Instrument for Financial Support for Border Management and Visa Policy (OJ L231, 30.6.2021, p 159).

[1] Regulation (EU) No 1303/2013 of the European Parliament and of the Council of 17 December 2013 laying down common provisions on the European Regional Development Fund, the European Social Fund, the Cohesion Fund, the European Agricultural Fund for Rural Development and the European Maritime and Fisheries Fund and laying down general provisions on the European Regional Development Fund, the European Social Fund, the Cohesion Fund and the European Maritime and Fisheries Fund and repealing Council Regulation (EC) No 1083/2006 (OJ L347, 20.12.2013, p 320).

[5.71]

Article 8 Cumulation

1. In determining whether the notification thresholds in Article 4 and the maximum aid intensities in Chapter III are respected, the total amount of State aid for the aided activity or project or undertaking shall be taken into account.

2. Where Union funding centrally managed by the institutions, agencies, joint undertakings or other bodies of the Union that is not directly or indirectly under the control of the Member State is combined with State aid, only the latter shall be considered for determining whether notification thresholds and maximum aid intensities or maximum aid amounts are respected, provided that the total amount of public funding granted in relation to the same eligible costs does not exceed the most favourable funding rate laid down in the applicable rules of Union law.

3. Aid with identifiable eligible costs exempted by this Regulation may be cumulated with:

(a) any other State aid, as long as those measures concern different identifiable eligible costs,

[(b) any other State aid, in relation to the same eligible costs, partly or fully overlapping, only if such cumulation does not result in exceeding the highest aid intensity or aid amount applicable to this aid under this Regulation.

Financing provided to the final beneficiaries with support from the InvestEU Fund covered by Section 16 of Chapter III and the cost covered by this financing shall not be considered for determining compliance with the cumulation provisions laid down in the first sentence of this point. Instead, the amount relevant for determining compliance with the cumulation provisions of the first sentence of this point shall be calculated as follows. First, the nominal amount of the financing supported by the InvestEU Fund shall be deducted from the total eligible project costs, obtaining the total remaining eligible costs; second, the maximum aid shall be calculated by applying the relevant highest aid intensity or aid amount only to the total remaining eligible costs.

In cases of Articles for which the notification threshold is expressed as a maximum aid amount, the nominal amount of financing provided to the final beneficiaries with the support from the InvestEU Fund shall also not be considered for determining whether the notification thresholds in Article 4 are respected.

Alternatively, for senior loans or guarantees on senior loans supported by the InvestEU Fund under Section 16 of Chapter III, the gross grant equivalent of the aid entailed in such loans or guarantees provided to the final beneficiaries may be calculated in accordance with Article 5(2), point (b) or (c), as appropriate. This gross grant equivalent of the aid can be used for ensuring, in line with the first sentence of this point, that cumulation with any other aid for the same identifiable eligible costs does not result in exceeding the highest aid intensity or aid amount applicable to the aid under this Regulation or the relevant notification threshold under this Regulation.]

[4. Aid without identifiable eligible costs exempted under Article 19b, 20a, 21, 22 or 23, Article 56e(5), point (a)(ii) or (iii), Article 56e(8), point (d), Article 56e(10) and Article 56f may be cumulated with any other State aid with identifiable eligible costs. Aid without identifiable eligible costs may be cumulated with any other State aid without identifiable eligible costs, up to the highest relevant total financing threshold fixed in the specific circumstances of each case by this or another block exemption regulation or decision adopted by the Commission. Aid without identifiable eligible costs exempted under Article 56e(5), point (a)(ii) or (iii), Article 56e(8), point (d), Article 56e(10) and Article 56f may be cumulated with other aid without identifiable eligible costs exempted under those Articles.]

5. State aid exempted under this Regulation shall not be cumulated with any de minimis aid in respect of the same eligible costs if such cumulation would result in an aid intensity exceeding those laid down in Chapter III of this Regulation.

6. By way of derogation from paragraph 3(b), aid in favour of workers with disabilities, as provided for in Articles 33 and 34 may be cumulated with other aid exempted under this Regulation in relation to the same eligible costs above the highest applicable threshold under this Regulation, provided that such cumulation does not result in an aid intensity exceeding 100% of the relevant costs over any period for which the workers concerned are employed.

[7. By way of derogation from paragraphs 1 to 6, in determining whether the ceilings for regional operating aid in outermost regions, as set out in Article 15(4), are respected, only regional operating aid in outermost regions implemented under this Regulation shall be taken into account.]

NOTES

Para 3: words in square brackets substituted by Commission Regulation 2021/1237/EU, Art 1(7)(a), as from 1 August 2021.

Para 4: substituted by Commission Regulation 2021/1237/EU, Art 1(7)(b), as from 1 August 2021.

Para 7: added by Commission Regulation 2017/1084/EU, Art 1(7).

Repeal of this Regulation in relation to the UK: this Regulation is repealed in relation to the UK (as from IP completion day); see the introductory notes to this Regulation *ante*.

[5.72]

Article 9 Publication and information

[1. The Member State concerned shall ensure the publication on a comprehensive State aid website, at national or regional level of:

(a) the summary information referred to in Article 11 in the standardised format laid down in Annex II or a link providing access to it;

(b) the full text of each aid measure, as referred to in Article 11 or a link providing access to the full text;

(c) the information referred to in Annex III on each individual aid award exceeding EUR 500,000, or for beneficiaries active in primary agricultural production, other than those to which Section 2a applies, each individual aid award for such production exceeding EUR 60,000 and for beneficiaries active in the fishery and aquaculture sector, other than those to which Section 2a applies, each individual aid award exceeding EUR 30,000.

As regards aid granted to European Territorial Cooperation projects referred to in Article 20, the information referred to in this paragraph shall be placed on the website of the Member State in which the Managing Authority concerned, as defined in Article 21 of Regulation (EU) No 1299/2013 of the European Parliament and of the Council,[1] *or Article 45 of Regulation (EU) 2021/1059 of the European Parliament and of the Council,*[2] *whichever is applicable, is located. Alternatively, the participating Member States may decide that each of them shall provide the information relating to the aid measures within their territory on the respective websites.*

The publication obligations laid down in the first subparagraph shall not apply to aid granted to European Territorial Cooperation projects referred to in Article 20a, as well as European Innovation Partnership for agricultural productivity and sustainability ("EIP") Operational Group projects and community-led local development ("CLLD") projects under Article 19b.

2. For schemes in the form of tax advantages, and for schemes covered by Article 16 and 21[3] *the conditions set out in paragraph 1, first subparagraph, point (c) of this Article shall be considered fulfilled if Member States publish the required information on individual aid amounts in the following ranges (in EUR million):*

0.03-0.5 (only for fishery and aquaculture);
0.06-0.5 (only for primary agricultural production); 0.5-1;
1-2;
2-5;
5-10;
10-30; and
30 and more.]

3. For schemes under Article 51 of this Regulation, the publication obligations laid down in this article shall not apply to final consumers.

[3a. If a financial product has been implemented by a Member State under the InvestEU Member State compartment or by a national promotional bank acting as an implementing partner or acting as a financial intermediary under InvestEU, the Member State remains under the obligation to ensure the publication of information as laid down in paragraph 1, first subparagraph, point (c). However, this obligation is deemed to be fulfilled if the implementing partner provides to the Commission the information as laid down in paragraph 1, first subparagraph, point (c), no later than 30 June of the year following the financial year in which the aid was granted and if the guarantee agreement signed between the Commission and the implementing partner stipulates the requirement to provide to the Commission the information as laid down in paragraph 1, first subparagraph, point (c).]

4. The information referred to in paragraph 1(c) of this Article shall be organised and accessible in a standardised manner, as described in Annex III, and shall allow for effective search and download functions. The information referred to in paragraph 1 shall be published within 6 months from the date the aid was granted, or for aid in the form of tax advantage, within 1 year from the date the tax declaration is due, and shall be available for at least 10 years from the date on which the aid was granted.

5. The Commission shall publish on its website:

(a) the links to the State aid websites referred to in paragraph 1 of this Article;

(b) the summary information referred to in Article 11.

6. Member States shall comply with the provisions of this Article at the latest within two years after the entry into force of this Regulation.

NOTES

Paras 1, 2 substituted, and para 3a inserted, by Commission Regulation 2021/1237/EU, Art 1(8), as from 1 August 2021.

Repeal of this Regulation in relation to the UK: this Regulation is repealed in relation to the UK (as from IP completion day); see the introductory notes to this Regulation *ante*.

[1] Regulation (EU) No 1299/2013 of the European Parliament and of the Council of 17 December 2013 on specific provisions for the support from the European Regional Development Fund to the European territorial cooperation goal (OJ L 347, 20.12.2013, p. 259).

[2] Regulation (EU) 2021/1059 of the European Parliament and of the Council of 24 June 2021 on specific provisions for the European territorial cooperation goal (Interreg) supported by the European Regional Development Fund and external financing instruments (OJ L 231, 30.6.2021, p. 94).

[30] For schemes under Article 16 and 21 of the present Regulation, the requirement to publish information on each individual award exceeding EUR 500,000 can be waived with respect to SMEs which have not carried out any commercial sale in

any market.

CHAPTER II MONITORING

[5.73]

Article 10 Withdrawal of the benefit of the block exemption

Where a Member State grants aid allegedly exempted from the notification requirement under this Regulation without fulfilling the conditions set out in Chapters I to III, the Commission may, after having provided the Member State concerned with the possibility to make its views known, adopt a decision stating that all or some of the future aid measures adopted by the Member State concerned which would otherwise fulfil the requirements of this Regulation, are to be notified to the Commission in accordance with Article 108(3) of the Treaty. The measures to be notified may be limited to the measures granting certain types of aid or in favour of certain beneficiaries or aid measures adopted by certain authorities of the Member State concerned.

NOTES

Repeal of this Regulation in relation to the UK: this Regulation is repealed in relation to the UK (as from IP completion day); see the introductory notes to this Regulation *ante*.

[5.74]

[Article 11 Reporting

[1. Member States, or in the case of aid granted to European Territorial Cooperation projects under Article 20, alternatively the Member State in which the Managing Authority, as defined in Article 21 of Regulation (EU) No 1299/2013, or Article 45 of Regulation (EU) 2021/1059, whichever is applicable, is located, shall transmit to the Commission:

(a) via the Commission's electronic notification system, the summary information about each aid measure exempted under this Regulation in the standardised format laid down in Annex II, together with a link providing access to the full text of the aid measure, including its amendments, within 20 working days following its entry into force; and

(b) an annual report, as referred to in Commission Regulation (EC) No 794/2004[1] *in electronic form, on the application of this Regulation, containing the information indicated in that Regulation, in respect of each whole year or each part of the year during which this Regulation applies. For financial products implemented by a Member State under the InvestEU Member State compartment or by a national promotional bank acting as an implementing partner or acting as a financial intermediary under InvestEU, this obligation of the Member State is deemed to be fulfilled if the implementing partner provides the annual reports to the Commission, in accordance with the relevant reporting requirements laid down in the guarantee agreement signed between the Commission and the implementing partner.*

This first subparagraph shall not apply in respect of aid granted to European Territorial Cooperation projects referred to in Article 20a, as well as to European Innovation Partnership for agricultural productivity and sustainability ("EIP") Operational Group projects and to community-led local development ("CLLD") projects as referred to Article 19b.]

2. Where, as a consequence of the extension of the application period of this Regulation until 31 December 2023 by Commission Regulation (EU) 2020/972,[2] *a Member State plans to extend measures in respect of which the summary information was submitted to the Commission in accordance with paragraph 1 of this Article, that Member State shall update that summary information regarding the extension of those measures and communicate that update to the Commission within 20 working days following the entry into force of the act which extends the respective measure by the Member State.*

NOTES

Substituted by Commission Regulation 2020/972/EU, Art 2(3).

Para 1: substituted by Commission Regulation 2021/1237/EU, Art 1(9), as from 1 August 2021.

Repeal of this Regulation in relation to the UK: this Regulation is repealed in relation to the UK (as from IP completion day); see the introductory notes to this Regulation *ante*.

[1] Commission Regulation (EC) No 794/2004 of 21 April 2004 implementing Council Regulation (EU) 2015/1589 laying down detailed rules for the application of Article 108 of the Treaty on the Functioning of the European Union (OJ L140, 30.4.2004, p 1).

[1] Commission Regulation (EU) 2020/972 of 2 July 2020 amending Regulation (EU) No 1407/2013 as regards its prolongation and amending Regulation (EU) No 651/2014 as regards its prolongation and relevant adjustments (OJ L215, 7.7.2020, p 3).

[5.75]

[Article 12 Monitoring

[1. In order to enable the Commission to monitor the aid exempted from notification by this Regulation, Member States, or alternatively, in the case of aid granted to European Territorial Cooperation projects referred to in Article 20, the Member State in which the Managing Authority is located, shall maintain detailed records with the information and supporting documentation necessary to establish that all the conditions laid down in this Regulation are fulfilled. Such records shall be kept for 10 years from the date on which the ad hoc aid was granted or the last aid was granted under the scheme.

The first subparagraph shall not apply in respect of aid granted to European Territorial Cooperation projects referred to in Article 20a, as well as to European Innovation Partnership for agricultural productivity and sustainability Operational Group projects and to community-led local development ("CLLD") projects as referred to Article 19b.]

2. In the case of schemes under which fiscal aid is granted automatically, such as those based on tax declarations of the beneficiaries, and where there is no ex ante verification that all compatibility conditions are met for each beneficiary, Member States shall regularly verify, at least ex post and on a sample basis, that all compatibility conditions are met, and draw the necessary conclusions. Member States shall maintain detailed records of the verifications for at least 10 years from the date of the controls.

3. The Commission may request, from each Member State, all the information and supporting documentation which the Commission considers necessary to monitor the application of this Regulation, including the information mentioned in paragraphs 1 and 2. The Member State concerned shall provide the Commission with the requested information and supporting documents within a period of 20 working days from receipt of the request or such longer period as may be fixed in the request.]

NOTES

Substituted by Commission Regulation 2017/1084/EU, Art 1(8).

Para 1: substituted by Commission Regulation 2021/1237/EU, Art 1(10), as from 1 August 2021.

Repeal of this Regulation in relation to the UK: this Regulation is repealed in relation to the UK (as from IP completion day); see the introductory notes to this Regulation *ante*.

CHAPTER III SPECIFIC PROVISIONS FOR DIFFERENT CATEGORIES OF AID

SECTION 1 REGIONAL AID

SUBSECTION A REGIONAL INVESTMENT AND OPERATING AID

[5.76]

[Article 13 Scope of regional aid

This Section shall not apply to:

- *(a) aid which favours activities in the steel sector, the coal sector, the shipbuilding sector or the synthetic fibres sector;*
- *(b) aid to the transport sector as well as the related infrastructure, and aid for energy generation, distribution and infrastructure, except for regional investment aid in outermost regions and regional operating aid schemes;*
- *(c) regional aid in the form of schemes which are targeted at a limited number of specific sectors of economic activity; schemes aimed at tourism activities, broadband infrastructures or processing and marketing of agricultural products are not considered to be targeted at specific sectors of economic activity;*
- *(d) regional operating aid granted to undertakings whose principal activities fall under Section K "Financial and insurance activities" of the NACE Rev. 2 or to undertakings that perform intra-group activities whose principal activities fall under classes 70.10 "Activities of head offices" or 70.22 "Business and other management consultancy activities" of NACE Rev. 2.]*

NOTES

Substituted by Commission Regulation 2017/1084/EU, Art 1(9).

Repeal of this Regulation in relation to the UK: this Regulation is repealed in relation to the UK (as from IP completion day); see the introductory notes to this Regulation *ante*.

[5.77]

Article 14 Regional investment aid

1. Regional investment aid measures shall be compatible with the internal market within the meaning of Article 107(3) of the Treaty and shall be exempted from the notification requirement of Article 108(3) of the Treaty, provided that the conditions laid down in this Article and in Chapter I are fulfilled.

2. The aid shall be granted in assisted areas.

3. In assisted areas fulfilling the conditions of Article 107(3)(a) of the Treaty, the aid may be granted for an initial investment regardless of the size of the beneficiary. In assisted areas fulfilling the conditions of Article 107(3)(c) of the Treaty, the aid may be granted to SMEs for any form of initial investment. Aid to large enterprises shall only be granted for an initial investment in favour of new economic activity in the area concerned.

4. The eligible costs shall be as follows:

- *(a) investment costs in tangible and intangible assets;*
- *(b) the estimated wage costs arising from job creation as a result of an initial investment, calculated over a period of two years; or*
- *(c) a combination of points (a) and (b) not exceeding the amount of (a) or (b), whichever is higher.*

5. The investment shall be maintained in the recipient area for at least five years, or at least three years in the case of SMEs, after completion of the investment. This shall not prevent the replacement of plant or equipment that has become outdated or broken within this period, provided that the economic activity is retained in the area concerned for the relevant minimum period.

6. The assets acquired shall be new except for SMEs and for the acquisition of an establishment. Costs related to the lease of tangible assets may be taken into account under the following conditions:

- *(a) for land and buildings, the lease must continue for at least five years after the expected date of completion of the investment project for large undertakings or three years in the case of SMEs;*
- *(b) for plant or machinery, the lease must take the form of financial leasing and must contain an obligation for the beneficiary of the aid to purchase the asset upon expiry of the term of the lease.*

[In the case of acquisition of the assets of an establishment within the meaning of point 49 or point 51 of Article 2, only the costs of buying the assets from third parties unrelated to the buyer shall be taken into consideration.] The transaction shall take place under market conditions. If aid has already been granted for the acquisition of assets prior to their purchase, the costs of those assets shall be deducted from the eligible costs related to the acquisition of an establishment. Where a member of the family of the original owner, or an employee, takes over a small enterprise, the condition that the assets be bought from third parties unrelated to the buyer shall be waived. The acquisition of shares does not constitute initial investment.

7. [For aid granted to large undertakings for a fundamental change in the production process, the eligible costs must exceed the depreciation of the assets linked to the activity to be modernised in the course of the preceding three fiscal years.] For aid granted for a diversification of an existing establishment, the eligible costs must exceed by at least 200% the book value of the assets that are reused, as registered in the fiscal year preceding the start of works.

8. Intangible assets are eligible for the calculation of investment costs if they fulfil the following conditions:

(a) they must be used exclusively in the establishment receiving the aid;

(b) they must be amortisable;

(c) they must be purchased under market conditions from third parties unrelated to the buyer; and

(d) they must be included in the assets of the undertaking receiving the aid and must remain associated with the project for which the aid is granted for at least five years or three years in the case of SMEs.

For large undertakings, costs of intangible assets are eligible only up to a limit of 50% of the total eligible investment costs for the initial investment.

9. Where eligible costs are calculated by reference to the estimated wage costs as referred to in paragraph 4(b), the following conditions shall be fulfilled:

(a) the investment project shall lead to a net increase in the number of employees in the establishment concerned, compared with the average over the previous 12 months, meaning that any job lost shall be deducted from the apparent created number of jobs during that period;

(b) each post shall be filled within three years of completion of works; and

[(c) each job created through the investment shall be maintained in the area concerned for a period of at least five years from the date the post was first filled, or three years in the case of SMEs, except if the job is lost between 1 January 2020 and 30 June 2021].

10. Regional aid for broadband network development shall fulfil the following conditions:

(a) aid shall be granted only in areas where there is no network of the same category (either basic broadband or NGA) and where no such network is likely to be developed on commercial terms within three years from the decision to grant the aid; and

(b) the subsidised network operator must offer active and passive wholesale access under fair and non-discriminatory conditions including physical unbundling in the case of NGA networks; and

(c) aid shall be allocated on the basis of a competitive selection process.

11. Regional aid for research infrastructures shall be granted only if the aid is made conditional on giving transparent and non-discriminatory access to the aided infrastructure.

12. The aid intensity in gross grant equivalent shall not exceed the maximum aid intensity established in the regional aid map which is in force at the time the aid is granted in the area concerned. Where the aid intensity is calculated on the basis of paragraph 4(c), the maximum aid intensity shall not exceed the most favourable amount resulting from the application of that intensity on the basis of investment costs or wage costs. For large investment projects the aid amount shall not exceed the adjusted aid amount calculated in accordance with the mechanism defined in Article 2, point 20;

13. Any initial investment started by the same beneficiary (at group level) within a period of three years from the date of start of works on another aided investment in the same level 3 region of the Nomenclature of Territorial Units for Statistics shall be considered to be part of a single investment project. Where such single investment project is a large investment project, the total aid amount for the single investment project shall not exceed the adjusted aid amount for large investment projects.

14. The aid beneficiary must provide a financial contribution of at least 25% of the eligible costs, either through its own resources or by external financing, in a form, which is free of any public support. In the outermost regions an investment made by an SME may receive an aid with a maximum aid intensity above 75%, in such situations the remainder shall be provided by way of a financial contribution from the aid beneficiary.

[15. For an initial investment linked to European territorial cooperation projects covered by Regulation (EU) No 1299/2013, or Regulation (EU) 2021/1059, the aid intensity of the area in which the initial investment is located shall apply to all beneficiaries participating in the project. If the initial investment is located in two or more assisted areas, the maximum aid intensity shall be the one applicable in the assisted area where the highest amount of eligible costs is incurred. In assisted areas eligible for aid under Article 107(3)(c) of the Treaty, this provision shall apply to large undertakings only if the initial investment concerns a new economic activity.]

[16. The beneficiary shall confirm that it has not carried out a relocation to the establishment in which the initial investment for which aid is requested is to take place, in the two years preceding the application for aid and give a commitment that it will not do so up to a period of two years after the initial investment for which aid is requested is completed. [With regard to commitments given prior to 31 December 2019, any loss of jobs, in the same or similar activity in one of the initial establishments of the beneficiary in the EEA, occurring between 1 January 2020 and 30 June 2021, shall not be considered a transfer within the meaning of Article 2(61a) of this Regulation.]

17. In the fisheries and aquaculture sector, aid shall not be granted to undertakings that have committed one or more of the infringements set out in Article 10(1)(a) to (d) and Article 10(3) of Regulation (EU) No 508/2014 of the European Parliament and of the Council[1] and for operations of Article 11 of that Regulation.]

NOTES

Paras 6, 7: words in square brackets substituted by Commission Regulation 2017/1084/EU, Art 1(10)(a), (b).

Para 9: point (c) substituted by Commission Regulation 2021/1237/EU, Art 1(11)(a), as from 1 August 2021.

Para 15: substituted by Commission Regulation 2021/1237/EU, Art 1(11)(b), as from 1 August 2021.

Paras 16, 17: added by Commission Regulation 2017/1084/EU, Art 1(10)(c). Words in square brackets in para 16 added by Commission Regulation 2020/972/EU, Art 2(4).

Repeal of this Regulation in relation to the UK: this Regulation is repealed in relation to the UK (as from IP completion day); see the introductory notes to this Regulation *ante*.

[1] Regulation (EU) No 508/2014 of the European Parliament and of the Council of 15 May 2014 on the European Maritime and Fisheries Fund and repealing Council Regulations (EC) No 2328/2003, (EC) No 861/2006, (EC) No 1198/2006 and (EC) No 791/2007 and Regulation (EU) No 1255/2011 of the European Parliament and of the Council (OJ L149,

20.5.2014, p 1).

[5.78]

[Article 15 Regional operating aid

1. Regional operating aid schemes in outermost regions, sparsely populated areas and very sparsely populated areas shall be compatible with the internal market within the meaning of Article 107(3) of the Treaty and shall be exempted from the notification requirement of Article 108(3) of the Treaty, provided that the conditions laid down in this Article and in Chapter II are fulfilled.

2. In sparsely populated areas, the regional operating aid schemes shall compensate for the additional transport costs of goods which have been produced in areas eligible for operating aid, as well as additional transport costs of goods that are further processed in those areas, under the following conditions:

- *(a) the aid is objectively quantifiable in advance on the basis of a fixed sum or per tonne/kilometre ratio or any other relevant unit;*
- *(b) the additional transport costs are calculated on the basis of the journey of the goods inside the national border of the Member State concerned using the means of transport which results in the lowest costs for the beneficiary.*

The aid intensity shall not exceed 100% of the additional transport costs as set out in this paragraph.

3. In very sparsely populated areas, the regional operating aid schemes shall prevent or reduce depopulation under the following conditions:

- *(a) the beneficiaries have their economic activity in the area concerned;*
- *(b) the annual aid amount per beneficiary under all operating aid schemes does not exceed 20% of the annual labour costs incurred by the beneficiary in the area concerned.*

4. In outermost regions, the operating aid schemes shall compensate for the additional operating costs incurred in those regions as a direct result of one or several of the permanent handicaps referred to in Article 349 of the Treaty, where the beneficiaries have their economic activity in an outermost region provided that the annual aid amount per beneficiary under all operating aid schemes implemented under this Regulation does not exceed any of the following percentages:

- *(a) 35% of the gross value added annually created by the beneficiary in the outermost region concerned;*
- *(b) 40% of the annual labour costs incurred by the beneficiary in the outermost region concerned;*
- *(c) 30% of the annual turnover of the beneficiary realised in the outermost region concerned.]*

NOTES

Substituted by Commission Regulation 2017/1084/EU, Art 1(11).

Repeal of this Regulation in relation to the UK: this Regulation is repealed in relation to the UK (as from IP completion day); see the introductory notes to this Regulation *ante*.

SUBSECTION B URBAN DEVELOPMENT AID

[5.79]

Article 16 Regional urban development aid

1. Regional urban development aid shall be compatible with the internal market within the meaning of Article 107(3) of the Treaty and shall be exempted from the notification requirement of Article 108(3) of the Treaty, provided that the conditions laid down in this Article and in Chapter I are fulfilled.

2. Urban development projects shall fulfil the following criteria:

- *(a) they are implemented via urban development funds in assisted areas;*
- *(b) they are co-financed by the European Structural and Investment Funds;*
- *(c) they support the implementation of an 'integrated sustainable urban development strategy';*

3. The total investment in an urban development project under any urban development aid measure shall not exceed EUR 20 million.

[4. The eligible costs shall be the overall costs of the urban development project to the extent that they comply with Articles 37 and 65 of Regulation (EU) No 1303/2013, or Articles 67 and 68 of Regulation (EU) 2021/1060, whichever is applicable.]

5. Aid granted by an urban development fund to the eligible urban development projects may take the form of equity, quasi-equity, loans, guarantees, or a mix thereof.

6. The urban development aid shall leverage additional investment from private investors at the level of the urban development funds or the urban development projects, so as to achieve an aggregate amount reaching minimum 30% of the total financing provided to an urban development project.

7. Private and public investors may provide cash or an in-kind contribution or a combination of those for the implementation of an urban development project. An in-kind contribution shall be taken into account at its market value, as certified by an independent qualified expert or duly authorised official body.

8. The urban development measures shall fulfil the following conditions:

- *(a) urban development fund managers shall be selected through an open, transparent and non-discriminatory call in accordance with the applicable Union and national laws. In particular, there shall be no discrimination between urban development fund managers on the basis of their place of establishment or incorporation in any Member State. Urban development fund managers may be required to fulfil predefined criteria objectively justified by the nature of the investments;*
- *(b) the independent private investors shall be selected through an open, transparent and non-discriminatory call in accordance with applicable Union and national laws aimed at establishing the appropriate risk-reward sharing arrangements whereby, for investments other than guarantees, asymmetric profit-sharing shall be given preference over downside protection. If the private investors are not selected by such a call, the fair rate of return to the private investors shall be established by an independent expert selected via an open, transparent and non-discriminatory call;*

(c) in the case of asymmetric loss-sharing between public and private investors, the first loss assumed by the public investor shall be capped at 25% of the total investment;

(d) in the case of guarantees to private investors in urban development projects, the guarantee rate shall be limited to 80% and total losses assumed by a Member State shall be capped at 25% of the underlying guaranteed portfolio;

(e) the investors shall be allowed to be represented in the governance bodies of the urban development fund, such as the supervisory board or the advisory committee;

(f) the urban development fund shall be established according to the applicable laws. The Member State shall provide for a due diligence process in order to ensure a commercially sound investment strategy for the purpose of implementing the urban development aid measure.

9. Urban development funds shall be managed on a commercial basis and shall ensure profit-driven financing decisions. This is considered to be the case when the managers of the urban development fund fulfil the following conditions:

(a) the managers of urban development funds shall be obliged by law or contract to act with the diligence of a professional manager in good faith and avoiding conflicts of interest; best practices and regulatory supervision shall apply;

(b) the remuneration of the managers of urban development funds shall conform to market practices. This requirement is considered to be met where a manager is selected through an open, transparent and non-discriminatory call, based on objective criteria linked to experience, expertise and operational and financial capacity;

(c) the managers of urban development funds shall receive a remuneration linked to performance, or shall share part of the investment risks by co-investing own resources so as to ensure that their interests are permanently aligned with the interests of the public investors;

(d) the managers of urban development funds shall set out an investment strategy, criteria and the proposed timing of investments in urban development projects, establishing the ex ante financial viability and their expected impact on urban development;

(e) a clear and realistic exit strategy shall exist for each equity and quasi-equity investment.

10. Where an urban development fund provides loans or guarantees to urban development projects, the following conditions shall be fulfilled:

(a) in the case of loans, the nominal amount of the loan is taken into account in calculating the maximum investment amount for the purposes of paragraph 3 of this Article;

(b) in the case of guarantees, the nominal amount of the underlying loan is taken into account in calculating the maximum investment amount for the purposes of paragraph 3 of this Article.

11. The Member State may assign the implementation of the urban development aid measure to an entrusted entity.

NOTES

Para 4: substituted by Commission Regulation 2021/1237/EU, Art 1(12), as from 1 August 2021.

Repeal of this Regulation in relation to the UK: this Regulation is repealed in relation to the UK (as from IP completion day); see the introductory notes to this Regulation *ante*.

SECTION 2 AID TO SMES

[5.80]

Article 17 Investment aid to SMEs

1. Investment aid to SMEs operating inside or outside the territory of the Union shall be compatible with the internal market within the meaning of Article 107(3) of the Treaty and shall be exempted from the notification requirement of Article 108(3) of the Treaty, provided that the conditions laid down in this Article and in Chapter I are fulfilled.

2. The eligible costs shall be either or both of the following:

(a) the costs of investment in tangible and intangible assets;

(b) the estimated wage costs of employment directly created by the investment project, calculated over a period of two years.

3. In order to be considered an eligible cost for the purposes of this Article, an investment shall consist of the following:

(a) an investment in tangible and/or intangible assets relating to the setting-up of a new establishment, the extension of an existing establishment, diversification of the output of an establishment into new additional products or a fundamental change in the overall production process of an existing establishment; or

(b) the acquisition of the assets belonging to an establishment, where the following conditions are fulfilled:

— *the establishment has closed or would have closed had it not been purchased;*

— *the assets are purchased from third parties unrelated to the buyer;*

— *the transaction takes place under market conditions.*

Where a member of the family of the original owner, or an employee, takes over a small enterprise, the condition that the assets shall be bought from third parties unrelated to the buyer shall be waived. The sole acquisition of the shares of an undertaking shall not constitute investment.

4. Intangible assets shall fulfil all of the following conditions:

(a) they shall be used exclusively in the establishment receiving the aid;

(b) they shall be regarded as amortizable assets;

(c) they shall be purchased under market conditions from third parties unrelated to the buyer;

(d) they shall be included in the assets of the undertaking for at least three years;

5. Employment directly created by an investment project shall fulfil the following conditions:

(a) it shall be created within three years of completion of the investment;

(b) there shall be a net increase in the number of employees in the establishment concerned, compared with the average over the previous 12 months;

(c) it shall be maintained during a minimum period of three years from the date the post was first filled.

6. The aid intensity shall not exceed:

(a) 20% of the eligible costs in the case of small enterprises;

(b) 10% of the eligible costs in the case of medium-sized enterprises.

NOTES

Repeal of this Regulation in relation to the UK: this Regulation is repealed in relation to the UK (as from IP completion day); see the introductory notes to this Regulation *ante*.

[5.81]

Article 18 Aid for consultancy in favour of SMEs

1. Aid for consultancy in favour of SMEs shall be compatible with the internal market within the meaning of Article 107(3) of the Treaty and shall be exempted from the notification requirement of Article 108(3) of the Treaty, provided that the conditions laid down in this Article and in Chapter I are fulfilled.

2. The aid intensity shall not exceed 50% of the eligible costs.

3. The eligible costs shall be the costs of consultancy services provided by external consultants.

4. The services concerned shall not be a continuous or periodic activity nor relate to the undertaking's usual operating costs, such as routine tax consultancy services, regular legal services or advertising.

NOTES

Repeal of this Regulation in relation to the UK: this Regulation is repealed in relation to the UK (as from IP completion day); see the introductory notes to this Regulation *ante*.

[5.82]

Article 19 Aid to SMEs for participation in fairs

1. Aid to SMEs for participation in fairs shall be compatible with the internal market within the meaning of Article 107(3) of the Treaty and shall be exempted from the notification requirement of Article 108(3) of the Treaty, provided that the conditions laid down in this Article and in Chapter I are fulfilled.

2. The eligible costs shall be the costs incurred for renting, setting up and running the stand for the participation of an undertaking in any particular fair or exhibition.

3. The aid intensity shall not exceed 50% of the eligible costs.

NOTES

Repeal of this Regulation in relation to the UK: this Regulation is repealed in relation to the UK (as from IP completion day); see the introductory notes to this Regulation *ante*.

[5.83]

[Article 19a Aid for costs incurred by SMEs participating in community-led local development ("CLLD") or European Innovation Partnership for agricultural productivity and sustainability ("EIP") Operational Group projects

1. Aid for costs incurred by SMEs participating in CLLD projects, designated as LEADER local development under the European Agricultural Fund for Rural Development, covered by Regulation (EU) No 1303/2013 or Regulation (EU) 2021/1060, as well as for EIP Operational Group projects covered by Article 35 of Regulation (EU) No 1305/2013, shall be compatible with the internal market within the meaning of Article 107(3) of the Treaty and shall be exempted from the notification requirement of Article 108(3) of the Treaty, provided the conditions laid down in this Article and in Chapter I are fulfilled.

2. The following costs, set out in Article 35(1) of Regulation (EU) No 1303/2013 or Article 34(1) of Regulation (EU) 2021/1060, whichever is applicable, shall be eligible for CLLD and EIP Operational Group projects:

(a) the costs of preparatory support, capacity building, training and networking with a view of preparing and implementing a CLLD strategy or an EIP Operational Group project;

(b) implementation of approved operations;

(c) preparation and implementation of the group's cooperation activities;

(d) running costs linked to the management of the implementation of the CLLD strategy or of the EIP Operational Group project;

(e) animation of the EIP community or the CLLD strategy in order to facilitate exchange between stakeholders to provide information and to promote the strategy and the projects, and to support potential beneficiaries with a view of developing operations and preparing applications.

3. The aid intensity shall not exceed the maximum co-financing rates provided for in the Fund specific Regulations supporting CLLD and EIP Operational Groups.]

NOTES

Inserted by Commission Regulation 2021/1237/EU, Art 1(13), as from 1 August 2021.

Repeal of this Regulation in relation to the UK: this Regulation is repealed in relation to the UK (as from IP completion day); see the introductory notes to this Regulation *ante*.

[5.84]

[Article 19b Limited amounts of aid to SMEs benefitting from community-led local development ("CLLD") or European Innovation Partnership for agricultural productivity and sustainability ("EIP") Operational Group projects

1. Aid to undertakings participating in, or benefitting from, CLLD or EIP Operational Group projects, as referred to in Article 19a(1), shall be compatible with the internal market within the meaning of Article 107(3) of the Treaty and shall be exempted from the notification requirement of Article 108(3) of the Treaty, provided the conditions laid down in this Article and in Chapter I are fulfilled.

2. The total amount of aid under this Article granted per project shall not exceed EUR 200,000 for CLLD projects, and EUR 350,000 for EIP Operational Group projects.]

NOTES

Inserted by Commission Regulation 2021/1237/EU, Art 1(13), as from 1 August 2021.

Repeal of this Regulation in relation to the UK: this Regulation is repealed in relation to the UK (as from IP completion day); see the introductory notes to this Regulation *ante*.

[SECTION 2A AID FOR EUROPEAN TERRITORIAL COOPERATION]

NOTES

The Section heading above was inserted by Commission Regulation 2021/1237/EU, Art 1(14), as from 1 August 2021.

[5.85]

[Article 20 Aid for costs incurred by undertakings participating in European Territorial Cooperation project

1. Aid for costs incurred by undertakings participating in European Territorial Cooperation projects covered by Regulation (EU) No 1299/2013 or Regulation (EU) 2021/1059 shall be compatible with the internal market within the meaning of Article 107(3) of the Treaty and shall be exempted from the notification requirement of Article 108(3) of the Treaty, provided the conditions laid down in this Article and in Chapter I are fulfilled.

2. To the extent that they are linked to the cooperation project, the following costs, which shall have the meaning ascribed to them in Commission Delegated Regulation (EU) No 481/2014,[1] or Articles 38 to 44 of Regulation (EU) 2021/1059, whichever is applicable, shall be eligible costs:

- *(a) staff costs;*
- *(b) office and administrative costs;*
- *(c) travel and accommodation costs;*
- *(d) external expertise and services costs;*
- *(e) equipment costs;*
- *(f) costs for infrastructure and works.*

3. The aid intensity shall not exceed the maximum co-financing rate provided for in Regulation (EU) No 1303/2013 or Regulation (EU) 2021/1060 and/or Regulation (EU) 2021/1059, whichever is applicable.]

NOTES

Substituted by Commission Regulation 2021/1237/EU, Art 1(15), as from 1 August 2021.

Repeal of this Regulation in relation to the UK: this Regulation is repealed in relation to the UK (as from IP completion day); see the introductory notes to this Regulation *ante*.

[1] Commission Delegated Regulation (EU) No 481/2014 of 4 March 2014 supplementing Regulation (EU) No 1299/2013 of the European Parliament and of the Council with regard to specific rules on eligibility of expenditure for cooperation programmes (OJ L 138, 13.5.2014, p. 45).';

[5.86]

[Article 20a Limited amounts of aid to undertakings for participation in European Territorial Cooperation projects

1. Aid to undertakings for their participation in European Territorial Cooperation projects covered by Regulation (EU) No 1299/2013 or by Regulation (EU) 2021/1059 shall be compatible with the internal market within the meaning of Article 107(3) of the Treaty and shall be exempted from the notification requirement of Article 108(3) of the Treaty, provided the conditions laid down in this Article and in Chapter I are fulfilled.

2. The total amount of aid under this Article granted to an undertaking per project shall not exceed EUR 20,000.]

NOTES

Inserted by Commission Regulation 2021/1237/EU, Art 1(16), as from 1 August 2021.

Repeal of this Regulation in relation to the UK: this Regulation is repealed in relation to the UK (as from IP completion day); see the introductory notes to this Regulation *ante*.

SECTION 3 AID FOR ACCESS TO FINANCE FOR SMES

[5.87]

Article 21 Risk finance aid

1. Risk finance aid schemes in favour of SMEs shall be compatible with the internal market within the meaning of Article 107(3) of the Treaty and shall be exempted from the notification requirement of Article 108(3) of the Treaty, provided the conditions laid down in this Article and in Chapter I are fulfilled.

2. At the level of financial intermediaries, risk finance aid to independent private investors may take one of the following forms:

- *(a) equity or quasi-equity, or financial endowment to provide risk finance investments directly or indirectly to eligible undertakings;*
- *(b) loans to provide risk finance investments directly or indirectly to eligible undertakings;*
- *(c) guarantees to cover losses from risk finance investments directly or indirectly to eligible undertakings.*

3. At the level of independent private investors, risk finance aid may take the forms mentioned in paragraph 2 of this Article, or be in the form of tax incentives to private investors who are natural persons providing risk finance directly or indirectly to eligible undertakings.

4. At the level of eligible undertakings, risk finance aid may take the form of equity, quasi-equity investments, loans, guarantees, or a mix thereof.

5. Eligible undertakings shall be undertakings which at the time of the initial risk finance investment are unlisted SMEs and fulfil at least one of the following conditions:

- *(a) they have not been operating in any market;*
- *(b) they have been operating in any market for less than 7 years following their first commercial sale;*

(c) *they require an initial risk finance investment which, based on a business plan prepared in view of entering a new product or geographical market, is higher than 50% of their average annual turnover in the preceding 5 years.*

6. The risk finance aid may also cover follow-on investments made in eligible undertakings, including after the 7 year period mentioned in paragraph 5(b), if the following cumulative conditions are fulfilled:

(a) *the total amount of risk finance mentioned in paragraph 9 is not exceeded;*

(b) *the possibility of follow-on investments was foreseen in the original business plan;*

(c) *the undertaking receiving follow-on investments has not become linked, within the meaning of Article 3(3) of Annex I with another undertaking other than the financial intermediary or the independent private investor providing risk finance under the measure, unless the new entity fulfils the conditions of the SME definition.*

7. For equity and quasi-equity investments in eligible undertakings, a risk finance measure may provide support for replacement capital only if the latter is combined with new capital representing at least 50% of each investment round into the eligible undertakings.

8. For equity and quasi-equity investments as referred to in paragraph 2(a), no more than 30% of the financial intermediary's aggregate capital contributions and uncalled committed capital may be used for liquidity management purposes.

9. The total amount of risk finance referred to in paragraph 4 shall not exceed EUR 15 million per eligible undertaking under any risk finance measure.

10. For risk finance measures providing equity, quasi-equity or loan investments to eligible undertakings, the risk finance measure shall leverage additional finance from independent private investors at the level of the financial intermediaries or the eligible undertakings, so as to achieve an aggregate private participation rate reaching the following minimum thresholds:

(a) *10% of the risk finance provided to the eligible undertakings prior to their first commercial sale on any market;*

(b) *40% of the risk finance provided to the eligible undertakings referred to in paragraph 5(b) of this Article;*

(c) *60% of the risk finance for investment provided to eligible undertakings mentioned in paragraph 5(c) and for follow-on investments in eligible undertakings after the 7-year period mentioned in paragraph 5(b).*

11. Where a risk finance measure is implemented through a financial intermediary targeting eligible undertakings at different development stages as referred to in paragraph 10 and does not provide for private capital participation at the level of the eligible undertakings the financial intermediary shall achieve a private participation rate that represents at least the weighted average based on the volume of the individual investments in the underlying portfolio and resulting from the application of the minimum participation rates to such investments as referred to in paragraph 10.

12. A risk finance measure shall not discriminate between financial intermediaries on the basis of their place of establishment or incorporation in any Member State. Financial intermediaries may be required to fulfil predefined criteria objectively justified by the nature of the investments.

13. A risk finance measure shall fulfil the following conditions:

(a) *it shall be implemented via one or more financial intermediaries, except for tax incentives to private investors in respect of their direct investments into eligible undertakings;*

(b) *financial intermediaries, as well as investors or fund managers shall be selected through an open, transparent and non-discriminatory call which is made in accordance with applicable Union and national laws and aimed at establishing appropriate risk-reward sharing arrangements whereby, for investments other than guarantees, asymmetric profit sharing shall be given preference over downside protection;*

(c) *in the case of asymmetric loss-sharing between public and private investors, the first loss assumed by the public investor shall be capped at 25% of the total investment;*

(d) *in the case of guarantees falling under point 2(c), the guarantee rate shall be limited to 80% and total losses assumed by a Member State shall be capped at a maximum of 25% of the underlying guaranteed portfolio. Only guarantees covering expected losses of the underlying guaranteed portfolio can be provided for free. If a guarantee also comprises coverage of unexpected losses, the financial intermediary shall pay, for the part of the guarantee covering unexpected losses, a market-conform guarantee premium.*

14. Risk finance measures shall ensure profit-driven financing decisions. This is considered to be the case where all of the following conditions are fulfilled:

(a) *financial intermediaries shall be established according to the applicable laws.*

(b) *the Member State, or the entity entrusted with the implementation of the measure, shall provide for a due diligence process in order to ensure a commercially sound investment strategy for the purpose of implementing the risk finance measure, including an appropriate risk diversification policy aimed at achieving economic viability and efficient scale in terms of size and territorial scope of the relevant portfolio of investments;*

(c) *risk finance provided to the eligible undertakings shall be based on a viable business plan, containing details of product, sales and profitability development, establishing ex-ante financial viability;*

(d) *a clear and realistic exit strategy shall exist for each equity and quasi-equity investment.*

15. Financial intermediaries shall be managed on a commercial basis. This requirement is considered to be fulfilled where the financial intermediary and, depending on the type of risk finance measure, the fund manager, fulfil the following conditions:

(a) *they shall be obliged by law or contract to act with the diligence of a professional manager in good faith and avoiding conflicts of interest; best practices and regulatory supervision shall apply;*

(b) *their remuneration shall conform to market practices. This requirement is presumed to be met where the manager or the financial intermediary is selected through an open, transparent and non-discriminatory selection call, based on objective criteria linked to experience, expertise and operational and financial capacity;*

(c) *they shall receive a remuneration linked to performance, or shall share part of the investment risks by co-investing own resources so as to ensure that their interests are permanently aligned with the interests of the public investor;*

(d) *they shall set out an investment strategy, criteria and the proposed timing of investments;*

(e) *investors shall be allowed to be represented in the governance bodies of the investment fund, such as the supervisory board or the advisory committee.*

16. *[A risk finance measure providing guarantees or loans to eligible undertakings or providing quasi-equity investments structured as debt in eligible undertakings, shall fulfil the following conditions:]*

(a) *as a result of the measure, the financial intermediary shall undertake investments that would not have been carried out or would have been carried out in a restricted or different manner without the aid. The financial intermediary shall be able to demonstrate that it operates a mechanism that ensures that all the advantages are passed on to the largest extent to the final beneficiaries in the form of higher volumes of financing, riskier portfolios, lower collateral requirements, lower guarantee premiums or lower interest rates;*

[(b) *in the case of loans and quasi-equity investments structured as debt, the nominal amount of the instrument is taken into account in calculating the maximum investment amount for the purposes of paragraph 9;]*

(c) *in the case of guarantees, the nominal amount of the underlying loan is taken into account in calculating the maximum investment amount for the purposes of paragraph 9. The guarantee shall not exceed 80% of the underlying loan.*

17. *A Member State may assign the implementation of a risk finance measure to an entrusted entity.*

18. *Risk finance aid for SMEs that do not fulfil the conditions laid down in paragraph 5 shall be compatible with the internal market within the meaning of Article 107(3) of the Treaty and shall be exempted from the notification requirement of Article 108(3) of the Treaty, provided that*

(a) *at the level of the SMEs, the aid fulfils the conditions laid down in Regulation (EU) No 1407/2013; and*

(b) *all the conditions laid down in the present Article, with the exception of those set out in paragraphs 5, 6, 9, 10, and 11, are fulfilled; and*

(c) *for risk finance measures providing equity, quasi-equity or loan investments to eligible undertakings, the measure shall leverage additional financing from independent private investors at the level of the financial intermediaries or the SMEs, so as to achieve an aggregate private participation rate reaching at least 60% of the risk finance provided to the SMEs.*

NOTES

Para 16: words in square brackets substituted by Commission Regulation 2017/1084/EU, Art 1(12).

Repeal of this Regulation in relation to the UK: this Regulation is repealed in relation to the UK (as from IP completion day); see the introductory notes to this Regulation *ante*.

[5.88]

Article 22 Aid for start-ups

1. *Start-up aid schemes shall be compatible with the internal market within the meaning of Article 107(3) of the Treaty and shall be exempted from the notification requirement of Article 108(3) of the Treaty, provided the conditions laid down in this Article and in Chapter I are fulfilled.*

[2. Eligible undertakings shall be any unlisted small enterprise up to five years following its registration, which fulfils the following conditions:

(a) *it has not taken over the activity of another enterprise;*

(b) *it has not yet distributed profits;*

(c) *it has not been formed through a merger.*

For eligible undertakings that are not subject to registration, the five year eligibility period may be considered to start from the moment when the enterprise either starts its economic activity or is liable to tax for its economic activity.

By way of derogation from point (c) of the first subparagraph, enterprises formed through a merger between undertakings eligible for aid under this Article shall also be considered eligible undertakings up to five years from the date of registration of the oldest enterprise participating in the merger.]

3. *Start-up aid shall take the form of:*

(a) *loans with interest rates which are not conform with market conditions, with a duration of 10 years and up to a maximum nominal amount of EUR 1 million, or EUR 1.5 million for undertakings established in assisted areas fulfilling the conditions of Article 107(3)(c) of the Treaty, or EUR 2 million for undertakings established in assisted areas fulfilling the conditions of Article 107(3)(a) of the Treaty. For loans with a duration comprised between 5 and 10 years the maximum amounts may be adjusted by multiplying the amounts above by the ratio between 10 years and the actual duration of the loan. For loans with a duration of less than 5 years, the maximum amount shall be the same as for loans with a duration of 5 years;*

(b) *guarantees with premiums which are not conform with market conditions, with a duration of 10 years and up to maximum EUR 1.5 million of amount guaranteed, or EUR 2.25 million for undertakings established in assisted areas fulfilling the conditions of Article 107(3)(c) of the Treaty, or EUR 3 million for undertakings established in assisted areas fulfilling the conditions of Article 107(3)(a) of the Treaty. For guarantees with a duration comprised between 5 and 10 years the maximum amount guaranteed amounts may be adjusted by multiplying the amounts above by the ratio between 10 years and the actual duration of the guarantee. For guarantees with a duration of less than 5 years, the maximum amount guaranteed shall be the same as for guarantees with a duration of 5 years. The guarantee shall not exceed 80% of the underlying loan.*

(c) *grants, including equity or quasi equity investment, interests rate and guarantee premium reductions up to EUR 0.4 million gross grant equivalent or EUR 0.6 million for undertakings established in assisted areas fulfilling the conditions of Article 107(3)(c) of the Treaty, or EUR 0.8 million for undertakings established in assisted areas fulfilling the conditions of Article 107(3)(a) of the Treaty.*

4. A beneficiary can receive support through a mix of the aid instruments referred to in paragraph 3 of this Article, provided that the proportion of the amount granted through one aid instrument, calculated on the basis of the maximum aid amount allowed for that instrument, is taken into account in order to determine the residual proportion of the maximum aid amount allowed for the other instruments forming part of such a mixed instrument.

5. For small and innovative enterprises, the maximum amounts set out in paragraph 3 may be doubled.

NOTES

Para 2: substituted by Commission Regulation 2017/1084/EU, Art 1(13).

Repeal of this Regulation in relation to the UK: this Regulation is repealed in relation to the UK (as from IP completion day); see the introductory notes to this Regulation *ante*.

[5.89]

Article 23 Aid to alternative trading platforms specialised in SMEs

1. Aid in favour of alternative trading platforms specialised in SMEs shall be compatible with the internal market within the meaning of Article 107(3) of the Treaty and shall be exempted from the notification requirement of Article 108(3) of the Treaty, provided the conditions laid down in this Article and in Chapter I are fulfilled.

2. Where the platform operator is a small enterprise, the aid measure may take the form of start-up aid to the platform operator, in which case the conditions laid down in Article 22 shall apply.

The aid measure may take the form of tax incentives to independent private investors that are natural persons in respect of their risk finance investments made through an alternative trading platform into undertakings eligible under the conditions laid down in Article 21.

NOTES

Repeal of this Regulation in relation to the UK: this Regulation is repealed in relation to the UK (as from IP completion day); see the introductory notes to this Regulation *ante*.

[5.90]

Article 24 Aid for scouting costs

1. Aid for scouting costs shall be compatible with the internal market within the meaning of Article 107(3) of the Treaty and shall be exempted from the notification requirement of Article 108(3) of the Treaty, provided the conditions laid down in this Article and in Chapter I are fulfilled.

2. The eligible costs shall be the costs for initial screening and formal due diligence undertaken by managers of financial intermediaries or investors to identify eligible undertakings pursuant to Articles 21 and 22.

3. The aid intensity shall not exceed 50% of the eligible costs.

NOTES

Repeal of this Regulation in relation to the UK: this Regulation is repealed in relation to the UK (as from IP completion day); see the introductory notes to this Regulation *ante*.

SECTION 4 AID FOR RESEARCH AND DEVELOPMENT AND INNOVATION

[5.91]

Article 25 Aid for research and development projects

[1. Aid for research and development projects, including research and development projects having received a Seal of Excellence quality label under the Horizon 2020 or under the Horizon Europe programme and co-funded research and development projects and, where applicable, aid for co-funded Teaming actions, shall be compatible with the internal market within the meaning of Article 107(3) of the Treaty and shall be exempted from the notification requirement of Article 108(3) of the Treaty, provided that the conditions laid down in this Article and in Chapter I are fulfilled.]

2. The aided part of the research and development project shall completely fall within one or more of the following categories:

- *(a) fundamental research;*
- *(b) industrial research;*
- *(c) experimental development;*
- *(d) feasibility studies.*

3. The eligible costs of research and development projects shall be allocated to a specific category of research and development and shall be the following:

- *(a) personnel costs: researchers, technicians and other supporting staff to the extent employed on the project;*
- *(b) costs of instruments and equipment to the extent and for the period used for the project. Where such instruments and equipment are not used for their full life for the project, only the depreciation costs corresponding to the life of the project, as calculated on the basis of generally accepted accounting principles are considered as eligible.*
- *(c) Costs for of buildings and land, to the extent and for the duration period used for the project. With regard to buildings, only the depreciation costs corresponding to the life of the project, as calculated on the basis of generally accepted accounting principles are considered as eligible. For land, costs of commercial transfer or actually incurred capital costs are eligible.*
- *(d) costs of contractual research, knowledge and patents bought or licensed from outside sources at arm's length conditions, as well as costs of consultancy and equivalent services used exclusively for the project;*
- *(e) additional overheads and other operating expenses, including costs of materials, supplies and similar products, incurred directly as a result of the project;*

4. The eligible costs for feasibility studies shall be the costs of the study.

5. The aid intensity for each beneficiary shall not exceed:

- *(a) 100% of the eligible costs for fundamental research;*
- *(b) 50% of the eligible costs for industrial research;*

(c) 25% of the eligible costs for experimental development;
(d) 50% of the eligible costs for feasibility studies.

6. The aid intensities for industrial research and experimental development may be increased up to a maximum aid intensity of 80% of the eligible costs as follows:

(a) by 10 percentage points for medium-sized enterprises and by 20 percentage points for small enterprises;
(b) by 15 percentage points if one of the following conditions is fulfilled:
  (i) the project involves effective collaboration:
    — between undertakings among which at least one is an SME, or is carried out in at least two Member States, or in a Member State and in a Contracting Party of the EEA Agreement, and no single undertaking bears more than 70% of the eligible costs, or
    — between an undertaking and one or more research and knowledge-dissemination organisations, where the latter bear at least 10% of the eligible costs and have the right to publish their own research results;
  (ii) the results of the project are widely disseminated through conferences, publication, open access repositories, or free or open source software.

7. The aid intensities for feasibility studies may be increased by 10 percentage points for medium-sized enterprises and by 20 percentage points for small enterprises;

NOTES

Para 1: substituted by Commission Regulation 2021/1237/EU, Art 1(17), as from 1 August 2021.

Repeal of this Regulation in relation to the UK: this Regulation is repealed in relation to the UK (as from IP completion day); see the introductory notes to this Regulation *ante*.

[5.92]

[Article 25a Aid for projects awarded a Seal of Excellence quality label

1. Aid for SMEs for research and development projects as well as feasibility studies awarded a Seal of Excellence quality label under the Horizon 2020 or the Horizon Europe programme, shall be compatible with the internal market within the meaning of Article 107(3) of the Treaty and shall be exempted from the notification requirement of Article 108(3) of the Treaty, provided that the conditions laid down in this Article and in Chapter I are fulfilled.

2. The eligible activities of the aided research and development project or feasibility study shall be those defined as eligible under the Horizon 2020 or the Horizon Europe programme rules, excluding activities going beyond experimental development activities.

3. The categories, maximum amounts and methods of calculation of eligible costs of the aided research and development project or feasibility study shall be those defined as eligible under the Horizon 2020 or Horizon Europe programme rules.

4. The maximum aid amount shall not exceed EUR 2,5 million per SME per research and development project or feasibility study.

5. The total public funding provided for each research and development project or feasibility study shall not exceed the funding rate set out for that research and development project or feasibility study under the Horizon 2020 or under the Horizon Europe programme rules.]

NOTES

Inserted by Commission Regulation 2021/1237/EU, Art 1(18), as from 1 August 2021.

Repeal of this Regulation in relation to the UK: this Regulation is repealed in relation to the UK (as from IP completion day); see the introductory notes to this Regulation *ante*.

[5.93]

[Article 25b Aid for Marie Skłodowska-Curie actions and ERC Proof of Concept actions

1. Aid for Marie Skłodowska-Curie actions and ERC Proof of Concept actions awarded a Seal of Excellence quality label under the Horizon 2020 or the Horizon Europe programme shall be compatible with the internal market within the meaning of Article 107(3) of the Treaty and shall be exempted from the notification requirement of Article 108(3) of the Treaty, provided that the conditions laid down in this Article and in Chapter I are fulfilled.

2. The eligible activities of the aided action shall be those defined as eligible under the Horizon 2020 or the Horizon Europe programme rules.

3. The categories, maximum amounts and methods of calculation of eligible costs of the aided action shall be those defined as eligible under the Horizon 2020 or Horizon Europe programme rules.

4. The total public funding provided for each aided action shall not exceed the maximum level of support provided for in the Horizon 2020 or the Horizon Europe programme.]

NOTES

Inserted by Commission Regulation 2021/1237/EU, Art 1(18), as from 1 August 2021.

Repeal of this Regulation in relation to the UK: this Regulation is repealed in relation to the UK (as from IP completion day); see the introductory notes to this Regulation *ante*.

[5.94]

[Article 25c Aid involved in co-funded research and development projects

1. Aid provided to a co-funded research and development project or a feasibility study (including research and development projects implemented under a European institutionalised Partnership based on Article 185 or Article 187 of the Treaty or a programme co-fund action, as defined in the Horizon Europe programme rules) which is implemented by at least three Member States, or alternatively two Member States and at least one associated country, and selected on the basis of the evaluation and ranking made by independent experts following transnational calls in line with the Horizon 2020 or Horizon Europe programme rules, shall be compatible with the internal market within the meaning of Article 107(3) of the Treaty and shall be exempted from the notification requirement of Article 108(3) of the Treaty provided that the conditions laid down in this Article and in Chapter I are fulfilled.

2. The eligible activities of the aided research and development project or feasibility study shall be those defined as eligible under the Horizon 2020 or the Horizon Europe programme rules, excluding activities going beyond experimental development activities.

3. The categories, maximum amounts and methods of calculation of eligible costs shall be those defined as eligible under the Horizon 2020 or the Horizon Europe programme rules.

4. The total public funding provided shall not exceed the funding rate established for the research and development project or feasibility study following the selection, ranking and evaluation under the Horizon 2020 or Horizon Europe programme rules.

5. The funding provided by the Horizon 2020 or Horizon Europe programme shall cover at least 30% of the total eligible costs of a research and innovation action or an innovation action as defined under the Horizon 2020 or Horizon Europe programme.]

NOTES

Inserted by Commission Regulation 2021/1237/EU, Art 1(18), as from 1 August 2021.

Repeal of this Regulation in relation to the UK: this Regulation is repealed in relation to the UK (as from IP completion day); see the introductory notes to this Regulation *ante*.

[5.95]

[Article 25d Aid for Teaming actions

1. Aid provided to co-funded Teaming actions, involving at least two Member States and selected on the basis of the evaluation and ranking made by independent experts following transnational calls under the Horizon 2020 or the Horizon Europe programme rules, shall be compatible with the internal market within the meaning of Article 107(3) of the Treaty and shall be exempted from the notification requirement of Article 108(3) of the Treaty provided that the conditions laid down in this Article and in Chapter I are fulfilled.

2. The eligible activities of the co-funded Teaming action shall be those defined as eligible under the Horizon 2020 or Horizon Europe programme rules. Activities going beyond experimental development activities are excluded.

3. The categories, maximum amounts and methods of calculation of eligible costs shall be those defined as eligible under the Horizon 2020 or the Horizon Europe programme rules. In addition, investment costs in project-related tangible and intangible assets shall be eligible.

4. The total public funding provided shall not exceed the funding rate established for the Teaming action following the selection, ranking and evaluation under the Horizon 2020 or the Horizon Europe programme rules. In addition, for investments in project related tangible and intangible assets the aid shall not exceed 70% of the investment costs.

5. For investment aid for infrastructures under a Teaming action the following additional conditions shall apply:

- *(a) where the infrastructure pursues both economic and non-economic activities, the financing, costs and revenues of each type of activity shall be accounted for separately on the basis of consistently applied and objectively justifiable cost accounting principles;*
- *(b) the price charged for the operation or use of the infrastructure shall correspond to a market price;*
- *(c) access to the infrastructure shall be open to several users and be granted on a transparent and non-discriminatory basis. Undertakings which have financed at least 10% of the investment costs of the infrastructure may be granted preferential access under more favourable conditions. In order to avoid overcompensation, such access shall be proportional to the undertaking's contribution to the investment costs and these conditions shall be made publicly available;*
- *(d) where the infrastructure receives public funding for both economic and non-economic activities, Member States shall put in place a monitoring and claw-back mechanism in order to ensure that the applicable aid intensity is not exceeded as a result of an increase in the share of economic activities compared to the situation envisaged at the time of awarding the aid.]*

NOTES

Inserted by Commission Regulation 2021/1237/EU, Art 1(18), as from 1 August 2021.

Repeal of this Regulation in relation to the UK: this Regulation is repealed in relation to the UK (as from IP completion day); see the introductory notes to this Regulation *ante*.

[5.96]

Article 26 Investment aid for research infrastructures

1. Aid for the construction or upgrade of research infrastructures that perform economic activities shall be compatible with the internal market within the meaning of Article 107(3) of the Treaty and shall be exempted from the notification requirement of Article 108(3) of the Treaty, provided that the conditions laid down in this Article and in Chapter I are fulfilled.

2. Where a research infrastructure pursues both economic and non-economic activities, the financing, costs and revenues of each type of activity shall be accounted for separately on the basis of consistently applied and objectively justifiable cost accounting principles.

3. The price charged for the operation or use of the infrastructure shall correspond to a market price.

4. Access to the infrastructure shall be open to several users and be granted on a transparent and non-discriminatory basis. Undertakings which have financed at least 10% of the investment costs of the infrastructure may be granted preferential access under more favourable conditions. In order to avoid overcompensation, such access shall be proportional to the undertaking's contribution to the investment costs and these conditions shall be made publicly available.

5. The eligible costs shall be the investment costs in intangible and tangible assets.

6. The aid intensity shall not exceed 50% of the eligible costs.

7. Where a research infrastructure receives public funding for both economic and non-economic activities, Member States shall put in place a monitoring and claw-back mechanism in order to ensure that the applicable aid intensity is not exceeded as a result of an increase in the share of economic activities compared to the situation envisaged at the time of awarding the aid.

NOTES

Repeal of this Regulation in relation to the UK: this Regulation is repealed in relation to the UK (as from IP completion day); see the introductory notes to this Regulation *ante*.

[5.97]

Article 27 Aid for innovation clusters

1. Aid for innovation clusters shall be compatible with the internal market within the meaning of Article 107(3) of the Treaty and shall be exempted from the notification requirement of Article 108(3) of the Treaty, provided that the conditions laid down in this Article and in Chapter I are fulfilled.

2. Aid for innovation clusters shall be granted exclusively to the legal entity operating the innovation cluster (cluster organisation).

3. Access to the cluster's premises, facilities and activities shall be open to several users and be granted on a transparent and non-discriminatory basis. Undertakings which have financed at least 10% of the investment costs of the innovation cluster may be granted preferential access under more favourable conditions. In order to avoid overcompensation, such access shall be proportional to the undertaking's contribution to the investment costs and these conditions shall be made publicly available.

4. The fees charged for using the cluster's facilities and for participating in the cluster's activities shall correspond to the market price or reflect their costs.

5. Investment aid may be granted for the construction or upgrade of innovation clusters. The eligible costs shall be the investment costs in intangible and tangible assets.

6. The aid intensity of investment aid for innovation clusters shall not exceed 50% of the eligible costs. The aid intensity may be increased by 15 percentage points for innovation clusters located in assisted areas fulfilling the conditions of Article 107(3)(a) of the Treaty and by 5 percentage points for innovation clusters located in assisted areas fulfilling the conditions of Article 107(3)(c) of the Treaty

7. Operating aid may be granted for the operation of innovation clusters. It shall not exceed 10 years.

8. The eligible costs of operating aid for innovation clusters shall be the personnel and administrative costs (including overhead costs) relating to:

- *(a) animation of the cluster to facilitate collaboration, information sharing and the provision or channelling of specialised and customised business support services;*
- *(b) marketing of the cluster to increase participation of new undertakings or organisations and to increase visibility;*
- *(c) management of the cluster's facilities; organisation of training programmes, workshops and conferences to support knowledge sharing and networking and transnational cooperation.*

9. The aid intensity of operating aid shall not exceed 50% of the total eligible costs during the period over which the aid is granted.

NOTES

Repeal of this Regulation in relation to the UK: this Regulation is repealed in relation to the UK (as from IP completion day); see the introductory notes to this Regulation *ante*.

[5.98]

Article 28 Innovation aid for SMEs

1. Innovation aid for SMEs shall be compatible with the internal market within the meaning of Article 107(3) of the Treaty and shall be exempted from the notification requirement of Article 108(3) of the Treaty, provided the conditions laid down in this Article and in Chapter I are fulfilled:

2. The eligible costs shall be the following:

- *(a) costs for obtaining, validating and defending patents and other intangible assets;*
- *(b) costs for secondment of highly qualified personnel from a research and knowledge-dissemination organization or a large enterprise, working on research, development and innovation activities in a newly created function within the beneficiary and not replacing other personnel;*
- *(c) costs for innovation advisory and support services;*

3. The aid intensity shall not exceed 50% of the eligible costs.

4. In the particular case of aid for innovation advisory and support services the aid intensity can be increased up to 100% of the eligible costs provided that the total amount of aid for innovation advisory and support services does not exceed EUR 200,000 per undertaking within any three year period.

NOTES

Repeal of this Regulation in relation to the UK: this Regulation is repealed in relation to the UK (as from IP completion day); see the introductory notes to this Regulation *ante*.

[5.99]

Article 29 Aid for process and organisational innovation

1. Aid for process and organisational innovation shall be compatible with the internal market within the meaning of Article 107(3) of the Treaty and shall be exempted from the notification requirement of Article 108(3) of the Treaty, provided the conditions laid down in this Article and in Chapter I are fulfilled.

2. Aid to large undertakings shall only be compatible if they effectively collaborate with SMEs in the aided activity and the collaborating SMEs incur at least 30% of the total eligible costs.

3. The eligible costs shall be the following:

- *(a) personnel costs;*
- *(b) costs of instruments, equipment, buildings and land to the extent and for the period used for the project;*
- *(c) costs of contractual research, knowledge and patents bought or licensed from outside sources at arm's length conditions;*

(d) additional overheads and other operating costs, including costs of materials, supplies and similar products, incurred directly as a result of the project.

4. The aid intensity shall not exceed 15% of the eligible costs for large undertakings and 50% of the eligible costs for SMEs.

NOTES

Repeal of this Regulation in relation to the UK: this Regulation is repealed in relation to the UK (as from IP completion day); see the introductory notes to this Regulation *ante*.

[5.100]

Article 30 Aid for research and development in the fishery and aquaculture sector

1. Aid for research and development in the fishery and aquaculture sector shall be compatible with the internal market within the meaning of Article 107(3) of the Treaty and shall be exempted from the notification requirement of Article 108(3) of the Treaty, provided that the conditions laid down in this Article and in Chapter I are fulfilled.

2. The aided project shall be of interest to all undertakings in the particular sector or sub-sector concerned.

3. Prior to the date of the start of the aided project the following information shall be published on the internet:

(a) that the aided project will be carried out;

(b) the goals of the aided project;

(c) the approximate date for the publication of the results expected from the aided project and its place of publication on the internet;

(d) a reference that the results of the aided project will be available to all undertakings active in the particular sector or sub-sector concerned at no cost.

4. The results of the aided project shall be made available on internet from the end date of the aided project or the date on which any information concerning those results is given to members of any particular organisation, whatever comes first. The results shall remain available on internet for a period of at least 5 years starting from the end date of the aided project.

5. Aid shall be granted directly to the research and knowledge-dissemination organisation and shall not involve the direct granting of non-research related aid to an undertaking producing, processing or marketing fishery or aquaculture products.

6. The eligible costs shall be those provided in Article 25(3).

7. The aid intensity shall not exceed 100% of the eligible costs.

NOTES

Repeal of this Regulation in relation to the UK: this Regulation is repealed in relation to the UK (as from IP completion day); see the introductory notes to this Regulation *ante*.

SECTION 5 TRAINING AID

[5.101]

Article 31 Training aid

1. Training aid shall be compatible with the internal market within the meaning of Article 107(3) of the Treaty and shall be exempted from the notification requirement of Article 108(3) of the Treaty, provided that the conditions laid down in this Article and in Chapter I are fulfilled.

2. Aid shall not be granted for training which undertakings carry out to comply with national mandatory standards on training.

3. The eligible costs shall be the following:

(a) trainers' personnel costs, for the hours during which the trainers participate in the training;

[(b) trainers' and trainees' operating costs directly relating to the training project such as travel expenses, accommodation costs, materials and supplies directly related to the project, depreciation of tools and equipment, to the extent that they are used exclusively for the training project;]

(c) costs of advisory services linked to the training project;

(d) trainees' personnel costs and general indirect costs (administrative costs, rent, overheads) for the hours during which the trainees participate in the training.

4. The aid intensity shall not exceed 50% of the eligible costs. It may be increased, up to a maximum aid intensity of 70% of the eligible costs, as follows:

(a) by 10 percentage points if the training is given to workers with disabilities or disadvantaged workers;

(b) by 10 percentage points if the aid is granted to medium-sized enterprises and by 20 percentage points if the aid is granted to small enterprises.

5. Where the aid is granted in the maritime transport sector, the aid intensity may be increased to 100% of the eligible costs provided that the following conditions are met:

(a) the trainees are not active members of the crew but are supernumerary on board; and

(b) the training is carried out on board of ships entered in Union registers.

NOTES

Para 3: point (b) substituted by Commission Regulation 2017/1084/EU, Art 1(15).

Repeal of this Regulation in relation to the UK: this Regulation is repealed in relation to the UK (as from IP completion day); see the introductory notes to this Regulation *ante*.

SECTION 6 AID FOR DISADVANTAGED WORKERS AND FOR WORKERS WITH DISABILITIES

[5.102]

Article 32 Aid for the recruitment of disadvantaged workers in the form of wage subsidies

1. Aid schemes for the recruitment of disadvantaged workers shall be compatible with the internal market within the meaning of Article 107(3) of the Treaty and shall be exempted from the notification requirement of Article 108(3) of the Treaty, provided the conditions laid down in this Article and in Chapter I are fulfilled.

2. Eligible costs shall be the wage costs over a maximum period of 12 months following recruitment of a disadvantaged worker. Where the worker concerned is a severely disadvantaged worker, eligible costs shall be the wage costs over a maximum period of 24 months following recruitment.

3. Where the recruitment does not represent a net increase, compared with the average over the previous 12 months, in the number of employees in the undertaking concerned, the post or posts shall have fallen vacant following voluntary departure, disability, retirement on grounds of age, voluntary reduction of working time or lawful dismissal for misconduct and not as a result of redundancy.

4. Except in the case of lawful dismissal for misconduct, the disadvantaged workers shall be entitled to continuous employment for a minimum period consistent with the national legislation concerned or any collective agreements governing employment contracts.

5. If the period of employment is shorter than 12 months, or 24 months in the case of severely disadvantaged workers, the aid shall be reduced pro rata accordingly.

6. The aid intensity shall not exceed 50% of the eligible costs.

NOTES

Repeal of this Regulation in relation to the UK: this Regulation is repealed in relation to the UK (as from IP completion day); see the introductory notes to this Regulation *ante*.

[5.103]

Article 33 Aid for the employment of workers with disabilities in the form of wage subsidies

1. Aid for the employment of workers with disabilities shall be compatible with the internal market within the meaning of Article 107(3) of the Treaty and shall be exempted from the notification requirement of Article 108(3) of the Treaty, provided the conditions laid down in this Article and in Chapter I are fulfilled.

2. Eligible costs shall be the wage costs over any given period during which the worker with disabilities is employed.

3. Where the recruitment does not represent a net increase, compared with the average over the previous 12 months, in the number of employees in the undertaking concerned, the post or posts shall have fallen vacant following voluntary departure, disabilities, retirement on grounds of age, voluntary reduction of working time or lawful dismissal for misconduct and not as a result of redundancy.

4. Except in the case of lawful dismissal for misconduct, the workers with disabilities shall be entitled to continuous employment for a minimum period consistent with the national legislation concerned or any collective agreements which are legally binding for the undertaking and governing employment contracts.

5. The aid intensity shall not exceed 75% of the eligible costs.

NOTES

Repeal of this Regulation in relation to the UK: this Regulation is repealed in relation to the UK (as from IP completion day); see the introductory notes to this Regulation *ante*.

[5.104]

Article 34 Aid for compensating the additional costs of employing workers with disabilities

1. Aid for compensating the additional costs of employing workers with disabilities shall be compatible with the internal market within the meaning of Article 107(3) of the Treaty and shall be exempted from the notification requirement of Article 108(3) of the Treaty, provided the conditions laid down in this Article and in Chapter I are fulfilled.

2. The eligible costs shall be the following:

- *(a) costs of adapting the premises;*
- *(b) costs of employing staff solely for time spent on the assistance of the workers with disabilities and of training such staff to assist workers with disabilities;*
- *(c) costs of adapting or acquiring equipment, or acquiring and validating software for use by workers with disabilities, including adapted or assistive technology facilities, which are additional to those which the beneficiary would have incurred had it employed workers who are not workers with disabilities;*
- *(d) costs directly linked to transport of workers with disabilities to the working place and for work related activities;*
- *(e) wage costs for the hours spent by a worker with disabilities on rehabilitation;*
- *(f) where the beneficiary provides sheltered employment, the costs of constructing, installing or modernising the production units of the undertaking concerned, and any costs of administration and transport, provided that such costs result directly from the employment of workers with disabilities.*

3. The aid intensity shall not exceed 100% of the eligible costs.

NOTES

Repeal of this Regulation in relation to the UK: this Regulation is repealed in relation to the UK (as from IP completion day); see the introductory notes to this Regulation *ante*.

[5.105]

Article 35 Aid for compensating the costs of assistance provided to disadvantaged workers

1. Aid for compensating the costs of assistance provided to disadvantaged workers shall be compatible with the internal market within the meaning of Article 107(3) of the Treaty and shall be exempt from the notification requirement of Article 108(3) of the Treaty, provided the conditions laid down in this Article and in Chapter I are fulfilled.

2. The eligible costs shall be the costs of:

- *(a) employing staff solely for time spent on the assistance of the disadvantaged workers over a maximum period of 12 months following recruitment of a disadvantaged worker or over a maximum period of 24 months following recruitment of a severely disadvantaged worker;*
- *(b) of training such staff to assist disadvantaged workers.*

3. The assistance provided shall consist of measures to support the disadvantaged worker's autonomy and adaptation to the work environment, in accompanying the worker in social and administrative procedures, facilitation of communication with the entrepreneur and managing conflicts.

4. The aid intensity shall not exceed 50% of the eligible costs.

NOTES

Repeal of this Regulation in relation to the UK: this Regulation is repealed in relation to the UK (as from IP completion day); see the introductory notes to this Regulation *ante*.

SECTION 7 AID FOR ENVIRONMENTAL PROTECTION

[5.106]

Article 36 Investment aid enabling undertakings to go beyond Union standards for environmental protection or to increase the level of environmental protection in the absence of Union standards

1. Investment aid enabling undertakings to go beyond Union standards for environmental protection or to increase the level of environmental protection in the absence of Union standards shall be compatible with the internal market within the meaning of Article 107(3) of the Treaty and shall be exempted from the notification requirement of Article 108(3) of the Treaty, provided that the conditions laid down in this Article and in Chapter I are fulfilled.

2. The investment shall fulfil one of the following conditions:

(a) it shall enable the beneficiary to increase the level of environmental protection resulting from its activities by going beyond the applicable Union standards, irrespective of the presence of mandatory national standards that are more stringent than the Union standards;

(b) it shall enable the beneficiary to increase the level of environmental protection resulting from its activities in the absence of Union standards.

3. Aid shall not be granted where investments are undertaken to ensure that undertakings comply with Union standards already adopted and not yet in force.

4. By way of derogation from paragraph 3, aid may be granted for

(a) the acquisition of new transport vehicles for road, railway, inland waterway and maritime transport complying with adopted Union standards, provided that the acquisition occurs before those standards enter into force and that, once mandatory, they do not apply to vehicles already purchased before that date.

(b) retrofitting of existing transport vehicles for road, railway, inland waterway and maritime transport, provided that the Union standards were not yet in force at the date of entry into operation of those vehicles and that, once mandatory, they do not apply retroactively to those vehicles.

5. The eligible costs shall be the extra investment costs necessary to go beyond the applicable Union standards or to increase the level of environmental protection in the absence of Union standards. They shall be determined as follows:

(a) where the costs of investing in environmental protection can be identified in the total investment cost as a separate investment, this environmental protection-related cost shall constitute the eligible costs;

(b) in all other cases, the costs of investing in environmental protection are identified by reference to a similar, less environmentally friendly investment that would have been credibly carried out without the aid. The difference between the costs of both investments identifies the environmental protection-related cost and constitutes the eligible costs.

The costs not directly linked to the achievement of a higher level of environmental protection shall not be eligible.

6. The aid intensity shall not exceed 40% of the eligible costs.

7. The aid intensity may be increased by 10 percentage points for aid granted to medium sized undertakings and by 20 percentage points for aid granted to small undertakings.

8. The aid intensity may be increased by 15 percentage points for investments located in assisted areas fulfilling the conditions of Article 107(3)(a) of the Treaty and by 5 percentage points for investments located in assisted areas fulfilling the conditions of Article 107(3)(c) of the Treaty.

NOTES

Repeal of this Regulation in relation to the UK: this Regulation is repealed in relation to the UK (as from IP completion day); see the introductory notes to this Regulation *ante*.

[5.107]

[Article 36a Investment aid for publicly accessible recharging or refuelling infrastructure for zero and low emission road vehicles

1. Aid for the deployment of recharging or refuelling infrastructure for the supply of energy to zero and low emission road vehicles for transport purposes shall be compatible with the internal market within the meaning of Article 107(3) of the Treaty and shall be exempted from the notification requirement of Article 108(3) of the Treaty, provided that the conditions laid down in this Article and in Chapter I are fulfilled.

2. This Article shall only cover aid granted for the deployment of recharging or refuelling infrastructures that supply vehicles with electricity or renewable hydrogen for transport purposes. The Member State shall ensure that the requirement to supply renewable hydrogen is complied with throughout the economic lifetime of the infrastructure.

3. The eligible costs shall be the costs of the construction, installation or upgrade of the recharging or refuelling infrastructure. These may include the costs of the recharging or refuelling infrastructure itself, installation of or upgrades to electrical or other components, including power transformers that are required for connecting the recharging or refuelling infrastructure to the grid or to a local electricity or hydrogen production or storage unit, as well as related technical equipment, civil engineering works, land or road adaptations, installation costs and costs for obtaining related permits. The costs of local production or storage units generating or storing the electricity and the costs of local hydrogen production units are excluded.

4. Aid under this Article shall be granted in a competitive bidding process on the basis of clear, transparent and non-discriminatory criteria and the aid intensity may reach up to 100% of the eligible costs.

5. The aid granted to any one beneficiary shall not exceed 40% of the overall budget of the scheme concerned.

6. Aid under this Article shall only be granted for the construction, installation or upgrade of recharging or refuelling infrastructure accessible to the public and providing non-discriminatory access to users, including in relation to tariffs, authentication and payment methods and other terms and conditions of use.
7. The necessity of aid to incentivise the deployment of recharging or refuelling infrastructure of the same category (for example, for recharging infrastructure: normal or high power) shall be verified through an ex ante open public consultation or an independent market study. In particular, it shall be verified that no such infrastructure is likely to be deployed on commercial terms within three years from the publication of the aid measure.
8. By way of derogation from paragraph 7, the necessity of aid for recharging or refuelling infrastructure can be presumed where either battery electric vehicles (for recharging infrastructures) or hydrogen vehicles (for refuelling infrastructures) represent respectively less than 2% of the total number of vehicles of the same category registered in the Member State concerned. For the purpose of this paragraph, passenger cars and light commercial vehicles shall be considered as being part of the same category of vehicles.
9. Any concession or other entrustment to a third party to operate the supported recharging or refuelling infrastructure shall be assigned on a competitive, transparent and non-discriminatory basis, having due regard to the applicable procurement rules.]

NOTES

Inserted by Commission Regulation 2021/1237/EU, Art 1(19), as from 1 August 2021.

Repeal of this Regulation in relation to the UK: this Regulation is repealed in relation to the UK (as from IP completion day); see the introductory notes to this Regulation *ante*.

[5.108]

Article 37 Investment aid for early adaptation to future Union standards

1. Aid encouraging undertakings to comply with new Union standards which increase the level of environmental protection and are not yet in force shall be compatible with the internal market within the meaning of Article 107(3) of the Treaty and shall be exempted from the notification requirement of Article 108(3) of the Treaty, provided that the conditions laid down in this Article and in Chapter I are fulfilled.
2. The Union standards shall have been adopted and the investment shall be implemented and finalised at least one year before the date of entry into force of the standard concerned.
3. The eligible costs shall be the extra investment costs necessary to go beyond the applicable Union standards. They shall be determined as follows:

(a) where the costs of investing in environmental protection can be identified in the total investment cost as a separate investment, this environmental protection-related cost shall constitute the eligible costs;
(b) in all other cases, the costs of investing in environmental protection are identified by reference to a similar, less environmentally friendly investment that would have been credibly carried out without the aid. The difference between the costs of both investments identifies the environmental protection-related cost and constitutes the eligible costs.

The costs not directly linked to the achievement of a higher level of environmental protection shall not be eligible.
4. The aid intensity shall not exceed the following:

(a) 20% of the eligible costs for small undertakings, 15% of the eligible costs for medium-sized undertakings and 10% of the eligible costs for large undertakings if the implementation and finalisation of the investment take place more than three years before the date of entry into force of the new Union standard;
(b) 15% of the eligible costs for small undertakings, 10% of the eligible costs for medium-sized undertakings and 5% of the eligible costs for large undertakings if the implementation and finalisation of the investment take place between one and three years before the date of entry into force of the new Union standard.

5. The aid intensity may be increased by 15 percentage points for investments located in assisted areas fulfilling the conditions of Article 107(3)(a) of the Treaty and by 5 percentage points for investments located in assisted areas fulfilling the conditions of Article 107(3)(c) of the Treaty.

NOTES

Repeal of this Regulation in relation to the UK: this Regulation is repealed in relation to the UK (as from IP completion day); see the introductory notes to this Regulation *ante*.

[5.109]

Article 38 Investment aid for energy efficiency measures

1. Investment aid enabling undertakings to achieve energy efficiency shall be compatible with the internal market within the meaning of Article 107(3) of the Treaty and shall be exempted from the notification requirement of Article 108(3) of the Treaty, provided that the conditions laid down in this Article and in Chapter I are fulfilled.
2. Aid shall not be granted under this Article where improvements are undertaken to ensure that undertakings comply with Union standards already adopted, even if they are not yet in force.
[3. The eligible costs shall be the extra investment costs necessary to achieve the higher level of energy efficiency. They shall be determined as follows:

(a) where the costs of investing in energy efficiency can be identified in the total investment cost as a separate investment, this energy efficiency-related cost shall constitute the eligible costs;
(b) where the investment relates to the improvement of the energy efficiency of (i) residential buildings; (ii) buildings dedicated to the provision of education or social services; (iii) buildings dedicated to activities related to public administration or to justice, police or fire-fighting services; or (iv) buildings referred to in points (i), (ii) or (iii) and in which activities other than those mentioned in those points occupy less than 35% of the internal floor area, the entire investment costs necessary to achieve a higher level of energy efficiency shall constitute the eligible costs, provided that the energy efficiency improvements lead to a reduction in primary energy demand of at least 20% in the case of renovation and to primary energy savings of at least 10% compared to threshold set for the nearly zero-energy building requirements in national measures

implementing Directive 2010/31/EU of the European Parliament and of the Council[1] *in the case of new buildings. The initial primary energy demand and the estimated improvement shall be established by reference to an Energy Performance Certificate as defined in Article 2(12) of Directive 2010/31/EU;*

(c) *in all other cases, the costs of investing in energy efficiency shall be identified by reference to a similar, less energy efficient investment that would have been credibly carried out without the aid. The difference between the costs of the two investments identifies the energy efficiency-related cost and constitutes the eligible costs.*

The costs not directly linked to the achievement of a higher level of energy efficiency shall not be eligible.]

[3a. For the buildings referred to in paragraph 3, point (b), the investment in improving the energy efficiency of the building may be combined with investments in any or all of the following:

(a) *integrated on-site renewable energy installations generating electricity and/or heat;*

(b) *equipment for the storage of the energy generated by the on-site renewable energy installation;*

(c) *equipment and related infrastructure incorporated in the building for the recharging of electric vehicles of the building's users;*

(d) *investments in the digitalisation of the building, in particular to increase its smart readiness. Eligible investments may include interventions limited to passive in-house wiring or structured cabling for data networks and, if necessary, the ancillary part of the passive network on the private property outside the building. Wiring or cabling for data networks outside the private property is excluded.*

In case of any such combined works as set out in the first subparagraph, points (a) to (d), the entire investment cost of the various pieces of equipment shall constitute the eligible costs.

The aid may be granted either to the building owner(s) or to the tenant(s), depending on who is commissioning the energy efficiency works.]

4. The aid intensity shall not exceed 30% of the eligible costs.

5. The aid intensity may be increased by 20 percentage points for aid granted to small undertakings and by 10 percentage points for aid granted to medium-sized undertakings.

6. The aid intensity may be increased by 15 percentage points for investments located in assisted areas fulfilling the conditions of Article 107(3)(a) of the Treaty and by 5 percentage points for investments located in assisted areas fulfilling the conditions of Article 107(3)(c) of the Treaty.

[7. Aid for measures that improve the energy efficiency of buildings may also relate to the facilitation of energy performance contracts subject to the following cumulative conditions:

(a) *the support takes the form of a loan or guarantee to the provider of the energy efficiency improvement measures under an energy performance contract, or consists in a financial product aimed to refinance the respective provider (e.g. factoring, forfeiting);*

(b) *the nominal amount of total outstanding financing provided under this paragraph per beneficiary does not exceed EUR 30 million;*

(c) *the support is provided to SMEs or small mid-caps;*

(d) *the support is provided for energy performance contracting within the meaning of Article 2, point (27) of Directive 2012/27/EU;*

(e) *the energy performance contracting relates to a building referred to in paragraph 3, point (b).]*

NOTES

Para 3: substituted by Commission Regulation 2021/1237/EU, Art 1(20)(a), as from 1 August 2021.

Para 3a: inserted by Commission Regulation 2021/1237/EU, Art 1(20)(b), as from 1 August 2021.

Para 7: added by Commission Regulation 2021/1237/EU, Art 1(20)(c), as from 1 August 2021.

Repeal of this Regulation in relation to the UK: this Regulation is repealed in relation to the UK (as from IP completion day); see the introductory notes to this Regulation *ante*.

[1] Directive 2010/31/EU of the European Parliament and of the Council of 19 May 2010 on the energy performance of buildings (OJ L153, 18.6.2010, p 13).

[5.110]

Article 39 [Investment aid for energy efficiency projects in buildings in the form of financial instruments]

1. Investment aid for energy efficiency projects in buildings shall be compatible with the internal market within the meaning of Article 107(3) of the Treaty and shall be exempted from the notification requirement of Article 108(3) of the Treaty, provided that the conditions laid down in this Article and in Chapter I are fulfilled.

2. Eligible for aid under the present Article are energy efficiency projects relating to buildings.

[2a. Where the investment relates to the improvement of the energy efficiency of (i) residential buildings; (ii) buildings dedicated to the provision of education or social services; (iii) buildings dedicated to activities related to public administration or to justice, police or fire-fighting services; or (iv) buildings referred to in points (i), (ii) or (iii) and in which activities other than those mentioned in those points occupy less than 35% of the floor area, energy efficiency projects under this Article may also be combined with any of the following investments:

(a) *integrated on-site renewable energy installation generating electricity and/or heat;*

(b) *equipment for the storage of the energy generated from the on-site renewable energy installation;*

(c) *equipment and related infrastructure incorporated in the building for the charging of electric vehicles of the building users;*

(d) *investments in the digitalisation of the building, in particular to increase its smart readiness. Eligible investments may include interventions limited to passive in-house wiring or structured cabling for data networks and, if necessary, the ancillary part of the passive network on the private property outside the building. Wiring or cabling for data networks outside the private property is excluded.]*

[3. The eligible costs shall be the overall costs of the energy efficiency project, except for buildings referred to in paragraph 2a, where the eligible costs shall be the overall costs of the energy efficiency project as well as the investment cost of the various pieces of equipment listed in paragraph 2a.

4. The aid shall be granted in the form of an endowment, equity, a guarantee or a loan to an energy efficiency fund or other financial intermediary, which shall pass it on to the largest extent possible to the final beneficiaries, being the building owners or tenants, in the form of higher volumes of financing, lower collateral requirements, lower guarantee premiums or lower interest rates.

5. The aid granted by the energy efficiency fund or other financial intermediary to the eligible energy efficiency projects may take the form of loans or guarantees. The nominal value of the loan or the amount guaranteed shall not exceed EUR 15 million per project at the level of the final beneficiaries, except in the case of combined investments referred to in paragraph 2a, where it shall not exceed EUR 30 million. The guarantee shall not exceed 80% of the underlying loan.]

6. The repayment by the building owners to the energy efficiency fund or other financial intermediary shall not be less than the nominal value of the loan.

7. The energy efficiency aid shall leverage additional investment from private investors reaching at minimum 30% of the total financing provided to an energy efficiency project. When the aid is provided by an energy efficiency fund, the leverage of private investment can be done at the level of the energy efficiency fund and/or at the level of the energy efficiency projects, so as to achieve an aggregate minimum 30% of the total financing provided to an energy efficiency project.

8. Member States can set up energy efficiency funds and/or can use financial intermediaries when providing energy efficiency aid. The following conditions must then be fulfilled:

- *(a) Financial intermediary managers, as well as energy efficiency fund managers shall be selected through an open, transparent and non-discriminatory call in accordance with applicable Union and national laws. In particular, there shall be no discrimination on the basis of their place of establishment or incorporation in any Member State. Financial intermediaries and energy efficiency fund managers may be required to fulfil predefined criteria objectively justified by the nature of the investments;*
- *(b) The independent private investors shall be selected through an open, transparent and non-discriminatory call in accordance with applicable Union and national laws aimed at establishing the appropriate risk-reward sharing arrangements whereby, for investments other than guarantees, asymmetric profit-sharing shall be given preference over downside protection. If the private investors are not selected by such a call, the fair rate of return to the private investors shall be established by an independent expert selected via an open, transparent and non-discriminatory call;*
- *(c) In the case of asymmetric loss-sharing between public and private investors, the first loss assumed by the public investor shall be capped at 25% of the total investment;*
- *(d) In the case of guarantees, the guarantee rate shall be limited to 80% and total losses assumed by a Member State shall be capped at 25% of the underlying guaranteed portfolio. Only guarantees covering the expected losses of the underlying guaranteed portfolio can be provided for free. If a guarantee also comprises coverage of unexpected losses, the financial intermediary shall pay, for the part of the guarantee covering unexpected losses, a market conform guarantee premium;*
- *(e) The investors shall be allowed to be represented in the governance bodies of the energy efficiency fund or financial intermediary, such as the supervisory board or the advisory committee;*
- *(f) The energy efficiency fund or financial intermediary shall be established according to the applicable laws and the Member State shall provide for a due diligence process in order to ensure a commercially sound investment strategy for the purpose of implementing the energy efficiency aid measure.*

9. Financial intermediaries, including energy efficiency funds shall be managed on a commercial basis and shall ensure profit-driven financing decisions. This is considered to be the case when the financial intermediary and, as the case may be, the managers of the energy efficiency fund fulfil the following conditions:

- *(a) they are obliged by law or contract to act with the diligence of a professional manager in good faith and avoiding conflicts of interest; best practices and regulatory supervision shall apply;*
- *(b) their remuneration conforms with market practices. This requirement is considered to be met where the manager is selected through an open, transparent and non-discriminatory call, based on objective criteria linked to experience, expertise and operational and financial capacity;*
- *(c) they shall receive a remuneration linked to performance, or shall share part of the investment risks by co-investing own resources so as to ensure that their interests are permanently aligned with the interests of the public investor;*
- *(d) they shall set out an investment strategy, criteria and the proposed timing of investments in energy efficiency projects, establishing the ex-ante financial viability and their expected impact on energy efficiency.*
- *(e) a clear and realistic exit strategy shall exist for the public funds invested in the energy efficiency fund or granted to the financial intermediary, allowing the market to finance energy efficiency projects when the market is ready to do so.*

10. Energy efficiency improvements undertaken to ensure that the beneficiary complies with Union standards which have already been adopted shall not be exempted from the notification requirement under this Article.

NOTES

The Article title was substituted, para 2a was inserted, and paras 3–5 were substituted, by Commission Regulation 2021/1237/EU, Art 1(21), as from 1 August 2021.

Repeal of this Regulation in relation to the UK: this Regulation is repealed in relation to the UK (as from IP completion day); see the introductory notes to this Regulation *ante*.

[5.111]

Article 40 Investment aid for high-efficiency cogeneration

1. Investment aid for high-efficiency cogeneration shall be compatible with the internal market within the meaning of Article 107(3) of the Treaty and shall be exempted from the notification requirement of Article 108(3) of the Treaty, provided that the conditions laid down in this Article and in Chapter I are fulfilled.

2. The investment aid shall be granted in respect of newly installed or refurbished capacities only.

3. The new cogeneration unit shall provide overall primary energy savings compared to separate production of heat and electricity as provided for by Directive 2012/27/EU of the European Parliament and of the Council of 25 October 2012 on energy efficiency, amending Directives 2009/125/EC and 2010/30/EU and repealing Directives 2004/8/EC and 2006/32/EC.[1] *The improvement of an existing cogeneration unit or conversion of an existing power generation unit into a cogeneration unit shall result in primary energy savings compared to the original situation.*

4. The eligible costs shall be the extra investment costs for the equipment needed for the installation to operate as a high-efficiency cogeneration installation, compared to conventional electricity or heating installations of the same capacity or the extra investment cost to upgrade to a higher efficiency when an existing installation already meets the high efficiency threshold.

5. The aid intensity shall not exceed 45% of the eligible costs. The aid intensity may be increased by 20 percentage points for aid granted to small undertakings and by 10 percentage points for aid granted to medium-sized undertakings.

6. The aid intensity may be increased by 15 percentage points for investments located in assisted areas fulfilling the conditions of Article 107(3)(a) of the Treaty and by 5 percentage points for investments located in assisted areas fulfilling the conditions of Article 107(3)(c) of the Treaty.

NOTES

Repeal of this Regulation in relation to the UK: this Regulation is repealed in relation to the UK (as from IP completion day); see the introductory notes to this Regulation *ante*.

[1] OJ L315, 14.11.2012, p 1.

[5.112]

Article 41 Investment aid for the promotion of energy from renewable sources

1. Investment aid for the promotion of energy from renewable energy sources shall be compatible with the internal market within the meaning of Article 107(3) of the Treaty and shall be exempted from the notification requirement of Article 108(3) of the Treaty, provided that the conditions laid down in this Article and in Chapter I are fulfilled.

2. Investment aid for the production of biofuels shall be exempted from the notification requirement only to the extent that the aided investments are used for the production of sustainable biofuels other than food-based biofuels. However, investment aid to convert existing food-based biofuel plants into advanced biofuel plants shall be exempted under this Article, provided that the food-based production would be reduced commensurate to the new capacity.

3. Aid shall not be granted for biofuels which are subject to a supply or blending obligation.

4. Aid shall not be granted for hydropower installations that do not comply with Directive 2000/60/EC of the European Parliament.

5. The investment aid shall be granted to new installations only. No aid shall be granted or paid out after the installation started operations and aid shall be independent from the output.

6. The eligible costs shall be the extra investment costs necessary to promote the production of energy from renewable sources. They shall be determined as follows:

(a) where the costs of investing in the production of energy from renewable sources can be identified in the total investment cost as a separate investment, for instance as a readily identifiable add-on component to a pre-existing facility, this renewable energy-related cost shall constitute the eligible costs;

(b) where the costs of investing in the production of energy from renewable sources can be identified by reference to a similar, less environmentally friendly investment that would have been credibly carried out without the aid, this difference between the costs of both investments identifies the renewable energy-related cost and constitutes the eligible costs;

(c) for certain small installations where a less environmentally friendly investment cannot be established as plants of a limited size do not exist, the total investment costs to achieve a higher level of environmental protection shall constitute the eligible costs.

The costs not directly linked to the achievement of a higher level of environmental protection shall not be eligible.

7. The aid intensity shall not exceed:

(a) 45% of the eligible costs if the eligible costs are calculated on the basis of point (6)(a) or point (6)(b);

(b) 30% of the eligible cost if the eligible costs are calculated on the basis of point (6)(c).

8. The aid intensity may be increased by 20 percentage points for aid granted to small undertakings and by 10 percentage points for aid granted to medium-sized undertakings.

9. The aid intensity may be increased by 15 percentage points for investments located in assisted areas fulfilling the conditions of Article 107(3)(a) of the Treaty and by 5 percentage points for investments located in assisted areas fulfilling the conditions of Article 107(3)(c) of the Treaty.

10. Where aid is granted in a competitive bidding process on the basis of clear, transparent and non-discriminatory criteria, the aid intensity may reach 100% of the eligible costs. Such a bidding process shall be non-discriminatory and provide for the participation of all interested undertakings. The budget related to the bidding process shall be a binding constraint in the sense that not all participants can receive aid and the aid shall be granted on the basis of the initial bid submitted by the bidder, therefore excluding subsequent negotiations.

NOTES

Repeal of this Regulation in relation to the UK: this Regulation is repealed in relation to the UK (as from IP completion day); see the introductory notes to this Regulation *ante*.

[5.113]

Article 42 Operating aid for the promotion of electricity from renewable sources

1. Operating aid for the promotion of electricity from renewable energy sources shall be compatible with the internal market within the meaning of Article 107(3) of the Treaty and shall be exempted from the notification requirement of Article 108(3) of the Treaty, provided that the conditions laid down in this Article and in Chapter I are fulfilled.

2. Aid shall be granted in a competitive bidding process on the basis of clear, transparent and non-discriminatory criteria which shall be open to all generators producing electricity from renewable energy sources on a non-discriminatory basis.

3. The bidding process can be limited to specific technologies where a process open to all generators would lead to a suboptimal result which cannot be addressed in the process design in view of in particular:

(i) the longer-term potential of a given new and innovative technology; or

(ii) the need to achieve diversification; or

(iii) network constraints and grid stability; or

(iv) system (integration) costs; or

(v) the need to avoid distortions on the raw material markets from biomass support

Member States shall carry out a detailed assessment of the applicability of such conditions and report it to the Commission according to the modalities described in Article 11 (a).

4. Aid shall be granted to new and innovative renewable energy technologies in a competitive bidding process open to at least one such technology on the basis of clear, transparent and non-discriminatory criteria. Such aid shall not be granted for more than 5% of the planned new electricity capacity from renewable energy sources per year in total.

5. Aid shall be granted as a premium in addition to the market price whereby the generators sell their electricity directly in the market.

6. Aid beneficiaries shall be subject to standard balancing responsibilities. Beneficiaries may outsource balancing responsibilities to other undertakings on their behalf, such as aggregators.

7. Aid shall not be granted when prices are negative.

8. Aid may be granted in the absence of a competitive bidding process as described in paragraph 2 to installations with an installed electricity capacity of less than 1 MW for the production of electricity from all renewable sources except for wind energy, where aid may be granted in the absence of a competitive bidding process as described in paragraph 2 to installations with an installed electricity capacity of less than 6 MW or to installations with less than 6 generation units. Without prejudice to paragraph 9, when aid is granted in the absence of a competitive bidding process, the conditions under paragraphs 5, 6 and 7 shall be respected. In addition, when aid is granted in the absence of a competitive bidding process, the conditions under Article 43 paragraphs 5, 6 and 7 shall be applicable.

9. The conditions under paragraphs 5, 6 and 7 shall not apply to operating aid granted to installations with an installed electricity capacity of less than 500 kW for the production of electricity from all renewable sources except for wind energy, where these conditions shall not apply to operating aid granted to installations with an installed electricity capacity of less than 3 MW or to installations with less than 3 generation units.

10. For the purpose of calculating the above maximum capacities referred to in paragraphs 8 and 9, installations with a common connection point to the electricity grid shall be considered as one installation.

11. Aid shall only be granted until the plant generating the electricity from renewable sources has been fully depreciated according to generally accepted accounting principles. Any investment aid previously received must be deducted from the operating aid.

NOTES

Repeal of this Regulation in relation to the UK: this Regulation is repealed in relation to the UK (as from IP completion day); see the introductory notes to this Regulation *ante*.

[5.114]

Article 43 Operating aid for the promotion of energy from renewable sources in small scale installations

1. Operating aid for the promotion of energy from renewable energy sources in small scale installations shall be compatible with the internal market within the meaning of Article 107(3) of the Treaty and shall be exempted from the notification requirement of Article 108(3) of the Treaty, provided that the conditions laid down in this Article and in Chapter I are fulfilled.

2. Aid shall only be granted to installations with an installed capacity of less than 500 kW for the production of energy from all renewable sources except for wind energy, for which aid shall be granted to installations with an installed capacity of less than 3 MW or with less than 3 generation units and for biofuels, for which aid shall be granted to installations with an installed capacity of less than 50,000 tonnes/year. For the purpose of calculating those maximum capacities, small scale installations with a common connection point to the electricity grid shall be considered as one installation.

3. Aid shall only be granted to installations producing sustainable biofuels other than food-based biofuels. However, operating aid to plants producing food-based biofuels that have started operation before 31 December 2013 and are not yet fully depreciated shall be exempted under this Article but in any event no later than 2020.

4. Aid shall not be granted for biofuels which are subject to a supply or blending obligation.

5. The aid per unit of energy shall not exceed the difference between the total levelized costs of producing energy from the renewable source in question and the market price of the form of energy concerned. The levelized costs shall be updated regularly and at least every year.

6. The maximum rate of return used in the levelized cost calculation shall not exceed the relevant swap rate plus a premium of 100 basis points. The relevant swap rate shall be the swap rate of the currency in which the aid is granted for a maturity that reflects the depreciation period of the installations supported.

7. Aid shall only be granted until the installation has been fully depreciated according to generally accepted accounting principles. Any investment aid granted to an installation shall be deducted from the operating aid.

NOTES

Repeal of this Regulation in relation to the UK: this Regulation is repealed in relation to the UK (as from IP completion day); see the introductory notes to this Regulation *ante*.

[5.115]

Article 44 Aid in the form of reductions in environmental taxes under Directive 2003/96/EC

1. Aid schemes in the form of reductions in environmental taxes fulfilling the conditions of Council Directive 2003/96/EC of 27 October 2003 restructuring the Community framework for the taxation of energy products and electricity[1] shall be compatible with the internal market within the meaning of Article 107(3) of the Treaty and shall be exempted from the notification requirement of Article 108(3) of the Treaty, provided that the conditions laid down in this Article and in Chapter I are fulfilled.

2. The beneficiaries of the tax reduction shall be selected on the basis of transparent and objective criteria and shall pay at least the respective minimum level of taxation set by Directive 2003/96/EC.

3. Aid schemes in the form of tax reductions shall be based on a reduction of the applicable environmental tax rate or on the payment of a fixed compensation amount or on a combination of these mechanisms.

4. Aid shall not be granted for biofuels which are subject to a supply or blending obligation.

NOTES

Repeal of this Regulation in relation to the UK: this Regulation is repealed in relation to the UK (as from IP completion day); see the introductory notes to this Regulation *ante*.

[1] OJ L283, 31.10.2003, p 51.

[5.116]

Article 45 Investment aid for remediation of contaminated sites

1. Investment aid to undertakings repairing environmental damage by remediating contaminated sites shall be compatible with the internal market within the meaning of Article 107(3) of the Treaty and shall be exempted from the notification requirement of Article 108(3) of the Treaty, provided that the conditions laid down in this Article and in Chapter I are fulfilled.

2. The investment shall lead to the repair of the environmental damage, including damage to the quality of the soil or of surface water or groundwater.

3. Where the legal or physical person liable for the environmental damage under the law applicable in each Member State without prejudice to the Union rules in this matter — in particular Directive 2004/35/EC of the European Parliament and of the Council of 21 April 2004 on environmental liability with regard to the prevention and remedying of environmental damage[2] as amended by Directive 2006/21/EC of the European Parliament and of the Council of 15 March 2006 on the management of waste from extractive industries,[3] Directive 2009/31/EC of the European Parliament and of the Council of 23 April 2009 on the geological storage of carbon dioxide and amending Council Directive 85/337/EEC, European Parliament and Council Directives 2000/60/EC, 2001/80/EC, 2004/35/EC, 2006/12/EC, 2008/1/EC and Regulation (EC) No 1013/2006[4] and Directive 2013/30/EU of the European Parliament and of the Council of 12 June 2013 on safety of offshore oil and gas operations and amending Directive 2004/35/EC[5] — is identified, that person must finance the remediation in accordance with the 'polluter pays' principle, and no State aid shall be granted. Where the person liable under the applicable law is not identified or cannot be made to bear the costs, the person responsible for the remediation or decontamination work may receive State aid.

4. The eligible costs shall be the costs incurred for the remediation work, less the increase in the value of the land. All expenditure incurred by an undertaking in remediating its site, whether or not such expenditure can be shown as a fixed asset on its balance sheet, may be considered as eligible investment in the case of the remediation of contaminated sites.

5. Evaluations of the increase in value of the land resulting from remediation shall be carried out by an independent expert.

6. The aid intensity shall not exceed 100% of the eligible costs.

NOTES

Repeal of this Regulation in relation to the UK: this Regulation is repealed in relation to the UK (as from IP completion day); see the introductory notes to this Regulation *ante*.

[2] OJ L143, 30.4.2004, p 56.

[3] OJ L102, 11.4.2006, p 1.

[4] OJ L140, 5.6.2009, p 114.

[5] OJ L178, 28.6.2013, p 66.

[5.117]

Article 46 Investment aid for energy efficient district heating and cooling

1. Investment aid for the installation of energy efficient district heating and cooling system shall be compatible with the internal market within the meaning of Article 107(3) of the Treaty and shall be exempted from the notification requirement of Article 108(3) of the Treaty, provided that the conditions laid down in this Article and in Chapter I are fulfilled.

2. The eligible costs for the production plant shall be the extra costs needed for the construction, expansion and refurbishment of one or more generation units to operate as an energy efficient district heating and cooling system compared to a conventional production plant. The investment shall be an integral part of the energy efficient district heating and cooling system.

3. The aid intensity for the production plant shall not exceed 45% of the eligible costs. The aid intensity may be increased by 20 percentage points for aid granted to small undertakings and by 10 percentage points for aid granted to medium-sized undertakings.

4. The aid intensity for the production plant may be increased by 15 percentage points for investments located in assisted areas fulfilling the conditions of Article 107(3)(a) of the Treaty and by 5 percentage points for investments located in assisted areas fulfilling the conditions of Article 107(3)(c) of the Treaty.

5. The eligible costs for the distribution network shall be the investment costs.

6. The aid amount for the distribution network shall not exceed the difference between the eligible costs and the operating profit. The operating profit shall be deducted from the eligible costs ex ante or through a claw-back mechanism.

NOTES

Repeal of this Regulation in relation to the UK: this Regulation is repealed in relation to the UK (as from IP completion day); see the introductory notes to this Regulation *ante*.

[5.118]

Article 47 Investment aid for waste recycling and re-utilisation

1. Investment aid for waste recycling and re-utilisation shall be compatible with the internal market within the meaning of Article 107(3) of the Treaty and shall be exempted from the notification requirement of Article 108(3) of the Treaty, provided that the conditions laid down in this Article and in Chapter I are fulfilled.

2. The investment aid shall be granted for the recycling and re-utilisation of waste generated by other undertakings.

3. The recycled or re-used materials treated would otherwise be disposed of, or be treated in a less environmentally friendly manner. Aid to waste recovery operations other than recycling shall not be block exempted under this Article.

4. The aid shall not indirectly relieve the polluters from a burden that should be borne by them under Union law, or from a burden that should be considered a normal company cost.

5. The investment shall not merely increase demand for the materials to be recycled without increasing collection of those materials.

6. The investment shall go beyond the state of the art.

7. The eligible costs shall be the extra investment costs necessary to realise an investment leading to better or more efficient recycling or re-use activities compared to a conventional process of re-use and recycling activities with the same capacity that would be constructed in the absence the aid.

8. The aid intensity shall not exceed 35% of the eligible costs. The aid intensity may be increased by 20 percentage points for aid granted to small undertakings and by 10 percentage points for aid granted to medium-sized undertakings.

9. The aid intensity may be increased by 15 percentage points for investments located in assisted areas fulfilling the conditions of Article 107(3)(a) of the Treaty and by 5 percentage points for investments located in assisted areas fulfilling the conditions of Article 107(3)(c) of the Treaty.

10. Aid for investments relating to the recycling and re-utilisation of the beneficiary's own waste shall not be exempt from the notification requirement under this Article.

NOTES

Repeal of this Regulation in relation to the UK: this Regulation is repealed in relation to the UK (as from IP completion day); see the introductory notes to this Regulation *ante*.

[5.119]

Article 48 Investment aid for energy infrastructure

1. Investment aid for the construction or upgrade of energy infrastructure shall be compatible with the internal market within the meaning of Article 107(3) of the Treaty and shall be exempted from the notification requirement of Article 108(3) of the Treaty, provided that the conditions laid down in this Article and in Chapter I are fulfilled.

2. Aid shall be granted for energy infrastructure located in assisted areas.

3. The energy infrastructure shall be subject to full tariff and access regulation according to internal energy market legislation.

4. The eligible costs shall be the investment costs.

5. The aid amount shall not exceed the difference between the eligible costs and the operating profit of the investment. The operating profit shall be deducted from the eligible costs ex ante or through a claw-back mechanism.

6. Aid for investments in electricity and gas storage projects and oil infrastructure shall not be exempt from the notification requirement under this Article.

NOTES

Repeal of this Regulation in relation to the UK: this Regulation is repealed in relation to the UK (as from IP completion day); see the introductory notes to this Regulation *ante*.

[5.120]

Article 49 Aid for environmental studies

1. Aid for studies, including energy audits, directly linked to investments referred to in this Section shall be compatible with the internal market within the meaning of Article 107(3) of the Treaty and shall be exempted from the notification requirement of Article 108(3) of the Treaty, provided that the conditions laid down in this Article and in Chapter I are fulfilled.

2. The eligible costs shall be the costs of the studies referred to in paragraph 1.

3. The aid intensity shall not exceed 50% of the eligible costs.

4. The aid intensity may be increased by 20 percentage points for studies undertaken on behalf of small enterprises and by 10 percentage points for studies undertaken on behalf of medium size enterprises.

5. Aid shall not be granted to large undertakings for energy audits carried out under Article 8(4) of the Directive 2012/27/EU, unless the energy audit is carried out in addition to the mandatory energy audit under that Directive.

NOTES

Repeal of this Regulation in relation to the UK: this Regulation is repealed in relation to the UK (as from IP completion day); see the introductory notes to this Regulation *ante*.

SECTION 8 AID TO MAKE GOOD THE DAMAGE CAUSED BY CERTAIN NATURAL DISASTERS

[5.121]

Article 50 Aid schemes to make good the damage caused by certain natural disasters

1. Aid schemes to make good the damage caused by earthquakes, avalanches, landslides, floods, tornadoes, hurricanes, volcanic eruptions and wild fires of natural origin shall be compatible with the internal market within the meaning of Article 107(2)(b) of the Treaty and shall be exempted from the notification requirement of Article 108(3) of the Treaty, provided that the conditions laid down in this Article and in Chapter I are fulfilled.

2. Aid shall be granted subject to the following conditions:

(a) the competent public authorities of a Member State have formally recognised the character of the event as a natural disaster; and

(b) there is a direct causal link between the natural disaster and the damages suffered by the affected undertaking.

3. Aid schemes related to a specific natural disaster shall be introduced within three years following the occurrence of the event. Aid on the basis of such schemes shall be granted within four years following the occurrence.

4. The costs arising from the damage incurred as a direct consequence of the natural disaster, as assessed by an independent expert recognised by the competent national authority or by an insurance undertaking shall be eligible costs. Such damage may include material damage to assets such as buildings, equipment, machinery or stocks and loss of income due to the full or partial suspension of activity for a period not exceeding six months from the occurrence of the disaster. The calculation of the material damage shall be based on the repair cost or economic value of the affected asset before the disaster. It shall not exceed the repair cost or the decrease in fair market value caused by the disaster, that is to say the difference between the property's value immediately before and immediately after the occurrence of the disaster. Loss of income shall be calculated on the basis of financial data of the affected undertaking (earnings before interest and taxes (EBIT), depreciation and labour costs related only to the establishment affected by the natural disaster) by comparing the financial data for the six months after the occurrence of the disaster with the average of three years chosen among the five years preceding the occurrence of the disaster (by excluding the two years giving the best and the worst financial result) and calculated for the same six months period of the year. The damage shall be calculated at the level of the individual beneficiary.

5. The aid and any other payments received to compensate for the damage, including payments under insurance policies, shall not exceed 100% of the eligible costs.

NOTES

Repeal of this Regulation in relation to the UK: this Regulation is repealed in relation to the UK (as from IP completion day); see the introductory notes to this Regulation *ante*.

SECTION 9 SOCIAL AID FOR TRANSPORT FOR RESIDENTS OF REMOTE REGIONS

[5.122]

Article 51 Social aid for transport for residents of remote regions

1. Aid for air and maritime passenger transport shall be compatible with the internal market pursuant to Article 107(2)(a) of the Treaty and shall be exempted from the notification requirement of Article 108(3) of the Treaty, provided that the conditions laid down in this Article and in Chapter I are fulfilled.

2. The entire aid shall be for the benefit of final consumers who have their normal residence in remote regions.

3. The aid shall be granted for passenger transport on a route linking an airport or port in a remote region with another airport or port within the European Economic Area.

4. The aid shall be granted without discrimination as to the identity of the carrier or type of service and without limitation as to the precise route to or from the remote region.

5. The eligible costs shall be the price of a return ticket from or to the remote region, including all taxes and charges invoiced by the carrier to the consumer.

6. The aid intensity shall not exceed 100% of the eligible costs.

NOTES

Repeal of this Regulation in relation to the UK: this Regulation is repealed in relation to the UK (as from IP completion day); see the introductory notes to this Regulation *ante*.

SECTION 10 AID FOR BROADBAND INFRASTRUCTURES

[5.123]

[Article 52 Aid for fixed broadband networks

1. Aid for fixed broadband network deployment shall be compatible with the internal market pursuant to Article 107(3) of the Treaty and shall be exempted from the notification requirement of Article 108(3) of the Treaty, provided that the conditions laid down in this Article and in Chapter I are fulfilled.

2. The eligible costs shall be all costs for the construction, management and operation of a fixed broadband network. The maximum aid amount for a project shall be established on the basis of a competitive selection process as set out in paragraph 6, point (a). Where an investment is carried out in accordance with paragraph 6, point (b), without a competitive selection process, the aid amount shall not exceed the difference between the eligible costs and the operating profit of the investment. The operating profit shall be deducted from the eligible costs ex ante on the basis of reasonable projections and verified ex post through a claw-back mechanism.

3. The following alternative types of investment are eligible:

(a) fixed broadband network deployment to connect households and socioeconomic drivers in areas where there is no network able to reliably provide speeds of at least 30 Mbps download (threshold speeds) present or credibly planned to be deployed within three years from the moment of publication of the planned aid measure or within the same time horizon as the deployment of the subsidised network, which shall not be shorter than two years. This shall be verified by mapping and public consultation in accordance with paragraph 4. Areas

with at least one present or credibly planned network able to reliably provide speeds of at least 30 Mbps download shall be excluded. The aided network shall ensure at least a doubling of download and upload speeds compared to the present or credibly planned networks and shall be able to reliably provide at least 30 Mbps download speeds (target speeds);

(b) *fixed broadband network deployment to connect households and socioeconomic drivers in areas where there is no network able to reliably provide speeds of at least 100 Mbps download (threshold speeds) present or credibly planned to be deployed within three years from the moment of publication of the planned aid measure or within the same time horizon as the deployment of the subsidised network, which shall not be shorter than two years. This shall be verified by mapping and public consultation in accordance with paragraph 4. Areas with at least one present or credibly planned network able to reliably provide speeds of at least 100 Mbps download shall be excluded. The aided network shall ensure at least a doubling of download and upload speeds compared to the present or credibly planned networks and shall be able to reliably provide at least 300 Mbps download and 100 Mbps upload speeds (target speeds);*

(c) *fixed broadband network deployment to connect only socioeconomic drivers in areas where there is only one network able to reliably provide speeds of at least 100 Mbps download but below 300 Mbps download (threshold speeds) present or credibly planned to be deployed within three years from the moment of publication of the planned aid measure or within the same time horizon as the deployment of the subsidised network, which shall not be shorter than two years. This shall be verified by mapping and public consultation in accordance with paragraph 4. Areas with at least one present or credibly planned network able to reliably provide speeds of at least 300 Mbps download shall be excluded. Areas with at least two present or credibly planned networks able to reliably provide speeds of at least 100 Mbps download shall also be excluded. The aided network shall ensure at least a doubling of download and upload speeds compared to the present or credibly planned networks and shall be able to reliably provide at least 1 Gbps download speeds (target speeds).*

4. *The mapping and public consultation referred to in paragraph 3 shall meet all the following requirements:*

(a) *the mapping shall identify the geographic target areas envisaged to be covered under the public intervention and shall take into account all present public and private networks able to reliably provide the threshold speeds identified in paragraph 3 depending on the type of investment. The mapping shall be performed: (i) for purely fixed networks, at address level on the basis of premises passed and (ii) for fixed wireless access networks, at address level on the basis of premises passed or on the basis of maximum 100 x100 metre grids. For points (i) and (ii) the mapping shall always be verified through a public consultation;*

(b) *the public consultation shall be carried out by the competent public authority through publication of the main characteristics of the planned measure and the list of geographic target areas identified in the mapping exercise in accordance with point (a) on an appropriate website (including at national level). The public consultation shall invite interested parties to comment on the measure and to submit substantiated information in accordance with point (a) regarding their networks able to reliably provide the threshold speeds set out in paragraph 3 in the target area that are present or credibly planned to be deployed within three years from the moment of publication of the planned aid measure. If the granting authority takes a shorter or longer time horizon than three years for the deployment of the subsidised infrastructure, the same time horizon, which cannot be shorter than two years, must also be used to assess whether networks referred to in the previous sentence are credibly planned to be deployed. The public consultation shall last at least 30 days.*

5. *The aided project shall bring a significant improvement (step change) compared to networks present or credibly planned to be deployed within three years from the moment of publication of the planned aid measure or within the same time horizon as the deployment of the subsidised network, which cannot be shorter than two years, in accordance with paragraph 4. A step change takes place if, as a result of the subsidised intervention, a significant new investment in the broadband network is undertaken and the subsidised network brings significant new capabilities to the market in terms of broadband internet access service availability and capacity, speeds and competition compared to the present or credibly planned networks. The project must include substantial investments in passive infrastructure going beyond marginal investments related merely to the upgrade of the active elements of the network.*

6. *The aid shall be granted as follows:*

(a) *the aid shall be allocated to providers of electronic communications networks and services on the basis of an open, transparent and non-discriminatory competitive selection procedure in line with the principles of public procurement rules and respecting the principle of technology neutrality, without prejudice to the applicable public procurement rules, based on the most economically advantageous offer. For the purposes of the competitive selection procedure, the aid granting authority shall establish in advance objective, transparent and non-discriminatory qualitative award criteria that have to be weighed against the requested aid amount. At similar quality conditions the bidder with the lowest amount of aid requested shall be awarded the aid;*

(b) *when the aid is granted without a competitive selection procedure to a public authority to deploy and manage, directly or through an in-house entity, a fixed broadband network, the public authority or the in-house entity, as the case may be, shall provide only wholesale services using the subsidised network. The public authority shall ensure accounting separation between the funds used for the operation of the network and other funds at its disposal. Any concession or other entrustment to a third party to build or operate the network shall be allocated through an open, transparent and non-discriminatory competitive selection procedure, in line with the principles of public procurement rules and respecting the principle of technology neutrality, without prejudice to the to the applicable public procurement rules, based on the most economically advantageous offer.*

7. *The operation of the subsidised network shall offer the widest possible active and passive wholesale access, in accordance with Article 2, point (139), under fair and non-discriminatory conditions, including physical unbundling. A project may offer virtual unbundling instead of physical unbundling if the virtual access product is declared as equivalent to physical unbundling by the national regulatory authority. Active wholesale access shall be granted for at least seven years and the wholesale access to the physical infrastructure including ducts or poles shall not be limited in time. The same access conditions shall apply to the entirety of the subsidised network, including on parts*

of the network where existing infrastructures have been used. The access obligations shall be enforced irrespective of any change in ownership, management or operation of the subsidised network. In the case of aid for the construction of ducts, the ducts shall be large enough to cater for at least three networks and different network topologies.

8. The wholesale access price shall be based on one of the following benchmarks: (i) the average published wholesale prices that prevail in other comparable, more competitive areas of the Member State or the Union; or (ii) in the absence of such published prices, the regulated prices already set or approved by the national regulatory authority for the markets and services concerned; or (iii) in the absence of such published or regulated prices, the pricing shall comply with cost orientation and the methodology mandated in accordance with the sectorial regulatory framework. Without prejudice to the competences of the national regulatory authority under the regulatory framework, the national regulatory authority shall be consulted on the terms and conditions for access, including on prices, and on disputes related to the application of this Article.

9. Member States shall put in place a monitoring and claw-back mechanism if the amount of aid granted to the project exceeds EUR 10 million.]

NOTES

Substituted by Commission Regulation 2021/1237/EU, Art 1(22), as from 1 August 2021.

Repeal of this Regulation in relation to the UK: this Regulation is repealed in relation to the UK (as from IP completion day); see the introductory notes to this Regulation *ante*.

[5.124]

[Article 52a Aid for 4G and 5G mobile networks

1. Aid for 4G and 5G mobile network deployment shall be compatible with the internal market pursuant to Article 107(3) of the Treaty and shall be exempted from the notification requirement of Article 108(3) of the Treaty, provided that the conditions laid down in this Article and in Chapter I are fulfilled.

2. The eligible costs shall be all costs for the construction, management and operation of a passive mobile network. The maximum aid amount for a project shall be established on the basis of a competitive selection process as set out in paragraph 7, point (a). Where an investment is carried out in accordance with paragraph 7, point (b), without a competitive selection process, the aid amount shall not exceed the difference between the eligible costs and the operating profit of the investment. The operating profit shall be deducted from the eligible costs ex ante on the basis of reasonable projections and verified ex post through a claw-back mechanism.

3. 5G investment shall be located in areas where mobile networks have not been deployed or where only mobile networks able to support mobile services of up to 3G are available and where there are no 4G and no 5G mobile networks present or credibly planned to be deployed within three years from the moment of publication of the planned aid measure or within the same time horizon as the deployment of the subsidised network, which shall not be shorter than two years. This shall be verified by mapping and public consultation in accordance with paragraph 4. 4G investment shall be located in areas where mobile networks have not been deployed or where only mobile networks able to support mobile services of up to 2G are available and where there are no 3G, 4G or 5G mobile networks present or credibly planned to be deployed within three years from the moment of publication of the planned aid measure or within the same time horizon as the deployment of the subsidised network, which shall not be shorter than two years. This shall be verified by mapping and public consultation in accordance with paragraph 4.

4. The mapping and public consultation referred to in paragraph 3 shall meet all the following requirements:

(a) the mapping shall clearly identify the geographic target areas envisaged to be covered under the public intervention and shall take into account all present mobile networks, depending on the type of investment. Mapping shall be performed on the basis of maximum 100 x100 metre grids. Mapping shall always be verified through a public consultation;

(b) the public consultation shall be carried out by the competent public authority through publication of the main characteristics of the planned measure and the list of geographic target areas identified in the mapping exercise in accordance with point (a) on an appropriate website (including at national level). The public consultation shall invite interested parties to comment on the measure and to submit substantiated information in accordance with point (a) regarding their mobile networks in the target area that are present or credibly planned to be deployed within three years from the moment of publication of the planned aid measure. If the granting authority takes a shorter or longer time horizon than three years for the deployment of the subsidised infrastructure, the same time horizon, which cannot be shorter than two years, must also be used to assess whether networks referred to in the previous sentence are credibly planned to be deployed. The public consultation shall last at least 30 days.

5. The aided infrastructure shall not be taken into account to meet the coverage obligations of the mobile networks operators that arise out of conditions attached to rights of use of 4G and 5G spectrum.

6. The supported project shall bring a significant improvement (step change) compared to mobile networks present or credibly planned to be deployed within three years from the moment of publication of the planned aid measure or within the same time horizon as the deployment of the subsidised network, which cannot be shorter than two years, in accordance with paragraph 4. A step change takes place if, as a result of the subsidised intervention, a significant new investment in the mobile network is undertaken and the subsidised network brings significant new capabilities to the market in terms of mobile service availability, capacity, speeds and competition compared to the present or credibly planned networks. The project must include substantial investments in passive infrastructure going beyond marginal investments related merely to the upgrade of the active elements of the network.

7. The aid shall be granted as follows:

(a) the aid shall be allocated to providers of electronic communications networks and services on the basis of an open, transparent and non-discriminatory competitive selection process in line with the principles of public procurement rules and respecting the principle of technology neutrality, without prejudice to the applicable public procurement rules, based on the most economically advantageous offer. For the purposes of the

competitive selection procedure, the aid granting authority shall establish in advance objective, transparent and non-discriminatory qualitative award criteria that have to be weighed against the requested aid amount. At similar quality conditions the bidder with the lowest amount of aid requested shall be awarded the aid;

(b) *when the aid is granted without a competitive selection procedure to a public authority to deploy and manage, directly or through an in-house entity, a passive mobile network, the public authority or the in-house entity, as the case may be, shall provide only wholesale services using the subsidised network. The public authority shall ensure accounting separation between the funds used for the operation of the network and other funds at the disposal of the public authority. Any concession or other entrustment to a third party to build or operate the network shall be allocated through an open, transparent and non-discriminatory competitive selection process, in line with the principles of public procurement rules and respecting the principle of technology neutrality without prejudice to the to the applicable public procurement rules, based on the most economically advantageous offer.*

8. The operation of the subsidised network shall offer the widest possible active and passive wholesale access, in accordance with Article 2, point (139), under fair and non-discriminatory conditions. Active wholesale access shall be granted for at least seven years and wholesale access to the physical infrastructure including ducts or poles shall not be limited in time. The same access conditions shall apply on the entirety of the subsidised network, including on the parts of such network where existing infrastructures have been used. The access obligations shall be enforced irrespective of any change in ownership, management or operation of the subsidised network. In the case of aid for the construction of ducts, the ducts shall be large enough to cater at least for all existing mobile networks operators.

9. The wholesale access price shall be based on one of the following benchmarks: (i) the average published wholesale prices that prevail in other comparable, more competitive areas of the Member State or the Union; or (ii) in the absence of such published prices, the regulated prices already set or approved by the national regulatory authority for the markets and services concerned; or (iii) in the absence of such published or regulated prices, the pricing shall comply with the cost orientation and the methodology mandated in accordance with the sectorial regulatory framework. Without prejudice to the competences of the national regulatory authority under the regulatory framework, the national regulatory authority shall be consulted on the terms and conditions for access, including on prices, and on disputes related to the application of this Article.

10. Member States shall put in place a monitoring and claw-back mechanism if the amount of aid granted to the project exceeds EUR 10 million.

11. The use of the publicly funded 4G or the 5G network to provide fixed wireless access services shall only be allowed as follows:

(a) *in areas where there is no network able to reliably provide speeds of at least 30 Mbps download present or credibly planned to be deployed within three years from the moment of publication of the planned aid measure or within the same time horizon as the deployment of the subsidised network, which cannot be shorter than two years, if the following cumulative conditions are met: (i) the mapping and public consultation exercise also takes into account the fixed broadband networks present or credibly planned determined according to Article 52(4);*

(ii) *the supported 4G or 5G fixed wireless access solution is able to reliably provide speeds of at least 30 Mbps download and at least a doubling of download and upload speed compared to the fixed networks present or credibly planned in those areas;*

(b) *in areas where there is no network able to reliably provide speeds of at least 100 Mbps download present or credibly planned to be deployed within three years from the moment of publication of the planned aid measure or within the same time horizon as the deployment of the subsidised network, which cannot be shorter than two years, if the following cumulative conditions are met: (i) the mapping and public consultation exercise takes also into account the fixed broadband networks present or credibly planned determined according to Article 52(4);*

(ii) *the supported 4G or 5G fixed wireless access solution is able to reliably provide speeds of at least 300 Mbps download and 100 Mbps upload and at least a doubling of download and upload speed compared to the fixed networks present or credibly planned in those areas.]*

NOTES

Inserted by Commission Regulation 2021/1237/EU, Art 1(23), as from 1 August 2021.

Repeal of this Regulation in relation to the UK: this Regulation is repealed in relation to the UK (as from IP completion day); see the introductory notes to this Regulation *ante*.

[5.125]

[Article 52b Aid for projects of common interest in the area of trans-European digital connectivity infrastructure

1. Aid for projects of common interest in the area of trans-European digital connectivity infrastructure financed under Regulation (EU) 2021/1153 or awarded a Seal of Excellence quality label under that Regulation shall be compatible with the internal market within the meaning of Article 107(3) of the Treaty and shall be exempted from the notification requirement of Article 108(3) of the Treaty provided that the conditions laid down in this Article and in Chapter I are fulfilled.

2. Projects shall fulfil the cumulative general compatibility conditions laid down in paragraph 3. They shall, in addition, fall under one of the categories of eligible projects laid down in paragraph 4 and shall fulfil all specific compatibility conditions for the relevant category laid down in that paragraph. Only projects which refer solely to the elements and entities specified under each relevant category in paragraph 4 shall fall within the scope of the exemption in paragraph 1.

3. The general cumulative compatibility conditions shall be the following:

(a) *the beneficiary must provide a financial contribution of at least 25% of the eligible costs through its own resources or through external financing not containing any public financial support. When the 25%*

contribution of the beneficiary is provided through external financing via an investment platform combining different sources of financing, the condition that external financing must not contain any public financial support laid down in the previous sentence is replaced by the requirement of a presence in the platform of at least 30% of private investment;

(b) *only costs that are eligible investment costs under Regulation (EU) 2021/1153 for the deployment of the infrastructure are eligible for aid;*

(c) *the project must be selected in compliance with Regulation (EU) 2021/1153 in one of the following ways:*

(i) *by an independent financial intermediary appointed by the Commission on the basis of commonly agreed investment guidelines;*

(ii) *by the Commission through a competitive bidding process based on clear, transparent and non-discriminatory criteria;*

(iii) *by independent experts appointed by the Commission;*

(d) *the project must enable connectivity capabilities going beyond the requirements relating to any existing legal obligations, such as those attached to a right to use spectrum;*

(e) *the project must ensure third party open wholesale access including unbundling under fair, reasonable and non-discriminatory conditions in accordance with Article 52(7) and (8) or Article 52a(8) and (9) as appropriate.*

4. The categories of eligible projects and the specific cumulative compatibility conditions applicable to them shall be the following:

(a) *investments in the deployment of a cross-border section of a 5G corridor along a transport corridor identified in the trans-European transport network guidelines as laid down in Regulation (EU) No 1315/2013 (TEN-T corridors) that meet the following specific cumulative conditions:*

(i) *the project consists of a cross-border section of a 5G corridor which crosses the border between two or more Member States, or crosses the border of at least one Member State and at least one European Economic Area country;*

(ii) *the total cross-border sections of 5G corridors located in a Member State shall not represent more than 15% of the total length of the 5G corridors along the trans-European transport core network in that Member State that are not covered by any existing legal obligations, such as those attached to a right to use spectrum. Exceptionally, if a Member State supports the deployment of cross-border 5G corridors along its trans-European transport comprehensive network, the total cross-border sections of 5G corridors located in that Member State shall not represent more than 15% of the total length of the 5G corridors along the trans-European transport comprehensive network in that Member State that are not covered by any existing legal obligations, such as those attached to a right to use spectrum;*

(iii) *the project ensures a significant new investment in the 5G mobile network suitable for connected and automated mobility services going beyond marginal investments related merely to the upgrade of the active elements of the network;*

(iv) *the project supports the deployment of new passive infrastructure only if existing passive infrastructure cannot be reused;*

(b) *investments in the deployment of a cross-border section of a pan-European terabit backbone network supporting the objectives of the European High-Performance Computing Joint Undertaking by interconnecting certain computing facilities, supercomputing facilities and data infrastructures that meet the following specific cumulative conditions:*

(i) *the project shall deploy or acquire connectivity assets, including Indefeasible Rights of Use, dark fibre or equipment, for building a cross-border section of a pan-European backbone network that supports the interconnection with unconstrained end to end connectivity of a minimum of 1 Tbps, of at least two computing facilities, supercomputing facilities or data infrastructures that: (1) are hosting entities of the European High Performance Computing Joint Undertaking established in accordance with Council Regulation (EU) 2018/1488,[1] or are research infrastructures and other computing and data infrastructures supporting research flagships and missions set out in Regulation (EU) 2021/695 of the European Parliament and of the Council[2] and Council Regulation (EC) No 723/2009 that contribute to the objectives of the European High-Performance Computing Joint Undertaking; and (2) are located in at least two Member States or at least one Member State and at least one member of the European Research Area;*

(ii) *the project ensures a significant new investment in the backbone network going beyond marginal investments, such as investments related to mere software upgrades or licensing;*

(iii) *the acquisition of connectivity assets is carried out through public procurement;*

(iv) *the project supports the deployment of new passive infrastructure only if existing passive infrastructure cannot be reused;*

(c) *investments in the deployment of a cross-border section of a backbone network interconnecting cloud infrastructures of certain socioeconomic drivers that meet the following specific cumulative conditions:*

(i) *the project interconnects cloud infrastructures of socioeconomic drivers that are public administrations or public or private entities entrusted with the operation of services of general interest or of services of general economic interest within the meaning of Article 106(2) of the Treaty;*

(ii) *the project consists of a cross-border section of the deployment of new cross-border backbone networks or a significant upgrade of existing ones that (1) crosses the border between two or more Member States; or (2) crosses the border between at least one Member State and at least one European Economic Area country;*

(iii) *the project covers at least two eligible socioeconomic drivers under point (i), each operating in a different Member State or in one Member State and one European Economic Area country;*

(iv) *the project ensures a significant new investment in the backbone network going beyond marginal investments, such as investments related to mere software upgrades or licensing. The project shall be able to reliably provide symmetric download and upload speeds of at least multiples of 10 Gbps;*

(v) *the project supports the deployment of new passive infrastructure only if existing passive infrastructure cannot be reused;*

(d) *investments in the deployment of a submarine cable network that meet the following specific cumulative conditions:*

(i) *the project consists of a cross-border section of a submarine cable network which (1) crosses the border between two or more Member States; or (2) crosses the border of at least one Member State and at least one European Economic Area country. Alternatively, the entity receiving aid shall only ensure the provision of wholesale services and the supported infrastructure shall improve the connectivity of European outermost regions, overseas territories, or island regions, even within a single Member State;*

(ii) *the project must not concern routes served already by at least two present or credibly planned backbone infrastructures;*

(iii) *the project ensures a significant new investment in the submarine cable network, by rolling-out a new submarine cable or connection to an existing submarine cable, addressing redundancy issues and going beyond marginal investments. The project shall be able to reliably provide symmetric download and upload speeds of at least 1 Gbps;*

(iv) *the project supports the deployment of new passive infrastructure only if existing passive infrastructure cannot be reused.]*

NOTES

Inserted by Commission Regulation 2021/1237/EU, Art 1(23), as from 1 August 2021.

Repeal of this Regulation in relation to the UK: this Regulation is repealed in relation to the UK (as from IP completion day); see the introductory notes to this Regulation *ante*.

[1] Council Regulation (EU) 2018/1488 of 28 September 2018 establishing the European High Performance Computing Joint Undertaking (OJ L252, 8.10.2018, p 1).

[2] Regulation (EU) 2021/695 of the European Parliament and of the Council of 28 April 2021 establishing Horizon Europe – the Framework Programme for Research and Innovation, laying down its rules for participation and dissemination, and repealing Regulations (EU) No 1290/2013 and (EU) No 1291/2013 (OJ L170, 12.5.2021, p 1).

[5.126]

[Article 52c Connectivity vouchers

1. Aid in the form of a connectivity voucher scheme for consumers in order to facilitate teleworking, online education, training services or for SMEs shall be compatible with the internal market pursuant to Article 107(3) of the Treaty and shall be exempted from the notification requirement of Article 108(3) of the Treaty, provided that the conditions laid down in this Article and in Chapter I are fulfilled.

2. The duration of a voucher scheme shall not exceed 24 months.

3. The following categories of voucher schemes shall be eligible:

(a) *voucher schemes available to consumers for subscribing to a new broadband internet access service or upgrading the current subscription to a service providing speeds of at least 30 Mbps download, provided that all providers of electronic communications services able to reliably provide speeds of at least 30 Mbps download are eligible under the vouchers scheme, whereas vouchers shall not be awarded for switching providers providing the same speeds or for upgrades of an existing subscription of at least 30 Mbps download;*

(b) *voucher schemes available to SMEs for subscribing to a new broadband internet access service or upgrading the current subscription to a service providing speeds of at least 100 Mbps download, provided that all providers able to reliably provide speeds of at least 100 Mbps download are eligible under the vouchers scheme, whereas vouchers shall not be awarded for switching providers providing the same speeds or upgrades of an existing subscription of at least 100 Mbs download.*

4. The vouchers shall cover up to 50% of the total set-up costs and monthly fee to subscribe to a broadband internet access service with the speeds specified in paragraph 3, whether on a stand-alone basis or as part of a bundle of services, which include at least the necessary terminal equipment (modem/router) for access to the internet with the speed specified in paragraph 3. The voucher shall be paid by the public authorities directly to the end-users or directly to the service provider chosen by the end-users, in which case the amount of the voucher shall be deducted from the end-users' invoice.

5. The vouchers shall be available to consumers or SMEs only in areas where there is at least one existing network able to reliably provide the speeds specified in paragraph 3, which shall be verified by mapping and public consultation. The mapping exercise and the public consultation shall identify the geographic target areas covered by at least one network able to reliably provide the speed specified in paragraph 3 for the duration of the vouchers scheme, the eligible providers present in the area and collect information to calculate their market share. The mapping shall be performed (i) for wireline-based fixed networks at address level on the basis of premises passed; and (ii) for fixed wireless access networks or mobile networks at address level on the basis of premises passed or on the basis of maximum 100 x100 metre grids. The mapping shall always be verified through a public consultation. The public consultation shall be carried out by the competent public authority through publication of the main characteristics of the planned measure and the list of geographic target areas identified in the mapping exercise on an appropriate website, including at national level. The public consultation shall invite interested parties to comment on the draft measure and to submit substantiated information regarding their existing networks able to reliably provide the speed specified in paragraph 3. The public consultation shall last at least 30 days.

6. The voucher scheme shall comply with the principle of technological neutrality, in the sense that the vouchers can be used for subscriptions to services of any operators able to reliably provide the speeds specified in paragraph 3 over an existing broadband network, irrespective of the technologies used. In order to facilitate the choice of the consumers or SMEs, the list of eligible providers for each of the geographic target areas shall be published on-line and every interested providers shall be able to apply for being included on the basis of open, transparent and non-discriminatory criteria.

7. In order to be eligible, in cases where the provider of the broadband internet access service is vertically integrated and has a retail market share above 25%, it must offer on the corresponding wholesale access market to any electronic communication services provider at least one wholesale access product able to ensure that the access-seeker will be able to reliably provide a retail service at the speed specified in paragraph 3, under open, transparent and non-discriminatory conditions. The wholesale access price shall be set on one of the following benchmarks: (i) the average published wholesale prices that prevail in other comparable, more competitive areas of the Member State or the Union; or (ii) in the absence of such published prices, the regulated prices already set or approved by the national regulatory authority for the markets and services concerned; or (iii) in the absence of such published or regulated prices, the pricing shall comply with the cost orientation and the methodology mandated in accordance with the sectorial regulatory framework. Without prejudice to the competences of the national regulatory authority under the regulatory framework, the national regulatory authority shall be consulted on the terms and conditions for access, including on prices, and on disputes related to the application of this Article.]

NOTES

Inserted by Commission Regulation 2021/1237/EU, Art 1(23), as from 1 August 2021.

Repeal of this Regulation in relation to the UK: this Regulation is repealed in relation to the UK (as from IP completion day); see the introductory notes to this Regulation *ante*.

SECTION 11 AID FOR CULTURE AND HERITAGE CONSERVATION

[5.127]

Article 53 Aid for culture and heritage conservation

1. Aid for culture and heritage conservation shall be compatible with the internal market within the meaning of Article 107(3) of the Treaty and shall be exempted from the notification requirement of Article 108(3) of the Treaty, provided the conditions laid down in this Article and in Chapter I are fulfilled.

2. The aid shall be granted for the following cultural purposes and activities:

[(a) museums, archives, libraries, artistic and cultural centres or spaces, theatres, cinemas, opera houses, concert halls, other live performance organisations, film heritage institutions and other similar artistic and cultural infrastructures, organisations and institutions;]

(b) tangible heritage including all forms of movable or immovable cultural heritage and archaeological sites, monuments, historical sites and buildings; natural heritage linked to cultural heritage or if formally recognized as cultural or natural heritage by the competent public authorities of a Member State;

(c) intangible heritage in any form, including folklorist customs and crafts;

(d) art or cultural events and performances, festivals, exhibitions and other similar cultural activities;

(e) cultural and artistic education activities as well as promotion of the understanding of the importance of protection and promotion of the diversity of cultural expressions through educational and greater public awareness programs, including with the use of new technologies;

(f) writing, editing, production, distribution, digitisation and publishing of music and literature, including translations.

3. The aid may take the form of:

(a) investment aid, including aid for the construction or upgrade of culture infrastructure;

(b) operating aid.

4. For investment aid, the eligible costs shall be the investment costs in tangible and intangible assets, including:

(a) costs for the construction, upgrade, acquisition, conservation or improvement of infrastructure, if at least 80% of either the time or the space capacity per year is used for cultural purposes;

(b) costs for the acquisition, including leasing, transfer of possession or physical relocation of cultural heritage;

(c) costs for safeguarding, preservation, restoration and rehabilitation of tangible and intangible cultural heritage, including extra costs for storage under appropriate conditions, special tools, materials and costs for documentation, research, digitalisation and publication;

(d) costs for improving the accessibility of cultural heritage to the public, including costs for digitisation and other new technologies, costs to improve accessibility for persons with special needs (in particular, ramps and lifts for disabled persons, braille indications and hands-on exhibits in museums) and for promoting cultural diversity with respect to presentations, programmes and visitors;

(e) costs for cultural projects and activities, cooperation and exchange programmes and grants including costs for selection procedures, costs for promotion and costs incurred directly as a result of the project;

5. For operating aid, the eligible costs shall be the following:

(a) the cultural institution's or heritage site's costs linked to continuous or periodic activities including exhibitions, performances and events and similar cultural activities that occur in the ordinary course of business;

(b) costs of cultural and artistic education activities as well as promotion of the understanding of the importance of protection and promotion of the diversity of cultural expressions through educational and greater public awareness programs, including with the use of new technologies;

(c) costs of the improvement of public access to the cultural institution or heritage sites and activities including costs of digitisation and of use of new technologies as well as costs of improving accessibility for persons with disabilities;

(d) operating costs directly relating to the cultural project or activity, such as rent or lease of real estate and cultural venues, travel expenses, materials and supplies directly related to the cultural project or activity,

architectural structures for exhibitions and stage sets, loan, lease and depreciation of tools, software and equipment, costs for access rights to copyright works and other related intellectual property rights protected contents, costs for promotion and costs incurred directly as a result of the project or activity; depreciation charges and the costs of financing are only eligible if they have not been covered by investment aid;

(e) costs for personnel working for the cultural institution or heritage site or for a project;

(f) costs for advisory and support services provided by outside consultants and service providers, incurred directly as a result of the project.

6. For investment aid, the aid amount shall not exceed the difference between the eligible costs and the operating profit of the investment The operating profit shall be deducted from the eligible costs ex ante, on the basis of reasonable projections, or through a claw-back mechanism. The operator of the infrastructure is allowed to keep a reasonable profit over the relevant period.

7. For operating aid, the aid amount shall not exceed what is necessary to cover the operating losses and a reasonable profit over the relevant period. This shall be ensured ex ante, on the basis of reasonable projections, or through a clawback mechanism.

[8. For aid not exceeding EUR 2 million, the maximum amount of aid may be set at 80% of eligible costs, as an alternative to application of the method referred to in paragraphs 6 and 7.]

9. [For the activities defined in paragraph 2(f), the maximum aid amount shall not exceed either the difference between the eligible costs and the project's discounted revenues or 70% of the eligible costs.] The revenues shall be deducted from the eligible costs ex ante or through a clawback mechanism. The eligible costs shall be the costs for publishing of music and literature, including the authors' fees (copyright costs), translators' fees, editors' fees, other editorial costs (proofreading, correcting, reviewing), layout and pre-press costs and printing or e-publication costs.

10. Aid to press and magazines, whether they are published in print or electronically, shall not be eligible under this Article.

NOTES

Para 2: point (a) substituted by Commission Regulation 2017/1084/EU, Art 1(17)(a).

Para 8: substituted by Commission Regulation 2017/1084/EU, Art 1(17)(b).

Para 9: words in square brackets substituted by Commission Regulation 2017/1084/EU, Art 1(17)(c).

Repeal of this Regulation in relation to the UK: this Regulation is repealed in relation to the UK (as from IP completion day); see the introductory notes to this Regulation *ante*.

[5.128]

Article 54 Aid schemes for audiovisual works

1. Aid schemes to support the script-writing, development, production, distribution and promotion of audiovisual works shall be compatible with the internal market pursuant to Article 107(3) of the Treaty and shall be exempted from the notification requirement of Article 108(3) of the Treaty, provided the conditions laid down in this Article and in Chapter I are fulfilled.

2. Aid shall support a cultural product. To avoid manifest errors in the qualification of a product as cultural, each Member State shall establish effective processes, such as selection of proposals by one or more persons entrusted with the selection or verification against a predetermined list of cultural criteria.

3. Aid may take the form of:

(a) aid to the production of audiovisual works;

(b) pre-production aid; and

(c) distribution aid.

4. Where a Member States makes the aid subject to territorial spending obligations, aid schemes for the production of audiovisual works may either:

(a) require that up to 160% of the aid granted to the production of a given audiovisual work is spent in the territory of the Member State granting the aid; or

(b) calculate the aid granted to the production of a given audiovisual work as a percentage of the expenditure on production activities in the granting Member State, typically in case of aid schemes in the form of tax incentives.

[In both cases, the maximum expenditure subject to territorial spending obligations shall in no case exceed 80% of the overall production budget.

For projects to be eligible for aid, a Member State may also require a minimum level of production activity in the territory concerned, but that level shall not exceed 50% of the overall production budget.]

5. The eligible costs shall be the following:

(a) for production aid: the overall costs of production of audiovisual works including costs to improve accessibility for persons with disabilities.

(b) for pre-production aid: the costs of script-writing and the development of audiovisual works.

(c) for distribution aid: the costs of distribution and promotion of audiovisual works.

6. The aid intensity for the production of audiovisual works shall not exceed 50% of the eligible costs.

7. The aid intensity may be increased as follows:

(a) to 60% of the eligible costs for cross-border productions funded by more than one Member State and involving producers from more than one Member State;

(b) to 100% of the eligible costs for difficult audiovisual works and co-productions involving countries from the Development Assistance Committee (DAC) List of the OECD.

8. The aid intensity for pre-production shall not exceed 100% of the eligible costs. If the resulting script or project is made into an audiovisual work such as a film, the pre-production costs shall be incorporated in the overall budget and taken into account when calculating the aid intensity. The aid intensity for distribution shall be the same as the aid intensity for production.

9. Aid shall not be reserved for specific production activities or individual parts of the production value chain. Aid for film studio infrastructures shall not be eligible under this Article.

10. Aid shall not be reserved exclusively for nationals and beneficiaries shall not be required to have the status of undertaking established under national commercial law.

NOTES

Para 4: words in square brackets substituted by Commission Regulation 2017/1084/EU, Art 1(18).

Repeal of this Regulation in relation to the UK: this Regulation is repealed in relation to the UK (as from IP completion day); see the introductory notes to this Regulation *ante*.

SECTION 12 AID FOR SPORT AND MULTIFUNCTIONAL RECREATIONAL INFRASTRUCTURES

[5.129]

Article 55 Aid for sport and multifunctional recreational infrastructures

1. Aid for sport and multifunctional recreational infrastructures shall be compatible with the internal market within the meaning of Article 107(3) of the Treaty and shall be exempted from the notification requirement of Article 108(3) of the Treaty, provided that the conditions laid down in this Article and in Chapter I are fulfilled.

2. Sport infrastructure shall not be used exclusively by a single professional sport user. Use of the sport infrastructure by other professional or non-professional sport users shall annually account for at least 20% of time capacity. If the infrastructure is used by several users simultaneously, corresponding fractions of time capacity usage shall be calculated.

3. Multifunctional recreational infrastructure shall consist of recreational facilities with a multi-functional character offering, in particular, cultural and recreational services with the exception of leisure parks and hotel facilities.

4. Access to the sport or multifunctional recreational infrastructures shall be open to several users and be granted on a transparent and non-discriminatory basis. Undertakings which have financed at least 30% of the investment costs of the infrastructure may be granted preferential access under more favourable conditions, provided those conditions are made publicly available.

5. If sport infrastructure is used by professional sport clubs, Member States shall ensure that the pricing conditions for its use are made publicly available.

6. Any concession or other entrustment to a third party to construct, upgrade and/or operate the sport or multifunctional recreational infrastructure shall be assigned on a open, transparent and non-discriminatory basis, having due regard to the applicable procurement rules.

7. The aid may take the form of:

(a) investment aid, including aid for the construction or upgrade of sport and multifunctional recreational infrastructure;

(b) operating aid for sport infrastructure;

8. For investment aid for sport and multifunctional recreational infrastructure the eligible costs shall be the investment costs in tangible and intangible assets.

9. For operating aid for sport infrastructure the eligible costs shall be the operating costs of the provision of services by the infrastructure. Those operating costs include costs such as personnel costs, materials, contracted services, communications, energy, maintenance, rent, administration, etc., but exclude depreciation charges and the costs of financing if these have been covered by investment aid.

10. For investment aid for sport and multifunctional recreational infrastructure, the aid amount shall not exceed the difference between the eligible costs and the operating profit of the investment. The operating profit shall be deducted from the eligible costs ex ante, on the basis of reasonable projections, or through a claw-back mechanism.

11. For operating aid for sport infrastructure, the aid amount shall not exceed the operating losses over the relevant period. This shall be ensured ex ante, on the basis of reasonable projections, or through a claw-back mechanism.

[12. For aid not exceeding EUR 2 million, the maximum amount of aid may be set at 80% of eligible costs, as an alternative to application of the method referred to in paragraphs 10 and 11.]

NOTES

Para 12: substituted by Commission Regulation 2017/1084/EU, Art 1(19).

Repeal of this Regulation in relation to the UK: this Regulation is repealed in relation to the UK (as from IP completion day); see the introductory notes to this Regulation *ante*.

SECTION 13 AID FOR LOCAL INFRASTRUCTURES

[5.130]

Article 56 Investment aid for local infrastructures

1. Financing for the construction or upgrade of local infrastructures which concerns infrastructure that contribute at a local level to improving the business and consumer environment and modernising and developing the industrial base shall be compatible with the internal market within the meaning of Article 107(3) of the Treaty and shall be exempt from the notification requirement of Article 108(3) of the Treaty, provided that the conditions laid down in this Article and in Chapter I are fulfilled.

2. This Article shall not apply to aid for infrastructures that is covered by other sections of Chapter III of this Regulation with the exception of Section 1 — Regional aid. This Article shall also not apply to airport infrastructure and port infrastructure.

3. The infrastructure shall be made available to interested users on an open, transparent and non-discriminatory basis. The price charged for the use or the sale of the infrastructure shall correspond to market price.

4. Any concession or other entrustment to a third party to operate the infrastructure shall be assigned on an open, transparent and non-discriminatory basis, having due regard to the applicable procurement rules.

5. The eligible costs shall be the investment costs in tangible and intangible assets.

6. The aid amount shall not exceed the difference between the eligible costs and the operating profit of the investment. The operating profit shall be deducted from the eligible costs ex ante, on the basis of reasonable projections, or through a claw-back mechanism.

7. Dedicated infrastructure shall not be exempted under this Article.

NOTES

Repeal of this Regulation in relation to the UK: this Regulation is repealed in relation to the UK (as from IP completion day); see the introductory notes to this Regulation *ante*.

[SECTION 14 AID FOR REGIONAL AIRPORTS

[5.131]

Article 56a Aid for regional airports

1. Investment aid to an airport shall be compatible with the internal market within the meaning of Article 107(3) of the Treaty and shall be exempted from the notification requirement of Article 108(3) of the Treaty, provided that the conditions laid down in paragraphs 3 to 14 of this Article and in Chapter II are fulfilled.

2. Operating aid to an airport shall be compatible with the internal market within the meaning of Article 107(3) of the Treaty and shall be exempted from the notification requirement of Article 108(3) of the Treaty, provided that the conditions laid down in paragraphs 3, 4, 10 and 15 to 18 of this Article and in Chapter II are fulfilled.

3. The airport shall be open to all potential users. In the case of physical limitation of capacity, the allocation shall take place on the basis of pertinent, objective, transparent and non-discriminatory criteria.

4. The aid shall not be granted for the relocation of existing airports or for the creation of a new passenger airport, including the conversion of an existing airfield into a passenger airport.

5. The investment concerned shall not exceed what is necessary to accommodate the medium-term expected traffic on the basis of reasonable traffic forecasts.

6. The investment aid shall not be granted to an airport located within 100 kilometres or 60 minutes travelling time by car, bus, train or high-speed train from an existing airport from which scheduled air services, within the meaning of Article 2(16) of Regulation (EC) No 1008/2008, are operated.

7. Paragraphs 5 and 6 shall not apply to airports with average annual passenger traffic of up to 200,000 passengers during the two financial years preceding the year in which aid is actually granted if the investment aid is not expected to result in the airport increasing its average annual passenger traffic to above 200,000 passengers within two financial years following the granting of the aid. Investment aid granted to such airports shall comply either with paragraph 11 or with paragraphs 13 and 14.

8. Paragraph 6 shall not apply where the investment aid is granted to an airport situated within 100 kilometres from existing airports from which scheduled air services, within the meaning of Article 2(16) of Regulation (EC) No 1008/2008, are operated, provided the route between each of these other existing airports and the airport receiving the aid necessarily involves either a total travelling time by maritime transportation of at least 90 minutes or air transportation.

9. The investment aid shall not be granted to airports with average annual passenger traffic of more than three million passengers during the two financial years preceding the year in which aid is actually granted. The investment aid shall not be expected to result in the airport increasing its average annual traffic to above three million passengers within two financial years following the granting of the aid.

10. The aid shall not be granted to airports with average annual freight traffic of more than 200,000 tonnes during the two financial years preceding the year in which aid is actually granted. The aid shall not be expected to result in the airport increasing its average annual freight traffic to above 200,000 tonnes within two financial years following the granting of the aid.

11. The investment aid amount shall not exceed the difference between the eligible costs and the operating profit of the investment. The operating profit shall be deducted from the eligible costs ex ante, on the basis of reasonable projections, or through a claw-back mechanism.

12. The eligible costs shall be the costs relating to the investments in airport infrastructure, including planning costs.

13. The investment aid amount shall not exceed:

(a) 50% of eligible costs for airports with an average annual passenger traffic of one to three million passengers during the two financial years preceding the year in which aid is actually granted;

(b) 75% of the eligible costs for airports with average annual passenger traffic of up to one million passengers during the two financial years preceding the year in which aid is actually granted.

14. The maximum aid intensities set out in paragraph 13 may be increased by 20 percentage points for airports located in remote regions.

15. Operating aid shall not be granted to airports with average annual passenger traffic of more than 200,000 passengers during the two financial years preceding the year in which aid is actually granted.

16. The amount of operating aid shall not exceed what is necessary to cover the operating losses and a reasonable profit over the relevant period. The aid shall be granted either in the form of periodic instalments fixed ex ante, which shall not be increased during the period for which the aid is granted, or in the form of amounts defined ex post based on the observed operating losses.

17. Operating aid shall not be paid out in respect of any calendar year during which the annual passenger traffic of the airport exceeds 200,000 passengers.

18. The granting of the operating aid shall not be made conditional upon the conclusion of arrangements with specific airlines relating to airport charges, marketing payments or other financial aspects of the airlines' operations at the airport concerned.]

NOTES

Inserted (together with Arts 56b, 56c and preceding section headings) by Commission Regulation 2017/1084/EU, Art 1(20).

Repeal of this Regulation in relation to the UK: this Regulation is repealed in relation to the UK (as from IP completion day); see the introductory notes to this Regulation *ante*.

[SECTION 15 AID FOR PORTS

[5.132]

Article 56b Aid for maritime ports

1. Aid for maritime ports shall be compatible with the internal market within the meaning of Article 107(3) of the Treaty and shall be exempted from the notification requirement of Article 108(3) of the Treaty, provided that the conditions laid down in this Article and in Chapter I are fulfilled.

2. The eligible costs shall be the costs, including planning costs, of:

(a) investments for the construction, replacement or upgrade of port infrastructures;

(b) investments for the construction, replacement or upgrade of access infrastructure;

(c) dredging.

3. Costs relating to non-transport related activities, including industrial production facilities active in a port, offices or shops, as well as for port superstructures shall not be eligible costs.

4. The aid amount shall not exceed the difference between the eligible costs and the operating profit of the investment or dredging. The operating profit shall be deducted from the eligible costs ex ante, on the basis of reasonable projections, or through a claw-back mechanism.

5. The aid intensity per investment referred to in point (a) of paragraph 2 shall not exceed

(a) 100% of the eligible costs where total eligible costs of the project are up to EUR 20 million;

(b) 80% of the eligible costs where total eligible costs of the project are above EUR 20 million and up to EUR 50 million;

(c) 60% of the eligible costs where total eligible costs of the project are above EUR 50 million and up to the amount laid down in point (ee) of Article 4(1).

The aid intensity shall not exceed 100% of the eligible costs determined in point (b) of paragraph 2 and point (c) of paragraph 2 up to the amount laid down in point (ee) of Article 4(1).

6. The aid intensities laid down in points (b) and (c) of the first subparagraph of paragraph 5 may be increased by 10 percentage points for investments located in assisted areas fulfilling the conditions of point (a) of Article 107(3) of the Treaty and by 5 percentage points for investments located in assisted areas fulfilling the conditions of point (c) of Article 107(3) of the Treaty.

7. Any concession or other entrustment to a third party to construct, upgrade, operate or rent aided port infrastructure shall be assigned on a competitive, transparent, non-discriminatory and unconditional basis.

8. The aided port infrastructure shall be made available to interested users on an equal and non-discriminatory basis on market terms.

9. For aid not exceeding EUR 5 million, the maximum amount of aid may be set at 80% of eligible costs, as an alternative to application of the method referred to in paragraphs 4, 5 and 6.]

NOTES

Inserted as noted to Art 56a at **[5.131]**.

Repeal of this Regulation in relation to the UK: this Regulation is repealed in relation to the UK (as from IP completion day); see the introductory notes to this Regulation *ante*.

[5.133]

[Article 56c Aid for inland ports

1. Aid for inland ports shall be compatible with the internal market within the meaning of Article 107(3) of the Treaty and shall be exempted from the notification requirement of Article 108(3) of the Treaty, provided that the conditions laid down in this Article and in Chapter II are fulfilled.

2. The eligible costs shall be the costs, including planning costs, of:

(a) investments for the construction, replacement or upgrade of port infrastructures;

(b) investments for the construction, replacement or upgrade of access infrastructure;

(c) dredging.

3. Costs relating to non-transport related activities, including industrial production facilities active in a port, offices or shops, as well as for port superstructures shall not be eligible costs.

4. The aid amount shall not exceed the difference between the eligible costs and the operating profit of the investment or dredging. The operating profit shall be deducted from the eligible costs ex ante, on the basis of reasonable projections, or through a claw-back mechanism.

5. The maximum aid intensity shall not exceed 100% of the eligible costs up to the amount laid down in point (ff) of Article 4(1).

6. Any concession or other entrustment to a third party to construct, upgrade, operate or rent aided port infrastructure shall be assigned on a competitive, transparent, non-discriminatory and unconditional basis.

7. The aided port infrastructure shall be made available to interested users on an equal and non-discriminatory basis on market terms.

8. For aid not exceeding EUR 2 million, the maximum amount of aid may be set at 80% of eligible costs, as an alternative to application of the method referred to in paragraphs 4 and 5.]

NOTES

Inserted as noted to Art 56a at **[5.131]**.

Repeal of this Regulation in relation to the UK: this Regulation is repealed in relation to the UK (as from IP completion day); see the introductory notes to this Regulation *ante*.

[SECTION 16 AID INVOLVED IN FINANCIAL PRODUCTS SUPPORTED BY THE INVESTEU FUND

[5.134]

Article 56d Scope and common conditions

1. This Section shall apply to aid involved in financial products supported by the InvestEU Fund that provide aid to implementing partners, financial intermediaries or final beneficiaries.

2. The aid shall be compatible with the internal market within the meaning of Article 107(3) of the Treaty and shall be exempted from the notification requirement of Article 108(3) of the Treaty, provided that the conditions laid down in Chapter I, this Article, and either Article 56e or Article 56f are fulfilled.

3. The aid shall comply with all applicable conditions laid down in Regulation (EU) 2021/523 and the InvestEU Investment Guidelines laid down in the Annex to Commission Delegated Regulation (EU) 2021/1078.[1]

4. The maximum thresholds laid down in Articles 56e and 56f shall apply to the total outstanding financing, in so far as that financing provided under any financial product supported by the InvestEU Fund contains aid. The maximum thresholds shall apply:

- *(a) per project in the case of aid covered by Article 56e(2) and (4), Article 56e(5), point (a)(i), Article 56e(6) and (7), Article 56e(8), points (a) and (b), and Article 56e(9);*
- *(b) per final beneficiary in the case of aid covered by Article 56e(5), points (a)(ii) and (iii), Article 56e(8), point (d), Article 56e(10) and Article 56f.*

5. Aid shall not be granted in the form of refinancing of or guarantees on existing portfolios of financial intermediaries.]

NOTES

Section 16 (Articles 56d–56f) inserted by Commission Regulation 2021/1237/EU, Art 1(24), as from 1 August 2021.

Repeal of this Regulation in relation to the UK: this Regulation is repealed in relation to the UK (as from IP completion day); see the introductory notes to this Regulation *ante*.

[1] Commission Delegated Regulation (EU) 2021/1078 of 14 April 2021 supplementing Regulation (EU) 2021/523 of the European Parliament and of the Council by setting out the investment guidelines for the InvestEU Fund (OJ L234, 2.7.2021, p 18).

[5.135]

[Article 56e Conditions for aid involved in financial products supported by the InvestEU Fund

1. Aid to the final beneficiary under a financial product supported by the InvestEU Fund shall:

- *(a) comply with the conditions set out in one of paragraphs 2 to 9; and*
- *(b) where the financing is provided in the form of loans to the final beneficiary, have an interest rate that corresponds at least to the base rate of the reference rate applicable at the time of the granting of the loan.*

2. Aid for projects of common interest in the area of trans-European digital connectivity infrastructure financed under Regulation (EU) 2021/1153 or awarded a Seal of Excellence quality label under that Regulation shall only be granted to projects fulfilling all general and specific compatibility conditions laid down in Article 52b. The nominal amount of total financing provided to any final beneficiary per project under the support of the InvestEU Fund shall not exceed EUR 150 million.

3. Aid for investments in fixed broadband networks to connect only certain eligible socioeconomic drivers shall comply with the following conditions:

- *(a) aid shall only be granted to projects fulfilling all compatibility conditions laid down in Article 52 unless indicated otherwise in points (c) and (d) of this paragraph;*
- *(b) the nominal amount of total financing provided to any final beneficiary per project under the support of the InvestEU Fund shall not exceed EUR 150 million;*
- *(c) the project connects only socioeconomic drivers that are public administrations or public or private entities entrusted with the operation of services of general interest or of services of general economic interest within the meaning of Article 106(2) of the Treaty. Projects including elements or entities other than those specified under this point are excluded;*
- *(d) by way of derogation from Article 52(4), the identified market failure must be verified either by available appropriate mapping or, when such mapping is not available, by a public consultation, as follows:*
  - *(i) the mapping can be considered appropriate if it is not older than 18 months and includes all networks able to reliably provide speeds of at least 100 Mbps download but below 300 Mbps download (threshold speeds) that pass the premises of an eligible socioeconomic driver identified in point (c). This mapping must be carried out by the competent public authority, must take into account all networks able to reliably provide the threshold speeds present or credibly planned in the next three years or within the same time horizon as the planned supported intervention, which cannot be shorter than two years, and must be performed (i) for purely fixed networks at address level on the basis of premises passed; and (ii) for fixed wireless access networks at address level on the basis of premises passed or on the basis of maximum 100 x100 metre grids;*
  - *(ii) the public consultation must be carried out by the competent public authority through publication on an appropriate website inviting interested parties to comment on the draft measure and to submit substantiated information regarding networks able to reliably provide speeds of at least 100 Mbps download but below 300 Mbps download (threshold speeds) present or credibly planned in the next three years or within the same time horizon as the planned supported intervention, which cannot be shorter than two years, that pass the premises of an eligible socioeconomic driver as referred to in point (c), based on information: (i) for purely fixed networks, at address level on the basis of premises passed; and (ii) for fixed wireless access networks, at address level on the basis of premises passed or on the basis of maximum 100 x100 metre grids. The public consultation shall last at least 30 days.*

4. Aid for energy generation and energy infrastructure shall comply with the following conditions:

- *(a) aid shall only be granted for investments in energy infrastructure in gas and electricity not exempted from third party access, tariff regulation and unbundling, based on the internal energy market legislation for the following categories of projects:*
  - *(i) as regards gas infrastructure, projects included in the prevailing Union list of Projects of Common Interest in Annex VII to Regulation (EU) No 347/2013 of the European Parliament and of the Council;*[1]
  - *(ii) as regards electricity infrastructure:*

(1) smart grids, including investments in the development, smartening and modernisation of electricity transmission and distribution infrastructure;

(2) other projects:

— which fulfil any of the criteria laid down in Article 4(1)(c) of Regulation (EU) No 347/2013, or

— which are included in the prevailing Union list of Projects of Common Interest in Annex VII to Regulation (EU) No 347/2013;

(3) other projects, with the exclusion of electricity storage, in assisted areas;

(iii) electricity storage projects, based on new and innovative technology, irrespective of the voltage level of the connection to the network;

(b) investment aid for generation of energy from renewable energy sources shall comply with the following requirements:

(i) aid shall only be granted for new installations selected on a competitive, transparent, objective and non-discriminatory basis;

(ii) aid may be granted to new installations also in combination with storage equipment or hydrogen electrolysers, provided that both the electricity or hydrogen storage equipment and the hydrogen electrolysers only use the energy generated by renewable energy installation(s);

(iii) aid shall not be granted for hydropower installations that do not comply with the conditions laid down in Directive 2000/60/EC;

(iv) in case of installations producing biofuels, aid shall only be granted for installations producing sustainable biofuels other than food based biofuels.

(c) The nominal amount of total financing provided to any final beneficiary per project referred to in point (a) under the support of the InvestEU Fund shall not exceed EUR 150 million. The nominal amount of total financing provided to any final beneficiary per project referred to in point (b) under the support of the InvestEU Fund shall not exceed EUR 75 million.

5. Aid for social, educational, cultural and natural heritage infrastructure and activities shall comply with the following conditions:

(a) the nominal amount of total financing provided to any final beneficiary under the support of the InvestEU Fund shall not exceed:

(i) EUR 100 million per project for investments in infrastructure used for the provision of social services and for education; EUR 150 million per project for cultural and heritage conservation purposes and activities set out in Article 53(2), including natural heritage;

(ii) EUR 30 million for activities related to social services;

(iii) EUR 75 million for activities related to culture and heritage conservation; and

(iv) EUR 5 million for education and training.

(b) aid shall not be granted for training aimed at complying with mandatory national training requirements.

6. Aid for transport and transport infrastructures shall comply with the following conditions:

(a) aid for infrastructure, except ports, shall be provided only to the following projects:

(i) projects of common interest as defined in Article 3, point (a), of Regulation (EU) No 1315/2013, except for projects concerning port or airport infrastructure;

(ii) connections to Trans-European transport network urban nodes;

(iii) rolling stock only for the provision of rail transport services not covered by a public service contract within the meaning of Regulation (EC) No 1370/2007 of the European Parliament and of the Council,[2] provided the beneficiary is a new entrant;

(iv) urban transport;

(v) recharging or refuelling infrastructure that supplies vehicles with electricity or renewable hydrogen;

(b) aid for port infrastructure projects shall comply with the following requirements:

(i) aid may only be provided for investments in access infrastructure and port infrastructure that are made available to interested users on an equal and non-discriminatory basis on market terms;

(ii) any concession or other entrustment to a third party to construct, upgrade, operate or rent aided port infrastructure shall be assigned on a competitive, transparent, non-discriminatory and unconditional basis;

(iii) aid shall not be granted for investments in port superstructures.

(c) the nominal amount of total financing provided under point (a) or (b) to any final beneficiary per project under the support of the InvestEU Fund shall not exceed EUR 150 million.

7. Aid for other infrastructures shall comply with the following conditions:

(a) aid shall be provided only to the following projects:

(i) investment in water supply and waste water infrastructure for the general public;

(ii) investment in waste recycling and preparation for re-use in line with Article 47(1) to (6), insofar as it is aimed at managing waste generated by other undertakings;

(iii) investment in research infrastructure;

(iv) investment in the construction or upgrade of innovation cluster facilities;

(b) the nominal amount of total financing provided to any final beneficiary per project under the support of the InvestEU Fund shall not exceed EUR 100 million.

8. Aid for environmental protection, including climate protection, shall comply with the following conditions:

(a) aid shall be provided only to the following projects:

(i) investments enabling undertakings to remedy or prevent damage to physical surroundings (including climate change) or natural resources by a beneficiary's own activities, insofar as the investment goes beyond Union standards for environmental protection or increases the level of environmental protection in the absence of Union standards or constitutes an early adaptation to future Union standards for environmental protection;

(ii) measures improving the energy efficiency of an undertaking, insofar as the energy efficiency improvements are not undertaken to ensure that the undertaking complies with Union standards already adopted, even if they are not yet in force;

(iii) remediation of contaminated sites, insofar as no legal or physical person liable for the environmental damage under the applicable law is identified in line with the "polluter pays" principle as referred to in Article 45(3);

(iv) environmental studies;

(v) enhancement and restoration of biodiversity and ecosystems where that activity contributes to protecting, conserving or restoring biodiversity and to achieving the good condition of ecosystems, or to protecting ecosystems that are already in good condition;

(b) without prejudice to point (a), where the aid measure relates to the improvement of the energy efficiency of (1) residential buildings; (2) buildings dedicated to the provision of education or social services or to activities related to justice, police or fire-fighting services; (3) buildings dedicated to activities related to public administration; or (4) buildings referred to in (1), (2) or (3) and in which activities other than those mentioned in (1), (2) or (3) occupy less than 35% of the internal floor area, aid may also be granted for measures that simultaneously improve the energy efficiency of those buildings and integrate any or all of the following investments:

(i) integrated installations generating renewable energy on-site of the building concerned by the energy efficiency aid measure. The integrated on-site renewable energy installation relates to production of electricity and/or heat. It may be combined with equipment for the storage of the renewable energy generated on-site;

(ii) on-site storage installations;

(iii) equipment and related infrastructure incorporated to the building for the recharging of electric vehicles of the building's users;

(iv) investments for the digitalisation of the building, in particular to increase its smart readiness. The investments for the digitalisation of the building may include interventions limited to passive in-house wiring or structured cabling for data networks and, if necessary, the ancillary part of the passive network on the private property outside the building. Wiring or cabling for data networks outside the private property is excluded;

The final beneficiary of the aid may be either building owner(s) or tenant(s), depending on who obtains the financing for the project;

(c) the nominal amount of total financing provided to any final beneficiary per project referred to in point (a) under the support of the InvestEU Fund shall not exceed EUR 50 million;

(d) the nominal amount of total financing provided per project referred to in point (b) under the support of the InvestEU Fund shall not exceed EUR 50 million per final beneficiary and building;

(e) aid for measures that improve the energy efficiency of buildings referred to in point (b) may also relate to the facilitation of energy performance contracts subject to the following conditions:

(i) the support takes the form of a loan or guarantee to the provider of the energy efficiency improvement measures under an energy performance contract, or consists in a financial product aimed to refinance the respective provider (e.g. factoring, forfeiting);

(ii) the nominal amount of total financing provided under the support of the InvestEU Fund does not exceed EUR 30 million;

(iii) the support is provided to SMEs or small mid-caps;

(iv) the support is provided for energy performance contracting within the meaning of Article 2(27) of Directive 2012/27/EU;

(v) the energy performance contracting relates to a building referred to in paragraph 8, point (b).

9. Aid for research, development, innovation and digitalisation shall comply with the following conditions:

(a) aid may be granted for:

(i) fundamental research;

(ii) industrial research;

(iii) experimental development;

(iv) process innovation or organisational innovation for SMEs;

(v) innovation advisory services and innovation support services for SMEs;

(vi) digitalisation for SMEs;

(b) for projects falling under points (a) (i), (ii) and (iii), the nominal amount of total financing provided to any final beneficiary per project under the support of the InvestEU Fund shall not exceed EUR 75 million. For projects falling under point (a) (iv), (v) and (vi), the nominal amount of total financing provided to any final beneficiary per project under the support of the InvestEU Fund shall not exceed EUR 30 million.

10. SMEs or, where applicable, small mid-caps may, in addition to the categories of aid provided for in paragraphs 2 to 9, also receive aid in the form of financing supported by the InvestEU Fund provided that one of the following conditions are fulfilled:

(a) the nominal amount of total financing provided per final beneficiary under the support of the InvestEU Fund does not exceed EUR 15 million and is provided to:

(i) unlisted SMEs that have not yet been operating in any market or have been operating for less than 7 years following their first commercial sale;

(ii) unlisted SMEs entering a new product or geographical market, where the initial investment for entering into a new product or geographical market must be higher than 50% of the average annual turnover in the preceding 5 years;

(iii) SMEs and small mid-caps that are innovative enterprises as defined in Article 2, point (80);

(b) *the nominal amount of total financing provided per final beneficiary under the support of the InvestEU Fund does not exceed EUR 15 million and is provided to SMEs or small mid-caps whose principal activities are located in assisted areas provided that the financing is not used for relocation of activities as defined in Article 2, point (61a);*

(c) *the nominal amount of total financing provided per final beneficiary under the support of the InvestEU Fund does not exceed EUR 2 million and is provided to SMEs or small mid-caps.]*

NOTES

Section 16 (Articles 56d–56f) inserted by Commission Regulation 2021/1237/EU, Art 1(24), as from 1 August 2021.

Repeal of this Regulation in relation to the UK: this Regulation is repealed in relation to the UK (as from IP completion day); see the introductory notes to this Regulation *ante*.

1 Regulation (EU) No 347/2013 of the European Parliament and of the Council of 17 April 2013 on guidelines for trans-European energy infrastructure and repealing Decision No 1364/2006/EC and amending Regulations (EC) No 713/2009, (EC) No 714/2009 and (EC) No 715/2009 (OJ L115, 25.4.2013, p 39).

2 Regulation (EC) No 1370/2007 of the European Parliament and of the Council of 23 October 2007 on public passenger transport services by rail and by road and repealing Council Regulations (EEC) No 1191/69 and (EEC) No 1107/70 (OJ L315, 3.12.2007, p 1).

[5.136]

[Article 56f Conditions for aid involved in intermediated commercially-driven financial products supported by the InvestEU Fund

1. Financing to the final beneficiaries shall be provided by commercial financial intermediaries which shall be selected in an open, transparent and non-discriminatory way based on objective criteria.

2. The commercial financial intermediary that provides financing to the final beneficiary shall retain a minimum risk exposure of 20% of each financing transaction.

3. The nominal amount of total financing provided to each final beneficiary through the commercial financial intermediary shall not exceed EUR 7,5 million.]

NOTES

Section 16 (Articles 56d–56f) inserted by Commission Regulation 2021/1237/EU, Art 1(24), as from 1 August 2021.

Repeal of this Regulation in relation to the UK: this Regulation is repealed in relation to the UK (as from IP completion day); see the introductory notes to this Regulation *ante*.

CHAPTER IV FINAL PROVISIONS

[5.137]

Article 57 Repeal

Regulation (EC) No 800/2008 shall be repealed.

NOTES

Repeal of this Regulation in relation to the UK: this Regulation is repealed in relation to the UK (as from IP completion day); see the introductory notes to this Regulation *ante*.

[5.138]

Article 58 Transitional provisions

[1. This Regulation shall apply to individual aid granted before the respective provisions of this Regulation have entered into force where the aid fulfils all the conditions laid down in this Regulation, with the exception of Article 9.]

2. Any aid not exempted from the notification requirement of Article 108(3) of the Treaty by virtue of this Regulation or other regulations adopted pursuant to Article 1 of Regulation (EC) No 994/98 previously in force shall be assessed by the Commission in accordance with the relevant frameworks, guidelines, communications and notices.

3. Any individual aid granted before 1 January 2015 by virtue of any regulation adopted pursuant to Article 1 of Regulation (EC) No 994/98 in force at the time of granting the aid shall be compatible with the internal market and exempted from the notification requirement of Article 108(3) of the Treaty with the exclusion of regional aid. Risk capital aid schemes in favour of SMEs set up before 1 July 2014 and exempted from the notification requirement of Article 108(3) of the Treaty under Regulation (EC) No 800/2008, shall remain exempted and compatible with the internal market until the termination of the funding agreement, provided the commitment of the public funding into the supported private equity investment fund, on the basis of such agreement, was made before 1 January 2015 and the other conditions for exemption remain fulfilled.

[3a. Any individual aid granted between 1 July 2014and 2 August 2021in accordance with the provisions of this Regulation as applicable at the time of granting the aid shall be compatible with the internal market and exempted from the notification requirement of Article 108(3) of the Treaty. Any individual aid granted before 1 July 2014in accordance with the provisions of this Regulation, with the exception of Article 9, as applicable either before or after 10 July 2017, or before or after 3 August 2021, shall be compatible with the internal market and exempted from the notification requirement of Article 108(3) of the Treaty.]

4. At the end of the period of validity of this Regulation, any aid schemes exempted under this Regulation shall remain exempted during an adjustment period of six months, with the exception of regional aid schemes. The exemption of regional aid schemes shall expire on the date of expiry of the approved regional aid maps. The exemption of risk finance aid exempted pursuant to Article 21(2)(a) shall expire at the end of the period foreseen in the funding agreement, provided the commitment of public funding to the supported private equity investment fund was made on the basis of such agreement within 6 months from the end of the period of validity of this Regulation and all other conditions for exemption remain fulfilled.

[5. If this Regulation is amended, any aid scheme exempted under this Regulation as applicable at the time of the entry into force of the scheme shall remain exempted during an adjustment period of six months.]

NOTES

Para 1: substituted by Commission Regulation 2017/1084/EU, Art 1(21)(a).

Para 3a: originally inserted by Commission Regulation 2017/1084/EU, Art 1(21)(b). Subsequently substituted by Commission Regulation 2021/1237/EU, Art 1(25), as from 1 August 2021.

Para 5: added by Commission Regulation 2017/1084/EU, Art 1(21)(c).

Repeal of this Regulation in relation to the UK: this Regulation is repealed in relation to the UK (as from IP completion day); see the introductory notes to this Regulation *ante*.

[5.139]

Article 59

This Regulation shall enter into force on 1 July 2014.

[It shall apply until 31 December 2023.]

This Regulation shall be binding in its entirety and directly applicable in all Member States.

NOTES

Words in square brackets substituted by Commission Regulation 2020/972/EU, Art 2(5).

Repeal of this Regulation in relation to the UK: this Regulation is repealed in relation to the UK (as from IP completion day); see the introductory notes to this Regulation *ante*.

ANNEXES

ANNEX I
SME DEFINITION

[5.140]

Article 1 Enterprise

An enterprise is considered to be any entity engaged in an economic activity, irrespective of its legal form. This includes, in particular, self-employed persons and family businesses engaged in craft or other activities, and partnerships or associations regularly engaged in an economic activity.

Article 2 Staff headcount and financial thresholds determining enterprise categories

1. The category of micro, small and medium-sized enterprises ('SMEs') is made up of enterprises which employ fewer than 250 persons and which have an annual turnover not exceeding EUR 50 million, and/or an annual balance sheet total not exceeding EUR 43 million.

2. Within the SME category, a small enterprise is defined as an enterprise which employs fewer than 50 persons and whose annual turnover and/or annual balance sheet total does not exceed EUR 10 million.

3. Within the SME category, a micro-enterprise is defined as an enterprise which employs fewer than 10 persons and whose annual turnover and/or annual balance sheet total does not exceed EUR 2 million.

Article 3 Types of enterprise taken into consideration in calculating staff numbers and financial amounts

1. An 'autonomous enterprise' is any enterprise which is not classified as a partner enterprise within the meaning of paragraph 2 or as a linked enterprise within the meaning of paragraph 3.

2. 'Partner enterprises' are all enterprises which are not classified as linked enterprises within the meaning of paragraph 3 and between which there is the following relationship: an enterprise (upstream enterprise) holds, either solely or jointly with one or more linked enterprises within the meaning of paragraph 3, 25% or more of the capital or voting rights of another enterprise (downstream enterprise).

However, an enterprise may be ranked as autonomous, and thus as not having any partner enterprises, even if this 25% threshold is reached or exceeded by the following investors, provided that those investors are not linked, within the meaning of paragraph 3, either individually or jointly to the enterprise in question:

(a) public investment corporations, venture capital companies, individuals or groups of individuals with a regular venture capital investment activity who invest equity capital in unquoted businesses (business angels), provided the total investment of those business angels in the same enterprise is less than EUR 1,250,000;

(b) universities or non-profit research centres;

(c) institutional investors, including regional development funds;

(d) autonomous local authorities with an annual budget of less than EUR 10 million and less than 5,000 inhabitants.

3. 'Linked enterprises' are enterprises which have any of the following relationships with each other:

(a) an enterprise has a majority of the shareholders' or members' voting rights in another enterprise;

(b) an enterprise has the right to appoint or remove a majority of the members of the administrative, management or supervisory body of another enterprise;

(c) an enterprise has the right to exercise a dominant influence over another enterprise pursuant to a contract entered into with that enterprise or to a provision in its memorandum or articles of association;

(d) an enterprise, which is a shareholder in or member of another enterprise, controls alone, pursuant to an agreement with other shareholders in or members of that enterprise, a majority of shareholders' or members' voting rights in that enterprise.

There is a presumption that no dominant influence exists if the investors listed in the second subparagraph of paragraph 2 are not involving themselves directly or indirectly in the management of the enterprise in question, without prejudice to their rights as shareholders.

Enterprises having any of the relationships described in the first subparagraph through one or more other enterprises, or any one of the investors mentioned in paragraph 2, are also considered to be linked.

Enterprises which have one or other of such relationships through a natural person or group of natural persons acting jointly are also considered linked enterprises if they engage in their activity or in part of their activity in the same relevant market or in adjacent markets.

An 'adjacent market' is considered to be the market for a product or service situated directly upstream or downstream of the relevant market.

4. Except in the cases set out in paragraph 2, second subparagraph, an enterprise cannot be considered an SME if 25% or more of the capital or voting rights are directly or indirectly controlled, jointly or individually, by one or more public bodies.

5. Enterprises may make a declaration of status as an autonomous enterprise, partner enterprise or linked enterprise, including the data regarding the thresholds set out in Article 2. The declaration may be made even if the capital is spread in such a way that it is not possible to determine exactly by whom it is held, in which case the enterprise may declare in good faith that it can legitimately presume that it is not owned as to 25% or more by one enterprise or jointly by enterprises linked to one another. Such declarations are made without prejudice to the checks and investigations provided for by national or Union rules.

Article 4 Data used for the staff headcount and the financial amounts and reference period

1. The data to apply to the headcount of staff and the financial amounts are those relating to the latest approved accounting period and calculated on an annual basis. They are taken into account from the date of closure of the accounts. The amount selected for the turnover is calculated excluding value added tax (VAT) and other indirect taxes.

2. Where, at the date of closure of the accounts, an enterprise finds that, on an annual basis, it has exceeded or fallen below the headcount or financial thresholds stated in Article 2, this will not result in the loss or acquisition of the status of medium-sized, small or micro-enterprise unless those thresholds are exceeded over two consecutive accounting periods.

3. In the case of newly-established enterprises whose accounts have not yet been approved, the data to apply is to be derived from a bona fide estimate made in the course of the financial year.

Article 5 Staff headcount

The headcount corresponds to the number of annual work units (AWU), i.e. the number of persons who worked full-time within the enterprise in question or on its behalf during the entire reference year under consideration. The work of persons who have not worked the full year, the work of those who have worked part-time, regardless of duration, and the work of seasonal workers are counted as fractions of AWU. The staff consists of:

- *(a) employees;*
- *(b) persons working for the enterprise being subordinated to it and deemed to be employees under national law;*
- *(c) owner-managers;*
- *(d) partners engaging in a regular activity in the enterprise and benefiting from financial advantages from the enterprise.*

Apprentices or students engaged in vocational training with an apprenticeship or vocational training contract are not included as staff. The duration of maternity or parental leaves is not counted.

Article 6 Establishing the data of an enterprise

1. In the case of an autonomous enterprise, the data, including the number of staff, are determined exclusively on the basis of the accounts of that enterprise.

2. The data, including the headcount, of an enterprise having partner enterprises or linked enterprises are determined on the basis of the accounts and other data of the enterprise or, where they exist, the consolidated accounts of the enterprise, or the consolidated accounts in which the enterprise is included through consolidation.

To the data referred to in the first subparagraph are added the data of any partner enterprise of the enterprise in question situated immediately upstream or downstream from it. Aggregation is proportional to the percentage interest in the capital or voting rights (whichever is greater). In the case of cross-holdings, the greater percentage applies.

To the data referred to in the first and second subparagraph are added 100% of the data of any enterprise, which is linked directly or indirectly to the enterprise in question, where the data were not already included through consolidation in the accounts.

3. For the application of paragraph 2, the data of the partner enterprises of the enterprise in question are derived from their accounts and their other data, consolidated if they exist. To these are added 100% of the data of enterprises which are linked to these partner enterprises, unless their accounts data are already included through consolidation.

For the application of the same paragraph 2, the data of the enterprises which are linked to the enterprise in question are to be derived from their accounts and their other data, consolidated if they exist. To these are added, pro rata, the data of any possible partner enterprise of that linked enterprise, situated immediately upstream or downstream from it, unless it has already been included in the consolidated accounts with a percentage at least proportional to the percentage identified under the second subparagraph of paragraph 2.

4. Where in the consolidated accounts no staff data appear for a given enterprise, staff figures are calculated by aggregating proportionally the data from its partner enterprises and by adding the data from the enterprises to which the enterprise in question is linked.

NOTES

Repeal of this Regulation in relation to the UK: this Regulation is repealed in relation to the UK (as from IP completion day); see the introductory notes to this Regulation *ante*.

ANNEX II
INFORMATION REGARDING STATE AID EXEMPT UNDER THE CONDITIONS OF THIS REGULATION

PART I TO BE PROVIDED THROUGH THE ESTABLISHED COMMISSION IT APPLICATION AS LAID DOWN IN ARTICLE 11

[5.141]

Aid reference	*(to be completed by the Commission)*	
Member State	. . . .	
Member State reference number	. . . .	
Region	***Name of the Region(s) (NUTS[1])***	***Regional aid status[2]***
	. . . .	. . . .
Granting authority	*Name*	. . . .
	Postal address	. . . .
	Web address	. . . .
Title of the aid measure	. . . .	
National legal basis (Reference to the relevant national official publication)	. . . .	
Web link to the full text of the aid measure	. . . .	
Type of measure	☐ ***Scheme***	
	☐ ***Ad hoc aid***	***Name of the beneficiary and the group[3] it belongs to***
		. . . .
Amendment of an existing aid scheme or ad hoc aid		***Commission aid reference***
	☐ ***Prolongation***	. . . .
	☐ ***Modification***	. . . .
Duration[4]	☐ ***Scheme***	*dd/mm/yyyy to dd/mm/yyyy*
Date of granting[5]	☐ ***Ad hoc aid***	*dd/mm/yyyy*
Economic sector(s) concerned	☐ ***All economic sectors eligible to receive aid***	
	☐ ***Limited to certain sectors: Please specify at NACE group level[6]***	
		. . . .
Type of beneficiary	☐ ***SME***	
	☐ ***Large undertakings***	
Budget	***Total annual amount of the budget planned under the scheme[7]***	***National currency*** . . . . ***(full amounts)***
	Overall amount of the ad hoc aid awarded to the undertaking[8]	***National currency (full amounts)***
		. . . .
	☐ ***For guarantees[9]***	***National currency (full amounts)*** . . . .
Aid instrument	☐ ***Grant/Interest rate subsidy***	
	☐ ***Loan/Repayable advances***	
	☐ ***Guarantee (where appropriate with a reference to the Commission decision[10])***	
	☐ ***Tax advantage or tax exemption***	
	☐ ***Provision of risk finance***	
	☐ ***Other (please specify)***	
	. . . .	
	Indicate to which broad category below it would fit best in terms of its effect/function:	

	☐ **Grant** ☐ **Loan** ☐ **Guarantee** ☐ **Tax advantage** ☐ **Provision of risk finance**		
☐ ***If co-financed by EU fund(s)***	***Name of EU fund(s):***	***Amount of funding (as per EU fund)***	***National currency . . . . (full amounts)*** . . . .

NOTES

1 NUTS — Nomenclature of Territorial Units for Statistics. Typically, the region is specified at level 2.

2 Article 107(3)(a) TFEU (status 'A'), Article 107(3)(c) TFEU (status 'C'), unassisted areas i.e. areas not eligible for regional aid (status 'N').

3 An undertaking for the purposes of rules on competition laid down in the Treaty and for the purposes of this Regulation is any entity engaged in an economic activity, regardless of its legal status and the way in which it is financed. The Court of Justice has ruled that entities which are controlled (on a legal or on a de facto basis) by the same entity should be considered as one undertaking.

4 Period during which the granting authority can commit itself to grant the aid.

5 Determined in line with Article 2, point 27 of the Regulation.

6 NACE Rev. 2 – Statistical classification of Economic Activities in the European Community. Typically, the sector shall be specified at group level.

7 In case of an aid scheme: Indicate the annual overall amount of the budget planned under the scheme or the estimated tax loss per year for all aid instruments contained in the scheme.

8 In case of an *ad hoc* aid award: Indicate the overall aid amount/tax loss.

9 For guarantees, indicate the (maximum) amount of loans guaranteed.

10 Where appropriate, reference to the Commission decision approving the methodology to calculate the gross grant equivalent, in line with article 5(2)(c) of the Regulation.

[PART II TO BE PROVIDED THROUGH THE ESTABLISHED COMMISSION ELECTRONIC NOTIFICATION SYSTEM AS LAID DOWN IN ARTICLE 11

Please indicate under which provision of the GBER the aid measure is implemented.

[5.142]

Primary Objective – General Objectives (list)	*Objectives (list)*	*Maximum aid intensity in% or Maximum annual aid amount in national currency (in full amounts)*	*SME – bonuses in%*
Regional aid – investment aid[1] (Art. 14)	☐ *Scheme*	. . . %	. . . %
	☐ *Ad hoc aid*	. . . %	. . . %
Regional aid – operating aid (Art. 15)	☐ *In sparsely populated areas (Art. 15(2))*	. . . %	. . . %
	☐ *In very sparsely populated areas (Art. 15(3))*	. . . %	. . . %
	☐ *In outermost regions (Art. 15(4))*	. . . %	. . . %
☐ *Regional urban development aid (Art. 16)*		. . . .*national currency*	. . . %
SME aid (Arts. 17 – 19b)	☐ *Investment aid to SMEs (Art. 17)*	. . . %	. . . %
	☐ *Aid for consultancy in favour of SMEs (Art. 18)*	. . . %	. . . %
	☐ *Aid to SMEs for participation in fairs (Art. 19)*	. . . %	. . . %
	☐ *Aid for costs incurred by SMEs participating in community-led local development ("CLLD") or European Innovation Partnership for agricultural productivity and sustainability ("EIP") Operational Group projects (Art. 19a)*	. . . %	. . . %
	☐ *Limited amounts of aid to SMEs benefitting from community-led local development ("CLLD") or European Innovation Partnership for agricultural productivity and sustainability ("EIP") Operational Group projects (Art 19b)[2]*	. . . *national currency*	. . . %
Aid for European Territorial Cooperation (Arts. 20 – 20a)	☐ *Aid for costs incurred by undertakings participating in European Territorial Cooperation projects (Art. 20)*	. . . %	. . . %
	☐ *Limited amounts of aid to undertakings for participation in European Territorial Cooperation projects (Art. 20a)[3]*	. . . *national currency*	. . . %

Primary Objective – General Objectives (list)	*Objectives (list)*		*Maximum aid intensity in% or Maximum annual aid amount in national currency (in full amounts)*	*SME – bonuses in%*
SME aid – SMEs' access to finance (Arts. 21-22)	☐ *Risk finance aid (Art. 21)*		. . . *national currency*	. . . %
	☐ *Aid for start-ups (Art. 22)*		. . . *national currency*	. . . %
☐ *SME aid – Aid to alternative trading platforms specialised in SMEs (Art. 23)*			. . . %; *in case the aid measure takes the form of start-up aid:* . . . *national currency*	. . . %
☐ *SME aid – Aid for scouting costs (Art. 24)*			. . . %	. . . %
Aid for research, development and innovation (Arts. 25 – 30)	*Aid for research and development projects (Art. 25)*	☐ *Fundamental research (Art. 25(2)(a))*	. . . %	. . . %
		☐ *Industrial research (Art. 25(2) b))*	. . . %	. . . %
		☐ *Experimental development (Art. 25(2)(c))*	. . . %	. . . %
		☐ *Feasibility studies (Art. 25(2)(d))*	. . . %	. . . %
	☐ *Aid for projects awarded a Seal of Excellence quality label (Art. 25a)*		. . . *national currency*	. . . %
	☐ *Aid for Marie Skł odowska-Curie actions and European Research Council Proof of Concept actions (Art. 25b)*		. . . *national currency*	. . . %
	☐ *Aid involved in co-funded research and development projects (Art. 25c)*		. . . %	. . . %
	☐ *Aid for Teaming actions (Art. 25d)*		. . . %	. . . %
	☐ *Investment aid for research infrastructures (Art. 26)*		. . . %	. . . %
	☐ *Aid for innovation clusters (Art. 27)*		. . . %	. . . %
	☐ *Innovation aid for SMEs (Art. 28)*		. . . %	. . . %
	☐ *Aid for process and organisational innovation (Article 29)*		. . . %	. . . %
	☐ *Aid for research and development in the fishery and aquaculture sector (Art. 30)*		. . . %	. . . %
☐ *Training aid (Art. 31)*			. . . %	. . . %
Aid for disadvantaged workers and workers with disabilities (Arts. 32-35)	☐ *Aid for the recruitment of disadvantaged workers in the form of wage subsidies (Art. 32)*		. . . %	. . . %
	☐ *Aid for the employment of workers with disabilities in the form of wage subsidies (Art. 33)*		. . . %	. . . %
	☐ *Aid for compensating the additional costs of employing workers with disabilities (Art. 34)*		. . . %	. . . %
	☐ *Aid for compensating the costs of assistance provided to disadvantaged workers (Art.35)*		. . . %	. . . %

Primary Objective – General Objectives (list)	*Objectives (list)*	*Maximum aid intensity in% or Maximum annual aid amount in national currency (in full amounts)*	*SME – bonuses in%*
Aid for Environmental protection (Arts. 36-49)	☐ *Investment aid enabling undertakings to go beyond Union standards for environmental protection or increase the level of environmental protection in the absence of Union standards (Art. 36)*	. . . %	. . . %
	☐ *Investment aid for publicly accessible recharging or refuelling infrastructure for zero and low emission road vehicles (Art. 36a)*	. . . %	. . . %
	☐ *Investment aid for early adaptation to future Union standards (Art. 37)*	. . . %	. . . %
	☐ *Investment aid for energy efficiency measures (Art. 38)*	. . . %	. . . %
	☐ *Investment aid for energy efficiency projects in buildings in the form of financial instruments (Art. 39)*	. . . national currency	. . . %
	☐ *Investment aid for high-efficiency cogeneration (Art. 40)*	. . . %	. . . %
	☐ *Investment aid for the promotion of energy from renewable sources (Art. 41)*	. . . %	. . . %
	☐ *Operating aid for the promotion of electricity from renewable sources (Art. 42)*	. . . %	. . . %
	☐ *Operating aid for the promotion of energy from renewable sources in small scale installation (Art. 43)*	. . . %	. . . %
	☐ *Aid in the form of reductions in environmental taxes under Council Directive 2003/96/EC (Art. 44 of this Regulation)*	. . . %	. . . %
	☐ *Investment aid for remediation of contaminated sites (Art. 45)*	. . . %	. . . %
	☐ *Investment aid for energy efficient district heating and cooling (Art. 46)*	. . . %	. . . %
	☐ *Investment aid for waste recycling and re-utilisation (Art. 47)*	. . . %	. . . %
	☐ *Investment aid for energy infrastructure (Art. 48)*	. . . %	. . . %
	☐ *Aid for environmental studies (Art. 49)*	. . . %	. . . %
☐ *Aid schemes to make good the damage caused by certain natural disasters (Art. 50)*	*Maximum aid intensity*	. . . %	. . . %
	Type of natural disaster	☐ *earthquake* ☐ *avalanche* ☐ *landslide* ☐ *flood* ☐ *tornado* ☐ *hurricane* ☐ *volcanic eruption* ☐ *wild fire*	
	Date of occurrence of the natural disaster	*dd/mm/yyyy to dd/mm/yyyy*	
☐ *Social aid for transport for residents of remote regions (Art. 51)*		. . . %	. . . %
☐ *Aid for fixed broadband networks (Art. 52)*		. . . national currency	. . . %
☐ *Aid for 4G and 5G mobile networks (Art. 52a)*		. . . national currency	. . . %
☐ *Aid for projects of common interest in the area of trans-European digital connectivity infrastructure (Art. 52b)*		. . . national currency	. . . %
☐ *Connectivity vouchers (Art. 52c)*		. . . %	. . . %
☐ *Aid for culture and heritage conservation (Art. 53)*		. . . %	. . . %
☐ *Aid schemes for audiovisual works (Art. 54)*		. . . %	. . . %
☐ *Aid for sport and multifunctional recreational infrastructures (Art. 55)*		. . . %	. . . %
☐ *Investment aid for local infrastructures (Art. 56)*		. . . %	. . . %
☐ *Aid for regional airports (Art. 56a)*		. . . %	. . . %
☐ *Aid for maritime ports (Art. 56b)*		. . . %	. . . %
☐ *Aid for inland ports (Art. 56c)*		. . . %	. . . %

Primary Objective – General Objectives (list)	Objectives (list)		Maximum aid intensity in% or Maximum annual aid amount in national currency (in full amounts)	SME – bonuses in%
Aid involved in financial products supported by the InvestEU Fund (Arts. 56d-56f)	Art. 56e	☐ Aid for projects of common interest in the area of trans-European digital connectivity infrastructure financed under Regulation (EU) 2021/1153 or awarded a Seal of Excellence quality label under that Regulation (Art. 56e(2))	. . . national currency	. . . %
		☐ Aid for investments in fixed broadband networks to connect only certain eligible socio-economic drivers (Art. 56e(3))	. . . national currency	. . . %
		☐ Aid for energy generation and energy infrastructure (Art. 56e(4))	. . . national currency	. . . %
		☐ Aid for social, educational, cultural and natural heritage infrastructure and activities (Art. 56e(5))	. . . national currency	. . . %
		☐ Aid for transport and transport infrastructures (Art. 56e(6))	. . . national currency	. . . %
		☐ Aid for other infrastructures (Art. 56e(7))	. . . national currency	. . . %
		☐ Aid for environmental protection, including climate protection (Art. 56e(8))	. . . national currency	. . . %
		☐ Aid for research, development, innovation and digitalisation (Art. 56e(9))	. . . national currency	. . . %
		☐ Aid in the form of financing supported by the InvestEU Fund provided to SMEs or small mid-caps (Art 56e(10))	. . . national currency	. . . %
	☐ Aid involved in intermediated commercially-driven financial products supported by the InvestEU Fund (Art. 56f)		. . . national currency	. . . %]

NOTES

Substituted by Commission Regulation 2021/1237/EU, Art 1(26), Annex, as from 1 August 2021.

Repeal of this Regulation in relation to the UK: this Regulation is repealed in relation to the UK (as from IP completion day); see the introductory notes to this Regulation *ante*.

1 In the case of ad hoc regional aid supplementing aid awarded under aid scheme(s), please indicate both the aid intensity granted under the scheme and the intensity of the ad hoc aid.

2 According to Article 11(1), reporting on aid granted under Article 19b is not mandatory. Reporting on such aid is, therefore, merely optional.

3 According to Article 11(1), reporting on aid granted under Article 20a is not mandatory. Reporting on such aid is, therefore, merely optional.

ANNEX III
PROVISIONS FOR THE PUBLICATION OF INFORMATION AS LAID DOWN IN ARTICLE 9(1)

[5.143]

Member States shall organise their comprehensive State aid websites, on which the information laid down in Article 9(1) is to be published, in such a way as to allow easy access to the information. Information shall be published in a spreadsheet data format, which allows data to be searched, extracted and easily published on the internet, for instance in CSV or XML format. Access to the website shall be allowed to any interested party without restrictions. No prior user registration shall be required to access the website.

The following information on individual awards as laid down in Article 9(1)(c) shall be published:

— *Name of the beneficiary*
— *Beneficiary's identifier*
— *Type of enterprise (SME/large) at the time of granting*
— *Region in which the beneficiary is located, at NUTS level II*[1]
— *Sector of activity at NACE group level*[2]
— *Aid element, expressed as full amount in national currency*[3]
— *Aid instrument*[4] *(Grant/Interest rate subsidy, Loan/Repayable advances/Reimbursable grant, Guarantee, Tax advantage or tax exemption, Risk finance, Other (please specify))*
— *Date of granting*
— *Objective of the aid*
— *Granting authority*
— *For schemes under Articles 16 and 21, name of the entrusted entity, and the names of the selected financial intermediaries*
— *Reference of the aid measure.*[5]

NOTES

In footnotes 2, 3 below, words in square brackets substituted by Commission Regulation 2017/1084/EU, Art 1(23).

Repeal of this Regulation in relation to the UK: this Regulation is repealed in relation to the UK (as from IP completion day); see the introductory notes to this Regulation *ante*.

[1] NUTS — Nomenclature of Territorial Units for Statistics. Typically, the region is specified at level 2.

[2] [Regulation (EC) No 1893/2006 of the European Parliament and of the Council of 20 December 2006 establishing the statistical classification of economic activities NACE Revision 2 and amending Council Regulation (EEC) No 3037/90 as well as certain EC Regulations on specific statistical domains (OJ L393, 30.12.2006, p 1).]

[3] [Gross grant equivalent, or for measures under Articles 16, 21, 22 or 39 of this Regulation, the amount of the investment.] For operating aid, the annual amount of aid per beneficiary can be provided. For fiscal schemes and for schemes under Articles 16 (Regional urban development aid) and 21 (Risk finance aid), this amount can be provided by the ranges set out in Article 9(2) of this Regulation.

[4] If the aid is granted through multiple aid instruments, the aid amount shall be provided by instrument.

[5] As provided by the Commission under the electronic procedure referred to in Article 11 of this Regulation.

GENERAL BLOCK EXEMPTION REGULATION (GBER): FREQUENTLY ASKED QUESTIONS

Date of publication
Q&A to Articles 1 to 35: July 2015
Q&A to Articles 36 to 58: March 2016

[5.144]

NOTES

This document is available on the European Commission website at https://ec.europa.eu/competition/state_aid/legislation/block.html.

Note that the General Block Exemption Regulation (Regulation 651/2014/EU) is repealed, in relation to the UK, by the State Aid (Revocations and Amendments) (EU Exit) Regulations 2020, SI 2020/1470, reg 5, as from IP completion day (as defined in the European Union (Withdrawal Agreement) Act 2020, s 39). See **[5.63]**.

State funding that meets the criteria established in Article 107(1) TFEU constitutes State aid. As a general rule, State aid must be notified to and cleared by the Commission before it is granted. The General Block Exemption Regulation (hereafter the GBER or the Regulation) exempts Member States from this notification obligation, as long as all the GBER criteria are fulfilled. The Regulation simplifies the procedure for aid-granting authorities at national, regional and local level. It allows them to provide measures ranging from job creation and boosting competitiveness to measures that create a favourable environment for the Small and Medium Enterprises (hereafter SMEs).

The new GBER significantly extends the possibilities for Member States to grant "good aid" to companies without prior Commission scrutiny, simplifies the award of State aid and reduces the duration of processes for aid beneficiaries. It also introduces ex-post requirements for Member States such as the requirement to evaluate large aid schemes and to ensure greater transparency on aid awards.

The new GBER is a cornerstone of the State Aid Modernisation (SAM) agenda (see IP/12/458), which is a broad reform of State aid rules aimed at facilitating sustainable, smart and inclusive growth, focusing on cases with the biggest impact on the internal market and streamlining the rules to adopt faster and better informed decisions. The review of the GBER contributes to all SAM objectives, with a particular focus on simplification and dealing as a priority with cases that matter most for competition in the internal market. In addition, the GBER imposes conditions which aim to ensure that the beneficiary will indeed undertake the project or activity which he would not have undertaken had the aid not been granted (incentive effect). Lastly, the Regulation will lead to increased transparency, allowing all stakeholders to have a better grasp of the aid that has been granted and of its impact.

Member States will have a major role to play in designing and implementing schemes without prior notification. The purpose of this document – which is in fact a compilation of questions mainly received from the national administrations – is to offer guidance concerning the implementation of the GBER. This FAQs document does not intend to tackle all the interpretation questions that may arise, only the most common ones raised so far.

This document is a working paper prepared by the Commission services and is not binding on the European Commission as an institution. The FAQ follow the structure of the GBER and all references to Articles and recitals relate to the GBER unless otherwise stated.

1. CHAPTER I – COMMON PROVISIONS

Article 1

[5.145]

1. **In order to assess whether an aid scheme reaches the threshold for evaluation foreseen in Article 1(2)(a), ie ″average annual State aid budget exceeding EUR 150 million″, what is the correct assessment method for the aid component in the cases of aid comprised in loans, in guarantees and in the case of tax schemes?**

Only the State aid component of the budget is relevant for the evaluation threshold of Article 1(2)(a). Article 5 GBER on the transparency of aid states that the ″Regulation shall apply only to aid in respect of which it is possible to calculate precisely the gross grant equivalent of the aid ex ante without any need to undertake a risk assessment″.

For calculating the aid element comprised in loans, two provisions are relevant: Article 5(2)(b) GBER and the Communication from the Commission on the revision of the method for setting the reference and discount rates – 2008/C14/02.

For calculating the aid element comprised in guarantees, two provisions are relevant: Article 5(2)(c) GBER and the Commission Notice on the application of Articles 87 and 88 of the EC Treaty to State aid in the form of guarantees – 2008/C155/02.

In the case of a tax scheme, the budget corresponds to the estimated tax loss, per year, for all aid instruments contained in the scheme.

2. **What is the relation between the EUR 150 million thresholds set in Article 1(2)(a) (obligation to provide an evaluation plan) and Article 4(1)(v) – notification threshold for operating aid for energy produced from renewable energy sources?**

According to Article 1(2) and recital (8) of the GBER, in view of their greater potential impact, certain schemes with an annual budget exceeding EUR 150 million will be subject to State aid evaluation with the obligation for the Member State to submit an evaluation plan. The evaluation aims at verifying whether the assumptions and conditions underlying the compatibility of the scheme have been achieved and should provide indications on the impact of the scheme on competition and trade. In contrast to that obligation, the particular provision of operating aid for renewable energy in Article 4(1)(v) GBER, obliges Member States to notify to the Commission State aid exceeding EUR 150 million per year. This is to be calculated taking into account the combined budget of all schemes falling under Article 42 GBER, per Member State.

Therefore the two thresholds have different purposes. The first threshold concerns the expected average annual budget for a scheme within certain categories of the GBER that triggers a requirement of evaluation of such large scheme, and for which an evaluation plan has to be submitted within twenty working days after the scheme was put into effect. The second threshold refers to the expected aggregated annual aid to be granted by a Member State under all schemes falling under Article 42 that, if exceeded, triggers an ex ante notification obligation to the Commission, before putting into effect the aid measure.

The scheme concerning energy produced from renewable energy sources leading to a budget exceeding EUR 150 million will have therefore to be notified individually to the Commission. In reason of their different application, an operating aid scheme concerning energy produced from renewable energy sources and that is subject to the evaluation requirement, will also necessarily be caught by the notification obligation in Article 4(1)(v).

3. **Article 1(3) of the GBER states that aid can be granted to (a) the fishery and aquaculture sector and (b) the primary agricultural production sector for "aid for research and development, innovation aid for SMEs". Can the provisions of Section 4 – Aid for research and development and innovation be used to support relevant activities in (a) the fishery and aquaculture sector and (b) the primary agricultural production sector?**

As long as there is no distinction within Article 1(3) a and b as to the type of aid or instrument, all Articles within the Section 4 are applicable to aid in the fishery and aquaculture sector. Except for Article 30 that deals with a particular type of aid to research organisations for undertaking studies in the fisheries and aquaculture sector, all other Articles of Section 4 apply to the primary agricultural production sector as well.

4. **What is the relevance of the GBER for regional aid in view of the exclusion enshrined in Article 1(3)(e)?**

Article 1 defines the scope of the GBER. According to Article 1(3)(e), the GBER does not apply to the certain categories of regional aid listed in Art 13. Article 13 excludes the application of Section 1 (Regional aid) of the GBER to certain aid measures listed there-in, but it does not preclude that such aid could not at all be exempted under another section of the GBER, provided it fulfils both general and specific conditions of the GBER.

5. **Article 1(4)(c) prohibits the granting of aid to undertakings in difficulty and Article 2(18) defines such undertakings. In case the aid beneficiary is a daughter company of the group, does it mean that the aid grantor has to control the whole concern? And if eg another daughter of the concern is in difficulty then no aid can be granted to the group and other companies belonging to it?**

In accordance with the case law, an undertaking is defined as a single economic entity having a common source of control. Therefore, as long as the group acts as a single economic unit, it shall be considered as one undertaking and the economic situation of all the legal persons part of the group shall be considered when granting aid under the GBER. Otherwise, a company that is in difficulty might bypass the GBER prohibition of aid to enterprises in difficulty, by simply setting up a wholly owned subsidiary and transferring its liabilities to that company.

6. **Can a State aid scheme impose as a condition of eligibility requirements relating to the headquarters of potential aid beneficiaries? Could the scheme require that the potential beneficiary is registered within that Member State?**

The rationale of the Article 1(5) GBER originates from the basic EU freedom of establishment for nationals of a Member State in the territory of another Member State as stated in the Article 49 TFEU. The same freedom of establishment extends to legal persons that may set up branches in any other Member States and are therefore free to carry out their activity from different Member States, across the internal market. Any restrictions to this freedom to set up an establishment and carry out economic activity from that establishment is therefore contrary to the Treaty. Consequently, the provision of State aid should not be designed in such a way that would effectively prohibit undertakings from carrying out their activities in other Member States.

For the same reason, according to the Article 1(5)(a) GBER, if the aid schemes provides that it is only available for undertakings having their headquarters in a certain Member State, the GBER would not apply. However, the requirement to have an establishment or branch in the aid granting Member State at the moment of payment of the aid is permitted. Therefore, to the extent that the condition to 'be registered' (by means of a branch or an establishment) is a necessary condition for carrying an aided activity in such Member State, it would appear to be coherent with the GBER.

7. **With regard to the Article 1(5)(a) of GBER what is meant by "the beneficiary that is predominantly established in the Member State"? Could the scheme provide for a requirement that the beneficiary is registered in the granting Member State?**

The provision of State aid by one Member State should not be designed in such a way that would effectively prohibit undertakings from carrying out their activities in other Member States. This could, for example, be done by requiring the beneficiary to achieve a certain part of its turnover in the granting Member States. Also, it would not be allowed under the GBER to make the grant of aid subject to the obligation for the beneficiary to have its headquarters in the granting Member State (or in a certain region or municipality). However, the requirement to have an establishment or branch or activity in the granting Member State at the moment of payment of the aid is permitted. Therefore, to the extent that the condition to 'be registered' is a necessary condition for carrying an activity in such Member State, it would appear to be coherent with the GBER. Otherwise, such requirement would likely infringe internal market rules.

8. **Is it possible to require that a company is formally established in the granting Member State at the time when the application for aid is made?**

The GBER states in Article 1(5)a that a Member State might require that the company has an establishment in its territory at the time of payment of the aid. This cannot be interpreted as also meaning a requirement to have an establishment at the time of application for the aid as it would limit the possibility of companies located outside the granting Member State to apply for an aid and therefore carry out a particular project/investment.

9. **What is the evaluation plan decision procedure under GBER and its possible outcomes?**

Large aid schemes referred to in Article 1(2)(a) of the GBER can be implemented immediately by the Member States. However, for such schemes, the exemption under the Regulation expires six months following their entry into force.

The Member State is required to notify the evaluation plan within the first 20 working days following the entry into force of the scheme. Until a final notification form is adopted by the Commission as an annex to the Implementing regulation No 794/2004, Member States are encouraged to use the provisional supplementary information sheet for the notification of an evaluation plan, published on the DG Competition website. The Commission services will immediately start assessing the completeness and appropriateness of the evaluation plan.

The Commission should receive from the Member State the necessary information to be able to carry out the assessment of the evaluation plan and will request additional information without undue delay allowing the Member State to complete the missing elements for the Commission to adopt a decision.

Following the assessment of the evaluation plan, the Commission could exceptionally adopt a decision prolonging the exemption of the scheme beyond the initial six months.

If the Commission does not adopt a decision on the evaluation plan within the six months period, the scheme will no longer be exempted under the GBER. In this scenario, the concerned Member State will have to suspend its application until the evaluation plan has been approved.

Alternatively, Member States can notify the measure for a detailed assessment of its compatibility under the relevant State aid guidelines. Such assessment will review the whole scheme and the need for an adequate evaluation plan in line with the relevant State aid guidelines.

10. **When does the 6 months period referred to in Article 1(2)a begin? Is it 6 months after the evaluation plan has been sent or 6 months from the starting date of the scheme?**

The six months period begins from the date when the State aid scheme was put into effect.

11. **Are there any short guidelines, practical information on how an evaluation plan subject to notification should be designed?**

The Commission Staff Working Document "Common methodology for State aid evaluation" has been published on 28 May 2014 and is available on DG Competition's website https://ec.europa.eu/competition/state_aid/modernisation/state_aid_evaluation_methodology_en.pdf

The Staff Working Document provides guidance and best practices on the drafting of an evaluation plan and provides a description of its key elements. Member States are invited to take this guidance into account as much as possible.[1]

Article 2: Definitions

12. **What is meant by "without further implementing measures being required" in the definition of an aid scheme (Article 2(15))?**

The wording regarding the measures that constitute a scheme for the purposes of Article 2(15) of the GBER is meant to clarify that, in order for a State aid measure to be considered a scheme, the legal basis is detailed enough to determine the group of beneficiaries and under which conditions they may benefit of the aid measures.

13. **Does an undertaking subject to "collective insolvency proceeding" as described in Article 2(18)(c) GBER and in point 20 (c) of the Rescue and Restructuring Guidelines automatically qualify as "undertaking in difficulty"?**

Article 2(18)(c) of GBER and point 20(c) of the Rescue and Restructuring Guidelines refer to national insolvency proceedings. Thus, it is for the national law to define the conditions under which an undertaking is to be regarded as insolvent. Whenever an undertaking, under this national definition, is (1) subject to collective insolvency proceedings or (2) fulfils the criteria for being placed under such proceedings at the request of its creditors, it shall be regarded as an "undertaking in difficulty" under point 20(c) of the Guidelines.

14. **Can an undertaking subject to collective insolvency proceedings - whose continuation of the activity under a restructuring plan is approved and remains under the control of the (commercial) court – and which does not qualify in any other way as a firm in difficulty benefit from other types of aid?**

A firm subject to collective insolvency proceedings under national law fulfils the criterion of Article 2(18)(c) and therefore must be assessed as undertaking in difficulty, even if it does not meet any of the remaining criteria of Article 2(18), and thus is excluded from aid granted in application of the GBER. The only aid category available to undertakings in difficulty under the GBER is aid to compensate for damages of natural disasters.

15. **It is possible to choose the most favourable criteria among the ones of Article 2(18) of the GBER, or one must consider an undertaking to be in difficulty once at least one of the criteria is met?**

According to Article 2(18) of the GBER, an "undertaking in difficulty" means an undertaking in respect of which at least one (emphasis added) of the circumstances described in points (a) – (e) occurs. Therefore, it is not possible to choose an assessment criterion. As soon as a firm fulfils at least one of the criteria of Article 2(18) of the GBER, it must be considered as being in difficulty and thus, pursuant to Article 1(4)(c), the undertaking is not eligible for the categories of aid covered by the GBER, with the exception of aid schemes to make good the damage caused by certain natural disasters.

16. **What is meant by the term "debt" in the debt to equity ratio referred to in Article 2(18)(e)(1) of GBER?**

The term "debt" should be understood as the book value of short-term and long-term financial liabilities.

17. **Within the definition of "start of works" in Article 2(23) what is meant by "commitment that makes the investment irreversible"? Is a clause allowing for unilateral termination sufficient to make a contract reversible?**

'Start of work' is either the start of construction work or the first firm commitment to order equipment, excluding preliminary feasibility studies. Whether the agreements and payments made on the basis of these agreements can be considered a "first firm commitment" to start the project does not necessarily depend on the formal classification of the agreements in question, but on the terms of those agreements. If contractual obligations make it difficult from an economic standpoint to abandon the project in a given case, particularly because a considerable sum of money would be lost, work will be deemed to have started. A more detailed examination of the specific circumstances of the case would be needed to see if this is indeed the case.

As most contracts will have a clause allowing for unilateral termination under some conditions, this cannot be a sole factor for determining the nature of the commitment. However, if for instance the termination of that contract entails significant financial losses for the aid beneficiary, the contract may still be considered as a firm commitment to pursue the investment in the absence of State aid.

18. **Taking into account the new provision in the Article 2(23) GBER regarding "start of works", can the acquisition of a land which has been acquired before the aid application has been submitted be considered (in total or partially) a financial contribution of at least 25% of the eligible costs pursuant to the Article 14(14) GBER?**

According to the Article 2(23) of GBER buying land and preparatory works such as obtaining permits and conducting feasibility studies are not considered start of works. However, this provision does not preclude the possibility to accept the acquired land as own contribution. Article 14(14) GBER provides that the aid beneficiary must provide a financial contribution of at least 25% of the eligible costs, either through its own resources or by external financing, in a form, which is free of any public support. Given the fact that land is eligible cost under the RAG and under the condition this land has been acquired on market terms, it is not considered to be aid and may well be accepted as own contribution in the meaning of the paragraph (38) RAG 2014-20.

19. **What is meant by "the relevant lifetime of the investment" in Article 2(39)?**

The lifetime of the investment that can be assimilated to the depreciation period in most accounting systems.

20. **What is meant by 'transport related infrastructure' in Article 2(45)?**

The transport sector is defined in Article 2(45) of the GBER as meaning

"the following activities in terms of NACE Rev. 2:

(a) NACE 49: Land transport and transport via pipelines, excluding NACE 49.32 Taxi operation, 49.42 Removal services, 49.5 Transport via pipeline;

(b) NACE 50: Water transport;

(c) NACE 51: Air transport, excluding NACE 51.22 Space transport."

Therefore, the transport related infrastructure excluded from the scope of application of regional aid under the GBER refers to infrastructure that is needed for and used to provide the transport activities listed in Article 2(45) of the GBER. Aid to the transport sector is subject to special rules and specific guidelines apply. For example, the regional aid provisions of the GBER will not apply to State aid granted to airports and the related airport infrastructure given that this type of aid is assessed under the recently adopted Guidelines on State aid to airports and airlines (OJ C99, 4.4.2014, p 3.)

21. **Does the definition of 'transport sector' under the new GBER cover the cruise ship sector?**

The transport sector is defined in Article 2(45) of the GBER as "the transport of passengers by aircraft, maritime transport, road or rail and by inland waterway or freight transport services for hire or reward; more specifically the 'transport sector' means the following activities in terms of NACE Rev. 2 (. . .).

(a) NACE 49: Land transport and transport via pipelines, excluding NACE 49.32 Taxi operation, 49.42 Removal services, 49.5 Transport via pipeline;

(b) NACE 50: Water transport;

(c) NACE 51: Air transport, excluding NACE 51.22 Space transport."

Therefore, all the activities that fall under NACE 50 code are excluded from the scope of application of regional aid under the GBER. Cruise ships would normally fall under the water transport NACE code 50 and would consequently be excluded from regional aid under the GBER.

22. **What is meant by "new products" in Article 2(49)? Does a "new product" mean a different NACE classification?**

According to Article 2 (49) of the GBER, a "diversification" project is an initial investment if it is "diversification of the output of an establishment into products not previously produced in the establishment". The important condition for qualifying a "diversification" project as an "initial investment" is that the products were not produced in that establishment before the project. However, the "product" is not defined by reference to NACE codes. NACE codes are used for the definition of the „same or similar activity" (Article 2(50) of the GBER). If the activity resulting into the new product falls under a different four digit numerical NACE code, it can also be considered as diversification into a new product. However, not in all cases would the activities resulting into new products have to fall under different four digit numerical NACE codes.

[*Example*: NACE code C.1089 – Manufacture of other food products n.e.c. If the company was producing soups and broths and now it decides to produce artificial honey, we could consider it a new product, despite of the fact the activities resulting into these products fall under the same NACE codes.]

23. **What is meant by "initial investment in favour of a new economic activity" in Article 2(51)?**

"Initial investment in favour of a new economic activity" means an investment carried out by an undertaking introducing a new activity, which is not the same or similar activity to the activity previously performed in the establishment. An investment in an existing establishment is not considered initial investment in favour of new economic activity unless it introduces a new activity, which is not the same or similar activity to the activity previously performed in the establishment. Therefore, if the new activity falls under the same four-digit numerical code of the NACE as the activity pursued so far in the establishment, it cannot be considered initial investment in favour of new economic activity. The definition is relevant for regional aid to large enterprises in that the GBER allows for exemption from the notification requirement of such aid only for initial investments in favour of new economic activity of large enterprises in 'c' regions.

24. **What is the meaning of "a new establishment" in the context of Article 2(51)?**

If a large enterprise sets up a new establishment, which is self-standing and is not just a simple extension of the production capacity of an existing establishment, it could be considered as initial investment in favour of new economic activity.

However, if the investment project cannot be considered as one that is setting up a new establishment, but the project could qualify as a diversification of the existing establishment into a new product, it could fall under the Regional Aid Guidelines 2014-2020[2] (hereafter "RAG"). In that case, the Member State would have to notify such a project to the Commission, and the Commission will assess it on the basis of the RAG.

25. **What is meant by a "fundamental" change in the production process? How is it to be distinguished from a non-fundamental change?**

Initial investment in the form of a fundamental change in the overall production process of an existing establishment means the implementation of a fundamental (as opposed to routine) process innovation. The simple replacement of individual assets without fundamentally changing the overall production process constitutes a replacement investment which is not eligible for regional investment aid as it does not qualify as a fundamental change of an overall production process, and thus is not considered to constitute an initial investment. The fact of having replaced individual items of equipment by others that are more performing (unless this leads to a fundamental change on the overall production process) would also be considered a non-eligible replacement investment.

26. **What is meant by "extension of the capacity of an existing establishment"? Is this to be taken to mean production of a greater volume of all products?**

The extension of capacity of an existing establishment means that the existing establishment is put into a situation where it can manufacture more volume of at least one of the products already produced in the establishment, whilst the underlying overall production process is not fundamentally changed.

27. **If depreciation of "assets linked to the activity to be modernised" is to include all assets, however peripherally linked they are to production (such as the assembly hall premises, shared lighting etc.), how is the percentage share of these depreciations to be determined in order to be compared against the eligible expenditure? On the basis of the floor surface area of the assembly hall, the percentage use of the machines, the share of sales?**

The term assets in the context of initial investments refers both to tangible and intangible assets (see Article 2(49)(a) and Article 2(51)(a) GBER). Tangible assets consist of land, buildings and plant, machinery and equipment (see Article 2(28) GBER). Therefore, the buildings for manufacturing or storing manufactured products are covered by Article 14(7) 2nd sentence of the GBER if these assets are linked to the activity to be modernised. Member State can carry out a pro rata calculation. The GBER does not prescribe the method to be applied by the Member State for that purpose, ie the Member State can rely on a bona fide approach that takes into account the specific situation and characteristics of the establishment and activity concerned and normal general depreciation rules.

28. **What is meant by "diversification of the activity of an establishment" under the condition that the new activity is not the same or similar activity to the previously performed in the establishment?**

According to Article 2(51) of the GBER an investment related to the "diversification of the of the output of an existing establishment" into products not previously produced in the establishment qualifies as "initial investment in favour of new economic activity", if the additional product results from a production activity that falls under a different class (four-digit numerical code) of the NACE Rev.2 statistical classification of economic activities than the activity that was performed before the project in the establishment.

29. **Under the old Shipbuilding framework, the definition of ship building covered repair and maintenance of vessels; this framework also exempted smaller vessels under 100gt or less than 365KW in the case of tugs. Do the definitions of ship building under the old ship building framework still apply under the new GBER and if so would it be possible to grant aid to a project that supported the refurbishment and development of infrastructure (quays, docks and workspace) to maintain and repair small vessels under the new GBER?**

The GBER does not provide a new definition of ″shipbuilding″. Therefore, the most recent relevant definitions are provided in the 2011 Framework on State Aid to Shipbuilding[3] According to paragraph 12 of the Shipbuilding Framework, 'ship repair' means the repair or reconditioning, in the Union, of self-propelled commercial vessels. Paragraph 12 of the Framework also defines 'self-propelled commercial vessel'. If a vessel does not fall under the definition of 'self-propelled commercial vessel', its repair can be eligible for regional aid under the GBER. Therefore, as long as the infrastructure is used exclusively for this type of small vessels which do not fall under the definition of 'self-propelled commercial vessel', investments in the infrastructure could be eligible for regional aid granted under the GBER, unless they fall within the transport sector (including related infrastructure), which is excluded in Article 13(a) GBER

Such aid may fall under the scope of Article 56 GBER (local infrastructure), which however excludes port infrastructure.

30. **What is meant by ″establishment″ in the context of an initial investment?**

Based on the wording of definitions in Article 2(49) and (51) of the GBER, ″establishment″ in the context of an initial investment is understood as a production unit, and not a legal entity.

31. **What is meant by the ″scientific community″ in the definition of ″research infrastructure″ in Article 2(91)?**

The term ″scientific community″ corresponds to the term used in Council Regulation (EC) No 723/2009 of 25 June 2009 on the Community legal framework for a European Research Infrastructure Consortium[4] and relates to any structured or unstructured group or network of persons engaging in a systematic activity to acquire knowledge.

32. **Are project feasibility studies considered "knowledge transfer" under Article 2(91)? When are knowledge transfer activities considered as economic or non-economic?**

Technical and economic feasibility studies cannot qualify as ″knowledge transfer″ but may be eligible for aid under the conditions laid down for ″feasibility studies″.

Insofar as only Small and Medium Enterprises (SMEs) are eligible for aid for obtaining, validating and defending patents and other intangible assets, and as was the case under the previous RDI State aid rules, public research organisations that do not qualify as such cannot benefit from such aid.

The qualification of knowledge transfer activities as economic or non-economic does not depend on the selection process of the recipients but rather on whether those activities are conducted by a research organisation or research infrastructure (or jointly with, or on behalf of other such entities) and all profits from activities are reinvested in the primary activities of the relevant research organisation or research infrastructure (ie education for more and better skilled human resources, independent research and development for more knowledge and better understanding, wide dissemination of research results on a non-exclusive and non-discriminatory basis).

33. **The term ″smart grids″ is defined in Article (2) paragraph (130)(a)(v) in GBER. The definition refers to equipment, lines, cables and installations. Are intangible assets related to the infrastructure and essential to its proper functioning also eligible (eg software enabling the management and monitoring of the grid and communication between different installations)?**

The definition of ″smart grids″ is provided in Article 2(130)(a)(v). The eligible costs pursuant to Article 48(4) are those investment costs necessary to develop the said infrastructure and may include the costs of software.

Article 4

34. **How to proceed in cases where the same entity will implement several projects for which it has received funding under separate contracts which, for example because of the geographical proximity, have economic or technological links? In such a case, will it be necessary to sum up the values of these projects or each of them will be treated separately?**

The determining factor is whether there were separate investment decisions or all projects are based on one transaction or several inter-linked transactions. If the only linking element is economic or technological synergies it might not be sufficient to conclude that the entire investment is part of one single project. The national authorities are often in a good position to judge whether it is one investment decision or several ones as such projects are subject to a variety of permits (construction, environmental, etc.) from which the initial investment decision becomes clearer. More detailed rules apply for regional aid.

35. **How should we read the notification thresholds for investment aid in Articles 4(1)(bb) and (cc)? Are the two ceilings alternative or cumulative?**

The Regulation shall not apply to aid or projects which exceed any of the two thresholds. For example, in order for a local infrastructure project to be covered by the GBER, the aid shall not exceed 10 Mio Euro and the overall cost of the project shall not exceed 20 Mio Euro.

Article 5

36. **Is aid in the form of "equity" or "semi-equity" considered to be a transparent form of aid?**

Aid in the form of "equity" and/or "quasi-equity" is not listed under Article 5 (2) of the GBER as categories of aid that would be considered to be transparent. According to recital 17 of the preamble to the GBER "Capital injections should not be considered transparent aid, without prejudice to specific conditions concerning risk finance and start-up aid." However, such form of aid would be allowed in the following situations:

—specific provisions of the GBER allow such aid (see the GBER provisions concerning risk finance and start-up aid), or

—the nominal value of the capital injection is itself below the applicable threshold (be it de minimis or the individual notification threshold under the GBER).

In such cases, there is no risk of circumvention of the applicable thresholds, despite the fact that the GGE of the measure cannot be defined ex ante, since the nominal value of the capital injection is itself below the applicable thresholds.

Article 6

37. **What is the meaning of the term "incentive effect" in the Article 6 (2)(e) GBER? Are there different tests for different company sizes?**

Article 6(1) GBER requires for the aid to have incentive effect in order to qualify for the exemption under the GBER. According to recital 18, aid has insufficient incentive effect where the beneficiary would already engage under market conditions alone in activities or projects. For measures under the GBER, the aid is deemed to have an incentive effect if the beneficiary has submitted a written application for the aid to the Member State concerned before work on the project or activity starts. Furthermore, the obligatory elements of the aid application are listed in the Article 6(2), which among others requires the description of the type of aid (grant, loan, guarantee, repayable advance, equity injection or other) and denomination of the amount of public funding needed for the project.

In addition to the requirement that the beneficiary has submitted an application for the aid to the Member State concerned before work on the project or activity has started, in the situation of ad hoc aid to large enterprises, the Member State concerned must verify that documentation prepared by the beneficiary establishes one or more of the conditions set out in points (a) and (b) of Article 6.

38. **Article 6(3)(a) states that the regional ad hoc aid is compatible when the beneficiary demonstrates that – without the aid – either the project would not have been carried out in the area or would not have been sufficiently profitable for the beneficiary in the area concerned. Is the project deemed not sufficiently profitable when the return of investment (IRR) is objectively low or when carrying out the investment at that moment does not bring enough profits for the beneficiary - in a wider context?**

The notion that the investment would not have been sufficiently profitable for the beneficiary in the area concerned should be understood by analogy to scenario 1 (investment decision) described in the RAG. Consequently, the profitability of the project – also when aid is granted under the GBER – should be evaluated by reference to methodologies which are standard practice in the particular industry concerned, and which may include methods to evaluate the net present value of the project (NPV), the internal rate of return (IRR) or the average return on capital employed (ROCE). The profitability of the project is to be compared with normal rates of return applied by the company in other investment projects of a similar kind. Where these rates are not available, the profitability of the project is to be compared with the cost of capital of the company as a whole or with the rates of return commonly observed in the industry concerned.

39. **What are the applicable rules in case of combined regional investment aid and aid for consultancy services granted to a beneficiary in relation to the same project, including the requirements for the presence of incentive effect?**

In this respect, we note that regional investment aid under the new GBER can be granted in line with its Article 14, while consultancy aid – for SMEs only – under the Article 18. These types of aid have a different scopes and can be granted for different eligible costs. It can thus be considered that while regional aid under Article 14 relates to the physical investment in the project, aid under Article 18 relates to the activity of providing consultancy services for the phase prior to the investment. Consequently, it can be considered that in order to comply with the criteria of Article 6 of the new GBER, and thus to have incentive effect, the beneficiary concerned should have applied for the regional investment aid before the start of works on the – physical – investment project, and in case of an ad-hoc aid it should have also complied with the conditions of Article 6(3)(a) and should have applied for the consultancy aid before signing the consultancy contract. In line with Art. 2(23), it does not seem necessary in such case to have applied for the regional investment aid before the start of the preparatory (consultancy) activities.

40. **Is Article 6(2) applicable to both SMEs and large companies under schemes?**

Yes, both aid schemes for SMEs and large undertakings shall comply with the incentive effect conditions described in Article 6(2). The provisions in Article 6(3) apply only for ad hoc aid to large enterprises.

41. **Does Article 6(5)(h) of the GBER apply to all aid for culture and heritage conservation covered by the GBER?**

Article 6(5)(h) applies to aid for culture and heritage conservation as defined in Article 53. It specifically refers to this Article only and does not apply to Article 54 (Aid schemes for audiovisual works).

42. **How is the incentive effect met when aid is granted in the form of interest rate subsidies?**

The incentive effect is met if the aid application for an interest rate subsidy is made before start of works and before signature of a legally binding loan contract allowing to finance a part of the project costs. In this case, the signature of the loan with the subsidised interest rate is the aid granting moment. Making a request after this point would not qualify as meeting the incentive effect requirement as the aid would be considered granted at the time of the signature. Therefore, in order to meet the incentive effect, the request should be made before the loan is signed. Investments may not start before such request for aid is made.

In addition to the requirement that the beneficiary has submitted an application for the aid to the Member State concerned before work on the project or activity has started, in the situation of ad hoc aid to large enterprises, the Member State concerned must verify that documentation prepared by the beneficiary establishes one or more of the conditions set out in points (a) and (b) of Article 6.

43. **Article 6(2)(c) of the GBER states that the application for aid shall contain certain information, inter alia "location of the project". What is meant under "the location of the project"? How precisely the location has to be specified (eg in the town/village or county)? In case the measure includes the visits to foreign trade fairs will the location of the project be the place of the fair?**

The location of the project should be as specific as possible, including the town/village if this is known. If aid is given for participation in fairs, the location of the fair shall be mentioned.

Article 7

44. **Is Value Added Tax on productive and non-productive assets and services eligible for support under the GBER?**

According to Recital (23) GBER, all figures used should be taken before any deduction of taxes or other charges. The principle is that if the Value Added Tax (hereafter VAT) is a real cost in the sense that it cannot be recovered, then it is part of the eligible cost and therefore eligible for support under the GBER. If the VAT can be recovered, is not considered a real cost and therefore shall not be considered as eligible cost under GBER.

45. **With reference to Article 7(4) of the GBER which stipulates "where aid is granted by means of tax advantages, discounting of aid tranches shall take place on the basis of the discount rates applicable at the various times the tax advantage takes effect", what is the basis for calculation of the aid element?**

Discounting of aid amounts means the calculation of the net present value of each aid tranche (in the case of tax advantages, the aid tranche represents the gross grant equivalent of the tax advantage granted to the undertaking). The discount rate to be used for each such aid tranche will depend on the time when such aid is granted. The rate to be used for discounting purposes is indicated in the Communication from the Commission on the revision of the method for setting the reference and discount rates (2008/C14/02).

46. **What evidence can be adduced to prove that the beneficiary spent the money to finance eligible costs?**

According to Recital (23) of the GBER, Member States shall require that the identification of eligible costs shall be supported by documentary evidence which shall be clear, specific and contemporary. In addition, pursuant to Article 12 of the GBER, Member States have the obligation to maintain detailed records with the information and supporting documentation necessary to establish that all the conditions laid down in the GBER are fulfilled. Such records should be kept for a period of 10 years. Therefore, in the context of the monitoring exercise on a particular GBER scheme, Member States may be requested to provide to the Commission all the relevant documentation to show that beneficiaries used the aid to finance projects that fulfil all GBER conditions, including the eligible costs.

Article 8

47. **Cumulation of aid under GBER with any other State aid in respect of the same eligible costs is acceptable if such cumulation does not result in exceeding the highest aid intensity or aid amount applicable to this aid under GBER. How to proceed when cumulation refers to aid granted under GBER with aid for which the Commission issued a decision approving some higher intensity than set forth in GBER?**

Article 8 refers to cumulation under the GBER. Of course, if the Commission approved higher aid intensities in a Commission decision, such aid is allowed for that specific project. Any aid already granted under the GBER for the same eligible cost will have to be taken into account when giving the additional aid under the decision but the total aid may reach the intensity specified in the Commission decision.

48. **How is it possible to comply with the rule on the cumulation of aid for a single project that includes several different categories of eligible costs, falling under several Articles of the GBER?**

If there is no overlap between the eligible expenditures under each of the Articles mentioned, the aid intensity for each relevant expenditure may indeed go up to the maximum foreseen for the specific Article.

49. **Does the term "public funding" in Article 8(2) mean State aid only or the amount of State aid and EU funding together?**

The term "public funding" refers to State aid and EU funding together. Please note that EU funding is to be understood as centrally managed EU funding which is outside the direct and indirect control of a Member State; this notion does not include funding under the Structural Funds (ERDF, Cohesion Fund?). Structural Funds are managed and controlled by the Member States and therefore would qualify as State aid. As a consequence, they would need to be taken into account for the calculation of the notification threshold, aid intensity under the GBER etc.

50. **Does "funding rate" in this Article 8(2) mean "aid intensity"?**

The term "funding rate" is broader than "aid intensity". It refers to the ratio of the total amount of public funding to the eligible costs for a specific project.

51. **How should one understand "the most favourable funding rate laid down in the applicable rules of Union law" in Article 8(2)?**

If we take for example a project with eligible costs of 100, that is eligible for aid under both a centrally managed EU funding program and a State aid scheme, with the State aid rules providing for a maximum intensity of 50% while the centrally managed EU funding program provides for a maximum intensity of 70%. In this example, the amount of State aid granted should not exceed 50% and the total public funding should not exceed an intensity of 70%.

Therefore the project could receive 50% State aid and an additional 20% from the EU funding. The amount of EU funding is not taken into account for the calculation of notification thresholds and aid intensities under the State aid rules.

52. **Investment aid enabling undertakings to achieve energy efficiency may be supported with 30% of the eligible costs (Article 38 GBER). Investment aid for the construction or upgrade of research infrastructure may be supported with 50% of the eligible costs (Article 26 GBER). Would it be in line with Article 26 of the GBER to support the investment cost of energy efficiency measures relating to research infrastructures with 50% of the eligible costs?**

Yes, the cumulation rules laid down in Article 8(3)(b) of the GBER apply to the extent that those investments costs are borne in the context of the construction or upgrade of research infrastructures.

Article 9

53. **Article 9(6) of the new GBER provides that Member States have two years within which to comply with the provisions of Article 9. Does the requirement in Article 9(1)(c) - ie to publish details on a State Aid website of each individual aid award exceeding EUR 500,000 - apply to all such awards from the 1st July 2014, or only to such awards from the date on which the website is established?**

Member States have the obligation to comply with the transparency provisions of Article 9 at the latest within two years after the entry into force of Commission Regulation (EU) No 651/2014. In practical terms this means that Member State have to publish information on their national or regional transparency website on individual aid awards above EUR 500,000 that were awarded after 01.07.2016. On the transparency requirements in general, please refer to the relevant Commission Communication, available here: (http://eur-lex.europa.eu/legal- content/EN/TXT/?qid=1405601594344&uri=CELEX:52014XC0627(02)).

54. **Is aid information to be published with the date the aid was granted on the central website as soon as possible starting from 1 July 2016. Does the reporting obligation after 1 July 2016 concern only individual aid under schemes notified to the Commission after 1 July 2016 or also to individual aid granted after 1 July 2016 for schemes notified before that date?**

Individual aid awards above EUR 500,000 granted after 1st of July 2016 have to be published at the national or regional transparency webpage. This concerns both, schemes that were notified before and after 1st of July 2016. There is no obligation to publish individual awards granted before that date. However, on voluntarily basis, Member States can publish this information earlier.

55. **Is the summary information referred to in Article 11 and laid down in Annex II (or a link to that information) or the full text of each aid measure, as referred to Article 11 (or a link to the full text) not to be published on the central website provided that no individual aid award under the scheme exceeds EUR 500,000?**

The obligation to publish the summary information sheet referred to in Article 11 and laid down in Annex II (or a link to that information) and the full text of each aid measure, as referred to Article 11 (or a link to the full text) concerns all aid measures that are put in place under the GBER, by each Member State. Such publication obligation deriving from Articles 9(1)(a) and (b) should be fulfilled once the respective schemes are in place, independent of the amount of individual aid awards to be granted. Once an individual aid award above Euro 500,000 is granted under a specific scheme, it shall also be published on the transparency web page, within the deadlines foreseen in Article 9(4).

56. **With regard to Article 9(4), what types of aid does the deadline for publication apply to?**

The obligation to publish the summary information sheet referred to in Article 11 and laid down in Annex II (or a link to that information) and the full text of each aid measure, as referred to Article 11 (or a link to the full text) concerns all aid measures that are put in place by Member States. Once an individual aid awards above Euro 500,000 is published on the transparency page, it shall be linked to the summary information sheet of the aid measure under which it was granted.

NOTES

1 Additional Frequently asked questions about State aid evaluation are available on the DG Competition website: https://ec.europa.eu/competition/state_aid/modernisation/evaluation_faq_en.pdf

2 Guidelines on regional State aid for 2014-2020, OJ C209, 23.07.2013.

3 Framework on State aid for shipbuilding, OJ C364 of 14.12.2011, p 9-13.

4 Council Regulation (EC) No 723/2009 of 25 June 2009 on the Community Legal Framework for a European Research Infrastructure Consortium (ERIC), OJ L 206, 8.8.2009, p 1.

2. CHAPTER II – MONITORING

Article 10

[5.146]

57. **Since the transparency condition is one of the general conditions for the applicability of the GBER, does the failure to comply with this condition render the measure incompatible with the internal market? What other possible sanctions are linked to a failure to publish aid on the central website?**

As stated in Article 10, failure to comply with the GBER conditions (including publication and information) might lead to a Commission decision that all or some of the future aid measures adopted by the Member State in question, that otherwise fulfil the GBER requirements, are to be notified to the Commission in accordance with Article 108(3) of the Treaty.

58. **Regarding sanctions foreseen in Article 10, will they be automatic?**

As provided under Article 10, the application of such sanction can only be done following a Commission decision, to this specific purpose. As stated in Recital (29) the sanction would have to be applied in a proportionate way compared with the number of occurrences and the gravity of the failure to comply with the GBER compatibility criteria by the relevant Member State.

Article 11

59. **Article 11 stipulates: "Member States, or in the case of aid granted to European Territorial Cooperation projects, alternatively the Member State in which the Managing Authority, as defined in Article 21 of Regulation (EC) No 1299/2013 of the European Parliament and of the Council, is located, shall transmit to the Commission (. . .) the summary information in the standardised format laid down in Annex II...". Does it mean that in case of European Territorial Cooperation (ETC) projects Member States can choose whether the Managing Authority or each Member State separately will send the summary information to the Commission?**

In order to avoid duplication of efforts, in case of ETC projects summary information can be sent by the Member State in which the Managing Authority is located (not necessarily by the Managing Authority itself) via the usual channels used for State aid notification. The other participating Member States may also place the information on their website (Article 9(1) of the GBER).

3. CHAPTER III – SPECIFIC PROVISIONS FOR DIFFERENT CATEGORIES OF AID

Article 13

[5.147]

60. **According to the provisions of Article 13, regional aid shall not apply in the energy generation, distribution and infrastructure sector. What are the NACE code references that this exclusion concerns?**

In more precise terms, only NACE division 35 is excluded from the regional aid provisions of GBER. This includes the following economic activities:

35 - Electricity, gas, steam and air conditioning supply

35.1 - Electric power generation, transmission and distribution

35.1.1 - Production of electricity

35.1.2 - Transmission of electricity

35.1.3 - Distribution of electricity

35.1.4 - Trade of electricity

35.2 - Manufacture of gas; distribution of gaseous fuels through mains

35.2.1 - Manufacture of gas

35.2.2 - Distribution of gaseous fuels through mains

35.2.3 - Trade of gas through mains

35.3 - Steam and air conditioning supply

35.3.0 - Steam and air conditioning supply.

When deciding whether the aid favours energy generation, distribution activities or energy infrastructure, the activity that is target of financing/investment will be the main criterion of the assessment.

61. **In a situation where relocation was caused by a compelling reason such as a flood protection measure, would the subsequent regional aid measure still fall outside the GBER?**

Yes, a notification of such aid measure would be necessary.

62. **How is the term ″concrete plans″ in Article 13(d) to be interpreted and how should be the existence of such concrete plans proven?**

The term ″concrete plans″ should be evaluated on a case-by-case basis. The granting authority could also envisage, for example, a declaration form, where the beneficiary would need to make a declaration that no such plans exist, and a monitoring mechanism that would verify that no relocation took place.

63. **Should the word beneficiary in Article 13(d) be interpreted as beneficiary at group level or only the beneficiary as legal entity?**

The assessment shall be done at the level of the economic unit (group level) and not only at the level of a subsidiary (given legal entity).

64. **Article 13 of the General Block Exemption Regulation (GBER)[5] states that ″Regional investment and operating aid ″ . . . shall not apply to: . . . (d) individual regional investment aid to a beneficiary that has closed down the same or a similar activity in the European Economic Area in the two years preceding its application for regional investment aid or which, at the time of the aid application, has concrete plans to close down such an activity within a period of up to two years after the initial investment for which aid is requested is completed in the area concerned.″**

The implementation of the provision concerning the notification obligation raises the following important interpretation questions: (i) At what level is the beneficiary considered; (ii) What is the area of reference for "closing down the same or similar activity";[6] (iii) What is the geographical scope of the provision, ie what is the relation between the location of the closed activity and the location of the new investment; (iv) What is the concept of "closing down an activity"?; and (v) What period of the closure should be taken into account for the notification obligation?

1. The beneficiary is to be defined at ″group level″, which is considered to be an economic entity with a common source of control rather than just a single subsidiary (a single legal entity).

2. The "closure of the same or similar activity" is to be looked at the level of the given establishment, rather than at the level of a region or a Member State. In other words, the activity would be considered to be closed down if the beneficiary closes down this activity in a particular establishment (even if he continues the same or similar activity elsewhere in the region or in the MS).

3. The provision applies only if the closure/relocation involves different EEA countries, ie the closure happens in one EEA country and the aided investment is carried out in another EEA country. Aid given to a beneficiary who has (partially) closed the same or similar activity elsewhere in the same Member State is not excluded from the benefit of the GBER.

4. The concept of closing down means that the activity is fully (100%) closed at the establishment concerned or that the activity is partially closed when this results in substantial job losses. For the purpose of this provision substantial job losses are defined as losses of at least 100 jobs or as a job reduction of at least 50% of the workforce in the establishment on the date of the application (compared to the average employment in the establishment in any of the two years preceding the date of application). Consequently, notification is necessary in all cases of full closures and if at least one of the two thresholds is exceeded in case of partial closures.

5. The notification of the aid measure is necessary if the beneficiary has closed down the same or similar activity within two years before the date of application or if the beneficiary plans to close such an activity over the entire period from the date of the application and two years after the completion of the initial investment.

65. **Article 13 excludes the transport sector from the scope of regional aid. Is this sector also excluded from the regional operating aid schemes in these regions?**

Pursuant to Article 13 (a) GBER, the transport sector is excluded from the scope of application of regional aid. The rationale for excluding the transport sector from the regional aid provisions in the GBER is to prevent the application of the regional aid rules instead of the more appropriate sector- specific rules. Both regional investment aid and operating aid are concerned by the exclusion.

66. **Can the activities listed in Article 13 (c) benefit of regional operating aid when intended to compensate additional costs, other than transport costs, in the outermost regions?**

Article 13(c) lists a number of sectors for which Member States cannot grant regional operating aid compensating for the transport costs in outermost regions. However, Article 1(3)(b) stipulates that the GBER applies to aid granted in the primary agricultural production sector, intended to compensate for additional costs (other than transport costs) in outermost regions as provided in Article 15(2)(b).

The other sectors mentioned in Article 13 (c) are either excluded from the scope of the GBER altogether (eg fisheries as per Article 1(3)(a)), or are subject to sector-specific rules (eg electricity, gas).

67. **Is it correct that regional investment aid for port infrastructure cannot be granted under the GBER, as the Regulation does not apply to the transport sector as well as the related infrastructure?**

Correct.

68. **Are yachts considered to be part of shipbuilding in the meaning of the GBER?**

As shipbuilding is not defined in the RAG or in the GBER and as RAG makes a reference to the former Framework on State Aid to Shipbuilding, the definitions given in the latter are still considered to be relevant. According to paragraph 12 of Framework on State aid to shipbuilding, 'shipbuilding' means the building, in the Union, of self-propelled commercial vessels. Yachts do not seem to be caught by the 'Self-propelled commercial vessel' definition, therefore construction of yachts could be considered eligible under the GBER.

Article 14

69. **Is it possible to grant aid under Article 14 of the GBER or under RAG for production of bioenergy or biofuels?**

According to Article 13(1)(a) of the GBER the regional aid section does not apply to aid which favours activities in / . . . / energy generation, distribution and infrastructure.

According to recital 33 to the GBER energy generation, distribution and infrastructure are subject to sector-specific internal market legislation, which is reflected in the criteria for ensuring that aid in these areas is compatible with the internal market and consistent with the Union's environmental and energy policies. Regional aid granted under Section 1 of the GBER pursues economic development and cohesion objectives, and is therefore subject to very different compatibility conditions. The provisions of this Regulation on regional aid should therefore not apply to measures concerning energy generation, distribution and infrastructure. Section 7 of the GBER contains specific rules for production of renewable energy, including biofuels. Since the GBER contains specific rules for energy production, including biofuels, investment aid for production of renewable energy and biofuels would not be covered by the regional aid provisions of the GBER.

70. **What is meant by ″single investment project″?**

The rule regarding the single investment project aims to avoid artificial splitting of an aided project into sub-projects in order to escape the notification obligation and/or to escape the capping of the aid amount in accordance with Article 2(20) of the GBER.

As defined by Article 14(13) of the GBER, the date of start of works of two investments concerned is decisive for the qualification of a single investment project. If the date of start of works of the aided projects are started within the period of three years, if the investments are made in the same NUTS 3 region and if the companies making the investments belong to the same group, then the investments concerned form a single investment project. Please note that in order to belong to same group, the companies need to form a collection of parent and subsidiary corporations that function as a single economic entity through a common source of control.

Please note that the "initial investment" is defined in Article 2 (49) of the GBER and that the 'start of works" is defined in Article 2(23) of the GBER.

71. **May the same beneficiary (at group level) commence a new initial investment only after three years from the date of start of works on the previous initial investment for which aid was granted in the same NUTS 3 region, in order to avoid the division of projects into sub-projects?**

Article 14(13) of the GBER does not restrict commencing a new initial investment project but provides when such projects are considered to be part of a single investment project (SIP) and clarifies the total amount of aid that may be granted if such a SIP amounts to a large investment project.

72. **Does the three years rule apply if works on the first aided investment in the same NUTS 3 region started before 1 July 2014 (before the GBER enters into force) and works on another aided investment started after 1 July 2014 (but within a period of three years)?**

For measures that fall under GBER 2014, ie the aid was granted after 30 June 2014, the rules on the single investment project as defined under Article 14(13) of the GBER 2014 apply. For this purpose the 3 years rule applies from the date of start of works of the aided projects carried out by the same beneficiary (at group level) in the same NUTS 3 region regardless of the fact whether those happened before the entry into force of the GBER, ie before 01/07/02014.

For measures that fall under GBER 2008, ie the aid was granted before 1 July 2014, the rules on the single investment project as defined under Article 13(10) of the GBER 2008 apply, regardless of the fact whether the works started before or after 1 July 2014.

73. **In the GBER there is no longer a reference to Regulation No 139/2004. Why has the reference been removed and does this mean that in the grant implementation process the same conditions as given by the Regulation No 139/2004 can be used?**

According to Article 3 (2) of Regulation 139/2004 control shall be constituted by rights, contracts or any other means which, either separately or in combination and having regard to the considerations of fact or law involved, confer the possibility of exercising decisive influence on an undertaking, in particular by: - ownership or the right to use all or part of the assets of an undertaking; - rights or contracts which confer decisive influence on the composition, voting or decisions of the organs of an undertaking.

Article 14(8)(c) provides as one of the conditions for eligibility of costs of intangible assets that the assets ″must be purchased under market conditions from third parties unrelated to the buyer.″ Unrelated parties are referred to also in other provisions of the GBER in connection with acquisition of assets (eg Articles 2(49) and (51), 14(4) and 17(3)(b)).

Since the GBER does not refer to control in terms of Article 3 of Regulation 139/2004, but to ″parties unrelated to the buyer ″, the fact that the buyer does not control the seller, is not sufficient for fulfilling the criteria of the relevant Articles of the GBER. The parties have to be unrelated. For that, there should be, at the very least, no influence (decisive or not) on the composition, voting or decisions of the organs of an undertaking. That is why even a very small equity participation (eg 1%) would mean that the parties are not unrelated.

74. **If an individual grant for broadband respects the regional aid map and the aid intensities set forth therein, and there has been a tender open to all types of projects, including broadband projects, could this type of wide tender be accepted as a "competitive selection process" under Article 14(10) of the GBER?**

The regional aid section of the GBER has the horizontal objective of promoting regional development rather than focusing on a specific sector. Therefore, public procurement procedures which are open to all sectors and all type of projects that fall under the scope of regional aid could be accepted as long as the ″competitive selection process″ carried out by the Member State complies with EU Public Procurement Rules.

75. **Is the net present value (NPV) of eligible costs of investments subject to the single investment project rule to be calculated as the sum of the three NPVs calculated on the date of starting the different investments, or the NPVs should be calculated for the same date (first investment or last investment)?**

The sub-projects of the investment do not happen at simultaneous times. The values of the eligible costs of and the aid to the sub-projects need to become time-consistent and hence comparable in order to be able to carry out the addition of the eligible costs and of the aid amounts of the sub- projects. Therefore, the NPV should be calculated to the time of one investment sub-project. Based on the case practice, all sub-projects should be discounted to the date of granting the aid for the first sub-project.

76. **What is meant by ″group″?**

In general, a corporate group or group of companies is understood as a collection of parent and subsidiary corporations that function as a single economic entity through a common source of control. The definition of 'single undertaking' included in the Regulation №1407/2013 is only relevant in the context of that Regulation.

77. **What are the effects of cumulating the provisions of Article 14 with Article 17?**

The cumulation rules of Article 14 apply only for regional investment aid within the borders of the regional aid map and using the regional aid intensities as defined for large enterprises and for SMEs.

Under Article 17, SME investment aid can be granted to SMEs irrespective of their location and for both types of eligible costs at the same moment, but only at the SMEs intensities of 20% for small and 10% for medium sized enterprises.

78. **What is meant by ″the assets that are reused″?**

Article 14(7) 2nd sentence of the GBER reads as follows: ″For aid granted for a diversification of an existing establishment, the eligible costs must exceed by at least 200% the book value of the assets that are reused, as registered in the fiscal year preceding the start of works.″

This sentence concerns initial investment for diversification of the output of an establishment into products not previously produced in the establishment (see Article 2(49)(a) GBER), and initial investment in favour of new economic activity for diversification of the activity of an establishment (see Article 2(51)(a) GBER). The term ″assets″

includes in the context of initial investments both tangible and intangible assets (see Article 2 (49)(a) and Article 2 (51)(a) GBER). Tangible assets consist of land, buildings and plant, machinery and equipment (see Article 2 (29) GBER).

In a "diversification" project certain assets used for producing a previously produced product would continue to be used for production of a new product. For instance, land and buildings that were used for producing product "A" could completely or partially be used for producing product "B". Such assets are the "reused assets".

The GBER does not require that assets used in an abandoned production are reused. However, pursuant to Article 14 (7) of the GBER, where existing and new assets are combined in a new production activity, the value of the new assets must exceed by at least 200% the book value of the assets that are reused, as registered in the fiscal year preceding the start of works. It means that the eligible costs must be at least three times as high as the book value of the "reused assets". The book value is the residual value of these assets as entered to the books of the beneficiary in the end of the fiscal year that precedes the start of works. If an asset (eg, a building) is only partially reused, the book value of the asset can be taken into account "pro rata". If the condition in Article 14 (7) is not fulfilled, the investment is not considered to constitute an initial investment in the form of diversification of an existing establishment diversification of the output of an establishment into products not previously produced in the establishment (Article 2 (49) of the GBER).

79. **What is meant by "the book value of assets"?**

The book value of assets refers to the net book value (ie the cost of the asset minus the accumulated depreciation).

In case of a "fundamental change in the manufacturing process", the value of the eligible costs has to exceed the value of the depreciation for the last 3 years prior to the start of works counting from the date of the granting of the aid.

In a "diversification of an existing establishment" scenario, the eligible costs must exceed by at least 200% the book value of the assets that are reused, as registered in the fiscal year preceding the start of works. It means that the eligible costs have to be more than three times higher than the book value of the "reused assets". The book value is the residual value of these assets as entered to the books of the beneficiary in the end of the fiscal year that precedes the start of works.

80. **Regarding the notion of "fundamental change in the production process": does it mean that during the modernisation (fundamental change) all the assets (or some of the assets) have to be replaced by the new assets and the costs of the new assets have to be at least the same as the depreciation of the old assets during the preceding 3 years entered in the accounts?**

Initial investment in the form of a fundamental change in the overall production process of an existing establishment means the implementation of a fundamental (as opposed to routine) process innovation. The GBER does not define the notion of fundamental change. However, the GBER requires that the eligible expenditure to be incurred for investments in tangible and intangible assets necessary for the implementation of this process innovation exceeds a certain threshold. Under Article 14(7) of the GBER this threshold is defined as "the depreciation of the assets linked to the activity to be modernised in the course of the preceding three fiscal years." The sum of depreciation is calculated over the three fiscal years that preceded the start of works of the project. "Start of works" is defined in Article 2(23) of the GBER.

The simple replacement of individual assets without fundamentally changing the overall production process constitutes a replacement investment which is not eligible for regional investment aid as it does not qualify as a fundamental change of an overall production process, and thus is not considered to constitute an initial investment. This holds also if individual items of equipment are replaced by others that are more performing unless this leads to a fundamental change on the overall production process. Under Article 14(4) eligible costs are investment costs in tangible and intangible assets. Under Article 14(8) for large undertakings the costs of intangible assets are eligible only up to a limit of 50% of the total eligible investment costs for the initial investment. Under Article 14(6) the assets acquired have to be new, except for SMEs.

81. **Do the assets that are re-used in the case of State aid to a diversification of an existing establishment qualify as eligible costs?**

In principle, only new assets can qualify as eligible costs for all types of initial investments foreseen by regional aid provisions of the new GBER (except for SMEs and for the acquisition of an establishment, as specified in Article 14(6) of the GBER, where used assets purchased from a third party can be eligible as well). In the diversification of an existing establishment (being a particular type of initial investment) there is one additional requirement. This investment project as such can be composed of two types of assets: 1) already belonging to the company and re-used for the project (and not being eligible for aid) and 2) new or- in special circumstances mentioned above- purchased from a third party used assets (eligible for aid). However, for the project to be considered eligible for aid, the value of its new assets (or purchased from a third party used assets) must exceed by at least 200% the book value of re-used assets as registered in the fiscal year preceding the start of works. As only the new assets (or – in special circumstances mentioned above – purchased from a third party used assets) are eligible for aid, the total aid will be calculated with reference to the amount of these assets.

82. **If depreciation of "assets linked to the activity to be modernised" is to include all assets, however peripherally linked they are to production (such as the assembly hall premises, shared lighting etc.), how is the percentage share of these depreciations to be determined in order to be compared against the eligible expenditure? On the basis of the floor surface area of the assembly hall, the percentage use of the machines, the share of sales?**

The term assets in the context of initial investments refers both to tangible and intangible assets (see Article 2 (49)(a) and Article 2 (51)(a) GBER). Tangible assets consist of land, buildings and plant, machinery and equipment (see Article 2 (28) GBER). Therefore, the buildings for manufacturing or storing manufactured products are covered by Article 14 (7) 2nd sentence of the GBER if these assets are linked to the activity to be modernised. Member State can carry out a pro rata calculation. The GBER does not prescribe the method to be applied by the Member State for that purpose, ie the Member State can rely on a bona fide approach that takes into account the specific situation and characteristics of the establishment and activity concerned.

83. **How is asset depreciation to be calculated for companies that have existed for less than three years?**

The Member State can apply a bona fide estimate, taking into account standard depreciation rules under its fiscal law.

84. **What can be the financial contribution "in the form free of any public support"?**

The financial contribution free of any public support means funding derived from the own resources of the company or loans obtained in the market on commercial terms, and not covered by State guarantees. The shareholder structure of the company is not relevant in this case.

The centrally managed Union funding is considered public support, even if it is not State aid.

85. **Is there any best practice on how to demonstrate that the assets of an establishment were acquired on market conditions, especially in the case of acquisitions of entire establishments (undertakings) and intangible assets?**

We would consider as best practice the expertise conducted by an independent company, or proving that the acquisition of an establishment takes place between independent companies or in full respect of the "arm's length" principle.

86. **In the case of regional aid, does the condition regarding the provision of wholesale access to build broadband infrastructure only apply to NGA networks, or also to basic broadband networks?**

The subsidized network operator must offer active and passive wholesale access under fair and non-discriminatory conditions both in cases of basic broadband and NGA.

87. **How is Article 14 to be applied in relation to undertakings' investments consisting in the construction and equipping of research laboratories?**

Article 14(11) GBER specifies that if the aid is granted for research infrastructure, the access to the latter needs to be transparent and non-discriminatory. This provision would therefore not be applicable in case of a laboratory infrastructure of undertakings which use this infrastructure for solely for their own purposes.

88. **What should be the adopted maximum limits of regional investment aid for a single investment project implemented in stages?**

According to Article 14(13) of the GBER, any initial investment started by the same beneficiary at group level within a period of three years from the date of start of works on another aided investment in the same NUTS 3 region shall be considered to be part of a single investment project. The applicable aid intensity for each partial project is the aid intensity applicable under the regional aid map in force at the time of awarding the aid (adjusted by scaling down, where applicable).

Article 15

89. **How are the thresholds in Article 15 to be applied?**

When the aid per beneficiary under all operating aid schemes does not exceed the amount resulting from one of the alternative methods to determine the additional operational costs (other than transports costs) referred to in Article 15(2)(b)ii of the GBER, the aid can be considered justified in terms of contributing to regional development and proportionate to the handicaps that undertakings face in the outermost regions.

90. **Can the regions covered by the measure choose to apply only one of the criteria or any criterion of Article 15(2)(b)ii, which ever would be the most favourable to the beneficiary?**

The regions covered by the measure may apply only one of these criteria. They may apply any criterion of Article 15(2)(b)ii, which is most favourable to the beneficiary. In any case, Member States shall ensure that the applicable threshold is respected.

91. **If the level of aid to be granted under a scheme does not exceed the limits provided in Article 15, can the aid be considered compatible with the internal market and exempt from notification?**

In order for operating aid to be considered compatible with the internal market and exempt from notification, it has to be ensured that aid from all operating aid schemes granted to the same beneficiary does not exceed the limits provided in Article 15 of the GBER and that other, specific and general conditions laid down in the GBER are respected.

Member States need to introduce in the national legislation specific provisions and effective mechanisms for control in order to ensure that the aid granted under all operating aid schemes per beneficiary does not exceed the limits laid down in the GBER and the respect of the other GBER conditions. Thus Member States shall also monitor cumulation with other operating aid schemes under which the beneficiaries can receive aid.

92. **To calculate the requirement laid down in point ii) of paragraph a), of number 2, of Article 15 of GBER, will it be acceptable to consider an average value calculated on the basis of a consultation to several freight forwarders operating in an outermost region?**

Article 15(2)(a)(ii) allows for the granting of operating aid aimed to compensate for aid which is objectively quantifiable in advance on the basis of a fixed sum or per tonne/kilometre ratio or any other relevant unit. In this respect, the Commission services consider that an average value calculated on the basis of a consultation to several freight forwarders would enable the beneficiaries to later choose for the lowest possible offer from freight forwarders. Therefore, we consider that for the purpose of calculating these costs, the Member State should take into account the lowest possible offer.

Ideally, those additional transport costs should be compensated on the basis of the actual costs incurred by the beneficiaries as demonstrated by an invoice.

93. **What is meant by "journey"?**

The definition of a "journey" as referred to in Article 15(2)(a) of the GBER should be understood to mean "the movement of goods from the point of origin to the point of destination, including intermediary sections or stages within or outside the Member State concerned, made using one or more means of transport". The 'point of destination' is defined as "the place where the goods are unloaded" (Article 2(53) of the GBER), whereas the 'point of origin' is defined as "the place where the goods are loaded for transport" (Article 2(54) GBER). Therefore, the additional transport costs should be calculated on the basis of the journey from the place of production (factory) to the place of delivery to the distributor/customer.

Article 16

94. **Urban development projects must be implemented via urban development funds in assisted areas. What is the connection between point 8 and 11 of Article 16?**

The possibility to "assign the implementation of the urban development aid measure to an entrusted entity" laid down in Article 16(11) of the GBER means that a Member State may entrust the implementation of a public financial instrument (ie the provision of equity, quasi-equity, loans or guarantees on behalf of the State) to a financial institution. To the extent that analogous provisions are laid down in Article 21 for risk finance aid, it can in this context be considered that qualifying financial institutions are those which are referred to in Article 2(79) of the GBER. In any case, urban development fund managers must be selected through an open, transparent and non-discriminatory call.

Article 17

95. **Does the term "third parties which are unrelated to the buyer" only relates to structural relationships or to contractual relationships such as supplier contracts between the buyer and the seller?**

For the parties to be unrelated, there should be, at the very least, no influence (decisive or not) on the composition, voting or decisions of the organs of an undertaking. That is why even a very small equity participation (eg, 1%) would mean that the parties are not unrelated. A typical contractual relationship without such a participation would not be considered to be within the scope of this provision.

Article 18

96. **Can internal services be financed in the context of preparatory works?**

Article 18(3) of the new GBER specifically states that: "The eligible costs shall be the costs of consultancy services provided by external consultants". Consequently, it is not possible to grant aid for internal consultancy services.

97. **Can the costs of preparatory studies and consultancy related to the investment project be included in the eligible costs of the investment even if they were encountered before the application for aid?**

As such treatment of consultancy costs is not specifically foreseen in the provisions of the new GBER, this is not allowed. Any aid for consultancy (for SMEs) should be granted under Article 18 of the new GBER.

Article 19

98. **How is the incentive effect to be applied in relation to participation in fairs?**

In order to comply with the provisions of Article 19 GBER regarding maximum aid intensity and the requirements regarding incentive effect, beneficiaries under the call will have to submit (maybe after an initial pre-selection phase) a request detailing the relevant eligible costs of fairs in which they intend to participate. It should be possible in the same request to identify the location. The incentive effect condition in this case must be met before any binding commitment to participate in the fair(s) is made.

Article 20

99. **What is meant by "investment expenditure directly related to the project"?**

Based on the comments received in the public consultation on the GBER, an effort was made to harmonise the wording of Article 20(2) with European Territorial Cooperation rules and extra- territorial cooperation cost categories as mentioned in the European Territorial Cooperation Regulation (Regulation (EU) No 1299/2013 of the European Parliament and of the Council of 17 December 2013 on specific provisions for the support from the European Regional Development Fund to the European territorial cooperation goal). The investment expenditure directly related to the project should be interpreted as meaning investment costs in tangible and intangible assets that are undertaken by the project-partners and are directly related to the European Territorial Cooperation project.

100. **Does aid intensity refer to the entire eligible costs of the project budget or the budgets of individual beneficiaries?**

The aid intensities are established at the level of individual beneficiaries. Please note that in case of participants of the project which are not engaged in economic activity, their funding is not considered State aid and therefore the maximum aid intensity requirement does not apply to them.

Article 21

101. **Is it correct that in the context of a follow-on investment under Art. 21 para 6 GBER it is not required that an independent investor makes the investment?**

Correct, the private investor making the follow-on investment should be the same as the investor who made the initial investment. The requirement of "independent private investor" as defined in GBER Article 2(72) relates to the time of the initial investment.

102. **Can the requirement in Article 21(7) that generation of new capital should reach "at least 50% of each investment round" be clarified?**

This provision addresses a situation where the aided investment involves the replacement of existing shareholders. In this case, out of the entire amount of each investment round involving such capital replacement operations, at least 50% must be invested in newly issued shares. One should not take into account previous investment rounds. Eg where 1m EUR is invested under a risk finance measure (private and public funds combined), 500,000 EUR of that can be used as replacement capital but the other 500,000 EUR must serve as new capital for the undertaking.

103. **What does it mean that private investors should be chosen in the framework of an open, transparent, non-discriminatory call?**

Art. 21 para 13(b) GBER makes reference to a genuine call to select private investors. The documents published for such a call should not define in detail the financial conditions under which the risk finance investment will be made, but should rather leave them open for independent private investors to make proposals. The outcome of the call should be specific on the conditions under which independent private investors are willing to invest alongside the public investor (cf. Art. 21 para 13 (b): "a call, which is [..] aimed at establishing appropriate risk-reward sharing arrangements").

The call is aimed at finding independent private investors that will invest with fresh funds as part of the risk finance provided together with the public investor. The purpose of risk finance measures is for the public investment to constitute a proportionate incentive for independent private investors.

104. **Does the GBER allow Member States to design risk finance measures with a downside protection mechanism other than by way of guarantees?**

Article 21.13(b) GBER requires that, for instruments other than guarantees, the open call aimed at establishing the risk-reward sharing arrangements favours selection criteria based on asymmetric profit sharing over downside protection. However, if the result of the call is that asymmetric profit sharing is not possible, Article 13 (b) does not prohibit downside protection.

Article 21.13(c) GBER does not apply to guarantees, but to all other financial instruments, such as loans and equity. It can for instance be agreed that the public investor will cover the first loss piece, but in that case this first loss piece must be limited to 25% of the total investment. Please note that the 25% cap does not limit the public investment to 25% of the total investment, but only limits the first loss taken by the public investor.

In this context, please note that paragraph 48 of the Risk Finance guidelines requires, amongst other, that, for instruments other than guarantees, where the public investor would cover a first loss higher than 25% or where the open call favours selection criteria based on downside protection over upside incentives, the risk finance measure needs to be notified and will be assessed under the Risk Finance Guidelines.

105. **What are consequences of the situation in which the task to implement a risk finance measure is assigned to the entity entrusted with the task?**

The Member State may entrust the implementation of a risk finance measure (e. g. providing the State financing or the State guarantees on behalf of the State) to an entrusted entity, which acts as the State.

In some cases it occurs that the entrusted entity shares risk with the State under the measure by co-investing own financial resources. Where it co-invests, the entrusted entity acts in its own capacity as a financial institution by taking risk on its own balance sheet, and is no longer subject to the risk finance rules on entrusted entities, but must respect the risk finance rules on financial intermediaries.

What is important to note is that the notion of an "entrusted entity" refers to its role (acting on behalf of the State), but not to the process of selecting such institution, ie entrustment does not necessarily imply an appointment. In other words, the State may select or appoint a financial institution to act as its entrusted entity.

106. **How shall the remuneration of the financial intermediaries be calculated?**

A market conform remuneration should be established on the basis of a competitive procedure for the selection of the financial intermediary. Any other additional advantage granted to the financial intermediary through the measure would have to be passed on to the investee undertakings or capped at the de-minimis level.

107. **Can the Commission clarify whether the levels of required investment of GBER Article 21(10) a-c also apply to follow-on investments in so far as the target undertaking meets the relevant criteria in GBER Article 21 (6) a-c?**

Follow-on investments under the risk finance rules are only allowed for eligible undertakings that have received an initial risk finance investment in the period prior to their first commercial sale up to 7 years thereafter. If a follow-on investment is made in the period prior to first commercial sale, the aggregate private participation rate of Article 21, paragraph 10(a) applies. If a follow-on investment is made in the period up to 7 years after first commercial sale, the aggregate private participation rate of Article 21, paragraph 10 (b) applies. A follow-on investment may be made even after the initial 7-year period, but in this case, pursuant to Article 21, paragraph 10(c), the risk finance measure must leverage additional independent private finance representing at least 60% of the follow-on risk finance investment.

108. **Does the GBER cover the situation where the entrusted entity co-finances and manages the fund?**

According to Article 21(17), "a Member State may assign the implementation of a risk finance measure to an entrusted entity". This means the Member State may entrust the implementation of a public financial instrument (ie the provision of a loan or equity financing or guarantees on behalf of the State) to a financial institution, in which case the financial institution acts as an entrusted entity of the State. GBER Article 2(79) specifies the types of qualifying financial institutions that may be entrusted by the State.

According to point 20 of the Risk Finance guidelines, the State and the entity acting on its behalf may not finance the SMEs directly. This means that financing to SMEs must be provided by financial intermediaries (they carry out credit risk assessment or investment due diligence), as per Article 17(13)a. The financial intermediaries must be selected through an open, transparent and non-discriminatory call as per Article 17(13)b.

109. **Should Article 21(18)(a) be interpreted as meaning that also the de minimis threshold has to be respected by the SMEs covered by this provision?**

According to recital (19) of the de minimis Regulation, where a de minimis aid scheme is implemented through financial intermediaries, it should be ensured that the latter do not receive any State aid. This can be achieved, for example, by requiring financial intermediaries that benefit from a State guarantee to pay a market- conform premium or to fully pass on any advantage to the final beneficiaries, or by respecting the de minimis ceiling and other conditions of this Regulation also at the level of the intermediaries.

In the light of the above, Article 21(18)(a) GBER is meant to address situations where aid is present at several levels, not only at the level of the final beneficiary (SME-level in this case). As regards the SME level, all the conditions under the de minimis Regulation (including the aid ceiling) should be applied. However, the risk scheme as such (including aid at the level of the financial intermediary and at the level of the SME) would still have to be designed in accordance with the GBER provisions or in accordance with the prescriptions of recital (19) in order to be exempted from notification.

Article 22

110. **Can start-up aid be made available through initial investments and follow on investments, provided that the total of the start-up aid to any one eligible undertaking respects the overall limits?**

Yes, start-up aid can be given for a total up to the maximum amounts mentioned in paragraphs 3(c) and 5, as long as the eligible undertaking remains at the moment of granting within the definition in paragraph 2 (ie within the 5 year period).

111. **For the awarding of aid for start-ups, the GBER does not require a call for tender. Is this the same in case the aid for start-ups is given by a fund, or must the fund management in this case be selected in accordance with Article 21 GBER in an open, transparent call?**

Article 22 GBER requires neither that the aid is awarded via a financial intermediary, nor that, if a financial intermediary is used, it must be selected in an open, transparent call.

However, if start-up aid is granted via a financial intermediary, it needs to be ensured that no aid remains at the level of the financial intermediary. If the financial intermediary is selected through an open, transparent, non-discriminatory call, then the presence of aid at the level of the financial intermediary can be excluded, provided that, in case of debt instruments, the financial intermediary is subject to the obligation to pass on in full to the final beneficiary any advantage stemming from the instrument; if not, the Member State needs ensure in another way that there is no aid at that level.

112. **Does the concept of ″entrusted entity″ also apply in the case of aid for start-ups?**

The rules on entrusted entities only apply within the scope of Article 21, which encompasses underlying basic principles that apply to aid for risk finance aid. It should be noted in this connection that the status of ″entrusted entity″ as defined in Article 2(79) of the GBER excludes that such entity intervenes or co-invests in a risk finance aid measure, as in such a case the entity concerned would rather have the status of a ″financial intermediary″. As regards start-up aid granted pursuant to Article 22 of the GBER, the concept of ″entrusted entity″ is not relevant as this provision does not require aid to be deployed via intermediated financial products.

113. **Can start-up aid be provided at different times and through a mix of aid instruments?**

Yes, start-up aid can be provided at different times, as long as at the time of granting the beneficiary complies with the eligibility conditions.

The maximum amount of start-up aid that can be given is not equal to the maximum nominal amount allowed for loans (eg 1 million EUR), plus the maximum guaranteed amount for guarantees (eg 1.5 million EUR), plus the maximum gross grant equivalent amount (eg 0.4 million EUR).

The calculation of the amounts that can be granted in case of a mix of aid instruments is on a proportional basis as described in paragraph 4 (″[..] the proportion of the amount granted through one aid instrument, calculated on the basis of the maximum aid amount allowed for that instrument, is taken into account in order to determine the residual proportion of the maximum aid amount allowed for the other instruments forming part of such a mixed instrument″).

If we take as an example a company in a non-assisted area that does not qualify as an 'innovative enterprise', to which the authorities wish to give a mix of start-up support in the form of a loan with duration of 10 years, in the form of a guarantee with duration of 10 years and in the form of a grant:

For the part in form of loan, the maximum nominal amount is 1 million EUR, so if 200,000 EUR is given as nominal loan amount, this represents 20% of the maximum nominal amount for loans.

For the part in form of guarantee, the maximum guaranteed amount is 1.5m EUR, so if 600,000 EUR is guaranteed, this represents 40% of the maximum guaranteed amount.

Therefore the support in form of grant is allowed up to 40% of the gross grant equivalent amount of 0.4 million EUR, which means that 160,000 EUR of gross grant equivalent is allowed.

114. **Article 5.4 of the old Research and Development and Innovation guidelines (2007- June 2014) restricted a beneficiary of young innovative enterprise aid to Research and Development aid and risk capital aid for a period of 3 years after receipt of the aid. There does not appear to be any similar restriction on a beneficiary under Article 22 of the GBER.**

The restriction was discontinued. The cumulation rules laid down in Article 8(4) GBER however apply.

Article 25

115. **Can the Commission confirm that when the beneficiary has obligation of maintenance under national legal basis or the provisions of Structural Funds, this maintenance period can be taken into consideration as part of the project, therefore depreciation costs occurred during this period are also eligible?**

No, regardless of any specific obligation laid down in the national legal basis or the provisions of Structural Funds, costs of buildings and land are only eligible to the extent and for the duration period used for the aided Research and Development project.

116. **Can the Commission confirm that the following costs are eligible, if they are directly linked to the research and development project: costs of participation of conferences related to the project such as travelling costs, accommodation costs, participation fees?**

Yes, such costs can be eligible as additional overheads and other operating expenses if they are incurred directly as a result of the project.

117. **How should Article 25.6(b)(i), second indent, be interpreted? What contribution should provide the research and knowledge-dissemination organisation, and what is the maximum funding rate for the entire project in case of collaboration?**

Article 25.6(b)(i), second indent, of the GBER provides for a possible increase in aid intensities for Research and Development projects which are carried out through effective collaboration (in the meaning of Article 2(90) of the GBER) between undertakings and research and knowledge- dissemination organisations. In particular, aid intensities may thus be increased by up to 15 percentage points, under the condition that the collaborating research and knowledge-dissemination organisations bear at least 10% of the eligible costs and have the right to publish their own research results. Since aid intensities must be established for each beneficiary of aid, including in the case of collaborative projects, the maximum funding rate for a specific project will however depend on the number and type of collaborating parties, as well as on the categories of research activities carried out and share of eligible costs borne by each one of them.

118. **Can you confirm that the aid for process and organisational innovation concern both products and services?**

Yes.

119. **Under which applicable rules can large undertakings receive aid for industrial property rights?**

Aid for obtaining, validating and defending patents and other intangible assets can only be granted to SMEs. However, large undertakings could for instance receive aid for the "costs of knowledge and patents bought or licensed from outside sources at arm´s length conditions" in the context of aid for Research and Development projects (Article 25 GBER).

120. **C an investment aid be granted for Research and Development projects aiming at improving technical and utility value of products, technologies and services?**

All R&D&I aid should in principle lead to increased technical and practical value of products, technologies or services. Please note that routine or periodic changes made to existing products, production lines, manufacturing processes, services and other operations in progress, even if those changes may represent improvements, are not eligible for funding.

Article 26

121. **What is meant by research infrastructure?**

Research infrastructures are defined by their content on the basis of Regulation No. 723/2009.[7]

122. **Is it possible to grant State aid to research organisations for construction or upgrade of research infrastructure if the use of the infrastructure is not linked to any concrete Research and Development and Innovation project?**

Yes.

123. **Can research organisations be aid beneficiaries of the investment aid for construction and upgrade of research infrastructure?**

Yes.

124. **Can investment aid be granted for research infrastructure covered under Art 26 GBER to undertakings, which will have exclusive right to use it?**

No. State aid for construction and upgrade of research infrastructure is in accordance with Art.26 of GBER compatible with the internal market, only if the access to such infrastructure is granted to several users on a transparent and non-discriminatory basis. Preferential access under more favourable conditions to the publicly co-financed infrastructure could only be granted to undertakings which have financed at least 10% of the investment costs. The access must be in proportion with their contribution to the investment costs and the conditions of access must be made public. Therefore, an exclusive use of publicly funded infrastructure by an undertaking or a group of undertakings (dedicated infrastructure) is not in line with Article 26 of GBER.

125. **Would it be in line with GBER to support the investment cost of energy efficiency measures relating to research infrastructures with 50% of the eligible costs?**

Yes, to the extent that those investments costs are borne in the context of the construction or upgrade of research infrastructures the cumulation rules laid down in Article 8.3(b) of the GBER apply.

126. **Can the users of publicly supported infrastructure receive de minimis aid?**

Yes, users of publicly supported infrastructure may receive de minimis aid, provided that all the applicable conditions are respected.

127. **How are the eligible investment cost calculated? What about cases that may require the re-assignment of existing assets?**

Article 26 of the GBER lays down the rules applying to investment aid for research infrastructures, that is to say aid for the construction or upgrade of research infrastructures that perform economic activities. In this context, the eligible costs referred to in Article 26(5) are the investment costs in tangible and intangible assets, as defined in Articles 2(29) and (30) of the GBER.

As a rule, and insofar as the aid relates to the construction and upgrade of research infrastructures, it is therefore expected that the eligible investment costs relate to the acquisition of new assets that will be used for performing economic activities, of which at least 50% have indeed to be borne by the aid beneficiary.

In those cases that may exceptionally require the re-assignment of existing assets (such as land and buildings) from non-economic to economic activities, and to the extent that such assets would qualify as eligible costs, this has to be done on the basis of a proper separation of the financing, costs and revenues of each type of activity. Under these circumstances, existing assets that have been provided or financed by the State for non-economic activities before the Aéroports de Paris judgment of 12 December 2000 (Case T-128/98 Aéroports de Paris v Commission ECLI:EU:T:2000:290) may generally be considered as not including State aid. Otherwise, such assets may be considered for the purpose of determining the "own contribution" from the aid beneficiary only if they have been fully depreciated by the date of their re-assignment or a compensation for their use equivalent to the market price is due by the economic "division" of the aid beneficiary to its non-economic "division".

128. **What conditions should be met to consider the bonus for the dissemination of the results reasonable?**

Taking account of the national specificity and the individual character of each R&D project, the Member State should define the optimal process for the research results (and not merely the overall deliveries of the project) to be disseminated to the widest extent possible, at national as well as EU level.

129. **May this provision provide the basis for the financing of R&D infrastructure in undertakings and in the case of projects implemented by the scientific and industrial consortia in which an undertaking will be the leader/applicant?**

Subject to compliance with the definition of "research infrastructure" laid down in Article 2(91) of the GBER, the R&D&I State aid rules do not contain any limitations relating to ownership (public or private) or nature of activities (economic or non-economic) of the relevant infrastructure.

However, in line with the said definition, the research infrastructure eligible for support under Article 26 of the GBER needs to be used by the scientific community, where the expression "scientific community" is used in the same sense as in Council Regulation (EC) No 723/2009 of 25 June 2009 on the Community legal framework for a European Research Infrastructure Consortium (ERIC)[8] and relates to any structured or unstructured group or network of persons engaging in a systematic activity to acquire knowledge. Furthermore, in line with Article 26 of the GBER, it is essential that access to the infrastructure is granted to several users on a transparent and non-discriminatory basis.

In light of the above, support for a research infrastructure used by one undertaking for its own purpose (therefore excluding its use by the "scientific community" on a non-discriminatory basis) falls outside the scope of Article 26.

130. **In what period should the monitoring be carried out?**

The monitoring mechanism applies where a research infrastructures receives public funding for both economic and non-economic activities and should be carried out for the economic life of the infrastructure, ie for the depreciation period of the relevant assets.

Article 27

131. **Are the costs referred to in Article 2(42), (personnel costs, materials, contracted services, communications, energy, maintenance, rent, administration, etc.) also applicable to Article 27?**

The cost categories mentioned in Article 2(42) of the GBER are directly relevant for regional operating aid only. Insofar as operating aid for innovation clusters is concerned, eligible costs are limited to the personnel and administrative costs related to the eligible activities listed in Article 27. Therefore, any costs that do not fall under the relevant categories (personnel and administrative costs) cannot be considered as eligible for this purpose.

132. **Since which moment is the 10 years period computed?**

The period during which operating aid may be granted for innovation clusters starts at the moment when such operating aid is granted for the first time.

133. **Besides costs of salaries, holiday pay, health checks and taxes, may personnel costs include costs of staff training and travelling to market the cluster?**

Yes, to the extent that such costs are clearly and strictly linked to the marketing of the cluster.

134. **When organising training programmes, workshops and conferences, are costs of buying materials and services also eligible (catering, renting a room, etc.)? Or travel costs for bringing over a speaker?**

Yes, to the extent that such costs are clearly and strictly linked to the organisation of a specific training/workshop/conference.

135. **What is considered eligible for marketing purposes? Does marketing of the cluster include travelling abroad (for personnel) and organising an event there (eg to meet other clusters, to market what the cluster has to offer) or participating in a fair?**

Eligible costs for marketing purposes are those personnel and administrative costs (including overheads) which are incurred with a view to increase participation of new undertakings or organisations, as well as visibility of the relevant cluster. To the extent this is the case, eligible costs can thus refer to travelling abroad, organising an event or participating in a fair.

136. **May operating aid be provided both to existing clusters and to new ones?**

Yes. Since operating aid is limited to a maximum of 10 years, for existing clusters this however means that any past aid needs to be taken into account, ie the starting date for the calculation is the date of the first aid granted.

137. **May the operating costs listed in Article 27(8), points a), b) and c) be implemented by companies outside the cluster, as eligible costs?**

As follows from Article 27(2) of the GBER, operating aid for innovation clusters shall be granted exclusively to the legal entity operating the cluster. The eligible costs are limited to the personnel and administrative costs incurred by the cluster operator and relating to the eligible activities listed in Article 27(8). Therefore, any costs that do not fall under the relevant categories (personnel and administrative costs) cannot be considered as eligible for this purpose.

138. **How is Article 27(4) of the GBER to be interpreted? May there be an "exemption from the payment obligation" for cluster members or users?**

As follows from Article 27(1) of the GBER, aid for innovation clusters is reserved to the legal entity operating the innovation cluster (and not eg its members or users) and can only be block exempted if all the necessary conditions are fulfilled. One of these conditions is that fees charged for using the clusters' facilities and for participating in their activities correspond to the market price or reflect costs.

However, although there may not be an "exemption from the payment obligation", cluster members or users can benefit from aid granted in compliance with other GBER provisions (typically, aid for start-ups under Article 22 and aid for innovation advisory and support services under Article 28) or the de minimis regulation to purchase the clusters' services.

Article 28

139. **May aid associated with obtaining and defending intellectual property rights cover only the costs associated with obtaining such rights to research results and processes carried out by the undertaking/beneficiary on his own, or also the acquisition of rights of a third party who carried out the research and patented its outcome?**

The eligible costs listed in Article 28(2)(a) of the GBER are costs for obtaining, validating and defending patents and other intangible assets and have to be incurred by the beneficiary directly. Costs linked to acquisition of rights from a third party can only be eligible under Articles 25 ("aid for research and development projects") or 29 ("aid for process and organisational innovation") of the GBER, provided they are incurred in the framework of an eligible R&D&I project or activity.

Article 30

140. **Can the Commission confirm which Articles within Section 4 – Aid for research and development and innovation can be used to support relevant activities in (a) the fishery and aquaculture sector and (b) the primary agricultural production sector?**

As long as there is no distinction within Article 1(3)(a) and (b) as to the type of aid or instrument, all Articles within the Section 4 are applicable to aid in the fishery and aquaculture sector. Except for Article 30 that deals with a particular type of aid to research organisations for undertaking studies in the fisheries and aquaculture sector, all other Articles of Section 4 apply to the primary agricultural production sector as well.

Article 31

141. **How is Article 31(2) to be interpreted?**

Aid for training which is mandatory under national law lacks incentive effect as it would be pursued even in the absence of public funding, and, therefore, cannot be block exempted. In this regard, it is irrelevant whether the training is carried out to comply with national standards which are mandatory for the undertaking in question or for its employees and also whether the training is carried out by the undertaking itself or an external trainer. As long as the State is paying for this training, which is mandatory under national law, and the training benefits the undertaking directly or indirectly (in case the employees are trained outside the undertaking), the aid is covered by Article 31(2) and cannot be granted.

142. **Can accommodation costs of seafarers be exceptionally covered regarding training aid in maritime transport?**

Article 31(3)(b) explicitly excludes accommodation from eligible costs (in contrast with the previous GBER). Article 31(5) (applicable only to maritime transport) requires that training is conducted on board of ships and trainees are supernumerary (ie not active crew members). In order to comply with those two conditions trainees have to stay on board of a ship during training. Thus, in the case of training on board of ships accommodation costs are operating costs directly relating to the training project. Accommodation cost may be found compatible should a training aid be notified and assessed under the Maritime Guidelines.

143. **Which is the maximum aid intensity for mid-sized businesses and small enterprise, for the training to workers with disabilities or disadvantaged workers?**

As stated in point 4 of Article 31, the aid intensity shall not exceed 50% of the eligible costs. It may be increased, up to a maximum aid intensity of 70% of the eligible costs, as follows:

(a) by 10% if the training is given to workers with disabilities or disadvantaged workers;

(b) by 10% if the aid is granted to medium-sized enterprises and by 20% if the aid is granted to small enterprises;

The maximum aid intensity for training to workers with disabilities or disadvantaged workers is thus

50%+10% = 60%;

The maximum aid intensity for training to workers with disabilities or disadvantaged workers in mediums sized enterprises is thus 50%+10%+10% = 70%;

The maximum aid intensity for training to workers with disabilities or disadvantaged workers in small enterprises is thus 50%+10%+20% = 80% but limited to the maximum aid intensity of 70%.

144. **Which types of training would be covered by Article 31 and what does the Commission mean by 'national mandatory standards on training'?**

The purpose of Article 31(2) is to allow for the support of training measures undertaken by enterprises with the purpose of developing and updating the knowledge of their workforce (eg management trainings, language trainings). However, trainings that are mandatory under the national system for example health and safety training would have to be pursued anyway, even in the absence of the aid. Aid for such trainings, thus, lacks incentive effect and can, therefore and in accordance with Article 31(2), not be block exempted

145. **What is meant under "trainers' personnel costs" and "wage costs" – only salaries or all related non-wage costs (social insurance contributions, additional remuneration, allowances, etc.)? How should eligible personnel costs be calculated – gross (before social security contributions and other non-wage costs that shall be paid by the employer) or net?**

″Trainers' personnel costs″ are identified in Article 31 point 3 (a) of GBER as ″the hours during which the trainers participate in the training″. This can be either the fees paid to the trainers or, if they are in-house trainers, an allocation pro-rata of their salaries to the hours spent on training. According to the recital (23) of the GBER: ″(. . .) The identification of eligible costs should be supported by clear, specific and up-to date documentary evidence. All figures used should be taken before any deduction of tax or other charges. (. . .)″ Therefore all sums should be calculated on the basis of gross amounts.

The notion of ″wage costs″ is not defined in the GBER in relation to training aid but is applicable to regional aid measures or aid measures for certain categories of employees. The notion of ″wage costs″ may however be relevant for training aid under ″trainees' personnel costs for the hours during which the trainees participate in the training″ (see above). Article 2 point 31 of GBER defines 'wage cost' as ″the total amount actually payable by the beneficiary of the aid in respect of the employment concerned, comprising over a defined period of time the gross wage before tax and compulsory contributions such as social security, child care and parent care costs″.

As regards ″allowances″ or ″additional remuneration″, pursuant to Article 31(3)(b) of the GBER additional costs not related to the trainers' or trainees' personnel costs may only be covered, if they qualify as ″operating costs directly relating to the training project″. Therefore, if ″allowances″ or ″additional remuneration″ are considered for example as necessary travel expenses, then they can be covered by this category.

146. **Do the costs of advisory services linked to the training project include consultancy fees for the preparation of the project proposal?**

Consultancy fees for the preparation of the project proposal can be considered as ″costs of advisory services linked to the training project″ and therefore falling within the list of eligible costs as defined in Article 31 point 3 (c) if this project proposal has been eventually chosen.

Article 32

147. **How should Articles 32(3) and 33(3) be interpreted?**

These paragraphs intend to clarify in what circumstances the recruitment or wage costs of newly employed personnel shall be eligible for support, even in case of no net increase in the number of total employees of the undertaking (and without prejudice to the net increase in another establishment of that undertaking). Therefore, as the beneficiary of the aid will be the undertaking, the conditions concerning the net increase should apply at the level of the undertaking.

148. **May firms acquire grants for the recruitment of disadvantaged workers in less than 12 months, if there is a net increase in the number of employees?**

The condition in paragraph (3) of Article 32 is meant to ensure that no employees are made redundant with the objective of re-hire of disadvantaged workers in order to benefit from the State aid. If the company is in existence for less than 12 months, the average number of workers shall be calculated over the period for which the company was in existence. The firm may thus acquire grants for the recruitment of disadvantaged workers if there is a net increase in the number of employees.

149. **What is the meaning of ″regular employment″? Is State subsidised employment considered to be regular employment?**

State subsidised employment may also be considered as regular employment. The reason for requiring the worker not to be in regular employment is linked to the definition of 'disadvantaged worker'. In this context, the type of work or financing shall not change the nature of 'regular employment', meaning lasting a certain minimum duration. The other conditions in Article 32 regarding the net increase in the number of workers shall also be complied with.

Articles 33–34

150. **For what duration may State aid for the employment of workers with disabilities be granted?**

Article 33 and 34 may be used to compensate the additional costs of employing workers with disabilities and the scope of the scheme may limit the benefit to one or more undertakings based on objective criteria. The duration however will have to be limited to the GBER duration and the aid will have to be capped ex ante (to the notification threshold) to ensure that the aid amount remains transparent.

151. **If the beneficiary provides sheltered employment, eligible costs may be, among others, the costs of constructing, installing or modernising the production units of the undertaking concerned. Does this investment mean the rooms in which the employer offering sheltered employment carries out production, or should it be understood broadly - as all units that the employer uses to conduct economic activity, eg to provide services, as well as other rooms, eg rest and social base as required under national law?**

This eligible cost shall be understood broadly as covering all units that the employer uses to conduct economic activity.

152. **Could it be considered aid to keep disabled workers in their posts when the recruitment has taken place one or two years before the date of granting the aid?**

If at the time of employment the workers was not disabled but becomes disabled during the validity of the contract, the company employing him may receive support under Article 33 of the GBER starting with the moment when the worker becomes disabled. If however the worker is already employed for two years before the company requests support, it is doubtful whether the condition of Article 33(4) is fulfilled.

153. **Could the term "any given period" mean that a limited period is required or could the term "any given period" also be interpreted in the sense of a period of time as long as the validity of the employment contract?**

Any given period in the context of Article 33(2) shall be interpreted as a period of time as long as the validity of the employment contract. The eligible cost base in Article 32(2) is stricter as this refers to the recruitment of disadvantaged workers that, after a certain period, are considered to have been duly integrated in the working market and no need of additional support exists.

Article 36:

154. **How is the maximum aid intensity established in collaboration projects if the partners are undertakings of different sizes?**

Investment aid granted under Article 36 for undertakings going beyond standards for environmental protection can be granted with a maximum aid intensity of 40% of the eligible costs. This intensity can be increased by 20 percentage points for small enterprises and by 10 percentage points for medium enterprises. Regional bonuses can be added depending on the location of the investment.

The aid intensity shall be established **for each beneficiary**, see e.g. the fact that the relevant notification threshold is set per undertaking. This interpretation is further supported by the Research and Development and Innovation (RDI) State aid rules which typically involve collaboration projects (see Article 31(3) of the GBER 2008 "The aid intensity shall be established for each beneficiary of aid, including in a collaboration project, [. . .]" and point 15(c) of the 2014 RDI Framework "The aid intensity is calculated per beneficiary"). This means that, when the aid is calculated, first, the eligible costs of each partner must be identified, then, the relevant maximum aid intensity (50% for the medium-sized company and 60% for the small company) can be used to calculate the maximum aid amount.

155. **Should only the purchase price of a vehicle be subsidised or are also the lease costs covered?**

The purchase price of a transport vehicle can be covered by investment aid under Article 36 of the GBER provided that the vehicle complies with adopted Union standards and its acquisition takes place before those standards enter into force. If the vehicle complying with Union standards is purchased after the Union standards have entered into force, its acquisition costs are not eligible for investment aid.

GBER allows lease costs to be covered by investment aid only when it is in the form of financial leasing, which contains an obligation to purchase the asset at the expiry of the term of the lease.

156. **Are best available techniques conclusions considered to be the Union standards applicable according to the Article 2(102) of the new GBER?**

According to Article 2(102), Union standards are defined as the obligation under Directive 2010/75/EU of the European Parliament and of the Council to use the best available techniques (BAT) and ensure that emission levels of pollutants are not higher than they would be when applying BAT.

In light of the above, the BAT conclusions set the Union standard for Member States. Only after a period of four years following the publication date of BAT conclusions, the Union standards become mandatory for undertakings. During this 4-year period, the BAT conclusions are considered, for the purposes of Article 36(3), adopted Union standards but not yet in force.

157. **As to what moment in the process of project submission/evaluation/implementation is the amount of eligible costs determined? Taking into consideration the Article 36(3) of the new GBER, is the amount of eligible costs to be re-evaluated if in the process of project implementation new Union standards are adopted?**

For the purposes of Article 36(3) of the GBER, the evaluation of eligible costs (and the applicable Union standards) shall be made at the moment of the project "evaluation", meaning when the project is assessed by the national authorities in view of deciding if aid would be granted for it. If new standards are adopted after the aid has been granted, during the implementation of the project, there is no need to re-evaluate the eligible costs of the aid amounts. However, when new standards are adopted before the aid is granted, these should be taken into account in the evaluation of the project and the eligible costs and amounts of aid should be adjusted accordingly (for example the measure could be converted in "earlier adaptation to future Union standards").

158. **What is the meaning of the concept of extra investment costs under Article 36(5) of the GBER?**

In Article 36(5) the extra investment costs refer to the additional investment costs necessary and directly linked to the investment that enable going beyond the applicable Union standards or ensuring an increased level of environmental protection in the absence of Union standards.

They could be identified as the difference between the investment costs of a project guaranteeing higher level of environmental protection (allowing the undertaking to go beyond the applicable Union standards) and the investment costs of another technologically comparable project that achieves a lower level of environmental protection (allowing the undertaking to simply meet the applicable Union standards).

159. **Is it necessary to take into account the operating costs and benefits, for calculating the eligible costs for investment aid for environmental protection?**

According to Article 36(5) of the GBER the extra investment costs refer to the additional investment costs necessary and directly linked to the investment that enable going beyond the applicable Union standards or ensuring an increased level of environmental protection in the absence of Union standards.

They represent the difference between the investment costs of a project guaranteeing higher level of environmental protection (allowing the undertaking to go beyond the applicable Union standards) and the investment costs of another technologically comparable project that achieves a lower level of environmental protection (allowing the undertaking to simply meet the applicable Union standards). Operating costs and benefits do not need to be taken into account.

Article 37:

160. **How should the end of the investment be understood? Is this the physical completion, or maybe performance of start-up, or putting into actual use and its beginning?**

Under Article 37(2) of the GBER investment aid for early adaptation to future Union standards is permissible if the investment is implemented and finalised at least one year before the date of entry into force of the standard concerned.

An investment shall be considered implemented and finalised when the measures it is aimed at are put in place and can deliver a result, guaranteeing the achievement of the Union standards.

161. **Can investment aid to comply with the Union standards be granted under Article 37 for energy efficiency measures that are excluded under Article 38(2)?**

Article 38(2) of the GBER states that aid shall not be granted under this Article where improvements are undertaken to ensure that undertakings comply with Union standards already adopted, even if they are not yet in force.

Article 37 can be used to provide aid for early adaptation to standards already adopted, including for energy measures that would not qualify for aid under Article 38(2). Of course, all the conditions foreseen in Article 37 should be complied with.

Article 38:

162. **Does this provision include aid for mobility actions aimed at the achievement of energy saving like vehicle fleet management systems or mobility plans in undertakings, when the criteria established by Article 38(3) are fulfilled?**

According to GBER, "energy efficiency" means an amount of saved energy determined by measuring and/or estimating consumption before and after implementation of an energy efficiency improvement measure, whilst ensuring normalisation for external conditions that affect energy consumption.

Aid measures directed to vehicle fleet management systems or mobility plans of undertakings can be granted under Article 38 of the GBER, provided the measures lead to reduced energy consumption, in line with the definition of the GBER for energy efficiency.

163. **What is the best way to deal with investments where there is an increase in capacity as compared with the counterfactual scenario?**

According to Article 38(3)(b), the reference investment should be a "similar, less energy-efficient investment". This should be read in light of the purpose of the provision. The purpose of comparing the planned investment with a reference investment is to ensure that aid is only granted to cover costs resulting from the higher level of energy-efficiency. Thus, Article 38(3)(b) explicitly states that "the costs not directly linked to the achievement of a higher level of energy efficiency shall not be eligible".

By calculating the eligible costs on the basis of a comparison between the planned investment and an alternative investment with a significantly lower capacity, costs not directly linked to the achievement of a higher level of energy efficiency, i.e. costs related to the higher production capacity, would be included in the eligible costs. Hence, such an investment would not be acceptable as a reference investment under Article 38(3)(b) of the GBER.

The reference investment should be similar in terms of size and capacity. In this respect, point 73 of the EEAG and in particular footnote 49 clarify that the reference investment should be "a technically comparable investment", meaning "an investment with the same production capacity and all other technical characteristics (except those directly related to the extra investment for the targeted objective)".

164. **For the purpose of Article 38, is it possible to consider total investment costs as eligible costs?**

We confirm that in certain situations, when the energy efficiency project is exclusively aimed at increasing the energy efficiency (and no investment would have been necessary to be made by the beneficiary in the absence of the aid) it is possible to consider the total investment costs as eligible costs.

165. **Does Article 38 also apply to savings made in power and heat generation, for example by acquiring more efficient sources (boilers), since in such cases there is a fuel saving and thereby a saving in primary energy?**

Investment aid for energy efficiency measures can be granted under Article 38 of the GBER. According to the GBER, "energy efficiency" means an amount of saved energy determined by measuring and/or estimating consumption before and after implementation of an energy efficiency improvement measure, whilst ensuring normalisation for external conditions that affect energy consumption.

It follows that measures aimed at fuel savings in power and heat generation (including cogeneration units) could, in principle, be covered under this Article, provided the measures lead to reduced energy consumption, in line with the definition of the GBER for energy efficiency.

166. **How do standards concerning the financing of energy efficiency projects apply?**

Aid under Article 38 of the GBER can only be granted for energy efficiency projects that are not necessary to comply with Union standards. The provision refers in general to all standards applicable to the beneficiaries, not specifically to standards imposing a certain level of energy efficiency.

Union standards are defined in Article 2(102) of the GBER as:

(a) a mandatory Union standard setting the levels to be attained in environmental terms by individual undertakings; or

(b) the obligation under Directive 2010/75/EU of the European Parliament and of the Council to use the best available techniques (BAT) and ensure that emission levels of pollutants are not higher than they would be when applying BAT; for the cases where emission levels associated with the BAT have been defined in implementing acts adopted under Directive 2010/75/EU, those levels will be applicable for the purpose of this Regulation; where those levels are expressed as a range, the limit where the BAT is first achieved will be applicable.

As a general rule, if the beneficiary already complies with all the Union standards applicable to it (including standards adopted but not yet in force), aid for energy efficiency projects can be granted to the respective beneficiary. If however the beneficiary does not comply with all the standards applicable to it, it must be checked that the energy efficiency project for which aid is required would not be necessary for the beneficiary to comply with those standards. If a project is necessary to comply with a Union standard, the beneficiary would be obliged to undertake the respective project (or an equivalent project) anyway and the aid would have no incentive effect.

167. **Could installations of undertakings whose primary activity is not electricity/heat production benefit from aid granted under Article 38 of the GBER given that they enable undertakings to achieve energy efficiency?**

According to Article 2(103) of the GBER, "energy efficiency" means an amount of saved energy determined by measuring and/or estimating consumption before and after implementation of an energy-efficiency improvement measure, whilst ensuring normalisation for external conditions that affect energy consumption.

Aid for measures aimed at enabling installations (regardless of the nature of their activity) to achieve energy efficiency can be granted under Article 38 of the GBER, provided the measures lead to reduced energy consumption, in line with the definition of the GBER for energy efficiency.

Nevertheless aid shall not be granted where improvements are undertaken to ensure that the undertakings comply with Union standards already adopted, even if they are not yet in force (Article 38(2) of the GBER).

Article 39:

168. **What is meant by "efficiency fund managers"?**

The energy efficiency fund manager is defined in Article 2(106) of the GBER as "a professional management company with a legal personality, selecting and making investments in eligible energy efficiency projects". Any company complying with the definition provided in GBER can be an energy efficiency fund manager.

According to Article 39 of the GBER, "the aid shall be granted in the form of an endowment, equity, a guarantee or loan to an energy efficiency fund or other financial intermediary, which shall fully pass it on to the final beneficiaries being the building owners or tenants. The aid granted by the energy efficiency fund or other financial intermediary to the eligible energy efficiency projects may take the form of loans or guarantees." There is therefore a distinction between energy efficiency funds and other financial intermediaries.

An energy efficiency fund is defined in Article 2(105) of the GBER as "a specialised investment vehicle set up for the purpose of investing in energy efficiency projects aimed at improving the energy efficiency of buildings in both the domestic and non-domestic sectors." An energy efficiency fund will be managed by an energy efficiency fund manager, who will make investments from the fund. It is not excluded that energy efficiency fund managers use the services of financial intermediaries under certain circumstances.

A bank (or another financial intermediary) setting up a unit to grant aid to final beneficiaries for energy efficiency measures in buildings will most likely qualify as a financial intermediary, but not as an energy efficiency fund.

169. **In what form can energy efficiency funds or other financial intermediaries grant aid to final beneficiaries? Can the aid be in the form of a grant?**

Under Article 39(5) aid granted by energy efficiency funds or other financial intermediaries may take the form of loans or guarantees.

Article 2 of the GBER provides the following definitions for loans and guarantees:

- loan is defined in point 82 as "an agreement which obliges the lender to make available to the borrower an agreed amount of money for an agreed period of time and under which the borrower is obliged to repay the amount within the agreed period";
- guarantee is defined in point 67 as "a written commitment to assume responsibility for all or part of a third party's newly originated loan transactions".

Grants are a form of aid which is not expected to be repaid by the recipient. They therefore do not fall within the mentioned definitions, nor comply with Article 39(6), which states that the repayment shall not be less than the nominal value of the loan. In this context grants are consequently excluded as a form of aid that could be granted through energy efficiency funds or other financial intermediaries.

Article 40:

170. **Does the reference to "conventional electricity and heating installations" include conventional electricity and thermal energy installations?**

According to Article 40(4), the eligible costs shall be the extra investment costs for the equipment needed for the installation to operate as a high-efficiency cogeneration installation, compared to conventional electricity or heating installations of the same capacity or the extra investment cost to upgrade to a higher efficiency when an existing installation already meets the high-efficiency threshold.

According to Article 2(108) of the GBER "cogeneration" or combined heat and power (CHP) means the simultaneous generation in one process of thermal energy and electrical and/or mechanical energy.

From the stated above it follows that conventional electricity and thermal energy installations can be used for the calculation of the eligible costs provided that the principles of calculating the eligible costs, set out in Article 7 of the GBER, are respected.

171. **Does this article apply to support for the construction of biogas plants that use biowaste?**

Investment aid for high-efficiency cogeneration can be granted under Article 40 of the GBER. According to Article 40(4), the eligible costs shall be the extra investment costs for the equipment needed for the installation to operate as a high efficiency cogeneration installation, compared to conventional electricity or heating installations of the same capacity or the extra investment cost to upgrade to a higher efficiency when an existing installation already meets the high-efficiency threshold. If follows that the costs of the fuel, or of the installation producing the fuel used by the cogeneration units cannot be covered by aid granted under this provision of the GBER.

172. **Could installations of undertakings whose primary activity is not electricity/heat production be treated equally to those belonging to undertakings from the energy sector and benefit from aid for the promotion of energy from renewable sources under Article 41 of the GBER (biomass) or aid for high-efficiency cogeneration under Article 40 of the GBER (gas) respectively?**

If the conditions set out in Articles 41 and 40, as well as in Chapter I, are complied with, aid can be granted to eligible installations, regardless of which is the primary activity of the undertaking.

Article 41:

173. **What is the best way to determine the difference between the costs of both investments as long as investments in the renewable energy field are environmentally friendly by default, therefore one could consider the base scenario as being "no investment" at all, instead of a "similar" investment?**

Indeed, investments in renewable energy production facilities are environmentally friendly. The reference investment would normally be a less environmentally friendly energy production facility with the same capacity.

Please note in this context that Annex 2 of the EEAG provides a list of typical counterfactual (reference) investments. In case of doubt, we suggest referring to the examples provided in this Annex to establish the correct counterfactual also for the environmental measures designed under the GBER.

174. **Granting of investment aid is limited to new installations. Does this limit refer to "new installation" or rather to "new investment"? Are costs for reconstruction or expansion of renewable installation eligible under Article 41(5)?**

Under Article 41(5) of the GBER the investment aid can cover part of the upfront costs (depending on the amount of the eligible costs) of new renewable installations.

Reconstruction works (upgrading or refurbishment) of an existing plant can also be eligible for investment aid under Article 41(5) of the GBER if this operation concerns considerable parts of the plant and is prolonging its expected lifetime.

However, maintenance operations and replacement of small parts and components of a plant, that are normally done during the expected lifetime of the plant, would not qualify for investment aid under Article 41(5) of the GBER.

175. **How should the expression "no aid shall be granted or paid out after the installation started operations" be understood?**

Article 41 of the GBER specifies the rules for granting investment aid in favour of renewable energy. Articles 42 and 43 of the GBER detail the rules which are applicable to operating aid in favour of renewable energy.

Article 41(5) states that "no aid shall be granted or paid out after the installation started operations and aid shall be independent from output". This provision serves to distinguish between investment aid and operating aid and thus whether Article 41 of the GBER is applicable or whether the provisions of Article 42 respectively Article 43 of the GBER need to be complied with.

Moreover one of the general conditions for the application of the GBER is that the aid has a clear incentive effect (Recital 5 of the GBER). Please note that the Commission considers that aid does not present an incentive effect for the beneficiary in all cases where work on the project had already started prior to the aid application by the beneficiary.

However, when the aid (or part of it) is paid within a short period of time after the completion of the project in order to allow the authorities to carry out necessary verifications that the project complies with all the applicable criteria (e.g. verify that the project has been finalised, verify that the alleged expenses have been incurred by beneficiaries), such aid would still qualify as investment aid that can be granted under Article 41(5) of the GBER, as long as all the other conditions are complied with (in particular the aid amount should be totally independent from the output).

176. **Does Article 41(5) prohibit to pay out the last tranche of investment aid if the plant started operation?**

Article 41 applies to aid granted for compensating part of the upfront investment costs only, whereas Articles 42 and 43 applies to aid paid out over the depreciation period (economic life time). Article 41(5) does therefore not prohibit to pay out the last tranche of investment aid as a balance payment to match differences between anticipated and actual expenditure in order to avoid overcompensation.

177. **Biofuels are made from raw material that is agricultural or forest based biomass. Agricultural biomass is manure, agricultural residues (straw), food crops residues, oilseed rape, cereals and sugar beet. Forest based biomass is wood wastes. Which of these raw materials can be used for food-based biofuels, which are defined as biofuels produced from cereal and other starch rich crops, sugars and oil crops?**

Only the last three categories mentioned as agriculture biomass, namely oilseed rape, cereals and sugar beet, should be considered food-based. Biofuels from residues (even food crops residues) qualify as second generation biofuels.

178. **What is meant by "aid shall be independent from the output"? In relation with boiler houses under what circumstances can aid be regarded as independent from the output?**

Investment aid should be established in connection with the eligible investment costs. It should be independent from the output in the sense that its amount cannot vary depending on the quantity of energy produced.

For example, aid calculated as X% of the eligible investment costs is independent from the output (and therefore acceptable under Article 41 of the GBER), while an aid calculated as Y EUR/MWh is not independent from the output (and therefore not acceptable under Article 41 of the GBER).

179. **Can credit tax be granted as investment aid?**

Investment aid for the promotion of energy from renewable sources should be, in line with Article 41(5) only granted to new installations. It should be granted and paid out before the installations start to operate.

Aid that is paid out in tranches, during a certain period of time after the installations have started to operate, in different forms (including tax credits) is usually not considered investment aid, but operating aid, even if it is meant to cover (also) investment costs.

180. **What is meant by "small installation" in Article 41(6)(c)?**

There is no strict definition of a small installation, referred to by Article 41(6)(c). This possibility is included to acknowledge that some investments to promote energy produced from renewable sources might be very small so that there are no technically comparable conventional power plants that could be used as reference investment. Article 41(6)(c) applies to only such investments. Normally these are cases where the installations producing energy from renewable sources are not the only installations used by the beneficiary to produce energy, but are rather used as secondary installations to complement the energy available from other sources (e.g. secondary installations that are used when renewable sources are available, aimed to reduce the use of the main conventional energy installations). In such cases it is possible that in the absence of the aid the most credible counterfactual scenario would be an increased use of the other (less environmental friendly) existing installations or sources of energy.

This would be the case, for example, when small installations producing energy from renewable sources are part of an integrated system producing energy, and in the absence of the aid the beneficiary would be able to use the rest of the respective integrated system and no other investment would be necessary.

181. **Is Article 41 for granting aid to boiler houses which currently use conventional energy for producing heat for conversion to energy from renewable sources?**

Yes, investment aid can be granted under Article 41 of the GBER for the conversion of conventional energy boilers to energy from renewable sources. More in general, large investments made to an existing plant can be eligible for investment aid under Article 41 of the GBER, if they concern considerable parts of the plant and are prolonging the expected lifetime of the plant, or are necessary to allow the plant to produce energy from renewable sources. However, maintenance operations and replacement of small parts and components of the plant, that are normally replaced during the expected lifetime of the plant, would not qualify for investment aid under Article 41 of the GBER.

182. **In case an existing oil-using boiler house is rebuilt into a boiler house using renewable energy sources, could the costs of the whole investment be regarded as extra investment costs?**

In line with Article 41(6) the eligible costs shall be the extra investment costs necessary to promote the production of energy from renewable sources. Where the costs of investing in the production of energy from renewable sources can be identified in the total investment cost as a separate investment, this renewable energy-related cost shall constitute the eligible costs. Where the costs of investing in the production of energy from renewable sources can be identified by reference to a similar, less environmentally friendly investment that would have been credibly carried out without the aid, this difference between the costs of both investments identifies the environmental protection-related cost and constitutes the eligible costs.

Taking the example of an existing oil-using boiler house that is rebuilt into a boiler house using renewable energy sources, it would be necessary first to establish what the counterfactual scenario would be – what would happen in the absence of the aid. If the existing oil-using boiler house already complies with all the necessary standards, and could continue to operate using oil, without requiring any investments in the foreseeable future, then the costs of the whole investment to convert it into a boiler house using renewable energy sources could be regarded as extra investment costs and would constitute the eligible costs. If however the existing oil-using boiler house would need certain investments in the absence of the aid, in order to continue to operate (e.g. investments necessary to comply with certain standards or investments to replace depreciated parts of it) the eligible costs should be calculated by reference to the respective counterfactual scenario, and the respective costs (that the beneficiary would incur in the absence of the aid) should be deducted.

183. **Article 41(1) provides for the possibility to grant investment aid for the promotion of renewable energy. Can this legal basis be used for granting aid to boiler houses which currently use conventional energy for conversion to renewable energy?**

It is in principle permitted to grant aid for the conversion of an already existing boiler house which uses conventional energy sources (e.g. oil) to a boiler house that uses renewable energy sources (e.g. wood chips), but only in relation to the investment costs necessary for the respective conversion.

184. **Is the modernisation of a plant already in operation, known as repowering, eligible for investment aid under Article 41 of the GBER?**

Modernisation (upgrading or refurbishment) of an existing plant can be eligible for investment aid under Article 41 of the GBER, if this operation concerns considerable parts of the plant and is prolonging the expected lifetime of the plant.

However, maintenance operations and replacement of small parts and components of the plant, that are normally replaced during the expected lifetime of the plant, would not qualify for investment aid under Article 41 of the GBER.

Article 42:

185. **What are the "generally accepted accounting principles"?**

The GBER does not specify the depreciation method. Depreciation of the plant would normally be understood in accounting terms applied during the economic life of the plant and equipment, rather than as tax depreciation. As indicative reference, you may want to see the International accounting standard 16 in Regulation (EC) No 2002/1606 on the application of international accounting or Article 12(5) and (6) of the Accounting Directive 2013/34/EU.

The actual depreciation method can vary from one Member State to another. Past case practice shows that in many Member States the depreciation period applied refers to the economic lifetime of the plant. The calculation of the aid amount should also follow this period. The Commission will assess the overall duration of the aid case by case in the light of the method used and the overall design of the measure.

186. **What is understood by "common connection point" in Article 42(10)? Will multiple installations be considered as one if the connection point has a single owner? What about if the installations have different owners but a common connection point?**

Under Article 42(10) installations with a common connection point to the electricity grid shall normally be considered as one installation. The ownership of the actual connection point is irrelevant for determining the total size of the installation.

When separate legal entities own installations with a common connection point, the possibility of considering these installations as one shall be evaluated on case by case basis, depending on:

- The types of installations involved: if they are installations of a similar kind, using the same type of primary energy source;
- The relationship between the legal entities: if they are unrelated or are related through a certain form of common ownership (part of a holding company, subsidiary and a parent company, etc.);
- The authorisation process: if it is necessary to obtain one authorisation for each installation or if one authorisation is enough for all of them;
- The way the installations are (inter)connected, the way the costs for the connection to the grid are split.

This assessment is normally done by the national authorities, which are well placed to verify all these aspects and decide if there are separate projects or components of a single project.

187. **What is understood by a "competitive bidding process"?**

Article 42(2) requires that operating aid promoting renewable energies is subject to a competitive bidding process on the basis of clear, transparent and nondiscriminatory criteria which are open to all generators producing electricity from renewable energy on a non-discriminatory basis.

Article 2(38) of the GBER defines a competitive bidding process as "a nondiscriminatory bidding process that provides for the participation of a sufficient number of undertakings and where the aid is granted on the basis of either the initial bid submitted by the bidder or a clearing price. In addition, the budget or volume related to the bidding process is a binding constraint leading to a situation where not all bidders can receive aid".

These requirements are therefore applicable to Article 42(3) and Article 42(4) which deal with some specific cases.

188. **What is meant by "negative prices"?**

"Negative prices" are wholesale electricity prices, whose values are below zero (0).

189. **What approach should the granting authority take when levelised costs are difficult to establish in practice?**

If the levelised costs are difficult to establish in practice, the calculation of the total levelised production costs could be based on the average costs of all plants to which the scheme applies where this provides for the correct typical representative production costs.

190. **Should a competitive bidding process be introduced in all circumstances?**

The intention to set up a competitive bidding process is in line with the requirements of Article 42(2) of the GBER. Please note that the bidding process can be limited to specific technologies only in specific circumstances, if the conditions under Article 42(3) apply.

191. **If the government guarantees to buy the produced energy at an agreed tariff above the market rate, is this considered State aid?**

A publicly supported purchase of energy at a level above market price is likely to constitute State aid. The aid element would in principle amount to the difference between the price paid and the market price of the energy concerned. The GBER contains provisions on operating aid for renewables in Articles 42 and 43. Provided that all the applicable conditions set out in the GBER are met, such State aid could in principle be handled under this Regulation.

192. **If a tender procedure is open to all technologies, but sets limits in the form of efficiency thresholds is the justification for applying such thresholds also subject to reporting to the Commission pursuant to Article 11(a)?**

Under Article 11(a) of the GBER the Member State must submit to the Commission via the Commission's electronic notification system a summary information about each aid measure exempted under GBER together with a link to the full text of the aid measure, including its amendments, within 20 working days following its entry into force.

In this context all key features and requirements of the aid measure must be communicated to the Commission.

Article 42(3) allows for some limitations in the bidding process but extends the scope of the reporting obligation for aid which is granted on the basis of such a limited bidding process. For such aid measures the information that must be submitted to the Commission includes also a detailed assessment of any restrictive conditions introduced to limit the competitive bidding process. When certain limits are imposed, the justification for the respective limits should therefore be included in the information sent to the Commission.

Article 43:

193. **Does Article 43(5) permit that the total levelised costs of producing energy from the counterfactual fuel are used as a proxy where there is no market price for the form of energy concerned? If so, is it for the Member State to identify the appropriate counterfactual fuel?**

The GBER only refers to the market price of the energy concerned in Article 43(5) to which there is a cross reference in Article 42(8). Article 43 specifies the conditions for granting operating aid to renewable energy in small scale installations.

Article 43(5) essentially caps the aid to the difference between the production costs of renewable energy and the market price of the energy concerned. In most cases market prices are readily available, notably in the case of electricity prices.

In some cases the market price may not be readily available. In such case the best proxy for the market price should be taken. Such best proxy could be the total levelised costs of the counterfactual form of energy.

Article 43(5) does not define the market price of the energy concerned. It is for the Member State to identify the correct market price in line with the rules set out in Article 43.

194. **Can it be presumed that where a market does not exist (and therefore neither a futures market or relevant swap rate) that Article 43(6) does not apply?**

Article 43 specifies the conditions for granting operating aid to renewable energy in small scale installations. Article 43(5) limits the aid amount to the difference between the total levelised costs of producing renewable energy and the market price of the energy concerned.

The calculation of the total levelised production costs is sensitive to the rate of return used. Therefore, Article 43(6) caps that rate of return that can be used for the calculation of the total levelised costs. Article 43(6) is phrased in a general way referring to generally available swap rates and does not require to identify a rate for a specific market (e.g. heat market).

In order to benefit from the GBER, all conditions of the Articles need to be respected, including Article 43(6). If these conditions are not respected and the Member State would still put in place the measure, such measure would need to be notified.

195. **Where the GBER is used for a scheme rather than ad hoc aid, do the "total levelised costs" in Article 43(5) refer to average costs of all plants to which the scheme applies?**

Article 43 specifies the conditions for granting operating aid to renewable energy in small scale installations. Article 43(5) limits the aid amount to the difference between the total levelised costs of producing renewable energy and the market price of the energy concerned.

In case of a scheme the total levelised production costs can be based on typical representative production costs of producing renewable energy for each relevant category of renewable energy.

The calculation of the total levelised production costs could be based on the average costs of all plants to which the scheme applies where this provides for the correct typical representative production costs. The plants to which the scheme applies should be a relevant category ensuring that the calculated production costs can be considered typical and representative for all plants.

196. **Where the GBER is being used for a scheme allowing to pay out the aid over a set period (e.g. 20 years), does the requirement to update levelised costs regularly apply only in relation to the setting of support levels for future applications for aid?**

Article 43 specifies that the levelised costs need to be updated at least every year. The update of the levelised costs impacts on the maximum amount of aid that can be granted. Once the aid is granted to an installation, payment of the aid can take place in line with the support period set out in the conditions of the scheme (until depreciation). Adjustments in the levelised costs would therefore only impact on new applications for which the aid was not yet granted.

197. **Is cost plus methodology appropriate for a calculation of the internal rate of return?**

Member States are not restricted to using a specific calculation methodology for the determination of the internal rate of return. However, in setting the level of return, Member States must respect the limits set out in Article 43(6) of the GBER.

Article 44:

198. **In which circumstances would Article 44(2) of the GBER apply?**

Aid in the form of reductions in environmental taxes under Directive 2003/96/EC can be exempted from the notification requirement contained in Article 108(3) TFEU if the conditions contained in Article 44 of the GBER are fulfilled. Article 44(2) of the GBER provides that beneficiaries must at least still pay the applicable minimum level of taxation set by the ETD. The minimum level of taxation referred to in the GBER is the respective minimum level listed in Annex I to the ETD. In other words, Article 44 of the GBER can only be applied in cases where tax reductions are given to some undertakings or groups of undertakings while these still pay taxes equal or above the minimum levels contained in Annex I to the ETD. In such cases, all other conditions of Article 44 of the GBER should equally be complied with.

Article 45:

199. **Can the definition of "hazardous substances" and/or "environmental damage" include concrete and other materials associated with permanent structures in order to clear derelict or brownfield land?**

Article 45 of the GBER specifies the conditions for granting aid for the remediation of contaminated sites. A contaminated site is defined in Article 2(121) as a site where there is a confirmed presence, caused by man, of hazardous substances of such a level that they pose a significant risk to human health or the environment taking into account current and approved future use of the land.

The eligible costs are defined in Article 45(4) as the costs incurred for the remediation work, less the increase in the value of the land. All expenditure incurred by an undertaking in remediating its site, whether or not such expenditure can be shown as a fixed asset on its balance sheet, may be considered as eligible investment in the case of the remediation of contaminated sites.

For determining whether a site is eligible for support, it is required that there are hazardous substances of such a level that they pose a significant risk to human health or the environment. The GBER does not provide further specific conditions and therefore it does not exclude that such risk relates from derelict or brownfield land, as long as they pose a significant risk to human health or the environment.

200. **Would a derelict building in a dangerous state of repair be a hazard to health?**

Under this provision, it is required that there are hazardous substances present at the site, making it a contaminated site. Only decontamination (i.e. the removal of these hazardous substances) of contaminated sites could be caught by the notification exemption contained in Article 45 of the GBER.

Article 46:

201. **Is Article 46 applicable to aid for a heating distribution network favouring greenhouses? If so, can all the investments costs in order to use and transport the waste heat from an existing power plant to the users be considered as costs for the "distribution network"?**

The scope of Article 46 is not limited to cities and can also relate to the heating of business areas/industrial zones. The expansion of district heating to industrial zones is encouraged and promoted under the Energy Efficiency Directive (see Annex VIII). However, the district heating network needs to be energy efficient as defined in Article 2(124) of the GBER.

In the event of an existing power plant, the additional investment costs can be considered as the costs of the distribution network as long as the investment is not an integral part of the production plant and the investment serves the purpose of a (controlled) distribution of heat to all the users. The network should benefit all users and indirect beneficiaries of the aid should be excluded, see for instance paragraph 35 of Commission decision N208/2010.

202. **Can the duration of any clawback mechanism for operating profit not only equal the operating lifetime of the asset but also be shorter than this subject to the specific circumstances of a project?**

Article 46 specifies the conditions for granting aid to district heating and cooling. The Article distinguishes between aid for the production plant and aid for the distribution network.

Article 46(5) caps the eligible costs for the distribution network to the investment costs. Article 46(6) limits the aid amount to the difference between the investment costs and the operating profit.

The clawback mechanism referred to in Article 46(6) serves to avoid that the aid amount exceeds the above mentioned difference. The GBER does not specify the design or duration of the clawback mechanism, but rather the purpose of a clawback mechanism and what it needs to ensure.

In view of the purpose of a clawback mechanism the duration of a clawback mechanism would logically equal the operating lifetime of the asset. Without excluding the possibility of a shorter duration, general circumstances that justify a shorter duration of the clawback mechanism cannot be identified ex ante.

203. **Can the funding gap method be used under the GBER?**

The criteria of identification of the eligible costs, at least for the distribution network of energy efficient district cooling and heating projects as set out in the GBER diverge from the "funding gap approach" as defined in point 32 of the EEAG as follows:

a) the GBER considers the *eligible costs* as the total investment costs less the operating profit (as defined in Article 2(39) of the GBER);

b) the EEAG, for the distribution network (point 76) enable to consider as eligible costs the difference between the positive and negative cash flows over the lifetime of the investment, discounted to their current value (typically using the cost of capital).

Regarding the eligible costs under the GBER (point a above), it should be noted that, as stated in Article 2(39) of the GBER, only a positive operating profit is taken into account. If the operating profit of the investment over its lifetime is equal to zero (operating cost=operating benefit), the entire investment cost may be subsidised. If the operating profit is negative (operating cost > operating benefit), only the total investment costs may be subsidised.

204. **In the case of district heating, should there be deducted one year operating profit or should there be taken into account costs during the first five years of the investments (as it was mentioned in the Community Guidelines on State aid for environmental protection (2008/C 82/01), point 82) or the entire lifetime of the investment (20 years)?**

Aid for energy infrastructure, as well as for district heating network infrastructure under the GBER, cannot exceed the difference between the investment cost and the operating profit of such infrastructure. The operating profit shall be estimated over the entire economic lifetime of the investment.

205. **Does this article apply to any heat generation facilities connected to a heat supply network?**

Energy efficient district heating and cooling is defined in Article 2(124) of the GBER as "district heating and cooling which satisfies the definition of efficient district heating and cooling system set out in Article 2(41) and (42) of Directive 2012/27/EU. The definition includes the heating/cooling production plants and the network (including related facilities) necessary to distribute the heat/cooling from the production units to the customer premises." Article 46 of the GBER allows, under certain conditions, aid to be granted for energy efficient district heating and cooling.

If an investor is considering investment in both the production plant and the connecting distribution networks, these should be assessed as two separate investments, specific rules and specific aid intensities applying to each of them: the aid intensities under paragraph 3 would apply for the production plant and under paragraphs 6 would apply for the distribution network. The eligible costs for the respective parts are also different, as defined by paragraphs 2 (for the production plant) and 5 (for the distribution network).

Article 47:

206. **What would an acceptable method for evaluating a "state of the art" investment be?**

The state of the art is defined in Article 2(129) of the GBER as "a process in which the re-use of a waste product to manufacture an end product is economically profitable normal practice." According to the GBER, where appropriate, the concept of state of the art must be interpreted from a Union technological and internal market perspective.

Beyond the state of the art would normally refer to new and innovative technologies, meaning new and unproven technologies compared to the state of the art in the industry, which carry a risk of technological or industrial failure and are not optimisation or scaling up of an existing technology.

For an example of a measure approved by the Commission in the waste sector, as going beyond the state of the art, please see the decision adopted in the case SA.37380, available on our website, http://ec.europa.eu/competition/state_aid/cases/249982/249982_1562944_119_2.pdf.

207. **What is meant by "a conventional process"?**

A conventional process should be understood as a process normally used by the recycling industry and which is economically profitable (corresponding to what is the state of the art).

Article 48:

208. **How is the aid amount under Article 48(5) calculated?**

In the case of investment aid for energy infrastructure the eligible costs are the investment costs.

The aid amount shall not exceed the difference between the eligible costs and the operating profit of the investment (i.e. aid amount = the investment costs – operating profit). Operating profit is defined in Article 2(39) of the GBER as "the difference between the discounted revenues and the discounted operating costs over the relevant lifetime of the investment, where this difference is positive", meaning that operating losses cannot be covered by aid.

Where an estimation of future operating profits is not possible ex ante, a clawback may be put in place.

209. **If the electric line part of a project is eligible for aid under Article 48 of the GBER, how should the operating profit be calculated?**

Operating profit is defined in Article 2(39) of the GBER as "the difference between the discounted revenues and the discounted operating costs over the relevant lifetime of the investment, where this difference is positive", meaning that operating losses cannot be covered by aid.

Under Article 2(39) of the GBER operating costs shall include costs such as personnel costs, materials, contracted services, communications, energy, maintenance, rent, administration, but exclude depreciation charges and the costs of financing of these.

Where an estimation of future operating profits is not possible ex ante, a clawback may be put in place.

210. **How to ensure that the energy infrastructure projects are not split artificially in order to comply with the GBER notification threshold?**

Energy infrastructure is defined in Article 2(130), but there are no pre-established criteria for the delimitation on an energy infrastructure project. Each project must be assessed individually, taking into account in particular the technical features of the projects, as well as its economic and administrative aspects.

It is not allowed to artificially split one project into pieces (e.g. with the aim of remaining under the notification threshold).

National authorities (and national energy regulators) must assess whether several projects receiving aid are separate projects, or if they are parts of a single project that was split artificially, on the basis of the detailed information they usually receive about the respective projects, including approvals, accreditations or licences for certain projects.

Article 49:

211. **Is this provision applicable to financing risk analyses before starting clean-up of a contaminated location, specifying suitable clean-up methods, clean-up limits and usually alternative clean-up scenarios as well?**

Aid under Article 49 of the GBER can be granted to finance risk analyses before starting clean-up of a contaminated location.

212. **Do the environmental studies have to be related to a specific investment for environmental protection in order to comply with the requirement of Article 49(1)?**

Article 49(1) clarifies that aid for environmental studies can only be granted if it serves the specific purpose for environmentally friendly investments mentioned in Section 7 of the GBER. Article 49(1) does not require that the study is linked to an individual investment.

Article 50:

213. **What is the meaning of "wild fires of natural origin"?**

Article 50 of the GBER only covers aid to compensate for damage caused by certain natural disasters. Wild fires caused by forest activity are excluded from the scope of the GBER, as they are not of natural origin, but are caused by accident, with civil damage liability of the human or company that caused it. In most cases where the Commission approved aid to compensate for damage caused by forest fires, declaring it compatible with Article 107(2)(b) TFEU, these events were qualified as exceptional occurrence (in cases of fires resulting in widespread loss) and not as natural disaster.

214. **What is meant by "competent authority"?**

"Competent public authorities" within the meaning of Article 50(2)(a) are public authorities or agencies responsible or entrusted to declare an event as a natural disaster. In its decisions, the Commission has accepted as competent authorities both national and regional authorities, as well as national or regional civil protection services or agencies.

215. **Can we consider damage caused by exceptional snowfalls within the definition of avalanches?**

The list provided in the GBER is comprehensive and includes all types of natural disaster for which aid can be exempted from the notification obligation. Exceptional snowfalls are not included in that list and cannot be considered as avalanches. Therefore, compensation measures for damage caused by heavy or exceptional snowfall would need to be assessed on a case by case basis following notification.

Article 52:

216. **How is the funding gap approach to be implemented under the new GBER given that in past decision-making practice the costs to be taken into consideration (investment costs only or investments plus operating costs) were considered differently?**

Article 52 of the GBER defines as eligible costs only the investment costs.

If a Member State would like to use a funding gap approach, it would still need to ensure that only investment costs are financed. A funding gap should therefore be calculated as follows: either (i) as investment costs - revenue = funding gap ; or (ii) if the Member State wishes to include operating costs in the formula, which is only possible if the operating costs do not exceed the revenues: investment costs + operating costs – revenue = funding gap (provided it is ensured that operating costs < revenues).

217. **Can Article 52 be interpreted in the sense that economic funding gaps can also be considered as investment costs eligible for State aid? Can the aid be submitted in the form of a grant and is it limited to the amount of the gap or can it be higher?**

Provided that all conditions of Article 52 are met (see also the preceding question and answer), the calculation of the aid to investment costs as the "economic funding gaps" is possible. It can be granted in the form of a grant. However, the aid has to be limited to the minimum and has to be established on the basis of an open tendering procedure.

218. **Can one apply the Broadband Guidelines by analogy? Does this also include the application of the access criteria?**

Article 52(4) of the GBER requires that the network operator grants fair and nondiscriminatory access to the network and as widely as possible (i.e. passive and active). Where appropriate, Article 52 of the GBER should be read consistently with the relevant provision of the Broadband Guidelines. The Broadband Guidelines, in particular points 42, 78(g) and (h) and point 80 specify in more detail the requirements which need to be met to fulfil the access criterion. These requirements therefore have to be applied as well to State aid granted for broadband networks under the GBER.

219. **Can the Commission confirm that the active elements of a broadband network (optical systems, WDMA equipment, routers, etc.) are eligible on the basis of Article 52(2)(c) and (d)?**

We agree with the proposed interpretation. Investment costs for the deployment of basic broadband or next generation access (NGA) networks can include costs relating to passive and active elements of a broadband network.

220. **Can the Commission confirm that granting aid for the active elements in case of upgrading a basic broadband infrastructure to an NGA network is also allowed on the basis of Article 52(3)?**

The upgrade of a basic broadband infrastructure to an NGA network can be eligible for State aid under Article 52 of the GBER provided that the area of intervention is NGA white, as required under Article 52(3) of the GBER – and also respecting the other conditions described in the GBER – in particular with regard to full and effective unbundling.

221. **Could the GBER be used to provide aid directed at broadband infrastructure built in white intervention areas under certain compatibility or threshold conditions? The Commission has indicated that the duct access obligation that must be met for NGA deployments must be met on an "open access" basis i.e. the duct infrastructure in the white NGA intervention area must be available by the supplier for any wholesale communications service regardless of whether it is for the purpose of delivering NGA or business connectivity services.**

For aid granted under the GBER, the network operator must offer the widest possible active and passive wholesale access, under fair and non-discriminatory conditions. The network operator should therefore ensure access to the passive infrastructure – duct access in your question – for any wholesale communications service, regardless of whether it is for the purpose of delivering NGA, or business connectivity services.

222. **What are the applicable tender rules and procedure?**

The requirement to observe a "competitive selection process" in granting State aid in accordance with the provisions of the GBER should be interpreted consistently with the EU Guidelines for the application of State aid rules in relation to the rapid deployment of broadband networks. As stated in Article 52(4), the selection process has to respect the principle of technology neutrality.

For reference, among the relevant provisions of the Broadband Guidelines, more notably point 78(c) of the Broadband Guidelines specifies that: "Competitive selection process: Whenever the granting authorities select a third-party operator to deploy and operate the subsidised infrastructure, the selection process shall be conducted in line with the spirit and the principles of the EU Public Procurement Directives. It ensures that there is transparency for all investors wishing to bid for the implementation and/or management of the subsidised project. Equal and nondiscriminatory treatment of all bidders and objective evaluation criteria are indispensable conditions. The competitive tender is a method to reduce budgetary costs, to minimise the potential State aid involved and at the same time reduces the selective nature of the measure insofar as the choice of the beneficiary is not known in advance. Member States shall ensure a transparent process and a competitive outcome and shall use a dedicated central website at the national level to publish all on-going tender procedures on broadband State aid measures."

223. **Is it possible to provide aid for implementation of projects involving the upgrade of NGA network to the standard of highspeed networks with parameters of at least 100 Mbps to the end user?**

The question concerns whether Article 52(3) of the GBER, which states that investment aid for broadband networks is possible for investments located in areas where there is no infrastructure of the same category (either basic broadband or NGA network) and where no such infrastructure is likely to be developed on commercial terms within three years, should be interpreted as allowing aid under the GBER for the deployment of an "ultra-fast" NGA network in an area where regular NGA infrastructure exists.

The GBER is silent as regards "ultra-fast" NGA networks, and a literal reading of the GBER would exclude a legal basis to accept such an interpretation. Article 2(138) of the GBER describes NGA networks as advanced networks which have certain characteristics including very high speed (but without providing any figure in terms of Mbps). The

GBER further sets out that at the current stage of market and technological development, NGA networks are: (a) fibre-based access networks (FTTx), (b) advanced upgraded cable networks and (c) certain advanced wireless access networks capable of delivering reliable high-speeds per subscriber. "Ultrafast" NGA networks would fall under these categories. In this case, the GBER makes no distinction between "ultra-fast" NGA networks and regular NGA networks, and thus Article 52(3) could not be used as a legal basis to allow aid for investment into "ultra-fast" NGA networks where there exists regular NGA infrastructure.

Moreover, the GBER should cover only those cases where the aid is not expected to significantly distort competition. In the case of upgrading of regular NGA infrastructure to "ultra-fast" NGA, there may be a risk that incumbents are favoured because they can use the GBER aid to upgrade their infrastructure. For these reasons the GBER would not be adequate.

224. **Do the costs of purchase, lease or rent of existing (new or used) infrastructure (in particular the long-term lease on the basis of IRU agreement) shall be considered as eligible costs within the meaning of Article 52(2) of the GBER?**

Such costs shall be considered as eligible costs and therefore falling within the scope of Article 52(2) of the GBER since the list of eligible costs as defined in this Article include all investment costs which refer to the deployment of basic broadband networks, next generation access networks and a passive broadband infrastructure. Please note however that such investment shall take place in areas which are either "basic white" or "NGA white", as required under Article 52(3) of the GBER.

Article 53:

225. **What is meant by "cultural and natural heritage"?**

The formal recognition as cultural or natural heritage by the competent public authorities constitutes a condition for granting aid under Article 53(2)(c) . The GBER does not define such recognition procedure as this does not fall within the remit of the European institutions. Therefore, it is for the concerned Member State to decide which projects or activities can be declared as cultural or natural heritage. As soon as that project or activity is formally recognized as cultural or natural heritage by a competent public authority of this Member State, the condition for application of Article 53 would be deemed to be fulfilled.

226. **Is it possible to apply the provisions of this Regulation on the aid for culture and heritage conservation concerning zoos?**

In light of the obligations imposed on zoos by Council Directive 1999/22/EC of 29 March 1999 relating to the keeping of wild animals in zoos, and the recognised importance of natural habits and species (as evidenced e.g. by the Habitats Directive (Council Directive 92/43/EEC of 21 May 1992 on the conservation of natural habitats and of wild fauna and flora)) we consider that zoos can qualify as natural heritage, provided they are formally recognised as such by the relevant public authorities.

227. **Is it possible to provide support under this Article to an international summer academy for culture and arts at an university?**

An international summer academy for culture and arts taught at a university could a priori be considered as a cultural and artistic education activity in the meaning of Article 53(2)(e) of the GBER. Aid granted to support such academy could therefore be considered compatible with the internal market and exempted from the notification requirement of Article 108(3) TFEU, provided that it fulfils all the other conditions of Article 53 and of Chapter I of the GBER. In particular, teaching related to fashion and design, pursuant to Recital 72 of the GBER, cannot be considered as cultural.

Considering the nature of the activities described in your question (educational activities), we would also like to remind you that State aid rules, in the meaning of Article 107(1) TFUE, do not apply to measures concerning non-economic activities. Public education, i.e. education supervised and predominantly funded by the State, may be considered as a non-economic activity. The fact that students have to pay tuition or enrolment fees would not change the non-economic nature of public education, provided that the service remains predominantly funded by the State. This also concerns universities.

228. **Which authorities could qualify as "competent public authorities" in the meaning of Article 53(2)(b)?**

Public authorities of a Member State can qualify as "competent authorities" within the meaning of Article 53(2)(b), provided national rules entrust them with the responsibilities to decide on the status of an activity as cultural and/or natural heritage.

229. **Does Article 6(5)(h) of the GBER apply to all aid for culture and heritage conservation covered by the GBER or does it only apply to Article 53 (aid for culture and heritage conservation)?**

Article 6(5)(h) applies to aid for culture and heritage conservation as defined in Article 53. It specifically refers to this Article only and does not apply to Article 54.

230. **What is the best way to determine the fulfilment of the conditions referred to in Article 53 (4)(a)?**

The wording of Article 53(4)(a) of the GBER indicates that space and time capacity are alternative indicators of the eligible costs of the infrastructure, not cumulative ones. Indeed, the provision states that:

For investment aid, the eligible costs shall be the investment costs in tangible and intangible assets, including:

(a) costs for the construction, upgrade, acquisition, conservation or improvement of infrastructure, if at least 80% of either the time or the space capacity per year is used for cultural purposes.

It follows from this wording that the costs listed in point (a) will be eligible either if 80% or more of the infrastructure's surface is used for cultural purposes (space capacity) or if during 80% or more of its total number of opening hours per year, the funded infrastructure is used for cultural activities (time capacity).

Taking the example of a museum with a souvenir shop and a café, the space capacity would be the relevant indicator, given that there are, inside one infrastructure, different spaces dedicated to cultural and non-cultural activities. The time capacity would be used if the same infrastructure is used at different points in time for cultural and non-cultural purposes (e.g. a concert hall is rented out for conferences).

231. **Does the provision in the last sentence of Article 53(6) only apply if the creator/owner of cultural infrastructure is also the operator of the infrastructure?**

Article 53(6) solely relates to investment aid to the creator/owner of cultural infrastructure and to the limitation of the aid amount that the creator/owner can maximally receive. Where the creator/owner of cultural infrastructure and the operator of that infrastructure are different entities Article 53(6) must be read as relating only to the creator/owner. The reference to "operating profit of the investment" in Article 53(6) would accordingly relate to the revenue generated by the creator/owner of the infrastructure (e.g. by renting the infrastructure to the separate operator). Likewise, where the creator/owner of cultural infrastructure is different from the operator of that infrastructure, it would be the creator/owner who would constitute the "operator" in the sense of the last sentence of Article 53(6) and who is allowed to keep a reasonable profit.

Where the creator/owner of cultural infrastructure and the operator of that infrastructure are different entities, it may be the case that investment aid to the creator/owner leads to operating aid being granted to the operator. If the separate operator receives operating aid, that operating aid would be subject to Article 53(7) and the operator would be allowed to keep at most a reasonable profit under that provision. However, investment aid to the creator/owner does not lead to operating aid to the separate operator if the operator has been chosen in an open, transparent and non-discriminatory tender procedure.

232. **When is the formal recognition considered to be met?**

A body of evidence consisting of factual circumstances and acts adopted by a local authority in an administrative or civil law context (such as a contract, a grant decision, or a donation act which specifies the objective of conserving natural heritage) should be sufficient. It is not required to have a formal recognition act adopted at national central level.

233. **Regarding Article 53(6) and Article 55(10), are the two points cumulative or alternative?**

The methods are alternative. Either the Member State operates an ex-ante deduction of future operating profit based on reasonable estimates or, when this is not possible, through the setting up of a clawback mechanism ex post.

234. **What are the eligible costs for the purpose of the aid for culture and heritage conservation?**

The GBER foresees alternative calculation methodologies as regards operating aid for culture and heritage conservation. A Member State can therefore choose to apply either Article 53(7) (i.e. amount of aid capped to operating losses and a reasonable profit over the relevant period) or Article 53(8) (maximum amount of aid capped at 80% of the eligible costs, if the aid does not exceed EUR 1 million) depending on the specifics of the situation at hand.

The authorities of a Member State are free to design their schemes under the GBER, provided that they comply with all the relevant requirements (general and specific conditions of the GBER). Therefore, Member States may choose to limit the type of eligible costs covered by operating aid in the context of a particular scheme.

235. **How should the reasonable profit be determined according to Article 2(142)?**

According to Article 2(142), the reasonable profit shall be determined with respect to the typical profit for the sector concerned. Such definition grants certain flexibility to Member States for the determination of the reasonable profit. Therefore, any of the different indicators mentioned in the SGEI package (rate of return on capital, return on capital employed, return on equity, return on assets or return on sales) can be used. However, regardless of the choice of the indicator, this needs to be justified by a benchmarking against the typical profits in the sector concerned.

For example, for museums and other cultural institutions, rate of return on sales may be easier to use. In this case, it should be ensured that the beneficiary does not achieve, after having received the aid, a return on sales that is higher than the typical return on sales achieved by purely commercial operators in the sector concerned.

In addition, the definition of reasonable profit in Article 2(142) also includes a safe harbour, defined as a rate of return on capital that does not exceed the relevant swap rate plus a premium of 100 basis points. In the absence of other profit indicators benchmarked against the typical profits of the sector, this safe harbour will in any event be considered to be reasonable.

236. **How is the reasonable profit based on the swap rate (Article 2(142)) calculated correctly? Does one take the swap rate which is valid at the moment when the contract starts for the whole approved period and does one leave this rate at that level? Or would one adapt the swap rate after each change by the Commission respectively with effect for the future? (Alternatively, is there a choice?)**

Article 2(142) reads as follows: "'reasonable profit' shall be determined with respect to the typical profit for the sector concerned. In any event, a rate of return on capital that does not exceed the relevant swap rate plus a premium of 100 basis points will be considered to be reasonable."

Article 2(142) makes clear that a reasonable profit is normally dependent on the sector concerned and hence does not have to be limited to the swap rate plus a premium of 100 basis points. However, it also contains the safe harbour provision that a profit of not more than the relevant swap rate plus 100 basis points is in any event reasonable. If the latter approach is chosen to determine a reasonable profit, the swap rate will depend on the compensation mechanism:

- if the compensation is determined ex ante, on the basis of reasonable projections, the swap rate that is valid at that moment (i.e. when the aid is granted) is to be used and can be kept at that level for the whole period.
- if the compensation is however determined ex post, on the basis of the actual incurred costs, the swap rates for each relevant period have to be applied (rather than one constant rate).
- likewise, if a clawback mechanism is used (and hence an ex post calculation is performed based on the actual figures), the swap rates for each relevant period have to be applied.

237. **Is this provision applicable to the promotion of measures for energy-saving and energy-efficiency measures in cultural institutions?**

As a general rule Articles 38 and/or 39 of the GBER (on energy efficiency) are the relevant articles to address investment aid for the promotion of energy-saving and energy-efficiency measures.

Where energy efficiency measures are carried out for the benefit of cultural institutions, they may also be covered by Article 53 (investment aid for upgrade of the cultural infrastructure). If the measures were to be considered as cultural aid in the meaning of Article 53, they would need to fulfil all the conditions of Article 53 and of Chapter I of the GBER in order to be considered compatible with the internal market and to be exempted from the notification requirement of Article 108(3) TFEU.

Article 54:

238. **How much of the eligible costs can be covered?**

Article 54 lists the specific compatibility criteria applicable to aid schemes for audiovisual works. Its paragraph 7 clarifies that aid intensities of more than 50% of the eligible costs are possible for difficult audiovisual works. Article 2(140) defines "difficult audiovisual works" as works identified as such by Member States on the basis of pre-defined criteria. These may include works whose sole original version is in a language of a Member State with a small territory or population or in a language that is only used in part of a Member State or only by a part of the population of a Member State.

239. **Is it envisioned that audiovisual works, as covered by Article 54 of the GBER, can include aid to video game companies for products which are judged to meet the culture test as set out by the national tax scheme?**

No, Article 54 of the GBER (aid schemes for audiovisual works) does not apply to aid for video games. Recital 72 of the GBER clearly states that " [. . .] In general, activities which, although they may present a cultural aspect, have a predominantly commercial character because of the higher potential for competition distortions, such as press and magazines (written or electronic), should not be covered. Furthermore, the list of eligible cultural purposes and activities should not include commercial activities such as fashion, design or video games."

240. **Article 54(4) lists conditions with regard to territorial spending obligations. Reference is made to the "minimum level of production activity in the territory". Does this refer to local expenses or to the percentage of film shooting taking place in that territory?**

Territorial conditions requiring a minimum level of production activity in the territory of the Member State or part of it can be imposed in various ways:

- A film fund may require a certain level of local spending (direct territorial conditions).
- A film fund may also impose territorial spending conditions in an indirect way, for example by requiring a certain part of the film shooting to take place in the territory of the Member State or part of it.

Both types of territorial conditions are covered by the "minimum level of production activity". The minimum level of production activity is always expressed as a percentage of the overall production budget of the film – therefore, any film shooting activity requirement must be "translated" into the corresponding share of the film's overall production budget.

When setting territorial requirements (in particular indirect ones), Member States must ensure that this does not mean that the aid is reserved for specific production activities or individual parts of the production value chain (Art. 54(9) of the GBER). For instance, whereas the Commission's services generally accept the requirement for a certain part of the film shooting to take place in the territory of the Member State or part of it, it is not possible to link the aid to the requirement that specific post-production activities take place in the territory or that specific studio infrastructures are used.

Article 55:

241. **Can aid for sport and multifunctional recreational infrastructures (marinas) be granted under the GBER?**

Marinas are usable for sports such as amateur sailing and could also provide for other recreational activities (tourism, culture).

Article 55 of the GBER allows investment aid sport and multifunctional recreational infrastructures (except for hotels and leisure parks).

Under Article 55(10) of the GBER the aid amount may cover the funding gap so that the aid intensity would normally be higher than under the applicable regional aid rules.

Article 55(12) of the GBER also provides for an alternative (optional) method for calculating maximum amount of aid (80% of eligible costs in case of aid not exceeding EUR 1 million) but in that case the remaining 20% of financing has to be aid free.

242. **Does the GBER also cover investments in sport infrastructure in the form of creating possibilities for accommodation of athletes and their accompanying personnel, sauna, gym, massage rooms as well as seminar rooms and cafeterias?**

This type of investment would be covered by Article 55 provided that it is directly linked to the sports infrastructure and that it fulfils the conditions specified in the GBER (Article 55 and the general requirements).

243. **Is it possible to use rules for operating aid for sport and multifunctional recreational infrastructure to finance the operation of existing sport infrastructure (e.g. swimming pool, stadium)?**

It is possible to use the provisions on operating aid of Article 55 of the GBER to finance the operation of existing sport infrastructure, provided it complies with that Article and the general requirements set out in the GBER. In this respect, particular attention is drawn to the fact that Article 6 of the GBER (and in particular its paragraph 2) must be complied with. If the beneficiary is a large enterprise, the condition laid down in Article 6(3)(b) of the GBER applies.

244. **Is it possible to provide operating aid for sport infrastructure to an entity which has the infrastructure in its lease? If so, is it possible that the period of the lease of the infrastructure is shorter than a year?**

It is possible to provide operating aid for sport infrastructure to an entity which leases the sport infrastructure. According to Article 55(9) of the GBER: "For operating aid for sport infrastructure the eligible costs shall be the operating costs of the provision of services by the infrastructure. Those operating costs include costs such as [. . .] rent, administration, etc., but exclude depreciation charges and the costs of financing if these have been covered by investment aid". On this basis, rent costs are accepted as eligible operating costs. Please note that the maximum allowed under Article 4(1)(bb) of the GBER amounts to EUR 2 million per infrastructure per year. It is possible that the period of lease of the infrastructure is shorter than a year but the overall aid granted to the infrastructure must always remain below EUR 2 million and therefore must be adapted pro rata.

Article 56:

245. **Is this article applicable to the construction of water management infrastructure where the subsequent operation of the infrastructure is carried out by the aid recipient (the investor) without delegating operation to a third party? Could both public entities (such as municipalities) and private entities be aid beneficiaries?**

The provisions of Article 56 cover only the granting of investment aid to the infrastructure owner. Therefore, an "in house" operator benefitting from the aid must comply with the provisions of Article 56(3). The conditions of Article 56(4) apply only when the owner of a given infrastructure entrusts its operations to "a third party".

246. **Can this article be applied to the construction of business incubators for SMEs which provide favourable conditions for renting office space and advice for budding entrepreneurs?**

The Article block-exempts the aid granted to the infrastructure owner. We understand that by referring to "favourable conditions", you refer to State aid that might be granted to SMEs renting such office spaces at conditions that are not market conform. Any State aid involved in the granting of favourable conditions to entrepreneurs (e.g. start-up aid) will have to comply with the relevant GBER provisions or be notified. Please note that this should not be a bespoke investment.

In addition, please note that Article 56 only applies if no other provision of the GBER applies, such as specific provisions for infrastructure funding.

247. **Can the Commission define the relationship between Article 56 and Decision SA.36346 (2013/N), which found that the development of land on industrial sites does not involve State aid?**

The existence of State aid in a particular situation is outside the scope of the GBER, as the latter only concerns compatibility requirements for investments that are aid. Only when State aid cannot be excluded at the level of the infrastructure owner could the provisions of the GBER be applicable if all the other requirements are met.

In the case SA.36346, the Commission concluded that no aid was involved on the basis of the following characteristics of the measure. Firstly, the financial transfers from the federal level to the communes is considered an intrastate transfer and therefore outside the scope of Article 107(1) TFEU. In addition, activities that fall within the public remit are not considered economic activities and again outside the scope of Article 107(1) TFEU. In case the operator (in the case of the GRW decision, the "developer") is chosen via a tender procedure, it does not benefit of any aid either. Last but not least, as regards bodies implementing the measure that were not municipalities, they have a legal obligation to pass on/refund any advantage derived from the sale of the land.

In these circumstances, the Commission concluded that that particular measure did not constitute State aid. In other cases, aid may be involved but it can be considered compatible provided the conditions of the GBER provision are met.

248. **Is this provision applicable to investment in the rehabilitation/modernisation of old rails station buildings? If yes, can it be applied in cases where the buildings are owned by private transport operators?**

Yes, this article should be applicable if State aid is involved at the level of the infrastructure owner, independent of whether this is a public or private owner.

249. **Is this provision applicable to infrastructure investment aid relating to the construction of normal rental housing?**

Yes, provided that all the conditions regarding the operators and users of the infrastructure are met and that the thresholds are not exceeded.

250. **Are the users of the infrastructure covered by the GBER exemption from notification?**

Infrastructure users that pay a market price are not considered aid beneficiaries. The market price can be determined via a tender procedure (rather seldom on the user level) or via benchmarking consisting on a comparison of charges across a sufficient number of suitable comparable infrastructures or via the incremental cost approach.

In principle a scheme for aid granted to municipalities and other public institutions for preparation of industrial zones and related to technical infrastructure (buying, preparation and revitalization of land, ensuring its connection to utilities, construction and modernization of transport infrastructure and buildings) would indeed be a scheme that, if involving State aid, would seem to be covered by Article 56 of the GBER. Please note, however, that Article 56 only applies if no other more specific provision of the GBER applies, such as Article 48 relating to energy infrastructure. Also note that all the requirements of Article 56 should be met, including the prohibition as regards dedicated infrastructure and the total investment cost of maximum EUR 20 million (eligible cost also is capped at EUR 10 million).

251. **Is this provision applicable to financing of building or modernization of water management infrastructures, like sewage treatment plants, sewerage system and water pipelines?**

As long as the investment is not covered by other provisions of the GBER (e.g. Article 47 regarding waste management), Article 56 could be applicable. However, the modernisation of the infrastructure implies that the operator should also pay proportionately more for being allowed to use and operate the new/modernised infrastructure. If there is no new procurement procedure, there is a risk that the operator receives an advantage as it would not pay "market-conform" operating fees in accordance with the upgraded infrastructure. If the payment of a "market-conform" price cannot be ensured, the operator would receive operating aid which would in principle not fall under the GBER.

252. **Can the electric car charging stations (on a highway) be financed under the provision of local infrastructure?**

Electric car charging infrastructures cannot be considered as energy infrastructures within the meaning of GBER (Article 2(130) of the GBER defines what constitutes an energy infrastructure). Therefore Article 48 of the GBER, investment aid for energy infrastructure, does not apply. Article 56, investment aid for local infrastructure, may be applicable for such investments as long as the requirements of that Article and GBER Section 1 are respected.

253. **Is it correct that for merely the sale of a building and the grant of a guarantee the local authority is not obliged to organize an open, transparent and non-discriminatory procedure? If this is not correct could you please indicate the conditions for this procedure?**

The documents mentioned above address different scenarios. In the Commission Communication on State aid elements in the sales of land and buildings by public authorities as well as the Commission Notice on the application of Articles 87 and 88 of the EC Treaty to State aid in the form of guarantees, the Commissions shares its assessment of conditions that should be met in order for a measure not to involve State aid. The GBER sets out criteria to be met by measures which are State aid in order to be found compatible.

Therefore, if the conditions of the two documents mentioned in the previous paragraph are fulfilled, the Commission considers that there is no State aid involved in the measure. Furthermore, Article 56 refers to the situation where infrastructure is being constructed or upgraded (and not to the simple sale of land).

254. **Could a project regarding the realization of a park & ride provision for railway travellers be considered a local infrastructure?**

Provided that the measure entails the granting of State aid for the owner of that infrastructure, the referenced type of infrastructure could be covered by Article 56 of the GBER.

255. **Please confirm that for the purpose of calculating the eligible cost under paragraph 6, it is possible to use the method identified by the European Commission in the context of the Structural Funds for revenue-generating projects.**

In line with other measures concerning investment aid to an infrastructure project, in order to be covered by the GBER, the eligible costs shall be calculated in accordance with the following methodology: Total investment costs less operating profit (as defined in Article 2(39) of the GBER). That difference may be subsidised with State aid. As stated in Article 2(39), only a positive operating profit is taken into account. If the operating profit of the investment over its lifetime is equal to zero (operating cost=operating benefit), the entire investment cost may be subsidised. If the operating profit is negative (operating cost > operating benefit), only the total investment costs may be subsidised.

In line with previous practice for cases co-financed by structural funds, the Commission can accept, for the calculation of operating profit for the purpose of Article 56 GBER, a discount rate of 4%.

NOTES

5 OJ L187, 26.06.2014, p 1.

6 Article 2(50) of the GBER stipulates that the "same or a similar activity" means an activity falling under the same class (four-digit numerical code) of the NACE Rev. 2 statistical classification of economic activities as laid down in Regulation (EC) No 1893/2006 of the European Parliament and of the Council of 20 December 2006 establishing the statistical classification of economic activities NACE Revision 2 and amending Council Regulation (EEC) No 3037/90 as well as certain EC Regulations on specific statistical domains.

7 Council Regulation (EC) No 723/2009 of 25 June 2009 on the Community legal framework for a European Research Infrastructure Consortium (ERIC), OJ L206, 8.8.2009, p 1.

8 OJ L206, 8.8.2009, p 1.

4. CHAPTER IV – FINAL PROVISIONS

Article 58:

[5.148]

256. **How should this provision be read in conjunction with the "applicability provisions" of various Frameworks and Guidelines, which typically specify that "unlawful aid will be assessed in accordance with the rules applicable at the date on which the aid was granted"?**

According to the provisions of Article 58(1), the GBER will apply to any individual aid granted before 1 July 2014 (being generally more generous than the previous GBER). The GBER is a higher ranking legal instrument, having precedence over specific Guidelines. Therefore, only for cases which cannot be covered by the current GBER, the Commission services would apply the Guidelines in force at the time of the granting of the aid (such Guidelines should still be more favourable for the Member States than the new Guidelines, which are generally stricter).

257. **What are the provisions for the transitional period?**

The GBER entered in force on 1 July 2014. Its entry into force was immediate, without a transitional period. According to its Article 58(1), it can be applied for individual aid measures also before its entry into force, provided that the measures in question fulfil all its conditions.

258. **Do individual aids granted before the entry into force of this Regulation need to fulfil the obligation of communication laid down in Article 11(a)?**

According to Article 3, the GBER applies to aid that fulfils all the conditions of its Chapters I and III. As regards the individual aid granted before its entry into force, Article 58(1) would derogate from this application of Chapters I and III only with regard to the application of Article 9 (publication and information obligations). However, we would stress that this interpretation is only for the benefit of the application of the GBER to a particular individual aid. As regards new aid measures, the Member States should also comply with Chapter II of the Regulation to be able to effectively monitor how the GBER conditions are complied with.

COUNCIL REGULATION

(2015/1588/EU)

of 13 July 2015

on the application of Articles 107 and 108 of the Treaty on the Functioning of the European Union to certain categories of horizontal State aid (codification) (Enabling Regulation)

(Text with EEA relevance)

[5.149]

NOTES

Date of publication in OJ: OJ L248, 24.9.2015, p 1.

Repeal of this Regulation in relation to the UK: this Regulation is repealed, in relation to the UK, by the State Aid (Revocations and Amendments) (EU Exit) Regulations 2020, SI 2020/1470, reg 5, as from IP completion day (as defined in the European Union (Withdrawal Agreement) Act 2020, s 39) (for transitional provisions and savings in relation to claims before a court or tribunal relating to State aid infringement before IP completion day, see Sch 3 to those Regulations at **[7.89]**).

THE COUNCIL OF THE EUROPEAN UNION,

Having regard to the Treaty on the Functioning of the European Union, and in particular Article 109 thereof,

Having regard to the proposal from the European Commission,

Having regard to the opinion of the European Parliament,[1]

Whereas:

(1) Council Regulation (EC) No 994/98[2] *has been substantially amended.*[3] *In the interests of clarity and rationality that Regulation should be codified.*

(2) Under the Treaty on the Functioning of the European Union (TFEU), the assessment of compatibility of aid with the internal market essentially rests with the Commission.

(3) The proper functioning of the internal market requires strict and efficient application of the rules of competition with regard to State aid.

(4) The Commission should be enabled to declare by means of regulations, in areas where the Commission has sufficient experience to define general compatibility criteria, that certain specified categories of aid are compatible with the internal market pursuant to one or more of the provisions of Article 107(2) and (3) TFEU and are exempted from the procedure provided for in Article 108(3) thereof.

(5) Block exemption regulations ensure transparency and legal certainty. They can be directly applied by national courts, without prejudice to Article 4(3) of the Treaty on European Union and to Article 267 TFEU.

(6) State aid is an objective notion defined in Article 107(1) TFEU. The power of the Commission to adopt block exemptions as provided for in this Regulation only applies to measures that fulfil all the criteria of Article 107(1) TFEU and therefore constitute State aid. Inclusion of a certain category of aid in this Regulation or in an exemption regulation does not predetermine the qualification of a measure as State aid within the meaning of Article 107(1) TFEU.

(7) The Commission should be enabled to declare that, under certain conditions, aid to small and medium-sized enterprises, aid in favour of research, development and innovation, aid in favour of environmental protection, aid in favour of employment and training, and aid that complies with the map approved by the Commission for each Member State for the grant of regional aid is compatible with the internal market and not subject to the notification requirement.

(8) Innovation has become a Union policy priority in the context of 'Innovation Union', one of the Europe 2020 flagship initiatives. Moreover, many aid measures for innovation are relatively small and create no significant distortions of competition.

(9) In the culture and heritage conservation sector, a number of measures taken by Member States might not constitute aid because they do not fulfil all the criteria of Article 107(1)TFEU, for example because the beneficiary does not carry out an economic activity or because there is no effect on trade between Member States. However, to the extent measures in the field of culture and heritage conservation do constitute State aid within the meaning of Article 107(1) TFEU, the Commission should be enabled to declare that, under certain conditions, that aid is compatible with the internal market and not subject to the notification requirement in Article 108(3) TFEU. Small culture, creation and heritage conservation projects do not typically give rise to any significant distortion, and recent cases have shown that such aid has limited effects on trade.

(10) Exemptions in the culture and heritage conservation sector could be designed on the basis of the Commission's experience as set out in guidelines, such as for cinematographic and audiovisual works, or developed case by case. When drafting such block exemptions, the Commission should take into account that they should only cover measures constituting State aid, that they should in principle focus on measures that contribute to the objectives of 'EU State aid modernisation', and that only aid in respect of which the Commission has already substantial experience is block-exempted. Furthermore, the primary competence of the Member States in the area of culture, the special protection enjoyed by cultural diversity under Article 167(1) TFEU and the special nature of culture should be taken into account.

(11) As regards State aid measures to make good the damage caused by natural disasters, as well as State aid measures to make good the damage caused by certain adverse weather conditions in fisheries, the amounts granted in those areas are usually limited, and clear compatibility conditions can be defined. This Regulation should enable the Commission to exempt such aid from the notification requirement. In the Commission's experience, such aid does not give rise to any significant distortion, and clear compatibility conditions can be defined on the basis of the experience acquired.

(12) In accordance with Article 42 TFEU, State aid rules do not apply under certain conditions to certain aid measures in favour of agriculture products listed in Annex I to the TFEU. Article 42 does not apply to forestry or to products not listed in that Annex. The Commission should be able to exempt certain types of aid in favour of forestry, including aid contained in the rural development programmes and also that in favour of promoting and advertising food sector products not listed in Annex I to the TFEU, where, according to the Commission's experience, the distortions of competition are limited and clear compatibility conditions can be defined.

(13) According to Article 7 of Council Regulation (EC) No 1198/2006,[4] Articles 107, 108 and 109 TFEU apply to aid granted by the Member States to enterprises in the fisheries sector, except for payments made by Member States pursuant to, and in conformity with, Regulation (EC) No 1198/2006. Additional State aid for the conservation of marine and freshwater biological resources usually has limited effects on trade between Member States, contributes to the Union's objectives in the field of maritime and fisheries policy, and does not create serious distortions of competition. The amounts granted are usually limited and clear compatibility conditions can be defined.

(14) In the sports sector, in particular in the field of amateur sport, a number of measures taken by Member States might not constitute aid because they do not fulfil all the criteria of Article 107(1) TFEU, for example because the beneficiary does not carry out an economic activity, or because there is no effect on trade between Member States. However, to the extent that measures in the field of sports do constitute State aid within the meaning of Article 107(1) TFEU, the Commission should be enabled to declare that, under certain conditions, that aid is compatible with the internal market and not subject to the notification requirement. State aid measures for sport, in particular those in the field of amateur sport or those that are small-scale, often have limited effects on trade between Member States and do not create serious distortions of competition. The amounts granted are typically also limited. Clear compatibility conditions can be defined on the basis of the experience acquired so as to ensure that aid to sports does not give rise to any significant distortion.

(15) In relation to aid concerning air and maritime transport, in the Commission's experience, aid having a social character for the transport of residents of remote regions such as outermost regions and islands, including single region island Member States and sparsely populated areas, does not give rise to any significant distortion, provided that it is granted without discrimination related to the identity of the carrier. Moreover, clear compatibility conditions can be defined.

(16) In the field of aid to broadband infrastructure, the Commission has in recent years acquired vast experience and has devised guidelines.[5] In the Commission's experience, aid for certain types of broadband infrastructure does not give rise to any significant distortion and could benefit from a block exemption, provided that certain compatibility conditions are met and that the infrastructure is deployed in 'white areas', being areas where there is no infrastructure of the same category (either broadband or very high-speed next-generation access, 'NGA') and where none is likely to be developed in the near future, as outlined in the criteria developed in the guidelines. This is true of aid covering the provision of basic broadband, as well as of aid for small individual measures covering NGA networks, and of aid to broadband-related civil engineering works and passive broadband infrastructure.

(17) As regards infrastructure, a number of measures taken by Member States might not constitute aid because they do not fulfil all the criteria of Article 107(1) TFEU, for example because the beneficiary does not carry out an economic activity, because there is no effect on trade between Member States, or because the measure consists of compensation for a service of general economic interest which fulfils all the criteria of the Altmark case-law.[6] However, to the extent that the financing of infrastructure constitutes State aid within the meaning of Article 107(1) TFEU, the Commission should be enabled to declare that, under certain conditions, that aid is compatible with the internal market and not subject to the notification requirement. With regard to infrastructure, small amounts of aid for infrastructure projects can be an efficient way of supporting the Union's objectives, to the extent that the aid minimises costs and the potential distortion of competition is limited. The Commission should therefore be able to exempt State aid for infrastructure projects that are in support of the objectives mentioned in this Regulation and in support of other objectives of common interest, in particular the Europe 2020 objectives.[7] This could include support for projects involving multi-sectoral networks or facilities where relatively small amounts of aid are necessary. However, block exemptions can only be granted for infrastructure projects where the Commission has enough experience to define clear and strict compatibility criteria, ensuring that the risk of potential distortion of competition is limited and that large amounts of aid remain subject to notification pursuant to Article 108(3) TFEU.

(18) It is appropriate that the Commission, when it adopts regulations exempting categories of aid from the obligation to notify provided for in Article 108(3) TFEU, specifies the purpose of the aid, the categories of beneficiaries and thresholds limiting the exempted aid, the conditions governing the cumulation of aid and the conditions of monitoring, in order to ensure the compatibility with the internal market of aid covered by this Regulation.

(19) Thresholds for each category of aid in respect of which the Commission adopts a block exemption regulation can be expressed in terms of aid intensities in relation to a set of eligible costs, or in terms of maximum aid amounts. Moreover, the Commission should also be enabled to issue block exemptions for certain types of measures involving State aid which, because of the specific way in which they are designed, cannot be expressed precisely in terms of the aid intensities or maximum amounts of aid, such as financial engineering instruments or certain forms of measures aimed to promote risk capital investments. Such complex measures may involve aid at different levels: direct beneficiaries, intermediate beneficiaries and indirect beneficiaries. Given the increasing importance of such measures and their contribution to the Union's objectives, it should be possible to exempt them. It should therefore be possible, in the case of such measures, to define the thresholds for a particular award of aid in terms of the maximum level of state support in or related to that measure. The maximum level of state support may comprise an element of support, which may not be State aid, provided that the measure includes at least some elements that contain State aid within the meaning of Article 107(1) TFEU and which elements are not marginal.

(20) It may be useful to set thresholds or other appropriate conditions requiring the notification of awards of aid in order to allow the Commission to examine individually the effect of certain aid on competition and trade between Member States and its compatibility with the internal market.

(21) It is appropriate to enable the Commission, when it adopts regulations exempting certain categories of aid from the obligation to notify in Article 108(3) TFEU, to attach further detailed conditions in order to ensure the compatibility with the internal market of aid covered by this Regulation.

(22) The Commission, having regard to the development and the functioning of the internal market, should be enabled to establish by means of a regulation that certain aid does not fulfil all the criteria of Article 107(1) TFEU and is therefore exempted from the notification procedure laid down in Article 108(3) TFEU, provided that aid granted to the same undertaking over a given period of time does not exceed a certain fixed amount.

(23) In accordance with Article 108(1) TFEU the Commission is under an obligation, in cooperation with Member States, to keep under constant review all systems of existing aid. For this purpose and in order to ensure the largest possible degree of transparency and adequate control it is desirable that the Commission ensures the establishment of a reliable system of recording and storing information about the application of the regulations it adopts, to which all Member States have access, and that it receives all necessary information from the Member States on the implementation of aid exempted from notification to fulfil this obligation, which may be examined and evaluated with the Member States within the Advisory Committee on State aid. For this purpose it is also desirable that the Commission may require such information to be supplied as is necessary to ensure the efficiency of such review.

(24) Member States should provide summaries of information concerning aid implemented by them which is covered by an exemption regulation. The publication of those summaries is necessary to ensure the transparency of the measures adopted by the Member States. With the growth of electronic communication media, publication of the summaries on the website of the Commission is a fast and effective method ensuring transparency for the benefit of interested parties. Therefore, those summaries should be published on the website of the Commission.

(25) The control of the granting of aid involves factual, legal and economic issues of a very complex nature and great variety in a constantly evolving environment. The Commission should therefore regularly review the categories of aid which should be exempted from notification. The Commission should be able to repeal or amend regulations it has adopted pursuant to this Regulation where circumstances have changed with respect to any important element which constituted grounds for their adoption or where the progressive development or the functioning of the internal market so requires.

(26) The Commission, in close and constant liaison with the Member States, should be able to define precisely the scope of those regulations and the conditions attached to them. In order to provide for cooperation between the Commission and the competent authorities of the Member States, it is appropriate that the Advisory Committee on State aid be consulted before the Commission adopts regulations pursuant to this Regulation.

(27) Draft regulations and other documents to be examined by the Advisory Committee on State aid in accordance with this Regulation should be published on the website of the Commission to ensure transparency.

(28) The Advisory Committee on State aid should be consulted before publication of a draft regulation. However, in the interest of transparency, the draft regulation should be published on the website of the Commission at the same time as the Commission consults the Advisory Committee for the first time,

NOTES

Repeal of this Regulation in relation to the UK: this Regulation is repealed in relation to the UK (as from IP completion day); see the introductory notes to this Regulation *ante*.

[1] Opinion of 29 April 2015 (not yet published in the Official Journal).

[2] Council Regulation (EC) No 994/98 of 7 May 1998 on the application of Articles 107 and 108 of the Treaty on the Functioning of the European Union to certain categories of horizontal State aid (OJ L142, 14.5.1998, p 1).

[3] See Annex I.

4 Council Regulation (EC) No 1198/2006 of 27 July 2006 on the European Fisheries Fund (OJ L223, 15.8.2006, p 1).

5 Communication from the Commission — EU Guidelines for the application of State aid rules in relation to the rapid deployment of broadband networks (OJ C25, 26.1.2013, p 1).

6 Judgment of the Court of Justice of 24 July 2003 in Case C-280/00, *Altmark Trans GmbH and Regierungspräsidium Magdeburg v Nahverkehrsgesellschaft Altmark GmbH* ([2003] ECR I-7747).

7 See Council Recommendation 2010/410/EU of 13 July 2010 on broad guidelines for the economic policies of the Member States and of the Union (OJ L191, 23.7.2010, p 28) and Council Decision 2010/707/EU of 21 October 2010 on guidelines for the employment policies of the Member States (OJ L308, 24.11.2010, p 46).

HAS ADOPTED THIS REGULATION:

[5.150]

Article 1 Block exemptions

1. The Commission may, by means of regulations adopted in accordance with the procedure laid down in Article 8 of this Regulation and in accordance with Article 107 TFEU, declare that the following categories of aid are compatible with the internal market and are not subject to the notification requirements of Article 108(3) TFEU:

(a) aid in favour of:

(i) small and medium-sized enterprises;

(ii) research, development and innovation;

(iii) environmental protection;

(iv) employment and training;

(v) culture and heritage conservation;

(vi) making good the damage caused by natural disasters;

(vii) making good the damage caused by certain adverse weather conditions in fisheries;

(viii) forestry;

(ix) promotion of food sector products not listed in Annex I of the TFEU;

(x) conservation of marine and freshwater biological resources;

(xi) sports;

(xii) residents of remote regions, for transport, when this aid has a social character and is granted without discrimination related to the identity of the carrier;

(xiii) basic broadband infrastructure, small individual infrastructure measures covering next-generation access networks, broadband-related civil engineering works and passive broadband infrastructure, in areas where there is either no such infrastructure or where no such infrastructure is likely to be developed in the near future;

(xiv) infrastructure in support of the objectives listed in points (i) to (xiii) as well as in point (b) of this paragraph and in support of other objectives of common interest, in particular the Europe 2020 objectives;

[(xv) financing channelled through or supported by EU centrally-managed financial instruments or budgetary guarantees, where the aid consists in the form of additional funding provided through State resources;

(xvi) projects supported by EU European Territorial Cooperation programmes;]

(b) aid that complies with the map approved by the Commission for each Member State for the grant of regional aid.

2. The regulations referred to in paragraph 1 shall specify for each category of aid:

(a) the purpose of the aid;

(b) the categories of beneficiaries;

(c) thresholds expressed in terms of aid intensities in relation to a set of eligible costs or in terms of maximum aid amounts or, for certain types of aid where it may be difficult to identify the aid intensity or amount of aid precisely, in particular financial engineering instruments or risk capital investments or those of a similar nature, in terms of the maximum level of state support in or related to that measure, without prejudice to the qualification of the measures concerned in the light of Article 107(1) TFEU;

(d) the conditions governing the cumulation of aid;

(e) the conditions of monitoring as specified in Article 3.

3. In addition, the regulations referred to in paragraph 1 may, in particular:

(a) set thresholds or other conditions for the notification of awards of individual aid;

(b) exclude certain sectors from their scope;

(c) attach further conditions for the compatibility of aid exempted under such regulations.

NOTES

Para 1: points (a)(xv) and (xvi) added by Council Regulation 2018/1911/EU, Art 1.

Repeal of this Regulation in relation to the UK: this Regulation is repealed in relation to the UK (as from IP completion day); see the introductory notes to this Regulation *ante*.

[5.151]

Article 2 De minimis

1. The Commission may, by means of a regulation adopted in accordance with the procedure laid down in Article 8 of this Regulation, decide that, having regard to the development and functioning of the internal market, certain aid does not meet all the criteria of Article 107(1) TFEU and that it is therefore exempted from the notification procedure provided for in Article 108(3) TFEU, provided that aid granted to the same undertaking over a given period of time does not exceed a certain fixed amount.

2. At the Commission's request, Member States shall, at any time, communicate to it any additional information relating to aid exempted under paragraph 1.

NOTES

Repeal of this Regulation in relation to the UK: this Regulation is repealed in relation to the UK (as from IP completion day); see the introductory notes to this Regulation *ante*.

[5.152]

Article 3 Transparency and monitoring

1. When adopting regulations pursuant to Article 1, the Commission shall impose detailed rules upon Member States to ensure transparency and monitoring of the aid exempted from notification in accordance with those regulations. Such rules shall consist, in particular, of the requirements laid down in paragraphs 2, 3 and 4.

2. Upon implementing aid systems or individual aids granted outside any system, which have been exempted pursuant to regulations referred to in Article 1(1), Member States shall forward to the Commission, with a view to publication on the website of the Commission, summaries of the information regarding such systems of aid or such individual aids as are not covered by exempted aid systems.

3. Member States shall record and compile all the information regarding the application of the block exemptions. If the Commission has information which leads it to doubt that an exemption regulation is being applied properly, the Member States shall forward to it any information it considers necessary to assess whether an aid complies with that regulation.

4. At least once a year, Member States shall supply the Commission with a report on the application of block exemptions, in accordance with the Commission's specific requirements, preferably in computerised form. The Commission shall make access to those reports available to all the Member States. The Committee referred to in Article 7 shall examine and evaluate those reports once a year.

NOTES

Repeal of this Regulation in relation to the UK: this Regulation is repealed in relation to the UK (as from IP completion day); see the introductory notes to this Regulation *ante*.

[5.153]

Article 4 Period of validity and amendment of regulations

1. Regulations adopted pursuant to Articles 1 and 2 shall apply for a specific period. Aid exempted by a regulation adopted pursuant to Articles 1 and 2 shall be exempted for the period of validity of that regulation and for the adjustment period provided for in paragraphs 2 and 3 of this Article.

2. Regulations adopted pursuant to Articles 1 and 2 may be repealed or amended where circumstances have changed with respect to any important element that constituted grounds for their adoption or where the progressive development or the functioning of the internal market so requires. In that case the new regulation shall set a period of adjustment of six months for the adjustment of aid covered by the previous regulation.

3. Regulations adopted pursuant to Articles 1 and 2 shall provide for a period as referred to in paragraph 2 of this Article, should their application not be extended when they expire.

NOTES

Repeal of this Regulation in relation to the UK: this Regulation is repealed in relation to the UK (as from IP completion day); see the introductory notes to this Regulation *ante*.

[5.154]

Article 5 Evaluation report

Every five years the Commission shall submit a report to the European Parliament and to the Council on the application of this Regulation. It shall submit a draft report for consideration by the Committee referred to in Article 7.

NOTES

Repeal of this Regulation in relation to the UK: this Regulation is repealed in relation to the UK (as from IP completion day); see the introductory notes to this Regulation *ante*.

[5.155]

Article 6 Hearing of interested parties

Where the Commission intends to adopt a regulation, it shall publish a draft thereof to enable all interested persons and organisations to submit their comments to it within a reasonable time limit to be fixed by the Commission and which may not under any circumstances be less than one month.

NOTES

Repeal of this Regulation in relation to the UK: this Regulation is repealed in relation to the UK (as from IP completion day); see the introductory notes to this Regulation *ante*.

[5.156]

Article 7 Advisory Committee on State aid

The Advisory Committee on State aid ('the Committee') shall be set up. It shall be composed of representatives of the Member States and chaired by a representative of the Commission.

NOTES

Repeal of this Regulation in relation to the UK: this Regulation is repealed in relation to the UK (as from IP completion day); see the introductory notes to this Regulation *ante*.

[5.157]

Article 8 Consultation of the Committee

1. The Commission shall consult the Committee:

(a) at the same time as publishing any draft regulation in accordance with Article 6;

(b) before adopting any regulation.

2. Consultation of the Committee shall take place at a meeting called by the Commission. The drafts and documents to be examined shall be annexed to the notification and may be published on the Commission website. The meeting shall take place no earlier than two months after notification has been sent.

This period may be reduced in the case of the consultations referred to in paragraph 1(b), when urgent or for simple extension of a regulation.

3. The representative of the Commission shall submit to the Committee a draft of the measures to be taken. The Committee shall deliver its opinion on the draft, within a time limit which the chairman may lay down according to the urgency of the matter, if necessary by taking a vote.

4. The opinion shall be recorded in the minutes. In addition, each Member State shall have the right to ask to have its position recorded in the minutes. The Committee may recommend the publication of the opinion in the Official Journal of the European Union.

5. The Commission shall take the utmost account of the opinion delivered by the Committee. It shall inform the Committee of the manner in which its opinion has been taken into account.

NOTES

Repeal of this Regulation in relation to the UK: this Regulation is repealed in relation to the UK (as from IP completion day); see the introductory notes to this Regulation *ante*.

[5.158]

Article 9 Repeal

Regulation (EC) No 994/98 is repealed.

References to the repealed Regulation shall be construed as references to this Regulation and shall be read in accordance with the correlation table in Annex II.

NOTES

Repeal of this Regulation in relation to the UK: this Regulation is repealed in relation to the UK (as from IP completion day); see the introductory notes to this Regulation *ante*.

[5.159]

Article 10 Entry into force

This Regulation shall enter into force on the twentieth day following that of its publication in the Official Journal of the European Union.

NOTES

Repeal of this Regulation in relation to the UK: this Regulation is repealed in relation to the UK (as from IP completion day); see the introductory notes to this Regulation *ante*.

ANNEXES

ANNEX I
REPEALED REGULATION WITH ITS AMENDMENT

[5.160]

Council Regulation (EC) No 994/98	*(OJ L142, 14.5.1998, p 1).*
Council Regulation (EU) No 733/2013	*(OJ L204, 31.7.2013, p 11).*

NOTES

Repeal of this Regulation in relation to the UK: this Regulation is repealed in relation to the UK (as from IP completion day); see the introductory notes to this Regulation *ante*.

ANNEX II
CORRELATION TABLE

[5.161]

Regulation (EC) No 994/98	***This Regulation***
Articles 1 to 8	*Articles 1 to 8*
—	*Article 9*
Article 9	*Article 10*
—	*Annex I*
—	*Annex II*

NOTES

Repeal of this Regulation in relation to the UK: this Regulation is repealed in relation to the UK (as from IP completion day); see the introductory notes to this Regulation *ante*.

COUNCIL REGULATION

(2015/1589/EU)

of 13 July 2015

laying down detailed rules for the application of Article 108 of the Treaty on the Functioning of the European Union (codification) (Procedural Regulation)

(Text with EEA relevance)

[5.162]

NOTES

Date of publication in OJ: OJ L248, 24.9.2015, p 9.

Repeal of this Regulation in relation to the UK: this Regulation is repealed, in relation to the UK, by the State Aid (Revocations and Amendments) (EU Exit) Regulations 2020, SI 2020/1470, reg 5, as from IP completion day (as defined in the European Union (Withdrawal Agreement) Act 2020, s 39) (for transitional provisions and savings in relation to claims before a court or tribunal relating to State aid infringement before IP completion day, see Sch 3 to those Regulations at **[7.89]**).

THE COUNCIL OF THE EUROPEAN UNION,

Having regard to the Treaty on the Functioning of the European Union, and in particular Article 109 thereof,

Having regard to the proposal from the European Commission,

Having regard to the opinion of the European Parliament,[1]

Whereas:

(1) Council Regulation (EC) No 659/1999[2] has been substantially amended several times.[3] In the interests of clarity and rationality, that Regulation should be codified.

(2) Without prejudice to special procedural rules laid down in regulations for certain sectors, this Regulation should apply to aid in all sectors. For the purpose of applying Articles 93 and 107 of the Treaty on the Functioning of the European Union (TFEU), the Commission has specific competence under Article 108 thereof to decide on the compatibility of State aid with the internal market when reviewing existing aid, when taking decisions on new or altered aid and when taking action regarding non-compliance with its decisions or with the requirement as to notification.

(3) In the context of a modernised system of State aid rules, to contribute both to the implementation of the Europe 2020 strategy for growth and to budgetary consolidation, Article 107 of the TFEU should be applied effectively and uniformly throughout the Union. Regulation (EC) No 659/1999 consolidated and reinforced the Commission's previous practice of increasing legal certainty and supporting the development of State aid policy in a transparent environment.

(4) In order to ensure legal certainty, it is appropriate that the circumstances under which aid is to be considered as existing aid be defined. The completion and enhancement of the internal market is a gradual process, reflected in the permanent development of State aid policy. Following those developments, certain measures, which at the moment they were put into effect did not constitute State aid, may since have become aid.

(5) In accordance with Article 108(3) TFEU, any plans to grant new aid are to be notified to the Commission and should not be put into effect before the Commission has authorised it.

(6) In accordance with Article 4(3) of the Treaty on European Union (TEU), Member States are under an obligation to cooperate with the Commission and to provide it with all information required to allow the Commission to carry out its duties under this Regulation.

(7) The period within which the Commission is to conclude the preliminary examination of notified aid should be set at 2 months from the receipt of a complete notification or from the receipt of a duly reasoned statement of the Member State concerned that it considers the notification to be complete because the additional information requested by the Commission is not available or has already been provided. For reasons of legal certainty, that examination should be brought to an end by a decision.

(8) In all cases where, as a result of the preliminary examination, the Commission cannot find that the aid is compatible with the internal market, the formal investigation procedure should be opened in order to enable the Commission to gather all the information it needs to assess the compatibility of the aid and to allow the interested parties to submit their comments. The rights of the interested parties can best be safeguarded within the framework of the formal investigation procedure provided for in Article 108(2) TFEU.

(9) In order to assess the compatibility with the internal market of any notified or unlawful State aid for which the Commission has exclusive competence under Article 108 TFEU, it is appropriate to ensure that the Commission has the power, for the purposes of enforcing the State aid rules, to request all necessary market information from any Member State, undertaking or association of undertakings whenever it has doubts as to the compatibility of the measure concerned with the Union rules, and has therefore initiated the formal investigation procedure. In particular, the Commission should use this power in cases in which a complex substantive assessment appears necessary. In deciding whether to use this power, the Commission should take due account of the duration of the preliminary examination.

(10) For the purpose of assessing the compatibility of an aid measure after the initiation of the formal investigation procedure, in particular as regards technically complex cases subject to substantive assessment, the Commission should be able, by simple request or by decision, to require any Member State, undertaking or association of undertakings to provide all market information necessary for completing its assessment, if the information provided by the Member State concerned during the course of the preliminary examination is not sufficient, taking due account of the principle of proportionality, in particular for small and medium-sized enterprises.

(11) In the light of the special relationship between aid beneficiaries and the Member State concerned, the Commission should be able to request information from an aid beneficiary only in agreement with the Member State concerned. The provision of information by the beneficiary of the aid measure in question does not constitute a legal basis for bilateral negotiations between the Commission and the beneficiary in question.

(12) The Commission should select the addressees of information requests on the basis of objective criteria appropriate to each case, while ensuring that, when the request is addressed to a sample of undertakings or associations thereof, the sample of respondents is representative within each category. The information sought should consist, in particular, of factual company and market data and facts-based analysis of the functioning of the market.

(13) The Commission, as the initiator of the procedure, should be responsible for verifying both the information transmission by the Member States, undertakings or associations of undertakings, and the purported confidentiality of the information to be disclosed.

(14) The Commission should be able to enforce compliance with the requests for information it addresses to any undertaking or association of undertakings, as appropriate, by means of proportionate fines and periodic penalty payments. In setting the amounts of fines and periodic penalty payments, the Commission should take due account of the principles of proportionality and appropriateness, in particular as regards small and medium-sized enterprises. The rights of the parties requested to provide information should be safeguarded by giving them the opportunity to make known their views before any decision imposing fines or periodic penalty payments is taken. The Court of Justice of the European Union should have unlimited jurisdiction with regard to such fines and periodic penalties pursuant to Article 261 TFEU.

(15) Taking due account of the principles of proportionality and appropriateness, the Commission should be able to reduce the periodic penalty payments or waive them entirely, when addressees of requests provide the information requested, albeit after the expiry of the deadline.

(16) Fines and periodic penalty payments are not applicable to Member States, since they are under a duty to cooperate sincerely with the Commission in accordance with Article 4(3) TEU, and to provide the Commission with all information required to allow it to carry out its duties under this Regulation.

(17) After having considered the comments submitted by the interested parties, the Commission should conclude its examination by means of a final decision as soon as the doubts have been removed. It is appropriate, should this examination not be concluded after a period of 18 months from the opening of the procedure, that the Member State concerned has the opportunity to request a decision, which the Commission should take within 2 months.

(18) In order to safeguard the rights of defence of the Member State concerned, it should be provided with copies of the requests for information sent to other Member States, undertakings or associations of undertakings, and be able to submit its observations on the comments received. It should also be informed of the names of the undertakings and the associations of undertakings requested, to the extent that these entities have not demonstrated a legitimate interest in the protection of their identity.

(19) The Commission should take due account of the legitimate interests of undertakings in the protection of their business secrets. It should not be able to use confidential information provided by respondents, which cannot be aggregated or otherwise be anonymised, in any decision unless it has previously obtained their agreement to disclose that information to the Member State concerned.

(20) In cases where information marked as confidential does not seem to be covered by obligations of professional secrecy, it is appropriate to have a mechanism in place according to which the Commission can decide the extent to which such information can be disclosed. Any such decision to reject a claim that information is confidential should indicate a period at the end of which the information will be disclosed, so that the respondent can make use of any judicial protection available to it, including any interim measure.

(21) In order to ensure that the State aid rules are applied correctly and effectively, the Commission should have the opportunity of revoking a decision which was based on incorrect information.

(22) In order to ensure compliance with Article 108 TFEU, and in particular with the notification obligation and the standstill clause in Article 108(3), the Commission should examine all cases of unlawful aid. In the interests of transparency and legal certainty, the procedures to be followed in such cases should be laid down. When a Member State has not respected the notification obligation or the standstill clause, the Commission should not be bound by time limits.

(23) The Commission should be able, on its own initiative, to examine information on unlawful aid, from whatever source, in order to ensure compliance with Article 108 TFEU, and in particular with the notification obligation and standstill clause laid down in Article 108(3) TFEU, and to assess the compatibility of an aid with the internal market.

(24) In cases of unlawful aid, the Commission should have the right to obtain all necessary information enabling it to take a decision and to restore immediately, where appropriate, undistorted competition. It is therefore appropriate to enable the Commission to adopt interim measures addressed to the Member State concerned. The interim measures may take the form of information injunctions,

suspension injunctions and recovery injunctions. The Commission should be enabled, in the event of non-compliance with an information injunction, to decide on the basis of the information available and, in the event of non-compliance with suspension and recovery injunctions, to refer the matter to the Court of Justice directly, in accordance with the second subparagraph of Article 108(2) TFEU.

(25) In cases of unlawful aid which is not compatible with the internal market, effective competition should be restored. For this purpose it is necessary that the aid, including interest, be recovered without delay. It is appropriate that recovery be effected in accordance with the procedures of national law. The application of those procedures should not, by preventing the immediate and effective execution of the Commission decision, impede the restoration of effective competition. To achieve this result, Member States should take all necessary measures ensuring the effectiveness of the Commission decision.

(26) For reasons of legal certainty it is appropriate to provide for a period of limitation of 10 years with regard to unlawful aid, after the expiry of which no recovery can be ordered.

(27) For reasons of legal certainty, it is appropriate to provide for limitation periods for the imposition and enforcement of fines and periodic penalty payments.

(28) Misuse of aid may have effects on the functioning of the internal market which are similar to those of unlawful aid and should thus be treated according to similar procedures. Unlike unlawful aid, aid which has possibly been misused is aid which has been previously approved by the Commission. Therefore the Commission should not be allowed to use a recovery injunction with regard to misuse of aid.

(29) In accordance with Article 108(1) TFEU, the Commission is under an obligation, in cooperation with Member States, to keep under constant review all systems of existing aid. In the interests of transparency and legal certainty, it is appropriate to specify the scope of cooperation under that Article.

(30) In order to ensure compatibility of existing aid schemes with the internal market and in accordance with Article 108(1) TFEU, the Commission should propose appropriate measures where an existing aid scheme is not, or is no longer, compatible with the internal market and should initiate the procedure provided for in Article 108(2) TFEU if the Member State concerned declines to implement the proposed measures.

(31) It is appropriate to set out all the possibilities which third parties have to defend their interests in State aid procedures.

(32) Complaints are an essential source of information for detecting infringements of the Union rules on State aid. To ensure the quality of the complaints submitted to the Commission, and at the same time transparency and legal certainty, it is appropriate to lay down the conditions that a complaint should fulfil in order to put the Commission in possession of information regarding alleged unlawful aid and set in motion the preliminary examination. Submissions not meeting those conditions should be treated as general market information, and should not necessarily lead to ex officio investigations.

(33) Complainants should be required to demonstrate that they are interested parties within the meaning of Article 108(2) TFEU and of Article 1(h) of this Regulation. They should also be required to provide a certain amount of information in a form that the Commission should be empowered to set out in an implementing provision. In order not to discourage prospective complainants, that implementing provision should take into account that the demands on interested parties for lodging a complaint should not be burdensome.

(34) In order to ensure that the Commission addresses similar issues in a consistent manner across the internal market, it is appropriate to provide for a specific legal basis to launch investigations into sectors of the economy or into certain aid instruments across several Member States. For reasons of proportionality and in the light of the high administrative burden entailed by such investigations, sector inquiries should be carried out only when the information available substantiates a reasonable suspicion that State aid measures in a particular sector could materially restrict or distort competition within the internal market in several Member States, or that existing aid measures in a particular sector in several Member States are not, or are no longer, compatible with the internal market. Such inquiries would enable the Commission to deal in an efficient and transparent way with horizontal State aid issues and to obtain an ex ante overview of the sector concerned.

(35) In order to allow the Commission to monitor effectively compliance with Commission decisions and to facilitate cooperation between the Commission and Member States for the purpose of the constant review of all existing aid schemes in the Member States in accordance with Article 108(1) TFEU, it is necessary that a general reporting obligation with regard to all existing aid schemes be laid down.

(36) Where the Commission has serious doubts as to whether its decisions are being complied with, it should have at its disposal additional instruments allowing it to obtain the information necessary to verify that its decisions are being effectively complied with. For this purpose on-site monitoring visits are an appropriate and useful instrument, in particular for cases where aid might have been misused. Therefore the Commission should be empowered to undertake on-site monitoring visits and should obtain the cooperation of the competent authorities of the Member States where an undertaking opposes such a visit.

(37) Consistency in the application of the State aid rules requires that arrangements be established for cooperation between the courts of the Member States and the Commission. Such cooperation is relevant for all courts of the Member States that apply Article 107(1) and Article 108 TFEU. In particular, national courts should be able to ask the Commission for information or for its opinion on points

concerning the application of State aid rules. The Commission should also be able to submit written or oral observations to courts which are called upon to apply Article 107(1) or Article 108 TFEU. When assisting national courts in this respect, the Commission should act in accordance with its duty to defend the public interest.

(38) Those observations and opinions of the Commission should be without prejudice to Article 267 TFEU and not legally bind the national courts. They should be submitted within the framework of national procedural rules and practices including those safeguarding the rights of the parties, in full respect of the independence of the national courts. Observations submitted by the Commission on its own initiative should be limited to cases that are important for the coherent application of Article 107(1) or Article 108 TFEU, in particular to cases which are significant for the enforcement or the further development of Union State aid case law.

(39) In the interests of transparency and legal certainty, it is appropriate to give public information on Commission decisions while, at the same time, maintaining the principle that decisions in State aid cases are addressed to the Member State concerned. It is therefore appropriate to publish all decisions which might affect the interests of interested parties either in full or in a summary form or to make copies of such decisions available to interested parties, where they have not been published or where they have not been published in full.

(40) The Commission, when publishing its decisions, should respect the rules on professional secrecy, including the protection of all confidential information and personal data, in accordance with Article 339 TFEU.

(41) The Commission, in close liaison with the Advisory Committee on State aid, should be able to adopt implementing provisions laying down detailed rules concerning the procedures under this Regulation,

NOTES

Repeal of this Regulation in relation to the UK: this Regulation is repealed in relation to the UK (as from IP completion day); see the introductory notes to this Regulation *ante*.

[1] Opinion of 29 April 2015 (not yet published in the Official Journal).

[2] Council Regulation (EC) No 659/1999 of 22 March 1999 laying down detailed rules for the application of Article 108 of the Treaty on the Functioning of the European Union (OJ L83, 27.3.1999, p 1).

[3] See Annex I.

HAS ADOPTED THIS REGULATION:

CHAPTER I GENERAL

[5.163]

Article 1 Definitions

For the purposes of this Regulation, the following definitions shall apply:

- *(a) 'aid' means any measure fulfilling all the criteria laid down in Article 107(1) TFEU;*
- *(b) 'existing aid' means:*
  - *(i) without prejudice to Articles 144 and 172 of the Act of Accession of Austria, Finland and Sweden, to point 3 and the Appendix of Annex IV to the Act of Accession of the Czech Republic, Estonia, Cyprus, Latvia, Lithuania, Hungary, Malta, Poland, Slovenia and Slovakia, to points 2 and 3(b) and the Appendix of Annex V to the Act of Accession of Bulgaria and Romania, and to points 2 and 3(b) and the Appendix of Annex IV to the Act of Accession of Croatia, all aid which existed prior to the entry into force of the TFEU in the respective Member States, that is to say, aid schemes and individual aid which were put into effect before, and are still applicable after, the entry into force of the TFEU in the respective Member States;*
  - *(ii) authorised aid, that is to say, aid schemes and individual aid which have been authorised by the Commission or by the Council;*
  - *(iii) aid which is deemed to have been authorised pursuant to Article 4(6) of Regulation (EC) No 659/1999 or to Article 4(6) of this Regulation, or prior to Regulation (EC) No 659/1999 but in accordance with this procedure;*
  - *(iv) aid which is deemed to be existing aid pursuant to Article 17 of this Regulation;*
  - *(v) aid which is deemed to be an existing aid because it can be established that at the time it was put into effect it did not constitute an aid, and subsequently became an aid due to the evolution of the internal market and without having been altered by the Member State. Where certain measures become aid following the liberalisation of an activity by Union law, such measures shall not be considered as existing aid after the date fixed for liberalisation;*
- *(c) 'new aid' means all aid, that is to say, aid schemes and individual aid, which is not existing aid, including alterations to existing aid;*
- *(d) 'aid scheme' means any act on the basis of which, without further implementing measures being required, individual aid awards may be made to undertakings defined within the act in a general and abstract manner and any act on the basis of which aid which is not linked to a specific project may be awarded to one or several undertakings for an indefinite period of time and/or for an indefinite amount;*
- *(e) 'individual aid' means aid that is not awarded on the basis of an aid scheme and notifiable awards of aid on the basis of an aid scheme;*
- *(f) 'unlawful aid' means new aid put into effect in contravention of Article 108(3) TFEU;*
- *(g) 'misuse of aid' means aid used by the beneficiary in contravention of a decision taken pursuant to Article 4(3) or Article 7(3) or (4) of Regulation (EC) No 659/1999 or Article 4(3) or Article 9(3) or (4) of this Regulation;*

(h) *'interested party' means any Member State and any person, undertaking or association of undertakings whose interests might be affected by the granting of aid, in particular the beneficiary of the aid, competing undertakings and trade associations.*

NOTES

Repeal of this Regulation in relation to the UK: this Regulation is repealed in relation to the UK (as from IP completion day); see the introductory notes to this Regulation *ante*.

CHAPTER II PROCEDURE REGARDING NOTIFIED AID

[5.164]

Article 2 Notification of new aid

1. Save as otherwise provided in regulations made pursuant to Article 109 TFEU or to other relevant provisions thereof, any plans to grant new aid shall be notified to the Commission in sufficient time by the Member State concerned. The Commission shall inform the Member State concerned without delay of the receipt of a notification.

2. In a notification, the Member State concerned shall provide all necessary information in order to enable the Commission to take a decision pursuant to Articles 4 and 9 ('complete notification').

NOTES

Repeal of this Regulation in relation to the UK: this Regulation is repealed in relation to the UK (as from IP completion day); see the introductory notes to this Regulation *ante*.

[5.165]

Article 3 Standstill clause

Aid notifiable pursuant to Article 2(1) shall not be put into effect before the Commission has taken, or is deemed to have taken, a decision authorising such aid.

NOTES

Repeal of this Regulation in relation to the UK: this Regulation is repealed in relation to the UK (as from IP completion day); see the introductory notes to this Regulation *ante*.

[5.166]

Article 4 Preliminary examination of the notification and decisions of the Commission

1. The Commission shall examine the notification as soon as it is received. Without prejudice to Article 10, the Commission shall take a decision pursuant to paragraphs 2, 3 or 4 of this Article.

2. Where the Commission, after a preliminary examination, finds that the notified measure does not constitute aid, it shall record that finding by way of a decision.

3. Where the Commission, after a preliminary examination, finds that no doubts are raised as to the compatibility with the internal market of a notified measure, in so far as it falls within the scope of Article 107(1) TFEU, it shall decide that the measure is compatible with the internal market ('decision not to raise objections'). The decision shall specify which exception under the TFEU has been applied.

4. Where the Commission, after a preliminary examination, finds that doubts are raised as to the compatibility with the internal market of a notified measure, it shall decide to initiate proceedings pursuant to Article 108(2) TFEU ('decision to initiate the formal investigation procedure').

5. The decisions referred to in paragraphs 2, 3 and 4 of this Article shall be taken within 2 months. That period shall begin on the day following the receipt of a complete notification. The notification shall be considered as complete if, within 2 months from its receipt, or from the receipt of any additional information requested, the Commission does not request any further information. The period can be extended with the consent of both the Commission and the Member State concerned. Where appropriate, the Commission may fix shorter time limits.

6. Where the Commission has not taken a decision in accordance with paragraphs 2, 3 or 4 within the period laid down in paragraph 5, the aid shall be deemed to have been authorised by the Commission. The Member State concerned may thereupon implement the measures in question after giving the Commission prior notice thereof, unless the Commission takes a decision pursuant to this Article within a period of 15 working days following receipt of the notice.

NOTES

Repeal of this Regulation in relation to the UK: this Regulation is repealed in relation to the UK (as from IP completion day); see the introductory notes to this Regulation *ante*.

[5.167]

Article 5 Request for information made to the notifying Member State

1. Where the Commission considers that information provided by the Member State concerned with regard to a measure notified pursuant to Article 2 is incomplete, it shall request all necessary additional information. Where a Member State responds to such a request, the Commission shall inform the Member State of the receipt of the response.

2. Where the Member State concerned does not provide the information requested within the period prescribed by the Commission or provides incomplete information, the Commission shall send a reminder, allowing an appropriate additional period within which the information shall be provided.

3. The notification shall be deemed to be withdrawn if the requested information is not provided within the prescribed period, unless, before the expiry of that period, either the period has been extended with the consent of both the Commission and the Member State concerned, or the Member State concerned, in a duly reasoned statement, informs the Commission that it considers the notification to be complete because the additional information requested is not available or has already been provided. In that case, the period referred to in Article 4(5) shall begin on the day following receipt of the statement. If the notification is deemed to be withdrawn, the Commission shall inform the Member State thereof.

NOTES

Repeal of this Regulation in relation to the UK: this Regulation is repealed in relation to the UK (as from IP completion day); see the introductory notes to this Regulation *ante*.

[5.168]

Article 6 Formal investigation procedure

1. The decision to initiate the formal investigation procedure shall summarise the relevant issues of fact and law, shall include a preliminary assessment of the Commission as to the aid character of the proposed measure and shall set out the doubts as to its compatibility with the internal market. The decision shall call upon the Member State concerned and upon other interested parties to submit comments within a prescribed period which shall normally not exceed 1 month. In duly justified cases, the Commission may extend the prescribed period.

2. The comments received shall be submitted to the Member State concerned. If an interested party so requests, on grounds of potential damage, its identity shall be withheld from the Member State concerned. The Member State concerned may reply to the comments submitted within a prescribed period which shall normally not exceed 1 month. In duly justified cases, the Commission may extend the prescribed period.

NOTES

Repeal of this Regulation in relation to the UK: this Regulation is repealed in relation to the UK (as from IP completion day); see the introductory notes to this Regulation *ante*.

[5.169]

Article 7 Request for information made to other sources

1. After the initiation of the formal investigation procedure provided for in Article 6, in particular as regards technically complex cases subject to substantive assessment, the Commission may, if the information provided by a Member State concerned during the course of the preliminary examination is not sufficient, request any other Member State, an undertaking or an association of undertakings to provide all market information necessary to enable the Commission to complete its assessment of the measure at stake taking due account of the principle of proportionality, in particular for small and medium-sized enterprises.

2. The Commission may request information only:

(a) if it is limited to formal investigation procedures that have been identified by the Commission as being ineffective to date; and

(b) in so far as aid beneficiaries are concerned, if the Member State concerned agrees to the request.

3. The undertakings or associations of undertakings providing information following a Commission's request for market information based on paragraphs 6 and 7 shall submit their answer simultaneously to the Commission and to the Member State concerned, to the extent that the documents provided do not include information that is confidential vis-à-vis that Member State.

The Commission shall steer and monitor the information transmission between the Member States, undertakings or associations of undertakings concerned, and verify the purported confidentiality of the information transmitted.

4. The Commission shall request only information that is at the disposal of the Member State, undertaking or association of undertakings concerned by the request.

5. Member States shall provide the information on the basis of a simple request and within a time limit prescribed by the Commission which should normally not exceed 1 month. Where a Member State does not provide the information requested within that period or provides incomplete information, the Commission shall send a reminder.

6. The Commission may, by simple request, require an undertaking or an association of undertakings to provide information. Where the Commission sends a simple request for information to an undertaking or an association of undertakings, it shall state the legal basis and the purpose of the request, specify what information is required and prescribe a proportionate time limit within which the information is to be provided. It shall also refer to the fines provided for in Article 8(1) for supplying incorrect or misleading information.

7. The Commission may, by decision, require an undertaking or an association of undertakings to provide information. Where the Commission, by decision, requires an undertaking or an association of undertakings to supply information, it shall state the legal basis, the purpose of the request, specify what information is required and prescribe a proportionate time limit within which the information is to be provided. It shall also indicate the fines provided for in Article 8(1) and shall indicate or impose the periodic penalties payments provided for in Article 8(2), as appropriate. In addition, it shall indicate the right of the undertaking or association of undertakings to have the decision reviewed by the Court of Justice of the European Union.

8. When issuing a request under paragraph 1 or 6 of this Article, or adopting a decision under paragraph 7, the Commission shall also simultaneously provide the Member State concerned with a copy thereof. The Commission shall indicate the criteria by which it selected the recipients of the request or decision.

9. The owners of the undertakings or their representatives, or, in the case of legal persons, companies, firms or associations without legal personality, the persons authorised to represent them by law or by their constitution, shall supply on their behalf the information requested or required. Persons duly authorised to act may supply the information on behalf of their clients. The latter shall nevertheless be held fully responsible if the information supplied is incorrect, incomplete or misleading.

NOTES

Repeal of this Regulation in relation to the UK: this Regulation is repealed in relation to the UK (as from IP completion day); see the introductory notes to this Regulation *ante*.

[5.170]

Article 8 Fines and periodic penalty payments

1. The Commission may, if deemed necessary and proportionate, impose by decision on undertakings or associations of undertakings fines not exceeding 1 % of their total turnover in the preceding business year where they, intentionally or through gross negligence:

(a) supply incorrect or misleading information in response to a request made pursuant to Article 7(6);

(b) supply incorrect, incomplete or misleading information in response to a decision adopted pursuant to Article 7(7), or do not supply the information within the prescribed time limit.

2. The Commission may, by decision, impose on undertakings or associations of undertakings periodic penalty payments where an undertaking or association of undertakings fails to supply complete and correct information as requested by the Commission by decision adopted pursuant to Article 7(7).

The periodic penalty payments shall not exceed 5 % of the average daily turnover of the undertaking or association concerned in the preceding business year for each working day of delay, calculated from the date established in the decision, until it supplies complete and correct information as requested or required by the Commission.

3. In fixing the amount of the fine or periodic penalty payment, regard shall be had to the nature, gravity and duration of the infringement, taking due account of the principles of proportionality and appropriateness, in particular for small and medium-sized enterprises.

4. Where the undertakings or associations of undertakings have satisfied the obligation which the periodic penalty payment was intended to enforce, the Commission may reduce the definitive amount of the periodic penalty payment compared to that under the original decision imposing periodic penalty payments. The Commission may also waive any periodic penalty payment.

5. Before adopting any decision in accordance with paragraph 1 or 2 of this Article, the Commission shall set a final deadline of 2 weeks to receive the missing market information from the undertakings or associations of undertakings concerned and also give them the opportunity of making known their views.

6. The Court of Justice of the European Union shall have unlimited jurisdiction within the meaning of Article 261 TFEU to review fines or periodic penalty payments imposed by the Commission. It may cancel, reduce or increase the fine or periodic penalty payment imposed.

NOTES

Repeal of this Regulation in relation to the UK: this Regulation is repealed in relation to the UK (as from IP completion day); see the introductory notes to this Regulation *ante*.

[5.171]

Article 9 Decisions of the Commission to close the formal investigation procedure

1. Without prejudice to Article 10, the formal investigation procedure shall be closed by means of a decision as provided for in paragraphs 2 to 5 of this Article.

2. Where the Commission finds that, where appropriate following modification by the Member State concerned, the notified measure does not constitute aid, it shall record that finding by way of a decision.

3. Where the Commission finds that, where appropriate following modification by the Member State concerned, the doubts as to the compatibility of the notified measure with the internal market have been removed, it shall decide that the aid is compatible with the internal market ('positive decision'). That decision shall specify which exception under the TFEU has been applied.

4. The Commission may attach to a positive decision conditions subject to which aid may be considered compatible with the internal market and may lay down obligations to enable compliance with the decision to be monitored ('conditional decision').

5. Where the Commission finds that the notified aid is not compatible with the internal market, it shall decide that the aid shall not be put into effect ('negative decision').

6. Decisions taken pursuant to paragraphs 2 to 5 shall be taken as soon as the doubts referred to in Article 4(4) have been removed. The Commission shall as far as possible endeavour to adopt a decision within a period of 18 months from the opening of the procedure. This time limit may be extended by common agreement between the Commission and the Member State concerned.

7. Once the time limit referred to in paragraph 6 of this Article has expired, and should the Member State concerned so request, the Commission shall, within 2 months, take a decision on the basis of the information available to it. If appropriate, where the information provided is not sufficient to establish compatibility, the Commission shall take a negative decision.

8. Before adopting any decision in accordance with paragraphs 2 to 5, the Commission shall give the Member State concerned the opportunity of making known its views, within a time-limit that shall not normally exceed 1 month, on the information received by the Commission and provided to the Member State concerned pursuant to Article 7(3).

9. The Commission shall not use confidential information provided by respondents, which cannot be aggregated or otherwise be anonymised, in any decision taken in accordance with paragraphs 2 to 5 of this Article, unless it has obtained their agreement to disclose that information to the Member State concerned. The Commission may take a reasoned decision, which shall be notified to the undertaking or association of undertakings concerned, finding that information provided by a respondent and marked as confidential is not protected, and setting a date after which the information will be disclosed. That period shall not be less than 1 month.

10. The Commission shall take due account of the legitimate interests of undertakings in the protection of their business secrets and other confidential information. An undertaking or an association of undertakings providing information pursuant to Article 7, and which is not a beneficiary of the State aid measure in question, may request, on grounds of potential damage, that its identity be withheld from the Member State concerned.

NOTES

Repeal of this Regulation in relation to the UK: this Regulation is repealed in relation to the UK (as from IP completion day); see the introductory notes to this Regulation *ante*.

[5.172]

Article 10 Withdrawal of notification

1. The Member State concerned may withdraw the notification within the meaning of Article 2 in due time before the Commission has taken a decision pursuant to Article 4 or to Article 9.

2. In cases where the Commission initiated the formal investigation procedure, the Commission shall close that procedure.

NOTES

Repeal of this Regulation in relation to the UK: this Regulation is repealed in relation to the UK (as from IP completion day); see the introductory notes to this Regulation *ante*.

[5.173]

Article 11 Revocation of a decision

The Commission may revoke a decision taken pursuant to Article 4(2) or (3), or Article 9(2), (3) or (4), after having given the Member State concerned the opportunity to submit its comments, where the decision was based on incorrect information provided during the procedure which was a determining factor for the decision. Before revoking a decision and taking a new decision, the Commission shall open the formal investigation procedure pursuant to Article 4(4). Articles 6, 9 and 12, Article 13(1) and Articles 15, 16 and 17 shall apply mutatis mutandis.

NOTES

Repeal of this Regulation in relation to the UK: this Regulation is repealed in relation to the UK (as from IP completion day); see the introductory notes to this Regulation *ante*.

CHAPTER III PROCEDURE REGARDING UNLAWFUL AID

[5.174]

Article 12 Examination, request for information and information injunction

1. Without prejudice to Article 24, the Commission may on its own initiative examine information regarding alleged unlawful aid from whatever source.

The Commission shall examine without undue delay any complaint submitted by any interested party in accordance with Article 24(2) and shall ensure that the Member State concerned is kept fully and regularly informed of the progress and outcome of the examination.

2. If necessary, the Commission shall request information from the Member State concerned. Article 2(2) and Article 5(1) and (2) shall apply mutatis mutandis.

After the initiation of the formal investigation procedure, the Commission may also request information from any other Member State, from an undertaking, or association of undertakings in accordance with Articles 7 and 8, which shall apply mutatis mutandis.

3. Where, despite a reminder pursuant to Article 5(2), the Member State concerned does not provide the information requested within the period prescribed by the Commission, or where it provides incomplete information, the Commission shall by decision require the information to be provided ('information injunction'). The decision shall specify what information is required and prescribe an appropriate period within which it is to be supplied.

NOTES

Repeal of this Regulation in relation to the UK: this Regulation is repealed in relation to the UK (as from IP completion day); see the introductory notes to this Regulation *ante*.

[5.175]

Article 13 Injunction to suspend or provisionally recover aid

1. The Commission may, after giving the Member State concerned the opportunity to submit its comments, adopt a decision requiring the Member State to suspend any unlawful aid until the Commission has taken a decision on the compatibility of the aid with the internal market ('suspension injunction').

2. The Commission may, after giving the Member State concerned the opportunity to submit its comments, adopt a decision requiring the Member State provisionally to recover any unlawful aid until the Commission has taken a decision on the compatibility of the aid with the internal market ('recovery injunction'), if all the following criteria are fulfilled:

- *(a) according to an established practice there are no doubts about the aid character of the measure concerned;*
- *(b) there is an urgency to act;*
- *(c) there is a serious risk of substantial and irreparable damage to a competitor.*

Recovery shall be effected in accordance with the procedure set out in Article 16(2) and (3). After the aid has been effectively recovered, the Commission shall take a decision within the time limits applicable to notified aid.

The Commission may authorise the Member State to couple the refunding of the aid with the payment of rescue aid to the firm concerned.

The provisions of this paragraph shall be applicable only to unlawful aid implemented after the entry into force of Regulation (EC) No 659/1999.

NOTES

Repeal of this Regulation in relation to the UK: this Regulation is repealed in relation to the UK (as from IP completion day); see the introductory notes to this Regulation *ante*.

[5.176]

Article 14 Non-compliance with an injunction decision

If the Member State fails to comply with a suspension injunction or a recovery injunction, the Commission shall be entitled, while carrying out the examination on the substance of the matter on the basis of the information available, to refer the matter to the Court of Justice of the European Union directly and apply for a declaration that the failure to comply constitutes an infringement of the TFEU.

NOTES

Repeal of this Regulation in relation to the UK: this Regulation is repealed in relation to the UK (as from IP completion day); see the introductory notes to this Regulation *ante*.

[5.177]

Article 15 Decisions of the Commission

1. The examination of possible unlawful aid shall result in a decision pursuant to Article 4(2), (3) or (4). In the case of decisions to initiate the formal investigation procedure, proceedings shall be closed by means of a decision pursuant to Article 9. If a Member State fails to comply with an information injunction, that decision shall be taken on the basis of the information available.

2. In cases of possible unlawful aid and without prejudice to Article 13(2), the Commission shall not be bound by the time-limit set out in Articles 4(5), 9(6) and 9(7).

3. Article 11 shall apply mutatis mutandis.

NOTES

Repeal of this Regulation in relation to the UK: this Regulation is repealed in relation to the UK (as from IP completion day); see the introductory notes to this Regulation *ante*.

[5.178]

Article 16 Recovery of aid

1. Where negative decisions are taken in cases of unlawful aid, the Commission shall decide that the Member State concerned shall take all necessary measures to recover the aid from the beneficiary ('recovery decision'). The Commission shall not require recovery of the aid if this would be contrary to a general principle of Union law.

2. The aid to be recovered pursuant to a recovery decision shall include interest at an appropriate rate fixed by the Commission. Interest shall be payable from the date on which the unlawful aid was at the disposal of the beneficiary until the date of its recovery.

3. Without prejudice to any order of the Court of Justice of the European Union pursuant to Article 278 TFEU, recovery shall be effected without delay and in accordance with the procedures under the national law of the Member State concerned, provided that they allow the immediate and effective execution of the Commission's decision. To this effect and in the event of a procedure before national courts, the Member States concerned shall take all necessary steps which are available in their respective legal systems, including provisional measures, without prejudice to Union law.

NOTES

Repeal of this Regulation in relation to the UK: this Regulation is repealed in relation to the UK (as from IP completion day); see the introductory notes to this Regulation *ante*.

CHAPTER IV LIMITATION PERIODS

[5.179]

Article 17 Limitation period for the recovery of aid

1. The powers of the Commission to recover aid shall be subject to a limitation period of 10 years.

2. The limitation period shall begin on the day on which the unlawful aid is awarded to the beneficiary either as individual aid or as aid under an aid scheme. Any action taken by the Commission or by a Member State, acting at the request of the Commission, with regard to the unlawful aid shall interrupt the limitation period. Each interruption shall start time running afresh. The limitation period shall be suspended for as long as the decision of the Commission is the subject of proceedings pending before the Court of Justice of the European Union.

3. Any aid with regard to which the limitation period has expired shall be deemed to be existing aid.

NOTES

Repeal of this Regulation in relation to the UK: this Regulation is repealed in relation to the UK (as from IP completion day); see the introductory notes to this Regulation *ante*.

[5.180]

Article 18 Limitation period for the imposition of fines and periodic penalty payments

1. The powers conferred on the Commission by Article 8 shall be subject to a limitation period of 3 years.

2. The period provided for in paragraph 1 shall start on the day on which the infringement referred to in Article 8 is committed. However, in the case of continuing or repeated infringements, the period shall begin on the day on which the infringement ceases.

3. Any action taken by the Commission for the purpose of the investigation or proceedings in respect of an infringement referred to in Article 8 shall interrupt the limitation period for the imposition of fines or periodic penalty payments, with effect from the date on which the action is notified to the undertaking or association of undertakings concerned.

4. After each interruption, the limitation period shall start running afresh. However, the limitation period shall expire at the latest on the day on which a period of 6 years has elapsed without the Commission having imposed a fine or a periodic penalty payment. That period shall be extended by the time during which the limitation period is suspended in accordance with paragraph 5 of this Article.

5. The limitation period for the imposition of fines or periodic penalty payments shall be suspended for as long as the decision of the Commission is the subject of proceedings pending before the Court of Justice of the European Union.

NOTES

Repeal of this Regulation in relation to the UK: this Regulation is repealed in relation to the UK (as from IP completion day); see the introductory notes to this Regulation *ante*.

[5.181]
Article 19 Limitation periods for the enforcement of fines and periodic penalty payments

1. The powers of the Commission to enforce decisions adopted pursuant to Article 8 shall be subject to a limitation period of 5 years.

2. The period provided for in paragraph 1 shall start on the day on which the decision taken pursuant to Article 8 becomes final.

3. The limitation period provided for in paragraph 1 of this Article shall be interrupted:

(a) by notification of a decision modifying the original amount of the fine or periodic penalty payment or refusing an application for modification;

(b) by any action of a Member State, acting at the request of the Commission, or of the Commission, intended to enforce payment of the fine or periodic penalty payment.

4. After each interruption, the limitation period shall start running afresh.

5. The limitation period provided for in paragraph 1 shall be suspended for so long as:

(a) the respondent is allowed time to pay;

(b) the enforcement of payment is suspended pursuant to a decision of the Court of Justice of the European Union.

NOTES

Repeal of this Regulation in relation to the UK: this Regulation is repealed in relation to the UK (as from IP completion day); see the introductory notes to this Regulation *ante*.

CHAPTER V PROCEDURE REGARDING MISUSE OF AID

[5.182]
Article 20 Misuse of aid

Without prejudice to Article 28, the Commission may, in cases of misuse of aid, initiate the formal investigation procedure pursuant to Article 4(4). Articles 6 to 9, 11 and 12, Article 13(1) and Articles 14 to 17 shall apply mutatis mutandis.

NOTES

Repeal of this Regulation in relation to the UK: this Regulation is repealed in relation to the UK (as from IP completion day); see the introductory notes to this Regulation *ante*.

CHAPTER VI PROCEDURE REGARDING EXISTING AID SCHEMES

[5.183]
Article 21 Cooperation pursuant to Article 108(1) TFEU

1. The Commission shall obtain from the Member State concerned all necessary information for the review, in cooperation with the Member State, of existing aid schemes pursuant to Article 108(1) TFEU.

2. Where the Commission considers that an existing aid scheme is not, or is no longer, compatible with the internal market, it shall inform the Member State concerned of its preliminary view and give the Member State concerned the opportunity to submit its comments within a period of 1 month. In duly justified cases, the Commission may extend this period.

NOTES

Repeal of this Regulation in relation to the UK: this Regulation is repealed in relation to the UK (as from IP completion day); see the introductory notes to this Regulation *ante*.

[5.184]
Article 22 Proposal for appropriate measures

Where the Commission, in the light of the information submitted by the Member State pursuant to Article 21, concludes that the existing aid scheme is not, or is no longer, compatible with the internal market, it shall issue a recommendation proposing appropriate measures to the Member State concerned. The recommendation may propose, in particular:

(a) substantive amendment of the aid scheme; or

(b) introduction of procedural requirements; or

(c) abolition of the aid scheme.

NOTES

Repeal of this Regulation in relation to the UK: this Regulation is repealed in relation to the UK (as from IP completion day); see the introductory notes to this Regulation *ante*.

[5.185]
Article 23 Legal consequences of a proposal for appropriate measures

1. Where the Member State concerned accepts the proposed measures and informs the Commission thereof, the Commission shall record that finding and inform the Member State thereof. The Member State shall be bound by its acceptance to implement the appropriate measures.

2. Where the Member State concerned does not accept the proposed measures and the Commission, having taken into account the arguments of the Member State concerned, still considers that those measures are necessary, it shall initiate proceedings pursuant to Article 4(4). Articles 6, 9 and 11 shall apply mutatis mutandis.

NOTES

Repeal of this Regulation in relation to the UK: this Regulation is repealed in relation to the UK (as from IP completion day); see the introductory notes to this Regulation *ante*.

CHAPTER VII INTERESTED PARTIES

[5.186]

Article 24 Rights of interested parties

1. Any interested party may submit comments pursuant to Article 6 following a Commission decision to initiate the formal investigation procedure. Any interested party which has submitted such comments and any beneficiary of individual aid shall be sent a copy of the decision taken by the Commission pursuant to Article 9.

2. Any interested party may submit a complaint to inform the Commission of any alleged unlawful aid or any alleged misuse of aid. To that effect, the interested party shall duly complete a form that has been set out in an implementing provision referred to in Article 33 and shall provide the mandatory information requested therein.

Where the Commission considers that the interested party does not comply with the compulsory complaint form, or that the facts and points of law put forward by the interested party do not provide sufficient grounds to show, on the basis of a prima facie examination, the existence of unlawful aid or misuse of aid, it shall inform the interested party thereof and call upon it to submit comments within a prescribed period which shall not normally exceed 1 month. If the interested party fails to make known its views within the prescribed period, the complaint shall be deemed to have been withdrawn. The Commission shall inform the Member State concerned when a complaint has been deemed to have been withdrawn.

The Commission shall send a copy of the decision on a case concerning the subject matter of the complaint to the complainant.

3. At its request, any interested party shall obtain a copy of any decision pursuant to Articles 4 and 9, Article 12(3) and Article 13.

NOTES

Repeal of this Regulation in relation to the UK: this Regulation is repealed in relation to the UK (as from IP completion day); see the introductory notes to this Regulation *ante*.

CHAPTER VIII INVESTIGATIONS INTO SECTORS OF THE ECONOMY AND INTO AID INSTRUMENTS

[5.187]

Article 25 Investigations into sectors of the economy and into aid instruments

1. Where the information available substantiates a reasonable suspicion that State aid measures in a particular sector or based on a particular aid instrument may materially restrict or distort competition within the internal market in several Member States, or that existing aid measures in a particular sector in several Member States are not, or no longer, compatible with the internal market, the Commission may conduct an inquiry across various Member States into the sector of the economy or the use of the aid instrument concerned. In the course of that inquiry, the Commission may request the Member States and/or the undertakings or associations of undertakings concerned to supply the necessary information for the application of Articles 107 and 108 TFEU, taking due account of the principle of proportionality.

The Commission shall state the reasons for the inquiry and for the choice of addressees in all requests for information sent under this Article.

The Commission shall publish a report on the results of its inquiry into particular sectors of the economy or particular aid instruments across various Member States and shall invite the Member States and any undertakings or associations of undertakings concerned to submit comments.

2. Information obtained from sector inquiries may be used in the framework of procedures under this Regulation.

3. Articles 5, 7 and 8 of this Regulation shall apply mutatis mutandis.

NOTES

Repeal of this Regulation in relation to the UK: this Regulation is repealed in relation to the UK (as from IP completion day); see the introductory notes to this Regulation *ante*.

CHAPTER IX MONITORING

[5.188]

Article 26 Annual reports

1. Member States shall submit to the Commission annual reports on all existing aid schemes with regard to which no specific reporting obligations have been imposed in a conditional decision pursuant to Article 9(4).

2. Where, despite a reminder, the Member State concerned fails to submit an annual report, the Commission may proceed in accordance with Article 22 with regard to the aid scheme concerned.

NOTES

Repeal of this Regulation in relation to the UK: this Regulation is repealed in relation to the UK (as from IP completion day); see the introductory notes to this Regulation *ante*.

[5.189]

Article 27 On-site monitoring

1. Where the Commission has serious doubts as to whether decisions not to raise objections, positive decisions or conditional decisions with regard to individual aid are being complied with, the Member State concerned, after having been given the opportunity to submit its comments, shall allow the Commission to undertake on-site monitoring visits.

2. The officials authorised by the Commission shall be empowered, in order to verify compliance with the decision concerned:

- *(a) to enter any premises and land of the undertaking concerned;*
- *(b) to ask for oral explanations on the spot;*
- *(c) to examine books and other business records and take, or demand, copies.*

The Commission may be assisted if necessary by independent experts.

3. The Commission shall inform the Member State concerned, in good time and in writing, of the on-site monitoring visit and of the identities of the authorised officials and experts. If the Member State has duly justified objections to the Commission's choice of experts, the experts shall be appointed in common agreement with the Member State. The officials of the Commission and the experts authorised to carry out the on-site monitoring shall produce an authorisation in writing specifying the subject-matter and purpose of the visit.

4. Officials authorised by the Member State in whose territory the monitoring visit is to be made may be present at the monitoring visit.

5. The Commission shall provide the Member State with a copy of any report produced as a result of the monitoring visit.

6. Where an undertaking opposes a monitoring visit ordered by a Commission decision pursuant to this Article, the Member State concerned shall afford the necessary assistance to the officials and experts authorised by the Commission to enable them to carry out the monitoring visit.

NOTES

Repeal of this Regulation in relation to the UK: this Regulation is repealed in relation to the UK (as from IP completion day); see the introductory notes to this Regulation *ante*.

[5.190]

Article 28 Non-compliance with decisions and judgments

1. Where the Member State concerned does not comply with conditional or negative decisions, in particular in cases referred to in Article 16 of this Regulation, the Commission may refer the matter to the Court of Justice of the European Union directly in accordance with Article 108(2) TFEU.

2. If the Commission considers that the Member State concerned has not complied with a judgment of the Court of Justice of the European Union, the Commission may pursue the matter in accordance with Article 260 TFEU.

NOTES

Repeal of this Regulation in relation to the UK: this Regulation is repealed in relation to the UK (as from IP completion day); see the introductory notes to this Regulation *ante*.

CHAPTER X COOPERATION WITH NATIONAL COURTS

[5.191]

Article 29 Cooperation with national courts

1. For the application of Article 107(1) and Article 108 TFEU, the courts of the Member States may ask the Commission to transmit to them information in its possession or its opinion on questions concerning the application of State aid rules.

2. Where the coherent application of Article 107(1) or Article 108 TFEU so requires, the Commission, acting on its own initiative, may submit written observations to the courts of the Member States that are responsible for applying the State aid rules. It may, with the permission of the court in question, also make oral observations.

The Commission shall inform the Member State concerned of its intention to submit observations before formally doing so.

For the exclusive purpose of preparing its observations, the Commission may request the relevant court of the Member State to transmit documents at the disposal of the court, necessary for the Commission's assessment of the matter.

NOTES

Repeal of this Regulation in relation to the UK: this Regulation is repealed in relation to the UK (as from IP completion day); see the introductory notes to this Regulation *ante*.

CHAPTER XI COMMON PROVISIONS

[5.192]

Article 30 Professional secrecy

The Commission and the Member States, their officials and other servants, including independent experts appointed by the Commission, shall not disclose information which they have acquired through the application of this Regulation and which is covered by the obligation of professional secrecy.

NOTES

Repeal of this Regulation in relation to the UK: this Regulation is repealed in relation to the UK (as from IP completion day); see the introductory notes to this Regulation *ante*.

[5.193]

Article 31 Addressee of decisions

1. The decisions taken pursuant to Article 7(7), Article 8(1) and (2), and Article 9(9) shall be addressed to the undertaking or association of undertakings concerned. The Commission shall notify the decision to the addressee without delay and shall give the addressee the opportunity to indicate to the Commission which information it considers to be covered by the obligation of professional secrecy.

2. All other decisions of the Commission taken pursuant to Chapters II, III, V, VI and IX shall be addressed to the Member State concerned. The Commission shall notify them to the Member State concerned without delay and shall give that Member State the opportunity to indicate to the Commission which information it considers to be covered by the obligation of professional secrecy.

NOTES

Repeal of this Regulation in relation to the UK: this Regulation is repealed in relation to the UK (as from IP completion day); see the introductory notes to this Regulation *ante*.

[5.194]

Article 32 Publication of decisions

1. The Commission shall publish in the Official Journal of the European Union a summary notice of the decisions which it takes pursuant to Article 4(2) and (3) and Article 22 in conjunction with Article 23(1). The summary notice shall state that a copy of the decision may be obtained in the authentic language version or versions.

2. The Commission shall publish in the Official Journal of the European Union the decisions which it takes pursuant to Article 4(4) in their authentic language version. In the Official Journal published in languages other than the authentic language version, the authentic language version shall be accompanied by a meaningful summary in the language of that Official Journal.

3. The Commission shall publish in the Official Journal of the European Union the decisions which it takes pursuant to Article 8(1) and (2) and Article 9.

4. In cases where Article 4(6) or Article 10(2) applies, a short notice shall be published in the Official Journal of the European Union.

5. The Council, acting unanimously, may decide to publish decisions pursuant to the third subparagraph of Article 108(2) TFEU in the Official Journal of the European Union.

NOTES

Repeal of this Regulation in relation to the UK: this Regulation is repealed in relation to the UK (as from IP completion day); see the introductory notes to this Regulation *ante*.

[5.195]

Article 33 Implementing provisions

The Commission, acting in accordance with the procedure laid down in Article 34, shall have the power to adopt implementing provisions concerning:

(a) the form, content and other details of notifications;
(b) the form, content and other details of annual reports;
(c) the form, content and other details of complaints submitted in accordance with Article 12(1) and Article 24(2);
(d) details of time-limits and the calculation of time-limits; and
(e) the interest rate referred to in Article 16(2).

NOTES

Repeal of this Regulation in relation to the UK: this Regulation is repealed in relation to the UK (as from IP completion day); see the introductory notes to this Regulation *ante*.

[5.196]

Article 34 Consultation of the Advisory Committee on State aid

1. Before adopting any implementing provision pursuant to Article 33 the Commission shall consult the Advisory Committee on State aid set up by Council Regulation (EU) 2015/1588[1] ('the Committee').

2. Consultation of the Committee shall take place at a meeting called by the Commission. The drafts and documents to be examined shall be annexed to the notification. The meeting shall take place no earlier than 2 months after notification has been sent. This period may be reduced in the case of urgency.

3. The representative of the Commission shall submit to the Committee a draft of the measures to be taken. The Committee shall deliver an opinion on the draft, within a time-limit which the chairman may lay down according to the urgency of the matter, if necessary by taking a vote.

4. The opinion shall be recorded in the minutes. In addition, each Member State shall have the right to ask to have its position recorded in the minutes. The Committee may recommend the publication of the opinion in the Official Journal of the European Union.

5. The Commission shall take the utmost account of the opinion delivered by the Committee. It shall inform the Committee on the manner in which its opinion has been taken into account.

NOTES

Repeal of this Regulation in relation to the UK: this Regulation is repealed in relation to the UK (as from IP completion day); see the introductory notes to this Regulation *ante*.

[1] Council Regulation (EU) 2015/1588 of 13 July 2015 on the application of Articles 107 and 108 of the Treaty on the Functioning of the European Union to certain categories of horizontal State aid (see page 1 of this Official Journal).

[5.197]

Article 35 Repeal

Regulation (EC) No 659/1999 is repealed.

References to the repealed Regulation shall be construed as references to this Regulation and shall be read in accordance with the correlation table in Annex II.

NOTES

Repeal of this Regulation in relation to the UK: this Regulation is repealed in relation to the UK (as from IP completion day); see the introductory notes to this Regulation *ante*.

[5.198]

Article 36 Entry into force

This Regulation shall enter into force on the twentieth day following that of its publication in the Official Journal of the European Union.

NOTES

Repeal of this Regulation in relation to the UK: this Regulation is repealed in relation to the UK (as from IP completion day); see the introductory notes to this Regulation *ante*.

ANNEXES

ANNEX I
REPEALED REGULATION WITH LIST OF ITS SUCCESSIVE AMENDMENTS

[5.199]

Council Regulation (EC) No 659/1999	*(OJ L83, 27.3.1999, p 1).*
Point 5(6) of Annex II to the 2003 Act of Accession	
Council Regulation (EC) No 1791/2006	*(OJ L363, 20.12.2006, p 1).*
Council Regulation (EU) No 517/2013	*(OJ L158, 10.6.2013, p 1).*
Council Regulation (EU) No 734/2013	*(OJ L204, 31.7.2013, p 15).*

NOTES

Repeal of this Regulation in relation to the UK: this Regulation is repealed in relation to the UK (as from IP completion day); see the introductory notes to this Regulation *ante*.

ANNEX II
CORRELATION TABLE

[5.200]

Regulation (EC) No 659/1999	***This Regulation***
Articles 1 to 6	*Articles 1 to 6*
Article 6a	*Article 7*
Article 6b	*Article 8*
Article 7	*Article 9*
Article 8	*Article 10*
Article 9	*Article 11*
Article 10	*Article 12*
Article 11(1)	*Article 13(1)*
Article 11(2), first subparagraph, introductory wording	*Article 13(2), first subparagraph, introductory wording*
Article 11(2), first subparagraph, first indent	*Article 13(2), first subparagraph, point (a)*
Article 11(2), first subparagraph, second indent	*Article 13(2), first subparagraph, point (b)*
Article 11(2), first subparagraph, third indent	*Article 13(2), first subparagraph, point (c)*
Article 11(2), second, third and fourth subparagraphs	*Article 13(2), second, third and fourth subparagraphs*
Article 12	*Article 14*
Article 13	*Article 15*
Article 14	*Article 16*
Article 15	*Article 17*
Article 15a	*Article 18*
Article 15b	*Article 19*
Article 16	*Article 20*
Article 17	*Article 21*
Article 18	*Article 22*
Article 19	*Article 23*
Article 20	*Article 24*
Article 20a	*Article 25*
Article 21	*Article 26*
Article 22	*Article 27*
Article 23	*Article 28*
Article 23a	*Article 29*
Article 24	*Article 30*
Article 25	*Article 31*
Article 26(1) and (2)	*Article 32(1) and (2)*
Article 26(2)a	*Article 32(3)*
Article 26(3)	*Article 32(3)*
Article 26(4)	*Article 32(4)*
Article 26(5)	*Article 32(5)*
Article 27	*Article 33*

Regulation (EC) No 659/1999	*This Regulation*
Article 28	—
Article 29	*Article 34*
—	*Article 35*
Article 30	*Article 36*
—	*Annex I*
—	*Annex II*

NOTES

Repeal of this Regulation in relation to the UK: this Regulation is repealed in relation to the UK (as from IP completion day); see the introductory notes to this Regulation *ante*.

COMMISSION NOTICE

(2016/C262/01)

on the Notion of State aid as referred to in Article 107(1) of the Treaty on the Functioning of the European Union

[5.201]

NOTES

Date of publication in OJ: OJ C262, 19.7.2016, p 1.

1. INTRODUCTION

[5.202]

1. In the context of the State aid modernisation, the Commission wishes to provide further clarification on the key concepts relating to the notion of State aid as referred to in Article 107(1) of the Treaty on the Functioning of the European Union, with a view to contributing to an easier, more transparent and more consistent application of this notion across the Union.

2. This Notice only concerns the notion of State aid as referred to in Article 107(1) of the Treaty, which both the Commission and national authorities (including national courts) have to apply in conjunction with the notification and standstill obligations provided for in Article 108(3) of the Treaty. It does not concern the compatibility of State aid with the internal market pursuant to Article 107(2) and (3) and Article 106(2) of the Treaty, which is for the Commission to assess.

3. Given that the notion of State aid is an objective and legal concept defined directly by the Treaty,[1] this Notice clarifies the Commission's understanding of Article 107(1) of the Treaty, as interpreted by the Court of Justice and the General Court ('the Union Courts'). On issues that have not yet been considered by the Union Courts, the Commission will set out how it considers that the notion of State aid should be construed. The views set out in this Notice are without prejudice to the interpretation of the notion of State aid by the Union Courts;[2] the primary reference for interpreting the Treaty is always the case-law of the Union Courts.

4. It should be stressed that the Commission is bound by this objective notion and enjoys only a limited margin of discretion in applying it, namely where the appraisals by the Commission are technical or complex in nature, in particular in situations involving complex economic assessments.[3]

5. Article 107(1) of the Treaty defines State aid as 'any aid granted by a Member State or through State resources in any form whatsoever which distorts or threatens to distort competition by favouring certain undertakings or the production of certain goods [. . .], in so far as it affects trade between Member States'.[4] This Notice will clarify the different constituent elements of the notion of State aid: the existence of an undertaking, the imputability of the measure to the State, its financing through State resources, the granting of an advantage, the selectivity of the measure and its effect on competition and trade between Member States. In addition, given the need for specific guidance expressed by Member States, this Notice provides specific clarification with respect to public funding of infrastructure.

NOTES

1 See Judgment of the Court of Justice of 22 December 2008, *British Aggregates v Commission*, C-487/06 P, ECLI:EU:C:2008:757, paragraph 111.

2 See Judgment of the Court of Justice of 21 July 2011, *Alcoa Trasformazioni v Commission*, C-194/09 P, ECLI:EU:C:2011:497, paragraph 125.

3 See Judgment of the Court of Justice of 22 December 2008, *British Aggregates v Commission*, C-487/06 P, ECLI:EU:C:2008:757, paragraph 114, and Judgment of the Court of Justice of 2 September 2010, *Commission v Scott*, C-290/07 P, ECLI:EU:C:2010:480, paragraph 66.

4 The rules on State aid apply to production of and trade in agricultural products, which under Article 38(1) of the Treaty include fisheries products, only to the extent determined by the European Parliament and the Council (Article 42 of the Treaty).

2. NOTION OF UNDERTAKING AND ECONOMIC ACTIVITY

[5.203]

6. The State aid rules only apply where the beneficiary of a measure is an 'undertaking'.

2.1. GENERAL PRINCIPLES

7. The Court of Justice has consistently defined undertakings as entities engaged in an economic activity, regardless of their legal status and the way in which they are financed.[5] The classification of a particular entity as an undertaking thus depends entirely on the nature of its activities. This general principle has three important consequences.

8. First, the status of the entity under national law is not decisive. For example, an entity that is classified as an association or a sports club under national law may nevertheless have to be regarded as an undertaking within the meaning of Article 107(1) of the Treaty. The same applies to an entity that is formally part of the public administration. The only relevant criterion is whether it carries out an economic activity.

9. Second, the application of the State aid rules does not depend on whether the entity is set up to generate profits. Non-profit entities can also offer goods and services on a market.[6] Where this is not the case, non-profit entities remain outside the scope of State aid control.

10. Third, the classification of an entity as an undertaking is always relative to a specific activity. An entity that carries out both economic and non-economic activities is to be regarded as an undertaking only with regard to the former.[7]

11. Several separate legal entities may be considered to form one economic unit for the purposes of the application of State aid rules. That economic unit is then considered to be the relevant undertaking. In this respect, the Court of Justice considers the existence of a controlling share and other functional, economic and organic links to be relevant.[8]

12. To clarify the distinction between economic and non-economic activities, the Court of Justice has consistently held that any activity consisting in offering goods and services on a market is an economic activity.[9]

13. The question whether a market exists for certain services may depend on the way those services are organised in the Member State concerned[10] and may thus vary from one Member State to another. Moreover, due to political choice or economic developments, the classification of a given activity can change over time. What is not an economic activity today may become one in the future, and vice versa.

14. The decision of a public authority not to allow third parties to provide a certain service (for example, because it wishes to provide the service in-house) does not rule out the existence of an economic activity. In spite of such market closure, an economic activity can exist where other operators would be willing and able to provide the service in the market concerned. More generally, the fact that a particular service is provided in-house has no relevance for the economic nature of the activity.[11]

15. Since the distinction between economic and non-economic activities depends to some extent on political choices and economic developments in a given Member State, it is not possible to draw up an exhaustive list of activities that a priori would never be economic. Such a list would not provide genuine legal certainty and would thus be of little use. Paragraphs 17 to 37 instead seek to clarify the distinction with respect to a number of important areas.

16. The simple fact that an entity holds shares, even a majority shareholding, in an undertaking providing goods or services on a market does not mean that that entity should automatically be considered an undertaking for the purposes of Article 107(1) of the Treaty. Where that shareholding only gives rise to the exercise of rights attached to the status of shareholder as well as, if appropriate, the receipt of dividends, which are merely the fruits of the ownership of an asset, that entity will not be considered an undertaking if it does not itself provide goods or services on a market.[12]

2.2. EXERCISE OF PUBLIC POWERS

17. Article 107(1) of the Treaty does not apply where the State acts 'by exercising public power'[13] or where public entities act 'in their capacity as public authorities'.[14] An entity may be deemed to act by exercising public power where the activity in question forms part of the essential functions of the State or is connected with those functions by its nature, its aim and the rules to which it is subject.[15] Generally speaking, unless the Member State concerned has decided to introduce market mechanisms, activities that intrinsically form part of the prerogatives of official authority and are performed by the State do not constitute economic activities. Examples of such activities are the following:

(a) the army or the police;[16]
(b) air navigation safety and control;[17]
(c) maritime traffic control and safety;[18]
(d) anti-pollution surveillance;[19]
(e) the organisation, financing and enforcement of prison sentences;[20]
(f) the development and revitalization of public land by public authorities;[21] and
(g) the collection of data to be used for public purposes on the basis of a statutory obligation imposed on the undertakings concerned to disclose such data.[22]

18. In so far as a public entity exercises an economic activity which can be separated from the exercise of public powers, that entity acts as an undertaking in relation to that activity. In contrast, if that economic activity cannot be separated from the exercise of public powers, the activities exercised by that entity as a whole remain connected with the exercise of those public powers and therefore fall outside the notion of undertaking.[23]

2.3. SOCIAL SECURITY

19. Whether schemes in the area of social security are to be classified as involving an economic activity depends on the way they are set up and structured. In essence, the case-law distinguishes between schemes based on the principle of solidarity and economic schemes.

20. Solidarity-based social security schemes that do not involve an economic activity typically have the following characteristics:

(a) affiliation with the scheme is compulsory;[24]
(b) the scheme pursues an exclusively social purpose;[25]
(c) the scheme is non-profit;[26]
(d) the benefits are independent of the contributions made;[27]
(e) the benefits paid are not necessarily proportionate to the earnings of the person insured;[28] and
(f) the scheme is supervised by the State.[29]

21. Such solidarity-based schemes must be distinguished from schemes that involve an economic activity.[30] The latter are regularly characterised by:

(a) optional membership;[31]
(b) the principle of capitalisation (dependency of entitlements on the contributions paid and the financial results of the scheme);[32]
(c) their profit-making nature;[33] and
(d) the provision of entitlements which are supplementary to those under a basic scheme.[34]

22. Some schemes combine features of both categories. In such cases, the classification of the scheme depends on an analysis of different elements and their respective importance.[35]

2.4. HEALTH CARE

23. In the Union, health care systems differ significantly between Member States. Whether and to what degree different health care providers compete with each other depends on these national specificities.

24. In some Member States, public hospitals are an integral part of a national health service and are almost entirely based on the principle of solidarity.[36] Such hospitals are directly funded from social security contributions and other State resources and provide their services free of charge on the basis of universal coverage.[37] The Union Courts have confirmed that, where such a structure exists, the relevant organisations do not act as undertakings.[38]

25. Where that structure exists, even activities that in themselves could be of an economic nature, but are carried out merely for the purpose of providing another non-economic service, are not of an economic nature. An organisation that purchases goods — even in large quantities — for the purpose of offering a non-economic service does not act as an undertaking simply because it is a purchaser in a given market.[39]

26. In many other Member States, hospitals and other health care providers offer their services for remuneration, be it directly from patients or from their insurance.[40] In such systems, there is a certain degree of competition between hospitals concerning the provision of health care services. Where this is the case, the fact that a health service is provided by a public hospital is not sufficient for the activity to be classified as non-economic.

27. The Union Courts have also clarified that health care services which independent doctors and other private practitioners provide for remuneration at their own risk are to be regarded as an economic activity.[41] The same principles apply to pharmacies.

2.5. EDUCATION AND RESEARCH ACTIVITIES

28. Public education organised within the national educational system funded and supervised by the State may be considered as a non-economic activity. The Court of Justice held that the State: 'by establishing and maintaining such a system of public education and financed entirely or mainly by public funds and not by pupils or their parents [. . .] does not intend to become involved in activities for remuneration, but carries out its task towards its population in the social, cultural and educational areas'.[42]

29. The non-economic nature of public education is in principle not affected by the fact that pupils or their parents sometimes have to pay tuition or enrolment fees which contribute to the operating expenses of the system. Such financial contributions often only cover a fraction of the true costs of the service and can thus not be considered as remuneration for the service provided. They therefore do not alter the non-economic nature of a general education service predominantly funded by the public purse.[43] These principles can cover public educational services such as vocational training,[44] private and public primary schools[45] and kindergartens,[46] secondary teaching activities in universities[47] and the provision of education in universities.[48]

30. Such public education services must be distinguished from services financed predominantly by parents or pupils or commercial revenues. For example, higher education financed entirely by students clearly fall within the latter category. In certain Member States public entities can also offer educational services which, due to their nature, financing structure and the existence of competing private organisations, are to be regarded as economic.

31. In the light of the principles set out in paragraphs 28, 29 and 30, the Commission considers that certain activities of universities and research organisations fall outside the scope of the State aid rules. This concerns their primary activities, namely:

(a) education for more and better skilled human resources;
(b) the conduct of independent research and development for more knowledge and better understanding, including collaborative research and development;
(c) the dissemination of research results.

32. The Commission considers that knowledge transfer activities (licensing, creation of spin-off, or other forms of management of knowledge created by the research organisation or infrastructure) are non-economic where they are conducted either by the research organisation or research infrastructure (including their departments or subsidiaries) or jointly with, or on behalf of other such entities, and all income from those activities is reinvested in the primary activities of the research organisations or infrastructures concerned.[49]

2.6. CULTURE AND HERITAGE CONSERVATION, INCLUDING NATURE CONSERVATION

33. Culture is a vehicle of identities, values and meanings that mirror and shape the Union's societies. The area of culture and heritage conservation covers a vast array of purposes and activities, inter alia, museums, archives, libraries, artistic and cultural centres or spaces, theatres, opera houses, concert halls, archaeological sites, monuments, historical sites and buildings, traditional customs and crafts, festivals and exhibitions, as well as cultural and artistic education activities. Europe's rich natural heritage, including conservation of biodiversity, habitats and species further provides valuable benefits for societies in the Union.

34. Taking into account their particular nature, certain activities related to culture, heritage and nature conservation may be organised in a non-commercial way and thus be non-economic in nature. Public funding thereof may therefore not constitute State aid. The Commission considers that public funding of a cultural or heritage conservation activity accessible to the general public free of charge fulfils a purely social and cultural purpose which is non-economic in nature. In the same vein, the fact that visitors of a cultural institution or participants in a cultural or heritage conservation activity, including nature conservation, open to the general public are required to pay a monetary contribution that only covers a fraction of the true costs does not alter the non-economic nature of that activity, as it cannot be considered genuine remuneration for the service provided.

35. In contrast, cultural or heritage conservation activities (including nature conservation) predominantly financed by visitor or user fees or by other commercial means (for example, commercial exhibitions, cinemas, commercial music performances and festivals and arts schools predominantly financed from tuition fees) should be qualified as economic in nature. Similarly, heritage conservation or cultural activities benefitting exclusively certain undertakings rather than the general public (for example, the restoration of a historical building used by a private company) should normally be qualified as economic in nature.

36. Moreover, many cultural or heritage conservation activities are objectively non-substitutable (for example, keeping public archives holding unique documents) and thus exclude the existence of a genuine market. In the Commission's view, such activities would also qualify as non-economic in nature.

37. In cases where an entity carries out cultural or heritage conservation activities, some of which are non-economic activities as set out in paragraphs 34 and 36 and some of which are economic activities, public funding it receives will fall under the State aid rules only insofar as it covers the costs linked to the economic activities.[50]

NOTES

5 Judgment of the Court of Justice of 12 September 2000, *Pavlov and Others*, Joined Cases C-180/98 to C-184/98, ECLI:EU:C:2000:428, paragraph 74; Judgment of the Court of Justice of 10 January 2006, *Cassa di Risparmio di Firenze SpA and Others*, C-222/04, ECLI:EU: C:2006:8, paragraph 107.

6 Judgment of the Court of Justice of 29 October 1980, *Van Landewyck*, Joined Cases 209/78 to 215/78 and 218/78, ECLI:EU:C:1980:248, paragraph 88; Judgment of the Court of Justice of 16 November 1995, *FFSA and Others*, C-244/94, ECLI:EU:C:1995:392, paragraph 21; Judgment of the Court of Justice of 1 July 2008, MOTOE, C-49/07, ECLI:EU:C:2008:376, paragraphs 27 and 28.

7 Judgment of the General Court of 12 December 2000, *Aéroports de Paris v Commission*, T-128/98, ECLI-:EU:T:2000:290, paragraph 108.

8 Judgment of the Court of Justice of 16 December 2010, *AceaElectrabel Produzione SpA v Commission*, C-480/09 P, ECLI:EU:C:2010:787, paragraphs 47 to 55; Judgment of the Court of Justice of 10 January 2006, *Cassa di Risparmio di Firenze SpA and Others*, C-222/04, ECLI: EU:C:2006:8, paragraph 112.

9 See Judgment of the Court of Justice of 16 June 1987, *Commission v Italy*, 118/85, ECLI:EU:C:1987:283, paragraph 7; Judgment of the Court of Justice of 18 June 1998, *Commission v Italy*, C-35/96, ECLI:EU:C:1998:303, paragraph 36; Judgment of the Court of Justice of 12 September 2000, *Pavlov and Others*, Joined Cases C-180/98 to C-184/98, ECLI:EU:C:2000:428, paragraph 75.

10 Judgment of the Court of Justice of 17 February 1993, *Poucet and Pistre*, Joined Cases C-159/91 and C-160/91, ECLI:EU:C:1993:63, paragraphs 16 to 20.

11 See Opinion of Advocate General Geelhoed of 28 September 2006, *Asociación Nacional de Empresas Forestales (Asemfo)*, C-295/05, ECLI: EU:C:2006:619, paragraphs 110 to 116; Regulation (EC) No 1370/2007 of the European Parliament and of the Council of 23 October 2007 on public passenger transport services by rail and by road and repealing Council Regulations (EEC) Nos 1191/69 and 1107/70 (OJ L315, 3.12.2007, p 1), Articles 5(2) and 6(1); Commission Decision 2011/501/EU of 23 February 2011 on State aid C-58/06 (ex NN 98/05) implemented by Germany for Bahnen der Stadt Monheim (BSM) and Rheinische Bahngesellschaft (RBG) in the Verkehrsverbund Rhein-Ruhr (OJ L210, 17.8.2011, p 1) recitals 208 and 209.

12 Judgment of the Court of Justice of 10 January 2006, *Cassa di Risparmio di Firenze SpA and Others*, C-222/04, ECLI:EU:C:2006:8, paragraphs 107 to 118 and 125.

13 Judgment of the Court of Justice of 16 June 1987, *Commission v Italy*, 118/85, ECLI:EU:C:1987:283, paragraphs 7 and 8.

14 Judgment of the Court of Justice of 4 May 1988, *Bodson*, 30/87, ECLI:EU:C:1988:225, paragraph 18.

15 See, in particular, Judgment of the Court of Justice of 19 January 1994, *SAT/Eurocontrol*, C-364/92, ECLI-:EU:C:1994:7, paragraph 30 and Judgment of the Court of Justice of 18 March 1997, *Calì & Figli*, C-343/95, ECLI:EU:C:1997:160, paragraphs 22 and 23.

16 Commission Decision of 7 December 2011 on State aid SA.32820 (2011/NN) — United Kingdom –Aid to Forensic Science Services (OJ C29, 2.2.2012, p 4), paragraph 8.

17 Judgment of the Court of Justice of 19 January 1994, *SAT/Eurocontrol*, C-364/92, ECLI:EU:C:1994:7, paragraph 27; Judgment of the Court of Justice of 26 March 2009, *Selex Sistemi Integrati v Commission*, C-113/07 P, ECLI:EU:C:2009:191, paragraph 71.

18 Commission Decision of 16 October 2002 on State aid N 438/02 — Belgium — Aid to port authorities, (OJ C284, 21.11.2002, p 2).

19 Judgment of the Court of Justice of 18 March 1997, *Calì & Figli*, C-343/95, ECLI:EU:C:1997:160, paragraph 22.

20 Commission Decision of 19 July 2006 on State aid N 140/06 — Lithuania — Allotment of subsidies to the State Enterprises at the Correction Houses (OJ C244, 11.10.2006, p 12).

[21] Commission decision of 27 March 2014 on State aid SA.36346 — Germany — GRW land development scheme for industrial and commercial use (OJ C141, 9.5.2014, p 1). In the context of a measure that supported the revitalisation (including decontamination) of public land by local authorities, the Commission found that making public terrain ready to build upon and ensuring that it is connected to utilities (water, gas, sewage and electricity) and transport networks (rail and roads) did not constitute an economic activity, but was part of the public tasks of the State, namely the provision and supervision of land in line with local urban and spatial development plans.

[22] Judgment of the Court of Justice of 12 July 2012, *Compass-Datenbank GmbH*, C-138/11, ECLI:EU:C:2012:449, paragraph 40.

[23] Judgment of the Court of Justice of 12 July 2012, *Compass-Datenbank GmbH*, C-138/11, ECLI:EU:C:2012:449, paragraph 38, and Judgment of the Court of Justice of 26 March 2009, *Selex Sistemi Integrati v Commission*, C-113/07 P, ECLI:EU:C:2009:191, paragraphs 72 et seq.

[24] Judgment of the Court of Justice of 17 February 1993, *Poucet and Pistre*, Joined Cases C-159/91 and C-160/91, ECLI:EU:C:1993:63, paragraph 13.

[25] Judgment of the Court of Justice of 22 January 2002, *Cisal and INAIL*, C-218/00, ECLI:EU:C:2002:36, paragraph 45.

[26] Judgment of the Court of Justice of 16 March 2004, *AOK Bundesverband*, Joined Cases C-264/01, C-306/01, C-354/01 and C-355/01, ECLI:EU:C:2004:150, paragraphs 47 to 55.

[27] Judgment of the Court of Justice of 17 February 1993, *Poucet and Pistre*, Joined Cases C-159/91 and C-160/91, ECLI:EU:C:1993:63, paragraphs 15 to 18.

[28] Judgment of the Court of Justice of 22 January 2002, *Cisal and INAIL*, C-218/00, ECLI:EU:C:2002:36, paragraph 40.

[29] Judgment of the Court of Justice of 17 February 1993, *Poucet and Pistre*, Joined Cases C-159/91 and C-160/91, ECLI:EU:C:1993:63, paragraph 14; Judgment of the Court of Justice of 22 January 2002, *Cisal and INAIL*, C-218/00, ECLI:EU:C:2002:36, paragraphs 43 to 48; Judgment of the Court of Justice of 16 March 2004, *AOK Bundesverband*, Joined Cases C-264/01, C-306/01, C-354/01 and C-355/01, ECLI:EU:C:2004:150, paragraphs 51 to 55.

[30] See, in particular, Judgment of the Court of Justice of 16 November 1995, *FFSA and Others*, C-244/94, ECLI:EU:C:1995:392, paragraph 19.

[31] Judgment of the Court of Justice of 21 September 1999, *Albany*, C-67/96, ECLI:EU:C:1999:430, paragraphs 80 to 87.

[32] Judgment of the Court of Justice of 16 November 1995, *FFSA and Others*, C-244/94, ECLI:EU:C:1995:392, paragraphs 9 and 17 to 20; Judgment of the Court of Justice of 21 September 1999, *Albany*, C-67/96, ECLI:EU:C:1999:430, paragraphs 81 to 85; see also Judgment of the Court of Justice of 21 September 1999, *Brentjens*, Joined Cases C-115/97 to C-117/97, ECLI:EU:C:1999:434 paragraphs 81 to 85; Judgment of the Court of Justice of 21 September 1999, *Drijvende Bokken*, C-219/97, ECLI:EU:C:1999:437, paragraphs 71 to 75, and Judgment of the Court of Justice of 12 September 2000, *Pavlov and Others*, Joined Cases C-180/98 to C-184/98, ECLI:EU:C:2000:428, paragraphs 114 and 115.

[33] Judgment of the Court of Justice of 21 September 1999, *Brentjens*, Joined Cases C-115/97 to C-117/97, ECLI:EU:C:1999:434, paragraphs 74 to 85.

[34] Judgment of the Court of Justice of 12 September 2000, *Pavlov and Others*, Joined Cases C-180/98 to C-184/98, ECLI:EU:C:2000:428, paragraphs 67 to 70.

[35] Judgment of the Court of Justice of 5 March 2009, *Kattner Stahlbau*, C-350/07, ECLI:EU:C:2009:127, paragraphs 33 et seq.

[36] A prominent example is the Spanish National Health System (see Judgment of the General Court of 4 March 2003, *FENIN*, T-319/99, ECLI:EU:T:2003:50 and Judgment of the Court of Justice of 11 July 2006, *FENIN*, C-205/03 P, ECLI:EU:C:2006:453, paragraphs 25 to 28).

[37] Depending on the overall characteristics of the system, charges which only cover a small fraction of the true cost of the service may not affect its classification as non-economic.

[38] Judgment of the General Court of 4 March 2003, *FENIN*, T-319/99, ECLI:EU:T:2003:50, paragraph 39; and Judgment of the Court of Justice of 11 July 2006, *FENIN*, C-205/03 P, ECLI:EU:C:2006:453, paragraphs 25 to 28.

[39] Judgment of the General Court of 4 March 2003, *FENIN*, T-319/99, ECLI:EU:T:2003:50, paragraph 40.

[40] See, for instance, Judgment of the Court of Justice of 12 July 2001, *Geraets-Smits and Others*, C-157/99, ECLI:EU:C:2001:404, paragraphs 53 to 58.

[41] See Judgment of the Court of Justice of 12 September 2000, *Pavlov and Others*, Joined Cases C-180/98 to C-184/98, ECLI:EU: C:2000:428, paragraphs 75 and 77.

[42] Judgment of the Court of Justice of 11 September 2007, *Commission v Germany*, C-318/05, ECLI:EU:C:2007:495, paragraph 68. See also Commission Decision of 25 April 2001 on State aid N 118/00 Subvention publiques aux clubs sportifs professionnels (OJ C333 28.11.2001, p 6).

[43] Judgment of the EFTA Court of 21 February 2008 in Case E-5/07 *Private Barnehagers Landsforbund v EFTA Surveillance Authority* EFTA Ct. Rep [2008] p 62, paragraph 83.

[44] Judgment of the Court of Justice of 27 September 1988, *Humbel*, 263/86, ECLI:EU:C:1988:451, paragraph 18.

[45] Judgment of the Court of Justice of 11 September 2007, *Commission v Germany*, C-318/05, ECLI:EU:C:2007:495, paragraphs 65 to 71; Judgment of the Court of Justice of 11 September 2007, *Schwarz*, C-76/05, ECLI-:EU:C:2007:492, paragraphs 37 to 47.

[46] Judgment of the EFTA Court of 21 February 2008 in Case E-5/07 *Private Barnehagers Landsforbund v EFTA Surveillance Authority EFTA* Ct. Rep [2008] p 62.

[47] Judgment of the Court of Justice of 18 December 2007, *Jundt*, C-281/06, ECLI:EU:C:2007:816, paragraphs 28 to 39.

[48] Judgment of the Court of Justice of 7 December 1993, *Wirth*, C-109/92, ECLI:EU:C:1993:916, paragraphs 14 to 22.

[49] See point 19 of the Framework for State aid for research and development and innovation (OJ C198, 27.6.2014, p 1).

[50] As explained in paragraph 207, the Commission considers that public financing provided to customary amenities (such

as restaurants, shops or paid parking) of infrastructures that are almost exclusively used for a non-economic activity normally has no effect on trade between Member States. Similarly, the Commission considers that public financing to customary amenities that are provided in the context of non-economic culture and heritage conservation activities (for instance, a shop, bar, or paid cloakroom in a museum) normally has no effect on trade between Member States.

3. STATE ORIGIN

[5.204]

38. The granting of an advantage directly or indirectly through State resources and the imputability of such a measure to the State are two separate and cumulative conditions for State aid to exist.[51] However, they are often considered together when assessing a measure under Article 107(1) of the Treaty, as they both relate to the public origin of the measure in question.

3.1. IMPUTABILITY

39. In cases where a public authority grants an advantage to a beneficiary, the measure is by definition imputable to the State, even if the authority in question enjoys legal autonomy from other public authorities. The same applies if a public authority designates a private or public body to administer a measure conferring an advantage. Indeed, Union law cannot permit the rules on State aid to be circumvented through the creation of autonomous institutions charged with allocating aid.[52]

40. Imputability is less evident, however, if the advantage is granted through public undertakings.[53] In such cases, it is necessary to determine whether the public authorities can be regarded as having been involved, in one way or another, in adopting the measure.[54]

41. The mere fact that a measure is taken by a public undertaking is not *per se* sufficient to consider it imputable to the State.[55] However, it does not need to be demonstrated that, in a particular case, the public authorities specifically incited the public undertaking to take the measure in question.[56] In fact, since relations between the State and public undertakings are necessarily close, there is a real risk that State aid may be granted through the intermediary of those undertakings in a non-transparent manner and in breach of the rules on State aid laid down by the Treaty.[57] Moreover, precisely because of the privileged relations that exist between the State and public undertakings, it will, as a general rule, be very difficult for a third party to demonstrate that measures taken by such an undertaking were in fact adopted on the instructions of the public authorities in a particular case.[58]

42. For these reasons, the imputability to the State of a measure taken by a public undertaking may be inferred from a set of indicators arising from the circumstances of the case and the context in which the measure was taken.[59]

3.1.1. INDICATORS FOR IMPUTABILITY

43. Possible indicators to establish whether a measure is imputable include the following:[60]

(a) the fact that the body in question could not take the contested decision without taking account of the requirements of the public authorities;
(b) the presence of factors of an organic nature which link the public undertaking to the State;
(c) the fact that the undertaking through which aid was granted had to take account of directives issued by governmental bodies;[61]
(d) the integration of the public undertaking into the structures of the public administration;
(e) the nature of the public undertaking's activities[62] and their exercise on the market in normal conditions of competition with private operators;
(f) the legal status of the undertaking (whether it is subject to public law or ordinary company law), although the mere fact that a public undertaking has been constituted in the form of a capital company under ordinary law cannot be regarded as sufficient reason to exclude imputability,[63] having regard to the autonomy which that legal form confers on it;
(g) the degree of supervision that the public authorities exercise over the management of the undertaking;
(h) any other indicator showing the involvement of the public authorities in adopting the measure in question or the unlikelihood of their not being involved, taking account of the scope of the measure, its content or the conditions it contains.

3.1.2. IMPUTABILITY AND OBLIGATIONS UNDER UNION LAW

44. A measure is not imputable to a Member State if the Member State is under an obligation to implement it under Union law without any discretion. In that case, the measure stems from an act of the Union legislature and is not imputable to the State.[64]

45. However, this is not the case in situations where Union law simply allows for certain national measures and the Member State enjoys discretion (i) as to whether to adopt the measures in question or (ii) in establishing the characteristics of the concrete measure which are relevant from a State aid perspective.[65]

46. Measures that are adopted jointly by several Member States are imputable to all the Member States concerned pursuant to Article 107(1) of the Treaty.[66]

3.2. STATE RESOURCES

3.2.1. GENERAL PRINCIPLES

47. Only advantages granted directly or indirectly through State resources can constitute State aid within the meaning of Article 107(1) of the Treaty.[67]

48. State resources include all resources of the public sector,[68] including resources of intra-State entities (decentralised, federated, regional or other)[69] and, under certain circumstances, resources of private bodies (see paragraphs 57 and 58). It is irrelevant whether or not an institution within the public sector is autonomous.[70] Funds provided by the central bank of a Member State to specific credit institutions generally imply the transfer of State resources.[71]

49. Resources of public undertakings also constitute State resources within the meaning of Article 107(1) of the Treaty because the State is capable of directing the use of these resources.[72] For the purposes of State aid law, transfers within a public group may also constitute State aid if, for example, resources are transferred from the parent company to its subsidiary (even if they constitute a single undertaking from an economic point of view).[73] The question of whether the transfer of such resources is imputable to the State is addressed in section 3.1. The fact that a public undertaking is a beneficiary of an aid measure does not mean it may not grant aid to another beneficiary by way of a different aid measure.[74]

50. The fact that a measure granting an advantage is not financed directly by the State, but by a public or private body established or appointed by the State to administer the aid, does not necessarily mean that the measure is not financed through State resources.[75] A measure adopted by a public authority and favouring certain undertakings or products does not lose the character of a gratuitous advantage by virtue of the fact that it is wholly or partially financed by contributions imposed by the public authority and levied on the undertakings concerned.[76]

51. The transfer of State resources may take many forms, such as direct grants, loans, guarantees, direct investment in the capital of companies and benefits in kind. A firm and concrete commitment to make State resources available at a later point in time is also considered a transfer of State resources. A positive transfer of funds does not have to occur; foregoing State revenue is sufficient. Waiving revenue which would otherwise have been paid to the State constitutes a transfer of State resources.[77] For example, a 'shortfall' in tax and social security revenue due to exemptions or reductions in taxes or social security contributions granted by the Member State, or exemptions from the obligation to pay fines or other pecuniary penalties, fulfils the State resources requirement of Article 107(1) of the Treaty.[78] The creation of a concrete risk of imposing an additional burden on the State in the future, by a guarantee or by a contractual offer, is sufficient for the purposes of Article 107(1).[79]

52. If public authorities or public undertakings provide goods or services at a price below market rates, or invest in an undertaking in a manner that is inconsistent with the market economy operator test, as described from paragraph 73 onwards, this implies foregoing State resources (as well as the granting of an advantage).

53. Granting access to a public domain or natural resources, or granting special or exclusive rights[80] without adequate remuneration in line with market rates, can constitute foregoing State revenues (as well as the granting of an advantage).[81]

54. In these cases it needs to be established whether the State, in addition to its role of manager of the public assets in question, acts as a regulator that pursues policy objectives by making the selection process of the undertakings concerned subject to qualitative criteria (established *ex ante* in a transparent and non-discriminatory manner).[82] When the State acts as a regulator, it can decide legitimately not to maximise the revenues which could otherwise have been achieved without falling under the scope of State aid rules, provided that all the operators concerned are treated in line with the principle of non-discrimination, and that there is an inherent link between achieving the regulatory purpose and the foregoing of revenue.[83]

55. In any event, a transfer of State resources is present if, in a given case, the public authorities do not charge the normal amount under their general system for access to the public domain or natural resources, or for granting certain special or exclusive rights.

56. A negative indirect effect on State revenues stemming from regulatory measures does not constitute a transfer of State resources where it is an inherent feature of the measure.[84] For example, a derogation from employment law provisions altering the framework for contractual relations between undertakings and employees does not constitute a transfer of State resources, despite the fact that it may reduce social security contributions or taxes payable to the State.[85] Similarly, national regulation which sets a minimum price for certain goods does not entail the transfer of State resources.[86]

3.2.2. Controlling influence over the resources

57. The origin of the resources is not relevant provided that, before being directly or indirectly transferred to the beneficiaries, they come under public control and are therefore available to the national authorities,[87] even if the resources do not become the property of the public authority.[88]

58. Thus, subsidies financed through parafiscal charges or compulsory contributions imposed by the State and managed and apportioned in accordance with the provisions of public rules imply a transfer of State resources, even if not administered by the public authorities.[89] Moreover, the mere fact that the subsidies are financed in part by voluntary private contributions is not sufficient to rule out the presence of State resources, since the relevant factor is not the origin of the resources but the degree of intervention of the public authority within the definition of the measure and its method of financing.[90] The transfer of State resources can only be ruled out in very specific circumstances, notably if resources from the members of a trade association are earmarked for funding a specific purpose in the interest of the members, are decided on by a private organisation and have a purely commercial purpose, and if the Member State is simply acting as a vehicle in order to make the contribution introduced by the trade organisation compulsory.[91]

59. A transfer of State resources is also present if the resources are at the joint disposal of several Member States who decide jointly on the use of those resources.[92] This would be the case, for example, for funds from the European Stability Mechanism (ESM).

60. Resources coming from the Union (for example from structural funds), from the European Investment Bank or the European Investment Fund, or from international financial institutions, such as the International Monetary Fund or the European Bank for Reconstruction and Development, are considered as State resources if national authorities have discretion as to the use of these resources (in particular the selection of beneficiaries).[93] By contrast, if such resources are awarded directly by the Union, by the European Investment Bank or by the European Investment Fund, with no discretion on the part of the national authorities, they do not constitute State resources (for example funding awarded in direct management under the Horizon 2020 framework programme, the EU programme for the Competitiveness of Enterprises and Small and Medium-sized Enterprises (COSME) or the Trans-European Transport Network (TEN-T) funds).

3.2.3. State involvement in redistribution between private entities

61. Regulation that leads to financial redistribution from one private entity to another without any further involvement of the State does not, in principle, entail a transfer of State resources if the money flows directly from one private entity to another, without passing through a public or private body designated by the State to administer the transfer.[94]

62. For example, an obligation imposed by a Member State on private electricity suppliers to purchase electricity produced from renewable energy sources at fixed minimum prices does not entail the direct or indirect transfer of State resources to undertakings which produce that type of electricity.[95] In this case, the undertakings concerned (that is to say the private electricity suppliers) are not appointed by the State to manage an aid scheme, but are only bound by an obligation to purchase a specific type of electricity with their own financial resources.

63. However, a transfer of State resources is present where the charges paid by private persons transit through a public or private entity designated to channel them to the beneficiaries.

64. For example, this is the case even where a private entity is appointed by law to collect such charges on behalf of the State and to channel them to the beneficiaries, but is not allowed to use the proceeds from the charges for purposes other than those provided for by the law. In this case, the sums in question remain under public control and are therefore available to the national authorities, which is sufficient reason for them to be considered State resources.[96] Since this principle applies both to public bodies and private entities appointed to collect the charges and process the payments, changing the status of the intermediary from a public to a private entity has no relevance for the State resources criterion if the State continues to strictly monitor that entity.[97]

65. Moreover, a mechanism for offsetting in full the additional costs imposed on undertakings because of an obligation to purchase a product from certain providers at a price higher than the market price that is financed by all final consumers of the said product also constitutes an intervention through State resources, even when this mechanism is partly based on a direct transfer of resources between private entities.[98]

NOTES

51 See, for instance, Judgment of the Court of Justice of 16 May 2002, *France v Commission (Stardust)*, C-482/99, ECLI:EU:C:2002:294, paragraph 24; Judgment of the General Court of 5 April 2006, *Deutsche Bahn AG v Commission*, T-351/02, ECLI:EU:T:2006:104, paragraph 103.

52 Judgment of the General Court of 12 December 1996, *Air France v Commission*, T-358/94, ECLI:EU:T:1996:194, paragraph 62.

53 The concept of public undertakings can be defined by reference to Commission Directive 2006/111/EC, of 16 November 2006, on the transparency of financial relations between Member States and public undertakings as well as on financial transparency within certain undertakings (OJ L318, 17.11.2006, p 17). Article 2(b) of this Directive states that 'public undertakings' means any undertaking over which the public authorities may exercise directly or indirectly a dominant influence by virtue of their ownership of it, their financial participation therein, or the rules which govern it'.

54 Judgment of the Court of Justice of 16 May 2002, *France v Commission (Stardust)*, C-482/99, ECLI-:EU:C:2002:294, paragraph 52.

55 Judgment of the Court of Justice of 16 May 2002, *France v Commission (Stardust)*, C-482/99, ECLI-:EU:C:2002:294. See also Judgment of the General Court of 26 June 2008, *SIC v Commission*, T-442/03, ECLI:EU:T:2008:228, paragraphs 93 to 100.

56 It is, furthermore, not necessary to demonstrate that, in a particular case, the public undertaking's conduct would have been different if it had acted autonomously, see Judgment of the General Court of 25 June 2015, *SACE and Sace BT v Commission*, T-305/13, ECLI:EU: T:2015:435, paragraph 48.

57 Judgment of the Court of Justice of 16 May 2002, *France v Commission (Stardust)*, C-482/99, ECLI-:EU:C:2002:294, paragraph 53.

58 Judgment of the Court of Justice of 16 May 2002, *France v Commission (Stardust)*, C-482/99, ECLI-:EU:C:2002:294, paragraph 54.

59 Judgment of the Court of Justice of 16 May 2002, *France v Commission (Stardust)*, C-482/99, ECLI-:EU:C:2002:294, paragraph 55.

60 Judgment of the Court of Justice of 16 May 2002, *France v Commission (Stardust)*, C-482/99, ECLI-:EU:C:2002:294, paragraphs 55 and 56. See also the Opinion of Advocate General Jacobs of 13 December 2001, *France v Commission (Stardust)*, C-482/99, ECLI:EU: C:2001/685, paragraphs 65 to 68.

61 Judgment of the Court of Justice of 23 October 2014, *Commerz Nederland*, C-242/13, ECLI:EU:C:2014:2224, paragraph 35.

62 For instance, when measures are taken by public development banks pursuing public policy objectives (Judgment of the General Court of 27 February 2013, *Nitrogenmuvek Vegyipari, Zrt. v Commission*, T-387/11, ECLI:EU:T:2013:98, paragraph 63) or when measures are taken by privatisation agencies or public pension funds (Judgment of the General Court of 28 January 2016, *Slovenia v Commission* ('ELAN'), T-507/12, ECLI:EU:T:2016:35, paragraph 86).

63 Judgment of the Court of Justice of 16 May 2002, *France v Commission (Stardust)*, C-482/99, ECLI-:EU:C:2002:294, paragraph 57.

64 See Judgment of the Court of Justice of 23 April 2009, *Puffer*, C-460/07, ECLI:EU:C:2009:254, paragraph 70,

on the right to tax deductions under the VAT system set up by the Union, and Judgment of the General Court of 5 April 2006, *Deutsche Bahn AG v Commission*, T-351/02, ECLI:EU:T:2006:104, paragraph 102, on tax exemptions required by Union law.

65 See Judgment of the Court of Justice of 10 December 2013, *Commission v Ireland and Others*, C-272/12 P, ECLI:EU:C:2013:812, paragraphs 45 to 53, on an authorisation granted to a Member State by a Council decision to introduce certain tax exemptions. The judgment also clarifies that the fact that a Council decision in the area of harmonisation of legislation was adopted on a proposal by the Commission is irrelevant because the notion of State aid is an objective notion.

66 Commission Decision 2010/606/EU of 26 February 2010 on State aid C9/2009 (ex NN 45/08, NN 49/08 and NN 50/08) implemented by the Kingdom of Belgium, the French Republic and the Grand Duchy of Luxembourg for Dexia SA (OJ L274, 19.10.2010, p 54).

67 Judgment of the Court of Justice of 24 January 1978, *Van Tiggele*, 82/77, ECLI:EU:C:1978:10, paragraphs 25 and 26; Judgment of the General Court of 12 December 1996, *Air France v Commission*, T-358/94, ECLI-:EU:T:1996:194, paragraph 63.

68 Judgment of the General Court of 12 December 1996, *Air France v Commission*, T-358/94, ECLI:EU:T:1996:194, paragraph 56.

69 Judgment of the Court of Justice of 14 October 1987, *Germany v Commission*, 248/84, ECLI:EU:C:1987:437, paragraph 17; Judgment of the General Court of 6 March 2002, *Territorio Histórico de Álava and Others v Commission*, Joined Cases T-92/00 and 103/00, ECLI:EU: T:2002:61, paragraph 57.

70 Judgment of the General Court of 12 December 1996, *Air France v Commission*, T-358/94, ECLI:EU:T:1996:194, paragraphs 58 to 62.

71 See Communication from the Commission on the application, from 1 August 2013, of State aid rules to support measures in favour of banks in the context of the financial crisis ('Banking Communication') (OJ C216, 30.7.2013, p 1), in particular point 62. However, the Commission clarified that where a central bank reacts to a banking crisis with general measures open to all comparable market players in the market (for example lending to the whole market on equal terms) rather than with selective measures in favour of individual banks, such general measures often fall outside the scope of State aid control.

72 Judgment of the Court of Justice of 16 May 2002, *France v Commission (Stardust)*, C-482/99, ECLI-:EU:C:2002:294, paragraph 38. See also Judgment of the Court of Justice of 29 April 2004, *Greece v Commission*, C-278/00, ECLI:EU:C:2004:239, paragraphs 53 and 54, and Judgment of the Court of Justice of 8 May 2003, *Italy and SIM 2 Multimedia SpA v Commission*, Joined Cases C-328/99 and C-399/00, ECLI:EU:C:2003:252, paragraphs 33 and 34.

73 Judgment of the Court of Justice of 11 July 1996, *SFEI and Others*, C-39/94, ECLI:EU:C:1996:285, paragraph 62.

74 Judgment of the General Court of 24 March 2011, *Freistaat Sachsen and Land Sachsen-Anhalt and Others v Commission*, Joined Cases T-443/08 and T-455/08, ECLI:EU:T:2011:117, paragraph 143.

75 Judgment of the Court of Justice of 22 March 1977, *Steinike & Weinlig*, 78/76, ECLI:EU:C:1977:52, paragraph 21.

76 Judgment of the Court of Justice of 22 March 1977, *Steinike & Weinlig*, 78/76, ECLI:EU:C:1977:52, paragraph 22.

77 Judgment of the Court of Justice of 16 May 2000, *France v Ladbroke Racing Ltd and Commission*, C-83/98 P, ECLI:EU:C:2000:248, paragraphs 48 to 51.

78 Judgment of the Court of Justice of 15 March 1994, *Banco Exterior de España*, C-387/92, ECLI:EU:C:1994:100, paragraph 14 on tax exemptions. Furthermore, derogations from the normal insolvency rules, which allow undertakings to continue trading in circumstances under which they would not be allowed if the ordinary insolvency rules were applied, may involve an additional burden for the State if public bodies are among the principal creditors of those undertaking or where such action amounts to a de facto waiver of public debts. See Judgment of the Court of Justice of 17 June 1999, *Piaggio*, C-295/97, ECLI:EU:C:1999:313, paragraphs 40 to 43 and Judgment of the Court of Justice of 1 December 1998, *Ecotrade*, C-200/97, ECLI:EU:C:1998:579, paragraph 45.

79 Judgment of the Court of Justice of 1 December 1998, *Ecotrade*, C-200/97, ECLI:EU:C:1998:579, paragraph 41 and Judgment of the Court of Justice of 19 March 2013, *Bouygues and Bouygues Télécom v Commission and Others*, Joined Cases C-399/10 P and C-401/10 P, ECLI:EU:C:2013:175, paragraphs 137, 138 and 139.

80 As defined in Article 2 (f) and (g) of Commission Directive 2006/111/EC of 16 November 2006 on the transparency of financial relations between Member States and public undertakings as well as on financial transparency within certain undertakings (OJ L318, 17.11.2006, p 17).

81 See also Communication from the Commission on the application of the European Union State aid rules to compensation granted for the provision of services of general economic interest (OJ C8, 11.1.2012, p 4), paragraph 33.

82 See Judgment of the General Court of 4 July 2007, *Bouygues SA v Commission*, T-475/04, ECLI:EU:T:2007:196, where the General Court noted that, in granting access to a scarce public resource such as the radio spectrum, national authorities simultaneously performed the roles of telecommunications regulator and manager of such public resources, paragraph 104.

83 See to that effect Commission Decision of 20 July 2004 on State aid NN 42/2004 — France — Modification of payments due from Orange and SFR for UMTS licences (OJ C275, 8.11.2005, p 3), recitals 28, 29 and 30, upheld by the Union courts (Judgment of the General Court of 4 July 2007, *Bouygues SA v Commission*, T-475/04, ECLI:EU:T:2007:196, paragraphs 108 to 111 and 123, and Judgment of the Court of Justice of 2 April 2009, *Bouygues and Bouygues Télécom v Commission*, C-431/07 P, ECLI:EU:C:2009:223, paragraphs 94 to 98 and 125). In this case, as regards the granting of UMTS radio spectrum licences, the State simultaneously performed the roles of telecommunications regulator and manager of these public resources and pursued the regulatory objectives set out in Directive 97/13/EC of the European Parliament and of the Council of 10 April 1997 on a common framework for general authorisations and individual licences in the field of telecommunication services (OJ L117, 7.5.1997, p 15). In such a situation, the Union Courts confirmed that the award of licences without maximising the revenues which could have been achieved did not involve the granting of State aid, given that the measures in question were justified by the regulatory objectives set out in Directive 97/13/EC and complied with the principle of non-discrimination. In contrast, in the Judgment of the Court of Justice of 8 September 2011, *Commission v Netherlands*, C-279/08 P, ECLI-:EU:C:2011:551, paragraphs 88 et seq. the Court did not identify regulatory reasons that would have justified the award without consideration of freely tradable emission rights. See also Judgment of the Court of Justice of 14 January 2015, *Eventech v The Parking Adjudicator*, C-518/13, ECLI:EU:C:2015:9, paragraphs 46 et seq.

84 Judgment of the Court of Justice of 13 March 2001, *PreussenElektra*, C-379/98, ECLI:EU:C:2001:160, paragraph 62.

85 Judgment of the Court of Justice of 17 March 1993, *Sloman Neptun Schiffahrts*, Joined Cases C-72/91 and C-73/91, ECLI:EU:C:1993:97, paragraphs 20 and 21. See also Judgment of the Court of Justice of 7 May 1998, *Viscido et al.*, Joined Cases C-52/97, C-53/97 and C-54/97, ECLI:EU:C:1998:209, paragraphs 13 and 14 and Judgment of the Court of Justice of 30 November 1993, *Kirsammer-Hack*, C-189/91, ECLI:EU:C:1993:907, paragraphs 17 and 18, on the fact that the non-application of certain provisions of employment law does not constitute a transfer of State resources.

86 Judgment of the Court of Justice of 24 January 1978, *Van Tiggele*, 82/77, ECLI:EU:C:1978:10, paragraphs 25 and 26.

87 See, for instance Judgment of the Court of Justice of 17 July 2008, *Essent Netwerk Noord*, C-206/06, ECLI-:EU:C:2008:413, paragraph 70; Judgment of the Court of Justice of 16 May 2000, *France v Ladbroke Racing Ltd and Commission*, C-83/98 P, ECLI:EU:C:2000:248, paragraph 50.

88 See Judgment of the General Court of 12 December 1996, *Air France v Commission*, T-358/94, ECLI-:EU:T:1996:194, paragraphs 65, 66 and 67, concerning an aid granted by the Caisse des Dépôts et Consignations which was financed with the voluntary deposits of private citizens which could be withdrawn at any time. That did not affect the conclusion that those funds were State resources because the Caisse was able to use them from the balance produced by deposits and withdrawals as if they were permanently at its disposal. See also Judgment of the Court of Justice of 16 May 2000, *France v Ladbroke Racing Ltd and Commission*, C-83/98 P, ECLI:EU:C:2000:248, paragraph 50.

89 Judgment of the Court of Justice of 2 July 1974, *Italy v Commission*, 173/73, ECLI:EU:C:1974:71, paragraph 16; Judgment of the Court of Justice of 11 March 1992, *Compagnie Commerciale de l'Ouest*, Joined Cases C-78/90 to C-83/90, ECLI:EU:C:1992:118, paragraph 35; Judgment of the Court of Justice of 17 July 2008, *Essent Netwerk Noord*, C-206/06, ECLI:EU:C:2008:413, paragraphs 58 to 74.

90 Judgment of the General Court of 27 September 2012, *France et al. v Commission*, Joined Cases T-139/09, T-243/09 and T-328/09, ECLI:EU:T:2012:496, paragraphs 63 and 64.

91 See Judgment of the Court of Justice of 15 July 2004, *Pearle*, C-345/02, ECLI:EU:C:2004:448, paragraph 41 and Judgment of the Court of Justice of 30 May 2013, *Doux élevages SNC et al*, C-677/11, ECLI:EU:C:2013:348.

92 Commission Decision 2010/606/EU of 26 February 2010 on State aid C9/2009 (ex NN 45/08, NN 49/08 and NN 50/08) implemented by the Kingdom of Belgium, the French Republic and the Grand Duchy of Luxembourg for Dexia SA (OJ L274, 19.10.2010, p 54).

93 See, for instance, concerning structural funds, Commission Decision of 22 November 2006 on State aid N 157/06, United Kingdom South Yorkshire Digital Region Broadband Project, recitals 21 and 29 on a measure partly financed by the European Regional Development Fund (ERDF) (OJ C80, 13.4.2007, p 2). As regards financing for the production of and trade in agricultural products, the scope of application of the State aid rules is limited by Article 42 of the Treaty.

94 Judgment of the Court of Justice of 24 January 1978, *Van Tiggele*, 82/77, ECLI:EU:C:1978:10, paragraphs 25 and 26.

95 Judgment of the Court of Justice of 13 March 2001, *PreussenElektra*, C-379/98, ECLI:EU:C:2001:160, paragraphs 59 to 62. The Court held that the imposition of a purchase obligation on private undertakings does not constitute a direct or indirect transfer of State resources, and that this qualification does not change because of the lower revenues of the undertakings subject to that obligation which is likely to cause a diminution of tax revenues, because this constitutes an inherent feature of the measure. See also Judgment of the Court of Justice of 5 March 2009, UTECA, C-222/07, ECLI:EU:C:2009:124, paragraphs 43 to 47, on compulsory contributions imposed on broadcasters in favour of film production not involving a transfer of State resources.

96 Judgment of the Court of Justice of 17 July 2008, *Essent Netwerk Noord*, C-206/06, ECLI:EU:C:2008:413, paragraphs 69 to 75.

97 Commission Decision 2011/528/EU on State aid C-24/09 (ex NN 446/08) — Austria — Green Electricity Act (OJ L235, 10.9.2011, p 42), recital 76.

98 Judgment of the Court of Justice of 19 December 2013, *Vent de Colère and Others*, C-262/12, ECLI-:EU:C:2013:851, paragraphs 25 and 26.

4. ADVANTAGE

4.1. THE NOTION OF ADVANTAGE IN GENERAL

[5.205]

66. An advantage, within the meaning of Article 107(1) of the Treaty, is any economic benefit which an undertaking could not have obtained under normal market conditions, that is to say in the absence of State intervention.[99] Section 4.2 of this Communication provides detailed guidance on the question whether a benefit can be considered to be obtained under normal market conditions.

67. Only the effect of the measure on the undertaking is relevant, and not the cause or the objective of the State intervention.[100] Whenever the financial situation of an undertaking is improved as a result of State intervention[101] on terms differing from normal market conditions, an advantage is present. To assess this, the financial situation of the undertaking following the measure should be compared with its financial situation if the measure had not been taken.[102] Since only the effect of the measure on the undertaking matters, it is irrelevant whether the advantage is compulsory for the undertaking in that it could not avoid or refuse it.[103]

68. The precise form of the measure is also irrelevant in establishing whether it confers an economic advantage on the undertaking.[104] Not only the granting of positive economic advantages is relevant for the notion of State aid, but relief from economic burdens[105] can also constitute an advantage. The latter is a broad category which comprises any mitigation of charges normally included in the budget of an undertaking.[106] This covers all situations in which economic operators are relieved of the inherent costs of their economic activities.[107] For instance, if a Member State pays part of the costs of the employees of a specific undertaking, it relieves that undertaking from costs that are inherent of its economic activities. An advantage also exists where public authorities pay a salary supplement to the

workers of a specific undertaking, even if the undertaking was under no legal obligation to pay such a supplement.[108] It also covers situations where some operators do not have to bear costs that other comparable operators normally do under a given legal order, regardless of the non-economic nature of the activity to which the costs relate.[109]

69. Costs arising from regulatory obligations imposed by the State[110] can in principle be considered to relate to the inherent costs of the economic activity, so that any compensation for these costs confers an advantage on the undertaking.[111] This means that the existence of an advantage is in principle not excluded by the fact that the benefit does not go beyond compensation for a cost stemming from the imposition of a regulatory obligation. The same applies to relief for costs that the undertaking would not have incurred had there been no incentive stemming from the State measure because without this incentive it would have structured its activities differently.[112] The existence of an advantage is also not excluded if a measure compensates charges of a different nature that are unconnected with that measure.[113]

70. As regards compensation for costs incurred to provide a service of general economic interest, the Court made clear in the *Altmark* judgment that the granting of an advantage can be excluded if four cumulative conditions are met.[114] First, the recipient undertaking must actually have public service obligations to discharge, and the obligations must be clearly defined. Second, the parameters on the basis of which the compensation is calculated must be established in advance in an objective and transparent manner. Third, the compensation cannot exceed what is necessary to cover all or part of the costs incurred in the discharge of public service obligations, taking into account the relevant receipts and a reasonable profit. Fourth, where the undertaking that is to discharge public service obligations is not chosen following a public procurement procedure to select a tenderer capable of providing these services at the least cost to the community, the level of compensation needed must be determined on the basis of an analysis of the costs which a typical undertaking, well-run and adequately provided with means to meet the public service requirements, would have incurred in discharging those obligations, taking into account the relevant receipts and a reasonable profit for discharging the obligations. The Commission has further elaborated its understanding of these conditions in its Communication on the application of the European Union State aid rules to compensation granted for the provision of services of general economic interest.[115]

71. The existence of an advantage is excluded in the case of a reimbursement of illegally levied taxes,[116] an obligation for the national authorities to compensate for damage they have caused to certain undertakings[117] or the payment of compensation for an expropriation.[118]

72. The existence of an advantage is not ruled out by the mere fact that competing undertakings in other Member States are in a more favourable position,[119] because the notion of advantage is based on an analysis of the financial situation of an undertaking in its own legal and factual context with and without the particular measure.

4.2. THE MARKET ECONOMY OPERATOR (MEO) TEST

4.2.1. INTRODUCTION

73. The Union legal order is neutral with regard to the system of property ownership[120] and does not in any way prejudice the right of Member States to act as economic operators. However, when public authorities directly or indirectly carry out economic transactions in any form,[121] they are subject to Union State aid rules.

74. Economic transactions carried out by public bodies (including public undertakings) do not confer an advantage on its counterpart, and therefore do not constitute aid, if they are carried out in line with normal market conditions.[122] This principle has been developed with regard to different economic transactions. The Union courts have developed the '*market economy investor principle*' to identify the presence of State aid in cases of public investment (in particular, capital injections): to determine whether a public body's investment constitutes State aid, it is necessary to assess whether, in similar circumstances, a private investor of a comparable size operating in normal conditions of a market economy could have been prompted to make the investment in question.[123] Similarly, the Union courts have developed the '*private creditor test*' to examine whether debt renegotiations by public creditors involve State aid, comparing the behaviour of a public creditor to that of hypothetical private creditors that find themselves in a similar situation.[124] Finally, the Union courts have developed the '*private vendor test*' to assess whether a sale carried out by a public body involves State aid, considering whether a private vendor, under normal market conditions, could have obtained the same or a better price.[125]

75. Those tests are variations of the same basic concept that the behaviour of public bodies should be compared to that of similar private economic operators under normal market conditions to determine whether the economic transactions carried out by such bodies grant an advantage to their counterparts. In this Communication, the Commission will therefore refer, in general terms, to the '*market economy operator*' (MEO) test as the relevant method to assess whether a range of economic transactions carried out by public bodies take place under normal market conditions and, therefore, whether they involve the granting of an advantage (which would not have occurred in normal market conditions) to their counterparts. The general principles and the relevant criteria for applying the MEO test are set out in sections 4.2.2. and 4.2.3.

4.2.2. GENERAL PRINCIPLES

76. The purpose of the MEO test is to assess whether the State has granted an advantage to an undertaking by not acting like a market economy operator with regard to a certain transaction. In that respect, it is not relevant whether the intervention constitutes a rational means for the public bodies to pursue public policy (for example employment) considerations. Similarly, the profitability or unprofitability of the beneficiary is not in itself a decisive indicator for establishing whether or not the economic transaction in question is in line with market conditions. The decisive element is whether the public bodies acted as a market economy operator would have done in a similar situation. If this is not the case, the beneficiary undertaking has received an economic advantage which it would not have obtained under normal market conditions,[126] placing it in a more favourable position compared to that of its competitors.[127]

77. For the purpose of the MEO test, only the benefits and obligations linked to the role of the State as an economic operator — to the exclusion of those linked to its role as a public authority — are to be taken into account.[128] Indeed, the MEO test is normally not applicable if the State acts as a public authority rather than as an economic operator. For example, if a State intervention is driven by public policy reasons (for instance, for reasons of social or regional development), the State's behaviour, while being rational from a public policy perspective, may at the same time include considerations which a market economy operator would normally not consider. Accordingly, the MEO test should be applied leaving aside all considerations which exclusively relate to a Member State's role as a public authority (for example social, regional or sectoral policy considerations).[129]

78. Whether a State intervention is in line with market conditions must be examined on an *ex-ante* basis, having regard to the information available at the time the intervention was decided upon.[130] In fact, any prudent market economy operator would normally carry out its own ex-ante assessment of the strategy and financial prospects of a project,[131] for instance, by means of a business plan. It is not enough to rely on *ex-post* economic evaluations entailing a retrospective finding that the investment made by the Member State concerned was actually profitable.[132]

79. If a Member State argues that it acted as a market economy operator it must, where there is doubt, provide evidence showing that the decision to carry out the transaction was taken on the basis of economic evaluations comparable to those which, in similar circumstances, a rational market economy operator (with characteristics similar to those of the public body concerned) would have had carried out to determine the profitability or economic advantages of the transaction.[133]

80. Whether a transaction is in line with market conditions must be established through a global assessment of the effects of the transaction on the undertaking concerned without considering whether the specific means used to carry out that transaction would be available to market economy operators. For instance, the applicability of the MEO test cannot be ruled out simply because the means employed by the State are fiscal in nature.[134]

81. In certain cases, several consecutive measures of State intervention may, for the purposes of Article 107(1) of the Treaty, be regarded as a single intervention. This could be the case, in particular, where consecutive interventions are so closely linked to each other, especially having regard to their chronology, their purpose and the circumstances of the undertaking at the time of those interventions, that they are inseparable.[135] For instance, a series of State interventions which take place in relation to the same undertaking in a relatively short period of time, are linked to each other, or were all planned or foreseeable at the time of the first intervention, may be assessed as one intervention. On the other hand, when the later intervention was a result of unforeseen events at the time of the earlier intervention[136] the two measures should normally be assessed separately.

82. To assess whether certain transactions are in line with market conditions all the relevant circumstances of the particular case should be considered. For instance, there can be exceptional circumstances in which the purchase of goods or services by a public authority, even if carried out at market prices, may not be considered in line with market conditions.[137]

4.2.3. ESTABLISHING COMPLIANCE WITH MARKET CONDITIONS

83. When applying the MEO test, it is useful to distinguish between situations in which the transaction's compliance with market conditions can be directly established through transaction-specific market data and situations in which, due to the absence of such data, the transaction's compliance with market conditions has to be assessed on the basis of other available methods.

4.2.3.1.
Cases where compliance with market conditions can be directly established

84. A transaction's compliance with market conditions can be directly established through transaction-specific market information in the following situations

(i) where the transaction is carried out '*pari passu*' by public entities and private operators; or

(ii) where it concerns the sale and purchase of assets, goods and services (or other comparable transactions) carried out through a competitive, transparent non-discriminatory and unconditional tender procedure.

85. In such cases, if the specific market information concerning the transaction shows that it does not comply with market conditions, it would not normally be appropriate to use other assessment methodologies to reach a different conclusion.[138]

(i) *Pari passu* transactions

86. When a transaction is carried out under the same terms and conditions (and therefore with the same level of risk and rewards) by public bodies and private operators who are in a comparable situation (a '*pari passu*' transaction),[139] as may occur in public private partnerships, it can normally be inferred that such a transaction is in line with market conditions.[140] In contrast, if a public body and private operators who are in a comparable situation take part in the same transaction at the same time but under different terms or conditions, this normally indicates that the intervention of the public body is not in line with market conditions.[141]

87. In particular, to consider a transaction '*pari passu*', the following criteria should be assessed:

(a) whether the intervention of the public bodies and private operators is decided and carried out at the same time or whether there has been a time lapse and a change of economic circumstances between those interventions;

(b) whether the terms and conditions of the transaction are the same for the public bodies and all private operators involved, also taking into account the possibility of increasing or decreasing the level of risk over time;

(c) whether the intervention of the private operators has real economic significance and is not merely symbolic or marginal;[142] and

(d) whether the starting position of the public bodies and the private operators involved is comparable with regard to the transaction, taking into account, for instance, their prior economic exposure vis-à-vis the undertakings concerned (see section 4.2.3.3), the possible synergies which can be achieved,[143] the extent to which the different investors bear similar transaction costs,[144] or any other circumstance specific to the public body or private operator which could distort the comparison.

88. The '*pari passu*' condition may not be applicable in some cases where the public involvement (in view of its unique nature or magnitude) is such that it could in practice not be replicated by a market economy operator.

(ii) The sale and purchase of assets, goods and services (or other comparable transactions) through competitive, transparent, non-discriminatory and unconditional tenders

89. If the sale and purchase of assets, goods and services (or other comparable transactions[145]) are carried out following a competitive[146], transparent, non-discriminatory and unconditional tender procedure in line with the principles of the TFEU on public procurement[147] (see paragraphs 90 to 94), it can be presumed that those transactions are in line with market conditions, provided that the appropriate criteria for selecting the buyer or seller as set out in paragraphs 95 and 96 have been used. In contrast, if a Member States decides to provide support, for public policy reasons, to a certain activity and tenders out, for example, the amount of funding provided, such as in the case of support to the production of renewable energy or to the mere availability of electricity generation capacity, this would not fall in the scope of this sub-section (ii). In such a situation a tender can only minimize the amount granted but cannot exclude an advantage.

90. A tender procedure has to be competitive to allow all interested and qualified bidders to participate in the process.

91. The procedure has to be transparent to allow all interested tenderers to be equally and duly informed at each stage of the tender procedure. Accessibility of information, sufficient time for interested tenderers, and the clarity of the selection and award criteria are all crucial elements for a transparent selection procedure. A tender has to be sufficiently well-publicised, so that all potential bidders can take note of it. The degree of publicity needed to ensure sufficient publication in a given case depends on the characteristics of the assets, goods and services. Assets, goods and services which may attract bidders operating on a Europe-wide or international scale in view of their high value or other features should be publicised in such a manner as to attract potential bidders operating on a Europe-wide or international scale.

92. Non-discriminatory treatment of all bidders at all stages of the procedure and objective selection and award criteria specified in advance of the process are indispensable conditions for ensuring that the resulting transaction is in line with market conditions. To guarantee equal treatment, the criteria for the award of the contract should enable tenders to be compared and assessed objectively.

93. Using and complying with the procedures provided for in the Public Procurement Directives[148] can be considered sufficient to meet the requirements above provided that all the conditions for the use of the respective procedure are fulfilled. This does not apply in specific circumstances that make it impossible to establish a market price, such as the use of the negotiated procedure without publication of a contract notice. If only one bid is submitted, the procedure would not normally be sufficient to ensure a market price, unless either (i) there are particularly strong safeguards in the design of the procedure ensuring genuine and effective competition and it is not apparent that only one operator is realistically able to submit a credible bid or (ii) the public authorities verify through additional means that the outcome corresponds to the market price.

94. A tender for the sale of assets, goods or services is unconditional when a potential buyer is generally free to acquire the assets, goods or services to be sold and to use them for its own purposes irrespective of whether or not it runs certain businesses. If there is a condition that the buyer is to assume special obligations for the benefit of the public authorities or in the general public interest, which a private seller would not have demanded — other than those arising from general domestic law or a decision of the planning authorities —, the tender cannot be considered unconditional.

95. When public bodies sell assets, goods and services, the only relevant criterion for selecting the buyer should be the highest price,[149] also taking into account the requested contractual arrangements (for example the vendor's sales guarantee or other post-sale commitments). Only credible[150] and binding offers should be considered.[151]

96. When public bodies buy assets, goods and services, any specific conditions attached to the tender should be non-discriminatory and closely and objectively related to the subject matter and to the specific economic objective of the contract. They should allow for the most economically advantageous offer to match the value of the market. The criteria therefore should be defined in such a way as to allow for an effectively competitive tendering procedure which leaves the successful bidder with a normal return, not more. In practice, this implies the use of tenders which put significant weight on the 'price' component of the bid or which are otherwise likely to achieve a competitive outcome (e.g. certain reverse tenders with sufficiently clear-cut award criteria).

4.2.3.2.
Establishing whether a transaction is in line with market conditions on the basis of benchmarking or other assessment methods

97. If a transaction has been realised through a tender or on '*pari passu*' terms, this provides direct and specific evidence of compliance with market conditions. However, if a transaction has not been realised through a tender, or if the intervention of the public bodies is not '*pari passu*' with that of private operators, this does not automatically mean that the transaction does not comply with market conditions.[152] In such cases compliance with market conditions can still be assessed through (i) benchmarking or (ii) other assessment methods.[153]

(i) Benchmarking

98. To establish whether a transaction is in compliance with market conditions, that transaction can be assessed in the light of the terms under which comparable transactions carried out by comparable private operators have taken place in comparable situations (benchmarking).

99. To identify an appropriate benchmark, it is necessary to pay particular attention to the kind of operator concerned (for example a group holding, a speculative fund, or a long-term investor seeking to secure profits in the longer run), the type of transaction at stake (for example equity participation or debt transaction) and the market or markets concerned (for example financial markets, fast-growing technology markets, utility or infrastructure markets). The timing of the transactions is also particularly relevant when significant economic developments have taken place. Where appropriate, the available market benchmarks may need to be adjusted according to the specific features of the State transaction (for instance, the situation of the beneficiary undertaking and of the relevant market).[154] Benchmarking may not be an appropriate method to establish market prices if the available benchmarks have not been defined with regard to market considerations or the existing prices are significantly distorted by public interventions.

100. Benchmarking often does not establish one precise reference value but rather establishes a range of possible values by assessing a set of comparable transactions. Where the aim of the assessment is to consider whether the State intervention is in line with market conditions, it is normally appropriate to consider measures of central tendency such as the average or the median of the set of comparable transactions.

(ii) Other assessment methods

101. Whether a transaction is in line with market conditions can also be established on the basis of a generally-accepted, standard assessment methodology.[155] Such a methodology must be based on the available objective, verifiable and reliable data,[156] which should be sufficiently detailed and should reflect the economic situation at the time at which the transaction was decided, taking into account the level of risk and future expectations.[157] Depending on the value of the transaction, the robustness of the evaluation should normally be corroborated by performing a sensitivity analysis, assessing different business scenarios, preparing contingency plans and comparing the results with alternative evaluation methodologies. A new (*ex-ante*) valuation may need to be carried out if the transaction is delayed and it is necessary to take into account recent changes in market conditions.

102. A widely accepted standard methodology to determine the (annual) return on investments is to calculate the internal rate of return (IRR).[158] One can also evaluate the investment decision in terms of its net present value (NPV),[159] which produces results equivalent to the IRR in most cases.[160] To assess whether the investment is carried out on market terms, the return on the investment must be compared to the normal expected market return. A normal expected return (or cost of capital of the investment) can be defined as the average expected return that the market requires from the investment on the basis of generally accepted criteria, in particular the risk of the investment, taking into account the financial position of the company and the specific features of the sector, region or country. If this normal return cannot be reasonably expected, then the investment would most likely not be pursued on market terms. In general, the riskier the project, the higher the rate of return that fund providers will demand, that is to say the higher the cost of capital.

103. The appropriate assessment methodology may depend on the market situation,[161] data availability or the type of transaction. For instance, whereas an investor seeks to generate a profit by investing in undertakings (in which case IRR or NPV are likely to be the most appropriate method), a creditor seeks to obtain payment of sums owed to it (the principal sum and any interest) by a debtor within the contractually and legally determined period[162] (in which case the evaluation of collateral, for example the asset value, could be more relevant). In the case of sales of land, an independent expert evaluation prior to the sale negotiations to establish the market value on the basis of generally accepted market indicators and valuation standards is in principle satisfactory.[163]

104. Methods to establish the IRR or NPV of an investment do not typically result in one precise value that could be accepted, but rather in a range of possible values (depending on the economic, legal and other specific circumstances of the transaction inherent in the assessment method). Where the aim of the assessment is to consider whether the State intervention is in line with market conditions, it is normally appropriate to consider measures of central tendency, such as the average or the median of the set of comparable transactions.

105. Prudent market economy operators typically assess their interventions by using several different methodologies to corroborate the estimates (for instance, NPV calculations are validated by benchmarking methods). The different methodologies converging at the same value will provide a further indication for establishing a genuine market price. Thus, the presence of complementary valuation methodologies corroborating each other's findings will be considered a positive indication when assessing whether a transaction is in line with market conditions.

4.2.3.3.
Counterfactual analysis in the case of prior economic exposure to the undertaking concerned

106. The fact that the public body concerned has prior economic exposure to an undertaking should be taken into consideration when examining whether a transaction is in line with market conditions, provided that a comparable private operator could have such prior exposure (for example in its capacity of shareholder of an undertaking).[164]

107. Prior exposure must be considered in the framework of counterfactual scenarios for the purpose of the MEO test. For instance, in the case of an equity or debt intervention in a public undertaking in difficulty, the expected return on such an investment should be compared with the expected return in the counterfactual scenario of the liquidation of the company. In the event that liquidation provides higher gains or lower losses, a prudent market economy operator would choose that option.[165] For this purpose, the liquidation costs to be considered should not include costs linked to the responsibilities of the public authorities, but only costs that a rational market economy operator would incur,[166] also taking into account the evolution of the social, economic and environmental context in which it operates.[167]

4.2.3.4.
Specific considerations to establish whether the terms for loans and guarantees are in line with market terms

108. In the same way as any other transaction, loans and guarantees granted by public bodies (including public undertakings) may entail State aid if they are not in line with market terms.

109. For guarantees, a triangular situation involving a public entity as a guarantor, a borrower and a lender normally has to be analysed.[168] In most cases, aid can only be present at the level of the borrower, as the public guarantee may grant it an advantage, by enabling it to borrow at a rate that would not have been obtainable on the market without the guarantee[169] (or to borrow in a situation where, exceptionally, no loan could have been obtained on the market at any rate). However, under certain specific circumstances, the granting of a public guarantee might also entail aid to the lender, in particular where the guarantee is given *ex post* on an existing obligation between lender and borrower, where a complete passing on of the advantage to the borrower is not ensured[170] or where a guaranteed loan is used to pay back a non-guaranteed one.[171]

110. Any guarantee granted on terms that are more favourable than market conditions, taking into account the economic situation of the borrower, confers an advantage on the latter (who pays a fee that does not appropriately reflect the risk that the guarantor assumes).[172] In general, unlimited guarantees are not in line with normal market conditions. This also applies to implicit guarantees stemming from State liability for the debts of insolvent undertakings sheltered from ordinary bankruptcy rules.[173]

111. In the absence of specific market information on a given debt transaction, the debt instrument's compliance with market conditions may be established on the basis of a comparison with comparable market transactions (that is to say through benchmarking). In the case of loans and guarantees, information on the financing costs of the undertaking may, for example, be obtained from other (recent) loans taken by the undertaking in question, from yields on bonds issued by the undertaking or from credit default swap spreads on that undertaking. Comparable market transactions may also be similar loan or guarantee transactions undertaken by a sample of comparator companies, bonds issued by a sample of comparator companies or credit default swap spreads on a sample of comparator companies. In the case of guarantees, if no corresponding price benchmark can be found on the financial markets, the total financing cost of the guaranteed loan, including the interest rate of the loan and the guarantee premium, should be compared to the market price of a similar non-guaranteed loan. Benchmarking methods may be complemented with assessment methods based on the return on capital.[174]

112. To facilitate assessment of whether a measure complies with the MEO test, the Commission has developed proxies to determine the aid character of loans and guarantees.

113. For loans, the methodology to calculate a reference rate, to act as a proxy for the market price in situations where comparable market transactions are not easy to identify (something that is more likely to apply to transactions involving limited amounts and/or transactions involving small and medium sized undertakings (SMEs)) is set out in the Reference Rate Communication.[175] It should be recalled that this reference rate is only a proxy.[176] If comparable transactions have typically taken place at a lower price than that indicated as a proxy by the reference rate, the Member State can consider this lower price to be the market price. If, on the other hand, the same company has carried out recent similar transactions at a higher price than the reference rate, and its financial situation and the market environment have remained substantially unchanged, the reference rate may not constitute a valid proxy of market rates for that specific case.

114. The Commission has developed detailed guidance on proxies (and irrebuttable presumptions ('safe harbours') for SMEs) relating to guarantees in the Notice on Guarantees.[177] According to that Notice, in order to rule out the presence of aid, it is normally sufficient that the borrower is not in financial difficulty, that the guarantee is linked to a specific transaction, that the lender bears part of the risk and that the borrower pays a market-oriented price for the guarantee.

4.3. INDIRECT ADVANTAGE

115. An advantage can be conferred on undertakings other than those to which State resources are directly transferred (indirect advantage).[178] A measure can also constitute both a direct advantage to the recipient undertaking and an indirect advantage to other undertakings, for instance, undertakings operating at subsequent levels of activity.[179] The direct recipient of the advantage can be either an undertaking or an entity (natural or legal person) not engaged in any economic activity.[180]

116. Such indirect advantages should be distinguished from mere secondary economic effects that are inherent in almost all State aid measures (for example through an increase of output). For this purpose, the foreseeable effects of the measure should be examined from an *ex ante* point of view. An indirect advantage is present if the measure is designed in such a way as to channel its secondary effects towards identifiable undertakings or groups of undertakings. This is the case, for example, if the direct aid is, *de facto* or *de jure*, made conditional on the purchase of goods or services produced by certain undertakings only (for example only undertakings established in certain areas).[181]

NOTES

99 Judgment of the Court of Justice of 11 July 1996, *SFEI and Others*, C-39/94, ECLI:EU:C:1996:285, paragraph 60; Judgment of the Court of Justice of 29 April 1999, *Spain v Commission*, C-342/96, ECLI:EU:C:1999:210, paragraph 41.

100 Judgment of the Court of Justice of 2 July 1974, *Italy v Commission*, 173/73, ECLI:EU:C:1974:71, paragraph 13.

101 The term 'State interventions' does not only refer to positive actions by the State but also covers the fact that the authorities do not take measures in certain circumstances, for example to enforce debts. See for example Judgment of the Court of Justice of 12 October 2000, *Magefesa*, C-480/98, ECLI:EU:C:2000:559, paragraphs 19 and 20.

102 Judgment of the Court of Justice of 2 July 1974, *Italy v Commission*, 173/73, ECLI:EU:C:1974:71, paragraph 13.

103 Commission Decision 2004/339/EC of 15 October 2003 on the measures implemented by Italy for RAI SpA (OJ L119, 23.4.2004, p 1), recital 69; Opinion of Advocate General Fennelly of 26 November 1998, *France v Commission*, C-251/97, ECLI:EU:C:1998:572, paragraph 26.

104 Judgment of the Court of Justice of 24 July 2003, *Altmark Trans*, C-280/00, ECLI:EU:C:2003:415, paragraph 84.

105 Such as, for example, tax advantages or reductions of social security contributions.

106 Judgment of the Court of Justice of 15 March 1994, *Banco Exterior de España*, C-387/92, ECLI:EU:C:1994:100, paragraph 13; Judgment of the Court of Justice of 19 September 2000, *Germany v Commission*, C-156/98, ECLI:EU:C:2000:467, paragraph 25; Judgment of the Court of Justice of 19 May 1999, *Italy v Commission*,

C-6/97, ECLI:EU:C:1999:251, paragraph 15; Judgment of the Court of Justice of 3 March 2005, *Heiser*, C-172/03, ECLI:EU:C:2005:130, paragraph 36.

107 Judgment of the Court of Justice of 20 November 2003, *GEMO SA*, C-126/01, ECLI:EU:C:2003:622, paragraphs 28 to 31 on the free collection and disposal of waste.

108 Judgment of the Court of Justice of 26 September 1996, *France v Commission*, C-241/94, ECLI:EU:C:1996:353, paragraph 40; Judgment of the Court of Justice of 12 December 2002, *Belgium v Commission*, C-5/01, ECLI:EU:C:2002:754, paragraphs 38 and 39; Judgment of the General Court of 11 September 2012, *Corsica Ferries France SAS v Commission*, T-565/08, ECLI:EU:T:2012:415, paragraphs 137 and 138, upheld on appeal, see Judgment of the Court of Justice of 4 September 2014, *SNCM and France v Commission*, Joined Cases C-533/12 P and C-536/12 P, ECLI:EU:C:2014:2142.

109 See the Guidelines on State aid to airports and airlines (OJ C99, 4.4.2014, p 3), recital 37.

110 As regards the agricultural sector, examples for an imposition of a regulatory obligation would be veterinary or food-safety checks and tests that are imposed on the agricultural producers. In contrast, checks and tests carried out and financed by public bodies and not prescribed by law to be carried out or financed by the agricultural producers are not considered regulatory obligations imposed on the undertakings. See Commission Decisions of 18 September 2015 on State aid SA.35484, milk quality tests pursuant to the Milk and Fat Law and of 4 April 2016 on State aid SA.35484, general healthcare control activities pursuant to the Milk and Fat Law.

111 Judgment of the General Court of 25 March 2015, *Belgium v Commission*, T-538/11, ECLI:EU:T:2015:188, paragraphs 74 to 78.

112 For instance, if a company receives a subsidy to carry out an investment in an assisted region, it cannot be argued that this does not mitigate costs normally included in the budget of the undertaking given that, in the absence of the subsidy, the company would not have carried out the investment.

113 Judgment of the Court of Justice of 8 December 2011, *France Télécom SA v Commission*, C-81/10 P, ECLI-:EU:C:2011:811, paragraphs 43 to 50. This logically applies to the relief of costs incurred by an undertaking to replace the status of officials with the status of employees comparable to that of its competitors, which confers an advantage on the undertaking concerned (on which there was some previous uncertainty following the judgment of the General Court of 16 March 2004, *Danske Busvognmænd v Commission*, T-157/01, ECLI:EU: T:2004:76, paragraph 57). On compensation for stranded costs, see also Judgment of the General Court of 11 February 2009, *Iride SpA and Iride Energia SpA v Commission*, T-25/07, ECLI:EU:T:2009:33, paragraphs 46 to 56.

114 Judgment of the Court of Justice of 24 July 2003, *Altmark Trans*, C-280/00, ECLI:EU:C:2003:415, paragraph 87 to 95.

115 OJ C8, 11.1.2012, p 4.

116 Judgment of the Court of Justice of 27 March 1980, *Amministrazione delle finanze dello Stato*, 61/79, ECLI-:EU:C:1980:100, paragraphs 29 to 32.

117 Judgment of the Court of Justice of 27 September 1988, *Asteris AE and Others v Greece*, Joined Cases 106 to 120/87, ECLI:EU: C:1988:457, paragraphs 23 and 24.

118 Judgment of the General Court of 1 July 2010, *Nuova Terni Industrie Chimiche SpA v Commission*, T-64/08, ECLI:EU:T:2010:270, paragraphs 59 to 63 and 140 to 141, clarifying that while the payment of compensation for an expropriation does not grant an advantage, an extension ex post of such compensation can constitute State aid.

119 Judgment of the Court of Justice of 2 July 1974, *Italy v Commission*, 173/73, ECLI:EU:C:1974:71, paragraph 17. See also Judgment of the General Court of 29 September 2000, *Confederación Espanola de Transporte de Mercancías v Commission*, T-55/99, ECLI:EU: T:2000:223, paragraph 85.

120 Article 345 of the Treaty provides that '*The Treaties shall in no way prejudice the rules in Member States governing the system of property ownership*'.

121 See, for instance, Judgment of the Court of Justice of 10 July 1986, *Belgium v Commission*, 40/85, ECLI-:EU:C:1986:305, paragraph 12.

122 Judgment of the Court of Justice of 11 July 1996, *SFEI and Others*, C-39/94, ECLI:EU:C:1996:285, paragraphs 60 and 61.

123 See, for instance, Judgment of the Court of Justice of 21 March 1990, *Belgium v Commission ('Tubemeuse')*, C-142/87, ECLI:EU: C:1990:125, paragraph 29; Judgment of the Court of Justice of 21 March 1991, *Italy v Commission ('ALFA Romeo')*, C-305/89, ECLI:EU: C:1991:142, paragraphs 18 and 19; Judgment of the General Court of 30 April 1998, *Cityflyer Express v Commission*, T-16/96, ECLI:EU: T:1998:78, paragraph 51; Judgment of the General Court of 21 January 1999, *Neue Maxhütte Stahlwerke and Lech-Stahlwerke v Commission*, Joined Cases T-129/95, T-2/96 and T-97/96, ECLI:EU:T:1999:7, paragraph 104; Judgment of the General Court of 6 March 2003, *Westdeutsche Landesbank Girozentrale and Land Nordrhein-Westfalen v Commission*, Joined Cases T-228/99 and T-233/99, ECLI:EU: T:2003:57.

124 Judgment of the Court of Justice of 22 November 2007, Spain v Commission, C-525/04 P, ECLI:EU:C:2007:698; Judgment of the Court of Justice of 24 January 2013, *Frucona v Commission*, C-73/11 P, ECLI:EU:C:2013:32; Judgment of the Court of Justice of 29 June 1999, *DMTransport*, C-256/97, ECLI:EU:C:1999:332.

125 Judgment of the General Court of 28 February 2012, *Land Burgenland and Austria v Commission*, Joined Cases T-268/08 and T-281/08, ECLI:EU:T:2012:90.

126 Judgment of the General Court of 6 March 2003, *Westdeutsche Landesbank Girozentrale and Land Nordrhein-Westfalen v Commission*, Joined Cases T-228/99 and T-233/99, ECLI:EU:T:2003:57, paragraph 208.

127 See, to that effect, Judgment of the Court of Justice of 5 June 2012, *Commission v EDF*, C-124/10 P, ECLI:EU:C:2012:318, paragraph 90; Judgment of the Court of Justice of 15 March 1994, *Banco Exterior de España*, C-387/92, ECLI:EU:C:1994:100, paragraph 14; Judgment of the Court of Justice of 19 May 1999, *Italy v Commission*, C-6/97, ECLI:EU:C:1999:251, paragraph 16.

128 Judgment of the Court of Justice of 5 June 2012, *Commission v EDF*, C-124/10 P, ECLI:EU:C:2012:318, paragraphs 79 to 81; Judgment of the Court of Justice of 10 July 1986, *Belgium v Commission*, 234/84, ECLI:EU:C:1986:302, paragraph 14; Judgment of the Court of Justice of 10 July 1986, *Belgium v Commission*, 40/85, ECLI:EU:C:1986:305, paragraph 13; Judgment of the Court of Justice of 14 September 1994, *Spain v Commission*, Joined Cases C-278/92 to C-280/92, ECLI:EU:C:1994:325, paragraph 22; Judgment of the Court of Justice of 28 January 2003, *Germany v Commission*, C-334/99, ECLI:EU:C:2003:55, paragraph 134.

129 Judgment of the Court of Justice of 5 June 2012, *Commission v EDF*, C-124/10 P, ECLI:EU:C:2012:318,

paragraphs 79, 80 and 81; Judgment of the Court of Justice of 10 July 1986, *Belgium v Commission*, 234/84, ECLI:EU:C:1986:302, paragraph 14; Judgment of the Court of Justice of 10 July 1986, *Belgium v Commission*, 40/85, ECLI:EU:C:1986:305, paragraph 13; Judgment of the Court of Justice of 14 September 1994, *Spain v Commission*, Joined Cases C-278/92 to C-280/92, ECLI:EU:C:1994:325, paragraph 22; Judgment of the Court of Justice of 28 January 2003, *Germany v Commission*, C-334/99, ECLI:EU:C:2003:55, paragraph 134; Judgment of the General Court of 6 March 2003, *Westdeutsche Landesbank Girozentrale and Land Nordrhein-Westfalen v Commission*, Joined Cases T-228/99 and T-233/99, ECLI:EU:T:2003:57; Judgment of the General Court of 24 September 2008, *Kahla Thüringen Porzellan v Commission*, T-20/03, ECLI:EU:T:2008:395; Judgment of the General Court of 17 October 2002, *Linde v Commission*, T-98/00, ECLI:EU:T:2002:248.

Judgment of the Court of Justice of 5 June 2012, *Commission v EDF*, C-124/10 P, ECLI:EU:C:2012:318, paragraphs 79, 80 and 81; Judgment of the Court of Justice of 10 July 1986, *Belgium v Commission*, 234/84, ECLI:EU:C:1986:302, paragraph 14; Judgment of the Court of Justice of 10 July 1986, *Belgium v Commission*, 40/85, ECLI:EU:C:1986:305, paragraph 13; Judgment of the Court of Justice of 14 September 1994, *Spain v Commission*, Joined Cases C-278/92 to C-280/92, ECLI:EU:C:1994:325, paragraph 22; Judgment of the Court of Justice of 28 January 2003, *Germany v Commission*, C-334/99, ECLI:EU:C:2003:55, paragraph 134; Judgment of the General Court of 6 March 2003, *Westdeutsche Landesbank Girozentrale and Land Nordrhein-Westfalen v Commission*, Joined Cases T-228/99 and T-233/99, ECLI:EU:T:2003:57; Judgment of the General Court of 24 September 2008, *Kahla Thüringen Porzellan v Commission*, T-20/03, ECLI:EU:T:2008:395; Judgment of the General Court of 17 October 2002, *Linde v Commission*, T-98/00, ECLI:EU:T:2002:248.

130 Judgment of the Court of Justice of 5 June 2012, *Commission v EDF*, C-124/10 P, ECLI:EU:C:2012:318, paragraphs 83, 84 and 85 and 105; Judgment of the Court of Justice of 16 May 2002, *France v Commission (Stardust)*, C-482/99, ECLI:EU:C:2002:294, paragraphs 71 and 72; Judgment of the General Court of 30 April 1998, *Cityflyer Express v Commission*, T-16/96, ECLI:EU:T:1998:78, paragraph 76.

131 Judgment of the Court of Justice of 5 June 2012, *Commission v EDF*, C-124/10 P, ECLI:EU:C:2012:318, paragraphs 82 to 85 and 105.

132 Judgment of the Court of Justice of 5 June 2012, *Commission v EDF*, C-124/10 P, ECLI:EU:C:2012:318, paragraph 85.

133 Judgment of the Court of Justice of 5 June 2012, *Commission v EDF*, C-124/10 P, ECLI:EU:C:2012:318, paragraphs 82 to 85. See also Judgment of the Court of Justice of 24 October 2013, *Land Burgenland v Commission*, Joined Cases C-214/12 P, C-215/12 P and C-223/12 P, ECLI:EU:C:2013:682, paragraph 61. The level of sophistication of such an ex ante assessment may vary depending on the complexity of the transaction concerned and the value of the assets, goods or services involved. Normally, such ex ante evaluations should be carried out with the support of experts with appropriate skills and experience. Such evaluations should always be based on objective criteria and should not be affected by policy considerations. Evaluations conducted by independent experts may provide an additional corroboration for the credibility of the assessment.

134 Judgment of the Court of Justice of 5 June 2012, *Commission v EDF*, C-124/10 P, ECLI:EU:C:2012:318, paragraph 88.

135 Judgment of the Court of Justice of 19 March 2013, *Bouygues and Bouygues Télécom v Commission and Others*, Joined Cases C-399/10 P and C-401/10 P, ECLI:EU:C:2013:175, paragraph 104; Judgment of the General Court of 13 September 2010, *Greece and Others v Commission*, Joined Cases T-415/05, T-416/05 and T-423/05, ECLI:EU:T:2010:386, paragraph 177; Judgment of the General Court of 15 September 1998, *BP Chemicals v Commission*, T-11/95, ECLI:EU:T:1998:199, paragraphs 170 and 171.

136 Commission Decision of 19 December 2012 in Case SA.35378 Financing of Berlin Brandenburg Airport, Germany (OJ C36, 8.2.2013, p 10), recitals 14 to 33.

137 In Judgment of the General Court of 28 January 1999, *BAI v Commission*, T-14/96, ECLI:EU:T:1999:12, paragraphs 74 to 79, the General Court held that, in the light of specific circumstances of the case, it could be concluded that the purchase of travel vouchers by national authorities from P&O Ferries did not meet an actual need, and thus the national authorities did not act in a manner similar to that of a private operator acting under normal market economy conditions. Accordingly, that purchase conferred an advantage on P&O Ferries which it would not have obtained under normal market conditions and all the sums paid in the fulfilment of the purchase agreement constituted State aid.

138 See to that effect, Judgment of the Court of Justice of 24 October 2013, *Land Burgenland v Commission*, Joined Cases C-214/12 P, C-215/12 P and C-223/12 P, ECLI:EU:C:2013:682, paragraphs 94 and 95. In that case, the Court held in particular that, where a public authority proceeds to sell an undertaking through a proper tender, it can be presumed that the market price corresponds to the highest (binding and credible) offer, without the necessity to resort to other valuation methods, such as independent studies.

139 The terms and conditions cannot be considered to be the same if public bodies and private operators intervene on the same terms but at different moments, following a change in the economic situation that is relevant to the transaction.

140 See, in that regard, Judgment of the General Court of 12 December 2000, *Alitalia v Commission*, T-296/97, ECLI:EU:T:2000:289, paragraph 81.

141 However, if the transactions are different and are not carried out at the same time, the mere fact that the terms and conditions are different does not provide any decisive indication (positive or negative) as to whether the transaction carried out by the public body is in line with market conditions.

142 For instance, in the Citynet Amsterdam case, the Commission considered that two private operators taking up one-third of the total equity investments in a company (considering also the overall shareholding structure and that their shares are sufficient to form a blocking minority regarding any strategic decision of the company) could be considered economically significant (see Commission Decision 2008/729/EC of 11 December 2007 on State aid C-53/2006 Citynet Amsterdam, the Netherlands (OJ L247, 16.9.2008, p 27), recitals 96 to 100). By contrast, in case N 429/2010 Agricultural Bank of Greece (ATE) (OJ C317, 29.10.2011, p 5), the private participation reached only 10% of the investment, as opposed to 90% by the State, so that the Commission concluded that '*pari passu*' conditions were not met since the capital injected by the State was neither accompanied by a comparable participation of a private shareholder nor proportionate to the number of shares held by the State. See also Judgment of the General Court of 12 December 2000, *Alitalia v Commission*, T-296/97, ECLI:EU:T:2000:289, paragraph 81.

143 They must also have the same industrial rationale; see Commission Decision 2005/137/EC on State aid C-25/2002 Walloon region's financial stake in Carsid SA (OJ L47, 18.2.2005, p 28), recitals 67 to 70.

144 Transaction costs may relate to the costs that the respective investors incur for the purpose of screening and selecting the investment project, arranging the terms of the contract or monitoring the performance over the lifetime of the contract. For instance, where publicly owned banks consistently bear the costs of screening investment projects for loan financing, the mere fact that private investors co-invest at the same interest rate is not sufficient to exclude aid.

145 For instance, the lease of certain goods or the grant of concessions for the commercial exploitation of natural resources.

146 The Union Courts often refer, in the context of State aid, to an 'open' tender procedure (see for example Judgment of the General Court of 5 August 2003, *P & O European Ferries (Vizcaya) v Commission*, Joined Cases T-116/01 and T-118/01, ECLI:EU:T:2003:217, paragraphs 117 and 118; Judgment of the Court of Justice of 24 October 2013, *Land Burgenland v Commission*, Joined Cases C-214/12 P, C-215/12 P and C-223/12 P, ECLI:EU:C:2013:682, paragraph 94). The use of the word 'open', however, does not refer to a specific procedure under Directive 2014/24/EU of the European Parliament and of the Council of 26 February 2014 on public procurement and repealing Directive 2004/18/EC and Directive 2014/25/EU of the European Parliament and of the Council of 26 February 2014 on procurement by entities operating in the water, energy, transport and postal services sectors and repealing Directive 2004/17/EC. Therefore, the word 'competitive' appears more appropriate. It is not intended to deviate from the substantive conditions set out in the case law.

147 Judgment of the Court of Justice of 7 December 2000, *Telaustria*, C-324/98, ECLI:EU:C:2000:669, paragraph 62; Judgment of the Court of Justice of 3 December 2001, *Bent Mousten Vestergaard*, C-59/00, ECLI:EU:C:2001:654, paragraph 20. See also Commission Interpretative Communication on the Community law applicable to contract awards not or not fully subject to the provisions of the Public Procurement Directives (OJ C179, 1.8.2006, p 2).

148 Directive 2014/24/EU of the European Parliament and of the Council of 26 February 2014 on public procurement and repealing Directive 2004/18/EC; Directive 2014/25/EU of the European Parliament and of the Council of 26 February 2014 on procurement by entities operating in the water, energy, transport and postal services sectors and repealing Directive 2004/17/EC.

149 Judgment of the General Court of 28 February 2012, *Land Burgenland and Austria v Commission*, Joined Cases T-268/08 and T-281/08, ECLI:EU:T:2012:90, paragraph 87.

150 An unsolicited bid can also be credible, depending on the circumstances of the case, and in particular if the bid is binding (see Judgment of the General Court of 13 December 2011, *Konsum Nord v Commission*, T-244/08, ECLI:EU:T:2011:732, paragraphs 73, 74 and 75).

151 For instance, mere announcements without legally binding requirements would not be given consideration in the tender procedure; see Judgment of the General Court of 28 February 2012, *Land Burgenland and Austria v Commission*, Joined Cases T-268/08 and T-281/08, ECLI:EU:T:2012:90, paragraph 87 and Judgment of the General Court of 13 December 2011, *Konsum Nord v Commission*, T-244/08, ECLI:EU:T:2011:732, paragraphs 67 and 75.

152 See Judgment of the General Court of 12 June 2014, *Sarc v Commission*, T-488/11, ECLI:EU:T:2014:497, paragraph 98.

153 When the market price is set through '*pari passu*' or tender transactions, these results cannot be disputed by other assessment methodologies, such as by independent studies (see Judgment of the Court of Justice of 24 October 2013, *Land Burgenland v Commission*, Joined Cases C-214/12 P, C-215/12 P and C-223/12 P, ECLI:EU:C:2013:682, paragraphs 94 and 95).

154 See Judgment of the General Court of 6 March 2003, *Westdeutsche Landesbank Girozentrale and Land Nordrhein-Westfalen v Commission*, Joined Cases T-228/99 and T-233/99, ECLI:EU:T:2003:57, paragraph 251.

155 See Judgment of the General Court of 29 March 2007, *Scott v Commission*, T-366/00, ECLI:EU:T:2007:99, paragraph 134, and Judgment of the Court of Justice of 16 December 2010, *Seydaland Vereinigte Agrarbetriebe*, C-239/09, ECLI:EU:C:2010:778, paragraph 39.

156 See Judgment of the General Court of 16 September 2004, *Valmont Nederland BV v Commission*, T-274/01, ECLI:EU:T:2004:266, paragraph 71.

157 See Judgment of the General Court of 29 March 2007, *Scott v Commission*, T-366/00, ECLI:EU:T:2007:99, paragraph 158.

158 The IRR is not based on accounting earnings in a given year, but takes into account the stream of future cash flows that the investor expects to receive over the entire lifetime of the investment. It is defined as the discount rate for which the NPV of a stream of cash flows equals zero.

159 The NPV is the difference between the positive and negative cash flows over the lifetime of the investment, discounted at the appropriate return (the cost of capital).

160 There is a perfect correlation between NPV and IRR in cases where the IRR is equal to the opportunity cost to the investor. Where the NPV of an investment is positive, this implies that the project has an IRR that exceeds the required rate of return (opportunity cost to the investor). In this case, the investment is worth carrying out. If the project has an NPV that is equal to zero, the IRR of the project equals the required rate of return. In this case, it is immaterial whether the investor makes the investment or invests elsewhere. Where the NPV is negative, the IRR is below the cost of capital. The investment is not profitable enough as better opportunities exist elsewhere. Where the IRR and the NPV lead to different investment decisions (such a difference in result could arise, in particular, in mutually exclusive projects), in principle the NPV method should be preferred in line with market practice, unless there is significant uncertainty as to the appropriate discount rate.

161 For instance, in the case of liquidation of a company, a valuation based on liquidation value or on asset value could be the most appropriate assessment methods.

162 See, for instance, Judgment of the Court of Justice of 29 April 1999, *Spain v Commission*, C-342/96, ECLI-:EU:C:1999:210, paragraph 46, and Judgment of the Court of Justice of 29 June 1999, *DMTransport*, C-256/97, ECLI:EU:C:1999:332, paragraph 24.

163 If the comparative method (benchmarking) is not appropriate and other generally accepted methods appear to fail to accurately establish the land value, an alternative method could be employed, such as the Vergleichspreissystem valuation method proposed by Germany (endorsed for agricultural and forestry land in Commission Decision on State aid SA.33167 Proposed alternative method to evaluate agriculture and forestry land in Germany when sold by public authorities (OJ C43, 15.2.2013, p 7)). On the limitations of other methods see Judgment of the Court of Justice of 16 December 2010, *Seydaland Vereinigte Agrarbetriebe*, C-239/09, ECLI:EU: C:2010:778, paragraph 52.

164 See Judgment of the Court of Justice of 3 April 2014, *ING Groep NV*, C-224/12 P, ECLI:EU:C:2014:213,

paragraphs 29 to 37. However the prior exposure should not be taken into account if it results from a measure which, on a global assessment of all aspects of that measure, could not have been undertaken by a private investor seeking a profit (Judgment of the Court of Justice of 24 October 2013, *Land Burgenland v Commission*, Joined Cases C-214/12 P, C-215/12 P and C-223/12 P, ECLI:EU:C:2013:682, paragraphs 52 to 61.

165 See, to that effect, Judgment of the General Court of 12 December 2000, *Alitalia v Commission*, T-296/97, ECLI:EU:T:2000:289, or Judgment of the Court of Justice of 24 January 2013, *Frucona v Commission*, C-73/11 P, ECLI:EU:C:2013:32, paragraphs 79 and 80.

166 Judgment of the Court of Justice of 28 January 2003, *Germany v Commission*, C-334/99, ECLI:EU:C:2003:55, paragraph 140.

167 Judgment of the General Court of 11 September 2012, *Corsica Ferries France SAS v Commission*, T-565/08, ECLI:EU:T:2012:415, paragraphs 79 to 84, upheld on appeal, see Judgment of the Court of Justice of 4 September 2014, *SNCM and France v Commission*, Joined Cases C-533/12 P and C-536/12 P, ECLI:EU:C:2014:2142, paragraphs 40 and 41. The Courts confirmed in this case that, in principle, it might be economically rational in the long term for private investors, in particular larger groups of companies, to pay complementary indemnities (for instance, to protect the brand image of a group). However, the necessity of paying such complementary indemnities should be demonstrated thoroughly in the concrete case in which the protection of the image is needed and it should also be demonstrated that such payments are an established practice amongst private companies in similar circumstances (mere examples are not sufficient).

168 For information on the assessment to be carried out concerning the possible grant of State aid in the form of a guarantee, see also the Commission Notice on the application of Articles 87 and 88 of the EC Treaty to State aid in the form of guarantees (OJ C155, 20.6.2008, p 10). That Notice is not replaced by this Notice.

169 See Judgment of the Court of Justice of 8 December 2011, *Residex Capital v Gemeente Rotterdam*, C-275/10, ECLI:EU:C:2011:814, paragraph 39.

170 See Judgment of the Court of Justice of 19 March 2015, *OTP Bank Nyrt v Magyar Állam and Others*, C-672/13, ECLI:EU:C:2015:185.

171 See Judgment of the Court of Justice of 8 December 2011, *Residex Capital v Gemeente Rotterdam*, C-275/10, ECLI:EU:C:2011:814, paragraph 42.

172 See Judgment of the Court of Justice of 3 April 2014, *France v Commission*, C-559/12 P, ECLI:EU:C:2014:217, paragraph 96.

173 See Judgment of the Court of Justice of 3 April 2014, *France v Commission*, C-559/12 P, ECLI:EU:C:2014:217, paragraph 98.

174 For instance, through RAROC (Risk Adjusted Return on Capital), which is what lenders and investors require for providing finance of similar benchmark risk and maturity to an undertaking active in the same sector.

175 See the Communication from the Commission on the revision of the method for setting the reference and discount rates (OJ C14, 19.1.2008, p 6). For subordinated loans, which are not covered in the Reference Rate Communication, the methodology set out in Commission Decision of 11 December 2008 on State aid N 55/2008, GA/EFRE Nachrangdarlehen, (OJ C9, 14.1.2009, p 1), can be used.

176 However, where Commission regulations or Commission decisions on aid schemes refer to the reference rate for the identification of the aid amount, the Commission will consider it as a fixed no-aid benchmark (safe-harbour).

177 Commission Notice on the application of Articles 87 and 88 of the EC Treaty to State aid in the form of guarantees (OJ C155, 20.6.2008, p 10).

178 Judgment of the Court of Justice of 19 September 2000, *Germany v Commission*, C-156/98, ECLI:EU:C:2000:467, paragraphs 26 and 27; Judgment of the Court of Justice of 28 July 2011, *Mediaset SpA v Commission*, C-403/10 P, ECLI:EU:C:2011:533, paragraphs 73 to 77; Judgment of the Court of Justice of 13 June 2002, *Netherlands v Commission*, C-382/99, ECLI:EU:C:2002:363, paragraphs 60 to 66; Judgment of the General Court of 4 March 2009, *Italy v Commission*, T-424/05, ECLI:EU:T:2009:49, paragraphs 136 to 147. See also Article 107(2)(a) of the Treaty.

179 In case an intermediary undertaking is a mere vehicle for transferring the advantage to the beneficiary and it does not retain any advantage, it should not normally be considered as a recipient of State aid.

180 Judgment of the Court of Justice of 19 September 2000, *Germany v Commission*, C-156/98, ECLI:EU:C:2000:467, paragraphs 26 and 27; Judgment of the Court of Justice of 28 July 2011, *Mediaset SpA v Commission*, C-403/10 P, ECLI:EU:C:2011:533, paragraph 81.

181 By contrast, a mere secondary economic effect in the form of increased output (which does not amount to indirect aid) can be found where the aid is simply channelled through an undertaking (for example a financial intermediary) which passes it on in full to the aid beneficiary.

5. SELECTIVITY

5.1. GENERAL PRINCIPLES

[5.206]

117. To fall within the scope of Article 107(1) of the Treaty, a State measure must favour 'certain undertakings or the production of certain goods'. Hence, not all measures which favour economic operators fall under the notion of aid, but only those which grant an advantage in a selective way to certain undertakings or categories of undertakings or to certain economic sectors.

118. Measures of purely general application which do not favour certain undertakings only or the production of certain goods only do not fall within the scope of Article 107(1) of the Treaty. However, the case-law has made it clear that even interventions which, at first appearance, apply to undertakings in general may be selective to a certain extent and, accordingly, be regarded as measures designed to favour certain undertakings or the production of certain goods.[182] Neither a large number of eligible undertakings (which can even include all undertakings of a given sector), nor the diversity and size of the sectors to which they belong, provide grounds for concluding that a State measure constitutes a general measure of economic policy, if not all economic sectors can benefit from it.[183] The fact that the

aid is not aimed at one or more specific recipients defined in advance, but that it is subject to a series of objective criteria according to which it may be granted, within the framework of a predetermined overall budget allocation, to an indefinite number of beneficiaries who are not initially individually identified, is insufficient to call into question the selective nature of the measure.[184]

119. To clarify the notion of selectivity under State aid law, it is useful to distinguish between material and regional selectivity. Moreover, it is useful to provide further guidance on certain issues specific to tax (or similar) measures.

5.2. MATERIAL SELECTIVITY

120. The material selectivity of a measure implies that the measure applies only to certain (groups of) undertakings or certain sectors of the economy in a given Member State. Material selectivity can be established *de jure* or *de facto*.

5.2.1. DE JURE AND DE FACTO SELECTIVITY

121. De jure selectivity results directly from the legal criteria for granting a measure that is formally reserved for certain undertakings only (for instance: those having a certain size, active in certain sectors or having a certain legal form;[185] companies incorporated or newly listed on a regulated market during a particular period;[186] companies belonging to a group having certain characteristics or entrusted with certain functions within a group;[187] ailing companies;[188] or export undertakings or undertakings performing export-related activities).[189] *De facto* selectivity can be established in cases where, although the formal criteria for the application of the measure are formulated in general and objective terms, the structure of the measure is such that its effects significantly favour a particular group of undertakings (as in the examples in the preceding sentence).[190]

122. *De facto* selectivity may be the result of conditions or barriers imposed by Member States preventing certain undertakings from benefiting from the measure. For example, applying a tax measure (for example a tax credit) only to investments exceeding a certain threshold (other than a minor threshold for reasons of administrative expediency) may mean that the measure is de facto reserved for undertakings with significant financial resources.[191] A measure granting certain advantages for a brief period only may also be de facto selective.[192]

5.2.2. SELECTIVITY STEMMING FROM DISCRETIONARY ADMINISTRATIVE PRACTICES

123. General measures which *prima facie* apply to all undertakings but are limited by the discretionary power of the public administration are selective.[193] This is the case where meeting the given criteria does not automatically result in an entitlement to the measure.

124. Public administrations have discretionary power in applying a measure, in particular, where the criteria for granting the aid are formulated in a very general or vague manner that necessarily involves a margin of discretion in the assessment. One example would be that the tax administration can vary the conditions for granting a tax concession according to the characteristics of the investment project submitted to it for assessment. Similarly, if the tax administration has broad discretion to determine the beneficiaries or the conditions under which a tax advantage is granted on the basis of criteria unrelated to the tax system, such as maintaining employment, the exercise of that discretion must then be regarded as favouring 'certain undertakings or the production of certain goods'.[194]

125. The fact that a tax relief requires prior administrative authorisation does not automatically mean that it constitutes a selective measure. This is not the case where a prior administrative authorisation is based on objective, non-discriminatory criteria which are known in advance, thus circumscribing the exercise of the public administrations' discretion. Such a prior administrative authorisation scheme must also be based on a procedural system which is easily accessible and capable of ensuring that a request for authorisation will be dealt with objectively and impartially within a reasonable time and refusals to grant authorisation must also be capable of being challenged in judicial or quasi-judicial proceedings.[195]

5.2.3. THE ASSESSMENT OF MATERIAL SELECTIVITY FOR MEASURES MITIGATING THE NORMAL CHARGES OF UNDERTAKINGS

126. When Member States adopt ad hoc positive measures benefiting one or more identified undertakings (for instance, granting money or assets to certain undertakings), it is normally easy to conclude that such measures have a selective character, as they reserve favourable treatment for one or a few undertakings.[196]

127. The situation is usually less clear when Member States adopt broader measures applicable to all undertakings fulfilling certain criteria, which mitigate the charges that those undertakings would normally have to bear (for instance, tax or social security exemptions for undertakings fulfilling certain criteria).

128. In such cases, the selectivity of the measures should normally be assessed by means of a three-step analysis. First, the system of reference must be identified. Second, it should be determined whether a given measure constitutes a derogation from that system insofar as it differentiates between economic operators who, in light of the objectives intrinsic to the system, are in a comparable factual and legal situation. Assessing whether a derogation exists is the key element of this part of the test and allows a conclusion to be drawn as to whether the measure is *prima facie* selective. If the measure in question does not constitute a derogation from the reference system, it is not selective. However, if it does (and therefore is *prima facie* selective), it needs to be established, in the third step of the test, whether the derogation is justified by the nature or the general scheme of the (reference) system.[197] If a *prima facie* selective measure is justified by the nature or the general scheme of the system, it will not be considered selective and will thus fall outside the scope of Article 107(1) of the Treaty.[198]

129. However, the three-step analysis cannot be applied in certain cases, taking into account the practical effects of the measures concerned. It must be emphasised that Article 107(1) of the Treaty does not distinguish between measures of State intervention in terms of their causes or aims, but defines them in relation to their effects, independently of the techniques used.[199] This means that in certain exceptional cases it is not sufficient to examine whether a given measure derogates from the rules of the reference system as defined by the Member State concerned.

It is also necessary to evaluate whether the boundaries of the system of reference have been designed in a consistent manner or, conversely, in a clearly arbitrary or biased way, so as to favour certain undertakings which are in a comparable situation with regard to the underlying logic of the system in question.

130. Thus, in Joined Cases C-106/09 P and C-107/09 P[200] concerning the Gibraltar tax reform, the Court of Justice found that the reference system as defined by the Member State concerned, although founded on criteria that were of a general nature, discriminated in practice between companies which were in a comparable situation with regard to the objective of the tax reform, resulting in a selective advantage being conferred on offshore companies.[201] In this respect, the Court found that the fact that offshore companies were not taxed was not a random consequence of the regime, but the inevitable consequence of the fact that the bases of assessment were specifically designed so that offshore companies had no tax base.[202]

131. Similar verification may also be necessary in certain cases concerning special-purpose levies, where there are elements indicating that the boundaries of the levy have been designed in a clearly arbitrary or biased way, so as to favour certain products or certain activities which are in a comparable situation with regard to the underlying logic of the levies in question. For instance, in *Ferring*,[203] the Court of Justice considered that a levy imposed on the direct sale of medicinal products by pharmaceutical laboratories but not on the sale by wholesalers was selective. In the light of the particular factual circumstances — such as the clear objective of the measure and its effects — the Court did not simply examine whether the measure in question would lead to a derogation from the reference system constituted by the levy. It also compared the situations of the pharmaceutical laboratories (subject to the levy) and of the wholesalers (excluded), concluding that the non-imposition of the tax on the direct sales by the wholesalers equated to granting them a *prima facie* selective tax exemption.[204]

5.2.3.1.
Identification of the reference system

132. The reference system constitutes the benchmark against which the selectivity of a measure is assessed.

133. The reference system is composed of a consistent set of rules that generally apply — on the basis of objective criteria — to all undertakings falling within its scope as defined by its objective. Typically, those rules define not only the scope of the system, but also the conditions under which the system applies, the rights and obligations of undertakings subject to it and the technicalities of the functioning of the system.

134. In the case of taxes, the reference system is based on such elements as the tax base, the taxable persons, the taxable event and the tax rates. For example, a reference system could be identified with regard to the corporate income tax system,[205] the VAT system,[206] or the general system of taxation of insurance.[207] The same applies to special-purpose (stand-alone) levies, such as levies on certain products or activities having a negative impact on the environment or health, which do not really form part of a wider taxation system. As a result, and subject to special cases illustrated in paragraphs 129 to 131 above, the reference system is, in principle, the levy itself.[208]

5.2.3.2.
Derogation from the system of reference

135. Once the reference system has been established, the next step of the analysis consists in examining whether a given measure differentiates between undertakings in derogation from that system. To do this, it is necessary to determine whether the measure is liable to favour certain undertakings or the production of certain goods as compared with other undertakings which are in a similar factual and legal situation, in the light of the intrinsic objective of the system of reference.[209] External policy objectives — such as regional, environmental or industrial policy objectives — cannot be relied upon by the Member State to justify the differentiated treatment of undertakings.[210]

136. The structure of certain special-purpose levies (and in particular their tax bases), such as environmental and health taxes imposed to discourage certain activities or products that have an adverse effect on the environment or human health, will normally integrate the policy objectives pursued. In such cases, a differentiated treatment for activities or products whose situation is different from the situation of those activities or products which are subject to the tax as regards the intrinsic objective pursued, does not constitute a derogation.[211]

137. If a measure favours certain undertakings or the production of certain goods which are in a comparable legal and factual situation, the measure is *prima facie* selective.

5.2.3.3.
Justification by the nature or general scheme of the system of reference

138. A measure which derogates from the reference system (*prima facie selectivity*) is non-selective if it is justified by the nature or general scheme of that system. This is the case where a measure derives directly from the intrinsic basic or guiding principles of the reference system or where it is the result of inherent mechanisms necessary for the functioning and effectiveness of the system.[212] In contrast, it is not possible to rely on external policy objectives which are not inherent to the system.[213]

139. The basis for a possible justification could, for instance, be the need to fight fraud or tax evasion, the need to take into account specific accounting requirements, administrative manageability, the principle of tax neutrality[214], the progressive nature of income tax and its redistributive purpose, the need to avoid double taxation,[215] or the objective of optimising the recovery of fiscal debts.

140. Member States should, however, introduce and apply appropriate control and monitoring procedures to ensure that derogations are consistent with the logic and general scheme of the tax system.[216] For derogations to be justified by the nature or general scheme of the system, it is also necessary to ensure that those measures are proportionate and do not go beyond what is necessary to achieve the legitimate objective being pursued, in that the objective could not be attained by less far-reaching measures.[217]

141. A Member State which introduces a differentiation between undertakings needs to be able to show that this differentiation is actually justified by the nature and general scheme of the system in question.[218]

5.3. REGIONAL SELECTIVITY

142. In principle, only measures that apply within the entire territory of the Member State escape the regional selectivity criterion laid down in Article 107(1) of the Treaty. However, as outlined below, the reference system does not necessarily have to be defined as the entire Member State.[219] It follows that not all measures that apply only to certain parts of the territory of a Member State are automatically selective.

143. As established by the case-law,[220] measures with a regional or local scope of application may not be selective if certain requirements are fulfilled. This case-law has so far only dealt with tax measures. However, as regional selectivity is a general concept, the principles set out by the Union Courts as regards tax measures apply to other types of measures as well.

144. In order to assess regional selectivity, three scenarios must be distinguished:[221]

(1) In the first scenario, which results in the regional selectivity of a measure, the central government of a Member State unilaterally decides to apply a lower level of taxation within a defined geographical area.

(2) The second scenario corresponds to symmetrical devolution of tax powers[222] — a model of distribution of tax competences in which all infra-State authorities at a particular level (regions, districts or others) of a Member State have the same autonomous power in law to decide the applicable tax rate within their territory of competence, independently of the central government. In this case, the measures decided by the infra-State authorities are not selective as it is impossible to determine a normal tax rate capable of constituting the reference framework.

(3) In the third scenario — the asymmetrical devolution of tax powers[223] — only certain regional or local authorities can adopt tax measures applicable within their territory. In this case, the assessment of the selective nature of the measure at stake depends on whether the authority concerned is sufficiently autonomous from the central government of the Member State.[224] This is the case when three cumulative criteria of autonomy are fulfilled: institutional, procedural and economic and financial autonomy.[225] If all of these criteria of autonomy are present when a regional or local authority decides to adopt a tax measure applicable only within its territory, then the region in question, not the Member State, constitutes the geographical reference framework.

5.3.1. INSTITUTIONAL AUTONOMY

145. The existence of institutional autonomy can be established where the tax measure decision has been taken by a regional or local authority with its own constitutional, political and administrative status that is separate from that of the central government. In the *Azores* case, the Court observed that the Portuguese Constitution recognised the Azores as an autonomous region with its own political and administrative status and self- governing institutions, which also have their own fiscal competence, and the power to adapt national fiscal provisions to particular regional features.[226]

146. The assessment of whether this criterion has been fulfilled in each individual case should include, in particular, examination of the constitution and other relevant laws of a given Member State so as to verify whether a given region indeed has its own separate political and administrative status and whether it has its own self- governing institutions which have the power to exercise their own fiscal competence.

5.3.2. PROCEDURAL AUTONOMY

147. The existence of procedural autonomy can be established where a tax measure decision has been adopted without the central government being able to directly intervene in determining its content.

148. The essential criterion for determining whether procedural autonomy exists is not the extent of the competence that the infra-State body is recognised as having, but the capability of that body, in view of its competence, to adopt a decision on a tax measure independently, that is to say without the central government being able to intervene directly as regards its content.

149. The fact that a consultation or conciliation procedure exists between the central and regional (or local) authorities to avoid conflicts does not automatically mean that an infra-State body does not have procedural autonomy, provided that that body, and not the central government, has the final word on the adoption of the measure at stake.[227]

150. The mere fact that the acts which an infra-State body adopts are subject to judicial review does not in itself mean that that body lacks procedural autonomy, since the existence of such review is an inherent feature of the rule of law.[228]

151. A regional (or local) tax measure does not have to be completely separate from a more general tax system for it not to constitute State aid. In particular, it is not necessary that the tax system in question (bases of assessment, tax rates, tax recovery rules and exemptions) is fully devolved to the infra-State body.[229] For example, corporate tax devolution limited to the power to vary rates within a limited range, without devolving the power to change the bases of assessment (tax allowances and exemptions, etc.), could be considered as fulfilling the procedural autonomy condition if the pre-defined rate bracket allows the region concerned to exercise meaningful autonomous powers of taxation, without the central government being able to directly intervene as regards content.

5.3.3. ECONOMIC AND FINANCIAL AUTONOMY

152. The existence of economic and financial autonomy can be established where an infra-State body assumes responsibility for the political and financial consequences of a tax reduction measure. This cannot be the case if the infra-State body is not responsible for managing a budget, that is to say when it does not have control of both revenue and expenditure.

153. Therefore, in establishing the existence of economic and financial autonomy, the financial consequences of the tax measure in the region must not be offset by aid or subsidies from other regions or the central government. Hence, the existence of a direct causal link between the tax measure adopted by the infra-State body and the financial support from other regions or the central government of the Member State concerned rules out the existence of such autonomy.[230]

154. The existence of economic and financial autonomy is not undermined by the fact that a shortfall in tax revenues as a result of the implementation of devolved tax powers (for example a lower tax rate) is offset by a parallel increase in the same revenues due to the arrival of new businesses attracted by the lower rates.

155. The autonomy criteria do not require the rules governing tax collection to be devolved to the regional or local authorities, nor do they require the tax revenues to actually be collected by those authorities. The central government may continue to be responsible for collecting devolved taxes if the collection costs are borne by the infra-State authority.

5.4. SPECIFIC ISSUES CONCERNING TAX MEASURES

156. Member States are free to decide on the economic policy which they consider most appropriate and, in particular, to spread the tax burden as they see fit across the various factors of production. Nonetheless, Member States must exercise this competence in accordance with Union law.[231]

5.4.1. COOPERATIVE SOCIETIES

157. In principle, genuine cooperative societies conform to operating principles which distinguish them from other economic operators.[232] In particular, they are subject to specific membership requirements and their activities are conducted for the mutual benefit of their members,[233] not in the interest of outside investors. In addition, reserves and assets are non-distributable and must be dedicated to the common interest of the members. Finally, cooperatives generally have limited access to equity markets and generate low profit margins.

158. In the light of these particular features, cooperatives can be regarded as not being in a comparable factual and legal situation to that of commercial companies, so that preferential tax treatment for cooperatives may fall outside the scope of the State aid rules provided that:[234]

— they act in the economic interest of their members;
— their relations with members are not purely commercial, but personal and individual;
— the members are actively involved in the running of the business;
— they are entitled to equitable distribution of the results of economic performance.

159. If, however, the cooperative society under examination is found to be comparable to commercial companies, it should be included in the same reference framework as commercial companies and undergo the three-step analysis as set out in paragraphs 128 to 141. The third step of that analysis requires an analysis of whether the tax regime in question is justified by the logic of the tax system.[235]

160. For this purpose, it should be noted that the measure needs to be in line with the basic or guiding principles of the Member State's tax system (by reference to the mechanisms inherent to that system). A derogation for cooperative societies in the sense that they are not taxed themselves as cooperatives can, for example, be justified by the fact that they distribute all their profits to their members and that tax is then levied on those individual members. In any event, the reduced taxation must be proportionate and not go beyond what is necessary. Moreover, appropriate control and monitoring procedures must be applied by the Member State concerned.[236]

5.4.2. UNDERTAKINGS FOR COLLECTIVE INVESTMENT[237]

161. It is generally accepted that investment vehicles, such as undertakings for collective investment,[238] should be subject to an appropriate level of taxation since they basically operate as intermediary bodies between (third party) investors and the target companies that are the subject of investment. The absence of special tax rules governing investment funds or companies could result in an investment fund being treated as a separate taxpayer — with an additional layer of tax being imposed on any income or gains by the intermediary vehicle. In this context, Member States generally seek to reduce adverse taxation effects on investments through investment funds or companies compared to direct investments by individual investors and, as far as possible, to ensure that the overall final tax burden on the basket of various types of investments is about the same, irrespective of the vehicle used for the investment.

162. Tax measures aimed at ensuring tax neutrality for investments in collective investment funds or companies should not be viewed as selective where those measures do not have the effect of favouring certain undertakings for collective investment or certain types of investments,[239] but rather of reducing or eliminating double economic taxation in accordance with the overall principles inherent to the tax system in question. For the purpose of this section, tax neutrality means that taxpayers are treated the same whether they invest in assets, such as government securities and the shares of joint-stock companies, directly or indirectly through investment funds. Accordingly, a tax regime for undertakings for collective investment respecting the purpose of fiscal transparency at the level of the intermediary vehicle may be justified by the logic of the tax system in question, provided that the prevention of double economic taxation constitutes a principle inherent to the tax system in question. By contrast, preferential tax treatment limited to well-defined investment vehicles which fulfil specific conditions[240] to the detriment of other investment vehicles that are in a comparable legal and factual situation should be viewed as selective,[241] for instance, where tax rules would provide for a favourable treatment of national venture, social impact or long-term investment funds and omit EU- harmonised EuVECA,[242] EuSEF[243] or ELTIF[244] funds.

163. However, tax neutrality does not mean that such investment vehicles should be entirely exempt from any tax or that the fund managers should be exempt from tax on the fees charged by them for managing the underlying assets being invested into by the funds.[245] Nor does it justify a more beneficial tax treatment of a collective investment than of an individual investment for the tax regimes in question.[246] In such cases, the tax regime would be disproportionate and would go beyond what is necessary to achieve the objective of preventing double taxation and would therefore constitute a selective measure.

5.4.3. Tax amnesties

164. Tax amnesties commonly involve immunity from criminal penalties, fines and (some or all) interest payments. While certain amnesties require payment in full of tax amounts due,[247] others entail a partial waiver of the amount of tax due.[248]

165. In general, a tax amnesty measure that applies to undertakings can be considered a general measure if the conditions below are met.[249]

166. First, the measure is effectively open to any undertaking of any sector or size that has outstanding tax liabilities due at the date set by the measure, without favouring any pre-defined group of undertakings. Second, it does not entail any *de facto* selectivity in favour of certain undertakings or sectors. Third, the tax administration's action is limited to administering the implementation of the tax amnesty without any discretionary power to intervene in the granting or intensity of the measure. Finally, the measure does not entail a waiver from verification.

167. The limited temporal application of tax amnesties, which apply only for a short period[250] to tax liabilities which were due before a pre-defined date and which are still due at the time of the introduction of the tax amnesty, is inherent to the concept of a tax amnesty that aims to improve both the collection of taxes and taxpayers' compliance.

168. Tax amnesty measures may also be considered as general measures if they follow the national legislature's objective of ensuring compliance with a general principle of law, such as the principle that a judgment must be given within a reasonable period of time.[251]

5.4.4. Tax rulings and settlements

5.4.4.1. Administrative tax rulings

169. The function of a tax ruling is to establish in advance the application of the ordinary tax system to a particular case in view of its specific facts and circumstances. For reasons of legal certainty, many national tax authorities provide prior administrative rulings on how specific transactions will be treated fiscally.[252] This may be done to establish in advance how the provisions of a bilateral tax treaty or national fiscal provisions will be applied to a particular case or how 'arm's-length profits' will be set for related party transactions where uncertainty justifies an advance ruling to ascertain whether certain intra-group transactions are priced at arm's length.[253] Member States can provide their taxpayers with legal certainty and predictability on the application of general tax rules, which is best ensured if its administrative ruling practice is transparent and the rulings are published.

170. The grant of a tax ruling must, however, respect the State aid rules. Where a tax ruling endorses a result that does not reflect in a reliable manner what would result from a normal application of the ordinary tax system, that ruling may confer a selective advantage upon the addressee, in so far as that selective treatment results in a lowering of that addressee's tax liability in the Member State as compared to companies in a similar factual and legal situation.

171. The Court of Justice has held that a reduction in the taxable base of an undertaking that results from a tax measure that enables a taxpayer to employ transfer prices in intra-group transactions that do not resemble prices which would be charged in conditions of free competition between independent undertakings negotiating under comparable circumstances at arm's length confers a selective advantage on that taxpayer, by virtue of the fact that its tax liability under the ordinary tax system is reduced as compared to independent companies which rely on their actually recorded profit to determine their taxable base.[254] Accordingly, a tax ruling which endorses a transfer pricing methodology for determining a corporate group entity's taxable profit that does not result in a reliable approximation of a market-based outcome in line with the arm's length principle confers a selective advantage upon its recipient. The search for a 'reliable approximation of a market- based outcome' means that any deviation from the best estimate of a market-based outcome must be limited and proportionate to the uncertainty inherent in the transfer pricing method chosen or the statistical tools employed for that approximation exercise.

172. This arm's length principle necessarily forms part of the Commission's assessment of tax measures granted to group companies under Article 107(1) of the Treaty, independently of whether a Member State has incorporated this principle into its national legal system and in what form. It is used to establish whether the taxable profit of a group company for corporate income tax purposes has been determined on the basis of a methodology that produces a reliable approximation of a market-based outcome. A tax ruling endorsing such a methodology ensures that that company is not treated favourably under the ordinary rules of corporate taxation of profits in the Member State concerned as compared to standalone companies who are taxed on their accounting profit, which reflects prices determined on the market negotiated at arm's length. The arm's length principle the Commission applies in assessing transfer pricing rulings under the State aid rules is therefore an application of Article 107(1) of the Treaty, which prohibits unequal treatment in taxation of undertakings in a similar factual and legal situation. This principle binds the Member States and the national tax rules are not excluded from its scope.[255]

173. When examining whether a transfer pricing ruling complies with the arm's length principle inherent in Article 107(1) of the Treaty, the Commission may have regard to the guidance provided by the Organisation for Economic Cooperation and Development ('OECD'), in particular the 'OECD Transfer Pricing Guidelines for Multinational Enterprises and Tax Administrations'. Those guidelines do not deal with matters of State aid per se, but they capture the international consensus on transfer pricing and provide useful guidance to tax administrations and multinational enterprises on how to ensure that a transfer pricing methodology produces an outcome in line with market conditions. Consequently, if a transfer pricing arrangement complies with the guidance provided by the OECD Transfer Pricing Guidelines, including the guidance on the choice of the most appropriate method and leading to a reliable approximation of a market based outcome, a tax ruling endorsing that arrangement is unlikely to give rise to State aid.

174. In sum, tax rulings confer a selective advantage on their addressees in particular where:

(a) the ruling misapplies national tax law and this results in a lower amount of tax;[256]
(b) the ruling is not available to undertakings in a similar legal and factual situation;[257] or

(c) the administration applies a more 'favourable' tax treatment compared with other taxpayers in a similar factual and legal situation. This could, for instance, be the case where the tax authority accepts a transfer pricing arrangement which is not at arm's length because the methodology endorsed by that ruling produces an outcome that departs from a reliable approximation of a market-based outcome.[258] The same applies if the ruling allows its addressee to use alternative, more indirect methods for calculating taxable profits, for example the use of fixed margins for a cost-plus or resale-minus method for determining an appropriate transfer pricing, while more direct ones are available.[259]

5.4.4.2. Tax settlements

175. Tax settlements generally occur in the context of disputes between a taxpayer and the tax authorities concerning the amount of tax owed. They constitute a common practice in a number of Member States. The conclusion of such tax settlements allows tax authorities to avoid long-standing legal disputes before national jurisdictions and to ensure quick recovery of the tax due. While the competence of Member States in this field is not in dispute, State aid may be involved in the conclusion of a tax settlement, in particular where it appears that the amount of tax due has been reduced without clear justification (such as optimising the recovery of debt) or in a disproportionate manner to the benefit of the taxpayer.[260]

176. In this context, a transaction between the tax administration and a taxpayer may in particular entail a selective advantage where:[261]

(a) in making disproportionate concessions to a taxpayer, the administration applies a more 'favourable' discretionary tax treatment compared to other taxpayers in a similar factual and legal situation;

(b) the settlement is contrary to the applicable tax provisions and has resulted in a lower amount of tax, outside a reasonable range. This might be the case, for example, where established facts should have led to a different assessment of the tax on the basis of the applicable provisions (but the amount of tax due has been unlawfully reduced).

5.4.5. Depreciation/amortisation rules

177. In general, tax measures of a purely technical nature such as depreciation/amortisation rules do not constitute State aid. The method of calculating asset depreciation varies from one Member State to another, but such methods may be inherent to the tax systems to which they belong.

178. The difficulty in assessing possible selectivity with regard to the depreciation rate of certain assets lies in the requirement to establish a benchmark (from which a specific rate or depreciation method would possibly derogate). While in accounting terms, the purpose of this exercise is generally to reflect the economic depreciation of the assets with the aim of presenting a fair view of the financial situation of the company, the fiscal process follows different purposes such as allowing companies to spread deductible expenses over time.

179. Depreciation incentives (such as a shorter term of depreciation, a more favourable depreciation method,[262] early depreciation, etc.) for certain types of assets or undertakings, which are not based on the guiding principles of the depreciation rules in question, may give rise to the existence of State aid. In contrast, accelerated and early depreciation rules for leased assets may be seen as general measures if the lease contracts in question are really accessible to companies of all sectors and sizes.[263]

180. If the tax authority has discretionary power to set different depreciation periods or different valuation methods, firm by firm or sector by sector, there is obviously a presumption of selectivity. Likewise, prior authorisation from a tax administration as a condition for applying a depreciation scheme involves selectivity if the authorisation is not limited to the prior verification of the legal requirements.[264]

5.4.6. Fixed basis tax regime for specific activities

181. Specific provisions that do not contain discretionary elements, allowing, for example, income tax to be determined on a fixed basis, may be justified by the nature and general scheme of the system where, for instance, they take account of specific accounting requirements or of the importance of land in assets which are specific to certain sectors.

182. Such provisions are therefore not selective, if the following conditions are fulfilled:

(a) the fixed basis regime is justified by the concern to avoid disproportionate administrative burden on certain types of undertakings because of their small size or sector of activity (for example in the agriculture or fisheries sectors);

(b) on average, the fixed basis regime does not have the effect of implying a lower tax burden for those undertakings as compared to other undertakings excluded from its scope and does not entail advantages for a sub-category of beneficiaries of the regime.

5.4.7. Anti-abuse rules

183. The provision of anti-abuse rules may be justified as measures to prevent tax avoidance by taxpayers.[265] However, such rules might be selective if they provide for a derogation (non-application of the anti-abuse rules) to specific undertakings or transactions, which would not be consistent with the logic underlying the anti- abuse rules in question.[266]

5.4.8. Excise duties

184. Although excise duties are largely harmonised at Union level (which may affect the imputability criterion),[267] this does not automatically imply that any duty relief in these areas would fall outside the scope of the State aid rules. In fact, a reduced excise duty can grant a selective advantage to the undertakings which use the product in question as an input or sell it on the market.[268]

NOTES

182 Judgment of the Court of Justice of 29 June 1999, *DMTransport*, C-256/97, ECLI:EU:C:1999:332, paragraph 27; Judgment of the General Court of 6 March 2002, *Territorio Histórico de Álava — Diputación Foral de Álava et aL. v Commission*, Joined Cases T-127/99, T-129/99 and T-148/99, ECLI:EU:T:2002:59, paragraph 149.

183 See, for instance, Judgment of the Court of Justice of 17 June 1999, *Belgium v Commission*, C-75/97, ECLI-:EU:C:1999:311, paragraph 32; Judgment of the Court of Justice of 8 November 2001, *Adria-Wien Pipeline*, C-143/99, ECLI:EU:C:2001:598, paragraph 48.

184 Judgment of the General Court of 29 September 2000, *Confederación Espanola de Transporte de Mercancías v Commission*, T-55/99, ECLI: EU:T:2000:223, paragraph 40. See also Judgment of the General Court of 13 September 2012, *Italy v Commission*, T-379/09, ECLI:EU: T:2012:422, paragraph 47. The measure in question in that case was a partial exemption from excise duty on the diesel used for the heating of greenhouses. The General Court indicated that the fact that the exemption could benefit all undertakings choosing greenhouse production was not sufficient to establish the general character of the measure.

185 Judgment of the Court of Justice of 8 September 2011, *Paint Graphos and others*, Joined Cases C-78/08 to C-80/08, ECLI:EU:C:2011:550, paragraph 52.

186 Judgment of the General Court of 4 September 2009, *Italy v Commission*, T-211/05, ECLI:EU:T:2009:304, paragraph 120, and Judgment of the Court of Justice of 24 November 2011, *Italy v Commission*, C-458/09 P, ECLI:EU:C:2011:769, paragraphs 59 and 60.

187 Judgment of the Court of Justice of 22 June 2006, *Belgium and Forum 187 v Commission*, Joined Cases C-182/03 and C-217/03, ECLI: EU:C:2006:416, paragraph 122.

188 Judgment of the General Court of 4 February 2016, *Heitkamp Bauholding v Commission*, T-287/11, ECLI-:EU:T:2016:60, paragraph 129 et seq.

189 Judgment of the Court of Justice of 10 December 1969, *Commission v France*, Joined Cases6 and 11/69, ECLI:EU:C:1969:68, paragraph 3; Judgment of the Court of Justice of 7 June 1988, *Greece v Commission*, 57/86, ECLI:EU:C:1988:284, paragraph 8; Judgment of the Court of Justice of 15 July 2004, *Spain v Commission*, C-501/00, ECLI:EU:C:2004:438, paragraph 92.

190 This was the case in the Judgment of the Court of Justice of 15 November 2011, *Commission and Spain v Government of Gibraltar and United Kingdom*, Joined Cases C-106/09 P and C-107/09 P, ECLI:EU:C:2011:732, concerning the Gibraltar tax reform, which de facto favoured offshore companies. See paragraphs 101 et seq. of that judgment. The reform introduced a system consisting of three taxes applicable to all Gibraltar companies, namely a payroll tax, a business property occupation tax (BPOT) and a registration fee. Liability for payroll tax and BPOT would have been capped at 15% of profits. The Court found that such a combination of taxes excluded from the outset any taxation of offshore companies as they had no taxable basis due to the lack of employees and lack of business property in Gibraltar.

191 See, for instance, Judgment of the General Court of 6 March 2002, *Ramondin SA and Ramondín Cápsulas SA v Commission*, Joined Cases T-92/00 and T-103/00, ECLI:EU:T:2002:61, paragraph 39.

192 Judgment of the General Court of 12 September 2007, *Italy and Brandt Italia v Commission*, Joined Cases T-239/04 and T-323/04, ECLI: EU:T:2007:260, paragraph 66; Judgment of the General Court of 4 September 2009, *Italy v Commission*, T-211/05, ECLI:EU: T:2009:304, paragraph 120; Judgment of the Court of Justice of 24 November 2011, *Italy v Commission*, C-458/09 P, ECLI:EU: C:2011:769, paragraphs 59 and 60.

193 See Judgment of the Court of Justice of 29 June 1999, *DMTransport*, C-256/97, ECLI:EU:C:1999:332, paragraph 27.

194 See Judgment of the Court of Justice of 18 July 2013, *P Oy*, C-6/12, ECLI:EU:C:2013:525, paragraph 27.

195 See Judgment of the Court of Justice of 12 July 2001, *Smits and Peerbooms*, C-157/99, ECLI:EU:C:2001:404, paragraph 90; Judgment of the Court of Justice of 3 June 2010, *Sporting Exchange Ltd, trading 'Betfair' v Minister van Justitie*, C-203/08, ECLI:EU:C:2010:307, paragraph 50.

196 See Judgment of the Court of Justice of 4 June 2015, *Commission v MOL*, C-15/14 P, ECLI:EU:C:2015:362, paragraphs 60 et seq.; Opinion of Advocate General Mengozzi of 27 June 2013, *Deutsche Lufthansa*, C-284/12, ECLI:EU:C:2013:442, paragraph 52.

197 See, for instance, Judgment of the Court of Justice of 8 September 2011, *Commission v Netherlands*, C-279/08 P, ECLI:EU:C:2011:551, paragraph 62; Judgment of the Court of Justice of 8 November 2001, *Adria-Wien Pipeline*, C-143/99, ECLI:EU:C:2001:598.

198 See, for instance, Judgment of the Court of Justice of 8 September 2011, *Paint Graphos and others*, Joined Cases C-78/08 to C-80/08, ECLI:EU:C:2011:550, paragraph 49 et seq.; Judgment of the Court of Justice of 29 April 2004, *GIL Insurance*, C-308/01, ECLI:EU: C:2004:252.

199 See Judgment of the Court of Justice of 22 December 2008, *British Aggregates v Commission*, C-487/06 P, ECLI:EU:C:2008:757, paragraphs 85 and 89 and the case-law cited; Judgment of the Court of Justice of 8 September 2011, *Commission v Netherlands*, C-279/08 P, ECLI:EU:C:2011:551, paragraphs 51; Judgment of the Court of Justice of 15 November 2011, *Commission and Spain v Government of Gibraltar and United Kingdom*, Joined Cases C-106/09 P and C-107/09 P, ECLI:EU:C:2011:732, paragraph 87.

200 Judgment of the Court of Justice of 15 November 2011, *Commission and Spain v Government of Gibraltar and United Kingdom*, Joined Cases C-106/09 P and C-107/09 P, ECLI:EU:C:2011:732.

201 Judgment of the Court of Justice of 15 November 2011, *Commission and Spain v Government of Gibraltar and United Kingdom*, Joined Cases C-106/09 P and C-107/09 P, ECLI:EU:C:2011:732, paragraphs 101 et seq.

202 Judgment of the Court of Justice of 15 November 2011, *Commission and Spain v Government of Gibraltar and United Kingdom*, Joined Cases C-106/09 P and C-107/09 P, ECLI:EU:C:2011:732, paragraph 106.

203 Judgment of the Court of Justice of 22 November 2001, *Ferring*, C-53/00, ECLI:EU:C:2001:627, paragraph 20.

204 Judgment of the Court of Justice of 22 November 2001, *Ferring*, C-53/00, ECLI:EU:C:2001:627, paragraphs 19 and 20.

205 See Judgment of the Court of Justice of 8 September 2011, *Paint Graphos and others*, Joined Cases C-78/08 to C-80/08, ECLI:EU: C:2011:550, paragraph 50. The Court sometimes applies in this context the term of 'the ordinary tax system' (see Judgment of the Court of Justice of 22 June 2006, *Belgium and Forum 187 v Commission*, Joined Cases C-182/03 and C-217/03, ECLI:EU:C:2006:416, paragraph 95) or 'the general tax scheme' (see

Judgment of the Court of Justice of 15 December 2005, *Italy v Commission*, C-66/02, ECLI:EU:C:2005:768, paragraph 100).

206 See the Court's reasoning concerning selectivity in Judgment of the Court of Justice of 3 March 2005, *Heiser*, C-172/03, ECLI:EU: C:2005:130, paragraphs 40 et seq.

207 See Judgment of the Court of Justice of 29 April 2004, *GIL Insurance*, C-308/01, ECLI:EU:C:2004:252, paragraphs 75 and 78.

208 See Judgment of the General Court of 7 March 2012, *British Aggregates Association v Commission*, T-210/02 RENV, ECLI:EU:T:2012:110, paragraphs 49 and 50. Even if a levy is introduced in the national legal system to transpose a Union directive, that levy remains the system of reference.

209 In its *Paint Graphos* judgment, the Court has indicated however that, in light of the peculiarities of cooperative societies which have to conform to particular operating principles, those undertakings cannot be regarded as being in a comparable factual and legal situation to that of commercial companies, provided that they act in the economic interest of their members and their relations with their members are not purely commercial but personal and individual, the members being actively involved in the running of the business and entitled to equitable distribution of the results of economic performance (See Judgment of the Court of Justice of 8 September 2011, *Paint Graphos and others*, Joined Cases C-78/08 to C-80/08, ECLI:EU:C:2011:550, paragraph 61).

210 Judgment of the Court of Justice of 18 July 2013, *P Oy*, C-6/12, ECLI:EU:C:2013:525, paragraph 27 et seq.

211 A levy introduced in the national legal system transposing an EU directive which provides within its scope for differentiated treatment for certain activities/products can indicate that such activities/products are in a different situation as regards the intrinsic objective pursued.

212 See for example Judgment of the Court of Justice of 8 September 2011, *Paint Graphos and others*, Joined Cases C-78/08 to C-80/08, ECLI: EU:C:2011:550, paragraph 69.

213 See Judgment of the Court of Justice of 8 September 2011, *Paint Graphos and others*, Joined Cases C-78/08 to C-80/08, ECLI:EU: C:2011:550, paragraphs 69 and 70; Judgment of the Court of Justice of 6 September 2006, *Portugal v Commission*, C-88/03, ECLI:EU: C:2006:511, paragraph 81; Judgment of the Court of Justice of 8 September 2011, *Commission v Netherlands*, C-279/08 P, ECLI:EU: C:2011:551; Judgment of the Court of Justice of 22 December 2008, *British Aggregates v Commission*, C-487/06 P, ECLI:EU:C:2008:757; Judgment of the Court of Justice of 18 July 2013, *P Oy*, C-6/12, ECLI:EU:C:2013:525, paragraphs 27 et seq.

214 For undertakings for collective investment; see section 5.4.2.

215 In Judgment of the Court of Justice of 8 September 2011, *Paint Graphos and others*, Joined Cases C-78/08 to C-80/08, ECLI:EU: C:2011:550, the Court referred to the possibility of relying on the nature or general scheme of the national tax system as a justification for the fact that cooperative societies which distribute all their profits to their members are not taxed themselves as cooperatives, provided that tax is levied on the individual members (paragraph 71).

216 Judgment of the Court of Justice of 8 September 2011, *Paint Graphos and others*, Joined Cases C-78/08 to C-80/08, ECLI:EU:C:2011:550, paragraph 74.

217 Judgment of the Court of Justice of 8 September 2011, *Paint Graphos and others*, Joined Cases C-78/08 to C-80/08, ECLI:EU:C:2011:550, paragraph 75.

218 See Judgment of the Court of Justice of 15 November 2011, *Commission and Spain v Government of Gibraltar and United Kingdom*, Joined Cases C-106/09 P and C-107/09 P, ECLI:EU:C:2011:732, paragraph 146; Judgment of the Court of Justice of 29 April 2004, *Netherlands v Commission*, C-159/01, ECLI:EU:C:2004:246, paragraph 43; Judgment of the Court of Justice of 6 September 2006, *Portugal v Commission*, C-88/03, ECLI:EU:C:2006:511.

219 Judgment of the Court of Justice of 6 September 2006, *Portugal v Commission*, C-88/03, ECLI:EU:C:2006:511, paragraph 57; Judgment of the Court of Justice of 11 September 2008, *Unión General de Trabajadores de La Rioja*, Joined Cases C-428/06 to C-434/06, ECLI:EU: C:2008:488, paragraph 47.

220 Judgment of the Court of Justice of 6 September 2006, *Portugal v Commission*, C-88/03, ECLI:EU:C:2006:511, paragraphs 57 et seq.; Judgment of the Court of Justice of 11 September 2008, *Unión General de Trabajadores de La Rioja*, Joined Cases C-428/06 to C-434/06, ECLI:EU:C:2008:488, paragraphs 47 et seq.

221 Judgment of the Court of Justice of 6 September 2006, *Portugal v Commission*, C-88/03, ECLI:EU:C:2006:511, paragraphs 63 to 66.

222 See Opinion of Advocate General Geelhoed of 20 October 2005, *Portugal v Commission*, C-88/03, ECLI-:EU:C:2005:618, paragraph 60.

223 Opinion of Advocate General Geelhoed of 20 October 2005, *Portugal v Commission*, C-88/03, ECLI-:EU:C:2005:618, paragraph 60.

224 Judgment of the Court of Justice of 6 September 2006, *Portugal v Commission*, C-88/03, ECLI:EU:C:2006:511, paragraph 58: '*It is possible that an infra-state body enjoys legal and factual status which makes it sufficiently autonomous in relation to the central government of a Member State, with the result that, by the measures it adopts, it is that body and not the central government which plays a fundamental role in the definition of the political and economic environment in which undertakings operate.*'

Judgment of the Court of Justice of 6 September 2006, *Portugal v Commission*, C-88/03, ECLI:EU:C:2006:511, paragraph 58: '*It is possible that an infra-state body enjoys legal and factual status which makes it sufficiently autonomous in relation to the central government of a Member State, with the result that, by the measures it adopts, it is that body and not the central government which plays a fundamental role in the definition of the political and economic environment in which undertakings operate.*'

225 Judgment of the Court of Justice of 6 September 2006, *Portugal v Commission*, C-88/03, ECLI:EU:C:2006:511, paragraph 67.

226 Judgment of the Court of Justice of 6 September 2006, *Portugal v Commission*, C-88/03, ECLI:EU:C:2006:511, paragraph 70.

227 Judgment of the Court of Justice of 11 September 2008, *Unión General de Trabajadores de La Rioja*, Joined Cases C-428/06 to C-434/06, ECLI:EU:C:2008:488, paragraphs 96 to 100.

228 Judgment of the Court of Justice of 11 September 2008, *Unión General de Trabajadores de La Rioja*, Joined Cases C-428/06 to C-434/06, ECLI:EU:C:2008:488, paragraphs 80 to 83.

229 Judgment of the Court of Justice of 6 September 2006, *Portugal v Commission*, C-88/03, ECLI:EU:C:2006:511.

230 Judgment of the Court of Justice of 11 September 2008, *Unión General de Trabajadores de La Rioja*, Joined Cases C-428/06 to C-434/06, ECLI:EU:C:2008:488, paragraphs 129 et seq.

231 In particular, Member States must not introduce or maintain legislation which entails incompatible State aid or discrimination that is contrary to the fundamental freedoms. See, for instance, Judgment of the Court of Justice of 17 September 2009, *Glaxo Wellcome*, C-182/08, ECLI:EU:C:2009:559, paragraph 34 and the case-law cited.

232 See preamble to Council Regulation (EC) No 1435/2003 of 22 July 2003 on the Statute for a European Cooperative Society.

233 Control of cooperatives is vested equally in its members, as reflected in the 'one person, one vote' rule.

234 See Judgment of the Court of Justice of 8 September 2011, *Paint Graphos and others*, Joined Cases C-78/08 to C-80/08, ECLI:EU: C:2011:550, paragraphs 55 and 61.

235 See Judgment of the Court of Justice of 8 September 2011, *Paint Graphos and others*, Joined Cases C-78/08 to C-80/08, ECLI:EU: C:2011:550, paragraphs 69 to 75.

236 See Judgment of the Court of Justice of 8 September 2011, *Paint Graphos and others*, Joined Cases C-78/08 to C-80/08, ECLI:EU: C:2011:550, paragraphs 74 and 75.

237 This section is not limited to undertakings for collective investment subject to Directive 2009/65/EC of the European Parliament and of the Council on the coordination of laws, regulations and administrative provisions relating to undertakings for collective investment in transferable securities (UCITS). It also covers other types of collective investment undertakings not covered by that Directive, such as — among others — Alternative Investment Funds as defined by Directive 2011/61/EU of the European Parliament and of the Council (OJ L174, 1.7.2011, p 1).

238 Such undertakings may be constituted under the law of contract (as common funds managed by management companies) or trust law (as unit trusts) or under statute (as investment companies). See Article 1(3) of the UCITS Directive.

239 See Judgment of the General Court of 4 March 2009, *Associazione italiana del risparmio gestito and Fineco Asset Management v Commission*, T-445/05, ECLI:EU:T:2009:50, paragraph 78 et seq. where the General Court upheld Commission Decision 2006/638/EC of 6 September 2005 (OJ L268, 27.9.2006, p 1), declaring as incompatible with the common market an aid scheme that provides certain undertakings with tax incentives for collective investment in transferable securities specialising in shares of small or medium-sized capitalisation companies which may be traded on the regulated European market.

240 For example, preferential tax treatment at the investment vehicle level being conditional upon the investment of three-quarters of the fund's assets in SMEs.

241 See Judgment of the General Court of 4 March 2009, *Associazione italiana del risparmio gestito and Fineco Asset Management v Commission*, T-445/05, ECLI:EU:T:2009:50, paragraph 150.

242 Regulation (EU) No 345/2013 of the European Parliament and of the Council of 17 April 2013 on European venture capital funds (OJ L115, 25.4.2013, p 1).

243 Regulation (EU) No 346/2013 of the European Parliament and of the Council of 17 April 2013 on European social entrepreneurship funds (OJ L115, 25.4.2013, p 18).

244 Regulation (EU) 2015/760 of the European Parliament and of the Council of 29 April 2015 on European long-term investment funds (OJ L123, 19.5.2015, p 98).

245 The logic of neutrality behind the special taxation of investment undertakings applies to the fund capital, but not to the management companies' own revenues and capital. See State aid Decision of the EFTA Surveillance Authority of 18 March 2009 with regard to the taxation of investment undertakings in Liechtenstein.

246 See Commission Decision of 12 May 2010, N 131/2009, Finland, Residential Real Estate Investment Trust (REIT) scheme (OJ C178, 3.7.2010, p 1), recital 33.

247 Tax amnesties may also provide the possibility to report undeclared assets or incomes.

248 See Judgment of the Court of Justice of 29 March 2012, *Ministero dell'Economia e delle Finanze*, C-417/10, ECLI:EU:C:2012:184, paragraph 12.

249 See Commission Decision of 11 July 2012 on the tax amnesty measure notified by Latvia, SA.33183 (OJ C1, 4.1.2013, p 6).

250 The period of application should be sufficient to allow all taxpayers to whom the measure applies to seek to benefit from it.

251 See Judgment of the Court of Justice of 29 March 2012, *Ministero dell'Economia e delle Finanze*, C-417/10, ECLI:EU:C:2012:184, paragraphs 40, 41 and 42.

252 Some Member States have adopted circulars regulating the scope and extent of their ruling practices. Some of them also publish their rulings.

253 See Commission Decision of 21 October 2015 in Case SA.38374, Starbucks, not yet published, Commission Decision of 21 October 2015 in Case SA.38375, Fiat, not yet published, Commission Decision of 11 January 2016 in Case SA.37667, excess profit exemption state aid scheme, not yet published, all cases are under appeal.

254 See Judgment of the Court of Justice of 22 June 2006, *Belgium and Forum 187 v Commission*, Joined Cases C-182/03 and C-217/03, ECLI:EU:C:2006:416. In that judgment on the Belgian tax regime for coordination centres, the Court of Justice assessed a challenge to a Commission decision (Commission Decision 2003/757/EC of 17 February 2003 on the aid scheme implemented by Belgium for coordination centres established in Belgium (OJ L282, 30.10.2003, p 25)) which concluded, inter alia, that the method for determining taxable income under that regime conferred a selective advantage on those centres. Under that regime, taxable profit was established at a flat-rate amount which represented a percentage of the full amount of operating costs and expenses, from which staff costs and financial charges were excluded. According to the Court, '*in order to decide whether a method of assessment of taxable income such as that laid down under the regime for coordination centres confers an advantage on them, it is necessary, [. . .], to compare that regime with the ordinary tax system, based on the difference between profit and outgoings of an undertaking carrying on its activities in conditions of free competition.*' The Court then held that 'the effect of the exclusion of [staff costs and the financial costs] from the expenditure which serves to determine the taxable income of the centres is that the transfer prices do not resemble those which would be charged in conditions of free competition', which the Court found to '[confer] an advantage on the coordination centres' (paragraphs 96 and 97).

255 See Judgment of the Court of Justice of 22 June 2006, *Belgium and Forum 187 v Commission*[Joined Cases C-182/03 and C-217/03, ECLI:EU:C:2006:416, paragraph 81. See also Judgment of the General Court of 25 March 2015, *Belgium v Commission*, T-538/11, ECLI: EU:T:2015:188, paragraphs 65 and 66 and the case-law cited.

256 See Commission Decision 2003/601/EC of 17 February 2003 on the Foreign Income aid scheme implemented by Ireland (OJ L204, 13.8.2003, p 51), recitals 33 to 35.

257 For example, this would be the case if some undertakings involved in transactions with controlled entities are not allowed to request such rulings, contrary to a pre-defined category of undertakings. See in this respect Commission Decision 2004/77/EC of 24 June 2003 on the tax ruling system for US foreign sales corporations (OJ L23, 28.1.2004, p 14), recitals 56 to 62.

258 See Commission Decision of 21 October 2015 in Case SA.38374, Starbucks, not yet published, Commission Decision of 21 October 2015 in Case SA.38375, *Fiat*, not yet published, Commission Decision of 11 January 2016 in Case SA.37667, excess profit exemption state aid scheme, not yet published, all cases are under appeal.

259 See Commission Decision 2003/438/EC of 16 October 2002 on State aid C50/2001, Luxembourg Finance Companies (OJ L153, 20.6.2003, p 40), recitals 43 and 44; Commission Decision 2003/501/EC of 16 October 2002 on State aid C49/2001, Luxembourg Coordination centres (OJ L170, 9.7.2003, p 20), recitals 46, 47 and 50; Commission Decision 2003/757/EC of 17 February 2003, Belgian Coordination centres (OJ L 282, 30.10.2003, p 25), recitals 89 to 95 and the related Judgment of the Court of Justice of 22 June 2006, *Belgium and Forum 187 v Commission*, Joined Cases C-182/03 and C-217/03, ECLI:EU:C:2006:416, paragraphs 96 and 97; Commission Decision 2004/76/EC of 13 May 2003, French Headquarters and Logistic Centres (OJ L23, 28.1.2004, p 1), recitals 50 and 53; Commission Decision of 21 October 2015 in Case SA.38374, *Starbucks*, not yet published, under appeal, recitals 282 to 285; Commission Decision of 21 October 2015 in Case SA.38375, Fiat, not yet published, under appeal, recital 245.

260 See Commission Decision 2011/276/EU of 26 May 2010 on State aid C-76/03, Umicore SA (OJ L122, 11.5.2011, p 76).

261 See Commission Decision 2011/276/EU of 26 May 2010 on State aid C-76/03, Umicore SA (OJ L122, 11.5.2011, p 76), recital 155.

262 Declining-balance method or the sum-of-the-years' digits method as opposed to the most common straight-line method.

263 See Commission Decision of 20 November 2012 on SA.34736 on the early depreciation of certain assets acquired through a financial leasing (OJ C384, 13.12.2012, p 1).

264 See Commission Decision of 20 December 2006 on the aid scheme implemented by France under Article 39 CA of the General Tax Code (OJ L112, 30.4.2007, p 41), recital 122.

265 Judgment of the Court of Justice of 29 April 2004, *GIL Insurance*, C-308/01, ECLI:EU:C:2004:252, paragraphs 65 et seq.

266 See Commission Decision 2007/256/EC of 20 December 2006 on the aid scheme implemented by France under Article 39 CA of the General Tax Code (OJ L112, 30.4.2007, p 41), recital 81 et seq.

267 See section 3.1.

268 See, for instance, Commission Decision 1999/779/EC of 3 February 1999 on an Austrian aid granted in the form of an exemption from beverage tax of wine and other fermented beverages sold directly on the place of production to the consumer (OJ L305, 30.11.1999, p 27).

6. EFFECT ON TRADE AND COMPETITION

6.1. GENERAL PRINCIPLES

[5.207]

185. Public support to undertakings only constitutes State aid under Article 107(1) of the Treaty if it 'distorts or threatens to distort competition by favouring certain undertakings or the production of certain goods' and only insofar as it 'affects trade between Member States'.

186. These are two distinct and necessary elements of the notion of aid. In practice, however, these criteria are often treated jointly in the assessment of State aid as they are, as a rule, considered inextricably linked.[269]

6.2. DISTORTION OF COMPETITION

187. A measure granted by the State is considered to distort or threaten to distort competition when it is liable to improve the competitive position of the recipient compared to other undertakings with which it competes.[270] For all practical purposes, a distortion of competition within the meaning of Article 107(1) of the Treaty is generally found to exist when the State grants a financial advantage to an undertaking in a liberalised sector where there is, or could be, competition.[271]

188. The fact that the authorities assign a public service to an in-house provider (even if they were free to entrust that service to third parties) does not as such exclude a possible distortion of competition. However, a possible distortion of competition is excluded if the following cumulative conditions are met:

(a) a service is subject to a legal monopoly (established in compliance with EU law);[272]

(b) the legal monopoly not only excludes competition on the market, but also for the market, in that it excludes any possible competition to become the exclusive provider of the service in question;[273]

(c) the service is not in competition with other services; and

(d) if the service provider is active in another (geographical or product) market that is open to competition, cross-subsidisation has to be excluded. This requires that separate accounts are used, costs and revenues are allocated in an appropriate way and public funding provided for the service subject to the legal monopoly cannot benefit other activities.

189. Public support is liable to distort competition even if it does not help the recipient undertaking to expand and gain market share. It is enough that the aid allows it to maintain a stronger competitive position than it would have had if the aid had not been provided. In this context, for aid to be considered to distort competition, it is normally sufficient that the aid gives the beneficiary an advantage by relieving it of expenses it would otherwise have had to bear in the course of its day-to-day business operations.[274] The definition of State aid does not require that the distortion of competition or effect on trade is significant or material. The fact that the amount of aid is low or the recipient undertaking is small will not in itself rule out a distortion of competition or the threat thereof,[275] provided however that the likelihood of such a distortion is not merely hypothetical.[276]

6.3. EFFECT ON TRADE

190. Public support to undertakings only constitutes State aid under Article 107(1) of the Treaty insofar as it 'affects trade between Member States'. In that respect, it is not necessary to establish that the aid has an actual effect on trade between Member States but only whether the aid is liable to affect such trade.[277] In particular, the Union Courts have ruled that 'where State financial aid strengthens the position of an undertaking as compared with other undertakings competing in intra-[Union] trade, the latter must be regarded as affected by the aid.'[278]

191. Public support can be considered capable of having an effect on trade between Member States even if the recipient is not directly involved in cross-border trade. For instance, the subsidy may make it more difficult for operators in other Member States to enter the market by maintaining or increasing local supply.[279]

192. The relatively small amount of aid or the relatively small size of the undertaking which receives it does not as such exclude the possibility that trade between Member States might be affected.[280] A public subsidy granted to an undertaking which provides only local or regional services and does not provide any services outside its State of origin may nonetheless have an effect on trade between Member States where undertakings from other Member States could provide such services (also through the right of establishment) and that possibility is not merely hypothetical. For example, where a Member State grants a public subsidy to an undertaking for supplying transport services, the supply of those services may, by virtue of the subsidy, be maintained or increased with the result that undertakings established in other Member States have less of a chance of providing their transport services in the market in that Member State.[281] Such an effect may, however, be less likely where the scope of the economic activity is very small, as may for instance be evidenced by a very low turnover.

193. In principle, an effect on trade can also occur even if the recipient exports all or most of its production outside the Union, but in such situations the effect is less immediate and cannot be assumed from the mere fact that the market is open to competition.[282]

194. In establishing an effect on trade, it is not necessary to define the market or to investigate in detail the impact of the measure on the competitive position of the beneficiary and its competitors.[283]

195. However, an effect on trade between Member States cannot be merely hypothetical or presumed. It must be established why the measure distorts or threatens to distort competition and is liable to have an effect on trade between Member States, based on the foreseeable effects of the measure.[284]

196. The Commission has in a number of decisions considered, in view of the specific circumstances of the cases, that the measure had a purely local impact and consequently had no effect on trade between Member States. In those cases the Commission ascertained in particular that the beneficiary supplied goods or services to a limited area within a Member State and was unlikely to attract customers from other Member States, and that it could not be foreseen that the measure would have more than a marginal effect on the conditions of cross-border investments or establishment.

197. While it is not possible to define general categories of measures that typically meet these criteria, past decisions provide examples of situations where the Commission found, in the light of the specific circumstances of the case, that public support was not liable to affect trade between Member States. Some examples of such cases are:

(a) sports and leisure facilities serving predominantly a local audience and unlikely to attract customers or investment from other Member States;[285]

(b) cultural events and entities performing economic activities[286] which however are unlikely to attract users or visitors away from similar offers in other Member States;[287] the Commission considers that only funding granted to large and renowned cultural institutions and events in a Member State which are widely promoted outside their home region has the potential to affect trade between Member States;

(c) hospitals and other health care facilities providing the usual range of medical services aimed at a local population and unlikely to attract customers or investment from other Member States;[288]

(d) news media and/or cultural products which, for linguistic and geographical reasons, have a locally restricted audience;[289]

(e) a conference centre, where its location and the potential effect of the aid on prices is genuinely unlikely to divert users from other centres in other Member States;[290]

(f) an information and networking platform to directly address problems of unemployment and social conflicts in a predefined and very small local area;[291]

(g) small airports[292] or ports[293] that predominately serve local users, thereby limiting competition for the services offered to a local level, and for which the impact on cross-border investment is genuinely no more than marginal;

(h) the financing of certain cable ways (and in particular ski lifts) in areas with few facilities and limited tourism capability. The Commission has clarified that the following factors are typically taken into account to draw a distinction between installations supporting an activity capable of attracting non-local users, which are generally considered to have an effect on trade, and sport-related installations in areas with few facilities and limited tourism capability, where public support may not have an effect on trade between Member States:[294] a) the location of the installation (for example within cities or linking villages); b) operating time; c) predominantly local users (proportion of daily as opposed to weekly passes); d) the total number and capacity of installations relative to the number of resident users; e) other tourism-related facilities in the area. Similar factors could, with the necessary adjustments, also be relevant for other types of facilities.

198. Even if the circumstances in which the aid is granted are in most cases sufficient to show that the aid is capable of affecting trade between Member States and of distorting or threatening to distort competition, those circumstances should be appropriately set out. In the case of aid schemes, it is normally sufficient to examine the characteristics of the particular scheme.[295]

NOTES

269 Judgment of the General Court of 15 June 2000, *Alzetta*, Joined Cases T-298/97, T-312/97 etc., ECLI-:EU:T:2000:151, paragraph 81.

270 Judgment of the Court of Justice of 17 September 1980, *Philip Morris*, 730/79, ECLI:EU:C:1980:209, paragraph 11; Judgment of the General Court of 15 June 2000, *Alzetta*, Joined Cases T-298/97, T-312/97 etc., ECLI:EU:T:2000:151, paragraph 80.

271 Judgment of the General Court of 15 June 2000, *Alzetta*, Joined Cases T-298/97, T-312/97 etc., ECLI-:EU:T:2000:151, paragraphs 141 to 147; Judgment of the Court of Justice of 24 July 2003, *Altmark Trans*, C-280/00, ECLI:EU:C:2003:415.

272 A legal monopoly exists where a given service is reserved by law or regulatory measures to an exclusive provider, with a clear prohibition for any other operator to provide such service (not even to satisfy a possible residual demand from certain customer groups). However, the mere fact that the provision of a public service is entrusted to a specific undertaking does not mean that such undertaking enjoys a legal monopoly.

273 Judgment of the General Court of 16 July 2014, *Germany v Commission*, T-295/12, ECLI:EU:T:2014:675, paragraph 158; Commission Decision of 7 July 2002 on State aid No N 356/2002 — United Kingdom — Network Rail (OJ C232, 28.9.2002, p 2), recitals 75, 76 and 77. For example, if a concession is awarded through a competitive procedure there is competition for the market.

274 Judgment of the Court of Justice of 3 March 2005, *Heiser*, C-172/03, ECLI:EU:C:2005:130, paragraph 55.

275 Judgment of the General Court of 29 September 2000, *Confederación Espanola de Transporte de Mercancías v Commission*, T-55/99, ECLI: EU:T:2000:223, paragraph 89; Judgment of the Court of Justice of 24 July 2003, *Altmark Trans*, C-280/00, ECLI:EU:C:2003:415, paragraph 81.

276 Judgment of the Court of Justice of 24 July 2003, *Altmark Trans*, C-280/00, ECLI:EU:C:2003:415, paragraph 79.

277 Judgment of the Court of Justice of 14 January 2015, *Eventech v The Parking Adjudicator*, C-518/13, ECLI-:EU:C:2015:9, paragraph 65; Judgment of the Court of Justice of 8 May 2013, *Libert and others*, Joined Cases C-197/11 and C-203/11, ECLI:EU:C:2013:288, paragraph 76.

278 Judgment of the Court of Justice of 14 January 2015, *Eventech v The Parking Adjudicator*, C-518/13, ECLI-:EU:C:2015:9, paragraph 66; Judgment of the Court of Justice of 8 May 2013, *Libert and others*, Joined Cases C-197/11 and C-203/11, ECLI:EU:C:2013:288, paragraph 77; Judgment of the General Court of 4 April 2001, *Friulia Venezia Giulia*, T-288/97, ECLI:EU:T:2001:115, paragraph 41.

279 Judgment of the Court of Justice of 14 January 2015, *Eventech v The Parking Adjudicator*, C-518/13, ECLI-:EU:C:2015:9, paragraph 67; Judgment of the Court of Justice of 8 May 2013, *Libert and others*, Joined Cases C-197/11 and C-203/11, ECLI:EU:C:2013:288, paragraph 78; Judgment of the Court of Justice of 24 July 2003, *Altmark Trans*, C-280/00, ECLI:EU:C:2003:415, paragraph 78.

280 Judgment of the Court of Justice of 14 January 2015, *Eventech v The Parking Adjudicator*, C-518/13, ECLI-:EU:C:2015:9, paragraph 68.

281 Judgment of the Court of Justice of 24 July 2003, *Altmark Trans*, C-280/00, ECLI:EU:C:2003:415, paragraphs 77 and 78.

282 Judgment of the Court of Justice of 21 March 1990, *Belgium v Commission ('Tubemeuse')*, C-142/87, ECLI-:EU:C:1990:125, paragraph 35; Judgment of the Court of Justice of 30 April 2009, *Commission v Italian Republic and Wam SpA*, C-494/06 P, ECLI:EU:C:2009:272, paragraph 62.

283 Judgment of the Court of Justice of 17 September 1980, *Philip Morris*, 730/79, ECLI:EU:C:1980:209; Judgment of the General Court of 4 September 2009, *Italy v Commission*, T-211/05, ECLI:EU:T:2009:304, paragraphs 157 to 160; Judgment of the General Court of 15 June 2000, *Alzetta*, Joined Cases T-298/97, T-312/97 etc., ECLI:EU:T:2000:151, paragraph 95.

284 Judgment of the General Court of 6 July 1995, *AITEC and others v Commission*, Joined Cases T-447/93, T-448/93 and T-449/93, ECLI: EU:T:1995:130, paragraph 141.

285 See, for instance, Commission Decisions on State aid cases in N 258/2000 Leisure Pool Dorsten (OJ C172, 16.6.2001, p 16); C10/2003 — Netherlands — Non-profit harbours for recreational crafts (OJ L34, 6.2.2004, p 63); SA.37963 — United Kingdom — Alleged State aid to Glenmore Lodge (OJ C277, 21.8.2015, p 3); SA.38208 — United Kingdom — Alleged State aid to UK member-owned golf clubs (OJ C277, 21.8.2015, p 4).

286 See section 2.6 for the conditions under which cultural or heritage conservation activities are economic in nature in the meaning of Article 107(1) of the Treaty. For cultural or heritage conservation activities which are not economic in nature an assessment whether possible public funding may have an effect on trade is not necessary.

287 See, for instance, the Commission decisions in State aid cases N 630/2003 Local Museums Sardinia (OJ C275, 8.11.2005, p 3); SA.34466 Cyprus — Center for Visual Arts and Research (OJ C1, 4.1.2013, p 10); SA.36581 Greece — Construction of Archaeological Museum, Messara, Crete (OJ C353, 3.12.2013, p 4); SA.35909 (2012/N) — Czech Republic — Infrastructure for tourism (NUTS II region Southeast) (OJ C306, 22.10.2013, p 4); SA.34891 (2012/N) — Poland — State support to Związek Gmin Fortecznych Twierdzy Przemyśl (OJ C293, 9.10.2013, p 1).

288 See, for instance, Commission Decisions in State aid cases N 543/2001 Ireland — Capital allowances for hospitals (OJ C154, 28.6.2002, p 4); SA.34576 Portugal — Jean Piaget North-east Continuing Care Unit (OJ C73, 13.3.2013, p 1); SA.37432 — Czech Republic — Funding to public hospitals in the Hradec Králové Region (OJ C203, 19.6.2015, p 2); SA.37904 — Germany — Alleged State aid to medical center in Durmersheim (OJ C188, 5.6.2015, p 2); SA.38035 — Germany — Alleged aid to a specialised rehabilitation clinic for orthopaedic medicine and trauma surgery (OJ C188, 5.6.2015, p 3).

289 See, for instance, Commission Decisions in State aid cases N 257/2007 Subsidies for theatre productions in the Basque country (OJ C173, 26.7.2007, p 1); N 458/2004 Editorial Andaluza Holding (OJ C131, 28.5.2005, p 1); SA.33243 Jornal da Madeira (OJ C16, 19.1.2013, p 1).

290 See, for instance, the Commission Decision in State aid case N 486/2002 Sweden — Congress hall in Visby (OJ C75, 27.3.2003, p 2).

291 See Commission Decision on State aid in SA.33149 — Germany — Alleged unlawful State aid for the Städtische Projekt 'Wirtschaftsbür Gaarden' — Kiel (OJ C188, 5.6.2015, p 1).

292 See, for instance, Commission Decision in State aid in case SA.38441 — United Kingdom — Isles of Scilly Air links (OJ C5, 9.1.2015, p 4).

293 See, for instance, Commission Decisions in State aid cases SA.39403 — Netherlands — Investment in the port of Lauwersoog (OJ C259, 7.8.2015, p 4); SA.42219 — Germany — Refurbishment of the Schuhmacher-quay in the port of Maasholm (OJ C426, 18.12.2015, p 5).

294 Commission communication to the Member States and other interested parties concerning State aid N 376/01 — Aid scheme for cableways (OJ C172, 18.7.2002, p 2).

295 See, for instance, Judgment of the Court of Justice of 14 October 1987, *Germany v Commission*, 248/84, ECLI:EU:C:1987:437, paragraph 18.

7. INFRASTRUCTURE: SOME SPECIFIC CLARIFICATIONS

7.1. INTRODUCTION

[5.208]

199. The guidance regarding the notion of State aid as set out in this Notice applies to the public funding of infrastructure having an economic use, as it applies to any other public funding that favours an economic activity.[296] However, given the strategic importance of public funding of infrastructure, not least for the promotion of growth, and the questions which it often raises, it is appropriate to provide specific guidance on when public funding of infrastructure favours an undertaking, grants an advantage and has an effect on competition and on trade between Member States.

200. Infrastructure projects often involve several categories of actors and any State aid involved may potentially benefit the construction (including extensions or improvements), the operation or the use of the infrastructure.[297] For the purposes of this section, it is, therefore, useful to distinguish between the developer and/or first owner ('developer/owner')[298] of an infrastructure, the operators (that is to say undertakings who make direct use of the infrastructure to provide services to end-users, including undertakings which acquire the infrastructure from the developer/owner to exploit it economically or which obtain a concession or lease for the use and operation of the infrastructure), and the end-users of an infrastructure, although these functions may in some cases overlap.

7.2. AID TO THE DEVELOPER/OWNER

7.2.1. ECONOMIC ACTIVITY VERSUS NON-ECONOMIC ACTIVITY

201. The public funding of much infrastructure was traditionally considered to fall outside the State aid rules since their construction and operation were considered to constitute general measures of public policy and not an economic activity.[299] More recently, several factors, such as liberalisation, privatisation, market integration and technological progress have, however, increased the scope for commercial exploitation of infrastructures.

202. In the *Aéroports de Paris* judgment[300] the General Court acknowledged this evolution, clarifying that the operation of an airport had to be seen as an economic activity. More recently, the *Leipzig/Halle* judgment[301] confirmed that the construction of a commercial airport runway is an economic activity in itself. While these cases relate specifically to airports, the principles developed by the Union Courts appear to be of broader interpretation and thus applicable to the construction of other infrastructures that are indissociably linked to an economic activity.[302]

203. On the other hand, the funding of infrastructure that is not meant to be commercially exploited is in principle excluded from the application of the State aid rules. This concerns, for instance, infrastructure that is used for activities that the State normally performs in the exercise of its public powers (for instance, military facilities, air traffic control in airports, lighthouses and other equipment for the needs of general navigation including on inland waterways, flood protection and low water management in the public interest, police and customs) or that is not used for offering goods or services on a market (for instance roads made available for free public use). Such activities are not of an economic nature and consequently fall outside the scope of the State aid rules, as does, accordingly, the public funding of the related infrastructure.[303]

204. Where an infrastructure originally used for non-economic activities is later re-assigned to economic use (for example where a military airport is converted to civilian use), only the costs incurred for the conversion of the infrastructure to economic use will be taken into account for the assessment under the State aid rules.[304]

205. If an infrastructure is used for both economic and non-economic activities, public funding for its construction will fall under the State aid rules only insofar as it covers the costs linked to the economic activities.

206. If an entity is engaged in economic and non-economic activities, Member States have to ensure that the public funding provided for the non-economic activities cannot be used to cross-subsidize the economic activities. This can notably be ensured by limiting the public funding to the net cost (including the cost of capital) of the non-economic activities, to be identified on the basis of a clear separation of accounts.

207. If, in cases of mixed use, the infrastructure is used almost exclusively for a non-economic activity, the Commission considers that its funding may fall outside the State aid rules in its entirety, provided the economic use remains purely ancillary, that is to say an activity which is directly related to and necessary for the operation of the infrastructure, or intrinsically linked to its main non-economic use. This should be considered to be the case when the economic activities consume the same inputs as the primary non-economic activities, for example material, equipment, labour or fixed capital. Ancillary economic activities must remain limited in scope, as regards the capacity of the infrastructure.[305] Examples of such ancillary economic activities may include a research organisation occasionally renting out its equipment and laboratories to industrial partners.[306] The Commission also considers that public financing provided to customary amenities (such as restaurants, shops or paid parking) of infrastructures that are almost exclusively used for a non-economic activity normally has no effect on trade between Member States since those customary amenities are unlikely to attract customers from other Member States and their financing is unlikely to have a more than marginal effect on cross-border investment or establishment.

208. As the Court of Justice acknowledged in its *Leipzig/Halle* judgment, the construction of an infrastructure, or part of it, can fall within the State's exercise of public powers.[307] In such a case the public funding of the infrastructure (or the relevant part of the infrastructure) is not subject to State aid rules.

209. Due to the uncertainty that existed prior to the *Aéroports de Paris* judgment, public authorities could legitimately consider that the public funding of infrastructure granted prior to that judgment did not constitute State aid and that, accordingly, such measures did not need to be notified to the Commission. It follows that the Commission cannot put such funding measures definitively adopted before the *Aéroports de Paris* judgment into question on the basis of State aid rules.[308] This does not imply any presumption as regards the presence or absence of State aid or legitimate expectations as regards funding measures not definitively adopted before the *Aéroports de Paris* judgment, which will have to be verified on a case by case basis.[309]

7.2.2. Distortion of competition and effect on trade

210. The rationale underlying the cases in which the Commission considered that certain measures were not capable of affecting trade between Member States as set out in paragraphs 196 and 197 can also be relevant for certain public funding of infrastructure, particularly local or municipal infrastructure, even if it is commercially exploited. One pertinent characteristic of such cases would be a predominately local catchment area as well as evidence that cross-border investment is unlikely to be affected more than marginally. For example, the construction of local leisure installations, health care facilities, small airports or ports that predominately serve local users and for which the impact on cross-border investment is marginal are unlikely to affect trade. Evidence to demonstrate that there is no effect on trade could include data showing that there is only limited use of the infrastructure from outside the Member State and that cross-border investments in the market under consideration are minimal or unlikely to be adversely affected.

211. There are circumstances in which certain infrastructures do not face direct competition from other infrastructures of the same kind or other infrastructures of a different kind offering services with a significant degree of substitutability, or with such services directly[310]. The absence of direct competition between infrastructures is likely the case for comprehensive network infrastructures[311] that are natural monopolies, that is to say for which a replication would be uneconomical. Similarly, there may be sectors where private financing for the construction of infrastructures is insignificant.[312] The Commission considers that an effect on trade between Member States or a distortion of competition is normally excluded as regards the construction of the infrastructure in cases where at the same time (i) an infrastructure typically faces no direct competition, (ii) private financing is insignificant in the sector and Member State concerned and (iii) the infrastructure is not designed to selectively favour a specific undertaking or sector but provides benefits for society at large.

212. In order for the entire public funding of a given project to fall outside State aid rules, Member States have to ensure that the funding provided for the construction of the infrastructures in the situations mentioned in paragraph 211 cannot be used to cross-subsidize or indirectly subsidize other economic activities, including the operation of the infrastructure. Cross-subsidization can be excluded by ensuring that the infrastructure owner does not engage in any other economic activity or — if the infrastructure owner is engaged in any other economic activity — by keeping separate accounts, allocating costs and revenues in an appropriate way and ensuring that any public funding does not benefit other activities. The absence of indirect aid, in particular to the operator of the infrastructure, can be ensured, for example, by tendering out the operation.

7.2.3. Aid to the developer/owner of an infrastructure — an overview sector-by-sector

213. This section provides an overview of how the Commission intends to assess the State aid nature of the funding of infrastructure in different sectors, having regard to the main features that public infrastructure financing typically and currently shows in the different sectors with respect to the conditions identified above. It is without prejudice to the outcome of the concrete case by case assessment of projects in the light of their specific characteristics, the way a given Member State has organised the provision of services linked to the use of the infrastructure and the development of the commercial services and of the internal market. It is not intended to replace an individual assessment of whether all the elements of the notion of State aid are fulfilled in respect of the concrete financing measure of a specific infrastructure. The Commission has also provided more detailed guidance on specific sectors in some of its Guidelines and Frameworks.

214. **Airport infrastructure** consists of different types of infrastructure. Based on the case law of the Union courts, it is well established that most airport infrastructure[313] is intended for the provision of airport services to airlines against payment,[314] which qualify as economic activities, and that therefore their funding is subject to the State aid rules. Similarly, if an infrastructure is intended for non-aeronautical commercial services to other users, its public funding is subject to the State aid rules.[315] Since airports often compete with one another, the financing of airport infrastructure is also likely to affect trade between Member States. In contrast, public funding of infrastructures intended for activities that fall under the responsibility of the State in the exercise of its public powers does not fall under the State aid rules. Air traffic control, aircraft rescue and firefighting, police, customs and activities necessary to safeguard civil aviation at an airport against acts of unlawful interference are in general considered to be of such a non-economic nature.

215. Similarly, as follows from the Commission's decision-making practice,[316] public funding of **port infrastructure** favours an economic activity and is hence in principle subject to State aid rules. As is the case with airports, ports may compete with one another and the financing of port infrastructure is therefore also likely to affect trade between Member States. However, investment for infrastructure that is necessary for activities that fall under the responsibility of the State in the exercise of its public powers are not subject to State aid control. Maritime traffic control, firefighting, police and customs are in general of such non-economic nature.

216. **Broadband infrastructure** is used to enable the provision of telecommunication connectivity to end-users. Providing connectivity to end-users against payment is an economic activity. Broadband infrastructure is in many instances built by operators without any State funding, which is evidence of significant market financing, and in many geographical zones several networks of different operators compete.[317] Broadband infrastructures are part of large, interconnected and commercially exploited networks. For these reasons, public funding of broadband infrastructure

for the provision of connectivity to end-users is subject to State aid rules, as set out in the Guidelines for the application of State aid rules in relation to the rapid deployment of broadband networks.[318] In contrast, connecting only public authorities is a non-economic activity and the public funding of so called 'closed networks' therefore does not constitute State aid.[319]

217. **Energy infrastructure**[320] is used for the provision of energy services against payment, which amounts to an economic activity. Energy infrastructure is, to a large extent, built by market actors, which is evidence of significant market financing, and financed through user tariffs. Public funding of energy infrastructure therefore favours an economic activity and is likely to have an effect on trade between Member States and is hence in principle subject to State aid rules.[321]

218. Public funding of **research infrastructures** can favour an economic activity and is hence subject to State aid rules insofar as the infrastructure is in fact intended for the performance of economic activities (such as renting out equipment or laboratories to undertakings, supplying services to undertakings or performing contract research). Public funding of research infrastructures used for non-economic activities, such as independent research for increased knowledge and better understanding, in contrast, does not fall under the State aid rules. For more detailed guidance on the distinction between economic and non-economic activities in the area of research, see the explanations provided in the Framework for State aid for research and development and innovation.[322]

219. While the operation of **railway infrastructure**[323] may constitute an economic activity,[324] the construction of railway infrastructure which is made available to potential users on equal and non-discriminatory terms — as opposed to the operation of the infrastructure — typically fulfils the conditions set out in paragraph 211 and its financing therefore typically does not affect trade between Member States or distort competition. To ensure that the entire funding of a given project is not subject to State aid rules, Member States also have to ensure that the conditions set out in paragraph 212 are fulfilled. The same reasoning applies to investments in **railway bridges, railway tunnels** and **urban transport infrastructure.**[325]

220. While **roads** made available for free public use are general infrastructures and their public funding does not fall under State aid rules, the operation of a toll-road constitutes in many instances an economic activity. However, the construction as such of road infrastructure,[326] including toll-roads — as opposed to the operation of a toll-road and provided that it does not constitute dedicated infrastructure — typically fulfils the conditions set out in paragraph 211 and its financing therefore typically does not affect trade between Member States or distort competition.[327] To ensure that the entire public funding of a given project is not subject to State aid rules Member States also have to ensure that the conditions set out in paragraph 212 are fulfilled. The same reasoning applies to investments in **bridges, tunnels** and **inland waterways (for example rivers and canals).**

221. While the operation of **water supply and waste water networks**[328] constitutes an economic activity, the construction of a comprehensive water supply and waste water network as such typically fulfils the conditions set out in paragraph 211 and its financing therefore typically does not distort competition or affect trade between Member States. To ensure that the entire funding of a given project is not subject to State aid rules Member States also have to ensure that the conditions set out in paragraph 212 are fulfilled.

7.3. AID TO OPERATORS

222. Where all the elements of Article 107(1) of the Treaty are fulfilled as regards the developer/owner of an infrastructure, State aid to the developer/owner is present, irrespective of whether they make direct use of the infrastructure to provide goods or services themselves or make the infrastructure available to a third party operator who in turn provides services to end-users of the infrastructure (for example, where the owner of an airport grants a concession for the provision of services in the airport).

223. Operators who make use of the aided infrastructure to provide services to end-users receive an advantage if the use of the infrastructure provides them with an economic benefit that they would not have obtained under normal market conditions. This normally applies if what they pay for the right to exploit the infrastructure is less than what they would pay for a comparable infrastructure under normal market conditions. Guidance on how to establish whether the terms of operation comply with market conditions is provided in section 4.2. In line with that section, the Commission considers that an economic advantage to the operator can in particular be excluded if the concession to operate the infrastructure (or parts of it) is assigned for a positive price through a tender that meets all the relevant conditions set out in paragraphs 90 to 96.[329]

224. However, the Commission recalls that if a Member State does not comply with its notification obligation and there are doubts as to the compatibility of the aid to the developer/owner with the internal market, the Commission may issue an injunction requiring the Member State to suspend the implementation of the measure and to provisionally recover any money paid until it has taken a decision on its compatibility. In addition, national judges are under an obligation to do so as well at the request of competitors. Furthermore, if, following its assessment of the measure, the Commission adopts a decision declaring the aid to be incompatible with the internal market and orders its recovery, an impact on the operator of the infrastructure cannot be excluded.

7.4. AID TO END-USERS

225. If the operator of an infrastructure has received State aid or if its resources constitute State resources, it is in a position to grant an advantage to the users of the infrastructure (if they are undertakings) unless the terms of use comply with the MEO test, that is to say the infrastructure is made available to the users on market terms.

226. In accordance with the general principles explained in section 4.2, an advantage to users in such cases can be excluded where the fees for use of the infrastructure have been set through a tender that meets all the relevant conditions set out in paragraphs 90 to 96.

227. As explained in section 4.2, where such specific evidence is not available, the question of whether a transaction is in line with market conditions can be assessed in the light of the terms and conditions under which the use of comparable infrastructure is granted by comparable private operators in comparable situations (benchmarking), provided such a comparison is possible.

228. If none of the above assessment criteria can be applied, the fact that a transaction is in line with market conditions can be established on the basis of a generally accepted, standard assessment methodology. The Commission considers that the MEO test can be satisfied for public funding of open infrastructures not dedicated to any specific user(s) where their users incrementally contribute, from an *ex ante* viewpoint, to the profitability of the project/operator. This is the case where the operator of the infrastructure establishes commercial arrangements with individual users that allow covering all costs stemming from such arrangements, including a reasonable profit margin on the basis of sound medium-term prospect. This assessment should take into account all incremental revenues and expected incremental costs incurred by the operator in relation to the activity of the specific user.[330]

NOTES

296 'Public funding to infrastructure' is meant to include all forms of provision of State resources for the construction, acquisition or operation of infrastructure.

297 This section does not concern potential aid to contractors involved in the construction of infrastructure.

298 'Owner' includes any entity exercising the effective ownership rights over the infrastructure and enjoying the economic benefits thereof. For example, in case the owner delegates its ownership rights to a separate entity (for example to a port authority) who manages the infrastructure on behalf of the owner, this can be seen as replacing the owner for the purposes of State aid control.

299 Twenty-Fifth Report on Competition Policy, 1995, pt. 175.

300 Judgment of the General Court of 12 December 2000, *Aéroports de Paris v Commission,* T-128/98, ECLI-:EU:T:2000:290, paragraph 125, confirmed on appeal in Judgment of the Court of Justice of 24 October 2002, *Aéroports de Paris v Commission*, C-82/01 P, ECLI:EU: C:2002:617. See also Judgment of the General Court of 17 December 2008, *Ryanair v Commission*, T-196/04, ECLI:EU:T:2008:585, paragraph 88.

301 Judgment of the General Court of 24 March 2011, *Freistaat Sachsen and Land Sachsen-Anhalt and Others v Commission*, Joined Cases T-443/08 and T-455/08, ECLI:EU:T:2011:117, in particular paragraphs 93 and 94, upheld on appeal in Judgment of the Court of Justice of 19 December 2012, *Mitteldeutsche Flughafen AG and Flughafen Leipzig-Halle GmbH v Commission*, C-288/11 P, ECLI:EU: C:2012:821, in particular paragraphs 40 to 43, 47.

302 Judgment of the Court of Justice of 19 December 2012, *Mitteldeutsche Flughafen AG and Flughafen Leipzig-Halle GmbH v Commission*, C-288/11 P, ECLI:EU:C:2012:821, paragraphs 43 and 44. Judgment of the Court of Justice of 14 January 2015, *Eventech v The Parking Adjudicator*, C-518/13, ECLI:EU:C:2015:9, paragraph 40.

303 Judgment of the Court of Justice of 16 June 1987, *Commission v Italy*, C-118/85, ECLI:EU:C:1987:283, paragraphs 7 and 8. Judgment of the Court of Justice of 4 May 1988, *Bodson/Pompes funèbres des régions libérées*, C-30/87, ECLI:EU:C:1988:225, paragraph 18; Judgment of the General Court of 24 March 2011, *Freistaat Sachsen and Land Sachsen-Anhalt and Others v Commission*, Joined Cases T-443/08 and T-455/08, ECLI-:EU:T:2011:117, paragraph 98.

304 See Commission Decision on State aid SA.23324 — Tampere-Pirkkala Airport (OJ L309, 13.11.2013, p 27), and on State aid SA.35388 — Poland — Setting up the Gdynia-Kosakowo Airport.

305 In this respect, the economic use of the infrastructure may be considered ancillary when the capacity allocated each year to such activity does not exceed 20 per cent of the infrastructure's overall annual capacity.

306 If the activities do not remain ancillary, also secondary economic activities can be subject to the State aid rules (see Judgment of the General Court of 12 September 2013, *Germany v Commission*, T-347/09, ECLI:EU:T:2013:418 on the selling of wood and tourism activities of nature conservation organizations).

307 Judgment of the Court of Justice of 19 December 2012, *Mitteldeutsche Flughafen AG and Flughafen Leipzig-Halle GmbH v Commission*, C-288/11 P, ECLI:EU:C:2012:821, paragraph 47.

308 Commission Decision of 3 October 2012 on State aid case SA.23600, Financing Arrangements for Munich Airport Terminal 2 (OJ L319, 29.11.2013, p 8), recitals 74 to 81. The Commission's 1994 Aviation guidelines stated that '*[t]he construction [or] enlargement of infrastructure projects (such as airports, motorways, bridges, etc.) represents a general measure of economic policy which cannot be controlled by the Commission under the Treaty rules on State aids*' (OJ C350, 10.12.1994, p 5), paragraph 12.

309 These clarifications are without prejudice to the application of Cohesion Policy rules in these circumstances, on which guidance has been provided in other instances. See for example the Commission's guidance note to the COCOF: Verification of compliance with State Aids in infrastructure cases, available under http://ec.europa.eu/regional_policy/sources/docoffic/cocof/2012/cocof_12_0059_01_en.pdf.

310 For example services offered by commercial ferry operators can be in competition with a toll bridge or tunnel.

311 In a network infrastructure different elements of the network complement each other, instead of competing with one another.

312 The question whether there is only insignificant market financing in a given sector has to be assessed at the level of the Member State concerned rather than a regional or local level, similarly to the assessment of the existence of a market in a Member State (see, for example, Judgment of the General Court of 26 November 2015, *Spain v Commission*, T-461/13, ECLI:EU:T:2015:891, paragraph 44).

313 Such as runways and their lighting systems, terminals, aprons, taxiways or centralised ground handling infrastructure such as baggage belts.

314 Guidelines on State aid to airports and airlines (OJ C99, 4.4.2014, p 3), recital 31.

315 Guidelines on State aid to airports and airlines (OJ C99, 4.4.2014, p 3), recital 33.

316 Commission Decision of 27 March 2014 on State aid SA.38302 — Italy — Port of Salerno; Commission Decision of 22 February 2012 on State aid SA.30742 (N/2010) — Lithuania — Construction of infrastructure for the passenger and cargo ferries terminal in Klaipeda (OJ C121, 26.4.2012, p 1); Commission Decision of 2 July 2013 on State Aid SA.35418 (2012/N) — Greece — Extension of Piraeus Port (OJ C256, 5.9.2013, p 2).

317 As stated in paragraph 211 and footnote 312, the question whether there is only insignificant market financing in a given

sector has to be assessed at the level of the Member State concerned rather than at regional or local level.

318 OJ C25, 26.1.2013, p 1. The guidelines explain that the broadband sector is characterised by specific features, in particular by the fact that a broadband network can host several operators of telecommunication services and can therefore provide an opportunity for the presence of competing operators.

319 EU Guidelines for the application of State aid rules in relation to the rapid deployment of broadband networks (OJ C25, 26.1.2013, p 1), recital 11 and footnote 14.

320 Energy infrastructure includes, in particular, transmission, distribution and storage infrastructures for electricity, gas and oil. For more details, see the definition in Guidelines on State aid for environmental protection and energy 2014-2020 (OJ C200, 28.6.2014, p 1), recital 31.

321 Guidelines on State aid for environmental protection and energy 2014-2020 (OJ C 200, 28.6.2014, p 1), section 3.8; Commission Decision of 10.7.2014 on State aid no SA.36290 — United Kingdom — Northern Ireland Gas Pipeline; extension to the West and the North West.

322 OJ C198, 27.6.2014, p 1, recitals 17 et seq.

323 Such as rail tracks and train stations.

324 This observation is without any prejudice to the question of whether any advantage granted to the infrastructure operator by the State amounts to State aid. For instance, if the operation of the infrastructure is subject to a legal monopoly and if competition for the market to operate the infrastructure is excluded, an advantage granted to the infrastructure operator by the State cannot distort competition and therefore does not constitute State aid. See paragraph 188 of this Communication and Commission Decision of 17 July 2002 on State aid N 356/2002 — United Kingdom Network Rail and Commission Decision of 2 May 2013 on SA.35948 — Czech Republic — Prolongation of interoperability scheme in railway transport. As explained in paragraph 188, if the owner or operator is active in another liberalised market, it should, in order to prevent cross-subsidisation, maintain separate accounts, allocate costs and revenues in an appropriate way and ensure that any public funding does not benefit other activities.

325 Such as tracks for trams or underground public transport.

326 Including roads for the connection of commercially exploitable land, see Commission Decision of 1 October 2014 on SA.36147 — Alleged infrastructure aid for Propapier and Commission Decision of 8 January 2016 on SA.36019 — Road infrastructure measures in the vicinity of a real estate project — Uplace.

327 An atypical situation in which State aid cannot be excluded would, for example, be a bridge or tunnel between two Member States, offering a largely substitutable service to the service offered by commercial ferry operators or the construction of a toll-road in direct competition with another toll-road (for example two toll-roads running in parallel to each other, thereby offering largely substitutable services).

328 Water supply and waste water networks include the infrastructure for the distribution of water and the transportation of waste water, such as the respective pipes.

329 See Commission Decision of 1 October 2014 on SA.38478 — Hungary — Development of the Győr-Gönyű National Public Port. In contrast, an advantage for the developer/owner of an infrastructure cannot be excluded by a tender and the tender only minimizes the aid granted.

330 See for example Commission Decision of 1 October 2014 on SA.36147, Alleged infrastructure aid for Propapier. See also the Guidelines on State aid to airports and airlines (OJ C99, 4.4.2014, p 3), recitals 61 to 64.

8. FINAL PROVISIONS

[5.209]

229. This Communication replaces the following Commission Communications and Notices:

— Commission Communication to the Member States 93/C-307/03 on the application of Articles 92 and 93 of the EEC Treaty and of Article 5 of Commission Directive 80/723/EEC to public undertakings in the manufacturing sector;[331]

— Commission Communication on State aid elements in sales of land and buildings by public authorities;[332]

— Commission Notice on the application of the State aid rules to measures relating to direct business taxation.[333]

230. The present Communication replaces any opposing statements relating to the notion of State aid included in any existing Commission Communications and Frameworks, save for statements pertaining to specific sectors and justified by their particular features.

NOTES

331 OJ C307, 13.11.1993, p 3.

332 OJ C209, 10.7.1997, p 3.

333 OJ C307, 13.11.1993, p 3.

COMMUNICATION FROM THE COMMISSION

(2018/C253/05)

Code of Best Practices for the conduct of State aid control procedures

[5.210]

NOTES

Date of publication in OJ: OJ C253, 19.7.2018, p 14.

TABLE OF CONTENTS

1. SCOPE AND PURPOSE OF THE CODE

[5.211]
1. Over recent years, the Commission has implemented a State Aid Modernisation agenda ('SAM') to focus its State aid control on measures which genuinely affect competition in the Internal Market, while at the same time simplifying and streamlining rules and procedures. This has facilitated public investments, by empowering Member States to grant public support without prior scrutiny by the Commission and by speeding up decision-making in State aid procedures.

1. The Commission has, in particular, adopted:
- A Notice on the Notion of State Aid ('NoA')[1] clarifying the types of public support that do not involve State aid. This is the case, for example, for funding of economic activities on market terms, investments in infrastructure such as railways, motorways, inland waterways and water distribution systems which do not compete with similar infrastructures, investments in small-scale infrastructures and funding of essentially local services.
- A General Block Exemption Regulation ('GBER')[2] allowing Member States to implement a wide range of State aid measures without prior Commission approval which are unlikely to distort competition. More than 97% of newly implemented State aid measures fall under the GBER and, therefore, are implemented without prior Commission approval[3].
- A revised Procedural State Aid Regulation, including rules on complaint-handling and on market information tools to target State aid control on cases which are most liable to distort competition in the Internal Market[4].
- A series of decisions in specific cases confirming that Member States can support many small-scale projects without State aid control, due to their local nature and very limited impact on the Internal Market[5].

2. The effort to focus and streamline EU State aid rules is continuing. In the context of the Multiannual Financial Framework 2021-2027, the Commission has proposed a revision of the EU State aid Enabling Regulation to make it easier (i) to combine EU Funding which is paid in the form of financial instruments with Member States funding and (ii) streamline the conditions for Member States to support certain projects under EU structural and investment funds[6].

4. To make the most of those modernised State aid rules, this Communication ('Best Practices Code') provides guidance to Member States, aid beneficiaries and other stakeholders, on how State aid procedures work in practice[7]. It aims to make State aid procedures as transparent, simple, clear, predictable and timely as possible. It replaces the Notice on a Code of Best Practices adopted in 2009[8] and integrates the Simplified Procedure Notice of 2009[9].

5. To achieve the goals pursued by this Communication and to ensure the correct and efficient application of the State aid rules, Member States and the Commission should closely cooperate as partners. In this context, the Commission services will continue to offer pre-notification contacts concerning potential State aid measures that the Member States are considering implementing. They will work with the Member States to define priorities with regard to the procedural handling of cases. Furthermore, they will have in place a network of country coordinators and offer support to Member States in the form of guidance and training on the application of the State aid rules. As part of stepping up its effort to strengthen its cooperation and partnership with Member States, the Commission services will encourage them to share experiences with it and each other on best practices and challenges encountered in applying the State aid rules.

6. This Best Practices Code also seeks to improve the procedure for dealing with State aid complaints. It clarifies the conditions under which the Commission services will consider a case to be a formal complaint and provides indicative deadlines for the handling of formal complaints.

7. The specific features of an individual case may however require an adaptation of, or deviation from this code. The specificities of the fishery and aquaculture sectors and of the activities in the primary production, marketing or processing of agricultural products may also justify a deviation from this code.

NOTES

1 Commission Notice on the notion of State aid as referred to in Article 107(1) of the Treaty on the Functioning of the European Union, OJ C 262, 19.7.2016, p. 1-50.

2 Commission Regulation (EU) No. 651/2014 of 17 June 2014, OJ L 187, 26.06.2014, p. 1-78, as further amended by Commission Regulation (EU) 2017/1084 of 14 June 2017, OJ L 156, 20.6.2017, p. 1-18.

3 Commission State Aid Scoreboard 2017, Results, trends and observations regarding EU28 State Aid expenditure reports for 2016, 29.11.17, p. 14.

4 Council Regulation (EU) 2015/1589 of 13 July 2015 laying down detailed rules for the application of Article 108 of the Treaty on the Functioning of the European Union , OJ L 248, 24.9.2015, p. 9-29.

5 See Commission Press Release, State aid: Commission gives guidance on local public support measures that do not

constitute State aid, IP/16/3141, 21 September 2016; Commission Press Release, State Aid: Commission gives guidance on local public support measures that can be granted without prior Commission approval, IP/15/4889, 29 April 2015.

6 Commission Proposal for a Council Regulation amending Council Regulation (EU) 2015/1588 of 13 July 2015 on the application of Articles 107 and 108 of the Treaty on the Functioning of the European Union to certain categories of horizontal State aid, COM/2018/398 final - 2018/0222, 06/06/2018.

7 Since a significant part of the measures covered by Simplified Procedure Notice are now exempted from State aid notification and the use of that procedure is thus very limited, the Simplified Procedure Notice has been integrated into the present Best Practices Code.

8 Commission Notice on a Code of Best Practice for the conduct of State aid control procedures, OJ C 136, 16.6.2009, p. 13-20.

9 Commission Notice on a Simplified procedure for the treatment of certain types of State aid, OJ C 136, 16.6.2009, p. 3-12.

2. RELATIONSHIP TO EU LAW

[5.212]

8. This code describes and clarifies the procedures followed by the Commission services when assessing State aid cases. It does not provide an exhaustive overview of EU State aid rules, but should rather be read together with all other documents containing those rules. The code does not create any new rights in addition to those laid down in the Treaty on the Functioning of the European Union ('the Treaty'), the Procedural Regulation[10] and the Implementing Regulation[11] and their interpretation by the EU Courts. It also does not alter those rights in any way.

NOTES

10 Council Regulation (EU) 2015/1589 of 13 July 2015 laying down detailed rules for the application of Article 108 of the Treaty on the Functioning of the European Union, OJ L 248, 24.9.2015, p. 9.

11 Commission Regulation (EC) No 794/2004 of 21 April 2004 implementing Council Regulation (EU) 2015/1589 laying down detailed rules for the application of Article 108 of the Treaty on the Functioning of the European Union, as last amended by Commission Regulation (EU) 2015/2282 of 27 November 2015, OJ L 325, 10.12.2015, p 1.

3. PRE-NOTIFICATION

3.1. OBJECTIVES

[5.213]

9. The Commission services invite the Member States to contact them before formally notifying potential State aid measures to the Commission ('pre-notification contacts'). These 'pre-notification contacts' have several objectives.

10. First, during these pre-notification contacts, the Commission services and the Member State can discuss what information is needed for the notification of the State aid measure in question to be considered as complete. Thus, pre-notification contacts generally lead to better and more complete notifications. This in turn speeds up the handling of such notifications, generally allowing the Commission to adopt decisions within 2 months of the date of notification[12].

11. Second, during the pre-notification contacts, the Commission services and the Member State can discuss the legal and economic aspects of a proposed measure in an informal and confidential[13] manner before it is formally notified. In particular, the pre-notification phase can provide an opportunity to address those aspects of a proposed measure that might not be fully in line with the State aid rules, including in cases where significant changes to the measure are necessary.

12. Third, during the pre-notification phase the Commission services will make a first assessment of whether or not a case qualifies for application of the streamlined procedure (see Section 6).

3.2. SCOPE

13. The Commission services will engage in pre-notification contacts whenever a Member State requests them. The Commission services strongly recommends that Member States engage in such contacts in cases which have novel aspects or features or complexity which justify prior informal discussions with the Commission services. Pre-notification contacts can also be useful for projects of common interest with high EU relevance, such as the Trans-European Network for Transport (TEN-T) core network projects, to the extent that their funding is likely to constitute State aid.

3.3. TIMING

14. To ensure that the pre-notification contacts are efficient, Member States should provide the Commission services with all information necessary for assessing a proposed State aid measure, in the form of a draft notification. Informal pre-notification contacts will then take place typically by email, telephone or conference call to speed up the process. Where necessary, or at the request of the Member State, meetings between the Commission services and the Member State may also take place.

15. For particularly complex cases (such as those on restructuring aid, or large or complex individual aid measures), the Commission services recommend that Member States initiate pre-notification contacts as early as possible to allow for a fruitful discussion. Such contacts can also be useful in some seemingly less problematic cases, in order to validate Member States' own initial assessment and establish the information the Commission services would need to assess the case.

16. The timing and format of pre-notification contacts largely depend on the complexity of the case. Although such contacts may last several months, they should, as a general rule, not last more than 6 months.

17. After the conclusion of the pre-notification contacts, the Member State should be able to submit a complete notification. In cases where the Commission services consider that pre-notification contacts do not bring satisfactory results, they may close the pre-notification phase. This does not prevent the Member State from pre-notifying or notifying a similar measure again.

3.4. CONTENT

18. Based on its experience, especially in cases with major technical, financial and project-related implications, the Commission recommends involving the beneficiaries of individual measures in pre-notification contacts. Nevertheless, the decision on whether or not to involve the beneficiary rests with the Member State.

19. For measures involving several Member States (for instance, important projects of common European interest), the participating Member States are generally encouraged to discuss between themselves before initiating pre-notification contacts, to ensure a consistent approach to the measure and to establish a realistic timeline.

20. The Commission services will try to provide the Member State with an informal preliminary assessment of the measure at the end of the pre-notification phase. That preliminary assessment comprises non-binding guidance from the Commission services on the completeness of the draft notification and an informal and non-binding assessment[14] of whether the measure constitutes State aid and whether or not it is compatible with the internal market.

21. In particularly novel or complex cases, the Commission services might not provide an informal preliminary assessment at the end of the pre-notification phase. In such cases, at the request of the Member State, they may indicate in writing what information still needs to be provided to enable them to carry out an assessment of the measure.

22. Pre-notification contacts are voluntary and confidential. They do not affect the assessment of the case after its formal notification. In particular, the fact that pre-notification contacts have taken place does not mean that the Commission services cannot request the Member State to provide further information after the formal notification.

NOTES

12 See Article 4(5) referring to decisions under Articles 4(2), 4(3) and 4(4) of the Procedural Regulation. That deadline cannot be respected where the Commission's services has to issue several requests for information due to incomplete notifications.

13 Based on Article 30 of the Procedural Regulation the Commission is bound by professional secrecy in all State aid proceedings. This is backed by the general obligation of professional secrecy laid down in Article 339 of the Treaty.

14 Thus, it does not constitute or prejudge an official position of the Commission.

4. CASE PORTFOLIO APPROACH AND MUTUALLY AGREED PLANNING

4.1. CASE PORTFOLIO APPROACH

[5.214]

23. Member States may ask the Commission services to treat cases that they consider of priority with more predictable timelines. To that end, they can participate in the 'portfolio exercise' offered by the Commission services. Twice per year[15], the Commission services will ask the Member States to inform them which notified cases in their portfolio they consider to be of high or low priority. If they wish to participate in the exercise, Member States should reply to the request within the given timeline. Once it has received that information, and with due regard to available resources and other pending cases involving the Member State making the request, the Commission services may propose a Mutually Agreed Planning for those cases to ensure they are dealt with promptly and predictably.

4.2. MUTUALLY AGREED PLANNING

4.2.1. OBJECTIVE AND CONTENT

24. Mutually Agreed Planning is a tool which can be used to increase the transparency and predictability of the likely duration of a State aid investigation. This tool allows the Commission services and the Member State to agree on the expected timeline of an investigation in a specific case, and in some cases also on the likely course of the investigation. This can be particularly useful in cases which have novel aspects, which are related to TEN-T core network projects or which are technically complex, urgent or sensitive.

25. In particular the Commission services and the Member State could agree on the following:

- Priority treatment of the case as part of the portfolio exercise. Where necessary for planning or resource purposes[16], priority treatment can be granted in return for the Member State's formal acceptance of the suspension or the extension of the time limit of the examination[17] of other cases from its portfolio.
- Which information[18] the Member State and/or the intended aid beneficiary should provide to the Commission services, and which type of unilateral information-gathering the Commission services intend to use in the case.
- The likely form and duration of the assessment of the case by the Commission services after its notification.

26. If the Member State promptly provides all information agreed upon, the Commission services will endeavour to comply with the mutually agreed time frame for their investigation of the case. Nevertheless, it may not be possible to work within that time frame in cases where the information provided by the Member State or third parties raises further issues.

4.2.2. SCOPE AND TIMING

27. Mutually Agreed Planning will, in particular, be used in cases which involve very novel aspects, or are technically difficult or sensitive. In these cases, Mutually Agreed Planning will take place at the end of the pre-notification phase, and be followed by the formal notification.

28. Mutually Agreed Planning can also take place at the beginning of the formal investigation procedure. In such cases, the Member State should request Mutually Agreed Planning for further treatment of the case.

NOTES

15 Currently at the end of January and the end of September of each year.

16 For instance, in cases where the financial institutions of the European Union act as holding fund.

17 See Article 4(5) of the Procedural Regulation.

[18] For example studies or external expertise.

5. THE PRELIMINARY EXAMINATION OF NOTIFIED MEASURES

5.1. REQUESTS FOR INFORMATION

[5.215]

29. The Commission services start their preliminary examination of each notified measure when they receive its notification. If they need further information after an aid measure has been notified, they will send a request for information to the Member State. Because the Commission services try to group requests for information and because pre-notification contacts should ensure that Member States submit complete notifications[19], one comprehensive request for information will generally be enough. The request explains which information is needed and will normally be sent within 4 weeks following the formal notification.

30. After receiving the Member State's response, the Commission services may raise additional questions depending on the content of the answers and on the nature of the case. This does not necessarily mean that the Commission has serious difficulties in assessing the case.

31. If the Member State does not provide the requested information within the deadline, the Commission services will send a reminder. If, after one reminder, the Member State still does not send the information, the Commission services will inform the Member State that the notification is considered as withdrawn[20], unless there are exceptional circumstances. If a notification is considered to have been withdrawn, the Member State may subsequently re-notify the measure with the missing information added.

32. When the conditions to open the formal investigation procedure are met, the Commission will generally open that procedure after, at the most, two rounds of questions. However, in some cases more requests for information may be issued before the formal investigation procedure is opened, depending on the nature of the case and the completeness and complexity of the information provided by the Member State.

5.2. AGREED SUSPENSION OF THE PRELIMINARY EXAMINATION

33. The Commission services may suspend the preliminary examination, for example when a Member State requests a suspension in order to change the aid measure to bring it in line with State aid rules, or by common agreement.

34. The period of suspension will be agreed in advance. If the Member State has not submitted a complete notification which complies with the State aid rules at the end of this period, the Commission services will continue the procedure from the point at which it was suspended. The Commission services will usually then inform the Member State that the notification is considered to have been withdrawn, or immediately open the formal investigation procedure due to serious doubts as to whether the aid measure complies with the State aid rules and hence its compatibility with the internal market.

5.3. 'STATE OF PLAY' CONTACTS AND CONTACTS WITH THE AID BENEFICIARY

35. Upon request, the Commission services will inform the Member State of the state of play of the preliminary examination of the notification.

36. The Member State may decide to involve the beneficiary of a potential (individual) State aid measure in the 'state of play' contacts with the Commission, especially in cases with major technical, financial and project-related implications. The Commission services recommend the beneficiary becomes involved in such contacts. Nevertheless, the decision on whether or not to involve the beneficiary rests with the Member State.

NOTES

[19] Unless otherwise agreed in Mutually Agreed Planning.

[20] On the basis of Article 5(3) of the Procedural Regulation.

6. STREAMLINED PROCEDURE IN STRAIGHTFORWARD CASES

6.1. CASES THAT MAY BE SUBJECT TO THE STREAMLINED PROCEDURE

[5.216]

37. If a case is straightforward and certain conditions are fulfilled, the Commission may agree to handle it under a streamlined procedure. In such cases, the Commission will, within 25 days from the date of notification, endeavour to adopt a short-form decision finding that the notified measure does not constitute aid or a decision not to raise objections[21].

38. If a Member State asks for the streamlined procedure to be applied, the Commission services will decide whether the case is suitable for this procedural treatment. This may, in particular, be the case when a measure is sufficiently similar to other measures which were approved in at least three Commission decisions adopted in the 10 years preceding the date of pre-notification ('precedent decisions'). To decide whether the measure is sufficiently similar to those assessed in the precedent decisions, the Commission services will look at all applicable substantive and procedural conditions, and in particular at the objectives and overall set-up of the measure, the types of beneficiaries, eligible costs, individual notification ceilings, aid intensities and applicable bonuses (if any), cumulation provisions, incentive effect and transparency requirements.

39. Generally, where at least three precedent decisions are available, it is clear that the measure does not constitute aid or that the aid measure is compatible with the internal market. Nevertheless, this may not be the case in certain circumstances, for example if the Commission is reassessing the precedent decisions in the light of recent case-law. As such cases need to be closely examined, the Commission services will usually refuse to apply the streamlined procedure.

40. The Commission services may also refuse to apply the streamlined procedure in cases where the aid measure could benefit a company which is under an obligation to repay State aid that the Commission held to be illegal and incompatible with the internal market[22].

6.2. PRE-NOTIFICATION CONTACTS IN DETERMINING THE USE OF STREAMLINED PROCEDURE

41. The Commission services will only agree to apply the streamlined procedure if pre-notification contacts have taken place on the aid measure in question. In this context, the Member State should submit a draft notification form containing all relevant information, including references to precedent decisions, and a draft summary of the notification[23], which is intended for publication on the website of DG Competition.

42. The Commission services will only apply the streamlined procedure if they consider the notification form to be, in principle, complete. This means that the Commission services in principle would have enough information to approve the measure, if the Member State bases its notification on the draft notification form including the results of the pre-notification contacts.

6.3. NOTIFICATION AND PUBLICATION OF THE SHORT SUMMARY

43. The time limit of 25 days for the adoption of a short-form decision (see Point 38) starts when the Member State submits the notification. The standard notification forms[24] are used in the streamlined procedure.

44. After having received the notification, the Commission services will publish a summary of the notification[25] on DG Competition's website and will state that the aid measure may qualify for the application of the streamlined procedure. Interested parties will then have 10 working days to comment, particularly on circumstances which might require more thorough examination. If an interested party raises concerns which are at first sight well founded, the Commission services will apply the normal procedure. They will inform the Member State and the interested parties thereof.

6.4. SHORT-FORM DECISION

45. In cases where the streamlined procedure is applied, the Commission will normally issue a short-form decision. The Commission will endeavour to adopt a decision finding that the notified measure does not constitute aid or a decision not to raise objections[26] within 25 working days from notification.

46. The short-form decision contains the summary published at the time of notification and a short assessment of the measure under Article 107(1) of the Treaty and, where applicable, mentions that it is in line with the Commission's previous decision-making practice. The public version of the decision will be published on DG Competition's website.

NOTES

21 Pursuant to Article 4(2) or 4(3) of the Procedural Regulation.

22 On the basis of an outstanding recovery order of the Member States, see Judgment of the ECJ of 9 March 1994, Case C-188/92, TWD Textilwerke Deggendorf, ECLI:EU:C:1994:90.

23 Annex to this Best Practices Code.

24 Annex I of the Implementing Regulation.

25 This summary is based on the standard form provided in the Annex of this Best Practices Code.

26 Based on Article 4(2) or 4(3) of the Procedural Regulation.

7. THE FORMAL INVESTIGATION PROCEDURE

[5.217]

47. The Commission aims to improve the transparency, predictability and efficiency of the treatment of the complex cases which are handled under the formal investigation procedure. To this end, it will efficiently use all procedural means it has on the basis of the Procedural Regulation.

7.1 PUBLICATION OF THE DECISIONS AND MEANINGFUL SUMMARIES

48. The Commission endeavours to publish its decision to open the formal investigation procedure ('opening decision'), together with a meaningful summary[27] within 2 months of its adoption in cases where the Member State does not ask for confidential information to be removed from the decision.

49. Where there is disagreement between the Commission services and the Member State about removal of confidential information from the opening decision, the Commission will apply the principles of the Communication on professional secrecy[28] and will publish the decision as soon as possible after its adoption[29]. The same practice applies to the publication of all final decisions[30].

7.2. INTERESTED PARTIES' COMMENTS

50. Interested parties, including the beneficiary of the aid, may comment on the opening decision within 1 month of its publication[31]. The Commission services will, in principle, not extend that deadline or accept submissions after it has passed[32]. The Commission services can grant an extension only in exceptional and duly justified cases, for example if the interested party intends to submit particularly voluminous factual information or if there has been contact with the interested party before the deadline expires.

51. In very complex cases, the Commission services may send a copy of the opening decision to interested parties, including trade or business associations, and ask them to comment on specific aspects of the case[33]. Interested parties' cooperation is voluntary. In their letter, the Commission services will invite interested parties to reply within 1 month to ensure that the procedure is efficient. The Commission will send the same invitation to comment to the aid beneficiary.

52. In order to respect the rights of defence[34], the Commission services will forward a non-confidential version of any comments received from interested parties to the Member State concerned and invite the Member State to reply within 1 month. If there are no comments from interested parties, the Commission services will inform the Member State to that effect.

53. The Commission services invite the Member States to accept comments from interested parties in their original language, so that they can be forwarded as quickly as possible. Nevertheless, the Commission services will provide a translation if a Member State asks for it. This may result in the procedure taking longer.

7.3. MEMBER STATES' COMMENTS

54. The Commission services strive to complete the formal investigation procedure as quickly as possible. Therefore, they strictly apply the deadlines laid down in the Procedural Regulation. If a Member State does not submit comments on the opening decision or on third-party comments within 1 month[35], the Commission services may extend the deadline by another month, if the request from the Member State is justified, stating that, except in exceptional circumstances, no further extension will be granted. If the Member State does not send a sufficient and meaningful reply, the Commission may take a decision on the basis of the information available to it[36].

55. If information which is essential for the Commission in order to come to a final decision is missing in the case of unlawful aid (that is to say if new aid put into effect is in breach of Article 108(3) of the Treaty), the Commission might issue an information injunction[37] requiring the Member State to provide the information. If the Member State does not respond to the injunction within the prescribed period, the Commission may take a decision based on the information available to it.

7.4. REQUESTS FOR ADDITIONAL INFORMATION FROM THE MEMBER STATE CONCERNED

56. In very complex cases, the Commission services may need to send a further request for information after the Member State's comments on the opening decision have been received. The deadline for the Member State to reply is normally 1 month.

57. If a Member State does not reply by the deadline, the Commission services will send a reminder, setting a final deadline, which is usually 20 working days. They will also inform the Member State that, in the absence of a suitable response by the deadline, the Commission has several options according to the characteristics of the case. It may observe that the notification is withdrawn[38]. It may send a request for information to other sources[39]. For cases of unlawful aid, the Commission may issue an information injunction. It may also take a decision based on the information available to it[40].

7.5. REQUESTS FOR INFORMATION MADE TO OTHER SOURCES

58. After initiating the formal investigation procedure in cases where it has been formally concluded that the Member State has not provided sufficient information during the preliminary examination, the Commission may issue a request for information to sources other than the Member State[41].

59. If the Commission services want to request information from the aid beneficiary, they need to obtain the Member State's express consent. The Member State will typically have a short deadline to reply to such a request for consent.

60. The Commission services will respect the principle of proportionality[42] and only request information from other sources if that information is at the disposal of those parties. Interested parties will have a reasonable period, usually no more than 1 month, to provide the information.

61. Besides requests for information from other sources, the Commission also has the power to investigate and collect information based on the case-law of EU courts[43]. This power is not affected by the specific rules governing requests for information to other sources.

7.6. JUSTIFIED SUSPENSION OF A FORMAL INVESTIGATION

62. The Commission services will only suspend a formal investigation in exceptional circumstances and in agreement with the Member State. This could be the case if the Member State asks for a suspension to bring its project in line with the State aid rules, or where the judgment in a case pending before EU courts is likely to have an impact on the assessment of the case.

63. Formal suspension will normally only be granted once, and for a period agreed in advance between the Commission services and the Member State.

7.7. ADOPTION OF THE FINAL DECISION AND JUSTIFIED EXTENSION OF THE FORMAL INVESTIGATION

64. The Commission always endeavours to adopt a final decision expeditiously and, as far as possible, within 18 months from the opening of the procedure[44]. That time limit may be extended by agreement between the Commission services and the Member State. An extension may be appropriate if the case concerns a novel aid measure or raises novel legal issues.

65. To ensure that this 18-month deadline is complied with, the Commission will endeavour to adopt the final decision no later than 6 months after the Member State submits the last piece of information, or after the last deadline expires.

NOTES

27 The 'meaningful summary' is intended to be a short summary of the grounds on which the Commission has decided to open the procedure. The meaningful summary is translated into all official languages of the EU and published together with the full text of the opening decision in the Official Journal.

28 Commission communication on professional secrecy in State aid decisions (OJ C 297, 9.12.2003, p. 6).

29 In line with paragraph 33 of the Communication on professional secrecy.

30 In line with paragraph 34 of the Communication on professional secrecy.

31 Article 6 of the Procedural Regulation.

32 Without prejudice to Article 12(1) of the Procedural Regulation.

33 According to settled case law, the Commission is entitled to send the decision to open the formal investigation to identified interested parties; see for example Case T-198/01, *Technische Glaswerke Ilmenau v. Commission*, ECLI:EU:T:2004:222, paragraph 195; Joined Cases C-74/00 P and C-75/00 P, *Falck Spa and others v. Commission*, ECLI:EU:C:2002:524, paragraph 83.

34 And in accordance with Article 6(2) of the Procedural Regulation.

35 Article 6(1) of the Procedural Regulation.

36 In line with Article 9(7) and 15(1) of the Procedural Regulation.

37 Article 12 of the Procedural Regulation.

38 Article 5(3) of the Procedural Regulation.

39 Article 7 of the Procedural Regulation.

40 Articles 9(7) and 15(1) of the Procedural Regulation.

41 Article 7 of the Procedural Regulation.

42 Article 7 of the Procedural Regulation.

43 For instance, in Case T-198/01 Technische Glaswerke Ilmenau v Commission, ECLI:EU:T:2004:222, the Court of First Instance recognised implicitly that the Commission was entitled to put questions to one of the firms that made comments following the decision to open the formal investigation procedure. Similarly, in Case T-296/97 *Alitalia v Commission*, ECLI:EU:T:2000:289, the Court of First Instance also implicitly accepted that the Commission could, via its appointed expert consultants, contact institutional investors in order to assess the conditions of investment of the Italian State in Alitalia.

44 Article 9(6) of the Procedural Regulation. Pursuant to Article 15(2) of that Regulation, the Commission is not bound by the deadline in the case of unlawful aid.

8. INVESTIGATIONS INTO SECTORS OF THE ECONOMY AND INTO AID INSTRUMENTS

[5.218]

66. The Commission has the power to conduct sector inquires, in which it will respect the principle of proportionality[45]. At the end of such an inquiry, the Commission will publish a report on the results of its investigation on DG Competition's website. The Commission will inform Member States and invite them and other concerned parties to comment on the report within a period of no more than 1 month.

67. The information obtained through the sector inquiry may be used in State aid procedures, and could lead to the Commission launching investigations into State aid measures on its own initiative.

NOTES

45 Article 25 of the Procedural Regulation.

9. FORMAL COMPLAINTS

[5.219]

68. The Commission services endeavours to handle complaints from interested parties as efficiently and transparently as possible, using the best practices described below.

9.1. THE COMPLAINT FORM AND OBLIGATION TO SHOW AFFECTED INTEREST

69. Article 1(h) of the Procedural Regulation defines interested parties as any Member State and any person, undertaking or association of undertakings whose interests might be affected by the granting of aid, in particular the beneficiary of the aid, competing undertakings and trade associations. Interested parties wanting to submit a formal complaint to the Commission should fill out the complaint form[46] and provide all the requested information, together with a non-confidential version of the complaint[47]. If the complaint form is complete and the submitting party shows that its interests might be affected by the granting of the aid pursuant to Article 1(h) of the Procedural Regulation[48], the Commission services will register the case as a formal complaint.

70. If the submitting party does not provide all information required by the complaint form or does not show that it has an interest to act, the Commission services will treat the submission as market information[49]. The Commission services will inform the submitting party to that effect. Market information may lead to further investigation by the Commission.

9.2. INDICATIVE TIME FRAME AND OUTCOME OF THE INVESTIGATION OF A FORMAL COMPLAINT

71. The Commission services endeavour to investigate a formal complaint within a non-binding time limit of 12 months from when they are registered. The investigation could be longer based on the circumstances of the case, for example if the Commission services need to ask the complainant, Member State or third parties for further information.

3. If a complaint is unsubstantiated, the Commission services will try to inform the complainant within 2 months from its registration that there are insufficient grounds for taking a view on the case. They will invite the complainant to submit further substantive comments within 1 month. If the complainant does not provide further comments within the deadline, the complaint will be considered to have been withdrawn.

73. With regard to complaints on approved aid and/or aid measures which do not need to be notified, the Commission services will also try to reply to the complainant within 2 months from receipt of the complaint.

74. Depending on its workload and in applying its right to set the priorities for investigations[50], the Commission services will try to carry out one of the following within 12 months following the registration of the complaint:

- adopt a decision[51], and send a copy to the complainant;
- send a letter to the complainant setting out its preliminary views on the measure based on the available information ('preliminary assessment letter'); this letter is not an official position of the Commission.

75. If the preliminary assessment letter provisionally concludes that there is no incompatible aid, the complainant can comment on it within 1 month. If the complainant does not comment within the deadline, the complaint will be considered to have been withdrawn.

76. If a complaint concerns unlawful aid, the Commission services will remind the complainant that it is possible to start proceedings before national courts which can order that such aid be suspended or recovered[52]. The Commission services may treat formal complaints on aid measures which are being challenged before national courts as a low priority for the duration of those proceedings.

77. The Commission services will usually, but not necessarily, forward the non-confidential version of the substantiated complaints to the Member State for comments. The Commission services will invite the Member State concerned to meet the deadlines for commenting and providing information on complaints. Complaints will normally be sent to the Member State in their original language. Nevertheless, the Commission services will provide a translation if the Member State asks for it. This may result in the procedure taking longer.

78. The Commission services will systematically keep Member States and complainants informed of the processing or closure of complaints.

NOTES

46 Annex IV to the Implementing Regulation.

47 See Article 24(2) of the Procedural Regulation.

48 'Interested party' means any Member State and any person, undertaking or association of undertakings whose interests might be affected by the granting of aid, in particular the beneficiary of the aid, competing undertakings and trade associations.

49 As explained in Recital 32 in the preamble to the Procedural Regulation, '[t]o ensure the quality of the complaints submitted to the Commission, and at the same time transparency and legal certainty, it is appropriate to lay down the conditions that a complaint should fulfil in order to put the Commission in possession of information regarding alleged unlawful aid and set in motion the preliminary examination. Submissions not meeting those conditions should be treated as general market information, and should not necessarily lead to ex officio investigations.

50 Case T-475/04, *Bouygues SA v Commission*, ECLI:EU:T:2007:196, paragraphs 158 and 159.

51 Article 4 of the Procedural Regulation.

52 See Commission Notice on the Enforcement of State Aid Law by National Courts (OJ C 85, 9.4.2009, p. 1-22).

10. EVALUATION PLANS

[5.220]

79. The positive effects of State aid should outweigh its potential negative effects on competition and trade. To ensure that this is the case, the Commission encourages an effective *ex post* evaluation of aid schemes which could lead to substantial distortions of competition. This includes aid schemes with large budgets or novel characteristics, and schemes in markets where significant market, technology or regulatory changes are expected. The Commission services will decide during the pre-notification phase whether an evaluation is necessary. They will inform the Member State as soon as possible, so that it has enough time to prepare an evaluation plan.

80. For schemes that must be evaluated on the basis of the GBER[53], the Member State must notify its evaluation plan to the Commission within 20 working days from the scheme's entry into force. The Commission will assess the evaluation plan and, if it meets the conditions, approve it as soon as possible. It will also then extend the period for which the scheme can be implemented under the GBER.

81. For notified schemes that must be evaluated, the Member State must submit its evaluation plan to the Commission at the same time as the notification. The Commission will assess the evaluation plan alongside the scheme itself, and its decision will cover both the plan and the scheme. All procedural requirements from the Procedural Regulation apply in full.

NOTES

53 Article 1(2)(a) of the GBER excludes from the scope of the block-exemption aid schemes with annual budgets exceeding EUR 150 million, from 6 months of their entry into force, unless the Commission has prolonged that period following the approval of an evaluation plan.

11. MONITORING

[5.221]

82. The Commission keeps all systems of aid that exist in the Member States under constant review[54]. The review takes place in cooperation with the Member States, which must provide all the necessary information to the Commission[55].

83. Since SAM, Member States have had greater possibilities to grant aid without notifying it to the Commission, mainly because GBER now applies to more measures. To ensure that those measures comply with the rules in a consistent way throughout the EU, it is increasingly important for the Commission to monitor how Member States apply existing or exempted aid schemes. Therefore, the Commission services have set up an annual monitoring process during which they select a sample of State aid cases for further scrutiny.

84. The Commission services check both the compliance of the selected schemes with their legal basis and their implementation[56].

85. The Commission services obtain the necessary information for the monitoring process through requests for information to the Member States. Member States usually have 20 working days to reply to these requests. In justified cases, for example where an exceptionally large amount of information needs to be provided, that period may be longer.

86. If the information provided is not sufficient to conclude whether the measure is correctly designed and implemented, the Commission services will send further requests for information to the Member State.

87. The Commission services will try to complete the monitoring of a State aid measure within 12 months from the first request for information and inform the Member State concerned of the outcome.

NOTES

[54] On the basis of Article 108(1) of the Treaty.

[55] In accordance with Article 21(1) of the Procedural Regulation.

[56] If the scheme was actually implemented.

12. BETTER COORDINATION AND PARTNERSHIP WITH MEMBER STATES

[5.222]

88. Since SAM, Member States have had greater responsibility in State aid control and more possibilities to grant aid without notifying it to the Commission. Therefore, cooperation between the Commission and the Member States on the application of the new State aid rules has become more important.

89. To foster closer working relationships with Member States, the Commission services have set up several working groups bringing together representatives from both the Member States and the Commission. These working groups meet on a regular basis and are meant to exchange information on practical aspects and lessons learned in the application of State aid rules. The Commission services provide the secretariat for the working groups.

90. In addition, the Commission services are also ready to support Member States, for example by providing informal guidance on the interpretation of the new rules. The Commission services also try to provide training sessions for Member States on State aid topics when asked for by the Member States.

91. The Commission services have also set up a network of country coordinators to facilitate day-to-day contacts with the Member States. The country coordinator is a contact point for Member States that wish to reach out to the Commission services on the handling of cases and other aspects of the application of State aid rules. The country coordinators should be kept in copy of electronic communication on cross-cutting issues, especially on the case portfolio approach.

13. FUTURE REVIEW

[5.223]

92. The Commission will apply this Best Practices Code to notified measures and measures which were otherwise brought to its attention 30 days after it is published in the *Official Journal of the European Union.*

93. This Best Practices Code may be revised to reflect:

– changes to legislative, interpretative and administrative measures;
– the relevant case-law of the EU Courts; or
– experience gained in its application.

94. The Commission will engage, on a regular basis, in dialogue with the Member States and other stakeholders on the application of the Procedural Regulation in general, and this Best Practices Code in particular.

ANNEX
SUMMARY OF NOTIFICATION: INVITATION TO THIRD PARTIES TO SUBMIT COMMENTS NOTIFICATION OF A STATE AID MEASURE

[5.224]

On . . . the Commission received a notification of an aid measure pursuant to Article 108 of the Treaty on the Functioning of the European Union. On preliminary examination, the Commission finds that the notified measure could fall within the scope of the Streamlined Procedure pursuant to Section 6 of Communication from the Commission on a Code of Best Practices for the conduct of State aid control procedures (OJ C . . . xx.xx.2018, p. . . .).

The Commission invites interested third parties to submit their possible observations on the proposed measure to the Commission.

The main features of the aid measure are the following:

Reference number of the aid: SA . . .

Member State:

Member State reference number:

Region:

Granting authority:

Title of the aid measure:

National legal basis:

Proposed Union basis for assessment: . . . guidelines or established Commission practice as highlighted in Commission Decision (1, 2 and 3).

Type of measure: Aid scheme/Ad hoc aid

Amendment of an existing aid measure:

Duration (scheme):

Date of granting:

Economic sector(s) concerned:

Type of beneficiary (SMEs/large enterprises):

Budget:

Aid instrument (grant, interest rate subsidy, . . .):

Observations raising competition issues relating to the notified measure must reach the Commission no later than 10 working days following the date of this publication and include a non-confidential version of these observations to be provided to the Member State concerned and/or other interested parties. Observations can be sent to the Commission by fax, by post or email under reference number SA . . . to the following address:

European Commission

Directorate-General for Competition

State Aid Registry

1049 Bruxelles/Brussels

BELGIQUE/BELGIË

Fax +32 22961242

Email: stateaidgreffe@ec.europa.eu

COMMUNICATION FROM THE COMMISSION

(2019/C247/01)

Commission Notice on the recovery of unlawful and incompatible State aid

[5.225]

NOTES

Date of publication in OJ: OJ C247, 23.7.2019, p 1.

TABLE OF CONTENTS

1. INTRODUCTION

[5.226]

1. Since 2012, the European Commission ('Commission') has implemented the State Aid Modernisation Agenda ('SAM').[1] Under the SAM, the Commission has streamlined and consolidated a number of guidelines. A package of legislation has also strengthened the Member States' responsibility and increased cooperation between the Commission and Member States in the field of State aid enforcement. As a result, Member States grant more aid without prior control by the Commission. The Juncker Commission has put particular focus on this matter and since 2015, more than 96 % of new aid measures for which expenditure was reported for the first time was covered by the General Block Exemption Regulation ('GBER')[2] — an absolute increase of about 28 percentage points compared to 2013.[3] The Commission, for its part, has enhanced the downstream monitoring to ensure that Member States remove distortions to competition by recovering the aid which is paid in breach of the State aid rules. This is an important part of the Commission's overall enforcement agenda.

2. The purpose of this Notice is to explain the European Union rules and procedures governing the recovery of State aid, and how the Commission works with Member States to ensure compliance with their obligations under European Union law. It is addressed to the authorities of the Member States in charge of implementing a decision by which the Commission has ordered the recovery of State aid (a 'recovery decision').

3. In 1973, the Court of Justice of the European Union (the 'Court of Justice') established for the first time that the Commission has the power to decide that a Member State must alter or abolish a State aid found incompatible with the internal market and to require repayment of that aid.[4] In 1983[5] the Commission informed the Member States that it had decided to use all measures at its disposal to ensure that Member States fulfil their obligations under current Article 108(3) of the Treaty on the Functioning of the European Union ('TFEU'),[6] including the requirement to recover aid granted in breach of European Union State aid rules.

4. In the second half of the 1980s and in the 1990s, the Commission started ordering more systematically that Member States recover incompatible aid. In 1999, Council Regulation (EC) No 659/1999,[7] now replaced by Council Regulation (EU) 2015/1589[8] (the 'Procedural Regulation'), introduced basic rules on recovery. More detailed implementing provisions were laid down in Commission Regulation (EC) No 794/2004[9] (the 'Implementing Regulation').

5. In 2007, the Commission explained its policy and practice in the Notice 'Towards an effective implementation of Commission decisions ordering Member States to recover unlawful and incompatible State aid' (the '2007 Recovery Notice').[10]

6. Since then, the Commission's practice and the case law of the General Court and the Court of Justice (together, the 'Union Courts') has evolved. This Notice explains those developments and replaces the 2007 Recovery Notice.

7. This Notice forms part of the modernised State aid control framework introduced by the SAM, by assisting Member States in their responsibilities for ensuring the correct enforcement of State aid rules, promoting better cooperation between the Commission and Member States, and increasing further the predictability of the Commission's actions.

8. Furthermore, this Notice aims to contribute to a robust enforcement of competition policy, in line with the Commission's priority to remedy distortions of competition that undermine the level playing field in the internal market. On the one hand, the enforcement of recovery policy spurs efficiency and growth in the internal market. On the other hand, enhanced cooperation between the Commission and Member States may reduce the recourse to infringement proceedings.

9. This Notice does not create or alter any right or obligation as compared to those laid down in the Treaty on the Functioning of the European Union, the Procedural Regulation and the Implementing Regulation as interpreted by the Union Courts.

NOTES

1 Communication from the Commission to the European Parliament, the Council, the European Economic and Social Committee and the Committee of the Regions – EU State Aid Modernisation (SAM), COM/2012/0209 final.

2 Commission Regulation (EU) No 651/2014 of 17 June 2014 declaring certain categories of aid compatible with the internal market in application of Articles 107 and 108 of the Treaty (OJ L187, 26.6.2014, p 1).

3 See http://ec.europa.eu/competition/state_aid/scoreboard/index_en.html

4 See Judgment of the Court of Justice of 12 July 1973, *Commission v Germany ('Kohlegesetz')*, C-70/72, ECLI-:EU:C:1973:87, paragraph 13.

5 Commission communication (OJ C318, 24.11.1983, p 3).

6 OJ C202, 7.6.2016, p 47.

7 Council Regulation (EC) No 659/1999 of 22 March 1999 laying down detailed rules for the application of Article 93 of the EC Treaty (OJ L83, 27.3.1999, p 1).

8 Council Regulation (EU) 2015/1589 of 13 July 2015 laying down detailed rules for the application of Article 108 of the Treaty on the Functioning of the European Union (codification) (OJ L248, 24.9.2015, p 9).

9 Commission Regulation (EC) No 794/2004 of 21 April 2004 implementing Council Regulation (EC) No 659/1999 laying down detailed rules for the application of Article 93 of the EC Treaty (OJ L140, 30.4.2004, p 1).

10 OJ C272, 15.11.2007, p 4.

2. GENERAL PRINCIPLES

[5.227]

10. The TFEU prevents Member States from giving financial advantages to undertakings in a way which could distort competition in the internal market. Under Article 107(1) TFEU, State aid is incompatible with the internal market, unless it falls within the categories of exceptions laid down in paragraphs (2) and (3) of that same Article. Articles 42, 93, 106(2), 108(2) and 108(4) TFEU also provide for conditions under which State aid is or may be considered compatible with the internal market.

11. Under Article 108(2) TFEU, the Commission has exclusive competence to assess the compatibility of an aid measure with the internal market.[11] The assessment of the Commission is subject to review by the General Court and the Court of Justice.[12]

12. Article 108(3) TFEU provides that each Member State must notify in advance to the Commission any plans to grant or alter aid. It prohibits Member States from putting into effect the proposed aid measure before the Commission has adopted a final decision on its compatibility with the internal market (the so-called 'standstill obligation').

13. New aid[13] implemented without notification to the Commission or before its approval is unlawful.[14] As the standstill obligation has direct effect,[15] national courts must draw all consequences from the unlawfulness of the aid. In particular, the Member State concerned must in principle put an end to its implementation and, when already implemented, order its recovery in the absence of exceptional circumstances.[16] The Commission, for its part, has also to establish the incompatibility of the unlawful aid with the internal market before ordering its recovery.[17]

14. While the TFEU does not contain any explicit provision on the recovery of unlawful State aid, the Court of Justice has ruled that recovery is the necessary corollary of the general prohibition of State aid established by Article 107(1) TFEU and protects the effectiveness of the standstill obligation enshrined in Article 108(3) TFEU.[18]

15. The Union Courts have subsequently provided further guidance on the scope of the recovery obligation and on how to meet it. The rules and procedures in the Procedural Regulation and the Implementing Regulation are based on that case law.

2.1. THE PURPOSE AND SCOPE OF RECOVERY

16. The purpose of recovery is to restore the situation which existed in the internal market before the aid was paid.[19] By paying back the unlawful aid, in fact, its recipient forfeits the advantage which it has enjoyed over its competitors.[20] To eliminate any advantages incidental to the unlawful aid, interest on the aid amount unlawfully granted (the 'recovery interest') is also to be recovered. By paying the recovery interest the aid beneficiary forfeits the financial advantage arising from the availability of the aid in question, free of charge, from the date it was put at the disposal of the beneficiary until it is paid back.[21]

17. Article 16(1) of the Procedural Regulation requires the Commission to order recovery of unlawful and incompatible aid unless that would be contrary to a general principle of European Union law. The Commission orders a Member State to recover the aid through a recovery decision.

18. Article 16(2) of the Procedural Regulation establishes that the aid must be recovered together with the interest accrued until the date of its effective recovery; the Implementing Regulation sets out the method for calculating the recovery interest (see section 4.4.2).

19. Lastly, Article 16(3) of the Procedural Regulation states that 'recovery shall be effected without delay and in accordance with the procedures under the national law of the Member State concerned, provided that they allow for the immediate and effective execution of the Commission decision'.

2.2. THE PRINCIPLE OF SINCERE COOPERATION

2.2.1. The general principle

20. Article 4(3) of the Treaty on European Union[22] ('TEU') requires Member States to facilitate the achievement of the European Union's tasks. Pursuant to the principle of sincere cooperation, the European Union and Member States must assist each other in carrying out those tasks, with a view to attaining the objectives of the European Union.

21. This principle, which is applicable in all relations between the Commission and the Member States, is particularly important for the State aid recovery policy.[23]

22. The Commission and the Member States must cooperate in good faith in all phases of State aid proceedings, especially during an investigation pursuant to Article 108(2) TFEU. Good cooperation already during the investigation may allow for easier and faster execution of a recovery decision.

2.2.2. The principle applied to the sharing of information

23. The Member State concerned by a recovery decision must report to the Commission regularly about its implementation. That cooperation allows the Commission to assess the correct execution of a recovery decision and to better identify any need for assistance.

24. In particular, the Commission may share examples of spreadsheets for the Member State to provide information on aid beneficiaries and aid amounts. The Commission may also share mock calculations of aid to be recovered, based on the formulae or methodologies established in the relevant recovery decision.

25. In that context, the Commission, in line with the recovery decision, may assist the Member State concerned by elaborating on the standard of proof and the type of evidence required to determine, among other things, the identity of the aid beneficiaries, the amount of aid subject to recovery and the amounts finally recovered. The Commission may also share examples of escrow agreements (see paragraph 118).

2.3. THE OBLIGATION TO RECOVER

26. Recovery of State aid is not a penalty[24] but rather the logical consequence of the finding that it is unlawful,[25] and it cannot depend on the form in which the aid was granted.[26] Recovery can therefore neither be regarded as disproportionate to the objectives of the TFEU with regard to State aid,[27] nor as entailing unjust enrichment for the Member State concerned, since it merely provides for the restitution of an amount that should not have been paid to the beneficiary.[28]

27. Pursuant to Article 13(2) of the Procedural Regulation, the Commission can use its discretion and adopt a recovery injunction already during its investigation of the aid measures concerned — i.e. before adopting a final decision on the compatibility of the aid measures with the internal market — provided a series of cumulative criteria are fulfilled.

28. On the contrary, where adopting a decision finding that aid is incompatible with the internal market ('negative decision'), the Commission has no discretion and must order the recovery of the aid[29] unless that would be contrary to a general principle of European Union law. For this reason, once the Commission has established that an aid measure is unlawful and incompatible with the internal market, it is not required to state additional reasons to order its recovery.[30]

29. Irrespective of the source of the recovery obligation, be that a recovery injunction or a recovery decision, the Member State concerned must implement recovery effectively and immediately, in accordance with Article 16(2) and Article 16(3) of the Procedural Regulation. The measures taken by the Member State cannot only aim at an immediate and effective execution of the recovery decision, but must actually attain it.[31]

2.4. LIMITS TO THE OBLIGATION TO RECOVER

2.4.1. General principles of European Union law

30. Under Article 288 TFEU, decisions are binding in their entirety upon those to whom they are addressed. In the case of State aid, the Commission addresses its decision to the Member State concerned, which is obliged to execute it[32] by making use of all the measures necessary to ensure its implementation, including interim measures.[33] Commission decisions are presumed to be lawful and remain binding in all respects also while proceedings before the Union Courts are pending.[34]

31. In line with the Union Courts' case law and Article 16(1) of the Procedural Regulation, the Commission does not require recovery of State aid if this would be contrary to a general principle of European Union law.

32. Neither the TEU nor the TFEU identify or list the general principles of European Union law; instead, the Union Courts have derived them from the general principles common to the laws of the Member States. The following paragraphs deal with the general principles of European Union law most frequently invoked in the context of the implementation of the recovery obligation.

33. While these principles inspire the whole European Union legal framework, in the context of State aid recovery policy they are subject to a restrictive interpretation.[35] Therefore, generic claims about an alleged infringement of a general principle of European Union law cannot be accepted.

2.4.1.1.
The principle of legal certainty

34. The principle of legal certainty requires that legal rules be clear, precise and predictable in their effect, so that interested parties can ascertain their position in situations and legal relationships governed by European Union law.[36] Therefore, Member States and aid beneficiaries are afforded protection against a recovery order in case of a breach of legal certainty.

35. The Union Courts have given a restrictive interpretation of the principle of legal certainty and have accepted that recovery be limited only in exceptional circumstances, to be assessed on a case-by-case basis.

36. Where State aid has been granted in breach of the standstill obligation, a delay by the Commission in exercising its supervisory powers and ordering recovery of the aid is not a sufficient legal ground to limit or exclude recovery.[37]

37. In addition, the principles of the primacy and effectiveness of European Union law mean that Member States and aid beneficiaries cannot rely on the principle of legal certainty to limit recovery in case of an alleged conflict between national and European Union law. European Union law prevails and national rules must be left unapplied or interpreted in a way that preserves the effectiveness of European Union law.[38]

38. Under the law of certain Member States, the national legal basis of an aid measure becomes null and void from the date of its entry into force as a consequence of the adoption of a Commission recovery decision. In light of the principle of effectiveness, any such provision under national law cannot affect the lawfulness of the Commission decision and the obligation to recover. Recovery cannot depend on the consequences under national law of the failure to comply with the standstill obligation.[39]

2.4.1.2.
The principle of the protection of legitimate expectations

39. The principle of the protection of legitimate expectations[40] is a corollary of the principle of legal certainty and the Union Courts have applied them in conjunction. It concerns any person who can entertain expectations which are justified and well founded, having received precise, unconditional and consistent assurances from the competent institutions of the European Union. Those assurances must be given in accordance with the applicable rules.[41] Thus, this principle protects justified expectations of Member States and aid beneficiaries that the Commission will not order the recovery of aid.

40. In view of the mandatory nature of Article 108(3) TFEU, a Member State whose authorities have granted aid in breach of the standstill obligation may not plead that that infringement creates a legitimate expectation for a beneficiary that the aid would not be recovered. Otherwise, Article 107 and Article 108 TFEU would be deprived of any effect.[42]

41. Similarly, in case of breach of the standstill obligation, the aid beneficiary cannot claim to entertain legitimate expectations that the grant of the aid was lawful, unless exceptional circumstances apply.[43] A diligent business operator should be able to determine whether the aid was duly approved by the Commission.[44] This principle also applies to small undertakings.[45]

42. The Union Courts have identified a series of situations which do not give rise to legitimate expectations and which, therefore, cannot limit or preclude recovery of the aid concerned. In particular, the following situations do not create legitimate expectations:

— the silence of the Commission on an aid measure notified to it;[46]
— any apparent failure of the Commission to react to an aid measure which was not notified;[47]
— the adoption of a decision opening a formal investigation pursuant to Article 6 of the Procedural Regulation, in which the Commission merely carries out a provisional assessment of the aid measures at issue, since an aid beneficiary cannot base legitimate expectations on a provisional decision;[48]
— absence of action by the Commission for a relatively long period;[49]
— an earlier decision from the Commission;[50]
— the adoption of several successive Commission decisions authorising the grant of aid, subsequently annulled by the Union Courts;[51]
— a proposal for a decision from the Commission submitted to the Council.[52]

2.4.1.3.
The principle of res judicata

43. The principle of *res judicata* establishes that 'judicial decisions which have become definitive after all rights of appeal have been exhausted or after expiry of the time limits provided to exercise those rights can no longer be called into question'.[53]

44. The Court of Justice recognised the importance of this principle in both the legal order of the European Union and the legal systems of the Member States.[54] However, since its application cannot undermine the primacy and effectiveness of European Union law, the principle of *res judicata* cannot be used to justify an infringement of European Union law and to preclude the recovery of State aid.[55]

45. Under the principle of primacy of European Union law, European Union State aid rules prevail over conflicting national laws, which must be left unapplied. This holds true also for national rules and judicial rulings whose effect is that the application of the principle of *res judicata* breaches European Union State aid rules.

46. With specific regard to unlawful aid, while the rules implementing the principle of res judicata are a matter for the legal system of each Member State in accordance with the principle of procedural autonomy, they cannot render any final decision by a national court an obstacle, nor can they have the consequence of making it impossible for the national courts or authorities to drawing the necessary consequences from the breach of the standstill obligation.[56]

2.4.1.4.
Absolute impossibility to recover

47. The principle that 'no one is obliged to do the impossible' is among the general principles of European Union law.[57] The existence of exceptional circumstances which make it absolutely impossible for a Member State to implement the recovery decision is the only situation recognised by the Court of Justice as justifying the Member State's failure to implement that decision.[58]

48. Absolute impossibility has been construed by the Union Courts in a restrictive manner. A Member State must demonstrate that it attempted, in good faith, to recover the aid and it must cooperate with the Commission in accordance with Article 4(3) TEU, with a view to overcoming the difficulties encountered.[59]

49. The burden of proof is on the Member State to demonstrate the existence of reasons justifying the absence of recovery[60] or only partial recovery of the incompatible aid. The type of evidence necessary to prove absolute impossibility to recover depends on the specific features of each case.

50. The Member State concerned cannot demonstrate the absolute impossibility of implementing a recovery decision by merely informing the Commission of legal, political, practical or internal difficulties.[61]

51. Thus, the Member State concerned, in order to justify its failure to comply with a recovery decision, cannot plead the existence of absolute impossibility based on requirements of national law, such as national limitation periods,[62] the absence of a right under national law to impose recovery[63] or a legal vacuum.[64] Equally, a Member State cannot plead provisions, practices or situations prevailing in its domestic legal order, including concerns of social unrest,[65] to justify its failure to observe obligations arising from European Union law.[66] Only in very specific cases may the basis for an absolute impossibility be a legal one, provided that it complies with European Union law.[67]

52. The Member State must identify and adopt the necessary measures without delay.[68] To attain that result, the Member State concerned may have to adopt new legal acts, including legislation, or to set aside provisions of national law which do not allow for a swift removal of the difficulties encountered. Lastly, the attempts to recover must be exhaustive and duly substantiated with evidence.[69]

53. Nor is the obligation to recover the aid affected by the economic situation of the beneficiary. The fact that an undertaking is in financial difficulties or even insolvent does not constitute proof that recovery is impossible,[70] unless it has been liquidated and no assets are recoverable[71] (see section 4.8). In addition, the aid is impossible to recover where the beneficiary has already ceased to exist, without any legal and economic successor (see paragraph 135).

54. The aim of recovery is not to maximise the Member States' return but to restore the situation that existed in the internal market before the aid was granted. Consequently, possible losses for a Member State in its capacity as a shareholder or creditor do not justify its failure to fulfil the recovery obligation.

55. While the absolute impossibility to recover is typically an issue which arises during the execution of a recovery decision, the absolute impossibility to recover may already be established during the Commission's formal investigation pursuant to Article 6 of the Procedural Regulation.[72]

2.4.2. LIMITATION PERIOD

56. Article 17(1) of the Procedural Regulation establishes that the powers of the Commission to order the recovery of aid are subject to a limitation period of 10 years (the 'limitation period').

57. Pursuant to Article 17(2) of the Procedural Regulation, the limitation period begins on the day on which the unlawful aid is awarded to the beneficiary,[73] either as individual aid or as aid under an aid scheme.[74] In the case of an aid scheme, the limitation period does not run from the date of adoption of its legal basis but from the moment the individual aid is granted under that scheme.[75]

58. The date on which aid was granted depends on the nature of the aid in question. For a multiannual scheme entailing payments or other financial advantages granted on a periodic basis, the date of adoption of the legal basis of the aid scheme and the date on which the undertakings concerned will actually be granted the aid may be a considerable period of time apart. In this case, for the purpose of calculating the limitation period the aid must be regarded as not having been awarded to the beneficiary until the date on which it was actually received by the beneficiary.[76]

59. The principle referred to in paragraph 58 also applies to an aid scheme entailing fiscal measures granted on a periodic basis (for instance, tax reliefs on every annual or biannual tax declaration, etc.), for which the limitation period starts running for each fiscal exercise on the date on which the tax is due.

60. To enforce a recovery decision, the Member State concerned may have to perform controls, for example tax audits of certain fiscal years, even when that would be time-barred under national law. In that case, national prescription rules cannot justify a failure to fulfil the recovery obligation and must be left unapplied, if need be.[77]

61. Since the investigation of an aid measure is a bilateral procedure between the Member State and the Commission, after the limitation period has started running it can be interrupted by any action undertaken by the Commission or by the Member State at the Commission's request.[78] This is the case irrespective of whether the action has been notified to the aid beneficiary[79] or has come to its knowledge. If a decision of the Commission is subject to proceedings before the Union Courts, the limitation period remains suspended until the end of the proceedings.

62. Article 17(3) of the Procedural Regulation provides that 'any aid with regard to which the limitation period has expired shall be deemed to be existing aid'. The limitation period provided for by the Procedural Regulation 'merely precludes recovery of aid awarded more than 10 years before the Commission first intervened'.[80]

2.5. THE APPLICATION OF NATIONAL LAW AND THE IMMEDIATE AND EFFECTIVE EXECUTION OF THE COMMISSION'S RECOVERY DECISIONS

63. Article 16(3) of the Procedural Regulation codified the requirements of the principle of effectiveness.[81] The recovery obligation is met only when the Member State concerned has effectively recovered the amount of incompatible aid, including the recovery interest[82] (the 'full recovery amount').

64. The Member State concerned can choose the means to meet its obligation to recover aid, provided that they comply with the principle of effectiveness[83] and the principle of equivalence.[84] The question whether the Member State concerned has given immediate and effective execution of the recovery obligation in accordance with those principles can be assessed only on a case-by-case basis.[85]

NOTES

11 See Judgment of the Court of Justice of 21 November 1991, *Fédération nationale du commerce extérieur des produits alimentaires and Others v France ('Saumon')*, C-354/90, ECLI:EU:C:1991:440, paragraph 14; Judgment of the Court of Justice of 15 December 2005, *Unicredito Italiano*, C-148/04, ECLI:EU:C:2005:774, paragraph 42.

12 See Judgment of the Court of Justice of 8 December 2011, *Residex Capital IV*, C-275/10, ECLI:EU:C:2011:814, paragraph 27.

13 See Article 1(c) of Council Regulation (EU) 2015/1589 of 13 July 2015 laying down detailed rules for the application of Article 108 of the Treaty on the Functioning of the European Union (codification) (OJ L248, 24.9.2015, p 9).

14 Under Articles 109 and 108(4) TFEU, some categories of State aid may be exempted from the obligation to notify it to the Commission, under the so-called 'exemption Regulations'. Any aid granted pursuant to an exemption Regulation without meeting the conditions for exemption from notification established therein is also unlawful. See Judgment of the Court of Justice of 5 March 2019, *Eesti Pagar*, C-349/17, ECLI:EU:C:2019:172, paragraphs 84-87. Article 108(2) TFEU also provides for the exceptional and specific case in which the Council may decide that aid is compatible with the internal market. See Judgment of the Court of Justice of 4 December 2013, *Commission v Council*, C-117/10, ECLI:EU:C:2013:786, paragraph 51.

15 See Judgment of the Court of Justice of 21 November 1991, *Fédération nationale du commerce extérieur des produits alimentaires and Others v France ('Saumon')*, C-354/90, ECLI:EU:C:1991:440, paragraph 11,; Judgment of the Court of Justice of 21 November 2013, *Deutsche Lufthansa*, C-284/12, ECLI:EU:C:2013:755, paragraph 29.

16 To that effect, see Judgment of the Court of Justice of 11 July 1996, *SFEI and Others*, C-39/94, ECLI:EU:C:1996:285, paragraphs 68-71. See also Judgment of the Court of Justice of 5 March 2019, *Eesti Pagar*, C-349/17, ECLI-:EU:C:2019:172, paragraphs 92-94. For additional information on the role of national courts in the enforcement of State aid rules, see the Commission Notice on the enforcement of State aid law by national courts (OJ C85, 9.4.2009, p 1), or any legal act amending or replacing it.

17 The Court has clarified that the Commission cannot request recovery of unlawful aid without first examining the compatibility of the aid with the internal market under the procedure provided for by Article 108(2) TFEU. To that effect, see Judgment of the Court of Justice of 14 February 1990, *France v Commission ('Boussac')*, C-301/87, ECLI-:EU:C:1990:67, paragraphs 9, 10–22. This does not preclude the possibility for the Commission to issue a recovery injunction in specific cases, see paragraph 27.

18 See Judgment of the Court of Justice of 11 December 1973, *Lorenz GmbH v Bundesrepublik Deutschland and Others*, C-120/73, ECLI:EU:C:1973:152, paragraphs 3 and 4.

19 See Judgment of the Court of Justice of 11 December 2012, *Commission v Spain ('Magefesa II')*, C-610/10, ECLI:EU:C:2012:781, paragraph 105.

20 See Judgment of the Court of Justice of 4 April 1995, *Commission v Italy ('ALFA Romeo')*, C-348/93, ECLI-:EU:C:1995:95, paragraph 27.

21 See Judgment of the Court of First Instance of 8 June 1995, *Siemens v Commission*, T-459/93, ECLI:EU:T:1995:100, paragraphs 9-101.

22 OJ C202, 7.6.2016, p 13.

23 See Judgment of the Court of Justice of 11 September 2014, *Commission v Germany ('Biria Gruppe')*, C-527/12, ECLI:EU:C:2014:2193, paragraph 51 and 56.

24 See Judgment of the Court of Justice of 17 June 1999, *Belgium v Commission ('Maribel bis/ter scheme')*, C-75/97, ECLI:EU:C:1999:311, paragraph 65.

25 See Judgment of the Court of Justice of 21 December 2016, *Commission v Aer Lingus*, C-164/15 P and C-165/15 P, ECLI:EU:C:2016:990, paragraphs 114 and 116.

26 See Judgment of the Court of Justice of 17 September 2015, *Commission v Italy ('Venice and Chioggia II')*, C-367/14, ECLI:EU:C:2015:611, paragraph 41.

27 See Judgment of the Court of Justice of 21 March 1990, *Belgium v Commission ('Tubemeuse')*, C-142/87, ECLI:EU:C:1990:125, paragraph 66.

28 See Judgment of the General Court of 1 March 2017, *SNCM v Commission*, T-454/13, ECLI:EU:T:2017:134, paragraph 269.

29 See Judgment of the Court of Justice of 7 March 2002, *Italy v Commission ('Employment Measures I')*, C-310/99, ECLI:EU:C:2002:143, paragraph 99.

30 See Judgment of the General Court of 20 September 2011, *Regione autonoma della Sardegna and Others v Commission*, T-394/08, T-408/08, T-453/08 and T-454/08, ECLI:EU:T:2011:493, paragraph 152.

31 See Judgment of the Court of Justice of 29 March 2012, *Commission v Italy ('Hotel industry in Sardinia')*, C-243/10, ECLI:EU:C:2012:182, paragraph 35.

32 See Article 31(2) of the Procedural Regulation, stating that negative decisions shall be addressed to the Member State concerned.

33 See Judgment of the Court of Justice of 14 November 2018, *Commission v Greece ('Hellenic Shipyards II')*, C-93/17, ECLI:EU:C:2018:903, paragraph 69.

34 See Judgment of the Court of Justice of 9 July 2015, *Commission v France ('Lignes maritimes Marseille-Corse')*, C-63/14, ECLI:EU:C:2015:458, paragraph 44.

35 See Judgment of the General Court of 20 September 2011, *Regione autonoma della Sardegna and Others v Commission*, T-394/08, T-408/08, T-453/08 and T-454/08, ECLI:EU:T:2011:493, paragraph 283.

36 See Judgment of the Court of Justice of 15 February 1996, *Duff and Others*, C-63/93, ECLI:EU:C:1996:51, paragraph 20.

37 The principle of legal certainty has the effect of preventing the Commission from indefinitely delaying the exercise of its powers. However, the Court of Justice established that 'a delay by the Commission in exercising its supervisory powers and ordering recovery of the aid does not render that recovery decision unlawful, except in exceptional cases which show that the Commission manifestly failed to act and clearly breached its duty of diligence': see Judgment of the Court of Justice of 22 April 2008, *Commission v Salzgitter*, C-408/04 P, ECLI:EU:C:2008:236, paragraph 106. In the *GIE Fiscaux* case, the Commission decided that due to the specific combination of exceptional circumstances in that case, recovery had to be limited to the aid granted after the date of the Commission decision to initiate the formal investigation pursuant to Article 6 of the Procedural Regulation, in order to protect the principle of legal certainty. See Commission Decision of 20 December 2006 on the aid scheme implemented by France under Article 39 CA of the General Tax Code — State aid C 46/2004 (ex NN 65/2004) (OJ L112, 30.4.2007, p 41).

38 See Judgment of the Court of Justice of 5 October 2006, *Commission v France ('Scott')*, C-232/05, ECLI-:EU:C:2006:651, paragraphs 50-53.

39 See Judgment of the General Court of 7 October 2010, *DHL Aviation and DHL Hub Leipzig v Commission*, T-452/08, ECLI:EU:T:2010:427, paragraphs 34 and 41.

40 On the principle of the protection of legitimate expectations, see Judgment of the Court of Justice of 20 September 1990, *Commission v Germany*, C-5/89, ECLI:EU:C:1990:320, paragraphs 13 and 14.

41 See Judgment of the Court of Justice of 24 March 2011, *ISD Polska and Others v Commission*, C-369/09 P, ECLI:EU:C:2011:175, paragraph 123; Judgment of the Court of Justice of 16 December 2010, *Kahla Thüringen Porzellan v Commission*, C-537/08 P, ECLI:EU:C:2010:769, paragraph 63; Judgment of the Court of Justice of 16 December 2008, *Masdar (UK) v Commission*, C-47/07 P, ECLI:EU:C:2008:726, paragraphs 34 and 81.

42 See Judgment of the Court of Justice of 9 June 2011, *Diputación Foral de Vizcaya and Others v Commission*, C-465/09 P to C-470/09 P, ECLI:EU:C:2011:372, paragraph 150.

43 See Judgment of the General Court of 15 November 2018, *Deutsche Telekom v Commission*, T-207/10, ECLI-:EU:T:2018:786, paragraph 42. The Court of Justice has recognised the existence of legitimate expectations of an aid beneficiary only once, in the RSV judgment. See Judgment of the Court of Justice of 24 November 1987, *RSV v Commission*, C-223/85, ECLI:EU:C:1987:502. However, the Union Courts have underlined the exceptional circumstances of that case, by refusing to extend the protection of legitimate expectations beyond the exceptional situation identified in RSV; for instance, see Judgment of the Court of First Instance of 14 January 2004, Fleuren *Compost v Commission*, T-109/01, ECLI:EU:T:2004:4, paragraphs 145-148 and Judgment of the Court of Justice of 29 April 2004, *Italy v Commission*, C-298/00 P, ECLI:EU:C:2004:240, paragraph 90.

44 See Judgment of the Court of Justice of 20 March 1997, *Land Rheinland-Pfalz v Alcan Deutschland*, C-24/95, ECLI:EU:C:1997:163, paragraph 25.

45 See Judgment of the Court of Justice of 29 April 2004, *Italy v Commission*, C-298/00 P, ECLI:EU:C:2004:240, paragraph 88.

46 See Judgment of the Court of First Instance of 30 November 2009, *France v Commission*, T-427/04 and T-17/05, ECLI:EU:T:2009:474, paragraph 261.

47 See Judgment of the Court of Justice of 8 December 2011, *France Télécom v Commission*, C-81/10 P, ECLI-:EU:C:2011:811, paragraphs 58-60.

48 See Judgment of the General Court of 27 February 2013, *Nitrogénmuvek Vegyipari v Commission*, T-387/11, ECLI:EU:T:2013:98, paragraph 121; Judgment of the Court of First Instance of 25 March 2009, *Alcoa Trasformazioni v Commission*, T-332/06, ECLI:EU:T:2009:79, paragraph 61.

49 See Judgment of the Court of Justice of 28 July 2011, *Diputación Foral de Vizcaya and Others v Commission*, C-471/09 P to C-473/09 P, ECLI:EU:C:2011:521, paragraphs 64-65, 68, 75-77.

50 A previous decision finding that a certain measure does not constitute State aid or declaring a certain State aid measure compatible with the internal market must be read as strictly applicable to the particular facts and circumstances of that specific case. Each case must be assessed on its own merits. Thus, for instance, the Court of Justice held that an earlier decision declaring a measure as not constituting State aid for a limited duration and based on the circumstances prevailing at a given time cannot give rise to legitimate expectations as to the future assessment of the State aid nature of a similar measure. See Judgment of the Court of Justice of 21 July 2011, *Alcoa Trasformazioni v Commission*, C-194/09 P, ECLI:EU:C:2011:497, paragraphs 72-75. A different situation occurs if the Commission alters its appraisal of a measure on the basis only of a more rigorous application of the Treaty rules on State aid. In this circumstance, the Court concluded that the aid beneficiaries were entitled to expect that a Commission decision reversing its previous approach would give them the time necessary to address that change and therefore they benefit from the protection of legitimate expectations. To that effect, see Judgment of the Court of Justice of 22 June 2006, *Belgium v Commission ('Forum 187')*, C-182/03 and C-217/03, ECLI:EU:C:2006:416, paragraph 71.

51 In the *CELF II* judgment, the Court of Justice held that the unusual succession of annulments reflects, in principle, the difficulty of the case and, far from giving rise to legitimate expectations, would rather appear likely to increase the aid beneficiary's doubts as to the compatibility of the disputed aid. See Judgment of the Court of Justice of 11 March 2010, *CELF and ministre de la Culture et de la Communication ('CELF II')*, C-1/09, ECLI:EU:C:2010:136, paragraphs 51-52 and 55.

52 See Judgment of the Court of Justice of 24 March 2011, *ISD Polska and Others v Commission*, C-369/09 P, ECLI:EU:C:2011:175, paragraph 124.

53 See Judgment of the Court of Justice of 22 December 2010, *Commission v Slovakia ('Frucona Košice')*, C-507/08, ECLI:EU:C:2010:802, paragraph 59.

54 See Judgment of the Court of Justice of 24 January 2013, *Commission v Spain ('Magefesa')*, C-529/09, ECLI-:EU:C:2013:31, paragraph 64.

55 See Judgment of the Court of Justice of 18 July 2007, *Lucchini*, C-119/05, ECLI:EU:C:2007:434, paragraphs 61-63; Judgment of the Court of Justice of 11 November 2015, *Klausner Holz Niedersachsen*, C-505/14, ECLI:EU:C:2015:742, paragraph 45.

56 See Judgment of the Court of Justice of 11 November 2015, *Klausner Holz Niedersachsen*, C-505/14, ECLI-:EU:C:2015:742, paragraph 40; see also Judgment of the Court of Justice of 5 March 2019, *Eesti Pagar*, C-349/17, ECLI:EU:C:2019:172, paragraph 138 and 139.

57 Judgment of the Court of Justice of 6 November 2018, *Scuola Elementare Maria Montessori v Commission*, C-622/16 P to C-624/16 P, ECLI:EU:C:2018:873, paragraph 79.

58 See Judgment of the Court of Justice of 9 November 2017, *Commission v Greece ('Larco')*, C-481/16, ECLI-:EU:C:2017:845, paragraph 28.

59 See Judgment of the Court of Justice of 12 February 2015, *Commission v France ('Plans de Campagne')*, C-37/14, ECLI:EU:C:2015:90, paragraph 67.

60 See, to that effect, Judgment of the Court of Justice of 9 July 2015, *Commission v France ('Lignes maritimes Marseille-Corse')*, C-63/14, ECLI:EU:C:2015:458, paragraphs 52 and 53.

61 See Judgment of the Court of Justice of 9 November 2017, *Commission v Greece ('Larco')*, C-481/16, ECLI-:EU:C:2017:845, paragraph 29; see also Judgment of the Court of Justice of 6 November 2018, *Scuola Elementare Maria Montessori v Commission*, C-622/16 P to C-624/16 P, ECLI:EU:C:2018:873, paragraphs 91 and 95.

62 See Judgment of the Court of Justice of 20 March 1997, *Land Rheinland-Pfalz v Alcan Deutschland*, C-24/95, ECLI:EU:C:1997:163, paragraphs 34-37.

63 See Judgment of the Court of Justice of 21 March 1991, *Italy v Commission ('Lanerossi')*, C-303/88, ECLI-:EU:C:1991:136, paragraphs 52 and 60.

64 See Judgment of the Court of Justice of 17 October 2013, *Commission v Greece ('Ellinikos Xrysos')*, C-263/12, ECLI:EU:C:2013:673, paragraph 36.

65 To that effect, the Court has clarified that 'as regards the possible outbreak of social unrest which might jeopardise public order, the Court has consistently held, as the Advocate General noted in paragraph 86 of his Opinion, that where such unrest is threatened, it is for the Member State to adopt all appropriate measures to guarantee the full scope and effect of European Union law so as to ensure its proper implementation in the interests of all economic operators, concerned unless it can show that action on its part would have consequences for public order with which it could not cope by using the means at its disposal'. See Judgment of the Court of Justice of 9 July 2015, *Commission v France ('Lignes maritimes Marseille-Corse')*, C-63/14, ECLI:EU:C:2015:458, paragraph 52.

66 See Judgment of the Court of Justice of 17 September 2015, *Commission v Italy ('Venice and Chioggia II')*, C-367/14, ECLI:EU:C:2015:611, paragraph 51.

67 See Judgment of the Court of Justice of 11 September 2014, *Commission v Germany ('Biria Gruppe')*, C-527/12, ECLI:EU:C:2014:2193, paragraph 49.

68 See Judgment of the Court of Justice of 9 July 2015, *Commission v France ('Lignes maritimes Marseille-Corse')*, C-63/14, ECLI:EU:C:2015:458, paragraph 49.

69 See Judgment of the Court of Justice of 9 July 2015, *Commission v France ('Lignes maritimes Marseille-Corse')*, C-63/14, ECLI:EU:C:2015:458, paragraph 57.

70 See Judgment of the Court of Justice of 15 January 1986, *Commission v Belgium*, C-52/84, ECLI:EU:C:1986:3, paragraph 14.

71 See Judgment of the Court of Justice of 2 July 2002, *Commission v Spain*, C-499/99, ECLI:EU:C:2002:408, paragraph 37.

72 See Judgment of the Court of Justice of 6 November 2018, *Scuola Elementare Maria Montessori v Commission*, C-622/16 P to C-624/16 P, ECLI:EU:C:2018:873, paragraphs 82 and 84.

73 Judgment of the General Court of 25 January 2018, *BSCA v Commission*, T-818/14, ECLI:EU:T:2018:33, paragraph 72.

74 The notions of 'aid scheme' and 'individual aid' are defined, respectively, in Article 1(d) and (e) of the Procedural Regulation.

75 See Judgment of the Court of Justice of 8 December 2011, *France Télécom v Commission*, C-81/10 P, ECLI-:EU:C:2011:811, paragraph 80.

76 See Judgment of the Court of Justice of 8 December 2011, *France Télécom v Commission*, C-81/10 P, ECLI-:EU:C:2011:811, paragraph 82.

77 See Judgment of the Court of Justice of 20 March 1997, *Land Rheinland-Pfalz v Alcan Deutschland*, C-24/95, ECLI:EU:C:1997:163, paragraphs 34-37.

78 For example, a request for information from the Commission to the Member State concerned interrupts the limitation period and starts time running afresh. See Judgment of the Court of Justice of 26 April 2018, ANGED, C-233/16, ECLI:EU:C:2018:280, paragraphs 84 and 85.

79 See Judgment of the Court of Justice of 6 October 2005, *Scott v Commission*, C-276/03 P, ECLI:EU:C:2005:590, paragraphs 27 and 36.

80 Judgment of the Court of Justice of 23 January 2019, *Fallimento Traghetti del Mediterraneo*, C-387/17, ECLI-:EU:C:2019:51, paragraph 52; Judgment of the Court of First Instance of 30 April 2002, Gibraltar v Commission, T-195/01 and T-207/01, ECLI:EU:T:2002:111, paragraph 130.

81 See Judgment of the Court of Justice of 11 September 2014, *Commission v Germany ('Biria Gruppe')*, C-527/12, ECLI:EU:C:2014:2193, paragraphs 39 and 41.

82 To that effect, see Judgment of the Court of Justice of 6 October 2011, *Commission v Italy ('Venice and Chioggia I')*, C-302/09, ECLI:EU:C:2011:634, paragraphs 38 and 39.

83 See Judgment of the Court of Justice of 5 October 2006, *Commission v France ('Scott')*, C-232/05, ECLI-:EU:C:2006:651, paragraph 49.

84 Pursuant to the principle of equivalence, national law must be applied in a non-discriminatory manner as compared to similar cases which are governed solely by national legislation. See Judgment of the Court of Justice of 13 June 2002, *Netherlands v Commission*, C-382/99, ECLI:EU:C:2002:363, paragraph 90.

85 See Judgment of the Court of Justice of 11 September 2014, *Commission v Germany ('Biria Gruppe')*, C-527/12, ECLI:EU:C:2014:2193, paragraph 43.

3. THE RESPECTIVE ROLES OF THE COMMISSION AND THE MEMBER STATE CONCERNED

[5.228]
65. Both the Commission and the Member States have an essential role to play in implementing recovery decisions and must contribute to the effective enforcement of recovery policy. A robust enforcement of recovery policy, coupled with close and proactive cooperation, effectively remedies distortions of competition in the internal market and promotes its full potential.

3.1. THE ROLE OF THE COMMISSION

66. The Commission endeavours in its recovery decisions to identify the beneficiaries of the incompatible aid and quantify the aid to be recovered.[86] This allows recovery decisions to be implemented more swiftly and facilitates the fulfilment of the recovery obligation. If that is not possible, the Commission describes in the recovery decision the methodology by which the Member State has to identify the beneficiaries and determine the aid amount to be recovered.[87]

67. Pursuant to the principle of sincere cooperation, the Commission assists the Member State concerned in implementing the recovery decision, among other things, by:

— sharing examples of spreadsheets for the Member State concerned to provide information on aid beneficiaries and aid amounts (see paragraphs 24 and 25);
— assessing requests to extend the deadline to execute a recovery decision (see section 4.1);
— organising a kick-off meeting (see section 4.2);
— providing a tool to calculate recovery interest (see paragraph 111);
— sharing examples of escrow agreements suitable for the provisional recovery of aid (see paragraph 118);
— informing the Member State concerned about the provisional or definitive closure of a recovery procedure (see section 4.9).

3.2. THE ROLE OF THE MEMBER STATE

68. Member States play a crucial role in rendering recovery policy effective. In particular, by providing accurate and complete information in the course of the formal investigation pursuant to Article 6 of the Procedural Regulation, Member States can contribute to the adoption of recovery decisions that are more easily enforceable and prevent or reduce the risk that recovery is not immediate and effective. In particular, a Member State may submit specific circumstances that, in its view, should be taken into account by the Commission when establishing the deadline to implement the recovery obligation (see paragraphs 71 and 72).

69. Pursuant to Article 16(1) of the Procedural Regulation, the Member State concerned is required to take all necessary measures to recover the aid from the beneficiary. Based on the legal system of the Member State concerned, several authorities, either at local, regional or national level, may be concerned by the recovery process. A Commission decision addressed to a Member State is binding on all the organs of that State, including its courts.[88]

70. In the absence of pertinent provisions of European Union law, it is for each Member State to implement a recovery decision by applying the rules and procedures laid down by national law.[89] Whilst each Member State designates the actual entity responsible for the implementation of the recovery decision, some Member States have entrusted a single body with the task of coordinating and overseeing the national recovery process. In the experience of the Commission, a single coordinating body contributes to the immediate and effective execution of recovery decisions, by collecting and disseminating knowledge at national level and by creating a stable channel of communication with the Commission's services.

NOTES

86 Whilst it is generally not complex to identify the beneficiary of individual aid, the Commission is generally not in the position to identify each and all of the beneficiaries of an incompatible aid scheme, let alone the exact amount of aid received.

87 The Commission is not legally required to spell out in its recovery decision the exact amount to be recovered. It is sufficient for the Commission to include in it information enabling the Member State to quantify that amount without overmuch difficulty. See Judgment of the Court of Justice of 28 July 2011, *Mediaset v Commission*, C-403/10 P, ECLI:EU:C:2011: 533, paragraph 126.

88 See Judgment of the Court of Justice of 21 May 1987, *Albako v BALM*, C-249/85, ECLI:EU:C:1987:245, paragraph 17. See also Judgment of the Court of Justice of 5 March 2019, Eesti Pagar, C-349/17, ECLI:EU:C:2019:172, paragraph 90.

89 See Judgment of the Court of Justice of 13 June 2002, *Netherlands v Commission ('Service stations')*, C-382/99, ECLI:EU:C:2002:363, paragraph 90.

4. IMPLEMENTING THE RECOVERY DECISION

[5.229]
71. Where the Commission concludes that aid already granted is incompatible with the internal market and orders its recovery, the Member State concerned must abolish the aid[90] and recover it, where relevant,[91] within the deadline set by the Commission (the 'recovery deadline'). Recovery after the recovery deadline cannot satisfy the requirements of European Union law and represents a failure to execute the recovery decision.[92] In any event, the Member State concerned remains under an obligation to enforce the recovery of the unlawful aid and to put an end to the infringement of European Union law as close as possible after the expiry of the recovery deadline.

72. In its recovery decision, the Commission sets two deadlines for the Member State concerned to (i) submit precise information on the measures it has planned and already undertaken to execute the recovery decision (generally within 2 months of its service); and (ii) fulfil the recovery obligation (generally within 4 months of its service).[93] In particular, within the first deadline the Member State is generally required to provide complete information on the identity of the beneficiaries, if not already identified in the recovery decision, the amount to be recovered and the national procedure applicable to fulfil the recovery obligation.

73. The Member State concerned is free to choose the national procedure to implement a recovery decision, provided that it allows for the immediate and effective execution of the recovery decision.[94] In the experience of the Commission, fast-track, specialised administrative procedures can be very effective and allow Member States to duly comply with their obligations. Irrespective of the national procedure chosen to implement a recovery decision, the competent authority or court is under a duty to give full effect to European Union law[95]

4.1. REQUEST FOR AN EXTENSION OF THE DEADLINE TO EXECUTE THE DECISION

74. If a Member State encounters difficulties in executing the recovery decision within the recovery deadline, it is under a duty to submit those difficulties for consideration to the Commission, in sufficient time to enable the latter to assess the situation, together with proposals for suitable solutions.[96] This may include a proposal to extend the recovery deadline.

75. In these cases, the Commission and the Member State concerned must work together in good faith to overcome the difficulties while fully complying with European Union law.[97] In the same way, the Member State concerned must provide the Commission with all the information enabling it to establish that the means chosen will lead to the correct implementation of the recovery decision.[98]

76. The Commission's practice is to grant an extension of the deadline to execute its decision only in exceptional circumstances if the Member State demonstrates with conclusive evidence that all other possible measures that could lead to timely implementation of the Commission decision would not be effective.

77. Requests for extension of the recovery deadline are not granted where the delay in recovery is due to the ways and means chosen by the Member State, where faster options were available.

78. Requests to extend the recovery deadline once it has elapsed cannot be granted retroactively[99] (see paragraph 71).

4.2. KICK-OFF MEETING

79. The Commission customarily offers a kick-off meeting to the authorities of the Member States concerned shortly after the service of a recovery decision. This is preferably held within one month and in any case before the expiry of the first deadline to provide information, as referred to in paragraph 72.

80. The kick-off meeting aims to facilitate and accelerate the recovery process by establishing a collaborative and transparent relationship between the Commission and the authorities of the Member State concerned. The Commission also explains the tools that it can offer the Member State to facilitate the recovery.

81. The Commission endeavours to give, during the kick-off meeting, initial feedback about the recovery strategy and the implementing measures that the Member State concerned has planned to ensure compliance with the recovery decision.

82. While participating in a kick-off meeting is not compulsory, the Commission strongly encourages Member States to avail themselves of this possibility to receive guidance on the main aspects of recovery and to anticipate any request for clarifications they may need.

4.3. IDENTIFICATION OF THE BENEFICIARIES FROM WHOM THE AID MUST BE RECOVERED

83. Unlawful aid found to be incompatible with the internal market must be recovered from the beneficiaries that actually benefitted from it.[100] When the aid beneficiaries are not identified in the recovery decision, the Member State concerned must look at the individual situation of each undertaking concerned.[101]

84. Pursuant to Article 345 TFEU, private and public undertakings are subject to the same State aid rules; therefore there is no difference between them when it comes to recovering unlawful aid.

4.3.1. Identification of the aid beneficiary belonging to a group of undertakings

85. Generally, the identification of the aid beneficiary is not complex. In some cases, however, the Commission may have to assess which undertaking within a group of undertakings forming an economic unit benefitted from the aid.

86. Where certain transactions occurred within a group of undertakings, the Commission may still limit the scope of recovery to only one aid beneficiary within the group. However, the Commission may conclude in its recovery decision that undertakings belonging to a group, even if they are qualified under national law as separate legal entities, form an economic unit for the purposes of competition law[102] and have benefitted from the aid. The Commission may also conclude that other undertakings of such group have benefitted from the aid.

87. In the case referred to in paragraph 86, the recovery decision may order the Member State concerned to recover the aid not only from the undertaking which directly benefitted from it but also from the whole group of undertakings forming an economic unit or from some of the legal entities belonging to it[103] that also benefitted from the aid.

88. In implementing such a recovery decision, the Member State concerned must prove to the Commission that it has correctly recovered the aid either from its direct beneficiary or from the other undertakings subject to the recovery obligation.

4.3.2. Extension of the recovery order; economic continuity

89. If, at the implementation stage of a recovery decision, the aid cannot be recovered from the original beneficiary and it was transferred to another undertaking, the Member State should extend recovery to the undertaking that effectively enjoys the advantage following the transfer of activities and ensure that the recovery obligation is not circumvented.[104]

90. The Court of Justice has drawn a distinction between two means to transfer the activities of an undertaking. These are (i) the sale of all or part of its assets, following which the activity is no longer carried out by the same legal entity ('asset deal'); and (ii) the sale of its shares, following which the undertaking which has benefitted from the aid retains its legal personality and continues to carry out its activities ('share deal').[105]

4.3.2.1.
Asset deal

91. Where the beneficiary of incompatible aid creates a new company or transfers its assets to another undertaking to continue some or all of its activities, the continuation of those activities may prolong the distortion of competition brought about by the aid. Accordingly, the newly created company or the buyer of the assets may, if it retains that advantage, be required to pay back the aid in question.

92. In an asset deal scenario, the Commission assesses the existence of economic continuity between undertakings on a case-by-case basis, using an open set of non-cumulative criteria. In particular, the Commission may take into account the following criteria:[106] (i) the scope of the transfer (assets[107] and liabilities, maintenance of the workforce and/or management); (ii) the price of the transfer;[108] (iii) the identity of the shareholders or the owners of the seller and of the buyer; (iv) the time at which the transfer takes place (during the preliminary investigation pursuant to Article 4 of the Procedural Regulation or the formal investigation pursuant to Article 6 of the that Regulation, or after adoption of the recovery decision); (v) the economic logic of the operation.[109]

4.3.2.2.
Share deal

93. The sale to a third party of shares in a beneficiary of incompatible aid does not affect the obligation of the beneficiary to reimburse such aid.[110]

94. Where the shares of the undertaking to which unlawful State aid was granted are sold, but the undertaking retains its legal personality and continues to carry out the activities subsidised by the State aid, the Member State must recover the aid from it.[111] In fact, it is that undertaking which maintains an advantage over its competitors.

4.2.3.3.
Mergers and other business reorganisations

95. Besides asset and share deals, a Member State may be called upon to determine from which undertaking the aid must be recovered following a merger or another form of business reorganisation. In these cases, the Member State concerned must identify the legal successor of the original aid beneficiary and recover the aid from the surviving entity.[112]

4.3.3. THE AID BENEFICIARIES OF TAX MEASURES

96. As regards the specific case of schemes granting tax reliefs, the Member State concerned must identify the undertakings that have benefitted from the advantage granted through the scheme and recover the aid from them.

97. For the purpose of identifying a beneficiary it is not relevant whether the aid measure has been applied correctly by the relevant undertaking in its tax declaration or, instead, in breach of the applicable national rules.[113] The relevant question is whether an undertaking has enjoyed the tax relief found to constitute State aid incompatible with the internal market. National procedures to address the misapplication or abuse of national tax rules cannot jeopardise the immediate and effective recovery of State aid.

4.4. QUANTIFICATION OF THE AMOUNT TO BE RECOVERED

98. Where the Commission decision already quantifies the aid amount, a Member State is bound to implement the decision as adopted by the Commission. If the Member State disputes the quantification of the aid amount, the issue has to be brought before the Union Courts. It follows that the Member State must recover the aid amount as established in the recovery decision, unless and until it has been suspended or annulled by the General Court or the Court of Justice.

99. If the Commission has not quantified the precise amount of aid to be recovered in the recovery decision, the Member State concerned must quantify the aid to be recovered from each of the beneficiaries, based on the methodology set out in the recovery decision.[114]

100. In principle, the Commission requires the Member State to recover all aid, unless at the time it was granted the aid met the applicable requirements established by (i) a regulation declaring certain categories of aid compatible with the internal market in application of Article 107 and Article 108 TFEU (a 'Block Exemption Regulation'); (ii) a regulation establishing that some public support does not meet all the criteria of Article 107(1) TFEU and is therefore exempted from the notification provided for in Article 108(3) TFEU ('*de minimis* Regulation'); (iii) a different, previous decision of the Commission.[115]

101. The Commission can accept the retrospective application of the *de minimis* rule to an aid beneficiary, under the following conditions:

— the entire amount of aid must be below the *de minimis* ceiling;[116] in this regard, the use of average amounts per beneficiary is not acceptable, since it does not ensure that no undertaking benefitted from a total amount that exceeded that ceiling;[117]

— when verifying retrospectively the amount of *de minimis* aid granted over any period of 3 fiscal years, a Member State must consider each 3 fiscal year period which includes the date on which the aid which should purportedly be excluded from recovery was granted;[118] and

— all the conditions laid down in the applicable Regulation, which can be applied retrospectively must be met.[119]

102. To calculate the amount to be recovered, a Member State can also take into account whether the beneficiary has paid taxes on the aid received. If that is the case, (i.e. the gross aid does not equal the net aid), the Member State may, in accordance with its national tax rules, take account of the earlier payment of taxes by recovering only the net amount received by the aid beneficiary.

103. By contrast, where a beneficiary of unlawful and incompatible aid has not paid taxes on the aid received (i.e. the gross aid equals the net aid), the beneficiary must pay back the gross amount of aid received.

104. In any case, the Member State concerned must ensure that the aid beneficiary will not be able to enjoy a further tax relief by claiming that the reimbursement has reduced his taxable income.

4.4.1. Tax measures

105. In the context of a State aid granted through tax relief, 're-establishing the *status quo ante* means returning, as far as possible, to the situation which would have prevailed if the operations at issue had been carried out without the tax reduction'.[120]

106. Therefore, the Member State concerned must calculate the correct tax amount that an undertaking should have paid without the unlawful aid measure. This quantification can only be based on the choices actually made in the past, without taking into account alternative, hypothetical choices which would have been available.[121] Only automatically applicable deductions provided for by national and international law, if applicable, or by the recovery decision can be taken into account.

107. For instance, if a Member State implements a recovery decision by increasing the tax base of the aid beneficiary, other tax reliefs which were already available at the time the initial tax was due could in principle still be applied.[122]

108. Based on the obligation of professional secrecy established by Article 339 TFEU and Article 30 of the Procedural Regulation, the confidentiality of tax documents is not a valid justification for not providing the requested evidence in this context.

109. Pursuant to national law, in order to collect tax amounts (including State aid granted in the form of tax reliefs), the tax authorities of the Member State concerned might have to carry out internal tax audits prior to the actual recovery. Such tax audits are acceptable provided that (i) they lead to recovery within the recovery deadline; and (ii) the methodology set out in the decision for quantifying the aid to be recovered is followed.

4.4.2. Calculation of recovery interest

110. Under Article 16(2) of the Procedural Regulation, the aid to be recovered pursuant to a recovery decision includes interest from the date when the aid was made available to the beneficiary until its recovery.[123] Pursuant to the Implementing Regulation interest must be applied on a compound basis.[124]

111. It is the task of the Member State concerned to quantify the exact amount of interest to be recovered. To facilitate that task, the Commission has made available to Member States a tool to calculate interest according to the rules established by the Implementing Regulation.[125]

4.5. THE SERVICE OF RECOVERY ORDERS

112. The Member State to which a recovery decision is addressed must order the beneficiary to pay back the aid incompatible with the internal market within the time period prescribed in the decision. An immediate service of the recovery order, imposing the repayment of the State aid within the recovery deadline, is crucial to guarantee that the requirements established by Article 16(3) of the Procedural Regulation are met (see paragraph 19).

113. The nature and features of a recovery order may vary depending on, among other things, the granting authority, the way the incompatible aid was granted, its amount. Without prejudice to the peculiarities of the relevant national legal system, in the experience of the Commission standardised forms and procedures for the service of recovery orders may contribute to a timely and effective execution of recovery decisions.

114. The reference to national law also implies that in principle all rules and procedures in the legal order of the Member State concerned shall apply, irrespective of their source. Therefore, for aid beneficiaries not having their seat or a permanent establishment in the territory of the Member State concerned, the service of recovery orders may be governed by the rules and procedures established in international agreements or private international law applicable in that Member State.

115. In accordance with the principle of sincere cooperation, Member States must warn the Commission at the earliest opportunity if they expect difficulties in serving a recovery order.

4.6. PROVISIONAL IMPLEMENTATION OF RECOVERY

116. Where a recovery decision is still subject to legal challenges, a Member State may accept provisional repayment of the aid to be recovered.

117. The Member State concerned may consider provisional recovery insofar as it is adequate to ensure the full, albeit provisional, removal of the distortion of competition brought about by the incompatible aid. To that end, the Member State concerned must ensure that the advantage linked to the unlawful and incompatible aid leaves the beneficiary. The Member State concerned should justify to the Commission the need for provisional measures and submit an exhaustive description of the provisional measures envisaged.

118. Provisional implementation of the recovery decision can be achieved, for instance, by way of a payment by the beneficiary of the full recovery amount into an escrow account.[126] The Commission is ready to share examples of suitable escrow agreements. A Member State may also submit to the Commission a specific escrow account agreement complying with the conditions cited in paragraph 117.

119. Conversely, the provision of guarantees for the future payment of the recovery amount is not an adequate provisional measure since the aid is meanwhile left at the disposal of the beneficiary.

120. Alternatively, if provided for by national law, a beneficiary can choose to pay back the aid amount and the recovery interest to the Member State under a special clause by which the aid returns to the beneficiary if the final outcome of the ongoing litigation is favourable to the latter.

121. Other means of provisional implementation may also be used in exceptional cases, as long as the principles described above are respected. In the absence of immediate final recovery, Member States should make use of any existing provision in their legal order allowing their authorities to order an interim payment of the aid,[127] even when that provision is not designed for the specific purpose of recovering State aid.[128]

4.7. ALTERNATIVE MEANS OF RECOVERY

122. Where a Member State recovers aid by means other than a cash payment, it must provide the Commission with the information enabling it to establish that the means chosen constitute an appropriate means to implement the decision.[129] The Commission accepts alternative means of recovery only if: (i) they are a suitable instrument for re-establishing the market conditions that have been distorted by the unlawful aid measure; (ii) they are capable of being identified as such by the Commission and other interested parties;[130] and (iii) the Member State proves that they have an equivalent effect to a cash payment.

123. The Commission regularly receives requests to accept recovery implemented through alternative means, such as recovery in kind or offsetting of State aid claims against the existing credits held by the aid beneficiary against the Member State concerned.

124. The Commission can accept recovery in kind only in exceptional cases, if the conditions cited in paragraph 122 are met and if the Member State concerned acts in compliance with the following basic principles.

- The value of the assets must be established in an objective manner in order to allow the Commission to conclude that the value is equivalent to the recovery amount, including the appropriate recovery interest.
- Recovery in kind must be allowed under national law. The Member State must inform the Commission of the relevant legal provisions at national level which provide for recovery in kind.
- It must be avoided that economic activities are carried out using the beneficiary's assets for a certain period of time after the decision (for instance at least until full depreciation of those assets according to standard accounting rules). On this point, reference is made to the criteria for evaluating the existence of economic continuity set out in paragraph 92.

125. The Commission can accept offsetting of claims only in exceptional cases, if the Member State concerned acts in compliance with the following basic principles.

- The possibility of offsetting claims is provided for by national law;[131]
- The claims offset are certain, of a fixed amount and due; and
- The measures taken are fully transparent in order to enable the Commission to satisfy itself that they are suitable for the purpose of eliminating the distortion to competition caused by the aid.

126. Deferrals of recovery or payments in instalments beyond the recovery deadline would imply that the recovery obligation is not implemented without delay, and are therefore not allowed, even if they would maximise the return of the Member State concerned (see paragraph 54).

4.8. INSOLVENCY PROCEEDINGS

127. An aid beneficiary which is not able to pay back the aid and the recovery interest due is in principle surviving in the market only because of the aid it received. Therefore, to restore the situation in the internal market retrospectively through the removal of the aid, that aid beneficiary must exit the internal market. If the aid beneficiary exits the market but a portion or all of the advantage is transferred to a legal and economic successor, the recovery obligation should be extended to the latter (see section 4.3.2).

128. In order to recover the aid from an insolvent beneficiary, the Member State can only proceed to seize the assets of the aid beneficiary and to cause its liquidation if the latter is unable to pay back the aid or to take any other measure enabling the aid to be recovered, as provided for under its national law.[132] In this regard, recovering the aid by means of proceedings aimed at winding up the beneficiary cannot in principle be regarded as disproportionate to the objectives of the TFEU.[133] Therefore, the Member State concerned must bring those proceedings in its capacity as a creditor or shareholder, where it has this latter position.[134]

129. From the moment the aid beneficiary is undergoing insolvency proceedings, restoration of the previous situation and elimination of the distortion of competition resulting from the aid can be achieved through registration of the claim relating to the aid to be recovered in the schedule of liabilities[135] within the recovery deadline. In that case, the registration of the claim must be followed by (i) recovery of the full recovery amount, or, if that can not achieved, (ii) the winding-up of the undertaking and the definitive cessation of its activities.[136]

130. As regards the first condition cited in paragraph 129, the Member State concerned must register the amount to be recovered, i.e. the incompatible aid, together with recovery interest accrued until full repayment or until an earlier date if under national law interest stops accruing for all creditors on that earlier date (for instance, the date of opening of the insolvency proceedings). As recovery interest forfeits the financial advantage arising from the availability of the aid (see paragraph 16) and, as such, its recovery serves the same purpose of the recovery of the aid principal, Member States must register the aid principal amount and recovery interest with the same ranking.

131. As regards the second condition cited in paragraph 129, certain Member States provide for proceedings aimed at the restructuring or temporary continuation of some or all of the activities of insolvent undertakings. However, such proceedings must be left unapplied insofar as, in absence of timely recovery of the full recovery amount, they prevent the winding up and cessation of activities of the aid beneficiary.[137]

132. Thus, where a plan providing for the continuation of the activity of the aid beneficiary is proposed to the creditors' committee, the authorities of the Member State concerned can support that plan only if it ensures recovery of the full recovery amount within the recovery deadline. A Member State cannot waive part of its recovery claim if the aid beneficiary continues its activity after the recovery deadline.

133. There might be cases where the shareholders of an aid beneficiary decide to voluntarily liquidate it, outside a procedure administered by or under the surveillance of a court. Irrespective of the procedure chosen, the same principles outlined in this section apply.

134. All the organs of the Member State concerned, including its courts, must leave unapplied all provisions under the national insolvency proceedings or the national rules governing voluntary liquidation which, by keeping the aid to be recovered at the disposal of the beneficiary, do not ensure immediate and effective execution of a Commission recovery decision. In the same way, the Commission considers that the Member State must challenge any decision adopted by its national courts in breach of European Union law.[138]

135. For the purpose of the fulfilment of the recovery obligation, an aid beneficiary is liquidated when its activities cease and its assets and interests are sold under market conditions.[139] While national rules apply, the sale must be carried out through an open, transparent and non-discriminatory procedure.[140] The evaluation of the assets should be carried out by an independent expert. Based on the Commission's experience, these requirements are generally met in the case of bankruptcy proceedings under the surveillance of a court. To prevent the buyer of the assets from being liable to pay back the aid, the Member State must ensure that there is no economic continuity (see section 4.3.2).

4.9. PROVISIONAL AND DEFINITIVE CLOSURE OF RECOVERY PROCEDURES

136. Over recent years, the Commission has developed the internal practice of 'provisional closure' of recovery procedures. This applies to situations where a recovery decision has been provisionally implemented by a Member State but cannot be considered as definitively executed due to: (i) pending litigation at European Union or national level; (ii) ongoing national administrative procedures that may still affect the fulfilment of the recovery obligation; or (iii) still pending insolvency proceedings in which the State aid claims have been properly registered at the appropriate rank.

137. Pursuant to the principle of sincere cooperation, the Commission endeavours to communicate to the Member State concerned when it provisionally closes a recovery procedure.

138. Following the provisional closure of a recovery procedure, the Member State concerned must keep the Commission updated and continue providing information and evidence on request and at least once per year until the Commission concludes that the Member State concerned has definitively executed the recovery decision.

139. The Commission also continues to inform the Member State concerned about its assessment of the state of the procedure. By letter from its services, it also informs the Member State when the recovery procedure is definitively closed. At that stage, the recovery procedure is also removed from the list of State aid cases with pending recovery procedures published on the website of the Commission's Directorate-General for Competition.[141]

140. Neither the provisional nor the definitive closure of a recovery procedure precludes the Commission from resuming closer scrutiny of the matter or reopening the procedure. That would be the case if new facts change the situation that had led the Commission to the closure.

NOTES

90 This implies that a Member State must take all the measures necessary to restore the situation which existed before the aid was granted, including, for instance, by cancelling a contract. See Judgment of the Court of Justice of 8 December 2011, Residex Capital IV, C-275/10, ECLI:EU:C:2011:814, paragraphs 45-47.

91 See Judgment of the Court of Justice of 20 March 1997, *Land Rheinland-Pfalz v Alcan Deutschland*, C-24/95, ECLI:EU:C:1997:163, paragraph 34.

92 To that effect, see Judgment of the Court of Justice of 22 December 2010, *Commission v Italy ('Newly listed companies')*, C-304/09, ECLI:EU:C:2010:812, paragraph 32.

93 The Commission may set a different recovery deadline, based on the specific circumstances of the case. See paragraph 68.

94 See Judgment of the Court of Justice of 11 September 2014, *Commission v Germany ('Biria Gruppe')*, C-527/12, ECLI:EU:C:2014:2193, paragraph 41.

95 See Judgment of the Court of Justice of 5 March 2019, Eesti Pagar, C-349/17, ECLI:EU:C:2019:172, paragraph 91.

96 See Judgment of the Court of Justice of 9 November 2017, *Commission v Greece ('Larco')*, C-481/16, ECLI-:EU:C:2017:845, paragraph 29.

97 See Judgment of the Court of Justice of 20 March 2014, *Rousse Industry v Commission*, C-271/13 P, ECLI-:EU:C:2014:175, paragraph 78.

98 For an illustration of proposals for implementation, see Judgment of the Court of Justice of 12 December 2002, *Commission v Germany*, C-209/00, ECLI:EU:C:2002:747, paragraphs 40-44.

99 In that sense, see Judgment of the Court of Justice of 9 July 2015, *Commission v France ('Lignes maritimes Marseille-Corse')*, C-63/14, ECLI:EU:C:2015:458, paragraph 45.

100 See Judgment of the Court of Justice of 29 April 2004, *Germany v Commission ('SMI')*, C-277/00, ECLI-:EU:C:2004:238, paragraph 75.

101 See Judgment of the Court of Justice of 13 February 2014, *Mediaset*, C-69/13, ECLI:EU:C:2014:71, paragraph 22.

102 According to the case law of the Court of Justice, where legally distinct natural or legal persons constitute an economic unit, they must be treated as a single undertaking for the purposes of European Union competition law. See Judgment of the Court of Justice of 12 July 1984, *Hydrotherm*, C-170/83, ECLI:EU:C:1984:271, paragraph 11. The Commission has a broad discretion to determine whether undertakings of a group should be considered as an economic unit or separate entities for the purpose of State aid law. See Judgment of the General Court of 29 June 2000, *DSG v Commission*, T-234/95, ECLI:EU:T:2000:174, paragraph 124.

103 See Judgment of the Court of First Instance of 29 June 2000, *DSG v Commission*, T-234/95, ECLI:EU:T:2000:174, paragraph 124.

104 See Judgment of the General Court of 13 September 2010, *Greece v Commission*, T-415/05, T-416/05 and T-423/05, ECLI:EU:T:2010:386, paragraphs 143-146.

105 See Judgment of the Court of Justice of 29 April 2004, *Germany v Commission ('SMI')*, C-277/00, ECLI-:EU:C:2004:238, paragraphs 78 and 84.

106 The Commission is not required to take into account all of the criteria. To that effect, see Judgment of the General Court of 28 March 2012, *Ryanair v Commission*, T-123/09, ECLI:EU:T:2012:164, paragraphs 155 and 156.

107 As regards the scope of the transaction, in principle the assets sold have to be only a part of those owned by the aid

beneficiary. The larger the share of the original business that is transferred to a new entity, the higher the likelihood that the economic activity related to the assets sold continues to benefit from the incompatible aid. See Commission Decision (EU) 2015/1826 of 15 October 2014 on the State aid SA.33797 — (2013/C) (ex 2013/NN) (ex 2011/CP) implemented by Slovakia for NCHZ (OJ L269, 15.10.2015, p 71). As regards economic continuity, see Commission Decision of 17 September 2008, State aid N 321/08, N 322/08 and N 323/08 — Greece — *Vente de certains actifs d'Olympic Airlines/Olympic Airways Services*; Commission decision of 12 November 2008 State aid N 510/2008 — Italy — Sale of assets of Alitalia; Commission decision of 4 April 2012 SA.34547 — France — *Reprise des actifs du groupe SERNAM dans le cadre de son redressement judiciaire*.

108 Where the assets are sold through an open, transparent, non-discriminatory and non-conditional tender to the highest bidder, the price paid is generally presumed to be the market price. This principle was followed by the Commission in Commission Decision of 1.10.2014 on the State aid SA.31550 (2012/C) (ex 2012/NN) implemented by Germany for Nürburgring; Commission Decision of 27.3.2014 on the State aid SA.34572 (13/C) (ex 13/NN) implemented by Greece for Larco General Mining & Metallurgical Company S.A.; Commission Decision of 7.5.2015 on the State aid SA.35546 (2013/C) (ex 2012/NN) implemented by Portugal for Estaleiros Navais de Viana do Castelo S.A.

109 The Commission found economic continuity in cases where there would be no change in the way the business was run, in the scope of the activity or in production. For instance, see Commission Decision (EU) 2015/1826 of 15 October 2014 on the State aid SA.33797 — (2013/C) (ex 2013/NN) (ex 2011/CP) implemented by Slovakia for NCHZ (OJ L269, 15.10.2015, p 71). Conversely, in cases where significant changes in the activity or the business strategy were demonstrated, the Commission took the view that there was no economic continuity. See Commission Decision (EU) 2016/151 of 1 October 2014 on the State aid SA.31550 (2012/C) (ex 2012/NN) implemented by Germany for Nürburgring (OJ L34, 10.2.2016, p 1); Commission Decision (EU) 2016/152 of 1 October 2014 on State aid SA 27339 (12/C) (ex 11/NN) implemented by Germany for Zweibrücken airport and airlines using the airport (OJ L34, 10.2.2016, p 68). In any event, economic logic alone has not been considered a conclusive element when looking for economic continuity between two undertakings.

110 See Judgment of the Court of Justice of 29 April 2004, *Germany v Commission ('SMI')*, C-277/00, ECLI-:EU:C:2004:238, paragraph 81.

111 See Judgment of the Court of Justice of 1 October 2015, *Electrabel and Dunamenti Eromu v Commission*, C-357/14 P, ECLI:EU:C:2015:642, paragraph 113.

112 To that effect, see Judgment of the Court of Justice of 7 March 2018, *SNCF Mobilités v Commission*, C-127/16 P, ECLI:EU:C:2018:165.

113 See Judgment of the Court of Justice of 14 July 2011, *Commission v Italy ('Tremonti bis')*, C-303/09, ECLI-:EU:C:2011:483, paragraph 43.

114 See Judgment of the Court of Justice of 13 February 2014, *Mediaset*, C-69/13, ECLI:EU:C:2014:71, paragraph 21. See also paragraph 66 above.

115 For instance, see Commission Decision of 11 July 2001 on the State aid scheme applied by Spain to certain newly established firms in Álava (OJ L314, 18.11.2002, p 1), Recital 90.

116 See Judgment of the General Court of 20 September 2011, *Regione autonoma della Sardegna and Others v Commission*, T-394/08, T-408/08, T-453/08 and T-454/08, ECLI:EU:T:2011:493, paragraphs 310-312, as upheld by Judgment of the Court of Justice of 13 June 2013, *HGA and Others v Commission*, C-630/11 P to C-633/11 P, ECLI:EU:C:2013:387.

117 See Judgment of the Court of Justice of 13 September 2017, *Commission v Belgium*, C-591/14, ECLI:EU:C:2017:670, paragraph 46.

118 For instance, if a Member State is claiming in 2018 that an advantage granted on 31 December 2014 could be retrospectively considered as *de minimis* aid, that Member State must prove that also when including that new *de minimis* aid, the relevant ceiling is not exceeded in any of the following three-year periods: 2012-2014, 2013-2015 and 2014-2016. It follows that the Commission can allow the retrospective inclusion of that alleged *de minimis* aid only on the condition that the relevant *de minimis* ceiling is never exceeded.

119 As also established by Commission Regulation (EU) No 1407/2013 of 18 December 2013 on the application of Articles 107 and 108 of the Treaty on the Functioning of the European Union to *de minimis* aid (OJ L352, 24.12.2013, p 1).

120 See Judgment of the Court of Justice of 15 December 2005, *Unicredito Italiano*, C-148/04, ECLI:EU:C:2005:774, paragraph 117.

121 See Judgment of the Court of Justice of 15 December 2005, *Unicredito Italiano*, C-148/04, ECLI:EU:C:2005:774, paragraphs 118-119.

122 In that instance, the following conditions relating to the other tax reliefs must be fulfilled: (i) they shall not lead to any (new) State aid; (ii) they should concern all taxpayers in the same way; (iii) they shall apply by way of a rule that existed at the time the incompatible aid was granted; and (iv) the undertakings eligible to the reliefs must benefit from them automatically (i.e. the application of the relief does not require prior authorisation from the Member State nor the activation of an option in due time by the taxpayer).

123 In the case of recovery decisions subject to court proceedings, the recovery interest shall be calculated also for the periods during which the decision was suspended by a court order or annulled by a first instance judgment then overturned by the Court of Justice. To that effect, see Judgment of the Court of Justice of 12 February 2008, *CELF and ministre de la Culture et de la Communication ('CELF I')*, C-199/06, ECLI:EU:C:2008:79, paragraphs 56-58 and 69.

124 Reference and discount rates (in %) since 1 August 1997 are published on the website of the Directorate-General for Competition of the Commission.

125 Access to the tool is granted following a registration process at both national and European Union level. This registration ensures that only the authorised officials of the authorities of the Member State concerned and of the Commission's services can access the tool.

126 The payment of the total amount of aid including recovery interest on an escrow account may be governed by a specific agreement, signed by the Member State, a bank or a trustee and the aid beneficiary, by which the parties agree that the amount paid in escrow will be released in favour of one or other party, depending on the final outcome of the litigation. Should the final ruling of the Union Courts only partially uphold the recovery decision in a way that it entails the reduction of the recovery amount, the funds held in escrow, including any potential gain or loss, must be transferred to the Member State concerned and the aid beneficiary pro quota.

127 For instance, French law provides for national courts to order the provisional payment of the aid (i.e. pending the outcome of the proceedings on the merits of the case) if the obligation to pay back the aid cannot be seriously called into question. This interim request for payment (called *'référé-provision'*) can be granted for a recovery order issued following a Commission decision.

128 For instance, some Member States do not have provisions allowing their authorities responsible for recovery to order provisional payments under tax law, but do have similar provisions under civil law. In those cases, a Member State should make use of the rules allowing the provisional implementation of the decision, irrespective of the procedure chosen to execute it.

129 See Judgment of the Court of Justice of 7 July 2009, *Commission v Greece ('Olympic Airways II')*, C-369/07, ECLI:EU:C:2009:428, paragraph 79.

130 See Judgment of the Court of Justice of 12 December 2002, *Commission v Germany*, C-209/00, ECLI:EU:C:2002:747, paragraphs 57-58.

131 See Judgment of the Court of Justice of 7 July 2009, *Commission v Greece ('Olympic Airways II')*, C-369/07, ECLI:EU:C:2009:428, paragraph 68.

132 See Judgment of the Court of Justice of 17 January 2018, *Commission v Greece ('United Textiles')*, C-363/16, ECLI:EU:C:2018:12, paragraph 36.

133 See Judgment of the Court of Justice of 21 March 1990, *Belgium v Commission ('Tubemeuse')*, C-142/87, ECLI:EU:C:1990:125, paragraphs 65-66.

134 See Judgment of the Court of Justice of 17 January 2018, *Commission v Greece ('United Textiles')*, C-363/16, ECLI:EU:C:2018:12, paragraph 38.

135 As recovery is effected in accordance with the procedures under the national law of the Member State concerned, national law governs the ranking of the State aid claim in the schedule of liabilities, provided the ranking complies with the principle of effectiveness and the principle of equivalence. See paragraph 64. In any event, the State aid claim cannot be ranked lower than ordinary unsecured claims.

136 See Judgment of the Court of Justice of 11 December 2012, *Commission v Spain ('Magefesa II')*, C-610/10, ECLI:EU:C:2012:781, paragraphs 72 and 104.

137 To that effect, see Judgment of the General Court of 21 October 2014, *Italy v Commission*, T-268/13, ECLI-:EU:T:2014:900, paragraphs 62-64.

138 To that effect, see Judgment of the Court of Justice of 17 November 2011, *Commission v Italy ('Employment Measures II')*, C-496/09, ECLI:EU:C:2011:740, paragraph 74.

139 See Judgment of the Court of Justice of 29 April 2004, *Germany v Commission ('SMI')*, C-277/00, ECLI-:EU:C:2004:238, paragraph 86.

140 In that sense, see the Commission Notice on the notion of State aid as referred to in Article 107(1) of the Treaty on the Functioning of the European Union (OJ C262, 19.7.2016, p 1), paragraphs 89-96.

141 See http://ec.europa.eu/competition/state_aid/studies_reports/recovery.html

5. LITIGATION BEFORE NATIONAL COURTS

[5.230]

141. The implementation of recovery decisions can give rise to litigation before national courts.[142] In the experience of the Commission, proceedings before administrative courts, where available, tend to guarantee a faster enforcement of recovery orders than proceedings before civil courts.

142. Two main categories of recovery-related litigation can be distinguished: (i) actions brought by the recovering authority seeking a court order to force an unwilling beneficiary to pay back the aid; and (ii) actions brought by beneficiaries contesting the recovery order, including individual measures to ensure recovery.

143. There is a risk of the execution of a recovery decision being delayed where the national measures taken to implement it are challenged in court.[143]

144. If the aid beneficiary requests interim relief against the national measures adopted to implement the recovery decision because of an alleged illegality of that decision, the national court has to assess whether the case at hand fulfils the conditions established by the Court of Justice in the cases *Zuckerfabrik*[144] and *Atlanta*.[145] Under that case law, interim relief can be granted by a national court only if the following cumulative conditions are met:[146]

(i) that court entertains serious doubts as to the validity of the European Union act and, if the validity of the contested act is not already in issue before the Court of Justice, the national court itself refers the question to the Court of Justice;[147]

(ii) there is urgency, in that the interim relief is necessary to avoid serious and irreparable damage being caused to the party seeking the relief;

(iii) the national court takes due account of the interest of the European Union; and

(iv) in its assessment of all those conditions, it respects any decisions of the Court of Justice or the General Court ruling on the lawfulness of the European Union act or on an application for interim measures seeking similar interim relief at European level.

145. Where the conditions set out in paragraph 144 are not met, the Member State concerned cannot rely on interim measures granted by national courts to justify its failure to implement the decision.[148] In that context, it is for the Member State to prove that all the conditions are satisfied.[149]

NOTES

142 For additional information on the role of national courts in the enforcement of State aid rules, see the Commission Notice on the enforcement of State aid law by national courts (OJ C85, 9.4.2009, p 1), or any legal act amending or replacing it.

143 The national court concerned may cooperate with the Commission by using the cooperation tools provided for by Article 29(1) of the Procedural Regulation.

144 See Judgment of the Court of Justice of 21 February 1991, *Zuckerfabrik Süderdithmarschen and Zuckerfabrik Soest v*

Hauptzollamt Itzehoe and Hauptzollamt Paderborn, C-143/88 and C-92/89, ECLI:EU:C:1991:65, paragraph 23 and following.

145 See Judgment of the Court of Justice of 9 November 1995, *Atlanta Fruchthandelsgesellschaft and Others (I) v Bundesamt für Ernährung und Forstwirtschaft*, C-465/93, ECLI:EU:C:1995:369, paragraph 51.

146 See Judgment of the Court of Justice of 29 March 2012, *Commission v Italy ('Hotel industry in Sardinia')*, C-243/10, ECLI:EU:C:2012:182, paragraph 48.

147 See Judgment of the Court of Justice of 14 July 2011, *Commission v Italy ('Tremonti bis')*, C-303/09, ECLI-:EU:C:2011:483, paragraph 46.

148 See Judgment of the Court of Justice of 6 October 2011, *Commission v Italy ('Venice and Chioggia I')*, C-302/09, ECLI:EU:C:2011:634, paragraph 50.

149 See Judgment of the Court of Justice of 17 September 2015, *Commission v Italy ('Venice and Chioggia II')*, C-367/14, ECLI:EU:C:2015:611, paragraph 50.

6. CONSEQUENCES OF A FAILURE TO IMPLEMENT A COMMISSION RECOVERY DECISION

[5.231]

146. Where the Member State concerned has not complied with a recovery decision, and has not been able to demonstrate the existence of absolute impossibility, the Commission may initiate infringement proceedings. In addition, it may make the payment of new compatible aid to the beneficiary or beneficiaries concerned conditional to the recovery of the previous aid found unlawful and incompatible.

6.1. INFRINGEMENT PROCEEDINGS

147. Infringements of provisions of the TFEU concerning State aid affect trade and directly harm the interests of other players in the markets concerned, who do not benefit from the same type of support.

6.1.1. Action pursuant to Article 108(2) TFEU

148. Due to the importance of State aid rules for protecting competition and for the effective functioning of the internal market, Article 108(2) TFEU provides that if the Member State concerned does not comply with the recovery decision within the recovery deadline, the Commission may directly refer the matter to the Court of Justice. In fact, in contrast to Article 258 TFEU, Article 108(2) TFEU does not provide for a pre-litigation phase.[150]

149. In order to refer a matter under Article 108(2) TFEU to the Court of Justice, the Commission must first establish which obligation imposed on the Member State by the recovery decision was not fulfilled. Generally, the recovery decision includes two different types of obligations: (i) to inform the Commission of the measures taken or to be taken to implement the decision and keep it informed about the state of play of the case following the recovery deadline; and (ii) to execute the obligation to recover the State aid within the recovery deadline.

150. Consequently, the infringement of either of these obligations, as well as of any other obligation established in the recovery decision, may lead to an action pursuant to Article 108(2) TFEU. While the infringement is established if the relevant obligation was not fulfilled by the recovery deadline, Member States also remain under an obligation to enforce the recovery of the unlawful aid after its expiry.

151. The recovery obligation is an obligation of results. To remove the distortion of competition caused by the aid, Member States must succeed in actually recovering the full recovery amount.[151]

152. The Commission systematically considers launching a court action if recovery is not achieved, irrespective of the reasons for that failure[152] and of the national administration or organ which internally bears responsibility for the failure to comply with the recovery obligation.[153]

153. The decision to launch a court action is at the discretion of the Commission. It is taken on a case-by-case basis in light of objective grounds, the commitment of the Member State and of the actions already taken to implement the decision.[154] The Commission may also take into account whether the aid has been partially recovered and, if so, what percentage.

6.1.2. Actions on the basis of Article 260(2) TFEU

154. Article 260(2) TFEU provides that, if the Commission considers that the Member State has failed to fulfil the obligations established in a judgment pursuant to Article 108(2) TFEU, the Commission may bring the matter to the Court of Justice, after giving that State the opportunity to submit its observations.

155. The reference date for assessing the existence of an infringement for the purposes of Article 260(2) TFEU is the deadline set in the letter of formal notice issued in accordance with the first subparagraph of Article 260(2) TFEU.[155]

156. The procedure laid down in Article 260(2) TFEU aims to induce a defaulting Member State to comply with a previous judgment establishing a failure to fulfil obligations, thereby ensuring that European Union law is in fact applied. Both sanctions provided for by that provision, namely a lump sum and a penalty payment, are intended to achieve this objective.

157. The sanctions are decided by the Court of Justice on the basis of a proposal from the Commission (which is not binding on the Court of Justice). This proposal of sanctions under an Article 260(2) TFEU action follows the criteria set out in a Communication from the Commission[156] which is regularly updated. According to that Communication, when imposing a financial sanction on a Member State, three fundamental criteria must be taken into account: (i) the seriousness of the infringement; (ii) its duration; and (iii) the need to ensure that the sanction itself acts as a deterrent to further infringements. The Commission considers that the infringement of the recovery obligation is always a serious infringement.[157]

158. The Commission systematically considers referring to the Court of Justice, pursuant to Article 260(2) TFEU, cases where the Member State concerned has failed to comply with a judgment pursuant to Article 108(2) TFEU.[158]

6.2. THE DEGGENDORF CASE LAW

159. In its judgment in the Deggendorf case, the Court of Justice held that the Commission may declare aid to an undertaking compatible with the internal market on condition that the undertaking pays back previous unlawful aid, given the cumulative effect of the aids in question.[159]

160. Where legally distinct natural or legal persons constitute an economic unit, they are to be treated as a single undertaking for the purposes of European Union competition law. In such cases, for the purpose of assessing the cumulative effect of previous and planned new aids, the Commission must consider the group of which the aid beneficiary forms part.[160]

NOTES

150 See Judgment of the Court of Justice of 3 July 2001, *Commission v Belgium*, C-378/98, ECLI:EU:C:2001:370, paragraph 26.

151 See Judgment of the Court of Justice of 17 January 2018, *Commission v Greece ('United Textiles')*, C-363/16, ECLI:EU:C:2018:12, paragraph 34; Judgment of the Court of Justice of 24 January 2013, *Commission v Spain ('Magefesa')*, C-529/09, ECLI:EU:C:2013:31, paragraph 91. Clearly, that is without prejudice to the limits to the obligation to recover: see Section 2.4.

152 This is without prejudice to a demonstrated absolute impossibility to recover the aid.

153 See Judgment of the Court of Justice of 30 September 2003, Köbler, C-224/01, ECLI:EU:C:2003:513, paragraphs 31-33.

154 Since the adoption of the 2007 Recovery Notice, the Court of Justice has decided on several matters referred to it by the Commission under Article 108(2) TFEU. See Judgment of the Court of Justice of 17 January 2018, *Commission v Greece ('United Textiles')*, C-363/16, ECLI:EU:C:2018:12; Judgment of the Court of Justice of 9 November 2017, *Commission v Greece ('Larco')*, C-481/16, ECLI:EU:C:2017:845; Judgment of the Court of Justice of 9 July 2015, *Commission v France ('Lignes maritimes Marseille-Corse')*, C-63/14, ECLI:EU:C:2015:458; Judgment of the Court of Justice of 6 May 2015, *Commission v Germany ('Deutsche Post')*, C-674/13, ECLI:EU:C:2015:302; Judgment of the Court of Justice of 11 September 2014, *Commission v Germany ('Biria Gruppe')*, C-527/12, ECLI-:EU:C:2014:2193; Judgment of the Court of Justice of 5 June 2014, *Commission v Italy ('Exemption from excise duty')*, C-547/11, ECLI:EU:C:2014:1319; Judgment of the Court of Justice of 12 December 2013, *Commission v Italy ('Preferential electrical tariff')*, C-411/12, ECLI:EU:C:2013:832; Judgment of the Court of Justice of 17 October 2013, *Commission v Italy ('Alcoa')*, C-344/12, ECLI:EU:C:2013:667; Judgment of the Court of Justice of 17 October 2013, *Commission v Greece ('Ellinikos Xrysos')*, C-263/12, ECLI:EU:C:2013:673; Judgment of the Court of Justice of 10 October 2013, *Commission v Italy ('Ixfin')*, C-353/12, ECLI:EU:C:2013:651; Judgment of the Court of Justice of 21 March 2013, *Commission v Italy ('Sardinia Ferries')*, C-613/11, ECLI:EU:C:2013:192; Judgment of the Court of Justice of 28 June 2012, *Commission v Greece ('Hellenic Shipyards I')*, C-485/10, ECLI:EU:C:2012:395; Judgment of the Court of Justice of 29 March 2012, *Commission v Italy ('Hotel industry in Sardinia')*, C-243/10, ECLI-:EU:C:2012:182; Judgment of the Court of Justice of 1 March 2012, *Commission v Greece ('Tax-exempt reserve fund')*, C-354/10, ECLI:EU:C:2012:109; Judgment of the Court of Justice of 13 October 2011, *Commission v Italy ('New Interline')*, C-454/09, ECLI:EU:C:2011:650; Judgment of the Court of Justice of 6 October 2011, *Commission v Italy ('Venice and Chioggia I')*, C-302/09, ECLI:EU:C:2011:634; Judgment of the Court of Justice of 14 July 2011, *Commission v Italy ('Tremonti bis')*, C-303/09, ECLI:EU:C:2011:483; Judgment of the Court of Justice of 5 May 2011, *Commission v Italy ('Trade fairs')*, C-305/09, ECLI:EU:C:2011:274; Judgment of the Court of Justice of 14 April 2011, *Commission v Poland ('Technologie Buczek')*, C-331/09, ECLI:EU:C:2011:250; Judgment of the Court of Justice of 22 December 2010, *Commission v Slovakia ('Frucona Košice')*, C-507/08, ECLI:EU:C:2010:802; Judgment of the Court of Justice of 22 December 2010, *Commission v Italy ('Newly listed companies')*, C-304/09, ECLI-:EU:C:2010:812; Judgment of the Court of Justice of 13 November 2008, *Commission v France ('Article 44-septies CGI')*, C-214/07, ECLI:EU:C:2008:619; Judgment of the Court of Justice of 19 June 2008, *Commission v Germany ('Kahla/Thüringen')*, C-39/06, ECLI:EU:C:2008:349; Judgment of the Court of Justice of 14 February 2008, *Commission v Greece ('Olympic Airways I')*, C-419/06, ECLI:EU:C:2008:89; Judgment of the Court of Justice of 6 December 2007, *Commission v Italy ('Mesures urgentes en faveur de l'emploi')*, C-280/05, ECLI:EU:C:2007:753.

155 See Judgment of the Court of Justice of 17 September 2015, *Commission v Italy ('Venice and Chioggia II')*, C-367/14, ECLI:EU:C:2015:611, paragraph 35.

156 Communication from the Commission on the Application of Article 228 of the EC Treaty, SEC(2005) 1658 (OJ C126, 7.6.2007, p 15), as amended and updated by the communications published on the website of the Commission.

157 See Judgment of the Court of Justice of 13 May 2014, Commission v Spain ('Basque fiscal aid'), C-184/11, ECLI:EU:C:2014:316, paragraph 69.

158 Since the adoption of the 2007 Recovery Notice, the Court of Justice has decided on several matters referred to it by the Commission under Article 260(2) TFEU. See Judgment of the Court of Justice of 14 November 2018, *Commission v Greece ('Hellenic Shipyards II')*, C-93/17, ECLI:EU:C:2018:903; Judgment of the Court of Justice of 17 September 2015, *Commission v Italy ('Venice and Chioggia II')*, C-367/14, ECLI:EU:C:2015:611; Judgment of the Court of Justice of 17 November 2011, *Commission v Italy ('Employment Measures II')*, C-496/09, ECLI:EU:C:2011:740; Judgment of the Court of Justice of 13 May 2014, *Commission v Spain ('Basque fiscal aid')*, C-184/11, ECLI:EU:C:2014:316; Judgment of the Court of Justice of 7 July 2009, *Commission v Greece ('Olympic Airways II')*, C-369/07, ECLI:EU:C:2009:428; Judgment of the Court of Justice of 11 December 2012, *Commission v Spain ('Magefesa II')*, C-610/10, ECLI:EU:C:2012:781. In all these judgments, except the Basque fiscal aid, the Court of Justice imposed both a lump sum and a penalty payment. In particular, in *Hellenic Shipyards*, the Court imposed a penalty payment of EUR 7,294,000 for every 6 months of delay in implementing the necessary measures to comply with the judgment of the Court and a lump sum of EUR 10 million; in *Venice and Chioggia II*, the Court imposed a penalty payment of EUR 12 million for every 6 months of delay in implementing the necessary measures to comply with the judgment of the Court and a lump sum of EUR 30 million; in *Employment Measures II* the Court imposed a penalty payment of an amount calculated by multiplying the basic amount of EUR 30 million by the percentage of the unlawful aid that has not yet been recovered, or not shown to have been recovered, at the end of the period concerned, compared to the total amount not yet recovered on the date of delivery of that judgment, for every 6 months of delay in implementing the necessary measures to comply with the judgment of the Court under Article 108 TFEU (paragraph 68), plus a lump sum of EUR 30 million (paragraph 97); in *Basque fiscal aid*, the Court imposed a lump sum of EUR 30 million (paragraph 84); in *Olympic Airways II* the Court imposed a penalty payment of EUR 16,000 for each

day of delay in adopting the measures necessary to comply with the judgment of the Court (paragraph 127) and a lump sum of EUR 2 million (paragraph 150); in *Magefesa II* the Court imposed a penalty payment of EUR 50,000 for each day of delay in adopting the measures necessary to comply with the judgment of the Court (paragraph 136) and a lump sum of EUR 20 million (paragraph 148).

159 See Judgment of the Court of Justice of 15 May 1997, *TWD v Commission*, C-355/95 P, ECLI:EU:C:1997:241, paragraphs 25 and 26.

160 See Judgment of the Court of First Instance of 8 September 2009, *AceaElectrabel v Commission*, T-303/05, ECLI:EU:T:2009:312, paragraph 163, as upheld by Judgment of the Court of Justice of 16 December 2010, *AceaElectrabel v Commission*, C-480/09 P, ECLI:EU:C:2010:787.

7. FINAL PROVISIONS

[5.232]

161. This Notice replaces the 2007 Recovery Notice.

162. The Commission may review this Notice on the basis of future important developments in its practice on the recovery of State aid or relevant modifications of the applicable European Union rules or case law.

163. The authorities of the Member States may contact the Commission's single contact point for queries about the recovery of State aid: comp-recovery-state-aid@ec.europa.eu

COMMISSION RECOMMENDATION

of 14 July 2020

on making State financial support to undertakings in the Union conditional on the absence of links to non-cooperative jurisdictions

Brussels, 14.7.2020 C(2020) 4885 final

[5.233]

NOTES

Date of publication in OJ: OJ L227, 16.7.2020, p 76.

THE EUROPEAN COMMISSION,

Having regard to the Treaty on the Functioning of the European Union, and in particular Article 292 thereof,

Whereas:

(1) The diversion of financial aid to tax havens can damage the integrity of Member States' public finances as well as the proper functioning of the Union financial system and the internal market of the Union. The Commission has taken a clear stance against tax havens in recent years through its External Strategy for Effective Taxation.[1]

(2) The COVID-19 outbreak has prompted unprecedented action at national and Union level to support Member States' economies and facilitate their recovery. This includes State intervention to ensure liquidity and access to finance for undertakings, considerable part of which has been subject to Union State aid rules.

(3) The volume of financial support, in particular liquidity support, granted to undertakings in the current COVID-19 related circumstances, calls for immediate and coordinated action to prevent the misuse of public financing. Such action so far has mostly been undertaken in the context of Union State aid rules. Furthermore and beyond the COVID-19 related circumstances, the granting of financial support should address the need for tackling tax avoidance and fraud as well as the abuse of national and Union budgets at the expense of taxpayers and social security systems.

(4) In order to effectively pursue the efforts to curb tax avoidance, fraud and abuse, it is equally important to cater for the proper functioning of the internal market. For that purpose, Member States should coordinate their action, to prevent their tax bases from being unduly eroded and ensure that they adopt solutions which do not create significant discrepancies or market distortions.

(5) The Union list of non-cooperative jurisdictions for tax purposes ('EU list of non-cooperative jurisdictions')[2] is designed to address threats to EU Member States' tax bases. Against that background, it would be appropriate to recommend that Member States make their financial support to undertakings in the Union conditional on the absence of links between those undertakings and jurisdictions that feature on the Union list. Moreover, the Commission observes that, in the context of granting State aid in the form of recapitalisations, several Member States have indicated their intention to create a strong link between financial support and a fair share of tax paid by the beneficiary.

(6) Nonetheless, it is critical that Member States protect genuine economic activities in listed non-cooperative jurisdictions and guarantee that those economic activities are not inadvertently affected. For this purpose, Member States should include appropriate exceptions in their laws, in order to ensure that financial support not be prevented where there is real economic activity.

(7) In order to ensure that the financial support can flow to eligible undertakings, Member States should establish reasonable requirements to demonstrate the absence of links to a jurisdiction that features on the EU list of non-cooperative jurisdictions. At the same time, it is essential to guarantee that undertakings cannot circumvent the requirements for entitlement to financial support.

(8) In an effort to create a comprehensive framework, Member States should extend the conditions for granting State financial support to undertakings beyond the absence of links to listed non-cooperative jurisdictions, in order to include cases where it has been established that an undertaking or its owners have been the subject of a conviction to a serious crime or in breach of obligations relating to the payment of taxes or social security contributions.

NOTES

[1] Communication from the Commission to the European Parliament and the Council on an External Strategy for Effective Taxation, 28 January 2016 (https://eur-lex.europa.eu/resource.html?uri=cellar:b5aef3db-c5a7-11e5-a4b5-01aa75ed71a1.0018.02/DOC_1&format=PDF).

[2] Jurisdictions featuring in Annex I of the relevant Council Conclusions (so-called "black list"). The list is regularly updated: https://ec.europa.eu/taxation_customs/tax-common-eu-list_en.

HAS ADOPTED THIS RECOMMENDATION:

[5.234]

1. Subject-matter and scope

This Recommendation sets out a coordinated approach to making the granting of financial support by Member States conditional on the absence of links between the recipient undertaking and jurisdictions which feature on the EU list of non-cooperative jurisdictions.

[5.235]

2. Definitions

"Ownership" means direct and indirect holdings, as well as the beneficial owner, as defined in Article 3 point 6 of Directive 2015/849 of 20 May 2015.[3]

'Financial support' means any type of financial assistance available to all undertakings or selective measures, including State aid granted pursuant to the new State Aid Temporary Framework.[4]

'Undertaking' means any entity or natural person engaged in economic activities regardless of its legal form or sector of activity.

NOTES

[3] Directive (EU) 2015/849 of the European Parliament and of the Council of 20 May 2015 on the prevention of the use of the financial system for the purpose of money laundering or terrorist financing, OJ L141, 5.6.2015, p 73.

[4] Communication from the Commission Temporary Framework for State aid measures to support the economy in the current COVID-19 outbreak C/2020/1863, OJ C91I, 20.3.2020, p 1, as amended on 3 April, 8 May and 29 June 2020.

[5.236]

3. Making State financial support to undertakings in the Union conditional on the absence of links to jurisdictions which feature on the EU list of non-cooperative jurisdictions

Where Member States adopt measures that provide financial support to eligible undertakings in their jurisdiction, they should make the entitlement to such financial support contingent upon a number of conditions. Therefore, the undertakings that receive the financial support should not:

(a) be resident for tax purposes in, or incorporated under the laws of, jurisdictions that feature on the EU list of non-cooperative jurisdictions;

(b) be controlled, directly or indirectly, by shareholders in jurisdictions that feature on the EU list of non-cooperative jurisdictions, up to the beneficial owner, as defined in Article 3 point 6 of Directive 2015/849;

(c) control, directly or indirectly, subsidiaries or own permanent establishments in jurisdictions that feature on the EU list of non-cooperative jurisdictions; and

(d) share ownership with undertakings in jurisdictions that feature on the EU list of non-cooperative jurisdictions.

In order to verify compliance with the rule prescribing the absence of links to jurisdictions that feature on the EU list of non-cooperative jurisdictions, Member States should ensure that not only the immediate shareholders but also the ultimate owner and all other undertakings under the same ownership are not tax resident in, or incorporated under the laws of, such a jurisdiction. The owners of the undertaking that receives financial support may be legal entities (e.g. corporations, partnerships, etc.), legal arrangements (e.g. trusts) or natural persons.

For the purpose of determining whether an undertaking may be granted financial support, it should be irrelevant how many tiers of legal entities or legal arrangements may sit between the undertaking established in the Member State that grants the financial support and the entity in a jurisdiction that features on the EU list.

[5.237]

4. Carve-outs

Member States may disregard the existence of links to the listed non-cooperative jurisdictions, when the undertaking provides evidence that one of the following circumstances is met:

(a) where the level of the tax liability in the Member State granting the support over a given period of time (e.g. the last three years) is considered adequate when compared to the overall turnover or level of activities of the undertaking receiving the support, at domestic and group level, over the same period.

(b) where the undertaking makes legally binding commitments to remove its ties to EU listed non-cooperative jurisdictions within a short timeframe, subject to appropriate follow-up and sanctions in case of non-compliance.

Member States should disregard the existence of links to the listed non-cooperative jurisdictions where the undertaking has substantial economic presence (supported by staff, equipment, assets and premises, as evidenced by relevant facts and circumstances) and performs a substantive economic activity in listed non-cooperative jurisdictions. Member States should not apply those exceptions if they are not in a position to verify the accuracy of the information. This could be due to the insufficient exchange of information on request with the third country concerned, in particular the absence of a tax treaty allowing exchange of information or the lack of cooperation from the third country jurisdiction concerned.

[5.238]

5. Implementation and enforcement

Member States should agree to reasonable requirements demonstrating the absence of links to a jurisdiction that features on the EU list of non-cooperative jurisdictions. The following principles aim at assisting Member States in ensuring swift implementation and effective enforcement of the requirements:

(a) In order to simplify procedures and facilitate access to financial support, Member States could accept self-certifications by the applicants as evidence that they are fully compliant with the requirements for receiving the financial support. That process should be complemented with enhanced audits/controls at a later stage making full use of the tools available in order to mitigate the risk of non-compliance such as country by country reports, automatic exchange of financial account information, exchange of information on request or access to beneficial ownership information.

(b) Member States should provide for effective, proportionate and dissuasive sanctions in order to discourage false or inaccurate information by the applicants, including, as a minimum, the recovery of unduly granted financial support.

(c) Member States should not allow self-certification and should carry out enhanced verifications where the undertaking in question has links to EU listed jurisdictions and claims the benefit of a carve-out.

[5.239]

6. Other restrictions

Member States should refrain from providing financial support to undertakings in the following cases:

- where it has been established that an undertaking or its owners have been the subject of a conviction by final judgment for any of the crimes laid down in Article 57(1) of Directive 2014/24/EU of the European Parliament and of the Council;[5]
- where it has been established by final judgment or final administrative decision that an undertaking or its owners is in breach of its obligations relating to the payment of taxes or social security contributions in accordance with the applicable law.

NOTES

5 Directive 2014/24/EU of the European Parliament and of the Council of 26 February 2014 on public procurement, OJ L94, 28.3.2014, p 65-242.

[5.240]

7. Follow-up

Member States are requested to inform the Commission about the measures taken further to the present Recommendation.

The Commission is ready to discuss with Member States their plans for ensuring that the granting of State aid, in particular in the form of recapitalisations, should be limited to undertakings paying their fair share of tax.

The Commission will publish a report on the application of this Recommendation within three years after its adoption.

COMMUNICATION FROM THE COMMISSION

(2021/C305/01)

Commission Notice on the enforcement of State aid rules by national courts

[5.241]

NOTES

Date of publication in OJ: OJ L305, 30.7.2021, p 1.

TABLE OF CONTENTS

1. INTRODUCTION

[5.242]

(1) Since 2012, the Commission has implemented the State aid modernisation agenda.[1] Under this agenda, the Commission has adopted a package of legislation, guidelines and notices for assessing State aid measures. This package has allowed the Commission to focus its *ex ante* scrutiny on cases with the biggest impact on the internal market, while developing closer cooperation with the Member States in State aid enforcement. To that end, the Commission has introduced more possibilities for the Member States to grant aid without prior Commission scrutiny by providing additional exemptions from the obligation to notify the Commission of any planned State aid measure. As a result, the amount of aid granted on the basis of block exemptions has increased.[2] In this context, the role of national courts in ensuring compliance with State aid rules has become even more prominent.

(2) In 2019, the Commission published a study on the enforcement of State aid rules and decisions by national courts in 28 Member States[3] (the 'Enforcement Study').[4] The Enforcement Study reviewed over 750 national judgements falling into two categories: 1) cases where national courts are involved in drawing the consequences of the unlawful implementation of aid ('private enforcement') and 2) cases where national courts are involved in implementing Commission decisions ordering recovery ('public enforcement').

(3) The Enforcement Study revealed that the number of State aid cases addressed to national courts increased between 2007 and 2017. Despite this increase, national courts only awarded remedies on rare occasions, and claims for damages represent a small minority of cases. In addition, the means of cooperation between the Commission and national courts, which were introduced in 2009 by the Commission Notice on the enforcement of State aid law by national courts (the '2009 Enforcement Notice')[5] and in 2015 by Council Regulation (EU) 2015/1589 (the 'Procedural Regulation')[6] have not been widely used.

(4) This notice provides national courts and other interested parties with practical information on the enforcement of State aid rules at national level. It takes into account the questions raised by these courts in the context of the Enforcement Study or in cases referred for preliminary rulings to the Court of Justice of the European Union ('Court of Justice'). Some examples are the coherence between the procedures before the Commission and national court proceedings, or the questions raised by the incorrect application of block exemption regulations.

(5) This notice is intended to provide guidance to courts and tribunals of the Member States within the meaning of Article 267 of the Treaty on the Functioning of the European Union ('TFEU')[7] and to encourage closer cooperation between the Commission and national courts by laying down all the available tools of cooperation.

It does not bind the national courts or affect their independence.[8] The main focus of this notice is private enforcement. The Commission Notice on the Recovery of unlawful and incompatible State aid[9] ('Recovery Notice') addresses the aspects related to public enforcement.

(6) Since the 2009 Enforcement Notice, the case-law of the General Court and the Court of Justice (together, the 'Union Courts') has evolved. This notice incorporates those developments and replaces the 2009 Enforcement Notice.

1.1. THE SYSTEM OF STATE AID CONTROL

(7) State aid is a legal concept defined directly by the TFEU, which must be interpreted on the basis of objective factors.[10] According to Article 107(1) TFEU, 'any aid granted by a Member State or through State resources in any form whatsoever which distorts or threatens to distort competition by favouring certain undertakings or the production of certain goods shall, in so far as it affects trade between Member States, be incompatible with the internal market'. The Commission has provided guidance on how to interpret the notion of State aid.[11]

(8) The general prohibition of State aid relies on a double system of *ex ante* and *ex post* control of interventions involving State aid. Pursuant to Article 108 TFEU, the Commission must keep under constant review all systems of existing aid and assess any plans by a Member State to grant new aid or alter existing aid. For the Commission to perform this review effectively, Member States must cooperate by providing any relevant information and by notifying State aid measures.

(9) Member States are under an obligation, first, to notify the Commission of any measure intended to grant new aid or alter existing aid and, second, not to put into effect such measure until the Commission has assessed its compatibility with the internal market ('standstill obligation').[12] The standstill obligation stemming from Article 108(3) TFEU has direct effect:[13] it confers rights on individuals, which they can rely on before national courts.

(10) It follows that the implementation of the system of State aid control, of which the provision of Article 108(3) TFEU constitutes a fundamental feature, is a matter for both the Commission and the national courts, their respective roles being complementary but separate. While the Commission has exclusive competence for assessing the compatibility of aid measures with the internal market, it is for the national courts to safeguard the rights of individuals faced with a possible breach of Article 108(3) TFEU.[14]

1.2. THE STANDSTILL OBLIGATION

(11) The immediate enforceability of Article 108(3) TFEU implies that national courts must take all appropriate actions, in accordance with their national law, to address the consequences of an infringement of that provision.[15]

(12) For a measure to be subject to the standstill requirement of Article 108(3) TFEU, two conditions need to be satisfied: first, the measure qualifies as new aid, including alterations of an existing aid;[16] and second, the measure must be subject to the prior notification obligation of Article 108(3) TFEU.

(13) Therefore, where a measure does not constitute new aid, Member States can implement it without prior notification to the Commission. Moreover, Member States may implement aid measures that fulfil all the conditions to benefit from an exemption from the notification obligation.

(14) By *de minimis* regulations,[17] the Commission set the conditions according to which aid is deemed not to affect trade between Member States and not to distort or threaten to distort competition.[18]

(15) The Commission has also adopted block exemption regulations – such as the General Block Exemption Regulation[19] – setting out the conditions according to which aid measures must or can be considered compatible with the internal market under Article 107(2) or (3).[20] If an aid measure fulfils all the relevant conditions provided for in these regulations, the Member State concerned is exempted from its obligation to notify the Commission of the aid.

(16) Moreover, Commission Decision 2012/21/EU,[21] with regard to State aid for Services of General Economic Interest in general, and the Regulation (EC) No 1370/2007 of the European Parliament and of the Council,[22] with particular regard to public passenger transport services by rail and by road, set conditions according to which the compensations for public service obligations are considered compatible with the internal market pursuant to Articles 106(2) and 93 TFEU. Also in these cases, the measures concerned are not subject to the standstill obligation.

NOTES

1 Communication from the Commission to the European Parliament, the Council, the European Economic and Social Committee and the Committee of the Regions – EU State Aid Modernisation (SAM), COM/2012/0209 final.

2 Since 2015, more than 96 % of new aid measures for which expenditure was reported for the first time was covered by a block exemption regulation. See http://ec.europa.eu/competition/state_aid/scoreboard/index_en.html

3 The Enforcement Study was conducted before the Agreement on the withdrawal of the United Kingdom of Great Britain and Northern Ireland from the European Union and the European Atomic Energy Community was signed (24 January 2020) and before it entered into force (1 February 2020). All reference to Member States in the Enforcement Study is to be intended as also referring to the United Kingdom.

4 See 'Final Study on the enforcement of State aid rules and decisions by national courts (COMP/2018/001)', Publications Office of the European Union, Luxemburg, 2019.

5 Commission Notice on the enforcement of State aid law by national courts (OJ C 85, 9.4.2009, p. 1).

6 Council Regulation (EU) 2015/1589 of 13 July 2015 laying down detailed rules for the application of Article 108 of the Treaty on the Functioning of the European Union (codification) (OJ L 248, 24.9.2015, p. 9).

7 To determine whether a body is a court or tribunal for the purposes of Article 267 TFEU, the Court of Justice takes into account a number of factors, such as whether the body is established by law, whether it is permanent, whether its jurisdiction is compulsory, whether its procedure is *inter partes*, whether it applies rules of law and whether it is independent. In that sense, see Judgment of the Court of Justice of 21 January 2020, *Banco de Santander*, C-274/14, ECLI:EU:C:2020:17, paragraph 51. Arbitral tribunals may not be considered as courts or tribunals within the meaning of Article 267 TFEU where the parties are under no obligation, in law or in fact, to refer their disputes to arbitration and where the public authorities of the Member State concerned are not involved in the decision to opt for arbitration nor required to intervene in the proceedings before the arbitrator. However, the Court has held admissible preliminary questions referred to it by an arbitral tribunal, where that tribunal had been established by law, its decisions were binding on the parties and its jurisdiction did not depend on their agreement. See order of the Court of Justice of 13 February 2014, *Merck Canada*, C-555/13, paragraphs 17 and 18 and the case-law cited therein.

8 However, even if those guidelines are not intended to produce binding effects, the national courts are required to take them into consideration in order to decide disputes submitted to them. See Judgment of the Court of Justice of 3 September 2014, *Baltlanta*, C-410/13, EU:C:2014:2134, paragraph 64 and Judgment of the Court of Justice of 13 December 1989, *Grimaldi*, C-322/88, ECLI:EU:C:1989:646, paragraph 18; Judgment of the Court of Justice of 13 February 2014, *Mediaset*, C-69/13, ECLI:EU:C:2014:71, paragraph 31.

9 OJ C 247, 23.7.2019, p. 1.

10 Judgment of the Court of Justice of 22 December 2008, *British Aggregates v Commission*, C-487/06 P, ECLI-:EU:C:2008:757, paragraph 111; Judgment of the Court of Justice of 16 May 2000, *France v Ladbroke Racing and Commission*, C-83/98 P, ECLI:EU: C:2000:248, paragraph 25.

11 See, for instance, Commission Notice on the notion of State aid as referred to in Article 107(1) of the Treaty on the Functioning of the European Union (OJ C 262, 19.7.2016, p. 1); Communication from the Commission on the application of the European Union State aid rules to compensation granted for the provision of services of general economic interest (OJ C 8, 11.1.2012, p. 4); Commission Notice on the application of Articles 87 and 88 of the EC Treaty to State aid in the form of guarantees (OJ C 155, 20.6.2008, p. 10); Communication from the Commission — Framework for State aid for research and development and innovation (OJ C 198, 27.6.2014, p. 1).

12 Judgment of the Court of Justice of 14 November 2019, *Dilly's Wellnesshotel*, C-585/17, ECLI:EU:C:2019:969, paragraph 54.

13 Judgment of the Court of Justice of 5 March 2019, *Eesti Pagar*, C-349/17, ECLI:EU:C:2019:172, paragraph 88; Judgment of the Court of Justice of 3 March 2020, *Vodafone Magyarország*, C-75/18, ECLI:EU:C:2020:139, paragraph 22; Judgment of the Court of Justice of 21 November 2013, *Deutsche Lufthansa*, C-284/12, ECLI:EU:C:2013:755, paragraph 29.

14 Judgment of the Court of Justice of 5 October 2006, *Transalpine Ölleitung in Österreich*, C-368/04, ECLI-:EU:C:2006:644, paragraph 38; Judgment of the Court of Justice of 11 March 2010, *CELF et ministre de la Culture et de la Communication*, C-1/09, ECLI:EU:C:2010:136, paragraph 26; Judgment of the Court of Justice of 11 November 2015, *Klausner Holz Niedersachsen*, C-505/14, ECLI:EU:C:2015:742, paragraph 21; Judgment of the Court of Justice of 3 March 2020, *Vodafone Magyarország*, C-75/18, ECLI:EU:C:2020:139, paragraph 21.

15 Judgment of the Court of Justice of 5 March 2019, *Eesti Pagar*, C-349/17, ECLI:EU:C:2019:172, paragraphs 88 to 89; Judgment of the Court of Justice of 3 March 2020, *Vodafone Magyarország*, C-75/18, ECLI:EU:C:2020:139, paragraphs 22 to 23.

16 By virtue of Article 1(c) of the Procedural Regulation, 'new aid' is defined as 'all aid, that is to say, aid schemes and individual aid, which is not existing aid, including alterations to existing aid'. Since that provision is established in broad terms, it is capable of covering not only the alteration itself, but also the aid concerned by that alteration. In addition, according to Article 1(b)(ii) of the Procedural Regulation, 'existing aid' is understood as being, *inter alia*, 'authorised aid, that is to say, aid schemes and individual aid which have been authorised by the Commission or by the Council'. Thus, aid which was the subject of an authorisation decision and which, as a result of an alteration that did not satisfy a condition laid down by that decision in order to ensure the compatibility of that aid with the internal market, is no longer covered by the decision which authorised it, may constitute new aid. See Judgment of the Court of Justice of 25 October 2017, C-467/15 P, *Commission v Italy*, ECLI:EU:C:2017:799, paragraphs 46 and 47. See also Section 4.2.2.2. of this notice.

17 Commission Regulation (EU) No 1407/2013 of 18 December 2013 on the application of Articles 107 and 108 of the Treaty on the Functioning of the European Union to *de minimis* aid (OJ L 352, 24.12.2013, p. 1); Commission Regulation (EU) No 360/2012 of 25 April 2012 on the application of Articles 107 and 108 of the Treaty on the Functioning of the European Union to de minimis aid granted to undertakings providing services of general economic interest (OJ L 114, 26.4.2012, p. 8); Commission Regulation (EU) No 1408/2013 of 18 December 2013 on the application of Articles 107 and 108 of the Treaty on the Functioning of the European Union to *de minimis aid* in the agriculture sector (OJ L 352, 24.12.2013, p. 9); Commission Regulation (EU) No 717/2014 of 27 June 2014 on the application of Articles 107 and 108 of the Treaty on the Functioning of the European Union to de minimis aid in the fishery and aquaculture sector (OJ L 190, 28.6.2014, p. 45).

18 Such regulations are adopted on the basis of the enabling Council Regulation (EU) 2015/1588 of 13 July 2015 on the

application of Articles 107 and 108 of the Treaty on the Functioning of the European Union to certain categories of horizontal State aid (OJ L 248, 24.9.2015, p. 1).

[19] Commission Regulation (EU) No 651/2014 of 17 June 2014 declaring certain categories of aid compatible with the internal market in application of Articles 107 and 108 of the Treaty (OJ L 187, 26.6.2014, p. 1).

[20] Pursuant to Article 109 TFEU, the Council of the European Union may adopt regulations for the application of Articles 107 and 108 TFEU and determine categories of aid that are exempted from the notification obligation. As provided for in Article 108(4) TFEU, the Commission may then adopt regulations relating to the categories of State aid that the Council has determined, pursuant to Article 109 TFEU.

[21] Commission Decision 2012/21/EU of 20 December 2011 on the application of Article 106(2) of the Treaty on the Functioning of the European Union to State aid in the form of public service compensation granted to certain undertakings entrusted with the operation of services of general economic interest (notified under document C(2011) 9380) (OJ L 7, 11.1.2012, p. 3).

[22] Regulation (EC) No 1370/2007 of the European Parliament and of the Council of 23 October 2007 on public passenger transport services by rail and by road (OJ L 315, 3.12.2007, p. 1).

2. GENERAL PRINCIPLES OF THE ENFORCEMENT OF STATE AID RULES

2.1. THE PRINCIPLE OF SINCERE COOPERATION

[5.243]

(17) Article 4(3) of the Treaty on European Union[23] ('TEU') requires Member States to facilitate the achievement of the Union's tasks. Pursuant to the principle of sincere cooperation enshrined in this Article, the Union and Member States, acting within the scope of their jurisdiction, must assist each other in carrying out those tasks.

(18) The obligation of mutual assistance stemming from Article 4(3) TEU also applies to national courts.[24] This means that the Commission assists national courts when they apply Union law,[25] and that, conversely, national courts assist the Commission in the fulfilment of its tasks. National courts must, therefore, take all the necessary measures to ensure fulfilment of their obligations under Union law and refrain from taking decisions which may jeopardise the attainment of the objectives of the TEU and the TFEU (together, the 'Treaties').[26]

2.2. THE PRINCIPLES OF EQUIVALENCE AND EFFECTIVENESS APPLIED TO NATIONAL PROCEDURES

(19) The Court of Justice has consistently recognised the principle of procedural autonomy in the enforcement of State aid rules.[27] According to this principle, in the absence of Union legislation on the subject, Member States are free to choose how they fulfil their obligations stemming from the Treaties, provided that the means they use do not adversely affect the scope and effectiveness of Union law.

(20) In accordance with the Union Courts' case-law, the applicable national legislation must not be less favourable when applying Article 108(3) TFEU than the one governing similar domestic situations ('principle of equivalence') and must not be framed in such a way as to make it in practice impossible or excessively difficult to exercise the rights conferred by the Union law ('principle of effectiveness').[28] Sections 2.2.1., 2.2.2. and 2.2.3. explain the interplay between the principle of procedural autonomy on the one hand, and the principles of equivalence and effectiveness, on the other, in relation to legal standing, the national courts' jurisdiction and the principle of res judicata.[29]

2.2.1. Legal standing

(21) In application of the principle of procedural autonomy, Member States apply their national rules on legal standing to national litigation concerning State aid, provided that they respect the principles of equivalence and effectiveness.

(22) Pursuant to the principle of effectiveness, national rules on individuals' legal standing and interest in bringing proceedings should not undermine their right to effective judicial protection of the rights conferred on them by Union law.[30]

(23) The Enforcement Study showed that national courts rule mostly on cases brought by competitors of the aid beneficiary, which are directly affected by the distortion of competition arising from the implementation of the unlawful aid.[31]

(24) However, when applying the national rules on standing, national courts have to take into account their duty to protect the interest of any parties having a sufficient legal interest in initiating proceedings ('third parties'), irrespective of whether they have been directly affected by the distortion of competition arising from the unlawful implementation of the aid measure.

(25) National courts have to consider further elements when assessing third parties' legal standing in cases concerning State aid granted through fiscal measures. Third party taxpayers may be regarded as having an interest in bringing an action to obtain the refund of the amount levied in breach of the standstill obligation only where the tax or levy to which they are subject forms part of the financing of the unlawful State aid.[32] Their legal standing does not rely on the existence of a competitive relationship with the aid beneficiary.[33]

(26) Conversely, third party taxpayers cannot rely on the unlawfulness of an aid measure exempting from taxation certain undertakings or sectors to avoid payment of that tax or levy or to obtain its reimbursement, unless the tax revenue is reserved exclusively for funding the unlawful State aid as indicated in paragraph (25). This is also the case where they operate in competition with the beneficiaries.[34] Such a solution would result in increasing the anticompetitive effects of the State aid as it would enlarge the number of undertakings benefitting from a tax exemption constituting unlawful State aid.[35]

(27) Finally, the requirement for national court to ensure effective judicial protection can go beyond the strict enforcement of Article 108(3) TFEU. In light of Article 47 of the Charter of Fundamental Rights of the European Union, individuals and organisations with no standing to request the annulment of a State aid decision under Article 263 TFEU should be given the opportunity to challenge the aid or measures implementing the aid before

national courts and trigger a reference under Article 267 TFEU to the Court of Justice for a preliminary ruling on the interpretation or validity of the Commission decision authorising that aid.[36] In that situation, not only economic interests, but also other interests of individuals and organisations can be relevant to establish their standing in proceedings relating to the national measures implementing the aid, depending on the measures and national procedures in question.[37]

2.2.2. JURISDICTION

(28) The principle of procedural autonomy implies that it is for the national legal system of each Member State to designate the courts that have jurisdiction in proceedings concerning the granting of unlawful aid. It also implies that Member States determine the detailed procedural rules governing these legal actions, provided that the principles of equivalence and effectiveness are complied with.[38]

(29) In the absence of specific rules under Union law, the structure of the Member States' judicial systems varies widely. While a few Member States have set up specialised courts for State aid matters, others have assigned exclusive jurisdiction to chambers of existing courts or adopted procedural rules clarifying the courts' jurisdiction in public and private enforcement cases.[39] In the majority of the Member States, civil and administrative courts are competent in the application of State aid rules.[40]

2.2.3. THE PRINCIPLE OF RES JUDICATA

(30) The principle of *res judicata* states that judgements that have become definitive cannot be called into question anymore. This is the case where all rights of appeal have been exhausted or where the time limits to exercise those rights have expired. The principle of *res judicata* aims to guarantee the stability of law and legal relations, as well as the sound administration of justice, and it is enshrined both in the legal order of the Union and in national legal systems.[41] According to case-law, in the absence of EU legislation in this area, the rules implementing the principle of *res judicata* are a matter for the national legal order, in accordance with the principle of the procedural autonomy of the Member States. However, such procedural rules must abide by the principles of equivalence and effectiveness.[42]

(31) Under the principle of primacy of Union law,[43] national courts are under a duty to give full effect to the provisions of Union law, including, if needed, by refusing on their own motion to apply any conflicting provision of national legislation. This also applies to national rules enshrining the principle of res judicata.[44]

(32) The case-law of the Union Courts has limited the force of the principle of *res judicata* in the field of State aid. The principle of the primacy of Union law prevents the application of the principle of *res judicata* from limiting the exclusive competence conferred on the Commission by the TFEU to assess State aid compatibility.[45] Further, the circumstance that a national court has ruled out the existence of State aid in relation to a measure cannot prevent the Commission from finding later that the measure at stake constitutes unlawful and incompatible State aid.[46] This holds even in case of a judgment by a national court adjudicating at last instance.[47] This applies also where national rules on *res judicata* extend to pleas in law that could have been, but were not, invoked in court proceedings.[48]

NOTES

23 OJ C 202, 7.6.2016, p. 13.

24 Judgment of the Court of Justice of 22 October 2002, *Roquette Frères*, C-94/00, ECLI:EU:C:2002:603, paragraph 31.

25 Judgment of the Court of Justice of 11 July 1996, *SFEI and Others*, C-39/94, ECLI:EU:C:1996:285, paragraph 50; Judgment of the Court of Justice of 28 February 1991, *Delimitis v Henninger Bräu*, C-234/89, ECLI:EU:C:1991:91, paragraph 53.

26 Judgment of the Court of Justice of 11 September 2014, *Commission v Germany*, C-527/12, ECLI:EU:C:2014:2193, paragraph 56; Judgment of the Court of Justice of 21 November 2013, *Deutsche Lufthansa*, C-284/12, ECLI-:EU:C:2013:755, paragraph 41.

27 Judgment of the Court of Justice of 21 September 1983, *Deutsche Milchkontor GmbH*, C-205/82, ECLI-:EU:C:1983:233, paragraphs 22 to 23; Judgment of the Court of Justice of 13 June 2002, *Netherlands v Commission*, C-382/99, ECLI:EU:C:2002:363, paragraph 90; Judgment of the Court of Justice of 11 September 2014, *Commission v Germany*, C-527/12, ECLI:EU:C:2014:2193, paragraphs 39 to 42; Judgment of the Court of Justice of 23 January 2019, *Fallimento Traghetti del Mediterraneo*, C-387/17, ECLI:EU:C:2019:51, paragraph 72; Judgment of the Court of Justice of 11 November 2015, *Klausner Holz Niedersachsen*, C-505/14, ECLI:EU:C:2015:742, paragraphs 40 to 41; Judgment of the Court of Justice of 5 March 2019, *Eesti Pagar*, C-349/17, ECLI:EU:C:2019:172, paragraph 135.

28 Compliance with the principle of effectiveness must be addressed by analysing the particular features of that provision and its role in the relevant procedure. In that sense, see Judgment of the Court of Justice of 11 November 2015, *Klausner Holz Niedersachsen*, C-505/14, ECLI:EU:C:2015:742, paragraph 40; Judgment of the Court of Justice of 5 March 2019, *Eesti Pagar*, C-349/17, ECLI:EU: C:2019:172, paragraphs 138 to 140.

29 The compliance of applicable domestic procedural rules with the principles of equivalence and effectiveness can, however, relate to any other aspects of the national legislation, including, for instance, the level of costs associated with the private enforcement of State aid before national courts.

30 Judgment of the Court of Justice of 13 January 2005, *Streekgewest*, C-174/02, ECLI:EU:C:2005:10, paragraph 18.

31 For example, in Romania, any person who is affected by an unlawful State aid measure has legal standing in court. See Annex 3: Country reports of the 'Final Study on the enforcement of State aid rules and decisions by national courts (COMP/2018/001)', Publications Office of the European Union, Luxemburg, 2019, p. 404. Also, in Latvia, legal standing is directly based on Article 108(3) TFEU and thus national courts may rely on the definition of 'interested party' of the Procedural Regulation to determine whether a person has legal standing in a case. See Annex 3: Country reports of the 'Final Study on the enforcement of State aid rules and decisions by national courts (COMP/2018/001)', Publications Office of the European Union, Luxemburg, 2019, p. 300.

32 Reference is made, for instance, to cases where the unlawful aid is financed by a levy to which the plaintiff is subject. The position is, however, different where the dispute concerns not an application to be exempted from the contested tax, but the legality of the rules relating to that tax. See in that sense Judgment of the Court of Justice of 3 March 2020, Vodafone Magyarország, C-75/18, ECLI:EU: C:2020:139, paragraph 25 and Judgment of the Court of Justice of 26 April 2018, ANGED, C-233/16, ECLI:EU:C:2018:280, paragraph 26.

33 Judgment of the Court of Justice of 13 January 2005, *Streekgewest*, C-174/02, ECLI:EU:C:2005:10, paragraph 19.

34 Judgment of the Court of Justice of 10 November 2016, *DTS Distribuidora de Televisión Digital v Commission*, C-449/14 P, ECLI:EU: C:2016:848, paragraphs 81 to 82; Judgment of the Court of Justice of 21 December 2016, *Commission v Aer Lingus*, C-164/15 P, ECLI:EU:C:2016:990, paragraph 121; Judgment of the Court of Justice of 3 March 2020, *Vodafone Magyarország*, C-75/18, ECLI:EU: C:2020:139, paragraphs 24 to 28.

35 Judgment of the Court of Justice of 15 June 2006, *Air Liquide Industries Belgium*, C-393/04, ECLI:EU:C:2006:403, paragraph 45.

36 See, to this effect, order of the Court of Justice of 10 October 2017, *Greenpeace energy v Commission*, C-640/16 P, ECLI:EU:C:2017:752, paragraphs 61 to 63.

37 This may be the case, for instance, for environmental protection. See, to that effect, Judgment of the Court of Justice of 22 September 2020, *Austria v Commission*, C-594/18, ECLI:EU:C:2020:742, paragraph 100, in respect of aid approved under Article 107(3)(c) TFEU in the nuclear sector. See also paragraphs 38 to 42 of Commission Notice on access to justice in environmental matters (OJ C 275, 18.8.2017, p. 1) with regard to recognition of the standing of environmental organisations promoting environmental protection in the context of the Aarhus Convention on access to information, public participation in decision-making and access to justice in environmental matters.

38 Judgment of the Court of Justice of 23 January 2019, *Fallimento Traghetti del Mediterraneo*, C-387/17, ECLI-:EU:C:2019:51, paragraph 72.

39 For example, Ireland has attributed exclusive jurisdiction to the Competition List of the High Court to hear competition law disputes, including State aid cases. Also, in Italy, the administrative courts of the country have been attributed nearly exclusive competence to hear cases concerning public and private enforcement of State aid rules from 19 January 2013. Civil courts have kept their competence regarding certain types of proceedings and actions. See Annex 3: Country reports of the 'Final Study on the enforcement of State aid rules and decisions by national courts (COMP/2018/001)', Publications Office of the European Union, Luxemburg, 2019, pp. 253 and 263 to 264. See, also, 'Final Study on the enforcement of State aid rules and decisions by national courts (COMP/2018/001)', pp. 103 to 104.

40 In particular, in most Member States, administrative courts are competent when the plaintiff challenges an act of the public authority, such as the order implementing the recovery or awarding the aid, while civil courts are competent for issues related to the recovery of State aid in the context of insolvency proceedings or to the award of damages. See 'Final Study on the enforcement of State aid rules and decisions by national courts (COMP/2018/001)', Publications Office of the European Union, Luxemburg, 2019, p. 64.

41 Judgment of the Court of Justice of 11 November 2015, *Klausner Holz Niedersachsen*, C-505/14, ECLI-:EU:C:2015:742, paragraph 38.

42 Judgment of the Court of Justice of 3 September 2009, *Fallimento Olimpiclub*, C-2/08, EU:C:2009:506, paragraph 24. Judgment of the Court of Justice of 10 July 2014, *Impresa Pizzarotti*, C-213/13, EU:C:2014:2067, paragraph 54 ; Judgment of the Court of Justice of 4 May 2020, *Telecom Italia*, C-34/19; ECLI:EU:C:2020:148, paragraph 58.

43 Judgment of the Court of Justice of 5 February 1963, *Van Gend en Loos v Administratie der Belastingen*, C-26/62, ECLI:EU:C:1963:1; Judgment of the Court of Justice of 15 July 1964, *Costa v E.N.E.L.*, C-6/64, ECLI-:EU:C:1964:66; Judgment of the Court of Justice of 9 March 1978, *Amministrazione delle finanze dello Stato v Simmenthal*, C-106/77, ECLI:EU:C:1978:49.

44 Judgment of the Court of Justice of 18 July 2007, *Lucchini*, C-119/05, ECLI:EU:C:2007:434, paragraphs 60 and 61.

45 Judgment of the Court of Justice of 18 July 2007, *Lucchini*, C-119/05, ECLI:EU:C:2007:434, paragraph 61 to 63; Judgment of the Court of Justice of 11 November 2015, *Klausner Holz Niedersachsen*, C-505/14, ECLI-:EU:C:2015:742, paragraph 44; Judgment of the Court of Justice of 4 March 2020, *Buonotourist v Commission*, C-586/18 P, ECLI:EU:C:2020:152, paragraphs 92 to 96; Judgment of the Court of Justice of 4 March 2020, *CSTP Azienda della Mobilità v Commission*, C-587/18 P, ECLI:EU:C:2020:150, paragraphs 92 to 96; Judgment of the Court of Justice of 3 September 2009, *Fallimento Olimpiclub*, C-2/08, EU:C:2009:506, paragraphs 22-25.

46 'A national rule which prevents the national court from drawing all the consequences of a breach of the third sentence of Article 108(3) TFEU because of a decision of a national court, which is res judicata, given in a dispute which does not have the same subject- matter and which did not concern the State aid characteristics of the contracts at issue must be regarded as being incompatible with the principle of effectiveness', Judgment of the Court of Justice of 11 November 2015, *Klausner Holz Niedersachsen*, C-505/14, ECLI: EU:C:2015:742, paragraph 45.

47 Judgment of the Court of Justice of 4 March 2020, *Buonotourist v Commission*, C-586/18 P, ECLI:EU:C:2020:152, paragraphs 92 to 96.

48 Judgment of the Court of Justice of 11 November 2015, *Klausner Holz Niedersachsen*, C-505/14, ECLI-:EU:C:2015:742, paragraphs 30 and 42 to 43.

3. THE ROLE OF THE COMMISSION

[5.244]

(33) The aim of the system of prior control established by Article 108(3) TFEU is to ensure that only compatible aid can be implemented.[49] In order to achieve that aim, the implementation of planned aid that is not block exempted is to be deferred until the Commission adopts a decision on its compatibility with the internal market.[50]

3.1. THE EXCLUSIVE COMPETENCE OF THE COMMISSION

(34) The Commission generally exercises its competence to assess the compatibility of an aid measure in two steps. First, the Commission assesses whether the measure qualifies as State aid under Article 107(1) TFEU;[51] second, it examines whether the measure is compatible with the internal market. The first step, consisting of the assessment of the existence of aid, is a competence exercised by both the Commission and national courts, as the latter may have to establish if a measure is subject to the standstill obligation[52] (see Sections 4.2.1 and 4.2.2). The second step, consisting of the compatibility assessment, falls within the Commission's exclusive responsibility. The compatibility assessment must be included in a decision,[53] which is subject to review by the Union Courts.[54]

(35) The Commission can conclude on a measure's compatibility with the internal market either following a preliminary examination (where it has no doubts as to the measure's compatibility with the internal market)[55] or following a formal investigation (where, in the context of the preliminary examination it had doubts as to the

measure's compatibility with the internal market).[56] When it initiates a formal investigation, the Commission adopts a decision in which it sets out its preliminary assessment as to the aid character of the measure and its doubts as to the measure's compatibility with the internal market ('opening decision').[57]

(36) The Commission's exclusive power to assess State aid compatibility can limit national courts in the exercise of their competence of applying Articles 107(1) and 108(3) TFEU (see Section 4.1).[58] This is true of opening decisions, which, pending the assessment of the measure's compatibility, have certain legal consequences on the proceedings before national courts (see Section 4.1.3)

(37) Prior final Commission decisions are binding on national courts, and national courts must follow the Commission's assessment on the existence of aid.[59] Conversely, if a national court rules prior to any Commission decision, this ruling, even if having the force of *res judicata*, cannot prevent the Commission from exercising at some point in time the exclusive competence conferred on it by the TFEU (see Section 2.2.3).[60]

3.2. THE COMMISSION'S POWERS TO ENFORCE STATE AID RULES

(38) As a general rule, in order to impose remedies for the violation of State aid rules, when it concludes that the measure examined constitutes unlawful and incompatible State aid, the Commission needs to adopt a final decision which concludes the formal investigation and orders the recovery of this aid ('recovery decision').[61]

(39) By adopting rules of procedure in the field of State aid, the Commission has codified its enforcement powers.[62] Pursuant to Article 16 of the Procedural Regulation, the Commission must order the recovery of unlawful and incompatible aid by adopting a decision. When it establishes in a decision that an aid measure is unlawful and incompatible with the internal market, the Commission has no discretion and must order its recovery,[63] unless that would be contrary to a general principle of Union law.[64] In addition, the Commission's powers to order recovery are subject to a limitation period of 10 years from the day on which the unlawful aid was awarded to the beneficiary.[65]

(40) In some instances, pursuant to Article 13 of the Procedural Regulation, the Commission could, at its discretion, adopt provisional measures while it completes the compatibility assessment. In particular, the Commission may issue suspension or recovery injunctions, provided that a number of conditions are fulfilled.[66] These measures seek to limit the damage associated with the implementation of the aid in breach of the notification and standstill obligations.[67]

NOTES

49 Judgment of the Court of Justice of 3 March 2020, *Vodafone Magyarország*, C-75/18, ECLI:EU:C:2020:139, paragraph 19.

50 Judgment of the Court of Justice of 21 November 2013, *Deutsche Lufthansa*, C-284/12, ECLI:EU:C:2013:755, paragraphs 25 to 26; Judgment of the Court of Justice of 18 May 2017, *Fondul Proprietatea*, C-150/16, ECLI-:EU:C:2017:388, paragraph 40; Judgment of the Court of Justice of 5 March 2019, *Eesti Pagar*, C-349/17, ECLI:EU:C:2019:172, paragraph 84.

51 Commission Notice on the notion of State aid as referred to in Article 107(1) of the Treaty on the Functioning of the European Union (OJ C 262, 19.7.2016, p. 1).

52 Judgment of the Court of Justice of 4 March 2020, *Buonotourist v Commission*, C-586/18 P, ECLI:EU:C:2020:152, paragraph 90.

53 See Articles 4 and 9 of the Procedural Regulation.

54 Judgment of the Court of Justice of 19 July 2016, *Kotnik and Others*, C-526/14, ECLI:EU:C:2016:570, paragraph 37.

55 Decision not to raise objection, Procedural Regulation, Article 4(3).

56 See the notions of 'positive decision' and 'negative decision' respectively in Article 9(3) and (5) of the Procedural Regulation.

57 See Article 4(3) and (4) of the Procedural Regulation.

58 See Judgment of the Court of Justice of 4 March 2020, *Buonotourist v Commission*, C-586/18 P, ECLI-:EU:C:2020:152, paragraphs 93 to 94 'the exercise of such a power implies that the Commission may examine, pursuant to Article 108 TFEU, whether a measure constitutes State aid which should have been notified to it, in accordance with paragraph 3 of that article, in a situation where the authorities of a Member State have taken the view that that measure did not satisfy the conditions laid down in Article 107(1) TFEU, including where those authorities have complied, in that regard, with the assessment of a national court. That conclusion cannot be invalidated by the fact that that court has adopted a decision having the force of *res judicata*. It should be emphasised that the rule of exclusive competence of the Commission is necessary in the internal legal order as a consequence of the principle of the primacy of Union law'.

59 Judgment of the Court of Justice of 15 September 2016, *PGE*, C-574/14, ECLI:EU:C:2016:686, paragraphs 33 and 36 to 37.

60 Judgment of the Court of Justice of 4 March 2020, *Buonotourist v Commission*, C-586/18 P, ECLI:EU:C:2020:152, paragraphs 92 to 96; Judgment of the Court of Justice of 4 March 2020, *CSTP Azienda della Mobilità v Commission*, C-587/18 P, ECLI:EU:C:2020:150, paragraphs 92 to 96.

61 Judgment of the Court of Justice of 14 February 1990, *France v Commission* ('*Boussac*'), C-301/87, ECLI-:EU:C:1990:67, paragraphs 9 to 22. This does not preclude the possibility for the Commission to issue a recovery injunction before it has completed the compatibility assessment, in specific cases provided for under Article 13(2) of the Procedural Regulation.

62 Judgment of the Court of Justice of 23 January 2019, *Fallimento Traghetti del Mediterraneo*, C-387/17, ECLI-:EU:C:2019:51, paragraph 66; Judgment of the Court of Justice of 5 March 2019, *Eesti Pagar*, C-349/17, ECLI:EU:C:2019:172, paragraph 110. In both instances, the Court of Justice was referring to the Procedural Regulation which, in so far as it contains rules of a procedural nature which apply to all administrative procedures in the matter of State aid pending before the Commission, it codifies and reinforces the Commission's practice in reviewing State aid.

63 Judgment of the Court of Justice of 7 March 2002, *Italy v Commission*, C-310/99, ECLI:EU:C:2002:143, paragraph 99.

64 See Article 16(1) of the Procedural Regulation.

65 See Article 17(1) of the Procedural Regulation.

[66] Judgment of the Court of Justice of 14 February 1990, *France v Commission*, C-301/87, ECLI:EU:C:1990:67, paragraphs 19 to 20; Judgment of the Court of Justice of 21 March 1991, *Italy v Commission*, C-303/88, ECLI:EU:C:1991:136, paragraph 46. If the Member State fails to comply with a suspension or a recovery injunction, the Commission is entitled, while carrying out the examination on the substance of the matter, to bring the matter directly before the Court of Justice by applying for a declaration that such failure constitutes an infringement of the TFEU, pursuant to Article 14 of the Procedural Regulation.

[67] See Article 13(1) and (2) of the Procedural Regulation.

4. THE ROLE OF NATIONAL COURTS

[5.245]

(41) While the Commission must examine the compatibility of an aid measure with the internal market, even where it has established its implementation in breach of Article 108(3) TFEU, the primary role of national courts is to preserve the rights of individuals faced with that breach.[68]

(42) National courts have the responsibility to offer effective legal protection to third parties.[69] Their contribution to the State aid control system is especially necessary in cases where unlawful aid is granted, in the absence of a final Commission decision on the same measure or until the adoption of such decision, as well as in cases where a possibly compatible aid has been granted in violation of the standstill obligation.[70]

4.1. DELIMITATION OF THE COMPETENCES OF NATIONAL COURTS IN THE APPLICATION OF STATE AID RULES

(43) National courts have the power to interpret and apply Articles 107(1) and 108(3) TFEU. In particular, in the absence of a Commission decision regarding the same measure,[71] national courts are bound only by the objective notion of State aid when exercising their competence to assess the existence of State aid.[72]

(44) The Commission also assesses the existence of State aid, which is normally a first step before assessing its compatibility. Therefore, any proceedings before the Commission, prior or subsequent to those before national courts, could affect the latter,[73] as explained in Sections 4.1.1 to 4.1.3.

4.1.1. Following a decision by the Commission

(45) National courts must refrain from taking decisions which conflict with a decision of the Commission[74] and must therefore abide by the Commission's assessment on the existence of State aid. National courts also have no jurisdiction to declare Commission decisions invalid.[75] The Union Courts alone have that jurisdiction pursuant to Article 263 TFEU.[76]

(46) If a national court has doubts about the interpretation or the validity of a Commission decision, that court may seek clarification from the Commission (see Section 5.1) or, depending on the circumstances, may or must[77] refer a question to the Court of Justice for a preliminary ruling, in accordance with Article 267 TFEU.[78]

4.1.1.1. Following a Commission decision declaring the aid compatible

(47) A final Commission decision recognising the compatibility of unlawful aid after it has been granted does not have the effect of regularising *ex post facto* the implementing measures which had been adopted in breach of the standstill obligation provided for by the TFEU.[79]

(48) In this context, national courts must offer individuals the certain prospect that all appropriate conclusions will be drawn[80] from the infringement of the standstill obligation, including by ordering the recovery of the interest in respect of the period of unlawfulness, in accordance with their national law.[81]

(49) It follows that, where a third party seeks before a national court the elimination of advantages linked to the premature implementation of the aid, the court should uphold its action even if the Commission has already declared the aid in question compatible. Any other interpretation would have the effect of allowing the Member States to disregard the provisions of the TFEU and thus deprive them of their effectiveness.[82]

4.1.1.2. Following an opening decision by the Commission

(50) The situation is different when the Commission has merely initiated, pursuant to Article 108(2) TFEU, an investigation procedure regarding an aid measure brought before a national court. In the opening decision, the Commission, in principle, expresses doubts as to whether an aid measure is compatible with the internal market. While these doubts generally concern the compatibility of the aid, the assessment of the existence of aid is preliminary in nature and is drawn from an initial examination of the measure in question.[83]

(51) In accordance with Article 4(3) TEU, national courts must take into account the legal situation resulting from the ongoing procedures before the Commission, even if it is provisional.

(52) This means that, while the investigation procedure is ongoing, national courts must draw legal consequences from the opening decision itself. Following an opening decision, a national court cannot hold that this measure does not constitute aid within the meaning of Article 107(1) TFEU, otherwise the effectiveness of Article 108(3) TFEU would be compromised.[84]

(53) To that end, it is the responsibility of national courts to take all appropriate action to address the potential breach of the standstill obligation. National courts may decide to suspend the implementation of the measure in question and order the recovery of payments already made. They may also decide to order other provisional measures in order to safeguard both the interests of the parties concerned and the effectiveness of the Commission's opening decision.[85]

(54) In addition, the national courts cannot simply stay their proceedings until the Commission has reached a final decision,[86] as this would amount to maintaining the advantage on the market in spite of the potential breach of the standstill obligation.

(55) The same constraints may apply to national courts when a final Commission decision[87] has been annulled by the Union Courts, either by a judgment which may be appealed or by a final judgement, as the Commission is not required to recommence the procedure from the start but can resume from the point at which the illegality occurred.[88] The opening decision may therefore stand until the Commission takes a new final decision. In those circumstances, national courts are therefore bound to ensure compliance with the stand-still obligation resulting from the opening of the formal procedure, for instance preventing the recovered aid from being paid back.

4.2. THE COMPETENCES OF NATIONAL COURTS

(56) As stated in paragraphs (11) to (13), national courts must establish whether State aid has been granted in accordance with Article 108(3) TFEU within the limits set by the Commission's exclusive competence to assess the aid's compatibility and any pre-existing Commission decision on the same measure.

(57) National courts carry out their assessment in two steps: first, they assess the nature of the measure to establish whether it qualifies as State aid under Article 107(1) TFEU; second, if the national courts find that the measure constitutes State aid, they have to conclude whether the measure is subject to the standstill obligation. Where national courts find a breach of the standstill obligation, they must adopt appropriate remedies to safeguard the rights of individuals affected by such breach.

4.2.1. ASSESSING THE EXISTENCE OF AID

(58) The Union Courts have confirmed that, as is the case for the Commission, national courts have jurisdiction to interpret the notion of State aid.[89]

(59) To ascertain the existence of State aid, a series of complex issues often needs to be assessed (see paragraph (14)). In its notice on the notion of State aid, as referred to in Article 107(1) TFEU,[90] the Commission issued detailed guidance that can provide assistance to national courts.

(60) Where doubts arise as to the existence of State aid elements, national courts may ask the Commission to provide its opinion (see Section 5.1.1.2). National courts also have the possibility or the obligation to refer the matter to the Court of Justice for a preliminary ruling under Article 267 TFEU.

4.2.2. ASSESSING WHETHER THERE IS A BREACH OF THE STANDSTILL OBLIGATION

(61) In the context of assessing whether an aid measure is subject to the standstill obligation, national courts must consider whether the measure falls under one of the exceptions from the notification obligation (see Section 1.2). In particular, national courts evaluate whether the measure concerned fulfils the criteria set out in a block exemption regulation or constitutes existing aid.

(62) If an aid measure fulfils all the conditions provided in a block exemption regulation, it is exempted from prior notification to the Commission and it is deemed to be compatible with the internal market.

(63) Existing aid is not subject to the notification obligation of Member States under Article 108(3) TFEU, but is subject to a different system of review by the Commission under Article 108(1) TFEU. However, alterations to existing aid within the meaning of Article 1(c) of the Procedural Regulation do not fall within the notion of existing aid.

4.2.2.1.
Applying the conditions of block exemption regulations

(64) Member States may rely on a measure being exempted from the notification requirement if it fulfils the general and specific conditions provided for in block exemption regulations. However, if a Member State implements an aid measure that does not meet all conditions of the applicable block exemption without prior notification to the Commission, the implementation of that aid is unlawful.

(65) The notification and standstill obligations stemming from the TFEU are binding not merely on national courts but also on all administrative bodies of the Member States.[91]

(66) When national courts assess if a State aid measure has been lawfully implemented, they must verify whether the conditions of a block exemption regulation were complied with to establish that the measure was exempt from the notification obligation. The Court of Justice has defined the scope of the competences of national courts when they establish whether the conditions of the General Block Exemption Regulation were correctly applied,[92] that is to say, the extent to which national courts can interpret its provisions.

(67) The adoption of block exemption regulations does not intend to transfer to Member States the assessment of State aid compatibility with the internal market, which remains the exclusive competence of the Commission.[93] It is, however, the duty of national courts to ascertain whether national authorities have granted aid that fully complies with the general and specific conditions of the applicable block exemption regulation, strictly interpreted.[94]

(68) Where aid has been implemented under a block exemption regulation without satisfying all applicable conditions, the recipient of this aid cannot have at that time a legitimate expectation that the granting of the aid was lawful.[95] This is because national authorities are not vested with the power to adopt final decisions finding that there is no obligation to notify the aid.[96]

4.2.2.2.
Existing aid

(69) As stated in paragraph (63), contrary to new aid, existing aid is not subject to the notification obligation. It is exclusively for the Commission to assess whether an existing aid is still compatible with the internal market and propose appropriate measures where it considers that a scheme is no longer compatible. When implementing State aid rules, the role of the national courts is limited to assessing whether an aid measure constitutes existing aid within the meaning of Article 108(1) TFEU. If the measure is existing aid, there is no question of breach of Article 108(3) TFEU to be remedied by the national court.

(70) The Treaties do not provide any guidance on the classification of an aid measure as existing aid. It is in the provisions of the Procedural Regulation where the circumstances under which aid is to be considered as existing are defined.[97] However, the Procedural Regulation does not contain any provision relating to the powers and obligations of national courts, which continue to be governed by the provisions of the TFEU, as interpreted by the Court of Justice.[98]

4.2.3. SAFEGUARDING THE RIGHTS OF INDIVIDUALS FACED WITH THE BREACH OF THE STANDSTILL OBLIGATION

(71) To safeguard the rights of individuals against the unlawful implementation of State aid, national courts can adopt different types of remedies, depending on the situation. For instance, they may decide to suspend or terminate the implementation of the measure (Section 4.2.3.1), order the recovery of the sums already disbursed (Section 4.2.3.2) or adopt different provisional measures to otherwise safeguard the interests of the parties concerned (Section 4.2.3.3).[99] Finally, they may be asked to rule on compensation for damages suffered by third parties as a consequence of the unlawful implementation of the State aid (Section 4.2.3.4). In any event, national courts must offer to individuals the certainty that all appropriate action will be taken, in accordance with their national law, to address the consequences of the infringement of Article 108(3) TFEU.[100]

4.2.3.1 SUSPENSION OR TERMINATION OF THE IMPLEMENTATION OF THE MEASURE

(72) Where a State authority has not yet implemented a State aid measure granted in violation of Article 108(3) TFEU, national courts must prevent that implementation, either by suspending it or by terminating it. Such remedy might also be appropriate in cases where the State aid measure has entered into force, but the aid has not yet been disbursed (fully or partly), notwithstanding the need for additional remedies for the part of the aid that has already been paid.

(73) Union law does not impose any specific conclusion that the national courts must necessarily draw about the validity of the act granting the unlawful State aid. It solely requires that they take effective measures to prevent the disbursement of the unlawful aid to the beneficiary. However, there may be situations under national law where the unlawful implementation of the measure can be suspended by annulling the granting act.[101]

(74) Accordingly, national courts may declare the contract by which the aid is granted null and void, annul the decision of the Member State's authorities granting the aid, or suspend its implementation (for instance, in cases where the aid is granted in the form of access to a facility or service).

(75) When the aid is granted in instalments, national courts should order the suspension of future payments.

4.2.3.2.
Recovery

(76) When the unlawful aid has already been paid to the beneficiary, national courts must, in principle, and in the absence of a Commission decision declaring the aid compatible, order the full recovery of the unlawfully paid amount.[102] Removal of the aid by means of recovery is the logical consequence of its unlawfulness.[103]

(77) To restore the situation existing before the aid was granted, national courts must abolish completely the advantage unlawfully conferred on the beneficiary. Such advantage encompasses the aid (the 'aid principal') as well as the non-payment of the interest that the undertaking would have paid had it had to borrow the amount of the aid on the market during the period of the unlawfulness, which results in the improvement of its competitive position over that period ('illegality interest').[104] Therefore, national courts must order the recovery of both the aid principal and the illegality interest.

(78) If there are parallel procedures before a national court and before the Commission, and if the Commission declares the aid incompatible, the national court should draw the appropriate consequences from it, according to national rules governing the execution of recovery decisions.[105]

(79) As indicated in paragraph (48), if the Commission declares the aid compatible, Union law only requires Member States to recover the illegality interest in respect of the period of unlawfulness,[106] which runs from the aid's payment until the declaration of its compatibility.

(80) If a Commission decision declaring the measure compatible is annulled, this measure cannot be considered cleared by the Commission, and its implementation is considered unlawful.[107] In that case, the recipient is not entitled to invoke any legitimate expectation that the aid was lawful, given that an action for the annulment of the positive decision had been brought.[108]

(81) For calculating the illegality interest, neither Article 16(2) of the Procedural Regulation nor Articles 9 and 11 of Commission Regulation (EC) No 794/2004[109] apply to the recovery of unlawful aid by a Member State in the absence of a Commission recovery decision. Therefore, in such cases, the authorities of the Member State concerned must calculate the illegality interest in accordance with the applicable rules of national law, provided that two conditions are fulfilled. First, these rules must respect the principles of equivalence and effectiveness (see Section 2.2); and, second, the illegality interest must be calculated, at the minimum, at a rate equivalent to that which would have been applied if the beneficiary had had to borrow the amount of the aid at issue on the market within that period.[110]

(82) With regard to the prescription period applied to national courts' powers to order recovery, the Union Courts have ruled that the ten-year limitation period provided for by the Procedural Regulation applies solely to the Commission.[111] As long as national procedures provide for a longer prescription period, a national judge must order the recovery of aid granted in violation of the standstill obligation, even after the limitation period provided for the Commission has expired. National prescription periods shorter than 10 years also bind national courts, unless there is a Commission recovery decision.[112] Where the Commission adopts a recovery decision, Member States cannot justify their failure to implement that decision on the basis of requirements of national law, such as national prescription periods.[113]

4.2.3.3. Interim measures

(83) As part of their obligations under Article 108(3) TFEU, national courts are required to take interim measures where this is appropriate to safeguard the rights of individuals and the direct effect of Article 108(3) TFEU.[114] National courts adopt these measures, which aim to eliminate the anti-competitive effects of the aid on a provisional basis,[115] in accordance with their national law, provided that the conditions of equivalence and effectiveness are fulfilled (see Section 2.2).

(84) National courts may choose to take interim measures where presumably unlawful aid has already been paid[116] or is about to be paid. In the first case, national courts may order either the repayment of the aid with illegality interest or the provisional transfer of the aid, including interest for the period between the implementation of the aid and its transfer, on a blocked account. These options ensure that the advantage linked to the presumably unlawful aid does not remain further at the disposal of the beneficiary. Where there is a risk of imminent payment of the aid, the court may issue an interim order preventing the disbursement of the presumably unlawful aid until the substance of the matter is resolved.[117]

(85) An ongoing Commission investigation does not release the national court from its obligation to protect rights of individuals under Article 108(3).[118] The national court may therefore adopt appropriate interim measures as a way to address the consequences of a potential infringement of the standstill obligation.

(86) National courts have an obligation to adopt interim measures if the following conditions are satisfied: (a) there is no doubt regarding the existence of State aid; (b) the aid is about to be, or has been, implemented; and (c) no exceptional circumstances have been found, which would make recovery inappropriate.[119]

4.2.3.4. Action for damages

(87) As part of their role under Article 108(3) TFEU, national courts may also be required to adjudicate on claims for compensation for damages caused to third parties by unlawful State aid. If successful, such claims provide the claimants with direct financial compensation for the loss suffered.

(88) The Court of Justice has repeatedly held that affected third parties can bring such actions for compensation for damages before national courts, in accordance with national law,[120] which should comply with the principles of equivalence and effectiveness (see Section 2.2).

(89) Based on the '*Francovich*'[121] and '*Brasserie du Pêcheur*'[122] case-law of the Court of Justice,[123] Member States are required to compensate for loss and damage caused to individuals as a result of breaches of Union law for which the State is responsible.[124] Such liability exists where the following requirements are met: (a) the rule of law infringed is intended to confer rights on individuals; (b) the breach is sufficiently serious; and (c) there is a direct causal link between the breach of the Member State's obligation and the damage suffered by the injured parties.[125]

(90) The first two requirements set out in paragraph (89) will generally be met in relation to violations of Article 108(3) TFEU. The Court of Justice has confirmed the existence of rights of individuals under this provision and clarified that the protection of these rights is the genuine role of national courts.[126]

(91) Similarly, as Member State authorities are, in principle, under an obligation to notify State aid measures prior to their implementation, the infringement of Article 108(3) TFEU will in most cases be sufficient to establish the existence of a serious breach under the case-law of the Union Courts. In the presence of State aid, Member State authorities cannot normally argue that they were not aware of the standstill obligation, as there is sufficient case-law and Commission guidance on the application of Articles 107(1) and 108(3) TFEU. In case of doubt and for reasons of legal certainty, Member States can always notify the measure to the Commission prior to its implementation.[127]

(92) The third requirement set out in paragraph (89), that the breach of Union law must have caused actual and certain financial damage to the claimant, can be met in various ways. The Enforcement Study pointed out that national courts have rarely awarded damages, specifying that the damage quantification and the establishment of the causal link between the harm and the unlawful aid represent major obstacles for claimants.[128]

(93) Claimants will often argue that the aid directly caused a loss of profit. When confronted with such claims, national courts should take into account the following considerations:

(a) by virtue of Union legal requirements of equivalence and effectiveness, national rules may not exclude a Member State's liability for loss of profit.[129] Should national law contain such an exclusion, the national court should leave that provision unapplied as regards damage claims for breach of Article 108(3) TFEU;

(b) determining the actual amount of lost profit will be easier where the unlawful aid enabled the beneficiary to win over a contract or a specific business opportunity from the claimant and the latter has already been executed by the beneficiary;

(c) more complicated damage quantifications are required where the aid merely leads to a loss of market share. One possible way for dealing with such cases could be to compare the claimant's actual income situation (based on the profit and loss account) with the hypothetical income situation had the unlawful aid not been granted;[130]

(d) there may be circumstances where the damage suffered by the claimant exceeds the lost profit. This could be the case where, as a consequence of the unlawful aid, the claimant is forced out of business.

(94) National procedural rules will sometimes allow national courts to seek the advice of experts for the purpose of determining the actual amount of damage compensation. Where that is the case, and provided the principle of effectiveness[131] is respected, the use of such estimates would also be possible for claims for damages arising under Article 108(3) TFEU.

(95) The possibility to claim damages is, in principle, independent of any parallel Commission investigation concerning the same aid measure. Any ongoing investigation by the Commission does not release national courts from their obligation to safeguard rights of individuals under Article 108(3) TFEU.[132] Since claimants may be able to

demonstrate that they suffered a loss due to the aid's premature implementation and, more specifically, as a result of the beneficiary's illegal time advantage, successful damage claims are also not ruled out where the Commission has already declared the aid compatible by the time the national court decides.[133]

(96) The Court of Justice recalled that State aid is fundamentally different in its legal nature from damages that national authorities may be ordered to pay to individuals in compensation for the damage they have caused (Asteris case-law).[134] However, when ruling on the compensation to third parties for the costs incurred as a direct result of an unlawful aid, national courts must be careful not to adopt decisions having the effect of granting an aid[135] or enlarging the circle of beneficiaries.[136]

(97) While individuals may request national courts to order the payment of damages which they consider to be entitled to, such actions cannot have the effect of circumventing the effective application of EU State aid rules.[137] In particular, individuals who might be entitled under national law to receive aid which has not been notified to and approved by the Commission, but who have not received such aid, cannot claim as compensation for damages the equivalent of the sum of the non-received aid, since this would constitute an indirect grant of unlawful aid.[138] It follows that the Asteris case-law does not concern cases where the applicant requests a national court to award to it previous State aid, which the applicant has not received for whatever reason.[139]

(98) Beneficiaries of unlawful aid sometimes try to claim damages from the State after having been ordered to reimburse the amount. Usually, these beneficiaries put forward arguments concerning the alleged breach of their legitimate expectations. Nevertheless, the Court of Justice held that an unlawfully granted measure could not generate any legitimate expectation for the beneficiary, which should be able to determine whether the correct procedure for the granting of the aid has been followed.[140] Their claims should therefore be rejected.

(99) While the case-law has recognised an EU right to seek damages against the Member State concerned by third parties that suffered losses because of the unlawful implementation of an aid, actions for damages against beneficiaries of aid are allowed but not required as a matter of EU State aid law, since Articles 107 and 108 TFEU do not impose any direct obligations on beneficiaries. In the 'SFEI' judgment, the Court of Justice concluded that, because Article 108(3) TFEU does not impose any direct obligations on the beneficiary, the breach of that Article is not a sufficient basis for the recipient to incur liability.[141] This is without prejudice to the possibility of bringing an action for damages against the beneficiary in accordance with national law, for instance on the basis of national provisions governing non-contractual liability.[142]

NOTES

68 Judgment of the Court of Justice of 12 February 2008, *CELF et ministre de la Culture et de la Communication*, C-199/06, ECLI:EU: C:2008:79, paragraph 38; Judgment of the Court of Justice of 21 November 1991, *Fédération nationale du commerce extérieur des produits alimentaires and Others v France*, C-354/90, ECLI:EU:C:1991:440, paragraphs 11 to 12.

69 Judgment of the Court of Justice of 11 December 1973, *Lorenz GmbH v Bundesrepublik Deutschland and Others*, C-120/73, ECLI:EU: C:1973:152, paragraph 8; Judgment of the Court of Justice of 21 November 1991, *Fédération nationale du commerce extérieur des produits alimentaires and Others v France*, C-354/90, ECLI:EU:C:1991:440, paragraph 11; Judgment of the Court of Justice of 11 July 1996, *SFEI and Others*, C-39/94, ECLI:EU:C:1996:285, paragraph 39.

70 For the role of national courts in the public enforcement of State aid, see the Recovery Notice (OJ C 247, 23.7.2019, p. 1).

71 See also Judgement of the General Court of 20 June 2019, *A&O hostel and hotel Berlin v Commission*, T-578/17, ECLI:EU:T:2019:437, paragraph 72.

72 To that effect, see Judgment of the Court of 22 March 1977, *Steineke e Weinlig*, 78/76, ECLI:EU:C:1977:52, paragraph 14.

73 Judgment of the Court of Justice of 4 March 2020, CSTP *Azienda della Mobilità v Commission*, C-587/18 P, ECLI:EU:C:2020:150, paragraphs 92 to 93; Judgment of the Court of Justice of 4 March 2020, *Buonotourist v Commission*, C-586/18 P, ECLI:EU:C:2020:152, paragraph 96.

74 Judgment of the Court of Justice of 21 November 2013, *Deutsche Lufthansa*, C-284/12, ECLI:EU:C:2013:755, paragraph 41.

75 Judgment of the Court of Justice of 22 October 1987, *Foto-Frost v Hauptzollamt Lübeck-Ost*, C-314/85, ECLI-:EU:C:1987:452, paragraph 20.

76 Judgment of the Court of Justice of 21 February 1991, *Zuckerfabrik Süderdithmarschen and Zuckerfabrik Soest v Hauptzollamt Itzehoe and Hauptzollamt Paderborn*, C-143/88 and C-92/89, ECLI:EU:C:1991:65, paragraph 23; Judgment of the Court of Justice of 9 November 1995, *Atlanta Fruchthandelsgesellschaft and Others (I) v Bundesamt für Ernährung und Forstwirtschaft*, C-465/93, ECLI:EU:C:1995:369, paragraph 51; Judgment of the Court of Justice of 18 July 2007, *Lucchini*, C-119/05, ECLI:EU:C:2007:434, paragraph 53.

77 Based on Article 267 TFEU, a national court whose decision is not subject to further judicial review is under an obligation to initiate a preliminary reference to the Court of Justice in certain circumstances. Where the interpretation of Union law may be clearly deduced from existing case-law or where it leaves no scope for reasonable doubt, a court against whose decisions there is no judicial remedy under national law is not required to refer the case for a preliminary ruling by the Court of Justice, although it is free to do so. See Judgment of the Court of Justice of 6 October 1982, *CILFIT v Ministero della Sanità*, C-283/81, ECLI:EU:C:1982:335, paragraphs 14 to 20; Judgment of the Court of Justice of 11 September 2008, *Unión General de Trabajadores de la Rioja*, C-428/06 to C-434/06, ECLI-:EU:C:2008:488, paragraphs 42 and 43; Judgment of the Court of Justice of 28 July 2016, *Association France Nature Environnement*, C-379/15, ECLI:EU:C:2016:603, paragraphs 47 to 50; Judgment of the Court of Justice of 15 September 2016, *PGE*, C-574/14, ECLI:EU:C:2016:686, paragraph 40; Judgment of the Court of Justice of 4 October 2018, *Commission v France (Advance Payment)*, C-416/17, ECLI:EU:C:2018:811, paragraphs 108 et seq.

78 Judgment of the Court of Justice of 11 July 1996, *SFEI and Others*, C-39/94, ECLI:EU:C:1996:285, paragraphs 50 to 51; Judgment of the Court of Justice of 21 November 2013, *Deutsche Lufthansa*, C-284/12, ECLI:EU:C:2013:755, paragraph 44.

79 Judgment of the Court of Justice of 12 February 2008, *CELF et ministre de la Culture et de la Communication*, C-199/06,

ECLI:EU:C:2008:79, paragraph 40; Judgment of the Court of Justice of 19 March 2015, *OTP Bank*, C-672/13, ECLI:EU:C:2015:185, paragraph 76; Judgment of the Court of Justice of 23 January 2019, *Fallimento Traghetti del Mediterraneo*, C-387/17, ECLI:EU:C:2019:51, paragraph 59.

80 Judgment of the Court of Justice of 21 November 2013, *Deutsche Lufthansa*, C-284/12, ECLI:EU:C:2013:755, paragraph 30; Judgment of the Court of Justice of 5 March 2019, *Eesti Pagar*, C-349/17, ECLI:EU:C:2019:172, paragraph 89; Judgment of the Court of Justice of 3 March 2020, *Vodafone Magyarország*, C-75/18, ECLI-:EU:C:2020:139, paragraph 23; Judgment of the Court of Justice of 13 December 2018, *Rittinger and Others*, C-492/17, ECLI:EU:C:2018:1019, paragraph 42.

81 Judgment of the Court of Justice of 12 February 2008, *CELF et ministre de la Culture et de la Communication*, C-199/06, ECLI:EU: C:2008:79, paragraphs 52 to 55. Within the framework of its domestic law, the national court may, if appropriate, also order the recovery of the unlawful aid, without prejudice to the Member State's right to reimplement it subsequently. It may also be required to uphold claims for compensation for damage caused by reason of the unlawful nature of the aid (*Ibid.*, paragraph 53).

82 See, to that effect, Judgment of the Court of Justice of 19 December 2019, *Arriva Italia and Others*, C-385/18, ECLI:EU:C:2019:1121, paragraph 85.

83 Judgment of the Court of Justice of 21 November 2013, *Deutsche Lufthansa*, C-284/12, ECLI:EU:C:2013:755, paragraphs 37 to 40.

84 Judgment of the Court of Justice of 21 November 2013, *Deutsche Lufthansa*, C-284/12, ECLI:EU:C:2013:755, paragraph 38.

85 Judgment of the Court of Justice of 21 November 2013, *Deutsche Lufthansa*, C-284/12, ECLI:EU:C:2013:755, paragraphs 41 to 43.

86 Judgment of the Court of Justice of 11 March 2010, *CELF et ministre de la Culture et de la Communication*, C-1/09, ECLI:EU:C:2010:136, paragraphs 31 et seq.; Order of the Court of Justice of 4 April 2014, *Flughafen Lübeck*, C-27/13, ECLI:EU:C:2014:240, paragraph 30.

87 I.e. a decision closing the formal investigation based on Article 9 of the Procedural Regulation.

88 See, to that effect, Judgment of the Court of Justice of 12 November 1998, *Spain v Commission*, C-415/96, EU:C:1998:533, paragraph 31; Judgment of the Court of Justice of 3 October 2000, *Industrie des poudres sphériques v Council*, C-458/98 P, EU: C:2000:531, paragraph 82; Judgment of the Court of Justice of 9 July 2008, *Alitalia v Commission*, T-301/01, EU:T:2008:262, paragraphs 99 and 142.

89 Judgment of the Court of Justice of 22 March 1977, *Steinike & Weinlig*, C-78/76, ECLI:EU:C:1977:52, paragraph 14; Judgment of the Court of Justice of 11 July 1996, *SFEI and Others*, C-39/94, ECLI:EU:C:1996:285, paragraph 49; Judgment of the Court of Justice of 21 November 1991, *Fédération nationale du commerce extérieur des produits alimentaires and Others v France*, C-354/90, ECLI:EU: C:1991:440, paragraph 10; Judgment of the Court of Justice of 18 July 2007, *Lucchini*, C-119/05, ECLI:EU:C:2007:434, paragraph 50; Judgment of the Court of Justice of 5 October 2006, *Transalpine Ölleitung in Österreich*, C-368/04, ECLI:EU:C:2006:644, paragraph 39.

90 OJ C 262, 19.7.2016, p. 1.

91 Judgment of the Court of Justice of 5 March 2019, *Eesti Pagar*, C-349/17, ECLI:EU:C:2019:172, paragraphs 90 to 92.

92 Judgment of the Court of Justice of 5 March 2019, *Eesti Pagar*, C-349/17, ECLI:EU:C:2019:172, paragraph 101; Judgment of the Court of Justice of 29 July 2019, *BMW v Commission*, C-654/17 P, ECLI:EU:C:2019:634, paragraph 151.

93 Judgment of the Court of Justice of 29 July 2019, *BMW v Commission*, C-654/17 P, ECLI:EU:C:2019:634, paragraphs 132 and 133; Judgment of the Court of Justice of 5 March 2019, *Eesti Pagar*, C-349/17, ECLI-:EU:C:2019:172, paragraph 67.

94 Judgment of the Court of Justice of 5 March 2019, *Eesti Pagar*, C-349/17, ECLI:EU:C:2019:172, paragraph 60. In this respect, the Court has clarified that the criteria for the application of the exemption must be clear and easily enforceable and their verification by national courts should not necessitate complex economic assessments on a case-by-case basis (Ibid. paragraphs 61 and 68).

95 Judgment of the Court of Justice of 15 December 2005, *Unicredito Italiano*, C-148/04, ECLI:EU:C:2005:774, paragraph 104; Judgment of the Court of Justice of 19 March 2015, *OTP Bank*, C-672/13, ECLI:EU:C:2015:185, paragraph 77; Judgment of the Court of Justice of 5 March 2019, *Eesti Pagar*, C-349/17, ECLI:EU:C:2019:172, paragraph 104.

96 Judgment of the Court of Justice of 5 March 2019, *Eesti Pagar*, C-349/17, ECLI:EU:C:2019:172, paragraph 101; Judgment of the Court of Justice of 29 July 2019, *BMW v Commission*, C-654/17 P, ECLI:EU:C:2019:634, paragraph 151.

97 Procedural Regulation, Articles 1(b) and 17(3).

98 Judgment of the Court of Justice of 23 January 2019, *Fallimento Traghetti del Mediterraneo*, C-387/17, ECLI-:EU:C:2019:51, paragraph 66; Judgment of the Court of Justice of 5 March 2019, *Eesti Pagar*, C-349/17, ECLI:EU:C:2019:172, paragraph 110. For instance, Article 17(1) of the Procedural Regulation, which establishes that the powers of the Commission to recover aid are subject to a limitation period of 10 years, and paragraph 3 of that Article, which provides that 'any aid with regard to which the limitation period has expired shall be deemed to be existing aid', do not lay down a general principle that is applicable to national courts (see paragraph (82) below).

99 Judgment of the Court of Justice of 21 November 2013, *Deutsche Lufthansa*, C-284/12, ECLI:EU:C:2013:755, paragraph 43; Judgment of the Court of Justice of 21 December 2016, *Commission v Hansestadt Lübeck*, C-524/14 P, ECLI:EU:C:2016:971, paragraph 29.

100 Judgment of the Court of Justice of 3 March 2020, *Vodafone Magyarország*, C-75/18, ECLI:EU:C:2020:139, paragraph 23; Judgment of the Court of Justice of 19 December 2019, *Arriva Italia and Others*, C-385/18, ECLI:EU:C:2019:1121, paragraph 84.

101 Judgment of the Court of Justice of 8 December 2011, *Residex Capital IV*, C-275/10, ECLI:EU:C:2011:814, paragraphs 44-47.

102 Judgment of the Court of Justice of 21 July 2005, *Xunta de Galicia*, C-71/04, ECLI:EU:C:2005:493, paragraph 49; Judgment of the Court of Justice of 11 July 1996, *SFEI and Others*, C-39/94, ECLI:EU:C:1996:285, paragraphs 40 and 68; Judgment of the Court of Justice of 21 November 1991, *Fédération nationale du commerce extérieur des produits alimentaires and Others v France*, C-354/90, ECLI: EU:C:1991:440, paragraph 12; Judgment of the Court

of Justice of 8 December 2011, *Residex Capital IV*, C-275/10, ECLI:EU: C:2011:814, paragraph 43.

103 Judgment of the Court of Justice of 21 December 2016, *Commission v Aer Lingus*, C-164/15 P and C-165/15 P, ECLI:EU:C:2016:990, paragraph 116; Judgment of the Court of Justice of 19 March 2015, *OTP Bank*, C-672/13, ECLI:EU:C:2015:185, paragraph 70; Judgment of the Court of Justice of 8 December 2011, *Residex Capital IV*, C-275/10, ECLI:EU:C:2011:814, paragraph 33.

104 Judgment of the Court of Justice of 5 March 2019, *Eesti Pagar*, C-349/17, ECLI:EU:C:2019:172, paragraph 132; Judgment of the Court of Justice of 8 December 2011, *Residex Capital IV*, C-275/10, ECLI:EU:C:2011:814, paragraph 39.

105 In that sense, see the Recovery Notice (OJ C 247, 23.7.2019, p. 1).

106 Judgment of the Court of Justice of 5 March 2019, *Eesti Pagar*, C-349/17, ECLI:EU:C:2019:172, paragraph 134.

107 Judgment of the Court of Justice of 12 February 2008, *CELF et ministre de la Culture et de la Communication*, C-199/06, ECLI:EU: C:2008:79, paragraph 63.

108 Judgment of the Court of Justice of 12 February 2008, *CELF et ministre de la Culture et de la Communication*, C-199/06, ECLI:EU: C:2008:79, paragraph 68.

109 Commission Regulation (EC) No 794/2004 of 21 April 2004 implementing Council Regulation (EC) No 659/1999 laying down detailed rules for the application of Article 93 of the EC Treaty (OJ L 140, 30.4.2004, p. 1).

110 Judgment of the Court of Justice of 5 March 2019, *Eesti Pagar*, C-349/17, ECLI:EU:C:2019:172, paragraph 141.

111 Judgment of the Court of Justice of 23 January 2019, *Fallimento Traghetti del Mediterraneo*, C-387/17, ECLI-:EU:C:2019:51, paragraph 61.

112 Judgment of the Court of Justice of 23 January 2019, *Fallimento Traghetti del Mediterraneo*, C-387/17, ECLI-:EU:C:2019:51, paragraphs 71 to 75.

113 Judgment of the Court of Justice of 20 March 1997, *Land Rheinland-Pfalz v Alcan Deutschland*, C-24/95, ECLI:EU:C:1997:163, paragraphs 34 to 37; Judgment of the Court of Justice of 29 March 2012, *Commission v Italy*, C-243/10, ECLI:EU:C:2012:182, paragraph 35; Judgment of the Court of Justice of 30 April 2020, *Nelson Antunes da Cunha*, C-627/18, ECLI:EU:C:2020:321, paragraph 60.

114 Judgment of the Court of Justice of 21 November 1991, *Fédération nationale du commerce extérieur des produits alimentaires and Others v France*, C-354/90, ECLI:EU:C:1991:440, paragraph 12; Judgment of the Court of Justice of 21 December 2016, *Commission v Hansestadt Lübeck*, C-524/14 P, ECLI:EU:C:2016:971, paragraph 29; Judgment of the Court of Justice of 11 July 1996, *SFEI and Others*, C-39/94, ECLI:EU:C:1996:285, paragraph 52; Judgment of the Court of Justice of 5 October 2006, *Transalpine Ölleitung in Österreich*, C-368/04, ECLI-:EU:C:2006:644, paragraph 46.

115 Judgment of the Court of Justice of 11 July 1996, *SFEI and Others*, C-39/94, ECLI:EU:C:1996:285, paragraph 52; Judgment of the Court of Justice of 5 October 2006, *Transalpine Ölleitung in Österreich*, C-368/04, ECLI-:EU:C:2006:644, paragraph 46.

116 An interesting French court order following a negative decision of the Commission was reported in the Enforcement Study: in order to compensate for the automatic suspensory effect of an appeal against the recovery order, the national court ordered the beneficiary to pay the sums due on a blocked account. In doing so, the court used a provision of French law by which provisional payment is possible in cases where the obligation to pay cannot be seriously called into question. See Annex 3: Country reports of the 'Final Study on the enforcement of State aid rules and decisions by national courts (COMP/2018/001)', Publications Office of the European Union, Luxemburg, 2019, p. 156, Case Summary FR8: *Cour administrative d'appel de Bordeaux*, 10 December 2015.

117 Judgment of the Court of Justice of 26 October 2016, *DEI and Commission v Alouminion tis Ellados*, C-590/14 P, ECLI:EU:C:2016:797, paragraph 101.

118 National courts may also choose to take provisional measures while awaiting an opinion or information from the Commission, or a judgement from a higher national court or from the Union Courts.

119 Judgment of the Court of Justice of 11 March 2010, *CELF et ministre de la Culture et de la Communication*, C-1/09, ECLI:EU:C:2010:136, paragraph 36; Order of the General Court of 3 March 2015, *Gemeente Nijmegen v Commission*, T-251/13, ECLI:EU:T:2015:142, paragraph 45.

120 Judgment of the Court of Justice of 12 February 2008, *CELF et ministre de la Culture et de la Communication*, C-199/06, ECLI:EU: C:2008:79, paragraph 55; Judgment of the Court of Justice of 5 October 2006, *Transalpine Ölleitung in Österreich*, C-368/04, ECLI:EU: C:2006:644, paragraph 56; Judgment of the Court of Justice of 11 July 1996, *SFEI and Others*, C-39/94, ECLI:EU:C:1996:285, paragraph 75; Judgment of the Court of Justice of 23 January 2019, *Fallimento Traghetti del Mediterraneo*, C-387/17, ECLI:EU: C:2019:51, paragraph 56.

121 Judgment of the Court of Justice of 19 November 1991, *Francovich and Bonifaci v Italy*, C-6/90 and C-9/90, ECLI:EU:C:1991:428, paragraphs 30 to 46.

122 Judgment of the Court of Justice of 5 March 1996, *Brasserie du pêcheur v Bundesrepublik Deutschland and The Queen / Secretary of State for Transport, ex parte Factortame and Others*, C-46/93 and C-48/93, ECLI:EU:C:1991:428, paragraph 51.

123 Judgment of the Court of Justice of 13 June 2006, *Traghetti del Mediterraneo*, C-173/03, ECLI:EU:C:2006:391, paragraph 41.

124 Judgment of the Court of Justice of 19 November 1991, *Francovich and Bonifaci v Italy*, C-6/90 and C-9/90, ECLI:EU:C:1991:428, paragraphs 31 to 37; Judgment of the Court of Justice of 5 March 1996, *Brasserie du pêcheur v Bundesrepublik Deutschland and The Queen / Secretary of State for Transport, ex parte Factortame and Others*, C-46/93 and C-48/93, ECLI:EU:C:1991:428, paragraph 31.

125 Judgment of the Court of Justice of 13 June 2006, *Traghetti del Mediterraneo*, C-173/03, ECLI:EU:C:2006:391, paragraph 45.

126 Judgment of the Court of Justice of 21 November 1991, *Fédération nationale du commerce extérieur des produits alimentaires and Others v France*, C-354/90, ECLI:EU:C:1991:440, paragraphs 12 to 14; Judgment of the Court of Justice of 21 October 2003, *van Calster and Cleeren*, C-261/01 and C-262/01, ECLI:EU:C:2003:571, paragraph 53; Judgment of the Court of Justice of 12 February 2008, *CELF et ministre de la Culture et de la Communication*, C-199/06, ECLI:EU:C:2008:79, paragraph 38.

127 In some cases, however, the Union Courts have taken the view that, in order to determine whether a mere infringement of Union law by a Member State constitutes a sufficiently serious breach, national courts must take account of several factors, such as the excusability of the relevant breach or the fact that the position taken by a Union institution may have

contributed to that breach. In that sense, see Judgment of the Court of Justice of 25 January 2007, *Robins and Others*, C-278/05, ECLI:EU:C:2007:56, paragraph 71; Judgment of the Court of Justice of 4 July 2000, *Haim*, C-424/97, ECLI:EU:C:2000:357, paragraph 38; Judgment of the Court of Justice of 23 May 1996, *The Queen v Ministry of Agriculture, Fisheries and Food, ex parte Hedley Lomas (Ireland)*, C-5/94, ECLI:EU: C:1996:205, paragraph 28.

128 In some cases, however, the national courts accepted the principle of responsibility of the State. In that sense, see Administrative Court of Appeal of Marseille, *CTC v Corsica Ferries France*, 12 February 2018; Rapport d'expertise, *CTC v Corsica Ferries France*, 28 February 2019, N/REF: 500060, Annex 3: Country reports of the 'Final Study on the enforcement of State aid rules and decisions by national courts (COMP/2018/001)', Publications Office of the European Union, Luxemburg, 2019, p. 152.

129 Judgment of the Court of Justice of 5 March 1996, *Brasserie du pêcheur v Bundesrepublik Deutschland and The Queen / Secretary of State for Transport, ex parte Factortame and Others*, C-46/93 and C-48/93, ECLI:EU:C:1991:428, paragraphs 87 and 90.

130 An interesting case was reported in the Enforcement Study where a French administrative court, following a Commission decision ordering recovery of incompatible aid, decided to award damages for loss of market share to the main competitor of the beneficiary. The court of appeal partially quashed the previous judgement on the estimation of damages and consequently appointed an independent expert to calculate the exact amount of compensation. The expert assessed the number of customers that had shifted from the complainant to the beneficiary because of the incompatible aid and quantified the amount of income subsequently lost. Such quantification is often complex and will depend on the characteristics of the market and the number of competitors. See Annex 3: Country reports of the 'Final Study on the enforcement of State aid rules and decisions by national courts (COMP/2018/001)', Publications Office of the European Union, Luxemburg, 2019, p. 152, Case Summary FR6: Tribunal administratif de Bastia, 23 February 2017. See also, Court of Appeal of Marseille, *CTC v Corsica Ferries France*, 12 February 2018; Rapport d'expertise, *CTC v Corsica Ferries France*, 28 February 2019, N/REF: 500060.

131 See Section 2.2.

132 Judgment of the Court of Justice of 11 July 1996, *SFEI and Others*, C-39/94, ECLI:EU:C:1996:285, paragraph 44; Judgment of the Court of Justice of 23 January 2019, *Fallimento Traghetti del Mediterraneo*, C-387/17, ECLI-:EU:C:2019:51, paragraphs 57 to 58.

133 Judgment of the Court of Justice of 12 February 2008, *CELF et ministre de la Culture et de la Communication*, C-199/06, ECLI:EU: C:2008:79, paragraphs 53 and 55; Judgment of the Court of Justice of 23 January 2019, *Fallimento Traghetti del Mediterraneo*, C-387/17, ECLI:EU:C:2019:51, paragraph 60.

134 Judgment of the Court of Justice of 27 September 1988, *Asteris and Others v Greece and EEC*, C-106 to 120/87, ECLI:EU:C:1988:457, paragraph 23; Judgment of the Court of Justice of 21 December 2016, *Commission v Aer Lingus*, C-164/15 P and C-165/15 P, ECLI: EU:C:2016:990, paragraph 72.

135 See Commission Decision 2014/201/EU of 2 October 2013 on compensation to be paid to SIMET SpA for public transport services provided between 1987 and 2003 (State aid measure SA.33037 (2012/C) Italy) (OJ 2014 L 114, p. 67), upheld on this point by Judgment of the General Court of 3 March 2016, *Simet v Commission*, Case T-15/14, ECLI:EU:T:2016:124, paragraphs 102 to 104. See also Commission Decision (EU) 2015/1470 of 30 March 2015 on State aid SA.38517 (2014/C) (ex 2014/NN) implemented by Romania — Arbitral award Micula v Romania of 11 December 2013 (OJ L 232, 4.9.2015, p. 43), annulled by Judgment of the General Court of 18 June 2019, *European Food and Others v Commission*, T-624/15 ECLI:EU:T:2019:423, currently under review by the Court of Justice in case C-638/19 P, *Commission v European Food and Others*.

136 Judgment of the Court of Justice of 5 October 2006, *Transalpine Ölleitung in Österreich*, C-368/04, ECLI-:EU:C:2006:644, paragraph 57.

137 Judgment of the Court of Justice of 29 June 2004, *Commission v Council*, C-110/02, ECLI:EU:C:2004:395, paragraph 43; Judgment of the Court of Justice of 18 July 2007, *Lucchini*, C-119/05, ECLI:EU:C:2007:434, paragraphs 59 to 63; Judgment of the Court of Justice of 11 November 2015, *Klausner Holz Niedersachsen*, C-505/14, ECLI:EU:C:2015:742, paragraphs 42 to 44.

138 See also, in this respect, the opinion of Advocate General Ruiz-Jarabo Colomer of 28 April 2005 in Joined Cases C-346/03 and C-529/03 *Atzeni and Others*, EU:C:2005:256, paragraph 198.

139 Instead, the *Asteris* case-law covers cases where the applicant simply requests compensation (e.g. rectification of damage caused unlawfully by public authorities) that any other person in a similar situation would be entitled to in that Member State. In that latter case, the mere fact that the defendant is a public entity does not transform into State aid the compensation that any litigant would have received in a similar situation, such as in similar litigation between two private entities.

140 Judgment of the Court of Justice of 5 March 2019, *Eesti Pagar*, C-349/17, ECLI:EU:C:2019:172, paragraphs 98 to 104; Judgment of the Court of Justice of 15 December 2005, *Unicredito Italiano*, C-148/04, ECLI:EU:C:2005:774, paragraph 104; Judgment of the Court of Justice of 19 March 2015, *OTP Bank*, C-672/13, ECLI:EU:C:2015:185, paragraph 77.

141 Judgment of the Court of Justice of 11 July 1996, *SFEI and Others*, C-39/94, ECLI:EU:C:1996:285, paragraphs 72 to 74.

142 Judgment of the Court of Justice of 11 July 1996, *SFEI and Others*, C-39/94, ECLI:EU:C:1996:285, paragraph 75. In situations involving a conflict of laws, the law applicable is determined by Regulation (EC) No 864/2007 of the European Parliament and of the Council of 11 July 2007 on the law applicable to non-contractual obligations (Rome II) (OJ L 199, 31.7.2007, p. 40).

5. COOPERATION BETWEEN THE COMMISSION AND NATIONAL COURTS

[5.246]

(100) The Commission must support national courts in fulfilling their key role in the enforcement of State aid rules, pursuant to Article 4(3) TEU. Conversely, national courts can request the Commission's assistance when applying these rules in the context of a pending case. Close cooperation between the national courts and the Commission contributes to an increased level of consistency[143] and effectiveness in the application of State aid rules across the Union.

5.1. COMMISSION'S ASSISTANCE TO NATIONAL COURTS

(101) When supporting national courts, the Commission must respect its duty of professional secrecy and safeguard its own functioning and independence.[144] In fulfilling its duty under Article 4(3) TEU towards national courts, the Commission is committed to remaining neutral and objective. The Commission may ask national courts to transmit the information and documents necessary to provide the requested assistance. When the Commission assists national courts, it will not serve the private interests of the parties. The Commission's contribution is, indeed, part of its duty to ensure that State aid rules are correctly implemented and to defend the public interest.[145] The Commission will, therefore, not hear any of the parties involved in the national proceedings.

(102) The support offered to national courts under Article 29 of the Procedural Regulation is without prejudice to the possibility or obligation[146] for national courts to ask the Court of Justice for a preliminary ruling[147] on the interpretation or the validity of Union law in accordance with Article 267 TFEU.[148] However, it is no longer possible to question the validity of the Commission decision by way of a preliminary ruling where the claimant could undoubtedly have challenged the Commission decision before the Union Courts under Article 263 TFEU but failed to do so.[149]

5.1.1. THE MEANS OF COOPERATION

(103) Article 29 of the Procedural Regulation codified three means of cooperation between the Commission and national courts. Sections 5.1.1.1, 5.1.1.2 and 5.1.1.3 of this notice explain in further detail these means of cooperation.

5.1.1.1.
Transmission of information to national courts

(104) Pursuant to Article 29 of the Procedural Regulation, national courts may ask the Commission to transmit to them information in its possession.[150]

(105) National courts may ask the Commission to provide information on State aid procedures before it. This includes, for instance, information on: (a) whether a procedure regarding a State aid measure is pending before the Commission; (b) whether a Member State has duly notified a certain aid measure in accordance with Article 108(3) TFEU; (c) whether the Commission has initiated a formal investigation; and (d) whether the Commission has already adopted a decision.[151]

(106) In addition, national courts may request that the Commission transmits documents in its possession. This can include copies of existing Commission decisions if these decisions have not already been published on the Commission's website, factual data, statistics, market studies and economic analyses.

(107) The duty of sincere cooperation enshrined in Article 4(3) TEU requires the Commission to provide national courts with whatever information they may seek.[152] That also includes information covered by the obligation of professional secrecy.

(108) In transmitting information to national courts, the Commission must uphold the guarantees given to natural and legal persons under Article 339 TFEU.[153] Article 339 TFEU prevents members, officials and other servants of the Commission from disclosing information that is covered by the obligation of professional secrecy. That can include confidential information and business secrets.

(109) Where the Commission intends to transmit information covered by professional secrecy to a national court, it will ask the national court to confirm that it will guarantee the protection of such confidential information and business secrets. Where the national court offers such a guarantee (e.g. by referring to the national legal basis for it), the Commission will transmit the information requested, indicating those parts that are covered by professional secrecy and should therefore not be disclosed. Where, on the other hand, the national court cannot offer such a guarantee, the Commission will refrain from transmitting the information concerned.[154]

(110) The Commission may also not be able to disclose information to national courts in other situations. In particular, the Commission may refuse to transmit information to a court of a Member State where such transmission would interfere with the functioning and independence of the Union. This would be the case where disclosure would jeopardise the accomplishment of the tasks entrusted to the Commission[155] (for example, information concerning the Commission's internal decision-making process).

(111) To ensure efficiency in its cooperation with national courts, the Commission endeavours to provide national courts with the requested information within one month from the date of the request. Where the Commission needs to ask national courts for further clarifications on their initial requests or to consult third parties directly affected by the transmission of the information, the one-month period starts to run afresh from the moment the clarification is received or the consultation concluded.[156]

5.1.1.2.
Transmission of opinions on the application of State aid rules

(112) Article 29 of the Procedural Regulation also provides the possibility for national courts to ask the Commission to provide its opinion on questions concerning the application of State aid rules.[157]

(113) When applying State aid rules to a case pending before them, national courts must respect the relevant Union rules and case-law of the Union Courts. Without prejudice to the ultimate interpretation of the Treaties by the Union Courts, national courts may find guidance on the application of State aid rules in the Commission's decision-making practice, as well as in the relevant Commission notices and guidelines. National courts may also find guidance on previous Commission opinions or observations published on the Commission's website, when the issues at stake present elements of analogy with those faced by other national courts.[158]

(114) However, there may be circumstances in which previous Commission decisions or opinions and Commission notices and guidelines do not provide sufficient guidance to the national courts. In accordance with the principle of sincere cooperation enshrined in Article 4(3) TEU, and given the essential role played by national courts in State aid enforcement, the Commission offers the national courts the opportunity to request the Commission's opinion on relevant issues concerning the application of State aid rules.[159]

(115) Requests for a Commission opinion may, in principle, cover all economic, factual or legal matters relating to State aid that arise in the context of the national proceedings. The national courts may ask the Commission, among other things:

(a) whether a certain measure has aid elements within the meaning of Article 107(1) TFEU and, if so, request guidance on how to quantify the amount of the aid. Such requests can relate to a specific State aid element under Article 107 TFEU (namely, notion of undertaking, existence of a selective advantage, imputability of the measure to the Member State and involvement of State resources, possible distortion of competition and effect on trade between Member States).

(b) whether a certain aid measure fulfils a requirement of a block exemption regulation or a requirement of a *de minimis* regulation, which would mean that prior notification to the Commission is not necessary and the standstill obligation provided in Article 108(3) TFEU does not apply.

(c) whether an individual aid falls under an aid scheme notified to the Commission and declared compatible with the internal market by a Commission decision, or otherwise qualifies as existing aid, and hence the standstill obligation under Article 108(3) TFEU does not apply.

(d) whether exceptional circumstances,[160] which would prevent the national court from ordering full recovery under Union law, exist.

(e) what the legal prerequisites are for damage claims under Union law and guidance on how to quantify the damage incurred.

(f) how to calculate the amount of the aid to be recovered and how to calculate the recovery interest.

(116) National courts do not have jurisdiction to assess the compatibility of an aid measure on the basis of Article 107(2), Article 107(3), Article 106(2) and Article 93 TFEU.[161] Therefore, they cannot ask the Commission to provide its opinion on the compatibility of a certain aid measure with the internal market. National courts can, however, ask the Commission whether it is already assessing the compatibility of a certain aid measure, as explained in Section 5.1.1.1.

(117) When giving its opinion, the Commission, in line with the principle of sincere co-operation of Article 4(3) TEU, will provide the national court with the factual information or economic or legal clarification sought. Unlike the authoritative interpretation of Union law by the Union Courts, the Commission's opinion does not legally bind the national court.

(118) The Commission will provide its opinion to national courts in accordance with their procedural rules and practices. To ensure effective cooperation with the national courts, the Commission will endeavour to provide the national court with the requested opinion within 4 months from the date of the request. Where the Commission needs to ask the national court for further clarifications concerning its request, this four-month period may be extended.

(119) National courts must protect rights of individuals under Article 108(3) TFEU also during the period in which the Commission prepares the requested opinion. As set out above,[162] the national court's obligation to protect rights of individuals under Article 108(3) TFEU, including by way of interim measures, applies irrespective of an outstanding Commission opinion.

5.1.1.3.
Submission of amicus curiae observations

(120) Pursuant to Article 29(2) of the Procedural Regulation, the Commission may submit written observations to national courts applying State aid rules. It may also make oral observations with the permission of the national court in question. These observations are also known as '*amicus curiae* observations'. The Commission submits *amicus curiae* observations on its own initiative.

(121) The national courts or the parties to a case pending before a national court may, however, ask the Commission to provide *amicus curiae* observations in a case where State aid matters are at stake. The decision to intervene as *amicus curiae* in a case before a national court is an exclusive prerogative of the Commission and falls entirely within its discretion. However, with a view to allowing national courts to plan their proceedings, the Commission will inform them without delay on its intention to intervene as *amicus curiae*.

(122) The Commission submits *amicus curiae* observations in the context of national judicial proceedings to ensure a coherent application of Articles 107(1) or 108(3) TFEU.[163] To evaluate the necessity and appropriateness of its contribution, the Commission may consider, among other things:

(a) whether the case is expected to have a significance beyond the specific case at hand (for example, where the case involves a general question of State aid);

(b) whether the observations from the Commission may contribute to the effectiveness of the enforcement of State aid rules by the concerned national courts;

(c) if the case involves a novel question of substance, which is not covered by the Commission decision-making practice or notices and guidelines; or

(d) whether the case is pending before a court whose judgment cannot be subject to further appeals.

(123) The Commission fully respects the independence and functioning of national courts. As for the Commission's opinions referred to in Section 5.1.1.2 above, *amicus curiae* observations are not binding on the national court adjudicating the case in which the Commission intervened. Before submitting on its own initiative *amicus curiae* observations, the Commission informs the Member State concerned by sending a letter to its Permanent Representation to the Union.

(124) In order to be able to submit useful observations, the Commission may request the relevant national court to transmit documents at its disposal that are necessary for the Commission's assessment of the matter. The Commission will only use those documents for the purpose of preparing its observations.

(125) The Procedural Regulation does not provide for a procedural framework within which the *amicus curiae* observations are to be submitted. Therefore, the Commission submits its observations in accordance with the Member States' procedural rules and practices, including those safeguarding the rights of the parties. Where a Member State has not yet established the relevant procedural framework, it is for the national court to determine which procedural rules should be followed for the submission of *amicus curiae* observations in the case pending before it, bearing in mind that these submissions are based on Article 29 of the Procedural Regulation.

(126) The national procedural framework should respect the principles set out in Section 2.2 of this notice. This implies that the national procedural framework for the submission of observations on issues concerning the application of Articles 107(1) and 108(3) TFEU cannot make the submission of such observations (a) excessively difficult or practically impossible (in line with the principle of effectiveness); and (b) more difficult than the submission of observations in court proceedings where equivalent national law is applied (pursuant to the principle of equivalence).

5.1.2. Single contact point and publication of opinions and amicus curiae observations

(127) For more effective cooperation and communication with the national courts, the Commission has established a single contact point to which national courts or parties can address their requests:

European Commission
Directorate General for Competition COMP Amicus State Aid
1049 Bruxelles/Brussel BELGIQUE/BELGIË Tel. +32 22976271
Fax +32 22953584
Email: COMP-AMICUS-STATE-AID@ec.europa.eu

(128) The Commission invites national courts to continue using this single contact point to convey to the Commission any information or request in accordance with Section 5.1.1 of this notice. National courts can send their submissions in any of the 24 official languages of the Union.[164]

(129) The Commission will report on its cooperation with national courts in its annual report on competition policy. It will also make its opinions and observations in the context of amicus curiae interventions available on its website.

(130) When submitting opinions or *amicus curiae* observations, the Commission asks national courts to authorise their publication. This allows the Commission to publish on its website the opinions and amicus curiae observations submitted by the Commission and, when available, the judgments rendered by the national court concerned.

5.2. NATIONAL COURTS' ASSISTANCE TO THE COMMISSION

(131) The duty of sincere cooperation enshrined in Article 4(3) TEU also implies that Member States, including their judicial authorities, have to assist the Union institutions in attaining the objectives of the Union.

(132) To ensure the effective enforcement of State aid rules, national courts are invited to forward to the Commission without delay a copy of any written judgment they have issued following the provision by the Commission of information or an opinion, or its submission of *amicus curiae* observations. This enables the Commission to become aware in a timely fashion of cases for which it might be appropriate to submit observations, should one of the parties lodge an appeal against the judgment. When sending a judgment, national courts indicate to the Commission whether they give their authorisation for that judgment to be published on the Commission's website.

(133) For a more effective and consistent application of State aid rules, the Commission encourages the Member States to set up coordination points for national judges dealing with State aid issues. These coordination points should match with the administrative structure of the Member States and respect the independence of the judicial authority. The Commission also takes the view that the creation of formal or informal networks of judges dealing with State aid matters, either at national or European level, may be particularly important for knowledge sharing. Central coordination points and networks of judges may allow national judges to share best practices in the field of State aid and facilitate the conveyance of information by the Commission on any recent developments in State aid policy by way of, for instance, training courses and newsletters.

NOTES

143 Recital 37 of the Procedural Regulation.

144 Order of the Court of Justice of 6 December 1990, *Zwartveld and Others*, C-2/88 Imm., ECLI:EU:C:1990:440, paragraphs 10 and 11; Judgment of the General Court of 18 September 1996, *Postbank v Commission*, T-353/94, ECLI:EU:T:1996:119, paragraph 93.

145 Recital 37 of the Procedural Regulation.

146 See Judgment of the Court of Justice of 6 October 1982, *CILFIT v Ministero della Sanità*, C-283/81, ECLI-:EU:C:1982:335, paragraphs 14 to 20; Judgment of the Court of Justice of 11 September 2008, *Unión General de Trabajadores de la Rioja*, C-428/06 to C-434/06, ECLI:EU:C:2008:488, paragraphs 42 to 43; Judgment of the Court of Justice of 28 July 2016, *Association France Nature Environnement*, C-379/15, ECLI:EU:C:2016:603, paragraphs 47 to 50; Judgment of the Court of Justice of 15 September 2016, *PGE*, C-574/14, ECLI: EU:C:2016:686, paragraph 40; Judgment of the Court of Justice of 4 October 2018, *Commission v France (Advance Payment)*, C-416/17, ECLI:EU:C:2018:811, paragraphs 108 et seq.

147 Requests for information or an opinion have the advantage of being less formalistic, and can always be complemented by a request for a preliminary ruling – see, in that respect, Judgement of the Court of Justice of 28 October 2020, *INAIL*, C-608/19, ECLI:EU: C:2020:865, where both possibilities have been used.

148 Judgment of the Court of Justice of 21 November 2013, *Deutsche Lufthansa*, C-284/12, ECLI:EU:C:2013:755, paragraph 44; Judgment of the Court of Justice of 15 September 2016, *PGE*, C-574/14, ECLI:EU:C:2016:686, paragraph 40.

149 Judgment of the Court of Justice of 9 March 1994, *TWD Textilwerke Deggendorf v Germany*, C-188/92,

ECLI:EU:C:1994:90, paragraphs 17, 25 and 26; see also Judgement of the Court of Justice of 23 February 2006, *Atzeni and Others*, C-346/03 and C-529/03, ECLI:EU: C:2006:130, paragraph 31; and Judgement of the Court of 5 October 2006, *Commission v France, ('Scott')*, C-232/05, ECLI:EU: C:2006:651, paragraph 59; Judgment of the Court of Justice of 25 July 2018, *Georgsmarienhütte and Others*, C-135/16, ECLI:EU: C:2018:582, paragraph 17.

150 Procedural Regulation, Article 29(1), first part.

151 Upon receipt of this information, the requesting national court may ask for regular updates on the state of play.

152 Judgment of the General Court of 18 September 1996, *Postbank v Commission*, T-353/94, ECLI:EU:T:1996:119, paragraph 64; Order of the Court of Justice of 13 July 1990, *Zwartveld and Others*, C-2/88 Imm., ECLI-:EU:C:1990:315, paragraphs 16 to 22.

153 Judgment of the Court of Justice of 28 February 1991, *Delimitis v Henninger Bräu*, C-234/89, ECLI:EU:C:1991:91, paragraph 53; Judgment of the General Court of 18 September 1996, *Postbank v Commission*, T-353/94, ECLI-:EU:T:1996:119, paragraph 90.

154 Judgment of the General Court of 18 September 1996, *Postbank v Commission*, T-353/94, ECLI:EU:T:1996:119, paragraph 93; Order of the Court of Justice of 6 December 1990, *Zwartveld and Others*, C-2/88 Imm., ECLI-:EU:C:1990:440, paragraphs 10 and 11.

155 Order of the Court of Justice of 6 December 1990, *Zwartveld and Others*, C-2/88 Imm., ECLI:EU:C:1990:440, paragraph 11; Judgment of the Court of Justice of 26 November 2002, *First and Franex*, C-275/00, ECLI-:EU:C:2002:711, paragraph 49; Judgment of the General Court of 18 September 1996, *Postbank v Commission*, T-353/94, ECLI:EU:T:1996:119, paragraph 93.

156 This could be the case, for example, for certain types of information submitted by a private person, or where information submitted by one Member State is being requested by a court of a different Member State.

157 Procedural Regulation, Article 29(1), second part.

158 See Section 5.1.2.

159 Judgment of the Court of Justice of 11 July 1996, *SFEI and Others*, C-39/94, ECLI:EU:C:1996:285, paragraph 50.

160 To that effect, see Judgment of the Court of Justice of 11 July 1996, *SFEI and Others*, C-39/94, EU:C:1996:285, paragraphs 68 to 71.

161 Judgment of the Court of Justice of 4 March 2020, *CSTP Azienda della Mobilità v Commission*, C-587/18 P, EU:C:2020:150, paragraph 90; Judgment of the Court of Justice of 19 July 2007, *Lucchini*, C-119/05, EU:C:2007:434, paragraphs 50 to 52.

162 See *supra*, Section 4.2.3.3.

163 Since 2014, the Commission has submitted *amicus curiae* observations about the existence of aid, the definition of service of general economic interest, the execution of the Commission's recovery decisions and guidance on whether to use national or Union law. In that sense, see 'Final Study on the enforcement of State aid rules and decisions by national courts (COMP/2018/001)', Publications Office of the European Union, Luxemburg, 2019, p. 111.

164 A complete list of the Union official languages is provided in Article 55(1) TEU.

6. CONSEQUENCES OF THE FAILURE TO IMPLEMENT STATE AID RULES AND DECISIONS

[5.247]

(134) As indicated in Sections 4.2.1 and 4.2.2 of this notice, national courts may be called upon to apply directly in their national legal systems the provisions of Articles 107(1) and 108(3) TFEU. Where national courts, by their judgments, grant new aid in breach of the standstill obligation, the Commission may initiate an investigation procedure pursuant to Article 12 of the Procedural Regulation to assess the compatibility of the unlawful State aid with the internal market. In addition, where the national courts fail to ensure compliance with the obligations stemming from a Commission recovery decision or the Treaties,[165] the Commission may initiate infringement proceedings against the Member States concerned.

(135) As organs of the Member States, national courts are called upon to take appropriate measures to ensure that recovery decisions are effectively implemented. The consequences of Member States' failure to implement Commission recovery decisions are outlined in the Recovery Notice.[166]

(136) National courts must also safeguard the rights of individuals faced with a possible breach of the standstill obligation.[167] As indicated in Section 6.2 of this Notice, Member States, including their national courts, which fail to safeguard these rights fail to fulfil their obligations under Union law.[168]

6.1. PROCEDURES BEFORE THE COMMISSION REGARDING UNLAWFUL AID

(137) National courts may infringe directly Article 108(3) TFEU by granting new aid in the context of their proceedings. This can occur where a national court issues a judgment affecting the implementation of an act granting State aid. This is the case for instance, where the interpretation of a contract or an aid-granting decision has the effect of prolonging the original duration of an aid measure.[169]

(138) As a result, national courts have to comply with Article 108(3) TFEU and accordingly make sure that any of their decisions that results in amending or prolonging an act granting State aid, for instance by way of interpretation,[170] is notified before its implementation, in accordance with applicable administrative rules in force in the Member State.

(139) If the national court does not ensure compliance with the standstill obligation and the new aid is not notified, subject to the Commission's review, the Commission may initiate an investigation concerning the unlawful State aid on its own initiative or after receipt of a complaint from any interested party pursuant to Article 12 of the Procedural Regulation.

6.2. INFRINGEMENT PROCEEDINGS

(140) Pursuant to Article 258 TFEU, if the Commission considers that a Member State has failed to fulfil an obligation under the Treaties, it may launch an infringement procedure. The purpose of the procedure is to end the infringement. The Commission may refer the matter to the Court of Justice following a pre-litigation phase where it delivers a reasoned opinion after a formal exchange of views with the Member State concerned.[171]

(141) When national courts do not draw the appropriate consequences from the breach of Article 108(3) TFEU, they infringe their obligations under the Treaties. This may be the case where national courts do not prevent an unlawful measure from being implemented or do not order its recovery.[172]

(142) Failure by national courts to safeguard the rights of individuals in violation of their obligations stemming from Article 108(3) TFEU may also give rise to liability on the part of the Member State. The Court of Justice has held that Member States are liable for damage resulting from infringements of Union law, including infringements stemming from a decision of a national court adjudicating at last instance.[173]

NOTES

165 Judgment of the Court of Justice of 11 September 2014, *Commission v Germany*, C-527/12, ECLI:EU:C:2014:2193, paragraph 56.

166 See Recovery Notice (OJ C 247, 23.7.2019, p. 1), Section 6.

167 Judgment of the Court of Justice of 5 October 2006, *Transalpine Ölleitung in Österreich*, C-368/04, ECLI-:EU:C:2006:644, paragraph 38; Judgment of the Court of Justice of 21 November 2013, *Deutsche Lufthansa*, C-284/12, ECLI:EU:C:2013:755, paragraph 28.

168 Judgment of the Court of Justice of 23 January 2019, *Fallimento Traghetti del Mediterraneo*, C-387/17, ECLI-:EU:C:2019:51, paragraph 66; Judgment of the Court of Justice of 5 March 2019, *Eesti Pagar*, C-349/17, ECLI:EU:C:2019:172, paragraph 110.

169 Whether the national court delivers its judgment in the context of interlocutory proceedings or substantive procedures is irrelevant, as in both cases the judgment may be liable to affect the aid measure, even if only temporarily.

170 Judgment of the Court of Justice of 26 October 2016, *DEI and Commission v Alouminion tis Ellados*, C-590/14 P, ECLI:EU:C:2016:797, paragraphs 107 and 108.

171 If the Commission considers that the Member State has failed to fulfil the obligations established in a judgment pursuant to Article 258(2) TFEU, the Commission may bring the matter to the Court of Justice pursuant to Article 260(2) TFEU, after giving the Member State concerned the opportunity to submit its observations.

172 Judgment of the Court of Justice of 21 November 1991, *Fédération nationale du commerce extérieur des produits alimentaires and Others v France*, C-354/90, ECLI:EU:C:1991:440, paragraph 12; Judgment of the Court of Justice of 11 July 1996, *SFEI and Others*, C-39/94, ECLI:EU:C:1996:285, paragraph 70.

173 Judgment of the Court of Justice of 30 September 2003, *Köbler*, C-224/01, ECLI:EU:C:2003:513, paragraph 50.

7. FINAL PROVISIONS

[5.248]

(143) This notice replaces the 2009 Enforcement Notice.

(144) This notice aims to provide guidance to national courts in the application of the State aid rules. It does not bind the national courts or affect their independence.

(145) The Commission may review this Notice, when it considers it appropriate, *inter alia*, on the basis of modifications of the applicable Union rules or future developments in the case-law.

DEPARTMENT FOR BUSINESS, ENERGY & INDUSTRIAL STRATEGY: GUIDANCE ON THE UK'S INTERNATIONAL SUBSIDY CONTROL COMMITMENTS (UPDATED 24 JUNE 2021)

[5.249]

NOTES

This document is available on the BEIS website at: https://www.gov.uk/government/publications/complying-with-the-uks-international-obligations-on-subsidy-control-guidance-for-public-authorities.

See also *Annex 1: Examples of continuity and other Free Trade Agreement commitments* and *Annex 2: Public authorities' assessment of how individual subsidies comply with UK-EU Trade and Cooperation Agreement principles* (both on the same webpage as above).

TABLE OF CONTENTS

SECTION 1: OVERVIEW

[5.250]

This guidance draws together information on the provision of subsidies in the UK from 1 January 2021. The EU State aid rules, which were developed and adopted to support the EU 'Single Market', no longer apply to subsidies granted in the UK. The only exception is aid within scope of the Withdrawal Agreement, specifically Article 10 of the Northern Ireland Protocol, and Article 138 in relation to aid for ongoing EU programmes and activities within the UK's share of the previous Multiannual Financial Framework (2014 – 2020). This guidance is therefore designed to help public authorities understand the UK's international commitments on subsidy control, in advance of the development of the UK's own subsidy control regime, following the Government's consultation which closed on 31 March 2021. All public authorities should read this guidance and assure themselves they understand the UK's commitments and comply with their obligations in relation to the award of subsidies from 1 January 2021.

The overview below summarises the key steps public authorities should take when awarding subsidies after 1 January 2021. However public authorities should also refer to the detail of our commitments as set out in the chapters covering the World Trade Organisation's Agreement on Subsidies and Countervailing Measures (ASCM), the UK-EU Trade and Co-operation Agreement, and the Northern Ireland Protocol. And where the guidance does not address a specific subsidy scenario, public authorities can also request advice from the Department for Business, Energy and Industrial Strategy (BEIS), Department for International Trade (DIT) and Department for Environment, Food and Rural Affairs (DEFRA) if required, and the Subsidy Control teams in the devolved administrations.

Contacts for further advice

UK Subsidy Control team subsidycontrol@beis.gov.uk

Defra Subsidy Control team: nick.howard@environment-agency.gov.uk

State Aid Unit (Northern Ireland): stateaid@economy-ni.gov.uk

DAERA State Aid Unit (Northern Ireland – Agriculture) stateaid@daera-ni.gov.uk

Subsidy Control Division (Scotland): subsidycontrol@gov.scot

Subsidy Control Team (Wales): State.Aid@gov.wales

DIT WTO team: wtocommitteeinbox@trade.gov.uk

Defra WTO team: wto.team@defra.gov.uk

The guidance is addressed to public authorities, but potential subsidy recipients may also wish to read this guidance to understand existing and new obligations placed on public authorities and how it affects them.

KEY STEPS PUBLIC AUTHORITIES SHOULD TAKE WHEN AWARDING SUBSIDIES

Step 1: Are you giving a subsidy and if so, what international obligations apply?

In general terms, and for the purposes of our international commitments, a subsidy is a measure which:

- is given by a public authority. This can be at any level – central, devolved, regional or local government or a public body;
- makes a contribution (this could be a financial or an in kind contribution) to an enterprise, conferring an economic advantage that is not available on market terms. Examples of a contribution are grants, loans at below market rate, or a loan guarantee at below market rate or allowing a company to use publicly owned office space rent free. An enterprise is anyone who puts goods or services on a market. An enterprise could be a government department or a charity if they are acting commercially; and
- affects international trade. This can be trade with any World Trade Organisation member or, more specifically, between the UK and a country with whom it has a Free Trade Agreement. For example, if the subsidy is going towards a good or a service which is traded between the UK and the EU this could affect trade between the EU and the UK. Please note that you are not being asked whether the subsidy could harm trade but merely whether there could be some sort of effect. Subsidies to truly local companies or a small tourist attraction are unlikely to be caught as this is unlikely to affect international trade.

All of these tests must be met for a measure to be a subsidy. If the measure meets the definition of a subsidy, then you should consider which international obligations apply. Not all measures will be subsidies that are in scope of international agreements. Subsidies for services are outside the scope of the World Trade Organisation (WTO) Agreement on Subsidies and Countervailing Measures (ASCM). The WTO ASCM is most likely to be of relevance to subsidies in sensitive sectors such as aerospace, steel or automotive. Attention also needs to be given to the Free Trade Agreements (FTAs) the UK has agreed, notably the UK-EU Trade and Cooperation Agreement (TCA), which has its own exemptions and does not cover some small amounts of financial assistance. These contain important obligations which must be met, where applicable. Note however that neither for the WTO or the TCA is there an approval process by an independent body before a subsidy may be granted. Please consult Section 5 of the technical guidance for more information on the TCA, and Section 6 for details on the WTO ASCM.

Public authorities also need to consider the implications of Article 10 of the Northern Ireland Protocol. The Protocol sets out that the EU State aid rules will apply in certain, limited cases where this is relevant to trade between Northern Ireland and the EU. Please consult Section 6 of the guidance for more information on the Northern Ireland Protocol.

Step 2: Is the proposed measure a prohibited subsidy?

The WTO ASCM contains two categories of prohibited subsidies, which may not be given in any circumstances:

- subsidies dependent on export performance – for example giving a subsidy to a widget manufacturer linked to exporting a certain tonnage of widgets to another country
- subsidies contingent on the use of domestic content – for example stating that the beneficiary must use 50% UK manufactured widgets in their product

These are not new obligations. The UK, as a member of the WTO, has been following the WTO ASCM rules since 1994. Therefore, any existing subsidies for goods should already be designed to be compliant with these obligations.

In addition, several FTAs – including the TCA – expand the above prohibitions to cover services and include additional prohibitions. These include a ban on giving:

— unlimited State guarantees
— restructuring subsidy if the beneficiary does not have a valid plan in place to return the company to viability

The UK-EU TCA includes some additional conditions for subsidies given to air carriers, energy/environment and large cross border or international projects. These are not prohibitions but conditions which must be met.

Step 3: If you are within scope of the TCA, you must ensure that the subsidy meets the terms of the principles

The UK-EU TCA sets out principles which all subsidies of more than 325,000 Special Drawing Rights (SDR) given to a single beneficiary over three years. Special Drawing Rights are an IMF unit and 325,000 SDR is currently approximately £332,000. Any subsidies below this amount are out of scope of the TCA's obligation to apply the principles. Further detail is set out in Section 5.

The only exceptions are subsidies to compensate for natural disasters, subsidies for agriculture and fisheries and subsidies for audio visual goods and services. If in scope, you must consider these principles in the design and granting of subsidies on a case-by-case basis. Failure to do so could leave a public authority open to judicial review in the UK.

The principles in Article 366 are that:

— subsidies should pursue a specific public policy objective to remedy an identified market failure or to address an equity rationale such as social difficulties or distributional concerns ("the objective")
— subsidies should be proportionate and limited to what is necessary to achieve the objective.
— subsidies should be designed to bring about a change of economic behaviour of the beneficiary that is conducive to achieving the objective and that would not be achieved in the absence of subsidies being provided.
— subsidies should not normally compensate for the costs the beneficiary would have funded in the absence of any subsidy.
— subsidies should be an appropriate policy instrument to achieve a public policy objective and that objective cannot be achieved through other less distortive means.
— subsidies' positive contributions to achieving the objective should outweigh any negative effects, in particular the negative effects on trade or investment between the Parties.

It is important to note that all the principles should be met. Public authorities should use the template in the Annex of the guidance to record their consideration of the principles. They may be required to provide this to the UK government if asked as part of the consultation or remedial measures processes in the UK-EU TCA or if they are subject to judicial review in the UK courts.

For the avoidance of doubt, public authorities can still pay out subsidies under previously approved schemes as these will be in line with the principles. This includes subsidies related to COVID-19 that have previously been given under the State aid Temporary Framework. Public authorities should keep these schemes under review and apply the principles to any changes made to these schemes.

Step 4: Assess the likelihood of triggering a dispute or unilateral remedies under WTO ASCM rules and other FTAs

This is where consideration needs to be given as to whether the subsidy could harm international trade or investment rather than merely affect it. The bar for WTO action is high and is only likely to affect large subsidies in sensitive sectors. Subsidies in these sectors may also be relevant under the other FTAs – especially the UK-EU TCA.

When thinking about this, in addition to the sector, public authorities should consider:

— value of the subsidy and the intervention rate: very substantial subsidies (e.g, £hundreds of millions) are more likely to attract attention than small subsidies. The same is true for high intervention rates (e.g, 70% of project costs)
— international competitors: how many competitors are there? How easy is it to enter this market internationally? Are there only one or two competitors in the market who are likely to have concerns about any amount of subsidy?
— impact on trade: does this subsidy make it less likely that competitors can enter the UK market? Does it make it more likely that the beneficiary (or beneficiaries) can undercut in other markets? Does it make it more likely that the beneficiaries can win orders in markets abroad?

Public authorities should take a proportionate view when considering whether a subsidy could trigger action. Small sums to small companies are unlikely to do so. In the event that you think that you may be granting a subsidy that is at high risk, please contact the DIT WTO SCM or BEIS Subsidy Control team as appropriate.

Step 5: Record the award of the subsidy

BEIS maintains a transparency database for public authorities to record information on relevant subsidies. This is beneficial not only for providing transparency in a domestic context but will also help deliver compliance with our international reporting requirements. It is therefore very important that subsidies are recorded in a timely way. View the database (https://searchforuksubsidies.beis.gov.uk/).

SECTION 2: DESCRIPTION OF THE UK'S INTERNATIONAL SUBSIDY COMMITMENTS

[5.251]

The UK has several international obligations in relation to subsidies[1]:

— the UK-EU Trade and Cooperation Agreement (TCA) contains a chapter on subsidies which is aimed at ensuring that the granting of subsidies does not have a detrimental effect on trade between the Parties. The chapter ensures that each Party will have in place its own independent system of subsidy control and that neither Party is bound to follow the rules of the other. This agreement will be of most relevance to public authorities that are granting subsidies. It includes some broad principles against which public authorities should make an assessment when they grant subsidies that are in scope of the TCA. Unlike the EU State aid regime, there is no requirement for approval from an independent body to be secured before a subsidy can be granted. Further information including FAQs is provided in Section 5 for managing subsidies that are in scope of the TCA. Annex 2 contains a short form to help public authorities assess compliance for when subsidies are in scope

— there are also commitments on subsidies arising from the UK's continued membership of the World Trade Organisation (WTO). These are primarily set out in the Agreement on Subsidies and Countervailing Measures (ASCM) as well as the Agreement on Trade-Related Investment Measures (TRIMS)[2], the General Agreement on Trade in Services (GATS)[3] and the Agreement on Agriculture (AoA)[4]. These are not new commitments – the UK was subject to the WTO rules when it was a Member State of the EU

— the UK has also signed Free Trade Agreements (FTAs) with other countries and some of these agreements contain provisions on subsidies[5]. Future FTAs that the UK agrees with trade partners may likewise include obligations relating to subsidies

— the Northern Ireland Protocol states that EU State aid rules will apply in certain, limited circumstances to aid that affects trade in goods and electricity between Northern Ireland and the EU. Subsidies are only within scope of the State aid rules in the Protocol where there is a 'genuine and direct' link to Northern Ireland, and a 'real foreseeable' impact on trade between Northern Ireland and EU[6]. Public authorities should consult Section 6 of this guidance, which is published by the Secretary of State under section 48 of the United Kingdom Internal Market Act 2020.

— there are other limited circumstances in the UK-EU Withdrawal Agreement where State aid rules continue to be relevant.[7]

From 1 January 2021 public authorities will need to determine whether their subsidy carries any appreciable risk of triggering a dispute with a trade partner under the terms of the TCA, the WTO ASCM rules or the UK's other FTAs. This is in addition to assessing whether the proposed subsidy falls within scope of domestic law obligations relevant to subsidy control. There is no change to the WTO ASCM assessment public authorities need to make, which was also necessary when the UK was a Member State of the EU.

Public authorities who are considering giving subsidies in scope of the UK-EU TCA subsidies chapter must comply with these obligations from 1 January 2021. They should also consider whether their subsidy carries any appreciable risk of triggering a dispute with a trade partner under the terms of the WTO ASCM rules or the UK's other FTAs. The subsidy specific elements of the UK-EU Withdrawal Agreement – notably Article 10 of the Northern Ireland Protocol – are incorporated in UK law through the European Union (Withdrawal Agreement) Act 2020. Further information on the Northern Ireland Protocol can be found at Section 6.

The UK Government has consulted on how best to design a bespoke approach to subsidy control that works for the UK economy and will subject to the outcome of the consultation, which closed on 31 March, bring forward primary legislation to establish in domestic law a system of subsidy control which works throughout the UK and ensures effective implementation of our international obligations. The Government will respond to the consultation in due course.

NOTES

1 The material in this guidance sets out subsidy-related provisions in international agreements. The detail outlined is without prejudice to any wider, overarching provisions or 'exemptions' contained in those agreements.

2 For instance, if a public body were to apply a trade-related investment measure (in the form of local content requirement), as a condition for the receipt of a subsidy, that measure would also be a violation of Article 2 the TRIMs Agreement.

3 The UK is also bound by National Treatment obligations in relation to services subsidies under the GATS. GATS Article II (Most Favoured Nation treatment) applies to services subsidies where they are measures by Members that affect trade in services as defined by Article I (Scope and Definition). Moreover, in sectors, sub-sectors, and/or modes of supply in which a Member has scheduled a GATS commitment, Article XVII (National Treatment) disciplines also apply to subsidy practices. Subsidies must be granted on a national treatment basis unless limitations have been specifically inscribed in the UK's schedule of commitments.

4 The AoA sets out obligations and limits on some types of subsidies (domestic support) given to producers of most agricultural (and some horticultural and forestry) products.

5 These can be found at https://www.gov.uk/guidance/uk-trade-agreements-with-non-eu-countries.

6 https://www.gov.uk/government/publications/the-northern-ireland-protocol.

7 See footnote 1

SECTION 3 AWARDING A SUBSIDY

[5.252]

This section of the guidance focuses on helping public authorities to understand how they can award subsidies that are compliant with the WTO ASCM rules and the TCA and other FTAs.

In addition, public authorities must continue to award subsidies in line within any relevant legislation and consult where necessary the relevant guidance on general spending controls, value for money, and appropriate use of public money. For example, 'Green Book'[8] and 'Managing Public Money'[9] documents and supplementary guidance which are mostly relevant for public authorities in England.

With respect to ensuring they are compliant with the UK's international subsidy obligations; public authorities should consult and follow the 'five step' process outlined below. The 'five steps' have been designed to help public authorities award subsidies within the UK's international obligations and relevant domestic law.

(1) Determine whether a measure is a subsidy and what international obligations are relevant.

(2) Evaluate whether the measure is a prohibited subsidy.

(3) If you are in scope of the UK-EU Trade and Cooperation Agreement, assess the subsidy against the principles.

(4) Assess the likelihood of triggering a dispute under WTO ASCM rules and other FTAs.

(5) Record the award of the subsidy.

STEP 1: DETERMINE WHETHER A MEASURE IS A SUBSIDY AND WHAT INTERNATIONAL OBLIGATIONS ARE RELEVANT.

The definition of a subsidy differs subtly between the UK's international agreements. The WTO ASCM sets out a baseline definition, with FTAs (most notably the TCA) building on this definition in different ways. For the limited measures in scope of the Northern Ireland Protocol, the relevant definition is the one utilised by EU State aid rules.

However, in simple terms, there are four key characteristics of a support measure that are likely to indicate that it would be considered a subsidy, which all need to be met:

— a subsidy must constitute a financial (or in kind) contribution such as a grant, loan or guarantee
— in addition, the financial contribution must be provided by a 'public authority', including, but not limited to, central, devolved, regional or local government
— thirdly, the award of the subsidy must also confer a benefit on the recipient in the sense of an economic advantage that is not available on market terms
— finally, the subsidy must cause a distortion in or harm to competition, trade or investment.[10]

Further information on the exact definition of a subsidy within each agreement can be found in the relevant sections in this guidance. Once public authorities have identified what international agreements, they may be in scope of they should consult the relevant section in the guidance to learn more about the specific definitions for each agreement. Public authorities can then make a final assessment on what agreements they are in scope of based on this additional detail. If the proposed measure does not have any of these characteristics, then it is unlikely to be considered a subsidy.

Decision tree: what international agreements could be relevant to your proposed measure?

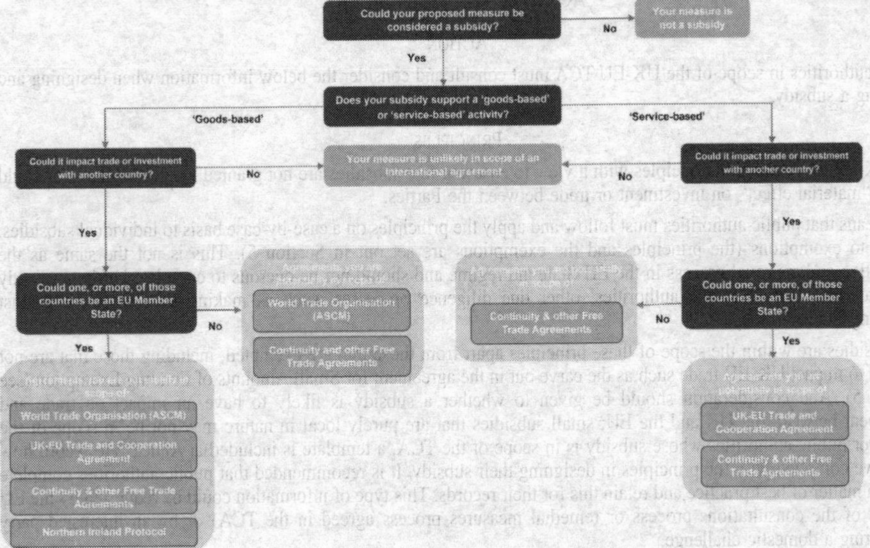

As set out in Section 2, one of the key issues a public authority needs to understand for the purposes of the WTO ASCM is whether the subsidy supports 'goods-based' or 'service-based' activity. The WTO ASCM only applies to trade in 'goods' and as such challenges under the 'actionable subsidy' route cannot be used when the subsidy is given to a 'service'[11]. Where public authorities are subsidising a 'service' they should, however, continue to assess their obligations under the terms of FTAs that extend their provisions to services, in particular the UK-EU TCA.

To determine whether the subsidy is being given to a 'good' or a 'service', public authorities should assess whether the product in question is in scope of the General Agreement on Tariffs and Trade (and therefore a 'good') or the General Agreement on Trade in Services (and is therefore a 'service').

Whilst it is not a definitive rule, and there are grey areas due to issues such as servitisation[12], making such an assessment is likely to provide public authorities with a strong indication on what 'label' is attached to the subsidy. If a public authority is unclear on whether their subsidy is supporting a 'goods-' or a 'service-based' activity, and are otherwise concerned about compliance with international agreements, they should contact subsidycontrol@beis.gov.uk. Please find further information on examples of FTAs that extend their provisions to services at Annex 1.

STEP 2: EVALUATE WHETHER THE MEASURE IS A PROHIBITED SUBSIDY OR SUBJECT TO CONDITIONS

All public authorities have a responsibility to ensure that they are compliant with the relevant domestic provisions implementing the UK's international obligations. As set out in Section 5 and Section 6, the UK has commitments under WTO ASCM rules, the UK-EU TCA, and some FTAs, that it should not award certain types of subsides (referred to as "prohibited subsidies") or award them subject to certain conditions.

Accordingly, public authorities should assess whether their proposed subsidy could be considered prohibited under the WTO ASCM or under relevant FTAs.

Article 3 of the ASCM sets out two categories of subsidies which WTO members are prohibited from awarding, given their impact on trade. Firstly, public authorities should not provide subsidies where the award is dependent upon export performance[13]. This would include subsidies that are linked to exported quantities, assistance to establish or operate a distribution network, and other current expenditure directly linked to exporting. Secondly, the ASCM prohibits subsidies which make the award of the subsidy contingent on the recipient using domestic rather than imported goods[14]. This would include subsidies that are provided to a manufacturer with the condition that domestically produced components are used.

In addition to the ASCM prohibited subsidies, several FTAs (including the UK-EU TCA) prohibit two additional types of subsidies in so far as they materially impact trade (or in the case of UK-EU TCA, trade and investment) between the UK and the other country/Party:

a. Subsidies in the form of unlimited state guarantees

b. Subsidies for restructuring an ailing or insolvent enterprise without a credible plan being in place to return the enterprise to viability (including specific rules for subsidies to restructure banks, credit institutions and insurance companies).

The UK-EU TCA also sets out a small number of subsidies which are subject to conditions. Subsidy givers must follow the conditions when designing and awarding these subsidies. These relate to subsidies granted to air carriers, subsidies to energy and the environment, and subsidies granted in the context of large cross border or international cooperation projects. Public authorities should consult Article 367 [Prohibited subsidies and subsidies subject to conditions] of the UK-EU TCA for further information.

STEP 3: IF YOU ARE IN SCOPE OF THE UK-EU TCA, ASSESS THE SUBSIDY AGAINST THE PRINCIPLES

ACTION

Public authorities in scope of the UK-EU TCA must consult and consider the below information when designing and awarding a subsidy.

PRINCIPLES

The UK-EU TCA contains principles with a view to ensuring that subsidies are not granted where they have or could have a "material effect" on investment or trade between the Parties.

This means that public authorities must follow and apply the principles on a case-by-case basis to individual subsidies, subject to exemptions (the principles and the exemptions are set out in Section 5). This is not the same as the notification and approval process in the EU State aid regime and should not be onerous to complete before a subsidy is awarded as part of public authorities' other due diligence processes, such as making an assessment against Managing Public Money.

All subsidies are within the scope of these principles apart from those that are exempted, including those that are not deemed to impact UK-EU trade such as the carve out in the agreement for Small Amounts of Funding Exemption (see Section 5). And consideration should be given to whether a subsidy is likely to have an impact on trade and investment between the UK and the EU; small subsidies that are purely local in nature may not be in scope of the TCA. For public authorities whose subsidy is in scope of the TCA, a template is included at Annex 2 to record how they have complied with the principles in designing their subsidy. It is recommended that public authorities complete this as a matter of best practice and retain this for their records. This type of information could be requested by the EU (as part of the consultations process or remedial measures process agreed in the TCA) or by an interested party considering a domestic challenge.

ENFORCEMENT AND THE ROLE OF COURTS

The TCA requires both parties to establish or maintain an independent body with an appropriate role in their respective subsidy systems, while retaining full discretion over any functions that body may have. The Government has consulted on the role and functions of an independent body in its consultation which closed on 31 March 2021.

The TCA also includes provisions on the role of domestic courts in reviewing domestic subsidy decisions by way of judicial review. Public authorities should be mindful of the possibility that some complainants will challenge subsidy awards by reference to the principles and their effect in domestic law by virtue of provisions in the European Union (Future Relationship) Act 2020. The UK and EU have also agreed that, in certain circumstances, domestic courts should have the power to order the recovery of subsidies that have been improperly granted under domestic law (e.g, a subsidy that was in scope of, but did not comply with the principles). This may be done through established UK processes for judicial review with recovery of subsidies only being a remedy, provided that the successful judicial review was commenced within the strict time periods specified in the TCA (Please see Section 4 for details).

STEP 4: ASSESS THE LIKELIHOOD OF TRIGGERING A DISPUTE OR UNILATERAL REMEDIES UNDER THE TCA, WTO ASCM RULES AND OTHER FTAS

In this context, public authorities should assess the subsidy against the WTO ASCM rules and other UK FTAs regardless of whether their measure is in scope of, and compliant with, the terms of the UK-EU TCA. However, as previously noted, in practice the risk of disputes under the WTO ASCM and other FTAs is likely to be small apart from subsidies to sensitive sectors operating at scale in international markets. And in relation to the TCA following the principles may mitigate the risk of the TCA dispute procedure being triggered leading to remedial measures being applied to the UK under the mechanism set out below.

Under the TCA, the UK and the EU have agreed a reciprocal mechanism that allows either side to take rapid unilateral action (or "remedial measures") where a subsidy granted by the other Party is causing, or there is a serious risk that it will cause, a significant negative effect on trade or investment between the Parties. The UK will be able to challenge the EU subsidies granted at the supranational level (e.g, funding given by EU institutions), and subsidies granted by EU Member States where these harm the UK. These measures can be challenged using an accelerated arbitration procedure and there is the possibility of compensation if a Party has used these measures in a significantly unnecessary or disproportionate manner.

It should be noted that even where a public authority has assured itself of the compatibility of the subsidy with the terms of the TCA a trade partner can raise concerns about a subsidy the UK has given through the WTO actionable subsidy route or, where available the terms of another FTA.

Where a public authority has deemed itself out of scope of the TCA but is within scope of the WTO ASCM or another FTA, they should also consider the below material. Each subsidy carries its own individual risk, so the possibility of a subsidy triggering WTO action must be assessed on a case-by-case basis and past disputes should not be considered a reliable guide to what subsidies may concern other WTO members.

Under the WTO actionable subsidy provisions, members can dispute the award of a subsidy if they can demonstrate the subsidy causes actual adverse effects on their interests. As set out in Section 6, any subsidy which is not prohibited could potentially be actionable and subject to challenge by another WTO member if the subsidy causes injury to their domestic industry or 'serious prejudice' to their interests. There are specific factors that are likely to increase the risk of a subsidy being challenged through WTO or FTA routes where available.

Public authorities are encouraged to consult the checklist below to help guide their assessment of potential WTO ASCM and FTA risks. The 'checklist' sets out several issues which may make a subsidy more likely to be challenged by another country if they can prove it causes adverse effects (or significant negative effect) on their interests and those of their domestic firms. The more items on the checklist that apply to a public authority's proposed subsidy, the more likely that the measure presents a potential risk.

A) VALUE OF THE SUBSIDY

If the subsidy is of high value, then it is more likely to raise concerns with another WTO member or an FTA trading partner. For example, any subsidies that fall below the value threshold of 325k SDR to be registered on the UK's transparency database are unlikely to carry any appreciable risk of WTO or FTA action. This is not a 'legal exemption' and WTO members are still entitled to challenge these subsidies if they can prove harm, even if the actual risk is considered very low. However, even above this threshold, many subsidies will not carry any considerable WTO risks but of course, the higher the value of the subsidy, the more the risk potentially increases. In addition, as outlined in Section 5, the TCA and other FTAs include value thresholds where subsidies below that amount are exempt from certain obligations and this could be used as a guide on the magnitude of subsidies that may cause concern where there are no value thresholds.

B) HISTORICALLY SENSITIVE SECTORS

There are a small number of 'historically sensitive' sectors which have previously been the focus of WTO action. If a subsidy is targeted at these sectors this is likely to increase the risk of trade partners deciding to start a dispute. Examples of these sectors include steel, automotive and aerospace. Action taken under the terms of an FTA are rare, with countries preferring to use the WTO, but this does not mean the risk of an FTA should be ignored.

C) INTERNATIONAL COMPETITORS

If enterprises within the sector that the subsidy is targeted at usually compete with companies from outside the UK this will increase the risk of WTO or FTA action. This applies to all sectors of the economy and not just 'historically sensitive' sectors. Public authorities should consider both the number of international competitors but also the size of those firms and the importance to their country's economy.

D) IMPACT ON TRADE

Public authorities should consider whether the subsidy they are proposing may impact the sales volume, prices or profits of international producers of similar goods, in the UK or foreign markets. If a subsidy impacts international producers in this way this will raise the risk of WTO or FTA action. In the case of the UK-EU TCA, impact on investment should also be considered.

There are no pre-defined mixtures of these characteristic of a subsidy that would guarantee a trade partner would or would not act under WTO ASCM rules or, where available to them, FTA terms. Each subsidy carries its own risk of potentially triggering WTO or FTA action. The more of these characteristics that apply to a proposed subsidy the greater the likelihood is that a trade partner could decide to take action against the subsidy.

Public authorities should adopt a proportionate approach when it comes to conducting analysis to determine WTO and FTA risk. The level of analysis required to satisfy a public authority that there are no, or minimal, appreciable WTO risks will need to be decided on a case-by-case basis, as will the decision as to whether they should contact BEIS to discuss the matter further. Where available, analytical and legal professionals should be consulted as part of these considerations.

If, after conducting an internal risk assessment, a public authority believes the subsidy they are proposing carries a credible risk of a trade partner invoking action through WTO ASCM rules or under FTA terms they should contact Department for International Trade.

STEP 5: RECORD THE AWARD OF THE SUBSIDY

BEIS maintains a transparency database where public authorities should register information on the subsidies they award. This is beneficial not only for providing transparency in a domestic context but will also help deliver compliance with our international reporting requirements with regards to the UK-EU TCA, WTO ASCM and other FTAs.

For example, the UK-EU TCA states that information on relevant subsidies should be made transparent by being made publicly available, on an official website or a public database, within 6 months[15] of granting a subsidy. The information, which will be collected via the transparency database, covers:

— the legal basis and policy objective or purpose of the subsidy;
— the name of the recipient of the subsidy when available;
— the date of the grant of the subsidy, the duration of the subsidy and any other time limits attached to the subsidy; and
— the amount of the subsidy or the amount budgeted for the subsidy

In addition, under the TCA terms interested parties can request an explanation of how a subsidy respects the principles within 28 days of a request being made in writing. Interested parties include the beneficiary, competitors of the beneficiary and relevant trade associations.

AGRICULTURAL SUBSIDIES

The process set out above is for industrial subsidies. If a proposed measure is within scope of the World Trade Organisation Agreement on Agriculture (Domestic Support) 2020 (AoA), then the WTO Regulations apply (see Section 6). This covers subsidies given to producers of most agricultural, and some forestry and horticulture, products. The Regulations set out the process for deciding the classification of the support, and recording and categorising subsidies, for the purposes of the AoA. For further information, please contact DEFRA at wto.team@defra.gov.uk.

NOTES

8 The Green Book: appraisal and evaluation in central government.

9 Managing Public Money (https://www.gov.uk/government/publications/managing-public-money).

10 Strictly speaking, harm is not an element of the definition of subsidy in the WTO ASCM but subsidies must be harmful before they are actionable by other States.

11 There may be cases where the benefit of the subsidy is "passed through" to an enterprise supplying goods.

12 Servitisation is the term used to describe the trend of an increasing overlap, and link between, the sale of 'goods' and 'services'. For example, a company may sell a physical good as part of a 'bundle' with an ongoing maintenance package (which would be considered a 'service').

13 "subsidies contingent, in law or in fact, whether solely or as one of several other conditions, upon export performance". It is worth noting that the concept of 'contingency' is broader than just 'conditionality'. A subsidy which induces greater exportation than would otherwise be the case may be found to be de facto contingent on export performance, even where the subsidy is not directly conditioned on exports.

14 "subsidies contingent, whether solely or as one of several other conditions, upon the use of domestic over imported goods".

15 For subsidies in the form of tax measures, the information shall be made public within one year from the date the tax declaration is due and the information required on the amount may be provided as a range.

SECTION 4: UK-EU TRADE AND CO-OPERATION AGREEMENT AND OTHER FTAS

[5.253]

Alongside the UK's commitments on subsidies under the WTO, the UK has made agreements with trading partners which contain provisions on subsidies, including as part of the UK's 'trade agreement continuity' programme[16]. Further information on the content of a selection of these agreements can be found at Annex 1. On 24 December 2020, the UK and EU announced an agreement had been reached on the UK-EU Trade and Cooperation Agreement (TCA)[17].

This section focuses on the UK-EU TCA and should be followed once it has been determined that a subsidy may be in scope of this agreement using the guidance and decision tree set out in Section 3 above.

DEFINITION AND SCOPE

The subsidies chapter within the UK-EU TCA provides the definition of a subsidy for the purpose of the chapter that is bespoke to the Agreement. This definition set out in Article 363 builds upon the WTO ASCM and draws in elements that are common to the EU State aid rules. It states there will be a subsidy where:

i. there is financial assistance arising from resources of the Parties (followed by a non-exhaustive list);

ii. which confers an economic advantage on one or more economic actors;

iii. which is specific insofar as it benefits certain economic actors over others in relation to the production of certain goods or services; and iv. has or could have an effect on trade or investment between the UK and the EU.

The phrase "economic actor" relates to an entity or group of entities engaged in an economic activity by offering goods or services on the market; it is similar in meaning to the WTO ASCM term "enterprise" and the EU term "undertaking". There are detailed provisions to assess whether a tax measure (if it comprises financial assistance under the first limb of the definition) is "specific" for the purposes of the UK-EU TCA. The fourth element requires that the subsidy has, or could have, an effect on trade or investment between the UK and EU; this is relevant only to the definition of a subsidy (i.e., whether the subsidy chapter applies), the requirement to be transparent about the subsidy, and relevant thresholds.

In common with other FTAs, the TCA has 'value' thresholds whereby the subsidy chapter does not apply to certain subsidies based on the value of the subsidy or do not apply to subsidies value at below a certain amount. The UK-EU TCA subsidies chapter only applies to subsidies over the value of 325,000 Special Drawing Rights, which is an IMF unit, per beneficiary over a three-year period (TCA Article 364), ("Small Amounts of Funding Exemption"); this threshold is set higher, at 750,000 Special Drawing Rights, for Services of Public Economic interest (Article 365)[18]. The scope and exemptions of the TCA are set out in Article 364.

It is also common for subsidy chapters to have agreed areas that are exempt. Annex 1 sets out where continuity agreements and other FTAs have 'exemptions'. The UK-EU TCA includes the following exceptions:

— certain agricultural subsidies, and subsidies related to trade in fish and fish products which are covered by the WTO Agreement on Agriculture, and subsidies for audio-visual services are excluded from the provisions of the subsidies chapter;

— subsidies for natural disasters or other exceptional non-economic occurrences are subject to the transparency provisions and consultations provisions, but are outside the provisions on prohibited subsidies/subsidies subject to conditions, principles and remedial measures;

— temporary subsidies to address the effects of a national or global economic emergency are allowed as long as they are targeted and proportionate. They must follow the principles and the transparency provisions. However, they are exempt from remedial measures and from the provisions under prohibited subsidies.

These provisions in the UK-EU TCA are relevant for Covid-19 related subsidies. Covid-19 schemes in operation before the 1 January 2021 will already be compliant and will not need to be amended. Going forward, subsidies that provide compensation for actual costs incurred because of Covid-19 are provided for under Article 364(1) (to compensate the damage caused by natural disasters or other exceptional non-economic occurrences). These are subject to the provisions on transparency and consultations but are not subject to the provisions on prohibited subsidies, principles and remedial measures. Subsidies that provide support to industry are provided for under Article 364 (3) temporary subsidies to respond to a national or global economic emergency) if they are targeted, proportionate and effective. They must follow the principles and the transparency provisions. However, they are exempt from remedial measures and from the provisions under Article 367 (prohibited subsidies and subsidies subject to conditions). Covid-19 related subsidies in Northern Ireland will continue to follow the terms of the Temporary Framework to the extent that they are within scope of the Northern Ireland Protocol.

ACTION

Public authorities are encouraged to refer to the text of the TCA and where necessary, contact subsidycontrol@beis.gov.uk if they need further advice on whether their measure is within scope of the relevant subsidy chapter.

AWARDING A SUBSIDY IN SCOPE OF THE TCA - APPLICATION OF THE PRINCIPLES

The TCA contains principles in Article 366 with a view to ensuring that subsidies are not granted where they have or could have a "material effect" on investment or trade between the Parties. This means that public authorities must follow and apply the principles on a case-by-case basis to individual subsidies, subject to exemptions.

The principles to be respected are as follows:

a) subsidies pursue a specific public policy objective to remedy an identified market failure or to address an equity rationale such as social difficulties or distributional concerns ("the objective");

b) subsidies are proportionate and limited to what is necessary to achieve the objective;

c) subsidies are designed to bring about a change of economic behaviour of the beneficiary that is conducive to achieving the objective and that would not be achieved in the absence of subsidies being provided;

d) subsidies should not normally compensate for the costs the beneficiary would have funded in the absence of any subsidy;

e) subsidies are an appropriate policy instrument to achieve a public policy objective and that objective cannot be achieved through other less distortive means;

f) subsidies' positive contributions to achieving the objective outweigh any negative effects, in particular the negative effects on trade or investment between the Parties.

For subsidies that are in scope of the principles, a template is included at Annex 2 for public authorities to record how they have complied with the principles in designing their subsidy. It is highly recommended that public authorities complete this as a matter of best practice and retain this for their records. This type of information could be requested by the EU (as part of the consultations process or remedial measures process agreed in the TCA) or by an interested party considering a domestic challenge.

The UK-EU TCA includes a separate joint declaration that provides non-binding guidance on additional sectors which either side may take into consideration in their respective systems of subsidy control. These relate to: subsidies for the development of disadvantaged areas (regional aid); subsidies for transport (airports, roads and ports); monetary policy, and subsidies for research and development.

Subsidies of Public Economic Interest (SPEIs) – which are subsidies provided to deliver public services such as the Post Office network - must meet the terms of the principles[19] if their value is over 750,000 Special Drawing Rights, and the terms of Article 365 of the TCA covering SPEIs. SPEI are public services whose end user are private citizens, which the market would not normally provide or not to the extent required. Article 365 sets out conditions for such subsidies, including that compensation is limited to what is necessary to cover all or part of the costs incurred in the discharge of the public interest task, taking into account the relevant receipts and a reasonable profit for discharging that task. Public authorities must ensure that any subsidy for SPEI is not used to cross-subsidise the beneficiary's commercial activities. The SPEI task must be assigned in advance in a transparent manner.

PROHIBITED SUBSIDIES

Public authorities should pay particular attention to the set of FTAs which include obligations related to additional categories of prohibited subsidies. In these instances, the UK has agreed with a trade partner to go beyond the two categories of prohibited subsidies contained within the WTO ASCM. Where they exist the categories of additional prohibitions can be broadly defined as:

— 'unlimited guarantees' – these are subsidies where public authorities cover debts or liabilities of enterprise without any limitation (including amount and duration).
— 'rescue without a credible restructuring plan' – these are subsidies to an 'insolvent or ailing enterprise' without establishing a credible restructuring plan to bring the enterprise back to long-term viability within a reasonable time period.

The UK-EU TCA mirrors several the prohibitions above and in the WTO ASCM rules (the latter extended to cover services as well as goods). There are also more detailed provisions on export subsidies and rescue and restructuring (including in the case of banks, credit institutions and insurance companies). The UK-EU TCA also sets out a small number of subsidies which are subject to conditions. These relate to subsidies granted to air carriers, subsidies to energy and the environment and subsidies granted in the context of large cross border or international cooperation projects. Public authorities should consult Article 367 (Prohibited subsidies and subsidies subject to conditions) of the UK-EU TCA for further information and should contact subsidycontrol@beis.gov.uk if they believe their proposed subsidy could fall within scope of these prohibitions.

TRANSPARENCY

A frequent component of FTAs is to include, in addition to the commitments under the WTO ASCM rules, subsidy specific transparency commitments, and public authorities are directed towards Article 369 of the TCA which will be relevant for most subsidy grantors. They commit the parties to report information on subsidies to the other party. The commitments may go further than the ASCM transparency requirements in terms of timing, details or sector. For example, where an FTA has expanded the definition of a subsidy to cover services, then these need to be included as part of the transparency commitments.

These FTA reporting commitments normally need to be fulfilled on a recurring basis (the frequency of reporting varies between agreements but is normally either every 1 or 2 years). These conditions can either be met through directly reporting to the trade partner or, in some instances, the obligation can be met through the publication of the subsidies on a publicly accessible transparency database. The transparency database being developed by BEIS will meet the majority of these requirements. Public authorities should be mindful that there are some international reporting requirements that will not be captured by the transparency database and subsidy information may need to be provided separately in the unlikely event that it is required by an FTA.

Article 369 of the TCA states that information on relevant subsidies should be made transparent by being made publicly available, on an official website or a public database, within 6 months[20] of granting a subsidy. The information, which will be collected via the transparency database, includes:

— the legal basis and policy objective or purpose of the subsidy;
— the name of the recipient of the subsidy when available;
— the date of the grant of the subsidy, the duration of the subsidy and any other time limits attached to the subsidy; and
— the amount of the subsidy or the amount budgeted for the subsidy

In addition, interested parties can request an explanation of how a subsidy respects the principles within 28 days of a request being made in writing. Interested parties include the beneficiary, competitors of the beneficiary and relevant trade associations.

CONSULTATION

Alongside transparency commitments, many FTAs contain obligations that provide for consultation between parties about particular schemes or individual subsidies, and in the case of the TCA this may be requested for subsidies that have not yet been provided. These consultations, where requested, will take place at an international level between the UK Government and the trading partner in question. The results of these consultations are not typically binding although there are obligations to provide information about the subsidy in question if requested and often obligations to make attempts to find mutual resolution.

There is the possibility that a trade partner may wish to discuss with the UK a particular scheme or subsidy that has been awarded by a public authority. In these instances, the UK Government will refer initially to the information provided on the transparency database and then liaise with the relevant public authority to provide the trading partner with the necessary information (e.g, information on how the subsidy complies with UK-EU TCA principles, which public authorities are highly recommended to record on the template at Annex 2 and retain for their records). In the situation where a trade partner contacts the UK Government about a particular subsidy then contact will be made with the relevant public authority.

ENFORCEMENT, DISPUTE SETTLEMENT AND REMEDIAL MEASURES

In addition to potentially actionable subsidies under the WTO, FTAs have mechanisms to ensure compliance with the subsidy provisions in each agreement. In general, these take the form of dispute resolution for specific provisions. This means that the UK, or the relevant trade partner, can use the agreement's dispute resolution process to raise an issue if one partner believes the other is failing to meet their obligations. In the case of the TCA, whether the system of subsidy control ensures the principles, prohibited subsidies and subsidies subject to conditions are applied is subject to the Agreement's dispute settlement mechanism. However, how these elements have been applied by a public authority on an individual award of a subsidy is not subject to the dispute settlement mechanism.

TCA Article 371 requires both parties to establish or maintain an independent body with an appropriate role in their respective subsidy systems, while retaining full discretion over any functions that body may have. Read details of the Government's consultation on the domestic subsidy regime, which concluded on 31 March 2021 (https://www.gov.uk/government/consultations/subsidy-control-designing-a-new-approach-for-the-uk).

The Agreement also includes provisions in Article 372 on the role of domestic courts in reviewing domestic subsidy decisions by way of judicial review which may be bought by interested parties. This means any natural or legal person, economic actor or association of economic actors whose interest might be affected by the granting of a subsidy, in particular the beneficiary, economic actors competing with the beneficiary or relevant trade associations (Article 369). The UK Government will legislate in the Subsidy Control Bill to give clarity on the role of the courts in subsidy cases (including as regards recovery of subsidies) but public authorities should be mindful of the possibility that some complainants will challenge subsidy awards by reference to the principles and their effect in domestic law by virtue of provisions in the European Union (Future Relationship) Act 2020. The UK and EU have also agreed that, in certain circumstances, domestic courts should have the power to order the recovery of subsidies that have been improperly granted under domestic law (e.g, a subsidy that was in scope of, but did not comply with the principles). Recovery could follow from a successful judicial review of the decision to grant the subsidy, provided that the judicial review was commenced within the time period specified in the TCA. This is one month from the date that information in Article 369(1) and (2) is "made available" on the transparency database or other public site. This is extended by a month if the interested party requests the fuller information set out in Article 369(5)(b).

The UK and the EU have agreed a reciprocal mechanism that allows either side to take rapid unilateral action (or "remedial measures") where a subsidy granted by the other Party is causing, or there is a serious risk that it will cause, a significant negative effect on trade or investment between the Parties. These measures can be challenged using an accelerated arbitration procedure and there is the possibility of compensation if a Party has used these measures in a manner that is neither proportionate nor strictly necessary. This is set out in Article 374.

Rebalancing Measures, set out in Article 411 may be applied where significant divergences in the subsidy control regime have had a material impact on trade or investment between the UK and the EU.

UK-EU TRADE AND COOPERATION AGREEMENT FREQUENTLY ASKED QUESTIONS

Article 363 Definitions: How should public authorities determine when a group of companies constitutes a single economic actor?

A company with subsidiaries or branches should be regarded as a single economic actor, and the level of subsidy should be assessed at group level, unless the subsidiaries are effectively autonomous of the group and cannot rely on it for resources/financing.

In relation to what is meant by a 'subsidy', Article 363 (1) (b) suggests that a 'subsidy' means financial assistance which arises from the resources of the Parties that is used to provide goods or services, or to purchase goods or services. However, if the goods or services are provided or purchased at a market rate, is this still a 'subsidy'?

If financial assistance is provided on a commercial basis, or goods or services that are required by the state are purchased at a market rate then there will be no subsidy.

Under Article 363 (2)(c) can a measure be considered non-specific if the exemption is justified by 'objective criteria'?

A measure may be justified as non-specific if it is available to all enterprises who are in the same legal and factual position on the same terms. This provision is designed to provide clarity on how levy schemes can be designed to fall outside the scope of the TCA.

Article 364 Scope and exceptions: Does Article 364 (3) provide cover for Covid measures?

Subsidies granted to respond to Covid can be granted under Article 364(3) where they meet the relevant conditions e.g, that they are temporary. Such subsidies are excluded from the commitments on prohibited subsidies and subsidies subject to conditions. Furthermore, they cannot result in retaliatory measures.

Existing Covid-19 schemes that were approved under the EU State aid rules can continue, though note that public authorities are no longer bound to follow the limits set out in the EU State aid rules. When public authorities implement new schemes and subsidies, or amend an existing scheme, which could not be done under the terms of EU State aid rules, then an assessment will need to be made against the principles set out in Article 366 This is so that the public authority can satisfy itself of TCA compliance.

Note that only measures that compensate for actual damage caused by a natural disaster or other exception non-economic occurrences are exempt from the application of the principles per Article 364(1), as opposed to general business support to deal with the impact of such occurrences.

In relation to the Small Amounts of Funding Exemption below 325,000 Special Drawing Rights (SDR), how do public authorities determine the Sterling equivalent amount?

Public authorities should use the International Monetary Fund SDR convertor (https://www.imf.org/external/np/fin/data/rms_five.aspx).

Support below this level is not subject to compliance with the principles under the TCA agreement.

On what basis is the 3-year limit to be calculated – consecutive fiscal years or rolling 3 x 365 days?

Small Amounts of Funding of less than 325,000 SDR are calculated over a three-year consecutive fiscal period.

How long will public authorities need to keep records on those subsidies under the threshold for De Minimis and Small Amounts of Funding Exemption?

Public authorities must keep records of De Minimis aid granted in the ten years prior to the end of the transition period. The approach for the Small Amounts of Funding Exemption will be determined in the Subsidy Control Bill .

Does any de minimis aid provided to a company in Northern Ireland that has GB 'partners' or 'links' to GB companies count towards the 325,000 Special Drawing Rights (SDR) ceiling of a beneficiary / single economic actor? (and vice versa)

De Minimis aid and support under the Small Amounts of Funding Exemption need to be cumulated and not exceed the applicable thresholds i.e., De Minimis for aid that is in scope of the NI Protocol, and support under the Small Amounts of Funding Exemption under the TCA. Where De Minimis aid is granted, this would count towards the Small Amounts of Funding Exemption threshold where companies in receipt of support are a single economic actor. The question of whether aid is in scope of the NI Protocol, needs to be tested in line with Chapter 7 of this guidance.

It should also be noted that any De Minimis Aid and support under the Small Amounts of Funding Exemption will also count towards the limit of 750,000 SDR that can be granted outside the TCA for Small Amounts of Funding for Services of Public Economic Interest (SPEI).

What is meant by 'supranational' level subsidies?

Supranational subsidies include those provided by EU institutions from centrally-managed EU resources (which are not imputable to Member States and therefore constitute State aid under the EU's State aid regime).

From 1 January 2021, are public authorities allowed to provide subsidies in scope of the TCA to companies that are not located in the UK's Assisted Areas map? (http://www.ukassistedareasmap.com/)

Yes. The Government is consulting on its approach to subsidies for the development of disadvantaged or deprived areas or regions, but under the TCA subsidies may be granted as long as the principles are met. These areas are not defined, there is no equivalent of the assisted areas map as there is for EU Regional aid, and there are no set limits on the amount of subsidy which may be provided, either as an absolute amount or as a percentage of investment costs. Public authorities should also take note of the UK-EU Declarations of 24 December 2020[21] which include a non-binding declaration on subsidy control policies. This provides guidance on subsidies for the development of disadvantaged areas, which states that when determining the amount of subsidy, the following may be considered:

— the socio-economic situation of the disadvantaged area
— the size of the beneficiary
— the size of the investment project

The declaration also provides guidance on the beneficiary's contribution, which must be substantial. Moreover, the subsidy should not have, as its main purpose or effect, to incentivise movement of the beneficiary from one Party to the other.

Article 366 Principles: What are examples of specific public policy objectives to remedy identified market failures?

Examples might include the failure of the market without subsidy to meet climate goals, deliver business finance to SMEs, or to meet the UK's objective to increase broadband coverage.

What is meant by 'equity rationale' such as social difficulties or distributional concerns?

Equity objectives arise where a subsidy granter seeks to reduce inequalities. This provides a basis on which subsidies may be provided to support levelling up and ensure that disadvantaged groups or regions have increased economic opportunity. This could be through support for example for a particular disadvantaged region or for wage subsidies to incentivise companies to hire the long term unemployed. Another example would be where the state steps in to support public services at the level that is required for citizens, such as rural public transport, where the market fails to do so on a commercial basis.

Rescue subsidies to avoid serious local difficulties arising may also serve an equity rationale, though note that such subsidies need to follow an additional set of conditions in the TCA for rescue and restructuring (Article 367).

Is a record of compliance with the principles required for every individual subsidy under a scheme or is it intended to be completed at "scheme" level?

It should be sufficient to do a thorough compliance check with the principles at scheme level. It will, however, be important to ensure that all beneficiaries and subsidy awards are then completely within the terms of the scheme.

Article 367 Prohibited subsidies and subsidies subject to conditions: What constitutes a reasonable time in the context of a restructuring plan for a company to be restored to viability?

This will depend on the size of the company and the sector it is involved in and how extensive any restructuring needs to be. For advice on a particular case, then public authorities should contact BEIS Subsidy Control Team at subsidycontrol@beis.gov.uk.

What is meant by a small and medium-sized enterprise (SME)?

Granting authorities should apply the definition of SME contained in the Companies Act 2006.

Small companies are defined in section 382.

Medium sized companies are defined in section 465.

What is meant by 'significant funds' in the context of companies needing to make a contribution to the cost of restructuring?

Public authorities should assess what constitutes significant funds on a case-by-case basis. For advice on a particular case, then public authorities should contact BEIS Subsidy Control Team subsidycontrol@beis.gov.uk.

What is meant by social hardship and severe market failure?

Public authorities should assess what is classed as social hardship and severe market failure on a case-by-case basis. For advice on a particular case, then public authorities should contact BEIS Subsidy Control Team subsidycontrol@beis.gov.uk.

Article 369 Transparency: Where will the details of TCA subsidies be recorded?

A UK database is available (https://searchforuksubsidies.beis.gov.uk/) and information on subsidy awards must be uploaded onto it within 6 months of the award being made.

Public authorities that require access to the database should contact BEIS Subsidy Control Team subsidycontrol@beis.gov.uk.

Does the requirement to upload subsidy information apply at scheme level or per award?

Details of schemes and awards above the values set out below need to be uploaded.

Currently, each subsidy award of £500,000 or more that is provided under a scheme must be entered onto the database. A subsidy award of less than £500,000 under a scheme must also be entered if it would cumulate with other awards for the same costs to an amount of £500,000 or over for a single recipient.

Ad hoc subsidy awards provided on an individual, one off basis outside schemes must be declared if the award would result in the recipient having received more than 325,000 SDR of non-scheme subsidies or de minimis State aid in the preceding three years.

Compensation above 15 million SDR for services of public economic interest must also be declared on the database.

Will details of all grants awarded after 31 December 2020 but provided under schemes previously set up under the Temporary Framework be required to be published?

Details of schemes that were live as at 01/01/2021 have been extracted from the EU's electronic notification system (SANI) system and uploaded onto the new database by BEIS.

Do subsidies below 325,000 SDR have to be uploaded to the database?

Subsidies below 325,000 SDR over three years are exempt from the transparency obligations under the TCA, they do not need to be uploaded.

Article 371 Independent authority or body and cooperation: When and how will the UK establish or maintain an operationally independent authority or body?

Under the terms of the TCA, an independent authority will have an 'appropriate role' in the UK. Our options on the role of the independent body remain open. The exact role, function and powers of the independent body is being considered as part of the wider consultation on the new domestic subsidy control regime.

Article 372 Courts and tribunals: How is an interested party defined for the purposes of the TCA?

The TCA defines an interested party as any natural or legal person, economic actor, or association of economic actors whose interest might be affected by the granting of a subsidy. This could include the beneficiary, competitors of the beneficiary and relevant trade associations.

Article 373 Recovery: Has the TCA changed the period within which a challenge must be brought against aid awards made in the EU (i.e., by the Commission, Member States, or competitors in the European Union)?

No, the TCA has not changed the substance or procedure of the EU State aid regime. Interested parties will still be able to complain to the European Commission if they believe there has been unlawful aid granted in the EU (or for aid in scope of the NI Protocol).

How can public authorities manage the risk of recovery of subsidies?

As previously noted, recovery is a time limited remedy and only applies where subsidies do not follow the TCA principles. Therefore, public authorities should ensure that the subsidy meets the principles, making an assessment using the form provided in the annex to this guidance, which should evidence how the principles are met, and they should also upload the required subsidy information promptly on the UK subsidy database, to minimise the risk of recovery for any potential beneficiaries.

NOTES

16 Further information about 'continuity' agreements can be found at https://www.gov.uk/guidance/uk-trade-agreements-with-non-eu-countries.

17 https://www.gov.uk/government/publications/agreements-reached-between-the-united-kingdom-of-great-britain-and-northern-ireland-and-the-european-union.

18 Special drawing rights (SDR) are supplementary international reserve assets defined and maintained by the International Monetary Fund (IMF).

19 Insofar as the application of the principles in Article 364 does not obstruct the performance in law or fact of the particular task assigned to the economic actor concerned.

20 For subsidies in the form of tax measures, the information shall be made public within one year from the date the tax

declaration is due, and the information required on the amount may be provided as a range.

21 https://assets.publishing.service.gov.uk/government/uploads/system/uploads/attachment_data/file/948105/EU-UK_Declarations_24.12.2020.pdf.

SECTION 5: WORLD TRADE ORGANISATION AGREEMENTS

[5.254]
This section explains the obligations contained in the WTO agreements. Even if a subsidy is compliant with the UK's commitments with the EU they could still be challenged under the UK's WTO ASCM (and FTA subsidy commitments) and therefore a WTO assessment should still be made.

WTO AGREEMENT ON SUBSIDIES & COUNTERVAILING MEASURES (ASCM)

The WTO ASCM came into force in 1995 and sets a framework for how subsidies given by WTO members interact with international trade and competition[22]. The terms of this agreement only apply in relation to trade in goods.

For the purposes of the WTO ASCM a subsidy is defined as a financial contribution[23] provided by a public authority[24] – which includes, but is not limited to, central, devolved, regional and local government – that provides a benefit to the recipient[25].

Examples of financial contributions include but are not limited to:

a) the direct transfer of funds from a public authority to an organisation through measures such as a grant or loan;

b) the potential direct transfer of funds or liabilities, for example through a loan guarantee, between a public authority and the recipient;

c) a public authority forgoing revenue otherwise due from an enterprise. This could be in the form of financial incentives such as tax credits;

d) where a public authority provides a good or service to an enterprise (apart from those considered general infrastructure), or purchases goods[26];

e) where a public authority uses a funding mechanism or private entity to undertake one or more of the above functions in a way which is no different to the public authority conducting the activity which would normally be vested in the government (or other state entity) and the practice, in no real sense, differs from practices normally followed by governments.

Any support must provide the recipient with a benefit in order to be considered a subsidy, i.e., the recipient becomes 'better off' as a result of the financial contribution. In general, a 'benefit' exists if the recipient is advantaged in what they could have received from the market (in the absence of the subsidy). The existence of a benefit is determined by the situation of the recipient, rather than the cost to the public authority. For example, if the financial contribution is in the form of:

a) a grant – does the award of the grant provide a recipient with funds that it otherwise would not have had access to?

b) a loan or equity investment – are the terms of that loan or investment more favourable than the recipient could have received from a commercial lender or investor?

c) a loan guarantee – are the repayment terms more favourable to the recipient than it otherwise would have been able to receive without a public authority guaranteeing the loan?

d) provision of a goods or services – is the provision of a good or service by a public authority being provided at a cost which is below that the recipient could be expected to pay if they obtained the good or service from another provider?

However, in order for a subsidy to be subject to challenge under the WTO ASCM rules[27] it must be 'specific'[28]. This means that a subsidy has been, in fact or in law, targeted at one of the following by a public authority:

— a particular enterprise or enterprises; or
— a particular sector or industry; or
— a particular region.[29]

Article 2.1(b) of the ASCM states that certain subsidies are not deemed specific if they set out objective criteria or conditions[30] governing the eligibility for, and the amount of, the subsidy. This is subject to providing that eligibility is automatic, the criteria or conditions are strictly adhered to and the criteria or conditions are clearly spelt out in an official document. In addition, the ASCM states that "the setting or change of generally applicable tax rates by all levels of government entitled to do so shall not be deemed to be a specific subsidy".

Public authorities should be aware that a subsidy may be specific 'in fact' even if upon initial analysis it does not seem to meet the criteria. A subsidy that appears open to all enterprises, sectors and regions could still be considered specific if:

a) a subsidy programme is used by a limited number of enterprises,

b) there is predominant use by certain enterprises,

c) disproportionately large amounts of subsidy have been granted to certain enterprises, or

d) the manner in which discretion has been exercised by the granting authority in the decision to grant a subsidy suggests targeting in fact.

Public authorities should note that it is the activity that an organisation is engaged in, not its intentions, that define whether any support provided could be considered a subsidy. For example, non-profit organisations, charities, and public bodies can receive support that is defined as a subsidy if they are engaged in certain activities, such as the competitive provisions of goods and services. Support to these types of organisation when they are not engaged in such activities is not considered a subsidy. As such, support to individuals through the social security system is not a subsidy and neither is support given to publicly funded healthcare or school-age education.

WTO ASCM rules do not explicitly define an enterprise, industry, sector or region but WTO case law does set out more information on these concepts[31]. If public authorities remain unsure if their subsidy is being given to an enterprise, industry sector or region they should contact subsidycontrol@beis.gov.uk.

The diagram below gives a simple view of how a subsidy is defined under WTO ASCM rules and whether it is 'specific'.

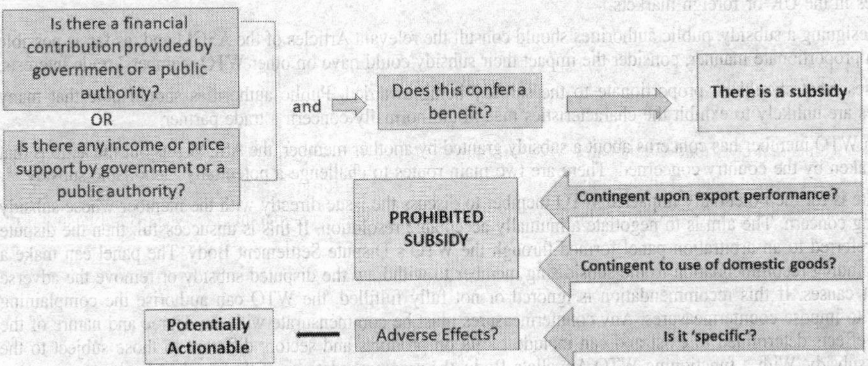

Figure A: definition of a subsidy

WTO AGREEMENT ON AGRICULTURE (AOA)

Subsidies given to producers of most agricultural, and some forestry and horticulture, products fall within the scope of the WTO AoA. Such subsidies, often referred to as 'domestic support' are excluded from the WTO ASCM and often exempted from FTA subsidy chapters.

Whilst the AoA does not provide a specific definition of a subsidy, the definitions in the ASCM should be read across to the AoA where possible. The AoA defines what is in scope of the Agreement by specifying the product coverage. Financial support given to producers of the products listed in Annex 1 of the Agreement is within scope. If producers of any of these products are eligible for the support, then the support is likely to be within scope of the AoA, and related commitments in the agreement, as well as in scope of the UK's relevant secondary legislation[32].

The design and implementation of agricultural support schemes is devolved with DEFRA being the lead Department in England. For further information on the AoA, and reporting and notification requirements under the AoA, please contact DEFRA WTO Policy Team: wto.team@defra.gov.uk. If your organisation is based in Northern Ireland, Scotland, or Wales, please contact the equivalent department in the relevant Devolved Administration.

The ASCM prohibits the granting of two types of subsidies, while most other subsides are, in principle, permitted but potentially "actionable" if another WTO Member State can evidence that they cause harm. The agreement contains processes to deal with the situation where a WTO member grants a prohibited subsidy and where disputes relating to potentially actionable subsidies between trading partners arise. It also has provisions on the use of countervailing measures which are primarily tariffs used to offset the damage subsidies can cause.

Unlike EU State aid rules, there is no obligation to notify subsidies to a body for approval before giving the subsidy[33]. The ASCM used to have categories of "non-actionable" subsidy which would always be safe from challenge, but these no longer exist. Therefore, it is not possible to provide a full guarantee against the risk of potential challenge from another WTO state. This should not, however, necessarily stop public authorities proceeding to award their subsidies.

Instead, the key issues to consider under ASCM are:

a. whether your subsidy falls into the "prohibited" category;

b. accepting that 'specific' subsidies are potentially "actionable", assess (as far as possible) the adverse effects of the subsidy on other WTO members and their potential appetite to bring a challenge against the UK on the basis of the subsidy

PROHIBITED SUBSIDIES UNDER THE ASCM

Article 3 of the ASCM sets out two categories of subsidies which WTO members are prohibited from awarding, given their impact on trade.

Firstly, public authorities should not provide subsidies where the award is dependent upon export performance[34]. An example could be a subsidy that is conditional on a company increasing its exports by 5%. Annex 1 of the ASCM includes a number of illustrative examples of what constitutes an 'export subsidy'. This would include, for example, tax breaks on exported products that are more favourable than those offered to similar domestically consumed products[35]]. Secondly, the ASCM prohibits subsidies which make the award of the subsidy contingent on the recipient using domestic rather than imported goods[36].

There is a dispute resolution process that can be triggered if there are concerns that a particular subsidy given within the territory of a WTO member is prohibited by the ASCM.

SUBSIDIES THAT ARE POTENTIALLY ACTIONABLE UNDER THE ASCM

Other types of subsidies, as long as they are "specific", are potentially "actionable" under the ASCM. Although they are not prohibited, other WTO members can dispute their award if they can demonstrate the subsidy causes adverse effects on another member's interests[37]. In practice, a subsidy is likely to be considered to cause injury or 'serious prejudice' if it leads to market displacement, price undercutting, or significant price suppression, price depression or lost sales in the UK or foreign markets.

When designing a subsidy, public authorities should consult the relevant Articles of the ASCM and, as far as possible and in a proportionate manner, consider the impact their subsidy could have on other WTO members' trade interests.

Any assessment should be proportionate to the subsidy being awarded. Public authorities should note that many subsidies are unlikely to exhibit the characteristics that would normally concern a trade partner.

Where a WTO member has concerns about a subsidy granted by another member, the ASCM sets out the actions that can be taken by the country concerned. There are two main routes to challenge a potentially 'actionable subsidy'[38].

One route is for the potentially impacted WTO member to discuss the issue directly with the member whose subsidy is causing concern. The aim is to negotiate a mutually acceptable resolution. If this is unsuccessful, then the dispute can be referred to an arbitration panel formed through the WTO's Dispute Settlement Body. The panel can make a legally binding recommendation to the subsidising member to withdraw the disputed subsidy or remove the adverse effects it causes. If this recommendation is ignored or not fully fulfilled, the WTO can authorise the complaining member to impose countermeasures. Any countermeasures must be commensurate with the degree and nature of the adverse effects determined to exist and can include tariffs on products and sectors different to those subject to the original subsidy. With a functioning WTO Appellate Body, the recommendations of the panel and subsequent action can be appealed.

The alternative route is for the WTO member to launch its own investigation into the subsidy and produce evidence of the harm caused to their domestic industry. Following this investigation, the member can impose 'countervailing duties' but only on imports of the item whose production has been subsidised and limited to offsetting the harm caused by the offending subsidy. The imposition of countervailing measures can be appealed through the establishment of an arbitration panel and then, if functioning, the WTO Appellate Body.

TRANSPARENCY COMMITMENTS UNDER THE ASCM

Within the ASCM there is an obligation on WTO members to notify subsidies for goods which builds upon a similar obligation contained in the WTO General Agreement on Tariffs and Trade (GATT).

WTO members are required to notify all subsidies that are directed to specific enterprises as well as all actions taken against another member. These can range from the initiation of an anti-subsidy investigation through to the imposition of countervailing measures as well as any relevant domestic legislation. The WTO also requires notification of any subsidy that directly or indirectly causes trade effects. Subsidy notifications are reviewed at regular meetings of the WTO Committee on Subsidies and Countervailing Measures, where members may, among other things, raise another member's failure to submit a notification or ask questions about another member's subsidy programmes.

In 2021 and beyond, the UK Government will need to provide a full subsidy notification to the WTO by 30 June of every odd-numbered year. DIT are responsible for reporting under the ASCM to the WTO, whilst DEFRA is responsible for reporting under the obligations of the AoA.

WTO AGREEMENT ON AGRICULTURE (AOA)

The AoA came into effect in 1995 and details the obligations in relation to agricultural subsidies. As a founding member of the WTO, the UK is a signatory to the AoA. Domestic support given to producers of most agricultural (and some forestry and horticultural) products falls within scope of the AoA.

Classifications of support under the AoA

— Green box support is support which is considered to be non-trade-distorting.
— blue box support is support considered trade-distorting (because it is coupled to levels of production) but with limited impacts because it is coupled to limited levels of production.
— amber box support is support which is considered to be potentially trade distorting.

Domestic support within the scope of the AoA is treated differently depending on whether it is considered trade distorting or not, and the different classifications are set out in the box above. Only support that is classified as trade-distorting ('amber box' support) is subject to limits, but all support given in favour of agricultural producers within the scope of the AoA must be recorded and notified to the WTO. UK regulations[39] made under the powers in the Agriculture Act 2020 set out the processes for classifying and notifying domestic support that falls within scope of the AoA, as well as limits for each part of the UK on amber box support.

Green box and blue box support are exempt from the reduction commitment and is not subject to limits under the AoA. Permitted support that does not meet the green box or blue box requirements is by default amber box and is subject to limits. This limit applies to the UK as a whole. For transparency, all (green, blue, and amber box) domestic support awarded to agricultural producers in the UK must be notified to the WTO on an annual basis. Domestic regulations and non-legislative agreements have been put in place to ensure UK-wide compliance with these obligations.

NOTES

22 Further information on the ASCM can be found in the relevant WTO Analytical Index which includes article-by-article guides on the interpretation and application of WTO agreements: https://www.wto.org/english/res_e/publications_e/ai17_e/subsidies_e.htm.

23 This includes income and/or price support and the contribution can be 'in kind'.

24 An organisation is considered a public authority (or public body under ASCM terminology) if it is controlled by the government (or other public bodies), or where it performs governmental functions, whether or not a statute or a legal instrument confers governmental authority on such a body. For example, this includes an agency or organisation acting on behalf of the government.

25 Footnote 1 of the ASCM gives effect to a particular "carve out" from the definition of a subsidy related to duties or taxes on exported products.

26 This would only be considered a subsidy where the remuneration for the good or service was not in line with prevailing market conditions (e.g. if a public authority purchases a good at a much higher value than other organisations are offering the same or similar good or service for). Note that government purchases of goods and services may also be also within scope of the UK's commitments under the Government Procurement Agreement and domestic procurement rules.

27 Subsidies contingent upon export performance or on the use of domestic over imported goods are deemed specific under WTO ASCM rules and are prohibited (see Section 6 for more information).

28 Public authorities should consult Section 5 to understand how the UK-EU TCA builds upon the concept of 'specificity'.

29 Regional specificity is where a subsidy targets producers in specified parts of a member's territory.

30 Objective criteria or conditions are defined in the ASCM as neutral, which do not favour certain enterprises over others, and which are economic in nature and horizontal in application, such as number of employees or size of enterprise.

31 The WTO analytical index sets out article-by-article guides of each WTO agreement. The entry on subsidies sets out how wider WTO case law on these concepts is applied to the ASCM. https://www.wto.org/english/res_e/publications_e/ai17_e/subsidies_e.htm.

32 World Trade Organisation Agreement on Agriculture (Domestic Support) Regulations 2020.

33 This is without prejudice to the requirement for public authorities to register their subsidies on the UK's transparency database. This does not constitute an 'approval' mechanism and it is not necessary to register the subsidy on the database prior to the award of a subsidy.

34 "subsidies contingent, in law or in fact, whether solely or as one of several other conditions, upon export performance". It is worth noting that the concept of 'contingency' is broader than just 'conditionality'. A subsidy which induces greater exportation than would otherwise be the case may be found to be de facto contingent on export performance, even where the subsidy is not directly conditioned on exports.

35 Annex I also includes certain carve-outs from the prohibition on export subsidies (e.g. footnote 59 and the second paragraph of item (k), Annex I to the ASCM).

36 "subsidies contingent, whether solely or as one of several other conditions, upon the use of domestic over imported goods".

37 The WTO member challenging the subsidy needs to demonstrate actual adverse effects would be caused by the subsidy rather than just the subsidy having potential to have such an impact.

38 At the time of writing, however, the WTO Appellate Body is currently not functional as it does not have the necessary number of judges to be quorate. The Appellate Body is the final destination for all WTO disputes and, as such, its non-functioning limits the extent to which a WTO Member could rely on the WTO's Dispute Settlement Body to resolve a dispute.

39 The World Trade Organisation Agreement on Agriculture (Domestic Support) Regulations 2020.

SECTION 6: NORTHERN IRELAND PROTOCOL

SUMMARY

[5.255]

As set out in previous sections, from 1 January 2021 the Government will follow the World Trade Organisation rules for subsidy control and any related commitments the Government has agreed in Free Trade Agreements. In addition, the arrangements agreed in the Northern Ireland Protocol (NI Protocol) to the Withdrawal Agreement, to avoid a hard border on the island of Ireland, include obligations with respect to State aid at Article 10. The UK has given effect to these commitments in domestic law under section 7A of the European Union (Withdrawal) Act 2018.

Article 10 of the NI Protocol provides that EU State aid rules will continue to apply to the UK in respect of measures which affect trade in goods and electricity between NI and the EU. This means that for the substantial majority of subsidies in Great Britain the Protocol will not be engaged It is important to note that Article 10 does not directly apply to services so NI will enjoy new freedoms to provide subsidies for services, subject to the UK's own independent subsidy control regime.

This section is guidance about the practical application of Article 10 of the NI Protocol and is published by the Secretary of State for the purposes of section 48 of the United Kingdom Internal Market Act 2020. All public authorities in the UK with functions relating to the implementation of Article 10, such as providing financial assistance or other subsidies, must have regard to this guidance when exercising such functions.

The State aid provisions of Article 10 will, in practice, primarily apply to aid for manufacturers and sellers of goods located in NI that trade with the EU. In certain limited circumstances, these provisions may also apply to aid measures granted in the rest of the UK, if these could have an effect on trade between Northern Ireland and the EU. Such aid will need to be granted in compliance with EU State aid rules.

Article 10 of the Protocol has been subject to specific further consideration as part of the work of the UK-EU Joint Committee overseeing the implementation of the Protocol. This was in line with the UK Government's view, expressed in its policy statement of 17 September 2020, that there should be protections to avoid any "insistence that the EU's state aid provisions should apply in GB in circumstances when there is no link or only a trivial one to commercial operations taking place in NI".

This concern has now been addressed through declarations in the Joint Committee, which have legal force in interpreting the Protocol. The EU's declaration states that:

"When applying Art. 107 TFEU to situations referred to in Art. 10(1) of the Protocol, the European Union will have due regard to Northern Ireland's integral place in the United Kingdom internal market. The European Union underlines that, in any event, an effect on trade between Northern Ireland and the Union which is subject to this Protocol cannot merely be hypothetical, presumed or without a genuine, direct link to Northern Ireland. It must be established why the measure is liable to have such an effect on trade between Northern Ireland and the Union, based on the real foreseeable effects of the measure."

In practical terms, this declaration means that subsidies granted in Great Britain are only in scope of Article 10 where there is a clear benefit from and a genuine, direct link between the subsidy and companies in Northern Ireland.

This guidance is intended to help public authorities reach a view on whether the NI Protocol applies to subsidies granted in Northern Ireland and the rest of the UK. However, public authorities will need to decide, before granting any aid either individually or via a scheme, whether the aid is outside the scope of the Protocol. The guidance suggests a number of ways in which this may be done.

However, this guidance cannot provide legal certainty or address every potential circumstance a public authority may encounter. Therefore, if there is any doubt about whether the NI Protocol applies, advice should be sought from the BEIS or DEFRA Subsidy Control teams, for industrial and agricultural measures respectively. The UK will only notify measures to the Commission when public authorities and the relevant Department's Subsidy Control team agree that this is legally required. This approach should be taken both to notifications that need to be approved by the Commission, and those which are made pursuant to Block Exemption Regulations.

This section of the guidance only concerns measures that constitute a State aid. Those measures that do not constitute a State aid do not need to be considered for the purposes of Article 10 of the NI Protocol. Accordingly, the first question that public authorities should consider is whether they are giving a State aid before consideration of whether a particular measure falls within scope of Article 10. Most public spending in the UK falls outside State aid rules entirely, such as social security, support for the NHS and Higher Education, and the building of general infrastructure, such as public roads or flood defences.

The European Commission's interpretation of EU case law on what does and does not constitute State aid is set out in its Notice on the Notion of Aid. It is important to note however that the notion of aid, for the purposes of Article 10, is to be understood differently, taking into account the Joint Committee declaration. Therefore, in relation to subsidy measures outside Northern Ireland, these will only have an effect on trade between Northern Ireland and the EU, and hence constitute State aid within the meaning of Article 10, if there is a genuine, direct link to Northern Ireland (see the 'Application of Article 10 beyond Northern Ireland' heading below).

APPLICATION OF ARTICLE 10 IN NORTHERN IRELAND

Aid for goods and electricity

Article 10 will apply to aid granted to manufacturers of goods located in Northern Ireland, where this could affect trade between Northern Ireland and the EU. In these circumstances, public authorities should take the steps they would have done before 1 January 2021 to comply with State aid rules. This could be either using de minimis rules, or a General Block Exemption, or seeking approval from the Commission before granting the aid (similar rules and exemptions are also available for agriculture and fisheries as expanded under the next heading). Public authorities are also encouraged to consider whether support may be provided on a no-aid basis, such as through the provision of commercial loan guarantees, or making support available on a non-selective basis. Furthermore, subsidies that have a purely local effect do not constitute State aid.

Article 10 will also apply to aid measures in respect of wholesale electricity markets insofar as they apply to the generation, transmission, distribution, and supply of electricity, trading in wholesale electricity or cross-border exchanges in electricity.

Aid for agriculture and fisheries

Once a public authority has determined that it is providing aid relating to agriculture or fisheries, consideration must be given as to whether it is also in scope of Article 10 of the NI Protocol.

This is important as Article 10(2) of the protocol provides for an exemption for aid to agriculture and fisheries – within certain limits – to EU State aid rules which would otherwise be applied. The UK is responsible for monitoring and reporting on compliance with the NI Protocol, including use of the exemption for agriculture and fisheries subsidies. As such, public authorities should contact the Northern Ireland's Department of Agriculture, Environment and Rural Affairs (DAERA) if they believe that spending may relate to agriculture and fisheries, and that spending falls within scope of Article 10 of the NI Protocol.

Article 10(2) sets out that EU State aid rules will not apply in respect to measures taken by the UK to support the production of, and trade in, agricultural and fisheries products in Northern Ireland. The UK-EU Joint Committee has reached a binding Decision as to the limits that apply in this regard[40]. This exemption applies to spend up to a total of £382.2 million per annum for agriculture, and up to a total of £16.93m over five years for fisheries, with a maximum spend of £4.01m annually (provided that the spending does not fall within the prohibited categories set out in the Joint Committee's Decision on the limits that apply). Furthermore, for domestic support relating to agriculture, 83% of this exempted 10(2) limit must comply with the provisions of Annex 2 to the WTO AoA, also known as 'Green Box'. To be Green Box compliant, the support needs to be considered non-trade-distorting.

Beyond the 10(2) limit, EU State aid rules as detailed in Article 10(1) and Annex 5, will apply. This means that public authorities will need to be aware of EU State aid rules and the relevant notification processes. Even under Article 10(1), public authorities spending money on agriculture and fisheries will be able to utilise certain measures to give state aid lawfully such as de minimis limits and general, agricultural, and fisheries block exemptions.

Any public authority seeking to provide aid relating to agriculture or fisheries which is within scope of Article 10 of the NI Protocol should consult DAERA, both to confirm whether a full exemption may apply under Article 10(2) or a limited exemption applies under Article 10(1), and so that reporting can take place in compliance with the NI Protocol.

AID FOR SERVICES

As the Protocol only applies to aid that affects NI-EU trade in goods and electricity, then in principle aid that is granted to service providers, should not be covered. NI will therefore enjoy greater flexibilities for its service industries under domestic subsidy arrangements than is the case under the EU State aid rules. However, subsidies for services will still need to follow the requirements under our other FTAs including the UK-EU TCA, where applicable.

There may, however, be certain extremely limited circumstances in which subsidies to a services provider could still distort competition or affect trade of a particular good between Northern Ireland and the EU[41]. This may arise where a company provides services that are specifically tailored to the needs of a particular company or a sector that manufactures or trades in goods. This is referred to as the 'servitisation' of goods. When designing a subsidy scheme for a service provider, public authorities should examine the form of the service provision in order to establish whether it is likely to be in scope of Article 10 of the Protocol.

Public authorities giving capital investment support to companies that produce both goods and services also need to consider the implications of Article 10. General training aid and support for research and development may, for example, offset costs related to both goods and services. However, public authorities should seek to establish through due diligence whether the costs that are being offset are in respect of goods or services, and where possible to separate these out, as only the aid for goods should be in scope of Article 10.

UNDERTAKINGS IN DIFFICULTY

In applying the 'undertaking in difficulty' test for aid that is within scope of Article 10 to determine whether a recipient is eligible for support, public authorities should note that accounts will need to be examined at the level of the parent company. This includes where aid is granted to a NI company, but the parent company is in Great Britain.

APPLICATION OF ARTICLE 10 BEYOND NORTHERN IRELAND

The NI Protocol will principally be of relevance to aid granted in Northern Ireland. However, UK public authorities that grant subsidies should consider the extent to which these could affect trade between Northern Ireland and the EU, and therefore whether Article 10 could apply to aid.

It will be important for public authorities to carefully consider whether subsidies granted are in scope of Article 10 in light of this guidance. The starting assumption for subsidies granted to recipients outside of Northern Ireland should be that the NI Protocol does not apply. This is bolstered by the EU Unilateral Declaration in the Joint Committee, which has legal force in interpreting the Protocol. This underlines the need for a "genuine and direct" link between the aid and the effect on NI-EU trade; and makes clear that this has to be the "real foreseeable" effect of the measure.

To determine whether Article 10 applies, it will be necessary to assess each case on its individual facts to establish whether the subsidy could affect trade in goods between NI and the EU. For example, to the extent that a UK-wide measure benefits NI companies, or a subsidy is given to a company in GB with a subsidiary or branch in NI (without appropriate separation between those entities), it is likely to fall within the scope of Article 10. Even where these conditions are met, however, it may be possible through scheme design, or separate accounting to ensure that such subsidies do not engage Article 10.

It may also be necessary to assess the factual circumstances where a subsidy is given to a company in GB which produces goods exported to NI. While Article 10 is highly unlikely to apply, subsidies that have the effect of channelling advantages to one or a select group of enterprises in Northern Ireland may need to be considered further. Secondary economic effects, such as a general increase in economic output, do not constitute State aid and are therefore outside of Article 10. Therefore, where a subsidy is provided, and a company then simply places goods on the NI market alongside other markets then this subsidy will not be in scope of Article 10. Please contact subsidycontrol@beis.gov.uk for further advice if necessary.

As noted above, there should be a very strong assumption that aid to services cannot be relevant to Article 10. Servitisation will usually be a secondary effect, and it is only where there is a direct foreseeable link between the subsidy of a service, and the production of goods affecting trade between NI and the EU that consideration needs to be given as to whether the subsidy is aid in scope of Article 10. Making the distinction between subsidies that could be caught and a secondary effect, which will not be caught, can be difficult and will turn on the individual facts of the case, e.g. the amount of aid, its purpose, and the contractual and selling arrangements of the recipient, but public authorities should seek advice from subsidycontrol@beis.gov.uk.

MANAGING THE APPLICATION OF THE NI PROTOCOL

The above provides a general guide as to the potential application of Article 10. It is important to undertake a robust assessment in each case as to whether aid falls within scope of the Protocol or not and consider practical steps to manage how subsidies are granted. The table below suggests how public authorities might manage the application of the Protocol in some areas where it might be engaged.

Measure in potential scope	*Management*
UK-wide measures if NI manufacturing companies benefit	Schemes operating UK wide may be designed in a way that ring-fences aid to GB, without engaging Article 10. Only the NI element of the scheme would then need to be notified
Subsidy to a company in GB with a subsidiary in NI trading in goods/energy	Maintenance of separate accounts for GB and NI would provide confidence that the subsidy provided for investment in GB cannot cross subsidise commercial goods operations in NI that affect trade with the EU. Article 10 might apply if a company in GB is able to directly cross subsidise commercial operations in NI.
Subsidy to a company in GB simply producing goods that are exported to NI	There is a presumption that this is out of scope because there would need to be a genuine and direct link between the aid and the effect on trade between NI and the EU. Where a subsidy is provided, and a company then simply places goods on the NI market alongside other markets then this subsidy will not be in scope of Article 10. goods
Servitisation of goods, where a subsidy for a service contributes to a lower price for a good caught by Article 10, e.g, a subsidy to a GB logistics firm with tailored services to a NI client	If there is no real direct foreseeable link between subsidy for a service and effect on trade in goods, between NI and the EU, i.e., the service is not dedicated to the production or trade of goods, Article 10 should not apply.

In those limited circumstances where aid measures are in scope of Article 10, the following requirements will apply:

— notification and stand-still obligations in respect of relevant new aid;
— any reporting obligations in respect of relevant aid measures; and
— any decision adopted by the Commission addressed to the UK.

SEEKING ADVICE AND MANAGING NOTIFICATIONS

Public authorities should contact subsidycontrol@beis.gov.uk or the DEFRA Subsidy Control team if they are planning a subsidy measure which they consider may fall within scope of Article 10. The teams can provide a view on whether Article 10 applies, and where that is the case advise on what is needed to comply. Any notifications of aid to the Commission must be made via the BEIS or DEFRA Subsidy Control team, which must agree that they are legally required.

NOTES

40 https://assets.publishing.service.gov.uk/government/uploads/system/uploads/attachment_data/file/946277/Decision_of_the_Withdrawal_Agreement_Joint_Committee_on_agricultural_subsidies.pdf.

41 The EU State aid rules apply to subsidies whether directed at recipients trading in goods or services. Therefore, the legislation and case law has not had to set out the circumstances in which the granting of aid to a services provider nevertheless potentially threatens to distort competition or affect trade of particular goods between Member States.

SECTION 7: UPDATES AND FURTHER INFORMATION

[5.256]
The content of this document will be reviewed on a regular basis to ensure it remains up to date. The accuracy of the guidance, however, with respect to its coverage of the UK's international subsidy commitments cannot be guaranteed at all times. For example, Section 5 and Section 6 may not instantly be updated to fully capture all the relevant obligations where agreements are updated or interpreted through WTO case law, or new FTAs are entered into with subsidy provisions.

Please contact subsidycontrol@beis.gov.uk if you have any queries or feedback in relation to this guidance. The Department for Business, Energy and Industrial Strategy, Department for International Trade or Department for Environment, Food and Rural Affairs are not able to provide advice to public authorities on the design of their subsidy outside of reviewing compliance with the UK's international commitments and related domestic law obligations.

B. TEMPORARY RULES ESTABLISHED IN RESPONSE TO THE ECONOMIC AND FINANCIAL CRISIS

COMMUNICATION FROM THE COMMISSION

(2009/C10/03)

The recapitalisation of financial institutions[1] in the current financial crisis: limitation of aid to the minimum necessary and safeguards against undue distortions of competition (Note)

(Text with EEA relevance)

[5.257]

NOTES

This Communication has been omitted from this edition of the Handbook due to constraints on the amount of available space. Customers who wish to refer to this Communication are advised to retain the 26th edition (2020) of this Handbook. This Communication is available on the European Commission's website at https://ec.europa.eu/competition-policy/sectors/financial-services/legislation_en.

Date of publication in OJ: OJ C10, 15.01.2009, p 2.

COMMUNICATION FROM THE COMMISSION

(2009/C72/01)

on the treatment of impaired assets in the Community banking sector (Note)

[5.258]

NOTES

This Communication has been omitted from this edition of the Handbook due to constraints on the amount of available space. Customers who wish to refer to this Communication are advised to retain the 26th edition (2020) of this Handbook. This Communication is available on the European Commission's website at https://ec.europa.eu/competition-policy/sectors/financial-services/legislation_en.

Date of publication in OJ: OJ C72, 26.3.2009, p 1.

COMMUNICATION FROM THE COMMISSION

(2009/C195/04)

on the return to viability and the assessment of restructuring measures in the financial sector in the current crisis under the State aid rules (Note)

(Text with EEA relevance)

[5.259]

NOTES

This Communication has been omitted from this edition of the Handbook due to constraints on the amount of available space. Customers who wish to refer to this Communication are advised to retain the 26th edition (2020) of this Handbook. This Communication is available on the European Commission's website at https://ec.europa.eu/competition-policy/sectors/financial-services/legislation_en.

Date of publication in OJ: OJ C195, 19.8.2009, p 9.

COMMUNICATION FROM THE COMMISSION

(2010/C329/07)

On the application, from 1 January 2011, of State aid rules to support measures in favour of banks in the context of the financial crisis (Note)

(Text with EEA relevance)

[5.260]

NOTES

This Communication has been omitted from this edition of the Handbook due to constraints on the amount of available space. Customers who wish to refer to this Communication are advised to retain the 26th edition (2020) of this Handbook. This Communication is available on the European Commission's website at https://ec.europa.eu/competition-policy/sectors/financial-services/legislation_en.

Date of publication in OJ: OJ C329, 7.12.2010, p 7.

DG COMPETITION STAFF WORKING DOCUMENT THE APPLICATION OF STATE AID RULES TO GOVERNMENT GUARANTEE SCHEMES COVERING BANK DEBT TO BE ISSUED AFTER 30 JUNE 2011 (NOTE)

[5.261]

NOTES

This document has been omitted from this edition of the Handbook due to constraints on the amount of available space. Customers who wish to refer to this document are advised to retain the 26th edition (2020) of this Handbook. This document is available on the European Commission's website at ec.europa.eu/competition-policy/sectors/financial-services/legislation_en.

COMMUNICATION FROM THE COMMISSION

on the application, from 1 January 2012, of State aid rules to support measures in favour of banks in the context of the financial crisis (Note)

Brussels, 1.12.2011 C(2011) 8744 final

(Text with EEA relevance)

[5.262]

NOTES

This Communication has been omitted from this edition of the Handbook due to constraints on the amount of available space. Customers who wish to refer to this Communication are advised to retain the 26th edition (2020) of this Handbook. This Communication is available on the European Commission's website at https://ec.europa.eu/competition-policy/sectors/financial-services/legislation_en.

Date of publication in OJ: OJ C356, 6.12.2011, p 7.

COMMUNICATION FROM THE COMMISSION

(2013/C216/01)

on the application, from 1 August 2013, of State aid rules to support measures in favour of banks in the context of the financial crisis ('Banking Communication') (Note)

(Text with EEA relevance)

[5.263]

NOTES

This Communication has been omitted from this edition of the Handbook due to constraints on the amount of available space. Customers who wish to refer to this Communication are advised to retain the 26th edition (2020) of this Handbook. This Communication is available on the European Commission's website at https://ec.europa.eu/competition-policy/sectors/financial-services/legislation_en.

Date of publication in OJ: OJ C216, 30.7.2013, p 1.

C. HORIZONTAL RULES

1. TRAINING AID

COMMUNICATION FROM THE COMMISSION

(2009/C188/01)

Criteria for the analysis of the compatibility of State aid for training subject to individual notification

[5.264]

NOTES

Date of publication in OJ: OJ C188, 11.8.2009, p 1.

Note: with effect from 1 December 2009, the EC Treaty was replaced by the Treaty on the Functioning of the European Union. References in this document to provisions of the EC Treaty should be construed accordingly.

1. INTRODUCTION

[5.265]

1. The Lisbon European Council in March 2000 set a strategic goal for the European Union to become the most competitive and dynamic knowledge-based economy in the world. The Lisbon conclusions stressed the central role of education and training as the main instruments to increase human capital and its impact on growth, productivity and employment. Training usually has positive external effects for society as a whole since it increases the pool of skilled workers from which undertakings can draw and it improves the competitiveness of the economy and promotes a knowledge society capable of embracing a more innovative development path.

2. Undertakings may, however, provide less than a socially optimal level of training if employees are free to change employers and other undertakings can benefit from recruiting employees trained by them. This is particularly true of training targeted at skills that are transferable between undertakings. State aid may help to create additional incentives for employers to provide training at a level that is socially desirable.

3. This Communication sets out guidance as to the criteria the Commission will apply for the assessment of training aid measures. This guidance is intended to make the Commission's reasoning transparent and to create predictability and legal certainty. Pursuant to Article 6(1)(g) of Commission Regulation (EC) No 800/2008 of 6 August 2008 declaring certain categories of aid compatible with the common market in application of Articles 87 and 88 of the Treaty (General block exemption Regulation)[1] any individual training aid, whether granted ad hoc or on the basis of a scheme, will be subject to this guidance when its grant equivalent exceeds EUR 2 million per training project.

4. The criteria set out in this guidance will not be applied mechanically. The level of the Commission's assessment and the kind of information it may require will be proportional to the risk of distortion of competition. The scope of the analysis will depend on the nature of the case.

NOTES

[1] OJ L214, 9.8.2008, p 3. For ad-hoc training aid to a large undertaking below the threshold of EUR 2 million, the Commission will *mutatis mutandis* apply the principles as outlined in this Communication, though in a less detailed manner.

2. POSITIVE EFFECTS OF THE AID

2.1. EXISTENCE OF MARKET FAILURES

[5.266]

5. Skilled workers contribute to increasing the productivity and competitiveness of undertakings. Nevertheless, employers and employees may under-invest in training for a number of reasons. Employees may limit their investment in training if they are risk averse, suffer from financial constraints or have difficulties signalling the level of their acquired knowledge to future employers.

6. Undertakings may refrain from training their workforce at the level that would be optimal for society as a whole. This is due to the market failure linked with the positive externalities of training and to difficulties in appropriating the rents if employees are free to change employers. Undertakings may invest less into training, if they are concerned that once trained, an employee will leave before the undertaking has recouped its investment. Undertakings may be reluctant to provide sufficient training to their workers unless training pays off quickly or is rather specific to the needs of the undertaking concerned, or unless contractual clauses can prevent the trained employee from leaving the undertaking before the training cost have been amortised or (part of) the training expenses have been reimbursed.

7. Under-investment in training may even occur if the undertaking can fully recoup its investment but its private benefits are smaller than the benefits for society as a whole. Such positive externalities of training may arise in particular if training improves transferable skills; that is to say, skills that can be used in more than one undertaking. In contrast, specific training only yields productivity gains in a specific undertaking and can be easily appropriated by undertakings[1]. Thus the scope for positive externalities of specific training is less pronounced than the scope for such externalities of general training.

8. Where undertakings are faced with higher costs and uncertain benefits for training disadvantaged or disabled workers[2] there may be an incentive to provide less training to those groups. However, training disadvantaged or disabled workers can usually be expected to produce positive externalities for society as a whole[3].

9. Member States should demonstrate that there is a market failure justifying the aid. In its analysis, the Commission will, among other things, consider the following elements:

1. The nature of the training — whether it is specific or general within the meaning of Article 38 of Regulation (EC) No 800/2008; a single training project can comprise both general and specific elements; general training will produce more positive externalities.
2. The transferability of the skills acquired during the training; the more transferable the skills the higher the likelihood of positive externalities training will be considered to provide transferable skills if, for example:
   - (a) training is jointly organised by several independent undertakings, or if employees of different undertakings may benefit from the training;
   - (b) training is certified, leads to a recognised diploma or is validated by public authorities or institutions;
   - (c) training targets the categories of employees that are characterised by a high turnover in the undertaking and in the sector concerned;
   - (d) training could be valuable for the employee beyond his current job (future occupations in another undertaking, social life, well-being etc.).
3. The participants in the training: the inclusion of disabled or disadvantages workers may increase the positive externalities of the training.

NOTES

1 However, externalities of general training can also be appropriated by the undertakings through special clauses in contracts requiring the trained employee to remain in the undertaking for a defined period of time after he had received such training.

2 Disabled and disadvantaged workers are defined in Article 2 of Regulation (EC) No 800/2008.

3 For example, society will attach more value to training received by young and low skilled workers than an undertaking will do due to a perceived or real lower productivity.

2.2. STATE AID AS AN APPROPRIATE POLICY INSTRUMENT

10. State aid is not the only policy instrument available to Member States to encourage training. Most training is provided through education systems (for example, universities, schools, vocational training carried out or sponsored by state authorities). Training can also be undertaken by the individuals themselves, with or without the support of their employers.

11. Where the Member State has considered other policy options, and the advantages of using a selective instrument such as State aid for a specific undertaking are established, the measures concerned are considered to constitute an appropriate instrument. The Commission will in particular take account of any impact assessment of the proposed measure the Member State may have made.

2.3. INCENTIVE EFFECT AND NECESSITY OF THE AID

12. State aid for training must result in the aid beneficiary changing its behaviour so that it provides more and/or better training than would have been the case without the aid. If such an increase in the quantity or quality of planned training activities does not take place, the aid is considered not to have an incentive effect.

13. Incentive effect is identified by counterfactual analysis, comparing the levels of intended training with aid and without aid. Most employers find it necessary to train their workforce in order to ensure the proper functioning of their undertakings. It cannot be presumed that State aid for training, especially for specific training, is always needed.

14. Member States should demonstrate to the Commission the existence of the incentive effect and the necessity of the aid. First, the beneficiary must have submitted an application for the aid to the Member State concerned before it started the training project. Second, the Member State must demonstrate that the State aid leads to an increase, by comparison to the situation without aid, in the size, quality, scope or targeted participants of the training project. The additional amount of training offered with aid can be shown, for example, by higher number of training hours or courses, higher numbers of participants, shifting from undertaking-specific to general training, or increasing the participation of certain categories of disadvantaged or disabled workers.

15. In its analysis, the Commission will consider, among other things, the following elements:

- (a) internal documents of the aid beneficiary on training costs, budgets, participants, content and scheduling for two scenarios: training with aid and training without aid;
- (b) the existence of a legal obligation for employers to provide a certain type of training (for example, safety): if such an obligation exists, the Commission will normally conclude that there is no incentive effect;
- (c) the credibility of the project submitted, for example, by referring to and comparing it with training budgets for previous years;
- (d) the relationship between the training programme and the business activities of the aid beneficiary: the closer the relationship, the less likely the incentive effect. For example, training on the introduction of a new technology in a specific sector is unlikely to have an incentive effect since undertakings have no choice but to train their workforce on the newly introduced technology.

2.4. PROPORTIONALITY OF THE AID

16. The Member State must demonstrate that the aid is necessary and the amount is kept to the minimum in order to achieve the objective of the aid.

Eligible costs must be calculated in accordance with Article 39 of Regulation (EC) No 800/2008 and be limited to the costs arising from training activities which would not be undertaken without aid.

Member States should provide evidence that the aid amount does not exceed the part of the eligible costs that cannot be appropriated by the undertaking[1]. In any case, aid intensities must never exceed those laid down in Article 39 of Regulation (EC) No 800/2008 and will be applied to the eligible costs[2].

NOTES

1 This equals the part of the extra costs of the training that the undertaking cannot recover by benefiting directly from the skills acquired by its employees during the training.

2 See also current case practice, for example, C 35/2007, Training aid to Volvo Cars in Gent, Commission Decision 2008/948/EC of 23 July 2008 on measures by Germany to assist DHL and Leipzig Halle airport (OJ L346, 23.12.2008, p 1) and Commission Decision 2007/612/EC of 4 April 2007 on State aid C 14/06 which Belgium is planning to implement for General Motors Belgium in Antwerp (OJ L243, 18.9.2007, p 71).

3. NEGATIVE EFFECTS OF THE AID

[5.267]

17. If the aid is proportionate to achieve the objective of the aid the negative effects of the aid are likely to be limited and an analysis of the negative effects may not be necessary[1]. However, in some cases, even where aid is necessary and proportionate for a specific undertaking to increase the amount of training provided, the aid may result in a change in the behaviour of the beneficiary which significantly distorts competition. In those cases the Commission will conduct a thorough analysis of the distortion of competition. The extent of the distortion of competition caused by the aid can vary depending on the characteristics of the aid and of the markets affected[2].

18. The aid characteristics that may affect the likelihood and the extent of the distortion are:

(a) selectivity;
(b) the size of the aid;
(c) the repetition and duration of the aid;
(d) the effect of the aid on the undertaking's costs.

19. For example, a training scheme used to encourage undertakings in general in a Member State to undertake more training is likely to have a different effect on the market than a large amount of aid given to a single undertaking to enable it to increase its training. The latter is likely to distort competition more significantly as the aid beneficiary's competitors become less able to compete[3]. The distortion will be even greater if the training costs in the beneficiary's business represent a high share of the total costs.

20. In assessing the market characteristics, which can give a much more accurate picture of the likely impact of an aid, the Commission will among other things consider:

(a) the structure of the market; and
(b) the characteristics of the sector or industry.

21. The structure of the market will be assessed through the concentration of the market, the size of undertakings[4], importance of product differentiation[5] and barriers to entry and exit. Market shares and concentration ratios will be calculated once the relevant market has been defined. In general, the fewer undertakings there are, the larger their share of the market, and the less competition one would expect to observe[6]. If the affected market is concentrated with high barriers to entry[7] and the aid beneficiary is a major player on it then it is more likely that competitors will have to alter their behaviour in response to the aid.

22. While examining the characteristics of the sector the Commission will look among other things at the importance of the trained workforce for the business, the existence of overcapacity, whether the markets in the industry are growing, mature or declining, financing strategies of competitors for training (State aid, employees, employers). For example, training aid in a declining industry may increase the risk of a distortion of competition by keeping an inefficient undertaking afloat.

23. Training aid may, in particular cases, lead to distortions of competition in respect of market entry and exit, effect on trade flows and crowding out of training investment.

MARKET ENTRY AND EXIT

24. In a competitive market undertakings sell products that generate profits. By altering costs, State aid alters profitability, and can therefore affect the undertaking's decision to offer a product or not. For example, State aid that would reduce the ongoing costs of production such as training for staff would make entry more appealing and enable undertakings with otherwise poor commercial prospects to enter a market or introduce new products to the detriment of more efficient competitors.

25. The availability of State aid may also affect an undertaking's decision to leave a market where it is already operating. State aid for training could reduce the size of losses and enable an undertaking to stay in the market for longer — which may mean that other, more efficient undertakings that do not get aid are forced to exit instead.

EFFECT ON TRADE FLOWS

26. State aid for training may result in some territories benefiting from more favourable production conditions than others. This may result in the displacement of trade flows in favour of the regions where such aid is given.

CROWDING OUT OF TRAINING INVESTMENT

27. To survive in the marketplace and maximize profits, undertakings have incentives to invest in training of staff. The amount of investment in training which each undertaking is willing to make also depends on how much its competitors invest. Undertakings which are subsidised by the state may reduce their own investment. Alternatively, if the aid induces the aid beneficiary to invest more, competitors may react by reducing their own expenditure in training. If, to achieve the same objective, aid beneficiaries or their competitors spend less in the presence of the aid than in its absence, their private investment in training of staff is crowded out by the aid.

NOTES

1 In addition, if the labour market functioned perfectly, employees could always extract a larger salary for their better skills due to the training received and internalise positive externalities of the training.

2 A number of markets can be affected by the aid, because the impact of the aid may not be restricted to the markets where the aid beneficiary is active but it can extend to other markets, for example input markets.

3 It should be noted however, that training aid given to a whole sector in one Member State may lead to a distortion on trade between Member States.

4 Size of the undertaking can be expressed in the terms of market shares as well as turnover and/or employment.

5 The lower the degree of product differentiation, the greater the effect of the aid on competitors' profits will be.

6 It is important to note however, that some markets are competitive despite there being few undertakings present.

7 It should be noted however, that sometimes granting of an aid helps to overcome entry barriers and allows new undertakings to enter a market.

4. BALANCING AND DECISION

[5.268]

28. The last step in the analysis is to evaluate the extent to which the positive effects of the aid outweigh its negative effects. This will be done on a case-by-case basis. In order to balance the positive and the negative effects, the Commission will assess them and make an overall assessment of their impact on producers and consumers in each of the markets affected. Unless quantitative information is readily available the Commission will use qualitative information for the purposes of the assessment.

29. The Commission is likely to take a more positive stance and therefore accept a higher degree of distortion of competition, if the aid is necessary, well targeted and proportionate for a specific undertaking to increase its training activities and society benefits from the extra training provided more than the aid beneficiary.

2. EMPLOYMENT AID

COMMUNICATION FROM THE COMMISSION

(2009/C188/02)

Criteria for the analysis of the compatibility of State aid for the employment of disadvantaged and disabled workers subject to individual notification

[5.269]

NOTES

Date of publication in OJ: OJ C188, 11.8.2009, p 6.

Note: with effect from 1 December 2009, the EC Treaty was replaced by the Treaty on the Functioning of the European Union. References in this document to provisions of the EC Treaty should be construed accordingly.

1. INTRODUCTION

[5.270]

1. The promotion of employment and social cohesion is a central aim of the economic and social policies of the Community and of its Member States. Unemployment and, in particular, structural unemployment, remains a significant problem in some parts of the Community, and certain categories of workers still encounter difficulties in entering the labour market. State aid in the form of subsidies to wage costs, where wage cost means the total amount actually payable by the beneficiary of the aid in respect of the employment concerned, comprising: (a) the gross wage, before tax; and (b) the compulsory contributions, such as social security charges; and (c) child care and parent care costs ('wage subsidies') can provide additional incentives to undertakings to increase their levels of employment of disadvantaged and disabled workers. The objective of such aid is thus to encourage the recruitment of the targeted categories of worker.

2. This Communication sets out guidance as to the criteria the Commission will apply for the assessment of State aid in the form of wage subsidies that needs to be notified individually pursuant to Article 6(1)(h) and (i) of the Commission Regulation (EC) No 800/2008 of 6 August 2008 declaring certain categories of aid compatible with the common market in application of Articles 87 and 88 of the Treaty (General block exemption Regulation[1]). This guidance is intended to make the Commission's reasoning transparent and to create predictability and legal certainty.

3. This guidance applies to State aid in the form of wage subsidies for disadvantaged workers, severely disadvantaged workers and disabled workers within the meaning of Article 2(18), (19) and (20) of Regulation (EC) No 800/2008. Any individual measure, whether granted ad hoc or on the basis of a scheme, will be subject to this guidance when its grant equivalent exceeds EUR 5 million per undertaking per year for the employment of disadvantaged workers and severely disadvantaged workers (hereinafter referred to together as 'disadvantaged workers') and EUR 10 million per undertaking per year for the employment of disabled workers[2].

4. The criteria set out in this guidance will not be applied mechanically. The level of the Commission's assessment and the kind of information it may require will be proportional to the risk of distortion of competition. The scope of the analysis will depend on the nature of the case.

NOTES

1 OJ L214, 9.8.2008, p 3.

2 Due to their specific nature, individual measures applying to the compensation for the additional cost of employing disabled workers and additional costs incurred by social enterprises of which the grant equivalent exceeds EUR 10 million per undertaking per year will be assessed on the basis of Article 87(3)(c) of the Treaty establishing the European Community. For ad-hoc aid for the employment of disadvantaged workers below EUR 5 million and ad-hoc aid to large undertakings for the employment of disabled workers below EUR 10 million, the Commission will *mutatis mutandis* apply the principles as outlined in this guidance, though in a less detailed manner.

2. POSITIVE EFFECTS OF THE AID

2.1. EXISTENCE OF AN OBJECTIVE OF COMMON INTEREST

[5.271]

5. Certain categories of worker experience particular difficulty in finding jobs, because employers consider them to be less productive or have prejudices against them. This perceived or real lower productivity may be due either to lack of recent experience in employment (for example, young workers or long-term unemployed) or to a permanent disability. Because of their perceived or real lower productivity the workers are likely to be excluded from the labour market unless employers are offered compensation for their employment.

6. It is socially desirable that all categories of workers are integrated in the labour market. This means that a share of the domestic income may be redistributed to the categories of workers concerned by the measures. State aid may help disadvantaged and disabled workers to enter the labour market or stay in the labour market by covering the extra costs resulting from their perceived or real lower productivity.

7. Member States should demonstrate that the aid will address the objective of common interest. In its analysis, the Commission will, among other things, consider the following elements:

(a) the number and categories of workers concerned by the measure;

(b) employment rates of the categories of workers concerned by the measure on the national and/or regional level and in the undertaking or undertakings concerned;

(c) unemployment rates for the categories of workers concerned by the measure on the national and/or regional level;

(d) particularly marginalised sub-groups within the broader categories of disabled and disadvantaged workers.

2.2. STATE AID AS AN APPROPRIATE POLICY INSTRUMENT

8. State aid in the form of wage subsidies is not the only policy instrument available to Member States to encourage employment of disadvantaged and disabled workers. Member States can also use general measures such as reduction of the taxation of labour and social costs, boosting investment in education and training, measures to provide guidance and counselling, assistance and training for the unemployed and improvements in labour law.

9. Where the Member State has considered other policy options, and the advantages of using a selective instrument such as State aid for a specific undertaking are established, the measures concerned are considered to constitute an appropriate instrument. The Commission will in particular take account of any impact assessment of the proposed measure the Member State may have made.

2.3. INCENTIVE EFFECT AND NECESSITY OF THE AID

10. State aid for the employment of disadvantaged and disabled workers must result in the aid beneficiary changing its behaviour so that the aid results in a net increase in the number of disadvantaged or disabled employees in the undertaking concerned. Newly recruited disadvantaged or disabled employees should only fill newly created posts or posts that have fallen vacant following voluntary departure, disability, retirement on grounds of age, voluntary reduction of working time or lawful dismissal for misconduct. Posts resulting from redundancy are not to be filled with subsidised disadvantaged or disabled workers. Thus State aid cannot be used to replace workers in respect of whom the undertaking no longer receives a subsidy and who have consequently been dismissed.

11. Member States should demonstrate to the Commission the existence of the incentive effect and the necessity of the aid. First, the beneficiary must have submitted an application for the aid to the Member State concerned before the categories of workers concerned by the measures were employed. Second, the Member State must demonstrate that the aid is paid in respect of a disadvantaged or disabled worker in an undertaking, where the recruitment would have not occurred without the aid.

12. In its analysis, the Commission will consider, among other things, the following elements:

(a) internal documents of the aid beneficiary on employment costs in relation to the categories of workers concerned by the measure for two scenarios: with aid and without aid;

(b) existing or past wage subsidies in the undertaking concerned: categories and number of workers subject to subsidies;

(c) annual turnover of the categories of workers concerned by the measure.

2.4. PROPORTIONALITY OF THE AID

13. The Member State must demonstrate that the aid is necessary and the amount is kept to the minimum in order to achieve the objective of the aid.

Member States should provide evidence that the aid amount does not exceed the net additional costs of employing the categories of workers concerned by the measure compared to the costs of employing workers who are not disadvantaged or disabled[1].

In any case, aid intensities must never exceed those laid down in Articles 40[2] and 41[3] of Regulation (EC) No 800/2008. Eligible costs, to which aid intensities are to be applied, must be calculated in accordance with Articles 40[4] and 41[5] of Regulation (EC) No 800/2008.

NOTES

1 Net additional costs take into account the costs corresponding to the employment of the targeted categories of disadvantaged or disabled workers (for example, due to lower productivity) and benefits, which the aid beneficiary extracts from this employment (for example, due to an improvement of the image of the undertaking).

2 The aid intensity for disadvantaged workers must not exceed 50% of the eligible costs.

3 The aid intensity for disabled workers must not exceed 75% of the eligible costs.

4 For the employment of disadvantaged workers eligible costs are the wage costs over a maximum period of 12 months following recruitment. However, where the worker concerned is a severely disadvantaged worker, eligible costs are the wage costs over a maximum period of 24 months following recruitment.

5 For the employment of disabled workers eligible costs are the wage costs over any given duration during which the disabled worker is being employed.

3. NEGATIVE EFFECTS OF THE AID

[5.272]

14. If the aid is proportionate to achieve the objective of the aid, the negative effects of the aid are likely to be limited and an analysis of the negative effects may not be necessary. However, in some cases, even where the aid is necessary and proportionate for a specific undertaking to increase the employment of categories of workers concerned by the measure, the aid may result in a change in the behaviour of the beneficiary which significantly distorts competition. In those cases the Commission will conduct an analysis of the distortion of competition. The extent of the distortion of competition caused by the aid can vary depending on the characteristics of the aid and of the markets affected[1].

15. The aid characteristics that may affect the likelihood and the extent of the distortion are:

(a) selectivity;

(b) the size of the aid;

(c) the repetition and duration of the aid;

(d) the effect of the aid on the undertaking's costs.

16. For example, an aid scheme used to encourage undertakings in general in a Member State to employ more disadvantaged or disabled workers is likely to have a different effect on the market than a large amount of aid given ad hoc to a single undertaking to enable it to increase its employment of a certain category of workers. The latter is likely to distort competition more significantly as the aid beneficiary's competitors become less able to compete. The distortion will be even greater if the labour costs in the beneficiary's business represent a high share of the total costs.

17. In assessing the market characteristics, which can give a much more accurate picture of the likely impact of an aid, the Commission will among other things consider:

(a) the structure of the market;
(b) the characteristics of the sector or industry;
(c) the situation on the national/regional labour market.

18. The structure of the market will be assessed through the concentration of the market, the size of undertakings[2], importance of product differentiation[3], and barriers to entry and exit. Market shares and concentration ratios will be calculated once the relevant market has been defined. In general, the fewer undertakings there are, the larger their share of the market, and the less competition one would expect to observe[4]. If the affected market is concentrated with high barriers to entry[5] and the aid beneficiary is a major player on it then it is more likely that competitors will have to alter their behaviour in response to the aid, for example postpone or abandon the introduction of a new product or technology or exit the market all together.

19. The Commission will also look at the characteristics of the sector, such as the existence of overcapacity and whether the markets in the industry are growing[6], mature or declining. For example, the presence of overcapacity or of mature markets in an industry may increase the risk of aid leading to inefficiency and displacement of output among undertakings which do not have subsidised workers.

20. Finally, the measure will be placed in the context of the situation on the labour market, that is to say, unemployment and employment rates, wage levels, and labour law.

21. Wage subsidies may in particular cases lead to the distortions of competition discussed in paragraphs 22 to 27.

SUBSTITUTION AND DISPLACEMENT EFFECT

22. The substitution effect relates to the situation where jobs given to a certain category of workers simply replace jobs for other categories. A wage subsidy which targets a specific subgroup of workers splits the labour force into subsidised workers and unsubsidised workers, and may induce undertakings to replace unsubsidised workers with subsidised workers. This occurs because relative wage costs for subsidised and unsubsidised workers are changed[7].

23. Since undertakings which employ subsidised workers, compete in the same markets for goods or services as those which do not employ subsidised workers, wage subsidies can contribute to the reduction of jobs elsewhere in the economy. Such a situation occurs when an undertaking employing subsidised workers increases output, but displaces output among undertakings who do not employ subsidised workers and, as a result, the aid crowds-out unsubsidised employment.

MARKET ENTRY AND EXIT

24. Employment costs form part of the normal operating costs of any undertaking. It is therefore particularly important that aid should have a positive effect on employment and should not merely enable undertakings to reduce costs which they would otherwise bear. For example, wage subsidies reduce the ongoing costs of production and thus would make entry more appealing and enable undertakings with otherwise poor commercial prospects to enter a market or introduce new products to the detriment of more efficient competitors.

25. The availability of State aid may also affect an undertaking's decision to leave a market where it is already operating. Wage subsidies could reduce the size of losses and enable an undertaking to stay in the market for longer — which may mean that other, more efficient undertakings that do not receive aid are forced to exit instead.

INVESTMENT INCENTIVES

26. In the markets where wage subsidies are granted undertakings are discouraged from competing and may reduce their investments and attempts to increase efficiency and innovation. There may be a delay in the introduction of new less labour intensive technologies by the aid beneficiary due to the change in relative costs for labour intensive and technology intensive production methods. Manufacturers of competing or complementary products may also decrease or delay their investment. As a consequence, the overall investment level in the industry concerned will decline.

EFFECT ON TRADE FLOWS

27. Wage subsidies within a particular region may result in some territories benefiting from more favourable production conditions than others. This may result in the displacement of trade flows in favour of the regions where such aid is given.

NOTES

1 A number of markets can be affected by the aid, because the impact of the aid may not be restricted to the markets where the aid beneficiary is active but can extend to other markets, for example input markets.

2 Size of the undertaking can be expressed in the terms of market shares as well as turnover and/or employment.

3 The lower the degree of product differentiation, the greater the effect of the aid on competitors' profits will be.

4 However, some markets are competitive despite there being few undertakings present.

5 However, granting aid sometimes helps to overcome entry barriers and allows new undertakings to enter a market.

6 The existence of growing markets will usually lead to a less pronounced effect of the aid on competitors.

7 Such substitution effect depends on the elasticity of demand for labour, both for subsidised and unsubsidised workers.

4. BALANCING AND DECISION

[5.273]

28. The last step in the analysis is to evaluate the extent to which the positive effects of the aid outweigh its negative effects. This will be done on a case-by-case basis for all individual measures. In order to balance the positive and the negative effects, the Commission will assess them and make an overall assessment of their impact on producers and consumers in each of the markets affected. Unless quantitative information is readily available the Commission will use qualitative information for the purposes of the assessment.

29. The Commission is likely to take a more positive stance and therefore accept a higher degree of distortion of competition if the aid is necessary and well targeted to achieve the objective of the aid and is limited to the net extra costs of compensating for the lower productivity of the categories of workers concerned by the measure.

3. REGIONAL AID

GUIDELINES ON REGIONAL STATE AID FOR 2014–2020 (NOTE)

(2013/C209/01)

(Text with EEA relevance)

[5.274]

NOTES

Date of publication in OJ: OJ C209, 23.7.2013, p 1.

Editorial note: these Guidelines were due to expire on 31 December 2020, but were extended to 31 December 2021 by Communication from the Commission concerning the prolongation and the amendments of the Guidelines on Regional State Aid for 2014-2020, Guidelines on State Aid to Promote Risk Finance Investments, Guidelines on State Aid for Environmental Protection and Energy 2014-2020, Guidelines on State aid for rescuing and restructuring non-financial undertakings in difficulty, Communication on the Criteria for the Analysis of the Compatibility with the Internal Market of State Aid to Promote the Execution of Important Projects of Common European Interest, Communication from the Commission – Framework for State aid for research and development and innovation and Communication from the Commission to the Member States on the application of Articles 107 and 108 of the Treaty on the Functioning of the European Union to short-term export-credit insurance (2020/C224/02).

These Guidelines are applicable until the end of 2021, but have been omitted from this edition of the Handbook due to constraints on the amount of available space. Customers who wish to refer to the Guidelines are advised to retain the 26th edition (2020) of this Handbook.

Note also that new Guidelines have been published covering the period 2022–2027. See **[5.276]** *post*.

GUIDELINES ON REGIONAL STATE AID FOR 2014–2020: ACCEPTANCE OF THE PROPOSED APPROPRIATE MEASURES PURSUANT TO ARTICLE 108(1) OF THE TREATY ON THE FUNCTIONING OF THE EUROPEAN UNION BY ALL MEMBER STATES

(2014/C101/03)

[5.275]

NOTES

Date of publication in OJ: OJ C101, 5.4.2014, p 3.

In paragraph 191 of the Guidelines on regional State aid for 2014-2020,[1] the Commission proposed to Member States to accept as appropriate measures the limitation of the application of all existing regional aid schemes which are not covered under a block exemption regulation and of all regional aid maps to aid intended to be awarded on or before 30 June 2014, as well as the amendment of other existing horizontal aid schemes providing specific treatment for aid to projects in assisted areas in order to ensure that aid to be awarded after 30 June 2014 complies with the regional aid map applicable on the date the aid is awarded. Member States were requested to confirm their acceptance of the proposed appropriate measures by 31 December 2013.

Pursuant to Article 19(1) of Council Regulation (EC) No 659/1999 of 22 March 1999 laying down detailed rules for the application of Article 93 EC,[2] the Commission recorded the unconditional and explicit agreement to the appropriate measures by all Member States.

NOTES

[1] OJ C209, 23.7.2013, p 1.

[2] OJ L83, 27.3.1999, p 1.

GUIDELINES ON REGIONAL STATE AID

(2021/C153/01))

[5.276]

NOTES

Date of publication in OJ: OJ C209, 23.7.2013, p 1.

TABLE OF CONTENTS

1. INTRODUCTION

[5.277]

1. The Commission may consider the following types of State aid compatible with the internal market, on the basis of Article 107(3)(a) and (c) of the Treaty on the Functioning of the European Union:

(a) State aid to promote the economic development of areas where the standard of living is abnormally low or where there is serious underemployment, and to promote the development of the regions referred to in Article 349 of the Treaty; and

(b) State aid to facilitate the development of certain economic areas in the European Union.[1]

These types of State aid are known as regional aid.

2. These Guidelines set out the conditions under which regional aid may be considered to be compatible with the internal market. They also set out the criteria for identifying the areas that fulfil the conditions of compatibility under Article 107(3)(a) and (c) of the Treaty.

3. The primary objective of State aid control in the field of regional aid is to ensure that aid for regional development and territorial cohesion[2] does not to an undue extent adversely affect trading conditions between Member States.[3] In particular, it aims at preventing subsidy races that may occur when Member States seek to attract or retain businesses in assisted areas of the EU, and to limit the effects of regional aid on trade and competition to the minimum necessary.

4. The objective of regional development and territorial cohesion distinguishes regional aid from other forms of aid, such as aid for research, development and innovation, employment, training, energy or for environmental protection, which pursue other objectives of economic development under Article 107(3) of the Treaty. In some circumstances, higher aid intensities may be allowed for those other types of aid when granted to undertakings established in assisted areas, in recognition of the specific difficulties they face in these areas.[4]

5. Regional aid can only play an effective role if it is used sparingly and proportionately and is focused on assisted areas in the EU.[5] In particular, the permissible aid ceilings should reflect the extent of the problems affecting the development of the areas concerned. The advantages of the aid in terms of the development of an assisted area must outweigh the distortion of competition and trade that it may result in.[6] The weight given to the positive effects of the aid is likely to vary according to the derogation under Article 107(3) of the Treaty, which means that a greater distortion of competition can be accepted in the most disadvantaged areas covered by Article 107(3)(a) than in areas covered by Article 107(3)(c).[7]

6. Furthermore, regional aid can only be effective in promoting or facilitating the economic development of assisted areas, provided that it is awarded to stimulate additional investment or economic activity in those areas. In certain very limited, well-identified cases, the obstacles faced by these areas in attracting or maintaining economic activity may be so severe or permanent that investment aid may not be sufficient to enable the area to develop. In this situation may regional investment aid be supplemented by regional operating aid.

7. In 2019, the Commission launched an evaluation of the regional aid framework to assess whether the regional aid guidelines were still fit for purpose. The results[8] showed that, in principle, the rules work well, but they require some improvements to reflect economic developments. In addition, the 'European Green Deal',[9] the 'A new industrial strategy for Europe'[10] and 'Shaping Europe's digital future',[11] may be taken into account by the Commission when assessing the impact of regional aid, which require making some amendments to the rules. In this context, also other State aid rules are undergoing a revision process and the Commission is paying particular attention to the scope of each of the thematic guidelines and also to the possibilities to potentially combine different kinds of aid for the same investment. As such, support for initial investments for new environmentally friendly technologies that contribute to the decarbonisation of production processes in industry, including energy-intensive industries such as steel, can be assessed, depending on their exact features, in particular under the State aid rules for research, development and innovation or for environmental protection and energy. Regional aid can also be combined with other types of aid. It is possible, for example, for the same investment project, to combine regional aid with support under the State aid rules for environmental protection and energy if that investment project facilitates the development

of an assisted area and at the same time increases the level of environmental protection to an extent that the investment or part of it qualifies for support under both thematic rules and the provisions of both sets of rules are complied with. In this way, Member States can incentivise reaching both objectives in an optimal way, while avoiding overcompensation. The Commission also included in these guidelines specific provisions to facilitate support in the context of the Just Transition Fund (JTF) in line with cohesion principles. The JTF is one of the pillars of the Just Transition Mechanism to be implemented under cohesion policy[12] to contribute to addressing the social, economic and environmental consequences that may accompany the ambitious objective of the transition towards a climate neutral Union by 2050. The aims of the JTF are to mitigate the adverse effects of the climate transition by supporting the most affected territories and workers concerned and to promote a balanced socio-economic transition.

8. In response to the economic disturbance created by the COVID-19 pandemic, the Commission has put in place targeted instruments, such as the Temporary Framework for State aid measures.[13] The pandemic may have more long-lasting effects in certain areas than in others. At this point in time, it is too early to predict the impact of the pandemic over the mid-to long-term and to identify which areas will be particularly affected. The Commission therefore plans a mid-term review of the regional aid maps in 2023, which will take into account the latest available statistics.

NOTES

1 Areas eligible for regional aid under Article 107(3)(a) of the Treaty, commonly referred to as 'a' areas, tend to be the most disadvantaged in the EU in terms of economic development. Areas eligible under Article 107(3)(c) of the Treaty, referred to as 'c' areas, also tend to be disadvantaged, but to a lesser extent.

2 Under Article 174(1) and (2) of the Treaty '*In order to promote its overall harmonious development, the Union shall develop and pursue its actions leading to the strengthening of its economic, social and territorial cohesion. In particular, the Union shall aim at reducing disparities between the levels of development of the various regions and the backwardness of the least favoured regions.*'

3 For the purpose of these Guidelines, when mentioning 'Member States' the Commission includes the territory of Northern Ireland as agreed within the 'Protocol on Ireland/Northern Ireland' annexed to the Agreement on the withdrawal of the United Kingdom of Great Britain and Northern Ireland from the European Union and the European Atomic Energy Community.

4 Regional top-ups for aid granted for such purposes are therefore not considered as regional aid.

5 Member States can identify these areas in a regional aid map, following the conditions laid down in Section 7.

6 See judgment of 17 September 1980, *Philip Morris Holland BV v Commission of the European Communities*, Case 730/79, ECLI:EU: C:1980:209, paragraph 17, and judgment of 14 January 1997, Spain v Commission, C-169/95, ECLI:EU:C:1997:10, paragraph 20.

7 See judgment of 12 December 1996, *AIUFFASS and AKT v Commission*, T-380/94, ECLI:EU:T:1996:195, paragraph 54.

8 See the Commission staff working document on the results of the Fitness Check of 30 October 2020 – SWD(2020) 257 final.

9 Communication from the Commission to the European Parliament, the European Council, the Council, the European Economic and Social Committee and the Committee of the Regions of 11 December 2019 – COM (2019) 640 final.

10 Communication from the Commission to the European Parliament, the European Council, the Council, the European Economic and Social Committee and the Committee of the Regions of 10 March 2020 – COM (2020) 102 final.

11 Communication from the Commission to the European Parliament, the Council, the European Economic and Social Committee and the Committee of the Regions of 19 February 2020 – COM (2020) 67 final.

12 Proposal for a Regulation of the European Parliament and of the Council establishing the Just Transition Fund – COM (2020) 22 final.

13 OJ C91 I, 20.3.2020, p 1.

2. SCOPE AND DEFINITIONS

2.1. SCOPE OF REGIONAL AID

[5.278]

9. The compatibility conditions set out in these Guidelines are applicable both to notifiable regional aid schemes and notifiable individual aid.

10. These Guidelines do not cover State aid granted to the steel,[14] lignite[15] and coal[16] sectors.

11. The Commission will apply the principles set out in these Guidelines to regional aid in all other sectors of economic activity, apart from sectors that are subject to specific State aid rules, in particular, in fisheries and aquaculture,[17] agriculture,[18] transport,[19] broadband,[20] and energy,[21] save where State aid is granted in those sectors as part of a horizontal regional operating aid scheme.

12. The Commission will apply the principles set out in these Guidelines in respect of processing and marketing of agricultural products into non-agricultural products and in respect of aid measures that support activities outside the scope of Article 42 of the Treaty but are either co-financed by the European Agriculture Fund for Rural Development (EAFRD)[22] or are granted as additional national financing to such co-financed measures, unless the sectoral rules state otherwise.

13. Large enterprises tend to be less affected than small and medium sized enterprises (SMEs) by regional constraints to investing or maintaining economic activity in an assisted area. Firstly, large enterprises can more easily obtain capital and credit on global markets and are less constrained by the more limited offer of financial services in assisted areas. Secondly, investments by large enterprises can produce economies of scale that reduce location-specific initial costs and, in many respects, are not tied to the area in which the investment takes place. Thirdly, large enterprises that plan investments usually have considerable bargaining power vis-à-vis the authorities, which may lead to aid being awarded without need or due justification. Lastly, large enterprises are more likely to be significant players on the market concerned and, as a result, the investment for which the aid is awarded may distort competition and trade on the internal market.

14. Since regional aid to large enterprises for their investments is unlikely to have an incentive effect, as a rule it cannot be considered as compatible with the internal market under Article 107(3)(c) of the Treaty, unless it is granted for initial investments that create new economic activities in these 'c' areas in line with the criteria laid down in these guidelines. However, in the territories most affected by the climate transition, the structural advantages available to large enterprises might not be sufficient to reach the level of investment vital to ensure a balanced socio-economic transition and offer sufficient employment opportunities to offset job losses stemming from the closure of economic activities triggered by the transition. Therefore, by way of derogation[23] to the first sentence of this paragraph, regional aid to large enterprises can also be considered as compatible with the internal market in line with the criteria of these guidelines, if it is granted for the diversification of the output of an establishment into products not previously produced in the establishment or for a fundamental change in the overall production process of the product(s) concerned by the investment in the establishment, provided (1) that it concerns an initial investment in a territory identified for co-financed support from the JTF in a 'c' area that has a GDP per capita below 100% of the EU-27 average; (2) that the investment and the beneficiary are identified in the territorial just transition plan[24] of a Member State approved by the Commission; and (3) that the State aid for the investment is covered by the JTF to the maximum allowed.

15. Regional aid aimed at reducing the current expenses of an undertaking constitutes operating aid. Operating aid may be considered compatible only if it can be shown that it is necessary for the development of the area, for instance if it aims to reduce certain specific difficulties faced by SMEs in the most disadvantaged areas (under Article 107(3)(a) of the Treaty), if it compensates for additional costs incurred in pursuing an economic activity in outermost regions, or if it prevents or reduces depopulation in sparsely and very sparsely populated areas.

16. These Guidelines do not cover operating aid awarded to undertakings whose principal activity falls under Section K 'Financial and insurance activities' of the NACE Rev. 2 statistical classification of economic activities[25] or to undertakings that perform intra-group activities and whose principal activity falls under classes 70.10 'Activities of head offices' or 70.22 'Business and other management consultancy activities' of NACE Rev. 2.

17. Regional aid may not be awarded to undertakings in difficulty, as defined for the purpose of these Guidelines by the Guidelines on State aid for rescuing and restructuring non-financial undertakings in difficulty.[26]

18. When assessing regional aid awarded to an undertaking that is subject to an outstanding recovery order following a previous Commission decision declaring an aid illegal and incompatible with the internal market, the Commission will take account of any aid still to be recovered.[27]

2.2. DEFINITIONS

19. For the purposes of these Guidelines, the following definitions apply:

(1) '"a" areas' mean areas designated in a regional aid map in accordance with Article 107(3)(a) of the Treaty and '"c" areas' mean areas designated in a regional aid map in accordance with Article 107(3)(c) of the Treaty;

(2) 'ad hoc aid' means aid that is not awarded on the basis of a scheme;

(3) 'adjusted aid amount' means the maximum permissible aid amount for a large investment project, calculated according to the following formula:

3.1. adjusted aid amount = $R \times (A + 0.50 \times B + 0.34 \times C)$

3.2. where: R is the maximum aid intensity applicable in the area concerned, excluding the increased aid intensity for SMEs. A is the part of eligible costs equal to EUR 50 million, B is the part of eligible costs between EUR 50 million and EUR 100 million, and C is the part of eligible costs above EUR 100 million;

(4) 'aid intensity' means the gross grant equivalent expressed as a percentage of the eligible costs;

(5) 'assisted area' means either an '"a" area' or a '"c" area';

(6) 'completion of the investment' means the moment when the investment is considered by the national authorities as completed or three years after the start of works, whichever is earlier;

(7) 'date of award of the aid' means the date when the legal right to receive the aid is conferred on the aid beneficiary under the applicable national legal regime;

(8) 'EU-27' means all 27 Member States (excluding Northern Ireland);

(9) 'evaluation plan' means a document covering one or more aid schemes and containing at least the following minimum aspects: the objectives to be evaluated, the evaluation questions, the result indicators, the envisaged method to conduct the evaluation, the data collection requirements, the proposed timing of the evaluation including the date of submission of the interim and the final evaluation reports, the description of the independent body that will carry out the evaluation or the criteria that will be used for its selection and the modalities for making the evaluation publicly available;

(10) 'gross grant equivalent' means the discounted amount of the aid equivalent to what it would amount to if provided in the form of a grant to the aid beneficiary, before taxes or other charges, as calculated at the date of award of the aid or at the time the aid is notified to the Commission, whichever is earlier, on the basis of the reference rate applicable on that date;

(11) 'horizontal regional operating aid scheme' means an act on the basis of which, without further implementing measures, individual operating aid may be granted to undertakings defined in the act in a general and abstract manner. For the purpose of this definition, a sectoral aid scheme cannot be considered as a horizontal regional operating aid scheme;

(12) 'individual aid' means ad hoc aid or awards of aid to individual beneficiaries on the basis of an aid scheme;

(13) 'initial investment' means:

(a) an investment in tangible and intangible assets related to one or more of the following:

— the setting-up of a new establishment;

— the extension of the capacity of an existing establishment;

— the diversification of the output of an establishment into products[28] not previously produced in the establishment; or

— a fundamental change in the overall production process of the product(s) concerned by the investment in the establishment; or

(b) an acquisition of assets belonging to an establishment that has closed or would have closed had it not been purchased. Sole acquisition of the shares of an undertaking does not qualify as initial investment.

Replacement investment thus does not constitute initial investment.

(14) 'initial investment that creates a new economic activity' means:

(a) an investment in tangible and intangible assets related to one or more of the following:

— the setting up of a new establishment; or

— the diversification of the activity of an establishment, under the condition that the new activity is not the same or a similar activity to the activity previously performed in the establishment; or

(b) an acquisition of assets belonging to an establishment that has closed or would have closed had it not been purchased, provided that the new activity to be carried out using the acquired assets is not the same or a similar activity than the one carried out in the establishment before the acquisition. Sole acquisition of the shares of an undertaking does not qualify as initial investment that creates a new economic activity.

(15) 'intangible assets' means assets that do not have a physical or financial embodiment such as patent rights, licences, know-how or other intellectual property;

(16) 'job creation' means a net increase in the number of employees in the establishment concerned compared with the average over the previous 12 months, after deducting from the number of jobs created, any job losses that occurred during that period, expressed in annual labour units;

(17) 'large enterprises' means undertakings that do not fulfil the conditions to qualify as SMEs in accordance with point;[28]

(18) 'large investment project' means an initial investment with eligible costs exceeding EUR 50 million;

(19) 'maximum aid intensity' means the aid intensity reflected in the regional aid maps set out in subsection 7.4, including the increased aid intensity for SMEs;

(20) 'number of employees' means the number of annual labour units, namely the numbers of persons employed full-time in one year; persons working part-time or employed in seasonal work are counted in annual labour unit fractions;

(21) 'outermost regions' means the regions referred to in Article 349 of the Treaty;[29]

(22) 'operating aid' means aid aimed to reduce an undertaking's current expenditure, including categories such as personnel costs, materials, contracted services, communications, energy, maintenance, rent and administration, but excluding depreciation charges and the costs of financing if these have been included in the eligible costs when granting regional investment aid;

(23) 'regional aid map' means the list of areas designated by a Member State in line with the conditions laid down in these Guidelines and approved by the Commission;

(24) 'relocation' means a transfer of the same or a similar activity or part thereof from an establishment in one contracting party to the EEA Agreement (initial establishment) to the establishment in which the aided investment takes place in another contracting party to the EEA Agreement (aided establishment). There is a transfer if the product in the initial and in the aided establishments serves at least partly the same purposes and meets the demands or needs of the same type of customers and jobs are lost in the same or similar activity in one of the initial establishments of the aid beneficiary in the EEA;

(25) 'same or a similar activity' means an activity in the same class (four-digit numerical code) of the NACE Rev. 2 statistical classification of economic activities;

(26) 'sectoral aid scheme' means a scheme that covers activities falling within the scope of fewer than five classes (four-digit numerical code) of the NACE Rev.2 statistical classification;

(27) 'single investment project' means any initial investment related to the same or a similar activity started by the aid beneficiary at group level within three years of the date of start of works on another aided investment in the same NUTS 3[30] region;

(28) 'SMEs' means undertakings that fulfil the conditions laid down in Commission Recommendation of 6 May 2003 concerning the definition of micro, small and medium-sized enterprises;[31]

(29) 'start of works' means either the start of construction works relating to the investment, or the first legally binding commitment to order equipment or any other commitment that makes the investment irreversible, whichever is earlier. Buying land and preparatory works such as obtaining permits and conducting preliminary feasibility studies are not considered as start of works. For takeovers, 'start of works' means the date when the assets directly linked to the acquired establishment were acquired;

(30) 'sparsely populated areas' mean the areas designated by the Member State concerned in line with paragraph 169;

(31) 'tangible assets' means assets such as land, buildings, and plant, machinery and equipment;

(32) 'very sparsely populated areas' mean the NUTS 2 regions with fewer than eight inhabitants per km^2 or parts of NUTS 2 regions designated by the Member State concerned in line with paragraph 169;

(33) 'wage costs' means the total amount actually payable by the aid beneficiary in respect of the employment concerned, comprising gross wages before tax and compulsory contributions such as social security, child care and parent care costs over a defined period of time.

NOTES

14 As defined in Annex VI.

15 'Lignite' means low-rank C or Ortho-lignite and low-rank B or Meta lignite as defined by the international codification system for coal established by the United Nations Economic Commission for Europe.

16 'Coal' means high-grade, medium grade and low grade category A and B coal as defined by the international codification system for coal established by the United Nations Economic Commission for Europe and clarified in the Council

decision of 10 December 2010 on State aid to facilitate the closure of uncompetitive coal mines (OJ L336, 21.12.2010, p 24).

17 As covered by Regulation (EU) No 1379/2013 of the European Parliament and of the Council of 11 December 2013 on the common organisation of the markets in fishery and aquaculture products, amending Council Regulations (EC) No 1184/2006 and (EC) No 1224/2009 and repealing Council Regulation (EC) No 104/2000 (OJ L354, 28.12.2013, p 1).

18 State aid for the primary production, processing and marketing of agricultural products resulting in agricultural products listed in Annex I to the Treaty and forestry is subject to rules laid down in the Guidelines for State aid in the agricultural sector (OJ C204, 1.7.2014, p 1).

19 Transport means the transport of passengers by aircraft, maritime transport, road, railway and by inland waterway or freight transport services for hire or reward. Transport infrastructure covered by specific guidelines, such as airports, is also excluded from these Guidelines (see the Communication from the Commission – Guidelines on State aid to airports and airlines (OJ C99, 4.4.2014, p 3).

20 EU Guidelines for the application of State aid rules in relation to the rapid deployment of broadband networks (OJ C25, 26.1.2013, p 1).

21 The Commission will assess the compatibility of State aid to the energy sector on the basis of the Guidelines on State aid for environmental protection and energy 2014-2020 (OJ C200, 28.6.2014, p 1).

22 Covered by Regulation (EU) No 1305/2013 of the European Parliament and of the Council of 17 December 2013 on support for rural development by the European Agricultural Fund for Rural Development (EARDF) (OJ L347, 20.12.2013, p 487).

23 This derogation will only apply if a regulation is adopted following the Commission's proposal referred to in footnote 12 and is temporary for the duration of the JTF.

24 It should be demonstrated in the territorial just transition plan that investments in these enterprises are necessary to compensate for the loss of jobs due to the transition that cannot be compensated by the creation of jobs in SMEs.

25 Regulation (EC) No 1893/2006 of the European Parliament and of the Council of 20 December 2006 establishing the statistical classification of economic activities NACE Revision 2 and amending Council Regulation (EEC) No 3037/90 as well as certain EC Regulations on specific statistical domains (OJ L393, 30.12.2006, p 1).

26 Guidelines on State aid for rescuing and restructuring non-financial undertakings in difficulty (OJ C249, 31.7.2014, p 1). As explained in point 23 of those guidelines, given that its very existence is in danger, an undertaking in difficulty cannot be considered an appropriate vehicle for promoting other public policy objectives until such time as its viability is assured.

27 See judgment of 13 September 1995, *TWD Textilwerke Deggendorf GmbH v Commission of the European Communities*, Joined cases T-244/93 and T-486/93, ECLI:EU:T:1995:160, paragraph 56.

28 The concept of product also covers services in the context of these Guidelines.

29 Currently: Guadeloupe, French Guiana, Martinique, Mayotte, Réunion, Saint-Martin, the Azores, Madeira and the Canary Islands (OJ C202, 7.6.2016, p 195). Saint-Martin is not included in the NUTS 2021.

30 Regulation (EC) No 1059/2003 of the European Parliament and of the Council on the establishment of a common classification of territorial units for statistics (NUTS) (OJ L154, 21.6.2003, p 1) as amended by Commission Delegated Regulation (EU) 2019/1755 (OJ L270, 24.10.2019, p 1). The data used in these Guidelines are based on this NUTS 2021 nomenclature.

31 Commission Recommendation of 6 May 2003 concerning the definition of micro, small and medium-sized enterprises (OJ L124, 20.5.2003, p 36).

3. NOTIFIABLE REGIONAL AID

[5.279]

20. In principle, Member States must notify regional aid under Article 108(3) of the Treaty, with the exception of measures that fulfil the conditions laid down in a Block Exemption Regulation adopted by the Commission under Article 1 of Council Regulation (EU) 2015/1588.[32]

21. The Commission will apply these Guidelines to notifiable regional aid schemes and notifiable individual regional aid.

22. Individual aid granted under a notified scheme remains subject to the notification obligation under Article 108(3) of the Treaty if the aid from all sources exceeds the individual notification threshold laid down in the General Block Exemption Regulation[33] ('GBER') for regional investment aid.

23. Individual aid granted under a notified scheme also remains subject to the notification obligation under Article 108(3) of the Treaty unless the beneficiary:

(a) has confirmed that in the 2 years preceding the application for aid, it has not carried out a relocation to the establishment in which the aided initial investment is to take place; and
(b) has committed not to carry out such relocation up to a period of two years after completion of the initial investment.

NOTES

32 Council Regulation (EU) 2015/1588 of 13 July 2015 on the application of Articles 107 and 108 of the Treaty on the Functioning of the European Union to certain categories of horizontal State aid (OJ L248, 24.9.2015, p 1).

33 Commission Regulation (EU) No 651/2014 of 17 June 2014 declaring certain categories of aid compatible with the internal market in application of Articles 107 and 108 of the Treaty (OJ L187, 26.6.2014, p 1).

4. ELIGIBLE COSTS

4.1. INVESTMENT AID

[5.280]

24. The eligible costs are as follows:

(1) investment costs in tangible and intangible assets; or

(2) the estimated wage costs arising from job creation as a result of an initial investment, calculated over two years; or

(3) a combination of part of the costs referred to in point (1) and (2) but not exceeding the amount of (1) or (2), whichever is higher.

25. If the eligible costs are drawn up on the basis of investment costs in tangible and intangible assets, only the costs of assets that form part of the initial investment in the establishment of the aid beneficiary located in the targeted assisted area are eligible.

26. By way of derogation from the condition in paragraph 25, vendor tooling[34] assets can be included in the eligible costs of the undertaking that acquired (or produced) them if they are used over the full minimum maintenance period of five years for large enterprises, and three years for SMEs, for a processing or assembly operation of the aid beneficiary directly linked to a production process based on the aided initial investment of the aid beneficiary. This derogation is applicable provided the supplier's establishment is located in an assisted area, the supplier itself does not receive regional investment aid or investment aid for SMEs pursuant to Article 17 GBER for the assets concerned, and the aid intensity does not exceed the relevant maximum aid intensity applicable to the location of the supplier's establishment. Any adjustment of the aid intensity for large investment projects also applies to the aid calculated for the costs of the vendor tooling assets, which are considered to form part of the overall investment cost of the initial investment.

4.1.1. ELIGIBLE COSTS CALCULATED ON THE BASIS OF INVESTMENT COSTS

27. The assets acquired must be new, except for SMEs or for the acquisition of an establishment.[35]

28. For SMEs, up to 50% of the costs of preparatory studies or consultancy costs linked to the investment may also be considered as eligible costs.

29. For aid granted to large enterprises for a fundamental change in the production process, the eligible costs must exceed the depreciation of the assets linked to the activity to be modernised over the preceding three fiscal years.

30. For aid awarded for a diversification of an existing establishment, the eligible costs must exceed by at least 200% the book value of the reused assets, as registered in the fiscal year preceding the start of works.

31. Costs related to the lease of tangible assets may be taken into account under the following conditions:

(1) for land and buildings, the lease must continue for at least five years after the expected date of completion of the investment for large enterprises, and three years for SMEs;

(2) for plant or machinery, the lease must take the form of financial leasing and must contain an obligation for the aid beneficiary to purchase the asset at the expiry of the term of the lease.

32. In case of an initial investment as referred to in paragraph 19(13)(b) or 19(14)(b), in principle only the costs of buying the assets from third parties unrelated to the buyer should be taken into consideration. However, if a member of the family of the original owner, or an employee, takes over a small enterprise, the condition that the assets must be bought from third parties unrelated to the buyer does not apply. The transaction must take place under market conditions. If the acquisition of the assets of an establishment is accompanied by an additional investment eligible for regional aid, the eligible costs of that additional investment should be added to the cost of acquisition of the assets of the establishment.

33. For large enterprises, the costs of intangible assets are eligible only up to 50% of the total eligible investment costs for the initial investment. For SMEs, 100% of the costs of intangible assets are eligible.

34. Intangible assets that can be taken into account for the calculation of the investment costs must remain associated with the area concerned and must not be transferred to other areas. To this end, the intangible assets must fulfil the following conditions:

(1) they must be used exclusively in the establishment receiving the aid;

(2) they must be amortisable;

(3) they must be purchased under market conditions from third parties unrelated to the buyer;

(4) they must be included in the assets of the undertaking that receives the aid and must remain associated with the project for which the aid is awarded for at least five years (three years for SMEs).

4.1.2. ELIGIBLE COSTS CALCULATED ON THE BASIS OF WAGE COSTS

35. Regional aid may also be calculated by reference to the estimated wage costs arising from job creation as a result of an initial investment. The aid may compensate only the wage costs related to job creation, calculated over two years, and the resulting aid intensity must not exceed the maximum applicable aid intensity in the area concerned.

36. Where eligible costs are calculated by reference to the estimated wage costs as referred to in paragraph 35, the following conditions must be fulfilled:

(1) the investment project must lead to job creation;

(2) each post must be filled within three years of the completion of the investment;

(3) each job created through the investment must be maintained in the area concerned for at least five years from the date the post was first filled, or three years for SMEs.

4.2. OPERATING AID

37. Eligible costs for operating aid schemes must be predefined and fully attributable to the problems that the aid is intended to address, as demonstrated by the Member State.

38. In outermost regions, the operating aid schemes can compensate for the additional operating costs incurred in those regions as a direct result of one or several of the permanent constraints mentioned in Article 349 of the Treaty. These additional costs must be quantified and compared with the cost incurred by similar undertakings established in other regions of the Member State concerned.

NOTES

34 Vendor tooling is the acquisition (or auto-production) of machines, tools or equipment and related software by an undertaking (at group level), which are acquired (or produced) not for use on one of its premises (at group level), but made available to selected suppliers for the production of products to be manufactured on the supplier's premises, which will serve as intermediary products for the production process of the undertaking. Vendor tooling assets remain the property of the acquiring undertaking, but are made available to the supplier for the tasks and under the conditions defined in a supply contract or similar agreement. They are linked to well-defined processing or assembly operations in one or several of the undertaking's (at group level) premises, and may have to be returned to the owner after completion of the order, or expiry or termination of a framework contract.

35 Defined in paragraph 19 (13) and (14).

5. COMPATIBILITY ASSESSMENT OF REGIONAL AID

[5.281]

39. The Commission will consider a regional aid measure compatible with Article 107(3) of the Treaty only if the aid contributes to regional development and cohesion. The aim must be either to promote the economic development of 'a' areas or to facilitate the development of 'c' areas (Section 5.1) and in addition it must meet each of the following criteria:

(1) incentive effect: the aid must change the behaviour of the undertakings concerned in such a way that they carry out an additional activity which they would not carry out without the aid or would carry out in a restricted or different manner or location; (Section 5.2)

(2) need for State intervention: a State aid measure must be targeted towards a situation where aid can bring about a material improvement that the market cannot deliver itself, for example by remedying a market failure or addressing an equity or cohesion concern; (Section 5.3)

(3) appropriateness of the aid measure: the proposed aid measure must be an appropriate policy instrument to meet its objective; (Section 5.4)

(4) proportionality of the aid (aid to the minimum): the aid amount must be limited to the minimum needed to stimulate the additional investment or activity in the area concerned; (Section 5.5)

(5) avoidance of undue negative effects on competition and trade between Member States: the negative effects of the aid on competition and trade must be outweighed by the positive effects; (Section 5.6)

(6) transparency of the aid: Member States, the Commission, economic operators, and the public, must have easy access to all relevant acts and information on the aid awarded (Section 5.7).

40. The overall balance of certain categories of schemes may also be made subject to the requirement to carry out an *ex post* evaluation, as described in Section 6. In such cases, the Commission may limit the duration of the schemes (typically to four years or less), with the option to re-notify their prolongation afterwards.

41. If a State aid measure, the conditions attached to it (including its financing method when the financing method forms an integral part of the State aid measure), or the activity it finances entail a violation of a relevant provision of EU law, the aid cannot be declared compatible with the internal market.[36]

5.1. CONTRIBUTION TO REGIONAL DEVELOPMENT AND TERRITORIAL COHESION

42. The primary objective of regional aid is the economic development of the EU's disadvantaged areas. By promoting and facilitating the sustainable development of assisted areas, the aid contributes to the EU's territorial cohesion policy, which aims to improve economic and social cohesion by reducing disparities in the level of development between areas.

5.1.1. INVESTMENT AID SCHEMES

43. Regional aid schemes should form an integral part of a regional development strategy with clearly defined objectives.

44. Member States must demonstrate that the scheme is consistent with and contributes to the development strategy of the area concerned. For this purpose, Member States can refer to evaluations of past State aid schemes, impact assessments made by the granting authorities, or expert opinions. To ensure that the aid scheme contributes to the development strategy, it must include a method that enables the granting authorities to prioritise and select the investment projects that meet the objectives of the scheme (for example, by using a formal scoring method).

45. Regional aid schemes may be put in place in 'a' areas to support initial investments made by SMEs or large enterprises. In 'c' areas, schemes may be put in place to support initial investments made by SMEs and initial investments that create a new economic activity made by large enterprises.

46. When awarding aid to individual investment projects on the basis of a scheme, the granting authority must verify that the selected project will contribute towards the scheme's objective and thus towards the development strategy in the area concerned. For this purpose, Member States should refer to the information provided by the aid applicant in the aid application form describing the positive effects of the investment on the development of the area concerned.[37]

47. To ensure that the investment makes a real and sustained contribution to the development of the area concerned, the investment must be maintained in that area for at least five years, or three years for SMEs, after the completion of the investment.[38]

48. To ensure that the investment is viable, the Member State must ensure that the aid beneficiary provides a financial contribution of at least 25%[39] of the eligible costs, through its own resources or by external financing, in a form that is free of any public support.[40]

49. To avoid State aid measures leading to environmental harm, Member States must also ensure compliance with EU environmental legislation, including in particular the need to carry out an environmental impact assessment when required by law and to obtain all relevant permits.

5.1.2. Notifiable individual investment aid

50. To demonstrate the contribution of notifiable individual investment aid to regional development, Member States may use a variety of indicators such as the ones mentioned below that can be both direct (for example, direct jobs created) and indirect (for example, local innovation):

(1) The number of direct jobs created by the investment is an important indicator of the contribution to regional development and territorial cohesion. The quality and durability of the jobs created and the required skill level should also be considered.

(2) An even higher number of new jobs might be created in the local (sub-) supplier network, helping to better integrate the investment in the area concerned and ensuring more widespread spillover effects. The number of indirect jobs created is therefore also an indicator to be taken into account.

(3) A commitment by the aid beneficiary to enter into widespread training activities to improve the skills (general and specific) of its workforce will be considered as a factor that contributes to regional development and territorial cohesion. Emphasis will also be put on providing traineeships or apprenticeships, especially for young people and on training that improves the knowledge and employability of workers outside the undertaking.

(4) External economies of scale or other benefits from a regional development viewpoint may arise as a result of proximity (clustering effect). Clustering of undertakings in the same industry allows individual plants to specialise more, which leads to increased efficiency. However, the importance of this indicator in determining the contribution to regional development and territorial cohesion depends on the state of development of the cluster.

(5) Investments embody technical knowledge and can be the source of a significant transfer of technology (knowledge spillovers). Investments taking place in technology intensive industries are more likely to involve technology transfer to the area concerned. The level and the specificity of the knowledge dissemination are also important in this regard.

(6) The projects' contribution to the area's ability to create new technology through local innovation can also be considered. Co-operation with local research and knowledge-dissemination organisations, such as universities or research institutes can be considered positively in this respect.

(7) The duration of the investment and possible future follow-on investments are an indication of a durable engagement of an undertaking in the area concerned.

51. Member States can refer to the business plan of the aid beneficiary which could provide information on the number of jobs to be created, salaries to be paid (increase in household wealth as spill-over effect), volume of acquisition from local producers, turnover generated by the investment and benefiting the area possibly through additional tax revenues.

52. For notifiable individual investment aid, requirements laid down in paragraphs 47 to 49 apply.

53. For ad hoc aid,[41] Member States must demonstrate, in addition to the requirements laid down in paragraphs 50 to 52, that the project is coherent with and contributes to the development strategy of the area concerned.

5.1.3. Operating aid schemes

54. Operating aid schemes promote the development of assisted areas only if the challenges that those areas face are clearly identified in advance. The obstacles to attracting or maintaining economic activity may be so severe or permanent that investment aid alone is not sufficient for these areas to develop.

55. For aid to reduce certain specific difficulties faced by SMEs in 'a' areas, Member States must demonstrate the existence and scale of those specific difficulties and must demonstrate that an operating aid scheme is needed as those specific difficulties cannot be overcome with investment aid.

56. As regards operating aid to offset specific additional costs in the outermost regions, the types of permanent constraints that severely restrain the development of the outermost regions are set out in Article 349 of the Treaty. They include remoteness, insularity, small size, difficult topography and climate, and economic dependence on a few products. Member States must identify the specific additional costs related to these permanent constraints that the operating aid scheme is intended to compensate.

57. As regards operating aid to prevent or reduce depopulation in sparsely and very sparsely populated areas, Member States must demonstrate the risk of depopulation in the event that operating aid is not granted.

5.2. INCENTIVE EFFECT

5.2.1. Investment aid

58. Regional aid can only be found compatible with the internal market if it has an incentive effect. State aid is considered to have an incentive effect when it changes the behaviour of an undertaking in a way that it carries out additional activity contributing to the development of an area that it would not have carried out, or would only have done in a limited or different manner or in another location, if the aid was not granted. The aid must not subsidise the costs of an activity that an undertaking would carry out in any event and must not compensate for the normal business risk of an economic activity.

59. The incentive effect can be proven in two ways:

(1) the aid gives an incentive to take a positive decision to invest in the area concerned because otherwise the investment would not be sufficiently profitable for the aid beneficiary anywhere in the EEA[42] (*scenario 1, investment decision*);

(2) the aid gives an incentive to locate a planned investment in the area concerned rather than elsewhere because it offsets the net disadvantages and costs of investing in a location in the area concerned (*scenario 2, location decision*).

60. If the aid does not change the behaviour of the aid beneficiary by stimulating (additional) initial investment in the area concerned, it can be considered that the same investment would be made in the area even without the aid. The aid therefore lacks an incentive effect to achieve the regional development and territorial cohesion objective and cannot be approved as compatible with the internal market under these Guidelines.

61. However, for regional aid awarded through cohesion policy funds or the EAFRD in 'a' areas to investments necessary to achieve standards set by EU law, the aid may be considered to have incentive effect, if in absence of the aid, it would not have been sufficiently profitable for the aid beneficiary to make the investment in the area concerned, leading to the closure of an existing establishment in that area.

5.2.1.1.
Investment aid schemes

62. Works on an individual investment can start only after the application form for aid is submitted.

63. If works start before the application form for aid is submitted, any aid awarded for that individual investment will not be considered compatible with the internal market.

64. Member States must submit a standard aid application form that contains, as a minimum, all the information listed in Annex VII. In the application form, SMEs and large enterprises must explain counterfactually what would happen if they were not granted aid, indicating the applicable scenario described in paragraph 59.

65. In addition, large enterprises must submit documentary evidence to underpin the counterfactual described in the application form. SMEs are not subject to such obligation in respect of non-notifiable aid granted under a scheme.

66. The granting authority must carry out a credibility check of the counterfactual and verify that regional aid has the required incentive effect corresponding to one of the scenarios described in paragraph 59. A counterfactual is credible if it is genuine and relates to the decision-making factors prevalent at the time of the decision by the aid beneficiary regarding the investment.

5.2.1.2.
Notifiable individual investment aid

67. In addition to the requirements of paragraphs 62 to 66, for notifiable individual aid, Member States must provide clear evidence that the aid has an impact on the investment decision or on the choice of location (43). They must specify which scenario described in paragraph 59 applies. To enable a comprehensive assessment to be made, Member States must provide not only information on the project but also a comprehensive description of the counterfactual scenario, in which the applicant receives no aid from any public authority in the EEA.

68. In *scenario 1*, Member States could prove that the aid has an incentive effect by providing the undertaking's documents that show that the investment would not be sufficiently profitable without the aid.

69. In *scenario 2*, Member States could prove that the aid has an incentive effect by providing the undertaking's documents showing that a comparison has been made between the costs and benefits of locating in the area concerned and those in alternative area(s). The Commission verifies whether these comparisons are realistic.

70. Member States are invited to draw on genuine and official board documents, risk assessments (including the assessment of location-specific risks), financial reports, internal business plans, expert opinions and other studies related to the investment project under assessment. Those documents need to be contemporary to the decision making process concerning the investment or its location. Documents containing information on demand forecasts, cost forecasts, financial forecasts, documents submitted to an investment committee and that elaborate on investment scenarios, or documents provided to the financial institutions could help Member States to demonstrate the incentive effect.

71. In this context, and in particular in *scenario 1*, the level of profitability can be evaluated by using methods that are standard practice in the given industry, which may include methods to evaluate the net present value of the project (NPV),[44] the internal rate of return (IRR)[45] or the average return on capital employed (ROCE). The profitability of the project is to be compared with normal rates of return applied by the beneficiary in other investment projects of a similar kind. Where these rates are not available, the profitability of the project must be compared with the cost of capital of the beneficiary as a whole or with the rates of return commonly observed in the industry concerned.

72. If the aid does not change the behaviour of the aid beneficiary by stimulating (additional) investment in the area, there is no positive effect for the area. Therefore, aid will not be considered compatible with the internal market if it appears that the same investment would be made in the area even without aid being granted.

5.2.2. Operating aid schemes

73. For operating aid schemes, the aid is considered to have an incentive effect if it is likely that, in the absence of aid, the level of economic activity in the area concerned would be significantly reduced due to the problems that the aid aims to tackle.

74. The Commission will therefore consider that the operating aid provides an incentive to additional economic activity in the area, if the Member State has demonstrated the existence and substantial nature of those problems in that area (see paragraphs 54 to 57).

5.3. NEED FOR STATE INTERVENTION

75. To assess whether State aid is necessary to achieve the objective of regional development and territorial cohesion, it is necessary first to diagnose the problem. State aid should be targeted to situations where aid can bring about a material improvement that the market cannot deliver. This is especially important in a context of scarce public resources.

76. State aid measures can, under certain conditions, correct market failures and thereby contribute to the efficient functioning of markets and boost competitiveness. Where markets do provide efficient outcomes but such outcomes are deemed unsatisfactory in terms of equity or cohesion, State aid may be used to obtain a more desirable, equitable market outcome.

77. As regards aid granted for the development of areas included in the regional aid map in line with the rules in Section 7 of these Guidelines, the Commission considers that in those areas, the market does not deliver outcomes resulting in a sufficient level of economic development of the region and territorial cohesion without State intervention. Therefore, aid granted in those areas is considered necessary.

5.4. APPROPRIATENESS OF REGIONAL AID

78. The aid measure must be an appropriate policy instrument to address the policy objective concerned. An aid measure will not be considered compatible if other less distortive policy instruments or other less distortive types of aid instrument make it possible to achieve the same positive contribution to regional development and territorial cohesion.

5.4.1. APPROPRIATENESS AMONG ALTERNATIVE POLICY INSTRUMENTS

5.4.1.1. Investment aid

79. Regional investment aid is not the only policy instrument available to Member States to boost investment and job creation in assisted areas. Member States can use other measures such as infrastructure development, enhancing the quality of education and training, or improving the business environment.

80. When notifying an investment aid scheme, Member States must indicate why regional aid is an appropriate instrument to help develop the area.

81. If a Member State decides to put in place a sectoral aid scheme, it must demonstrate the advantages of doing so instead of using a multi-sectoral scheme or other policy options.

82. In particular, the Commission will take account of impact assessments of the proposed aid scheme that Member States make available. Likewise, it may take into account the results of *ex post* evaluations described in Section 6 to assess the appropriateness of the proposed scheme.

83. In the case of ad hoc investment aid, Member States must demonstrate how the aid can better contribute to the development of the area than aid under a scheme or other types of measures.

5.4.1.2. Operating aid schemes

84. Member States must demonstrate that the aid is appropriate to achieve the objective of the scheme for the problems that the aid aims to address. To demonstrate that the aid is appropriate, Member States may calculate the aid amount *ex ante* as a fixed sum covering the expected additional costs over a given period, to encourage undertakings to contain costs and develop their business in a more efficient manner over time.[46]

5.4.2. APPROPRIATENESS AMONG DIFFERENT AID INSTRUMENTS

85. Regional aid can be awarded in several forms. Member States must however, ensure that the aid is awarded in the form likely to have the lowest impact in distorting trade and competition. If the aid is awarded in forms that provide a direct pecuniary advantage (for example, direct grants, exemptions or reductions in taxes, social security or other compulsory charges, or the supply of land, goods or services at favourable prices), Member States must demonstrate why other potentially less distortive forms of aid such as repayable advances or aid based on debt or equity instruments (for example, low-interest loans or interest rebates, State guarantees, the purchase of a share-holding or an alternative injection of capital on favourable terms) are not appropriate.

86. The results of *ex post* evaluations as described in Section 6 may be taken into account to assess the appropriateness of the proposed aid instrument.

5.5. PROPORTIONALITY OF THE AID AMOUNT (LIMITING AID TO THE MINIMUM NEEDED)

5.5.1. INVESTMENT AID

87. The amount of regional aid must be limited to the minimum needed to stimulate additional investment or activity in the area concerned.

88. To ensure predictability and a level playing field, the Commission applies maximum aid intensities[47] for investment aid.

89. For an initial investment project, the maximum aid intensity and maximum aid amount[48] (adjusted aid amount[49] and the related reduced aid intensity for a large investment project) must be calculated by the granting authority when awarding the aid or notifying the aid to the Commission, whichever is earlier.

90. Since large investment projects are likely to give rise to greater distortions of competition and trade, the aid amount for these projects must not exceed the adjusted aid amount.

91. Where the initial investment is part of a single investment project and that single investment project is a large investment project, the aid amount for the single investment project must not exceed the adjusted aid amount. The exchange rate and discount rate to be applied for the purpose of this rule are those applicable at the date of award of the aid for the first project in the single investment project.

92. The maximum aid intensities serve a dual purpose.

93. First, for notifiable schemes, these maximum aid intensities serve as safe harbours for SMEs: provided that the aid intensity remains below the maximum permissible, the aid is deemed proportionate.

94. Second, for all other cases, the maximum aid intensities are used as a cap to the net-extra costs approach described in paragraphs 95 to 97.

95. As a general rule, the Commission will consider notifiable individual aid to be limited to the minimum, if the aid amount corresponds to the net-extra costs of investing in the area concerned, compared to the counterfactual in the absence of aid,[50] with maximum aid intensities as a cap. Likewise, for investment aid granted to large enterprises under notifiable schemes, Member States must ensure that the aid amount is limited to the minimum on the basis of a 'net-extra cost approach', with maximum aid intensities as a cap.

96. For *scenario 1* situations (investment decisions), the aid amount should therefore not exceed the minimum necessary to render the project sufficiently profitable, for example to increase its IRR above the normal rate applied by the undertaking in other investment projects of a similar kind or, when available, to increase its IRR above the cost of capital of the beneficiary as a whole or above the rates of return commonly achieved in that industry.

97. For *scenario 2* situations (location incentives), the aid amount should not exceed the difference between the NPV of the investment in the target area with the NPV in the alternative location. All relevant costs and benefits must be taken into account, including for example administrative costs, transport costs, training costs not covered by training aid and wage differences. However, if the alternative location is in the EEA, subsidies in that location cannot be taken into account.

98. Calculations used to analyse the incentive effect can also be used to assess whether the aid is proportionate. Member States must demonstrate proportionality with documentation, such as that referred to in paragraph 70.

99. Investment aid may be awarded concurrently under several regional aid schemes or cumulated with ad hoc regional aid, provided that the total aid from all sources does not exceed the maximum aid intensity per project, which must be calculated in advance by the first granting authority. Any other State aid in relation to the same eligible costs, partly or fully overlapping, may be cumulated only if it does not result in exceeding the highest aid intensity or aid amount applicable to this aid under the applicable thematic rules. Cumulation checks must be carried out both when the aid is granted and when the aid is paid.[51] If the Member State allows State aid under one scheme to be cumulated with State aid under other schemes, it must specify, for each scheme, the method to ensure compliance with the conditions in this paragraph.

100. For an initial investment linked to European Territorial Cooperation (ETC) projects meeting the criteria of the Regulation laying down the specific provisions for the European Territorial Cooperation goal (Interreg),[52] the aid intensity applicable to the area in which the initial investment is located applies to all beneficiaries participating in the project. If the initial investment is located in two or more assisted areas, the maximum aid intensity for the initial investment is the one applicable in the assisted area where the highest amount of the eligible costs is incurred. Initial investments carried out by large enterprises in 'c' areas may only receive regional aid in the context of ETC projects if they are initial investments that create a new economic activity.

5.5.2. Operating aid schemes

101. Member States must demonstrate that the level of the aid is proportionate to the problems that the aid aims to address.

102. In particular, Member States must meet the following conditions:

(1) the aid must be calculated in relation to a predefined set of eligible costs that are fully attributable to the problems that the aid aims to address, as demonstrated by the Member State;

(2) the aid must be limited to a certain proportion of that predefined set of eligible costs and must not exceed these costs;

(3) the aid amount per aid beneficiary must be proportional to the level of the problems actually experienced by each aid beneficiary.

103. As regards aid to reduce certain specific difficulties faced by SMEs in 'a' areas, the level of the aid must be progressively reduced over the duration of the scheme.[53] This does not apply to schemes to prevent depopulation in sparsely and very sparsely populated areas and to schemes compensating for the additional operating costs incurred in outermost regions as a direct result of one or several permanent constraints referred to in Article 349 of the Treaty.

5.6. AVOIDING UNDUE NEGATIVE EFFECTS ON COMPETITION AND TRADE

104. For the aid to be compatible, the negative effects of the aid measure in terms of distortions of competition and impact on trade between Member States must be limited and must not outweigh the positive effects of the aid to an extent that would be contrary to the common interest.

5.6.1. General considerations

105. In the overall balancing of the positive effects of the aid (Section 5.1) against its negative effects on competition and trade, the Commission may take into account, where relevant, the circumstance that on top of its contribution to regional development and cohesion, the aid produces other positive effects. Such may be the case for instance where it is established that the initial investment, in addition to creating local jobs, introducing new activities and/or generating local revenues, contributes substantially in particular to the digital transition or transition towards environmentally sustainable activities, including low carbon, climate neutral or climate-resilient activities. The Commission will pay particular attention to Article 3 of the EU Taxonomy Regulation (EU) 2020/852 of the European Parliament and of the Council,[54] including the 'Do no significant harm' principle, or other comparable methodologies. Furthermore, as part of the assessment of negative effects on competition and trade, the Commission may take into account, where relevant, negative externalities of the aided activity where such externalities adversely affect competition and trade between Member States to an extent contrary to the common interest by creating or aggravating market inefficiencies.[55]

106. In terms of negative effects, regional aid can give rise to two main types of potential distortion of competition and trade. These are product market distortions and location effects. Both types of distortion can lead to allocative inefficiencies (undermining the economic performance of the internal market) and to distributional concerns (distribution of economic activity across areas).

107. One potentially harmful effect of State aid is that it prevents the market from delivering efficient outcomes by rewarding the most efficient producers and putting pressure on the least efficient to improve, restructure or exit the market. State aid that gives rise to a substantial capacity expansion in an underperforming market can unduly distort competition, as the creation or maintenance of overcapacity can squeeze profit margins, reduce competitors' investments or even result in competitors exiting the market. This can lead to a situation where competitors that would otherwise be able to compete on the market are forced out of the market. It may also prevent undertakings from entering or expanding in the market and it may weaken the incentives for competitors to innovate. This may result in inefficient market structures that are also detrimental to consumers in the long term. Making aid available may also encourage complacent or unduly risky behaviour on the part of potential beneficiaries. It is likely to have a negative long-term effect on the overall performance of the sector.

108. Aid may also have distortive effects in terms of increasing or maintaining substantial market power for the aid beneficiary. Even where aid does not strengthen substantial market power directly, it may do so indirectly by discouraging existing competitors from expanding, resulting in their exit from the market or discouraging the entry of new competitors.

109. Apart from distortions on the product markets, by its very nature, regional aid also affects the location of economic activity. If one area attracts investment due to the aid, another area loses out on that opportunity. These negative effects in the areas adversely affected by aid may be felt through lost economic activity and lost jobs, including jobs for subcontractors. Negative effects may also be felt in a loss of positive externalities (for example, the cluster effect, knowledge spillovers, education and training).

110. The geographical specificity of regional aid distinguishes it from other forms of horizontal aid. A specific characteristic of regional aid is that it aims to influence the choice made by investors about where to locate investment projects. When regional aid offsets the additional costs stemming from regional constraints and supports additional investment in assisted areas without attracting it away from other equally or less developed assisted areas, it contributes not only to the development of the area, but also to cohesion and ultimately benefits the whole EU. The potential negative location effects of regional aid are already limited to a certain degree by regional aid maps, which define the areas where regional aid may be granted, in line with the regional economic development and cohesion policy objectives, and the maximum permissible aid intensities. However, it remains important to understand what would happen in the absence of the aid to assess the impact of the aid on the development of the area and on territorial cohesion.

5.6.2. Manifest negative effects on competition and trade

111. The Commission identifies a number of situations where the negative effects of regional investment aid on competition and trade between Member States manifestly outweigh any positive effects, meaning that the aid is unlikely to be declared compatible with the internal market.

5.6.2.1.
Creating overcapacity in a market in absolute decline

112. As pointed out in paragraph 107, to assess the negative effects of aid, the Commission takes account of the additional production capacity created by the project when the market under-performs.

113. Where investments adding production capacity in a market are made possible because of State aid, there is a risk that production or investment in other areas of the EEA may be negatively affected. This is particularly likely if the capacity increase exceeds market growth or takes place in a market with overcapacity.

114. Therefore, where the investment leads to the creation or increase of overcapacity in a market that is structurally in absolute decline (i.e. the market is contracting),[56] the Commission considers the aid to have a negative effect, which is unlikely to be compensated by any positive effect. This applies in particular to scenario 1 situations (investment decisions).

115. For scenario 2 situations (location decisions), where the investment would be made in any event in the same geographical market or, exceptionally, in a different geographical market, but where sales target the same geographical market, the aid – provided it is limited to the minimum necessary to compensate for the locational disadvantage and does not give additional liquidity to the aid beneficiary – only influences the location decision. In this situation, the investment would add additional capacity on the given geographical market independently of the aid. Therefore, possible outcomes in terms of overcapacity would, in principle, be the same regardless of the aid. However, if the alternative investment location is in a different geographical market, and the aid leads to the creation of overcapacity on a market structurally in absolute decline, the conclusions of paragraph 114 apply.

5.6.2.2.
Counter-cohesion effects

116. As stated in paragraphs 109 and 110, to assess the negative effects of the aid, the Commission must take account of the effects on the location of the economic activity.

117. In scenario 2 situations (location decisions), where without aid the investment would have been located in an area with a regional aid intensity[57] that is higher or the same as in the target area, this constitutes a negative effect that is unlikely to be compensated by any positive effect because it runs counter to the very rationale of regional aid.

5.6.2.3. Relocation

118. When evaluating the notifiable measures, the Commission will request all necessary information to consider whether the State aid is likely to result in a substantial loss of jobs in existing locations within the EEA. In this situation, and if the investment enables the aid beneficiary to relocate an activity to the target area, if there is a causal link between the aid and the relocation, this constitutes a negative effect that is unlikely to be compensated by any positive effects.

5.6.3. Investment aid schemes

119. Investment aid schemes must not lead to significant distortions of competition and trade. In particular, even where distortions may be considered limited at an individual level (provided all conditions for investment aid are fulfilled), on a cumulative basis schemes might still lead to high levels of distortions. Such distortions could affect output markets by creating or aggravating a situation of overcapacity or creating, increasing or maintaining the substantial market power of some recipients in a way that negatively affects dynamic incentives. Aid available under schemes could also lead to a significant loss of economic activity in other areas of the EEA. If a scheme focuses on certain sectors, the risk of such distortions is even more pronounced.

120. Therefore, Member States must demonstrate that these negative effects will be limited to the minimum, taking into account, for example, the size of the projects, the individual and cumulative aid amounts, the expected beneficiaries and the characteristics of the targeted sectors. For the Commission to assess the likely negative effects, Member States can submit all available impact assessment and *ex post* evaluations carried out for similar predecessor schemes.

121. When awarding aid under a scheme to individual projects, the granting authority must verify and confirm that the aid does not result in manifest negative effects, as described in paragraphs 111 to 118. This verification can be based on the information received from the aid beneficiary when applying for aid and on the declaration made in the standard application form for aid, which should indicate the alternative location in the scenario that aid is not granted.

5.6.4. Notifiable individual investment aid

122. When evaluating the negative effects of individual aid, the Commission distinguishes between the two counterfactual scenarios described in paragraphs 96 and 97.

5.6.4.1. Scenario 1 situations (investment decision)

123. Under scenario 1 situations, the Commission places particular emphasis on the negative effects linked with the build-up of overcapacity in declining markets, the prevention of exit, and the concept of substantial market power. These negative effects are described in paragraphs 124 to 133 and must be counterbalanced with the positive effects of the aid. However, if it is established that the aid would result in the manifest negative effects described in paragraph 114, the aid is unlikely to be compensated by any positive effect and thus to be found compatible with the internal market.

124. To identify and assess potential distortion of competition and trade, Member States should provide evidence permitting the Commission to identify the product markets concerned (products affected by the change in behaviour of the aid beneficiary) and identify the competitors and customers/consumers affected. The product concerned is typically the product covered by the investment project.[58] When the project concerns an intermediate product and a significant part of the output is not sold on the market, the product concerned may be the downstream product. The relevant product market includes the product concerned and its substitutes considered to be such, either by the consumer (by reason of the product's characteristics, prices, or intended use) or by the producer (by reason of flexibility of production installations).

125. The Commission will use multiple criteria to assess these potential distortions, such as market structure of the product concerned, performance of the market (declining or growing market), the process for selecting the aid beneficiary, entry and exit barriers and product differentiation.

126. A systematic reliance on State aid by an undertaking could indicate that the undertaking is unable to withstand competition on its own or that it derives undue advantages compared to its competitors.

127. The Commission distinguishes two main sources of potential negative effects on product markets:

(1) cases of capacity expansion which leads to or deteriorates an existing situation of overcapacity, especially in a declining market;

(2) cases where the aid beneficiary holds substantial market power.

128. To evaluate whether the aid serves to create or maintain inefficient market structures, the Commission will take into account the additional production capacity created by the project and whether the market is underperforming.

129. If the market in question is growing, there is typically less cause for concern that the aid will negatively affect dynamic incentives or will unduly impede market exit or entry.

130. More concern is warranted when markets are in decline. The Commission distinguishes between cases for which, with a long-term outlook, the market is structurally in decline (i.e. it is contracting), and cases for which the market is in relative decline (i.e. it is still growing, but does not exceed a benchmark growth rate).

131. Underperformance of the market is typically measured against the EEA gross domestic product (GDP) over the three years before the start of the project (benchmark rate). It can also be measured on the basis of projected growth rates for the next three to five years. Indicators may include the expected future growth of the market concerned, the resulting expected capacity utilisation rates, and the likely impact of the capacity increase on competitors in terms of prices and profit margins.

132. In certain cases, assessing the growth of the product market in the EEA may not be appropriate to assess all the effects of aid, in particular if the geographic market is global. In such cases, the Commission will consider the effect of the aid on the market structures concerned, in particular, its potential to crowd out producers in the EEA.

133. To evaluate the existence of substantial market power, the Commission will take into account the position of the aid beneficiary over a period of time before receiving the aid and the expected market position after finalising the investment. The Commission will take account of market shares of the aid beneficiary, as well as of market shares of its competitors and other relevant factors. For example, it will assess the market structure by looking at market concentration, potential barriers to entry,[59] buyer power[60] and barriers to expansion or exit.

5.6.4.2. Scenario 2 situations (location decision)

134. If the counterfactual analysis suggests that without the aid the investment would have gone ahead in another location (scenario 2) in the same geographical market for the product concerned, and if the aid is proportional, the outcome in terms of overcapacity or substantial market power is in principle likely to be the same regardless of the aid. In such cases, the positive effects of the aid are likely to outweigh the limited negative effects on competition. However, if the alternative location is in the EEA, the Commission is particularly concerned with negative effects linked with the alternative location. Therefore, if the aid results in a manifest negative effect as described in paragraphs 117 and 118, it is unlikely to be compensated by any positive effects and thus is unlikely to be found compatible with the internal market.

5.6.5. Operating aid schemes

135. If the aid is necessary and proportional to achieve the contribution to regional development and territorial cohesion described in subsection 5.1.3, the negative effects of the aid on competition and trade between Member States are likely to be compensated by positive effects. However, in some cases, the aid may result in changes to the structure of the market or to the characteristics of a sector or industry which could significantly distort competition through barriers to market entry or exit, substitution effects, or displacement of trade flows. In those cases, the negative effects are unlikely to be compensated by any positive effects.

5.7. TRANSPARENCY

136. Member States must publish the following information in the European Commission's transparency award module[61] or on a comprehensive State aid website, at national or regional level:

(1) the full text of the individual aid granting decision or the approved aid scheme and its implementing provisions, or a link to it;

(2) information on each individual aid award exceeding EUR 100,000, using the structure in Annex VIII.

137. As regards aid granted to ETC projects, the information referred to in paragraph 136 must be placed on the website of the Member State in which the Managing Authority[62] concerned is located. Alternatively, the participating Member States may decide that each of them is to provide the information relating to the aid measures within their territory on the respective websites.

138. Member States must organise their comprehensive State aid websites, as referred to in paragraph 136, in such a way as to allow easy access to the information. Information must be published in a non-proprietary spreadsheet data format, which allows data to be effectively searched, extracted, downloaded and easily published on the internet, for instance in CSV or XML format. The general public must be allowed to access the website without any restrictions, including prior user registration.

139. For schemes in the form of tax advantages, the conditions set out in paragraph 136.2 will be considered to be fulfilled if Member States publish the required information on individual aid amounts in the following ranges (in EUR million):

0.1-0.5;
0.5-1;
1-2;
2-5;
5-10;
10-30;
30-60;
60-100;
100-250; and
250 and over.

140. The information referred to in paragraph 136.2 must be published within six months from the date of award of the aid, or, for aid in the form of tax advantages, within one year from the date the tax declaration is due.[63] For aid that is unlawful but subsequently found to be compatible, Member States must publish this information within six months from the date of the Commission's decision declaring the aid compatible. To enable the enforcement of State aid rules under the Treaty, the information must be available for at least 10 years from the date on which the aid was granted.

141. The Commission will publish on its website the link to the State aid website referred to in paragraph 136.

NOTES

36 See the Court judgments of 19 September 2000, *Germany v Commission*, C-156/98, ECLI:EU:C:2000:467, paragraph 78, and of 22 December 2008, *Régie Networks v Rhone Alpes Bourgogne*, C-333/07, ECLI-:EU:C:2008:764, paragraphs 94 to 116.

37 See Annex VII.

38 The obligation to maintain the investment in the area concerned for a minimum period of five years (three years for SMEs) should not prevent the replacement of plant or equipment that has become outdated or broken within this period,

provided that the economic activity is retained in the area concerned for the minimum period. However, regional aid may not be awarded to replace that plant or equipment.

39 The 25% own contribution requirement in paragraph 48 does not apply to investment aid granted for investments in outermost regions insofar as a lower contribution is necessary to fully accommodate the maximum aid intensity.

40 This is not the case for example for subsidised loans, public equity-capital loans or public participations which do not meet the market investor principle, State guarantees containing elements of aid, or public support granted within the scope of the *de minimis* rule.

41 Ad hoc aid is subject to the same requirements as individual aid granted on the basis of a scheme, unless otherwise mentioned.

42 Such investments may create the conditions for further investments that are viable without additional aid.

43 The counterfactual scenarios are described in paragraph 64.

44 The NPV of a project is the difference between the positive and negative cash flows over the lifetime of the investment, discounted to their current value (typically using the cost of capital).

45 The IRR is not based on accounting earnings in a given year, but takes into account the stream of future cash flows that the investor expects to receive over the entire lifetime of the investment. It is defined as the discount rate for which the NPV of a stream of cash flows equals zero.

46 However, where future costs and revenue developments are surrounded by a high degree of uncertainty and there is a strong asymmetry of information, the public authority may also wish to adopt compensation models that are not entirely *ex ante*, but a mix of *ex ante* and *ex post* (for example, using claw backs such as to allow sharing of unanticipated gains).

47 See Section 7.4 on regional aid maps.

48 Expressed as gross grant equivalent.

49 Idem.

50 When comparing counterfactual scenarios, the aid is to be discounted by the same factor as the corresponding investment and counterfactual scenarios.

51 The requirement that the maximum permissible aid intensity per project must be calculated in advance by the first granting authority does not apply when the aid is granted via automatic aid scheme(s) in the form of a tax advantage. In this situation, cumulation checks are in principle not possible when the aid is granted and should be carried out when the aid is paid out.

52 Regulation (EU) No 1299/2013 of the European Parliament and of the Council of 17 December 2013 on specific provisions for the support from the European Regional Development Fund to the European territorial cooperation goal (OJ L347, 20.12.2013, p 259) or a Regulation containing specific provisions for the European territorial cooperation goal (Interreg) applicable to the 2021-2027 programming period, whichever applies to a given initial investment.

53 Including when operating aid schemes are notified to prolong existing aid measures.

54 Regulation (EU) 2020/852 of the European Parliament and of the Council of 18 June 2020 on the establishment of a framework to facilitate sustainable investment, and amending Regulation (EU) 2019/2088 (OJ L198, 22.6.2020, p 13).

55 This could also be the case where the aid distorts the operation of economic instruments put in place to internalise such negative externalities (e.g. by affecting price signals given by the EU Emissions Trading System or a similar instrument).

56 The Commission will assess this both in terms of volume and value and will take into account the business cycle.

57 To verify this, the standard applicable aid ceiling in 'c' areas bordering 'a' areas should be used regardless of the increased aid intensities, in accordance with paragraph 184.

58 For investment projects that involve the production of several different products, each product must be assessed.

59 These entry barriers include legal barriers (in particular intellectual property rights), economies of scale and scope, and access barriers to networks and infrastructure. If the aid concerns a market where the aid beneficiary is an incumbent, potential barriers to entry may exacerbate the potential substantial market power wielded by the aid beneficiary and thus the possible negative effects of that market power.

60 Where there are strong buyers in the market, it is less likely that an aid beneficiary can increase prices vis-à-vis these strong buyers.

61 'State Aid Transparency Public Search', available at the following website: https://webgate.ec.europa.eu/competition/transparency/ public?lang=en.

62 As defined in Article 21 of Regulation (EC) No 1299/2013.

63 If there is no formal requirement for an annual declaration, 31 December of the year for which the aid was granted will be considered as the granting date for encoding purposes.

6. EVALUATION

[5.282]

142. To further ensure that distortion of competition and trade is limited, the Commission may require that aid schemes as referred to in paragraph 143 are subject to an ex post evaluation. Evaluations will be carried out for schemes where the potential distortion of competition and trade is particularly high, i.e. that may risk significantly restricting or distorting competition if implementation is not reviewed in due time.

143. *Ex post* evaluation may be required for schemes with large aid budgets, or containing novel characteristics, or when significant market, technology or regulatory changes are foreseen. In any case, evaluation will be required for schemes with a State aid budget or accounted expenditure over EUR 150 million in any given year or EUR 750 million over their total duration, i.e. the combined duration of the scheme and any predecessor scheme covering a similar objective and geographical area, starting from 1 January 2022. Given the objectives of the evaluation, and to avoid putting a disproportionate burden on Member States, ex post evaluations are only required for aid schemes the total duration of which exceeds three years, starting from 1 January 2022.

144. The *ex post* evaluation requirement may be waived for aid schemes that are an immediate successor of a scheme covering a similar objective and geographical area that has been subject to an evaluation, delivered a final evaluation report in compliance with the evaluation plan approved by the Commission and has not generated any negative findings. Where the final evaluation report of a scheme is not in compliance with the approved evaluation plan, that scheme must be suspended with immediate effect.

145. The aim of the evaluation should be to verify whether the assumptions and conditions underlying the compatibility of the scheme have been achieved, in particular the necessity and the effectiveness of the aid measure in the light of its general and specific objectives. It should also assess the impact of the scheme on competition and trade.

146. For aid schemes subject to the evaluation requirement according to paragraph 143, Member States must notify a draft evaluation plan, which will form an integral part of the Commission's assessment of the scheme, as follows:

(1) together with the aid scheme, if the State aid budget of the scheme exceeds EUR 150 million in any given year or EUR 750 million over its total duration;

(2) within 30 working days following a significant change that increases the budget of the scheme to over EUR 150 million in any given year or EUR 750 million over the total duration of the scheme;

(3) within 30 working days following the recording in official accounts of expenditure under the scheme in excess of EUR 150 million in any year.

147. The draft evaluation plan must be in line with the common methodological principles provided by the Commission.[64] Member States must publish the evaluation plan approved by the Commission.

148. The *ex post* evaluation must be carried out by an expert independent from the aid granting authority on the basis of the evaluation plan. Each evaluation must include at least one interim and one final evaluation report. Member States must publish both reports.

149. The final evaluation report must be submitted to the Commission in due time to assess any prolongation of the aid scheme and at the latest nine months before its expiry. That period may be reduced for schemes triggering the evaluation requirement in their last two years of implementation. The precise scope and arrangements for each evaluation will be set out in the decision approving the aid scheme. The notification of any subsequent aid measure with a similar objective must describe how the results of the evaluation have been taken into account.

NOTES

[64] Commission staff working document, Common methodology for State aid evaluation, Brussels, 28.5.2014, SWD(2014) 179 final, or any of its successors.

7. REGIONAL AID MAPS

[5.283]

150. In this section, the Commission lays down criteria for identifying the areas that fulfil the conditions of Article 107(3)(a) and (c) of the Treaty. The areas that fulfil those conditions and which Member States wish to designate as 'a' or 'c' areas[65] must be identified in a regional aid map which must be notified to and approved by the Commission before regional aid can be awarded to undertakings located in the designated areas.

151. The maps must also specify the maximum aid intensities that apply in those areas during the period of validity of the approved map.

152. To maintain the incentive effect of the aid, where aid applications for discretionary aid measures were introduced already before the start of the period of validity of the map, the 'aid amount deemed necessary' identified in the original aid application must not be amended retroactively after the start of works on the project to justify a higher aid intensity that might be available under these Guidelines.

153. For automatic aid schemes in the form of a tax advantage, the maximum aid intensities available under these Guidelines may only be applied to projects started on or after the date on which the increase of the relevant maximum aid intensity became applicable under the relevant national rules. For projects started before that date, the maximum aid intensity approved under the previous regional aid map will continue to apply.

7.1. POPULATION COVERAGE ELIGIBLE FOR REGIONAL AID

154. Given that the award of regional State aid derogates from the general prohibition of State aid laid down in Article 107(1) of the Treaty, the Commission considers that the combined population of 'a' and 'c' areas in the EU-27 must be lower than that in non-designated areas. The total coverage of designated areas should therefore be less than 50% of the EU-27's population.

155. In the Guidelines on regional State aid for 2014-2020[66] the overall coverage of 'a' and 'c' areas was set at 47% of the EU28 population. Given the withdrawal of the United Kingdom of Great Britain and Northern Ireland from the EU, the Commission considers that an increase to 48% of the overall EU-27 population coverage is appropriate.

156. Accordingly, the overall maximum coverage of 'a' and 'c' areas should be set at 48% of the EU-27 population.[67]

7.2. THE DEROGATION IN ARTICLE 107(3)(A)

157. Article 107(3)(a) of the Treaty provides that 'aid to promote the economic development of areas where the standard of living is abnormally low or where there is serious underemployment, and of the regions referred to in Article 349, in view of their structural, economic and social situation' may be considered to be compatible with the internal market. According to the Court of Justice, 'the use of the words "abnormally" and "serious" in Article (107)(3)(a) shows that the exemption concerns only areas where the economic situation is extremely unfavourable in relation to the [Union] as a whole'.[68]

158. The Commission considers that the conditions of Article 107(3)(a) of the Treaty are fulfilled in NUTS 2 regions that have a gross domestic product (GDP) per capita below or equal to 75% of the EU-27 average.[69]

159. Therefore Member States may designate the following areas as 'a' areas:

(1) NUTS 2 regions whose GDP per capita in purchasing power standard[70] is below or equal to 75% of the EU-27 average (based on the average of the last three years for which Eurostat data are available)[71];

(2) the outermost regions.

160. Annex I sets out the eligible 'a' areas by Member State. Some of those 'a' areas, at the level of NUTS 3, also qualify as sparsely populated areas under paragraph 166(2).

7.3. THE DEROGATION IN ARTICLE 107(3)(C)

161. Article 107(3)(c) of the Treaty provides that 'aid to facilitate the development of certain economic activities or of certain economic areas, where such aid does not adversely affect trading conditions to an extent contrary to the common interest' may be considered to be compatible with the internal market. According to the Court of Justice, '[t]he exemption in Article (107)(3)(c) [. . .] permits the development of certain areas without being restricted by the economic conditions laid down in Article [107](3)(a), provided such aid "does not adversely affect trading conditions to an extent contrary to the common interest. That provision gives the Commission power to authorise aid intended to further the economic development of areas of a Member State which are disadvantaged in relation to the national average"'.[72]

162. The maximum coverage for 'c' areas in the EU-27 ('"c" coverage') is obtained by subtracting the population of the eligible 'a' areas in the EU-27 from the overall maximum coverage laid down in paragraph 156.

163. There are two categories of 'c' areas:

(1) areas that fulfil certain set conditions and that a Member State may therefore designate as 'c' areas without any further justification ('predefined "c" areas');

(2) areas that a Member State may, at its own discretion, designate as 'c' areas provided that the Member State demonstrates that such areas fulfil certain socioeconomic criteria ('non-predefined "c" areas').

7.3.1. PREDEFINED 'C' AREAS

7.3.1.1.
Specific allocation of 'c' coverage for predefined 'c' areas

164. The Commission considers that Member States must have sufficient 'c' coverage to be able to designate as 'c' areas the areas which had 'a' status in the regional aid map in 2017-2020[73] but that no longer qualify as an 'a' area.

165. The Commission also considers that Member States must have sufficient 'c' coverage to be able to designate as 'c' areas the areas with low population density.

166. The following areas are considered as predefined 'c' areas:

(1) former 'a' areas: NUTS 2 regions designated as 'a' areas in 2017-2020;

(2) sparsely populated areas: NUTS 2 regions with fewer than 8 inhabitants per km^2 or NUTS 3 regions with fewer than 12.5 inhabitants per km2 (based on Eurostat data on population density for 2018).

167. Annex I sets out the specific allocation of predefined 'c' coverage by Member State. This population allocation may only be used to designate predefined 'c' areas.

7.3.1.2.
Designation of predefined 'c' areas

168. Member States may designate as 'c' areas the predefined 'c' areas referred to in paragraph 166.

169. For sparsely populated areas, Member States should in principle designate NUTS 2 regions with fewer than 8 inhabitants per km2 or NUTS 3 regions with fewer than 12.5 inhabitants per km2. However, Member States may designate parts of NUTS 3 regions with fewer than 12.5 inhabitants per km2 or other contiguous areas adjacent to those NUTS 3 regions, provided that these areas have fewer than 12.5 inhabitants per km2. For very sparsely populated areas, Member States may designate NUTS 2 regions with fewer than 8 inhabitants per km2 or other smaller contiguous areas adjacent to those NUTS 2 regions, provided that these areas have fewer than 8 inhabitants per km2 and that the population of the very sparsely populated areas taken together with the sparsely populated areas does not exceed the specific allocation of 'c' coverage referred to in paragraph 167.

7.3.2. NON-PREDEFINED 'C' AREAS

7.3.2.1.
Method for allocating non-predefined 'c' coverage among Member States

170. The maximum coverage for non-predefined 'c' areas in the EU-27 is obtained by subtracting the population of the eligible 'a' areas and of the predefined 'c' areas from the overall maximum coverage laid down in paragraph 156. The non-predefined 'c' coverage is allocated among the EU-27 by applying the method set out in Annex III.

7.3.2.2.
Safety net and minimum population coverage

171. To ensure continuity in the regional aid maps and a minimum scope of action for all Member States, the Commission considers that no Member State should lose more than 30% of its total coverage compared to the period 2017-2020 and that all Member States should have a minimum population coverage.

172. Therefore, by way of derogation from the overall maximum coverage laid down in paragraph 156, the 'c' coverage for each Member State is increased as necessary so that:

(1) the total 'a' and 'c' coverage of each Member State concerned is not reduced by more than 30% compared to the period 2017-2020;[74]

(2) all Member States have a population coverage of at least 7.5% of the national population[75].

173. Annex I and II set out the non-predefined 'c' coverage, including the safety net and the minimum population coverage, by Member State.

7.3.2.3.
Designation of non-predefined 'c' areas

174. The Commission considers that the criteria used by Member States for designating 'c' areas should reflect the range of situations in which granting regional aid may be justified. The criteria should therefore address the socioeconomic, geographical or structural problems likely to be encountered in 'c' areas and should provide sufficient safeguards that granting regional State aid will not affect trading conditions to an extent contrary to the common interest.

175. Therefore, Member States may designate as 'c' areas the non-predefined 'c' areas defined on the basis of the following criteria:

(1) Criterion 1: contiguous areas of at least 100,000 inhabitants.[76] These are to be located in NUTS 2 or NUTS 3 regions that have:
 (i) a GDP per capita below or equal to the EU-27 average; or
 (ii) an unemployment rate above or equal to 115% of the national average.[77]

(2) Criterion 2: NUTS 3 regions of fewer than 100,000 inhabitants that have:
 (i) a GDP per capita below or equal to the EU-27 average; or
 (ii) an unemployment rate above or equal to 115% of the national average.

(3) Criterion 3: islands or contiguous areas characterised by similar geographical isolation (for example, peninsulas or mountain areas) that have:
 (i) a GDP per capita below or equal to the EU-27 average;[78] or
 (ii) an unemployment rate above or equal to 115% of the national average;[79] or
 (iii) fewer than 5,000 inhabitants.

(4) Criterion 4: NUTS 3 regions, or parts of NUTS 3 regions that form contiguous areas, that are adjacent to an 'a' area or that share a land border with a country outside the EEA or the European Free Trade Association (EFTA).

(5) Criterion 5: contiguous areas of at least 50,000 inhabitants[80] that are undergoing major structural change or are in serious relative decline, provided that such areas are not located in NUTS 3 regions or contiguous areas that fulfil the conditions to be designated as predefined areas or under Criteria 1 to 4.[81]

176. For the purpose of applying the criteria set out in paragraph 175, the concept of contiguous areas refers to whole local administrative units (LAU)[82] or to a group of LAU.[83] A group of LAU will be considered to form a contiguous area if each area in the group shares an administrative border with another area in the group.[84]

177. Compliance with the population coverage allowed for each Member State will be assessed on the basis of the most recent data on the total resident population of the areas concerned, as published by the national statistical office.

7.4. MAXIMUM AID INTENSITIES APPLICABLE TO REGIONAL INVESTMENT AID

178. The Commission considers that the maximum aid intensities applicable to regional investment aid must take into account the nature and scope of the disparities between the levels of development of the different areas in the EU. The aid intensities should therefore be higher in 'a' areas than in 'c' areas.

7.4.1. MAXIMUM AID INTENSITIES IN 'A' AREAS

179. The aid intensity for large enterprises in 'a' areas must not exceed:

(1) 50% in NUTS 2 regions whose GDP per capita is below or equal to 55% of the EU-27 average;
(2) 40% in NUTS 2 regions whose GDP per capita is above 55% and below or equal to 65% of the EU-27 average;
(3) 30% in NUTS 2 regions with a GDP per capita above 65% of the EU-27 average.

180. The aid intensities set in paragraph 179 may be increased by up to 20 percentage points in outermost regions that have a GDP per capita below or equal to 75% of the EU-27 average or by up to 10 percentage points in other outermost regions.

181. The aid intensities set in paragraph 179 may also be increased in the areas referred to in Sections 7.4.4 and 7.4.5 to the extent that the aid intensity for large enterprises in the area concerned does not exceed 70%.

7.4.2. MAXIMUM AID INTENSITIES IN 'C' AREAS

182. The aid intensity for large enterprises must not exceed:

(1) 20% in sparsely populated areas and in areas (NUTS 3 regions or parts of NUTS 3 regions) that share a land border with a country outside the EEA or the EFTA;
(2) 15% in former 'a' areas;
(3) 10% in non-predefined 'c' areas that have a GDP per capita above 100% of the EU-27 average and an unemployment rate below 100% of the EU-27 average;
(4) 15% in other non-predefined 'c' areas.

183. In former 'a' areas, the aid intensity of 15% set in paragraph 182(2) may be increased by up to 5 percentage points until 31 December 2024.

184. If a 'c' area is adjacent to an 'a' area, the aid intensities set in paragraph 182 in the NUTS 3 regions or parts of NUTS 3 regions within that 'c' area which are adjacent to the 'a' area may be increased as necessary so that the difference in aid intensity between the two areas does not exceed 15 percentage points.

185. The aid intensities set in paragraph 182 may also be increased in the areas referred to in Section 7.4.5.

7.4.3. INCREASED AID INTENSITIES FOR SMES

186. The aid intensities laid down in subsections 7.4.1 and 7.4.2 may be increased by up to 20 percentage points for small enterprises or by up to 10 percentage points for medium-sized enterprises.[85]

7.4.4. Increased aid intensities for territories identified for support from the JTF[86]

187. The maximum aid intensities laid down in subsection 7.4.1 may be increased by 10 percentage points for territories identified for support from the JTF in a territorial just transition plan of a Member State approved by the Commission on the condition that those territories are located in assisted areas according to Article 107(3)(a) of the Treaty.[87]

7.4.5. Increased aid intensities for regions experiencing population loss

188. The maximum aid intensities laid down in subsection 7.4.1 may be increased by 10 percentage points and the maximum aid intensities laid down in subsection 7.4.2 may be increased by 5 percentage points for NUTS 3 regions experiencing population loss of more than 10% over the period 2009-2018.[88]

7.5. NOTIFICATION OF REGIONAL AID MAPS AND THEIR ASSESSMENT

189. Following the publication of these Guidelines in the *Official Journal of the European Union*, each Member State should notify to the Commission a single regional aid map applicable from 1 January 2022 to 31 December 2027. Each notification should include the information specified in Annex V.

190. The Commission will examine for each Member State its notified regional aid map and, if the map meets the conditions laid down in these Guidelines, it will adopt a decision approving it. All regional aid maps will be published in the Official Journal of the European Union and will constitute an integral part of these Guidelines.

7.6. AMENDMENTS

7.6.1. Population reserve

191. On its own initiative, a Member State may decide to establish a reserve of national population coverage consisting of the difference between the maximum population coverage for that Member State, as allocated by the Commission,[89] and the coverage used for the 'a' and 'c' areas designated in its regional aid map.

192. If a Member State decides to create this reserve, it may, at any time, use the reserve to add new 'c' areas in its map until it reaches the national maximum coverage. For this purpose, the Member State may use the most recent socioeconomic data provided by Eurostat or by its national statistical office or other recognised sources. The population of the 'c' areas concerned should be calculated on the basis of the population data used to draw up the initial map.

193. The Member State must notify the Commission each time it intends to use its population reserve to add new 'c' areas before making such amendments.

7.6.2. Mid-term review

194. A mid-term review of the regional aid maps, taking into account updated statistics, will be carried out in 2023. By June 2023, the Commission will communicate the details on that mid-term review.

NOTES

65 Sparsely populated and very sparsely populated areas should also be identified on the regional aid map.

66 OJ C209, 23.7.2013, p 1.

67 This ceiling is set using Eurostat population data for 2018. The ceiling will correspond to 48.00% of the EU27_2020 – (European Union – 27 countries (from 2020)).

68 Judgment of 14 October 1987, *Germany v Commission*, Case 248/84, EU:C:1987:437, paragraph 19; judgment of 14 January 1997, *Spain v Commission*, C-169/95, EU:C:1997:10, paragraph 15; and judgment of 7 March 2002, *Italy v Commission*, C-310/99, EU:C:2002:143, paragraph 77.

69 The reference to regions with a GDP per capita below 75% of the EU-27 average was made in the Commission communication on the method for the application of Article 92(3)(a) and (c) to regional aid (OJ C212, 12.8.1988, p 2).

70 In all subsequent references to GDP per capita, GDP is measured in PPS.

71 The data cover the period 2016-2018. In all subsequent references to GDP per capita in relation to the EU-27 average, data are based on the average of Eurostat regional data for 2016-2018 (as updated on 23.3.2020).

72 *Germany v Commission*, Case 248/84, *op. cit.*, paragraph 19.

73 The list of 'a' areas was amended in 2016. See Communication from the Commission amending Annex I to the Guidelines on regional State aid for 2014-2020 (Mid-term review of the regional aid maps) (OJ C231, 25.6.2016, p 1).

74 This aspect of the safety net applies to Germany, Ireland, Malta and Slovenia.

75 This minimum population coverage applies to Denmark and Luxembourg.

76 This population threshold will be reduced to 50,000 inhabitants for Member States that have a non-predefined 'c' coverage of less than 1 million inhabitants or to 10,000 inhabitants for Member States whose national population is below 1 million inhabitants.

77 For unemployment, calculations should be based on regional data published by the national statistical office, using the average of the last three years for which such data are available (at the moment of the notification of the regional aid map). Except as otherwise indicated in these Guidelines, the unemployment rate in relation to the national average is calculated on this basis.

78 To calculate whether such islands or contiguous areas have a GDP per capita below or equal to the EU-27 average, the Member State may use data provided by their national statistical office or other recognised sources.

79 To calculate whether such islands or contiguous areas have an unemployment rate above or equal to 115% of the national average, Member States may use data provided by their national statistical office or other recognised sources.

80 This population threshold will be reduced to 25,000 inhabitants for Member States that have a non-predefined 'c' coverage of fewer than 1 million inhabitants, to 10,000 inhabitants for Member States whose total population is below 1 million inhabitants, or to 5,000 inhabitants for islands or contiguous areas characterised by similar geographical isolation.

81 For the purpose of applying Criterion 5, Member States must demonstrate that the area is undergoing major structural change or is in serious relative decline by comparing the areas concerned with the situation of other areas in the same

Member State or in other Member States on the basis of socioeconomic indicators concerning structural business statistics, labour markets, household accounts, education, or other similar indicators. For this purpose, Member States may use data provided by their national statistical office or other recognised sources. For territories identified for support from the JTF in a territorial just transition plan of a Member State approved by the Commission, this justification is not required as the structural change is considered to be demonstrated as part of the just transition plan.

82 The Local Administrative Units (LAU) are defined in Annex III of Regulation (EC) No 1059/2003 of the European Parliament and of the Council on the establishment of a common classification of territorial units for statistics (NUTS) as amended by the Commission Delegated Regulation (EU) 2019/1755.

83 The Member State may nevertheless designate parts of a LAU, provided that the population of the LAU concerned exceeds the minimum population required for contiguous areas under Criteria 1 or 5 (including the reduced population thresholds for those criteria) and that the population of the parts of that LAU is at least 50% of the minimum population required under the applicable criterion.

84 For islands, administrative borders include maritime borders with other administrative units of the Member State concerned.

85 The increased aid intensities for SMEs will not apply to aid awarded for large investment projects.

86 This section will only apply if a regulation is adopted following the Commission's proposal referred to in footnote 12.

87 The regional aid maps can be updated on that basis if the areas are not yet known when the map is adopted.

88 See Annex IV.

89 See Annex I.

8. AMENDMENT OF THE GUIDELINES ON REGIONAL STATE AID FOR 2014-2020

[5.284]

195. In its notification under paragraph 189, a Member State may also include an amendment to its regional aid map for 2014-2021[90] to replace the areas eligible for aid under the Guidelines on regional State aid for 2014-2020 with the areas eligible for aid in the map to be approved by the Commission under paragraph 190 of these Guidelines. The reviewed regional aid map will be valid from the date of adoption of the Commission decision on the notified amendment of the regional aid map for 2014-2021 until 31 December 2021. That decision will also indicate the maximum aid intensities applicable in the areas eligible for aid under the amended regional aid map for 2014-2021, corresponding to the maximum aid intensities set out in the Guidelines on regional State aid for 2014-2020. The amended map will constitute an integral part of the Guidelines on regional State aid for 2014-2020, in line with paragraph 179 of those Guidelines.

196. The Guidelines on regional State aid for 2014-2020 are amended as follows:

(1) paragraph 20(r) is replaced with the following:

'"regional aid map" means the list of areas designated by a Member State in line with the conditions laid down in these Guidelines, or the Guidelines on regional State aid applicable as from 1 January 2022, and approved by the Commission;';

(2) the following paragraph 185a is inserted after paragraph 185:

'5.6.3. AMENDMENT FOLLOWING THE GUIDELINES ON REGIONAL STATE AID APPLICABLE AS FROM 1 JANUARY 2022

185a. A Member State may request an amendment to its regional aid map in line with Section 7.6 of the Guidelines on regional State aid applicable as from 1 January 2022.'

NOTES

90 The regional aid map approved by the Commission under the Guidelines on regional State aid for 2014-2020 that is applicable for the period 1 July 2014 to 31 December 2021.

9. APPLICABILITY OF REGIONAL AID RULES

[5.285]

197. The Commission will apply the principles set out in these Guidelines to assess the compatibility of all notifiable regional aid awarded or intended to be awarded after 31 December 2021.

198. Notifications of regional aid schemes or of aid measures to be awarded after 31 December 2021 cannot be considered complete until the Commission has adopted a decision approving the regional aid map for the Member State concerned, in line with the arrangements described in subsection 7.5.

199. The implementation of these Guidelines will lead to some changes in the rules applicable to regional aid in the EU. Therefore, it is necessary to review the continuing justification for and effectiveness of all existing[91] regional aid schemes, including investment aid and operating aid schemes, that are due to extend beyond 2021.

200. For these reasons, the Commission proposes the following appropriate measures to Member States, under Article 108(1) of the Treaty:

(1) Member States must limit the application of all existing regional aid schemes to aid intended to be awarded by 31 December 2021 at the latest;

(2) Member States must amend other existing horizontal aid schemes that give specific treatment for aid to projects in assisted areas in order to ensure that aid to be awarded after 31 December 2021 is in line with the regional aid map applicable on the date the aid is awarded;

(3) Member States should confirm acceptance of the measures proposed in points (1) and (2) within one month of publication of these Guidelines in the *Official Journal of the European Union*.

NOTES

91 Aid measures put into effect under the GBER do not qualify as existing aid schemes. Aid schemes put into effect in breach of Article 108(3) of the Treaty do not qualify as existing aid schemes except when they are deemed to be existing

aid under Article 17(3) of Council Regulation (EU) 2015/1589 of 13 July 2015 laying down detailed rules for the application of Article 108 of the Treaty on the Functioning of the European Union (OJ L248, 24.9.2015, p 9).

10. REPORTING AND MONITORING

[5.286]

201. Under Council Regulation (EU) 2015/1589[92] and Commission Regulation (EC) No 794/2004,[93] Member States must submit annual reports to the Commission.

202. Member States must maintain detailed records regarding all aid measures. These records must contain all information necessary to establish that the conditions regarding eligible costs and maximum aid intensities have been fulfilled. Member States must maintain those records for 10 years from the date of award of the aid and must provide them to the Commission upon request.

NOTES

[92] Council Regulation (EU) 2015/1589.

[93] Commission Regulation (EC) No 794/2004 of 21 April 2004 implementing Council Regulation (EC) No 659/1999 laying down detailed rules for the application of Article 93 of the EC Treaty (OJ L140, 30.4.2004, p 1).

11. REVISION

[5.287]

203. The Commission may decide to modify these Guidelines at any time if necessary for reasons associated with competition policy or to take account of other EU policies and international commitments or for any other justified reason.

ANNEX I
REGIONAL AID COVERAGE BY MEMBER STATE FOR 2022–2027

[5.288]

Belgium	**NUTS regions**	**GDP per capita**[1]	**Percentage of national population**[2]
'a' areas	BE34 Prov. Luxembourg (BE)	73.00	2.50%
Non-predefined 'c' areas	—	—	23.33%
Total population coverage 2022-2027	—	—	25.83%

Bulgaria	**NUTS regions**	**GDP per capita**	**Percentage of national population**
'a' areas	BG31 Северозападен / Severozapaden	31.67	10.66%
	BG32 Северен централен / Severen tsentralen	34.33	11.24%
	BG33 Североизточен / Severoiztochen	40.33	13.26%
	BG34 Югоизточен / Yugoiztochen	43.00	14.74%
	BG42 Южен централен / Yuzhen tsentralen	35.00	20.13%
Predefined 'c' areas (former 'a' areas)	BG41 Югозападен / Yugozapaden	81.33	29.97%
Total population coverage 2022-2027	—	—	100.00%

Czechia	**NUTS regions**	**GDP per capita**	**Percentage of national population**
'a' areas	CZ04 Severozápad	63.67	10.50%
	CZ05 Severovýchod	75.00	14.22%
	CZ07 Střední Morava	73.33	11.43%
	CZ08 Moravskoslezsko	74.33	11.33%
Predefined 'c' areas (former 'a' areas)	CZ02 Střední Cechy	82.67	12.81%
	CZ03 Jihozápad	78.00	11.52%
	CZ06 Jihovýchod	82.67	15.94%
Total population coverage 2022-2027	—	—	87.76%

Denmark	**NUTS regions**	**GDP per capita**	**Percentage of national population**
Non-predefined 'c' areas	—	—	7.50%
Total population coverage 2022-2027	—	—	7.50%

Germany	**NUTS regions**	**GDP per capita**	**Percentage of national population**
Non-predefined 'c' areas	—	—	18.10%
Total population coverage 2022-2027	—	—	18.10%

Estonia	**NUTS regions**	**GDP per capita**	**Percentage of national population**
Predefined 'c' areas (former 'a' areas)	EE00 Eesti	79.33	100.00%
Total population coverage 2022-2027	—	—	100.00%

Ireland	**NUTS regions**	**GDP per capita**	**Percentage of national population**
Non-predefined 'c' areas	—	—	35.90%
Total population coverage 2022-2027	—	—	35.90%

Greece	**NUTS regions**	**GDP per capita**	**Percentage of national population**
'a' areas	EL41 Βόρειο Αιγαίο / Voreio Aigaio	49.00	2.01%
	EL42 Νότιο Αιγαίο / Notio Aigaio	73.67	3.19%
	EL43 Κρήτη / Kriti	58.33	5.91%
	EL51 Ανατολική Μακεδονία, Θράκη / Anatoliki Makedonia. Thraki	47.67	5.59%
	EL52 Κεντρική Μακεδονία / Kentriki Makedonia	53.67	17.47%
	EL53 Δυτική Μακεδονία / Dytiki Makedonia	59.67	2.50%
	EL54 Ήπειρος / Ipeiros	48.67	3.11%
	EL61 Θεσσαλία / Thessalia	52.67	6.71%
	EL62 Ιόνια Νησιά / Ionia Nisia	63.33	1.90%
	EL63 Δυτική Ελλάδα / Dytiki Elláda [EL643 Ευρυτανία / Evrytania Sparsely populated area]	50.33	6.12%
	EL64 Στερεά Ελλάδα / Sterea Elláda	62.33	5.18%
	EL65 Πελοπόννησος / Peloponnisos	56.67	5.36%
Non-predefined 'c' areas	—	—	17.28%
Total population coverage 2022-2027			82.34%

Spain	**NUTS regions**	**GDP per capita**	**Percentage of national population**
'a' areas	ES42 Castilla-La Mancha [ES423 Cuenca Sparsely Populated Area]	72.33	4.35%
	ES43 Extremadura	66.67	2.28%

Spain	NUTS regions	GDP per capita	Percentage of national population
	ES61 Andalucía	68.33	17.99%
	ES63 Ciudad de Ceuta	72.67	0.18%
	ES64 Ciudad de Melilla	67.00	0.18%
	ES70 Canarias	75.00	4.68%
Predefined 'c' areas (former 'a' areas)	ES62 Región de Murcia	76.67	3.17%
Predefined 'c' areas (sparsely populated areas)	ES242 Teruel	—	0.29%
	ES417 Soria	—	0.19%
Non-predefined 'c' areas	—	—	32.99%
Total population coverage 2022-2027	—	—	66.29%
Spain	NUTS regions	GDP per capita	Percentage of national population
'a' areas	ES42 Castilla-La Mancha [ES423 Cuenca Sparsely Populated Area]	72.33	4.35%
	ES43 Extremadura	66.67	2.28%
	ES61 Andalucía	68.33	17.99%
	ES63 Ciudad de Ceuta	72.67	0.18%
	ES64 Ciudad de Melilla	67.00	0.18%
	ES70 Canarias	75.00	4.68%
Predefined 'c' areas (former 'a' areas)	ES62 Región de Murcia	76.67	3.17%
Predefined 'c' areas (sparsely populated areas)	ES242 Teruel	—	0.29%
	ES417 Soria	—	0.19%
Non-predefined 'c' areas	—	—	32.99%
Total population coverage 2022-2027	—	—	66.29%

France	NUTS regions	GDP per capita	Percentage of national population
'a' areas	FRY1 Guadeloupe	73.00	0.63%
	FRY2 Martinique	77.00	0.55%
	FRY3 Guyane	50.33	0.42%
	FRY4 La Réunion	70.00	1.28%
	FRY5 Mayotte	32.67:	0.40%:
	Saint-Martin *	:	:
Non-predefined 'c' areas	—	—	28.68%
Total population coverage 2022-2027	—	—	31.95%

Croatia	NUTS regions	GDP per capita	Percentage of national population
'a' areas	HR02 Panonska Hrvatska	41.58	27.02%
	HR03 Jadranska Hrvatska [HR032 Licko-senjska županija Sparsely Populated Area]	60.33	33.48%
	HR06 Sjeverna Hrvatska	48.43	20.04%
Predefined 'c' areas (former 'a' areas)	HR05 Grad Zagreb	109.24	19.46%
Total population coverage 2022-2027	—	—	100.00%

Italy	NUTS regions	GDP per capita	Percentage of national population
'a' areas	ITF2 Molise	69.33	0.51%
	ITF3 Campania	62.67	9.62%

Italy	**NUTS regions**	**GDP per capita**	**Percentage of national population**
	ITF4 Puglia	63.33	6.68%
	ITF5 Basilicata	74.67	0.94%
	ITF6 Calabria	57.33	3.23%
	ITG1 Sicilia	59.67	8.30%
	ITG2 Sardegna	70.33	2.72%
Non-predefined 'c' areas	—	—	9.99%
Total population coverage 2022-2027	—	—	41.99%

Cyprus	**NUTS regions**	**GDP per capita**	**Percentage of national population**
Non-predefined 'c' areas	—	—	49.46%
Total population coverage 2022-2027	—	—	49.46%

Latvia	**NUTS regions**	**GDP per capita**	**Percentage of national population**
'a' areas	LV00 Latvija [LV008 Vidzeme Sparsely Populated Area]	67.00	100.00%
Total population coverage 2022-2027	—	—	100.00%

Lithuania	**NUTS regions**	**GDP per capita**	**Percentage of national population**
'a' areas	LT02 Vidurio ir vakaru Lietuvos regionas	65.00	71.16%
Predefined 'c' areas (former 'a' areas)	LT01 Sostines regionas	113.67	28.84%
Total population coverage 2022-2027	—	—	100.00%

Luxembourg	**NUTS regions**	**GDP per capita**	**Percentage of national population**
Non-predefined 'c' areas	—	—	7.50%
Total population coverage 2022-2027	—	—	7.50%

Hungary	**NUTS regions**	**GDP per capita**	**Percentage of national population**
'a' areas	HU12 Pest	55.00	13.00%
	HU21 Közép-Dunántúl	65.33	10.81%
	HU22 Nyugat-Dunántúl	72.67	10.10%
	HU23 Dél-Dunántúl	47.33	9.03%
	HU31 Észak-Magyarország	47.67	11.57%
	HU32 Észak-Alföld	44.33	14.89%
	HU33 Dél-Alföld	50.00	12.69%
Total population coverage 2022-2027	—	—	82.09%

Malta	**NUTS regions**	**GDP per capita**	**Percentage of national population**
Non-predefined 'c' areas	—		70.00%
Total population coverage 2022-2027	—		70.00%

Netherlands	**NUTS regions**	**GDP per capita**	**Percentage of national population**
Non-predefined 'c' areas	—	—	8.98%

Netherlands	NUTS regions	GDP per capita	Percentage of national population
Total population coverage 2022-2027	—	—	8.98%

Austria	NUTS regions	GDP per capita	Percentage of national population
Non-predefined 'c' areas	—	—	22.42%
Total population coverage 2022-2027	—	—	22.42%

Poland	NUTS regions	GDP per capita	Percentage of national population
'a' areas	PL21 Malopolskie	63.67	8.84%
	PL22 Śląskie	72.33	11.82%
	PL42 Zachodniopomorskie	58.33	4.43%
	PL43 Lubuskie	58.00	2.64%
	PL52 Opolskie	55.33	2.57%
	PL61 Kujawsko-Pomorskie	56.33	5.41%
	PL62 Warmińsko-Mazurskie	49.00	3.73%
	PL63 Pomorskie	67.67	6.06%
	PL71 Łódzkie	65.00	6.43%
	PL72 Świętokrzyskie	50.00	3.24%
	PL81 Lubelski	47.67	5.52%
	PL82 Podkarpackie	49.33	5.54%
	PL84 Podlaskie	49.67	3.08%
	PL92 Mazowiecki regionalny	59.33	6.12%
Predefined 'c' areas (former 'a' areas)	PL41 Wielkopolskie	75.67	9.09%
	PL51 Dolnośląskie	77.00	7.55%
Non-predefined 'c' areas	—	—	0.82%
Total population coverage 2022-2027	—	—	92.90%

Portugal	NUTS regions	GDP per capita	Percentage of national population
'a' areas	PT11 Norte	65.67	34.76%
	PT16 Centro (PT)	67.33	21.63%
	PT18 Alentejo	72.67	6.89%
	PT20 Região Autónoma dos Açores	69.00	2.37%
	PT30 Região Autónoma da Madeira	76.00	2.47%
Non-predefined 'c' areas	—	—	2.11%
Total population coverage 2022-2027	—	—	70.23%

Romania	NUTS regions	GDP per capita	Percentage of national population
'a' areas	RO11 Nord-Vest	58.33	13.13%
	RO12 Centru	60.00	11.93%
	RO21 Nord-Est	39.67	16.48%
	RO22 Sud-Est	52.67	12.37%
	RO31 Sud – Muntenia	49.33	15.14%
	RO41 Sud-Vest Oltenia	46.67	9.96%
	RO42 Vest	66.00	9.15%
Non-predefined 'c' areas	—	—	1.19%
Total population coverage 2022-2027	—	—	89.34%

Slovenia	**NUTS regions**	**GDP per capita**	**Percentage of national population**
'a' areas	SI03 Vzhodna Slovenija	70.67	52.71%
Non-predefined 'c' areas	—	—	17.29%
Total population coverage 2022-2027	—	—	70.00%

Slovakia	**NUTS regions**	**GDP per capita**	**Percentage of national population**
'a' areas	SK02 Západné Slovensko	66.67	33.55%
	SK03 Stredné Slovensko	58.00	24.60%
	SK04 Východné Slovensko	52.00	29.82%
Total population coverage 2022-2027	—	—	87.97%

Finland	**NUTS regions**	**GDP per capita**	**Percentage of national population**
Predefined 'c' areas (sparsely populated areas)	FI1D1 Etelä-Savo	—	2.67%
	FI1D2 Pohjois-Savo	—	4.46%
	FI1D3 Pohjois-Karjala	—	2.95%
	FI1D5 Keski-Pohjanmaa	—	1.24%
	FI1D7 Lappi	—	3.24%
	FI1D8 Kainuu	—	1.34%
	FI1D9 Pohjois-Pohjanmaa	—	7.43%
Non-predefined 'c' areas	—	—	3.52%
Total population coverage 2022-2027	—	—	26.86%

Sweden	**NUTS regions**	**GDP per capita**	**Percentage of national population**
Predefined 'c' areas (sparsely populated areas)	SE312 Dalarnas län	—	2.81%
	SE321 Västernorrlands län	—	2.42%
	SE322 Jämtlands län	—	1.27%
	SE331 Västerbottens län	—	2.63%
	SE332 Norrbottens län	—	2.48%
Non-predefined 'c' areas	—	—	9.98%
Total population coverage 2022-2027	—	—	21.60%

NOTES

[1] Measured in PPS, three-year average for 2016-2018 (EU-27 = 100) (as updated on 23.3.2020).

[2] Based on Eurostat population data for 2018.

ANNEX II
REGIONAL AID COVERAGE FOR NORTHERN IRELAND

[5.289]

Northern Ireland*	**NUTS regions**	**GDP per capita**	**Percentage of population[1]**
Non-predefined 'c' areas	—	—	100.00%
Total population coverage 2022-2027	—	—	100.00%

* These Guidelines apply also to Northern Ireland as agreed within the Protocol on Ireland/Northern Ireland annexed to the Withdrawal Agreement (Agreement on the withdrawal of the United Kingdom of Great Britain and Northern Ireland from the European Union and the European Atomic Energy Community (OJ L29, 31.1.2020, p 7).

NOTES

[1] To ensure continuity in the regional aid map of Northern Ireland in light of the structural impact of the withdrawal of the United Kingdom from the European Union, Northern Ireland should exceptionally keep its current coverage (100%).

ANNEX III
METHOD TO BE USED FOR ALLOCATING NON-PREDEFINED 'C' COVERAGE AMONG MEMBER STATES

[5.290]

The Commission will calculate the non-predefined 'c' coverage for each Member State by applying the following method:

(1) The Commission will identify any NUTS 3 regions in the Member States that are not in any of the following areas:
- eligible 'a' areas set out in Annex I;
- former 'a' areas set out in Annex I;
- sparsely populated areas set out in Annex I.

(2) Among the NUTS 3 regions identified under Step 1, the Commission will identify those that have either:
- a GDP per capita[1] below or equal to the national GDP per capita disparity threshold[2] or;
- an unemployment[3] rate above or equal to the national unemployment disparity threshold,[4] or above or equal to 150% of the national average or;
- a GDP per capita below or equal to 90% of the EU-27 average or;
- an unemployment rate above or equal to 125% of the EU-27 average.

(3) The allocation of non-predefined 'c' coverage for Member State *i* (A^i) is calculated by using the following formula (expressed as a percentage of the EU-27 population):

$A_i = p_i / P \times 100$ where:

p_i is the population[5] of the NUTS 3 regions in Member State *i* identified under Step 2.

P is the sum of the population of the NUTS 3 regions in the EU-27 identified under Step 2.

NOTES

1 All GDP per capita referred to in this Annex are based on the average over the last three years for which Eurostat data are available, i.e. 2016-2018.

2 The national GDP per capita disparity threshold for Member State i (TGi) is calculated using the following formula (expressed as a percentage of national GDP per capita):
$(TG)_i = 85 \times ((1 + 100 / g_i) / 2)$
where: g_i is the GDP per capita of Member State i, expressed as a percentage of the EU-27 average.

3 All unemployment data referred to in this Annex are based on the average of the last three years for which Eurostat data are available, i.e. 2017-2019. However, these data do not contain information at NUTS 3 level and therefore unemployment data for the NUTS 2 region in which those NUTS 3 regions are located are used.

4 The national unemployment rate disparity threshold for Member State i (TUi) is calculated using the following formula (expressed as a percentage of the national unemployment rate):
$(TU)_i = 115 \times ((1 + 100 / ui) / 2)$
where: u_i is the national unemployment rate of Member State i, expressed as a percentage of the EU-27 average.

5 Population figures for NUTS 3 regions are calculated on the basis of the population data used by Eurostat to calculate the regional GDP per capita for 2018.

ANNEX IV
METHOD TO DEFINE ASSISTED AREAS EXPERIENCING POPULATION LOSS AS REFERRED TO IN SECTION 7.4.5

[5.291]

In accordance with paragraph 188, Member States may identify the areas experiencing a population loss as follows:
- Member States must identify assisted areas at the level of NUTS3 under Article 107(3) (a) and (c) of the Treaty;
- Eurostat data on population density for the period 2009-2018 must be used, based on the most recent NUTS classification available;
- Member States must demonstrate a population loss of more than 10% over the period 2009-2018.
- Where the NUTS classification was changed during the previous 10 years, then Member States must use the data on population density for the longest available time period.

Member States must include the areas thus identified when issuing a notification under paragraph 189.

ANNEX V
INFORMATION TO BE PROVIDED WHEN NOTIFYING A REGIONAL AID MAP

[5.292]

(1) Member States must provide information for each of the following categories of areas proposed for designation, if applicable:
- 'a' areas;
- former 'a' areas;
- sparsely populated areas;
- very sparsely populated areas;
- territories identified for support from the Just Transition Fund as referred to in section 7.4.4;
- assisted areas experiencing population loss as referred to in section 7.4.5;
- non-predefined areas 'c' areas designated on the basis of Criterion 1;
- non-predefined areas 'c' areas designated on the basis of Criterion 2;
- non-predefined areas 'c' areas designated on the basis of Criterion 3;
- non-predefined areas 'c' areas designated on the basis of Criterion 4;
- non-predefined areas 'c' areas designated on the basis of Criterion 5;

(2) Under each category, Member States must provide the following information for each proposed area:

- identification of the area (using the NUTS 2 or NUTS 3 region code of the area, the LAU code of the areas that form the contiguous area or other official denominations of the administrative units concerned);
- the proposed aid intensity in the area for the period 2022-2027 or, for former 'a' areas, for the periods 2022-2024 and 2025-2027 (indicating any increase of aid intensity as under paragraphs 180, 181, 183 or 184, 185 and 186, if applicable);
- the total resident population of the area, as stated in paragraph 177.

(3) For the designation of sparsely and very sparsely populated areas, Member States must provide sufficient proof that the applicable conditions in paragraph 169 are met.

(4) For non-predefined areas designated on the basis of Criteria 1-5, Member States must provide sufficient proof that all applicable conditions laid down in paragraphs 175, 176 and 177 are met.

ANNEX VI
DEFINITION OF THE STEEL SECTOR

[5.293]

For the purpose of these Guidelines, 'steel sector' means the production of one or more of the following:

(a) pig iron and ferro-alloys: pig iron for steelmaking, foundry and other pig iron, spiegeleisen and high-carbon ferro-manganese, not including other ferro-alloys;

(b) crude and semi-finished products of iron, ordinary steel or special steel: liquid steel cast or not cast into ingots, including ingots for forging semi-finished products: blooms, billets and slabs; sheet bars and tinplate bars; hot-rolled wide coils, with the exception of the production of liquid steel for castings from small and medium-sized foundries;

(c) hot finished products of iron, ordinary steel or special steel: rails, sleepers, fishplates, soleplates, joists, heavy sections of 80 mm and over, sheet piling, bars and sections of less than 80 mm and flats of less than 150 mm, wire rod, tube rounds and squares, hot-rolled hoop and strip (including tube strip), hot-rolled sheet (coated or uncoated), plates and sheets of 3 mm thickness and over, universal plates of 150 mm and over, with the exception of wire and wire products, bright bars and iron castings;

(d) cold finished products: tinplate, terneplate, blackplate, galvanised sheets, other coated sheets, cold-rolled sheets, electrical sheets and strip for tinplate, cold-rolled plate, in coil and in strip;

(e) tubes: all seamless steel tubes, welded steel tubes with a diameter of over 406.4 mm.

ANNEX VII
INFORMATION TO BE INCLUDED IN THE APPLICATION FORM FOR REGIONAL INVESTMENT AID

[5.294]

1. Information about the aid beneficiary:
   - Name, registered address of main seat, main sector of activity (NACE code).
   - Declaration that the firm is not in difficulty, as defined under the rescue and restructuring guidelines.
   - Declaration detailing the aid (both *de minimis* and State aid) already received for other investments over the last three years in the same NUTS 3 region where the new investment will be located. Declaration specifying regional aid received or to be received for the same project by other granting authorities.
   - Declaration specifying whether the beneficiary has closed a same or similar activity in the EEA two years preceding the date of this application.
   - Declaration specifying whether the beneficiary has the intention to close down such an activity at the moment of aid application within a period of two years after the investment to be subsidised is completed.
   - For aid granted under a scheme: non-relocation declaration and commitment.
2. Information about the investment to be supported:
   - Short description of the investment.
   - Short description of expected positive effects for the area concerned (for example, number of jobs created or safeguarded, R&D&I activities, training, creation of a cluster and project's possible contribution to the green (1) and digital transition of the regional economy).
   - Applicable legal basis (national, EU or both).
   - Planned start of works and completion of the investment.
   - Location(s) of the investment.
3. Information about the financing of the investment:
   - Investment costs and other associated costs, cost benefit analysis for the notified aid measure.
   - Total eligible costs.
   - Aid amount needed to carry out the investment.
   - Aid intensity.
4. Information on the need for aid and its expected impact:
   - Short explanation of the need for aid and its impact on the investment decision or location decision. This must include an explanation of the alternative investment or location decision if aid is not granted.
   - Declaration of absence of an irreversible agreement between the aid beneficiary and contractors to carry out the investment.

ANNEX VIII
INFORMATION REFERRED TO IN PARAGRAPH 136

[5.295]

The information on individual awards referred to in paragraph 136.2 of the Guidelines must include the following:

— Identity of the individual aid beneficiary[1]
    — name
    — aid beneficiary's identifier
— Type of aid beneficiary at the time of application:
    — SME
    — large enterprise
— Region in which the aid beneficiary is located, at NUTS level II or below
— The main sector or activity of the aid beneficiary for the given aid, identified by the, NACE group (three-digit numerical code)[2]
— Aid element expressed in full in the national currency
— Where different from the aid element, the nominal aid amount, expressed in full in the national currency[3]
— Aid instrument:[4]
    — grant/interest rate subsidy/debt write-off
    — loan/repayable advances/reimbursable grant
    — guarantee
    — tax advantage or tax exemption
    — risk finance
    — other (please specify)
— Date of award and date of publication
— Objective of the aid
— Identity of the granting authority or authorities
— Where applicable, name of the entrusted entity, and the names of the selected financial intermediaries
— Reference of the aid measure[5]

NOTES

1 With the exception of business secrets and other confidential information in duly justified cases and subject to the Commission's agreement (Commission communication of 1.12.2003 on professional secrecy in State aid decisions, C(2003) 4582 (OJ C297, 9.12.2003, p 6)).

2 Regulation (EC) No 1893/2006 of the European Parliament and of the Council of 20 December 2006 establishing the statistical classification of economic activities NACE Revision 2 and amending Council Regulation (EEC) No 3037/90 as well as certain regulations governing specific statistical domains (OJ L393, 30.12.2006, p 1).

3 Gross grant equivalent, or where applicable, the amount of the investment. For operating aid, the annual aid amount per aid beneficiary can be provided. For fiscal schemes, this amount can be provided by the ranges set out in paragraph 139. The amount to be published is the maximum allowed tax benefit and not the amount deducted each year (e.g. in the context of a tax credit, the maximum allowed tax credit must be published rather than the actual amount, which might depend on the taxable revenue and vary each year).

4 If the aid is granted through multiple aid instruments, the aid amount must be specified by instrument.

5 As provided by the Commission under the notification procedure referred to in Section 3.

4. RESEARCH AND DEVELOPMENT AND INNOVATION AID

COMMUNICATION FROM THE COMMISSION FRAMEWORK FOR STATE AID FOR RESEARCH AND DEVELOPMENT AND INNOVATION

(2014/C198/01)

[5.296]

NOTES

Date of publication in OJ: OJ C198, 27.06.2014, p 1.

See also the list of consultations and draft documents in the Appendix at **[A1]**.

INTRODUCTION

[5.297]

1. In order to prevent State subsidies from distorting competition in the internal market and affecting trade between Member States in a manner contrary to the common interest, Article 107(1) of the Treaty on the Functioning of the European Union ('the Treaty') lays down the principle that State aid is prohibited. In certain cases, however, such aid may be compatible with the internal market on the basis of Articles 107(2) and 107(3) of the Treaty.

2. Promoting research and development and innovation ('R&D&I') is an important Union objective laid down in Article 179 of the Treaty, which states that '[t]he Union shall have the objective of strengthening the scientific and technological bases by achieving a European research area in which researchers, scientific knowledge and technology circulate freely, and encouraging it to become more competitive, including in its industry, while promoting all the research activities deemed necessary (. . .)'. Articles 180 to 190 of the Treaty determine the activities to be carried out in that respect and the scope and implementation of the multiannual framework programme.

3. The Europe 2020 strategy[1] identifies research and development ('R&D') as a key driver for achieving the objectives of smart, sustainable and inclusive growth. To that effect, the Commission set out the headline target according to which 3% of the Union's gross domestic product ('GDP') should be invested in R&D by 2020. In order to foster progress in the field of R&D&I, the Europe 2020 strategy in particular puts forward the 'Innovation Union' flagship initiative[2] aiming at improving framework conditions and access to finance for research and innovation in order to ensure that innovative ideas can be turned into products and services that create growth and jobs.[3] The Europe 2020 communication noted that State aid policy can 'actively and positively contribute . . . by prompting and supporting initiatives for more innovative, efficient and greener technologies, while facilitating access to public support for investment, risk capital and funding for research and development'.

4. Whereas it is generally accepted that competitive markets tend to bring about efficient results in terms of prices, output and use of resources, in the presence of market failures[4] State intervention may improve the functioning of markets and, thereby, contribute to smart, sustainable and inclusive growth. In the context of R&D&I, market failures may arise for instance because market actors do not normally take into account the (positive) externalities that ensue on other actors in the economy, and therefore engage in a level of R&D&I activities which is too low from the point of view of society. Likewise, R&D&I projects might suffer from insufficient access to finance (due to asymmetric information) or from coordination problems among firms. Therefore, State aid for R&D&I can be compatible with the internal market where it can be expected to alleviate a market failure in promoting the execution of an important project of common European interest or facilitating the development of certain economic activities, and where the ensuing distortion of competition and trade is not contrary to the common interest.

5. Aid for R&D&I will primarily be justified on the basis of Articles 107(3)(b) and 107(3)(c) of the Treaty, according to which the Commission may consider compatible with the internal market State aid to promote the execution of an important project of common European interest or to facilitate the development of certain economic activities within the Union, where such aid does not adversely affect trading conditions to an extent which goes contrary to the common interest.

6. In the communication on State aid modernisation,[5] the Commission announced three objectives to be pursued through the modernisation of State aid control:

(a) fostering sustainable, smart and inclusive growth in a competitive internal market;

(b) focusing *ex ante* scrutiny on cases with the biggest impact on the internal market while strengthening the cooperation with Member States in State aid enforcement;

(c) streamlining the rules and providing for faster decisions.

7. In particular, the communication called for a common approach in the revision of the different guidelines and frameworks based on strengthening the internal market, promoting more effectiveness in public spending through a better contribution by State aid to objectives of common interest, and exercising greater scrutiny on the incentive effect, on limiting the aid to the minimum, and on the potential negative effects of the aid on competition and trade. The compatibility conditions set out in this framework are based on that common approach.

NOTES

1 Communication from the Commission, 'Europe 2020 – A strategy for smart, sustainable and inclusive growth', COM(2010) 2020 final, 3.3.2010.

2 Communication from the Commission to the European Parliament, the Council, the European Economic and

Social Committee and the Committee of the Regions, 'European 2020 Flagship Initiative – Innovation Union', COM(2010) 546 final, 6.10.2010.

3 Overall R&D expenditure within the Union (of which roughly 1/3 is public and 2/3 private) stood at 2.06% of GDP in 2012, and increased by 0.24 percentage points since 2005 (Eurostat Statistics on headline indicators: https://ec.europa.eu/eurostat/web/main/home). Even though private expenditure in R&D as a share of GDP has slightly increased since 2008, there are however large differences among Member States, industrial sectors and individual actors (European Commission, 'Research and Innovation performance in EU Member States and Associated Countries 2013').

4 The term 'market failure' refers to situations in which markets, where left to their own devices, are unlikely to produce efficient outcomes.

5 Communication from the Commission to the European Parliament, the Council, the European Economic and Social Committee and the Committee of the regions, 'EU State Aid Modernisation (SAM)', COM(2012) 209 final, 8.5.2012.

1. SCOPE OF APPLICATION AND DEFINITIONS

1.1. SCOPE OF APPLICATION

[5.298]

8. The principles set out in this framework apply to State aid for R&D&I in all sectors governed by the Treaty. It therefore applies to those sectors which are subject to specific Union rules on State aid, unless such rules provide otherwise.

9. Union funding centrally managed by the institutions, agencies, joint undertakings or other bodies of the Union that is not directly or indirectly under the control of Member States[1] does not constitute State aid. Where such Union funding is combined with State aid, only the latter will be considered for determining whether notification thresholds and maximum aid intensities are respected or, in the context of this framework, subject to a compatibility assessment.

10. Aid for R&D&I for firms in difficulty, as defined for the purposes of this framework by the Community guidelines on State aid for rescuing and restructuring firms in difficulty,[2] as amended or replaced, is excluded from the scope of this framework. [This Framework shall, however, apply to undertakings which were not in difficulty on 31 December 2019 but became undertakings in difficulty in the period from 1 January 2020 to 30 June 2021.]

11. When assessing R&D&I aid in favour of a beneficiary that is subject to an outstanding recovery order following a previous Commission decision declaring an aid illegal and incompatible with the internal market, the Commission will take account of the amount of aid still to be recovered.[3]

NOTES

Point 10: words in square brackets inserted by Communication from the Commission (2020/C224/02), para (15).

1 Such as funding provided under Horizon 2020 or the EU programme for the Competitiveness of Enterprises and Small and Medium-sized Enterprises (COSME).

2 Community guidelines on State aid for rescuing and restructuring firms in difficulty (OJ C244, 1.10.2004, p 2).

3 See Joined Cases T-244/93 and T-486/93 TWD *Textilwerke Deggendorf GmbH v Commission* [1995] ECR II-02265.

1.2. AID MEASURES COVERED BY THE FRAMEWORK

12. The Commission has identified a series of R&D&I measures for which State aid may, under specific conditions, be compatible with the internal market:

(a) ***aid for R&D projects*** where the aided part of the research project falls within the categories of fundamental research and applied research, of which the latter can be divided into industrial research and experimental development.[1] Such aid is mainly targeted at the market failure related to positive externalities (knowledge spill-overs), but may also address a market failure caused by imperfect and asymmetric information or (mainly in collaboration projects) a coordination failure;

(b) ***aid for feasibility studies*** related to R&D projects, which aims at overcoming a market failure primarily related to imperfect and asymmetric information;

(c) ***aid for the construction and upgrade of research infrastructures***, which mainly addresses the market failure stemming from coordination difficulties. High-quality research infrastructures are increasingly necessary for ground-breaking research, as they attract global talent and are essential for example for information and communication technologies and key enabling technologies;[2]

(d) ***aid for innovation activities***, which is mainly targeted at market failures related to positive externalities (knowledge spill-overs), coordination difficulties and, to a lesser extent, asymmetric information. With respect to small and medium-sized enterprises ('SMEs') such innovation aid may be awarded for obtaining, validating and defending patents and other intangible assets, for the secondment of highly qualified personnel, and for acquiring innovation advisory and support services. Moreover, in order to encourage large enterprises to collaborate with SMEs in process and organisational innovation activities, the costs incurred by both SMEs and large enterprises for such activities may also be supported;

(e) ***aid for innovation clusters***, which aims at tackling market failures linked with coordination problems hampering the development of clusters, or limiting the interactions and knowledge flows within and between clusters. State aid could contribute to resolving this problem, first by supporting the investment in open and shared infrastructures for innovation clusters, and second by supporting, for no longer than 10 years, the operation of clusters for the enhancement of collaboration, networking and learning.

13. Member States must notify R&D&I aid pursuant to Article 108(3) of the Treaty, with the exception of measures that fulfil the conditions laid down in a block exemption Regulation adopted by the Commission pursuant to Article 1 of Council Regulation (EC) No 994/98.[3]

14. This framework sets out the compatibility criteria for R&D&I aid schemes and individual aid which are subject to the notification requirement and must be assessed on the basis of Article 107(3)(c) of the Treaty.[4]

NOTES

[1] The Commission considers that it is useful to maintain different categories of R&D activities regardless of the fact that those activities may follow an interactive model rather than a linear model.

[2] Key enabling technologies are defined and identified in the communication from the Commission to the European Parliament, the Council, the European Economic and Social Committee and the Committee of the regions, 'A European strategy for Key Enabling Technologies — A bridge to growth and jobs', COM(2012) 341 final, 26.6.2012.

[3] Council Regulation (EC) No 994/98 of 7 May 1998 on the application of Articles 92 and 93 of the Treaty establishing the European Community to certain categories of horizontal State aid (OJ L142, 14.5.1998, p 1), as amended by Council Regulation (EU) No 733/2013 of 22 July 2013 (OJ L204, 31.7.2013, p 15).

[4] The criteria for the analysis of the compatibility with the internal market of State aid to promote the execution of important projects of common European interest, including R&D&I aid assessed on the basis of Article 107(3)(b) of the Treaty, are laid down in a separate communication from the Commission.

1.3. DEFINITIONS

15. For the purposes of this framework, the following definitions apply:

(a) '***ad hoc aid***' means aid not awarded on the basis of an aid scheme;

(b) '**aid**' means any measure fulfilling the criteria laid down in Article 107(1) of the Treaty;

(c) '**aid intensity**' means the gross aid amount expressed as a percentage of the eligible costs, before any deduction of tax or other charge. Where aid is awarded in a form other than a grant, the aid amount is the grant equivalent of the aid. Aid payable in several instalments is discounted to its value at the date of award. The interest rate to be used for this purpose is the discount rate[1] applicable at the date of award. The aid intensity is calculated per beneficiary;

(d) '**aid scheme**' means any act on the basis of which, without further implementing measures being required, individual aid may be awarded to undertakings defined therein in a general and abstract manner and any act on the basis of which aid which is not linked to a specific project may be awarded to one or several undertakings;

(e) '**applied research**' means industrial research, experimental development, or any combination of both;

(f) '**arm's length**' means that the conditions of the transaction between the contracting parties do not differ from those which would be stipulated between independent enterprises and contain no element of collusion. Any transaction that results from an open, transparent and non-discriminatory procedure is considered as meeting the arm's length principle;

(g) '**date of award of the aid**' means the date on which the legal right to receive the aid is conferred on the beneficiary under the applicable national legal regime;

(h) '**effective collaboration**' means collaboration between at least two independent parties to exchange knowledge or technology, or to achieve a common objective based on the division of labour where the parties jointly define the scope of the collaborative project, contribute to its implementation and share its risks, as well as its results. One or several parties may bear the full costs of the project and thus relieve other parties of its financial risks. Contract research and provision of research services are not considered forms of collaboration.

(i) '**exclusive development**' means the public procurement of research and development services of which all benefits accrue exclusively to the contracting authority or contracting entity, and which it may use in the conduct of its own affairs on condition that it fully remunerates them;

(j) '**experimental development**' means acquiring, combining, shaping and using existing scientific, technological, business and other relevant knowledge and skills with the aim of developing new or improved products, processes or services. This may also include, for example, activities aiming at the conceptual definition, planning and documentation of new products, processes or services. Experimental development may comprise prototyping, demonstrating, piloting, testing and validation of new or improved products, processes or services in environments representative of real life operating conditions where the primary objective is to make further technical improvements on products, processes or services that are not substantially set. This may include the development of a commercially usable prototype or pilot which is necessarily the final commercial product and which is too expensive to produce for it to be used only for demonstration and validation purposes. Experimental development does not include routine or periodic changes made to existing products, production lines, manufacturing processes, services and other operations in progress, even if those changes may represent improvements;

(k) '**feasibility study**' means the evaluation and analysis of the potential of a project, which aims at supporting the process of decision making by objectively and rationally uncovering its strengths and weaknesses, opportunities and threats, as well as identifying the resources required to carry it through and ultimately its prospects for success;

(l) '**full allocation**' means that the research organisation, research infrastructure or public purchaser enjoys the full economic benefit of intellectual property rights by retaining the right to make unrestricted use of them, particularly the right of ownership and the right to license. This may also be the case where the research organisation or research infrastructure (respectively, public purchaser) decides to conclude further contracts concerning those rights, including licensing them to a collaboration partner (respectively, under takings).

(m) '**fundamental research**' means experimental or theoretical work undertaken primarily to acquire new knowledge of the underlying foundations of phenomena and observable facts, without any direct commercial application or use in view;

(n) '**gross grant equivalent**' means the amount of the aid if it had been awarded in the form of a grant, before any deduction of tax or other charge;

(o) '**highly qualified personnel**' means staff having a tertiary education degree and at least five years of relevant professional experience which may also include doctoral training;

(p) '**individual aid**' means aid awarded to a specific undertaking and includes ad hoc aid and aid awarded on the basis of an aid scheme;

(q) '**industrial research**' means the planned research or critical investigation aimed at the acquisition of new knowledge and skills for developing new products, processes or services or for bringing about a significant improvement in existing products, processes or services. It comprises the creation of components parts of complex systems, and may include the construction of prototypes in a laboratory environment or in an environment with simulated interfaces to existing systems as well as of pilot lines, when necessary for the industrial research and notably for generic technology validation;

(r) '**innovation advisory services**' means consultancy, assistance and training in the fields of knowledge transfer, acquisition, protection and exploitation of intangible assets, use of standards and regulations embedding them;

(s) '**innovation clusters**' means structures or organised groups of independent parties (such as innovative start-ups, small, medium and large enterprises, as well as research and knowledge dissemination organisations, non-for-profit organisations and other related economic actors) designed to stimulate innovative activity by promoting sharing of facilities and exchange of knowledge and expertise and by contributing effectively to knowledge transfer, networking, information dissemination and collaboration among the undertakings and other organisations in the cluster;

(t) '**innovation support services**' means the provision of office space, data banks, libraries, market research, laboratories, quality labelling, testing and certification for the purpose of developing more effective products, processes or services;

(u) '**intangible assets**' means assets that do not have a physical or financial embodiment such as patents, licences, know-how or other intellectual property;

(v) '**knowledge transfer**' means any process which has the aim of acquiring, collecting and sharing explicit and tacit knowledge, including skills and competence in both economic and non-economic activities such as research collaborations, consultancy, licensing, spin-off creation, publication and mobility of researchers and other personnel involved in those activities. Besides scientific and technological knowledge, it includes other kinds of knowledge such as knowledge on the use of standards and regulations embedding them and on conditions of real life operating environments and methods for organisational innovation, as well as management of knowledge related to identifying, acquiring, protecting, defending and exploiting intangible assets;

(w) '**large enterprises**' means undertakings which do not fall within the definition of small and medium-sized enterprises;

(x) '**net extra costs**' means the difference between the expected net present values of the aided project or activity and a viable counterfactual investment that the beneficiary would have carried out in the absence of aid;

(y) '**organisational innovation**' means the implementation of a new organisational method in an undertaking's business practices, workplace organisation or external relations, excluding changes that are based on organisational methods already in use in the undertaking, changes in management strategy, mergers and acquisitions, ceasing to use a process, simple capital replacement or extension, changes resulting purely from changes in factor prices, customisation, localisation, regular, seasonal and other cyclical changes and trading of new or significantly improved products;

(z) '**personnel costs**' means the cost of researchers, technicians and other supporting staff to the extent employed on the relevant project or activity;

(aa) '**pre-commercial procurement**' means the public procurement of research and development services where the contracting authority or contracting entity does not reserve all the results and benefits of the contract exclusively for itself for use in the conduct of its own affairs, but shares them with the providers under market conditions. The contract, the object of which falls within one or several categories of research and development defined in this framework, must be of limited duration and may include the development of prototypes or limited volumes of first products or services in the form of a test series. The purchase of commercial volumes of products or services must not be an object of the same contract;

(bb) '**process innovation**' means the implementation of a new or significantly improved production or delivery method (including significant changes in techniques, equipment or software), excluding minor changes or improvements, increases in production or service capabilities through the addition of manufacturing or logistical systems which are very similar to those already in use, ceasing to use a process, simple capital replacement or extension, changes resulting purely from changes in factor prices, customisation, localisation, regular, seasonal and other cyclical changes and trading of new or significantly improved products;

(cc) '**R&D project**' means an operation that includes activities spanning over one or several categories of research and development defined in this framework, and that is intended to accomplish an indivisible task of a precise economic, scientific or technical nature with clearly pre-defined goals. A R&D project may consist of several work packages, activities or services, and includes clear objectives, activities to be carried out to achieve those objectives (including their expected costs), and concrete deliverables to identify the outcomes of those activities and compare them with the relevant objectives. When two or more R&D projects are not clearly separable from each other and in particular when they do not have independent probabilities of technological success, they are considered as a single project.

(dd) '**repayable advance**' means a loan for a project which is paid in one or more instalments and the conditions for the reimbursement of which depend on the outcome of the project;

(ee) '**research and knowledge dissemination organisation**' or 'research organisation' means an entity (such as universities or research institutes, technology transfer agencies, innovation intermediaries, research-oriented physical or virtual collaborative entities), irrespective of its legal status (organised under public or private law) or way of financing, whose primary goal is to independently conduct fundamental research, industrial research or experimental development or to widely disseminate the results of such activities by way of teaching, publication or knowledge transfer. Where such entity also pursues economic activities, the financing, the costs and the revenues of those economic activities must be accounted for separately. Undertakings that can exert a decisive influence upon such an entity, for example in the quality of shareholders or members, may not enjoy a preferential access to the results generated by it.

(ff) '**research infrastructure**' means facilities, resources and related services that are used by the scientific community to conduct research in their respective fields and covers scientific equipment or set of instruments, knowledge-based resources such as collections, archives or structured scientific information, enabling information and communication technology-based infrastructures such as grid, computing, software and communication, or any other entity of a unique nature essential to conduct research. Such infrastructures may be 'single-sited' or 'distributed' (an organised network of resources);[2]

(gg) '**secondment**' means temporary employment of staff by a beneficiary with the right for the staff to return to the previous employer;

(hh) '**small and medium-sized enterprises**' or 'SMEs', 'small enterprises' and 'medium-sized enterprises' means undertakings fulfilling the criteria laid down in the Commission recommendation on the definition of micro, small and medium-sized enterprises;[3]

(ii) '**start of works**' or 'start of the project' means either the start of R&D&I activities, or the first agreement between the beneficiary and the contractors to conduct the project, whichever comes first. Preparatory works such as obtaining permits and conducting feasibility studies are not considered as start of works;

(jj) '**tangible assets**' means assets consisting of land, buildings and plants, machinery and equipment.

NOTES

1 See the communication from the Commission on the revision of the method for setting the reference and discount rates (OJ C14, 19.1.2008, p 6).

2 See Article 2(a) of Council Regulation (EC) No 723/2009 of 25 June 2009 on the Community legal framework for a European Research Infrastructure Consortium (ERIC) (OJ L206, 8.8.2009, p 1).

3 Commission Recommendation of 6 May 2003 concerning the definition of micro, small and medium-sized enterprises (OJ L124, 20.5.2003, p 36).

2. STATE AID WITHIN THE MEANING OF ARTICLE 107(1) OF THE TREATY

[5.299]

16. Generally, any measure meeting the criteria of Article 107(1) of the Treaty constitutes State aid. Whilst a separate Commission notice on the notion of State aid clarifies how the Commission understands the notion of State aid in general, situations typically arising in the field of R&D&I activities are considered in this Section without prejudice to the interpretation of the Court of Justice of the European Union.

2.1. RESEARCH AND KNOWLEDGE DISSEMINATION ORGANISATIONS AND RESEARCH INFRASTRUCTURES AS RECIPIENTS OF STATE AID

17. Research and knowledge dissemination organisations ('research organisations') and research infrastructures are recipients of State aid if their public funding fulfils all conditions of Article 107(1) of the Treaty. As explained in the Notice on the notion of State aid, and in accordance with the case-law of the Court of Justice, the beneficiary must qualify as an undertaking, but that qualification does not depend upon its legal status, that is to say whether it is organised under public or private law, or its economic nature, that is to say whether it seeks to make profits or not. Rather, what is decisive for that qualification as an undertaking is whether it carries out an economic activity consisting of offering products or services on a given market.[1]

NOTES

1 Case C-118/85 *Commission v Italy* [1987] ECR 2599, paragraph 7; Case C-35/96 *Commission v Italy* [1998] ECR I-3851 paragraph 36; Case C-309/99 *Wouters* [2002] ECR I-1577, paragraph 46.

2.1.1. PUBLIC FUNDING OF NON-ECONOMIC ACTIVITIES

18. Where the same entity carries out activities of both economic and non-economic nature, the public funding of the non-economic activities will not fall under Article 107(1) of the Treaty if the two kinds of activities and their costs, funding and revenues can be clearly separated so that cross-subsidisation of the economic activity is effectively avoided. Evidence of due allocation of costs, funding and revenues can consist of annual financial statements of the relevant entity.

19. The Commission considers that the following activities are generally of a non-economic character:

(a) primary activities of research organisations and research infrastructures, in particular:

— education for more and better skilled human resources. In line with case-law[1] and decisional practice of the Commission,[2] and as explained in the Notice on the notion of State aid and the SGEI Communication,[3] public education organised within the national educational system, predominantly or entirely funded by the State and supervised by the State is considered as a non-economic activity;[4]

— independent R&D for more knowledge and better understanding, including collaborative R&D where the research organisation or research infrastructure engages in effective collaboration;[5]

— wide dissemination of research results on a non-exclusive and non-discriminatory basis, for example through teaching, open-access databases, open publications or open software.

(b) knowledge transfer activities, where they are conducted either by the research organisation or research infra structure (including their departments or subsidiaries) or jointly with, or on behalf of other such entities, and where all profits from those activities are reinvested in the primary activities of the research organisation or research infrastructure. The non-economic nature of those activities is not prejudiced by contracting the provision of corresponding services to third parties by way of open tenders.

20. Where a research organisation or research infrastructure is used for both economic and non-economic activities, public funding falls under State aid rules only insofar as it covers costs linked to the economic activities.[6] Where the research organisation or research infrastructure is used almost exclusively for a non-economic activity, its funding may fall outside State aid rules in its entirety, provided that the economic use remains purely ancillary, that is to say corresponds to an activity which is directly related to and necessary for the operation of the research organisation or research infrastructure or intrinsically linked to its main non-economic use, and which is limited in scope. For the purposes of this framework, the Commission will consider this to be the case where the economic activities consume exactly the same inputs (such as material, equipment, labour and fixed capital) as the non-economic activities and the capacity allocated each year to such economic activities does not exceed 20% of the relevant entity's overall annual capacity.

2.1.2. PUBLIC FUNDING OF ECONOMIC ACTIVITIES

21. Without prejudice to point 20, where research organisations or research infrastructures are used to perform economic activities, such as renting out equipment or laboratories to undertakings, supplying services to undertakings or performing contract research, public funding of those economic activities will generally be considered State aid.

22. However, the Commission will not consider the research organisation or research infrastructure to be a beneficiary of State aid if it acts as a mere intermediary for passing on to the final recipients the totality of the public funding and any advantage acquired through such funding. This is generally the case where:

(a) both the public funding and any advantage acquired through such funding are quantifiable and demonstrable, and there is an appropriate mechanism which ensures that they are fully passed on to the final recipients, for example through reduced prices, and

(b) no further advantage is awarded to the intermediary because it is either selected through an open tender procedure or the public funding is available to all entities which satisfy the necessary objective conditions, so that customers as final recipients are entitled to acquire equivalent services from any relevant intermediary.

23. Where the conditions in point 22 are fulfilled, State aid rules apply at the level of the final recipients.

NOTES

1 Case C-263/86 *Humble and Edel* [1988] ECR I-5365, paragraphs 9–10, 15–18; Case C-109/92 *Wirth* [1993] ECR I-06447, paragraph 15.

2 See for instance cases NN54/2006, *Pøerov logistics College*, and N 343/2008, *Individual aid to the College of Nyíregyháza for the development of the Partium Knowledge Centre*.

3 See points 26–29 of the communication from the Commission on the application of the European Union State aid rules to compensation granted for the provision of services of general economic interest (OJ C8, 11.1.2012, p 4).

4 Workforce training, in the sense of State aid rules for training aid, does not qualify as a non-economic primary activity of research organisations.

5 Provision of R&D services and R&D carried out on behalf of undertakings are not considered as independent R&D.

6 Where a research organisation or research infrastructure is both publicly and privately funded, the Commission will consider this to be the case where the public funding allocated to the relevant entity for a specific accounting period exceeds the costs of non-economic activities incurred in that period.

2.2. INDIRECT STATE AID TO UNDERTAKINGS THROUGH PUBLIC FUNDED RESEARCH AND KNOWLEDGE DISSEMINATION ORGANISATIONS AND RESEARCH INFRASTRUCTURES

24. The question of whether and under which conditions undertakings obtain an advantage within the meaning of Article 107(1) of the Treaty in cases of contract research or research services provided by a research organisation or research infrastructure, as well as in cases of collaboration with a research organisation or research infrastructure must be answered in accordance with general State aid principles. To this purpose, as explained in the Notice on the notion of State aid, it may in particular be necessary to assess whether the behaviour of the research organisation or research infrastructure can be imputed to the State.[1]

2.2.1. RESEARCH ON BEHALF OF UNDERTAKINGS (CONTRACT RESEARCH OR RESEARCH SERVICES)

25. Where a research organisation or research infrastructure is used to perform contract research or provide a research service to an undertaking, which typically specifies the terms and conditions of the contract, owns the results of the research activities and carries the risk of failure, no State aid will usually be passed to the under taking if the research organisation or research infrastructure receive payment of an adequate remuneration for its services, particularly where one of the following conditions is fulfilled:

(a) the research organisation or research infrastructure provides its research service or contract research at market price,[2] or

(b) where there is no market price, the research organisation or research infrastructure provides its research service or contract research at a price which:

— reflects the full costs of the service and generally includes a margin established by reference to those commonly applied by undertakings active in the sector of the service concerned, or

— is the result of arm's length negotiations where the research organisation or research infrastructure, in its capacity as service provider, negotiates in order to obtain the maximum economic benefit at the moment when the contract is concluded and covers at least its marginal costs.

26. Where the ownership of, or access rights to intellectual property rights ('IPR') remain with the research organisation or research infrastructure, their market value may be deducted from the price payable for the services concerned.

2.2.2. COLLABORATION WITH UNDERTAKINGS

27. A project is considered to be carried out through effective collaboration where at least two independent parties pursue a common objective based on the division of labour and jointly define its scope, participate in its design, contribute to its implementation and share its financial, technological, scientific and other risks, as well as its results. One or several parties may bear the full costs of the project and thus relieve other parties of its financial risks. The terms and conditions of a collaboration project, in particular as regards contributions to its costs, the sharing of risks and results, the dissemination of results, access to and rules for allocation of IPR, must be concluded prior to the start of the project.[3] Contract research and provision of research services are not considered to be forms of collaboration.

28. Where collaboration projects are carried out jointly by undertakings and research organisations or research infrastructures, the Commission considers that no indirect State aid is awarded to the participating undertakings through those entities due to favourable conditions of the collaboration if one of the following conditions is fulfilled:

(a) the participating undertakings bear the full cost of the project, or

(b) the results of the collaboration which do not give rise to IPR may be widely disseminated and any IPR resulting from the activities of research organisations or research infrastructures are fully allocated to those entities, or

(c) any IPR resulting from the project, as well as related access rights are allocated to the different collaboration partners in a manner which adequately reflects their work packages, contributions and respective interests, or

(d) the research organisations or research infrastructures receive compensation equivalent to the market price for the IPR which result from their activities and are assigned to the participating undertakings, or to which participating undertakings are allocated access rights. The absolute amount of the value of any contribution, both financial and non-financial, of the participating undertakings to the costs of the research organisations or research infrastructures' activities that resulted in the IPR concerned, may be deducted from that compensation.

29. For the purpose of point 28(d), the Commission will consider that the compensation received is equivalent to the market price if it enables the research organisations or research infrastructures concerned to enjoy the full economic benefit of those rights, where one of the following conditions is fulfilled:

(a) the amount of the compensation has been established by means of an open, transparent and non-discriminatory competitive sale procedure, or

(b) an independent expert valuation confirms that the amount of the compensation is at least equal to the market price, or

(c) the research organisation or research infrastructure, as seller, can demonstrate that it effectively negotiated the compensation, at arm's length conditions, in order to obtain the maximum economic benefit at the moment when the contract is concluded, while considering its statutory objectives, or

(d) in cases where the collaboration agreement provides the collaborating undertaking with a right of first refusal as regards IPR generated by the collaborating research organisations or research infrastructures, where those entities exercise a reciprocal right to solicit more economically advantageous offers from third parties so that the collaborating undertaking has to match its offer accordingly.

30. If none of the conditions in point 28 are fulfilled, the full value of the contribution of the research organisations or research infrastructures to the project will be considered as an advantage for the collaborating undertakings, to which State aid rules apply.

NOTES

1 See Case C-482/99 *France v Commission* [2002] ECR I-4397, paragraph 24.

2 Where the research organisation or research infrastructure provides a specific research service or carries out contract research for the first time on behalf of a given undertaking, on a trial basis and during a clearly limited period of time, the Commission will normally consider the price charged as a market price where that research service or contract research is unique and it can be shown that there is no market for it.

3 This does not include definite agreements on the market value of resulting IPR and the value of contributions to the project.

2.3. PUBLIC PROCUREMENT OF RESEARCH AND DEVELOPMENT SERVICES

31. Public purchasers may procure research and development services from undertakings, through both exclusive development and pre-commercial procurement procedures.[1]

32. As long as an open tender procedure for the public procurement is carried out in accordance with the applicable directives,[2] the Commission will generally consider that no State aid within the meaning of Article 107(1) of the Treaty is awarded to the undertakings delivering the relevant services.[3]

33. In all other cases, including pre-commercial procurement, the Commission will consider that no State aid is awarded to undertakings where the price paid for the relevant services fully reflects the market value of the benefits received by the public purchaser and the risks taken by the participating providers, in particular where all of the following conditions are fulfilled:

(a) the selection procedure is open, transparent and non-discriminatory, and is based on objective selection and award criteria specified in advance of the bidding procedure;

(b) the envisaged contractual arrangements describing all rights and obligations of the parties, including with regard to IPR, are made available to all interested bidders in advance of the bidding procedure;

(c) the procurement does not give any of the participant providers any preferential treatment in the supply of commercial volumes of the final products or services to a public purchaser in the Member State concerned;[4] and

(d) one of the following conditions is fulfilled:

- all results which do not give rise to IPR may be widely disseminated, for example through publication, teaching or contribution to standardisation bodies in a way that allows other undertakings to reproduce them, and any IPR are fully allocated to the public purchaser, or
- any service provider to which results giving rise to IPR are allocated is required to grant the public purchaser unlimited access to those results free of charge, and to grant access to third parties, for example by way of non-exclusive licenses, under market conditions.

34. Where the conditions in point 33 are not fulfilled, Member States may rely on an individual assessment of the terms of the contract between the public purchaser and the undertaking, without prejudice to the general obligation to notify R&D&I aid pursuant to Article 108(3) of the Treaty.

NOTES

1 See the communication and associated staff working document — communication from the Commission to the European Parliament, the Council, the European Economic and Social Committee and the Committee of the Region, 'Pre-commercial procurement: driving innovation to ensure sustainable high quality public services in Europe', COM(2007) 799 final, 14.12.2007.

2 See Article 27 of Directive 2014/24/EU of the European Parliament and of the Council of 26 February 2014 on public procurement and repealing Directive 2004/18/EC (OJ L94, 28.3.2014, p 65) and Article 45 of Directive 2014/25/EU of the European Parliament and of the Council of 26 February 2014 on procurement by entities operating in the water, energy, transport and postal services sectors and repealing Directive 2004/17/EC (OJ L94, 28.3.2014, p 243). Likewise, in the case of a restricted procedure within the meaning of respectively Articles 28 of Directive 2014/24/EU and 46 of Directive 2014/25/EU, the Commission will also consider that no State aid is awarded to undertakings, unless interested providers are prevented from tendering without valid reasons.

3 This will also be the case where public purchasers procure innovative solutions resulting from a preceding R&D procurement, or non-R&D products and services that are to be delivered to a performance level requiring a product, process or organisational innovation.

4 Without prejudice to procedures that cover both the development and the subsequent purchase of unique or specialised products or services.

3. COMMON ASSESSMENT PRINCIPLES

[5.300]

35. To assess whether a notified aid measure can be considered compatible with the internal market, the Commission generally analyses whether the design of the aid measure ensures that the positive impact of the aid towards an objective of common interest exceeds its potential negative effects on trade and competition.

36. The communication on State aid modernisation of 8 May 2012 called for the identification and definition of common principles applicable to the assessment of compatibility of all the aid measures carried out by the Commission. For this purpose, the Commission will consider an aid measure compatible with the Treaty only if it satisfies each of the following criteria:

(a) *contribution to a well-defined objective of common interest*: a State aid measure must aim at an objective of common interest in accordance with Article 107(3) of the Treaty (Section 4.1);

(b) *need for State intervention*: a State aid measure must be targeted towards a situation where aid can bring about a material improvement that the market cannot deliver itself, for example by remedying a market failure or addressing an equity or cohesion concern (Section 4.2);

(c) *appropriateness of the aid measure*: the proposed aid measure must be an appropriate policy instrument to address the objective of common interest (Section 4.3);

(d) *incentive effect*: the aid must change the behaviour of the undertaking(s) concerned in such a way that it engages in additional activity, which it would not carry out without the aid or would carry out in a restricted or different manner or location (Section 4.4);

(e) *proportionality of the aid (aid to the minimum)*: the amount and intensity of the aid must be limited to the minimum needed to induce the additional investment or activity by the undertaking(s) concerned (Section 4.5);

(f) *avoidance of undue negative effects on competition and trade between Member States*: the negative effects of aid must be sufficiently limited, so that the overall balance of the measure is positive (Section 4.6);

(g) *transparency of aid*: Member States, the Commission, economic operators, and the public, must have easy access to all relevant acts and to pertinent information about the aid awarded thereunder (Section 4.7).

37. The overall balance of certain categories of aid schemes may further be made subject to a requirement of ex post evaluation as described in Section 5. In such cases, the Commission may limit the duration of those schemes (normally to four years or less) with a possibility to re-notify their prolongation afterwards.

38. If a State aid measure or the conditions attached to it (including its financing method when it forms an integral part of the measure) entail a non-severable violation of Union law, the aid cannot be declared compatible with the internal market.[1]

39. In assessing the compatibility of any individual aid with the internal market, the Commission will take account of any proceedings concerning infringement to Articles 101 or 102 of the Treaty which may concern the beneficiary of the aid and which may be relevant for its assessment under Article 107(3) of the Treaty.[2]

NOTES

1 See for instance Case C-156/98 *Germany v Commission* [2000] ECR I-6857, paragraph 78 and Case C-333/07 *Régie Networks v Rhone Alpes Bourgogne* [2008] ECR I-10807, paragraphs 94–116.

2 See Case C-225/91 *Matra v Commission* [1993] ECR I-3203, paragraph 42.

4. COMPATIBILITY ASSESSMENT OF R&D&I AID

[5.301]

40. State aid for R&D&I can be declared compatible with the internal market within the meaning of Article 107(3)(c) of the Treaty where, on the basis of the common assessment principles set out in Section 3, it leads to increased R&D&I activities without adversely affecting trading conditions in a manner contrary to the common interest.

41. In this section, the Commission clarifies how it will apply those common assessment principles and, where applicable, lays down specific conditions for aid schemes and additional ones for individual aid which are subject to the notification obligation.[1]

NOTES

[1] The compatibility conditions laid down in a block exemption Regulation remain fully applicable to all other cases of individual aid, including where such aid is awarded on the basis of an aid scheme which is subject to the notification obligation.

4.1. CONTRIBUTION TO A WELL-DEFINED OBJECTIVE OF COMMON INTEREST

4.1.1. General conditions

42. The general objective of R&D&I aid is the promotion of R&D&I in the Union. In doing so, R&D&I aid should contribute to the achievement of the Europe 2020 strategy of delivering smart, sustainable and inclusive growth.

43. Member States considering awarding State aid for R&D&I, must precisely define the objective pursued, and in particular explain how the measure intends to promote R&D&I. For measures co-financed by the European Structural and Investments Funds, Member States may rely on the reasoning in the relevant Operational Programmes.

44. With respect to aid schemes subject to the notification obligation ('notifiable aid schemes'), the Commission takes a favourable view of aid measures which are an integral part of a comprehensive programme or action plan to stimulate R&D&I activities or smart specialisation strategies, and are supported by rigorous evaluations of similar past aid measures demonstrating their effectiveness.

45. With respect to State aid which is awarded for projects or activities that are also financed by the Union, either directly or indirectly (that is to say by the Commission, by its executive agencies, by joint undertakings established on the basis of Articles 185 and 187 of the Treaty, or by any other implementing bodies where the Union funding is not directly or indirectly under the control of Member States), the Commission will consider that the contribution to a well-defined objective of common interest has been established.

4.1.2. Additional conditions for individual aid

46. To demonstrate that individual aid subject to the notification obligation ('notifiable individual aid') contributes to an increased level of R&D&I activities, Member States may use the following indicators, together with other relevant quantitative or qualitative elements:

(a) *increase in project size*: increase in the total project costs (without a decrease in spending by the aid beneficiary when compared to the situation without aid); increase in the number of people assigned to R&D&I activities;

(b) *increase in scope*: increase in the number of the expected deliverables of the project; increase in the level of ambition of the project evidenced by a higher number of partners involved, a higher probability of a scientific or technological break-through or a higher risk of failure (notably linked to the long-term nature of the project and uncertainty about its results);

(c) *increase in speed*: the completion of the project requires less time when compared to the completion time necessary for the same project carried out without aid;

(d) *increase in total amount spent*: increase in total R&D&I spending by the aid beneficiary, in absolute terms or as a proportion of turnover; changes in the committed budget for the project (without a corresponding decrease in the budget allocated to other projects).

47. In order to conclude that the aid contributes to increasing the level of R&D&I in the Union, the Commission will consider not only the net increase of R&D&I carried out by the undertaking, but also the contribution of the aid to the overall increase of R&D&I spending in the sector concerned, as well as to the improvement of the Union situation with regard to R&D&I in the international context. A favourable view will be taken regarding aid measures, for which a publicly available ex post evaluation of their contribution to the common interest is envisaged.

4.2. NEED FOR STATE INTERVENTION

4.2.1. General conditions

48. As explained in Section 3, State aid may be necessary to increase R&D&I in the Union in a situation where the market, on its own, fails to deliver an efficient outcome. In order to assess whether State aid is effective in reaching the objective of common interest, it is first necessary to identify the problem, which needs to be addressed. State aid should be targeted towards situations where it can bring about a material improvement that the market cannot deliver on its own. Member States should explain how the aid measure can effectively mitigate the market failure associated with reaching the objective of common interest without that aid.

49. R&D&I takes place through a series of activities, which are usually upstream to a number of product markets and exploit available capabilities to develop new or improved products, services and processes in those product markets or completely new ones, thereby fostering growth in the economy, contributing to territorial and social cohesion or furthering the general consumer interest. However, given the available R&D&I capabilities, market failures may be an obstacle to reaching the optimal output and may lead to an inefficient outcome for the following reasons:

— **positive externalities/knowledge spillovers**: R&D&I often generate benefits for society in the form of positive spill-over effects, for example knowledge spillovers or enhanced opportunities for other economic actors to develop complementary products and services. However, if left to the market, a number of projects might have an unattractive rate of return from a private perspective, although they would be beneficial for society, because profit seeking undertakings cannot sufficiently appropriate the benefits of their actions when deciding about the amount of R&D&I they should carry out. State aid may therefore contribute to the implementation of projects which result in an overall societal or economic benefit and which would other wise not be pursued.

However, neither are all benefits of R&D&I activities externalities, nor does the presence of externalities alone automatically mean that State aid is compatible with the internal market. In general, consumers are willing to pay for the direct benefit of new products and services while firms can appropriate the benefits from their investment through other existing instruments, such as IPR. In some cases, however, those means are imperfect and leave a residual market failure that may be corrected by State aid. For instance, as is often argued for fundamental research, it may be difficult to exclude others from gaining access to the results of some activities, which might therefore have a public good character. On the other hand, more specific knowledge related to production can often be well protected, for example through patents, allowing the inventor to reap a higher return on the invention,

— **imperfect and asymmetric information**: R&D&I activities are characterised by a high degree of uncertainty. Under certain circumstances, due to imperfect and asymmetric information, private investors may be reluctant to finance valuable projects and highly-qualified personnel may be unaware of recruitment possibilities in innovative undertakings. As a result, the allocation of human and financial resources may not be adequate and projects which may be valuable for society or the economy may not be carried out.

In certain cases, imperfect and asymmetric information may also hamper access to finance. However, imperfect information and the presence of risk do not automatically justify the need for State aid. Projects with lower private returns on investments not being financed can very well be a sign of market efficiency. More over, risk is part of every business activity and is not a market failure in itself. However, in a context of asymmetric information, risk may exacerbate financing problems,

— **coordination and network failures**: the ability of undertakings to coordinate with each other or to inter act in order to deliver R&D&I may be impaired for various reasons, including difficulties in coordinating among a large number of collaboration partners where some of them have diverging interests, problems in designing contracts, and difficulties in coordinating collaboration due for example to sensitive information being shared.

4.2.2. Additional conditions for individual aid

50. Whilst certain market failures may hamper the overall level of R&D&I in the Union, not all undertakings and sectors in the economy are affected by them to the same extent. Consequently, for notifiable individual aid, Member States should provide adequate information about whether the aid addresses a general market failure regarding R&D&I in the Union, or a specific market failure regarding, for example, a particular sector or line of business.

51. Depending on the specific market failure to be addressed, the Commission will take into consideration the following elements:

— **knowledge spillovers**: level of knowledge dissemination envisaged; specificity of the knowledge created; availability of IPR protection; degree of complementarity with other products and services,

— **imperfect and asymmetric information**: level of risk and complexity of R&D&I activities; need for external finance; characteristics of the aid beneficiary regarding access to external finance,

— **coordination failures**: number of collaborating undertakings; intensity of collaboration; diverging interests among collaborating partners; problems in designing contracts; problems to coordinate collaboration.

52. In its analysis of an alleged market failure the Commission will in particular take into account any available sectoral comparisons and other studies, which should be provided by the Member State concerned.

53. When notifying investment or operating aid for clusters, Member States must provide information on the planned or expected specialisation of the innovation cluster, existing regional potential and presence of clusters in the Union with similar purposes.

54. With respect to State aid which is awarded for projects or activities that are also financed by the Union, either directly or indirectly (that is to say by the Commission, by its executive agencies, by joint undertakings established on the basis of Articles 185 and 187 of the Treaty, or by any other implementing bodies where the Union funding is not directly or indirectly under the control of Member States), the Commission will consider that the need for State intervention has been established.

55. On the other hand, where State aid is awarded for projects or activities which, with respect to their technological content, level of risk and size, are similar to those already delivered within the Union at market conditions, the Commission will in principle presume that no market failure is present and will require further evidence of and justification for the need for State intervention.

4.3. APPROPRIATENESS OF THE AID MEASURE

4.3.1. Appropriateness among alternative policy instruments

56. State aid is not the only policy instrument available to Member States to promote R&D&I activities. It is important to keep in mind that there may be other, better placed instruments such as demand-side measures involving regulation, public procurement or standardisation, as well as an increase in funding of public research and education and general fiscal measures. The appropriateness of a policy instrument in a given situation is normally linked to the nature of the problem that is being addressed. For instance, reducing market barriers may be more appropriate than State aid to deal with a new entrant's difficulty to appropriate R&D&I results. Increased investment in education may be more appropriate to deal with a lack of qualified personnel than awarding State aid.

57. Aid for R&D&I can be authorised as an exception to the general prohibition of State aid, when it is necessary to achieve an objective of common interest. An important element in this respect is therefore whether and to what extent aid for R&D&I can be considered an appropriate instrument to increase R&D&I activities, given that other less distortive instruments may achieve the same results.

58. In its compatibility analysis, the Commission will take particular account of any impact assessment of the proposed measure carried out by the Member State concerned. Measures, for which Member States have considered other policy options and for which the advantages of using a selective instrument such as State aid are established and submitted to the Commission, are considered to constitute an appropriate instrument.

59. With respect to State aid which is awarded for projects or activities that are also financed by the Union, either directly or indirectly (that is to say by the Commission, by its executive agencies, by joint undertakings established on the basis of Articles 185 and 187 of the Treaty, or by any other implementing bodies where the Union funding is not directly or indirectly under the control of Member States), the Commission will consider that the appropriateness of the aid measure has been established.

4.3.2. Appropriateness among different aid instruments

60. State aid for R&D&I can be awarded in various forms. Member States should therefore ensure that the aid is awarded in the form that is likely to generate the least distortions of competition and trade. In this respect, where the aid is awarded in forms that provide a direct pecuniary advantage (such as direct grants, exemptions or reductions in taxes or other compulsory charges, or the supply of land, products or services at favourable prices), the Member State concerned must include an analysis of other options and explain why or how other potentially less distortive forms of aid such as repayable advances or forms of aid that are based on debt or equity instruments (such as State guarantees, the purchase of a share-holding or an alternative provision of debt or capital on favourable terms) are less appropriate.

61. The choice of the aid instrument should be made in view of the market failure which it seeks to address. For instance, where the underlying market failure is a problem of access to external debt finance due to asymmetric information, Member States should normally resort to aid in the form of liquidity support, such as a loan or guarantee, rather than a grant. Where it is also necessary to provide the firm with a certain degree of risk sharing, a repayable advance should normally be the aid instrument of choice. In particular, where aid is awarded in a form other than liquidity support or a repayable advance for activities that are close to the market, Member States must justify the appropriateness of the chosen instrument for tackling the specific market failure in question. For aid schemes implementing the objectives and priorities of Operational Programmes, the financing instrument chosen in those programmes is in principle presumed to be an appropriate instrument.

4.4. INCENTIVE EFFECT

4.4.1. General conditions

62. R&D&I aid can only be found compatible with the internal market if it has an incentive effect. An incentive effect occurs where the aid changes the behaviour of an undertaking in such a way that it engages in additional activities, which it would not carry out or it would carry out in a restricted or different manner without the aid. The aid must however not subsidise the costs of an activity that an undertaking would anyhow incur and must not compensate for the normal business risk of an economic activity.[1]

63. The Commission considers that aid does not present an incentive for the beneficiary wherever work on the relevant R&D&I activity[2] has already started prior to the aid application by the beneficiary to the national authorities.[3] Where start of works takes place before the aid application is submitted by the beneficiary to the national authorities, the project will not be eligible for aid.

64. The aid application must include at least the applicant's name and size, a description of the project, including its location and start and end dates, the amount of public support needed to carry it out, and a list of eligible costs.

65. To the extent they constitute State aid, the Commission may consider that fiscal measures have an incentive effect, by stimulating higher R&D&I spending by undertakings, on the basis of evaluation studies[4] provided by Member States.

NOTES

1 Joined Cases C-630/11 P to C-633/11 P *HGA and Others v Commission* (not yet published).

2 If the aid application is for an R&D project, this does not exclude that the potential beneficiary would have already carried out feasibility studies which are not covered by the request for aid.

3 In the case of aid for projects or activities that are carried out in successive phases which may be subject to separate aid awarding procedures, this means that start of works must not take place before the first aid application. In the case of aid awarded under an automatic fiscal aid scheme, such scheme must have been adopted and entered into force before any work on the aided project or activity starts.

4 Even though this may not be possible *ex ante* for a newly introduced measure, Member States will be expected to provide evaluation studies on the incentive effect of their own fiscal aid schemes (so that planned or intended methodologies for *ex post* evaluations should normally be part of the design of such measures). In the absence of any evaluation studies, the incentive effect of fiscal aid schemes maybe presumed only for incremental measures.

4.4.2. Additional conditions for individual aid

66. For notifiable individual aid, Member States must demonstrate to the Commission that the aid has an incentive effect and therefore need to provide clear evidence that the aid has a positive impact on the decision of the undertaking to pursue R&D&I activities which would otherwise not have been pursued. To enable the Commission to carry out a comprehensive assessment of the aid measure in question, the Member State concerned must provide not only information concerning the aided project but also, to the extent possible, a comprehensive description of what would have happened or could reasonably have been expected to happen without aid, that is to say the counterfactual

scenario. The counterfactual scenario may consist in the absence of an alternative project or in a clearly defined and sufficiently predictable alternative project considered by the beneficiary in its internal decision making, and may relate to an alternative project that is wholly or partly carried out outside the Union.

67. In its analysis, the Commission will take into consideration the following elements:

— **specification of intended change**: the change in behaviour which is expected to result from State aid, that is to say whether a new project is triggered, or the size, scope or speed of a project is enhanced, has to be well specified,
— **counterfactual analysis**: the change of behaviour has to be identified by comparing what the expected outcome and level of intended activity would be with and without aid. The difference between the two scenarios shows the impact of the aid measure and its incentive effect,
— **level of profitability**: where a project would not, in itself, be profitable to carry out for an undertaking, but would generate important benefits for society, it is more likely that the aid has an incentive effect;
— **amount of investment and time-frame of cash flows**: a high start-up investment, a low level of appropriable cash flows and a significant fraction of the cash flow arising in the very far future or in a very uncertain manner, will be considered positive elements in assessing the incentive effect,
— **level of risk involved**: the assessment of risk will in particular take into account the irreversibility of the investment, the probability of commercial failure, the risk that the project will be less productive than expected, the risk that the project undermines other activities of the aid beneficiary and the risk that the project costs undermine its financial viability.

68. Member States are in particular invited to rely on board documents, risk assessments, financial reports, internal business plans, expert opinions and other studies related to the project under assessment. Documents containing information on demand forecasts, cost forecasts, financial forecasts, documents that are submitted to an investment committee and that describe in detail various investment scenarios, or documents provided to financial institutions could help Member States demonstrate the incentive effect.

69. In order to ensure that the incentive effect is established on an objective basis, the Commission may in its assessment compare company-specific data with data concerning the industry in which the aid beneficiary is active. In particular, Member States should where possible provide industry-specific data demonstrating that the beneficiary's counterfactual scenario, its required level of profitability and its expected cash-flows are reasonable.

70. In that context, the level of profitability can be evaluated by reference to methodologies which are demonstrably used by the beneficiary undertaking or are standard practice in the particular industry concerned, and which may include methods for evaluating the net present value of the project (NPV),[1] the internal rate of return (IRR)[2] or the average return on capital employed (ROCE).

71. If the aid does not change the behaviour of the beneficiary by stimulating additional R&D&I activities, it has no positive effects in terms of promoting R&D&I in the Union. Therefore, aid will not be considered compatible with the internal market in cases where it appears that the same activities could and would be pursued even without the aid.

NOTES

1 The net present value of a project is the difference between the positive and negative cash flows over the lifetime of the investment, discounted to their current value (using the cost of capital).

2 The IRR is not based on accounting earnings in a given year, but takes into account the stream of future cash flows that the investor expects to receive over the entire lifetime of the investment. It is defined as the discount rate for which the NPV of a stream of cash flows equals zero.

4.5. PROPORTIONALITY OF THE AID

4.5.1. General conditions

72. For any R&D&I aid to be considered proportional, its amount must be limited to the minimum needed for carrying out the aided activity.

4.5.1.1. Maximum aid intensities

73. In order to ensure that the level of aid is proportionate to the market failures which it is intended to address, the aid must be determined in relation to a predefined set of eligible costs and limited to a certain proportion of those eligible costs ('aid intensity'). The aid intensity must be established for each beneficiary of aid, including in a collaboration project.

74. To ensure predictability and a level playing field, the Commission applies maximum aid intensities for R&D&I aid, which are established on the basis of three criteria: (i) the closeness of the aid to the market, as a proxy for its expected negative effects and the need for it, taking into account the potential higher revenues that can be expected from the aided activities; (ii) the size of the beneficiary as a proxy for the more acute difficulties generally faced by smaller undertakings to finance a risky project; and (iii) the acuteness of the market failure, such as the expected externalities in terms of dissemination of knowledge. Therefore, aid intensities should generally be lower for activities linked to development and innovation than for research activities.

75. The eligible costs for each aid measure covered by this framework are set out in Annex I. When an R&D project encompasses different tasks, each eligible task must fall under the categories of fundamental research, industrial research or experimental development.[1] When classifying different activities according to the relevant category, the Commission will refer to its own practice as well as to the specific examples and explanations provided in the OECD Frascati Manual.[2]

76. The maximum aid intensities generally applicable to all eligible R&D&I measures are set out in Annex II.[3]

77. In the case of State aid for a project being carried out in collaboration between research organisations and undertakings, the combination of direct public support and, where they constitute aid, contributions from research organisations to the same project must not exceed the applicable aid intensities for each beneficiary undertaking.

NOTES

[1] This qualification does not necessarily need to follow a chronological approach, moving sequentially over time from fundamental research to activities closer to the market. Accordingly, nothing will prevent the Commission from classifying a task which is carried out at a later stage of a project as industrial research, while finding that an activity carried out at an earlier stage constitutes experimental development or is not research at all.

[2] 'The Measurement of Scientific and Technological Activities, Proposed Standard Practice for Surveys on Research and Experimental Development', Frascati Manual, OECD, 2002, as amended or replaced. For practical purposes, and unless it is shown that a different scale should be used in individual cases, the different R&D categories can also be considered to correspond to Technology Readiness Levels 1 (fundamental research), 2–4 (industrial research) and 5–8 (experimental development) – see communication from the Commission to the European Parliament, the Council, the European Economic and Social Committee and the Committee of the regions, 'A European strategy for Key Enabling Technologies – A bridge to growth and jobs', COM(2012) 341 final of 26.6.2012.

[3] Without prejudice to specific provisions applying to aid for research and development in the agricultural and fisheries sectors, as laid down in a block exemption Regulation.

4.5.1.2.
Repayable advances

78. If a Member State awards a repayable advance which qualifies as State aid within the meaning of Article 107(1) of the Treaty, the rules laid down in this section apply.

79. Where a Member State can demonstrate, on the basis of a valid methodology based on sufficient verifiable data, that it is possible to calculate the gross grant equivalent of a repayable advance, it may notify an aid scheme and the associated methodology to the Commission. If the Commission accepts the methodology and deems the scheme compatible, the aid may be awarded on the basis of the gross grant equivalent of the repayable advance, up to the aid intensities laid down in Annex II.

80. In all other cases, the repayable advance is expressed as a percentage of the eligible costs and may exceed the applicable maximum aid intensities by 10 percentage points, provided that the following conditions are fulfilled:

(a) in case of a successful outcome, the measure must provide that the advance is to be repaid with an interest rate not less than the discount rate resulting from the application of the communication from the Commission on the revision of the method for setting the reference and discount rates;[1]

(b) in case of a success exceeding the outcome defined as successful, the Member State concerned should request payments beyond repayment of the advance amount including interest according to the applicable discount rate;

(c) in case the project fails, the advance does not have to be fully repaid. In case of partial success, the repayment should be proportional to the degree of success achieved.

81. For the Commission to assess the measure, it must include detailed provisions on the repayment in case of success, which clearly define what will be considered as a successful outcome, on the basis of reasonable and prudent hypothesis.

NOTES

[1] Communication from the Commission on the revision of the method for setting the reference and discount rates (OJ C14, 19.1.2008, p 6).

4.5.1.3.
Fiscal measures

82. To the extent it constitutes State aid, the aid intensity of a fiscal measure can be calculated either on the basis of individual projects or, at the level of an undertaking, as the ratio between the overall tax relief and the sum of all eligible R&D&I costs incurred in a period not exceeding three consecutive fiscal years. In the latter case, the fiscal measure may apply without distinction to all eligible activities, but must not exceed the applicable aid intensity for experimental development.[1]

NOTES

[1] Conversely, where a fiscal aid measure distinguishes between different R&D categories, the relevant aid intensities must not be exceeded.

4.5.1.4.
Cumulation of aid

83. Aid may be awarded concurrently under several aid schemes or cumulated with ad hoc aid, provided that the total amount of State aid for an activity or project does not exceed the aid ceilings laid down in this framework. As recalled in point 9, Union funding centrally managed by the institutions, agencies, joint under takings or other bodies of the Union that is not directly or indirectly under the control of Member States does not constitute State aid and should not be taken into account. Where such Union funding is combined with State aid, the total amount of public funding awarded in relation to the same eligible costs must however not exceed the most favourable funding rate laid down in the applicable rules of Union law.

84. Where the expenditure eligible for R&D&I aid is also potentially eligible in whole or in part for aid for other purposes, the overlapping portion will be subject to the most favourable ceiling under any of the relevant rules.

85. Aid for R&D&I may not be cumulated with de minimis support in respect of the same eligible costs if that would result in an aid intensity exceeding those laid down in this framework.

4.5.2. Additional conditions for individual aid

86. For notifiable individual aid, mere compliance with a set of predefined maximum aid intensities is not sufficient to ensure proportionality.

87. As a general rule, and in order to establish whether the aid is proportional, the Commission will verify that its amount does not exceed the minimum necessary for the aided project to be sufficiently profitable, for example by making possible to achieve an IRR corresponding to the sector or firm specific benchmark or hurdle rate. Normal rates of return required by the beneficiary in other R&D&I projects, its cost of capital as a whole or returns commonly observed in the industry concerned may also be used for this purpose. All relevant expected costs and benefits must be considered over the lifetime of the project, including the costs and revenues stemming from the results of R&D&I activities.

88. Where it is shown, for example by means of internal company documents, that the aid beneficiary faces a clear choice between carrying out either an aided project or an alternative one without aid, the aid will be considered to be limited to the minimum only if its amount does not exceed the net extra costs of implementing the activities concerned, compared to the counterfactual project that would be carried out in the absence of aid. In order to establish the net extra costs, the Commission will compare the expected net present values of the investment in the aided project and the counterfactual project, account being taken of the probabilities of different business scenarios occurring.[1]

NOTES

[1] In the particular case where aid merely allows for an increase in the speed of completion of the project, the comparison should mostly reflect the different timelines in terms of cash flows and delayed entry in the market.

89. Where aid is awarded for R&D projects or for the construction or upgrade of research infrastructures and the Commission can establish, on the basis of the methodology laid down in points 87 or 88, that the aid is strictly limited to the minimum necessary, higher maximum aid intensities than those laid down in Annex II may be allowed, up to the levels set out in the following table.

	Small enterprise	**Medium-sized enterprise**	**Large enterprise**
Aid for R&D projects			
Fundamental research	100%	100%	100%
Applied research	80%	70%	60%
—subject to effective collaboration between undertakings (for large enterprises cross-border or with at least one SME) or between an undertaking and a research organisation, or —subject to wide dissemination of results	90%	80%	70%
Aid for the construction and upgrade of research infrastructures	60%	60%	60%

90. In order to demonstrate that aid is limited to the minimum necessary, Member States must explain how the aid amount has been established. Documentation and calculations used for the analysis of the incentive effect can also be used to assess whether the aid is proportionate. Insofar as the identified need for aid relates mainly to difficulties in attracting debt finance from the market, rather than to a lack of profitability, a particularly apt way to ensure that the aid is kept to the minimum may be to provide it in the form of a loan, guarantee or repayable advance instead of a non-repayable form, such as a grant.

91. Where there are multiple potential candidates for carrying out the aided activity, the proportionality requirement is more likely to be met if the aid is awarded on the basis of transparent, objective and non-discriminatory criteria.

92. In order to address actual or potential direct or indirect distortions of international trade, higher intensities than generally permissible under this framework may be authorised if, directly or indirectly, competitors located outside the Union have received in the last three years or are going to receive aid of an equivalent intensity for similar projects. However, where distortions of international trade are likely to occur after more than three years, given the particular nature of the sector in question, the reference period may be extended accordingly. Where possible, the Member State concerned will provide the Commission with sufficient information to enable it to assess the situation, in particular the need to take account of the competitive advantage enjoyed by a third country competitor. Where the Commission does not have evidence concerning the awarded or proposed aid, it may also base its decision on circumstantial evidence.

93. When gathering evidence, the Commission may use its investigative powers.[1]

NOTES

[1] See Article 1(3) of Council Regulation (EU) No 734/2013 of 22 July 2013 (OJ L204, 31.7.2013, p 15).

4.6. AVOIDANCE OF UNDUE NEGATIVE EFFECTS ON COMPETITION AND TRADE

4.6.1. General considerations

94. For R&D&I aid to be compatible with the internal market, the negative effects of the aid measure in terms of distortions of competition and impact on trade between Member States must be limited and outweighed by the positive effects in terms of contribution to the objective of common interest.

95. The Commission identifies two main potential distortions of competition and trade between Member States caused by R&D&I aid, namely product market distortions and location effects. Both types may lead to allocative inefficiencies, undermining the economic performance of the internal market, and distributional concerns, in that the aid affects the distribution of economic activity across regions.

96. As far as distortions on the product markets are concerned, State aid for R&D&I may have an impact on competition in innovation processes and in the product markets where the results of the R&D&I activities are exploited.

4.6.1.1.
Effects on product markets

97. State aid for R&D&I can hamper competition in innovation processes and product markets in three ways, namely by distorting the competitive entry and exit process, by distorting dynamic investment incentives and by creating or maintaining market power.

(i)
Distorting the competitive entry and exit processes

98. R&D&I aid may prevent the market mechanism from rewarding the most efficient producers and putting pressure on the least efficient to improve, restructure or exit the market. That might lead to a situation where, due to the aid awarded, competitors that would otherwise be able to stay on are forced out of the market, or never enter in the first place. Similarly, State aid can prevent inefficient firms from leaving the market or even induce them to enter and gain market shares from otherwise more efficient competitors. If not correctly targeted, R&D&I aid may therefore support inefficient undertakings and lead to market structures in which many players operate significantly below efficient scale. In the long run, interfering with the competitive entry and exit processes may stifle innovation and slow down industry-wide productivity improvements.

(ii)
Distorting dynamic incentives

99. R&D&I aid may distort the dynamic incentives to invest of competitors of the aid beneficiary. When an undertaking receives aid, the likelihood of successful R&D&I activities on its part generally increases, leading to an increased presence on the relevant product market(s) in the future. That increased presence may lead competitors to reduce the scope of their original investment plans (crowding out effect).

100. Furthermore, the presence of aid may make potential beneficiaries complacent or more risk seeking. The long term effect on the overall performance of the sector is in this case likely to be negative. R&D&I aid may therefore, if not correctly targeted, support inefficient undertakings and lead to market structures where many market players operate significantly below efficient scale.

(iii)
Creating or maintaining market power

101. Aid for R&D&I may also have distortive effects in terms of increasing or maintaining the degree of market power in product markets. Market power is the power to influence market prices, output, the variety or quality of products and services, or other parameters of competition for a significant period of time, to the detriment of consumers. Even where aid does not strengthen market power directly, it may do so indirectly, by discouraging the expansion of existing competitors or inducing their exit or discouraging the entry of new competitors.

4.6.1.2.
Effects on trade and location choice

102. State aid for R&D&I may also give rise to distortions of competition when it influences the choice of a location. Those distortions can arise across Member States, either when firms compete across borders or consider different locations. Aid aimed at relocating an activity in another region within the internal market may not lead directly to a distortion in the product market, but it displaces activities or investments from one region into another.

4.6.1.3.
Manifest negative effects

103. In principle, an aid measure and the context in which it is applied need to be analysed to identify the extent to which it can be deemed distortive. However, certain situations can be identified where the negative effects manifestly outweigh any positive effects, meaning that aid cannot be found compatible with the internal market.

104. In particular, according to the general principles of the Treaty, State aid cannot be considered compatible with the internal market if the aid measure is discriminatory to an extent not justified by its State aid character. As explained in Section 3, the Commission will thus not allow any measure where such measure or the conditions attached to it entail a non-severable violation of Union law. This is particularly the case for aid measures where the award of aid is subject to the obligation for the beneficiary to have its central seat in the relevant Member State (or to be predominantly established in that Member State) or to use national products or services, as well as for aid measures restricting the possibility for the beneficiary to exploit the R&D&I results in other Member States.

105. Likewise, aid that merely leads to a change in location of R&D&I activities within the internal market without changing the nature, size or scope of the project will not be considered compatible.

4.6.2. AID SCHEMES

106. In order to be compatible with the internal market, notifiable aid schemes must not lead to significant distortions of competition and trade. In particular, even where distortions may be considered limited at individual level (provided the aid is necessary and proportional to achieve the common objective), on a cumulative basis aid schemes might still lead to high levels of distortions. Such distortions may for instance result from aid that negatively affects dynamic incentives to innovate on the part of competitors. In the case of a scheme focusing on certain sectors, the risk of that kind of distortions is even more pronounced.

107. Without prejudice to point 122, Member States therefore must demonstrate that any negative effects will be limited to the minimum taking into account, for example, the size of the projects concerned, the individual and cumulative aid amounts, the number of expected beneficiaries as well as the characteristics of the targeted sectors. In order to enable the Commission to assess the likely negative effects of notifiable aid schemes, Member States may submit any impact assessment as well as ex-post evaluations carried out for similar predecessor schemes.

4.6.3. ADDITIONAL CONDITIONS FOR INDIVIDUAL AID

4.6.3.1.
Distortions in product markets

108. For notifiable individual aid, in order to enable the Commission to identify and assess potential distortions of competition and trade, Member States should provide information on (i) the product markets concerned, that is to say the markets affected by the change in behaviour of the aid beneficiary, and (ii) the competitors and customers or consumers affected.

109. In assessing the negative effects of the aid measure, the Commission will focus its analysis of the distortions of competition on the foreseeable impact of the R&D&I aid on competition between undertakings in the product markets concerned. The Commission will give more weight to risks for competition and trade that arise in the near future and with particular likelihood.

110. To the extent that a specific innovative activity will be associated with multiple future product markets, the impact of State aid will be looked upon on the set of markets concerned. In certain cases the results of R&D&I activities, for example in the form of IPR, are themselves traded in technology markets, for instance through patent licensing or trading. In those cases, the Commission may also consider the effect of the aid on competition in technology markets.

111. The Commission will use various criteria to assess the potential distortions of competition, namely distorting dynamic incentives, creating or maintaining market power, and maintaining inefficient market structures.

(i)
Distorting dynamic incentives

112. In its analysis of the potential distortion of dynamic incentives, the Commission will consider the following elements:

— *Market growth*: the more the market is expected to grow in the future, the less likely that the competitors' incentives will be negatively affected by the aid, given that there remain ample opportunities to develop a profitable business,

— *Aid amount*: aid measures which involve significant amounts of aid are more likely to lead to significant crowding out effects. The significance of the aid amount will be measured mainly with reference to the amount spent by the main market players on projects of a similar kind,

— *Closeness to the market/category of the aid*: the more the aid measure is aimed at activities close to the market, the more it is liable to develop significant crowding out effects,

— *Open selection process*: where the aid is awarded on the basis of transparent, objective and non-discriminatory criteria, the Commission will take a more positive stance,

— *Exit barriers*: competitors are more likely to maintain, or even to increase their investment plans when exit barriers to the innovation process are high. That may be the case when many of the competitors' past investments are locked in to a particular R&D&I trajectory,

— *Incentives to compete for a future market*: R&D&I aid may lead to a situation where competitors of the aid beneficiary renounce competing for a future 'winner takes all' market, because the advantage provided by the aid, in terms of degree of technological advance, economies of scale, network effects or timing, reduces their possibility to potentially successfully enter that future market,

— *Product differentiation and intensity of competition*: where product innovation is rather about developing differentiated products, related for example to distinct brands, standards, technologies or consumer groups, competitors are less likely to be affected. The same situation arises where there are many effective competitors in the market.

(ii)
Creating or maintaining market power

113. The Commission is concerned mainly about those R&D&I measures which enable the aid beneficiary to strengthen market power held on existing product markets or to transfer it to future product markets. The Commission is therefore unlikely to identify competition concerns related to market power in cases where the aid beneficiary has a market share below 25% and in markets with a market concentration below 2,000 on the Herfindahl-Hirschman Index (HHI).

114. In its analysis of market power, the Commission will consider the following elements:

— *Market power of the aid beneficiary and market structure*: where the aid recipient is already dominant on a product market, the aid measure may reinforce that dominance by further weakening the competitive constraint that competitors can exert on the recipient undertaking. Similarly, State aid measures may have a significant impact in oligopolistic markets where only a few players are active,
— *Level of entry barriers*: in the field of R&D&I, there may be significant barriers to entry for new entrants. Those barriers include legal entry barriers (in particular in respect of IPR), economies of scale and scope, access barriers to networks and infrastructure, and other strategic barriers to entry or expansion,
— *Buyer power*: the market power of an undertaking may also be limited by the market position of the buyers. The presence of strong buyers can serve to counter a finding of a strong market position if it is likely that the buyers will seek to preserve sufficient competition in the market,
— *Selection process*: aid measures which allow undertakings with a strong market position to influence the selection process, for example by having the right to recommend undertakings in the selection process or influencing the research path in a way which disfavours alternative paths on unjustified grounds, are liable to raise concern by the Commission.

(iii)
Maintaining inefficient market structures

115. In its analysis of market structures, the Commission will consider whether the aid is awarded in markets featuring overcapacity or in declining industries. Situations where the market is growing or where State aid for R&D&I is likely to change the overall growth dynamics of the sector, notably by introducing new technologies, are less likely to give rise to concerns.

4.6.3.2.
Location effects

116. In particular where R&D&I aid is close to the market, it may result in some territories benefiting from more favourable conditions in respect of subsequent production, particularly because of comparatively lower production costs as a result of the aid or due to higher levels of R&D&I activities pursued through the aid. This may lead undertakings to re-locate to those territories.

117. Location effects may also be relevant to research infrastructures. If aid is mainly used to attract an infrastructure to a particular region at the expense of another, it will not contribute to promoting further R&D&I activities in the Union.

118. In its analysis of notifiable individual aid, the Commission will accordingly take into account any evidence that the aid beneficiary has considered alternative locations.

4.7. TRANSPARENCY

119. As from 1 July 2016, and with the exception of individual aid awards below EUR 500,000, Member States must publish on a comprehensive State aid website, at national or regional level, at least the following information on notified State aid measures: the full text of the aid scheme and its implementing provisions or legal basis for individual aid, or a link to it; the identity of the aid awarding authority; the identity of individual beneficiaries; the form and amount of aid awarded to each beneficiary; the date of award; the type of beneficiary (SME or large enterprise); the region in which the beneficiary is located (at NUTS level II); and the principal economic sector in which the beneficiary has its activities (at NACE group level).[1] Such information must be published within six months after the awarding decision has been taken or, for fiscal measures, within one year from the date of the tax declaration, must be kept for at least 10 years and must be available to the general public without restrictions.[2]

NOTES

[1] With the exception of business secrets and other confidential information in duly justified cases and subject to the Commission's agreement (Commission communication of 1.12.2003 on professional secrecy in State aid decisions, C(2003) 4582 (OJ C297, 9.12.2003, p 6)). For fiscal measures, the information on individual aid amounts can be provided in the following ranges (in EUR million): [0.5–1];[1–2]; [2–5]; [5–10]; [10–30]; [30 and more].

[2] In case of unlawful aid, Member States will be required to ensure the *ex post* publication of the same information, at the latest six months after the date of the Commission decision. This information should be available in a format which allows data to be searched, extracted, and easily published on the internet, for instance in CSV or XML format.

5. EVALUATION

[5.302]

120. To further ensure that distortions of competition and trade are limited, the Commission may require that notifiable aid schemes be subject to a time limitation and to the evaluation referred to in point 37. Evaluations should in particular be carried out for schemes where the potential distortions are particularly high, that is to say schemes that may risk to significantly restrict competition if their implementation is not reviewed in due time.

121. Given its objectives and in order not to put a disproportionate burden on Member States and on smaller aid measures, the requirement referred to in point 120 will apply only for aid schemes with large budgets, containing novel characteristics or when significant market, technology or regulatory changes are fore seen. The evaluation must be carried out by an expert independent from the aid awarding authority on the basis of a common methodology provided by the Commission[1] and must be made public. Member States must notify, together with the relevant aid scheme, a draft evaluation plan, which will be an integral part of the Commission assessment of the scheme.

122. In the case of aid schemes excluded from the scope of a block exemption Regulation exclusively on the grounds of their large budget, the Commission will assess their compatibility solely on the basis of the evaluation plan.

123. The evaluation must be submitted to the Commission in due time to allow for the assessment of the possible prolongation of the aid scheme and in any case upon its expiry. The precise scope and modalities of each evaluation will be defined in the decision approving the aid scheme. Any subsequent aid measure with a similar objective, including any alteration of aid schemes referred to in point 122, must take into account the results of the evaluation.

NOTES

1 See the separate communication from the Commission on common methodological guidance on State aid evaluation.

6. REPORTING AND MONITORING

[5.303]

124. In accordance with Council Regulation (EC) No 659/1999[1] and Commission Regulation (EC) No 794/2004[2] and their subsequent amendments, Member States must submit annual reports to the Commission.

125. Member States must maintain detailed records regarding all aid measures. Such records must contain all information necessary to establish that the conditions regarding eligible costs and maximum aid intensities have been fulfilled. Those records must be maintained for 10 years from the date of award of the aid and must be provided to the Commission upon request.

NOTES

1 Council Regulation (EC) No 659/1999 laying down detailed rules for the application of Article 93 of the EC Treaty (OJ L83, 27.3.1999, p 1).

2 Commission Regulation (EC) No 794/2004 of 21 April 2004 implementing Council Regulation (EC) No 659/1999 laying down detailed rules for the application of Article 93 of the EC Treaty (OJ L140, 30.4.2004, p 1).

7. APPLICABILITY

[5.304]

126. The Commission will apply the principles set out in this framework for the compatibility assessment of all notified R&D&I aid in respect of which it is called upon to take a decision after 1 July 2016. Unlawful R&D&I aid will be assessed in accordance with the rules applicable at the date on which the aid was awarded.

127. Pursuant to Article 108(1) of the Treaty, the Commission proposes that Member States amend, where necessary, their existing R&D&I aid schemes in order to bring them into line with this framework no later than 1 January 2015.

128. Member States are invited to give their explicit unconditional agreement to the appropriate measures proposed in point 127 within two months from the date of publication of this framework in the *Official Journal of the European Union*. In the absence of a reply from any of the Member States, the Commission will assume that the Member State in question does not agree with the proposed measures.

8. REVISION

[5.305]

129. The Commission may decide to review or amend this framework at any time should it be necessary for reasons associated with competition policy or in order to take account of other Union policies and international commitments or for any other justified reason.

ANNEX I
ELIGIBLE COSTS

[5.306]

Aid for R&D projects	(a) Personnel costs: researchers, technicians and other supporting staff to the extent employed on the project. (b) Costs of instruments and equipment to the extent and for the period used for the project. If such instruments and equipment are not used for their full life for the project, only the depreciation costs corresponding to the life of the project, as calculated on the basis of good accounting practice, are considered as eligible. (c) Costs of buildings and land, to the extent and for the period used for the project. With regard to buildings, only the depreciation costs corresponding to the life of the project, as calculated on the basis of good accounting practice are considered as eligible. For land, costs of commercial transfer or actually incurred capital costs are eligible. (d) Cost of contractual research, knowledge and patents bought or licensed from outside sources at arm's length conditions, as well as costs of consultancy and equivalent services used exclusively for the project. (e) Additional overheads incurred directly as a result of the project. (f) Other operating expenses, including costs of materials, supplies and similar products incurred directly as a result of the project.
Aid for feasibility studies	Costs of study.

Aid for the construction and upgrade of research infrastructures	Investment costs in intangible and tangible assets.
Innovation aid for SMEs	(a) Costs for obtaining, validating and defending patents and other intangible assets. (b) Costs for secondment of highly qualified personnel from a research and knowledge dissemination organisation or a large enterprise, working on R&D&I activities in a newly created function within the beneficiary and not replacing other personnel. (c) Costs for innovation advisory and support services.
Aid for process and organisational innovation	Personnel costs; costs of instruments, equipment, buildings and land to the extent and for the period used for the project; costs of contractual research, knowledge and patents bought or licensed from outside sources at arm's length conditions; additional overheads and other operating costs, including costs of materials, supplies and similar products, incurred directly as a result of the project.
Aid for innovation clusters	
Investment aid	Investment costs in tangible and intangible assets.
Operating aid	Personnel and administrative costs (including overhead costs) relating to: (a) animation of the cluster to facilitate collaboration, information sharing and the provision or channel ling of specialised and customised business support services; (b) marketing of the cluster to increase participation of new undertakings or organisations and to increase visibility; (c) management of the cluster's facilities; and (d) organisation of training programmes, workshops and conferences to support knowledge sharing and networking and transnational cooperation.

ANNEX II
MAXIMUM AID INTENSITIES

[5.307]

	Small enterprise	**Medium-sized enterprise**	**Large enterprise**
Aid for R&D projects			
Fundamental research	100%	100%	100%
Industrial research	70%	60%	50%
— subject to effective collaboration between undertakings (for large enterprises, cross-border or with at least one SME) or between an undertaking and a research organisation, or — subject to wide dissemination of results	80%	75%	65%
Experimental development	45%	35%	25%
— subject to effective collaboration between undertakings (for large enterprises, cross-border or with at least one SME) or between an undertaking and a research organisation, or — subject to wide dissemination of results	60%	50%	40%
Aid for feasibility studies	70%	60%	50%
Aid for the construction and upgrade of research infrastructures	50%	50%	50%
Innovation aid for SMEs	50%	50%	-
Aid for process and organisational innovation	50%	50%	15%
Aid for innovation clusters			
Investment aid	50%	50%	50%
— in assisted regions fulfilling the conditions of Article 107(3)(c) of the Treaty,	55%	55%	55%
— in assisted regions fulfilling the conditions of Article 107(3)(a) of the Treaty	65%	65%	65%
Operating aid	50%	50%	50%

5. ENVIRONMENTAL AID

COMMUNICATION FROM THE COMMISSION

(2014/C200/01)

Guidelines on State aid for environmental protection and energy 2014–2020 (Note)

[5.308]

NOTES

Date of publication in OJ: OJ C200, 28.06.2014, p 1. The text of this Communication was corrected by a corrigendum published in OJ C290, 10.8.2016, p 11.

Editorial note: these Guidelines were due to expire on 31 December 2020, but were extended to 31 December 2021 by Communication from the Commission concerning the prolongation and the amendments of the Guidelines on Regional State Aid for 2014-2020, Guidelines on State Aid to Promote Risk Finance Investments, Guidelines on State Aid for Environmental Protection and Energy 2014-2020, Guidelines on State aid for rescuing and restructuring non-financial undertakings in difficulty, Communication on the Criteria for the Analysis of the Compatibility with the Internal Market of State Aid to Promote the Execution of Important Projects of Common European Interest, Communication from the Commission – Framework for State aid for research and development and innovation and Communication from the Commission to the Member States on the application of Articles 107 and 108 of the Treaty on the Functioning of the European Union to short-term export-credit insurance (2020/C224/02).

These Guidelines are applicable until the end of 2021, but have been omitted from this edition of the Handbook due to constraints on the amount of available space. Customers who wish to refer to the Guidelines are advised to retain the 26th edition (2020) of this Handbook. Revised guidelines are due to be published before the end of the year (see also the list of consultations and draft documents in the Appendix at **[A1]**).

COMMUNICATION FROM THE COMMISSION

Guidelines on certain State aid measures in the context of the system for greenhouse gas emission allowance trading post 2021

Brussels, 21.9.2020 C(2020) 6400 final

[5.309]

NOTES

Date of publication in OJ: OJ C317, 25.9.2020, p 5.

TABLE OF CONTENTS

INTRODUCTION

[5.310]

1. In order to prevent State aid from distorting competition in the internal market and affecting trade between Member States in a way which is contrary to the common interest, Article 107(1) of the Treaty on the Functioning of the European Union ('the Treaty') lays down the principle that State aid is prohibited unless it falls within the categories of exceptions laid down in Article 107(2) of the Treaty or is declared by the Commission compatible with the internal market pursuant to Article 107(3) of the Treaty. Articles 42 and 93, Article 106(2) and Article 108(2) and (4) of the Treaty also provide for conditions under which State aid is or may be considered compatible with the internal market.

2. On the basis of Article 107(3)(c) of the Treaty, the Commission may consider State aid to facilitate the development of certain economic activities compatible with the internal market, where such aid does not adversely affect trading conditions to an extent contrary to the common interest.

3. Directive 2003/87/EC of the European Parliament and of the Council[1] established a system for greenhouse gas emission allowance trading within the Union (hereinafter referred to as the 'EU ETS'), in order to promote reductions of greenhouse gas emissions in a cost-effective and economically efficient manner. Directive 2003/87/EC was amended in 2018[2] to improve and extend the EU ETS for the period 2021-2030.

4. On 11 December 2019, the Commission published the European Green Deal Communication,[3] outlining the policies to achieve climate-neutrality in Europe by 2050 and to address other environmental problems. To deliver the European Green Deal, there is a need to rethink policies for clean energy supply across the economy, including industry, production and consumption, large-scale infrastructure, transport, food and agriculture, construction, as well as taxation and social benefits.

5. As long as many international partners do not share the same ambition as the Union, there is a risk of carbon leakage, either because production is transferred from the Union to other countries with lower ambition for emission reduction, or because Union products are replaced by more carbon-intensive imports. If this risk materialises, there will be no reduction in global emissions, and this will frustrate the efforts of the Union and its industries to meet the global climate objectives of the Paris Agreement,[4] adopted on 12 December 2015, following the 21st Conference of the Parties to the United Nations Framework Convention on Climate Change (the 'Paris Agreement').

6. The primary objective of State aid control in the context of implementation of the EU ETS is to ensure that the positive effects of the aid outweigh its negative effects in terms of distortions of competition in the internal market. State aid must be necessary to achieve the environmental objective of the EU ETS (necessity of the aid) and must be limited to the minimum needed to achieve the environmental protection sought (proportionality of the aid) without creating undue distortions of competition and trade in the internal market.

7. In these Guidelines, the Commission sets out the conditions under which aid measures in the context of the EU ETS may be considered compatible with the internal market under Article 107(3)(c) of the Treaty. Following the review and possible revision of all climate-related policy instruments (notably of the Directive 2003/87/EC) to deliver additional greenhouse gas emissions reductions for 2030, reflecting the Climate Target Plan, and the initiative for the creation of a Carbon Border Adjustment Mechanism, the Commission will check whether any revision or adaptation of these Guidelines is necessary to ensure consistency with, and contribute to, the fulfilment of the climate neutrality objective while respecting a level playing field.[5]

8. These Guidelines also take into account the specificities of European small and medium enterprises (SMEs), in line with the SME Strategy for a sustainable and digital Europe.[6]

NOTES

1 Directive 2003/87/EC of the European Parliament and of the Council of 13 October 2003 establishing a system for greenhouse gas emission allowance trading within the Union and amending Council Directive 96/61/EC (OJ L275, 25.10.2003, p 32).

2 Directive (EU) 2018/410 of the European Parliament and of the Council of 14 March 2018 amending Directive 2003/87/EC to enhance cost-effective emission reductions and low-carbon investments, and Decision (EU) 2015/1814 (OJ L76, 19.3.2018, p 3).

3 Communication from the Commission to the European Parliament, the European Council, the Council, the European Economic and Social Committee and the Committee of the Regions, The European Green Deal, COM(2019) 640 final

4 OJ L282, 19.10.2016, p 4.

5 See conclusions adopted by the European Council at the meeting of 12 December 2019.

6 Communication from the Commission to the European Parliament, the Council, the European Economic and Social Committee and the Committee of the Regions, An SME Strategy for a sustainable and digital Europe, COM(2020) 103 final.

1. SCOPE AND DEFINITIONS

1.1. SCOPE OF APPLICATION

[5.311]

9. The principles set out in these Guidelines apply only to the specific aid measures provided for in Articles 10a(6) and 10b of the Directive 2003/87/EC.

10. Aid may not be awarded to firms in difficulty within the meaning of the Guidelines on State aid for rescuing and restructuring firms in difficulty.[7]

11. When assessing aid in favour of an undertaking which is subject to an outstanding recovery order following a previous Commission decision declaring aid to be illegal and incompatible with the internal market, the Commission will take account of the amount of aid still to be recovered.[8] In practice, it will assess the cumulative effect of both aid measures and may suspend the payment of the new aid until the outstanding recovery order is implemented.

1.2. AID MEASURES COVERED BY THESE GUIDELINES

1.2.1. AID TO COMPENSATE FOR INCREASES IN ELECTRICITY PRICES RESULTING FROM THE INCLUSION OF THE COSTS OF GREENHOUSE GAS EMISSIONS DUE TO THE EU ETS (COMMONLY REFERRED TO AS 'INDIRECT EMISSION COSTS')

12. Under Article 10a(6) of Directive 2003/87/EC, Member States should adopt financial measures in favour of sectors or subsectors which are exposed to a genuine risk of carbon leakage due to significant indirect costs that are actually incurred from greenhouse gas emission costs passed on in electricity prices, provided that such financial measures are in accordance with State aid rules, and in particular do not cause undue distortions of competition in the internal market.

1.2.2. AID INVOLVED IN THE OPTIONAL TRANSITIONAL FREE ALLOCATION FOR THE MODERNISATION OF THE ENERGY SECTOR

13. Under Article 10c of Directive 2003/87/EC, Member States fulfilling certain conditions relating to the level of GDP per capita in comparison to the Union average, may derogate from the principle set out in the second subparagraph of Article 10a(1) of Directive 2003/87/EC that no free allocation is to be made in respect of any electricity production. Those Member States may give a transitional free allocation to installations for electricity generation for the modernisation, diversification and sustainable transformation of the energy sector.

14. As already established in a number of Commission decisions,[9] the granting of transitional free allowances to the energy sector involves State aid within the meaning of Article 107(1) of the Treaty, because Member States forego revenues by granting free allowances and give a selective advantage to energy actors. Those actors may compete with energy actors in other Member States, which may, as a result, distort or threaten to distort competition and affect trade in the internal market.

1.3. DEFINITIONS

15. For the purposes of these Guidelines the following definitions apply:

(1) 'aid' means any measure fulfilling all the criteria laid down in Article 107(1) of the Treaty;

(2) 'aid granting period' means one or more years within the period 2021-2030. If a Member State wishes to grant aid corresponding to a shorter period, it should take as a reference a business year of the beneficiaries and grant aid on a yearly basis;

(3) 'carbon leakage' means the prospect of an increase in global greenhouse gas emissions when companies shift production outside the Union because they cannot pass on the cost increases induced by the EU ETS to their customers without significant loss of market share;

(4) 'maximum aid intensity' means the total aid amount expressed as a percentage of the eligible costs;

(5) 'auto generation' means generation of electricity by an installation that does not qualify as an 'electricity generator' within the meaning of point (u) of Article 3 of Directive 2003/87/EC;

(6) 'beneficiary' means an undertaking receiving aid;

(7) 'European Union Allowance' (EUA) means a transferable allowance to emit one tonne of CO_2 equivalent during a specified period;

(8) 'gross value added' (GVA) means gross value added at factor costs, which is GVA at market prices less any indirect taxes plus any subsidies.

(9) 'EUA forward price', in euros, means the simple average of the daily one-year forward EUA prices (closing offer prices) for delivery in December of the year for which the aid is granted, as observed in a given EU carbon exchange from 1 January to 31 December of the year preceding the year for which the aid is granted.[10]

(10) 'CO_2 emission factor', in tCO_2/MWh, means the weighted average of the CO_2 intensity of electricity produced from fossil fuels in different geographic areas. The weight reflects the production mix of the fossil fuels in the given geographic area. The CO_2 factor is the result of the division of the CO_2 equivalent emission data of the energy industry divided by the gross electricity generation based on fossil fuels in TWh. For the purposes of these Guidelines,[11] the areas are defined as geographic zones (a) which consist of submarkets coupled through power exchanges, or (b) within which no declared congestion exists and, in both cases, hourly day-ahead power exchange prices within the zones showing price divergence in euros (using daily ECB exchange rates) of maximum 1% in significant number of all hours in a year. Such regional differentiation reflects the significance of fossil fuel plants for the final price set on the wholesale market and their role as marginal plants in the merit order. The mere fact that electricity is traded between two Member States does not automatically mean that they constitute a supranational region. Given the lack of relevant data at sub-national level, the geographic areas comprise the entire territory of one or more Member States. On this basis, the following geographic areas can be identified: Adriatic (Croatia and Slovenia), Nordic (Sweden and Finland), Baltic (Lithuania, Latvia and Estonia), Central Western Europe (Austria, Germany and Luxembourg), Iberia (Portugal and Spain), Czechia and Slovakia (Czechia and Slovakia) and all other Member States separately. The corresponding maximum regional CO_2 factors, which apply as maximal values when the notifying Member State has not established an assessment of the market based CO_2 factor pursuant to point (11) below, are listed in Annex III. In order to ensure equal treatment of sources of electricity and avoid possible abuses, the same CO_2 emission factor applies to all sources of electricity supply (auto generation, electricity supply contracts or grid supply) and to all aid beneficiaries in the Member State concerned;

(11) 'market-based CO_2 emission factor', in tCO_2/MWh. Member States intending to grant indirect cost compensation may, as part of the notification of the relevant scheme, request that the applicable CO_2 emission factor be established based on a study of the CO_2 content of the actual margin setting technology in the electricity market. Such a notification of a market-based CO_2 emission factor must demonstrate the appropriateness of the retained market-based CO_2 emission factor based on a model of the electrical system simulating price formation and observed data on the margin setting technology over the entire year t-1 (including the hours when imports were margin setting). This report must be submitted to the national regulatory authority for approval and transmitted to the Commission when the State aid measure is notified to the Commission pursuant to Article 108(3) of the Treaty. The Commission assesses the appropriateness of the study and the resulting market-based CO_2 emission factor as parts of its compatibility analysis under Article 107(3)(c) of the Treaty and the present guidelines;

(12) 'actual output', in tonnes per year, means the installation's actual production in year t, determined *ex post* in year t+1;

(13) 'actual electricity consumption', in MWh, means the actual electricity consumption at the installation (including electricity consumption for the production of out-sourced products eligible for aid) in year t, determined *ex post* in year t+1;

(14) 'electricity consumption efficiency benchmark', in MWh/tonne of output and defined at Prodcom 8 level,[12] means the product-specific electricity consumption per tonne of output achieved by the most electricity-efficient methods of production for the product considered. The electricity consumption efficiency benchmark update needs to be consistent with Article 10a(2) of Directive 2003/87/EC. For products within the eligible sectors for which fuel and electricity exchangeability has been established in section 2 of Annex I to Commission Delegated Regulation (EU) 2019/331,[13] electricity consumption efficiency benchmarks are determined within the same system boundaries, taking into account only the share of electricity for the determination of the aid amount. The corresponding electricity consumption benchmarks for products covered by eligible sectors are listed in Annex II to these Guidelines;

(15) 'fall back electricity consumption efficiency benchmark' means [. . .] per cent of actual electricity consumption, determined by Commission decision together with the electricity consumption efficiency benchmarks. It corresponds to the average reduction effort imposed by the application of the electricity consumption efficiency benchmarks (benchmark electricity consumption/*ex-ante* electricity consumption). It is applied for all products which fall within the eligible sectors, but for which an electricity consumption efficiency benchmark is not defined.

NOTES

7 Guidelines on State aid for rescuing and restructuring non-financial undertakings in difficulty (OJ C249, 31.7.2014, p 1).

8 See in this respect the joint Cases T-244/93 and T-486/93, TWD *Textilwerke Deggendorf GmbH v Commission* ECLI:EU:T:1995:160, and the Notice from the Commission — Towards an effective implementation of Commission decisions ordering Member States to recover unlawful and incompatible State aid (OJ C272, 15.11.2007, p 4).

9 See for example, Commission decision SA.34385 — Bulgaria — Allocation of free greenhouse gas emission allowances in line with Article 10c of Directive 2003/87/EC in exchange for investments in installations for electricity production and in energy infrastructure (OJ C63, 20.2.2015, p 1); Commission decision SA.34674 — Poland — Free allowances to power generators under Article 10c of Directive 2003/87/EC (OJ C24, 23.1.2015, p 1).

10 For example, for aid granted for 2023, it is the simple average of the December 2023 EUA closing offer prices observed from 1 January 2022 to 31 December 2022 in a given EU carbon exchange.

11 These Guidelines do not qualify as legislative instruments and therefore do not have to be incorporated into the EEA Agreement by the EEA Joint Committee. The EFTA Surveillance Authority is responsible for setting the relevant rules applicable for EFTA States, including the methodology for setting the CO_2 factors.

12 The Prodcom list is a European list of products from extractive and manufacturing industries: https://ec.europa.eu/eurostat/ramon/nomenclatures/index.cfm?TargetUrl=LST_NOM&StrGroupCode=CLASSIFIC&StrLanguageCode=EN&IntFamilyCode=&TxtSearch=prodcom&IntCurrentPage=1.

13 Commission Delegated Regulation (EU) 2019/331 of 19 December 2018 determining transitional Union-wide rules for harmonised free allocation of emission allowances pursuant to Article 10a of Directive 2003/87/EC of the European Parliament and of the Council (OJ L59, 27.2.2019, p 8).

2. COMMON ASSESSMENT PRINCIPLES

[5.312]

16. To assess whether a notified aid measure can be considered compatible with the internal market, the Commission generally analyses whether the design of the aid measure ensures that the positive impact of the aid towards the achievement of an objective of common interest exceeds its potential negative effects on trade and competition.

17. The communication on State aid modernisation of 8 May 2012[14] called for the identification and definition of common principles applicable to the assessment of compatibility of all the aid measures carried out by the Commission. The Commission will therefore consider an aid measure compatible with the Treaty only if it satisfies each of the following criteria: it must contribute to an objective of common interest in accordance with Article 107(3) of the Treaty; it must be targeted towards a situation where aid can bring about a material improvement that the market cannot deliver itself, for example by remedying a market failure or addressing an equity or cohesion concern; it must be an appropriate policy instrument to address the objective of common interest; it must change the behaviour of the undertakings concerned in such a way that they engage in additional activity, which they would not carry out without the aid or would carry out in a restricted or different manner or location; the amount and intensity of the aid must be limited to the minimum needed; the negative effects of the aid must be sufficiently limited; Member States, the Commission, economic operators and the public must have easy access to all relevant acts and to pertinent information about the aid awarded thereunder.

18. Sections 3.1 and 3.2 explain how these general criteria translate into specific compatibility requirements to be met for the purposes of the aid measures covered by these Guidelines.

NOTES

14 COM/2012/0209 final

3. COMPATIBILITY ASSESSMENT UNDER ARTICLE 107(3)(C) OF THE TREATY

3.1. AID TO UNDERTAKINGS IN SECTORS DEEMED TO BE EXPOSED TO A GENUINE RISK OF CARBON LEAKAGE DUE TO SIGNIFICANT INDIRECT COSTS THAT ARE ACTUALLY INCURRED FROM GREENHOUSE GAS EMISSION COSTS PASSED ON IN ELECTRICITY PRICES (AID FOR INDIRECT EMISSION COSTS)

[5.313]

19. Aid for indirect emission costs will be considered compatible with the internal market within the meaning of Article 107(3)(c) of the Treaty provided that the conditions below are met.

20. The objective of this type of aid is to prevent a significant risk of carbon leakage, in particular due to EUA costs passed on in electricity prices supported by the beneficiary, if its competitors from third countries do not face similar costs in their electricity prices and the beneficiary is unable to pass on those costs to product prices without losing significant market share. Addressing the risk of carbon leakage, by assisting beneficiaries to reduce their exposure to this risk, serves an environmental objective, since the aid aims to avoid an increase in global greenhouse gas emissions due to shifts of production outside the Union, in the absence of a binding international agreement on reduction of greenhouse gas emissions.

21. To limit the risk of competition distortion within the internal market, the aid must be limited to sectors that are exposed to a genuine risk of carbon leakage due to significant indirect costs that are actually incurred as a consequence of greenhouse gas emission costs being passed on in electricity prices. For the purpose of these Guidelines, a genuine risk of carbon leakage is considered to exist only if the beneficiary is active in a sector listed in Annex I.

22. If Member States decide to grant the aid only to some of the sectors listed in Annex I, the choice of sectors must be made on the basis of objective, non-discriminatory and transparent criteria.

23. Within the eligible sector, Member States need to ensure that the choice of beneficiaries is made on the basis of objective, non-discriminatory and transparent criteria and that the aid is granted in principle in the same way for all competitors in the same sector if they are in a similar factual situation.

24. For the purpose of compensating indirect ETS costs, State aid is considered an appropriate instrument independently of the form in which it is granted. In this context, compensation taking the form of a direct grant is considered an appropriate instrument.

25. The aid is compatible with the internal market only if it has an incentive effect. For the aid to have an incentive effect and actually prevent carbon leakage, it must be applied for and paid to the beneficiary in the year in which the costs are incurred or in the following year.

26. If aid is paid in the year in which the costs are incurred, an ex-post payment adjustment mechanism must be in place to ensure that any over-payment of aid will be repaid before 1 July in the following year.

27. The aid is proportionate and has a sufficiently limited negative effect on competition and trade if it does not exceed 75% of the indirect emission costs incurred. The electricity consumption efficiency benchmark ensures that support to inefficient production processes remains limited and maintains the incentive for dissemination of most energy-efficient technologies.

28. The maximum aid payable per installation for the manufacture of products within the sectors listed in Annex I must be calculated according to the following formula:

(a) Where electricity consumption efficiency benchmarks listed in Annex II are applicable to the products manufactured by the beneficiary, the maximum aid payable per installation for costs incurred in year t equals:
$Amax_t = Ai \times C_t \times P_{t-1} \times E \times AO_t$
In this formula, Ai is the aid intensity, expressed as a fraction (e.g. 0.75); C_t is the applicable CO_2 emission factor or market-based CO_2 emission factor (tCO_2/MWh) (at year t); P_{t-1} is the EUA forward price at year t-1 (EUR/tCO_2); E is the applicable product-specific electricity consumption efficiency benchmark defined in Annex II; and AO_t is the actual output in year t. These concepts are defined in section 1.3.

(b) Where electricity consumption efficiency benchmarks listed in Annex II are not applicable to the products manufactured by the beneficiary, the maximum aid payable per installation for costs incurred in year t equals:
$Amax_t = Ai \times C_t \times P_{t-1} \times EF \times AEC_t$
In this formula, Ai is the aid intensity, expressed as a fraction (e.g. 0.75); C_t is the applicable CO_2 emission factor (tCO_2/MWh) (at year t); P_{t-1} is the EUA forward price at year t-1 (EUR/tCO_2); EF is the fall-back electricity consumption efficiency benchmark as defined in Annex II; and AEC is the actual electricity consumption (MWh) in year t. These concepts are defined in section 1.3.

29. If an installation manufactures products for which an electricity consumption efficiency benchmark listed in Annex II is applicable and products for which the fall back electricity consumption efficiency benchmark is applicable, the electricity consumption for each product must be apportioned according to the respective tonnage of production of each product.

30. If an installation manufactures products that are eligible for aid (that is to say, they fall within the eligible sectors listed in Annex I) and products that are not eligible for aid, the maximum aid payable must be calculated only for the products that are eligible for aid.

31. Given that for some sectors the aid intensity of 75% might not be sufficient to ensure that there is adequate protection against the risk of carbon leakage, when needed, Member States may limit the amount of the indirect costs to be paid at undertaking level to 1.5% of the gross value added of the undertaking concerned in year t. The gross value added of the undertaking must be calculated as turnover, plus capitalised production, plus other operating income, plus or minus changes in stocks, minus purchases of goods and services (which shall not include personnel costs), minus other taxes on products that are linked to turnover but not deductible, minus duties and taxes linked to production. Alternatively, it can be calculated from gross operating surplus by adding personnel costs. Income and expenditure classified as financial or extraordinary in company accounts is excluded from value added. Value added at factor costs is calculated at gross level, as value adjustments (such as depreciation) are not subtracted.[15]

32. When Member States decide to limit the amount of the indirect costs to be paid at undertaking level to 1.5% of gross value added, that limitation must apply to all eligible undertakings in the relevant sector. If Member States decide to apply the limitation of 1.5% of gross value added only to some of the sectors listed in Annex I, the choice of sectors must be made on the basis of objective, non-discriminatory and transparent criteria.

33. The aid may be cumulated with:

(a) any other State aid in relation to different identifiable eligible costs,

(b) any other State aid, in relation to the same eligible costs, partly or fully overlapping, and any other State aid without identifiable eligible costs, only if such cumulation does not result in exceeding the maximum aid intensity or aid amount applicable to the aid under this section.

34. Union funding centrally managed by the Commission that is not directly or indirectly under the control of the Member State, does not constitute State aid. Where such Union funding is combined with State aid, only the latter is considered for determining whether notification thresholds and maximum aid intensities are respected, provided that the total amount of public funding granted in relation to the same eligible costs does not exceed the maximum funding rate(s) laid down in the applicable rules of Union law.

35. Aid must not be cumulated with *de minimis* aid in respect of the same eligible costs if such cumulation would result in an aid intensity exceeding that laid down in this section.

36. The duration of aid schemes under which the aid is granted must not be longer than the duration of these Guidelines (2021–2030).

3.2. AID INVOLVED IN OPTIONAL TRANSITIONAL FREE ALLOWANCES FOR THE MODERNISATION OF ELECTRICITY GENERATION

37. State aid involved in the optional transitional free allowances for the modernisation of electricity generation, in accordance with Article 10c of Directive 2003/87/EC, is compatible with the internal market within the meaning of Article 107(3)(c) of the Treaty provided the conditions set out below are met.

38. The objective of the aid must be the modernisation, diversification and sustainable transformation of the energy sector. The investments supported must be consistent with the transition to a safe and sustainable low-carbon economy, the objectives of the Union's 2030 climate and energy policy framework, the European Green Deal, and the long-term objectives expressed in the Paris Agreement.

39. Where an investment leads to additional electricity generation capacity, the operator concerned must also demonstrate that a corresponding amount of electricity-generation capacity with higher emission intensity has been decommissioned by it or another associated operator by the start of operation of the additional capacity.

40. The aid is compatible with the internal market only if it has an incentive effect. An incentive effect occurs when the aid induces the beneficiary to change its behaviour, a change in behaviour which it would not undertake without the aid. The aid must not subsidise the costs of an activity that an undertaking would anyhow incur and must not compensate for the normal business risk of an economic activity.

41. When receiving an aid application, the granting authority must check that the aid would have the required incentive effect.

42. Aid can be paid out in the form of allocations to operators only where it is demonstrated that an investment selected in accordance with the rules of a competitive bidding process has been carried out.

43. For projects involving a total amount of investment exceeding EUR 12.5 million, aid can only be granted on the basis of a competitive bidding process, to take place in one or more rounds between 2021 and 2030. That competitive bidding process must:

(a) comply with the principles of transparency, non-discrimination, equal treatment and sound financial management;

(b) ensure that only projects which contribute to the diversification of their energy mix and sources of supply, the necessary restructuring, environmental upgrading and retrofitting of the infrastructure, clean technologies, such as renewable energy technologies, or modernisation of the energy production sector, such as efficient and sustainable district heating, and of the transmission and distribution sector, are eligible to bid;

(c) define clear, objective, transparent and non-discriminatory selection criteria for the ranking of projects, so as to ensure that only projects are selected which:

(i) on the basis of a cost-benefit analysis, ensure a net positive gain in terms of emission reduction and realise a pre-determined significant level of CO_2 reductions taking into account the size of the project;

(ii) are additional, clearly respond to replacement and modernisation needs and do not supply a market-driven increase in energy demand;

(iii) offer the best value for money;

(iv) do not contribute to or improve the financial viability of highly emission-intensive electricity generation or increase dependency on emission-intensive fossil fuels.

44. For projects involving a total amount of investment with a value of less than EUR 12.5 million, aid can be granted without a competitive bidding process. The selection of the projects must in this case be based on objective and transparent criteria. The results of the selection process must be published for public comments. Where more than one investment is carried out within the same installation, the investments must be assessed as a whole to establish whether or not the threshold of EUR 12.5 million is exceeded, unless those investments are, independently, technically or financially viable.

45. The Commission will consider the aid to be proportionate if the aid intensity does not exceed 70% of the relevant costs of the investment. All figures used must be taken before any deduction of tax or other charges. Where aid is awarded in a form other than a grant, the aid amount must be the equivalent of the grant in terms of value. Aid payable in several instalments must be calculated at its total net present value at the moment of granting the first instalment, using the relevant Commission reference rate for discounting the value over time. The aid intensity is calculated per beneficiary.

46. The aid must not adversely affect trading conditions to an extent contrary to the common interest, in particular where aid is concentrated on a limited number of beneficiaries or where the aid is likely to reinforce the beneficiaries' market position (at the group level).

47. The aid may be cumulated with:
   (a) any other State aid in relation to different identifiable eligible costs,
   (b) any other State aid, in relation to the same eligible costs, partly or fully overlapping, and any other State aid without identifiable eligible costs, only if such cumulation does not result in exceeding the maximum aid intensity or aid amount applicable to this aid under this section.

48. Aid may be awarded concurrently under several aid schemes or cumulated with *ad hoc* aid, provided that the total amount of State aid for an activity or project does not exceed the aid ceilings laid down in this section. Union funding centrally managed by the Commission that is not directly or indirectly under the control of a Member State, does not constitute State aid. Where such Union funding is combined with State aid, only the latter is considered for determining whether notification thresholds and maximum aid intensities are respected, provided that the total amount of public funding granted in relation to the same eligible costs does not exceed the maximum funding rate(s) laid down in the applicable rules of Union law.

49. Aid is not to be cumulated with *de minimis* aid in respect of the same eligible costs if such cumulation would result in an aid intensity exceeding that laid down in this section.

50. The duration of aid schemes under which the aid is granted must not be longer than the duration of these Guidelines (2021–2030).

NOTES

[15] Code 12 15 0 within the legal framework set out by Regulation (EC) No 295/2008 of the European Parliament and of the Council of 11 March 2008 concerning structural business statistics (OJ L97, 9.4.2008, p 13).

4. EVALUATION

[5.314]

51. To further ensure that distortion of competition is limited, the Commission may require that certain aid schemes are subject to an *ex post* evaluation. Evaluations will need to be carried out for schemes where the potential distortion of competition is particularly high, that is to say, that may risk significantly restricting or distorting competition if their implementation is not reviewed in due time.

52. Given its objectives, and in order not to put disproportionate burden on Member States and on smaller aid projects, evaluation is only required for aid schemes with large aid budgets, containing novel characteristics or when significant market, technology or regulatory changes are foreseen. The evaluation must be carried out by an expert independent from the aid granting authority on the basis of a common methodology provided by the Commission. It must be made public. The Member State must notify, together with the aid scheme, a draft evaluation plan, which will be an integral part of the Commission's assessment of the scheme.

53. The evaluation must be submitted to the Commission in due time to allow for the assessment of the possible prolongation of the aid scheme and in any case upon its expiry. The precise scope and rules/requirements concerning each evaluation will be defined in the decision approving the aid scheme. Any subsequent aid measure with a similar objective must take into account the results of the evaluation.

5. ENERGY AUDITS AND MANAGEMENT SYSTEMS

[5.315]

54. For aid covered by Section 3.1, Member States commit to verifying that the beneficiary complies with its obligation to conduct an energy audit in the sense of Article 8 of Directive 2012/27/EU of the European Parliament and of the Council,[16] either as a stand alone energy audit or within the framework of a certified Energy Management System or Environmental Management System, for example the EU eco-management and audit scheme (EMAS).[17]

55. Member States also commit to monitoring that beneficiaries covered by the obligation to conduct an energy audit under Article 8(4) of Directive 2012/27/EU will:
   (a) implement recommendations of the audit report, to the extent that the pay-back time for the relevant investments does not exceed 3 years and that the costs of their investments is proportionate; or alternatively
   (b) reduce the carbon footprint of their electricity consumption, so as to cover at least 30% of their electricity consumption from carbon-free sources; or alternatively
   (c) invest a significant share of at least 50% of the aid amount in projects that lead to substantial reductions of the installation's greenhouse gas emissions and well below the applicable benchmark used for free allocation in the EU Emissions Trading System.

NOTES

[16] Directive 2012/27/EU of the European Parliament and of the Council of 25 October 2012 on energy efficiency, amending Directives 2009/125/EC and 2010/30/EU and repealing Directives 2004/8/EC and 2006/32/EC (OJ L315, 14.11.2012, p 1).

[17] Regulation (EC) No 1221/2009 on the voluntary participation by organisations in a Community eco-management and audit scheme (EMAS) (OJ L342, 22.12.2009, p 1).

6. TRANSPARENCY

[5.316]

56. Member States must ensure that the following information is published in the Commission's transparency award module[18] or on a comprehensive State aid website, at national or regional level:
   (a) the full text of the approved aid scheme or the individual aid granting decision and its implementing provisions, or a link to it;
   (b) the identity of the granting authority or authorities;

(c) the name and the identifier of each beneficiary, except business secrets and other confidential information in duly justified cases and subject to the Commission's agreement in accordance with Commission communication on professional secrecy in State aid decisions;[19]
(d) the aid instrument,[20] the aid element and, where different, the nominal amount of aid, expressed as full amount in national currency[21] granted to each beneficiary;
(e) the date of granting[22] and the date of publication;
(f) the type of undertaking (small or medium sized enterprise/large company);
(g) the region in which the beneficiary is located (at NUTS level II or below);
(h) the principal economic sector in which the beneficiary has its activities (at NACE group level);
(i) the objective of the aid.

57. Such a requirement applies with respect to individual aid awards exceeding EUR 500,000.

58. Such information must be published after the decision to grant the aid has been taken, must be kept for at least 10 years and must be available to the general public without restrictions.[23]

NOTES

[18] https://webgate.ec.europa.eu/competition/transparency/public?lang=en.

[19] C(2003) 4582 (OJ C297, 9.12.2003, p 6).

[20] Grant/Interest rate subsidy; Loan/Repayable advances/Reimbursable grant; Guarantee; Tax advantage or tax exemption; Risk finance; Other (please specify). If the aid is granted through multiple aid instruments, the aid amount must be provided by instrument.

[21] Gross grant equivalent. For operating aid, the annual amount of aid per beneficiary can be provided.

[22] The date when the legal right to receive the aid is conferred on the beneficiary under the applicable national legal regime.

[23] This information must be published within 6 months from the date of granting. In case of unlawful aid, Member States will be required to ensure the publication of this information ex post within 6 months from the date of the Commission decision. The information must be available in a format which allows data to be searched, extracted, and easily published on the internet, for instance in CSV or XML format.

7. REPORTING AND MONITORING

[5.317]

59. In accordance with Council Regulation (EU) 2015/1589[24] and Commission Regulation (EC) No 794/2004,[25] Member States must submit annual reports to the Commission.

60. Beyond the requirement laid down in those Regulations, Member States must include in their annual reports the following information by using the standard form provided by the Commission:
(a) the name of each beneficiary and the aided installations under its ownership;
(b) the sector(s) in which each beneficiary is active (identified by NACE-4 code);
(c) the year for which the aid is granted and the year in which it is being paid;
(d) the actual output for each aided installation in the pertinent sector;
(e) the actual electricity consumption for each aided installation (if any aid is given using a fall back electricity consumption efficiency benchmark);
(f) the EUA forward price used to compute the aid amount per beneficiary;
(g) the aid intensity;
(h) the national CO2 emission factor.

61. Member States must ensure that detailed records regarding all measures involving the granting of aid are maintained. Such records must contain all information necessary to establish that the conditions regarding, where applicable, eligible costs and maximum allowable aid intensity have been observed. Those records must be maintained for 10 years from the date on which the aid was granted and be provided to the Commission upon request.

62. In any year in which the budget of the aid schemes referred to by section 3.1 exceeds 25% of the revenues generated from the auctioning of allowances, the Member State concerned must publish a report setting out the reasons for exceeding that amount, in accordance with Article 10a(6) of Directive 2003/87/EC. The report must include relevant information on electricity prices for large industrial consumers benefiting from the scheme, without prejudice to requirements regarding the protection of confidential information. The report must also include information on whether due consideration has been given to other measures to sustainably lower indirect carbon costs in the medium to long term.

63. Electricity generators and network operators benefiting from aid covered by section 3.2 must report, by 28 February of each year, on the implementation of their selected investments, including the balance of free allocation and investment expenditure incurred and the types of investments supported.

NOTES

[24] OJ L 248, 24.9.2015, p. 9.

[25] OJ L 140, 30.4.2004, p. 1.

8. PERIOD OF APPLICATION AND REVISION

[5.318]

64. These Guidelines replace the Guidelines on certain State aid measures in the context of the greenhouse gas emission allowance trading scheme post 2012 published on 5 June 2012,[26] as of 1 January 2021.

65. The Commission will apply the principles set out in these Guidelines from 1 January 2021 until 31 December 2030.

66. The Commission will apply the principles set out in these Guidelines to all notified aid measures in respect of which it is called upon to take a decision, from the 1 January 2021, even where the projects were notified prior to their publication. Unlawful aid will be assessed in accordance with the rules in force on the date on which the aid was granted in accordance with the Commission notice on the determination of the applicable rules for the assessment of unlawful State aid.[27]

67. The Commission will adapt these Guidelines to update the electricity consumption efficiency benchmarks, the geographic areas, and the CO_2 emission factors in 2025. In 2025, the Commission will also assess whether additional data is available allowing to improve the methodology used to calculate the CO_2 emission factors as described in Annex III, that is to say to take into account the increasingly important price-setting role of climate neutral technologies in Union electricity markets and the conclusions of the assessments notified to the Commission pursuant to point 15(11) above. Consequently, Member States may have to adapt their respective schemes in order to bring them into line with the adapted guidelines.

68. The Commission may decide to review or adapt these Guidelines at any time if this should be necessary for reasons associated with competition policy or in order to take account of other Union policies, international commitments or material market developments. Member States may have to adapt their respective schemes in order to bring them into line with the adapted guidelines.

NOTES

[26] OJ C158, 5.6.2012, p 4.

[27] OJ C119, 22.5.2002, p 22.

ANNEX I
SECTORS DEEMED TO BE EXPOSED TO A GENUINE RISK OF CARBON LEAKAGE DUE TO INDIRECT EMISSION COSTS

[5.319]

	NACE code	Description
1.	14.11	Manufacture of leather clothes
2.	24.42	Aluminium production
3.	20.13	Manufacture of other inorganic basic chemicals
4.	24.43	Lead, zinc and tin production
5.	17.11	Manufacture of pulp
6.	17.12	Manufacture of paper and paperboard
7.	24.10	Manufacture of basic iron and steel and ferro-alloys
8.	19.20	Manufacture of refined petroleum products
9.	24.44	Copper production
10.	24.45	Other non-ferrous metal production
11.		The following subsectors within the plastics sector (20.16):
	20.16.40.15	Polyethylene in primary forms
12.		All product categories in the casting of iron sector (24.51)
13.		The following subsectors within the glass fibre sector (23.14):
	23.14.12.10 23.14.12.30	Glass fibre mats Glass fibre voiles
14.		The following subsectors within the industrial gases sector (20.11):
	20.11.11.50 20.11.12.90	Hydrogen Inorganic oxygen compounds of non-metals

ANNEX II
ELECTRICITY CONSUMPTION EFFICIENCY BENCHMARKS FOR PRODUCTS COVERED BY THE NACE CODES IN ANNEX I

[5.320]

This Annex was blank in the original document. The explanatory note accompanying the draft ETS Guidelines provides that the electricity consumption efficiency benchmarks, which represent the product-specific electricity consumption per tonne of output achieved by the most electricity-efficient methods of production for the product considered, will be updated at the beginning of the next ETS trading period (1 January 2021). They will also be updated once in the middle of the next trading period.

See https://ec.europa.eu/competition/consultations/2020_ets_stateaid_guidelines/explanatory_note_en.pdf.

ANNEX III
MAXIMUM REGIONAL CO_2 EMISSIONS FACTORS IN DIFFERENT GEOGRAPHIC AREAS (TCO_2/MWH)

[5.321]

Zones		**Applicable CO_2 emission factor**
Adriatic	Croatia, Slovenia	[. . .]
Iberia	Spain, Portugal	[. . .]
Baltic	Lithuania, Latvia, Estonia	[. . .]
Central Western Europe	Austria, Germany, Luxembourg	[. . .]
Nordic	Sweden, Finland	[. . .]
Czechia-Slovakia	Czechia, Slovakia	[. . .]
Belgium		[. . .]
Bulgaria		[. . .]
Denmark		[. . .]
Ireland		[. . .]
Greece		[. . .]
France		[. . .]
Italy		[. . .]
Cyprus		[. . .]
Hungary		[. . .]
Malta		[. . .]
Netherlands		[. . .]
Poland		[. . .]
Romania		[. . .]

6. RISK CAPITAL AID

COMMUNICATION FROM THE COMMISSION

(2014/C19/04)

Guidelines on State aid to promote risk finance investments (Note)

[5.322]

NOTES

Date of publication in OJ: OJ C19, 22.01.2014, p 4.

Editorial note: these Guidelines were due to expire on 31 December 2020, but were extended to 31 December 2021 by Communication from the Commission concerning the prolongation and the amendments of the Guidelines on Regional State Aid for 2014-2020, Guidelines on State Aid to Promote Risk Finance Investments, Guidelines on State Aid for Environmental Protection and Energy 2014-2020, Guidelines on State aid for rescuing and restructuring non-financial undertakings in difficulty, Communication on the Criteria for the Analysis of the Compatibility with the Internal Market of State Aid to Promote the Execution of Important Projects of Common European Interest, Communication from the Commission – Framework for State aid for research and development and innovation and Communication from the Commission to the Member States on the application of Articles 107 and 108 of the Treaty on the Functioning of the European Union to short-term export-credit insurance (2020/C224/02).

These Guidelines are applicable until the end of 2021, but have been omitted from this edition of the Handbook due to constraints on the amount of available space. Customers who wish to refer to the Guidelines are advised to retain the 26th edition (2020) of this Handbook. Revised guidelines are due to be published before the end of the year (see also the list of consultations and draft documents in the Appendix at **[A1]**).

---

7. RESCUE AND RESTRUCTURING AID

COMMUNICATION FROM THE COMMISSION

(2014/C249/01)

Guidelines on State aid for rescuing and restructuring non-financial undertakings in difficulty

[5.323]

NOTES

Date of publication in OJ: OJ C249, 31.07.2014, p 1.

Editorial note: these Guidelines were due to expire on 31 December 2020, but were extended to 31 December 2023 by Communication from the Commission concerning the prolongation and the amendments of the Guidelines on Regional State Aid for 2014-2020, Guidelines on State Aid to Promote Risk Finance Investments, Guidelines on State Aid for Environmental Protection and Energy 2014-2020, Guidelines on State aid for rescuing and restructuring non-financial undertakings in difficulty, Communication on the Criteria for the Analysis of the Compatibility with the Internal Market of State Aid to Promote the Execution of Important Projects of Common European Interest, Communication from the Commission – Framework for State aid for research and development and innovation and Communication from the Commission to the Member States on the application of Articles 107 and 108 of the Treaty on the Functioning of the European Union to short-term export-credit insurance (2020/C224/02).

1. INTRODUCTION

[5.324]

1. In these guidelines, the Commission sets out the conditions under which State aid for rescuing and restructuring non-financial undertakings in difficulty may be considered to be compatible with the internal market on the basis of Article 107(3)(c) of the Treaty on the Functioning of the European Union.

2. The Commission adopted its original Guidelines on State aid for rescuing and restructuring firms in difficulty[1] in 1994. In 1997, the Commission added specific rules for agriculture.[2] A modified version of the guidelines was adopted in 1999.[3] In 2004 the Commission adopted new guidelines,[4] the validity of which was first extended until 9 October 2012[5] and subsequently until their replacement by new rules[6] in line with the reform programme set out in the Commission Communication of 8 May 2012 on EU State aid modernisation.[7]

3. In that Communication, the Commission announced three objectives in respect of modernising State aid control:

(a) to foster sustainable, smart and inclusive growth in a competitive internal market;

(b) to focus Commission *ex ante* scrutiny on cases with the biggest impact on the internal market while strengthening the cooperation with Member States in State aid enforcement;

(c) to streamline the rules and provide for faster decisions.

4. In particular, the Communication called for a common approach to the revision of the different guidelines and frameworks, based on strengthening the internal market, promoting more effectiveness in public spending through a better contribution of State aid to objectives of common interest and greater scrutiny of the incentive effect, limiting aid to the minimum and avoiding the potential negative effects of the aid on competition and trade.

5. The Commission has reviewed the guidelines concerning the rescue and restructuring of firms in difficulty on the basis of its experience in applying the existing rules and in line with the common approach referred to above. The revision also takes into account the Europe 2020 strategy adopted by the Commission[8] and the fact that the negative effects of State aid might interfere with the need to boost productivity and growth, preserve equal opportunities for undertakings and combat national protectionism.

6. Rescue and restructuring aid are among the most distortive types of State aid. It is well established that successful sectors of the economy witness productivity growth not because all the undertakings present in the market gain in productivity, but rather because the more efficient and technologically advanced undertakings grow at the expense of those that are less efficient or have obsolete products. Exit of less efficient undertakings allows their more efficient competitors to grow and returns assets to the market, where they can be applied to more productive uses. By interfering with this process, rescue and restructuring aid may significantly slow economic growth in the sectors concerned.

7. Where parts of a failing undertaking remain essentially viable, the undertaking may be able to carry out a restructuring that leads to its exit from certain structurally loss-making activities and allows the remaining activities to be reorganised on a basis that gives a reasonable prospect of long-term viability. Such restructuring should usually be possible without State aid, through agreements with creditors or by means of insolvency or reorganisation proceedings. Modern insolvency law should help sound companies to survive, help safeguard jobs and enable suppliers to keep their customers, and allow owners to retain value in viable companies.[9] Insolvency proceedings may also return a viable undertaking to the market by way of acquisition by third parties, whether of the undertaking as a going concern or its various production assets.

8. It follows that undertakings should only be eligible for State aid when they have exhausted all market options and where such aid is necessary in order to achieve a well-defined objective of common interest. Undertakings should be allowed to receive aid under these guidelines only once within 10 years (the 'one time, last time' principle).

9. A further concern is the moral hazard problem created by State aid. Undertakings anticipating that they are likely to be rescued when they run into difficulty may embark upon excessively risky and unsustainable business strategies. In addition, the prospect of rescue and restructuring aid for a given undertaking may artificially reduce its cost of capital, giving it an undue competitive advantage in the marketplace.

10. State aid for rescuing and restructuring undertakings in difficulty may also undermine the internal market by shifting an unfair share of the burden of structural adjustment and the attendant social and economic problems to other Member States. This is undesirable in itself and may set off a wasteful subsidy race among Member States. Such aid may also lead to the creation of entry barriers and the undermining of incentives for cross-border activities, contrary to the objectives of the internal market.

11. It is therefore important to ensure that aid is only allowed under conditions that mitigate its potential harmful effects and promote effectiveness in public spending. In relation to restructuring aid, the requirements of return to viability, own contribution and measures to limit distortions of competition have proved their value in terms of mitigating the potential harmful effects of such aid. They continue to apply under these guidelines, adapted as necessary to take account of the Commission's recent experience. The notion of burden sharing has been introduced, *inter alia*, to better address the issue of moral hazard. In the case of rescue aid and temporary restructuring support, potential harmful effects are mitigated by means of restrictions on the duration and form of aid.

12. Where aid takes the form of liquidity assistance that is limited in both amount and duration, concerns about its potential harmful effects are much reduced, allowing it to be approved on less stringent conditions. While such aid could in principle be used to support an entire restructuring process, the limitation of the rescue aid period to six months means that this rarely happens; instead, rescue aid is commonly followed by restructuring aid.

13. To encourage the use of less distortive forms of aid, these guidelines introduce a new concept of 'temporary restructuring support'. In common with rescue aid, temporary restructuring support can only take the form of liquidity assistance that is limited in both amount and duration. To allow it to support an entire restructuring process, however, the maximum duration of temporary restructuring support is set at 18 months. Temporary restructuring support may only be granted to SMEs[10] and to smaller State-owned undertakings,[11] which face greater challenges than large undertakings in terms of access to liquidity.

14. Where aid to providers of services of general economic interest ('SGEI') in difficulty falls under these guidelines, the assessment should be carried out in accordance with the standard principles of the guidelines. However, the specific application of those principles should be adapted where necessary to take account of the specific nature of SGEI and, in particular, of the need to ensure continuity of service provision in accordance with Article 106(2) of the Treaty.

15. The Commission's Action Plan for a competitive and sustainable steel industry in Europe[12] ('Steel Action Plan'), sets out a series of actions that aim to promote a strong and competitive steel sector. The Steel Action Plan also identifies a number of areas in which State support is available to undertakings in the steel sector in accordance with the State aid rules. However, in the present conditions of significant European and global overcapacity,[13] State aid for rescuing and restructuring steel undertakings in difficulty is not justified. The steel sector should therefore be excluded from the scope of these guidelines.

16. Council Decision 2010/787/EU[14] sets out the conditions under which operating, social and environmental aid may be granted until 2027 to uncompetitive production in the coal sector.[15] The current rules follow previous sector-specific rules applied between 2002 and 2010[16] and 1993 and 2002,[17] which facilitated the restructuring of uncompetitive undertakings active in the coal sector. As a result, and in view of the persistent need to provide support for structural adjustment of coal production in the Union, the current rules are stricter than previous ones and require the permanent cessation of production and sale of aided coal production and the definitive closure of uncompetitive production units by 31 December 2018 at the latest. In application of those rules, several Member States have adopted and are implementing plans leading to the definitive closure of coal mines in difficulty operated by undertakings in this sector.[18] The coal sector should therefore be excluded from the scope of these guidelines.

17. The Commission's experience with the rescue and restructuring of financial institutions during the financial and economic crisis has shown that specific rules applicable to the financial sector can be beneficial in view of the specific characteristics of financial institutions and financial markets. Undertakings covered by dedicated rules for the financial sector are therefore excluded from the scope of these guidelines.

NOTES

1 Community guidelines on State aid for rescuing and restructuring firms in difficulty (OJ C368, 23.12.1994, p 12).

2 Community guidelines on State aid for rescuing and restructuring firms in difficulty (OJ C283, 19.9.1997, p 2).

3 Community guidelines on State aid for rescuing and restructuring firms in difficulty (OJ C288, 9.10.1999, p 2).

4 Community guidelines on State aid for rescuing and restructuring firms in difficulty (OJ C244, 1.10.2004, p 2).

5 Commission Communication concerning the prolongation of the Community Guidelines on State aid for Rescuing and Restructuring Firms in Difficulty (OJ C156, 9.7.2009, p 3).

6 Commission communication concerning the prolongation of the application of the Community guidelines on State aid for rescuing and restructuring firms in difficulty of 1 October 2004 (OJ C296, 2.10.2012, p 3).

7 Communication from the Commission to the European Parliament, the Council, the European Economic and Social Committee and the Committee of the Regions on EU State aid modernisation (SAM), COM(2012) 209 final.

8 Communication from the Commission: EUROPE 2020 — A strategy for smart, sustainable and inclusive growth, COM(2010) 2020 final.

9 Communication from the Commission to the European Parliament, the Council and the European Economic and Social Committee: A new European approach to business failure and insolvency, COM(2012) 742 final. See also Commission Recommendation of 12.3.2014 on a new approach to business failure and insolvency, C(2014) 1500 final, in particular recital 12.

10 For the purposes of these guidelines, 'SME', 'small enterprise' and 'medium-sized enterprise' have the meanings given to those terms in Commission Recommendation 2003/361/EC of 6 May 2003 concerning the definition of micro, small and medium-sized enterprises (OJ L124, 20.5.2003, p 36) and 'large undertaking' means an undertaking that is not an SME.

11 For the purposes of these guidelines, to avoid discrimination between public and private ownership of undertakings, 'smaller State-owned undertakings' are economic units with an independent power of decision that would qualify as

small or medium-sized enterprises under Recommendation 2003/361/EC but for the fact that 25% or more of the capital or voting rights are directly or indirectly controlled, jointly or individually, by one or more public bodies.

12 Communication from the Commission to the Parliament, the Council, the European Economic and Social Committee and the Committee of the Regions: Action Plan for a competitive and sustainable steel industry in Europe, COM(2013) 407.

13 Steel Action Plan, p. 3.

14 Council Decision 2010/787/EU of 10 December 2010 on State aid to facilitate the closure of uncompetitive coal mines (OJ L336, 21.12.2010, p 24).

15 OJ L336, 21.12.2010, p 24.

16 Council Regulation (EC) No 1407/2002 of 23 July 2002 on State aid to the coal industry (OJ L205, 2.8.2002, p 1).

17 Commission Decision No 3632/93/ECSC of 28 December 1993 establishing Community rules for state aid to the Coal Industry (OJ L329, 30.12.1993, p 12).

18 See Commission Decisions in cases N 175/2010 — Slovenia, SA.33013 — Poland, N 708/2007 — Germany, SA.33033 — Romania and SA.33861 — Hungary.

2. SCOPE OF THE GUIDELINES

2.1. SECTORAL SCOPE

[5.325]

18. The Commission will apply these guidelines to aid for all undertakings in difficulty, except to those operating in the coal sector[19] or the steel sector[20] and those covered by specific rules for financial institutions,[21] without prejudice to any specific rules relating to undertakings in difficulty in a particular sector.[22] The Commission will apply these guidelines to the fisheries and aquaculture sector, subject to compliance with the specific rules laid down in the Guidelines for the examination of State aid to fisheries and aquaculture,[23] and to the agricultural sector, including the primary agricultural production sector.[24]

2.2. MATERIAL SCOPE: MEANING OF 'UNDERTAKING IN DIFFICULTY'

19. A Member State which proposes to grant aid in accordance with these guidelines to an undertaking must demonstrate on objective grounds that the undertaking concerned is in difficulty within the meaning of this section, subject to the specific provisions for rescue aid and temporary restructuring support under point 29.

20. For the purposes of these guidelines, an undertaking is considered to be in difficulty when, without intervention by the State, it will almost certainly be condemned to going out of business in the short or medium term. Therefore, an undertaking is considered to be in difficulty if at least one of the following circumstances occurs:

(a) In the case of a limited liability company,[25] where more than half of its subscribed share capital[26] has disappeared as a result of accumulated losses. This is the case when deduction of accumulated losses from reserves (and all other elements generally considered as part of the own funds of the company) leads to a negative cumulative amount that exceeds half of the subscribed share capital.

(b) In the case of a company where at least some members have unlimited liability for the debt of the company,[27] where more than half of its capital as shown in the company accounts has disappeared as a result of accumulated losses.

(c) Where the undertaking is subject to collective insolvency proceedings or fulfils the criteria under its domestic law for being placed in collective insolvency proceedings at the request of its creditors.

(d) In the case of an undertaking that is not an SME, where, for the past two years:

i. the undertaking's book debt to equity ratio has been greater than 7.5 and

ii. the undertaking's EBITDA interest coverage ratio has been below 1.0.

21. A newly created undertaking is not eligible for aid under these guidelines even if its initial financial position is insecure. This is the case, for instance, where a new undertaking emerges from the liquidation of a previous undertaking or merely takes over that undertaking's assets. An undertaking will in principle be considered as newly created for the first three years following the start of operations in the relevant field of activity. Only after that period will it become eligible for aid under these guidelines, provided that:

(a) it qualifies as an undertaking in difficulty within the meaning of these guidelines, and

(b) it does not form part of a larger business group[28] except under the conditions laid down in point 22.

22. A company belonging to or being taken over by a larger business group is not normally eligible for aid under these guidelines, except where it can be demonstrated that the company's difficulties are intrinsic and are not the result of an arbitrary allocation of costs within the group, and that the difficulties are too serious to be dealt with by the group itself. Where a company in difficulty creates a subsidiary, the subsidiary, together with the company in difficulty controlling it, will be regarded as a group and may receive aid under the conditions laid down in this point.

23. Given that its very existence is in danger, an undertaking in difficulty cannot be considered an appropriate vehicle for promoting other public policy objectives until such time as its viability is assured. Consequently, the Commission considers that aid to undertakings in difficulty may contribute to the development of economic activities without adversely affecting trade to an extent contrary to the common interest only if the conditions set out in these guidelines are met, even if such aid is granted in accordance with a scheme that has already been authorised.

24. A number of regulations and communications in the field of State aid and elsewhere therefore prohibit undertakings in difficulty from receiving aid. For the purposes of such regulations and communications, and unless otherwise defined therein:

(a) 'undertakings in difficulty' or 'firms in difficulty' should be understood to mean undertakings in difficulty within the meaning of point 20 of these guidelines, and

(b) an SME that has been in existence for less than three years will not be considered to be in difficulty unless it meets the condition set out in point 20(c).

2.3. RESCUE AID, RESTRUCTURING AID AND TEMPORARY RESTRUCTURING SUPPORT

25. These guidelines deal with three types of aid: rescue aid, restructuring aid and temporary restructuring support.

26. Rescue aid is by nature urgent and temporary assistance. Its primary objective is to make it possible to keep an ailing undertaking afloat for the short time needed to work out a restructuring or liquidation plan. The general principle is that rescue aid makes it possible to provide temporary support to an undertaking facing a serious deterioration of its financial situation, involving an acute liquidity crisis or technical insolvency. Such temporary support should allow time to analyse the circumstances which gave rise to the difficulties and to develop an appropriate plan to remedy those difficulties.

27. Restructuring aid often involves more permanent assistance and must restore the long-term viability of the beneficiary on the basis of a feasible, coherent and far-reaching restructuring plan, while at the same time allowing for adequate own contribution and burden sharing and limiting the potential distortions of competition.

28. Temporary restructuring support is liquidity assistance designed to support the restructuring of an undertaking by providing the conditions needed for the beneficiary to design and implement appropriate action to restore its long-term viability. Temporary restructuring support may only be granted to SMEs and smaller State-owned undertakings.

29. By way of derogation to point 19, rescue aid as well as, in the case of SMEs and smaller State-owned undertakings, temporary restructuring support may also be granted to undertakings that are not in difficulty within the meaning of point 20 but that are facing acute liquidity needs due to exceptional and unforeseen circumstances.

2.4. AID TO COVER THE SOCIAL COSTS OF RESTRUCTURING

30. Restructuring normally entails reductions in or abandonment of the affected activities. Such retrenchments are often necessary in the interests of rationalisation and efficiency, quite apart from any capacity reductions that may be required as a condition for granting aid. Regardless of the underlying reasons, such measures will generally lead to reductions in the beneficiary's workforce.

31. Member States' labour legislation may include general social security schemes under which certain benefits are paid directly to redundant employees. Such schemes are not to be regarded as State aid falling within the scope of Article 107(1) of the Treaty.

32. Besides such social security benefits for employees, general social support schemes frequently provide for the government to cover the cost of benefits which an undertaking grants to redundant workers and which go beyond its statutory or contractual obligations. Where such schemes are available generally without sectoral limitations to any worker meeting predefined and automatic eligibility conditions, they are not deemed to involve aid under Article 107(1) for undertakings carrying out restructuring. On the other hand, if the schemes are used to support restructuring in particular industries, they may well involve aid because of the selective way in which they are used.[29]

33. The obligations an undertaking itself bears under employment legislation or collective agreements with trade unions to provide certain benefits to redundant workers, such as redundancy payments or measures to increase their employability, are part of the normal costs of business which an undertaking must meet from its own resources. That being so, any contribution by the State to those costs must be counted as aid. This is true regardless of whether the payments are made directly to the undertaking or are administered through a government agency to the employees.

34. The Commission has no *a priori* objection to such aid when it is granted to an undertaking in difficulty, for it brings economic benefits above and beyond the interests of the undertaking concerned, facilitating structural change and reducing hardship.

35. Besides providing direct financial support, such aid is commonly provided in connection with a particular restructuring scheme for training, counselling and practical help with finding alternative employment, assistance with relocation, and professional training and assistance for employees wishing to start new businesses. Given that such measures, which increase the employability of redundant workers, further the objective of reducing social hardship, the Commission consistently takes a favourable view of such aid when it is granted to undertakings in difficulty.

NOTES

[19] As defined in Decision 2010/787/EU.

[20] As defined in Annex IV to the Communication from the Commission: Guidelines on regional state aid for 2014–2020 (OJ C209, 23.7.2013, p 1).

[21] Communication from the Commission on the application, from 1 August 2013, of the State aid rules to support measures in favour of banks in the context of the financial crisis ('Banking Communication') (OJ C216, 30.7.2013, p 1).

[22] Specific rules of this nature exist for the rail freight sector — see Community guidelines on State aid for railway undertakings (OJ C184, 22.7.2008, p 13).

[23] Guidelines for the examination of State aid to fisheries and aquaculture (OJ C84, 3.4.2008, p 10).

[24] For the purposes of these Guidelines, 'primary agricultural production' means production of products of the soil and of stock farming, listed in Annex I to the Treaty, without performing any further operation changing the nature of such products.

[25] This refers in particular to the types of company mentioned in Annex I of Directive 2013/34/EU of the European Parliament and of the Council of 26 June 2013 on the annual financial statements, consolidated financial statements and related reports of certain types of undertakings, amending Directive 2006/43/EC of the European Parliament and of the Council and repealing Council Directives 78/660/EEC and 83/349/EEC (OJ L182, 29.6.2013, p 19).

[26] Where relevant, 'share capital' includes any share premium.

[27] This refers in particular to the types of company mentioned in Annex II of Directive 2013/34/EU.

[28] To determine whether a company is independent or forms part of a group, the criteria laid down in Annex I to Recommendation 2003/361/EC will be taken into account.

[29] In its judgment in Case C-241/94 *France v Commission* [1996] ECR I-4551 (Kimberly Clark Sopalin), the Court of Justice confirmed that the system of financing on a discretionary basis by the French authorities, through the National Employment Fund, was liable to place certain undertakings in a more favourable situation than others and thus to qualify as aid within the meaning of Article 107(1) of the Treaty. The Court's judgment did not call into question the Commission's conclusion that the aid was compatible with the internal market.

3. COMPATIBILITY WITH THE INTERNAL MARKET

[5.326]

36. The circumstances in which State aid to undertakings in difficulty may be approved as compatible with the internal market are set out in Article 107(2) and (3) of the Treaty. Under Article 107(3)(c), the Commission has the power to authorise 'aid to facilitate the development of certain economic activities (. . .) where such aid does not adversely affect trading conditions to an extent contrary to the common interest'. In particular, this could be the case where the aid is necessary to correct disparities caused by market failures or to ensure economic and social cohesion.

37. Aid measures in favour of large undertakings must be notified individually to the Commission. Under certain conditions, the Commission may authorise schemes for smaller amounts of aid to SMEs and smaller State-owned undertakings: those conditions are set out in Chapter 6.[30]

38. In assessing whether notified aid can be declared compatible with the internal market, the Commission will consider whether each of the following criteria is met:

(a) contribution to a well-defined objective of common interest: a State aid measure must aim at an objective of common interest in accordance with Article 107(3) of the Treaty (section 3.1).

(b) need for State intervention: a State aid measure must be targeted towards a situation where aid can bring about a material improvement that the market cannot deliver itself, for example by remedying a market failure or addressing an equity or cohesion concern (section 3.2).

(c) appropriateness of the aid measure: an aid measure will not be considered compatible if other, less distortive measures allow the same objective to be achieved (section 3.3).

(d) incentive effect: it must be shown that in the absence of the aid, the beneficiary would have been restructured, sold or wound up in a way that would not have achieved the objective of common interest(section 3.4).

(e) proportionality of the aid (aid limited to the minimum): the aid must not exceed the minimum needed to achieve the objective of common interest (section 3.5).

(f) avoidance of undue negative effects on competition and trade between Member States: the negative effects of aid must be sufficiently limited, so that the overall balance of the measure is positive (section 3.6).

(g) transparency of aid: Member States, the Commission, economic operators and the public must have easy access to all relevant acts and pertinent information about the aid awarded (section 3.7).

39. If any of the above criteria is not met, the aid will not be considered to be compatible with the internal market.

40. The overall balance of certain categories of schemes may also be made subject to a requirement of *ex post* evaluation, as described in points 118, 119 and 120 of these guidelines.

41. Moreover, if an aid measure or the conditions attached to it (including its financing method when that forms an integral part of the aid measure) entails a non-severable violation of Union law, the aid cannot be declared compatible with the internal market.[31]

42. In this Chapter, the Commission sets out the conditions under which it will assess each of the criteria referred to in point 38.

3.1. CONTRIBUTION TO AN OBJECTIVE OF COMMON INTEREST

43. Given the importance of market exit to the process of productivity growth, merely preventing an undertaking from exiting the market does not constitute a sufficient justification for aid. Clear evidence should be provided that aid pursues an objective of common interest, in that it aims to prevent social hardship or address market failure (section 3.1.1) by restoring the long-term viability of the undertaking (section 3.1.2).

3.1.1. Demonstration of social hardship or market failure

44. Member States must demonstrate that the failure of the beneficiary would be likely to involve serious social hardship or severe market failure, in particular by showing that:

(a) the unemployment rate in the region or regions concerned (at NUTS level II) is either:

  i. higher than the Union average, persistent and accompanied by difficulty in creating new employment in the region or regions concerned, or

  ii. higher than the national average, persistent and accompanied by difficulty in creating new employment in the region(s) concerned;

(b) there is a risk of disruption to an important service which is hard to replicate and where it would be difficult for any competitor simply to step in (for example, a national infrastructure provider);

(c) the exit of an undertaking with an important systemic role in a particular region or sector would have potential negative consequences (for example as a supplier of an important input);

(d) there is a risk of interruption to the continuity of provision of an SGEI;

(e) the failure or adverse incentives of credit markets would push an otherwise viable undertaking into bankruptcy;

(f) the exit of the undertaking concerned from the market would lead to an irremediable loss of important technical knowledge or expertise; or

(g) similar situations of severe hardship duly substantiated by the Member State concerned would arise.

3.1.2. Restructuring plan and return to long-term viability

45. Restructuring aid within the scope of these guidelines cannot be limited to financial aid designed to make good past losses without tackling the reasons for those losses. In the case of restructuring aid, therefore, the Commission will require that the Member State concerned submit a feasible, coherent and far-reaching restructuring plan to restore the beneficiary's long-term viability.[32] Restructuring may involve one or more of the following elements: the reorganisation and rationalisation of the beneficiary's activities on to a more efficient basis, typically involving

withdrawal from loss-making activities, restructuring of those existing activities that can be made competitive again and, possibly, diversification towards new and viable activities. It typically also involves financial restructuring in the form of capital injections by new or existing shareholders and debt reduction by existing creditors.

46. The granting of the aid must therefore be conditional on implementation of the restructuring plan, which must be endorsed by the Commission in all cases of ad hoc aid.

47. The restructuring plan must restore the long-term viability of the beneficiary within a reasonable timescale and on the basis of realistic assumptions as to future operating conditions that should exclude any further State aid not covered by the restructuring plan. The restructuring period should be as short as possible. The restructuring plan must be submitted in all relevant detail to the Commission and must include, in particular, the information set out in this section 3.1.2.

48. The restructuring plan must identify the causes of the beneficiary's difficulties and the beneficiary's own weaknesses, and outline how the proposed restructuring measures will remedy the beneficiary's underlying problems.

49. The restructuring plan must provide information on the business model of the beneficiary, demonstrating how the plan will foster its long-term viability. This should include, in particular, information on the beneficiary's organisational structure, funding, corporate governance and all other relevant aspects. The restructuring plan should assess whether the beneficiary's difficulties could have been avoided through appropriate and timely management action and, where that is the case, should demonstrate that appropriate management changes have been made. Where the beneficiary's difficulties stem from flaws in its business model or corporate governance system, appropriate changes will be required.

50. The expected results of the planned restructuring should be demonstrated in a baseline scenario as well as in a pessimistic (or worst-case) scenario. For this purpose, the restructuring plan should take account, inter alia, of the current state and future prospects of supply and demand on the relevant product market and the main cost drivers of the industry, reflecting baseline and adverse scenario assumptions, as well as the beneficiary's specific strengths and weaknesses. Assumptions should be compared with appropriate sector-wide benchmarks and should, where appropriate, be adapted to cater for country- and sector-specific circumstances. The beneficiary should provide a market survey and a sensitivity analysis identifying the driving parameters of the beneficiary's performance and the main risk factors going forward.

51. The beneficiary's return to viability should derive mainly from internal measures, entailing in particular withdrawal from activities which would remain structurally loss-making in the medium term. The return to viability must not be dependent on optimistic assumptions about external factors such as variation in prices, demand or supply of scarce resources, nor can it be linked to the beneficiary outperforming the market and its competitors or entering and expanding into new activities where it has no experience and track record (unless duly justified and required for reasons of diversification and viability).

52. Long-term viability is achieved when an undertaking is able to provide an appropriate projected return on capital after having covered all its costs including depreciation and financial charges. The restructured undertaking should be able to compete in the marketplace on its own merits.

3.2. NEED FOR STATE INTERVENTION

53. Member States that intend to grant restructuring aid must provide a comparison with a credible alternative scenario not involving State aid, demonstrating how the relevant objective or objectives in section 3.1.1 would not be attained, or would be attained to a lesser degree, in the case of that alternative scenario. Such scenarios may, for example, include debt reorganisation, asset disposal, private capital raising, sale to a competitor or break-up, in each case either through entry into an insolvency or reorganisation procedure or otherwise.

3.3. APPROPRIATENESS

54. Member States should ensure that aid is awarded in the form that allows the objective to be achieved in the least distortive way. In the case of undertakings in difficulty, that can be achieved by ensuring that aid is in the appropriate form to address the beneficiary's difficulties and that it is properly remunerated. This section sets out the requirements that must be complied with in order to demonstrate that an aid measure is appropriate.

3.3.1. RESCUE AID

55. In order to be approved by the Commission, rescue aid must fulfil the following conditions:

(a) it must consist of temporary liquidity support in the form of loan guarantees or loans;

(b) the financial cost of the loan or, in the case of loan guarantees, the total financial cost of the guaranteed loan, including the interest rate of the loan and the guarantee premium, must comply with point 56;

(c) except as otherwise specified in point (d) below, any loan must be reimbursed and any guarantee must come to an end within a period of not more than six months after disbursement of the first instalment to the beneficiary;

(d) Member States must undertake to communicate to the Commission, not later than six months after the rescue aid measure has been authorised or, in the case of non-notified aid, not later than six months after disbursement of the first instalment to the beneficiary;

   i. proof that the loan has been reimbursed in full and/or that the guarantee has been terminated; or

   ii. provided that the beneficiary qualifies an undertaking in difficulty (and not only faces acute liquidity needs in the circumstances foreseen in point 29 above), a restructuring plan as set out in section 3.1.2; upon submission of a restructuring plan, the authorisation of the rescue aid will be automatically extended until the Commission reaches its final decision on the restructuring plan, unless the Commission decides that such extension is not justified or should be limited in time or scope; once a restructuring plan for which aid has been requested has been put in place and is being implemented, all further aid will be considered as restructuring aid; or

iii. a liquidation plan setting out in a substantiated way the steps leading to the liquidation of the beneficiary within a reasonable time frame without further aid.

(e) Rescue aid may not be used to finance structural measures, such as acquisition of significant businesses or assets, unless they are required during the rescue period for the survival of the beneficiary.

56. The level of remuneration that a beneficiary is required to pay for rescue aid should reflect the underlying creditworthiness of the beneficiary, discounting the temporary effects of both liquidity difficulties and State support, and should provide incentives for the beneficiary to repay the aid as soon as possible. The Commission will therefore require remuneration to be set at a rate not less than the reference rate set out in the Reference Rate Communication[33] for weak undertakings offering normal levels of collateralisation (currently 1-year IBOR plus 400 basis points)[34] and to be increased by at least 50 basis points for rescue aid the authorisation of which is extended in accordance with point 55(d)ii.

57. Where there is evidence that the rate identified in point 56 does not represent an appropriate benchmark, for example where it differs substantially from the market pricing of similar instruments recently issued by the beneficiary, the Commission may adapt the required level of remuneration accordingly.

3.3.2. Restructuring aid

58. Member States are free to choose the form that restructuring aid takes. However, in doing so, they should ensure that the instrument chosen is appropriate to the issue that it is intended to address. In particular, Member States should assess whether beneficiaries' problems relate to liquidity or solvency and select appropriate instruments to address the problems identified. For instance, in the case of solvency problems, increasing assets through recapitalisation might be appropriate, whereas in a situation where the problems mainly relate to liquidity, assistance through loans or loan guarantees might be sufficient.

3.4. INCENTIVE EFFECT

59. Member States that intend to grant restructuring aid must demonstrate that in the absence of the aid, the beneficiary would have been restructured, sold or wound up in a way that would not have achieved the objective of common interest identified in section 3.1.1. This demonstration can form part of the analysis presented in accordance with point 53.

3.5. PROPORTIONALITY OF THE AID/AID LIMITED TO THE MINIMUM

3.5.1. Rescue aid

60. Rescue aid must be restricted to the amount needed to keep the beneficiary in business for six months. In determining that amount, regard will be had to the outcome of the formula set out in Annex I. Any aid exceeding the result of that calculation will only be authorised if it is duly justified by the provision of a liquidity plan setting out the beneficiary's liquidity needs for the coming six months.

3.5.2. Restructuring aid

61. The amount and intensity of restructuring aid must be limited to the strict minimum necessary to enable restructuring to be undertaken, in the light of the existing financial resources of the beneficiary, its shareholders or the business group to which it belongs. In particular, a sufficient level of own contribution to the costs of the restructuring and burden sharing must be ensured, as set out in more detail in this section (3.5.2). Such assessment will take account of any rescue aid granted beforehand.

3.5.2.1.
Own contribution

62. A significant contribution[35] to the restructuring costs is required from the own resources of the aid beneficiary, its shareholders or creditors or the business group to which it belongs, or from new investors. Such own contribution should normally be comparable to the aid granted in terms of effects on the solvency or liquidity position of the beneficiary. For example, where the aid to be granted enhances the beneficiary's equity position, the own contribution should similarly include measures that are equity-enhancing, such as raising fresh equity from incumbent shareholders, the write-down of existing debt and capital notes or the conversion of existing debt to equity, or the raising of new external equity on market terms. The Commission will take account of the extent to which own contribution has a comparable effect to the aid granted when assessing the necessary extent of the measures to limit distortions of competition in accordance with point 90.

63. Contributions must be real, that is to say actual, excluding future expected profits such as cash flow, and must be as high as possible. Contribution by the State or a public company may only be taken into account provided that it is free of aid. That could be the case, in particular, where the contribution is made by an entity which is independent from the aid-granting authority (such as a State-owned bank or public holding company) and that takes the decision to invest on the basis of its own commercial interests.[36]

64. Own contribution will normally be considered to be adequate if it amounts to at least 50% of the restructuring costs. In exceptional circumstances and in cases of particular hardship, which must be demonstrated by the Member State, the Commission may accept a contribution that does not reach 50% of the restructuring costs, provided that the amount of that contribution remains significant.

3.5.2.2.
Burden sharing

65. Where State support is given in a form that enhances the beneficiary's equity position, for example where the State provides grants, injects capital or writes off debt, this can have the effect of protecting shareholders and subordinated creditors from the consequences of their choice to invest in the beneficiary. That can create moral hazard and undermine market discipline. Consequently, aid to cover losses should only be granted on terms which involve adequate burden sharing by existing investors.

66. Adequate burden sharing will normally mean that incumbent shareholders and, where necessary, subordinated creditors must absorb losses in full. Subordinated creditors should contribute to the absorption of losses either via conversion into equity or write-down of the principal of the relevant instruments. Therefore, State intervention should only take place after losses have been fully accounted for and attributed to the existing shareholders and subordinated debt holders.[37] In any case, cash outflows from the beneficiary to holders of equity or subordinated debt should be prevented during the restructuring period to the extent legally possible, unless that would disproportionately affect those that have injected fresh equity.

67. Adequate burden sharing will also mean that any State aid that enhances the beneficiary's equity position should be granted on terms that afford the State a reasonable share of future gains in value of the beneficiary, in view of the amount of State equity injected in comparison with the remaining equity of the company after losses have been accounted for.

68. The Commission may allow exceptions from full implementation of the measures set out in point 66 where those measures would otherwise lead to disproportionate results. Such situations could include cases where the aid amount is small in comparison with the own contribution, or the Member State concerned demonstrates that subordinated creditors would receive less in economic terms than under normal insolvency proceedings and if no State aid were granted.

69. The Commission will not systematically require a contribution by senior debt holders to restoring a beneficiary's equity position. However, it may treat any such contribution as grounds for a reduction in the necessary extent of measures to limit distortions of competition in accordance with point 90.

3.6. NEGATIVE EFFECTS

3.6.1. 'ONE TIME, LAST TIME' PRINCIPLE

70. In order to reduce moral hazard, excessive risk-taking incentives and potential competitive distortions, aid should be granted to undertakings in difficulty in respect of only one restructuring operation. This is referred to as the 'one time, last time' principle. The need for an undertaking that has already received aid pursuant to these guidelines to obtain further such aid demonstrates that the undertaking's difficulties are either of a recurrent nature or were not dealt with adequately when the earlier aid was granted. Repeated State interventions are likely to lead to problems of moral hazard and distortions of competition that are contrary to the common interest.

71. When planned rescue or restructuring aid is notified to the Commission, the Member State must specify whether the undertaking concerned has already received rescue aid, restructuring aid or temporary restructuring support in the past, including any such aid granted before the entry into force of these guidelines and any non-notified aid.[38] If so, and where less than 10 years[39] have elapsed since the aid was granted or the restructuring period came to an end or implementation of the restructuring plan was halted (whichever occurred the latest), the Commission will not allow further aid pursuant to these guidelines.

72. Exceptions to that rule are permitted in the following cases:

(a) where restructuring aid follows the granting of rescue aid as part of a single restructuring operation;

(b) where rescue aid or temporary restructuring support has been granted in accordance with these guidelines and that aid was not followed by restructuring aid, if:

  i. it could reasonably have been believed that the beneficiary would be viable in the long term when the aid pursuant to these guidelines was granted, and

  ii. new rescue or restructuring aid becomes necessary after at least five years due to unforeseeable circumstances[40] for which the beneficiary is not responsible;

(c) in exceptional and unforeseeable circumstances for which the beneficiary is not responsible.

73. The application of the one time, last time principle will in no way be affected by any changes in ownership of the beneficiary following the grant of aid or by any judicial or administrative procedure which has the effect of putting its balance sheet on a sounder footing, reducing its liabilities or wiping out its previous debts where it is the same undertaking that is continuing in business.

74. Where a business group has received rescue aid, restructuring aid or temporary restructuring support, the Commission will normally not allow further rescue or restructuring aid to the group itself or any of the entities belonging to the group unless 10 years have elapsed since the aid was granted or the restructuring period came to an end or implementation of the restructuring plan was halted, whichever occurred the latest. Where an entity belonging to a business group has received rescue aid, restructuring aid or temporary restructuring support, the group as a whole as well as the other entities of the group remain eligible for rescue or restructuring aid (subject to compliance with the other provisions of these guidelines), with the exception of the earlier beneficiary of the aid. Member States must demonstrate that no aid will be passed on from the group or other group entities to the earlier beneficiary of the aid.

75. Where an undertaking takes over assets of another undertaking, and in particular one that has been the subject of one of the procedures referred to in point 73 or of collective insolvency proceedings brought under national law and has already received rescue or restructuring aid or temporary restructuring support, the purchaser is not subject to the 'one time, last time' principle, provided that there is no economic continuity between the old undertaking and the purchaser.[41]

3.6.2. MEASURES TO LIMIT DISTORTIONS OF COMPETITION

76. When restructuring aid is granted, measures must be taken to limit distortions of competition, so that adverse effects on trading conditions are minimised as much as possible and positive effects outweigh any adverse ones. The Commission will assess the appropriate form and scope of such measures in accordance with this section (3.6.2).

3.6.2.1.
Nature and form of measures to limit distortions of competition

77. Without prejudice to point 84, measures to limit distortions of competition will usually take the form of structural measures. Where appropriate to address the distortions of competition in particular cases, the Commission may accept behavioural measures other than those set out in point 84 or market opening measures in place of some or all of the structural measures that would otherwise be required.

Structural measures – divestments and reduction of business activities

78. On the basis of an assessment in accordance with the criteria for calibration of measures to limit distortions of competition (set out in section 3.6.2.2), undertakings benefiting from restructuring aid may be required to divest assets or reduce capacity or market presence. Such measures should take place in particular in the market or markets where the undertaking will have a significant market position after restructuring, in particular those where there is significant excess capacity. Divestments to limit distortions of competition should take place without undue delay, taking into account the type of asset being divested and any obstacles to its disposal,[42] and in any case within the duration of the restructuring plan. Divestments, write-offs and closure of loss-making activities which would at any rate be necessary to restore long-term viability will generally not be considered sufficient, in the light of the principles set out in section 3.6.2.2, to address distortions of competition.

79. In order for such measures to strengthen competition and contribute to the internal market, they should favour the entry of new competitors, the expansion of existing small competitors or cross-border activity. Retrenchment within national borders and fragmentation of the internal market should be avoided.

80. Measures to limit distortions of competition should not lead to a deterioration in the structure of the market. Structural measures should therefore normally take the form of divestments on a going concern basis of viable stand-alone businesses that, if operated by a suitable purchaser, can compete effectively in the long term. In the event that such an entity is not available, the beneficiary could carve out and subsequently divest an existing and appropriately funded activity, creating a new and viable entity that should be able to compete in the market. Structural measures that take the form of divestment of assets alone and do not involve the creation of a viable entity able to compete in the market are less effective in preserving competition and will therefore only be accepted in exceptional cases where the Member State concerned demonstrates that no other form of structural measures would be feasible or that other structural measures would seriously jeopardise the economic viability of the undertaking.

81. The beneficiary should facilitate divestitures, for example through ring-fencing of activities and by agreeing not to solicit clients of the divested business.

82. Where it appears that it may be difficult to find a buyer for the assets which a beneficiary proposes to divest, it will be required, as soon as it becomes aware of such difficulties, to identify alternative divestments or measures to be taken in relation to the market or markets concerned if the primary divestment fails.

Behavioural measures

83. Behavioural measures aim at ensuring that aid is used only to finance the restoration of long-term viability and that it is not abused to prolong serious and persistent market structure distortions or to shield the beneficiary from healthy competition.

84. The following behavioural measures must be applied in all cases, to avoid undermining the effects of structural measures, and should in principle be imposed for the duration of the restructuring plan:

(a) Beneficiaries must be required to refrain from acquiring shares in any company during the restructuring period, except where indispensable to ensure the long-term viability of the beneficiary. This aims at ensuring that the aid is used to restore viability and not to fund investments or to expand the beneficiary's presence in existing or new markets. Upon notification, any such acquisitions may be authorised by the Commission as part of the restructuring plan;

(b) Beneficiaries must be required to refrain from publicising State support as a competitive advantage when marketing their products and services.

85. Under exceptional circumstances, it may be necessary to require beneficiaries to refrain from engaging in commercial behaviour aimed at a rapid expansion of their market share relating to specific products or geographic markets by offering terms (for example as regards prices and other commercial conditions) which cannot be matched by competitors that are not in receipt of State aid. Such restrictions will only be applied where no other remedy, structural or behavioural, can adequately address the competition distortions identified, and where such a measure will not itself restrict competition in the market concerned. For the purposes of applying such a requirement, the Commission will compare the terms offered by the beneficiary with those offered by credible competitors with a substantial market share.

Market opening measures

86. In its overall assessment, the Commission will consider possible commitments from the Member State concerning the adoption of measures, either by the Member State itself or by the beneficiary, that are aimed at promoting more open, sound and competitive markets, for instance by favouring entry and exit. This could in particular include measures to open up certain markets directly or indirectly linked to the beneficiary's activities to other Union operators, in compliance with Union law. Such initiatives may replace other measures to limit distortions of competition that would normally be required of the beneficiary.

3.6.2.2.
Calibration of measures to limit distortions of competition

87. Measures to limit distortions of competition should address both moral hazard concerns and possible distortions in the markets where the beneficiary operates. The extent of such measures will depend on several factors, such as, in particular: the size and nature of the aid and the conditions and circumstances under which it was granted; the size[43] and the relative importance of the beneficiary in the market and the characteristics of the market concerned; and the extent to which moral hazard concerns remain following the application of own contribution and burden-sharing measures.

88. In particular, the Commission will consider the size, where appropriate by means of approximations, and nature of the aid both in absolute terms and in relation to the beneficiary's assets and the size of the market as a whole.

89. As regards the size and the relative importance of the beneficiary on its market or markets both before and after the restructuring, The Commission will assess them in order to evaluate the likely effects of the aid on those markets as compared to the likely outcome in the absence of State aid. The measures will be tailored to market characteristics[44] to make sure that effective competition is preserved.

90. With regard to moral hazard concerns, the Commission will also assess the degree of own contribution and burden sharing. Greater degrees of own contribution and burden sharing than those required under section 3.5.2, by limiting the amount of aid and moral hazard, may reduce the necessary extent of measures to limit distortions of competition.

91. Since restructuring activities may threaten to undermine the internal market, measures to limit distortions of competition that help to ensure that national markets remain open and contestable will be considered positively.

92. Measures limiting distortions of competition should not compromise the prospects of the beneficiary's return to viability, which might be the case if a measure is very costly to execute or, in exceptional cases duly substantiated by the Member State concerned, would reduce the activity of the beneficiary to such an extent that its return to viability would be compromised, nor should they come at the expense of consumers and competition.

93. Aid to cover the social costs of restructuring of the type described in points 32 to 35 must be clearly identified in the restructuring plan, since aid for social measures exclusively for the benefit of redundant employees will be disregarded for the purposes of determining the extent of measures to limit distortions of competition. In the common interest the Commission will ensure, in the context of the restructuring plan, that the social effects of the restructuring in Member States other than the one granting aid are kept to the minimum.

3.6.3. Recipients of previous unlawful aid

94. Where unlawful aid has previously been granted to the undertaking in difficulty, in respect of which the Commission has adopted a negative decision with a recovery order, and where no such recovery has taken place in violation of Article 14 of Council Regulation (EC) No 659/1999,[45] the assessment of any aid pursuant to these guidelines to be granted to the same undertaking will take into account, first, the cumulative effect of the old aid and of the new aid and, secondly, the fact that the old aid has not been repaid.[46]

3.6.4. Specific conditions attached to approval of aid

95. The Commission may impose any conditions and obligations it considers necessary to ensure that the aid does not distort competition to an extent contrary to the common interest, in the event that the Member State concerned has not given a commitment that it will adopt such provisions. For example, it may require the Member State to take certain measures itself, to impose certain obligations on the beneficiary or to refrain from granting other types of aid to the beneficiary during the restructuring period.

3.7. TRANSPARENCY

96. Member States shall ensure the publication of the following information on a comprehensive State aid website, at national or regional level:

— the full text of the approved aid scheme or the individual aid granting decision and its implementing provisions, or a link to it,

— the identity of the granting authority/(ies),

— the identity of the individual beneficiaries, the form and amount of aid granted to each beneficiary, the date of granting, the type of undertaking (SME/large company), the region in which the beneficiary is located (at NUTS level II) and the principal economic sector in which the beneficiary has its activities (at NACE group level).[47]

Such a requirement can be waived with respect to individual aid awards below EUR 500,000 (EUR 60,000 for beneficiaries active in the primary agricultural production sector). For schemes in the form of tax advantage, the information on individual aid amounts[48] can be provided in the following ranges (in EUR million): [0.06–0.5] (for beneficiaries active in the primary agricultural production sector); [0.5–1]; [1–2]; [2–5]; [5–10]; [10–30]; [30 and more].

Such information must be published after the decision to grant the aid has been taken, must be kept for at least 10 years and must be available to the general public without restrictions.[49] Member States will not be required to publish the abovementioned information before 1 July 2016.[50]

NOTES

30 For the avoidance of doubt, this does not prevent Member States from notifying individually aid to SMEs and smaller State-owned undertakings. In such cases, the Commission will assess the aid under the principles established in these guidelines.

31 See for instance Case C-156/98 *Germany v Commission* [2000] ECR I-6857, paragraph 78 and Case C-333/07 *Régie Networks v Rhone Alpes Bourgogne*[2008] ECR I-10807, paragraphs 94–116.

32 An indicative model restructuring plan is set out in Annex II.

33 Communication from the Commission on the revision of the method for setting the reference and discount rates (OJ C14, 19.1.2008, p 6).

34 For the avoidance of doubt, the note regarding remuneration of rescue aid to the table of loan margins contained in that communication will not apply to aid assessed under these guidelines.

35 This contribution must not contain any aid. This is not the case, for instance, where a loan carries an interest-rate subsidy or is backed by government guarantees containing elements of aid.

36 See for example Commission Decision in Case SA.32698 *Air Åland.*

37 For this purpose, the firm's balance-sheet situation will have to be established at the time of the provision of the aid.

38 With regard to non-notified aid, the Commission will take account in its appraisal of the possibility that the aid could have been declared compatible with the internal market otherwise than as rescue or restructuring aid.

39 Five years in the case of the primary agricultural production sector.

40 An unforeseeable circumstance is one which could in no way be anticipated by the beneficiary's management when the restructuring plan was drawn up and which is not due to negligence or errors of the beneficiary's management or decisions of the group to which it belongs.

41 See Joined Cases C-328/99 and C-399/00 *Italy and SIM 2 Multimedia v Commission* [2003] ECR I-4035; Joined Cases T-415/05, T-416/05 and T-423/05 *Greece and others v Commission* [2010] ECR II-4749; Case T-123/09 *Ryanair v Commission*, not yet reported (confirmed on appeal by the European Court of Justice in Case C-287/12 P, not yet reported).

42 For example, sale of a portfolio or of individual assets may be possible, and should therefore take place, in a significantly shorter time than sale of a business as a going concern, particularly when that business must first be carved out from a wider entity.

43 In this respect the Commission may also take into account whether the beneficiary is a medium-sized or a large enterprise.

44 In particular, concentration levels, capacity constraints, the level of profitability and barriers to entry and to expansion may be taken into account.

45 Council Regulation (EC) No 659/1999 of 22 March 1999 laying down detailed rules for the application of Article 93 of the EC Treaty(OJ L83, 27.3.1999, p 1).

46 Case C-355/95 P, *Textilwerke Deggendorf v Commission and others*[1997] ECR I-2549.

47 With the exception of business secrets and other confidential information in duly justified cases and subject to the Commission's agreement (Commission communication on professional secrecy in State aid decisions, C(2003) 4582, OJ C297, 9.12.2003, p 6).

48 The amount to be published is the maximum allowed tax benefit and not the amount deducted each year (e.g. in the context of a tax credit, the maximum allowed tax credit shall be published rather than the actual amount which might depend on the taxable revenues and vary each year).

49 This information shall be published within 6 months from the date of granting (or, for aid in the form of tax advantage, within 1 year from the date the tax declaration is due). In case of unlawful aid, the Member States will be required to ensure the publication of this information *ex post*, at least within 6 months from the date of the Commission decision. The information shall be available in a format which allows data to be searched, extracted, and easily published on the internet, for instance in CSV or XML format.

50 Publication of information on aid awards granted before 1 July 2016 and, for fiscal aid, publication for aid claimed or granted before 1 July 2016, will not be required.

4. RESTRUCTURING AID IN ASSISTED AREAS

[5.327]

97. Economic and social cohesion is a priority objective of the European Union under Article 174 of the Treaty and other policies are required to contribute to this objective under Article 175.[51] The Commission will therefore take the needs of regional development into account when assessing restructuring aid in assisted areas. The fact that an ailing undertaking is located in an assisted area does not, however, justify a permissive approach to aid for restructuring: in the medium to long term it does not help a region to prop up companies artificially. Furthermore, in order to promote regional development it is in the region's own best interests to apply its resources in such a way as to rapidly develop activities that are viable and sustainable. Finally, distortions of competition must be minimised even in the case of aid to undertakings in assisted areas. In this context, regard must also be had to possible harmful spill-over effects which could occur in the area concerned and other assisted areas.

98. Thus, the criteria listed in Chapter 3 are equally applicable to assisted areas, even when the needs of regional development are considered. In assisted areas, however, and unless otherwise stipulated in rules on State aid in a particular sector, the Commission will apply the provisions of section 3.6.2 on measures to limit distortions of competition in such a way as to limit the negative systemic impacts for the region. That could, in particular, involve less stringent requirements in terms of reductions of capacity or market presence. A distinction will be drawn in such cases between areas eligible for regional aid under Article 107(3)(a) of the Treaty and those eligible under Article 107(3)(c), to take account of the greater severity of the regional problems in the former areas. Where the specific circumstances of assisted areas so require, for example where a beneficiary faces particular difficulties in raising new market financing as a result of its location in an assisted area, the Commission may accept a contribution which is less than 50% of the restructuring costs for the purposes of point 64.

NOTES

51 Article 175 of the Treaty provides, inter alia, that 'the formulation and implementation of the Union's policies and actions and the implementation of the internal market shall take into account the objectives set out in Article 174 and shall contribute to their achievement'.

5. AID TO SGEI PROVIDERS IN DIFFICULTY

[5.328]

99. In assessing State aid to SGEI providers in difficulty, the Commission will take account of the specific nature of SGEI and, in particular, of the need to ensure continuity of service provision in accordance with Article 106(2) of the Treaty.

100. SGEI providers may require State aid in order to continue to provide SGEI on terms that are compatible with their long-term viability. For the purposes of point 47, therefore, the restoration of long-term viability may be based on the assumption, in particular, that any State aid that meets the compatibility requirements of the SGEI Framework,[52] the SGEI Decision,[53] Regulation (EC) No 1370/2007 of the Parliament and the Council,[54] Regulation (EC) No 1008/2008 of the Parliament and the Council[55] and the Aviation Guidelines[56] or Council Regulation (EEC) No 3577/92[57] and the Maritime Guidelines,[58] will continue to be available for the duration of any entrustment entered into before or during the restructuring period.

101. Where the Commission assesses aid to SGEI providers in difficulty under these guidelines, it will take into account all State aid received by the provider in question, including any compensation for public service obligations. However, since SGEI providers can derive a large proportion of their normal revenues from public service compensation, the total amount of aid determined in this manner may be very large in comparison with the size of the beneficiary and may overstate the burden on the State in relation to the beneficiary's restructuring. When determining the own contribution required under section 3.5.2.1, therefore, the Commission will disregard any public service compensation that meets the compatibility requirements of the SGEI Framework, the SGEI Decision or Regulation (EC) No 1370/2007 or Regulation (EC) No 1008/2008 and the Aviation Guidelines or Council Regulation (EEC) No 3577/92 and the Maritime Guidelines.

102. To the extent that assets are necessary for the provision of SGEI, it may not be practicable to require the divestment of such assets by way of measures to limit distortions of competition for the purposes of section 3.6.2. In such cases, the Commission may require alternative measures to be taken to ensure that competition is not distorted to an extent contrary to the common interest, in particular by introducing fair competition in respect of the SGEI in question as soon as possible.

103. Where an SGEI provider is not able to comply with the conditions of these guidelines, the aid in question cannot be found compatible. In such cases, however, the Commission may authorise the payment of such aid as is necessary to ensure continuity of the SGEI until a new provider is entrusted with the service. The Commission will only authorise aid where the Member State concerned demonstrates on objective grounds that the aid is strictly limited to the amount and duration indispensable to entrust a new provider with the service.

NOTES

52 Communication from the Commission — European Union framework for State aid in the form of public service compensation (2011)(OJ C8, 11.1.2012, p 15).

53 Commission Decision 2012/21/EU of 20 December 2011 on the application of Article 106(2) of the Treaty on the Functioning of the European Union to State aid in the form of public service compensation granted to certain undertakings entrusted with the operation of services of general economic interest (OJ L7, 11.1.2012, p 3).

54 Regulation (EC) No 1370/2007 of the European Parliament and of the Council of 23 October 2007 on public passenger transport services by rail and by road and repealing Council Regulations (EEC) Nos 1191/69 and 1107/70 (OJ L315, 3.12.2007, p 1).

55 Regulation (EC) No 1008/2008 of the European Parliament and of the Council of 24 September 2008 on common rules for the operation of air services in the Community (OJ L293, 31.10.2008, p 3), Articles 16, 17 and 18.

56 Communication from the Commission: Guidelines on State aid to airports and airlines (OJ C99, 4.4.2014, p 3).

57 Council Regulation (EEC) No 3577/92 of 7 December applying the principles of freedom to provide services to maritime transport within Member States (OJ L364, 12.12.1992, p 7).

58 Commission communication C(2004) 43 — Community guidelines on State aid to maritime transport (OJ C13, 17.1.2004, p 3).

6. AID SCHEMES FOR SMALLER AID AMOUNTS AND BENEFICIARIES

6.1. GENERAL CONDITIONS

[5.329]

104. Should Member States wish to provide aid pursuant to these guidelines to SMEs or smaller State-owned undertakings, such aid should normally be granted under schemes. The use of schemes helps to limit distortions of competition linked to moral hazard, by allowing a Member State to make a clear statement *ex ante* concerning the terms on which it may decide to grant aid to undertakings in difficulty.

105. Schemes must specify the maximum amount of aid that can be awarded to any one undertaking as part of an operation to provide rescue aid, restructuring aid or temporary restructuring support, including where the plan is modified. The maximum total amount of aid granted to any one undertaking may not be more than EUR 10 million, including any aid obtained from other sources or under other schemes.

106. Whilst the compatibility of such schemes will in general be assessed in the light of the conditions set out in Chapters 3, 4 and 5, it is appropriate to provide for simplified conditions in certain respects, to enable Member States to apply those conditions without further reference to the Commission and to reduce the burden on SMEs and smaller State-owned undertakings of providing the information required. In view of the small size of the aid amounts and the beneficiaries at stake, the Commission considers that the potential for significant distortions of competitions is more limited in such cases. Therefore, the provisions of Chapters 3, 4 and 5 apply to such schemes *mutatis mutandis*, except as provided otherwise in sections 6.2, 6.3, 6.4 and 6.5. This Chapter also includes provisions on temporary restructuring support and on the duration and evaluation of schemes.

6.2. OBJECTIVE OF COMMON INTEREST

107. Whilst the failure of an individual SME[59] is unlikely to involve the degree of social hardship or market failure required for the purposes of point 44, there is a greater concern in relation to SMEs that value may be destroyed when SMEs that have the potential to restructure so as to restore their long-term viability are denied the chance to do so by liquidity problems. As regards the grant of aid under schemes, therefore, it is sufficient for a Member State to determine that the failure of the beneficiary would likely involve social hardship or a market failure, in particular that:

(a) the exit of an innovative SME or an SME with high growth potential would have potential negative consequences;
(b) the exit of an undertaking with extensive links to other local or regional undertakings, particularly other SMEs, would have potential negative consequences;
(c) the failure or adverse incentives of credit markets would push an otherwise viable undertaking into bankruptcy; or
(d) similar situations of hardship duly substantiated by the beneficiary would arise.

108. By way of derogation from point 50, beneficiaries under schemes will not be required to submit a market survey.

6.3. APPROPRIATENESS

109. The requirement set out in point 55(d) will be deemed to have been satisfied provided that rescue aid is granted for no longer than six months, during which time an analysis must be made of the beneficiary's position. Before the end of that period:

(a) the Member State must approve a restructuring plan or liquidation plan, or
(b) the beneficiary must submit a simplified restructuring plan, pursuant to point 115, or
(c) the loan must be reimbursed or the guarantee terminated.

110. By way of derogation from point 57, Member States will not be required to assess whether the remuneration as determined in accordance with point 56 represents an appropriate benchmark.

6.4. PROPORTIONALITY OF THE AID/AID LIMITED TO THE MINIMUM

111. By way of derogation from point 64, Member States may consider an own contribution to be adequate if it amounts to at least 40% of the restructuring costs in the case of medium-sized enterprises or 25% of the restructuring costs in the case of small enterprises.

6.5. NEGATIVE EFFECTS

112. A Member State that intends to grant rescue aid, restructuring aid or temporary restructuring support must verify whether the 'one time, last time' principle set out in section 3.6.1 is complied with. For that purpose, the Member State must determine whether the undertaking concerned has already received rescue aid, restructuring aid or temporary restructuring support in the past, including any such aid granted before the entry into force of these guidelines and any non-notified aid. If so, and where less than 10 years[60] have elapsed since the rescue aid or temporary restructuring support was granted or the restructuring period came to an end or implementation of the restructuring plan was halted (whichever occurred the latest), further rescue aid, restructuring aid or temporary restructuring support must not be granted, except:

(a) where temporary restructuring support follows the granting of rescue aid as part of a single restructuring operation;
(b) where restructuring aid follows the granting of rescue aid or temporary restructuring support as part of a single restructuring operation;
(c) where rescue aid or temporary restructuring support has been granted in accordance with these guidelines and that aid was not followed by restructuring aid, if:
   i. it could reasonably have been believed that the beneficiary would be viable in the long term when the aid pursuant to these guidelines was granted, and
   ii. new rescue or restructuring aid or temporary restructuring support becomes necessary after at least five years due to unforeseeable circumstances for which the beneficiary is not responsible;
(d) in exceptional and unforeseeable circumstances for which the beneficiary is not responsible.

113. Measures limiting distortions of competition are likely to have a disproportionate impact on small enterprises, particularly given the burden of carrying out such measures. By way of derogation from point 76, therefore, Member States are not obliged to require such measures from small enterprises, except where otherwise provided by rules on State aid in a particular sector. However, small enterprises should not normally increase their capacity during a restructuring period.

6.6. TEMPORARY RESTRUCTURING SUPPORT

114. In certain cases, it may be possible for an undertaking to complete restructuring without the need for restructuring aid, provided that it is able to obtain liquidity support of a longer duration than is available under the terms of rescue aid. Member States may put in place schemes that allow liquidity aid for a longer period than six months (referred to as 'temporary restructuring support'), on the conditions set out below.

115. Temporary restructuring support must fulfil the following conditions:

(a) The support must consist of aid in the form of loan guarantees or loans.
(b) The financial cost of the loan or, in the case of loan guarantees, the total financial cost of the guaranteed loan, including the interest rate of the loan and the guarantee premium, must comply with point 116.
(c) Temporary restructuring support must comply with the provisions of Chapter 3 of these guidelines, as modified by this chapter.
(d) Temporary restructuring support may be granted for a period not exceeding 18 months, less any immediately preceding period of rescue aid. Before the end of that period:
   i. the Member State must approve a restructuring plan as foreseen in point 55(d)(ii) above, or liquidation plan, or

ii. the loan must be reimbursed or the guarantee terminated,

(e) Not later than six months after disbursement of the first instalment to the beneficiary, less any immediately preceding period of rescue aid, the Member State must approve a simplified restructuring plan. That plan need not contain all the elements set out in points 47 to 52, but must, as a minimum, identify the actions that the beneficiary must take to restore its long-term viability without State support.

116. Remuneration for temporary restructuring support should be set at a rate not less than the reference rate set out in the Communication from the Commission on the revision of the method for setting the reference and discount rates for weak undertakings offering normal levels of collateralisation (currently 1-year IBOR plus 400 basis points).[61] To provide incentives for exit, the rate should increase by not less than 50 basis points once 12 months have elapsed from the time of disbursement of the first instalment to the beneficiary (less any immediately preceding period of rescue aid).

117. Temporary restructuring support must be restricted to the amount needed to keep the beneficiary in business for 18 months; in determining that amount regard should be had to the outcome of the formula set out in Annex I; any aid exceeding the result of that calculation can only be granted if it is duly justified by the provision of a liquidity plan setting out the beneficiary's liquidity needs for the coming 18 months.

6.7. DURATION AND EVALUATION

118. The Commission may require Member States to limit the duration of certain schemes (normally to four years or less) and to conduct an evaluation of those schemes.

119. Evaluations will be required for schemes where the potential distortions are particularly high, that is to say schemes where there is a risk of significant restrictions of competition if their implementation is not reviewed in due time.

120. Given the objectives and in order not to impose disproportionate burdens on Member States in respect of smaller aid projects, this only applies to aid schemes with large budgets or containing novel characteristics, or when significant market, technology or regulatory changes are anticipated. The evaluation must be carried out by an expert independent from the State aid granting authority, on the basis of a common methodology,[62] and must be made public. The evaluation must be submitted to the Commission in due time to allow for the assessment of possible extension of the aid scheme and in any case upon expiry of the scheme. The precise scope of the evaluation and how it is to be carried out will be defined in the decision approving the aid measure. Any subsequent aid measure with a similar objective must take into account the results of the evaluation.

NOTES

59 For the purposes of Chapter 6, 'SME' includes smaller State-owned undertakings.

60 Five years in the case of the primary agricultural production sector.

61 For the avoidance of doubt, the note regarding remuneration of rescue aid to the table of loan margins contained in that communication will not apply to aid assessed under these guidelines.

62 Such a common methodology may be provided by the Commission (see footnote 34).

7. PROCEDURES

7.1. ACCELERATED PROCEDURE FOR RESCUE AID

[5.330]

121. The Commission will as far as possible endeavour to take a decision within a period of one month in respect of rescue aid that complies with all of the conditions set out in Chapter 3 and with the following cumulative requirements:

(a) the rescue aid is limited to the amount resulting from the formula set out in Annex I and does not exceed EUR 10 million;

(b) the aid is not granted in the situations mentioned in point 72(b) or (c).

7.2. PROCEDURES RELATED TO RESTRUCTURING PLANS

7.2.1. Implementation of the restructuring plan

122. The beneficiary must fully implement the restructuring plan and must discharge any other obligations laid down in the Commission decision authorising the aid. The Commission will regard any failure to implement the plan or to fulfil the other obligations as misuse of the aid, without prejudice to Article 23 of Regulation (EC) No 659/1999 or to the possibility of an action before the Court of Justice pursuant to the second subparagraph of Article 108(2) of the Treaty.

123. Where restructuring operations cover several years and involve substantial amounts of aid, the Commission may require payment of the restructuring aid to be split into instalments and may make payment of each instalment subject to:

(a) confirmation, prior to each payment, of the satisfactory implementation of each stage in the restructuring plan, in accordance with the planned timetable; or

(b) its approval, prior to each payment, after verification that the plan is being satisfactorily implemented.

7.2.2. Amendment of the restructuring plan

124. Where restructuring aid has been approved, the Member State concerned may, during the restructuring period, ask the Commission to agree to changes to the restructuring plan and the amount of the aid. The Commission may allow such changes where they meet the following conditions:

(a) the revised plan must still show a return to viability within a reasonable time scale;

(b) if the restructuring costs are increased, the own contribution must increase correspondingly;

(c) if the amount of the aid is increased, measures to limit distortions of competition must be more extensive than those initially imposed;
(d) if the proposed measures to limit distortions of competition are more limited than those initially imposed, the amount of the aid must be correspondingly reduced;
(e) the new timetable for implementation of the measures to limit distortions of competition may be delayed with respect to the timetable initially adopted only for reasons outside the beneficiary's or the Member State's control: if that is not the case, the amount of the aid must be correspondingly reduced.

125. If the conditions imposed by the Commission or the commitments given by the Member State are relaxed, the amount of aid must be correspondingly reduced or other conditions may be imposed.

126. Should the Member State concerned introduce changes to an approved restructuring plan without duly informing the Commission, or should the beneficiary depart from the approved restructuring plan, the Commission will initiate proceedings under Article 108(2) of the Treaty, as provided for by Article 16 of Regulation (EC) No 659/1999 (misuse of aid), without prejudice to Article 23 of Regulation (EC) No 659/1999 and to the possibility of an action before the Court of Justice pursuant to the second subparagraph of Article 108(2) of the Treaty.

7.2.3. NEED TO NOTIFY TO THE COMMISSION ANY AID GRANTED TO THE BENEFICIARY DURING THE RESTRUCTURING PERIOD

127. Where restructuring aid is examined under these guidelines, the grant of any other aid during the restructuring period, even in accordance with a scheme that has already been authorised, is liable to influence the Commission's assessment concerning the necessary extent of the measures to limit distortions of competition.

128. Therefore, notifications of restructuring aid must indicate all other aid of any kind which is planned to be granted to the beneficiary during the restructuring period, unless it is covered by the *de minimis* rule or by exemption regulations. The Commission shall take such aid into account when assessing the restructuring aid.

129. Any aid actually granted during the restructuring period, including aid granted in accordance with an approved scheme, must be notified individually to the Commission to the extent that the latter was not informed thereof at the time of its decision on the restructuring aid.

130. The Commission shall ensure that the grant of aid under approved schemes is not liable to circumvent the requirements of these guidelines.

8. REPORTING AND MONITORING

[5.331]
131. In accordance with Regulation (EC) No 659/1999 and Commission Regulation (EC) No 794/2004 of 21 April 2004,[63] Member States must submit annual reports to the Commission. Those annual reports will be published on the Commission's website.

132. When adopting a decision under these guidelines the Commission may impose additional reporting obligations regarding the aid granted in order to be able to check whether the decision approving the aid measure has been respected. In certain cases, the Commission may require the appointment of a monitoring trustee, a divestment trustee or both, to ensure compliance with any conditions and obligations linked to the approval of the aid.

NOTES

[63] Commission Regulation (EC) No 794/2004 of 21 April 2004 implementing Council Regulation (EC) No 659/1999 laying down detailed rules for the application of Article 93 of the EC Treaty (OJ L140, 30.4.2004, p 1).

9. APPROPRIATE MEASURES AS REFERRED TO IN ARTICLE 108(1) TFEU

[5.332]
133. Pursuant to Article 108(1) of the Treaty, the Commission proposes that Member States amend, where necessary, their existing aid schemes in order to bring them into line with these guidelines no later than 1 February 2015.The Commission will make authorisation of any future scheme conditional on compliance with those provisions.

134. Member States are invited to give their explicit unconditional agreement to the appropriate measures proposed in point 133 within two months from the date of publication of these guidelines in the *Official Journal of the European Union*. In the absence of a reply from any of the Member States, the Commission will assume that the Member State in question does not agree with the proposed measures.

10. DATE OF APPLICATION AND DURATION

[5.333]
[135. The Commission will apply these guidelines with effect from 1 August 2014 until 31 December 2023.]

136. Notifications registered by the Commission prior to 1 August 2014 will be examined in the light of the criteria in force at the time of notification.

137. The Commission will examine the compatibility with the internal market of any rescue or restructuring aid granted without its authorisation and therefore in breach of Article 108(3) of the Treaty on the basis of these guidelines if some or all of the aid is granted after their publication in the *Official Journal of the European Union*.

138. In all other cases it will conduct the examination on the basis of the guidelines which applied at the time the aid was granted.

139. Notwithstanding the provisions of points 136, 137 and 138, the Commission will apply the provisions of Chapter 5 from 1 August 2014 when examining aid to SGEI providers in difficulty, regardless of when that aid was notified or granted.

140. Where, by virtue of paragraph 9 of the SGEI Framework, the Commission examines under these guidelines any aid granted before 31 January 2012 to an SGEI provider in difficulty, it will deem such aid to be compatible with the internal market if it complies with the provisions of the SGEI Framework, with the exception of paragraphs 9, 14, 19, 20, 24, 39 and 60.

NOTES

Para 135: substituted by Communication from the Commission (2020/C224/02), para (12).

ANNEX I

FORMULA[1] FOR CALCULATION OF THE MAXIMUM AMOUNT OF RESCUE AID OR TEMPORARY RESTRUCTURING SUPPORT PER SIX-MONTH PERIOD

[5.334]

$$\frac{EBIT_t + depreciation_t - (working\ \ capital_t - working\ \ capital_{t-1})}{2}$$

The formula is based on the operating results of the beneficiary (EBIT, earnings before interest and taxes) recorded in the year before granting/notifying the aid (indicated as t). To this amount depreciation has been added back. Then changes in working capital must be subtracted from the total. The change in working capital is calculated as the change in the difference between the current assets and current liabilities[2] for the latest closed accounting periods. Similarly, any provisions at the level of the operating result will need to be clearly indicated and the result should not include such provisions.

The formula aims at estimating the negative operating cash flow of the beneficiary in the year preceding the application for the aid (or before award of the aid in the case of non-notified aid). Half of this amount should keep the beneficiary in business for a six-month period. Thus the result of the formula has to be divided by 2 for the purposes of point 60. For the purposes of point 117, the result of the formula has to be multiplied by 1.5.

This formula can only be applied where the result is a negative amount. If it leads to a positive result, a detailed explanation will need to be submitted demonstrating that the beneficiary is an undertaking in difficulty as defined in point 20.

Example:

Earnings before interest and taxes (EUR million)	(12)	
Depreciation (EUR million)	2	
Balance sheet (EUR million)	December 31, t	December 31, t-1
Current assets		
Cash or equivalents	10	5
Accounts receivable	30	20
Inventories	50	45
Prepaid expenses	20	10
Other current assets	20	20
Total current assets	**130**	**100**
Current liabilities		
Accounts payable	20	25
Accrued expenses	15	10
Deferred income	5	5
Total current liabilities	**40**	**40**
Working capital	90	60
Change in working capital	30	

$$[-12+2-30]/2 = -\text{EUR}\ \ 20\ \ \text{million}.$$

As the outcome of the formula is higher than EUR 10 million, the accelerated procedure described in point 121 cannot be used. In addition, in this example, if the amount of rescue aid exceeds EUR 20 million or the amount of temporary restructuring support exceeds EUR 60 million, the amount of aid must be duly justified by the provision of a liquidity plan setting out the beneficiary's liquidity needs.

NOTES

1 To EBIT must be added back depreciation in the same period plus the changes in working capital over a two-year period (year before the application and preceding year), divided by two to determine an amount over six months.

2 Current assets: liquid funds, receivables (client and debtor accounts), other current assets and prepaid expenses, inventories. Current liabilities: financial debt, trade accounts payable (supplier and creditor accounts) and other current liabilities, deferred income, other accrued liabilities, tax liabilities.

ANNEX II
INDICATIVE MODEL RESTRUCTURING PLAN

[5.335]

This Annex sets out an indicative table of contents for a restructuring plan, to assist Member States and the Commission in preparing and reviewing restructuring plans as efficiently as possible.

The information set out below is without prejudice to the more detailed requirements set out in the guidelines concerning the content of a restructuring plan and the other matters to be demonstrated by the Member State concerned.

1. Description of the beneficiary
2. Description of the market or markets where the beneficiary operates
3. Demonstration of the social hardship that the aid aims to prevent or the market failure that it aims to address, comparison with a credible alternative scenario not involving State aid, demonstrating how such objective or objectives would not be attained, or would be attained to a lesser degree, in the case of the alternative scenario
4. Description of the sources of the beneficiary's difficulties (including an assessment of the role of any flaws in the beneficiary's business model or corporate governance system in causing those difficulties and the extent to which the difficulties could have been avoided through appropriate and timely management action) and SWOT analysis
5. Description of possible plans to remedy the beneficiary's problems and comparison of those plans in terms of the amount of State aid required and the anticipated results of those plans
6. Description of the State intervention, full details of each State measure (including the form, amount and remuneration of each measure) and demonstration that the State aid instruments chosen are appropriate to the issues that they are intended to address
7. Outline of the process for implementing the preferred plan with a view to restoring the beneficiary's long-term viability within a reasonable timescale (in principle, not to exceed three years), including a timetable of actions and a calculation of the costs of each action
8. Business plan setting out financial projections for the next five years and demonstrating the return to long-term viability
9. Demonstration of the return to viability under both a baseline and a pessimistic scenario, presentation and justification on the basis of a market survey of the assumptions used and sensitivity analysis
10. Proposed own contribution and burden-sharing measures
11. Proposed measures to limit distortions of competition

8. PROJECTS OF COMMON EUROPEAN INTEREST

COMMUNICATION FROM THE COMMISSION

(2014/C188/02)

Criteria for the analysis of the compatibility with the internal market of State aid to promote the execution of important projects of common European interest (Note)

[5.336]

NOTES

Date of publication in OJ: OJ C188, 20.06.2014, p 4.

Editorial note: this Communication was due to expire on 31 December 2020, but were extended to 31 December 2021 by Communication from the Commission concerning the prolongation and the amendments of the Guidelines on Regional State Aid for 2014-2020, Guidelines on State Aid to Promote Risk Finance Investments, Guidelines on State Aid for Environmental Protection and Energy 2014-2020, Guidelines on State aid for rescuing and restructuring non-financial undertakings in difficulty, Communication on the Criteria for the Analysis of the Compatibility with the Internal Market of State Aid to Promote the Execution of Important Projects of Common European Interest, Communication from the Commission – Framework for State aid for research and development and innovation and Communication from the Commission to the Member States on the application of Articles 107 and 108 of the Treaty on the Functioning of the European Union to short-term export-credit insurance (2020/C224/02).

This Communication is applicable until the end of 2021, but has been omitted from this edition of the Handbook due to constraints on the amount of available space. Customers who wish to refer to the Communication are advised to retain the 26th edition (2020) of this Handbook.

The Guidelines that apply from 1 January 2022 are set out below.

COMMUNICATION FROM THE COMMISSION

(C(2021) 8481 final)

Criteria for the analysis of the compatibility with the internal market of State aid to promote the execution of important projects of common European interest

[5.336A]

NOTES

Brussels, 25.11.2021.

1. INTRODUCTION

1. This Communication gives guidance on the assessment of public financing of important projects of common European interest (IPCEIs) under Union State aid rules.

2. IPCEIs can make a very important contribution to sustainable economic growth, jobs, competitiveness and resilience for industry and the economy in the Union and strengthen its open strategic autonomy, by enabling breakthrough innovation and infrastructure projects through cross-border cooperation and with positive spill-over effects on the internal market and the society as a whole.

3. IPCEIs make it possible to bring together knowledge, expertise, financial resources and economic actors from across the Union, in a bid to address important market or systemic failures or societal challenges that could not otherwise be addressed. They are designed to bring together the public and private sectors to undertake large-scale projects of significant benefit to the Union and its citizens.

4. IPCEIs can underpin all policies and actions that seek to achieve common European objectives, in particular the European Green Deal[1], the Digital Strategy[2] and the Digital Decade[3], the New Industrial Strategy for Europe[4] and its update[5], the European Strategy for Data[6] and Next Generation EU[7]. IPCEIs can also contribute to a sustainable recovery following serious economic disturbances such as those caused by the COVID-19 pandemic and support efforts to strengthen the Union's social and economic resilience.

5. Taking into account the updated New Industrial Strategy and the Small and Medium-sized Enterprise (SME) Strategy[8], it is important that SMEs and start-ups can participate in IPCEIs and benefit from them. The Commission will take into account in its assessment any circumstances which indicate that the notified aid is less likely to unduly distort competition, for example due to its amount.

6. The deployment of IPCEIs often requires a significant participation from public authorities whenever the market would not otherwise finance such projects. This Communication sets out the rules that apply where public financing of such projects constitutes State aid, in order for State aid for IPCEIs to be considered to be compatible with the internal market. Notably, the rules aim at ensuring that such aid will not to an undue extent adversely affect trading conditions between Member States, and at limiting the effects of such aid on trade and competition to the minimum necessary.

7. Article 107(3), point (b) of the Treaty on the Functioning of the European Union provides that aid to promote the execution of an important project of common European interest may be considered to be compatible with the internal market. Accordingly, this Communication sets out guidance on the criteria the Commission will apply for assessing State aid granted to promote the execution of IPCEIs. It first sets out its scope and then provides a list of

criteria the Commission will use to assess the nature and the importance of IPCEIs for the purposes of applying Article 107(3), point (b) of the Treaty. It then explains how the Commission will assess the compatibility of the public financing of IPCEIs with State aid rules.

8. This Communication does not exclude the possibility that aid to promote the execution of IPCEIs may also be found compatible with the internal market on the basis of other Treaty provisions, in particular Article 107(3), point (c) of the Treaty. However, those Treaty provisions may not fully address the relevance, specificities and features of IPCEIs. These may require specific eligibility, compatibility and procedural rules, as set out in this Communication.

NOTES

1 Communication from the Commission to the European Parliament, the European Council, the Council, the European Economic and Social Committee and the Committee of the Regions – 'The European Green Deal', COM(2019) 640 final, 11 December 2019.

2 Communication from the Commission to the European Parliament, the Council, the European Economic and Social Committee and the Committee of the Regions – 'Shaping Europe's digital future', COM(2020) 67 final, 19 February 2020.

3 Communication from the Commission to the European Parliament, the Council, the European Economic and Social Committee and the Committee of the Regions – '2030 Digital Compass: the European way for the Digital Decade', COM(2021), 118 final, 9 March 2021.

4 Communication from the Commission to the European Parliament, the European Council, the Council, the European Economic and Social Committee and the Committee of the Regions – 'A New Industrial Strategy for Europe', COM(2020) 102 final, 10 March 2020.

5 Communication from the Commission to the European Parliament, the European Council, the Council, the European Economic and Social Committee and the Committee of the Regions – 'Updating the 2020 New Industrial Strategy: Building a stronger Single Market for Europe's recovery', COM(2021) 350 final, 5 May 2021.

6 Communication from the Commission to the European Parliament, the Council, the European Economic and Social Committee and the Committee of the Regions – 'A European strategy for data', COM(2020) 66 final, 19 February 2020.

7 Communication from the Commission to the European Parliament, the European Council, the Council, the European Economic and Social Committee and the Committee of the Regions – 'Europe's moment: Repair and Prepare for the Next Generation', COM(2020) 456 final, 27 May 2020.

8 Communication from the Commission to the European Parliament, the Council, the European Economic and Social Committee and the Committee of the Regions – 'An SME Strategy for a sustainable and digital Europe', COM(2020) 103 final, 10 March 2020.

2. SCOPE

9. The Commission will apply the principles set out in this Communication to IPCEIs in all sectors of economic activity.

10. Those principles do not apply to:

(a) measures consisting of aid for undertakings in difficulty, as defined in the rescue and restructuring guidelines[9] or any successor guidelines, with the exception of undertakings which were not in difficulty on 31 December 2019 but became undertakings in difficulty on or after 1 January 2020 for as long as the Temporary Framework[10] is applied;

(b) measures consisting of aid for undertakings which are subject to an outstanding recovery order following a previous Commission decision declaring aid illegal and incompatible with the internal market;

(c) aid measures that constitute by themselves, by virtue of the conditions attached to them or of their financing method, a non-severable violation of Union law[11], in particular:

(i) aid measures in accordance with which the granting of aid is subject to the obligation for the beneficiary to have its headquarters in the Member State concerned or be predominantly established in that Member State,

(ii) aid measures in accordance with which the granting of aid is subject to the obligation for the beneficiary to use nationally produced goods or national services,

(iii) aid measures restricting the possibility for the beneficiary to use the obtained research, development and innovation results in other Member States.

NOTES

9 Guidelines on State aid for rescuing and restructuring non-financial undertakings in difficulty (OJ C 249, 31.7.2014, p 1). As explained in paragraph 23 of those guidelines, given that its very existence is in danger, an undertaking in difficulty cannot be considered an appropriate vehicle for promoting other public policy objectives until such time as its viability is assured.

10 Communication from the Commission - Temporary framework for State aid measures to support the economy in the current COVID-19 outbreak, OJ C 91I, 20.3.2020, p 1, and its amendments.

11 See for instance *Case C-156/98 Germany v Commission [2000]* ECLI:EU:C:2000:467, paragraph 78 and *Case C-333/07 Régie Networks v Rhone Alpes Bourgogne [2008]* ECLI:EU:C:2008:764, paragraphs 94 to 116.

3. ELIGIBILITY CRITERIA

11. In determining whether or not a project falls within the scope of Article 107(3), point (b) of the Treaty, the Commission will apply the criteria set out in sections 3.1, 3.2 and 3.3 of this Communication.

3.1. DEFINITION OF A PROJECT

12. The aid proposal must concern a single project, which is clearly defined in respect of its objectives as well as the terms of its implementation, including its participants and its funding[12].

13. The Commission may also consider eligible an 'integrated project', that is to say, a group of single projects inserted in a common structure, roadmap or programme aiming at the same objective and based on a coherent systemic approach. The individual components of the integrated project may relate to separate levels of the supply chain but must be complementary and significantly add value in their contribution towards the achievement of the European objective[13].

3.2. COMMON EUROPEAN INTEREST

3.2.1. General cumulative criteria

14. The project must represent a concrete, clear and identifiable important contribution to the Union's objectives or strategies and must have a significant impact on sustainable growth, for example by being of major importance for the European Green Deal, the Digital Strategy, the Digital Decade and European Strategy for Data, the New Industrial Strategy for Europe and its update, Next Generation EU, the European Health Union[14], the new European Research Area for research and innovation[15], the new Circular Economy Action Plan[16], or the Union's objective to become climate neutral by 2050, among others.

15. The project must demonstrate that it is designed to overcome important market or systemic failures, preventing the project from being carried out to the same extent or in the same manner in the absence of the aid, or societal challenges, which would not otherwise be adequately addressed or remedied.

16. Unless a smaller number is justified by the nature of the project[17], the project must ordinarily involve at least four Member States and its benefits must not be confined to the financing Member States, but extend to a wider part of the Union. The benefits of the project must be clearly defined in a concrete and identifiable manner[18].

17. All Member States must be given a genuine opportunity to participate in an emerging project. Notifying Member States must demonstrate that all Member States were informed of the possible emergence of a project, for example by way of contacts, alliances, meetings, or match-making events, also involving SMEs and start-ups, and given opportunity to participate.

18. The benefits of the project must not be limited to the undertakings or to the sector concerned but must be of wider relevance and application to the economy or society in the Union through positive spillover effects (such as having systemic effects on multiple levels of the value chain, or up- or downstream markets, or having alternative uses in other sectors or modal shift) which are clearly defined in a concrete and identifiable manner.

19. The project must involve important co-financing by the beneficiary[19].

20. Member States must provide evidence as to whether the project complies with the principle of 'do no significant harm' within the meaning of Article 17 of Regulation (EU) 2020/852, or other comparable methodologies[20]. In the overall balancing of the positive effects of the aid against its negative effects on competition and trade, the Commission will consider compliance with this principle as an important factor in its assessment. In general, investments that do significant harm to environmental objectives within the meaning of Article 17 of Regulation (EU) 2020/852 are unlikely to have sufficient positive effects to outweigh their negative effects on competition and trade. The positive effects of a project in addressing important market or systemic failures or societal challenges that could not otherwise be addressed are in all cases subject to individualised assessment.

3.2.2. General positive indicators

21. In addition to the cumulative criteria in Section 3.2.1, the Commission will take positive note of the following suggested elements by Member States:

(a) the design of the project involves the Commission or any legal body to which the Commission has delegated its powers, such as the European Investment Bank and the European Investment Fund;
(b) the selection of the project involves the Commission or any legal body to which the Commission has delegated its power, provided that that body is acting for that purpose as an implementing structure;
(c) the governance structure of the project involves the Commission or any legal body to which the Commission has delegated its powers, and the participating Member States;
(d) the project involves important collaborative interactions in terms of number of partners, involvement of organisations from different sectors, or the involvement of undertakings of different sizes and, in particular, cooperation between large enterprises and SMEs, including start-ups, in different Member States and supports the development of more disadvantaged regions;
(e) the project involves co-funding or co-financing from an Union fund[21] in direct, indirect or shared management;
(f) the project involves a significant contribution by independent private investors[22];
(g) the project addresses a clearly identified and significant strategic dependency.

3.2.3. Specific criteria

22. Research & Development & Innovation ("R&D&I") projects must be of a major innovative nature or constitute an important added value in terms of R&D&I in the light of the state of the art in the sector concerned[23].

23. Projects comprising of first industrial deployment must allow for the development of a new product or service with high research and innovation content or the deployment of a fundamentally innovative production process. Regular upgrades without an innovative dimension of existing facilities and the development of newer versions of existing products do not qualify as first industrial deployment.

24. For the purpose of this Communication, first industrial deployment means the upscaling of pilot facilities, demonstration plants or of the first-in-kind equipment and facilities covering the steps subsequent to the pilot line including the testing phase and bringing batch production to scale, but not mass production or commercial activities[24]. The end of first industrial deployment is determined taking into account, inter alia, the relevant R&D&I-related performance indicators pointing at the ability to start mass production. First industrial deployment activities can be

financed with State aid as long as the first industrial deployment follows on from an R&D&I activity and itself contains an important R&D&I component which constitutes an integral and necessary element for the successful implementation of the project. The first industrial deployment does not need to be carried out by the same entity that carried out the R&D&I activity, as long as that entity acquires the rights to use the results from the previous R&D&I activity, and the R&D&I activity and the first industrial deployment are both described in the project.

25. Infrastructure projects in the environmental, energy, transport, health or digital sectors, to the extent that they are not covered by points 22 and 23, must be of great importance for the environmental, climate, energy (including security of energy supply), transport, health, industrial or digital strategies of the Union or contribute significantly to the internal market, including, but not limited to those specific sectors, and can be supported for the period until becoming fully operational following construction.

3.3. IMPORTANCE OF THE PROJECT

26. In order to qualify as an IPCEI, a project must be important quantitatively or qualitatively. It should be particularly important in size or scope or imply a very considerable level of technological or financial risk, or both. To determine the importance of a project, the Commission will take into account the criteria set out in section 3.2.

NOTES

12 In the case of research and development, when two or more projects are not clearly separable from each other and, in particular when they do not have independent probabilities of technological success, they must be considered as a single project.

13 Hereafter a single project and an integrated project are referred to as a 'project'.

14 Communication from the Commission to the European Parliament, the European Council, the Council, the European Economic and Social Committee and the Committee of the Regions – 'Building a European Health Union - preparedness and resilience', COM/2020/724 final, 11 November 2020.

15 Communication from the Commission to the European Parliament, the Council, the European Economic and Social Committee and the Committee of the Regions – 'A new ERA for Research and Innovation', COM(2020) 628 final, 30 September 2020.

16 Communication from the Commission to the European Parliament, the Council, the European Economic and Social Committee and the Committee of the Regions – 'A new Circular Economy Action Plan For a cleaner and more competitive Europe', COM(2020) 98 final, 11 March 2020.

17 A smaller number of Member States, but not less than two, may be exceptionally justified in duly motivated circumstances, for example, if the project concerns interconnected research infrastructures, TEN-E and TEN-T projects that are of fundamentally transnational importance because they are part of a physically connected cross-border network or are essential to enhance cross-border traffic management or interoperability; or the project is financed from EU funds, in relation to which legal provisions on Member States' collaboration require a lower number of participating Member States. In all cases, projects must be designed in a transparent manner in line with point 17.

18 The mere fact that the project is carried out by undertakings in different countries, or that a research infrastructure is subsequently used by undertakings established in different Member States, is not sufficient for a project to qualify as an IPCEI. The Court has upheld the Commission's policy of considering that a project may be described as being of common European interest for the purposes of Article 107(3), point (b) when it forms part of a transnational European programme supported jointly by a number of governments of the Member States, or arises from concerted action by a number of Member States to combat a common threat. *Joined Cases C-62/87 and 72/87 Exécutif regional wallon and SA Glaverbel v Commission [1988]* ECLI:EU:C:1988:132, paragraph 22.

19 When assessing the extent of co-financing, the Commission will take into account the specificities of certain sectors and of SMEs. In exceptional, and duly motivated circumstances, the Commission may consider that aid is justified even in the absence of important co-financing by the beneficiary.

20 Regulation (EU) 2020/852 of the European Parliament and of the Council of 18 June 2020 on the establishment of a framework to facilitate sustainable investment, OJ L 198, 22.6.2020, p 13. For measures which are identical to measures within Recovery and Resilience Plans as approved by the Council, their compliance with the 'Do no significant harm' principle is considered fulfilled as this has already been verified.

21 Union funding centrally managed by the institutions, agencies, joint undertakings or other bodies of the EU that is not directly or indirectly under the control of the Member State does not constitute State aid. State aid can be cumulated with financing from a Union fund provided that the condition in point 35 is complied with.

22 Contribution of tangible and intangible assets, as well as land, must be accounted at market price.

23 This might include, when relevant, progressively advancing towards the state of the art, to the extent that a participating project clearly and credibly aims at and describes how it will go beyond such state of the art.

24 Limited sales, when necessary in the specific sector, related to the testing phase, including sample or feedback or certification sales, are excluded from the notion of "commercial activities".

4. COMPATIBILITY CRITERIA

27. When assessing the compatibility with the internal market of aid to promote the execution of an IPCEI on the basis of Article 107(3), point (b) of the Treaty, the Commission will take into account the criteria[25] set out in sections 4.1, 4.2 and 4.3 of this Communication.

28. The Commission will carry out, in the meaning of section 4.2., a balancing test to assess whether the expected positive effects of the aid outweigh the possible negative effects.

29. Taking into account the nature of the project, the Commission may consider that the presence of important market or systemic failures or societal challenges, as well as the contribution to a common European interest, can be presumed for the individual components of an integrated project where the project fulfils the eligibility criteria set out in Section 3.

4.1. NECESSITY AND PROPORTIONALITY OF THE AID

30. The aid must not subsidise the costs of a project that an undertaking would anyhow incur and must not compensate for the normal business risk of an economic activity. Without the aid, the realisation of the project should be impossible, or should only be possible on a smaller scale, with a more narrow scope, or not with sufficient speed, or in a different manner that would significantly restrict its expected benefits[26]. Aid will only be considered proportionate if the same result could not be achieved with less aid.

31. The Member States must provide the Commission with adequate information concerning the aided project as well as a comprehensive description of the counterfactual scenario, which corresponds to the situation where no aid is awarded by any Member State[27]. The counterfactual scenario may consist in the absence of an alternative project, where evidence supports that this is the most likely counterfactual, or in an alternative project considered by the beneficiaries in their internal decision-making, and may relate to an alternative project that is wholly or partly carried out outside the Union. To demonstrate the credibility of the counterfactual scenario presented by the beneficiaries, the notifying Member States are invited to provide relevant internal documents of the beneficiaries, such as board presentations, analyses, reports and studies[28].

32. In the absence of an alternative project, the Commission will verify that the aid amount does not exceed the minimum necessary for the aided project to be sufficiently profitable, for example by making it possible to achieve an internal rate of return corresponding to the sector or firm specific benchmark or hurdle rate. Normal rates of return required by the beneficiaries in other investment projects of a similar kind, their cost of capital as a whole or returns commonly observed in the industry concerned may also be used for this purpose. All relevant expected costs and benefits over the lifetime of the project must be considered.

33. The maximum permitted aid level will be determined with regard to the identified funding gap in relation to the eligible costs. If justified by the funding gap analysis, the aid intensity could cover all of the eligible costs. The funding gap refers to the difference between the positive and negative cash flows over the lifetime of the investment, discounted to their current value on the basis of an appropriate discount factor reflecting the rate of return necessary for the beneficiary to carry out the project, notably in view of the risks involved. The eligible costs are set out in the Annex[29].

34. Where it is shown, for example by means of internal company documents, that the aid beneficiary faces a clear choice between carrying out either an aided project or an alternative one without aid, the Commission will compare the expected net present values of the investment in the aided project and the counterfactual project, account being taken of the probabilities of the different business scenarios occurring.

35. State aid to promote the execution of IPCEIs may be cumulated with Union funding or other State aid, provided that the total amount of public funding granted in relation to the same eligible costs does not exceed the most favourable funding rate laid down in the applicable rules of Union law.

36. As an additional safeguard to ensure that the State aid remains proportionate and limited to the necessary, the Commission may request the notifying Member State to implement a claw-back mechanism[30]. The claw-back mechanism should ensure a balanced distribution of additional gains when the project is more profitable than forecasted in the notified funding gap analysis and should apply only to those investments which reach, based on the ex post cash flow results and of State aid disbursements, a rate of return exceeding the beneficiaries' cost of capital. Any such claw-back mechanism should be clearly defined in advance in order to provide financial predictability for beneficiaries at the moment of decision-making on participation in the project. Such mechanism should be designed in such a way as to maintain strong incentives for beneficiaries to maximise their investment and project performance.

37. In its analysis, the Commission will take into consideration the following elements:

(a) specification of intended change: the Member State must clearly specify the change in behaviour which is expected to result from the State aid, that is to say whether a new project will be triggered, or the size, scope, speed or cross-border dimension of a project will be enhanced. The change of behaviour has to be identified by comparing the expected outcome and level of intended activity with and without aid. The difference between the two scenarios shows the impact of the aid measure and its incentive effect;

(b) level of profitability: where a project would not in itself be sufficiently profitable for a private undertaking to undertake, but would generate important benefits for society, it is more likely that the aid has an incentive effect.

38. In order to address actual or potential direct or indirect distortions of international trade, the Commission may take account of the fact that, directly or indirectly, competitors located outside the Union have received, in the last three years, or are going to receive, aid of an equivalent intensity for similar projects. However, where distortions of international trade are likely to occur after more than three years, given the particular nature of the sector in question, the reference period may be extended accordingly. If at all possible, the Member State concerned will provide the Commission with sufficient information to enable it to assess the situation, in particular the need to take account of the competitive advantage enjoyed by a third country competitor. If the Commission does not have evidence concerning the awarded or proposed aid, it may also base its decision on circumstantial evidence. The Commission may also take appropriate action to address competition distortions arising from subsidies received outside the Union.

39. When gathering evidence, the Commission may use its investigative powers[31].

40. The choice of the aid instrument must be made with a view to the market failure or other important systemic failures which it seeks to address. For instance, where the underlying problem is lack of access to finance, Member States should normally resort to aid in the form of liquidity support, such as a loan or guarantee[32]. Where it is also necessary to provide the undertaking with a certain degree of risk-sharing, a repayable advance should normally be the aid instrument of choice. Repayable aid instruments will generally be considered as a positive indicator.

41. The selection of beneficiaries through a competitive, transparent and non-discriminatory procedure will be considered as a positive indicator.

4.2. PREVENTION OF UNDUE DISTORTIONS OF COMPETITION AND BALANCING TEST

42. The Member States must provide evidence that the proposed aid measure constitutes the appropriate policy instrument to address the objective of the project. An aid measure will not be considered appropriate if other less distortive policy instruments or other less distortive types of aid instruments make it possible to achieve the same result.

43. For the aid to be compatible, the negative effects of the aid measure in terms of distortions of competition and impact on trade between Member States must be limited and outweighed by the positive effects in terms of contribution to the objective of common European interest.

44. In assessing the negative effects of the aid measure, the Commission will focus its analysis on the foreseeable impact the aid may have on competition between undertakings in the product markets concerned, including up- or downstream markets, and on the risk of overcapacity.

45. The Commission will assess the risk of market foreclosure and dominance. Projects involving the construction of an infrastructure[33] must comply with principles of open and non-discriminatory access to the infrastructure and non-discriminatory pricing and network operation, including those laid down in Union law[34].

46. The Commission will assess the potential negative effects on trade including the risk of a subsidy race between Member States, which may arise in particular with respect to the choice of a location.

47. In its assessment of the potential negative effects on trade, the Commission will consider whether aid is conditional on the relocation of a production activity or any other activity of the beneficiary from another Contracting Party to the EEA Agreement to the territory of the Member State granting the aid. Such a condition would appear to be harmful to the internal market, irrespective of the number of job losses actually incurred in the initial establishment of the beneficiary in the EEA, and unlikely to be compensated by any positive effects.

4.3. TRANSPARENCY

48. Member States must ensure that the following information is published in the Commission's transparency award module or on a comprehensive State aid website, at national or regional level:

(a) the full text of the individual aid granting decision and its implementing provisions, or a link to it;
(b) the identity of the granting authority or authorities;
(c) the name and the identifier of each beneficiary, except business secrets and other confidential information in duly justified cases and subject to the Commission's agreement in accordance with Commission communication on professional secrecy in State aid decisions[35];
(d) the aid instrument[36], the aid element and, where different, the nominal amount of aid, expressed as the full amount in national currency granted to each beneficiary;
(e) the date of granting and the date of publication;
(f) the type of beneficiary (SME/large company/start-up);
(g) the region in which the beneficiary is located (at NUTS level II or below);
(h) the principal economic sector in which the beneficiary has its activities (at NACE group level);
(i) the objective of the aid.

49. The requirement to publish information applies with respect to individual aid awards exceeding EUR 100 000. Such information must be published after the decision to grant the aid has been taken, must be kept for at least 10 years and must be available to the general public without restrictions[37].

NOTES

25 According to the Court of Justice, the Commission enjoys discretion as regards the assessment of the compatibility of IPCEIs. *Joined Cases C-62/87 and 72/87 Exécutif regional wallon and SA Glaverbel v Commission [1988]* ECLI:EU:C:1988:132, paragraph 21.

26 The aid application must precede the starts of the works, which is either the start of construction works on the investment or the first firm commitment to order equipment or other commitment that makes the investment irreversible, whichever is the first in time. Buying of land and preparatory works such as obtaining permits and conducting preliminary feasibility studies are not considered as start of works.

27 For projects by SMEs, the counterfactual scenario may consist in the absence of an alternative project as referred to in point 32.

28 Where the information provided is covered by the obligation of professional secrecy, it is to be handled in accordance with Article 30 of Council Regulation (EU) 2015/1589 of 13 July 2015 laying down detailed rules for the application of Article 108 of the Treaty on the Functioning of the European Union (OJ L 248, 24.9.2015, p 9).

29 In case of an integrated project, the eligible costs must be detailed at the level of each individual project.

30 For projects by SMEs, no claw-back mechanism needs to be implemented unless in exceptional circumstances, in particular in consideration to the amounts of aid notified for such projects.

31 See Article 25 of Council Regulation (EU) 2015/1589 of 13 July 2015 laying down detailed rules for the application of Article 108 of the Treaty on the Functioning of the European Union (OJ L 248, 24.9.2015, p 9–29).

32 Aid in the form of guarantees must be limited in time, and aid in the form of loans must be subject to repayment periods.

33 For avoidance of doubt, pilot lines are not considered as infrastructures.

34 Where the project involves an energy infrastructure, it shall be subject to the tariff and access regulation and to the unbundling requirements where required by internal market legislation.

35 C(2003) 4582 (OJ C 297, 9.12.2003, p 6).

36 Grant/Interest rate subsidy; Loan/Repayable advances/Reimbursable grant; Guarantee; Tax advantage or tax exemption; Risk finance; Other. If the aid is granted through multiple aid instruments, the aid amount must be provided by instrument.

37 This information must be published within 6 months from the date of granting. In case of unlawful aid, Member States will be required to ensure the publication of this information ex post within 6 months from the date of the Commission decision. The information must be available in a format which allows data to be searched, extracted, and easily published

on the internet, for instance in CSV or XML format.

5. NOTIFICATION, REPORTING AND APPLICATION

5.1. NOTIFICATION OBLIGATION

50. According to Article 108(3) of the Treaty, Member States must notify the Commission in advance of any plans to grant or alter State aid, including aid for an IPCEI.

51. Member States involved in the same IPCEI are invited, whenever possible, to submit a common notification to the Commission including a joint text describing the IPCEI and demonstrating its eligibility.

5.2. EX POST EVALUATION AND REPORTING

52. The execution of the project must be subject to regular reporting. Where appropriate, the Commission may ask for an ex post evaluation to be conducted.

5.3. APPLICATION

53. The Commission will apply the principles set out in this Communication from 1 January 2022.

54. It will apply those principles to all notified aid projects in respect of which it is called upon to take a decision on or after 1 January 2022, even where the projects were notified prior to that date.

55. In line with the Notice on the determination of the applicable rules for the assessment of unlawful State aid[38], in the case of non-notified aid, the Commission will apply the principles set out in this Communication if the aid was granted on or after 1 January 2022, and the rules in force at the time when the aid was granted in all other cases.

NOTES

38 Commission notice on the determination of the applicable rules for the assessment of unlawful State aid (OJ C 119, 22.5.2002, p 22).

ANNEX
ELIGIBLE COSTS

a) Feasibility studies, including preparatory technical studies, and the costs of obtaining the permissions necessary for the realisation of the project.

b) Costs of instruments and equipment (including installations and transport vehicles) to the extent and for the period used for the project. If such instruments and equipment are not used for their full life for the project, only the depreciation costs corresponding to the life of the project, as calculated on the basis of good accounting practice, are considered as eligible.

c) Costs of the acquisition (or construction) of buildings, infrastructure and land, to the extent and for the period used for the project. Where these costs are determined with regard to the commercial transfer value or the actually incurred capital costs, as opposed to the depreciation costs, the residual value of the land, building or infrastructure should be deducted from the funding gap, either ex ante or ex post.

d) Costs of other materials, supplies and similar products necessary for the project.

e) Costs for obtaining, validating and defending patents and other intangible assets. Costs of contractual research, knowledge and patents bought or licensed from outside sources at arm's length conditions, as well as costs of consultancy and equivalent services used exclusively for the project.

f) Personnel and administrative costs (including overheads) directly incurred for the R&D&I activities, including those R&D&I activities related to first industrial deployment, or in the case of an infrastructure project, incurred during the construction of the infrastructure.

g) In case of aid to a project of first industrial deployment, the capital and operating expenditures to the extent and for the period used for the project, as long as the industrial deployment follows on from an R&D&I activity and itself contains an important R&D&I component which constitutes an integral and necessary element for the successful implementation of the project. The operating expenditures must be related to such component of the project.

h) Other costs may be accepted if justified, and where they are inextricably linked to the realisation of the project, to the exclusion of operating costs not covered by point (g).

D. SECTOR-SPECIFIC RULES

1. AUDIOVISUAL PRODUCTION

COMMUNICATION FROM THE COMMISSION ON STATE AID FOR FILMS AND OTHER AUDIOVISUAL WORKS

(2013/C 332/01)

(Text with EEA relevance)

[5.337]

NOTES

Date of publication in OJ: OJ C332, 15.11.2013, p 1.

Note that the Commission Communication on certain legal aspects relating to cinematographic and other audiovisual works (OJ C43, 16.2.2002, p 6) was included in previous editions of this Handbook (together with the Commission Communication on the follow-up to the Commission Communication on certain legal aspects relating to cinematographic and other audiovisual works (OJ C123, 30.4.2004, p 1)) and still applies to unlawful aid granted up to 15 November 2013.

1. INTRODUCTION

1. Audiovisual works, particularly films, play an important role in shaping European identities. They reflect the cultural diversity of the different traditions and histories of the EU Member States and regions. Audiovisual works are both economic goods, offering important opportunities for the creation of wealth and employment, and cultural goods which mirror and shape our societies.

2. Amongst audiovisual works, films still have a particular prominence, because of their cost of production and cultural importance. Film production budgets are substantially higher than for other audiovisual content, they are more frequently the subject of international co-production, and the duration of their exploitation life is longer. Films in particular face strong competition from outside Europe. On the other hand, there is little circulation of European audiovisual works outside their country of origin.

3. This limited circulation results from the fragmentation of the European audiovisual sector into national or even regional markets. While this is related to Europe's linguistic and cultural diversity, proximity is also built into the public support for European audiovisual works, with which national, regional and local funding schemes subsidise many small production companies.

4. It is generally accepted that aid is important to sustain European audiovisual production. It is difficult for film producers to obtain a sufficient level of upfront commercial backing to put together a financial package so that production projects can proceed. The high risk associated with their businesses and projects, together with the perceived lack of profitability of the sector, make it dependent on State aid. Left purely to the market, many of these films would not have been made because of a combination of the high investment required and the limited audience for European audiovisual works. In these circumstances, the fostering of audiovisual production by the Commission and the Member States have a role to ensure that their culture and creative capacity can be expressed and the diversity and richness of European culture reflected.

5. MEDIA, the European Union's support programme for the film, television and new media industries, offers a variety of funding schemes, each targeting different areas of the audiovisual sector, including schemes for producers, distributors, sales agents, organisers of training courses, operators in new digital technologies, operators of video-on-demand (VoD) platforms, exhibitors and organisers of festivals, markets and promotional events. It encourages the circulation and promotion of European films with particular emphasis on non-national European films. These actions will be continued in the MEDIA Sub-programme within Creative Europe, the new European support programme for the cultural and creative sectors.

2. WHY CONTROL STATE AID FOR FILMS AND OTHER AUDIOVISUAL WORKS?

6. Member States implemented a wide range of support measures for the production of films, TV programmes and other audiovisual works. Altogether, Member States provide an estimated EUR 3 billion of film support per year.[1] This funding is provided through over 600 national, regional and local support schemes. The rationale behind these measures is based on both cultural and industrial considerations. They have the primary cultural aim of ensuring that the national and regional cultures and creative potential are expressed in the audiovisual media of film and television. On the other hand, they aim to generate the critical mass of activity that is required to create the dynamic for the development and consolidation of the industry through the creation of soundly based production undertakings and the development of a permanent pool of human skills and experience.

7. With this support, the EU has become one of the largest producers of films in the world. The EU cinema industry produced 1 299 feature films in 2012 compared to 817 in the US (2011), or 1 255 in India (2011). In 2012, Europe counted 933.3 million cinema admissions.[2] In 2008, the European audiovisual market for filmed entertainment was valued at EUR 17 billion.[3] Over one million people are employed in the audiovisual sector in the European Union.[4]

8. This makes film production and distribution not only a cultural but also a significant economic activity. Furthermore, film producers are active on an international level and audiovisual works are traded internationally. This means that such aid in the form of grants, tax incentives or other types of financial support is liable to affect trade between Member States. The producers and audiovisual works which receive such support are likely to have a financial and hence competitive advantage over those which do not. Consequently, such support may distort competition and is regarded as State aid pursuant to Article 107(1) TFEU. According to Article 108 TFEU the Commission is therefore obliged to assess the compatibility of aid to the audiovisual sector with the internal market, as it does with State aid measures in other sectors.

9. In this context, it is important to stipulate that the Treaty recognises the utmost importance of promoting culture for the European Union and its Member States by incorporating culture among the Union's policies specifically referred to in the Treaty on the Functioning of the European Union (TFEU). Article 167(2) TFEU provides that:

> 'Action by the Union shall be aimed at encouraging cooperation between Member States and, if necessary, supporting and supplementing their action in the following areas:
> [. . .]
> — artistic and literary creation, including in the audiovisual sector.'

10. Article 167(4) TFEU provides that:

> 'The Union shall take cultural aspects into account in its action under other provisions of the Treaties, in particular in order to respect and to promote the diversity of its cultures.'

11. Article 107(1) TFEU prohibits aid granted by the State or through State resources, which distorts or threatens to distort competition and trade between Member States. However, the Commission may exempt certain State aid from this prohibition. One of these exemptions is Article 107(3)(d) TFEU for aid to promote culture, where such aid does not affect competition and trading conditions to an extent contrary to the common interest.

12. The Treaty rules on State aid control acknowledge the specificities of culture and the economic activities related to it. Audiovisual aid contributes to the medium- to long-term sustainability of the European film and audiovisual sectors across all Member States and increases the cultural diversity of the choice of works available to European audiences.

13. As Party to the UNESCO Convention on the Protection and the Promotion of the Diversity of Cultural Expressions, the European Union, alongside the EU Member States, is committed to integrating the cultural dimension as a vital element in its policies.

NOTES

1 EUR 2.1 billion of support is provided annually by European film funds (www.obs.coe.int/about/oea/pr/fundingreport2011.html). According to the study into the economic and cultural impact of territorial conditions in film support schemes, a further, estimated EUR 1 billion is provided annually by Member States through film tax incentives (ec.europa.eu/avpolicy/info_centre/library/studies/index_en.htm#territorialisation).

2 Source: *Focus 2012 — World film market trends*, European Audiovisual Observatory, May 2012.

3 PWC Global Entertainment and Media Outlook 2009–2013, June 2009, p 193.

4 Study by KEA European Affairs, Multi-Territory Licensing of Audiovisual Works in the European Union, Final Report prepared for the European Commission, Directorate-General for the Information Society and Media, October 2010, p 21 (www.keanet.eu/docs/mtl%20-%20full%20report%20en.pdf)

3. DEVELOPMENTS SINCE 2001

14. The assessment criteria for State aid for the production of films and other audiovisual works were originally set out in the 2001 Cinema Communication.[1] The validity of these criteria was extended in 2004,[2] 2007[3] and 2009[4] and expired on 31 December 2012. This Communication pursues the main lines of the 2001 Communication, whilst responding to a number of trends which have emerged since 2001.

15. The aid schemes approved by the Commission since the 2001 rules came into force show that Member States use a wide variety of aid mechanisms and conditions. Most schemes follow the model for which the assessment criteria of the 2001 Communication were designed, namely grants awarded to selected film productions, where the maximum aid is determined as a percentage of the production budget of the aid beneficiary. However, a growing number of Member States introduced schemes which define the aid amount as a percentage of the expenditure on production activity undertaken in the granting Member State only. These schemes are often designed in the form of a tax reduction or otherwise in a way which applies automatically to a film which fulfils certain criteria for its eligibility for aid. Compared to film funds which individually award support to single films upon application, these schemes with their automatic application allow film producers to factor in a foreseeable amount of funding already in the film planning and development phase.

16. Regarding the scope of aided activities, some Member States also offer aid to activities other than film production. This includes aid to film distribution or to cinemas, for example to support rural cinemas or arthouse cinemas in general or to cover their renovation and modernisation, including their transition to digital projection. Some Member States support audiovisual projects which go beyond the traditional concept of film and TV productions, in particular interactive products like transmedia or games. In these cases, the Commission applied the criteria of the Cinema Communication as a reference to assess the necessity, proportionality and adequacy of the aid, whenever such aid was notified to it. The Commission also noted a competition among Member States to use State aid to attract inward investment from large-scale film production companies of third countries. These issues were not addressed in the 2001 Communication.

17. Already the 2001 Communication announced that the Commission would review the maximum level of territorial spending obligations in this sector permitted under the State aid rules. Territorial spending obligations in film-funding schemes require a certain part of the supported film budget to be spent in the Member State granting the aid. The 2004

extension identified territorial spending obligations in film funding schemes as an issue which needs to be further assessed in view of its compliance with the internal market principles of the Treaty. Case law of the Court of Justice, adopted since 2001 on the importance of the internal market with regard to rules on the origin of goods and services, also needs to be taken into account.[5]

18. Also the application of the 'cultural test' has raised issues in practice. The compatibility of aid to film production is assessed under Article 107(3)(d) TFEU which provides for the possibility to grant aid 'to promote culture'. The 2001 Communication required that the aid was directed towards a cultural product. However, the Commission's detailed scrutiny of cultural criteria in film support schemes has been controversial with Member States, particularly in view of the subsidiarity principle.

19. Accordingly, when extending the State aid assessment criteria of the 2001 Cinema Communication in 2009, the Commission noted the need for further reflection on the implications of these developments and a review of the assessment criteria.

NOTES

[1] Communication from the Commission to the Council, the European Parliament, the Economic and Social Committee and the Committee of the Regions on certain legal aspects relating to cinematographic and other audiovisual works (OJ C43, 16.2.2002, p 6).

[2] OJ C123, 30.4.2004, p 1.

[3] OJ C134, 16.6.2007, p 5.

[4] OJ C31, 7.2.2009, p 1.

[5] In particular the Judgment of the Court of Justice of 10 March 2005 in Case *Laboratoires Fournier* (C-39/04), ECR 2005 I-2057.

4. SPECIFIC CHANGES

20. This Communication addresses the issues above and introduces amendments to the criteria of the 2001 Communication. In particular, it covers State aid for a wider scope of activities, highlights the principle of subsidiarity in the area of cultural policy and the respect of internal market principles, introduces a higher maximum aid intensity level for cross-border productions and caters for the protection of and access to film heritage. The Commission believes that these changes are necessary in view of the developments since 2001 and will help European works to be more competitive and pan-European in future.

4.1. SCOPE OF ACTIVITIES

21. Regarding the scope of activities to which this Communication applies, the State aid criteria of the 2001 Cinema Communication focused on the production of films. As noted, some Member States however offer also support for other related activities, such as scriptwriting, development, film distribution, or film promotion (including film festivals). The objective of protecting and promoting Europe's cultural diversity through audiovisual works can only be achieved if these works are seen by audiences. Aid to production alone risks stimulating the supply of audiovisual content without ensuring that the resulting audiovisual work is properly distributed and promoted. It is therefore appropriate that aid may cover all aspects of film creation, from story concept to delivery to the audience.

22. Regarding aid to cinemas, usually the amounts involved are small, so that for example rural and arthouse cinemas should be sufficiently served by the levels of aid which fall under the *de minimis* Regulation.[1] However, if a Member State can justify that more support to cinemas is required, the aid will be assessed under the present Communication as aid to promote culture in the meaning of Article 107(3)(d) TFEU. Aid for cinemas promotes culture because the principle purpose of cinemas is the exhibition of the cultural product of film.

23. Some Member States considered support to audiovisual projects which go beyond the traditional concept of film and TV productions. Transmedia storytelling (also known as multi-platform storytelling or cross-media storytelling) is the technique of telling stories across multiple platforms and formats using digital technologies, like films and games. Importantly, these pieces of content are linked together.[2] Since transmedia projects are inevitably linked to the production of a film, the film production component is considered to be an audiovisual work within the scope of this Communication.

24. Conversely, although games may represent one of the fastest-growing form of mass media in the coming years, not all games necessarily qualify as audiovisual works or cultural products. They have other characteristics regarding production, distribution, marketing, and consumption than films. Therefore, the rules designed for film production cannot apply automatically to games. Furthermore, contrary to the film and television sector, the Commission does not have a critical mass of decisions on State aid to games. Consequently, this Communication does not cover aid granted to games. Any aid measures in support of games not meeting the conditions of the General Block Exemption Regulation (GBER)[3] or the *de minimis* Regulation will continue to be addressed on a case-by-case basis. To the extent that the necessity of an aid scheme targeted at games which serve a cultural or educational purpose can be demonstrated, the Commission will apply the aid intensity criteria of this Communication by analogy.

NOTES

[1] Commission Regulation (EC) No 1998/2006 of 15 December 2006 on the application of Articles 87 and 88 of the Treaty to *de minimis* aid (OJ L379, 28.12.2006, p 5).

[2] Not to be confused with traditional cross-platform media franchises, sequels or adaptations.

[3] Commission Regulation (EC) No 800/2008 of 6 August 2008 declaring certain categories of aid compatible with the common market in application of Articles 87 and 88 of the Treaty (General Block Exemption Regulation) (OJ L214, 9.8.2008, p 3).

4.2. CULTURAL CRITERION

25. To be compatible with Article 107(3)(d) TFEU, aid to the audiovisual sector needs to promote culture. In line with the subsidiarity principle enshrined in Article 5 TEU, the definition of cultural activities is primarily a responsibility of the Member States. In assessing an audiovisual support scheme, the Commission acknowledges that its task is limited to verifying whether a Member State has a relevant, effective verification mechanism in place able to avoid manifest error. This would be achieved through the existence of either a cultural selection process to determine which audiovisual works should benefit from aid or a cultural profile to be fulfilled by all audiovisual works as a condition of the aid. In line with the UNESCO Convention on the Protection and Promotion of the Diversity of Cultural Expressions of 2005,[1] the Commission notes that the fact that a film is commercial does not prevent it from being cultural.

26. Linguistic diversity is an important element of cultural diversity; hence, defending and promoting the use of one or several of the languages of a Member State also serves the promotion of culture.[2] According to the well-established caselaw of the Court, both the promotion of a language of a Member State[3] and cultural policy[4] may constitute an overriding requirement relating to the general interest which justifies a restriction on the freedom to provide services. Therefore, Member States may require, as condition for the aid, inter alia, that the film is produced in a certain language, when it is established that this requirement is necessary and adequate to pursue a cultural objective in the audiovisual sector, which can also favour the freedom of expression of the different social, religious, philosophical or linguistic components which exist in a given region. The fact that such a criterion may constitute in practice an advantage for cinema production undertakings which work in the language covered by that criterion appears inherent to the objective pursued.[5]

NOTES

1 The Convention states in Article 4(4): 'Cultural activities, goods and services refers to those activities, goods and services, which . . . embody or convey cultural expressions, irrespective of the commercial value they may have. Cultural activities may be an end in themselves, or they may contribute to the production of cultural goods and services.'.

2 Judgment of the Court of 5 March 2009, *UTECA*, Case C-222/07, paragraphs 27–33.

3 Judgment of the Court of 13 December 2007, *United Pan-Europe Communications Belgium*, Case C-250/06, paragraph 43.

4 Judgment of the Court of 28 October 1999, *ARD*, Case C-6/98, paragraph 50.

5 Judgment of the Court of 5 March 2009, *UTECA*, Case C-222/07, paragraphs 34, 36.

4.3. TERRITORIAL SPENDING OBLIGATIONS

27. Obligations imposed by the authorities granting the aid on film producers to spend a certain part of the film production budget in a particular territory (territorial spending obligations) have been subject to particular attention since the Commission started looking into film support schemes. The 2001 Cinema Communication allowed Member States to require that up to 80% of the entire film budget needed to be spent on their territory. The schemes which define the aid amount as a percentage of the expenditure on production activity undertaken in the granting Member State do try already by their design to draw as much production activity as possible to the aid granting Member State and contain an inherent element of territorialisation of expenditure. The Cinema Communication needs to take into account these different types of aid schemes now in place.

28. Territorial spending obligations constitute a restriction of the internal market for audiovisual production. Therefore, the Commission commissioned an external study on territorial conditions imposed on audiovisual production which was completed in 2008.[1] As stated in the 2009 extension of the Cinema Communication, overall, the study was inconclusive: it could not judge whether or not the positive effects of territorial conditions outweighed the negative effects.

29. However, the study found that the costs of film production seem to be higher in those countries which apply territorial conditions than in those which do not. The study also found that territorial conditions may cause some obstacles to co-productions and may make them less efficient. Overall, the study found that the more restrictive territorial spending obligations do not lead to sufficient positive effects to justify maintaining the current levels of restrictions. It also did not demonstrate the necessity of these conditions in view of the objectives pursued.

30. A national measure which hampers the exercise of fundamental freedoms guaranteed by the Treaty may only be acceptable when complying with several conditions: it has to pursue an overriding reason of general interest, it has to be suitable for securing the attainment of the objective which it pursues and must not go beyond what is necessary in order to attain it.[2] The specific characteristics of the film industry, in particular the extreme mobility of productions, and the promotion of cultural diversity and national culture and languages, may constitute an overriding requirement of general interest capable of justifying a restriction on the exercise of the fundamental freedoms. Therefore, the Commission continues to acknowledge that, to a certain extent, such conditions may be necessary to maintain a critical mass of infrastructure for film production in the Member State or region granting the aid.

31. Hardly any Member States impose territorial spending obligations up to the ceiling of 80% of the production budget allowed by the 2001 Communication. Several Member States do not have territorial spending obligations at all in their schemes. Many regional schemes are linked to the aid amount and require that 100% or 150% of this amount must or should be spent in the granting Member State, without being specific on the origin of the subcontracted services or the origin of goods used in the production. In some schemes, the producer receiving the aid is free to spend at least 20% of the production budget outside that Member State. Certain Member States design the film aid as a percentage of just the local expenditure.

32. The amount of expenditure which is subject to territorial spending obligations should at least be proportionate to the actual financial commitment of a Member State and not with the overall production budget. This was not necessarily the case with the territorial criterion of the 2001 Communication.[3]

33. There are essentially two, distinct aid mechanisms applied by Member States awarding aid for film production:

— aid awarded — for example by a selection panel — as direct grants, for example defined as a percentage of the production budget; and
— aid awarded and defined as a proportion of the production expenditure in the granting Member State (e.g. a tax incentive).

34. Paragraph 50 sets the limits for each mechanism within which the Commission can accept that a Member State is applying territorial spending obligations which could be still considered as necessary and proportionate to a cultural objective.

35. In the case of aid awarded as grants, the maximum territorial spending obligation should be limited to 160% of the aid amount. This corresponds to the previous '80% of the production budget' rule when the aid intensity reaches the general maximum stated in paragraph 52(2), namely 50% of the production budget.[4]

36. In the case of aid awarded as a percentage of the expenditure on production activity in the granting Member State, there is an incentive to spend more in the Member State to receive more aid. Limiting the eligible production activity to that which takes place in the Member State granting the aid is a territorial restriction. Consequently, to establish a limit which is comparable to the limit for grants, the maximum expenditure subject to territorial spending obligations is 80% of the production budget.

37. In addition, under either mechanism, any scheme may have an eligibility criterion requiring a minimum level of production activity in the territory of the granting Member State. This level shall not exceed 50% of the production budget.

38. In any case, under EU law, Member States are under no obligation to impose territorial spending obligations.

NOTES

1 2008 Study on the Economic and Cultural Impact, notably on Co-productions, of Territorialisation Clauses of state aid Schemes for Films and Audiovisual Productions (ec.europa.eu/avpolicy/docs/library/studies/territ/final_rep.pdf).

2 Judgment *UTECA*, Case C-222/07, §25.

3 For example: a producer is making a film with a budget of EUR 10 million and applies for aid to a scheme offering at most EUR 1 million per film. It is disproportionate to exclude the film from the scheme on the grounds that the producer does not expect to spend at least EUR 8 million of the production budget in the territory offering the aid.

4 For example: a producer is making a film with a budget of EUR 10 million and applies for aid to a scheme offering at most EUR 1 million per film. The producer can only be expected to spend EUR 1.6 million of the production budget in the territory offering the aid. However, if the film budget had been EUR 2 million and received the maximum aid amount, the producer would face a territorial spending obligation corresponding to 80% of the production budget.

4.4. COMPETITION TO ATTRACT MAJOR FOREIGN PRODUCTIONS

39. When the 2001 Cinema Communication was adopted, few Member States tried to use film aid to attract major foreign film projects to be produced in their territory. Since then, several Member States have introduced schemes with the objective to attract high profile productions to Europe, in global competition with the locations and facilities elsewhere, such as in Australia, Canada, New Zealand, or the United States. Contributors to the public consultations preceding the present Communication agreed that these productions were necessary to maintain a high-quality audiovisual infrastructure, to contribute to the employment of high class studio facilities, equipment and staff, and to contribute to transfer of technology, know-how and expertise. The partial employment of facilities by foreign productions would also help to have the capacities to realise high quality and high profile European productions.

40. Regarding the possible effect on the European audiovisual sector, foreign production may have a lasting impact as it usually makes wide use of this local infrastructure and of local cast. Overall, this may thus have a positive effect on the national audiovisual sector. It should also be noted that many of the films which are considered to be major third country projects are in fact co-productions involving also European producers. Thereby, these subsidies would contribute also to the promotion of European audiovisual works and to sustaining facilities for national productions.

41. Therefore, the Commission considers that such aid may in principle be compatible with Article 107(3)(d) TFEU as aid to promote culture under the same conditions as aid for European production. However, as the amounts of aid for major international productions can be very high, the Commission will monitor the further development of this type of aid to ensure that competition takes place primarily on the basis of quality and price, rather than on the basis of State aid.

4.5. CROSS-BORDER PRODUCTIONS

42. Few European films are distributed outside their production territories. The likelihood that a European film is released in several Member States is higher in the case of co-productions involving producers from several countries. In view of the importance of co-operation of producers from different Member States for the production of European works which are seen across several Member States, the Commission considers that a higher aid intensity is justified for co-productions funded by more than one Member State and involving producers from more than one Member State.

4.6. FILM HERITAGE

43. Films should be collected, preserved and accessible for future generations for cultural and educational purposes.[1] The Education, Youth, Culture and Sports Council Conclusions on European film heritage of 18 November 2010[2] invited Member States to ensure that films that have been supported by State aid are deposited with a film heritage institution, together with all related material, where feasible, and the appropriate rights in relation to the preservation and cultural and non-commercial use of films and related material.

44. Some Member States have introduced the practice of paying the last instalment of the aid after the film heritage institution has certified the deposit of the aided film. This has proved to be an efficient instrument for enforcing the contractual deposit obligation.

45. Some Member States have also introduced provisions in their grant agreements to allow the use of publicly funded films for specified purposes in the execution of the public interest missions of the film heritage institutions after an agreed period of time and provided that this does not interfere with the normal use of the film.

46. Therefore, Member States should encourage and support producers to deposit a copy of the aided film in the film heritage institution designated by the funding body for preservation,[3] as well as for specified non-commercial use agreed with the right holder(s) in compliance with intellectual property rights and without prejudice to fair remuneration for the right holder(s) after an agreed period of time set in the grant agreement and such that this does not interfere with the normal use of the film.

NOTES

1 European Parliament and Council Recommendation on film heritage (OJ L323, 9.12.2005, p 57).

2 OJ C324, 1.12.2010, p 1.

3 Film Heritage Institutions are designated by Member States in order to collect, preserve and make available film heritage for cultural and educational purposes. In application of the 2005 European Parliament and Council Recommendation on film heritage, Member States have listed their Film Heritage Institutions. The current list is available online (https://ec.europa.eu/archives/information_society/avpolicy/docs/reg/cinema/institutions.pdf).

5. ASSESSING THE COMPATIBILITY OF THE AID

47. When it assesses aid for films and other audiovisual works, the Commission verifies on the basis of the above considerations.

— First, whether the aid scheme respects the 'general legality' principle, i.e. the Commission must verify that the scheme does not contain clauses that would be contrary to provisions of the TFEU in fields other than State aid.

— Secondly, whether the scheme fulfils the specific compatibility criteria for aid, set out below.

5.1. GENERAL LEGALITY

48. The Commission must first verify that the aid respects the 'general legality' principle and that the eligibility conditions and award criteria do not contain clauses contrary to the TFEU in fields other than State aid. This includes ensuring that the TFEU principles prohibiting discrimination on the grounds of nationality, free movement of goods, free movement of workers, freedom of establishment, freedom to provide services and freedom of movement of capital have been respected (Articles 18, 34, 36, 45, 49, 54, 56 and 63 TFEU). The Commission enforces these principles in conjunction with the application of competition rules when the provisions in breach of these principles are inseparable from the operation of the scheme.

49. In compliance with the above principles, aid schemes must not, for example, reserve the aid exclusively for nationals; require beneficiaries to have the status of national undertaking established under national commercial law (undertakings established in one Member State and operating in another by means of a permanent branch or agency must be eligible for aid; furthermore the agency requirement should only be enforceable upon payment of the aid); or oblige foreign companies providing filmmaking services to circumvent the terms and conditions of Directive 96/71/EC with respect to their posted workers.[1]

50. In view of the specific situation of the European film sector, film production support schemes may either:

— require that up to 160% of the aid amount awarded to the production of a given audiovisual work is spent in the territory granting the aid, or

— calculate the aid amount awarded to the production of a given audiovisual work as a percentage of the expenditure on film production activities in the granting Member State, typically in case of support schemes in the form of tax incentives.

In both cases, Member States may require a minimum level of production activity in their territory for projects to be eligible for any aid. This level cannot, however, exceed 50% of the overall production budget. In addition, the territorial linking shall in no case exceed 80% of the overall production budget.

NOTES

1 Directive 96/71/EC of the European Parliament and of the Council of 16 December 1996 concerning the posting of workers in the framework of the provision of services (OJ L18, 21.1.1997, p 1).

5.2. SPECIFIC ASSESSMENT CRITERIA UNDER ARTICLE 107(3)(D) TFEU

51. The objective for supporting the production of European audiovisual works and ensuring the existence of the infrastructure necessary for their production and exhibition is the shaping of European cultural identities and the enhancement of cultural diversity. Therefore, the purpose of the aid is the promotion of culture. Such aid may be compatible with the Treaty in accordance with Article 107(3)(d) TFEU. Undertakings in the film and TV programme production sector may also benefit from other aid types granted under Article 107(3)(a) and (c) TFEU (e.g. regional aid, aid for SME, Research and Development, training, or employment), within the maximum aid intensities in the case of cumulation of aid.

52. In the case of schemes designed to support the scriptwriting, development, production, distribution and promotion of audiovisual works covered by this Communication, the Commission will examine the following criteria with reference to the audiovisual work which will benefit from the aid to assess whether the scheme is compatible with the Treaty under Article 107(3)(d) TFEU.

1. The aid is directed to a cultural product. Each Member State ensures that the content of the aided production is cultural according to its own national criteria, through an effective verification process to avoid a manifest error: either through the selection of film proposals, for example by a panel or a person entrusted with the selection, or, in the absence of such a selection process, by establishing a list of cultural criteria against which each audiovisual work will be verified.

2. The aid intensity must in principle be limited to 50% of the production budget, with a view to stimulating normal commercial initiatives. The aid intensity for cross-border productions funded by more than one Member State and involving producers from more than one Member State may be up to 60% of the production budget. Difficult audiovisual works[1] and co-productions involving countries from the DAC List of the OECD[2] are excluded from these limits. Films whose sole original version is in an official language of a Member State with a limited territory, population or language area may be regarded as difficult audiovisual works in this context.
3. In principle, there is no limit for aid to scriptwriting or development. However, if the resulting script or project is ultimately made into a film, the costs of scriptwriting and development are subsequently included in the production budget and taken into account for calculating the maximum aid intensity for the audiovisual work as set out in sub-paragraph 2 above.
4. The costs of distributing and promoting audiovisual works which are eligible for production support may be supported with the same aid intensity as they were or could have been for their production.
5. Apart from scriptwriting, development, distribution or promotion, aid granted for specific production activities is not allowed. Consequently, the aid must not be reserved for individual parts of the production value chain. Any aid granted to the production of a specific audiovisual work should contribute to its overall budget. The producer should be free to choose the items of the budget that will be spent in other Member States. This is to ensure that the aid has a neutral incentive effect. The earmarking of aid to specific individual items of a film budget could turn such aid into a national preference to the sectors providing the specific aided items, which would be incompatible with the Treaty.
6. Member States should encourage and support producers to deposit a copy of the aided film in the film heritage institution designated by the funding body for preservation, as well as for specified non-commercial use agreed with the right holder(s) in compliance with intellectual property rights and without prejudice to fair remuneration for the right holder(s) after an agreed period of time set in the grant agreement and such that this does not interfere with the normal use of the film.

[7. Member States shall ensure the publication of the following information on a comprehensive State aid website, at national or regional level:

— the full text of the approved aid scheme or the individual aid granting decision and its implementing provisions, or a link to it,

— the identity of the granting authority/(ies),

— the identity of the individual beneficiaries, the form and amount of aid granted to each beneficiary, the date of granting, the type of undertaking (SME/large company), the region in which the beneficiary is located (at NUTS level II) and the principal economic sector in which the beneficiary has its activities (at NACE group level).[3]

Such a requirement can be waived with respect to individual aid awards below EUR 500,000. For schemes in the form of tax advantage, the information on individual aid amounts[3a] can be provided in the following ranges (in EUR million): [0.5–1]; [1–2]; [2–5]; [5–10]; [10–30]; [30 and more].

Such information must be published after the decision to grant the aid has been taken, must be kept for at least 10 years and must be available to the general public without restrictions.[3b] Member States will not be required to publish the abovementioned information before 1 July 2016.[3c]]

53. The modernisation of cinemas, including their digitisation, may be aided where the Member States can justify the necessity, proportionality and adequacy of such aid. On this basis, the Commission would assess whether the scheme is compatible with the Treaty under Article 107(3)(d) TFEU.

54. In determining whether the maximum aid intensity is respected, the total amount of public support measures of Member States for the aided activity or project shall be taken into account, regardless of whether that support is financed from local, regional, national or Union sources. However, funds awarded directly by EU programmes like MEDIA, without the involvement of Member States in the award decision, are not State resources. Therefore, their assistance does not count for the purposes of respecting the aid ceilings.

NOTES

Para 52: point 7 substituted, together with associated footnotes, by Commission Communication 2014/C198/02.

1 Such as short films, films by first-time and second-time directors, documentaries, or low budget or otherwise commercially difficult works. Under the subsidiarity principle, it is up to each Member State to establish a definition of difficult film according to national parameters.

2 The DAC list shows all countries and territories eligible to receive official development assistance. These consist of all low and middle-income countries based on gross national income (GNI) per capita as published by the World Bank, with the exception of G8 members, EU members, and countries with a firm date for entry into the EU. The list also includes all of the Least Developed Countries (LDCs) as defined by the United Nations (www.oecd.org/document/45/0,3746,en_2649_34447_2093101_1_1_1_1,00.html)

3 With the exception of business secrets and other confidential information in duly justified cases and subject to the Commission's agreement (Commission communication on professional secrecy in State aid decisions, C(2003) 4582 (OJ C297, 9.12.2003, p 6)).

3a The amount to be published is the maximum allowed tax benefit and not the amount deducted each year (e.g. in the context of tax credit, the maximum allowed tax credit shall be published rather than the actual amount which might depend on the taxable revenues and vary each year).

3b This information shall be published within 6 months from the date of granting (or, for aid in the form of tax advantage, within 1 year from the date the tax declaration is due). In case of unlawful aid, Member States will be required to ensure the publication of this information ex post, at least within 6 months from the date of the Commission decision. The information shall be available in a format which allows data to be searched, extracted, and easily published on the internet, for instance in CSV or XML format.

3c Publication of information on aid awards granted before 1 July 2016 and, for fiscal aid, publication for aid claimed or granted before 1 July 2016, will not be required.

6. APPROPRIATE MEASURES

55. The Commission proposes as appropriate measures for the purposes of Article 108(1) TFEU that Member States bring their existing schemes regarding film funding in line with this Communication within 2 years of its publication in the *Official Journal of the European Union*. Member States should confirm to the Commission within one month of publication of this Communication in the Official Journal that they agree to the appropriate measures proposed. In the absence of any reply, the Commission will take it that the Member State concerned does not agree.

7. APPLICATION

56. This Communication will be applied from the first day following its publication in the *Official Journal of the European Union*.

57. The Commission will apply this Communication to all notified aid measures in respect of which it is called upon to take a decision after the Communication is published in the Official Journal, even where the aid measures were notified prior to that date.

58. In accordance with the Commission notice on the determination of the applicable rules for the assessment of unlawful State aid,[1] in the case of non-notified aid the Commission will apply:

(a) this Communication, if the aid was granted after its publication in the *Official Journal of the European Union*;
(b) the 2001 Cinema Communication in all other cases.

NOTES

[1] OJ C119, 22.5.2002, p 22.

2. BROADCASTING

COMMUNICATION FROM THE COMMISSION

(2009/C257/01)

on the application of state aid rules to public service broadcasting

(Text with EEA relevance)

[5.338]

NOTES

Date of publication in OJ: OJ C257, 27.10.2009, p 1.

Note: with effect from 1 December 2009, the EC Treaty was replaced by the Treaty on the Functioning of the European Union. References in this document to provisions of the EC Treaty should be construed accordingly.

1. INTRODUCTION AND SCOPE OF THE COMMUNICATION

[5.339]

1. Over the last three decades, broadcasting has undergone important changes. The abolition of monopolies, the emergence of new players and rapid technological developments have fundamentally altered the competitive environment. Television broadcasting was traditionally a reserved activity. Since its inception, it has mostly been provided by public undertakings under a monopoly regime, mainly as a consequence of the limited availability of broadcasting frequencies and the high barriers to entry.

2. In the 1970s, however, economic and technological developments made it increasingly possible for Member States to allow other operators to broadcast. Member States have therefore decided to introduce competition in the market. This has led to a wider choice for consumers, as many additional channels and new services became available; it has also favoured the emergence and growth of strong European operators, the development of new technologies, and a larger degree of pluralism in the sector, which means more than a simple availability of additional channels and services. Whilst opening the market to competition, Member States considered that public service broadcasting ought to be maintained, as a way to ensure the coverage of a number of areas and the satisfaction of needs and public policy objectives that would otherwise not necessarily be fulfilled to the optimal extent. This was confirmed in the interpretative protocol on the system of public broadcasting in the Member States, annexed to the EC Treaty (hereinafter referred to as the Amsterdam Protocol).

3. At the same time, the increased competition, together with the presence of State-funded operators, has also led to growing concerns for a level playing field, which have been brought to the Commission's attention by private operators. The complaints allege infringements of Articles 86 and 87 of the EC Treaty in relation to public funding of public service broadcasters.

4. The 2001 Communication from the Commission on the application of State aid rules to public service broadcasting[1] has first set out the framework governing State funding of public service broadcasting. The 2001 Communication has served as a good basis for the Commission to develop significant decision-making practice in the field. Since 2001, more than 20 decisions have been adopted concerning the financing of public service broadcasters.

5. In the meantime, technological changes have fundamentally altered the broadcasting and audiovisual markets. There has been a multiplication of distribution platforms and technologies, such as digital television, IPTV, mobile TV and video on demand. This has led to an increase in competition with new players, such as network operators and Internet companies, entering the market. Technological developments have also allowed the emergence of new media services such as online information services and non-linear or on-demand services. The provision of audiovisual services is converging, with consumers being increasingly able to obtain multiple services on a single platform or device or to obtain any given service on multiple platforms or devices. The increasing variety of options for consumers to access media content has led to the multiplication of audiovisual services offered and the fragmentation of audiences. New technologies have enabled improved consumer participation. The traditional passive consumption model has been gradually turning into active participation and control over content by consumers. In order to keep up with the new challenges, both public and private broadcasters have been diversifying their activities, moving to new distribution platforms and expanding the range of their services. Most recently, this diversification of the publicly funded activities of public service broadcasters (such as online content, special interest channels) prompted a number of complaints by other market players also including publishers.

6. Since 2001, important legal developments have also taken place, which have an impact on the broadcasting field. In the 2003 Altmark judgment[2], the European Court of Justice defined the conditions under which public service compensation does not constitute State aid. In 2005, the Commission adopted a new decision[3] and framework[4] on State aid in the form of public service compensation. In 2007, the Commission adopted a Communication accompanying the Communication on 'A single market for 21st century Europe' — Services of general interest, including social services of general interest: a new European Commitment[5]. Furthermore, in December 2007, the Audiovisual Media Services Directive[6] entered into force, extending the scope of the EU audiovisual regulation to emerging media services.

7. These changes in the market and in the legal environment have called for an update to the 2001 Communication on State aid for public broadcasting. The Commission's 2005 State Aid Action Plan[7] announced that the Commission would 'revisit its Communication on the application of State aid rules to public service broadcasting. Notably with the development of new digital technologies and of Internet-based services, new issues have arisen regarding the scope of public service activities'.

8. In the course of 2008 and 2009, the Commission held several public consultations on the review of the 2001 Broadcasting Communication. The present Communication consolidates the Commission's case practice in the field of State aid in a future-orientated manner based on the comments received in the public consultations. It clarifies the principles followed by the Commission in the application of Articles 87 and 86(2) of the EC Treaty to the public funding of audiovisual services in the broadcasting sector[8], taking into account recent market and legal developments. The present Communication is without prejudice to the application of the internal market rules and fundamental freedoms in the field of broadcasting.

NOTES

1 OJ C320, 15.11.2001, p 5.

2 Judgment in Case C-280/2000 *Altmark Trans GmbH* and *Regierungspräsidium Magdeburg v Nahverkehrsgesellschaft Altmark GmbH (Altmark)* (2003) ECR I-7747.

3 Commission Decision of 28 November 2005 on the application of Article 86(2) of the EC Treaty to State aid in the form of public service compensation granted to certain undertakings entrusted with the operation of services of general economic interest (OJ L312, 29.11.2005, p 67).

4 Community framework for State aid in the form of public service compensation (OJ C297, 29.11.2005, p 4).

5 COM(2007) 725 final.

6 Directive 2007/65/EC of the European Parliament and of the Council of 11 December 2007 amending Council Directive 89/552/EEC on the coordination of certain provisions laid down by law, regulation or administrative action in Member States concerning the pursuit of television broadcasting activities (OJ L332, 18.12.2007, p 27.

7 COM(2005) 107 final.

8 For the purpose of the present communication, the notion 'audiovisual service(s)' refers to the linear and/or non-linear distribution of audio and/or audiovisual content and of other neighbouring services such as online text-based information services. This notion of 'audiovisual service(s)' must be distinguished from the narrower concept of 'audiovisual media service(s)', as defined in Article 1(a) of the Audiovisual Media Services Directive.

2. THE ROLE OF PUBLIC SERVICE BROADCASTING

[5.340]

9. Public service broadcasting, although having a clear economic relevance, is not comparable to a public service in any other economic sector. There is no other service that at the same time has access to such a wide sector of the population, provides it with so much information and content, and by doing so conveys and influences both individual and public opinion.

10. Furthermore, broadcasting is generally perceived as a very reliable source of information and represents, for a not inconsiderable proportion of the population, the main source of information. It thus enriches public debate and ultimately can ensure that all citizens participate to a fair degree in public life. In this connection, safeguards for the independence of broadcasting are of key importance, in line with the general principle of freedom of expression as embodied in Article 11 of the Charter of Fundamental Rights of the European Union[9] and Article 10 of the European Convention of Human Rights, a general principle of law the respect of which is ensured by the European Courts[10].

11. The role of the public service[11] in general is recognised by the Treaty, in particular Articles 16 and 86(2). The interpretation of these provisions in the light of the particular nature of the broadcasting sector is outlined in the Amsterdam Protocol, which, after considering 'that the system of public broadcasting in the Member States is directly related to the democratic, social and cultural needs of each society and to the need to preserve media pluralism', states that 'the provisions of the Treaty establishing the European Community shall be without prejudice to the competence of Member States to provide for the funding of public service broadcasting insofar as such funding is granted to broadcasting organisations for the fulfilment of the public service remit as conferred, defined and organised by each Member State, and insofar as such funding does not affect trading conditions and competition in the Community to an extent which would be contrary to the common interest, while the realisation of the remit of that public service shall be taken into account'.

12. The importance of public service broadcasting for social, democratic and cultural life in the Union was reaffirmed in the Council Resolution concerning public service broadcasting. As underlined by the Resolution 'broad public access, without discrimination and on the basis of equal opportunities, to various channels and services is a necessary precondition for fulfilling the special obligation of public service broadcasting'. Moreover, public service broadcasting needs to 'benefit from technological progress', bring 'the public the benefits of the new audiovisual and information services and the new technologies' and to undertake 'the development and diversification of activities in the digital age'. Finally, 'public service broadcasting must be able to continue to provide a wide range of programming in accordance with its remit as defined by the Member States in order to address society as a whole; in this context it is legitimate for public service broadcasting to seek to reach wide audiences'[12].

13. The role of public service broadcasting in promoting cultural diversity was also recognised by the 2005 Unesco Convention on the Protection and Promotion of the Diversity of Cultural Expressions, which was approved by the Council on behalf of the Community and thus forms part of EC law[13]. The Convention states that each party may adopt 'measures aimed at protecting and promoting the diversity of cultural expressions within its territory'. Such measures may include, among others, 'measures aimed at enhancing diversity of the media, including through public service broadcasting'[14].

14. These values of public broadcasting are equally important in the rapidly changing new media environment. This has also been highlighted in the recommendations of the Council of Europe concerning media pluralism and diversity of media content[15], and the remit of public service media in the information society[16]. The latter recommendation calls upon the members of the Council of Europe to 'guarantee public service media (. . .) in a transparent and accountable manner' and to 'enable public service media to respond fully and effectively to the challenges of the information society, respecting the public/private dual structure of the European electronic media landscape and paying attention to market and competition questions'

15. In its Resolution on concentration and pluralism in the media in the European Union, the European Parliament has recommended that 'regulations governing State aid are devised and implemented in a way which allow the public service and community media to fulfil their function in a dynamic environment, while ensuring that public service media carry out the function entrusted to them by Member States in a transparent and accountable manner, avoiding the abuse of public funding for reasons of political or economic expediency'[17].

16. At the same time and notwithstanding the above, it must be noted that commercial broadcasters, of whom a number are subject to public service requirements, also play a significant role in achieving the objectives of the Amsterdam Protocol to the extent that they contribute to pluralism, enrich cultural and political debate and widen the choice of programmes. Moreover, newspaper publishers and other print media are also important guarantors of an objectively informed public and of democracy. Given that these operators are now competing with broadcasters on the Internet, all these commercial media providers are concerned by the potential negative effects that State aid to public service broadcasters could have on the development of new business models. As recalled by the Audiovisual Media Services Directive[18], 'the coexistence of private and public audiovisual media service providers is a feature which distinguishes the European audiovisual media market.' Indeed, it is in the common interest to maintain a plurality of balanced public and private media offer also in the current dynamic media environment.

NOTES

9 OJ C364, 18.12.2000, p 1.

10 Judgment in Case C-260/89 ERT, (1991) ECR I-2925.

11 For the purpose of the present communication, and in accordance with Article 16 of the EC Treaty and the declaration (No 13) annexed to the final act of Amsterdam, the term 'public service' as of the Protocol on the system of public broadcasting in the Member States has to be intended as referring to the term 'service of general economic interest' used in Article 86(2).

12 Resolution of the Council and of the Representatives of the Governments of the Member States, meeting within the Council of 25 January 1999 (OJ C30, 5.2.1999, p 1).

13 Unesco Convention on the Protection and Promotion of the Diversity of Cultural Expressions, approved by Council Decision 2006/515/EC of 18 May 2006. In accordance with Annex 2 to of the Council Decision, 'the Community is bound by the Convention and will ensure its implementation.'

14 Unesco Convention on the Protection and Promotion of the Diversity of Cultural Expressions, Article 6(1) and (2)(h).

15 Recommendation CM/Rec(2007)2 of the Committee of the Ministers to Member States on media pluralism and diversity of media content, adopted on 31 January 2007 at the 985th meeting of the Ministers' Deputies.

16 Recommendation CM/Rec(2007)3 of the Committee of Ministers to Member States on the remit of public service media in the information society, adopted on 31 January 2007 at the 985th meeting of the Ministers' Deputies.

17 European Parliament Resolution of 25 September 2008 on concentration and pluralism in the media in the European Union, 2007/2253(INI).

18 Cf. footnote 6 above.

3. THE LEGAL CONTEXT

[5.341]

17. The application of State aid rules to public service broadcasting has to take into account a wide number of different elements. The State aid assessment is based on Articles 87 and 88 on State aid and Article 86(2) on the application of the rules of the Treaty and the competition rules, in particular, to services of general economic interest. The Treaty of Maastricht introduced Article 151 concerning culture and Article 87(3)(d) on aid to promote culture. The Treaty of Amsterdam introduced a specific provision (Article 16) on services of general economic interest and the Amsterdam Protocol on the system of public broadcasting in the Member States.

18. The regulatory framework concerning 'audiovisual media services' is coordinated at European level by the Audiovisual Media Services Directive. The financial transparency requirements concerning public undertakings are regulated by the Transparency Directive[19].

19. These rules are interpreted by the Court of Justice and the Court of First Instance. The Commission has also adopted several communications on the application of the State aid rules. In particular, in 2005, the Commission adopted the Services of General Economic Interest Framework[20] and Decision[21] clarifying the requirements of Article 86(2) of the EC Treaty. The latter is also applicable in the field of broadcasting, to the extent that the conditions provided in Article 2(1)(a) of the Decision are met[22].

NOTES

19 Commission Directive 2006/111/EC of 16 November 2006.

20 Cf. footnote 4 above.

21 Cf. footnote 3 above.

22 According to Article 2(1)(a) of the Decision, it applies to State aid in the form of 'public service compensation granted to undertakings with an average annual turnover before tax, all activities included, of less than EUR 100 million during the two financial years preceding that in which the service of general economic interest was assigned, which receive annual compensation for the service in question of less than EUR 30 million'.

4. APPLICABILITY OF ARTICLE 87(1)

4.1. THE STATE AID CHARACTER OF STATE FINANCING OF PUBLIC SERVICE BROADCASTERS

[5.342]

20. In line with Article 87(1), the concept of State aid includes the following conditions: (a) there must be an intervention by the State or by means of State resources; (b) the intervention must be liable to affect trade between Member States; (c) it must confer an advantage of the beneficiary; (d) it must distort or threaten to distort competition[23]. The existence of State aid has to be assessed on an objective basis, taking into account the jurisprudence of the Community Courts.

21. The effect of State intervention, not its purpose, is the decisive element in any assessment of its State aid content under Article 87(1). Public service broadcasters are normally financed out of the State budget or through a levy on broadcasting equipment holders. In certain specific circumstances, the State makes capital injections or debt cancellations in favour of public service broadcasters. These financial measures are normally attributable to the public authorities and involve the transfer of State resources[24].

22. State financing of public service broadcasters can also be generally considered to affect trade between Member States. As the Court of Justice has observed, 'when aid granted by the State or through State resources strengthens the position of an undertaking compared with other undertakings competing in intra-Community trade the latter must be regarded as affected by that aid'[25]. This is clearly the position as regards the acquisition and sale of programme rights, which often takes place at an international level. Advertising, too, in the case of public service broadcasters who are allowed to sell advertising space, has a cross-border effect, especially for homogeneous linguistic areas across national boundaries. Moreover, the ownership structure of commercial broadcasters may extend to more than one Member State. Furthermore, services provided on the internet normally have a global reach.

23. Regarding the existence of an advantage, the Court of justice clarified in the Altmark case[26] that public service compensation does not constitute State aid provided that four cumulative conditions are met. First, the recipient undertaking must actually have public service obligations to discharge, and the obligations must be clearly defined. Second, the parameters on the basis of which the compensation is calculated must be established in advance in an objective and transparent manner. Third, the compensation cannot exceed what is necessary to cover all or part of the costs incurred in the discharge of the public service obligations, taking into account the relevant receipts and a reasonable profit. Finally, where the undertaking which is to discharge public service obligations, in a specific case, is not chosen pursuant to a public procurement procedure which would allow for the selection of the bidder capable of providing those services at the least cost to the community, the level of compensation must be determined on the basis of an analysis of the costs which a typical undertaking, well run and adequately equipped so as to be able to meet the necessary public service requirements, would have incurred in discharging those obligations.

24. To the extent that the funding fails to satisfy the above conditions, it would be considered as selectively favouring only certain broadcasters and thereby distorting or threatening to distort competition.

4.2. NATURE OF THE AID: EXISTING AID AS OPPOSED TO NEW AID

25. The funding schemes currently in place in most of the Member States were introduced a long time ago. As a first step, therefore, the Commission must determine whether these schemes may be regarded as 'existing aid' within the meaning of Article 88(1). In line with this provision, 'the Commission shall, in cooperation with Member States, keep under constant review all systems of aid existing in those States. It shall propose to the latter any appropriate measures required by the progressive development or by the functioning of the common market'.

26. Pursuant to Article 1(b)(i) of the Procedural Regulation[27], existing aid includes ' . . . all aid which existed prior to the entry into force of the Treaty in the respective Member States, that is to say, aid schemes and individual aid which were put into effect before, and are still applicable after, the entry into force of the Treaty'.

27. In the cases of Austria, Finland and Sweden, State aid measures introduced before the entry into force of the EEA Agreement on 1 January 1994 in these countries is regarded as existing aid. Regarding the 10 Member States which acceded in 2004 (the Czech Republic, Estonia, Cyprus, Latvia, Lithuania, Hungary, Malta, Poland, Slovenia and Slovakia) and Bulgaria and Romania which acceded in 2007, measures put into effect before 10 December 1994, those included in the list annexed to the Treaty of Accession and those approved under the so-called 'interim procedure' are considered as existing aid.

28. Pursuant to Article 1(b)(v) of the Procedural Regulation, existing aid also includes 'aid which is deemed to be an existing aid because it can be established that at the time it was put into effect it did not constitute an aid, and subsequently became an aid due to the evolution of the common market and without having been altered by the Member State'.

29. In accordance with the case law of the Court[28], the Commission must verify whether or not the legal framework under which the aid is granted has changed since its introduction. The Commission believes that a case by case approach is the most appropriate[29], taking into account all the elements related to the broadcasting system of a given Member State.

30. According to the case law in Gibraltar[30], not every alteration to existing aid should be regarded as changing the existing aid into new aid. According to the Court of First Instance, 'it is only where the alteration affects the actual substance of the original scheme that the latter is transformed into a new aid scheme. There can be no question of such a substantive alteration where the new element is clearly severable from the initial scheme.'

31. In light of the above considerations, in its decision-making practice the Commission has generally examined: (a) whether the original financing regime for public service broadcasters is existing aid in line with the rules indicated in paragraphs 26 and 27 above; (b) whether subsequent modifications affect the actual substance of the original measure (ie, the nature of the advantage or the source of financing, the purpose of the aid, the beneficiaries or the scope of activities of the beneficiaries) or whether these modifications are rather of a purely formal or administrative nature;

and (c) in case subsequent modifications are substantial, whether they are severable from the original measure, in which case they can be assessed separately, or whether they are not severable from the original measure so that the original measure is as a whole transformed into a new aid.

NOTES

23 Judgment in joined Cases T-309/04, T-317/04, T-329/04 and T-336/04 'TV2' at 156.

24 Regarding the qualification of licence fee funding as State resources, see judgment in joined Cases T-09/04, T-317/04, T-329/04 and T-336/04 'TV2' at 158-159.

25 Cases C-730/79, Philip Morris Holland v Commission (1980) ECR 2671, paragraph 11; C-303/88, Italy v Commission (1991) ECR I- 1433, paragraph 27; C-156/98, Germany v Commission (2000) ECR I-6857, paragraph 33.

26 Case C-280/2000, cf. footnote 2 above.

27 Council Regulation (EC) No 659/1999 of 22 March 1999 laying down detailed rules for the application of Article 93 of the EC Treaty (OJ L83, 27.3.1999, p 1).

28 Case C-44/93, *Namur-Les Assurances du Crédit SA v Office National du Ducroire and the Belgian State* (1994) ECR I-3829.

29 See, for example, the decisions of the Commission in the following cases: E 8/06, State funding for Flemish public service broadcaster VRT (OJ C143, 10.6.2008, p 7); E 4/05, State aid financing of RTE and TNAG (TG4) (OJ C121, 17.5.2008, p 5); E 9/05, Licence fee payments to RAI (OJ C235, 23.9.2005, p 3); E 10/2005, Licence fee payments to France 2 and 3 (OJ C240, 30.9.2005, p 20); E 8/05, Spanish national public service broadcaster RTVE (OJ C239, 4.10.2006, p 17); C 2/04, Ad hoc financing of Dutch public broadcasters (OJ L49, 22.2.2008, p 1); C 60/99 Commission Decision of 10 December 2003 on State aid implemented by France for France 2 and France 3 (OJ L361, 8.12.2004, p 21); C 62/99 Commission Decision of 15 October 2003 on the measures implemented by Italy for RAI SpA (OJ L119, 23.4.2004, p 1); NN 88/98, Financing of a 24-hour advertising-free news channel with licence fee by the BBC (OJ C78, 18.3.2000, p 6) and NN 70/98, State aid to public broadcasting channels Kinderkanal and Phoenix (OJ C238, 21.8.1999, p 3).

30 Joined Cases T-195/01 and T-207/01, (2002) ECR II-2309.

5. ASSESSMENT OF THE COMPATIBILITY OF STATE AID UNDER ARTICLE 87(3)

[5.343]

32. Although compensation for public service broadcasting is typically assessed under Article 86(2) of the Treaty, the derogations listed in Article 87(3) may in principle also apply in the field of broadcasting, provided that the relevant conditions are met.

33. In accordance with Article 151(4) of the Treaty, the Community is to take cultural aspects into account in its action under other provisions of the Treaty, in particular in order to respect and to promote the diversity of its cultures. Article 87(3)(d) of the Treaty allows the Commission to regard aid to promote culture as compatible with the common market where such aid does not affect trading conditions and competition in the Community to an extent that is contrary to the common interest.

34. It is the Commission's task to decide on the actual application of that provision in the same way as for the other exemption clauses in Article 87(3). It should be recalled that the provisions granting exemption from the prohibition of State aid have to be applied strictly. Accordingly, the Commission considers that the cultural derogation may be applied in those cases where the cultural product is clearly identified or identifiable[31]. Moreover, the Commission takes the view that the notion of culture must be applied to the content and nature of the product in question, and not to the medium or its distribution per se[32]. Furthermore, the educational and democratic needs of a Member State have to be regarded as distinct from the promotion of culture under Article 87(3)(d)[33].

35. State aid to public service broadcasters usually does not differentiate between cultural, democratic and educational needs of society. Unless a funding measure is specifically aimed at promoting cultural objectives, Article 87(3)(d) would generally not be relevant. State aid to public service broadcasters is generally provided in the form of compensation for the fulfilment of the public service mandate and is assessed under Article 86(2), on the basis of the criteria set out in the present Communication.

NOTES

31 For example, Commission Decisions NN 88/98 BBC 24-hours (OJ C78, 18.3.2000), NN 70/98 'Kinderkanal and Phoenix' (OJ C238, 21.8.1999).

32 For example, Commission Decision N 458/2004 State aid to Espacio Editorial Andaluza Holding sl., OJ C131, 29.5.2005.

33 NN 70/98, State aid to public broadcasting channels Kinderkanal and Phoenix (OJ C238, 21.8.1999, p 3).

6. ASSESSMENT OF THE COMPATIBILITY OF STATE AID UNDER ARTICLE 86(2)

[5.344]

36. In accordance with Article 86(2), 'undertakings entrusted with the operation of services of general economic interest or having the character of revenue-producing monopoly shall be subject to the rules contained in this Treaty, in particular to the rules on competition, in so far as the application of such rules does not obstruct the performance, in law or in fact, of the particular tasks assigned to them. The development of trade must not be affected to such an extent as would be contrary to the interests of the Community.'

37. The Court has consistently held that Article 86 provides for a derogation and must therefore be interpreted restrictively. The Court has clarified that in order for a measure to benefit from such a derogation, it is necessary that all the following conditions be fulfilled:

(i) the service in question must be a service of general economic interest and clearly defined as such by the Member State (definition)[34];

(ii) the undertaking in question must be explicitly entrusted by the Member State with the provision of that service (entrustment)[35];

(iii) the application of the competition rules of the Treaty (in this case, the ban on State aid) must obstruct the performance of the particular tasks assigned to the undertaking and the exemption from such rules must not affect the development of trade to an extent that would be contrary to the interests of the Community (proportionality test)[36].

38. In the specific case of public broadcasting the above approach has to be adapted in the light of the interpretative provisions of the Amsterdam Protocol, which refers to the 'public service remit as conferred, defined and organised by each Member State' (definition and entrustment) and provides for a derogation from the Treaty rules in the case of the funding of public service broadcasting 'insofar as such funding is granted to broadcasting organisations for the fulfilment of the public service remit (. . .) and (. . .) does not affect trading conditions and competition in the Community to an extent which would be contrary to the common interest, while the realisation of the remit of that public service shall be taken into account' (proportionality).

39. It is for the Commission, as guardian of the Treaty, to assess, on the basis of evidence provided by the Member States, whether these criteria are satisfied. As regards the definition of the public service remit, the role of the Commission is to check for manifest errors (see Section 6.1). The Commission further verifies whether there is an explicit entrustment and effective supervision of the fulfilment of the public service obligations (see Section 6.2).

40. In carrying out the proportionality test, the Commission considers whether or not any distortion of competition arising from the public service compensation can be justified in terms of the need to perform the public service and to provide for its funding. The Commission assesses, in particular on the basis of the evidence that Member States are bound to provide whether there are sufficient guarantees to avoid disproportionate effects of public funding, overcompensation and cross-subsidisation, and to ensure that public service broadcasters respect market conditions in their commercial activities (see Section 6.3 and following).

41. The analysis of the compliance with the State aid requirements must be based on the specific characteristics of each national system. The Commission is aware of the differences in the national broadcasting systems and in the other characteristics of the Member States' media markets. Therefore, the assessment of the compatibility of State aid to public service broadcasters under Article 86(2) is made on a case-by-case basis, according to Commission practice[37], in line with the basic principles set out in the following sections.

42. The Commission will also take into account the difficulty some smaller Member States may have to collect the necessary funds, if costs per inhabitant of the public service are, *ceteris paribus*, higher[38] while equally considering potential concerns of other media in these Member States.

6.1. DEFINITION OF PUBLIC SERVICE REMIT

43. In order to meet the condition mentioned in point 37(i) for application of Article 86(2), it is necessary to establish an official definition of the public service mandate. Only then can the Commission assess with sufficient legal certainty whether the derogation under Article 86(2) is applicable.

44. Definition of the public service mandate falls within the competence of the Member States, which can decide at national, regional or local level, in accordance with their national legal order. Generally speaking, in exercising that competence, account must be taken of the Community concept of 'services of general economic interest'.

45. The definition of the public service mandate by the Member States should be as precise as possible. It should leave no doubt as to whether a certain activity performed by the entrusted operator is intended by the Member State to be included in the public service remit or not. Without a clear and precise definition of the obligations imposed upon the public service broadcaster, the Commission would not be able to carry out its tasks under Article 86(2) and, therefore, could not grant any exemption under that provision.

46. Clear identification of the activities covered by the public service remit is also important for non-public service operators, so that they can plan their activities. Moreover, the terms of the public service remit should be sufficiently precise, so that Member States' authorities can effectively monitor compliance, as described in the following chapter.

47. At the same time, given the specific nature of the broadcasting sector, and the need to safeguard the editorial independence of the public service broadcasters, a qualitative definition entrusting a given broadcaster with the obligation to provide a wide range of programming and a balanced and varied broadcasting offer is generally considered, in view of the interpretative provisions of the Amsterdam Protocol, legitimate under Article 86(2)[39]. Such a definition is generally considered consistent with the objective of fulfilling the democratic, social and cultural needs of a particular society and guaranteeing pluralism, including cultural and linguistic diversity. As expressed by the Court of First Instance, the legitimacy of such a widely defined public service remit rests upon the qualitative requirements for the services offered by a public service broadcaster[40]. The definition of the public service remit may also reflect the development and diversification of activities in the digital age and include audiovisual services on all distribution platforms.

48. As regards the definition of the public service in the broadcasting sector, the role of the Commission is limited to checking for manifest error. It is not for the Commission to decide which programmes are to be provided and financed as a service of general economic interest, nor to question the nature or the quality of a certain product. The definition of the public service remit would, however, be in manifest error if it included activities that could not reasonably be considered to meet — in the wording of the Amsterdam Protocol — the 'democratic, social and cultural needs of each society'. That would normally be the position in the case of advertising, e-commerce, teleshopping, the use of premium rate numbers in prize games[41], sponsoring or merchandising, for example. Moreover, a manifest error could occur where State aid is used to finance activities which do not bring added value in terms of serving the social, democratic and cultural needs of society.

49. In this context, it must be recalled that the public service remit describes the services offered to the public in the general interest. The question of the definition of the public service remit must not be confused with the question of the financing mechanism chosen to provide these services. Therefore, whilst public service broadcasters may perform commercial activities such as the sale of advertising space in order to obtain revenue, such activities cannot be viewed as part of the public service remit[42].

6.2. ENTRUSTMENT AND SUPERVISION

50. In order to benefit from the exemption under Article 86(2), the public service remit should be entrusted to one or more undertakings by means of an official act (for example, by legislation, contract or binding terms of reference).

51. The entrustment act(s) shall specify the precise nature of the public service obligations in line with Section 6.1 above, and shall set out the conditions for providing the compensation, as well as the arrangements for avoiding and repaying any overcompensation.

52. Whenever the scope of the public service remit is extended to cover new services, the definition and entrustment Act(s) should be modified accordingly, within the limits of Article 86(2). In the interest of allowing public service broadcasters to react swiftly to new technological developments, Member States may also foresee that the entrustment with a new service is provided following the assessment outlined in Part 6.7 below, before the original entrustment Act is formally consolidated.

53. It is not sufficient, however, that the public service broadcaster be formally entrusted with the provision of a well-defined public service. It is also necessary that the public service be actually supplied as provided for in the formal agreement between the State and the entrusted undertaking. It is therefore desirable that an appropriate authority or appointed body monitors its application in a transparent and effective manner. The need for such an appropriate authority or body in charge of supervision is apparent in the case of quality standards imposed on the entrusted operator. In accordance with the Commission communication on the principles and guidelines for the Community's audiovisual policy in the digital era[43], it is not for the Commission to judge on the fulfilment of quality standards: it must be able to rely on appropriate supervision by the Member States of compliance by the broadcaster with its public service remit including the qualitative standards set out in that remit[44].

54. In line with the Amsterdam Protocol, it is within the competence of the Member State to choose the mechanism to ensure effective supervision of the fulfilment of the public service obligations, therefore enabling the Commission to carry out its tasks under Article 86(2). Such supervision would only seem effective if carried out by a body effectively independent from the management of the public service broadcaster, which has the powers and the necessary capacity and resources to carry out supervision regularly, and which leads to the imposition of appropriate remedies insofar it is necessary to ensure respect of the public service obligations.

55. In the absence of sufficient and reliable indications that the public service is actually supplied as mandated, the Commission would not be able to carry out its tasks under Article 86(2) and, therefore, could not grant any exemption under that provision.

6.3. CHOICE OF FUNDING OF PUBLIC SERVICE BROADCASTING

56. Public service duties may be either quantitative or qualitative or both. Whatever their form, they could justify compensation, as long as they entail supplementary costs that the broadcaster would normally not have incurred.

57. Funding schemes can be divided into two broad categories 'single-funding' and 'dual-funding'. The 'single-funding' category comprises those systems in which public service broadcasting is financed only through public funds, in whatever form. 'Dual-funding' systems comprise a wide range of schemes, where public service broadcasting is financed by different combinations of State funds and revenues from commercial or public service activities, such as the sale of advertising space or programmes and the offering of services against payment.

58. As stated in the Amsterdam Protocol: 'The provisions of the Treaty establishing the European Community shall be without prejudice to the competence of Member States to provide for the funding of public service broadcasting (. . .)'. The Commission has therefore no objection in principle to the choice of a dual financing scheme rather than a single funding scheme.

59. While Member States are free to choose the means of financing public service broadcasting, the Commission has to verify, under Article 86(2), that the State funding does not affect competition in the common market in a disproportionate manner, as referred to in paragraph 38 above.

6.4. TRANSPARENCY REQUIREMENTS FOR THE STATE AID ASSESSMENT

60. The State aid assessment by the Commission requires a clear and precise definition of the public service remit and a clear and appropriate separation between public service activities and non-public service activities including a clear separation of accounts.

61. Separation of accounts between public service activities and non-public service activities is normally already required at national level as it is essential to ensure transparency and accountability when using public funds. A separation of accounts provides a tool for examining alleged cross-subsidisation and for defending justified compensation payments for general economic interest tasks. Only on the basis of proper cost and revenue allocation can it be determined whether the public financing is actually limited to the net costs of the public service remit and thus acceptable under Article 86(2) and the Amsterdam Protocol.

62. Member States are required by Directive 2006/111/EC to take transparency measures in the case of any undertaking granted special or exclusive rights or entrusted with the operation of a service of general economic interest and receiving public service compensation in any form whatsoever in relation to such service and which carries out other activities, that is to say, non-public service activities. These transparency requirements are: (a) the

internal accounts corresponding to different activities, ie, public service and non-public service activities must be separate; (b) all costs and revenues must be correctly assigned or allocated on the basis of consistently applied and objectively justifiable cost accounting principles; and (c) the cost-accounting principles according to which separate accounts are maintained must be clearly established[45].

63. These general transparency requirements apply also to broadcasters, insofar as they are entrusted with the operation of a service of general economic interest, receive public compensation in relation to such service, and also carry out other, non-public-service activities.

64. In the broadcasting sector, separation of accounts poses no particular problem on the revenue side. For this reason, the Commission considers that, on the revenue side, broadcasting operators should give detailed account of the sources and amount of all income accruing from the performance of public and non-public service activities.

65. On the cost side, all the expenses incurred in the operation of the public service may be taken into consideration. Where the undertaking carries out activities falling outside the scope of the public service, only the costs associated with the public service may be taken into consideration. The Commission recognises that, in the public broadcasting sector, separation of accounts may be more difficult on the cost side. This is because, in particular in the field of traditional broadcasting, Member States may consider the whole programming of a broadcaster covered by the public service remit, while at the same time allowing for its commercial exploitation. In other words, public service and non-public service activities may share the same inputs to a large extent and the costs may not always be severable in a proportionate manner.

66. Costs specific to non-public service activities (eg, the marketing cost of advertising) should always be clearly identified and separately accounted. In addition, input costs which are intended to serve the development of activities in the field of public and non-public services simultaneously should be allocated proportionately to public service and non-public service activities respectively, whenever it is possible in a meaningful way.

67. In other cases, whenever the same resources are used to perform public service and non-public service tasks, the common input costs should be allocated on the basis of the difference in the firm's total costs with and without non-public service activities[46]. In such cases, costs that are entirely attributable to public service activities, while benefiting also non-public service activities, need not be apportioned between the two and can be entirely allocated to the public service activity. This difference to the approach generally followed in other utilities sectors is explained by the specificities of the public broadcasting sector. In the field of public broadcasting, the net benefits of commercial activities related to the public service activities have to be taken into account for the purpose of calculating the net public service costs and therefore to reduce the public service compensation level. This reduces the risk of cross-subsidisation by means of accounting common costs to public service activities.

68. The main example for the situation described in the preceding paragraph would be the cost of producing programmes in the framework of the public service mission of the broadcaster. These programmes serve both to fulfil the public service remit and to generate audience for selling advertising space. However, it is virtually impossible to quantify with a sufficient degree of precision how much of the program viewing fulfils the public service remit and how much generates advertising revenue. For this reason, the distribution of the cost of programming between the two activities risks being arbitrary and not meaningful.

69. The Commission considers that financial transparency can be further enhanced by an adequate separation between public service and non-public service activities at the level of the organisation of the public service broadcaster. Functional or structural separation normally makes it easier to avoid cross-subsidisation of commercial activities from the outset and to ensure transfer pricing and the respect of the arm's length principle. Therefore, the Commission invites Member States to consider functional or structural separation of significant and severable commercial activities, as a form of best practice.

6.5. NET COST PRINCIPLE AND OVERCOMPENSATION

70. As a matter of principle, since overcompensation is not necessary for the operation of the service of general economic interest, it constitutes incompatible State aid that must be repaid to the State subject to the clarifications provided in the present chapter with regard to public service broadcasting.

71. The Commission starts from the consideration that the State funding is normally necessary for the undertaking to carry out its public service tasks. However, in order to satisfy the proportionality test, it is as a general rule necessary that the amount of public compensation does not exceed the net costs of the public service mission, taking also into account other direct or indirect revenues derived from the public service mission. For this reason, the net benefit of all commercial activities related to the public service activity will be taken into account in determining the net public service costs.

72. Undertakings receiving compensation for the performance of a public service task may, in general, enjoy a reasonable profit. This profit consists of a rate of return on own capital that takes account of the risk, or absence of risk, incurred by the undertaking. In the broadcasting sector the public service mission is often carried out by broadcasters that are not profit oriented or that do not have to remunerate the capital employed and do not perform any other activity than the provision of the public service. The Commission considers that in these situations, it is not reasonable to include a profit element in the amount of compensation for the fulfilment of the public service mission[47]. However, in other cases, for example where specific public service obligations are entrusted to commercially run undertakings which need to remunerate the capital invested in them, a profit element which represents the fair remuneration of capital taking into account risk may be considered reasonable, if duly justified and provided that it is necessary for the fulfilment of the public service obligations.

73. Public service broadcasters may retain yearly overcompensation above the net costs of the public service (as public service reserves) to the extent that this is necessary for securing the financing of their public service obligations. In general, the Commission considers that an amount of up to 10% of the annual budgeted expenses of the public service mission may be deemed necessary to withstand cost and revenue fluctuations. As a rule, overcompensation above this limit must be recovered without undue delay.

74. By way of exception, public service broadcasters may be allowed to keep an amount in excess of 10% of the annual budgeted expenses of their public service mission in duly justified cases. This is only acceptable provided that this overcompensation is specifically earmarked in advance of and in a binding way for the purpose of a non-recurring, major expense necessary for the fulfilment of the public service mission[48]. The use of such clearly earmarked overcompensation should also be limited in time depending on its dedication.

75. In order to allow the Commission to exercise its duties, Member States shall lay down the conditions under which the above overcompensation may be used by the public service broadcasters.

76. The overcompensation mentioned above shall be used for the purpose of financing public service activities, only. Cross-subsidisation of commercial activities is not justified and constitutes incompatible State aid.

6.6. FINANCIAL CONTROL MECHANISMS

77. Member States shall provide for appropriate mechanisms to ensure that there is no overcompensation, subject to the provisions of paragraphs 72 to 76. They shall ensure regular and effective control of the use of public funding, to prevent overcompensation and cross-subsidisation, and to scrutinise the level and the use of 'public service reserves'. It is within the competence of Member States to choose the most appropriate and effective control mechanisms in their national broadcasting systems, taking also into account the need to ensure coherence with the mechanisms in place for the supervision of the fulfilment of the public service remit.

78. Such control mechanisms would only seem effective if carried out by an external body independent from the public service broadcaster at regular intervals, preferably on a yearly basis. Member States shall make sure that effective measures can be put in place to recover overcompensation going beyond the provisions of the previous Chapter 6.5 and cross-subsidisation.

79. The financial situation of the public service broadcasters should be subject to an in-depth review at the end of each financing period as provided for in the national broadcasting systems of the Member States, or in the absence thereof, a time period which normally should not exceed four years. Any 'public service reserves' existing at the end of the financing period, or of an equivalent period as provided above, shall be taken into account for the calculation of the financial needs of the public service broadcaster for the next period. In case of 'public service reserves' exceeding 10% of the annual public service costs on a recurring basis, Member States shall review whether the level of funding is adjusted to the public service broadcasters' actual financial needs.

6.7. DIVERSIFICATION OF PUBLIC BROADCASTING SERVICES

80. In recent years, audiovisual markets have undergone important changes, which have led to the ongoing development and diversification of the broadcasting offer. This has raised new questions concerning the application of the State aid rules to audiovisual services which go beyond broadcasting activities in the traditional sense.

81. In this respect, the Commission considers that public service broadcasters should be able to use the opportunities offered by digitisation and the diversification of distribution platforms on a technology neutral basis, to the benefit of society. In order to guarantee the fundamental role of public service broadcasters in the new digital environment, public service broadcasters may use State aid to provide audiovisual services over new distribution platforms, catering for the general public as well as for special interests, provided that they are addressing the same democratic, social and cultural needs of the society in question, and do not entail disproportionate effects on the market, which are not necessary for the fulfilment of the public service remit.

82. In parallel with the rapid evolution of the broadcasting markets, the business models of broadcasters are also undergoing changes. In fulfilling their public service remit, broadcasters are increasingly turning to new sources of financing, such as online advertising or the provision of services against payment (so-called pay-services, like access to archives for a fee, special interest TV channels on a pay-per-view basis, access to mobile services for a lump sum payment, deferred access to TV programmes for a fee, paid online content downloads, etc.). The remuneration element in pay services can be related, for example, to the payment of network distribution fees or copyrights by broadcasters (for example if services over mobile platforms are provided against payment of a mobile distribution fee).

83. Although public broadcasting services have traditionally been free-to-air, the Commission considers that a direct remuneration element in such services — while having an impact on access by viewers[49] — does not necessarily mean that these services are manifestly not part of the public service remit provided that the pay element does not compromise the distinctive character of the public service in terms of serving the social, democratic and cultural needs of citizens, which distinguishes public services from purely commercial activities[50]. The element of remuneration is one of the aspects to be taken into account when deciding on the inclusion of such services in the public service remit, as it may affect the universality and the overall design of the service provided as well as its impact on the market. Provided that the given service with a pay element satisfies specific social, democratic and cultural needs of society without leading to disproportionate effects on competition and cross-border trade, Member States may entrust public service broadcasters with such a service as part of their public service remit.

84. As set out above, State aid to public service broadcasters may be used for distributing audiovisual services on all platforms provided that the material requirements of the Amsterdam Protocol are met. To this end, Member States shall consider, by means of a prior evaluation procedure based on an open public consultation, whether significant new audiovisual services envisaged by public service broadcasters meet the requirements of the Amsterdam Protocol, ie, whether they serve the democratic, social and cultural needs of the society, while duly taking into account its potential effects on trading conditions and competition.

85. It is up to the Member States to determine, taking into account the characteristics and the evolution of the broadcasting market, as well as the range of services already offered by the public service broadcaster, what shall qualify as 'significant new service'. The 'new' nature of an activity may depend among others on its content as well as on the modalities of consumption[51]. The 'significance' of the service may take into account for instance the financial resources required for its development and the expected impact on demand. Significant modifications to existing services shall be subject to the same assessment as significant new services.

86. It is within the competence of the Member States to choose the most appropriate mechanism to ensure the consistency of audiovisual services with the material conditions of the Amsterdam Protocol, taking into account the specificities of their national broadcasting systems, and the need to safeguard editorial independence of public service broadcasters.

87. In the interest of transparency and of obtaining all relevant information necessary to arrive at a balanced decision, interested stakeholders shall have the opportunity to give their views on the envisaged significant new service in the context of an open consultation. The outcome of the consultation, its assessment as well as the grounds for the decision shall be made publicly available.

88. In order to ensure that the public funding of significant new audiovisual services does not distort trade and competition to an extent contrary to the common interest, Member States shall assess, based on the outcome of the open consultation, the overall impact of a new service on the market by comparing the situation in the presence and in the absence of the planned new service. In assessing the impact on the market, relevant aspects include, for example, the existence of similar or substitutable offers, editorial competition, market structure, market position of the public service broadcaster, level of competition and potential impact on private initiatives. This impact needs to be balanced with the value of the services in question for society. In the case of predominantly negative effects on the market, State funding for audiovisual services would appear proportionate only if it is justified by the added value in terms of serving the social, democratic and cultural needs of society[52], taking also into account the existing overall public service offer.

89. Such an assessment would only be objective if carried out by a body which is effectively independent from the management of the public service broadcaster, also with regard to the appointment and removal of its members, and has sufficient capacity and resources to exercise its duties. Member States shall be able to design a procedure which is proportionate to the size of the market and the market position of the public service broadcaster.

90. The considerations outlined above shall not prevent public service broadcasters from testing innovative new services (eg, in the form of pilot projects) on a limited scale (eg, in terms of time and audience) and for the purpose of gathering information on the feasibility of and the value added by the foreseen service, insofar as such test phase does not amount to the introduction of a fully-fledged, significant new audiovisual service.

91. The Commission considers that the above assessment at the national level will contribute to ensuring compliance with the EC State aid rules. This is without prejudice to the competences of the Commission to verify that Member States respect the Treaty provisions, and to its right to act, whenever necessary, also on the basis of complaints or on its own initiative.

6.8. PROPORTIONALITY AND MARKET BEHAVIOUR

92. In accordance with the Amsterdam Protocol, public service broadcasters shall not engage in activities which would result in disproportionate distortions of competition that are not necessary for fulfilling the public service mission. For example, the acquisition of premium content as part of the overall public service mission of public service broadcasters is generally considered legitimate. However, disproportionate market distortions would arise in the event that public service broadcasters were to maintain exclusive premium rights unused without offering to sublicense them in a transparent and timely manner. Therefore, the Commission invites Member States to ensure that public service broadcasters respect the principle of proportionality also with regard to the acquisition of premium rights, and to provide rules for the sub-licensing of unused exclusive premium rights by public service broadcasters.

93. When carrying out commercial activities, public service broadcasters shall be bound to respect market principles and, when they act through commercial subsidiaries, they shall keep arm's length relations with these subsidiaries. Member States shall ensure that public service broadcasters respect the arm's length principle, undertake their commercial investments in line with the market economy investor principle, and do not engage in anti-competitive practices with regard to their competitors, based on their public funding.

94. An example of anti-competitive practice may be price undercutting. A public service broadcaster might be tempted to depress the prices of advertising or other non-public service activities (such as commercial pay services) below what can reasonably be considered to be market-conform, so as to reduce the revenue of competitors, insofar as the resulting lower revenues are covered by the public compensation. Such conduct cannot be considered as intrinsic to the public service mission attributed to the broadcaster and would in any event 'affect trading conditions and competition in the Community to an extent which would be contrary to the common interest' and thus infringe the Amsterdam Protocol.

95. In view of the differences between the market situations, the respect of the market principles by public service broadcasters, in particular the questions whether public service broadcasters are undercutting prices in their commercial offer, or whether they are respecting the principle of proportionality with regard to the acquisition of premium rights[53], shall be assessed on a case-by-case basis, taking into account the specificities of the market and of the service concerned.

96. The Commission considers that it is, in the first place, up to the national authorities to ensure that public service broadcasters respect market principles. To this end, Member States shall have appropriate mechanisms in place which allow assessing any potential complaint in an effective way at the national level.

97. Notwithstanding the preceding paragraph, where necessary, the Commission may take action on the basis of Articles 81, 82, 86 and 87 of the EC Treaty.

NOTES

[34] Judgment in the Case 172/80 *Zuechner*; (1981) 2021.

[35] Judgment in the Case C-242/95 *GT-Link*; (1997) 4449.

[36] Judgment in the Case C-159/94 *EDF and GDF*; (1997) I-5815.

[37] See, for example, the recent decisions of the Commission in the following cases: E 8/06, State funding for Flemish public service broadcaster VRT (OJ C143, 10.6.2008, p 7); E 4/05, State aid financing of RTE and TNAG (TG4) (OJ C121, 17.5.2008, p 5); E 3/05, Aid to the German public service broadcasters (OJ C185, 8.8.2007, p 1); E 9/05, Licence fee payments to RAI (OJ CC 235, 23.9.2005, p 3); E 10/05, Licence fee payments to France 2 and 3 (OJ C240, 30.9.2005, p 20); State aid E8/05, Spanish national public service broadcaster RTVE (OJ C239, 4.10.2006, p 17); C 2/04, Ad hoc financing of Dutch public service broadcasters (OJ L49, 22.2.2008, p 1).

[38] Similar difficulties may also be encountered when public service broadcasting is addressed to linguistic minorities or to local needs.

[39] Judgment in the Case T-442/03, SIC v Commission, (2008), paragraph 201, Judgement in joined Cases T-309/04, T-317/04, T-329/04 and T-336/04 TV2/Denmark v Commission (2008) at 122 to 124.

[40] These qualitative criteria are according to the Court of First Instance 'the justification for the existence of broadcasting SGEIs in the national audiovisual sector'. There is 'no reason for a widely defined broadcasting SGEI which sacrifices compliance with those qualitative requirements in order to adopt the conduct of a commercial operator', T-442/03, SIC v Commission, paragraph 211.

[41] Regarding the qualification, under the Audiovisual Media Services Directive, of prize games including the dialling of a premium rate number as teleshopping or advertising, see the judgment of the Court in Case C-195/06 *KommAustria v ORF* of 18 October 2007.

[42] See judgment in joined Cases T-309/04, T-317/04, T-329/04 and T-336/04 TV2 (2008) at 107-108.

[43] COM(1999) 657 final, Section 3(6).

[44] See judgment in the Case T-442/03 SIC/Commission (2008) at 212.

[45] Article 4 of Directive 2006/111/EC.

[46] This implies reference to the hypothetical situation in which the non-public service activities were to be discontinued: the costs that would be so avoided represent the amount of common costs to be allocated to non-public service activities.

[47] Of course, this provision does not preclude public service broadcasters from earning profits with their commercial activities outside the public service remit.

[48] Such special reserves may be justified for major technological investments (such as digitisation) which are foreseen to occur at a certain point in time and are necessary for the fulfilment of the public service remit; or for major restructuring measures necessary to maintain the continuous operation of a public service broadcaster within a well-defined time period.

[49] As the Council of Europe provided, in its Recommendation on the remit of public service media in the information society, '(. . .) Member States may consider complementary funding solutions paying due attention to market and competition questions. In particular, in the case of new personalised services, Member States may consider allowing public service media to collect remunerations (. . .). However, none of these solutions should endanger the principle of universality of public service media or lead to discrimination between different groups of society (. . .) When developing new funding systems, Member States should pay due attention to the nature of the content provided in the interest of the public and in the common interest.'

[50] For example, the Commission considers that requiring direct payment from users for the provision of a specialised premium content offer would normally qualify as commercial activity. On the other hand, the Commission, for example, considers that the charging of pure transmission fees for broadcasting a balanced and varied programming over new platforms such as mobile devices would not transform the offer into a commercial activity.

[51] For example, the Commission considers that some forms of linear transmission, such as the simultaneous transmission of the evening TV news on other platforms (eg, Internet, mobile devices), may be qualified as not being 'new' for the purposes of this Communication. Whether other forms of retransmission of public broadcasters' programs on other platforms qualify as significant new services, should be determined by Member States, taking into account the specificities and the features of the services in question.

[52] See also at footnote 40 on the justification of a broadcasting SGEI.

[53] For example, one of the relevant issues may be to consider whether public service broadcasters are consistently overbidding for premium programme rights in a way which goes beyond the needs of the public service mandate and results in disproportionate distortions on the marketplace.

7. TEMPORAL APPLICATION

[5.345]

98. This Communication will be applied from the first day following its publication in the *Official Journal of the European Union*. It will replace the 2001 Communication from the Commission on the application of State aid rules to public service broadcasting.

99. The Commission will apply this Communication to all notified aid measures in respect of which it is called upon to take a decision after the Communication is published in the Official Journal, even where the projects were notified prior to that date.

100. In accordance with the Commission notice on the determination of the applicable rules for the assessment of unlawful State aid[54], the Commission will apply, in the case of non-notified aid,

(a) this Communication, if the aid was granted after its publication;

(b) the 2001 Communication in all other cases.

NOTES

[54] OJ C119, 22.5.2002, p 22.

3. BROADBAND

COMMUNICATION FROM THE COMMISSION

(2013/C25/01)

EU Guidelines for the application of State aid rules in relation to the rapid deployment of broadband networks

[5.346]

NOTES

Date of publication in OJ: OJ C25, 26.1.2013, p 1.

The Commission Communication on Community Guidelines for the application of State aid rules in relation to rapid deployment of broadband networks (OJ C235, 30.9.2009, p 7) was included in previous editions of this Handbook and continues to apply to unlawful aid granted until 31 December 2013.

See also the list of consultations and draft documents in the Appendix at **[A1]**.

1. INTRODUCTION

[5.347]

(1) Broadband connectivity is of strategic importance for European growth and innovation in all sectors of the economy and for social and for territorial cohesion. The Europe 2020 Strategy (EU2020) underlines the importance of broadband deployment as part of the EU's growth strategy for the coming decade and sets ambitious targets for broadband development. One of its flagship initiatives, the Digital Agenda for Europe (DAE)[1] acknowledges the socio-economic benefits of broadband, highlighting its importance for competitiveness, social inclusion and employment. The achievement of Europe 2020 objective of a smart, sustainable and inclusive growth depend also on the provision of widespread and affordable access to high-speed Internet infrastructure and services. Meeting the challenge of financing a good-quality and affordable broadband infrastructure is a crucial factor for Europe to increase its competitiveness and innovation, provide job opportunities for young people, prevent relocation of economic activity and attract inward investments. The DAE restates the objective of the EU2020 to bring basic broadband to all Europeans by 2013 and seeks to ensure that, by 2020, (i) all Europeans have access to much higher Internet speeds of above 30 Mbps and (ii) 50% or more of European households subscribe to Internet connections above 100 Mbps.

(2) To achieve the objective of access to Internet speeds of above 30 Mbps it is estimated[2] that up to EUR 60 billion of investment would be necessary and up to EUR 270 billion for at least 50% of households to take up Internet connections above 100 Mbps.[3] Such investments shall primarily come from commercial investors. However, the DAE objectives cannot be reached without the support of public funds. For this reason, the DAE calls on Member States to use 'public financing in line with EU competition and State aid rules' in order to meet the coverage, speed and take-up targets defined in EU2020.[4] Demand for capacity-intensive services is expected to increase in the future, as cloud computing, a more intense use of peer-to-peer technologies, social networks and video on demand services will develop further.

(3) The electronic communication sector has undergone a thorough liberalisation process and is now subject to sectoral regulation. The EU regulatory framework for electronic communications also provides harmonisation rules concerning broadband access.[5] With regard to legacy broadband networks, wholesale markets are to date subject to *ex ante* regulation in the majority of Member States. The regulatory approach has proved successful to foster competitive markets, to encourage investment and to increase consumer choice: for example, the highest broadband coverage and take-up is found in Member States with infrastructure competition, combined with effective *ex ante* regulation to promote service competition. Further deployment of broadband networks and in particular of Next Generation Access (NGA) networks continues to require the intervention of the national regulatory authorities (NRAs) due to their role in the electronic communications sector.

(4) It is all the more important that public funds are carefully used in this sector and that the Commission ensures that State aid is complementary and does not substitute investments of market players. Any State intervention should limit as much as possible the risk of crowding out private investments, of altering commercial investment incentives and ultimately of distorting competition contrary to the common interest of the European Union.

(5) In its Communication on State Aid Modernisation (SAM), the Commission notes that State aid policy should focus on facilitating well-designed aid targeted at market failures and objectives of common European interest.[6] State aid measures can, under certain conditions, correct market failures, thereby improving the efficient functioning of markets and enhancing competitiveness. Further, where markets provide efficient outcomes but these are deemed unsatisfactory from a cohesion policy point of view, State aid may be used to obtain a more desirable, equitable market outcome. In particular, a well-targeted State intervention in the broadband field can contribute to reducing the 'digital divide'[7] between areas or regions where affordable and competitive broadband services are on offer and areas where such services are not.

(6) However, if State aid for broadband were to be used in areas where market operators would normally choose to invest or have already invested, this could significantly undermine the incentives of commercial investors to invest in broadband in the first place. In such cases, State aid to broadband might become counterproductive to the objective pursued. The purpose of State aid control in the broadband sector is to ensure that State aid measures will result in a higher level, or a faster rate, of broadband coverage and penetration than would be the case without State aid, while supporting higher quality, more affordable services and pro-competitive investments. The positive effects of the aid should outweigh the distortions of competition.

(7) In response to the Commission's calling on them to do so in the DAE, most Member States developed national broadband strategies to achieve the DAE objectives in their respective territories. Most of these strategies envisage using public funds to extend broadband coverage in areas where there is no incentive for commercial operators to invest in and accelerate the deployment of very high speed, next generation access networks.

(8) These guidelines summarise the principles of the Commission's policy in applying the State aid rules of the Treaty to measures that support the deployment of broadband networks in general (Section 2). They explain the application of these principles in the assessment of aid measures for the rapid roll-out of basic broadband and very high speed, next generation access (NGA) networks (in Section 3). The Commission will apply the guidelines in the assessment of State aid for broadband. This will increase the legal certainty and transparency of its decision-making.

NOTES

1 Communication from the Commission to the European Parliament, the Council, the European Economic and Social Committee and the Committee of the Regions, COM(2010) 245 final, *A Digital Agenda for Europe*.

2 See Communication from the Commission to the European Parliament, the Council, the European Economic and Social Committee and the Committee of the Regions, European broadband: investing in digitally driven growth, COM(2010) 472 final.

3 The actual investments costs could be significantly lower depending on the reusability of existing infrastructures and depending on the market, technology and regulatory developments.

4 Paragraph 2.4, Key Action 8.

5 See Article 12(4) of Directive 2002/21/EC of the European Parliament and of the Council of 7 March 2002 on a common regulatory Framework for Electronic Communications Networks and Services (Framework Directive) (OJ L108, 24.4.2002, p 33), as amended by Directive 2009/140/EC (Better Regulation Directive) (OJ L337, 18.12.2009, p 37) and by Regulation (EC) No 544/2009 (OJ L167, 29.6.2009, p 12).

6 Communication from the Commission on EU State Aid Modernisation (SAM). Brussels, 8.5.2012. COM(2012) 209 final.

7 The term 'digital divide' is most commonly used to define the gap between those individuals and communities that have access to the information technologies and those that do not. Although there are several reasons for this 'digital divide', the most important is the lack of an adequate broadband infrastructure. From the regional point of view, the degree of urbanisation is an important factor for access to and use of ICTs. Internet penetration remains thus much lower in thinly populated areas throughout the European Union.

2. THE MAIN PRINCIPLES OF THE COMMISSION'S POLICY ON STATE AID FOR BROADBAND

[5.348]

(9) According to Article 107(1) of the Treaty on the Functioning of the European Union (TFEU), 'any aid granted by a Member State or through State resources in any form whatsoever which distorts or threatens to distort competition by favouring certain undertakings or the production of certain goods shall, insofar as it affects trade between Member States, be incompatible with the common market'. It follows that in order for a measure to qualify as State aid, the following cumulative conditions have to be met: (a) the measure has to be granted out of State resources, (b) it has to confer an economic advantage to undertakings, (c) the advantage has to be selective and (d) distort or threaten to distort competition, (e) the measure has to affect trade between Member States.

2.1. ARTICLE 107(1) TFEU: PRESENCE OF AID

(10) *The use of State resources*: The transfer of State resources may take many forms such as direct grants, tax rebates,[8] soft loans or other types of preferential financing conditions. State resources will also be involved if the State provides a benefit in kind, for instance investing in the construction of (part) of the broadband infrastructure. State resources can be used[9] at the national, regional or local level. Funding from European funds such as the European Agricultural Fund for Rural Development (EAFRD) and the European Regional Development Fund (ERDF)[10] will likewise constitute State resources, when these funds are allocated at a Member State's discretion.[11]

(11) *Undertaking*: State measures supporting broadband investments usually address the exercise of an economic activity, such as the construction, operation and granting of access to broadband infrastructure or enabling the provision of connectivity to end-users. Also, the State itself can carry out an economic activity when it operates and exploits (parts of) a broadband infrastructure, for instance via an in-house company or as part of the State administration. The construction of a broadband network infrastructure with a view of its future commercial exploitation by the State or third-party operators, will also constitute an economic activity.[12] The roll-out of a broadband network for non-commercial purposes might not constitute State aid,[13] because the network construction does not favour any undertaking.[14] However, if such a network is subsequently opened for the use of broadband investors or operators, State aid is likely to be involved.[15]

(12) *Advantage*: The aid is usually granted directly to investors of the network, which in most cases are chosen by means of a competitive tender process. When the State's contribution is not provided on normal market terms and consequently qualifies as State aid under the market economy investor principle (see paragraph 16 below), the use of a competitive selection process ensures that any aid is limited to the minimum amount necessary for the particular project. However, it does not eliminate the aid, as the public authority will still provide a subsidy to the winning bidder (for instance, in terms of 'gap funding' or in-kind contribution) and the purpose of such procedure is precisely the selection of the aid beneficiary. The financial support received will enable the successful bidder to conduct this commercial activity on conditions which would not otherwise be available on the market. Besides the direct beneficiary of the aid, third-party operators receiving wholesale access to the subsidised infrastructure may be indirect beneficiaries.[16]

(13) *Selectivity*: State measures supporting the deployment of broadband networks are selective in nature in that they target broadband investors and third-party operators which are active only in certain segments of the overall electronic communications services market. As regards the business end-users of the subsidised network,[17] by contrast, the measure might not be selective as long as the access to the subsidised infrastructure is open to all sectors of the

economy. Selectivity will exist if broadband deployment is specifically addressed to dedicated business users, for instance if the State support is geared toward the deployment of a broadband network in favour of predetermined companies which are not chosen according to general criteria applicable in the entire area for which the granting authority is responsible.[18]

(14) *Distortion of competition*: According to the case law of the Court of Justice of the European Union (the Court), financial support or support in kind distorts competition insofar as it strengthens the position of an undertaking compared with other undertakings.[19] Due to the State aid granted to a competitor, existing operators might reduce capacity or potential operators might decide not to enter into a new market or a geographic area. Distortions of competition are likely to be enhanced if the beneficiary of the aid has market power. Where the aid beneficiary is already dominant on a market, the aid measure may reinforce this dominance by further weakening the competitive constraint that competitors can exert.

(15) *Effect on trade*: Finally, insofar as the State intervention is liable to affect service providers from other Member States (also by discouraging their establishment in the Member States in question) it also has an effect on trade since the markets for electronic communications services (wholesale and retail broadband markets) are open to competition between operators and service providers.[20]

2.2. ABSENCE OF AID: THE APPLICATION OF THE MARKET ECONOMY INVESTOR PRINCIPLE

(16) Article 345 TFEU provides that 'this Treaty shall in no way prejudice the rules in Member States governing the system of property ownership'. According to the case law of the Court, it follows from the principle of equal treatment that capital placed by the State, directly or indirectly, at the disposal of an undertaking in circumstances which correspond to normal market conditions cannot be regarded as State aid. When equity participation or capital injections by a public investor do not present sufficient prospects of profitability, even in the long term, such intervention must be regarded as aid within the meaning of Article 107 TFEU, and its compatibility with the common market must be assessed on the basis solely of the criteria laid down in that provision.[21]

(17) In its Amsterdam decision, the Commission has examined the application of the principle of the market economy private investor in the broadband field.[22] As underlined in this decision, the conformity of a public investment with market terms has to be demonstrated thoroughly and comprehensively, either by means of a significant participation of private investors or the existence of a sound business plan showing an adequate return on investment. Where private investors take part in the project, it is a *sine qua non* condition that they would have to assume the commercial risk linked to the investment under the same terms and conditions as the public investor. This also applies to other forms of State supports such as soft loans or guarantees.[23]

2.3. STATE AID FOR BROADBAND DEPLOYMENT AS A SERVICE OF GENERAL ECONOMIC INTEREST — ALTMARK AND COMPATIBILITY UNDER ARTICLE 106(2) TFEU

(18) In some cases, Member States may consider that the provision of a broadband network should be regarded as a service of a general economic interest (SGEI) within the meaning of Article 106(2) TFEU[24] and the Altmark jurisprudence[25] and provide public funding on this basis. In such cases, Member States measures have to be assessed in line with the Commission Communication on the application of the EU State aid rules to compensation granted for the provision of services of general economic interest,[26] the Commission Decision of 20 December 2011 on the application of Article 106(2) of the Treaty on the Functioning of the European Union to State aid in the form of public service compensation granted to certain undertakings entrusted with the operation of services of general economic interest,[27] the Commission Communication on a European Union framework for State aid in the form of public service compensation (2011)[28] and the Commission Regulation of 25 April 2012 on the application of Articles 107 and 108 of the Treaty on the Functioning of the European Union to de minimis aid granted to undertakings providing services of general economic interest.[29] These Commission documents (referred to all together as the 'SGEI package'), indeed, also apply to State aid for broadband deployment. What follows will only illustrate the application of some of the principles clarified in these documents to broadband financing, in the light of certain sectoral specificities

The SGEI definition

(19) Concerning the SGEI definition, the Commission has already clarified, in general terms, that Member States cannot attach specific public service obligations to services that are already provided or can be provided satisfactorily and under conditions, such as price, objective quality characteristics, continuity and access to the service, consistent with the public interest, as defined by the State, by undertakings operating under normal market conditions.[30]

(20) Applying this principle to the broadband sector, the Commission considers that in areas where private investors have already invested in a broadband network infrastructure (or are further expanding the network) and are already providing competitive broadband services with an adequate broadband coverage, setting up a parallel competitive and publicly funded broadband infrastructure cannot be considered as an SGEI within the meaning of Article 106(2) TFEU.[31] However, where it can be demonstrated that private investors are not in a position to provide in the near future[32] adequate broadband coverage to all citizens or users, thus leaving a significant part of the population unconnected, a public service compensation may be granted to an undertaking entrusted with the operation of an SGEI provided the conditions of the SGEI communication cited above are fulfilled. In this respect, the networks to be taken into consideration for assessing the need for an SGEI should always be of comparable type, namely either basic broadband or NGA networks.

(21) Moreover, the deployment and the operation of a broadband infrastructure can qualify as an SGEI only if such infrastructure provides all users in a given area with universal connectivity, residential and business users alike. Support for connecting businesses only would not be sufficient.[33]

(22) The compulsory nature of the SGEI mission also implies that the provider of the network to be deployed will not be able to refuse wholesale access to the infrastructure on a discretionary and/or discriminatory basis (because, for instance, it may not be commercially profitable to provide access services to a given area).

(23) Given the degree of competition that has been achieved since the liberalisation of the electronic communications sector in the Union, and in particular the competition that exists today on the retail broadband market, a publicly funded network set up within the context of an SGEI should be available to all interested operators. Accordingly, the recognition of an SGEI mission for broadband deployment should be based on the provision of a passive,[34] neutral[35] and open infrastructure. Such a network should provide access seekers with all possible forms of network access and allow effective competition at the retail level, ensuring the provision of competitive and affordable services to end-users.[36]

(24) Therefore, the SGEI mission should only cover the deployment of a broadband network providing universal connectivity and the provision of the related wholesale access services, without including retail communication services.[37] Where the provider of the SGEI mission is also a vertically integrated broadband operator, adequate safeguards should be put in place to avoid any conflict of interest, undue discrimination and any other hidden indirect advantages.[38]

(25) Given that the market for electronic communications is fully liberalised, it follows that an SGEI mission for broadband deployment cannot be based on the award of an exclusive or special right to the provider of the SGEI within the meaning of Article 106(1) TFEU.

Calculation of the compensation and clawback

(26) For the calculation of the SGEI compensation the principles of the SGEI package fully apply. However, in the light of the specificities of the broadband sector, it is useful to add a clarification for SGEI intended to cover unconnected neighbourhoods or districts (so called white spots) within a broader area in which some operators have already deployed their own network infrastructure or may plan to do so in the near future. In cases in which the area for which the SGEI is entrusted is not limited just to the 'white spots', because of their size or location, the SGEI provider may need to deploy a network infrastructure also in the profitable areas already covered by commercial operators. In such situation, any compensation granted should only cover the costs of rolling out an infrastructure in the non-profitable white spots, taking into account relevant revenue and a reasonable profit.[39]

(27) In many circumstances, it may be appropriate to fix the compensation amount on an *ex ante* basis, so as to cover the expected funding gap over a given period, rather than to establish the compensation merely on the basis of costs and revenues as they occur. In the former model, there are typically more incentives for the company to contain costs and to develop the business over time.[40] Where an SGEI mission for the deployment of a broadband network is not based on the deployment of a publicly owned infrastructure adequate review and clawback mechanisms should be put in place to prevent the SGEI provider from obtaining an undue advantage by retaining ownership of the network that was financed with public funds when the SGEI concession expires.

2.4. ADMINISTRATIVE AND REGULATORY MEASURES SUPPORTING BROADBAND ROLL-OUT FALLING OUTSIDE THE SCOPE OF EU STATE AID RULES

(28) As also explained in the Commission's Broadband Communication,[41] Member States may choose several types of measures in order to accelerate the deployment of broadband and in particular NGA networks besides providing direct funding to companies. These measures do not necessarily need to involve State aid within the meaning of Article 107(1) TFEU.

(29) Given that generally a large part of the cost of deploying NGA networks is in the civil engineering work,[42] Member States may decide in accordance with the EU regulatory framework for electronic communications, for instance, to facilitate the acquisition process of rights of ways, to require that network operators coordinate their civil engineering works and/or that they share part of their infrastructure. In the same vein, Member States may also require that for any new constructions (including new water, energy, transport or sewage networks) and/or buildings a connection suitable for NGA should be in place. Third parties may also place at their own cost their passive network infrastructure when general civil engineering works are carried out in any event. This opportunity should be offered in a transparent and non-discriminatory way to all interested operators and should in principle be open to all potential users and not just electronic communications operators (i.e. electricity gas, water utilities, etc.).[43] A centralised inventory of the existing infrastructure (subsidised or otherwise), possibly also including planned works, could help the roll-out of commercial broadband.[44] Existing infrastructure does not only concern telecommunication infrastructure, such as wired, wireless or satellite infrastructure, but also alternative infrastructures (sewers, manholes, etc.) of other industries (such as utilities).[45]

2.5. THE COMPATIBILITY ASSESSMENT UNDER ARTICLE 107(3) TFEU

(30) Where State intervention to support broadband deployment fulfils the conditions defined in Section 2.1, its compatibility will generally be assessed by the Commission under Article 107(3)(c) TFEU.[46] To date, regional and local authorities have adopted different models of intervention. A non-exhaustive list of these models is provided in the Annex. Apart from those described in the Annex, public authorities may also develop other models of supporting broadband deployment.[47] For all types of intervention forms all the compatibility criteria set out in these Guidelines must be applied.[48]

(31) Broadband State aid projects may be implemented in assisted areas within the meaning of Article 107(3)(a) and (c) TFEU, and the Regional Aid specific rules.[49] In this case, aid for broadband may qualify as aid for an initial investment within the meaning of the regional aid rules. Where a measure falls within the scope of such rules, and where it is envisaged to grant individual ad hoc aid to a single firm, or aid confined to one area of activity, the Member State is responsible for demonstrating that the conditions of the regional aid rules have been fulfilled. This includes in particular that the project in question contributes towards a coherent regional development strategy and that, having regard to the nature and size of the project, it will not result in unacceptable distortions of competition.

Overview of the common principles of compatibility

(32) In the assessment under Article 107(3)(c) of the TFEU the Commission ensures that the positive impact of the aid measure in reaching an objective of common interest outweighs its potential negative side effects, such as distortions of trade and competition. This exercise is conducted in two steps.

(33) First, every aid measure has to comply with the below necessary conditions. Failure to comply with one of the following conditions will result in declaring the aid incompatible with the internal market.

1. Contribution to the achievement of objectives of common interest
2. Absence of market delivery due to market failures or important inequalities
3. Appropriateness of State aid as a policy instrument
4. Existence of incentive effect
5. Aid limited to the minimum necessary
6. Limited negative effects
7. Transparency

(34) Second, if all necessary conditions are met, the Commission balances the positive effects of the aid measure in reaching an objective of common interest against the potential negative effects.

(35) The individual steps of the Commission assessment in the field of broadband are set out in further detail in what follows.

1. Contribution to the achievement of objectives of common interest

(36) As regards the common interest objective, the Commission will assess to what extent the planned intervention will contribute to the achievement of the objectives of common interest explained above as further specified in the DAE.

2. Absence of market delivery due to market failures or important in equalities

(37) A 'market failure' exists if markets, left to their own devices, without intervention fail to deliver an efficient outcome for society. This may arise, for instance, when certain investments are not being undertaken even though the economic benefit for society exceeds the cost.[50] In such cases, the granting of State aid may produce positive effects and overall efficiency can be improved by adjusting the economic incentives for firms. In the broadband sector, one form of market failure is related to positive externalities. Such externalities arise where market players do not internalise the whole benefit of their actions. For example, the availability of broadband networks paves the way for the provision of more services and for innovation, both of these are likely to benefit more people than the immediate investors and subscribers to the network. The market outcome would therefore generate insufficient private investment in broadband networks.

(38) Due to economics of density, the deployment of broadband networks is generally more profitable where potential demand is higher and concentrated, i.e. in densely populated areas. Because of high fixed costs of investment, unit costs increase significantly as population densities drop.[51] Therefore, when deployed on commercial terms, broadband networks tend to profitably cover only part of the population. However, as acknowledged in the DAE, widespread and affordable access to broadband generates positive externalities because of its ability to accelerate growth and innovation in all sectors of the economy. Where the market does not provide sufficient broadband coverage or the access conditions are not adequate, State aid may therefore help to remedy such market failure.

(39) A second possible objective of common interest is related to equity. Governments may choose to intervene to correct social or regional inequalities generated by a market outcome. In certain cases, State aid for broadband may also be used to achieve equity objectives, i.e. as a way of improving access to an essential means of communication and participation in society as well as freedom of expression for all members of society, thereby improving social and territorial cohesion.

3. Appropriateness of State aid as a policy instrument and the design of the measure

(40) Public intervention in support of broadband networks may take place at State, regional or municipal level.[52] Therefore, coordination of the various interventions is essential to avoid duplications and incoherence. To ensure consistency and coordination of the local interventions, it is necessary to ensure a high level of transparency of local initiatives.

(41) Wherever possible and respecting competences and specificities, Member States are encouraged to design nationwide schemes containing the main principles underlying the public initiatives and to indicate the most relevant features of the planned networks.[53] National framework schemes for broadband development ensure coherency in the use of public funds, reduce administrative burden on smaller granting authorities and accelerate the implementation of the individual aid measures. Further, Member States are encouraged to give clear guidance at central level for the implementation of State aid-financed broadband projects.

(42) The role of NRAs in designing a pro-competitive State aid measure in support of broadband is particularly important. The NRAs have gained technical knowledge and expertise due to the crucial role assigned to them by sectoral regulation.[54] They are best placed to support public authorities with regard to the State aid schemes and should be consulted when target areas are being identified. NRAs should also be consulted with regard to determining the wholesale access prices and conditions and solving disputes between access seekers and the subsidised infrastructure operator. Member States are encouraged to provide NRAs with the resources they need to give such support. Where necessary, Member States should provide an appropriate legal basis for such involvement of NRAs

in State aid broadband projects. In keeping with best practice, NRAs should issue guidelines for local authorities which include recommendations on market analysis, wholesale access products and pricing principles taking into account the Electronic Communications Regulatory Framework and relative Recommendations issued by the Commission.[55]

(43) In addition to the involvement of NRAs, National Competition Authorities may also provide useful advice in particular in relation to large framework schemes to help establishing a level playing field for the bidding operators and to avoid that a disproportionately high share of State funds is earmarked to one operator, thereby strengthening its (possibly already dominant) market position.[56] In addition to the role of NRAs, some Member States set up national competence centres to help small, local authorities to design adequate State aid measures and ensure consistency in the application of the State aid rules as specified in these Guidelines.[57]

(44) So that the measure is properly designed, the balancing test further requires that State aid is an *appropriate* policy instrument to address the problem. In this respect, whilst *ex ante* regulation has in many cases facilitated broadband deployment in urban and more densely populated areas, it may not be a sufficient instrument to enable the supply of broadband service, especially in underserved areas where the inherent profitability of investment is low.[58] Likewise, although they can contribute positively to broadband penetration,[59] demand-side measures in favour of broadband (such as vouchers for end-users) cannot always solve the lack of broadband provision.[60] Hence, in some situations there may be no alternative to granting public funding to overcome the lack of broadband connectivity. Granting authorities shall also take into account spectrum (re-)allocations leading to possible network roll-out in the target areas that could achieve the objectives of the granting authorities without the provision of direct grants.

4.
Existence of incentive effect

(45) Regarding the *incentive effect* of the measure, it needs to be examined whether the broadband network investment concerned would not have been undertaken within the same time frame without any State aid. Where an operator is subject to certain obligations to cover the target area,[61] it may not be eligible for State aid, as the latter is unlikely to have an incentive effect.

5.
Aid limited to the minimum necessary

(46) In assessing the *proportional* character of the notified measures, the Commission has highlighted a number of necessary conditions to minimise the State aid involved and the potential distortions of competition as explained more in detail in the following sections.

6.
Limited negative effects

(47) The change in the beneficiary's behaviour because of the aid may also have negative effects on competition and trade, however. The significance of the distortion of competition can be assessed in terms of effects on competitors. If competitors see the profitability of their prior investment decreasing because of the aid, they may decide to reduce their own future investment or even withdraw from the market altogether.[62] Additionally, where the aid beneficiary to be chosen following the competitive selection process is likely to be an undertaking already dominant on a market or may become dominant due to the State funded investment, the aid measure could weaken the competitive constraint that competitors can exert. Moreover, if a State aid measure or the conditions attached to it (including its financing method when it forms an integral part of it) entail a non-severable violation of EU law, the aid cannot be declared compatible with the internal market.[63]

7.
Transparency

(48) Aid shall be awarded in a transparent manner; in particular, it must be ensured that the Member States, economic operators, the interested public and the Commission have easy access to all relevant acts and pertinent information about the aid awarded thereunder. The details of the transparency requirements are specified in paragraph 78.

8.
The over all balancing exercise and the compatibility conditions to limit the distortion of competition

(49) A carefully designed State aid scheme for broadband should ensure that the overall balance of the effects of the measure is positive.

(50) In this regard, the effect of the State aid measure can be described as a change of activity compared with what would have happened without the aid. The positive effects of the aid are directly linked to the change in the aid beneficiary's behaviour. This change should enable the achievement of the desired common interest goal. In the broadband sector, the aid leads to the rollout of a new infrastructure which would not have been there otherwise, thus delivering additional capacity and speed on the market as well as lower prices and better choice for consumers, higher quality and innovation. This would also result in more access for consumers to online resources and, together with increased consumer protection in this area, it is likely to stimulate an increase in demand. This will contribute to the completion of the Digital Single Market and bring benefits to the EU economy as a whole.

(51) A subsidised network should be able to ensure a 'step change' in terms of broadband availability. A 'step change' can be demonstrated if as the result of the public intervention (i) the selected bidder makes significant new investments in the broadband network[64] and (ii) the subsidised infrastructure brings significant new capabilities to the market in terms of broadband service availability and capacity,[65] speeds and competition.[66] The step change shall be compared to that of existing as well as concretely planned network roll-outs.

(52) Moreover, to ensure that the negative effects on competition are minimised, a number of conditions have to be fulfilled in the design of the aid measure, as specified below in Section 3.4.

(53) To further ensure that distortion of competition are limited, the Commission may require that certain schemes are subject to a time limitation (of normally 4 years or less) and to an evaluation in order to verify (i) whether the assumptions and conditions which led to the compatibility decision have been realised; (ii) the effectiveness of the aid measure in light of its predefined objectives; (iii) its impact on markets and competition and that no undue distortive effects arise under the duration of the aid scheme that is contrary to the interests of the Union.[67] Given its objectives and in order not to put disproportionate burden on Member States and on smaller aid projects, this only applies for national aid schemes and aid schemes with large aid budgets, containing novel characteristics or when significant market, technology or regulatory changes are foreseen. The evaluation shall be carried out by an expert independent from the State aid granting authority on the basis of a common methodology[68] and shall be made public. The evaluation shall be submitted to the Commission in due time to allow for the assessment of the possible prolongation of the aid measure and in any case upon expiry of the scheme. The precise scope and modalities of the evaluation shall be defined in the approval decision of the aid measure. Any subsequent aid measure with a similar objective shall take into account the results of that evaluation. [In the case of aid schemes excluded from the scope of a block exemption Regulation exclusively on the grounds of their large budget, the Commission will assess their compatibility solely on the basis of the evaluation plan.]

(54) If the balancing test shows that the negative effects outweigh the benefits, the Commission may prohibit the aid, or ask for remedial action, either in the design of the aid, or in the harm it does to competition.

NOTES

Para (53): words in square brackets added by Commission Communication 2014/C198/02.

8 See, for instance, Commission Decision N 398/05 — Hungary, *Development Tax Benefit for Broadband*.

9 Resources of a public undertaking constitute State resources within the meaning of Article 107 of the Treaty because the public authorities control these resources. Case C-482/99 *France v Commission*, [2002] ECR I-4397. In line with this judgment, it will further have to be assessed whether financing via a public undertaking is imputable to the State.

10 Regulation (EC) No 1698/2005 of 20 September 2005 on support for rural development by the European Agricultural Fund for Rural Development (EAFRD) (OJ L277, 21.10.2005, p 1), Regulation (EC) No 1080/2006 of 5 July 2006 on the European Regional Development Fund and repealing Regulation (EC) No 1783/1999 (OJ L210, 31.7.2006, p 1), Regulation (EC) No 1083/2006, of 11 July 2006 laying down general provisions on the European Regional Development Fund, the European Social Fund and the Cohesion Fund and repealing Regulation (EC) No 1260/1999 (OJ L210, 31.7.2006, p 25).

11 See, for instance, Commission Decision in Case N 157/06 — United Kingdom South Yorkshire *Digital Region Broadband Project*. The Court has confirmed that once financial means remain constantly under public control and are therefore available to the competent national authorities, this is sufficient for them to be categorised as State aid, see Case C-83/98 *P France v Ladbroke Racing Ltd and Commission* [2000] ECR I-3271, paragraph 50.

12 Case T-443/08 and T-455/08 *Freistaat Sachsen and Others v Commission* (not yet published), paragraphs (93) to (95).

13 See, for instance, Commission Decision in Case NN 24/07 — Czech Republic. *Prague Municipal Wireless Network*.

14 Similarly, if a network is constructed or broadband services are procured to satisfy the own needs of the public administration, under certain circumstances, such intervention might not confer advantage to economic undertakings. See Commission Decision in Case N 46/07 — United Kingdom, *Welsh Public Sector Network Scheme*.

15 Commission Decision in Case SA.31687(N 436/10) — Italy *Broadband in Friuli Venezia Giulia (Project Ermes)* and in Case N 407/09 — *Spain, Xarxa Oberta*.

16 It is likely that the benefit of the subsidy is at least partially passed on to third-party operators even if they pay a remuneration for the wholesale access. Indeed, wholesale prices are often regulated. Price regulation leads to a lower price than the one which the wholesaler could otherwise achieve on the market (which could be a monopoly price if there is no competition with other networks). Where prices are not regulated, the wholesaler will in any case be required to benchmark his prices on the average prices applied in other, more competitive areas (see paragraph 78 h) below) which is also likely to lead to a price lower than the one which the wholesaler could otherwise have achieved on the market.

17 Subsidies to residential users fall outside the scope of Article 107(1) TFEU.

18 An example would be aid to a business districts, see for instance, Commission Decision in Case N 626/09 — Italy, *NGA for industrial districts of Lucca*.

19 Case C-310/99, *Italian Republic v Commission* [2002] ECR-I-02289, paragraph 65.

20 See Commission Decision in Case N 237/08 — Germany, *Broadband support in Niedersachsen*.

21 Case C-303/88, *Italian Republic v Commission*, [1991] ECR I-1433, at paragraphs 20-22.

22 Commission Decision of 11 December 2007 in Case C 53/06 — The Netherlands, *Citynet Amsterdam — Investment by the city of Amsterdam in a fibre-to-the home (FttH) network* (OJ L247, 16.9.2008, p 27).

23 Commission Notice on the application of Articles 87 and 88 of the EC Treaty to State aid in the form of guarantees (OJ C155, 20.6.2008, p 10) and the Corrigendum to the Notice (OJ C244, 25.9.2008, p 32).

24 According to the case law, undertakings entrusted with the operation of services of general economic interest must have been assigned that task by an act of a public authority. In this respect, a service of general economic interest may be entrusted to an operator through the grant of a public service concession; see Joined Cases T-204/97 and T-270/97 EPAC — *Empresa para a Agroalimentação e Cereais, SA v Commission* [2000] ECR II-2267, paragraph 126 and Case T-17/02 *Fred Olsen, SA v Commission* [2005] ECR II-2031, paragraphs 186, 188-189.

25 Case C-280/00, *Altmark Trans GmbH and Regierungspräsidium Magdeburg v Nahverkehrsgesellschaft Altmark GmbH* [2003] ECR I-7747.

26 OJ C8, 11.1.2012, p 4.

27 OJ L7, 11.1.2012, p 3.

28 OJ C8, 11.1.2012, p 15.

29 OJ L114, 26.4.2012, p 8.

30 See point 48 of the Commission Communication on the application of the EU State aid rules to compensation granted for the provision of services of general economic interest and point 13 of the Commission Communication on a European Union framework for State aid in the form of public service compensation (2011).

31 See paragraphs 49 of the Commission Communication on the application of the EU State aid rules to compensation granted for the provision of services of general economic interest.

32 The term in the 'near future' should be understood as referring to a period of 3 years in line with paragraph 63 of these Guidelines.

33 In line with the principle expressed in paragraph 50 of the Commission Communication on the application of the EU State aid rules to compensation granted for the provision of services of general economic interest. See also Commission Decision N 284/05 — Ireland, Regional broadband Programme: *Metropolitan Area* Networks (MANs), phases II and III and N 890/06 — France, *Aide du Sicoval pour un réseau de très haut débit*.

34 The passive network infrastructure is basically the physical infrastructure of the networks. For a definition, see the Glossary.

35 A network should be technologically neutral and thus enable access seekers to use any of the available technologies to provide services to end-users.

36 In line with paragraph 78(g) of these Guidelines.

37 This limitation is justified by the fact that, once a broadband network providing universal connectivity has been deployed, the market forces are normally sufficient to provide communication services to all users at a competitive price.

38 Such safeguards should include, in particular, an obligation of accounting separation, and may also include the setting up of a structurally and legally separate entity from the vertically integrated operator. Such entity should have sole responsibility for complying with and delivering the SGEI mission assigned to it.

39 It is for Member States to devise, given the particularities of each case, the most appropriate methodology to ensure that the compensation granted will only cover the costs of discharging the SGEI mission in the white spots in line with the principles of the SGEI package, taking into account the relevant revenue and a reasonable profit. For instance, the compensation granted could be based on a comparison between revenues accruing from the commercial exploitation of the infrastructure in the profitable areas already covered by commercial operators and the revenues accruing from the commercial exploitation in the white spots. Any profit in excess of a reasonable profit, i.e. profits beyond the average industry return on capital for deploying a given broadband infrastructure, could be assigned to the financing of the SGEI in the non-profitable areas while the remaining profits could be part of the financial compensation granted. See Commission Decision in Case N 331/08, France — *THD Hauts de Seine*.

40 However, where future costs and revenue developments are surrounded by a high degree of uncertainty and there is a strong asymmetry of information, the public authority may also wish to adopt compensation models that are not entirely *ex ante*, but rather a mix of *ex ante* and *ex post* (e.g. using clawbacks such as to allow a balanced sharing of unanticipated gains).

41 For reference, see footnote 2.

42 For instance, digging, laying down cables, in-house wirings. In case of deploying fibre to the home networks, such costs could entail up to 70%-80% of the total investment costs.

43 See also N 383/09 — Germany — Amendment of N 150/08 Broadband in the rural areas of Saxony. This case concerned a situation where general civil engineering works, like road maintenances, did not constitute State aid. The measures taken by the German authorities constituted 'general civil engineering works' which would have been carried out by the State for maintenance purposes in any event. The possibility of placing ducts and broadband infrastructure at the occasion of the road maintenance — and at the costs of the operators — was announced publicly and not limited to or geared towards the broadband sector. However, it cannot be excluded that public funding of such works falls within the notion of aid of Article 107(1) TFEU if they are limited to or clearly geared towards the broadband sector.

44 See, for instance, the German NRA's 'Infrastrukturatlas', where operators voluntarily share information on the available and potential reusable infrastructures.

45 It should be recalled that the EU regulatory framework for e-communications gives the competent national authorities the possibility to require undertakings to provide the necessary information in order for these authorities to be able to establish, in conjunction with NRAs, a detailed inventory of the nature, availability and geographical location of network elements and facilities, and make it available to interested parties. See Article 12(4) of Directive 2002/21/EC of the European Parliament and of the Council of 7 March 2002 on a common regulatory Framework for Electronic Communications Networks and services (Framework Directive) as amended by Directive 2009/140/EC of the European Parliament and of the Council of 25 November 2009.

46 The list of all the Commission decisions taken under the State aid rules concerning broadband is available at ec.europa.eu/competition/sectors/telecommunications/broadband_decisions.pdf

47 For instance, loans (as opposed to grants) may be a useful tool to counteract the lack of credit for long-term infrastructure investments.

48 This is without prejudice to the possible application of the Regional Aid Guidelines as referred to in paragraph 31.

49 Guidelines on national regional aid applicable *ratione temporis* (e.g. Guidelines on national regional aid for 2007-2013 (OJ C54, 4.3.2006, p 13).

50 However, the fact that a specific company may not be capable of undertaking a project without aid does not mean that there is a market failure. For instance, the decision of a company not to invest in a project with low profitability or in a region with limited market demand and/or poor cost competitiveness may not be an indication of a market failure, but rather of a market that functions well.

51 Satellite systems also have unit costs, but in larger steps and, therefore, tend to be more independent of population density.

52 For municipal and regional funding, see Commission Decisions in Cases SA.33420 (11/N) — Germany, *Breitband Lohr am Main*, N 699/09 — Spain, *Desarrollo del programa de infraestructuras de telecomunicaciones en la Región de Murcia*.

53 Often Member States notify framework programmes which describe under which conditions municipal or regional funding can be granted to broadband deployment. See, for instance, N 62/10 — Finland, *High-speed broadband construction aid in sparsely populated areas of Finland*, N 53/10 — Germany, *Federal framework programme on duct support*, or N 30/10 — Sweden, *State aid to Broadband within the framework of the rural development program*.

54 For reference, see above footnote 5.

55 This would increase transparency, ease the administrative burden on local authorities and could mean that NRAs would not have to analyse each State aid case individually.

56 See, for instance, *Avis N° 12-A-02 du 17 janvier 2012 relatif à une demande d'avis de la commission de l'économie, du développement durable et de l'aménagement du territoire du Sénat concernant le cadre d'intervention des collectivités territoriales en matière de déploiement des réseaux à très haut débit* (French Competition Authority's opinion in relation

to the deployment of very high speed broadband networks).

57 See, for instance, Commission Decisions in Cases N 237/08 *Broadband support in Niedersachsen, Germany* or SA.33671 *Broadband Delivery UK, United Kingdom.*

58 See, for instance, Commission Decision N 473/07 — Italy, *Broadband connection for Alto Adige*, Decision N 570/07 — Germany, *Broadband in rural areas of Baden-Württemberg*.

59 In particular to promote take-up of already available broadband solutions, be they locally available terrestrial fixed or wireless networks or generally available satellite solutions.

60 See, for instance, Commission Decision N 222/06 — Italy, *Aid to bridge the digital divide in Sardinia*.

61 This may, for instance, apply to mobile LTE (long-term evolution) or LTE advanced operators with coverage targets under their licence conditions. in the target area. Similarly, if an operator designated with an universal service obligation (USO) receives public service compensation, no additional State aid can be granted to finance the same network.

62 This type of effects can be referred to as 'crowding out'.

63 See, for instance, Case C-156/98 *Germany v Commission* [2000] ECR I-6857, paragraph 78 and Case C-333/07 *Régie Networks* [2008] ECR I-10807, paragraphs 94-116.

64 For instance, marginal investments related merely to the upgrade of the active components of the network should not be considered eligible for State aid. Similarly, although certain copper enhancing technologies (such as vectoring) could increase the capabilities of the existing networks, they may not require significant investments in new infrastructure hence should not be eligible for State aid.

65 For instance, an upgrade from a basic to an NGA broadband network. Also certain upgrades of an NGA network (such as extension of fibre connectivity nearer to the end-user) could constitute a step change. In areas where broadband networks are already present, the application of the step change should ensure that the use of State aid does not lead to a duplication of existing infrastructure. Similarly, a small, gradual upgrade of existing infrastructures, for instance from 12 Mbps to 24 Mbps is unlikely to bring additional service capabilities (and would likely disproportionately favour the existing operator).

66 The subsidised network should be pro-competitive, i.e. allow for effective access at different levels of the infrastructure in the way indicated in paragraph 78 and, in the case of support to NGA deployment, also in paragraph 80.

67 See, for instance, Commission Decision in Case SA.33671 *Broadband Delivery UK, United Kingdom.*

68 Such a common methodology may be provided by the Commission.

3. THE ASSESSMENT OF STATE AID FOR BROADBAND

3.1. TYPES OF BROADBAND NETWORKS

[5.349]

(55) For the purposes of State aid assessment, the present Guidelines distinguish between basic and NGA networks.

(56) Several different technology platforms can be considered as basic broadband networks including asymmetric digital subscriber lines (up to ADSL2+ networks), non-enhanced cable (e.g. DOCSIS 2.0), mobile networks of third generation (UMTS) and satellite systems.

(57) At the current stage of market and technological development,[69] NGA networks are access networks which rely wholly or partly on optical elements[70] and which are capable of delivering broadband access services with enhanced characteristics as compared to existing basic broadband networks.[71]

(58) NGA networks are understood to have at least the following characteristics: (i) deliver services reliably at a very high speed per subscriber through optical (or equivalent technology) backhaul sufficiently close to user premises to guarantee the actual delivery of the very high speed; (ii) support a variety of advanced digital services including converged all-IP services; and (iii) have substantially higher upload speeds (compared to basic broadband networks). At the current stage of market and technological development, NGA networks are: (i) fibre-based access networks (FTTx);[72] (ii) advanced upgraded cable networks;[73] and (iii) certain advanced wireless access networks capable of delivering reliable high speeds per subscriber.[74]

(59) It is important to bear in mind that in the longer term NGA networks are expected to supersede existing basic broadband networks and not just to upgrade them. To the extent that NGA networks require a different network architecture, offering significantly better quality broadband services than today as well as the provision of multiple services that could not be supported by today's broadband networks, it is likely that in the future there will be marked differences emerging between areas that will be covered and areas that will not covered by NGA networks.[75]

(60) Member States can freely decide what form their intervention will take, provided it complies with State aid rules. In some cases, Member States might decide to finance so-called next generation networks (NGN), i.e. backhaul networks which do not reach the end-user. Backhaul networks are a necessary input for retail telecommunication operators to provide access services to the end-users. These types of networks are able to sustain both basic and NGA types of networks;[76] it is the (investment) choice of the telecommunication operators what type of 'last mile' infrastructure they wish to connect to the backhaul network.[77] Public authorities may also decide to undertake just civil engineering works (such as digging on public land, construction of ducts) in order to enable and accelerate the deployment by the operators concerned of their own network elements. Furthermore, when suitable, public authorities might also wish to take satellite solutions into account.

3.2. THE DISTINCTION BETWEEN WHITE, GREY AND BLACK AREAS FOR BASIC BROADBAND NETWORKS

(61) In order to assess market failure and equity objectives, a distinction can be made between the types of areas that may be targeted. This distinction is explained in the following sections. In the identification of the targeted areas, whenever the public intervention is limited to the backhaul part of the network, the State aid assessment will take into account the situation on both the backhaul markets and the access markets.[78]

(62) The different standards to justify public interventions in these geographical areas will be described below.

(63) For the purpose of identifying the geographical areas as white, grey or black as described below, the aid granting authority needs to determine whether broadband infrastructures exist in the targeted area. In order to further ensure that the public intervention does not disrupt private investments, the aid granting authorities should also verify whether private investors have concrete plans to roll out their own infrastructure in the near future. The term 'near future' should be understood as referring to a period of 3 years.[79] If the granting authority takes a longer time horizon for the deployment of the subsidised infrastructure, the same time horizon should also be used to assess the existence of commercial investment plans.

(64) To verify that there are no private investors planning to roll out their own infrastructure in the near future, the aid granting authority should publish a summary of the planned aid measure and invite interested parties to comment.

(65) There exists the risk that a mere 'expression of interest' by a private investor could delay delivery of broadband services in the target area if subsequently such investment does not take place while at the same time public intervention has been stalled. The aid granting authority could therefore require certain commitments from the private investor before deferring the public intervention. These commitments should ensure that significant progress in terms of coverage will be made within the 3-year period or for the longer period foreseen for the supported investment. It may further request the respective operator to enter into a corresponding contract which outlines the deployment commitments. This contract could foresee a number of 'milestones' which would have to be achieved during the 3-year period[80] and reporting on the progress made. If a milestone is not achieved, the granting authority may then go ahead with its public intervention plans. This rule applies both for basic and for NGA networks.

'WHITE AREAS': PROMOTING TERRITORIAL COHESION AND THE ECONOMIC DEVELOPMENT OBJECTIVE

(66) 'White areas' are those in which there is no broadband infrastructure and it is unlikely to be developed in the near future. The Commission targets for the DAE aim for a ubiquitous coverage of basic broadband services in the EU by 2013 and of at least 30 Mbps by 2020. It is therefore a priority to ensure timely investment in areas which are not yet sufficiently covered. The Commission acknowledges therefore that by providing financial support for the provision of broadband services in areas where broadband is currently not available, Member States pursue genuine cohesion and economic development objectives and thus, their intervention is likely to be in line with the common interest, provided the conditions set out in Section 3.4 below are fulfilled.[81]

'GREY AREAS': NEED FOR A MORE DETAILED ASSESSMENT

(67) 'Grey areas' are those in which one network operator is present and another network[82] is unlikely to be developed in the near future. The mere existence of one network operator[83] does not necessarily imply that no market failure or cohesion problem exists. If that operator has market power (monopoly) it may provide citizens with a suboptimal combination of service quality and prices. Certain categories of users may not be adequately served or, in the absence of regulated wholesale access tariffs, retail prices may be higher than those charged for the same services offered in more competitive but otherwise comparable areas or regions of the country. If, in addition, there are only limited prospects that alternative operators enter the market, the funding of an alternative infrastructure could be an appropriate measure.[84]

(68) On the other hand, in areas where there is already one broadband network operator, subsidies for the construction of an alternative network could distort market dynamics. Therefore, State support for the deployment of broadband networks in 'grey' areas is only justified when it can be clearly demonstrated that a market failure persists. A more detailed analysis and a thorough compatibility assessment will be necessary.

(69) Grey areas could be eligible for State support, provided the compatibility conditions of in Section 3.4 are met, if it is proved that (i) no affordable or adequate services are offered to satisfy the needs of citizens or business users[85] and that (ii) there are no less distortive measures available (including *ex ante* regulation) to reach the same goals.

(70) To establish (i) and (ii), the Commission will assess in particular whether:

(a) the overall market conditions are not adequate, by looking, inter alia, into the level of current broadband prices, the type of services offered to end-users (residential and business users) and the conditions attached thereto;

(b) in the absence of *ex ante* regulation imposed by an NRA, effective network access is not offered to third parties or access conditions are not conducive to effective competition;

(c) overall entry barriers preclude the potential entry of other electronic communication operators;[86] and

(d) any measures taken or remedies imposed by the competent national regulatory or competition authority with regard to the existing network provider have not been able to overcome such problems.

(71) Only grey areas that meet the eligibility criteria listed above will undergo the compatibility test described in Section 3.4.

'BLACK AREAS': NO NEED FOR STATE INTERVENTION

(72) When in a given geographical zone there are or there will be in the near future at least two basic broadband networks of different operators and broadband services are provided under competitive conditions (infrastructure-based competition,[87] it can be assumed that there is no market failure. Accordingly, there is very little scope for State intervention to bring further benefits. On the contrary, State support for the funding of the construction of an additional broadband network with comparable capabilities will, in principle, lead to an unacceptable distortion of competition, and the crowding out of private investors. Accordingly, in the absence of a clearly demonstrated market failure, the Commission will take a negative view of measures to fund the roll-out of an additional broadband infrastructure in a 'black area'.[88]

3.3. THE DISTINCTION BETWEEN WHITE, GREY AND BLACK AREAS FOR NGA NETWORKS

(73) The distinction made above in Section 3.2 between 'white', 'grey' and 'black' areas is relevant also for assessing whether State aid for NGA networks is compatible with the internal market under Article 107(3)(c).

(74) At present, by upgrading active equipment, certain advanced basic broadband networks can also support some broadband services which in the future are likely to be offered over NGA networks (such as triple play services) and thereby contribute to meeting the DAE targets. However, novel products or services which are not substitutable from the perspective of either demand or supply may emerge and will require capacity, reliability and substantially higher upload and download speeds beyond the upper physical limits of basic broadband infrastructure.

'WHITE NGA AREAS'

(75) Accordingly, for the purposes of assessing State aid for NGA networks, an area where NGA networks do not at present exist and where they are not likely to be built within 3 years in line with paragraphs 63 to 65 by private investors, should be considered to be a 'white NGA' area. Such an area is eligible for State aid to NGA provided the compatibility conditions indicated in Sections 3.4 and 3.5 are fulfilled.

'GREY NGA AREAS'

(76) An area should be considered a 'grey NGA' area where only one NGA network[89] is in place or is being deployed in the coming 3 years and there are no plans by any operator to deploy a NGA network in the coming 3 years. In assessing whether other network investors could deploy additional NGA networks in a given area, account should be taken of any existing regulatory or legislative measures that may have lowered barriers for such network deployments (access to ducts, sharing of infrastructure, etc.). The Commission will need to carry out a more detailed analysis in order to verify whether State intervention is needed since State intervention in such areas carries a high risk of crowding out existing investors and distorting competition. In this respect, the Commission will carry out its assessment on the basis of the compatibility conditions established in these Guidelines.

'BLACK NGA AREAS'

(77) If at least two NGA networks of different operators exist in a given area or will be deployed in the coming 3 years, such an area should be considered a 'black NGA' area. The Commission will consider that State support for an additional publicly funded, equivalent NGA network in such areas is likely to seriously distort competition and is incompatible with the internal market under Article 107(3)(c) of the TFEU.

3.4. DESIGN OF THE MEASURE AND THE NEED TO LIMIT DISTORTIONS OF COMPETITION

(78) Every State measure in support of broadband deployment should fulfil all compatibility principles described above in Section 2.5, including the common interest objective, the existence of market failure, the appropriateness and the incentive effect of the measure. As regards limiting the distortions of competition, besides the demonstration of how a 'step change' is achieved in all cases (in white, grey and black areas),[90] the following necessary conditions must be fulfilled to demonstrate the proportionality of the measure. Failure to meet any of these conditions would most likely require an in-depth assessment[91] which could result in a conclusion that the aid is incompatible with the internal market.

(a) Detailed *mapping and analysis of coverage*: Member States should clearly identify which geographic areas will be covered by the support measure in question,[92] whenever possible in cooperation with the competent national bodies. The consultation of the NRA is encouraged but optional. Best practice examples suggest creation of a central database of the available infrastructure at a national level thereby increasing transparency and reducing the costs for the implementation of smaller, local projects. Member States have the freedom to define the target areas, however, they are encouraged to take into account economic conditions in the definition of relevant regions before launching the tender.[93]

(b) *Public consultation*: Member States should give adequate publicity to the main characteristics of the measure and to the list of target areas by publishing the relevant information of the project and inviting to comment. A publication on a central web page at national level would in principle ensure that such information is made available to all interested stakeholders. By also verifying the results of the mapping in a public consultation Member States minimise distortions of competition with existing providers and with those who already have investment plans for the near future and enable these investors to plan their activities.[94] A detailed mapping exercise and a thorough consultation ensure not only a high degree of transparency but serve also as an essential tool for defining the existence of 'white', 'grey' and 'black' areas.[95]

(c) *Competitive selection process*: Whenever the granting authorities select a third-party operator to deploy and operate the subsidised infrastructure,[96] the selection process shall be conducted in line with spirit and the principles of the EU Public Procurement Directives.[97] It ensures that there is transparency for all investors wishing to bid for the implementation and/or management of the subsidised project. Equal and non-discriminatory treatment of all bidders and objective evaluation criteria are indispensable conditions. The competitive tender is a method to reduce budgetary costs, to minimise the potential State aid involved and at the same time reduces the selective nature of the measure insofar as the choice of the beneficiary is not known in advance.[98] Member States shall ensure a transparent process[99] and a competitive outcome[100] and shall use a dedicated central website at the national level to publish all on-going tender procedures on broadband State aid measures.[101]

(d) *Most economically advantageous offer*: Within the context of a competitive tender procedure, the aid granting authority shall establish qualitative award criteria on which the submitted bids are assessed. Relevant award criteria may include, for instance, the achieved geographical coverage,[102] sustainability of the technological approach or the impact of the proposed solution on competition.[103] Such qualitative criteria have to be weighed against the requested aid amount. In order to reduce the amount of aid to be granted, at similar if not identical quality conditions, the bidder with the lowest amount of aid requested should in principle receive more priority points within the overall assessment of its bid. The awarding authority shall always specify in advance the relative weighting which it will give to each of the (qualitative) criteria chosen.

(e) *Technological neutrality*: As different technological solutions exist to provide broadband services, the tender should not favour or exclude any particular technology or network platform. Bidders should be entitled to propose the provision of the required broadband services using or combining whatever technology they deem most suitable. On the basis of the objective tender criteria, the granting authority is then entitled to select the most suitable technological solution or mix of technology solutions. In principle, universal coverage of larger target areas can be reached with a mix of technologies.

(f) *Use of existing infrastructure*: Since the reusability of existing infrastructure is one of the main determinants for the cost of broadband roll-out, Member States should encourage bidders to have recourse to any available existing infrastructure so as to avoid unnecessary and wasteful duplication of resources and to reduce the amount of public funding. Any operator which owns or controls infrastructure (irrespective of whether it is actually used) in the target area and which wishes to participate in the tender, should fulfil the following conditions: (i) to inform the aid granting authority and the NRA about that infrastructure during the public consultation; (ii) to provide all relevant information to other bidders at a point in time which would allow the latter to include such infrastructure in their bid. Member States should setup a national database on the availability of existing infrastructures that could be reused for broadband roll-out.

(g) *Wholesale access*: Third parties' effective wholesale access to a subsidised broadband infrastructure is an indispensable component of any State measure supporting broadband. In particular, wholesale access enables third-party operators to compete with the selected bidder (when the latter is also present at the retail level), thereby strengthening choice and competition in the areas concerned by the measure while at the same time avoiding the creation of regional service monopolies. Applying only to State aid beneficiaries, this condition is not contingent on any prior market analysis within the meaning of Article 7 of the Framework Directive.[104] The type of wholesale access obligations imposed on a subsidised network should be aligned with the portfolio of access obligations laid down under the sectoral regulation.[105] In principle, subsidised companies should provide a wider range of wholesale access products than those mandated by NRAs under sectoral regulation to the operators who have significant market power[106] since the aid beneficiary is using not just its own resources but taxpayers' money to deploy its own infrastructure.[107] Such wholesale access should be granted as early as possible before starting the network operation.[108]

Effective wholesale access to the subsidised infrastructure[109] should be offered for at least a period of 7 years. If at the end of the 7-year period the operator of the infrastructure in question is designated by the NRA under the applicable regulatory framework as having significant market power (SMP) in the specific market concerned, access obligations would need to be imposed in accordance with the Electronic Communications Regulatory Framework. NRAs or other competent national bodies are encouraged to publish guidance for granting authorities on the principles to set wholesale access conditions and tariffs. In order to allow effective access, the same access conditions shall apply on the entirety of the subsidised network, including on the parts of such network where existing infrastructures have been used.[110] The access obligations shall be enforced irrespective of any change in ownership, management or operation of the subsidised infrastructure.

(h) *Wholesale access pricing*: Benchmarking is an important tool for ensuring that the aid granted will serve to replicate market conditions like those prevailing in other competitive broadband markets. Wholesale access price, should be based on the pricing principles set by the NRA and on benchmarks and should take into account the aid received by the network operator.[111] For the benchmark, the average published wholesale prices that prevail in other comparable, more competitive areas of the country or the Union shall be taken or, in the absence of such published prices, prices already set or approved by the NRA for the markets and services concerned. If there are no published or regulated prices available for certain wholesale access products to benchmark against, the pricing should follow the principles of cost orientation pursuant to the methodology established in accordance with the sectorial regulatory framework.[112] Given the complexity of benchmarking wholesale access prices, Member States are encouraged to provide a mandate and the necessary staffing to the NRA to advice aid granting authorities on such matters. A detailed description of the aid project should be sent to the NRA at least 2 months prior to the notification to allow the NRA to have a reasonable period of time to provide its opinion. Where the NRA has obtained such competence, the aid granting authority should seek advice from the NRA in setting the wholesale access prices and conditions. The benchmarking criteria should be clearly indicated in the tender documents.

(i) *Monitoring and clawback mechanism*: The granting authorities shall closely monitor the implementation of the broadband project during the entire duration of the project. Where the operator is selected on the basis of a competitive procurement procedure, there is typically less need to monitor the subsequent development of the profitability of the project. In many circumstances, it may be appropriate to fix the aid amount on an *ex ante* basis, so as to cover the expected funding gap over a given period, rather than to establish the aid amount on the basis of costs and revenues as they are incurred. In the former model, there are typically more incentives for the company to contain costs and to become more efficient over time. However, where future costs and revenue developments are surrounded by a high degree of uncertainty and there is a strong asymmetry of information, the public authority may also wish to adopt financing models that are not entirely *ex ante*, but rather a mix of *ex ante* and *ex post* (e.g. using clawbacks such as to allow a balanced sharing of unanticipated gains). In order not to put a disproportionally high burden on small, local projects, a minimum threshold may be justified for the clawback mechanism. Therefore, Member States should implement the clawback mechanism if the aid amount of the project is above EUR 10 million.[113] Granting authorities can foresee that any extra profit reclaimed from the selected bidder could be spent for further broadband network expansion within the framework scheme and at the same conditions of the original aid measure. An accounting separation obligation for the winning bidder as regards the subsidy received will make it easier for the granting authorities to monitor the implementation of the scheme as well as any extra profit generated.[114]

(j) *Transparency*: [Member States shall ensure the publication of the following information on a comprehensive State aid website, at national or regional level:

— the full text of the approved aid scheme or the individual aid granting decision and its implementing provisions, or a link to it,

— the identity of the granting authority/(ies),

— the identity of the individual beneficiaries, the form and amount of aid granted to each beneficiary, the date of granting, the type of undertaking (SME/large company), the region in which the beneficiary is located (at NUTS level II) and the principal economic sector in which the beneficiary has its activities (at NACE group level).[114A]

Such a requirement can be waived with respect to individual aid awards below EUR 500,000. For schemes in the form of tax advantage, the information on individual aid amounts[114B] can be provided in the following ranges (in EUR million): {0.5–1}; {1–2}; {2–5}; {5–10}; {10–30}; {30 and more}.

Such information must be published after the decision to grant the aid has been taken, must be kept for at least 10 years and must be available to the general public without restrictions.[114C] Member States will not be required to publish the abovementioned information before 1 July 2016.[114D]]

The aid beneficiary is obliged to provide entitled third parties with comprehensive and non-discriminatory access to information on its infrastructure (including, inter alia, ducts, street cabinets and fibre) deployed under a State aid measure.[115] This will enable other operators to easily ascertain the possibility to access such infrastructure and should provide all relevant information about the broadband network to a central register of broadband infrastructures, if such database exists within the Member State, and/or to the NRA.

(k) *Reporting*: Starting from the date when the network is put into use, for the duration of the aid measure, the State aid granting authority should report every 2 years key information on the aid projects to the European Commission.[116] In the case of national or regional framework schemes, the national or regional authorities should consolidate the information of the individual measures and report to the European Commission. When adopting a decision under these Guidelines the Commission may require additional reporting regarding the aid granted.

3.5. SUPPORTING THE RAPID DEPLOYMENT OF NGA NETWORKS

(79) As with the policy followed with respect to basic broadband deployment, State aid in favour of NGA network deployment may constitute an appropriate and justified instrument, provided that a number of fundamental conditions are fulfilled. While commercial operators take their investment decisions in NGA networks on the basis of the expected profitability, the choice of the public authority has to take into account also the public interest in funding an open and neutral platform on which multiple operators will be able to compete for the provision of services to the end-users.

(80) Any measure to support NGA deployment must fulfil the compatibility conditions indicated in Sections 2.5 and 3.4. In addition, the following conditions must be met, taking into account the specific situations in which the public investment in NGA networks will occur.

(a) *Wholesale access*: Due to the economics of NGAs, it is of utmost importance to ensure effective wholesale access for third-party operators. Especially in areas in which there are already competing basic broadband operators,[117] in which it has to be ensured that the competitive market situation which existed before the intervention is preserved. The access conditions described above in Section 3.4 are specified as follows. The subsidised network must therefore offer access under fair and non-discriminatory conditions to all operators who request it and will provide them with the possibility of effective and full unbundling.[118] Moreover, third-party operators must have access to passive and not only active[119] network infrastructure.[120] Apart from bitstream access and unbundled access to the local loop and sub-loop, the access obligation should therefore also include the right to use ducts and poles, dark fibre or street cabinets.[121] Effective wholesale access should be granted for at least 7 years and the right of access to ducts or poles should not be limited in time. This is without prejudice to any similar regulatory obligations that may be imposed by the NRA in the specific market concerned in order to foster effective competition or measures adopted during or after the expiry of that period.[122]

It may be the case that in areas with low population density, where there are limited broadband services, or for small local companies, the imposition of all types of access products might disproportionately increase investment costs[123] without delivering significant benefits in terms of increased competition.[124] In such a situation, one may envisage that access products requiring costly interventions on the subsidised infrastructure not otherwise foreseen (e.g. co-location in intermediary distribution points) be offered only in case of a reasonable demand from a third-party operator. The demand is considered reasonable if (i) the access seeker provides a coherent business plan which justifies the development of the product on the subsidised network and (ii) no comparable access product is already offered in the same geographic area by another operator at equivalent prices to those of more densely populated areas.[125]

By contrast, the preceding paragraph cannot be invoked in more densely populated areas where one may expect infrastructure competition to develop. Therefore, in such areas, the subsidised network should satisfy all types of network access products that operators may seek.[126]

(b) *Fair and non-discriminatory treatment*: The subsidised infrastructure must enable the provision of competitive and affordable services to end-users by competing operators. Where the network operator is vertically integrated, adequate safeguards must be put in place to prevent any conflict of interest, undue discrimination towards access seekers or content providers and any other hidden indirect advantages. In the same vein, the award criteria should contain the provision that bidders proposing a wholesale-only model, a passive-only model or both shall receive additional points.

(81) State aid projects aiming at the funding of backhaul networks[127] or limited to civil works open for access to all operators and technologies exhibit especially pro-competitive features. This feature will be taken into account in the assessment of such projects.

3.6. AID TO ULTRA-FAST BROADBAND NETWORKS

(82) In light of the Digital Agenda objectives, in particular achieving 50% penetration to Internet connections above 100 Mbps, and taking into account that especially in urban areas there may be higher performance needs compared to what commercial investors are willing to offer in the near future, by way of derogation to paragraph 77, public intervention could exceptionally be allowed for NGA networks able to provide ultra-fast speeds well above 100 Mbps.

(83) In 'black NGA' areas, such intervention could only be allowed if the 'step change' required by paragraph 51 is proved on the basis of the following cumulative criteria:

(a) the existing or planned[128] NGA networks do not reach the end-user premises with fibre networks;[129]
(b) the market situation is not evolving towards the achievement of a competitive provision of ultra-fast services[130] above 100 Mbit/s in the near future by the investment plans of commercial operators in accordance with paragraphs 63 to 65;
(c) there is expected demand for such qualitative improvements.[131]

(84) In the situation described in the previous paragraph, any new subsidised network must respect the compatibility conditions of paragraphs 78 and 80. In addition, the aid granting authority must also demonstrate that:

(a) the subsidised network exhibits significant enhanced technological characteristics and performance compared to the verifiable characteristics and performance of existing or planned networks;[132] and
(b) the subsidised network will be based on an open architecture operated as a wholesale only network; and
(c) the aid does not lead to an excessive distortion of competition with other NGA technologies that have recently been the subject of significant new infrastructure investments by market operators in the same target areas.[133]

(85) Only if these additional conditions are fulfilled, public funding of such networks might be considered compatible under the balancing test. In other words, such funding would have to lead to a significant, sustainable, pro-competitive and non-temporary technological advancement without creating disproportionate disincentives to private investments.

NOTES

Para (78): words in square brackets in point (j) substituted, together with associated footnotes, by Commission Communication 2014/C198/02.

69 Due to rapid technological development, in the future other technologies may also be able to deliver NGA services.

70 Coaxial, wireless and mobile technologies make use, to a certain extent, of a fibre support infrastructure, thereby making them conceptually similar to a wired network using copper to deliver the service for the part of the last mile not covered by fibre.

71 The final connection to the end-user may be ensured both by wired and wireless technologies. Given the rapid evolution of advanced wireless technologies such as LTE-Advanced and the intensifying market deployment of LTE or Wi-Fi, next generation fixed wireless access (e.g. based on possibly tailored mobile broadband technology) could be a viable alternative to certain wired NGA (FTTCab, for example) if certain conditions are met. Since the wireless medium is 'shared' (the speed per user depends on the number of connected users in the area covered) and is inherently subject to fluctuating environmental conditions, in order to provide reliably the minimum download speeds per subscriber that can be expected of an NGA, next generation fixed wireless networks may need to be deployed at a certain degree of density and/or with advanced configurations (such as directed and/or multiple antennas). Next generation wireless access based on tailored mobile broadband technology must also ensure the required quality of service level to users at a fixed location while serving any other nomadic subscribers in the area of interest.

72 The term FTTx refers to FFTC, FTTN, FTTP, FTTH and FTTB.

73 Using at least the 'DOCSIS 3.0' cable modem standard.

74 See, for instance, Commission Decision in Case SA.33671 *Broadband Delivery UK, United Kingdom.*

75 If today the differences between an area where only narrowband Internet is available (dial-up) and an area where broadband exists means that the former is a 'white' area, likewise an area that lacks a next generation broadband infrastructure, but may still have one basic broadband infrastructure in place should also be considered a 'white' NGA area.

76 In comparison to other networks which do not reach the end consumer (like FTTC), an important characteristic of NGN backhaul infrastructure is that it is open for interconnection with other networks.

77 Commission Decision in Case N 407/09 — Spain — *Optical fibre Catalonia (Xarxa Oberta).*

78 Commission Decisions in Cases N 407/09 — Spain — *Optical fibre Catalonia (Xarxa Oberta)* and SA.33438 — Poland, *Broadband network for Eastern Poland.*

79 The 3-year period would start from the moment of publication of the planned aid measure.

80 In this regard, an operator should be able to demonstrate that within the 3-year period it will cover a substantial part of the territory and of the population concerned thereby. For instance, the aid granting authority may request any operator who declares an interest in building its own infrastructure in the target area to deliver a credible business plan, supporting documents like bank loan agreements and a detailed calendar deployment plan within 2 months. In addition, within 12 months the investment should be started and permission should be obtained for most of the rights of ways necessary for the project. Additional milestones on the progress of the measure can be agreed for every 6-month period.

81 See, for instance, Commission Decisions in Cases N 607/09 — Ireland, *Rural Broadband Reach*, or N 172/09 — Slovenia, Broadband development in Slovenia.

82 The same company may operate separate fixed and mobile networks in the same area but this will not change the 'colour' of such area.

83 The competitive situation is assessed according to the number of existing infrastructure operators. In Commission Decision N 330/10 — France, *Programme national Très Haut Débit*, it was clarified that the existence of several retail providers on one network (including Local Loop Unbundling (LLU)) does not turn the area into a black area, but that the territory remains a grey area as only one infrastructure is present. At the same time, the existence of competing operators (at the retail level) will be considered an indication that, albeit grey, the area in question may not be problematic in terms of presence of a market failure. Convincing proof of access problems or quality of service will have to be supplied.

84 In its Decision N 131/05 — United Kingdom, *FibreSpeed Broadband Project Wales*, the Commission had to assess

whether the financial support given by the Welsh authorities for the construction of an open, carrier-neutral, fibre-optic network linking 14 business parks could still be declared compatible even if the target locations were already served by the incumbent network operator, who provided price regulated leased lines. The Commission found that the leased lines offer by the incumbent operator was very expensive, almost unaffordable for SMEs. See also Commission Decision N 890/06 — France, *Aide du Sicoval pour un réseau de très haut débit* and Commission Decision N 284/05 — Ireland, *Regional Broadband Programme: Metropolitan Area Networks (MANs), phases II and III.*

85 In addition to the specifications of paragraph 70, the granting authorities could take into consideration indicators such as: the penetration rate for services with the highest performance levels, excessively high prices for high-performance services (including leased lines for end-users as explained in the previous footnote) having the effect of discouraging take up and innovation, e-government services in the process of being developed which require performances beyond the ones offered on the existing network. Where in the target area a significant proportion of citizens and business users are already adequately served, it has to be ensured that the public intervention does not lead to an undue overbuilt of the existing infrastructure. In that case, the public intervention may be limited to 'gap-filling' measures only.

86 For instance, whether the broadband network already in place was built on the basis of a privileged use/access to ducts not accessible by or not shared with other network operators.

87 If only one infrastructure is present, even if this infrastructure is used — via unbundling (LLU) — by several electronic communication operators, such situation shall be considered to be a competitive grey area. It is not considered as a 'black area' within the meaning of these Guidelines. See also Commission Decision in Case SA.31316 *Programme national "Très haut débit"*, France.

88 See Commission Decision of 19 July 2006 on the measure C 35/05 (ex N 59/05) — The Netherlands Broadband infrastructure in *Appingedam* (OJ L86, 27.3.2007, p 1). In this decision, the Commission noted that the competitive forces of the specific market were not duly taken into account. In particular, that the Dutch broadband market was a fast-moving market in which providers of electronic communications services, including cable operators and Internet Service Providers, were in the process of introducing very high capacity broadband services without any State support.

89 The same company may operate separate fixed and wireless NGA networks in the same area but this will not change the 'colour' of such area.

90 See paragraph 51 above.

91 The detailed assessment could necessitate the opening of a procedure according to Article 108(2) TFEU.

92 This mapping should be done on the basis of homes passed by a particular network infrastructure and not on the basis of the actual number of homes or customers connected as subscribers.

93 For instance, target areas that are too small might not provide sufficient economic incentives for market players to bid for the aid, while areas that are too big might reduce the competitive outcome of the selection process. Several selection procedures also allow different potential undertakings to benefit from State aid thereby avoiding that one (already dominant) operators' market share is further strengthened by State aid measures by favouring large market players or discouraging technologies which would mainly be competitive in smaller target areas.

94 In case where it can be demonstrated that existing operators did not provide any meaningful information to a public authority for the purposes of the required mapping exercise, such authorities would have to rely only on whatever information has been made available to them.

95 See, for instance, Commission Decision in Case N 266/08 — Germany, *Broadband in rural areas of Bayern.*

96 The situation is different when the public authority decides to deploy and manage the network directly (or through a fully owned entity) such as in Commission Decision in Case N 330/10 — France *Programme national Très Haut Débit and* SA.33807 (11/N) — Italy, *National Broadband Plan*. In such cases, to safeguard the results of competition that have been achieved since the liberalisation of the electronic communications sector in the Union, and in particular the competition that exists today on the retail broadband market, in case of a publicly managed subsidised networks (i) the publicly owned network operators shall limit their activity on the predefined target areas and shall not expand to other commercially attractive regions; (ii) the public authority shall limit its activity to maintain the passive infrastructure and to grant access to it, but shall not engage in competition on the retail levels with commercial operators; and (iii) to have an accounting separation between the funds used for the operation of the networks and the other funds at the disposal of the public authority.

97 Directive 2004/18/EC of the European Parliament and of the Council of 31 March 2004 on the coordination of procedures for the award of public works contracts, public supply contracts and public service contracts (OJ L134, 30.4.2004, p 114).

98 See, for instance, Commission Decision N 475/07 — Ireland, 'National Broadband Scheme (NBS)', Commission Decision N 157/06 — United Kingdom, 'South Yorkshire Digital region Broadband Project'.

99 When the object of such a competitive selection process is a public contract covered by the EU public procurement directives 2004/17/EC or 2004/18/EC, the tender notice shall be published in the Official Journal in order to ensure European-wide competition, in accordance with the requirements of these directives. In all other cases, tender information should be publicised at least nationwide.

100 In the case that a competitive selection process does not generate a sufficient number of bidders, the cost calculation proposed by the winning bidder may be put to examination by an external auditor.

101 If for technical reasons, it is not feasible to set up a national website, regional websites should be put in place. Such regional websites should be interconnected.

102 In terms of the geographic area as defined in the call for the competitive selection process.

103 For instance, network topologies allowing full and effective unbundling could receive more points. It should be noted that at this stage of market development, a point-to-point topology are more conducive for long-term competition in comparison with point-to-multipoint topology, while the deployment costs are comparable especially in urban areas. Point-to-multipoint networks will be able to provide full and effective unbundling only once wavelength-division-multiplexed passive optical network (WDM-PON) access is standardised and requested under the applicable regulatory frameworks.

104 Moreover, whenever Member States opt for a management model whereby the subsidised broadband infrastructure offers only wholesale access services to third parties, not retail services, the likely distortions of competition are further reduced as such a network management model helps to avoid potentially complex issues of margin squeeze and hidden forms of access discrimination. See, for instance, SA.30317 High-speed broadband in Portugal.

105 Whenever the State aid measure covers the funding of new passive infrastructure elements such as ducts or poles, access

to those should also be granted and be unlimited in time. See, for instance, Commission Decisions in Cases N 53/10 — Germany, *Federal framework programme on ducts support*, N 596/09 — Italy — *Bridging the digital divide in Lombardia*, N 383/09 — Germany — Amendment of N 150/08 *Broadband in the rural areas of Saxony*, N 330/10 — France, *Programme national Très Haut Débit*.

106 For example, for NGA networks, the point of reference should be the list of access products included in the NGA recommendation.

107 If State aid is provided to fund the construction of ducts, the latter should be large enough to cater for several cable networks and to host point-to-multipoint as well as point-to-point solutions.

108 Where the network operator also provides retail services, in line with the NGA recommendation, this would normally imply granting access at least 6 months before the launch of such retail services.

109 Effective wholesale access to the subsidised infrastructure can be provided by means of the wholesale access products detailed in Annex II.

110 For instance, the usage of wholesale access by third parties cannot be limited only to retail broadband services.

111 To what extent the aid amount is taken into account may vary depending on the competitive situation in the competitive selection process and in the target area. The benchmark would therefore be the upper limit of the wholesale price.

112 So that operators do not artificially inflate their costs, Member States are encouraged to use contracts which incentivise firms to reduce their costs with time. For instance, in contrast to cost-plus contracts, a fixed-price contract would give the company the incentive to reduce costs over time.

113 The clawback is not necessary in case of publicly owned, wholesale only infrastructures, managed by the public authority with the sole purpose to grant fair and non-discriminatory access to all operators if the conditions specified in footnote 96 are met.

114 Best practice examples suggest monitoring and clawback for a minimum of 7 years, and any extra profit (i.e. profit higher than in the original business plan or the industry average) to be shared between the beneficiary and the public authorities according to the aid intensity of the measure.

114A With the exception of business secrets and other confidential information in duly justified cases and subject to the Commission's agreement (Commission communication on professional secrecy in State aid decisions, C(2003) 4582 (OJ C297, 9.12.2003, p 6)).

114B The amount to be published is the maximum allowed tax benefit and not the amount deducted each year (e.g. in the context of tax credit, the maximum allowed tax credit shall be published rather than the actual amount which might depend on the taxable revenues and vary each year).

114C This information shall be published within 6 months from the date of granting (or, for aid in the form of tax advantage, within 1 year from the date the tax declaration is due). In case of unlawful aid, Member States will be required to ensure the publication of this information ex post, at least within 6 months from the date of the Commission decision. The information shall be available in a format which allows data to be searched, extracted, and easily published on the internet, for instance in CSV or XML format.

114D Publication of information on aid awards granted before 1 July 2016 and, for fiscal aid, publication for aid claimed or granted before 1 July 2016, will not be required.

115 This information should be regularly updated (for example every 6 months) and shall be available in non-proprietary formats.

116 Such information should at least include: besides the information already made public following paragraph 78(j), the date when the network is put into use, the wholesale access products, the number of access seekers and service providers on the network, the number of houses passed, take-up rates.

117 Including LLU operators.

118 At this stage of market development, a point-to-point topology can be effectively unbundled. If the selected bidder rolls out a point-to-multipoint topology network, it shall have a clear obligation to provide effective unbundling via wavelength division multiplexing (WDM) as soon as the access is standardised and commercially available. Until WDM unbundling becomes effective, the selected bidder shall be required to provide access seekers with a virtual unbundling product, as close as possible to physical unbundling.

119 If they are indirect beneficiaries, when they obtain access at the wholesale level, third-party operators may have to give bitstream access themselves. In spite of the fact that aid was only granted for passive infrastructure, also active access was requested, for instance in Commission Decision in Case N 330/10 — France, *Programme national Très Haut Débit*.

120 Such as Customer premise equipment (CPEs) or other equipment needed to operate the network. If it proves necessary to upgrade certain parts of the network in order to provide effective access, this shall be foreseen in the granting authorities' plans, for example: foreseeing adequately sized ducts, increasing the size of street cabinets to provide effective unbundling.

121 A strong access obligation is all the more crucial in order to deal with the temporary substitution between the services offered by existing ADSL operators and those offered by future NGA network operators. The access obligation will ensure that competing ADSL operators can migrate their customers to a NGA network as soon as a subsidised network is in place and thus start planning their own future investments without suffering a competitive handicap. See, for instance, N 461/09 — United Kingdom, *Cornwall and Isles of Scilly Next Generation Broadband*.

122 In this regard, the possible persistence of the specific market conditions that justified the granting of an aid for the infrastructure in question should be taken into consideration.

123 The disproportionate increase in costs must be proved with detailed and objective cost calculations by the granting authority.

124 For instance, see Commission Decision in Case N 330/10 — France, *Programme national Très Haut Débit* and in Case SA.33671 — United Kingdom, *Broadband Delivery UK*.

125 Other conditions may be accepted by the Commission as part of the proportionality analysis in light of the specificities of the case and the overall balancing exercise. See for example, Commission Decision in Case N 330/10 — France, *Programme national Très Haut Débit* and in Case SA.33671 — United Kingdom, *Broadband Delivery UK*. If the conditions are fulfilled, access should be granted within a period which is customary for the particular market. In the case of conflict, the aid granting authority should ask the NRA or another competent national body for an advice.

126 For instance, in case of passive fixed networks it shall be able to support both point-to-point as well as point-to-multipoint topologies depending on the choice of the operators. In particular in the more densely populated areas, should they be eligible for State aid, it would not be considered in the public interest to grant aid for investments

in simple upgrades of existing networks not bringing a step change also in terms of competition.

127 See above paragraph 60. Interventions going beyond the central office level will be considered already NGA and not NGN. See Commission Decision in Case SA.34031 — *Next generation broadband in Valle d'Aosta.*

128 Based on credible investment plans for the near future of 3 years in accordance with paragraphs 63 to 65.

129 For instance, NGA networks do not reach end-user premises with fibre in case of FTTN networks, where fibre is installed only until the nodes (cabinets). Similarly, some cable networks are also using fibre until the cabinets and connect end-users with coaxial cables.

130 For example, in an area where there is an FTTC or equivalent network and an upgraded cable network (at least DOCSIS 3.0) the market conditions are generally considered competitive enough to be able to evolve towards the provision of ultra-fast services without the need of public intervention.

131 See for example the indicators in footnote 84 and 85.

132 See paragraphs 63 to 65 above.

133 This would normally be the case when, due to the aid, market operators cannot recoup the infrastructure investments undertaken in an appropriate period taking into account normal amortisation time. The following (interconnected) factors will in particular be taken into account: the size of the investment, how recent it is, the minimum period required in order to get an adequate return on the investment and the likely effect of the roll-out of the new subsidised ultra-fast network on the number of subscribers to the existing NGA networks and the relative subscription prices.

4. FINAL PROVISIONS

[5.350]

(86) These Guidelines will be applied from the first day following its publication in the *Official Journal of the European Union*.

(87) The Commission will apply these Guidelines to all notified aid measures in respect of which it is called upon to take a decision after the Guidelines are published in the Official Journal, even where the projects were notified prior to that date.

(88) In accordance with the Commission notice on the determination of the applicable rules for the assessment of unlawful State aid,[134] the Commission will apply to unlawful aid the rules in force at the time when the aid was granted. Accordingly, it will apply these Guidelines in the case of unlawful aid granted after its publication.

(89) The Commission herewith proposes to Member States, on the basis of Article 108(1) TFEU, to take appropriate measures and amend, where necessary, their existing aid schemes in order to bring them into line with the provisions of these Guidelines within 12 months after their publication in the *Official Journal of the European Union*.

(90) The Member States are invited to give their explicit unconditional agreement to these proposed appropriate measures within 2 months from the date of publication of the Guidelines in the *Official Journal of the European Union*. In the absence of any reply, the Commission will assume that the Member State in question does not agree with the proposed measures.

(91) The Commission may review the present Guidelines on the basis of future important market, technological and regulatory developments.

NOTES

134 OJ C119, 22.5.2002, p 22.

ANNEXES

ANNEX I
TYPICAL INTERVENTIONS FOR BROADBAND SUPPORT

[5.351]

In its case practice, the Commission has observed certain most recurrent funding mechanisms used by Member States to foster broadband deployment, assessed under Article 107(1) TFEU. The following list is illustrative and not exhaustive, as public authorities might develop different ways of supporting broadband deployment or deviate from the models described. The constellations typically involve State aid, unless the investment is carried out in line with the market economy investor principle (see Section 2.2).

1. *Monetary allocation* (gap funding):[1] In the majority of cases examined by the Commission, the Member State[2] awards direct monetary grants to broadband investors[3] to build, manage and commercially exploit a broadband network.[4] Such grants normally involve State aid within the meaning of Article 107(1) TFEU, as the grant is financed by State resources and gives an advantage to the investor to conduct a commercial activity under conditions which would not have been available on the market. In such cases both the network operators receiving the grant and the electronic communication providers seeking wholesale access to the subsidised network are beneficiaries of the aid.

2. *Support in kind*: In other cases, Member States support broadband deployment by financing the roll-out of a full broadband network (or parts thereof) which is subsequently put at the disposal of electronic communication investors which will use these network elements for their own broadband deployment project. This support can take many forms, with the most recurring being Member States providing broadband passive infrastructure by carrying out civil engineering work (for instance by digging up a road) or by placing ducts or dark fibre.[5] Such forms of support create an advantage for the broadband investors who save the respective investment costs[6] as well as for electronic communication providers which seek wholesale access to the subsidised network.

3. *State-operated broadband network or parts thereof*: State aid can also be involved if the State, instead of providing support to a broadband investor, constructs (parts of) a broadband network and operates it directly through a branch of the public administration or via an in-house company.[7] This model of intervention typically consists of the construction of a publicly owned passive network infrastructure, with a view of making it available to broadband

operators by granting wholesale access to the network on non-discriminatory terms. Operating the network and granting of wholesale access to it against remuneration is an economic activity within the meaning of Article 107(1) TFEU. The construction of a broadband network with a view to its commercial exploitation constitutes an economic activity according to case law (i.e. State aid within the meaning of Article 107(1) TFEU can already be present at the moment of the construction of the broadband network).[8] Electronic communication providers seeking wholesale access to the publicly operated network will also be considered aid beneficiaries.

4. *Broadband network, managed by a concessionary*: Member States may also fund the roll-out of a broadband network, that remains in public ownership, but whose operation will be offered through a competitive tender procedure to a commercial operator to manage and exploit it at the wholesale level.[9] Also in this case, as the network is constructed with a view to its exploitation, the measure may constitute State aid. The operator managing and exploiting the network as well as third-party electronic communication providers seeking wholesale access to the network will also be considered aid beneficiaries.

NOTES

1 'Gap funding' refers to the difference between investment costs and expected profits for private investors.

2 Or any other public authority granting the aid.

3 The term 'investors' denotes undertakings or electronic communications network operators that invest in the construction and deployment of broadband infrastructures.

4 Examples of gap funding are Commission decisions in Cases SA.33438 a.o — Poland — *Broadband network project in Eastern Poland*, SA.32866 — Greece — *Broadband development in Greek rural areas*, SA.31851 — Italy — *Broadband Marche*, N 368/09 — Germany — Amendment of State aid broadband scheme N 115/08 — *Broadband in the rural areas of Germany*.

5 Commission decisions in Cases N 53/10 — Germany, *Federal framework programme on ducts support*, N 596/09 — Italy — *Bridging the digital divide in Lombardia*, see also N 383/09 — Germany — Amendment of N 150/08 *Broadband in the rural areas of Saxony*.

6 Civil engineering costs and other investment in passive infrastructure can constitute up to 70% of the total cost of a broadband project.

7 Commission decision in Case N 330/10 — France — *Programme national Très Haut Débit*, which covered various intervention modalities, inter alia one in which the *collectivités territoriales* can operate their own broadband networks as a 'regie' operation.

8 Case T-443/08 and T-455/08 *Freistaat Sachsen v Commission* (not yet published).

9 Commission decisions in Cases N 497/10 — United Kingdom, SHEFA — 2 *Interconnect*, N 330/10 — France — *Programme national Très Haut Débit*, N 183/09 — Lithuania, RAIN *project*.

ANNEX II
GLOSSARY OF TECHNICAL TERMS

[5.352]

For the purpose of these Guidelines, the following definitions should apply. The definitions are without prejudice to further market, technological and regulatory changes.

Access segment: 'Last mile' segment connecting the backhaul network with the end-user premises.

Backhaul network: The part of the broadband network which constitutes the intermediate link between the backbone network and the access network and carries data to and from the global network.

Bitstream access: Wholesale access provider installs a high-speed access link to the customer premises and makes this access link available to third parties.

Dark fibre: Unlit fibre without transmission systems connected.

Duct: Underground pipe or conduit used to house (fibre, copper or coax) cables of a broadband network.

Full unbundling: Physical unbundling grants access to the end-consumer access line and allows the competitor's own transmission systems to directly transmit over it. In certain circumstances, virtual unbundling may be considered equivalent to physical unbundling.

FTTH: Fibre-to-the-home network, which reaches the end-user premises with fibre, i.e. an access network consisting of optical fibres lines in both the feeder and the drop segments of the access network (including in-house wiring).

FTTB: Fibre-to-the-building, which reaches the end-user premises with fibre, i.e. fibre is rolled out to the building, but copper, coax or LAN is used within the building.

FTTN: Fibre-to the nodes, the fibre is terminated in a street cabinet up to several kilometres away from the customer premises, with the final connection being copper (in fibre to the cabinet/VDSL networks) or coax (in the cable/DOCSIS 3 network). Fibre-to-the-node is often seen as a temporary, interim step towards full FTTH.

Neutral networks: Networks which can sustain any type of network topologies. In case of FTTH networks, the infrastructure shall be able to support both point-to-point and point-to-multipoint topologies.

Next Generation Access Network: Access networks which rely wholly or partly on optical elements and which are capable of delivering broadband access services with enhanced characteristics as compared to existing basic broadband networks.

Passive network: Broadband network without any active component. Typically comprises civil engineering infrastructure, ducts and dark fibre and street cabinets.

Passive wholesale access: Access to a transmission medium without any electronic component.

Point-to-multipoint: A network topology that has dedicated individual customer lines to an intermediate passive node (e.g. street cabinet) where these lines are aggregated onto a shared line. Aggregation could be either passive (with splitters such as in a PON architecture) or active (such as FTTC).

Point-to-point: Network topology whereby the customer lines remain dedicated all the way from the customer to the metropolitan point of presence.

Wholesale access products: Access enables an operator to utilise the facilities of another operator. The wholesale access products that can be provided over the subsidised network are the following.

— FTTH/FTTB network: ducts access, access to dark fibre, unbundled access to the local loop (WDM-PON or optical distribution frame (ODF) unbundling), and bitstream access.

— Cable networks: duct access and bitstream access.

— FTTC networks: duct access, sub-loop unbundling and bitstream access.

— Passive network infrastructure: duct access, access to dark fibre and/or unbundled access to the local loop. In case of an integrated operator: the access obligations (differing from the passive infrastructure access) shall be imposed in accordance with the provisions of the NGA Recommendation.

— ADSL-based broadband networks: unbundled access to the local loop, bitstream access.

— Mobile or wireless networks: bitstream, sharing of physical masts and access to the backhaul networks.

— Satellite platform: bitstream access.

4. TRANSPORT

COMMISSION COMMUNICATION

(2004/C13/03)

Community guidelines on State aid to maritime transport

[5.353]

NOTES

Date of publication in OJ: OJ C13, 17.1.2004, p 3.

Note: with effect from 1 December 2009, the EC Treaty was replaced by the Treaty on the Functioning of the European Union. References in this document to provisions of the EC Treaty should be construed accordingly.

1. INTRODUCTION

[5.354]

The White Paper 'European transport policy for 2010: time to decide' stresses the vital importance of maritime transport services for the Community economy. 90% of all trade between the Community and the rest of the world is transported by sea. Short sea shipping accounts for 69% of the volume of goods transported between the Member States (this percentage is 41% if domestic transport is included). Community maritime transport and its related activities remains one of the most important in the world.

The shipping companies of the Member States still manage about a third of the world fleet today. The accession of Cyprus and Malta[1] in 2004 will increase still further the Union's share of shipping, as the shipping registers of these two countries currently account for about 10% of world tonnage.

Since the 1970s the European fleet has been faced with competition from vessels registered in third countries which do not take much care to observe social and safety rules in force at international level.

The lack of competitiveness of Community-flagged vessels was recognised at the end of the 1980s and, in the absence of harmonised European measures, several Member States adopted different arrangements for aiding maritime transport. The strategies adopted and the budgets allocated to support measures differ from one Member State to the other in reflection of the attitude of those States to public aid or the importance they attach to the maritime sector.

In addition, to encourage the re-registering of vessels, Member States have relaxed rules concerning crews, notably through the creation of second registers.

Second registers comprise, firstly, 'offshore registers' belonging to territories which have a greater or lesser autonomy in relation to the Member State, and secondly, 'international registers', attached directly to the State which created them.

In spite of the efforts made, a large part of the Community fleet continues to be registered under the flags of third countries. This is because the registers of third countries which apply open registration policies — some of which are called 'flags of convenience' — have continued and are still continuing to enjoy a significant competitive edge over the registers of Member States.

AID TO THE SHIPPING INDUSTRY SINCE 1989

In the light of the differences between the aid systems adopted by Member States faced with more intense competition from non-Community flagged vessels, in 1989 the Commission defined its first guidelines on this subject to ensure a certain convergence between the actions of the Member States. This method nevertheless proved to be ineffective and the decline of Community fleets continued. The guidelines were accordingly reviewed, leading to a 1997 communication defining new Guidelines on State aid to maritime transport[2].

The major development in recent years concerning support measures from the Member States for maritime transport is the widespread extension in Europe of flat rate tonnage taxation systems ('tonnage tax'). Tonnage tax entered into force very early in Greece and was progressively extended to the Netherlands (1996), to Norway (1996), to Germany (1999), to the United Kingdom (2000), to Denmark, to Spain and to Finland (2002) and to Ireland (2002). Belgium and France also decided to adopt it in 2002, while the Italian Government is envisaging this possibility.

RESULTS OF MEASURES PROPOSED BY MEMBER STATES AND APPROVED BY THE COMMISSION COMPARED WITH THE GENERAL OBJECTIVES OF THE 1997 REVISED GUIDELINES

(A) TRENDS OF THE COMMUNITY-FLAGGED FLEET (COMPETITIVENESS OF THE FLEET)

According to the replies provided by the Member States mid-2002 to the Commission's questionnaire and to the most recent statistical data[3], Member States which have introduced aid measures, particularly in the form of tax relief, have obtained re-registration under the national flag of a significant volume of tonnage in all the registers taken together. In percentage terms, the fleet as entered in the registers of the Member States increased as follows: the number of vessels by 0,4% on average per year, tonnage by 1,5% and container ships by 12,4%. Even if, in the case of the first registers, the number of units entered declined practically everywhere in the period 1989 to 2001, these figures can be viewed as a reversal of the trend, observed up to 1997, of abandoning Community flags.

During the same period, however, the share of Member State registers in total world tonnage fell slightly. While world shipping increased, the growth of the Community-managed fleet registered under third-country flags was faster than that of the fleet registered under the flags of the Member States.

(B) EMPLOYMENT TRENDS

According to the most recent estimates, the number of seafarers on board Community-flagged vessels fell from 188,000 in 1996 to approximately 180,000 in 2001[4]. The total number of Community nationals employed on board vessels flying Community flags is currently about 120,000, a figure which is 40% lower than that of 1985, while the number of nationals of third countries employed on board Community vessels has gone up from 29,000 in 1983 to approximately 60,000 today. When assessing the drop in the total number of seafarers, the following factors must be taken into account:

— first, productivity per vessel has continued to increase. Accordingly, a smaller crew makes it possible to transport an equal if not higher volume than that carried in the past,

— secondly, the Community-flagged fleet was renewed in the period 1997 to 2001. The average age of vessels went down from 22,9 years to 17,2 years. 35% of the fleet in service on 1 January 2001 had been built in the period 1996 to 2000. New vessels, of more advanced technology, need better trained but smaller crews.

Notable differences between the Member States in the employment rate of Community seafarers are nevertheless apparent. However, nothing in these figures indicates a reversal of the trend whereby the Community-flagged fleet depends more and more on third-country seafarers. This trend was pointed out by the Commission in 2001 in its Communication on the training and recruitment of seafarers[5].

(C) CONTRIBUTION TO ECONOMIC ACTIVITY AS A WHOLE

Maritime industries are inextricably linked with maritime transport. This association is a strong argument in favour of positive measures whose aim is to maintain a fleet dependent on Community shipping. Since maritime transport is one of the links in the chain of transport in general and in the chain of the maritime industries in particular, measures seeking to maintain the competitiveness of the European fleet also have repercussions on investments on land in maritime-related industries[6] and on the contribution of maritime transport to the economy of the Community as a whole and to jobs in general.

The significance of shipping and the whole maritime cluster varies considerably with the countries under consideration. However, the importance of the European maritime cluster and its direct economic impact can be clearly illustrated by the following figures: 1,550 million direct employees, a turnover of EUR 160 billion in 1997 (about 2% of GDP in the Community)[7]. Data on Denmark (3% of the GDP generated by the maritime cluster), Greece (2,3%) and the Netherlands (2%) can be taken as a valid example.

In this context, therefore, it is not insignificant to note that the fleet managed by European operators based in the Community has stayed at a level of around 34% of world tonnage, while the latter increased by 10% during the period. Given the mobility of the maritime industry and the facilities offered by third countries, one may conclude that support measures for maritime transport may contribute to avoiding widespread displacement of allied industries.

To sum up, it can be affirmed that, where measures in line with the 1997 Guidelines have been adopted, the structural decline of the Community registers and the Community's fleet has been halted and the objectives set by the Commission have been attained, at least in part.

The share of open registers in world tonnage continued, however, to increase during the period, rising from 43% in 1996 to 54% in 2001, and nothing indicates any significant reversal of the trend whereby the fleet had, and is continuing to have, increasing recourse to seafarers from third countries. The campaign undertaken in recent years must be pursued but it must be better targeted. Measures to promote Community seafarers must in particular be the subject of more active monitoring.

The results of the measures taken by the Member States and authorised by the Commission will have to be systematically analysed.

As a consequence, and even though as a matter of principle operating aid should be exceptional, temporary, and degressive, the Commission estimates that State aid to the European shipping industry is still justified and that the approach followed by the 1997 Guidelines was correct. This communication is therefore based on the same basic approach.

NOTES

1 The sixth and the fifth world registers of ships in terms of tonnage respectively (vessels of more than 300 gt. Source: ISL 2001).

2 Community guidelines on State aid to maritime transport (97/C 205/05) (OJ C205, 5.7.1997, p 5).

3 ISL, Shipping Statistics 2001.

4 Total combined number of Community and non-Community seafarers.

5 Communication from the Commission on the training and recruitment of seafarers of 6 April 2001, COM(2001) 188 final.

6 These activities include port services, logistics, the construction, repair, maintenance, inspection and classification of vessels, ship management and brokerage, banking activities and international financial services, insurance, advice and professional services.

7 Study undertaken by the European Commission, DG Enterprise (published in the Europa internet site).

2. SCOPE AND GENERAL OBJECTIVES OF THE REVISED STATE AID GUIDELINES

[5.355]
This communication — replacing the 1997 Guidelines — aims at setting the parameters within which State aid to maritime transport will be approved, pursuant to Community State aid rules and procedures, by the Commission under Article 87(3)(c) and/or Article 86(2) of the Treaty.

Aid schemes should not be conducted at the expense of other Member States' economies and must be shown not to risk distortion of competition between Member States to an extent contrary to the common interest. State aid must always be restricted to what is necessary to achieve its purpose and be granted in a transparent manner. The cumulative effect of all aid granted by State authorities (including national, regional and local levels) must always be taken into account.

These Guidelines are applicable to 'maritime transport' activities as defined in Regulation (EEC) No 4055/86[8] and in Regulation (EEC) No 3577/92[9], that is to say, to the 'transport of goods and persons by sea'. They also, in specific parts, relate to towage and dredging.

2.1. SCOPE OF REVISED STATE AID GUIDELINES

These Guidelines cover any aid granted by Member States or through State resources in favour of maritime transport. This includes any financial advantage, conferred in any form whatsoever, funded by public authorities (whether at national, regional, provincial, departmental or local level). For these purposes, 'public authorities' may include public undertakings and State-controlled banks. Arrangements whereby the State guarantees loans or other funding by commercial banks may also fall within the definition of aid. The Guidelines draw no distinction between types of beneficiary in terms of their legal structure (whether companies, partnerships or individuals), nor between public or private ownership, and any reference to companies shall be taken to include all other types of legal entity.

These guidelines do not cover aid to shipbuilding (within the meaning of Council Regulation (EC) No 1540/98[10] or any subsequent instrument). Investments in infrastructure are not normally considered to involve State aid within the meaning of Article 87(1) of the Treaty if the State provides free and equal access to the infrastructure for the benefit of all operators concerned. However, the Commission may examine such investments if they could directly or indirectly benefit particular shipowners. Finally, the Commission has established the principle that no State aid is involved where public authorities contribute to a company on a basis that would be acceptable to a private investor operating under normal market-economy conditions.

2.2. GENERAL OBJECTIVES OF REVISED STATE AID GUIDELINES

The Commission has stressed that increased transparency of State aid is necessary so that not only national authorities in the broad sense but also companies and individuals are aware of their rights and obligations. These Guidelines are intended to contribute to this and to clarify what State aid schemes may be introduced in order to support the Community maritime interest, with the aim of:

— improving a safe, efficient, secure and environment friendly maritime transport,
— encouraging the flagging or re-flagging to Member States' registers,
— contributing to the consolidation of the maritime cluster established in the Member States while maintaining an overall competitive fleet on world markets,
— maintaining and improving maritime know-how and protecting and promoting employment for European seafarers, and
— contributing to the promotion of new services in the field of short sea shipping following the White Paper on Community transport policy.

State aid may generally be granted only in respect of ships entered in Member States' registers. In certain exceptional cases, however, aid may be granted in respect of ships entered in registers under point (3) of the Annex, provided that:

— they comply with the international standards and Community law, including those relating to security, safety, environmental performance and on-board working conditions,
— they are operated from the Community,
— their shipowner is established in the Community and the Member State concerned demonstrates that the register contributes directly to the objectives mentioned above.

Additionally, flag-neutral aid measures may be approved in certain exceptional cases where a benefit to the Community is clearly demonstrated.

NOTES

8 Council Regulation (EEC) No 4055/86 of 22 December 1986 applying the principle of freedom to provide services to maritime transport between Member States and between Member States and third countries (OJ L378, 31.12.1986, p 1).

9 Council Regulation (EEC) No 3577/92 of 7 December 1992 applying the principle of freedom to provide services to maritime transport within Member States (maritime cabotage) (OJ L364, 12.12.1992, p 7).

10 OJ L202, 18.7.1998, p 1.

3. FISCAL AND SOCIAL MEASURES TO IMPROVE COMPETITIVENESS

3.1. FISCAL TREATMENT OF SHIPOWNING COMPANIES

[5.356]

Many third countries have developed significant shipping registers, sometimes supported by an efficient international services infrastructure, attracting shipowners through a fiscal climate which is considerably milder than within Member States. The low-tax environment has resulted in there being an incentive for companies not only to flag out their vessels but also to consider corporate relocation. It should be emphasised that there are no effective international rules at present to curb such tax competition and few administrative, legal or technical barriers to moving a ship's registration from a Member State's register. In this context, the creation of conditions allowing fairer competition with flags of convenience seems the best way forward.

The question of fiscal competition between Member States should be addressed. At this stage, there is no evidence of schemes distorting competition in trade between Member States to an extent contrary to the common interest. In fact, there appears to be an increasing degree of convergence in Member States' approaches to shipping aid. Flagging out between Member States is a rare phenomenon. Fiscal competition is mainly an issue between Member States on the one hand and third countries on the other, since the cost savings available to shipowners through third country registers are considerable in comparison to the options available within the Community.

For this reason, many Member States have taken special measures to improve the fiscal climate for shipowning companies, including, for instance, accelerated depreciation on investment in ships or the right to reserve profits made on the sale of ships for a number of years on a tax-free basis, provided that these profits are reinvested in ships.

These tax relief measures which apply in a special way to shipping are considered to be State aid. Equally, the system of replacing the normal corporate tax system by a tonnage tax is a State aid. 'Tonnage tax' means that the shipowner pays an amount of tax linked directly to the tonnage operated. The tonnage tax will be payable irrespective of the company's actual profits or losses.

Such measures have been shown to safeguard high quality employment in the on-shore maritime sector, such as management directly related to shipping and also in associated activities (insurance, brokerage and finance). In view of the importance of such activities to the economy of the Community and in support of the objectives stated earlier, these types of fiscal incentive can generally be endorsed. Further, safeguarding quality employment and stimulating a competitive shipping industry established in a Member State through fiscal incentives, taken together with other initiatives on training and enhancement of safety, will facilitate the development of Community shipping in the global market.

The Commission is aware that the income of shipowners today is often obtained from the operation of ships under different flags — for instance, when making use of chartered vessels under foreign flags or by making use of partner vessels within alliances. It is also recognised that the incentive for expatriation of management and ancillary activities would continue if the shipowner obtained a significant financial benefit from maintaining different establishments and accounting separately for Community flag earnings and other earnings. This would be the case, for example, if the non-Community flag earnings were liable either to the full rate of corporate taxation in a Member State or to a low rate of tax overseas if overseas management could be demonstrated.

The objective of State aid within the common maritime transport policy is to promote the competitiveness of the Community fleets in the global shipping market. Consequently, tax relief schemes should, as a rule, require a link with a Community flag. However, they may also, exceptionally, be approved where they apply to the entire fleet operated by a shipowner established within a Member State's territory liable to corporate tax, provided that it is demonstrated that the strategic and commercial management of all ships concerned is actually carried out from within the territory and that this activity contributes substantially to economic activity and employment within the Community. The evidence furnished by the Member State concerned to demonstrate this economic link should include details of vessels owned and operated under Community registers, Community nationals employed on ships and in land-based activities and investments in fixed assets. It must be stressed that the aid must be necessary to promote the repatriation of the strategic and commercial management of all ships concerned in the Community and, in addition, that the beneficiaries of the schemes must be liable to corporate tax in the Community. In addition, the Commission would request any available evidence to show that all vessels operated by companies benefiting from these measures comply with the relevant international and Community safety standards, including those relating to onboard working conditions.

As was argued in the above paragraph, it should not be forgotten that, as a matter of principle, tax relief schemes require a link with the flag of one of the Member States. Before aid is exceptionally granted (or confirmed) to fleets which also comprise vessels flying other flags, Member States should ensure that beneficiary companies commit themselves to increasing or at least maintaining under the flag of one of the Member States the share of tonnage that they will be operating under such flags when this Communication becomes applicable. Whenever a company controls ship operating companies within the meaning of the Seventh Council Directive 83/349/EEC[11] (Article 1), the abovementioned tonnage share requirement will have to apply to the parent company and subsidiary companies taken together on a consolidated basis. Should a company (or group) fail to respect that requirement, the relevant Member State should not grant further tax relief with respect to additional non-Community flagged vessels operated by that company, unless the Community-flagged share of the global tonnage eligible for tax relief in that Member State has not decreased on average during the reporting period referred to in the next paragraph. The Member State must inform the Commission of the application of the derogation. The Community-tonnage share requirement set out in this paragraph does not apply to undertakings operating at least 60% of their tonnage under a Community flag.

In all cases, where fiscal schemes have been approved on the above exceptional basis and in order to allow the Member State concerned to prepare, every three years, the report required under Chapter 12 ('Final Remarks'), recipients must provide the Member State concerned with proof that all the conditions for the derogation from the flag link have been fulfilled during the period. Furthermore, evidence must be provided that, in the case of the beneficiary fleet, the tonnage share requirement laid down in the previous paragraph has been observed and that each vessel of that fleet complies with the relevant international and Community standards, including those relating to security, safety, environmental performance and on-board working conditions. Should recipients fail to provide such evidence, they will not be allowed to continue to benefit from the tax scheme.

It is also of interest to stipulate that whereas Community-based shipping companies are the natural recipients of the above tax schemes, certain ship management companies established in the Community may also qualify under the same provisions. Ship management companies are entities providing different kind of services to shipowners, such as technical survey, crew recruiting and training, crew management, and vessel operation. In some cases ship managers are assigned both technical and crewing management of vessels. In this case they act as classic 'shipowners' as far as transport operations are concerned. Moreover, as in the case of the shipping industry, this sector is experiencing strong and increasing competition at an international level. For these reasons, it seems appropriate to extend the possibility of tax relief to that category of ship managers.

Ship management companies may qualify for aid only in respect of vessels for which they have been assigned the entire crew and technical management. In particular, in order to be eligible, ship managers have to assume from the owner the full responsibility for the vessel's operation, as well as take over from the owner all the duties and responsibilities imposed by the ISM Code[12]. Should ship managers also provide other specialised services, even related to vessel operation, separate accounting for such activities, which do not qualify for the tax relief schemes, should be ensured. The requirement regarding Member States' flag share described above also applies to ship management companies[13].

These guidelines apply only to maritime transport. The Commission can accept that the towing at sea of other vessels, oil platforms, etc. falls under that definition.

The Commission has, however, become aware that in certain cases Member States allow tugboats which are designed for work at sea to benefit from aid even though they are not active at sea, or rarely so. Thus it is useful to state in these guidelines which line the Commission has taken and will take on this point.

'Towage' is covered by the scope of the Guidelines only if more than 50% of the towage activity effectively carried out by a tug during a given year constitutes 'maritime transport'. Waiting time may be proportionally assimilated to that part of total activity effectively carried out by a tug which constitutes 'maritime transport'. It should be emphasised that towage activities which are carried out *inter alia* in ports, or which consist in assisting a self-propelled vessel to reach port do not constitute 'maritime transport' for the purposes of this communication. No derogation from the flag link is possible in the case of towage.

Similarly in the case of dredging, the experience gained during the recent years suggests that some points should be made.

'Dredging' activities are, in principle, not eligible for aid to maritime transport. However, fiscal arrangements for companies (such as tonnage tax) may be applied to those dredgers whose activity consists in 'maritime transport' — that is, the transport at deep sea of extracted materials — for more than 50% of their annual operational time and only in respect of such transport activities. Eligible dredgers are only those registered in a Member State (no derogation from the flag link is possible). In such cases, separate accounting for maritime transport activities is required[14].

Finally, the method of assessing tonnage tax systems notified up to now has consisted of the following steps: a virtual profit for shipowners has been calculated by applying a notional profit rate to their tonnage; national corporate tax has been applied to the amount so determined. The resulting amount is the 'tonnage tax' to be paid.

The notional profit rates provided for by Member States have been homogeneous up to now. However, since corporate tax rates may vary significantly across the Community, the tonnage taxes to be paid for the same tonnage might be very uneven in the different Member States. In order to keep the present equitable balance, the Commission will only approve schemes giving rise to a tax-load for the same tonnage fairly in line with the schemes already approved.

In all cases, the benefits of schemes must facilitate the development of the shipping sector and employment in the Community interest. Consequently, the fiscal advantages mentioned above must be restricted to shipping activities; hence, in cases where a shipowning company is also engaged in other commercial activities, transparent accounting will be required in order to prevent 'spill-over' into non-shipping activities. This approach would help Community shipping to be competitive, with tax liabilities comparable to levels applying elsewhere in the world, but would preserve a Member State's normal tax levels for other activities and personal remuneration of shareholders and directors.

3.2. LABOUR-RELATED COSTS

As was mentioned earlier, maritime transport is a sector experiencing fierce international competition. Support measures for the maritime sector should, therefore, aim primarily at reducing fiscal and other costs and burdens borne by Community shipowners and Community seafarers towards levels in line with world norms. They should directly stimulate the development of the sector and employment, rather than provide general financial assistance.

In keeping with these objectives, the following action on employment costs should be allowed for Community shipping:

— reduced rates of contributions for the social protection of Community seafarers employed on board ships registered in a Member State,

— reduced rates of income tax for Community seafarers on board ships registered in a Member State.

For the purposes of this point, 'Community seafarers' is defined as:

— Community/EEA citizens, in the case of seafarers working on board vessels (including ro-ro ferries)[15] providing scheduled passenger services between ports of the Community,

— all seafarers liable to taxation and/or social security contributions in a Member State, in all other cases.

The previous 1997 Guidelines allowed such reductions for all seafarers working on board vessels registered in a Member State and subject to tax and or social security contributions in a Member State. However, since then it has become clear that pressure by international competition on European shipowners is very strong in the case of international freight transport, while it is lighter in the case of intra-Community scheduled passenger transport. Boosting the competitiveness of European shipping industry is therefore a prior objective of aid in the former case. Preventing Member States from granting tax relief to all seafarers in this case would have very negative effects on the competitiveness of European shipowners, which could be encouraged to flag-out. At the same time it has been noticed that employment of European citizens is significant, in percentage terms and in numbers, in intra-Community scheduled passenger transport. Protection of employment in the Community is therefore a priority for aid in this case.

For internal fiscal reasons some Member States prefer not to apply reduced rates as mentioned above, but instead may reimburse shipowners — partially or wholly — for the costs arising from these levies. Such an approach may generally be considered equivalent to the reduced-rate system as described above, provided that there is a clear link to these levies, no element of overcompensation, and that the system is transparent and not open to abuse.

For the maritime part of towage and dredging activities (maritime transport of materials), aid in favour of the employment of Community seafarers may be granted by analogy to the rules contained in this point, but only if the aid relates to Community seafarers working on board seagoing, self-propelled tugs and dredgers, registered in a Member State, carrying out maritime transport at sea for at least 50% of their operational time[16].

Finally, it should be recalled that aid to employment is covered by the block exemption provided for by Commission Regulation (EC) No 2204/2002 of 12 December 2002 on the application of Articles 87 and 88 of the EC Treaty to State aid for employment[17], which also applies to maritime transport.

NOTES

11 OJ L193, 18.7.1983, p 1.

12 'ISM Code', International Management Code for the Safe Operation of Ships and for Pollution Prevention, adopted by the International Maritime Organization (IMO) by resolution A.741(18).

13 The Commission will examine the effects of these provisions on ship management after three years of implementation of this communication.

14 The ships used by these operators also extract or dredge materials which they carry afterwards. Extraction or dredging as such do not qualify for State aid to maritime transport.

15 See Article 2, point (a), of Council Directive 1999/35/EC of 29 April 1999 on a system of mandatory surveys for the safe operation of regular ro-ro ferry and high-speed passenger craft services (OJ L138, 1.6.1999, p 1).

16 Thus dredging activities carried out, *inter alia*, mainly in ports will not qualify for aid in favour of employment of Community seafarers.

17 OJ L337, 13.12.2002, p 3.

4. CREW RELIEF

[5.357]
Aid for crew relief tends to reduce the costs of employing Community seafarers, especially those on ships operating in distant waters. Aid, which is subject to the ceiling (as set out in Chapter 11), may, therefore, be granted in the form of payment or reimbursement of the costs of repatriation of Community seafarers working on board ships entered in Member States' registers.

5. INVESTMENT AID

[5.358]
Subsidies for fleet renewal are not common in other transport modes such as road haulage and aviation. Since they tend to distort competition, the Commission has been reluctant to approve such schemes, except where they form part of a structural reform leading to reductions in overall fleet capacity.

Investment must comply with Regulation (EC) No 1540/98 or any other Community legislation that may replace it. Within the framework of these guidelines, other investment aid may, however, be permitted, in line with the Community safe seas policy, in certain restricted circumstances to improve equipment on board vessels entered in a Member State's registers or to promote the use of safe and clean ships. Thus aid may be permitted which provides incentives to upgrade Community-registered ships to standards which exceed the mandatory safety and environmental standards laid down in international conventions and anticipating agreed higher standards, thereby enhancing safety and environmental controls. Such aid must comply with the applicable Community provisions on shipbuilding.

Since shipping is essentially very mobile, regional aid for maritime companies in disadvantaged regions, which often take the form of investment aid to companies investing in the regions, may only be permitted where it is clear that the benefits will accrue to the region over a reasonable time period. This would, for example, be the case of investment related to the construction of dedicated warehouses or to the purchase of fixed transhipment equipment. Investment aid for maritime companies in disadvantaged regions may then only be permitted where it also complies with the regional aid rules (see Chapter 6).

6. REGIONAL AID ON THE BASIS OF ARTICLE 87(3)(A) AND (C)

[5.359]
In the context of regional aid schemes, the Commission will apply the general rules set out in its communications or other provisions on national regional aid or future amendments thereto.

7. TRAINING

[5.360]
It should be recalled, firstly, that aid to training is covered by the block exemption provided for by Commission Regulation (EC) No 68/2001 of 12 January 2001 on the application of Articles 87 and 88 of the EC Treaty to training aid[18], which also applies to maritime transport.

Moreover, many training schemes followed by seafarers and supported by the State are not considered to be State aid because they are of a general nature (whether vocational or academic). These are, therefore, not subject to notification and examination by the Commission.

If a scheme is to be regarded as including State aid, notification is, however, required. This may be the case if, for example, a particular scheme is specifically related to on-board training and the benefit of State financial support is received by the training organisation, the cadet, seafarer or shipowner. The Commission takes a favourable attitude towards aid, granted on a non-discriminatory basis, to training carried out on board ships registered in a Member State. Exceptionally, training on board other vessels may be supported where justified by objective criteria, such as the lack of available places on vessels in a Member State's register.

Where financial contributions are paid for on-board training, the trainee may not, in principle, be an active member of the crew but must be supernumerary. This provision is to ensure that net wage subsidies cannot be paid for seafarers occupied in normal crewing activities.

Similarly, to safeguard and develop maritime expertise in the Community and the competitive edge of the Community maritime industries, further extensive research and development efforts are necessary, with a focus on quality, productivity, safety and environmental protection. For such projects, State support may also be authorised within the limits set by the Treaty.

Aid aimed at enhancing and updating Community officers' skills may be allowed during their whole career. The aid may consist of a contribution to the cost of the training and/or compensation for the wage paid to the officer during the training period. The schemes must, however, be designed in a way which prevents the aid for training from being directly or indirectly diverted into a subsidy to officers' wages.

Aid aimed at professional retraining of high-sea fishermen willing to work as seafarers may also be allowed.

NOTES

18 OJ L10, 13.1.2001, p 20.

8. RESTRUCTURING AID

[5.361]
Although the Community guidelines on restructuring and rescuing firms in difficulty[19] apply to transport only to the extent that the specific nature of the sector is taken into account, the Commission will apply those guidelines or any other Community instrument replacing them in considering restructuring aid for maritime companies.

NOTES

19 OJ C288, 9.10.1999, p 2.

9. PUBLIC SERVICE OBLIGATIONS AND CONTRACTS

[5.362]
In the field of maritime cabotage, public service obligations (PSOs) may be imposed or public service contracts (PSCs) may be concluded for the services indicated in Article 4 of Regulation (EEC) No 3577/92. For those services, PSOs and PSCs as well as their compensation must fulfil the conditions of that provision and the Treaty rules and procedures governing State aid, as interpreted by the Court of Justice.

The Commission accepts that if an international transport service is necessary to meet imperative public transport needs, PSOs may be imposed or PSCs may be concluded, provided that any compensation is subject to the abovementioned Treaty rules and procedures.

The duration of public service contracts should be limited to a reasonable and not overlong period, normally in the order of six years, since contracts for significantly longer periods could entail the danger of creating a (private) monopoly.

10. AID TO SHORT SEA SHIPPING

[5.363]
There is no legal definition of 'Short Sea Shipping'. However, the communication from the Commission on the development of Short Sea Shipping in Europe of 29 June 1999[20] has provided a working definition of Short Sea Shipping, to be understood as 'the movement of cargo and passenger by sea between ports situated in geographical Europe or between those ports and ports situated in non-European countries having a coastline on the enclosed seas bordering Europe'[21]. In this communication the Commission underscored the role of this transport mode to promote sustainable and safe mobility, to strengthen cohesion within the Community and to improve transport efficiency as part of an intermodal approach. The Commission also recognises that the promotion of short-sea shipping must be carried out at all levels, whether Community, national or regional.

Since aid to Short Sea Shipping aims to improve the intermodal chain and to decongest roads in the Member States, the definition of Short Sea Shipping such as provided by the 1999 communication should, for the purposes of this communication, be restricted to transport between ports in the territory of the Member States.

The Commission recognises that launching short-sea shipping services may be accompanied by substantial financial difficulties which the Member States may wish to attenuate in order to ensure the promotion of such services.

When such is the case, the Commission will be able to approve aid of this kind, on condition that it is intended for shipowners within the meaning of Article 1 of Regulation (EEC) No 4055/86 in respect of ships flying the flag of one of the Member States. Aid of this kind will have to be notified and to fulfil the following conditions:

— the aid must not exceed three years in duration and its purpose must be to finance a shipping service connecting ports situated in the territory of the Member States,
— the service must be of such a kind as to permit transport (of cargo essentially) by road to be carried out wholly or partly by sea, without diverting maritime transport in a way which is contrary to the common interest,
— the aid must be directed at implementing a detailed project with a pre-established environmental impact, concerning a new route or the upgrading of services on an existing one, associating several shipowners if necessary, with no more than one project financed per line and with no renewal, extension or repetition of the project in question,
— the purpose of the aid must be to cover, either up to 30% of the operational costs of the service in question[22], or to finance the purchase of trans-shipment equipment to supply the planned service, up to a level of 10% in such investment,
— the aid to implement a project must be granted on the basis of transparent criteria applied in a non-discriminatory way to shipowners established in the Community. The aid should normally be granted for a project selected by the authorities of the Member State through a tender procedure in compliance with applicable Community rules,

— the service which is the subject of the project must be of a kind to be commercially viable after the period in which it is eligible for public funding,

— such aid must not be cumulated with public service compensation (obligations or contracts).

NOTES

20 Communication from the Commission to the European Parliament, the Council, the Economic and Social Committee and the Committee of Regions, 'The development of Short Sea Shipping in Europe: a dynamic alternative in a sustainable transport chain — Second two-yearly report', COM(1999) 317 final.

21 Communication, p 2.

22 In case of Community financing or eligibility under different aid schemes, the ceiling of 30% applies to the combined total of aid/financial support. It should be noticed that the aid intensity is the same as that provided for modal shift actions within the Marco Polo Community initiative: cf. Article 5(2) of Regulation (EC) No 1382/2003 (OJ L196, 2.8.2003, p 1).

11. CEILING

[5.364]
As was explained above, certain Member States support their maritime sectors through tax reduction whilst other Member States prefer to make direct payments — for instance, by providing reimbursement of seafarers' income tax. In view of the current lack of harmonisation between the fiscal systems of the Member States, it is felt that the two alternatives should remain possible. Obviously, those two approaches may, in some instances, be combined. However, this risks causing a cumulation of aid to levels which are disproportionate to the objectives of the Community common interest and could lead to a subsidy race between Member States.

A reduction to zero of taxation and social charges for seafarers and a reduction of corporate taxation of shipping activities such as is described in point 3.1 (penultimate paragraph) is the maximum level of aid which may be permitted. To avoid distortion of competition, other systems of aid may not provide any greater benefit than this. Moreover, although each aid scheme notified by a Member State will be examined on its own merits, it is considered that the total amount of aid granted under Chapters 3 to 6 should not exceed the total amount of taxes and social contributions collected from shipping activities and seafarers.

12. FINAL REMARKS

[5.365]
The Commission will continue to monitor regularly and closely the market conditions for shipping. Should the latter change, and should consequently the need for State aid be reduced or overcome, the Commission will take the necessary measures in good time.

All new proposals for measures notified to the Commission must include a calendar indicating, for the next six years, the expected quantified effects for each objective of point 2.2. In particular, the expected macro-economic return on the corresponding maritime cluster, together with an estimation of the number of jobs saved or created, is to be presented in such proposals.

For all the aid schemes — whether existing or new — falling within the scope of this Communication, Member States are to communicate to the Commission an assessment of their effects during their sixth year of implementation.

When aid has been approved and granted to a beneficiary, under the derogation from the flag link referred to in point 3.1, the relevant Member State must report to the Commission every three years starting from the date when the grant was granted. In its report, the Member State will quantify the effects produced and compare the results with the expected effects. The reporting requirements set out in this communication will enter into force upon its publication.

Furthermore, should it prove necessary, for example following a justified complaint, the Member State concerned must provide the Commission with evidence that the assistance granted to the respective beneficiary under an agreed scheme has been limited to the strict definition therein and has also produced the effects expected.

13. APPROPRIATE MEASURES

[5.366]
These guidelines will apply from the date of their publication in the *Official Journal of the European Union*. In accordance with Article 88(1) of the Treaty, the Commission proposes that Member States amend their existing aid schemes relating to State aid covered by these guidelines so as to comply with them by 30 June 2005 at the latest. Member States are invited to confirm that they accept these proposals for appropriate measures in writing by 30 June 2004 at the latest.

Should a Member State fail to confirm its acceptance in writing by that date, the Commission will apply Article 19(2) of Regulation (EC) No 659/1999 and, if necessary, initiate the proceedings referred to in that provision.

These guidelines will be reviewed within seven years of their date of application.

ANNEX
DEFINITION OF MEMBER STATES' REGISTERS

[5.367]
'Member States' registers' should be understood as meaning registers governed by the law of a Member State applying to their territories forming part of the European Community.

1. All the first registers of Member States are Member States' registers.

[2. In addition, registers located in Member States and subject to their laws, are Member States' registers, if they are located in and subject to the law of territories where the Treaty applies. For example, at the time these Guidelines were adopted, the following registers were considered to fall under this category:

— the Danish International Register of Shipping (DIS),

— the German International Shipping Register (ISR),
— the Italian International Shipping Register,
— the Madeira International Ship Register (MAR),
— the Canary Islands register.]

3. Other registers are not considered to be Member States' registers even if they serve in practice as a first alternative for shipowners based in that Member State. This is because they are located in and subject to the law of territories where the Treaty does not, in whole or in substantial part, apply. Hence, the following registers are not Member States' registers:

— the Kerguelen register (the Treaty does not apply to this territory),
— the Dutch Antilles' register (this territory is associated with the Community; and only Part IV of the Treaty applies to it; it is responsible for its own fiscal regime),
— the registers of:
  — Isle of Man (only specific parts of the Treaty apply to the Isle — see Article 299(6)(c) of the Treaty; the Isle of Man parliament has sole right to legislate on fiscal matters),
  — Bermuda and Cayman (they are part of the territories associated to the Community, and only Part IV of the Treaty applies to them; they enjoy a fiscal autonomy).

4. In the case of Gibraltar, the Treaty applies fully and the Gibraltar register is, for the purposes of these Guidelines, considered to be a Member State's register.

NOTES

Para 2: substituted by Commission Communication Updating the Annex to Commission Communication — Community guidelines on State aid to maritime transport (OJ C120, 13.04.2017, p 10).

EUROPEAN PARLIAMENT AND COUNCIL REGULATION

(1370/2007/EC)

of 23 October 2007

on public passenger transport services by rail and by road and repealing Council Regulations (EEC) Nos 1191/69 and 1107/70

[5.368]

NOTES

Date of publication in OJ: OJ L315, 3.12.2007, p 1.

Application of this Regulation in relation to the UK: in accordance with the European Union (Withdrawal) Act 2018, s 3 at **[7.5]**, this Regulation became domestic law on IP completion day (as defined in the European Union (Withdrawal Agreement) Act 2020, s 39). In so far as applying to the UK, this Regulation is amended by the Regulation (EC) No 1370/2007 (Public Service Obligations in Transport) (Amendment) (EU Exit) Regulations 2020, SI 2020/504, as from IP completion day, and by the State Aid (Revocations and Amendments) (EU Exit) Regulations 2020, SI 2020/1470 (as from the same date). The amendments are set out below. With regard to these amendments, note that Articles that are repealed are reproduced in italics and, in the case of other amendments, the amending provision from SI 2020/504 or SI 2020/1470 is set out in full in the Notes to the amended Article, and the text of the amended Article has not been altered. Note also that the amendments made by the State Aid (Revocations and Amendments) (EU Exit) Regulations 2020, SI 2020/1470 do not apply to Northern Ireland.

Note: with effect from 1 December 2009, the EC Treaty was replaced by the Treaty on the Functioning of the European Union. References in this document to provisions of the EC Treaty should be construed accordingly.

THE EUROPEAN PARLIAMENT AND THE COUNCIL OF THE EUROPEAN UNION,

Having regard to the Treaty establishing the European Community, and in particular Articles 71 and 89 thereof,

Having regard to the proposal from the Commission,

Having regard to the opinion of the European Economic and Social Committee[1],

Having regard to the opinion of the Committee of the Regions[2],

Acting in accordance with the procedure laid down in Article 251 of the Treaty[3],

Whereas:

(1) Article 16 of the Treaty confirms the place occupied by services of general economic interest in the shared values of the Union.

(2) Article 86(2) of the Treaty lays down that undertakings entrusted with the operation of services of general economic interest are subject to the rules contained in the Treaty, in particular to the rules on competition, in so far as the application of such rules does not obstruct the performance, in law or in fact, of the particular tasks assigned to them.

(3) Article 73 of the Treaty constitutes a *lex specialis* in relation to Article 86(2). It establishes rules applicable to the compensation of public service obligations in inland transport.

(4) The main objectives of the Commission's White Paper of 12 September 2001 'European transport policy for 2010: time to decide' are to guarantee safe, efficient and high-quality passenger transport services through regulated competition, guaranteeing also transparency and performance of public passenger transport services, having regard to social, environmental and regional development factors, or to offer specific tariff conditions to certain categories of traveller, such as pensioners, and to eliminate the disparities between transport undertakings from different Member States which may give rise to substantial distortions of competition.

(5) At the present time, many inland passenger transport services which are required in the general economic interest cannot be operated on a commercial basis. The competent authorities of the Member States must be able to

act to ensure that such services are provided. The mechanisms that they can use to ensure that public passenger transport services are provided include the following: the award of exclusive rights to public service operators, the grant of financial compensation to public service operators and the definition of general rules for the operation of public transport which are applicable to all operators. If Member States, in accordance with this Regulation, choose to exclude certain general rules from its scope, the general regime for State aid should apply.

(6) Many Member States have enacted legislation providing for the award of exclusive rights and public service contracts in at least part of their public transport market, on the basis of transparent and fair competitive award procedures. As a result, trade between Member States has developed significantly and several public service operators are now providing public passenger transport services in more than one Member State. However, developments in national legislation have led to disparities in the procedures applied and have created legal uncertainty as to the rights of public service operators and the duties of the competent authorities. Regulation (EEC) No 1191/69 of the Council of 26 June 1969 on action by Member States concerning the obligations inherent in the concept of a public service in transport by rail, road and inland waterway[4], does not deal with the way public service contracts are to be awarded in the Community, and in particular the circumstances in which they should be the subject of competitive tendering. The Community legal framework ought therefore to be updated.

(7) Studies carried out and the experience of Member States where competition in the public transport sector has been in place for a number of years show that, with appropriate safeguards, the introduction of regulated competition between operators leads to more attractive and innovative services at lower cost and is not likely to obstruct the performance of the specific tasks assigned to public service operators. This approach has been endorsed by the European Council under the Lisbon Process of 28 March 2000 which called on the Commission, the Council and the Member States, each in accordance with their respective powers, to 'speed up liberalisation in areas such as . . . transport'.

(8) Passenger transport markets which are deregulated and in which there are no exclusive rights should be allowed to maintain their characteristics and way of functioning in so far as these are compatible with Treaty requirements.

(9) In order to be able to organise their public passenger transport services in the manner best suited to the needs of the public, all competent authorities must be able to choose their public service operators freely, taking into account the interests of small and medium-sized enterprises, under the conditions stipulated in this Regulation. In order to guarantee the application of the principles of transparency, equal treatment of competing operators and proportionality, when compensation or exclusive rights are granted, it is essential that a public service contract between the competent authority and the chosen public service operator defines the nature of the public service obligations and the agreed reward. The form or designation of the contract may vary according to the legal systems of the Member States.

(10) Contrary to Regulation (EEC) No 1191/69, the scope of which extends to public passenger transport services by inland waterway, it is not considered advisable for this Regulation to cover the award of public service contracts in that specific sector. The organisation of public passenger transport services by inland waterway and, in so far as they are not covered by specific Community law, by national sea water is therefore subject to compliance with the general principles of the Treaty, unless Member States choose to apply this Regulation to those specific sectors. The provisions of this Regulation do not prevent the integration of services by inland waterway and national sea water into a wider urban, suburban or regional public passenger transport network.

(11) Contrary to Regulation (EEC) No 1191/69, the scope of which extends to freight transport services, it is not considered advisable for this Regulation to cover the award of public service contracts in that specific sector. Three years after the entry into force of this Regulation the organisation of freight transport services should therefore be made subject to compliance with the general principles of the Treaty.

(12) It is immaterial from the viewpoint of Community law whether public passenger transport services are operated by public or private undertakings. This Regulation is based on the principles of neutrality as regards the system of property ownership referred to in Article 295 of the Treaty, of the freedom of Member States to define services of general economic interest, referred to in Article 16 of the Treaty, and of subsidiarity and proportionality referred to in Article 5 of the Treaty.

(13) Some services, often linked to specific infrastructure, are operated mainly for their historical interest or tourist value. As the purpose of these operations is manifestly different from the provision of public passenger transport, they need not therefore be governed by the rules and procedures applicable to public service requirements.

(14) Where the competent authorities are responsible for organising the public transport network, apart from the actual operation of the transport service, this may cover a whole range of other activities and duties that the competent authorities must be free either to carry out themselves or entrust, in whole or in part, to a third party.

(15) Contracts of long duration can lead to market foreclosure for a longer period than is necessary, thus diminishing the benefits of competitive pressure. In order to minimise distortions of competition, while protecting the quality of services, public service contracts should be of limited duration. The extension of such contracts could be subject to positive confirmation from users. In this context, it is necessary to make provision for extending public service contracts by a maximum of half their initial duration where the public service operator must invest in assets for which the depreciation period is exceptional and, because of their special characteristics and constraints, in the case of the outermost regions as specified in Article 299 of the Treaty. In addition, where a public service operator makes investments in infrastructure or in rolling stock and vehicles which are exceptional in the sense that both concern high amounts of funds, and provided the contract is awarded after a fair competitive tendering procedure, an even longer extension should be possible.

(16) Where the conclusion of a public service contract may entail a change of public service operator, it should be possible for the competent authorities to ask the chosen public service operator to apply the provisions of Council Directive 2001/23/EC of 12 March 2001 on the approximation of the laws of the Member States relating to the safeguarding of employees' rights in the event of transfer of undertakings, businesses or parts of undertakings or businesses[5]. This Directive does not preclude Member States from safeguarding transfer conditions of employees' rights other than those covered by Directive 2001/23/EC and thereby, if appropriate, taking into account social

standards established by national laws, regulations or administrative provisions or collective agreements or agreements concluded between social partners.

(17) In keeping with the principle of subsidiarity, competent authorities are free to establish social and qualitative criteria in order to maintain and raise quality standards for public service obligations, for instance with regard to minimal working conditions, passenger rights, the needs of persons with reduced mobility, environmental protection, the security of passengers and employees as well as collective agreement obligations and other rules and agreements concerning workplaces and social protection at the place where the service is provided. In order to ensure transparent and comparable terms of competition between operators and to avert the risk of social dumping, competent authorities should be free to impose specific social and service quality standards.

(18) Subject to the relevant provisions of national law, any local authority or, in the absence thereof, any national authority may choose to provide its own public passenger transport services in the area it administers or to entrust them to an internal operator without competitive tendering. However, this self-provision option needs to be strictly controlled to ensure a level playing field. The competent authority or group of authorities providing integrated public passenger transport services, collectively or through its members, should exercise the required control. In addition, a competent authority providing its own transport services or an internal operator should be prohibited from taking part in competitive tendering procedures outside the territory of that authority. The authority controlling the internal operator should also be allowed to prohibit this operator from taking part in competitive tenders organised within its territory. Restrictions on the activities of an internal operator do not interfere with the possibility of directly awarding public service contracts where they concern transport by rail, with the exception of other track-based modes such as metro or tramways. Furthermore, the direct award of public service contracts for heavy rail does not preclude the possibility for competent authorities to award public service contracts for public passenger transport services on other track-based modes, such as metro and tramway, to an internal operator.

(19) Subcontracting can contribute to more efficient public passenger transport and makes it possible for undertakings to participate, other than the public service operator which was granted the public service contract. However, with a view to the best use of public funds, competent authorities should be able to determine the modalities for subcontracting their public passenger transport services, in particular in the case of services performed by an internal operator. Furthermore, a subcontractor should not be prevented from taking part in competitive tenders in the territory of any competent authority. The selection of a subcontractor by the competent authority or its internal operator needs to be carried out in accordance with Community law.

(20) Where a public authority chooses to entrust a general interest service to a third party, it must select the public service operator in accordance with Community law on public contracts and concessions, as established by Articles 43 to 49 of the Treaty, and the principles of transparency and equal treatment. In particular, the provisions of this Regulation are to be without prejudice to the obligations applicable to public authorities by virtue of the directives on the award of public contracts, where public service contracts fall within their scope.

(21) Effective legal protection should be guaranteed, not only for awards falling within the scope of Directive 2004/17/EC of the European Parliament and of the Council of 31 March 2004 coordinating the procurement procedures of entities operating in the water, energy, transport and postal services sectors[6] and Directive 2004/18/EC of the European Parliament and of the Council of 31 March 2004 on the coordination of procedures for the award of public works contracts, public supply contracts and public service contracts[7], but also for other contracts awarded under this Regulation. An effective review procedure is needed and should be comparable, where appropriate, to the relevant procedures set out in Council Directive 89/665/EEC of 21 December 1989 on the coordination of the laws, regulations and administrative provisions relating to the application of review procedures to the award of public supply and public works contracts[8] and Council Directive 92/13/EEC of 25 February 1992 coordinating the laws, regulations and administrative provisions relating to the application of Community rules on the procurement procedures of entities operating in the water, energy, transport and telecommunications sectors[9].

(22) Some invitations to tender require the competent authorities to define and describe complex systems. These authorities should therefore have power, when awarding contracts in such cases, to negotiate details with some or all of the potential public service operators once tenders have been submitted.

(23) Invitations to tender for the award of public service contracts should not be mandatory where the contract relates to modest amounts or distances. In this respect, greater amounts or distances should enable competent authorities to take into account the special interests of small and medium-sized enterprises. Competent authorities should not be permitted to split up contracts or networks in order to avoid tendering.

(24) Where there is a risk of disruption in the provision of services, the competent authorities should have power to introduce emergency short-term measures pending the award of a new public service contract which is in line with all the conditions for awarding a contract laid down in this Regulation.

(25) Public passenger transport by rail raises specific issues of investment burden and infrastructure cost. In March 2004, the Commission presented a proposal to amend Council Directive 91/440/EEC of 29 July 1991 on the development of the Community's railways[10] so as to guarantee access for all Community railway undertakings to the infrastructure of all Member States for the purpose of operating international passenger services. The aim of this Regulation is to establish a legal framework for compensation and/or exclusive rights for public service contracts and not the further opening of the market for railway services.

(26) In the case of public services, this Regulation allows each competent authority, within the context of a public service contract, to select its operator of public passenger transport services. Given the differences in the way Member States organise their territory in this respect, competent authorities may justifiably be allowed to award public service contracts directly for railway travel.

(27) The compensation granted by competent authorities to cover the costs incurred in discharging public service obligations should be calculated in a way that prevents overcompensation. Where a competent authority plans to award a public service contract without putting it out to competitive tender, it should also respect detailed rules ensuring that the amount of compensation is appropriate and reflecting a desire for efficiency and quality of service.

(28) By appropriately considering the effects of complying with the public service obligations on the demand for

public passenger transport services in the calculation scheme set out in the Annex, the competent authority and the public service operator can prove that overcompensation has been avoided.

(29) With a view to the award of public service contracts, with the exception of emergency measures and contracts relating to modest distances, the competent authorities should take the necessary measures to advertise, at least one year in advance, the fact that they intend to award such contracts, so as to enable potential public service operators to react.

(30) Directly awarded public service contracts should be subject to greater transparency.

(31) Given that competent authorities and public service operators will need time to adapt to the provisions of this Regulation, provision should be made for transitional arrangements. With a view to the gradual award of public service contracts in line with this Regulation, Member States should provide the Commission with a progress report within the six months following the first half of the transitional period. The Commission may propose appropriate measures on the basis of these reports.

(32) During the transitional period, the application of the provisions of this Regulation by the competent authorities may take place at different times. It may therefore be possible, during this period, that public service operators from markets not yet affected by the provisions of this Regulation tender for public service contracts in markets that have been opened to controlled competition more rapidly. In order to avoid, by means of proportionate action, any imbalance in the opening of the public transport market, competent authorities should be able to refuse, in the second half of the transitional period, tenders from undertakings, more than half the value of the public transport services performed by which are not granted in accordance with this Regulation, provided that this is applied without discrimination and decided in advance of an invitation to tender.

(33) In paragraphs 87 to 95 of its judgment of 24 July 2003 in Case C-280/00 Altmark Trans GmbH[11], the Court of Justice of the European Communities ruled that compensation for public service does not constitute an advantage within the meaning of Article 87 of the Treaty, provided that four cumulative conditions are satisfied. Where those conditions are not satisfied and the general conditions for the application of Article 87(1) of the Treaty are met, public service compensation constitutes State aid and is subject to Articles 73, 86, 87 and 88 of the Treaty.

(34) Compensation for public services may prove necessary in the inland passenger transport sector so that undertakings responsible for public services operate on the basis of principles and under conditions which allow them to carry out their tasks. Such compensation may be compatible with the Treaty pursuant to Article 73 under certain conditions. Firstly, it must be granted to ensure the provision of services which are services of general interest within the meaning of the Treaty. Secondly, in order to avoid unjustified distortions of competition, it may not exceed what is necessary to cover the net costs incurred through discharging the public service obligations, taking account of the revenue generated thereby and a reasonable profit.

(35) Compensation granted by the competent authorities in accordance with the provisions of this Regulation may therefore be exempted from the prior notification requirement of Article 88(3) of the Treaty.

(36) This Regulation replaces Regulation (EEC) No 1191/69, which should therefore be repealed. For public freight transport services, a transitional period of three years will assist the phasing out of compensation not authorised by the Commission in accordance with Articles 73, 86, 87 and 88 of the Treaty. Any compensation granted in relation to the provision of public passenger transport services other than those covered by this Regulation which risks involving State aid within the meaning of Article 87(1) of the Treaty should comply with the provisions of Articles 73, 86, 87 and 88 thereof, including any relevant interpretation by the Court of Justice of the European Communities and especially its ruling in Case C-280/00 Altmark Trans GmbH. When examining such cases, the Commission should therefore apply principles similar to those laid down in this Regulation or, where appropriate, other legislation in the field of services of general economic interest.

(37) The scope of Council Regulation (EEC) No 1107/70 of 4 June 1970 on the granting of aids for transport by rail, road and inland waterway[12] is covered by this Regulation. That Regulation is considered obsolete while limiting the application of Article 73 of the Treaty without granting an appropriate legal basis for authorising current investment schemes, in particular in relation to investment in transport infrastructure in a public private partnership. It should therefore be repealed in order for Article 73 of the Treaty to be properly applied to continuing developments in the sector without prejudice to this Regulation or Council Regulation (EEC) No 1192/69 of 26 June 1969 on common rules for the normalisation of the accounts of railway undertakings[13]. With a view to further facilitating the application of the relevant Community rules, the Commission will propose State aid guidelines for railway investment, including investment in infrastructure in 2007.

(38) With a view to assessing the implementation of this Regulation and the developments in the provision of public passenger transport in the Community, in particular the quality of public passenger transport services and the effects of granting public service contracts by direct award, the Commission should produce a report. This report may, if necessary, be accompanied by appropriate proposals for the amendment of this Regulation,

NOTES

1 OJ C195, 18.8.2006, p 20.

2 OJ C192, 16.8.2006, p 1.

3 Opinion of the European Parliament of 14 November 2001 (OJ C140 E, 13.6.2002, p 262), Council Common Position of 11 December 2006 (OJ C70 E, 27.3.2007, p 1) and Position of the European Parliament of 10 May 2007. Council Decision of 18 September 2007.

4 OJ L156, 28.6.1969, p 1. Regulation as last amended by Regulation (EEC) No 1893/91 (OJ L169, 29.6.1991, p 1).

5 OJ L82, 22.3.2001, p 16.

6 OJ L134, 30.4.2004, p 1. Directive as last amended by Council Directive 2006/97/EC (OJ L363, 20.12.2006, p 107).

7 OJ L134, 30.4.2004, p 114. Directive as last amended by Council Directive 2006/97/EC.

8 OJ L395, 30.12.1989, p 33. Directive as amended by Directive 92/50/EEC (OJ L209, 24.7.1992, p 1).

9 OJ L76, 23.3.1992, p 14. Directive as last amended by Directive 2006/97/EC.

10 OJ L237, 24.8.1991, p 25. Directive as last amended by Directive 2006/103/EC (OJ L363, 20.12.2006, p 344).

11 [2003] ECR I-7747.

12 OJ L130, 15.6.1970, p 1. Regulation as last amended by Regulation (EC) No 543/97 (OJ L84, 26.3.1997, p 6).

[13] OJ L156, 28.6.1969, p 8. Regulation as last amended by Regulation (EC) No 1791/2006 (OJ L363, 20.12.2006, p 1).

HAVE ADOPTED THIS REGULATION:

[5.369]

Article 1 Purpose and scope

1. The purpose of this Regulation is to define how, in accordance with the rules of Community law, competent authorities may act in the field of public passenger transport to guarantee the provision of services of general interest which are among other things more numerous, safer, of a higher quality or provided at lower cost than those that market forces alone would have allowed.

To this end, this Regulation lays down the conditions under which competent authorities, when imposing or contracting for public service obligations, compensate public service operators for costs incurred and/or grant exclusive rights in return for the discharge of public service obligations.

2. This Regulation shall apply to the national and international operation of public passenger transport services by rail and other track-based modes and by road, except for services which are operated mainly for their historical interest or their tourist value. Member States may apply this Regulation to public passenger transport by inland waterways and, without prejudice to Council Regulation (EEC) No 3577/92 of 7 December 1992 applying the principle of freedom to provide services to maritime transport within Member States (maritime cabotage)[1], national sea waters.

[Subject to agreement of the competent authorities of the Member States on whose territory the services are provided, public service obligations may concern public transport services at cross-border level, including those covering local and regional transport needs.]

3. This Regulation shall not apply to public works concessions within the meaning of Article 1(3)(a) of Directive 2004/17/EC or of Article 1(3) of Directive 2004/18/EC.

NOTES

Para 2: words in square brackets inserted by European Parliament and Council Regulation 2016/2338/EU, Art 1(1).

Application of this Article in relation to the UK: this Article is amended, in relation to the UK only, by the Regulation (EC) No 1370/2007 (Public Service Obligations in Transport) (Amendment) (EU Exit) Regulations 2020, SI 2020/504, reg 3, as from IP completion day (as defined in the European Union (Withdrawal Agreement) Act 2020, s 39), as follows—

"In Article 1 (purpose and scope)—

(a) in the first subparagraph of paragraph 1 omit ", in accordance with the rules of Community law,".

(b) in paragraph 2—

 (i) in the first subparagraph omit the second sentence;

 (ii) in the second subparagraph for "of the Member States on whose territory" substitute "in whose geographical area";

(c) for paragraph 3 substitute—

"3. This Regulation shall not apply to "works concession contracts" as defined for England and Wales in regulation 3(2) of the Concession Contracts Regulations 2016, and for Scotland in regulation 3(2) of the Concession Contracts (Scotland) Regulations 2016."."

Transitional provisions: the Regulation (EC) No 1370/2007 (Public Service Obligations in Transport) (Amendment) (EU Exit) Regulations 2020, SI 2020/504, reg 16 provides as follows—

"16 Transitional provision

Nothing in these Regulations affects the validity of the—

(a) award of a public service contract, or

(b) extension of a public service contract,

where an action in relation to the award or extension was taken before IP completion day in accordance with Regulation (EC) No 1370/2007 of the European Parliament and of the Council of 23 October 2007 on public passenger transport services by rail and by road and repealing Council Regulations (EEC) No 1191/69 and 1107/70 as it had effect in domestic law at that time.".

[1] OJ L364, 12.12.1992, p 7.

[5.370]

Article 2 Definitions

For the purpose of this Regulation:

(a) 'public passenger transport' means passenger transport services of general economic interest provided to the public on a non-discriminatory and continuous basis;

[(aa) 'public passenger transport services by rail' means public passenger transport by rail, excluding passenger transport by other track-based modes, such as metros or tramways;]

(b) 'competent authority' means any public authority or group of public authorities of a Member State or Member States which has the power to intervene in public passenger transport in a given geographical area or any body vested with such authority;

(c) 'competent local authority' means any competent authority whose geographical area of competence is not national;

(d) 'public service operator' means any public or private undertaking or group of such undertakings which operates public passenger transport services or any public body which provides public passenger transport services;

(e) 'public service obligation' means a requirement defined or determined by a competent authority in order to ensure public passenger transport services in the general interest that an operator, if it were considering its own commercial interests, would not assume or would not assume to the same extent or under the same conditions without reward;

(f) 'exclusive right' means a right entitling a public service operator to operate certain public passenger transport services on a particular route or network or in a particular area, to the exclusion of any other such operator;
(g) 'public service compensation' means any benefit, particularly financial, granted directly or indirectly by a competent authority from public funds during the period of implementation of a public service obligation or in connection with that period;
(h) 'direct award' means the award of a public service contract to a given public service operator without any prior competitive tendering procedure;
(i) 'public service contract' means one or more legally binding acts confirming the agreement between a competent authority and a public service operator to entrust to that public service operator the management and operation of public passenger transport services subject to public service obligations; depending on the law of the Member State, the contract may also consist of a decision adopted by the competent authority:
  — taking the form of an individual legislative or regulatory act, or
  — containing conditions under which the competent authority itself provides the services or entrusts the provision of such services to an internal operator;
(j) 'internal operator' means a legally distinct entity over which a competent local authority, or in the case of a group of authorities at least one competent local authority, exercises control similar to that exercised over its own departments;
(k) 'value' means the value of a service, a route, a public service contract, or a compensation scheme for public passenger transport corresponding to the total remuneration, before VAT, of the public service operator or operators, including compensation of whatever kind paid by the public authorities and revenue from the sale of tickets which is not repaid to the competent authority in question;
(l) 'general rule' means a measure which applies without discrimination to all public passenger transport services of the same type in a given geographical area for which a competent authority is responsible;
(m) 'integrated public passenger transport services' means interconnected transport services within a determined geographical area with a single information service, ticketing scheme and timetable.

NOTES

Para (aa) inserted by European Parliament and Council Regulation 2016/2338/EU, Art 1(2).

Application of this Article in relation to the UK: this Article is amended, in relation to the UK only, by the Regulation (EC) No 1370/2007 (Public Service Obligations in Transport) (Amendment) (EU Exit) Regulations 2020, SI 2020/504, reg 4, as from IP completion day (as defined in the European Union (Withdrawal Agreement) Act 2020, s 39), as follows—

"In Article 2 (definitions)—
(a) in paragraph (b), in the definition of "competent authority", omit "of a Member State or Member States";
(b) in paragraph (i), in the definition of "public service contract", omit "depending on the law of the Member State,".".

Transitional provisions, see the note to Art 1 at **[5.369]**.

[5.371]

[Article 2a Specification of public service obligations

1. The competent authority shall lay down specifications for public service obligations in the provision of public passenger transport services and the scope of their application in accordance with Article 2(e). This includes the possibility to group cost-covering services with non-cost-covering services.

When laying down those specifications and the scope of their application, the competent authority shall duly respect the principle of proportionality, in accordance with Union law.

The specifications shall be consistent with the policy objectives stated in public transport policy documents in the Member States.

The content and format of public transport policy documents and the procedures for consulting relevant stakeholders shall be determined in accordance with national law.

2. The specifications of the public service obligations and the related compensation of the net financial effect of public service obligations shall:
(a) achieve the objectives of the public transport policy in a cost-effective manner; and
(b) financially sustain the provision of public passenger transport, in accordance with the requirements laid down in the public transport policy in the long term.]

NOTES

Inserted by European Parliament and Council Regulation 2016/2338/EU, Art 1(3).

Application of this Article in relation to the UK: this Article is amended, in relation to the UK only, by the Regulation (EC) No 1370/2007 (Public Service Obligations in Transport) (Amendment) (EU Exit) Regulations 2020, SI 2020/504, reg 5, as from IP completion day (as defined in the European Union (Withdrawal Agreement) Act 2020, s 39), as follows—

"In Article 2a (specification of public service obligations), in paragraph (1)—
(a) in the second subparagraph omit ", in accordance with Union law";
(b) in the third subparagraph omit "in the Member States";
(c) omit the fourth subparagraph.".

Transitional provisions, see the note to Art 1 at **[5.369]**.

[5.372]

Article 3 Public service contracts and general rules

1. Where a competent authority decides to grant the operator of its choice an exclusive right and/or compensation, of whatever nature, in return for the discharge of public service obligations, it shall do so within the framework of a public service contract.

2. By way of derogation from paragraph 1, public service obligations which aim at establishing maximum tariffs for all passengers or for certain categories of passenger may also be the subject of general rules. In accordance with the principles set out in Articles 4 and 6 and in the Annex, the competent authority shall compensate the public service

operators for the net financial effect, positive or negative, on costs incurred and revenues generated in complying with the tariff obligations established through general rules in a way that prevents overcompensation. This shall be so notwithstanding the right of competent authorities to integrate public service obligations establishing maximum tariffs in public service contracts.

3. Without prejudice to the provisions of Articles 73, 86, 87 and 88 of the Treaty, Member States may exclude from the scope of this Regulation general rules on financial compensation for public service obligations which establish maximum tariffs for pupils, students, apprentices and persons with reduced mobility. These general rules shall be notified in accordance with Article 88 of the Treaty. Any such notification shall contain complete information on the measure and, in particular, details on the calculation method.

NOTES

Application of this Article in relation to the UK: this Article is amended, in relation to the UK only, by the Regulation (EC) No 1370/2007 (Public Service Obligations in Transport) (Amendment) (EU Exit) Regulations 2020, SI 2020/504, reg 6, as from IP completion day (as defined in the European Union (Withdrawal Agreement) Act 2020, s 39), as follows—

"In Article 3 (public service contracts and general rules) omit paragraph 3.".

Transitional provisions, see the note to Art 1 at **[5.369]**.

[5.373]

Article 4 Mandatory content of public service contracts and general rules

1. Public service contracts and general rules shall:

[(a) clearly set out the public service obligations, defined in this Regulation and specified in accordance with Article 2a thereof, with which the public service operator is to comply, and the geographical areas concerned;

(b) establish in advance, in an objective and transparent manner:

(i) the parameters on the basis of which the compensation payment, if any, is to be calculated; and

(ii) the nature and extent of any exclusive rights granted, in a way that prevents overcompensation.

In the case of public service contracts not awarded according to Article 5(1), (3) or (3b), these parameters shall be determined in such a way that no compensation payment may exceed the amount required to cover the net financial effect on costs incurred and revenues generated in discharging the public service obligations, taking account of revenue relating thereto kept by the public service operator and a reasonable profit;]

(c) determine the arrangements for the allocation of costs connected with the provision of services. These costs may include in particular the costs of staff, energy, infrastructure charges, maintenance and repair of public transport vehicles, rolling stock and installations necessary for operating the passenger transport services, fixed costs and a suitable return on capital.

2. Public service contracts and general rules shall determine the arrangements for the allocation of revenue from the sale of tickets which may be kept by the public service operator, repaid to the competent authority or shared between the two.

3. The duration of public service contracts shall be limited and shall not exceed 10 years for coach and bus services and 15 years for passenger transport services by rail or other track-based modes. The duration of public service contracts relating to several modes of transport shall be limited to 15 years if transport by rail or other track-based modes represents more than 50% of the value of the services in question.

4. If necessary, having regard to the conditions of asset depreciation, the duration of the public service contract may be extended by a maximum of 50% if the public service operator provides assets which are both significant in relation to the overall assets needed to carry out the passenger transport services covered by the public service contract and linked predominantly to the passenger transport services covered by the contract.

If justified by costs deriving from the particular geographical situation, the duration of public service contracts specified in paragraph 3 in the outermost regions may be extended by a maximum of 50%.

If justified by the amortisation of capital in relation to exceptional infrastructure, rolling stock or vehicular investment and if the public service contract is awarded in a fair competitive tendering procedure, a public service contract may have a longer duration. In order to ensure transparency in this case, the competent authority shall transmit to the Commission within one year of the conclusion of the contract the public service contract and elements justifying its longer duration.

[4a. In the performance of public service contracts, public service operators shall comply with obligations applicable in the field of social and labour law established by Union law, national law or collective agreements.

4b. Directive 2001/23/EC shall apply to a change of public service operator where such a change constitutes a transfer of undertaking within the meaning of that Directive.]

5. Without prejudice to national and Community law, including collective agreements between social partners, competent authorities may require the selected public service operator to grant staff previously taken on to provide services the rights to which they would have been entitled if there had been a transfer within the meaning of Directive 2001/23/EC. Where competent authorities require public service operators to comply with certain social standards, tender documents and public service contracts shall list the staff concerned and give transparent details of their contractual rights and the conditions under which employees are deemed to be linked to the services.

[6. Where competent authorities, in accordance with national law, require public service operators to comply with certain quality and social standards, or establish social and qualitative criteria, those standards and criteria shall be included in the tender documents and in the public service contracts. While respecting Directive 2001/23/EC, such tender documents and public service contracts shall, where applicable, also contain information on the rights and obligations relating to the transfer of staff taken on by the previous operator.]

7. Tender documents and public service contracts shall indicate, in a transparent manner, whether, and if so to what extent, subcontracting may be considered. If subcontracting takes place, the operator entrusted with the administration and performance of public passenger transport services in accordance with this Regulation shall be required to

perform a major part of the public passenger transport services itself. A public service contract covering at the same time design, construction and operation of public passenger transport services may allow full subcontracting for the operation of those services. The public service contract shall, in accordance with national and Community law, determine the conditions applicable to subcontracting.

[8. Public service contracts shall require the operator to provide the competent authority with the information essential for the award of public service contracts, while ensuring the legitimate protection of confidential business information. Competent authorities shall make available to all interested parties relevant information for the preparation of an offer under a competitive tendering procedure, while ensuring the legitimate protection of confidential business information. This shall include information on passenger demand, fares, costs and revenues related to the public passenger transport covered by the competitive tendering procedure and details of the infrastructure specifications relevant for the operation of the required vehicles or rolling stock to enable interested parties to draft well informed business plans. Rail infrastructure managers shall support competent authorities in providing all relevant infrastructure specifications. Non-compliance with the provisions set out above shall be subject to the legal review provided for in Article 5(7).]

NOTES

Points (a) and (b) of para 1, and para 6 were substituted, and paras 4a, 4b and 8 were inserted and added respectively, by European Parliament and Council Regulation 2016/2338/EU, Art 1(4).

Application of this Article in relation to the UK: this Article is amended, in relation to the UK only, by the Regulation (EC) No 1370/2007 (Public Service Obligations in Transport) (Amendment) (EU Exit) Regulations 2020, SI 2020/504, reg 7, as from IP completion day (as defined in the European Union (Withdrawal Agreement) Act 2020, s 39), as follows—

"In Article 4 (mandatory content of public service contracts and general rules)—

(a) in paragraph 4, in the third subparagraph, omit the second sentence;

(b) in paragraph 4a, for "Union law, national law", substitute "any enactment, rule of law";

(c) for paragraph 4b substitute—

"4b. The Transfer of Undertakings (Protection of Employment) Regulations 2006 shall apply to a change of public service operator where such a change constitutes a relevant transfer within the meaning of regulation 2(1) of those Regulations.";

(d) in paragraph 5—

(i) for "Without prejudice to national and Community law, including collective agreements" substitute "Without prejudice to any enactment, rule of law or collective agreements";

(ii) for "transfer within the meaning of Directive 2001/23/EC" substitute "relevant transfer as defined in regulation 2(1) of the Transfer of Undertakings (Protection of Employment) Regulations 2006";

(e) in paragraph 6 omit ", in accordance with national law," and for "While respecting Directive 2001/23/EC" substitute "While respecting the requirements of the Transfer of Undertakings (Protection of Employment) Regulations 2006";

(f) in paragraph 7 omit ", in accordance with national and Community law,".".

Transitional provisions, see the note to Art 1 at **[5.369]**.

[5.374]

Article 5 Award of public service contracts

1. Public service contracts shall be awarded in accordance with the rules laid down in this Regulation. However, service contracts or public service contracts as defined in Directives 2004/17/EC or 2004/18/EC for public passenger transport services by bus or tram shall be awarded in accordance with the procedures provided for under those Directives where such contracts do not take the form of service concessions contracts as defined in those Directives. Where contracts are to be awarded in accordance with Directives 2004/17/EC or 2004/18/EC, the provisions of paragraphs 2 to 6 of this Article shall not apply.

[2. Unless prohibited by national law, any competent local authority, whether or not it is an individual authority or a group of authorities providing integrated public passenger transport services may decide to provide public passenger transport services itself or to award public service contracts directly to a legally distinct entity over which the competent local authority, or, in the case of a group of authorities at least one competent local authority, exercises control similar to that exercised over its own departments.

In the case of public passenger transport services by rail, the group of authorities referred to in the first subparagraph may be composed only of local competent authorities whose geographical area of competence is not national. The public passenger transport service or the public service contract referred to in the first subparagraph may only cover the transport needs of urban agglomerations or rural areas, or both.

Where a competent local authority takes such a decision, the following shall apply:]

(a) for the purposes of determining whether the competent local authority exercises control, factors such as the degree of representation on administrative, management or supervisory bodies, specifications relating thereto in the articles of association, ownership, effective influence and control over strategic decisions and individual management decisions shall be taken into consideration. In accordance with Community law, 100% ownership by the competent public authority, in particular in the case of public-private partnerships, is not a mandatory requirement for establishing control within the meaning of this paragraph, provided that there is a dominant public influence and that control can be established on the basis of other criteria;

(b) the condition for applying this paragraph is that the internal operator and any entity over which this operator exerts even a minimal influence perform their public passenger transport activity within the territory of the competent local authority, notwithstanding any outgoing lines or other ancillary elements of that activity which enter the territory of neighbouring competent local authorities, and do not take part in competitive tenders concerning the provision of public passenger transport services organised outside the territory of the competent local authority;

(c) notwithstanding point (b), an internal operator may participate in fair competitive tenders as from two years before the end of its directly awarded public service contract under the condition that a final decision has been taken to submit the public passenger transport services covered by the internal operator contract to fair competitive tender and that the internal operator has not concluded any other directly awarded public service contract;

(d) in the absence of a competent local authority, points (a), (b) and (c) shall apply to a national authority for the benefit of a geographical area which is not national, provided that the internal operator does not take part in competitive tenders concerning the provision of public passenger transport services organised outside the area for which the public service contract has been granted;

(e) if subcontracting under Article 4(7) is being considered, the internal operator shall be required to perform the major part of the public passenger transport service itself.

[3. Any competent authority which has recourse to a third party other than an internal operator, shall award public service contracts on the basis of a competitive tendering procedure, except in the cases specified in paragraphs 3a, 4, 4a, 4b, 5 and 6. The procedure adopted for competitive tendering shall be open to all operators, shall be fair and shall observe the principles of transparency and non-discrimination. Following the submission of tenders and any preselection, the procedure may involve negotiations in accordance with these principles in order to determine how best to meet specific or complex requirements.]

[3a. Unless prohibited by national law, as regards public service contracts for public passenger transport services by rail awarded on the basis of a competitive tendering procedure, the competent authority may decide to temporarily award new contracts directly where the competent authority considers that the direct award is justified by exceptional circumstances. Such exceptional circumstances shall include situations where:

— there are a number of competitive tendering procedures that are already being run by the competent authority or other competent authorities which could affect the number and quality of bids likely to be received if the contract is the subject of a competitive tendering procedure, or

— changes to the scope of one or more public service contracts are required in order to optimise the provision of public services.

The competent authority shall issue a substantiated decision and shall inform the Commission thereof without undue delay.

The duration of contracts awarded pursuant to this paragraph shall be proportionate to the exceptional circumstance concerned and in any case shall not exceed 5 years.

The competent authority shall publish such contracts. In doing so, it shall take into consideration the legitimate protection of confidential business information and commercial interests.

The subsequent contract that concerns the same public service obligations shall not be awarded on the basis of this provision.

3b. In application of paragraph 3, competent authorities may decide to apply the following procedure:

Competent authorities may make public their intentions to award a public service contract for public passenger transport services by rail by publishing an information notice in the *Official Journal of the European Union*.

That information notice shall contain a detailed description of the services that are the subject of the contract to be awarded, as well as the type and the duration of the contract.

Operators may express their interest within a period fixed by the competent authority which shall not be less than 60 days following the publication of the information notice.

If after the expiration of that period:

(a) only one operator has expressed its interest in participating in the procedure to award the public service contract;

(b) that operator has duly proved that it will in fact be able to provide the transport service complying with the obligations established in the public service contract;

(c) the absence of competition is not the result of an artificial narrowing of the parameters of the procurement; and

(d) no reasonable alternative exists;

the competent authorities may start negotiations with this operator in order to award the contract without further publication of an open tendering procedure.]

[4. Unless prohibited by national law, the competent authority may decide to award public service contracts directly:

(a) where their average annual value is estimated at less than EUR 1,000,000 or, in the case of a public service contract including public passenger transport services by rail, less than EUR 7,500,000; or

(b) where they concern the annual provision of less than 300,000 kilometres of public passenger transport services or, in the case of a public service contract including public passenger transport services by rail, less than 500,000 kilometres.]

In the case of a public service contract directly awarded to a small or medium-sized enterprise operating not more than 23 road vehicles, those thresholds may be increased to either an average annual value estimated at less than EUR 2,000,000 or to an annual provision of less than 600,000 kilometres of public passenger transport services.]

[4a. Unless prohibited by national law, the competent authority may decide to award public service contracts for public passenger transport services by rail directly:

(a) where it considers that the direct award is justified by the relevant structural and geographical characteristics of the market and network concerned, and in particular size, demand characteristics, network complexity, technical and geographical isolation and the services covered by the contract, and

(b) where such a contract would result in an improvement in quality of services or cost-efficiency, or both, compared to the previously awarded public service contract.

On that basis, the competent authority shall publish a substantiated decision and shall inform the Commission thereof within one month of its publication. The competent authority may proceed with the award of the contract.

Member States for which on 24 December 2017 the maximum annual market volume is less than 23 million train-km and which have only one competent authority at national level and one public service contract covering the entire network shall be deemed to fulfil the condition set out in point (a). Where a competent authority of one of those Member States decides to award a public service contract directly, the Member State concerned shall inform the Commission thereof. The United Kingdom may decide to apply this subparagraph to Northern Ireland.

Where the competent authority decides to award a public service contract directly, it shall lay down measurable, transparent and verifiable performance requirements. Such requirements shall be included in the contract.

The performance requirements shall in particular cover punctuality of services, frequency of train operations, quality of rolling stock and transport capacity for passengers.

The contract shall include specific performance indicators enabling the competent authority to carry out periodic assessments. The contract shall also include effective and deterrent measures to be imposed in case the railway undertaking fails to meet the performance requirements.

The competent authority shall periodically assess whether the railway undertaking has achieved its targets for meeting the performance requirements as set in the contract and shall make its findings public. Such periodic assessments shall take place at least every 5 years. The competent authority shall take appropriate and timely measures, including the imposition of effective and deterrent contractual penalties if the required improvements in quality of services or cost-efficiency, or both, are not achieved. The competent authority may at any time wholly or partially suspend or terminate the contract awarded under this provision if the operator fails to meet the performance requirements.

4b. Unless prohibited by national law, the competent authority may decide to award public service contracts for public passenger transport services by rail directly where they concern operating only passenger rail services by an operator which manages simultaneously the entire or the major part of the railway infrastructure on which the services are provided, where that railway infrastructure is excluded from the application of Articles 7, 7a, 7b, 7c, 7d, 8, 13 and Chapter IV of Directive 2012/34/EU of the European Parliament and of the Council[1] in accordance with Article 2(3)(a) or (b) of that Directive.

By way of derogation from Article 4(3), the duration of directly awarded contracts pursuant to this paragraph and paragraph 4a of this Article shall not exceed 10 years, except where Article 4(4) applies.

Contracts awarded in accordance with this paragraph and paragraph 4a shall be published, while taking into consideration the legitimate protection of confidential business information and commercial interests.]

[5. In the event of a disruption of services or the immediate risk of such a situation, the competent authority may take emergency measures.

The emergency measures shall take the form of a direct award or a formal agreement to extend a public service contract or a requirement to provide certain public service obligations. The public service operator shall have the right to appeal against the decision to impose the provision of certain public service obligations. The period for which a public service contract is awarded, extended or imposed by emergency measures shall not exceed 2 years.]

6. Unless prohibited by national law, competent authorities may decide to make direct awards of public service contracts where they concern transport by rail, with the exception of other track-based modes such as metro or tramways. In derogation from Article 4(3), such contracts shall not exceed 10 years, except where Article 4(4) applies.

[6a. In order to increase competition between railway undertakings, competent authorities may decide that contracts for public passenger transport services by rail covering parts of the same network or package of routes are to be awarded to different railway undertakings. To this end, the competent authorities may, before launching the competitive tendering procedure, decide to limit the number of contracts to be awarded to the same railway undertaking.]

7. Member States shall take the necessary measures to ensure that decisions taken in accordance with paragraphs 2 to 6 may be reviewed effectively and rapidly, at the request of any person having or having had an interest in obtaining a particular contract and who has been or risks being harmed by an alleged infringement, on the grounds that such decisions have infringed Community law or national rules implementing that law.

[For cases covered by paragraphs 4a and 4b, such measures shall include the possibility to request an assessment of the substantiated decision taken by the competent authority by an independent body designated by the Member State concerned. The outcome of such assessment shall be made publicly available in accordance with national law.]

Where bodies responsible for review procedures are not judicial in character, written reasons for their decisions shall always be given. Furthermore, in such a case, provision must be made so that any alleged illegal measure taken by the review body or any alleged defect in the exercise of the powers conferred on it may be the subject of judicial review or review by another body which is a court or tribunal within the meaning of Article 234 of the Treaty and independent of both the contracting authority and the review body.

NOTES

All words in square brackets in this Article were substituted or inserted by European Parliament and Council Regulation 2016/2338/EU, Art 1(5).

Application of this Article in relation to the UK: this Article is amended, in relation to the UK only, by the Regulation (EC) No 1370/2007 (Public Service Obligations in Transport) (Amendment) (EU Exit) Regulations 2020, SI 2020/504, reg 8, as from IP completion day (as defined in the European Union (Withdrawal Agreement) Act 2020, s 39), as follows—

"In Article 5 (award of public service contracts)—

(a) for paragraph 1 substitute—

"1. Public service contracts shall be awarded in accordance with the rules laid down in this Regulation. However, service contracts as defined in the relevant utilities contracts regulations and public service contracts as defined in the relevant public contracts regulations for public passenger transport services by bus or tram shall be awarded in accordance with the procedures provided for under those Regulations where such contracts do not take the form of services concession contracts. Where such service contracts or public service contracts are to be awarded in accordance with those Regulations, the provisions of paragraphs 2 to 6 of this Article shall not apply.

For the purposes of this paragraph:

—the relevant utilities contracts regulations for England and Wales are the Utilities Contracts Regulations 2016 and for Scotland are the Utilities Contracts (Scotland) Regulations 2016;

—the relevant public contracts regulations for England and Wales are the Public Contracts Regulations 2015 and for Scotland are the Public Contracts (Scotland) Regulations 2015; and

—a "services concession contract" is as defined:

—for England and Wales, in regulation 2(1) of the Concession Contracts Regulations 2016;

—for Scotland, in regulation 2(1) of the Concession Contracts (Scotland) Regulations 2016.";

(b) in paragraph 2—

(i) in the first subparagraph for "Unless prohibited by national law" substitute "Unless prohibited by any enactment or rule of law";

(ii) in the third subparagraph, in point (a) omit "In accordance with Community law,";

(c) in paragraph 3a—

(i) in the first subparagraph for "Unless prohibited by national law" substitute "Unless prohibited by any enactment or rule of law";

(ii) in the second subparagraph omit "and shall inform the Commission thereof without undue delay";

(d) in paragraph 3b, in the second subparagraph for "in the *Official Journal of the European Union*" substitute "in such form and manner as they consider appropriate";

(e) in paragraph 4—

(i) in the first subparagraph for "Unless prohibited by national law" substitute "Unless prohibited by any enactment or rule of law", and in point (a) for "EUR 1 000 000" substitute "£875,000" and for "EUR 7 500 000" substitute £6,500,000";

(ii) in the second subparagraph for "EUR 2 000 000" substitute "£1,750,000";

(f) in paragraph 4a—

(i) in the first subparagraph for "Unless prohibited by national law" substitute "Unless prohibited by any enactment or rule of law";

(ii) in the second subparagraph omit "and shall inform the Commission thereof within one month of its publication";

(iii) omit the third subparagraph;

(g) in paragraph 4b, in the first subparagraph for "Unless prohibited by national law" substitute "Unless prohibited by any enactment or rule of law" and for the words from "is excluded" to the end substitute "comprises a network of the kind referred to in regulation 4(7)(a) or (b) of the Railways (Access, Management and Licensing of Railway Undertakings) Regulations 2016";

(h) in paragraph 6 for "Unless prohibited by national law" substitute "Unless prohibited by any enactment or rule of law"."

Transitional provisions, see the note to Art 1 at **[5.369]**.

[1] Directive 2012/34/EU of the European Parliament and of the Council of 21 November 2012 establishing a single European railway area (OJ L343, 14.12.2012, p 32).

[5.375]

[Article 5a Rail rolling stock

1. With a view to launching a competitive tendering procedure, competent authorities shall assess whether measures are necessary to ensure effective and non-discriminatory access to suitable rolling stock. This assessment shall take into account the presence of rolling-stock leasing companies, or of other market actors providing for the leasing of rolling stock, in the relevant market. The assessment report shall be made publicly available.

2. Competent authorities may decide, in accordance with national law and in compliance with State aid rules, to take appropriate measures to ensure effective and non-discriminatory access to suitable rolling stock. Such measures may include:

(a) the acquisition by the competent authority of the rolling stock used for the execution of the public service contract with a view to making it available to the selected public service operator at market price or as part of the public service contract pursuant to Article 4(1)(b), Article 6 and, if applicable, to the Annex;

(b) the provision by the competent authority of a guarantee for the financing of the rolling stock used for the execution of the public service contract at market price or as part of the public service contract pursuant to Article 4(1)(b), Article 6 and, if applicable, to the Annex, including a guarantee covering the residual value risk;

(c) a commitment by the competent authority in the public service contract to take over the rolling stock at predefined financial conditions at the end of the contract at market price; or

(d) cooperation with other competent authorities in order to create a larger pool of rolling stock.

3. If the rolling stock is made available to a new public transport operator, the competent authority shall include in the tender documents any available information about the cost of maintenance of the rolling stock and about its physical condition.]

NOTES

Inserted by European Parliament and Council Regulation 2016/2338/EU, Art 1(6).

Application of this Article in relation to the UK: this Article is amended, in relation to the UK only, by the Regulation (EC) No 1370/2007 (Public Service Obligations in Transport) (Amendment) (EU Exit) Regulations 2020, SI 2020/504, reg 9, as from IP completion day (as defined in the European Union (Withdrawal Agreement) Act 2020, s 39), as follows—

"In Article 5a (rail rolling stock), in paragraph 2 omit "in accordance with national law and".".

Transitional provisions, see the note to Art 1 at **[5.369]**.

This Article is also amended, in relation to the UK only, by the State Aid (Revocations and Amendments) (EU Exit) Regulations 2020, SI 2020/1470, reg 7(1), Sch 1, Pt 1, para 2(2), as from IP completion day (as defined in the European Union (Withdrawal Agreement) Act 2020, s 39), as follows—

"(2) In Article 5a, in paragraph 2—

(a) omit the comma after "decide";

(b) omit "in compliance with State aid rules,".".

Note that the amendment made by SI 2020/1470 does not extend to Northern Ireland (see reg 1(5) of the 2020 Regulations).

[5.376]

Article 6 Public service compensation

[1. All compensation connected with a general rule or a public service contract shall comply with Article 4, irrespective of how the contract was awarded. All compensation of whatever nature connected with a public service contract not awarded according to Article 5(1), (3) or (3b) or connected with a general rule shall also comply with the provisions laid down in the Annex.]

2. At the written request of the Commission, Member States shall communicate, within a period of three months or any longer period as may be fixed in that request, all the information that the Commission considers necessary to determine whether the compensation granted is compatible with this Regulation.

NOTES

Para 1: substituted by European Parliament and Council Regulation 2016/2338/EU, Art 1(7).

Application of this Article in relation to the UK: this Article is amended, in relation to the UK only, by the Regulation (EC) No 1370/2007 (Public Service Obligations in Transport) (Amendment) (EU Exit) Regulations 2020, SI 2020/504, reg 10, as from IP completion day (as defined in the European Union (Withdrawal Agreement) Act 2020, s 39), as follows—

"In Article 6 (public service compensation) omit paragraph 2.".

Transitional provisions, see the note to Art 1 at **[5.369]**.

[5.377]

Article 7 Publication

[1. Each competent authority shall make public once a year an aggregated report on the public service obligations for which it is responsible. That report shall include the starting date and duration of the public service contracts, the selected public service operators and the compensation payments and exclusive rights granted to those public service operators by way of reimbursement. The report shall distinguish between bus transport and rail transport, enable the performance, quality and financing of the public transport network to be monitored and assessed and, if appropriate, provide information on the nature and extent of any exclusive rights granted. The report shall also take into consideration the policy objectives as stated in public transport policy documents in the Member State concerned. Member States shall facilitate central access to these reports, for instance through a common web portal.]

2. Each competent authority shall take the necessary measures to ensure that, at least one year before the launch of the invitation to tender procedure or one year before the direct award, the following information at least is published in the *Official Journal of the European Union*:

(a) the name and address of the competent authority;

(b) the type of award envisaged;

(c) the services and areas potentially covered by the award;

[(d) the envisaged starting date and duration of the public service contract.]

Competent authorities may decide not to publish this information where a public service contract concerns an annual provision of less than 50,000 kilometres of public passenger transport services.

Should this information change after its publication, the competent authority shall publish a rectification accordingly as soon as possible. This rectification shall be without prejudice to the launching date of the direct award or of the invitation to tender.

This paragraph shall not apply to Article 5(5).

3. In the case of a direct award of public service contracts for transport by rail, as provided for in Article 5(6), the competent authority shall make public the following information within one year of granting the award:

(a) name of the contracting entity, its ownership and, if appropriate, the name of the party or parties exercising legal control;

(b) duration of the public service contract;

(c) description of the passenger transport services to be performed;

(d) description of the parameters of the financial compensation;

(e) quality targets, such as punctuality and reliability and rewards and penalties applicable;

(f) conditions relating to essential assets.

4. When so requested by an interested party, a competent authority shall forward to it the reasons for its decision for directly awarding a public service contract.

NOTES

Para 1 substituted, and point (d) of para 2 added, by European Parliament and Council Regulation 2016/2338/EU, Art 1(8).

Application of this Article in relation to the UK: this Article is amended, in relation to the UK only, by the Regulation (EC) No 1370/2007 (Public Service Obligations in Transport) (Amendment) (EU Exit) Regulations 2020, SI 2020/504, reg 11, as from IP completion day (as defined in the European Union (Withdrawal Agreement) Act 2020, s 39), as follows—

"In Article 7 (publication)—

(a) in paragraph 1 omit "in the Member State concerned" and omit the final sentence;

(b) in paragraph 2, for "in the *Official Journal of the European Union*" substitute "on its website".".

Transitional provisions, see the note to Art 1 at **[5.369]**.

[5.378]

Article 8 Transition

1. Public service contracts shall be awarded in accordance with the rules laid down in this Regulation. However, service contracts or public service contracts as defined in Directive 2004/17/EC or 2004/18/EC for public passenger transport services by bus or tram shall be awarded in accordance with the procedures provided for under those

Directives where such contracts do not take the form of service concessions contracts as defined in those Directives. Where contracts are to be awarded in accordance with Directives 2004/17/EC or 2004/18/EC, the provisions of paragraphs 2 to 4 of this Article shall not apply.

[2. Without prejudice to paragraph 3,

(i) Article 5 shall apply to the award of public service contracts for passenger transport services by road and by track-based modes other than rail such as metro or tramways from 3 December 2019.

(ii) Article 5 shall apply to public passenger transport services by rail from 3 December 2019.

(iii) Article 5(6) and Article 7(3) shall cease to apply from 25 December 2023.

The duration of contracts awarded in accordance with Article 5(6) between 3 December 2019 and 24 December 2023 shall not exceed 10 years.

Until 2 December 2019, Member States shall take measures to gradually comply with Article 5 in order to avoid serious structural problems in particular relating to transport capacity.

Within six months after 25 December 2020, Member States shall provide the Commission with a progress report, highlighting the implementation of any award of public service contracts that comply with Article 5. On the basis of the Member States' progress reports, the Commission shall carry out a review and, if appropriate, submit legislative proposals.]

[2a. Public service contracts for public passenger transport services by rail directly awarded on the basis of a procedure other than a fair competitive procedure as of 24 December 2017 until 2 December 2019 may continue until their expiry date. In derogation from Article 4(3), the duration of such contracts shall not exceed 10 years, except where Article 4(4) applies.]

3. In the application of paragraph 2, no account shall be taken of public service contracts awarded in accordance with Community and national law:

(a) before 26 July 2000 on the basis of a fair competitive tendering procedure;

(b) before 26 July 2000 on the basis of a procedure other than a fair competitive tendering procedure;

(c) as from 26 July 2000 and before 3 December 2009 on the basis of a fair competitive tendering procedure;

[(d) as from 26 July 2000 and before 24 December 2017 on the basis of a procedure other than a fair competitive tendering procedure.]

The contracts referred to in (a) may continue until they expire. The contracts referred to in (b) and (c) may continue until they expire, but for no longer than 30 years. The contracts referred to in (d) may continue until they expire, provided they are of limited duration comparable to the durations specified in Article 4.

Public service contracts may continue until they expire where their termination would entail undue legal or economic consequences and provided that the Commission has given its approval.

4. Without prejudice to paragraph 3, the competent authorities may opt, in the second half of the transitional period specified in paragraph 2, to exclude from participation in the award of contracts by invitation to tender those public service operators which cannot provide evidence that the value of the public transport services for which they are receiving compensation or enjoy an exclusive right granted in accordance with this Regulation represents at least half the value of all the public transport services for which they are receiving compensation or enjoy an exclusive right. Such exclusion shall not apply to public service operators running the services which are to be tendered. For the application of this criterion, no account shall be taken of public service contracts awarded by emergency measure as referred to in Article 5(5).

Where competent authorities make use of the option referred to in the first subparagraph, they shall do so without discrimination, exclude all potential public service operators meeting this criterion and inform the potential operators of their decision at the beginning of the procedure for the award of public service contracts.

The competent authorities concerned shall inform the Commission of their intention to apply this provision at least two months before the publication of the invitation to tender.

NOTES

Para 2 and point (d) of para 3 were substituted, and para 2a was inserted, by European Parliament and Council Regulation 2016/2338/EU, Art 1(9).

Application of this Article in relation to the UK: this Article is amended, in relation to the UK only, by the Regulation (EC) No 1370/2007 (Public Service Obligations in Transport) (Amendment) (EU Exit) Regulations 2020, SI 2020/504, reg 12, as from IP completion day (as defined in the European Union (Withdrawal Agreement) Act 2020, s 39), as follows—

"In Article 8 (transition)—

(a) for paragraph 1, substitute—

"1. Public service contracts shall be awarded in accordance with the rules laid down in this Regulation. However, service contracts as defined in the relevant utilities contracts regulations and public service contracts as defined in the relevant public contracts regulations for public passenger transport services by bus or tram shall be awarded in accordance with the procedures provided for under those Regulations where such contracts do not take the form of services concession contracts. Where such service contracts or public service contracts are to be awarded in accordance with those Regulations, the provisions of paragraphs 2 to 4 of this Article shall not apply.

For the purposes of this paragraph:

—the relevant utilities contracts regulations for England and Wales are the Utilities Contracts Regulations 2016 and for Scotland are the Utilities Contracts (Scotland) Regulations 2016;

—the relevant public contracts regulations for England and Wales are the Public Contracts Regulations 2015 and for Scotland are the Public Contracts (Scotland) Regulations 2015; and

—a "services concession contract" is as defined:

—for England and Wales, in regulation 2(1) of the Concession Contracts Regulations 2016;

—for Scotland, in regulation 2(1) of the Concession Contracts (Scotland) Regulations 2016.";

(b) in paragraph 2 omit the fourth subparagraph;

(c) in paragraph 3, in the third subparagraph omit "and provided that the Commission has given its prior approval";

(d) in paragraph 4 omit the third subparagraph.".

Transitional provisions, see the note to Art 1 at **[5.369]**.

[5.379]

Article 9 Compatibility with the Treaty

1. Public service compensation for the operation of public passenger transport services or for complying with tariff obligations established through general rules paid in accordance with this Regulation shall be compatible with the common market. Such compensation shall be exempt from the prior notification requirement laid down in Article 88(3) of the Treaty.

2. Without prejudice to Articles 73, 86, 87 and 88 of the Treaty, Member States may continue to grant aid for the transport sector pursuant to Article 73 of the Treaty which meets transport coordination needs or which represents reimbursement for the discharge of certain obligations inherent in the concept of a public service, other than those covered by this Regulation, and in particular:

(a) until the entry into force of common rules on the allocation of infrastructure costs, where aid is granted to undertakings which have to bear expenditure relating to the infrastructure used by them, while other undertakings are not subject to a like burden. In determining the amount of aid thus granted, account shall be taken of the infrastructure costs which competing modes of transport do not have to bear;

(b) where the purpose of the aid is to promote either research into, or development of, transport systems and technologies which are more economic for the Community in general. Such aid shall be restricted to the research and development stage and may not cover the commercial exploitation of such transport systems and technologies.

[5.380]

Article 10 Repeal

1. Regulation (EEC) No 1191/69 is hereby repealed. Its provisions shall however continue to apply to freight transport services for a period of three years after the entry into force of this Regulation.

2. Regulation (EEC) No 1107/70 is hereby repealed.

[5.381]

Article 11 Reports

After the end of the transitional period specified in Article 8(2), the Commission shall present a report on the implementation of this Regulation and on the developments in the provision of public passenger transport in the Community, assessing in particular the development of the quality of public passenger transport services and the effects of direct awards, accompanied, if necessary, by appropriate proposals for the amendment of this Regulation.

NOTES

Repeal of this Article in relation to the UK: this Article is repealed, in relation to the UK only, by the Regulation (EC) No 1370/2007 (Public Service Obligations in Transport) (Amendment) (EU Exit) Regulations 2020, SI 2020/504, reg 13, as from IP completion day (as defined in the European Union (Withdrawal Agreement) Act 2020, s 39).

Transitional provisions, see the note to Art 1 at **[5.369]**.

[5.382]

Article 12 Entry into force

This Regulation shall enter into force on 3 December 2009.

This Regulation shall be binding in its entirety and directly applicable in all Member States.

NOTES

Application of this Article in relation to the UK: this Article is amended, in relation to the UK only, by the Regulation (EC) No 1370/2007 (Public Service Obligations in Transport) (Amendment) (EU Exit) Regulations 2020, SI 2020/504, reg 14, as from IP completion day (as defined in the European Union (Withdrawal Agreement) Act 2020, s 39), as follows—

"In the text immediately after Article 12 (entry into force) omit "and directly applicable in all Member States".".

Transitional provisions, see the note to Art 1 at **[5.369]**.

ANNEX

RULES APPLICABLE TO COMPENSATION IN THE CASES REFERRED TO IN ARTICLE 6(1)

[5.383]

1. The compensation connected with public service contracts awarded directly in accordance with Article 5(2), (4), (5) or (6) or with a general rule must be calculated in accordance with the rules laid down in this Annex.

2. The compensation may not exceed an amount corresponding to the net financial effect equivalent to the total of the effects, positive or negative, of compliance with the public service obligation on the costs and revenue of the public service operator. The effects shall be assessed by comparing the situation where the public service obligation is met with the situation which would have existed if the obligation had not been met. In order to calculate the net financial effect, the competent authority shall be guided by the following scheme:

costs incurred in relation to a public service obligation or a bundle of public service obligations imposed by the competent authority/authorities, contained in a public service contract and/or in a general rule,

minus any positive financial effects generated within the network operated under the public service obligation(s) in question,

minus receipts from tariff or any other revenue generated while fulfilling the public service obligation(s) in question,

plus a reasonable profit,

equals net financial effect.

3. Compliance with the public service obligation may have an impact on possible transport activities of an operator beyond the public service obligation(s) in question. In order to avoid overcompensation or lack of compensation, quantifiable financial effects on the operator's networks concerned shall therefore be taken into account when calculating the net financial effect.

4. Costs and revenue must be calculated in accordance with the accounting and tax rules in force.

5. In order to increase transparency and avoid cross-subsidies, where a public service operator not only operates compensated services subject to public transport service obligations, but also engages in other activities, the accounts of the said public services must be separated so as to meet at least the following conditions:

— the operating accounts corresponding to each of these activities must be separate and the proportion of the corresponding assets and the fixed costs must be allocated in accordance with the accounting and tax rules in force,

— all variable costs, an appropriate contribution to the fixed costs and a reasonable profit connected with any other activity of the public service operator may under no circumstances be charged to the public service in question,

— the costs of the public service must be balanced by operating revenue and payments from public authorities, without any possibility of transfer of revenue to another sector of the public service operator's activity.

6. 'Reasonable profit' must be taken to mean a rate of return on capital that is normal for the sector in a given Member State and that takes account of the risk, or absence of risk, incurred by the public service operator by virtue of public authority intervention.

7. The method of compensation must promote the maintenance or development of:

— effective management by the public service operator, which can be the subject of an objective assessment, and

— the provision of passenger transport services of a sufficiently high standard.

NOTES

Application of this Annex in relation to the UK: this Annex is amended, in relation to the UK only, by the Regulation (EC) No 1370/2007 (Public Service Obligations in Transport) (Amendment) (EU Exit) Regulations 2020, SI 2020/504, reg 15, as from IP completion day (as defined in the European Union (Withdrawal Agreement) Act 2020, s 39), as follows—

"In the Annex, in paragraph 6 omit "in a given Member State".".

Transitional provisions, see the note to Art 1 at **[5.369]**.

COMMUNICATION FROM THE COMMISSION

(2008/C184/07)

Community guidelines on State aid for railway undertakings

[5.384]

NOTES

Date of publication in OJ: OJ C184, 22.7.2008, p 13.

Note: with effect from 1 December 2009, the EC Treaty was replaced by the Treaty on the Functioning of the European Union. References in this document to provisions of the EC Treaty should be construed accordingly.

1. INTRODUCTION

1.1. General context: the railway sector

[5.385]

1. The railways have unique advantages: they are a safe and clean mode of transport. Rail transport therefore has great potential for contributing to the development of sustainable transport in Europe.

2. The White Paper "European transport policy for 2010: time to decide"[1] and its mid-term review[2] underline to what extent a dynamic railway industry is necessary for establishing an efficient, clean and safe goods and passenger transport system that will contribute to the creation of a single European market enjoying lasting prosperity. The road congestion plaguing the towns and certain areas of the European Community, the need to face up to the challenges of climate change, and the increase in fuel prices show how necessary it is to stimulate the development of rail transport. In this respect it should be pointed out that the common transport policy also has to pursue the environmental objectives set by the Treaty.[3]

3. However, rail transport in Europe has an image problem, having declined steadily from the 1960s to the end of the 20th century. Both goods and passenger traffic volumes have fallen in relative terms compared with the other transport modes. Rail freight has even shown a decline in absolute terms: loads transported by rail were higher in 1970 than in 2000. The traditional railway undertakings were unable to offer the reliability and good timekeeping their customers expected of them, which led to a shift of traffic from rail to the other modes of transport, chiefly road.[4] Although passenger transport by rail might have continued to grow in absolute terms, this increase seems very limited compared with that of road and air transport.[5]

4. This trend seems to have reversed recently,[6] but there is still a long way to go for rail transport to become sound and competitive. Particularly in the rail freight transport sector there continue to be major difficulties which call for public-sector action.[7]

5. The relative decline in Europe's railway industry is largely due to the way transport supply has been organised historically, essentially on national and monopolistic lines.

6. First of all, in the absence of competition on the national networks, railway undertakings had no incentive to reduce their operating costs and develop new services. Their activities did not bring in sufficient revenue to cover all the costs and investments necessary. These essential investments were not always made and sometimes the Member States forced the national railway undertakings into making them when they were not in a position to finance them adequately from their own resources. The result was heavy indebtedness for these undertakings, which itself had a negative impact on their development.

7. Secondly, the development of rail transport in Europe was hamstrung by the lack of standardisation and interoperability on the networks, while road hauliers and air carriers had been able to develop a whole range of international services. The Community has inherited a mosaic of national rail networks characterised by different track gauges and incompatible signalling and safety systems, which do not allow the railway undertakings to benefit from the economies of scale which would result from designing infrastructure and rolling stock for a large single market rather than for 25[8] national markets.

8. The Community is conducting a three-pronged policy to revitalise the rail industry by:

(a) gradually introducing conditions fostering competition on the rail transport services markets;

(b) encouraging standardisation and technical harmonisation on the European rail networks, aiming at full interoperability at the European level;

(c) granting financial support at Community level (in the TEN-T programme and the Structural Funds framework).

9. The Community has thus gradually opened up the rail transport markets to competition. An initial liberalisation package was adopted in 2001 including Directive 2001/12/EC of the European Parliament and of the Council of 26 February 2001 amending Council Directive 91/440/EEC on the development of the Community's railways,[9] Directive 2001/13/EC of the European Parliament and of the Council of 26 February 2001 amending Council Directive 95/18/EC on the licensing of railway undertakings,[10] Directive 2001/14/EC of the European Parliament and of the Council of 26 February 2001 on the allocation of railway infrastructure capacity and the levying of charges for the use of railway infrastructure and safety certification.[11] That package was followed by a second package in 2004 the main instruments of which were Regulation (EC) No 881/2004 of the European Parliament and of the Council of 29 April 2004 establishing a European Railway Agency,[12] Directive 2004/49/EC of the European Parliament and of the Council of 29 April 2004 on safety on the Community's railways and amending Council Directive 95/18/EC on the licensing of railway undertakings and Directive 2001/14/EC on the allocation of railway infrastructure capacity and the levying of charges for the use of railway infrastructure and safety certification,[13] Directive 2004/50/EC of the European Parliament and of the Council of 29 April 2004 amending Council Directive 96/48/EC on the interoperability of the trans-European high-speed rail system and Directive 2001/16/EC of the European Parliament and of the Council on the interoperability of the trans-European conventional rail system[14] and Directive 2004/51/EC of the European Parliament and of the Council of 29 April 2004 amending Council Directive 91/440/EEC on the development of the Community's railways.[15] A third package was adopted in 2007 comprising Regulation (EC) No 1370/2007 of the European Parliament and of the Council of 23 October 2007 on public passenger transport services by rail and by road and repealing Council Regulations (EEC) No 1191/69 and (EEC) No 1107/70,[16] Regulation (EC) No 1371/2007 of the European Parliament and of the Council of 23 October 2007 on rail passengers' rights and obligations,[17] Directive 2007/58/EC of the European Parliament and of the Council of 23 October 2007 amending Council Directive 91/440/EEC on the development of the Community's railways, and Directive 2001/14/EC on the allocation of railway infrastructure capacity and the levying of charges for the use of railway infrastructure[18] and Directive 2007/59/EC of the European Parliament and of the Council of 23 October 2007 on the certification of train drivers operating locomotives and trains on the railway system in the Community.[19] As a result, the rail freight market was opened to competition on 15 March 2003 on the trans-European rail freight network, then on 1 January 2006 for international freight and finally from 1 January 2007 for rail cabotage. The third railway package sets 1 January 2010 as the date for opening up international passenger transport to competition. Some of the Member States, such as the United Kingdom, Germany, the Netherlands and Italy, have already (partially) opened up their domestic passenger transport markets.

10. The relevant provisions of Council Directive 91/440/EEC of 29 July 1991 on the development of the Community's railways,[20] put in place a new institutional and organisational framework for the players in the railway industry, involving:

(a) separating railway undertakings[21] from infrastructure managers[22] as regards accounts and organisation;

(b) management independence of railway undertakings;

(c) management of railway undertakings according to the principles which apply to commercial companies;

(d) financial equilibrium of railway undertakings according to a sound business plan;

(e) compatibility of Member States' financial measures with the State aid rules.[23]

11. Alongside this liberalisation process, the Commission has undertaken, on a second level, to promote the interoperability of European rail networks. This approach has been accompanied by Community initiatives to improve the safety standard of rail transport.[24]

12. The third level of public intervention in favour of the railway industry lies in the area of financial support. The Commission considers this support to be justified in certain circumstances in view of the substantial adaptation costs necessary in that industry.

13. The Commission notes, furthermore, that there has always been considerable injection of public funds in the rail transport sector. Since 2004 the States of the European Union when it comprised 25 Member States (EU-25) have overall contributed funds totalling some EUR 17 billion to the construction and maintenance of railway infrastructure.[25] The Member States pay railway undertakings EUR 15 billion annually in compensation for the provision of unprofitable passenger transport services.[25]

14. The granting of State aid to the railway industry can be authorised only where it contributes to the completion of an integrated European market, open to competition and interoperable and to Community objectives of sustainable mobility. The Commission will accordingly make sure that public sector financial support does not cause distortions of competition contrary to the common interest. Here the Commission will in certain cases be able to ask Member States for commitments on the Community objectives in return for the granting of aid.

1.2.
Objective and scope of these guidelines

15. The objective of these guidelines is to provide guidance on the compatibility with the Treaty of State aid to railway undertakings as it is defined in Directive 91/440/EEC and in the context described above. In addition, Chapter 3 also applies to urban, suburban and regional passenger transport undertakings. The guidelines are based in particular on the principles established by the Community legislator in the three successive railway packages. Their aim is to improve the transparency of public financing and legal certainty with regard to the Treaty rules in the context of the opening-up of the markets. These guidelines do not concern public financing intended for infrastructure managers.

16. Article 87(1) of the Treaty provides that in principle any aid granted by a Member State which threatens to distort competition by favouring certain undertakings or the production of certain goods is, in so far as it affects trade between Member States, incompatible with the common market. Nevertheless, such State aid may in certain situations be justified in the light of the common interest of the Community. Some of these situations are mentioned in Article 87(3) of the Treaty, and apply to the transport sector as they do to other sectors of the economy.

17. Also, Article 73 of the Treaty provides that aids are compatible with the common market "if they meet the needs of coordination of transport or if they represent reimbursement for the discharge of certain obligations inherent in the concept of a public service". This Article constitutes a lex specialis in the general scheme of the Treaty. On the basis of this Article the Community legislator has adopted two instruments specific to the transport sector: Council Regulation (EEC) No 1191/69 of 26 June 1969 on action by Member States concerning the obligations inherent in the concept of a public service in transport by rail, road and inland waterway[26] and Council Regulation (EEC) No 1107/70 of 4 June 1970 on the granting of aids for transport by rail, road and inland waterway.[27] Council Regulation (EEC) No 1192/69 of 26 June 1969 on common rules for the normalisation of the accounts of railway undertakings[28] likewise provides that certain compensation may be granted by Member States to railway undertakings.

18. Article 3 of Regulation (EEC) No 1107/70 provides that Member States are neither to take coordination measures nor to impose obligations inherent in the concept of a public service which involve the granting of aids pursuant to Article 73 of the Treaty except in the cases or circumstances provided for by the Regulation in question, without prejudice, however, to Regulations (EEC) No 1191/69 and (EEC) No 1192/69. According to the judgment of the Court of Justice of the European Communities in *Altmark*,[29] it follows that State aid which cannot be authorised on the basis of Regulations (EEC) No 1107/70, (EEC) No 1191/69 or (EEC) No 1192/69 cannot be declared compatible on the basis of Article 73 of the Treaty.[30] In addition, it should be recalled that public service compensation which does not respect provisions stemming from Article 73 of the Treaty cannot be declared compatible with the common market on the basis of Article 86(2) or any other provision of the Treaty.[31]

19. Regulation (EC) No 1370/2007 ("the PSO Regulation"), which will enter into force on 3 December 2009 and which repeals Regulations (EEC) No 1191/69 and (EEC) No 1107/70, will put in place a new legal framework. The aspects relating to public service compensation are therefore not covered by these guidelines.

20. After the entry into force of Regulation (EC) No 1370/2007, Article 73 of the Treaty will be directly applicable as a legal basis for establishing the compatibility of aid not covered by the PSO Regulation, and in particular aid for the coordination of freight transport. A general interpretation therefore needs to be developed for considering the compatibility of aid for coordination purposes with Article 73 of the Treaty. The aim of these guidelines is in particular to establish criteria for this examination and intensity thresholds. In view of the wording of Article 73, the Commission must nevertheless make it possible for Member States to show, where appropriate, the need for and proportionality of any measures which exceed the thresholds established.

21. These guidelines concern the application of Articles 73 and 87 of the Treaty and their implementation with regard to public funding for railway undertakings within the meaning of Directive 91/440/EEC. They deal with the following aspects: public financing of railway undertakings by means of infrastructure funding (Chapter 2), aid for the purchase and renewal of rolling stock (Chapter 3), debt cancellation by States with a view to the financial rejuvenation of railway undertakings (Chapter 4), aid for restructuring railway undertakings (Chapter 5), aid for the needs of transport coordination (Chapter 6), and State guarantees for railway undertakings (Chapter 7). However, these guidelines do not deal with the rules for the application of the PSO Regulation, for which the Commission has not yet developed any decision-making practice.[32]

NOTES

1 COM(2001) 370 of 12 September 2001, p 18.

2 Communication from the Commission "Keep Europe moving – Sustainable mobility for our continent – Mid-term review of the Transport White Paper" (COM(2006) 314, 22 June 2006, p 21).

3 Article 2 of the Treaty stipulates as one of the main objectives of the Community that of promoting "sustainable and non-inflationary growth" respecting the environment. These provisions are supplemented by specific objectives set out in

Article 174, which provides that Community environment policy shall contribute in particular to preserving, protecting and improving the quality of the environment. Article 6 of the Treaty provides that "Environmental protection requirements must be integrated into the definition and implementation of the Community policies and activities referred to in Article 3, in particular with a view to promoting sustainable development".

4 From 1995 to 2005 rail freight (expressed in tonne-km) increased by 0,9% per year on average, as against + 3,3% average annual growth for road during the same period (source: Eurostat).

5 From 1995 to 2004 passenger rail transport (expressed in passenger-km) increased by 0,9% per year on average, as against + 1,8% average annual growth for private vehicles during the same period (source: Eurostat).

6 Since 2002, particularly in those countries which have opened up their markets to competition. In 2006 there was a 3,7% growth on the year in rail freight performance and 3% in the performance of passenger transport. This improvement is likely to continue in 2007.

7 Communication from the Commission "Towards a rail network giving priority to freight" (SEC(2007) 1322, SEC(2007) 1324 and SEC(2007) 1325, 18 October 2007).

8 Malta and Cyprus do not have rail transport networks.

9 OJ L75, 15.3.2001, p 1.

10 OJ L75, 15.3.2001, p 26.

11 OJ L75, 15.3.2001, p 29. Directive as last amended by Directive 2007/58/EC (OJ L315, 3.12.2007, p 44).

12 OJ L164, 30.4.2004, p 1.

13 OJ L164, 30.4.2004, p 44.

14 OJ L164, 30.4.2004, p 114.

15 OJ L164, 30.4.2004, p 164.

16 OJ L315, 3.12.2007, p 1.

17 OJ L315, 3.12.2007, p 14.

18 OJ L315, 3.12.2007, p 44.

19 OJ L315, 3.12.2007, p 51.

20 OJ L237, 24.8.1991, p 25. Directive as last amended by Directive 2007/58/EC.

21 Article 3 of Directive 91/440/EEC defines a railway undertaking as "any public or private undertaking licensed according to applicable Community legislation, the principal business of which is to provide services for the transport of goods and/or passengers by rail with a requirement that the undertaking must ensure traction; this also includes undertakings which provide traction only".

22 Article 3 of Directive 91/440/EEC defines an infrastructure manager as "any body or undertaking responsible in particular for establishing and maintaining railway infrastructure. This may also include the management of infrastructure control and safety systems. The functions of the infrastructure manager on a network or part of a network may be allocated to different bodies or undertakings".

23 Article 9(3) of Directive 91/440/EEC states: "Aid accorded by Member States to cancel the debts referred to in this Article shall be granted in accordance with Articles 73, 87 and 88 of the Treaty".

24 In particular, Directive 2004/49/EC.

25 Source: European Commission, on the basis of the data communicated annually by the Member States. The figures may be even higher in that not all financial support has been notified, in particular co-financing through the Structural and Cohesion Funds.

26 OJ L156, 28.6.1969, p 1. Regulation as last amended by Regulation (EEC) No 1893/91 (OJ L169, 29.6.1991, p 1).

27 OJ L130, 15.6.1970, p 1.

28 OJ L156, 28.6.1969, p 8. Regulation as last amended by Regulation (EC) No 1791/2006 (OJ L363, 20.12.2006, p 1).

29 Judgment of the Court of Justice of 24 July 2003, Case C-280/00, *Altmark Trans GmbH and Regierungspräsidium Magdeburg v Nahverkehrsgesellschaft Altmark GmbH ("Altmark")* [2003] ECR I-7747.

30 Judgement in *Altmark*, paragraph 107.

31 See, in that regard, recital 17 of Commission Decision of 28 November 2005 on the application of Article 86(2) of the EC Treaty to State aid in the form of public service compensation granted to certain undertakings entrusted with the operation of services of general economic interest (OJ L312, 29.11.2005, p 67, point 17).

32 Nor do they concern the application of Regulation (EEC) No 1192/69.

2. PUBLIC FINANCING OF RAILWAY UNDERTAKINGS BY MEANS OF RAILWAY INFRASTRUCTURE FUNDING

[5.386]

22. Railway infrastructure is of major importance for the development of the railway sector in Europe. Whether for interoperability, safety or the development of high-speed rail, considerable investments will have to be made in this infrastructure.[1]

23. These guidelines apply only to railway undertakings. Their aim is therefore not to define, in the light of State aid rules, the legal framework which applies to the public financing of infrastructure. This Chapter only examines the effects of public financing of infrastructure on railway undertakings.

24. Moreover, public financing of infrastructure development can grant an advantage to railway undertakings indirectly and thereby constitute aid. According to the case-law of the Court of Justice, it should be evaluated whether the infrastructure measure has the economic effect of lightening the burden of charges normally encumbering railway undertakings' budgets.[2] For that to be the case, a selective advantage would have to be granted to the undertakings concerned, that advantage originating in the financing of the infrastructure in question.[3]

25. Where infrastructure use is open to all potential users in a fair and non-discriminatory manner, and access to that infrastructure is charged for at a rate in accordance with Community legislation (Directive 2001/14/EC), the Commission normally considers that public financing of the infrastructure does not constitute State aid to railway undertakings.[4]

26. The Commission also points out that, where public financing of railway infrastructure constitutes aid to one or more railway undertakings, it may be authorised, for example on the basis of Article 73 of the Treaty, if the infrastructure in question meets the needs of transport coordination. In this regard, Chapter 6 of these guidelines is a pertinent reference point for assessing compatibility.

NOTES

1 Communication from the Commission "Keep Europe moving – Sustainable mobility for our continent – Mid-term review of the Transport White Paper".

2 Judgment of the Court of Justice of 13 June 2002, Case C-382/99, *Netherlands v Commission* [2002] ECR I-5163.

3 Judgment of the Court of Justice of 19 September 2000, Case C-156/98, *Germany v Commission* [2000] ECR I-6857.

4 Commission Decision of 7 June 2006, N 478/04, Ireland – State guarantee for capital borrowings by Córas Iompair Éireann (CIÉ) for infrastructure investment (OJ C209, 31.8.2006, p 8); Decision of 8 March 2006, N 284/05, Ireland – Regional Broadband Programme (OJ C207, 30.8.2006, p 3), point 34; and the following Decisions: Decision 2003/227/EC of 2 August 2002 on various measures and the State aid invested by Spain in "Terra Mítica SA", a theme park near Benidorm (Alicante) (OJ L91, 8.4.2003, p 23), point 64; Decision of 20 April 2005, N 355/04 PPP, Belgium – Public-Private-Partnership for tunnelling the Krijgsbaan at Deurne; the development of industrial estates and the operation of Antwerp Airport (OJ C176, 16.7.2005, p 11), point 34; Decision of 11 December 2001, N 550/01, Belgium – Public-Private Partnership for loading and unloading facilities (OJ C24, 26.1.2002, p 2), point 24; Decision of 20 December 2001, N 649/01, United Kingdom – Freight Facilities Grant (OJ C45, 19.2.2002, p 2), point 45; Decision of 17 July 2002, N 356/02, United Kingdom – Network Rail (OJ C232, 28.9.2002, p 2), point 70; N 511/95, Jaguar Cars Ltd. See also, the Commission Guidelines on the application of Articles 92 and 93 of the EC Treaty and Article 61 of the EEA Agreement to State aids in the aviation sector (OJ C350, 10.12.1994, p 5), point 12; White Paper: Fair Payment for Infrastructure use (COM(1998) 466 final), point 43; Communication from the Commission to the European Parliament and the Council: "Reinforcing Quality Service in Sea Ports: A Key for European Transport" (COM(2001) 35 final, p 11).

3. AID FOR THE PURCHASE AND RENEWAL OF ROLLING STOCK

3.1. Objective

[5.387]

27. The fleet of locomotives and carriages used for passenger transport is ageing and in some cases worn out, especially in the new Member States. In 2005, 70% of the locomotives (diesel and electric) and 65% of the wagons of the EU-25 were more than 20 years old.[1] Taking only the Member States which joined the European Union in 2004, 82% of locomotives and 62% of wagons were more than 20 years old in 2005.[2] According to the information at its disposal, the Commission estimates that the annual rate of renewal of the fleet is around 1%.

28. This trend of course reflects the difficulties of the railway industry in general, which reduce the incentives for railway undertakings and their capacity to invest in an effort to modernise and/or renew their rolling stock. Such investment is indispensable to keeping rail transport competitive with other modes of transport which cause more pollution or entail higher external costs. It is also necessary to limit the impact of rail transport on the environment, particularly by reducing the noise pollution it causes, and to improve its safety. Finally, improving interoperability between the national networks means it is necessary to adapt the existing rolling stock in order to be able to maintain a coherent system.

29. In the light of the above it seems that under certain circumstances aid for the purchase and renewal of rolling stock can contribute to several types of objectives of common interest and therefore be considered compatible with the common market.

30. This Chapter seeks to define the conditions in which the Commission is to carry out such a compatibility assessment.

3.2. Compatibility

31. The compatibility assessment has to be made according to the common-interest objective to which the aid is contributing.

32. The Commission considers that in principle the need to modernise rolling stock can be sufficiently taken into account either in implementing the general State aid rules or by applying Article 73 of the Treaty where such aid is intended for transport coordination (see Chapter 6).

33. In assessing the compatibility of aid for rolling stock the Commission therefore generally applies the criteria defined for each of the following aid categories in these guidelines or in any other relevant document:

(a) aid for coordination of transport;[3]
(b) aid for restructuring railway undertakings;[4]
(c) aid for small and medium-sized enterprises;[5]
(d) aid for environmental protection;[6]
(e) aid to offset costs relating to public service obligations and in the framework of public service contracts;[7]
(f) regional aid.[8]

34. In the case of regional aid for initial investment, the Guidelines on national regional aid, "the regional aid guidelines", provide that "in the transport sector, expenditure on the purchase of transport equipment (movable assets) is not eligible for aid for initial investment" (point 50, footnote 48). The Commission considers that a derogation should be made from this rule with regard to rail passenger transport. This is due to the specific characteristics of this

mode of transport, and in particular to the fact that it is possible that the rolling stock in this sector may be permanently assigned to specific lines or services. Subject to certain conditions, defined below, the costs of acquisition of rolling stock in the rail passenger transport sector (or for other modes such as light rail, underground or tram) are deemed to be admissible expenditure within the meaning of the guidelines in question.[9] However, the costs of acquisition of rolling stock for exclusive use in freight transport are not admissible.

35. In view of the situation described in points 28 and 29, this derogation applies to any kind of investment in rolling stock, whether initial or for replacement purposes, so long as it is assigned to lines regularly serving a region eligible for aid under Article 87(3)(a) of the Treaty, an outermost region or a region of low population density within the meaning of points 80 and 81 of the regional aid guidelines.[10] In the other regions, the derogation applies only to aid for initial investment. For aid for investment for replacement purposes, the derogation applies only when all the rolling stock that the aid is used to modernise is more than 15 years old.

36. In order to avoid distortions of competition which would be contrary to the common interest, the Commission does, however, consider that such a derogation has to be made subject to four conditions, which have to be met cumulatively:

(a) the rolling stock concerned must be exclusively assigned to urban, suburban or regional passenger transport services in a specific region or for a specific line serving several different regions; For the purposes of these guidelines "urban and suburban transport services" is to be understood as transport services serving an urban centre or conurbation as well as those services between that centre or conurbation and its suburbs. "Regional transport services" is to be understood as transport services intended to meet the transport needs of one or more regions. Transport services serving several different regions, in one or more Member States, may therefore be covered by the scope of this point if it can be shown that there is an impact on the regional development of the regions served, in particular by the regular nature of the service. In this case, the Commission verifies that the aid does not compromise the effective opening of the international passenger transport market and cabotage following the entry into force of the third railway package;

(b) the rolling stock must remain exclusively assigned to the specific region or the specific line passing through several different regions for which it has received aid for at least ten years;

(c) the replacement rolling stock must meet the latest interoperability, safety and environmental standards[11] applicable to the network concerned;

(d) the Member State must prove that the project contributes to a coherent regional development strategy.

37. The Commission will take care to avoid undue distortions of competition, notably by taking account of the additional revenue that the replaced rolling stock on the line in question could procure for the enterprise aided, for example, through sales to a third party or use on other markets. To this end, the granting of the aid may be made subject to the obligation on the recipient undertaking to sell under normal market conditions all or part of the rolling stock it is no longer using, so as to allow its further use by other operators; in this case the proceeds from the sale of the old rolling stock will be deducted from the eligible costs.

38. More generally, the Commission will ensure that no improper use is made of the aid. The other conditions provided for in the regional aid guidelines, notably as regards the intensity ceilings and the regional aid maps and the rules on the cumulation of aid, apply. The Commission notes that the specific lines concerned may in certain cases pass through regions where there are different intensity ceilings in accordance with the regional aid maps. In this case the Commission will apply the highest rate of intensity of the regions regularly served by the line concerned in proportion to the regularity of such service.[12]

39. With regard to investment projects with eligible expenditure in excess of EUR 50 million, the Commission considers it appropriate, due to the specificities of the rail passenger transport sector, to derogate from points 60 to 70 of the regional aid guidelines. However, points 64 and 67 of those guidelines remain applicable when the investment project concerns rolling stock assigned to a specific line serving several regions.

40. If the recipient undertaking is entrusted with providing services of general economic interest that necessitate buying and/or renewing rolling stock and it already receives compensation for this, that compensation should be taken into account in the amount of regional aid that may be awarded to this undertaking, in order to avoid overcompensation.

NOTES

1 *Source:* UIC Rolling stock fleet in EU-25 + Norway (2005).

2 *Source:* CER (2005).

3 See Chapter 6.

4 Community guidelines on State aid for rescuing and restructuring firms in difficulty (OJ C244, 1.10.2004, p 2), and Chapter 5.

5 Commission Regulation (EC) No 70/2001 of 12 January 2001 on the application of Articles 87 and 88 of the EC Treaty to State aid to small and medium-sized enterprises (OJ L10, 13.1.2001, p 33). Regulation as last amended by Regulation (EC) No 1976/2006 (OJ L368, 23.12.2006, p 85).

6 Community guidelines on State aid for environmental protection (OJ C82, 1.4.2008, p 1).

7 Regulation (EEC) No 1191/69 cited above; PSO Regulation of the European Parliament and of the Council, cited above, in which attention should be drawn in particular to Article 3(1): "Where a competent authority decides to grant the operator of its choice an exclusive right and/or compensation, of whatever nature, in return for the discharge of public service obligations, it shall do so within the framework of a public service contract".

8 Guidelines on national regional aid for 2007–2013 (OJ C54, 4.3.2006, p 13), point 8.

9 The Commission notes that, depending on the specific circumstances of the case in point, this reasoning may be applied mutatis mutandis to vehicles used for the public transport of passengers by road, where such vehicles meet the latest Community standards applicable to new vehicles. Where that is the case, in the interests of equal treatment the Commission will, in such situations, apply the approach described here for railway rolling stock. The Commission encourages the Member State to support the least polluting technologies when awarding this type of aid and will study the extent to which specific financial aid leading to higher aid intensities for such technologies is appropriate.

10 The least populated regions represent or belong to regions at NUTS-II level with a population density of no more than 8 inhabitants per km2 and extend to adjacent and contiguous smaller areas meeting the same population density criterion.

11 Aid for the acquisition of new transport vehicles which go beyond Community standards or which increase the level of environmental protection in the absence of Community standards is possible within the Guidelines on State aid for environmental protection.

12 Where the line or specific service systematically (that is to say, on every journey) serves the region to which the highest rate applies, this rate is applied to all admissible expenditure. Where the region to which the highest rate applies is only occasionally served, this rate is applied only to the part of the admissible expenditure allocated to serving that region.

4. DEBT CANCELLATION

4.1. Objective

[5.388]

41. As mentioned in Section 1.1, railway undertakings have in the past experienced a state of imbalance between their revenues and their costs, especially their investment costs. This has led to major indebtedness, the financial servicing of which represents a very heavy burden on railway undertakings and limits their capacity to make the necessary investments in both infrastructure and renewal of rolling stock.

42. Directive 91/440/EEC explicitly took this situation into account. It is stated in the seventh recital thereto that Member States "should ensure in particular that existing publicly owned or controlled railway transport undertakings are given a sound financial structure" and envisages that a "financial rearrangement" might be necessary for this purpose. Article 9 of the Directive provides: "In conjunction with the existing publicly owned or controlled railway undertakings, Member States shall set up appropriate mechanisms to help reduce the indebtedness of such undertakings to a level which does not impede sound financial management and to improve their financial situation". Article 9(3) envisages the granting of State aid "to cancel the debts referred to in this Article", and provides that such aid must be granted in accordance with Articles 73, 87 and 88 of the Treaty.

43. At the beginning of the 1990s, following the entry into force of Directive 91/440/EEC, the Member States considerably reduced the debts of railway undertakings. The debt restructuring took different forms:

(a) transfer of all or part of the debt to the body responsible for managing the infrastructure, thus enabling the railway undertaking to operate on a sounder financial footing. It was possible to make this transfer when transport service activities were separated from infrastructure management;

(b) the creation of separate entities for the financing of infrastructure projects (for example, high-speed lines), making it possible to relieve railway undertakings of the future financial burden which the financing of this new infrastructure would have meant;

(c) financial restructuring of railway undertakings, notably by the cancellation of all or part of their debts.

44. These three types of action have helped to improve the financial situation of railway undertakings in the short term. Their indebtedness has been reduced compared with total liabilities, as has the share of interest repayments in the operating costs. In general the debt reduction has allowed railway undertakings to improve their financial situation through a reduction in their capital and interest repayments. Such reductions have also helped to lower the rates of interest, which has a substantial impact on the financial servicing of the debt.

45. However, the Commission notes that the level of indebtedness of many railway undertakings continues to give cause for concern. Several of these undertakings have a level of indebtedness higher than is acceptable for a commercial company, are still not capable of self-financing, and/or cannot finance their investment needs from the revenue from present and future transport operations. Also, in the Member States which joined the Community after 1 May 2004 the level of indebtedness of the companies in the sector is considerably higher than in the rest of the Community.

46. This fact is reflected in the Community legislator's choice not to amend the provisions of Directive 91/440/EEC when Directives 2001/12/EC and 2004/51/EC were adopted. These provisions therefore fall within the general framework formed by the successive railway packages.

47. This Chapter seeks to define how, in the light of this requirement of secondary legislation, the Commission intends to apply the Treaty rules on State aid to the mechanisms for reducing the indebtedness of railway undertakings.

4.2. Presence of State aid

48. The Commission notes first of all that the principle of incompatibility laid down in Article 87(1) of the Treaty applies only to aid "which distorts or threatens to distort competition by favouring certain undertakings or the production of certain goods" and only "insofar as it affects trade between Member States". Under established case-law, when State financial aid strengthens the position of an undertaking compared with other undertakings competing in intra-community trade, these undertakings must be regarded as affected by that aid.[1]

49. Any measure attributable to the State which leads to the complete or partial cancellation of debts specifically in favour of one or more railway undertakings and through State resources therefore falls within the scope of Article 87(1) of the Treaty, if the railway undertaking in question is active in markets open to competition and if this debt cancellation strengthens its position in at least one of those markets.

50. The Commission notes that Directive 2001/12/EC opened up the international rail freight services market to competition over the whole trans-European rail freight network from 15 March 2003. It therefore considers that, generally, the market was opened up to competition at the latest on 15 March 2003.

4.3.
Compatibility

51. When the cancellation of a railway undertaking's debt constitutes State aid covered by Article 87(1) of the Treaty it must be notified to the Commission in accordance with Article 88 of the Treaty.

52. Aid of this kind must generally be examined on the basis of the Community guidelines on State aid for rescuing and restructuring firms in difficulty of 2004 ("the 2004 guidelines on State aid for restructuring"), subject to Chapter 5 of these Guidelines.

53. In specific cases where the debts cancelled exclusively concern transport coordination, compensation of public service obligations or the setting of accounting standards, the compatibility of this aid will be examined on the basis of Article 73 of the Treaty, the regulations adopted for the implementation thereof and the rules for the normalisation of the accounts.[2]

54. In the light of Article 9 of Directive 91/440/EEC, the Commission also considers that, under certain circumstances, it should be possible to authorise this aid without financial restructuring if the cancellation concerns old debts incurred prior to the entry into force of Directive 2001/12/EC, which lays down the conditions for opening up the sector to competition.

55. The Commission takes the view that this type of aid may be compatible in so far as it seeks to ease the transition to an open rail market, as provided for by Article 9 of Directive 91/440/EEC.[3] Thus it considers that such aid may be regarded as compatible with Article 87(3)(c) of the Treaty,[4] provided that the following conditions are met.

56. Firstly, the aid must serve to offset clearly determined and individualised debts incurred prior to 15 March 2001, the date on which Directive 2001/12/EC entered into force. Under no circumstances may the aid exceed the amount of these debts. In cases where the Member States joined the Community after 15 March 2001, the relevant date is that of accession to the Community. The logic of Article 9 of Directive 91/440/EEC, repeated in subsequent Directives, was to address a level of debt accumulated at a time when a decision to open the market at Community level had yet to be taken.

57. Secondly, the debts concerned must be directly linked to the activity of rail transport or the activities of management, construction or use of railway infrastructure. Debts incurred for the purpose of investment not directly linked to transport and/or rail infrastructure are not eligible.

58. Thirdly, the cancellation of debts must be in favour of undertakings facing an excessive level of indebtedness which is hindering their sound financial management. The aid must be necessary to remedy this situation, insofar as the likely development of competition on the market would not allow them to rectify their financial situation within a foreseeable future. Assessment of this criterion has to take into account any productivity improvements which the undertaking can reasonably be expected to achieve.

59. Fourthly, the aid must not go beyond what is necessary for the purpose. In this regard, account must also be taken of future developments in competition. It should not, at any rate, place the undertaking in a situation more favourable than that of an average well-managed undertaking with the same activity profile.

60. Fifthly, cancellation of its debts must not give an undertaking a competitive advantage such that it prevents the development of effective competition on the market, for example by deterring outside undertakings or new players from entering certain national or regional markets. In particular, aid intended for cancelling debts cannot be financed from levies imposed on other rail operators.[5]

61. Where these conditions are met, the debt cancellation measures are contributing to the objective set in Article 9 of Directive 91/440/EEC, without unduly distorting competition and trade between Member States. They can thus be considered compatible with the common market.

NOTES

1 Judgment of the Court of Justice of 17 September 1980, Case 730/79, *Phillip Morris Holland v Commission* [1980] ECR 2671, paragraph 11.

2 Regulation (EEC) No 1192/69.

3 The Commission applies, by analogy, certain conditions laid down by the Commission communication relating to the methodology for analysing State aid linked to stranded costs of 26 July 2001, SEC(2001) 1238.

4 Without prejudice to the application of Regulations (EEC) No 1191/69, (EEC) No 1192/69 and (EEC) No 1107/70.

5 Without prejudice to the application of Directive 2001/14/EC.

5. AID FOR RESTRUCTURING RAILWAY UNDERTAKINGS – RESTRUCTURING A "FREIGHT" DIVISION

5.1.
Objective

[5.389]
62. Save where specifically provided otherwise, the Commission assesses the compatibility of State aid for restructuring firms in difficulty in the railway industry on the basis of the 2004 guidelines on State aid for restructuring. Those guidelines do not provide for any derogation for railway undertakings.

63. Generally speaking, a division of an undertaking, namely an economic entity without legal personality, is not eligible for restructuring aid. The 2004 guidelines on State aid for restructuring apply only to "firms in difficulty". They also state, at point 13, that a firm "belonging to or being taken over by a larger business group is not normally eligible for restructuring aid, except where it can be demonstrated that the firm's difficulties are intrinsic and are not the result of an arbitrary allocation of costs within the group, and that the difficulties are too serious to be dealt with by the group itself". It should be avoided, a fortiori, that artificial subdivision allows a loss-making activity within a given company to receive public funds.

64. However, the Commission considers that the European rail freight sector currently finds itself in a very specific situation making it necessary, in the common interest, to envisage that aid granted to a railway undertaking allowing it to overcome difficulties in the freight operations of that undertaking might, under certain circumstances, be considered compatible with the common market.

65. In today's railway industry, the competitive situation of freight transport operations is quite different from that which applies to passenger transport. The national freight markets are open to competition whereas the rail passenger transport markets are not going to be opened up before 1 January 2010.

66. This situation has a financial impact in so far as freight is in principle governed solely by the business relations between shippers and carriers. The financial equilibrium of passenger transport, on the other hand, may also depend on the public authorities taking action by way of public service compensation.

67. However, several European railway undertakings have not legally separated their passenger and freight transport activities, or have only just done so. Moreover, current Community legislation does not provide for the obligation to make this legal separation.

68. Furthermore, one of the central priorities of European transport policy has, for many years, been to breathe new life into the railway freight industry. The reasons for this are set out in Chapter 1 of these guidelines.

69. This specific characteristic of rail freight activities necessitates an adapted approach, as has been recognised in the Commission's decision-making practice[1] on the basis of the Community Guidelines on State aid for rescuing and restructuring firms in difficulty of 1999.[2]

70. This Chapter is intended to show, in the light of the Commission's decision-making practice and taking account of the amendments made by the 2004 guidelines on State aid for restructuring to the corresponding 1999 guidelines, the way in which the Commission intends to implement this approach in future.

71. In view of the risks highlighted above, this approach is justified and will be maintained only for the freight divisions of railway undertakings, and for a transitional period, namely for restructurings notified before 1 January 2010, the date on which the rail passenger transport market will be opened up to competition.

72. Furthermore, the Commission wishes to take account of the fact that, in a growing number of Member States, railway undertakings have adapted their organisation to specific developments in rail freight and passenger transport activities by taking steps to legally separate their freight transport activities. The Commission will therefore require, as part of the restructuring efforts and before awarding any aid, the legal separation of the freight division in question by transforming it into a commercial company under common commercial law. The Commission is of the view that this separation will, with other appropriate measures, help considerably to achieve two goals, namely to exclude all cross-subsidisation between the restructured division and the rest of the undertaking and to ensure that all financial relations between these two activities are carried out in a sustainable manner and on a commercial basis.

73. In order to avoid any doubt, the 2004 guidelines on State aid for restructuring will continue to apply in their entirety when examining the aid dealt with in this Chapter, except with regard to the express derogations set out below.

5.2. *Eligibility*

74. The eligibility criteria must be adapted to include the situation in which a freight division of a railway undertaking constitutes a coherent and permanent economic unit, which will be legally separated from the rest of the undertaking through the restructuring process before aid is granted, and faces difficulties such that, if it had been separated from the railway undertaking, it would be a "firm in difficulty" within the meaning of the 2004 restructuring guidelines.

75. This means, in particular, that that division of the undertaking would be facing serious difficulties of its own, which are not the result of an arbitrary allocation of costs within the railway undertaking.

76. In order for the division to be restructured to constitute a coherent and permanent economic unit it must comprise all the freight transport activities of the railway undertaking, whether industrial, commercial, accounting or financial. It must be possible to attribute to it a level of losses, as well as a level of own funds or capital, which sufficiently reflects the economic reality of the situation which the division faces in order to evaluate in a coherent manner the criteria fixed in point 10 of the 2004 guidelines on State aid for restructuring.[3]

77. When assessing whether a division is in difficulty as described above, the Commission will also take into account the ability of the rest of the railway undertaking to ensure the recovery of the division to be restructured.

78. The Commission is of the view that, although the situation described is not directly covered by the 2004 guidelines on State aid for restructuring, point 12 of which excludes newly created firms from the scope of the guidelines, restructuring aid may be granted in this context to enable the firm created by this legal separation to operate in viable market conditions. This is intended to apply only in situations where the firm to be created as a result

of legal separation includes the entire freight division, as described by the separate accounting established in accordance with Article 9 of Directive 91/440/EEC, and includes all the division's assets, liabilities, capital, off-balance sheet commitments and workforce.

79. The Commission considers that, for the same reasons, when a railway undertaking has recently legally separated its freight division, where this division fulfilled the above criteria, the firm in question must not be considered a newly created firm within the meaning of point 12 of the 2004 guidelines on State aid for restructuring, and is therefore not excluded from the scope of these guidelines.

5.3.
Return to long-term viability

80. The Commission will make sure not only that the criteria for a return to long-term viability as set out in the 2004 guidelines on State aid for restructuring are fulfilled,[4] but also that restructuring will ensure the freight activity is transformed from a protected activity enjoying exclusive rights into one which is competitive on the open market. This restructuring should therefore concern all aspects of the freight activity, whether industrial, commercial, or financial. The restructuring plan required by the restructuring guidelines[5] must make it possible to ensure a standard of quality, reliability and service which meets customers' requirements.

5.4.
Prevention of any excessive distortion of competition

81. In analysing the prevention of any excessive distortion of competition, as provided for by the guidelines on State aid for restructuring, the Commission will also base itself on:

(a) the difference between the economic models for rail and the other modes of transport;
(b) the Community objective of shifting the balance between modes of transport;
(c) the competitive situation on the market at the time of restructuring (degree of integration, growth potential, presence of competitors, likely trends).

5.5.
Aid limited to a minimum

82. The provisions of the 2004 guidelines on State aid for restructuring apply when verifying this criterion. To this end the firm's own contribution will include that of the freight division which will be legally separated from the railway undertaking. However, in the Commission's view, the very specific situation of the European rail freight industry, which is described above, may constitute an exceptional circumstance within the meaning of paragraph 44 of those guidelines. It may therefore accept lower own contributions than those provided for in the 2004 guidelines on State aid for restructuring provided that the freight division's own contribution is as high as possible without jeopardising the viability of the operation.

5.6.
"One time, last time" principle

83. The "one time, last time" principle applies to the legally separated firm, by taking account of the restructuring aid notified as initial restructuring aid received by the undertaking. However, restructuring aid authorised under the conditions set out in this Chapter does not affect application of the "one time, last time" principle with regard to the rest of the railway undertaking.

84. To avoid any doubt, if the railway undertaking as a whole has already received restructuring aid, the "one time, last time" principle means that aid as provided for in this Chapter may not be granted to restructure the freight division of the undertaking.

NOTES

1 See Commission Decision of 2 March 2005, N 386/04, Aid for restructuring SNCF Freight – France (OJ C172, 12.7.2005, p 3).

2 OJ C288, 9.10.1999, p 2.

3 Point 10 of the guidelines on State aid for restructuring states: "In particular, a firm is, in principle and irrespective of its size, regarded as being in difficulty for the purposes of these guidelines in the following circumstances:

— in the case of a limited liability company, where more than half of its registered capital has disappeared and more than one quarter of that capital has been lost over the preceding 12 months, or
— in the case of a company where at least some members have unlimited liability for the debt of the company, where more than half of its capital as shown in the company accounts has disappeared and more than one quarter of that capital has been lost over the preceding 12 months, or
— whatever the type of company concerned, where it fulfils the criteria under its domestic law for being the subject of collective insolvency proceedings".

4 See in particular points 34 to 37 of the guidelines on State aid for restructuring.

5 See in particular Section 3.2 of the restructuring guidelines.

6. AID FOR COORDINATION OF TRANSPORT

6.1.
Objective

[5.390]

85. As already stated, Article 73 of the Treaty was implemented by Regulations (EEC) No 1191/69 and (EEC) No 1107/70, which will be repealed by the PSO Regulation. The PSO Regulation will, however, apply only to land passenger transport. It will not cover rail freight transport, for which aid for coordination of transport will continue to be subject only to Article 73 of the Treaty.

86. In addition to this, Article 9 of the PSO Regulation concerning aid for coordination of transport and aid for research and development applies explicitly without prejudice to Article 73 of the Treaty, so it will be possible to use Article 73 directly for justifying the compatibility of aid for coordination of rail passenger transport.

87. The objective of this Chapter is therefore to establish criteria which will allow the Commission to assess the compatibility, on the basis of Article 73 of the Treaty, of aid for the coordination of transport, both generally (Section 6.2) and as regards certain specific forms of aid (Section 6.3). The Commission notes that, although the general implementing principles of Article 73 of the Treaty are relevant when assessing State aid under the PSO Regulation, these guidelines do not cover the detailed rules for the implementation of the Regulation in question.

6.2.
General considerations

88. Article 73 of the Treaty provides for compatibility of aid which meets the needs of coordination of transport. The Court of Justice has ruled that this Article "acknowledges that aid to transport is compatible with the Treaty only in well-defined cases which do not jeopardise the general interests of the Community".[1]

89. The concept of "coordination of transport" used in Article 73 of the Treaty has a significance which goes beyond the simple fact of facilitating the development of an economic activity. It implies an intervention by public authorities which is aimed at guiding the development of the transport sector in the common interest.

90. The progress made with liberalising the land transport sector has in some respects considerably reduced the need for coordination. In an efficient liberalised sector, coordination can in principle result from the action of market forces. As indicated above, however, the fact remains that investment in infrastructure development continues to be carried out by the public authorities. Moreover, even after the liberalisation of the sector, there may still be various market failures. These in particular are the failures which justify the intervention of the public authorities in this field.

91. Firstly, the transport sector entails major negative externalities, for example between users (congestion), or in respect of society as a whole (pollution). These externalities are difficult to take into account, notably due to the inherent limits to the possibility of including external costs, or even simply direct usage costs, in the pricing systems for access to transport infrastructure. As a result there may be disparities between the different modes of transport, which ought to be corrected by public authority support for those modes of transport which give rise to the lowest external costs.

92. Secondly, the transport sector may experience "coordination" difficulties in the economic sense of the term, for example in the adoption of a common interoperability standard for rail, or in the connections between different transport networks.

93. Thirdly, the railway undertakings may not be able to reap the full rewards of their research, development and innovation efforts (positive externalities), which also amounts to a failure of the market.

94. The presence of a specific provision in the Treaty making it possible to authorise aid which meets the needs of transport coordination shows how important these risks of market failures are and the negative impact they have on the development of the Community.

95. In principle, aid which meets the needs of transport coordination has to be considered compatible with the Treaty.

96. Nevertheless, for a given aid measure to be considered to "meet the needs" of transport coordination, it has to be necessary and proportionate to the intended objective. Furthermore, the distortion of competition which is inherent in aid must not jeopardise the general interests of the Community. By way of illustration, aid likely to shift traffic flows from short sea shipping to rail would fail to meet these criteria.

97. Finally, in view of the rapid development of the transport sector, and hence the need for coordinating it, any aid notified to the Commission for the purpose of obtaining a decision, on the basis of Article 73 of the Treaty, that the aid is compatible with the Treaty has to be limited[2] to a maximum of 5 years, in order to allow the Commission to re-examine it in the light of the results obtained and, where necessary, to authorise its renewal.[3]

98. As regards the railway industry more specifically, aid for the needs of transport coordination can take several forms:

(a) aid for infrastructure use, that is to say, aid granted to railway undertakings which have to pay charges for the infrastructure they use, while other undertakings providing transport services based on other modes of transport do not have to pay such charges;

(b) aid for reducing external costs, designed to encourage a modal shift to rail because it generates lower external costs than other modes such as road transport;

(c) aid for promoting interoperability, and, to the extent to which it meets the needs of transport coordination, aid for promoting greater safety, the removal of technical barriers and the reduction of noise pollution in the rail transport sector, hereinafter referred to as "interoperability aid";

(d) aid for research and development in response to the needs of transport coordination.

99. In the following Sections the Commission will specify the conditions which, from the point of view of its decision-making practice, make it possible to ensure, for these different types of aid for coordination of transport, that the aid concerned meets the conditions of compatibility mentioned in Article 73 of the Treaty. In view of the specific nature of research and development aid, the criteria applicable to this type of measure are dealt with separately.

6.3.
Criteria for aid for rail infrastructure use, reducing external costs and interoperability

100. The assessment of the compatibility of aid for infrastructure use, reducing external costs and interoperability with respect to Article 73 of the Treaty is in keeping with the Commission's decision-making practice pursuant to Article 3(1)(b) of Regulation (EEC) No 1107/70. In the light of this practice the conditions which follow appear sufficient for determining whether the aid is compatible.

6.3.1. Eligible costs

101. The eligible costs are determined on the basis of the following.

102. As regards **aid for rail infrastructure use**, the eligible costs are the additional costs for infrastructure use paid by rail transport but not by a more polluting competing transport mode.

103. As regards **aid for reducing external costs**, the eligible costs are the part of the external costs which rail transport makes it possible to avoid compared with competing transport modes.

104. In that regard, it should be recalled that Article 10 of Directive 2001/14/EC explicitly allows Member States to put in place a compensation scheme for the demonstrably unpaid environmental, accident-related and infrastructure costs of competing transport modes in so far as these costs exceed the equivalent costs of rail. If there is not yet any Community legislation which harmonises methods for calculating infrastructure access charges within or across land transport modes, the Commission will take account of the development of the rules governing the allocation of infrastructure costs and external costs when applying these guidelines.[4]

105. Both for aid for rail infrastructure use and for aid for reducing external costs, the Member State has to provide a transparent, reasoned and quantified comparative cost analysis between rail transport and the alternative options based on other modes of transport.[5] The methodology used and calculations performed must be made publicly available.[6]

106. As regards **interoperability aid**, the eligible costs cover, to the extent to which they contribute to the objective of coordinating transport, all investments relating to the installation of safety systems and interoperability,[7] or noise reduction both in rail infrastructure and in rolling stock. In particular they cover investment associated with the deployment of ERTMS (European Rail Traffic Management System) and any like measure which can help to remove the technical barriers in the European rail services market.[8]

6.3.2. Necessity and proportionality of the aid

107. The Commission considers that there is a presumption of necessity and proportionality of the aid when the intensity of the aid stays below the following values:

(a) for aid for rail infrastructure use, 30% of the total cost of rail transport, up to 100% of the eligible costs;[9]
(b) for aid for reducing external costs, 30%[10] of the total cost of rail transport, up to 50% of the eligible costs;[11]
(c) for interoperability aid, 50% of the eligible costs.

108. For aid above these thresholds, Member States must demonstrate the need and proportionality of the measures in question.[12]

109. For both aid for rail infrastructure use and aid for reducing external costs, the aid has to be strictly limited to compensation for opportunity costs connected with the use of rail transport rather than with the use of a more polluting mode of transport. Where there are several competing options which cause higher levels of pollution than rail transport, the limit chosen corresponds to the highest cost differential among the various options. Where the intensity thresholds referred to in point 108 are adhered to, it may be presumed that the "no overcompensation" criterion is met.

110. At any rate, where the aid recipient is a railway undertaking it must be proved that the aid really does have the effect of encouraging the modal shift to rail. In principle this will mean that the aid has to be reflected in the price demanded from the passenger or from the shipper, since it is they who make the choice between rail and the more polluting transport modes such as road.[13]

111. Finally, specifically as regards aid for rail infrastructure use and aid for reducing external costs, there must be realistic prospects of keeping the traffic transferred to rail so that the aid leads to a sustainable transfer of traffic.

6.3.3. Conclusion

112. Aid for rail infrastructure use, for reducing external costs or for interoperability that is necessary and proportionate and so does not distort competition contrary to the common interest must be considered compatible under Article 73 of the Treaty.

6.4.
Compatibility of aid for research and development

113. In the area of land transport, Article 3(1)(c) of Regulation (EEC) No 1107/70, adopted on the basis of Article 73 of the Treaty, provides for the possibility of granting aid to research and development. The Commission has recently developed a body of practice in the application of this provision.[14]

114. Article 9(2)(b) of the PSO Regulation adopts the text of Article 3(1)(c) of Regulation (EEC) No 1107/70. Under that provision, aid which has the purpose of promoting research into or development of rail passenger transport systems and technologies which are more economic for the community in general, which is restricted to the research and development stage and which does not cover the commercial exploitation of such transport systems and technologies, has to be regarded as meeting the needs of transport coordination.

115. Article 9(2)(b) of the PSO Regulation applies without prejudice to Article 87 of the Treaty. Thus, aid for research, development and innovation in the field of passenger transport, if not covered by Article 9 of the PSO Regulation, and aid which only concerns freight, may be considered compatible on the basis of Article 87(3)(c) of the Treaty.

116. In this regard the Commission has defined, in the Community framework for State aid for research and development and innovation[15] (hereinafter the "Community framework"), the conditions under which it will declare aid of that type compatible with the common market on the basis of Article 87(3)(c) of the Treaty. That framework applies "to aid to support research and development and innovation in all sectors governed by the Treaty. It also applies to those sectors which are subject to specific Community rules on State aid, unless such rules provide otherwise".[16] The framework therefore applies to aid for research, development and innovation in the railway transport sector which does not fall within the scope of Article 3(1)(c) of Regulation (EEC) No 1107/70 or Article 9 of the PSO Regulation (following the entry into force of that Regulation).

117. It is not excluded that the compatibility of aid for research and development may be analysed directly on the basis of Article 73 of the Treaty, if it is aimed at meeting the needs of transport coordination. In this case the abovementioned conditions should be checked, in particular the fact that the aid must be necessary and proportionate to the intended objective, and must not jeopardise the general interests of the Community. The Commission considers that the general principles set out in the Community framework are relevant in analysing these various criteria.

NOTES

1 [Editorial note: the original document does not contain a footnote numbered 1.].

2 Ibidem.

3 This period is increased to 10 years for measures which fall within the scope of Article 15(1)(e) of Council Directive 2003/96/EC of 27 October 2003 restructuring the Community framework for the taxation of energy products and electricity (OJ L283, 31.10.2003, p 51); Directive as last amended by Directive 2004/75/EC (OJ L157, 30.4.2004, p 100). See in particular Commission Decision of 2 April 2008, NN 46/B/06, Slovakia – Excise duty exemptions and reductions provided for by Council Directive 2003/96/EC (transport sector), not yet published.

4 In this connection the third paragraph of Article 11 of Directive 1999/62/EC of the European Parliament and of the Council of 17 June 1999 on the charging of heavy goods vehicles for the use of certain infrastructures (OJ L187, 20.7.1999, p 42), as amended by Directive 2006/103/EC (OJ L363, 20.12.2006, p 344), provides that "No later than 10 June 2008, the Commission shall present, after examining all options including environment, noise, congestion and health-related costs, a generally applicable, transparent and comprehensible model for the assessment of all external costs to serve as the basis for future calculations of infrastructure charges. This model shall be accompanied by an impact analysis of the internalisation of external costs for all modes of transport and a strategy for a stepwise implementation of the model for all modes of transport". During the preparation of a communication on the internalisation of external costs to comply with this objective, on 16 January 2008 the Commission published a handbook on the studies carried out so far on external costs in the transport sector (ec.europa.eu/transport/costs/handbook/index_en.htm). This handbook, which was compiled jointly by several transport research institutes, can be used, amongst other factors, to determine eligible costs. Furthermore, the Commission has published a White Paper COM(1998) 466, Fair payment for infrastructure use – A phased approach to a common transport infrastructure charging framework in the European Union (Bulletin of the EU – Supplement No 3/98).

5 Member States can find indications of the different methods for evaluating extra costs in Annex 2 to Commission Green Paper Towards fair and efficient pricing in transport – Policy options for internalising the external costs of transport in the European Union (Bulletin of the EU – Supplement No 2/96; COM(1995) 691 final) and in the study which the Commission published on 16 January 2008 (See Article 11 of Directive 1999/62/EC).

6 Article 10 of Directive 2001/14/EC.

7 See, in particular, Council Directive 96/48/EC of 23 July 1996 on the interoperability of the trans-European high-speed rail system (OJ L235, 17.9.1996, p 6). Directive as last amended by Directive 2007/32/EC (OJ L141, 25.6.2007, p 63) and Directive 2001/16/EC of the European Parliament and of the Council of 19 March 2001 on the interoperability of the trans-European conventional rail system (OJ L110, 20.4.2001, p 1). Directive as last amended by Directive 2007/32/EC.

8 Calculation of the eligible costs will take account of any changes made to charges for infrastructure use based on rolling stock performance (especially sound performance).

9 See, by way of illustration, Commission Decision of 22 December 2006, N 574/05, prolongation of existing aid scheme *N 335/03, Italy – Friuli Venezia Giulia* – Aid for the setting up of rolling-motorway services (OJ C133, 15.6.2007, p 6); Commission Decision of 12 October 2006, N 427/06, United Kingdom – Rail Environmental Benefit Procurement Scheme (REPS) (OJ C283, 21.11.2006, p 10).

10 Annex I to Regulation (EC) No 1692/2006 of the European Parliament and of the Council of 24 October 2006 establishing the second Marco Polo programme for the granting of Community financial assistance to improve the environmental performance of the freight transport system (Marco Polo II) and repealing Regulation (EC) No 1382/2003 (OJ L328, 24.11.2006, p 1) provides that Community financial assistance for modal shift actions is limited to a maximum of 35% of the total expenditure necessary to achieve the objectives of the action and incurred as a result of the action. In these guidelines, as regards State aid for transport coordination the criterion is 30% of the total cost of rail transport.

11 See, by way of illustration, Commission Decision of 22 December 2006, N 552/06, Denmark – Prolongation of environ-

mental aid scheme for the transport of goods by rail (OJ C133, 15.6.2007, p 5) and Commission Decision of 12 October 2006, N 427/06, United Kingdom – Rail Environmental Benefit Procurement Scheme (REPS), op. cit.

12 This could be the case with interoperability measures on the trans-European transport network as last defined by Decision No 884/2004/EC of the European Parliament and of the Council of 29 April 2004 amending Decision No 1692/96/EC on Community guidelines for the development of the trans-European transport network (OJ L167, 30.4.2004, p 1).

13 With regard to measures falling under Article 15(1)(e) of Directive 2003/96/EC, an impact on the price of transport may be taken for granted, unless there is proof to the contrary. See in particular the Commission Decision of 2 April 2008, NN 46/B/06, Slovakia – Excise duty exemptions and reductions provided for by Council Directive 2003/96/EC (transport sector), not yet published.

14 Commission Decision of 30 May 2007, N 780/06, The Netherlands – *Onderzoek en ontwikkeling composiet scheepsconstructie en multi-purpose laadruim*; het "CompoCaNord"-project (OJ C227, 27.9.2007, p 5); Commission Decision of 19 July 2006, N 556/05, The Netherlands – Environmental protection and innovation in public transport in the province of Gelderland (OJ C207, 30.8.2006); Commission Decision of 20 July 2005, N 63/05, Czech Republic – Programme for energy economics and use of alternative fuels in the transport sector (OJ C83, 6.4.2006).

15 OJ C323, 30.12.2006, p 1.

16 Ibidem, point 2.1.

7. STATE GUARANTEES FOR RAILWAY UNDERTAKINGS

[5.391]

118. The Commission Notice on the application of Articles 87 and 88 of the EC Treaty to State aid in the form of guarantees[1] sets out the legal requirements applicable to State guarantees, including in the rail transport field.

119. This notice states, in point 2.1.3, that the Commission "regards as aid in the form of a guarantee, the more favourable funding terms obtained by enterprises whose legal form rules out bankruptcy or other insolvency procedures or provides an explicit State guarantee or coverage of losses by the State".

120. The Commission's consistent practice has been to consider unlimited guarantees in a sector open to competition to be incompatible with the Treaty. In accordance with the proportionality principle they cannot in particular be justified by tasks of general interest. With an unlimited guarantee it is impossible to check whether the amount of aid exceeds the net costs of providing the public service.[2]

121. When the State guarantees are granted to undertakings with a presence on both competitive and non-competitive markets, the Commission's practice is to require the complete removal of the unlimited guarantee granted to the undertaking as a whole.[3]

122. Several railway undertakings are enjoying unlimited guarantees. These guarantees are generally a legacy of special cases of historic monopolies set up for railway undertakings before the Treaty entered into force or before the rail transport services market was opened up to competition.

123. According to the information available to the Commission, these guarantees do, to a large extent, constitute existing aid. The Member States concerned are invited to inform the Commission of the conditions for implementing the schemes for existing aid as well as of the measures envisaged for removing them, in accordance with the procedure defined in Section 8.3.

NOTES

1 OJ C71, 11.3.2000, p 14.

2 Commission Decision 2005/145/EC of 16 December 2003 on the State aid granted by France to EDF and the electricity and gas industries (OJ L49, 22.2.2005, p 9); Commission Decision of 24 April 2007, E-12/05, Poland – Unlimited guarantee for the Polish post office (*Poczta Polska*) (OJ C284, 27.11.2007, p 2); Commission Decision of 27 March 2002, E-10/00, Germany – State guarantees for public credit institutions in Germany (OJ C150, 22.6.2002, p 7).

3 Ibidem.

8. FINAL PROVISIONS

8.1.
Rules on the cumulation of aid

[5.392]

124. The aid ceilings stipulated in these guidelines are applicable irrespective of whether the aid in question is financed wholly or in part from State resources or from Community resources. Aid authorised under these guidelines may not be combined with other forms of State aid within the meaning of Article 87(1) of the Treaty or with other forms of Community financing if such combination produces a level of aid higher than that laid down in these guidelines.

125. In the case of aid serving different purposes and involving the same eligible costs, the most favourable aid ceiling will apply.

8.2.
Date of application

126. The Commission will apply these guidelines from the date of their publication in the *Official Journal of the European Union*. The Commission will apply these guidelines to all aid, whether or not notified, in respect of which it is called upon to take a decision after the date of their publication.

8.3.
Appropriate measures

127. In accordance with Article 88(1) of the Treaty, the Commission proposes that the Member States amend their existing aid schemes relating to State aid covered by these guidelines so as to comply with them at the latest two years after their publication in the *Official Journal of the European Union*, subject to the specific provisions in the Chapter on State guarantees. The Member States are invited to confirm that they accept these proposals for appropriate measures in writing at the latest one year after the date of publication in the *Official Journal of the European Union*.

128. Should a Member State fail to confirm its acceptance in writing by that date, the Commission will apply Article 19(2) of Council Regulation (EC) No 659/1999 of 22 March 1999 laying down detailed rules for the application of Article 93 of the EC Treaty[1] and, if necessary, initiate the proceedings referred to in that provision.

8.4.
Period of validity and reporting

129. The Commission reserves the right to amend these guidelines. It will present a report on their application before any amendment and at the latest five years after the date of their publication.

NOTES

[1] OJ L83, 27.3.1999, p 1. Regulation as last amended by Regulation (EC) No 1791/2006.

COMMUNICATION FROM THE COMMISSION

(2008/C317/08)

Providing guidance on State aid complementary to Community funding for the launching of the motorways of the sea

(Text with EEA relevance)

[5.393]

NOTES

Date of publication in OJ: OJ C317, 12.12.2008, p 10.

Note: with effect from 1 December 2009, the EC Treaty was replaced by the Treaty on the Functioning of the European Union. References in this document to provisions of the EC Treaty should be construed accordingly.

INTRODUCTION

[5.394]

1. The White Paper 'European transport policy for 2010: time to decide' of 2001[1] introduced the concept of 'motorways of the sea' as high quality transport services based on short sea shipping. Motorways of the sea are composed of infrastructure, facilities and services spanning at least two Member States. The motorways of the sea aim to shift significant shares of freight transport from road to sea. Their successful implementation will help achieving two main objectives of the European transport policy, that is, reduction of congestion on the roads and a reduced environmental impact of freight transport. The mid-term review of the White Paper[2] points to the increasing problem of road congestion, costing the Community about 1% of GDP, and to the threat of greenhouse gasses emissions from transport with respect to Kyoto targets and reconfirms the importance of the motorways of the sea.

NOTES

[1] COM(2001) 370.

[2] COM(2006) 314 final: Communication from the Commission to the Council and the European Parliament 'Keep Europe moving — Sustainable mobility for our continent — Mid-term review of the European Commission's 2001 Transport White Paper'.

COMPLEMENTARY STATE AID FOR MARCO POLO II 'MOTORWAYS OF THE SEA' PROJECTS

[5.395]

2. Chapter 10 of the Community Guidelines on State aid to maritime transport[3] allow, under certain conditions, for start-up aid to new or improved short sea shipping services with a maximum duration of three years and a maximum intensity of 30% of operational cost and 10% of investments costs.

3. The second 'Marco Polo' programme (further referred to as Marco Polo II) established by Regulation (EC) No 1692/2006 of the European Parliament and of the Council of 24 October 2006 establishing the second 'Marco Polo' programme for the granting of Community financial assistance to improve the environmental performance of the freight transport system (Marco Polo II) and repealing Regulation (EC) No 1382/2003[4] is one of the two Community funding instruments directly and explicitly supporting the motorways of the sea, as one out of the five actions that are supported for avoiding traffic or shifting traffic away from road. Marco Polo II provides support mainly to the services part of the motorways of the sea. That support is attributed through yearly calls for proposals directed to the industry players. The allocated financial support is constrained by the grants available under the Marco Polo programme. Funding to the motorways of the sea can also be provided through the Regional Policy.

4. Under Article 5(1)(b) of Regulation (EC) No 1692/2006, in the framework of Marco Polo II programme 'Motorways of the Sea Actions' are, under certain conditions, eligible to Community financial assistance with a maximum intensity of 35% of the total cost for establishing and operating the transport service and a maximum duration of 60 months, as fixed by Annex I, points 1(a) and 2(a) of column B.

5. Article 7 of Regulation (EC) No 1692/2006 reads: *Community financial assistance for the actions covered by the Programme shall not prevent those actions from being granted State aid at national, regional or local level, insofar as such aid is compatible with the State-aid arrangements laid down in the Treaty and within the cumulative limits established for each type of action set out in Annex I.*

6. According to Article 7 of Regulation (EC) No 1692/2006, therefore, Member States' authorities may complement Community financing by allocating their own financial resources to projects selected according to the criteria and procedures laid down in that Regulation, within the ceilings set out in the Regulation. The objective of Article 7 of Regulation (EC) No 1692/2006 is to make it possible for undertakings interested in a project to count on a predetermined amount of public funding irrespective of its origin. As a matter of fact, it may be the case that the Community financial resources allocated by the Regulation (EC) No 1692/2006 are not sufficient to provide all the selected projects with the maximum possible support. Actually, if a large number of valid projects are presented in a given year, some projects may be granted limited amounts of Community funding. While the fact of having a large number of selected projects would be a sign of success for Marco Polo II, this success would be jeopardised if the involved undertakings were to withdraw their submission or were discouraged from future submissions because of the lack of public funding, necessary for the start-up of the relevant services. Moreover, fixing a pre-determined amount of public funding that can be relied on is essential for potential bidders.

7. Against this background, the Commission has noticed that amongst stakeholders and Member States' authorities there are doubts about the possibility for the latter to grant complementary State aid to Marco Polo II projects going beyond what is allowed for short sea shipping under Chapter 10 of the Community Guidelines on State aid to maritime transport. Actually, the eligibility conditions for schemes under the Guidelines on State aid to maritime transport are slightly different from those of Marco Polo II. The Guidelines provide for a maximum intensity of 30% of operational costs (35% of the total expenditure in Marco Polo II) and a maximum duration of three years (in comparison to five years under Marco Polo II). Such differences have probably confused potential bidders for motorways of the sea actions.

8. For the above reasons, the Commission considers that maximum duration and intensity of State aid and Community funding for projects which have been selected under the Regulation should be the same. Therefore, on the basis of Article 87(3)(c) of the Treaty, in the absence of Community funding, or to the extent not covered by Community funding, the Commission will authorise State aid to the start-up of Marco Polo II 'Motorways of the Sea' projects with a maximum intensity of 35% of operational costs and a maximum duration of five years[5]. The same will apply to projects selected under Marco Polo II but for which funding is finally provided through the European Regional Development Fund (ERDF)[6] or the Cohesion Fund[7].

9. Start-up aid to operational costs may not exceed the above-mentioned duration and intensity, irrespective of the source of funding. Aid can not be cumulated with public service compensation. The Commission also recalls that the same eligible costs cannot benefit from two Community financial instruments.

10. Member States will have to notify to the Commission State aid that they intend to grant on the basis of the present communication to projects selected under Regulation (EC) No 1692/2006.

NOTES

3 Commission Communication C(2004) 43 (OJ C13, 17.1.2004, p 3).

4 OJ L328, 24.11.2006, p 1.

5 It should be noticed that the clause contained in Annex I(2)(b) of the Marco Polo II Regulation (about the limits to funding based on freight actually shifted from road) applies to Community funding, but not to complementary State aid addressed in the present communication.

6 Regulation (EC) No 1080/2006 of 5 July 2006 (OJ L210, 31.7.2006, p 1).

7 Regulation (EC) No 1084/2006 of 11 July 2006 (OJ L210, 31.7.2006, p 79).

COMPLEMENTARY STATE AID FOR TEN-T 'MOTORWAYS OF THE SEA' PROJECTS

[5.396]

11. Article 12a of Decision No 1692/96/EC of the European Parliament and of the Council of 23 July 1996 on Community guidelines for the development of the trans-European transport network[8] provides for the setting up of 'Motorways of the Sea' concentrating *flows of freight on sea-based logistical routes in such a way as to improve existing maritime links or to establish new viable regular and frequent maritime links for the transport of goods between Member States so as to reduce road congestion and/or to improve access to peripheral and islands regions and State.* The trans-European network of motorways of the sea must consist of facilities and infrastructure concerning at least two ports in two different Member States.

12. The Community guidelines for the development of the trans-European transport network concern Community support for the development of infrastructure, including in the case of the motorways of the sea. However, second indent of Article 12a(5) of Decision No 1692/96/EC, includes a possibility of granting Community support for start-up aid to a project, without prejudice to Articles 87 and 88 of the Treaty. This support may be granted to the extent *it is deemed necessary for the financial viability of the project.* In fact, the case may arise that the proposing consortium of ports and operators incurs start-up losses within the launching period of the motorways of the sea services.

13. Start-up support under the Community guidelines for the development of the trans-European transport network is limited to 'duly justified capital costs', to be understood as investment support. This may include the depreciation of ships allocated to the service[9]. Under the Community guidelines for the development of the trans-European transport network, start-up support is limited to two years with a maximum intensity of 30%.

14. In the framework of TEN-T projects, financial resources may be provided by Member States to the extent that Community funding is not available. In the case of start-up aid to shipping services, however, the second indent of Article 12a(5) of Decision No 1692/96/EC makes a reference to the provisions on State aid of the Treaty. Therefore, Member States may provide complementary aid to the extent that Community funding is not available, but they have to respect the rules on State aid while doing so. Since in the matter of aid to short sea shipping, guidance on the application of State aid rules has been provided by Chapter 10 of the Guidelines on State aid to maritime transport, the latter applies to complementary State aid. The Community Guidelines on State aid to maritime transport, however, allow for aid to investment with a maximum intensity of 10% during three years. As a result, if a motorway of the sea project is selected as a TEN-T project, but it is not granted the maximum Community support to investment, ie, 30% during two years, it may happen that public support will not achieve the maximum possible amount, if national State aid may not go beyond the 10% over three years authorised by the Community Guidelines on State aid to maritime transport. Furthermore, the difference in the maximum duration of the two schemes (two years under Decision No 1692/96/EC and three years under the Community Guidelines on State aid to maritime transport) is capable of generating uncertainty and confusion. For the sake of clarity and in order to allow for a pre-determined public support to undertakings taking part in a motorway of the sea TEN-T project, the maximum intensity and duration of complementary State aid to be provided by Member States should be the same as the maximum intensity and duration of Community funding.

15. For the above reasons, on the basis of Article 87(3)(c) of the Treaty, in the absence of Community funding for start-up aid or for the part not covered by Community funding, the Commission will authorise State aid to investment with a maximum intensity of 30% and a maximum duration of two years to projects corresponding to Article 12a of Decision 1692/96/EC and selected in accordance with the procedure laid down in Regulation (EC) No 680/2007 of the European Parliament and of the Council of 20 June 2007 laying down general rules for the granting of Community financial aid in the field of the trans-European transport and energy networks[10]. The same will apply where the Member States decide to fund the project through the European regional development Fund or the Cohesion Fund.

16. Start-up aid to investment may not exceed the duration and intensity referred to in this point, irrespective of the source of funding. It can not be cumulated with public service compensation. Also for this case, the Commission recalls that the same eligible costs cannot benefit from two Community financial instruments.

17. Member States will have to notify to the Commission State aid that they intend to grant on the basis of the present communication to projects selected under Regulation (EC) No 680/2007.

NOTES

[8] OJ L228, 9.9.1996, p 1.

[9] Vademecum of 28 February 2005 issued in conjunction with the call for proposals for the TEN-T 2005; paragraph 4.3 (Start-up aid related to capital costs).

[10] OJ L162, 22.6.2007, p 1.

APPLICATION

[5.397]

18. The Commission will apply the guidance provided for in this communication from the day following that of its publication in the Official Journal.

COMMUNICATION FROM THE COMMISSION

(2009/C132/06)

providing guidance on State aid to ship management companies

(Text with EEA relevance)

[5.398]

NOTES

Date of publication in OJ: OJ C132, 11.6.2009, p 6.

Note: with effect from 1 December 2009, the EC Treaty was replaced by the Treaty on the Functioning of the European Union. References in this document to provisions of the EC Treaty should be construed accordingly.

1. SCOPE

[5.399]

This Communication deals with the eligibility of crew and technical managers of ships for the reduction of corporate tax or the application of the tonnage tax under Section 3.1 of Commission Communication C(2004) 43 — Community guidelines on State aid to maritime transport[1] ('the Guidelines'). It does not deal with State aid to commercial managers of ships. This Communication applies to crew and technical management irrespectively of whether they are individually provided or jointly provided to the same ship.

NOTES

1 OJ C13, 17.1.2004, p 3.

2. INTRODUCTION

2.1 GENERAL CONTEXT

[5.400]

The Guidelines provide for the possibility that ship management companies qualify for the tonnage tax or other tax arrangements for shipping companies (Section 3.1). However, eligibility is limited to the joint provision of both technical and crew management for a same vessel ('full management'), while those activities are not eligible to the tonnage tax or other tax arrangements when provided individually.

The Guidelines stipulate that the Commission will examine the effects of the Guidelines on ship management after three years[2]. This Communication sets out the results of that fresh assessment and draws conclusions on the eligibility of ship management companies for State aid.

2.2. SHIP MANAGEMENT

Ship management companies are entities providing different services to shipowners, such as technical survey, crew recruiting and training, crew management and vessel operation. There are three main categories of ship management services: crew management, technical management and commercial management.

Crew management consists, in particular, in dealing with all the matters relating to crew, such as selecting and engaging suitably qualified seafarers, issuing payrolls, ensuring the appropriateness of the manning level of ships, checking the certifications of seafarers, providing for seafarers' accident and disability insurance coverage, taking care of travel and visa arrangements, handling medical claims, assessing the performance of the seafarers and, in some cases, training them. Crew management represents by far the largest part of the ship management industry worldwide.

Technical management consists in ensuring the seaworthiness of the vessel and its full compliance with technical, safety and security requirements. In particular, the technical manager is responsible for making decisions on the repair and maintenance of a ship. Technical management represents a significant part of the ship management industry, although much smaller than crew management.

Commercial management consists in promoting and ensuring the sale of ships' capacity, by means of chartering the ships, taking bookings for cargo or passengers, ensuring marketing and appointing agents. Commercial management represents a very small part of the ship management industry. To date the Commission does not have complete information about commercial management at its disposal. Commercial management is therefore not addressed by this Communication.

Like any maritime activity, ship management is a global business by nature. In the absence of international law regulating third party ship management, the standards in this field have been settled within the framework of private law agreements[3].

In the Community, ship management is mainly carried out in Cyprus. There are, however, ship management companies in the United Kingdom, Germany, Denmark, Belgium and the Netherlands. Outside the Community, ship management companies are mainly established in Hong Kong, Singapore, India, United Arab Emirates and the USA.

2.3. REVIEW OF THE ELIGIBILITY CONDITIONS FOR SHIP MANAGEMENT COMPANIES

Since the publication of the Guidelines in January 2004, several maritime countries have entered the Community, amongst them Cyprus, which features the largest ship management industry in the world.

The accession of Cyprus and its preliminary work for complying with the Guidelines, as well as a study realised by a consortium for the administration of that Member State[4], allowed for a more complete understanding of this activity and of its evolution. More awareness has been acquired in particular in respect of the link between technical and crew management on the one hand, and shipping on the other, as well as the possibility that crew and/or technical managers can help achieving the objectives of the Guidelines.

NOTES

2 See footnote 3 on page 7 of OJ C13, 17.1.2004.

3 An example is the *'BIMCO's Standard Ship Management Agreement SHIPMAN 98'* which is frequently used in relations between ship management companies and shipowners.

4 *Study on Ship Management in Cyprus and in the European Union* of 31 May 2008, carried out for the Cypriot government by a consortium under the direction of the Vienna University of Economics and Business Administration.

3. ASSESSMENT OF ELIGIBILITY OF SHIP MANAGEMENT COMPANIES

[5.401]

Unlike other maritime-related services, ship management is a standard core-activity of maritime carriers, normally provided in-house. Ship management is one of the most characteristic activities of ship operators. Nowadays, however, it is outsourced to third-party ship management companies in some cases. It is because of this link between ship management and shipping that third-party ship management companies are professional operators with the same background as shipowners, although segmented according to their specialisation, operating in their same business environment. Shipowners are the only customers of ship management companies.

Against this background the Commission considers that outsourcing of ship management should not be fiscally penalised with respect to in-house ship management, provided that the ship management companies meet the same requirements as are applicable to shipowners and that the provision of the aid to the former contributes to the achievement of the objectives of the Guidelines in the same way as the provision of aid to shipowners.

In particular the Commission considers that, precisely because of their specialisation and the nature of their core-business, ship management companies may substantially contribute to the achievement of the objectives of the Guidelines, in particular the achievement of an 'efficient, secure and environment friendly maritime transport' and of the 'consolidation of the maritime cluster established in the Member States'[5].

NOTES

[5] Section 2.2 of the Guidelines.

4. EXTENSION TO SHIP MANAGEMENT COMPANIES OF ELIGIBILITY TO STATE AID

[5.402]
On the basis of what has been explained in Section 3 above, the Commission will authorise under Article 87(3)(c) of the Treaty establishing the European Community, tax relief for ship management companies, as referred to in Section 3.1 of the Guidelines, with respect to joint or separate crew and technical management of ships, provided that the conditions set out in Sections 5 and 6 of this Communication are fulfilled.

5. CONDITIONS FOR ELIGIBILITY APPLICABLE TO BOTH TECHNICAL AND CREW MANAGERS

[5.403]
In order to qualify for aid ship management companies should present a clear link with the Community and its economy, in line with Section 3.1 of the Guidelines. Moreover, they should contribute to the objectives of the Guidelines, such as those laid down in Section 2.2 of the Guidelines. Technical and crew managers are eligible to State aid, provided that the ships they manage comply with all the requirements set out in Sections 5.1 to 5.4 of this Communication. Eligible activities must be entirely carried out from the territory of the Community.

5.1. CONTRIBUTION TO THE ECONOMY AND EMPLOYMENT WITHIN THE COMMUNITY

The economic link with the Community is proven by the fact that ship management is carried out in the territory of one or more Member States and that mainly Community nationals are employed in land-based activities or on ships.

5.2. ECONOMIC LINK BETWEEN THE MANAGED SHIPS AND THE COMMUNITY

Ship management companies may benefit from State aid with respect to ships entirely managed from the territory of the Community, irrespective of whether management is provided in-house or whether it is partially or totally outsourced to one or more ship management companies.

However, since ship management companies do not have full control of their customers, the above requirement is deemed to be fulfilled if at least two thirds of the tonnage of the managed ships is managed from the territory of the Community. Tonnage in excess of that percentage which is not entirely managed from the Community is not eligible[6].

5.3. COMPLIANCE WITH INTERNATIONAL AND COMMUNITY STANDARDS

Ship management companies are eligible if all the ships and crews they manage comply with international standards and Community law requirements are fulfilled, in particular those relating to security, safety, training and certification of seafarers, environmental performance and on-board working conditions.

5.4. FLAG-SHARE REQUIREMENT (FLAG LINK)

The flag-share requirement, as laid down in the eighth paragraph of Section 3.1 of the Guidelines applies to ship management companies. The share of Community flags to be considered as the benchmark is that of the day on which this Communication is published in the *Official Journal of the European Union*. For new companies the benchmark is to be calculated one year after the date on which they started activity.

NOTES

[6] While the fact of not complying with the 2/3 rule does not affect the eligibility of the ship management company as such.

6. ADDITIONAL REQUIREMENTS FOR CREW MANAGERS

6.1. TRAINING OF SEAFARERS

[5.404]
Crew managers are eligible for State aid as long as all seafarers working onboard managed ships are educated, trained and hold a certificate of competency in accordance with the Convention of the International Maritime Organisation on Standards of Training, Certification and Watchkeeping for Seafarers, 1978, as amended (STCW), and have successfully completed training for personal safety on board ship. Moreover, crew managers are eligible if they fulfil the STCW and Community law requirements regarding responsibilities of companies.

6.2 SOCIAL CONDITIONS

In order to be eligible for State aid, crew managers must ensure that on all managed ships the provisions of the Maritime Labour Convention, 2006, of the International Labour Organisation ('MLC')[7], are fully implemented by the seafarer's employer, be it the shipowner or the ship management companies. The ship management companies must ensure, in particular, that the provisions of the MLC concerning the seafarer's employment agreement[8], ship's loss or foundering[9] medical care[10], shipowner's liability including payment of wages in case of accident or sickness[11], and repatriation[12] are properly applied. Crew managers must also ensure that the international standards regarding hours of work and hours of rest provided for by the MLC are fully complied with.

Finally, in order to be eligible, crew managers must also provide financial security to assure compensation in the event of the death or long-term disability of seafarers due to an occupational injury, illness or hazard.

NOTES

7 It should be recalled that the European social partners adopted an agreement taking up the relevant part of the Maritime Labour Convention 2006 which has been integrated into Community law by Council Directive 2009/13/EC of 16 February 2009 implementing the Agreement concluded by the European Community Shipowners' Associations (ECSA) and the European Transport Workers' Federation (ETF) on the Maritime Labour Convention, 2006, and amending Directive 1999/63/EC (OJ L124, 20.5.2009, p 30).

8 Regulation 2.1 and Standard A2.1 (Seafarers' employment agreement) of Title 2 of MLC.

9 Ibid. Regulation 2.6 and Standard A2.6 (Seafarer compensation for the ship's loss or foundering) of Title 2.

10 Ibid. Regulation 4.1 and Standard A4.1 (Medical care on board ship and ashore Shipowners' liability); Regulation 4.3 and A4.3 (Health and safety protection and accident prevention); Regulation 4.4 (Access to shore-based welfare facilities) of Title 4.

11 Ibid. Regulation 4.2 and Standard A4.2 (Shipowners' liability) of Title 4.

12 Ibid. Regulation 2.5 and Standard A2.5 (Repatriation) of Title 2.

7. CALCULATION OF TAX

[5.405]

Also in the case of ship management companies the Commission will apply the principle contained in the Guidelines, according to which, in order to avoid distortion, it will only authorise schemes giving rise to a homogeneous tax-load across the Member States for the same activity or the same tonnage. This means that total exemption or equivalent schemes will not be authorised[13].

The tax base to be used for ship management companies can obviously not be the same as that applied to shipowners since, with respect to a given ship, the turnover of the ship management companies is much lower than that of the shipowner. According to the study mentioned in Section 2.3, as well as to notifications received in the past, the tax-base to be applied to ship management companies should be approximately 25% (in terms or tonnage or notional profit) of that which would apply to the shipowner for the same ship or tonnage. The Commission, therefore, requires that a percentage of no less than 25% is applied under ship management tonnage tax schemes[14].

If ship management companies engage in activities which are not eligible for State aid under the present Communication, they must keep separate accounts for those activities.

In case ship management companies subcontract part of their activity to third parties, the latter are not eligible to State aid.

NOTES

13 The Commission takes this opportunity within the present Communication to emphasise that the mechanism used to calculate the tax to be paid by both ship management companies and ship owners is irrelevant as such; in particular, it is irrelevant whether or not a system based on notional profit is applied.

14 The shipowner, if eligible, remains liable for the whole tonnage tax.

8. APPLICATION AND REVIEW

[5.406]

The Commission will apply the guidance provided for in this Communication from the day following that of its publication in the *Official Journal of the European Union*.

State aid to ship management companies will be included in the general revision of the Guidelines such as foreseen in Section 13 of the latter.

COMMUNICATION FROM THE COMMISSION

(2014/C92/01)

on interpretative guidelines concerning Regulation (EC) No 1370/2007 on public passenger transport services by rail and by road

[5.407]

NOTES

Date of publication in OJ: OJ C92, 29.3.2014, p 1.

1. INTRODUCTION

[5.408]

Regulation (EC) No 1370/2007 of the European Parliament and of the Council on public passenger transport services by rail and by road and repealing Council Regulations (EEC) No 1191/69 and 1107/70[1] was adopted on 23 October 2007. This Regulation, which entered into force on 3 December 2009, aims to create an internal market for the provision of public passenger transport services. It does so by complementing the general rules on public procurement. It also lays down the conditions under which compensation payments stipulated in contracts and concessions for public passenger transport services shall be deemed compatible with the internal market and exempt from prior State aid notification to the Commission.

Regulation (EC) No 1370/2007 is of major importance for the organisation and financing of public transport services by bus, tram, metro and rail in the Member States. A coherent and correct application of its provisions is economically and politically important. This is because the value added and employment in the public transport sector each correspond to about 1% of GDP and of total employment, respectively, of the Union. A well performing public transport sector is a cornerstone of effective social, economic and environmental policy.

Both an external ex-post assessment of the implementation of Regulation (EC) No 1370/2007[2] conducted by an external consultant as well as representatives of European associations and of Member States speaking at an EU-wide stakeholders' conference organised by the Commission on the implementation of that Regulation on 14 November 2011[3] called on the Commission to provide guidance on certain provisions of that Regulation. Diverging interpretations of provisions concerning the definition of public service obligations, the scope of public service contracts, the award of such contracts and the compensation of public service obligations can hamper the creation of an internal market for public transport and lead to undesired market distortions.

Before adopting this Communication, the Commission consulted Member States and stakeholders representing parties interested in this issue, such as European associations of the public transport sector, including transport staff and passenger organisations.

In this Communication, the Commission sheds light on its understanding of a number of provisions of the Regulation, inspired by best practices, to help Member States reap the full benefits of the internal market. This Communication does not aspire to cover all provisions in an exhaustive manner, nor does it create any new legislative rules. It should be noted that, in any event, the interpretation of Union law is ultimately the role of the Court of Justice of the European Union.

On 30 January 2013, the Commission adopted a proposal to amend Regulation (EC) No 1370/2007 in anticipation of the opening up of the market for domestic passenger transport services by rail.[4] Some of the provisions of the Regulation that the Commission proposed to modify, such as the provisions on the award of public service contracts in rail, are interpreted in the present Communication. As regards these provisions, the guidance provided in this document should be considered valid until any amendment to Regulation (EC) No 1370/2007 enters into force.

NOTES

1 OJ L315, 3.12.2007, p 1.

2 DLA Piper, Study on the implementation of Regulation (EC) No 1370/2007 on public passenger transport services by rail and by road, 31 October 2010, published at http://ec.europa.eu/transport/modes/rail/studies/rail_en.htm

3 Documents on the conference are published at http://ec.europa.eu/transport/modes/rail/events/2011-11-14-workshop_en.htm

4 Proposal for a Regulation of the European Parliament and of the Council amending Regulation (EC) No 1370/2007 concerning the opening of the market for domestic passenger transport services by rail, COM/2013/028 final.

2. THE COMMISSION'S UNDERSTANDING OF REGULATION (EC) NO 1370/2007

2.1. SCOPE OF REGULATION (EC) NO 1370/2007

[5.409]

This chapter on the scope of Regulation (EC) No 1370/2007 provides interpretative guidance on the relationship between this Regulation and the following directives: Directive 2014/24/EU of the European Parliament and the Council on public procurement and repealing Directive 2004/18/EC[5] ('Directive 2014/24/EU'); Directive 2014/25/EU on procurement by entities operating in the water, energy, transport and postal services sectors and repealing Directive 2004/17/EC[6] ('Directive 2014/25/EU'); and Directive 2014/23/EU on the award of concession contracts[7] ('Directive 2014/23/EU'). This chapter also clarifies the modalities of the Regulation's application to inland waterways and national seawaters, and clarifies its applicability to freight transport contracts until 2 December 2012.

2.1.1. ARTICLE 1(3) AND ARTICLE 5(1). RELATIONSHIP BETWEEN REGULATION (EC) NO 1370/2007 AND THE PUBLIC PROCUREMENT AND CONCESSION DIRECTIVES

Regulation (EC) No 1370/2007 governs the award of public service contracts, as defined in Article 2(i) thereof, in the field of public passenger transport by road and by rail. However, these public service contracts may also fall within the scope of the public procurement directives (Directive 2014/24/EU and Directive 2014/25/EU). Since the directives referred to in Regulation (EC) No 1370/2007 (Directive 2004/17/EC and Directive 2004/18/EC) have been repealed and replaced by the above-mentioned directives, the references in Regulation (EC) No 1370/2007 should be understood as relating to the new directives.

Article 1(3) provides that Regulation (EC) No 1370/2007 shall not apply to public works concessions within the meaning of Article 1(3)(a) of Directive 2004/17/EC or Article 1(3) of Directive 2004/18/EC. After the entry into force of Directive 2014/23/EU on the award of concession contracts, the term 'works concession' is defined in Art 5(1)(a) of this Directive. Therefore, works concessions for public passenger transport services by rail and other track-based modes and by road are governed solely by Directive 2014/23/EU.

For the relationship between Regulation (EC) No 1370/2007 and the public procurement directives as well as Directive 2014/23/EU, it is important to distinguish between service contracts and service concessions.

Article 2 points (1), (2) and (5) of Directive 2014/25/EU defines 'service contracts' as contracts for pecuniary interest concluded in writing between one or more contracting entities and one or more economic operators and having as their object the provision of services. When these contracts involve 'contracting authorities' within the meaning of Article 2(1) point (1) of Directive 2014/24/EU, they are considered as 'public service contracts' in accordance with Article 2(1) points (6) and (9) of Directive 2014/24/EU.

Article 5(1)(b) of Directive 2014/23/EU on the award of concession contracts defines a 'service concession' as 'a contract for pecuniary interest concluded in writing by means of which one or more contracting authorities or contracting entities entrust the provision and the management of services other than the execution of works referred to in point (a) to one or more economic operators, the consideration of which consists either solely in the right to exploit the services that are the subject of the contract or in that right together with payment'. Art 5(1) specifies further that 'the award of a works or services concession shall involve the transfer to the concessionaire of an operating risk in exploiting those works or services encompassing demand or supply risk or both. The concessionaire shall be deemed to assume operating risk where, under normal operating conditions, it is not guaranteed to recoup the investments made or the costs incurred in operating the works or the services which are the subject-matter of the concession. The part of the risk transferred to the concessionaire shall involve real exposure to the vagaries of the market, such that any potential estimated loss incurred by the concessionaire shall not be merely nominal or negligible'.

This distinction between (public) service contracts and concessions is important because according to Article 10(3) of Directive 2014/23/EU this Directive shall not apply to concessions for public passenger transport services within the meaning of Regulation (EC) No 1370/2007. The award of service concessions for these public passenger transport services is solely governed by Regulation (EC) No 1370/2007.

Article 5(1) of Regulation (EC) No 1370/2007 specifies that the award of (public) service contracts for transport services by bus or tram is governed by Directives 2004/17/EC[8] and 2004/18/EC,[9] except where such contracts take the form of service concessions. The award of (public) service contracts for public passenger services by bus or tram is thus solely governed by Directives 2014/24/EU and 2014/25/EU.

The award of (public) service contracts for public passenger transport services by railway and metro is governed by Regulation (EC) No 1370/2007 and excluded from the scope of Directive 2014/24/EU according to its Recital 27 and Article 10(i) and from the scope of Directive 2014/25/EU according to its Recital 35 and Article 21(g).

TableSummary of the applicable legal basis for contract awards by type of contractual arrangement and by transport mode

Public passenger services by	(Public) service contracts as defined in Directives 2014/24/EU and 2014/25/EU	Service concessions as defined in Directive 2014/23/EU
Bus and tram	Directives 2014/24/EU and 2014/25/EU	Regulation (EC) No 1370/2007
Railway and metro	Regulation (EC) No 1370/2007	Regulation (EC) No 1370/2007

2.1.2. Article 1(2). Application of Regulation (EC) No 1370/2007 to inland waterways and national seawaters

Article 1(2) states that Regulation (EC) No 1370/2007 shall apply to national and international public passenger transport services by rail, by other track-based modes and by road and that Member States may apply that Regulation to public passenger transport by inland waterways. To ensure legal certainty, a Member State's decision to apply Regulation (EC) No 1370/2007 to public passenger transport by inland waterways should be adopted in a transparent manner through a legally binding act. Applying Regulation (EC) No 1370/2007 to inland waterway passenger transport services may be especially useful where those services are integrated into a wider urban, suburban or regional public passenger transport network.

In the absence of a decision to apply Regulation (EC) No 1370/2007 to inland waterway passenger transport services, these services will be governed directly by Article 93 of the Treaty on the Functioning of the European Union (TFEU). Certain aspects of passenger transport by inland waterways are further covered by Council Regulation (EEC) No 3921/91 of 16 December 1991 laying down the conditions under which non-resident carriers may transport goods or passengers by inland waterways within a Member State[10] and by Council Regulation (EC) No 1356/96 of 8 July 1996 on common rules applicable to the transport of goods or passengers by inland waterway between Member States with a view to establishing freedom to provide such transport services.[11]

Article 1(2) also provides that Member States may apply Regulation (EC) No 1370/2007 to national seawater transport services only if this is without prejudice to Council Regulation (EEC) No 3577/92 of 7 December 1992 applying the principle of freedom to provide services to maritime transport within Member States (maritime cabotage).[12] Certain key provisions of that Regulation do not fully match with those of Regulation (EC) No 1370/2007 (such as the provisions on its application to freight transport, contract duration, exclusive rights and on the thresholds for directly awarding small-scale contracts). Applying Regulation (EC) No 1370/2007 to national seawaters raises a number of difficulties. In a Communication,[13] the Commission provides guidance on Regulation (EEC) No 3577/92, where these difficulties are addressed.

2.1.3. Article 10(1). Applicability of Regulation (EEC) No 1191/69 to freight transport contracts until 2 December 2012

In the past, some specific rail freight transport services may have been subject to public service obligations covered by Regulation (EEC) No 1191/69 of the Council of 26 June 1969 on action by Member States concerning the obligations inherent in the concept of a public service in transport by rail, road and inland waterway.[14] Regulation (EC) No 1370/2007, which repeals Regulation (EEC) No 1191/69, does not, however, apply to freight transport services. To help phase out compensation not authorised by the Commission in accordance with Articles 93, 107 and 108 TFEU, Article 10(1) of Regulation (EC) No 1370/2007 states that Regulation (EEC) No 1191/69 shall remain applicable to freight transport services for a period of three years after the entry into force of Regulation (EC) No 1370/2007 (i.e. until 2 December 2012). Freight transport services can only be qualified as services of general economic interest when the Member State concerned establishes that they have special characteristics compared to those of commercial freight services.[15] If Member States wish to keep State aid schemes in place for rail freight transport services which do not fulfil the specific conditions defined in the Altmark judgment,[16] they must notify those schemes to the Commission so that they can be approved in advance. Those schemes shall be assessed under

Article 93 TFEU directly. If those schemes are not notified in advance, they will constitute new and unlawful aid, as they will No longer be exempted from the obligation to notify State aid.

NOTES

5 OJ L94, 28.3.2014, p 65.

6 OJ L94, 28.3.2014, p 243.

7 OJ L94, 28.3.2014, p 1.

8 Repealed and replaced by Directive 2014/25/EU.

9 Repealed and replaced by Directive 2014/24/EU.

10 OJ L373, 31.12.1991, p 1.

11 OJ L175, 13.7.1996, p 7.

12 OJ L364, 12.12.1992, p 7.

13 Communication from the Commission on the interpretation of Council Regulation (EEC) No 3577/92 applying the principle of freedom to provide services to maritime transport within Member States (maritime cabotage) (not yet published in the Official Journal).

14 OJ L156, 28.6.1969, p 1.

15 Case C-179/90 *Merci Convenzionali Porto di Genova SpA v Siderurgica Gabrielli SpA* [1991] ECR I-5889, paragraph 27. Case C-242/95 *GT-Link A/S v De Danske Statsbaner (DSB)* [1997] ECR I-4449, paragraph 53. Case C-266/96 *Corsica Ferries France SA v Gruppo Antichi Ormeggiatori del Porto di Genova Coop, arl and Others* [1998] ECR I-3949, paragraph 45.

16 Case C-280/00 *Altmark Trans GmbH and Regierungspräsidium Magdeburg v Nahverkehrsgesellschaft Altmark GmbH, and Oberbundesanwalt beim Bundesverwaltungsgericht* [2003] ECR I-7747.

2.2. DEFINITION OF PUBLIC SERVICE OBLIGATIONS AND GENERAL RULES/CONTENTS OF PUBLIC SERVICE CONTRACTS

[5.410]

This chapter provides interpretative guidance on the constitutive features of public service contracts, key characteristics of general rules, and how competent authorities define the nature and extent of public service obligations and of exclusive rights in the context of Regulation (EC) No 1370/2007. Furthermore, it addresses the conditions under which extensions of the duration of public service contracts can be granted as well as the conditions for subcontracting, including in the case of internal operators.

2.2.1. Article 2(i). Constitutive features of a public service contract

According to Article 2(i), a public service contract consists of 'one or more legally binding acts confirming the agreement between a competent authority and a public service operator to entrust to that public service operator the management and operation of public passenger transport services subject to public service obligations'. The contract may also consist of a decision adopted by a competent authority taking the form of an individual legislative or regulatory act or containing conditions under which the competent authority itself provides the services or entrusts the provision of such services to an internal operator. The notion of 'public service contract' as defined by Regulation (EC) No 1370/2007 also covers public service concessions.

To take account of the different legal regimes and traditions in the Member States, the definition of a public service contract provided by Regulation (EC) No 1370/2007 is very broad and includes various types of legally binding acts. It thereby ensures that No legal situation escapes the scope of that Regulation, even if the relationship between the competent authority and the operator is not formally and strictly expressed in the form of a contract within the strictest meaning of the term. For this reason, the definition also includes public service contracts consisting of a decision taking the form of an individual legislative or regulatory act. A combination of a general legal act, assigning the operation of services to an operator, with an administrative act, setting out the detailed requirements concerning the services to be provided and the method of compensation calculation to be applied, can also constitute a public service contract. The definition also covers decisions adopted by the competent authority stating the conditions under which the authority itself provides the services or entrusts the provision of services to an internal operator.

2.2.2. Article 2(l). Characteristics and establishment process of general rules

General rules are defined in Article 2(l) as measures that apply 'without discrimination to all public passenger transport services of the same type in a given geographical area for which a competent authority is responsible'. General rules are therefore measures for one or several types of public transport services by road or by rail that may be imposed unilaterally by public authorities on public service operators in a non-discriminatory manner or that may be included in contracts concluded between the competent authority and the public service operators. The measure is restricted to the geographical area for which a competent authority is responsible, but does not necessarily need to cover the entire geographical area. A general rule can also be a regional or national law applicable to all existing or potential transport operators in a region or a Member State. It is therefore usually not negotiated with individual public service operators. Even if the general rule is imposed by a unilateral act, it is not excluded that public service operators are consulted in a transparent and non-discriminatory manner before general rules are established.

2.2.3. Article 3(2) and (3). Setting up general rules inside and outside a public service contract. Scope of general rules

Recital 17 of Regulation (EC) No 1370/2007 states that 'competent authorities are free to establish social and qualitative criteria in order to maintain and raise quality standards for public service obligations, for instance with regard to minimal working conditions, passenger rights, the needs of persons with reduced mobility, environmental protection, the security of passengers and employees as well as collective agreement obligations and other rules and agreements concerning workplaces and social protection at the place where the service is provided. In order to ensure transparent and comparable terms of competition between operators and to avert the risk of social dumping, competent authorities should be free to impose specific social and service quality standards'.

Member States and/or competent authorities may organise public transport through general rules such as laws, decrees or regulatory measures. However, when these general rules involve compensation or an exclusive right, there is an additional obligation to conclude a public service contract pursuant to Article 3(1) of Regulation (EC) No 1370/2007. This obligation does not exist when general rules establish maximum tariffs for all passengers or for certain categories of passengers pursuant to Article 3(2) of that Regulation. In that case, there is No obligation to conclude a public service contract and the compensation mechanism can be defined on a non-discriminatory, generally applicable basis.

A competent authority may decide to use general rules to establish social or qualitative standards in accordance with national law. If the general rules provide for compensation or if the competent authority thinks that the implementation of the general rules requires compensation, a public service contract or public service contracts defining the obligations and the parameters of the compensation of their net financial effect will also have to be concluded, in accordance with Articles 4 and 6 as well as with the Annex to Regulation (EC) No 1370/2007.

2.2.4. Article 3(3). Notification under Union rules on State aid of general rules on maximum tariff schemes for transport of pupils, students, apprentices and persons with reduced mobility that are outside the scope of Regulation (EC) No 1370/2007

Article 3(3) allows the Member States to exclude from the scope of Regulation (EC) No 1370/2007 general rules on financial compensation for public service obligations which establish maximum tariffs for the transport of pupils, students, apprentices and persons with reduced mobility. If a Member State decides to do so, the national authorities must assess the compensation provisions under the Treaty rules instead, in particular those relating to State aid. If those general rules constitute State aid, the Member State must notify those rules to the Commission in accordance with Article 108 TFEU.

2.2.5. Article 2(e) and Article 4(1). Definition by competent authorities of the nature and extent of public service obligations and of the scope of public service contracts

Article 14 TFEU and Protocol No 26 on services of general interest annexed to the TFEU lay out the general principles of how Member States define and provide services of general economic interest. Article 14 TFEU states that 'the Union and the Member States, each within their respective powers and within the scope of application of the Treaties, shall take care that such services (of general economic interest (SGEI)) operate on the basis of principles and conditions, particularly economic and financial conditions, which enable them to fulfil their missions'. According to Protocol No 26, national, regional and local authorities play an essential role and have wide discretion in providing, commissioning and organising SGEIs tailored as closely as possible to the needs of the users. It is a shared value of the Union that SGEIs strive for a high level of quality, safety, affordability, equal treatment and the promotion of universal access and the rights of users. The possibilities for Member States to provide, commission and organise SGEIs in the field of public passenger transport by rail and by road are regulated by Regulation (EC) No 1370/2007. Article 1 of Regulation (EC) No 1370/2007 states that its purpose 'is to define how, in accordance with the rules of Union law, competent authorities may act in the field of public passenger transport to guarantee the provision of services of general interest which are among other things more numerous, safer, of a higher quality or provided at lower cost than those that market forces alone would have allowed'. As mentioned in Article 2(e) of Regulation (EC) No 1370/2007, a public service obligation is a requirement to ensure public passenger transport services in the general interest that an operator, if it were considering its own commercial interests, would not assume or would not assume to the same extent or under the same conditions without reward.[17] Thus, within the framework laid down by Regulation (EC) No 1370/2007, Member States have wide discretion to define public service obligations in line with the needs of end users.

Typically but not exclusively, public service obligations can refer to specific requirements placed on the public service operator as regards, for instance, the frequency of services, service quality, service provision in particular at smaller intermediate stations which may not be commercially attractive, and the provision of early morning and late evening trains. As an illustrative example, the Commission considers that the services to be classified as public services must be addressed to citizens or be in the interest of society as a whole. Competent authorities define the nature and scope of public service obligations while respecting general principles of the Treaty. To achieve the objectives of the Regulation, which means to guarantee safe, cost-effective and high-quality passenger transport services, competent authorities have to strive for an economically and financially sustainable provision of these services. In the context of contractualisation as defined by Article 3(1) of Regulation (EC) No 1370/2007, both parties to the contract can expect their rights to be respected and must fulfil their contractual obligations. These rights and obligations include financial ones. The geographical scope of public service contracts should enable competent authorities to optimise the economics of public transport services operated under their responsibility including, where appropriate, local, regional and sub-national network effects. Reaping network effects allows for a cost-effective provision of public transport services due to the cross-financing between more than cost-covering services and not cost-covering services. This should in turn enable the authorities to achieve established transport policy objectives whilst guaranteeing, where applicable, the conditions for effective and fair competition on the network, for instance, potentially for some high-speed rail services.

2.2.6. Article 2(f) and Article 3(1). Definition of the nature and extent of exclusive rights to ensure compliance with Union law

Under Article 3(1), a public service contract must be concluded if a competent authority decides to grant an operator an exclusive right and/or compensation in return for the discharge of public service obligations. An exclusive right is defined in Article 2(f) as 'a right entitling a public service operator to operate certain public passenger transport services on a particular route or network or in a particular area, to the exclusion of any other such operator'. This right may be established in a legislative, regulatory or administrative instrument. Very often, the public service contract specifies the conditions for exercising the exclusive right, in particular the geographical scope and the duration of the exclusive right. Exclusivity protects the undertaking from competition by other operators in a specific market in so far as No other undertaking may provide the same service. However, Member States may grant certain rights that appear non-exclusive but de facto prevent other undertakings from participating in the market through legal rules or administrative practices. For example, administrative arrangements granting authorisation to operate public transport services subject to criteria, such as relating to a desirable volume and quality of such services, could have the practical effect of limiting the number of operators on the market. The Commission considers that the notion of exclusivity used in Regulation (EC) No 1370/2007 also covers the latter situation.

To ensure the smooth functioning of the internal market for public transport services, the competent authorities should give a precise definition of exclusive rights as rights that do not exceed what is necessary to provide the required economic protection for the services in question, while leaving room, where possible, for other types of services. In this context, recital 8 of Regulation (EC) No 1370/2007 states that 'passenger transport markets which are deregulated and in which there are No exclusive rights should be allowed to maintain their characteristics and way of functioning in so far as these are compatible with Treaty requirements'. The Commission would like to point out, however, that even under a deregulated system, introducing contractual arrangements to promote the accessibility of bus services to certain segments of the population constitutes a public service obligation. This obligation falls under Regulation (EC) No 1370/2007.[18]

If all conditions for the application of Regulation (EC) No 1370/2007 apply, including the condition that a public transport operator benefits from an exclusive right, the public service contract that has to be concluded may be directly awarded, for instance in the case of a small value contract and in the case of a small and medium sized operating company, if the conditions of Article 5(4) are met.

2.2.7. Article 4(4). Conditions under which a 50% extension of the duration of the public service contract can be granted

Article 4(3) states that the maximum duration of a public service contract shall be '10 years for coach and bus services and 15 years for passenger transport services by rail or other track-based modes'. Article 4(4) allows for an extension of the duration of a public service contract by 50%, if necessary, having regard to the conditions of asset depreciation. Such an extension can be granted if the public service operator provides assets that are significant in relation to the overall assets needed to carry out the passenger transport services covered by the public service contract and are predominantly linked to the passenger transport services covered by the contract.

The interpretation of these two conditions depends on the particular circumstances of each case. As recital 15 of Regulation (EC) No 1370/2007 underlines, 'contracts of long duration can lead to market foreclosure for a longer period than is necessary, thus diminishing the benefits of competitive pressure. In order to minimise distortions of competition, while protecting the quality of services, public service contracts should be of limited duration'. Additionally, in the case of very long contract durations it becomes difficult to correctly attribute risks between the operator and the authority due to increasing uncertainties. On the other hand, recital 15 explains that 'it is necessary to make provision for extending public service contracts by a maximum of half their initial duration where the public service operator must invest in assets for which the depreciation period is exceptional and, because of their special characteristics and constraints, in the case of the outermost regions as specified in Article 349 TFEU'.

Any decision about extending the duration of a public service contract by 50% should be subject to the following considerations: the public service contract must oblige the operator to invest in assets such as rolling stock, maintenance facilities or infrastructure for which the depreciation period is exceptionally long.

Normally, the competent authority will decide to extend the contract's duration before the award of a new contract. If an extension of the duration needs to be decided while the contract is running, because intended investments in new rolling stock are made not at the beginning of the contract period but, for instance, due to technical reasons at a later stage, this possibility shall be clearly indicated in the tender documents and this option shall be adequately reflected in terms of compensation. In any event, the total contract extension must not exceed 50% of the duration stipulated in Article 4(4).

2.2.8. Article 4(5). Available options to competent authorities, if they consider desirable to take measures of staff protection in case of a change of operator

Article 4(5) provides that 'without prejudice to national and Community law, including collective agreements between social partners, competent authorities may require the selected public service operator to grant staff previously taken on to provide services the rights to which they would have been entitled if there had been a transfer within the meaning of Council Directive 2001/23/EC of 12 March 2001 on the approximation of the laws of the Member States relating to the safeguarding of employees' rights in the event of transfers of undertakings, businesses or parts of undertakings or businesses.[19] Where competent authorities require public service operators to comply with certain social standards, tender documents and public service contracts shall list the staff concerned and give transparent details of their contractual rights and the conditions under which employees are deemed to be linked to the services'. In compliance with the principle of subsidiarity and as set out in recitals 16 and 17, competent authorities basically have the following options in the case of a change of operator as regards staff protection:

(i) Not to take any specific action. In this case, employees' rights such as a transfer of staff only have to be granted where the conditions for the application of Directive 2001/23/EC are fulfilled, for instance, where there is transfer of significant tangible assets such as rolling stock.[20]

(ii) To require a transfer of staff previously taken on to provide services with the rights to which the staff would have been entitled, whether or not Directive 2001/23/EC applies, if there has been a transfer within the meaning of Directive 2001/23/EC. Recital 16 of Regulation (EC) No 1370/2007 explains that 'this Directive does not preclude Member States from safeguarding transfer conditions of employees' rights other than those covered by Directive 2001/23/EC and thereby, if appropriate, taking into account social standards established by national laws, regulations or administrative provisions or collective agreements or agreements concluded between social partners'.

(iii) To require the public transport operator to respect certain social standards for all staff involved in the provision of public transport services 'in order to ensure transparent and comparable terms of competition between operators and to avert the risk of social dumping' as set out in recital 17 of Regulation (EC) No 1370/2007. For instance, these standards could possibly relate to a collective agreement at company level or a collective agreement concluded for the relevant market segment.

(iv) To apply a combination of options (ii) and (iii).

In order to ensure transparency of employment conditions, competent authorities have the obligation, if they require a transfer of staff or impose certain social standards, to clearly specify these obligations in detail in the tender documents and the public service contracts.

2.2.9. Article 5(2)(e). Conditions of subcontracting in the case of public service contracts awarded by internal operators

Public service contracts directly awarded to an internal operator may be subcontracted under strict conditions. In such a case, pursuant to Article 5(2)(e), the internal operator must provide 'the major part' of the public passenger transport services itself. With this provision, the legislator intended to avoid that the concept of an 'internal operator' under the control of the competent authority would be devoid of meaning, since the internal operator would otherwise be allowed to subcontract all or a very important share of the transport services to another entity. Article 5(2)(e) therefore aims to avoid the establishment of false internal operators. The provision of public passenger transport services by an internal operator is an exception to the principle set out in Article 5(3), according to which public service contracts shall be awarded 'on the basis of a competitive tendering procedure'. According to recital 7 of Regulation (EC) No 1370/2007, 'the introduction of regulated competition between operators leads to more attractive and innovative services at lower cost'. Without prejudice to a case-by-case analysis, it would seem reasonable to consider that subcontracting more than one third of the public transport services would require a strong justification, in particular in view of the objectives of Article 5(2)(e) as explained. Typically, these transport services are expressed in value terms. In any case, subcontracting by internal operators must be carried out respecting relevant public procurement legislation.

Finally, Regulation (EC) No 1370/2007 does not prevent the public service contract from stipulating a minimum percentage of transport services in value terms to be subcontracted by the operator under a public service contract. The contract can stipulate this, provided the provisions of that Regulation are respected, especially those on the maximum share of a public service contract that may be subcontracted.

NOTES

17 This approach is consistent with the Commission's general approach to Services of General Economic Interest in other sectors. See, in particular, point 48 of the Communication from the Commission on the application of the European Union State aid rules to compensation granted for the provision of services of general economic interest (OJ C8, 11.1.2012, p 4).

18 See Commission Decision N 588/2002 — United Kingdom, BSO — Grant for long-distance bus services.

19 OJ L82, 22.3.2001, p 16.

20 In accordance with the case-law of the Court of Justice of the European Union, Directive 2001/23/EC is applicable to a transfer of undertaking which takes place following a tendering procedure for the award of a public service contract. In sectors of activity based on tangible assets, such as bus or rail transport, the Directive applies if significant tangible assets are transferred. The existence of a transfer within the meaning of Directive 2001/23/EC is not precluded by the fact that ownership of the tangible assets previously used by a transferor and taken over by a transferee is not transferred, for example in case the tangible assets taken over by the new contractor did not belong to its predecessor but were provided by the contracting authority; see in this regard Commission Memorandum on rights of workers in cases of transfers of undertakings at: ec.europa.eu/social/main.jsp?catId=707&langId=en&intPageId=208

2.3. AWARD OF PUBLIC SERVICE CONTRACTS

[5.411]

This chapter provides interpretative guidance on a number of provisions related to the award of public services contracts. The guidance covers the conditions under which public service contracts can be directly awarded as well as the procedural requirements for the competitive tendering of contracts.

2.3.1. Article 5(2)(b). Conditions under which a public service contract may be directly awarded to an internal operator

Regulation (EC) No 1370/2007 allows local competent authorities to provide public passenger transport services by rail and by road themselves or to award a public service contract directly to an internal operator. However, if they choose the second option, they must respect a number of strict rules and conditions set out in Article 5(2). The Commission notes the following:

(i) Article 5(2) provides that a public service contract may be awarded directly to internal operators by a competent local authority or a group of such authorities providing integrated public passenger transport services. This means that the public passenger transport services under a contract directly awarded by a group of competent local authorities must be integrated from a geographical, transport or tariff point of view across the territory for which such a group of authorities is responsible. The Commission also considers that the geographical scope of such services provided under the responsibility of a competent local authority or a group of such authorities should be defined in a manner that, typically, these local services would serve the needs of an urban agglomeration and/or a rural district.

(ii) The rules on control of the internal operator by the competent authority defined in Article 2(j) and specified in Article 5(2) must in any event be respected. An internal operator must be 'a legally distinct entity over which a competent local authority [. . .] exercises control similar to that exercised over its own departments'. Article 5(2)(a) lays down a set of criteria that shall be taken into consideration in assessing whether a competent authority effectively controls its internal operator. These criteria are 'the degree of representation on administrative, management or supervisory bodies, specifications relating to this representation in the articles of association, ownership, effective influence and control over strategic decisions and individual management decisions'. The assessment of control must be based on all the criteria, if relevant.

With regard to the ownership criterion, Regulation (EC) No 1370/2007 does not require the competent authorities to hold 100% of the internal operator's capital. This could be relevant, for example, in cases of public-private partnerships. In this respect, Regulation (EC) No 1370/2007 interprets 'in-house' operator more broadly than the Court of Justice of the European Union in its case-law.[21] However, effective control by the competent authority has to be proven by other criteria as mentioned in Article 5(2)(a).

(iii) To reduce distortions of competition, Article 5(2)(b) requires that the transport activities of internal operators and any body or bodies under their control should be geographically confined within the competent authority's territory or jointly controlled by a local competent authority. Thus, these operators or bodies may not participate in competitive tender procedures related to the provision of public passenger transport services organised outside the territory of the competent authority. Article 5(2)(b) is deliberately drafted in broad terms to prevent the creation of corporate structures that aim to circumvent this geographical confinement. Without prejudice to the provisions on outgoing lines, as mentioned in point (v), the Commission will be particularly strict in the application of this provision on geographical confinement, in particular when the internal operator and another body providing transport services are both controlled by a local competent authority.

(iv) By analogy with the case-law on public procurement and concessions which provides that the in-house operator's activities should not be 'market-oriented',[22] the condition of Article 5(2)(b) that 'the internal operator [. . .] perform their public passenger transport activity within the territory of the competent local authority, [. . .] and do not take part in competitive tenders concerning the provision of public passenger transport services organised outside the territory of the competent local authority' should be interpreted as follows: the internal operator or the entity influenced by the internal operator must not operate public passenger transport services, including as a subcontractor, or participate in tender procedures outside the competent authority's territory within the Union or, due to a possible indirect effect on the internal market, elsewhere in the world.

(v) Article 5(2)(b) allows internal operators to operate 'outgoing lines or other ancillary elements of that activity which enter the territory of neighbouring competent local authorities'. This provision provides some flexibility by catering for transport between neighbouring regions. Internal operators may therefore operate services beyond the territory of their competent local authority to a certain extent. To assess whether the services under public service contract are compliant with this provision, the following criteria should be applied: whether those services connect the territory of the competent authority in question to a neighbouring territory and whether they are ancillary rather than the main purpose of the public transport activities under public service contract. The Commission will assess whether the public transport activities are of a secondary nature by comparing their volume in vehicle or train km with the total volume of the public transport activities covered by the internal operator's contract(s).

2.3.2. Article 5(3). Procedural requirements for the competitive tendering of public service contracts

Article 5(3) stipulates that, if a competent authority uses a third party other than an internal operator to provide public passenger transport services, it shall award public service contracts through a fair, open, transparent and non-discriminatory competitive tendering procedure.

Article 5(3) provides few other details on the conditions under which a competitive tendering procedure should be organised. As laid out under point 2.4.1, contract award procedures must be designed so as to create conditions for effective competition. The application of the general principles of the Treaty, such as the principles of transparency and non-discrimination, implies, for instance, that the assessment criteria for the selection of offers must be published with the tender documents. The more detailed procedural rules of Union public procurement legislation, such as Directives 2014/24/EU and 2014/25/EU, or Directive 2014/23/EU on concessions, although not required, may be applied if Member States so wish.

However, according to Article 5(3) of Regulation (EC) No 1370/2007, the competent authority may also choose to negotiate with the pre-selected parties, after a pre-selection of tenders, in the case of specific or complex requirements. An example of this is when bidding operators must come up with technologically innovative transport solutions to meet the requirements published in the tender documents. Even when using pre-selection and negotiation, the selection and award procedure must nevertheless comply with all the conditions set out in Article 5(3).

In order to provide potential tenderers with fair and equal opportunities, the period between the launching of the competitive tendering procedure and the submission of the offers, as well as the period between the launching of the competitive tendering procedure and the moment from which the operation of the transport services has to start, shall be of appropriate and reasonable length.

To make the competitive tendering procedure more transparent, competent authorities should provide all the relevant technical and financial data, including information about the allocation of costs and revenues if available, to potential bidders to assist in the preparation of their offers. However, this shared information cannot undermine the legitimate protection of the commercial interests of third parties. Railway undertakings, rail infrastructure managers and all other relevant parties should make available appropriate accurate data to the competent authorities to enable them to comply with their information obligation.

2.3.3. Article 5(4). Conditions under which a competent authority may directly award a public service contract in case of a small contract volume or a SME

In the case of a direct award of a public service contract of small value or to a small or medium-sized operator (Article 5(4)), the competent authority may directly award the contract without a competitive tendering procedure. A public service contract is considered to be of small value if its average annual value is less than EUR 1 million or if it involves the annual provision of less than 300,000 kilometres of public passenger transport services. A small or medium-sized operator is an enterprise operating not more than 23 vehicles. In this case, the thresholds may be increased to an average annual value estimated at less than EUR 2 million or the annual provision of less than 600,000 kilometres of public transport services.

The SME threshold defined in terms of 'vehicles' indicates that this provision is geared to the transport by bus, but not to transport by tram, metro or train. The threshold of 23 vehicles has to be interpreted in a restrictive manner to avoid abuse of the exceptional character of Article 5(4). Therefore, the terms 'vehicles being operated' must be interpreted as referring to the total number of vehicles being operated by the public transport operator and not the number of vehicles operated for services covered by a particular public service contract.

However, the national legislator may decide to oblige its competent authority to apply to such cases the rule that public service contracts should be awarded in a fair, open, transparent and non-discriminatory competitive tendering process.

2.3.4. Article 5(4). Possibility of Member States to set lower thresholds allowing for a direct award in the case of contracts of small value or small and medium-sized operators

To the same extent that Article 5(4) allows the Member States (i) to oblige their competent authorities to apply the rule that public service contracts should be awarded in a fair, open, transparent and non-discriminatory competitive tendering procedure in the case of contracts of small value or small and medium-sized operators, the Member States may also decide (ii) to lower the thresholds set out in that provision for direct awards of such contracts or (iii) to use the thresholds provided for in Article 5(4) of Regulation (EC) No 1370/2007.

2.3.5. Article 5(6). Rail services that qualify for the direct award procedure

Article 5(6) allows competent authorities to award public service contracts directly for rail transport, 'with the exception of other track-based modes such as metro and tramways'.

The award by an authority of contracts for the provision of services of general interest to a third party has to respect general Treaty principles, such as transparency and equal treatment.[23] Contracts directly awarded under Article 5(6) are not exonerated from compliance with these Treaty principles. This is the reason why Regulation (EC) No 1370/2007 requires notably, in Article 7(2) and (3), that competent authorities publish certain information about directly awarded public service contracts in rail at least one year before and one year after the award.

The exception to the general rule of a competitive award procedure must also be applied restrictively. Rail substitute services, for instance, by bus and coach that may be contractually required from the public service operator in cases of disruption of the rail network cannot be considered as rail transport services and thus do not fall under Article 5(6). Subcontracting such rail substitute services by bus and coach according to relevant public procurement legislation is thus required.

Whether certain types of urban or suburban rail transport systems, such as the S-Bahn (in Austria, Germany and Denmark) and the RER (in France), or modes of transport that are similar to 'other track based modes' (for instance, metro or tram services), such as tram-train services and certain automatic train services operated under optical guidance systems, are included in the rail exemption of Article 5(6) must be assessed on a case-by-case basis, applying suitable criteria. In particular, this will depend on factors such as whether the systems in question are normally interoperable and/or share infrastructure with the traditional heavy rail network. Although tram-train services do use heavy rail infrastructure, their special characteristics mean they should nonetheless be regarded as an 'other track based mode'.

2.3.6. Modifications of public service contracts

Where a running public service contract needs to be amended, for instance where the transport service volume and corresponding compensation amount need to be adapted due to an extension of a metro line, the question arises whether the competent authority should start a new award procedure or whether the contract can be amended without a new award.

The Court of Justice has held that in the case of minor, non-substantial modifications a new award may not be necessary to ensure that general Treaty principles such as transparency and non-discrimination are complied with and a simple amendment of the contract may be sufficient.[24] According to the Court, in order to ensure transparency of procedures and equal treatment of tenderers, substantial amendments to essential provisions of a service concession contract or to contracts subject to the public procurement directives require the award of a new contract in certain cases. This is the case, in particular, if the new provisions are materially different in character from the original contract and are therefore such as to demonstrate the intention of the parties to renegotiate the essential terms of that contract

According to the Court, an amendment to a contract during its term may be regarded as substantial if it introduces conditions which, if they had been part of the original award procedure, would have allowed for the admission of tenderers other than those originally admitted or would have allowed for the acceptance of an offer other than that originally accepted.

In the absence of specific provisions in Regulation (EC) No 1370/2007, the principles of the above case-law are fully applicable to modifications of public service contracts covered by that Regulation. In order to determine what constitutes non-substantial modifications, a case-by-case assessment based on objective criteria is required.[25]

NOTES

21 Case C-324/07 *Coditel Brabant SA v Commune d'Uccle and Région de Bruxelles-Capitale* [2008] ECR I-8457, paragraph 30.

22 The case-law related to 'in-house' undertakings does not refer to a condition prohibiting those undertakings from taking part in competitive tenders outside the territory of the competent authority. However, the case-law has clearly indicated that an undertaking that becomes market-oriented renders the municipality's control tenuous (see, Case C-458/03 *Parking Brixen GmbH v Gemeinde Brixen and Stadtwerke Brixen* AG [2005] ECR I-08585.)

[23] See for instance recital 20 of Regulation (EC) No 1370/2007: 'Where a public authority chooses to entrust a general interest service to a third party, it must select the public service operator in accordance with Community law on public contracts and concessions, as established by Articles 43 to 49 of the Treaty, and the principles of transparency and equal treatment'.

[24] Case C-337/98 Commission v France [2000] ECR I-8377, paragraphs 44 and 46, Case C-454/06 *pressetext Nachrich-tenagentur* [2008] ECR I-4401, paragraph 34) and Case C-91/08 Wall AG [2010] ECR I-02815, paragraph 37 and 38.

[25] The Court of Justice pointed out in the Wall AG case that a change of subcontractor, even if the possibility of a change is provided for in the contract, may in exceptional cases constitute a substantial amendment to one of the essential provisions of a concession contract where the use of one subcontractor rather than another was, in view of the particular characteristics of the services concerned, a decisive factor in concluding the contract, which is in any event for the referring court to ascertain.

2.4. PUBLIC SERVICE COMPENSATION

[5.412]

The rules on compensation laid down in Regulation (EC) No 1370/2007 ensure the absence of overcompensation and compliance with the Treaty rules. They also address the concepts of reasonable profit and efficiency incentive, the issues of cross-subsidisation of commercial activities with compensation paid for public service obligations and of under-compensation, and the Commission's ex ante and ex post investigation procedures regarding public service compensation.

2.4.1. ARTICLE 4(1) AND ARTICLE 5(3). ABSENCE OF OVERCOMPENSATION IN THE CASE OF A PUBLIC SERVICE CONTRACT AWARDED ON THE BASIS OF AN OPEN AND COMPETITIVE PUBLIC TENDERING PROCEDURE

Unlike other economic sectors, Article 106(2) TFEU does not apply in cases where compensation is paid for public service obligations in land transport. Rather, such compensation is covered by Article 93 TFEU. Accordingly, the Union rules regarding compensation for services of general economic interest[26] which are based on Article 106(2) TFEU, do not apply to inland transport.[27]

In the case of public passenger transport services by rail and by road, provided that compensation for those services is paid in accordance with Regulation (EC) No 1370/2007, such compensation shall be deemed compatible with the internal market and shall be exempt from the prior notification requirement laid down in Article 108(3) TFEU, in accordance with Article 9(1) of that Regulation.

This presumption of compatibility and exemption from the notification requirement does not address the question of the possible State aid character of the compensation paid for the provision of public transport services. In order not to constitute State aid, such compensation would have to respect the four conditions laid down by the European Court of Justice in the Altmark judgement.[28]

An open, transparent and non-discriminatory competitive tendering procedure within the meaning of Article 5(3) will minimise the public compensation that the competent authorities will need to pay to the service provider to obtain the level of public service imposed in the tender, thus preventing overcompensation. In such a case, there is No need to apply the detailed rules on compensation set out in the annex.

In order to comply with Article 5(3), public procurement procedures must be designed in such a way that they create conditions for effective competition. The exact characteristics of the tender can vary in accordance with Article 5(3) which allows, for example, for a certain margin of negotiation between the competent authority and companies having submitted bids in the tender procedure. However, such negotiations must be fair and respect the principles of transparency and non-discrimination. For example, a purely negotiated procedure without prior publication of a contract notice is against the principles of transparency and non-discrimination of Article 5(3). Therefore, such a procedure does not comply with Article 5(3). Similarly, a tender procedure which is designed in such a way as to unduly restrict the number of potential bidders does not comply with Article 5(3). In this context, competent authorities should be particularly vigilant when they have clear indications of non-effective competition, in particular, for instance, when only one bid is submitted. In such cases, the Commission is also more likely to enquire about the specific circumstances of the tender procedure.

The selection criteria, including for example quality related, environmental or social criteria, should be closely related to the subject-matter of the service provided. The awarding authority is not prevented from setting qualitative standards to be met by all economic operators or from taking qualitative aspects related to the different proposals into account in its award decision.

Finally, there can be circumstances where a procurement procedure in accordance with Article 5(3) does not give rise to a sufficiently open and genuine competition. This could be the case, for example, due to the complexity or extent of the services to be provided or to the necessary infrastructure or assets owned by a particular service provider or to be provided for the execution of the contract.

2.4.2. ARTICLE 6. ABSENCE OF OVERCOMPENSATION IN THE CASE OF DIRECTLY AWARDED PUBLIC SERVICE CONTRACTS

The direct award of a public service contract in accordance with Article 5(2), (4), (5) or (6), or the imposition of general rules within the meaning of Article 3(2), do not guarantee that the level of compensation is reduced to the minimum. This is because that direct award will not result from the interaction of competitive market forces, but rather from a direct negotiation between the competent authority and the service provider.

Article 6(1) provides that in the case of directly awarded public service contracts or general rules compensation must comply with the provisions of Regulation (EC) No 1370/2007 as well as with its Annex to ensure the absence of overcompensation. The Annex to that Regulation establishes an ex post check to ensure that the compensatory payments are not higher than the actual net cost for the provision of the public service over the lifetime of the contract.

Additionally, the Commission considers that regular checks are in principle needed during the lifetime of the contract in order to detect and avoid at an early stage clear overcompensation situations from developing. This is the case, in particular, for long-term contracts.

Compensation must be limited to the net financial effect of the public service obligation. This is calculated as costs minus revenues generated by the public service operations, minus potential revenues induced by network effects, plus a reasonable profit.

On the cost side, all costs directly linked to the provision of the public service can be taken into account (such as train drivers' salaries, traction current, rolling stock maintenance, overhead costs (such as cost of management and administration) and contract-related costs of affiliated undertakings). Where the undertaking also carries out activities that fall outside the scope of the public service, an appropriate part of the costs that are shared between public service and other activities (such as office rental costs, the salaries of accountants or administrative personnel) may also be taken into account on top of the direct costs necessary to discharge the public service. Where the undertaking holds several public service contracts, the common costs must not only be allocated between the public service contracts and other activities, but also between the different public service contracts. To determine the appropriate proportion of common costs to be taken into account in the public service costs, market prices for using the resources, if available, may be taken as a benchmark. If such prices are not available, other methodologies may be used where appropriate. Revenues directly or indirectly related to the provision of the public service, such as revenues from the sale of tickets or from the sale of food and drinks, must be deducted from the costs for which compensation is claimed.

The operation of public passenger transport services under a public service contract by a transport undertaking also involved in other commercial operations may bring about positive induced network effects. For example, by serving a certain network under a public service contract which links to other routes operated under commercial terms, an operator may be able to increase its client base. The Commission welcomes induced network effects such as those brought about by through-ticketing and integrated timetabling, provided they are designed to benefit passengers. The Commission is also aware of the practical difficulties in quantifying these potential network effects. Nevertheless, in accordance with the Annex to Regulation (EC) No 1370/2007, any such quantifiable financial benefits shall be deducted from the costs for which compensation is claimed.

2.4.3. ARTICLE 4(1) AND THE ANNEX. THE NOTION OF 'REASONABLE PROFIT'

Article 4(1)(c) provides that the costs to be taken into account in a public service contract may include 'a suitable return on capital'. The Annex specifies that compensation for a public service obligation may not exceed the net financial effect of the obligation, defined as costs minus revenues generated by public service operations, minus potential induced network revenues, plus a 'reasonable profit'.

The Annex states that ' "reasonable profit" must be taken to mean a rate of return on capital that is normal for the sector in a given Member State and that takes account of the risk, or absence of risk, incurred by the public service operator by virtue of public authority intervention'. However, No further guidance is offered on the correct level of 'return on capital' or 'reasonable profit'.

While the Communication from the Commission on the application of the European Union State aid rules to compensation granted for the provision of services of general economic interest[29] (SGEI Communication) is based on a different legal basis than Regulation (EC) No 1370/2007 and thus not applicable in cases where compensation is paid for public service obligations in land transport, it provides some guidance on the determination of the level of reasonable profit that may serve as an indicator for competent authorities when awarding public service contracts under Regulation (EC) No 1370/2007.[30] The SGEI Communication explains that 'where generally accepted market remuneration exists for a given service, that market remuneration provides the best benchmark for the compensation in the absence of a tender'.[31] Such benchmarks would ideally be found in contracts in the same sector of activity, with similar characteristics and in the same Member State. The reasonable profit must therefore be in line with normal market conditions and should not exceed what is necessary to reflect the level of risk of the service provided.

However, such market benchmarks do not always exist. In that case, the level of reasonable profit could be determined by comparing the profit margin required by a typical well run undertaking active in the same sector to provide the service in question.[32]

A standard way in which to measure the return on capital of a public service contract is to consider the internal rate of return (IRR) that the company makes on its invested capital over the lifetime of the project, that is to say the IRR on the cash flows of the contract. However, accounting measures, such as the return on equity (ROE), the return on capital employed (ROCE) or other generally accepted economic indicators for the return on capital may also be used.

It should be noted that indicators may be influenced by the accounting methods used by the company and reflect the company situation only in a given year. Where this is the case, it should be ensured that the accounting practices of the company reflect the long-term economic reality of the public service contract. In that context, whenever feasible, the level of reasonable profit should be assessed over the lifetime of the public service contract. The differences in the economic models of railways, tramways, metro and bus transport should also be taken into account. For example, while railway transport is generally very capital-intensive, bus transport tends to be more dependent on personnel costs.

In any event, depending on the particular circumstances of each public service contract, a case-by-case assessment by the competent authority is needed to determine the adequate level of reasonable profit. Among other things, it must take into account the specific characteristics of the undertaking in question, the normal market remuneration for similar services and the level of risk involved in each public service contract. For example, a public service contract that includes specific provisions protecting the level of compensation in the case of unforeseen costs is less risky than a public service contract that does not contain such guarantees. All other things being equal, the reasonable profit in the former contract should therefore be lower than in the latter contract.

The use of efficiency incentives in the compensation mechanism is generally to be encouraged.[33] It should be underlined that compensation schemes which simply cover actual costs as they occur provide few incentives for the transport company to contain costs or to become more efficient over time. Their use is therefore better confined to instances where uncertainty about costs is large and the transport provider needs a high degree of protection against uncertainty.

2.4.4. Article 4(1) and (2) and the Annex. Preventing compensation received for a public service obligation from being used to cross-subsidise commercial activities

When a public service provider also carries out commercial activities, it is necessary to ensure that the public compensation it receives is not used to strengthen its competitive position in its commercial activities. In this context, the Annex lays down rules to avoid the cross-subsidisation of commercial activities with revenues from public service operations. These rules essentially consist of accounting separation between the two types of activities (public service and commercial) and a sound cost allocation method reflecting the real costs of providing the public service.

Article 4(1) and (2), together with the rules laid down in the Annex, require costs and revenues pertaining to the provision of services under each public service contract awarded to a transport undertaking and to commercial activities to be correctly allocated between the two types of activities. This is to effectively monitor public compensation and possible cross-subsidisation between the two activities. The adequacy of the cost-sharing and ring-fencing measures between the public service obligation and the commercial activities are crucial in this respect. For example, when means of transport (such as rail rolling stock or buses) or other assets or services needed to discharge the public service obligation (such as offices, personnel or stations) are shared between public service and commercial activities, the costs of each must be allocated to the two different types of activities in proportion to their relative weight in the overall transport services provided by the transport undertaking.

If, for example, the public service and the commercial activities of the same transport undertaking made use of services in stations, but the full costs of those services were allocated only to the public service activities, this would constitute a cross-subsidisation incompatible with Regulation (EC) No 1370/2007. Directive 2012/34/EC of the European Parliament and of the Council of 21 November 2012 establishing a single European railway area[34] also lays down specific obligations for the separation of accounts of railway undertakings.

Each public service contract should contain specific rules on compensation and should give rise to specific accounting entries. In other words, if the same undertaking has entered into several public service contracts, the accounts of the transport undertakings should specify which public compensation corresponds to which public service contract. At the written request of the Commission, these accounts must be made available in accordance with Article 6(2) of Regulation (EC) No 1370/2007.

2.4.5. Article 4(1). Design of compensation schemes to promote efficiency

Recital 27 of Regulation (EC) No 1370/2007 states that in the case of a direct award or general rules, the parameters for compensation should be set in such a way that compensation is appropriate and reflects a 'desire for efficiency and quality of service'. This means that the competent authorities should, through the compensation mechanism, encourage the service providers to become more efficient, by providing the required level and quality of service with the fewest resources possible.

The rules on compensation in Regulation (EC) No 1370/2007 leave some leeway for the competent authorities to design incentive schemes for the public service provider. In any event, competent authorities are obliged to 'promote the maintenance or development of effective management by the public service operator, which can be the subject of an objective assessment' (point 7 of the Annex). This implies that the compensation system must be designed to ensure at least a certain improvement in efficiency over time.

Efficiency incentives should nevertheless be proportionate and remain within a reasonable level, taking into account the difficulty in attaining the efficiency objectives. This may, for example, be ensured through a balanced sharing of any rewards linked to efficiency gains between the operator, the public authorities and/or the users. In any event, a system must be put in place to ensure that the undertaking is not allowed to retain disproportionate efficiency benefits. In addition, the parameters of these incentive schemes must be fully and precisely defined in the public service contract.

Incentives to provide public services more efficiently should not, however, prevent the provision of high-quality services. In the context of Regulation (EC) No 1370/2007, efficiency must be understood as the relation between the quality or level of the public services and the resources used to provide those services. Efficiency incentives should therefore focus on reducing costs and/or increasing the quality or level of service.

2.4.6. Article 6(1). Circumstances under which the Commission will investigate whether a compensation scheme complies with Regulation (EC) No 1370/2007

Public service compensation paid in accordance with Regulation (EC) No 1370/2007 is exempt from the requirement to notify State aid before it is implemented as laid down in Article 108(3) TFEU. Nevertheless, the Commission may be asked to assess a compensation scheme for reasons of legal certainty if a Member State is not sure whether the scheme complies with the Regulation. The Commission may also assess a compensation scheme on the basis of a complaint or an ex officio investigation if it is aware of evidence pointing to the non-compliance of that scheme with the compensation rules of the Regulation.

2.4.7. Article 6(1). Differences between the Commission's ex ante and ex post investigations into compensation schemes

The main difference between the Commission's ex ante and ex post investigations into compensation schemes relates to the time at which the Commission assesses the scheme, not in the method used for analysing whether overcompensation is present.

When assessing whether a compensation scheme prevents overcompensation ex ante, for example in the context of a notification, the Commission will assess, among other things, the precise compensation parameters. In particular, it will pay attention to the cost categories that are taken into account for the calculation of the compensation, as well as to the proposed level of reasonable profit. Furthermore, it will consider whether an adequate mechanism is in place to ensure that, in the event revenues from the provision of public services are higher than expected over the lifetime of the public service contract, the operator is not allowed to keep any excessive compensation over and above the actual net costs, a reasonable profit margin and any rewards for efficiency gains stipulated in the contract.

The public service contract must also in principle provide for regular checks during the lifetime of the contract in order to detect and avoid at an early stage clear overcompensation situations from arising, in particular in the case of long-term contracts. The competent authorities are obliged to verify compliance with the terms of the public service contract during the lifetime of the contract. Computerised tools can be developed to help perform these checks in a standardised manner. Overcompensation must be assessed separately for each public service contract to avoid excessive profits for individual public services that are averaged out across several contracts.

In the case of an ex post investigation, whether the compensation received exceeds the net financial effect of the public service as defined in the annex to Regulation (EC) No 1370/2007 can be assessed on the basis of actual financial revenue and cost data, since the compensation schemes have already been put in place. The method does not change however: compensation should not exceed the compensation amount to which the undertaking was entitled according to the parameters set out in the contract in advance, even if this amount is not sufficient to cover the actual net costs.

2.4.8. ARTICLE 1(1) AND ARTICLE 6(1). ENSURING THAT COMPETENT AUTHORITIES WILL PAY OPERATORS 'APPROPRIATE' COMPENSATION FOR THE DISCHARGE OF PUBLIC SERVICE OBLIGATIONS

According to Article 1 of Regulation (EC) No 1370/2007, 'the purpose of this Regulation is to define how, in accordance with the rules of [Union] law, competent authorities may act in the field of public passenger transport to guarantee the provision of services of general interest which are among other things more numerous, safer, of a higher quality or provided at lower cost than those that market forces alone would have allowed. To this end, this Regulation lays down the conditions under which competent authorities, when imposing or contracting for public service obligations, compensate public service operators for costs incurred and/or grant exclusive rights in return for the discharge of public service obligations'. Moreover, according to point 7 of the Annex to Regulation (EC) No 1370/2007, 'the method of compensation must promote the maintenance or development of [. . .] the provision of passenger transport services of a sufficiently high standard'.

This means that not only do the rules of Regulation (EC) No 1370/2007 aim to prevent any possible overcompensation for public service obligations, but also that they aim to ensure that the offer of public services defined in the public service contract is financially sustainable to reach and maintain a high level of service quality. The public service obligation should therefore be appropriately compensated so that the operator's own funds under a public service contract are not eroded in the long run, preventing the efficient fulfilment of its obligations under the contract and the maintenance of the provision of passenger transport services of a high standard as referred to in point 7 of the Annex to Regulation (EC) No 1370/2007.

In any event, if the competent authority does not pay appropriate compensation, it risks reducing the number of bids submitted in response to a competitive tendering procedure for the award of a public service contract, creating serious financial difficulties for the operator if the public service contract is awarded directly and/or reducing the overall level and quality of the public services provided during the lifetime of the contract.

NOTES

26 Notably Commission Decision on the application of Article 106(2) TFEU to State aid in the form of public service compensation granted to certain undertakings entrusted with the operation of services of general economic interest (OJ L7, 11.1.2012, p 3) and EU framework for State aid in the form of public service compensation (OJ C8, 11.1.2012, p 15).

27 However, Commission Regulation (EU) No 360/2012 on the application of Articles 107 and 108 to de minimis aid granted to undertakings providing services of general economic (OJ L114, 26.4.2012, p 8) does apply to land transport.

28 Case C-280/00 *Altmark Trans GmbH and Regierungspräsidium Magdeburg v Nahverkehrsgesellschaft Altmark GmbH* [2003] ECR I-7747. See, in particular, section 3 of the Communication from the Commission on the application of the European Union State aid rules to compensation granted for the provision of services of general economic interest (OJ C8, 11.1.2012, p 4).

29 OJ C8, 11.1.2012, p 4.

30 See in particular point 61 of the SGEI Communication.

31 Point 69 of the SGEI Communication.

32 Further guidance is given in the SGEI Communication on what is to be considered a 'typical well-run undertaking'. See in particular points 70-76.

33 See in particular point 7 of the Annex to the Regulation.

34 OJ L343, 14.12.2012, p 32. See Article 6 on the separation of accounts of railway undertakings and railway infrastructure managers.

2.5. PUBLICATION AND TRANSPARENCY

[5.413]

The interpretative guidance provided in this chapter covers the obligation of competent authorities to publish annual reports on the public service contracts they are responsible for, as well as their obligations to ensure transparency about the award of public service contracts before and after the award procedure.

2.5.1. Article 7(1). Publication obligations of competent authorities with regard to their annual reports on public service contracts under their responsibility

Article 7(1) requires each competent authority to publish an aggregated report once a year on the public service obligations for which it is responsible, the selected public service operators, and the compensation payments and exclusive rights granted to public service operators by way of reimbursement. This report shall distinguish between bus transport and rail transport, allow the performance, quality and financing of the public transport network to be monitored and assessed, and, if appropriate, provide information on the nature and extent of any exclusive rights granted.

The Commission understands the term 'aggregated report' in the sense that a competent authority should publish a comprehensive report about all the public service contracts it has awarded, while these contracts should all be individually identified. The information provided should therefore, besides the total values, refer to each contract, while ensuring the protection of the legitimate commercial interests of the operators concerned.

The public transport operators must provide all information and data to the competent authority in order to enable the latter to comply with its publication obligations.

To achieve the objective of this provision, which is to enable the monitoring and assessment of the public transport network in a meaningful manner allowing for a comparison with other public transport networks in a transparent, structured framework, the Commission encourages Member States and their authorities to voluntarily ensure ease of access to this information and to allow useful comparisons to be made. This could mean, for instance, that the information is published on a central website, such as that of an association of competent authorities or that of the transport ministry. The information and data should also be prepared in a methodologically consistent manner and presented in common units of measure.

2.5.2. Article 7(2) and (3). Possibilities of competent authorities to discharge their publication obligations concerning public service contracts pursuant to Article 7(2) and (3)

Competent authorities have certain obligations under Article 7 of Regulation (EC) No 1370/2007 to publish the intended (and concluded) award of public service contracts in the Official Journal of the European Union.

Article 7(2) states that at least one year before the publication of an invitation to tender or the direct award of a public service contract, competent authorities shall publish certain information on the contract envisaged in the Official Journal of the European Union.

Article 7(3) states that within one year of the direct award of a public service contract for rail services, competent authorities shall publish certain information on the awarded contract.

The Commission services have developed model forms and procedures that allow competent authorities to comply with these publication requirements. Through the possibility to reuse data, the forms and the publication procedure should also allow competent authorities, if they so wish, to reap synergies with the publication of a public tender for services pursuant to Article 5(3) of Regulation (EC) No 1370/2007.

The forms have been designed to fulfil the following requirements:

— to allow authorities easy access to the web application, to navigate the web application and to be comprehensible and clear;

— to clearly distinguish the publication requirements under Regulation (EC) No 1370/2007 from publication requirements under Directives 2014/23/EU, 2014/24/EU and 2014/25/EU;

— to request a level of detail of information that is not perceived as burdensome and thus can be acceptable to authorities;

— to be suitable for generating useful statistics on the award procedure of public service contracts and hence on the effective implementation of Regulation (EC) No 1370/2007.

During 2013, the Publications Office made an online publication procedure available on 'eNotices'.[35] The procedure is based on these model forms for publication in the Official Journal of the European Union, in accordance with Article 7(2) and (3) of Regulation (EC) No 1370/2007. The publication of information about directly awarded public service contracts for rail transport in the Official Journal of the European Union according to Article 7(3) is done on a voluntary basis.

2.5.3. Article 7(4). Right of interested parties to request information on public service contracts to be awarded directly before the actual date of award

Article 7(4) provides that a competent authority, when so requested by an interested party, shall forward to it the reasons for directly awarding a public service contract. Recital 30 states that 'directly awarded public service contracts should be subject to greater transparency'. This needs to be read in conjunction with recital 29, which states the need to publish the intention to award a contract and to enable potential public service operators to react. A competent authority must determine its intention to award a contract directly at least one year in advance, since this information must be published in the Official Journal of the European Union (Article 7(2), in particular point (b)). Thus, interested parties are placed in a position to formulate questions a long time before the contract is awarded, which will be one year later at the earliest. In order to grant effective legal protection, the information requested in accordance with Article 7(4) should be provided without undue delay.

Making contracts more transparent is, by definition, also related to the procedure for awarding a contract. The greater transparency required by recital 30 therefore not only implies transparency after the award of the contract, but also relates to the procedure before the contract is actually awarded to the public transport operator concerned.

(1)

NOTES

[35] https://enotices.ted.europa.eu/contentView?page=index

2.6. TRANSITIONAL ARRANGEMENTS

[5.414]
This chapter provides interpretative guidance on some aspects of the provisions on transitional arrangements concerning contracts awarded before the entry into force of Regulation (EC) No 1370/2007 and those awarded during the transitional period from 2009 until December 2019.

2.6.1. ARTICLE 8(2). SCOPE OF APPLICATION OF THE TRANSITIONAL PERIOD OF 10 YEARS STARTING FROM 3 DECEMBER 2009

Article 8(2) states that, without prejudice to its paragraph 3, 'the award of public service contracts by rail and by road shall comply with Article 5 as from 3 December 2019'. During this transitional period, Member States shall take measures to gradually comply with Article 5 to avoid serious structural problems, in particular relating to transport capacity.

Article 8(2) refers to Article 5 in its entirety. However, the Commission considers that only Article 5(3) concerning the obligation to apply open, transparent, non-discriminatory and fair procedures when granting public service contracts seems pertinent in this context. As stated in recital 31, the objective of the transitional provisions is to give competent authorities and public service operators enough time to adapt to the provisions of Regulation (EC) No 1370/2007. The obligation imposed on Member States to gradually comply with Article 5 is reasonable only if it concerns the obligation to apply open, transparent, non-discriminatory and fair procedures when granting public service contracts. It does not make sense that Member States 'gradually' apply the notion of internal operator or the exceptions defined in paragraphs 4, 5 and 6 of Article 5 of Regulation (EC) No 1370/2007 as they introduce more lenient provisions compared to the general Treaty principles and corresponding case-law. It does also not seem reasonable to say that the legislator wanted to postpone the full application of Article 5(7) concerning procedural guarantees and judicial review until 3 December 2019.

2.6.2. ARTICLE 8(2). OBLIGATIONS OF MEMBER STATES DURING THE TRANSITIONAL PERIOD UNTIL 2 DECEMBER 2019

Article 8(2) states that within six months of the first half of the transitional period (by 3 May 2015), 'Member States shall provide the Commission with a progress report, highlighting the implementation of any gradual award of public service contracts in line with Article 5'. This clearly indicates that Member States cannot wait until 2 December 2019 before starting to comply with the general rule of ensuring competitive tendering procedures for public service contracts that are open to all operators on a fair, transparent and non-discriminatory basis. Member States should take appropriate measures to gradually comply with that requirement during the transitional period to avoid a situation in which available transport capacity in the public transport market will not allow transport operators to satisfactorily respond to all competitive tendering procedures that would be launched at the end of the transitional period.

2.6.3. ARTICLE 8(3). MEANING OF 'LIMITED DURATION COMPARABLE TO THE DURATIONS SPECIFIED IN ARTICLE 4'

Article 8(3)(d) states that public service contracts awarded 'as from 26 July 2000 and before 3 December 2009 on the basis of a procedure other than a fair competitive tendering procedure [. . .] may continue until they expire, provided they are of limited duration comparable to the durations specified in Article 4'.

The Commission considers that the term 'comparable to the durations specified in Article 4' should be interpreted restrictively, so as to ensure that Member States work towards achieving the objectives of the Regulation from the date of its entry into force on 3 December 2009. The Commission therefore takes the view that it would be sensible to consider that the duration of public service contracts should be similar to those indicated in Article 4.

COMMUNICATION FROM THE COMMISSION

(2014/C99/03)

Guidelines on State aid to airports and airlines

[5.415]

NOTES

Date of publication in OJ: OJ C99, 4.4.2014, p 3.

See also *Overview of the State aid rules and public service obligations rules applicable to the air transport sector during the COVID-19 outbreak* at: https://ec.europa.eu/competition/sectors/transport/legislation_air_state_aid.html.

1. INTRODUCTION: STATE AID POLICY IN THE AVIATION SECTOR

[5.416]
1. Linking people and regions, air transport plays a vital role in the integration and the competitiveness of the European Union, as well as its interaction with the world. Air transport contributes significantly to the Union's economy, with more than 15 million annual commercial movements, 822 million passengers transported to and from Union airports in 2011, 150 scheduled airlines, a network of over 460 airports and 60 air navigation service providers.[1] The Union benefits from its position as a global aviation hub, with airlines and airports alone contributing more than EUR 140 thousand million to the Union's Gross Domestic Product each year. The aviation sector employs some 2.3 million people in the Union.[2]

2. The Europe 2020 Strategy[3] ('EU 2020') underlines the importance of transport infrastructure as part of the Union's sustainable growth strategy for the coming decade. In particular, the Commission has emphasised in its White Paper 'Roadmap to a Single Transport Area'[4] that the internalisation of externalities, the elimination of unjustified subsidies and free and undistorted competition are an essential part of the effort to align market choices with sustainability needs. The 'Roadmap to a Single Transport Area' also emphasises the importance of an efficient use of resources. In practice, transport has to use less and cleaner energy, better exploit a modern infrastructure and reduce its negative impact on the climate and the environment and, in particular, on key natural assets like water, land and ecosystems.

3. The gradual completion of the internal market has led to the removal of all commercial restrictions for airlines flying within the Union, such as restrictions on routes or number of flights and the setting of fares. Since the liberalisation of air transport in 1997,[5] the industry has expanded as never before, and this has contributed to economic growth and job creation. This has also paved the way for the emergence of low-cost carriers, operating a new business model based on quick turn-around times and very efficient fleet use. This development has generated a tremendous increase in traffic, with low-cost carriers' traffic growing at a fast pace since 2005. In 2012, for the first time, low-cost airlines (44.8%) exceeded the market share of incumbent air carriers (42.4%), a trend which continued in 2013 (45.94% for low-cost and 40.42% for incumbent).

4. While still predominantly publicly owned and managed,[6] airports across the Union are currently witnessing growing involvement of private undertakings. New markets have been created in the last decade through partial privatisation of certain airports, as well as through competition for the management of publicly owned airports, including regional airports.

5. Smaller airports display the greatest proportion of public ownership[7] and most often rely on public support to finance their operations. The prices of these airports tend not to be determined with regard to market considerations and in particular sound ex ante profitability prospects, but essentially having regard to local or regional considerations. Under the current market conditions the profitability prospects of commercially run airports also remain highly dependent[8] on the level of throughput, with airports that have fewer than 1 million passengers per annum typically struggling to cover their operating costs. Consequently the vast majority of regional airports are subsidised by public authorities on a regular basis.

6. Certain regions are still hampered by poor accessibility from the rest of the Union, and major hubs are facing increasing levels of congestion.[9] At the same time, the density of regional airports in certain regions of the Union has led to substantial overcapacity of airport infrastructure relative to passenger demand and airline needs.

7. The pricing system in most Union airports has traditionally been designed as a published scheme of airport charges based on passenger numbers and aircraft weight.[10] However, the evolution of the market and the close cooperation between airports and airlines have gradually paved the way for a wide variety of commercial practices, including long-term contracts with differentiated tariffs and sometimes substantial amounts of incentives and marketing support paid by airports and/or local authorities to airlines. In particular, public funds earmarked for supporting airport operations may be channelled to airlines in order to attract more commercial traffic, thereby distorting air transport markets.[11]

8. In its Communication on State Aid Modernisation (SAM),[12] the Commission points out that State aid policy should focus on facilitating well-designed aid targeted at market failures and objectives of common interest of the Union, and avoiding waste of public resources. State aid measures can indeed, under certain conditions, correct market failures, thereby contributing to the efficient functioning of markets and enhancing competitiveness. Furthermore, where markets provide efficient outcomes but these are deemed unsatisfactory from a cohesion policy point of view, State aid may be used to obtain a more desirable, equitable market outcome. However, State aid may have negative effects, such as distorting competition between undertakings and affecting trade between Member States to an extent contrary to the common interests of the Union. State aid control in the airport and air transport sectors should therefore promote sound use of public resources for growth-oriented policies, while limiting competition distortions that would undermine a level playing field in the internal market, in particular by avoiding duplication of unprofitable airports in the same catchment area and creation of overcapacities.

9. The application of State aid rules to the airport and air transport sectors constitutes part of the Commission's efforts aimed at improving the competitiveness and growth potential of the Union airport and airline industries.[13] A level-playing field among airlines and airports in the Union is of paramount importance for those objectives, as well as for the entire internal market. At the same time, regional airports can prove important both for local development and for the accessibility of certain regions, in particular against the backdrop of positive traffic forecasts for air transport in the Union.

10. As part of the general plan to create a single airspace of the Union and taking account of market developments, in 2005 the Commission adopted guidelines on financing of airports and start-up aid to airlines departing from regional airports[14] (the '2005 Aviation guidelines'). Those guidelines specified the conditions under which certain categories of State aid to airports and airlines could be declared compatible with the internal market. They supplemented the 1994 Aviation guidelines,[15] which mainly contained provisions with regard to the restructuring of flag carriers and social aid for the benefit of Union citizens.

11. These guidelines take stock of the new legal and economic situation concerning the public financing of airports and airlines and specify the conditions under which such public financing may constitute State aid within the meaning of Article 107(1) of the Treaty on the Functioning of the European Union and, when it does constitute State aid, the conditions under which it can be declared compatible with the internal market pursuant to Article 107(3)(c) of the Treaty. The Commission's assessment is based on its experience and decision-making practice, as well as on its analysis of current market conditions in the airport and air transport sectors. It is therefore without prejudice to its approach in respect of other infrastructures or sectors. In particular, the Commission considers that the mere fact that

an airport operator receives or has received State aid does not automatically imply that its customer airlines are also aid beneficiaries. If the conditions offered to an airline at a given airport would have been offered by a profit-driven airport operator, the airline cannot be deemed to receive an advantage for the purposes of State aid rules.

12. Where public support constitutes State aid, the Commission considers that under certain conditions, certain categories of aid to regional airports and airlines using those airports can be justified, in particular to develop new services and contribute to local accessibility and economic development. Nevertheless, distortions of competition on all markets concerned should be taken into consideration and only State aid which is proportional and necessary to contribute to an objective of common interest can be acceptable.

13. In this context, it should be pointed out that operating aid constitutes, in principle, a very distortive form of aid and can only be authorised under exceptional circumstances. The Commission considers that airports and airlines should normally bear their own operating costs. Nevertheless, the gradual shift to a new market reality, as described in points 3 to 7, explains the fact that regional airports have received widespread operating support from public authorities prior to the adoption of these guidelines. Against this backdrop, for a transitional period, and to enable the aviation industry to adapt to the new market situation, certain categories of operating aid to airports might still be justified under certain conditions. As explained in point 5, under the current market conditions the available data and industry consensus point to a link between an airport's financial situation and its traffic levels, with financing needs normally being proportionately greater for smaller airports. In the light of their contribution to economic development and territorial cohesion in the Union, managers of smaller regional airports should therefore be given time to adjust to the new market environment, for example, by gradually increasing airport charges to airlines, by introducing rationalisation measures, by differentiating their business models or by attracting new airlines and customers to fill their idle capacity.

14. At the end of the transitional period, airports should no longer be granted operating aid and they should finance their operations from their own resources. Whilst the provision of compensation for uncovered operating costs of services of general economic interest should remain possible for small airports or to allow for connectivity of all regions with particular requirements, the market changes stimulated by these guidelines should allow airports to cover their costs as in any other industry.

15. Development of new air traffic should, in principle, be based on a sound business case. However, without appropriate incentives, airlines are not always prepared to run the risk of opening new routes from unknown and untested small airports. Therefore, under certain conditions, airlines may be granted start-up aid during and even after the transitional period, if this provides them with the necessary incentive to create new routes from regional airports, increases the mobility of the citizens of the Union by establishing access points for intra-Union flights and stimulates regional development. As remote regions are penalised by their poor accessibility, start-up aid for routes from those regions is subject to more flexible compatibility criteria.

16. The allocation of airport capacity to airlines should therefore gradually become more efficient (that is to say demand-oriented), and there should be less need for public funding of airports as private investment becomes more widespread. If a genuine transport need and positive externalities for a region can be established, investment aid to airports should nevertheless continue to be accepted after the transitional period, with maximum aid intensities ensuring a level-playing field across the Union.

17. Against this backdrop these guidelines introduce a new approach to the assessment of compatibility of aid to airports:

(a) whereas the 2005 Aviation guidelines left open the issue of investment aid, these revised guidelines define maximum permissible aid intensities depending on the size of the airport;

(b) however, for large airports with a passenger volume of over 5 million per annum, investment aid should in principle not be declared compatible with the internal market pursuant to Article 107(3)(c) of the Treaty, except in very exceptional circumstances, such as relocation of an existing airport, where the need for State intervention is characterised by a clear market failure, taking into account the exceptional circumstances, the magnitude of the investment and the limited competition distortions;

(c) the maximum permissible aid intensities for investment aid are increased by up to 20% for airports located in remote regions;

(d) for a transitional period of 10 years, operating aid to regional airports can be declared compatible with the internal market pursuant to Article 107(3)(c) of the Treaty; however, with regard to airports with passenger traffic of less than 700,000 per annum the Commission will, after a period of four years, reassess the profitability prospects of this category of airport in order to evaluate whether special rules should be devised to assess the compatibility with the internal market of operating aid in favour of those airports.

18. In addition, the compatibility conditions for start-up aid to airlines have been streamlined and adapted to recent market developments.

19. The Commission will apply a balanced approach which is neutral vis-à-vis the various business models of airports and airlines, and takes into account the growth prospects of air traffic, the need for regional development and accessibility and the positive contribution of the low-cost carriers' business model to the development of some regional airports. But at the same time, a gradual move towards a market-oriented approach is undoubtedly warranted; except in duly justified and limited cases, airports should be able to cover their operating costs and any public investment should be used to finance the construction of viable airports meeting the demand of airlines and passengers; distortions of competition between airports and between airlines, as well as duplication of unprofitable airports should be avoided. This balanced approach should be transparent, easily understood and straightforward to apply.

20. These guidelines are without prejudice to Member States duty to comply with Union law. In particular, to avoid that the investment would lead to environmental harm, Member States must also ensure compliance with Union environmental legislation, including the need to carry out an environmental impact assessment where appropriate and ensure all relevant permits.

NOTES

1 Sources: Eurostat, Association of European Airlines, International Air Transport Association.

2 Study on the effects of the implementation of the EU aviation common market on employment and working conditions in the Air Transport Sector over the period 1997/2010. Steer Davies Gleave for the European Commission, DG MOVE. Final report of August 2012.

3 Communication from the Commission – Europe 2020 – A strategy for smart, sustainable and inclusive growth, COM(2010) 2020 final of 3 March 2010.

4 Roadmap to a Single Transport Area – Towards a competitive and resource efficient transport system, COM(2011) 144.

5 Council Regulation (EEC) No 2407/92 of 23 July 1992 on licensing of air carriers (OJ L240, 24.8.1992, p 1), Council Regulation (EEC) No 2408/92 of 23 July 1992 on access for Community air carriers to intra-Community air routes (OJ L240, 24.8.1992, p 8), and Council Regulation (EEC) No 2409/92 of 23 July 1992 on fares and rates for air services (OJ L240, 24.8.1992, p 15).

6 According to Airport Council International Europe, 77% of airports were fully publicly owned in 2010, while 9% were fully privately owned, see Airport Council International Europe: The Ownership of Europe's Airports 2010.

7 This is exemplified by the fact that, although in 2010 their share of the overall number of airports amounted to 77%, publicly owned airports accounted for only 52% of total passenger traffic.

8 As shown in 2002 by the 'Study on competition between airports and the application of State aid rules' – Cranfield University, June 2002, and subsequently confirmed by industry reports.

9 13 airports in the Union are forecasted to be operating at full capacity eight hours a day every day of the year in 2030, compared to 2007 when only 5 airports were operating at or near capacity 100% of the time (see Communication from the European Commission to the European Parliament, the Council, the European Economic and Social Committee and the Committee of the Regions on Airport policy in the European Union – addressing capacity and quality to promote growth, connectivity and sustainable mobility of 1 December 2011, COM(2011) 823) ('the Communication on Airport policy in the European Union').

10 As evidenced by the International Civil Aviation Organization's policies on charges for airports and navigations services (Document 9082), last revised in April 2012.

11 In particular where aid is determined on the basis of ex post calculations (making good for any deficits as they arise), airports may not have much incentive to contain costs and charge airport charges that are sufficient to cover costs.

12 Communication from the Commission to the European Parliament, the Council, the European Economic and Social Committee and the Committee of the Regions on EU State Aid Modernisation (SAM), COM(2012) 209 final.

13 See the Communication on Airport policy in the European Union.

14 Communication from the Commission – Community guidelines on financing of airports and start-up aid to airlines departing from regional airports (OJ C312, 9.12.2005, p 1).

15 Application of Articles 92 and 93 of the EC Treaty and Article 61 of the EEA Agreement to State aids in the aviation sector (OJ C350, 10.12.1994, p 5).

2. SCOPE AND DEFINITIONS

2.1. SCOPE

[5.417]

21. The principles set out in these guidelines apply to State aid to airports and airlines.[16] They will be applied in accordance with the Treaty and secondary legislation adopted pursuant to the Treaty as well as other Union guidelines on State aid.[17]

22. Some airports and airlines are specialised in freight transport. The Commission does not yet have sufficient experience in assessing the compatibility of aid to airports and airlines specialised in freight transport to summarise its practice in the form of specific compatibility criteria. For those categories of undertakings, the Commission will apply the common principles of compatibility as set out in section 5 through a case-by-case analysis.

23. The Commission will not apply the principles set out in the Guidelines on national regional aid for 2007–2013[18] and the Guidelines on regional State aid for 2014–2020[19] or any future guidelines on regional aid to State aid granted for airport infrastructure.

24. These guidelines replace the 1994 and 2005 Aviation guidelines.

2.2. DEFINITIONS

25. For the purpose of these guidelines:

(1) 'aid' means any measure fulfilling all the criteria laid down in Article 107(1) of the Treaty;

(2) 'aid intensity' means the total aid amount expressed as a percentage of eligible costs, both figures expressed in net present value terms at the moment the aid is granted and before any deduction of tax or other charges;

(3) 'airline' means any airline with a valid operating licence issued by a Member State or a Member of the Common European Aviation Area pursuant to Regulation (EC) No 1008/2008 of the European Parliament and of the Council;[20]

(4) 'airport charge' means a price or a levy collected for the benefit of the airport and paid by the airport users for the use of facilities and services which are exclusively provided by the airport and which are related to landing, take-off, lighting and parking of aircraft, and processing of passengers and freight, including charges or fees paid for ground handling services and fees for centralised ground handling infrastructure;

(5) 'airport infrastructure' means infrastructure and equipment for the provision of airport services by the airport to airlines and the various service providers, including runways, terminals, aprons, taxiways, centralised ground handling infrastructure and any other facilities that directly support the airport services, excluding infrastructure and equipment which is primarily necessary for pursuing non-aeronautical activities, such as car parks, shops and restaurants;

(6) 'airport' means an entity or group of entities performing the economic activity of providing airport services to airlines;

(7) 'airport revenue' means the revenue from airport charges net of marketing support or any incentives provided by the airport to the airlines, taking into account revenue stemming from non-aeronautical activities (free of any public support), excluding any public support and compensation for tasks falling within public policy remit, or services of general economic interest;

(8) 'airport services' means services provided to airlines by an airport or any of its subsidiaries, to ensure the handling of aircraft, from landing to take-off, and of passengers and freight, so as to enable airlines to provide air transport services, including the provision of ground handling services and the provision of centralised ground handling infrastructure;

(9) 'average annual passenger traffic' means a figure determined on the basis of the inbound and outbound passenger traffic during the two financial years preceding that in which the aid is notified or granted in the case of non-notified aid;

(10) 'capital costs' means the depreciation of the eligible investment costs into airport infrastructure and equipment, including the underlying costs of financing;

(11) 'capital costs funding gap' means the net present value of the difference between the positive and negative cash flows, including investment costs, over the lifetime of the investment in fixed capital assets;

(12) 'catchment area of an airport' means a geographic market boundary that is normally set at around 100 kilometres or around 60 minutes travelling time by car, bus, train or high-speed train; however, the catchment area of a given airport may be different and needs to take into account the specificities of each particular airport. The size and shape of the catchment area varies from airport to airport, and depends on various characteristics of the airport, including its business model, location and the destinations it serves;

(13) 'costs of financing' means the costs related to debt and equity financing of the eligible costs of the investment; in other words, the costs of financing take into account the proportion of total interest and own capital remuneration that corresponds to the financing of eligible costs of the investment, excluding the financing of working capital, investments in non-aeronautical activities or other investment projects;

(14) 'date of grant of the aid' means the date when the Member State took a legally binding commitment to award the aid that can be invoked before a national court;

(15) 'eligible investment costs' means the costs relating to investments in airport infrastructure, including planning costs, but excluding investment costs for non-aeronautical activities, investment costs in relation to equipment for ground handling services, ordinary maintenance costs and costs for tasks falling within the public policy remit;

(16) 'ground handling services' means services provided to airport users at airports as described in the Annex to Directive 96/67/EC, and any subsequent legislation on access to the ground handling market at airports;

(17) 'high-speed train' means a train capable of reaching speeds of over 200 km/h;

(18) 'investment aid' means aid to finance fixed capital assets, specifically, to cover the capital costs funding gap;

(19) 'net present value' means the difference between the positive and negative cash flows over the lifetime of the investment, discounted to their current value using the cost of capital, that is to say, the normal required rate of return applied by the company in other investment projects of a similar kind or, where not available, the cost of capital of the company as a whole, or expected returns commonly observed in the airport sector;

(20) 'non-aeronautical activities' means commercial services to airlines or other users of the airport, such as ancillary services to passengers, freight forwarders or other service providers, renting out of offices and shops, car parking and hotels;

(21) 'operating aid' means aid to cover the 'operating funding gap', either in the form of an upfront payment or in the form of periodic instalments to cover expected operating costs (periodic lump sum payments);

(22) 'operating costs' means the underlying costs of an airport in respect of the provision of airport services, including cost categories such as cost of personnel, contracted services, communications, waste, energy, maintenance, rent and administration, but excluding the capital costs, marketing support or any other incentives granted to airlines by the airport, and costs falling within a public policy remit;

(23) 'operating funding gap' means the operating losses of an airport over the relevant period, discounted to their current value using the cost of capital, that is to say the shortfall (in Net Present Value terms) between airport revenues and operating costs of the airport;

(24) 'outermost regions' means the regions referred to in Article 349 of the Treaty;[21]

(25) 'reasonable profit margin' means a rate of return on capital, for example, measured as an Internal Rate of Return (IRR), that the undertaking is normally expected to make on investments with a similar degree of risk;

(26) 'regional airport' means an airport with annual passenger traffic volume of up to 3 million;

(27) 'remote regions' mean outermost regions, Malta, Cyprus, Ceuta, Mellila, islands which are part of the territory of a Member State, and sparsely populated areas;

(28) 'sparsely populated areas' mean NUTS 2 regions with less than 8 inhabitants per km^2 or NUTS 3 regions with less than 12.5 inhabitants per km^2 (based on Eurostat data on population density);

(29) 'start of works' means either the start of construction works on the investment, or the first firm commitment to order equipment or other commitment that makes the investment irreversible, whichever comes first, and does not include preparatory works, such as obtaining permits and conducting preliminary feasibility studies.

NOTES

16 The principles set out in these guidelines do not apply to aid for the provision of ground handling services regardless of whether they are provided by the airport itself, by an airline or by a supplier of ground handling services to third parties; such aid will be assessed on the basis of the relevant general rules. Pursuant to Council Directive 96/67/EC of 15 October 1996 on access to the groundhandling market at Community airports (OJ L272, 25.10.1996, p 36), or any subsequent legislation on access to the ground handling market at Union's airports, airports that carry out ground handling are required to keep separate accounts of their ground handling activities and other activities. Moreover, an airport may not subsidise its ground handling activities from the revenue it derives from its airport activities. These guidelines also do not apply to undertakings which, though active at an airport, are engaged in non-aeronautical activities.

17 Notably, but not exclusively, Regulation (EC) No 1008/2008 of the European Parliament and of the Council of 24 September 2008 on common rules for the operation of air services in the Community (OJ L293, 31.10.2008, p 3),

Directive 96/67/EC, Directive 2009/12/EC of the European Parliament and of the Council of 11 March 2009 on airport charges (OJ L70, 14.3.2009, p 11), and any subsequent legislation on airport charges.

18 Guidelines on national regional aid for 2007–2013 (OJ C54, 4.3.2006, p 13).

19 Guidelines on regional State aid for 2014–2020 (OJ C209, 23.7.2013, p 1).

20 Regulation (EC) No 1008/2008 of the European Parliament and of the Council of 24 September 2008 on common rules for the operation of air services in the Community (OJ L293, 31.10.2008, p 3).

21 Currently: Guadeloupe, French Guiana, Martinique, Réunion, Saint-Martin, Mayotte, the Azores, Madeira and the Canary Islands. In accordance with European Council Decision (2010/718/EU) of 29 October 2010 amending the status with regard to the European Union of the island of Saint-Barthélemy (OJ L325, 9.12.2010, p 4), from 1 January 2012, Saint-Barthélemy ceased to be an outermost region and became an overseas country or territory referred to in Part Four of the Treaty. In accordance with European Council Decision (2012/419/EU) of 11 July 2012 amending the status of Mayotte with regard to the European Union (OJ L204, 31.7.2012, p 131), from 1 January 2014, Mayotte ceased to be an overseas country or territory and became an outermost region.

3. PRESENCE OF STATE AID WITHIN THE MEANING OF ARTICLE 107(1) OF THE TREATY

3.1. NOTION OF UNDERTAKING AND ECONOMIC ACTIVITY

[5.418]

26. In accordance with Article 107(1) of the Treaty, State aid rules apply only where the recipient is an 'undertaking'. The Court of Justice of the European Union has consistently defined undertakings as entities engaged in an economic activity, regardless of their legal status or ownership and the way in which they are financed.[22] Any activity consisting in offering goods and services on a market is an economic activity.[23] The economic nature of an activity as such does not depend on whether the activity generates profits.[24]

27. It is now clear that the activity of airlines which consists in providing transport services to passengers or undertakings constitutes an economic activity. The 1994 Aviation guidelines, however, still reflected the view that '*[t]he construction [or] enlargement of infrastructure projects (such as airports, motorways, bridges, etc.) represents a general measure of economic policy which cannot be controlled by the Commission under the Treaty rules on State aids*.' In '*Aéroports de Paris*',[25] the Union Courts ruled against this view and held that the operation of an airport consisting in the provision of airport services to airlines and to the various service providers also constitutes an economic activity. In its judgment in the '*Leipzig-Halle airport*' case,[26] the General Court clarified that the operation of an airport is an economic activity, of which the construction of airport infrastructure is an inseparable part.

28. As far as past financing measures are concerned, the gradual development of market forces in the airport sector[27] does not allow for a precise date to be determined, from which the operation of an airport should without doubt be considered as an economic activity. However, the Union Courts have recognised the evolution in the nature of airport activities. In '*Leipzig/Halle airport*', the General Court held that, from 2000, the application of State aid rules to the financing of airport infrastructure could no longer be excluded.[28] Consequently, from the date of the judgment in '*Aéroports de Paris*' (12 December 2000), the operation and construction of airport infrastructure must be considered as falling within the ambit of State aid control.

29. Conversely, due to the uncertainty that existed prior to the judgment in '*Aéroports de Paris*', public authorities could legitimately consider that the financing of airport infrastructure did not constitute State aid and, accordingly, that such measures did not need to be notified to the Commission. It follows that the Commission cannot now bring into question, on the basis of State aid rules, financing measures granted[29] before the '*Aéroports de Paris*' judgment.[30]

30. In any event, measures that were granted before any competition developed in the airport sector did not constitute State aid when granted, but could be considered as existing aid pursuant to Article 1 (b) (v) of Council Regulation (EC) No 659/1999[31] if the conditions of Article 107(1) of the Treaty are met.

31. The entity or group of entities performing the economic activity of providing airport services to airlines, that is to say, the handling of aircraft, from landing to take-off, and of passengers and freight, so as to enable airlines to provide air transport services,[32] will be referred to as the 'airport'.[33] An airport provides a range of services ('airport services') to airlines, in exchange for payment ('airport charges'). While the exact extent of the services provided by airports, as well as the labelling of charges as 'fees' or 'taxes' varies across the Union, the provision of airport services to airlines in exchange for airport charges constitutes an economic activity in all Member States.

32. The legal and regulatory framework within which individual airports are owned and operated varies from airport to airport across the Union. In particular, regional airports are often managed in close cooperation with public authorities. In this respect, the Court has ruled that several entities can be deemed to perform an economic activity together, thereby constituting an economic unit, under specific conditions.[34] In the field of aviation, the Commission considers that significant involvement in an airport's commercial strategy, such as through the direct conclusion of agreements with airlines or the setting of airport charges, would constitute a strong indication that, alone or jointly, the relevant entity performs the economic activity of operating the airport.[35]

33. In addition to airport services, an airport may also provide other commercial services to airlines or other users of the airport, such as ancillary services to passengers, freight forwarders or other service providers (for example, through the rental of premises to shop and restaurant managers, parking operators, etc.). These economic activities will be collectively referred to as 'non-aeronautical activities'.

34. However, not all the activities of an airport are necessarily of an economic nature.[36] Since the classification of an entity as an undertaking is always in relation to a specific activity, it is necessary to distinguish between the activities of a given airport and to establish to what extent those activities are of an economic nature. If an airport carries out both economic and non-economic activities, it is to be regarded as an undertaking only with regard to the former.

35. The Court has held that activities that normally fall under the responsibility of the State in the exercise of its official powers as a public authority are not of an economic nature and in general do not fall within the scope of the rules on State aid.[37] At an airport, activities such as air traffic control, police, customs, firefighting, activities necessary to safeguard civil aviation against acts of unlawful interference and the investments relating to the infrastructure and equipment necessary to perform those activities are considered in general to be of a non-economic nature.[38]

36. The public funding of such non-economic activities does not constitute State aid, but should be strictly limited to compensating the costs to which they give rise and may not be used to finance other activities.[39] Any possible overcompensation by public authorities of costs incurred in relation to non-economic activities may constitute State aid. Moreover, if an airport is engaged in non-economic activities, alongside its economic activities, separated cost accounting is required in order to avoid any transfer of public funds between the non-economic and economic activities.

37. Public financing of non-economic activities must not lead to undue discrimination between airports. Indeed, it is established case law that there is an advantage when public authorities relieve undertakings of the costs inherent to their economic activities.[40] Therefore, when it is normal under a given legal order that civil airports have to bear certain costs inherent to their operation, whereas other civil airports do not, the latter might be granted an advantage, regardless of whether or not those costs relate to an activity which in general is considered to be of a non-economic nature.

3.2. USE OF STATE RESOURCES AND IMPUTABILITY TO THE STATE

38. The transfer of State resources may take many forms such as direct grants, tax rebates,[41] soft loans or other types of preferential financing conditions. State resources will also be involved if the State provides a benefit in kind or in the form of subsidised services,[42] such as airport services. State resources can be used[43] at national, regional or local level. Funding from Union funds will likewise constitute State resources, when those funds are allocated at a Member State's discretion.[44]

39. The Court has also ruled that even if the State is in a position to control a public undertaking and to exercise a dominant influence over its operations, actual exercise of that control in a particular case cannot be automatically presumed.[45] Therefore, it needs to be assessed whether measures granted by public undertakings are imputable to the State. The Court has indicated that the imputability to the State of a measure granted by a public undertaking may be inferred from a set of indicators arising from the circumstances of the case and the context in which that measure was taken.[46]

40. Against this background, the resources of a public airport constitute public resources. Consequently, a public airport may grant aid to an airline using the airport if the decision to grant the measure is imputable to the State and the other conditions of Article 107(1) of the Treaty are met. The Court has also ruled that whether a measure is granted directly by the State or by public or private bodies established or appointed by it to administer the measure is irrelevant to whether it is considered to be State aid.[47]

3.3. DISTORTION OF COMPETITION AND EFFECT ON TRADE

41. According to the case law of the Court, financial support distorts competition in so far as it strengthens the position of an undertaking compared with other undertakings.[48]

42. In general, when an advantage granted by a Member State strengthens the position of an undertaking compared with other undertakings competing in a given Union market, trade between Member States must be regarded as being affected by that advantage.[49]

43. Competition between airports can be assessed in the light of airlines' criteria of choice, and in particular by comparing factors such as the type of airport services provided and the clients concerned, population or economic activity, congestion, whether there is access by land, and the level of charges and overall commercial conditions for use of airport infrastructure and services. The charge level is a key factor, since public funding granted to an airport could be used to maintain airport charges at an artificially low level in order to attract airlines and may thus significantly distort competition.

44. The Commission further notes that airports are in competition for the management of airport infrastructure, including at local and regional airports. The public funding of an airport may therefore distort competition in the markets for airport infrastructure operation. Moreover, public funding to both airports and airlines can distort competition and have an effect on trade in air transport markets across the Union. Finally, intermodal competition may also be affected by public funding to airports or airlines.

45. The Court held in the *Altmark* judgment[50] that even public funding granted to an undertaking which provides only local or regional transport services may have an effect on trade between Member States, as the supply of transport services by that undertaking may thereby be maintained or increased with the result that undertakings established in other Member States have less chance of providing their transport services. Even the fact that the amount of aid is small or the relatively small size of the undertaking which receives public funding does not, as such, exclude the possibility that trade between Member States might be affected. Consequently, the public financing of airports or airlines operating services from those airports might affect trade between Member States.

3.4. PUBLIC FUNDING OF AIRPORTS AND THE APPLICATION OF THE MARKET ECONOMY OPERATOR PRINCIPLE

46. Article 345 of the Treaty states that the Treaty in no way prejudices the rules in Member States governing the system of property ownership. Member States can accordingly own and manage undertakings, and can purchase shares or other interests in public or private undertakings.

47. Consequently, these guidelines make no distinction between the different types of beneficiaries in terms of their legal structure or whether they belong to the public or private sector, and all references to airlines and airports or the companies which manage them encompass all types of legal entity.

48. In order to assess whether an undertaking has benefited from an economic advantage, the so-called Market Economy Operator ('MEO') test is applied. This test should be based on available information and foreseeable developments at the time when the public funding was granted and it should not rely on any analysis based on a later situation.[51]

49. Consequently, when an airport benefits from public funding, the Commission will assess whether such funding constitutes aid by considering whether in similar circumstances a private operator, having regard to the foreseeability of obtaining a return and leaving aside all social, regional-policy and sectoral considerations,[52] would have granted the same funding. Public funding granted in circumstances which correspond to normal market conditions is not regarded as State aid.[53]

50. The Court has also ruled that the conduct of a public investor may be compared with that of a private investor guided by prospects of profitability in the longer term,[54] over the lifetime of the investment. These considerations are particularly pertinent to investment in infrastructure, which often involve large amounts of financial resources and can produce a positive return only after many years. Any assessment of the profitability of an airport must take into account airport revenues.

51. Consequently, as regards public financing to airports, the analysis of conformity with the MEO test should be based on sound *ex ante* profitability prospects for the entity granting the financing.[55] Any traffic forecasts used for that purpose should be realistic and subject to a reasonable sensitivity analysis. The absence of a business plan constitutes an indication that the MEO test may not be met.[56] In the absence of a business plan, Member States can provide analysis or internal documents from the public authorities or from the airport concerned showing clearly that an analysis conducted before the granting of the public financing demonstrates that the MEO test is satisfied.

52. Airports can play an important role in fostering local development or accessibility. Nevertheless regional or policy considerations cannot be taken into account for the purposes of the MEO test.[57] Such considerations can, however, under certain conditions, be taken into account when assessing the compatibility of aid.

3.5. FINANCIAL RELATIONSHIPS BETWEEN AIRPORTS AND AIRLINES

53. Where an airport has public resources at its disposal, aid to an airline using the airport can, in principle, be excluded where the relationship between the airport and that airline satisfies the MEO test. This is normally the case if:

(a) the price charged for the airport services corresponds to the market price (see section 3.5.1); or
(b) it can be demonstrated through an ex ante analysis that the airport/airline arrangement will lead to a positive incremental profit contribution for the airport (see section 3.5.2).

3.5.1. COMPARISON WITH THE MARKET PRICE

54. One approach to the assessment of the presence of aid to airlines involves establishing whether the price charged by an airport to a particular airline corresponds to the market price. On the basis of available and relevant market prices, an appropriate benchmark can be identified, taking into account the elements set out in point 60.

55. The identification of a benchmark requires, first, that a sufficient number of comparable airports providing comparable services under normal market conditions can be selected.

56. In this respect the Commission notes that for the moment, a large majority of Union airports benefit from public funding to cover investment and operating costs. Most of those airports can only remain on the market with public support.

57. Publicly owned airports have traditionally been considered by public authorities as infrastructures for facilitating local development and not as undertakings operating in accordance with market rules. Those airports' prices consequently tend not to be determined with regard to market considerations and in particular sound *ex ante* profitability prospects, but essentially having regard to social or regional considerations.

58. Even if some airports are privately owned or managed without social or regional considerations, the prices charged by those airports can be strongly influenced by the prices charged by the majority of publicly subsidised airports as the latter prices are taken into account by airlines during their negotiations with the privately owned or managed airports.

59. In those circumstances, the Commission has strong doubts that at the present time, an appropriate benchmark can be identified to establish a true market price for services provided by airports. This situation may change or evolve in the future, in particular once the State aid rules apply in full to public financing of airports.

60. In any event, the Commission considers that a benchmarking exercise should be based on a comparison of airport charges, net of any benefits provided to the airline (such as marketing support, discounts or any other incentive), across a sufficient number of suitable 'comparator airports', whose managers behave as market economy operators. In particular, the following indicators should be used:

(a) traffic volume;
(b) type of traffic (business or leisure or outbound destination), the relative importance of freight and the relative importance of revenue stemming from the non-aeronautical activities of the airport;
(c) type and level of airport services provided;
(d) proximity of the airport to a large city;
(e) number of inhabitants in the catchment area of the airport;
(f) prosperity of the surrounding area (GDP per capita);
(g) different geographical areas from which passengers could be attracted.

3.5.2. EX ANTE PROFITABILITY ANALYSIS

61. At present the Commission considers *ex ante* incremental profitability analysis to be the most relevant criterion for the assessment of arrangements concluded by airports with individual airlines.

62. In this respect, the Commission considers that price differentiation is a standard business practice, as long as it complies with all relevant competition and sectoral legislation.[58] Nevertheless, such differentiated pricing policies should be commercially justified to satisfy the MEO test.[59]

63. The Commission considers that arrangements concluded between airlines and an airport can be deemed to satisfy the MEO test when they incrementally contribute, from an *ex ante* standpoint, to the profitability of the airport. The airport should demonstrate that, when setting up an arrangement with an airline (for example, an individual contract or an overall scheme of airport charges), it is capable of covering all costs stemming from the arrangement, over the duration of the arrangement, with a reasonable profit margin[60] on the basis of sound medium-term prospects.[61]

64. In order to assess whether an arrangement concluded by an airport with an airline satisfies the MEO test, expected non-aeronautical revenues stemming from the airline's activity should be taken into consideration together with airport charges, net of any rebates, marketing support or incentive schemes.[62] Similarly, all expected costs incrementally incurred by the airport in relation to the airline's activity at the airport should be taken into account.[63] Such incremental costs could encompass all categories of expenses or investments, such as incremental personnel, equipment and investment costs induced by the presence of the airline at the airport. For instance, if the airport needs to expand or build a new terminal or other facilities mainly to accommodate the needs of a specific airline, such costs should be taken into consideration when calculating the incremental costs. In contrast, costs which the airport would have to incur anyway independently from the arrangement with the airline should not be taken into account in the MEO test.

65. Where an airport operator benefits from compatible aid, the advantage resulting from such aid is not passed on to a specific airline[64] if the following conditions are met: the infrastructure is open to all airlines[65] (this includes infrastructure which is more likely to be used by certain categories, like low cost operators or charters) and not dedicated to a specific airline; and the airlines pay tariffs covering at least the incremental costs as defined in point 64. Furthermore, the Commission considers that under such conditions, even if there would have been State aid to the airlines, such aid would in any event have been compatible with the internal market for the same reasons that justify the compatibility of the aid at the level of the airport. Where an airport operator benefits from incompatible investment aid, the advantage resulting from such aid is not passed on to a specific airline if the following conditions are met: the infrastructure is open to all airlines and not dedicated to a specific airline; and the airlines pay tariffs covering at least the incremental cost as defined in point 64. The Commission considers that under such conditions a sectorial advantage to the airline industry or other users cannot be excluded but should not lead to recovery from specific airlines or other users.

66. When assessing airport/airline arrangements, the Commission will also take into account the extent to which the arrangements under assessment can be considered part of the implementation of an overall strategy of the airport expected to lead to profitability at least in the long term.

NOTES

22 See Communication from the Commission on the application of the European Union State aid rules to compensation granted for the provision of services of general economic interest (OJ C8, 11.1.2012, p 4) part 2.1 and associated case law, in particular joined Cases C-180/98 to C-184/98 *Pavlov and Others*, [2000] ECR I-6451.

23 Case 118/85 *Commission v Italy*, [1987] ECR 2599, paragraph 7; Case C-35/96 *Commission v Italy*, [1998] ECR I-3851, paragraph 36; *Pavlov and Others*, paragraph 75.

24 Joined Cases 209/78 to 215/78 and 218/78 *Van Landewyck*, [1980] ECR 3125, paragraph 88; Case C-244/94 *FFSA and Others*, [1995] ECR I-4013, paragraph 21; and Case C-49/07 *MOTOE*, [2008] ECR I-4863, paragraphs 27 and 28.

25 Case T-128/98 *Aéroports de Paris v Commission*, [2000] ECR II-3929, confirmed by Case C-82/01, [2002] ECR I-9297, paragraphs 75–79.

26 Joined Cases T-443/08 and T-455/08 *Mitteldeutsche Flughafen AG and Flughafen Leipzig Halle GmbH v Commission*, ('*Leipzig-Halle airport*' judgment), [2011] ECR II-1311, in particular paragraphs 93 and 94; confirmed by Case C-288/11 P *Mitteldeutsche Flughafen and Flughafen Leipzig-Halle v Commission*, [2012] not yet reported.

27 See point 3, and Leipzig-Halle airport judgment, paragraph 105.

28 See Leipzig-Halle airport judgment, paragraph 106.

29 The relevant criterion for the date at which a possible aid measure is deemed to have been granted is the date of the legally binding act by which public authorities undertake to award the measure at stake to its beneficiary. See Case T-358/94 *Compagnie Nationale Air France v Commission*, [1996] ECR II-2109, paragraph 79, Case T-109/01, *Fleuren Compost BV v Commission*, [2004] ECR II-127, paragraph 74 and Joined Cases T-362/05 and T-363/05 *Nuova Agricast v Commission*, [2008] ECR II-297, paragraph 80, and Joined Cases T-427/04 and T-17/05, *France and France Télécom v Commission*, [2009] ECR II-4315, paragraph 321.

30 Decision C 38/2008 of 3 October 2012 on Munich airport Terminal 2, (OJ L319, 29.11.2013, p 8), paragraphs 74 to 81.

31 Council Regulation (EC) No 659/1999 of 22 March 1999 laying down detailed rules for the application of Article 108 of the Treaty on the Functioning of the European Union (OJ L83, 27.3.1999, p 1).

32 See Directive 2009/12/EC, recital 1.

33 The airport may or may not be the same entity that owns the airport.

34 The joint exercise of an economic activity is normally assessed by analysing the existence of functional, economic and organic links between the entities. See for instance, Case C-480/09 P *AceaElectrabel Produzione SpA v Commission*, [2010] ECR I-13355, paragraphs 47 to 55; Case C-222/04 *Ministero dell'Economia e delle Finanze v. Cassa di Risparmio di Firenze SpA and Others*, [2006] ECR I-289, paragraph 112.

35 Case T-196/04 *Ryanair Ltd v Commission*, [2008] ECR II-3643 ('*Charleroi*' judgment), paragraph 88.

36 Leipzig-Halle airport judgment, paragraph 98.

37 Case C-118/85 *Commission v Italy*, [1987] ECR 2599, paragraphs 7 and 8, and Case C-30/87 *Bodson/Pompes funèbres des régions libérées*, [1988] ECR 2479, paragraph 18.

38 See, in particular, Case C-364/92 *SAT/Eurocontrol*, [1994] ECR I-43, paragraph 30 and Case C-113/07 P *Selex Sistemi Integrati v Commission*, [2009] ECR I-2207, paragraph 71.

[39] Case C-343/95 *Cali & Figli v Servizi ecologici porto di Genova*, [1997] ECR I-1547. Commission Decision N 309/2002 of 19 March 2003, Aviation security — compensation for costs incurred following the attacks of 11 September 2001, (OJ C148, 25.6.2003, p 7). Commission Decision N 438/2002 of 16 October 2002, Aid in support of public authority functions in the port sector, (OJ C284, 21.11.2002, p 2).

[40] See among others Case C-172/03 *Wolfgang Heiser v Finanzamt Innsbruck*, [2005] ECR I-01627, paragraph 36, and case-law cited in that judgment.

[41] See Decision N 324/2006 of 24 October 2006 – France, Aid in support of the charter of an ATR 72–500 by Air Caraïbes, (OJ C300, 9.12.2006, p 10).

[42] See Case C-126/01 *Ministère de l'Économie, des Finances et de l'Industrie v GEMO SA* [2003] ECR I-13769, paragraph 29.

[43] Resources of a public undertaking constitute State resources within the meaning of Article 107(1) of the Treaty because the public authorities control these resources. See Case C-482/99 *France v Commission*, [2002] ECR I-4397 ('*Stardust Marine*' judgment).

[44] The Court has confirmed that once financial means remain constantly under public control and are therefore available to the competent national authorities, this is sufficient for them to be categorized as State aid, see Case C-83/98 P *France v Ladbroke Racing Ltd and Commission*, [2000] ECR I-3271, paragraph 50.

[45] See Stardust Marine judgment, paragraph 52.

[46] See Stardust Marine judgement, paragraphs 55 and 56.

[47] Case 78/76, *Steinike & Weinlig v Germany*, [1977] ECR 595, paragraph 21.

[48] Case C-310/99, *Italy v Commission*, [2002] ECR-I-2289, paragraph 65.

[49] Case C-280/00 *Altmark Trans GmbH and Regierungspräsidium Magdeburg v Nahverkehrsgesellschaft Altmark GmbH* ('*Altmark*' judgment), [2003] ECR I-7747.

[50] See Altmark judgment, paragraphs 77 to 82.

[51] Stardust Marine judgment, paragraph 71. Case C-124/10P *European Commission v EDF*, [2012], not yet reported, paragraphs 84, 85 and 105.

[52] Cases T-129/95, T-2/96 and T-97/96 *Neue Maxhütte Stahlwerke and Lech Stahlwerke v Commission*, [1999] ECR II-17, paragraph 120. See also case C-40/85, *Belgium v Commission*, [1986] ECR 02321, paragraph 13.

[53] Stardust Marine judgment, paragraph 69. See also Case C-303/88 *Italy v Commission*, [1991] ECR I-1433, paragraph 20.

[54] Case C-305/89 *Italy v Commission* ('*Alfa Romeo*' judgment), [1991] ECR I-1603, paragraph 20. Case T-228/99 *Westdeutsche Landesbank Girozentrale v Commission*, [2003] ECR II-435, paragraph 250–270.

[55] See Commission Decision in Case C 25/2007 – *Finland – Tampere Pirkkala airport and Ryanair*, (OJ L309, 19.11.2013, p 27).

[56] Case C-124/10 P *Commission v EDF* [2012], not yet reported, paragraphs 84, 85 and 105.

[57] Cases T-129/95, T-2/96 and T-97/96 *Neue Maxhütte Stahlwerke and Lech Stahlwerke v Commission*, [1999] ECR II-17, paragraph 120. See also case C-40/85 *Belgium v Commission*, [1986] ECR 02321, paragraph 13.

[58] Relevant provisions include Articles 101 and 102 of the Treaty, and Directive 2009/12/EC.

[59] See Commission Decision in Case C 12/2008 – *Slovakia – Agreement between Bratislava Airport and Ryanair* (OJ L27, 1.2.2011, p 24), and Commission Decision in Case C 25/2007 – *Finland – Tampere Pirkkala airport and Ryanair*, (OJ L309, 19.11.2013, p 27).

[60] A reasonable profit margin is a 'normal' rate of return on capital, that is to say, a rate of return that would be required by a typical company for an investment of similar risk. The return is measured as an Internal Rate of Return ('IRR') over the envisaged cash flows induced by the arrangement with the airline.

[61] This does not preclude foreseeing that future benefits over the duration of the arrangements may offset initial losses.

[62] Any public support, such as for example marketing agreements directly concluded between public authorities and the airline, designed to offset part of the normal costs incurred by the airport in relation to the airport/airline arrangement will likewise be taken into account. This is irrespective of whether such support is directly granted to the airline concerned, or channelled through the airport or another entity.

[63] Charleroi judgment, paragraph 59.

[64] What is said in this paragraph about airlines applies in the same way to other users of the airport.

[65] See notably joined Cases T-443/08 and T-455/08 *Mitteldeutsche Flughafen AG and Flughafen Leipzig Halle GmbH v Commission*, [2011] ECR II-1311, paragraph 109.

4. PUBLIC FUNDING OF SERVICES OF GENERAL ECONOMIC INTEREST

[5.419]

67. In some cases, public authorities may define certain economic activities carried out by airports or airlines as services of general economic interest ('SGEI') within the meaning of Article 106(2) of the Treaty and the *Altmark* case-law,[66] and provide compensation for discharging such services.

68. In such cases, the SGEI Communication[67] and Commission Regulation (EU) No 360/2012[68] provide guidance on the conditions under which the public financing of an SGEI constitutes State aid within the meaning of Article 107(1) of the Treaty. Aid in the form of public service compensation will be assessed under Commission Decision 2012/21/EU[69] and the SGEI framework.[70] Together those four documents form the 'SGEI package', which also applies to compensation granted to airports and airlines. What follows illustrates the application of some of the principles set out in the SGEI package in the light of certain sectoral specificities.

4.1. DEFINITION OF A SERVICE OF GENERAL ECONOMIC INTEREST IN THE AIRPORT AND AIR TRANSPORT SECTORS

69. The first *Altmark* criterion requires a clear definition of the tasks which constitute a service of general economic interest. This requirement coincides with that of Article 106(2) of the Treaty.[71] According to case law,[72] undertakings entrusted with the operation of an SGEI must have received that task by an act of a public authority. The Commission

has also clarified[73] that, for an activity to be considered as an SGEI, it should exhibit special characteristics as compared with ordinary economic activities, and that the general interest objective pursued by public authorities cannot simply be that of the development of certain economic activities or economic areas provided for in Article 107(3)(c) of the Treaty.[74]

70. As regards air transport services, public service obligations can only be imposed in accordance with Regulation (EC) No 1008/2008.[75] In particular, such obligations can only be imposed with regard to a specific route or group of routes,[76] and not with regard to any generic route originating from a given airport, city or region. Moreover, public service obligations can only be imposed with regard to a route to fulfil transport needs which cannot be adequately met by an existing air route or by other means of transport.[77]

71. In this respect, it should be stressed that compliance with the substantive and procedural requirements of Regulation (EC) No 1008/2008 does not eliminate the need for the Member State(s) concerned to assess compliance with Article 107(1) of the Treaty.

72. As far as airports are concerned, the Commission considers that it is possible for the overall management of an airport, in well-justified cases, to be considered an SGEI. In the light of the principles outlined in point 69, the Commission considers that this can only be the case if part of the area potentially served by the airport would, without the airport, be isolated from the rest of the Union to an extent that would prejudice its social and economic development. Such an assessment should take due account of other modes of transport, and in particular of high-speed rail services or maritime links served by ferries. In such cases, public authorities may impose a public service obligation on an airport to ensure that the airport remains open to commercial traffic. The Commission notes that certain airports have an important role to play in terms of regional connectivity of isolated, remote or peripheral regions of the Union. Such a situation may, in particular, occur in respect of the outermost regions, as well as islands or other areas of the Union. Subject to a case-by-case assessment and depending on the particular characteristics of each airport and the region which it serves, it may be justified to define SGEI obligations in those airports.[78]

73. In the light of the specific requirements attached to public service obligations for air transport services,[78] and in view of the complete liberalisation of air transport markets, the Commission considers that the scope of public service obligations imposed on airports should not encompass the development of commercial air transport services.

4.2. COMPATIBILITY OF AID IN THE FORM OF PUBLIC SERVICE COMPENSATION

74. If one of the cumulative criteria of the *Altmark* judgment is not fulfilled, public service compensation provides an economic advantage to its beneficiary, and might constitute State aid within the meaning of Article 107(1) of the Treaty. Such State aid may be regarded as compatible with the internal market pursuant to Article 106(2) of the Treaty, if all the compatibility criteria developed for the application of that paragraph are met.

75. State aid in the form of public service compensation is exempt from the notification requirement of Article 108(3) of the Treaty if the requirements set out in Decision 2012/21/EU are met. The scope of Decision 2012/21/EU covers public service compensation granted to:

(a) airports where the average annual traffic does not exceed 200,000 passengers[79] over the duration of the SGEI entrustment; and

(b) airlines, as regards air links to islands where the average annual traffic does not exceed 300,000 passengers.[80]

76. State aid not covered by Decision 2012/21/EU can be declared compatible pursuant to Article 106(2) of the Treaty, if the conditions of the SGEI Framework are met. However, it should be noted that for assessment under both Decision 2012/21/EU and the SGEI Framework, the considerations on the definition of public service obligations imposed on airports or airlines in points 69 to 73 of these guidelines will apply.

NOTES

66 See Altmark judgment, paragraphs 86 to 93. Public funding for the provision of an SGEI does not entail a selective advantage within the meaning of Article 107(1) of the Treaty if the following four conditions are met: (a) the beneficiary of a State funding mechanism for an SGEI must be formally entrusted with the provision and discharge of an SGEI, the obligations of which must be clearly defined (b) the parameters for calculating the compensation must be established beforehand in an objective and transparent manner; (c) the compensation cannot exceed what is necessary to cover all or part of the costs incurred in the discharge of the SGEI, taking into account the relevant receipts and a reasonable profit for discharging those obligations and (d) where the beneficiary is not chosen pursuant to a public procurement procedure, that allows for the provision of the service at the least cost to the community, the level of compensation granted must be determined on the basis of an analysis of the costs which a typical undertaking, well run, would have incurred in discharging those obligations, taking into account the relevant receipts and a reasonable profit.

67 See footnote 22.

68 Commission Regulation (EU) No 360/2012 of 25 April 2012 on the application of Articles 107 and 108 of the Treaty on the Functioning of the European Union to *de minimis* aid granted to undertakings providing services of general economic interest (OJ L114, 26.4.2012, p 8).

69 Commission Decision 2012/21/EU of 20 December 2011 on the application of Article 106(2) of the Treaty on the Functioning of the European Union to State aid in the form of public service compensation granted to certain undertakings entrusted with the operation of services of general economic interest (OJ L7, 11.1.2012, p 3).

70 Commission Communication on a European Union framework for State aid in the form of public service compensation (2011) (OJ C8, 11.1.2012, p 15).

71 Case T-289/03 *British United Provident Association Ltd (BUPA) v Commission* [2008], ECR II-81, paragraphs 171 and 224.

72 See Joined Cases T-204/97 and T-270/97 EPAC — *Empresa para a Agroalimentação e Cereais, SA v Commission* [2000] ECR II-2267, paragraph 126 and Case T-17/02 *Fred Olsen, SA v Commission* [2005] ECR II-2031, paragraphs 186, 188–189.

73 See SGEI Communication, paragraph 45.

74 See decision N 381/04 – France, Project for a high capacity telecommunications network in the Pyrénées-Atlantiques (DORSAL), (OJ C162, 2.7.2005, p 5).

[75] Articles 16, 17 and 18.

[76] Both origin and destination airports must be clearly identified see Article 16(1) of Regulation (EC) No 1008/2008.

[77] In particular, the Commission considers that it would be difficult to justify PSOs on a route to a given airport if there are already similar services notably in terms of transport time, frequencies, level and quality of service, to another airport serving the same catchment area.

[78] See point 70 and Regulation (EC) No 1008/2008, recital 12 and articles 16 to 18.

[79] This threshold refers to a one-way count, that is to say, a passenger flying from the airport and back to the airport would be counted twice. If an airport is part of a group of airports, the passenger volume is established on the basis of each individual airport.

[80] This threshold refers to a one-way count, that is to say, a passenger flying to the island and back would be counted twice. It applies to individual routes between an airport on the island and an airport on the mainland.

5. COMPATIBILITY OF AID UNDER ARTICLE 107(3)(C) OF THE TREATY

[5.420]

77. If public funding granted to airports and/or airlines constitutes aid, that aid can be considered compatible with the internal market pursuant to Article 107(3)(c) of the Treaty provided that it complies with the compatibility criteria for airports in section 5.1 of these guidelines and for airlines in section 5.2. State aid granted to airlines which incrementally decreases the profitability of the airport (see points 63 and 64 of these guidelines) will be deemed incompatible with the internal market pursuant to Article 107(1) of the Treaty, unless the compatibility conditions for start-up aid set out in section 5.2 of these guidelines are met.

78. To assess whether a State aid measure can be considered compatible with the internal market pursuant to Article 107(3)(c) of the Treaty, the Commission generally analyses whether the design of the aid measure ensures that the positive impact towards an objective of common interest exceeds its potential negative effects on trade and competition.

79. The Communication on State Aid Modernisation (SAM) called for the identification and definition of common principles applicable to the assessment of compatibility of all aid measures carried out by the Commission. An aid measure will be considered compatible with the internal market pursuant to Article 107(3) of the Treaty provided that the following cumulative conditions are met:

(a) contribution to a well-defined objective of common interest: a State aid measure must have an objective of common interest in accordance with Article 107(3) Treaty;

(b) need for State intervention: a State aid measure must be targeted towards a situation where aid can bring about a material improvement that the market cannot deliver itself, for example by remedying a market failure or addressing an equity or cohesion concern;

(c) appropriateness of the aid measure: the aid measure must be an appropriate policy instrument to address the objective of common interest;

(d) incentive effect: the aid must change the behaviour of the undertakings concerned in such a way that they engage in additional activity which they would not carry out without the aid or they would carry out in a restricted or different manner or location;

(e) proportionality of the aid (aid limited to the minimum): the aid amount must be limited to the minimum needed to induce the additional investment or activity in the area concerned;

(f) avoidance of undue negative effects on competition and trade between Member States: the negative effects of the aid must be sufficiently limited, so that the overall balance of the measure is positive;

(g) transparency of aid: Member States, the Commission, economic operators, and the interested public, must have easy access to all relevant acts and to pertinent information about the aid awarded thereunder as outlined in section 8.2.

80. As regards State aid in the aviation sector, the Commission considers that those common principles are respected when State aid granted to airports or airlines meets all the conditions outlined respectively in sections 5.1 and 5.2. Therefore, compliance with those conditions implies compatibility of the aid with the internal market pursuant to Article 107(3)(c) of the Treaty.

81. However, if an inseparable aspect of a State aid measure and the conditions attached to it (including its financing method when the financing method forms an integral part of the State aid measure) entail a violation of Union law, the aid cannot be declared compatible with the internal market.[81]

82. Moreover, in assessing the compatibility of any State aid with the internal market, the Commission will take account of any proceedings concerning infringements of Article 101 or 102 of the Treaty which may concern the beneficiary of the aid and which may be relevant for its assessment under Article 107(3) of the Treaty.[82]

5.1. AID TO AIRPORTS

5.1.1. INVESTMENT AID TO AIRPORTS

83. Investment aid granted to airports either as individual aid or under an aid scheme will be considered compatible with the internal market pursuant to Article 107(3)(c) of the Treaty provided that the cumulative conditions in point 79 are fulfilled as set out in points 84 to 108.

(a)

Contribution to a well-defined objective of common interest

84. Investment aid to airports will be considered to contribute to the achievement of an objective of common interest, if it:

(a) increases the mobility of Union citizens and the connectivity of the regions by establishing access points for intra-Union flights; or

(b) combats air traffic congestion at major Union hub airports; or

(c) facilitates regional development.

85. Nevertheless, the duplication of unprofitable airports or the creation of additional unused capacity does not contribute to an objective of common interest. If an investment project is primarily aimed at creating new airport capacity, the new infrastructure must, in the medium-term, meet the forecasted demand of the airlines, passengers and freight forwarders in the catchment area of the airport. Any investment which does not have satisfactory medium-term prospects for use, or diminishes the medium-term prospects for use of existing infrastructure in the catchment area, cannot be considered to serve an objective of common interest.

86. Accordingly, the Commission will have doubts as to the medium-term prospects for use of airport infrastructure at an airport located in the catchment area of an existing airport where the existing airport is not operating at or near full capacity. The medium-term prospects for use must be demonstrated on the basis of sound passenger and freight traffic forecasts incorporated in an ex ante business plan and must identify the likely effect of the investment on the use of existing infrastructure, such as another airport or other modes of transport, in particular high-speed train connections.

(b)
Need for State intervention

87. In order to assess whether State aid is effective in achieving an objective of common interest, it is necessary to identify the problem to be addressed. State aid should be targeted towards situations where such aid can bring about a material improvement that the market itself cannot deliver.

88. The conditions that smaller airports face when developing their services and in attracting private financing of their infrastructure investments are often less favourable than those faced by the major airports in the Union. For those reasons, under present market conditions, smaller airports may have difficulties in ensuring the financing of their investments without public funding.

89. The need for public funding to finance infrastructure investments will, due to high fixed costs,[83] vary according to the size of an airport and will normally be greater for smaller airports. The Commission considers that, under current market conditions, the following categories of airports,[84] and their relative financial viabilities, can be identified:

(a) airports with up to 200,000 passengers per annum may not be able to cover their capital costs to a large extent;
(b) airports with annual passenger traffic of between 200,000 and 1 million are usually not able to cover their capital costs to a large extent;
(c) airports with annual passenger traffic of 1–3 million should, on average, be able to cover their capital costs to a greater extent;
(d) airports with annual passenger traffic of above 3 and up to 5 million should, in principle, be able to cover, to a large extent, all their costs (including operating costs and capital costs) but, under certain case-specific circumstances, public support might be necessary to finance some of their capital costs;
(e) airports with annual passenger traffic above 5 million are usually profitable and are able to cover all of their costs, except in very exceptional circumstances.

(c)
Appropriateness of State aid as a policy instrument

90. The Member States must demonstrate that the aid measure is an appropriate policy instrument to achieve the intended objective or resolve the problems intended to be addressed by the aid. An aid measure will not be considered compatible with the internal market if other less distortive policy instruments or aid instruments allow the same objective to be reached.

91. The Member States can make different choices with regard to the use of different policy instruments and forms of aid. In general, where a Member State has considered other policy options and the use of a selective instrument, such as State aid in the form of a direct grant, has been compared with less distortive forms of aid (such as loans, guarantees or repayable advances), the measures concerned are considered to constitute an appropriate instrument.

92. Wherever possible, Member States are encouraged to design national schemes that reflect the main principles underlying public financing and indicate the most relevant features of the planned public funding of airports. Framework schemes ensure coherence in the use of public funds, reduce the administrative burden on smaller granting authorities and accelerate the implementation of individual aid measures. Further, Member States are encouraged to give clear guidance for the implementation of State aid financing for regional airports.

(d)
Existence of incentive effect

93. Works on an individual investment can start only after an application has been submitted to the granting authority. If works start before an application is submitted to the granting authority, any aid awarded in respect of that individual investment will not be considered compatible with the internal market.

94. An investment project at an airport may be economically attractive in its own right. Therefore, it needs to be verified that the investment would not have been undertaken or would not have been undertaken to the same extent without any State aid. If this is confirmed, the Commission will consider that the aid measure has an incentive effect.

95. The incentive effect is identified through counterfactual analysis, comparing the levels of intended activity with aid and without aid.

96. Where no specific counterfactual is known, the incentive effect can be assumed when there is a capital cost funding gap, that is to say, when on the basis of an *ex ante* business plan, it can be shown that there is a difference between the positive and negative cash flows (including investment costs into fixed capital assets) over the lifetime of the investment in net present value terms.[85]

(e)
Proportionality of the aid amount (aid limited to the minimum)

97. The maximum permissible amount of State aid is expressed as a percentage of eligible costs (the maximum aid intensity). Eligible costs are the costs relating to the investments in airport infrastructure, including planning costs, ground handling infrastructure (such as baggage belts, etc.) and airport equipment. Investment costs relating to non-aeronautical activities (in particular parking, hotels, restaurants, and offices) are ineligible.[86]

98. The investment costs relating to the provision of ground handling services (such as buses, vehicles, etc.) are ineligible, insofar as they are not part of ground handling infrastructure.[87]

99. In order to be proportionate, investment aid to airports must be limited to the extra costs (net of extra revenues) which result from undertaking the aided project/activity rather than the alternative project/activity that the beneficiary would have undertaken in the counterfactual scenario, that is to say, if it had not received the aid. Where no specific counterfactual is known, in order to be proportionate, the amount of the aid should not exceed the funding gap of the investment project (so-called 'capital cost funding gap'), which is determined on the basis of an ex ante business plan as the net present value of the difference between the positive and negative cash flows (including investment costs) over the lifetime of the investment. For investment aid the business plan should cover the period of the economic utilisation of the asset.

100. As the funding gap will vary according to the size of the airport and is normally wider for smaller airports, the Commission will use a range of permissible maximum aid intensities to ensure overall proportionality. The aid intensity must not exceed the maximum permissible investment aid intensity and should, in any case, not go beyond the actual funding gap of the investment project.

101. The following table summarises the maximum permissible aid intensity depending on the size of the airport as measured by the number of passengers per annum.[88]

Size of airport based on average passenger traffic (passengers per annum)	Maximum investment aid intensity
>3–5 million	up to 25%
1–3 million	up to 50%
<1 million	up to 75%

102. The maximum aid intensities for investment aid to finance airport infrastructure may be increased by up to 20% for airports located in remote regions irrespective of their size.

103. Airports with average traffic below 1 million passengers per annum should contribute at least 25% to the financing of the total eligible investment costs. However, investment projects at certain airports with average traffic below 1 million passengers per annum located in peripheral regions of the Union may result in a funding gap which is higher than the maximum permissible aid intensities. Subject to a case-by-case assessment and depending on the particular characteristics of each airport, investment project and the region served, intensity exceeding 75% may be justified in exceptional circumstances for airports with traffic volume below 1 million passengers per annum.

104. In order to take account of the specific circumstances regarding the relocation of an existing airport and cessation of airport activities at an existing site, the Commission will assess, in particular, the proportionality, the necessity and the maximum aid intensity of the State aid granted on the basis of the funding gap analysis or the counterfactual scenario of each specific case, regardless of the average passenger traffic of that airport.

105. Additionally, under very exceptional circumstances, characterised by a clear market failure and taking into account the magnitude of the investment, the impossibility to finance the investment on capital markets, a very high level of positive externalities and the competition distortions, airports with average traffic over 5 million passengers per annum may receive aid to finance airport infrastructure. However, in such cases, the Commission will always carry out an in-depth assessment, in particular on the proportionality, the necessity and the maximum aid intensity of the State aid granted on the basis of the funding gap analysis and the counterfactual scenario of each specific case, regardless of the average passenger traffic of that airport.

(f)
Avoidance of undue negative effects on competition and trade

106. In particular, the duplication of unprofitable airports or the creation of additional unused capacity in the catchment area of existing infrastructure might have distortive effects. Accordingly, the Commission will, in principle, have doubts as to the compatibility of investment into airport infrastructure at an airport located in the catchment area of an existing airport[89] where the existing airport is not operating at or near full capacity.

107. Further, in order to avoid the negative effects of aid that may arise where airports face soft budget constraints,[90] investment aid to airports with traffic of up to 5 million passengers can be granted either as an upfront fixed amount to cover eligible investment costs or in annual instalments to compensate for the capital cost funding gap resulting from the business plan of the airport.

108. In order to further limit any distortions, the airport, including any investment for which aid is granted, must be open to all potential users and must not be dedicated to one specific user. In the case of physical limitation of capacity, the allocation should be done on the basis of pertinent, objective, transparent and non-discriminatory criteria.

Notification requirements for aid schemes and individual aid measures:

109. Member States are encouraged to notify State aid schemes for investment aid for airports with average annual traffic below 3 million passengers.

110. When assessing an aid scheme, the conditions relating to the necessity of the aid, the incentive effect and the proportionality of the aid will be considered to be satisfied if the Member State has committed itself to granting individual aid under the approved aid scheme only after it has verified that the cumulative conditions in this section are met.

111. Due to a higher risk of distortion of competition, the following aid measures should always be notified individually:

(a) investment aid to airports with average annual traffic above 3 million passengers;
(b) investment aid with an aid intensity exceeding 75% to an airport with average annual traffic below 1 million passengers, with the exception of airports located in remote regions;
(c) investment aid granted for the relocation of airports;
(d) investment aid financing a mixed passenger/freight airport handling more than 200,000 tonnes of freight during the two financial years preceding that in which the aid is notified;
(e) investment aid aimed at the creation of a new passenger airport (including the conversion of an existing airfield into a passenger airport);
(f) investment aid aimed at the creation or development of an airport located within 100 kilometres distance or 60 minutes travelling time by car, bus, train or high-speed train from an existing airport.

5.1.2. Operating aid to airports

112. Operating aid granted to airports either as individual aid or under an aid scheme will be considered compatible with the internal market pursuant to Article 107(3)(c) of the Treaty for a transitional period of 10 years starting from 4 April 2014provided that the cumulative conditions in point 79 are fulfilled as set out in points 113 to 134.

(a)
Contribution to a well-defined objective of common interest

113. As stated in point 13, in order to give airports time to adjust to new market realities and to avoid any disruptions in the air traffic and connectivity of the regions, operating aid to airports will be considered to contribute to the achievement of an objective of common interest for a transitional period of 10 years, if it:

(a) increases the mobility of Union citizens and the connectivity of the regions by establishing access points for intra-Union flights; or
(b) combats air traffic congestion at major Union hub airports; or
(c) facilitates regional development.

114. Nevertheless, the duplication of unprofitable airports does not contribute to an objective of common interest. Where an airport is located in the same catchment area as another airport with spare capacity, the business plan, based on sound passenger and freight traffic forecasts, must identify the likely effect on the traffic of the other airport located in that catchment area.

115. Accordingly, the Commission will have doubts as to the prospects for an unprofitable airport to achieve full operating cost coverage at the end of the transitional period, if another airport is located in the same catchment area.

(b)
Need for State intervention

116. In order to assess whether State aid is effective in achieving an objective of common interest, it is necessary to identify the problem to be addressed. State aid should be targeted towards situations where such aid can bring about a material improvement that the market itself cannot deliver.

117. The conditions that smaller airports face when developing their services and in attracting private financing are often less favourable than those faced by the major airports in the Union. Therefore, under present market conditions, smaller airports may have difficulties in ensuring the financing of their operation without public funding.

118. Under current market conditions, the need for public funding to finance operating costs will, due to high fixed costs, vary according to the size of an airport and will normally be proportionately greater for smaller airports. The Commission considers that, under current market conditions, the following categories of airports, and their relative financial viabilities, can be identified:

(a) airports with up to 200,000 passengers per annum may not be able to cover their operating costs to a large extent;
(b) airports with annual passenger traffic between 200,000 and 700,000 passengers may not be able to cover their operating costs to a substantial extent;
(c) airports with annual passenger traffic of 700,000 to 1 million should in general be able to cover their operating costs to a greater extent;
(d) airports with annual passenger traffic of 1–3 million should, on average, be able to cover the majority of their operating costs;
(e) airports with annual passenger traffic above 3 million are usually profitable at operating level and should be able to cover their operating costs.

119. Therefore, the Commission considers that in order to be eligible for operating aid, the annual traffic of the airport must not exceed 3 million passengers[91]

(c)
Appropriateness of State aid as a policy instrument

120. The Member States must demonstrate that the aid is appropriate to achieve the intended objective or resolve the problems intended to be addressed by the aid. An aid measure will not be considered compatible with the internal market if other less distortive policy instruments or aid instruments allow the same objective to be reached.[92]

121. In order to provide proper incentives for efficient management of an airport, the aid amount is, in principle, to be established ex ante as a fixed sum covering the expected operating funding gap (determined on the basis of an ex ante business plan) during a transitional period of 10 years. For these reasons no ex post increase of the aid amount should, in principle, be considered compatible with the internal market. The Member State may pay the ex-ante fixed amount as an up-front lump sum or in instalments, for instance on an annual basis.

122. In exceptional circumstances, where future costs and revenue developments are surrounded by a particularly high degree of uncertainty and the public authority faces important information asymmetries, the public authority may calculate the maximum amount of compatible operating aid according to a model based on the initial operating funding gap at the beginning of the transitional period. The initial operating funding gap is the average of the operating funding gaps (that is to say the amount of operating costs not covered by revenues) during the five years preceding the beginning of the transitional period (2009 to 2013).

123. Wherever possible, Member States are encouraged to design national schemes that reflect the main principles underlying public financing and indicate the most relevant features of the planned public funding of airports. Framework schemes ensure coherence in the use of public funds, reduce the administrative burden on smaller granting authorities and accelerate the implementation of individual aid measures. Furthermore, Member States are encouraged to give clear guidance for the implementation of State aid financing for regional airports and airlines using those airports.

(d)
Existence of incentive effect

124. Operating aid has an incentive effect if it is likely that, in the absence of the operating aid, and taking into account the possible presence of investment aid and the level of traffic, the level of economic activity of the airport concerned would be significantly reduced.

(e)
Proportionality of the aid amount (aid limited to the minimum necessary):

125. In order to be proportionate, operating aid to airports must be limited to the minimum necessary for the aided activity to take place.

126. The business plan of the airport must pave the way towards full operating cost coverage at the end of the transitional period. The key parameters of this business plan form an integral part of the Commission's compatibility assessment.

127. The path towards full operating cost coverage will be different for every airport and will depend on the initial operating funding gap of the airport at the beginning of the transitional period. The transitional period will start from 4 April 2014.

128. In any event, the maximum permissible aid amount during the whole transitional period will be limited to 50% of the initial funding gap for a period of 10 years.[93] For instance, if the annual average funding gap of a given airport over the period 2009 to 2013 is equal to EUR 1 million, the maximum amount of operating aid that the airport could receive as an ex-ante established fixed sum would be EUR 5 million over ten years (50% x 1 million x 10). No further operating aid will be considered compatible for that airport.

129. By 10 years after the beginning of the transitional period at the latest, all airports must have reached full coverage of their operating costs and no operating aid to airports will be considered compatible with the internal market after that date, with the exception of operating aid granted in accordance with horizontal State aid rules, such as rules applicable to the financing of SGEIs.

130. Under the current market conditions, airports with annual passenger traffic of up to 700,000 may face increased difficulties in achieving the full cost coverage during the 10-year transitional period. For this reason, the maximum permissible aid amount for airports with up to 700,000 passengers per annum will be 80% of the initial operating funding gap for a period of five years after the beginning of the transitional period. For instance, if the annual average funding gap of a small airport over the period 2009 to 2013 is equal to EUR 1 million, the maximum amount of operating aid that the airport could receive as an ex-ante established fixed sum would be EUR 4 million over five years (80% x 1 million x 5). The Commission will reassess the need for continued specific treatment and the future prospects for full operating cost coverage for this category of airport, in particular with regard to the change of market conditions and profitability prospects.

(f)
Avoidance of undue negative effects on competition and trade

131. When assessing the compatibility of operating aid the Commission will take account of the distortions of competition and the effects on trade. Where an airport is located in the same catchment area as another airport with spare capacity, the business plan, based on sound passenger and freight traffic forecasts, must identify the likely effect on the traffic of the other airports located in that catchment area.

132. Operating aid for an airport located in the same catchment area will be considered compatible with the internal market only when the Member State demonstrates that all airports in the same catchment area will be able to achieve full operating cost coverage at the end of the transitional period.

133. In order to limit further the distortions of competition, the airport must be open to all potential users and not be dedicated to one specific user. In the case of physical limitation of capacity, the allocation should be done on the basis of pertinent, objective, transparent and non-discriminatory criteria.

134. Further, in order to limit the negative effects on competition and trade, the Commission will approve operating aid to airports for a transitional period of 10 years beginning from 4 April 2014. The Commission will reassess the situation of airports with annual passenger traffic of up to 700,000 four years after the beginning of the transitional period.

Notification requirements for aid schemes and individual aid measures

135. Member States are strongly encouraged to notify national schemes for operating aid for the financing of airports, rather than individual aid measures for each airport. This is intended to reduce the administrative burden both for the Member States' authorities and for the Commission.

136. Due to a higher risk of distortion of competition, the following aid measures should always be notified individually:

(a) operating aid financing a mixed passenger/freight airport handling more than 200,000 tonnes of freight during the two financial years preceding that in which the aid is notified;

(b) operating aid to an airport, if other airports are located within 100 kilometres or 60 minutes travelling time by car, bus, train or high-speed train.

Aid granted before the beginning of the transitional period

137. Operating aid granted before the beginning of the transitional period (including aid paid before 4 April 2014) may be declared compatible to the full extent of uncovered operating costs provided that the conditions in section 5.1.2 are met, with the exception of points 115, 119, 121, 122, 123, 126 to 130, 132, 133 and 134. In particular, when assessing the compatibility of operating aid granted before 4 April 2014, the Commission will take account of the distortions of competition.

5.2. START-UP AID TO AIRLINES

138. As mentioned in point 15, State aid granted to airlines for launching a new route with the aim of increasing the connectivity of a region will be considered compatible with the internal market pursuant to Article 107(3)(c) of the Treaty, if the cumulative conditions in point 79 are fulfilled as set out in points 139 to 153.

(a)
Contribution to a well-defined objective of common interest

139. Start-up aid to airlines will be considered to contribute to the achievement of an objective of common interest, if it:

(a) increases the mobility of Union citizens and the connectivity of the regions by opening new routes; or

(b) facilitates regional development of remote regions.

140. When a connection which will be operated by the new air route is already operated by a high-speed rail service or from another airport in the same catchment area under comparable conditions, in particular in terms of length of journey, it cannot be considered to contribute to a well-defined objective of common interest.

(b)
Need for State intervention

141. The conditions that smaller airports face when developing their services are often less favourable than those faced by the major airports in the Union. Also, airlines are not always prepared to run the risk of opening new routes from unknown and untested airports, and may not have appropriate incentives to do so.

142. On this basis, start-up aid will only be considered compatible for routes linking an airport with less than 3 million passengers per annum[94] to another airport within the Common European Aviation Area.[95]

143. Start-up aid for routes linking an airport located in a remote region to another airport (within or outside the Common European Aviation Area) will be compatible irrespective of the size of the airports concerned.

144. Start-up aid for routes linking an airport with more than 3 million passengers *per annum*[96] and less than 5 million passengers per annum not located in remote regions can be considered compatible with the internal market only in duly substantiated exceptional cases.

145. Start-up aid for routes linking an airport with more than 5 million passengers per annum not located in remote regions cannot be considered compatible with the internal market.

(c)
Appropriateness of State aid as policy instrument

146. The Member States must demonstrate that the aid is appropriate to achieve the intended objective or resolve the problems intended to be addressed by the aid. An aid measure will not be considered compatible with the internal market if other less distortive policy instruments or aid instruments allow the same objective to be reached.[97]

147. An ex ante business plan prepared by the airline should establish that the route receiving the aid has prospects of becoming profitable for the airline without public funding after 3 years. In the absence of a business plan for a route, the airlines must provide an irrevocable commitment to the airport to operate the route for a period at least equal to the period during which it received start-up aid.

(d)
Existence of incentive effect

148. Start-up aid to airlines has an incentive effect if it is likely that, in the absence of the aid, the level of economic activity of the airline at the airport concerned would not be expanded. For example the new route would not have been launched.

149. The new route must start only after the application for aid has been submitted to the granting authority. If the new route begins before the application for aid is submitted to the granting authority, any aid awarded in respect of that individual route will not be considered compatible with the internal market.

(e)
Proportionality of the aid amount (aid limited to the minimum necessary)

150. Start-up aid may cover up to 50% of airport charges in respect of a route for a maximum period of three years. The eligible costs are the airport charges in respect of the route.

(f)
Avoidance of undue negative effects on competition and trade

151. In order to avoid undue negative effects on competition and trade, where a connection (for example, city-pair) which will be operated by the new air route is already operated by a high-speed rail service or by another airport in the same catchment area under comparable conditions, notably in terms of length of journey, such air route will not be eligible for start-up aid.

152. Any public body which plans to grant start-up aid to an airline for a new route, whether or not via an airport, must make its plans public in good time and with adequate publicity to enable all interested airlines to offer their services.

153. Start-up aid cannot be combined with any other type of State aid granted for the operation of a route.

Notification requirements for aid schemes and individual aid measures:

154. Member States are strongly encouraged to notify national schemes for start-up aid to airlines, rather than individual aid measures for each airport. This is intended to reduce the administrative burden both for the Member States' authorities and for the Commission.

155. Due to the higher risk of distortion of competition, start-up aid to airports not located in remote regions with average annual traffic above 3 million passengers should always be notified individually.

NOTES

81 See for instance Case C-156/98 *Germany v Commission* [2000] ECR I-6857, paragraph 78 and Case C-333/07 *Régie Networks v Rhone Alpes Bourgogne* [2008] ECR I-10807, paragraphs 94–116.

82 See Case C-225/91 *Matra v Commission*, [1993] ECR I-3203, paragraph 42.

83 Between 70% and 90% of the airport's costs are fixed.

84 The categories of airports for the purposes of these guidelines are based on the available industry data.

85 This does not preclude foreseeing that future benefits may offset initial losses.

86 Financing of such activities is not covered by these guidelines, as they are of a non-transport character, and will thus be assessed on the basis of the relevant sectoral and general rules.

87 The principles set out in these guidelines do not apply to aid for the provision of ground handling services regardless whether they are provided by the airport itself, by an airline or by a supplier of ground handling services to third parties; such aid will be assessed on the basis of the relevant general rules.

88 Actual average annual passenger traffic during the two financial years preceding that in which the aid is notified or actually granted or paid in the case of non-notified aid. In the case of a newly created passenger airport, the forecasted average annual passenger traffic during the two financial years after the beginning of the operation of commercial passenger air traffic should be considered. These thresholds refer to a one-way count. This means a passenger flying, for example, to the airport and back would be counted twice; it applies to individual routes. If an airport is part of a group of airports, the passenger volume is established on the basis of each individual airport.

89 See Section 5.1.1(a).

90 If the aid were to be determined on the basis of ex post calculations (making good for any deficits as they arise), airports might not have much incentive to contain costs and charge airport charges that are adequate to cover costs.

91 91 Actual average annual passenger traffic during the two financial years preceding that in which the aid is notified or actually granted or paid in the case of non-notified aid. In the case of a newly created passenger airport the forecasted average annual passenger traffic during the two financial years after the beginning of the operation of commercial passenger air traffic should be considered. These thresholds refer to a one-way count. This means a passenger flying for example to the airport and back would be counted twice; it applies to individual routes. If an airport is part of a group of airports, the passenger volume is established on the basis of each individual airport.

92 See also point 91.

93 The 50% intensity corresponds to the funding gap over 10 years for an airport which, starting from the initial operating cost coverage at the beginning of the transition period, achieves full operating cost coverage after 10 years.

94 Actual average annual passenger traffic during the two financial years preceding that in which the aid is notified or actually granted or paid in the case of non-notified aid. In the case of a newly created passenger airport, the forecasted average annual passenger traffic during the two financial years after the beginning of the operation of commercial passenger air traffic should be considered. These thresholds refer to a one-way count. This means a passenger flying for example to the airport and back would be counted twice; it applies to individual routes.

95 Decision 2006/682/EC of the Council and of the Representatives of the Member States meeting within the Council on the signature and provisional application of the Multilateral Agreement between the European Community and its Member States, the Republic of Albania, Bosnia and Herzegovina, the Republic of Bulgaria, the Republic of Croatia, the former Yugoslav Republic of Macedonia, the Republic of Iceland, the Republic of Montenegro, the Kingdom of Norway, Romania, the Republic of Serbia and the United Nations Interim Administration Mission in Kosovo on the Establishment of a European Common Aviation Area (ECAA) (OJ L285, 16.10.2006, p 1).

96 See also footnote 94.

97 See also point 91.

6. AID OF A SOCIAL CHARACTER UNDER ARTICLE 107(2)(A) OF THE TREATY

[5.421]

156. Aid of a social character for air transport services will be considered compatible with the internal market pursuant to Article 107(2)(a) of the Treaty, provided that the following cumulative conditions are met:[98]

(a) the aid must effectively be for the benefit of final consumers;

(b) the aid must have a social character, that is, it must, in principle, only cover certain categories of passengers travelling on a route (for instance passengers with particular needs like children, people with disabilities, people on low incomes, students, elderly people, etc.); however, where the route concerned links remote regions, such as outermost regions, islands, and sparsely populated areas, the aid could cover the entire population of that region;

(c) the aid must be granted without discrimination as to the origin of the services, meaning irrespective of the airline which is operating the services.

157. Member States are strongly encouraged to notify national schemes for aid of a social character, rather than individual aid measures.

NOTES

[98] See for example, as regards the assessment of aid of a social character granted to individual consumers, Commission decision of 16 May 2006, N 169/2006 – United Kingdom – Aid of social character air services in the Highlands and Islands of Scotland (OJ C272, 9.11.2006, p 10); Commission decision of 11 December 2007, N 471/2007 – Portugal – Social allowances to passengers residing in the Autonomous Region of Madeira and students, in air transport services between mainland Portugal and the Autonomous Region (OJ C46, 19.2.2008, p 2); and Commission decision of 5 January 2011, N 426/2010 – France – Aid of a social character for certain categories of passenger on air services between La Réunion and metropolitan France (OJ C71, 5.3.2011, p 5).

7. CUMULATION

[5.422]

158. The maximum aid intensities applicable under these guidelines apply regardless of whether the aid is financed entirely from State resources or is partly financed by the Union.

159. Aid authorised under these guidelines may not be combined with other State aid, *de minimis* aid or other forms of Union financing, if such a combination results in an aid intensity higher than that laid down in these guidelines.

8. FINAL PROVISIONS

8.1. ANNUAL REPORTING

[5.423]

160. In accordance with Regulation (EC) No 659/1999 and Commission Regulation (EC) No 794/2004,[99] Member States must submit annual reports to the Commission. The annual reports will be published on the internet site of the Commission.

8.2. TRANSPARENCY

161. The Commission considers that further measures are necessary to improve the transparency of State aid in the Union. In particular, steps must be taken to ensure that the Member States, economic operators, the interested public and the Commission have easy access to the full text of all applicable aid schemes in the aviation sector and to pertinent information about individual aid measures.

[162. Member States shall ensure the publication of the following information on a comprehensive State aid website, at national or regional level:

— the full text of the approved aid scheme or the individual aid granting decision and its implementing provisions, or a link to it,

— the identity of the granting authority/(ies),

— the identity of the individual beneficiaries, the form and amount of aid granted to each beneficiary, the date of granting, the type of undertaking (SME/large company), the region in which the beneficiary is located (at NUTS level II) and the principal economic sector in which the beneficiary has its activities (at NACE group level).[100]

Such a requirement can be waived with respect to individual aid awards below EUR 500,000. For schemes in the form of tax advantage, the information on individual aid amounts[100A] can be provided in the following ranges (in EUR million): [0.5–1]; [1–2]; [2–5]; [5–10]; [10–30]; [30 and more].

Such information must be published after the decision to grant the aid has been taken, must be kept for at least 10 years and must be available to the general public without restrictions.[100B] Member States will not be required to publish the abovementioned information before 1 July 2016.[100C]]

8.3. MONITORING

164. Member States must ensure that detailed records are kept regarding all measures involving the granting of State aid in accordance with these guidelines. Such records must contain all information necessary to establish that the compatibility conditions have been observed, in particular, those regarding eligible costs and maximum allowable aid intensity, where applicable. Those records must be maintained for 10 years from the date on which the aid is granted and be provided to the Commission upon request.

165. In order to allow the Commission to monitor the progress of the phasing out of operating aid to airports and its impact on competition, Member States must submit a regular report (on a yearly basis) on the progress in terms of reduction of operating aid for each airport benefiting from such aid. In certain cases, a monitoring trustee may be appointed to ensure compliance with any conditions and obligations underpinning the authorisation of the aid.

8.4. EVALUATION

166. To further ensure that distortions of competition and trade are limited, the Commission may require that certain schemes be subject to a limited duration and to an evaluation. Evaluations should, in particular, be carried out for schemes where the potential distortions are particularly high, that is to say schemes that may risk significantly restricting competition if their implementation is not reviewed in due time.

167. Given its objectives and in order not to put a disproportionate burden on Member States and on smaller aid measures, this requirement applies only in respect of aid schemes with large aid budgets, containing novel characteristics or where significant market, technology or regulatory changes are foreseen. The evaluation must be carried out by an expert independent from the aid granting authority on the basis of a common methodology[101] and must be made public. [In the case of aid schemes excluded from the scope of a block exemption Regulation exclusively on the grounds of their large budget, the Commission will assess their compatibility solely on the basis of the evaluation plan.]

168. The evaluation must be submitted to the Commission in due time to allow for the assessment of the possible prolongation of the aid scheme and in any case upon expiry of the scheme. The precise scope and methodology of the evaluation that is to be carried out will be defined in the decision approving the aid scheme. Any subsequent aid measure with a similar objective must take into account the results of that evaluation.

8.5. APPROPRIATE MEASURES

169. Member States should, where necessary, amend their existing schemes in order to bring them into line with these guidelines by 12 months at the latest after 4 April 2014.

170. Member States are invited to give their explicit unconditional agreement to these guidelines within two months following 4 April 2014. In the absence of any reply, the Commission will assume that the Member State in question does not agree with the proposed measures.

8.6. APPLICATION

171. The principles in these guidelines will be applied from 4 April 2014. These guidelines replace the 1994 Aviation Guidelines and the 2005 Aviation Guidelines from that date.

172. In the light of the development of the aviation sector, and in particular its liberalisation, the Commission considers that the provisions of its notice on the determination of the applicable rules for the assessment of unlawful State Aid[102] should not apply to pending cases of illegal operating aid to airports granted prior to 4 April 2014. Instead, the Commission will apply the principles set out in these guidelines to all cases concerning operating aid (pending notifications and unlawful non-notified aid) to airports even if the aid was granted before 4 April 2014 and the beginning of the transitional period.

173. As regards investment aid to airports, the Commission will apply the principles set out in these guidelines to all notified investment aid measures in respect of which it is called upon to take a decision from 4 April 2014, even where the projects were notified prior to that date. In accordance with the Commission notice on the determination of the applicable rules for the assessment of unlawful State aid, the Commission will apply to unlawful investment aid to airports the rules in force at the time when the aid was granted. Accordingly, it will not apply the principles set out in these guidelines in the case of unlawful investment aid to airports granted before 4 April 2014.

174. As regards start-up aid to airlines, the Commission will apply the principles set out in these guidelines to all notified start-up aid measures in respect of which it is called upon to take a decision from 4 April 2014, even where the measures were notified prior to that date. In accordance with the Commission notice on the determination of the applicable rules for the assessment of unlawful State aid, the Commission will apply to unlawful start-up aid to airlines the rules in force at the time when the aid was granted. Accordingly, it will not apply the principles set out in these guidelines in the case of unlawful start-up aid to airlines granted before 4 April 2014.

8.7. REVIEW

175. The Commission may undertake an evaluation of these guidelines at any time and will do so at the latest six years after 4 April 2014. That evaluation will be based on factual information and the results of wide-ranging consultations conducted by the Commission on the basis of data provided by Member States and stakeholders. The Commission will reassess the situation of airports with annual passenger traffic up to 700,000 in order to determine the need for continued specific compatibility rules on operating aid in favour of this category of airport in the light of the future prospects for full operating cost coverage, in particular with regard to the change of market conditions and profitability prospects.

176. After consulting Member States, the Commission may replace or supplement these guidelines on the basis of important competition policy or transport policy considerations.

NOTES

Para 162: substituted, together with associated footnotes (for the original paras 162, 163), by Commission Communication 2014/C198/02.

Para 167: words in square brackets added by Commission Communication 2014/C198/02.

[99] Commission Regulation (EC) No 794/2004 of 21 April 2004 implementing Council Regulation (EC) No 659/1999 laying down detailed rules for the application of Article 93 of the EC Treaty (OJ L140, 30.4.2004, p 1).

[100] With the exception of business secrets and other confidential information in duly justified cases and subject to the Commission's agreement (Commission communication on professional secrecy in State aid decisions, C(2003) 4582 (OJ C297, 9.12.2003, p 6)).

[100A] The amount to be published is the maximum allowed tax benefit and not the amount deducted each year (e.g. in the context of tax credit, the maximum allowed tax credit shall be published rather than the actual amount which might depend on the taxable revenues and vary each year).

[100B] This information shall be published within 6 months from the date of granting (or, for aid in the form of tax advantage, within 1 year from the date the tax declaration is due). In case of unlawful aid, Member States will be required to ensure the publication of this information ex post, at least within 6 months from the date of the Commission decision. The information shall be available in a format which allows data to be searched, extracted, and easily published on the internet, for instance in CSV or XML format.

[100C] Publication of information on aid awards granted before 1 July 2016 and, for fiscal aid, publication for aid claimed or granted before 1 July 2016, will not be required.

101 Such a common methodology may be provided by the Commission.

102 Commission notice on the determination of the applicable rules for the assessment of unlawful State aid (OJ C119, 22.5.2002, p 22).

ANNEX
SUMMARY OF THE COMPATIBILITY CONDITIONS

TABLE 1 OVERVIEW OF COMPATIBILITY CONDITIONS FOR AID TO AIRPORTS

[5.424]

Compatibility conditions	Investment aid to the airport	Operating aid to the airport
a) **Contribution to a well-defined objective of common interest**	— Increasing mobility by establishing access points for intra-EU flights — Combating congestion at major hubs — Facilitating regional development	
	Duplication of airports and unused capacity in absence of satisfactory medium-term prospects for use does not contribute to a well defined objective of common interest.	
b) **Need for State intervention**	< 3 million passengers > 3–5 million passengers under certain case-specific circumstances > 5 million passengers only in very exceptional circumstances	< 3 million passengers
c) **Appropriateness of the aid measure**	The aid measure must be an appropriate policy instrument to address the objective of common interest	
	Consideration of less distortive aid instruments (guarantees, soft loans etc.)	Ex ante as a fixed sum covering the expected funding gap of operating costs (determined on the basis of an ex ante business plan) during a 10 year transitional period.
d) **Incentive effect**	Present, if the investment would not have been undertaken or to a different extent (counterfactual or funding gap analysis based on ex ante business plan)	Present, if the level of economic activity of the airport would be significantly reduced in its absence
e) **Proportionality of the aid (aid limited to the minimum)**		
Eligible costs:	Costs relating to investments in airport infrastructure and equipment, except investment costs for non-aeronautical activities	Operating funding gap of the airport
Maximum permissible aid intensities:	> 3–5 million up to 25% 1–3 million up to 50% < 1 million up to 75%	**During the transitional period**: 50% of the initial average operating funding gap calculated as average of 5 years preceding the transitional period (2009–2013) **After transitional period of 10 years**: no operating aid allowed (except if granted under horizontal rules)
Exceptions:	**For airports located in remote regions (irrespective of their size)** the maximum aid intensities for investment aid to finance airport infrastructure may be increased by up to 20% **For airports < 1 million passengers per annum located in a peripheral region**: intensity may exceed 75% in exceptional circumstances subject to case-by-case assessment **In case of relocation**: proportionality, necessity and maximum aid intensity will be assessed regardless of average traffic	**For airports < 700,000 passengers per annum**: 80% of the initial average operating funding gap for 5 years after the beginning of the transitional period

Compatibility conditions	Investment aid to the airport	Operating aid to the airport
	For airports over 5 million passengers per annum: only under very exceptional circumstances, characterised by a clear market failure and taking into account the magnitude of the investment and the competition distortions	
f) **Avoidance of undue negative effects on competition and trade between Member States**	Open to all potential users and not dedicated to one specific user Airports < 5 million passengers per annum: upfront fixed amount or annual instalments to compensate for capital cost funding gap resulting from airport business plan	Assessment of distortion of competition and effect on trade Open to all potential users and not dedicated to one specific user Airports < 700,000 passengers per annum: reassessed four years after the beginning of the transitional period
Notification requirements for aid schemes and individual aid measures	Aid schemes: — airports < 3 million passengers per annum Individual notifications: — airports > 3 million passengers per annum — investment aid to an airport < 1 million passengers per annum exceeding 75% aid intensity — investment aid granted for the relocation of airports — mixed passenger/freight airports > 200,000 tonnes of freight during two financial years preceding the notification year — creation of a new passenger airport (including conversion of existing airfield) — creation or development of an airport located within 100 kilometres or 60 minutes travelling time from an existing airport	Aid schemes: — airports < 3 million passengers per annum Individual notifications: — mixed passenger/freight airports > 200,000 tonnes of freight during two financial years preceding the notification year — operating aid to an airport within 100 kilometres or 60 minutes travelling time from other airports

TABLE 2 OVERVIEW OF COMPATIBILITY CONDITIONS FOR START-UP AID TO AIRLINES

Compatibility conditions	Start-up aid to airlines
a) **Contribution to a well-defined objective of common interest**	— Increasing mobility by establishing access points for intra-EU flights — Facilitating regional development No duplication of existing comparable connection operated by a high-speed rail service or by another airport in the same catchment area under comparable conditions
b) **Need for State intervention**	— Airports < 3 million passengers per annum — Airports located in remote regions irrespective of their size — Airports between > 3–5 million passengers per annum only in exceptional circumstances — No start-up aid for air links from airports above 5 million passengers per annum
c) **Appropriateness of the aid measure**	— Not eligible if the route is already operated by a high-speed rail service or another airport in the same catchment area under the same conditions — Ex ante business plan showing profitability of the route at least after 3 years or irrevocable commitment from the airline to operate the route least for a period as long as the period during which it received start-up aid

Compatibility conditions	Start-up aid to airlines
d) **Incentive effect**	Present, if in the absence of the aid, the level of economic activity of the airline at the airport concerned would be significantly reduced (for example the new route would not have been launched). The new route or the new schedule can start only after submitting the application form for aid from the granting authority.
e) **Proportionality of the aid (aid limited to the minimum)**	
— *Eligible costs*:	Airport charges in respect of a route
— *Maximum permissible aid intensities*:	50% for a maximum period of 3 years
f) **Avoidance of undue negative effects on competition and trade between Member States**	— Public authorities must make plans public in good time to enable all interested airlines to offer services — No cumulation with other types of State aid for operation of a route
Notification requirements for aid schemes and individual aid measures	Aid schemes: — Airports < 3 million passengers per annum and airports located in remote regions Individual notifications: — Airports > 3 million passengers per annum, except airports located in remote regions

TABLE 3 SOCIAL AID

COMPATIBILITY CONDITIONS

a) Effectively for the benefit of final consumers

b) Of a social character:

Only covering certain categories of passengers (e.g. with particular needs like children, people with disabilities, people on low incomes, students, elderly people etc.)

Except: where the route links remote regions (e.g. outermost regions, islands, sparsely populated areas), the aid can cover the entire population of a region

c) Without discrimination as to the origin of the airline operating the services

TABLE 4 COMPATIBILITY OF AID IN THE FORM OF PUBLIC SERVICE COMPENSATION

Size of airport based on average traffic (passengers per annum)	Applicable legal framework	Notification requirement
Airport managers at airports < 200,000 passengers per annum over the duration of the SGEI entrustment Airlines as regards air links to islands were traffic < 300,000 passengers per annum	Article 106(2) of the Treaty Decision 2012/21/EU	Exempt from the notification requirement
Airports above 200,000 passengers per annum over the duration of the SGEI entrustment	Article 106(2) of the Treaty SGEI Framework	Notification required

COMMUNICATION FROM THE COMMISSION

(2018/C456/06)

concerning the prolongation of the specific regime for operating aid for airports with up to 700,000 passengers per annum provided for in the Guidelines on State aid to airports and airlines

[5.425]

NOTES

Date of publication in OJ: OJ C456, 18.12.2018, p 27.

1. The Guidelines on State aid to airports and airlines[1] ('the Guidelines') specify the conditions under which public financing of airports and airlines may constitute State aid within the meaning of Article 107(1) of the Treaty on the Functioning of the European Union, and when it does constitute State aid, the conditions under which it can be declared compatible with the internal market.

2. In principle, operating aid constitutes a very distortive form of aid and can only be authorised under exceptional circumstances. The Commission considers that airports and airlines should normally bear their own operating costs. Nevertheless, to enable the aviation industry to adapt to new market situations, such as increased competition between airports to attract airlines, certain categories of operating aid to airports might still be justified under certain conditions.

3. In this context, the Guidelines foresee a transitional period of 10 years from 4 April 2014 during which airports with annual average traffic of up to 3 million passengers per annum can receive operating aid. By the end of the transitional period in 2024, all airports must have reached full coverage of their operating costs and no operating aid to airports will be considered compatible with the internal market after that date, with the exception of operating aid granted in accordance with horizontal State aid rules, such as rules applicable to the financing of services of general economic interest.[2]

4. The Guidelines recognise that airports with annual passenger traffic of up to 700,000 may face increased difficulties in achieving full cost coverage during the 10-year transitional period. They therefore provide for a specific regime for such airports for an initial period of five years until 3 April 2019.

5. For the purposes of that specific regime, the aid amount is, in principle, to be established ex-ante as a fixed sum covering the expected operating funding gap (determined on the basis of an ex-ante business plan).[3] In any event, the maximum permissible aid amount during the whole transitional period is limited to 80% of the initial operating funding gap for a period of five years.4[4]

6. The Guidelines state that the Commission will reassess the need for continued specific treatment and the future prospects for full operating cost coverage for this category of airports, in particular with regard to changes in market conditions and profitability prospects after four years. The Guidelines contain no specific rules as regards operating aid for this category of airports beyond 3 April 2019.

7. In point 175 of the Guidelines, the Commission states that it will undertake a general evaluation of the Guidelines by 4 April 2020, including the rules on operating aid for airports.

8. As a review of the specific rules for smaller airports together with the remaining rules on operating aid will allow for a more comprehensive assessment of the market situation, it is appropriate to carry out the reassessment of this specific regime in the context of the overall evaluation of the Guidelines, which will be undertaken by 4 April 2020. This will also allow the Commission to assess the appropriateness of the Guidelines as a whole and, if necessary, to propose a consistent package of changes concerning all categories of airports and all types of aid.

9. As a consequence of postponing the evaluation of the specific regime for airports with up to 700,000 passengers per annum, the existing rules need to be prolonged which will provide for continuity and legal certainty in the treatment of this type of aid. Therefore, the specific regime set out in point 130 of the Guidelines is extended until 3 April 2024, aligning the transitional period for the application of the rules for smaller airports with that applicable for airports with more than 700,000 passengers per annum.

10. Thus, as of the date of the publication of this Communication in the *Official Journal of the European Union*, the maximum permissible aid amount for airports with up to 700,000 passengers per annum will be 80% of the initial operating funding gap for a period of 10 years after the beginning of the transitional period. For instance, if the annual average funding gap of a small airport over the period 2009 to 2013 is equal to EUR 1 million, the maximum amount of operating aid that the airport could receive as an *ex-ante* established fixed sum would be EUR 8 million over 10 years (80% x 1 million x 10).

NOTES

1. OJ C99, 4.4.2014, p 3.
2. See Commission Decision 2012/21/EU of 20 December 2011 on the application of Article 106(2) of the Treaty on the Functioning of the European Union to State aid in the form of public service compensation granted to certain undertakings entrusted with the operation of services of general economic interest (OJ L7, 11.1.2012, p 3); Commission Communication on a European Union framework for State aid in the form of public service compensation (2011) (OJ C8, 11.1.2012, p 15).
3. See point 121 of the Guidelines.
4. See point 130 of the Guidelines.

5. ELECTRICITY (STRANDED COSTS)

COMMISSION COMMUNICATION

relating to the methodology for analysing State aid linked to stranded costs

[5.426]

NOTES

This Communication is available on the European Commission's website at: https://ec.europa.eu/competition/state_aid/legislation/specific_rules.html.

Note: with effect from 1 December 2009, the EC Treaty was replaced by the Treaty on the Functioning of the European Union. References in this document to provisions of the EC Treaty should be construed accordingly.

1. INTRODUCTION

[5.427]

European Parliament and Council Directive 96/92/EC of 19 December 1996 concerning common rules for the internal market in electricity[1] laid down the principles for opening up the European electricity industry to competition. The Commission attaches utmost importance to deepening the common market in electricity, this being a significant step towards completing the internal market in energy.

The gradual transition from a situation of largely restricted competition to one of genuine competition at European level must take place under acceptable economic conditions that take account of the specific characteristics of the electricity industry. This concern is already reflected to a very large extent in the text of the Directive itself.

In order to enable them to cope with a number of very specific situations, Article 24 allows Member States to defer application of some of the provisions of the Directive for a transitional period. A number of Member States also wish to introduce State aid mechanisms designed to allow their electricity undertakings to adapt to the introduction of competition under favourable conditions; such aid mechanisms do not fall within the scope of the derogations provided for in Article 24.

The purpose of this Notice is to clarify how the Commission intends, in the light of Directive 96/92/EC, to apply the rules of the Treaty to State aid of this kind.

This Notice does not prejudice the rules on State aid that result from the ECSC Treaty, the Euratom Treaty and the relevant Commission frameworks, guidelines or notices. In particular, the Commission will continue to authorise regional aid and environmental aid in accordance with the respective guidelines. Similarly, aid that could not be authorised under Article 87 of the EC Treaty will, where appropriate, be open to examination in the light of Article 86(2).

NOTES

[1] OJ L27, 30.1.1997, p 20.

2. TRANSITIONAL MEASURES AND STATE AID

[5.428]

With the exception of Belgium, Greece and Ireland, the Member States were required to transpose Directive 96/92/EC into national law by 19 February 1999 at the latest. Belgium and Ireland were required to do so by 19 February 2000 at the latest and Greece by 19 February 2001 at the latest.

Article 24 of the Directive stipulates, however, that transitional measures derogating temporarily from the Directive may be authorised by the Commission:

"*1. Those Member States in which commitments or guarantees of operation given before the entry into force of this Directive may not be honoured on account of the provisions of this Directive may apply for a transitional regime which may be granted to them by the Commission, taking into account, amongst other things, the size of the system concerned, the level of interconnection of the system and the structure of its electricity industry. The Commission shall inform the Member States of those applications before it takes a decision, taking into account respect for confidentiality. This decision shall be published in the Official Journal of the European Communities.*

2. The transitional regime shall be of limited duration and shall be linked to expiry of the commitments or guarantees referred to in paragraph 1. The transitional regime may cover derogations from Chapters IV, VI and VII of this Directive. Applications for a transitional regime must be notified to the Commission no later than one year after the entry into force of this Directive."

Most Member States wished to avail themselves of Article 24 and have, therefore, notified the Commission of transitional measures. It transpires that in several Member States the measures notified do not fall within the scope of Article 24[2].

Given the present state of play, the Commission considers that decisions taken by it pursuant to Article 24 can create a transitional regime only where it has previously found that the measures notified by the Member States pursuant to that Article are incompatible with the Directive's provisions set out in Chapters IV, V, VI and VII. Under Article 24, the Commission alone may authorise derogations from those provisions.

Accordingly, a system of levies introduced by a Member State via a fund to offset the costs of commitments or guarantees that might not be honoured on account of the application of Directive 96/92/EC does not constitute a measure that could benefit from a Commission decision granting a transitional regime under Article 24 of that

Directive; such a measure does not require a derogation from the relevant chapters of the Directive. It may, on the other hand, constitute State aid, which is covered by Articles 87 and 88 of the Treaty, without prejudice to the ECSC and Euratom Treaties.

The purpose of this Notice is to show how the Commission intends to apply the Treaty rules on State aid in the case of aid measures designed to compensate for the cost of commitments or guarantees that it might no longer be possible to honour on account of Directive 96/92/EC. In particular, the Notice does not apply to measures that could not be classified as State aid within the meaning of Article 87(1) of the EC Treaty pursuant to the ruling of the Court of Justice of 13 March 2001 in Case C-379/98, *PreussenElektra AG v Schleswag AG*[3].

NOTES

[2] See in particular Commission Decisions 1999/791/EC, 1999/792/EC, 1999/795/EC, 1999/796/EC, 1999/797/EC, and 1999/798/EC, concerning respectively the United Kingdom, France, Austria, the Netherlands, Spain and Denmark, pursuant to Article 24 of Directive 96/92/EC (OJ L319, 11.12.1999).

[3] [2001] ECR I- . . . .

3. DEFINITION OF ELIGIBLE STRANDED COSTS

[5.429]

Such commitments or guarantees of operation are normally referred to as "stranded costs". They may, in practice, take a variety of forms: long-term purchase contracts, investments undertaken with an implicit or explicit guarantee of sale, investments undertaken outside the scope of normal activity, etc. In order to rank as eligible stranded costs that could be recognised by the Commission, such commitments or guarantees must satisfy the following criteria:

3.1 The "commitments or guarantees of operation" that could give rise to stranded costs must predate 19 February 1997, the date of entry into force of Directive 96/92/EC.

3.2 The existence and validity of such commitments or guarantees will be substantiated in the light of the underlying legal and contractual provisions and of the legislative context in which they were made.

3.3 Such commitments or guarantees of operation must run the risk of not being honoured on account of the provisions of Directive 96/92/EC. In order to qualify as stranded costs, commitments or guarantees must consequently become non-economical on account of the effects of the Directive and must significantly affect the competitiveness of the undertaking concerned. Among other things, this must result in that undertaking's making accounting entries (eg, provisions) designed to reflect the foreseeable impact of the commitment or guarantee.

Especially where, as a result of the commitments or guarantees in question, the viability of the undertakings might be jeopardised in the absence of aid or any transitional measures, the commitments or guarantees are deemed to meet the requirements laid down in the preceding paragraph.

The effect of such commitments or guarantees on the competitiveness or viability of the undertakings concerned will be assessed at the consolidated level. For commitments or guarantees to constitute stranded costs, it must be possible to establish a cause-and-effect relationship between the entry into force of Directive 96/92/EC and the difficulty that the undertakings concerned have in honouring or securing compliance with such commitments or guarantees. In order to establish such cause-and-effect relationship, the Commission will take into account any fall in electricity prices or market share losses suffered by the undertakings concerned. Commitments or guarantees that could not have been honoured irrespective of the entry into force of the Directive do not constitute stranded costs.

3.4 Such commitments or guarantees must be irrevocable. Should an undertaking have the possibility of revoking against payment, or modifying, such commitments or guarantees, account will have to be taken of this fact in calculating the eligible stranded costs.

3.5 Commitments or guarantees linking enterprises belonging to one and the same group cannot, as a rule, qualify as stranded costs.

3.6 Stranded costs are economic costs that must correspond to the actual sums invested, paid or payable by virtue of the commitments or guarantees from which they result: flat-rate calculations cannot, therefore, be accepted unless it can be shown that they reflect economic realities.

3.7 Stranded costs must be net of the income, profits or added value associated with the commitments or guarantees from which they arise.

3.8 Stranded costs must be valued net of any aid paid or payable in respect of the assets to which they relate. In particular, where a commitment or a guarantee of operation corresponds to an investment which is the subject of State aid, the value of the aid must be deducted from any stranded costs resulting from the commitment or guarantee.

3.9 Wherever stranded costs arise from commitments or guarantees that are difficult to honour on account of Directive 96/92/EC, calculation of the eligible stranded costs will take account of the actual change over time in the economic and competitive conditions prevailing on the national and Community electricity markets. In particular, where commitments or guarantees could constitute stranded costs because of the foreseeable fall in electricity prices, calculation of the stranded costs must take account of actual movements in electricity prices.

3.10 Costs depreciated before the transposition of Directive 96/92/EC into national law cannot give rise to stranded costs. However, provisions or depreciation of assets entered in the balance sheet of the undertakings concerned with the explicit aim of taking account of the foreseeable effects of the Directive may correspond to stranded costs.

3.11 Eligible stranded costs may not exceed the minimum level necessary to allow the undertakings concerned to continue to honour or secure compliance with the commitments or guarantees called into question by Directive 96/92/EC[4]*. Consequently, they will have to be calculated by taking into account the most economic solution (in the absence* *of any aid) from the point of view of the undertakings concerned. This may involve, among other things, the termination of commitments or guarantees giving rise to stranded costs or the disposal of all or some of the assets giving rise to stranded costs (where this does not run counter to the very principles of the commitments or guarantees themselves).*

3.12 Costs which some undertakings may have to bear after the time horizon indicated in Article 26 of the Directive (18 February 2006) cannot, as a rule, constitute eligible stranded costs within the meaning of this methodology[5]*. However, if it appears necessary, the Commission may in due course take into account such commitments or guarantees and, if appropriate, consider them as eligible stranded costs during the next stage of opening up the Community electricity market.*

For Member States which open up their market more quickly than is required by the Directive, the Commission may agree to regard as eligible stranded costs under this methodology costs which some undertakings may have to bear after the time horizon indicated in Article 26 of the Directive if such costs result from commitments or guarantees which meet the criteria under points 3.1. to 3.12. and provided that they are limited to a period not extending beyond 31 December 2010.

NOTES

4 In the case of a long-term contract of sale or purchase, the stranded costs will, therefore, be calculated by comparison with the conditions on which, in a liberalised market, the undertaking would normally have been able to sell or purchase the product under consideration, all things being equal.

5 It must be understood that investments which cannot be recouped or are not economically viable as a result of the liberalisation of the internal market in electricity may constitute stranded costs within the meaning of this methodology, including in cases where they are, in principle, to extend beyond 2006. Furthermore, commitments or guarantees which must absolutely continue to be honoured after 18 February 2006 because failure to do so might give rise to major risks concerning protection of the environment, public safety, social protection of workers or the security of the electricity network may, if duly justified, constitute eligible stranded costs according to this methodology.

4. STRANDED COSTS AND STATE AID

[5.430]

The general principle laid down in Article 87(1) of the EC Treaty is that State aid is prohibited. However, paragraphs 2 and 3 of that Article provide for a number of derogations from this general rule. Furthermore, in accordance with Article 86(2), "undertakings entrusted with the operation of services of general economic interest or having the character of a revenue-enhancing monopoly" are subject to the rules contained in the Treaty, in particular the rules on competition, in so far as the application of those rules does not obstruct the performance, in law or in fact, of the particular tasks assigned to them. In any event, trade must not be affected to an extent contrary to the interests of the Community.

The State aid corresponding to the eligible stranded costs defined in this Notice is designed to facilitate the transition for electricity undertakings to a competitive electricity market. The Commission may take a favourable view of such aid to the extent that the distortion of competition is counterbalanced by the contribution made by the aid to the attainment of a Community objective which market forces could not achieve. Indeed, the distortion of competition that results from aid paid to facilitate the transition for electricity undertakings from a largely closed market to one that has been partially liberalised cannot be contrary to the common interest where it is limited in time and in its effects, since liberalisation of the electricity market is in the general interest of the common market in accordance with Articles 2 and 3(1)(t) of the EC Treaty and supplements moves to establish the internal market. The Commission also takes the view that aid granted for stranded costs enables electricity undertakings to reduce the risks relating to their historic commitments or investments and may thus encourage them to maintain their investments in the long term. Finally, if there were no compensation for stranded costs, there would be a greater risk that the undertakings concerned might pass on the entire cost of their non-economical commitments or guarantees to their captive customers.

Aid to compensate for stranded costs in the electricity industry can be further justified in relation to other liberalised sectors by the fact that liberalisation of the electricity market has not been accompanied by either faster technological progress or increased demand and by the fact that it is hardly conceivable, in the interests of environmental protection, security of supply and the smooth operation of the Community's economy, to wait until electricity undertakings encounter difficulties before considering whether to grant them state support.

In this context, the Commission takes the view that aid designed to offset stranded costs normally qualifies for the derogation under Article 87(3)(c) if it facilitates the development of certain economic activities without adversely affecting trading conditions to an extent contrary to the common interest.

Without prejudice to the specific provisions resulting from the ECSC and Euratom Treaties and from the Commission notices on State aid, including the Guidelines on State aid for environmental protection[6], the Commission may, in principle, accept as being compatible with Article 87(3)(c) of the EC Treaty aid designed to offset eligible stranded costs which satisfied the following criteria:

4.1 The aid must serve to offset eligible stranded costs that have been clearly determined and isolated. It may under no circumstances exceed the amount of the eligible stranded costs.

4.2 The arrangements for paying the aid must allow account to be taken of future developments in competition. Such developments may be gauged in particular by way of quantifiable factors (prices, market shares, other relevant factors indicated by the Member State). Since changes in the conditions of competition have a direct effect on the amount of eligible stranded costs, the amount of the aid paid will necessarily be conditional on the development of genuine competition, and the calculation of aid paid over time will have to take account of changes in the relevant factors in order to gauge the degree of competition achieved.

4.3 The Member State must undertake to send to the Commission an annual report that, in particular, describes developments in the competitive situation on its electricity market by indicating among other things the changes observed in the relevant quantifiable factors. The annual report will give details of how the stranded costs taken into account for the relevant year have been calculated and will specify the amounts of aid paid.

4.4 The degressive nature of aid intended to offset stranded costs will be viewed favourably by the Commission when making its assessment; it will, in fact, help the undertaking concerned to speed up its preparations for a liberalised electricity market[7].

4.5 The maximum amount of aid that can be paid to an undertaking to offset stranded costs must be specified in advance. It must take account of productivity gains that may be achieved by the undertaking.

Similarly, the detailed arrangements for calculating and financing aid designed to offset stranded costs and the maximum period for which such aid can be granted must be clearly spelt out in advance. Notification of the aid will specify in particular how calculation of the stranded costs will take account of changes in the various factors mentioned in point 4.2.

4.6 In order to avoid any cumulation of aid, the Member State will undertake in advance not to pay any rescue or restructuring aid to undertakings that are to benefit from aid in respect of stranded costs. The Commission takes the view that the payment of compensation for stranded costs linked to investments in assets that offer no prospects of long-term viability does not facilitate the transition of the electricity industry to a liberalised market and cannot therefore qualify for the derogation under Article 87(3)(c) of the EC Treaty.

However, the Commission entertains the most serious misgivings regarding aid intended to offset stranded costs which do not satisfy the above criteria or which are likely to give rise to distortions of competition contrary to the common interest for the following reasons:

4.7 The aid is not linked to eligible stranded costs that meet the above definition or to clearly defined and individualised stranded costs or exceeds the amount of eligible stranded costs.

4.8 The aid is intended to safeguard all or some of the income pre-dating the entry into force of Directive 96/92/EC, without taking strictly into account the eligible stranded costs that might result from the introduction of competition.

4.9 The amount of aid is not likely to be adjusted to take due account of the differences between the economic and market assumptions initially made when estimating stranded costs and real changes in them over time.

NOTES

[6] OJ C72, 10.3.1994, p 3.

5. METHOD OF FINANCING AID INTENDED TO OFFSET STRANDED COSTS

[5.431]

Member States are free to choose the methods of financing aid intended to offset stranded costs which they consider to be the most appropriate. However, in order to authorise such aid, the Commission will make sure that the financing arrangements do not give rise to effects that conflict with the objectives of Directive 96/92/EC or with the Community interest. The Community interest takes into account, among other things, consumer protection, free movement of goods and services, and competition.

Consequently, the financing arrangements must not have the effect of deterring outside undertakings or new players from entering certain national or regional markets. In particular, aid intended to offset stranded costs cannot be financed out of levies on electricity in transit between Member States or from levies linked to the distance between the producer and the consumer[8].

The Commission will also ensure that the arrangements for financing aid intended to offset stranded costs result in fair treatment for eligible and non-eligible consumers. To this end, the annual report referred to in point 4.3 will give the breakdown by eligible and non-eligible consumers of the sources of finance intended to offset the stranded costs. Where non-eligible consumers participate in the financing of stranded costs directly through the tariff for the purchase of electricity, this must be clearly stated. The contribution imposed on either group (eligible or non-eligible) must not exceed the proportion of stranded costs to be offset that corresponds to the market share accounted for by those consumers.

Where funds are raised by private undertakings with a view to financing aid mechanisms designed to offset stranded costs, the management of those funds will have to be clearly separate from that of the normal resources of those undertakings. Such investments must not benefit the undertakings managing them.

6. OTHER ASSESSMENT FACTORS

[5.432]

In examining State aid intended to offset stranded costs, the Commission takes particular account of the size and level of interconnection of the network concerned and of the structure of the electricity industry. Aid for a small network with a low degree of interconnection with the rest of the Community will be less likely to give rise to substantial distortions of competition.

This methodology for stranded costs is without prejudice to the application, in the regions covered by Article 87(3)(a), of the guidelines on national regional aid.[7] Pursuant to Article 86(2) of the EC Treaty, where application of the rules on State aid to stranded costs obstructs the performance, in law or in fact, of the particular tasks assigned to undertakings entrusted with the operation of services of general economic interest or having the character of a revenue-producing monopoly, those rules may be derogated from provided that trade is not affected to an extent contrary to the interests of the Community.

The rules laid down in this methodology for State aid intended to offset stranded costs arising from Directive 96/92/EC apply independently of the public or private ownership of the undertakings concerned.

NOTES

[7] OJ C74, 10.3.1998, p 9. [note that this footnote was erroneously numbered as footnote number nine in the original version]

6. POSTAL SERVICES

COMMISSION NOTICE

(98/C39/02)

on the application of the competition rules to the postal sector and on the assessment of certain State measures relating to postal services

(Text with EEA relevance)

[5.433]

NOTES

Date of publication in OJ: OJ C39, 6.2.1998, p 2.

Note: with effect from 1 December 2009, the EC Treaty was replaced by the Treaty on the Functioning of the European Union. References in this document to provisions of the EC Treaty should be construed accordingly.

PREFACE

[5.434]

Subsequent to the submission by the Commission of a Green Paper on the development of the single market for postal services[1] and of a communication to the European Parliament and the Council, setting out the results of the consultations on the Green Paper and the measures advocated by the Commission[2], a substantial discussion has taken place on the future regulatory environment for the postal sector in the Community. By Resolution of 7 February 1994 on the development of Community postal services[3], the Council invited the Commission to propose measures defining a harmonised universal service and the postal services which could be reserved. In July 1995, the Commission proposed a package of measures concerning postal services which consisted of a proposal for a Directive of the European Parliament and the Council on common rules for the development of Community postal services and the improvement of quality of service[4] and a draft of the present Notice on the application of the competition rules[5].

This notice, which complements the harmonisation measures proposed by the Commission, builds on the results of those discussions in accordance with the principles established in the Resolution of 7 February 1994. It takes account of the comments received during the public consultation on the draft of this notice published in December 1995, of the European Parliament's resolution[6] on this draft adopted on 12 December 1996, as well as of the discussions on the proposed Directive in the European Parliament and in Council.

The Commission considers that because they are an essential vehicle of communication and trade, postal services are vital for all economic and social activities. New postal services are emerging and market certainty is needed to favour investment and the creation of new employment in the sector. As recognized by the Court of Justice of the European Communities, Community law, and in particular the competition rules of the EC Treaty, apply to the post sector[7]. The Court stated that 'in the case of public undertakings to which Member States grant special or exclusive rights, they are neither to enact nor to maintain in force any measure contrary to the rules contained in the Treaty with regard to competition' and that those rules 'must be read in conjunction with Article 90(2) which provides that undertakings entrusted with the operation of services of general economic interest are to be subject to the rules on competition in so far as the application of such rules does not obstruct the performance, in law or in fact, of the particular tasks assigned to them.' Questions are therefore frequently put to the Commission on the attitude it intends to take, for purposes of the implementation of the competition rules contained in the Treaty, with regard to the behaviour of postal operators and with regard to State measures relating to public undertakings and undertakings to which the Member States grant special or exclusive rights in the postal sector.

This notice sets out the Commission's interpretation of the relevant Treaty provisions and the guiding principles according to which the Commission intends to apply the competition rules of the Treaty to the postal sector in individual cases, while maintaining the necessary safeguards for the provision of a universal service, and gives to enterprises and Member States clear guidelines so as to avoid infringements of the Treaty. This Notice is without prejudice to any interpretation to be given by the Court of Justice of the European Communities.

Furthermore, this Notice sets out the approach the Commission intends to take when applying the competition rules to the behaviour of postal operators and when assessing the compatibility of State measures restricting the freedom to provide service and/or to compete in the postal markets with the competition rules and other rules of the Treaty. In addition, it addresses the issue of non-discriminatory access to the postal network and the safeguards required to ensure fair competition in the sector.

Especially on account of the development of new postal services by private and public operators, certain Member States have revised, or are revising, their postal legislation in order to restrict the monopoly of their postal organisations to what is considered necessary for the realisation of the public-interest objective. At the same time, the Commission is faced with a growing number of complaints and cases under competition law on which it must take position. At this stage, a notice is therefore the appropriate instrument to provide guidance to Member States and postal operators, including those enjoying special or exclusive rights, to ensure correct implementation of the competition rules. This Notice, although it cannot be exhaustive, aims to provide the necessary guidance for the correct interpretation, in particular, of Articles 59, 85, 86, 90, and 92 of the Treaty in individual cases. By issuing the present notice, the Commission is taking steps to bring transparency and to facilitate investment decisions of all postal operators, in the interest of the users of postal services in the European Union.

As the Commission explained in its communication of 11 September 1996 on 'Services of general interest in Europe'[8], solidarity and equal treatment within a market economy are fundamental Community objectives. Those objectives are furthered by services of general interest. Europeans have come to expect high-quality services at affordable prices, and many of them even view services of general interest as social rights.

As regards, in particular, the postal sector, consumers are becoming increasingly assertive in exercising their rights and wishes. Worldwide competition is forcing companies using such services to seek out better price deals comparable to those enjoyed by their competitors. New technologies, such as fax or electronic mail, are putting enormous pressures on the traditional postal services. Those developments have given rise to worries about the future of those services accompanied by concerns over employment and economic and social cohesion. The economic importance of those services is considerable. Hence the importance of modernising and developing services of general interest, since they contribute so much to European competitiveness, social solidarity and quality of life.

The Community's aim is to support the competitiveness of the European economy in an increasingly competitive world and to give consumers more choice, better quality and lower prices, while at the same time helping, through its policies, to strengthen economic and social cohesion between the Member States and to reduce certain inequalities. Postal services have a key role to play here. The Community is committed to promoting their functions of general economic interest, as solemnly confirmed in the new Article 7d, introduced by the Amsterdam Treaty, while improving their efficiency. Market forces produce a better allocation of resources and greater effectiveness in the supply of services, the principal beneficiary being the consumer, who gets better quality at a lower price. However, those mechanisms sometimes have their limits; as a result the potential benefits might not extend to the entire population and the objective of promoting social and territorial cohesion in the Union may not be attained. The public authority must then ensure that the general interest is taken into account.

The traditional structures of some services of general economic interest, which are organised on the basis of national monopolies, constitute a challenge for European economic integration. This includes postal monopolies, even where they are justified, which may obstruct the smooth functioning of the market, in particular by sealing off a particular market sector.

The real challenge is to ensure smooth interplay between the requirements of the single market in terms of free movement, economic performance and dynamism, free competition, and the general interest objectives. This interplay must benefit individual citizens and society as a whole. This is a difficult balancing act, since the goalposts are constantly moving: the single market is continuing to expand and public services, far from being fixed, are having to adapt to new requirements.

The basic concept of universal service, which was originated by the Commission[9], is to ensure the provision of high-quality service to all prices everyone can afford. Universal service is defined in terms of principles: equality, universality, continuity and adaptability; and in terms of sound practices: openness in management, price-setting and funding and scrutiny by bodies independent of those operating the services. Those criteria are not always all met at national level, but where they have been introduced using the concept of European universal service, there have been positive effects for the development of general interest services. Universal service is the expression in Europe of the requirements and special features of the European model of society in a policy which combines a dynamic market, cohesion and solidarity.

High-quality universal postal services are of great importance for private and business customers alike. In view of the development of electronic commerce their importance will even increase in the very near future. Postal services have a valuable role to play here.

As regards the postal sector, Directive 97/67/EC has been adopted by the European Parliament and the Council (hereinafter referred to as 'the Postal Directive'). It aims to introduce common rules for developing the postal sector and improving the quality of service, as well as gradually opening up the markets in a controlled way.

The aim of the Postal Directive is to safeguard the postal service as a universal service in the long term. It imposes on Member States a minimum harmonised standard of universal services including a high-quality service countrywide with regular guaranteed deliveries at prices everyone can afford. This involves the collection, transport, sorting and delivery of letters as well as catalogues and parcels within certain price and weight limits. It also covers registered and insured (valeur déclarée) items and applies to both domestic and cross-border deliveries. Due regard is given to considerations of continuity, confidentiality, impartiality and equal treatment as well as adaptability.

To guarantee the funding of the universal service, a sector may be reserved for the operators of this universal service. The scope of the reserved sector has been harmonised in the Postal Directive According to the Postal Directive, Member States can only grant exclusive rights for the provision of postal services to the extent that this is necessary to guarantee the maintenance of the universal service. Moreover, the Postal Directive establishes the maximum scope that Member States may reserve in order to achieve this objective. Any additional funding which may be required for the universal service may be found by writing certain obligations into commercial operator's franchises; for example, they may be required to make financial contributions to a compensation fund administered for this purpose by a body independent of the beneficiary or beneficiaries, as foreseen in Article 9 of the Postal Directive.

The Postal Directive lays down a minimum common standard of universal services and establishes common rules concerning the reserved area. It therefore increases legal certainty as regards the legality of some exclusive and special rights in the postal sector. There are, however State measures that are not dealt with in it and that can be in conflict with the Treaty rules addressed to Member States. The autonomous behaviour of the postal operators also remains subject to the competition rules in the Treaty.

Article 90(2) of the Treaty provides that suppliers of services of general interest may be exempted from the rules in the Treaty, to the extent that the application of those rules would obstruct the performance of the general interest tasks for which they are responsible. That exemption from the Treaty rules is however subject to the principle of proportionality. That principle is designed to ensure the best match between the duty to provide general interest services and the way in which the services are actually provided, so that the means used are in proportion to the ends pursued. The principle is formulated to allow for a flexible and context-sensitive balance that takes account of the technical and budgetary constraints that may vary from one sector to another. It also makes for the best possible interaction between market efficiency and general interest requirements, by ensuring that the means used to satisfy the requirements do not unduly interfere with the smooth running of the single European market and do not affect trade to an extent that would be contrary to the Community interest[10].

The application of the Treaty rules, including the possible application of the Article 90(2) exemption, as regards both behaviour of undertakings and State measures can only be done on a case-by-case basis. It seems, however, highly desirable, in order to increase legal certainty as regards measures not covered by the Postal Directive, to explain the Commission's interpretation of the Treaty and the approach that it aims to follow in its future application of those rules. In particular, the Commission considers that, subject to the provisions of Article 90(2) in relation to the provision of the universal service, the application of the Treaty rules would promote the competitiveness of the undertakings active in the postal sector, benefit consumers and contribute in a positive way to the objectives of general interest.

The postal sector in the European Union is characterised by areas which Member States have reserved in order to guarantee universal service and which are now being harmonised by the Postal Directive in order to limit distortive effects between Member States. The Commission must, according to the Treaty, ensure that postal monopolies comply with the rules of the Treaty, and in particular the competition rules, in order to ensure maximum benefit and limit any distortive effects for the consumers. In pursuing this objective by applying the competition rules to the sector on a case-by-case-basis, the Commission will ensure that monopoly power is not used for extending a protected dominant position into liberalised activities or for unjustified discrimination in favour of big accounts at the expense of small users. The Commission will also ensure that postal monopolies granted in the area of cross-border services are not used for creating or maintaining illicit price cartels harming the interest of companies and consumers in the European Union.

This notice explains to the players on the market the practical consequences of the applicability of the competition rules to the postal sector, and the possible derogations from the principles. It sets out the position the Commission would adopt, in the context set by the continuing existence of special and exclusive rights as harmonised by the Postal Directive, in assessing individual cases or before the Court of Justice in cases referred to the Court by national courts under Article 177 of the Treaty.

NOTES

1 COM(91) 476 final.

2 'Guidelines for the development of Community postal services' (COM(93) 247 of 2 June 1993).

3 OJ C48, 16.2.1994, p 3.

4 OJ C322, 2.12.1995, p 22.

5 OJ C322, 2.12.1995, p 3.

6 OJ C20, 20.1.1997, p 159.

7 In particular in Joined Cases C-48/90 and C-66/90, *Netherlands and Koninklijke PTT Nederland* and *PTT Post BV v Commission* [1992] ECR I-565 and Case C-320/91 *Procureur du Roi v Paul Corbea*u [1993] ECR I-2533.

8 COM(96) 443 final.

9 See footnote 8.

10 See judgment of 23 October 1997 in Cases C-157/94 to C-160/94 'Member State Obligations — Electricity' Commission v Netherlands (157/94), Italy (158/94). France (154/94), Spain (160/94).

1. DEFINITIONS

[5.435]
In the context of this notice, the following definitions shall apply[11]:

'postal services:' services involving the clearance, sorting, transport and delivery of postal items;

'public postal network': the system of organisation and resources of all kinds used by the universal service provider(s) for the purposes in particular of:

- the clearance of postal items covered by a universal service obligation from access points throughout the territory,
- the routing and handling of those items from the postal network access point to the distribution centre,
- distribution to the addresses shown on items;

'access points': physical facilities, including letter boxes provided for the public either on the public highway or at the premises of the universal service provider, where postal items may be deposited with the public postal network by customers;

'clearance': the operation of collecting postal items deposited at access points;

'distribution': the process from sorting at the distribution centre to delivery of postal items to their addresses;

'postal item': an item addressed in the final form in which it is to be carried by the universal service provider. In addition to items of correspondence, such items also include for instance books, catalogues, newspapers, periodicals and postal packages containing merchandise with or without commercial value;

'item of correspondence': a communication in written form on any kind of physical medium to be conveyed and delivered at the address indicated by the sender on the item itself or on its wrapping. Books, catalogues, newspapers and periodicals shall not be regarded as items of correspondence;

'direct mail': a communication consisting solely of advertising, marketing or publicity material and comprising an identical message, except for the addressee's name, address and identifying number as well as other modifications which do not alter the nature of the message, which is sent to a significant number of addresses, to be conveyed and delivered at the address indicated by the sender on the item itself or on its wrapping. The National Regulatory Authority should interpret the term 'significant number of addressees' within each Member State and publish an appropriate definition. Bills, invoices, financial statements and other non-identical messages should not be regarded as direct mail. A communication combining direct mail with other items within the same wrapping should not be regarded as direct mail. Direct mail includes cross-border as well as domestic direct mail;

'document exchange': provision of means, including the supply of ad hoc premises as well as transportation by a third party, allowing self-delivery by mutual exchange of postal items between users subscribing to this service;

'express mail service': a service featuring, in addition to greater speed and reliability in the collection, distribution, and delivery of items, all or some of the following supplementary facilities: guarantee of delivery by a fixed date; collection from point of origin; personal delivery to addressee; possibility of changing the destination and address in transit; confirmation to sender of receipt of the item dispatched; monitoring and tracking of items dispatched; personalised service for customers and provision of an à la carte service, as and when required. Customers are in principle prepared to pay a higher price for this service;

'universal service provider': the public or private entity providing a universal postal service or parts thereof within a Member State, the identity of which has been notified to the Commission;

'exclusive rights': rights granted by a Member State which reserve the provision of postal services to one undertaking through any legislative, regulatory or administrative instrument and reserve to it the right to provide a postal service, or to undertake an activity, within a given geographical area;

'special rights': rights granted by a Member State to a limited number of undertakings through any legislative, regulatory or administrative instrument which, within a given geographical area:

- limits, on a discretionary basis, to two or more the number of such undertakings authorised to provide a service or undertake an activity, otherwise than according to objective, proportional and non-discriminatory criteria, or
- designates, otherwise than according to such criteria, several competing undertakings as undertakings authorised to provide a service or undertake an activity, or
- confers on any undertaking or undertakings, otherwise than according to such criteria, legal or regulatory advantages which substantially affect the ability of any other undertaking to provide the same service or undertake the same activity in the same geographical area under substantially comparable conditions;

'terminal dues': the remuneration of universal service providers for the distribution of incoming cross-border mail comprising postal items from another Member State or from a third country;

'intermediary': any economical operator who acts between the sender and the universal service provider, by clearing, routing and/or pre-sorting postal items, before channelling them into the public postal network of the same or of another country;

'national regulatory authority': the body or bodies, in each Member State, to which the Member State entrusts, inter alia, the regulatory functions falling within the scope of the Postal Directive;

'essential requirements': general non-economic reasons which can induce a Member State to impose conditions on the supply of postal services[12]. These reasons are: the confidentiality of correspondence, security of the network as regards the transport of dangerous goods and, where justified, data protection, environmental protection and regional planning.

Data protection may include personal data protection, the confidentiality of information transmitted or stored and protection of privacy.

NOTES

11 The definitions will be interpreted in the light of the Postal Directive and any changes resulting from review of that Directive.

12 The meaning of this important phrase in the context of Community competition law is explained in paragraph 5.3.

2. MARKED DEFINITION AND POSITION ON THE POSTAL MARKET

(A) GEOGRAPHICAL AND PRODUCT MARKET DEFINITION

[5.436]

2.1. Articles 85 and 86 of the Treaty prohibit as incompatible with the common market any conduct by one or more undertakings that may negatively affect trade between Member States which involves the prevention, restriction, or distortion of competition and/or an abuse of a dominant position within the common market or a substantial part of it. The territories of the Member States constitute separate geographical markets with regard to the delivery of domestic mail and also with regard to the domestic delivery of inward cross-border mail, owing primarily to the exclusive rights of the operators referred to in point 4.2 and to the restrictions imposed on the provision of postal services. Each of the geographical markets constitutes a substantial part of the common market. For the determination of 'relevant market', the country of origin of inward cross-border mail is immaterial.

2.2. As regards the product markets, the differences in practice between Member States demonstrate that recognition of several distinct markets is necessary in some cases. Separation of different product-markets is relevant, among, other things, to special or exclusive rights granted. In its assessment of individual cases on the basis of the different market and regulatory situations in the Member States and on the basis of a harmonised framework provided by the Postal Directive, the Commission will in principle consider that a number of distinct product markets exist, like the clearance, sorting, transport and delivery of mail, and for example direct mail, and cross-border mail. The Commission will take into account the fact that these markets are wholly or partly liberalised in a number of Member States. The Commission will consider the following markets when assessing individual cases.

2.3. The general letter service concerns the delivery of items of correspondence to the addresses shown on the items. It does not include self-provision, that is the provision of postal services by the natural or legal person (including a sister or subsidiary organisation) who is the originator of the mail.

Also excluded, in accordance with practice in many Member States, are such postal items as are not considered items of correspondence, since they consist of identical copies of the same written communication and have not been altered by additions, deletions or indications other than the name of the addressee and his address. Such items are magazines, newspapers, printed periodicals catalogues, as well as goods or documents accompanying and relating to such items.

Direct mail is covered by the definition of items of correspondence. However, direct mail items do not contain personalised messages. Direct mail addresses the needs of specific operators for commercial communications services, as a complement to advertising in the media. Moreover, the senders of direct mail do not necessarily require the same short delivery times, priced at first-class letter tariffs, asked for by customers requesting services on the market as referred to above. The fact that both services are not always directly interchangeable indicates the possibility of distinct markets.

2.4. Other distinct markets include, for example, the express mail market, the document exchange market, as well as the market for new services (services quite distinct from conventional services). Activities combining the new telecommunications technologies and some elements of the postal services may be, but are not necessarily, new services within the meaning of the Postal Directive. Indeed, they may reflect the adaptability of traditional services.

A document exchange differs from the market referred to in point 2.3 since it does not include the collection and the delivery to the addressee of the postal items transported. It involves only means, including the supply of ad hoc premises as well as transportation by a third party, allowing self-delivery by mutual exchange of postal items between users subscribing to this service. The users of a document exchange are members of a closed user group.

The express mail service also differs from the market referred to in point 2.3 owing to the value added by comparison with the basic postal service[13]. In addition to faster and more reliable collection, transportation and delivery of the postal items, an express mail service is characterised by the provision of some or all of the following supplementary services: guarantee of delivery by a given date; collection from the sender's address; delivery to the addressee in person; possibility of a change of destination and addressee in transit; conformation to the sender of delivery; tracking and tracing; personalised treatment for customers and the offer of a range of services according to requirements. Customers are in principle prepared to pay a higher price for this service. The reservable services as defined in the Postal Directive may include accelerated delivery of items of domestic correspondence falling within the prescribed price and weight limits.

2.5. Without prejudice to the definition of reservable services given in the Postal Directive, different activities can be recognised, within the general letter service, which meet distinct needs and should in principle be considered as different markets; the markets for the clearance and for the sorting of mail, the market for the transport of mail and, finally, the delivery of mail (domestic or inward cross-border). Different categories of customers must be distinguished in this respect. Private customers demand the distinct products or services as one integrated service. However, business customers, which represent most of the revenues of the operators referred to in point 4.2, actively pursue the possibilities of substituting for distinct components of the final service alternative solutions (with regard to quality of service levels and/or costs incurred) which are in some cases provided by, or sub-contracted to, different operators. Business customers want to balance the advantages and disadvantages of self-provision versus provision by the postal operator. The existing monopolies limit the external supply of those individual services, but they would otherwise limit the external supply of those individual according to market conditions. That market reality supports the opinion that clearance, sorting, transport and delivery of postal items constitute different markets[14]. From a competition-law point of view, the distinction between the four markets may be relevant.

That is the case for cross-border mail where the clearance and transport will be done by a postal operator other than the one providing the distribution. This is also the case as regards domestic mail, since most postal operators permit major customers to undertake sorting of bulk traffic in return for discounts, based on their public tariffs. The deposit and collection of mail and method of payment also vary in these circumstances. Mail rooms of larger companies are now often operated by intermediaries, which prepare and pre-sort mail before handing it over to the postal operator for final distribution. Moreover, all postal operators allow some kind of downstream access to distribution. Moreover, all postal operators allow some kind of downstream access to their postal network, for instance by allowing or even demanding (sorted) mail to be deposited at an expediting or sorting centre. This permits in many cases a higher reliability (quality of service) by bypassing any sources of failure in the postal network upstream.

(B) DOMINANT POSITION

2.6. Since in most Member States the operator referred to in point 4.2 is, by virtue of the exclusive rights granted to him, the only operator controlling a public postal network covering the whole territory of the Member State, such an operator has a dominant position within the meaning of Article 86 of the Treaty on the national market for the distribution of items of correspondence. Distribution is the service to the user which allows for important economies of scale, and the operator providing this service is in most cases also dominant on the markets for the clearance, sorting and transport of mail. In addition, the enterprise which provides distribution, particularly if it also operates post office premises, has the important advantage of being regarded by the users as the principal postal enterprise, because it is the most conspicuous one, and is therefore the natural first choice. Moreover, this dominant position also includes, in most Member States, services such as registered mail or special delivery services, and/or some sectors of the parcels market.

(C) DUTIES OF DOMINANT POSTAL OPERATORS

2.7. According to point (b) of the second paragraph of Article 86 of the Treaty, an abuse may consist in limiting the performance of the relevant service to the prejudice of its consumers. Where a Member State grants exclusive rights to an operator referred to in point 4.2 for services which it does not offer, or offers in conditions not satisfying the needs of customers in the same way as the services which competitive economic operators would have offered, the Member State induces those operators, by the simple exercise of the exclusive right which has been conferred on them, to limit the supply of the relevant service, as the effective exercise of those activities by private companies is, in this case, impossible. This is particularly the case where measures adopted to protect the postal service restrict the provision of other distinct services on distinct or neighbouring markets such as the express mail market. The Commission has requested several Member States to abolish restrictions resulting from exclusive rights regarding the provision of express mail services by international couriers[15].

Another type of possible abuse involves providing a seriously inefficient service and failing to take advantage of technical developments. This harms customers who are prevented from choosing between alternative suppliers. For instance, a report prepared for the Commission[16] in 1994 showed that, where they have not been subject to competition, the public postal operators in the Member States have not made any significant progress since 1990 in the standardisation of dimensions and weights. The report also showed that some postal operators practised hidden cross-subsidies between reserved and non-reserved services (see points 3.1 and 3.4), which explained, according to that study, most of the price disparities between Member States in 1994, especially penalising residential users who do not qualify for any discounts schemes, since they make use of reserved services that are priced at a higher level than necessary.

The examples given illustrate the possibility that, where they are granted special or exclusive rights, postal operators may let the quality of the service decline[17] and omit to take necessary steps to improve service quality. In such cases, the Commission may be induced to act taking account of the conditions explained in point 8.3.

As regards cross-border postal services, the study referred to above showed that the quality of those services needed to be improved significantly in order to meet the needs of customers, and in particular of residential customers who cannot afford to use the services of courier companies or facsimile transmission instead. Independent measurements carried out in 1995 and 1996 show an improvement of quality of service since 1994. However, those measurements only concern first class mail, and the most recent measurements show that the quality has gone down slightly again.

The majority of Community public postal operators have notified an agreement on terminal dues to the Commission for assessment under the competition rules of the Treaty. The parties to the agreement have explained that their aim is to establish fair compensation for the delivery of cross-border mail reflecting more closely the real costs incurred and to improve the quality of cross-border mail services.

2.8. Unjustified refusal to supply is also an abuse prohibited by Article 86 of the Treaty. Such behaviour would lead to a limitation of services within the meaning of Article 86, second paragraph, (b) and, if applied only to some users, result in discrimination contrary to Article 86, second paragraph, (c), which requires that no dissimilar conditions be applied to equivalent transactions. In most of the Member States, the operators referred to in point 4.2 provide access at various access points of their postal networks to intermediaries. Conditions of access, and in particular the tariffs applied, are however, often confidential and may facilitate the application of discriminatory conditions. Member States should ensure that their postal legislation does not encourage postal operators to differentiate injustifiably as regards the conditions applied or to exclude certain companies.

2.9. While a dominant firm is entitled to defend its position by competing with rivals, it has a special responsibility not to further diminish the degree of competition remaining on the market. Exclusionary practices may be directed against existing competitors on the market or intended to impede market access by new entrants. Examples of such illegal behaviour include: refusal to deal as a means of eliminating a competitor by a firm which is the sole or dominant source of supply of a product or controls access to an essential technology or infrastructure; predatory pricing and selective price cutting (see section 3); exclusionary dealing agreements; discrimination as part of a wider pattern of monopolizing conduct designed to exclude competitors; and exclusionary rebate schemes.

NOTES

13 Commission Decisions 90/16/EEC (OJ L10, 12.1.1990, p 47) and 90/456/EEC (OJ L233, 28.8.1990, p 19).

14 See Commission Notice on the definition of the relevant market for the purpose of the application of Community competition law (OJ C372, 9.12.1997, p 5).

15 See footnote 13.

16 UFC — Que Choisir, Postal services in the European Union, April 1994.

17 In many Member States users could, some decades ago, still rely on this service to receive in the afternoon, standard letters posted in the morning. Since then, a continuous decline in the quality of the service has been observed, and in particular of the number of daily rounds of the postmen, which were reduced from five to one (or two in some cities of the European Union). The exclusive rights of the postal organisations favoured a fall in quality, since they prevented other companies from entering the market. As a consequence the postal organisations failed to compensate for wage increases and reduction of the working hours by introducing modern technology, as was done by enterprises in industries open to competition.

3. CROSS-SUBSIDISATION

(A) BASIC PRINCIPLES

[5.437]

3.1. Cross-subsidisation means that an undertaking bears or allocates all or part of the costs of its activity in one geographical or product market to its activity in another geographical or product market. Under certain circumstances, cross-subsidisation in the postal sector, where nearly all operators provide reserved and non-reserved services, can distort competition and lead to competitors being beaten by offers which are made possible not by efficiency (including economies of scope) and performance but by cross-subsidies. Avoiding cross-subsidisation leading to unfair competition is crucial for the development of the postal sector.

3.2. Cross-subsidisation does not distort competition when the costs of reserved activities are subsidised by the revenue generated by other reserved services since there is no competition possible as to these services. This form of subsidisation may sometimes be necessary, to enable the operators referred to in point 4.2 to perform their obligation to provide a service universally, and on the same conditions to everybody[18]. For instance, unprofitable mail delivery in rural areas is subsidised through revenues from profitable mail delivery in urban areas. The same could be said of subsidising the provision of reserved services through revenues generated by activities open to competition. Moreover, cross-subsidisation between non-reserved activities is not in itself abusive.

3.3. By contrast, subsidising activities open to competition by allocating their costs to reserved services is likely to distort competition in breach of Article 86. It could amount to an abuse by an undertaking holding a dominant position within the Community. Moreover, users of activities covered by a monopoly would have to bear costs which are unrelated to the provision of those activities. Nonetheless, dominant companies too many compete on price, or improve their cash flow and obtain only partial contribution to their fixed (overhead) costs, unless the prices are predatory or go against relevant national or Community regulations.

(B) CONSEQUENCES

3.4. A reference to cross-subsidisation was made in point 2.7; duties of dominant postal operators. The operators referred to in point 4.2 should not use the income from the reserved area to cross-subsidise activities in areas open to competition. Such a practice could prevent, restrict or distort competition in the non-reserved area. However, in some justified cases, subject to the provisions of Article 90(2), cross-subsidisation can be regarded as lawful, for example for cultural mail[19], as long as it is applied in a non-discriminatory manner, or for particular services to the socially, medically and economically disadvantaged. When necessary, the Commission will indicate what other exemptions the Treaty would allow to be made. In all other cases, taking into account the indications given in point 3.3, the price of competitive services offered by the operator referred to in point 4.2 should, because of the difficulty of allocating common costs, in principle be at least equal to the average total costs of provision. This means covering the direct costs plus an appropriate proportion of the common and overhead costs of the operator. Objective criteria, such as volumes, time (labour) usage, or intensity of usage, should be used to determine the appropriate proportion. When using the turnover generated by the services involved as a criterion in a case of cross-subsidisation, allowance should be made for the fact that in such a scenario the turnover of the relevant activity is being kept artificially low. Demand-influenced factors, such as revenues or profits, are themselves influenced by predation. If services were offered systematically and selectively at a price below average total cost, the Commission would, on a case-by-case basis, investigate the matter under Article 86, or under Article 86 and Article 90(1) or under Article 92.

NOTES

[18] See these Postal Directive, recitals 16 and 28, and Chapter 5.

[19] Referred to by UPU as 'work of the mind', comprising books, newspapers, periodicals and journals.

4. PUBLIC UNDERTAKINGS AND SPECIAL OR EXCLUSIVE RIGHTS

[5.438]

4.1. The treaty obliges the Member States, in respect of public undertakings and undertakings to which they grant special or exclusive rights, neither to enact nor maintain in force any measures contrary to the Treaty rules (Article 90(1)). The expression 'undertaking' includes every person or legal entity exercising an economic activity, irrespective of the legal status of the entity and the way in which it is financed. The clearance, sorting, transportation and distribution of postal items constitute economic activities, and these services are normally supplied for reward.

The term 'public undertaking' includes every undertaking over which the public authorities may exercise directly or indirectly a dominant influence by virtue of ownership of it, their financial participation in it or the rules which govern it[20]. A dominant influence on the part of the public authorities may in particular be presumed when the public authorities hold, directly or indirectly, the majority of the subscribed capital of the undertaking, control the majority of the voting rights attached to shares issued by the undertaking or can appoint more than half of the members of the administrative, managerial or supervisory body. Bodies which are part of the Member State's administration and which provide in an organised manner postal services for third parties against remuneration are to be regarded as such undertakings. Undertakings to which special or exclusive rights are granted can, according to Article 90(1), be public as well as private.

4.2. National regulations concerning postal operators to which the Member States have granted special or exclusive rights to provide certain postal services are 'measures' within the meaning of Article 90(1) of the Treaty and must be assessed under the Treaty provisions to which that Article refers.

In addition to Member States' obligations under Article 90(1), public undertakings and undertakings that have been granted special or exclusive rights are subject to Articles 85 and 86.

4.3. In most Member States, special and exclusive rights apply to services such as the clearance, transportation and distribution of certain postal items, as well as the way in which those services are provided, such as the exclusive right to place letter boxes along the public highway or to issue stamps bearing the name of the country in question.

NOTES

[20] Commission Directive 80/723/EEC on the transparency of financial relations between Member States and public undertakings, OJ L195, 29.7.1980, p 35.

5. FREEDOM TO PROVIDE SERVICES

(A) BASIC PRINCIPLES

[5.439]

5.1. The granting of special or exclusive rights to one or more operators referred to in point 4.2 to carry out the clearance, including public collection, transport and distribution of certain categories of postal items inevitably restricts the provision of such services, both by companies established in other Member States and by undertakings established in the Member State concerned. This restriction has a transborder character when the addresses or the senders of the postal items handled by those undertakings are established in other Member States. In practice, restrictions on the provision of postal services, within the meaning of Article 59 of the Treaty[21], comprise prohibiting the conveyance of certain categories of postal items to other Member States including by intermediaries, as well as the prohibition on distributing gross-border mail. The Postal Directive lays down the justified restrictions on the provision of postal services.

5.2. Article 66, read in conjunction with Article 55 and 56 of the Treaty, sets out exceptions from Article 59. Since they are exceptions to a fundamental principle, they must be interpreted restrictively. As regards postal services, the exception under Article 55 only applies to the conveyance and distribution of a special kind of mail, that is mail generated in the curse of judicial or administrative procedures, connected, even occasionally, with the exercise of official authority, in particular notifications in pursuance of any judicial or administrative procedures. The conveyance and distribution of such items on a Member State's territory may therefore be subjected at a licensing requirement (see point 5.5) in order to protect the public interest. The conditions of the other derogations from the Treaty listed in those provisions will not normally be fulfilled in relation to postal services. Such services cannot, in themselves, threaten public policy and cannot affect public health.

5.3. The case-law of the Court of Justice allows, in principle, further derogations on the basis of mandatory requirements, provided that they fulfil non-economic essential requirements in the general interest, are applied without discrimination, and are appropriate and proportionate to the objective to be achieved. As regards postal services, the essential requirements which the Commission would consider as justifying restrictions on the freedom to provide postal services are data protection subject to approximation measures taken in this field, the confidentiality of correspondence, security of the network as regards the transport of dangerous goods, as well as, where justified under the provisions of the Treaty, environmental protection and regional planning. Conversely, the Commission would not consider it justified to impose restrictions on the freedom to provide postal services for reasons of consumer protection since this general interest requirement can be met by the general legislation on fair trade practices and consumer protection. Benefits to consumers are enhanced by the freedom to provide postal services, provided that universal service obligations are well defined on the basis of the Postal Directive and can be fulfilled.

5.4. The Commission therefore considers that the maintenance of any special or exclusive right which limits cross-border provision of postal services needs to be justified in the light of Articles 90 and 59 of the Treaty. At present, the special or exclusive rights whose scope does not go beyond the reserved services as defined in the Postal Directive are prima facie justified under Article 90(2). Outward cross-border mail is de jure or de facto liberalised in some Member States, such as Denmark, the Netherlands, Finland, Sweden, and the United Kingdom.

(B) CONSEQUENCES

5.5. The adoption of the measures contained in the Postal Directive requires Member States to regulate postal services. Where Member States restrict postal services to ensure the achievement of universal service and essential requirements, the content of such regulation must correspond to the objective pursued. Obligations should, as a general rule, be enforced within the framework of class licences and declaration procedures by which operators of postal services supply their name, legal form, title and address as well as a short description of the services they offer to the public. Individual licensing should only be applied for specific postal services, where it is demonstrated that less restrictive procedures cannot ensure those objectives. Member States may be invited, on a case-by-case basis, to notify the measures they adopt to the Commission to enable it to assess their proportionality.

NOTES

[21] For a general explanation of the principles deriving from Article 59, see Commission interpretative communication concerning the free movement of services across frontiers (OJ C334, 9.12.1993, p 3).

6. MEASURES ADOPTED BY MEMBER STATES

(A) BASIC PRINCIPLES

[5.440]

6.1. Member States have the freedom to define what are general interest services, to grant the special or exclusive rights that are necessary for providing them, to regulate their management and, where appropriate, to fund them. However, under Article 90(1) of the Treaty, Member States must, in the case of public undertakings and undertakings to which they have granted special or exclusive rights, neither enact nor maintain in force any measure contrary to the Treaty rules, and in particular its competition rules.

(B) CONSEQUENCES

6.2. The operation of a universal clearance and distribution network confers significant advantages on the operator referred to in point 4.2 in offering not only reserved or liberalised services falling within the definition of universal service, but also other (non-universal postal) services. The prohibition under Articles 90(1), read in conjunction with Article 86(b), applies to the use, without objective justification, of a dominant position on one market to obtain market power on related or neighbouring markets which are distinct from the former, at the risk of eliminating competition on those markets. In countries where local delivery of items of correspondence is liberalised, such as Spain, and the monopoly is limited to inter-city transport and delivery, the use of a dominant position to extend the monopoly from the latter market to the former would therefore be incompatible with the Treaty provisions, in the absence of specific justification, if the functioning of services in the general economic interest was not previously endangered. The Commission considers that it would be appropriate for Member States to inform the Commission of any extension of special or exclusive rights and of the justification therefor.

6.3. There is a potential effect on the trade between Member States from restrictions on the provision of postal services, since the postal services offered by operators other than the operators referred to in point 4.2 can cover mailings to or from other Member States, and restrictions may impede cross-border activities of operators in other Member States.

6.4. As explained in point 8(b)(vii), Member States must monitor access conditions and the exercise of special and exclusive rights. They need not necessarily set up new bodies to do this but they should not give to their operator[22] as referred to in point 4.2, or to a body which is related (legally, administratively and structurally) to that operator, the power of supervision of the exclusive rights granted and of the activities of postal operators generally. An enterprise in a dominant position must not be allowed to have such a power over its competitors. The independence, both in theory and in practice, of the supervisory authority from all the enterprise supervised is essential. The system of undistorted competition required by the Treaty can only be ensured if equal opportunities for the different economic operators, including confidentiality of sensitive business information, are guaranteed. To allow an operator to check the declarations of its competitors or to assign to an undertaking the power to supervise the activities of its competitors or to be associated in the granting of licences means that such undertaking is given commercial information about its competitors and thus has the opportunity to influence the activity of those competitors.

NOTES

[22] See in particular, Case C-18/88 *RTT v GB-Inno-BM* [1991] ECR I-5981, paragraphs 25 to 28.

7. POSTAL OPERATORS AND STATE AID

(A) PRINCIPLES

[5.441]

While a few operators referred to in point 4.2 are highly profitable, the majority appear to be operating either in financial deficit or at close to break-even in postal operations, although information on underlying financial performance is limited, as relatively few operators publish relevant information of an auditable standard on a regular basis. However, direct financial support in the form of subsidies or indirect support such as tax exemptions is being given to fund some postal services, even if the actual amounts are often not transparent.

The Treaty makes the Commission responsible for enforcing Article 92, which declares State aid that affects trade between Member States of the Community to be incompatible with the common market except in certain circumstances where an exemption is, or may be, granted. Without prejudice to Article 90(2), Articles 92 and 93 are applicable to postal services[23].

Pursuant to Article 93(3), Member States are required to notify to the Commission for approval all plans to grant aid or to alter existing aid arrangements. Moreover, the Commission is required to monitor aid which it has previously authorised or which dates from before the entry into force of the Treaty or before the accession of the Member State concerned.

All universal service providers currently fall within the scope of Commission Directive 80/723/EEC of 25 June 1980 on the transparency of financial relations between Member States and public undertakings[24], as last amended by Directive 93/84/EEC[25]. In addition to the general transparency requirement for the accounts of operators referred to in point 4.2 as discussed in point 8(b)(vi), Member States must therefore ensure that financial relations between them and those operators are transparent as required by the Directive, so that the following are clearly shown:

(a) public funds made available directly, including tax exemptions or reductions;
(b) public funds made available through other public undertakings or financial institutions;
(c) the use to which those public funds are actually put.

The Commission regards, in particular, the following as making available public funds:

(a) the setting-off of operating losses;
(b) the provision of capital;
(c) non-refundable grants or loans on privileged terms;
(d) the granting of financial advantages by forgoing profits or the recovery of sums due;
(e) the forgoing of a normal return on public funds used;
(f) compensation for financial burdens imposed by the public authorities.

(B) APPLICATION OF ARTICLES 90 AND 92

The Commission has been called upon to examine a number of tax advantages granted to a postal operator on the basis of Article 92 in connection with Article 90 of the Treaty. The Commission sought to check whether that privileged tax treatment could be used to cross-subsidize that operator's operations in sectors open to competition. At that time, the postal operator did not have an analytical cost-accounting system serving to enable the Commission to distinguish between the reserved activities and the competitive ones. Accordingly, the Commission, on the basis of the findings of studies carried out in that area, assessed the additional costs due to universal-service obligations borne by that postal operator and compared those costs with the tax advantages. The Commission concluded that the costs exceeded those advantages and therefore decided that the tax system under examination could not lead to cross-subsidization of that operator's operations in the competitive areas[26].

It is worth noting that in its decision the Commission invited the Member State concerned to make sure that the postal operator adopted an analytical cost-accounting system and requested an annual report which would allow the monitoring of compliance with Community law.

The Court of First Instance ha endorsed the Commission's decision and has stated that the tax advantages to that postal operator are State aid which benefit from an exemption from the prohibition set out in Article 92(1) on the basis of Article 90(2)[27].

NOTES

[23] Case C-387/92 *Banco de Credito Industrial v Ayuntamiento Valencia* [1994] ECR I-877.

[24] OJ L195, 29.7.1980, p 35.

[25] OJ L254, 12.10.1993, p 16.

[26] Case NN 135/92, OJ C262, 7.10.1995, p 11.

[27] Case T-106/95 *FFSA v Commission* [1997] ECR II-229.

8. SERVICE OF GENERAL ECONOMIC INTEREST

(A) BASIC PRINCIPLES

[5.442]

8.1. Article 90(2) of the Treaty allows an exception from the application of the Treaty rules where the application of those rules obstructs, in law or in fact, the performance of the particular task assigned to the operators referred to in point 4.2 for the provision of a service of general economic interest. Without prejudice to the rights of the Member States to define particular requirements of services of general interest, that task consists primarily in the provision and the maintenance of a universal public postal service, guaranteeing at affordable, cost-effective and transparent tariffs nationwide access to the public postal network within a reasonable distance and during adequate opening hours, including the clearance of postal items from accessible postal boxes or collection points throughout the territory and the timely delivery of such items to the address indicated, as well as associated services entrusted by measures of a regulatory nature to those operators for universal delivery at a specified quality. The universal service is to evolve in response to the social, economical and technical environment and to the demands of users.

The general interest involved requires the availability in the Community of a genuinely integrated public postal network, allowing efficient circulation of information and thereby fostering, on the one hand, the competitiveness of European industry and the development of trade and greater cohesion between the regions and Member States, and on the other, the improvement of social contacts between the citizens of the Union. The definition of the reserved area has to take into account the financial resources necessary for the provision of the service of general economic interest.

8.2. The financial resources for the maintenance and improvement of that public network still derive mainly from the activities referred to in point 2.3. Currently, and in the absence of harmonisation at Community level, most Member States have fixed the limits of the monopoly by reference to the weight of the item. Some Member States apply a combined weight and price limit whereas one Member State applies a price limit only. Information collected by the Commission on the revenues obtained from mail flows in the Member States seems to indicate that the maintenance of special or exclusive rights with regard to this market could, in the absence of exceptional circumstances, be sufficient to guarantee the improvement an maintenance of the public postal network.

The service for which Member States can reserve exclusive or special rights, to the extent necessary to ensure the maintenance of the universal service, is harmonised in the Postal Directive. To the extent to which Member States grant special or exclusive rights for this service, the service is to be considered a separate product-market in the assessment of individual cases in particular with regard to direct mail, the distribution of inward cross-border mail, outward cross-border mail, as well as with regard to the collection, sorting and transport of mail. The Commission will take account of the fact that those markets are wholly or partly liberalised in a number of Member States.

8.3. When applying the competition rules and other relevant Treaty rules to the postal sector, the Commission, acting upon a complaint or upon its own initiative, will take account of the harmonized definition set out in the Postal Directive in assessing whether the scope of the reserved area can be justified under Article 90(2). The point of departure will be a presumption that, to the extent that they fall within the limits of the reserved area as defined in the Postal Directive, the special or exclusive rights will be prima facie justified under Article 90(2). That presumption can, however, be rebutted if the facts in a case show that a restriction does not fulfil the conditions of Article 90(2)[28].

8.4. The direct mail market is still developing at a different pace from one Member State to the other, which makes it difficult for the Commission, at this stage, to specify in a general way the obligations of the Member States regarding that service. The two principal issues in relation to direct mail are potential abuse by customers of its tariffication and of its liberalisation (reserved items being delivered by an alternative operators as if they were non-reserved direct mail items) so as to circumvent the reserved services referred to in point 8.2. Evidence from the Member States which do not restrict direct mail services, such as Spain, Italy, the Netherlands, Austria, Sweden and Finland, is still inconclusive and does not yet allow a definitive general assessment. In view of that uncertainty, it is considered appropriate to proceed temporarily on a case-by-case basis. If particular circumstances make it necessary, and without prejudice to point 8.3, Member States may maintain certain existing restrictions on direct mail services or introduce licensing in order to avoid artificial traffic distortions and substantial destabilisation of revenues.

8.5. As regards the distribution of inward cross-border mail, the system of terminal dues received by the postal operator of the Member State of delivery of cross-border mail from the operator of the Member State of origin is currently under revision to adapt terminal dues, which are in many cases too low, to actual costs of delivery.

Without prejudice to point 8.3, Member States may maintain certain existing restrictions on the distribution of inward cross-border mail[29], so as to avoid artificial diversion of traffic, which would inflate the share of cross-border mail in Community traffic. Such restrictions may only concern items falling under the reservable area of services. In assessing the situation in the framework of individual cases, the Commission will take into account the relevant, specific circumstances in the Member States.

8.6. The clearance, sorting and transport of postal items has been or is currently increasingly being opened up to third parties by postal operators in a number of Member States. Given that the revenue effects of such opening up may vary according to the situation in the different Member States, certain Member States may, if particular circumstances make it necessary, and without prejudice to point 8.3, maintain certain existing restrictions on the clearance, sorting and transport of postal items by intermediaries[30], so as to allow for the necessary restructuring of the operator referred to in point 4.2 However, such restrictions should in principle be applied only to postal items covered by the existing monopolies, should not limit what is already accepted in the Member State concerned, and should be compatible with the principle of non-discriminatory access to the postal network as set out in point 8(b)(vii).

(B) CONDITIONS FOR THE APPLICATION OF ARTICLE 90(2) TO THE POSTAL SECTOR

The following conditions should apply with regard to the exception under Article 90(2):

(I) LIBERALISATION OF OTHER POSTAL SERVICES

Except for those services for which reservation is necessary, and which the Postal Directive allows to be reserved, Member States should withdraw all special or exclusive rights for the supply of postal services to the extent that the performance of the particular task assigned to the operators referred to in point 4.2 for the provision of a service of a general economic interest is not obstructed in law or in fact, with the exception of mail connected to the exercise of official authority, and they should take all necessary measures to guarantee the right of all economic operators to supply postal services.

This does not prevent Member States from making, where necessary, the supply of such services subject to declaration procedures or class licences and, when necessary, to individual licensing procedures aimed at the enforcement of essential requirements and at safeguarding the universal service. Member States should, in that event, ensure that the conditions set out in those procedures are transparent, objective, and without discriminatory effect, and that there is an efficient procedure of appealing to the courts against any refusal.

(II) ABSENCE OF LESS RESTRICTIVE MEANS TO ENSURE THE SERVICES IN THE GENERAL ECONOMIC INTEREST

Exclusive rights may be granted or maintained only where they are indispensable for ensuring the functioning of the tasks of general economic interest. In many areas the entry of new companies into the market could, on the basis of their specific skills and expertise, contribute to the realisation of the services of general economic interest.

If the operator referred to in point 4.2 fails to provide satisfactorily all of the elements of the universal service required by the Postal Directive (such as the possibility of every citizen in the Member State concerned, and in particular those living in remote areas, to have access to newspapers, magazines and books), even with the benefit of a universal postal network and of special or exclusive rights, the Member State concerned must take action[31]. Instead of extending the rights already granted, Member States should create the possibility that services are provided by competitors and for this purpose may impose obligations on those competitors in addition to essential requirements. All of those obligations should be objective, non-discriminatory and transparent.

(III) PROPORTIONALITY

Member States should moreover ensure that the scope of any special and exclusive rights granted is in proportion to the general economic interest which is pursued through those rights. Prohibiting self-delivery, that is the provision of postal services by the natural or legal person (including a sister or subsidiary organisation) who is the originator of the mail, or collection and transport of such items by a third party acting solely on its behalf, would for example not be proportionate to the objective of guaranteeing adequate resources for the public postal network. Member States must also adjust the scope of those special or exclusive rights, according to changes in the needs and the conditions under which postal services are provided and taking account of any State aid granted to the operator referred to in point 4.2.

(IV) MONITORING BY AN INDEPENDENT REGULATORY BODY

The monitoring of the performance of the public-service tasks of the operators referred to in point 4.2 and of open access to the public postal network and, where applicable, the grant of licences or the control of declarations as well as the observance by economic operators of the special or exclusive rights of operators referred to in point 4.2 should be ensured by a body or bodies independent of the latter[32].

That body should in particular ensure: that contracts for the provision of reserved services are made fully transparent, are separately invoiced and distinguished from non-reserved services, such as printing, labelling and enveloping; that terms and conditions for services which are in part reserved and in part liberalised are separate; and that the reserved element is open to all postal users, irrespective of whether or not the non-reserved component is purchased.

(V) EFFECTIVE MONITORING OF RESERVED SERVICES

The tasks excluded from the scope of competition should be effectively monitored by the Member State according to published service targets and performance levels and there should be regular and public reporting on their fulfilment.

(VI) TRANSPARENCY OF ACCOUNTING

Each operator referred to in point 4.2 uses a single postal network to compete in a variety of markets. Price and service discrimination between or within classes of customers can easily be practised by operators running a universal postal network, given the significant overheads which cannot be fully and precisely assigned to any one service in particular. It is therefore extremely difficult to determine cross-subsidies within them, both between the different stages of the handling of postal items in the public postal network and between the reserved services and the services provided under conditions of competition. Moreover, a number of operators offer preferential tariffs for cultural items which clearly do not cover the average total costs. Member States are obliged by Article 5 and 90 to ensure that Community law is fully complied with. The Commission considers that the most appropriate way of fulfilling that obligation would be for Member States to require operators referred to in point 4.2 to keep separate financial records, identifying separately, inter alia, costs and revenues associated with the provision of the services supplied under their exclusive rights and those provided under competitive conditions, and making it possible to assess fully the conditions applied at the various access points of the public postal network. Services made up of elements falling within the reserved and competitive services should also distinguish between the costs of each element. Internal accounting systems should operate on the basis of consistently applied and objectively justified cost-accounting principles. The financial accounts should be drawn up, audited by an independent auditor, which may be appointed by the National Regulatory Authority, and be published in accordance with the relevant Community and national legislation applying to commercial organisations.

(VII) NON-DISCRIMINATORY ACCESS TO THE POSTAL NETWORK

Operators should provide the universal postal service by affording non-discriminatory access to customers or intermediaries at appropriate public points of access, in accordance with the needs of those users. Access conditions including contracts (when offered) should be transparent, published in an appropriate manner and offered on a non-discriminatory basis.

Preferential tariffs appear to be offered by some operators to particular groups of customers in a non-transparent fashion. Member States should monitor the access conditions to the network with a view to ensuring that there is no discrimination either in the conditions of use or in the charges payable. It should in particular be ensured that intermediaries, including operators from other Member States, can choose from amongst available access points to the public postal network and obtain access within a reasonable period at price conditions based on costs, that take into account the actual services required.

The obligation to provide non-discriminatory access to the public postal network does not mean that Member States are required to ensure access for items of correspondence from its territory, which were conveyed by commercial companies to another State, in breach of a postal monopoly, to be introduced in the public postal network via a postal operator of that other State, for the sole purpose of taking advantage of lower postal tariffs. Other economic reasons, such as production costs and facilities, added values or the level of service offered in other Member States are not regarded as improper. Fraud can be made subject to penalties by the independent regulatory body.

At present cross-border access to postal networks is occasionally rejected, or only allowed subject to conditions, for postal items whose production process includes cross-border data transmission before those postal items were given physical form. Those cases are usually called non-physical remail. In the present circumstances there may indeed be an economic problem for the postal operator that delivers the mail, due to the level of terminal dues applied between postal operators. The operators seek to resolve this problem by the introduction of an appropriate terminal dues system.

The Commission may request Member States, in accordance with the first paragraph of Article 5 of the Treaty, to inform the Commission of the conditions of access applied and of the reasons for them. The Commission is not to disclose information acquired as a result of such requests to the extent that it is covered by the obligation of professional secrecy.

NOTES

28 In relation to the limits on the application of the exception set out in Article 90(2), see the position taken by the Court of Justice in the following cases: Case C-179/90 *Merci convenzionali porto di Genova v Siderurgica Gabrielli* [1991] ECR I-1979; Case C-41/90 *Klaus Höfner and Fritz Elser v Macroton* [1991] ECR I-5889.

29 This may in particular concern mail from one State which has been conveyed by commercial companies to another State to be introduced in the public postal network via a postal operator of that other State.

30 Even in a monopoly situation, senders will have the freedom to make use of particular services provided by an intermediary, such as (pre-)sorting before deposit with the postal operator.

31 According to Article 3 of the Postal Directive, Member States are to ensure that users enjoy the right to a universal service.

32 See in particular Articles 9 and 22 of the Postal Directive.

9. REVIEW

[5.443]

This notice is adopted at Community level to facilitate the assessment of certain behaviour of undertakings and certain State measures relating to postal services. It is appropriate that after a certain period of development, possibly by the year 2000, the Commission should carry out an evaluation of the postal sector with regard to the Treaty rules, to establish whether modifications of the views set out in this notice are required on the basis of social, economic or technological considerations and on the basis of experience with cases in the postal sector. In due time the Commission will carry out a global evaluation of the situation in the postal sector in the light of the aims of this notice.

7. STEEL

COMMUNICATION FROM THE COMMISSION

(2002/C152/03)

concerning certain aspects of the treatment of competition cases resulting from the expiry of the ECSC Treaty

(Text with EEA relevance)

[5.444]

NOTES

Date of publication in OJ: OJ C152, 26.6.2002, p 5.

Note: with effect from 1 December 2009, the EC Treaty was replaced by the Treaty on the Functioning of the European Union. References in this document to provisions of the EC Treaty should be construed accordingly.

1. INTRODUCTION

[5.445]

1. By virtue of its Article 97, the Treaty establishing the European Coal and Steel Community (ECSC Treaty) expires on 23 July 2002[1]. This means in principle that as from 24 July 2002 the sectors previously covered by the ECSC Treaty and the procedural rules and other secondary legislation derived from the ECSC Treaty will be subject to the rules of the EC Treaty as well as the procedural rules and other secondary legislation derived from the EC Treaty[2].

2. The purposes of this Communication are

— in its section 2, to summarise for economic operators and Member States, in so far as they are concerned by the ECSC Treaty and its related secondary legislation, the most important changes with regard to the applicable substantive and procedural law arising from the transition to the EC regime,

— in its section 3, to explain how the Commission intends to deal with specific issues raised by the transition from the ECSC regime to the EC regime in the areas of antitrust[3], merger control[4] and State aid control.

3. The principles that underlie the competition rules of the two Treaties are similar. Articles 81 and 82 of the EC Treaty are clearly inspired by the corresponding Articles 65 and 66(7) of the ECSC Treaty. Furthermore, practices under the two Treaties have been converging for many years. In its Twentieth Report on Competition Policy (1990)[5], the Commission announced that the time had come to align the enforcement of ECSC competition rules as much as possible with the practice under the EC Treaty. In 1998, it published a notice[6] dealing with the alignment of procedures for processing mergers under the ECSC and EC Treaties. In practical terms, the changes, both substantial and procedural, arising from the expiry of the ECSC Treaty are likely to be limited in scope. The objective of this Communication is to facilitate the changeover by setting out how certain situations will be dealt with in the transition from the ECSC to the EC regime. This Communication is made without prejudice to the interpretation of the ECSC rules and EC rules by the Court of First Instance and the European Court of Justice.

NOTES

1 Article 97 ECSC Treaty provides: 'This Treaty is concluded for a period of 50 years from its entry into force.'.

2 The question which rules are applicable to individual cases, which started before the expiry of the ECSC Treaty and are not fully completed by 23.7.2002, is tackled under section 3 below.

3 In this Communication, the term 'antitrust' refers to the prohibition of restrictive agreements between undertakings, decisions by associations of undertakings and concerted practices, as well as the prohibition of abuses of dominant positions (Articles 65 and 66(7) ECSC Treaty; Articles 81 and 82 EC Treaty).

4 In this communication, the term 'merger control' refers to the control of any concentrations no matter whether they are effected by mergers between previously independent undertakings or acquisition of control of other undertakings (see Article 66(1) ECSC Treaty and Article 3 Council Regulation (EEC) No 4064/89 as amended by Regulation (EC) No 1310/97).

5 European Commission, Twentieth Report on Competition Policy (1990), paragraph 122.

6 Commission notice concerning alignment of procedures for processing mergers under the ECSC and EC Treaties (OJ C66, 2.3.1998, p 36).

2. THE MOST IMPORTANT CHANGES DUE TO THE EXPIRY OF THE ECSC TREATY

2.1. ANTITRUST

2.1.1. JURISDICTION

[5.446]

4. Under the ECSC regime, as the Commission had exclusive jurisdiction, the national competition authorities and national courts could not apply either Articles 65 and 66 ECSC Treaty[7] or their national competition rules to deal with coal and steel cases.

5. With the transition to the EC regime, the national authorities and courts responsible for competition will become competent[8] to apply the European competition rules in the coal and steel sectors as the relevant provisions of the EC Treaty have direct effect, with the exception of Article 81(3), for which the Commission retains at present sole competence[9]. Thus, under the principles of the EC regime, the Commission and the national authorities and courts will have parallel powers to apply Community competition law[10].

6. It should also be noted that, unlike Articles 65 and 66(7) ECSC Treaty, which did not include any conditions relating to effect on trade, Articles 81 and 82 EC Treaty apply only if trade between Member States is affected. Thus, where agreements or practices restricting competition, or an abuse of a dominant position, do not affect trade between Member States, the national competition authorities and the national courts will, from 24 July 2002, be authorised to apply their national competition rules in the field of coal and steel[11].

7. The national competition authorities and the national courts, which had no powers to apply competition law under the ECSC regime, will now be able to apply either national law and Community law or, where trade between Member States is not affected, only the relevant national law.

2.1.2. Substantive antitrust rules

8. As regards the question of an appreciable restriction of competition under Article 81(1) of the EC Treaty, the Commission would first point out that the policy concerning agreements of minor importance in terms of market share[12] (agreements that are not therefore covered by Article 81(1)[13]) will apply in full to the coal and steel sectors as from 24 July 2002.

9. Under the ECSC regime, joint ventures have generally been regarded as being covered by the provisions on concentrations (Article 66(1) to (6) of the ECSC Treaty)[14]. Joint ventures notified after 23 July 2002 that do not have the characteristics of a 'full-function' joint venture within the meaning of Regulation (EEC) No 4064/89[15] will be regarded as agreements within the meaning of Article 81 EC Treaty[16]. Agreements concluded by such undertakings will therefore be covered by the relevant provisions of Regulation No 17[17].

10. The system requiring price lists and conditions of sale to be notified to the Commission and made public will be abolished[18]. Effectively, the undertakings concerned will no longer be required systematically to communicate such data to the Commission before making use of it[19].

2.1.3. Procedural rules relating to antitrust

11. The Commission has for many years[20] endeavoured to apply the same principles, *inter alia* at procedural level, to practices under the ECSC Treaty and to those under the EC Treaty: thus important procedural features such as access to the file, hearings or the closing of a case with a comfort letter were introduced into ECSC practice on the basis of EC practice. The transition to the EC regime will enhance the transparency of these practices.

12. As regards agreements restricting competition, two innovative factors will be introduced into the sectors concerned: the requirement, where parties apply to the Commission for negative clearance or exemption, that the agreements be notified on form A/B[21] will be officially introduced[22]. In addition, prior consultation of an Advisory Committee will be required before the adoption of any Commission decision mentioned in Article 10 of Regulation No 17.

13. Undertakings are also informed that the provisions implementing the ban on abuse of a dominant position are more straightforward under the EC regime than under the ECSC regime. Indeed, under the Article 82 EC Treaty procedure, the Commission can immediately adopt directly applicable decisions, whereas under Article 66(7) ECSC Treaty, it must first send the undertaking concerned an ECSC recommendation and only then can it take a decision in consultation with the Member State concerned.

2.2. MERGER CONTROL

2.2.1. Jurisdiction

14. As far as jurisdiction is concerned, the ECSC Treaty gives the Commission exclusive jurisdiction over all concentrations involving coal and steel undertakings. On the other hand, the EC Merger Regulation[23] gives the Commission jurisdiction only over concentrations involving undertakings whose turnover exceeds certain thresholds. Therefore, some operations which would have required prior authorisation from the Commission under ECSC rules, but do not meet the thresholds under the EC Merger Regulation, will after the expiry of the ECSC Treaty fall outside the Commission's jurisdiction and fall to be examined by the national authorities in so far as national merger rules exist.

2.2.2. Substantive law relating to concentrations

15. In relation to substance, the tests under Article 66(2) ECSC Treaty[24] and under Article 2 EC Merger Regulation[25] though not expressed in the same language, are similar.

2.2.3. Procedural law relating to concentrations

16. The procedures for the treatment of concentrations have been aligned to a large extent since March 1998 when the Commission started to apply the provisions of its Notice concerning alignment of procedures for processing mergers under the ECSC and EC Treaties[26].

17. However, the timing of notifications under the ECSC regime and the EC regime is different. The ECSC rules allow notification at any time, while the proposed concentration cannot, however, be legally completed without the prior authorisation of the Commission. The EC Merger Regulation requires parties to notify within one week of the 'triggering event', ie, the moment when the operation becomes irrevocable. The Commission must then adopt its decision(s) within the time limits prescribed by the EC Merger Regulation, otherwise the proposed operation is automatically authorised.

2.3. CONTROL OF STATE AID TO THE STEEL INDUSTRY

2.3.1. SUBSTANTIVE RULES RELATING TO STEEL AID

18. As for the notion of State aid, Article 4(c) ECSC Treaty does not require the affectation of trade between Member States for a measure to be considered State aid, contrary to Article 87 EC Treaty. In practice, this difference will be, however, of very limited importance given the intense trade between Member States in steel products.

19. Under the EC rules, the criteria for assessment of compatibility of State aid with the common market will be in summary the following:

— Regional investment aid will continue to be forbidden[27]. This prohibition also covers the granting of regional aid supplements to small and medium-sized enterprises (SMEs).

— Rescue and restructuring aid will continue to be forbidden[28].

— Under the ECSC rules, environment aid was permitted in accordance with the Community guidelines on State aid for environmental protection adopted in 1994[29] and with the annex to the Steel Aid Code[30]. From 24 July 2002, the Community guidelines on State aid for environmental protection adopted in 2000 will apply[31]. The most important difference of these guidelines in comparison with the guidelines applicable to the steel industry before the expiry of the ECSC Treaty is that aid granted for conforming with standards will no longer be allowed (except for aid to SMEs in limited conditions).

— Research and development aid will continue to be permitted in line with the Community framework for State aid for research and development[32].

— Aid in connection with closures will continue to be permitted[33].

— Aid for small and medium-sized enterprises at aid rates of up to 15% and 7,5% respectively will be permitted in line with Commission Regulation(EC) No 70/2001[34] (except for large individual aid grants as defined in Article 6 of that Regulation which will continue to be forbidden).

— *De-minimis* aid will be permitted in line with Commission Regulation (EC) No 69/2001[35].

— Training aid will be permitted in line with Commission Regulation (EC) No 68/2001[36].

— Employment aid will be permitted in line with the guidelines on aid to employment[37].

2.3.2. PROCEDURAL RULES RELATING TO STEEL AID

20. Council Regulation (EC) No 659/1999[38] will apply as from 24 July 2002. This will not entail major changes as compared with the provisions established in Article 6 of the Steel Aid Code[39].

21. As for notification requirements, unless otherwise established, aid granted to the steel industry under schemes authorised by the Commission will no longer be subject to the prior notification requirement established in the Steel Aid Code. The same applies to aid block-exempted by virtue of Commission Regulations (EC) No 70/2001[40] and (EC) No 68/2001[41].

2.4. CONTROL OF STATE AID TO THE COAL INDUSTRY

2.4.1. SUBSTANTIVE RULES RELATING TO STEEL AID

22. Until the expiry of the ECSC Treaty, State aid to the coal industry will be assessed on the basis of the rules as laid down in Decision 3632/93/ECSC[42].

23. On 25 July 2001, the Commission adopted a proposal for a Council Regulation on State aid for the coal industry after the expiry of the ECSC Treaty[43]. The proposal is based on Articles 87(3)(e) and 89 EC Treaty. It has to be adopted by the Council, after an opinion from the European Parliament[44]. It would apply from 24 July 2002. The draft Regulation stipulates that aid covering costs for the year 2002 will, on the basis of a reasoned request by the Member State, continue to be subject to the rules and principles laid down in Decision No 3632/93/ECSC.

2.4.2. PROCEDURAL RULES RELATING TO COAL AID

24. According to the proposal adopted by the Commission on 25 July 2001, in addition to the provisions of Article 88 EC Treaty and Council Regulation (EC) No 659/1999, State aid to the coal industry would be subject to special rules of notification, appraisal and authorisation as laid down in the State aid regime proposed by the Commission.

NOTES

7 See judgment of the European Court of Justice (ECJ) of 13.4.1994, Case C-128/92, *Banks*, [1994] ECR I-1209 at paragraphs 17 and 18.

8 Where national administrations are concerned, on condition that their national law allows them to apply Community law.

9 The proposed amendment of Council Regulation No 17 (COM(2000) 582 final of 27.9.2000), currently before the Council and the European Parliament, foresees to give the national competition authorities and the national courts the power to apply Articles 81 and 82 EC Treaty in full.

10 The details of the cooperation between the Commission and the competent national authorities are defined in the Notice on cooperation between the national courts and the Commission in applying Articles 85 and 86 of the EEC Treaty (OJ C39, 13.2.1993, p 6) and in the Commission notice on cooperation between national competition authorities and the Commission in handling cases falling within the scope of Articles 85 or 86 of the EC Treaty (OJ C313, 15.10.1997, p 3).

11 This does not of course prevent national law from applying in parallel with Community law where the condition of effect on trade is satisfied.

12 Commission notice on agreements of minor importance which do not appreciably restrict competition under Article 81(1) of the Treaty establishing the European Community (*de minimis*) (OJ C368, 22.12.2001, p 13).

13 Provided they do not contain any 'hard core' restrictions.

14 However, in the case of undertakings whose object was a joint buying or a joint selling agreement, a specialisation

agreement or agreements analogous to specialisation agreements, Article 65(2) ECSC Treaty was applicable.

15 Concept described in the Commission notice on the concept of full-function joint ventures under Regulation (EEC) No 4064/89 on the control of concentrations between undertakings (OJ C66, 2.3.1998).

16 The sole exception will be transactions which benefited from an exemption from the requirement of prior authorisation under Article 66 of the ECSC Treaty and which have become irrevocable before 24 July 2002; see paragraph 36 below.

17 This will involve a modification of the timetable (there being much fewer rules on the time limits for the examination of such agreements by the Commission than for 'merger'-type procedures, except in the specific case of cooperative joint ventures 'of a structural character' where an accelerated procedure is established by Commission Regulation (EC) No 3385/94 of 21 December 1994), and of the criterion of compatibility of the agreement.

18 Pursuant to Article 60(2) ECSC Treaty, Decision No 4-53 of 12.2.1953 (OJ of the High Authority of 12.2.1953, p 3) and, as regards coal only, Decision 72/443/ECSC of 22.12.1972 on alignment of prices for sales of coal in the common market (OJ L297, 30.12.1972, p 45). In practice, the implementation of this obligation had been gradually relaxed, but certain undertakings in the coal sector nonetheless continued to send this information to the Commission.

19 The removal of this requirement is without prejudice to the Commission's power to seek from the undertakings concerned all the information it requires to carry out the tasks assigned to it by the Treaty and Community law.

20 European Commission, Twentieth Report on Competition Policy (1990), paragraph 122.

21 Commission Regulation (EC) No 3385/94 of 21 December 1994.

22 The Commission had already asked the undertakings concerned to use a simplified form for their applications for authorisation (Twenty-first Report on Competition Policy (1991), paragraph 138).

23 Council Regulation (EEC) No 4064/89 as amended by Regulation (EC) No 1310/97.

24 Article 66(2) ECSC Treaty provides: 'The Commission shall grant the authorisation referred to in the preceding paragraph if it finds that the proposed transaction will not give to the persons or undertakings concerned the power, in respect of the product or products within its jurisdiction:

— to determine prices, to control or restrict production or distribution or to hinder effective competition in a substantial part of the market for those products, or

— to evade the rules of competition instituted under this Treaty, in particular by establishing an artificially privileged position involving a substantial advantage in access to supplies or markets'.

25 Article 2(2) EC Merger Regulation provides: 'A concentration which does not create or strengthen a dominant position as a result of which effective competition would be significantly impeded in the common market or in a substantial part of it shall be declared compatible with the common market'.

26 OJ C66, 2.3.1998, p 36.

27 Communication from the Commission, Multisectoral framework on regional aid for large investment projects (OJ C70, 19.3.2002, p 8).

28 Communication from the Commission, Rescue and restructuring aid and closure aid for the steel sector, (OJ C70, 19.3.2002, p 21).

29 OJ C72, 10.3.1994, p 3.

30 Commission Decision No 2496/96/ECSC of 18.12.1996 establishing Community rules for State aid to the steel industry (OJ L338, 28.12.1996, p 42).

31 OJ C37, 3.2.2001, p 3.

32 OJ C45, 17.2.1996, p 5.

33 Communication from the Commission, Rescue and restructuring aid and closure aid for the steel sector, OJ C70, 19.3.2002, p 21.

34 OJ L10, 13.1.2001, p 33.

35 OJ L10, 13.1.2001, p 30.

36 OJ L10, 13.1.2001, p 20.

37 OJ C334, 12.12.1995, p 4. New rules are under preparation.

38 Council Regulation (EC) No 659/1999 of 22.3.1999 laying down detailed rules for the application of Article 93 of the EC Treaty (OJ L83, 27.3.1999, p 1).

39 Commission Decision No 2496/96/ECSC of 18 December 1996 establishing Community rules for State aid to the steel industry (OJ L338, 28.12.1996, p 42).

40 OJ L10, 13.1.2001, p 33.

41 OJ L10, 13.1.2001, p 20.

42 Commission Decision No 3632/93/ECSC of 28 December 1993 establishing Community rules for State aid to the coal industry (OJ L329, 30.12.1993, p 12).

43 OJ C304, 30.10.2001, p 202.

44 The Council reached a political agreement on this proposal on 7 June 2002.

3. SPECIFIC ISSUES RAISED BY THE TRANSITION FROM THE ECSC REGIME TO THE EC REGIME

[5.447]

25. When assessing the impact of the expiry of the ECSC Treaty on cases which would so far have been covered by the ECSC rules, three situations have to be distinguished:

— First, cases, which have been completed in all factual and legal respects on or before 23 July 2002, will be subject to the ECSC rules only and are therefore unproblematic.

— Second, cases, in which all the relevant events occur after 23 July 2002, will be subject to the EC rules only and are therefore unproblematic, too.

— Third, cases, which from a factual or legal point of view started before the expiry of the ECSC Treaty and which in some way or other continue after the expiry, may raise issues specifically caused by the expiry of the ECSC Treaty. The remaining part of this Communication sets out how the Commission intends to deal with such cases.

26. With regard to procedural law, the basic principle for all three areas (antitrust, merger control, State aid control) is that the rules applicable are those in force at the time of taking the procedural step in question[45]. This means that as from 24 July 2002 on, the Commission will exclusively apply the EC procedural rules in all pending and new cases. Unless otherwise stated in this Communication, procedural steps validly taken under the ECSC rules before expiry of the ECSC Treaty will after the expiry be taken to have fulfilled the requirements of the equivalent procedural step under the EC rules.

3.1. ANTITRUST

3.1.1. THE POSITION WHICH RESTRICTIVE AGREEMENTS/CONCERTED PRACTICES EXEMPTED BY THE COMMISSION ON THE BASIS OF ARTICLE 65(2) ECSC TREATY BEFORE OR ON 23 JULY 2002 WILL HAVE AFTER 23 JULY 2002

27. From 24 July 2002, all the EC competition rules will apply to those agreements or practices which have previously been authorised or the subject of a comfort letter adopted under the ECSC rules. Authorisations granted under the ECSC regime will also cease to be valid upon expiry of the ECSC Treaty.

28. It will therefore be for the undertakings concerned to review the legality of their agreements or practices in the light of Articles 81 and 82 EC Treaty. The Commission draws attention to the many block exemptions and guidelines applicable in this area. In addition, in view of the similarity of Articles 65(2) ECSC Treaty and 81(3) EC Treaty and the convergence policy applied by the Commission when examining ECSC cases over the years, the Commission informs undertakings that it does not intend, after 23 July 2002, to initiate proceedings under Article 81 EC Treaty in respect of agreements previously authorised under the ECSC regime and that, under the circumstances, it does not intend to impose any financial penalty on undertakings which are party to such agreements. This presupposes that, where Commission approval was subject to conditions or obligations, these continue to be complied with by the parties concerned.

29. The Commission reserves the right, however, under the EC rules, to initiate proceedings in respect of the future implementation of the practices and agreements referred to in the preceding paragraph if, owing to substantial factual or legal developments, such practices and agreements are clearly not eligible for exemption under Article 81(3) EC Treaty. In that case, the Commission would respect the legitimate expectation of the undertakings concerned and would intervene only in the following cases: where there has been a change in any of the facts which were basic to the making of the authorising decision; where the parties commit a breach of any condition or obligation attached to the decision; where the decision is based on incorrect information or was induced by deceit; where the parties abuse the authorisation pursuant to Article 65(2) of the ECSC Treaty granted to them by the decision.

3.1.2. NOTIFICATION CASES IN WHICH THE COMMISSION STARTED ITS PROCEDURE BEFORE EXPIRY OF THE ECSC TREATY AND IN WHICH THIS PROCEDURE IS STILL PENDING AFTER 23 JULY 2002

30. As regards notifications made under the ECSC regime that are still being examined at the time of the transition, the Commission will apply Article 65(2) of the ECSC Treaty as regards the period before the date of expiry of that Treaty and Article 81(3) of the EC Treaty as regards the period thereafter. In any event, as regards procedure, the law applicable after the expiry of the ECSC Treaty will be the EC law.

3.1.3. APPLICATION OF ARTICLES 65 ECSC TREATY AND 81 EC TREATY TO OTHER TYPES OF AGREEMENTS

31. If the Commission, when applying the Community competition rules to agreements, identifies an infringement in a field covered by the ECSC Treaty, the substantive law applicable will be, irrespective of when such application takes place, the law in force at the time when the facts constituting the infringement occurred. In any event, as regards procedure, the law applicable after the expiry of the ECSC Treaty will be the EC law[46]

3.2. MERGER CONTROL

3.2.1. CLEARANCE DECISIONS WITH CONDITIONS/OBLIGATIONS ADOPTED BY THE COMMISSION UNDER THE ECSC TREATY BEFORE EXPIRY OF THAT TREATY, COMPLIANCE WITH THESE CONDITIONS/OBLIGATIONS TO BE MONITORED AFTER 23 JULY 2002

32. Where a concentration has been cleared under the ECSC Treaty subject to conditions and/or obligations, which continue after 23 July 2002, and these conditions and/or obligations are not satisfactorily fulfilled after 23 July 2002, the Commission will take action under the appropriate provisions of the EC Merger Regulation[47].

33. Similarly, if it proves necessary to modify after 23 July 2002 conditions and/or obligations based on commitments given by undertakings in order to secure the authorisation of their concentrations prior to the expiry of the ECSC Treaty, the Commission will take action as if the original authorisation decision had been adopted under the EC Merger Regulation.

3.2.2. CONCENTRATIONS NOTIFIED UNDER THE ECSC TREATY AND PENDING AT THE EXPIRY OF THIS TREATY

34. Three principal possibilities arise in relation to concentrations notified under the ECSC Treaty and pending at the expiry of this Treaty:

— Where the notified ECSC case does not meet the thresholds of the EC Merger Regulation, there is no longer a case with the Commission. In this situation, the parties must as of 24 July 2002 notify the case to the competent national authorities, where appropriate.

— If the notified ECSC case meets the thresholds of the EC Merger Regulation, its instruction by the Commission will continue under the EC Merger Regulation and it will be treated as though it had been originally notified under that Regulation, if the triggering event in the sense of that Regulation took place on or before 23 July 2002. If the triggering event occurs afterwards, the operation should be renotified.

— In cases where a triggering event has occurred and a case which meets the thresholds under the EC Merger Regulation has entered the informal second phase (initiated by means of a letter setting out the Commission's concerns) at the expiry of the ECSC Treaty, but where a statement of objections has not yet been adopted, the Commission will adopt a decision under Article 6(1)(c) EC Merger Regulation as soon as is practicably possible after the expiry of the ECSC Treaty. The Commission will endeavour in such cases to adhere to the timetable set out in the EC Merger Regulation to the greatest extent possible, counting from the date of notification. In particular, it will endeavour to ensure that the statement of objections is sent out at the appropriate time and that the overall five-month deadline for the adoption of a final decision is respected.

3.2.3. Form of notification

35. The approach to pending notified ECSC transactions outlined above only applies to ECSC notifications made using Form CO and which are complete. Furthermore, it is clear from the EC Merger Regulation itself that its time periods only start to run once the Commission is in possession of a complete notification, in the form provided for[48].

3.2.4. Operations exempted from the requirement of prior authorisation under Article 66 ECSC Treaty

36. Decision No 25/67/ECSC[49] exempts certain operations from the requirement of prior authorisation under Article 66 ECSC Treaty. However neither the ECSC Treaty nor Decision No 25/67/ECSC set out when the exemption takes effect. There is no equivalent under the ECSC rules of the 'triggering event' under the EC Merger Regulation[50]. When an operation, which is exempted by Decision No 25/67/ECSC, has reached an irrevocable stage (for instance if the sale and purchase agreements have been finalised and signed) on or before 23 July 2002, then this operation remains exempted from the requirement of prior authorisation under the EC Merger Regulation. On the other hand, if the operation has not reached an irrevocable stage before 24 July 2002, the operation must be notified if necessary to the Commission under the EC Merger Regulation upon the occurrence of the triggering event.

3.2.5. Non-exempted ECSC transaction that has not been notified before expiry of the ECSC Treaty

37. Where a transaction which is not exempted from the requirement of prior authorisation under Article 66 ECSC Treaty has not been notified before expiry of that Treaty, the parties must notify the transaction under the EC Merger Regulation if the conditions for such notification are satisfied. Where the transaction is not notified in such circumstances, fines may be imposed for non-notification in accordance with Article 14(1)(a) of the EC Merger Regulation as of 31 July 2002 (ie, one week after the EC Merger Regulation applied).

3.2.6. Non-exempted ECSC transaction that has been implemented and not been notified before expiry of the ECSC Treaty

38. Where a transaction, which in the sense of the preceding point 3.2.5. is not exempted from the requirement of prior authorisation under Article 66 ECSC Treaty and has not been notified, has in addition been implemented before the expiry of the ECSC Treaty, fines may be imposed for non-authorised implementation of the concentration in accordance with Article 14(2)(b) of the EC Merger Regulation as of 24 July 2002, provided the transaction comes within the scope of that Regulation[51].

3.2.7. Joint ventures

39. The practice under the ECSC Treaty has been to treat most joint ventures (with the exception of joint buying, joint selling and specialisation agreements and agreements strictly analogous to them) as concentrations under the provisions of Article 66. Therefore, certain operations which are subject to the requirement of prior authorisation under Article 66 ECSC Treaty may not be notifiable under the EC Merger Regulation, for example if they are not full function[52]. If notifications of such joint ventures which would not be notifiable under the EC Merger Regulation are pending at the time of the expiry of the ECSC Treaty, the notifications could, in appropriate cases be converted under the provisions of Article 5 of the Implementing Regulation[53] into notifications under Regulation No 17.

40. The expiry of the ECSC Treaty will have no effect on joint ventures (full function or otherwise) authorised under Article 66(2) ECSC Treaty on or before 23 July 2002 or benefiting from an exemption within the meaning of paragraph 36 above.

41. After the expiry of the ECSC Treaty, Article 2(4) of the EC Merger Regulation will be applied to concentrations in the coal and steel sectors which fall within the scope of that Regulation. This Article, which has no equivalent in the ECSC rules, provides that where the creation of a full function joint venture constituting a concentration in the sense of that Regulation has as its object or effect the co-ordination of the competitive behaviour of undertakings that remain independent, such co-ordination shall be appraised in accordance with the criteria of Article 81 EC Treaty[54].

3.3. CONTROL OF STATE AID TO THE STEEL INDUSTRY

42. With regard to State aid authorised by the Commission under the Steel Aid Code[55] or Article 95 ECSC Treaty subject to conditions, the Commission will after 23 July 2002 continue to monitor their fulfilment. In case of non-compliance, Article 88 EC Treaty will be applicable.

43. Where the aid was notified before or on 31 December 2001[56] and the Commission has initiated the procedure of Article 6(5) of the Steel Aid Code, it will endeavour to adopt a decision at the latest on 23 July 2002 on the basis of the information available to it. However, if for objective reasons, this is not possible, the Commission will continue the investigation under the provisions of Regulation (EC) No 659/1999 and adopt a final decision under Article 88(2) EC Treaty.

44. When taking decisions after 23 July 2002 in respect of State aid put into effect on or before that date without prior Commission approval, the Commission will proceed in accordance with the Commission notice on the determination of the applicable rules for the assessment of unlawful State aid[57]. According to this notice, the Commission shall always assess the compatibility of unlawful State aid with the common market in accordance with the substantive criteria set out in any instrument in force at the time when the aid was granted.

3.4. CONTROL OF STATE AID TO THE COAL INDUSTRY

45. After the expiry of the ECSC Treaty, the Commission will continue to monitor the application by the Member States of the decisions authorising State aid adopted under Decision No 3632/93/ECSC[58]. In case of non-compliance, the case will be investigated following the procedures as laid down in Regulation (EC) No 659/1999.

46. It is expected that the majority of State aid which covers costs prior to 23 July 2002 will be the subject of Commission decisions before the expiry of the ECSC Treaty. However, there may be cases where the Commission is not in a position to adopt a decision before the expiry of the ECSC Treaty. These possible cases, and the Commission's proposed course of action in respect of them, are as follows.

— In accordance with Article 9(4) of Decision No 3632/93/ECSC, the Commission has to decide on the measures notified by a Member State within three months of receipt of notification. It may consequently happen that aid notified less than three months before the expiry of the ECSC Treaty (ie, notification after 23 April 2002) is not the subject of a Commission decision before the expiry of this Treaty. This could also be the case of a notification made earlier, if the Commission considered that the notification was insufficient and requested further information from the Member State or, having doubts about the compatibility of the aid, decided to initiate the procedure provided for under Article 88 ECSC Treaty.

— If there has been no Commission decision when three months from notification have passed, the expiry of the ECSC Treaty means that the Member State does not have the right to implement the notified measure at the end of the three-month period referred to above, as it would have had were Article 9(4) Decision No 3632/93/ECSC still in force. Indeed, any notification presented by the Member State before the expiry of the ECSC Treaty, which has not been the subject of a formal Commission decision, will have to be considered obsolete (ie, non-existent from a legal point of view) after 23 July 2002.

— The Member State would have to proceed with a new notification under the provisions of the EC Treaty and of the possible new Council Regulation[59] which, once adopted, would be applicable as from 24 July 2002. Alternatively, and more simply, the Member State could inform the Commission that the initial notification can be regarded as a newly submitted notification. The period in which the Commission will have to decide would start to run as of the date of this (new) notification. If such a case arose, the Commission would make the utmost efforts to ensure that a decision on the measure is adopted as soon as possible.

— The draft Council Regulation[60], currently under discussion[61] and intended to be applicable after the expiry of the ECSC Treaty, stipulates that Member States will be able to opt, for aid covering costs for 2002, for the application of the rules and of the principles laid down in Decision No 3632/93/ECSC.

47. When taking decisions after 23 July 2002 in respect of State aid put into effect on or before that date without prior Commission approval, the Commission will proceed in accordance with the specific provisions in the Council Regulation currently under discussion[62]. When assessing aid, which does not fall under that Regulation and which has been granted on or before that date without prior Commission approval, the Commission will proceed in accordance with the Commission notice on the determination of the applicable rules for the assessment of unlawful State aid[63]. According to this notice, the Commission shall always assess the compatibility of unlawful State aid with the common market in accordance with the substantive criteria set out in any instrument in force at the time when the aid was granted.

NOTES

45 Judgment of the ECJ of 6.7.1993 in Joined Cases C-121/91 and C-122/91, *CT Control v Commission*, [1993] ECR I-3873 at paragraph 22; Judgment of the ECJ of 12.11.1981 in Joined Cases 212 to 217/80, *Amminstrazione delle finanze dello Stato v Salumi*, [1981] ECR 2735 at paragraph 9.

46 Including the Commission notice on immunity from fines and reduction of fines in cartel cases (OJ C45, 19.2.2002, p 3).

47 Articles 6(3) and 8(5) of the EC Merger Regulation.

48 Article 10(1) EC Merger Regulation, Articles 3 and 4 of the Implementing Regulation (Commission Regulation (EC) No 447/98 of 1 March 1998 on the notifications, time limits and hearings provided for in Council Regulation (EEC) No 4064/89 on the control of concentrations between undertakings (OJ L61, 2.3.1998, p 1)).

49 Decision No 25-67 of 22 June 1967 laying down in implementation of Article 66(3) of the ECSC Treaty a regulation concerning exemption from prior authorisation (OJ 154, 14.7.1967, p 11). English special edition: Series-I 67, p 186.

50 The 'triggering event' within the meaning of the EC Merger Regulation is defined as the moment when the operation becomes irrevocable, see above paragraph 17.

51 As regards implementation without notification or prior authorisation of a non-exempted ECSC concentration, see also Article 66(6) of the ECSC Treaty.

52 Commission notice on the concept of full function joint ventures under Council Regulation (EEC) No 4064/89 on the control of concentrations between undertakings (OJ C66, 2.3.1998, p 1).

53 Commission Regulation (EC) No 447/98 of 1 March 1998 on the notifications, time limits and hearings provided for in Regulation (EEC) No 4064/89 on the control of concentrations between undertakings (OJ L61, 2.3.1998, p 1).

54 Where a concentration in the coal or steel sectors was implemented without authorisation before expiry of the ECSC Treaty and the undertakings involved actually engaged in anti-competitive practices inconsistent with Article 65 ECSC Treaty, the principles set out in point 3.1.3 will apply.

55 Commission Decision No 2496/96/ECSC of 18 December 1996 establishing Community rules for State aid to the steel industry (OJ L338, 28.12.1996, p 42).

56 Under Article 6(1) and (2) of the Steel Aid Code notifications of aid plans must be lodged with the Commission at the latest by 31 December 2001.

57 OJ C119, 22.5.2002, p 22.

58 Commission Decision No 3632/93/ECSC of 28 December 1993 establishing Community rules for State aid to the coal industry (OJ L329, 30.12.1993, p 12).

59 See paragraph 23 above.

60 See paragraph 23 above.

61 See footnote 44.

62 See paragraph 23 above.

63 OJ C119, 22.5.2002, p 22.

8. COAL

COUNCIL DECISION

(2010/787/EU)

of 10 December 2010

on State aid to facilitate the closure of uncompetitive coal mines

[5.448]

NOTES

Date of publication in OJ: OJ L336, 21.12.2010, p 24.

Repeal of this Decision in relation to the UK: this Decision is repealed, in relation to the UK, by the State Aid (Revocations and Amendments) (EU Exit) Regulations 2020, SI 2020/1470, reg 6, as from IP completion day (as defined in the European Union (Withdrawal Agreement) Act 2020, s 39) (for transitional provisions and savings in relation to claims before a court or tribunal relating to State aid infringement before IP completion day, see Sch 3 to those Regulations at **[7.89]**).

THE COUNCIL OF THE EUROPEAN UNION,

Having regard to the Treaty on the Functioning of the European Union, and in particular point (e) of Article 107(3) thereof,

Having regard to the proposal from the European Commission,

Having regard to the opinion of the European Parliament[1],

Whereas:

(1) Council Regulation (EC) No 1407/2002 of 23 July 2002 on State aid to the coal industry[2] *expires on 31 December 2010.*

(2) The small contribution of subsidised coal to the overall energy mix no longer justifies the maintenance of such subsidies for securing the supply of energy in the Union.

(3) The Union's policy of encouraging renewable energy sources and a sustainable and safe low-carbon economy does not justify the indefinite support for uncompetitive coal mines. The categories of aid permitted by Regulation (EC) No 1407/2002 should therefore not be continued indefinitely.

(4) However, in the absence of sector-specific State aid rules, only the general State aid rules apply to coal. In this context, uncompetitive coal mines, currently benefiting from aid under Regulation (EC) No 1407/2002, may no longer be eligible for aid and may be forced to close.

(5) Without prejudice to the general State aid rules, Member States should be able to take measures to alleviate the social and regional consequences of the closure of those mines, that is to say the orderly winding down of activities in the context of an irrevocable closure plan and/or the financing of exceptional costs, in particular inherited liabilities.

(6) This Decision marks the transition, for the coal sector, from the application of sector-specific rules to the application of general State aid rules which are applicable to all sectors.

(7) In order to minimise the distortion of competition in the internal market resulting from State aid to facilitate the closure of uncompetitive coal mines, such aid should be degressive and strictly limited to coal production units that are irrevocably planned for closure.

(8) In order to mitigate the environmental impact of the production of coal by coal production units to which closure aid is granted, the Member States should establish a plan of appropriate measures, for example in the field of energy efficiency, renewable energy or carbon capture and storage.

(9) Undertakings should be eligible for aid to cover costs which, in accordance with normal accounting practice, do not directly affect the cost of production. Such aid is intended to cover exceptional costs that arise from the closure of their coal production units. In order to avoid such aid from unduly benefiting undertakings that close only some of their production sites, the undertakings concerned should keep separate accounts for each of their coal production units.

(10) In accomplishing its task under this Decision, the Commission should ensure that normal conditions of competition are established, maintained and complied with. With regard, more especially, to the electricity market, aid to the coal industry should not be such as to affect electricity producers' choice of sources of primary energy supply. Consequently, the prices and quantities of coal should be freely agreed between the contracting parties in the light of prevailing conditions on the world market.

(11) The application of this Decision should not exclude that aid to the coal industry may be found compatible with the internal market on other grounds. In this context, other specific rules, in particular those concerning aid for research, development and innovation, aid for environmental protection and aid for training activities, continue to apply within the limits of the maximum aid intensities, unless they provide otherwise.

(12) The Commission should assess the measures notified on the basis of this Decision and take decisions in accordance with Council Regulation (EC) No 659/1999 of 22 March 1999 laying down detailed rules for the application of Article 93 of the EC Treaty[3].

(13) To avoid any discontinuity between measures envisaged in Regulation (EC) No 1407/2002 and the measures foreseen in this Decision, this Decision should apply from 1 January 2011,

NOTES

Repeal of this Decision in relation to the UK: this Decision is repealed in relation to the UK (as from IP completion day); see the introductory notes to this Decision *ante*.

[1] Opinion of 23 November 2010 (not yet published in the Official Journal).

2 OJ L205, 2.8.2002, p 1.
3 OJ L83, 27.3.1999, p 1.

HAS ADOPTED THIS DECISION:

CHAPTER 1 INTRODUCTORY PROVISIONS

[5.449]
Article 1
Definitions

For the purposes of this Decision, the following definitions shall apply:

(a) *'coal' means high-grade, medium-grade and low-grade category A and B coal within the meaning of the international codification system for coal laid down by the United Nations Economic Commission for Europe*[1]*;*
(b) *'closure' means the permanent cessation of production and sale of coal;*
(c) *'closure plan' means a plan drawn up by a Member State providing for measures culminating in the definitive closure of coal production units;*
(d) *'coal production unit' means underground or opencast coal workings and related infrastructure capable of producing raw coal independently of other parts of the undertaking;*
(e) *'coal year' means calendar year or another 12-month period used as a reference for contracts in the coal industry;*
(f) *'production costs' means total costs related to current production, including mining operations, operations for the dressing of coal, in particular washing, sizing and sorting, and transport to the utilization point, normal depreciation and market-based interest charges on borrowed capital;*
(g) *'current production losses' means the positive difference between the coal production cost and the selling price at utilisation point freely agreed between the contracting parties in the light of the conditions prevailing on the world market.*

NOTES

Repeal of this Decision in relation to the UK: this Decision is repealed in relation to the UK (as from IP completion day); see the introductory notes to this Decision *ante*.

1 International system for the codification of medium-grade and high-grade coal (1998), International classification of coal in seam (1998) and International system of codification for low-grade coal (1999).

CHAPTER 2 COMPATIBILITY OF AID

[5.450]
Article 2
Principle

1. In the context of closure of uncompetitive mines, aid to the coal industry may be considered compatible with the proper functioning of the internal market if it complies with the provisions of this Decision.
2. Aid shall cover only costs in connection with coal for the production of electricity, the combined production of heat and electricity, the production of coke and the fuelling of blast furnaces in the steel industry, where such use takes place in the Union.

NOTES

Repeal of this Decision in relation to the UK: this Decision is repealed in relation to the UK (as from IP completion day); see the introductory notes to this Decision *ante*.

[5.451]
Article 3
Closure aid

1. Aid to an undertaking intended specifically to cover the current production losses of coal production units may be considered compatible with the internal market only if it satisfies the following conditions:

(a) *the operation of the coal production units concerned must form part of a closure plan the deadline of which does not extend beyond 31 December 2018;*
(b) *the coal production units concerned must be closed definitively in accordance with the closure plan;*
(c) *the aid notified must not exceed the difference between the foreseeable production costs and the foreseeable revenue for a coal year. The aid actually paid must be subject to annual correction, based on the actual costs and revenue, at the latest by the end of the coal production year following the year for which the aid was granted;*
(d) *the amount of aid per tonne coal equivalent must not cause prices for Union coal at utilisation point to be lower than those for coal of a similar quality from third countries;*
(e) *the coal production units concerned must have been in activity on 31 December 2009;*
(f) *the overall amount of closure aid granted by a Member State must follow a downward trend: by the end of 2013 the reduction must not be less than 25%, by the end of 2015 not less than 40%, by the end of 2016 not less than 60% and by the end of 2017 not less than 75% of the aid granted in 2011;*
(g) *the overall amount of closure aid to the coal industry of a Member State must not exceed, for any year after 2010, the amount of aid granted by that Member State and authorised by the Commission in accordance with Articles 4 and 5 of Regulation (EC) No 1407/2002 for the year 2010;*
(h) *the Member States must establish a plan to take measures aimed at mitigating the environmental impact of the production of coal by production units to which aid is granted pursuant to this Article, for example in the field of energy efficiency, renewable energy or carbon capture and storage.*

2. The inclusion of measures constituting State aid within the meaning of Article 107(1) of the Treaty in a plan as referred to in point (h) of paragraph 1 shall be without prejudice to the notification and standstill obligations imposed on Member States with respect to such measures by Article 108(3) of the Treaty, and to the compatibility of such measures with the internal market.

3. If the coal production units to which aid is granted pursuant to paragraph 1 are not closed at the date fixed in the closure plan as authorised by the Commission, the Member State concerned shall recover all aid granted in respect of the whole period covered by the closure plan.

NOTES

Repeal of this Decision in relation to the UK: this Decision is repealed in relation to the UK (as from IP completion day); see the introductory notes to this Decision *ante*.

[5.452]

Article 4

Aid to cover exceptional costs

1. State aid granted to undertakings which carry out or have carried out an activity in connection with coal production to enable them to cover the costs arising from or having arisen from the closure of coal production units and which are not related to current production, may be considered compatible with the internal market provided that the amount paid does not exceed such costs. Such aid may be used to cover:

(a) the costs incurred and cost provisions made only by undertakings which are closing or have closed coal production units, including undertakings benefiting from closure aid;

(b) the costs incurred by several undertakings.

2. The categories of costs covered by paragraph 1 are defined in the Annex. Paragraph 1 shall not apply to costs resulting from non-compliance with environmental regulations.

NOTES

Repeal of this Decision in relation to the UK: this Decision is repealed in relation to the UK (as from IP completion day); see the introductory notes to this Decision *ante*.

[5.453]

Article 5

Cumulation

1. The maximum amount of aid authorised under this Decision shall apply regardless of whether the aid is financed entirely by Member States or is partly financed by the Union.

2. Aid authorised under this Decision shall not be combined with other State aid within the meaning of Article 107(1) of the Treaty or with other forms of Union financing for the same eligible costs if such overlapping results in an aid amount higher than that authorised under this Decision.

NOTES

Repeal of this Decision in relation to the UK: this Decision is repealed in relation to the UK (as from IP completion day); see the introductory notes to this Decision *ante*.

[5.454]

Article 6

Separation of accounts

All aid received by undertakings shall be shown in the profit-and-loss accounts as a separate item of revenue distinct from turnover. Where undertakings benefiting from aid under this Decision continue trading or operating after closing down some or all of their coal production units they shall keep precise and separate accounts for each of their coal production units and for other economic activities which are not related to coal mining. The aid granted under this Decision shall be managed in such a way that there is no possibility of it being transferred to other coal production units which are not part of the closure plan or to other economic activities of the same undertaking.

NOTES

Repeal of this Decision in relation to the UK: this Decision is repealed in relation to the UK (as from IP completion day); see the introductory notes to this Decision *ante*.

CHAPTER 3 PROCEDURES

[5.455]

Article 7

Information to be provided by Member States

1. In addition to Regulation (EC) No 659/1999, aid as referred to in this Decision shall be subject to the special rules laid down in paragraphs 2 to 6.

2. Member States which intend to grant closure aid as referred to in Article 3 shall notify a closure plan for the coal production units concerned to the Commission. The plan shall contain at least the following:

(a) identification of the coal production units;

(b) the real or estimated production costs for each coal production unit per coal year;

(c) estimated coal production, per coal year, of coal production units forming the subject of a closure plan;

(d) the estimated amount of closure aid per coal year.

3. Member States shall notify any amendments to the closure plan to the Commission.

4. Member States shall notify all the aid which they intend to grant to the coal industry under this Decision during a coal year. They shall submit to the Commission all details relevant to the calculation of the foreseeable production costs and their relationship to the closure plans notified to the Commission pursuant to paragraph 2.

5. Member States shall inform the Commission of the amount, and of the calculation of the aid actually paid during a coal year, no later than six months after the end of the year in question. Where any corrections are made to the amounts originally paid during a given coal year, Member States shall inform the Commission before the end of the following coal year.

6. When notifying aid as referred to in Articles 3 and 4 and when informing the Commission on aid actually paid, Member States shall supply all the information necessary for the Commission to verify that the provisions of this Decision are complied with.

NOTES

Repeal of this Decision in relation to the UK: this Decision is repealed in relation to the UK (as from IP completion day); see the introductory notes to this Decision *ante*.

CHAPTER 4 FINAL PROVISIONS

[5.456]

Article 8

Implementing measures

The Commission shall take all necessary measures for the implementation of this Decision. It may, within the limits laid down by this Decision, establish a joint framework for communication of the information referred to in Article 7.

NOTES

Repeal of this Decision in relation to the UK: this Decision is repealed in relation to the UK (as from IP completion day); see the introductory notes to this Decision *ante*.

[5.457]

Article 9

Entry into force

This Decision shall enter into force on the day following that of its publication in the Official Journal of the European Union.

It shall apply from 1 January 2011.

It shall expire on 31 December 2027.

NOTES

Repeal of this Decision in relation to the UK: this Decision is repealed in relation to the UK (as from IP completion day); see the introductory notes to this Decision *ante*.

ANNEX
DEFINITION OF COSTS REFERRED TO IN ARTICLE 4

[5.458]

1. Costs incurred and cost provisions made only by undertakings which have closed or are closing coal production units

The following cost categories exclusively, and only if they result from the closure of coal production units:

- *(a) the cost of paying social welfare benefits resulting from the pensioning-off of workers before they reach statutory retirement age;*
- *(b) other exceptional expenditure on workers who have lost or who lose their jobs;*
- *(c) the payment of pensions and allowances outside the statutory system to workers who have lost or who lose their jobs and to workers entitled to such payments before the closure;*
- *(d) the cost covered by the undertakings for the readaptation of workers in order to help them find new jobs outside the coal industry, especially training costs;*
- *(e) the supply of free coal to workers who have lost or who lose their jobs and to workers entitled to such supply before the closure, or the monetary equivalent;*
- *(f) residual costs resulting from administrative, legal or tax provisions which are specific to the coal industry;*
- *(g) additional underground safety work resulting from the closure of coal production units;*
- *(h) mining damage, provided that it has been caused by the coal production units which have been closed or which are being closed;*
- *(i) all duly justified costs related to the rehabilitation of former coal mining sites, including:*
  - *— residual costs resulting from contributions to bodies responsible for water supplies and for the removal of waste water,*
  - *— other residual costs resulting from water supplies and the removal of waste water;*
- *(j) residual costs to cover former miners' health insurance;*
- *(k) costs related to the cancelling or modification of ongoing contracts (for a maximum value of 6 months of production);*
- *(l) exceptional intrinsic depreciation provided that it results from the closure of coal production units;*
- *(m) costs of surface recultivation.*

The increase in the value of the land shall be deducted from the eligible costs for the cost categories referred to in points (g), (h), (i) and (m).

2. Costs incurred and cost provisions made by several undertakings

The following cost categories exclusively:

- *(a) increase in contributions, outside the statutory system, to cover social security costs as a result of the drop, following closure of coal production units, in the number of contributors;*
- *(b) expenditure, resulting from the closure of coal production units, on the supply of water and the removal of waste water;*

(c) *increase in contributions to bodies responsible for supplying water and removing waste water, provided that this increase is the result of a reduction, following the closure of coal production units, in the coal production subject to levy.*

NOTES

Repeal of this Decision in relation to the UK: this Decision is repealed in relation to the UK (as from IP completion day); see the introductory notes to this Decision *ante*.

9. AGRICULTURE

COMMISSION REGULATION

(1408/2013/EU)

of 18 December 2013

on the application of Articles 107 and 108 of the Treaty on the Functioning of the European Union to *de minimis* aid in the agriculture sector

[5.459]

NOTES

Date of publication in OJ: OJ L352, 24.12.2013, p 9.

Repeal of this Regulation in relation to the UK: this Regulation is repealed, in relation to the UK, by the State Aid (Revocations and Amendments) (EU Exit) Regulations 2020, SI 2020/1470, reg 5, as from IP completion day (as defined in the European Union (Withdrawal Agreement) Act 2020, s 39) (for transitional provisions and savings in relation to claims before a court or tribunal relating to State aid infringement before IP completion day, see Sch 3 to those Regulations at **[7.89]**).

THE EUROPEAN COMMISSION,

Having regard to the Treaty on the Functioning of the European Union, and in particular Article 108(4) thereof,

Having regard to Council Regulation (EC) No 994/98 of 7 May 1998 on the application of Articles 107 and 108 of the Treaty on the Functioning of the European Union to certain categories of horizontal State aid.[1]

Having published a draft of this Regulation.[2]

After consulting the Advisory Committee on State Aid,

Whereas:

(1) State funding meeting the criteria in Article 107(1) of the Treaty constitutes State aid and requires notification to the Commission by virtue of Article 108(3) of the Treaty. However, under Article 109 of the Treaty, the Council may determine categories of aid that are exempted from this notification requirement. In accordance with Article 108(4) of the Treaty, the Commission may adopt regulations relating to those categories of State aid. By virtue of Regulation (EC) No 994/98 the Council decided, in accordance with Article 109 of the Treaty, that de minimis aid could constitute one such category. On that basis, de minimis aid, being aid granted to a single undertaking over a given period of time that does not exceed a certain fixed amount, is deemed not to meet all the criteria laid down in Article 107(1) of the Treaty and is therefore not subject to the notification procedure.

(2) The Commission has, in numerous decisions, clarified the notion of aid within the meaning of Article 107(1) of the Treaty. The Commission has also stated its policy with regard to a de minimis ceiling below which Article 107(1) of the Treaty can be considered not to apply, initially in its notice on the de minimis rule for State aid[3] *and subsequently in Commission Regulations (EC) No 69/2001*[4] *and (EC) No 1998/2006.*[5] *In view of the special rules which apply in the agriculture sector and of the risk that even low levels of aid could fulfil the criteria laid down in Article 107(1) of the Treaty, the agriculture sector or parts of it were excluded from the scope of those Regulations. The Commission has already adopted a number of Regulations providing rules on de minimis aid granted in the agriculture sector, the latest of which was Regulation (EC) No 1535/2007.*[6] *In the light of the experience gained in applying Regulation (EC) No 1535/2007, it is appropriate to revise some of the conditions laid down in that Regulation and to replace it.*

(3) In the light of the Commission's experience in applying Regulation (EC) No 1535/2007, the maximum amount of aid to a single undertaking over a period of 3 years should be increased to EUR 15,000 and the national cap increased to 1% of annual output. Those new ceilings still ensure that any measure falling under this Regulation can be deemed not to have any effect on trade between Member States and not to distort or threaten to distort competition.

(4) For the purposes of the rules on competition laid down in the Treaty an undertaking is any entity engaged in an economic activity, regardless of its legal status and the way in which it is financed.[7] *The Court of Justice of the European Union has ruled that all entities which are controlled (on a legal or on a de facto basis) by the same entity should be considered as a single undertaking.*[8] *For the sake of legal certainty and to reduce the administrative burden, this Regulation should provide an exhaustive list of clear criteria for determining when two or more enterprises within the same Member State are to be considered as a single undertaking. The Commission has selected from the well-established criteria for defining 'linked enterprises' in the definition of small or medium-sized enterprises (SMEs) in Commission Recommendation 2003/361/EC*[9] *and in Annex I to Commission Regulation (EC) No 800/2008*[10] *those criteria that are appropriate for the purposes of this Regulation. The criteria are already familiar to public authorities and should be applicable, given the scope of this Regulation, to both SMEs and large undertakings. Those criteria should ensure that a group of linked enterprises is considered as one single undertaking for the application of the de minimis rule, but that enterprises which have no relationship with each other except for the fact that each of them has a direct link to the same public body or bodies are not treated as being linked to each other. The specific situation of enterprises controlled by the same public body or bodies, which may have an independent power of decision, is therefore taken into account. Similarly, those criteria should ensure that individual members of a legal person or group of natural or legal persons are not, for that reason alone, treated as being linked where national law provides for such individual members to assume rights and obligations comparable to those of individual farmers who have the status of head of holding, in particular as regards their economic, social and tax status and where those individual members have contributed to strengthening the agricultural structures of the legal persons or groups concerned.*

(5) Considering the similarities between the processing and marketing of agricultural products and of non-agricultural products, processing and marketing of agricultural products are included in the scope of Commission Regulation (EU) No 1407/2013.[11]

(6) The Court of Justice of the European Union has established that, once the Union has legislated for the

establishment of a common organisation of the market in a given sector of agriculture, Member States are under an obligation to refrain from taking any measure which might undermine or create exceptions to it.[12] *For that reason, this Regulation should not apply to aid the amount of which is fixed on the basis of the price or quantity of products purchased or put on the market. Nor should it apply to support which is linked to an obligation to share the aid with primary producers.*

(7) This Regulation should not apply to export aid or aid contingent upon the use of domestic over imported products. In particular, it should not apply to aid financing the establishment and operation of a distribution network in other Member States or in third countries. Aid towards the costs of participating in trade fairs, or of studies or consultancy services needed for the launch of a new or existing product on a new market in another Member State or a third country does not normally constitute export aid.

(8) The period of 3 years to be taken into account for the purposes of this Regulation should be assessed on a rolling basis so that, for each new grant of de minimis aid, the total amount of de minimis aid granted in the fiscal year concerned and during the previous 2 fiscal years needs to be taken into account.

(9) Where an undertaking is active in the primary production of agricultural products and is also active in other sectors or has other activities falling within the scope of Regulation (EU) No 1407/2013, the provisions of that Regulation should apply to aid granted in respect of those other sectors or activities, provided that the Member State concerned ensures, by appropriate means such as separation of activities or distinction of costs, that the primary production of agricultural products does not benefit from de minimis aid granted in accordance with that Regulation.

(10) Where an undertaking is active in the primary production of agricultural products as well as in the fishery and aquaculture sector, Commission Regulation (EC) No 875/2007[13] *should apply to aid granted in respect of the latter sector, provided that the Member State concerned ensures, by appropriate means such as separation of activities or distinction of costs, that the primary production of agricultural products does not benefit from de minimis aid granted in accordance with that Regulation.*

(11) This Regulation should lay down rules to ensure that it is not possible to circumvent maximum aid intensities laid down in specific regulations or Commission decisions. It should also provide for clear rules on cumulation that are easy to apply.

(12) This Regulation does not exclude the possibility that a measure might be considered not to be State aid within the meaning of Article 107(1) of the Treaty on grounds other than those set out in this Regulation, for instance because the measure complies with the market economy operator principle or because the measure does not involve a transfer of State resources. In particular, Union funding centrally managed by the Commission which is not directly or indirectly under the control of the Member State, does not constitute State aid and should not be taken into account in determining whether the relevant ceiling or the national cap is respected.

(13) For the purposes of transparency, equal treatment and effective monitoring, this Regulation should apply only to de minimis aid for which it is possible to calculate precisely the gross grant equivalent ex ante without any need to undertake a risk assessment ('transparent aid'). Such a precise calculation can, for instance, be made for grants, interest rate subsidies, capped tax exemptions or other instruments that provide for a cap ensuring that the relevant ceiling is not exceeded. Providing for a cap means that as long as the precise amount of aid is not, or not yet, known, the Member State has to assume that the amount equals the cap in order to ensure that several aid measures together do not exceed the ceiling set out in this Regulation and to apply the rules on cumulation.

(14) For the purposes of transparency, equal treatment and the correct application of the de minimis ceiling, all Member States should apply the same method of calculation. In order to facilitate such calculation, aid amounts not taking the form of a cash grant should be converted into their gross grant equivalent. Calculation of the gross grant equivalent of transparent types of aid other than grants and of aid payable in several instalments requires the use of market interest rates prevailing at the time such aid is granted. With a view to uniform, transparent and simple application of the State aid rules, the market rates applicable for the purposes of this Regulation should be the reference rates, as set out in the Communication from the Commission on the revision of the method for setting the reference and discount rates.[14]

(15) Aid comprised in loans, including de minimis risk finance aid taking the form of loans, should be considered transparent de minimis aid if the gross grant equivalent has been calculated on the basis of market interest rates prevailing at the time the aid is granted. In order to simplify the treatment of small loans of short duration, this Regulation should provide for a clear rule that is easy to apply and takes into account both the amount of the loan and its duration. Based on the Commission's experience, loans that are secured by collateral covering at least 50% of the loan and that do not exceed either EUR 75,000 and a duration of 5 years or EUR 37 500 and a duration of 10 years can be considered as having a gross grant equivalent not exceeding the de minimis ceiling. Given the difficulties linked to determining the gross grant equivalent of aid granted to undertakings that may not be able to repay the loan, this rule should not apply to such undertakings.

(16) Aid comprised in capital injections should not be considered as transparent de minimis aid, unless the total amount of the public injection does not exceed the de minimis ceiling. Aid comprised in risk finance measures taking the form of equity or quasi-equity investments, as referred to in the risk finance guidelines.[15] *should not be considered as transparent de minimis aid unless the measure concerned provides capital not exceeding the de minimis ceiling.*

(17) Aid comprised in guarantees, including de minimis risk finance aid taking the form of guarantees, should be considered as transparent if the gross grant equivalent has been calculated on the basis of safe-harbour premiums laid down in a Commission notice for the type of undertaking concerned.[16] *In order to simplify the treatment of guarantees of short duration securing up to 80% of a relatively small loan, this Regulation should provide for a clear rule that is easy to apply and takes into account both the amount of the underlying loan and the duration of the guarantee. This rule should not apply to guarantees on underlying transactions not constituting a loan, such as guarantees on equity transactions. Where the guarantee does not exceed 80% of the underlying loan, the amount guaranteed does not exceed EUR 112 500 and the duration of the guarantee does not exceed 5 years the guarantee can be considered as having a gross grant equivalent not exceeding the de minimis ceiling. The same applies where the guarantee does not exceed 80% of the underlying loan, the amount guaranteed does not exceed EUR 56 250 and the duration of the guarantee*

does not exceed 10 years. In addition, Member States can use a methodology to calculate the gross grant equivalent of guarantees which has been notified to the Commission under another Commission Regulation in the State aid area applicable at that time and which has been accepted by the Commission as being in line with the Guarantee Notice, or any successor notice, provided that the accepted methodology explicitly addresses the type of guarantee and the type of underlying transaction at stake in the context of the application of this Regulation. Given the difficulties linked to determining the gross grant equivalent of aid granted to undertakings that may not be able to repay the loan, this rule should not apply to such undertakings.

(18) Where a de minimis aid scheme is implemented through financial intermediaries, it should be ensured that the latter do not receive any State aid. This can be done, for example by requiring financial intermediaries that benefit from a State guarantee to pay a market-conform premium or to fully pass on any advantage to the final beneficiaries, or by respecting the de minimis ceiling and other conditions of this Regulation also at the level of the intermediaries.

(19) Upon notification by a Member State, the Commission may examine whether a measure which does not consist of a grant, loan, guarantee, capital injection or risk finance measure taking the form of an equity or quasi-equity investment, leads to a gross grant equivalent that does not exceed the de minimis ceiling and could therefore fall within the scope of this Regulation.

(20) The Commission has a duty to ensure that State aid rules are complied with and in accordance with the cooperation principle laid down in Article 4(3) of the Treaty on European Union, Member States should facilitate the fulfilment of this task by establishing the necessary tools in order to ensure that the total amount of de minimis aid granted to a single undertaking under the de minimis rule does not exceed the overall permissible ceiling. To that end, when granting a de minimis aid, Member States should inform the undertaking concerned of the amount of de minimis aid granted and of its de minimis character and should make express reference to this Regulation. Member States should be required to monitor aid granted to ensure the relevant ceilings are not exceeded and the cumulation rules are complied with. To comply with that obligation, before granting such aid, the Member State concerned should obtain from the undertaking a declaration about other de minimis aid covered by this Regulation or by other de minimis regulations received during the fiscal year concerned and the previous 2 fiscal years. Alternatively it should be possible for Member States to set up a central register with complete information on de minimis aid granted and check that any new grant of aid does not exceed the relevant ceiling.

(21) Before granting any new de minimis aid each Member State should verify that neither the de minimis ceiling nor the national cap will be exceeded in that Member State by the new de minimis aid and that the other conditions of this Regulation are complied with.

(22) Having regard to the Commission's experience and in particular the frequency with which it is generally necessary to revise State aid policy, the period of application of this Regulation should be limited. If this Regulation expires without being extended, Member States should have an adjustment period of 6 months with regard to de minimis aid covered by this Regulation,

NOTES

Repeal of this Regulation in relation to the UK: this Regulation is repealed in relation to the UK (as from IP completion day); see the introductory notes to this Regulation *ante*.

1 OJ L142, 14.5.1998, p 1.

2 OJ C227, 6.8.2013, p 3.

3 Commission notice on the *de minimis* rule for State aid (OJ C68, 6.3.1996, p 9).

4 Commission Regulation (EC) No 69/2001 of 12 January 2001 on the application of Articles 87 and 88 of the EC Treaty to *de minimis* aid (OJ L10, 13.1.2001, p 30).

5 Commission Regulation (EC) No 1998/2006 of 15 December 2006 on the application of Articles 87 and 88 of the EC Treaty to *de minimis* aid (OJ L379, 28.12.2006, p 5).

6 Commission Regulation (EC) No 1535/2007 of 20 December 2007 on the application of Articles 87 and 88 of the Treaty to *de minimis* aid in the sector of agricultural production (OJ L337, 21.12.2007, p 35).

7 Case C-222/04 *Ministero dell'Economia e delle Finanze v Cassa di Risparmio di Firenze SpA et al.* [2006] ECR I-289.

8 Case C-382/99 *Netherlands v Commission* [2002] ECR I-5163.

9 Commission Recommendation 2003/361/EC of 6 May 2003 concerning the definition of micro, small and medium-sized enterprises (OJ L124, 20.5.2003, p 36).

10 Commission Regulation (EC) No 800/2008 of 6 August 2008 declaring certain categories of aid compatible with the common market in application of Articles 87 and 88 of the Treaty (OJ L214, 9.8.2008, p 3).

11 Commission Regulation (EU) No 1407/2013 of 18 December 2013, on the application of Articles 107 and 108 of the Treaty on the Functioning of the European Union to *de minimis* aid (see page 1 of this Official Journal).

12 Case C-456/00 *France v Commission* [2002] I-11949.

13 Commission Regulation (EC) No 875/2007 of 24 July 2007 on the application of Articles 87 and 88 of the EC Treaty to *de minimis* aid in the fisheries sector and amending Regulation (EC) No 1860/2004 (OJ L193, 25.7.2007, p 6).

14 Communication from the Commission on the revision of the method for setting the reference and discount rates (OJ C14, 19.1.2008, p 6).

15 Community guidelines on State aid to promote risk capital investments in small and medium-sized enterprises (OJ C194, 18.8.2006, p 2).

16 For instance, Commission Notice on the application of Articles 87 and 88 of the EC Treaty to State aid in the form of guarantees (OJ C155, 20.6.2008, p 10).

HAS ADOPTED THIS REGULATION:

[5.460]

Article 1 Scope

1. This Regulation applies to aid granted to undertakings active in the primary production of agricultural products, with the exception of:

(a) aid the amount of which is fixed on the basis of the price or quantity of products put on the market;

(b) *aid to export-related activities towards third countries or Member States, namely aid directly linked to the quantities exported, to the establishment and operation of a distribution network or to other current expenditure linked to the export activity;*

(c) *aid contingent upon the use of domestic over imported goods.*

2. Where an undertaking is active in the primary production of agricultural products and is also active in one or more of the sectors or has other activities falling within the scope of Regulation (EU) No 1407/2013, that Regulation shall apply to aid granted in respect of the latter sectors or activities, provided that the Member State concerned ensures, by appropriate means such as separation of activities or distinction of costs, that the primary production of agricultural products does not benefit from de minimis aid granted in accordance with that Regulation.

3. Where an undertaking is active in the primary production of agricultural products as well as in the fishery and aquaculture sector, the provisions of Regulation (EC) No 875/2007 shall apply to aid granted in respect of the latter sector, provided that the Member State concerned ensures, by appropriate means such as separation of activities or distinction of costs, that the primary production of agricultural products does not benefit from de minimis aid granted in accordance with that Regulation.

NOTES

Repeal of this Regulation in relation to the UK: this Regulation is repealed in relation to the UK (as from IP completion day); see the introductory notes to this Regulation *ante*.

[5.461]

Article 2 Definitions

1. For the purposes of this Regulation, 'agricultural products' means products listed in Annex I to the Treaty, with the exception of fishery and aquaculture products covered by Council Regulation (EC) No 104/2000.[1]

2. 'Single undertaking' includes, for the purposes of this Regulation, all enterprises having at least one of the following relationships with each other:

(a) *one enterprise has a majority of the shareholders' or members' voting rights in another enterprise;*

(b) *one enterprise has the right to appoint or remove a majority of the members of the administrative, management or supervisory body of another enterprise;*

(c) *one enterprise has the right to exercise a dominant influence over another enterprise pursuant to a contract entered into with that enterprise or to a provision in its memorandum or articles of association;*

(d) *one enterprise, which is a shareholder in or member of another enterprise, controls alone, pursuant to an agreement with other shareholders in or members of that enterprise, a majority of shareholders' or members' voting rights in that enterprise.*

Enterprises having any of the relationships referred to in points (a) to (d) of the first subparagraph through one or more other enterprises shall also be considered to be a single undertaking.

[3. For the purposes of this Regulation, "product sector" means a sector listed in Article 1(2)(a) to (w) of Regulation (EU) No 1308/2013 of the European Parliament and of the Council.[2]

4. For the purposes of this Regulation, "sector cap" means a maximum cumulative aid amount applying to aid measures which benefit only one single product sector, which corresponds to 50% of the maximum amount of de minimis aid granted per Member State set out in Annex II.]

NOTES

Paras 3, 4: added by Commission Regulation 2019/316/EU, Art 1(1).

Repeal of this Regulation in relation to the UK: this Regulation is repealed in relation to the UK (as from IP completion day); see the introductory notes to this Regulation *ante*.

[1] Council Regulation (EC) No 104/2000 of 17 December 1999 on the common organisation of the markets in fishery and aquaculture products (OJ L17, 21.1.2000, p 22).

[2] Regulation (EU) No 1308/2013 of the European Parliament and of the Council of 17 December 2013 establishing a common organisation of the markets in agricultural products and repealing Council Regulations (EEC) No 922/72, (EEC) No 234/79, (EC) No 1037/2001 and (EC) No 1234/2007 (OJ L347, 20.12.2013, p 671).

[5.462]

[Article 3 De minimis aid

1. Aid measures shall be deemed not to meet all the criteria in Article 107(1) of the Treaty, and shall therefore be exempt from the notification requirement in Article 108(3) of the Treaty, if they fulfil the conditions laid down in this Regulation.

2. The total amount of de minimis aid granted per Member State to a single undertaking shall not exceed EUR 20,000 over any period of 3 fiscal years.

3. The cumulative amount of de minimis aid granted per Member State to undertakings active in the primary production of agricultural products over any period of 3 fiscal years shall not exceed the national cap set out in Annex I.

3a. By way of derogation from paragraphs 2 and 3, a Member State may decide that the total amount of de minimis aid granted to a single undertaking shall not exceed EUR 25,000 over any period of 3 fiscal years and that the total cumulative amount of de minimis aid granted over any period of 3 fiscal years shall not exceed the national cap set out in Annex II, subject to the following conditions:

(a) *for aid measures which benefit only one single product sector, the total cumulative amount granted over any period of 3 fiscal years shall not exceed the sector cap defined in Article 2(4);*

(b) *the Member State shall have in place a national central register in accordance with Article 6(2).*

4. De minimis aid shall be deemed granted at the moment the legal right to receive the aid is conferred on the undertaking under the applicable national legal regime, irrespective of the date of payment of the de minimis aid to the undertaking.

5. The de minimis ceilings and the national and sector caps referred to in paragraphs 2, 3 and 3a shall apply irrespective of the form of the de minimis aid or the objective pursued and regardless of whether the aid granted by the Member State is financed entirely or partly by resources of Union origin. The period of 3 fiscal years shall be determined by reference to the fiscal years used by the undertaking in the Member State concerned.

6. For the purposes of the de minimis ceilings and the national and sector caps referred to in paragraphs 2, 3 and 3a, aid shall be expressed as a cash grant. All figures used shall be gross, that is, before any deduction of tax or other charge. Where aid is granted in a form other than a grant, the aid amount shall be the gross grant equivalent of the aid.

Aid payable in several instalments shall be discounted to its value at the moment it is granted. The interest rate to be used for discounting purposes shall be the discount rate applicable at the time the aid is granted.

7. Where the de minimis ceilings, the national caps or the sector cap referred to in paragraphs 2, 3 and 3a would be exceeded by the grant of new de minimis aid, none of that new aid may benefit from this Regulation.

8. In the case of mergers or acquisitions, all prior de minimis aid granted to any of the merging undertakings shall be taken into account in determining whether any new de minimis aid to the new or the acquiring undertaking exceeds the relevant de minimis ceilings, the relevant national cap or the sector cap. De minimis aid lawfully granted before the merger or acquisition shall remain lawful.

9. If one undertaking splits into two or more separate undertakings, de minimis aid granted prior to the split shall be allocated to the undertaking that benefited from it, which is in principle the undertaking taking over the activities for which the de minimis aid was used. If such an allocation is not possible, the de minimis aid shall be allocated proportionately on the basis of the book value of the equity capital of the new undertakings at the effective date of the split.]

NOTES

Substituted by Commission Regulation 2019/316/EU, Art 1(2).

Repeal of this Regulation in relation to the UK: this Regulation is repealed in relation to the UK (as from IP completion day); see the introductory notes to this Regulation *ante*.

[5.463]

Article 4 Calculation of gross grant equivalent

1. This Regulation shall apply only to aid in respect of which it is possible to calculate precisely the gross grant equivalent of the aid ex ante without any need to undertake a risk assessment ('transparent aid').

2. Aid comprised in grants or interest rate subsidies shall be considered as transparent de minimis aid.

3. Aid comprised in loans shall be considered as transparent de minimis aid if:

- *(a) the beneficiary is not subject to collective insolvency proceedings nor fulfils the criteria under its domestic law for being placed in collective insolvency proceedings at the request of its creditors. In case of large undertakings, the beneficiary shall be in a situation comparable to a credit rating of at least B-; and*
- *[(b) for measures falling under Article 3(2), the loan is secured by collateral covering at least 50% of the loan and the loan amounts to either EUR 100,000 over 5 years or EUR 50,000 over 10 years, or, for measures falling under Article 3(3a), to either EUR 125,000 over 5 years or EUR 62,500 over 10 years; if a loan is for less than those amounts and/or if it is granted for a period of less than 5 or 10 years respectively, the gross grant equivalent of that loan shall be calculated as a corresponding proportion of the de minimis ceilings laid down in Article 3(2) or (3a); or]*
- *(c) the gross grant equivalent has been calculated on the basis of the reference rate applicable at the time of the grant.*

[4. Aid comprised in capital injections shall only be considered as transparent de minimis aid if the total amount of the public injection does not exceed the relevant de minimis ceiling.]

[5. Aid comprised in risk finance measures taking the form of equity or quasi-equity investments shall only be considered as transparent de minimis aid if the capital provided to a single undertaking does not exceed the relevant de minimis ceiling.]

6. Aid comprised in guarantees shall be treated as transparent de minimis aid if:

- *(a) the beneficiary is not subject to collective insolvency proceedings nor fulfils the criteria under its domestic law for being placed in collective insolvency proceedings at the request of its creditors. In case of large undertakings, the beneficiary shall be in a situation comparable to a credit rating of at least B-; and*
- *[(b) for measures falling under Article 3(2), the guarantee does not exceed 80% of the underlying loan and either the amount guaranteed is EUR 150,000 and the duration of the guarantee is 5 years or the amount guaranteed is EUR 75,000 and the duration of the guarantee is 10 years, or, for measures falling under Article 3(3a), the guarantee does not exceed 80% of the underlying loan and either the amount guaranteed is EUR 187,500 and the duration of the guarantee is 5 years or the amount guaranteed is EUR 93,750 and the duration of the guarantee is 10 years; if the amount guaranteed is lower than these amounts and/or if the guarantee is for a period of less than 5 or 10 years respectively, the gross grant equivalent of that guarantee shall be calculated as a corresponding proportion of the de minimis ceilings laid down in Article 3(2) or (3a); or]*
- *(c) the gross grant equivalent has been calculated on the basis of safe-harbour premiums laid down in a Commission notice; or*
- *(d) before implementation,*
  - *(i) the methodology used to calculate the gross grant equivalent of the guarantee has been notified to the Commission under another Commission Regulation in the State aid area applicable at that time and accepted by the Commission as being in line with the Guarantee Notice, or any successor Notice; and*
  - *(ii) that methodology explicitly addresses the type of guarantee and the type of underlying transaction at stake in the context of the application of this Regulation.*

7. Aid comprised in other instruments shall be considered as transparent de minimis aid if the instrument provides for a cap ensuring that the relevant ceiling is not exceeded.

NOTES

All words in square brackets were substituted by Commission Regulation 2019/316/EU, Art 1(3).

Repeal of this Regulation in relation to the UK: this Regulation is repealed in relation to the UK (as from IP completion day); see the introductory notes to this Regulation *ante*.

[5.464]

Article 5 Cumulation

1. Where an undertaking is active in the primary production of agricultural products and is also active in one or more of the sectors or has other activities falling within the scope of Regulation (EU) No 1407/2013, de minimis aid granted for activities in the sector of agricultural production in accordance with this Regulation may be cumulated with de minimis aid granted in respect of the latter sector(s) or activities up to the relevant ceiling laid down in Article 3(2) of Regulation (EU) No 1407/2013, provided that the Member State concerned ensures, by appropriate means such as separation of activities or distinction of costs, that the primary production of agricultural products does not benefit from de minimis aid granted in accordance with Regulation (EU) No 1407/2013.

2. Where an undertaking is active in the primary production of agricultural products as well as in the fishery and aquaculture sector, de minimis aid granted for activities in the sector of agricultural production in accordance with this Regulation may be cumulated with de minimis aid for activities in the latter sector in accordance with Regulation (EC) No 875/2007 up to the ceiling laid down in that Regulation, provided that the Member State concerned ensures, by appropriate means such as separation of activities or distinction of costs, that the primary production of agricultural products does not benefit from de minimis aid granted in accordance with Regulation (EC) No 875/2007.

3. De minimis aid shall not be cumulated with State aid in relation to the same eligible costs or with State aid for the same risk finance measure, if such cumulation would exceed the highest relevant aid intensity or aid amount fixed in the specific circumstances of each case by a block exemption regulation or a decision adopted by the Commission. De minimis aid which is not granted for or attributable to specific eligible costs may be cumulated with other State aid granted under a block exemption regulation or a decision adopted by the Commission.

NOTES

Repeal of this Regulation in relation to the UK: this Regulation is repealed in relation to the UK (as from IP completion day); see the introductory notes to this Regulation *ante*.

[5.465]

Article 6 Monitoring

1. Where a Member State intends to grant de minimis aid in accordance with this Regulation to an undertaking, it shall inform that undertaking in writing of the prospective amount of the aid expressed as a gross grant equivalent and of its de minimis character, making express reference to this Regulation and citing its title and publication reference in the Official Journal of the European Union. Where de minimis aid is granted in accordance with this Regulation to different undertakings on the basis of a scheme and different amounts of individual aid are granted to those undertakings under that scheme, the Member State concerned may choose to fulfil that obligation by informing the undertakings of a fixed sum corresponding to the maximum aid amount to be granted under that scheme. In such case, the fixed sum shall be used for determining whether the ceiling laid down in Article 3(2) is reached and the national cap referred to in Article 3(3) is not exceeded. Before granting the aid, the Member State shall obtain a declaration from the undertaking concerned, in written or electronic form, about any other de minimis aid received to which this Regulation or other de minimis regulations apply during the previous 2 fiscal years and the current fiscal year.

2. Where a Member State has set up a central register of de minimis aid containing complete information on all de minimis aid granted by any authority within that Member State, paragraph 1 shall cease to apply from the moment the register covers a period of 3 fiscal years.

[Where a Member State grants aid in accordance with Article 3(3a), it shall have in place a central register of de minimis aid containing complete information on all de minimis aid granted by any authority within that Member State. Paragraph 1 shall cease to apply from the moment the register covers a period of 3 fiscal years.]

[3. A Member State shall grant new de minimis aid in accordance with this Regulation only after having checked that this will not raise the total amount of de minimis aid granted to the undertaking concerned to a level above the relevant ceilings and national caps and the sector cap referred to in Article 3(2), (3) and (3a) and that all the conditions laid down in this Regulation are complied with.]

4. Member States shall record and compile all the information regarding the application of this Regulation. Such records shall contain all information necessary to demonstrate that the conditions of this Regulation have been complied with. Records regarding individual de minimis aid shall be maintained for 10 fiscal years from the date on which the aid was granted. Records regarding a de minimis aid scheme shall be maintained for 10 fiscal years from the date on which the last individual aid was granted under such a scheme.

5. On written request, the Member State concerned shall provide the Commission, within a period of 20 working days or such longer period as may be fixed in the request, with all the information that the Commission considers necessary for assessing whether the conditions of this Regulation have been complied with, and in particular the total amount of de minimis aid within the meaning of this Regulation and of other de minimis regulations received by any undertaking.

NOTES

The second sub-paragraph of para 2 was added, and para 3 was substituted, by Commission Regulation 2019/316/EU, Art 1(4).

Repeal of this Regulation in relation to the UK: this Regulation is repealed in relation to the UK (as from IP completion day); see the introductory notes to this Regulation *ante*.

[5.466]

Article 7 Transitional provisions

1. This Regulation shall apply to aid granted before its entry into force if the aid fulfils all the conditions laid down in this Regulation. Any aid which does not fulfil those conditions will be assessed by the Commission in accordance with the relevant frameworks, guidelines, communications and notices.

2. Any individual de minimis aid which was granted between 1 January 2005 and 30 June 2008, and which fulfils the conditions of Regulation (EC) No 1860/2004 shall be deemed not to meet all the criteria in Article 107(1) of the Treaty and shall therefore be exempt from the notification requirement in Article 108(3) of the Treaty.

3. Any individual de minimis aid granted between 1 January 2008 and 30 June 2014 and which fulfils the conditions of Regulation (EC) No 1535/2007, shall be deemed not to meet all the criteria in Article 107(1) of the Treaty and shall therefore be exempt from the notification requirement in Article 108(3) of the Treaty.

4. At the end of the period of validity of this Regulation, any de minimis aid scheme which fulfils the conditions of this Regulation shall remain covered by this Regulation for a further period of 6 months.

NOTES

Repeal of this Regulation in relation to the UK: this Regulation is repealed in relation to the UK (as from IP completion day); see the introductory notes to this Regulation *ante*.

[5.467]

Article 8 Entry into force and period of application

This Regulation shall enter into force on 1 January 2014.

[It shall apply until 31 December 2027.]

This Regulation shall be binding in its entirety and directly applicable in all Member States.

NOTES

Words in square brackets substituted by Commission Regulation 2019/316/EU, Art 1(5). The previous date of expiry was 31 December 2020.

Repeal of this Regulation in relation to the UK: this Regulation is repealed in relation to the UK (as from IP completion day); see the introductory notes to this Regulation *ante*.

ANNEXES

[ANNEX I

MAXIMUM CUMULATIVE AMOUNTS OF DE MINIMIS AID GRANTED PER MEMBER STATE TO UNDERTAKINGS ACTIVE IN THE PRIMARY PRODUCTION OF AGRICULTURAL PRODUCTS REFERRED TO IN ARTICLE 3(3)

(EUR)

Member State	*Maximum amounts of de minimis aid*[1]
Belgium	*106,269,708*
Bulgaria	*53,020,042*
Czechia	*61,865,750*
Denmark	*141,464,625*
Germany	*732,848,458*
Estonia	*11,375,375*
Ireland	*98,460,375*
Greece	*134,272,042*
Spain	*592,962,542*
France	*932,709,458*
Croatia	*28,920,958*
Italy	*700,419,125*
Cyprus	*8,934,792*
Latvia	*16,853,708*
Lithuania	*34,649,958*
Luxembourg	*5,474,083*
Hungary	*99,582,208*
Malta	*1,603,917*
Netherlands	*352,512,625*
Austria	*89,745,208*
Poland	*295,932,125*
Portugal	*87,570,583*
Romania	*215,447,583*
Slovenia	*15,523,667*
Slovakia	*29,947,167*

(EUR)

Member State	*Maximum amounts of de minimis aid*[1]
Finland	*55,693,958*
Sweden	*79,184,750*
United Kingdom	*394,587,292]*

NOTES

The original Annex was substituted by new Annexes I and II by Commission Regulation 2019/316/EU, Art 1(6), Annex.

Repeal of this Regulation in relation to the UK: this Regulation is repealed in relation to the UK (as from IP completion day); see the introductory notes to this Regulation *ante*.

[1] The maximum amounts are calculated on the basis of averaging the three highest values of annual agricultural production of each Member State in the period 2012-2017. The calculation method ensures that all Member States are treated equally and that none of the national average values is less than the maximum amounts previously established for the period 2014-2020.

[ANNEX II

MAXIMUM CUMULATIVE AMOUNTS OF DE MINIMIS AID GRANTED PER MEMBER STATE TO UNDERTAKINGS ACTIVE IN THE PRIMARY PRODUCTION OF AGRICULTURAL PRODUCTS REFERRED TO IN ARTICLE 3(3A)

(EUR)

Member State	*Maximum amounts of de minimis aid*[1]
Belgium	*127,523,650*
Bulgaria	*63,624,050*
Czechia	*74,238,900*
Denmark	*169,757,550*
Germany	*879,418,150*
Estonia	*13,650,450*
Ireland	*118,152,450*
Greece	*161,126,450*
Spain	*711,555,050*
France	*1,119,251,350*
Croatia	*34,705,150*
Italy	*840,502,950*
Cyprus	*10,721,750*
Latvia	*20,224,450*
Lithuania	*41,579,950*
Luxembourg	*6,568,900*
Hungary	*119,498,650*
Malta	*1,924,700*
Netherlands	*423,015,150*
Austria	*107,694,250*
Poland	*355,118,550*
Portugal	*105,084,700*
Romania	*258,537,100*
Slovenia	*18,628,400*
Slovakia	*35,936,600*
Finland	*66,832,750*
Sweden	*95,021,700*
United Kingdom	*473,504,750]*

NOTES

The original Annex was substituted by new Annexes I and II by Commission Regulation 2019/316/EU, Art 1(6), Annex.

Repeal of this Regulation in relation to the UK: this Regulation is repealed in relation to the UK (as from IP completion day); see the introductory notes to this Regulation *ante*.

[1] The maximum amounts are calculated on the basis of averaging the three highest values of annual agricultural production of each Member State in the period 2012-2017. The calculation method ensures that all Member States are treated equally and that none of the national average values is less than the maximum amounts previously established for the period 2014-2020.

COMMISSION REGULATION

(702/2014/EU)

of 25 June 2014

declaring certain categories of aid in the agricultural and forestry sectors and in rural areas compatible with the internal market in application of Articles 107 and 108 of the Treaty on the Functioning of the European Union

[5.468]

NOTES

Date of publication in OJ: OJ L193, 01.07.2014, p 1.

Repeal of this Regulation in relation to the UK: this Regulation is repealed, in relation to the UK, by the State Aid (Revocations and Amendments) (EU Exit) Regulations 2020, SI 2020/1470, reg 5, as from IP completion day (as defined in the European Union (Withdrawal Agreement) Act 2020, s 39) (for transitional provisions and savings in relation to claims before a court or tribunal relating to State aid infringement before IP completion day, see Sch 3 to those Regulations at **[7.89]**).

THE EUROPEAN COMMISSION,

Having regard to the Treaty on the Functioning of the European Union, and in particular Article 108(4) thereof,

Having regard to Council Regulation (EC) No 994/98 of 7 May 1998 on the application of Articles 107 and 108 of the Treaty on the Functioning of the European Union to certain categories of horizontal State aid[1] *and in particular Article 1(1)(a) and (b) thereof,*

Having published a draft of this Regulation in accordance with Article 6 and Article 8(2) of Regulation (EC) No 994/98,

Having consulted the Advisory Committee on State Aid,

Whereas:

(1) State funding meeting the criteria laid down in Article 107(1) of the Treaty constitutes State aid and requires notification to the Commission by virtue of Article 108(3) thereof. However, pursuant to Article 109 of the Treaty, the Council may determine categories of aid that are exempted from that notification requirement. In accordance with Article 108(4) of the Treaty the Commission may adopt regulations relating to those categories of aid. Regulation (EC) No 994/98 empowers the Commission to declare, in accordance with Article 109 of the Treaty, that certain categories of aid may be exempted from the notification requirement of Article 108(3) of the Treaty. On the basis of that Regulation, the Commission adopted Commission Regulation (EC) No 1857/2006[2] *which applies until 30 June 2014.*

(2) On 22 July 2013 Regulation (EC) No 994/98 was amended by Regulation (EU) No 733/2013[3] *to empower the Commission to extend the block exemption to new categories of aid in respect of which clear compatibility conditions can be defined. Such new categories of aid in the agricultural and forestry sectors should include: aid in favour of heritage conservation, aid in favour of making good the damage caused by natural disasters and aid in favour of forestry which can, under certain conditions, be exempted from the notification requirement of Article 108(3) of the Treaty.*

(3) Article 42 of the Treaty provides that the rules on competition apply to the production of and trade in agricultural products only to the extent determined by the European Parliament and the Council. Article 211(1) of Regulation (EU) No 1308/2013 of the European Parliament and the Council[4] *provides that State aid rules apply to aid for the production of and trade in agricultural products, subject to specific derogations. Article 211(2) of Regulation (EU) No 1308/2013 provides that State aid rules do not apply to payments made by Member States for measures provided for in that Regulation which are partly or wholly financed by the Union and for measures included in Articles 213 to 218 of that Regulation. Moreover, State aid rules do not apply to payments made by Member States pursuant to Regulation (EU) No 1305/2013 of the European Parliament and of the Council*[5] *nor to additional national financing, within the scope of Article 42 of the Treaty. Such payments intended to provide additional national financing within the scope of Article 42 of the Treaty, have to comply with the criteria of Regulation (EU) No 1305/2013 in order to be approved by the Commission as part of the rural development programme of a given Member State. Nevertheless, State aid rules apply, both to the part co-financed under the European Agricultural Fund for Rural Development (EAFRD) and to additional national financing for measures falling outside the scope of Article 42 of the Treaty.*

(4) As the economic effects of aid do not change depending on whether or not it is partly financed by the Union, or whether it is financed by a Member State alone, there should be consistency and coherence between the Commission's policy in respect of the control of State aid, and the support which is granted under the Union's own common agricultural and rural development policy.

(5) The scope of this Regulation should therefore be aligned with that of Regulation (EU) No 1305/2013, in particular as regards aid in favour of the forestry sector and aid in favour of micro and small and medium-sized enterprises (SMEs) active in rural areas. This Regulation should apply to aid measures in favour of forestry and in favour of SMEs active in the rural areas which fall outside the scope of Article 42 of the Treaty which are covered by Regulation (EU) No 1305/2013 only and insofar as those measures are included in the rural development programmes and are co-financed by the EAFRD. On the other hand, this Regulation should not apply to aid to undertakings in rural areas for activities falling outside the scope of Article 42 of the Treaty or to the forestry sector where there is no direct link to the rural development programmes and no co-financing from the EAFRD. However, aid for knowledge transfer and information actions in the forestry sector and aid for advisory services in the forestry sector should be possible to be granted outside the rural development programmes wholly financed by the Member States, provided that they comply with the respective compatibility conditions laid down in this Regulation.

(6) A simplified procedure should be made available for Member States when they are required to obtain State

aid clearance for both the co-financed part and the additional financing of their national rural development programmes, in accordance with Article 81(1) of Regulation (EU) No 1305/2013. In that respect such aid should be exempted from the notification requirement of Article 108(3) of the Treaty provided that it complies with the respective compatibility conditions laid down in this Regulation.

(7) With the Communication of 8 May 2012 from the Commission to the European Parliament, the Council, the European Economic and Social Committee and the Committee on the Regions — EU State Aid Modernisation (SAM),[6] *the Commission launched a wider review of the State aid rules. The main objectives of this modernisation are: (i) to achieve sustainable, smart and inclusive growth in a competitive internal market, while contributing to Member State efforts towards a more efficient use of public finances; (ii) to focus Commission ex ante scrutiny on cases with the biggest impact on the internal market, while strengthening Member State cooperation in State aid enforcement; and (iii) to streamline the rules and provide for faster, better informed and more robust decisions based on a clear economic rationale, a common approach and clear obligations.*

(8) This Regulation should allow for a better prioritisation of State aid enforcement activities, and greater simplification and should enhance transparency, effective evaluation and the control of compliance with the State aid rules at national and Union levels, while preserving the institutional competences of the Commission and the Member States. In accordance with the principle of proportionality this Regulation does not go beyond what is necessary in order to achieve those objectives.

(9) The Commission has applied Articles 107 and 108 of the Treaty to SMEs active in the production, processing and marketing of agricultural products in numerous cases, in particular in the framework of Regulation (EC) No 1857/2006, Commission Regulation (EC) No 800/2008[7] *and the Community Guidelines on State aid in the agriculture and forestry sector 2007 to 2013.*[8] *It has thus gained considerable experience in this field. The Commission's experience has allowed it, on the one hand, to better define the conditions under which certain categories of aid can be considered compatible with the internal market and to extend the scope of block exemptions and, on the other hand, made clear the necessity to strengthen transparency as well as monitoring and allow for a proper evaluation of large schemes in light of their effect on competition in the internal market.*

(10) The general conditions for the application of this Regulation should be defined on the basis of a set of common principles that ensure that the aid serves a purpose of common interest, has a clear incentive effect, is appropriate and proportionate, is granted in full transparency and subject to a control mechanism and regular evaluation, and does not adversely affect trading conditions to extent that is contrary to the common interest.

(11) Aid that fulfils all the conditions laid down in this Regulation, both general and specific to the relevant categories of aid, should be exempted from the notification requirement laid down in Article 108(3) of the Treaty. With a view to ensuring efficient supervision and simplifying administration, but without weakening Commission monitoring, exempted aid (aid schemes and individual aids) should contain an express reference to this Regulation.

(12) State aid within the meaning of Article 107(1) of the Treaty not covered by this Regulation remains subject to the notification requirement of Article 108(3) of the Treaty. This Regulation is without prejudice to the possibility for Member States to notify aid the objectives of which correspond to objectives covered by this Regulation.

(13) In view of the greater potential impact of large schemes on trade and competition, aid schemes with an average annual State aid budget exceeding a threshold based on an absolute value should in principle be subject to State aid evaluation. The evaluation should aim at verifying whether the assumptions and conditions underlying the compatibility of the scheme have been achieved, as well as the effectiveness of the aid measure in the light of its general and specific objectives and should provide indications on the impact of the scheme on competition and trade. In order to ensure equal treatment, State aid evaluation should be carried out on the basis of an evaluation plan approved by the Commission. While such plan should normally be drawn up at the moment of the design of the scheme and approved in time for the scheme to enter into force, this may not be possible in all cases. Therefore, in order not to delay their entry into force, this Regulation will apply to such schemes for a maximum period of six months. The Commission may decide to extend this period, upon approval of the evaluation plan. To this end, the evaluation plan should be notified to the Commission within 20 working days following the entry into force of the scheme. The Commission can also exceptionally decide that an evaluation is not necessary given the specificities of the case. The Commission should receive from the Member State the necessary information to be able to carry out the assessment of the evaluation plan and request additional information without undue delay allowing the Member State to complete the missing elements for the Commission to take a decision. In view of the novelty of this process, the Commission will provide, in a separate document, a detailed guidance on the procedure applicable during the 6 months period for the approval of the evaluation plan and the relevant templates through which the evaluation plans will have to be submitted. Alterations of schemes subject to evaluation, other than modifications which cannot affect the compatibility of the aid scheme under this Regulation or cannot significantly affect the content of the approved evaluation plan, should be assessed taking account of the outcome of such evaluation and should be excluded from the scope of this Regulation. The alterations such as purely formal modifications, administrative modifications or alterations carried out within the framework of the EU co-financed measures should not, in principle, be considered as significantly affecting the content of the approved evaluation plan.

(14) This Regulation should not apply to aid contingent upon the use of domestic over imported products or aid to export-related activities. In particular, it should not apply to aid financing the establishment and operation of a distribution network in another Member State or third country. Aid towards the cost of participating in trade fairs or of studies or consultancy services needed for the launch of a new or existing product on a new market in another Member State or third country should not normally constitute aid to export-related activities.

(15) The Commission should ensure that authorised aid does not adversely affect trading conditions to an extent that is contrary to the general interest. Therefore, aid in favour of a beneficiary which is subject to an outstanding recovery order following a previous Commission decision declaring an aid illegal and incompatible with the internal market should be excluded from the scope of this Regulation with the exception of aid to make good the damage caused by certain natural disasters.

(16) Aid granted to undertakings in difficulty should be excluded from the scope of this Regulation, since such aid should be assessed under the Guidelines on State aid for rescuing and restructuring firms in difficulty[9] *or their*

successor Guidelines in order to avoid their circumvention, with the exception, under certain conditions, of aid granted to compensate for damages caused by natural disasters, by an adverse climatic event which can be assimilated to a natural disaster, by animal disease or plants pest and aid for the restoration of damage to forests from fires, natural disasters, adverse climatic events, pests, diseases, catastrophic events and climate change related events, as stipulated by this Regulation. In addition, for reasons of public health protection and having in mind the emergency situation no distinction should be made, under certain conditions, as to the economic situation of an undertaking for aid for the costs of the eradication of animal diseases and for aid for the destruction and removal of fallen stock. In order to provide legal certainty, it is appropriate to establish clear criteria that do not require an assessment of all the particularities of the situation of an undertaking to determine whether an undertaking is considered to be in difficulty for the purposes of this Regulation.

(17) If a State aid or the conditions attached to it, including its financing method when it forms an integral part of it, entail a non-severable violation of Union legislation, the aid may not be declared compatible with the internal market. This Regulation should therefore not apply to aid which entails a non-severable violation of Union legislation.

(18) State aid enforcement is highly dependent on the cooperation of Member States. Therefore, Member States should take all necessary measures to ensure compliance with this Regulation, including compliance of individual aid granted under block-exempted schemes.

(19) Due to the high risk of adversely affecting trading conditions, large amounts of aid granted either individually or cumulatively should be assessed by the Commission upon notification. Thresholds by maximum aid amount should therefore be set for certain categories of investment aid falling within the scope of this Regulation at a level which takes into account the category of aid concerned and its likely effect on trading conditions. Any aid granted above those thresholds should remain subject to the notification requirement of Article 108(3) of the Treaty. The thresholds laid down in this Regulation should not be circumvented by the artificial splitting up of aid schemes or aid projects, for example into several aid schemes or projects with similar characteristics, objectives or beneficiaries. Other categories of aid, to the extent that the compatibility conditions and the maximum aid intensities or the maximum aid amounts laid down in this Regulation are respected, should not be considered as having a high risk of adversely affecting trading conditions.

(20) For the purpose of transparency, equal treatment and effective monitoring, this Regulation should apply only to aid in respect of which it is possible to calculate precisely the gross grant equivalent ex ante without the need to undertake a risk assessment ('transparent aid').

(21) For certain specific aid instruments, such as loans, guarantees, tax measures and, in particular, repayable advances, this Regulation should define the conditions under which they can be considered transparent. Aid comprised in guarantees should be considered as transparent if the gross grant equivalent has been calculated on the basis of safe-harbour premiums laid down for the respective type of undertaking. For instance, for SMEs the Commission Notice on the application of Articles 87 and 88 of the EC Treaty to State aid in the form of guarantees[10] indicates levels of annual premium above which a State guarantee would be deemed not to constitute aid. It should also be considered transparent if before the implementation of the measure, the methodology used to calculate the aid intensity of the state guarantee has been notified to and approved by the Commission in line with the Commission Notice on the application of Articles 87 and 88 of the EC Treaty to State aid in the form of guarantees. For the purpose of this Regulation, aid comprised in risk finance measures and capital injections should not be considered as transparent aid.

(22) Aid which would otherwise fall within the scope of this Regulation but is not transparent should always be notified to the Commission. Notification of non-transparent aid should be assessed by the Commission in particular in the light of the criteria set out in the European Union Guidelines for State aid in the agricultural and forestry sectors and in rural areas 2014 to 2020[11] or the other relevant frameworks, guidelines, communications and notices.

(23) In order to ensure that the aid is necessary and acts as an incentive to further develop activities or projects, this Regulation should not apply to aid for activities or projects in which the beneficiary would in any case engage even in the absence of the aid. No aid should be granted retroactively in respect of activities or projects which have already been undertaken by the beneficiary. Aid should only be exempted from the notification requirement of Article 108(3) of the Treaty in accordance with this Regulation where the activity or the work on the aided project starts after the beneficiary has submitted a written application for the aid.

(24) As regards any ad hoc aid covered by this Regulation granted to a beneficiary which is a large enterprise, the Member State should, in addition to the conditions on the incentive effect applicable to SMEs, also ensure that the beneficiary has analysed, in an internal document, the viability of the aided project or activity with aid and without aid. The Member State should verify that this internal document confirms a material increase in the scope of the project or activity, a material increase in the total amount spent by the beneficiary on the aided project or activity or a material increase in the speed of completion of the project or activity concerned. It should also be possible to establish the incentive effect on the basis of the fact that the investment project or the activity would not have been carried out as such in the rural area concerned in the absence of the aid.

(25) Automatic aid schemes in the form of tax advantages should continue to be subject to a specific condition concerning the incentive effect, in the light of the fact that the aid resulting from such aid schemes is granted within the framework of different procedures than other categories of aid. That specific condition means that those aid schemes should have been adopted before the activity or the work on the aided project/activity started. However, this condition should not apply in the case of fiscal successor schemes provided the activity was already covered by the previous fiscal schemes in the form of tax advantages. For the assessment of the incentive effect of such aid schemes, the crucial moment is the moment when the tax measure was set out for the first time in the original scheme, which is then replaced by the successor scheme.

(26) As regards aid for land consolidation, promotion measures in form of publications aimed at raising awareness of agricultural products among the wider public, aid to compensate for losses caused by adverse climatic event which can be assimilated to a natural disaster, aid to compensate for the costs of the eradication of animal diseases and plant pests and for losses caused by those animal diseases or plant pests, aid to cover the costs of the removal and destruction of fallen stock, aid for research and development, aid to make good the damage caused by natural disaster and aid for investments in favour of conservation of cultural and natural heritage on the agricultural

holding the existence of an incentive effect should not be required or should be deemed to be present if the specific conditions set out for those categories of aid in this Regulation are fulfilled.

(27) With a view to ensuring that aid is proportionate and limited to the amount necessary, the maximum aid amounts should, whenever possible, be expressed in terms of aid intensities in relation to a set of eligible costs. Where the maximum aid intensity cannot be set, because the eligible costs cannot be identified or in order to provide simpler instruments for small amounts, maximum aid amounts defined in nominal terms should be set out in order to ensure proportionality of the aid. The aid intensity and the maximum aid amounts should be fixed, in the light of the Commission's experience, at a level that minimises distortions of competition in the aided sector while appropriately addressing the objective of facilitating the development of the economic activities of the beneficiaries in the agricultural sector, the rural areas, or the forestry sector. In the interests of coherence with Union-financed rural development measures, the ceilings should be harmonised with those set out in Regulation (EU) No 1305/2013 insofar as this is in line with the State aid principles.

(28) For the calculation of the aid intensity, only eligible costs should be included. The Regulation should not exempt aid which exceeds the relevant aid intensity as a result of including ineligible costs. The identification of the eligible costs should be supported by clear, specific and contemporary documentary evidence. All figures used should be taken before any deduction of tax or other charges. Aid payable in several instalments should be discounted to its value on the date of granting the aid. The eligible costs should also be discounted to their value on the date of granting the aid. The interest rate to be used for discounting purposes and for calculating the amount of aid in the case of aid which does not take the form of a grant should be respectively the discount rate and the reference rate applicable on the date of granting the aid, as laid down in the Communication from the Commission on the revision of the method for setting the reference and discount rates.[12] Where aid is granted in a form other than a grant, the aid amount should be expressed in gross grant equivalent. Where aid is granted by means of tax advantages, aid tranches should be discounted on the basis of the discount rates applicable on the various dates when the tax advantages become effective. The use of aid in the form of repayable advances should be promoted, since such risk-sharing instruments are conducive to a strengthened incentive effect of the aid. It is therefore appropriate to establish that where aid is granted in the form of repayable advances the applicable aid intensities laid down in this Regulation may be increased.

(29) In the case of tax advantages on future taxes, the applicable discount rate and the exact amount of the aid tranches may not be known in advance. In such a case, Member States should set in advance a cap on the discounted value of the aid respecting the applicable aid intensity. Subsequently, when the amount of the aid tranche at a given date becomes known, discounting can take place on the basis of the discount rate applicable at that time. The discounted value of each aid tranche should be deducted from the overall amount of the cap ('capped amount').

(30) To determine whether the individual notification thresholds and the maximum aid intensities or the maximum aid amounts laid down in this Regulation are respected, the total amount of the State aid for the aided activity or project should be taken into account. Moreover, this Regulation should specify the circumstances under which different categories of aid may be cumulated. Aid exempted from notification by this Regulation and any other compatible aid exempted under other Regulation or approved by the Commission may be cumulated as long as those measures concern different identifiable eligible costs. Where different sources of aid are related to the same — partly or fully overlapping — identifiable eligible costs, cumulation should be allowed up to the highest aid intensity or aid amount applicable to that aid under this Regulation. This Regulation should also set out special rules for cumulation of aid with and without identifiable eligible costs, and for cumulation with de minimis aid. De minimis aid is often not granted for or attributable to specific identifiable eligible costs. In such a case it should be possible to freely cumulate de minimis aid with State aid exempted under this Regulation. Where, however, de minimis aid is granted for the same identifiable eligible costs as State aid exempted under this Regulation, cumulation should only be allowed up to the maximum aid intensity as set out in Chapter III of this Regulation.

(31) Union funding centrally managed by the institutions, agencies, joint undertakings or other bodies of the Union, that is not directly or indirectly under the control of Member States, does not constitute State aid. Where such Union funding is combined with State aid, only the latter should be considered for determining whether notification thresholds and maximum aid intensities or maximum aid amounts are respected, provided the total amount of public funding granted in relation to the same eligible costs does not exceed the most favourable funding rate laid down in the applicable rules of Union law.

(32) Given that State aid within the meaning of Article 107(1) of the Treaty is, in principle, prohibited, it is important that for all parties to be able to check whether an aid is granted in compliance with the applicable rules. Transparency of State aid is, therefore, essential for the correct application of Treaty rules and leads to better compliance, greater accountability, peer review and ultimately more effective public spending. To ensure transparency, Member States should be required to establish comprehensive State aid websites, at regional or national level, setting out summary information about each aid measure exempted under this Regulation That obligation should be a condition for the compatibility of the individual aid with the internal market. Following the standard practice regarding publication of information in Directive 2013/37/EU of the European Parliament and of the Council,[13] a standard format should be used which allows the information to be searched, downloaded and easily published on the internet. The links to the State aid websites of all the Member States should be published on the Commission's website. In accordance with Article 3(2) of Regulation (EC) No 994/98, as amended by Regulation (EU) No 733/2013, summary information on each aid measure exempted under this Regulation should be published on the website of the Commission.

(33) As regards the publication of information on individual aid awards it is appropriate to set thresholds above which that publication may be considered proportionate taking into account the importance of the aid. Based on the assessment of investment aid schemes in the primary agricultural sector with the highest annual expenditure reported in the framework of the Annual Report exercise 2013 which can be considered to be more distortive than the other categories of aid the Commission has established an average aid amount per beneficiary of EUR 59 596. In order to limit the administrative burden on Member States, it is therefore appropriate to set the threshold for publication of information on individual aid awards to primary agricultural producers at the level of EUR 60,000. Taking into account that the processing of agricultural products and the marketing of agricultural products is similar to that of

industrial products, it is appropriate to align the threshold for the publication of information on individual aid awards to beneficiaries in those sub-sectors, as well as in the forestry sector and for activities falling outside the scope of Article 42 of the Treaty, to that set in Commission Regulation (EU) No 651/2014.[14]

(34) To ensure effective monitoring, it is appropriate in accordance with Article 3(2) of Regulation (EC) No 994/98, to establish a standard format in which Member States should provide the Commission with summary information whenever, in accordance with this Regulation, an aid scheme is implemented or an individual aid is granted outside any aid scheme. Moreover, it is appropriate in accordance with Article 5 of Commission Regulation (EC) No 794/2004[15] *and Article 3(4) of Regulation (EC) No 994/98 to establish rules concerning annual reporting on aid exempted from the notification requirement of Article 108(3) of the Treaty in accordance with the conditions laid down in this Regulation, including specific requirements for certain categories of aid, to be submitted to the Commission by Member States.*

(35) In view of the wide availability of the necessary technology, the summary information and the annual report should be in computerised format and transmitted to the Commission via the Commission electronic systems.

(36) Moreover, it is appropriate in accordance with Article 3(3) of Regulation (EC) No 994/98 to establish rules concerning the records that Member States should keep regarding the aid exempted from the notification requirement of Article 108(3) of the Treaty by this Regulation, in the light of the limitation period established by Article 15 of Council Regulation (EC) No 659/1999.[16]

(37) To reinforce the effectiveness of compatibility conditions set out in this Regulation, it should be possible for the Commission to withdraw the benefit of the block exemption for the future aid measures in the event of failure to comply with these requirements. The Commission should be able to restrict the withdrawal of the benefit of the block exemption to certain types of aid, certain beneficiaries or aid measures adopted by certain authorities, where non-compliance with this Regulation affects only a limited group of measures or certain authorities. Such a targeted withdrawal should provide a proportionate remedy directly linked to the identified non-compliance with this Regulation. In case of failure to meet compatibility conditions set out in Chapters I and III, aid granted is not covered by this Regulation and, as a consequence, constitutes unlawful aid, which the Commission will examine in the framework of the relevant procedure as set out in Regulation No (EC) No 659/1999. In case of failure to fulfil the requirements of Chapter II, the withdrawal of the benefit of the block exemption in respect of the future aid measures does not affect the fact that the past measures complying with this Regulation were block exempted.

(38) Having regard to Article 107(3)(c) of the Treaty, aid should not have the sole effect of continuously or periodically reducing the operating costs which the beneficiary would normally have to bear, and should be proportionate to the handicaps that have to be overcome in order to secure the socioeconomic benefits deemed to be in the Union interest. Unilateral State aid which simply seeks to improve the financial situation of producers but which in no way contributes to the development of the sector, and in particular aid which is granted solely on the basis of price, quantity, unit of production or unit of means of production should be considered to constitute operating aid which is incompatible with the internal market. Furthermore, if granted in the agricultural sector, such aid is also likely to interfere with the mechanisms of the common organisations of the markets. It is therefore appropriate to limit the scope of this Regulation to certain types of aid.

(39) SMEs play a decisive role in job creation and, more generally, act as a factor of social stability and drive the economy. However, their development may be limited by market failures, leading to SMEs suffering from typical handicaps. SMEs often have difficulty in obtaining capital or loans, given the risk-averse nature of certain financial markets and the limited collateral that they may be able to offer. Their limited resources may also restrict their access to information, notably as regards new technology and potential markets. To facilitate the development of the economic activities of SMEs, this Regulation should therefore exempt certain categories of aid in favour of SMEs from the notification requirement of Article 108(3) of the Treaty.

(40) To eliminate differences that might give rise to distortions of competition and to facilitate coordination between different Union and national initiatives concerning SMEs as well as for reasons of administrative clarity and legal certainty, the definition of SME used for the purpose of this Regulation should be based on the definitions laid down in Commission Recommendation 2003/361/EC.[17]

(41) To ensure coherence with the rural development policy and to achieve simplification of the rules based on the experience already gained by the Commission in the light of the application of Regulation (EU) No 1857/2006 and Regulation (EU) No 800/2008, it is appropriate to exempt from the notification requirement of Article 108 (3) of the Treaty, different categories of aid in favour of SMEs active in primary agricultural production, the processing of agricultural products and the marketing of agricultural products.

(42) Those categories of aid should in particular encompass investment aid such as investments in tangible assets or intangible assets or for the relocation of farm buildings, aid for business start-ups and business opportunities such as aid for young farmers and small farms, aid for producer groups, as well as aid for participation in quality schemes, aid to facilitate business development, such as aid for knowledge transfer and information actions, aid for advisory services, aid for promotion activities, aid for farm replacement services, risk and crisis management aid such as aid to compensate for losses caused by adverse climatic events which can be assimilated to a natural disaster, aid for the costs of the prevention and eradication of animal diseases and plant pests and aid for insurance premiums, as well as aid for the livestock sector pursuing common public objectives such as the preservation of the genetic quality and the protection of animal and public health. That aid should be especially aimed at enhancing the competitiveness and the viability of the whole agricultural sector.

(43) Moreover, aids granted in favour of SMEs active in rural areas should also be exempted from the notification requirement of Article 108(3) of the Treaty under this Regulation. In this regard, and in order to ensure coherence between rural development measures co-financed under the EAFRD and measures financed from additional national resources the rules laid down in this Regulation should be consistent as far as possible with the rules laid down in Regulation (EU) No 1305/2013 and in the delegated and implementing acts adopted pursuant to that Regulation.

(44) Other categories of aid such as aid for research and development in the agricultural and forestry sectors, aid to make good the damage caused by natural disaster in the agricultural sector, aid for investments in favour of the

conservation of cultural and natural heritage located on agricultural holdings and aid in favour of forestry granted to both, SMEs and large enterprises should be exempted from the notification requirement of Article 108 (3) of the Treaty. In particular, as regard aid in favour of forestry and in order to ensure coherence between rural development measures co-financed under the EAFRD and measures financed from additional national resources or measures financed purely through State aid, the rules laid down in this Regulation should be consistent as far as possible with the rules laid down in Regulation (EU) No 1305/2013 and in the delegated and implementing acts.

(45) Aid granted to SMEs active in the primary agricultural production, in the processing of agricultural products and in the marketing of agricultural products, aid for research and development, aid in favour of the forestry sector or aid in favour of SMEs in the rural areas for activities falling outside the scope of Article 42 of the Treaty may also be exempted from the notification requirements of Article 108(3) of the Treaty in accordance with the conditions laid down in Regulation (EU) No 651/2014. Where Member States deem it more appropriate, they may alternatively choose to grant aid falling under the above mentioned categories in accordance with the conditions laid down in Regulation (EU) No 651/2014. In particular, Member State may choose to grant to SMEs active in the primary agricultural production regional operating aid to compensate additional costs other than transport costs in outermost regions, aid for consultancy in favour of SMEs risk finance aid, aid for research and development, innovation aid for SMEs, environmental aid, training aid and aid for disadvantaged workers in accordance with the conditions laid down in Regulation (EU) No 651/2014. In that context and in order to clarify the relation between the scope of application of this Regulation and Regulation (EU) No 651/2014, it should be noted that the objectives, the categories of aid and the aid conditions laid down in the two Regulations are different although they may target the same type of beneficiaries.

(46) To improve the economic and environmental performance and efficiency of the SMEs active in the agricultural sector and to provide the infrastructure needed for the development of agriculture and to support non-remunerative investments necessary to achieve environmental aims, aid should be provided for investments in tangible or intangible assets contributing to those objectives. Those investments should comply with Union legislation and with the national laws of the Member States concerned on the environmental protection. Furthermore, for investments requiring an environmental impact assessment under Directive 2011/92/EU of the European Parliament and of the Council[18] *the aid should be subject to the condition that such assessment shall have been carried out and the development consent should have been granted for the investment project concerned, before the date of granting the individual aid.*

(47) Because of the risk of distortions of competition resulting from targeted investment aid in the sector of primary agricultural production, investment aid exempted from the notification requirement of Article 108(3) of the Treaty under this Regulation should not be limited to a specific agricultural product. This condition should not prevent a Member State from excluding certain agricultural products from the scope of a particular aid, notably where no normal market outlets can be found. Moreover, aid to certain types of investment should per se not qualify for exemption from the notification requirement of Article 108(3) of the Treaty under this Regulation.

(48) To ensure the appropriate balance between minimising distortions of competition and promoting energy and resource efficiency, in case of investments on agricultural holdings linked to primary agricultural production this Regulation should provide that aid should be granted only for investment linked to the production on farm-level of biofuels or energy from renewable sources and only where that production does not exceed the average annual consumption of fuel or energy of the farm. In such case aid to biofuels should only be covered in so far as it is granted for sustainable biofuels in line with the Directive 2009/28/EC of the European Parliament and the Council.[19]

(49) In order to incentivise the shift towards the production of more advanced forms of biofuels, as foreseen by the horizontal environmental and energy State aid rules, aid for food based biofuels should be excluded from this Regulation in case of aid for investments in connection with the processing of agricultural products.

(50) To encourage and to facilitate the initial establishment of young farmers and the development of small farms which are potentially economically viable, it is appropriate to exempt from the notification requirement of Article 108(3) of the Treaty start-up aid. In order to ensure the viability of the newly established agricultural activities, the aid should be made conditional on the submission of a business plan. The start-up aid should cover only the initial period of the existence of a business and not become operating aid.

(51) To help the agricultural sector to face the challenges posed by increased competition and consolidation of downstream markets in relation to the marketing of the agricultural products, including in local markets, the setting up of producer groups and organisations should be encouraged. It is therefore appropriate to exempt from the notification requirement of Article 108(3) of the Treaty start up aid to producer groups and organisations. Only producer groups and organisations that qualify as SMEs should benefit from the aid. In order to ensure that the producer group and organisation becomes a viable entity, a business plan should be submitted to the competent authority as a condition for the official recognition of a producer group by Member States. To avoid providing operating aid and maintain the incentive effect, the maximum aid duration should be limited to five years.

(52) To enhance market opportunities and to achieve added value for the agricultural products concerned it is appropriate to encourage SMEs to participate in Union or national quality schemes and therefore aid for participation in quality schemes should be exempted from the notification requirement of Article 108(3) of the Treaty. Given that it is at the moment of entering such quality schemes and in the early years of their participation that additional costs and obligations imposed on the SMEs as a result of their participation are not fully remunerated by the market, the direct aid to the beneficiary should be limited to new participation and cover a period of not more than five years. In addition, aid in the form of subsidised services should be granted towards the costs for compulsory control measures in relation to the quality schemes or towards the costs for market research activities or for preparation of application for recognition of Union quality scheme.

(53) To enhance competitiveness and resource efficiency and to improve the environmental performance, the sustainable management and overall performance of the SMEs it is appropriate to exempt from the notification requirement of Article 108(3) of the Treaty aid for knowledge transfer, information actions and farm advisory services as well as promotion measures.

(54) Good risk and crisis management is a key tool for a sustainable and competitive agricultural sector. Primary agricultural production is exposed to particular natural, climatic and health risks and crises. Therefore, risk and crisis

management aid and the aid for the livestock sector should be limited to SMEs active in primary agricultural production. State aid for making good losses caused by adverse climatic events that can be assimilated to natural disasters, aid for combating animal diseases and plant pests and aid for paying insurance premiums should be limited to helping beneficiaries facing particular difficulties despite having undertaken reasonable efforts to minimise such risks. State aid should not have as its effect to entice beneficiaries into taking unnecessary risks. SMEs active in primary agricultural production should themselves bear the consequences of imprudent choices of production methods or products.

(55) The Commission has applied Articles 107 and 108 of the Treaty to aid in favour of the conservation of natural and cultural heritage in numerous cases, in particular in the framework of the Community Guidelines for State aid in the agriculture and forestry sector 2007 to 2013 and Regulation (EC) No 1857/2006. In the period from 2007 to 2013, investment aid for the conservation of traditional landscapes and buildings in favour of SMEs has been exempted from the notification requirement under Regulation (EC) No 1857/2006, while investment aid for the conservation of traditional landscapes and buildings in favour of large enterprise has been subject to the notification requirement and approved by the Commission in accordance with the Community Guidelines for State aid in the agriculture and forestry sector 2007 to 2013. During that period the Commission has assessed more than 87 investment aids concerning the conservation of traditional landscapes and buildings located on agricultural holdings. Heritage conservation projects, even carried out by large enterprises, do not typically give rise to any significant distortion of competition. It is therefore appropriate that the Commission should make use of the powers conferred on it by Regulation (EC) No 994/98, as regards aids in favour of the conservation of natural and cultural heritage.

(56) For aid in favour of the conservation of cultural and natural heritage to be exempted from the notification requirement under this Regulation, it should be granted for investments in tangible assets or capital works aimed at the conservation of the cultural or natural heritage. The cultural or natural heritage should be located on the agricultural holding of the beneficiary and should be officially recognised as such by the competent public authority in the Member State. Given the notification threshold for this aid of EUR 500,000 per investment project provided for by this Regulation which is considered a small scale infrastructure under the European Union Guidelines for State aid in the agricultural and forestry sectors and in rural areas 2014 to 2020, it is appropriate, under this Regulation, to set the aid intensity at up to 100% of the eligible costs.

(57) Emergency situations caused by natural disasters require urgent action by the granting authorities. It is therefore important to ensure a swift implementation of the envisaged aid. The Commission has applied Articles 107 and 108 of the Treaty in a considerable number of decisions concerning compensation for damage caused to the agricultural sector by natural disasters. The Community Guidelines for State aid in the agriculture and forestry sector 2007 to 2013 already covered the possibility to authorise aid schemes to compensate for damages caused by natural disasters. In the period from 2007 to 2012 and in application of the Community Guidelines on State aid in the agriculture and forestry sector 2007 to 2013, the Commission approved more than 25 aids regarding compensation for damages caused by natural disasters to the agricultural sector. The Commission's experience has shown that such measures need to be implemented swiftly in order to be effective. Accordingly, it is necessary to simplify the notification procedure for such aids. Moreover, they do not give raise to a significant distortion of competition in the internal market due to their compensatory nature and the existence of clear criteria for compatibility with the internal market. It is therefore appropriate that the Commission should also make use of the powers conferred on it by Regulation (EC) No 994/98 as regards aids for compensation for damage caused by natural disasters in the agricultural sector.

(58) Aid to make good damage caused by natural disasters should therefore be available to undertakings in the whole agricultural sector and be granted to both SMEs and large enterprises. The conditions to exempt aid to make good damage caused by natural disasters follow the already established practice and relate to the formal recognition by the Member States' authorities of the character of the event as a natural disaster, to the existence of a direct causal link between the natural disaster and the damage suffered by the beneficiary and should ensure that overcompensation is avoided. In particular, Member States should avoid overcompensation as a result of the combination of such aid with other compensations received by the beneficiaries including payments received under an insurance scheme.

(59) Aid for research and development can contribute to sustainable economic growth and strengthen competitiveness. Based on the Commission's experience in applying the Community Guidelines for State aid in the agriculture and forestry sector 2007 to 2013, the Community Framework for State aid for research and development and innovation[20] *and Regulation (EC) No 800/2008 to aid for research and development in the agricultural and forestry sectors, it is appropriate to exempt from the notification requirement of Article 108(3) of the Treaty aid for research and development which fulfils the conditions laid down in this Regulation. Since the promotion of research and development is an important objective in the common interest, this Regulation should require that the research project is of interest of all undertakings active in a particular agricultural or forestry sector or sub-sector. The information on the research project and the results of it should be made publicly available on internet. Moreover, the results of the research should be available to interested undertakings at no costs.*

(60) Forestry is an integral part of rural development. The Commission has applied Articles 107 and 108 of the Treaty to undertakings active in the forestry sector in numerous decisions, in particular in the framework of the Community Guidelines on State aid in the agriculture and forestry sector 2007 to 2013. In the period from 2007 to 2012 the Commission approved 140 aids in favour of the forestry sector in accordance with those Guidelines. In the light of the considerable experience gained by the Commission in the context of applying those Guidelines to undertakings active in the forestry sector, it is appropriate, with a view to simplifying procedures but at the same time ensuring efficient supervision and Commission monitoring, that the Commission should also make use of the powers conferred on it by Regulation (EC) No 994/98 as regards aid in favour of the forestry sector. According to the Commission's experience aid granted in the forestry sector for measures that are part of the rural development programmes and which is either co-financed by the EAFRD or granted as an additional national financing to such co-financed measures does not significantly distort competition in the internal market. Moreover, aid for knowledge transfer in the forestry sector and aid for advisory services in the forestry sector do not significantly distort competition in the internal market even though they are granted outside the rural development programmes. Clear conditions for the compatibility of such measures with the internal market should be defined in this Regulation. Those conditions

should be consistent as far as possible with the rules laid down in Regulation (EU) No 1305/2013 and in the delegated and implementing acts adopted pursuant to that Regulation.

(61) Those categories of aid should, in particular, encompass aid for afforestation and the creation of woodland, aid for agroforestry systems, aid for the prevention and restoration of forests damaged by fire, natural disasters, adverse climatic events, plant pests or catastrophic events, aid for investments improving the resilience and environmental value of forest ecosystems, aid for disadvantages related to Natura 2000 forest areas as defined in Article 3 of Council Directive 92/43/EEC[21] *and in Article 3 of Directive 2009/147/EC of the European Parliament and of the Council,*[22] *aid for forest-environmental and climate services and for forest conservation, aid for knowledge transfer and information actions, aid for advisory services, aid for infrastructure investments and aid for investments in forestry technologies and in the processing mobilising and marketing of forestry products. The aid to the forestry sector should avoid distorting competition and be market neutral.*

(62) In order to ensure coherence with Regulation (EU) No 1305/2013 and to achieve simplification of the rules to obtain State aid clearance for the co-financed part and the additional financing of the national rural development programmes, the aid in favour of the forestry sector exempted from the notification requirement of Article 108 (3) of the Treaty under this Regulation should be identical to the underlying rural development measures and the exempted aid should only be granted pursuant to and in conformity with the rural development programme of the Member State concerned. However, the aid intensities and the eligible costs should also be in line with the general Union State aid principles and the State aid rules applicable to the agricultural sector. Therefore, costs such as working capital that is ancillary to, and linked to new investment should not be eligible for aid under this Regulation. In line with the respective rural development programmes as approved by the Commission, the investment operations included in the forestry measures could also encompass one-off forestry treatments needed to prepare the investment where the objective of the relevant rural development provision so permits. It should be possible for aid for knowledge transfer, aid for advisory services and aid for forestry land consolidation to be granted irrespective of whether such aid is integrated in the national rural development programme.

(63) Economic diversification and the creation of new economic activities are essential for the development and competitiveness of rural areas and in particular for the SMEs which are the backbone of the Union rural economy. Regulation (EU) No 1305/2013 provides for measures to support non-agricultural business development in rural areas aimed at employment promotion, the setting up of quality jobs in rural areas, the maintenance of already existing jobs, a reduction of seasonality fluctuations in employment, development of non-agricultural sectors outside agriculture and food processing while fostering at the same time business integration and local inter-sectoral links.

(64) To ensure coherence with Regulation (EU) No 1305/2013 and to achieve simplification of the rules to obtain State aid clearance for the co-financed part and the additional national financing of the rural development programmes, this Regulation should exempt from the notification requirement of Article 108(3) of the Treaty different categories of aid in favour of SMEs active in rural areas. Those categories of aid should, in particular, encompass aid for investments concerning the processing of agricultural products into non-agricultural products or the production of cotton, aid for business start-ups for non-agricultural activities, aid for advisory services, aid for knowledge transfer and information actions and aid for the new participation of farmers in quality schemes for cotton and foodstuff and promotion measures in favour of foodstuffs. The aid to be exempted from the notification requirement of Article 108(3) of the Treaty under this Regulation should be identical to the underlying rural development measures and the exempted aid should only be granted pursuant to and in conformity with the rural development programme of the Member State concerned. However, the aid intensities and the eligible costs should also be in line with the general Union State aid principles and the horizontal State aid rules. Therefore, costs such as working capital that is ancillary to, and linked to new investment should not be eligible for aid under this Regulation.

(65) As regards aid for investments concerning the processing of agricultural products into non-agricultural products, it should be specified that investments linked to the production of biofuel or energy from renewable sources should not be eligible for aid under this Regulation. In principle, the horizontal environmental and energy State aid rules should apply to such investments.

(66) In the case of several categories of aid such as: (a) aid towards the costs of market research activities, product conception and design and for the preparation of applications for recognition of quality schemes; (b) aid towards the costs for compulsory control measures in relation to the quality schemes; (c) aid for knowledge transfer and information actions; (d) aid for advisory services; (e) aid for farm replacements services; (f) aid for promotion measures; (g) aid to compensate for the costs of the prevention and eradication of animal diseases and plant pests and (h) aid for the livestock sector the aid is granted to the final aid beneficiaries indirectly, in kind, by means of subsidised services. In such cases the aid should be paid to the provider of the service or activity in question. When selecting the provider due regard should be given to the respective applicable public procurement rules and to the principles of transparency, openness and non-discrimination in the selection procedure.

(67) In the light of the Commission's experience in this area, it is in principle necessary to periodically revise State aid policy. That is why the period of application of this Regulation should be limited. It is therefore appropriate to lay down transitional provisions, including the rules on an adjustment period at the end of validity of this Regulation for exempted aid schemes. Such rules should give Member States time to adapt to the possibly new regime,

NOTES

Repeal of this Regulation in relation to the UK: this Regulation is repealed in relation to the UK (as from IP completion day); see the introductory notes to this Regulation *ante*.

1 OJ L142, 14.5.1998, p 1.

2 Commission Regulation (EC) No 1857/2006 of 15 December 2006 on the application of Articles 87 and 88 of the Treaty to State aid to small and medium-sized enterprises active in the production of agricultural products and amending Regulation (EC) No 70/2001 (OJ L358, 16.12.2006, p 3), as amended by Commission Regulation (EU) No 1114/2013 of 7 November 2013 amending Regulation (EC) No 1857/2006 as regards its period of application (OJ L298, 8.11.2013, p 34).

3 Council Regulation (EU) No 733/2013 of 22 July 2013 amending Regulation (EC) No 994/98 on the application of

Articles 92 and 93 of the Treaty establishing the European Community to certain categories of horizontal State aid (OJ L204, 31.7.2013, p 11).

4 Regulation (EU) No 1308/2013 of the European Parliament and of the Council of 17 December 2013 establishing a common organisation of the markets in agricultural products and repealing Council Regulation (EEC) No 922/72, (EEC) No 234/79, (EC) No 1037/2001 and (EC) No 1234/2007 (OJ L347, 20.12.2013, p 671).

5 Regulation (EU) No 1305/2013 of the European Parliament and of the Council of 17 December 2013 on support for rural development by the European Agricultural Fund for Rural Development (EAFRD) and repealing Council Regulation (EC) No 1698/2005 (OJ L347, 20.12.2013, p 487).

6 COM(2012) 209 final.

7 Commission Regulation (EC) No 800/2008 of 6 August 2008 declaring certain categories of aid compatible with the common market in application of Articles 87 and 88 of the Treaty (General block exemption Regulation) (OJ L214, 9.8.2008, p 3).

8 OJ C319, 27.12.2006, p 1.

9 OJ C244, 1.10.2004, p 2.

10 OJ C155, 20.6.2008, p 10.

11 OJ C204, 1.7.2014, p 1.

12 OJ C14, 19.1.2008, p 6.

13 Directive 2013/37/EU of the European Parliament and of the Council of 26 June 2013 amending Directive 2003/98/EC on the re-use of public sector information (OJ L175, 27.6.2013, p 1).

14 Commission Regulation (EU) No 651/2014 of 17 June 2014 declaring certain categories of aid compatible with the internal market in application of Articles 107 and 108 of the Treaty (OJ L187, 26.6.2014, p 1).

15 Commission Regulation (EC) No 794/2004 of 21 April 2004 implementing Council Regulation (EC) No 659/1999 laying down detailed rules for the application of Article 93 of the EC Treaty (OJ L140, 30.4.2004, p 1).

16 Council Regulation (EC) No 659/1999 laying down detailed rules for the application of Article 93 of the EC Treaty (OJ L83, 27.3.1999, p 1).

17 Commission Recommendation 2003/361/EC concerning the definition of micro, small and medium-sized enterprises (OJ L124, 20.5.2003, p 36).

18 Directive 2011/92/EU of the European Parliament and of the Council of 13 December 2011 on the assessment of the effects of certain public and private projects on the environment (OJ L26, 28.1.2012, p 1).

19 Directive 2009/28/EC of the European Parliament and of the Council of 23 April 2009 on the promotion of the use of energy from renewable sources and amending and subsequently repealing Directives 2001/77/EC and 2003/30/EC (OJ L140, 5.6.2009, p 16).

20 OJ C323, 30.12.2006, p 1.

21 Council Directive 92/43/EEC of 21 May 1992 on the conservation of natural habitats and of wild fauna and flora (OJ L206, 22.7.1992, p 7).

22 Directive 2009/147/EC of the European Parliament and of the Council of 30 November 2009 on the conservation of wild birds (OJ L20, 26.1.2010, p 7).

HAS ADOPTED THIS REGULATION:

CHAPTER I COMMON PROVISIONS

[5.469]

Article 1 Scope

1. This Regulation shall apply to the following categories of aid:

(a) aid in favour of micro, small and medium sized enterprises (SMEs):

(i) active in the agricultural sector, namely primary agricultural production, the processing of agricultural products and the marketing of agricultural products, with the exception of Articles 14, 15, 16, 18 and 23 and Articles 25 to 28 which shall only apply to SMEs active in the primary agricultural production;

(ii) for activities falling outside the scope of Article 42 of the Treaty insofar as such aid is granted in accordance with Regulation (EU) No 1305/2013 and is either co-financed by the European Agricultural Fund for Rural Development (EAFRD) or granted as additional national financing for such co-financed measures.

(b) aid for investments for the conservation of cultural and natural heritage located on agricultural holdings;

(c) aid in favour of making good the damage caused by natural disasters in the agricultural sector;

(d) aid for research and development in the agricultural and forestry sectors;

(e) aid in favour of forestry.

2. Where Member States deem it appropriate, they may choose to grant aid referred to in paragraphs 1(a), 1(d) and 1 (e) of this Article under the conditions and in compliance with Regulation (EU) No 651/2014.

3. This Regulation shall not apply to aid in favour of:

(a) the forestry sector which is not co-financed by the EAFRD or granted as additional national financing for such co-financed measures, with the exception of Articles 31, 38, 39 and 43;

(b) SMEs for activities falling outside the scope of Article 42 of the Treaty which is not co-financed by the EAFRD or granted as additional national financing for such co-financed measure.

4. This Regulation shall not apply to:

(a) aid schemes provided for in Articles 17, 32 and 33, Article 34(5)(a) to (c), and Articles 35, 40, 41, and 44 of this Regulation, if the average annual State aid budget exceeds EUR 150 million, from six months after their entry into force. The Commission may decide that this Regulation shall continue to apply for a longer period to any of these aid schemes after having assessed the relevant evaluation plan notified by the Member State to the Commission, within 20 working days from the scheme's entry into force;

(b) any alterations of schemes referred to in paragraph 4(a) of this Article, other than modifications which cannot affect the compatibility of the aid scheme under this Regulation or cannot significantly affect the content of the approved evaluation plan;

(c) aid to export-related activities towards third countries or Member States, namely aid directly linked to the quantities exported, to the establishment and operation of a distribution network or to other current costs linked to export activity;

(d) aid contingent upon the use of domestic over imported goods.

5. With the exception of Article 30, this Regulation shall not apply to:

[(a) aid schemes which do not explicitly exclude the payment of individual aid in favour of an undertaking which is subject to an outstanding recovery order following a previous Commission decision declaring an aid granted by the same Member State illegal and incompatible with the internal market;

(b) ad hoc aid to an undertaking referred to in point (a)].

6. This Regulation shall not apply to aid to undertakings in difficulty with the exception of:

(a) aid to make good the damage caused by natural disasters in accordance with Article 30, aid for the costs of the eradication of animal diseases in accordance with Article 26(8) and aid for removal and destruction of fallen stock in accordance with Article 27(1)(c), (d) and (e);

(b) aid for the following events provided that the undertaking became an undertaking in difficulty due to losses or damages caused by the event in question:

(i) to compensate for losses caused by an adverse climatic event which can be assimilated to a natural disaster in accordance with Article 25;

(ii) aid for the costs of the eradication of plant pests and for making good the damage caused by animal diseases and plant pests in accordance with Article 26(8) and (9);

(iii) aid for the restoration of damage to forests from fires, natural disasters, adverse climatic events which can be assimilated to a natural disaster, other adverse climatic events, plant pests, catastrophic events and climate change related events in accordance with Article 34(5)(d);

[(c) aid to undertakings which were not in difficulty on 31 December 2019 but became undertakings in difficulty in the period from 1 January 2020 to 30 June 2021.]

7. This Regulation shall not apply to aids which entail, by themselves, by the conditions attached to them or by their financing method a non-severable violation of Union law, in particular to:

(a) aid where the grant of aid is subject to the obligation for the beneficiary to have its headquarters in the relevant Member State or to be predominantly established in that Member State;

(b) aid where the grant of aid is subject to the obligation for the beneficiary to use nationally produced goods or national services;

(c) aid restricting the possibility for the beneficiaries to exploit the research, development and innovation results in other Member States.

NOTES

Para 5: points (a), (b) substituted by Commission Regulation 2019/289/EU, Art 1(1).

Para 6: point (c) added by Commission Regulation 2020/2008/EU, Art 1(1).

Repeal of this Regulation in relation to the UK: this Regulation is repealed in relation to the UK (as from IP completion day); see the introductory notes to this Regulation *ante*.

[5.470]

Article 2 Definitions

For the purpose of this Regulation the following definitions shall apply:

(1) 'aid' means any measure fulfilling all the criteria laid down in Article 107(1) of the Treaty;

(2) 'SME' or 'micro, small and medium-sized enterprises' means undertakings fulfilling the criteria laid down in Annex I;

(3) 'agricultural sector' means all undertakings active in primary agricultural production, processing and marketing of agricultural products;

(4) 'agricultural product' means the products listed in Annex I to the Treaty, except the fishery and aquaculture products listed in Annex I to Regulation (EU) No 1379/2013 of the European Parliament and of the Council;[1]

(5) 'primary agricultural production' means the production of products of the soil and of stock farming, listed in Annex I to the Treaty, without performing any further operation changing the nature of such products;

(6) 'processing of agricultural products' means any operation on an agricultural product resulting in a product which is also an agricultural product, except on-farm activities necessary for preparing an animal or plant product for first sale;

(7) 'marketing of agricultural products' means holding or display with a view to sale, offering for sale, delivery or any other manner of placing on the market, except the first sale by a primary producer to resellers or processors and any activity preparing a product for such first sale; a sale by a primary producer to final consumers is considered as marketing of agricultural products if it takes place in separate premises reserved for that purpose;

(8) 'agricultural holding' means a unit comprising of land, premises and facilities used for primary agricultural production;

(9) 'natural disasters' means earthquakes, avalanches, landslides and floods, tornadoes, hurricanes, volcanic eruptions and wild fires of natural origin;

(10) 'aid scheme' means any act on the basis of which, without further implementing measures being required, individual aid awards may be made to undertakings defined within the act in a general and abstract manner and any act on the basis of which aid which is not linked to a specific project may be granted to one or several undertakings for an indefinite period of time and for an indefinite amount;

(11) 'evaluation plan' means a document containing at least the following minimum elements: the objectives of the aid scheme to be evaluated; the evaluation questions; the result indicators; the envisaged methodology to conduct the evaluation; the data collection requirements; the proposed timing of the evaluation, including the date of submission of the final evaluation report; the description of the independent body conducting the evaluation or the criteria that will be used for its selection and the modalities for ensuring the publicity of the evaluation;

(12) 'individual aid' means:

(a) ad hoc aid; and

(b) awards of aid to individual beneficiaries on the basis of an aid scheme;

(13) 'ad hoc aid' means aid not granted on the basis of an aid scheme;

(14) 'undertaking in difficulty' means an undertaking in respect of which at least one of the following circumstances occurs:

(a) in the case of a limited liability company (other than an SME that has been in existence for less than three years), where more than half of its subscribed share capital has disappeared as a result of accumulated losses. This is the case when deduction of accumulated losses from reserves (and all other elements generally considered as part of the own funds of the company) leads to a negative cumulative amount that exceeds half of the subscribed share capital. For the purposes of this provision, 'limited liability company' refers in particular to the types of company mentioned in Annex I of Directive 2013/34/EU of the European Parliament and of the Council[2] and 'share capital' includes, where relevant, any share premium;

(b) in the case of a company where at least some members have unlimited liability for the debt of the company (other than an SME that has been in existence for less than three), where more than half of its capital as shown in the company accounts has disappeared as a result of accumulated losses. For the purposes of this provision, 'a company where at least some members have unlimited liability for the debt of the company' refers in particular to the types of company mentioned in Annex II to Directive 2013/34/EU;

(c) where the undertaking is subject to collective insolvency proceedings or fulfils the criteria under its domestic law for being placed in collective insolvency proceedings at the request of its creditors;

(d) where the undertaking has received rescue aid and has not yet reimbursed the loan or terminated the guarantee, or has received restructuring aid and is still subject to a restructuring plan;

(e) in the case of an undertaking that is not an SME, where, for the past two years:

(i) the undertaking's book debt to equity ratio has been greater than 7.5 and

(ii) the undertaking's EBITDA interest coverage ratio has been below 1,0;

(15) 'fallen stock' means animals which have been killed by euthanasia with or without a definite diagnosis or which have died, including stillborn and unborn animals, on a farm or on any premises or during transport, but which have not been slaughtered for human consumption;

(16) 'adverse climatic event which can be assimilated to a natural disaster' means unfavourable weather conditions such as frost, storms and hail, ice, heavy or persistent rain or severe drought which destroy more than 30% of the average of the production calculated on the basis of:

(a) the preceding three-year period; or

(b) a three-year average based on the preceding five-year period, excluding the highest and the lowest entry;

(17) 'other adverse climatic events' means unfavourable weather conditions which do not meet the conditions of Article 2(16) of this Regulation;

(18) 'plant pest' means harmful organisms as defined in Article 2(1)(e) of Council Directive 2000/29/EC;[3]

(19) 'catastrophic event' means an unforeseen event of biotic or abiotic nature caused by human action that leads to important disturbances of forest structures, eventually causing important economic damage to the forest sectors;

(20) 'gross grant equivalent' means the amount of the aid if it had been provided in the form of a grant to the beneficiary, before any deduction of tax or other charges;

(21) 'tangible assets' means assets consisting of land, buildings and plant, machinery and equipment;

(22) 'intangible assets' means assets that do not have a physical or financial embodiment such as patents, licences, know-how or other intellectual property;

(23) 'agroforestry systems' means land use systems where trees are grown in combination with agriculture on the same land;

(24) 'repayable advance' means a loan for a project which is paid in one or more instalments and the conditions for the reimbursement of which depend on the outcome of the project;

(25) 'start of works on the project or activity' means the earlier of either the start of the activities or the construction works relating to the investment, or the first legally binding commitment to order equipment or employ services or any other commitment that makes the project or activity irreversible; buying land and preparatory works such as obtaining permits and conducting feasibility studies are not considered start of works or activity;

(26) 'large enterprises' means undertakings not fulfilling the criteria laid down in Annex I;

(27) 'fiscal successor scheme' means a scheme in the form of tax advantages which constitutes an amended version of a previously existing scheme in the form of tax advantages and which replaces it;

(28) 'aid intensity' means the gross aid amount expressed as a percentage of the eligible costs, before any deduction of tax or other charge;

(29) 'date of granting the aid' means the date when the legal right to receive the aid is conferred on the beneficiary under the applicable national legal regime;

(30) 'Union standard' means mandatory standard laid down in Union legislation setting the level which individual undertakings must achieve, in particular as regards the environment, hygiene and animal welfare; however, standards or targets set at Union level which are binding for Member States but not for individual undertakings are not deemed to be Union standards;

(31) 'rural development programme' means rural development programme as provided for in Article 6(1) of Regulation (EU) No 1305/2013;

(32) 'non-productive investment' means investment which does not lead to a significant increase in the value or profitability of the holding;

(33) 'investments to comply with an Union standard' means investments made to comply with an Union standard after the expiry of the transitional period provided for in Union legislation;

(34) 'young farmer' means a person who is no more than 40 years of age on the date of submitting the aid application, possesses adequate occupational skills and competences and is setting up for the first time in an agricultural holding as a head of that holding;

(35) 'outermost regions' means the regions referred to in the first paragraph of Article 349 of the Treaty;

(36) 'smaller Aegean islands' means the smaller islands referred to in Article 1(2) of Regulation (EU) No 229/2013 of the European Parliament and of the Council;[4]

(37) 'less developed regions' means regions where the gross domestic product (GDP) per capita is less than 75% of average GDP of the EU-27;

(38) 'EU-25' means the 25 Member States of the Union who were Member States of the Union in May 2005;

(39) 'EU-27' means the 27 Member States of the Union who were Member States of the Union in January 2007;

(40) 'capital works' means works, undertaken by the farmer personally or by the farmer's workers, that create an asset;

(41) 'food based biofuel' means a biofuel produced from cereal and other starch rich crops, sugars and oil crops as defined in the Commission's Proposal for a Directive of the European Parliament and of the Council amending Directive 98/70/EC relating to the quality of petrol and diesel fuels and amending Directive 2009/28/EC on the promotion of the use of energy from renewable sources;[5]

(42) 'active farmer' means an active farmer within the meaning of Article 9 of Regulation (EU) No 1307/2013[6] of the European Parliament and of the Council;

(43) 'producer group and organisation' means a group or organisation set up for the purpose of:

(a) adapting the production and output of producers who are members of such producer groups or organisations to market requirements; or

(b) jointly placing goods on the market, including the preparation for sale, centralisation of sales and supply to bulk buyers; or

(c) establishing common rules on production information, with particular regard to harvesting and availability; or

(d) other activities that may be carried out by producer groups or organisations, such as the development of business and marketing skills and the organisation and facilitation of innovation processes;

(44) 'fixed costs arising from participation in quality scheme' means the costs incurred for entering a supported quality scheme and the annual contribution for participating in that quality scheme, including, where necessary, expenditure on checks required to verify compliance with the specifications of the quality scheme;

(45) 'advice' means complete advice given in the framework of one and the same contract;

(46) 'member of a farm household' means a natural or legal person or a group of natural or legal persons, whatever legal status is granted to the group and its members by national law, with the exception of farm workers;

(47) 'Transmissible Spongiform Encephalopathy (TSE) and Bovine Spongiform Encephalopathy (BSE) test costs' means all costs, including those for test kits and for the taking, transporting, testing, storing and destruction of samples necessary for sampling and laboratory testing in accordance with Chapter C of Annex X to Regulation (EC) No 999/2001 of the European Parliament and of the Council;[7]

(48) 'herd book' means any book, register, file or data medium:

(a) which is maintained by a breeders' organisation or association officially recognised by a Member State in which the breeders' organisation or association was constituted; and

(b) in which pure-bred breeding animals of a given breed are entered or registered with mention of their ancestors;

(49) 'protected animal' means any animal protected either by Union or by national legislation;

(50) 'research and knowledge-dissemination organisation' means an entity (such as universities or research institutes, technology transfer agencies, innovation intermediaries, research-oriented physical or virtual collaborative entities), irrespective of its legal status (organised under public or private law) or way of financing, whose primary goal is to independently conduct fundamental research, industrial research or experimental development, or to widely disseminate the results of such activities by way of teaching, publication or knowledge transfer. Where such entity also pursues economic activities the financing, the costs and the revenues of those economic activities must be accounted for separately. Undertakings that can exert influence upon such an entity, in the quality of, for example, shareholders or members, may not enjoy a preferential access to its research capacities or to the results generated by it;

(51) 'arm's length' means that the conditions of the transaction between the contracting parties do not differ from those which would be stipulated between independent undertakings and contain no element of collusion. Any transaction that results from an open, transparent and unconditional procedure is considered as meeting the arm's length principle;

(52) 'fast growing trees' means a short rotation forest, where the minimum time before felling is set to be not less than 8 years and the maximum time before felling is set not to exceed 20 years;

(53) 'trees for short rotation coppicing' means tree species of CN code 06 02 9041 to be defined by Member States that consist of woody, perennial crops, the rootstock or stools of which remain in the ground after harvesting, with new shoots emerging in the following season and with a maximum harvest cycle to be determined by the Member States;

(54) 'transaction cost' means an additional cost linked to fulfilling a commitment, but not directly attributable to its implementation or not included in the costs or income foregone that are compensated directly; and which can be calculated on a standard cost basis;

(55) 'other land manager' means an undertaking which manages land other than undertaking active in the agricultural sector;

(56) 'processing of agricultural products into non-agricultural products' means any operation on an agricultural product resulting in a product which is not covered by Annex I to the Treaty;

(57) '"a" areas' means those areas designated in an approved regional aid map for the period from 1 July 2014 to 31 December 2020 in application of the provisions of Article 107(3)(a) of the Treaty;

(58) '"c" areas' means those areas designated in an approved regional aid map for the period 1 July 2014 to 31 December 2020 in application of the provisions of Article 107(3)(c) of the Treaty;
(59) 'sparsely populated areas' means areas accepted by the Commission as such in the individual decisions on regional aid maps for the period from 1 July 2014 to 31 December 2020;
(60) 'NUTS 3 area' means a region specified at level 3 of a common classification of territorial units for statistics in accordance with Regulation (EC) No 1059/2003 of the European Parliament and of the Council;[8]
(61) 'non-predefined "c" areas' means areas that a Member State at its own discretion designates as 'c' areas provided that the Member State demonstrates that such areas fulfil certain socioeconomic criteria and that those areas are designated in an approved regional aid map for the period 1 July 2014 to 31 December 2020 in application of the provisions of Article 107(3)(c) of the Treaty;
(62) 'former "a" areas' means those areas designated as 'a' areas in an approved regional map for the period from 1 January 2011 to 30 June 2014;
(63) 'foodstuffs' means foodstuffs which are not agricultural products and which are listed in Annex I to Regulation (EU) No 1151/2012 of the European Parliament and of the Council.[9]

NOTES

Repeal of this Regulation in relation to the UK: this Regulation is repealed in relation to the UK (as from IP completion day); see the introductory notes to this Regulation *ante*.

1 Regulation (EU) No 1379/2013 of the European Parliament and of the Council on the common organisation of the markets in fishery and aquaculture products, amending Council Regulations (EC) No 1184/2006 and (EC) No 1224/2009 and repealing Council Regulation (EC) No 104/2000 (OJ L354, 28.12.2013, p 1).

2 Directive 2013/34/EU of the European Parliament and of the Council of 26 June 2013 on the annual financial statements, consolidated financial statements and related reports of certain types of undertakings, amending Directive 2006/43/EC of the European Parliament and of the Council and repealing Council Directives 78/660/EEC and 83/349/EEC (OJ L182, 29.6.2013, p 19).

3 Council Directive 2000/29/EC of 8 May 2000 on protective measures against the introduction into the Community of organisms harmful to plants or plant products and against their spread within the Community (OJ L169, 10.7.2000, p 1).

4 Regulation (EU) No 229/2013 of the European Parliament and of the Council of 13 March 2013 laying down specific measures for agriculture in favour of the smaller Aegean islands and repealing Council Regulation (EC) No 1405/2006 (OJ L78, 20.3.2013, p 41).

5 COM(2012) 595, 17.10.2012.

6 Regulation (EU) No 1307/2013 of the European Parliament and of the Council of 17 December 2013 establishing rules for direct payments to farmers under support schemes within the framework of the common agricultural policy and repealing Council Regulation (EC) No 637/2008 and Council Regulation (EC) No 73/2009 (OJ L347, 20.12.2013, p 608).

7 Regulation (EC) No 999/2001 of the European Parliament and of the Council of 22 May 2001 laying down rules for the prevention, control and eradication of certain transmissible spongiform encephalopathies (OJ L147, 31.5.2001, p 1).

8 Regulation (EC) No 1059/2003 of the European Parliament and of the Council of 26 May 2003 on the establishment of a common classification of territorial units for statistics (NUTS) (OJ L154, 21.6.2003, p 1).

9 Regulation (EU) No 1151/2012 of the European Parliament and of the Council of 21 November 2012 on quality schemes for agricultural products and foodstuffs (OJ L343, 14.12.2012, p 1).

[5.471]
Article 3 Conditions for exemption

Aid schemes, individual aid granted under aid schemes and ad hoc aid shall be compatible with the internal market within the meaning of Article 107(2) or (3) of the Treaty and shall be exempted from the notification requirement of Article 108(3) of the Treaty provided that such aid fulfils all the conditions laid down in Chapter I of this Regulation, as well as the specific conditions for the relevant category of aid laid down in Chapter III of this Regulation.

NOTES

Repeal of this Regulation in relation to the UK: this Regulation is repealed in relation to the UK (as from IP completion day); see the introductory notes to this Regulation *ante*.

[5.472]
Article 4 Notification thresholds

1. This Regulation shall not apply to any individual aid, the gross grant equivalent of which exceeds the following thresholds:

- *(a) aid for investments in tangible assets or intangible assets on agricultural holdings linked to primary agricultural production as referred to in Article 14: EUR 500,000 per undertaking per investment project;*
- *(b) aid for investments concerning the relocation of a farm building resulting in the modernisation of facilities or in an increase in production capacity as referred to in Article 16(4): EUR 500,000 per undertaking per investment project;*
- *(c) aid for investments in connection with the processing of agricultural products and the marketing of agricultural products as referred to in Article 17: EUR 7.5 million per undertaking per investment project;*
- *(d) aid for investments in favour of the conservation of cultural and natural heritage located on the agricultural holding as referred to in Article 29: EUR 500,000 per undertaking per investment project;*
- *(e) aid for research and development in the agricultural and forestry sectors as referred to in Article 31: EUR 7.5 million per project;*
- *(f) aid for afforestation and the creation of woodland as referred to in Article 32: EUR 7.5 million per establishment project;*
- *(g) aid for agroforestry systems as referred to Article 33: EUR 7.5 million per agroforestry system establishment project;*
- *(h) aid for investments improving the resilience and environmental value of forest ecosystems as referred to in Article 35: EUR 7.5 million per investment project;*

(i) *aid for investments in infrastructure related to the development, modernisation or adaptation of the forestry sector as referred to in Article 40: EUR 7.5 million per investment project;*

(j) *aid for investments in forestry technologies and in the processing, mobilising and marketing of forestry products as referred to in Article 41: EUR 7.5 million per investment project;*

(k) *aid for investments concerning the processing of agricultural products into non-agricultural products or the production of cotton as referred to in Article 44: EUR 7.5 million per investment project.*

2. The thresholds set out in paragraph 1 shall not be circumvented by the artificial splitting up of the aid schemes or aid projects.

NOTES

Repeal of this Regulation in relation to the UK: this Regulation is repealed in relation to the UK (as from IP completion day); see the introductory notes to this Regulation *ante*.

[5.473]

Article 5 Transparency of aid

1. This Regulation shall apply only to aid in respect of which it is possible to calculate precisely the gross grant equivalent ex ante without need to undertake a risk assessment ('transparent aid').

2. The following categories of aid shall be considered to be transparent aid:

(a) *aid comprised in grants and interest rate subsidies;*

(b) *aid comprised in loans, where the gross grant equivalent has been calculated on the basis of the reference rate prevailing at the time of the grant;*

(c) *aid comprised in guarantees:*

(i) *where the gross grant equivalent has been calculated on the basis of safe-harbour premiums laid down in a Commission Notice; or*

(ii) *where before the implementation of the aid, the methodology to calculate the gross grant equivalent of the guarantee has been accepted on the basis of the Commission Notice on the application of Articles 87 and 88 of the EC Treaty to State aid in the form of guarantees, or any successor notice, following notification of that methodology to the Commission under any regulation adopted by the Commission in the State aid area applicable at the time, and the approved methodology explicitly addresses the type of guarantee and the type of underlying transaction at stake in the context of the application of this Regulation;*

(d) *aid in the form of tax advantages, where the measure provides for a cap ensuring that the applicable threshold is not exceeded;*

(e) *aid in the form of repayable advances, if the total nominal amount of the repayable advance does not exceed the thresholds applicable under this Regulation or if, before implementation of the measure, the methodology to calculate the gross grant equivalent of the repayable advance has been accepted following its notification to the Commission.*

3. For the purpose of this Regulation, the following categories of aid shall not be considered to be transparent aid:

(a) *aid comprised in capital injections;*

(b) *aid comprised in risk finance measures.*

NOTES

Repeal of this Regulation in relation to the UK: this Regulation is repealed in relation to the UK (as from IP completion day); see the introductory notes to this Regulation *ante*.

Article 6 Incentive effect

1. This Regulation shall apply only to aid which has an incentive effect.

2. Aid shall be considered to have an incentive effect if the beneficiary has submitted a written application for the aid to the Member State concerned before work on the project or activity has started. The application for the aid shall contain at least the following information:

(a) *undertaking's name and size;*

(b) *description of the project or the activity, including its start and end dates;*

(c) *location of the project or the activity;*

(d) *list of eligible costs;*

(e) *type (grant, loan, guarantee, repayable advance or other) and amount of public funding needed for the project/ activity.*

3. Ad hoc aid granted to large enterprises shall be considered to have an incentive effect if, in addition to ensuring that the condition laid down in paragraph 2 is fulfilled, the Member State has verified, before granting the ad hoc aid concerned, that documentation prepared by the beneficiary establishes that the aid will result in one or more of the following:

(a) *a material increase in the scope of the project or activity due to the aid;*

(b) *a material increase in the total amount spent by the beneficiary on the project or activity due to the aid;*

(c) *a material increase in the speed of completion of the project or activity concerned;*

(d) *in the case of investment ad hoc aid, that the project or activity would not have been carried out as such in the rural area concerned or would not have been sufficiently profitable for the beneficiary in the rural area concerned in the absence of the aid.*

4. By way of derogation from paragraphs 2 and 3, measures in the form of tax advantages shall be deemed to have an incentive effect if the following conditions are fulfilled:

(a) *the measure establishes a right to aid in accordance with objective criteria and without further exercise of discretion by the Member State; and*

(b) *the measure has been adopted and in force before work on the aided project or activity has started, except in the case of fiscal successor schemes where the activity was already covered by the previous schemes in the form of tax advantages.*

5. By way of derogation of paragraphs 2, 3 and 4 the following categories of aid are not required to have or shall be deemed to have an incentive effect:

(a) *aid schemes for land consolidation where the conditions laid down in Article 15 or Article 43 are fulfilled and where:*
   (i) *the aid scheme establishes a right to aid in accordance with objective criteria and without further exercise of discretion by the Member State; and*
   (ii) *the aid scheme has been adopted and in force before eligible costs under Article 15 or Article 43 are incurred by the beneficiary;*

(b) *aid for promotion measures in the form of publications aimed at raising awareness of agricultural products among the wider public where the conditions laid down in Article 24(2)(b) are fulfilled;*

(c) *aid to compensate for losses caused by adverse climatic event which can be assimilated to a natural disaster where the conditions laid down in Article 25 are fulfilled;*

(d) *aid to compensate for the costs of the eradication of animal diseases and plant pests and for losses caused by those animal diseases or plant pests where the conditions laid down in Article 26(9) and (10) are fulfilled;*

(e) *aid to cover the costs of the removal and destruction of fallen stock where the conditions laid down in Article 27(1) (c), (d) and (e) are fulfilled;*

(f) *aid for investments in favour of the conservation of cultural and natural heritage located on agricultural holdings in accordance with Article 29;*

(g) *aid to make good the damage caused by natural disasters where the conditions laid down in Article 30 are fulfilled;*

(h) *aid for research and development in the agricultural and forestry sectors where the conditions laid down in Article 31 are fulfilled;*

(i) *aid for the restoration of damage to forests from fires, natural disasters, adverse climatic events, plant pests, animal diseases, catastrophic events and climate change related events in accordance with Article 34(5)(d) where the conditions laid down in Article 34 are fulfilled;*

[(j) *aid for the participation of active farmers in quality schemes for cotton and foodstuffs where the conditions laid down in Article 48 are fulfilled*].

NOTES

Para 5: point (j) added by Commission Regulation 2019/289/EU, Art 1(2).

Repeal of this Regulation in relation to the UK: this Regulation is repealed in relation to the UK (as from IP completion day); see the introductory notes to this Regulation *ante*.

[5.474]

Article 7 Aid intensity and eligible costs

1. For the purposes of calculating the aid intensity and the eligible costs, all figures used shall be taken before any deduction of tax or other charge. The eligible costs shall be supported by documentary evidence which shall be clear, specific and contemporary. [The amounts of eligible costs may be calculated in accordance with the simplified cost options set out in Regulation (EU) No 1303/2013 of the European Parliament and of the Council,[1] *provided that the operation is at least partly financed through the EAFRD and that the category of costs is eligible according to the relevant exemption provision.]*

2. Value added tax (VAT) shall not be eligible for aid, except where it is non-recoverable under national VAT legislation.

3. Where aid is granted in a form other than a grant, the aid amount shall be the gross grant equivalent of the aid.

4. Aid payable in several instalments shall be discounted to its value on the date of granting the aid. The eligible costs shall be discounted to their value on the date of granting the aid. The interest rate to be used for discounting purposes shall be the discount rate applicable on the date of granting the aid.

5. Where aid is granted by means of tax advantages, the discounting of aid tranches shall take place on the basis of the discount rates applicable at the various times the tax advantage takes effect.

6. Where aid is granted in the form of repayable advances which, in the absence of an accepted methodology to calculate their gross grant equivalent, are expressed as a percentage of the eligible costs and the measure provides that in the case of a successful outcome of the project, as defined on the basis of reasonable and prudent hypothesis, the advances shall be repaid with an interest rate at least equal to the discount rate applicable on the date of granting the aid, the maximum aid intensities laid down in Chapter III may be increased by 10 percentage points.

NOTES

Para 1: words in square brackets inserted by Commission Regulation 2017/1084/EU, Art 2.

Repeal of this Regulation in relation to the UK: this Regulation is repealed in relation to the UK (as from IP completion day); see the introductory notes to this Regulation *ante*.

[1] Regulation (EU) No 1303/2013 of the European Parliament and of the Council of 17 December 2013 laying down common provisions on the European Regional Development Fund, the European Social Fund, the Cohesion Fund, the European Agricultural Fund for Rural Development and the European Maritime and Fisheries Fund and laying down general provisions on the European Regional Development Fund, the European Social Fund, the Cohesion Fund and the European Maritime and Fisheries Fund and repealing Council Regulation (EC) No 1083/2006 (OJ L347, 20.12.2013, p 320).

[5.475]

Article 8 Cumulation

1. In determining whether the notification thresholds provided for in Article 4 and the maximum aid intensities and maximum aid amounts laid down in Chapter III are respected, the total amount of State aid for the aided activity or project or undertaking shall be taken into account.

2. Where Union funding centrally managed by the institutions, agencies, joint undertakings or other bodies of the Union that is not directly or indirectly under the control of the Member State is combined with State aid, only the latter shall be considered for determining whether notification thresholds and maximum aid intensities and ceilings are respected, provided that the total amount of public funding granted in relation to the same eligible costs does not exceed the most favourable funding rates laid down in the applicable rules of Union law.

3. Aid with identifiable eligible costs, exempted from the notification requirement of Article 108(3) of the Treaty under this Regulation, may be cumulated with:

- *(a) any other State aid, as long as those measures concern different identifiable eligible costs;*
- *(b) any other State aid, in relation to the same eligible costs, partly or fully overlapping, only if such cumulation does not result in exceeding the highest aid intensity or aid amount applicable to this aid under this Regulation.*

4. Aid without identifiable eligible costs exempted under Articles 18 and 45 of this Regulation may be cumulated with any other State aid with identifiable eligible costs.

Aid without identifiable eligible costs may be cumulated with other State aid without identifiable eligible costs, up to the highest relevant total financing threshold fixed in the specific circumstances of each case by this or another block exemption regulation or decision adopted by the Commission.

5. State aid exempted under Sections 1, 2 and 3 of Chapter III of this Regulation shall not be cumulated with payments referred to in Articles 81(2) and 82 of Regulation (EU) No 1305/2013 in respect of the same eligible costs if such cumulation would result in an aid intensity or aid amount exceeding those laid down in this Regulation.

6. State aid exempted under this Regulation shall not be cumulated with any de minimis aid in respect of the same eligible costs if such cumulation would result in an aid intensity or aid amount exceeding those laid down in Chapter III.

7. Aid for investments aimed at the restoration of agricultural production potential as referred to in Article 14(3)(e) shall not be cumulated with aid for compensation for material damage referred to in Articles 25, 26 and 30 of this Regulation.

8. Start-up aid for producer groups and organisations in the agricultural sector as referred to in Article 19 of this Regulation shall not be cumulated with aid for setting-up of producers groups and organisations in the agricultural sector as referred to in Article 27 of Regulation (EU) No 1305/2013.

Start-up aid for young farmers and start-up aid for the development of small farms as referred to in Article 18 of this Regulation shall not be cumulated with business start-up aid for young farmers or the development of small farms as referred to in Article 19(1)(a)(i) and (iii) of Regulation (EU) No 1305/20013 if such cumulation would result in an aid amount exceeding those laid down in this Regulation.

NOTES

Repeal of this Regulation in relation to the UK: this Regulation is repealed in relation to the UK (as from IP completion day); see the introductory notes to this Regulation *ante*.

[5.476]

Article 9 Publication and information

1. At the latest 10 working days before the date of entry into force of an aid scheme exempted from the notification requirement of Article 108(3) of the Treaty under this Regulation, or the granting of ad hoc aid exempted under this Regulation, Member States shall transmit to the Commission, via the Commission's web notification application in accordance with Article 3 of Regulation (EC) No 794/2004, a summary information regarding such aid in the standardised format set out in Annex II to this Regulation.

Within 10 working days of receipt of that summary information, the Commission shall send to the Member State a notice of receipt with an identification number of the aid.

2. The Member State concerned shall ensure the publication on a comprehensive State aid website at national or regional level, of:

- *(a) the summary information referred to in paragraph 1 or a link to it;*
- *(b) the full text of each aid referred to in paragraph 1, including its amendments, or a link providing access to the full text;*
- *(c) the information referred to in Annex III to this Regulation on each individual aid award exceeding the following:*
  - *(i) EUR 60,000 for beneficiaries active in the primary agricultural production;*
  - *(ii) EUR 500,000 for beneficiaries active in the sectors of the processing of agricultural products, the marketing of agricultural products, the forestry sector or activities falling outside the scope of Article 42 of the Treaty.*

3. For aid schemes in the form of tax advantages, that conditions shall be considered fulfilled if Member States publish the required information on individual aid amounts in the following ranges in EUR million:

- *(a) 0.06–0.5 only for primary agricultural production;*
- *(b) 0.5–1;*
- *(c) 1 to 2;*
- *(d) 2 to 5;*
- *(e) 5 to 10;*
- *(f) 10 to 30; and*
- *(g) 30 and more.*

4. The information referred to in paragraph 2(c) above shall be organised and accessible in a standardised manner, as described in Annex III and shall allow for effective search and download functions. The information referred to in paragraph 2 shall be published within six months from the date the aid was granted or, for aid in the form of tax advantage, within one year from the date the tax declaration is due, and shall be available for at least 10 years from the date of granting the aid.

5. The full text of the aid scheme or of the ad hoc aid referred to in paragraph 1 shall include, in particular, an explicit reference to this Regulation, by citing its title and publication reference in the Official Journal of the European Union and to the specific provisions of Chapter III concerned by that act, or where applicable, to the national law which ensures that the relevant provisions of this Regulation are complied with. It shall be accompanied by its implementing provisions and its amendments.

6. The Commission shall publish on its website:

(a) the summary information referred to in paragraph 1;

(b) the links to the State aid websites of all Member States referred to in paragraph 2.

7. Member States shall comply with the provisions of paragraphs 2, 3 and 4 within two years from the date of entry into force of this Regulation at the latest.

[8. By way of derogation from paragraphs 1, 2 and 6, where a Member State wishes to prolong measures in respect of which summary information was submitted to the Commission, summary information regarding the prolongation of those measures shall be deemed to have been communicated to the Commission and published, provided that no substantive amendment, other than a budget increase, is made to the measures concerned.]

NOTES

Para 8: added by Commission Regulation 2020/2008/EU, Art 1(2).

Repeal of this Regulation in relation to the UK: this Regulation is repealed in relation to the UK (as from IP completion day); see the introductory notes to this Regulation *ante*.

[5.477]

Article 10 Avoidance of double publication

If the individual aid award falls within the scope of Regulation (EU) No 1305/2013 and is either co-financed by the EAFRD or granted as additional national financing for such co-financed measures, the Member State may choose not to publish it on the State aid website referred to in Article 9(2) of this Regulation, provided that the individual aid award has already been published in accordance with Articles 111, 112 and 113 of Regulation (EU) No 1306/2013 of the European Parliament and the Council.[1] *In that case, the Member State shall make a reference to the website referred to in Article 111 of Regulation (EU) No 1306/2013 on the State aid website referred to Article 9(2) of this Regulation.*

NOTES

Repeal of this Regulation in relation to the UK: this Regulation is repealed in relation to the UK (as from IP completion day); see the introductory notes to this Regulation *ante*.

[1] Regulation (EU) No 1306/2013 of the European Parliament and of the Council of 17 December 2013 on the financing, management and monitoring of the common agricultural policy and repealing Council Regulations (EEC) No 352/78, (EC) No 165/94, (EC) No 2799/98, (EC) No 814/2000, (EC) No 1290/2005 and (EC) No 485/2008 (OJ L347, 20.12.2013, p 549).

CHAPTER II PROCEDURAL REQUIREMENTS

[5.478]

Article 11 Withdrawal of the benefit of the block exemption

Where the Member State grants aid allegedly exempted from the notification requirement of Article 108(3) of the Treaty under this Regulation without fulfilling the conditions set out in Chapters I to III, the Commission may, after having provided the Member State concerned with the possibility to make its views known, adopt a decision stating that all or some of the future aid measures adopted by the Member State concerned which would otherwise fulfil the requirements of this Regulation, are to be notified to the Commission in accordance with Article 108(3) of the Treaty. The aids to be notified may be limited to certain types of aids, to aid granted in favour of certain beneficiaries or to aid adopted by certain authorities of the Member State concerned.

NOTES

Repeal of this Regulation in relation to the UK: this Regulation is repealed in relation to the UK (as from IP completion day); see the introductory notes to this Regulation *ante*.

[5.479]

Article 12 Reporting

1. Member States shall transmit to the Commission in electronic form an annual report, as referred to in Chapter III of Regulation (EC) No 794/2004, on the application of this Regulation in respect of each whole year or each part of the year during which this Regulation applies.

2. The annual report shall contain also the information concerning the following:

(a) animal diseases or plant pest as referred to in Article 26;

(b) meteorological information on the type, timing, relative magnitude and location of climatic events which can be assimilated to a natural disaster as referred to in Article 25 or natural disasters in the agricultural sector as referred to in Article 30.

NOTES

Repeal of this Regulation in relation to the UK: this Regulation is repealed in relation to the UK (as from IP completion day); see the introductory notes to this Regulation *ante*.

[5.480]

Article 13 Monitoring

Member States shall maintain detailed records with the information and supporting documentation necessary to establish that all the conditions laid down in this Regulation are fulfilled. Such records shall be kept for 10 years from the date on which the ad hoc aid was granted or the last aid was granted under an aid scheme. The Member State concerned shall provide the Commission, within a period of 20 working days or such longer period as may be fixed in the request, with all the information and supporting documentation which the Commission considers necessary to monitor the application of this Regulation.

NOTES

Repeal of this Regulation in relation to the UK: this Regulation is repealed in relation to the UK (as from IP completion day); see the introductory notes to this Regulation *ante*.

CHAPTER III CATEGORIES OF AID

SECTION 1 AID IN FAVOUR OF SMES ACTIVE IN PRIMARY AGRICULTURAL PRODUCTION, THE PROCESSING OF AGRICULTURAL PRODUCTS AND THE MARKETING OF AGRICULTURAL PRODUCTS

[5.481]

Article 14 Aid for investments in tangible assets or intangible assets on agricultural holdings linked to primary agricultural production

1. Aid for investments in tangible assets or intangible assets on agricultural holdings linked to the primary agricultural production shall be compatible with the internal market within the meaning of Article 107(3)(c) of the Treaty and shall be exempted from the notification requirement of Article 108(3) thereof where it fulfils the conditions laid down in paragraphs 2 to 14 of this Article and in Chapter I.

2. The investment may be carried out by one or more beneficiaries or concern a tangible asset or intangible asset used by one or more beneficiaries.

3. The investment shall pursue at least one of the following objectives:

(a) the improvement of the overall performance and sustainability of the agricultural holding, in particular through a reduction of production costs or the improvement and re-deployment of production;

(b) the improvement of the natural environment, hygiene conditions or animal welfare standards, provided that the investment concerned goes beyond Union standards in force;

(c) the creation and improvement of infrastructure related to the development, adaptation and modernisation of agriculture, including access to farm land, land consolidation and improvement, the supply and saving of energy and water;

(d) the achievement of agri-environmental-climate objectives, including the biodiversity conservation status of species and habitat as well as enhancing the public amenity value of a Natura 2000 area or other high nature value systems, defined in the national or regional rural development programmes of Member States, as long as investments are non-productive;

(e) the restoration of production potential damaged by natural disasters, adverse climatic events which can be assimilated to natural disasters, animal diseases and plant pests and the prevention of damages caused by those events.

4. The investment may be linked to the production at farm-level of biofuels or of energy from renewable sources, provided that such production does not exceed the average annual consumption of fuels or energy of the given farm.

Where the investment is made for the production of biofuels, the production capacity of the production facilities shall be no more than the equivalent to the annual average transport fuel consumption of the agricultural holding and the produced biofuel shall not be sold on the market.

Where the investment is made for the production of thermal energy and electricity from renewable sources on agricultural holdings, the production facilities shall serve only the beneficiary's own energy needs and their production capacity shall be no more than the equivalent to the combined average annual energy consumption of thermal energy and electricity on the agricultural holding, including the farm household. The selling of electricity into the grid shall only be allowed as far as the annual self-consumption limit is respected.

Where the investment is carried out by more beneficiaries with the purpose to serve their own biofuel and energy needs, the annual average consumption shall be accumulated to the amount equivalent to the average annual consumption of all beneficiaries.

The investments in renewable energy infrastructure that consume or produce energy shall comply with minimum standards for energy efficiency, where such standards exist at national level.

Investments in installations, the primary purpose of which is electricity production from biomass, shall not be eligible for aid unless a minimum percentage of heat energy, to be determined by the Member States, is utilised.

Member States shall establish thresholds for the maximum proportions of cereals and other starch rich crops, sugars and oil crops used for bioenergy production, including biofuels, for different types of installations. Aid to bioenergy investment projects shall be limited to bioenergy meeting the applicable sustainability criteria laid down in Union legislation, including in Article 17(2) to (6) of Directive 2009/28/EC.

5. The investment shall be in conformity with Union legislation and with the national laws of the Member State concerned on environmental protection. For investment requiring an environmental impact assessment under Directive 2011/92/EU the aid shall be subject to the condition that such assessment shall have been carried out and the development consent shall have been granted for the investment project concerned before the date of granting the individual aid.

6. The aid shall cover the following eligible costs:

(a) the costs for the construction, acquisition, including leasing, or improvement of immovable property, with land only being eligible to an extent not exceeding 10% of the total eligible costs of the operation concerned;

(b) the purchase or lease purchase of machinery and equipment up to the market value of the asset;

(c) the general costs linked to the expenditure referred to in points (a) and (b), such as architect, engineer and consultation fees, fees relating to advice on environmental and economic sustainability, including feasibility studies; feasibility studies shall remain eligible expenditure even where, based on their results, no expenditure under points (a) and (b) is incurred;

(d) the acquisition or development of computer software and the acquisition of patents, licences, copyrights and trademarks;

(e) expenses for non-productive investments linked to the objectives referred to in paragraph 3(d);

(f) in the case of irrigation, the costs for investments that fulfil the following conditions:

(i) a river basin management plan, as required by Article 13 of Directive 2000/60/EC of the European Parliament and of the Council,[1] must have been notified to the Commission for the entire area in which the investment is to take place, as well as in any other areas whose environment may be affected by the investment. The measures taking effect under the river basin management plan in accordance with Article 11 of that Directive and of relevance to the agricultural sector must be specified in the relevant programme of measures. Water metering enabling measurement of water use at the level of the supported investment must be in place or must be put in place as part of the investment;

(ii) the investment must lead to a reduction of previous water use of at least 25%;

However, as regards point (f) investments affecting bodies of ground- or surface water whose status has been identified as less than good in the relevant river basin management plan for reasons related to water quantity as well as investments resulting in a net increase of the irrigated area affecting a given body of ground- or surface water shall not be eligible for aid under this Article.

The conditions of point (f) (i) and (ii) above shall not apply to an investment in an existing installation which affects only energy efficiency or to an investment in the creation of a reservoir or to an investment in the use of recycled water which does not affect a body of ground- or surface water;

(g) in the case of investments aimed at the restoration of agricultural production potential damaged by natural disasters, adverse climatic events which can be assimilated to natural disasters, animal diseases or plant pests the eligible costs may include the costs incurred for restoring the agricultural production potential up to the level it was at before the occurrence of those events;

(h) in the case of investments aimed at the prevention of damages caused by natural disasters, adverse climatic events which can be assimilated to natural disasters, animal diseases or plant pests, the eligible costs may include the costs of specific preventive actions.

7. Costs, other than those referred to in paragraph 6(a) and (b) connected with leasing contracts, such as lessor's margin, interest refinancing costs, overheads and insurance charges shall not be considered to be eligible costs.

Working capital shall not be considered to be an eligible cost.

8. From 1 January 2017, in the case of irrigation, aid shall be paid only by Member States which ensure, in respect of the river basin district in which the investment takes place, a contribution of the different water uses to the recovery of the costs of water services by the agricultural sector consistent with Article 9(1) first indent of Directive 2000/60/EC having regard where appropriate, to the social, environmental and economic effects of the recovery as well as the geographic and climatic conditions of the region or regions affected.

9. Aid shall not be granted in respect of the following:

(a) the purchase of production rights, payment entitlements and annual plants;

(b) the planting of annual plants;

(c) drainage works;

(d) investments to comply with Union standards, with exception of aid granted to young farmers within 24 months from the date of their setting-up;

(e) the purchase of animals, with exception of aid granted for investments pursuant to paragraph 3(e).

10. The aid shall not be limited to specific agricultural products and must therefore be available either to all sectors of the primary agricultural production or to the whole plant production sector or to the whole animal production sector. However, Member States may exclude certain products because of overcapacity in the internal market or a lack of market outlets.

11. The aid referred to in paragraph 1 shall not be granted in contravention of any prohibition or restriction laid down in Regulation (EU) No 1308/2013, even where such prohibitions and restrictions only refer to the Union support provided for in that regulation.

12. The aid intensity shall be limited to:

(a) 75% of the amount of the eligible costs in outermost regions;

(b) 75% of the amount of the eligible costs in the smaller Aegean islands;

(c) 50% of the amount of the eligible costs in less developed regions and in all regions whose GDP per capita for the period from 1 January 2007 to 31 December 2013 was less than 75% of the average of the EU-25 for the reference period but whose GDP per capita is above 75% of the GDP average of the EU-27;

(d) 40% of the amount of the eligible costs in other regions.

13. The rates provided for in paragraph 12 may be increased by 20 percentage points, provided that the maximum aid intensity does not exceed 90% for:

(a) young farmers, or farmers who have set up during the five years preceding the date of application for aid;

(b) collective investments, such as storage facilities which are used by a group of farmers or facilities to prepare the agricultural products before marketing, and integrated projects covering several measures provided for in Regulation (EU) No 1305/2013, including those linked to a merger of producer organisations;

(c) investments in areas facing natural and other specific constraints;

(d) operations supported in the framework of the European Innovation Partnership (EIP), such as an investment in a new stable, allowing the testing of a new practice of animal housing, which has been developed in an operational group composed of farmers, scientists, and animal welfare non-governmental organisation;

(e) investments for the improvement of the natural environment, hygiene conditions or animal welfare standards, as referred to in paragraph 3(b); in this case the increased rate as provided for in this paragraph shall only apply to the additional costs necessary to obtain a level exceeding the Union standards in force and not leading to an increase in production capacity.

14. As regards non-productive investments referred to in paragraph 3(d) and investments for the restoration of production potential referred to in paragraph 3(e), the maximum aid intensity shall not exceed 100%.

For investments in relation to preventive measures, referred to in paragraph 3(e), the maximum aid intensity shall not exceed 80%. However, it may be increased to up to 100% if the investment is carried out collectively by more than one beneficiary.

NOTES

Repeal of this Regulation in relation to the UK: this Regulation is repealed in relation to the UK (as from IP completion day); see the introductory notes to this Regulation *ante*.

[1] Directive 2000/60/EC of the European Parliament and of the Council of 23 October 2000 establishing a framework for Community action in the field of water policy (OJ L327, 22.12.2000, p 1).

[5.482]

Article 15 Aid for agricultural land consolidation

Aid for agricultural land consolidation shall be compatible with the internal market within the meaning of Article 107 (3)(c) of the Treaty and shall be exempted from the notification requirement of Article 108(3) thereof where it fulfils the conditions laid down in Chapter I and is granted towards and limited to the legal and administrative costs, including survey costs, up to 100% of the real costs incurred.

NOTES

Repeal of this Regulation in relation to the UK: this Regulation is repealed in relation to the UK (as from IP completion day); see the introductory notes to this Regulation *ante*.

[5.483]

Article 16 Aid for investments concerning the relocation of farm buildings

1. Aid for investments concerning the relocation of farm buildings shall be compatible with the internal market within the meaning of Article 107(3)(c) of the Treaty and shall be exempted from the notification requirement of Article 108(3) thereof where it fulfils the conditions laid down in paragraphs 2 to 5 of this Article and in Chapter I.

2. The relocation of the farm building shall pursue an objective of public interest.

The public interest invoked to justify the granting of aid under this Article shall be specified in the relevant provisions of the Member State concerned.

3. Where the relocation of a farm building consists of the dismantling, removal and re-building of existing facilities the aid intensity shall be limited to 100% of the real costs incurred for such activities.

4. Where, in addition to the dismantling, removal and re-building of existing facilities as referred to in paragraph 3, the relocation results in a modernisation of these facilities or in an increase in production capacity the aid intensities for investments referred to in Article 14(12) and (13) shall apply in respect to the costs relating to the modernisation of the facilities or the increase in the production capacity.

For the purpose of this paragraph, the pure replacement of an existing building or facilities by a new up-to-date building or facilities without fundamentally changing the production or the technology involved shall not be considered to be related to the modernisation.

5. The maximum aid intensity may reach up to 100% of the eligible costs where the relocation concerns activities close to rural settlements, with a view to improving the quality of life or increasing the environmental performance of the rural settlement.

NOTES

Repeal of this Regulation in relation to the UK: this Regulation is repealed in relation to the UK (as from IP completion day); see the introductory notes to this Regulation *ante*.

[5.484]

Article 17 Aid for investments in connection with the processing of agricultural products and the marketing of agricultural products

1. Aid for investments in tangible assets or intangible assets in connection with the processing of agricultural products and the marketing of agricultural products shall be compatible with the internal market within the meaning of Article 107(3)(c) of the Treaty and shall be exempted from the notification requirement of Article 108(3) thereof where it fulfils the conditions laid down in paragraphs 2 to 10 of this Article and in Chapter I.

2. The investment shall concern the processing of agricultural products or the marketing of agricultural products.

3. Investments in connection with the production of food based biofuels shall not be eligible for aid under this Article.

4. The investment shall be in conformity with Union legislation and with the national laws of the Member State concerned on environmental protection. For investment requiring an environmental impact assessment under Directive 2011/92/EU the aid shall be subject to the condition that such assessment shall have been carried out and the development consent shall have been granted for the investment project concerned before the date of granting the individual aid.

5. The aid shall cover the following eligible costs:

(a) the construction, acquisition, including leasing, or improvement of immovable property, with land only being eligible to an extent not exceeding 10% of total eligible costs of the operation concerned;

(b) the purchase or lease purchase of machinery and equipment up to the market value of the asset;

(c) general costs linked to expenditure referred to in points (a) and (b), such as architect, engineer and consultation fees, fees relating to advice on environmental and economic sustainability, including feasibility studies; feasibility studies shall remain eligible expenditure even where, based on their results, no expenditure under in points (a) and (b) is incurred;

(d) *acquisition or development of computer software and acquisitions of patents, licenses, copyrights, trademarks.*

6. Costs, other than those referred to in paragraph 5(a) and (b), connected with leasing contracts, such as lessor's margin, interest refinancing costs, overheads and insurance charges shall not be considered to be eligible costs.

Working capital shall not be considered to be an eligible cost.

7. Aid shall not be granted in respect of investments to comply with Union standards in force.

8. Aid shall not be granted in contravention of any prohibition or restriction laid down in Regulation (EU) No 1308/2013, even where such prohibitions and restrictions only refer to Union support provided for in that Regulation.

9. The aid intensity shall not exceed:

- (a) *75% of the amount of the eligible costs in outermost regions;*
- (b) *75% of the amount of the eligible costs in the smaller Aegean islands;*
- (c) *50% of the amount of the eligible costs in less developed regions and in all regions whose GDP per capita for the 2007–2013 period was less than 75% of the average of the EU-25 for the reference period but whose GDP per capita is above 75% of the GDP average of the EU-27;*
- (d) *40% of the amount of the eligible costs in other regions.*

10. The rates referred to in paragraph 9 may be increased by 20 percentage points, provided that the maximum aid intensity does not exceed 90% for operations:

- (a) *linked to a merger of producer organisations; or*
- (b) *supported in the framework of the EIP.*

NOTES

Repeal of this Regulation in relation to the UK: this Regulation is repealed in relation to the UK (as from IP completion day); see the introductory notes to this Regulation *ante*.

[5.485]

Article 18 Start-up aid for young farmers and the development of small farms

1. Start-up aid for young farmers and start-up aid for the development of small farms shall be compatible with the internal market within the meaning of Article 107(3)(c) of the Treaty and shall be exempted from the notification requirement of Article 108(3) thereof where it fulfils the conditions laid down in paragraphs 2 to 7 of this Article and in Chapter I.

2. The aid shall be granted to young farmers as defined in Article 2(34) of this Regulation or to small farms as defined by Member States.

The definition of small farms by the Member States shall be the one included and approved by the Commission in the respective rural development programmes.

Member States shall define upper and lower thresholds for access to start-up aid for young farmers and the development of small farms in terms of the production potential of the agricultural holding, measured in standard output, as defined in Article 5 of Commission Regulation (EC) No 1242/2008,[1] *or an equivalent. The lower threshold for access to start-up aid for young farmers shall be higher than the upper threshold for access to aid for the development of small farms.*

Aid shall be limited to micro and small enterprises.

3. Where the aid is granted to a young farmer who is setting up a holding in the form of a legal person, the young farmer shall exercise effective and long-term control over the legal person in terms of decisions related to management, benefits and financial risks. Where several natural persons, including persons who are not young farmers, participate in the capital or management of the legal person, the young farmer shall be capable of exercising such effective and long-term control either solely or jointly together with other persons. Where a legal person is solely or jointly controlled by another legal person, those requirements shall apply to any natural person having control over that other legal person.

4. The aid shall be conditional on the submission of a business plan to the competent authority of the Member State concerned, the implementation of which shall start within nine months from the date of the adoption of the decision granting the aid.

The business plan shall describe at least the following:

- (a) *in the case of start-up aid to young farmers:*
  - (i) *the initial situation of the agricultural holding;*
  - (ii) *milestones and targets for the development of the activities of the agricultural holding;*
  - (iii) *details of the actions, including those related to environmental sustainability and resource efficiency, required for the development of the activities of the agricultural holding, such as investments, training, advice;*
- (b) *in the case of start-up aid for the development of small farms:*
  - (i) *the initial situation of the agricultural holding;*
  - (ii) *details of actions, including those related to environmental sustainability and resource efficiency, that could support the achievement of economic viability, such as investments, training, cooperation.*

5. For young farmers the business plan referred to in paragraph 4(a) of this Article shall provide that the beneficiary is required to fall within the definition of active farmer provided for in Article 2(42) within 18 months from the date of setting up. However, where the beneficiary does not possess adequate occupational skills and competences to fall within that definition, the beneficiary shall be entitled to receive aid, provided that the beneficiary makes a commitment to acquire those occupational skills and competences within 36 months from the date of the adoption of the decision granting the aid. That commitment must be included in the business plan.

6. Aid shall be provided or paid in at least two tranches or instalments over a maximum period of five years.

For young farmers, the last aid tranche or instalment of the aid shall be conditional upon the correct implementation of the business plan referred to in paragraph 4(a).

7. The aid amount per young farmer shall be based on the socioeconomic situation of the Member State concerned and shall be limited to EUR 70,000.
The aid amount per small farm shall be limited to EUR 15,000.

NOTES

Repeal of this Regulation in relation to the UK: this Regulation is repealed in relation to the UK (as from IP completion day); see the introductory notes to this Regulation *ante*.

1 Commission Regulation (EC) No 1242/2008 of 8 December 2008 establishing a Community typology for agricultural holdings (OJ L335, 13.12.2008, p 3).

[5.486]
Article 19 Start-up aid for producer groups and organisations in the agricultural sector

1. Start-up aid for producer groups and organisations shall be compatible with the internal market within the meaning of Article 107(3)(c) of the Treaty and shall be exempted from the notification requirement of Article 108(3) thereof where it fulfils the conditions laid down in paragraphs 2 to 9 of this Article and in Chapter I.

2. Only producer groups or organisations that have been officially recognised by the competent authority of the Member State concerned on the basis of a submission of a business plan shall be eligible for aid.

3. The aid shall be granted subject to the obligation of the Member State concerned to verify that the objectives of the business plan referred to in paragraph 2 have been reached within a period of five years from the date of the official recognition of the producer group or organisation.

4. The agreements, decisions and concerted practices concluded in the framework of the producer group or organisation shall comply with the competition rules as they apply by virtue of Articles 206 to 210 of Regulation (EU) No 1308/2013.

5. Aid shall not be granted to:

(a) production organisations, entities or bodies such as companies or cooperatives, the objective of which is the management of one or more agricultural holdings and which are therefore in effect single producers;

(b) agricultural associations, which undertake tasks such as mutual support and farm relief and farm management services, in the members' holdings without being involved in the joint adaptation of supply to the market;

(c) producer groups, organisations or associations the objectives of which are incompatible with Article 152(1)(c) and (3) and Article 156 of Regulation (EU) No 1308/2013.

6. The aid shall cover the following eligible costs: the costs of the rental of suitable premises, the acquisition of office equipment, including computer hardware and software, administrative staff costs, overheads and legal and administrative fees.
Where premises are purchased, the eligible costs for premises shall be limited to rental costs at market rates.

7. The aid shall be paid as a flat rate aid in annual instalments for the first five years from the date on which the producer group or organisation was officially recognised by the competent authority on the basis of the business plan referred to in paragraph 2.
Member States shall only pay the last instalment after having verified the correct implementation of that business plan.
The aid shall be degressive.

8. The aid intensity shall be limited to 100% of the eligible costs.

9. The aid amount shall be limited to EUR 500,000.

NOTES

Repeal of this Regulation in relation to the UK: this Regulation is repealed in relation to the UK (as from IP completion day); see the introductory notes to this Regulation *ante*.

[5.487]
Article 20 Aid for the participation of producers of agricultural products in quality schemes

1. The following categories of aid to producers of agricultural products shall be compatible with the internal market within the meaning of Article 107(3)(c) of the Treaty and shall be exempted from the notification requirement of Article 108(3) thereof:

(a) aid for new participation in quality schemes where it fulfils the conditions laid down in paragraphs 2 to and 6 of this Article and in Chapter I;

(b) aid towards the costs for compulsory control measures in relation to the quality schemes undertaken pursuant to Union or national legislation by or on behalf of the competent authority, where it fulfils the conditions laid down in paragraphs 2, 4, 6, 7 and 8 of this Article and in Chapter I;

(c) aid towards the costs of market research activities, product conception and design and for preparation of applications for the recognition of quality schemes where it fulfils the conditions laid down in paragraphs 2, 6, 7 and 8 of this Article and in Chapter I.

2. The aid referred to in paragraph 1 shall be granted in respect to the following quality schemes:

(a) quality schemes established under the following Regulations and provisions:

(i) Part II, Title II, Chapter I, Section 2 of Regulation (EU) No 1308/2013 as concerns wine;

(ii) Regulation (EU) No 1151/2012;

(iii) Council Regulation (EC) No 834/2007;[1]

(iv) Regulation (EC) No 110/2008 of the European Parliament and of the Council;[2]

(v) Regulation (EU) No 251/2014 of the European Parliament and of the Council;[3]

(b) quality schemes, including farm certification schemes, for agricultural products recognised by the Member States as complying with the following criteria:

(i) the specificity of the final product produced under such quality schemes must be derived from a clear obligations to guarantee:

— specific product characteristics, or

— *specific farming or production methods, or*

— *the quality of the final product that goes significantly beyond the commercial commodity standards as regards public, animal or plant health, animal welfare or environmental protection;*

(ii) *the quality scheme must be open to all producers;*

(iii) *the quality scheme must involve binding final product specifications and compliance with those specifications must be verified by public authorities or by an independent inspection body;*

(iv) *the quality scheme must be transparent and assure complete traceability of agricultural products;*

(c) *voluntary agricultural product certification schemes recognised by the Member State concerned as meeting the requirements laid down in the Commission Communication — EU best practice guidelines for voluntary certification schemes for agricultural products and foodstuffs.*[4]

3. The aid referred to in paragraph 1(a) shall be granted to producers of agricultural products in the form of an annual incentive payment, the level of which shall be determined according to the level of the fixed costs arising from participation in the quality schemes.

4. The aid referred to in paragraph 1(a) and (b) shall not be granted towards the cost of controls undertaken by the beneficiary itself, or where Union legislation provides that the cost of controls is to be met by producers of agricultural products and groups thereof, without specifying the actual level of charges.

5. The aid referred to in paragraph 1(a) shall be granted for a maximum period of five years and shall be limited to EUR 3,000 per beneficiary per year.

6. The aid shall be accessible to all those eligible undertakings in the area concerned, based on objectively defined conditions.

7. The aid referred to in paragraph 1(b) and (c) shall not involve direct payments to the beneficiaries.

The aid referred to in paragraph 1(b) and (c) shall be paid to the body responsible for control measures, the research provider or the consultancy provider.

8. The aid referred to in paragraph 1(b) and (c) shall be limited to 100% of the real costs incurred.

NOTES

Repeal of this Regulation in relation to the UK: this Regulation is repealed in relation to the UK (as from IP completion day); see the introductory notes to this Regulation *ante*.

1 Council Regulation (EC) No 834/2007 of 28 June 2007 on organic production and labelling of organic products and repealing Regulation (EEC) No 2092/91 (OJ L189, 20.7.2007, p 1).

2 Regulation (EC) No 110/2008 of the European Parliament and of the Council of 15 January 2008 on the definition, description, presentation, labelling and the protection of geographical indications of spirit drinks and repealing Council Regulation (EEC) No 1576/89 (OJ L39, 13.2.2008, p 16).

3 Regulation (EU) No 251/2014 of the European Parliament and of the Council of 26 February 2014 on the definition, description, presentation, labelling and the protection of geographical indications of aromatised wine products and repealing Council Regulation (EEC) No 1601/91 (OJ L84, 20.3.2014, p 14).

4 OJ C341, 16.12.2010, p 5.

[5.488]

Article 21 Aid for knowledge transfer and information actions

1. Aid for knowledge transfer and information actions shall be compatible with the internal market within the meaning of Article 107(3)(c) of the Treaty and shall be exempted from the notification requirement of Article 108(3) thereof where it fulfils the conditions laid down in paragraphs 2 to 8 of this Article and in Chapter I.

2. Aid shall cover vocational training and skills acquisition actions, including training courses, workshops and coaching, demonstration activities and information actions.

Aid may also cover short-term farm management exchange and farm visits.

Aid to demonstration activities may cover relevant investment costs.

3. The aid shall cover the following eligible costs:

(a) *the costs of organising the vocational training, skills acquisition actions, including training courses, workshops and coaching, demonstration activities or information actions;*

(b) *the costs for travel, accommodation and per diem expenses of the participants;*

(c) *the cost of the provision of replacement services during the absence of the participants;*

(d) *in the case of demonstration projects in relation to investments:*

(i) *the construction, acquisition, including leasing, or improvement of immovable property, with land only being eligible to an extent not exceeding 10% of total eligible costs of the operation concerned;*

(ii) *the purchase or lease purchase of machinery and equipment up to the market value of the asset;*

(iii) *general costs linked to expenditure referred to in points (i) and (ii), such as architect, engineer and consultation fees, fees relating to advice on environmental and economic sustainability, including feasibility studies; feasibility studies shall remain eligible expenditure even where, based on their results, no expenditure under in points (i) and (ii) is incurred;*

(iv) *the acquisition or development of computer software and the acquisitions of patents, licences, copyrights and trademarks.*

4. The costs referred to in paragraph 3(d) shall only be eligible to the extent used for the demonstration project and for the duration period of the demonstration project.

Only the depreciation costs corresponding to the life of the demonstration project, as calculated on the basis of generally accepted accounting principles, shall be considered as eligible.

5. Aid referred to in paragraph 3(a) and (c) shall not involve direct payments to the beneficiaries.

The aid referred to in paragraph 3(a) and (c) shall be paid to the provider of the knowledge transfer and information actions.

6. Bodies providing knowledge transfer and information actions shall have the appropriate capacities in the form of staff qualifications and regular training to carry out those tasks.

The provision of the activities referred to in paragraph 2 may be undertaken by producer groups or other organisations, regardless of their size.

7. The aid shall be accessible to all those eligible undertakings in the area concerned, based on objectively defined conditions.

Where the provision of the activities referred to in paragraph 2 is undertaken by producer groups and organisations, membership of such groups or organisations shall not be a condition for access to those activities.

Any contribution of non-members towards the administrative costs of the producer group or organisation concerned shall be limited to the costs of providing the activities referred to in paragraph 2.

8. The aid intensity shall be limited to 100% of the eligible costs.

In the case of demonstration projects referred to in paragraph 3(d) the maximum aid amount shall be limited to EUR 100,000 over 3 fiscal years.

NOTES

Repeal of this Regulation in relation to the UK: this Regulation is repealed in relation to the UK (as from IP completion day); see the introductory notes to this Regulation *ante*.

[5.489]

Article 22 Aid for advisory services

1. Aid for advisory services shall be compatible with the internal market within the meaning of Article 107(3)(c) of the Treaty and shall be exempted from the notification requirement of Article 108(3) thereof where it fulfils the conditions laid down in paragraphs 2 to 8 of this Article and in Chapter I.

2. The aid shall be designed to help undertakings active in the agricultural sector and young farmers benefit from the use of advisory services for the improvement of the economic and environmental performance as well as the climate friendliness and resilience of their undertaking or investment.

3. The advice shall be linked to at least one Union priority for rural development in accordance with Article 5 of Regulation (EU) No 1305/2013 and shall cover as a minimum one of the following elements:

- *(a) obligations deriving from the statutory management requirements or standards for good agricultural and environmental conditions provided for in Chapter I of Title VI of Regulation (EU) No 1306/2013;*
- *(b) where applicable, the agricultural practices beneficial for the climate and the environment laid down in Chapter 3 of Title III of Regulation (EU) No 1307/2013 and the maintenance of the agricultural area referred to in Article 4(1)(c) of that Regulation;*
- *(c) measures aiming at modernisation, competitiveness building, sectoral integration, innovation, market orientation as well as the promotion of entrepreneurship;*
- *(d) requirements as defined by Member States for implementing Article 11(3) of Directive 2000/60/EC of the European Parliament and of the Council;*
- *(e) requirements as defined by Member States for implementing Article 55 of Regulation (EC) No 1107/2009 of the European Parliament and of the Council,[1] and in particular the compliance with the general principles of integrated pest management as referred to in Article 14 of Directive 2009/128/EC of the European Parliament and of the Council;[2]*
- *(f) where relevant, occupational safety standards or safety standards linked to the farm;*
- *(g) specific advice for farmers setting up for the first time, including advice on economic and environmental sustainability.*

4. Advice may also cover issues, other than those referred to in paragraph 3 of this Article, related to climate change mitigation and adaptation, biodiversity and protection of water as laid down in Annex I to Regulation (EU) No 1307/2013 or linked to the economic and environmental performance of the agricultural holding including competitiveness aspects. This may include advice for the development of short supply chains, organic farming and health aspects of animal husbandry.

5. The aid shall not involve direct payments to the beneficiaries. The aid shall be paid to the advisory service provider.

6. The bodies selected to provide the advisory service shall have the appropriate resources in the form of regularly trained and qualified staff and advisory experience and reliability with respect to the fields they advise in.

The provision of advisory service may be undertaken by producer groups or other organisations, regardless of their size.

When providing advice, the provider of the advisory service shall respect the non-disclosure obligations referred to in Article 13(2) of Regulation (EU) No 1306/2013.

7. The aid shall be accessible to all those eligible undertakings in the area concerned, based on objectively defined conditions.

Where the provision of advisory services is undertaken by producer groups and organisations, membership of such groups or organisations shall not be a condition for access to the service.

Any contribution of non-members towards the administrative costs of the group or organisation concerned shall be limited to the costs of providing the advisory service.

8. The amount of aid shall be limited to EUR 1 500 per advice.

NOTES

Repeal of this Regulation in relation to the UK: this Regulation is repealed in relation to the UK (as from IP completion day); see the introductory notes to this Regulation *ante*.

1 Regulation (EC) No 1107/2009 of the European Parliament and of the Council of 21 October 2009 concerning the placing of plant protection products on the market and repealing Council Directives 79/117/EEC and 91/414/EEC (OJ L309, 24.11.2009, p 1).

2 Directive 2009/128/EC of the European Parliament and of the Council of 21 October 2009 establishing a framework for Community action to achieve the sustainable use of pesticides (OJ L309, 24.11.2009, p 71).

[5.490]

Article 23 Aid for farm replacement services

1. Aid for farm replacement services shall be compatible with the internal market within the meaning of Article 107 (3)(c) of the Treaty and shall be exempted from the notification requirement of Article 108(3) thereof where it fulfils the conditions laid down in paragraphs 2 to 5 of this Article and in Chapter I.

2. The aid shall cover the real costs incurred for the replacement of a farmer, a natural person who is a member of the farm household, or a farm worker, during their absence from work due to illness, including illness of their child, holidays, maternity and parental leave or in case of death.

3. The total duration of the replacement shall be limited to 3 months per year per beneficiary, with the exception of replacement for maternity and parental leave which shall be limited to 6 months in each case.

4. The aid shall not involve direct payments to the beneficiaries.

The aid shall be paid to the provider of the farm replacement service.

The provision of farm replacement services may be undertaken by producer groups and organisations, regardless of their size. In such case, membership of such groups or organisations shall not be a condition for access to the service.

5. The aid intensity shall be limited to 100% of the real costs incurred.

NOTES

Repeal of this Regulation in relation to the UK: this Regulation is repealed in relation to the UK (as from IP completion day); see the introductory notes to this Regulation *ante*.

[5.491]

Article 24 Aid for promotion measures in favour of agricultural products

1. Aid for promotion measures in favour of agricultural products shall be compatible with the internal market within the meaning of Article 107(3)(c) of the Treaty and shall be exempted from the notification requirement of Article 108(3) thereof where it fulfils the conditions laid down in paragraphs 2 to 8 of this Article and in Chapter I.

2. The aid shall cover the costs for:

- *(a) the organisation of and participation in competitions, trade fairs and exhibitions;*
- *(b) publications aimed at raising awareness of agricultural products among the wider public.*

3. The publications referred to in paragraph 2(b) shall not refer to any particular undertaking, brand name or origin. However that restriction shall not apply to reference to the origin of agricultural products covered by:

- *(a) quality schemes as referred to in Article 20(2)(a), provided that the reference corresponds exactly to that protected by the Union;*
- *(b) quality schemes as referred to in Article 20(2)(b) and (c), provided that the reference is secondary in the message.*

4. The aid shall cover the following eligible costs for the organisation of and participation in competitions, trade fairs and exhibitions referred to in paragraph 2(a):

- *(a) participation fees;*
- *(b) travel costs and costs for the transportation of animals;*
- *(c) costs of publications and websites announcing the event;*
- *(d) the rent of exhibition premises and stands and costs of their installation and dismantling;*
- *(e) symbolic prizes up to a value of EUR 1,000 per prize and per winner of a competition.*

5. The aid shall cover the following eligible cost for publications aimed at raising awareness of agricultural products among the wider public referred to in paragraph 2(b):

- *(a) costs of publications in print- and electronic media, websites, and spots in electronic media, on radio or television, aimed at presenting factual information on beneficiaries from a given region or producing a given agricultural product, provided that the information is neutral and that all beneficiaries concerned have equal opportunities to be represented in the publication;*
- *(b) costs for the dissemination of scientific knowledge and factual information on:*
  - *(i) quality schemes as referred to in Article 20(2) open to agricultural products from other Member States and third countries;*
  - *(ii) generic agricultural products and their nutritional benefits and suggested uses for them.*

6. The aid shall be granted:

- *(a) in kind; or*
- *(b) on the basis of the reimbursement of the real costs incurred by the beneficiary.*

Where the aid is granted in kind the aid shall not include direct payments to the beneficiaries but shall be paid to the provider of the promotion measures.

The provision of promotion measures may be undertaken by producer groups or other organisations, regardless of their size.

The aid for symbolic prizes referred to in paragraph 4(e) shall only be paid to the provider of the promotion measures if the prize has been actually awarded and upon presentation of a proof of the award.

7. Aid for promotion measures shall be accessible to all eligible undertakings in the area concerned, based on objectively defined conditions.

Where the promotion measure is undertaken by producer groups and organisations, participation shall not be subject to membership of these groups or organisations and any contribution in terms of administration fees for the group or organisation shall be limited to the cost of providing the promotion measures.

8. The aid intensity shall be limited to 100% of the eligible costs.

NOTES

Repeal of this Regulation in relation to the UK: this Regulation is repealed in relation to the UK (as from IP completion day); see the introductory notes to this Regulation *ante*.

[5.492]

Article 25 Aid to compensate for damage caused by adverse climatic event which can be assimilated to a natural disaster

1. Aid to compensate SMEs active in the primary agricultural production for damage caused by an adverse climatic event which can be assimilated to a natural disaster shall be compatible with the internal market within the meaning of Article 107(3)(c) of the Treaty and shall be exempted from the notification requirement of Article 108(3) thereof where it fulfils the conditions laid down in paragraphs 2 to 10 of this Article and in Chapter I.

2. Aid granted under this Article shall be subject to the following conditions:

(a) the competent authority of the Member State has formally recognised the character of the event as an adverse climatic event which can be assimilated to a natural disaster; and

(b) there is a direct causal link between the adverse climatic event which can be assimilated to a natural disaster and the damage suffered by the undertaking.

3. The aid shall be paid directly to the undertaking concerned or to a producer group or organisation of which that undertaking is a member.

Where the aid is paid to a producer group or organisation, the amount of aid shall not exceed the amount of aid to which that undertaking is eligible.

4. Aid schemes shall be established within three years from the date of the occurrence of the adverse climatic event which can be assimilated to a natural disaster.

The aid shall be paid out within four years from that date.

5. The eligible costs shall be the damage incurred as a direct consequence of the adverse climatic event which can be assimilated to a natural disaster, as assessed either by a public authority, by an independent expert recognised by the granting authority or by an insurance undertaking.

That damage shall include the following:

(a) the loss of income from the full or partial destruction of the agricultural production and the means of production as referred to in paragraph 6;

(b) the material damage as referred to in paragraph 7.

6. The loss of income shall be calculated by subtracting:

(a) the result of multiplying the quantity of the agricultural products produced in the year of the adverse climatic event which can be assimilated to a natural disaster, or each following year affected by the full or partial destruction of the means of production, by the average selling price obtained during that year;

from

(b) the result of multiplying the average annual quantity of agricultural products produced in the three-year period preceding the adverse climatic event which can be assimilated to a natural disaster, or a three-year average based on the five-year period preceding the adverse climatic event which can be assimilated to a natural disaster, excluding the highest and lowest entry by the average selling price obtained.

That reduction may be calculated either at annual farm production level or at crop or livestock level.

That amount may be increased by other costs incurred by the beneficiary due to the adverse climatic event which can be assimilated to a natural disaster.

That amount shall be reduced by any costs not incurred because of the adverse climatic event which can be assimilated to a natural disaster.

Indexes may be used in order to calculate the agricultural production of the beneficiary provided that the calculation method used permits the determination of the real loss of the beneficiary in the given year.

7. The material damage to assets such as farm buildings, equipment and machinery, stocks and means of production caused by the adverse climatic event which can be assimilated to a natural disaster shall be calculated on the basis of the repair cost or economic value of the affected asset before the adverse climatic event that can be assimilated to a natural disaster.

It shall not exceed the repair cost or the decrease in fair market value caused by the disaster, namely the difference between the asset's value immediately before and immediately after the adverse climatic event which can be assimilated to a natural disaster.

Where the reduction of the beneficiary's income referred to in paragraph 6 is calculated on the basis of crop or livestock level, only the material damage related to that crop or livestock shall be taken into account.

8. The calculation of the damage incurred due to the adverse climatic event which can be assimilated to a natural disaster shall be made at the level of the individual beneficiary.

9. Aid granted under this Article shall be reduced by 50% unless it is granted to beneficiaries who have taken out insurance covering at least 50% of their average annual production or production-related income and the statistically most frequent climatic risks in the Member State or region concerned for which insurance coverage is provided.

10. The aid and any other payments received to compensate for the losses, including payments under other national or Union measures or insurance policies for the damage receiving aid, shall be limited to 80% of the eligible costs. The aid intensity may be increased to 90% in areas facing natural constraints.

NOTES

Repeal of this Regulation in relation to the UK: this Regulation is repealed in relation to the UK (as from IP completion day); see the introductory notes to this Regulation *ante*.

[5.493]

Article 26 Aid for the costs of the prevention, control and eradication of animal diseases and plant pests and aid to make good the damage caused by animal diseases or plant pests

1. Aid to SMEs active in primary agricultural production for the costs of the prevention, control and eradication of animal diseases or plant pests and aid to compensate such undertakings for losses caused by those animal diseases or plant pests shall be compatible with the internal market within the meaning of Article 107(3)(c) of the Treaty and shall be exempted from the notification requirement of Article 108(3) thereof where it fulfils the conditions laid down in paragraphs 2 to 13 of this Article and in Chapter I.

2. Aid shall only be paid:

(a) in relation to animal diseases or plant pests for which Union or national rules exist, whether laid down by law, regulation or administrative action; and

(b) as part of:

(i) a public programme at Union, national or regional level for the prevention, control or eradication of the animal disease or the plant pest concerned; or

(ii) emergency measure imposed by competent authority; or

(iii) measures to eradicate or contain a plant pest implemented in accordance with Council Directive 2000/29/EC.

The programme and measures referred to in point (b) shall contain a description of the prevention, control or eradication measures concerned.

3. The aid shall not relate to measures in respect of which Union legislation provides that the cost of such measures is to be borne by the beneficiary, unless the cost of such measures is entirely offset by compulsory charges on the beneficiaries.

4. As regards animal diseases, the aid shall only be granted in respect of animal diseases referred to in the list of animal diseases established by the World Organisation for Animal Health or the animal diseases and zoonoses listed in Annexes I and II to Regulation (EU) No YYY/2014 of the European Parliament and of the Council.[1]

5. Aid shall be paid directly to the undertaking concerned or to a producer group or organisation of which that undertaking is a member.

Where the aid is paid to a producer group or organisation, the amount of aid shall not exceed the amount of aid to which that undertaking is eligible.

6. Aid schemes shall be introduced within three years from the date of the occurrence of the cost or loss caused by the animal disease or plant pest.

Aid shall be paid out within four years from that date.

7. In the case of prevention measures, the aid shall cover the following eligible costs:

(a) health checks;

(b) analyses, including in-vitro diagnostics;

(c) tests and other screening measures, including TSE and BSE tests;

(d) the purchase, storage, administration and distribution of vaccines, medicines, substances for the treatment of animals and plant protection products;

(e) the preventive slaughtering or culling of animals or the destruction of animal products and plants and the cleaning and disinfection of the holding and equipment.

8. In the case of control and eradication measures, the aid shall cover the following eligible costs:

(a) tests and other screening measures in case of animal diseases, including TSE and BSE tests;

(b) the purchase, storage, administration and distribution of vaccines, medicines, substances for the treatment of animals and plant protection products;

(c) the slaughter or culling and destruction of animals and the destruction of products linked to them, or destruction of plants, including those that die or are destroyed as a result of vaccinations or other measures ordered by the competent authorities and the cleaning and disinfection of the holding and equipment.

9. In the case of aid to make good the damage caused by animal diseases or plant pests, compensation shall be calculated only in relation to:

(a) the market value of the animals slaughtered or culled or that have died or the products, linked to them, or the plants destroyed:

(i) as a result of the animal disease or the plant pest;

(ii) as part of a public programme or measure as referred to in paragraph 2(b).

That market value shall be established on the basis of the value of the animals, products and plants immediately before any suspicion of the animal disease or plant pest arose or was confirmed.

(b) the loss of income due to quarantine obligations, difficulties in restocking or replanting and obligatory crop-rotation imposed as part of a public programme or measure as referred to in paragraph 2(b).

That amount shall be reduced by any costs not directly incurred due to the animal disease or plant pest which would otherwise have been incurred by the beneficiary.

10. The aid to make good the damage caused by animal diseases or plant pests shall be limited to costs and damage caused by animal diseases and plant pests for which the competent authority:

(a) has formally recognised an outbreak, in the case of an animal disease; or

(b) has formally acknowledged their presence, in the case of plants pests.

11. Aid in relation to the eligible costs referred to in paragraph 7 and 8 shall be granted in kind and shall be paid to the provider of the prevention and eradication measures.

By way of derogation from the first subparagraph of this paragraph, aid in relation to the eligible costs referred to in the following paragraphs may be granted directly to the beneficiary on the basis of reimbursement of the real costs incurred by the beneficiary:

(a) paragraphs 7(d) and 8(b) in the case of animal diseases or plant pests; and

(b) paragraphs 7(e) and 8(c) in the case of plant pests and for the cleaning and disinfection of the holding and equipment.

12. No individual aid shall be granted where it is established that the animal disease or the infestation with the plant pest was caused deliberately or by the negligence of the beneficiary.

13. The aid and any other payments received by the beneficiary, including payments under other national or Union measures or insurance policies for the same eligible costs as referred to in paragraphs 7, 8 and 9 shall be limited to 100% of the eligible costs.

NOTES

Repeal of this Regulation in relation to the UK: this Regulation is repealed in relation to the UK (as from IP completion day); see the introductory notes to this Regulation *ante*.

[1] Regulation (EU) No 652/2014 of the European Parliament and of the Council of 15 May 2014 laying down provisions for the management of expenditure relating to the food chain, animal health and animal welfare, and relating to plant health and plant reproductive material, amending Council Directives 98/56/EC, 2000/29/EC and 2008/90/EC, Regulations (EC) No 178/2002, (EC) No 882/2004 and (EC) No 396/2005 of the European Parliament and of the Council, Directive 2009/128/EC of the European Parliament and of the Council and Regulation (EC) No 1107/2009 of the European Parliament and of the Council and repealing Council Decisions 66/399/EEC, 76/894/EEC and 2009/470/EC (OJ L189, 27.6.2014, p 1).

[5.494]

Article 27 Aids to the livestock sector and aid for fallen stock

1. The following aid to livestock breeders shall be compatible with the internal market within the meaning of Article 107(3)(c) of the Treaty and shall be exempted from the notification requirement of Article 108(3) thereof where it fulfils the conditions laid down in paragraphs 2 and 3 of this Article and in Chapter I:

- *(a) aid at a rate of up to 100% of the administrative costs of the establishment and maintenance of herd books;*
- *(b) aid at a rate of up to 70% of the costs of tests performed by or on behalf of third parties, to determine the genetic quality or yield of livestock, with the exception of controls undertaken by the owner of the livestock and routine controls of milk quality;*
- *(c) aid at a rate of up to 100% of the costs of the removal of fallen stock, and 75% of the costs of the destruction of such fallen stock, or aid up to an equivalent aid intensity towards the costs of premiums paid by farmers for insurance covering the costs of the removal and destruction of fallen stock;*
- *(d) aid at a rate of up to 100% of the costs of the removal and destruction of fallen stock where the aid is financed through fees or through compulsory contributions destined for the financing of the destruction of such fallen stock, provided that such fees or contributions are limited to and directly imposed on the meat sector;*
- *(e) aid at a rate of 100% for the costs of the removal and destruction of fallen stock where there is an obligation to perform TSE tests on the fallen stock concerned or in case of an outbreak of an animal disease referred to in Article 26(4).*

2. The aid referred to in paragraph 1(c), (d) and (e) shall be conditional on the existence of a consistent monitoring programme which ensures the safe disposal of all fallen stock in the Member State.

The aid towards the costs of premiums paid by farmers for insurance covering the costs of the removal and destruction of fallen stock referred to in paragraph 1(c) of this Article shall comply with the conditions laid down in Article 28(2).

3. The aid shall be provided in kind and shall not involve direct payments to the beneficiaries.

In order to facilitate the administration of the aid referred to in paragraph 1(c), (d) and (e) the aid may be paid to economic operators or bodies that:

- *(a) are active downstream from the undertakings active in the livestock sector; and*
- *(b) provide services linked to the removal and destruction of fallen stock.*

NOTES

Repeal of this Regulation in relation to the UK: this Regulation is repealed in relation to the UK (as from IP completion day); see the introductory notes to this Regulation *ante*.

[5.495]

Article 28 Aid for the payment of insurance premiums

1. Aid granted to SMEs active in primary agricultural production for the payment of insurance premiums shall be compatible with the internal market within the meaning of Article 107(3)(c) of the Treaty and shall be exempted from the notification requirement of Article 108(3) thereof where it fulfils the conditions laid down in paragraphs 2 to 6 of this Article and in Chapter I.

2. The aid shall not:

- *(a) constitute a barrier to the operation of the internal market for insurance services;*
- *(b) be limited to insurance provided by a single insurance company or group of companies;*
- *(c) be made subject to the condition that the insurance contract be taken out with a company established in the Member State concerned.*

3. The insurance shall be intended to cover losses caused by any of the following:

- *(a) natural disasters;*
- *(b) an adverse climatic event which can be assimilated to a natural disaster and other adverse climatic events;*
- *(c) animal diseases or plant pest;*
- *(d) protected animals.*

4. The insurance shall:

- *(a) compensate only the cost of making good the losses referred to in paragraph 3;*
- *(b) not require or specify the type or quantity of future agricultural production.*

5. Member States may limit the amount of the insurance premium that is eligible for aid by applying appropriate ceilings.

6. The aid intensity shall be limited to 65% of the costs of the insurance premium.

NOTES

Repeal of this Regulation in relation to the UK: this Regulation is repealed in relation to the UK (as from IP completion day); see the introductory notes to this Regulation *ante*.

SECTION 2 AID FOR INVESTMENTS IN FAVOUR OF CONSERVATION OF CULTURAL AND NATURAL HERITAGE LOCATED ON AGRICULTURAL HOLDINGS

[5.496]

Article 29 Aid for investments in favour of the conservation of cultural and natural heritage located on agricultural holdings

1. Aid for investments aimed at the conservation of cultural and natural heritage located on the agricultural holding shall be compatible with the internal market within the meaning of Article 107(3) of the Treaty and shall be exempted from the notification requirement of Article 108(3) thereof where it fulfils the conditions laid down in paragraphs 2 to 6 of this Article and in Chapter I.

2. The investment shall comply with Union legislation and with the national laws of the Member State concerned.

3. The aid shall be granted for cultural and natural heritage in form of natural landscapes and buildings which is formally recognised as cultural or natural heritage by the competent public authorities of the Member State concerned.

4. The aid shall cover the following eligible costs intended for the conservation of cultural and natural heritage:

(a) investment costs in tangible assets;

(b) capital works.

5. The aid intensity shall be limited to 100% of the eligible costs.

6. Aid for capital works shall be limited to EUR 10,000 per year.

NOTES

Repeal of this Regulation in relation to the UK: this Regulation is repealed in relation to the UK (as from IP completion day); see the introductory notes to this Regulation *ante*.

SECTION 3 AID TO MAKE GOOD THE DAMAGE CAUSED BY NATURAL DISASTERS IN THE AGRICULTURAL SECTOR

[5.497]

Article 30 Aid to make good the damage caused by natural disasters in the agricultural sector

1. Aid schemes to make good the damage caused by natural disasters shall be compatible with the internal market within the meaning of Article 107(2)(b) of the Treaty and shall be exempted from the notification requirement of Article 108(3) thereof where it fulfils the conditions laid down in paragraphs 2 to 8 of this Article and in Chapter I.

2. Aid granted under this Article shall be subject to the following conditions:

(a) the competent authority of the Member State has formally recognised the character of the event as a natural disaster; and

(b) there is a direct causal link between the natural disaster and the damage suffered by the undertaking.

3. Aid shall be paid directly to the undertaking concerned or to a producer group or organisation of which that undertaking is a member.

Where the aid is paid to a producer group or organisation, the amount of aid shall not exceed the amount of aid to which that undertaking is eligible.

4. Aid schemes related to a specific natural disaster shall be established within three years from the date of the occurrence of the natural disaster.

The aid shall be paid out within four years from that date.

5. The eligible costs shall be the damage incurred as a direct consequence of the natural disaster, as assessed either by a public authority, by an independent expert recognised by the granting authority or by an insurance undertaking. That damage may include the following:

(a) material damage to assets, such as buildings, equipment, machinery, stocks and means of production;

(b) loss of income resulting from the full or partial destruction of the agricultural production and the means of agricultural production.

The damage shall be calculated at the level of the individual beneficiary.

6. The calculation of the material damage shall be based on the repair cost or economic value of the affected asset before the disaster. It shall not exceed the repair cost or the decrease in fair market value caused by the disaster, namely the difference between the property's value immediately before and immediately after the disaster.

7. The loss of income shall be calculated by subtracting:

(a) the result of multiplying the quantity of the agricultural products produced in the year of the natural disaster, or in each following year affected by the full or partial destruction of the means of production, by the average selling price obtained during that year,

from

(b) the result of multiplying the average annual quantity of agricultural products produced in the three-year period preceding the natural disaster or a three year average based on the five-year period preceding the natural disaster, excluding the highest and lowest entry by the average selling price obtained.

That amount may be increased by other costs incurred by the beneficiary due to the adverse climatic event which can be assimilated to a natural disaster.

That amount shall be reduced by any costs not incurred because of the natural disaster.

Indexes may be used in order to calculate the annual agricultural production of the beneficiary provided that the calculation method used permits the determination of the real loss of the beneficiary in the given year.

8. The aid and any other payments received to compensate the damage, including payments under insurance policies, shall be limited to 100% of the eligible costs.

NOTES

Repeal of this Regulation in relation to the UK: this Regulation is repealed in relation to the UK (as from IP completion day); see the introductory notes to this Regulation *ante*.

SECTION 4 AID FOR RESEARCH AND DEVELOPMENT IN THE AGRICULTURAL AND FORESTRY SECTORS

[5.498]

Article 31 Aid for research and development in the agricultural and forestry sectors

1. Aid for research and development in the agricultural and forestry sectors shall be compatible with the internal market within the meaning of Article 107(3) of the Treaty and shall be exempted from the notification requirement of Article 108(3) thereof where it fulfils the conditions laid down in paragraphs 2 to 7 of this Article and in Chapter I.

2. The aided project shall be of interest to all undertakings active in the particular agricultural or forestry sector or sub-sector concerned.

3. Prior to the date of the start of the aided project the following information shall be published on the internet:

- *(a) that the aided project is to be carried out;*
- *(b) the goals of the aided project;*
- *(c) an approximate date for the publication of the results expected from the aided project;*
- *(d) the place of publication of the results expected from the aided project on the internet;*
- *(e) a reference that the results of the aided project are available to all undertakings active in the particular agricultural and forestry sector or sub-sector concerned at no cost.*

4. The results of the aided project shall be made available on internet from the end date of the aided project or the date, on which any information concerning those results is given to members of any particular organisation, whatever comes first. The results shall remain available on internet for a period of at least 5 years starting from the end date of the aided project.

5. Aid shall be granted directly to the research and knowledge-dissemination organisation.

The aid shall not involve payments to undertakings active in the agricultural sector based on the price of the agricultural products.

6. The eligible costs shall be the following:

- *(a) personnel costs related to researchers, technicians and other supporting staff to the extent employed on the project;*
- *(b) costs of instruments and equipment to the extent and for the period used for the project. Where such instruments and equipment are not used for their full life for the project, only the depreciation costs corresponding to the life of the project, as calculated on the basis of generally accepted accounting principles are considered as eligible;*
- *(c) costs of buildings and land, to the extent and for the duration period used for the project. With regard to buildings, only the depreciation costs corresponding to the life of the project, as calculated on the basis of generally accepted accounting principles, are considered as eligible. For land, costs of commercial transfer or actually incurred capital costs are eligible;*
- *(d) costs of contractual research, knowledge and patents bought or licensed from outside sources at arm's length conditions, as well as costs of consultancy and equivalent services used exclusively for the project;*
- *(e) additional overheads and other operating expenses, including costs of materials, supplies and similar products, incurred directly as a result of the project.*

7. The aid intensity shall be limited to 100% of the eligible costs.

NOTES

Repeal of this Regulation in relation to the UK: this Regulation is repealed in relation to the UK (as from IP completion day); see the introductory notes to this Regulation *ante*.

SECTION 5 AID IN FAVOUR OF FORESTRY

[5.499]

Article 32 Aid for afforestation and the creation of woodland

1. Aid for afforestation and the creation of woodland granted to public and private land holders and their associations shall be compatible with the internal market within the meaning of Article 107(3)(c) of the Treaty and shall be exempted from the notification requirement of Article 108(3) thereof where it fulfils the conditions laid down in paragraphs 2 to 16 of this Article and in Chapter I.

2. The aid shall:

- *(a) be granted in the framework of a rural development programme in accordance with Regulation (EU) No 1305/2013 and the delegated and implementing acts adopted by the Commission pursuant to that Regulation either:*
  - *(i) as aid co-financed by the EAFRD; or*
  - *(ii) as additional national financing to the aid referred to in point (i);*

  and
- *(b) be identical to the underlying rural development measure provided for in the rural development programme referred to in point (a).*

3. The legal basis for the aid shall specify that the aid shall not be put into effect before the approval of the relevant rural development programme by the Commission.

4. In the case of afforestation of State-owned land, aid shall only be granted if the body managing such land is a private body or a municipality.

5. Limitations on ownership of forests, referred to in paragraph 4 shall not apply to the tropical or subtropical forests and to the wooded areas of the territories of the Azores, Madeira, the Canary islands, the smaller Aegean islands and the French overseas departments.

6. Aid shall be granted for afforestation and the creation of woodland on agricultural land and on non-agricultural land.

7. The aid for afforestation and the creation of woodland shall cover the costs of establishment and an annual premium per hectare.

The aid for afforestation and the creation of woodland may cover investment operations.

Aid for afforestation of land owned by public authorities or for fast growing trees shall cover only the costs of establishment.

8. [Save where support is provided in the form of financial instruments, aid for afforestation and the creation of woodland related to investment operations shall cover the following eligible costs:]

- *(a) the construction, acquisition, including leasing, or improvement of immovable property, with land only being eligible to an extent not exceeding 10% of the total eligible costs of the operation concerned;*
- *(b) the purchase or lease purchase of machinery and equipment up to the market value of the asset;*
- *(c) general costs linked to the expenditure referred to in points (a) and (b), such as architect, engineer and consultation fees, fees relating to advice on environmental and economic sustainability, including feasibility studies; feasibility studies shall remain eligible expenditure even where, based on their results, no expenditure under in points (a) and (b) is being incurred;*
- *(d) the acquisition or development of computer software and the acquisitions of patents, licences, copyrights, trademarks;*
- *(e) the costs of establishing forest management plans or equivalent instrument.*

Working capital shall not be considered to be an eligible cost.

9. The investment operations shall be in conformity with Union legislation and with national laws of the Member State concerned on environmental protection. For investment operations requiring an environmental impact assessment under Directive 2011/92/EU the aid shall be subject to the condition that such assessment shall have been carried out and the development consent shall have been granted for the investment project concerned before the date of granting the individual aid.

[The first subparagraph shall not apply to aid which is granted in the form of financial instruments.]

10. The following costs of establishment may be eligible:

- *(a) the costs of the plantation and propagation material;*
- *(b) the plantation costs and the costs directly linked to the plantation;*
- *(c) the cost for other related operations such as storing and treatments of seedlings with the necessary prevention and protection materials;*
- *(d) the costs for replanting necessary during the first year of afforestation.*

11. The annual premium per hectare shall cover the costs for the agricultural income foregone and for maintenance, including early and late cleansings, and shall be paid for a maximum period of 12 years from the date of granting the aid.

12. Aid shall not be granted for planting the following trees:

- *(a) trees for short rotation coppicing;*
- *(b) Christmas trees; or*
- *(c) fast growing trees for energy production.*

13. The species planted shall be adapted to the environmental and climatic conditions of the area and comply with minimum environmental requirements.

14. In areas where afforestation is difficult due to severe pedo-climatic conditions aid may be provided for planting perennial woody species such as shrubs or bushes suitable to the local conditions.

15. For beneficiaries above a certain size, to be determined by the Member States in the rural development programmes, the aid shall be conditional on the presentation of the relevant information from a forest management plan or equivalent instrument in line with sustainable forest management as defined by the Second Ministerial Conference on the Protection of Forests in Europe of 1993.

16. The aid intensity shall be limited to 100% of the eligible costs.

NOTES

The words in square brackets in para 8 were substituted, and the words in square brackets in para 9 were added, by Commission Regulation 2019/289/EU, Art 1(3).

Repeal of this Regulation in relation to the UK: this Regulation is repealed in relation to the UK (as from IP completion day); see the introductory notes to this Regulation *ante*.

[5.500]

Article 33 Aid for agroforestry systems

1. Aid for agroforestry systems granted to private land holders, municipalities and their associations shall be compatible with the internal market within the meaning of Article 107(3)(c) of the Treaty and shall be exempted from the notification requirement of Article 108(3) thereof where it fulfils the conditions laid down in paragraphs 2 to 11 of this Article and in Chapter I.

2. The aid shall:

- *(a) be granted in the framework of a rural development programme in accordance with Regulation (EU) No 1305/2013 and the delegated and implementing acts adopted by the Commission pursuant to that Regulation either:*
  - *(i) as aid co-financed by the EAFRD; or*
  - *(ii) as additional national financing to the aid referred to in point (i);*

  and
- *(b) be identical to the underlying rural development measure provided for in the rural development programme referred to in point (a).*

3. The legal basis for the aid shall specify that the aid shall not be put into effect before the approval of the relevant rural development programme by the Commission.

4. [The aid for agroforestry systems shall cover the costs of establishment, regeneration or renovation and an annual premium per hectare.]

The aid for agroforestry systems may cover investment operations.

5. [Save where support is provided in the form of financial instruments, the aid for agroforestry systems related to investment operations shall cover the following eligible costs:]

(a) the construction, acquisition, including leasing, or improvement of immovable property, with land only being eligible to an extent not exceeding 10% of the total eligible costs of the operation concerned;

(b) the purchase or lease purchase of machinery and equipment up to the market value of the asset;

(c) general costs linked to the expenditure referred to in points (a) and (b), such as architect, engineer and consultation fees, fees relating to advice on environmental and economic sustainability, including feasibility studies; feasibility studies shall remain eligible expenditure even where, based on their results, no expenditure under in points (a) and (b) is being incurred;

(d) the acquisition or development of computer software and the acquisitions of patents, licences, copyrights, trademarks;

(e) the costs of establishing forest management plans or equivalent instrument.

Working capital shall not be considered to be an eligible cost.

6. The investment operations shall be in conformity with Union legislation and with national laws of the Member State concerned on environmental protection. For investment operations requiring an environmental impact assessment under Directive 2011/92/EU the aid shall be subject to the condition that such assessment shall have been carried out and the development consent shall have been granted for the investment project concerned before the date of granting the individual aid.

[The first subparagraph shall not apply to aid which is provided in the form of financial instruments.]

[7. The following costs for establishment, regeneration or renovation of the agroforestry system may be eligible:

(a) the costs for planting trees, including the costs of the plantation material, the plantation, the storing and the treatments of seedlings with the necessary prevention and protection materials;

(b) the costs for converting existing forests or other wooded land, including the costs for felling trees, thinning and pruning and protection against grazing animals;

(c) other costs directly linked to the establishment, regeneration or renovation of an agroforestry system, such as costs for feasibility studies, establishment plan, soil examination, soil preparation and protection;

(d) the costs of silvopastoral, namely, grazing system watering and protective facilities;

(e) the costs of the necessary treatment connected to the establishment, regeneration or renovation of an agroforestry system, including watering and cutting;

(f) the costs for replanting during the first year after the establishment, regeneration or renovation of an agroforestry system.]

8. The annual premium per hectare shall cover the costs of maintenance of the agroforestry system, and shall be paid for a maximum period of five years from the date of granting the aid.

The eligible costs of maintenance may relate to the established tree belts, the weeding, pruning and thinning and protective actions and investments such as fences or individual protection tubes.

9. [Member States shall determine the minimum and maximum number of trees per hectare, taking account of the following:]

(a) local pedo-climatic and environmental conditions;

(b) forestry species; and

(c) the need to ensure sustainable agricultural use of the land.

10. For beneficiaries above a certain size, to be determined by the Member States, the aid shall be conditional on the presentation of the relevant information from a forest management plan or equivalent instrument in line with sustainable forest management as defined by the Second Ministerial Conference on the Protection of Forests in Europe of 1993.

11. The maximum aid intensity shall be limited to:

[(a) 80% of the eligible costs for investment operations and of the costs for establishment, regeneration or renovation referred to in paragraphs 5 and 7; and]

(b) 100% of the annual premium referred to in paragraph 8.

NOTES

All words in square brackets were substituted or inserted by Commission Regulation 2019/289/EU, Art 1(4).

Repeal of this Regulation in relation to the UK: this Regulation is repealed in relation to the UK (as from IP completion day); see the introductory notes to this Regulation *ante*.

[5.501]

Article 34 Aid for the prevention and restoration of damage to forests from forest fire, natural disasters, adverse climatic events which can be assimilated to a natural disaster, other adverse climatic events, plant pests and catastrophic events

1. Aid for the prevention and restoration of damage to forests from forest fire, natural disasters, adverse climatic events, which can be assimilated to a natural disaster, other adverse climatic events, plant pests and catastrophic events and climate change events pursuant to Article 24 of Regulation (EU) No 1305/2013 granted to private and public forest holders, and other private law and public bodies and their associations shall be compatible with the internal market within the meaning of Article 107(2)(b) or, as the case may be, Article 107(3)(c) of the Treaty and shall be exempted from the notification requirement of Article 108(3) thereof where it fulfils the conditions laid down in paragraphs 2 to 12 of this Article and in Chapter I.

2. The aid shall:

(a) be granted in the framework of a rural development programme in accordance with Regulation (EU) No 1305/2013 and the delegated and implementing acts adopted by the Commission pursuant to that Regulation either:

(i) as aid co-financed by the EAFRD; or

(ii) as additional national financing to the aid referred to in point (i);

and

(b) be identical to the underlying rural development measure provided for in the rural development programme referred to in point (a).

3. The legal basis for the aid shall specify that the aid shall not be put into effect before the approval of the relevant rural development programme by the Commission.

4. Only forest areas which are classified as a medium to high forest fire risk according to the forest protection plan established by the Member State concerned shall be eligible for aid for prevention of fire.

5. The aid shall cover the following eligible costs:

- *(a) the establishment of protective infrastructure;*
- *(b) local, small scale prevention activities against fire, or other natural hazards, including the use of grazing animals;*
- *(c) establishing and improving forest fire, pest and diseases monitoring facilities and communication equipment;*
- *(d) restoring forest potential damaged from fires, natural disasters, adverse climatic events, which can be assimilated to a natural disaster, other adverse climatic events, plant pests, catastrophic events and climate change related events.*

6. The aid may cover maintenance costs in the case of firebreaks.

7. The aid shall not be granted for agricultural related activities in areas covered by agri-environmental commitments.

8. In the case of the restoration of forest potential referred to in paragraph 5(d) the aid shall be subject to the formal recognition by the competent authorities of the Member State concerned that:

- *(a) the fire, natural disaster, adverse climatic event which can be assimilated to a natural disaster, other adverse climatic event, plant pest, catastrophic event or climate change related event has occurred; and*
- *(b) the event referred to in point (a) of this paragraph, including measures adopted in accordance with Directive 2000/29/EC to eradicate or contain a plant pest, has caused the destruction of at least 20% of the relevant forest potential.*

9. In the case of aid for prevention of damage to a forest from plant pests, the risk of occurrence of the plant pest shall be supported by scientific evidence and acknowledged by a scientific public organisation.

The list of species of harmful organisms which may cause a plant pest shall be provided for in the rural development programme of the Member State concerned.

10. The aided activities or projects shall be consistent with the forest protection plan established by the Member State.

For beneficiaries above a certain size, to be determined by the Member States, the aid shall be conditional on the presentation of the relevant information from a forest management plan or equivalent instrument in line with sustainable forest management as defined by the Second Ministerial Conference on the Protection of Forests in Europe of 1993, detailing the preventive objectives.

Costs other than those referred to in paragraph 5 related to the particularities of the forestry sector may be considered to be eligible costs.

11. Aid shall not be granted for loss of income resulting from fire, natural disasters, adverse climatic events, which can be assimilated to a natural disaster, other adverse climatic events, plant pests and catastrophic events.

12. The aid intensity shall be limited to 100% of the eligible costs.

Aid granted for the eligible costs as referred to in paragraph 5(d) and any other payments received by the beneficiary, including payments under other national or Union measures or insurance policies for the same eligible costs shall be limited to 100% of the eligible costs.

NOTES

Repeal of this Regulation in relation to the UK: this Regulation is repealed in relation to the UK (as from IP completion day); see the introductory notes to this Regulation *ante*.

[5.502]

Article 35 Aid for investments improving the resilience and environmental value of forest ecosystems

1. Aid for investments improving the resilience and environmental value of forest ecosystems granted to natural persons, private and public forest holders, private law and public bodies and their associations shall be compatible with the internal market within the meaning of Article 107(3)(c) of the Treaty and shall be exempted from the notification requirement of Article 108(3) thereof where it fulfils the conditions laid down in paragraphs 2 to 8 of this Article and in Chapter I.

2. The aid shall:

- *(a) be granted in the framework of a rural development programme in accordance with Regulation (EU) No 1305/2013 and the delegated and implementing acts adopted by the Commission pursuant to that Regulation either:*
  - *(i) as aid co-financed by the EAFRD; or*
  - *(ii) as additional national financing to the aid referred to in point (i);*

  and
- *(b) be identical to the underlying rural development measure provided for in the rural development programme referred to in point (a).*

3. The legal basis for the aid shall specify that the aid shall not be put into effect before the approval of the relevant rural development programme by the Commission.

4. Investments shall be aimed at the achievement of commitments for environmental aims, for provision of ecosystem services or enhancement of the public amenity value of forest and wooded land in the area concerned or the improvement of the climate change mitigation potential of ecosystems, without excluding economic benefits in the long term.

5. The investment shall be in conformity with Union legislation and with national laws of the Member State concerned on environmental protection. For investment requiring an environmental impact assessment under Directive 2011/92/EU the aid shall be subject to the condition that such assessment shall have been carried out and the development consent shall have been granted for the investment project concerned before the date of granting the individual aid.

[The first subparagraph shall not apply to aid which is provided in the form of financial instruments.]

6. [Save where support is provided in the form of financial instruments, the aid shall cover the following eligible costs:]

- *(a) the construction, acquisition, including leasing, or improvement of immovable property, with land only being eligible to an extent not exceeding 10% of the total eligible costs of the operation concerned;*
- *(b) the purchase or lease purchase of machinery and equipment up to the market value of the asset;*
- *(c) general costs linked to expenditure referred to in points (a) and (b), such as architect, engineer and consultation fees, fees relating to advice on environmental and economic sustainability, including feasibility studies; feasibility studies shall remain eligible expenditure even where, based on their results, no expenditure under points (a) and (b) is incurred;*
- *(d) the acquisition or development of computer software and the acquisitions of patents, licenses, copyrights and trademarks;*
- *(e) the costs of establishing forest management plans or equivalent instrument.*

7. [Save where support is provided in the form of financial instruments, costs other than those referred to in paragraph 6(a) and (b) connected with leasing contracts, such as lessor's margin, interest refinancing costs, overheads and insurance charges shall not be considered to be eligible costs.]

Working capital shall not be considered to be an eligible cost.

8. The aid intensity shall be limited to 100% of the eligible costs.

NOTES

The words in square brackets in para 5 were inserted, and the words in square brackets in paras 6 and 7 were substituted, by Commission Regulation 2019/289/EU, Art 1(5).

Repeal of this Regulation in relation to the UK: this Regulation is repealed in relation to the UK (as from IP completion day); see the introductory notes to this Regulation *ante*.

[5.503]

Article 36 Aid for disadvantages related to Natura 2000 forest areas

1. Aid for disadvantages related to Natura 2000 forest areas as defined in Article 3 of Directive 92/43/EEC and in Article 3 Directive 2009/147/EC granted to private forest holders and associations of private forest holders shall be compatible with the internal market within the meaning of Article 107(3)(c) of the Treaty and shall be exempted from the notification requirement of Article 108(3) thereof where it fulfils the conditions laid down in paragraphs 2 to 6 of this Article and in Chapter I.

2. The aid shall:

- *(a) be granted in the framework of a rural development programme in accordance with Regulation (EU) No 1305/2013 and the delegated and implementing acts adopted by the Commission pursuant to that Regulation either:*
  - *(i) as aid co-financed by the EAFRD; or*
  - *(ii) as additional national financing to the aid referred to in point (i);*

  and
- *(b) be identical to the underlying rural development measure provided for in the rural development programme referred to in point (a).*

3. The legal basis for the aid shall specify that the aid shall not be put into effect before the approval of the relevant rural development programme by the Commission.

4. The aid shall be granted annually and per hectare of forest in order to compensate beneficiaries for additional costs and income foregone resulting from disadvantages in the forest areas referred to in paragraph 5 of this Article, related to the implementation of Directive 92/43/EEC and Directive 2009/147/EC.

5. The following forest areas shall be eligible for aid:

- *(a) Natura 2000 forest areas in accordance with Article 3 of Directive 92/43/EEC and Article 3 of Directive 2009/147/EC;*
- *(b) features of the landscape which contribute to the implementation of Article 10 of Directive 92/43/EEC; those areas shall not exceed 5% of the areas included in Natura 2000 network covered by the territorial scope of the rural development programme concerned.*

6. The aid shall be limited to the maximum amount of EUR 500 per hectare per year in the initial period not exceeding five years and to EUR 200 per hectare per year afterwards.

Those amounts may be increased in exceptional cases taking into account specific circumstances to be justified in the rural development programmes.

Member States shall deduct from the aid the necessary amount in order to exclude double funding of the practices referred to in Article 29 of Regulation (EU) No 1307/2013.

NOTES

Repeal of this Regulation in relation to the UK: this Regulation is repealed in relation to the UK (as from IP completion day); see the introductory notes to this Regulation *ante*.

[5.504]

Article 37 Aid for forest-environmental and climate services and forest conservation

1. Aid for forest-environmental and climate services and for forest conservation granted to public or private forest holders, private law or public bodies and their associations shall be compatible with the internal market within the meaning of Article 107(3)(c) of the Treaty and shall be exempted from the notification requirement of Article 108(3) thereof where it fulfils the conditions laid down in paragraphs 2 to 9 of this Article and in Chapter I.

2. The aid shall:

- *(a) be granted in the framework of a rural development programme in accordance with Regulation (EU) No 1305/2013 and the delegated and implementing acts adopted by the Commission pursuant to that Regulation either:*

(i) *as aid co-financed by the EAFRD; or*
(ii) *as additional national financing to the aid referred to in point (i);*
and

(b) *be identical to the underlying rural development measure provided for in the rural development programme referred to in point (a).*

3. The legal basis for the aid shall specify that the aid shall not be put into effect before the approval of the relevant rural development programme by the Commission.

4. In the case of forest-environmental and climate services and forest conservation of State-owned land, aid shall only be granted if the body managing such land is a private body or a municipality.

5. For forest holdings above a certain threshold to be determined by Member States, aid shall be conditional on the presentation of the relevant information from of a forest management plan or equivalent instrument in line with sustainable forest management as defined by the Second Ministerial Conference on the Protection of Forests in Europe of 1993.

6. The aid shall be granted per hectare of forest land.

7. Aid shall cover only commitments which go beyond the mandatory requirements established by national forestry act or other relevant national or Union legislation. The mandatory national requirements shall be clearly identified. Commitments shall be undertaken for a period of between five and seven years. However, where necessary and duly justified, Member States may determine a longer period for particular types of commitments.

8. The aid shall compensate beneficiaries for all or part of the additional costs and income foregone resulting from undertaking the commitments referred to in paragraph 7.

Where necessary the aid may cover transaction costs up to a value of 20% of the aid.

In duly justified cases for operations concerning environmental conservation, the aid for commitments to renounce commercial use of trees and forests may be granted as a flat rate or as an one-off payment per unit calculated on the basis of additional costs and income foregone.

9. The aid shall be limited to the maximum amount of EUR 200 per hectare per year.

That maximum amount may be increased in exceptional cases taking into account specific circumstances to be justified in the rural development programmes.

NOTES

Repeal of this Regulation in relation to the UK: this Regulation is repealed in relation to the UK (as from IP completion day); see the introductory notes to this Regulation *ante*.

[5.505]

Article 38 Aid for knowledge transfer and information actions in the forestry sector

1. Aid for knowledge transfer and information actions granted in favour of undertakings active in the forestry sector shall be compatible with the internal market within the meaning of Article 107(3)(c) of the Treaty and shall be exempted from the notification requirement of Article 108(3) thereof where it fulfils the conditions laid down in paragraphs 2 to 6 of this Article and in Chapter I.

2. The aid shall cover vocational training and skills acquisition actions, including training courses, workshops and coaching, demonstration activities and information actions. [Infrastructure installed as a result of demonstration may be used after the operation is completed.]

Aid may also cover short-term forest management exchanges and forest visits.

Aid to demonstration activities may cover relevant investment costs.

[Aid for demonstration projects which is co-financed under the EAFRD or granted as additional national financing to such aid, and which is provided in the form of financial instruments, may cover eligible costs other than those referred to in paragraph 3(b), provided that the costs are fully eligible under Regulation (EU) No 1305/2013 and that the aid is identical to the underlying measure included in the rural development programme approved under that Regulation.]

3. The aid shall cover the following eligible costs:

(a) *the costs of organising and delivering the knowledge transfer or information action;*

(b) *in the case of demonstration projects related to investments:*
 (i) *the construction, acquisition, including leasing, or improvement of immovable property, with land only being eligible to an extent not exceeding 10% of total eligible costs of the operation concerned;*
 (ii) *the purchase or lease purchase of machinery and equipment up to the market value of the asset;*
 (iii) *general costs linked to expenditure referred to in points (i) and (ii), such as architect, engineer and consultation fees, fees relating to advice on environmental and economic sustainability, including feasibility studies; feasibility studies shall remain eligible expenditure even where, based on their results, no expenditure under in points (i) and (ii) is incurred;*
 (iv) *acquisition or development of computer software and acquisitions of patents, licenses, copyrights and trademarks;*

(c) *the costs for travel, accommodation and per diem expenses of the participants.*

4. The aid referred to in paragraph 3(a) and (b) shall not involve direct payments to the beneficiaries. The aid shall be paid to the knowledge transfer and information actions provider.

5. Bodies providing knowledge transfer and information actions shall have the appropriate capacities in the form of staff qualifications and regular training to carry out such tasks.

6. The aid intensity shall be limited to 100% of the eligible costs.

NOTES

Para 2: words in square brackets inserted by Commission Regulation 2019/289/EU, Art 1(6).

Repeal of this Regulation in relation to the UK: this Regulation is repealed in relation to the UK (as from IP completion day); see the introductory notes to this Regulation *ante*.

[5.506]

Article 39 Aid for advisory services in the forestry sector

1. Aid for advisory services granted in favour of forest holders and other land managers shall be compatible with the internal market within the meaning of Article 107(3)(c) of the Treaty and shall be exempted from the notification requirement of Article 108(3) thereof where it fulfils the conditions laid down in paragraphs 2 to 7 of this Article and in Chapter I.

2. Aid shall be granted to help forest holders and other land managers benefit from the use of advisory services for the improvement of the economic and environmental performance and climate friendliness and resilience of their holdings, enterprise or investment.

3. The advice shall cover as a minimum issues related to the implementation of Directives 92/43/EEC, Directive 2000/60/EC and Directive 2009/147/EC.

The advice may also cover issues linked to the economic and environmental performance of forestry holdings.

4. The aid shall not involve direct payments to the beneficiaries. The aid shall be paid to the provider of the advisory services.

The provider of advisory service shall have the appropriate resources in the form of regularly trained and qualified staff and advisory experience and reliability with respect to the fields they advise in.

[Aid which is co-financed under the EAFRD, or granted as additional national financing to such co-financed aid, may be paid to the Managing Authority referred to in point (a) of Article 65(2) of Regulation (EU) No 1305/2013.]

5. When providing advice, the provider of advisory services shall respect the non-disclosure obligations referred to in Article 13(2) of Regulation (EU) No 1306/2013.

6. Where justified and appropriate, the advice may be partly provided in group, while taking into account the situation of the individual beneficiaries of the advisory services.

7. The aid shall be limited to EUR 1 500 per advice.

NOTES

Para 4: words in square brackets inserted by Commission Regulation 2019/289/EU, Art 1(7).

Repeal of this Regulation in relation to the UK: this Regulation is repealed in relation to the UK (as from IP completion day); see the introductory notes to this Regulation *ante*.

[5.507]

Article 40 Aid for investments in infrastructure related to the development, modernisation or adaptation of the forestry sector

1. Aid for investments in infrastructure related to the development, modernisation or adaptation of the forestry sector granted to undertakings active in the forest sector shall be compatible with the internal market within the meaning of Article 107(3)(c) of the Treaty and shall be exempted from the notification requirement of Article 108(3) thereof where it fulfils the conditions laid down in paragraphs 2 to 9 of this Article and in Chapter I.

2. The aid shall:

- *(a) be granted in the framework of a rural development programme in accordance with Regulation (EU) No 1305/2013 and the delegated and implementing acts adopted by the Commission pursuant to that Regulation either:*
  - *(i) as aid co-financed by the EAFRD; or*
  - *(ii) as additional national financing to the aid referred to in point (i);*

  and
- *(b) be identical to the underlying rural development measure provided for in the rural development programme referred to in point (a).*

3. The legal basis for the aid shall specify that the aid shall not be put into effect before the approval of the relevant rural development programme by the Commission.

4. The investment shall be in conformity with Union legislation and with national laws of the Member State concerned on environmental protection. For investment requiring an environmental impact assessment under Directive 2011/92/EU the aid shall be subject to the condition that such assessment shall have been carried out and the development consent shall have been granted for the investment project concerned before the date of granting the individual aid.

[The first subparagraph shall not apply to aid which is provided in the form of financial instruments.]

5. The aid shall cover investments in tangible assets and intangible assets which concern infrastructure related to the development, modernisation or adaptation of forests, including the following:

- *(a) access to forest land;*
- *(b) land consolidation and improvement;*
- *(c) supply of energy and water.*

6. [Save where support is provided in the form of financial instruments, the aid shall cover the following eligible costs:]

- *(a) the construction, acquisition, including leasing, or improvement of immovable property, with land only being eligible to an extent not exceeding 10% of the total eligible costs of the operation concerned;*
- *(b) the purchase or lease purchase of machinery and equipment up to the market value of the asset;*
- *(c) general costs linked to the expenditure referred to in points (a) and (b), such as architect, engineer and consultation fees, fees relating to advice on environmental and economic sustainability, including feasibility studies; feasibility studies shall remain eligible expenditure even where, based on their results, no expenditure under points (a) and (b) is incurred;*
- *(d) acquisition or development of computer software and acquisitions of patents, licenses, copyrights and trademarks;*
- *(e) the costs of establishing forest management plans and their equivalent instruments.*

7. [Save where support is provided in the form of financial instruments, costs other than those referred to in paragraph 6(a) and (b) connected with leasing contracts, such as lessor's margin, interest refinancing costs, overheads and insurance charges shall not be considered to be eligible costs.]

Working capital shall not be considered to be an eligible cost.

8. In the case of non-productive investments, investments aimed exclusively at improving the environmental value of forests and investments for forest roads, which are open to the public free of charge and which serve the multifunctional aspects of forest the aid intensity shall be limited to 100% of the eligible costs.

9. In the case of investments, which improve the short or long term economic potential of forests, the aid intensity shall be limited to the following rates:

- *(a) 75% of the amount of the eligible costs for investment in outermost regions;*
- *(b) 75% of the amount of the eligible costs for investment in the smaller Aegean islands;*
- *(c) 50% of the amount of the eligible costs for investment in less developed regions and in all regions whose GDP per capita for the period from 1 January 2007 to 31 December 2013 period was less than 75% of the average of the EU-25 for the reference period but whose GDP per capita is above 75% of the GDP average of the EU-27;*
- *(d) 40% of the amount of the eligible costs for investment in other regions.*

NOTES

The words in square brackets in para 4 were inserted, and the words in square brackets in paras 6 and 7 were substituted, by Commission Regulation 2019/289/EU, Art 1(8).

Repeal of this Regulation in relation to the UK: this Regulation is repealed in relation to the UK (as from IP completion day); see the introductory notes to this Regulation *ante*.

[5.508]

Article 41 Aid for investments in forestry technologies and in processing, mobilising and marketing of forestry products

1. Aid for investments in forestry technologies and in the processing, mobilising and marketing of forestry products granted to private forest holders, municipalities and their associations and to SMEs shall be compatible with the internal market within the meaning of Article 107(3)(c) of the Treaty and shall be exempted from the notification requirement of Article 108(3) thereof where it fulfils the conditions laid down in paragraphs 2 to 11 of this Article and in Chapter I.

2. The aid shall:

- *(a) be granted in the framework of a rural development programme in accordance with Regulation (EU) No 1305/2013 and the delegated and implementing acts adopted by the Commission pursuant to that Regulation either:*
  - *(i) as aid co-financed by the EAFRD; or*
  - *(ii) as additional national financing to the aid referred to in point (i);*

  and
- *(b) be identical to the underlying rural development measure provided for in the rural development programme referred to in point (a).*

3. The legal basis for the aid shall specify that the aid shall not be put into effect before the approval of the relevant rural development programme by the Commission.

4. The investment shall be in conformity with Union legislation and with national laws of the Member State concerned on environmental protection. For investment requiring an environmental impact assessment under Directive 2011/92/EU the aid shall be subject to the condition that such assessment shall have been carried out and the development consent shall have been granted for the investment project concerned before the date of granting the individual aid.

[The first subparagraph shall not apply to aid which is provided in the form of financial instruments.]

5. In the territories of the Azores, Madeira, the Canary islands, the smaller Aegean islands and the French overseas departments aid may also be granted to undertakings that are not SMEs.

6. [Save where support is provided in the form of financial instruments, the aid shall cover the following eligible costs:]

- *(a) the construction, acquisition, including leasing, or improvement of immovable property, with land only being eligible to an extent not exceeding 10% of the total eligible costs of the operation concerned;*
- *(b) the purchase or lease purchase of machinery and equipment up to the market value of the asset;*
- *(c) general costs linked to the expenditure referred to in points (a) and (b), such as architect, engineer and consultation fees, fees relating to advice on environmental and economic sustainability, including feasibility studies; feasibility studies shall remain eligible expenditure even where, based on their results, no expenditure under points (a) and (b) is incurred;*
- *(d) acquisition or development of computer software and acquisitions of patents, licenses, copyrights and trademarks;*
- *(e) the costs of establishing forest management plans and their equivalent.*

7. [Save where support is provided in the form of financial instruments, costs other than those referred to in paragraph 6(a) and (b) connected with leasing contracts, such as lessor's margin, interest refinancing costs, overheads and insurance charges shall not be considered to be eligible costs.]

Working capital shall not be considered to be an eligible cost.

8. Investments related to the improvement of the economic value of forests shall be justified in relation to expected improvements to forests on one or more holdings and may include investments for soil and resource friendly harvesting machinery and practices.

9. Investments related to the use of wood as a raw material or energy source shall be limited to all working operations prior to industrial processing.

[Save where support is provided in the form of financial instruments, the following conditions shall apply:

(a) *the investments in renewable energy infrastructure that consume or produce energy shall comply with minimum standards for energy efficiency for, where such standards exist at national level;*

(b) *investments in installations, the primary purpose of which is electricity production from biomass, shall not be eligible for aid unless a minimum percentage of heat energy, to be determined by the Member States, is utilised;*

(c) *aid to bioenergy investment projects shall be limited to bioenergy meeting the applicable sustainability criteria laid down in Union legislation, including in Article 17(2) to (6) of Directive 2009/28/EC.]*

10. For forest holdings above a certain threshold to be determined by Member States, aid shall be conditional on the presentation of the relevant information from of a forest management plan or equivalent instrument in line with sustainable forest management as defined by the Second Ministerial Conference on the Protection of Forests in Europe of 1993.

11. The aid intensity shall be limited to the following rates:

(a) *75% of the amount of the eligible costs for investment in outermost regions;*

(b) *75% of the amount of the eligible costs for investment in the smaller Aegean islands;*

(c) *50% of the amount of the eligible costs for investment in less developed regions and in all regions whose GDP per capita for the period from 1 January 2007 to 31 December 2013 period was less than 75% of the average of the EU-25 for the reference period but whose GDP per capita is above 75% of the GDP average of the EU-27;*

(d) *40% of the amount of the eligible costs for investment in other regions.*

NOTES

All words in square brackets were inserted or substituted by Commission Regulation 2019/289/EU, Art 1(9).

Repeal of this Regulation in relation to the UK: this Regulation is repealed in relation to the UK (as from IP completion day); see the introductory notes to this Regulation *ante*.

[5.509]

Article 42 Conservation of genetic resources in forestry

1. Aid for the conservation of genetic resources in forestry, linked to forest-environmental and climate services and forest conservation, granted to public or private entities shall be compatible with the internal market within the meaning of Article 107(3)(c) of the Treaty and shall be exempted from the notification requirement of Article 108(3) thereof where it fulfils the conditions laid down in paragraphs 2 to 6 of this Article and in Chapter I.

2. The aid shall:

(a) *be granted in the framework of a rural development programme in accordance with Regulation (EU) No 1305/2013 and the delegated and implementing acts adopted by the Commission pursuant to that Regulation either:*

(i) *as aid co-financed by the EAFRD; or*

(ii) *as additional national financing to the aid referred to in point (i);*

and

(b) *be identical to the underlying rural development measure provided for in the rural development programme referred to in point (a).*

3. The legal basis for the aid shall specify that the aid shall not be put into effect before the approval of the relevant rural development programme by the Commission.

4. For the purposes of this Article the following definitions shall apply:

(a) *'in situ conservation' means the conservation of genetic material in ecosystems and natural habitats and the maintenance and recovery of viable population of species in their natural surroundings;*

(b) *'on-forest holding conservation' means in situ conservation and development at forest holding level;*

(c) *'ex situ conservation' means the conservation of genetic material for forestry outside their natural habitat;*

(d) *'ex situ collection' means a collection of genetic material for forestry maintained outside their natural habitat.*

5. The aid shall cover the costs for the following operations:

(a) *targeted actions: actions promoting the in situ and ex situ conservation, characterisation, collection and utilisation of genetic resources in forestry, including web-based inventories of genetic resources currently conserved in situ, including on-forest holding conservation, and of ex situ collections and databases;*

(b) *concerted actions: actions promoting the exchange of information for the conservation, characterisation, collection and utilisation of genetic resources in Union forestry, among competent organisations in the Member States;*

(c) *accompanying actions: information, dissemination and advisory actions involving non-governmental organisations and other relevant stakeholders, training courses and preparation of technical reports.*

6. The aid shall be limited to 100% of the eligible costs.

NOTES

Repeal of this Regulation in relation to the UK: this Regulation is repealed in relation to the UK (as from IP completion day); see the introductory notes to this Regulation *ante*.

[5.510]

Article 43 Aid for forestry land consolidation

Aid for forestry land consolidation shall be compatible with the internal market within the meaning of Article 107(3)(c) of the Treaty and shall be exempted from the notification requirement of Article 108(3) thereof where it fulfils the conditions laid down in Chapter I and it is granted:

(a) *to private forestry holders that are SMEs; and*

(b) *towards and limited to the legal and administrative costs, including survey costs; and*

(c) *up to 100% of the real costs incurred.*

NOTES

Repeal of this Regulation in relation to the UK: this Regulation is repealed in relation to the UK (as from IP completion day); see the introductory notes to this Regulation *ante*.

SECTION 6 AIDS IN FAVOUR OF SMES IN RURAL AREAS CO-FINANCED BY THE EAFRD OR GRANTED AS ADDITIONAL NATIONAL FINANCING TO SUCH CO-FINANCED MEASURES

[5.511]

Article 44 Aid for investments concerning the processing of agricultural products into non-agricultural products or the production of cotton

1. Aid for investments concerning the processing of agricultural products into non-agricultural products or the production of cotton, including the activities of ginning, granted to SMEs, shall be compatible with the internal market within the meaning of Article 107(3)(c) of the Treaty and shall be exempted from the notification requirement of Article 108(3) thereof where it fulfils the conditions laid down in paragraphs 2 to 10 of this Article and in Chapter I.

2. The aid shall:

(a) be granted in the framework of a rural development programme in accordance with Regulation (EU) No 1305/2013 and the delegated and implementing acts adopted by the Commission pursuant to that Regulation either:

(i) as aid co-financed by the EAFRD; or

(ii) as additional national financing to the aid referred to in point (i);

and

(b) be identical to the underlying rural development measure provided for in the rural development programme referred to in point (a).

3. The legal basis for the aid shall specify that the aid shall not be put into effect before the approval of the relevant rural development programme by the Commission.

4. Investment linked to the production of biofuel or energy from renewable sources shall not be eligible for aid under this Article.

5. The investment shall be in conformity with Union legislation and with national laws of the Member State concerned on environmental protection. For investment requiring an environmental impact assessment under Directive 2011/92/EU the aid shall be subject to the condition that such assessment shall have been carried out and the development consent shall have been granted for the investment project concerned before the date of granting the individual aid.

[The first subparagraph shall not apply to aid which is provided in the form of financial instruments.]

6. The aid shall cover investments in tangible and intangible assets.

7. [Save where support is provided in the form of financial instruments, the aid shall cover the following eligible costs:]

(a) the construction, acquisition, including leasing, or improvement of immovable property, with land only being eligible to an extent not exceeding 10% of the total eligible costs of the operation concerned;

(b) the purchase or lease purchase of machinery and equipment up to the market value of the asset;

(c) general costs linked to expenditure referred to in points (a) and (b), such as architect, engineer and consultation fees, fees relating to advice on environmental and economic sustainability, including feasibility studies; feasibility studies shall remain eligible expenditure even where, based on their results, no expenditure under points (a) and (b) is incurred;

(d) acquisition or development of computer software and acquisitions of patents, licenses, copyrights and trademarks.

8. [Save where support is provided in the form of financial instruments, costs other than those referred to in paragraph 7(a) and (b) connected with leasing contracts, such as lessor's margin, interest refinancing costs, overheads and insurance charges shall not be considered to be eligible costs.]

Working capital shall not be considered to be an eligible cost.

9. The aid intensity shall be limited to the following rates:

(a) in the outermost regions:

(i) 80% of the amount of the eligible costs for investment in regions whose GDP per capita is below or equal to 45% of the EU-27 average;

(ii) 65% of the amount of the eligible costs for investment in regions whose GDP per capita is between or equal to 45% and 60% of the EU-27 average;

(iii) 55% of the amount of the eligible costs for investment in regions with a GDP per capita between or equal to 60% and 75% of the EU-27 average;

(iv) 45% of the amount of the eligible costs for investment in other outermost regions;

(b) in less developed regions:

(i) 60% of the amount of the eligible costs for investment in regions whose GDP per capita is below or equal to 45% of the EU-27 average;

(ii) 45% of the amount of the eligible costs for investment in regions whose GDP per capita is between or equal to 45% and 60% of the EU-27 average;

(iii) 35% of the amount of the eligible costs for investment in regions with a GDP per capita above 60% of the EU-27 average;

(c) in 'c' areas:

(i) 25% of the amount of the eligible costs for investment in sparsely populated areas and in NUTS 3 regions or parts of NUTS 3 regions that share a land border with a country outside the European Economic Area or the European Free Trade Association;

(ii) 20% of the amount of the eligible costs for investment in non-predefined 'c' areas;

(iii) in the former 'a' areas the aid intensities may be increased by up to 5 percentage points during the period from 1 July 2014 to 31 December 2017;

(iv) where a 'c' area is adjacent to an 'a' area, the maximum aid intensity allowed in the NUTS 3 areas or parts of NUTS 3 areas within that 'c' area which are adjacent to the 'a' area may be increased as necessary so that the difference in aid intensity between both areas does not exceed 15 percentage points;

(d) 10% of the amount of the eligible costs for investment in all other regions.

10. The maximum aid intensities provided for in paragraph 9 may be increased by up to 10 percentage points for micro and small enterprises.

NOTES

The words in square brackets in para 5 were inserted, and the words in square brackets in paras 7 and 8 were substituted, by Commission Regulation 2019/289/EU, Art 1(10).

Repeal of this Regulation in relation to the UK: this Regulation is repealed in relation to the UK (as from IP completion day); see the introductory notes to this Regulation *ante*.

[5.512]

Article 45 Business start-up aid for non-agricultural activities in rural areas

1. Business start-up aid for non-agricultural activities in rural areas granted to SMEs shall be compatible with the internal market within the meaning of Article 107(3)(c) of the Treaty and shall be exempted from the notification requirement of Article 108(3) thereof where it fulfils the conditions laid down in paragraphs 2 to 9 of this Article and in Chapter I.

2. The aid shall:

(a) be granted in the framework of a rural development programme in accordance with Regulation (EU) No 1305/2013 and the delegated and implementing acts adopted by the Commission pursuant to that Regulation either:

(i) as aid co-financed by the EAFRD; or

(ii) as additional national financing to the aid referred to in point (i);

and

(b) be identical to the underlying rural development measure provided for in the rural development programme referred to in point (a).

3. The legal basis for the aid shall specify that the aid shall not be put into effect before the approval of the relevant rural development programme by the Commission.

4. Aid shall be granted to the following categories of beneficiaries:

(a) farmers or members of a farm household in rural areas diversifying into non-agricultural activities;

(b) micro and small enterprises in rural areas; and

(c) natural persons in rural areas.

5. Where the member of a farm household referred to in paragraph 4(a) is a legal person or a group of legal persons it must exercise an agricultural activity on the farm at the time of the submission of the application for the aid.

6. The aid shall be conditional on the submission of a business plan to the competent authority of the Member State concerned. The implementation of that business plan shall start within nine months from the date of the decision granting the aid.

The business plan shall describe the following:

(a) the initial economic situation of the beneficiary;

(b) milestones and targets for the development of the new activities of the beneficiary;

(c) details of the actions required for the development of the activities of the beneficiary, such as details of investments, training, advice.

[The business plan shall have a maximum duration of five years.]

7. [The aid shall be paid in at least two instalments.]

The instalments may be degressive.

The payment of the last instalment shall be conditional upon the correct implementation of the business plan referred to in paragraph 6.

8. Member States shall define the amount of aid taking into account the socioeconomic situation of the area covered by the rural development programme.

9. The aid shall be limited to EUR 70,000 per beneficiary.

NOTES

The words in square brackets in para 6 were inserted, and the words in square brackets in para 7 were substituted, by Commission Regulation 2019/289/EU, Art 1(11).

Repeal of this Regulation in relation to the UK: this Regulation is repealed in relation to the UK (as from IP completion day); see the introductory notes to this Regulation *ante*.

[5.513]

Article 46 Aid for advisory services for SMEs in rural areas

1. Aid for advisory services for SMEs in rural areas shall be compatible with the internal market within the meaning of Article 107(3)(c) of the Treaty and shall be exempted from the notification requirement of Article 108(3) thereof where it fulfils the conditions laid down in paragraphs 2 to 9 of this Article and in Chapter I.

2. The aid shall:

(a) be granted in the framework of a rural development programme in accordance with Regulation (EU) No 1305/2013 and the delegated and implementing acts adopted by the Commission pursuant to that Regulation either:

(i) as aid co-financed by the EAFRD; or

(ii) as additional national financing to the aid referred to in point (i);

and

(b) be identical to the underlying rural development measure provided for in the rural development programme referred to in point (a).

3. The aid shall be granted to help SMEs in rural areas benefit from the use of advisory services for the improvement of the economic and environmental performance, climate friendliness and resilience of their enterprise and investment.

4. The advice may cover issues linked to the economic and environmental performance of the beneficiary.

5. The aid shall not involve direct payment to the beneficiaries. [The aid shall be paid to the provider of the advisory services or to the Managing Authority referred to in point (a) of Article 65(2) of Regulation (EU) No 1305/2013.]

6. The provider of the advisory services shall have the appropriate resources in the form of regularly trained and qualified staff and advisory experience and reliability in the fields they advise in.

7. When providing advice, the providers of advisory services shall respect the non-disclosure obligations referred to in Article 13(2) of Regulation (EU) No 1306/2013.

8. Where appropriate, advice may be partly provided in groups, while taking into account the situations of the individual user of the advisory services.

9. The amount of aid shall be limited to EUR 1 500 per advice.

NOTES

Para 5: words in square brackets substituted by Commission Regulation 2019/289/EU, Art 1(12).

Repeal of this Regulation in relation to the UK: this Regulation is repealed in relation to the UK (as from IP completion day); see the introductory notes to this Regulation *ante*.

[5.514]

Article 47 Aid for knowledge transfer and information actions in favour of SMEs in rural areas

1. Aid for knowledge transfer and information actions in favour of SMEs in rural areas shall be compatible with the internal market within the meaning of Article 107(3)(c) of the Treaty and shall be exempted from the notification requirement of Article 108(3) thereof where it fulfils the conditions laid down in paragraphs 2 to 7 of this Article and in Chapter I.

2. The aid shall:

(a) be granted in the framework of a rural development programme in accordance with Regulation (EU) No 1305/2013 and the delegated and implementing acts adopted by the Commission pursuant to that Regulation either:

(i) as aid co-financed by the EAFRD; or

(ii) as additional national financing to the aid referred to in point (i);

and

(b) be identical to the underlying rural development measure provided for in the rural development programme referred to in point (a).

3. The aid shall cover vocational training and skills acquisition actions, including training courses, workshops and coaching, demonstration activities and information actions. [Infrastructure installed as a result of demonstration may be used after the operation is completed.]

Aid to demonstration activities may cover relevant investment costs.

[Aid for demonstration projects which is provided in the form of financial instruments may cover other eligible costs than those referred to in point (b) of paragraph 4, provided that the costs are fully eligible under Regulation (EU) No 1305/2013.]

4. The aid shall cover the following eligible costs:

(a) the costs of organising and delivering the knowledge transfer or information action;

(b) in case of demonstration projects related to investments:

(i) the construction, acquisition, including leasing, or improvement of immovable property, with land only being eligible to an extent not exceeding 10% of total eligible costs of the operation concerned;

(ii) the purchase or lease purchase of machinery and equipment up to the market value of the asset;

(iii) general costs linked to expenditure referred to in points (i) and (ii), such as architect, engineer and consultation fees, fees relating to advice on environmental and economic sustainability, including feasibility studies; feasibility studies shall remain eligible expenditure even where, based on their results, no expenditure under points (i) and (ii) is incurred;

(iv) acquisition or development of computer software and acquisitions of patents, licenses, copyright and, trademarks;

(c) costs for travel, accommodation and per diem expenses of participants.

5. The aid shall not involve direct payments to the beneficiaries.

That aid shall be paid to the provider of the knowledge transfer and information actions.

Bodies providing knowledge transfer and information actions shall have the appropriate capacities in the form of staff qualifications and regular training to carry out those tasks.

6. The aid shall be accessible to all those eligible undertakings active in the rural area concerned, based on objectively defined conditions.

7. The aid intensity shall be limited to the following rates:

(a) 60% of the eligible costs in the case of medium-sized enterprises;

(b) 70% of the eligible costs in the case of micro and small enterprises.

NOTES

Para 3: words in square brackets inserted by Commission Regulation 2019/289/EU, Art 1(13).

Repeal of this Regulation in relation to the UK: this Regulation is repealed in relation to the UK (as from IP completion day); see the introductory notes to this Regulation *ante*.

[5.515]

Article 48 Aid for new participation of active farmers in quality schemes for cotton and foodstuffs

[1. Aid for new participation, or participation in the five preceding years, of active farmers and groups of farmers that operate as SMEs, in quality schemes for cotton and foodstuffs shall be compatible with the internal market within the meaning of Article 107(3)(c) of the Treaty and shall be exempted from the notification requirement of Article 108(3) thereof where it fulfils the conditions laid down in paragraphs 2 to 7 of this Article and in Chapter I of this Regulation.]

2. The aid shall:

(a) be granted in the framework of a rural development programme in accordance with Regulation (EU) No 1305/2013 and the delegated and implementing acts adopted by the Commission pursuant to that Regulation either:

(i) as aid co-financed by the EAFRD; or

(ii) as additional national financing to the aid referred to in point (i);

and

(b) be identical to the underlying rural development measure provided for in the rural development programme referred to in point (a).

3. The legal basis for the aid shall specify that the aid shall not be put into effect before the approval of the relevant rural development programme by the Commission.

4. Aid shall be granted for new participation in one of the following types of quality schemes:

(a) quality schemes for cotton and foodstuffs established under Regulation (EU) No 1151/2012;

(b) quality schemes for cotton and foodstuffs, including certification schemes, recognised by the Member States as complying with the following criteria:

(i) the specificity of the final product produced under such quality schemes is derived from clear obligations to guarantee:

— specific product characteristics,

— specific farming or production methods, or

— a quality of the final product that goes significantly beyond the commercial commodity standards as regards public, animal or plant health, animal welfare or environmental protection;

(ii) the scheme is open to all producers;

(iii) the scheme involves binding final product specifications and compliance with those specifications is verified by public authorities or by an independent inspection body;

(iv) the scheme is transparent and assures complete traceability of agricultural products;

(c) voluntary foodstuff certification schemes recognised by the Member State concerned as meeting the requirements laid down in the Commission Communication — EU best practice guidelines for voluntary certification schemes for agricultural products and foodstuffs.

5. The aid shall be granted in the form of an annual incentive payment, the level of which shall be determined according to the level of the fixed costs arising from participation in quality schemes.

6. The aid shall be granted for a maximum period of five years.

[If the initial participation in the quality scheme started before the application for support, the maximum period of five years shall be reduced by the number of years which have elapsed between that initial participation and the time of the application for support.]

7. The aid shall be limited to EUR 3,000 per beneficiary per year.

NOTES

Para 1 was substituted, and the words in square brackets in para 6 were inserted, by Commission Regulation 2019/289/EU, Art 1(14).

Repeal of this Regulation in relation to the UK: this Regulation is repealed in relation to the UK (as from IP completion day); see the introductory notes to this Regulation *ante*.

[5.516]

Article 49 Aid for information and promotion activities concerning cotton and foodstuffs covered by a quality scheme

1. Aid for information and promotion activities concerning cotton and foodstuffs covered by a quality scheme shall be compatible with the internal market within the meaning of Article 107(3)(c) of the Treaty and shall be exempted from the notification requirement of Article 108(3) thereof where it fulfils the conditions laid down in paragraphs 2 to 11 of this Article and in Chapter I.

2. The aid shall:

(a) be granted in the framework of a rural development programme in accordance with Regulation (EU) No 1305/2013 and the delegated and implementing acts adopted by the Commission pursuant to that Regulation either:

(i) as aid co-financed by the EAFRD; or

(ii) as additional national financing to the aid referred to in point (i);

and

(b) be identical to the underlying rural development measure provided for in the rural development programme referred to in point (a).

3. The legal basis for the aid shall specify that the aid shall not be put into effect before the approval of the relevant rural development programme by the Commission.

4. The aid shall be granted to groups of producers implementing the information and promotion activities.

5. Only information and promotion activities that are implemented in the internal market shall be eligible for aid

6. The aid shall be granted for information and promotion activities concerning cotton and foodstuffs which are covered by a quality scheme and for which aid is granted in accordance with Article 48 of this Regulation.

7. The aid shall cover the costs for actions having the following characteristics:

(a) be designed to induce consumers to buy the foodstuffs or the cotton covered by a quality scheme as referred to in Article 48(4) of this Regulation;

(b) draw attention to specific features or advantages of the foodstuff or the cotton, notably to the quality, specific production method, high animal welfare standards and respect for the environment linked to the quality scheme concerned.

8. The actions referred to in paragraph 6 of this article shall not incite consumers to buy a foodstuff or cotton due to their particular origin, except for those covered by the quality schemes set out in Title II of Regulation (EU) No 1151/2012.

9. The origin of the foodstuff or cotton may be indicated, provided that the mention of the origin is subordinate to the main message.

10. Information and promotion activities related to particular undertakings or of commercial brands shall not be eligible for aid.

11. The aid intensity shall be limited to 70% of the eligible costs.

NOTES

Repeal of this Regulation in relation to the UK: this Regulation is repealed in relation to the UK (as from IP completion day); see the introductory notes to this Regulation *ante*.

CHAPTER IV TRANSITIONAL AND FINAL PROVISIONS

[5.517]

Article 50 Repeal

1. Regulation (EC) No 1857/2006 shall be repealed.

2. By way of derogation from paragraph 1 of this Article, Regulation (EC) No 1857/2006 shall continue to apply until 31 December 2015 to aid granted in connection with Council Regulation (EC) No 1698/2005[1] *and its implementing rules.*

NOTES

Repeal of this Regulation in relation to the UK: this Regulation is repealed in relation to the UK (as from IP completion day); see the introductory notes to this Regulation *ante*.

1 Council Regulation (EC) No 1698/2005 of 20 September 2005 on support for rural development by the European Agricultural Fund for Rural Development (*EAFRD*) (OJ L277, 21.10.2005, p 1).

[5.518]

Article 51 Transitional provisions

1. This Regulation shall apply to individual aid granted before the date of entry into force of this Regulation, if that individual aid fulfils all the conditions laid down in this Regulation, with the exception of Articles 9 and 10.

2. Any aid not exempted from the notification requirement of Article 108(3) of the Treaty by virtue of this Regulation or other regulations adopted pursuant to Article 1 of Regulation (EC) No 994/98 previously in force shall be assessed by the Commission in accordance with the European Union Guidelines for State aid in the agricultural and forestry sectors and in rural areas 2014 to 2020 and the other relevant frameworks, guidelines, communications and notices.

3. Any individual aid granted before 1 January 2015 by virtue of any regulation adopted pursuant to Article 1 of Regulation (EC) No 994/98 in force at the time of granting the aid shall be compatible with the internal market and exempted from the notification requirement of Article 108(3) of the Treaty.

4. At the end of the period of validity of this Regulation, any aid schemes exempted under this Regulation shall remain exempted during an adjustment period of six months.

By way of derogation from the first subparagraph, at the end of the period of validity of this Regulation aid schemes falling within the scope of Regulation (EU) No 1305/2013 and either co-financed by EAFRD or granted as additional national financing for such co-financed measures shall remain exempted for the duration of the programming period in accordance with Regulation (EU) No 1305/2013 and its implementing rules.

NOTES

Repeal of this Regulation in relation to the UK: this Regulation is repealed in relation to the UK (as from IP completion day); see the introductory notes to this Regulation *ante*.

[5.519]

Article 52 Entry into force and applicability

This Regulation shall enter into force on 1 July 2014.

[It shall apply until 31 December 2022.]

This Regulation shall be binding in its entirety and directly applicable in all Member States.

NOTES

Words in square brackets substituted by Commission Regulation 2020/2008/EU, Art 1(3). Note that previously this Regulation was due to expire on 31 December 2020.

Repeal of this Regulation in relation to the UK: this Regulation is repealed in relation to the UK (as from IP completion day); see the introductory notes to this Regulation *ante*.

ANNEXES

ANNEX I
DEFINITION OF MICRO, SMALL AND MEDIUM-SIZED ENTERPRISES

[5.520]

Article 1 Enterprise

An enterprise is considered to be any entity engaged in an economic activity, irrespective of its legal form. This includes, in particular, self-employed persons and family businesses engaged in craft or other activities, and partnerships or associations regularly engaged in an economic activity.

Article 2 Staff headcount and financial ceilings determining enterprise categories

1. The category of micro, small and medium-sized enterprises (SMEs) is made up of enterprises which employ fewer than 250 persons and which have an annual turnover not exceeding EUR 50 million, and/or an annual balance sheet total not exceeding EUR 43 million.

2. Within the SME category, a small enterprise is defined as an enterprise which employs fewer than 50 persons and whose annual turnover and/or annual balance sheet total does not exceed EUR 10 million.

3. Within the SME category, a microenterprise is defined as an enterprise which employs fewer than 10 persons and whose annual turnover and/or annual balance sheet total does not exceed EUR 2 million.

Article 3 Types of enterprise taken into consideration in calculating staff numbers and financial amounts

1. An 'autonomous enterprise' is any enterprise which is not classified as a partner enterprise within the meaning of paragraph 2 or as a linked enterprise within the meaning of paragraph 3.

2. 'Partner enterprises' are all enterprises which are not classified as linked enterprises within the meaning of paragraph 3 and between which there is the following relationship: an enterprise (upstream enterprise) holds, either solely or jointly with one or more linked enterprises within the meaning of paragraph 3, 25% or more of the capital or voting rights of another enterprise (downstream enterprise).

However, an enterprise may be ranked as autonomous, and thus as not having any partner enterprises, even if this 25% threshold is reached or exceeded by the following investors, provided that those investors are not linked, within the meaning of paragraph 3, either individually or jointly to the enterprise in question:

- *(a) public investment corporations, venture capital companies, individuals or groups of individuals with a regular venture capital investment activity who invest equity capital in unquoted businesses ('business angels'), provided the total investment of those business angels in the same enterprise is less than EUR 1 250,000;*
- *(b) universities or non-profit research centres;*
- *(c) institutional investors, including regional development funds;*
- *(d) autonomous local authorities with an annual budget of less than EUR 10 million and fewer than 5000 inhabitants.*

3. 'Linked enterprises' are enterprises which have any of the following relationships with each other:

- *(a) an enterprise has a majority of the shareholders' or members' voting rights in another enterprise;*
- *(b) an enterprise has the right to appoint or remove a majority of the members of the administrative, management or supervisory body of another enterprise;*
- *(c) an enterprise has the right to exercise a dominant influence over another enterprise pursuant to a contract entered into with that enterprise or to a provision in its memorandum or articles of association;*
- *(d) an enterprise, which is a shareholder in or member of another enterprise, controls alone, pursuant to an agreement with other shareholders in or members of that enterprise, a majority of shareholders' or members' voting rights in that enterprise.*

There is a presumption that no dominant influence exists if the investors listed in the second subparagraph of paragraph 2 are not involving themselves directly or indirectly in the management of the enterprise in question, without prejudice to their rights as stakeholders.

Enterprises having any of the relationships described in the first subparagraph through one or more other enterprises, or any one of the investors mentioned in paragraph 2, are also considered to be linked.

Enterprises which have one or other of such relationships through a natural person or group of natural persons acting jointly are also considered linked enterprises if they engage in their activity or in part of their activity in the same relevant market or in adjacent markets.

An 'adjacent market' is considered to be the market for a product or service situated directly upstream or downstream of the relevant market.

4. Except in the cases set out in paragraph 2, second subparagraph, an enterprise cannot be considered an SME if 25% or more of the capital or voting rights are directly or indirectly controlled, jointly or individually, by one or more public bodies.

5. Enterprises may make a declaration of status as an autonomous enterprise, partner enterprise or linked enterprise, including the data regarding the ceilings set out in Article 2. The declaration may be made even if the capital is spread in such a way that it is not possible to determine exactly by whom it is held, in which case the enterprise may declare in good faith that it can legitimately presume that it is not owned as to 25% or more by one enterprise or jointly by enterprises linked to one another. Such declarations are made without prejudice to the checks and investigations provided for by national or Union rules.

Article 4 Data used for the staff headcount and the financial amounts and reference period

1. The data to apply to the headcount of staff and the financial amounts are those relating to the latest approved accounting period and calculated on an annual basis. They are taken into account from the date of closure of the accounts. The amount selected for the turnover is calculated excluding value added tax (VAT) and other indirect taxes.

2. Where, at the date of closure of the accounts, an enterprise finds that, on an annual basis, it has exceeded or fallen below the headcount or financial ceilings stated in Article 2, this will not result in the loss or acquisition of the status of medium-sized, small or microenterprise unless those ceilings are exceeded over two consecutive accounting periods.

3. In the case of newly established enterprises whose accounts have not yet been approved, the data to apply is to be derived from a bona fide estimate made in the course of the financial year.

Article 5 Staff headcount

The headcount corresponds to the number of annual work units (AWU), i.e. the number of persons who worked full-time within the enterprise in question or on its behalf during the entire reference year under consideration. The work of persons who have not worked the full year, the work of those who have worked part-time, regardless of duration, and the work of seasonal workers are counted as fractions of AWU. The staff consists of:

(a) employees;
(b) persons working for the enterprise being subordinated to it and deemed to be employees under national law;
(c) owner-managers;
(d) partners engaging in a regular activity in the enterprise and benefiting from financial advantages from the enterprise.

Apprentices or students engaged in vocational training with an apprenticeship or vocational training contract are not included as staff. The duration of maternity or parental leaves is not counted.

Article 6 Establishing the data of an enterprise

1. In the case of an autonomous enterprise, the data, including the number of staff, are determined exclusively on the basis of the accounts of that enterprise.

2. The data, including the headcount, of an enterprise having partner enterprises or linked enterprises are determined on the basis of the accounts and other data of the enterprise or, where they exist, the consolidated accounts of the enterprise, or the consolidated accounts in which the enterprise is included through consolidation.

To the data referred to in the first subparagraph are added the data of any partner enterprise of the enterprise in question situated immediately upstream or downstream from it. Aggregation is proportional to the percentage interest in the capital or voting rights (whichever is greater). In the case of cross-holdings, the greater percentage applies.

To the data referred to in the first and second subparagraph is added 100% of the data of any enterprise, which is linked directly or indirectly to the enterprise in question, where the data were not already included through consolidation in the accounts.

3. For the application of paragraph 2, the data of the partner enterprises of the enterprise in question are derived from their accounts and their other data, consolidated if they exist. To these is added 100% of the data of enterprises which are linked to these partner enterprises, unless their accounts data are already included through consolidation.

For the application of the same paragraph 2, the data of the enterprises which are linked to the enterprise in question are to be derived from their accounts and their other data, consolidated if they exist. To these is added, pro rata, the data of any possible partner enterprise of that linked enterprise, situated immediately upstream or downstream from it, unless it has already been included in the consolidated accounts with a percentage at least proportional to the percentage identified under the second subparagraph of paragraph 2.

4. Where in the consolidated accounts no staff data appear for a given enterprise, staff figures are calculated by aggregating proportionally the data from its partner enterprises and by adding the data from the enterprises to which the enterprise in question is linked.

NOTES

Repeal of this Regulation in relation to the UK: this Regulation is repealed in relation to the UK (as from IP completion day); see the introductory notes to this Regulation *ante*.

ANNEX II

INFORMATION REGARDING STATE AID EXEMPTED UNDER THIS REGULATION

as provided for in Article 9(1)

(Text with EEA relevance)[1]

NOTES

[1] Applicable only to aid concerning the forestry sector and products not listed in Annex I to the Treaty.

PART I

[5.521]

Aid reference	*(to be completed by the Commission)*	
Member State	. . . .	
Member State reference number	. . . .	
Region	***Name of the Region (NUTS)***[1]	***Regional aid status***[2]
	. . . .	. . . .
	. . . .	. . . .
Granting authority	***Name***	. . . .
	Postal address	. . . .
	Web address	. . . .

Title of the aid measure	. . . .		
National legal basis (Reference to the relevant national official publication)	. . . .		
Web link to the full text of the aid measure	. . . .		
Type of measure	☐ ***Scheme***		
	☐ ***Ad hoc aid***	***Name of the beneficiary and the group[3] it belongs to***	
		. . . .	
Amendment of an existing aid scheme or ad hocaid		***Commission aid reference***	
	☐ ***Prolongation***	. . . .	
	☐ ***Modification***	. . . .	
Duration[4]	☐ ***Scheme***	*dd/mm/yyyy to dd/mm/yyyy*	
Date of granting	☐ ***Ad hoc aid***	*dd/mm/yyyy*	
Economic sector(s) concerned	***Please specify at NACE group level[5]***	. . . .	
Type of beneficiary	☐ ***SME***		
	☐ ***Large enterprises***		
Budget			
	☐ ***Scheme: Overall amount[6]***	***National currency . . . (full amounts)***	
		. . . .	
	☐ ***Ad hoc aid: Overall amount[7]***	***National currency . . . (full amounts)***	
		. . . .	
	For guarantees[8]	***National currency . . . (full amounts)***	
		. . . .	
Aid instrument	☐ ***Direct grant/ Interest rate subsidy***		
	☐ ***Subsidised services***		
	☐ ***Loan/ Repayable advances***		
	☐ ***Guarantee (where appropriate with a reference to the Commission decision)[9]***		
	☐ ***Tax advantage or tax exemption***		
	☐ ***Other (please specify)***		
	. . . .		
	Indicate to which broad category below it would fit best in terms of its effect/function:		
	☐ ***Grant***		
	☐ ***Loan***		
	☐ ***Guarantee***		
	☐ ***Tax advantage***		
If co-financed by EU fund(s)	***Name of EU fund(s):***	***Amount of funding (as per EU fund)***	***National currency . . . (full amounts)***
	. . . .	. . . .	. . . .
Other information			

NOTES

Repeal of this Regulation in relation to the UK: this Regulation is repealed in relation to the UK (as from IP completion day); see the introductory notes to this Regulation *ante*.

1 NUTS — Nomenclature of Territorial Units for Statistics. Typically, the region is specified at level 2.

2 Article 107(3)(a) of the Treaty on the Functioning of the European Union (status 'A'), Article 107(3)(c) of the Treaty on the Functioning of the European Union (status 'C'), unassisted areas namely areas that are not eligible for regional aid (status 'N').

3 An undertaking for the purposes of rules on competition laid down in the Treaty on the Functioning of the European Union and for the purposes of this Regulation is any entity engaged in an economic activity, regardless of its legal status

and the way in which it is financed. The Court of Justice has ruled that entities which are controlled (on a legal or on a de facto basis) by the same entity should be considered as one undertaking.

4 Period during which the granting authority can commit itself to grant the aid.

5 NACE Rev. 2 – Statistical classification of Economic Activities in the European Union. Typically, the sector shall be specified at group level.

6 In the case of an aid scheme: Indicate the overall amount of the budget planned under the scheme or the estimated tax loss for its whole duration for all aid instruments contained in the scheme.

7 In case of an *ad hoc* aid award: Indicate the overall aid amount or tax loss.

8 For guarantees, indicate the maximum amount of loans guaranteed.

9 Where appropriate, reference to the Commission decision approving the methodology to calculate the gross grant equivalent, in accordance with Article 5(2)(c)(ii) of this Regulation.

PART II PLEASE INDICATE UNDER WHICH PROVISION OF THIS REGULATION THE AID IS IMPLEMENTED

[5.522]

Primary objectives[1]	***Maximum aid intensity in%***	***Maximum aid amount in national currency (in full amounts)***
☐ ***Aid for investments in tangible assets or intangible assets in agricultural holding linked to primary agricultural production (Article 14)***		
☐ ***Aid for agricultural land consolidation (Article 15)***		
☐ ***Aid for investments concerning the relocation of farm buildings (Article 16)***		
☐ ***Aid for investments in connection with the processing of agricultural products and marketing of agricultural products (Article 17)***		
☐ ***Start-up aid for young farmers and the development of small farms (Article 18)***		
☐ ***Start-up aid for producer groups and organisations in the agricultural sector (Article 19)***		
☐ ***Aid for participation of producers of agricultural products in quality schemes (Article 20)***		
☐ ***Aid for knowledge transfer and information actions in the agricultural sector (Article 21)***		
☐ ***Aid for advisory services in the agricultural sector (Article 22)***		
☐ ***Aid for farm replacement services (Article 23)***		
☐ ***Aid for the promotional measures in favour of agricultural products (Article 24)***		
☐ ***Aid to compensate for damage caused by adverse climatic events which can be assimilated to a natural disaster (Article 25)***		
☐ ***Aid for the costs of the prevention, control and eradication of animal diseases and plant pests and aid to make good the damage caused by animal diseases and plant pests (Article 26)***		
☐ ***Aid to the livestock sector (Article 27(1)(a) or (b))***		
☐ ***Aid for removal of fallen stock (Article 27(1)(c), (d) or (e))***		
☐ ***Aid for the payment of insurance premiums (Article 28)***		
☐ ***Aid for investments in favour of conservation of cultural and natural heritage located on the agricultural holding (Article 29)***		
☐ ***Aid to make good the damage caused by natural disaster in the agricultural sector (Article 30)***		
Type of natural disaster	☐ *earthquake* ☐ *avalanche* ☐ *landslide* ☐ *flood* ☐ *tornado* ☐ *hurricane* ☐ *volcanic eruption*	

Primary objectives[1]	*Maximum aid intensity in%*	*Maximum aid amount in national currency (in full amounts)*
	☐ *wild fire*	
Date of occurrence of the natural disaster	*From dd/mm/yyyy to dd/mm/yyyy*	
☐ *Aid for research and development in the agricultural sector (Article 31)*		
☐ *Aid for research and development in the forestry sector (Article 31)*		
☐ *Aid for afforestation and creation of woodland (Article 32)*		
☐ *Aid for agroforestry systems (Article 33)*		
☐ *Aid for prevention and restoration of damage to forests from forest fire, natural disasters, adverse climatic events, plant pests and catastrophic events (Article 34)*		
☐ *Aid for investments improving the resilience and environmental value of forest ecosystems (Article 35)*		
☐ *Aid for disadvantages related to Natura 2000 forest areas (Article 36)*		
☐ *Aid for forest-environmental and climate services and forest conservation (Article 37)*		
☐ *Aid for knowledge transfer and information actions in the forestry sector (Article 38)*		
☐ *Aid for advisory services in the forestry sector (Article 39)*		
☐ *Aid for investments in infrastructure related to development, modernisation or adaptation of forestry sector(Article 40)*		
☐ *Aid for investments in forestry technologies and in processing, mobilising and marketing of forestry products (Article 41)*		
☐ *Aid for conservation of genetic resources in forestry (Article 42)*		
☐ *Aid for forestry land consolidation (Article 43)*		
☐ *Aid for investments concerning the processing of agricultural products into non-agricultural products or the production of cotton (Article 44)*		
☐ *Business start-up aid for non-agricultural activities in rural areas (Article 45)*		
☐ *Aid for advisory services for SMEs in rural areas (Article 46)*		
☐ *Aid for knowledge transfer and information actions in favour of SMEs in rural areas (Article 47)*		
☐ *Aid for new participation of active farmers in quality schemes for cotton or foodstuff (Article 48)*		
☐ *Aid for information and promotion activities concerning cotton and foodstuffs covered by a quality scheme (Article 49)*		

NOTES

Repeal of this Regulation in relation to the UK: this Regulation is repealed in relation to the UK (as from IP completion day); see the introductory notes to this Regulation *ante*.

[1] Multiple objectives are possible; in this case indicate all objectives

ANNEX III

PROVISIONS FOR THE PUBLICATION OF INFORMATION AS LAID DOWN IN ARTICLE 9(2)

[5.523]

Member States shall organise their comprehensive State aid websites, on which the information provided for in Article 9 (2) shall be published, in such a way as to allow easy access to that information. Information shall be published in a spreadsheet data format, which allows data to be searched, extracted and easily published on the Internet, such as CSV or XML format. Access to the State aid website shall be allowed to any interested party without restrictions. No prior user registration shall be required to access the State aid website.

The following information on individual aid award as laid down in Article 9(2)(c) shall be published:

a. *Reference of the identification number of the aid;*[1]
b. *Name of the beneficiary;*
c. *Type of enterprise (SME/large) at the date of granting the aid;*
d. *Region in which the beneficiary is located, at NUTS level II;*[2]
e. *Sector of activity at NACE group level;*[3]
f. *Aid element, expressed as full amount in national currency;*[4]
g. *Aid instrument*[5] *(Grant/Interest rate subsidy, Loan/Repayable advances/Reimbursable grant, Guarantee, Tax advantage or tax exemption, Risk finance, Other (please specify));*
h. *Date of granting the aid;*
i. *Objective of the aid;*[6]
j. *Granting authority;*

NOTES

Repeal of this Regulation in relation to the UK: this Regulation is repealed in relation to the UK (as from IP completion day); see the introductory notes to this Regulation *ante*.

1 As provided by the Commission under the procedure as referred to in Article 9(1) of this Regulation.

2 NUTS — Nomenclature of Territorial Units for Statistics. Typically, the region shall be specified at level 2.

3 Council Regulation (EEC) No 3037/90 of 9 October 1990 on the statistical classification of economic activities in the European Community (OJ No L293, 24.10.1990, p 1) as amended by Commission Regulation (EEC) No 761/93 of 24 March 1993 (OJ No L83, 3.4.1993, p 1, and corrigendum (OJ No L159, 11.7.1995, p 31).

4 Gross grant equivalent

5 If the aid is granted through multiple aid instruments, the aid amount shall be provided by an aid instrument

6 If the aid has multiple objectives, the aid amount shall be provided by an objective.

COMMISSION NOTICE

(2014/C204/01)

European Union Guidelines for State aid in the agricultural and forestry sectors and in rural areas 2014 to 2020

[5.524]

NOTES

Date of publication in OJ: OJ C204, 01.07.2014, p 1.

PART I. COMMON PROVISIONS

CHAPTER 1. INTRODUCTION

[5.525]

(1) Article 107(1) of the Treaty on the Functioning of the European Union ('the Treaty') stipulates that, '(s)ave as otherwise provided in the Treaties, any aid granted by a Member State or through State resources in any form whatsoever which distorts or threatens to distort competition by favouring certain undertakings or the production of certain goods shall, in so far as it affects trade between Member States, be incompatible with the internal market.'

(2) However, despite that general prohibition State aid may be necessary to address market failures in order to ensure a well-functioning and equitable economy. Therefore, the Treaty leaves room for the granting of State aid in respect of several policy objectives. With particular relevance to the agricultural sector and forestry, firstly in accordance with Articles 107(2)(b) of the Treaty, aid to make good the damage caused by natural disasters or exceptional occurrences shall be compatible with the internal market. Secondly, on the basis of Articles 107(3)(c) of the Treaty, the Commission may consider compatible with the internal market State aid to promote the economic development of the agricultural and forestry sectors and of rural areas, provided that it does not adversely affect trading conditions.

(3) Furthermore, due to the specificities of the agricultural sector, Article 42 of the Treaty provides that the rules on competition apply to production of and trade in agricultural products only to the extent determined by the European Parliament and the Council.

(4) In these Guidelines, the Commission sets out the conditions and criteria under which aid for the agricultural and forestry sectors and for rural areas will be considered to be compatible with the internal market and establishes the criteria for identifying the areas that fulfil the conditions of Article 107(3) of the Treaty. As regards aid granted pursuant to Article 107(2)(b), the Commission hereby sets out the conditions which will be verified in order to determine whether a measure constituting aid to make good the damage caused by natural disasters or exceptional occurrences is indeed covered by that Article.

(5) State aid to promote the economic development of the agricultural and forestry sectors and of rural areas is embedded in the broader common agricultural policy ('the CAP'). Within the CAP, the Union provides financial support to the agricultural and forestry sectors and to rural areas. As the economic effects of State aid do not change depending on whether it is (even partly) financed by the Union, or whether it is financed by a Member State alone, the Commission considers that there should in principle be consistency and coherence between its policy in respect of the control of State aid and the support which is granted under the Union's own common agricultural policy. Consequently, the use of State aid can be justified only if it is in line with the objectives of this policy and, in particular, the underlying objectives of the CAP reform towards 2020.[1] Therefore, when the Commission applies and interprets the rules of these Guidelines for specific aid schemes, it takes into consideration the CAP rules and policies.

(6) The following European instruments are of particular relevance for State aid considerations related to the CAP:

[(a) Regulation (EU) No 1144/2014 of the European Parliament and of the Council of 22 October 2014 on information provision and promotion measures concerning agricultural products implemented in the internal market and in third countries and repealing Council Regulation (EC) No 3/2008;[2]]

(b) Regulation (EU) No 228/2013 of the European Parliament and of the Council of 13 March 2013 laying down specific measures for agriculture in the outermost regions of the Union and repealing Council Regulation (EC) No 247/2006[3] and Regulation (EU) No 229/2013 of the European Parliament and of the Council of 13 March 2013 laying down specific measures for agriculture in favour of the smaller Aegean islands and repealing Council Regulation (EC) No 1405/2006.[4] Pursuant to those Regulations, support programmes can be established to take account of the geographical and economic handicaps of those regions;

(c) Regulation (EU) No 1303/2013 of the European Parliament and of the Council of 17 December 2013 laying down common provisions on the European Regional Development Fund, the European Social Fund, the Cohesion Fund, the European Agricultural Fund for Rural Development and the European Maritime and Fisheries Fund and laying down general provisions on the European Regional Development Fund, the European Social Fund, the Cohesion Fund and the European Maritime and Fisheries Fund and repealing Council Regulation (EC) No 1083/2006;[5]

(d) Regulation (EU) No 1305/2013 of the European Parliament and of the Council of 17 December 2013 on support for rural development by the European Agricultural Fund for Rural Development (EAFRD) and repealing Council Regulation (EC) No 1698/2005,[6] which aims at promoting sustainable rural development throughout the Union in a complementary manner to the other instruments of the CAP, such as direct payments and market measures. It contributes to the development of a more territorially and environmentally balanced, climate-friendly and resilient, competitive and innovative Union agricultural sector and to the development of rural territories;

(e) Regulation (EU) No 1306/2013 of the European Parliament and of the Council of 17 December 2013 on the financing, management and monitoring of the common agricultural policy and repealing Council Regulations (EEC) No 352/78, (EC) No 165/94, (EC) No 2799/98, (EC) No 814/2000, (EC) No 1290/2005 and (EC) No 485/2008;[7]

(f) Regulation (EU) No 1307/2013 of the European Parliament and of the Council of 17 December 2013 establishing rules for direct payments to farmers under support schemes within the framework of the common agricultural policy and repealing Council Regulation (EC) No 637/2008 and Council Regulation (EC) No 73/2009[8] which lays down rules on direct payments granted directly to farmers in the form of a basic income support under certain support schemes;

(g) Regulation (EU) No 1308/2013 of the European Parliament and of the Council of 17 December 2013 establishing a common organisation of the markets in agricultural products and repealing Council Regulations (EEC) No 922/72, (EEC) No 234/79, (EC) No 1037/2001 and (EC) No 1234/2007,[9] which lays down common rules for agricultural markets. In particular, those rules concern public intervention in the markets, quota and aid schemes, marketing and production standards, and trade with third countries.

(7) [The CAP is based on two pillars: the first pillar consists of instruments related to the functioning of agricultural markets and the food supply chain (Regulation (EU) No 228/2013, Regulation (EU) No 229/2013, Regulation (EU) No 1308/2013 and Regulation (EU) No 1144/2014) and to direct payments (Regulation (EU) No 1307/2013) conditional upon statutory management requirements, good agricultural and environmental conditions.] Combined, those measures provide a fundamental layer of support to farmers in the Union, creating the basis for keeping sustainable farming in place throughout the Union. The first pillar measures are mandatory for Member States and, with very few exceptions, there is no co-financing. This ensures the application of a common policy within the internal market. The second pillar of the CAP is the rural development policy which is governed by Regulation (EU) No 1305/2013 which aims at improving the competitiveness of agriculture, the sustainable management of natural resources and climate action and a balanced territorial development of rural areas. Rural development measures are largely voluntary, contractual in nature, co-financed and delivered within a strategic framework and implemented via rural development programmes meeting the Union's priorities for rural development at national, regional and local level.

(8) According to Article 39(1) of the Treaty, the objectives of the CAP are to increase agricultural productivity, to ensure a fair standard of living for the agricultural community, to stabilise markets, to assure the availability of supplies reaching the consumer at reasonable prices. According to Article 39(2) of the Treaty, in working out the CAP and the special methods for its application, account has to be taken of the particular nature of agricultural activity, which results from the social structure of agriculture and from structural and natural disparities between the various agricultural regions, the need to effect the appropriate adjustments by degrees and the fact that agriculture constitutes a sector closely linked with the economy as a whole.

(9) Agriculture has to adapt to new realities and to face challenges in terms of food security, environment, climate change and keeping the rural economy alive. In order to address those major challenges, in the Communication on the CAP towards 2020[10] the Commission has outlined the following objectives for the CAP 2014–2020: (1) viable food production; (2) sustainable management of natural resources and climate action; and (3) balanced territorial development.

(10) As an integral part of the CAP, the rural development policy 2014–2020 shall contribute to achieving the following objectives: (1) fostering the competitiveness of agriculture; (2) ensuring the sustainable management of natural resources, and climate action; and (3) achieving a balanced territorial development of rural economies and communities including the creation and maintenance of employment. The achievement of these objectives of rural development shall be pursued through the following Union priorities for rural development: (1) fostering knowledge transfer and innovation in agriculture, forestry, and rural areas; (2) enhancing farm viability and competitiveness of all types of agriculture in all regions and promoting innovative farm technologies and sustainable management of forests; (3) promoting food chain organisation, including processing and marketing of agricultural products, animal welfare

and risk management in agriculture; (4) restoring, preserving and enhancing ecosystems related to agriculture and forestry; (5) promoting resource efficiency and supporting the shift towards a low carbon and climate resilient economy in agriculture, food and forestry sectors; and (6) promoting social inclusion, poverty reduction and economic development in rural areas.[11]

(11) The CAP's objectives also fall within the scope of the objectives set out in the Communication from the Commission of 3 March 2010 'Europe 2020 – A strategy for smart, sustainable and inclusive growth'[12] and its flagship initiative for a resource-efficient Europe,[13] which set targets in areas such as competitiveness, climate, energy and biodiversity.

(12) State aid policy in the agricultural and forestry sectors and in rural areas also has to be embedded into the overall State aid modernisation initiative of the Commission. In its Communication on State aid modernisation,[14] the Commission announced three objectives to be pursued through the modernisation of State aid control: (1) to foster sustainable, smart and inclusive growth in a competitive internal market; (2) to focus Commission ex ante scrutiny on cases with the biggest impact on the internal market while strengthening the cooperation with Member States in State aid enforcement; and (3) to streamline the rules and provide for faster decisions. In particular, the Communication called for a common approach in the revision of the different Guidelines and frameworks with a view to strengthening the internal market, promoting more effectiveness in public spending through a better contribution of State aid to the objectives of common interest, greater scrutiny on the incentive effect, limiting the aid to the minimum, and avoiding the potential negative effects of aid on competition and trade. The compatibility conditions set out in these Guidelines are based on those common assessment principles and are applicable to notifiable aid schemes and individual aid.

CHAPTER 2. SCOPE AND DEFINITIONS

2.1. Effect of the CAP and the rural development policy on the scope of application

(13) In accordance with Article 42 of the Treaty, in so far as agricultural products listed in Annex I to the Treaty are concerned, the rules on State aid laid down in Articles 107 to 109 of the Treaty apply only to the extent determined by the European Parliament and the Council.

(14) As a general rule, pursuant to Article 211(1) of Regulation (EU) No 1308/2013 the rules on State aid are applicable to the production of and trade in agricultural products. [However, there are various derogations from this general principle which are laid down, amongst others, in Article 23 of Regulation (EU) No 228/2013, Article 17 of Regulation (EU) No 229/2013, Article 13 of Regulation (EU) No 1307/2013, Article 211(2) of Regulation (EU) No 1308/2013 and Article 27 of Regulation (EU) No 1144/2014.]

(15) As regards support for rural development, the general principle of the applicability of State aid rules in that context is set out in Article 81(1) of Regulation (EU) No 1305/2013. Articles 81(2) and 82 of that Regulation stipulate that the State aid rules do not apply to payments made by Member States pursuant to, and in conformity with Regulation (EU) No 1305/2013 or to additional national financing within the scope of Article 42 of the Treaty.

(16) Therefore, State aid rules do not apply to the co-financing of rural development support (both the EAFRD part and the national part) or to additional national financing on top of such support, provided that the measure in question is related to an agricultural activity falling within the scope of Article 42 of the Treaty and forms a part of the rural development programme.

(17) However, State aid rules apply fully to all co-financed aid measures (both the EAFRD part and the national part) and to the additional national financing for such measures which fall outside the scope of Article 42 of the Treaty, envisaged in Regulation (EU) No 1305/2013 in the following cases: (a) measures supporting activities in the rural areas and (b) forestry measures.

(18) If a Member State intends to finance exclusively from national funds (that is to say, without any EAFRD co-financing) a measure which is designed largely in accordance with the conditions of a given rural development measure ('rural development like measure'), State aid rules fully apply, regardless of whether the measure falls within or outside the scope of Article 42 of the Treaty.

2.2. Scope of application

(19) The Commission will apply these Guidelines to aid schemes and individual aid.

(20) These Guidelines apply to State aid for the primary agricultural production, the processing of agricultural products resulting in another agricultural product and the marketing of agricultural products.

(21) Based on the general considerations described in Section 2.1. of Part I of these Guidelines, in order to ensure coherence with the rural development policy and to achieve simplification for compliance with State aid rules, it is appropriate to also include in these Guidelines certain rural development measures falling outside the scope of Article 42 of the Treaty, whether co-financed by the EAFRD or additional national financing, as well as rural development like measures financed exclusively from national funds. Therefore, in addition to the agricultural sector, these Guidelines set out the compatibility criteria for State aid to the forestry sector and aid to undertakings active in rural areas which otherwise fall outside the scope of Article 42 of the Treaty.

(22) When analysing State aid and its compatibility with the general principles on State aid, the Commission will take into account, to the extent possible, the conditions laid down in Regulation (EU) No 1305/2013 and its implementing provisions and delegated act.

(23) In view of the aforementioned considerations, these Guidelines cover the following categories of aid:

(a) measures in the agricultural sector, financed exclusively from national funds, which consist of:

(i) rural development like measures falling outside the framework of a rural development programme (Section 1.1 of Part II of these Guidelines);

(ii) measures other than those referred to in (i) which fall outside the scope of Regulation (EU) No 1305/2013, such as certain risk and crisis management measures, aid for the livestock sector and certain promotion measures (Sections 1.2 and 1.3 of Part II of these Guidelines);

(b) aid for the forestry sector, which can be:
   (i) granted as part of a rural development programme or as additional national financing for such rural development measure (Sections 2.1 to 2.7 of Part II of these Guidelines);
   (ii) financed exclusively from national resources, in the form of
      — a rural development like forestry measure foreseen in Regulation (EU) No 1305/2013 and granted in accordance with the conditions of these Guidelines (Sections 2.1 to 2.7 of Part II of these Guidelines);
      — other aid in the forestry sector with ecological, protective and recreational objectives (Section 2.8 of Part II of these Guidelines);
      — aid in the forestry sector aligned with agricultural aid measures (Section 2.9 of Part II of these Guidelines);

(c) aid for undertakings active in rural areas which can be granted as:
   (i) an aid measure included in a rural development programme, co-financed by the EAFRD pursuant to, and in conformity with Regulation (EU) No 1305/2013, where the notifiable State aid measure is identical with the measure in the rural development programme (Chapter 3 of Part II of these Guidelines); or
   (ii) additional national financing related to a measure in the framework of a rural development programme (Chapter 3 of Part II of these Guidelines).

(24) Aid for LEADER local development referred to in Article 35 of Regulation (EU) No 1303/2013 and in Articles 42 to 45 of Regulation (EU) No 1305/2013, which involves individual projects designed and executed by local partnerships to address specific local problems, may be covered by these Guidelines to the extent that it meets the conditions of the related rural development measures as laid down in these Guidelines.

(25) These Guidelines apply in principle to aid to SMEs and to large enterprises. Large enterprises tend to be less affected by market failures than SMEs. Moreover, large enterprises in the agricultural and forestry sectors and in rural areas are more likely to be significant players on the market and, consequently, in specific cases, aid granted to large enterprises may particularly distort competition and trade in the internal market. As aid to large enterprises in the agricultural and forestry sectors and in rural areas and to other large enterprises can potentially cause similar distortions of competition, State aid rules for large enterprises in these Guidelines should be harmonised with the general State aid rules, and should be subject to the common assessment principles as laid down in Chapter 3 of Part I of these Guidelines. Without prejudice to those common assessment principles, as regards rural development measures for reasons of consistency and coherence with the rural development policy, the State aid rules for large enterprises should be aligned with the relevant rules of Regulation (EU) No 1305/2013. As regards aid measures for the livestock sector, which do not fall within the scope of Regulation (EU) No 1305/2013, the Commission maintains its previous policy that large enterprises should be able to finance the costs of these measures themselves. Therefore, aid in the livestock sector should be limited to SMEs.

[(26) Undertakings in difficulty[15] are excluded from the scope of these Guidelines, subject to the exceptions set out in this point. The Commission considers that when an undertaking is in financial difficulty, given that its very existence is in danger, it cannot be considered an appropriate vehicle for promoting other public policy objectives until such time as its viability is assured. Therefore, where the beneficiary of the aid is in financial difficulty within the meaning of point (35)15, the aid will be assessed in accordance with the Community Guidelines on State aid for rescuing and restructuring firms in difficulty,[16] as amended or replaced. This principle does not apply to compensatory aid for damage caused by natural disasters and exceptional occurrences referred to in Sections 1.2.1.1 and 2.1.3 of Part II of these Guidelines which is compatible with the internal market under Article 107(2)(b) of the Treaty. If the financial difficulty of an undertaking active in the agricultural and forestry sectors has been caused by the risk event referred to in Sections 1.2.1.2, 1.2.1.3, 1.2.1.5, 2.1.3, 2.8.1 or 2.8.5 of Part II of these Guidelines, aid to compensate for or restore the losses or damage caused by such risk events and to cover the costs of eradication of plant pests can be granted in line with these Guidelines and may be still found compatible with the internal market under Article 107(3)(c) of the Treaty. In addition, for reasons of public health protection and having in mind the emergency situation, no distinction should be made, under certain conditions, as to the economic situation of an undertaking for aid for destruction and removal of fallen stock in Section 1.2.1.4 and for aid for control and eradication measures in the case of animal diseases referred to in point (375) of Section 1.2.1.3 of Part II of these Guidelines. Moreover, undertakings that were not in difficulty on 31 December 2019 but became undertakings in difficulty in the period from 1 January 2020 until 30 June 2021 remain eligible for aid under these Guidelines.]

(27) When assessing aid granted to an undertaking which is subject to an outstanding recovery order following a previous Commission decision declaring an aid illegal and incompatible with the internal market, the Commission will take account of the amount of aid still to be recovered.[17] [This does not apply to aid to make good the damage caused by natural disasters and exceptional occurrences under Article 107(2)(b) of the Treaty.]

(28) The Commission will not authorise aid for export-related activities to third countries or to Member States which would be directly linked to the quantities exported, aid contingent upon the use of domestic over imported goods, or aid to establish and operate a distribution network or to cover any other expenditure linked to export activities. Aid towards the cost of participating in trade fairs, or of studies or consultancy services needed for the launch of a new or existing product on a new market in principle does not constitute export aid.

(29) Member States are reminded that the system of financing, for example, by parafiscal levies, should be notified, when the system forms an integral part of the aid measure (see paragraphs 41 to 44 of Case T-275/11).[18]

(30) The Commission will assess any aid measures not covered by these Guidelines or by any other relevant State aid rules on a case by case basis directly on the basis of Article 107(3) of the Treaty, taking into account the rules laid down in Articles 107, 108 and 109 of the Treaty, the CAP and by analogy these Guidelines, where possible. Member States notifying State aid not covered by the scope of these Guidelines will have to demonstrate that the State

aid in question meets the common assessment principles as laid down in Chapter 3 of Part I of these Guidelines. The Commission will only approve such measures if the positive contribution to the development of the sector clearly outweighs the risks of distorting competition in the internal market and affecting trade between Member States.

2.3. Horizontal rules and aid instruments applicable to the agricultural and forestry sectors and to rural areas

(31) In principle, to streamline State aid rules and due to the similarities between undertakings active in the agricultural and forestry sectors and in rural areas and other undertakings, the general State aid instruments laying down the criteria for compatibility of aid are applicable to the sectors covered by these Guidelines. This concerns in particular the Community guidelines on State aid for rescuing and restructuring firms in difficulty, the Framework for state aid for research and development and innovation[19] as amended or replaced, the Guidelines on State aid for environmental protection and energy 2014–2020[20] as amended or replaced, the EU Guidelines for the application of State aid rules in relation to the rapid deployment of broadband networks[21] as amended or replaced, the Guidelines on State aid to promote risk finance investments[22] as amended or replaced, the Communication from the Commission – Criteria for the compatibility analysis of training State aid cases subject to individual notification[23] as amended or replaced, the Communication from the Commission – Criteria for the compatibility analysis of State aid to disadvantaged and disabled workers subject to individual notification[24] as amended or replaced and the instruments related to services of general economic interest.[25]

(32) The above horizontal instruments apply to the production, processing and marketing of agricultural products unless the present Guidelines provide specific rules. These Guidelines provide for specific environmental aid measures, such as aid for agri-environment-climate and animal welfare commitments (Section 1.1.5 of Part II), aid for disadvantages related to Natura 2000 areas and to the Water Framework Directive[26] (Section 1.1.6 of Part II) and aid for organic farming (Section 1.1.8 of Part II). Aids for investments to pursue environmental objectives in the field of primary agricultural production are evaluated in accordance with the rules set out in Section 1.1.1.1. of Part II of these Guidelines. Aid for environmental protection in favour of undertakings active in the processing of agricultural products and the marketing of agricultural products will be declared compatible with the internal market under Article 107(3)(c) of the Treaty if it fulfils the conditions of the Guidelines on State aid for environmental protection and energy 2014–2020. Aid for investments in energy saving, biofuel and energy from renewable sources are excluded from the scope of Chapters 2 and 3 of Part II of these Guidelines as such aid should comply with the Guidelines on State aid for environmental protection and energy 2014–2020, unless it is exempted from notification obligation. However aid for investments linked to primary agricultural production related to the production of energy from renewable sources or to the production of biofuels on holdings can fall within the scope of these Guidelines provided that such production does not exceed the average annual consumption of fuels or energy of the agricultural holding in question (Section 1.1.1.1).

(33) The Guidelines on regional State aid for 2014–2020[27] do not apply to aid for the production of primary agricultural products due to the specificities of the sector. They do however apply to the processing of agricultural products and the marketing of agricultural products to the extent set out in these Guidelines.

(34) Both the general State aid rules and the more specific provisions of these Guidelines may concern undertakings active in the forestry sector or in rural areas. Where applicable, aid to undertakings active in the forestry sector or in rural areas may also be found compatible under the conditions and in compliance with general Union rules on State aid (in particular, with the Guidelines on regional State aid for 2014–2020, the Framework for state aid for research and development and innovation and the Guidelines on State aid for environmental protection and energy 2014–2020).

2.4. Definitions

(35) For the purposes of these Guidelines:

1. 'aid' means any measure fulfilling all the criteria laid down in Article 107(1) of the Treaty;
2. 'agricultural sector' means all undertakings active in primary production, processing and marketing of agricultural products;
3. 'agricultural product' means the products listed in Annex I to the Treaty, except fishery and aquaculture products listed in Annex I to Regulation (EU) No 1379/2013 of the European Parliament and of the Council;[28]
4. 'aid scheme' means any act on the basis of which, without further implementing measures being required, individual aid awards may be made to undertakings defined within the act in a general and abstract manner and any act on the basis of which aid which is not linked to a specific project may be granted to one or several undertakings for an indefinite period of time and/or for an indefinite amount;
5. 'outermost regions' means the regions referred to in the first paragraph of Article 349 of the Treaty;
6. 'smaller Aegean islands' means the smaller islands referred to in Article 1(2) of Regulation (EU) No 229/2013;[29]
7. 'rural development programme' means a rural development programme as provided for in Article 6(1) of Regulation (EU) No 1305/2013;
8. 'agricultural activity' means the production, processing and marketing of agricultural products;
9. 'forest' means an area of land spanning more than 0.5 hectares with trees higher than 5 meters and a canopy cover of more than 10%, or trees able to reach these thresholds in situ; and does not include land that is predominantly under agricultural or urban land use. A Member State or region may choose to apply another forest definition based on existing national legislation or inventory system. The Member States or regions must provide such definition in the notification and when it relates to a rural development measure, it should be provided in the rural development programme;
10. 'primary agricultural production' means the production of products of the soil and of stock farming, listed in Annex I to the Treaty, without performing any further operation changing the nature of such products;

11. 'processing of agricultural products' means any operation on an agricultural product resulting in a product which is also an agricultural product, except on-farm activities necessary for preparing an animal or plant product for first sale;
12. 'marketing of agricultural products' means holding or display with a view to sale, offering for sale, delivery or any other manner of placing on the market, except the first sale by a primary producer to resellers or processors and any activity preparing a product for such first sale; a sale by a primary producer to final consumers is considered as marketing of agricultural products if it takes place in separate premises reserved for that purpose;
13. 'SME' or 'micro, small and medium-sized enterprises' means undertakings fulfilling the criteria laid down in Annex I to Commission Regulation (EU) No 702/2014;[30]
14. 'large enterprises' means undertakings not fulfilling the criteria laid down in Annex I to Regulation (EU) No 702/2014;
15. 'undertaking in difficulty' means an undertaking in respect of which at least one of the following circumstances occurs:
    (a) in the case of limited liability company (other than SME that has been in existence for less than three years), where more than half of its subscribed share capital has disappeared as a result of accumulated losses. This is the case when deduction of accumulated losses from reserves (and all other elements generally considered as part of the own funds of the company) leads to a negative cumulative amount that exceeds half of the subscribed share capital. For the purposes of this provision 'limited liability company' refers in particular to the types of company mentioned in Annex I of Directive 2013/34/EU of the European Parliament and of the Council[31] and 'share capital' includes, where relevant, any share premium;
    (b) in the case of a company where at least some members have unlimited liability for the debt of the company (other than an SME that has been in existence for less than three years), where more than half of its capital as shown in the company accounts has disappeared as a result of accumulated losses. For the purposes of this provision, 'a company where at least some members have unlimited liability for the debt of the company' refers in particular to the types of company mentioned in Annex II of Directive 2013/34/EU;
    (c) where the undertaking is subject to collective insolvency proceedings or fulfils the criteria under its domestic law for being placed in collective insolvency proceedings at the request of its creditors;
    (d) where the undertaking has received rescue aid and has not yet reimbursed the loan or terminated the guarantee, or has received restructuring aid and is still subject to a restructuring plan;
    (e) in the case of an undertaking that is not an SME, where, for the past two years:
        (i) the undertaking's book debt to equity ratio has been greater than 7.5; and
        (ii) the undertaking's EBITDA interest coverage ratio has been below 1,0.
16. 'agricultural holding' means a unit comprising of land, premises and facilities used for primary agricultural production;
17. 'aid intensity' means the gross aid amount expressed as a percentage of the eligible costs, before any deduction of tax or other charge;
18. 'individual aid' means ad hoc aid and awards of aid to individual beneficiaries on the basis of an aid scheme;
19. 'ad hoc aid' means aid not granted on the basis of an aid scheme;
20. 'gross grant equivalent' means the amount of the aid if it had been provided in the form of a grant to the beneficiary, before any deduction of tax or other charges;
21. 'date of granting the aid' means the date when the legal right to receive the aid is conferred on the beneficiary under the applicable national legal regime.
22. 'producer group and organisation' means a group or organisation set up for the purpose of:
    (a) adapting the production and output of producers who are members of such producer group or organisation to market requirements, or
    (b) jointly placing goods on the market, including the preparation for sale, centralisation of sales and supply to bulk buyers; or
    (c) establishing common rules on production information, with particular regard to harvesting and availability; or
    (d) other activities that may be carried out by producer groups or organisations, such as the development of business and marketing skills and the organisation and facilitation of innovation processes;
23. 'repayable advance' means a loan for a project which is paid in one or more instalments and the conditions for the reimbursement of which depend on the outcome of the project;
24. 'plant pest' means harmful organisms as defined in point (e) of Article 2(1) of Council Directive 2000/29/EC;[32]
25. 'start of works on the project or activity' means the earlier of, either the start of the activities, or the construction works relating to the investment, or the first legally binding commitment to order equipment or employ services or any other commitment that makes the project or activity irreversible; buying land and preparatory works such as obtaining permits and conducting feasibility studies are not considered start of works or activity. The purchase of land referred to in point (144)(a) second sentence, (502)(a) second sentence and (635)(a) where the eligible costs for the land purchase equals 100% of the eligible investment costs, is considered to be the start of works on project or activity;
26. 'fiscal successor scheme' means a scheme in the form of tax advantages which constitutes an amended version of a previously existing scheme in the form of tax advantages and which replaces it;
27. 'fallen stock' means animals which have been killed by euthanasia with or without a definite diagnosis or which have died, including stillborn and unborn animals, on a farm or on any premises or during transport, but which have not been slaughtered for human consumption;
28. 'protected animal' means any animal protected either by Union or by national legislation;

29. 'young farmer' means a person who is no more than 40 years of age on the date of submitting the aid application, possesses adequate occupational skills and competences and is setting up for the first time in an agricultural holding as head of that holding;
30. 'large investment project' means an investment in rural areas, as referred to in Chapter 3 of Part II of these Guidelines, with eligible costs exceeding EUR 50 million, calculated at prices and exchange rates on the date of granting the aid;
31. 'adjusted aid amount' means the maximum permissible aid amount for a large investment project, calculated according to the following formula: maximum aid amount = R × (50 + 0.50 × B + 0.34 × C), where R is the maximum aid intensity applicable in the area concerned, excluding the increased aid intensity for SMEs. B is the part of eligible costs between EUR 50 million and EUR 100 million. C is the part of eligible costs above EUR 100 million;
32. 'tangible assets' means assets consisting of land, buildings and plant, machinery and equipment;
33. 'intangible assets' means assets that do not have a physical or financial embodiment such as patents, licences, know-how or other intellectual property;
34. 'adverse climatic event which can be assimilated to a natural disaster' means unfavourable weather conditions such as frost, storms and hail, ice, heavy or persistent rain or severe drought which destroy more than 30% of the average of the production calculated on the basis of the preceding three-year period or a three-year average based on the preceding five-year period, excluding the highest and the lowest entry;
35. 'other adverse climatic event' means unfavourable weather conditions which do not meet the conditions of point (35)34 of these Guidelines;
36. 'environmental incident' means a specific occurrence of pollution, contamination or degradation in the quality of the environment which is related to a specific event and is of limited geographical scope, which destroys more than 30% of the average annual production of the undertaking active in the agricultural sector in the preceding three-year period or a three-year average based on the preceding five-year period, excluding the highest and lowest entry. It does not cover general environmental risks not connected with a specific event, such as climate change or atmospheric pollution;
37. 'catastrophic event' means an unforeseen event of biotic or abiotic nature caused by human action that leads to important disturbances in forest structures, eventually causing important economic damage to the forestry sectors;
38. 'Union standard' means mandatory standard laid down in Union legislation setting the level which individual undertakings must achieve, in particular as regards the environment, hygiene and animal welfare; consequently, standards or targets set at Union level which are binding for Member States but not for individual undertakings are not deemed to be Union standards;
39. 'non-productive investment' means an investment which does not lead to a significant increase in the value or profitability of the holding;
40. 'investments to comply with an Union standard' means investments made to comply with an Union standard after the expiry of the transitional period provided for in Union legislation;
41. 'advice' means complete advice given in the framework of one and the same contract;
42. 'herd book' means any book, register, file or data medium:
    (a) which is maintained by a breeders' organisation or association officially recognised by a Member State in which the breeders' organisation or association was constituted; and
    (b) in which pure-bred breeding animals of a given breed are entered or registered with mention of their ancestors;
43. 'active farmer' means an active farmer within the meaning of Article 9 of Regulation (EU) No 1307/2013;
44. 'less developed regions' means regions where the gross domestic product (GDP) per capita is less than 75% of the average GDP of the EU-27;
45. 'EU-25' means the 25 Member States of the Union who were Member States of the Union in May 2005;
46. 'EU-27' means the 27 Member States of the Union who were Member States of the Union in January 2007;
47. 'capital works' means works, undertaken by the farmer personally or by the farmer's workers that create an asset;
48. 'small-scale infrastructure' means infrastructure with eligible costs limited to EUR 2 million;
49. 'food based biofuel' means a biofuel produced from cereal and other starch rich crops, sugars and oil crops as defined in the Commission's Proposal for a Directive of the European Parliament and of the Council amending Directive 98/70/EC relating to the quality of petrol and diesel fuels and amending Directive 2009/28/EC on the promotion of the use of energy from renewable sources;[33]
50. 'agricultural area' means any area taken up by arable land, permanent grassland and permanent pasture or permanent crops as defined in Article 4 of Regulation (EU) No 1307/2013;
51. 'other land manager' means an undertaking which manages land other than an undertaking active in the agricultural sector;
52. 'transaction cost' means an additional cost linked to fulfilling a commitment, but not directly attributable to its implementation or not included in the costs or income foregone that are compensated directly; and which can be calculated on a standard cost basis;
53. for the purposes of conservation of genetic resources in agriculture and in forestry:
    (a) 'in situ conservation' in agriculture means the conservation of genetic material in ecosystems and natural habitats and the maintenance and recovery of viable population of species or feral breeds in their natural surroundings and, in the case of domesticated animal breeds or cultivated plant species, in the farmed environment where they have developed their distinctive properties;
    (b) 'in situ conservation' in forestry means the conservation of genetic material in ecosystems and natural habitats and the maintenance and recovery of viable population of species in their natural surroundings;
    (c) 'on-farm or on-forest holding conservation' means in situ conservation and development at farm or forest holding level;

(d) 'ex situ conservation' means the conservation of genetic material for agriculture or forestry outside their natural habitat;

(e) 'ex situ collection' means a collection of genetic material for agriculture or forestry maintained outside their natural habitat;

54. 'foodstuffs' means foodstuffs which are not agricultural products and which are listed in Annex I to Regulation (EU) No 1151/2012 of the European Parliament and of the Council;[34]

55. 'fixed costs arising from participation in quality scheme' means the costs incurred for entering a supported quality scheme and the annual contribution for participating in that quality scheme, including, where necessary, expenditure on checks required to verify compliance with the specifications of the quality scheme;

56. 'short supply chain' means a supply chain involving a limited number of economic operators, committed to co-operation, local economic development, and close geographical and social relations between producers, processors and consumers;

57. 'member of a farm household' means a natural or legal person or a group of natural or legal persons, whatever legal status is granted to the group and its members by national law, with the exception of farm workers. Where a legal person or a group of legal persons is considered as a member of the farm household, that member must exercise an agricultural activity on the farm at the time of the aid application;

58. 'cluster' means a grouping of independent undertakings, including start-ups, small, medium and large enterprises as well as advisory bodies and/or research organisations designed to stimulate economic/innovative activity by promoting intensive interactions, the sharing of facilities and the exchange of knowledge and expertise, as well as contributing effectively to knowledge transfer, networking and information dissemination among the undertakings in the cluster;

59. 'small operator' means a microenterprise as defined in Commission Recommendation 2003/361,[35] or a natural person not engaged in economic activity at the moment of applying for aid;

60. 'local markets' means:

(a) markets in radius of 75 km from the farm of origin of the product, within which the activities of processing and sale to the final consumer have to take place; or

(b) markets for which the respective rural development programme sets out a kilometric radius from the farm of origin of the product, within which the activities of processing and sale to the final consumer have to take place; or

(c) markets for which the respective rural development programme sets out an convincing alternative definition;

61. 'Transmissible Spongiform Encephalopathy (TSE) and Bovine Spongiform Encephalopathy (BSE) test costs' means all costs, including those for test kits and for the taking, transporting, testing, storing and destruction of samples, necessary sampling and laboratory testing in accordance with Chapter C of Annex X to Regulation (EC) No 999/2001 of the European Parliament and of the Council;[36]

62. 'research and knowledge-dissemination organisation' means an entity (such as universities or research institutes, technology-transfer agencies, innovation intermediaries, research-oriented physical and/or virtual collaborative entities), irrespective of its legal status (organised under public or private law) or way of financing, whose primary goal is to independently conduct fundamental research, industrial research or experimental development, as defined in the Framework for state aid for research and development and innovation or to widely disseminate the results of such activities by way of teaching, publication or knowledge transfer. Where such entity also pursues economic activities, the financing, the costs and the revenues of economic activities must be accounted for separately. Undertakings that can exert influence upon such an entity, in the quality of, for example, shareholders or members, may not enjoy preferential access to its research capacities of such an entity or to the results generated by it;

63. 'arm's length' means that the conditions of the transaction between the contracting parties do not differ from those which would be stipulated between independent undertakings and contain no element of collusion. Any transaction that results from an open, transparent and unconditional procedure is considered as meeting the arm's length principle;

64. 'sustainable forest management' means using forests and forest land in a way and at a rate that maintains their biodiversity, productivity, regeneration capacity, vitality and their potential to fulfil now and in the future relevant ecological, economic and social functions at local, national and global levels and that does not cause damage to other ecosystems;

65. 'agro-forestry systems' means land use systems in which trees are grown in combination with agriculture on the same land;

66. 'fast growing trees' means a short rotation forest, where the minimum time before felling is set to be not less than 8 years and the maximum time before felling is set not to exceed 20 years;

67. 'trees for short rotation coppicing' means tree species of CN code 0602 90 41 to be defined by Member States that consist of woody, perennial crops, the rootstock or stools of which remain in the ground after harvesting, with new shoots emerging in the following season and with a maximum harvest cycle to be determined by the Member States as established in Article 4(1)(k) of Regulation (EU) No 1307/2013;

68. 'sparsely populated areas' means areas accepted by the Commission as such in the individual decisions on regional aid maps for the period 1 July 2014 to 31 December 2020;

69. '"a" areas' means those areas designated in an approved regional aid map for the period from 1 July 2014 to 31 December 2020 in application of the provisions of Article 107(3)(a) of the Treaty;

70. '"c" areas' means those areas designated in an approved regional aid map for the period 1 July 2014 to 31 December 2020 in application of the provisions of Article 107(3)(c) of the Treaty;

71. 'NUTS 3 area' means a region specified at level 3 of a common classification of territorial units for statistics in accordance with Regulation (EC) No 1059/2003 of the European Parliament and of the Council;[37]

72. 'non-predefined "c" areas' means areas that a Member State at its own discretion designate as 'c' areas provided that the Member States demonstrates that such areas fulfil certain socioeconomic criteria and that

those areas are designated in an approved regional aid map for the period of 1 July 2014 to 31 December 2020 in application of the provisions of Article 107(3)(c) of the Treaty;

73. 'former "a" areas' means those areas designated as 'a' areas in an approved regional map for the period from 1 January 2011 to 30 June 2014;

74. 'regional aid map' means the list of areas designated by a Member State in accordance with the conditions laid down in the Guidelines on regional State aid for 2014–2020 and approved by the Commission;

75. 'processing of agricultural products into non-agricultural products' means any operation on an agricultural product resulting in a product which is not an agricultural product;

76. 'evaluation plan' means a document containing at least the following minimum elements: the objectives of the aid scheme to be evaluated; the evaluation questions; the results indicators; the envisaged methodology to conduct the evaluation; the data collection requirements; the proposed timing of the evaluation, including the date of submission of the final evaluation report; the description of the independent body conducting the evaluation or the criteria that will be used for its selection and the modalities for ensuring the publicity of the evaluation.

2.5. NOTIFIABLE AID

(36) Where the conditions of Article 107(1) of the Treaty are met, Member States must notify to the Commission aid in the agricultural and forestry sectors and in rural areas pursuant to Article 108(3) of the Treaty and shall not put the proposed measure into effect until this procedure resulted in a final decision, with the exception of measures that fulfil the conditions laid down in a block exemption regulation.

(37) Individual aid granted on the basis of an aid scheme remains subject to the notification obligation pursuant to Article 108(3) of the Treaty, if the aid exceeds the following notification thresholds:

(a) for individual investment aid for the processing of agricultural products and the marketing of agricultural products under Section 1.1.1.4 of Part II of these Guidelines: eligible costs in excess of EUR 25 million, or where the gross grant equivalent exceeds EUR 12 million;

(b) for aid for promotion campaigns under Section 1.3.2. of Part II of these Guidelines: promotion campaigns with an annual budget in excess of EUR 5 million;

(c) for individual investment aid granted under Sections 3.1, 3.2, 3.6 and 3.10 of Chapter 3 of Part II of these Guidelines:

Aid intensity	Notification threshold
10%	EUR 7.5 million
15%	EUR 11.25 million
25%	EUR 18.75 million
35%	EUR 26.25 million
50% and above	EUR 37.5 million

CHAPTER 3. COMMON ASSESSMENT PRINCIPLES

(38) To assess whether a notified aid measure can be considered compatible with the internal market under Article 107(3) of the Treaty, the Commission generally analyses whether the design of the aid measure ensures that the positive impact of the aid towards an objective of common interest exceeds its potential negative effects on trade and competition.

(39) The Communication on State aid modernisation called for the identification and definition of common principles applicable to the assessment of compatibility of all the aid measures carried out by the Commission. For this purpose, the Commission will consider an aid measure compatible with the Treaty only if it satisfies each of the following criteria:

(a) contribution to a well-defined objective of common interest: a State aid measure must aim at an objective of common interest in accordance with Article 107(3) Treaty;

(b) need for State intervention: a State aid measure must be targeted towards a situation where aid can bring about a material improvement that the market cannot deliver itself, by remedying a well-defined market failure;

(c) appropriateness of the aid measure: the proposed aid measure must be an appropriate policy instrument to address the objective of common interest;

(d) incentive effect: the aid must change the behaviour of the undertaking(s) concerned in such a way that it engages in additional activity which it would not carry out without the aid or it would carry out in a restricted or different manner;

(e) proportionality of the aid (aid limited to the minimum necessary): the aid amount must be limited to the minimum needed to induce the activity in the sector concerned;

(f) avoidance of major undue negative effects on competition and trade between Member States: the negative effects of aid must be sufficiently limited, so that the overall balance of the measure is positive;

(g) transparency of aid: Member States, the Commission, economic operators, and the public must have easy access to all relevant acts and to pertinent information about the aid granted thereunder.

(40) The overall balance of certain categories of schemes may further be made subject to a requirement of ex post evaluation as described in points (720) to (723). In such cases, the Commission may limit the duration of those schemes (normally to four years or less) with a possibility to re-notify their prolongation afterwards.

(41) Moreover, if a State aid measure or the conditions attached to it (including its financing method when it forms an integral part of it) entail a non-severable violation of Union law, the aid cannot be declared compatible with the internal market.[38] In particular, the following aid is considered to entail a non-severable violation of EU law:

(a) aid the granting of which is subject to the obligation for the beneficiary to have its headquarters in the relevant Member State or to be predominantly established in that Member State;

(b) aid the granting of which is subject to the obligation for the beneficiary to use nationally produced goods or national services;

(c) aid restricting the possibility for the beneficiaries to exploit the research, development and innovation results in other Member States.

(42) The common assessment principles have to be seen in the specific context of the CAP. Therefore, these general competition policy considerations apply to all aid under these Guidelines, unless derogations are provided for in Sections 3.1. to 3.7 of Part I of these Guidelines, due to particular considerations applicable in the agricultural sector.

3.1. CONTRIBUTION TO A COMMON OBJECTIVE

(43) The objectives of aid in the agricultural and forestry sectors and in rural areas are to ensure viable food production and to promote the efficient and sustainable use of resources in order to achieve intelligent and sustainable growth.

(44) Aid in the agricultural and forestry sectors and in rural areas should relate closely to the CAP, should be consistent with the rural development objectives referred to in point (10) of these Guidelines and should be compatible with the rules on the common organisation of the markets in agricultural products.

Rural development objectives

(45) The rural development objectives taken jointly with the general principles on State aid will be taken into account for the assessment of compatibility of the aid.

(46) The Commission considers that measures, implemented pursuant to and in conformity with Regulation (EU) No 1305/2013 and its implementing and delegated acts or as an additional national financing in the framework of a rural development programme, are per se consistent with and contribute to the objectives of rural development.

(47) As regards rural development like measures financed exclusively from national funds, in order to ensure coherence with the rural development measures co-financed by the EAFRD under rural development programmes, Member States should demonstrate how the State aid under consideration fits into and is consistent with the relevant rural development programmes. Every notification must be accompanied by such documentation.

[(48) The Commission considers that the principle of contribution to the objectives of rural development is met regarding the aid measures in Sections 1.1.10.3, 1.2, 1.3, 2.8 and 2.9 of Part II of these Guidelines, which are outside the scope of rural development, since the Commission has gained sufficient experience as to the contribution of those measures to the rural development objectives.]

Additional conditions for individually notifiable aid on the basis of a scheme

(49) When awarding aid to individually notifiable investment projects on the basis of a scheme, the granting authority must demonstrate that the selected project will contribute towards the objective of the scheme and thus towards the objectives of aid in the agricultural and forestry sectors and in rural areas. For this purpose, Member States can rely on the information provided by the applicant for aid where the positive effects of the investment must be described.

Rules of the common organisation of the markets in agricultural products

(50) Due to the specificity of the agricultural sector,[39] although State aid rules are generally applicable to this sector, their application nevertheless remains subject to the provisions laid down in the regulations of the first pillar of the CAP. In other words, Member States' recourse to State aid measures cannot take precedence over Regulation (EU) No 1308/2013.[40] Therefore, the Commission will not authorise State aid which is incompatible with the provisions governing the common organisation of the market or which would interfere with the proper functioning of the common organisation.

(51) Further, specific conditions on the compliance with the principles of the common organisation of the markets in agricultural products are set out in Section 1.1.1.1 on investment aid on agricultural holdings linked to the primary agricultural production, in Section 1.1.4. on start-up aid for producer groups and organisations and in Section 1.2.2. on aid for closing of production capacity, of Part II of these Guidelines.

Environmental objectives

(52) Article 11 of the Treaty provides that 'Environmental protection requirements must be integrated into the definition and implementation of the Union's policies and activities, in particular with a view to promoting sustainable development.' The legal basis for the substantial environmental measures in the first and second pillars of the CAP is Article 11 of the Treaty. In line with this requirement, the Union's priorities for rural development should be pursued in the framework of sustainable development. The Union's promotion of the aim of protecting the environment as set out in Article 11 of the Treaty also takes into account the polluter pays principle.[41] Therefore, particular attention should be given to environmental issues in future State aid notifications. All State aid notifications should in the future contain an assessment on whether or not the aided activity is expected to have any environmental impact. In cases where there is an environmental impact, State aid notifications should provide information demonstrating that the aid measure will not result in an infringement of applicable Union environmental protection legislation. [For example, in the case of an aid scheme for investments which are intended to increase production, and which involve an increased use of scarce resources or an increase in pollution, it will be necessary to show that the scheme will not result in an infringement of the applicable Union legislation, including environmental protection legislation,[42] and the Good Agricultural and Environmental Conditions (GAECs) of cross-compliance under Regulation (EU) No 1306/2013.] Where State aid is notified, which forms part of the rural development programme, the environmental requirement for such State aid measure should be identical with the environmental requirement of the rural development measure.

3.2. Need for State intervention

(53) In order to assess whether State aid is necessary to achieve the objective of common interest, it is necessary first to diagnose the problem to be addressed. State aid should be targeted towards situations where it can bring about a material improvement that the market cannot deliver on its own.

(54) State aid measures can indeed, under certain conditions, correct market failures thereby contributing to the efficient functioning of markets and enhancing competitiveness. Furthermore, where markets provide efficient outcomes but these are deemed unsatisfactory from an equity or cohesion point of view, State aid may be used to obtain a more desirable, equitable market outcome.

(55) For the purposes of these Guidelines, the Commission considers that the market is not delivering the expected objectives without State intervention concerning the aid measures fulfilling the specific conditions laid down in Part II of these Guidelines. Therefore, such aid should be considered necessary to achieve the objectives of common interest specified under Section 3.1. of Part I of these Guidelines.

3.3. Appropriateness of aid

(56) The proposed aid measure must be an appropriate policy instrument to address the policy objective concerned. An aid measure will not be considered compatible if other less distortive policy instruments or other less distortive types of aid make it possible to achieve the same positive contribution to the objectives of CAP and in particular of rural development. It is important to keep in mind that there may be other, better placed instruments such as regulation, market-based instruments, infrastructure development and improvement in the business environment to achieve those objectives.

Appropriateness among alternative policy instruments

(57) The Commission considers that aid granted in the agricultural and forestry sectors and in rural areas, which fulfils the specific conditions laid down in the relevant Sections of Part II of these Guidelines, is an appropriate policy instrument.

(58) Where a Member State decides to put in place a rural development like aid measure financed exclusively from national funds, when at the same time the same measure is provided for in the relevant rural development programme, the Member State should demonstrate the advantages of such a national aid instrument compared to the rural development programme measure at stake.

Appropriateness among different aid instruments

(59) Aid can be granted in various forms. The Member State should however ensure that the aid is granted in the form that is likely to generate the least distortions of trade and competition.

(60) Where a specific form is foreseen for an aid measure described in Part II of these Guidelines, such form is considered as an appropriate aid instrument for the purpose of these Guidelines.

(61) The Commission further considers as regards rural development measures, co-financed by EAFRD or granted as an additional financing for such co-financed rural development measures, that aid granted in the form provided for in the respective rural development measure is an appropriate aid instrument.

(62) As regards investment aid not covered by Regulation (EU) No 1305/2013 as part of the rural development programme or as additional financing for such a rural development measure, where the aid is granted in forms that provide a direct pecuniary advantage (for example, direct grants, exemptions or reductions in taxes, social security or other compulsory charges, etc.), the Member State must demonstrate why other potentially less distortive forms of aid such as repayable advances or forms of aid that are based on debt or equity instruments (for example, low-interest loans or interest rebates, State guarantees or an alternative provision of capital on favourable terms) are less appropriate.

(63) With regard to forestry measures in Section 2.8 of Part II of these Guidelines, Member States must demonstrate that the ecological, protective and recreational objectives they are aiming for cannot be achieved with the rural development like forestry measures in Chapters 2.1 to 2.7 of Part II of these Guidelines.

(64) In the case of several categories of aid, such as aid towards the costs of market research activities, product conception and design and for the preparation of applications for the recognition of quality schemes, aid for knowledge transfer and information actions, aid for advisory services, aid for farm replacement services, aid for promotion measures, aid to compensate for the costs of the prevention and eradication of animal diseases and plant pest and aid to the livestock sector, the aid must be granted to the final aid beneficiaries indirectly, in kind, by means of subsidised services. In these cases the aid is paid to the provider of the service or activity in question.

(65) The compatibility assessment of an aid measure with the internal market is without prejudice to the applicable public procurement rules and to the principles of transparency and openness and non-discrimination in the selection process of a service provider.

3.4. Incentive effect and need for aid

(66) Aid in the agricultural and forestry sectors and in rural areas can only be found compatible with the internal market, if it has an incentive effect. An incentive effect is present when the aid changes the behaviour of an undertaking in such a way that it engages in additional activity contributing to the development of the sector which it would not have engaged in without the aid or in which would only have engaged in a restricted or different manner. The aid must however not subsidise the costs of an activity that an undertaking would have incurred in any event and must not compensate for the normal business risk of an economic activity.

(67) Unless exceptions are expressly provided for in Union legislation or in these Guidelines, unilateral State aid measures which are simply intended to improve the financial situation of undertakings but which in no way contribute to the development of the sector, and in particular aid which is granted solely on the basis of price, quantity, unit of

production or unit of the means of production are considered to constitute operating aid which is incompatible with the internal market. Furthermore, by its very nature, such aid is also likely to interfere with the mechanisms regulating the organisation of the internal market.

(68) These same reasons have led the Commission to authorise aid to facilitate compliance with obligatory standards only to the extent that it meets the objectives of rural development policy.

(69) For the same grounds, aid granted under Sections 1.2. and 2.8.5 of Part II of these Guidelines should be limited to helping undertakings active in the agricultural and forestry sectors facing various difficulties despite having undertaken reasonable efforts to minimise such risks. State aid should not have as an effect to entice undertakings into taking unnecessary risk. Undertakings active in the agricultural and forestry sectors should themselves bear the consequences of imprudent choices of production methods or products.

(70) For the same reasons, the Commission considers that aid does not present an incentive for the beneficiary wherever work on the relevant project or activity has already started prior to the aid application by the beneficiary to the national authorities.

(71) The aid application must include at least the applicant's name and the size of the undertaking, a description of the project or activity, including its location and start and end dates, the amount of aid needed to carry it out and the eligible costs.

(72) In addition, large enterprises must describe in the application, the situation without the aid, which situation is referred to as the counterfactual scenario or alternative project or activity and submit documentary evidence in support of the counterfactual described in the application.

(73) When receiving an application, the granting authority must carry out a credibility check of the counterfactual and confirm that the aid has the required incentive effect. A counterfactual is credible if it is genuine and relates to the decision-making factors prevalent at the time of the decision by the beneficiary regarding the project or activity concerned.

(74) By derogation from points (70) to (73), aid in the form of tax advantages granted to SMEs is deemed to have an incentive effect if the aid scheme establishes a right to aid in accordance with objective criteria and without further exercise of discretion by the Member State and if the aid scheme has been adopted and in force before work on the aided project or activity has started. The latter requirement does not apply in the case of fiscal successor schemes provided the activity was already covered by the previous schemes in the form of tax advantages.

(75) By way of derogation from points (70) to (74), the following categories of aid of these Guidelines are not required or are deemed to have an incentive effect:

(a) aid schemes for land consolidation in accordance with Section 1.3.4. and Section 2.9.2. and aid schemes with ecological, protective and recreational objectives in accordance with Section 2.8 of Part II and where:
  - (i) the aid scheme establishes a right to aid in accordance with objective criteria and without further exercise of discretion by the Member State;
  - (ii) the aid scheme has been adopted and in force before eligible costs under Sections 1.3.4, 2.9.2 and 2.8. are incurred by the beneficiary; and
  - (iii) the aid scheme only covers SMEs;

(b) aid for disadvantages related to Natura 2000 areas and to the Water framework directive granted to SMEs in accordance with Section 1.1.6 of Part II;

(c) aid to areas facing natural or other specific constraints in accordance with Section 1.1.7 of Part II;

(d) aid to make good the damage caused by natural disasters or exceptional occurrences in accordance with Section 1.2.1.1 of Part II;

(e) aid to compensate for the damage caused by adverse climatic events which can be assimilated to natural disaster in accordance with Section 1.2.1.2 of Part II;

[(f) aid to compensate for the costs of the prevention, control and eradication of animal diseases and plant pests and for losses caused by those animal diseases and plant pests in accordance with Section 1.2.1.3 of Part II;]

(g) aid to cover the costs of the removal and destruction of fallen stock in accordance with Section 1.2.1.4 of Part II;

(h) aid to compensate for the damage caused by protected animals in accordance with Section 1.2.1.5 of Part II;

(i) aid to make good the damage in forests caused by animals regulated by law in accordance with Section 2.8.5 of Part II;

(j) investment aid for meeting standards in accordance with point (148)(a) and (b);

(k) investment aid for meeting standards granted to SMEs in accordance with point (148)(c); investment aid for meeting standards to large enterprises in accordance with point (148)(c) may be considered to have an incentive effect, where the undertaking concerned can prove that without the aid, it would face the risk of closure.

(l) aid for investments in favour of conservation of cultural and natural heritage on the agricultural holding in accordance with Section 1.1.1.2 of Part II, with the exception of individual aid which exceeds EUR 500,000 per undertaking per investment project;

[(m) aid for promotion measures in accordance with point (464)(b), (c) and (d);]

(n) aid for research and development in the agricultural and forestry sectors in accordance with Section 1.3.6 and Section 2.9.1. of Part II;

(o) aid for the maintenance, restoration and upgrading of the cultural and natural heritage of villages, rural landscapes and high nature value sites in accordance with point (644)(e); this derogation does not apply to investment aid associated with the cultural and natural heritage of villages, rural landscapes and high nature value sites, which exceeds the notification thresholds set out in point (37)(c);

(p) aid for the drawing up and updating of plans for the development of municipalities and villages in rural areas and their basic services and of protection and management plans relating to Natura 2000 sites and other areas of high nature value, in accordance with point (644)(a);

(q) aid for the restoration of damage to forests from fires, natural disasters, adverse climatic events, plant pests, animal diseases, catastrophic events and climate change related events in accordance with Section 2.1.3 of Part II;

[(r) aid for the costs of treatment and preventing the spreading of pests and tree diseases and aid to make good the damage caused by the pests and tree diseases in accordance with Section 2.8.1 of Part II.]

[(s) aid for participation of active farmers in quality schemes for cotton and foodstuffs, in accordance with Section 3.8 of Part II.]

Additional conditions for individually notifiable investment aid

(76) In addition to the requirements set out above, for individually notifiable investment aid, the Member State must provide clear evidence that the aid effectively has an impact on the investment choice. To allow for a comprehensive assessment, the Member State must provide not only information concerning the aided project but also a comprehensive description of the counterfactual scenario, in which no aid is granted to the beneficiary by any public authority.

(77) The Member States are invited to rely on documents, such as official board documents, risk assessments, including the assessment of location-specific risks, financial reports, internal business plans, expert opinions and other studies related to the investment project under assessment. Documents containing information on demand forecasts, cost forecasts, financial forecasts, documents that are submitted to an investment committee and that elaborate on various investment scenarios, or documents provided to the financial institutions could help the Member States to demonstrate the incentive effect.

(78) In this context the level of profitability may be evaluated by reference to methodologies which are standard practice in the sector concerned and which may include methods to evaluate the net present value of the project (NPV),[43] the internal rate of return (IRR)[44] or the average return on capital employed (ROCE). The profitability of the project is to be compared with normal rates of return applied by the undertaking in other investment projects of a similar kind. Where these rates are not available, the profitability of the project is to be compared with the cost of capital of the undertaking as a whole or with the rates of return commonly observed in the sector concerned.

(79) Where no specific counterfactual scenario is known, the incentive effect can be assumed when there is a funding gap, that is to say when the investment costs exceed the NPV of the expected operating profits of the investment on the basis of an ex ante business plan.

(80) If the aid does not change the behaviour of the beneficiary by stimulating additional investment, it has no positive effects for development of the sector concerned. Therefore, aid will not be approved in cases where it appears that the same investment would still be pursued without the aid.

3.5. Proportionality of the aid

(81) Aid in the agricultural and forestry sectors and in rural areas is considered to be proportionate if the aid amount per beneficiary is limited to the minimum needed to achieve the common objective aimed for.

Maximum aid intensities and maximum aid amounts

(82) In principle, in order for the aid to be proportionate, the Commission considers that the aid amount should not exceed the eligible costs. This is without prejudice to rules for environmental or other public incentives that are expressively provided for in Sections 1.1.3 and 1.2.2 of Part II of these Guidelines.

(83) In order to ensure predictability and a level playing field, in these Guidelines the Commission further applies maximum aid intensities for aid. Where the maximum aid intensity cannot be set, for example in the case of start-up aid for young farmers and the development of small farms, maximum aid amounts defined in nominal terms are set out in order to ensure the proportionality of the aid.

(84) If the eligible costs are correctly calculated and the maximum aid intensities or maximum aid amounts set out in Part II of these Guidelines are respected, the criterion of proportionality is deemed to be fulfilled.

(85) The maximum aid intensity and aid amount must be calculated by the granting authority when granting the aid. The eligible costs must be supported by documentary evidence which should be clear, specific and contemporary. For the purposes of calculating the aid intensity and the eligible costs, all figures used must be taken before any deduction of tax or other charge.

(86) Value added tax (VAT) is not eligible for aid, except where it is not-recoverable under national VAT legislation.

(87) Where aid is granted in a form other than a grant, the aid amount is the gross grant equivalent of the aid.

(88) Aid payable in several instalments is discounted to its value at the moment of granting the aid. The eligible costs are discounted to their value at the moment of granting the aid. The interest rate to be used for discounting purposes is the discount rate applicable on the date of granting the aid.

(89) Where aid is granted by means of tax advantages, the discounting of aid tranches takes place on the basis of the discount rates applicable at the various times the tax advantage takes effect.

(90) As regards investment aid in rural areas, the maximum aid intensity for large investment projects must be scaled down to the adjusted aid amount as defined in point (35).31. In addition, large investment projects cannot benefit from the increased aid intensities for SMEs.

(91) Where commitments under Sections 1.1.5.1, 1.1.8, 2.3 and 3.4 of Part II of these Guidelines are expressed in units other than those set out in Annex II to Regulation (EU) No 1305/2013, Member States may calculate payments on the basis of those other units. In such cases, the Member States must ensure that the maximum amounts per year are complied with.

(92) Except for aid for commitments for the rearing of local breeds in danger of being lost to farming referred to in Section 1.1.5.1, aid under Sections 1.1.5.1, 1.1.8, 2.3 and 3.4 of Part II of these Guidelines cannot be granted per livestock unit. The conversion rates of the various categories of animals to livestock units are set out in Annex II of the implementing act to Regulation (EU) No 1305/2013.

(93) [Member States may fix the aid amount for the measures or types of operations referred to in Sections 1.1.5, 1.1.6, 1.1.7, 1.1.8, 2.1.1, 2.1.2, 2.2, 2.3, 3.4 and 3.5 of Part II of these Guidelines on the basis of standard assumptions of additional costs and income foregone.] Member States should ensure that the calculations and the corresponding aid (a) contain only elements that are verifiable; (b) are based on figures established by appropriate expertise; (c) indicate clearly the source of the figures used; (d) are differentiated to take account of regional or local site conditions and actual land use, where applicable; and (e) do not contain elements linked to investment costs.

(94) When assessing the compatibility of aid, the Commission will consider any insurance taken out, or which could have been taken out by the aid beneficiary. Regarding aid to compensate for losses caused by adverse climatic events which can be assimilated to a natural disaster, in order to avoid the risk of distorting competition, aid at the maximum aid intensity should be granted only to an undertaking that cannot be covered for such losses by insurance. This is why, in order to further improve risk management, beneficiaries must be encouraged to take out insurance wherever possible.

Additional conditions for individually notifiable investment aid and investment aid to large enterprises under notified schemes

(95) As a general rule, individually notifiable investment aid will be considered to be limited to the minimum, if the aid amount corresponds to the net extra costs of implementing the investment in the area concerned, compared to the counterfactual scenario in the absence of aid. Likewise, in the case of investment aid granted to large enterprises under notified schemes, Member States must ensure that the aid amount is limited to the minimum on the basis of a 'net-extra cost approach'.

(96) The aid amount should not exceed the minimum necessary to render the project sufficiently profitable, for example, it should not lead to an increase of its IRR beyond the normal rates of return applied by the undertaking concerned in other investment projects of a similar kind or, if these rates are not available, to an increase of its IRR beyond the cost of capital of the undertaking as a whole or beyond the rates of return commonly observed in the sector concerned.

(97) For investment aid to large enterprises under notified schemes, the Member State must ensure that the aid amount corresponds to the net extra costs of implementing the investment in the area concerned, compared to the counterfactual scenario in the absence of aid. The method explained in point (96) must be used together with maximum aid intensities as a cap.

(98) As regards individually notifiable investment aid, the Commission will verify whether the aid amount exceeds the minimum necessary to render the project sufficiently profitable, by using the method set out in point (96). Calculations used for the analysis of the incentive effect can also be used to assess if the aid is proportionate. The Member State must demonstrate the proportionality on the basis of documentation such as that referred to in point (77). This requirement does not apply to investment aid related to the primary agricultural production.

Cumulation of aid

(99) Aid may be granted concurrently under several schemes or cumulated with ad hoc aid, provided that the total amount of State aid for an activity or project does not exceed the aid ceilings laid down in these Guidelines.

(100) Aid with identifiable eligible costs may be cumulated with any other State aid, as long as those aids concern different identifiable eligible costs. Aid with identifiable eligible costs may be cumulated with any other State aid, in relation to the same eligible costs, partly or fully overlapping, only if such cumulation does not result in exceeding the highest aid intensity or aid amount applicable to this type of aid under these Guidelines.

(101) Aid without identifiable eligible costs under Sections 1.1.2 and 3.3. of Part II of these Guidelines may be cumulated with any other State aid measure with identifiable eligible costs. Aid without identifiable eligible costs may be cumulated with other State aid without identifiable eligible costs, up to the highest relevant total financing threshold fixed in the specific circumstances of each case by these Guidelines or other State aid guidelines, a block exemption regulation or a decision adopted by the Commission.

(102) State aid in favour of the agricultural sector should not be cumulated with payments referred to in Articles 81(2) and 82 of Regulation (EU) 1305/2013 in respect of the same eligible costs if such cumulation would result in an aid intensity or aid amount exceeding those laid down in these Guidelines.

(103) Where Union funding centrally managed by the institutions, agencies, joint undertakings or other bodies of the Union that is not directly or indirectly under the control of the Member State is combined with State aid, only the latter will be considered for determining whether notification thresholds and maximum aid intensities and ceilings are respected, provided that the total amount of public funding granted in relation to the same eligible costs does not exceed the most favourable funding rate(s) laid down in the applicable rules of Union law.

(104) Aid authorised under these Guidelines should not be cumulated with any de minimis aid in respect of the same eligible costs if such cumulation would result in an aid intensity or aid amount exceeding that fixed in these Guidelines.

(105) Aid for investments aimed at the restoration of agricultural production potential as referred to in point (143)(e) should not cumulated with aid for the compensation of material damage referred to in Sections 1.2.1.1, 1.2.1.2 and 1.2.1.3 of these Guidelines.

(106) Double funding of agricultural practices beneficial for the climate and the environment under Sections 1.1.5.1., 1.1.6, 1.1.8 and 3.5 of Part II of these Guidelines and equivalent practices referred to in Article 43 of Regulation (EU) No 1307/2013 should be excluded. The revision clause foreseen in point (724) of these Guidelines should also ensure avoiding double funding.

(107) Start-up aid for producer groups and organisations in the agricultural sector as referred to in Section 1.1.4 of Part II of these Guidelines should not be cumulated with aid for the setting-up of producers groups and organisations in the agricultural sector laid down in Article 27 of Regulation (EU) No 1305/2013. Start-up aid for young farmers and start-up aid for the development of small farms as referred to in Section 1.1.2 should not be cumulated with business start-up aid for young farmers or the development of small farms as referred to in Article 19(1)(a)(i) and (iii) of Regulation (EU) No 1305/2013 if such cumulation would result in an aid amount exceeding those laid down in these Guidelines.

3.6. AVOIDANCE OF UNDUE NEGATIVE EFFECTS ON COMPETITION AND TRADE

(108) For the aid to be compatible, the negative effects of the aid measure in terms of distortions of competition and impact on trade between Member States must be limited and outweighed by the positive effects in terms of contribution to the objective of common interest.

General considerations

(109) In assessing the negative effects of the aid measure, the Commission will focus its analysis of the distortions of competition on the foreseeable impact the aid in the agricultural and forestry sectors and in rural areas has on competition between undertakings in the product markets affected.[45]

(110) As a starting point, if the aid is well targeted, proportionate and limited to the net extra costs, the negative impact of the aid is softened and the risk that the aid will unduly distort competition will be more limited. Second, the Commission establishes maximum aid intensities. These constitute a basic requirement for compatibility, the aim of which is to prevent the use of State aid for projects where the ratio between aid amount and eligible costs is to be deemed very high and particularly likely to be distortive. In general, the greater the positive effects the aided project is likely to give rise to and the higher the likely need for aid, the higher the cap on aid intensity.

(111) However, even where aid is necessary and proportionate, it may result in a change of the behaviour of the beneficiaries which distorts competition. This is more likely in the agricultural sector which differs from other markets by the specific structure of primary agricultural production that is characterized by a high number of small undertakings involved. On such markets the risk of distortion of competition is high even when only small amounts of aid are granted.

(112) Two main potential distortions of competition and trade may be caused by aid for the agricultural and forestry sectors and for rural areas. These are product market distortions and location effects. Both types may lead to allocative inefficiencies, undermining the economic performance of the internal market and distributional concerns, in that the aid affects the distribution of economic activity across regions.

(113) In principle, due to its positive effects on the development of the sector, the Commission considers that where an aid fulfils the conditions and does not exceed the relevant maximum aid intensities, laid down in the applicable Sections of Part II of these Guidelines, the negative effect on competition and trade is limited to the minimum.

(114) However, because investment aid to undertakings active in the processing of agricultural products and the marketing of agricultural products and to undertakings active in other sectors, for example, in the food processing sector,[46] tends to have similar distortive effects on competition and trade, the general competition policy considerations on the effect on competition and trade should apply equally to all those sectors. Therefore, the conditions described in points (115) to (127) must be respected as regards investment aid for the processing of agricultural products and for the marketing of agricultural products, in the forestry sector and in rural areas.

Investment aid schemes for the processing of agricultural products and the marketing of agricultural products, in the forestry sector and in rural areas

(115) Aid schemes must not lead to significant distortions of competition and trade. In particular, even where distortions may be considered limited at an individual level (provided all conditions for investment aid are fulfilled), on a cumulative basis investment aid schemes might still lead to high levels of distortion. Such distortions might concern the output markets by creating or aggravating a situation of overcapacity or creating, increasing or maintaining the substantial market power of some beneficiaries in a way that will negatively affect dynamic incentives. Aid available under investment aid schemes might also lead to a significant loss of economic activity in other areas of the European Economic Area (EEA). In the case of an investment aid scheme focusing on certain sectors, the risk of such distortions is even more pronounced.

(116) Therefore, the Member State concerned must demonstrate that any negative effects will be limited to the minimum taking into account, for example, the size of the projects concerned, the individual and cumulative aid amounts, the expected beneficiaries as well as the characteristics of the targeted sectors. In order to enable the Commission to assess the likely negative effects, the Member State is encouraged to submit any impact assessment at its disposal as well as ex-post evaluations carried out for similar predecessor schemes.

Individually notifiable investment aid for the processing of agricultural products and the marketing of agricultural products and in rural areas

(117) In appraising the negative effects of individual investment aid, the Commission places particular emphasis on the negative effects linked with the build-up of overcapacity in declining markets, the prevention of exit, and the notion of substantial market power. These negative effects are described in points (118) to (127) and must be counterbalanced with the positive effects of the aid.

(118) In order to identify and assess the potential distortions of competition and trade, Member States should provide evidence permitting the Commission to identify the product markets concerned (that is to say, products affected by the change in the behaviour of the aid beneficiary) and to identify the competitors and customers/consumers affected.

(119) The Commission uses various criteria to assess those potential distortions, such as market structure of the product concerned, performance of the market (declining or growing market), process for selection of the aid beneficiary, entry and exit barriers, product differentiation.

(120) A systematic reliance on State aid by an undertaking might indicate that the undertaking is not able to withstand competition on its own or that it enjoys undue advantages compared to its competitors.

(121) The Commission distinguishes two main sources of potential negative effects on product markets:

- (a) cases of significant capacity expansion which leads to or deteriorates an existing situation of overcapacity, especially in a declining market; and
- (b) cases where the aid beneficiary holds substantial market power.

(122) In order to evaluate whether the aid may serve to create or maintain inefficient market structures, the Commission will take into account the additional production capacity created by the project and whether the market is underperforming.

(123) Where the market in question is growing, there is normally less reason to be concerned that the aid will negatively affect dynamic incentives or will unduly impede exit or entry.

(124) More concern is warranted when markets are in decline. In this respect the Commission distinguishes between cases for which, from a long-term perspective, the relevant market is structurally in decline (that is to say, shows a negative growth rate), and cases for which the relevant market is in relative decline (that is to say, shows a positive growth rate, but does not exceed a benchmark growth rate).

(125) Underperformance of the market will normally be measured compared to the EEA GDP over the last three years before the start of the project (benchmark rate); it can also be established on the basis of projected growth rates in the coming three to five years. Indicators may include the foreseeable future growth of the market concerned and the resulting expected capacity utilisation rates, as well as the likely impact of the capacity increase on competitors through its effects on prices and profit margins.

(126) In certain cases, assessing the growth of the product market in the EEA may not be appropriate to entirely assess the effects of aid, in particular if the geographic market is worldwide. In such cases, the Commission will consider the effect of the aid on the market structures concerned, in particular, its potential to crowd out producers in the EEA.

(127) In order to evaluate the existence of substantial market power, the Commission will take into account the position of the beneficiary over a period of time before receiving the aid and the expected market position after finalising the investment. The Commission will take account of the market shares of the beneficiary, as well as of the market shares of its competitors and other relevant factors, including, for example the market structure by looking at the concentration in the market, possible barriers to entry,[47] buyer power[48] and barriers to expansion or exit.

3.7. TRANSPARENCY

(128) Member States must ensure the publication of the following information on a comprehensive State aid website at national or regional level:

- (a) the full text of the aid scheme and its implementing provisions or legal basis for individual aid, or a link to it;
- (b) the identity of the granting authority/(ies);
- (c) the identity of the individual beneficiaries, the form and amount of aid granted to each beneficiary, the date of granting, the type of undertaking (SME/ large enterprise), the region in which the beneficiary is located (at NUTS level II) and the principal economic sector in which the beneficiary has its activities (at NACE group level). Such a requirement can be waived with respect of individual aid awards not exceeding the following thresholds:
  - (i) EUR 60,000 for beneficiaries active in the primary agricultural production;
  - (ii) EUR 500,000 for beneficiaries in the sectors of the processing of agricultural products, the marketing of agricultural products, the forestry sector or activities falling outside the scope of Article 42 of the Treaty.

(129) For aid schemes in the form of tax advantages the information on individual aid amount can be provided in the following ranges (in EUR million): 0.06–0.5 only for primary agricultural production; 0.5–1; 1 to 2; 2 to 5; 5 to 10; 10 to 30; and 30 and more.

(130) If the individual aid award falls within the scope of Regulation (EU) No 1305/2013 and is either cofinanced by the EAFRD or granted as additional national financing for such co-financed measures, the Member State concerned may choose not to publish it on the State aid website referred to in point (128) provided that the individual aid award has already been published in accordance with Articles 111, 112 and 113 of Regulation (EU) No 1306/2013. In that case, the Member State should make a reference to the website referred to in Article 111 of Regulation (EU) No 1306/2013 on the State aid website referred to in point (128).

(131) Such information must be published after the decision to grant the aid has been taken, must be kept for at least 10 years and be available for the general public without restrictions.[49] Member States will not be required to publish the abovementioned information before 1 July 2016.[50]

(132) For reasons of transparency Member States must carry out reporting and revision as required in Chapter 2 of Part III of these Guidelines.

NOTES

Point (6): para (a) (and footnote 2 below) substituted by Commission Notice amending the European Union Guidelines for State aid in the agricultural and forestry sectors and in rural areas 2014 to 2020 (2015/C390/05).

Points (7), (14), (27): words in square brackets substituted by Commission Notice amending the European Union Guidelines for State aid in the agricultural and forestry sectors and in rural areas 2014 to 2020 (2015/C390/05).

Point (26): substituted by Commission Notice amending the European Union Guidelines for State aid in the agricultural and forestry sectors and in rural areas 2014 to 2020 as regards their period of application and making temporary adaptations to take into account the impact of the COVID-19 pandemic (2020/C424/05).

Point (48): substituted by Commission Notice amending the European Union Guidelines for State aid in the agricultural and forestry sectors and in rural areas 2014 to 2020 (2015/C390/05).

Point (52): words in square brackets (and footnote 42 below) substituted by Commission Notice amending the European Union Guidelines for State aid in the agricultural and forestry sectors and in rural areas 2014 to 2020 (2015/C390/05).

Point (75): paras (f) and (m) substituted, and para (r) added, by Commission Notice amending the European Union Guidelines for State aid in the agricultural and forestry sectors and in rural areas 2014 to 2020 (2015/C390/05). Para (s) added by Commission Notice amending the European Union Guidelines for State aid in the agricultural and forestry sectors and in rural areas 2014 to 2020 (2018/C139/02).

Point (93): words in square brackets substituted by Commission Notice amending the European Union Guidelines for State aid in the agricultural and forestry sectors and in rural areas 2014 to 2020 (2018/C139/02).

1 More details on the CAP reform are available at: https://ec.europa.eu/info/food-farming-fisheries/key-policies/common-agricultural-policy/cap-glance

2 OJ L317, 4.11.2014, p. 56.

3 OJ L78, 20.3.2013, p 23.

4 OJ L78, 20.3.2013, p 41.

5 OJ L347, 20.12.2013, p 320.

6 OJ L347, 20.12.2013, p 487.

7 OJ L347, 20.12.2013, p 549.

8 OJ L347, 20.12.2013, p 608.

9 OJ L347, 20.12.2013, p 671.

10 Communication of 18 November 2010 from the Commission to the European Parliament, the Council, the European Economic and Social Committee and the Committee of the Regions. The CAP towards 2020: Meeting the food, natural resources and territorial challenges of the future (COM(2010) 672 final).

11 As defined in Articles 4 and 5 of Regulation (EU) No 1305/2013.

12 COM(2010) 2020 final.

13 Communication from the Commission to the European Parliament, the Council, the European Economic and Social Committee and the Committee of the Regions (COM(2011) 21 final).

14 COM(2012) 209 of 8.5.2012.

15 See definition of undertaking in difficulty in point (35)15.

16 OJ C244, 1.10.2004, p 2. As prolonged by OJ C156, 9.7.2009, p 3 and OJ C296, 2.10.2012, p 3.

17 See in this respect joint Cases T-244/93 and T-486/93, *TWD Textilwerke Deggendorf GmbH v Commission*, [1995] ECR II-02265.

18 CaseT-275/11 *Télévision française 1 (TF1) v Commission* [2013] ECR; See inter alia. Case C-174/02 *Streekgewest Westelijk Noord-Brabant* [2005], ECR I-85; Case C-526/04 *Laboratoires Boiron* [2006] ECR I-7529; Joint Cases C-78/90, C-79/90, C-80/90, C-81/90, C-82/90 et C-83/90 *Compagnie commerciale de l'Ouest v. Receveur principal des douanes de La Pallice-Port* [1992], ECR I-1847; Case C-234/99 *Niels Nygård v Svineafgiftsfonden, and Ministeriet for Fødevarer* [2002] ECR I-3657.

19 OJ C198, 27.6.2014, p 1.

20 The text as adopted on 9.4.2014 is available at: https://ec.europa.eu/competition-policy/sectors/energy-and-environment_en

21 OJ C25, 26.1.2013, p 1.

22 OJ C19, 22.1.2014, p 4.

23 OJ C188, 11.8.2009, p 1.

24 OJ C188, 11.8.2009, p 6.

25 See Commission Decision of 20 December 2011 on the application of Article 106(2) of the Treaty on the Functioning of the European Union to State aid in the form of public service compensation granted to certain undertakings entrusted with the operation of services of general economic interest (OJ L7, 11.1.2012, p 3) and European Union framework for State aid in the form of public service compensation (OJ C8, 11.1.2012, p 15).

26 Directive 2000/60/EC of the European Parliament and of the Council of 23 October 2000 establishing a framework for Community action in the field of water policy ('the Water Framework Directive') (OJ L327, 22.12.2000, p 1).

27 OJ C209, 23.7.2013, p 1.

28 Regulation (EU) No 1379/2013 of the European Parliament and of the Council on the common organisation of the markets in fishery and aquaculture products, amending Council Regulations (EC) No 1184/2006 and (EC) No 1224/2009 and repealing Council Regulation (EC) No 104/2000 (OJ L354, 28.12.2013, p 1).

29 Regulation (EU) No 229/2013 of the European Parliament and of the Council of 13 March 2013 laying down specific measures for agriculture in favour of the smaller Aegean islands and repealing Council Regulation (EC) No 1405/2006 (OJ L78, 20.3.2013, p 41).

30 Commission Regulation (EU) No 702/2014 of 25 June 2014 declaring certain categories of aid in the agricultural and forestry sectors and in rural areas compatible with the internal market in application of Articles 107 and 108 of the Treaty on Functioning of the European Union and repealing Commission Regulation (EC) No 1857/2006 (OJ L193, 1.7.2014, p 1).

31 Directive 2013/34/EU of the European Parliament and of the Council of 26 June 2013 on the annual financial statements, consolidated financial statements and related reports of certain types of undertakings, amending Directive 2006/43/EC of the European Parliament and of the Council and repealing Council Directives 78/660/EEC and 83/349/EEC (OJ L182, 29.6.2013, p 19).

32 Council Directive 2000/29/EC of 8 May 2000 on protective measures against the introduction into the Community of organisms harmful to plants or plant products and against their spread within the Community (OJ L169, 10.7.2000, p 1).

33 COM (2012) 595, 17.10.2012.

[34] Regulation (EU) No 1151/2012 of the European Parliament and of the Council of 21 November 2012 on quality schemes for agricultural products and foodstuffs (OJ L343, 14.12.2012, p 1).

[35] Commission Recommendation of 6 May 2003 concerning the definition of micro, small and medium-sized enterprises (OJ L124, 20.5.2003, p 36).

[36] Regulation (EC) No 999/2001 of the European Parliament and of the Council of 22 May 2001 laying down rules for the prevention, control and eradication of certain transmissible spongiform encephalopathies (OJ L147, 31.5.2001, p 1).

[37] Regulation (EC) No 1059/2003 of the European Parliament and of the Council of 26 May 2003 on the establishment of a common classification of territorial units for statistics (NUTS) (OJ L154, 21.6.2003, p 1).

[38] See for instance Case C-156/98 *Germany v Commission* [2000] ECR I-6857, paragraph 78 and Case C-333/07 *Regie Networks v Rhone Alpes Bourgogne* [2008] ECR I-10807, paragraphs 94 to 116.

[39] See points (13) and (14) of these Guidelines.

[40] Judgement of the European Court of Justice in Case 177/78 *Pigs and Bacon Commission v. McCarren* [1979] ECR 2161, paragraph 11.

[41] Recital 5 of Regulation (EU) No 1305/2013.

[42] As regards the Union environmental legislation: Directive 2009/147/EC of the European Parliament and of the Council of 30 November 2009 on the conservation of wild birds (OJ L20, 26.1.2010, p 7) ("the Birds Directive"); Council Directive 92/43/EEC of 21 May 1992 on the conservation of natural habitats and of wild fauna and flora (OJ L206, 22.7.1992, p 7) ("the Habitats Directive"); Council Directive 91/676/EEC of 12 December 1991 concerning the protection of waters against pollution caused by nitrates from agricultural sources (OJ L375, 31.12.1991, p 1) ("the Nitrates Directive"); Directive 2000/60/EC of the European Parliament and of the Council of 23 October 2000 establishing a framework for Community action in the field of water policy (OJ L327, 22.12.2000, p 1) ("the Water Framework Directive"); Directive 2006/118/EC of the European Parliament and of the Council of 12 December 2006 on the protection of groundwater against pollution and deterioration (OJ L372, 27.12.2006, p 19) ("the Groundwater Directive"); Directive 2009/128/EC of the European Parliament and of the Council of 21 October 2009 establishing a framework for Community action to achieve the sustainable use of pesticides (OJ L309, 24.11.2009, p 71) ("the Sustainable Use of Pesticides Directive"); Regulation (EC) No 1107/2009 of the European Parliament and of the Council of 21 October 2009 concerning the placing of plant protection products on the market and repealing Council Directives 79/117/EEC and 91/414/EEC (OJ L309, 24.11.2009, p 1); Directive 2011/92/EU of the European Parliament and of the Council of 13 December 2011 on the assessment of the effects of certain public and private projects on the environment (OJ L26, 28.1.2012, p 1) ("the Environmental Impact Assessment Directive"); and where applicable Directive 2001/42/EC of the European Parliament and of the Council of 27 June 2001 on the assessment of the effects of certain plans and programmes on the environment (OJ L197, 21.7.2001, p 30) ("the Strategic Environmental Assessment Directive").

[43] The net present value (NPV) of a project is the difference between the positive and negative cash flows over the lifetime of the investment, discounted to their current value (typically using the cost of capital).

[44] The internal rate of return (IRR) is not based on accounting earnings in a given year, but takes into account the stream of future cash flows that the investor expects to receive over the entire lifetime of the investment. It is defined as the discount rate for which the NPV of a stream of cash flows equals zero.

[45] A number of markets may be affected by the aid, because the impact of the aid may not be restricted to the market corresponding to the activity that is supported but may extend to other markets, which are connected to that market either because they are upstream, downstream or complementary, or because the beneficiary is already present on them or may be so present in the near future.

[46] In the Community Guidelines for State aid in the agriculture and forestry sector 2007 to 2013 (OJ C319, 27.12.2006, p 1) rules applying to agricultural processing and marketing companies have been already harmonised with those applying to non-agricultural companies (point 17 of those Guidelines).

[47] These entry barriers include legal barriers (in particular intellectual property rights), economies of scale and scope, access barriers to networks and infrastructure. Where the aid concerns a market where the aid beneficiary is an incumbent, possible barriers to entry may exacerbate the potential substantial market power wielded by the aid beneficiary and thus the possible negative effects of that market power.

[48] Where there are strong buyers in the market, it is less likely that an aid beneficiary can increase prices vis-à-vis these strong buyers.

[49] This information must be published within six months from the date of granting the aid (or, for aid in the form of tax advantage, within one year from the date of the tax declaration). In the case of unlawful aid, Member States will be required to ensure the publication of this information ex post, at least within a period of six months from the date of the Commission decision. The information must be available in a format which allows data to be searched, extracted, and easily published on the internet, for instance in CSV or XML format.

[50] Publication of information on aid awards granted before 1st July 2016 and, for fiscal aid, publication for aid claimed or granted before 1st July 2016, will not be required.

PART II. CATEGORIES OF AID

CHAPTER 1. AID IN FAVOUR OF UNDERTAKINGS ACTIVE IN THE PRIMARY PRODUCTION, PROCESSING AND MARKETING OF AGRICULTURAL PRODUCTS

1.1. Rural development measures

1.1.1. Aid for investment

[5.526]
(133) This Section applies to investment in agricultural holdings linked to the primary agricultural production, to investment in connection with the processing of agricultural products and the marketing of agricultural products.

(134) All aid for investment under Sections 1.1.1.1, 1.1.1.2, 1.1.1.3. and 1.1.1.4. of Part II of these Guidelines must comply with the following condition: where a common market organisation, including direct support schemes, financed by the European Agricultural Guarantee Fund (EAGF) places restrictions on the production or limitations on Union support at the level of individual undertakings, holdings or processing plants, no investment which would increase production beyond those restrictions or limitations may receive State aid support.

1.1.1.1.
Aid for investment in tangible assets and intangible assets on agricultural holdings linked to primary agricultural production

(135) The Commission will consider aid for investment in tangible assets and intangible assets on agricultural holdings linked to primary agricultural production compatible with the internal market under Article 107(3)(c) of the Treaty if it complies with the common assessment principles of these Guidelines, the general condition for investment aid set out in point (134) of these Guidelines and with the following conditions.

(136) This Section applies to aid for investments in tangible assets and intangible assets on agricultural holdings linked to the primary agricultural production. The investment is carried out by one or more beneficiaries or concerns a tangible asset or intangible asset used by one or more beneficiaries.

(137) This Section also applies to investment in tangible assets and intangible assets linked to the production of biofuels or to the production of energy from renewable sources on holdings, which fulfils the following conditions:

- (a) where the investment is made for the production of biofuels within the meaning of Directive 2009/28/EC[51] on agricultural holdings, renewable energy production facilities are eligible for aid only if their production capacity is no more than equivalent to the annual average transport fuel consumption of the agricultural holding; the produced biofuel should not be sold on the market;
- (b) where the investment is made for the production of thermal energy and/or electricity from renewable sources on agricultural holdings, the renewable energy production facilities are eligible for aid only if the aim is to serve their own energy needs and their production capacity is no more than equivalent to the combined average annual energy consumption of thermal energy and electricity on the agricultural holding, including the farm household; regarding electricity, the selling of electricity is allowed into the grid as far as the annual self-consumption limit is respected.

[(138) Where more than one agricultural holding carry out the investment for the production of energy from renewable sources with the aim to serve their own energy needs or for the production of biofuels on holdings, the annual average consumption is equivalent to the sum of the annual average consumption of all beneficiaries.]

(139) Member States must require compliance with minimum standards for energy efficiency for investments in renewable energy infrastructure that consume or produce energy, where such standards exist at national level.

[(140) Investments in installations, the primary purpose of which is electricity production from biomass, are not eligible for aid unless a minimum percentage of the heat energy produced is utilised, to be determined by the Member States.]

(141) Member States must establish thresholds for the maximum proportions of cereals and other starch rich crops, sugar and oil crops used for bioenergy production, including biofuels, for different types of installations. Aid to bioenergy projects must be limited to bioenergy meeting the applicable sustainability criteria laid down in Union legislation including Article 17(2) to (6) of Directive 2009/28/EC of the European Parliament and of the Council.

(142) If the production capacity of the installation exceeds the average annual consumption of the beneficiary or beneficiaries as referred to in points (137) and (138) of these Guidelines, Member States must comply with the conditions laid down in the Guidelines on State aid for environmental protection and energy 2014–2020 unless such aid is exempt from notification obligation.

(143) The investment must pursue at least one of the following objectives:

- (a) improvement of the overall performance and sustainability of the agricultural holding, in particular through a reduction of production costs or the improvement and re-deployment of production;
- (b) the improvement of the natural environment, hygiene or animal welfare standards, provided that the investment concerned aims at going beyond the Union standard in force;
- (c) the creation and improvement of infrastructure related to the development, adaptation and modernisation of agriculture, including access to farm land, land consolidation and land improvement, the supply and saving of energy and water;
- (d) the achievement of agri-environment-climate objectives, including biodiversity conservation status of species and habitats as well as enhancing the public amenity value of a Natura 2000 area or other high natural value systems, as long as the investments are non-productive;
- (e) the restoration of agricultural production potential damaged by natural disasters, exceptional occurrences or adverse climatic events which can be assimilated to a natural disaster, animal diseases and plant pests, protected animals and the prevention and risk mitigation of damage caused by those before-mentioned events and factors;
- (f) meeting standards under the conditions specified in point (148) below.

Eligible costs

(144) The aid covers the following eligible costs:

- (a) the construction, acquisition, including leasing, or improvement of immovable property, with land purchased only being eligible to an extent not exceeding 10% of the total eligible costs of the operation concerned; in exceptional and duly justified cases, a higher percentage may be permitted for operations concerning environmental conservation;

(b) the purchase or lease purchase of machinery and equipment up to the market value of the assets;
(c) general costs linked to the expenditure referred to in points (a) and (b), such as architect, engineer and consultation fees, fees relating to advice on environmental and economic sustainability, including feasibility studies; feasibility studies remain eligible costs even where based on their results, no expenditure under point (a) and (b) is incurred;
(d) the acquisition or development of computer software and acquisition of patents, licences, copyrights and trademarks;
(e) expenses for non-productive investments linked to the objectives referred to in point (143)(d) above;
(f) in the case of investment aiming at the restoration of agricultural production potential damaged by natural disasters, exceptional occurrences or adverse climatic events which can be assimilated to a natural disaster, animal diseases or plant pests and protected animals the eligible costs may include the costs incurred for restoring the production potential up to the level as it was at before the occurrence of those events;
(g) in the case of investments aiming at the prevention of damage caused by natural disasters, exceptional occurrences, adverse climatic events which can be assimilated to a natural disaster, animal diseases and plant pests and by protected animals, the eligible costs may include the costs of specific prevention actions aiming at reducing the consequences of such probable events.

(145) Aid must not be granted in respect of the following:
(a) the purchase of production rights, payment entitlements and annual plants;
(b) the planting of annual plants;
(c) the purchase of animals;
(d) investments to comply with Union standards in force;
(e) costs, other than those referred to (144) connected with leasing contracts, such as lessor's margin, interest refinancing costs, overheads and insurance charges
(f) working capital.

(146) By derogation from point (145)(c) aid may be granted for the purchase of animals carried out for the objective of point (143)(e) of these Guidelines.

(147) By way of derogation from point (145)(c) aid might be granted for the purchase of breeding animals for the improvement of the genetic quality of the herd, provided that it complies with the following conditions:
(a) the Commission considers that the improvement of the genetic quality of herds can in general be achieved through artificial insemination with genetic material of high quality animals. However, it acknowledges that the management practices put certain limits on the use of artificial insemination in beef cattle, sheep and goats; aid may therefore be granted only for the purchase of breeding animals for the improvement of the genetic quality of the herd in beef cattle, sheep and goats;
(b) only investment intended to improve the genetic quality of the stock through the purchase of high quality breeding animals, both male and female which are registered in herd books should be eligible; in the case of the replacement of existing breeding stock aid may be granted only for the replacement of animals which were not registered in a herd book;
(c) only active farmers are eligible for aid;
(d) only animals which ensure optimal reproductive potential for a certain period of time should be purchased; to that end only females purchased before delivering their first offspring should be eligible;
(e) purchased animals are to be kept for a period of at least four years in the herd.

(148) By way of derogation from point (145)(d) aid for meeting standards may be granted subject to the following conditions:
(a) to young farmers setting up for the first time in an agricultural holding as head of the holding in respect of investments to comply with Union standards applying to agricultural production, including occupational safety; such aid may be granted for a maximum period of 24 months from the date of setting up;
(b) Croatia may grant aid for the implementation of the Nitrates Directive[52] within a maximum period of four years from the date of its Accession pursuant to Article 3(2) and Article 5(1) of that Directive;
(c) where Union law imposes new requirements on undertakings active in the primary agricultural production aid may be granted for investments to comply with those requirements for a maximum period of 12 months from the date on which they become mandatory for the undertaking concerned.

(149) As regards irrigation in new and existing irrigated areas, only investments that fulfil the following conditions will be considered to be eligible costs:
(a) a river basin management plan, as required under the terms of the Water Framework Directive has been communicated to the Commission for the entire area in which the investment is to take place, as well as in any other areas whose environment may be affected by the investment; the measures taking effect under the river basin management plan in accordance with Article 11 of that Directive and of relevance to the agricultural sector has been specified in the relevant programme of measures;
(b) water metering enabling the measurement of water use at the level of the supported investment is in place or must be put in place as part of the investment;
(c) an investment in an improvement to an existing irrigation installation or element of irrigation infra structure is eligible only if it is assessed ex-ante as offering potential water savings of a minimum of between 5% and 25% according to the technical parameters of the existing installations or infrastructure; if the investment affects bodies of ground-or-surface water whose status has been identified as less than good in the relevant river basin management plan for reasons related to water quantity:
(i) the investment must ensure an effective reduction in water use, at the level of the investment, amounting to at least 50% of the potential water saving made possible by the investment;

(ii) in the case of an investment on a single agricultural holding, it must also result in a reduction to the agricultural holding's total water use amounting to at least 50% of the potential water saving made possible at the level of the investment; the total water use of the holding must include water sold by the holding:

None of the conditions of point (c) should apply to an investment in an existing installation which affects only energy efficiency or to an investment in the creation of a reservoir or to an investment in the use of recycled water which does not affect a body of ground or surface water;

(d) an investment resulting in a net increase of the irrigated area affecting a given body of ground or surface water is eligible only if:

(i) the status of the water body has not been identified as less than good in the relevant river basin management plan for reasons related to water quantity; and

(ii) an environmental analysis shows that there will be no significant negative environmental impact from the investment. Such an environmental impact analysis must be either carried out or approved by the competent authority and may also refer to groups of holdings;

(e) by way of derogation from point (d)(i), investments resulting in a net increase of the irrigated area may still be eligible if:

(i) the investment is combined with an investment in an existing irrigation installation or element of irrigation infrastructure assessed ex-ante as offering potential water savings of a minimum of between 5% and 25% according to the technical parameters of the existing installation or infrastructure; and

(ii) the investment ensures an effective reduction in water use, at the level of the investment as a whole, amounting to at least 50% of the potential water saving made possible by the investment in the existing irrigation installation or element of infrastructure;

(f) by way of derogation from point (d)(i), the conditions set out in that provision do not apply to investments in the establishment of a new irrigation installation supplied with water from an existing reservoir approved by the competent authority before 31 October 2013, if the following conditions are met:

(i) the reservoir in question is identified in the relevant river basin management plan and is subject to the control requirements provided for in articles 11(3)(e) of the Water Framework Directive;

(ii) on 31 October 2013, there was in force either a maximum limit on total abstractions from the reservoir or a minimum required level of flow in water bodies affected by the reservoir;

(iii) that maximum limit or minimum required level of flow complies with the conditions set out in Article 4 of the Water Framework Directive; and

(iv) the investment in question does not result in abstractions beyond the maximum limit in force on 31 October 2013 or result in a reduction of the level of flow in affected water bodies below the minimum required level in force on 31 October 2013.

(150) Areas which are not irrigated but in which an irrigation installation was active in the recent past, to be established and justified by Member States, may be considered as irrigated areas for the purpose of determining the net increase of the irrigated area.

(151) From 1 January 2017, in the case of irrigation, aid can be paid only by Member States which ensure, in respect of the river basin district in which the investment takes place, a contribution of the different water uses to the recovery of the costs of water services by the agricultural sector consistent with Article 9(1) first indent of Directive 2000/60/EC having regard where appropriate, to the social, environmental and economic effects of the recovery as well as the geographic and climatic conditions of the region or regions affected.

Aid intensity

(152) The aid intensity must not exceed the following:

(a) 75% of the amount of the eligible costs in the outermost regions;

(b) 75% of the amount of the eligible costs in the smaller Aegean Islands;

(c) 75% of the amount of the eligible costs in Croatia for the implementation of the Nitrates Directive in accordance with point (148)(b) of these Guidelines;

(d) 50% of the amount of the eligible costs in less developed regions and in all regions whose gross domestic product (GDP) per capita for the period from 1 January 2007 to 31 December 2013 was less than 75% of the average of the EU-25 for the reference period but whose GDP per capita is above 75% of the GDP average of the EU-27;

(e) 40% of the amount of the eligible costs in other regions;

(f) 30% of the amount of the eligible costs for the purchase of breeding animals referred to in point (147).

(153) The aid intensity rates referred to in point (152) above may be increased by 20 percentage points provided that the maximum combined aid does not exceed 90% for the following:

(a) young farmers or farmers who have set up during the five years preceding the date of the application for aid;

(b) collective investments, such as storage facilities which are used by a group of farmers or facilities to prepare the agricultural products before marketing; and integrated projects covering several measures provided for in Regulation (EU) No 1305/2013, including those linked to the merger of producer organisations;

(c) investments in areas facing natural or other specific constraints pursuant to Article 32 of Regulation (EU) No 1305/2013;

(d) operations financed in the framework of the European Innovation Partnership (EIP), such as an investment in a new stable, allowing the testing of a new practice of animal housing, which have been developed in an operational group composed of farmers, scientists and animal welfare non-governmental organisations;

(e) investments aimed at the improvement of the natural environment, hygiene conditions or animal welfare standards, as referred to in point (143)(b) above; in that case, the increased aid intensity as provided for in this point only applies to the additional costs necessary to obtain a level exceeding the Union standards in force and not leading to an increase in production capacity;

(f) investments aimed at the improvement of the sustainability of the agricultural holding, as referred to in point (143)(a), which are linked to agri-environment-climate commitments and organic farming under Section 1.1.5.1. and Section 1.1.8 of Part II.

(154) As regards non-productive investments referred to in point (143)(d) and investments for the restoration of production potential referred to in point (143)(e), the maximum aid intensity must not exceed 100% of the eligible costs.

[(155) As regards investment with preventive objectives in point (143)(e), the maximum aid intensity must not exceed 80 %. However, it may be increased up to 100 % if the investment is carried out collectively by more than one beneficiary or if the objective is to prevent damage caused by protected animals.]

1.1.1.2.
Aid for investments in favour of the conservation of cultural and natural heritage located on agricultural holdings

(156) The Commission will consider aid for investments in favour of the conservation of cultural and natural heritage located on the agricultural holding compatible with the internal market under Article 107(3) of the Treaty if it complies with the common assessment principles, the general condition for investment aid set out in point (134) of these Guidelines and with the following conditions.

(157) This Section applies to undertakings active in the primary agricultural production.

(158) The aid should be granted for cultural and natural heritage in the form of natural landscapes and buildings which is formally recognised as cultural or natural heritage by the competent public authorities of the Member State.

Eligible costs

(159) The following costs intended for the conservation of cultural and natural heritage are eligible:
- (a) investment costs in tangible assets;
- (b) capital works.

Aid intensity

(160) The following aid intensities apply:
- (a) in the case of investments aimed at the conservation of productive heritage features located on agricultural holdings and provided that the investment does not entail any increase in the production capacity, the aid intensity must be limited to
  - (i) 80% of the real costs incurred in areas facing natural or other specific constraints pursuant to Article 32 of Regulation (EU) No 1305/2013;
  - (ii) 70% of the real costs incurred in less developed regions;
  - (iii) 60% of the real costs incurred on other areas;
- (b) where there is an increase in production capacity, the aid intensities for the investments referred to in points (152) and (153) apply;
- (c) additional aid may be granted at a rate of up to 100% of the eligible costs to cover the extra costs incurred by using traditional materials necessary to maintain the heritage features of buildings located on agricultural holdings;
- (d) notwithstanding the rules set out in points (a), (b) and (c), the maximum aid intensity may reach 100% of the eligible costs, where the investment concerns small-scale infrastructures;
- (e) in the case of investments aimed at the conservation of non-productive heritage features located on agricultural holdings, such as archaeological or historical features, the aid intensity may reach up to 100% of the real costs incurred;
- (f) the aid for capital works must be limited to EUR 10,000 per year.

1.1.1.3.
Aid for investment concerning the relocation of farm buildings

(161) The Commission will consider aid for investments concerning the relocation of farm buildings compatible with the internal market under Article 107(3)(c) of the Treaty if it complies with the common assessment principles of these Guidelines, the general condition for investment aid set out in point (134) and with the following conditions.

(162) This Section applies to undertakings active in the primary agricultural production.

(163) The relocation of the farm building must pursue an objective of public interest. The public interest invoked to justify the granting of aid under this Section must be specified in the relevant provisions of the Member State concerned.

Aid intensities in relation to eligible costs

(164) The following aid intensities apply:
- (a) where the relocation of farm building consists of the dismantling, removal and re-building of existing facilities the aid intensity may reach up to 100% of the real costs incurred for such activities;
- (b) where, in addition to point (a) above, the relocation results in a modernisation of the facilities or in an increase in production capacity, the aid intensities for investments as referred to in points (152) and (153) apply in respect to the costs relating to the modernisation of the facilities or the increase of the production capacity. For

the purposes of this point, the pure replacement of an existing building or facilities by a new up-to-date building or facilities without fundamentally changing the production or the technology involved is not be considered to be related to the modernisation;

(c) where the relocation concerns activities close to rural settlements, with a view to improving the quality of life or increasing the environmental performance of the rural settlement and concerns small-scale infrastructures, the aid intensity may reach up to 100% of the eligible costs.

1.1.1.4.
Aid for investments in connection with the processing of agricultural products and the marketing of agricultural products

(165) The Commission will consider aid for investments in connection with the processing of agricultural products and the marketing of agricultural products compatible with the internal market under Article 107(3)(c) of the Treaty if it complies with the common assessment principles of these Guidelines, the general condition for investment aid set out in point (134) and with the following conditions.

(166) Aid for food based biofuels should not be granted under this Section, in order to incentivise the shift towards the production of more advanced forms of biofuels, as foreseen by the horizontal environmental and energy State aid rules.

(167) This Section applies to aid for investments in tangible assets and intangible assets in connection with the processing of agricultural products and the marketing of agricultural products as referred in point (35)11 and point (35)12.

(168) Member States may grant aid for investments in connection with the processing of agricultural products and the marketing of agricultural products if the aid fulfils all the conditions of one of the following aid instruments:

(a) Commission Regulation (EU) No 651/2014 of 17 June 2014 declaring certain categories of aid compatible with the internal market in application of Articles 107 and 108 of the Treaty;[53] or

(b) Guidelines on regional State aid for 2014–2020; or

(c) the conditions of this Section of these Guidelines.

Eligible costs

(169) The eligible costs under Point (168)(c) must be limited to:

(a) the construction, acquisition, including leasing, or improvement of immoveable property, with land purchased only being eligible to an extent not exceeding 10% of total eligible costs of the operation concerned;

(b) the purchase or lease purchase of machinery and equipment up to the market value of the asset;

(c) general costs linked to the expenditure referred to in points (a) and (b), such as architect, engineer and consultation fees, fees relating to advice on environmental and economic sustainability, including feasibility studies; feasibility studies remain eligible expenditure even where, based on their results, no expenditure under points (a) and (b) is incurred;

(d) the acquisition or development of computer software and the acquisition of patents, licences, copyrights and trademarks.

(170) The following costs are not eligible:

(a) costs, other than those referred to point (169) connected with leasing contracts, such as lessor's margin, interest refinancing costs, overheads and insurance charges;

(b) working capital;

(c) costs related to investments to comply with Union standards in force.

Aid intensity

(171) The maximum aid intensity under these Guidelines must not exceed the following:

(a) 75% of the amount of the eligible costs in the outermost regions;

(b) 75% of the amount of the eligible investment costs in the smaller Aegean islands;

(c) 50% of the amount of the eligible investment costs in less developed regions and in all regions whose GDP per capita for the period from 1 January 2007 to 31 December 2013 was less than 75% of the average of the EU-25 for the reference period but whose GDP per capita is above 75% of the GDP average of the EU-27;

(d) 40% of the amount of the eligible investment costs in other regions.

(172) The aid rates referred to in point (171) above may be increased by 20 percentage points, provided that the maximum aid intensity does not exceed 90% for operations:

(a) linked to a merger of producer organisations; or

(b) supported in the framework of the EIP.

(173) Individual aid exceeding the notification threshold referred to in point (37)(a) must be notified to the Commission in accordance with Article 108(3) of the Treaty.

1.1.2.
Start-up aid for young farmers and for the development of small farms

(174) The Commission will consider start-up aid for young farmers and start-up aid for the development of small farms compatible with the internal market under Article 107(3)(c) of the Treaty if it complies with the common assessment principles of these Guidelines and with the following conditions.

(175) This Section applies to undertakings active in the primary agricultural production.

(176) The aid is granted to young farmers as defined in point (35).29 of these Guidelines, who are micro- and small undertakings or to small farms. Small farms must be defined by Member States based on objective criteria and must be limited to micro- and small undertakings.

[(177) Member States must define the upper and lower thresholds for access to start-up aid for young farmers and the development of small farms in terms of the production potential of the agricultural holding, measured in standard output, as defined in Article 5b of Council Regulation (EC) No 1217/2009[54] and Article 6 of Commission Implementing Regulation (EU) 2015/220,[54a] or an equivalent. The lower threshold for access to start-up aid for young farmers must be higher than the upper threshold for access to aid for the development of small farms.]

(178) Where the aid is granted to a young farmer who is setting up a holding in the form of a legal person, the young farmer must exercise effective and long-term control over the legal person in terms of decisions related to management, benefits and financial risks. Where several natural persons, including persons who are not young farmers, participate in the capital or management of the legal person, the young farmer must be capable of exercising such effective and long-term control either solely or jointly together with other persons. Where a legal person is solely or jointly controlled by another legal person, those requirements must apply to any natural person having control over that other legal person.

(179) The aid must be conditional on the submission of a business plan to the competent authority of the Member State concerned, the implementation of which must start within nine months from the date of the adoption of the decision granting the aid.

(180) In the case of aid for young farmers, the business plan must provide that the beneficiary has to comply with the definition of active farmer provided for in Article 9 of Regulation (EU) No 1307/2013, within 18 months from the date of setting up.

(181) Young farmers who do not possess adequate occupational skills and competences are entitled to receive aid provided that they make a commitment to acquire those occupational skills and competences within 36 months from the date of the adoption of the decision on granting the aid. That commitment must be included in the business plan.

(182) The business plan must describe at least the following:

- (a) in the case of start-up aid to young farmers:
  - (i) the initial situation of the agricultural holding;
  - (ii) milestones and targets for the development of the activities of the agricultural holding;
  - (iii) details of the actions including those related to environmental sustainability and resource efficiency, required for the development of the activities of the agricultural holding, such as investments, training, advice or any other activity;
- (b) in the case of start-up aid for the development of small farms:
  - (i) the initial situation of the agricultural holding; and
  - (ii) details of actions including those related to environmental sustainability and resource efficiency, that could support the achievement of economic viability, such as investments, training, co-operation or any other action.

(183) Aid must be provided or paid in at least in two tranches or instalments over a maximum period of five years. For young farmers, the last aid tranche or the last instalment of the aid must be conditional upon the correct implementation of the business plan referred to in point (179).

Aid intensity

(184) The maximum aid must be limited to EUR 70,000 per young farmer and EUR 15,000 per small farm. Member States must define the amount of aid for young farmers also taking into account the socio-economic situation of the area concerned.

1.1.3.
Aid for the transfer of agricultural holdings

(185) The Commission will consider aid for the transfer of agricultural holdings compatible with the internal market under Article 107(3)(c) of the Treaty if it complies with the common assessment principles of these Guidelines and with the following conditions.

(186) This Section applies to undertakings active in the primary agricultural production which permanently transfer their agricultural holding to another undertaking active in the primary agricultural production.

(187) Aid is granted to undertakings, eligible to participate in the small farmers scheme, established by Title V of Regulation (EU) No 1307/2013, which on the date of submitting their aid application, have been so eligible for a period of at least one year and which undertake to permanently transfer their entire agricultural holding and the corresponding payment entitlements to another undertaking.

(188) The aid must be paid either as annual payment or as a one-off payment.

(189) The aid must be paid from the date of the transfer of the agricultural holding until 31 December 2020.

Aid intensity

(190) The aid corresponds to 120% of the annual payment that the beneficiary is eligible to receive under the small farmer scheme.

1.1.4.
Start-up aid for producer groups and organisations in the agricultural sector

(191) The Commission takes a favourable view for start-up aid for producer groups and producer organisations as it creates an incentive for bringing together farmers. It will therefore consider start-up aid for producer groups and producer organisations compatible with the internal market under Article 107(3)(c) of the Treaty if it complies with the common assessment principles of these Guidelines and with the following conditions.

(192) This Section applies to the whole agricultural sector.[55]

(193) Only producer groups or organisations that have been officially recognised by the competent authority of the Member State concerned on the basis of a submission of a business plan are eligible for aid.

(194) The start-up aid must be granted subject to the obligation of the Member State to verify that the objectives of the business plan have been reached within a period of five years from the date of the official recognition of the producer group or organisation.

(195) The agreements, decisions and concerted practices concluded in the framework of the producer group or organisation must comply with the competition rules as they apply by virtue of Articles 206 to 210 of Regulation (EU) No 1308/2013.

(196) As an alternative to providing start-up aid to producer groups or organisations, aid up to the same overall amount may be granted directly to producers to offset their contributions to the costs of running the groups or organisations during a period of the first five years following the formation of the group or organisation.

(197) Member States may continue to grant start up aid for producer groups even after they have been recognised as producer organisations under the conditions of Regulation (EU) No 1308/2013.

(198) Aid must be limited to producer groups and producer organisations falling with the definition of SMEs.[56] The Commission will not authorise State aid towards the costs covered in this Section in favour of large enterprises.[57]

(199) Aid schemes authorised under this Section will be subject to a condition requiring them to adjust to take account of any changes in the regulations governing the common organisation of the markets in agricultural products.

Eligible costs

(200) The eligible costs may include the costs of the rental of suitable premises, the acquisition of office equipment, including computer hardware and software, administrative staff costs, overheads and legal and administrative fees. Where premises are purchased, the eligible costs for premises must be limited to rental costs at market rates.

(201) Aid must not be granted to:

(a) production organisations, entities or bodies, such as companies or co-operatives, the objective of which is the management of one or more agricultural holdings and which are therefore in effect single producers;

(b) agricultural associations, which undertake tasks, such as mutual support and farm relief and farm management services, in the members' holdings without being involved in the joint adaptation of supply to the market;

(c) producer groups, organisations or associations, the objectives of which are incompatible with Articles 152 (1)(c) and (3) and Article 156 of Regulation (EU) No 1308/2013.

(202) The aid must be paid as a flat rate aid in annual instalments for the first five years from the date on which the producer group or organisation was officially recognised by the competent authority on the basis of its business plan. Member States must only pay the last instalment after having verified the correct implementation of the business plan.

(203) Aids which are granted to producer group or organisations to cover expenses which are not linked to start-up costs, such as investments or promotion activities, will be assessed in accordance with the rules governing such type of aids.

Aid intensity

(204) The aid intensity must be limited to 100% of the eligible costs.

(205) The total amount of aid must be limited to EUR 500,000. The aid must be degressive.

1.1.5.
Aid for agri-environment-climate and animal welfare commitments

(206) This Section applies to undertakings active in the primary agricultural production.

1.1.5.1.
Aid for agri-environment-climate commitments

(207) The Commission will consider aid for agri-environment-climate commitments compatible with the internal market under Article 107(3)(c) of the Treaty if it complies with the common assessment principles of these Guidelines and with the following conditions.

(208) This Section applies to aid to undertakings and groups of such undertakings which undertake, on a voluntary basis, to carry out operations consisting of one or more agri-environment-climate commitments on agricultural land which is to be defined by Member States, including but not limited to the agricultural area as defined under point (35)50 of these Guidelines.

(209) The measure must aim at the preservation as well as at the promotion of the necessary changes to agricultural practices that make a positive contribution to the environment and climate.

(210) The aid will cover only those voluntary commitments going beyond the relevant mandatory standards established pursuant to Chapter I of Title VI of Regulation (EU) No 1306/2013, the relevant criteria and minimum activities as established pursuant to points (c)(ii) and (c)(iii) of Article 4(1) of Regulation (EU) No 1307/2013, and

relevant minimum requirements for fertiliser and plant protection products use as well as other relevant mandatory requirements established by national law. All such mandatory standards and requirements must be identified and described in the notification to the Commission.

(211) Member States should endeavour to ensure that the undertakings that undertake to carry out operations under this measure are provided with the knowledge and information required to implement them, such as by commitment-related expert advice and/or by making aid under this measure conditional on obtaining relevant training.

(212) Commitments under this measure must be undertaken for a period of five to seven years. However, where necessary in order to achieve or maintain the environmental benefits sought, Member States may determine a longer period for particular types of commitments, including by means of providing for their annual extension after the termination of the initial period.[58] For new commitments directly following the commitment performed in the initial period, Member States may determine a shorter period.

(213) Where relevant, the rules for area related payments provided for in Article 47 of Regulation (EU) No 1305/2013 and in any delegated act adopted pursuant to that provision should be complied with.

(214) Aid for agri-environment-climate commitments to other land managers and other groups of beneficiaries than undertakings active in the agricultural sector may be granted under Section 3.4 of Part II these Guidelines.

(215) Commitments under the agri-environment-climate measure to extensify livestock farming must comply with at least the following conditions:

(a) the whole grazed area of the holding must be managed and maintained to avoid over- and under-grazing;
(b) livestock density must be defined taking account of all grazing livestock kept on the farm or, in the case of a commitment to limit nutrient leaching, all animals kept on the farm which are relevant to the commitment in question.

(216) Commitments under the agri-environment-climate measure to rear local breeds in danger of being lost to farming or to preserve plant genetic resources under threat of genetic erosion must require:

(a) to rear farm animals of local breeds, genetically adapted to one or more traditional production systems or environments in the country, in danger of being lost to farming; or
(b) to preserve plant genetic resources naturally adapted to the local and regional conditions and under threat of genetic erosion.

(217) The following species of farm animals are eligible for aid: cattle; sheep; goats; equidae; pigs and birds.

(218) Local breeds will be considered as being in danger of being lost to farming if the following conditions are fulfilled and if those conditions are also described and included in the notification to the Commission:

(a) the number, at national level, of breeding females concerned is stated;
(b) that number and the endangered status of the listed breeds is certified by a duly recognised relevant scientific body;
(c) a duly recognised relevant technical body registers and keeps up-to-date the herd or flock book for the breed;
(d) the bodies concerned possess the necessary skills and knowledge to identify animals of the breeds in danger.

(219) Plant genetic resources will be considered as being under threat of genetic erosion on condition that sufficient evidence of genetic erosion, based upon scientific results or indicators for the reduction of landraces/primitive local varieties, their population diversity and, where relevant, for modifications in the prevailing agricultural practices at local level, is described and included in the notification to the Commission.

(220) Aid may be provided for the conservation and for the sustainable use and development of genetic resources in agriculture for operations not covered by the provisions under points (208) to (219) of this Section.

Eligible costs

(221) Aid, with the exception of aid for operations for the conservation of genetic resources as referred to in point (220), covers compensation to beneficiaries for all or part of the additional costs and income foregone resulting from the commitments they made. The aid must be granted annually.

(222) In duly justified cases, for operations concerning environmental conservation, aid may be granted as a flat-rate or as a one-off payment per unit for commitments to renounce the commercial use of areas, calculated on the basis of additional costs incurred and income foregone.

(223) Where necessary the aid may also cover transaction costs to a value of up to 20% of the premium paid for the agri-environment-climate commitments. Where commitments are undertaken by groups of undertakings, the maximum level must be 30%.

(224) However, if a Member State wants to compensate for transaction costs caused by entering into agri-environment-climate commitments, it must provide convincing proof of such costs, for example by presenting cost comparisons with undertakings not entering into such commitments. The Commission will therefore not normally authorise State aid for transaction costs for the continuation of commitments already entered into in the past, unless a Member State demonstrates that such costs continue to occur or that new transaction costs are being incurred.

(225) Where transaction costs are calculated on the basis of average costs and/or average farms, Member States should demonstrate that, in particular, large enterprises are not overcompensated. For the purpose of calculating compensation, Member States must take into account whether the transaction costs in question are incurred per undertaking or per hectare.

(226) No aid under this measure may be granted for commitments that are covered under the organic farming measure defined in Section 1.1.8 of Part II of these Guidelines.

(227) Aid for the conservation of genetic resources in agriculture covers the costs for the following operations:

(a) targeted actions: actions promoting the in situ and ex situ conservation, characterisation, collection and utilisation of genetic resources in agriculture, including web-based inventories of genetic resources currently conserved in situ, including in situ/ on-farm conservation, and of ex situ collections and databases;

(b) concerted actions: actions promoting the exchange of information for the conservation, characterisation, collection and utilisation of genetic resources in Union agriculture, among competent organisations in the Member States;

(c) accompanying actions: information, dissemination and advisory actions involving non-governmental organisations and other relevant stakeholders, training courses and preparation of technical reports.

Aid amount and aid intensity

(228) Aid, with the exception of aid for operations for the conservation of genetic resources as referred to in point (220), must be limited to the following maximum amounts: EUR 600 per hectare per year for annual crops; EUR 900 per hectare per year for specialised perennial crops; EUR 450 per hectare per year for other land uses; EUR 200 per livestock unit per year for local breeds in danger of being lost to farming.

(229) These amounts may be increased in duly substantiated cases taking into account specific circumstances to be justified in the notification to the Commission.

[(230) For the conservation of genetic resources in agriculture, the aid must be limited to 100% of the eligible costs.]

1.1.5.2.
Aid for animal welfare commitments

(231) The Commission will consider aid for animal welfare commitments compatible with the internal market under Article 107(3)(c) of the Treaty if it complies with the common assessment principles of these Guidelines and with the following conditions.

(232) This Section applies to aid to undertakings active in the primary agricultural production which undertake, on a voluntary basis, to carry out operations consisting of one or more animal welfare commitments and which are active farmers.

(233) The aid covers only those commitments going beyond the relevant mandatory standards established pursuant to Chapter I of Title VI of Regulation (EU) No 1306/2013 and other relevant mandatory requirements. These relevant requirements must be identified and described in the notification to the Commission.

(234) Animal welfare commitments eligible to receive aid must provide upgraded standards of production methods in one of the following areas:

(a) water, feed and animal care in accordance with the natural needs of animal husbandry;

(b) housing conditions, such as increased space allowances, flooring surfaces, enrichment materials, natural light;

(c) outdoor access;

(d) practices which avoid mutilation and/or castration of animals or in specific cases when mutilation or castration of animals is deemed necessary, provide for the use of anaesthetics, analgesia and anti-inflammatory medication or immunocastration.

(235) The animal welfare commitments must be undertaken for a renewable period of one to seven years.

(236) The renewal of a contract can be also automatic, if its details are described in the contract. The mechanism of renewal of the animal welfare commitments must be set up by the Member States in accordance with their relevant national rules. Such mechanism must be communicated to the Commission as part of the notification of State aid pursuant to this Section. The renewal must always be subject to respect of conditions approved by the Commission for aid pursuant to this Section.

Eligible costs

(237) The aid must be granted annually and may compensate undertakings active in primary agricultural production for all or part of the additional costs and income foregone resulting from the commitment made by them.

(238) Where necessary, they may also cover transaction costs to the value up to 20% of the premium paid for the animal welfare commitments. However, if a Member State wants to compensate for transaction costs caused by entering into animal welfare commitments, it must provide convincing proof of such costs, for example by presenting cost comparisons with undertakings not entering into such animal welfare commitments. The Commission will, therefore, not normally authorise State aid for transaction costs for the continuation of animal welfare commitments already entered into in the past, unless a Member State demonstrates that such costs continue to occur or that new transaction costs are being incurred.

(239) Where transaction costs are calculated on the basis of average costs and/or average farms, Member States should demonstrate that, in particular, large enterprises are not overcompensated. For the purpose of calculating compensation, Member States must take into account whether the transaction costs in question are incurred per undertaking or per hectare.

Aid amount

(240) Aid must be limited to EUR 500 per livestock unit.

1.1.6.
Aid for disadvantages related to Natura 2000 areas and to the Water Framework Directive

(241) The Commission will consider aid for disadvantages related to Natura 2000 areas and to the Water Framework Directive compatible with the internal market under Article 107(3)(c) of the Treaty if it complies with the common assessment principles of these Guidelines and with the following conditions.

(242) This Section applies to undertakings active in the primary agricultural production.

(243) Aid to other land managers other than undertakings active in the agricultural sector in duly justified cases may be granted in accordance with Section 3.5 of Part II of these Guidelines.

Eligible costs

(244) Aid covers compensation to beneficiaries for additional costs and income foregone resulting from disadvantages in the areas concerned, related to the implementation of the Habitats Directive, the Birds Directive and the Water Framework Directive.[59]

(245) Aid linked to the Habitats Directive and the Birds Directive may only be granted in relation to disadvantages resulting from requirements that go beyond the good agricultural and environmental condition provided for in Article 94 and Annex II of Council Regulation (EU) No 1306/2013 and the relevant criteria and minimum activities as established pursuant to points (c)(ii) and (iii) of Article 4(1) of Regulation (EU) No 1307/2013.

(246) Aid linked to the Water Framework Directive may only be granted in relation to specific requirements that:

(a) were introduced by the Water Framework Directive, are in accordance with the programmes of measures of the river basin management plans for the purpose of achieving the environmental objectives of that Directive and go beyond the measures required to implement other Union legislation for the protection of water;
(b) go beyond the statutory management requirements and the good agricultural and environmental condition provided for in Chapter I of Title VI of Regulation (EU) No 1306/2013 and the relevant criteria and minimum activities as established pursuant to points (c)(ii) and (iii) of Article 4(1) of Regulation (EU) No 1307/2013;
(c) go beyond the level of protection of the Union law existing at the time the Water Framework Directive was adopted as laid down in Article 4(9) of the that Directive; and
(d) impose major changes in the type of land use, and/or major restrictions in farming practice resulting in a significant loss of income.

(247) The requirements referred to in points (245) and (246) must be identified and described in the notification to the Commission.

(248) The following areas are eligible for aid:

(a) Natura 2000 agricultural areas designated pursuant to the Habitats Directive and the Birds Directive;
(b) other delimited nature protection areas with environmental restrictions applicable to farming which contribute to the implementation of Article 10 of the Habitats Directive; these areas must not exceed 5% of the designated Natura 2000 areas covered by the territorial scope of the relevant rural development programme;
(c) agricultural areas included in river basin management plans according to the Water Framework Directive.

Aid amount

(249) Aid must be limited to the following amounts: EUR 500 per hectare per year maximum in the initial period not exceeding five years; and EUR 200 per hectare per year maximum thereafter. Aid related to the Water Framework Directive must amount to a minimum of EUR 50 per hectare per year.

(250) The maximum amounts of EUR 500 and EUR 200 may be increased in exceptional cases taking into account specific circumstances to be justified. The minimum amount of EUR 50 for aid related to the Water Framework Directive may be decreased in duly substantiated cases taking into account specific circumstances to be justified.

1.1.7.
Aid to areas facing natural or other specific constraints

(251) The Commission will consider aid in mountain areas and other areas facing natural or other specific constraints compatible with the internal market under Article 107(3)(c) of the Treaty if it complies with the common assessment principles of these Guidelines and with the following conditions.

(252) This Section applies to undertakings active in the primary agricultural production.

(253) Aid may be granted to undertakings which undertake to pursue their farming activity in areas designated pursuant to Article 32 of Regulation (EU) No 1305/2013 and who are active farmers.

Eligible costs

(254) The aid covers compensation to undertakings active in the primary agricultural production for all or part of the additional costs and income foregone related to the constraints for agricultural production in the area concerned. Member States must demonstrate the constraints in question and provide proof that the amount of compensation to be paid does not go beyond income loss and additional costs resulting from those constraints.

[(255) Additional costs and income foregone must be calculated in comparison to areas which are not affected by natural or other specific constraints, taking into account payments pursuant to Chapter 4 of Title III of the Regulation (EU) No 1307/2013.]

(256) When calculating additional costs and income foregone, Member States may, where duly justified, differentiate the level of payment taking into account the following:

(a) the severity of the identified permanent natural constraint affecting farming activities;
(b) the farming system.

(257) The aid will be granted annually per hectare of agricultural area.

Aid amount

(258) Aid must be fixed between the following minimum and maximum amounts: EUR 25 minimum per hectare per year on average of the area of the beneficiary receiving aid, and EUR 250 maximum per hectare per year. However, the maximum amount may reach EUR 450 per hectare per year in mountain areas as defined in Article 32(2) of Regulation (EU) No 1305/2013.

(259) The maximum amounts may be increased in duly substantiated cases taking into account specific circumstances to be justified in the notification to the Commission.

(260) Member States must provide for degressivity of aid above a threshold level of area per holding, to be defined, except if the grant only concerns the minimum amount per hectare per year as laid down in point (258) of these Guidelines. To that effect, notifications should specify the size of the farm that will benefit from such aid.

(261) In the case of a legal person, or a group of natural or legal persons, Member States may apply the degressivity of aid at the level of the members of these legal persons or groups where national law provides for the individual members to assume rights and obligations comparable to those of individual farmers who have the status of head of holding, in particular as regards their economic, social and tax status, provided that they have contributed to strengthening the agricultural structures of the legal persons or groups concerned.

(262) In addition to the aid provided for in point (253) Member States may grant aid under this measure between 2014 and 2020 to beneficiaries in areas which were eligible under Article 36(a)(ii) of Regulation (EC) No 1698/2005[60] during the 2007–2013 rural development programming period. For beneficiaries in areas that are no longer eligible following the new delimitation referred to in Article 32(3) of Regulation (EU) No 1305/2013, this aid must be degressive over a maximum period of four years starting on the date the delimitation in accordance with Article 32(3) of Regulation (EU) No 1305/2013 is completed and at the latest in 2018. Those aid must start at no more than 80% of the average payment fixed in the rural development programme for the period 2007–2013 or, if the measure was granted exclusively from national funds, in the relevant State aid decision, in accordance with Article 36(a)(ii) of Regulation (EC) No 1698/2005, and must end in 2020 at the latest at no more than 20%. When the application of degressivity results in the level of the payment reaching EUR 25, the Member State can continue to grant aid at this level until the phasing out period is completed.

(263) Following completion of the delimitation, beneficiaries in the areas that remain eligible must receive full payment under this measure.

1.1.8.
Aid for organic farming

(264) The Commission will consider aid for organic farming compatible with the internal market under Article 107(3)(c) of the Treaty if it complies with the common assessment principles of these Guidelines and with the following conditions.

(265) This Section applies to undertakings active in the primary agricultural production.

(266) Aid per hectare of agricultural area may be granted to undertakings or groups of undertakings which undertake on a voluntarily basis to convert to or maintain organic farming practices and methods as defined in Council Regulation (EC) No 834/2007[61] and who are active farmers.

(267) Aid is granted only for commitments which go beyond the following standards and requirements which must be identified and described in the notification to the Commission:

(a) the relevant mandatory standards established under Chapter 1, Title VI of Regulation (EU) No 1306/2013;
(b) the relevant criteria and minimum activities as established pursuant to points (c)(ii) and (c)(iii) of Article 4(1) of Regulation (EU) No 1307/2013;
(c) the relevant minimum requirements applicable to the use of fertilisers and plant protection products; as well as
(d) other relevant mandatory requirements laid down in national law.

(268) Commitments must be carried out over an initial period of five to seven years. However, where aid is granted for conversion to organic farming Member States may determine a shorter initial period corresponding to the period of conversion. Where aid is granted for the maintenance of organic farming, Member States may provide for an annual extension after the termination of the initial period. For new commitments concerning maintenance directly following the commitment performed in the initial period, Member States may determine a shorter period.

(269) Where relevant, the rules for area related payments laid down in Article 47 of Regulation (EU) No 1305/2013 and any delegated act adopted pursuant to that provision should be complied with.

Eligible costs

(270) Aid covers compensation to beneficiaries for part of or all additional costs and loss of income resulting from the commitments.

(271) Where necessary, aid may also cover transaction costs with a maximum value of 20% of the premium paid for the commitment. Where commitments are undertaken by groups of undertakings the maximum level is 30%. This aid is granted on an annual basis.

(272) However, if a Member State wants to compensate for transaction costs caused by entering into organic farming commitments, it must provide convincing proof of such costs, for example by presenting cost comparisons with undertakings not entering into such commitments. The Commission will, therefore, not normally authorise State aid for transaction costs for the continuation of organic farming commitments already entered into in the past, unless a Member State demonstrates that such costs continue to occur or that new transaction costs are being incurred.

(273) Where transaction costs are calculated on the basis of average costs and/or average farms, Member States should demonstrate that in particular large enterprises are not overcompensated. For the purpose of calculating compensation, Member States should take into account whether the transaction costs in question are incurred per undertakings or per hectare.

(274) Aid may not be granted under this Section for commitments covered by the agri-environment-climate measure, or for costs covered by the Section on aid to encourage the participation of producers of agricultural products in quality systems.

(275) Aid for investment in primary production and the processing and marketing of organic products is subject to the provisions of the Sections on aid for investment.

Aid amount

(276) The maximum amount of aid is: EUR 600 per hectare per year for annual crops; EUR 900 per hectare per year for specialised perennial crops; EUR 450 per hectare per year for other land use.

(277) These ceilings may be exceeded in exceptional cases, taking into account specific circumstances which must be justified.

1.1.9.
Aid for the participation of producers of agricultural products in quality schemes

(278) The Commission will consider aid in favour of the participation of producers of agricultural products and groups thereof in quality schemes compatible with the internal market under Article 107(3)(c) of the Treaty if it complies with the common assessment principles of these Guidelines and with the following conditions:

(279) This Section applies to producers of agricultural products. Only active farmers are eligible for aid referred to in point (280)(a).

Eligible costs

(280) The aid covers the following eligible costs in relation to quality schemes as referred to in point (282) of these Guidelines:

(a) the costs for new participation in quality schemes;

(b) the costs for compulsory control measures in relation to the quality schemes undertaken pursuant to Union or national legislation by or on behalf of the competent authorities;

(c) the costs of market research activities, product conception and design and for the preparation of applications for recognition of quality schemes.

(281) The aid referred to in point (280)(a) and (b) must not be granted towards the costs of controls undertaken by the beneficiaries themselves, or where Union legislation provides that the costs of control are to be met by producers of agricultural products and group thereof, without specifying the actual level of charges.

(282) The quality schemes referred to in point (280)(a) of these Guidelines must be the following:

(a) quality scheme established under the following Regulations and provisions:

(i) Part II, Title II, Chapter I, Section 2 of Regulation (EU) No 1308/2013 as concerns wine;

(ii) Regulation (EU) No 1151/2012;

(iii) Regulation (EC) No 834/2007;[62]

(iv) Regulation (EC) No 110/2008 of the European Parliament and of the Council;[63]

(v) Regulation (EU) No 251/2014 of the European Parliament and of the Council;[64]

(b) quality schemes, including farm certification schemes, for agricultural products recognised by the Member States as complying with the following criteria:

(i) the specificity of the final product produced under such quality schemes must be derived from a clear obligations to guarantee

— specific product characteristics; or

— specific farming or production method; or

— a quality of the final product that goes significantly beyond the commercial commodity standards as regards public, animal or plant health, animal welfare or environmental protection;

(ii) the quality scheme must be open to all producers;

(iii) the quality scheme must involve binding final product specifications and compliance with those specifications must be verified by public authorities or by an independent inspection body;

[(iv) the quality scheme must be transparent and ensure complete traceability of agricultural products;]

(c) voluntary agricultural product certification schemes recognised by the Member States concerned as meeting the requirements laid down in Commission Communication – EU best practice guidelines voluntary certification schemes for agricultural products and foodstuffs.[65]

(283) The aid must be accessible to all those eligible undertakings in the area concerned, based on objectively defined conditions.

(284) The aid referred to in point (280)(b) and (c) of these Guidelines must not involve direct payments to the beneficiaries and must be paid to the body responsible for control measures, the research provider or the consultancy provider.

Aid amount

(285) The aid referred to in Point (280)(a) above must be granted for a maximum period of five years and must be limited to EUR 3,000 per beneficiary per year. It must be granted in the form of an annual incentive payment, the level of which is determined according to the level of the fixed costs arising from the participation in quality schemes.

(286) The aid referred to in Point (280)(b) and (c) may reach 100% of the real costs incurred.

1.1.10.
Aid for provision of technical support in the agricultural sector

(287) This Section covers aid for the provision of technical support in the agricultural sector, with the exception of aid for farm replacement services which can be granted only to undertakings active in the primary agricultural production.

(288) The provision of technical support may be undertaken by producer groups or other organisations, regardless of their size.

(289) The aid must be accessible to all those eligible in the area concerned, based on objectively defined conditions. Where the provision of technical support is undertaken by producer groups or organisations, membership of such groups or organisations must not be a condition for access to the service. Any contribution of non-members towards the administrative costs of the group or organization concerned must be limited to the costs of providing the service.

1.1.10.1.
Aid for knowledge transfer and information actions

(290) The Commission will consider aid for knowledge transfer and information actions compatible with the internal market under Article 107(3)(c) of the Treaty if it complies with the common assessment principles of these Guidelines, with the general conditions for aid for technical support and with the following conditions.

(291) The aid covers vocational training and skills acquisitions, including training courses, workshops and coaching, demonstration activities and information actions.

(292) The aid may also cover short-term farm management exchange and farm visits.

Eligible costs

(293) The aid covers the following eligible costs:

(a) the costs of organising vocational training, skills acquisition actions, demonstration activities or information actions;

(b) the costs of travel, accommodation and per diem expenses of the participants;

(c) the costs of the provision of replacement services during the absence of the participants;

(d) in the case of demonstration projects the following investment costs are also eligible:

(i) the construction, acquisition, including leasing, or improvement of immovable property, with land only being eligible to an extent not exceeding 10% of total eligible costs of the operation concerned;

(ii) the purchase or lease purchase of machinery and equipment up to the market value of the asset;

(iii) general costs linked to expenditure referred to in points (i) and (ii), such as architect, engineer and consultation fees, fees relating to advice on environmental and economic sustainability, including feasibility studies; feasibility studies remain eligible expenditure even where, based on their results, no expenditure under points (i) and (ii) is incurred;

(iv) acquisition or development of computer software and the acquisitions of patents, licences, copyrights and trademarks;

(v) where duly justified, aid for small-scale demonstration projects may be granted for additional expenses and income foregone relating to the demonstration project.

(294) The costs referred to in point (293)(d) (i) to (iv) are eligible to the extent used for the demonstration project and for the duration period of the demonstration project. Only the depreciation costs corresponding to the life of the demonstration project, as calculated on the basis of generally accepted accounting principles are considered as eligible.

(295) Bodies providing knowledge transfer and information services must have the appropriate capacities in the form of staff qualifications and regular training to carry out those tasks.

[(296) Aid referred to in point (293)(a) and (c) and (d)(i) to (iv) must not involve direct payments to the beneficiaries and must be paid to the provider of knowledge transfer and information action. Aid for the costs of the provision of replacement services referred to in point (293)(c) may, alternatively, be paid directly to the provider of the replacement services. Aid referred to in point (293)(d)(v) must be paid directly to the beneficiaries. Aid for small-scale demonstration projects, referred to in point (293)(d)(i) to (iv), may be paid directly to the beneficiaries.]

Aid intensity

(297) The aid intensity must be limited to 100% of the eligible costs.

(298) In the case of eligible costs referred to in point (293)(d) the maximum aid amount must be limited to EUR 100,000 over 3 fiscal years.

1.1.10.2.
Aid for advisory services

(299) The Commission will consider aid for the provision of advisory services compatible with the internal market under Article 107(3)(c) of the Treaty if it complies with the common assessment principles of these Guidelines, with the general conditions for aid for technical support and with the following conditions.

(300) The aid should be designed to help undertakings active the agricultural sector and young farmers benefit from the use of advisory services for the improvement of the economic and environmental performance as well as the climate friendliness and resilience of their undertaking and/or investment.

(301) The advice must be linked to at least one Union priority for rural development and must cover as a minimum one of the following elements:

(a) Obligations deriving from the statutory management requirements and/or standards for good agricultural and environmental conditions provided in Chapter I of Title VI of Regulation (EU) No 1306/2013;

(b) where applicable, the agricultural practices beneficial for the climate and the environment as laid down in Chapter 3 of Title III of Regulation (EU) No 1307/2013 and the maintenance of the agricultural area as referred to in point (c) of Article 4(1) of that Regulation;
(c) measures aiming at farm modernization, competitiveness building, sectoral integration, innovation and market orientation as well as the promotion of entrepreneurship;
(d) requirements defined by Member States for implementing Article 11(3) of the Water Framework Directive;
(e) requirements defined by Member States for implementing Article 55 of Regulation (EC) 1107/2009 of the European Parliament and of the Council,[66] and in particular compliance with the general principles of integrated pest management as referred to in Article 14 of Sustainable Use of Pesticides Directive;[66]
(f) where relevant occupational safety standards and safety standards linked to farms;
(g) specific advice for farmers setting up for the first time, including advice on economic and environmental sustainability.

[(302) Advice may cover other issues and in particular the information related to climate change mitigation and adaptation, biodiversity and protection of waters as laid down in Annex I to Regulation (EU) No 1306/2013 or issues linked to the economic and environmental performance of the agricultural holding, including competitiveness aspects. This may include advice for the development of short supply chains, organic farming and health aspects of animal husbandry.]

(303) The aid must not involve direct payments to the beneficiaries. The aid must be paid to the advisory services provider.

(304) The bodies selected to provide the advisory service must have the appropriate resources in the form of regularly trained and qualified staff and advisory experience and reliability with respect to the fields they advise in.

(305) When providing advice, the advisory service providers must respect the non-disclosure obligations referred to in Article 13(2) of Regulation (EU) No 1306/2013.

(306) Where duly justified and appropriate, the advice may be partly provided in group, while taking into account the situation of the individual user of advisory services.

Aid amount

(307) The amount of aid is limited to EUR 1 500 per advice.

1.1.10.3. *Aid for farm replacement services*

(308) The Commission will consider aid for farm replacement services compatible with the internal market under Article 107(3)(c) of the Treaty if it complies with the common assessment principles of these Guidelines, with the general conditions for aid for technical support and with the following conditions.

(309) The aid must not involve direct payments to the farmer. The aid must be paid to the provider of the farm replacement service.

Eligible costs

[(310) Aid covers the real costs incurred for the replacement of a farmer, a natural person who is a member of farm household, or a farm worker, during their absence from work due to illness, including illness of their child, holidays, maternity and parental leave, mandatory military service or in case of death.]

[(311) The total duration of the replacement should be limited to three months per year per beneficiary, with the exception of replacement for maternity and parental leave and replacement during mandatory military service. For maternity and parental leave, the duration of the replacement shall be limited to six months in each case. However, in duly justified cases the Commission may authorize a longer time period. For mandatory military service, the duration of the replacement shall be limited to the duration of the service.]

Aid intensity

(312) The aid intensity is limited to 100% of the eligible costs.

1.1.11. Aid for co-operation in the agricultural sector

(313) The Commission will consider aid for co-operation in the agricultural sector compatible with the internal market under Article 107(3)(c) of the Treaty if it complies with the common assessment principles of these Guidelines and with the following conditions.

(314) This Section applies to the whole agricultural sector.[67]

(315) Aid should be granted in order to promote forms of cooperation involving at least two entities irrespective of whether they are active in the agricultural sector, but subject to the cooperation benefitting only the agricultural sector, and in particular:
(a) co-operation approaches among different undertakings in the agricultural sector, food chain (only if the result of the processing is an agricultural product) and other actors active in the agricultural sector that contribute to achieving the objectives and priorities of rural development policy, including producer groups, cooperatives and inter-branch organisation;
(b) the creation of clusters and networks;
(c) the establishment and operation of operational groups of the EIP for agricultural productivity and sustainability as referred to in Article 56 of Regulation (EU) No 1305/2013.

(316) The aid will be granted for cooperation relating, in particular, to the following activities:

(a) pilot projects;
(b) the development of new products, practices, processes and technologies in the agricultural sector and food sector only as far as agricultural products are concerned;
(c) co-operation among small operators in the agricultural sector in organizing joint work processes and sharing facilities and resources;
(d) horizontal and vertical co-operation among supply chain actors for the establishment and development of short supply chains and local markets;
(e) promotion activities in a local context relating to the development of short supply chain and local markets;
(f) joint action undertaken with a view to mitigating or adapting to climate change;
(g) joint approaches to environmental projects and ongoing environmental practices including efficient water management, the use of renewable energy[68] and the preservation of agricultural landscapes;
(h) horizontal and vertical cooperation among supply chain actors in the sustainable provision of biomass for use in food production if the result is an agricultural product and energy production for own consumption;
(i) implementation, in particular by groups of public and private partners other than those defined in point (b) of Article 32(2) of Regulation (EU) No 1303/2013, of local development strategies other than those defined in Article 2(19) of Regulation (EU) No 1303/2013 addressing one or more of the Union priorities for rural development.

(317) Aid for the creation of clusters and networks must be granted only to newly formed clusters and networks and those commencing an activity that is new to them.

(318) Aid for the activities referred to in point (316)(a) and (b) may be granted also to individual actors. Where aid is granted to individual actors, the results of the supported project or activity must be disseminated.

(319) Aid for the establishment and development of short supply chains, as referred to in point (316)(d) and (e) must cover only supply chains involving no more than one intermediary between farmer and consumer.

(320) Aid under this Section should comply with the relevant provisions of competition law, in particular with Articles 101 and 102 of the Treaty, as they apply by virtue of Articles 206 to 210 of Regulation (EU) No 1308/2013.

Eligible costs

(321) Aid covers the following eligible costs in so far as they concern agricultural activities:
(a) the costs for studies of the area concerned, of feasibility studies, and of drawing up a business plan or local development strategy other than the one referred to in Article 33 of Regulation (EU) No 1303/2013;
(b) the costs of animation of the area concerned in order to make feasible a collective territorial project or a project to be carried out by an operational group of the EIP for Agricultural Productivity and Sustainability as referred to in Article 56 of Regulation (EU) No 1305/2013. In the case of clusters, animation may also concern the organisation of training, networking between members and the recruitment of new members;
(c) the running costs of co-operation, such as the salary of a 'co-ordinator';
(d) the direct costs of specific projects linked to the implementation of a business plan, environmental plan, a local development strategy other than the one referred to in Article 33 of Regulation (EU) No 1303/2013 or other actions aiming at innovation including testing; direct costs must be limited to the eligible costs of investment aid, as specified in Section 1.1.1.1 of Part II of these Guidelines on investment aid;
(e) the costs for promotion activities.

(322) Aid must be limited to a maximum period of seven years except for collective environmental action in duly justified cases.

Aid intensity

(323) The aid may reach up to 100% of the eligible costs.

(324) Direct costs, referred to in point (321)(d) above, must be limited to the maximum aid intensity of investment aid, as specified in the Section on investment aid.

1.2. Risk and crisis management

(325) The granting of State aid may be an appropriate means of support with regards to certain types of risks in the agricultural sector, as the agricultural activity as a whole is particularly exposed to risks and crises. Differences exist, however, between undertakings active in primary agricultural production and undertakings active in the processing of agricultural products and their marketing, which normally have better possibilities to hedge risks. Some categories of aid in this Section will therefore only be available for undertakings active in primary agricultural production.

(326) When granting State aid to activities affected by the risks and crises, the Commission will take into consideration the need to avoid undue distortions of competition, by requiring a minimum contribution from producers to losses or the cost of such aid measures or some other adequate measures which should be taken to mitigate the risk of distortion of competition and ensure that the State aid is proportionate to the losses suffered. In its assessment, the Commission will take into account the need for the beneficiary to take adequate preventive measures to minimise the total amount of aid granted.

1.2.1.
Aids to compensate for the damage to agricultural production or the means of agricultural production and to prevent damage

1.2.1.1.
Aid to make good the damage caused by natural disasters or exceptional occurrences

(327) The Commission will consider aid to make good the damage caused by natural disasters or exceptional occurrences compatible with the internal market under Article 107(2) (b) of the Treaty if it complies with the following conditions.

(328) This Section applies to the agricultural sector.[69]

(329) As they constitute exceptions to the general prohibition of State aid within the internal market laid down in Article 107(1) of the Treaty, the Commission has consistently held that the notions of 'natural disaster' and 'exceptional occurrence' referred to in Article 107(2)(b) of the Treaty must be interpreted restrictively.

This has been confirmed by the Court of Justice of the European Union.[70]

(330) To date, the Commission has accepted that earthquakes, avalanches, landslides and floods may constitute natural disasters. In addition, it takes account of the development within the framework of the State aid modernization initiative which permits to block exempt also the following categories of natural disaster events: tornadoes, hurricanes, volcanic eruptions and wild fires of natural origin. Exceptional occurrences which have been accepted in the past by the Commission include war, internal disturbances or strikes, and, with certain reservations and depending on their extent, major nuclear or industrial accidents and fires which result in widespread loss.[71] The Commission will continue to evaluate proposals to grant State aid in accordance with Article 107(2)(b) of the Treaty on a case by case basis, having regard to its previous practice in this field.

(331) Aid granted under this Section is subject to the following conditions:

(a) the competent authority of the Member State has formally recognized the character of the event as a natural disaster or as exceptional occurrence; and

(b) there is a direct causal link between the natural disaster or the exceptional occurrence and the damage suffered by the undertaking.

(332) Member States may, where appropriate, establish in advance criteria on the basis of which the formal recognition referred to in point (331)(a) is deemed to be granted.

(333) Aid must be paid directly to the undertaking concerned or to a producer group or organization of which that undertaking is a member. Where the aid is paid to a producer group and organization, the amount of aid must not exceed the amount of aid to which that undertaking is eligible.

[(334) The aid scheme must be established within three years from the date of the occurrence of the event, and the aid must be paid out within four years of that date. For a specific natural disaster or exceptional occurrence, the Commission will authorise separately notified aid that derogates from this rule in duly justified cases, for example due to the nature and/or extent of the event or delayed or continuing nature of the damage.]

(335) In order to facilitate rapid crisis management, the Commission will authorize ex-ante framework aid schemes to compensate for the damage caused by earthquakes, avalanches, landslides and floods as well as by tornadoes, hurricanes, volcanic eruptions and wild fires of natural origin, provided that the conditions under which aid can be granted in cases of such natural disasters are clearly stipulated.[72] In the case of ex-ante schemes Member States must comply with the reporting obligation set out in point (728).

(336) Aid granted to compensate for the damage caused by other types of natural disasters not mentioned in point (330) and for damage caused by exceptional occurrences, must be individually notified to the Commission.

Eligible costs

(337) The eligible costs are the costs of the damage incurred as a direct consequence of the natural disaster or exceptional occurrence, as assessed either by a public authority, by an independent expert recognized by the granting authority or by an insurance undertaking.

(338) The damage may include the following:

(a) material damage to assets such as buildings, equipment, machinery, stocks and means of production;

(b) loss of income resulting from the full or partial destruction of the agricultural production and the means of the agricultural production.

(339) The damage must be calculated at the level of the individual beneficiary.

(340) The calculation of the material damage must be based on the repair cost or economic value of the affected asset before the natural disaster or the exceptional occurrence. It must not exceed the repair cost or the decrease in fair market value caused by the natural disaster or by the exceptional occurrence, that is to say the difference between the property's value immediately before and immediately after the natural disaster or the exceptional occurrence.

(341) The loss of income must be calculated by subtracting:

(a) the result of multiplying the quantity of the agricultural products produced in the year of the natural disaster or the exceptional occurrence, or in each following year affected by the full or partial destruction of the means of production, by the average selling price obtained during that year;

from

(b) the result of multiplying the average annual quantity of agricultural products produced in the three-year period preceding the natural disaster or the exceptional occurrence or a three year average based on the five-year period preceding the natural disaster or the exceptional occurrence, excluding the highest and lowest entry by the average selling price obtained.

(342) That amount may be increased by other costs incurred by the beneficiary due to the natural disaster or the exceptional occurrence and it must be reduced by any costs not incurred because of the natural disaster or the exceptional occurrence which would otherwise have been incurred by the beneficiary.

(343) Indexes may be used in order to calculate the annual agricultural production of the beneficiary provided that the calculation method used permits the determination of the real loss of an individual beneficiary in a given year.

(344) The Commission will accept other methods for the calculation of damage provided it is satisfied that these are representative, not based on abnormally high yields and do not result in the overcompensation of any beneficiary. The measurement of the extent of the damage may be tailored to the specific characteristics of each type of product using:

(a) biological indexes (quantity of biomass loss) or equivalent yield loss indexes established at farm, local, regional or national level; or

(b) weather indexes (including quantity of rainfall and temperature) established at local, regional or national level.

Aid intensity

(345) The aid and any other payments received to compensate the damage, including payments under insurance policies, must be limited to 100% of the eligible costs.

1.2.1.2.
Aid to compensate for damage caused by adverse climatic event which can be assimilated to a natural disaster

(346) The Commission will consider aid to compensate for the damage caused by an adverse climatic event which can be assimilated to a natural disaster compatible with the internal market under Article 107(3)(c) of the Treaty if it complies with the common assessment principles and with the following conditions.

(347) This Section applies to aid granted to compensate for damage caused by an adverse climatic event which can be assimilated to a natural disaster as defined in [point (35).34] in these Guidelines. It applies only to undertakings active in the primary agricultural production.

(348) Aid granted under this Section is subject to the following conditions:

(a) the competent authority of the Member State concerned has formally recognized the character of the event as an adverse climatic event which can be assimilated to a natural disaster;

and

(b) there is a direct causal link between the adverse climatic event which can be assimilated to a natural disaster and the damage suffered by the undertaking.

(349) Member States may, where appropriate, establish in advance criteria on the basis of which the formal recognition referred to in point (348)(a) is deemed to be granted.

(350) In the case of ex-ante schemes, Member States must comply with the reporting obligation set out in point (728).

(351) The aid must be paid directly to the undertaking concerned or to a producer group or organization of which that undertaking is a member. Where the aid is paid to a producer group or organization, the amount of aid must not exceed the amount of aid to which that undertaking is eligible.

(352) Aid schemes must be established within three years from the date of the occurrence of the adverse climatic event which can be assimilated to a natural disaster. The aid must be paid out within four years from that date.

Eligible costs

(353) The eligible costs are the damage incurred as a direct consequence of the adverse climatic event which can be assimilated to a natural disaster, as assessed either by a public authority, by an independent expert recognised by the granting authority or by an insurance undertaking.

(354) The damage includes the following:

(a) the material damage to assets such as farm buildings, equipment and machinery, stocks and means of production;

(b) the loss of income from the full or partial destruction of the agricultural production and the means of production.

(355) The calculation of the damage incurred due to the adverse climatic event which can be assimilated to a natural disaster must be made at the level of the individual beneficiary.

(356) The material damage to assets caused by the adverse climatic event which can be assimilated to a natural disaster must be calculated on the basis of the repair cost or economic value of the affected asset before the adverse climatic event that can be assimilated to a natural disaster. It must not exceed the repair cost or the decrease in fair market value caused by the adverse climatic event which can be assimilated to a natural disaster, that is to say the difference between the asset's value immediately before and immediately after the adverse climatic event which can be assimilated to a natural disaster.

(357) Where the reduction of the beneficiary's income referred to in point (354) (b) is calculated on the basis of crop or livestock level, only the material damage related to that crop or livestock should be taken into account.

(358) The loss of income must be calculated either at annual farm production level or at crop or livestock level by subtracting:

(a) the result of multiplying the quantity of the agricultural products produced in the year of the adverse climatic event which can be assimilated to a natural disaster, or each following year affected by the full or partial destruction of the means of production, by the average selling price obtained during that year;

from

(b) the result of multiplying the average annual quantity of agricultural products produced in the three-year period preceding the adverse climatic event which can be assimilated to a natural disaster, or a three year average based on the five-year period preceding the adverse climatic event which can be assimilated to a natural disaster, excluding the highest and lowest entry by the average selling price obtained.

(359) That amount may be increased by other costs incurred by the beneficiary due to the adverse climatic event which can be assimilated to a natural disaster. That amount must be reduced by any costs not incurred because of the adverse climatic event which can be assimilated to a natural disaster which would otherwise have been incurred by the beneficiary.

(360) Indexes may be used in order to calculate the annual agricultural production of the beneficiary provided that the calculation method used permits the determination of the real loss of an individual beneficiary in a given year.

(361) The Commission will accept other methods for the calculation of damage provided that it is satisfied that these are representative, not based on abnormally high yields and do not result in overcompensation of any beneficiary. The measurement of the extent of the damage may be tailored to the specific characteristics of each type of product using:

(a) biological indexes (quantity of biomass loss) or equivalent yield loss indexes established at farm, local, regional or national level; or

(b) weather indexes (including quantity of rainfall and temperature) established at local, regional or national level.

Aid intensity

(362) The aid and any other payments received to compensate for the damage, including payments under other national or Union measures or insurance policies for the damage receiving aid, must be limited to 80% of the eligible costs. The aid intensity may be increased to 90% in areas facing natural constraints.

(363) Aid granted under this Section must be reduced by 50% unless it is given to beneficiaries who have taken out insurance covering at least 50% of their average annual production or production-related income and the statistically most frequent climatic risks in the Member State or region concerned for which insurance coverage is provided. Derogation from this condition is only possible if a Member State can convincingly show that, despite all reasonable efforts, affordable insurance covering the statistically most frequent climatic risks in the Member State or region concerned was not available at the time the damage occurred.

1.2.1.3.

Aid for the costs of the prevention, control and eradication of animal diseases and plant pests and aid to make good the damage caused by animal diseases and plant pests

(364) The Commission will consider aid for the costs of the prevention, control and eradication of animal diseases or plant pests and aid to make good the damage caused by those animal diseases or plant pests compatible with the internal market under Article 107(3)(c) of the Treaty if it complies with the common assessment principles of these Guidelines and with the following conditions.

(365) This Section applies to aid granted to undertakings active in the primary agricultural production.

(366) Aid may only be paid:

(a) in relation to animal diseases or plant pests for which Union or national rules exist, whether laid down by law, regulation or administrative action; and

(b) as part of:

(i) a public programme at Union, national or regional level for the prevention, control or eradication of the animal disease or the plant pest concerned; or

(ii) emergency measures imposed by the competent public authority; or

(iii) measures to eradicate or contain a plant pest implemented in accordance with Council Directive 2000/29/EC of 8 May 2000 on protective measures against the introduction into the Community of organisms harmful to plants or plant products and against their spread within the Community.[73]

(367) The programmes and measures referred to in point (366)(b) must contain a description of the prevention, control and eradication measures concerned.

(368) The aid must not relate to measures in respect of which Union legislation provides that the cost of such measures is to be borne by the beneficiary, unless the cost of such aid measures is entirely offset by compulsory charges on the beneficiaries.

(369) The aid must be paid directly to the undertaking concerned or to a producer group or organisation of which that undertaking is a member. Where the aid is paid to a producer group or organisation, the amount of aid must not exceed the amount of aid to which that undertaking is eligible.

(370) No individual aid should be granted where it is established that the disease or the infestation with the plant pest was caused deliberately or by the negligence of the beneficiary.

(371) As regards animal diseases, the aid may only be granted in respect of diseases referred to in the list of animal diseases established by the World Organisation for Animal Health or the animal diseases and zoo-noses listed in Annexes I and II to Regulation (EU) No 652/2014 of the European Parliament and of the Council.[74]

(372) Aid schemes must be introduced within three years from the date of the occurrence of the cost or damage caused by the animal disease or plant pest. Aid must be paid out within four years from that date.

(373) In the case of ex-ante schemes Member States must comply with the reporting obligation set out in point (728).

Eligible costs

(374) [In the case of prevention measures (i.e. measures regarding an animal disease or plant pest that has not yet occurred), the aid may cover the following eligible costs:]

- (a) health checks;
- (b) analyses including in vitro diagnostics;
- (c) tests and other screening measures including TSE and BSE tests;
- (d) the purchase, storage, administration and distribution of vaccines, medicines, substances for the treatment of animals and plant protection products;
- (e) the preventive slaughtering or culling of animals or the destruction of animal products and plants and the cleaning and disinfection of the holding and equipment;

(375) [In the case of control and eradication measures (i.e. measures regarding animal diseases for which a competent authority has formally recognised an outbreak, or plant pests for which a competent authority has formally acknowledged their presence), the aid may cover the following eligible costs:]

- (a) tests and other screening measures in the case of animal diseases, including TSE and BSE tests;
- (b) the purchase, storage, administration and distribution of vaccines, medicines, substances for the treatment of animals and plant protection products;
- (c) the slaughter or culling and destruction of animals and the destruction of products linked to them or destruction of plants, including those that die or are destroyed as a result of vaccination or other measures ordered by the competent public authorities and the cleaning and disinfection of the holding and equipment.

(376) The aid in relation to eligible costs referred to in points (374) and (375) must be granted in kind and must be paid to the provider of the prevention and eradication measures with the exception of eligible costs referred to in points (374)(d) and (375)(b) and eligible costs referred to in points (374)(e) and (375)(c) in the case of plant pests and for the cleaning and disinfection of the holding and equipment.

(377) In the case of aid to make good the damage caused by animal diseases or plant pests, compensation must be calculated only in relation to the following:

- (a) the market value of the animals slaughtered or culled or that have died or the products linked to them, or the plants destroyed:
  - (i) as a result of the animal disease or plant pest;
  - (ii) as part of a public programme or measure referred to in point (366)(b) of these Guidelines;
- (b) the loss of income due to quarantine obligations and difficulties in restocking or replanting and obligatory crop-rotation imposed as part of a public programme or measure as referred to in point (366)(b).

(378) That amount must be reduced by any costs not directly incurred due to the animal disease or plant pest which would otherwise have been incurred by the beneficiary.

(379) The market value referred to in point (377)(a) must be established on the basis of the value of the animals, products and plants immediately before any suspicion of the animal disease or plant pest arose or was confirmed.

(380) The aid referred to in point (377) must be limited to the costs and damage caused by animal diseases and plant pests for which the competent authority:

- (a) has formally recognised an outbreak, in the case of an animal disease; or
- (b) has formally acknowledged their presence, in the case of plant pests.

(381) In exceptional and duly justified cases, the Commission may accept the costs incurred in carrying out necessary measures other than those referred to in this Section.

Aid intensity

(382) The aid and any other payments received by the beneficiary, including payments under other national or Union measures or insurance policies for the same eligible costs, must be limited to 100% of the eligible costs.

1.2.1.4.
Aid for fallen stock

(383) The Commission will consider aid for fallen stock compatible with the internal market under Article 107(3)(c) of the Treaty if it complies with the common assessment principles of these Guidelines and with the following conditions.

(384) This Section applies to undertakings active in the primary agricultural production.

Aid intensity in relation to eligible costs:

(385) In relation to the below listed eligible costs, the following aid intensities apply:

- (a) aid at a rate of up to 100% of the costs for the removal of fallen stock, and 75% of the costs for the destruction of such fallen stock; aid towards the costs of premiums for insurance covering the costs of the removal and destruction of fallen stock may be granted in accordance with the provisions of Section 1.2.1.6 of Part II of these Guidelines;
- (b) aid at a rate of up to 100% of the costs for the removal and destruction of fallen stock where the aid is financed through fees or through compulsory contributions destined for the financing of the removal and destruction of such fallen stock, provided that such fees or contributions are limited to and directly imposed on the meat sector;
- (c) aid at a rate of 100% of the costs for the removal and destruction of fallen stock where there is an obligation to perform TSE tests on the fallen stock concerned or in the case of an outbreak of an animal disease referred to in point (371) of these guidelines;

(386) The aid must be conditional on the existence of a consistent monitoring programme which ensures the safe disposal of all fallen stock in the Member State concerned.

(387) The aid must be provided in kind and must not involve direct payments to the beneficiaries, except where the livestock breeder who is the beneficiary of the aid acts also as service provider.

(388) In order to facilitate the administration of the aid, the aid may be paid to economic operators or bodies that:

(a) are active downstream from the undertakings active in the livestock sector; and

(b) provide services linked to the removal and destruction of fallen stock.

(389) In relation to fallen stock and slaughterhouse waste, the Commission will maintain its policy not to authorise aid for fallen stock given to operators active in the processing of agricultural products and the marketing of agricultural products and aid towards the costs of disposal of slaughterhouse waste. State aid for investments undertaken in relation to the disposal of slaughterhouse waste will be examined under the relevant rules applying to investment aid.

1.2.1.5.
Aid to compensate for the damage caused by protected animals

(390) Damage to equipment, infrastructure, animals and plants caused by protected animals is a growing problem. The success of Union conservation policy depends partly on the effective management of conflicts between protected animals and farmers. As a consequence, and in respect of the principle of proportionality, the Commission will consider aid to compensate for the damage caused by protected animals compatible with the internal market under Article 107(3)(c) of the Treaty if it complies with the common assessment principles of these Guidelines and with the following conditions.

(391) This Section applies to undertakings active in the primary agricultural production.

(392) A minimum counterpart from the beneficiaries is requested to mitigate the risk of distortions of competition and to provide an incentive for minimising risk. This contribution must take the form of reasonable preventive measures, such as safety fences where possible, livestock guarding dogs, which are proportionate to the risk of damage caused by protected animals in the area concerned. If no reasonable preventive measures are possible, the Member State concerned should demonstrate the impossibility to take such preventive measures in order for the aid to be considered compatible.

(393) A direct causal link between the damage suffered and the behaviour of the protected animal must be established by the Member State.

(394) Aid must be paid directly to the undertaking concerned or to a producer group or organisation of which that undertaking is a member. Where the aid is paid to a producer group and organisation, the amount of aid must not exceed the amount of aid to which that undertaking is eligible.

(395) The aid scheme must be established within a period of three years from the date of the occurrence of the damaging event. The aid must be paid out within four years from that date.

Eligible costs

(396) The eligible costs are the costs of the damage incurred as a direct consequence of the event that caused the damage, as assessed either by a public authority, by an independent expert recognized by the granting authority or by an insurance undertaking.

(397) The damage may include the following:

(a) damage for animals killed or plants destroyed: the eligible costs are based on the market value of the animal killed or of the plants destroyed by the protected animals;

(b) indirect costs: veterinary costs resulting from the treatment of wounded animals and labour costs related to the search for missing animals;

(c) the material damage to the following assets: to farm equipment, machinery and farm buildings and stocks; the calculation of the material damage must be based on the repair cost or economic value of the affected asset before the event that caused the damage; it must not exceed the repair cost or the decrease in fair market value caused by the event causing the damage, that is to say the difference between the property's value immediately before and immediately after the event.

(398) The amount must be reduced by any costs not incurred because of the event causing the damage, which would otherwise have been incurred by the beneficiary.

(399) The damage must be calculated at the level of the individual beneficiary.

(400) Investments related to measures to prevent damage by protected animals, may be supported under the conditions of the Section 1.1.1.1 of Part II of these Guidelines on investment aid in agricultural holdings.

Aid intensity

(401) Compensation may be granted up to 100% of the eligible costs.

(402) . . .

[(403) The aid and any other payments received to compensate for the damage, including payments under other national or Union measures or insurance policies for the damage receiving aid, must be limited to 100 % of the eligible costs.]

1.2.1.6.
Aid for the payment of insurance premiums

(404) In many instances, insurance is a most helpful tool for good risk and crisis management. Therefore, and in view of the often reduced financing possibilities of farmers, the Commission takes a positive view as regards State aid for insurance premiums where the insurance concerns primary agricultural production.

(405) The Commission will consider aid for the payment of insurance premiums compatible with the internal market under Article 107(3)(c) of the Treaty if it complies with the common assessment principles of these Guidelines and with the following conditions.

(406) This Section applies to undertakings active in the primary agricultural production.

(407) The aid must not constitute a barrier to the operation of the internal market for insurance services. In particular, the aid must not be limited to insurance provided by a single insurance company or group of companies, or be made subject to the condition that the insurance contract be taken out with a company established in the Member State concerned.

(408) Reinsurance schemes will be examined on a case-by-case basis.

Eligible costs

(409) The eligible costs are the costs of insurance premiums for insurance to cover the damage caused by natural disasters or exceptional occurrences, adverse climatic events which can be assimilated to a natural disaster, animal diseases and plant pests, the removal and destruction of fallen stock and damage caused by protected animals, as specified in Sections 1.2.1.1, 1.2.1.2, 1.2.1.3, 1.2.1.4 and 1.2.1.5, as well as by other adverse climatic events and/or damage caused by environmental incidents.

(410) The insurance may compensate only the cost of making good the damage referred to in point (409) above and may not require or specify the type or quantity of future production.

(411) In respect of aid for insurance premiums for insurance against losses caused by environmental incidents, the following additional conditions must be fulfilled: the occurrence of an environmental incident must be formally recognised as such by the competent authority of the Member State concerned. Member States may, where appropriate, establish in advance criteria on the basis of which that formal recognition is deemed to be granted. Indexes referred to in points (360) and (361) may be used in order to calculate the annual agricultural production of the beneficiary and the extent of the loss.

Aid intensity

(412) The gross aid intensity must not exceed 65% of the cost of the insurance premium, with the exception of aid for the removal and destruction of fallen stock, where the aid intensity must not exceed 100% of the cost of the insurance premium as regards insurance premiums for the removal of fallen stock and 75% of the cost of the insurance premium as regards insurance premiums for the destruction of such fallen stock.

(413) Member States may limit the amount of the insurance premium that is eligible for aid by applying appropriate ceilings.

1.2.1.7.
Aid for financial contributions to mutual funds

(414) The Commission will consider aid for financial contributions to mutual funds to pay compensation to farmers for the damage caused by adverse climatic events which can be assimilated to a natural disaster, animal diseases and plant pests as specified in Sections 1.2.1.2. and 1.2.1.3. and/or for the damage caused by environmental incidents compatible with the internal market under Article 107(3)(c) of the Treaty if it complies with the common assessment principles of these Guidelines and with the following conditions.

(415) This Section applies to undertakings active in the primary agricultural production.

(416) The mutual fund concerned must:

(a) be accredited by the competent authority in accordance with national law;
(b) have a transparent policy towards payments into and withdrawals from the fund;
(c) have clear rules attributing responsibilities for any debts incurred.

(417) Member States must define the rules for the constitution and management of the mutual funds, in particular for the granting of compensation payments, as well as for the administration and monitoring of compliance with these rules. Member States must ensure that the fund arrangements provide for penalties in case of negligence on the part of the undertaking.

Eligible costs

(418) Eligible are the costs of financial contributions to mutual funds to pay compensation to farmers for the damage caused by adverse climatic events which can be assimilated to a natural disaster, animal diseases and plant pests as specified in Sections 1.2.1.2. and 1.2.1.3. and/or for the damage caused by environmental incidents. The financial contributions may only relate to the amounts paid by the mutual fund as financial compensation to undertakings active in the primary agricultural production.

(419) In respect of aid for financial contributions to mutual funds to pay compensation for the damage caused by environmental incidents, the following additional conditions apply: the occurrence of an environmental incident has to be formally recognised as such by the competent authority of the Member State concerned. Member States may,

where appropriate, establish in advance criteria on the basis of which the formal recognition referred to is deemed to be granted. Indexes referred to in points (360) and (361) may be used in order to calculate the annual agricultural production of the beneficiary and the extent of the loss.

Aid intensity

(420) The aid must be limited to 65% of the eligible costs.

(421) Member States may limit the costs that are eligible for aid by applying:
(a) ceilings per fund;
(b) appropriate per member/affiliate to the fund ceilings.

1.2.2.
Aid for Closing Production Capacity

(422) This Section applies to the whole of the agricultural sector.[75]

1.2.2.1.
Closing of capacity for animal, plant or human health, sanitary, ethical or environmental reasons

(423) The Commission will consider aid for the closing of capacity compatible with the internal market under Article 107(3)(c) of the Treaty if it complies with the common assessment principles of these Guidelines and with the following conditions.

(424) The closing of capacity is done for animal, plant or human health, sanitary, ethical or environmental reasons, such as the reduction of overall stocking densities.

(425) There must be a sufficient counterpart from the beneficiary of the aid. This counterpart will consist of a definitive and irrevocable decision to scrap or irrevocably close the production capacity concerned. This will involve either the complete closure of capacity by the undertaking concerned or where duly justified, the partial closure of capacity. Legally binding commitments must be obtained from the beneficiary that the closure of the production capacity concerned is definitive and irreversible and that the beneficiary will not start the same activity elsewhere. These commitments must also bind any future purchaser of the land or facility concerned.

(426) Only undertakings that have actually been producing, and only production capacities that have actually been in constant use over the past five years before the closing of capacity are eligible for aid. In cases where the production capacity has already closed definitively, or where such closure appears inevitable, there is no counterpart from the beneficiary, and aid may not be granted.

(427) The Commission reserves the right to attach additional conditions to the authorisation of the aid.

(428) Only undertakings fulfilling Union standards are eligible for aid. Undertakings which do not fulfil Union standards and which would be obliged to stop production anyway are excluded.

(429) In order to avoid erosion and other negative effects on the environment, open farmland taken out of production must in principle be afforested or turned into nature area within a period of two years and in such a way as to ensure that negative effects on the environment are avoided. Alternatively, open farmland may be re-used after 20 years following effective capacity closure. Until then, such farmland must be maintained in good agricultural and environmental condition, in accordance with Chapter I of Title VI of Regulation (EU) No 1306/2013, and with the relevant implementing rules. The closure of installations covered by Directive 2010/75/EU of the European Parliament and of the Council[76] must be carried out in accordance with Articles 11 and 22 of that Directive which requires that the necessary measures are taken to avoid any pollution risk and that the site of operation is returned to a satisfactory state.

(430) Aid granted under an aid scheme must be accessible to all eligible undertakings.

Eligible costs

(431) The aid covers the compensation for the loss of value of assets, measured as the current selling value of the assets.

(432) In addition to the compensation of loss of value of assets, for the closing of capacity for environmental reasons, an incentive payment, which may not exceed 20% of the value of the assets, may be given.

(433) Compensation may also be granted for the costs of the destruction of the production capacity.

(434) The aid may also be paid to offset the obligatory social costs resulting from the implementation of the closure decision.

(435) Aid for afforestation and conversion of land into nature areas must be granted in accordance with the rules set out in Sections 2.1.1. and 2.1.2 of Part II and the rules on non-productive investment set out in Section 1.1.1.1 of Part II.

Aid intensity

(436) The maximum aid amounts are as follows:
(a) up to 100% for compensation for the loss of value of assets, for compensation for the costs of the destruction of the production capacity and to offset the obligatory social costs resulting from the implementation of the closure decision;
(b) up to 120% for compensation for the loss of value of assets where the closure is done for environmental reasons.

1.2.2.2.
Closing of capacity for other reasons

(437) The Commission will consider aid for the closing of capacity for other reasons than those laid down in Section 1.2.2.1. compatible with the internal market under Article 107(3)(c) of the Treaty if it complies with the common assessment principles of these Guidelines and with the following conditions.

(438) The closure must be done for the restructuring of the sector, for diversification or for early retirement.

(439) The conditions in points (425) to (429) must be fulfilled.

(440) No aid may be granted which would interfere with the mechanisms of the common organisation of the markets in agricultural products. Aid schemes applying to sectors which are subject to production limits or quotas will be evaluated on a case-by-case basis.

(441) The aid must be part of a programme which has defined objectives and a specific timetable aimed at the restructuring of the sector, at diversification or at early retirement.

(442) In order to ensure a rapid impact on the market, the duration of aid schemes aimed at closing capacity should be limited to a period of not more than six months for collecting applications for participation, and a further period of twelve months for actually closing down. The Commission will not accept aid schemes with duration of more than three years, since experience shows that these may result in postponing the necessary changes.

(443) The aid scheme should be accessible to all economic operators in the sector concerned under the same conditions. In order to achieve maximum impact, the Member State should use a transparent system of calls for interest which publicly invites all potentially interested undertakings to participate; at the same time, the organisation of the aid scheme should be managed in such a way that it neither requires nor facilitates anticompetitive agreements or concerted practices between the undertakings concerned.

Eligible costs and aid intensity

(444) The provisions on eligible costs and on aid intensity of Section 1.2.2.1 of Part II of these Guidelines are applicable, with the exception of the costs under point (432).

1.3. Other types of aid in the agricultural sector

1.3.1.
Aid to the livestock sector

(445) The Commission takes a favourable view towards aid that contributes to the maintenance and improvement of the genetic quality of the Union livestock. It will therefore consider aid in the livestock sector compatible with the internal market under Article 107(3)(c) of the Treaty if it complies with the common assessment principles of these Guidelines and with the following conditions.

(446) This Section applies to SMEs active in the primary agricultural production. The Commission will not authorise State aid towards the costs covered by this Section in favour of large enterprises.

(447) The aid should be provided in kind and should not involve direct payments to the beneficiaries.

Eligible costs

(448) The aid covers the establishment and maintenance of herd books as well as tests performed by or on behalf of third parties, to determine the genetic quality or yield of livestock, with the exception of controls undertaken by the owner of the livestock and routine controls of milk quality.

(449) The eligible costs include:

(a) the following administrative costs of the establishment and maintenance of herd books referred to in point (448):
  - (i) the collection and administration of data on animals, for example, the. origin of an animal, its date of birth, its date of insemination, its date of death and reasons for it and the expert's evaluation, actualisation and processing of the data necessary for the establishment and maintenance of herd books;
  - (ii) the administrative works relating to the registration of relevant data on animals in the herd books;
  - (iii) the actualisation of software for managing data in the herd books;
  - (iv) the on-line publication of information about herd books and of data from the herd books; or
  - (v) other related administrative costs;

(b) the following costs for the tests to determine the genetic quality or yield of livestock referred to in point(448):
  - (i) the costs of tests or controls;
  - (ii) related costs of the collection and evaluation of the data received from such tests and controls with regard to increasing the animal health and the level of environmental protection;
  - (iii) related costs of the collection and evaluation of the data received from such tests and controls aiming at assessing the genetic quality of animals for the implementation of advanced breeding techniques and for keeping the genetic diversity; or
  - (iv) other related costs.

Aid intensity

(450) The aid may be authorised up to 100% for the financing of the administrative costs of the establishment and maintenance of herd books.

(451) The aid will be authorised up to 70% for the costs of tests performed by or on behalf of third parties, to determine the genetic quality or yield of livestock.

1.3.2.

Aid for promotion measures in favour of agricultural products

(452) The Commission will consider aid for the promotion of agricultural products compatible with the internal market under Article 107(3)(c) of the Treaty if it complies with the common assessment principles of these Guidelines and with the following conditions.

(453) This Section applies to the whole agricultural sector.[77] The beneficiaries of aid for the organisation of competitions, trade fairs or exhibitions, referred to in point (464)(a) must be limited to SMEs.

(454) The promotion activity must be designed either to inform the public about the characteristics of agricultural products, for example,. by organising competitions, by participating in trade fairs and public relations activities, by the vulgarisation of scientific knowledge, or by publications with factual information or to encourage economic operators or consumers to buy the agricultural product in question by way of promotion campaigns. [The promotion activity may be implemented in the internal market and in third countries.]

(455) The promotion campaign must be focused on products covered by quality schemes as referred to in point (282) or it must be generic in character and for the benefit of all producers of the type of product concerned.

[(456) The promotion campaign must comply with Regulation (EU) No 1169/2011 of the European Parliament and of the Council[78] and, where appropriate, with specific labelling rules.]

(457) Member States must send representative samples of promotion material when notifying an aid or an aid scheme for a promotion campaign. If that material is not available at the time of the notification, a commitment should be taken to provide it at a later stage and in any case before the launching of the promotion campaign.

(458) Promotion campaigns exceeding the notification threshold referred to in point (37)(b) must be notified individually.

(459) The provision of promotion measures may be undertaken by producer groups or other organisation regardless of their size. Where the promotion measure is undertaken by producer groups or other organisations, participation must not be subject to membership of those groups or organisations and any contribution in terms of administration fees for the group or organisation must be limited to the cost of providing the promotion measure.

(460) The aid must be granted:

- (a) in kind; or
- (b) on the basis of reimbursement of real costs incurred by the beneficiary.

(461) By way of derogation from point (460), aid for promotion campaigns must be granted only in kind by means of subsidised services.

(462) Where the aid is granted in kind, the aid must not include direct payments to the beneficiaries but must be paid to the provider of the promotion measures.

(463) The aid for symbolic prizes referred to in point (464)(a)(v) may only be paid to the provider of the promotion measures if the prize has been actually granted and upon presentation of a proof of the award.

Eligible costs

(464) The costs eligible for aid for the promotion of agricultural products within the Union are the following:

- (a) concerning the organisation of and participation in competitions, trade fairs and exhibitions, provided that aid is accessible to all those eligible in the area concerned, based on objectively defined conditions:
  - (i) participation fees;
  - (ii) travel costs and costs for the transportation of animals;
  - (iii) costs of publications and websites announcing the event;
  - (iv) the rent of premises and stands and costs of their installation and dismantling;
  - (v) symbolic prizes up to a value of EUR 1,000 per prize and per winner of a competition;
- (b) the costs of publications in print- and electronic media, websites, and spots in electronic media, on radio or television, aimed at presenting factual information about producers from a given region or producers of a given product, provided that the information is neutral and that all producers have equal opportunities to be represented in the publication;
- (c) the costs for the dissemination of scientific knowledge and factual information on
  - (i) quality schemes as referred to in point (282) open to agricultural products from other Member States and third countries;
  - (ii) generic agricultural products and their nutritional benefits and suggested uses for them;
- (d) the costs for consumer-targeted promotion campaigns organised in the media or at retail outlets as well as for all promotion material which is distributed directly to consumers.

Reference to particular undertaking, brand name or origin

[(465) The promotion activities referred to in point (464)(c) and promotion campaigns referred to in point (464)(d), and in particular promotion activities which are generic in character and for the benefit of all producers of the type of product concerned, must not mention any particular undertaking, brand name or origin. Promotion campaigns referred to in (464)(d) must not be earmarked for products of one or more particular company or companies. The Commission will not declare compatible State aid for promotion which risks endangering sales or denigrates products from other Member States.]

(466) However, the restriction on the reference to origin does not apply to promotion activities and promotion campaigns referred to in point (464)(c) and (d), focussed on products covered by quality schemes as referred to in point (282), provided the following conditions are fulfilled:

- (a) where the promotion activity focuses on Union-recognised denominations, it may refer to the origin of products provided that the reference corresponds exactly to that registered by the Union;

(b) where the activity concerns products covered by quality schemes other than schemes for Union-recognised denominations, the origin of the products may be mentioned provided it is secondary in the message. In order to determine whether the reference to origin is secondary, the Commission will take into account the overall amount of text and/or the size of the symbol including images as well as the general presentation referring to the origin as compared with the text and/or symbol referring to the key sales pitch, that is to say, the part of the promotion not focused on the origin of the product. The reference to the origin must not be discriminatory, must not aim at encouraging the consumption of the agricultural product on the sole ground of its origin, must respect the general principles of Union law and must not amount to a restriction of the free movement of agricultural products in breach of Article 34 of the Treaty.

Aid intensity

(467) The aid intensity for eligible costs, referred to in point (464)(a) to (c), will be up to 100% of the eligible costs.

[(468) The aid intensity for promotion campaigns focussed on products covered by quality schemes, referred to in point (464)(d) in conjunction with point (455), may not exceed 50% of the eligible costs of the campaign or 80% as regards promotion in third countries. If the sector contributes at least 50% of the costs, irrespective of the form of the contribution, for example special taxes, the aid intensity may be up to 100%.[79]]

(469) The aid intensity for generic promotion campaigns, referred to in point (464)(d) in conjunction with point (455), may cover up to 100% of eligible costs.

[Aid for promotion measures referred to in Article 45 of Regulation (EU) No 1308/2013]

[(470) The Commission will consider national payments granted by Member States for the promotion measures referred to in Article 45 of Regulation (EU) No 1308/2013 compatible with the internal market under Article 107(3)(c) of the Treaty if they comply with the common assessment principles of these Guidelines and with the rules on aid for the promotion measures set out in this Section, in particular points (453), second sentence, to (469).]

1.3.3.
Aid for the outermost regions and the smaller Aegean islands

(471) The Commission will consider aid for the outermost regions and the smaller Aegean islands compatible with the internal market under Article 107(3) of the Treaty if it complies with the common assessment principles of these Guidelines and with the following conditions.

(472) This Section applies to the whole agricultural sector.[80]

(473) With regard to the outermost regions, in accordance with Article 23(4) of Regulation (EU) No 228/2013, Articles 107, 108 and 109 of the Treaty do not apply as concerns the following aids granted by Member States in conformity with that Regulation:

(a) measures in favour of local agricultural productions under Chapter IV of that Regulation;
(b) aids granted by France to the sugar sector under Article 23(3) of that Regulation;
(c) aids for plant health programmes under Article 24 of that Regulation; and
(d) aids granted by Spain for the production of tobacco in the Canary Islands under Article 28 of that Regulation.

(474) Save in those cases, State aid rules do apply for measures with regard to the outermost regions, with the following particularity: Article 23(1) of Regulation (EU) No 228/2013 provides that the Commission may authorize operating aid in the sectors producing, processing and marketing of agricultural products falling within the scope of Annex I to the Treaty, to which Articles 107, 108 and 109 of the Treaty apply, with a view to alleviating the specific constraints on farming in the outermost regions as a result of their isolation, insularity and extreme remoteness.

(475) With regard to the smaller Aegean islands, in accordance with Article 17(3) of Regulation (EU) No 229/2013, Articles 107, 108 and 109 of the Treaty do not apply to payments made under Chapters III and IV of that Regulation by Greece in conformity with that Regulation.

(476) Save in those cases, State aid rules do apply for measures with regard to the smaller Aegean islands, with the following particularity: Article 17(1) of Regulation (EU) No 229/2013 provides that the Commission may authorize operating aid in the sectors producing, processing and marketing of agricultural products falling within the scope of Annex I of the Treaty, to which Articles 107, 108 and 109 of the Treaty apply, with a view to alleviating the specific constraints on farming in the smaller Aegean islands as a result of their insularity, small size, mountainous terrain and climate, their economic dependency on a small number of products and their distance from markets.

Eligible costs

(477) The additional transport costs of agricultural products which have been produced in the outermost regions and in the smaller Aegean islands are eligible for compensation subject to the following conditions:

(a) the beneficiaries have their production activity in the outermost regions or in the smaller Aegean islands;
(b) the aid is objectively quantifiable in advance on the basis of a fixed sum or per ton/kilometer ratio or any other relevant unit;
(c) the additional transport costs are calculated on the basis of the journey of the products inside the national border of the Member State concerned using the means of transport which results in the lowest costs for the beneficiary, taking into account the external costs to the environment;
(d) for outermost regions, the eligible additional transport costs may include the costs of transporting agricultural products from the place of their production to locations in outermost areas where they are further processed.

(478) The Commission will examine proposals to grant State aid for other costs than additional transport costs which is designed to meet the needs of the outermost regions and the smaller Aegean islands on a case-by-case basis, on the basis of the common assessment principles and the specific legal provisions applying to those regions, and having regard, if applicable, to the compatibility of the measures concerned with the rural development programmes for the regions concerned, and their effects on competition both in the regions concerned and in other parts of the Union.

1.3.4.
Aid for agricultural land consolidation

(479) The Commission will consider aid for agricultural land consolidation compatible with the internal market under Article 107(3)(c) of the Treaty if it complies with the common assessment principles of these Guidelines and with the following conditions.

Eligible costs

(480) The eligible costs must be limited to the legal, administrative and survey costs of land consolidation.

Aid intensity

(481) The aid intensity must be up to 100% of the real costs incurred.

1.3.5.
Aid for rescuing and restructuring undertakings in difficulty

[(482) Aid for rescuing and restructuring undertakings in difficulty in the agricultural sector will be assessed in accordance with the Guidelines on State aid for rescuing and restructuring non-financial undertakings in difficulty.[81]]

[(483) However, with regard to aid for rescuing and restructuring undertakings active in the primary agricultural production, instead of the period of 10 years set out in Section 3.6.1, point (71) of the Guidelines on State aid for rescuing and restructuring non-financial undertakings in difficulty, a five-year period will apply.]

1.3.6.
Aid for research and development in the agricultural sector

(484) The Commission will consider aid for research and development in the agricultural sector compatible with the internal market under Article 107(3) of the Treaty if it complies with the common assessment principles of these Guidelines and with the following conditions.

(485) This Section applies to the whole agricultural sector.[82]

(486) The aided project must be of interest to all undertakings active in the particular agricultural sector or sub-sector concerned.

(487) Prior to the date of the start of the aided project the following information must be published on the internet:

- (a) that the aided project is carried out;
- (b) the goals of the aided project;
- (c) an approximate date of the publication of the results expected from the aided project;
- (d) the place of publication on the internet of the results expected from the aided project on the internet;
- (e) reference that the results are available to all undertakings active in the particular agricultural sector or sub-sector concerned at no cost.

(488) The results of the aided project must be made available on internet from the end date of the aided project or the date on which any information concerning those results is given to members of any particular organisation, whatever comes first. The results must remain available on internet for a period of at least five years starting from the end date of the aided project.

(489) Aid must be granted directly to the research and knowledge-dissemination organisation. The measure must not involve the provision of aid based on the price of the agricultural products to undertakings active in the agricultural sector.

Eligible costs

(490) The eligible costs include the following:

- (a) personnel costs related to researchers, technicians and other supporting staff to the extent employed on the project;
- (b) costs of instruments and equipment to the extent and for the period used for the project. Where such instruments and equipment are not used for their full life for the project, only the depreciation costs corresponding to the life of the project, as calculated on the basis of generally accepted accounting principles are considered as eligible;
- (c) costs of buildings and land, to the extent and for the duration period used for the project. With regard to buildings, only the depreciation costs corresponding to the life of the project, as calculated on the basis of generally accepted accounting principles are considered as eligible. For land, costs of commercial transfer or actually incurred capital costs are eligible;
- (d) costs of contractual research, knowledge and patents bought or licensed from outside sources at arm's length conditions, as well as costs of consultancy and equivalent services used exclusively for the project;
- (e) additional overheads and other operating expenses, including costs of materials, supplies and similar products, incurred directly as a result of the project.

Aid intensity

(491) The aid intensity must be up to 100% of the eligible costs.

(492) Aid for research and development in the agricultural sector which does not fulfil the above conditions will be assessed in accordance with the Framework for state aid for research and development and innovation.[83]

CHAPTER 2. AID FOR THE FORESTRY SECTOR WHICH IS CO-FINANCED BY THE EAFRD, GRANTED AS ADDITIONAL NATIONAL FINANCING TO SUCH CO-FINANCED MEASURES OR GRANTED AS A PURE STATE AID

(493) The forestry sector falls outside of the scope of Article 42 of the Treaty and Annex I thereto. Articles 107, 108 and 109 of the Treaty apply to aid granted by Member States to the forestry sector. Despite the fact that the production of natural cork, unworked, crushed, granulated or ground, waste cork (CN heading 4501) and the production of castanea/chestnut (CN code 0802 41 00) falls under Annex I of the Treaty, aid for forestry activities related to those trees can fall under the present Chapter of the Guidelines.

(494) In line with the Union's objective under Recital 20, Article 4 and Article 5 of Regulation (EC) No 1305/2013 aid for sustainable and climate friendly land use includes forest area development and sustainable management of forests. These Guidelines aim ensuring coherence with Regulation (EU) No 1305/2013 and with its implementing and delegated acts and with the general State aid principles. These principles affect eligible costs and aid intensities under these Guidelines.

(495) The provisions of Chapter 2 of these Guidelines are without prejudice to the possibility of granting State aid for the forestry sector under Union rules common either to all sectors or to trade and industry, as referred in point (34) of these Guidelines. Aid for investments in energy saving and renewable energies are excluded from the scope of Chapter 2 of Part II of these Guidelines as such aid should comply with the Guidelines on State aid for environmental protection and energy 2014–2020, unless it is exempt from notification obligation. However, in line with Article 5(5)(c), Article 21(1)(e) and Article 26 of Regulation (EU) No 1305/2013, these Guidelines cover investments related to the use of wood as a raw material or energy source, which is limited to all working operations prior to industrial processing. These Guidelines do not apply to forest based industries.

(496) Under this Chapter the Commission will declare State aid for the forestry sector compatible with the internal market under Article 107(3)(c) of the Treaty if the aid complies with the common assessment principles of these Guidelines and the specific requirements laid down in Sections 2.1 to 2.9 below.

(497) The scope of this Chapter covers aid for the forestry sector as laid down in point (23)(b) of these Guidelines.

(498) The ownership structure and the management of forests across the Union is diverse. Articles 22 to 26 and Article 34 of Regulation (EU) No 1305/2013 lay down specific restrictions as to potential aid beneficiaries of EAFRD co-financed measures in the forestry sector. For forestry measures forming part of a rural development programme, benefiting from EAFRD support, the restrictions as to the scope of aid beneficiaries laid down in Regulation (EU) No 1305/2013 apply, except for the tropical or subtropical forests and to the woodland of the territories of the Azores, Madeira, the Canary Islands, the smaller Aegean islands within the meaning of Regulation (EU) No 229/2013 and of the French overseas departments, in Sections 2.1.1 to 2.1.5 of Part II of these Guidelines. In order to complement the EU rural development policy, the restrictions as to potential beneficiaries do not apply to rural development like forestry measures, which are funded exclusively from national resources nor to the specific aid measures of Section 2.8 and 2.9 of Part II of these Guidelines. However as to investments in forestry technologies and in processing, mobilising and marketing of forest products and start-up of producer group as referred to in Section 2.1.5 and Section 2.7, respectively the limitations as to the size of eligible beneficiaries should always apply in accordance with in Article 26 and Article 27 of Regulation (EU) No 1305/2013.

2.1. INVESTMENTS IN FOREST AREA DEVELOPMENT AND IMPROVEMENT OF THE VIABILITY OF FORESTS

(499) The Commission will consider aid for investments in forest area development and the improvement of viability of forests compatible with the internal market under Article 107(3)(c) of the Treaty if it complies with the common assessment principles of these Guidelines and with the following conditions.

(500) This Section concerns aid for afforestation and creation of woodland, the establishment of agro-forestry systems, the prevention and restoration of damage to forests from forest fires, natural disasters, adverse climatic events, catastrophic events, climate change related events, pest and disease outbreaks, investments improving the resilience and environmental value, as well as the mitigation potential of forest ecosystems and investments in forestry technologies and in the processing, in the mobilising and in the marketing of forest products.

(501) The EU Biodiversity 2020 strategy of 03 May 2011[84] encourages the establishment of forest management plans to ensure the sustainability of forestry, where Union funding is available. Therefore wherever Regulation (EU) No 1305/2013, so requires for specific forestry measure forming part of a rural development programme, for holdings above a certain size, to be determined by the Member States in their rural development programmes or otherwise, aid must be conditional on the presentation of the relevant information from a forest management plan or equivalent instrument in line with sustainable forest management as defined by the Ministerial Conference on the protection of Forests in Europe of 1993[85] ('sustainable forest management'). This requirement does not apply to forestry aid under these Guidelines which is funded exclusively from national budget.

Eligible costs

(502) Working capital should not be considered as eligible cost for investments in the forestry sector. The following common eligible costs for investments are laid down in Article 45 of Regulation (EU) No 1305/2013.

(a) the construction, acquisition, including leasing, or improvement of immovable property, with land purchased only being eligible to an extent not exceeding 10% of the total eligible costs of the operation concerned; in exceptional and duly justified cases, the limit may be raised above the percentage for operations concerning environmental conservation;

(b) the purchase or lease purchase of machinery and equipment up to the market value of the asset;

(c) general costs linked to the expenditure referred to in points (a) and (b), such as architect, engineer and consultation fees, fees relating to advice on environmental and economic sustainability, including feasibility studies; feasibility studies remain eligible expenditure even where, based on their results, no expenditure under in points (a) and (b) is incurred;

(d) acquisition or development of computer software and acquisitions of patents, licences, copyrights and trademarks;
(e) the costs of establishing forest management plans and their equivalent instruments;
(f) other costs connected to leasing contracts, such as lessor's margin, interest refinancing costs, overheads and insurance charges may not be eligible costs.

[(503) Aid for forestry investments which is co-financed under the EAFRD, or granted as additional national financing to such co-financed aid, may cover other eligible costs than those referred to in point (502)(a) to (e), provided that those costs are fully eligible under Regulation (EU) No 1305/2013 and that the aid is identical to the underlying measure included in the rural development programme approved under that Regulation. Where such aid is provided in the form of financial instruments, it may cover also the costs referred to in point 502(f).]

2.1.1. AID FOR AFFORESTATION AND CREATION OF WOODLAND

(504) The Commission will consider aid for afforestation and creation of woodland compatible with the internal market under Article 107(3)(c) of the Treaty if it complies with the common assessment principles of these Guidelines and with the following conditions.

Beneficiaries of the aid

(505) Aid for establishment costs and the annual premium may be granted to public and private land-holders and their associations.

(506) Aid for afforestation of land owned by public authorities or for fast growing trees covers only the costs of establishment. In the case of state-owned land, aid may be granted if the body managing such land is a private body or municipality.

Eligible costs

(507) Aid covers the costs of establishment of forest and woodland on agricultural and non-agricultural land. Aid in the form of an annual premium per hectare may furthermore be granted to cover the costs of agricultural income foregone and maintenance, including early and late cleanings, for a maximum period of twelve years.

(508) No aid may be granted for the planting of trees for short rotation coppicing, Christmas trees or fast growing trees for energy production. Species planted must be adapted to the environmental and climatic conditions of the area and comply with minimum environmental requirements.

(509) The following minimum environmental requirements apply in the context of the afforestation and creation of woodland:

(a) the selection of species to be planted, of areas and of methods to be used must avoid the inappropriate afforestation of sensitive habitats such as peat lands and wetlands and negative effects on areas of high ecological value including areas under high natural value farming. On sites designated as Natura 2000 pursuant to Council Directive 92/43/EEC[86] and Directive 2009/147/EC of the European Parliament and of the Council[87] only afforestation consistent with the management objectives of the sites concerned and agreed with the Member State's authority in charge of implementing Natura 2000 must be allowed;
(b) the selection of species, varieties, ecotypes and provenances of trees must take account of the need for resilience to climate change and to natural disasters and the pedologic and hydrologic condition of the area concerned, as well as of the potential invasive character of the species under local conditions as defined by Member States. The beneficiary must be required to protect and care for the forest at least during the period for which the premium for agricultural income foregone and maintenance is paid. This must include tending, thinning or grazing, as appropriate, in the interest of the future development of the forest and regulating competition with herbaceous vegetation and avoiding the building up of fire prone undergrowth material. As regards fast-growing species, Member States must define the minimum and maximum time before felling. The minimum time must not be less than 8 years and the maximum must not exceed 20 years;
(c) in cases where, due to difficult environmental or climatic conditions, including environmental degradation, the planting of perennial woody species cannot be expected to lead to the establishment of forest cover as defined under the applicable national legislation, the Member State may allow the beneficiary to establish other woody vegetation cover. The beneficiary must provide the same level of care and protection as applicable to forests;
(d) in the case of afforestation operations leading to the creation of forests of a size exceeding a certain threshold, to be defined by Member States, the operation must consist of either:
    (i) the exclusive planting of ecologically adapted species and/or species resilient to climate change in the bio-geographical area concerned, which have not been found, through an assessment of impacts, to threaten biodiversity and ecosystem services, or to have a negative impact on human health; or
    (ii) a mix of tree species which includes either at least 10% of broadleaved trees by area, or a minimum of three tree species or varieties, with the least abundant making up at least 10% of the area.

(510) In areas where afforestation is made difficult by severe pedo-climatic conditions aid may be provided for planting other perennial woody species such as shrubs or bushes suitable to the local conditions.

(511) The notification to the Commission should contain sound description demonstrating compliance with the conditions of point (509) above and justifications where any derogation applies.

Aid intensity

(512) Aid may be allowed up to 100% of the eligible costs.

2.1.2.
[Aid for the establishment, regeneration or renovation of agroforestry systems]

[(513) The Commission will consider aid for the establishment, regeneration or renovation of agro-forestry systems compatible with the internal market under Article 107(3)(c) of the Treaty if it complies with the common assessment principles of these Guidelines and with the following conditions.]

(514) The aid may be granted for establishing land use systems in which trees are grown in combination with agriculture on the same land as defined in point (35)65. of these Guidelines.

Beneficiaries of the aid

(515) The aid may be granted to private land-holders, municipalities and their associations.

Eligible costs

[(516) The aid covers the costs of the establishment, regeneration or renovation and an annual premium per hectare may be granted to cover the costs of the maintenance for a maximum period of five years.]

(517) Member States must determine the minimum and maximum number of trees per hectare, taking account of local pedo-climatic and environmental conditions, forestry species and the need to ensure sustainable agricultural use of the land.

Aid intensity

[(518) The aid may be up to 80% of the amount of the eligible investment costs for the establishment, regeneration or renovation of agro-forestry systems, and up to 100 % of the amount of the annual premium.]

2.1.3.
Aid for the prevention and restoration of damage to forests from forest fire, natural disasters, adverse climatic events which can be assimilated to natural disaster, other adverse climatic events, plant pests and catastrophic events

(519) The Commission will consider aid for the prevention and restoration of damage to forests from forest fire, natural disasters, adverse climatic events which can be assimilated to natural disaster, other adverse climatic events, plant pests, catastrophic events and climate change related events compatible with the internal market under Article 107(2)(b) or, as the case may be, Article 107(3)(c) of the Treaty if it complies with the common assessment principles of these Guidelines and with the following conditions.

Beneficiaries of the aid

(520) Aid may be granted to private and public forest holders and other private and public bodies and their associations.

Eligible costs

(521) The aid covers the costs for:

(a) the establishment of protective infrastructure; in the case of firebreaks aid may also cover aid contributing to maintenance costs; no aid may be granted for agricultural related activities in areas covered by agri-environment-climate commitments;

(b) local, small-scale prevention activities against fire or other natural hazards, including the use of grazing animals;

(c) establishing and improving forest fire, pest and diseases monitoring facilities and communication equipment;

(d) restoring forest potential damaged by fires, natural disasters, adverse climatic events which can be assimilated to natural disaster, other adverse climatic events, plant pests, catastrophic events and climate change related events.

(522) In the case of the restoration of forest potential, referred to point (521)(d), the aid must be subject to the formal recognition by the competent public authorities of the Member State that the before mentioned event has occurred and that either that event, or measures adopted in accordance with Directive 2000/29/EC to combat, eradicate or contain harmful organisms, has caused the destruction of at least 20% of the relevant forest potential.

(523) In the case of aid for prevention of damage to a forest from plant pests, the risk of the occurrence of the plant pest must be supported by scientific evidence and acknowledged by a scientific public organisation. Where relevant, the list of harmful organisms which may cause a plant pest must be provided in the notification.

(524) Eligible operations must be consistent with the forest protection plan established by the Member States. For holdings above a certain size, to be determined by the Member States in the rural development programme, where the measure is co-financed by EAFRD, the aid must be conditional on the presentation of the relevant information from a forest management plan or equivalent instrument in line with sustainable forest management as defined by the Ministerial Conference on the protection of Forests in Europe of 1993, detailing the preventive objectives.

(525) Only forest areas which are classified as a medium to high forest fire risk according to the forest protection plan established by the Member States should be eligible for aid for prevention of fire.

(526) No aid may be granted for loss of income resulting from fires, natural disasters, adverse climatic events which can be assimilated to natural disaster, other adverse climatic events, plant pests, catastrophic events and climate change related events.

Aid intensity

(527) Aid may be granted up to 100% of the eligible costs.

(528) Aid granted for the eligible costs as referred to in (521)(d) and any other payments received by the beneficiary, including payments under other national or Union measures or insurance policies for the same eligible costs, are limited to 100% of the eligible costs.

2.1.4.
Aid for investments improving the resilience and environmental value of forest ecosystems

(529) The Commission will consider aid for investments improving the resilience and environmental value of forest ecosystems compatible with the internal market under Article 107(3)(c) of the Treaty if complies with the common assessment principles of these Guidelines and with the following conditions.

Beneficiaries of the aid

(530) Aid may be granted to natural persons, private and public forest holders and other private law and public bodies and their associations.

Eligible costs

(531) Investments should be aimed at the achievements of commitments for environmental aims for the provisions of ecosystem services and/or for the enhancement of the public amenity value of forests and woodland in the area concerned or the improvement of the climate change mitigation potential of ecosystems, without excluding economic benefits in the long term.

Aid intensity

(532) Aid may be granted up to 100% of eligible costs.

2.1.5.
Aid for investments in forestry technologies and in processing, in mobilising and in marketing of forest products

(533) The Commission will consider aid for investments enhancing forestry potential or relating to processing, mobilising and marketing adding value to forest products compatible with the internal market under Article 107(3)(c) of the Treaty if it complies with the common assessment principles of these Guidelines and with the following conditions.

(534) Member States must require compliance with minimum standards for energy efficiency for supported investments in renewable energy infrastructure, that consume or produce energy, where such standards exist at national level.

[(535) Investments in installations, the primary purpose of which is electricity production from biomass, are not eligible for aid unless a minimum percentage of the heat energy produced is utilised, to be determined by the Member States.]

(536) Aid to bioenergy projects shall be limited to bioenergy meeting the applicable sustainability criteria laid down in Union legislation, including in Article 17(2) to (6) of Directive 2009/28/EC of the European Parliament and of the Council.

[(536a) The conditions laid down in points (534), (535) and (536) do not apply to aid which is co-financed under the EAFRD, or granted as additional national financing to such co-financed aid, and which is provided in the form of financial instruments.]

Beneficiaries of the aid

[(537) Aid may be granted to private forest holders, municipalities and their associations and to SMEs. In the territories of Azores, Madeira, the Canary islands, the smaller Aegean islands within the meaning of Regulation (EU) No 229/2013 and the French overseas departments, aid may also be granted to undertakings that are not SMEs.]

Eligible costs

(538) Aid may be granted for investments enhancing forestry potential or relating to processing, mobilising and marketing adding value to forest products.

(539) Investments related to the improvement of the economic value of forests must be justified in relation to the expected improvements to forests on one or more holdings and may include investments for soil-friendly and resource-friendly harvesting machinery and practices.

(540) Investments related to the use of wood as a raw material or energy source must be limited to all working operations prior to industrial processing.

Aid intensity

(541) The aid intensity must not exceed:

(a) 75% of the amount of the eligible costs in the outermost regions;
(b) 75% of the amount of the eligible costs in the smaller Aegean islands;
(c) 50% of the amount of the eligible costs in less developed regions and in all regions whose GDP per capita for the period of 1 January 2007 to 31 December 2013 was less than 75% of the average of the EU-25 for the reference period but whose GDP per capita is above 75% of the GDP average of the EU-27;
(d) 40% of the amount of the eligible costs in other regions.

2.1.6.
Aid for investments in infrastructure related to the development, modernisation or adaptation of forestry

(542) The Commission will consider aid for investments in infrastructure related to the development, modernisation or adaptation of forestry compatible with the internal market under Article 107(3)(c) of the Treaty if it complies with the common assessment principles of these Guidelines and with the following conditions.

Eligible costs

(543) The aid covers investment in tangible and intangible assets which concern infrastructure related to the development, modernisation or adaptation of forests, including access to forest land, land consolidation and improvement, and the supply and saving of energy and water.

Aid intensity

(544) In the case of non-productive investments, investments aimed exclusively at improving the environmental value of forests and investments for forest roads, which are open to the public free of charge and which serve the multifunctional aspects of forest the aid intensity is limited to 100% of the eligible costs.

(545) In the case of investments, which improve the short- or long term economic potential of forests, the aid intensity must be limited to:

(a) 75% of the amount of the eligible costs in the outermost regions;

(b) 75% of the amount of the eligible costs in the smaller Aegean islands;

(c) 50% of the amount of the eligible costs in less developed regions and in all regions whose GDP per capita for the period of 1 January 2007 to 31 December 2013 was less than 75% of the average of the EU-25 for the reference period but whose GDP per capita is above 75% of the GDP average of the EU-27;

(d) 40% of the amount of the eligible costs in other regions.

2.2. Aid for disadvantages related to Natura 2000 forest areas

(546) The Commission will consider Sate aid related to Natura 2000 forest areas compatible with the internal market under Article 107(3)(c) of the Treaty if it complies with the common assessment principles of these Guidelines and with the following conditions.

Beneficiaries of the aid

(547) Aid may be granted to private forest holders and associations of private forest holders.

Eligible costs

(548) Aid under this measure must be granted annually and per hectare of forest in order to compensate beneficiaries for the additional costs incurred and income foregone resulting from disadvantages in the areas concerned, related to the implementation of the Habitats Directive and the Birds Directive.

(549) The following areas may be eligible for aid:

(a) Natura 2000 forest areas designated pursuant to the Habitats Directive and the Birds Directive;

(b) other delimited nature protection areas with environmental restrictions applicable to forests which contribute to the implementation of Article 10 of the Habitats Directive; provided that, where the measure is co-financed by EAFRD as a rural development measure, per rural development programme, those areas do not exceed 5% of the designated Natura 2000 areas covered by its territorial scope; for aid measures financed exclusively from national funds, this latter territorial restriction does not apply.

Aid amount

(550) Aid must be limited to the following maximum amounts: EUR 500 per hectare per year maximum in the initial period not exceeding five years and EUR 200 per hectare per year maximum thereafter. These maximum amounts may be increased in duly substantiated cases taking into account specific circumstances to be justified in the rural development programmes or otherwise if the measure is financed exclusively from national funds.

2.3. Aid for forest-environment and climate services and forest conservation

(551) The Commission will consider aid for forest-environment and climate services and forest conservation compatible with the internal market under Article 107(3)(c) of the Treaty if it complies with the common assessment principles of these Guidelines and with the following conditions.

(552) Aid under this measure must be granted per hectare of forest. For forest holdings above a certain threshold to be determined by Member States in their rural development programmes, aid must be conditional on the presentation of the relevant information from a forest management plan or equivalent instrument in line with sustainable forest management as defined by the Ministerial Conference on the protection of Forests in Europe of 1993.

(553) Aid covers voluntary commitment(s) going beyond the relevant mandatory requirements established by the national forestry act or other relevant national legislation. In the case of an EAFRD co-financed rural development measure, the relevant mandatory requirement should be clearly identified and described in the rural development programme. In the case of aid measures financed exclusively from national funds, the relevant mandatory requirement should be identified and described in the State aid notification to the Commission.

(554) Commitments must be undertaken for a period between five and seven years. However, where necessary and duly justified, Member States may determine a longer period for particular types of commitments. In the case of EAFRD co-financed rural development measure, it should be specified in the rural development programme. In the case of aid measures financed exclusively from national funds, it should be identified in the State aid notification.

(555) Where relevant, the rules for area related payments laid down in Article 47 of Regulation (EU) No 1305/2013 and the relevant provisions of its delegated act should be complied with.

Beneficiaries of the aid

(556) Aid may be granted to public and private forest holders and other private law and public bodies and their associations. In the case of state-owned forests, aid may only be granted if the body managing such a forest is a private body or a municipality.

(557) Public and private entities are eligible for aid for the conservation and promotion of forest genetic resources for operations not covered otherwise in this Section.

Eligible costs and modalities of the aid

(558) The aid compensates beneficiaries for all or part of the additional costs and income foregone resulting from the commitments made. Where necessary it may also cover transaction costs to a value of up to 20% of the aid premium paid for the forest-environment commitments.

(559) In duly justified cases for operations concerning environmental conservation, aid may be granted as a flat-rate or one-off payment per unit for commitments to renounce the commercial use of trees and forests, calculated on the basis of additional costs incurred and income foregone.

(560) Aid may be provided for the conservation and promotion of forest genetic resources for operations not covered by the provisions under the above points within this Section.

(561) Operations for the conservation of genetic resources in forestry must include the following:

(a) targeted actions: actions promoting the in situ and ex situ conservation, characterisation, collection and utilisation of genetic resources in forestry, including web-based inventories of genetic resources currently conserved in situ, including on-forest holding conservation, and of ex situ collections and databases;

(b) concerted actions: actions promoting the exchange of information for the conservation, characterisation, collection and utilisation of genetic resources in Union forestry, among competent organisations in the Member States;

(c) accompanying actions: information, dissemination and advisory actions involving non-governmental organisations and other relevant stakeholders, training courses and the preparation of technical reports.

Aid amount

(562) The aid, with the exception of aid for operations for the conservation of genetic resources as referred to in point (560) must be limited to the maximum amount of EUR 200 per hectare per year. That amount may be increased in duly substantiated cases taking into account specific circumstances to be justified in the rural development programmes or otherwise in the notification to the Commission.

(563) For the conservation of forest genetic resources, the aid must be limited to 100% of the eligible costs.

2.4. Aid for knowledge transfer and information actions in the forestry sector

(564) The Commission will consider aid for knowledge transfer and information actions in the forestry sector compatible with the internal market under Article 107(3)(c) of the Treaty if it complies with the common assessment principles of these Guidelines and with the following conditions.

(565) Aid for knowledge transfer and information actions to benefit persons engaged in the forestry sector should comply with the applicable relevant conditions set out in Section 1.1.10.1 of Part II with the exception as to the conditions of point (294), the maximum aid amount included in point (298) and the possibility to pay the aid directly to the beneficiary in point (296). [Infrastructure installed as a result of demonstration may be used after the operation is completed.]

(566) The aid may cover short term forest management exchanges and forest visits.

(567) The duration and the content of the short-term forest management exchange schemes and forest visits must be defined, in the case of EAFRD co-financed measure in the rural development programme, and in the case of nationally financed scheme in the notification to the Commission. Such schemes and visits must focus, in particular, on sustainable forestry methods and/or technologies, the development of new business opportunities and new technologies, and on the improvement of forest resilience.

[(567a) Aid for demonstration projects which is co-financed under the EAFRD or granted as additional national financing to such co-financed aid, and which is provided in the form of financial instruments, may cover other eligible costs than those referred to in point (293)(d)(i) to (iv) of Section 1.1.10.1, provided that those costs are fully eligible under Regulation (EU) No 1305/2013 and that the aid is identical to the underlying measure included in the rural development programme approved under that regulation.]

2.5. Aid for advisory services in the forestry sector

(568) The Commission will consider aid for advisory services in the forestry sector compatible with the internal market under Article 107(3)(c) of the Treaty if it complies with the common assessment principles of these Guidelines and with the following conditions.

(569) Aid for advisory services in the forestry sector to forest holders must be granted in accordance with the applicable relevant conditions specified under point 1.1.10.2 of Part II of these Guidelines, with the following additional provisions relating to forestry.

[(569a) Aid which is co-financed under the EAFRD, or granted as additional national financing to such co-financed aid, may be paid to the Managing Authority referred to in point (a) of Article 65(2) of Regulation (EU) No 1305/2013.]

Eligible costs

(570) Aid will be granted to help forest holders to benefit from the use of advisory services for the improvement of the economic and environmental performance as well as climate friendliness and resilience of their holdings, enterprise and/or investment.

(571) Advice to forest holders must cover as a minimum the relevant obligations under the Habitats Directive, the Birds Directive and the Water Framework Directive. It may also cover issues linked to the economic and environmental performance of the forest holding.

2.6. AID FOR CO-OPERATION IN FORESTRY SECTOR

(572) The Commission will consider aid for co-operation in the forestry sector compatible with the internal market under Article 107(3)(c) of the Treaty if it complies with the common assessment principles of these Guidelines and with the following conditions.

(573) Aid for co-operation involving at least two entities in the forestry sector or in the forestry and agricultural sectors must be granted in accordance with the conditions set out in Section 1.1.11. of Part II.

(574) For the forestry sector the following additional provisions apply.

Eligible costs and aid intensities

(575) Without prejudice to the costs referred to in Sections 1.1.11 of Part II of these Guidelines, aid for cooperation in the forestry sector may also relate to drawing up of forest management plans or equivalent.

(576) Direct costs referred to in point (321)(d) and direct costs of specific projects linked to the implementation of a forest management plan or equivalent must be limited to the eligible costs and maximum aid intensities of investment aid in the forestry sector, as specified in Section 2.1 of Part II of these Guidelines on investment aid.

(577) Aid for cooperation in the forestry sector may also relate to horizontal and vertical cooperation among supply chain actors in the sustainable production of biomass for energy production and industrial processes in compliance with Chapter 3.10 of Part II of these Guidelines.

2.7. START-UP AID FOR PRODUCER GROUPS AND ORGANISATIONS IN THE FORESTRY SECTOR

(578) The Commission will consider start-up aid for producer groups and organisations in the forestry sector compatible with the internal market under Article 107(3)(c) of the Treaty if it complies with the common assessment principles of these Guidelines and with the following conditions.

(579) Only producer groups or organisations that have been officially recognised by the competent authority of the Member State concerned on the basis of a submission of a business plan may be eligible for aid. The aid must be granted subject to the obligation of the Member State to verify that the objectives of the business plan have been reached within a period of five years from the date of recognition of the producer group or organisation.

(580) The agreements, decisions and concerted practices concluded in the framework of the producer group or organisation must comply with the relevant provisions of competition law, and in particular with Articles 101 and 102 of the Treaty.

(581) The aid must not be granted to

(a) production organisations, entities or bodies, such as companies or co-operatives, the objective of which is the management of one or more forestry holdings and which are therefore in effect a single producers;

(b) other forestry associations which undertake tasks, such as mutual support and forestry management services, in the members' holding without being involved in the joint adaptation of supply to the market.

Beneficiaries of the aid

(582) Aid is limited to producer groups and organisations which are SMEs. The Commission will not authorise State aid towards the costs in this Section in favour of large enterprises.

(583) As an alternative to providing aid to producer groups or organisations, aid up to the same overall amount may be granted directly to producers to offset their contributions to the costs of running the groups or organisations during the first five years following the formation of the group.

Eligible costs

[(584) Where the aid is financed exclusively from national resources, the eligible costs may include the costs of the rental of suitable premises, the acquisition of office equipment, including computer hardware and software, administrative staff costs, overheads and legal and administrative fees. Where premises are purchased, the eligible costs for premises must be limited to rental costs at market rates. Aid must not be paid in respect of costs incurred after the fifth year after recognition of the producer group or organisation by the competent authority on the basis of its business plan.]

[(585) Aid which is granted as part of the rural development programme or as additional national financing for a rural development measure shall be calculated on the basis of the average marketed production of the group or organisation. In the absence of the data on the marketed production of the group or organisation, the support in the first year shall be calculated on the basis of the average marketed production of the members of the group or organisation over the last five years before the recognition, excluding the highest and the lowest value. It must be paid as a flat rate aid in annual instalments for no more than five years following the date on which the producer group or organisation was recognised by the competent authority on the basis of its business plan, and must be degressive.]

[(586) Where the aid is paid in annual instalments, Member States shall pay the last instalment only after having verified the correct implementation of the business plan.]

Aid intensity

[(587) The aid intensity may be up to 100% of the eligible costs specified in point (584).]

[(588) The total amount of aid must be limited to EUR 500,000.]

2.8. OTHER AID TO THE FORESTRY SECTOR WITH ECOLOGICAL, PROTECTIVE AND RECREATIONAL OBJECTIVES

(589) In accordance with its established policy during the period of from 1 January 2007 to 31 December 2013, in order to contribute to the maintenance and improvement of forests and to promote their ecological, protective and recreational function, the Commission will consider that State aid measures, with the primary objective to maintain, improve or restore ecological, protective and recreational functions of forests, biodiversity and a healthy forest ecosystem, are compatible with the internal market under Article 107(3)(c) of the Treaty, if the following conditions are fulfilled.

(590) Member States should demonstrate that the measures directly contribute to maintaining or restoring the ecological, protective and recreational functions of forests, biodiversity and a healthy forest ecosystem.

(591) No aid may be granted under this Section to forest based industries or for commercially viable extraction of timber or for transportation of timber or the processing of wood or other forestry resources into products or for energy generation. No aid may be granted for felling the primary purpose of which is the commercially viable extraction of timber or for restocking where the felled trees are replaced by equivalent ones.

Aid intensity

(592) Aid for all measures described in this Section may be granted up to 100% of the eligible costs.

Beneficiaries of the aid

(593) Aid may be granted to undertakings active in the forestry sector.

2.8.1.
Aid for specific forest actions and interventions with the primary objective to contribute to maintaining or to restoring forest ecosystem and biodiversity or the traditional landscape

[(594) The Commission will consider aid for planting, pruning, thinning and felling of trees and other vegetation in existing forests, the removal of fallen trees, and the planning costs of such measures, aid for the costs of treating and preventing the spreading of pests and tree diseases and aid to make good the damage caused by the pests and tree diseases compatible with the internal market under Article 107(3)(c) of the Treaty if the aid complies with the common assessment principles and the common provisions applicable to Section 2.8 of Part II of these Guidelines, and where the primary objective of such measures is to contribute to maintaining or to restoring forest ecosystem and biodiversity or the traditional landscape.]

[(594a) Aid for the costs of treating and preventing the spreading of pests and tree diseases and aid to make good the damage caused by the pests and tree diseases may be granted for the following eligible costs:

(a) preventive and treatment measures, including soil preparation for replanting, and the products, appliances and materials necessary for such measures. Biological, physical and other non-chemical mechanical prevention and treatment methods must be preferred to chemical methods, unless it can be shown that such methods are not sufficient to provide satisfactory control over the disease or pest in question;[87a]

(b) loss of stock and restocking costs up to the market value of the stock destroyed on the order of the authorities to fight the disease or pest in question. When calculating the increment loss, the potential increment of the stock destroyed until the normal felling age may be taken into consideration.]

2.8.2.
Aid for maintaining and improving the soil quality and ensuring a balanced and healthy tree growth in the forestry sector

(595) The Commission will consider aid for maintaining and improving the soil quality and ensuring a balanced and healthy tree growth in the forestry sector compatible with the internal market under Article 107(3)(c) of the Treaty if it complies with the common assessment principles of these Guidelines, the common provisions applicable to Section 2.8 of Part II of these Guidelines and with the following conditions.

(596) Aid may be granted for maintaining and improving the soil quality in forests and ensuring balanced and healthy tree growth.

(597) Measures may include soil improvement by fertilisation and other treatments to maintain its natural balance, reducing excessive vegetation density and ensuring sufficient water retention and proper drainage. Member States should demonstrate that the measures do not reduce biodiversity, cause nutrient leaching or adversely affect natural water ecosystems or water protection zones.

(598) Aid may cover the planning costs of such measures.

2.8.3.
Restoration and maintenance of natural pathways, landscape elements and features and natural habitat for animals in the forestry sector

(599) The Commission will consider aid for the restoration and maintenance of natural pathways, landscape elements and features and natural habitat for animals in the forestry sector compatible with the internal market under Article 107(3)(c) of the Treaty if it complies with the common assessment principles of these Guidelines, the common provisions applicable to Section 2.8 of Part II of these Guidelines and with the following conditions.

(600) Aid may be granted for the restoration and maintenance of natural pathways, landscape elements and features and the natural habitat for animals, including planning costs.

(601) Measures aiming at the implementation of the Habitats Directive and the Birds Directive are excluded from this type of aid, as they should be put in place in accordance with the conditions of Section 2.2. of Part II of these Guidelines.

2.8.4.
Aid for maintaining roads to prevent forest fires

(602) The Commission will consider aid for maintain roads compatible with the internal market under Article 107(3)(c) of the Treaty if it complies with the common assessment principles of these Guidelines, the common provisions applicable to Section 2.8 of Part II of these Guidelines and with the following conditions.

(603) Aid for maintaining roads should aim for preventing forest fires. The link between the objective of the aid and the road maintenance should be demonstrated in the notification to the Commission.

2.8.5.
Aid to make good the damage in forests caused by animals regulated by law

(604) The Commission will consider aid to make good the damage caused by animals regulated by law in forests compatible with the internal market under Article 107(3)(c) of the Treaty if it complies with the common assessment principles of these Guidelines, the common provisions applicable to Section 2.8 of Part II of these Guidelines and with the following conditions.

(605) For the forestry sector, animals regulated by law cover protected animals as defined in Point (35)28 and species subject to specific national legislation, where there is a demonstrated interest for preserving the population of the species.

(606) A minimum counterpart from the beneficiaries is required to mitigate the risk of distortions of competition and to provide an incentive for minimising risk. That contribution must take the form of reasonable preventive measures, such as safety fences where possible, which are proportionate to the risk of damage by the animals regulated in the forest area concerned. If no reasonable preventive measures are possible, Member State should demonstrate the impossibility to take such preventive measures in the notification to the Commission in order for the aid to be considered compatible.

(607) A direct causal link between the damage suffered and the behaviour of the animals must be established.

(608) Aid schemes related to a specific damaging event must be established within three years from the occurrence of the event causing the damage. The aid must be paid out within four years from that date.

(609) The damage must be calculated at the level of the individual beneficiary.

Eligible costs

(610) The eligible costs are the costs of the damage incurred as a direct consequence of the event causing the damage, as assessed either by a public authority, by an independent expert recognized by the granting authority or by an insurance undertaking.

(611) The damage may include the following:

(a) damage to living trees. The aid may be granted to compensate for loss of stock and for restocking costs up to the market value of the stock destroyed by the regulated animals. When calculating the market value of the increment loss, the potential increment of the stock destroyed until the normal felling age may be taken into consideration;

(b) other costs incurred by the beneficiary due to the event causing the damage, such as treatment measures, including soil preparation for replanting and the products, appliances and materials necessary for such operations;

(c) the material damage to the following assets: forestry equipment, machinery and buildings. The calculation of the material damage must be based on the repair cost or economic value of the affected asset before the event caused the damage. It must not exceed the repair cost or the decrease in fair market value caused by the event, that is to say the difference between the property's value immediately before and immediately after the event that caused the damage.

(612) The amount must be reduced by any costs not incurred because of the damaging event, which would otherwise have been incurred by the beneficiary.

(613) Preventive measures against damage done by animals in forests can be supported under Section 2.1.4 of Part II of these Guidelines as protection of habitats and biodiversity-related actions.

(614) Aid for restoring damage in forests caused by animals regulated by national law can be granted if the conditions of Section 2.1.3 are complied with.

Aid intensity

(615) Compensation is allowed up to 100% of the eligible costs.

(616) The aid and any other payments received to compensate the damage, including payments under national or Union measures or insurance policies, is limited to 100% of the eligible costs.

2.8.6.
Aid for establishing forest management plans

(617) The Commission will consider aid for forest management plans compatible with the internal market under Article 107(3)(c) of the Treaty if it complies with the common assessment principles of these Guidelines, the common provisions applicable to Section 2.8 of Part II of these Guidelines and with the following conditions.

(618) Since the 2014–2020 rural development policy makes forest management plans or equivalent instruments a pre-condition for eligibility for aid under several measures, with a view to enhance the achievements of the rural development objectives, the Commission maintains its current policy that aid may be given for the establishment of forest management plans.

[(619) Aid must comply with the conditions of aid for advisory services, as laid down in points (288), (289), and (303) to (306)). The service provider will be the body establishing the forest management plan.]

2.9. AID IN THE FORESTRY SECTOR ALIGNED WITH THE AGRICULTURAL AID MEASURES

(620) In the past, the Commission has established its policy that for specific, less distortive aid measures, rules are common for the agricultural and forestry sector.

(621) Following the tendency to align agricultural and forestry policies where the aid is considered to be less distortive, the Commission will consider aid for research and development in the forestry sector and aid for forest land consolidation compatible with the internal market if the specific conditions of these sections are met.

(622) The aid intensity must be limited to 100% of the eligible costs.

2.9.1.
Aid for research and development in the forest sector

(623) The Commission will consider aid for research and development in the forest sector compatible with the internal market under Article 107(3) of the Treaty if it complies with the common assessment principles of these Guidelines, with the condition of Section 2.9 and with the following conditions.

(624) The aided project should be of interest to all undertakings active in the particular forestry sectors or subsectors concerned.

(625) Prior to the date of the start of the aided project the following information must be published on the internet:
(a) that the aided project is to be carried out;
(b) the goals of the aided project;
(c) an approximate date for the publication of the results expected from the aided project;
(d) the place of publication of the results expected from the aided project on the internet;
(e) a reference that the results of the aided project are available to all undertakings active in the forestry sector or sub-sector concerned at no cost.

(626) The results of the aided project must be made available on internet from the end date of the aided project or the date on which any information concerning those results is given to members of any particular organisation, whatever comes first. The results must remain available on internet for a period of at least five years starting from the end date of the aided project

(627) The aid should be granted directly to the research and knowledge-dissemination organisation and should not involve the provision of aid based on the price of the forestry products to undertakings active in the forestry sector.

Eligible costs

(628) The aid must be limited to the following eligible costs:
(a) personnel costs related to researchers, technicians and other supporting staff to the extent employed on the project;
(b) costs of instruments and equipment to the extent and for the period used for the project. Where such instruments and equipment are not used for their full life for the project, only the depreciation costs corresponding to the life of the project, as calculated on the basis of generally accepted accounting principles are considered as eligible;
(c) costs of buildings and land, to the extent and for the duration period used for the project. With regard to buildings, only the depreciation costs corresponding to the life of the project, as calculated on the basis of generally accepted accounting principles are considered as eligible. For land, costs of commercial transfer or actually incurred capital costs are eligible;
(d) costs of contractual research, knowledge and patents bought or licensed from outside sources at arm's length conditions, as well as costs of consultancy and equivalent services used exclusively for the project;
(e) additional overheads and other operating expenses, including costs of materials, supplies and similar products, incurred directly as a result of the project.

2.9.2.
Aid for forestry land consolidation

(629) The Commission will consider aid for forest land consolidation compatible with the internal market under Article 107(3)(c) of the Treaty if it complies with the common assessment principles of these Guidelines, with the condition of Section 2.9 and with the following conditions.

Eligible costs

(630) The eligible costs must be limited to the incurred real legal, administrative and survey costs of land consolidation.

CHAPTER 3. AIDS IN RURAL AREAS WHICH ARE CO-FINANCED BY THE EAFRD OR GRANTED AS ADDITIONAL NATIONAL FINANCING TO SUCH CO-FINANCED MEASURES

Common provisions applicable to Chapter 3 of Part II of these Guidelines

(631) Aid under Chapter 3 of Part II of these Guidelines should meet the following common condition: the aid must be granted in the framework of a rural development programme pursuant to and in conformity with Regulation (EU) No 1305/2013 either as aid co-financed by the EAFRD or as additional national financing to such aid.

(632) The provisions of Chapter 3 are without prejudice to the possibility of granting State aid for rural areas under Union rules common either to all sectors or to trade and industry.

(633) As regards to investments under Sections 3.1, 3.2, 3.6 and 3.10 of Chapter 3 of Part II of these Guidelines, the aid must comply with the following common provisions set out in points (634) to (639).

(634) Investments in energy saving and renewable energies are excluded from the scope of Chapter 3 of Part II of these Guidelines. Such aid must comply with the Guidelines on State aid for environmental protection and energy 2014–2020, unless it is exempt from notification obligation.

Eligible costs for investments falling within the scope of Chapter 3 of Part II of these Guidelines

(635) [Save where aid is provided in the form of financial instruments, and unless specified otherwise, the eligible costs for investment aid measures falling within the scope of Chapter 3 of Part II of these Guidelines must be limited to the following costs:]

(a) the construction, acquisition, including leasing, or improvement of immovable property, with land purchased only being eligible to an extent not exceeding 10% of total eligible costs of the operation concerned; however in exceptional and duly justified cases, a higher percentage may be permitted for operations concerning environmental conservation;
(b) the purchase or lease purchase of machinery and equipment up to the market value of the asset;
(c) the general costs linked to expenditure referred to in point (635)(a) and (b), such as architect, engineer and consultation fees, fees relating to advice on environmental and economic sustainability, including feasibility studies; feasibility studies remain eligible expenditure even where, based on their results, no expenditure under point (635) (a) and (b) is incurred;
(d) investment in the following intangible assets: acquisition or development of computer software and acquisitions of patents, licences, copyrights and trademarks.

[(636) Save where aid is provided in the form of financial instruments, costs, other than those referred to in point (635), connected with leasing contracts, such as lessor's margin, interest refinancing costs, overheads and insurance charges will not be considered to be eligible costs.]

(637) Working capital is not eligible cost under Chapter 3 of Part II.

Aid intensity for investment measures under Chapter 3 of Part II of these Guidelines

(638) [Unless specified otherwise, the aid intensity must not exceed:]

(a) in less developed regions:
   (i) 50% of the amount of the eligible costs for investment in regions whose GDP per capita is below 45% of the EU-27 average;
   (ii) 35% of the amount of the eligible costs for investment in regions whose GDP per capita is between 45% and 60% of the EU-27 average;
   (iii) 25% of the amount of the eligible costs for investment in regions with a GDP per capita above 60% of the EU-27 average;
(b) in outermost regions: the maximum aid intensities set out in point (a) may be increased either by up to 20 percentage points in outermost regions that have a GDP per capita below or equal to 75% of the EU-27 average or by up to 10 percentage points in other outermost regions;
(c) in 'c' areas:
   (i) 15% of the amount of the eligible costs for investment in sparsely populated areas and in NUTS 3 regions or parts of NUTS 3 regions that share a land border with a country outside the EEA or the European Free Trade Association (EFTA);
   (ii) 10% of the amount of the eligible costs for investment in non-predefined 'c' areas;
   (iii) in the former 'a' areas the aid intensities may be increased by up to 5 percentage points for the period from 1 July 2014 to 31 December 2017;
   (iv) where a 'c' area is adjacent to an 'a' area, the maximum aid intensity allowed in the NUTS 3 areas or parts of NUTS 3 areas within that 'c' area which are adjacent to the 'a' area may be increased as necessary so that the difference in aid intensity between both areas does not exceed 15 percentage points;
(d) with the exception of aid granted in favour of large investment projects, the maximum aid intensities set out in points (a) to (c) above may be increased by up to 10 percentage points for medium-sized undertakings and by up to 20 percentage points for micro and small undertakings;
(e) in all other areas: 10% of the amount of eligible costs for investment for medium-sized undertakings and 20% of the amount of eligible costs for investment for micro and small undertakings;
(f) the maximum aid intensity for large investment projects must be scaled down to the adjusted aid amount as defined in [point (35).31] of these Guidelines.

(639) Individual investment aid granted under a notified scheme remains subject to the notification obligation pursuant to Article 108(3) of the Treaty, if the aid from all sources exceeds the notification threshold, as specified in point (37)(c).

3.1. AID FOR INVESTMENTS CONCERNING THE PROCESSING OF AGRICULTURAL PRODUCTS INTO NON-AGRICULTURAL PRODUCTS, THE PRODUCTION OF COTTON OR INVESTMENTS IN THE CREATION AND DEVELOPMENT OF NON-AGRICULTURAL ACTIVITIES

(640) The Commission will consider aid for investments concerning the processing of agricultural products into non-agricultural products, the production of cotton or investments in the creation and development of non-agricultural activities compatible with the internal market within the meaning of Article 107(3)(c) of the Treaty if it complies with the common assessment principles of these Guidelines, with the common provisions applicable to Chapter 3 of Part II of these Guidelines and with the following conditions.

(641) Aid under this measure covers investment in tangible and intangible assets.

(642) This Section applies to aid for:

(a) the processing of agricultural products where the output of the production process is a non-agricultural product;

(b) the production of cotton, including the activity of ginning;

(c) investments in non-agricultural activities which are granted to farmers or members of a farm household who diversify into non-agricultural activities and to micro and small undertakings and natural persons in rural areas.

[(642a) Where aid is provided in the form of financial instruments, the input to the production process may also be a non-agricultural product on condition that the investment contributes to one or more of the Union priorities for rural development.]

3.2. AID FOR BASIC SERVICES AND VILLAGE RENEWAL IN RURAL AREAS

(643) The Commission will consider aid for basic services[88] and village renewal in rural areas compatible with the internal market within the meaning of Article 107(3)(c) and Article 107(3)(d) of the Treaty if it complies with the common assessment principles of these Guidelines, with the common provisions applicable to Chapter 3 of Part II of these Guidelines and with the following conditions.

(644) Aid under this measure covers:

(a) the drawing up and updating of plans for the development of municipalities and villages in rural areas and their basic services and of protection and management plans relating to Natura 2000 sites and other areas of high nature value;

(b) investments in the creation, improvement or expansion of all types of small-scale infrastructures as defined in point (35)48, excluding investments in renewable energy and energy savings and broadband infrastructure;

(c) investments in the setting-up, improvement or expansion of local basic services for the rural population, including leisure and culture, and the related infrastructure;

(d) investments for public use in recreational infrastructure, tourist information and small-scale tourism infrastructure;

(e) studies and investments associated with the maintenance, restoration and upgrading of the cultural and natural heritage of villages, rural landscapes and high nature value sites, including related socio-economic aspects, as well as environmental awareness actions;

(f) investments targeting the relocation of activities and conversion of buildings or other facilities located inside or close to rural settlements, with a view to improving the quality of life or increasing the environmental performance of the settlement.

[(644a) With regard to the infrastructure investments referred to in point (644)(b), (d) and (e), where support is provided in the form of financial instruments, aid is not limited to small-scale infrastructure.]

(645) Investments under this measure are eligible for aid where the relevant operations are implemented in accordance with plans for the development of municipalities and villages in rural areas and their basic services, where such plans exist and must be consistent with any relevant local development strategy. [Such plans are not required with regard to investments for which the support is provided in the form of financial instruments.]

(646) Aid referred to in point (644)(e) should be granted for heritage which is formally recognised as cultural or natural heritage by the competent public authorities of a Member State.

Eligible costs

(647) The following costs are eligible:

(a) the costs of drawing up and updating of development and management plans relating to rural areas and their basic services, and to high nature value sites;

(b) investment costs for tangible and intangible assets;

(c) the costs for the preparation of studies associated with cultural and natural heritage, rural landscapes and high nature value sites; costs linked to environmental awareness actions;

(d) the costs of capital works may be also eligible for aid referred to in point (644)(e).

Aid intensity

(648) The aid intensity for the activities under point (644)(a) and (b) must not exceed 100% of the eligible costs.

(649) The aid intensity for activities under point (644)(c), (d) and (e) must not exceed 100% of the eligible costs. The net revenues must be deducted from the eligible costs ex ante or through a clawback mechanism.

(650) The aid intensity for activities under point (644)(f) must not exceed the following amounts:

(a) where the relocation of the activities or the conversion of buildings or other facilities consists of the dismantling, removal and re-building of existing facilities, 100% of real costs incurred for such activities;

(b) where the relocation of the activities or the conversion of buildings or other facilities results, in addition to the dismantling, removal and re-building of existing facilities as referred to in point (650)(a), in a modernisation of these facilities or in an increase in production capacity, the aid intensities for investments laid down in point (638) should apply in respect to the costs relating to the modernisation of the facilities or the increase of production capacity.

(651) For the purpose of point (650) (b), the pure replacement of an existing building or facilities by a new up-to date building or facilities without fundamentally changing the production or the technology involved will not be considered to be related to the modernisation.

3.3. Business start-up aid for non-agricultural activities in rural areas

(652) The Commission will consider business start-up aid for non-agricultural activities in rural areas compatible with the internal market within the meaning of Article 107(3)(c) of the Treaty if it complies with the common assessment principles of these Guidelines, with the common provisions applicable to Chapter 3 of Part II of these Guidelines and with the following conditions.

(653) Aid may be granted to farmers or members of the farm household diversifying into non-agricultural activities and to micro- and small undertakings and to natural persons in rural areas. Aid for the setting up of farm management, farm relief and farm advisory services, as well as forestry advisory services, including the Farm Advisory System referred to in Articles 12 to 14 of Regulation (EU) No 1306/2013 may be granted also to medium-sized and large enterprises in rural areas.

(654) The aid must be conditional on the submission of a business plan. Implementation of the business plan has to start within nine months from the date of the decision granting the aid. [The business plan shall have a maximum duration of five years.]

(655) The business plan must describe at least the following:
- (a) the initial economic situation of the beneficiary applying for aid;
- (b) milestones and targets for the development of the new activities of the beneficiary;
- (c) details of the actions required for the development of the activities of the beneficiary, such as details of investments, training, advice or other activity.

(656) [The aid must be paid in at least two instalments.] The instalments may be degressive. The payment of the last instalment must be conditional upon the correct implementation of the business plan.

(657) In determining the amount of aid, Member States must also take into account the socio-economic situation of the programme area.

Aid amount

(658) The aid amount must be limited to EUR 70,000 per undertaking. Member States must define the amount of aid also taking into account the socio-economic situation of the area concerned.

3.4. Aid for agri-environment-climate commitments to other land managers and undertakings in rural areas not active in the agricultural sector

(659) The Commission will consider aid for agri-environment-climate commitments to other land managers and to undertakings in rural areas not active in the agricultural sector compatible with the internal market under Article 107(3)(c) of the Treaty if it complies with the common assessment principles of these Guidelines, with the common provisions applicable to Chapter 3 of Part II of these Guidelines and with the following conditions.

(660) The aid must be granted in accordance with the applicable relevant conditions set out in point 1.1.5.1 of Part II of these Guidelines, with the following additional provisions relating to other land managers.

(661) Aid for agri-environment-climate commitments may be granted to groups formed of undertakings active in the agricultural sector and other land managers who undertake, on a voluntary basis, to carry out operations consisting of one or more agri-environment-climate commitments on agricultural land to be defined by Member States, including but not limited to the agricultural area as defined under (35).50 of these Guidelines.

(662) Where duly justified to achieve environmental objectives, aid for agri-environment-climate commitments may be granted to other land-managers or groups of other land-managers.

[(663) Aid to undertakings in rural areas which are not active in the agricultural sector may be provided for the conservation and for the sustainable use and development of genetic resources in agriculture, including non-indigenous resources, for operations not covered by the provisions under points (208) to (219) of Section 1.1.5.1 of Part II of these Guidelines]

3.5. Aid for disadvantages related to Natura 2000 areas to other land managers

(664) The Commission will consider aid for disadvantages related to Natura 2000 areas to other land managers compatible with the internal market under Article 107(3)(c) of the Treaty if it complies with the common assessment principles of these Guidelines, with the common provisions applicable to Chapter 3 of Part II of these Guidelines and with the following conditions.

(665) Aid may be granted to other land managers only in duly justified cases.

Eligible costs

(666) Aid may be granted to compensate other land managers for the additional costs and income foregone resulting from disadvantages in the areas concerned, related to the implementation of the Habitats Directive and the Birds Directive.

(667) Measures undertaken only in the following areas are eligible for aid:
- (a) Natura 2000 agricultural areas designated pursuant to Habitats Directive and the Birds Directive;
- (b) other delimited nature protection areas with environmental restrictions applicable to farming which contribute to the implementation of Article 10 of the Habitats Directive.

Aid amount

(668) Aid must be limited to the following amounts: EUR 500 per hectare per year maximum in the initial period not exceeding five years; EUR 200 per hectare per year maximum thereafter. The maximum amounts of EUR 500 and EUR 200 may be increased in exceptional cases taking into account specific circumstances to be justified.

3.6. AID FOR KNOWLEDGE TRANSFER AND INFORMATION ACTIONS IN RURAL AREAS

(669) The Commission will consider aid for knowledge transfer and information actions in rural areas compatible with the internal market under Article 107(3)(c) of the Treaty if it complies with the common assessment principles of these Guidelines, with the common provisions applicable to Chapter 3 of Part II of these Guidelines and with the following conditions.

(670) Aid under this measure covers vocational training and skills acquisition actions (including training courses, workshops and coaching), demonstration activities and information actions. Aid may be granted also for the training of advisors linked to the advisory services referred to in Section 1.1.10.2. and Sections 2.5. and 3.7. of Part II.

(671) Aid can be granted in favour of persons engaged in the food sector, other land managers than undertakings active in the agricultural sector and SMEs in rural areas. Aid for the training of advisors may be granted also in favour of large enterprises in rural areas.

(672) Aid may be granted in respect of the following eligible costs:
(a) the costs of organising and delivering the knowledge transfer or information action;
(b) in case of demonstration projects, aid may also cover relevant investment costs;
(c) the costs for travel, accommodation and per diem expenses of participants.

[(672a) Infrastructure installed as a result of demonstration may be used after the operation is completed.]

(673) The aid referred to in point (672)(a) and (b) must not involve direct payments to the beneficiaries. The aid must be paid to the provider of training or other knowledge transfer and information action. [However, aid for the training of advisers may be paid to the Managing Authority referred to in point (a) of Article 65(2) of Regulation (EU) No 1305/2013.]

(674) The aid must be accessible to all those eligible undertakings active in the rural area concerned, based on objectively defined conditions.

(675) Bodies providing knowledge transfer and information services must have the appropriate capacities in the form of staff qualifications and regular training to carry out this task.

Aid intensity

(676) The aid intensity must be limited to 50% of the eligible costs in the case of large enterprises, to 60% in the case of medium-sized enterprises and to 70% in the case of micro and small enterprises. Aid for training for advisors must be limited to EUR 200,000 per three years.

3.7. AID FOR ADVISORY SERVICES IN RURAL AREAS

(677) The Commission will consider aid for advisory services in rural areas compatible with the internal market under Article 107(3)(c) of the Treaty if it complies with the common assessment principles of these Guidelines, with the common provisions applicable to Chapter 3 of Part II of these Guidelines and with the following conditions.

(678) Aid should be granted to help other land managers and SMEs in rural areas benefit from the use of advisory services for the improvement of the economic and environmental performance as well as climate friendliness and resilience of their enterprise and/or investment.

(679) Advice to SMEs in rural areas may cover issues linked to the economic and environmental performance of the beneficiary.

(680) Advice to other land managers in rural areas should cover as a minimum one of the elements set out in point (301) of Section 1.1.10.2. of Part II of these Guidelines. It may also cover other issues, as referred to in point (302).

(681) The aid must not involve direct payments to the beneficiaries. [The aid must be paid to the provider of the advisory services or to the Managing Authority referred to in point (a) of Article 65(2) of Regulation (EU) No 1305/2013.]

(682) When providing advice, the providers of advisory services must respect the non-disclosure obligations referred to in Article 13(2) of Regulation (EU) No 1306/2013.

(683) Where justified and appropriate, the advice may be partly provided in group, while taking into account the situations of the individual user of advisory services.

Aid intensity

(684) Aid must be limited to EUR 1 500 per advice.

3.8. [AID FOR PARTICIPATION OF ACTIVE FARMERS IN QUALITY SCHEMES FOR COTTON OR FOODSTUFFS]

[(685) The Commission will consider aid for new participation, or participation in the five preceding years, of active farmers in quality schemes for cotton or foodstuffs compatible with the internal market under Article 107(3)(c) of the Treaty if it complies with the common assessment principles of these Guidelines, with the common provisions applicable to Chapter 3 of Part II of these Guidelines and with the following conditions.]

(686) The aid concerns the first participation of active farmers in one of the following categories of quality schemes:
(a) quality schemes for cotton or foodstuffs established by Union legislation;
(b) quality schemes for cotton or foodstuffs recognised by the Member States as complying with the following criteria:
(i) the specificity of the final product produced under such quality schemes must be derived from a clear obligations to guarantee
— specific product characteristics; or
— specific farming or production method; or

— a quality of the final product that goes significantly beyond the commercial commodity standards as regards public, animal or plant health, animal welfare or environmental protection;

(ii) the quality scheme must be open to all producers;

(iii) the quality scheme must involve binding final product specifications and compliance with those specifications must be verified by public authorities or by an independent inspection body;

[(iv) the quality scheme must be transparent and ensure complete traceability of agricultural products;]

(c) voluntary agricultural product certification schemes recognised by the Member States as meeting the Union best practice Guidelines for the operation of voluntary certification schemes relating to agricultural products.

Eligible costs

(687) The aid must be granted in the form of an annual incentive payment, to be determined according to the level of the fixed costs arising from participation in the quality schemes.

(688) The aid may be granted for a maximum period of five years. [If the initial participation in the quality scheme started before the application for support, the maximum period of five years shall be reduced by the number of years, which have elapsed between that initial participation and the time of the application for support.]

Aid amount

(689) The aid must be limited to EUR 3,000 per beneficiary per year.

3.9. AID FOR INFORMATION AND PROMOTION ACTIVITIES CONCERNING COTTON AND FOODSTUFFS COVERED BY A QUALITY SCHEME

(690) The Commission will consider aid for information and promotion activities concerning cotton and foodstuffs covered by a quality scheme compatible with the internal market within under Article 107(3)(c) of the Treaty if it complies with the common assessment principles of these Guidelines, with the common provisions applicable to Chapter 3 of Part II of these Guidelines and with the following conditions.

Eligible costs

(691) Aid may be granted for information and promotion activities concerning cotton and foodstuffs which are covered by a quality scheme for which aid is granted under Section 3.8. of Part II of these Guidelines.

(692) The aid may be granted to groups of producers implementing the information and promotion activities.

(693) The aid must cover the costs for actions having the following characteristics:

(a) be designed to induce consumers to buy the foodstuffs or the cotton covered by a quality scheme;

(b) draw attention to specific features or advantages of the foodstuff or the cotton, notably to the quality, specific production method, high animal welfare standards and respect for the environment linked to the quality scheme concerned.

(694) The actions referred to in point (693) must not incite consumers to buy a foodstuff or cotton due to their particular origin, except for those covered by the quality schemes introduced by Title II of Regulation (EU) No 1151/2012.

(695) The origin of the foodstuff or cotton may, nevertheless, be indicated, provided that the mention of the origin is subordinate to the main message.

(696) Information and promotion activities related to particular undertakings or of commercial brands are not eligible for aid.

(697) Only information and promotion activities implemented in the internal market are eligible.

Aid intensity

(698) The aid intensity must be up to 70% of the eligible costs.

3.10. AID FOR CO-OPERATION IN RURAL AREAS

(699) The Commission will consider aid for co-operation in rural areas compatible with the internal market under Article 107(3)(c) of the Treaty if it complies with the common assessment principles of these Guidelines, with the common provisions applicable to Chapter 3 of Part II of these Guidelines and with the following conditions.

(700) The aid should be granted in order to promote forms of co-operation among undertakings active in the agricultural sector, undertakings active in the food chain and other actors that contribute to achieving the objectives and priorities of rural development policy, including producer groups, cooperatives and inter-branch organizations, where the cooperation benefits rural areas.

(701) The co-operation must involve at least two entities, and may relate in particular to

(a) co-operation approaches;

(b) the creation of clusters and networks;

(c) the establishment and operation of operational groups of the EIP for agricultural productivity and sustainability as referred to in Article 56 of Regulation (EU) No 1305/2013.

(702) The aid may be granted to cooperation relating to the following activities:

(a) pilot projects;

(b) the development of new products, practices, processes and technologies in the food sector;

(c) co-operation among small operators in organizing joint work processes and sharing facilities and resources and for the development and/or marketing of tourism services relating to rural tourism;

(d) horizontal and vertical co-operation among supply chain actors for the establishment and development of short supply chains and local markets;

(e) promotion activities in a local context relating to the development of short supply chain and local markets;
(f) joint actions undertaken with a view to mitigating or adapting to climate change;
(g) joint approaches to environmental projects and ongoing environmental practices, including efficient water management, the use of renewable energy and the preservation of agricultural landscapes;
(h) horizontal and vertical cooperation among supply chain actors in the sustainable provision of biomass for use in food and energy production and industrial processes;
(i) implementation, in particular by groups of public and private partners other than those defined in point (b) of Article 32(2) of Regulation (EU) No 1303/2013, of local development strategies other than those defined in Article 2(19) of Regulation (EU) No 1303/2013 addressing one or more of the Union priorities for rural development;
(j) diversification of farming activities into activities concerning health care, social integration, community-supported agriculture and education about the environment and food.

(703) Aid for the creation of clusters and networks can be granted only to newly formed clusters and networks and those commencing an activity that is new to them.

(704) Aid for pilot projects referred to in point (702)(a) and for the development of new products, practices, processes and technologies in the food sector referred to in point (702)(b) may be granted also to individual actors where this possibility is provided for in the rural development programme. The results of pilot projects under point (702)(a) and activities under (702)(b) carried out by individual actors must be disseminated.

(705) Aid for the establishment and development of short supply chains, as referred to in point (702)(d) and (e) must cover only supply chains involving no more than one intermediary between farmer and consumer.

(706) Aid under this Section must comply with the relevant provisions of competition law, in particular with Articles 101 and 102 of the Treaty.

(707) Aid must be limited to a maximum period of seven years except for collective environmental action in duly justified cases.

Eligible costs

(708) Aid may be granted to cover the following eligible costs:
(a) costs for studies of the area concerned, feasibility studies, and the drawing up of a business plan or local development strategy other than the one referred to in Article 33 of Regulation (EU) No 1303/2013;
(b) costs for the animation of the area concerned in order to make feasible a collective territorial project or a project to be carried out by an operational group of the EIP for Agricultural Productivity and Sustainability as referred to in Article 56 of Regulation (EU) No 1305/2013; in the case of clusters, the animation may also concern networking between members and the recruitment of new members;
(c) the running costs of co-operation, such as the salary of a 'co-ordinator';
(d) the direct costs of specific projects linked to the implementation of a business plan, an environmental plan, a local development strategy other than the one referred to in Article 29 of Regulation (EU) No 1303/2013 or other actions targeted towards innovation, including testing;
(e) costs for promotion activities.

[(709) Save where aid is provided in the form of financial instruments, direct costs under point (708)(d) must be limited to the eligible costs of investment aid, as specified in points (635) and (636).]

Aid intensity

(710) The aid intensity for eligible costs referred to in point (708)(a), (b), (c) and (e) must not exceed 50%.

(711) The aid intensity for direct costs under point (708)(d) must not exceed those specified in point (638) of these Guidelines, including the scaling down mechanism for large investment projects. The aid intensity which applies to the area in which the investment is located will apply to all beneficiaries participating in the co-operation project. If the investment is located in two or more areas, the maximum aid intensity for the investment will be the one applicable in the area where the largest part of the eligible costs are incurred.

(712) The notification threshold referred to in point (639) applies to aid for direct costs related to investments under point (708)(d).

3.11. AID FOR SETTING-UP OF MUTUAL FUNDS

(713) The Commission will consider aid for the setting up of mutual funds compatible with the internal market under Article 107(3)(c) of the Treaty if it complies with the common assessment principles of these Guidelines, with the common provisions applicable to Chapter 3 of Part II of these Guidelines and with the following conditions.

(714) The mutual fund concerned must:
(a) be accredited by the competent authority in accordance with national law;
(b) have a transparent policy towards payments into and withdrawals from the fund;
(c) have clear rules attributing responsibilities for any debts incurred;
(d) pay financial contribution to undertakings active in the primary agricultural production for losses caused by adverse climatic events which can be assimilated to a natural disaster and animal diseases and plant pests as specified in Sections 1.2.1.2. and 1.2.1.3. of Part II of these Guidelines and/or losses caused by environmental incidents.

(715) Member States must define the rules for the constitution and management of the mutual funds, in particular for the granting of compensation payments as well as for the administration and monitoring of compliance with these rules. Member States must ensure that the fund arrangements provide for penalties in case of negligence on the part of the undertaking.

Eligible costs

[(716) Aid may be granted to cover only the following costs:

(a) the administrative costs of setting up the mutual fund, spread over a maximum period of three years in a degressive manner;

(b) the initial capital stock of the mutual fund.]

[(717) Member States may limit the eligible costs by applying ceilings per fund.]

Aid intensity

[(718) Aid must be limited to 70% of the eligible costs.]

NOTES

Points (138), (140), (230), (255), (296), (302), (310), (311), (334), (465), (483), (535), (537), (584)–(588), (594), (619): substituted by Commission Notice amending the European Union Guidelines for State aid in the agricultural and forestry sectors and in rural areas 2014 to 2020 (2015/C390/05).

Points (155) and (403) were substituted, and point (402) was repealed, by Commission notice amending the European Union Guidelines for State aid in the agricultural and forestry sectors and in rural areas 2014 to 2020 (2018/C403/06).

Point (177): substituted by Commission Notice amending the European Union Guidelines for State aid in the agricultural and forestry sectors and in rural areas 2014 to 2020 (2015/C390/05). Note that footnote 54 below was also substituted and footnote 54a was added.

Points (282), (347), (374), (375), (638), (686): words in square brackets substituted by Commission Notice amending the European Union Guidelines for State aid in the agricultural and forestry sectors and in rural areas 2014 to 2020 (2015/C390/05).

Points (454), (466): words in square brackets inserted by Commission Notice amending the European Union Guidelines for State aid in the agricultural and forestry sectors and in rural areas 2014 to 2020 (2015/C390/05).

Point (456): substituted by Commission Notice amending the European Union Guidelines for State aid in the agricultural and forestry sectors and in rural areas 2014 to 2020 (2015/C390/05). Note that footnote 78 below was also substituted.

Point (468): substituted by Commission Notice amending the European Union Guidelines for State aid in the agricultural and forestry sectors and in rural areas 2014 to 2020 (2015/C390/05). Note that footnote 79 below was also substituted.

Point (470): substituted by Commission Notice amending the European Union Guidelines for State aid in the agricultural and forestry sectors and in rural areas 2014 to 2020 (2015/C390/05). Note that the title preceding this point was also substituted.

Point (482): substituted by Commission Notice amending the European Union Guidelines for State aid in the agricultural and forestry sectors and in rural areas 2014 to 2020 (2015/C390/05). Note that footnote 81 below was also substituted.

Points (503), (513), (516), (518), (636), (663), (685), (709), (716), (717), (718): substituted by Commission Notice amending the European Union Guidelines for State aid in the agricultural and forestry sectors and in rural areas 2014 to 2020 (2018/C139/02).

Section 2.1.2 heading and section 3.8 heading substituted by Commission Notice amending the European Union Guidelines for State aid in the agricultural and forestry sectors and in rural areas 2014 to 2020 (2018/C139/02).

Points (536a), (567a), (569a), (642a), (644a), (672a): inserted by Commission Notice amending the European Union Guidelines for State aid in the agricultural and forestry sectors and in rural areas 2014 to 2020 (2018/C139/02).

Points (565), (645), (654), (673), (688): words in square brackets inserted by Commission Notice amending the European Union Guidelines for State aid in the agricultural and forestry sectors and in rural areas 2014 to 2020 (2018/C139/02).

Point (594a): inserted by Commission Notice amending the European Union Guidelines for State aid in the agricultural and forestry sectors and in rural areas 2014 to 2020 (2015/C390/05). Note that footnote 87a below was also inserted.

Point (635), (656), (681): words in square brackets substituted by Commission Notice amending the European Union Guidelines for State aid in the agricultural and forestry sectors and in rural areas 2014 to 2020 (2018/C139/02).

[51] Directive 2009/28/EC of the European Parliament and of the Council of 23 April 2009 on the promotion of the use of energy from renewable sources and amending and subsequently repealing Directives 2001/77/EC and 2003/30/EC (OJ L140, 5.6.2009, p 16).

[52] See footnote 42 of these Guidelines.

[53] OJ L187, 26.6.2014, p 1.

[54] Council Regulation (EC) No 1217/2009 of 30 November 2009 setting up a network for the collection of accountancy data on the incomes and business operation of agricultural holdings in the European Union (OJ L328, 15.12.2009, p 27).

[54a] Commission Implementing Regulation (EU) 2015/220 of 3 February 2015 laying down rules for the application of Council Regulation (EC) No 1217/2009 setting up a network for the collection of accountancy data on the incomes and business operation of agricultural holdings in the European Union (OJ L46, 19.2.2015, p 1).

[55] See definition of agricultural sector in point (35)2 of these Guidelines.

[56] See the definition of SME in point (35)13 of these Guidelines.

[57] See the definition of large enterprise in point (35)14 of these Guidelines.

[58] For instance, in the case of sub-measures aiming at restoring and maintaining wetland habitats, aid could be granted for a period of more than seven years given the complexity of meeting these objectives.

[59] See point (52) and footnote 42 of these Guidelines.

[60] Council Regulation (EC) No 1698/2005 of 20 September 2005 on support for rural development by the European Agricultural Fund for Rural Development (*EAFRD*) (OJ L277, 21.10.2005, p 1).

[61] Council Regulation (EC) No 834/2007 of 28 June 2007 on organic production and labelling of organic products and repealing Regulation (EEC) No 2092/91 (OJ L189, 20.7.2007, p 1).

[62] Council Regulation (EC) No 834/2007 of 28 June 2007 on organic production and labelling of organic products and repealing Regulation (EEC) No 2092/91 (OJ L189, 20.7.2007, p 1).

[63] Regulation (EC) No 110/2008 of the European Parliament and of the Council of 15 January 2008 on the definition, description, presentation, labelling and the protection of geographical indications of spirit drinks and repealing Council Regulation (EEC) No 1576/89 (OJ L39, 13.2.2008, p 16).

[64] Regulation (EU) No 251/2014 of the European Parliament and of the Council of 26 February 2014 on the definition, description, presentation, labelling and the protection of geographical indications of aromatised wine products and repealing Council Regulation (EEC) No 1601/91 (OJ L84, 20.3.2014, p 14).

[65] OJ C341, 16.12.2010, p 5.

[66] See footnote 42 of these Guidelines.

67 See definition of agricultural sector in point (35)2 of these Guidelines.

68 This applies to co-operation relating to the production of energy from renewable sources or the production of biofuels on holdings, provided that the conditions laid down in Section 1.1.1.1 of Part II of these Guidelines are complied with.

69 See definition of agricultural sector in point (35)2 of these Guidelines.

70 Court of Justice, 11.11.2004, C 73/03, Spain v. Commission, par. 37; Court of Justice, 23.2.2006, C-346/03 and C-529/03, *Giuseppe Atzeni and others*, par. 79.

71 The Commission did not accept that a fire at a single processing plant which was covered by normal commercial insurance could be considered as an exceptional occurrence. As a general rule the Commission does not accept that an outbreak of an animal disease or the occurrence of a plant pest may be considered as constituting natural disasters or exceptional occurrences. However, in one case the Commission did recognise the very widespread outbreak of a completely new animal disease as an exceptional occurrence.

72 Commission decisions on State aid in cases N 274b/2010, N 274a/2010, SA.33605, SA.33628, SA.36787.

73 Council Directive 2000/29/EC of 8 May 2000 on protective measures against the introduction into the Community of organisms harmful to plants or plant products and against their spread within the Community (OJ L169, 10.7.2000, p 1).

74 Regulation (EU) No 652/2014 of the European Parliament and of the Council of 15 May 2014 laying down provisions for the management of expenditure relating to the food chain, animal health and animal welfare, and relating to plant health and plant reproductive material, amending Council Directives 98/56/EC, 2000/29/EC and 2008/90/EC, Regulations (EC) No 178/2002, (EC) No 882/2004 and (EC) No 396/2005 of the European Parliament and of the Council, Directive 2009/128/EC of the European Parliament and of the Council and Regulation (EC) No 1107/2009 of the European Parliament and of the Council and repealing Council Decisions 66/399/ EEC, 76/894/EEC and 2009/470/EC (OJ L189, 27.6.2014, p 1).

75 See definition of agricultural sector at point (35)2 of these Guidelines.

76 Directive 2010/75/EU of the European Parliament and of the Council of 24 November 2010 on industrial emissions (integrated pollution prevention and control) (OJ L334, 17.12.2010, p 17).

77 See definition of agricultural sector in point (35)2 of these Guidelines.

78 Regulation (EU) No 1169/2011 of the European Parliament and of the Council of 25 October 2011 on the provision of food information to consumers, amending Regulations (EC) No 1924/2006 and (EC) No 1925/2006 of the European Parliament and of the Council, and repealing Commission Directive 87/250/EEC, Council Directive 90/496/EEC, Commission Directive 1999/10/EC, Directive 2000/13/EC of the European Parliament and of the Council, Commission Directives 2002/67/EC and 2008/5/EC and Commission Regulation (EC) No 608/2004 (OJ L304, 22.11.2011, p 18).

79 Case T-139/09, France v. Commission, ECLI:EU:T:2012:496.

80 See definition of agricultural sector in point (35)2 of these Guidelines.

81 OJ C249, 31.7.2014, p 1.

82 See definition of agricultural sector in point (35)2 of these Guidelines.

83 OJ C198, 27.6.2014, p 1.

84 See Communication from the Commission to the European Parliament, the Council, the Economic and Social Committee and the Committee of the Regions, Our life insurance, our natural capital: an EU biodiversity strategy to 2020, COM (2011) 244 final.

85 Second Ministerial Conference on the protection of Forests in Europe, 16–17 June 1993, Helsinki/Finland, 'Resolution H1 – General Guidelines for the Sustainable Management of Forests in Europe'.

86 Council Directive 92/43/EEC of 21 May 1992 on the conservation of natural habitats and of wild fauna and flora (OJ L206, 22.7.1992, p 7) ('Habitats Directive').

87 Directive 2009/147/EC of the European Parliament and of the Council of 30 November 2009 on the conservation of wild birds (OJ L20, 26.1.2010, p 7) ('Birds Directive').

87a This approach is required under the principles of Integrated Pest Management in Directive 2009/128/EC establishing a framework for Community action to achieve the sustainable use of pesticides.

88 Articles 107, 108 and 109 of the Treaty apply to aid for basic services in rural areas, in so far as they constitute State aid within the meaning of Article 107(1) of the Treaty, taking also into account the interpretation of State aid given in the forthcoming Commission notice on the notion of aid.

PART III. PROCEDURAL MATTERS

1. Duration of aid schemes and evaluation

[5.527]

(719) Following the established practice in its previous Guidelines, in order to contribute to transparency and to the regular review of all existing aid schemes, the Commission will only authorise aid schemes of limited duration. Schemes covering State aid for measures that can also benefit from EAFRD co-financing under Regulation (EU) No 1305/2013 should be limited to the duration of the programming period 2014–2020. Where Union law so allows, and in accordance with the conditions set out therein, Member States may continue to make new commitments for rural development on the basis of Regulation (EU) No 1305/2013 and its implementing regulation. The Commission will therefore apply these Guidelines also to such new commitments. Other aid schemes should not apply for a period of more than seven years.

(720) To further ensure that distortions of competition and trade are limited, the Commission may require that certain schemes are subject to a time limitation (of normally four years or less) and to the evaluation referred to in point (40). Evaluations will be carried out for schemes where the potential distortions of competition are particularly high, that is to say, that may risk to significantly restrict or distort competition if their implementation is not reviewed in due time.

(721) Given the objectives of the evaluation and in order not to impose a disproportionate burden on Member States in respect of smaller aid amounts, evaluation only applies for aid schemes with large aid budgets, containing novel characteristics or when significant market, technology or regulatory changes are foreseen. The evaluation must be

carried out by an expert independent from the aid granting authority on the basis of a common methodology and must be made public. Member States must notify, together with the relevant aid scheme, a draft evaluation plan, which will be an integral part of the Commission assessment of the scheme.

(722) . . .

(723) The evaluation must be submitted to the Commission in due time to allow for the assessment of the possible prolongation of the aid scheme and in any case upon its expiry. Any subsequent aid measure with a similar objective must take into account the results of the evaluation.

2. Revision clause

(724) A revision clause should be provided for operations undertaken pursuant to Sections 1.1.5.1 and 1.1.5.2., Section1.1.8 and Sections 2.3. and 3.4. of Part II, in order to ensure their adjustment in the case of amendments of the relevant mandatory standards, requirements or obligations referred to in those Sections beyond which the commitments referred to in those Sections have to go.

(725) Operations undertaken pursuant to Sections 1.1.5.1 and 1.1.5.2., Section 1.1.8 and Sections 2.3. and 3.4. of Part II which extend beyond the rural development programming period 2014–2020 should contain a revision clause in order to allow for their adjustment to the legal framework of the following programming period.

(726) If the adjustments referred to in points (724) and (725) are not accepted or not implemented by the beneficiary, the commitment will expire and the aid amount should be reduced to the aid amount corresponding for the period until the expiry of the commitment.

3. Reporting and monitoring

(727) In accordance with Council Regulation (EC) No 659/1999[89] and Commission Regulation (EC) No 794/2004[90] and their subsequent amendments, Member States must submit annual reports to the Commission.

(728) The annual report must contain also information concerning the following:

(a) animal diseases or plant pest concerned under Section 1.2.1.3;

(b) meteorological information on the type, timing, relative magnitude and location of the climatic event which can be assimilated to a natural disaster or natural disasters under Sections 1.2.1.1 and 1.2.1.2 respectively.

(729) The Commission reserves the right to seek additional information on existing aid schemes on a case by case basis, where this is necessary to enable it to fulfil its responsibilities under Article 108(1) of the Treaty.

(730) Member States must ensure that detailed records regarding all measures involving the granting of aid are maintained. Such records must contain all information necessary to establish that all conditions of these Guidelines regarding, where applicable, eligible costs and maximum allowable aid intensity have been observed. These records must be maintained for 10 years from the date of granting the aid and must be provided to the Commission upon request.

4. Application of these Guidelines

(731) The Commission will apply these Guidelines from 1 July 2014.

(732) The Commission will apply these Guidelines to all notified aid measures in respect of which it is called upon to take a decision after 1 July 2014, even where the aid was notified prior to that date. However, individual aid granted under approved aid schemes and notified to the Commission pursuant to an obligation to notify such aid individually will be assessed under the Guidelines that apply to the approved aid scheme on which the individual aid is based.

(733) Unlawful aid will be assessed in accordance with the rules in force on the date of granting the aid. Individual aid granted under an unlawful aid scheme will be assessed under the Guidelines that apply to the unlawful aid scheme at the time the individual aid was granted.

(734) The former Community Guidelines for State aid in the Agriculture and Forestry sector 2007 to 2013 are repealed as of the date of application of these Guidelines. For EAFRD co-financed rural development measures, where Union law so allows, and in accordance with the conditions set out in the rural development rules, Member States may continue to make new commitments under the former Guidelines for State aid in the Agriculture and Forestry sector 2007 to 2013 in accordance with its Point 189.[91]

5. Proposals for appropriate measures

(735) In accordance with Article 108(1) of the Treaty the Commission proposes that Member States amend their existing aid schemes to conform with these Guidelines by 30 June 2015 at the latest. With regard to this delay, the following derogations apply:

(a) existing aid schemes, where the compatibility assessment under the Community Guidelines for State aid in the Agriculture and Forestry sector 2007–2013 had been carried out by the Commission in line with Regulation (EC) No 1857/2006, have to conform with these Guidelines as of 1 January 2015, at the latest;

(b) existing aid schemes for meeting standards under Sub-chapter IV.E. of the Community Guidelines for State aid in the Agriculture and Forestry sector 2007–2013 and aid for purchase of forestry land used as nature protection areas have to be put to end by 30 June 2016;

(c) existing aid schemes for tax exemptions and reductions under Directive 2003/96/EC referred to in Sub-chapter VI.F of the Community Guidelines for State aid in the Agriculture and Forestry sector 2007–2013 have to conform with the applicable horizontal rules of the Guidelines on State aid for environmental protection and energy 2014–2020 by 30 June 2016 unless such aid is exempt from notification obligation;

(d) existing aid schemes for early retirement should be phased out by 31 December 2018, at the latest.

(736) The Member States are invited to give their explicit unconditional agreement to these proposed appropriate measures within two months from the date of publication of these Guidelines in the Official Journal of the European Union. In the absence of any reply, the Commission will assume that the Member State in question does not agree with the proposed measures.

6. EXPIRY

[(737) These Guidelines will be applicable until 31 December 2022. The Commission may decide to review or amend these Guidelines at any time if this should be necessary for reasons associated with competition policy or to take account of other Union policies, such as agricultural and rural development or human and animal health, plant protection and environmental policy considerations, and international commitments, or for any other justified reason.]

NOTES

Point (722): repealed by Commission Notice amending the European Union Guidelines for State aid in the agricultural and forestry sectors and in rural areas 2014 to 2020 (2015/C390/05).

Point (737): substituted by Commission Notice amending the European Union Guidelines for State aid in the agricultural and forestry sectors and in rural areas 2014 to 2020 as regards their period of application and making temporary adaptations to take into account the impact of the COVID-19 pandemic (2020/C424/05). Note that previously these Guidelines were due to expire on 31 December 2020.

[89] Council Regulation (EC) No 659/1999 of 22 March 1999 laying down detailed rules for the application of Article 93 of the EC Treaty (OJ L83, 27.3.1999, p 3).

[90] Commission Regulation (EC) No 794/2004 of 21 April 2004 implementing Council Regulation (EC) No 659/1999 laying down detailed rules for the application of Article 93 of the EC Treaty (OJ L140, 30.4.2004, p 1).

[91] As modified on 19 November 2013, OJ C339, 20.11.2013, p 1.

10. FISHERIES

COUNCIL REGULATION

(744/2008/EC)

of 24 July 2008

instituting a temporary specific action aiming to promote the restructuring of the European Community fishing fleets affected by the economic crisis

[5.528]

NOTES

Date of publication in OJ: OJ L202, 31.7.2008, p 1.

Note: with effect from 1 December 2009, the EC Treaty was replaced by the Treaty on the Functioning of the European Union. References in this document to provisions of the EC Treaty should be construed accordingly.

Application of this Regulation to the United Kingdom: in accordance with the European Union (Withdrawal) Act 2018, s 3 at **[7.5]**, this Regulation became domestic law on IP completion day (as defined in the European Union (Withdrawal Agreement) Act 2020, s 39).

THE COUNCIL OF THE EUROPEAN UNION,

Having regard to the Treaty establishing the European Community, and in particular Articles 36 and 37 thereof,

Having regard to the proposal from the Commission,

Having regard to the opinion of the European Parliament[1],

Whereas:

(1) Council Regulation (EC) No 1198/2006 of 27 July 2006 on the European Fisheries Fund[2] lays down the rules regarding Community structural assistance in the fisheries sector. In particular, Chapter I of Title IV of that Regulation lays down the terms on which the Member States may receive a financial contribution from the European Fisheries Fund (EFF) for the measures for the adaptation of the Community fishing fleet.

(2) The EFF aims to contribute to the steps that have been taken since the 2002 reform of the common fisheries policy (CFP) in view of reducing pressure on fish stocks, whilst ensuring sustainable social and economic conditions for the sector concerned.

(3) In the context of the recent economic situation, following in particular the drastic increase in fuel prices, there is an impending need to take additional measures aiming for a more rapid adaptation of the Community fishing fleet to the current situation, addressing the need to ensure sustainable social and economic conditions for the sector concerned. Such measures should contribute to attaining the general objectives set out in Article 33 of the Treaty and the CFP objectives as laid down in Council Regulation (EC) No 2371/2002 of 20 December 2002 on the conservation and sustainable exploitation of fisheries resources under the common fisheries policy[3]. In this context, those measures should address both the immediate situation of economic and social hardship while tackling systemic overcapacity.

(4) It is of importance to ensure that such measures will be equally available for all Member States and that they do not introduce any distortion of competition between Member States or fleets. They therefore need to be addressed and coordinated at Community level.

(5) Consequently, there is a need for a Community initiative supplementing and allowing for temporary derogations from certain provisions of Regulation (EC) No 1198/2006 and to temporarily derogate from certain provisions of Regulations (EC) No 2371/2002 and (EC) No 1198/2006. This initiative should therefore provide for specific measures of general nature and for the implementation of Fleet Adaptation Schemes in the Member States, which effectively address the current economic difficulties, whilst ensuring the long-term viability of fisheries sector.

(6) In view of the exceptional nature of those measures and of the economic hardship they intend to address, the duration of these measures should be limited to the shortest possible period sufficient to achieve the expected aims.

(7) These measures should be implemented by the Member States in the context of their operational programme under the EFF and financed from the funds allocated to them in that framework.

(8) Moreover, Member States should be entitled to supplement the measures benefiting from such funds by financing certain measures through solely national funds with no financing from Community financial instruments. In view of the need to rapidly tackle the serious situation faced by the fisheries sector, those measures, aimed at bringing about structural improvement and long-term economic viability of the sector, should not be subject to the application of Articles 87, 88 and 89 of the Treaty. In order to limit possible distortions of competition and effects on the internal market, those measures should be subject to certain limitations.

(9) This Regulation should provide for a Community contribution to measures for permanent and temporary cessation of fishing activities, for investments on board aiming to reduce fuel dependency of fishing vessels, for socio-economic compensation as well as for certain actions of a more collective nature. In order to ensure the effectiveness of those measures, as well as to allow Member States to make use of the available funds to the fullest extent possible, the thresholds for private participation in the financing of the measures should be lowered.

(10) In order to contribute to restructuring, the temporary cessation of fishing activities should be made available. Temporary cessation of fishing activities should in particular be aimed at enhancing economic benefits by supporting stock recovery or by promoting more favourable marketing conditions. To that effect, Member States should be encouraged to link the period of temporary cessation with considerations of biological dynamics, seasonality and market dynamics. In the context of the economic crisis, it is also necessary to facilitate the compensation to be granted to fishers that have temporary ceased their activities prior to the adoption of this Regulation.

(11) In view of assisting the fishing sector to adapt to less fuel consuming fishing techniques, it is appropriate to

facilitate the replacement of existing equipment on board fishing vessels in order to allow for new, less energy-consuming, fishing techniques. In this regard, additional possibilities for contributions to investments on board fishing vessels should be made available.

(12) A Community contribution should also be provided for collective actions aimed at delivering expertise to vessel owners in relation to energy audits for vessels, and expert advice on the development of restructuring and modernisation plans and Fleet Adaptation Schemes. Moreover, financing should be made available for pilot projects aiming at reducing energy consumption for vessels, engines, equipment or gear.

(13) In view of long-term viability of the fishing sector, a new instrument should be introduced allowing Member States to reduce capacity and to increase profitability of the fleets. This should take the form of Fleet Adaptation Schemes and concern fleets where the energy costs represent on average at least 30% of the production costs. These Fleet Adaptation Schemes should result in a capacity reduction of the fleets concerned of at least 30% expressed in GT and kW.

(14) Where measures are implemented by Member States in the context of Fleet Adaptation Schemes, with a view to ensuring the long-term viability of one or more of their fleets through capacity reduction, more favourable conditions should apply.

(15) There is a need to encourage Member States to further extend their permanent cessation schemes in order to adjust their fleets to the available resources. Consequently, it is appropriate to allow for further contribution possibilities to permanent cessation. In order to facilitate restructuring, further possibilities for temporary cessation of fishing activities should be allowed for fishers and vessel owners concerned by Fleet Adaptation Schemes.

(16) Furthermore, Member States having adopted a Fleet Adaptation Scheme should also be allowed to implement partial decommissioning measures ensuring a more cost-efficient use of funds available for reducing capacity and energy consumption of the fleet concerned. Within such partial decommissioning measures, vessel owners withdrawing one or more of their vessels from the fleet should be allowed to re-use part of the capacity withdrawn for a new smaller and less energy consuming vessel. In addition, Member States should be allowed to allocate a limited amount of the total capacity withdrawn under the Fleet Adaptation Scheme to new vessels. In such case, funds should be made available only for the part of the capacity which is permanently withdrawn.

(17) The obligations of Member States regarding management and control pursuant to Article 70 of Regulation (EC) No 1198/2006 and the mechanism for corrections pursuant to Article 97 of Regulation (EC) No 1198/2006 should apply in the framework of this Regulation.

(18) Failure to achieve the 30% minimum reduction in capacity laid down in a Fleet Adaptation Scheme or failure to comply with the rules on temporary cessation, permanent cessation or partial decommissioning should be regarded as irregularities within the meaning of Article 97 of Regulation (EC) No 1198/2006.

(19) In view of the urgency of the situation and the need for immediate action in all Member States, it is appropriate to increase the percentage of Community co-financing under the EFF of the measures under this initiative to 95%. In the same context, it is important that these funds are available to Member States within shorter delays than normally applicable and that expenditure is eligible from the date of the entry into force of this Regulation.

(20) Given the urgency of the situation, there is a compelling need to allow an exception to the six-week period referred to in Section I.3 of the Protocol on the role of national parliaments in the European Union, annexed to the Treaty on European Union and to the Treaties establishing the European Communities,

NOTES

1 Opinion delivered on 10 July 2008 (not yet published in the Official Journal).

2 OJ L223, 15.8.2006, p 1.

3 OJ L358, 31.12.2002, p 59. Regulation as amended by Regulation (EC) No 865/2007 (OJ L192, 24.7.2007, p 1).

HAS ADOPTED THIS REGULATION:

CHAPTER I GENERAL PROVISIONS

[5.529]

Article 1 Subject matter

1. This Regulation establishes a specific Community action designed to provide for exceptional and temporary support for the persons and enterprises active in the fisheries sector affected by the economic crisis induced by the increase of oil prices in 2008, as a special regime under the European Fisheries Fund (hereinafter referred to as EFF).

2. This specific action shall consist of:

(a) general measures supplementing and derogating from certain provisions of Regulation (EC) No 1198/2006, and

(b) special measures supplementing and derogating from certain provisions of Regulations (EC) No 2371/2002 and (EC) No 1198/2006 that are conditional upon the implementation of a Fleet Adaptation Scheme as referred to in Article 12.

[5.530]

Article 2 Scope

This Regulation shall apply only to public aid which has been the subject of an administrative decision by the relevant national authorities by 31 December 2010.

[5.531]

Article 3 Financial framework

1. The measures provided for under this Regulation may receive financial support from the EFF within the limits of the commitment appropriations defined for the period 2007–13.

2. Public aid granted under this specific action may not be cumulated with another public aid having the same purpose, and in particular that granted by the European Agricultural Fund for Rural Development (EAFRD), the European Regional Development Fund (ERDF), the European Social Fund (ESF), the Cohesion Fund, other Community financial instruments and national funds.

[5.532]

Article 4 Application of State aid rules

1. Without prejudice to paragraph 2 of this Article, Articles 87, 88 and 89 of the Treaty shall not apply to aid granted by Member States, pursuant to and in conformity with this Regulation within the scope of Article 36 of the Treaty.
2. Aid granted by Member States with no financing from Community financial instruments and exceeding the limits laid down in Article 1(3) of Commission Regulation (EC) No 736/2008 of 22 July 2008 on the application of Articles 87 and 88 of the Treaty to State aid to small and medium-sized enterprises active in the production, processing and marketing of fisheries products[1] shall be subject to the application of Articles 87, 88 and 89 of the Treaty.
3. Where aid is granted by Member States with no financing from Community financial instruments within the limits laid down in Article 1(3) of Regulation (EC) No 736/2008, they shall forward to the Commission a summary of the information regarding such aid prior to its implementation. Moreover, each year, by 1 July at the latest, Member States shall submit to the Commission a report on the aid granted under this paragraph.

NOTES

[1] OJ L201, 30.7.2008, p 16.

CHAPTER II GENERAL MEASURES

[5.533]

Article 5 General measures

Public aid to the persons and enterprises referred to in Article 1 may be granted until 31 December 2010 according to the rules set out in this Chapter.

[5.534]

Article 6 Temporary cessation of fishing activities

1. In addition to the measures provided for in Article 24 of Regulation (EC) No 1198/2006, the EFF may contribute to the financing of aid measures for the temporary cessation of fishing activities for fishers and owners of fishing vessels for a maximum duration of three months implemented during the period from 1 July 2008 to 31 December 2009, provided that:
   (a) the temporary cessation of fishing activities commenced before 31 December 2008, and
   (b) the beneficiary enterprises become subject until 31 January 2009 to restructuring measures such as Fleet Adaptation Schemes, fishing effort adjustment plans, national decommissioning schemes, catch plans, other restructuring/modernisation measures.

The management plans provided for in Articles 9 and 10 of Regulation (EC) No 2371/2002 shall be covered by this paragraph, insofar as they involve fishing effort adjustment plans pursuant to Article 21 of Regulation (EC) No 1198/2006.

2. The measures provided for in paragraph 1 may cover the following costs:
   (a) part of the fixed cost incurred by the vessel owners when the vessel is tied-up in the port (such as port charges, insurance cost, maintenance costs, financial costs related to loans);
   (b) part of the basic salary of the fishers.
3. The total public aid per Member State to the measures provided for in paragraph 1 shall not exceed the higher of the following two thresholds: EUR 6 million or an amount equal to 8% of the EFF financial assistance allocated to the sector in the Member State concerned.

[5.535]

Article 7 Investments on board fishing vessels and selectivity

By way of derogation from point (a) of Annex II to Regulation (EC) No 1198/2006 where a contribution is granted for the financing of equipment, including auxiliary motors, which significantly improves energy efficiency on board fishing vessels, including small scale coastal fishing vessels, and reduces emissions and contributes to the fight against climate change, the minimum private financial participation to that operation shall be 40%.

[5.536]

Article 8 Socio-economic compensation

In addition to the measures provided for in Article 27 of Regulation (EC) No 1198/2006, the EFF may contribute to the financing of early departure measures, including early retirement for workers in the fisheries sector, with the exception of workers in the aquaculture sector and in the sector of processing of fisheries and aquaculture products.

[5.537]

Article 9 Collective actions

1. In addition to the collective actions provided for in Article 37 of Regulation (EC) No 1198/2006, the EFF may contribute to the financing of measures providing assistance for:
   (a) carrying out energy audits for groups of vessels, and
   (b) expert advice on the development of restructuring or modernisation plans, including Fleet Adaptation Schemes referred to in Article 12.
2. By way of derogation from point (a) of Annex II to Regulation (EC) No 1198/2006, where a contribution is granted for the financing of measures referred to in paragraph 1 of this Article, the maximum rate for public contribution shall be 100%.

3. The EFF may contribute to the financing of compensation granted to producer organisations which are no longer entitled to benefit from aid under the second and third subparagraph of Article 10(1) of Council Regulation (EC) 104/2000 of 17 December 1999 on the common organisation of the markets in fishery and aquaculture products[1], in order to offset the costs arising from the obligations imposed on them under Article 9 of the same Regulation, and subject to the conditions laid down in Article 10, paragraphs 2, 3 and 4 of that Regulation.

NOTES

[1] Council Regulation (EC) No 104/2000 of 17 December 1999 on the common organisation of the markets in fishery and aquaculture products (OJ L17, 21.1.2000, p 22). Regulation as last amended by Regulation (EC) No 1759/2006 (OJ L335, 1.12.2006, p 3).

[5.538]

Article 10 Pilot projects

In addition to the measures provided for in Article 41(2) of Regulation (EC) No 1198/2006, the EFF may contribute to the financing of pilot projects testing technical improvements aiming at reducing energy consumption for vessels, engines, equipment or gear and at reducing emissions and contributing to the fight against climate change.

CHAPTER III SPECIAL MEASURES APPLICABLE ONLY TO FLEETS CONCERNED BY FLEET ADAPTATION SCHEMES

[5.539]

Article 11 Measures applicable only to fleets subject to Fleet Adaptation Schemes

Public aid to the persons and enterprises referred to in Article 1 may be granted until 31 December 2010, according to the rules set out in this Chapter, provided they are subject to a Fleet or Fleet Segment Adaptation Scheme referred to in Article 12.

[5.540]

Article 12 Fleet Adaptation Schemes

1. Member States may adopt and implement Fleet Adaptation Schemes aimed at restructuring the fishing fleets or fleet segments affected by the economic crisis.
2. Fleet Adaptation Schemes may include the measures provided for in Chapter I of Title IV of Regulation (EC) No 1198/2006 and those provided for in this Regulation.
3. A Fleet Adaptation Scheme shall concern only fleets or fleet segments where the energy costs represent on average at least 30% of the production costs, based on the trading account for the 12 months preceding 1 July 2008 for the fleet concerned by that scheme.
4. A Fleet Adaptation Scheme shall fulfil the following requirements:
  (a) it shall result, by 31 December 2012 at the latest, in a permanent reduction of at least 30% of the fishing capacity of the fleet or fleet segment covered by the scheme; that threshold may be lowered to a minimum of 20%, subject to the approval of the Commission, where the Fleet Adaptation Scheme concerns a Member State whose fleet is less than 100 active vessels, or less than 12,000 GT, or where a Fleet Adaptation Scheme covers only vessels of less than 12 metres, and a 30% reduction would disproportionately affect the viability of the fisheries related activities depending on it, and
  (b) it shall include the list of the vessels covered by the scheme, identified by their names and Community Fishing Fleet Register numbers.
5. Each fishing vessel may be included only in one Fleet Adaptation Scheme. The conditions for including a fishing vessel in a Fleet Adaptation Scheme shall be as follows:
  (a) vessels must have carried out a fishing activity of at least 120 days at sea during the two years preceding the date of the adoption of the Fleet Adaptation Scheme; and
  (b) vessels must be operational on 31 July 2008.
6. By 30 June 2009 at the latest, Member States shall communicate to the Commission the Fleet Adaptation Schemes adopted.
7. When a Member State requests a revision of its operational programme for the purpose of incorporating the Fleet Adaptation Schemes, Article 18 of Regulation (EC) No 1198/2006 shall apply accordingly.

[5.541]

Article 13 Compliance and audit of Fleet Adaptation Schemes

1. The reports mentioned in Article 67 of Regulation (EC) No 1198/2006 shall include the results achieved in implementation of the Fleet Adaptation Schemes.
2. The Commission may perform audits on the implementation of the Fleet Adaptation Schemes. To that purpose, it may be assisted by external experts financed by the EFF under the provisions of Article 46(1) of Regulation (EC) No 1198/2006.

[5.542]

Article 14 Permanent cessation of fishing activities

1. For the purposes of Article 23 of Regulation (EC) No 1198/2006, Fleet Adaptation Schemes are assimilated to the fishing effort adjustment plans referred to in that Article.
2. The provisions of Article 23(2) of Regulation (EC) No 1198/2006 shall not apply to permanent cessation measures adopted in the context of a Fleet Adaptation Scheme.
3. Within six months from the adoption of a Fleet Adaptation Scheme, the vessels listed for permanent cessation of fishing activities under this Fleet Adaptation Scheme shall cease permanently their fishing activities.

[5.543]

Article 15 Temporary cessation of fishing activities

1. In addition to the measures provided for by Article 24 of Regulation (EC) No 1198/2006 and in Article 6 of this Regulation, the EFF may contribute to the financing of aid measures for temporary cessation of fishing activities for fishers and owners of fishing vessels included in a Fleet Adaptation Scheme, provided that the temporary cessation is implemented during the period going from 1 January 2009 to 31 December 2009 and has a maximum duration of:

(a) three months prior to the permanent withdrawal of the vessel or during the period of engine replacement; a maximum of three additional months may be granted where the process of engine replacement is still ongoing;

(b) six weeks in the case of the other vessels included in a Fleet Adaptation Scheme when those vessels are subject to one of the other measures referred to in Article 12, paragraph 2.

2. The measures provided for in paragraph 1 may cover the following costs:

(a) the fixed cost incurred by the vessel owners when the vessel is tied-up in the port (such as port charges, insurance cost, maintenance costs, financial costs related to loans);

(b) part of the basic salary of the fishers.

3. The total public aid per Member State to the measures provided for in paragraph 1 shall not exceed the higher of the following two thresholds: EUR 6 million or an amount equal to 8% of the EFF financial assistance allocated to the sector in the Member State concerned.

[5.544]

Article 16 Investments on board fishing vessels and selectivity

1. By way of derogation from point (a) of Annex II to Regulation (EC) No 1198/2006, where a contribution is granted for the financing of equipment or of gear or engine replacement which significantly improves energy efficiency on board fishing vessels, including small scale coastal fishing vessels, and reduces emissions and contributes to the fight against climate change, the minimum private financial participation to that operation shall be 40% of the total of the eligible costs of the operation.

2. Member States shall fix the minimum private financial participation referred to in paragraph 1 on the basis of objective criteria such as the age of the vessel, the energy efficiency improvement, or the amount of capacity reduction included in the Fleet Adaptation Scheme.

3. The age limit referred to in Article 25(1) of Regulation (EC) No 1198/2006 shall not apply to the vessels receiving aid under this Article for equipment or gear replacement.

4. By way of derogation from Article 25(3)(c) of Regulation (EC) No 1198/2006, the EFF may contribute to one replacement of the engine per vessel of more than 24 metres in overall length included in a Fleet Adaptation Scheme, provided that the new engine has at least 20% less power than the old one and it increases energy efficiency.

5. By way of derogation from paragraph 7 of Article 25 of Regulation (EC) No 1198/2006, one additional replacement of gear shall be allowed to vessels included in a Fleet Adaptation Scheme under the condition that the new gear significantly improves energy efficiency. The conditions laid down in points (a) and (b) of that paragraph shall not apply.

CHAPTER IV MEASURES FOR PARTIAL DECOMMISSIONING UNDER FLEET ADAPTATION SCHEMES

[5.545]

Article 17 Partial decommissioning

Public aid to vessel owners permanently withdrawing one or more vessels included in a Fleet Adaptation Scheme in order to build a new vessel of lesser fishing capacity and lesser energy consumption (hereinafter referred to as partial decommissioning) may be granted until 31 December 2010 according to the rules laid down in this Chapter, and provided that the Fleet Adaptation Scheme fulfils the following two requirements:

(a) it includes vessels using one and the same fishing gear, and

(b) it includes vessels representing at least 70% of the capacity of the fleet using that gear in the Member State.

[5.546]

Article 18 Public aid for the permanent cessation of fishing in the case of partial decommissioning

1. In addition to Article 23 of Regulation (EC) No 1198/2006, vessel owners engaging in partial decommissioning shall be entitled to receive public aid for the permanent cessation of fishing activities for the difference between the capacity withdrawn and the capacity re-allocated to a new vessel.

2. The fishing capacity of the new vessel shall not be higher than 40% of the capacity withdrawn by the vessel owners.

3. Where appropriate, Member States shall adapt the fishing licence accordingly.

[5.547]

Article 19 Withdrawal and reallocation of fishing capacity

1. By way of derogation from Article 11, paragraphs 3 and 4, of Regulation (EC) No 2371/2002, Member States shall be entitled to reallocate up to 25% of the capacity permanently withdrawn in the context of a Fleet Adaptation Scheme to new vessels as referred to in Article 17 of this Regulation.

2. The reference levels referred to in Article 12 of Regulation (EC) No 2371/2002 are deducted by the difference between the capacity permanently withdrawn and the capacity reallocated.

3. The capacity reallocated under paragraph 1 of this Article need not be taken into account for the establishment of the balance of entries and exits by Member States under Article 13 of Regulation (EC) No 2371/2002.

4. In Fleet Adaptation Schemes where partial decommissioning is applied to more than 33% of initial fleet capacity, the total reduction in capacity under the Fleet Adaptation Scheme shall be of at least 66%.

CHAPTER V FINANCIAL PROVISIONS

[5.548]

Article 20 Financial provisions

1. By way of derogation from Article 53 of Regulation (EC) No 1198/2006, the contribution from the EFF to operations financed in the context of the specific action set out in this Regulation shall be subject to a ceiling of 95% of the total public expenditure and shall not be taken into account for the purposes of the ceilings referred to in Article 53(3) of the said Regulation.
2. By way of derogation from Article 55(1) and (3), second subparagraph, of Regulation (EC) No 1198/2006, the date of eligibility of expenditure for measures financed by this specific action shall be 31 July 2008.
3. By way of derogation from Article 81(1) of Regulation (EC) No 1198/2006, a second pre-financing amount representing 7% of the contribution from the EFF for the period 2007 to 2013 to the operational programme shall be paid by the Commission upon request by the Member State. For operational programmes adopted in 2007, the above request shall be submitted to the Commission at the latest by 31 October 2008. For operational programmes adopted in 2008, the above request shall be submitted to the Commission at the latest by 30 June 2009. It may be spread to two financial years in accordance with the available budget of the EFF.
4. By way of derogation from Article 81(2) of Regulation (EC) No 1198/2006, where the second pre-financing amount is paid in accordance with paragraph 2 of the said Article, the total amount paid as pre-financing shall be reimbursed to the Commission by the body designated by the Member State if no application for payment under the operational programme is sent within 24 months from the date on which the Commission paid the first instalment of the second pre-financing amount.

CHAPTER VI OBLIGATIONS OF MEMBER STATES AND OF THE COMMISSION

[5.549]

Article 21 Follow-up and financial corrections

1. Member States shall ensure that aid granted pursuant to Chapters II, III and IV of this Regulation complies with the conditions laid down in Article 70 of Regulation (EC) No 1198/2006.
2. The Commission shall undertake the financial corrections provided for in Article 97 of Regulation (EC) No 1198/2006) if Member States fail to comply with the conditions laid down in this Regulation, in particular:
   (a) the obligation of persons or enterprises receiving aid to undergo restructuring measures pursuant to Article 6(1)(b);
   (b) the obligations laid down to reduce fishing capacity, and the temporary or permanent cessation of fishing activities as laid down in a Fleet Adaptation Scheme pursuant to Articles 12, 14 and 15;
   (c) reductions in fishing capacity effected in the framework of partial decommissioning undertaken pursuant to Articles 17, 18 and 19.

The criteria for corrections laid down in Article 97 of Regulation (EC) No 1198/2006 shall apply accordingly.

[5.550]

Article 22 Report

The Commission shall report to the European Parliament and the Council on the application of the measures laid down in this Regulation by 31 December 2009 at the latest.

CHAPTER VII FINAL PROVISIONS

[5.551]

Article 23 Implementing rules

The implementing rules for this Regulation may be adopted in accordance with the procedure referred to in Article 101(3) of Regulation (EC) No 1198/2006.

[5.552]

Article 24 Entry into force

This Regulation shall enter into force on the day of its publication in the *Official Journal of the European Union.*

COMMISSION REGULATION

(717/2014/EU)

of 27 June 2014

on the application of Articles 107 and 108 of the Treaty on the Functioning of the European Union to *de minimis* aid in the fishery and aquaculture sector

[5.553]

NOTES

Date of publication in OJ: OJ L190, 28.06.2014, p 45.

Repeal of this Regulation in relation to the UK: this Regulation is repealed, in relation to the UK, by the State Aid (Revocations and Amendments) (EU Exit) Regulations 2020, SI 2020/1470, reg 5, as from IP completion day (as defined in the European Union (Withdrawal Agreement) Act 2020, s 39) (for transitional provisions and savings in relation to claims before a court or tribunal relating to State aid infringement before IP completion day, see Sch 3 to those Regulations at **[7.89]**).

See also the list of consultations and draft documents in the Appendix at **[A1]**.

THE EUROPEAN COMMISSION,

Having regard to the Treaty on the Functioning of the European Union, and in particular Article 108(4) thereof,

Having regard to Council Regulation (EC) No 994/98 of 7 May 1998 on the application of Articles 107 and 108 of the Treaty on the Functioning of the European Union to certain categories of horizontal State aid,[1]

Having published a draft of this Regulation,[2]

After consulting the Advisory Committee on State Aid,

Whereas:

(1) State funding meeting the criteria in Article 107(1) of the Treaty constitutes State aid and requires notification to the Commission by virtue of Article 108(3) of the Treaty. However, under Article 109 of the Treaty, the Council may determine categories of aid that are exempted from this notification requirement. In accordance with Article 108(4) of the Treaty, the Commission may adopt regulations relating to those categories of State aid. By virtue of Regulation (EC) No 994/98 the Council decided, in accordance with Article 109 of the Treaty, that de minimis aid could constitute one such category. On that basis, de minimis aid, being aid granted to a single undertaking over a given period of time that does not exceed a certain fixed amount, is deemed not to meet all the criteria laid down in Article 107(1) of the Treaty and is therefore not subject to the notification procedure.

(2) The Commission has, in numerous decisions, clarified the notion of aid within the meaning of Article 107(1) of the Treaty. The Commission has also stated its policy with regard to a de minimis ceiling below which Article 107(1) of the Treaty can be considered not to apply, initially in its notice on the de minimis rule for State aid[3] *and subsequently in Commission Regulations (EC) No 69/2001*[4] *and (EC) No 1998/2006.*[5] *In view of the special rules which apply in the fishery and aquaculture sector and of the risks that even low levels of aid could fulfil the criteria laid down in Article 107(1) of the Treaty, the fishery and aquaculture sector was excluded from the scope of those Regulations. The Commission has already adopted a number of Regulations providing rules on de minimis aid granted in the fishery and aquaculture sector, the latest of which was Regulation (EC) No 875/2007.*[6] *By virtue of that Regulation, the total amount of de minimis aid granted to one single undertaking active in the fisheries sector was regarded as not meeting all the criteria laid down in Article 87(1) of the EC Treaty where it did not exceed EUR 30,000 per beneficiary over any period of three fiscal years and below a cumulative amount laid down for each Member State representing 2.5% of annual fisheries output. In the light of the experience gained in applying Regulation (EC) No 875/2007, it is appropriate to revise some of the conditions laid down in that Regulation and to replace it.*

(3) It is appropriate to maintain the ceiling of EUR 30,000 as the amount of de minimis aid that a single undertaking may receive per Member State over any period of three years. That ceiling remains necessary to ensure that any measure falling under this Regulation can be deemed not to have any effect on trade between Member States and not to distort or threaten to distort competition where the total amount of such aid granted to all undertakings in the fishery and aquaculture sector over three years is below a cumulative amount laid down for each Member State representing 2.5% of the annual fisheries turnover i.e. of catching, processing and aquaculture activities (the national cap).

(4) For the purposes of the rules on competition laid down in the Treaty an undertaking is any entity engaged in an economic activity, regardless of its legal status and the way in which it is financed.[7] *The Court of Justice of the European Union has ruled that all entities which are controlled (on a legal or on a de facto basis) by the same entity should be considered as a single undertaking.*[8] *For the sake of legal certainty and to reduce the administrative burden, this Regulation should provide an exhaustive list of clear criteria for determining when two or more enterprises within the same Member State are to be considered as a single undertaking. The Commission has selected from the well-established criteria for defining 'linked enterprises' in the definition of small or medium-sized enterprises (SMEs) in Commission Recommendation 2003/361/EC*[9] *and in Annex I to Commission Regulation (EC) No 800/2008*[10] *those criteria that are appropriate for the purposes of this Regulation. The criteria are already familiar to public authorities and should be applicable, given the scope of this Regulation, to both SMEs and large undertakings. Those criteria should ensure that a group of linked enterprises is considered as one single undertaking for the application of the de minimis rule, but that enterprises which have no relationship with each other except for the fact that each of them has a direct link to the same public body or bodies are not treated as being linked to each other. The specific situation of enterprises controlled by the same public body or bodies, which may have an independent power of decision, is therefore taken into account.*

(5) Considering the scope of the common fisheries policy and the definition of the fishery and aquaculture sector laid down in Article 5 (d) of Regulation (EU) No 1379/2013 of the European Parliament and the Council,[11] *this Regulation should be applicable to undertakings active in production, processing and marketing of the fishery and aquaculture products.*

(6) It is a general principle that no aid should be granted in circumstances where EU law, and in particular rules of the common fisheries policy, are not complied with. This principle also applies to de minimis aid.

(7) In view of the need to ensure coherence with the objectives of the common fisheries policy and the European Maritime and Fisheries Fund, in particular aid for purchase of fishing vessels, aid for the modernisation or replacement of main or ancillary engines of fishing vessels and aid to any of the ineligible operations under Regulation (EU) No 508/2014 of the European Parliament and the Council[12] *should be excluded from the scope of this Regulation.*

(8) The Court of Justice of the European Union has established that, once the Union has legislated for the establishment of a common organisation of the market in a given sector of agriculture, Member States are under an obligation to refrain from taking any measure which might undermine or create exceptions to it.[13] *This principle also applies in the fishery and aquaculture sector. For that reason, this Regulation should not apply to aid the amount of which is fixed on the basis of the price or quantity of products purchased or put on the market. Nor should it apply to support which is linked to an obligation to share the aid with primary producers.*

(9) This Regulation should not apply to export aid or aid contingent upon the use of domestic over imported products. In particular, it should not apply to aid financing the establishment and operation of a distribution network in other Member States or in third countries. Aid towards the costs of participating in trade fairs, or of studies or consultancy services needed for the launch of a new or existing product on a new market in another Member State or a third country does not normally constitute export aid.

(10) Where an undertaking is active in the fishery and aquaculture sector and is also active in other sectors or has other activities falling within the scope of Commission Regulation (EU) No 1407/2013,[14] *the provisions of that*

Regulation should apply to aid granted in respect of those other sectors or activities, provided that the Member State concerned ensures, by appropriate means such as separation of activities or distinction of costs, that the activity in the fishery and aquaculture sector does not benefit from de minimis aid granted in accordance with that Regulation.

(11) Where an undertaking is active in the fishery and aquaculture sector as well as in the sector of primary production of agricultural products, the provisions of this Regulation shall apply to aid granted in respect of the former sector or activities, provided that the Member State concerned ensures, by appropriate means such as separation of activities or distinction of costs, that the primary production of agricultural products does not benefit from de minimis aid granted in accordance with this Regulation.

(12) This Regulation should lay down rules to ensure that it is not possible to circumvent maximum aid intensities laid down in specific regulations or Commission decisions. It should also provide for clear rules on cumulation that are easy to apply.

(13) The period of three years to be taken into account for the purposes of this Regulation should be assessed on a rolling basis so that, for each new grant of de minimis aid, the total amount of de minimis aid granted in the fiscal year concerned and during the previous two fiscal years needs to be taken into account.

(14) This Regulation does not exclude the possibility that a measure might be considered not to be State aid within the meaning of Article 107(1) of the Treaty on grounds other than those set out in this Regulation, for instance because the measure complies with the market economy operator principle or because the measure does not involve a transfer of State resources. In particular, Union funding centrally managed by the Commission which is not directly or indirectly under the control of the Member State, does not constitute State aid and should not be taken into account in determining whether the relevant ceiling or the national cap is respected.

(15) For the purposes of transparency, equal treatment and effective monitoring, this Regulation should apply only to de minimis aid for which it is possible to calculate precisely the gross grant equivalent ex ante without any need to undertake a risk assessment ('transparent aid'). Such a precise calculation can, for instance, be made for grants, interest rate subsidies, capped tax exemptions or other instruments that provide for a cap ensuring that the relevant ceiling is not exceeded. Providing for a cap means that as long as the precise amount of aid is not or not yet known, the Member State has to assume that the amount equals the cap in order to ensure that several aid measures together do not exceed the ceiling set out in this Regulation and to apply the rules on cumulation.

(16) For the purposes of transparency, equal treatment and the correct application of the de minimis ceiling, all Member States should apply the same method of calculation. In order to facilitate such calculation, aid amounts not taking the form of a cash grant should be converted into their gross grant equivalent. Calculation of the gross grant equivalent of transparent types of aid other than grants and of aid payable in several instalments requires the use of market interest rates prevailing at the time such aid is granted. With a view to uniform, transparent and simple application of the State aid rules, the market rates applicable for the purposes of this Regulation should be the reference rates, as set out in the Communication from the Commission on the revision of the method for setting the reference and discount rates.[15]

(17) Aid comprised in loans, including de minimis risk finance aid taking the form of loans, should be considered transparent de minimis aid if the gross grant equivalent has been calculated on the basis of market interest rates prevailing at the time the aid is granted. In order to simplify the treatment of small loans of short duration, this Regulation should provide for a clear rule that is easy to apply and takes into account both the amount of the loan and its duration. Based on the Commission's experience, loans that are secured by collateral covering at least 50% of the loan and that do not exceed either EUR 150,000 and a duration of five years or EUR 75,000 and a duration of 10 years can be considered as having a gross grant equivalent not exceeding the de minimis ceiling. Given the difficulties linked to determining the gross grant equivalent of aid granted to undertakings that may not be able to repay the loan, this rule should not apply to such undertakings.

(18) Aid comprised in capital injections should not be considered as transparent de minimis aid, unless the total amount of the public injection does not exceed the de minimis ceiling. Aid comprised in risk finance measures taking the form of equity or quasi-equity investments, as referred to in the risk finance guidelines,[16] *should not be considered as transparent de minimis aid unless the measure concerned provides capital not exceeding the de minimis ceiling.*

(19) Aid comprised in guarantees, including de minimis risk finance aid taking the form of guarantees, should be considered as transparent if the gross grant equivalent has been calculated on the basis of safe-harbour premiums laid down in a Commission notice for the type of undertaking concerned.[17] *In order to simplify the treatment of guarantees of short duration securing up to 80% of a relatively small loan, this Regulation should provide for a clear rule that is easy to apply and takes into account both the amount of the underlying loan and the duration of the guarantee. This rule should not apply to guarantees on underlying transactions not constituting a loan, such as guarantees on equity transactions. Where the guarantee does not exceed 80% of the underlying loan, the amount guaranteed does not exceed EUR 225,000 and the duration of the guarantee does not exceed five years, the guarantee can be considered as having a gross grant equivalent not exceeding the de minimis ceiling. The same applies where the guarantee does not exceed 80% of the underlying loan, the amount guaranteed does not exceed EUR 112 500 and the duration of the guarantee does not exceed 10 years. In addition, Member States can use a methodology to calculate the gross grant equivalent of guarantees which has been notified to the Commission under another Commission Regulation in the State aid area applicable at that time and which has been accepted by the Commission as being in line with the Guarantee Notice, or any successor notice, provided that the accepted methodology explicitly addresses the type of guarantee and the type of underlying transaction at stake in the context of the application of this Regulation. Given the difficulties linked to determining the gross grant equivalent of aid granted to undertakings that may not be able to repay the loan, this rule should not apply to such undertakings.*

(20) Where a de minimis aid scheme is implemented through financial intermediaries, it should be ensured that the latter do not receive any State aid. This can be done, for example, by requiring financial intermediaries that benefit from a State guarantee to pay a market-conform premium or to fully pass on any advantage to the final beneficiaries, or by respecting the de minimis ceiling and other conditions of this Regulation also at the level of the intermediaries.

(21) Upon notification by a Member State, the Commission may examine whether a measure which does not

consist of a grant, loan, guarantee, capital injection or risk finance measure taking the form of an equity or quasi-equity investment leads to a gross grant equivalent that does not exceed the de minimis ceiling and could therefore fall within the scope of this Regulation.

(22) The Commission has a duty to ensure that State aid rules are complied with and in accordance with the cooperation principle laid down in Article 4(3) of the Treaty on European Union, Member States should facilitate the fulfilment of this task by establishing the necessary tools in order to ensure that the total amount of de minimis aid granted to a single undertaking under the de minimis rule does not exceed the overall permissible ceiling. To that end, when granting de minimis aid, Member States should inform the undertaking concerned of the amount of de minimis aid granted and of its de minimis character and should make express reference to this Regulation. Member States should be required to monitor aid granted to ensure the relevant ceilings are not exceeded and the cumulation rules are complied with. To comply with that obligation, before granting such aid, the Member State concerned should obtain from the undertaking a declaration about other de minimis aid covered by this Regulation or by other de minimis regulations received during the fiscal year concerned and the previous two fiscal years. Alternatively it should be possible for Member States to set up a central register with complete information on de minimis aid granted and check that any new grant of aid does not exceed the relevant ceiling.

(23) Before granting any new de minimis aid, each Member State should verify that neither the de minimis ceiling nor the national cap will be exceeded in that Member State by the new de minimis aid and that the other conditions of this Regulation are complied with.

(24) Having regard to the Commission's experience and in particular the frequency with which it is generally necessary to revise State aid policy, the period of application of this Regulation should be limited. If this Regulation expires without being extended, Member States should have an adjustment period of six months with regard to de minimis aid covered by this Regulation,

NOTES

Repeal of this Regulation in relation to the UK: this Regulation is repealed in relation to the UK (as from IP completion day); see the introductory notes to this Regulation *ante*.

1 OJ L142, 14.5.1998, p 1.

2 OJ C92, 29.3.2014, p 22.

3 Commission notice on the *de minimis* rule for State aid (OJ C68, 6.3.1996, p 9).

4 Commission Regulation (EC) No 69/2001 of 12 January 2001 on the application of Articles 87 and 88 of the EC Treaty to *de minimis* aid (OJ L10, 13.1.2001, p 30).

5 Commission Regulation (EC) No 1998/2006 of 15 December 2006 on the application of Articles 87 and 88 of the EC Treaty to *de minimis* aid (OJ L379, 28.12.2006, p 5).

6 Commission Regulation (EC) No 875/2007 of 24 July 2007 on the application of Articles 87 and 88 of the EC Treaty to *de minimis* aid in the fisheries sector and amending Regulation (EC) No 1860/2004 (OJ L193, 25.7.2007, p 6).

7 Case C-222/04 *Ministero dell'Economia e delle Finanze* v *Cassa di Risparmio di Firenze SpA et al.* [2006] ECR I-289.

8 Case C-382/99 *Netherlands* v *Commission* [2002] ECR I-5163.

9 Commission Recommendation 2003/361/EC of 6 May 2003 concerning the definition of micro, small and medium-sized enterprises (OJ L124, 20.5.2003, p 36).

10 Commission Regulation (EC) No 800/2008 of 6 August 2008 declaring certain categories of aid compatible with the common market in application of Articles 87 and 88 of the Treaty (OJ L214, 9.8.2008, p 3).

11 Regulation (EU) No 1379/2013 of the European Parliament and of the Council of 11 December 2013 on the common organisation of the markets in the fishery and aquaculture products, amending Council Regulations (EC) No 1184/2006 and (EC) No 1224/2009 and repealing Council Regulation (EC) No 104/2000 (OJ L354, 28.12.2013, p 1).

12 Regulation EU No 508/2014 of the European Parliament and of the Council of 15 May 2014 on the European Maritime and Fisheries Fund and repealing Council Regulations (EC) No 2328/2003, (EC) No 861/2006, (EC) No 1198/2006 and (EC) No 791/2007 and Regulation (EU) No 1255/2011 of the European Parliament and of the Council (OJ L149, 20.5.2014, p 1).

13 Case C-456/00 *France* v *Commission* [2002] ECR I-11949.

14 Commission Regulation (EU) No 1407/2013 of 18 December 2013 on the application of Articles 107 and 108 of the Treaty on the Functioning of the European Union to *de minimis* aid (OJ L352, 24.12.2013, p 1).

15 Communication from the Commission on the revision of the method for setting the reference and discount rates (OJ C14, 19.1.2008, p 6).

16 Community guidelines on State aid to promote risk capital investments in small and medium-sized enterprises (OJ C194, 18.8.2006, p 2).

17 For instance, Commission notice on the application of Articles 87 and 88 of the EC Treaty to State aid in the form of guarantees (OJ C155, 20.6.2008, p 10).

HAS ADOPTED THIS REGULATION:

[5.554]

Article 1 **Scope**

1. This Regulation applies to aid granted to undertakings in the fishery and aquaculture sector, with the exception of:

(a) aid the amount of which is fixed on the basis of price or quantity of products purchased or put on the market;

(b) aid to export-related activities towards third countries or Member States, namely aid directly linked to the quantities exported, to the establishment and operation of a distribution network or to other current expenditure linked to the export activity;

(c) aid contingent upon the use of domestic over imported goods;

(d) aid for the purchase of fishing vessels;

(e) aid for the modernisation or replacement of main or ancillary engines of fishing vessels;

(f) aid to operations increasing the fishing capacity of a vessel or equipment increasing the ability of a vessel to find fish;

(g) aid for the construction of new fishing vessels or importation of fishing vessels;

(h) aid to the temporary or permanent cessation of fishing activities unless specifically provided for in the Regulation (EU) No 508/2014;
(i) aid to exploratory fishing;
(j) aid to the transfer of ownership of a business;
(k) aid to direct restocking, unless explicitly provided for as a conservation measure by a Union legal act or in the case of experimental restocking.

2. Where an undertaking is active in the fishery and aquaculture sector and is also active in one or more of the sectors or has other activities falling within the scope of Regulation (EU) No 1407/2013, that Regulation shall apply to aid granted in respect of the latter sectors or activities, provided that the Member State concerned ensures, by appropriate means such as separation of activities or distinction of costs, that the activities in the fishery and aquaculture sector do not benefit from the de minimis aid granted in accordance with that Regulation.

3. Where an undertaking is active in the fishery and aquaculture sector as well as in the primary production of agricultural products falling within the scope of Commission Regulation (EU) No 1408/2013,[1] this Regulation shall apply to aid granted in respect of the former sector provided that the Member State concerned ensures, by appropriate means such as separation of activities or distinction of costs, that the primary production of agricultural products does not benefit from de minimis aid granted in accordance with this Regulation.

NOTES

Repeal of this Regulation in relation to the UK: this Regulation is repealed in relation to the UK (as from IP completion day); see the introductory notes to this Regulation *ante*.

[1] Commission Regulation (EU) No 1408/2013 of 18 December 2013 on the application of Articles 107 and 108 of the Treaty on the Functioning of the European Union to *de minimis* aid in agriculture sector (OJ L352, 24.12.2013, p 9).

[5.555]

Article 2 Definitions

1. For the purposes of this Regulation the following definitions shall apply:
(a) 'undertakings in the fishery and aquaculture sector' means undertakings active in the production, processing and marketing of fishery and aquaculture products;
(b) 'fishery and aquaculture products' means the products defined in Article 5 (a) and (b) of Regulation (EU) No 1379/2013;
(c) 'processing and marketing' means all operations, including handling, treatment, production and distribution, performed between the time of landing or harvesting and the end-product stage.

2. 'Single undertaking' includes, for the purposes of this Regulation, all enterprises having at least one of the following relationships with each other:
(a) one enterprise has a majority of the shareholders' or members' voting rights in another enterprise;
(b) one enterprise has the right to appoint or remove a majority of the members of the administrative, management or supervisory body of another enterprise;
(c) one enterprise has the right to exercise a dominant influence over another enterprise pursuant to a contract entered into with that enterprise or to a provision in its memorandum or articles of association;
(d) one enterprise, which is a shareholder in or member of another enterprise, controls alone, pursuant to an agreement with other shareholders in or members of that enterprise, a majority of shareholders' or members' voting rights in that enterprise.

Enterprises having any of the relationships referred to in points (a) to (d) of the first subparagraph through one or more other enterprises shall also be considered to be a single undertaking.

NOTES

Repeal of this Regulation in relation to the UK: this Regulation is repealed in relation to the UK (as from IP completion day); see the introductory notes to this Regulation *ante*.

[5.556]

Article 3 De minimis aid

1. Aid measures shall be deemed not to meet all the criteria in Article 107(1) of the Treaty, and shall therefore be exempt from the notification requirement in Article 108(3) of the Treaty, if they fulfil the conditions laid down in this Regulation.

2. The total amount of de minimis aid granted per Member State to a single undertaking in the fishery and aquaculture sector shall not exceed EUR 30,000 over any period of three fiscal years.

3. The cumulative amount of de minimis aid granted per Member State to undertakings active in the fishery and aquaculture sector over any period of three fiscal years shall not exceed the national cap set out in the Annex.

4. De minimis aid shall be deemed granted at the moment the legal right to receive the aid is conferred on the undertaking under the applicable national legal regime irrespective of the date of payment of the de minimis aid to the undertaking.

5. The ceiling laid down in paragraph 2 and the national cap referred to in paragraph 3 shall apply irrespective of the form of the de minimis aid or the objective pursued and regardless of whether the aid granted by the Member State is financed entirely or partly by resources of Union origin. The period of three fiscal years shall be determined by reference to the fiscal years used by the undertaking in the Member State concerned.

6. For the purposes of the ceiling laid down in paragraph 2 and the national cap referred to in paragraph 3, aid shall be expressed as a cash grant. All figures used shall be gross, that is, before any deduction of tax or other charge. Where aid is granted in a form other than a grant, the aid amount shall be the gross grant equivalent of the aid. Aid payable in several instalments shall be discounted to its value at the moment it is granted. The interest rate to be used for discounting purposes shall be the discount rate applicable at the time the aid is granted.

7. Where the ceiling laid down in paragraph 2 or the national cap referred to in paragraph 3 would be exceeded by the grant of new de minimis aid, none of that new aid may benefit from this Regulation.

8. In the case of mergers or acquisitions, all prior de minimis aid granted to any of the merging undertakings shall be taken into account in determining whether any new de minimis aid to the new or the acquiring undertaking exceeds the ceiling or the national cap. De minimis aid lawfully granted before the merger or acquisition shall remain lawful.
9. If one undertaking splits into two or more separate undertakings, de minimis aid granted prior to the split shall be allocated to the undertaking that benefited from it, which is in principle the undertaking taking over the activities for which the de minimis aid was used. If such an allocation is not possible, the de minimis aid shall be allocated proportionately on the basis of the book value of the equity capital of the new undertakings at the effective date of the split.

NOTES

Repeal of this Regulation in relation to the UK: this Regulation is repealed in relation to the UK (as from IP completion day); see the introductory notes to this Regulation *ante*.

[5.557]
Article 4 Calculation of gross grant equivalent

1. This Regulation shall apply only to aid in respect of which it is possible to calculate precisely the gross grant equivalent of the aid ex ante without any need to undertake a risk assessment ('transparent aid').
2. Aid comprised in grants or interest rate subsidies shall be considered as transparent de minimis aid.
3. Aid comprised in loans shall be considered as transparent de minimis aid if:
(a) the beneficiary is not subject to collective insolvency proceedings nor fulfils the criteria under its domestic law for being placed in collective insolvency proceedings at the request of its creditors. In case of large undertakings, the beneficiary shall be in a situation comparable to a credit rating of at least B-; and
(b) the loan is secured by collateral covering at least 50% of the loan and the loan amounts to either EUR 150,000 over five years or EUR 75,000 over 10 years; if a loan is for less than those amounts and/or is granted for a period of less than five or 10 years respectively, the gross grant equivalent of that loan shall be calculated as a corresponding proportion of the ceiling laid down in Article 3(2); or
(c) the gross grant equivalent has been calculated on the basis of the reference rate applicable at the time of the grant.
4. Aid comprised in capital injections shall only be considered as transparent de minimis aid if the total amount of the public injection does not exceed the de minimis ceiling laid down in Article 3(2).
5. Aid comprised in risk finance measures taking the form of equity or quasi-equity investments shall only be considered as transparent de minimis aid if the capital provided to a single undertaking does not exceed the de minimis ceiling laid down in Article 3(2).
6. Aid comprised in guarantees shall be treated as transparent de minimis aid if:
(a) the beneficiary is not subject to collective insolvency proceedings nor fulfils the criteria under its domestic law for being placed in collective insolvency proceedings at the request of its creditors. In case of large undertakings, the beneficiary shall be in a situation comparable to a credit rating of at least B-; and
(b) the guarantee does not exceed 80% of the underlying loan and either the amount guaranteed does not exceed EUR 225,000 and the duration of the guarantee is five years or the amount guaranteed does not exceed EUR 112 500 and the duration of the guarantee is 10 years; if the amount guaranteed is lower than these amounts and/or the guarantee is for a period of less than five or 10 years respectively, the gross grant equivalent of that guarantee shall be calculated as a corresponding proportion of the ceiling laid down in Article 3(2); or
(c) the gross grant equivalent has been calculated on the basis of safe-harbour premiums laid down in a Commission notice; or
(d) before implementation:
(i) the methodology used to calculate the gross grant equivalent of the guarantee has been notified to the Commission under another Commission Regulation in the State aid area applicable at that time and accepted by the Commission as being in line with the Guarantee Notice, or any successor Notice, and
(ii) that methodology explicitly addresses the type of guarantee and the type of underlying transaction at stake in the context of the application of this Regulation.
7. Aid comprised in other instruments shall be considered as transparent de minimis aid if the instrument provides for a cap ensuring that the relevant ceiling is not exceeded.

NOTES

Repeal of this Regulation in relation to the UK: this Regulation is repealed in relation to the UK (as from IP completion day); see the introductory notes to this Regulation *ante*.

[5.558]
Article 5 Cumulation

1. Where an undertaking is active in the fishery and aquaculture sector and is also active in one or more of the sectors or has other activities falling within the scope of Regulation (EU) No 1407/2013, de minimis aid granted for activities in the fishery and aquaculture sector in accordance with this Regulation may be cumulated with de minimis aid granted in respect of the latter sector(s) or activities up to the relevant ceiling laid down in Article 3(2) of Regulation (EU) No 1407/2013, provided that the Member State concerned ensures, by appropriate means such as separation of activities or distinction of costs, that the activities in the fishery and aquaculture sector do not benefit from de minimis aid granted in accordance with Regulation (EU) No 1407/2013.
2. Where an undertaking is active in the fishery and aquaculture sector as well as in the primary production of agricultural products, de minimis aid granted in accordance with Regulation (EU) No 1408/2013 may be cumulated with de minimis aid in the fishery and aquaculture sector in accordance with this Regulation up to the ceiling laid down in this Regulation, provided that the Member State concerned ensures, by appropriate means such as separation of activities or distinction of costs, that the primary production of agricultural products does not benefit from de minimis aid granted in accordance with this Regulation.

3. De minimis aid shall not be cumulated with State aid in relation to the same eligible costs or with State aid for the same risk finance measure, if such cumulation would exceed the highest relevant aid intensity or aid amount fixed in the specific circumstances of each case by a block exemption regulation or a decision adopted by the Commission. De minimis aid which is not granted for or attributable to specific eligible costs may be cumulated with other State aid granted under a block exemption regulation or a decision adopted by the Commission.

NOTES

Repeal of this Regulation in relation to the UK: this Regulation is repealed in relation to the UK (as from IP completion day); see the introductory notes to this Regulation *ante*.

[5.559]

Article 6 Monitoring

1. Where a Member State intends to grant de minimis aid in accordance with this Regulation to an undertaking, it shall inform that undertaking in writing of the prospective amount of the aid expressed as a gross grant equivalent and of its de minimis character, making express reference to this Regulation and citing its title and publication reference in the Official Journal of the European Union. Where de minimis aid is granted in accordance with this Regulation to different undertakings on the basis of a scheme and different amounts of individual aid are granted to those undertakings under that scheme, the Member State concerned may choose to fulfil that obligation by informing the undertakings of a fixed sum corresponding to the maximum aid amount to be granted under that scheme. In such case, the fixed sum shall be used for determining whether the ceiling laid down in Article 3(2) is reached and the national cap referred to in Article 3(3) is not exceeded. Before granting the aid, the Member State shall obtain a declaration from the undertaking concerned, in written or electronic form, about any other de minimis aid received to which this Regulation or other de minimis regulations apply during the previous two fiscal years and the current fiscal year.

2. Where a Member State has set up a central register of de minimis aid containing complete information on all de minimis aid granted by any authority within that Member State, paragraph 1 shall cease to apply from the moment the register covers a period of three fiscal years.

3. A Member State shall grant new de minimis aid in accordance with this Regulation only after having checked that this will not raise the total amount of de minimis aid granted to the undertaking concerned to a level above the ceiling laid down in Article 3(2) and the national cap referred to in Article 3(3) and that all the conditions laid down in this Regulation are complied with.

4. Member States shall record and compile all the information regarding the application of this Regulation. Such records shall contain all information necessary to demonstrate that the conditions of this Regulation have been complied with. Records regarding individual de minimis aid shall be maintained for 10 fiscal years from the date on which the aid was granted. Records regarding a de minimis aid scheme shall be maintained for 10 fiscal years from the date on which the last individual aid was granted under such a scheme.

5. On written request, the Member State concerned shall provide the Commission, within a period of 20 working days or such longer period as may be fixed in the request, with all the information that the Commission considers necessary for assessing whether the conditions of this Regulation have been complied with, and in particular the total amount of de minimis aid within the meaning of this Regulation and of other de minimis regulations received by any undertaking.

NOTES

Repeal of this Regulation in relation to the UK: this Regulation is repealed in relation to the UK (as from IP completion day); see the introductory notes to this Regulation *ante*.

[5.560]

Article 7 Transitional provisions

1. This Regulation shall apply to aid granted before its entry into force if the aid fulfils all the conditions laid down in this Regulation. Any aid which does not fulfil those conditions will be assessed by the Commission in accordance with the relevant frameworks, guidelines, communications and notices.

2. Any individual de minimis aid which was granted between 1 January 2005 and 30 June 2008, and which fulfils the conditions of Regulation (EC) No 1860/2004 shall be deemed not to meet all the criteria in Article 107(1) of the Treaty and shall therefore be exempt from the notification requirement in Article 108(3) of the Treaty.

3. Any individual de minimis aid granted between 31 July 2007 and 30 June 2014 and which fulfils the conditions of Regulation (EC) No 875/2007 shall be deemed not to meet all the criteria in Article 107(1) of the Treaty and shall therefore be exempt from the notification requirement in Article 108(3) of the Treaty.

4. At the end of the period of validity of this Regulation, any de minimis aid scheme which fulfils the conditions of this Regulation shall remain covered by this Regulation for a further period of six months.

NOTES

Repeal of this Regulation in relation to the UK: this Regulation is repealed in relation to the UK (as from IP completion day); see the introductory notes to this Regulation *ante*.

[5.561]

Article 8 Entry into force and period of application

This Regulation shall enter into force on 1 July 2014.

[It shall apply until 31 December 2022.]

This Regulation shall be binding in its entirety and directly applicable in all Member States.

NOTES

Words in square brackets substituted by Commission Regulation 2020/2008/EU, Art 2. Note that previously this Regulation was due to expire on 31 December 2020.

Repeal of this Regulation in relation to the UK: this Regulation is repealed in relation to the UK (as from IP completion day); see the introductory notes to this Regulation *ante*.

ANNEX
NATIONAL CAP AS REFERRED TO IN ARTICLE 3(3)

[5.562]

Member State	*Maximum cumulative amount of de minimis aid granted per Member State in the fishery and aquaculture sector (EUR)*
Belgium	*11 240 000*
Bulgaria	*1 270 000*
Czech Republic	*3 020 000*
Denmark	*51 720 000*
Germany	*55 520 000*
Estonia	*3 930 000*
Ireland	*20 820 000*
Greece	*27 270 000*
Spain	*165 840 000*
France	*112 550 000*
Croatia	*6 260 000*
Italy	*96 310 000*
Cyprus	*1 090 000*
Latvia	*4 450 000*
Lithuania	*8 320 000*
Luxembourg	*0*
Hungary	*975 000*
Malta	*2 500 000*
Netherlands	*22 960 000*
Austria	*1 510 000*
Poland	*41 330 000*
Portugal	*29 200 000*
Romania	*2 460 000*
Slovenia	*990 000*
Slovakia	*860 000*
Finland	*7 450 000*
Sweden	*18 860 000*
United Kingdom	*114 780 000*

NOTES

Repeal of this Regulation in relation to the UK: this Regulation is repealed in relation to the UK (as from IP completion day); see the introductory notes to this Regulation *ante*.

COMMISSION REGULATION

(1388/2014/EU)

of 16 December 2014

declaring certain categories of aid to undertakings active in the production, processing and marketing of fishery and aquaculture products compatible with the internal market in application of Articles 107 and 108 of the Treaty on the Functioning of the European Union

[5.563]

NOTES

Date of publication in OJ: OJ L369, 24.12.2014, p 37.

Repeal of this Regulation in relation to the UK: this Regulation is repealed, in relation to the UK, by the State Aid (Revocations and Amendments) (EU Exit) Regulations 2020, SI 2020/1470, reg 5, as from IP completion day (as defined in the European Union (Withdrawal Agreement) Act 2020, s 39) (for transitional provisions and savings in relation to claims before a court or tribunal relating to State aid infringement before IP completion day, see Sch 3 to those Regulations at **[7.89]**).

See also the list of consultations and draft documents in the Appendix at **[A1]**.

THE EUROPEAN COMMISSION,

Having regard to the Treaty on the Functioning of the European Union, and in particular Article 108(4) thereof,

Having regard to Council Regulation (EC) No 994/98 of 7 May 1998 on the application of Articles 107 and 108 of the Treaty on the Functioning of the European Union to certain categories of horizontal State aid,[1] and in particular Article 1(1)(a)(i) and (vi) thereof,

Having published a draft of this Regulation,[2]

After consulting the Advisory Committee on State Aid, Whereas:

(1) State funding meeting the criteria laid down in Article 107(1) of the Treaty constitutes State aid and requires notification to the Commission by virtue of Article 108(3) thereof. However, pursuant to Article 109 of the Treaty, the Council may determine categories of aid that are exempted from this notification requirement. In accordance with Article 108(4) of the Treaty, the Commission may adopt regulations relating to those categories of aid.

(2) Regulation (EC) No 994/98 empowers the Commission to declare, in accordance with Article 109 of the Treaty, that certain categories of aid may, under certain conditions, be exempted from the notification requirement. On the basis of that Regulation, the Commission adopted Commission Regulation (EC) No 736/2008[3] which provided that, under certain conditions, aid to small and medium-sized enterprises ('SMEs') active in the production, processing and marketing of fisheries products is compatible with the internal market and not subject to the notification requirement of Article 108(3) of the Treaty. Regulation (EC) No 736/2008 applied until 31 December 2013.

(3) The Commission has applied Articles 107 and 108 of the Treaty to SMEs active in the production, processing and marketing of fishery and aquaculture products in numerous decisions. It has also stated its policy in guidelines specific to that sector. In the light of the Commission's experience in applying those provisions to SMEs, it is appropriate for the Commission to continue making use of the powers conferred by Regulation (EC) No 994/98 in order to exempt aid to that category of undertakings from the notification requirement of Article 108(3) of the Treaty under certain conditions.

(4) On 22 July 2013 Regulation (EC) No 994/98 was amended by Council Regulation (EU) No 733/2013[4] to empower the Commission to extend the block exemption to new categories of aid in respect of which clear compatibility conditions can be defined. In the fishery and aquaculture sector, this is the case for aid to make good the damage caused by certain natural disasters, in light of the Commission's experience in applying Article 107(2)(b) of the Treaty to this category of aid.

(5) The compatibility of State aid in the fishery and aquaculture sector is assessed by the Commission on the basis of the objectives of both the Competition Policy and the Common Fisheries Policy. In the interests of coherence with Union-financed support measures, the maximum intensity of public aid allowed under this Regulation should be equal to that fixed for the same kind of aid in Article 95 of Regulation (EU) No 508/2014 of the European Parliament and of the Council[5] and the implementing acts adopted pursuant to that Regulation.

(6) It is essential that no aid is granted in circumstances where Union law, and in particular rules of the Common Fisheries Policy, are not complied with. An aid may therefore only be granted by a Member State in the fishery and aquaculture sector if the measures financed and their effects comply with Union law. Member States should ensure that beneficiaries of State aid comply with the rules of the Common Fisheries Policy.

(7) With its Communication on EU State Aid Modernisation (SAM),[6] the Commission launched a wider review of the State aid rules. The main objectives of that modernisation are: (i) to achieve sustainable, smart and inclusive growth in a competitive internal market, while contributing to Member State efforts towards a more efficient use of public finances; (ii) to focus Commission ex ante scrutiny of aid measures on cases with the biggest impact on the internal market, while strengthening Member State cooperation in State aid enforcement; and (iii) to streamline the rules and provide for faster, better informed and more robust decisions based on a clear economic rationale, a common approach and clear obligations. This Regulation is part of the SAM programme.

(8) This Regulation should allow for better prioritisation of State aid enforcement activities and greater simplification and should enhance transparency, effective evaluation and the control of compliance with the State aid rules at national and Union levels, while preserving the institutional competences of the Commission and the Member States. In accordance with the principle of proportionality, this Regulation does not go beyond what is necessary in order to achieve those objectives.

(9) The general conditions for the application of this Regulation should be defined on the basis of a set of common principles that ensure that the aid serves a purpose of common interest, has a clear incentive effect, is appropriate and proportionate, is granted in full transparency and subject to a control mechanism and regular evaluation and does not adversely affect trading conditions to an extent that is contrary to the common interest.

(10) Aid that fulfils all the conditions laid down in this Regulation both general and specific to the relevant categories of aid should be considered compatible with the internal market and exempted from the notification requirement laid down in Article 108(3) of the Treaty.

(11) State aid within the meaning of Article 107(1) of the Treaty not covered by this Regulation or by other Regulations adopted pursuant to Article 1 of Regulation (EC) No 994/98 remains subject to the notification requirement of Article 108(3) of the Treaty. This Regulation is without prejudice for

Member States to notify aid potentially covered by this Regulation. Such aid should be assessed in the light of the Guidelines for the examination of State aid in the fishery and aquaculture sector or any successor guidelines.[7]

(12) This Regulation should not apply to aid contingent upon the use of domestic over imported products or aid to export-related activities. In particular, it should not apply to aid financing the establishment and operation of a distribution network in other Member States or third countries. Aid towards the cost of participating in trade fairs or of studies or consultancy services needed for the launch of a new or existing product on a new market in another Member State or third country should not normally constitute aid to export-related activities.

(13) The Commission should ensure that authorised aid does not adversely affect trading conditions to an extent that is contrary to the common interest. Therefore, aid in favour of a beneficiary which is subject to an outstanding recovery order following a previous Commission decision declaring an aid illegal and incompatible with the internal market should be excluded from the scope of this Regulation, with the exception of aid schemes to make good the damage caused by natural disasters.

(14) Aid granted to undertakings in difficulty should be excluded from the scope of this Regulation, since such aid should be assessed under the Guidelines on State aid for rescuing and restructuring non-financial undertakings in difficulty,[8] *in order to avoid their circumvention, with the exception of aid schemes to make good the damage caused by natural disasters. In order to provide legal certainty, it is appropriate to establish clear criteria that do not require an assessment of all the particularities of the situation of an undertaking to determine whether an undertaking is considered to be in difficulty for the purposes of this Regulation.*

(15) State aid enforcement is highly dependent on the cooperation of Member States. Therefore, Member States should take all necessary measures to ensure compliance with this Regulation, including compliance of individual aid granted under block-exempted schemes.

(16) In view of the need to strike the appropriate balance between minimising distortions of competition in the aided sector and the objectives of this Regulation, this Regulation should not exempt individual grants which exceed a fixed maximum amount, whether or not made under an aid scheme exempted by this Regulation.

(17) For the purpose of transparency, equal treatment and effective monitoring, this Regulation should apply only to aid in respect of which it is possible to calculate precisely the gross grant equivalent ex ante without the need to undertake a risk assessment ('transparent aid').

(18) This Regulation should define the conditions under which certain specific aid instruments, such as loans, guarantees, tax measures, and, in particular, repayable advances may be considered transparent. Aid comprised in guarantees should be considered as transparent if the gross grant equivalent has been calculated on the basis of safe-harbour premiums laid down for the respective type of undertaking. In the case of SMEs, the Commission Notice on the application of Articles 87 and 88 of the EC Treaty to State aid in the form of guarantees[9] *indicates levels of annual premium above which a State guarantee would be deemed not to constitute aid. For the purposes of this Regulation, capital injections and risk capital measures should not be considered transparent aid.*

(19) In order to ensure that the aid is necessary and acts as an incentive to further develop activities or projects, this Regulation should not apply to aid for activities in which the beneficiary would in any case engage even in the absence of the aid. Aid should only be exempted from notification requirement of Article 108(3) of the Treaty in accordance with this Regulation, where the activity or the work on the aided project starts after the beneficiary has submitted a written application for the aid.

(20) Automatic aid schemes in the form of tax advantages should continue to be subject to a specific condition concerning the incentive effect, due to the fact that this kind of aid is granted under different procedures than other categories of aid. Such schemes should already have been adopted before work on the aided project or activity started. However, this condition should not apply in the case of fiscal successor schemes provided the activity was already covered by the previous fiscal schemes in the form of tax advantages. For the assessment of the incentive effect of such schemes, the crucial moment is the moment when the tax measure was set out for the first time in the original scheme, which is then replaced by the successor scheme.

(21) For the calculation of aid intensity, only eligible costs should be included. This Regulation should not exempt aid which exceeds the relevant aid intensity as a result of including ineligible costs. The identification of eligible costs should be supported by clear, specific and up-to date documentary evidence. All figures used should be taken before any deduction of tax or other charges. Aid payable in several instalments should be discounted to its value on the date of granting of the aid. The eligible costs should also be discounted to their value on the date of granting. The interest rate to be used for discounting purposes and for calculating the amount of aid in the case of aid which does not take the form of a grant should be respectively the discount rate and the reference rate applicable at the time of the grant, as laid down in the Commission Communication on the revision of the method for setting the reference and discount rates.[10] *Where aid is granted by means of tax advantages, aid tranches should be discounted on the basis of the discount rates applicable on the various dates when the tax advantages become effective. The use of aid in the form of repayable advances should be promoted, since such risk-sharing instruments are conducive to strengthened incentive effect of aid. It is therefore appropriate to establish that where aid is granted in the form of repayable advances the applicable aid intensities referred to in this Regulation may be increased.*

(22) In the case of tax advantages on future taxes, the applicable discount rate and the exact amount of the aid tranches may not be known in advance. In such cases, Member States should set in advance a cap on the discounted value of the aid respecting the applicable aid intensity. Subsequently, when the

amount of the aid tranche at a given date becomes known, discounting can take place on the basis of the discount rate applicable at that time. The discounted value of each aid tranche should be deducted from the overall amount of the cap ('capped amount').

(23) To determine whether the notification thresholds and the maximum aid intensities referred to in this Regulation are respected, the total amount of public support for the aided activity or project should be taken into account. Moreover, this Regulation should specify the circumstances under which different categories of aid may be cumulated. Aid exempted by this Regulation and any other compatible aid exempted under other regulations or approved by the Commission may be cumulated as long as those measures concern different identifiable eligible costs. Where different sources of aid are related to the same — partly or fully overlapping — identifiable eligible costs, cumulation should be allowed up to the highest aid intensity or aid amount applicable to that aid under this Regulation. This Regulation should also set out special rules for cumulation of aid measures with de minimis aid. De minimis aid is often not granted for or attributable to specific identifiable eligible costs. In such a case, it should be possible to freely cumulate de minimis aid with State aid exempted under this Regulation. Where, however, de minimis aid is granted for the same identifiable eligible costs as State aid exempted under this Regulation, cumulation should only be allowed up to the maximum aid intensity as referred to in Chapter III of this Regulation.

(24) Given that State aid within the meaning of Article 107(1) of the Treaty is, in principle, prohibited, it is important for all parties to be able to check whether an aid is granted in compliance with the applicable rules. Transparency of State aid is, therefore, essential for the correct application of Treaty rules and leads to better compliance, greater accountability, peer review and ultimately more effective public spending. To ensure transparency, Member States should be required to establish comprehensive State aid websites, at regional or national level, setting out summary information about each aid measure exempted under this Regulation. That obligation should be a condition for the compatibility of the individual aid with the internal market. Following the standard practice regarding publication of information in Directive 2013/37/EU of the European Parliament and of the Council,[11] a standard format should be used which allows the information to be searched, downloaded and easily published on the Internet. The links to the State aid websites of all the Member States should be published on the Commission's website. In accordance with Article 3 of Regulation (EC) No 994/98, as amended by Regulation (EU) No 733/2013, summary information on each aid measure exempted under this Regulation should be published on the website of the Commission.

(25) To ensure effective monitoring of aid measures in accordance with Regulation (EC) No 994/98, as amended by Regulation (EU) No 733/2013, it is appropriate to establish requirements regarding the reporting by the Member States of aid measures which have been exempted pursuant to this Regulation and the application of this Regulation. Moreover, it is appropriate to establish rules concerning the records that Member States should keep regarding the aid exempted by this Regulation, in light of the limitation period established in Article 15 of Council Regulation (EC) No 659/1999.[12] Finally, each individual aid should contain an express reference to this Regulation.

(26) To reinforce the effectiveness of compatibility conditions set out in this Regulation, it should be possible for the Commission to withdraw the benefit of the block exemption for future aid measures in the event of failure to comply with these requirements. The Commission should be able to restrict the withdrawal of the benefit of the block exemption to certain types of aid, certain beneficiaries or aid measures adopted by certain authorities, where non-compliance with this Regulation affects only a limited group of measures or certain authorities. Such a targeted withdrawal should provide a proportionate remedy directly linked to the identified non-compliance with this Regulation. In case of failure to meet compatibility conditions set out in Chapters I and III, aid granted will not be covered by this Regulation and, as a consequence, will constitute unlawful aid, which the Commission will examine in the framework of the relevant procedure as set out in Regulation No (EC) No 659/1999. In case of failure to fulfil the requirements of Chapter II, the withdrawal of the benefit of the block exemption in respect of the future aid measures does not affect the fact that the past measures complying with this Regulation were block exempted.

(27) To eliminate differences that might give rise to distortions of competition and to facilitate coordination between different Union and national initiatives concerning SMEs, as well as for reasons of administrative clarity and legal certainty, the definition of SMEs used for the purpose of this Regulation should be based on the definition in Commission Recommendation 2003/361/EC.[13]

(28) This Regulation should cover types of aid granted in the fishery and aquaculture sector which have been systematically approved by the Commission for many years. This aid should not require a case-by-case assessment of its compatibility with the internal market from the Commission, provided that it complies with the conditions laid down in Regulation (EU) No 508/2014.

(29) In accordance with Article 107(2)(b) of the Treaty, aid to make good the damage caused by natural disasters is compatible with the internal market. In order to provide legal certainty, it is necessary to define the type of the events that may constitute a natural disaster exempted by this Regulation. For the purposes of this Regulation, earthquakes, landslides, floods, in particular floods brought about by waters overflowing river banks or lake shores, avalanches, tornadoes, hurricanes, volcanic eruptions and wildfires of natural origin should be considered events constituting a natural disaster. Damage caused by adverse weather conditions such as storms, frost, hail, ice, rain or drought, which occur on a more regular basis, should not be considered a natural disaster within the meaning of Article 107(2)(b) of the Treaty. In order to ensure that the exemption covers indeed aid granted to make good the damage caused by natural disasters, this Regulation should lay down, following established practice, the conditions under which such aid schemes may benefit from that block exemption. Those conditions should relate, in particular, to the formal recognition by the competent Member States'

authorities of the character of the event as a natural disaster and to a direct causal link between the natural disaster and the damages suffered by the beneficiary undertaking, which may include undertakings in difficulty, and should ensure that overcompensation is avoided. The compensation should not exceed what is necessary to enable the beneficiary to return to the situation prevailing before the disaster occurred.

(30) Pursuant to Article 15(1)(f) and Article 15(3) of Council Directive 2003/96/EC,[14] Member States may introduce tax exemptions or reductions applicable to inland fishing and piscicultural works. It is therefore appropriate to continue exempting those measures from the notification requirement of Article 108(3) of the Treaty where the conditions provided under that Directive are fulfilled. Tax exemptions applicable to fishing within EU waters which Member States are to introduce pursuant to Article 14(1)(c) of that Directive are not imputable to the State and therefore should not constitute State aid.

(31) In the light of the Commission's experience in this area, State aid policy should periodically be revised. The period of application of this Regulation should therefore be limited and transitional provisions should be laid down. Having regard to the fact that the conditions for granting aid under this Regulation have been aligned with the conditions established for the application of Regulation (EU) No 508/2014,[15] it is appropriate to ensure consistency between the period of application of this Regulation and the period of application of Regulation (EU) No 508/2014. Should this Regulation expire without being extended, aid schemes already exempted by this Regulation should continue to be exempted for six months.

NOTES

Repeal of this Regulation in relation to the UK: this Regulation is repealed in relation to the UK (as from IP completion day); see the introductory notes to this Regulation *ante*.

1 Council Regulation (EC) No 994/98 of 7 May 1998 on the application of Articles 107 and 108 of the Treaty on the Functioning of the European Union to certain categories of horizontal State aid (OJ L142, 14.5.1998, p 1).

2 OJ C258, 8.8.2014, p 1.

3 Commission Regulation (EC) No 736/2008 of 22 July 2008 on the application of Articles 87 and 88 of the Treaty to State aid to small and medium-sized enterprises active in the production, processing and marketing of fisheries products (OJ L201, 30.7.2008, p 16).

4 Council Regulation (EU) No 733/2013 of 22 July 2013 amending Regulation (EC) No 994/98 on the application of Articles 92 and 93 of the Treaty establishing the European Community to certain categories of horizontal State aid (OJ L204, 31.7.2013, p 11).

5 Regulation (EU) No 508/2014 of the European Parliament and of the Council of 15 May 2014 on the European Maritime and Fisheries Fund and repealing Council Regulations (EC) No 2328/2003, (EC) No 861/2006, (EC) No 1198/2006 and (EC) No 791/2007 and Regulation (EU) No 1255/2011 of the European Parliament and of the Council (OJ L149, 20.5.2014, p 1).

6 COM(2012)209, 8.5.2012.

7 OJ C84, 3.4.2008, p 10.

8 OJ C249, 31.7.2014, p 1.

9 OJ C155, 20.6.2008, p 10.

10 OJ C14, 19.1.2008, p 6.

11 Directive 2013/37/EU of the European Parliament and of the Council of 26 June 2013 amending Directive 2003/98/EC on the re-use of public sector information (OJ L175, 27.6.2013, p 1).

12 Council Regulation (EC) No 659/1999 of 22 March 1999 laying down detailed rules for the application of Article 93 of the EC Treaty (OJ L83, 27.3.1999, p 1).

13 Commission Recommendation 2003/361/EC of 6 May 2003 concerning the definition of micro, small and medium sized enterprises (OJ L124, 20.5.2003, p 36).

14 Council Directive 2003/96/EC of 27 October 2003 restructuring the Community framework for the taxation of energy products and electricity (OJ L283, 31.10.2003, p 51).

15 Regulation (EU) No 508/2014 of the European Parliament and of the Council of 15 May 2014 on the European Maritime and Fisheries Fund and repealing Council Regulations (EC) No 2328/2003, (EC) No 861/2006, (EC) No 1198/2006 and (EC) No 791/2007 and Regulation (EU) No 1255/2011 of the European Parliament and of the Council (OJ L149, 20.5.2014, p 1).

HAS ADOPTED THIS REGULATION:

CHAPTER I COMMON PROVISIONS

[5.564]

Article 1 Scope

1. This Regulation shall apply to aid granted to small and medium-sized enterprises (SMEs) active in the production, processing or marketing of fishery and aquaculture products.

2. This Regulation shall also apply to aid granted to undertakings active in the production, processing or marketing of fishery and aquaculture products to make good the damage caused by natural disasters in accordance with Article 44 independently of the size of the beneficiary of the aid.

3. This Regulation shall not apply to:

- *(a) aid the amount of which is fixed on the basis of price or quantity of products put on the market;*
- *(b) aid to export-related activities towards third countries or Member States, namely aid directly linked to the quantities exported, to the establishment and operation of a distribution network or to other current costs linked to the export activity;*
- *(c) aid contingent upon the use of domestic over imported goods;*

[(d) aid granted to undertakings in difficulty, with the exception of aid to make good the damage caused by natural disasters and aid to undertakings which were not in difficulty on 31 December 2019 but became undertakings in difficulty in the period from 1 January 2020 to 30 June 2021;]

(e) aid schemes which do not explicitly exclude the payment of individual aid in favour of an undertaking which is subject to an outstanding recovery order following a previous Commission decision declaring an aid illegal and incompatible with the internal market, with the exception of aid schemes to make good the damage caused by natural disasters;

(f) ad hoc aid in favour of an undertaking as referred to in point (e);

(g) aid granted to operations which would have been ineligible for support under Article 11 of Regulation (EU) No 508/2014;

(h) aid granted to undertakings that cannot apply for support from the European Maritime and Fisheries Fund on the grounds set out in Article 10(1)-(3) of Regulation (EU) No 508/2014.

4. This Regulation shall not apply to State aid measures, which entail, by themselves, by the conditions attached to them or by their financing method a non-severable violation of Union law, in particular:

(a) aid where the grant of aid is subject to the obligation for the beneficiary to have its headquarters in the relevant Member State or to be predominantly established in that Member State. However, the requirement to have an establishment or branch in the aid granting Member State at the moment of payment of the aid is allowed;

(b) aid where the grant of aid is subject to the obligation for the beneficiary to use nationally produced goods or national services;

(c) aid restricting the possibility for the beneficiaries to exploit the research, development and innovation results in other Member States.

NOTES

Para 3: point (d) substituted by Commission Regulation 2020/2008/EU, Art 3(1).

Application of references to Regulation (EU) No 508/2014: the references to provisions of Regulation (EU) No 508/2014 in Articles 1 and 13–43 of this Regulation shall be understood as references to the version of those provisions applicable on 31 December 2020, regardless of whether that Regulation is repealed.

Repeal of this Regulation in relation to the UK: this Regulation is repealed in relation to the UK (as from IP completion day); see the introductory notes to this Regulation *ante*.

[5.565]

Article 2 Notification threshold

1. This Regulation shall not apply to aid for any project with eligible costs in excess of EUR 2 million, or where the amount of aid exceeds EUR 1 million per beneficiary per year.

2. The thresholds set out in paragraph 1 shall not be circumvented by artificially splitting up the aid schemes or aid projects.

NOTES

Repeal of this Regulation in relation to the UK: this Regulation is repealed in relation to the UK (as from IP completion day); see the introductory notes to this Regulation *ante*.

[5.566]

Article 3 Definitions

For the purpose of this Regulation the following definitions shall apply:

(1) 'aid' means any measure fulfilling all the criteria laid down in Article 107(1) of the Treaty;

(2) 'small and medium-sized undertakings' or 'SMEs' means undertakings fulfilling the criteria laid down in Annex I;

(3) 'fishery and aquaculture products' means the products defined in Annex I of Regulation (EU) No 1379/2013 of the European Parliament and of the Council of 11 December 2013;[1]

(4) 'natural disasters' means earthquakes, avalanches, landslides and floods, tornadoes, hurricanes, volcanic eruptions and wild fires of natural origin;

(5) 'undertaking in difficulty' means an undertaking in respect of which at least one of the following circumstances occurs:

(a) in the case of a limited liability company (other than an SME that has been in existence for less than three years), where more than half of its subscribed share capital has disappeared as a result of accumulated losses. This is the case when deduction of accumulated losses from reserves (and all other elements generally considered as part of the own funds of the company) leads to a negative cumulative amount that exceeds half of the subscribed share capital. For the purposes of this provision, 'limited liability company' refers in particular to the types of company mentioned in Annex I of Directive 2013/34/EU of the European Parliament and of the Council[2] *and 'share capital' includes, where relevant, any share premium;*

(b) in the case of a company where at least some members have unlimited liability for the debt of the company (other than an SME that has been in existence for less than three years), where more than half of its capital as shown in the company accounts has disappeared as a result of accumulated losses. For the purposes of this provision, 'a company where at least some members have unlimited liability for the debt of the company' refers in particular to the types of company mentioned in Annex II to Directive 2013/34/EU;

(c) where the undertaking is subject to collective insolvency proceedings or fulfils the criteria under its domestic law for being placed in collective insolvency proceedings at the request of its creditors;

(d) where the undertaking has received rescue aid and has not yet reimbursed the loan or terminated the guarantee, or has received restructuring aid and is still subject to a restructuring plan;

(6) 'ad hoc aid' means aid not granted on the basis of an aid scheme;

(7) 'aid scheme' means any act on the basis of which, without further implementing measures being required, individual aid awards may be made to undertakings defined within the act in a general and abstract manner and any act on the basis of which aid which is not linked to a specific project may be granted to one or several undertakings for an indefinite period of time and/or for an indefinite amount;

(8) 'individual aid' means:

(a) ad hoc aid; and

(b) awards of aid to individual beneficiaries on the basis of an aid scheme;

(9) 'gross grant equivalent' means the amount of the aid if it had been provided in the form of a grant to the beneficiary, before any deduction of tax or other charges;

(10) 'repayable advance' means a loan for a project which is paid in one or more instalments and the conditions for the reimbursement of which depend on the outcome of the project;

(11) 'start of works' means the earlier of either the start of construction works relating to the investment, or the first legally binding commitment to order equipment or any other commitment that makes the investment irreversible. Buying land and preparatory works such as obtaining permits and conducting feasibility studies are not considered start of works. For take-overs, 'start of works' means the moment of acquiring assets directly linked to the acquired establishment;

(12) 'fiscal successor scheme' means a scheme in the form of tax advantages which constitutes an amended version of a previously existing scheme in the form of tax advantages and which replaces it;

(13) 'aid intensity' means the gross aid amount expressed as a percentage of the eligible costs, before any deduction of tax or other charge;

(14) 'date of granting the aid' means the date when the legal right to receive the aid is conferred on the beneficiary under the applicable national legal regime.

NOTES

Repeal of this Regulation in relation to the UK: this Regulation is repealed in relation to the UK (as from IP completion day); see the introductory notes to this Regulation *ante*.

[1] Regulation (EU) No 1379/2013 of the European Parliament and of the Council of 11 December 2013 on the common organisation of the markets in fishery and aquaculture products, amending Council Regulations (EC) No 1184/2006 and (EC) No 1224/2009 and repealing Council Regulation (EC) No 104/2000 (OJ L354, 28.12.2013, p 1).

[2] Directive 2013/34/EU of the European Parliament and of the Council of 26 June 2013 on the annual financial statements, consolidated financial statements and related reports of certain types of undertakings, amending Directive 2006/43/EC of the European Parliament and of the Council and repealing Council Directives 78/660/EEC and 83/349/EEC (OJ L182, 29.6.2013, p 19).

[5.567]

Article 4 Conditions for exemption

1. Aid schemes, individual aid granted under aid schemes and ad hoc aid shall be compatible with the internal market within the meaning of Article 107(2) or (3) of the Treaty and shall be exempted from the notification requirement of Article 108(3) of the Treaty provided that such aid fulfils the conditions laid down in Chapter I of this Regulation, as well as the specific conditions for the relevant category of aid laid down in Chapter III of this Regulation.

2. Aid measures shall only be exempted under this Regulation as far as they explicitly provide that, during the grant period, the beneficiaries of the aid shall comply with the rules of the Common Fisheries Policy and that, if during that period it is found that the beneficiary does not comply with rules of the Common Fisheries Policy, the aid shall be reimbursed in proportion to the gravity of the infringement.

NOTES

Repeal of this Regulation in relation to the UK: this Regulation is repealed in relation to the UK (as from IP completion day); see the introductory notes to this Regulation *ante*.

[5.568]

Article 5 Transparency of aid

1. This Regulation shall apply only to aid in respect of which it is possible to calculate precisely the gross grant equivalent of the aid ex ante without any need to undertake a risk assessment ('transparent aid').

2. The following categories of aid shall be considered to be transparent:

(a) aid comprised in grants and interest rate subsidies;

(b) aid comprised in loans where the gross grant equivalent has been calculated on the basis of the reference rate prevailing at the time of the grant;

(c) aid comprised in guarantees:

(i) where the gross grant equivalent has been calculated on the basis of safe-harbour premiums laid down in a Commission notice; or

(ii) where before the implementation of the measure, the methodology to calculate the gross grant equivalent of the guarantee has been accepted on the basis of the Commission Notice on the application of Articles 87 and 88 of the EC Treaty to State aid in the form of guarantees,[1] or any successor notice, following notification of that methodology to the Commission under any regulation adopted by the Commission in the State aid area applicable at the time, and the approved methodology explicitly addresses the type of guarantee and the type of underlying transaction at stake in the context of the application of this Regulation;

(d) aid in the form of tax advantages, where the measure provides for a cap ensuring that the applicable threshold is not exceeded;

(e) *aid in the form of repayable advances, if the total nominal amount of the repayable advance does not exceed the thresholds applicable under this Regulation or if, before implementation of the measure, the methodology to calculate the gross grant equivalent of the repayable advance has been accepted following its notification to the Commission.*

3. *For the purposes of this Regulation, the following categories of aid shall not be considered to be transparent aid:*

(a) *aid comprised in capital injections;*

(b) *aid comprised in risk finance measures.*

NOTES

Repeal of this Regulation in relation to the UK: this Regulation is repealed in relation to the UK (as from IP completion day); see the introductory notes to this Regulation *ante*.

[1] OJ C155, 20.6.2008, p 10.

[5.569]

Article 6 Incentive effect

1. *This Regulation shall apply only to aid which has an incentive effect.*

2. *Aid shall be considered to have an incentive effect if the beneficiary has submitted a written application for the aid to the Member State concerned before work on the project or activity starts. The application for the aid shall contain at least the following information:*

(a) *undertaking's name and size;*

(b) *description of the project or activity, including its start and end dates; (c)location of the project or activity;*

(d) *list of eligible costs;*

(e) *type of aid (grant, loan, guarantee, repayable advance or other) and amount of public funding needed for the project or activity.*

3. *By way of derogation from paragraph 2, measures in the form of tax advantages shall be deemed to have an incentive effect if the following conditions are fulfilled:*

(a) *the measure establishes a right to aid in accordance with objective criteria and without further exercise of discretion by the Member State; and*

(b) *the measure has been adopted and is in force before work on the aided project or activity has started, except in the case of fiscal successor schemes where the activity was already covered by the previous schemes in the form of tax advantages.*

4. *By way of derogation from paragraphs 1 and 2, the following categories of aid are not required to have or shall be deemed to have an incentive effect:*

(a) *aid to make good the damage caused by natural disasters, if the conditions laid down in Article 44 are fulfilled;*

(b) *aid in the form of tax exemptions or reductions adopted by the Member States pursuant to Article 15(1)(f) and Article 15(3) of Directive 2003/96/EC, if the conditions laid down in Article 45 of this Regulation are fulfilled.*

NOTES

Repeal of this Regulation in relation to the UK: this Regulation is repealed in relation to the UK (as from IP completion day); see the introductory notes to this Regulation *ante*.

[5.570]

Article 7 Aid intensity and eligible costs

1. *For the purpose of calculating aid intensity and eligible costs, all figures used shall be taken before any deduction of tax or other charge. The eligible costs shall be supported by documentary evidence which shall be clear, specific and contemporary.*

2. *Where aid is granted in a form other than a grant, the aid amount shall be the gross grant equivalent of the aid.*

3. *Aid payable in several instalments shall be discounted to its value on the date of granting the aid. The eligible costs shall be discounted to their value on the date of granting the aid. The interest rate to be used for discounting purposes shall be the discount rate applicable on the date of granting the aid.*

4. *Where aid is granted by means of tax advantages discounting of aid tranches shall take place on the basis of the discount rates applicable on the various dates when the tax advantage takes effect.*

5. *Where aid is granted in the form of repayable advances which, in the absence of an accepted methodology to calculate their gross grant equivalent, are expressed as a percentage of the eligible costs and the measure provides that in case of a successful outcome of the project, as defined on the basis of a reasonable and prudent hypothesis, the advances will be repaid with an interest rate at least equal to the discount rate applicable on the date of granting the aid, the maximum aid intensities laid down in Chapter III may be increased by 10 percentage points.*

6. *The eligible costs shall comply with the requirements of Articles 67 to 69 of Regulation (EU) No 1303/2013 of the European Parliament and of the Council.*[1]

NOTES

Repeal of this Regulation in relation to the UK: this Regulation is repealed in relation to the UK (as from IP completion day); see the introductory notes to this Regulation *ante*.

[1] Regulation (EU) No 1303/2013 of the European Parliament and of the Council of 17 December 2013 laying down common provisions on the European Regional Development Fund, the European Social Fund, the Cohesion Fund, the European Agricultural Fund for Rural Development and the European Maritime and Fisheries Fund and laying down general provisions on the European Regional Development Fund, the European Social Fund, the Cohesion Fund and the European Maritime and Fisheries Fund and repealing Council Regulation (EC) No 1083/2006 (OJ L347, 20.12.2013, p 320).

[5.571]

Article 8 Cumulation

1. In determining whether the notification thresholds in Article 2 and the maximum aid intensities in Chapter III are respected, the total amount of public support measures for the aided activity or project or undertaking shall be taken into account, regardless of whether that support is financed from local, regional, national or Union sources.

2. Aid exempted by this Regulation may be cumulated with:

- *(a) any other State aid, as long as those measures concern different identifiable eligible costs;*
- *(b) any other State aid, in relation to the same eligible costs, partly or fully overlapping, only if such cumulation does not result in exceeding the highest aid intensity or aid amount applicable to this aid under this Regulation.*

3. State aid exempted under this Regulation shall not be cumulated with any de minimis aid in respect of the same eligible costs if such cumulation would result in an aid intensity exceeding those referred to in Chapter III.

NOTES

Repeal of this Regulation in relation to the UK: this Regulation is repealed in relation to the UK (as from IP completion day); see the introductory notes to this Regulation *ante*.

[5.572]

Article 9 Publication and information

1. The Member State concerned shall ensure the publication on a comprehensive State aid website, at national or regional level of:

- *(a) the summary information referred to in Article 11 in the standardised format laid down in Annex II or a link providing access to it;*
- *(b) the full text of each aid measure as referred to in Article 11 or a link providing access to the full text;*
- *(c) the information referred to in Annex III on each individual aid award exceeding EUR 30,000.*

2. For schemes in the form of tax advantages, the conditions set out in paragraph 1(c) shall be considered fulfilled if Member States publish the required information on individual aid amounts in the following ranges (in EUR million):

- *(a) 0.03-0.2*
- *(b) 0.2-0.4*
- *(c) 0.4-0.6*
- *(d) 0.6-0.8*
- *(e) 0.8-1*

3. The information referred to in paragraph 1(c) shall be organised and accessible in a standardised manner, as described in Annex III, and shall allow for effective search and download functions. The information referred to in paragraph 1 shall be published within six months from the date the aid was granted, or for aid in the form of tax advantage, within one year from the date the tax declaration is due, and shall be available for at least 10 years from the date on which the aid was granted.

4. Each aid scheme and individual aid shall contain an explicit reference to this Regulation, by citing its title and publication reference in the Official Journal of the European Union, and to the specific provisions of Chapter III concerned by that act, or where applicable, to the national law which ensures that the relevant provisions of this Regulation are complied with. It shall be accompanied by its implementing provisions and its amendments.

5. The Commission shall publish on its website:

- *(a) the links to the State aid websites, referred to in paragraph 1 of this Article;*
- *(b) the summary information referred to in Article 11.*

6. Member States shall comply with the provisions of this Article at the latest within two years after the entry into force of this Regulation.

NOTES

Repeal of this Regulation in relation to the UK: this Regulation is repealed in relation to the UK (as from IP completion day); see the introductory notes to this Regulation *ante*.

CHAPTER II MONITORING

[5.573]

Article 10 Withdrawal of the benefit of the block exemption

Where a Member State grants aid allegedly exempted from the notification requirement under this Regulation without fulfilling the conditions set out in Chapters I, II and III, the Commission may, after having provided the Member State concerned with the possibility to make its views known, adopt a decision stating that all or some of the future aid measures adopted by the Member State concerned which would otherwise fulfil the requirements of this Regulation, are to be notified to the Commission in accordance with Article 108(3) of the Treaty. The measures to be notified may be limited to measures granting certain types of aid, in favour of certain beneficiaries or adopted by certain authorities of the Member State concerned.

NOTES

Repeal of this Regulation in relation to the UK: this Regulation is repealed in relation to the UK (as from IP completion day); see the introductory notes to this Regulation *ante*.

[5.574]

Article 11 Reporting

Member States shall transmit to the Commission:

- (a) *via the Commission's electronic notification system, the summary information about each aid measure exempted under this Regulation in the standardised format laid down in Annex II, together with a link providing access to the full text of the aid measure, including its amendments, within 20 working days following its entry into force;*
- (b) *an annual report, as referred to in Commission Regulation (EC) No 794/2004,[1] in electronic form, on the application of this Regulation, containing the information indicated in Regulation (EC) No 794/2004, in respect of each whole year or each part of the year during which this Regulation applies.*

NOTES

Repeal of this Regulation in relation to the UK: this Regulation is repealed in relation to the UK (as from IP completion day); see the introductory notes to this Regulation *ante*.

[1] Commission Regulation (EC) No 794/2004 of 21 April 2004 implementing Council Regulation (EC) No 659/1999 laying down detailed rules for the application of Article 93 of the EC Treaty (OJ L140, 30.4.2004, p 1).

[5.575]

Article 11a Derogation from information and publication requirements

By way of derogation from Article 9(5) and Article 11, point (a), where a Member State wishes to prolong measures in respect of which summary information was submitted to the Commission, summary information regarding the prolongation of those measures shall be deemed to have been communicated to the Commission and published, provided that no substantive amendment, other than a budget increase, is made to the measures concerned.

NOTES

Inserted by Commission Regulation 2020/2008/EU, Art 3(2).

Repeal of this Regulation in relation to the UK: this Regulation is repealed in relation to the UK (as from IP completion day); see the introductory notes to this Regulation *ante*.

[5.576]

Article 12 Monitoring

In order to enable the Commission to monitor the aid exempted from notification by this Regulation, Member States shall maintain detailed records with the information and supporting documentation necessary to establish that all the conditions laid down in this Regulation are fulfilled. Such records shall be kept for 10 years from the date on which the ad hoc aid was granted or the last aid was granted under the scheme. The Member State concerned shall provide the Commission within a period of 20 working days or such longer period as may be fixed in the request, with all the information and supporting documentation which the Commission considers necessary to monitor the application of this Regulation.

NOTES

Repeal of this Regulation in relation to the UK: this Regulation is repealed in relation to the UK (as from IP completion day); see the introductory notes to this Regulation *ante*.

CHAPTER III SPECIFIC PROVISIONS FOR DIFFERENT CATEGORIES OF AID

SECTION 1 SUSTAINABLE DEVELOPMENT OF FISHERIES

[5.577]

Article 13 Aid for innovation

Aid for innovation in fisheries fulfilling the conditions laid down in Chapter I shall be compatible with the internal market within the meaning of Article 107(3)(c) of the Treaty and shall be exempted from the notification requirement of Article 108(3) thereof provided that:

- (a) *the aid fulfils the conditions of Article 25(1) and (2) and Article 26 of Regulation (EU) No 508/2014; and*
- (b) *the amount of the aid does not exceed, in gross grant equivalent, the maximum intensity of public aid fixed by Article 95 of Regulation (EU) No 508/2014 and the implementing acts adopted on the basis of Article 95(5) of that Regulation.*

NOTES

Application of references to Regulation (EU) No 508/2014: see the note to Article 1 at **[5.564]**.

Repeal of this Regulation in relation to the UK: this Regulation is repealed in relation to the UK (as from IP completion day); see the introductory notes to this Regulation *ante*.

[5.578]

Article 14 Aid for advisory services

Aid for advisory services fulfilling the conditions laid down in Chapter I shall be compatible with the internal market within the meaning of Article 107(3)(c) of the Treaty and shall be exempted from the notification requirement of Article 108(3) thereof provided that:

- (a) *the aid fulfils the conditions of Article 25(1) and (2) and Article 27 of Regulation (EU) No 508/2014; and*
- (b) *the amount of the aid does not exceed, in gross grant equivalent, the maximum intensity of public aid fixed by Article 95 of Regulation (EU) No 508/2014 and the implementing acts adopted on the basis of Article 95(5) of that Regulation.*

NOTES

Application of references to Regulation (EU) No 508/2014: see the note to Article 1 at **[5.564]**.

Repeal of this Regulation in relation to the UK: this Regulation is repealed in relation to the UK (as from IP completion day); see the introductory notes to this Regulation *ante*.

[5.579]

Article 15 Aid for partnership between scientists and fishermen

Aid for partnership between scientists and fishermen fulfilling the conditions laid down in Chapter I shall be compatible with the internal market within the meaning of Article 107(3)(c) of the Treaty and shall be exempted from the notification requirement of Article 108(3) thereof provided that:

(a) *the aid fulfils the conditions of Article 25(1) and (2) and Article 28 of Regulation (EU) No 508/2014; and*

(b) *the amount of the aid does not exceed, in gross grant equivalent, the maximum intensity of public aid fixed by Article 95 of Regulation (EU) No 508/2014 and the implementing acts adopted on the basis of Article 95(5) of that Regulation.*

NOTES

Application of references to Regulation (EU) No 508/2014: see the note to Article 1 at **[5.564]**.

Repeal of this Regulation in relation to the UK: this Regulation is repealed in relation to the UK (as from IP completion day); see the introductory notes to this Regulation *ante*.

[5.580]

Article 16 Aid to promote human capital, job creation and social dialogue

Aid to promote human capital, job creation and social dialogue fulfilling the conditions laid down in Chapter I shall be compatible with the internal market within the meaning of Article 107(3)(c) of the Treaty and shall be exempted from the notification requirement of Article 108(3) thereof provided that:

(a) *the aid fulfils the conditions of Article 25(1) and (2) and Article 29 of Regulation (EU) No 508/2014; and*

(b) *the amount of the aid does not exceed, in gross grant equivalent, the maximum intensity of public aid fixed by Article 95 of Regulation (EU) No 508/2014 and the implementing acts adopted on the basis of Article 95(5) of that Regulation.*

NOTES

Application of references to Regulation (EU) No 508/2014: see the note to Article 1 at **[5.564]**.

Repeal of this Regulation in relation to the UK: this Regulation is repealed in relation to the UK (as from IP completion day); see the introductory notes to this Regulation *ante*.

[5.581]

Article 17 Aid to facilitate diversification and new forms of income

Aid to facilitate diversification and new forms of income fulfilling the conditions laid down in Chapter I shall be compatible with the internal market within the meaning of Article 107(3)(c) of the Treaty and shall be exempted from the notification requirement of Article 108(3) thereof provided that:

(a) *the aid fulfils the conditions of Article 25(1) and (2) and Article 30 of Regulation (EU) No 508/2014; and*

(b) *the amount of the aid does not exceed, in gross grant equivalent, the maximum intensity of public aid fixed by Article 95 of Regulation (EU) No 508/2014 and the implementing acts adopted on the basis of Article 95(5) of that Regulation.*

NOTES

Application of references to Regulation (EU) No 508/2014: see the note to Article 1 at **[5.564]**.

Repeal of this Regulation in relation to the UK: this Regulation is repealed in relation to the UK (as from IP completion day); see the introductory notes to this Regulation *ante*.

[5.582]

Article 18 Aid to start-up support for young fishermen

Aid to start-up support for young fishermen fulfilling the conditions laid down in Chapter I shall be compatible with the internal market within the meaning of Article 107(3)(c) of the Treaty and shall be exempted from the notification requirement of Article 108(3) thereof provided that:

(a) *the aid fulfils the conditions of Article 25(1) and (2) and Article 31 of Regulation (EU) No 508/2014; and*

(b) *the amount of the aid does not exceed, in gross grant equivalent, the maximum intensity of public aid fixed by Article 95 of Regulation (EU) No 508/2014 and the implementing acts adopted on the basis of Article 95(5) of that Regulation.*

NOTES

Application of references to Regulation (EU) No 508/2014: see the note to Article 1 at **[5.564]**.

Repeal of this Regulation in relation to the UK: this Regulation is repealed in relation to the UK (as from IP completion day); see the introductory notes to this Regulation *ante*.

[5.583]

Article 19 Aid to improve health and safety

Aid to improve health and safety fulfilling the conditions laid down in Chapter I shall be compatible with the internal market within the meaning of Article 107(3)(c) of the Treaty and shall be exempted from the notification requirement of Article 108(3) thereof provided that:

(a) *the aid fulfils the conditions of Article 25(1) and (2) and Article 32 of Regulation (EU) No 508/2014 and the delegated acts adopted on the basis of Article 32(4) of that Regulation; and*

(b) *the amount of the aid does not exceed, in gross grant equivalent, the maximum intensity of public aid fixed by Article 95 of Regulation (EU) No 508/2014 and the implementing acts adopted on the basis of Article 95(5) of that Regulation.*

NOTES

Application of references to Regulation (EU) No 508/2014: see the note to Article 1 at **[5.564]**.

Repeal of this Regulation in relation to the UK: this Regulation is repealed in relation to the UK (as from IP completion day); see the introductory notes to this Regulation *ante*.

[5.584]

Article 20 Aid to mutual funds for adverse climatic events and environmental incidents

Aid to mutual funds for adverse climatic events and environmental incidents fulfilling the conditions laid down in Chapter I shall be compatible with the internal market within the meaning of Article 107(3)(c) of the Treaty and shall be exempted from the notification requirement of Article 108(3) thereof provided that:

- *(a) the aid fulfils the conditions of Article 25(1) and (2) and Article 35 of Regulation (EU) No 508/2014; and*
- *(b) the amount of the aid does not exceed, in gross grant equivalent, the maximum intensity of public aid fixed by Article 95 of Regulation (EU) No 508/2014 and the implementing acts adopted on the basis of Article 95(5) of that Regulation.*

NOTES

Application of references to Regulation (EU) No 508/2014: see the note to Article 1 at **[5.564]**.

Repeal of this Regulation in relation to the UK: this Regulation is repealed in relation to the UK (as from IP completion day); see the introductory notes to this Regulation *ante*.

[5.585]

Article 21 Aid to support systems of allocation of fishing opportunities

Aid to support systems of allocation of fishing opportunities fulfilling the conditions laid down in Chapter I shall be compatible with the internal market within the meaning of Article 107(3)(c) of the Treaty and shall be exempted from the notification requirement of Article 108(3) thereof provided that:

- *(a) the aid fulfils the conditions of Article 25(1) and (2) and Article 36 of Regulation (EU) No 508/2014; and*
- *(b) the amount of the aid does not exceed, in gross grant equivalent, the maximum intensity of public aid fixed by Article 95 of Regulation (EU) No 508/2014 and the implementing acts adopted on the basis of Article 95(5) of that Regulation.*

NOTES

Application of references to Regulation (EU) No 508/2014: see the note to Article 1 at **[5.564]**.

Repeal of this Regulation in relation to the UK: this Regulation is repealed in relation to the UK (as from IP completion day); see the introductory notes to this Regulation *ante*.

[5.586]

Article 22 Aid to support the design and implementation of conservation measures and regional cooperation

Aid to support the design and implementation of conservation measures and regional cooperation fulfilling the conditions laid down in Chapter I shall be compatible with the internal market within the meaning of Article 107(3)(c) of the Treaty and shall be exempted from the notification requirement of Article 108(3) thereof provided that:

- *(a) the aid fulfils the conditions of Article 25(1) and (2) and Article 37 of Regulation (EU) No 508/2014; and*
- *(b) the amount of the aid does not exceed, in gross grant equivalent, the maximum intensity of public aid fixed by Article 95 of Regulation (EU) No 508/2014 and the implementing acts adopted on the basis of Article 95(5) of that Regulation.*

NOTES

Application of references to Regulation (EU) No 508/2014: see the note to Article 1 at **[5.564]**.

Repeal of this Regulation in relation to the UK: this Regulation is repealed in relation to the UK (as from IP completion day); see the introductory notes to this Regulation *ante*.

[5.587]

Article 23 Aid to limit the impact of fishing on the marine environment and adapt fishing to the protection of species

Aid to limit the impact of fishing on the marine environment and adapt fishing to the protection of species fulfilling the conditions laid down in Chapter I shall be compatible with the internal market within the meaning of Article 107(3)(c) of the Treaty and shall be exempted from the notification requirement of Article 108(3) thereof provided that:

- *(a) the aid fulfils the conditions of Article 25(1) and (2) and Article 38 of Regulation (EU) No 508/2014; and*
- *(b) the amount of the aid does not exceed, in gross grant equivalent, the maximum intensity of public aid fixed by Article 95 of Regulation (EU) No 508/2014 and the implementing acts adopted on the basis of Article 95(5) of that Regulation.*

NOTES

Application of references to Regulation (EU) No 508/2014: see the note to Article 1 at **[5.564]**.

Repeal of this Regulation in relation to the UK: this Regulation is repealed in relation to the UK (as from IP completion day); see the introductory notes to this Regulation *ante*.

[5.588]

Article 24 Aid to innovation linked to the conservation of marine biological resources

Aid to innovation linked to the conservation of marine biological resources fulfilling the conditions laid down in Chapter I shall be compatible with the internal market within the meaning of Article 107(3)(c) of the Treaty and shall be exempted from the notification requirement of Article 108(3) thereof provided that:

- *(a) the aid fulfils the conditions of Article 25(1) and (2) and Article 39 of Regulation (EU) No 508/2014; and*
- *(b) the amount of the aid does not exceed, in gross grant equivalent, the maximum intensity of public aid fixed by Article 95 of Regulation (EU) No 508/2014 and the implementing acts adopted on the basis of Article 95(5) of that Regulation.*

NOTES

Application of references to Regulation (EU) No 508/2014: see the note to Article 1 at **[5.564]**.

Repeal of this Regulation in relation to the UK: this Regulation is repealed in relation to the UK (as from IP completion day); see the introductory notes to this Regulation *ante*.

[5.589]

Article 25 Aid for the protection and restoration of marine biodiversity and ecosystems and compensation regimes in the framework of sustainable fishing activities

Aid for the protection and restoration of marine biodiversity and ecosystems and compensation regimes in the framework of sustainable fishing activities fulfilling the conditions laid down in Chapter I shall be compatible with the internal market within the meaning of Article 107(3)(c) of the Treaty and shall be exempted from the notification requirement of Article 108(3) thereof provided that:

- *(a) the aid fulfils the conditions of Article 25(1) and (2) and Article 40 of Regulation (EU) No 508/2014 and the delegated acts adopted on the basis of Article 40(4) of that Regulation; and*
- *(b) the amount of the aid does not exceed, in gross grant equivalent, the maximum intensity of public aid fixed by Article 95 of Regulation (EU) No 508/2014 and the implementing acts adopted on the basis of Article 95(5) of that Regulation.*

NOTES

Application of references to Regulation (EU) No 508/2014: see the note to Article 1 at **[5.564]**.

Repeal of this Regulation in relation to the UK: this Regulation is repealed in relation to the UK (as from IP completion day); see the introductory notes to this Regulation *ante*.

[5.590]

Article 26 Aid to improve energy efficiency and to mitigate the effects of climate change

Aid to improve energy efficiency and to mitigate the effects of climate change, with the exception of aid to replace or modernise engines, fulfilling the conditions laid down in Chapter I shall be compatible with the internal market within the meaning of Article 107(3)(c) of the Treaty and shall be exempted from the notification requirement of Article 108(3) thereof provided that:

- *(a) the aid fulfils the conditions of Article 25(1) and (2) and Article 41 of Regulation (EU) No 508/2014 and the delegated acts adopted on the basis of Article 41(10) of that Regulation; and*
- *(b) the amount of the aid does not exceed, in gross grant equivalent, the maximum intensity of public aid fixed by Article 95 of Regulation (EU) No 508/2014 and the implementing acts adopted on the basis of Article 95(5) of that Regulation.*

NOTES

Application of references to Regulation (EU) No 508/2014: see the note to Article 1 at **[5.564]**.

Repeal of this Regulation in relation to the UK: this Regulation is repealed in relation to the UK (as from IP completion day); see the introductory notes to this Regulation *ante*.

[5.591]

Article 27 Aid to added value, product quality and use of unwanted catches

Aid to added value, product quality and use of unwanted catches fulfilling the conditions laid down in Chapter I shall be compatible with the internal market within the meaning of Article 107(3)(c) of the Treaty and shall be exempted from the notification requirement of Article 108(3) thereof provided that:

- *(a) the aid fulfils the conditions of Article 25(1) and (2) and Article 42 of Regulation (EU) No 508/2014; and*
- *(b) the amount of the aid does not exceed, in gross grant equivalent, the maximum intensity of public aid fixed by Article 95 of Regulation (EU) No 508/2014 and the implementing acts adopted on the basis of Article 95(5) of that Regulation.*

NOTES

Application of references to Regulation (EU) No 508/2014: see the note to Article 1 at **[5.564]**.

Repeal of this Regulation in relation to the UK: this Regulation is repealed in relation to the UK (as from IP completion day); see the introductory notes to this Regulation *ante*.

[5.592]

Article 28 Aid to fishing ports, landing sites, auction halls and shelters

Aid to fishing ports, landing sites, auction halls and shelters fulfilling the conditions laid down in Chapter I shall be compatible with the internal market within the meaning of Article 107(3)(c) of the Treaty and shall be exempted from the notification requirement of Article 108(3) thereof provided that:

- *(a) the aid fulfils the conditions of Article 25(1) and (2) and Article 43 of Regulation (EU) No 508/2014; and*
- *(b) the amount of the aid does not exceed, in gross grant equivalent, the maximum intensity of public aid fixed by Article 95 of Regulation (EU) No 508/2014 and the implementing acts adopted on the basis of Article 95(5) of that Regulation.*

NOTES

Application of references to Regulation (EU) No 508/2014: see the note to Article 1 at **[5.564]**.

Repeal of this Regulation in relation to the UK: this Regulation is repealed in relation to the UK (as from IP completion day); see the introductory notes to this Regulation *ante*.

[5.593]

Article 29 Aid to inland fishing and inland aquatic fauna and flora

Aid to inland fishing and inland aquatic fauna and flora fulfilling the conditions laid down in Chapter I shall be compatible with the internal market within the meaning of Article 107(3)(c) of the Treaty and shall be exempted from the notification requirement of Article 108(3) thereof provided that:

- *(a) the aid fulfils the conditions of Article 25(1) and (2) and Article 44 of Regulation (EU) No 508/2014; and*
- *(b) the amount of the aid does not exceed, in gross grant equivalent, the maximum intensity of public aid fixed by Article 95 of Regulation (EU) No 508/2014 and the implementing acts adopted on the basis of Article 95(5) of that Regulation.*

NOTES

Application of references to Regulation (EU) No 508/2014: see the note to Article 1 at **[5.564]**.

Repeal of this Regulation in relation to the UK: this Regulation is repealed in relation to the UK (as from IP completion day); see the introductory notes to this Regulation *ante*.

SECTION 2 SUSTAINABLE DEVELOPMENT OF AQUACULTURE

[5.594]

Article 30 Aid for innovation in aquaculture

Aid for innovation in aquaculture fulfilling the conditions laid down in Chapter I shall be compatible with the internal market within the meaning of Article 107(3)(c) of the Treaty and shall be exempted from the notification requirement of Article 108(3) thereof provided that:

(a) the aid fulfils the conditions of Articles 46 and 47 of Regulation (EU) No 508/2014; and

(b) the amount of the aid does not exceed, in gross grant equivalent, the maximum intensity of public aid fixed by Article 95 of Regulation (EU) No 508/2014 and the implementing acts adopted on the basis of Article 95(5) of that Regulation.

NOTES

Application of references to Regulation (EU) No 508/2014: see the note to Article 1 at **[5.564]**.

Repeal of this Regulation in relation to the UK: this Regulation is repealed in relation to the UK (as from IP completion day); see the introductory notes to this Regulation *ante*.

[5.595]

Article 31 Aid to productive investments in aquaculture

Aid to productive investments in aquaculture fulfilling the conditions laid down in Chapter I shall be compatible with the internal market within the meaning of Article 107(3)(c) of the Treaty and shall be exempted from the notification requirement of Article 108(3) thereof provided that:

(a) the aid fulfils the conditions of Articles 46 and 48 of Regulation (EU) No 508/2014; and

(b) the amount of the aid does not exceed, in gross grant equivalent, the maximum intensity of public aid fixed by Article 95 of Regulation (EU) No 508/2014 and the implementing acts adopted on the basis of Article 95(5) of that Regulation.

NOTES

Application of references to Regulation (EU) No 508/2014: see the note to Article 1 at **[5.564]**.

Repeal of this Regulation in relation to the UK: this Regulation is repealed in relation to the UK (as from IP completion day); see the introductory notes to this Regulation *ante*.

[5.596]

Article 32 Aid to management, relief and advisory services for aquaculture farms

Aid to management, relief and advisory services for aquaculture farms fulfilling the conditions laid down in Chapter I shall be compatible with the internal market within the meaning of Article 107(3)(c) of the Treaty and shall be exempted from the notification requirement of Article 108(3) thereof provided that:

(a) the aid fulfils the conditions of Articles 46 and 49 of Regulation (EU) No 508/2014; and

(b) the amount of the aid does not exceed, in gross grant equivalent, the maximum intensity of public aid fixed by Article 95 of Regulation (EU) No 508/2014 and the implementing acts adopted on the basis of Article 95(5) of that Regulation.

NOTES

Application of references to Regulation (EU) No 508/2014: see the note to Article 1 at **[5.564]**.

Repeal of this Regulation in relation to the UK: this Regulation is repealed in relation to the UK (as from IP completion day); see the introductory notes to this Regulation *ante*.

[5.597]

Article 33 Aid to promote human capital and networking in aquaculture

Aid to promote human capital and networking in aquaculture fulfilling the conditions laid down in Chapter I shall be compatible with the internal market within the meaning of Article 107(3)(c) of the Treaty and shall be exempted from the notification requirement of Article 108(3) thereof provided that:

(a) the aid fulfils the conditions of Articles 46 and 50 of Regulation (EU) No 508/2014 and

(b) the amount of the aid does not exceed, in gross grant equivalent, the maximum intensity of public aid fixed by Article 95 of Regulation (EU) No 508/2014 and the implementing acts adopted on the basis of Article 95(5) of that Regulation.

NOTES

Application of references to Regulation (EU) No 508/2014: see the note to Article 1 at **[5.564]**.

Repeal of this Regulation in relation to the UK: this Regulation is repealed in relation to the UK (as from IP completion day); see the introductory notes to this Regulation *ante*.

[5.598]

Article 34 Aid to increase the potential of aquaculture sites

Aid to increase the potential of aquaculture sites fulfilling the conditions laid down in Chapter I shall be compatible with the internal market within the meaning of Article 107(3)(c) of the Treaty and shall be exempted from the notification requirement of Article 108(3) thereof provided that:

(a) the aid fulfils the conditions of Articles 46 and 51 of Regulation (EU) No 508/2014; and

(b) *the amount of the aid does not exceed, in gross grant equivalent, the maximum intensity of public aid fixed by Article 95 of Regulation (EU) No 508/2014 and the implementing acts adopted on the basis of Article 95(5) of that Regulation.*

NOTES

Application of references to Regulation (EU) No 508/2014: see the note to Article 1 at **[5.564]**.

Repeal of this Regulation in relation to the UK: this Regulation is repealed in relation to the UK (as from IP completion day); see the introductory notes to this Regulation *ante*.

[5.599]

Article 35 Aid to encourage new aquaculture farmers practising sustainable aquaculture

Aid to encourage new aquaculture farmers practising sustainable aquaculture fulfilling the conditions laid down in Chapter I shall be compatible with the internal market within the meaning of Article 107(3)(c) of the Treaty and shall be exempted from the notification requirement of Article 108(3) thereof provided that:

(a) *the aid fulfils the conditions of Articles 46 and 52 of Regulation (EU) No 508/2014; and*
(b) *the amount of the aid does not exceed, in gross grant equivalent, the maximum intensity of public aid fixed by Article 95 of Regulation (EU) No 508/2014 and the implementing acts adopted on the basis of Article 95(5) of that Regulation.*

NOTES

Application of references to Regulation (EU) No 508/2014: see the note to Article 1 at **[5.564]**.

Repeal of this Regulation in relation to the UK: this Regulation is repealed in relation to the UK (as from IP completion day); see the introductory notes to this Regulation *ante*.

[5.600]

Article 36 Aid for the conversion to eco-management and audit schemes and organic aquaculture

Aid for the conversion to eco-management and audit schemes and organic aquaculture fulfilling the conditions laid down in Chapter I shall be compatible with the internal market within the meaning of Article 107(3)(c) of the Treaty and shall be exempted from the notification requirement of Article 108(3) thereof provided that:

(a) *the aid fulfils the conditions of Articles 46 and 53 of Regulation (EU) No 508/2014; and*
(b) *the amount of the aid does not exceed, in gross grant equivalent, the maximum intensity of public aid fixed by Article 95 of Regulation (EU) No 508/2014 and the implementing acts adopted on the basis of Article 95(5) of that Regulation.*

NOTES

Application of references to Regulation (EU) No 508/2014: see the note to Article 1 at **[5.564]**.

Repeal of this Regulation in relation to the UK: this Regulation is repealed in relation to the UK (as from IP completion day); see the introductory notes to this Regulation *ante*.

[5.601]

Article 37 Aid to aquaculture providing environmental services

Aid to aquaculture providing environmental services fulfilling the conditions laid down in Chapter I shall be compatible with the internal market within the meaning of Article 107(3)(c) of the Treaty and shall be exempted from the notification requirement of Article 108(3) thereof provided that:

(a) *the aid fulfils the conditions of Articles 46 and 54 of Regulation (EU) No 508/2014; and*
(b) *the amount of the aid does not exceed, in gross grant equivalent, the maximum intensity of public aid fixed by Article 95 of Regulation (EU) No 508/2014 and the implementing acts adopted on the basis of Article 95(5) of that Regulation.*

NOTES

Application of references to Regulation (EU) No 508/2014: see the note to Article 1 at **[5.564]**.

Repeal of this Regulation in relation to the UK: this Regulation is repealed in relation to the UK (as from IP completion day); see the introductory notes to this Regulation *ante*.

[5.602]

Article 38 Aid for public health measures

Aid for public health measures fulfilling the conditions laid down in Chapter I shall be compatible with the internal market within the meaning of Article 107(3)(c) of the Treaty and shall be exempted from the notification requirement of Article 108(3) thereof provided that:

(a) *the aid fulfils the conditions of Articles 46 and 55 of Regulation (EU) No 508/2014; and*
(b) *the amount of the aid does not exceed, in gross grant equivalent, the maximum intensity of public aid fixed by Article 95 of Regulation (EU) No 508/2014 and the implementing acts adopted on the basis of Article 95(5) of that Regulation.*

NOTES

Application of references to Regulation (EU) No 508/2014: see the note to Article 1 at **[5.564]**.

Repeal of this Regulation in relation to the UK: this Regulation is repealed in relation to the UK (as from IP completion day); see the introductory notes to this Regulation *ante*.

[5.603]

Article 39 Aid for animal health and welfare measures

Aid for animal health and welfare measures fulfilling the conditions laid down in Chapter I shall be compatible with the internal market within the meaning of Article 107(3)(c) of the Treaty and shall be exempted from the notification requirement of Article 108(3) thereof provided that:

(a) *the aid fulfils the conditions of Articles 46 and 56 of Regulation (EU) No 508/2014; and*

(b) *the amount of the aid does not exceed, in gross grant equivalent, the maximum intensity of public aid fixed by Article 95 of Regulation (EU) No 508/2014 and the implementing acts adopted on the basis of Article 95(5) of that Regulation.*

NOTES

Application of references to Regulation (EU) No 508/2014: see the note to Article 1 at **[5.564]**.

Repeal of this Regulation in relation to the UK: this Regulation is repealed in relation to the UK (as from IP completion day); see the introductory notes to this Regulation *ante*.

[5.604]

Article 40 Aid for aquaculture stock insurance

Aid for aquaculture stock insurance fulfilling the conditions laid down in Chapter I shall be compatible with the internal market within the meaning of Article 107(3)(c) of the Treaty and shall be exempted from the notification requirement of Article 108(3) thereof provided that:

(a) *the aid fulfils the conditions of Articles 46 and 57 of Regulation (EU) No 508/2014; and*

(b) *the amount of the aid does not exceed, in gross grant equivalent, the maximum intensity of public aid fixed by Article 95 of Regulation (EU) No 508/2014 and the implementing acts adopted on the basis of Article 95(5) of that Regulation.*

NOTES

Application of references to Regulation (EU) No 508/2014: see the note to Article 1 at **[5.564]**.

Repeal of this Regulation in relation to the UK: this Regulation is repealed in relation to the UK (as from IP completion day); see the introductory notes to this Regulation *ante*.

SECTION 3 MARKETING AND PROCESSING RELATED MEASURES

[5.605]

Article 41 Aid for marketing measures

Aid for marketing measures fulfilling the conditions laid down in Chapter I shall be compatible with the internal market within the meaning of Article 107(3)(c) of the Treaty and shall be exempted from the notification requirement of Article 108(3) thereof provided that:

(a) *the aid fulfils the conditions of Article 68 of Regulation (EU) No 508/2014; and*

(b) *the amount of the aid does not exceed, in gross grant equivalent, the maximum intensity of public aid fixed by Article 95 of Regulation (EU) No 508/2014 and the implementing acts adopted on the basis of Article 95(5) of that Regulation.*

NOTES

Application of references to Regulation (EU) No 508/2014: see the note to Article 1 at **[5.564]**.

Repeal of this Regulation in relation to the UK: this Regulation is repealed in relation to the UK (as from IP completion day); see the introductory notes to this Regulation *ante*.

[5.606]

Article 42 Aid for the processing of fishery and aquaculture products

Aid for the processing of fishery and aquaculture products fulfilling the conditions laid down in Chapter I shall be compatible with the internal market within the meaning of Article 107(3)(c) of the Treaty and shall be exempted from the notification requirement of Article 108(3) thereof provided that:

(a) *the aid fulfils the conditions of Article 69 of Regulation (EU) No 508/2014; and*

(b) *the amount of the aid does not exceed, in gross grant equivalent, the maximum intensity of public aid fixed by Article 95 of Regulation (EU) No 508/2014 and the implementing acts adopted on the basis of Article 95(5) of that Regulation.*

NOTES

Application of references to Regulation (EU) No 508/2014: see the note to Article 1 at **[5.564]**.

Repeal of this Regulation in relation to the UK: this Regulation is repealed in relation to the UK (as from IP completion day); see the introductory notes to this Regulation *ante*.

SECTION 4 OTHER CATEGORIES OF AID

[5.607]

Article 43 Aid for data collection

Aid for data collection fulfilling the conditions laid down in Chapter I shall be compatible with the internal market within the meaning of Article 107(3)(c) of the Treaty and shall be exempted from the notification requirement of Article 108(3) thereof provided that:

(a) *the aid fulfils the conditions of Article 77 of Regulation (EU) No 508/2014; and*

(b) *the amount of the aid does not exceed, in gross grant equivalent, the maximum intensity of public aid fixed by Article 95 of Regulation (EU) No 508/2014 and the implementing acts adopted on the basis of Article 95(5) of that Regulation.*

NOTES

Application of references to Regulation (EU) No 508/2014: see the note to Article 1 at **[5.564]**.

Repeal of this Regulation in relation to the UK: this Regulation is repealed in relation to the UK (as from IP completion day); see the introductory notes to this Regulation *ante*.

[5.608]

Article 44 Aid to make good the damage caused by natural disasters

1. Aid schemes to make good the damage caused by natural disasters shall be compatible with the internal market within the meaning of Article 107(2)(b) of the Treaty and shall be exempted from the notification requirement of Article 108(3) thereof where it fulfils the conditions laid down in this Article and in Chapter I.

2. Aid granted under this Article shall be granted subject to the following conditions:

(a) the competent authority of the Member State has formally recognized the character of the event as a natural disaster; and

(b) there is a direct causal link between the natural disaster and the damage suffered by the undertaking.

3. Aid shall be paid directly to the undertaking concerned.

4. Aid schemes related to a specific natural disaster shall be established within three years from the date of the occurrence of the natural disaster. The aid shall be paid out within four years from that date.

5. The eligible costs shall be the damage incurred as a direct consequence of the natural disaster, as assessed either by a public authority, by an independent expert recognized by the granting authority or by an insurance undertaking. That damage may include the following:

(a) material damage to assets such as buildings, equipment, machinery, stocks and means of production;

(b) loss of income due to the full or partial suspension of activity for a period not exceeding six months from the occurrence of the disaster.

6. The calculation of the material damage shall be based on the repair cost or economic value of the affected asset before the disaster. It shall not exceed the repair cost or the decrease in fair market value caused by the disaster, namely the difference between the property's value immediately before and immediately after the disaster.

7. The loss of income shall be calculated by subtracting:

(a) the result of multiplying the quantity of the fishery and aquaculture products produced in the year of the natural disaster, or in each following year affected by the full or partial destruction of the means of production, by the average selling price obtained during that year; from

(b) the result of multiplying the average annual quantity of fishery and aquaculture products produced in the three-year period preceding the natural disaster, or a three year average based on the five-year period preceding the natural disaster, excluding the highest and lowest entry, by the average selling price obtained.

8. The damage shall be calculated at the level of the individual beneficiary.

9. The aid and any other payments received to compensate the damage, including payments under insurance policies, shall be limited to 100% of the eligible costs.

NOTES

Repeal of this Regulation in relation to the UK: this Regulation is repealed in relation to the UK (as from IP completion day); see the introductory notes to this Regulation *ante*.

[5.609]

Article 45 Tax exemptions and reductions in accordance with Directive 2003/96/EC

1. Aid in the form of tax exemptions or reductions adopted by the Member States pursuant to Article 15(1)(f) and Article 15(3) of Directive 2003/96/EC shall be compatible with the internal market within the meaning of Article 107(3)(c) and exempt from the notification requirement of Article 108(3) of the Treaty, provided that the conditions laid down in Directive 2003/96/EC and in Chapter I of this Regulation are fulfilled.

2. The beneficiaries of the tax exemptions or reductions shall be selected on the basis of transparent and objective criteria. Where applicable, they shall pay at least the respective minimum level of taxation set by Directive 2003/96/EC.

NOTES

Repeal of this Regulation in relation to the UK: this Regulation is repealed in relation to the UK (as from IP completion day); see the introductory notes to this Regulation *ante*.

CHAPTER IV TRANSITIONAL AND FINAL PROVISIONS

[5.610]

Article 46 Transitional provisions

1. This Regulation shall apply to individual aid granted before its entry into force, if the aid fulfils all the conditions laid down in this Regulation, with the exception of Article 9.

2. Any aid granted before 1 July 2014 by virtue of any regulation adopted pursuant to Article 1 of Regulation (EC) No 994/98 previously in force shall be compatible with the internal market and exempted from the notification requirement of Article 108(3) of the Treaty.

3. Any aid not exempted from the notification requirement of Article 108(3) of the Treaty by virtue of this Regulation or other regulations adopted pursuant to Article 1 of Regulation (EC) No 994/98 previously in force shall be assessed by the Commission in accordance with the relevant frameworks, guidelines, communications and notices.

4. At the end of the period of validity of this Regulation any aid schemes exempted under this Regulation shall remain exempted during an adjustment period of six months.

NOTES

Repeal of this Regulation in relation to the UK: this Regulation is repealed in relation to the UK (as from IP completion day); see the introductory notes to this Regulation *ante*.

[5.611]

Article 47 Entry into force and applicability

This Regulation shall enter into force on 1 January 2015.

[It shall apply until 31 December 2022.]

NOTES

Words in square brackets substituted by Commission Regulation 2020/2008/EU, Art 3(3). Note that previously this Regulation was due to expire on 31 December 2020.

Repeal of this Regulation in relation to the UK: this Regulation is repealed in relation to the UK (as from IP completion day); see the introductory notes to this Regulation *ante*.

ANNEXES

ANNEX I
SME DEFINITION

Article 1
Enterprise

[5.612]

An enterprise is considered to be any entity engaged in an economic activity, irrespective of its legal form. This includes, in particular, self-employed persons and family businesses engaged in craft or other activities, and partnerships or associations regularly engaged in an economic activity.

Article 2
Staff headcount and financial thresholds determining enterprise categories

1. The category of micro, small and medium-sized enterprises ('SMEs') is made up of enterprises which employ fewer than 250 persons and which have an annual turnover not exceeding EUR 50 million, and/or an annual balance sheet total not exceeding EUR 43 million.

2. Within the SME category, a small enterprise is defined as an enterprise which employs fewer than 50 persons and whose annual turnover and/or annual balance sheet total does not exceed EUR 10 million.

3. Within the SME category, a micro-enterprise is defined as an enterprise which employs fewer than 10 persons and whose annual turnover and/or annual balance sheet total does not exceed EUR 2 million.

Article 3
Types of enterprise taken into consideration in calculating staff numbers and financial amounts

1. An 'autonomous enterprise' is any enterprise which is not classified as a partner enterprise within the meaning of paragraph 2 or as a linked enterprise within the meaning of paragraph 3.

2. 'Partner enterprises' are all enterprises which are not classified as linked enterprises within the meaning of paragraph 3 and between which there is the following relationship: an enterprise (upstream enterprise) holds, either solely or jointly with one or more linked enterprises within the meaning of paragraph 3, 25% or more of the capital or voting rights of another enterprise (downstream enterprise).

However, an enterprise may be ranked as autonomous, and thus as not having any partner enterprises, even if this 25% threshold is reached or exceeded by the following investors, provided that those investors are not linked, within the meaning of paragraph 3, either individually or jointly to the enterprise in question:

- *(a) public investment corporations, venture capital companies, individuals or groups of individuals with a regular venture capital investment activity who invest equity capital in unquoted businesses (business angels), provided the total investment of those business angels in the same enterprise is less than EUR 1,250,000;*
- *(b) universities or non-profit research centres;*
- *(c) institutional investors, including regional development funds;*
- *(d) autonomous local authorities with an annual budget of less than EUR 10 million and less than 5000 inhabitants.*

3. 'Linked enterprises' are enterprises which have any of the following relationships with each other:

- *(a) an enterprise has a majority of the shareholders' or members' voting rights in another enterprise;*
- *(b) an enterprise has the right to appoint or remove a majority of the members of the administrative, management or supervisory body of another enterprise;*
- *(c) an enterprise has the right to exercise a dominant influence over another enterprise pursuant to a contract entered into with that enterprise or to a provision in its memorandum or articles of association;*
- *(d) an enterprise, which is a shareholder in or member of another enterprise, controls alone, pursuant to an agreement with other shareholders in or members of that enterprise, a majority of shareholders' or members' voting rights in that enterprise.*

There is a presumption that no dominant influence exists if the investors listed in the second subparagraph of paragraph 2 are not involving themselves directly or indirectly in the management of the enterprise in question, without prejudice to their rights as shareholders.

Enterprises having any of the relationships described in the first subparagraph through one or more other enterprises, or any one of the investors mentioned in paragraph 2, are also considered to be linked.

Enterprises which have one or other of such relationships through a natural person or group of natural persons acting jointly are also considered linked enterprises if they engage in their activity or in part of their activity in the same relevant market or in adjacent markets.

An 'adjacent market' is considered to be the market for a product or service situated directly upstream or downstream of the relevant market.

4. Except in the cases set out in paragraph 2, second subparagraph, an enterprise cannot be considered an SME if 5% or more of the capital or voting rights are directly or indirectly controlled, jointly or individually, by one or more public bodies.

5. Enterprises may make a declaration of status as an autonomous enterprise, partner enterprise or linked enterprise, including the data regarding the thresholds set out in Article 2. The declaration may be made even if the capital is spread in such a way that it is not possible to determine exactly by whom it is held, in which case the enterprise may declare in good faith that it can legitimately presume that it is not owned as to 25% or more by one enterprise or jointly by enterprises linked to one another. Such declarations are made without prejudice to the checks and investigations provided for by national or Union rules.

Article 4

Data used for the staff headcount and the financial amounts and reference period

1. The data to apply to the headcount of staff and the financial amounts are those relating to the latest approved accounting period and calculated on an annual basis. They are taken into account from the date of closure of the accounts. The amount selected for the turnover is calculated excluding value added tax (VAT) and other indirect taxes.

2. Where, at the date of closure of the accounts, an enterprise finds that, on an annual basis, it has exceeded or fallen below the headcount or financial thresholds stated in Article 2, this will not result in the loss or acquisition of the status of medium-sized, small or micro-enterprise unless those thresholds are exceeded over two consecutive accounting periods.

3. In the case of newly-established enterprises whose accounts have not yet been approved, the data to apply is to be derived from a bona fide estimate made in the course of the financial year.

Article 5

Staff headcount

The headcount corresponds to the number of annual work units (AWU), i.e. the number of persons who worked full-time within the enterprise in question or on its behalf during the entire reference year under consideration. The work of persons who have not worked the full year, the work of those who have worked part-time, regardless of duration, and the work of seasonal workers are counted as fractions of AWU. The staff consists of:

- *(a) employees;*
- *(b) persons working for the enterprise being subordinated to it and deemed to be employees under national law;*
- *(c) owner-managers;*
- *(d) partners engaging in a regular activity in the enterprise and benefiting from financial advantages from the enterprise.*

Apprentices or students engaged in vocational training with an apprenticeship or vocational training contract are not included as staff. The duration of maternity or parental leaves is not counted.

Article 6

Establishing the data of an enterprise

1. In the case of an autonomous enterprise, the data, including the number of staff, are determined exclusively on the basis of the accounts of that enterprise.

2. The data, including the headcount, of an enterprise having partner enterprises or linked enterprises are determined on the basis of the accounts and other data of the enterprise or, where they exist, the consolidated accounts of the enterprise, or the consolidated accounts in which the enterprise is included through consolidation.

To the data referred to in the first subparagraph are added the data of any partner enterprise of the enterprise in question situated immediately upstream or downstream from it. Aggregation is proportional to the percentage interest in the capital or voting rights (whichever is greater). In the case of cross-holdings, the greater percentage applies.

To the data referred to in the first and second subparagraph are added 100% of the data of any enterprise, which is linked directly or indirectly to the enterprise in question, where the data were not already included through consolidation in the accounts.

3. For the application of paragraph 2, the data of the partner enterprises of the enterprise in question are derived from their accounts and their other data, consolidated if they exist. To these are added 100% of the data of enterprises which are linked to these partner enterprises, unless their accounts data are already included through consolidation.

For the application of the same paragraph 2, the data of the enterprises which are linked to the enterprise in question are to be derived from their accounts and their other data, consolidated if they exist. To these are added, pro rata, the data of any possible partner enterprise of that linked enterprise, situated immediately upstream or downstream from it, unless it has already been included in the consolidated accounts with a percentage at least proportional to the percentage identified under the second subparagraph of paragraph 2.

4. Where in the consolidated accounts no staff data appear for a given enterprise, staff figures are calculated by aggregating proportionally the data from its partner enterprises and by adding the data from the enterprises to which the enterprise in question is linked.

NOTES

Repeal of this Regulation in relation to the UK: this Regulation is repealed in relation to the UK (as from IP completion day); see the introductory notes to this Regulation *ante*.

ANNEX II

INFORMATION REGARDING STATE AID EXEMPT UNDER THE CONDITIONS OF THIS REGULATION TO BE PROVIDED THROUGH THE ESTABLISHED COMMISSION IT APPLICATION AS LAID DOWN IN ARTICLE 11

[5.613]

Aid reference	*(to be completed by the Commission)*	
Member State	....	
Member State reference number	....	
Region	**Name of the Region(s) (*NUTS* (1))**	....
Granting authority	**Name**	....
	Postal address **Web address**	....
Title of the aid measure	....	
National legal basis (Reference to the relevant national official publication)	....	
Web link to the full text of the aid measure	....	
Type of measure	☐ **Scheme**	
	☐ ***Ad hoc* aid**	**Name of the beneficiary and the group (2) it belongs to** ....
Amendment of an existing aid scheme or *ad hoc* aid		**Commission aid reference**
	☐ **Prolongation**	....
	☐ **Modification**	....

Duration (3)	☐ Scheme	dd/mm/yyyy to dd/mm/yyyy
Date of granting	☐ *Ad hoc* aid	dd/mm/yyyy
Economic sector(s) concerned	☐ All economic sectors eligible to receive aid	
	☐ Limited to certain sectors: Please specify at NACE group level (4)	....
Type of beneficiary	☐ SME	
	☐ Large undertakings	
Budget	Total annual amount of the budget planned under the scheme (5)	National currency .... (full amounts) ....
	Overall amount of the *ad hoc* aid awarded to the undertaking (6)	National currency .... (full amounts) ....
	☐ For guarantees (7)	National currency .... (full amounts) ....
Aid instrument	☐ Grant/Interest rate subsidy	
	☐ Loan/Repayable advances	
	☐ Guarantee (where appropriate with a reference to the Commission decision (8))	
	☐ Tax advantage or tax exemption	
	☐ Other (please specify) .... Indicate to which broad category below it would fit best in terms of its effect/function: ☐ Grant ☐ Loan ☐ Guarantee ☐ Tax advantage	

Indicate which of Articles 13 to 45 is used	☐ list of Articles
Aid to make good the damage caused by natural disasters (Article 44)	**Type of natural disaster:** ☐ earthquake ☐ avalanche ☐ landslide ☐ flood ☐ tornado ☐ hurricane ☐ volcanic eruption ☐ wild fire **Date of the occurrence of the natural disaster** dd/mm/yyyy to dd/mm/yyyy
Motivation	**Indicate why a State aid scheme has been established or an ad-hoc aid has been granted, instead of assistance under the European Maritime and Fisheries Fund (EMFF):** ☐ measure not covered by the national operational programme; ☐ prioritisation in the allocation of funds under the national operational programme; ☐ funding no longer available under the EMFF; ☐ other (please specify)

NOTES

Repeal of this Regulation in relation to the UK: this Regulation is repealed in relation to the UK (as from IP completion day); see the introductory notes to this Regulation *ante*.

[1] NUTS — Nomenclature of Territorial Units for Statistics. Typically the region is specified at level 2.

[2] An undertaking for the purposes of rules on competition laid down in the Treaty and for the purposes of this Regulation is any entity engaged in an economic activity, regardless of its legal status and the way in which it is financed. The Court of Justice has ruled that entities which are controlled (on a legal or on a de facto basis) by the same entity should be considered as one undertaking.

[3] Period during which the granting authority can commit itself to grant the aid.

[4] NACE Rev 2 — Statistical classification of Economic Activities in the European Union. Typically, the sector shall be specified at group level.

[5] In case of an aid scheme: Indicate the annual overall amount of the budget planned under the scheme or the estimated tax loss per year for all aid instruments contained in the scheme.

[6] In case of an *ad hoc* aid award: Indicate the overall aid amount/tax loss.

[7] For guarantees, indicate the (maximum) amount of loans guaranteed.

[8] Where appropriate, reference to the Commission decision approving the methodology to calculate the gross grant equivalent, in accordance with Article 5(2)(c).

ANNEX III
PROVISIONS FOR THE PUBLICATION OF INFORMATION REFERRED TO IN ARTICLE 9(1)

[5.614]

Member States shall organise their comprehensive State aid websites, on which the information referred to in Article 9(1) is to be published, in a way to allow easy access to the information.

Information shall be published in a spreadsheet data format, which allows data to be searched, extracted and easily published on the Internet, for instance in CSV or XML format. Access to the website shall be allowed to any interested party without restrictions. No prior user registration shall be required to access the website.

The following information on individual awards as laid down in Article 9(1)(c) shall be published:

— *Name of the beneficiary*
— *Beneficiary's identifier*
— *Type of enterprise (SME/large) at the date of granting*
— *Region in which the beneficiary is located, at NUTS level II*[1]
— *Sector of activity at NACE group level*[2]
— *Aid element, expressed as full amount in national currency*[3]

— *Aid instrument*[4] *(grant/interest rate subsidy, loan/repayable advances/reimbursable grant, guarantee, tax advantage or tax exemption, other (please specify))*
— *Date of granting*
— *Objective of the aid*
— *Granting authority*

NOTES

Repeal of this Regulation in relation to the UK: this Regulation is repealed in relation to the UK (as from IP completion day); see the introductory notes to this Regulation *ante*.

1 NUTS — Nomenclature of Territorial Units for Statistics. Typically, the region is specified at level 2.

2 Council Regulation (EEC) No 3037/90 of 9 October 1990 on the statistical classification of economic activities in the European Community (OJ L293, 24.10.1990, p 1).

3 Gross grant equivalent. For fiscal schemes, this amount can be provided by the ranges set out in Article 9(2).

4 If the aid is granted through multiple aid instruments, the aid amount shall be provided by instrument.

COMMUNICATION FROM THE COMMISSION

(2015/C217/01)

Guidelines for the examination of State aid to the fishery and aquaculture sector

[5.615]

NOTES

Date of publication in OJ: OJ C217, 2.7.2015, p 1.

Note: the 2008 Guidelines for the examination of State aid to fisheries and aquaculture (OJ C84, 3.4.2008, p 10) reproduced in previous editions of this Handbook, continue to apply to unlawful aid granted until 1 July 2015.

1. INTRODUCTION

[5.616]

(1) Article 107(1) of the Treaty on the Functioning of the European Union ('the Treaty') stipulates that 'Save as otherwise provided in the Treaties, any aid granted by a Member State or through State resources in any form whatsoever which distorts or threatens to distort competition by favouring certain undertakings or the production of certain goods shall, in so far as it affects trade between Member States, be incompatible with the internal market'.

(2) Article 107(2) of the Treaty lists types of aid that are compatible with the internal market, including aid to make good the damage caused by natural disasters or exceptional occurrences referred to in point (b) of paragraph 2 of that Article. Article 107(3) of the Treaty enumerates types of aid that may be considered to be compatible with the internal market, including aid to facilitate the development of certain economic activities or of certain economic areas, where such aid does not adversely affect trading conditions to an extent contrary to the common interest referred to in point (c) of paragraph 3 of that Article.

(3) Under Article 108(1) and (2) of the Treaty the Commission, in cooperation with the Member States, has to keep under constant review all systems of aid existing in the Member States. Under Article 108(3) of the Treaty each Member State has to inform the Commission of any plans to grant or alter aid. Detailed procedural rules for the application of Article 108 of the Treaty are set out in Council Regulation (EC) No 659/1999[1] and Commission Regulation (EC) No 794/2004.[2]

(4) Article 42 of the Treaty stipulates that the provisions of the Treaty relating to the rules on competition, which include those on State aid, apply to production of and trade in agricultural products, which include products of the fishery and aquaculture sector, to the extent determined by the European Parliament and the Council. The extent to which provisions of the Treaty on State aid apply to aid granted to the fishery and aquaculture sector has been determined in Article 8 of Regulation (EU) No 508/2014 of the European Parliament and the Council,[3] which establishes the European Maritime and Fisheries Fund (EMFF).

(5) Article 8(1) of Regulation (EU) No 508/2014 sets out that Articles 107, 108 and 109 of the Treaty apply to aid granted by the Member States to the fishery and aquaculture sector. Article 8(2) of that Regulation provides for an exception to this general rule and foresees that Articles 107, 108 and 109 of the Treaty do not apply to payments to the fishery and aquaculture sector made by Member States pursuant to and in conformity with that Regulation. However, under Article 8(3) of that Regulation, the provisions of the Treaty on State aid apply, if national provisions set up public financing as regards the fishery and aquaculture sector that goes beyond the provisions of that Regulation. In that case, the State aid rules apply to the public financing as a whole.

(6) Some payments made by Member States under Regulation (EU) No 508/2014 do not constitute payments to the fishery and aquaculture sector and fall outside the sector, for example, payments under Chapter VIII of Title V of that Regulation, which relates to Integrated Maritime Policy (IMP) measures financed under shared management. Further, payments under Chapter III of Title V of that Regulation, which relates to the sustainable development of fisheries and aquaculture areas, in general also fall outside the fishery and aquaculture sector. However, if those payments relate to measures provided for in Chapters I, II, and IV of Title V of that Regulation, as set out in Article 63(2) of that Regulation, they fall within the fishery and aquaculture sector.

(7) Payments under Regulation (EU) 508/2014 that fall outside the fishery and aquaculture sector are subject to the State aid rules of the Treaty. Where those payments constitute State aid, they should be assessed under the relevant State aid instruments. In that case, these Guidelines, Commission Regulation (EU) No 1388/2014,[4] and Commission Regulation (EU) No 717/2014[5] do not apply.

(8) These Guidelines set out the principles that the Commission will apply when assessing whether aid to the fishery and aquaculture sector can be considered compatible with the internal market under Article 107(2) or Article 107(3) of the Treaty.

[(9) State aid to the fishery and aquaculture sector is embedded within the broader framework of the Common Fisheries Policy (CFP). Consequently, the use of State aid can only be justified if it is in line with the objectives of the CFP. Therefore, the Commission applies and interprets these Guidelines in accordance with the rules of the CFP. Within the CFP the Union provides financial support to the fishery and aquaculture sector through the EMFF. The social and economic impact of public support is the same, irrespective of whether it is (even partly) financed by the Union or by a Member State alone. The Commission therefore considers that there should be consistency and coherence between its policy of State aid control and the support which is granted under the CFP. While State aid should not, in principle, be granted to operations that are not eligible for support under the EMFF, certain State aid measures, due to their positive contribution to the objectives of the CFP in specific circumstances, could nevertheless be compatible with the internal market.]

(10) The CFP, the objectives of which are set out in Article 2 of Regulation (EU) No 1380/2013 of the European Parliament and the Council,[6] aims, amongst others, at ensuring that fishing and aquaculture activities are environmentally sustainable in the long term and are managed in a way that is consistent with the objectives of achieving economic, social and employment benefits, and of contributing to the availability of food supplies.

(11) Under Article 5 of Regulation (EU) No 508/2014 the objectives of the EMFF are to promote competitive, environmentally sustainable, economically viable and socially responsible fisheries and aquaculture, to foster the implementation of the CFP, to promote a balanced and inclusive territorial development of fisheries and aquaculture areas, as well as to foster the development and implementation of the Union's IMP in a manner complementary to cohesion policy and to the CFP. Overall, the pursuit of those objectives is not to result in an increase in fishing capacity.

(12) The EMFF provides financial support to various specific themes and areas identified in Regulation (EU) No 508/2014. Measures supported by the EMFF are implemented on the basis of either direct or shared management principles.

(13) In its communication on EU State Aid Modernisation (SAM) of 8 May 2012 (Communication on SAM)[7] the Commission announced three broad objectives of the modernisation of State aid control: (a) to foster sustainable, smart and inclusive growth in a competitive internal market; (b) to focus Commission *ex ante* scrutiny on cases with the biggest impact on the internal market whilst strengthening the cooperation with Member States in State aid enforcement; and (c) to streamline the rules and provide for faster decisions.

(14) In particular, the Commission called for a common approach to the revision of the different guidelines and frameworks with a view to strengthening the internal market, promoting more effectiveness in public spending through a better contribution of State aid to the objectives of common interest, greater scrutiny of the incentive effect, limiting the aid to the minimum, and avoiding the potential negative effects of the aid on competition and trade. The principles and conditions set out in these Guidelines are based on the objectives established in the Communication on SAM.

NOTES

Point (9): substituted by the Communication from the Commission amending the Guidelines for the examination of State aid to the fishery and aquaculture sector (2018/C422/01).

1 Council Regulation (EC) No 659/1999 of 22 March 1999 laying down detailed rules for the application of Article 108 of the Treaty on the Functioning of the European Union (OJ L83, 27.3.1999, p 1).

2 Commission Regulation (EC) No 794/2004 of 21 April 2004 implementing Council Regulation (EC) No 659/1999 laying down detailed rules for the application of Article 93 of the EC Treaty (OJ L140, 30.4.2004, p 1).

3 Regulation (EU) No 508/2014 of the European Parliament and of the Council of 15 May 2014 on the European Maritime and Fisheries Fund and repealing Council Regulations (EC) No 2328/2003, (EC) No 861/2006, (EC) No 1198/2006 and (EC) No 791/2007 and Regulation (EU) No 1255/2011 of the European Parliament and of the Council (OJ L 149, 20.5.2014, p 1).

4 Commission Regulation (EU) No 1388/2014 of 16 December 2014 declaring certain categories of aid to undertakings active in the production, processing and marketing of fishery and aquaculture products compatible with the internal market in application of Articles 107 and 108 of the Treaty on the Functioning of the European Union (OJ L 369, 24.12.2014, p 37).

5 Commission Regulation (EU) No 717/2014 of 27 June 2014 on the application of Articles 107 and 108 of the Treaty on the Functioning of the European Union to de minimis aid in the fishery and aquaculture sector (OJ L 190, 28.6.2014, p 45).

6 Regulation (EU) No 1380/2013 of the European Parliament and of the Council of 11 December 2013 on the Common Fisheries Policy, amending Council Regulations (EC) No 1954/2003 and (EC) No 1224/2009 and repealing Council Regulations (EC) No 2371/2002 and (EC) No 639/2004 and Council Decision 2004/585/EC (OJ L 354, 28.12.2013, p 22).

7 Communication of 8 May 2012 from the Commission to the European Parliament, the Council, the European Economic and Social Committee and the Committee of the Regions, EU State Aid Modernisation (SAM), COM(2012) 209 final.

2. SCOPE, DUTY TO NOTIFY AND DEFINITIONS

2.1. SCOPE

[5.617]

(15) These Guidelines apply to all aid granted to the fishery and aquaculture sector. They apply to aid schemes and to individual aid.

(16) These Guidelines apply to the components of regional aid that relate to the fishery and aquaculture sector.[1] They also apply to all other aid that is granted to the fishery and aquaculture sector within the framework of European Structural and Investment Funds (ESI Funds) other than the EMFF.

(17) These Guidelines do not apply to aid granted as additional financing for the implementation of the compensation plans referred to in Article 72 of Regulation (EU) No 508/2014. Such aid is approved as part of those plans in accordance with Article 73 of that Regulation.

2.2. DUTY TO NOTIFY

(18) The Commission reminds each Member State of its duty to notify any plans to grant new aid, as provided for in Article 108(3) of the Treaty and Article 2 of Regulation (EC) No 659/1999.

(19) A Member State is, however, not obliged to notify to the Commission:

(a) aid complying with one of the Regulations on group exemptions adopted on the basis of Article 1 of Council Regulation (EC) No 994/98,[2] if they apply to the fishery and aquaculture sector, in particular:

(i) aid complying with Regulation (EU) No 1388/2014; and

(ii) training aid, aid for SMEs' access to finance, aid in the field of research and development, innovation aid for SMEs, and aid for disadvantaged workers and workers with disabilities complying with Commission Regulation (EU) No 651/2014;[3]

(b) *de minimis* aid complying with Regulation (EU) No 717/2014.

(20) The Commission reminds each Member State that, when the system of financing of an aid measure, for example, by parafiscal levies, forms an integral part of the aid measure, it should also be notified.[4]

(21) The Commission reminds the Member States that aid granted as additional financing for the implementation of the compensation plans referred to in Article 72 of Regulation (EU) No 508/2014 must be notified to the Commission as part of the compensation plans. Under Article 73 of that Regulation State aid thus notified will be regarded as notified within the meaning of the first sentence of Article 108(3) of the Treaty.

2.3. DEFINITIONS

(22) For the purposes of these Guidelines, the following definitions apply:

(a) 'aid' means any measure fulfilling the criteria laid down in Article 107(1) of the Treaty;

(b) 'aid scheme' means any act on the basis of which, without further implementing measures being required, individual aid may be granted to undertakings defined within the act in a general and abstract manner and any act on the basis of which aid which is not linked to a specific project may be granted to one or several undertakings for an indefinite period of time and/or for an indefinite amount;

(c) '*ad hoc* aid' means aid not granted on the basis of a scheme;

(d) 'individual aid' means *ad hoc* aid and awards of aid to individual beneficiaries on the basis of an aid scheme;

(e) 'date of granting the aid' means the date when the legal right to receive the aid is conferred on the beneficiary under the applicable national legal regime;

(f) 'aid intensity' means the gross aid amount expressed as a percentage of the eligible costs, before any deduction of tax or other charge;

(g) 'fishery and aquaculture sector' means the sector of the economy which comprises all activities of production, processing, and marketing of fishery or aquaculture products;

(h) 'fishery and aquaculture products' means the products listed in Annex I to Regulation (EU) No 1379/2013 of the European Parliament and the Council;[5]

(i) 'SMEs' or 'small and medium-sized enterprises' means undertakings fulfilling the criteria set out in Annex I to Regulation (EU) No 1388/2014;

(j) 'large undertaking' means any undertaking not fulfilling the criteria set out in Annex I to Regulation (EU) No 1388/2014;

(k) 'outermost regions' means the regions referred to in Article 349 of the Treaty. Under European Council Decision 2010/718/EU,[6]Saint-Barthélemy ceased to be an outermost region from 1 January 2012 on. Under European Council Decision 2012/419/EU,[7] Mayotte became an outermost region on 1 January 2014;

(l) 'operating aid' means aid that is aimed at or has the effect of increasing the business liquidity of an undertaking, reducing its production costs, or improving its income, in particular aid that is calculated solely on the basis of the quantity produced or marketed, product prices, units produced or the means of production.

NOTES

1 Guidelines on regional State Aid for 2014-2020 (OJ C209, 23.7.2013, p 1). Those guidelines do not apply to the fishery and aquaculture sector.

2 Council Regulation (EC) No 994/98 of 7 May 1998 on the application of Articles 107 and 108 of the Treaty on the Functioning of the European Union to certain categories of horizontal State aid (OJ L142, 14.5.1998, p 1).

3 Commission Regulation (EU) No 651/2014 of 17 June 2014 declaring certain categories of aid compatible with the internal market in application of Articles 107 and 108 of the Treaty (OJ L 187, 26.6.2014, p 1).

4 Judgment of the General Court of 16 October 2013, *Télévision française 1 (TF1) v European Commission*, T-275/11, ECLI:EU:T:2013:535, paragraphs 41-44.

5 Regulation (EU) 1379/2013 of the European Parliament and of the Council of 11 December 2013 on the common organisation of the markets in fishery and aquaculture products, amending Council Regulations (EC) No 1184/2006 and (EC) No 1224/2009 and repealing Council Regulation (EC) No 104/2000 (OJ L354, 28.12.2013, p 1).

6 European Council Decision of 29 October 2010 amending the status with regard to the European Union of the island of Saint-Barthélemy (OJ L325, 9.12.2010, p 4).

7 European Council Decision of 11 July 2012 amending the status of Mayotte with regard to the European Union (OJ L204, 31.7.2012, p 131).

3. PRINCIPLES

3.1. COMMON ASSESSMENT PRINCIPLES

[5.618]

(23) To assess whether an aid measure notified to the Commission can be considered compatible with the internal market, the Commission analyses whether the design of the aid measure ensures that the positive impact of the aid on an objective of common interest exceeds its potential negative effects on trade and competition.

(24) The Communication on SAM called for the identification and definition of common principles applicable to the assessment of compatibility of all the aid measures carried out by the Commission. Thus, the Commission will consider an aid measure compatible with the internal market only if it complies with each of the following principles:

- (a) contribution to a well-defined objective of common interest: a State aid measure must aim at an objective of common interest in accordance with Article 107(3) of the Treaty (Section 3.3);
- (b) need for State intervention: a State aid measure must be targeted towards a situation where aid can bring about a material improvement that the market cannot deliver itself, for example, by remedying a market failure or addressing an equity or cohesion concern (Section 3.4);
- (c) appropriateness of the aid measure: the proposed aid measure must be an appropriate policy instrument to address the objective of common interest (Section 3.5);
- (d) incentive effect: the aid must change the behaviour of the undertaking(s) concerned in such a way that it engages in additional activity which it would not carry out without the aid or it would carry out in a restricted or different manner or location (Section 3.6);
- (e) proportionality of the aid (aid limited to the minimum necessary): the aid amount must be limited to the minimum needed to induce the additional investment or activity in the area concerned (Section 3.7);
- (f) avoidance of undue negative effects on competition and trade between Member States: the negative effects must be sufficiently limited, so that the overall balance of the measure is positive (Section 3.8);
- (g) transparency of the aid: Member States, the Commission, economic operators, and the public, must have easy access to all relevant acts and to pertinent information about the aid awarded thereunder (Section 3.9).

(25) Certain categories of aid schemes may further be made subject to an *ex post* evaluation as set out in points (118) to (121). The Commission may limit the duration of those schemes, normally to four years or less, with a possibility to re-notify their prolongation afterwards.

(26) If an aid measure or any conditions attached to it, including its financing method when that method constitutes a non-severable part of the measure, entail a violation of Union law, the aid is incompatible with the internal market.[1]

(27) Aid for export-related activities towards third countries or Member States, namely aid directly linked to the quantities exported, to the establishment and operation of a distribution network, or to other costs linked to the export activity and aid contingent upon the use of domestic over imported goods is incompatible with the internal market.

(28) When assessing aid granted to an undertaking which is subject to an outstanding recovery order following a previous Commission decision declaring an aid illegal and incompatible with the internal market, the Commission will take account of the amount of aid still to be recovered.[2] This does not apply, however, to aid to make good the damage caused by natural disasters under Article 107(2)(b) of the Treaty.

(29) The common assessment principles overall have to be applied taking into account the specific context of the CFP. They therefore apply to all aid under these Guidelines, unless Sections 4 and 5 provide for derogations due to particular considerations in the fishery and aquaculture sector.

3.2. SPECIFIC PRINCIPLES FOR THE FISHERY AND AQUACULTURE SECTOR

(30) In addition to the common assessment principles set out in Section 3.1, the Commission also applies the specific principles for the fishery and aquaculture sector set out in this Section.

(31) Each beneficiary of a State aid measure must comply with the rules of the CFP.

(32) An application for aid or, if no application is foreseen, an equivalent act must be considered inadmissible, if the competent authority referred to in Article 10(1) of Regulation (EU) No 508/2014 has determined that the operator concerned has committed one or more of the infringements or offences set out in Article 10(1) of that Regulation or a fraud as set out in Article 10(3) of that Regulation. The periods of inadmissibility set out in the delegated acts adopted on the basis of Article 10(4) of that Regulation apply. This principle does not apply in the case of aid that meets the specific conditions set out in Sections 4, 5.3, and 5.4 of these Guidelines.

(33) Each undertaking, after submitting an application for aid or, if no application is foreseen, an equivalent act must continue to comply with the rules of the CFP throughout the period of implementation of the project and for a period of five years after the final payment to the beneficiary. Aid measures must explicitly provide that during those periods the beneficiary or beneficiaries must comply with the rules of the CFP. If it is determined by the competent authority that a beneficiary has committed one or more of the infringements set out in Article 10(1) of Regulation (EU) No 508/2014 during those periods and has as a consequence become inadmissible to apply for aid, the aid must be reimbursed by the beneficiary.

(34) An aid measure of the same kind as an operation that is eligible for funding under Regulation (EU) No 508/2014 can only be considered compatible with the internal market if it complies with the relevant provisions of that Regulation for that kind of operation, in particular, with the provisions on the intensity of public aid. If an aid goes beyond the criteria set out in that Regulation, the Member State must demonstrate the justification for and the indispensability of the aid.

[(35) No aid must be granted for activities that correspond to ineligible operations under Article 11 of Regulation (EU) No 508/2014, unless otherwise stated in these Guidelines.]

3.3. CONTRIBUTION TO A COMMON OBJECTIVE

(36) An aid measure must contribute to achieving one or more of the objectives of common interest set out in Article 107(3) of the Treaty.

(37) Furthermore, each aid measure must identify the objectives of the CFP to the achievement of which it contributes and clearly demonstrate how it will contribute to achieving those objectives without negatively affecting other CFP objectives. The objectives of the CFP are set out in Article 2 of Regulation (EU) No 1380/2013 and include, amongst others, to ensure that fishing and aquaculture activities are environmentally sustainable in the long-term and are managed in a way that is consistent with the objectives of achieving economic, social and employment benefits, and of contributing to the availability of food supplies.

[(38) The Commission considers that aid measures fulfilling the specific conditions set out in Sections 4, 5.1, 5.3, 5.4, and 5.6a of these Guidelines contribute to achieving an objective of common interest.]

3.4. NEED FOR STATE INTERVENTION

(39) In order to assess whether State aid is necessary to achieve the objective of common interest, the problem to be addressed shall be identified first. State aid should be targeted towards situations where it can bring about a material improvement that the market cannot deliver on its own. This holds especially in a context of scarce public resources

(40) State aid measures can under certain conditions correct market failures and thereby contribute to the efficient functioning of markets and to enhance competitiveness. Furthermore, where markets provide efficient outcomes but these are deemed unsatisfactory from an equity or cohesion point of view, State aid may be used to obtain a more desirable, equitable market outcome.

(41) State aid must overall not be protective in its aim and effect and must promote the rationalisation and efficiency of the fishery and aquaculture sector. Any State aid must aim at permanent improvements in order for the sector to function on the basis of market factors.

[(42) For the purposes of these Guidelines, the Commission considers that the market is not achieving the expected objectives without State intervention and that there is therefore need for State intervention in the case of aid fulfilling the specific conditions laid down in Sections 4, 5.1, 5.3, 5.4, and 5.6a of these Guidelines.]

3.5. APPROPRIATENESS OF THE AID MEASURE

(43) The proposed aid measure must be an appropriate policy instrument to contribute to achieving the objectives concerned. An aid measure will not be considered compatible with the internal market if other less distortive policy instruments or other less distortive forms of aid make it possible to make the same positive contribution to the objectives of the CFP.

[(44) The Commission considers that aid which meets the specific conditions set out in Sections 4, 5.1, 5.3, 5.4, and 5.6a of these Guidelines is an appropriate policy instrument. In all other cases a Member State must demonstrate that no other less distortive policy instrument exists.]

(45) The Commission will in particular take account of any impact assessments of the proposed aid scheme that the Member State may make available. Likewise, the results of ex post evaluations as described in Section 6 may be taken into account to assess whether no other less distortive policy instrument exists.

(46) Aid can be awarded in various forms. Each Member State must ensure that the aid is granted in the form that is likely to generate the least distortions of competition and trade.

(47) Where the aid is granted in forms that provide a direct pecuniary advantage (for example, direct grants, exemptions or reductions in taxes, social security or other compulsory charges), the Member State must demonstrate why other potentially less distortive forms of aid such as repayable advances or forms of aid that are based on debt or equity instruments (for example, low-interest loans or interest rebates, state guarantees, the purchase of a shareholding or an alternative provision of capital on favourable terms) are less appropriate.

(48) The results of ex post evaluations as described in Section 6 may be taken into account to assess whether no other less distortive form of aid exists.

3.6. INCENTIVE EFFECT

(49) Aid can only be found compatible with the internal market if it has an incentive effect. Aid has an incentive effect if it changes the behaviour of an undertaking in such a way that it engages in additional activity which it would not have carried out without the aid or would have carried out in a restricted or different manner. The aid must not subsidise the costs of an activity that an undertaking would have incurred in any event and must not compensate for the normal business risk of an economic activity.[3]

(50) Operating aid and aid to facilitate the achievement of obligatory standards is in principle incompatible with the internal market, unless exceptions are expressly provided for in Union legislation or these Guidelines and in duly justified other cases.

(51) Aid which is granted in respect of an operation that the beneficiary has already begun to implement before the aid application was submitted by the beneficiary to the national authorities cannot be considered to have an incentive effect.

[(52) Aid that is compensatory in nature, such as aid that meets the specific conditions set out in Sections 4, 5.3, and 5.4, aid that meets the conditions set out in Section 5.6, and aid that meets the specific conditions set out in Section 5.6a are not required to have an incentive effect.]

(53) Aid in the form of tax advantages will be deemed to have an incentive effect, if the measure establishes a right to the aid in accordance with objective criteria and without further exercise of discretion by the Member State and if the measure has been adopted and is in force before work on the aided project or activity has started. The latter requirement shall not apply in the case of fiscal successor schemes, if the measure was already covered by the previous schemes in the form of tax advantages.

3.7. PROPORTIONALITY OF THE AID (AID LIMITED TO THE MINIMUM NECESSARY)

(54) Aid must be limited to the minimum needed to induce the beneficiary to carry out an activity.

(55) As a general rule, aid will be considered to be limited to the minimum, if the aid amount corresponds to the net extra costs of implementing the investment in the area concerned, compared to the counterfactual in the absence of the aid (net extra cost approach).

(56) The aid must therefore not exceed the minimum amount necessary to render the project profitable. The aid must, for example, not increase the project's internal rate of return (IRR)[4] beyond the normal rates of return applied by the undertaking concerned in other similar investment projects. If such rates are unavailable, the aid should not increase the project's IRR beyond the costs of capital of the company as a whole or beyond the rates of return commonly observed in the industry concerned.

(57) Where an aid measure is of the same kind as an operation that is eligible for funding under Regulation (EU) No 508/2014, the principle of proportionality of the aid is deemed to be respected if the amount of the aid does not exceed the applicable maximum intensity of public aid set out in Article 95 of and Annex I to that Regulation. Where the maximum aid intensity for public aid of a measure goes beyond that set out in those provisions, the principle of proportionality of the aid is deemed to be respected if the Member State demonstrates the justification for and the indispensability of the aid.

[(58) Aid that is compensatory in nature, such as aid that meets the specific conditions set out in Sections 4, 5.3, and 5.4, aid that meets the conditions set out in Section 5.6, and aid that meets the specific conditions set out in Section 5.6a are deemed to be proportional.]

(59) Aid may be granted concurrently under several schemes or cumulated with *ad hoc* aid, provided that the total amount of public funding for an activity does not exceed the relevant maximum aid intensities referred to in these Guidelines.

3.8. AVOIDANCE OF UNDUE NEGATIVE EFFECTS ON COMPETITION AND TRADE

(60) For the aid to be compatible with the internal market, the negative effects of the aid measure in terms of distortions of competition and impact on trade between Member States must be limited and outweighed by the positive effects in terms of contribution to achieving the objective of common interest.

3.8.1. GENERAL CONSIDERATIONS

(61) In principle, aid to the fishery and aquaculture sector can cause product market distortions and have location effects. It may therefore lead to allocative inefficiencies, undermining the economic performance of the internal market, and to distributional concerns, distorting the distribution of economic activity across different geographical areas.

[(62) Due to its positive effects on the development of the sector the Commission considers that, where aid fulfils the specific conditions set out in Sections 4, 5.1, 5.3, 5.4, and 5.6a, the negative effects on competition and trade are limited to the minimum.]

(63) The Commission will in general consider the effects on competition and trade to be more limited if the aid is proportionate (aid limited to the minimum necessary) and the smaller the amount of aid as compared to the overall eligible costs.

3.8.2. AID SCHEMES

(64) Aid schemes must not lead to significant distortions of competition and trade. In particular, even where distortions may be considered limited at an individual level, a scheme should not lead to high levels of distortions on a cumulative basis.

(65) The Member State therefore has to demonstrate that the negative effects of the aid will be limited to the minimum taking into account, for example, the size of the projects concerned, the individual and cumulative aid amounts, the expected beneficiaries, as well as the characteristics of the targeted sector. In order to enable the Commission to assess the effects of the aid, the Member State may submit any impact assessment at its disposal, as well as ex post evaluations carried out for similar predecessor schemes.

3.8.3. NOTIFIED INDIVIDUAL AID

(66) When appraising the effects of notified individual aid, the Commission places particular emphasis on the negative effects linked to the prevention of exit from the market and the notion of substantial market power. These negative effects must be counterbalanced with the positive effects of the aid.

(67) In order to identify and assess the potential distortions of competition and trade, each Member State should provide the Commission with evidence permitting to identify the relevant product market, that is, products affected by the change of behaviour of the aid beneficiary, the geographical market, the competitors, as well as the customers and consumers concerned.

(68) The Commission will use various criteria to assess potential distortions of competition and trade, such as the market structure of the product concerned, the performance of the market (declining or growing market), the process for selecting the aid beneficiary, and the market strategy of the beneficiary.

3.9. TRANSPARENCY

(69) Each Member State must publish at least the following information on a comprehensive State aid website at national or regional level:

- (a) the full text of the aid scheme and its implementing provisions or legal basis for individual aid, or a link to it;
- (b) the granting authority or authorities;
- (c) the identity of the individual beneficiaries, the form and amount of aid granted to each beneficiary, the date of granting the aid, the type of undertaking (SME/large enterprise), the region in which the beneficiary is located (at NUTS level II), and the principal economic sector in which the beneficiary has its activities (at NACE group level). Such publication requirement can be waved with respect to individual aid awards not exceeding EUR 30 000.[5]

(70) In the case of aid schemes in the form of tax advantages the information on individual aid amounts can be provided in the following ranges (in EUR million): 0.03-0.5; above 0.5-1; above 1-2; above 2.

(71) Such information must be published after the decision to grant the aid has been taken, must be kept for at least 10 years, and be available for the general public without restrictions.[6] Member States are not required to publish the information before 1 July 2017.[7]

NOTES

Points (35), (38), (42), (44), (52), (58), (62): substituted by the Communication from the Commission amending the Guidelines for the examination of State aid to the fishery and aquaculture sector (2018/C422/01).

1 See, for example, Judgment of the Court of Justice of 19 September 2000, *Germany v Commission*, C-156/98, ECLI:EU:C:2000:467, paragraph 78 and Judgment of the Court of Justice of 22 December 2008, Régie Networks, C-333/07, ECLI:EU:C:2008:764, paragraphs 94-116.

2 Judgment of the General Court of 13 September 1995, *TWD v Commission*, Joined Cases T-244/93 and T-486/93, ECLI:EU:T:1995:160, paragraphs 53-63.

3 Judgment of the Court of 13 June 2013, *HGA and others v Commission*, Joined Cases C-630/11 P to C-633/11 P, ECLI:EU:C:2013:387, paragraphs 103-123

4 The internal rate of return (IRR) is not based on accounting earnings in a given year, but takes into account the stream of future cash flows that the investor expects to receive over the entire lifetime of an investment. It is defined as the discount rate for which the net present value (NPV) of a stream of cash flows equals zero. The NPV of a project is the difference between the positive and negative cash flows over the lifetime of an investment, discounted to their current value (typically using the cost of capital).

5 The threshold of EUR 30 000 corresponds to the threshold for the publication of information set out in Article 9 of Regulation (EU) No 1388/2014. It is appropriate to set the same threshold in both that Regulation and these Guidelines in order to ensure coherence between the various State aid instruments applicable to the fishery and aquaculture sector and to reduce the administrative burden of the Member States. In view of the protection of personal data, which might be at stake, the requirement of publishing information on individual aid exceeding the threshold of EUR 30 000 is proportionate to the legitimate aim it pursues, in particular as regards transparency with respect to the use of public funds.

6 The information must be published within six months from the date of granting the aid (or, for aid in the form of tax advantage, within one year from the date when the tax declaration is due). In the case of unlawful aid, Member State must publish the information ex post, at least within a period of six months from the date of the Commission decision. The information must be available in a format which allows data to be searched, extracted, and easily published on the internet, for instance in CSV or XML format.

7 Publication of aid awards granted before 1 July 2017 and, for fiscal aid, publication for aid claimed or granted before 1 July 2017, will not be required.

4. AID THAT IS COMPATIBLE WITH THE INTERNAL MARKET

4.1. AID TO MAKE GOOD THE DAMAGE CAUSED BY NATURAL DISASTERS AND EXCEPTIONAL OCCURRENCES

[5.619]

(72) Aid to make good the damage caused by natural disasters and exceptional occurrences is compatible with the internal market if it respects the principles set out in Section 3 and meets the specific conditions set out in this Section.

(73) The notions of natural disasters and exceptional occurrences must be interpreted restrictively.[1]

(74) To date, in the field of State aid to the fishery and aquaculture sector, the Commission has accepted that exceptionally severe storms and floods may constitute natural disasters. In addition, Regulation (EU) No 1388/2014 permits to block exempt also the following types of natural disasters: earthquakes, avalanches, landslides, tornadoes, hurricanes, volcanic eruptions and wild fires of natural origin.

(75) The following events are examples of exceptional occurrences that have been recognised by the Commission in cases outside the fishery and aquaculture sector: war, internal disturbances, strikes, with certain reservations and depending on their extent, major industrial and nuclear accidents, and fires resulting in widespread loss. The outbreak of an animal disease or a plant pest does in general not constitute an exceptional occurrence. The Commission has, however, in specific cases concerning the fishery and aquaculture sector accepted the very widespread outbreak of a new animal disease as an exceptional occurrence.

(76) The Commission will continue to assess proposals to grant aid in accordance with Article 107(2)(b) of the Treaty on a case-by-case basis, having regard to its previous practice in the field.

(77) Aid granted under this Section must additionally meet the following conditions:

- (a) the competent authority of the Member State has formally recognised the character of the event as a natural disaster or as an exceptional occurrence;
- (b) there is a direct causal link between the natural disaster or the exceptional occurrence and the damage suffered by the undertaking.

(78) Aid must be paid directly to the undertaking concerned.

(79) Aid schemes related to a specific natural disaster or exceptional occurrence must be established within three years from the date of the occurrence of the event. The aid must be paid out within four years from that date.

(80) In order to facilitate rapid reaction, the Commission will authorize ex ante framework aid schemes to compensate for the damage caused by earthquakes, avalanches, landslides, floods, tornadoes, hurricanes, volcanic eruptions, and wild fires of natural origin, provided that the conditions under which aid can be granted in such cases of natural disasters are clearly stipulated. The Member States must in such cases comply with the reporting obligation set out in point (130).

(81) The eligible costs are the costs of the damage incurred as a direct consequence of the natural disaster or exceptional occurrence, as assessed by a public authority, by an independent expert recognised by the granting authority, or by an insurance undertaking. The damage may include:

- (a) material damage to assets (such as buildings, equipment, machinery, stocks, and means of production); and
- (b) loss of income due to the full or partial destruction of fishery or aquaculture production or the means of such production.

(82) The calculation of the material damage must be based on the repair cost or economic value of the affected asset before the natural disaster or exceptional occurrence. It must not exceed the repair cost or the decrease in fair market value caused by the natural disaster or the exceptional occurrence, that is to say the difference between the asset's value immediately before and immediately after the natural disaster or exceptional occurrence.

(83) The loss of income must be calculated by subtracting:

- (a) the result of multiplying the quantity of the fishery and aquaculture products produced in the year of the natural disaster or exceptional occurrence, or in each following year affected by the full or partial destruction of the means of production, by the average selling price obtained during that year, from
- (b) the result of multiplying the average annual quantity of fishery and aquaculture products produced in the three-year period preceding the natural disaster or exceptional occurrence or a three year average based on the five-year period preceding the natural disaster or exceptional occurrence, excluding the highest and lowest entry by the average selling price obtained.

(84) The damage must be calculated at the level of the individual beneficiary.

(85) The aid and any other payments received to compensate the damage, including payments under insurance policies, must be limited to 100 % of the eligible costs.

NOTES

[1] Judgment of the Court of Justice of 23 February 2006, *Giuseppe Atzeni and Others*, Joined Cases C-346/03 and C-529/03, ECLI:EU:C:2006:130, paragraph 79.

5. AID THAT MAY BE CONSIDERED COMPATIBLE WITH THE INTERNAL MARKET

5.1. AID FOR CATEGORIES OF MEASURES COVERED BY A BLOCK EXEMPTION REGULATION

[5.620]

(86) Where aid benefitting SMEs or large undertakings is of the same kind as aid falling within a category of aid that can be considered compatible with the internal market under one of the Regulations on group exemptions referred to in point (19)(a), the Commission will assess the aid on the basis of the principles set out in Section 3 of these Guidelines, this Section, and the criteria laid down for each category of aid set out in those Regulations.

(87) If aid does not fulfil all the criteria referred to in point (86), the Member State must demonstrate the justification for and the indispensability of the aid. The Commission will assess such aid on a case-by-case basis.

(88) As an exception to point (86), aid of the same kind as aid falling with the category of aid to make good the damage caused by natural disasters mentioned in Article 44 of Regulation (EU) No 1388/2014 is be compatible with the Treaty if it meets the specific conditions set out in Section 4 of these Guidelines.

5.2. AID FALLING WITHIN THE SCOPE OF CERTAIN HORIZONTAL GUIDELINES

(89) Where aid falls within the scope of certain horizontal guidelines or other instruments adopted by the Commission (1), the Commission will assess such aid on the basis of the principles set out in Section 3 of these Guidelines and the relevant Sections of those instruments.

5.3. AID TO MAKE GOOD THE DAMAGE CAUSED BY ADVERSE CLIMATIC EVENTS(

(90) Where aid aims to make good the damage caused by adverse climatic events, the Commission will assess the aid on the basis of the principles set out in Section 3 of these Guidelines and the specific conditions set out in this Section.

(91) As an exception to point (90), the Commission will assess aid of the same kind as aid falling within the category of aid to mutual funds for adverse climatic events mentioned in Article 20 of Regulation (EU) No 1388/2014 under Section 5.1 of these Guidelines.

(92) To date, in the field of State aid to the fishery and aquaculture sector, the Commission has accepted that storms, gusts of wind causing exceptionally high waves, heavy and persistent rainfall, floods, and exceptionally elevated water temperatures over a longer period may constitute adverse climatic events. The Commission will continue to assess proposals to grant aid to make good the damage caused by adverse climatic events on a case-by-case basis, having regard to its previous practice in the field.

(93) Aid granted under this Section must additionally meet the following conditions:

- (a) the damage caused by the adverse climatic event must amount to more than 30 % of the average annual turnover, calculated on the basis of the preceding three calendar years or a three year average based on the five-year period preceding the adverse climatic event, excluding the highest and lowest entry;

(b) there must be a direct causal link between the adverse climatic event and the damage suffered by the undertaking;

(c) in the case of losses caused by adverse climatic events referred to in Article 35(1) of Regulation (EU) No 508/2014, the Member State must justify why it intends to grant aid rather than financial compensation being paid through mutual funds for adverse climatic events under Article 35 of that Regulation.

(94) The Commission will authorise ex ante framework aid schemes to compensate for the damage caused by adverse climatic events, provided that the conditions under which aid can be granted are clearly stipulated. The Member States must in such cases comply with the reporting obligation set out in point (130).

(95) The aid must be paid directly to the undertaking concerned.

(96) Aid schemes related to adverse climatic events must be established within three years from the date of the occurrence of the event. The aid must be paid out within four years from that date.

(97) The eligible costs are the costs of the damage incurred as a direct consequence of the adverse climatic event, as assessed either by a public authority, by an independent expert recognised by the granting authority, or by an insurance undertaking. The damage may include:

(a) material damage to assets (such as buildings, vessels, equipment, machinery, stocks, and means of production); and

(b) loss of income due to the full or partial destruction of fishery or aquaculture production or the means of such production.

(98) In the case of material damage to assets, the damage must have resulted in a loss of production that amounts to more than 30 % of the average annual turnover, calculated on the basis of the preceding three calendar years or a three year average based on the five-year period preceding the adverse climatic event, excluding the highest and lowest entry.

(99) The calculation of the material damage must be based on the repair cost or economic value of the affected asset before the adverse climatic event. It must not exceed the repair cost or the decrease in fair market value caused by the adverse climatic event, that is to say the difference between the asset's value immediately before and immediately after the adverse climatic event.

(100) The loss of income must be calculated by subtracting:

(a) the result of multiplying the quantity of the fishery and aquaculture products produced in the year of the adverse climatic event, or in each following year affected by the full or partial destruction of the means of production, by the average selling price obtained during that year, from

(b) the result of multiplying the average annual quantity of fishery and aquaculture products produced in the three-year period preceding the adverse climatic event or a three year average based on the five-year period preceding the adverse climatic event, excluding the highest and lowest entry by the average selling price obtained.

(101) The damage must be calculated at the level of the individual beneficiary.

(102) The aid and any other payments received to compensate the damage, including payments under insurance policies, must be limited to 100 % of the eligible costs.

5.4. AID FOR THE COSTS OF PREVENTION, CONTROL AND ERADICATION OF ANIMAL DISEASES IN AQUACULTURE

(103) Where aid aims to support costs relating to the prevention, control and eradication of animal diseases in aquaculture, the Commission will assess the aid on the basis of the principles set out in Section 3 of these Guidelines and the conditions set out in this Section

(104) As an exception to point (103), the Commission will assess aid of the same kind as aid falling with the category of aid for animal health and welfare measures mentioned in Article 39 of Regulation (EU) No 1388/2014 under Section 5.1 of these Guidelines.

(105) Aid under this Section may only be granted:

(a) in respect of diseases included in the list of animal diseases of the World Organization for Animal Health, Annex II to Regulation (EU) No 652/2014 of the European Parliament and of the Council,[1] or Part II of Annex IV to Council Directive 2006/88/EC;[2] and

(b) as part of:

(i) a programme at Union, national, or regional level for the prevention, control or eradication of animal diseases; or

(ii) emergency measures imposed by the competent national authority.

(106) The aid must be paid directly to the undertaking concerned.

(107) No aid should be granted if it is established that the beneficiary caused the disease deliberately or by negligence.

(108) Aid schemes must be established within three years from the date of the occurrence of the costs caused by the animal disease. Aid must be paid out within four years from that date.

(109) The Commission will authorise ex ante framework schemes, provided that the conditions under which aid can be granted are clearly stipulated. The Member States must in such cases comply with the reporting obligation set out in point (130).

(110) Eligible costs are costs related to:

(a) health checks, analyses, tests, and other screening measures;

(b) the purchase, storage, administration or distribution of vaccines, medicines, and substances for the treatment of animals;

(c) the slaughtering, culling, and destruction of animals;
(d) the destruction of animal products and of products linked to them;
(e) the cleaning and disinfection of the holding and equipment;
(f) the damage incurred due to the slaughtering, culling or destruction of animals, animal products, and products linked to them, limited to the market value of such animals and products if they had not been affected by the disease;
(g) loss of income due to difficulties in restocking;
(h) in exceptional and duly justified cases, other costs incurred due to animal diseases in aquaculture.

(111) The aid and any other payments received to compensate the damage, including payments under insurance policies, must be limited to 100 % of the eligible costs.

5.5. AID FINANCED THROUGH PARAFISCAL CHARGES

(112) Where aid schemes are financed by special charges imposed on certain fishery or aquaculture products irrespective of their origin, in particular parafiscal charges, the Commission will assess the scheme on the basis of the principles set out in Section 3 and the conditions set out in this Section. Only aid that equally benefits domestic and imported products may be considered compatible with the internal market.

5.6. OPERATING AID IN OUTERMOST REGIONS

(113) Where aid constitutes operating aid granted in outermost regions with a view to alleviating the specific constraints in those regions as a result of their isolation, insularity, and extreme remoteness, the Commission will assess such aid on a case-by-case basis, on the basis of the principles set out in Section 3, the conditions of this Section, and the specific legal provisions applying to those regions. It will also have regard to, if applicable, the compatibility of the aid with measures under the EMFF for the region concerned and its effects on competition both in the regions concerned and in other parts of the Union.

(114) The aid must not go beyond what is necessary to alleviate the specific constraints in the outermost regions as a result of their isolation, insularity, and extreme remoteness. To avoid overcompensation, the Member State must take into account other types of public intervention, including, if applicable, the compensation of additional costs in outermost regions for fishery and aquaculture products under Articles 70 to 72 of Regulation (EU) No 508/2014 and aid for implementing compensation plans under Article 73 of that Regulation.

[5.6A. AID FOR THE RENEWAL OF THE FISHING FLEET IN OUTERMOST REGIONS

(114a) Considering the particular status of the outermost regions under Article 349 of the Treaty and the prevailing challenges to their socioeconomic development due to the specific factors set out in that Article, as follow-up to the Communication from the Commission on a stronger and renewed strategic partnership with the EU's outermost regions of 24 October 2017[*1]) which recognised the role of sustainable fisheries for the development of the blue economy of those regions, and in view of the positive contribution of aid to the CFP in the outermost regions, in particular, as regards environmentally sustainable fishing activities, economic, social and employment benefits, and the availability of food supplies, where aid aims to support costs relating to the acquisition of a new fishing vessel that will be registered in an outermost region, the Commission will assess the aid on the basis of the principles set out in Section 3 of these Guidelines and the specific conditions set out in this Section.

(114b) Aid for the acquisition of a new fishing vessel under this Section may only be granted if:
(a) the new fishing vessel complies with Union and national rules on hygiene, health, safety, and working conditions for work on board of fishing vessels and characteristics of fishing vessels; and
(b) at the date of applying for the aid the beneficiary has its main place of registration in the outermost region where the new vessel will be registered.

(114c) At the date of granting the aid, the most recent report prepared in accordance with Article 22(2) and (3) of Regulation (EU) No 1380/2013 before that date must demonstrate that there is balance between the fishing capacity and fishing opportunities in the fleet segment of the outermost region to which the new vessel will belong. No support shall be granted, if the assessment on the balance in that report for the fleet segment to which the vessel concerned will belong has not been prepared on the basis of the biological, economic and vessel use indicators set out in the common guidelines referred to in Article 22(2) of that Regulation.[*2]

(114d) The fishing capacity ceilings of each Member State and of each fleet segment of the outermost regions set out in Annex II to Regulation (EU) No 1380/2013, taking into account any possible reduction of those ceilings under Article 22(6) of that Regulation, must not be exceeded at any time. The entry into the fleet of new capacity acquired with aid must be carried out in full respect of these capacity ceilings and must not lead to a situation in which these ceiling are exceeded.

(114e) The aid must not be made conditional on the acquisition of the new vessel from a specific shipyard.

(114f) The maximum intensity of public aid must not be more than 60 % of the total eligible costs in the case of vessels with an overall length of less than 12 metres, must not be more than 50 % of the total eligible costs in the case of vessels with an overall length of 12 metres or more and less than 24 metres, and must not be more than 25 % of the total eligible costs in the case of vessels with an overall length of 24 metres and more.

(114g) The vessel acquired with aid must remain registered in the outermost region for at least 15 years from the date of granting the aid and must during that time land all of its catches in an outermost region. If that condition is not complied with, the aid must be reimbursed in an amount that is proportionate to the period or extent of non-compliance.]

5.7. AID FOR OTHER MEASURES

[(115) Where aid does not correspond to one of the types of aid mentioned in Sections 4 and 5.1 to 5.6a, it is in principle not compatible with the internal market.]

(116) If a Member State nevertheless intends to provide such aid or provides such aid, it must clearly demonstrate that the aid complies with the principles set out in Section 3. The Commission may declare the aid compatible with the internal market on the basis of a case-by-case assessment.

NOTES

Section 5.6a (ie, points (114a)–(114g) and the associated footnotes below) inserted by the Communication from the Commission amending the Guidelines for the examination of State aid to the fishery and aquaculture sector (2018/C422/01).

Point (115) substituted by the Communication from the Commission amending the Guidelines for the examination of State aid to the fishery and aquaculture sector (2018/C422/01).

[1] Regulation (EU) No 652/2014 of the European Parliament and of the Council of 15 May 2014 laying down provisions for the management of expenditure relating to the food chain, animal health and animal welfare, and relating to plant health and plant reproductive material, amending Council Directives 98/56/EC, 2000/29/EC and 2008/90/EC, Regulations (EC) No 178/2002, (EC) No 882/2004 and (EC) No 396/2005 of the European Parliament and of the Council, Directive 2009/128/EC of the European Parliament and of the Council and Regulation (EC) No 1107/2009 of the European Parliament and of the Council and repealing Council Decisions 66/399/EEC, 76/894/EEC and 2009/470/EC (OJ L189, 27.6.2014, p 1).

[2] Council Directive 2006/88/EC of 24 October 2006 on animal health requirements for aquaculture animals and products thereof, and on the prevention and control of certain diseases in aquatic animals (OJ L328, 24.11.2006, p 14).

[*1] Communication from the Commission to the European Parliament, the Council, the European Economic and Social Committee, the Committee of the Regions and the European Investment Bank — A stronger and renewed strategic partnership with the EU's outermost regions (COM(2017) 623 final).

[*2] Communication from the Commission to the European Parliament and the Council — Guidelines for the analysis of the balance between fishing capacity and fishing opportunities according to Art 22 of Regulation (EU) No 1380/2013 of the European Parliament and the Council on the Common Fisheries Policy (COM(2014) 545 final).

6. PROCEDURAL MATTERS

6.1. MAXIMUM DURATION OF AID SCHEMES AND EVALUATION(

[5.621]

(117) The Commission will only authorise aid schemes of limited duration. Aid schemes must in principle not apply for a period exceeding seven years.

(118) To further ensure that distortions of competition and trade are limited, the Commission may require that certain schemes are subject to an additional time limitation of normally four years or less and to the ex post evaluation referred to in point (25). Ex post evaluations will be carried out for schemes in the case of which the potential distortions of competition are particularly high, that is to say, that may risk to significantly restrict or distort competition if their implementation is not reviewed in due time.

(119) Given the objectives of the ex post evaluation and in order not to impose a disproportionate burden on Member States in respect of smaller aid amounts, the ex post evaluation requirement only applies to aid schemes with large aid budgets, containing novel characteristics or when significant market, technology or regulatory changes are foreseen. The ex post evaluation must be carried out by an expert independent from the aid granting authority on the basis of a common methodology and must be made public. Each Member States must notify, together with the relevant aid scheme, a draft evaluation plan, which will be an integral part of the assessment of the scheme by the Commission.

(120) In the case of aid schemes excluded from the scope of a block exemption Regulation exclusively on the grounds of their large budget, the Commission will assess their compatibility solely on the basis of the evaluation plan.

(121) The ex post evaluation must be submitted to the Commission in due time to allow for the assessment of the possible prolongation of the aid scheme and in any case upon its expiry. Any subsequent aid measure with a similar objective must take into account the results of the ex post evaluation.

6.2. APPLICATION OF THE GUIDELINES

(122) The Commission will apply these Guidelines in the assessment of all aid to be granted on and after 1 July 2015, irrespective of the date of notification.

(123) Individual aid granted on the basis of an approved aid scheme and notified to the Commission pursuant to an obligation to notify such aid individually will be assessed on the basis of the Guidelines that apply to the approved aid scheme.

(124) Aid granted unlawfully will be assessed on the basis of the Guidelines in force at the time of granting the aid.

(125) The Guidelines for the examination of State aid to fisheries and aquaculture adopted in 2008 will no longer apply after 30 June 2015, with the exception of the cases referred to in points (123) and (124).

6.3. PROPOSALS FOR APPROPRIATE MEASURES

(126) In accordance with Article 108(1) of the Treaty, the Commission proposes that each Member State amends its existing aid schemes to conform with these Guidelines by 31 December 2015.

(127) The Commission invites each Member State to give its explicit and unconditional agreement to the appropriate measures proposed in these Guidelines within two months from the date of publication of these Guidelines in the *Official Journal of the European Union*.

(128) If a Member State does not give its explicit and unconditional agreement within the foreseen period, the Commission will assume that the Member State disagrees with the proposed measures. If a Member State disagrees with the proposed measures, the Commission will proceed in accordance with Article 19(2) of Regulation (EC) No 659/1999.

6.4. REPORTING AND MONITORING

(129) The Commission reminds each Member State of its duty to submit annual reports to the Commission, as set out in Article 21 of Regulation (EC) No 659/1999 and Articles 5, 6, and 7 of Regulation (EC) No 794/2004.

(130) The annual report must also include meteorological information about the type, timing, relative magnitude, and location of the natural disaster or adverse climatic event under Sections 4 and 5.3 as well as on prevention, control, and eradication programmes under Section 5.4. This reporting obligation only relates to ex ante framework schemes.

(131) Each Member State must maintain detailed records on all of its aid measures. Such records must contain all information necessary to establish that the conditions set out in these Guidelines regarding, where applicable, eligibility and aid intensity have been observed. These records must be maintained for 10 years from the date of granting the aid and must be provided to the Commission upon request.

6.5. REVISION

(132) The Commission may decide to review or change these Guidelines at any time, if this is necessary for reasons related to competition policy, other Union policies, international commitments, developments in the markets, or for any other justified reason.

E. SPECIFIC AID INSTRUMENTS

1. STATE GUARANTEES

COMMISSION NOTICE

(2008/C155/02)

on the application of Articles 87 and 88 of the EC Treaty to State aid in the form of guarantees

[5.622]

NOTES

Date of publication in OJ: OJ C155, 20.6.2008, p 10. The text of this Notice incorporates the Corrigendum published in OJ C244, 25.9.2008, p 32. This Notice replaces the Commission Notice on the application of Articles 87 and 88 of the EC Treaty to State aid in the form of guarantees (OJ C71, 11.3.2000, p 14).

Note: with effect from 1 December 2009, the EC Treaty was replaced by the Treaty on the Functioning of the European Union. References in this document to provisions of the EC Treaty should be construed accordingly. As to Articles 87 and 88 of the EC Treaty, see now Articles 107 and 108 of the Treaty on the Functioning of the European Union.

1. INTRODUCTION

1.1 Background

[5.623]

This Notice updates the Commission's approach to State aid granted in the form of guarantees and aims to give Member States more detailed guidance about the principles on which the Commission intends to base its interpretation of Articles 87 and 88 and their application to State guarantees. These principles are currently laid down in the Commission Notice on the application of Articles 87 and 88 of the EC Treaty to State aid in the form of guarantees.[1] Experience gained in the application of this Notice since 2000 suggests that the Commission's policy in this area should be reviewed. In this connection, the Commission wishes to recall for instance its recent practice in various specific decisions[2] with respect to the need to undertake an individual assessment of the risk of losses related to each guarantee in the case of schemes. The Commission intends to further make its policy in this area as transparent as possible so that its decisions are predictable and that equal treatment is ensured. In particular, the Commission wishes to provide small and medium-sized enterprises (hereafter "SMEs") and Member States with safe-harbours predetermining, for a given company and on the basis of its financial rating, the minimum margin that should be charged for a State guarantee in order to be deemed as not constituting aid within the scope of Article 87(1) of the Treaty. Likewise, any shortfall in the premium charged in comparison with that level could be deemed as the aid element.

1.2 Types of guarantee

In their most common form, guarantees are associated with a loan or other financial obligation to be contracted by a borrower with a lender; they may be granted as individual guarantees or within guarantee schemes.

However, various forms of guarantee may exist, depending on their legal basis, the type of transaction covered, their duration, etc. Without the list being exhaustive, the following forms of guarantee can be identified:

- general guarantees, ie guarantees provided to undertakings as such as opposed to guarantees linked to a specific transaction, which may be a loan, an equity investment, etc,
- guarantees provided by a specific instrument as opposed to guarantees linked to the status of the undertaking itself,
- guarantees provided directly or counter guarantees provided to a first level guarantor,
- unlimited guarantees as opposed to guarantees limited in amount and/or time. The Commission also regards as aid in the form of a guarantee the more favourable funding terms obtained by enterprises whose legal form rules out bankruptcy or other insolvency procedures or provides an explicit State guarantee or coverage of losses by the State. The same applies to the acquisition by a State of a holding in an enterprise if unlimited liability is accepted instead of the usual limited liability,
- guarantees clearly originating from a contractual source (such as formal contracts, letters of comfort) or another legal source as opposed to guarantees whose form is less visible (such as side letters, oral commitments), possibly with various levels of comfort that can be provided by this guarantee.

Especially in the latter case, the lack of appropriate legal or accounting records often leads to very poor traceability. This is true both for the beneficiary and for the State or public body providing it and, as a result, for the information available to third parties.

1.3 Structure and scope of the Notice

For the purpose of this Notice:

(a) "guarantee scheme" means any tool on the basis of which, without further implementing measures being required, guarantees can be provided to undertakings respecting certain conditions of duration, amount, underlying transaction, type or size of undertakings (such as SMEs);

(b) "individual guarantee" means any guarantee provided to an undertaking and not awarded on the basis of a guarantee scheme.

Sections 3 and 4 of this Notice are designed to be directly applicable to guarantees linked to a specific financial transaction such as a loan. The Commission considers that, owing to their frequency and the fact that they can usually be quantified, these are the cases where guarantees most need to be classed as constituting State aid or otherwise.

As in most cases the transaction covered by a guarantee would be a loan, the Notice will further refer to the principal beneficiary of the guarantee as the "borrower" and to the body whose risk is diminished by the State guarantee as the "lender". The use of these two specific terms also aims to facilitate understanding of the rationale underpinning the text, since the basic principle of a loan is broadly understood. However, it does not ensue that Sections 3 and 4 are only applicable to a loan guarantee. They apply to all guarantees where a similar transfer of risk takes place such as an investment in the form of equity, provided the relevant risk profile (including the possible lack of collateralisation) is taken into account.

The Notice applies to all economic sectors, including the agriculture, fisheries and transport sectors without prejudice to specific rules relating to guarantees in the sector concerned.

This Notice does not apply to export credit guarantees.

1.4 Other types of guarantee

Where certain forms of guarantee (see point 1.2) involve a transfer of risk to the guarantor and where they do not display one or more of the specific features referred to in point 1.3, for instance insurance guarantees, a case-by-case analysis will have to be made for which, as far as is necessary, the applicable Sections or methodologies described in this Notice will be applied.

1.5 Neutrality

This Notice applies without prejudice to Article 295 of the Treaty and thus does not prejudice the rules in Member States governing the system of property ownership. The Commission is neutral as regards public and private ownership.

In particular, the mere fact that the ownership of an undertaking is largely in public hands is not sufficient in itself to constitute a State guarantee provided there are no explicit or implicit guarantee elements.

NOTES

1 OJ C71, 11.3.2000, p 14.

2 For example: Commission Decision 2003/706/EC of 23 April 2003 on the aid scheme implemented by Germany entitled "Guarantee schemes of the Land of Brandenburg for 1991 and 1994" – State aid C45/98 (ex NN 45/97) (OJ L263, 14.10.2003, p 1); Commission Decision of 16 December 2003 on the guarantee schemes in ship financing – Germany (N 512/03) (OJ C62, 11.3.2004, p 3); Commission Decision 2006/599/EC of 6 April 2005 on the aid scheme which Italy is planning to implement for ship financing (OJ L244, 7.9.2006, p 17).

2. APPLICABILITY OF ARTICLE 87(1)

2.1 General remarks

[5.624]
Article 87(1) of the Treaty states that any aid granted by a Member State or through State resources in any form whatsoever which distorts or threatens to distort competition by favouring certain undertakings or the production of certain goods shall, in so far as it affects trade between Member States, be incompatible with the common market.

These general criteria equally apply to guarantees. As for other forms of potential aid, guarantees given directly by the State, namely by central, regional or local authorities, as well as guarantees given through State resources by other State-controlled bodies such as undertakings and imputable to public authorities,[3] may constitute State aid.

In order to avoid any doubts, the notion of State resources should thus be clarified as regards State guarantees. The benefit of a State guarantee is that the risk associated with the guarantee is carried by the State. Such risk-carrying by the State should normally be remunerated by an appropriate premium. Where the State forgoes all or part of such a premium, there is both a benefit for the undertaking and a drain on the resources of the State. Thus, even if it turns out that no payments are ever made by the State under a guarantee, there may nevertheless be State aid under Article 87(1) of the Treaty. The aid is granted at the moment when the guarantee is given, not when the guarantee is invoked nor when payments are made under the terms of the guarantee. Whether or not a guarantee constitutes State aid, and, if so, what the amount of that State aid may be, must be assessed at the moment when the guarantee is given.

In this context the Commission points out that the analysis under State aid rules does not prejudge the compatibility of a given measure with other Treaty provisions.

2.2 Aid to the borrower

Usually, the aid beneficiary is the borrower. As indicated under point 2.1, risk-carrying should normally be remunerated by an appropriate premium. When the borrower does not need to pay the premium, or pays a low premium, it obtains an advantage. Compared to a situation without guarantee, the State guarantee enables the borrower to obtain better financial terms for a loan than those normally available on the financial markets. Typically, with the benefit of the State guarantee, the borrower can obtain lower rates and/or offer less security. In some cases, the borrower would not, without a State guarantee, find a financial institution prepared to lend on any terms. State guarantees may thus facilitate the creation of new business and enable certain undertakings to raise money in order to pursue new activities. Likewise, a State guarantee may help a failing firm remain active instead of being eliminated or restructured, thereby possibly creating distortions of competition.

2.3 Aid to the lender

2.3.1. Even if usually the aid beneficiary is the borrower, it cannot be ruled out that under certain circumstances the lender, too, will directly benefit from the aid. In particular, for example, if a State guarantee is given *ex post* in respect of a loan or other financial obligation already entered into without the terms of this loan or financial obligation being adjusted, or if one guaranteed loan is used to pay back another, non-guaranteed loan to the same credit institution, then there may also be aid to the lender, in so far as the security of the loans is increased. Where the guarantee contains aid to the lender, attention should be drawn to the fact that such aid might, in principle, constitute operating aid.

2.3.2. Guarantees differ from other State aid measures, such as grants or tax exemptions, in that, in the case of a guarantee, the State also enters into a legal relationship with the lender. Therefore, consideration has to be given to the possible consequences for third parties of State aid that has been illegally granted. In the case of State guarantees for loans, this concerns mainly the lending financial institutions. In the case of guarantees for bonds issued to obtain financing for undertakings, this concerns the financial institutions involved in the issuance of the bonds. The question whether the illegality of the aid affects the legal relations between the State and third parties is a matter which has to be examined under national law. National courts may have to examine whether national law prevents the guarantee contracts from being honoured, and in that assessment the Commission considers that they should take account of the breach of Community law. Accordingly, lenders may have an interest in verifying, as a standard precaution, that the Community rules on State aid have been observed whenever guarantees are granted. The Member State should be able to provide a case number issued by the Commission for an individual case or a scheme and possibly a non-confidential copy of the Commission's decision together with the relevant reference to the *Official Journal of the European Union*. The Commission for its part will do its utmost to make available in a transparent manner information on cases and schemes approved by it.

NOTES

[3] See Case C-482/99, *France v Commission (Stardust)* [2002] ECR I-4397.

3. CONDITIONS RULING OUT THE EXISTENCE OF AID

3.1 General considerations

[5.625]

If an individual guarantee or a guarantee scheme entered into by the State does not bring any advantage to an undertaking, it will not constitute State aid.

In this context, in order to determine whether an advantage is being granted through a guarantee or a guarantee scheme, the Court has confirmed in its recent judgments[4] that the Commission should base its assessment on the principle of an investor operating in a market economy (hereafter referred to as the "market economy investor principle"). Account should therefore be taken of the effective possibilities for a beneficiary undertaking to obtain equivalent financial resources by having recourse to the capital market. State aid is not involved where a new funding source is made available on conditions which would be acceptable for a private operator under the normal conditions of a market economy.[5]

In order to facilitate the assessment of whether the market economy investor principle is fulfilled for a given guarantee measure, the Commission sets out in this Section a number of sufficient conditions for the absence of aid. Individual guarantees are covered in point 3.2 with a simpler option for SMEs in point 3.3. Guarantee schemes are covered in point 3.4 with a simpler option for SMEs in point 3.5.

3.2 Individual guarantees

Regarding an individual State guarantee, the Commission considers that the fulfilment of all the following conditions will be sufficient to rule out the presence of State aid.

(a) The borrower is not in financial difficulty.

In order to decide whether the borrower is to be seen as being in financial difficulty, reference should be made to the definition set out in the Community guidelines on State aid for rescuing and restructuring firms in difficulty.[6] SMEs which have been incorporated for less than three years shall not be considered as being in difficulty for that period for the purposes of this Notice.

(b) The extent of the guarantee can be properly measured when it is granted. This means that the guarantee must be linked to a specific financial transaction, for a fixed maximum amount and limited in time.

(c) The guarantee does not cover more than 80% of the outstanding loan or other financial obligation; this limitation does not apply to guarantees covering debt securities.[7]

The Commission considers that if a financial obligation is wholly covered by a State guarantee, the lender has less incentive to properly assess, secure and minimise the risk arising from the lending operation, and in particular to properly assess the borrower's creditworthiness. Such risk assessment might, due to lack of means, not always be taken over by the State guarantor. This lack of incentive to minimise the risk of non-repayment of the loan might encourage lenders to contract loans with a greater than normal commercial risk and could thus increase the amount of higher-risk guarantees in the State's portfolio.

This limitation of 80% does not apply to a public guarantee granted to finance a company whose activity is solely constituted by a properly entrusted Service of General Economic Interest (SGEI)[8] and when this guarantee has been provided by the public authority having put in place this entrustment. The limitation of 80% applies if the company concerned provides other SGEIs or other economic activities.

In order to ensure that the lender effectively bears part of the risk, due attention must be given to the following two aspects:

— when the size of the loan or of the financial obligation decreases over time, for instance because the loan starts to be reimbursed, the guaranteed amount has to decrease proportionally, in such a way that at each moment in time the guarantee does not cover more than 80% of the outstanding loan or financial obligation,

— losses have to be sustained proportionally and in the same way by the lender and the guarantor. In the same manner, net recoveries (ie revenues excluding costs for claim handling) generated from the recuperation of the debt from the securities given by the borrower have to reduce proportionally the losses borne by the lender and the guarantor. First-loss guarantees, where losses are first attributed to the guarantor and only then to the lender, will be regarded as possibly involving aid.

If a Member State wishes to provide a guarantee above the 80% threshold and claims that it does not constitute aid, it should duly substantiate the claim, for instance on the basis of the arrangement of the whole transaction, and notify it to the Commission so that the guarantee can be properly assessed with regards to its possible State aid character.

(d) A market-oriented price is paid for the guarantee.

As indicated under point 2.1, risk-carrying should normally be remunerated by an appropriate premium on the guaranteed or counter-guaranteed amount. When the price paid for the guarantee is at least as high as the corresponding guarantee premium benchmark that can be found on the financial markets, the guarantee does not contain aid.

If no corresponding guarantee premium benchmark can be found on the financial markets, the total financial cost of the guaranteed loan, including the interest rate of the loan and the guarantee premium, has to be compared to the market price of a similar non-guaranteed loan.

In both cases, in order to determine the corresponding market price, the characteristics of the guarantee and of the underlying loan should be taken into consideration. This includes: the amount and duration of the transaction; the security given by the borrower and other experience affecting the recovery rate evaluation; the probability of default of the borrower due to its financial position, its sector of activity and prospects; as well as other economic conditions. This analysis should notably allow the borrower to be classified by means of a risk rating. This classification may be provided by an internationally recognised rating agency or, where available, by the internal rating used by the bank providing the underlying loan. The Commission points to the link between rating and default rate made by international financial institutions, whose work is also publicly available.[9] To assess whether the premium is in line with the market prices the Member State can carry out a comparison of prices paid by similarly rated undertakings on the market.

The Commission will therefore not accept that the guarantee premium is set at a single rate deemed to correspond to an overall industry standard.

3.3 Valuation of individual guarantees for SMEs

As an exception, if the borrower is an SME,[10] the Commission can by way of derogation from point 3.2(d) accept a simpler evaluation of whether or not a loan guarantee involves aid. In that case, and provided all the other conditions laid down in points 3.2(a), (b) and (c) are met, a State guarantee would be deemed as not constituting aid if the minimum annual premium ("safe-harbour premium"[11]) set out in the following table is charged on the amount effectively guaranteed by the State, based on the rating of the borrower:[12]

Credit quality	**Standard & Poor's**	**Fitch**	**Moody's**	**Annual safe-harbour premium**
Highest quality	AAA	AAA	Aaa	0,4%
Very strong payment capacity	AA + AA AA –	AA + AA AA –	Aa 1 Aa 2 Aa 3	0,4%
Strong payment capacity	A + A A –	A + A A –	A 1 A 2 A 3	0,55%
Adequate payment capacity	BBB + BBB BBB –	BBB + BBB BBB –	Baa 1 Baa 2 Baa 3	0,8%
Payment capacity is vulnerable to adverse conditions	BB + BB BB –	BB + BB BB –	Ba 1 Ba 2 Ba 3	2.0%
Payment capacity is likely to be impaired by adverse conditions	B + B B –	B + B B–	B 1 B 2 B 3	3,8% 6,3%

Credit quality	Standard & Poor's	Fitch	Moody's	Annual safe-harbour premium
Payment capacity is dependent upon sustained favourable conditions	CCC + CCC CCC – CC	CCC + CCC CCC – CC C	Caa 1 Caa 2 Caa 3	No safe-harbour annual premium can be provided
In or near default	SD D	DDD DD D	Ca C	No safe-harbour annual premium can be provided

The safe-harbour premiums apply to the amount effectively guaranteed or counter-guaranteed by the State at the beginning of each year concerned. They must be considered as the minimum to be applied with respect to a company whose credit rating is at least equal to those given in the table.[13]

In the case of a single upfront guarantee premium, the loan guarantee is deemed to be free of aid if it is at least equal to the present value of the future guarantee premiums as indicated above, the discount rate used being the corresponding reference rate.[14]

As outlined in the table above, companies with a rating corresponding to CCC/Caa or worse cannot benefit from this simplified methodology.

For SMEs which do not have a credit history or a rating based on a balance sheet approach, such as certain special purpose companies or start-up companies, the safe-harbour premium is set at 3,8% but this can never be lower than the premium which would be applicable to the parent company or companies.

These margins may be revised from time to time to take account of the market situation.

3.4 Guarantee schemes

For a State guarantee scheme, the Commission considers that the fulfilment of all the following conditions will rule out the presence of State aid:

(a) the scheme is closed to borrowers in financial difficulty (see details in point 3.2(a));

(b) the extent of the guarantees can be properly measured when they are granted. This means that the guarantees must be linked to specific financial transactions, for a fixed maximum amount and limited in time;

(c) the guarantees do not cover more than 80% of each outstanding loan or other financial obligation (see details and exceptions in point 3.2(c));

(d) the terms of the scheme are based on a realistic assessment of the risk so that the premiums paid by the beneficiaries make it, in all probability, self-financing. The self-financing nature of the scheme and the proper risk orientation are viewed by the Commission as indications that the guarantee premiums charged under the scheme are in line with market prices.

This entails that the risk of each new guarantee has to be assessed, on the basis of all the relevant factors (quality of the borrower, securities, duration of the guarantee, etc). On the basis of this risk analysis, risk classes[15] have to be defined, the guarantee has to be classified in one of these risk classes and the corresponding guarantee premium has to be charged on the guaranteed or counter-guaranteed amount;

(e) in order to have a proper and progressive evaluation of the self-financing aspect of the scheme, the adequacy of the level of the premiums has to be reviewed at least once a year on the basis of the effective loss rate of the scheme over an economically reasonable time horizon, and premiums adjusted accordingly if there is a risk that the scheme may no longer be self-financing. This adjustment may concern all issued and future guarantees or only the latter;

(f) in order to be viewed as being in line with market prices, the premiums charged have to cover the normal risks associated with granting the guarantee, the administrative costs of the scheme, and a yearly remuneration of an adequate capital, even if the latter is not at all or only partially constituted.

As regards administrative costs, these should include at least the specific initial risk assessment as well as the risk monitoring and risk management costs linked to the granting and administration of the guarantee.

As regards the remuneration of the capital, the Commission observes that usual guarantors are subject to capital requirement rules and, in accordance with these rules, are forced to constitute equity in order not to go bankrupt when there are variations in the yearly losses related to the guarantees. State guarantee schemes are normally not subject to these rules and thus do not need to constitute such reserves. In other words, each time the losses stemming from the guarantees exceed the revenues from the guarantee premiums, the deficit is simply covered by the State budget. This State guarantee to the scheme puts the latter in a more favourable situation than a usual guarantor. In order to avoid this disparity and to remunerate the State for the risk it is taking, the Commission considers that the guarantee premiums have to cover the remuneration of an adequate capital.

The Commission considers that this capital has to correspond to 8%[16] of the outstanding guarantees. For guarantees granted to undertakings whose rating is equivalent to AAA/AA – (Aaa/Aa3), the amount of capital to be remunerated can be reduced to 2% of the outstanding guarantees. Meanwhile, with regard to guarantees granted to undertakings whose rating is equivalent to A+/A – (A1/A3), the amount of capital to be remunerated can be reduced to 4% of the outstanding guarantees.

The normal remuneration of this capital is made up of a risk premium, possibly increased by the risk-free interest rate.

The risk premium must be paid to the State on the adequate amount of capital in all cases. Based on its practice, the Commission considers that a normal risk premium for equity amounts to at least 400 basis points and that such risk premium should be included in the guarantee premium charged to the beneficiaries.[17]

If, as in most State guarantee schemes, the capital is not provided to the scheme and therefore there is no cash contribution by the State, the risk-free interest rate does not have to be taken into account. Alternatively, if the underlying capital is effectively provided by the State, the State has to incur borrowing costs and the scheme benefits from this cash by possibly investing it. Therefore the risk-free interest rate has to be paid to the State on the amount provided. Moreover, this charge should be taken from the financial income of the scheme and does not necessarily have to impact the guarantee premiums.[18] The Commission considers that the yield of the 10-year government bond may be used as a suitable proxy for the risk-free rate taken as normal return on capital;

(g) in order to ensure transparency, the scheme must provide for the terms on which future guarantees will be granted, such as eligible companies in terms of rating and, when applicable, sector and size, maximum amount and duration of the guarantees.

3.5 Valuation of guarantee schemes for SMEs

In view of the specific situation of SMEs and in order to facilitate their access to finance, especially through the use of guarantee schemes, two specific possibilities exist for such companies:

— the use of safe-harbour premiums as defined for individual guarantees to SMEs,

— the valuation of guarantee schemes as such by allowing the application of a single premium and avoiding the need for individual ratings of beneficiary SMEs.

The conditions of use of both rules are defined as follows:

Use of safe-harbour premiums in guarantee schemes for SMEs

In line with what is proposed for simplification purposes in relation to individual guarantees, guarantee schemes in favour of SMEs can also, in principle, be deemed self-financing and not constitute State aid if the minimum safe-harbour premiums set out in point 3.3 and based on the ratings of undertakings are applied.[19] The other conditions set out in points 3.4(a), (b) and (c) as well as in point 3.4(g) still have to be fulfilled, and the conditions set out in points 3.4(d), (e) and (f) are deemed to be fulfilled by the use of the minimum annual premiums set out in point 3.3.

Use of single premiums in guarantee schemes for SMEs

The Commission is aware that carrying out an individual risk assessment of each borrower is a costly process, which may not be appropriate where a scheme covers a large number of small loans for which it represents a risk pooling tool.

Consequently, where a scheme only relates to guarantees for SMEs and the guaranteed amount does not exceed a threshold of EUR 2.5 million per company in that scheme, the Commission may accept, by way of derogation from point 3.4(d), a single yearly guarantee premium for all borrowers. However, in order for the guarantees granted under such a scheme to be regarded as not constituting State aid, the scheme has to remain self-financing and all the other conditions set out in points 3.4(a), (b) and (c) as well as in points 3.4(e), (f) and (g) still have to be fulfilled.

3.6 No automatic classification as State aid

Failure to comply with any one of the conditions set out in points 3.2 to 3.5 does not mean that the guarantee or guarantee scheme is automatically regarded as State aid. If there is any doubt as to whether a planned guarantee or guarantee scheme constitutes State aid, it should be notified to the Commission.

NOTES

4 See Case C-482/99 referred to in footnote 3.

5 See Commission Communication on the application of Article 92 and 93 of the EC Treaty to public shareholdings (Bulletin of the European Communities No 9-1984); Joined Cases 296/82 and 318/82, *Netherlands and Leeuwarder Papierwarenfabriek BV v Commission* [1985] ECR 809, paragraph 17. Commission Communication on the application of Articles 92 and 93 of the EC Treaty and Article 61 of the EEA Agreement to State aid in the aviation sector (OJ C350, 10.12.1994, p 5), points 25 and 26.

6 OJ C244, 1.10.2004, p 2.

7 For the definition of "debt securities", see Article 2(1)(b) of Directive 2004/109/EC of the European Parliament and of the Council of 15 December 2004 on the harmonisation of transparency requirements in relation to information about issuers whose securities are admitted to trading on a regulated market and amending Directive 2001/34/EC (OJ L390, 31.12.2004, p 38). Directive as last amended by Directive 2008/22/EC (OJ L76, 19.3.2008, p 50).

8 Such an SGEI must comply with Community rules such as Commission Decision 2005/842/EC of 28 November 2005 on the application of Article 86(2) of the EC Treaty to State aid in the form of public service compensation granted to certain undertakings entrusted with the operation of services of general economic interest (OJ L312, 29.11.2005, p 67), and the Community framework for State aid in the form of public service compensation (OJ C297, 29.11.2005, p 4).

9 Such as Table 1 on agencies' credit ratings to be found in the Bank for International Settlements Working Paper No 207, available at: www.bis.org/publ/work207.pdf

10 "SMEs" refer to small and medium-sized enterprises as defined in Annex I to Regulation (EC) No 70/2001 on the application of Articles 87 and 88 of the EC Treaty to State aid to small and medium-sized enterprises (OJ L10, 13.1.2001, p 33). Regulation as last amended by Regulation (EC) No 1976/2006 (OJ L368, 23.12.2006, p 85).

11 These safe-harbour premiums are established in line with the margins determined for loans to similarly rated undertakings

in the Communication from the Commission on the revision of the method for setting the reference and discount rates (OJ C14, 19.1.2008, p 6). Following the study commissioned by the Commission on that topic (see pages 23 and 156–159 of the study), a general reduction of 20 basis points has been taken into account. This reduction corresponds to the difference in margin for a similar risk between a loan and a guarantee in order to take into account the additional costs specifically linked to loans.

12 The table refers to the rating classes of Standard & Poor's, Fitch and Moody's, which are the rating agencies most frequently used by the banking sector in order to link their own rating system, as described in point 3.2(d). However, ratings do not need to be obtained from those specific rating agencies. National rating systems or rating systems used by banks to reflect default rates are equally acceptable provided they supply the one-year probability of default as this figure is used by rating agencies to rank companies. Other systems should allow for a similar classification through this ranking key.

13 For example, a company to which a bank assigns a credit rating corresponding to BBB-/Baa3 should be charged a yearly guarantee premium of at least 0,8% on the amount effectively guaranteed by the State at the beginning of each year.

14 See the Communication referred to in footnote 11 providing that: "*The reference rate is also to be used as a discount rate, for calculating present values. To that end, in principle, the base rate increased by a fixed margin of 100 basis points will be used*" (p 4).

15 See further details in footnote 12.

16 Corresponding to the capital requirements laid down in Article 75 of Directive 2006/48/EC of the European Parliament and of the Council of 14 June 2006 relating to the taking up and pursuit of the business of credit institutions (OJ L177, 30.6.2006, p 1) read in conjunction with Annex VI (paragraph 41 onwards) thereto.

17 For a guarantee to a BBB rated company amounting to 100, the reserves to be constituted thus amount to 8. Applying 400 basis points (or 4%) to this amount results in annual capital costs of 8% × 4% = 0,32% of the guaranteed amount, which will impact the price of the guarantee accordingly. If the one-year default rate anticipated by the scheme for this company is, for instance, 0,35% and the yearly administrative costs are estimated at 0,1%, the price of the guarantee deemed as non-aid will be 0,77% per year.

18 In that case, and provided the risk-free rate is deemed to be 5%, the annual cost of the reserves to be constituted will be, for the same guarantee of 100 and reserves of 8 to be constituted, 8% × (4% + 5%) = 0,72% of the guaranteed amount. Under the same assumptions (default rate of 0,35% and administrative costs of 0,1%), the price of the guarantee would be 0,77% per year and an additional charge of 0,4% should be paid by the scheme to the State.

19 This includes the provision whereby for SMEs which do not have a credit history or a rating based on a balance sheet approach, the safe-harbour premium is set at 3,8% but this can never be lower than the premium which would be applicable to the parent companies.

4. GUARANTEES WITH AN AID ELEMENT

4.1 General

[5.626]

Where an individual guarantee or a guarantee scheme does not comply with the market economy investor principle, it is deemed to entail State aid. The State aid element therefore needs to be quantified in order to check whether the aid may be found compatible under a specific State aid exemption. As a matter of principle, the State aid element will be deemed to be the difference between the appropriate market price of the guarantee provided individually or through a scheme and the actual price paid for that measure.

The resulting yearly cash grant equivalents should be discounted to their present value using the reference rate, then added up to obtain the total grant equivalent.

When calculating the aid element in a guarantee, the Commission will devote special attention to the following elements:

(a) whether in the case of individual guarantees the borrower is in financial difficulty. Whether in the case of guarantee schemes, the eligibility criteria of the scheme provide for exclusion of such undertakings (see details in point 3.2(a)).

The Commission notes that for companies in difficulty, a market guarantor, if any, would, at the time the guarantee is granted charge a high premium given the expected rate of default. If the likelihood that the borrower will not be able to repay the loan becomes particularly high, this market rate may not exist and in exceptional circumstances the aid element of the guarantee may turn out to be as high as the amount effectively covered by that guarantee;

(b) whether the extent of each guarantee can be properly measured when it is granted.

This means that the guarantees must be linked to a specific financial transaction, for a fixed maximum amount and limited in time. In this connection the Commission considers in principle that unlimited guarantees are incompatible with Article 87 of the Treaty;

(c) whether the guarantee covers more than 80% of each outstanding loan or other financial obligation (see details and exceptions in point 3.2(c)).

In order to ensure that the lender has a real incentive to properly assess, secure and minimise the risk arising from the lending operation, and in particular to assess properly the borrower's creditworthiness, the Commission considers that a percentage of at least 20% not covered by a State guarantee should be carried by the lender[20] to properly secure its loans and to minimise the risk associated with the transaction. The Commission will therefore, in general, examine more thoroughly any guarantee or guarantee scheme covering the entirety (or nearly the entirety) of a financial transaction except if a Member State duly justifies it, for instance, by the specific nature of the transaction;

(d) whether the specific characteristics of the guarantee and loan (or other financial obligation) have been taken into account when determining the market premium of the guarantee, from which the aid element is calculated by comparing it with the premium actually paid (see details in point 3.2(d)).

4.2 Aid element in individual guarantees

For an individual guarantee the cash grant equivalent of a guarantee should be calculated as the difference between the market price of the guarantee and the price actually paid.

Where the market does not provide guarantees for the type of transaction concerned, no market price for the guarantee is available. In that case, the aid element should be calculated in the same way as the grant equivalent of a soft loan, namely as the difference between the specific market interest rate this company would have borne without the guarantee and the interest rate obtained by means of the State guarantee after any premiums paid have been taken into account. If there is no market interest rate and if the Member State wishes to use the reference rate as a proxy, the Commission stresses that the conditions laid down in the communication on reference rates[21] are valid to calculate the aid intensity of an individual guarantee. This means that due attention must be paid to the top-up to be added to the base rate in order to take into account the relevant risk profile linked to the operation covered, the undertaking guaranteed and the collaterals provided.

4.3 Aid element in individual guarantees for SMEs

For SMEs, the simplified evaluation system outlined in point 3.3 can also be applied. In that case, if the premium for a given guarantee does not correspond to the value set as a minimum for its rating class, the difference between this minimum level and the premium charged will be regarded as aid. If the guarantee lasts more than a year, the yearly shortfalls are discounted using the relevant reference rate.[22]

Only in cases clearly evidenced and duly justified by the Member State concerned may the Commission accept a deviation from these rules. A risk-based approach still has to be respected in such cases.

4.4 Aid element in guarantee schemes

For guarantee schemes, the cash grant equivalent of each guarantee within the scheme is the difference between the premium effectively charged (if any) and the premium that should be charged in an equivalent non-aid scheme set up in accordance with the conditions laid down in point 3.4. The aforementioned theoretical premiums from which the aid element is calculated have therefore to cover the normal risks associated with the guarantee as well as the administrative and capital costs.[23] This way of calculating the grant equivalent is aimed at ensuring that, also over the medium and long term, the total aid granted under the scheme is equal to the money injected by the public authorities to cover the deficit of the scheme.

Since, in the case of State guarantee schemes, the specific features of the individual cases may not be known at the time when the scheme is to be assessed, the aid element must be assessed by reference to the provisions of the scheme.

Aid elements in guarantee schemes can also be calculated through methodologies already accepted by the Commission following their notification under a regulation adopted by the Commission in the field of State aid, such as Commission Regulation (EC) No 1628/2006 of 24 October 2006 on the application of Articles 87 and 88 of the Treaty to national regional investment aid[24] or Commission Regulation (EC) No 1857/2006 of 15 December 2006 on the application of Articles 87 and 88 of the Treaty to State aid to small and medium-sized enterprises active in the production of agricultural products and amending Regulation (EC) No 70/2001,[25] provided that the approved methodology explicitly addresses the type of guarantees and the type of underlying transactions at stake.

Only in cases clearly evidenced and duly justified by the Member State concerned may the Commission accept a deviation from these rules. A risk-based approach still has to be respected in such cases.

4.5 Aid element in guarantee schemes for SMEs

The two simplification tools outlined in point 3.5 and relating to guarantee schemes for SMEs can also be used for aid calculation purposes. The conditions of use of both rules are defined as follows:

Use of safe-harbour premiums in guarantee schemes for SMEs

For SMEs, the simplified evaluation system outlined above in point 3.5 can also be applied. In that case, if the premium for a given category in a guarantee scheme does not correspond to the value set as a minimum for its rating class,[26] the difference between this minimum level and the premium charged will be regarded as aid.[27] If the guarantee lasts more than a year, the yearly shortfalls are discounted using the reference rate.[28]

Use of single premiums in guarantee schemes for SMEs

In view of the more limited distortion of competition that may be caused by State aid provided in the framework of a guarantee scheme for SMEs, the Commission considers that if an aid scheme only relates to guarantees for SMEs, where the guaranteed amount does not exceed a threshold of EUR 2.5 million per company in this given scheme, the Commission may accept, by way of derogation from point 4.4, a valuation of the aid intensity of the scheme as such, without the need to carry out a valuation for each individual guarantee or risk class within the scheme.[29]

NOTES

20 This is based on the assumption that the corresponding level of security is provided by the company to the State and the credit institution.

21 See the Communication referred to in footnote 11.

22 See further details in footnote 14.

23 This calculation can be summarised, for each risk class, as the difference between (a) the outstanding sum guaranteed, multiplied by the risk factor of the risk class ("risk" being the probability of default after inclusion of administrative and capital costs), which represents the market premium, and (b) any premium paid, ie (guaranteed sum × risk) – premium paid.

24 OJ L302, 1.11.2006, p 29.

25 OJ L358, 16.12.2006, p 3.

[26] This includes the possibility whereby SMEs which do not have a credit history or a rating based on a balance sheet approach, the safe-harbour premium is set at 3,8% but this can never be lower than the premium which would be applicable to the parent company or companies.

[27] This calculation can be summarised, for each risk class, as the outstanding sum guaranteed multiplied by the difference between (a) the safe-harbour premium percentage of that risk class and (b) the premium percentage paid, ie guaranteed sum × (safe-harbour premium – premium paid).

[28] See further details in footnote 11.

[29] This calculation can be summarised, irrespective of the risk class, as the difference between (a) the outstanding sum guaranteed, multiplied by the risk factor of the scheme ("risk" being the probability of default after inclusion of administrative and capital costs), and (b) any premium paid, ie (guaranteed sum × risk) – premium paid.

5. COMPATIBILITY WITH THE COMMON MARKET OF STATE AID IN THE FORM OF GUARANTEES

5.1 General

[5.627]
State guarantees within the scope of Article 87(1) of the Treaty must be examined by the Commission with a view to determining whether or not they are compatible with the common market. Before such assessment of compatibility can be made, the beneficiary of the aid must be identified.

5.2 Assessment

Whether or not this aid is compatible with the common market will be examined by the Commission according to the same rules as are applied to aid measures taking other forms. The concrete criteria for the compatibility assessment have been clarified and detailed by the Commission in frameworks and guidelines concerning horizontal, regional and sectoral aid.[30] The examination will take into account, in particular, the aid intensity, the characteristics of the beneficiaries and the objectives pursued.

5.3 Conditions

The Commission will accept guarantees only if their mobilisation is contractually linked to specific conditions which may go as far as the compulsory declaration of bankruptcy of the beneficiary undertaking, or any similar procedure. These conditions will have to be agreed between the parties when the guarantee is initially granted. In the event that a Member State wants to mobilise the guarantee under conditions other than those initially agreed to at the granting stage, then the Commission will regard the mobilisation of the guarantee as creating new aid which has to be notified under Article 88(3) of the Treaty.

NOTES

[30] See Competition law applicable to State aid in the European Community: ec.europa.eu/comm/competition/state_aid/legislation/legislation.html For sector specific State aid legislation, see for agriculture: ec.europa.eu/agriculture/stateaid/leg/index_en.htm and for transport: https://ec.europa.eu/competition-policy/sectors/energy-and-environment_en

6. REPORTS TO BE PRESENTED TO THE COMMISSION BY THE MEMBER STATES

[5.628]
In accordance with general monitoring obligations,[31] in order to further monitor new developments on the financial markets and since the value of State guarantees is difficult to assess and changes over time, the constant review, pursuant to Article 88(1) of the Treaty, of State guarantee schemes approved by the Commission is of particular importance. Member States shall therefore submit reports to the Commission.

For aid guarantee schemes, these reports will have to be presented at least at the end of the period of validity of the guarantee scheme and for the notification of an amended scheme. The Commission may however consider it appropriate to request reports on a more frequent basis, depending on the case.

For guarantee schemes, for which the Commission has taken a non-aid decision, and especially when no solid historic data exists for the scheme, the Commission may request, when taking its non-aid decision for such reports to be presented, thereby clarifying on a case-by-case basis the frequency and the content of the reporting requirement.

Reports should include at least the following information:

(a) the number and amount of guarantees issued;
(b) the number and amount of guarantees outstanding at the end of the period;
(c) the number and value of defaulted guarantees (displayed individually) on a yearly basis;
(d) the yearly income:
    1. income from the premiums charged;
    2. income from recoveries;
    3. other revenues (eg interest received on deposits or investments);
(e) the yearly costs:
    1. administrative costs;
    2. indemnifications paid on mobilised guarantees;
(f) the yearly surplus or shortfall (difference between income and costs); and
(g) the accumulated surplus or shortfall since the beginning of the scheme.[32]

For individual guarantees, the relevant information, mainly that referred to in points (d) to (g), should be similarly reported.

In all cases, the Commission draws the attention of Member States to the fact that correct reporting at a remote date presupposes correct collection of the necessary data from the beginning of the use of the scheme and their aggregation on a yearly basis.

The attention of Member States is also drawn to the fact that for non-aid guarantees provided individually or under a scheme, although no notification obligation exists, the Commission may have to verify that the guarantee or scheme does not entail aid elements, for instance following a complaint. In that case, the Commission will request information similar to that set out above for reports from the Member State concerned.

Where reports already have to be presented following specific reporting obligations established by block exemption regulations, guidelines or frameworks applicable in the State aid field, those specific reports will replace the reports to be presented under the present guarantee reporting obligation provided the information listed above is included.

NOTES

31 Such as those laid down in particular by Commission Regulation (EC) No 794/2004 of 21 April 2004 implementing Council Regulation (EC) No 659/1999 laying down detailed rules for the application of Article 93 of the EC Treaty (OJ L140, 30.4.2004, p 1). Regulation as last amended by Regulation (EC) No 271/2008 (OJ L82, 25.3.2008, p 1).

32 If the scheme has been active for more than 10 years, only the last 10 annual amounts of shortfall or surplus are to be provided.

7. IMPLEMENTING MEASURES

[5.629]
The Commission invites Member States to adjust their existing guarantee measures to the stipulations of the present Notice by 1 January 2010 as far as new guarantees are concerned.

2. EXPORT CREDIT INSURANCE

COMMUNICATION FROM THE COMMISSION TO THE MEMBER STATES

(2012/C392/01)

on the application of Articles 107 and 108 of the Treaty on the Functioning of the European Union to short-term export-credit insurance

(Text with EEA relevance)

[5.630]

NOTES

Date of publication in OJ: OJ C392, 19.12.2012, p 1.

Editorial note: this Communication was due to expire on 31 December 2018, but its validity was extended by the Communication from the Commission concerning the prolongation of the Communication from the Commission to the Member States on the application of Articles 107 and 108 of the Treaty on the Functioning of the European Union to short-term export-credit insurance (2018/C457/04). Its validity was originally extended until 31 December 2020. Note, however, that the above-mentioned Communication was amended by a 2020 Commission Communication (2020/C224/02) and the date of validity was further extended until 31 December 2021.

See also the Communication from the Commission: Sixth Amendment to the Temporary Framework for State aid measures to support the economy in the current COVID-19 outbreak and amendment to the Annex to the Communication from the Commission to the Member States on the application of Articles 107 and 108 of the Treaty on the Functioning of the European Union to short-term export-credit insurance. Paragraph 62 of the Communication provides that the Commission considers that all commercial and political risks associated with exports to the countries listed in the Annex are temporarily non-marketable until 31 March 2022.

See also the list of consultations and draft documents in the Appendix at **[A1]**.

1. INTRODUCTION

1. Export subsidies can adversely affect competition in the marketplace among potential rival suppliers of goods and services. That is why the Commission, as the guardian of competition under the Treaty, has always strongly condemned export aid for intra-Union trade and for exports outside the Union. To prevent Member States' support for export-credit insurance from distorting competition, its assessment under Union State aid rules needs to be clarified.

2. The Commission has used its power to regulate State aid in the area of short-term export-credit insurance to address actual or potential distortions of competition in the internal market, not only among exporters in different Member States (in trade within and outside the Union), but also among export-credit insurers operating in the Union. In 1997, the Commission laid down the principles for State intervention in its Communication to the Member States pursuant to Article 93(1) of the EC Treaty applying Articles 92 and 93 of the Treaty to short-term export-credit insurance[1] ('the 1997 Communication'). The 1997 Communication was to be applied for a period of five years from 1 January 1998. It was subsequently amended and its period of application was prolonged in 2001,[2] 2004,[3] 2005[4] and 2010.[5] It now applies until 31 December 2012.

3. Experience gained in applying the 1997 Communication, in particular during the financial crisis between 2009 and 2011, suggests that the Commission's policy in this area should be reviewed.

4. The rules set out in this Communication will help to ensure that State aid does not distort competition among private and public or publicly supported export-credit insurers and to create a level-playing field among exporters.

5. It aims to give Member States more detailed guidance about the principles on which the Commission intends to base its interpretation of Articles 107 and 108 of the Treaty and their application to short-term export-credit insurance. It should make the Commission's policy in this area as transparent as possible and ensure predictability and equal treatment. To that end, it lays down a set of conditions that must be fulfilled when State insurers wish to enter the short-term export-credit insurance market for marketable risks.

6. Risks that are in principle non-marketable are outside the scope of this Communication.

7. Section 2 describes the scope of this Communication and the definitions used in it. Section 3 deals with the applicability of Article 107(1) of the Treaty and the general prohibition of State aid for the export-credit insurance of marketable risks. Finally, Section 4 provides for some exceptions from the definition of marketable risks and specifies the conditions for State intervention in the insurance of temporarily non-marketable risks.

NOTES

[1] OJ C281, 17.9.1997, p 4.

[2] OJ C217, 2.8.2001, p 2.

[3] OJ C307, 11.12.2004, p 12.

[4] OJ C325, 22.12.2005, p 22.

[5] OJ C329, 7.12.2010, p 6.

2. SCOPE OF THE COMMUNICATION AND DEFINITIONS

2.1. SCOPE

8. The Commission will apply the principles set out in this Communication only to export-credit insurance with a risk period of less than two years. All other export finance instruments are excluded from the scope of this Communication.

2.2. DEFINITIONS

9. For the purposes of this Communication the following definitions will apply:

'co-insurance' means the percentage of each insured loss that is not indemnified by the insurer but is borne by another insurer;

'credit period' means the period of time given to the buyer to pay for the delivered goods and services under an export-credit transaction;

'commercial risks' means risks including, in particular:

- arbitrary repudiation of a contract by a buyer, that is to say any arbitrary decision made by a non-public buyer to interrupt or terminate the contract without a legitimate reason,
- arbitrary refusal of a non-public buyer to accept the goods covered by the contract without a legitimate reason,
- insolvency of a non-public buyer and its guarantor,
- protracted default, that is to say non-payment by a non-public buyer and by its guarantor of a debt resulting from the contract,

'export-credit insurance' means an insurance product whereby the insurer provides insurance against a commercial and political risk related to payment obligations in an export transaction;

'manufacturing period' means the period between the date of an order and the delivery of the goods or services;

'marketable risks' means commercial and political risks with a maximum risk period of less than two years, on public and non-public buyers in the countries listed in the Annex; all other risks are considered non-marketable for the purposes of this Communication.

'political risks' means risks including, in particular:

- the risk that a public buyer or country prevents the completion of a transaction or does not pay on time,
- a risk that is beyond the scope of an individual buyer or falls outside the individual buyer's responsibility,
- the risk that a country fails to transfer to the country of the insured the money paid by buyers domiciled in that country,
- the risk that a case of force majeure occurs outside the country of the insurer, which could include warlike events, in so far as its effects are not otherwise insured,

'private credit insurer' means a company or organisation other than a State insurer that provides export-credit insurance;

'quota-share' means reinsurance that requires the insurer to transfer, and the reinsurer to accept, a given percentage of every risk within a defined category of business written by the insurer;

'reinsurance' means insurance that is purchased by an insurer from another insurer to manage risk by lowering its own risk;

'risk period' means the manufacturing period plus the credit period;

'single-risk cover' means cover for all sales to one buyer or for a single contract with one buyer;

'State insurer' means a company or other organisation that provides export-credit insurance with the support of, or on behalf of, a Member State, or a Member State that provides export-credit insurance;

'top-up cover' means additional cover over a credit limit established by another insurer;

'whole turnover policy' means a credit insurance policy other than single risk-cover; that is to say, a credit insurance policy that covers all or most of the credit sales of the insured as well as payment receivables from sales to multiple buyers.

3. APPLICABILITY OF ARTICLE 107(1) OF THE TREATY

3.1. GENERAL PRINCIPLES

10. Article 107(1) of the Treaty states that 'any aid granted by a Member State or through State resources in any form whatsoever which distorts or threatens to distort competition by favouring certain undertakings or the production of certain goods shall, in so far as it affects trade between Member States, be incompatible with the internal market'.

11. If export-credit insurance is provided by State insurers, it involves State resources. The involvement of the State may give the insurers and/or the exporters a selective advantage and could thereby distort or threaten to distort competition and affect trade between Member States. The following principles are designed to provide guidance on how such measures will be assessed under State aid rules.

3.2. AID FOR INSURERS

12. If State insurers have certain advantages compared to private credit insurers, State aid may be involved. The advantages can take different forms and might include, for example:

(a) State guarantees of borrowing and losses;

(b) exemption from the requirement to constitute adequate reserves and the other requirements stemming from the exclusion of export-credit insurance operations for the account of or guaranteed by the State from First Council Directive 73/239/EEC of 24 July 1973 on the coordination of laws, regulations and administrative provisions relating to the taking-up and pursuit of the business of direct insurance other than life assurance;[1]

(c) relief or exemption from taxes normally payable (such as company taxes and taxes levied on insurance policies);

(d) awards of aid or provisions of capital by the State or other forms of financing that are not in accordance with the market economy investor principle;

(e) provision by the State of services in kind, such as access to and use of State infrastructure, facilities or privileged information, on terms that do not reflect their market value;

(f) direct reinsurance by the State or a direct State reinsurance guarantee on terms more favourable than those available on the private reinsurance market, leading to under-pricing of the reinsurance cover or to the artificial creation of capacity that would not be forthcoming from the private market.

3.3. PROHIBITION OF STATE AID FOR EXPORT CREDITS

13. The advantages for State insurers listed in point 12 with regard to marketable risks affect intra-Union trade in credit insurance services. They lead to variations in the insurance cover available for marketable risks in different Member States. This distorts competition among insurers in different Member States and has secondary effects on intra-Union trade regardless of whether intra-Union exports or exports outside the Union are concerned.[2] It is necessary to define the conditions under which State insurers can operate if they have such advantages compared to private credit insurers, in order to ensure they do not benefit from State aid. This requires that they should not be able to insure marketable risks.

14. Advantages for State insurers are also sometimes passed on to exporters, at least in part. Such advantages may distort competition and trade and constitute State aid within the meaning of Article 107(1) of the Treaty. However, if the conditions for the provision of export-credit insurance for marketable risks, as set out in section 4.3 of this Communication, are fulfilled, the Commission will consider that no undue advantage has been passed on to exporters.

NOTES

[1] OJ L228, 16.8.1973, p 3.

[2] In its judgment in Case C-142/87 *Kingdom of Belgium* v *Commission of the European Communities*, the Court held that not only aid for intra-Union exports, but also aid for exports outside the Union, can influence intra-Union competition and trade. Both types of operation are insured by export-credit insurers and aid for both can therefore affect intra-Union competition and trade.

4. CONDITIONS FOR PROVIDING EXPORT-CREDIT INSURANCE FOR TEMPORARILY NON-MARKETABLE RISKS

4.1. GENERAL PRINCIPLES

15. As stated in point 13, if State insurers have any advantages compared to private credit insurers, as described in point 12, they must not insure marketable risks. If State insurers or their subsidiaries wish to insure marketable risks, it must be ensured that in so doing, they do not directly or indirectly benefit from State aid. To this end, they must have a certain amount of own funds (a solvency margin, including a guarantee fund) and technical provisions (an equalisation reserve) and must have obtained the required authorisation in accordance with Directive 73/239/EEC. They must also at least keep a separate administration account and separate accounts for their insurance of marketable risks and non-marketable risks for the account of or guaranteed by the State, to show that they do not receive State aid for their insurance of marketable risks. The accounts for businesses insured on the insurer's own account should comply with Council Directive 91/674/EEC of 19 December 1991 on the annual accounts and consolidated accounts of insurance undertakings.[1]

16. Member States providing reinsurance cover to an export-credit insurer by way of participation or involvement in private sector reinsurance treaties covering marketable and non-marketable risks, must be able to demonstrate that the arrangements do not involve State aid as referred to in point 12(f).

17. State insurers may provide export-credit insurance for temporarily non-marketable risks, subject to the conditions set out in this Communication.

4.2. EXCEPTIONS TO THE DEFINITION OF MARKETABLE RISKS: TEMPORARILY NON-MARKETABLE RISKS

18. Notwithstanding the definition of marketable risks, certain commercial and political risks on buyers established in the countries listed in the Annex, are considered temporarily non-marketable in the following cases:

(a) if the Commission decides to temporarily remove one or more countries from the list of marketable risk countries in the Annex, by means of the mechanism described in Section 5.2, because the capacity of the private insurance market in is insufficient to cover all economically justifiable risks in the country or countries concerned;

(b) if the Commission, after having received a notification from a Member State, decides that the risks incurred by small and medium-sized enterprises as defined by the Commission Recommendation of 6 May 2003 concerning the definition of micro, small and medium-sized enterprises,[2] with a total annual export turnover not exceeding EUR 2 million, are temporarily non-marketable for exporters in the notifying Member State;

(c) if the Commission, after having received a notification from a Member State, decides that single-risk cover with a risk period at least 181 days and less than two years is temporarily non-marketable for exporters in the notifying Member State;

(d) if the Commission, after having received a notification from a Member State, decides that due to a shortage of export-credit insurance, certain risks are temporarily non-marketable for exporters in the notifying Member State.

19. To minimise distortions of competition in the internal market, risks which are considered temporarily non-marketable in accordance with point 18 can be covered by State insurers, provided they fulfil the conditions in section 4.3.

4.3. CONDITIONS FOR PROVIDING COVER FOR TEMPORARILY NON-MARKETABLE RISKS

4.3.1. *QUALITY OF COVER*

20. The quality of cover offered by State insurers must be consistent with market standards. In particular, only economically justified risks, that is to say, risks that are acceptable on the basis of sound underwriting principles, can be covered. The maximum percentage of cover must be 95% for commercial risks and political risks and the claims waiting period must be a minimum of 90 days.

4.3.2. *UNDERWRITING PRINCIPLES*

21. Sound underwriting principles must always be applied to the assessment of risks. Accordingly, the risk of financially unsound transactions must not be eligible for cover under publicly supported schemes. With regard to such principles, risk acceptance criteria must be explicit. If a business relationship already exists, exporters must have a positive trading and/or payment experience. Buyers must have a clean claims record, the probability of the buyers' default must be acceptable and their internal and/or external financial ratings must also be acceptable.

4.3.3. *ADEQUATE PRICING*

22. Risk-carrying in the export-credit insurance contract must be remunerated by an adequate premium. To minimise the crowding out of private credit insurers, average premiums under publicly supported schemes must be higher than the average premiums charged by private credit insurers for similar risks. This requirement ensures the phasing out of State intervention, because the higher premium will ensure that exporters return to private credit insurers as soon as market conditions allow them to do so and the risk becomes marketable again.

23. Pricing is considered adequate if the minimum premium[3] ('safe-harbour premium') for the relevant buyers' risk category[4] as set out in the following table is charged. The safe-harbour premium applies unless Member States provide evidence that these rates are inadequate for the risk in question. For a whole turnover policy, the risk category must correspond to the average risk of buyers covered by the policy.

Risk category	Annual risk premium[5] (% of insured volume)
Excellent[6]	0.2-0.4
Good[7]	0.41-0.9
Satisfactory[8]	0.91-2.3
Weak[9]	2.31-4.5

24. For co-insurance, quota share and top-up cover, pricing is considered adequate only if the premium charged is at least 30% higher than the premium for the (original) cover provided by a private credit insurer.

25. An administration fee must be added to the risk premium regardless of the term of the contract in order for pricing to be considered adequate.

4.3.4. *TRANSPARENCY AND REPORTING*

26. Member States must publish the schemes put in place for risks which are considered temporarily non-marketable in accordance with point 18 on the websites of State insurers, specifying all applicable conditions.

27. They must submit annual reports to the Commission on risks which are considered temporarily non-marketable in accordance with point 18 and are covered by State insurers. They must do so at the latest on 31 July of the year following the intervention.

28. The report must contain information on use of each scheme, including in particular the total volume of credit limits granted, turnover insured, premiums charged, claims registered and paid, amounts recovered and the administrative costs of the scheme. The Commission will publish the reports on its website.

NOTES

1 OJ L374, 31.12.1991, p 7.

2 OJ L124, 20.5.2003, p 36.

3 For each relevant risk category, the safe-harbour risk premium range was established on the basis of one-year Credit Default Swap (CDS) spreads, based on a composite rating including ratings of all three main credit rating agencies (Standard & Poor, Moody's and Fitch), for the past five years (2007–2011), assuming that average recovery ratios for short-term export-credit insurance are 40%. The ranges were subsequently made continuous to better cater for the fact that risk premiums do not remain constant over time.

4 The buyers' risk categories are based on credit ratings. Ratings do not need to be obtained from specific rating agencies. National rating systems or rating systems used by banks are equally acceptable. For firms without a public rating, a rating based on verifiable information could be applied.

5 Safe harbour for a 30-day insurance contract can be obtained by dividing the annual risk premium by 12.

6 The excellent risk category includes risks equivalent to AAA, AA+, AA, AA-, A+, A, A- in Standard & Poor's credit ratings.

7 The good risk category includes risks equivalent to BBB+, BBB or BBB- in Standard & Poor's credit ratings.

8 The satisfactory risk category includes risks equivalent to BB+, BB or BB- in Standard & Poor's credit ratings.

9 The weak risk category includes risks equivalent to B+, B or B- in Standard & Poor's credit ratings.

5. PROCEDURAL ISSUES

5.1. GENERAL PRINCIPLES

29. The risks specified in point 18(a) can be covered by State insurers, subject to the conditions in section 4.3. The Commission does not have to be notified in such cases.

30. The risks specified in point 18(b), (c) and (d) can be covered by State insurers, subject to the conditions in section 4.3 and following notification to and approval by the Commission.

31. Failure to fulfil any one of the conditions set out in Section 4.3 does not mean that the export-credit insurance or insurance scheme is automatically prohibited. If a Member States wishes to deviate from any of the conditions or if there is any doubt about whether a planned export-credit insurance scheme fulfils the conditions set out in this Communication, the Member State must notify the scheme to the Commission.

32. Analysis under State aid rules does not prejudge the compatibility of a given measure with other Treaty provisions.

5.2. MODIFICATION OF THE LIST OF MARKETABLE RISK COUNTRIES

33. When determining whether the lack of sufficient private capacity justifies the temporary removal of a country from the list of marketable risk countries, as referred to in point 18(a), the Commission will take the following factors into account, in order of priority:

(a) contraction of private credit insurance capacity: in particular, the decision of a major credit insurer not to cover risks on buyers in the country concerned, a significant decrease in total insured amounts or a significant decrease in acceptance ratios for the country concerned within a six-month period;

(b) deterioration of sovereign sector ratings: in particular, sudden changes in credit ratings within a six-month period, for example multiple downgrading by independent rating agencies, or a big increase in Credit Default Swap spreads;

(c) deterioration of corporate sector performance: in particular, a sharp increase in insolvencies in the country concerned within a six-month period.

34. When market capacity becomes insufficient to cover all economically justifiable risks, the Commission may revise the list of marketable risk countries at the written request of at least three Member States or on its own initiative.

35. If the Commission intends to modify the list of marketable risk countries in the Annex, it will consult and seek information from Member States, private credit insurers and interested parties. The consultation and the type of information sought will be announced on the Commission's website. The consultation period will usually not be longer than 20 working days. When, on the basis of the information gathered, the Commission decides to modify the list of marketable risk countries, it will inform Member States in writing and announce the decision on its website.

36. The temporary removal of a country from the list of marketable risk countries will be valid for no less than 12 months. Insurance policies relating to the temporarily removed country which are signed during that period may be valid for a maximum of 180 days after the date on which the temporary removal ceases. New insurance policies may not be signed after that date. Three months before the temporary removal ceases, the Commission will consider whether to prolong the removal of the country concerned from the list. If the Commission determines that market capacity is still insufficient to cover all economically justifiable risks, taking into account the factors set out in point 33, it may prolong the temporary removal of the country from the list, in accordance with point 35.

5.3. NOTIFICATION OBLIGATION FOR EXCEPTIONS IN POINT 18(B) AND (C)

37. The evidence currently available to the Commission suggests that there is a market gap as regards the risks specified in point 18(b) and (c) and that those risks are therefore non-marketable. It must be borne in mind, however, that the lack of cover does not exist in every Member State and that the situation could change over time, as the private sector might become interested in this segment of the market. State intervention should only be allowed for risks which the market would otherwise not cover.

38. For these reasons, if a Member State wants to cover the risks specified in point 18(b) or (c), it must make a notification to the Commission pursuant to Article 108(3) of the Treaty and demonstrate in its notification that it has contacted the main credit insurers and brokers in that Member State[1] and given them an opportunity to provide evidence that cover for the risks concerned is available there. If the credit insurers concerned do not give the Member State or the Commission information about the conditions of cover and insured volumes for the type of risks the Member State wants to cover within 30 days of receiving a request from the Member State to do so, or if the information provided does not demonstrate that cover for the risks concerned is available in that Member State, the Commission will consider the risks temporarily non-marketable.

5.4. NOTIFICATION OBLIGATION IN OTHER CASES

39. As regards the risks specified in point 18(d), the Member State concerned must, in its notification to the Commission pursuant to Article 108(3) of the Treaty, demonstrate that cover is unavailable for exporters in that particular Member State due to a supply shock in the private insurance market, in particular the withdrawal of a major credit insurer from the Member State concerned, reduced capacity or a limited range of products compared to other Member States.

NOTES

1 The contacted credit insurers and brokers should be representative in terms of the products offered (for example, specialised providers for single risks) and the size of the market they cover (for example, representing jointly a minimum share of 50% of the market).

6. DATE OF APPLICATION AND DURATION

40. The Commission will apply the principles in this Communication from 1 January 2013 until 31 December 2018, except for point 18(a) and section 5.2, which will be applied from the date of adoption of this Communication.

NOTES

As to the prolongation of this Communication to 31 December 2021, see paragraph **[5.680]** *post*.

[ANNEX
LIST OF MARKETABLE RISK COUNTRIES

The Commission considers all commercial and political risks associated with exports to the countries listed below as temporarily non-marketable until 31 December 2021.

Belgium
Bulgaria
Czech Republic
Denmark
Germany
Estonia
Ireland
Greece
Spain
France
Croatia
Italy

Cyprus
Latvia
Lithuania
Luxembourg
Hungary
Malta
Netherlands
Austria
Poland
Portugal
Romania
Slovenia

Slovakia
Finland
Sweden
Australia
Canada
Iceland
Japan
New Zealand
Norway
Switzerland
United Kingdom
United States of America]

NOTES

This Annex was substituted by virtue of para 62 of the Communication from the Commission: Sixth Amendment to the Temporary Framework for State aid measures to support the economy in the current COVID-19 outbreak and amendment to the Annex to the Communication from the Commission to the Member States on the application of Articles 107 and 108 of the Treaty on the Functioning of the European Union to short-term export-credit insurance. That paragraph provides that the Commission considers that all commercial and political risks associated with exports to the countries listed above are temporarily non-marketable until 31 March 2022.

3. TAX RULINGS

DG COMPETITION WORKING PAPER ON STATE AID AND TAX RULINGS

DG Competition – Internal Working Paper – Background to the High Level Forum on State Aid of 3 June 2016

[5.631]

NOTES

This document is available on the European Commission's website at https://ec.europa.eu/competition-policy/state-aid/legislation/specific-aid-instruments_en.

INTRODUCTION

[5.632]

(1) A measure by which the public authorities grant certain undertakings a favourable tax treatment which places them in a more favourable financial position than other taxpayers amounts to State aid within the meaning of Article 107(1) of the Treaty on the Functioning of the European Union (TFEU).[1] Since 1958, the Member States of the European Union are obliged to inform the European Commission of any plans to grant State aid and the Commission has the responsibility to assess whether measures notified by the Member States to it constitute State aid and, if so, whether those measures can be deemed compatible with the internal market.

(2) While the Member States enjoy fiscal autonomy in the design of their direct taxation systems, any fiscal measure a Member State adopts must comply with the EU State aid rules, which bind the Member States and enjoy primacy over their domestic legislation.[2] As early as 1974, the Court of Justice of the European Union clarified that the Commission's competence in the field of State aid control also covers the area of direct business taxation.[3] As a rule, fiscal measures of a general nature that apply to all undertakings without distinction fall within the remit of the Member States' fiscal autonomy and cannot constitute State aid, since they do not selectively advantage certain undertakings over others. By contrast, fiscal measures that discriminate between taxpayers in a similar factual and legal situation constitute, in principle, State aid.[4]

(3) In 1998, the Commission adopted a Notice on the application of the State aid rules to measures relating to direct business taxation,[5] which also covers discretionary administrative practices. More specifically, since 2001 the Commission has conducted a series of investigations into Member States' fiscal schemes that appeared to benefit only certain companies. Since then, the Commission has adopted a series of negative decisions finding such schemes to selectively advantage multinational companies. These decisions have *inter alia*, concerned national schemes that accept multinational corporations pricing their intra-group transactions in a manner that does not reflect the conditions that apply between independent companies at arm's length.[6] This "arm's length principle" aims to ensure that all economic operators are treated in the same manner when determining their taxable base for corporate income tax purposes, regardless of whether they form part of an integrated corporate group or operate as standalone companies on the market.

(4) In 2006, the European Court of Justice endorsed the arm's length principle for determining whether a fiscal measure prescribing a method for an integrated group company to determine its taxable profit gives rise to a selective advantage for the purposes of Article 107(1) TFEU.[7] Accordingly, a fiscal measure that endorses a method for determining an integrated group company's taxable profit in a manner that does not result in a reliable approximation of a market-based outcome in line with the arm's length principle can confer a selective advantage upon its recipient. That would be the case where such a fiscal measure results in a reduced taxable profit, and thus reduced corporate income tax liability.

(5) The Commission does not call into question the granting of tax rulings by the tax administrations of the Member States. It recognises the importance of advance rulings as a tool to provide legal certainty to taxpayers. Provided they do not grant a selective advantage to specific economic operators, tax rulings do not raise issues under EU State aid law. Since 2013, the Commission's Directorate-General for Competition (DG Competition) has been carrying out an inquiry into tax ruling practices from this perspective of EU State aid rules.

(6) By the end of 2014, all Member States had been asked to provide information about their tax ruling practice and the legal framework underlying that practice, as well as a list of tax rulings issued in the years 2010 to 2012 (and partly 2013). On the basis of this information, DG Competition requested specific tax rulings. Overall, DG Competition has looked at more than 1,000 tax rulings.[8]

(7) The inquiry has focussed, in particular, on tax rulings which endorse transfer pricing arrangements proposed by the taxpayer for determining the taxable basis of an integrated group company. Transfer prices refer to the prices charged for intra-group transactions concerning the sale of goods or services between associated group companies. The Commission has also analysed "confirmatory rulings", which confirm the application, or the non-application, of a certain legislative provision to a specific situation.[9]

(8) The inquiry led, in mid-2014, to the opening of three formal State aid investigations by the Commission on tax rulings granted by Ireland (to Apple),[10] Luxembourg (to Fiat)[11] and the Netherlands (to Starbucks).[12] Further investigations were opened by the Commission later the same year and in 2015 on tax rulings granted by Luxembourg (to Amazon[13] and to McDonald's[14]) and by Belgium (the Excess Profit scheme).[15] At the end of 2015 and the beginning of 2016, the Commission adopted three negative decisions with recovery with respect to the tax ruling

granted by the Netherlands to Starbucks,[16] the tax ruling granted by Luxembourg to Fiat[17] and the Excess Profit Scheme in Belgium.[18] Those decisions provide further guidance to Member States' tax administrations and multinational corporate groups on how the Commission applies the EU State aid rules in this field. The Commission is continuing its investigations concerning the tax treatment of Apple by Ireland, and Amazon and McDonald's by Luxembourg. It will open further investigations if it has serious reasons to consider that State aid may have been granted by way of a tax ruling in other cases.

(9) The inquiry has provided DG Competition with a first overview of the tax ruling practice of the Member States and of tax planning strategies utilised by integrated corporate groups.

(10) This working paper of DG Competition aims to provide a short summary of its preliminary orientations. It does not bind the Commission and is without prejudice to any further cases the Commission may open.

NOTES

1 Case C-105/14 *Taricco and Others* EU:C:2015:555, paragraph 61; Case C-6/12 *P Oy* EU:C:2013:525, paragraph 18; Joined Cases C-106/09 P and C-107/09 P *Commission and Spain v Government of Gibraltar and United Kingdom*, paragraphs 72 and 73; Joined Cases C-78/08 to C-80/08 *Paint Graphos and Others* EU:C:2009:417, paragraph 46; and Case C-387/92 *Banco Exterior de España* EU:C:1994:100, paragraph 14.

2 See Joined Cases C-182/03 and C-217/03 *Belgium and Forum 187 ASBL v. Commission* EU:C:2006:416, paragraph 81; Joined Cases C-106/09 P and C-107/09 P *Commission v Government of Gibraltar and United Kingdom* EU:C:2011:732; Case C-417/10 *3M Italia* EU:C:2012:184, paragraph 25, and Order in Case C-529/10 *Safilo* EU:C:2012:188, paragraph 18; See also Case T-538/11 *Belgium v. Commission*, EU:T:2015:188, paragraph 66.

3 Case 173/73 *Italy v Commission* EU:C:1974:71.

4 Case C-6/12 *P Oy* EU:C:2013:525, paragraph 18 and the case-law cited.

5 OJ 1998 C384, p 3; this Notice was recently repealed and replaced by the Commission Notice on the Notion of State aid as referred to in Article 107(1) TFEU, which was adopted on 19 May 2016.

6 See, for example, Commission Decision of 22 August 2002 in Case C48/2001 (ex NN 43/2000) *on the aid scheme implemented by Spain in favour of coordination centres in Vizcaya*, OJ L31, 6.2.2003, p 26; Commission Decision of 5 September 2002 *on the aid scheme implemented by Germany for control and coordination centres*, OJ L177, 16.7.2003, p 17; Commission decision of 16 October 2002 on the State aid scheme C49/2001 (ex NN 46/2000) - *Coordination Centres - implemented by Luxembourg*, OJ L170, 9.7.2003, p 20, paragraph 53; and Commission Decision of 17 February 2003 *on the aid scheme implemented by Belgium for coordination centres established in Belgium*, OJ L282, 30.10.2003, p 25.

7 Joined Cases C-182/03 and C-217/03 *Belgium and Forum 187 ASBL v. Commission* EU:C:2006:416.

8 Including about 600 tax rulings which appeared in the public domain in November 2014 ("LuxLeaks").

9 For example, a ruling can confirm that a company has a branch, which means that the company will in principle be taxable in the jurisdiction of that branch.

10 Commission Decision of 11 June 2014, Case SA.38373 *Alleged aid to Apple*, available at https://ec.europa.eu/competition/elojade/isef/case_details.cfm?proc_code=3_SA_38373.

11 Commission Decision of 11 June 2014, Case SA.38375 *Alleged aid to FFT*, Decision of 11 June 2014 available at https://ec.europa.eu/competition/elojade/isef/case_details.cfm?proc_code=3_SA_38375.

12 Commission Decision of 11 June 2014, Case SA.38374 *Alleged aid to Starbucks*, Decision of 11 June 2014 available at https://ec.europa.eu/competition/elojade/isef/case_details.cfm?proc_code=3_SA_38374.

13 Commission Decision of 7 October 2014, Case SA.38944 *Alleged aid to Amazon*, available at https://ec.europa.eu/competition/elojade/isef/case_details.cfm?proc_code=3_SA_38944.

14 Commission Decision of 3 December 2015, Case SA.38945 *Alleged aid to McDonald's*, not yet published, see IP/15/6221 available at europa.eu/rapid/press-release_IP-15-6221_en.htm.

15 Commission Decision of 3 February 2015, Case SA.37667 *Excess profit tax ruling system in Belgium* available at https://ec.europa.eu/competition/elojade/isef/case_details.cfm?proc_code=3_SA_37667.

16 Commission Decision of 21 October 2015, Case SA.38374 *Aid to Starbucks*, not yet published.

17 Commission Decision of 21 October 2015, Case SA.38375 *Aid to Fiat*, not yet published.

18 Commission Decision of 11 January 2016, Case SA.37667 *Excess profit tax ruling system in Belgium*, available at https://ec.europa.eu/competition/elojade/isef/case_details.cfm?proc_code=3_SA_37667.

PRELIMINARY FINDINGS OF THE RULING INVESTIGATION WITH RESPECT TO TRANSFER PRICING RULINGS

DIFFERENT MEMBER STATES' PRACTICES

[5.633]

(11) The tax ruling practices of the Member States differ significantly in **quantitative terms** over the period investigated. Some Member States have issued thousands of rulings to economic operators every year, among which many are transfer pricing rulings. By contrast, five Member States (Bulgaria, Croatia, Latvia, Greece and Slovenia) have informed the Commission that they did not grant any transfer pricing rulings during the period under investigation.

(12) In terms of the **procedure**, most Member States follow closely the procedural guidance provided by the EU[19] and the Organisation for Economic Co-operation and Development (OECD) for granting a transfer pricing ruling. In particular, a majority of tax administrations systematically require ruling requests to be accompanied by transfer pricing reports to substantiate the choice of a transfer pricing method and the arm's length nature.

TAX RULINGS: HOW TO APPROXIMATE MARKET PRICES

(13) A considerable number of the rulings relate to transfer pricing arrangements that appear to reflect a reliable approximation of a market based outcome in line with the arm's length principle. In general, rulings that cover intra-group transactions between two different Member States, where both companies carry out genuine economic activities on which they are taxed, have been found to be unproblematic.

(14) However, some transfer pricing arrangements do not seem to reflect the arm's length principle when the outcome manifestly deviates from a reliable approximation of a market based outcome.

(15) This concerns, for example, a number of tax rulings regarding the remuneration of **financing companies** that are part of group companies. The only activity of such financing companies is the passing-on of funds or intellectual property (IP) rights from one group company to another. In some Member States with no withholding tax, there are tax rulings approving profit margins for these financing companies. In a Commission decision of 2002, a scheme previously operated by Luxembourg setting out such margins at 12.5 basis points of the loan amount was qualified as incompatible State aid.[20] By way of example, and without prejudice to a case-by-case assessment, the taxable profit of the financing company is still determined in these rulings in a uniform manner as a margin of the underlying transaction, without a clear economic analysis. Under such rulings, the company taking the loan can typically deduct the full interest payment from its taxable income, while the group financing company receiving the interest payment is taxed only on this margin, which represents a fraction of the overall interest received on this loan.

(16) Another example are rulings which endorse **tax deductions for payments** or charges between group companies, even where such payments are not actually made. Without prejudice to a case by case analysis, such virtual payments seem possible only in a group context and not between independent companies transacting on the market at arm's length.

(17) As regards selecting the most appropriate **transfer pricing method**, the OECD's Transfer Pricing Guidelines[21] describe five methods to approximate an arm's length pricing of transactions between companies of the same corporate group: (i) the comparable uncontrolled price method (CUP); (ii) the cost plus method; (iii) the resale minus method; (iv) the transaction net margin method (TNMM) and (v) the transactional profit split method. The OECD Guidelines draw a distinction between traditional transaction methods (the first three methods) and transactional profit methods (the last two methods) and declare a preference for traditional transaction methods, such as the CUP, over transactional methods, such as the TNMM, as a means to establish whether transfer pricing is at arm's length.[22] Those guidelines further explain that multinational corporations retain the freedom to apply methods not described in those Guidelines to establish transfer prices, provided those prices satisfy the arm's length principle.

(18) As set out in the Commission Notice on the Notion of State aid, the OECD Guidelines "*provide useful guidance to tax administrations and multinational enterprises on how to ensure that a transfer pricing methodology produces an outcome in line with market conditions. Consequently, if a transfer pricing arrangement complies with the guidance provided by the OECD Transfer Pricing Guidelines, including the guidance on the choice of the most appropriate method and leading to a reliable approximation of a market based outcome, a tax ruling endorsing that arrangement is unlikely to give rise to State aid.*"[23]

(19) Furthermore, the inquiry suggests that the use of certain transfer pricing methods provides a more reliable means to approximate a market based outcome than others. In particular, the CUP method sets prices for intragroup transactions by making direct comparisons with the price charged on the market for the same goods or services. However, in some cases, a ruling is based on the CUP method without any comparables being presented. In such situations, the use of the CUP method may not result in a reliable approximation of a market-based outcome in line with the arm's length principle.

(20) Some rulings are based on a **two-sided approach**, i.e. both companies to the intra-group transaction are analysed, where there is less room to deviate from a market outcome. This is, in particular, the case for the profit split method, where both sides of the transaction are allocated a share of the overall profit. The profit split method does not rely on a reference to comparable transactions in the market but will, if applied consistently by all jurisdictions involved, divide the full amount of profits between the two companies to the intra-group transaction. A two-sided approach is also in principle required in case of Bilateral Advance Pricing Agreements (BAPAs), where two countries accept a transfer pricing arrangement between group companies in these two countries.

(21) Other rulings are based on a **one-sided approach**, which determines the remuneration of only one party to the intra-group transaction, namely the taxpayer requesting the ruling. In practice, this refers to rulings endorsing a transfer pricing arrangement based on the TNMM. This type of transfer pricing arrangement generally determines the remuneration of that company based on its activity or function performed.[24] Based on that determination, the remaining profit (the residual profit) is automatically allocated by that company to another company in another tax jurisdiction, sometimes without any information about the activities of that other company. This method is often used when the group company located in the other tax jurisdiction holds IP.

(22) Where the TNMM is used, operating expenses are often retained when the taxable base is determined as a mark-up on a **performance indicator**.[25] In some cases, it seems that this choice of operating expenses as a performance indicator is made systematically, without necessarily representing the commercial value of the functions of the company.[26] An appropriate indicator is the one that best captures the commercial value of the activity.

(23) The approximate nature of the arm's length principle cannot be used to justify a transfer pricing analysis that is either methodologically inconsistent or based on an inadequate comparables selection. There are cases where finding a market outcome is not straightforward and requires the use of an approximation. This is not a concern as such, as long as the approximation is as precise as it can be under the circumstances. In other words, the "*search for a 'reliable approximation of a market-based outcome' means that any deviation from the best estimate of a market-based outcome must be limited and proportionate to the uncertainty inherent in the transfer pricing method chosen or the statistical tools employed for that approximation exercise.*"[27] Against this background, DG Competition's focus is on cases where there is a **manifest breach** of the arm's length principle.

NOTES

19 See e.g. Commission Communication on Advance Pricing Agreements (COM (2007) 71 final), which in its Annex specifies the required documents for transfer pricing rulings.

20 Case C50/01 Commission Decision of 16 October 2002 *Finance Companies Luxembourg*, OJ 2003 L153, p 40.

21 Transfer Pricing Guidelines for Multinational Enterprises and Tax Administrations, OECD, 22 July 2010.

22 Paragraph 2.3 of the 2010 OECD Guidelines provides: "*As a result, where, taking account of the criteria described at paragraph 2.2, a traditional transaction method and a transactional profit method can be applied in an equally reliable manner, the traditional transaction method is preferable to the transactional profit method.*"

23 Commission Notice on the Notion of State aid as referred to in Article 107(1) TFEU, paragraph 173.

24 Commission Decision of 21 October 2015, Case SA.38375 *Alleged aid to FFT*, op cit. Commission Decision of 21 October 2015, Case SA.38374 *Alleged aid to Starbucks*, op cit., Commission Decision of 11 January 2016, Case SA.37667 *Excess profit tax ruling system in Belgium.*

25 The performance indicator is defined as the ratio of pre-tax profits to operating expense.

26 A more appropriate indicator in those cases could be return on sales or return on equity. In Commission Decision of 21 October 2015 in Case SA.38375 *Alleged aid to FFT*, op cit., paragraph 247, the Commission accepted the use of the TNMM method and that a return on equity was an appropriate indicator as the company was engaging in genuine financing activity.

27 Commission Notice on the Notion of State aid as referred to in Article 107(1) TFEU, adopted on 19 May 2016, paragraph 171.

CONCLUSION

[5.634]

(24) State aid control in tax rulings follows from the Commission's competence in the field of State aid as set out in the EU Treaties to investigate cases under State aid rules with the objective to prevent distortions of competition through the granting of special tax advantages that are not available to all similarly situated taxpayers in a given Member State.

4. STATE-OWNED ENTERPRISES

COMMISSION STAFF WORKING DOCUMENT

Guidance Paper on state aid-compliant financing, restructuring and privatisation of State-owned enterprises

Brussels 10.2.2012 swd (2012) 14 final

[5.635]

NOTES

This document is available on the European Commission website at: ec.europa.eu/competition/state_aid/studies_reports/studies_reports.html.

INTRODUCTION

[5.636]

It has become apparent in the context of the current economic and financial crisis that some State-owned enterprises ("SOE") are loss-making and/or have accumulated significant amounts of debt, which makes their economic viability uncertain. In order to address the problems that SOE encounter, several Member States are taking measures in the form of financing (eg, capital injections, writing off of debts), restructuring and/or privatisation of SOE, which may potentially involve state aid. A measure constituting state aid shall not be implemented before it has been approved by the Commission. The compatibility of state aid measures needs to be assessed on the basis of the Treaty on the Functioning of the European Union ("TFEU").

The purpose of this Guidance Paper is to raise awareness in all Member States of EU state aid rules, which must be complied with when carrying out financing, restructuring and/or privatisation of SOE, and to provide clarifications on the way the Commission applies the main state aid principles. This Guidance Paper exclusively refers to existing rules and individual cases will be assessed on their own merits.

The Guidance Paper also aims at clarifying the impact that state aid rules could have on the policies and decisions of Member States undergoing economic adjustment programmes, which have committed to reducing the strain on public finances among others by restructuring and/or privatising SOE. Very particularly, the Commission encourages Member States that are implementing large privatisation programmes to closely liaise with it in order to ensure that any state aid issue that may appear during the implementation of the programme is satisfactorily addressed in a timely fashion. This will help to ensure to the maximum possible extent legal certainty and will most likely avoid litigation that could hinder the privatisation process.

This Guidance Paper is a European Commission staff working document for information purposes. It does not represent an official position of the Commission on this issue, nor does it anticipate such a position. It is not intended to constitute a statement of the law and is without prejudice to the interpretation of the Treaty provisions on state aid by the Court of Justice or the General Court of the European Union. Save otherwise mentioned, the principles referred to in this Guidance Paper are applicable not only to SOE, totally or partially owned by the State, but more generally to any stake or participation that a public authority may hold in a company, independently of whether the public authority effectively exercises control or not over it.

2. BASIC PRINCIPLES

WHEN DOES A MEASURE CONSTITUTE STATE AID?

[5.637]

Article 107(1) TFEU provides a general definition of state aid, which is composed of the four cumulative elements defined below:

(1) The measure must be granted by a Member State or through **State resources**.

Under state aid rules, the State is not only the central administration but all levels of government (eg, regions, municipalities, etc). Special attention should be paid to public undertakings, since their actions can in many cases be considered imputable to the State and State resources could be involved.

The measure can take the form of a positive transfer of State resources (eg, a loan or a grant), but also of a negative transfer, that is when the State foregoes revenue it would normally have received (eg, through a tax exemption or a debt waiver).

(2) There must be a **selective advantage** (it must favour certain undertakings, the production of certain goods or the provision of certain services).

The recipient of the measure must be an undertaking. Under state aid rules, this is a functional criterion: what matters is the economic nature of the activity and whether the beneficiary provides a good or service on the market, rather than its legal form or whether it is run for profit or not.

Article 107 TFEU *et seq.* on state aid apply indifferently to both private and public undertakings. This results from Article 345 TFEU, which enshrines the principle of neutrality with regard to the system of property ownership, as well as from the case-law of the EU Courts, which have also recognised the principle of equality between public and private undertakings.

A measure gives an advantage to the beneficiary undertaking when it provides a financial or commercial benefit that this undertaking would not have been able to secure on the market (typically because the State provided the benefit for free or against insufficient remuneration). Normal market behaviour is the benchmark used in assessing all kinds of economic transactions entered into by public authorities. In order to identify what constitutes normal market behaviour, the Commission applies the Market Economy Investor Principle test, which is further explained in section 5.

The advantage must also be selective, ie, it must favour certain undertakings, regions and/or economic activities in detriment of others. Note that a measure which is formally neutral (ie, on paper it is open to all) can be *de facto* selective if in practice it applies only to certain undertakings.

(3) There must be a (potential for) **distortion of competition**.

If a measure provided by the State reinforces (or would be capable of reinforcing) the competitive situation of the beneficiary undertaking compared to that of its competitors, then competition is considered to be distorted. According to the TFEU, which establishes that the measure must distort or threaten to distort competition, no actual distortion of competition is required.

(4) There must be **an effect on trade** between Member States.

This criterion has also been broadly interpreted by the EU Courts. Indeed, it is sufficient that the beneficiary undertaking trades a good or service which could be traded between Member States. Within this meaning, a measure may also affect trade even if the recipient undertaking is not involved in intra-EU trade.

In case a measure fulfils all four cumulative criteria, then it constitutes state aid, which is in principle prohibited by Article 107(1) TFEU. However, Articles 107(2) and (3) TFEU lay down a number of conditions under which a state aid shall or may be considered compatible with the internal market and could thus be authorised by the Commission (which has the exclusive competence to declare state aid compatible with the internal market). On the basis of these Articles the Commission has issued detailed instruments and guidance documents in order to clarify the criteria it applies when assessing the compatibility of state aid.[1]

HIGHLIGHTS OF STATE AID PROCEDURES BEFORE THE COMMISSION

- All state aid measures (individual measures and aid schemes) have to be notified to the Commission for approval and must not be put into effect before the Commission has taken a decision authorising them ("standstill obligation").[2] All aid implemented before approval of the Commission is considered unlawful aid and may have to be recovered from the recipient with interests.
- Once a measure is notified, the Commission has to take a decision within two months. This time-limit starts to count once the notification is complete and the Commission has at its disposal all necessary information.
- When the notification is complete, the Commission may decide (i) that the measure is no aid, (ii) that it is aid but compatible with the internal market (and is therefore authorised), or (iii) that it has doubts that the aid is compatible with the internal market and decides to open a formal investigation procedure.
- If the Commission decides to open a formal investigation procedure, it will carry out a detailed assessment of the measure and the possible grounds for compatibility. The opening of the formal investigation procedure does not prejudge the final decision of the Commission. There is no binding time-limit for the formal investigation procedure, although the Commission shall as far as possible endeavour to adopt a decision within a period of 18 months from the opening of the procedure.[3]
- A formal investigation is closed by a final Commission decision establishing (i) whether the measure is state aid, and if so, (ii) whether it is compatible with the internal market and can be safely implemented, or (iii) whether it is incompatible and must not be implemented (if already implemented, the Commission will normally order the Member State to recover the aid from the beneficiary).

The Commission will moreover consider complaints by competitors, citizens, etc., on potential state aid issues and can also initiate an investigation on its own initiative. Thus, if a support measure is not notified to the Commission for approval before granting it, there is a clear risk of litigation and potential problems in the implementation of the measure given that it could constitute unlawful state aid. It must also be noted that a national court called upon (for example, by a competitor) to assess whether a measure constitutes state aid may order the measure to be annulled or suspended, and the aid to be recovered.[4]

The Commission has also put in place a ***specific pre-notification procedure****, which aims at assisting Member States in an informal way to prepare their notifications. This procedure can also be used by Member States seeking advice to determine whether a measure should be considered state aid or not. Pre-notifications are carried out* ***informally*** *while duly respecting* ***confidentiality***.

NOTES

1 All rules can be found at https://ec.europa.eu/competition-policy/state-aid/legislation_en.

2 here are nonetheless some exceptions to the obligation of prior notification. See for instance Council Regulation (EC) No 994/98 of 7 May 1998 on the application of Articles 92 and 93 of the Treaty establishing the European Community to certain categories of horizontal State aid (OJ L142, 14.5.1998, p 1), and Commission Regulation (EC) No 800/2008 of 6 August 2008 declaring certain categories of aid compatible with the common market in application of Articles 87 and 88 of the Treaty – General Block Exemption Regulation (OJ L214, 9.8.2008, p 3).

3 See Article 7(6) of Council Regulation (EC) No 659/1999 of 22 March 1999 laying down detailed rules for the application of Article 93 of the EC Treaty (OJ L83, 27.3.1999, p 1). This time limit may be extended by common agreement between the Commission and the Member State concerned.

4 See Commission Notice on the enforcement of state aid law by national courts, OJ C85, 9.4.2009, p 1. The Notice gives guidance on possible remedies against violations of the standstill obligation, such as the repayment of unlawful aid, damages claims, interim measures or interest payments. It also establishes two consultation mechanisms for national courts, which

can ask the Commission for information in its possession and/or for its opinion on the application of state aid rules.

3. FINANCING OF SOE

[5.638]

Public authorities may decide to provide funding to SOE in the context of restructuring/privatisation processes. In this eventuality, measures provided on market terms and against a return that would be satisfactory for a private owner/investor in the same industry do not constitute state aid and need not be notified. This would not be the case where fresh capital is contributed in circumstances that would not be acceptable to a private investor operating under prevailing market conditions. For example, (i) where the financial position of the company, and particularly the structure and volume of its debt, is such that a normal return (in dividends or capital gains) cannot be expected within a reasonable time from the capital invested; (ii) where, because of its inadequate cash flow or for any other reason, the company would be unable to raise the funds needed for an investment programme on the capital markets; (iii) where the holding is a short-term one, with duration and selling price fixed in advance, so that the return to the provider of capital is considerably less than he could have expected from a capital market investment for a similar period; or (iv) where the public authorities' holding involves the taking over or the continuation of all or part of the non-viable operations of an ailing company through the formation of a new legal entity.

For those support measures fulfilling the necessary conditions for being considered state aid, there are a number of grounds on which the aid can be considered compatible with the internal market. It is beyond the scope of this Guidance Paper to summarize the numerous compatibility grounds, although the following ones appear potentially valid in the context of the economic adjustment programmes: rescue and restructuring aid,[5] regional aid,[6] training aid,[7] aid for research and development and innovation,[8] etc. Where those compatibility grounds are not met, the financing of SOE will in principle entail incompatible state aid. Particular rules apply to the financing of public services, identified in the Treaties as services of general economic interest ("SGEI"). The SGEI are economic activities that public authorities identify as being of particular importance to citizens and that would not be supplied (or would be supplied under different conditions) if there was no public intervention.[9] The Court of Justice detailed in its *Altmark* judgment the cumulative conditions under which compensation for the provision of SGEI does not constitute state aid.[10] The new SGEI Package, adopted by the Commission on 20 December 2011, clarifies the conditions under which state aid in the form of public service compensation can be considered compatible with the EU rules.[11]

In order for the presence or absence of overcompensation to be established, the Transparency Directive[12] provides that companies receiving compensation and operating both on public services and other markets must keep separate accounts for their different activities. In the case of public undertakings – defined in the Transparency Directive as undertakings over which the public authorities may exercise directly or indirectly a dominant influence – Member States must ensure transparency as to the public funds made available to such undertakings and the use to which these funds are actually put. This transparency requirement applies in particular to the setting off of operating losses, the provision of capital, non-refundable grants, or loans on privileged terms, the foregoing of a normal return on public funds used and compensation of financial burdens imposed by the public authorities.

NOTES

5 See the Community Guidelines on state aid for rescuing and restructuring firms in difficulty, OJ C244, 1.10.2004, p 2.

6 See in particular the Guidelines on national regional aid for 2007-2013, OJ C54, 4.3.2006, p 13.

7 See the Communication from the Commission on the criteria for the analysis of the compatibility of State aid for training subject to individual notification, OJ C188, 11.8.2009, p 1.

8 See the Community framework for state aid for research and development and innovation, OJ C323, 30.12.2006, p 1.

9 SGEI range from large commercial services (network industries such as postal services, energy supply, electronic communication services or public transport services) to a wide range of health and social services (eg, care services for elderly and disabled).

10 Judgment of the Court of Justice of 24.7.2003 in case C-280/00, *Altmark Trans GmbH* [2003] ECR I- 7747. Compensation for the provision of SGEI does not amount to state aid due to the absence of advantage – and is therefore not subject to prior notification to and approval by the Commission – if four cumulative conditions are met: (i) the beneficiary must be entrusted with a clearly defined public service mission; (ii) the parameters for calculating the compensation payments must be established in advance in an objective and transparent manner; (iii) the compensation must not exceed the cost incurred in the discharge of the public service minus the revenues earned with providing the service plus a reasonable profit; and (iv) the beneficiary is chosen in a public tender or compensation does not exceed the costs of a well-run undertaking that is adequately equipped with the means to provide the public service.

11 See the Communication from the Commission on the application of the European Union State aid rules to compensation granted for the provision of services of general economic interest, OJ C8, 11.1.2012, p 4; the Commission Decision on the application of Article 106(2) [TFEU] to State aid in the form of public service compensation granted to certain undertakings entrusted with the operation of services of general economic interest, OJ L7, 11.1.2012, p 3; and the Communication from the Commission – European Union framework for State aid in the form of public service compensation, OJ C8, 11.1.2012, p 15.

12 Commission Directive 2006/111/EC of 16 November 2006 on the transparency of financial relations between Member States and public undertakings as well as on financial transparency within certain undertakings, OJ L318, 17.11.2006, p 17.

4. RESTRUCTURING OF SOE

[5.639]

In certain cases, Member States may seek to maximise the proceeds resulting from privatisation through prior restructuring of the target company, in order to raise the interest with potential buyers. Therefore, a short summary of the main rules on restructuring aid appears appropriate in the context of SOE privatisation. As a general principle, state aid can be ruled out in the context of restructuring if the measures are provided at market conditions, ie, if the measures would have been commercially rational for private owners/creditors of the firm in similar circumstances. If state aid cannot be ruled out clearly, then notification to and prior approval of the Commission are necessary before the restructuring is implemented. The Commission assesses compatibility of the measure on the basis of the Community guidelines on state aid for rescuing and restructuring firms in difficulty ("R&R Guidelines").[13]

In order to be eligible for restructuring aid, the beneficiary firm must be a "**firm in difficulty**" in the sense of points 9 to 13 of the R&R Guidelines. In short, a company in difficulty is a company that is unable, whether through its own resources or with the funds it is able to obtain from its owner/shareholders or creditors, to stem losses which without outside intervention by public authorities will almost certainly condemn it to go out of business in the short or medium term.

The aid must be conditional on implementation of a restructuring plan aimed at **restoring the long-term viability** of the beneficiary on the basis of realistic assumptions and within a reasonable time-frame. The beneficiary undertaking must abandon those activities which would remain structurally loss-making even after restructuring. The Commission must authorise the restructuring plan before it is implemented.

The aid must also be **limited to the minimum** necessary. The beneficiary will be expected to provide a significant contribution to the restructuring from its own resources or from external financing at market conditions. Such contribution must be real, ie, actual, excluding all future expected profits such as cash flow, and must be as high as possible. The extent of own contribution for large firms should normally amount to at least 50% of the restructuring costs.[14]

Importantly, **compensatory measures** will also be required in order to ensure that competition is distorted to the least possible extent by the fact that the aid allows the firm to remain in business. These measures may include divestment of assets, reduction in capacity or market presence, reduction of entry barriers on the market, etc,[15] depending on the specific case at hand and the identified competition distortions. However, this condition will not normally apply to small enterprises, since it can be assumed that *ad hoc* aid to small enterprises does not normally distort competition to an extent contrary to the common interest.[16] Write-offs and closure of loss-making activities that would at any rate be necessary to restore viability do not qualify as compensatory measures.

Finally, also the "**one time, last time**" principle must be respected: restructuring aid cannot be provided to an undertaking which has benefited from restructuring aid in the previous 10 years.

A sale of a SOE may contribute to make restructuring aid compatible, provided that the acquiring party provides new financing to the company. Such funding may demonstrate the confidence of the market on the restoration of the long-term viability of the company. It can normally be considered as "real contribution" in the sense of point 43 of the R&R Guidelines.

Although the general principles of restructuring aid apply across the board to all sectors of the economy, particular rules and conditions apply to restructuring of undertakings in the agricultural,[17] fisheries,[18] financial,[19] and transport sectors.[20]

NOTES

13 Cf. footnote 5. Albeit under the R&R Guidelines rescue aid (in the form of a temporary and reversible assistance) is also possible, it appears unlikely that it will be particularly relevant for SOE.

14 For small enterprises it should be at least 25%, and for medium-sized enterprises at least 40%. For all types of undertakings, the Commission may accept a lower contribution in exceptional circumstances and in cases of particular hardship, which must be demonstrated by the Member State.

15 In areas eligible for regional aid under Articles 107(3)(a) and (c) TFEU, the conditions for authorising aid may be less stringent as regards the implementation of compensatory measures and the size of the beneficiary's own contribution. See points 55 and 56 of the R&R Guidelines.

16 See point 41 of the R&R Guidelines.

17 See in particular chapter 5 of the R&R Guidelines as well as the Community Guidelines for state aid in the agriculture and forestry sector – 2007 to 2013, OJ C319, 27.12.2006, p 1.

18 Guidelines for the examination of State aid to fisheries and aquaculture, OJ C84, 3.4.2008, p 10.

19 See in particular the Commission Communication on the return to viability and the assessment of restructuring measures in the financial sector in the current crisis under the State aid rules, OJ C095, 19.8.2009, p 9. Note that this Communication, as well as the rest of communications adopted for the financial sector in response to the economic and financial crisis, constitute temporary rules and have a different legal basis from the R&R Guidelines, namely Article 107(3)(b) TFEU.

20 See for instance the Community Guidelines on State aid for railway undertakings, OJ C184, 22.7.2008, p 13, or the guidelines on the Application of Articles 92 and 93 of the EC Treaty and Article 61 of the EEA Agreement to State aids in the aviation sector, OJ C350, 10.12.1994, p 5.

5. PRIVATISATION OF SOE

[5.640]

As explained above, normal market behaviour is the benchmark used for assessing the action of public authorities when involved in economic transactions. This general principle also applies to privatisations: for privatisations not to entail state aid, public authorities must ensure that they are done on market terms and that no advantage (typically in the form of foregone revenues) is given to the buyer and/or the sold undertaking. This is particularly the case for highly indebted companies, for which liquidation is a plausible option.

In order to identify or exclude the presence of state aid, the Commission relies on the so-called Market Economy Investor Principle (MEIP) test. In order to determine whether an advantage was provided and its extent, one should compare the action of the public authorities with what a normal market operator would have done under the same circumstances.[21] For the purposes of the MEIP assessment, only those costs that would have been borne by a private operator placed in the same situation will be considered and not the costs or losses that the State would bear as a public authority.[22]

If the test shows that a normal market operator would have done the same as the State, then the presence of an advantage can be excluded and thus no state aid is involved. When the State invests in a company jointly (concomitantly) with a private investor in comparable circumstances and under the same terms and conditions, this provides strong evidence that the MEIP test is met. It is however necessary that the private operator's investment be significant and that its behaviour is not influenced by the State's conduct.

In a privatisation context, the MEIP translates into the Market Economy Vendor Principle (MEVP), ie, the assumption that a private vendor that intends to sell his company would do so for the highest possible price and without imposing conditions that would be liable to depress the price. When selling (assets of) a publicly-owned company, the Member State – in order to exclude the presence of state aid – must in principle likewise behave as a market economy vendor, seeking to maximise the revenues (or minimise the loss) from the sale. If the Member State behaves differently, the privatisation may involve a foregoing of State resources to the benefit of the buyer or the privatised company, which presumably constitutes state aid.

PREPARATORY MEASURES TO FACILITATE THE SUBSEQUENT PRIVATISATION OF SOE

In order to make the company more interesting for potential buyers, Member States may decide to 'clean' or restructure the asset side and/or liability side of the company's balance sheet. These preparatory measures for the privatisation of SOE will in many instances entail state aid, possibly in the form of restructuring aid (see section 4) or as pure financial measures without any accompanying changes to the firm's business or corporate governance model (see section 3). In particular, write-off of State debt, debt-to-equity/asset conversion and capital increases before privatisation will constitute state aid if they do not adhere to the MEIP as explained above.

However, it cannot be excluded from the outset that public authorities provide support on market terms, thereby ruling out state aid as the MEIP test would be met. For instance, in the case of privatisation by Initial Public Offering ("IPO") or sale of shares on the stock exchange, debt may be written off or reduced without this giving rise to state aid in the specific case where the proceeds of the flotation exceed the reduction in debt.

The Commission decision on the measures implemented by Poland for PZL Hydral (C 40/2008) features an example of debt arrangement and privatisation.

The measures included a settlement of old debts by public creditors under the condition of the orderly sale of the assets of PZL Hydral, where the Commission was called to apply ex post the Market Economy Creditor Principle.[23] *After examining the counterfactual scenario of ordinary bankruptcy, taking into account the ranking and the collateral of the public creditors, the Commission concluded that "each public creditor [. . .] is better-off in case of the sale of all PZL Hydral assets, ie, recuperates a higher proportion of his outstanding liabilities, than in a bankruptcy scenario leading to liquidation".*

Furthermore, PZL Wroclaw, an associated undertaking, was granted loans by its public owner. With the undertaking's difficulties making the repayment uncertain, the owner/creditor decided to swap the loans into equity, with the aim to privatise the company and recover part of the debt. Taking into account the price obtained by the sale of the undertaking, the Commission concluded that the creditor "could not reasonably expect to recover more of his claims under bankruptcy proceedings".

Therefore the debt-to-equity swap was considered market-conform.

SALES PROCESS FOR ENTITIES, SHARES, RIGHTS, REAL ESTATE, AND LAND

The Commission's XXIII Report on Competition Policy[24] provides guidance on how the Commission interprets the conditions under which the State may be considered to behave as a market economy vendor in the context of privatisations.

When the privatisation is effected by an IPO or **sale of shares on the stock exchange**, it is generally assumed to be on market conditions (as the price will be the market price) and not to involve state aid. Therefore, there is no obligation to notify the operation to the Commission in advance. However, this method is not always applicable, and in a context of financial and economic crisis like the current one, it might lead to a low valuation of the company to be privatised.

When a company is privatised by a **trade sale**, ie, by sale of the company as a whole or in parts to other companies **outside the stock exchange**, the following cumulative conditions should be observed in order to exclude, without further examination, the presence of state aid and thus prior notification to the Commission:

• A competitive tender must be held that is open to all comers, transparent and not conditional on the performance of other acts such as the acquisition of assets other than those bid for or the continued operation of certain businesses;

• The company / assets must be sold to the highest bidder; and

• Bidders must be given enough time and information to carry out a proper valuation of the assets as the basis for their bid.

If the conditions above are not complied with, privatisations carried out by trade sales must be notified to the Commission. This is so in particular in case of (i) sales after negotiation with a single prospective purchaser or a number of selected bidders; (ii) sales preceded by the writing-off of debt by the State, other public enterprises or any public body, and sales preceded by the conversion of debt into equity or capital increases (see section above on preparatory measures); and (iii) sales on conditions that are not customary in comparable transactions between private parties.

In all cases, there must be no discrimination based on the nationality of prospective buyers of the shares or assets.

In order to minimise the risk that state aid is present, privatisations should be carried out – when possible – by ***sale of shares in the stock exchange****. In the alternative, the preferred method is a* ***competitive tender that is open, transparent and unconditional****, where the highest bidder gets the assets/company.*

The competitive tender must be sufficiently **well publicized**, ie, it must be advertised over a reasonably long period in the national press, estate gazettes and/or other appropriate publications. If the privatisation may attract investors operating on a Europe-wide or international scale, the tender should be announced in publications which have a regular international circulation. Such offers should also be made known through agents addressing clients on a Europe-wide or international scale.

The tender will be considered **unconditional** when any buyer, irrespective of whether or not he runs a business or of its nature, is generally free to acquire the assets or company and to use it for his own purposes. According to a well established Commission practice confirmed by the case-law,[25] attaching to the sale of a company conditions that a market operator would not impose justifies the presumption that state aid might be involved. A market economy vendor would normally sell his company for the highest price without imposing conditions that would depress the price. It will need to be demonstrated on a case-by-case basis that conditions imposed on the acquirer do not result in state aid.

For instance, conditions may be imposed to avoid purely speculative bids or to ensure swift and secure payment. The existence of such conditions is irrelevant from a state aid perspective and would not make a tender conditional. Also, conditions for the prevention of public nuisance or for reasons of environmental protection would not make a tender conditional if they merely require compliance with pre-existing obligations laid down in the law.

On the other hand, a tender will be considered conditional (and may thus entail state aid) if it deviates from best practise by artificially restricting the number of potential buyers, directing the sale in favour of any of them or discriminating between different business strategies. For instance, a tender including a condition that makes it practically impossible for a potential investor intending to follow a different industrial strategy to win the bid simply by offering the highest price will be considered conditional. The Commission will not only assess the conditions expressly referred to in the offer but will also look at *de facto* conditions.

*In order to avoid state aid implications, the conditions (express or de facto) related to privatisation must be of such kind that **all potential buyers would be able to meet them** and **must not be liable to lead to a lower sales price**.*

In Automobile Craiova (Commission decision C 46/2007), Romania attached conditions to the privatisation of the company in the form of awarding criteria, such as maintaining a production integration level and reaching a certain production level. After opening the formal investigation procedure, the Commission concluded that "the conditions attached [. . .] have lowered the sales price and deterred other potential bidders from submitting a bid. As a result, the State has forgone privatisation revenue".

Also, in its decision 1999/720/EC on the measures granted by Germany to Gröditzer Stahlwerke, the Commission concluded that the privatisation procedure of the company was not unconditional. Interested parties were asked to submit a business plan in which they were to put forward detailed commitments regarding jobs to be created or saved, future investment and financing. The Commission noted in its decision that the commitments ultimately entered into influenced the purchase price negotiated. As a result, it concluded that incompatible state aid was involved and ordered recovery.

Conversely, the Commission found in its decision on the privatisation of Tractorul (C 41/2007) that the conditions attached to the tender were simple best-effort clauses of non-binding nature, which did not deter potential bidders and did not lower the price.

Compliance with the state aid rules and principles in the privatisation processes, in particular holding competitive tenders open to all comers, transparent and unconditional, will ensure that no aid is present and a revenue-maximising approach to privatisations.

In the special case of a **sale characterised by a negative price** (eg, including where the State invests more to prepare the sale of the company than the proceeds obtained from privatisation), it must be noted that an open, transparent and unconditional tender is not in itself sufficient to rule out state aid. In such case, the negative price would still need to be compared to the outcome of a liquidation (or bankruptcy) of the SOE in order to ensure that the State has chosen the economically most rational option and has minimised its losses.

For the sale of publicly-owned land and buildings, when the public authorities do not intend to follow an unconditional bidding procedure, there also exists the possibility of establishing the market value of the asset sold by means of a valuation carried out by one or more independent asset valuers prior to the sale negotiations on the basis of generally accepted market indicators and valuation standards.[26]

It cannot be excluded that a procedure other than a sale of shares on the stock exchange or an open, transparent and unconditional tender could nevertheless guarantee that the MEVP is respected and that there is no advantage. Were this to be the case, the Commission would conclude that there is no state aid. In order to ensure no aid to the buyer and/or to the company, the Member State would need to make sure that the best legal option to maximize profit is pursued and that other alternatives would be sub-optimal.

NOTES

21 Note that the presence or absence of a dysfunctional market or market failure (eg, temporarily depressed prices due to negative externalities and excessive risk aversion) is irrelevant for determining the presence or absence of aid. However, market failures or other potential aid justifications can be taken into account when deciding on the compatibility of the aid.

22 The potential positive externalities of the measure are not relevant for the assessment of the presence of aid (which focuses on the presence of a selective advantage to the firm). They may however be considered in the subsequent compatibility assessment of the aid.

23 The MEIP test also needs to be performed when the State acts in the capacity of a creditor and is then called the Market Economy Creditor Principle (MECP).

24 Available at bookshop.europa.eu/is-bin/INTERSHOP.enfinity/WFS/EU-Bookshop-Site/en_GB/-/EUR/ViewPublication-Start?PublicationKey=CM8294650.

25 See Commission Decision of 25.3.1992 in case C 29/1990 (ex NN 88/1989), *Intelhorce SA – Spain*, OJ L176, 30.6.1992,

p 57; Commission Decision in case C 38/1992, *Alumix – Italy*, OJ C288, 1.10.1996 p 4; and Commission Decision of 8.9.1999 in case C 73/1997, *Stardust Marine – France*, OJ L206, 15.8.2000, p 6. The Court of Justice endorsed this principle in Joined cases C-278/92, C-279/92 and C- 280/92, *Spain v Commission*, [1994] ECR I-4103, para.28.

26 See Commission Communication on state aid elements in sales of land and buildings by public authorities, OJ C209, 10.7.1997, p 3.

6. CONCLUSIONS

[5.641]

• In order to safeguard the internal market, it is essential to **ensure respect of state aid rules** in all circumstances.[27] This is an obligation under the TFEU for all Member States.

• Member States are strongly encouraged to use **the pre-notification procedure** for all state aid they intend to grant to SOE. This procedure can also be used to seek advice on whether a given measure entails state aid or not.

• If notification is necessary, Member States are required to **submit notifications as complete and detailed as possible**. No state aid should be put into effect until the Commission has taken a decision authorising it (**standstill obligation**).

• For all types of privatisations, including the sale of land and buildings, the Commission strongly encourages Member States to follow **competitive tenders** and when possible best practice IPOs or sale of shares in the stock exchange. This will ensure a revenue-maximising approach to privatisations and legal certainty to the maximum possible extent.

• Where large-scale privatisations are envisaged, Member States are strongly encouraged to set up a **global strategy on SOE** (to be privatised or not, to be restructured or not) as soon as possible, involving all necessary levels of the public administration. This will also allow for early identification of potentially problematic cases from a state aid perspective. They should also consider establishing a **central contact point** for state aid and SOE-related issues to facilitate communication with the Commission and effective management of state aid.

NOTES

27 Compliance with state aid rules is without prejudice to the obligation to comply with other relevant EU rules, including internal market rules.

F. SERVICES OF GENERAL ECONOMIC INTEREST

COMMUNICATION FROM THE COMMISSION

(2012/C8/02)

on the application of the European Union State aid rules to compensation granted for the provision of services of general economic interest

(Text with EEA relevance)

[5.642]

NOTES

Date of publication in OJ: OJ C8, 11.1.2012, p 4.

See also the list of consultations and draft documents in the Appendix at **[A1]**.

1. PURPOSE AND SCOPE OF THE COMMUNICATION

[5.643]

1. Services of general economic interest (SGEIs) are not only rooted in the shared values of the Union but also play a central role in promoting social and territorial cohesion. The Union and the Member States, each within their respective powers, must take care that such services operate on the basis of principles and conditions which enable them to fulfil their missions.

2. Certain SGEIs can be provided by public or private undertakings[1] without specific financial support from Member States' authorities. Other services can only be provided if the authority concerned offers financial compensation to the provider. In the absence of specific Union rules, Member States are generally free to determine how their SGEIs should be organised and financed.

3. The purpose of this Communication is to clarify the key concepts underlying the application of the State aid rules to public service compensation.[2] It will therefore focus on those State aid requirements that are most relevant for public service compensation.

4. In parallel with this Communication, the Commission envisages adopting an SGEI-specific de minimis Regulation clarifying that certain compensation measures do not constitute State aid within the meaning of Article 107 of the Treaty,[3] and is issuing a Decision,[4] which declares certain types of SGEI compensation constituting State aid to be compatible with the Treaty pursuant to Article 106(2) of the Treaty and exempts them from the notification obligation under Article 108(3) of the Treaty, and a Framework,[5] which sets out the conditions under which State aid for SGEIs not covered by the Decision can be declared compatible under Article 106(2) of the Treaty.

5. This Communication is without prejudice to the application of other provisions of Union law, in particular those relating to public procurement and requirements flowing from the Treaty and from sectoral Union legislation. Where a public authority chooses to entrust a third party with the provision of a service, it is required to comply with Union law governing public procurement, stemming from Articles 49 to 56 of the Treaty, the Union Directives on public procurement (Directive 2004/17/EC of the European Parliament and of the Council of 31 March 2004 coordinating the procurement procedures of entities operating in the water, energy, transport and postal services sectors[6] and Directive 2004/18/EC of the European Parliament and of the Council of 31 March 2004 on the coordination of procedures for the award of public works contracts, public supply contracts and public service contracts[7]) and sectoral rules.[8] Also in cases where the Directives on public procurement are wholly or partially inapplicable (for example, for service concessions and service contracts listed in Annex IIB to Directive 2004/18/EC, including different types of social services), the award may nevertheless have to meet Treaty requirements of transparency, equality of treatment, proportionality and mutual recognition.[9]

6. In addition to the issues addressed in this Communication, the Decision 2012/21/EU and the Communication from the Commission on EU Framework for State aid in the form of public service compensation (2011), the Commission will answer individual questions that arise in the context of the application of the State aid rules to SGEIs. It will do so inter alia through its Interactive Information Service on Services of General Interest, which is accessible on the Commission's website.[10]

7. This Communication is without prejudice to the relevant case-law of the Court of Justice of the European Union.

NOTES

1 In accordance with Article 345 of the Treaty, the Treaties in no way prejudice the rules in Member States governing the system of property ownership. Consequently, the competition rules do not discriminate against companies based on whether they are in public or private ownership.

2 Further guidance is contained in the Guide to the application of the European Union rules on State aid, public procurement and the internal market to services of general economic interest, and in particular to social services of general interest, SEC(2010) 1545 final, 7 December 2010.

3 See page 23 of this Official Journal.

4 Commission Decision 2012/21/EU of 21 December 2011 on the application of Article 106(2) of the Treaty on the Functioning of the European Union to State aid in the form of public service compensation granted to certain undertakings entrusted with the operation of services of general economic interest (OJ L7, 11.1.2012, p 3).

5 See page 15 of this Official Journal.

6 OJ L134, 30.4.2004, p 1.

7 OJ L134, 30.4.2004, p 114.

8 See for example, Regulation (EC) No 1370/2007 of the European Parliament and of the Council of 23 October 2007 on public passenger transport services by rail and by road and repealing Council Regulations (EEC) Nos 1191/69 and 1107/70 (OJ L315, 3.12.2007, p 1).

9 Case C-324/98 *Telaustria Verlags GmbH and Telefonadress GmbH v Telekom Austria AG* [2000] ECR I-10745, paragraph 60 and Commission interpretative communication on the Community law applicable to contract awards not or not fully subject to the provisions of the Public Procurement Directives (OJ C179, 1.8.2006, p 2).

10 https://ec.europa.eu/info/topics/single-market/services-general-interest_en

2. GENERAL PROVISIONS RELATING TO THE CONCEPT OF STATE AID

2.1 CONCEPTS OF UNDERTAKING AND ECONOMIC ACTIVITY

[5.644]

8. Based on Article 107(1) of the Treaty, the State aid rules generally only apply where the recipient is an 'undertaking'. Whether or not the provider of a service of general interest is to be regarded as an undertaking is therefore fundamental for the application of the State aid rules.

2.1.1. GENERAL PRINCIPLES

9. The Court of Justice has consistently defined undertakings as entities engaged in an economic activity, regardless of their legal status and the way in which they are financed.[11] The classification of a particular entity as an undertaking thus depends entirely on the nature of its activities. This general principle has three important consequences:

First, the status of the entity under national law is not decisive. For example, an entity that is classified as an association or a sports club under national law may nevertheless have to be regarded as an undertaking within the meaning of Article 107(1) of the Treaty. The only relevant criterion in this respect is whether it carries out an economic activity.

Second, the application of the State aid rules as such does not depend on whether the entity is set up to generate profits. Based on the case-law of the Court of Justice and the General Court, non-profit entities can offer goods and services on a market too.[12] Where this is not the case, non-profit providers remain of course entirely outside of State aid control.

Third, the classification of an entity as an undertaking is always relative to a specific activity. An entity that carries out both economic and non-economic activities is to be regarded as an undertaking only with regard to the former.

10. Two separate legal entities may be considered to form one economic unit for the purposes of the application of State aid rules. That economic unit is then considered to be the relevant undertaking. In this respect, the Court of Justice looks at the existence of a controlling share or functional, economic and organic links.[13] On the other hand, an entity that in itself does not provide goods or services on a market is not an undertaking for the simple fact of holding shares, even a majority shareholding, when the shareholding gives rise only to the exercise of the rights attached to the status of shareholder or member as well as, if appropriate, the receipt of dividends, which are merely the fruits of the ownership of an asset.[14]

11. To clarify the distinction between economic and non-economic activities, the Court of Justice has consistently held that any activity consisting in offering goods and services on a market is an economic activity.[15]

12. The question whether a market exists for certain services may depend on the way those services are organised in the Member State concerned.[16] The State aid rules only apply where a certain activity is provided in a market environment. The economic nature of certain services can therefore differ from one Member State to another. Moreover, due to political choice or economic developments, the classification of a given service can change over time. What is not a market activity today may turn into one in the future, and vice versa.

13. The decision of an authority not to allow third parties to provide a certain service (for example, because it wishes to provide the service in-house) does not rule out the existence of an economic activity. In spite of such market closure, an economic activity can exist where other operators would be willing and able to provide the service in the market concerned. More generally, the fact that a particular service is provided in-house[17] has no relevance for the economic nature of the activity.[18]

14. Since the distinction between economic and non-economic services depends on political and economic specificities in a given Member State, it is not possible to draw up an exhaustive list of activities that *a priori* would never be economic. Such a list would not provide genuine legal certainty and would thus be of little use. The following paragraphs instead seek to clarify the distinction with respect to a number of important areas.

15. In the absence of a definition of economic activity in the Treaties, the case-law appears to offer different criteria for the application of internal market rules and for the application of competition law.[19]

2.1.2. EXERCISE OF PUBLIC POWERS

16. It follows from the Court of Justice case-law that Article 107 of the Treaty does not apply where the State acts 'by exercising public power'[20] or where authorities emanating from the State act 'in their capacity as public authorities'.[21] An entity may be deemed to act by exercising public powers where the activity in question is a task that forms part of the essential functions of the State or is connected with those functions by its nature, its aim and the rules to which it is subject.[22] Generally speaking, unless the Member State concerned has decided to introduce market mechanisms, activities that intrinsically form part of the prerogatives of official authority and are performed by the State do not constitute economic activities. Examples are activities related to:

(a) the army or the police;
(b) air navigation safety and control;[23]
(c) maritime traffic control and safety;[24]

(d) anti-pollution surveillance;[25] and
(e) the organisation, financing and enforcement of prison sentences.[26]

2.1.3. SOCIAL SECURITY

17. Whether schemes in the area of social security are to be classified as involving an economic activity depends on the way they are set up and structured. In essence, the Court of Justice and the General Court distinguish between schemes based on the principle of solidarity and economic schemes.

18. The Court of Justice and the General Court use a range of criteria to determine whether a social security scheme is solidarity-based and therefore does not involve an economic activity. A bundle of factors can be relevant in this respect:
(a) whether affiliation with the scheme is compulsory;[27]
(b) whether the scheme pursues an exclusively social purpose;[28]
(c) whether the scheme is non-profit;[29]
(d) whether the benefits are independent of the contributions made;[30]
(e) whether the benefits paid are not necessarily proportionate to the earnings of the person insured;[31] and
(f) whether the scheme is supervised by the State.[32]

19. Such solidarity-based schemes must be distinguished from economic schemes.[33] In contrast with solidarity-based schemes, economic schemes are regularly characterised by:
(a) optional membership;[34]
(b) the principle of capitalisation (dependency of entitlements on the contributions paid and the financial results of the scheme);[35]
(c) their profit-making nature;[36] and
(d) the provision of entitlements which are supplementary to those under a basic scheme.[37]

20. Some schemes combine features of both categories. In such cases, the classification of the scheme depends on an analysis of different elements and their respective importance.[38]

2.1.4. HEALTH CARE

21. In the Union, the health care systems differ significantly between Member States. The degree to which different health care providers compete with each other in a market environment largely depends on these national specificities.

22. In some Member States, public hospitals are an integral part of a national health service and are almost entirely based on the principle of solidarity.[39] Such hospitals are directly funded from social security contributions and other State resources and provide their services free of charge to affiliated persons on the basis of universal coverage.[40] The Court of Justice and the General Court have confirmed that, where such a structure exists, the relevant organisations do not act as undertakings.[41]

23. Where that structure exists, even activities that in themselves could be of an economic nature, but are carried out merely for the purpose of providing another non-economic service, are not of an economic nature. An organisation that purchases goods — even in large quantities — for the purpose of offering a non-economic service does not act as an undertaking simply because it is a purchaser in a given market.[42]

24. In many other Member States, hospitals and other health care providers offer their services for remuneration, be it directly from patients or from their insurance.[43] In such systems, there is a certain degree of competition between hospitals concerning the provision of health care services. Where this is the case, the fact that a health service is provided by a public hospital is not sufficient for the activity to be classified as non-economic.

25. The Court of Justice and the General Court have also clarified that health care services which independent doctors and other private practitioners provide for remuneration at their own risk are to be regarded as an economic activity.[44] The same principles would apply as regards independent pharmacies.

2.1.5. EDUCATION

26. Case-law of the Union has established that public education organised within the national educational system funded and supervised by the State may be considered as a non-economic activity. In this regard, the Court of Justice has indicated that the State:

> 'by establishing and maintaining such a system of public education and financed entirely or mainly by public funds and not by pupils or their parents . . . does not intend to become involved in activities for remuneration, but carries out its task towards its population in the social, cultural and educational areas'.[45]

27. According to the same case-law, the non-economic nature of public education is in principle not affected by the fact that pupils or their parents sometimes have to pay tuition or enrolment fees which contribute to the operating expenses of the system. Such financial contributions often only cover a fraction of the true costs of the service and can thus not be considered as remuneration for the service provided. They therefore do not alter the non-economic nature of a general education service predominantly funded by the public purse.[46] These principles can cover public educational services such as vocational training,[47] private and public primary schools[48] and kindergartens,[49] secondary teaching activities in universities[50] and the provision of education in universities.[51]

28. Such public provision of educational services must be distinguished from services financed predominantly by parents or pupils or commercial revenues. For example, commercial enterprises offering higher education financed entirely by students clearly fall within the latter category. In certain Member States public institutions can also offer educational services which, due to their nature, financing structure and the existence of competing private organisations, are to be regarded as economic.

29. In the Community Framework for State aid for research and development and innovation,[52] the Commission has clarified that certain activities of universities and research organisations fall outside the ambit of the State aid rules. This concerns the primary activities of research organisations, namely:
(a) education for more and better skilled human resources;

(b) the conduct of independent research and development for more knowledge and better understanding, including collaborative research and development; and

(c) the dissemination of research results.

30. The Commission has also clarified that technology transfer activities (licensing, spin-off creation or other forms of management of knowledge created by the research organisation) are non-economic where those activities are of an internal nature[53] and all income is reinvested in the primary activities of the research organisations concerned.[54]

2.2. STATE RESOURCES

31. Only advantages granted directly or indirectly through State resources can constitute State aid within the meaning of Article 107 of the Treaty.[55] Advantages financed from private resources may have the effect of strengthening the position of certain undertakings but do not fall within the scope of Article 107 of the Treaty.

32. This transfer of State resources may take many forms such as direct grants, tax credits and benefits in kind. In particular, the fact that the State does not charge market prices for certain services constitutes a waiver of State resources. In its judgment in Case C-482/99 France v Commission,[56] the Court of Justice also confirmed that the resources of a public undertaking constitute State resources within the meaning of Article 107 of the Treaty because the public authorities are capable of controlling these resources. In cases where an undertaking entrusted with the operation of an SGEI is financed by resources provided by a public undertaking and this financing is imputable to the State, such financing is thus capable of constituting State aid.

33. The granting, without tendering, of licences to occupy or use public domain, or of other special or exclusive rights having an economic value, may imply a waiver of State resources and create an advantage for the beneficiaries.[57]

34. Member States may, in some instances, finance an SGEI from charges or contributions paid by certain undertakings or users, the revenue from which is transferred to the undertakings entrusted with the operation of that SGEI. This type of financing arrangement has been examined by the Court of Justice, in particular in its judgment in Case 173/73 Italy v Commission,[58] in which it held that:

> 'As the funds in question are financed through compulsory contributions imposed by State legislation and as, as this case shows, they are managed and apportioned in accordance with the provisions of that legislation, they must be regarded as State resources within the meaning of Article (107 of the Treaty), even if they are administered by institutions distinct from the public authorities.'

35. Similarly, in its judgment in Joined Cases C-78/90 to C-83/90 *Compagnie Commerciale de l'Ouest*,[59] the Court of Justice confirmed that measures financed through parafiscal charges constitute measures financed through State resources.

36. Accordingly, compensatory payments for the operation of SGEIs which are financed through parafiscal charges or compulsory contributions imposed by the State and managed and apportioned in accordance with the provisions of the legislation are compensatory payments made through State resources.

2.3. EFFECT ON TRADE

37. In order to be caught by Article 107 of the Treaty, public service compensation must affect or threaten to affect trade between Member States. Such an effect generally presupposes the existence of a market open to competition. Therefore, where markets have been opened up to competition either by Union or national legislation or *de facto* by economic development, State aid rules apply. In such situations Member States retain their discretion as to how to define, organise and finance SGEIs, subject to State aid control where compensation is granted to the SGEI provider, be it private or public (including in-house). Where the market has been reserved for a single undertaking (including an in-house provider), the compensation granted to that undertaking is equally subject to State aid control. In fact, where economic activity has been opened up to competition, the decision to provide the SGEI by methods other than through a public procurement procedure that ensures the least cost to the community may lead to distortions in the form of preventing entry by competitors or making easier the expansion of the beneficiary in other markets. Distortions may also occur in the input markets. Aid granted to an undertaking operating on a non-liberalised market may affect trade if the recipient undertaking is also active on liberalised markets.[60]

38. Aid measures can also have an effect on trade where the recipient undertaking does not itself participate in cross-border activities. In such cases, domestic supply may be maintained or increased, with the consequence that the opportunities for undertakings established in other Member States to offer their services in that Member State are reduced.[61]

39. According to the case-law of the Court of Justice, there is no threshold or percentage below which trade between Member States can be regarded as not having been affected.[62] The relatively small amount of aid or the relatively small size of the recipient undertaking does not *a priori* mean that trade between Member States may not be affected.

40. On the other hand, the Commission has in several cases concluded that activities had a purely local character and did not affect trade between Member States. Examples are:

(a) swimming pools to be used predominantly by the local population;[63]

(b) local hospitals aimed exclusively at the local population;[64]

(c) local museums unlikely to attract cross-border visitors;[65] and

(d) local cultural events, whose potential audience is restricted locally.[66]

41. Finally, the Commission does not have to examine all financial support granted by Member States. Regulation (EC) No 1998/2006 of 15 December 2006 on the application of Articles 87 and 88 of the Treaty to *de minimis* aid[67] stipulates that aid amounting to less than EUR 200,000 per undertaking over any period of three years is not caught by Article 107(1) of the Treaty. Specific *de minimis* thresholds apply in the transport, fisheries and agricultural sectors[68] and the Commission envisages adopting a Regulation with a specific *de minimis* threshold for local services of general economic interest.

NOTES

[11] Joined Cases C-180/98 to C-184/98 *Pavlov and Others* [2000] ECR I-6451.

[12] Joined Cases 209/78 to 215/78 and 218/78 *Van Landewyck* [1980] ECR 3125, paragraph 21; Case C-244/94 *FFSA and Others* [1995] ECR I-4013; Case C-49/07 *MOTOE* [2008] ECR I-4863, paragraphs 27 and 28.

[13] Case C-480/09 P *AceaElectrabel Produzione SpA v Commission* [2010] ECR paragraphs 47 to 55; Case C-222/04 *Ministero dell'Economia e delle Finanze v Cassa di Risparmio di Firenze SpA and Others* [2006] ECR I-289, paragraph 112.

[14] Case C-222/04 *Ministero dell'Economia e delle Finanze v Cassa di Risparmio di Firenze SpA and Others* [2006] ECR I-289, paragraphs 107-118 and 125.

[15] Case 118/85 Commission v Italy [1987] ECR 2599, paragraph 7; Case C-35/96 Commission v Italy [1998] ECR I-3851, paragraph 36; Joined Cases C-180/98 to C-184/98 *Pavlov and Others*, paragraph 75.

[16] Joined Cases C-159/91 and C-160/91 *Poucet and Pistre* [1993] ECR I-637.

[17] See Opinion of Mr Advocate General Geelhoed in Case C-295/05 *Asociación Nacional de Empresas Forestales (Asemfo) v Transformación Agraria SA (Tragsa) and Administración del Estado* [2007] ECR I-2999, paragraphs 110 to 116; Regulation (EC) No 1370/2007 of the European Parliament and of the Council of 23 October 2007 on public passenger transport services by rail and by road and repealing Council Regulations (EEC) Nos 1191/69 and 1107/70, OJ L315, 3.12.2007, p 1, Articles 5(2) and 6(1); Commission Decision 2011/501/EU of 23 February 2011 on State aid C 58/06 (ex NN 98/05) implemented by Germany for Bahnen der Stadt Monheim (BSM) and Rheinische Bahngesellschaft (RBG) in the Verkehrsverbund Rhein-Ruhr, OJ L210, 17.8.2011, p 1, paragraphs 208-209.

[18] Neither has it any relevance for the question whether the service can be defined as SGEI; see section 3.2.

[19] Case C-519/04 P *David Meca-Medina and Igor Majcen v Commission* [2006] ECR I-6991, paragraphs 30 to 33; Case C-350/07 *Kattner Stahlbau* [2009] ECR I-1513, paragraphs 66, 72, 74 and 75; Opinion of Mr Advocate General Poiares Maduro delivered on 10 November 2005 in Case C-205/03 P *FENIN* [2006] ECR I-6295, paragraphs 50 and 51.

[20] Case C-118/85 *Commission v Italy*, paragraphs 7 and 8.

[21] Case C-30/87 *Bodson/Pompes funèbres des régions libérées* [1988] ECR I-2479, paragraph 18.

[22] See, in particular, Case C-364/92 *SAT/Eurocontrol* [1994] ECR I-43, paragraph 30.

[23] Case C-364/92 *SAT/Eurocontrol*, paragraph 27; Case C-113/07 P *Selex Sistemi Integrati v Commission* [2009] ECR I-2207, paragraph 71.

[24] Commission Decision of 16 October 2002 in Case N 438/02 — Belgium — Aid to port authorities, OJ C284, 21.11.2002.

[25] Case C-343/95 *Cali & Figli* [1997] ECR I-1547, paragraph 22.

[26] Commission Decision in Case N 140/06 — Lithuania — Allotment of subsidies to the State Enterprises at the Correction Houses, OJ C244, 11.10.2006.

[27] Joined Cases C-159/91 and C-160/91 *Poucet and Pistre* [1993] ECR I-637, paragraph 13.

[28] Case C-218/00 *Cisal and INAIL* [2002] ECR I-691, paragraph 45.

[29] Joined Cases C-264/01, C-306/01, C-354/01 and C-355/01 *AOK Bundesverband* [2004] ECR I-2493, paragraphs 47 to 55.

[30] Joined Cases C-159/91 and C-160/91 *Poucet and Pistre*, paragraphs 15 to 18.

[31] Case C-218/00 *Cisal and INAIL*, paragraph 40.

[32] Joined Cases C-159/91 and C-160/91 *Poucet and Pistre*, paragraph 14; Case C-218/00 *Cisal and INAIL*, paragraphs 43 to 48; Joined Cases C-264/01, C-306/01, C-354/01 and C-355/01 *AOK Bundesverband*, paragraphs 51 to 55.

[33] See, in particular, Case C-244/94 *FFSA and Others*, paragraph 19.

[34] Case C-67/96 Albany [1999] ECR I-5751, paragraphs 80-87.

[35] Case C-244/94 *FFSA and Others*, paragraphs 9 and 17 to 20; Case C-67/96 Albany, paragraphs 81 to 85; see also Joined Cases C-115/97 to C-117/97 *Brentjens* [1999] ECR I-6025, paragraphs 81 to 85, Case C-219/97 *Drijvende Bokken* [1999] ECR I-6121, paragraphs 71 to 75, and Joined Cases C-180/98 to C-184/98 *Pavlov and Others*, paragraphs 114 and 115.

[36] Joined Cases C-115/97 to C-117/97 *Brentjens*.

[37] Joined Cases C-180/98 to C-184/98 *Pavlov and Others*.

[38] Case C-350/07 *Kattner Stahlbau* [2009] ECR I-1513.

[39] Based on the case-law of the European Courts, a prominent example is the Spanish National Health System (see Case T-319/99 *FENIN* [2003] ECR II-357).

[40] Depending on the overall characteristics of the system, charges which only cover a small fraction of the true cost of the service may not affect its classification as non-economic.

[41] Case T-319/99 *FENIN* [2003] ECR II-357, paragraph 39.

[42] Case T-319/99 *FENIN*, paragraph 40.

[43] See, for example, Case C-244/94 *FFSA*, Case C-67/96 Albany, Joined Cases C-115/97, C-116/97 and C-117/97 *Brentjens*, and Case C-219/97 *Drijvende Bokken*.

[44] See Joined Cases C-180 to C-184/98 *Pavlov and Others*, paragraphs 75 and 77.

[45] See, among others, Case C-318/05 *Commission v Germany* [2007] ECR I-6957, paragraph 68. See also Decision of the Commission of 25 April 2001, N 118/00 Subvention publiques aux clubs sportifs professionnels and decision of the EFTA Surveillance Authority in Case 68123 Norway Nasjonal digital laeringsarena, 12.10.2011, p. 9.

[46] Judgment of the EFTA Court of 21 February 2008 in Case E-5/07.

[47] Case 263/86 *Humbel* [1988] ECR-5365.

[48] Case C-318/05 *Commission v Germany* [2007] ECR I-6957; Case C-76/05 *Schwartz* [2007] ECR-6849.

[49] Judgment of the EFTA Court of 21 February 2008 in Case E-5/07.

[50] Case C-281/06 *Jundt* [2007] ECR I-12231.

[51] Case 109/92 *Wirth* [1993] ECR I-6447.

[52] See Community Framework for State aid for research and development and innovation, OJ C323, 30.12.2006, p 1.

[53] According to footnote 25 of the Community Framework for State aid for research and development and innovation, 'internal nature' means a situation where the management of the knowledge of the research organisation is conducted

either by a department or a subsidiary of the research organisation or jointly with other research organisations. Contracting the provision of specific services to third parties by way of open tenders does not jeopardise the internal nature of such activities.

54 See paragraphs 3.1.1 and 3.1.2 of the Community Framework for State aid for research and development and innovation.

55 Joined Cases C-52/97 to C-54/97 *Viscido and Others* [1998] ECR I-2629, paragraph 13, and Case C-53/00 *Ferring* [2001] ECR I-9067, paragraph 16. See also Case C-379/98, *PreussenElektra v Schleswag* [2001] ECR I-2099.

56 [2002] ECR I-4397.

57 Case C-462/99 *Connect Austria Gesellschaft für Telekommunikation GmbH v Telekom-Control-Kommission, and Mobilkom Austria AG* [2003] ECR I-05197, paragraphs 92 and 93; Case T-475/04 *Bouygues and Bouygues Télécom SA v Commission* [2007] ECR II-02097, paragraphs 101, 104, 105 and 111.

58 Case 173/73 Italy v Commission [1974] ECR 709, paragraph 16. See also Case 78/79 *Steinike* [1977] ECR 595, paragraph 21, Case C206/06, *Essent Netwerk* [2008] 5497, paragraphs 47, 57 and 96.

59 *Compagnie Commerciale de l'Ouest and others v Receveur Principal des Douanes de La Pallice Port* [1992] ECR I-1847, paragraph 35. See also Joined Cases C-34/01 to C-38/01 *Enirisorse SpA v Ministero delle Finanze* [2003] ECR I-14243, paragraph 26.

60 Joined Cases T-298/97, T-312/97, T-313/97, T-315/97, T-600/97 to T-607/97, T-1/98, T-3/98 to T-6/98 and T-23/98, *Mauro Alzetta and others v Commission* [2000] ECR II-2319, paragraphs 143-147.

61 See, in particular, Case C-280/00 *Altmark Trans GmbH and Regierungspräsidium Magdeburg v Nahverkehrsgesellschaft Altmark GmbH* [2003] ECR I-7747.

62 Case C-280/00 *Altmark Trans GmbH and Regierungspräsidium Magdeburg v Nahverkehrsgesellschaft Altmark GmbH*, paragraph 81.

63 Commission Decision in Case N 258/00 — Germany — Leisure Pool Dorsten, OJ C172, 16.6.2001, p 16.

64 Commission Decision in Case N 543/01 — Ireland — Capital allowances for hospitals, OJ C154, 28.6.2002, p 4.

65 Commission Decision in Case N 630/03 — Italy — Local museums — Sardinia, OJ C275, 8.12.2005, p 3.

66 Commission Decision in Case N 257/07 — Spain — Grants for theatrical productions in the Basque Country, OJ C173, 26.7.2007, p 2.

67 Commission Regulation (EC) No 1998/2006 of 15 December 2006 on the application of Articles 87 and 88 of the EC Treaty to *de minimis* aid, OJ L379, 28.12.2006, p 5.

68 See Article 2(2) of Regulation (EC) No 1998/2006 for transport; Commission Regulation (EC) No 875/2007 of 24 July 2007 on the application of Articles 87 and 88 of the Treaty to *de minimis* aid in the fisheries sector and amending Regulation (EC) No 1860/2004 (OJ L193, 25.7.2007, p 6); and Commission Regulation (EC) No 1535/2007 of 20 December 2007 on the application of Articles 87 and 88 of the EC Treaty to *de minimis* aid in the sector of agricultural production (OJ L337, 21.12.2007, p 35).

3. CONDITIONS UNDER WHICH PUBLIC SERVICE COMPENSATION DOES NOT CONSTITUTE STATE AID

3.1. THE CRITERIA ESTABLISHED BY THE COURT OF JUSTICE

[5.645]

42. The Court of Justice, in its Altmark judgment,[69] provided further clarification regarding the conditions under which public service compensation does not constitute State aid owing to the absence of any advantage.

43. According to the Court of Justice,

'Where a State measure must be regarded as compensation for the services provided by the recipient undertakings in order to discharge public service obligations, so that those undertakings do not enjoy a real financial advantage and the measure thus does not have the effect of putting them in a more favourable competitive position than the undertakings competing with them, such a measure is not caught by Article (107(1) of the Treaty). However, for such compensation to escape qualification as State aid in a particular case, a number of conditions must be satisfied.

— . . . First, the recipient undertaking must actually have public service obligations to discharge, and the obligations must be clearly defined. . . .

— . . . Second, the parameters on the basis of which the compensation is calculated must be established in advance in an objective and transparent manner, to avoid it conferring an economic advantage which may favour the recipient undertaking over competing undertakings. . . . Payment by a Member State of compensation for the loss incurred by an undertaking without the parameters of such compensation having been established beforehand, where it turns out after the event that the operation of certain services in connection with the discharge of public service obligations was not economically viable, therefore constitutes a financial measure which falls within the concept of State aid within the meaning of Article (107(1) of the Treaty).

— . . . Third, the compensation cannot exceed what is necessary to cover all or part of the costs incurred in the discharge of public service obligations, taking into account the relevant receipts and a reasonable profit . . .

— . . . Fourth, where the undertaking which is to discharge public service obligations, in a specific case, is not chosen pursuant to a public procurement procedure which would allow for the selection of the tenderer capable of providing those services at the least cost to the community, the level of compensation needed must be determined on the basis of an analysis of the costs which a typical undertaking, well run and adequately provided with means of transport so as to be able to meet the necessary public service requirements, would have incurred in discharging those obligations, taking into account the relevant receipts and a reasonable profit for discharging the obligations'.[70]

44. Sections 3.2 to 3.6 will address the different requirements established in the *Altmark* case-law, namely the concept of a service of general economic interest for the purposes of Article 106 of the Treaty,[71] the need for an entrustment act,[72] the obligation to define the parameters of compensation,[73] the principles concerning the avoidance of overcompensation[74] and the principles concerning the selection of the provider.[75]

3.2. EXISTENCE OF A SERVICE OF GENERAL ECONOMIC INTEREST

45. The concept of service of general economic interest is an evolving notion that depends, among other things, on the needs of citizens, technological and market developments and social and political preferences in the Member State concerned. The Court of Justice has established that SGEIs are services that exhibit special characteristics as compared with those of other economic activities.[76]

46. In the absence of specific Union rules defining the scope for the existence of an SGEI, Member States have a wide margin of discretion in defining a given service as an SGEI and in granting compensation to the service provider. The Commission's competence in this respect is limited to checking whether the Member State has made a manifest error when defining the service as an SGEI[77] and to assessing any State aid involved in the compensation. Where specific Union rules exist, the Member States' discretion is further bound by those rules, without prejudice to the Commission's duty to carry out an assessment of whether the SGEI has been correctly defined for the purpose of State aid control.

47. The first Altmark criterion requires the definition of an SGEI task. This requirement coincides with that of Article 106(2) of the Treaty.[78] It transpires from Article 106(2) of the Treaty that undertakings entrusted with the operation of SGEIs are undertakings entrusted with 'a particular task'.[79] Generally speaking, the entrustment of a 'particular public service task' implies the supply of services which, if it were considering its own commercial interest, an undertaking would not assume or would not assume to the same extent or under the same conditions.[80] Applying a general interest criterion, Member States or the Union may attach specific obligations to such services.

48. The Commission thus considers that it would not be appropriate to attach specific public service obligations to an activity which is already provided or can be provided satisfactorily and under conditions, such as price, objective quality characteristics, continuity and access to the service, consistent with the public interest, as defined by the State, by undertakings operating under normal market conditions.[81] As for the question of whether a service can be provided by the market, the Commission's assessment is limited to checking whether the Member State has made a manifest error.

49. An important example of this principle is the broadband sector, for which the Commission has already given clear indications as to the types of activities that can be regarded as SGEIs. Most importantly, the Commission considers that in areas where private investors have already invested in broadband network infrastructure (or are in the process of expanding further their network infrastructure) and are already providing competitive broadband services with adequate coverage, setting up parallel broadband infrastructure should not be considered as an SGEI. In contrast, where investors are not in a position to provide adequate broadband coverage, SGEI compensation may be granted under certain conditions.[82]

50. The Commission also considers that the services to be classified as SGEIs must be addressed to citizens or be in the interest of society as a whole.

3.3. ENTRUSTMENT ACT

51. For Article 106(2) of the Treaty to apply, the operation of an SGEI must be entrusted to one or more undertakings. The undertakings in question must therefore have been entrusted with a special task by the State.[83] Also the first Altmark criterion requires that the undertaking has a public service obligation to discharge. Accordingly, in order to comply with the Altmark case-law, a public service assignment is necessary that defines the obligations of the undertakings in question and of the authority.

52. The public service task must be assigned by way of an act that, depending on the legislation in Member States, may take the form of a legislative or regulatory instrument or a contract. It may also be laid down in several acts. Based on the approach taken by the Commission in such cases, the act or series of acts must at least specify:

(a) the content and duration of the public service obligations;
(b) the undertaking and, where applicable, the territory concerned;
(c) the nature of any exclusive or special rights assigned to the undertaking by the authority in question;
(d) the parameters for calculating, controlling and reviewing the compensation; and
(e) the arrangements for avoiding and recovering any overcompensation.

53. The involvement of the service provider in the process by which it is entrusted with a public service task does not mean that that task does not derive from an act of public authority, even if the entrustment is issued at the request of the service provider.[84] In some Member States, it is not uncommon for authorities to finance services which were developed and proposed by the provider itself. However, the authority has to decide whether it approves the provider's proposal before it may grant any compensation. It is irrelevant whether the necessary elements of the entrustment act are inserted directly into the decision to accept the provider's proposal or whether a separate legal act, for example, a contract with the provider, is put in place.

3.4. PARAMETERS OF COMPENSATION

54. The parameters that serve as the basis for calculating compensation must be established in advance in an objective and transparent manner in order to ensure that they do not confer an economic advantage that could favour the recipient undertaking over competing undertakings.

55. The need to establish the compensation parameters in advance does not mean that the compensation has to be calculated on the basis of a specific formula (for example, a certain price per day, per meal, per passenger or per number of users). What matters is only that it is clear from the outset how the compensation is to be determined.

56. Where the authority decides to compensate all cost items of the provider, it must determine at the outset how those costs will be determined and calculated. Only the costs directly associated with the provision of the SGEI can be taken into account in that context. All the revenue accruing to the undertaking from the provision of the SGEI must be deducted.

57. Where the undertaking is offered a reasonable profit as part of its compensation, the entrustment act must also establish the criteria for calculating that profit.

58. Where a review of the amount of compensation during the entrustment period is provided for, the entrustment act must specify the arrangements for the review and any impact it may have on the total amount of compensation.

59. If the SGEI is assigned under a tendering procedure, the method for calculating the compensation must be included in the information provided to all the undertakings wishing to take part in the procedure.

3.5. AVOIDANCE OF OVERCOMPENSATION

60. According to the third Altmark criterion, the compensation must not exceed what is necessary to cover all or part of the costs incurred in the discharge of public service obligations, taking into account the relevant receipts and a reasonable profit. Therefore any mechanism concerning the selection of the service provider must be decided in such a way that the level of compensation is determined on the basis of these elements.

61. Reasonable profit should be taken to mean the rate of return on capital[85] that would be required by a typical company considering whether or not to provide the service of general economic interest for the whole duration of the period of entrustment, taking into account the level of risk. The level of risk depends on the sector concerned, the type of service and the characteristics of the compensation mechanism. The rate should be determined where possible by reference to the rate of return on capital that is achieved on similar types of public service contracts under competitive conditions (for example, contracts awarded under a tender). In sectors where there is no undertaking comparable to the undertaking entrusted with the operation of the service of general economic interest, reference can be made to comparable undertakings situated in other Member States, or if necessary, in other sectors, provided that the particular characteristics of each sector are taken into account. In determining what constitutes a reasonable profit, the Member States may introduce incentive criteria relating, in particular, to the quality of service provided and gains in productive efficiency. Efficiency gains cannot be achieved at the expense of the quality of the service provided.

3.6. SELECTION OF PROVIDER

62. In accordance with the fourth Altmark criterion, the compensation offered must either be the result of a public procurement procedure which allows for selection of the tenderer capable of providing those services at the least cost to the community, or the result of a benchmarking exercise with a typical undertaking, well run and adequately provided with the necessary means.

3.6.1. AMOUNT OF COMPENSATION WHERE THE SGEI IS ASSIGNED UNDER AN APPROPRIATE TENDERING PROCEDURE

63. The simplest way for public authorities to meet the fourth Altmark criterion is to conduct an open, transparent and non-discriminatory public procurement procedure in line with Directive 2004/17/EC of the European Parliament and of the Council of 31 March 2004 coordinating the procurement procedures of entities operating in the water, energy, transport and postal services sectors[86] and Directive 2004/18/EC of the European Parliament and of the Council of 31 March 2004 on the coordination of procedures for the award of public works contracts, public supply contracts and public service contracts,[87] as specified below.[88] As indicated in paragraph 5, the conduct of such a public procurement procedure is often a mandatory requirement under existing Union rules.

64. Also in cases where it is not a legal requirement, an open, transparent and non-discriminatory public procurement procedure is an appropriate method to compare different potential offers and set the compensation so as to exclude the presence of aid.

65. Based on the case law of the Court of Justice, a public procurement procedure only excludes the existence of State aid where it allows for the selection of the tenderer capable of providing the service at 'the least cost to the community'.

66. Concerning the characteristics of the tender, an open[89] procedure in line with the requirement of the public procurement rules is certainly acceptable, but also a restricted[90] procedure can satisfy the fourth Altmark criterion, unless interested operators are prevented to tender without valid reasons. On the other hand, a competitive dialogue[91] or a negotiated procedure with prior publication[92] confer a wide discretion upon the adjudicating authority and may restrict the participation of interested operators. Therefore, they can only be deemed sufficient to satisfy the fourth Altmark criterion in exceptional cases. The negotiated procedure without publication of a contract notice[93] cannot ensure that the procedure leads to the selection of the tenderer capable of providing those services at the least cost to the community.

67. As to the award criteria, the 'lowest price'[94] obviously satisfies the fourth Altmark criterion. Also the 'most economically advantageous tender'[95] is deemed sufficient, Provided that the award criteria, including environmental[96] or social ones, are closely related to the subject-matter of the service provided and allow for the most economically advantageous offer to match the value of the market.[97] Where such circumstances occur, a claw-back mechanism may be appropriate to minimise the risk of overcompensation ex ante. The awarding authority is not prevented from setting qualitative standards to be met by all economic operators or from taking qualitative aspects related to the different proposals into account in its award decision.

68. Finally, there can be circumstances where a procurement procedure cannot allow for the least cost to the community as it does not give rise to a sufficient open and genuine competition. This could be the case, for example, due to the particularities of the service in question, existing intellectual property rights or necessary infrastructure owned by a particular service provider. Similarly, in the case of procedures where only one bid is submitted, the tender cannot be deemed sufficient to ensure that the procedure leads to the least cost for the community.

3.6.2. AMOUNT OF COMPENSATION WHERE THE SGEI IS NOT ASSIGNED UNDER A TENDERING PROCEDURE

69. Where a generally accepted market remuneration exists for a given service, that market remuneration provides the best benchmark for the compensation in the absence of a tender.[98]

70. Where no such market remuneration exists, the amount of compensation must be determined on the basis of an analysis of the costs that a typical undertaking, well run and adequately provided with material means so as to be able to meet the necessary public service requirements, would have incurred in discharging those obligations, taking into account the relevant receipts and a reasonable profit for discharging those obligations. The aim is to ensure that the high costs of an inefficient undertaking are not taken as the benchmark.

71. As regards the concept of 'well run undertaking' and in the absence of any official definition, the Member States should apply objective criteria that are economically recognised as being representative of satisfactory management. The Commission considers that simply generating a profit is not a sufficient criterion for deeming an undertaking to be 'well run'. Account should also be taken of the fact that the financial results of undertakings, particularly in the sectors most often concerned by SGEIs, may be strongly influenced by their market power or by sectoral rules.

72. The Commission takes the view that the concept of 'well run undertaking' entails compliance with the national, Union or international accounting standards in force. The Member States may base their analysis, among other things, on analytical ratios representative of productivity (such as turnover to capital employed, total cost to turnover, turnover per employee, value added per employee or staff costs to value added). Member States can also use analytical ratios relating to the quality of supply as compared with user expectations. An undertaking entrusted with the operation of an SGEI that does not meet the qualitative criteria laid down by the Member State concerned does not constitute a well run undertaking even if its costs are low.

73. Undertakings with such analytical ratios representative of efficient management may be regarded as representative typical undertakings. However, the analysis and comparison of the cost structures must take into account the size of the undertaking in question and the fact that in certain sectors undertakings with very different cost structures may exist side by side.

74. The reference to the costs of a 'typical' undertaking in the sector under consideration implies that there are a sufficient number of undertakings whose costs may be taken into account. Those undertakings may be located in the same Member State or in other Member States. However, the Commission takes the view that reference cannot be made to the costs of an undertaking that enjoys a monopoly position or receives public service compensation granted on conditions that do not comply with Union law, as in both cases the cost level may be higher than normal. The costs to be taken into consideration are all the costs relating to the SGEI, that is to say, the direct costs necessary to discharge the SGEI and an appropriate contribution to the indirect costs common to both the SGEI and other activities.

75. If the Member State can show that the cost structure of the undertaking entrusted with the operation of the SGEI corresponds to the average cost structure of efficient and comparable undertakings in the sector under consideration, the amount of compensation that will allow the undertaking to cover its costs, including a reasonable profit, is deemed to comply with the fourth Altmark criterion.

76. The expression 'undertaking adequately provided with material means' should be taken to mean an undertaking which has the resources necessary for it to discharge immediately the public service obligations incumbent on the undertaking to be entrusted with the operation of the SGEI.

77. 'Reasonable profit' should be taken to mean the rate of return on capital[99] that would be required by a typical company considering whether or not to provide the service of general economic interest for the whole duration of the period of entrustment, taking into account the level of risk, as provided in section 3.5.

NOTES

69 Case C-280/00 *Altmark Trans GmbH and Regierungspräsidium Magdeburg v Nahverkehrsgesellschaft Altmark GmbH.*

70 Case C-280/00 *Altmark Trans GmbH and Regierungspräsidium Magdeburg v Nahverkehrsgesellschaft Altmark GmbH*, paragraphs 87 to 93.

71 See section 3.2.

72 See section 3.3.

73 See section 3.4.

74 See section 3.5.

75 See section 3.6.

76 Cases C-179/90 *Merci convenzionali porto di Genova* [1991] ECR I-5889, paragraph 27; Case C-242/95 *GT-Link A/S* [1997] ECR I-4449, paragraph 53; and Case C-266/96, *Corsica Ferries France SA* [1998] ECR I-3949, paragraph 45.

77 Case T-289/03 *BUPA and Others v Commission* [2008] ECR II-81, paragraphs 166-169 and 172; Case T-17/02 *Fred Olsen* [2005] ECR II-2031, paragraph 216.

78 Case T-289/03 *British United Provident Association Ltd (BUPA) v Commission* [2008], ECR II-81, paragraphs. 171 and 224.

79 See, in particular, Case C-127/73 *BRT v SABAM* [1974] ECR-313.

80 See, in particular, Article 2 of Regulation (EC) No 1370/2007 of the European Parliament and of the Council of 23 October 2007 on public passenger transport services by rail and by road and repealing Council Regulations (EEC) Nos 1191/69 and 1107/70 (OJ L315, 3.12.2007, p 1).

81 Case C-205/99 *Analir* [2001] ECR I-1271, paragraph 71.

82 For more detailed provisions see paragraphs 24 to 30 of the Communication from the Commission — Community Guidelines for the application of State aid rules in relation to rapid deployment of broadband networks (OJ C235, 30.9.2009, p 7).

83 See, in particular, Case C-127/73 *BRT v SABAM* [1974] ECR-313.

84 Case T-17/02 *Fred Olsen*, paragraph 188.

85 The rate of return on capital means the Internal Rate of Return (IRR) that the undertaking makes on its invested capital over the lifetime of the project, that is to say the IRR over the cash flows of the contract.

86 OJ L134, 30.4.2004, p 114.

87 OJ L134, 30.4.2004, p 1.

88 The Commission intends to amend this Communication once new Union rules on public procurement have been adopted

in order to clarify the relevance for State aid purposes of the use of the procedures foreseen in those new rules.

89 Article 1(11)(a) of Directive 2004/18EC, Article 1(9)(a) of Directive 2004/17/EC.

90 Article 1(11)(b) of Directive 2004/18/EC, Article 1(9)(b) of Directive 2004/17/EC.

91 Article 29 of Directive 2004/18/EC.

92 Article 30 of Directive 2004/18/EC, Article 1(9)(a) of Directive 2004/17/EC.

93 Article 31 of Directive 2004/18/EC. See also Article 40(3) of Directive 2004/17/EC.

94 Article 53(1)(b) of Directive 2004/18/EC, Article 55 (1)(b) of Directive 2004/17/EC.

95 Article 53(1)(a) of Directive 2004/18/EC, Article 55(1)(a) of Directive 2004/17/EC; Case 31/87 *Beentjes* [1988] ECR 4635 and Case C-225/98 Commission v France [2000] ECR I-7445; Case C-19/00 *SIAC Construction* [2001] ECR I-7725.

96 See for example a new edition of 'Buying Green! A Handbook on Green public procurement', available at: https://ec.europa.eu/environment/gpp/buying_handbook_en.htm

97 In other words, the criteria should be defined in such a way as to allow for an effective competition that minimises the advantage for the successful bidder.

98 See for example Commission Decision in Case C 49/06 — Italy — State aid scheme implemented by Italy to remunerate *Poste Italiane* for distributing postal savings certificates (OJ L189, 21.7.2009, p 3).

99 The rate of return on capital means the Internal Rate of Return (IRR) that the undertaking makes on its invested capital over the lifetime of the project, that is to say the IRR over the cash flows of the contract.

COMMISSION DECISION

(2012/21/EU)

of 20 December 2011

on the application of Article 106(2) of the Treaty on the Functioning of the European Union to State aid in the form of public service compensation granted to certain undertakings entrusted with the operation of services of general economic interest

(notified under document C(2011) 9380)

(Text with EEA relevance)

[5.646]

NOTES

Date of publication in OJ: OJ L7, 11.1.2012, p 3.

Repeal of this Decision in relation to the UK: this Decision is repealed, in relation to the UK, by the State Aid (Revocations and Amendments) (EU Exit) Regulations 2020, SI 2020/1470, reg 6, as from IP completion day (as defined in the European Union (Withdrawal Agreement) Act 2020, s 39) (for transitional provisions and savings in relation to claims before a court or tribunal relating to State aid infringement before IP completion day, see Sch 3 to those Regulations at **[7.89]**).

THE EUROPEAN COMMISSION,

Having regard to the Treaty on the Functioning of the European Union, and in particular Article 106(3) thereof,

Whereas:

(1) Article 14 of the Treaty requires the Union, without prejudice to Articles 93, 106 and 107 of the Treaty, to use its powers in such a way as to make sure that services of general economic interest operate on the basis of principles and conditions which enable them to fulfil their missions.

(2) For certain services of general economic interest to operate on the basis of principles and under conditions which enable them to fulfil their missions, financial support from the State may prove necessary to cover some or all of the specific costs resulting from the public service obligations. In accordance with Article 345 of the Treaty, as interpreted by the Court of Justice of the European Union, it is irrelevant whether such services of general economic interest are operated by public or private undertakings.

(3) Article 106(2) of the Treaty states in this respect that undertakings entrusted with the operation of services of general economic interest or having the character of a revenue-producing monopoly are subject to the rules contained in the Treaty, in particular to the rules on competition, in so far as the application of these rules does not obstruct, in law or in fact, the performance of the tasks entrusted. This should however not affect the development of trade to such an extent as would be contrary to the interests of the Union.

(4) In its judgment in Altmark,[1] the Court of Justice held that public service compensation does not constitute State aid within the meaning of Article 107 of the Treaty provided that four cumulative criteria are met. First, the recipient undertaking must actually have public service obligations to discharge, and the obligations must be clearly defined. Second, the parameters on the basis of which the compensation is calculated must be established in advance in an objective and transparent manner. Third, the compensation must not exceed what is necessary to cover all or part of the costs incurred in the discharge of the public service obligations, taking into account the relevant receipts and a reasonable profit. Finally, where the undertaking that is to discharge public service obligations, in a specific case, is not chosen pursuant to a public procurement procedure which would allow for the selection of the tenderer capable of providing those services at the least cost to the community, the level of compensation needed must be determined on the basis of an analysis of the costs that a typical undertaking, well-run and adequately provided with the relevant means, would have incurred.

(5) Where those criteria are not fulfilled and the general conditions for the applicability of Article 107(1) of the

Treaty are met, public service compensation constitutes State aid and is subject to Articles 93, 106, 107 and 108 of the Treaty.

(6) In addition to this Decision, three instruments are relevant for the application of the State aid rules to compensation granted for the provision of services of general economic interest:

(a) a new Communication on the application of the European Union State aid rules to compensation granted for the provision of services of general economic interest[2] clarifies the application of Article 107 of the Treaty and the criteria set by the Altmark ruling to such compensation;

(b) a new Regulation, which the Commission intends to adopt, on the application of Articles 107 and 108 of the Treaty to de minimis aid for the provision of SGEI lays down certain conditions – including the amount of the compensation – under which public service compensations shall be deemed not to meet all the criteria of Article 107(1);

(c) a revised framework for State aid in the form of public service compensation[3] specifies how the Commission will analyse cases that are not covered by this Decision and therefore have to be notified to the Commission.

(7) Commission Decision 2005/842/EC of 28 November 2005 on the application of Article 86(2) of the EC Treaty to State aid in the form of public service compensation granted to certain undertakings entrusted with the operation of services of general economic interest[4] specifies the meaning and extent of the exception pursuant to Article 106(2) of the Treaty and sets out rules intended to enable effective monitoring of the fulfilment of the criteria set out in that provision. This Decision replaces Decision 2005/842/EC and lays down the conditions under which State aid in the form of compensation for a service of general economic interest is not subject to the prior notification requirement of Article 108(3) of the Treaty as it can be deemed compatible with Article 106(2) of the Treaty.

(8) Such aid may be deemed compatible only if it is granted in order to ensure the provision of services of general economic interest as referred to in Article 106(2) of the Treaty. It is clear from the case-law that, in the absence of sectoral Union rules governing the matter, Member States have a wide margin of discretion in the definition of services that could be classified as being services of general economic interest. Thus the Commission's task is to ensure that there is no manifest error as regards the definition of services of general economic interest.

(9) Provided a number of conditions are met, limited amounts of compensation granted to undertakings entrusted with the provision of services of general economic interest do not affect the development of trade and competition to such an extent as would be contrary to the interests of the Union. An individual State aid notification should therefore not be required for compensation below a specified annual amount of compensation provided the requirements of this Decision are met.

(10) Given the development of intra-Union trade in the provision of services of general economic interest, demonstrated for instance by the strong development of multi-national providers in a number of sectors which are of great importance for the development of the internal market, it is appropriate to set a lower limit for the amount of compensation which can be exempted from the notification requirement in accordance with this Decision than what was set by Decision 2005/842/EC, while allowing for that amount to be computed as an annual average over the entrustment period.

(11) Hospitals and undertakings in charge of social services, which are entrusted with tasks of general economic interest, have specific characteristics that need to be taken into consideration. In particular, account should be taken of the fact that, in the present economic conditions and at the current stage of development of the internal market, social services may require an amount of aid beyond the threshold in this Decision to compensate for the public service costs. A larger amount of compensation for social services does thus not necessarily produce a greater risk of distortions of competition. Accordingly, undertakings in charge of social services, including the provision of social housing for disadvantaged citizens or socially less advantaged groups, who due to solvency constraints are unable to obtain housing at market conditions, should also benefit from the exemption from notification provided for in this Decision, even if the amount of compensation they receive exceeds the general compensation threshold laid down in this Decision. The same should apply to hospitals providing medical care, including, where applicable, emergency services and ancillary services directly related to their main activities, in particular in the field of research. In order to benefit from the exemption from notification, social services should be clearly identified services, meeting social needs as regards health and long-term care, childcare, access to and reintegration into the labour market, social housing and the care and social inclusion of vulnerable groups.

(12) The extent to which a particular compensation measure affects trade and competition depends not only on the average amount of compensation received per year and the sector concerned, but also on the overall duration of the period of entrustment. Unless a longer period is justified due to the need for a significant investment, for example in the area of social housing, the application of this Decision should therefore be limited to periods of entrustment not exceeding 10 years.

(13) In order for Article 106(2) of the Treaty to apply, the undertaking in question must have been specifically entrusted by the Member State with the operation of a particular service of general economic interest.

(14) In order to ensure that the criteria set out in Article 106(2) of the Treaty are met, it is necessary to lay down more precise conditions that must be fulfilled in respect of the entrustment of the operation of services of general economic interest. The amount of compensation can be properly calculated and checked only if the public service obligations incumbent on the undertakings and any obligations incumbent on the State are clearly set out in one or more acts of the competent public authorities in the Member State concerned. The form of the instrument may vary from one Member State to another but it should specify, at least, the undertakings concerned, the precise content and duration of and, where appropriate, the territory concerned by the public service obligations imposed, the granting of any exclusive or special rights, and describe the compensation mechanism and the parameters for determining the compensation and avoiding and recovering any possible overcompensation. In order to ensure transparency in relation to the application of this Decision, the act of entrustment should also include a reference to it.

(15) In order to avoid unjustified distortions of competition, the compensation should not exceed what is necessary to cover the net costs incurred by the undertaking in operating the service, including a reasonable profit.

(16) Compensation in excess of what is necessary to cover the net costs incurred by the undertaking concerned

in operating the service is not necessary for the operation of the service of general economic interest, and consequently constitutes incompatible State aid that should be repaid to the State. Compensation granted for the operation of a service of general economic interest but actually used by the undertaking concerned to operate on another market for purposes other than those specified in the act of entrustment is not necessary for the operation of the service of general economic interest, and may consequently also constitute incompatible State aid that should be repaid.

(17) The net cost to be taken into account should be calculated as the difference between the cost incurred in operating the service of general economic interest and the revenue earned from the service of general economic interest or, alternatively, as the difference between the net cost of operating with the public service obligation and the net cost or profit operating without the public service obligation. In particular, if the public service obligation leads to a reduction of the revenue, for instance due to regulated tariffs, but does not affect the costs, it should be possible to determine the net cost incurred in discharging the public service obligation on the basis of the foregone revenue. In order to avoid unjustified distortions of competition, all revenues earned from the service of general economic interest, that is to say, any revenues that the provider would not have obtained had it not been entrusted with the obligation should be taken into account for the purposes of calculating the amount of compensation. If the undertaking in question holds special or exclusive rights linked to activities, other than the service of general economic interest for which the aid is granted, that generate profits in excess of the reasonable profit, or benefits from other advantages granted by the State, these should be included in its revenue, irrespective of their classification for the purposes of Article 107 of the Treaty.

(18) Reasonable profit should be determined as a rate of return on capital that takes into account the degree of risk, or absence of risk, incurred. The rate of return on capital should be defined as the internal rate of return that the undertaking obtains on its invested capital over the duration of the period of entrustment.

(19) Profit not exceeding the relevant swap rate plus 100 basis points should not be regarded as unreasonable. In this context, the relevant swap rate is viewed as an appropriate rate of return for a risk-free investment. The premium of 100 basis points serves, inter alia, to compensate for liquidity risk related to the provision of capital which is committed for the operation of the service during the period of entrustment.

(20) In cases where the undertaking entrusted with a service of general economic interest does not bear a substantial degree of commercial risk, for instance because the costs it incurs in the operation of the service are compensated in full, profits exceeding the benchmark of the relevant swap rate plus 100 basis points should not be viewed as reasonable.

(21) Where, by reason of specific circumstances, it is not appropriate to use the rate of return on capital, Member States should be able to rely on other profit level indicators to determine what the reasonable profit should be, such as the average return on equity, return on capital employed, return on assets or return on sales.

(22) In determining what constitutes a reasonable profit, the Member States should be able to introduce incentive criteria relating, in particular, to the quality of service provided and gains in productive efficiency. Efficiency gains should not reduce the quality of the service provided. For instance, Member States should be able to define productive efficiency targets in the entrustment act whereby the level of compensation is made dependent upon the extent to which the targets have been met. The entrustment act may provide that if the undertaking does not meet the objectives, the compensation is to be reduced by applying a calculation method specified in the entrustment act, whereas if the undertaking exceeds the objectives, the compensation may be increased by applying a method specified in the entrustment act. Any rewards linked to productive efficiency gains should be set at a level such as to allow balanced sharing of those gains between the undertaking and the Member State and/or the users.

(23) Article 93 of the Treaty constitutes a lex specialis with regard to Article 106(2) of the Treaty. It lays down the rules applicable to public service compensation in the land transport sector. Article 93 has been interpreted by Regulation (EC) No 1370/2007 of the European Parliament and of the Council of 23 October 2007 on public passenger transport services by rail and by road and repealing Council Regulations (EEC) Nos 1191/69 and 1107/70,[5] which lays down the rules applicable to the compensation of public service obligations in public passenger traffic. Its application to inland waterway passenger traffic is at the discretion of the Member States. Regulation (EC) No 1370/2007 exempts from notification pursuant to Article 108(3) of the Treaty all compensation in the land transport sector that fulfils the conditions of that Regulation. In accordance with the judgment in Altmark, compensation in the land transport sector that does not comply with the provisions of Article 93 of the Treaty cannot be declared compatible with the Treaty on the basis of Article 106(2) of the Treaty, or on the basis of any other Treaty provision. Consequently, this Decision does not apply to the land transport sector.

(24) Unlike land transport, the maritime and air transport sectors are subject to Article 106(2) of the Treaty. Certain rules applicable to public service compensation in the air and maritime transport sectors are to be found in Regulation (EC) No 1008/2008 of the European Parliament and of the Council of 24 September 2008 on common rules for the operation of air services in the Community[6] and in Council Regulation (EEC) No 3577/92 of 7 December 1992 applying the principle of freedom to provide services to maritime transport within Member States (maritime cabotage).[7] However, unlike Regulation (EC) No 1370/2007, those Regulations do not refer to the compatibility of the possible State aid elements, nor do they provide for an exemption from the obligation to notify pursuant to Article 108(3) of the Treaty. This Decision should therefore apply to public service compensation in the air and maritime transport sectors provided that, in addition to fulfilling the conditions set out in this Decision, such compensation also complies with the sectoral rules contained in Regulations (EC) No 1008/2008 and (EEC) No 3577/92 where applicable.

(25) In the specific cases of public service compensation for air or maritime links to islands and for airports and ports which constitute services of general economic interest as referred to in Article 106(2) of the Treaty, it is appropriate to provide thresholds based on the average annual number of passengers as this more accurately reflects the economic reality of these activities and their character of services of general economic interest.

(26) Exemption from the requirement of prior notification for certain services of general economic interest does not rule out the possibility for Member States to notify a specific aid project. In the event of such a notification, or if the Commission assesses the compatibility of a specific aid measure following a complaint or ex officio, the Commission will assess whether the conditions of this Decision are met. If that is not the case, the measure will

be assessed in accordance with the principles contained in the Commission Communication on a framework for State aid in the form of public service compensation.

(27) This Decision should apply without prejudice to the provisions of Commission Directive 2006/111/EC of 16 November 2006 on the transparency of financial relations between Member States and public undertakings as well as on financial transparency within certain undertakings.[8]

(28) This Decision should apply without prejudice to the Union provisions in the field of competition, in particular Articles 101 and 102 of the Treaty.

(29) This Decision should apply without prejudice to the Union provisions in the field of public procurement.

(30) This Decision should apply without prejudice to stricter provisions relating to public service obligations that are contained in sectoral Union legislation.

(31) Transitional provisions should be laid down for individual aid that was granted before the entry into force of this Decision. Aid schemes put into effect in accordance with Decision 2005/842/EC before the entry into force of this Decision should continue to be compatible with the internal market and exempt from the notification requirement for a further period of 2 years. Aid put into effect before the entry into force of this Decision that was not awarded in accordance with Decision 2005/842/EC but fulfils the conditions laid down in this Decision should be compatible with the internal market and exempt from the notification requirement.

(32) The Commission intends to carry out a review of this Decision 5 years after its entry into force,

NOTES

Repeal of this Decision in relation to the UK: this Decision is repealed in relation to the UK (as from IP completion day); see the introductory notes to this Decision *ante*.

1 Case C-280/00 *Altmark Trans and Regierungspräsidium Magdeburg v Nahverkehrsgesellschaft Altmark* [2003] ECR I-7747.

2 OJ C8, 11.1.2012, p 4.

3 OJ C8, 11.1.2012, p 15.

4 OJ L312, 29.11.2005, p 67.

5 OJ L315, 3.12.2007, p 1.

6 OJ L293, 31.10.2008, p 3.

7 OJ L364, 12.12.1992, p 7.

8 OJ L318, 17.11.2006, p 17.

HAS ADOPTED THIS DECISION:

[5.647]

Article 1

Subject matter

This Decision sets out the conditions under which State aid in the form of public service compensation granted to certain undertakings entrusted with the operation of services of general economic interest is compatible with the internal market and exempt from the requirement of notification laid down in Article 108(3) of the Treaty.

NOTES

Repeal of this Decision in relation to the UK: this Decision is repealed in relation to the UK (as from IP completion day); see the introductory notes to this Decision *ante*.

[5.648]

Article 2

Scope

1. This Decision applies to State aid in the form of public service compensation, granted to undertakings entrusted with the operation of services of general economic interest as referred to in Article 106(2) of the Treaty, which falls within one of the following categories:

(a) compensation not exceeding an annual amount of EUR 15 million for the provision of services of general economic interest in areas other than transport and transport infrastructure;
where the amount of compensation varies over the duration of the entrustment, the annual amount shall be calculated as average of the annual amounts of compensation expected to be made over the entrustment period;

(b) compensation for the provision of services of general economic interest by hospitals providing medical care, including, where applicable, emergency services; the pursuit of ancillary activities directly related to the main activities, notably in the field of research, does not, however, prevent the application of this paragraph;

(c) compensation for the provision of services of general economic interest meeting social needs as regards health and long term care, childcare, access to and reintegration into the labour market, social housing and the care and social inclusion of vulnerable groups;

(d) compensation for the provision of services of general economic interest as regards air or maritime links to islands on which the average annual traffic during the 2 financial years preceding that in which the service of general economic interest was assigned does not exceed 300,000 passengers;

(e) compensation for the provision of services of general economic interest as regards airports and ports for which the average annual traffic during the 2 financial years preceding that in which the service of general economic interest was assigned does not exceed 200,000 passengers, in the case of airports, and 300,000 passengers, in the case of ports.

2. This Decision only applies where the period for which the undertaking is entrusted with the operation of the service of general economic interest does not exceed 10 years. Where the period of entrustment exceeds 10 years, this Decision only applies to the extent that a significant investment is required from the service provider that needs to be amortised over a longer period in accordance with generally accepted accounting principles.

3. If during the duration of the entrustment the conditions for the application of this Decision cease to be met, the aid shall be notified in accordance with Article 108(3) of the Treaty.

4. In the field of air and maritime transport, this Decision only applies to State aid in the form of public service compensation, granted to undertakings entrusted with the operation of services of general economic interest as referred to in Article 106(2) of the Treaty, which complies with Regulation (EC) No 1008/2008 and, respectively, Regulation (EEC) No 3577/92 where applicable.

5. This Decision does not apply to State aid in the form of public service compensation granted to undertakings in the field of land transport.

NOTES

Repeal of this Decision in relation to the UK: this Decision is repealed in relation to the UK (as from IP completion day); see the introductory notes to this Decision *ante*.

[5.649]
Article 3
Compatibility and exemption from notification

State aid in the form of public service compensation that meets the conditions laid down in this Decision shall be compatible with the internal market and shall be exempt from the prior notification obligation provided for in Article 108(3) of the Treaty provided that it also complies with the requirements flowing from the Treaty or from sectoral Union legislation.

NOTES

Repeal of this Decision in relation to the UK: this Decision is repealed in relation to the UK (as from IP completion day); see the introductory notes to this Decision *ante*.

[5.650]
Article 4
Entrustment

Operation of the service of general economic interest shall be entrusted to the undertaking concerned by way of one or more acts, the form of which may be determined by each Member State. The act or acts shall include, in particular:

- *(a) the content and duration of the public service obligations;*
- *(b) the undertaking and, where applicable, the territory concerned;*
- *(c) the nature of any exclusive or special rights assigned to the undertaking by the granting authority;*
- *(d) a description of the compensation mechanism and the parameters for calculating, controlling and reviewing the compensation;*
- *(e) the arrangements for avoiding and recovering any overcompensation; and*
- *(f) a reference to this Decision.*

NOTES

Repeal of this Decision in relation to the UK: this Decision is repealed in relation to the UK (as from IP completion day); see the introductory notes to this Decision *ante*.

[5.651]
Article 5
Compensation

1. The amount of compensation shall not exceed what is necessary to cover the net cost incurred in discharging the public service obligations, including a reasonable profit.

2. The net cost may be calculated as the difference between costs as defined in paragraph 3 and revenues as defined in paragraph 4. Alternatively, it may be calculated as the difference between the net cost for the undertaking of operating with the public service obligation and the net cost or profit of the same undertaking operating without the public service obligation.

3. The costs to be taken into consideration shall comprise all the costs incurred in operating the service of general economic interest. They shall be calculated on the basis of generally accepted cost accounting principles, as follows:

- *(a) where the activities of the undertaking in question are confined to the service of general economic interest, all its costs may be taken into consideration;*
- *(b) where the undertaking also carries out activities falling outside the scope of the service of general economic interest, only the costs related to the service of general economic interest shall be taken into consideration;*
- *(c) the costs allocated to the service of general economic interest may cover all the direct costs incurred in operating the service of general economic interest and an appropriate contribution to costs common to both the service of general economic interest and other activities;*
- *(d) the costs linked with investments, notably concerning infrastructure, may be taken into account when necessary for the operation of the service of general economic interest.*

4. The revenue to be taken into consideration shall include at least the entire revenue earned from the service of general economic interest, regardless of whether the revenue is classified as State aid within the meaning of Article 107 of the Treaty. If the undertaking in question holds special or exclusive rights linked to activities, other than the service of general economic interest for which the aid is granted, that generate profits in excess of the reasonable profit, or benefits from other advantages granted by the State, these shall be included in its revenue, irrespective of their classification for the purposes of Article 107 of the Treaty. The Member State concerned may decide that the profits accruing from other activities outside the scope of the service of general economic interest in question are to be assigned in whole or in part to the financing of the service of general economic interest.

5. For the purposes of this Decision, 'reasonable profit' means the rate of return on capital that would be required by a typical undertaking considering whether or not to provide the service of general economic interest for the whole period of entrustment, taking into account the level of risk. The 'rate of return on capital' means the internal rate of return that the undertaking makes on its invested capital over the duration of the period of entrustment. The level of risk depends on the sector concerned, the type of service and the characteristics of the compensation.

6. In determining what constitutes a reasonable profit, Member States may introduce incentive criteria relating, in particular, to the quality of service provided and gains in productive efficiency. Efficiency gains shall not reduce the quality of the service provided. Any rewards linked to productive efficiency gains shall be set at a level such as to allow balanced sharing of those gains between the undertaking and the Member State and/or the users.

7. For the purposes of this Decision, a rate of return on capital that does not exceed the relevant swap rate plus a premium of 100 basis points shall be regarded as reasonable in any event. The relevant swap rate shall be the swap rate the maturity and currency of which correspond to the duration and currency of the entrustment act. Where the provision of the service of general economic interest is not connected with a substantial commercial or contractual risk, in particular when the net cost incurred in providing the service of general economic interest is essentially compensated ex post in full, the reasonable profit may not exceed the relevant swap rate plus a premium of 100 basis points.

8. Where, by reasons of specific circumstances, it is not appropriate to use the rate of return on capital, Member States may rely on profit level indicators other than the rate of return on capital to determine what the reasonable profit should be, such as the average return on equity, return on capital employed, return on assets or return on sales. The 'return' means the earnings before interests and taxes in that year. The average return is computed using the discount factor over the life of the contract as specified by the Communication from the Commission on the revision of the method for setting the reference and discount rates.[1] *Whatever indicator is chosen, the Member State shall be able to provide the Commission upon request with evidence that the profit does not exceed what would be required by a typical undertaking considering whether or not to provide the service, for instance by providing references to returns achieved on similar types of contracts awarded under competitive conditions.*

9. Where an undertaking carries out activities falling both inside and outside the scope of the service of general economic interest, the internal accounts shall show separately the costs and receipts associated with the service of general economic interest and those of other services, as well as the parameters for allocating costs and revenues. The costs linked to any activities outside the scope of the service of general economic interest shall cover all the direct costs, an appropriate contribution to the common costs and an adequate return on capital. No compensation shall be granted in respect of those costs.

10. Member States shall require the undertaking concerned to repay any overcompensation received.

NOTES

Repeal of this Decision in relation to the UK: this Decision is repealed in relation to the UK (as from IP completion day); see the introductory notes to this Decision *ante*.

[1] OJ C14, 19.1.2008, p 6.

[5.652]
Article 6
Control of overcompensation

1. Member States shall ensure that the compensation granted for the operation of the service of general economic interest meets the requirements set out in this Decision and in particular that the undertaking does not receive compensation in excess of the amount determined in accordance with Article 5. They shall provide evidence upon request from the Commission. They shall carry out regular checks, or ensure that such checks are carried out, at least every 3 years during the period of entrustment and at the end of that period.

2. Where an undertaking has received compensation in excess of the amount determined in accordance with Article 5, the Member State shall require the undertaking concerned to repay any overcompensation received. The parameters for the calculation of the compensation shall be updated for the future. Where the amount of overcompensation does not exceed 10% of the amount of the average annual compensation, such overcompensation may be carried forward to the next period and deducted from the amount of compensation payable in respect of that period.

NOTES

Repeal of this Decision in relation to the UK: this Decision is repealed in relation to the UK (as from IP completion day); see the introductory notes to this Decision *ante*.

[5.653]
Article 7
Transparency

For compensation above EUR 15 million granted to an undertaking which also has activities outside the scope of the service of general economic interest, the Member State concerned shall publish the following information on the Internet or by other appropriate means:

(a) the entrustment act or a summary which includes the elements listed in Article 4;
(b) the amounts of aid granted to the undertaking on a yearly basis.

NOTES

Repeal of this Decision in relation to the UK: this Decision is repealed in relation to the UK (as from IP completion day); see the introductory notes to this Decision *ante*.

[5.654]
Article 8
Availability of information

The Member States shall keep available, during the period of entrustment and for at least 10 years from the end of the period of entrustment, all the information necessary to determine whether the compensation granted is compatible with this Decision.

On written request by the Commission, Member States shall provide the Commission with all the information that the latter considers necessary to determine whether the compensation measures in force are compatible with this Decision.

NOTES

Repeal of this Decision in relation to the UK: this Decision is repealed in relation to the UK (as from IP completion day); see the introductory notes to this Decision *ante*.

[5.655]
Article 9
Reports

Each Member State shall submit a report on the implementation of this Decision to the Commission every 2 years. The reports shall provide a detailed overview of the application of this Decision for the different categories of services referred to in Article 2(1), including:

(a) a description of the application of this Decision to the services falling within its scope, including in-house activities;

(b) the total amount of aid granted in accordance with this Decision, with a breakdown by the economic sector of the beneficiaries;

(c) an indication of whether, for a particular type of service, the application of this Decision has given rise to difficulties or complaints by third parties;

and

(d) any other information concerning the application of this Decision required by the Commission and to be specified in due time before the report is to be submitted.

The first report shall be submitted by 30 June 2014.

NOTES

Repeal of this Decision in relation to the UK: this Decision is repealed in relation to the UK (as from IP completion day); see the introductory notes to this Decision *ante*.

[5.656]
Article 10
Transitional provisions

This Decision shall apply to individual aid and aid schemes as follows:

(a) any aid scheme put into effect before the entry into force of this Decision that was compatible with the internal market and exempted from the notification requirement in accordance with Decision 2005/842/EC shall continue to be compatible with the internal market and exempt from the notification requirement for a further period of 2 years;

(b) any aid put into effect before the entry into force of this Decision that was not compatible with the internal market nor exempted from the notification requirement in accordance with Decision 2005/842/EC but fulfils the conditions laid down in this Decision shall be compatible with the internal market and exempt from the requirement of prior notification.

NOTES

Repeal of this Decision in relation to the UK: this Decision is repealed in relation to the UK (as from IP completion day); see the introductory notes to this Decision *ante*.

[5.657]
Article 11
Repeal

Decision 2005/842/EC is hereby repealed.

NOTES

Repeal of this Decision in relation to the UK: this Decision is repealed in relation to the UK (as from IP completion day); see the introductory notes to this Decision *ante*.

[5.658]
Article 12
Entry into force

This Decision shall enter into force on 31 January 2012.

NOTES

Repeal of this Decision in relation to the UK: this Decision is repealed in relation to the UK (as from IP completion day); see the introductory notes to this Decision *ante*.

[5.659]
Article 13
Addressees

This Decision is addressed to the Member States.

NOTES

Repeal of this Decision in relation to the UK: this Decision is repealed in relation to the UK (as from IP completion day); see the introductory notes to this Decision *ante*.

COMMUNICATION FROM THE COMMISSION

(2012/C8/03)

European Union framework for State aid in the form of public service compensation (2011)

(Text with EEA relevance)

[5.660]

NOTES

Date of publication in OJ: OJ C8, 11.1.2012, p 15. Note that the Official Journal version of this Communication contains the date '2011' in the title, but the document itself was published in 2012.

1. PURPOSE AND SCOPE

[5.661]

1. For certain services of general economic interest (SGEIs) to operate on the basis of principles and under conditions that enable them to fulfil their missions, financial support from the public authorities may prove necessary where revenues accruing from the provision of the service do not allow the costs resulting from the public service obligation to be covered.

2. It follows from the case-law of the Court of Justice of the European Union[1] that public service compensation does not constitute State aid within the meaning of Article 107(1) of the Treaty on the Functioning of the European Union if it fulfils a certain number of conditions.[2] Where those conditions are met, Article 108 of the Treaty does not apply.

3. Where public service compensation does not meet those conditions, and to the extent the general criteria for the applicability of Article 107(1) of the Treaty are satisfied, such compensation constitutes State aid and is subject to Articles 106, 107 and 108 of the Treaty.

4. In its Communication on the application of the European Union State aid rules to compensation granted for the provision of services of general economic interest,[3] the Commission has clarified the conditions under which public service compensation is to be regarded as State aid. Furthermore, in its Commission Regulation on the application of Articles 107 and 108 of the Treaty on the Functioning of the European Union to *de minimis* aid granted to undertakings providing services of general economic interest,[4] the Commission will set out the conditions under which small amounts of public service compensation should be deemed not to affect trade between Member States and/or not to distort or threaten to distort competition. In those circumstances, compensation is not caught by Article 107(1) of the Treaty and consequently does not fall under the notification procedure provided for in Article 108(3) of the Treaty.

5. Article 106(2) of the Treaty provides the legal basis for assessing the compatibility of State aid for SGEIs. It states that undertakings entrusted with the operation of SGEIs or having the character of a revenue-producing monopoly are subject to the rules contained in the Treaty, in particular to the rules on competition. However, Article 106(2) of the Treaty provides for an exception from the rules contained in the Treaty insofar as the application of the competition rules would obstruct, in law or in fact, the performance of the tasks assigned. This exception only applies where the development of trade is not affected to such an extent as would be contrary to the interests of the Union.

6. Commission Decision 2012/21/EU[5] on the application of Article 106(2) of the Treaty on the Functioning of the European Union to State aid in the form of public service compensation granted to certain undertakings entrusted with the operation of services of general economic interest[6] lays down the conditions under which certain types of public service compensation are to be regarded as compatible with the internal market pursuant to Article 106(2) of the Treaty and exempt from the requirement of prior notification under Article 108(3) of the Treaty.

7. The principles set out in this Communication apply to public service compensation only in so far as it constitutes State aid not covered by Decision 2012/21/EU. Such compensation is subject to the prior notification requirement under Article 108(3) of the Treaty. This Communication spells out the conditions under which such State aid can be found compatible with the internal market pursuant to Article 106(2) of the Treaty. It replaces the Community framework for State aid in the form of public service compensation.[7]

8. The principles set out in this Communication apply to public service compensation in the field of air and maritime transport, without prejudice to stricter specific provisions contained in sectoral Union legislation. They apply neither to the land transport sector, nor to the public service broadcasting sector, which is covered by the Communication from the Commission on the application of State aid rules to public service broadcasting.[8]

9. Aid for providers of SGEIs in difficulty will be assessed under the Community guidelines on State aid for rescuing and restructuring firms in difficulty.[9]

10. The principles set out in this Communication apply without prejudice to:

(a) requirements imposed by Union law in the field of competition (in particular Articles 101 and 102 of the Treaty);

(b) requirements imposed by Union law in the field of public procurement;

(c) the provisions of the Commission Directive 2006/111/EC of 16 November 2006 on the transparency of financial relations between Member States and public undertakings as well as on financial transparency within certain undertakings;[10]
(d) additional requirements flowing from the Treaty or from sectoral Union legislation.

NOTES

1 Judgments in Case C-280/00 *Altmark Trans GmbH and Regierungspräsidium Magdeburg v Nahverkehrsgesellschaft Altmark GmbH ('Altmark')* [2003] ECR I-7747 and Joined Cases C-34/01 to C-38/01 *Enirisorse SpA v Ministero delle Finanze* [2003] ECR I-14243.

2 In its judgment in Altmark, the Court of Justice held that public service compensation does not constitute State aid if four cumulative criteria are met. First, the recipient undertaking must actually have public service obligations to discharge, and the obligations must be clearly defined. Second, the parameters on the basis of which the compensation is calculated must be established in advance in an objective and transparent manner. Third, the compensation cannot exceed what is necessary to cover all or part of the costs incurred in the discharge of the public service obligations, taking into account the relevant receipts and a reasonable profit. Finally, where the undertaking which is to discharge public service obligations, in a specific case, is not chosen pursuant to a public procurement procedure which would allow for the selection of the tenderer capable of providing those services at the least cost to the community, the level of compensation needed must be determined on the basis of an analysis of the costs which a typical undertaking, well run and adequately provided with the relevant means, would have incurred.

3 See page 23 of this Official Journal.

4 See page 4 of this Official Journal.

5 OJ L7, 11.1.2012, p 3.

6 OJ L7, 11.1.2012.

7 OJ C297, 29.11.2005, p 4.

8 OJ C257, 27.10.2009, p 1.

9 OJ C244, 1.10.2004, p 2.

10 OJ L318, 17.11.2006, p 17.

2. CONDITIONS GOVERNING THE COMPATIBILITY OF PUBLIC SERVICE COMPENSATION THAT CONSTITUTES STATE AID

2.1. GENERAL PROVISIONS

[5.662]

11. At the current stage of development of the internal market, State aid falling outside the scope of Decision 2012/21/EU may be declared compatible with Article 106(2) of the Treaty if it is necessary for the operation of the service of general economic interest concerned and does not affect the development of trade to such an extent as to be contrary to the interests of the Union. The conditions set out in sections 2.2 to 2.10 must be met in order to achieve that balance.

2.2. GENUINE SERVICE OF GENERAL ECONOMIC INTEREST AS REFERRED TO IN ARTICLE 106 OF THE TREATY

12. The aid must be granted for a genuine and correctly defined service of general economic interest as referred to in Article 106(2) of the Treaty.

13. In its Communication on the application of the European Union State aid rules to compensation granted for the provision of services of general economic interest, the Commission has provided guidance on the requirements concerning the definition of a service of general economic interest. In particular, Member States cannot attach specific public service obligations to services that are already provided or can be provided satisfactorily and under conditions, such as price, objective quality characteristics, continuity and access to the service, consistent with the public interest, as defined by the State, by undertakings operating under normal market conditions. As for the question of whether a service can be provided by the market, the Commission's assessment is limited to checking whether the Member State's definition is vitiated by a manifest error, unless provisions of Union law provide a stricter standard.

14. For the scope of application of the principles set out in this Communication, Member States should show that they have given proper consideration to the public service needs supported by way of a public consultation or other appropriate instruments to take the interests of users and providers into account. This does not apply where it is clear that a new consultation will not bring any significant added value to a recent consultation.

2.3. NEED FOR AN ENTRUSTMENT ACT SPECIFYING THE PUBLIC SERVICE OBLIGATIONS AND THE METHODS OF CALCULATING COMPENSATION

15. Responsibility for the operation of the SGEI must be entrusted to the undertaking concerned by way of one or more acts, the form of which may be determined by each Member State. The term 'Member State' covers the central, regional and local authorities.

16. The act or acts must include, in particular:
(a) the content and duration of the public service obligations;
(b) the undertaking and, where applicable, the territory concerned;
(c) the nature of any exclusive or special rights assigned to the undertaking by the granting authority;
(d) the description of the compensation mechanism and the parameters for calculating, monitoring and reviewing the compensation; and
(e) the arrangements for avoiding and recovering any overcompensation.

2.4. DURATION OF THE PERIOD OF ENTRUSTMENT

17. The duration of the period of entrustment should be justified by reference to objective criteria such as the need to amortise non-transferable fixed assets. In principle, the duration of the period of entrustment should not exceed the period required for the depreciation of the most significant assets required to provide the SGEI.

2.5. COMPLIANCE WITH THE DIRECTIVE 2006/111/EC

18. Aid will be considered compatible with the internal market on the basis of Article 106(2) of the Treaty only where the undertaking complies, where applicable, with Directive 2006/111/EC.[11] Aid that does not comply with that Directive is considered to affect the development of trade to an extent that would be contrary to the interest of the Union within the meaning of Article 106(2) of the Treaty.

2.6. COMPLIANCE WITH UNION PUBLIC PROCUREMENT RULES

19. Aid will be considered compatible with the internal market on the basis of Article 106(2) of the Treaty only where the responsible authority, when entrusting the provision of the service to the undertaking in question, has complied or commits to comply with the applicable Union rules in the area of public procurement. This includes any requirements of transparency, equal treatment and non-discrimination resulting directly from the Treaty and, where applicable, secondary Union law. Aid that does not comply with such rules and requirements is considered to affect the development of trade to an extent that would be contrary to the interests of the Union within the meaning of Article 106(2) of the Treaty.

2.7. ABSENCE OF DISCRIMINATION

20. Where an authority assigns the provision of the same SGEI to several undertakings, the compensation should be calculated on the basis of the same method in respect of each undertaking.

2.8. AMOUNT OF COMPENSATION

21. The amount of compensation must not exceed what is necessary to cover the net cost[12] of discharging the public service obligations, including a reasonable profit.

22. The amount of compensation can be established on the basis of either the expected costs and revenues, or the costs and revenues actually incurred, or a combination of the two, depending on the efficiency incentives that the Member State wishes to provide from the outset, in accordance with paragraphs 40 and 41.

23. Where the compensation is based, in whole or in part, on expected costs and revenues, they must be specified in the entrustment act. They must be based on plausible and observable parameters concerning the economic environment in which the SGEI is being provided. They must rely, where appropriate, on the expertise of sector regulators or of other entities independent from the undertaking. Member States must indicate the sources on which these expectations are based.[13] The cost estimation must reflect the expectations of efficiency gains achieved by the SGEI provider over the lifetime of the entrustment.

Net cost necessary to discharge the public service obligations

24. The net cost necessary, or expected to be necessary, to discharge the public service obligations should be calculated using the net avoided cost methodology where this is required by Union or national legislation and in other cases where this is possible.

Net avoided cost methodology

25. Under the net avoided cost methodology, the net cost necessary, or expected to be necessary, to discharge the public service obligations is calculated as the difference between the net cost for the provider of operating with the public service obligation and the net cost or profit for the same provider of operating without that obligation. Due attention must be given to correctly assessing the costs that the service provider is expected to avoid and the revenues it is expected not to receive, in the absence of the public service obligation. The net cost calculation should assess the benefits, including intangible benefits as far as possible, to the SGEI provider.

26. Annex IV to Directive 2002/22/EC of the European Parliament and of the Council of 7 March 2002 on universal service and users' rights relating to electronic communications networks and services,[14] and Annex I to Directive 97/67/EC of the European Parliament and of the Council of 15 December 1997 on common rules for the development of the internal market of Community postal services and the improvement of quality of service,[15] contain more detailed guidance on how to apply the net avoided cost methodology.

27. Although the Commission regards the net avoided cost methodology as the most accurate method for determining the cost of a public service obligation, there may be cases where the use of that methodology is not feasible or appropriate. In such cases, where duly justified, the Commission can accept alternative methods for calculating the net cost necessary to discharge the public service obligations, such as the methodology based on cost allocation.

Methodology based on costal location

28. Under the cost allocation methodology, the net cost necessary to discharge the public service obligations can be calculated as the difference between the costs and the revenues for a designated provider of fulfilling the public service obligations, as specified and estimated in the entrustment act.

29. The costs to be taken into consideration include all the costs necessary to operate the SGEI.

30. Where the activities of the undertaking in question are confined to the SGEI, all its costs may be taken into consideration.

31. Where the undertaking also carries out activities falling outside the scope of the SGEI, the costs to be taken into consideration may cover all the direct costs necessary to discharge the public service obligations and an appropriate contribution to the indirect costs common to both the SGEI and other activities. The costs linked to any activities outside the scope of the SGEI must include all the direct costs and an appropriate contribution to the common costs.

To determine the appropriate contribution to the common costs, market prices for the use of the resources, where available, can be taken as a benchmark.[16] In the absence of such market prices, the appropriate contribution to the common costs can be determined by reference to the level of reasonable profit[17] the undertaking is expected to make on the activities falling outside the scope of the SGEI or by other methodologies where more appropriate.

Revenue

32. The revenue to be taken into account must include at least the entire revenue earned from the SGEI, as specified in the entrustment act, and the excessive profits generated from special or exclusive rights even if linked to other activities as provided in paragraph 45, regardless of whether those excessive profits are classified as State aid within the meaning of Article 107(1) of the Treaty.

Reasonable profit

33. Reasonable profit should be taken to mean the rate of return on capital[18] that would be required by a typical company considering whether or not to provide the service of general economic interest for the whole duration of the entrustment act, taking into account the level of risk. The level of risk depends on the sector concerned, the type of service and the characteristics of the compensation mechanism.

34. Where duly justified, profit level indicators other than the rate of return on capital can be used to determine what the reasonable profit should be, such as the average return on equity[19] over the entrustment period, the return on capital employed, the return on assets or the return on sales.

35. Whatever indicator is chosen, the Member State must provide the Commission with evidence that the projected profit does not exceed what would be required by a typical company considering whether or not to provide the service, for instance by providing references to returns achieved on similar types of contracts awarded under competitive conditions.

36. A rate of return on capital that does not exceed the relevant swap rate[20] plus a premium of 100 basis points[21] is regarded as reasonable in any event. The relevant swap rate is the swap rate whose maturity and currency correspond to the duration and currency of the entrustment act.

37. Where the provision of the SGEI is connected with a substantial commercial or contractual risk, for instance because the compensation takes the form of a fixed lump sum payment covering expected net costs and a reasonable profit and the undertaking operates in a competitive environment, the reasonable profit may not exceed the level that corresponds to a rate of return on capital that is commensurate with the level of risk. That rate should be determined where possible by reference to the rate of return on capital that is achieved on similar types of public service contracts awarded under competitive conditions (for example, contracts awarded under a tender). Where it is not possible to apply that method, other methods for establishing a return on capital may also be used, upon justification.[22]

38. Where the provision of the SGEI is not connected with a substantial commercial or contractual risk, for instance because the net cost incurred in providing the service of general economic interest is essentially compensated *ex post* in full, the reasonable profit may not exceed the level that corresponds to the level specified in paragraph 36. Such a compensation mechanism provides no efficiency incentives for the public service provider. Hence its use is strictly limited to cases where the Member State is able to justify that it is not feasible or appropriate to take into account productive efficiency and to have a contract design which gives incentives to achieve efficiency gains.

Efficiency incentives

39. In devising the method of compensation, Member States must introduce incentives for the efficient provision of SGEI of a high standard, unless they can duly justify that it is not feasible or appropriate to do so.

40. Efficiency incentives can be designed in different ways to best suit the specificity of each case or sector. For instance, Member States can define upfront a fixed compensation level which anticipates and incorporates the efficiency gains that the undertaking can be expected to make over the lifetime of the entrustment act.

41. Alternatively, Member States can define productive efficiency targets in the entrustment act whereby the level of compensation is made dependent upon the extent to which the targets have been met. If the undertaking does not meet the objectives, the compensation should be reduced following a calculation method specified in the entrustment act. In contrast, if the undertaking exceeds the objectives, the compensation should be increased following a method specified in the entrustment act. Rewards linked to productive efficiency gains are to be set at a level such as to allow balanced sharing of those gains between the undertaking and the Member State and/or the users.

42. Any such mechanism for incentivising efficiency improvements must be based on objective and measurable criteria set out in the entrustment act and subject to transparent *ex post* assessment carried out by an entity independent from the SGEI provider.

43. Efficiency gains should be achieved without prejudice to the quality of the service provided and should meet the standards laid down in Union legislation.

Provisions applicable to undertakings also carrying out activities outside the scope of the SGEI or providing several SGEIs

44. Where an undertaking carries out activities falling both inside and outside the scope of the SGEI, the internal accounts must show separately the costs and revenues associated with the SGEI and those of the other services in line with the principles set out in paragraph 31. Where an undertaking is entrusted with the operation of several SGEIs because the granting authority or the nature of the SGEI is different, the undertaking's internal accounts must make it possible to verify whether there has been any overcompensation at the level of each SGEI.

45. If the undertaking in question holds special or exclusive rights linked to activities, other than the SGEI for which aid is granted, that generate profits in excess of the reasonable profit, or benefits from other advantages granted by the State, these must be taken into consideration, irrespective of their classification for the purposes of Article 107(1)

of the Treaty, and added to the undertaking's revenue. The reasonable profit on the activities for which the undertaking holds special or exclusive rights has to be assessed from an *ex ante* perspective, in the light of the risk, or the absence of risk, incurred by the undertaking in question. That assessment also has to take into account the efficiency incentives that the Member State has introduced in relation to the provision of the services in question.

46. The Member State may decide that the profits accruing from other activities outside the scope of the SGEI, in particular those activities which rely on the infrastructure necessary to provide the SGEI, must be allocated in whole or in part to the financing of the SGEI.

Overcompensation

47. Overcompensation should be understood as compensation that the undertaking receives in excess of the amount of aid as defined in paragraph 21 for the whole duration of the contract. As stated in paragraphs 39 to 42, a surplus that results from higher than expected efficiency gains may be retained by the undertaking as additional reasonable profit as specified in the entrustment act.[23]

48. Since overcompensation is not necessary for the operation of the SGEI, it constitutes incompatible State aid.

49. Member States must ensure that the compensation granted for operating the SGEI meets the requirements set out in this Communication and in particular that undertakings are not receiving compensation in excess of the amount determined in accordance with this the requirements set out in this section. They must provide evidence upon request from the Commission. They must carry out regular checks, or ensure that such checks are carried out, at the end of the period of entrustment and, in any event, at intervals of not more than three years. For aid granted by means other than a public procurement procedure with publication,[24] checks should normally be made at least every two years.

50. Where the Member State has defined upfront a fixed compensation level which adequately anticipates and incorporates the efficiency gains that the public service provider can be expected to make over the period of entrustment, on the basis of a correct allocation of costs and revenues and of reasonable expectations as described in this section, the overcompensation check is in principle confined to verifying that the level of profit to which the provider is entitled in accordance with the entrustment act is indeed reasonable from an *ex ante* perspective.

2.9. ADDITIONAL REQUIREMENTS WHICH MAY BE NECESSARY TO ENSURE THAT THE DEVELOPMENT OF TRADE IS NOT AFFECTED TO AN EXTENT CONTRARY TO THE INTERESTS OF THE UNION

51. The requirements set out in sections 2.1 to 2.8 are usually sufficient to ensure that aid does not distort competition in a way that is contrary to the interests of the Union.

52. It is conceivable, however, that in some exceptional circumstances, serious competition distortions in the internal market could remain unaddressed and the aid could affect trade to such an extent as would be contrary to the interest of the Union.

53. In such a case, the Commission will examine whether such distortions can be mitigated by requiring conditions or requesting commitments from the Member State.

54. Serious competition distortions such as to be contrary to the interests of the Union are only expected to occur in exceptional circumstances. The Commission will restrict its attention to those distortions where the aid has significant adverse effects on other Member States and the functioning of the internal market, for example, because they deny undertakings in important sectors of the economy the possibility to achieve the scale of operations necessary to operate efficiently.

55. Such distortions may arise, for instance, where the entrustment either has a duration which cannot be justified by reference to objective criteria (such as the need to amortise non-transferable fixed assets) or bundles a series of tasks (typically subject to separate entrustments with no loss of social benefit and no additional costs in terms of efficiency and effectiveness in the provision of the services). In such a case, the Commission would examine whether the same public service could equally well be provided in a less distortive manner, for instance by way of a more limited entrustment in terms of duration or scope or through separate entrustments.

56. Another situation in which a more detailed assessment may be necessary is where the Member State entrusts a public service provider, without a competitive selection procedure, with the task of providing an SGEI in a non-reserved market where very similar services are already being provided or can be expected to be provided in the near future in the absence of the SGEI. Those adverse effects on the development of trade may be more pronounced where the SGEI is to be offered at a tariff below the costs of any actual or potential provider, so as to cause market foreclosure. The Commission, while fully respecting the Member State's wide margin of discretion to define the SGEI, may therefore require amendments, for instance in the allocation of the aid, where it can reasonably show that it would be possible to provide the same SGEI at equivalent conditions for the users, in a less distortive manner and at lower cost for the State.

57. Closer scrutiny is also warranted where the entrustment of the service obligation is connected with special or exclusive rights that seriously restrict competition in the internal market to an extent contrary to the interest of the Union. While the primary route for apprehending such a case remains Article 106(1) of the Treaty, the State aid may not be deemed compatible where the exclusive right provides for advantages that could not be properly assessed, quantified or apprehended according to the methodologies to calculate the net costs of the SGEI described in section 2.8.

58. The Commission will also pay attention to situations where the aid allows the undertaking to finance the creation or use of an infrastructure that is not replicable and enables it to foreclose the market where the SGEI is provided or related relevant markets. Where this is the case, it may be appropriate to require that competitors are given fair and non-discriminatory access to the infrastructure under appropriate conditions.

59. If distortions of competition are a consequence of the entrustment hindering effective implementation or enforcement of Union legislation aimed at safeguarding the proper functioning of the internal market, the Commission will examine whether the public service could equally well be provided in a less distortive manner, for instance by fully implementing the sectoral Union legislation.

2.10. TRANSPARENCY

60. For each SGEI compensation falling within the scope of this Communication, the Member State concerned must publish the following information on the internet or by other appropriate means:

(a) the results of the public consultation or other appropriate instruments referred to in paragraph 14;
(b) the content and duration of the public service obligations;
(c) the undertaking and, where applicable, the territory concerned;
(d) the amounts of aid granted to the undertaking on a yearly basis.

2.11. AID WHICH MEETS THE CONDITIONS LAID DOWN IN ARTICLE 2(1) OF DECISION 2012/21/EU

61. The principles set out in paragraphs 14, 19, 20, 24, 39, 51 to 59 and 60(a) do not apply to aid which meets the conditions laid down in Article 2(1) of Decision 2012/21/EU.

NOTES

11 Directive 2006/111/EC on the transparency of financial relations between Member States and public undertakings as well as on financial transparency within certain undertakings.

12 In this context, net cost means net cost as determined in paragraph 25 or costs minus revenues where the net avoided cost methodology cannot be applied.

13 Public sources of information, cost levels incurred by the SGEI provider in the past, cost levels of competitors, business plans, industry reports, etc.

14 OJ L108, 24.4.2002, p 51.

15 OJ L15, 21.1.1998, p 14.

16 In *Chronopost* (Joined Cases C-83/01 P, C-93/01 P and C-94/01 P *Chronopost SA* [2003] ECR I-6993), the European Court of Justice referred to 'normal market conditions': 'In the absence of any possibility of comparing the situation of La Poste with that of a private group of undertakings not operating in a reserved sector, "normal market conditions", which are necessarily hypothetical, must be assessed by reference to the objective and verifiable elements which are available'.

17 The reasonable profit will be assessed from an *ex ante* perspective (based on expected profits rather than on realised profits) in order not to remove the incentives for the undertaking to make efficiency gains when operating activities outside the SGEI.

18 The rate of return on capital is defined here as the Internal Rate of Return (IRR) that the company makes on its invested capital over the lifetime of the project, that is to say the IRR on the cash flows of the contract.

19 In any given year the accounting measure return on equity (ROE) is defined as the ratio between earnings before interests and taxes (EBIT) and equity capital in that year. The average annual return should be computed over the lifetime of the entrustment by applying as discount factor either the company's cost of capital or the rate set by the Commission Reference rate Communication, whatever more appropriate.

20 The swap rate is the longer maturity equivalent to the Inter-Bank Offered Rate (IBOR rate). It is used in the financial markets as a benchmark rate for establishing the funding rate.

21 The premium of 100 basis points serves, inter alia, to compensate for liquidity risk related to the fact that an SGEI provider that invests capital in an SGEI contract commits that capital for the duration of the entrustment act and will be unable to sell its stake as rapidly and at as low a cost as is the case with a widely held and liquid risk-free asset.

22 For instance, by comparing the return with the weighted average cost of capital (WACC) of the company in relation to the activity in question, or with the average return on capital for the sector in recent years, taking into account whether historical data can be appropriate for forward-looking purposes.

23 Similarly, a deficit which results from efficiency gains lower than expected should be partially borne by the undertaking when stipulated in the entrustment act.

24 Such as aid granted in relation to in-house contracts, concessions with no competitive allocation, public procurement procedures with no prior publication.

3. REPORTING AND EVALUATION

[5.663]

62. Member States shall report to the Commission on the compliance with this Communication every two years. The reports must provide an overview of the application of this Communication to the different sectors of service providers, including:

(a) a description of the application of the principles set out in this Communication to the services falling within its scope, including in-house activities;
(b) the total amount of aid granted to undertakings falling within the scope of this Communication with a breakdown by the economic sector of the beneficiaries;
(c) an indication of whether, for a particular type of service, the application of the principles set out in this Communication has given rise to difficulties or complaints by third parties; and
(d) any other information concerning the application of the principles set out in this Communication required by the Commission and to be specified in due time before the report is to be submitted.

The first report shall be submitted by 30 June 2014.

63. In addition, in accordance with the requirements of Council Regulation (EC) No 659/1999 of 22 March 1999 laying down detailed rules for the application of Article 93 of the EC Treaty[25] (now Article 108 of the Treaty) and Commission Regulation (EC) No 794/2004 of 21 April 2004 implementing Council Regulation (EC) No 659/1999 laying down detailed rules for the application of Article 93 of the EC Treaty,[26] Member States must submit annual reports to the Commission on the aid granted following a decision of the Commission based on this Communication.

64. The reports will be published on the internet site of the Commission.

65. The Commission intends to carry out a review of this Communication by 31 January 2017.

NOTES

[25] OJ L83, 27.3.1999, p 1.

[26] OJ L140, 30.4.2004, p 1.

4. CONDITIONS AND OBLIGATIONS ATTACHED TO COMMISSION DECISIONS

[5.664]

66. Pursuant to Article 7(4) of Regulation (EC) No 659/1999, the Commission may attach to a positive decision conditions subject to which aid may be considered compatible with the internal market, and lay down obligations to enable compliance with the decision to be monitored. In the field of SGEI, conditions and obligations may be necessary in particular to ensure that aid granted to the undertakings concerned does not lead to undue distortions of competition and trade in the internal market. In this context, periodic reports or other obligations may be necessary, in the light of the specific situation of each service of general economic interest.

5. APPLICATION

[5.665]

67. The Commission will apply the provisions of this Communication from 31 January 2012.

68. The Commission will apply the principles set out in this Communication to all aid projects notified to it and will take a decision on those projects in accordance with those principles, even if the projects were notified prior to 31 January 2012.

69. The Commission will apply the principles set out in this Communication to unlawful aid on which it takes a decision after 31 January 2012 even if the aid was granted before this date. However, where the aid was granted before 31 January 2012, the principles set out in paragraphs 14, 19, 20, 24, 39 and 60 do not apply.

6. APPROPRIATE MEASURES

[5.666]

70. The Commission proposes as appropriate measures for the purposes of Article 108(1) of the Treaty that Member States publish the list of existing aid schemes regarding public service compensation which have to be brought into line with this Communication by 31 January 2013, and that they bring those aid schemes into line with this Communication by 31 January 2014.

71. Member States should confirm to the Commission by 29 February 2012 that they agree to the appropriate measures proposed. In the absence of any reply, the Commission will take it that the Member State concerned does not agree.

COMMISSION REGULATION

(360/2012/EU)

of 25 April 2012

on the application of Articles 107 and 108 of the Treaty on the Functioning of the European Union to *de minimis* aid granted to undertakings providing services of general economic interest

(Text with EEA relevance)

[5.667]

NOTES

Date of publication in OJ: OJ L114, 26.4.2012, p 8.

Repeal of this Regulation in relation to the UK: this Regulation is repealed, in relation to the UK, by the State Aid (Revocations and Amendments) (EU Exit) Regulations 2020, SI 2020/1470, reg 5, as from IP completion day (as defined in the European Union (Withdrawal Agreement) Act 2020, s 39) (for transitional provisions and savings in relation to claims before a court or tribunal relating to State aid infringement before IP completion day, see Sch 3 to those Regulations at **[7.89]**).

THE EUROPEAN COMMISSION,

Having regard to the Treaty on the Functioning of the European Union,

Having regard to Council Regulation (EC) No 994/98 of 7 May 1998 on the application of Articles 92 and 93 of the Treaty establishing the European Community to certain categories of horizontal State aid,[1] and in particular Article 2(1) thereof,

Having published a draft of this Regulation,[2]

After consulting the Advisory Committee on State Aid,

Whereas:

(1) Regulation (EC) No 994/98 empowers the Commission to set out in a Regulation a threshold below which aid measures are considered not to meet all the criteria laid down in Article 107(1) of the Treaty and therefore do not fall under the notification procedure provided for in Article 108(3) of the Treaty.

(2) On the basis of that Regulation, the Commission has adopted, in particular, Regulation (EC) No 1998/2006 of 15 December 2006 on the application of Articles 87 and 88 of the Treaty to de minimis aid,[3] which sets a general de minimis ceiling of EUR 200,000 per beneficiary over a period of three fiscal years.

(3) The Commission's experience in applying the State aid rules to undertakings providing services of general economic interest within the meaning of Article 106(2) of the Treaty has shown that the ceiling below which advantages granted to such undertakings may be deemed not to affect trade between Member States and/or not to distort or threaten to distort competition can, in some cases, differ from the general de minimis ceiling established in Regulation (EC) No 1998/2006. Indeed, at least some of those advantages are likely to constitute compensation for additional costs linked to the provision of services of general economic interest. Moreover, many activities qualifying as the provision of services of general economic interest have a limited territorial scope. It is therefore appropriate to introduce, alongside Regulation (EC) No 1998/2006, a Regulation containing specific de minimis rules for undertakings providing services of general economic interest. A ceiling should be established for the amount of de minimis aid each undertaking may receive over a specific period of time.

(4) In the light of the Commission's experience, aid granted to undertakings providing a service of general economic interest should be deemed not to affect trade between Member States and/or not to distort or threaten to distort competition provided that the total amount of aid granted for the provision of services of general economic interest received by the beneficiary undertaking does not exceed EUR 500,000 over any period of three fiscal years. In view of the development of the road passenger transport sector and of the mostly local nature of services of general economic interest in this field, it is not appropriate to apply a lower ceiling to this sector and the ceiling of EUR 500,000 should apply.

(5) The years to be taken into account for the purpose of determining whether that ceiling is met should be the fiscal years as used for fiscal purposes by the undertaking in the Member State concerned. The relevant period of three years should be assessed on a rolling basis so that, for each new grant of de minimis aid, the total amount of de minimis aid granted in the fiscal year concerned, as well as during the previous two fiscal years, needs to be determined. Aid granted by a Member State should be taken into account for this purpose even when financed entirely or partly by resources of Union origin. It should not be possible for aid measures exceeding the de minimis ceiling to be broken down into a number of smaller parts in order to bring such parts within the scope of this Regulation.

(6) This Regulation should apply only to aid granted for the provision of a service of general economic interest. The beneficiary undertaking should therefore be entrusted in writing with the service of general economic interest in respect of which the aid is granted. While the entrustment act should inform the undertaking of the service of general economic interest in respect of which it is granted, it must not necessarily contain all the detailed information as set out in Commission Decision 2012/21/EU of 20 December 2011 on the application of Article 106(2) of the Treaty on the Functioning of the European Union to State aid in the form of public service compensation granted to certain undertakings entrusted with the operation of services of general economic interest.[4]

(7) In view of the special rules which apply in the sectors of primary production of agricultural products, fisheries, aquaculture and road freight transport, of the fact that undertakings in those sectors are rarely entrusted with services of general economic interest, and of the risk that amounts of aid below the ceiling set out in this Regulation could fulfil the criteria of Article 107(1) of the Treaty in those sectors, this Regulation should not apply to those sectors. However, if undertakings are active in the sectors of primary production of agricultural products, fisheries, aquaculture or road freight transport as well as in other sectors or activities, this Regulation should apply to those other sectors or activities (such as for example collection of litter at sea) provided that Member States ensure that the activities in the excluded sectors do not benefit from the de minimis aid under this Regulation, by appropriate means such as separation of activities or distinction of costs. Member States can fulfil this obligation, in particular, by limiting the amount of de minimis aid to the compensation of the costs of the provision of the service, including a reasonable profit. This Regulation should not apply to the coal sector, in view of its special characteristics and of fact that undertakings in those sectors are rarely entrusted with services of general economic interest.

(8) Considering the similarities between the processing and marketing of agricultural products, on the one hand, and of non-agricultural products, on the other, this Regulation should apply to the processing and marketing of agricultural products, provided that certain conditions are met. Neither on-farm activities necessary for preparing a product for the first sale, such as harvesting, cutting and threshing of cereals, or packing of eggs, nor the first sale to resellers or processors should be considered as processing or marketing in this respect.

(9) The Court of Justice has established[5] *that, once the Union has legislated for the establishment of a common organisation of the market in a given sector of agriculture, Member States are under an obligation to refrain from taking any measure which might undermine or create exceptions to it. For this reason, this Regulation should not apply to aid the amount of which is set on the basis of the price or quantity of products purchased or put on the market. Nor should it apply to de minimis support which is linked to an obligation to share the aid with primary producers.*

(10) This Regulation should not apply to de minimis export aid or de minimis aid favouring domestic over imported products.

(11) This Regulation should not apply to undertakings in difficulty within the meaning of the Community guidelines on State aid for rescuing and restructuring firms in difficulty[6] *since it is not appropriate to grant operating aid to firms in difficulty outside of a restructuring concept and there are difficulties linked to determining the gross grant equivalent of aid granted to undertakings of this type.*

(12) In accordance with the principles governing aid falling within Article 107(1) of the Treaty, de minimis aid should be considered to be granted at the moment the legal right to receive the aid is conferred on the undertaking under the applicable national legal regime.

(13) In order to avoid circumvention of maximum aid intensities laid down in different Union instruments, de minimis aid should not be cumulated with State aid in respect of the same eligible costs if such cumulation would result in an aid intensity exceeding that specified in the particular circumstances of each case by a block exemption regulation or decision adopted by the Commission.

(14) This Regulation should not restrict the application of Regulation (EC) No 1998/2006 to undertakings providing services of general economic interest. Member States should remain free to rely either on this Regulation or on Regulation (EC) No 1998/2006 as regards aid granted for the provision of services of general economic interest.

(15) The Court of Justice, in its Altmark judgment,[7] *has identified a number of conditions which must be fulfilled*

in order for compensation for the provision of a service of general economic interest not to constitute State aid. Those conditions ensure that compensation limited to the net costs incurred by efficient undertakings for the provision of a service of general economic interest does not constitute State aid within the meaning of Article 107(1) of the Treaty. Compensation in excess of those net costs constitutes State aid which may be declared compatible on the basis of the applicable Union rules. In order to avoid this Regulation being applied to circumvent the conditions identified in the Altmark judgment, and in order to avoid de minimis aid granted under this Regulation affecting trade due to its cumulation with other compensation for the same service of general economic interest, de minimis aid under this Regulation should not be cumulated with any other compensation in respect of the same service, regardless of whether or not it constitutes State aid under the Altmark judgment or compatible State aid under Decision 2012/21/EU or under the Communication from the Commission — European Union framework for State aid in the form of public service compensation (2011).[8] Therefore, this Regulation should not apply to compensation received for the provision of a service of general economic interest in respect of which other types of compensation are also being granted, except where that other compensation constitutes de minimis aid according to other de minimis regulations and the cumulation rules set out in this Regulation are complied with.

(16) For the purposes of transparency, equal treatment and correct application of the de minimis ceiling, all Member States should apply the same method of calculation. In order to facilitate such calculation and in accordance with present practice in applying the de minimis rule, aid amounts not taking the form of a cash grant should be converted into their gross grant equivalent. Calculation of the grant equivalent of transparent types of aid other than grants and of aid payable in several instalments requires the use of market rates prevailing at the time of granting such aid. With a view to uniform, transparent and simple application of the State aid rules, the market rates for the purposes of this Regulation should be deemed to be the reference rates, as currently set out in the Communication from the Commission on the revision of the method for setting the reference and discount rates.[9]

(17) For the purposes of transparency, equal treatment and effective monitoring, this Regulation should apply only to de minimis aid which is transparent. Transparent aid is aid for which it is possible to calculate precisely the gross grant equivalent ex ante without a need to undertake a risk assessment. Such a precise calculation can, for instance, be made for grants, interest rate subsidies and capped tax exemptions. Aid comprised in capital injections should not be considered as transparent de minimis aid, unless the total amount of the public injection is lower than the de minimis ceiling. Aid comprised in risk capital measures as referred to in the Community guidelines on State aid to promote risk capital investments in small and medium-sized enterprises[10] should not be considered as transparent de minimis aid, unless the risk capital scheme concerned provides capital only up to the de minimis ceiling to each target undertaking. Aid comprised in loans should be treated as transparent de minimis aid when the gross grant equivalent has been calculated on the basis of market interest rates prevailing at the time of grant.

(18) Legal certainty needs to be provided for guarantee schemes which do not have the potential to affect trade and distort competition and in respect of which sufficient data are available to assess any potential effects reliably. This Regulation should therefore transpose the de minimis ceiling of EUR 500,000 into a guarantee-specific ceiling based on the guaranteed amount of the individual loan underlying such guarantee. This specific ceiling should be calculated using a methodology assessing the State aid amount included in guarantee schemes covering loans in favour of viable undertakings. The methodology and the data used to calculate the guarantee-specific ceiling should exclude undertakings in difficulty as referred to in the Community guidelines on State aid for rescuing and restructuring firms in difficulty. This specific ceiling should therefore not apply to individual aid granted outside the scope of a guarantee scheme, to aid granted to undertakings in difficulty, or to guarantees on underlying transactions not constituting a loan, such as guarantees on equity transactions. The specific ceiling should be determined on the basis of the fact that taking account of a cap rate (net default rate) of 13%, representing a worst case scenario for guarantee schemes in the Union, a guarantee amounting to EUR 3 750,000 can be considered as having a gross grant equivalent identical to the EUR 500,000 de minimis ceiling. Only guarantees covering up to 80% of the underlying loan should be covered by these specific ceilings. A methodology accepted by the Commission following notification of such methodology on the basis of a Commission regulation in the State aid area may also be used by Member States for the purpose of assessing the gross grant equivalent contained in a guarantee, if the approved methodology explicitly addresses the type of guarantees and the type of underlying transactions at stake in the context of the application of this Regulation.

(19) Upon notification by a Member State, the Commission may examine whether an aid measure which does not consist in a grant, loan, guarantee, capital injection, risk capital measure or capped tax exemption leads to a gross grant equivalent that does not exceed the de minimis ceiling and could therefore be covered by the provisions of this Regulation.

(20) The Commission has a duty to ensure that State aid rules are complied with and in particular that aid granted under the de minimis rules adheres to the conditions thereof. In accordance with the cooperation principle laid down in Article 4(3) of the Treaty on European Union, Member States should facilitate the fulfilment of this task by establishing the necessary tools in order to ensure that the total amount of de minimis aid granted to the same undertaking for the provision of services of general economic interest does not exceed the overall permissible ceiling. To that end and to ensure compliance with the provisions on cumulation with de minimis aid under other de minimis regulations, when granting de minimis aid under this Regulation, Member States should inform the undertaking concerned of the amount of the aid and of its de minimis character by referring to this Regulation. Moreover, prior to granting such aid the Member State concerned should obtain from the undertaking a declaration about other de minimis aid covered by this Regulation or by other de minimis regulations received during the fiscal year concerned and the two previous fiscal years. Alternatively, the Member State should have the possibility to ensure that the ceiling is observed by means of a central register.

(21) This Regulation should apply without prejudice to the requirements of Union law in the area of public procurement or of additional requirements flowing from the Treaty or from sectoral Union legislation.

(22) This Regulation should apply to aid granted before its entry into force to undertakings providing services of general economic interest.

(23) The Commission intends to carry out a review of this Regulation five years after its entry into force,

NOTES

Repeal of this Regulation in relation to the UK: this Regulation is repealed in relation to the UK (as from IP completion day); see the introductory notes to this Regulation *ante*.

[1] OJ L142, 14.5.1998, p 1.

[2] OJ C8, 11.1.2012, p 23.

[3] OJ L379, 28.12.2006, p 5.

[4] OJ L7, 11.1.2012, p 3.

[5] Case C-456/00 *French Republic v Commission of the European Communities* [2002] I-11949.

[6] OJ C244, 1.10.2004, p 2.

[7] Case C-280/00 *Altmark Trans GmbH and Regierungspräsidium Magdeburg v Nahverkehrsgesellschaft Altmark GmbH, and Oberbundesanwalt beim Bundesverwaltungsgericht* [2003] ECR I-7747.

[8] OJ C8, 11.1.2012, p 15.

[9] OJ C14, 19.1.2008, p 6.

[10] OJ C194, 18.8.2006, p 2.

HAS ADOPTED THIS REGULATION:

[5.668]

Article 1 Scope and definitions

1. This Regulation applies to aid granted to undertakings providing a service of general economic interest within the meaning of Article 106(2) of the Treaty.

2. This Regulation does not apply to:

(a) aid granted to undertakings active in the fishery and aquaculture sectors, as covered by Council Regulation (EC) No 104/2000;[1]

(b) aid granted to undertakings active in the primary production of agricultural products;

(c) aid granted to undertakings active in the processing and marketing of agricultural products, in the following cases:

(i) when the amount of the aid is fixed on the basis of the price or quantity of such products purchased from primary producers or put on the market by the undertakings concerned,

(ii) when the aid is conditional on being partly or entirely passed on to primary producers;

(d) aid to export-related activities towards third countries or Member States, namely aid directly linked to the quantities exported, to the establishment and operation of a distribution network or to other current expenditure linked to the export activity;

(e) aid contingent upon the use of domestic over imported goods;

(f) aid granted to undertakings active in the coal sector, as defined in Council Decision 2010/787/EU;[2]

(g) aid granted to undertakings performing road freight transport for hire or reward;

(h) aid granted to undertakings in difficulty.

If undertakings are active in the sectors referred to in points (a), (b), (c) or (g) of the first subparagraph as well as in sectors not excluded from the scope of application of this Regulation, this Regulation applies only to aid granted in respect of those other sectors or activities, provided that Member States ensure that the activities in the excluded sectors do not benefit from the de minimis aid under this Regulation, by appropriate means such as separation of activities or distinction of costs.

[2a. By derogation from point (h) of paragraph 2, this Regulation shall apply to undertakings which were not in difficulty on 31 December 2019 but became undertakings in difficulty in the period from 1 January 2020 to 30 June 2021.]

3. For the purposes of this Regulation:

(a) 'agricultural products' means products listed in Annex I to the Treaty, with the exception of fishery products;

(b) 'processing of agricultural products' means any operation on an agricultural product resulting in a product which is also an agricultural product, except on-farm activities necessary for preparing an animal or plant product for the first sale;

(c) 'marketing of agricultural products' means holding or display with a view to sale, offering for sale, delivery or any other manner of placing on the market, except the first sale by a primary producer to resellers or processors and any activity preparing a product for such first sale; a sale by a primary producer to final consumers shall be considered as marketing if it takes place in separate premises reserved for that purpose.

NOTES

Para 2a: inserted by Commission Regulation 2020/1474/EU, Art 1(a).

Repeal of this Regulation in relation to the UK: this Regulation is repealed in relation to the UK (as from IP completion day); see the introductory notes to this Regulation *ante*.

[1] OJ L17, 21.1.2000, p 22.

[2] OJ L336, 21.12.2010, p 24.

[5.669]

Article 2 *De minimis **aid***

1. Aid granted to undertakings for the provision of a service of general economic interest shall be deemed not to meet all the criteria of Article 107(1) of the Treaty and shall therefore be exempt from the notification requirement of Article 108(3) of the Treaty if it fulfils the conditions laid down in paragraphs 2 to 8 of this Article.

2. The total amount of de minimis aid granted to any one undertaking providing services of general economic interest shall not exceed EUR 500,000 over any period of three fiscal years.

This ceiling shall apply irrespective of the form of the de minimis aid and regardless of whether the aid granted by the Member State is financed entirely or partly by resources of Union origin. The period shall be determined by reference to the fiscal years used by the undertaking in the Member State concerned.

3. The ceiling laid down in paragraph 2 shall be expressed as a cash grant. All figures used shall be gross, that is, before any deduction of tax or other charges. Where aid is awarded in a form other than a grant, the aid amount shall be the gross grant equivalent of the aid.

Aid payable in several instalments shall be discounted to its value at the moment of it being granted. The interest rate to be used for discounting purposes shall be the discount rate applicable at the time of grant.

4. This Regulation shall apply only to aid in respect of which it is possible to calculate precisely the gross grant equivalent of the aid ex ante without need to undertake a risk assessment ('transparent aid'). In particular:

- *(a) aid comprised in loans shall be considered as transparent de minimis aid when the gross grant equivalent has been calculated on the basis of the reference rate applicable at the time of the grant;*
- *(b) aid comprised in capital injections shall not be considered as transparent de minimis aid, unless the total amount of the public injection does not exceed the de minimis ceiling;*
- *(c) aid comprised in risk capital measures shall not be considered as transparent de minimis aid, unless the risk capital scheme concerned provides capital only up to the de minimis ceiling to each target undertaking;*
- *(d) individual aid provided under a guarantee scheme to undertakings which are not undertakings in difficulty shall be treated as transparent de minimis aid when the guaranteed part of the underlying loan provided under such scheme does not exceed EUR 3 750,000 per undertaking. If the guaranteed part of the underlying loan only accounts for a given proportion of this ceiling, the gross grant equivalent of that guarantee shall be deemed to correspond to the same proportion of the ceiling laid down in paragraph 2. The guarantee shall not exceed 80% of the underlying loan. Guarantee schemes shall also be considered as transparent if:*
  - *(i) before the implementation of the scheme, the methodology to calculate the gross grant equivalent of the guarantees has been accepted following notification of this methodology to the Commission under a regulation adopted by the Commission in the State aid area, and*
  - *(ii) the approved methodology explicitly addresses the type of guarantees and the type of underlying transactions at stake in the context of the application of this Regulation.*

5. Where the overall amount of de minimis aid under this Regulation granted to an undertaking for the provision of services of general economic interest exceeds the ceiling laid down in paragraph 2, that amount may not benefit from this Regulation, even for a fraction not exceeding that ceiling. In such a case, the benefit of this Regulation may not be claimed for this aid measure.

6. De minimis aid under this Regulation shall not be cumulated with State aid in respect of the same eligible costs if such cumulation would result in an aid intensity exceeding that stipulated in the specific circumstances of each case by a block exemption regulation or decision adopted by the Commission.

7. De minimis aid under this Regulation may be cumulated with de minimis aid under other de minimis regulations up to the ceiling laid down in paragraph 2.

8. De minimis aid under this Regulation shall not be cumulated with any compensation in respect of the same service of general economic interest, regardless of whether or not it constitutes State aid.

NOTES

Repeal of this Regulation in relation to the UK: this Regulation is repealed in relation to the UK (as from IP completion day); see the introductory notes to this Regulation *ante*.

[5.670]

Article 3 Monitoring

1. Where a Member State intends to grant de minimis aid under this Regulation to an undertaking, it shall inform that undertaking in writing of the prospective amount of the aid expressed as gross grant equivalent, of the service of general economic interest in respect of which it is granted and of the de minimis character of the aid, making express reference to this Regulation and citing its title and publication reference in the Official Journal of the European Union. Where de minimis aid under this Regulation is granted to different undertakings on the basis of a scheme and different amounts of individual aid are granted to those undertakings under that scheme, the Member State concerned may choose to fulfil that obligation by informing the undertakings of a fixed sum corresponding to the maximum aid amount to be granted under that scheme. In such case, the fixed sum shall be used for determining whether the ceiling laid down in Article 2(2) is met. Prior to granting the aid, the Member State shall also obtain a declaration from the undertaking providing the service of general economic interest, in written or electronic form, about any other de minimis aid received under this Regulation or under other de minimis regulations during the previous two fiscal years and the current fiscal year.

The Member State shall grant the new de minimis aid under this Regulation only after having checked that this will not raise the total amount of de minimis aid granted to the undertaking concerned to a level above the ceiling laid down in Article 2(2) and that the cumulation rules in Article 2(6), (7) and (8) are complied with.

2. Where a Member State has set up a central register of de minimis aid containing complete information on all de minimis aid granted to undertakings providing services of general economic interest by any authority within that Member State, the first subparagraph of paragraph 1 shall cease to apply from the moment the register covers a period of three years.

3. Member States shall record and compile all the information regarding the application of this Regulation. Such records shall contain all information necessary to demonstrate that the conditions of this Regulation have been complied with. Records regarding individual de minimis aid shall be maintained for 10 fiscal years from the date on which the aid was granted. Records regarding a de minimis aid scheme shall be maintained for 10 years from the date on which the last individual aid was granted under such a scheme. On written request, the Member State concerned shall provide the Commission, within a period of 20 working days or such longer period as may be fixed in the request, with all the information that the Commission considers necessary for assessing whether the conditions of this Regulation have been complied with, and in particular the total amount of de minimis aid under this Regulation and under other de minimis regulations received by any undertaking.

NOTES

Repeal of this Regulation in relation to the UK: this Regulation is repealed in relation to the UK (as from IP completion day); see the introductory notes to this Regulation *ante*.

[5.671]

Article 4 Transitional provisions

This Regulation shall apply to de minimis aid granted for the provision of services of general economic interest before its entry into force, provided that such aid fulfils the conditions laid down in Articles 1 and 2. Any aid for the provision of services of general economic interest which does not fulfil those conditions shall be assessed in accordance with the relevant decisions, frameworks, guidelines, communications and notices.

At the end of the period of validity of this Regulation, any de minimis aid which fulfils the conditions of this Regulation may be validly implemented for a further period of six months.

NOTES

Repeal of this Regulation in relation to the UK: this Regulation is repealed in relation to the UK (as from IP completion day); see the introductory notes to this Regulation *ante*.

[5.672]

Article 5 Entry into force and period of validity

This Regulation shall enter into force on the third day following that of its publication in the Official Journal of the European Union.

[It shall apply until 31 December 2023.]

This Regulation shall be binding in its entirety and directly applicable in all Member States.

NOTES

Words in square brackets substituted by Commission Regulation 2020/1474/EU, Art 1(b). As originally enacted, this Regulation would have expired on 31 December 2018. The expiry date was extended to 31 December 2020 by Commission Regulation 2018/1923/EU. It was further extended, to 31 December 2023, by Commission Regulation 2020/1474/EU.

Repeal of this Regulation in relation to the UK: this Regulation is repealed in relation to the UK (as from IP completion day); see the introductory notes to this Regulation *ante*.

COMMISSION STAFF WORKING DOCUMENT

Guide to the application of the European Union rules on state aid, public procurement and the internal market to services of general economic interest, and in particular to social services of general interest

Brussels, 29.4.2013 (SWD(2013) 53 final/2

[5.673]

NOTES

This document is available on the European Commission website at: https://ec.europa.eu/competition-policy/state-aid/legislation/sgei_en.

This document is a working paper prepared by the Commission's services. It provides technical explanations, in particular on the basis of concise and sometimes simplified summaries of the legislation and case law on state aid, public procurement and the internal market and, in relation to state aid, of Commission decisions on SGEIs and in particular SSGIs. This document is not binding on the European Commission as an institution.

1 INTRODUCTION

[5.674]

A number of questions have been raised by public authorities in the Member States, citizens, civil society organisations and other stakeholders on the **application of the EU rules, notably those on State aid, public procurement and the internal market, to services of general interest** and, in particular, to **social services of general interest (SSGIs)**. These questions concern the impact of these rules on the ways these services can be organised and financed by public authorities in the Member States, on the modalities of selection of the service providers, in case the provision is outsourced, and, more generally, on the regulatory framework concerning i.a. the types of providers or the access to and the quality of the services.[1]

As for the questions on **State aid rules**, they concern in the first place the precise conditions under which compensation for public service obligations constitutes State Aid, and secondly the conditions under which State Aid may be regarded as compatible with the Treaty on the Functioning of the European Union (TFEU). Clarification concerning the obligation to notify such aid to the Commission is also sought.

In its judgment in *Altmark Trans GmbH and Regierungspräsidium Magdeburg* v *Nahverkehrsgesellschaft Altmark GmbH* (*Altmark*),[2] the Court of Justice of the European Union (the Court) held that public service compensation did not constitute State Aid within the meaning of Article 107 of the TFEU provided that four cumulative criteria were met.[3]

Where the four criteria are met, public service compensation does not constitute State Aid, and Articles 107 and 108 TFEU do not apply. If the Member States do not comply with the criteria, and if the general conditions of Article 107(1) TFEU are met, public service compensation constitutes State Aid.

However, the Commission Regulation of 25 April 2012 on the application of Articles 107 and 108 TFEU to *de minimis* aid granted to undertakings providing services of general economic interest[4] (hereinafter: 'the SGEI *de minimis* Regulation') stipulates the conditions under which aid granted to undertakings for the provision of SGEIs will be deemed not to meet all the conditions of Article 107(1) TFEU. Therefore, public service compensation falling within the scope of the SGEI *de minimis* Regulation is deemed not to constitute State Aid.

Where public service compensation constitutes State Aid, Article 106 TFEU and, for land transport, Article 93 TFEU allow the Commission to declare compensation for SGEIs compatible with the internal market. The Commission Decision of 20 December 2011 on the application of Article 106(2) TFEU to State Aid in the form of public service compensation granted to certain undertakings entrusted with the operation of SGEIs[5] (hereinafter: 'the Decision') and, for land transport, Regulation (EC) No 1370/2007 of the European Parliament and of the Council[6] (hereinafter: 'Regulation 1370/2007') specify the conditions under which certain compensation arrangements are compatible with Article 106(2) and Article 93 respectively and are not subject to the prior notification requirement of Article 108(3) TFEU. Any other public service compensation must be notified to the Commission, which will assess its compatibility on the basis of the European Union framework for State Aid in the form of public service compensation (2011)[7] (hereinafter: 'the Framework') and, for land transport, Regulation 1370/2007.

The *Altmark* judgment, the Decision and the Framework have made a significant contribution to clarifying and simplifying the applicable rules. Nonetheless, governments and stakeholders have raised a number of questions about the practical application of the legal framework to specific cases. While reviewing the Decision and the Framework in 2011, the Commission therefore adopted an explicative Communication[8] (hereinafter: 'the Communication') clarifying the key concepts of State Aid relevant to SGEIs. In order to simplify further, the Commission supplemented the State Aid package for SGEIs with the SGEI *de minimis* Regulation.

The present guide seeks to provide specific clarification on certain issues that have been raised by public authorities in the Member States, service users and providers and other stakeholders. The section on State aid has been revised, compared to the 2010 version of the Guide[9] following the adoption of the new package of State aid rules for SGEIs. The questions and answers it contains refer specifically to social services of general economic interest and to transport, but they also apply to SGEIs in general.

As for the questions on the **application of the EU rules on public procurement, they focus in particular on SSGIs** and relate to the conditions under which public procurement rules apply to SSGIs, the scope of the rules and how the rules allow the specific features of SSGIs to be taken into account.

First of all, it should be stressed that the EU rules on public procurement do not require public authorities to outsource an SSGI. They are free to decide whether to provide the service themselves, directly or in-house. They may also decide to provide the service in cooperation with other public authorities under the conditions laid down by case law.

The rules on public procurement/concessions apply only if a public authority decides to entrust the provision of a service to a third party against remuneration.

Against this background, if a contracting authority or entity decides to award a public service or a service contract, the contract will fall within the scope of Directive 2004/18/EC or Directive 2004/17/EC only if the relevant threshold amounts for the application of the Directive are met.[10] However, social services and health contracts are not subject to all the provisions of Directive 2004/18/EC or Directive 2004/17/EC;[11] they are subject only to a very limited number of them,[12] and to the fundamental principles of EU law, such as the requirement to treat all economic operators in an equal and non-discriminatory manner and the principle of transparency.

Public service and service contracts[13] whose value is below the application thresholds of the Public Procurement Directives and service concessions (regardless of their amount) fall outside the scope of the Public Procurement Directives and are subject only to the fundamental principles of the TFEU (non-discrimination, equal treatment, transparency, etc.) in so far as the contracts have a certain cross-border interest. In the absence of a certain cross-border interest, the contracts also fall outside the scope of the TFEU.[14]

This guide seeks to provide greater clarification as to the conditions and arrangements for applying the rules on public procurement to SSGIs, by addressing all the issues raised most frequently in questions, such as the provision of services by an in-house organisation or as part of cooperation between public authorities, public-private sector partnerships, service concessions and the scope of the fundamental principles of the TFEU.

It aims also to provide a more detailed explanation of the many options available to public authorities when it comes to taking account in their public procurement of the specific features of SSGIs, in particular of all the qualitative requirements that they consider appropriate to meet the complex needs of users. We hope that these clarifications will answer the questions asked on this subject by the different stakeholders and will support and provide greater encouragement to public authorities endeavouring to ensure that citizens enjoy high-quality social services.

The Commission has adopted its proposal for new public procurement rules on 20.12.2011.[15] It is planned to update the public procurement section of this guide once the new public procurement rules have been adopted in order to bring it in line with the new provisions.

As for the answers to questions concerning the **application of the internal market rules**,[16] they focus mainly on SSGIs: these services are covered by the internal market rules laid down in the TFEU where they constitute an 'economic activity' within the meaning of the Court's case law on the interpretation of those provisions. Certain SSGIs may also be covered by the Services Directive.

The answers given on this matter are intended to clarify the options available to the Member States for determining how these services are to be provided in order to guarantee their accessibility and quality, and therefore take account of the specific nature of SGEIs, and of SSGIs in particular, whenever those rules are applied. This document also makes it clear that the Services Directive contains provisions that recognise and take account of the specific features of social services that have not been excluded from the scope of the Directive.

The application of EU rules to SGEI and, in particular to SSGI, and more generally the debate on SGEI has been the object of various Commission initiatives[17] and, most recently, of the Communication "A Quality Framework for Services of General Interest in Europe"[18] (hereinafter 'the Commission Quality Framework') adopted the same day as the new State aid package and the Commission's proposals on Public Procurement and Concessions.

NOTES

1 For the analysis of these questions, in relation to social services, see the First and Second Biennial Reports on social services of general interest, SEC(2008) 2179 of 2 July 2008, and SEC(2010) 1284 of 22 October 2010.

2 Case C-280/00 *Altmark* [2003] ECR I-7747.

3 For further details, see the answer provided to question 61.

4 Commission Regulation (EU) No 360/2012 of 25 April 2012 on the application of Articles 107 and 108 of the Treaty on the Functioning of the European Union to *de minimis* aid granted to undertakings providing services of general economic interest, OJ L114, 26.4.2012, p 8.

5 Commission Decision of 20 December 2011 on the application of Article 106(2) of the Treaty on the Functioning of the European Union to State aid in the form of public service compensation granted to certain undertakings entrusted with the operation of services of general economic interest, OJ L7, 11.1.2012, p 3.

6 Regulation (EC) No 1370/2007 of the European Parliament and of the Council of 23 October 2007 on public passenger transport services by rail and by road and repealing Council Regulations (EEC) Nos 1191/69 and 1107/70, OJ L315, 3.12.2007, p 1.

7 Communication from the Commission, European Union framework for State aid in the form of public service compensation (2011), OJ C8, 11.1.2012, p 15.

8 Communication from the Commission on the application of the European Union State aid rules to compensation granted for the provision of services of general economic interest, OJ C8, 11.1.2012, p 4.

9 Commission Staff Working Document SEC(2010) 1545 final of 7 December 2010.

10 Article 7 of Directive 2004/18/EC.

11 Social services and health services are among the services listed in Annex II B to Directive 2004/18/EC. Contracts for such services are subject only to a limited number of provisions of the Directive (on the distinction between the services listed in Annexes II A and II B, see Articles 20 and 21 of Directive 2004/18/EC). Annex II B also includes an explicit reference to social services and health services. The codes referred to therein may be consulted on the DG Internal Market website at www.simap.europa.eu.

12 The technical specifications must be laid down at the start of the procurement process, and the results of the tendering process must be published, as required by Article 21 of Directive 2004/18/EC read in conjunction with Articles 23 and 35(4) of Directive 2004/18/EC.

13 Irrespective of the nature of the services.

14 See Commission Interpretative Communication on the Community law applicable to contract awards not or not fully subject to the provisions of the Public Procurement Directives (2006), OJ 1.8.2006, C179, page 2.

15 Proposal for a Directive of the European Parliament and of the Council on public procurement, COM/2011/0896 final; Proposal for a Directive of the European Parliament and of the Council on procurement by entities operating in the water, energy, transport and postal services sectors, COM/2011/0895 final; Proposal for a Directive of the European Parliament and of the Council on the award of concession contracts, COM/2011/0897 final.

16 "Internal market rules" refers to the rules in the TFEU on the freedom of establishment and the freedom to provide services (Articles 49 and 56 TFEU) and in the Services Directive.

17 See i.a. the White paper on Services of General Interest (COM(2004) 374 of 12 May 2004), the Communication on social services of general interest "Implementing the Community Lisbon programme: Social services of general interest in the European Union" (COM(2006) 177 of 26 April 2006) and the Communication on "Services of general interest, including social services of general interest: a new European commitment" (COM(2007) 725 final of 20 November 2007).

18 COM(2011) 900 final of 20.12.2011.

2 CONCEPT OF SGEI

[5.675]

1. What is a service of general interest (SGI)?

Protocol No 26 to the TFEU concerns SGIs, but does not define the concept. The Commission has clarified the concept in its Quality Framework (p. 3), where it explains that they are services that public authorities of the Member States at national, regional or local level classify as being of general interest and, therefore, subject to specific public service obligations (PSO). The term covers both economic activities (see the definition of SGEI below) and non-economic services. The latter are not subject to specific EU legislation and are not covered by the internal market and competition rules of the Treaty. Some aspects of how these services are organised may however be subject to other general Treaty rules, such as the principle of non-discrimination.

2. What is a service of general economic interest (SGEI)? Do public authorities have to introduce this concept into their domestic law?

The concept of SGEI appears in Articles 14 and 106(2) TFEU and in Protocol No 26 to the TFEU, but it is not defined in the TFEU or in secondary legislation. The Commission has clarified in its Quality Framework that SGEIs are economic activities which deliver outcomes in the overall public good that would not be supplied (or would be supplied under different conditions in terms of objective quality, safety, affordability, equal treatment or universal access) by the market without public intervention. A PSO is imposed on the provider by way of an entrustment and on the basis of a general interest criterion which ensures that the service is provided under conditions allowing it to fulfil its mission.

The Court has established that SGEIs are services that exhibit special characteristics as compared with those of other economic activities.[19]

The concept may apply to different situations and terms, depending on the Member States, and EU law does not create any obligation to designate formally a task or a service as being of general economic interest, except when such obligation is laid out in Union legislation (e.g. universal service in the postal and telecommunication sectors). If the content of an SGEI – i.e. public service obligations – is clearly identified, it is not necessary for the service in question to be designated 'SGEI'. The same is true of the concept of social services of general interest (SSGIs) that are economic in nature.

3. What is a social service of general interest (SSGI)?

The concept of SSGI is not defined in the TFEU or in secondary legislation. The Communication *Implementing the Community Lisbon programme: Social services of general interest in the European Union*[20] identified two main groups of SSGIs in addition to health services:

- statutory and complementary social security schemes, organised in various ways (mutual or occupational organisations), covering the main risks of life, such as those linked to health, ageing, occupational accidents, unemployment, retirement and disability;
- other essential services provided directly to the person. These services that play a prevention and social cohesion role consist of customised assistance to facilitate social inclusion and safeguard fundamental rights. In the first place, they offer assistance to persons faced by personal challenges or crises (such as debt, unemployment, drug addiction or family breakdown). Secondly, they include activities to ensure that the people concerned are able to completely reintegrate into society (rehabilitation, language training for immigrants) and, in particular, return to the labour market (occupational training and reintegration). These services complement and support the role of families in caring for the youngest and oldest members of society in particular. Thirdly, these services include activities to integrate people with long-term health or disability problems. Fourthly, they also include social housing, which provides housing for disadvantaged citizens or socially less advantaged groups. Certain services can obviously include all four of these dimensions.

The Commission Quality Framework (p. 3 and 4) has also referred to this description.

Moreover, the Communication on *Services of general interest, including social services of general interest: a new European commitment*[21] highlighted the objectives and the organisational principles which characterise SSGIs.

As these two communications make clear, SSGIs may be of an economic or non-economic nature, depending on the activity involved. The fact that an activity is termed 'social' is not of itself enough[22] for it to avoid being regarded as an 'economic activity' within the meaning of the Court's case law. SSGIs that are economic in nature are SGEIs (see the answer to question 2).

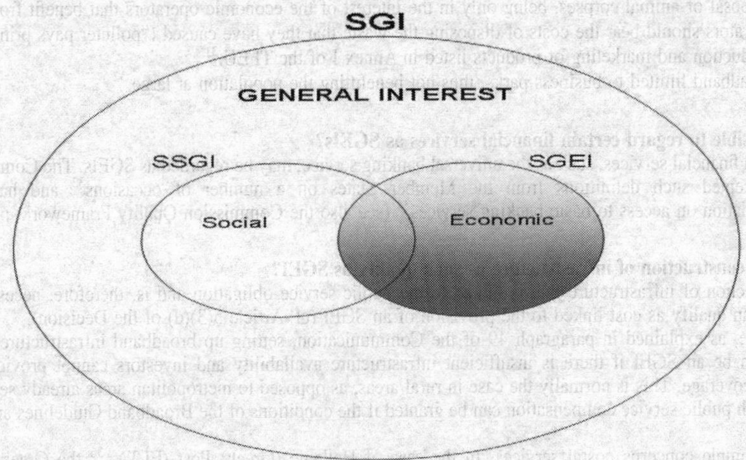

4. Do the Member States have any discretion when it comes to defining SGEIs?

Yes. As explained in the Communication,[23] public authorities in the Member States, whether at national, regional or local level, depending on the allocation of powers between them under national law, have considerable discretion when it comes to defining what they regard as services of general economic interest[24] (on the concept of SGEI, see the answer to question 2). The only limits are those imposed by EU law (see the answer to question 6) and manifest error of assessment (see the answer to question 7).

5. Can the Commission provide a list of criteria for the public authorities to use in determining whether a service is of general interest?

The scope and organisation of SGEIs vary considerably from one Member State to another, depending on the history and culture of public intervention in each Member State. SGEIs are therefore very diverse and disparities may exist in relation to users' needs and preferences because of different geographical, social and cultural situations. Accordingly, it is essentially the responsibility of the public authorities at national, regional or local level to decide the nature and scope of a service of general interest.

In accordance with the principles of subsidiarity and proportionality, the EU takes action only where necessary and within the limits of the powers conferred on it by the TFEU. Its action respects the diversity of situations in the Member States and the roles devolved to national, regional and local authorities to ensure the well-being of their citizens and promote social cohesion, while guaranteeing democratic choices in relation to the level of the quality of services, for example.

Therefore it is not for the Commission to provide a list of criteria for determining the general interest of a particular service. It is for the public authorities in the Member States to determine whether or not a service is in the general interest.

6. Does EU law impose limits on Member States' discretion when defining SGEIs?

Yes. In sectors which have been harmonised at Union level,[25] and where objectives of general interest have been taken into account,[26] the Member States' discretion cannot contradict the rules governing such harmonisation. Furthermore, Member States' discretion remains always subject to a control of manifest error.

Sectors harmonised at Union level:

- Where EU harmonisation rules refer only to certain specific services, the Member States have considerable discretion in defining additional services as SGEIs. For example, in the electronic communications sector, the Member States are required to lay down the universal service obligations provided for by the Directive, but they have discretion to go further than the Directive in defining electronic communication services as SGEIs.

7. Are there examples of manifest error of assessment by the Member States when defining SGEIs?

As explained in paragraph 46 of the Communication, the freedom of the Member States to define SGEIs is subject to review by the Commission and the Union's courts to check for manifest errors of assessment.[27]

The Court's case law and the Commission's decision-making practice illustrate certain limited examples of manifest error.

Examples:

- Port operations, i.e. the loading, unloading, transhipment, storage and movement in general of goods or any equipment in national ports, are not necessarily services of general economic interest, which exhibit special characteristics as compared with the general economic interest of other economic activities.[28]
- Activities consisting in advertising, e-commerce, the use of premium-rate telephone numbers in prize games, sponsoring or merchandising. Including them in the ambit of audio-visual public service is a manifest error of assessment.[29]
- Disposal of animal corpses, being only in the interest of the economic operators that benefit from it. These operators should bear the costs of disposing the waste that they have caused ("polluter pays principle").[30]
- Production and marketing of products listed in Annex I of the TFEU.[31]
- Broadband limited to business parks, thus not benefitting the population at large.[32]

8. Is it possible to regard certain financial services as SGEIs?

Yes. Certain financial services, such as the universal banking service, may be regarded as SGEIs. The Commission has already accepted such definitions from the Member States on a number of occasions[33] and has issued a Recommendation on access to basic banking services[34] (see also the Commission Quality Framework, p. 10).

9. Can the construction of infrastructure as such qualify as SGEI?

The construction of infrastructure that is linked to the public service obligation and is, therefore, necessary for its provision can qualify as cost linked to the provision of an SGEI (cf. Article 5(3)(d) of the Decision).

For example, as explained in paragraph 49 of the Communication, setting up broadband infrastructure in a given territory can be an SGEI if there is insufficient infrastructure availability and investors cannot provide adequate broadband coverage. This is normally the case in rural areas, as opposed to metropolitan areas already served by the market. Such public service compensation can be granted if the conditions of the Broadband Guidelines are complied with.[35]

Another example concerns postal services. In the case of Hellenic (Greek) Post (ELTA),[36] the Greek authorities defined the SGEI as a set of different services, including the postal universal service. The Commission verified that the authorities had not overcompensated the Greek Post for the net cost of providing the SGEI, including the depreciation costs of a new modernised infrastructure. Thus, the Greek Post was able to modernise its infrastructure and to improve the quality of the public service, in order to satisfy the requirements established by Directive 2002/39/EC.[37]

10. Can the creation and retention of jobs in an undertaking for the purposes of expanding its research and development activity (in biopharmacy, for example) be regarded as an SGEI?

It does not seem possible to regard the creation or retention of jobs in a given undertaking as an SGEI. SGEIs are services addressed to citizens or in the interest of society as a whole, an aspect which is not present in this case and cannot, therefore, be used to justify a measure under Article 106(2) TFEU.

On the other hand, the State may wish to participate in the financing of such activity, but that would constitute State Aid to the undertaking in question. Such participation may be perfectly compatible with EU law, for example under the Community framework for State Aid for research and development and innovation[38] or the general block exemption Regulation[39] for aid to employment, training or SMEs, depending on the intended purpose of the public intervention (support for research, development of employment or training, SMEs, etc.).

The rules on prior notification, eligible costs, eligibility conditions, etc. of the planned aid have to be assessed on the basis of the applicable texts, which will help to ensure that, where necessary, the aid is compatible with Article 107(3) TFEU.

11. Can a public authority classify a service as SGEI if a similar service is already provided by other operators in the market that are not entrusted with an SGEI?

Member States have a wide margin of discretion when it comes to defining SGEIs (see the answer to question 4). However, where there are other undertakings operating under normal market conditions, not entrusted with an SGEI, who already provide or can provide a service satisfactorily and under conditions, such as price, objective quality characteristics, continuity and access to the service, consistent with the public interest as defined by the State, the Commission considers that it would not be appropriate to attach a public service obligation to such a service.[40] Therefore, it is even more important that the Member States clearly specify the characteristics of the service in question, in particular the conditions for its provision and its target group. If a service is already provided by the market, albeit under conditions that are considered unsatisfactory by the Member State concerned, for instance because the market cannot provide it with the level of quality or at a price that public authorities might consider as being in the public interest (for example because transport fares are too expensive for low-income families), such a service can qualify as SGEI. This service must be offered on a non-discriminatory basis.

When the service is not already provided by the market, the question of whether it can be provided by the market is for the Member State to decide, while the Commission can only check for manifest error.

12. Can a service be defined as SGEI if the market would be able to provide it in the near future?

Where the classification of a service as SGEI is otherwise justified, the mere fact that the market may be able to provide it in the future would in principle not prevent a Member State from defining the service currently as an SGEI. However, in cases where it is clear that the market will be able to provide the service within a short time under the conditions (including price, quality, continuity and access to it) desired by the Member State, the public authorities should reduce the entrustment period accordingly and monitor the evolution of the market in order to be able to decide whether a new entrustment is still needed when the previous one expires. If the market is still failing to provide the service at the end of the entrustment period, and the Member State considers that the service still qualifies as an SGEI, a new entrustment compliant with Article 106 TFEU is possible.

As regards the question of whether it is clear that the market will be able to provide a particular service in the foreseeable future, the Commission's task is limited to checking for manifest errors in the Member State's assessment.

13. If a childcare provider, operating on market terms and not entrusted with the provision of an SGEI, gets into difficulties and risks going bankrupt, can the Member State at that moment entrust it with an SGEI in order to ensure continuity of the service (assuming there is a lack of other childcare providers in that area that could provide the service)?

With respect to childcare it should first of all be noted that under certain conditions the provision of this service can be considered as not involving an economic activity.[41] Where childcare services constitute an economic activity, they are often defined as an SGEI. A Member State can entrust a childcare provider with the provision of an SGEI if the public service obligation is clearly defined, and the entrustment is compliant with State Aid rules. It is possible that in a certain area, while often childcare providers are entrusted with an SGEI to provide childcare services at lower than market rates, others offer childcare services at market rates. If a childcare provider that has been operating on market terms risks going bankrupt and there are not sufficient alternative providers that could immediately step in, the Member State can entrust that provider with an SGEI under the Decision,[42] so as to ensure the continuity of the service (i.e. a sufficient number of childcare places). In such a specific situation related to capacity problems, however, the public authorities should consider limiting the duration of the SGEI entrustment to the time necessary to allow potential other market operators to take over the service at market terms.

Since no public service obligation has been entrusted to the childcare provider before, the SGEI compensation can in principle only cover future SGEI costs and has to be calculated on the basis of the parameters outlined in the entrustment act in accordance with the Decision.

As regards losses from the past, if the service provider cannot find private funding, these could be covered by rescue and restructuring aid, if the conditions of the R&R Guidelines[43] are fulfilled.

NOTES

19 Cases C-179/90 *Merci convenzionali porto di Genova* [1991] ECR I-5889, paragraph 27; Case C-242/95 *GT-Link A/S* [1997] ECR I-4449, paragraph 53; and Case C-266/96, *Corsica Ferries France SA* [1998] ECR I-3949, paragraph 45.

20 COM(2006) 177 final, 26 April 2006.

21 COM(2007) 725 final, 20 November 2007.

22 Joined Cases C-180/98 to C-184/98 *Pavlov* [2000] ECR I-6451, paragraph 118; Case C-218/00 *INAIL* [2002] ECR I-691, paragraph 37; and Case C-355/00 *Freskot* [2003] I-5263.

23 See paragraph 46 of the Communication.

24 Case T-17/02 *Fred Olsen* [2005] ECR II-2031, paragraph 216; Case T-289/03 *BUPA and Others* v *Commission* [2008] ECR II-81, paragraphs 166-169; Case T-309/04 *TV2* [2008] ECR II-2935, paragraphs 113 *et seq.*

25 For example, telecommunications and the postal and energy sectors have been harmonised at Union level. See Directive 2002/22/EC of the European Parliament and of the Council of 7 March 2002 on universal service and users' rights relating to electronic communications networks and services (Universal Service Directive), OJ L108, 24.4.2002, p 51 (as amended by Directive 2009/136/EC, OJ L337, 18.12.2009, p 11); Directive 97/67/EC of the European Parliament and of the Council of 15 December 1997 on common rules for the development of the internal market of Community postal services and the improvement of quality of service, OJ L15, 21.1.1998, p 14 (as amended by Directives 2002/39/EC, OJ L176, 5.7.2002, p 21 and 2008/06/EC, OJ L52, 27.2.2008, p 3); Directive 2009/72/EC of the European Parliament and of the Council of 13 July 2009 concerning common rules for the internal market in electricity, OJ L211, 14.8.2009, p 55.

26 Case C-206/98 *Commission* v *Belgium* [2000] ECR I-3509, paragraph 45.

27 Case T-17/02 *Fred Olsen* [2005] ECR II-2031, paragraph 216; Case T-289/03 *BUPA and Others* v *Commission* [2008] ECR II-81, paragraphs 165 *et seq.* Moreover, the Member States' discretion cannot be exercised in the face

of the applicable harmonisation rules – see the answer to question 6.

28 Case C-179/90, *Merci convenzionali porto di Genova* [1991] ECR I-5889, paragraph 27; Case C-242/95 *GT-Link* [1997] ECR I-4449, paragraph 53; and Joined Cases C-34/01 to C38/01 *Enirisorse* [2003] I-14243, paragraphs 33-34.

29 Communication from the Commission on the application of State aid rules to public service broadcasting, OJ C257, 27.10.2009, p 1.

30 Commission decision concerning State aid No SA.25051 – Germany – Association for disposal of dead animal bodies, OJ L236, 1.9.2012, eurlex.europa.eu/LexUriServ/LexUriServ.do?uri=OJ:L:2012:236:0001:0034:EN:PDF. See also Case C- 126/01 *Ministère de l'Economie, des Finances et de l'Industrie v GEMO* [2003] I-13769.

31 Commission decision concerning State aid No C 28/1998 – Italy – Centrale del Latte di Roma, OJ L265, 19.10.2000, eurlex. europa.eu/LexUriServ/LexUriServ.do?uri=OJ:L:2000:265:0015:0028:EN:PDF.

32 Commission decisions concerning State aid No N 890/2006 – France – SICOVAL, ec.europa.eu/competition/state_aid/cases/218142/218142_723454_30_2.pdf; State aid No. N 284/2005 – Ireland – Metropolitan Area Networks, ec.europa.eu/competition/state_aid/cases/199656/199656_581678_68_2.pdf.

33 Commission decisions concerning state aid No N 514/2001 – United Kingdom – Modernisation of the UK benefit payment system and provision of access to universal banking services through post offices, OJ C186, 6.8.2003, state aid No N 244/2003 – United Kingdom – Credit Union Provision of Access to Basic Financial Services, OJ C223, 10.9.2005, ; state aid No C 49/2006 — Italy — Poste Italiane — distribution of postal savings certificates, OJ L189, 21.7.2009, ; state aid No N 642/2005 — Sweden — Posten AB, OJ C291, 5.12.2007, ; state aid No N 650/2001 – Ireland – An Post, OJ C43, 27.2.2007.

34 Commission Recommendation on access to a basic payment account (C(2011)4977).

35 Communication from the Commission – Community Guidelines for the application of State aid rules in relation to rapid deployment of broadband networks, OJ C235, 30.9.2009, p 7.

36 Commission Decision on state aid SA.32562 – Greece – Aid to the Hellenic Post, OJ C99, 3.4.2012.

37 Directive 2002/39/EC of the European Parliament and of the Council of 10 June 2002 amending Directive 97/67/EC with regard to the further opening to competition of Community postal services, OJ L176, 5.7.2002, p 21.

38 Community framework for state aid for research and development and innovation, OJ C323, 30.12.2006, p 1.

39 Commission Regulation (EC) No 800/2008 of 6 August 2008 declaring certain categories of aid compatible with the common market in application of Articles 87 and 88 of the Treaty (Articles 107 and 108 TFEU), OJ L214, 9.8.2008, p 3.

40 Case C-205/99 *Analir* [2001] ECR I-1271, p 71. See also paragraph 48 of the Communication.

41 Judgment of the EFTA Court of 21 February 2008 in Case E-5/07.

42 Since homes for the elderly fall under the scope of application of the Decision (Article 2(1)(c)) irrespective of the amount of compensation, the SGEI Framework is not applicable.

43 Communication from the Commission – Community guidelines on State aid for rescuing and restructuring firms in difficulty, OJ C244, 1.10.2004, p 2.

3 THE NEW STATE AID SGEI PACKAGE

3.1 OVERVIEW OF THE NEW STATE AID SGEI PACKAGE

[5.676]

14. What instruments does the new State Aid SGEI package consist of?

The State Aid SGEI package consists of four instruments applicable to all authorities (national, regional, local) that grant compensation for the provision of SGEIs:

- The **Communication** clarifies basic concepts of State Aid which are relevant to SGEIs, such as the notions of aid, SGEI, economic activity, the relation between public procurement and State Aid rules, etc.
- The **SGEI *de minimis* Regulation** provides that SGEI compensation not exceeding EUR 500,000 over any period of three fiscal years does not fall under State Aid scrutiny.
- The revised **Decision** exempts Member States from the obligation to notify public service compensation to the Commission, if the compatibility conditions of the Decision are fulfilled.
- The revised **Framework** sets out the rules for assessing SGEI compensation that constitutes State Aid and is not exempted from notification by the Decision. Those cases have to be notified to the Commission and may be declared compatible if they meet the criteria of the Framework.

15. What is the purpose of the SGEI Communication?

The Communication gives a comprehensive and practical overview of the EU State Aid concepts relevant to SGEIs and provides explanations of key issues in a single document. It summarises the most relevant case law of the EU Courts and the Commission's decision-making practice. It aims at facilitating the application of State Aid rules for national, regional and local authorities as well as public service providers. The Commission has sought to provide as much clarity as possible on key concepts, such as the notion of economic activity, effect on trade or SGEI, as well as on the relation between State Aid and public procurement rules.

16. What is the SGEI de minimis Regulation?

Under the SGEI *de minimis* Regulation, public funding of SGEIs not exceeding EUR 500,000, granted over any period of three fiscal years, is not considered as State Aid. This is because the amount is so small that it can be deemed not to have an impact on cross-border trade or competition. Since the measures are not considered as State Aid, there is no obligation to ***notify them in advance to the Commission.***

17. What is the Decision about?

The Decision specifies the conditions under which compensation to companies for the provision of public services is compatible with the EU State Aid rules and does not have to be notified to the Commission in advance.

18. What is the Framework about?

The Framework specifies the conditions under which public service compensation not covered by the Decision is compatible with the EU State Aid rules. Such compensation will have to be notified to the Commission due to the higher risk of distortion of competition, so that the Commission can make an in-depth assessment and decide whether the measure in question is compatible with the internal market.

19. What are the respective objectives of the Decision and the Framework? What are the differences between the two?

Both texts specify the conditions under which public service compensation constituting State Aid is compatible with the TFEU.

The most important difference lies in the fact that public service compensation covered by the Decision **does not need to be notified** to the Commission. Once the criteria of the Decision are met, the Member State concerned may grant the compensation without delay. However, when the conditions set out in the Decision are not met, the compensation would fall under the Framework. This means that it must be notified in advance to the Commission so that it can check whether the State Aid concerned is compatible with the TFEU.

In addition, given that cases falling under the Framework are typically large cases that could potentially create more significant distortions of competition, the compatibility conditions are generally stricter than under the Decision. For more details on compatibility conditions, see section 3.5.2.

20. What are the logical steps of the analysis for public service compensation?

The graph below outlines the main steps to be followed for determining which instrument of the SGEI package may apply to public service compensation.

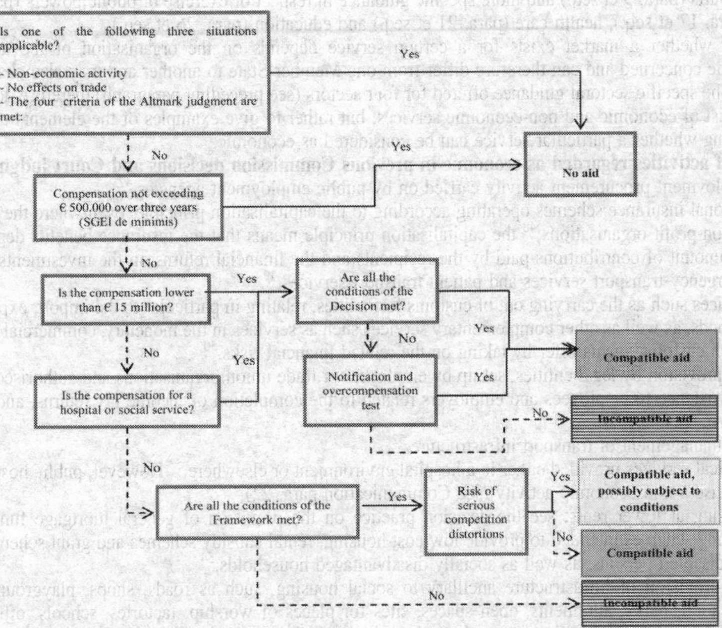

21. How can legal certainty be provided to SGEI providers? What if they do not know whether the compensation falls under the Decision, the Framework or the SGEI de minimis Regulation?

The State aid SGEI package and the Commission's decisions applying the Framework are published in the Official Journal and on the internet. The responsibility for making sure that any compensation for an SGEI is in compliance with the State Aid rules lies with the national authorities that entrust an undertaking with the provision of the SGEI. Where aid is granted under the Decision, the entrustment act must make reference to the Decision, so that the SGEI provider is informed about the legal basis and can check compliance with the Decision. If the entrustment act does not make reference to the Decision, the SGEI provider can ask the entrusting authority on what legal basis the aid is granted and check that, where the aid falls under the Framework, it is covered by an approval decision by the Commission.

22. Are there any legal obligations for SGEI providers?

The SGEI package does not impose any specific obligations on SGEI providers. The public authority entrusting the provider with the SGEI has to ensure that State Aid rules are respected. However, the conditions necessary to ensure that the compensation granted is in line with the State Aid rules should be reflected in the entrustment act so that the provider is fully aware of them. The provider ultimately bears the risk of having to reimburse the compensation if it is granted in violation of the State Aid rules.

23. Does the SGEI package establish the right of undertakings to receive aid in the form of public service compensation?

Under Article 107(1) TFEU State Aid is incompatible with the TFEU, except where the derogations provided for by the Treaty itself apply. Hence the principle is that State Aid is not permitted and can be granted only exceptionally in the cases and in compliance with the conditions provided for by Article 107(2) and (3) and Article 106(2) TFEU. Consequently, there is no right on the part of undertakings to State Aid.

The SGEI package does not establish the right of undertakings to receive aid in the form of public service compensation, but it defines compatibility conditions for such aid where the public authorities of the Member States decide to organise and finance SGEIs by means of State Aid.

3.2 COMMUNICATION

3.2.1 WHEN DO THE STATE AID RULES APPLY AND WHAT ARE THE CONSEQUENCES?

24. When do the State Aid rules laid down in the TFEU apply to the organisation and financing of SGEIs?

The State aid rules apply only to 'undertakings'. This concept covers any entity engaged in an economic activity, regardless of the entity's legal status or the way in which it is financed.[44] In particular, it is irrelevant whether the entity is set up to generate profits or not (Communication para. 9).

25. When does an activity qualify as 'economic' within the meaning of the competition rules?

Any activity consisting in offering goods and/or services in a given market is an economic activity within the meaning of the competition rules[45] (see Communication para. 11). In this context, the fact that the activity in question is termed 'social' or is carried on by a non-profit operator is not in itself enough[46] to avoid classification as an economic activity. The Communication provides both general guidance on the concept of economic activity as developed by the European courts (para. 9 et seq.) and more specific guidance in respect of exercise of public powers (para. 16), social security (para. 17 et seq.), health care (para. 21 et seq.) and education (para. 26 et seq.).

Importantly, whether a market exists for a certain service depends on the organisation of the activity by the Member State concerned and can therefore differ from one Member State to another and may also change over time (para. 12). The specific sectoral guidance offered for four sectors (see preceding paragraph) therefore does not seek to establish a list of economic and non-economic services, but rather to give examples of the elements that play a role in determining whether a particular service can be considered as economic.

Examples of activities regarded as economic in previous Commission decisions and Court judgments:

- Employment procurement activity carried on by public employment agencies.[47]
- Optional insurance schemes operating according to the capitalisation principle, even where they are managed by non-profit organisations;[48] the capitalisation principle means that the insurance benefits depend solely on the amount of contributions paid by the recipients and the financial returns on the investments made.
- Emergency transport services and patient transport services.[49]
- Services such as the carrying out of customs formalities, relating in particular to the import, export and transit of goods, as well as other complementary services such as services in the monetary, commercial and tax fields, which customs agents offer by taking on the related financial risks.[50]
- The provision by legal entities, set up by employers or trade union organisations and authorised by the State, of assistance to employees and employers related to the completion of income tax returns, and other related advice.[51]
- The management of transport infrastructure.[52]
- Medical services provided either in a hospital environment or elsewhere.[53] However, public hospitals can also exercise a non-economic activity (see Communication para. 22).
- Housing at lower rents; see the decision practice on the provision of general mortgage funds, affordable housing schemes intended to provide low-cost housing, rental subsidy schemes and grant schemes for elderly and disabled persons, as well as socially disadvantaged households.[54]
- The provision of infrastructure ancillary to social housing, such as roads, shops, playgrounds, places of recreation, parks, allotments, open spaces, sites for places of worship, factories, schools, offices and other buildings or land and such other works and services, which is needed to ensure a good environment for social housing.[55]

On the concept of economic activity within the meaning of the TFEU rules on the internal market, see the answer to question 223.

26. May members of a liberal profession constitute 'undertakings' within the meaning of the competition rules?

Yes. The Court of Justice has taken the view that medical specialists may provide, in their capacity as self-employed economic operators, services in a market, namely the market in specialist medical services, and thus constitute undertakings. The fact that they provide complex and technical services and the fact that the practice of their profession is regulated cannot alter that conclusion.[56]

27. When does an activity qualify as non-economic for the purposes of the competition rules?

Two relevant categories of activities which have been determined to be non-economic are:

Activities related to the exercise of state prerogatives

Activities linked to the exercise of state prerogatives by the State itself, or by authorities functioning within the limits of their public authority, do not constitute economic activities for the purposes of the competition rules. This exception is limited to those activities that intrinsically form part of the prerogatives of official authority and are performed by the State, i.e. for which the Member State concerned has not decided to introduce market mechanisms (Communication para. 16). In this context, it is irrelevant whether the State is acting directly through a body forming part of the State administration or by way of a separate body on which it has conferred special or exclusive rights.[57]

Examples of non-economic activities linked to the exercise of state prerogatives:

- Activities related to the army or the police.
- The maintenance and improvement of air navigation safety,[58] security,[59] air traffic control, maritime traffic control and safety.[60]
- Anti-pollution surveillance[61] is a task in the public interest that forms part of the essential functions of the State as regards protection of the environment in maritime areas.
- The organisation, financing and enforcement of prison sentences in order to ensure the operation of the penal system.[62]

Certain activities of a purely social nature

The case law has provided a set of criteria under which certain activities with a purely social function are considered non-economic.

Examples of non-economic activities of a purely social nature:

- The management under the control of the State of compulsory social security schemes pursuing an exclusively social objective, functioning according to the principle of solidarity, offering insurance benefits independently of contributions and of the earning of the insured person.[63] See para. 17 *et seq.* of the Communication on the factors distinguishing economic from non-economic social security schemes.
- The provision of childcare and public education financed as a general rule by the public purse and carrying out a public service task in the social, cultural and educational fields directed towards the population.[64] See para. 26 *et seq.* of the Communication on the factors distinguishing economic from non-economic activities in the area of education.
- The organisation of public hospitals which are an integral part of a national health service and are almost entirely based on the principle of solidarity, funded directly from social security contributions and other State resources, and which provide their services free of charge to affiliated persons on the basis of universal coverage.[65] See para. 21 *et seq.* of the Communication on the factors distinguishing economic from non-economic activities in the area of health care.

28. When a public authority provides information and advice to citizens within its area of responsibility, does it engage in an economic activity within the meaning of the competition rules?

The provision of general information by public authorities (at national, regional or local level) concerning the way in which the competent bodies apply the rules under their responsibility is inextricably linked to the exercise of their public authority. This activity is not regarded as economic within the meaning of the competition rules.

29. The Communication provides specific guidance on the distinction between economic and non-economic activity for four areas. Are all activities outside those four areas always economic?

No. The Communication offers guidance on when an activity is economic and when it is non-economic and builds on the case law of the European courts. In addition to the general principles (para. 9 *et seq.*), the Communication provides more specific guidance for certain areas, such as health care and education, and lists relevant factors for the test of whether a specific activity is economic.

Neither the examples given in the specific sections (such as the examples of areas that intrinsically form part of the exercise of public powers in para. 16) nor the selection of areas for which more specific guidance is provided suggest that these are exhaustive examples. This can be seen from the wording of the Communication, where in particular para. 14 clearly states that no exhaustive list can be drawn up. It is a consequence of the fact that the notion of economic activity can change over time (see following question 30). For activities that are not specifically referred to, the general principles contained in para. 9 *et seq.* provide guidance on whether an activity is economic or not.

30. Can classification as economic or non-economic change over time?

Yes. The classification of an activity may depend on the way in which the activity is organised in a Member State and it can change over time due to policy decisions on the way in which the activity is organised or as a result of market developments (Communication para. 12).

31. May the TFEU rules on State Aid apply to non-profit service providers?

Yes. The mere fact that an entity is non-profit-making does not mean that the activities which it carries on are not of an economic nature.[66] The legal status of an entity providing SSGIs does not affect the nature of the activity concerned. The relevant criterion is whether the entity pursues an economic activity (Communication para. 9).

For example, a non-profit association or a charitable organisation pursuing an economic activity will constitute an 'undertaking' only for that specific activity (Communication para. 9, last subparagraph). The competition rules will not apply to their non-economic activities.

Example:

The provision of emergency transport services and patient transport services by non-profit organisations may constitute an economic activity. Public service obligations may make the services provided by such organisations less competitive than comparable services rendered by other operators not bound by such obligations, but that fact cannot prevent the activities in question from being regarded as economic.[67]

32. Is it possible for a public authority to prefer some kinds of organisations (e.g. public/for profit/not for profit organisations) as the provider of an SGEI?

State aid rules do not impose specific criteria for the choice of the provider but they apply equally to public and private undertakings. Therefore, State aid rules in principle do not prevent Member States from giving preference to some types of providers. However, public authorities can be bound by other areas of EU law, such as in particular the rules on public procurement, the rules on the internal market or sectoral rules, such as those in the field of transport.

When EU public procurement rules are applicable, compliance with the specific requirements of these rules is also a condition for the compatibility of the aid in cases covered by the Framework (para. 19 of the Framework). On this issue, as far as public procurement and internal market rules are concerned, see sections 4 and 6, in particular questions 209 and 227.

33. Are social action centres which provide SSGIs (such as services for elderly and disabled people) subject to the State Aid rules?

One cannot generalise about whether or not local social assistance centres are subject to the competition law rules, and specifically to the State Aid rules, as this depends on the activities they carry out.

If a centre of this type runs a meals-on-wheels or home care service, for instance, and the same services could be provided by other service providers, whether public or private, then the centre is supplying services in a market and is thus performing an economic activity within the meaning of the competition rules (see the answer to question 25). This does not, however, imply that all the centre's activities should be classified as economic in nature; it may also perform an activity involving social protection only, such as making public welfare payments to people on benefits, which would not constitute an economic activity.

34. Does the distribution of vouchers by a municipality to certain categories of individual users to enable them to obtain SGEIs constitute State Aid?

The Member States, including local authorities, can provide this type of support to people using these services under the conditions laid down in Article 107(2)(a) of the TFEU, which stipulates that aid must have a social character and be granted to individual consumers without discrimination related to the origin of the products concerned.

35. Does social assistance granted to certain beneficiaries such as low-income households (depending, for example, on their actual expenditure on an SGEI and/or other objective criteria arising from their individual situation) and paid directly to the service provider under a 'third party pays' arrangement constitute State Aid?

If there is, for instance, a risk that the assistance provided may not fulfil its social purpose if it is paid directly to the beneficiary, a social organisation may decide to pay some or all of it to the party providing the service concerned (e.g. a social housing landlord or a school canteen for children).

Such a payment will not constitute State Aid to the service provider if the amount paid under a 'third party pays' arrangement and the basis on which it is calculated are clearly defined and closely linked to the final beneficiary, who must be a natural person. This implies that the transfer does not confer any other advantages on the service provider. For instance, the total amount of rent payable to the service provider must be established independently and in advance, so that the remaining rent payable by the beneficiary is genuinely reduced by the amount which the service provider has already received from the social organisation concerned.

36. SGEIs are often provided in a local context. Do they really affect trade between Member States?

In the field of State Aid law, the effect on trade does not depend on the local or regional character of the service supplied, or on the scale of the activity concerned. The relatively small amount of aid provided or the relatively small size of the entity which receives it do not in themselves rule out the possibility that trade between Member States might be affected.[68] Even a small amount of aid can boost the services supplied by one service provider, thereby making it more difficult for other European companies to supply the same services on the local market.

However, on the basis of its own experience, the Commission has established ceilings up to which it believes that aid will not affect trade or competition. For instance, aid for the provision of an SGEI not exceeding a ceiling of EUR 500,000 over any period of three years is, under the SGEI *de minimis* Regulation, deemed not to affect trade between Member States and/or not to distort or threaten to distort competition and therefore does not fall under Article 107(1) of the TFEU. Furthermore, under the general *de minimis* Regulation (Regulation 1998/2006) aid not exceeding a ceiling of EUR 200000 (EUR 100000 for undertakings active in the road transport sector) is deemed not to affect trade between Member States.[69]

Moreover, in certain cases there is indeed no effect on trade due to the local character of the service. The Communication provides examples of decisions taken by the Commission (para. 40), concerning for example swimming pools to be used predominantly by the local population[70] and local museums unlikely to attract crossborder visitors[71] (for more detail see question 38 below).

General example of effect on trade between Member States

Subsidies payable to Dutch service stations located near the German border, as a result of an increase in national fuel prices following a rise in excise duties in the Netherlands, affected trade between Member States, since their purpose was to mitigate the disparity between the level of excise duties payable in the Netherlands and the amount of excise duty levied on light oils in Germany.[72]

Example of effect on trade between Member States where SGEIs are concerned

Public subsidies for running regular coach services in the municipality of Stendal, Germany, paid to a company which provided only local or regional transport and did not provide any transport services outside its country of origin, could have an impact on trade between Member States.[73]

37. Is there really an effect on trade in cases where a single operator provides a specific SGEI in a region?

Even if an operator providing a specific SGEI (as in the case of specialised medical care or ambulance services) is the only operator within a region or local community because there are no others there, this does not rule out the possibility of operators from other Member States being interested in providing the SGEI in question. This means that one cannot rule out the possibility of there being a potential impact on trade between Member States.[74] Moreover, the regional operator could be active or plan to operate in other regions.

38. Are there any examples of local SGEIs which do not really seem to affect trade between Member States?

Yes. The Commission has taken a number of decisions on State Aid whereby measures designed to fund local services (irrespective of whether the latter are SGEIs, SSGIs of an economic nature or purely commercial services) have been deemed not to affect trade between Member States (see also Communication para. 40):

Examples of measures considered to have no effect on trade between Member States

- In the case of the Dorsten swimming pool,[75] it was considered that an annual subsidy for the construction and operation of a public swimming pool in Dorsten which would be used only by the local population could not affect trade between Member States.
- In the case of the Irish hospitals,[76] the view taken was that a system of capital allowances aiming at the creation of facilities for relatively small local public hospitals, serving a local hospital market with clear undercapacity, could not attract investment or customers from other Member States and could not, therefore, affect trade between Member States.
- In the case of service areas in Tenerife,[77] it was considered that subsidies granted for the construction by local road haulage associations of municipal service areas for their members could not affect trade between Member States, as they were for local use only.
- In the case of local museums in Sardinia,[78] the view taken was that funding museum-related projects of a limited size and budget would not affect trade between Member States, as – except in the case of a few major museums of international repute – people from other Member States were not liable to cross borders for the primary purpose of visiting these museums.
- It was ruled that funding for Basque theatrical productions[79] did not affect trade between Member States because these were small-scale productions put on by local micro-enterprises or small companies, their potential audience was restricted to a specific geographic and linguistic region, and they could not attract cross-border tourism.
- In a case concerning funding for a centre promoting the Cypriot culture and heritage conservation in Nicosia (Cyprus),[80] the Commission found that the local character and the geographical position of the centre together with the nature of the activity exclude any effect on trade between Member States.
- The Commission considered that support to build a medium- and long-term mental health care unit in the northeast of Portugal[81] does not affect trade between Member States because of the limited capacity of the unit (50 beds) that will almost entirely be used for the provision of services to residents of the area and because of the lack of interest of other entities to provide such services in this region.
- In a case concerning funding to a newspaper publisher publishing a daily newspaper in Madeira[82] the Commission concluded that there was no effect on trade. There are only two daily newspapers published in Madeira, none of which is published by a company from another Member State. Both publishers are not active in any other market where there is any competition with companies from other Member States.
- The Commission found that the sale of land by a Dutch municipality to a riding school[83] cannot have any effect on trade, even if sold at a lower than market price, because of the manifestly local character of the riding school.

39. What if an activity is economic and affects trade between Member States?

If an activity is economic and affects trade between Member States, it is covered by the competition rules.

40. Does the application of the competition rules mean that the Member States are required to change the ways in which their SGEIs are organised and run?

No. The fact that the competition rules apply does not mean that public authorities are required to ensure that there are a large number of service providers on the market. Nor does it mean that public authorities are obliged to abolish any special or exclusive rights already granted to service providers which are necessary for and proportionate to the performance of the SGEIs concerned. The public authorities can grant such rights provided that they do not go beyond what is necessary to enable service providers to carry out their task of providing services of general interest under economically acceptable conditions.[84] Similarly, the public authorities are not under any obligation to privatise providers of SGEIs (see also Communication para. 37).

41. What if a public authority provides compensation for a service of general interest which is deemed to be of an economic nature?

Public service compensation provided by a public authority to a service provider may constitute State Aid if the criteria established by the Court of Justice in its Altmark ruling are not cumulatively met (see the answers to the questions in section 3.2.3) and if the other State Aid[85] criteria are met. Nevertheless, the fact that public service compensation constitutes State Aid does not in itself mean that it is not permissible, as it may be compatible with the TFEU.

42. Do the State Aid rules impose a specific organisational model on the public authorities as regards SGEIs?

No. The public authorities have considerable discretion as regards the way in which they choose to manage the SGEIs which they put in place. Under the State Aid rules, the public authorities can organise and finance their SGEIs as they see fit, provided that the compensation they provide in this context does not go beyond what is necessary to ensure that the SGEIs are performed under economically acceptable conditions, in accordance with Article 106(2) of the TFEU.

43. Can the financial sums granted in connection with the transfer of powers between public bodies in the context of decentralisation be classified as State Aid?
No. The concept of State Aid draws no distinctions on the basis of the level (central, regional, local or other) at which it is granted. However, it applies only in the case of a transfer of resources to one or more undertakings which meet(s) the conditions laid down in Article 107(1) of the TFEU.
Where financial transfers are made within state structures on the other hand (from the state to regions, or from a department to municipalities, for example), purely in line with the transfer of public powers and in a way that does not relate to economic activity, there is no transfer of state resources such as to confer an advantage on an undertaking.

44. Does funding an in-house body — within the meaning of the rules on public procurement — which provides SGEIs imply ruling out the application of the State Aid rules?
No. The term 'in-house' is used in public procurement law, while the State Aid rules fall under competition law. Whether or not the competition rules, and in particular the State Aid rules, are applicable depends not on the legal status or the nature of the body providing SGEIs, but on the 'economic' character of the activity performed by that body (Communication para. 9). According to settled case law, any activity that consists in supplying goods and/or services in a particular market is an economic activity within the meaning of the competition rules (for examples of economic activities within the meaning of the competition rules, see the answer to question 25). Consequently, if the public funding of an economic activity performed by an in-house body within the meaning of the rules on public contracts meets the conditions laid down in Article 107(1) of the TFEU[86] and does not meet all the conditions set out in the *Altmark* judgment (for these conditions, see the answer to question 61), the State Aid rules are applicable (see Communication paras. 13 and 37). In this context, it should be borne in mind that when financial transfers are made within state structures (from the state to regions, or from a department to municipalities, for example), purely in line with the transfer of public powers and in a way that does not relate to any economic activity, there is no transfer of state resources to an undertaking, which means there is no State Aid (see question 43).

45. What are the consequences if compensation for an SGEI is indeed deemed to be State Aid?
The fact that public service compensation constitutes State Aid **does not mean that such compensation is forbidden.** This compensation is compatible with the TFEU when the conditions specified in the Decision[87] or the Framework[88] are met.[89]

3.2.2 Entrustment act

46. What is the objective of an 'act of entrustment'?
An act of entrustment (see Communication para. 51 et seq.) is the act which entrusts the provision of an SGEI to the undertaking concerned and spells out the nature of the task as well as the scope and the general operational conditions of the SGEI. A public service assignment is necessary in order to define the obligations of the undertaking and of the State. In the absence of such an act, the specific task of the undertaking is unknown and fair compensation cannot be determined.

47. What types of acts of entrustment are considered to be adequate?
An entrustment in the sense of Article 106(2) TFEU and in the sense of the Altmark judgment only requires that the act of entrustment take the form of one or more acts having binding legal force under national law. The specific form of the act (or acts) may be determined by each Member State, depending among other things on its political and/or administrative organisation.
According to the basic rules of administrative law, every local, regional or central public authority needs a legal basis in order to define an SGEI and finance it. Consequently, the notion of act of entrustment can largely correspond to the legal basis that the public authority concerned chooses in each case at its own discretion. It is not necessary for this act to bear the title of act of entrustment. It is also not necessary for Member States to establish a special legal framework for adopting so-called 'acts of entrustment'.
There is therefore no standard 'one size fits all' act of entrustment; it depends both on the public authority entrusting the service and on the activity concerned.
It should be noted that under the State Aid rules the requirements in respect of an act of entrustment are rather basic: this does not exclude the possibility that Member States' authorities may add more detail to the act of entrustment, such as, for example, quality requirements. However, certain elements have to be specified in the entrustment act, such as the content and the duration of the obligation, the parameters for calculating, controlling and reviewing the compensation and arrangements for avoiding and recovering any overcompensation (Communication para. 52).
Where State Aid for an SGEI is granted under the Decision or the Framework, the requirements for the entrustment act are set out explicitly and with additional details in Art. 4 and para. 16 respectively (i.e.: the undertaking and, where applicable, the territory concerned; the nature of any exclusive rights assigned to the undertaking by the granting authority; a description of the compensation mechanisms; reference to the Decision).
Approval or authorisation given by a public authority to a service provider, authorising the provision of certain services, does not correspond to the notion of act of entrustment. This is because it does not create an obligation for the operator to provide the services concerned, but just allows it to exercise an economic activity by offering certain services in a market. An example could be the authorisation given to an operator to open a childcare centre or a centre for elderly people based only on the operator's compliance with public health, safety or quality rules.
Examples of acts of entrustment:

- Concession contract[90] and public service contract
- Ministerial programme contracts[91]
- Ministerial instructions[92]
- Laws[93] and Acts[94]

- Yearly or multiannual performance contracts[95]
- Legislative decrees[96] and any kind of regulatory decisions, as well as municipal decisions or acts.

48. Is an act of entrustment necessary even for an SSGI?

The competition rules apply to services of general interest that are economic in nature (as regards the concept of economic activity for the purposes of the competition rules, see the answer to question 25). The fact that the activity in question may be called 'social' is not of itself enough to avoid classification as an 'economic activity' within the meaning of these rules. Thus, entrustment being one of the necessary conditions for public service compensation to be compatible with the Treaty, it is mandatory for operators that are responsible for SGEIs, including SSGIs of an economic nature.

49. Which authorities are entitled to entrust a company with an SGEI? Do municipal authorities have this competence?

It is a question of national law which authorities are entitled to entrust a company with an SGEI. EU law does not set any requirements in this respect. In general, any authority that has the competence to define and finance an SGEI would also have the competence to entrust an undertaking with the provision of this SGEI.

50. Can the SGEI provider itself, who often has specific knowledge, define the content of the entrustment act?

In certain Member States, it is not uncommon for providers to develop and propose services that are then discussed with and financed by the public authorities. The concept of entrustment act under Article 106(2) TFEU and EU State Aid law in general does not contain any limitation on the involvement of the provider in drawing up the entrustment act. However, the ultimate decision whether to entrust the provider has to come from the public authority. This requirement can be satisfied, for instance, by approving the proposal of the provider (Communication para. 53; see on this issue also question 59).

51. Does the concept of act of entrustment within the meaning of Article 106(2) TFEU and of the SGEI package correspond to the concept of 'provider mandated by the State' within the meaning of Article 2(2)(j) of the Services Directive?

No. The concept of act of entrustment within the meaning of Article 106(2) TFEU and the SGEI package and that of 'provider mandated by the State' referred to in Article 2(2)(j) of the Services Directive are two matching concepts, in that they presuppose the existence of an obligation for the SGEI provider to provide the service. The existence of an obligation to provide is an essential element of both concepts.

On the other hand, the two concepts have different functions. The first concept is one of the preconditions that have to be met before public service compensation can be regarded as compliant with the conditions of the *Altmark* case law or as compatible with Article 106(2) TFEU, and possibly exempted from notification (if it falls within the scope of the Decision), while the second concept aims at delimiting the scope of the exclusion of certain social services from the ambit of the Services Directive.

Thus, under the SGEI package, the act of entrustment corresponds to the act that entrusts an undertaking with providing an SGEI. In this case, besides establishing an obligation to provide the service, as indicated above, the act of entrustment must also define, inter alia, the nature and duration of the public service obligations, the entities entrusted with providing the services, the compensation calculation parameters, and the safeguards for avoiding overcompensation (see also questions 46 and 47).

In the context of the Services Directive, the Commission takes the view that for a provider to be regarded as 'mandated by the State' within the meaning of Article 2(2)(j) it must be under an obligation to provide a service entrusted to it by the State. A provider under an obligation to provide a service, for instance as a result of a public procurement procedure or service concession, can be regarded as a provider 'mandated by the State' within the meaning of the Services Directive. This also applies to any other type of measure taken by the State provided that it involves an obligation for the provider in question to furnish the service.

Consequently, an operator receiving an act of entrustment within the meaning of the SGEI package will also be regarded as 'mandated' within the meaning of the Services Directive. Under the State Aid rules, the act of entrustment will require, of course, compliance with additional conditions, relating in particular to the mechanisms implemented in order to ensure that the aid received does not exceed the costs incurred by the service provider.

52. Does the following constitute an act of entrustment within the meaning of the State Aid rules and the Services Directive: a decision by a regional public authority defining a vocational training social service of general interest and entrusting management of this service to one or more training entities?

A decision by a regional public authority, with binding legal force under national law, that defines (a) the nature and duration of the public service obligations, (b) the undertaking or undertakings entrusted with these obligations and the territory concerned, (c) the nature of any exclusive or special rights granted to the undertaking(s), (d) the parameters for calculating, controlling and reviewing the compensation, and (e) the arrangements for avoiding and repaying any overcompensation may constitute an act of entrustment within the meaning of the Decision (see also question 47 above).

Such a decision, constituting an act of entrustment within the meaning of the State Aid rules, also constitutes an act mandating the provider within the meaning of the Services Directive because it creates an obligation on the undertaking(s) in question to provide the service.

On the other hand, if the decision in question imposes an obligation to provide the service but does not include the elements mentioned above, it constitutes an act mandating the provider within the meaning of the Services Directive but not an act of entrustment within the meaning of the SGEI package.

As regards the application of the Services Directive, see section 7.

53. In the case of an SGEI co-financed by several public authorities, is it necessary for each of the public authorities concerned to adopt its own act of entrustment or is it possible to refer, when granting the compensation, to the act of entrustment issued by the SGEI's 'lead' or organising authority?

From the point of view of the State Aid rules, there is no template act of entrustment; this act must be adapted to the national law of the Member State concerned, under which it must establish the obligation of the selected provider to provide the service. Thus, the question whether an act of entrustment within the meaning of the SGEI package, adopted by a 'lead' public authority such as a region, is also valid for other authorities (for instance a municipality or another region) is a matter of national law.

Examples of acts which could constitute an 'act of entrustment' within the meaning of the SGEI package in the case of an SSGI/SGEI co-financed by several public authorities:

- An act issued by a region and then approved by a municipal council decision; the approving decision can also constitute an act of entrustment by the municipality concerned.
- An act of entrustment issued and approved jointly by a region, a county and a municipality or by two municipalities and two regions for a given SGEI to be provided by one or more specified providers.

As a general rule, once an act of entrustment establishes the conditions set out in para. 52 of the Communication, the chosen form of legal act and the number of public authorities concerned do not influence its nature as an act of entrustment within the meaning of the SGEI package.

54. Where a public authority wishes to entrust several SGEIs to one or more service providers, is it necessary for that authority to adopt several acts corresponding to individual SGEIs?

No. It is not necessary to adopt several acts of entrustment, each corresponding to one particular SGEI or service provider. Nevertheless, the act of entrustment must indicate the nature, duration and other necessary details of each public service obligation imposed on each operator by the public authority. It is not necessary to specify each individual service if the content and scope of each SGEI are sufficiently precise.

55. Should the act of entrustment specify a 'task' or 'specific activities' to be performed?

The act of entrustment does not have to specify each and every activity involved in the provision of an SGEI.

Where it is not possible to spell out the services concerned more precisely, a broad definition of the public service task can be accepted, as long as the scope of the task is clearly set out. Nevertheless, the more precisely an act of entrustment defines the task assigned, the greater the level of protection from challenge under the State Aid rules (for example by competitors) for the compensation granted.

It is also up to the public authorities, as well as being in their best interest, to make it clear how SGEI tasks are to be performed, for instance by specifying quality requirements.

56. How should an act of entrustment concerning services such as SSGIs that have to be on the one hand viewed globally, and on the other tailored to the specific needs of individual users, be drafted? Does the act of entrustment have to describe each service to be provided?

The act of entrustment has to specify the nature and duration of the public service obligations, the entities entrusted with the provision of the services, the parameters for calculating the compensation (but not the exact amount of compensation to be awarded), and the safeguards put in place to avoid overcompensation.

It is not always necessary to include in the act of entrustment each type of service to be provided. For instance, there is no need to refer to each type of healthcare service, and something along the lines of 'daily medical assistance at home for elderly people in the city of x' may be sufficient. However, the act of entrustment must allow the correct allocation of costs between the SGEI and non-SGEI activities which the service provider may offer.

Certain types of SGEIs, such as assistance to elderly or disadvantaged people, may require different types of service within the framework of an overall public service task. The purpose of the act of entrustment is not to restrict the way in which the provision of SGEIs is organised, but to set out a clear framework within which those SGEIs are provided and the scope of the services concerned.

The elements that have to be included in an act of entrustment for the purposes of the State Aid rules do not in any way limit the discretion public authorities have in defining and organising their SGEIs. Member States and public bodies have a wide margin of discretion when it comes to defining the public service tasks they want to put in place, and the precise/highly detailed services which form part of these tasks do not necessarily have to be specified.[97]

Public authorities can go beyond the basic act of entrustment requirements and specify criteria that they want to set for the purpose of improving the performance of the undertakings entrusted with SGEIs.

Examples:

- Where a public authority wants to set up a centre or home assistance service for elderly people, it will be sufficient to specify in the act of entrustment that the provider of the SSGI has been entrusted with the task of setting up a centre that will provide the assistance needed, taking into account the multiplicity of needs, in particular where necessary at the medical, psychological and social level or, in the case of assistance at home, services such as medical care, meal delivery, home cleaning services, etc.
- Where a public authority wants to set up a support centre for young unemployed people, it will be sufficient to specify that the service provider has been entrusted with the task of organising a support service for unemployed youth which will provide the necessary training but will also include other services directly related to the effective reintegration of the persons being assisted.

57. At the end of an entrustment period, can the same SGEI be entrusted to the same company again?

Yes. The same provider can subsequently be entrusted with the same SGEI. This is also true if the Decision or the Framework apply, which set specific limits as regards the entrustment period duration.

If the entrustment consists in a public contract or concession and the EU public procurement rules apply, the public authority must organise in principle a new tender procedure, which is of course open also to the existing provider.

58. How should an act of entrustment concerning services that have to be adapted in the process of delivery to changing circumstances in terms of care intensity, user profiles and user numbers be drawn up?

Public authorities and service providers have, most of the time, experience of the personalised services and specific needs that may present themselves during the provision of SGEIs, and of the changing situations that may occur. On the basis of their experience, they can make a reliable estimation of any additional needs that may arise and reflect this estimation in the act of entrustment.

There are two options:

- The public authority may include in the act of entrustment an *ex post* correction mechanism which will allow for periodic revision of the task entrusted.[98]
- The public authority may update the act of entrustment if it becomes clear that a specific service was not envisaged but could be supplied by the same entity.

Example:

A municipality would like to provide integrated services covering the various needs of elderly people (medical assistance at home, meal delivery, home cleaning services, etc.). What should be done to ensure that the municipality can compensate the service provider for the provision of additional services responding to needs which were not initially foreseen?

As indicated above, the municipality could make an estimation of such additional services from its prior experience in the field, or define *ex post* correction mechanisms for such needs. For instance, if the initial act of entrustment consists of a public contract, the estimation of additional services will generally take the form of an option for possible additional services indicated in the initial tender.

The municipality could also in principle update the act of entrustment if it becomes clear that a specific service was not envisaged and could be supplied by the same body. However, if the initial act of entrustment consisted of a public contract or a concession and the initial tender did not envisage an option for additional services, the contracting authority would not be able to modify the public contract or concession during its performance (see in this respect the answer to question 205 below), but would need to organise in principle a new tender procedure, this tender being of course open also to the provider of the initial services.

59. Does the requirement of an act of entrustment limit the autonomy and freedom of initiative of the service providers?

No. The requirement related to an act of entrustment does not limit the autonomy and freedom of initiative of entities which provide social services in any way at all. They are entirely free to take the initiative in developing or improving such services and to make proposals to public authorities.

The notion of act of entrustment is flexible enough to correspond in this case to the decision of the public authority approving and financing such proposals. Therefore, in the event that a public authority approves a proposal made by a service provider, in accordance with the provisions of the Decision, the definition of the SGEI task as well as the parameters for the calculation of compensation and the safeguards put in place to avoid overcompensation have to be included in the content of the decision/agreement or in the contract drawn up between the public authority and the service provider.

60. Does the requirement of an act of entrustment limit the autonomy of local branches of an SGEI provider duly mandated at national level in setting priorities?

In so far as a provider is assigned an SGEI at national level on the basis of an act of entrustment complying with the requirements as set out in para. 52 of the Communication, local branches of the provider may set priorities within the limits of the conditions laid down in the act of entrustment.

3.2.3 Aid-free compensation under the Altmark ruling

61. What does the Court state in the Altmark ruling?

In *Altmark*, the Court of Justice held that public service compensation **does not constitute State Aid** within the meaning of Article 107 of the TFEU provided that four cumulative criteria are met.

- First, the recipient undertaking must actually have public service obligations to discharge, and the obligations must be clearly defined.
- Second, the parameters on the basis of which the compensation is calculated must be established in advance in an objective and transparent manner.
- Third, the compensation cannot exceed what is necessary to cover all or part of the costs incurred in discharging the public service obligations, taking into account the relevant receipts and a reasonable profit.
- Finally, where the undertaking which is to discharge public service obligations, in a specific case, is not chosen pursuant to a public procurement procedure which would allow for the selection of the bidder capable of providing those services at the least cost to the community, the level of compensation needed must be determined on the basis of an analysis of the costs which a typical undertaking, if well run and adequately equipped, would have incurred.

Examples of cases where the Commission considered that the *Altmark* criteria were met and consequently the compensation did not constitute State Aid:

- The finance provided for a scheme promoting investments to ensure security of electricity supply in Ireland was not considered to be State Aid;
  - The provision of new electricity reserve generation capacity to cope with electricity demand at any time of the year, including in peak periods, was deemed to be an SGEI.
  - Moreover, the open, transparent and non-discriminatory competitive procedure had been organised in such a way as to guarantee that all of the other three conditions set out in the *Altmark* decision were met.[99]
- Subsidies financing broadband infrastructure in France were not deemed to be aid because:
  - Universal access to broadband (and high-speed broadband) infrastructure for the whole country was an SGEI.

- Specific parameters predefined the amount of compensation in the concession contract.
- There was no risk of overcompensation, as the parameters for calculating compensation were precisely defined in the operators' business plans, which were based on the specific data provided by the public authority itself. Another reason why there was no risk of overcompensation was the fact that the public authority had required the operators who were to provide the service to set up an *ad hoc* company for that purpose, which would guarantee the neutrality of the service provider concerned; moreover, there were better-fortune clauses in case profits were to rise above a given level.
- The needs of the project and what the candidates had to offer were analysed in depth and in detail. Moreover, the procedure chosen enabled the most efficient candidate offering the service at least cost to the community to be selected.[100]

- In the Dorsal case, the Commission considered that the fourth Altmark criterion was met because a thorough comparative analysis of the specific needs of the project and the candidates' tenders as well as the competitive procedure itself enabled compensation to be estimated on the basis of the costs that would be incurred by a well-run and adequately equipped undertaking.[101]
- The Commission found that the rated fees paid by 'Cassa Depositi e Prestiti' – a state-controlled financial body – to 'Poste Italiane' were not considered to be State Aid:
  - The distribution of postal savings books was deemed to be an SGEI.
  - The market fee was an appropriate estimate of the level of costs that would be incurred by a typical, well-run and adequately equipped undertaking in the same sector, taking into account receipts and a reasonable profit from discharging its obligations. The fourth *Altmark* criterion was thus met.[102]

62. Can a public authority escape the application of the State Aid rules by organising a tender, without checking whether all the criteria of the Altmark judgment are met?

No. The Court of Justice's Altmark judgment sets out four cumulative conditions that have to be fulfilled in order for compensation for the provision of an SGEI not to constitute State Aid. This being said, the contract and the tender documents can contain all necessary specifications so as to ensure compliance with the other 3 conditions.

63. Why should the provision of an SGEI be compensated according to the 'least cost to the community' criterion? Would this not lead to the provision of a poor-quality service?

The requirement of a public procurement procedure that allows for the provision of a service at the 'least cost to the community' has been set out by the Court of Justice in the Altmark judgment. The Communication clarifies that 'least cost to the community' is broader than lowest price and that a public procurement procedure does not necessarily have to entail the lowest price as the award criterion in order to fulfil the first alternative of the fourth Altmark criterion. Para. 67 of the Communication states that the 'most economically advantageous offer' can also be used, provided that the award criteria are closely related to the subject matter of the service to be provided and allow for the most economically advantageous offer to match the value of the market. This criterion allows a range of elements to be taken into account, including quality considerations (in addition to those provided in the technical specifications and the selection criteria) and social and environmental criteria, but the criteria have to be defined in advance in such a way as to allow for effective competition.

Furthermore, it should be noted that compensation not fulfilling the fourth Altmark criterion, and thus constituting State Aid, may still be compatible with Article 106 TFEU and exempted from notification under the Decision or approved by the Commission upon notification on the basis of the Framework.

64. Can you give an example of a situation where a clawback mechanism (as mentioned in para. 67 of the Communication) would be appropriate?

A clawback mechanism is a provision that requires the provider to pay back compensation under certain circumstances. When it is difficult to foresee the revenues that will be earned from the provision of a service, a clawback mechanism in the entrustment act can be an appropriate tool to reduce the risk that the provider is overcompensated (i.e. receiving compensation beyond net costs including a reasonable profit, taking account of the risks involved).

It should be noted that in cases where the provider assumes a high risk (e.g. certain types of concession contracts), the level of revenues can vary from negative (losses) to higher than usual. This does not automatically mean that in the latter case the provider would be overcompensated, as long as the level of profit is still reasonable in relation to the risk level. Member States could in such cases, however, also include a clawback clause in the compensation mechanism in order to put a cap on the maximum profit that will be paid.

65. What is an open procedure, in the sense of paragraph 66 of the Communication?

The open procedure referred to in paragraph 66 of the Communication means a public procurement procedure whereby any interested economic operator may submit a tender, as defined in Article 1(11)(a) of Directive 2004/18/EC and Article 1(9)(a) of Directive 2004/17/EC.

66. What is a restricted procedure in the sense of paragraph 66 of the Communication?

The restricted procedure referred to in paragraph 66 of the Communication means a public procurement procedure in which any economic operator may request to participate and whereby only those economic operators invited by the contracting authority or entity may submit a tender, as defined in Article 1(11)(b) of Directive 2004/18/EC and Article 1(9)(b) of Directive 2004/17/EC.

In restricted procedures for public contracts covered by Directive 2004/18/EC, contracting authorities may limit the number of suitable candidates they will invite to tender, provided a sufficient number of suitable candidates is available. The contracting authorities have also to indicate in the contract notice the objective and nondiscriminatory criteria or rules they intend to apply, the minimum number of candidates they intend to invite (which must be at least five) and, where appropriate, the maximum number. In any event the number of candidates invited must be sufficient to ensure genuine competition. The contracting authorities must invite a number of candidates at least equal to the minimum number set in advance. Where the number of candidates meeting the selection criteria and the minimum levels of ability fail to match the minimum number, the contracting authority may continue the procedure by inviting any candidate(s) with the required capabilities. The contracting authority may not include in the context of the same procedure other economic operators who did not request to participate, or candidates who do not have the required capabilities (see Article 44(3) of Directive 2004/18/EC).

Similar rules exist for restricted procedures for contracts in the utilities sectors covered by Directive 2004/17/EC (see Article 54 of Directive 2004/17/EC).

67. Why is the negotiated procedure considered to fulfil the fourth Altmark criterion only in exceptional circumstances?

The negotiated procedure with prior publication (as defined in Article 30 of Directive 2004/18 EC) involves negotiation with the potential providers of the SGEI and therefore confers a too wide discretion upon the public authority and may also restrict the participation of interested potential providers. For these reasons, it can only meet the first alternative of the fourth Altmark criterion in exceptional circumstances.[103]

As for the negotiated procedure without prior publication (as defined in Article 31 of Directive 2004/18/EC), it does not involve the prior publication of a contract notice and therefore does not provide enough safeguards as regards publicity and transparency to attract all potentially interested providers. It therefore cannot ensure the selection of the provider able to provide the service 'at the least cost to the community' (Communication para. 66).

However, it should be noted that compensation not fulfilling the fourth Altmark criterion, and thus constituting State Aid, may still be compatible with Article 106 TFEU and exempted from notification under the Decision or approved by the Commission upon notification on the basis of the Framework.

68. If only one bid is submitted, is that tender never deemed sufficient to ensure the provision of the service at the least cost to the community or can there also be cases where the tender may still be sufficient?

The Communication (para. 68) sets out the general principle that a procedure where only one bid is submitted is, in principle, insufficient to ensure compliance with the first alternative of the fourth Altmark criterion. However, it does not mean that there cannot be cases where, due to particularly strong safeguards in the design of the procedure, also a procedure where one bid is submitted can be sufficient to ensure the provision of the service at 'the least cost to the community'. In these situations, however, Member States are advised to notify the measure, if the measure is not exempted under the Decision.

69. What is the interplay between national public procurement rules and State Aid law? Can EU State Aid law lead to an obligation to always apply public procurement rules if a provider is entrusted with an SGEI?

Outside the scope of EU public procurement law, it is up to the Member States to set out the conditions under which national public procurement rules should apply. A Member State is free to design the scope of application of its national public procurement law in such a way that those rules in practice always apply if a provider is entrusted with an SGEI. If a Member States thus links EU State Aid law and public procurement law, however, that is an autonomous decision of the Member State and not a consequence of the application of EU law.

70. What happens if the scope of application of public procurement procedures that contain a negotiation element is changed in the currently ongoing reform of the EU public procurement rules?

The Communication explicitly states that the guidance is provided for the procedures and award criteria as defined in the EU public procurement directives currently in force. As long as the legislative process for the design of future public procurement rules is ongoing and the texts that would be adopted are not yet known, the Communication cannot give guidance as to whether any procedure that differs in scope from those foreseen in the Directives in force can ensure the provision of the service at 'the least cost to the community'.

71. What exactly does 'generally accepted market remuneration' mean? Can one expert opinion be sufficient to prove it?

The Communication states that generally accepted market remuneration provides the best benchmark for the amount of compensation that an efficient undertaking requires (second alternative of the fourth Altmark criterion). Generally accepted market remuneration requires that the services are indeed comparable in all respects and is therefore a rather strict concept. The Communication does not go into detail about how the existence of generally accepted market remuneration can be proven because this depends on all the particularities of each individual situation, in particular on the evidence and methodology used in the expert opinion, its quality and representativeness and how recent it is. A general statement that one expert opinion is sufficient evidence to establish generally accepted market remuneration is therefore not possible.

72. Can a Member State use a pre-established reference cost for the purpose of applying the criterion relating to the costs of a typical well-run undertaking?

The Member States have the option of using a pre-established reference cost with a view to applying the second element of the fourth *Altmark* criterion, provided that they can justify this. If this cost is arrived at in a reliable way, is based on sound data and is in line with market values, it can be considered to correspond to 'the costs incurred by a typical undertaking that is well run and suitably equipped' within the meaning of the fourth *Altmark* criterion.

Examples of Commission practice as regards reference costs

- The consideration paid to Poste Italiane for the distribution of postal savings books (*libretti postali*) was lower than the amounts for similar financial products on the market; the compensation paid in this context was therefore deemed to meet the criterion of a typical, well-run and suitably equipped undertaking, and did not constitute aid, while the other three *Altmark* criteria were also met.[104] However,
- As regards the use of predetermined statistical costs supplied by the Czech authorities in order to calculate the amount of compensation, no proof was provided that these costs were representative of those that would be incurred by a typical, well-run and suitably equipped undertaking.[105]

73. What are the consequences of the application or non-application of the Altmark criteria?
Where all the *Altmark* criteria are met, the public service compensation does not constitute State Aid.
Where at least one of the *Altmark* criteria is not met, but the other State Aid criteria[106] are fulfilled, the public service compensation constitutes State Aid. However, it may still be compatible with Article 106 TFEU and exempted from notification under the Decision or approved by the Commission upon notification on the basis of the Framework.

3.3 AID-FREE COMPENSATION UNDER THE DE MINIMIS REGULATIONS

74. What is the difference between the SGEI de minimis Regulation and the general de minimis Regulation?
The general *de minimis* Regulation (Regulation 1998/2006) provides that aid measures not exceeding EUR 200,000 over any period of three fiscal years per undertaking are outside the notion of aid (Article 107(1) TFEU) because they are deemed not to affect trade between Member States and/or not to distort or threaten to distort competition. This Regulation applies irrespective of the purpose for which the support is granted, provided the conditions of the Regulation are respected.
The SGEI *de minimis* Regulation provides for a higher threshold (EUR 500,000 over any period of three fiscal years per undertaking) as regards aid measures granted for the provision of an SGEI.
The SGEI *de minimis* Regulation is based on the principle that a higher threshold is justified for measures linked to the provision of an SGEI because at least part of the amount is granted as compensation for additional costs linked to the provision of the SGEI. The potential advantage for an SGEI provider is thus lower than the compensation amount actually granted, while under the general *de minimis* Regulation the advantage from the same amount would be higher. Therefore, the ceiling up to which there is no impact on competition and trade between Member States is higher for compensation for an SGEI.

75. How can it be ensured that the ceiling of EUR 500,000 is respected? Are there any checks for compliance?
The SGEI *de minimis* Regulation (in the same way as the general *de minimis* Regulation) provides for two alternative methods for ensuring that the total amount received by an undertaking remains within the ceiling. One option is that the Member State establishes a central register of all *de minimis* aid granted by all authorities within the Member State (Article 3(2)). Alternatively, the granting authority has to obtain a declaration from the undertaking about all *de minimis* aid received in order to check that the ceiling is respected (Article 3(1)).
Member States have to compile all the relevant information regarding *de minimis* aid granted in order to be able to demonstrate compliance with the Regulation. The Commission can request submission of the information to check whether all conditions of the SGEI *de minimis* Regulation are complied with (Article 3(3)).

76. Is an entrustment act in the sense of the Decision/Framework necessary also under the SGEI de minimis Regulation?
The SGEI *de minimis* Regulation only applies to aid granted for the provision of an SGEI. Therefore, the beneficiary undertaking has to be entrusted with a specific SGEI. This entrustment does not have to contain all the information required under the SGEI Decision or the SGEI Framework but, for reasons of legal certainty, it has to be in writing and has to inform the undertaking of the SGEI in respect of which the compensation is granted (see recital 6 of the SGEI *de minimis* Regulation).

77. What is the advantage of using the SGEI de minimis Regulation compared to the Decision?
The SGEI *de minimis* Regulation contains simplifications in two major respects. First, the conditions regarding both the entrustment and the entrustment act are lighter (see question 76). Second, the SGEI *de minimis* Regulation does not require verification of the costs incurred in providing the service and consequently no check for overcompensation is needed.

78. What are the rules on cumulation of aid granted under the two de minimis Regulations? More specifically, can an undertaking that has received general de minimis aid in the last years now also receive SGEI de minimis aid?
The SGEI *de minimis* Regulation allows cumulation of SGEI *de minimis* aid and *de minimis* aid granted under another Regulation up to the ceiling of EUR 500,000 (Article 2(7)). This means, for example, that if an undertaking has already received EUR 150,000 during the last three fiscal years, it can still receive up to EUR 350,000 under the SGEI *de minimis* Regulation.
The EUR 500,000 ceiling per undertaking is an absolute maximum for all types of *de minimis* aid added together. It applies irrespective of whether the amount granted under the general *de minimis* Regulation was granted for an SGEI or for a separate non-SGEI activity.

79. What are the rules on cumulation of compensation granted under the SGEI de minimis Regulation and compensation granted in compliance with the Altmark criteria?

The SGEI *de minimis* Regulation does not allow for one SGEI compensated in compliance with the Altmark criteria to also receive additional aid under the SGEI *de minimis* Regulation (Article 2(8)). Therefore, in order to avoid being classified as State Aid, the full amount of compensation granted for an SGEI has either to meet the conditions set out in the Altmark judgment or it must not exceed the SGEI *de minimis* threshold.

If one provider, in contrast, is entrusted with several SGEIs, it can be compensated for one of the SGEIs under the SGEI *de minimis* Regulation and may, for other SGEIs, receive compensation that meets all four Altmark conditions.

80. Can a company receive compensation for one SGEI under the Decision or the Framework, and de minimis aid for another SGEI under the SGEI de minimis Regulation?

Yes. The SGEI *de minimis* Regulation sets a ceiling of EUR 500,000 for all measures under that Regulation per undertaking, irrespective of whether they are granted for the same or for different SGEIs. It also provides that for the same SGEI, the provider cannot receive compensation both under the Decision or the Framework and under the SGEI *de minimis* Regulation (Article 2(8)), since this would lead to overcompensation. By contrast, receiving compensation under the Decision or Framework for one SGEI and SGEI *de minimis* aid for another SGEI is possible.

81. Can a service provider who has for a certain period of time received compensation under the Decision or the Framework be financed for another period of time under the SGEI de minimis Regulation for the same service?

Yes. If different periods of time are concerned, the costs incurred by the SGEI provider have not already been compensated under the Decision or the Framework and therefore the SGEI *de minimis* Regulation can be applied. However, a provider cannot receive for the same service and the same period of time compensation under the Decision or the Framework and under the SGEI *de minimis* Regulation (Article 2(8)). This provision is based on the fact that the SGEI *de minimis* Regulation provides for a higher threshold than the general *de minimis* Regulation because the provider incurs costs that the *de minimis* aid will at least in part compensate for, which is no longer true if the same costs are compensated under the Decision or the Framework (recitals 3 and 15). There is also no need for additional compensation under the de minimis Regulation, if compensation is already granted under the Decision or the Framework.

82. A service provider would like to establish a support service for unemployed young people which requires financial support of EUR 150,000: do the State Aid rules apply to such a grant by a public authority?)

Financing of this type may be granted without meeting the criteria laid down in the Decision, if the total amount of state resources provided over a three-year period does not exceed the ceiling laid down in the general *de minimis* Regulation (EUR 200,000) or the SGEI *de minimis* Regulation (EUR 500,000). If the amount does not exceed either of the ceilings, as is the case in this example, both Regulations can be used (recital 14). If the conditions of either of the two *de minimis* Regulations are met, such support does not constitute State Aid within the meaning of Article 107(1) TFEU and would not have to be notified to the Commission.

A public authority can, therefore, make such a grant of a limited amount without further concerns as to the application of the State Aid rules, even when the activity to be financed is deemed to be economic.

In all other circumstances, the measure will still be compatible if the criteria of the Decision are fulfilled.

83. Can a public authority finance a pilot initiative in order to define the content of SGEI tasks?

Yes, public authorities can launch a pilot initiative in order to define the task of the SGEI they want to put in place. In order to finance such pilot initiatives, public authorities can rely on the opportunities offered by the general *de minimis* Regulation, which stipulates that Article 107(1) does not apply to the grant of aid not exceeding EUR 200,000 over a period of three years. They cannot use the SGEI *de minimis* Regulation, in contrast, because the aid is not granted to an SGEI provider for a specific SGEI, as in the pilot initiative the SGEI tasks are still to be defined.

84. In the event that an SGEI is financed according to the general de minimis Regulation or the SGEI de minimis Regulation, does the amount of EUR 200,000 / EUR 500,000 refer to the SGEI or to the undertaking entrusted with the SGEI, taking into account other activities for which the undertaking receives state resources?

Both ceilings apply to the undertaking and not to each of the activities for which the undertaking receives state resources. According to Article 2(2)[107] of the general *de minimis* Regulation, the total amount of *de minimis* aid granted to one undertaking cannot exceed EUR 200,000 over any period of three fiscal years. Similarly, under the SGEI *de minimis* Regulation the total amount of *de minimis* aid granted to one undertaking cannot exceed EUR 500000. What matters is that the same undertaking must not receive more than EUR 200000 / EUR 500,000 over any period of three fiscal years.

85. In the case of a body entrusted with the provision of several SGEIs which draws up separate accounts for each SGEI, is it possible to apply the de minimis rule to each SGEI separately?

No. For both the general *de minimis* Regulation and the SGEI *de minimis* Regulation to apply, the total amount of state resources, irrespective of the objective pursued, granted to any one undertaking cannot exceed EUR 200,000 / EUR 500,000. Consequently, when an undertaking has a number of general economic interest tasks, the total amount that it can receive under the *de minimis* rule is EUR 200,000 (under the general *de minimis* Regulation) or EUR 500,000 (under the SGEI *de minimis* Regulation) over a period of three years. The fact that in accounting terms individual budgets exist for these tasks is of no significance for the application of the *de minimis* rule.

86. In the event that a body entrusted with the provision of an SGEI is also engaged in non-economic activities, is it necessary to deduct the amount of compensation paid for the non-economic SGIs for the purposes of the de minimis Regulations?

No. The financing of services of general interest of a non-economic nature does not come within the scope of the State Aid rules, which apply only to activities of an economic nature. The financing of non-economic general-interest tasks is therefore not regarded as financing within the meaning of the *de minimis* Regulations and does not need to be taken into account when the total amount is calculated for the purposes of applying those Regulations.

87. The budget for the investment outlay linked to an SSGI can be booked over a period extending from one to several years. In such circumstances, is it possible to apply the de minimis Regulations?

The investment outlay for an SSGI can be financed by public resources under the *de minimis* Regulations provided, however, that those resources do not exceed EUR 200000 (under the general *de minimis* Regulation) or EUR 500,000 (under the SGEI *de minimis* Regulation) over any three-year period, whatever the period of three consecutive fiscal years considered, as laid down in the Regulations.

In the event that the public resources exceed EUR 200000 / EUR 500,000 over any three fiscal years, they may benefit from application of the Decision or the Framework, provided that they fulfil the compatibility conditions (for these conditions, see sections 3.4.2 and 3.5.2).

88. Do the SGEI de minimis Regulation and the general de minimis Regulation apply to SGEI providers in difficulty?

No. Neither the general *de minimis* Regulation (Article 1(1)(h)) nor the SGEI *de minimis* Regulation (Article 1(2)(h)) applies to undertakings in difficulty within the meaning of the Community guidelines on State Aid for rescuing and restructuring firms in difficulty.[108]

3.4 COMPENSATION UNDER THE SGEI DECISION

3.4.1 SCOPE OF APPLICATION

89. In what cases is the Decision applicable?

The Decision applies to:

- public service compensation not exceeding EUR 15 million on an annual basis, granted for SGEIs in areas other than transport and transport infrastructure.
- public service compensation granted to hospitals providing medical care, including, where applicable, emergency services, irrespective of the amount.
- public service compensation for the provision of SGEIs meeting social needs as regards health and long-term care, childcare, access to and reintegration into the labour market, social housing and the care and social inclusion of vulnerable groups, irrespective of the amount.
- in the field of transport, only public service compensation for air or maritime links to islands granted in accordance with sectoral rules, on which annual traffic does not exceed 300,000 passengers; the Decision applies also to public service compensation for airports and ports whose average annual traffic during the two financial years preceding that in which the SGEI was assigned does not exceed 200,000 passengers in the case of airports and 300,000 passengers in the case of ports.

3.4.1.1
The EUR 15 million threshold

90. Is the threshold of EUR 15 million to be applied as net or gross value?

The threshold for the amount of compensation set out in Article 2(1)(a) of the Decision is EUR 15 million gross (i.e. without any deduction of taxes).

91. Does the threshold apply per SGEI entrustment or per undertaking? What if several undertakings jointly provide an SGEI?

The EUR 15 million threshold applies for each specific SGEI entrusted to a given undertaking.

If an undertaking is entrusted with three different SGEIs, the threshold applies for each of those SGEIs (i.e. the undertaking can receive total compensation up to a maximum of EUR 45 million under the Decision, provided that the compensation per SGEI does not exceed EUR 15 million). If the same SGEI is jointly entrusted to five undertakings, the threshold applies only once for that specific SGEI task (i.e. even if the amount of compensation per undertaking does not exceed EUR 15 million, the Decision does not apply if the aggregate compensation for the SGEI paid to all undertakings is above EUR 15 million).

3.4.1.2
Hospitals and social services

92. There is a provision on ancillary activity in Article 2(1)(b) for hospitals, but not in Article 2(1)(c) for social services. Does this mean that social services are treated less favourably?

No. The reference to ancillary activities in Article 2(1)(b) of the Decision is intended to mean that hospitals fall under the decision irrespective of the amount of compensation, also if they pursue other ancillary activities (such as research activity or a cafeteria). However, compensation can only be paid for services of general economic interest.

Article 2(1)(c) for social services does not contain a restriction to purely social service providers that have at the most an ancillary commercial activity. Therefore, social service providers can have other activities that are more than just ancillary, but they can receive compensation only for SGEI activities. The Decision is therefore in fact more lenient for social services than for hospitals.

93. Who can define the content of the notion of 'social services'?
The list of social services in Article 2(1)(c) is an exhaustive list. Since the Decision is directly applicable in all Member States, it does not need to be transposed into national law. Member States do not have competence to adopt legislation that could change or clarify the Decision. Nevertheless, as long as they stay within the scope of Article 2(1)(c), Member States can of course specify in more detail in the entrustment act the specific services they want to be provided, for example which types of childcare, under which conditions and for which beneficiaries. The definition of social services is very broad and covers the most important areas of social services. Moreover, by covering also SGEIs relating to 'the care and social inclusion of vulnerable groups', it offers the necessary flexibility to include, in accordance with the needs of each Member State, different types of services addressed to those groups of society that need them most.
The Court of Justice and national courts can be called upon to decide whether an aid is illegal or whether it falls under the exemption provision of Article 2(1)(c) of the Decision. However, they cannot change the content of the Decision.

94. Why is the list of exempted social services in the Decision exhaustive? What if a Member State wants to entrust a service provider with a social service of general interest that is not covered by this list?
Since the Decision is directly applicable in the Member States, it needs to contain clear and precise definitions, ensuring legal certainty. Therefore, the exempted aid measures must be comprehensively defined. However, the definition of social services is very broad and covers the most important areas of social services. Moreover, by including also SGEIs relating to 'the care and social inclusion of vulnerable groups' it gives the necessary flexibility to include, in accordance with the needs of each Member State, different types of services addressed to those groups of society that need them the most. Should a particular social service not be covered by the definition of social services in Article 2(1)(c), the compensation might still be exempted from notification under Article 2(1)(a) of the Decision, as long as the compensation does not exceed an annual amount of EUR 15 million.

95. How does the list of social services in the Decision relate to the lists of services in Annex II B of the public procurement Directive (Directive 2004/18/EC)?
The list of social services in Article 2(1)(c) of the Decision is different from the list of services in Annex II B of the public procurement Directive (Directive 2004/18/EC).
The list contained in the Decision enumerates the social services which are covered by the Decision, irrespective of the amount of compensation the service provider receives. This list is based on broad categories (for example 'care and social inclusion of vulnerable groups').
The list of services in Annex II B of the public procurement Directive is based on the Common Procurement Vocabulary (CPV) and has a different purpose. This list covers all categories of social services, but also other categories of services that are considered as less likely to be of certain cross-border interest for tenderers in other Member States and that, for this reason, are not subject to the full set of provisions of Directive 2004/18/EC, but only to a limited number of rules of this Directive and to the general principles of the TFEU. Directive 2004/18/EC thus offers a very flexible approach (as regards procurement rules) to social services and other services covered by Annex II B of this Directive (for more details on this point, see answer to question 200).

96. What does the term 'childcare' in Article 2(1)(c) cover?
The term 'childcare' is a broad concept that covers different forms of care for and supervision of children in different organisational settings. However, for the Decision to apply in the first place, the Member State must entrust the provider with a specific public service obligation.

97. Does the wording 'meeting social needs' restrict the type of social services that can be an SGEI, for example in the case of childcare, to childcare for families with financial difficulties?
The wording 'meeting social needs' in Article 2(1)(c) does not restrict the services mentioned in the list. As long as the services defined qualify as genuine SGEIs, the Decision can apply to all respective services. In the example, the Decision can be applied to all childcare services, not only if they are provided for families with financial difficulties.

98. What does the term 'social inclusion of vulnerable groups' in Article 2(1)(c) cover?
The term 'social inclusion of vulnerable groups' gives Member States the necessary flexibility to include, in accordance with the needs of each Member State, different types of services addressed to those groups of society that need them the most. It is a broad concept and could cover, for example, social integration services for people with disabilities, social assistance services for migrants, services for the homeless, parenting support services,[109] services supporting over-indebted persons or social services for the lesbian, gay, bisexual and transgender (LGBT) community.

99. What does the term 'access to and reintegration into the labour market' in Article 2(1)(c) cover? Is professional training part of it?
The term 'access to and reintegration into the labour market' refers to different types of services that aim at facilitating the employability. Professional training only falls under Article 2(1)(c) of the Decision if it allows access to or reintegration into the labour market or if it fosters the social inclusion of a vulnerable group. Therefore, for example, professional training for the long-term unemployed falls under Article 2(1)(c) of the Decision. If the professional

training, in contrast, is for persons already in employment, it would normally not fall under Article 2(1)(c) of the Decision, unless it were to provide for the inclusion of a vulnerable group. It should be noted, however, that State aid for professional training can be granted under the conditions set out in Article 38 and 39 of Regulation 800/2008/EC (General block exemption Regulation).

100. Can aid to social and work integration enterprises be covered by the Decision?
Social integration enterprises can have different characteristics and take different forms, but in general they offer employment opportunities to different groups of disadvantaged workers facilitating their access to and their reintegration into the labour market and promoting their social inclusion. They often benefit from support measures such as exemption or reduction of social contributions pursuant to national laws or regulations.
Such aid can under certain conditions be covered by the GBER[110] or the general *de minimis* Regulation.[111]
Public authorities in the Member States might also define social and work integration as a SSGI and entrust social and work integration enterprises with a SGEI. In these cases, the SGEI Decision applies to those services.

3.4.1.3
Duration of the entrustment period

101. Can the duration of the entrustment period exceed 10 years only if a significant investment has to be amortised over a longer period or also for other justified reasons? What does 'significant investment' mean?
The only case where the duration of the entrustment period may exceed 10 years is the depreciation of a significant investment. Whether an investment can be considered significant depends both on the absolute value and on the relative value of the investment that needs to be amortised over a period longer than 10 years compared to the value(s) of other assets needed for the provision of the service. The difference between the rules on the duration of the entrustment period in the Decision and the Framework is further explained in question 166.

102. Given the limitation of the entrustment period to 10 years in principle, is it no longer possible to authorise a provider for an unlimited period?
An authorisation to perform a certain activity without an obligation of the provider to provide a specific public service has to be distinguished from an entrustment act, which necessarily confers an obligation on the provider to provide a specific public service. The authorisation without the obligation is not relevant from a State Aid point of view. The State Aid rules therefore do not prevent Member States from authorising a provider for an unlimited period to perform an activity, but in order to be able to receive compensation for the provision of a service of general economic interest, the undertaking has to be entrusted with a specific public service obligation. As regards the duration of this entrustment, it is under the Decision in principle limited to 10 years (Article 2(2)). The Decision allows for a longer period of entrustment in cases where a significant investment is required that needs to be amortised over a period longer than ten years. Since the duration is closely linked to the period of time needed for amortisation of the asset, unlimited duration is not possible under the Decision. After the end of the period of entrustment, the same provider can be entrusted again with the provision of the service.

3.4.1.4
Application to the transport sector

103. What is the difference between Article 2(1)(d) and Article 2(1)(e) of the Decision?
Article 2(1)(d) of the Decision sets out the scope of application of the Decision to SGEIs providing air or maritime links, i.e. air or maritime transport services. Article 2(1)(e) of the Decision, in contrast, deals with the scope of application as regards the imposition of SGEI obligations on ports and airports, i.e. transport infrastructure.

104. What exactly does the 300,000 passenger threshold for air and maritime links to islands as set out in Article 2(1)(d) of the Decision refer to? Can the Decision also be applied to air/maritime routes that do not provide links to an island?
The threshold of 300,000 passengers for air and maritime links to islands refers to a one-way count, i.e. a passenger flying to the island and back counts twice. The threshold applies to the individual route between one airport/port on the island and one airport/port on the mainland, not to all air traffic from any airport/port on the island to any airport/port on the mainland.
As regards air/maritime routes, the Decision only applies in the case of air or maritime links to islands. It does not apply to air/maritime routes between two airports/ports on the **mainland.**

105. Do airports with more than 200,000 passengers or ports with more than 300,000 passengers fall within the scope of the Decision in cases where the public service compensation does not exceed EUR 15 million?
No. The general threshold of EUR 15 million does not apply to transport and transport infrastructure (Article 2(1)(a) of the Decision). If airports have more than 200000 passengers and ports have more than 300,000 passengers, aid for SGEI does not fall under the Decision and will be examined by the Commission after notification on the basis of the Framework. The passenger thresholds are to be interpreted as meaning arriving and departing passengers (one-way count).
In this context, it is important to note that State Aid to the air transport sector is governed by the Community guidelines on financing of airports and start-up aid to airlines departing from regional airports (hereinafter 'the 2005 Guidelines') and by Commission Communication 94/C 350/07 on the application of Articles 92 and 93 of the Treaty in the aviation sector. These guidelines allow to consider certain economic activities carried out by airports as constituting SGEIs. In exceptional cases, the overall management of an airport can be considered an SGEI as long as it is limited to activities linked to its basic activities.

Example:
A public authority might impose public service obligations on an airport located, for example, in an isolated region, and might decide to pay compensation for these obligations. It is important to note that the overall management of an airport as an SGEI should not cover activities which are not directly linked to its basic activities (that is to say, commercial activities, including construction, financing, use and renting of land and buildings, not only for offices and storage but also for hotels and industrial enterprises located within the airport perimeter, as well as shops, restaurants and car parks).

106. What is the relation between the Decision and Regulation (EC) No 1008/2008, in particular Article 16 of the Regulation? Could you give some examples of what kind of services could be defined as SGEIs for airports under Article 2(1)(e) of the Decision?
Article 2(4) of the Decision stipulates that the Decision can only be applied to air transport if the requirements set out in Regulation 1008/2008 as well as the requirements set out in the Decision are met.
Paragraphs 45 *et seq.* of the Communication give further guidance on the scope of the Member States to define SGEIs and the Commission's tasks. Regarding airports in particular, paragraphs 34 and 53 of the 2005 Guidelines on financing of airports provide guidance on what activities can be considered as SGEIs. In substance, the overall management of an airport can only be considered an SGEI in exceptional cases, such as isolated regions. In any case, the pursuit of commercial activities not directly linked to the airport's core activities cannot be included in the scope of an SGEI (see paragraph 53 (iv) of the 2005 Guidelines).

107. What is the relationship between the Decision and Regulation 1370/2007?
The Decision does not apply to public service compensation in the land transport sector (Article 2(5) of the Decision). Compensation for public service obligations in the rail and road passenger transport sector is governed by Regulation (EC) No 1370/2007 of the European Parliament and of the Council of 23 October 2007. Compensation granted in compliance with the provisions of this Regulation is exempted from the obligation of prior notification.

3.4.1.5
Undertakings in difficulty

108. Does the Decision also apply to firms in difficulty?
Yes. There is no provision that would prevent the Decision from being applied to firms in difficulty.

3.4.2 Compatibility conditions

3.4.2.1
General presentation

109. What are the main compatibility conditions established by the Decision?
The main compatibility conditions established by the Decision are the following:

- An act of entrustment specifying, in particular, the nature and duration of the public service obligations, the undertaking and the territory concerned, the nature of any exclusive or special rights assigned to the undertaking, the parameters for calculating, controlling and reviewing the compensation, the arrangements for avoiding and repaying any overcompensation and including a reference to the Decision.
- The compensation must not exceed what is necessary to cover the costs incurred in discharging the public service obligations including a reasonable profit; a calculation of all costs as well as any kind of revenue received is necessary to this end.
- Control of overcompensation by the Member States' public authorities.

110. What is the difference between the conditions of the Altmark judgment and the conditions laid down in the Decision?
The *Altmark* judgment establishes when a measure comes within the scope of the concept of State Aid, while the Decision and the Framework establish the conditions under which compensation constituting State Aid is compatible with the internal market. The main substantive difference between the judgment and the SGEI package concerns the amount/calculation of the compensation.
According to the fourth criterion of the *Altmark* judgment, in order not to constitute State Aid[112] the amount of the compensation must be defined:

- through an open, transparent and non-discriminatory public procurement procedure, allowing for selection of the tenderer capable of providing the services at the least cost to the community; or
- through a procedure whereby the public authorities have to determine the amount of compensation on the basis of an analysis of the costs of a typical undertaking, well run and adequately equipped.

In other words, the fourth Altmark criterion is fulfilled if the compensation is not set above the level that would be required by an efficient undertaking (capable of winning a tender or identified through a benchmarking exercise).
The **Decision** does not set efficiency requirements. The amount of the compensation does not necessarily have to be determined through a public procurement procedure, or by comparison with the costs of a typical well-run undertaking.
As long as the public authority proves that the compensation granted corresponds to the net costs estimated on the basis of the precisely defined parameters contained in the act of entrustment and that there is no overcompensation, the compensation in question is regarded as State Aid compatible with the TFEU rules.[113]
Example:
A public authority decides to entrust an operator with the provision of an SGEI and to provide it with financing for this service. There are three possible scenarios:

- The SGEI in question is provided by an operator selected through a tendering procedure complying with the fourth Altmark condition at a price of 90. If all other conditions of the *Altmark* judgment are met, the compensation of 90 will not constitute State Aid.
- The SGEI is provided by an operator at a net cost of 90. If this cost of 90 corresponds to that of a typical undertaking, well run and adequately equipped, in accordance with the fourth *Altmark* criterion, and if all other conditions of the *Altmark* judgment are met, the compensation of 90 will not constitute State Aid.
- The SGEI is provided by an operator that is not selected through a tendering procedure complying with the fourth Altmark criterion and net costs exceed 90 (e.g. 100). A compensation of 100 will be regarded by the Decision as compatible State Aid provided that the compensation does not go beyond what is necessary to cover the net cost actually incurred by the operator in providing the SGEI, including a reasonable profit. This obviously is possible if the SGEI in question falls under the categories defined in the Decision.

111. What are the main differences between the 2005 and 2011 Decisions as regards the compatibility conditions?

The differences between the 2005 and the 2011 Decisions mainly concern the scope of application (reduction of the compensation threshold from 30 to 15 million, removal of the service provider's turnover threshold, extension of the list of eligible social services regardless of amounts beyond hospital and social housing, limitation of the duration of the entrustment period).

As regards the compatibility conditions, there are only a few changes which are mainly aimed at simplifying the application of the rules and at increasing transparency.

In order to simplify the application of the rules, the new Decision allows for an overcompensation test over a longer time span.[114] It also introduces a safe harbour for reasonable profit,[115] which also constitutes a limit to the reasonable profit when the provision of the SGEI is not connected with a substantial risk.

As regards transparency, the new Decision introduces an obligation to make a reference to the Decision in the entrustment act[116] and to publish the entrustment act and the amount of aid granted for compensation above EUR 15 million.[117]

112. In the event that all market operators are entrusted with the same SGEI, should they all receive the same amount of compensation for provision of the SGEI within the meaning of the rules on State Aid?

Member States have a wide margin of discretion when it comes to organising and financing what they regard as an SGEI. The Decision allows Member States to finance in full the net costs incurred in providing SGEIs by their providers, but does not oblige them to do so. Member States can, if they so wish, decide to pay equal flat-rate compensation to all providers, so long as such compensation does not give rise to overcompensation for the operators concerned. They are also free to under-compensate, or not compensate at all, SGEI providers. Inasmuch as public service compensation granted to SGEI providers is calculated on the basis of their effective costs and relevant revenues and does not exceed what is necessary for discharging the SGEI, such compensation can be viewed as compatible within the meaning of the State Aid rules.

As explained in section 3.5.2 of the present guide, when the compatibility of the aid is assessed on the basis of the Framework, the method of calculating the compensation must be the same for all undertakings entrusted with the same SGEI.

113. Does the Decision require selection of the least expensive undertaking for the provision of SGEIs?

No, this is not required by the Decision. Member States are responsible for defining the SGEIs they want and, in particular, the quality of these services. Where the quality is higher, the costs of providing the service may be higher and the compensation can cover all the costs actually incurred by the company.

114. Is it correct that if a public authority classifies a service as SGEI and complies with the Decision, it does not need to comply with EU public procurement rules?

This is not correct. As provided by recital (29), the Decision applies without prejudice to the Union provisions in the field of public procurement. Applicable public procurement rules should thus be complied with. However, compliance with those rules is not a condition for the application of the Decision.

3.4.2.2
Entrustment act

115. Why is there a new requirement to add a reference to the Decision in the entrustment act (Article 4(f))?

By requiring public authorities to include a reference to the Decision in the entrustment act, the Commission intends to increase transparency and improve compliance with the rules. In particular, stakeholders will know what rules are applicable and which conditions the aid should meet to be compatible with the internal market. Thereby legal certainty is also increased.

116. The Decision requires parameters to calculate the amount of compensation to be defined in the act of entrustment. How is it possible to do so before offering the service?

It is often impossible to be aware of all the details of costs when an undertaking starts providing an SGEI. Consequently, the Decision does not ask for a detailed calculation of, for example, the price per day, per meal, per care category to be reimbursed by public funding, to be provided in advance, when this is not possible. Public authorities clearly remain free to specify such parameters if they so wish.

The Decision only requires the act of entrustment to include the basis for the future calculation of compensation: for example that compensation will be determined on the basis of a price per day, per meal, per care category, based on an estimation of the number of potential users, etc.

The compensation may cover the net cost incurred in providing the SGEI (compensation ex post in full), but in this case, pursuant to Article 5(7) of the Decision, the profit should be limited to the relevant swap rate + 100 basis points. What matters is that the basis on which the funding body (the State, the local authority) will finance the provider is clear. Such transparency is also beneficial to taxpayers.

Examples:

- In the event that a public authority wants to set up a centre for the elderly, the parameters for cost compensation could be:
  - the number of elderly people attending the centre over a one-year period;
  - the number of days spent in the centre during this period.
- In the event that a public authority wants to set up a youth unemployment support centre, the parameters for cost compensation could be:
  - the number of young unemployed people following a training course over a one-year period;
  - the equipment used and trainers' salaries over a one-year period.

117. Even for bodies experienced in providing SGEIs, there may be a high level of cost unpredictability and a risk of ex post losses: unpredictable changes in the level of care required, in users' profiles, in user numbers and in the level of revenues (non-payment of user fees, fluctuation in number of users, refusal of other public authorities to contribute). How can public bodies cope with this situation?

An undertaking assigned an SGEI, especially when it starts up its activity or is of a limited size, cannot commit itself to a fixed budget or a price per unit. Obviously, if there is an increase in the number of users, the costs will also rise; if some of them cannot pay a predefined contribution, revenues will be lower, etc.

However, this does not change the way the costs are incurred (salaries paid, rent, etc.) or can be established (per care category, etc.). It mainly means that the provider will face higher costs and the public body will have to pay higher compensation.

All these situations can be taken into account under the Decision. When an estimation of changing or unpredictable situations that may arise during the provision of an SGEI is not provided for in the act of entrustment, the definition of *ex post* mechanisms for correction of the estimated costs in comparison with the real costs may be one way of anticipating such situations.

Two options are possible for as long as the total amount of annual compensation does not exceed the threshold established by the Decision:

- the public authority may define in the act of entrustment an ex post correction mechanism which will allow for periodic revision of the cost parameters;
- the public authority may update the act of entrustment if it sees that a cost parameter has to be modified.

118. When the parameters for calculating the compensation are defined for a given body, should a comparison be made with other bodies? Should a judgment be made on efficiency? How can the value of pastoral care, spiritual guidance, additional time taken, etc. be compared?

It is for the public authority to define the extent of the remit concerned and if non-measurable tasks (for elderly or disabled people, etc.) have as a consequence a higher level of costs, for instance in terms of time spent by the people providing the service. These costs can of course be taken into account and compensated. The Decision does not require any assessment on efficiency, just as it leaves judgments on the quality of service required to the public authorities concerned.

For example, when two bodies provide SGEIs for which a different level of quality is defined in the acts of entrustment, each of the service providers will receive the compensation corresponding to its own costs incurred, which will differ as a result of the level of quality required.

119. How should the parameters for cost compensation be determined in the event that a given SGEI is financed by two or more public authorities?

If two or more public authorities (say, a town and a region) want to finance partially, for instance, a centre for disadvantaged persons, each authority may determine the parameters of compensation according to the service under consideration, possibly following discussions with the service provider.

The public authorities may determine their individual contributions to the compensation as they wish, as long as the total amount corresponding to all the different kinds of compensation received does not exceed the net cost incurred by the SGEI provider, including a reasonable profit.

120. In the event that a public authority wishes to finance only a part of the annual costs of a provider assigned an SGEI, how should the parameters for compensation be determined?

What counts is that the amount of compensation must not exceed what is necessary to cover the costs incurred in discharging the public service obligations, taking into account the relevant receipts and a reasonable profit.[118]

For instance, a public authority can provide in the entrustment act that it will compensate the provider for 60% of the net cost (costs minus revenues) incurred in providing the SGEI.

121. In the event that an SGEI is financed in part by the public authority and in part by its users, is it possible for a public authority to cover all costs if the SGEI is loss-making?
In the event that an SGEI is jointly financed by a public authority and by its users and it is making a loss, due, for example, to a decline in users' contributions, the loss may be compensated by the public authority in so far as it does not lead to overcompensation and if the parameters for calculating compensation set by the competent national authority so allow. Providing there is no overcompensation, the percentage of funding of the SGEI by the public authority may be freely determined by national legislation and is of no significance with respect to the rules on State Aid.

122. Is it possible for a public authority to establish in the act of entrustment that it will cover the operating losses incurred for each set period without defining any other parameters for calculating compensation?
For the purposes of compatibility with the Decision, Member States have to define in the act of entrustment the parameters on the basis of which compensation is calculated in order to enable the EU institutions to play their supervisory role.
Nevertheless, Member States have some leeway in defining the parameters of their choice in order to facilitate their financial planning, in so far as the method chosen allows for transparent and verifiable calculation of compensation. What matters in terms of compatibility with the State Aid rules is that they do not end up overcompensating SGEI operators. Member States are free to decide the manner and the level of financing of their SGEIs as long as they abide by the EU rules. In principle they can, therefore, define the compensation parameters in reference to covering operating losses provided that the calculation parameters make it possible to determine that there is no overcompensation. In this case, pursuant to Article 5(7) of the Decision, the profit should be limited to the relevant swap rate + 100 basis points.

3.4.2.3
Amount of compensation

123. What methodology should be used to calculate the net cost of the public service obligations pursuant to the Decision?
Article 5(2) of the Decision provides for two methodologies, either of which can be used to calculate the net costs of a public service obligation:

- as under the 2005 Decision, the net cost can be calculated as the difference between costs and revenues ('methodology based on cost allocation'); where the undertaking concerned also carries out activities falling outside the scope of the SGEI, only the costs related to the SGEI will be taken into consideration;
- alternatively, the net cost may be calculated as the difference between the net cost for the undertaking of operating with the public service obligation and the net cost or profit of the same undertaking operating without the public service obligation ('net avoided cost methodology'). This methodology can be appropriate for instance in the social housing sector: the net cost can be calculated as the sum of foregone rent (due to limitation of rent compared to market price) and the additional costs arising from the public service obligation (e.g. costs incurred in checking that tenants are eligible); revenues which would not have been received if the housing had been commercial should be subtracted.

In contrast to the Framework, the Decision does not impose a specific methodology: Member States can decide which methodology is the most appropriate for each specific case.

124. Could you provide some examples of the type of investment which could be supported as part of an SGEI? For example, can the costs linked to a ship engine be considered SGEI cost, knowing that the authority has entrusted the owner of the ship with a public service obligation to carry passengers?
Pursuant to Article 5(3)(d) of the Decision, the costs linked with investments necessary for the provision of the SGEI may be taken into account to determine the amount of the compensation. There is no limitative list of the type of investment concerned. The depreciation costs of an engine for a ship that is used exclusively for the provision of SGEIs are a valid example. If the ship is used also for non-SGEI activities, the costs can only partially be taken into account (see Article 5(3)(c)).

125. Is it necessary to attribute a specific amount of compensation to specific costs?
No. The rules on State Aid do not refer to the nature of SGEI costs (e.g. salaries, maintenance of premises, specific external expenses or purchases) but to their scope, that is whether the costs are associated with the operation of an SGEI or not. It is not necessary for the public authority to set aside a specific amount of compensation for specific services within the overall public service task.

126. In calculating compensation, is it possible to take into account both grants made by a public authority and services provided by a public authority to help a body discharge its public service obligations?
Yes. According to Article 5(4) of the Decision, the amount of compensation includes all the advantages granted by the State or through state resources in any form whatsoever. In this respect, the exact financial or material nature of the advantages provided by the public authorities (compensation, services, etc.) is of no significance.
Therefore the public authority should take into account both grants and services (or buildings or assets) provided below market prices, when calculating the compensation and checking for overcompensation. This means that a grant equivalent should be calculated for the provision of services (or buildings or assets) below market price.

127. How should the amount of compensation for a public service be calculated in the event that the SGEI providers hold special or exclusive rights related to the discharge of a number of public service tasks?

Article 5(4) of the Decision stipulates that profits in excess of a reasonable profit deriving from special or exclusive rights and any other advantage granted by the State to the undertaking operating the SGEI must be included in the revenue to be taken into account and therefore reduce the compensation. The same can be done for other profits deriving from other activities if the State so decides.

128. In the event that several public bodies, including a local authority, join together with private bodies in a legal entity in order to operate SGEIs jointly, how should the presence in that entity of members which are not public authorities be taken into account when calculating compensation?

Assuming that the members which are not public authorities provide the operator with financial contributions or some other form of support, what needs to be determined is whether such contributions must be characterised as State Aid within the meaning of Article 107(1) TFEU. The contribution made by a body governed by private law can indeed be characterised as State Aid if it is made by way of 'state resources'. That is the case, in particular, if the private law-governed body in question is a public undertaking within the meaning of the Transparency Directive[119] and, moreover, if the decision to grant the aid is imputable to a public authority.[120] If the contribution concerned is characterised as State Aid, it must be added to the other instances of State Aid and then it must be ascertained whether or not the total sum of State Aid exceeds what is necessary to cover the costs incurred in discharging the public service obligations, taking into account the relevant receipts and, where necessary, a reasonable profit for discharging those obligations.

Moreover, if the contribution made does constitute State Aid within the meaning of Article 107(1) TFEU, it must satisfy the conditions of the Decision or of the Framework, in particular in that it must satisfy the provisions of an act of entrustment. The body in question can finance the SGEI on the basis of the act of entrustment (with reference to the public service obligations established by the public authorities).

If the contribution made towards the public service obligations is not characterised as State Aid within the meaning of Article 107(1) TFEU, it does not need to be added to the calculation of the overall amount of State Aid; it is, however, to be added to the revenue relating to the public service obligations and thus reduces both the net costs resulting from the SGEI and therefore the basis for potential compensation. It does not, however, have to satisfy the conditions laid down in the Decision and the Framework.

129. Should tax benefits arising from the corporate status of a body be counted among revenues within the meaning of Article 5(4) of the Decision?

Compensation may cover the difference between the costs actually incurred in providing an SGEI and the relevant receipts. A tax benefit can be State aid and can be granted in the form of either revenue or cost reduction. Irrespective of its nature, it has to be taken into account when determining the amount of compensation necessary to provide the SGEI.

When the tax benefit consists of a cost reduction, this means that no compensation can be awarded for the amount corresponding to that reduction. When the tax benefit consists of revenue for the service provider, this means that it will have to be deducted from the compensation to be allocated.

130. Should payments made under a profit-and-loss transfer agreement within a public holding be counted as revenues within the meaning of Article 5(4) of the Decision?

In several Member States, public holding undertakings have profit-and-loss transfer agreements under which a profitable subsidiary has to transfer its profits to the holding company, which then uses these profits to cover losses generated by a loss-making subsidiary that performs SGEIs.

Such payments received to cover SGEI losses are to be counted among revenues within the meaning of Article 5(4) of the Decision and will accordingly reduce the net costs eligible for compensation.

131. What is the meaning of the term 'reasonable profit' for the calculation of compatible compensation?

According to Article 5(5) of the Decision, 'reasonable profit' means the rate of return on capital that would be required by a typical undertaking considering whether or not to provide the service of general economic interest for the whole period of entrustment, taking into account the level of risk. The 'rate of return on capital' means the internal rate of return that the undertaking makes on its invested capital over the duration of the period of entrustment. The level of risk depends on the sector concerned, the type of service and the characteristics of the compensation.

Article 5(8) of the Decision provides that '*Where, by reasons of specific circumstances, it is not appropriate to use the rate of return on capital, Member States may rely on profit level indicators other than the rate of return on capital to determine what the reasonable profit should be, such as the average return on equity, return on capital employed, return on assets or return on sales*'.

Article 5(7) of the Decision provides for a safe harbour provision, stating that a rate of return on capital that does not exceed the relevant swap rate plus a premium of 100 basis points shall be regarded as reasonable in any event. This rate is also the upper limit for reasonable profit if the provision of the service is not connected with a substantial risk.

132. How should 'risk' be defined? Can you give examples of what would constitute a risk for the provider?

Risk is to be understood as a factor which could reduce the expected profit (by reducing expected revenue and/or increasing expected costs).

Certain factors can be included in the parameters for the calculation of compensation (for instance oil price or number of passengers for a bus service); if those factors have been included in the parameters, they no longer constitute risk factors.

Article 5(5) of the Decision provides that the level of risk depends on the sector concerned, the type of service and the characteristics of the compensation.

The characteristics of the compensation mechanism are an important example of a factor which affects the risk. Where the net cost incurred in providing an SGEI is essentially compensated ex post in full, the level of risk will be negligible and the reasonable profit will therefore be limited. A contrario, a lump sum for the provision of the SGEI, determined ex ante, involves a higher risk for the provider.

The sector of the activity is another example of a risk factor. Competitive sectors, where demand and costs are volatile (unless already factored into the compensation parameters) or where assets are expensive and difficult to resell, are considered to be more risky. Therefore, a provider would require a higher return on capital to invest and provide the service in such cases.

133. For the purpose of calculating reasonable profit, the Decision refers to a rate of return on capital. Is it possible to use different methods to calculate reasonable profit?

Yes, under specific circumstances, as set out in Article 5(8) of the Decision.

The return on capital (meaning the 'internal rate of return' that the undertaking makes on its invested capital) may not be available or appropriate for a concrete case, whereas other profit level indicators, such as the return on sales, are available and more appropriate. In such circumstances, it is possible to use other profit indicators, like those mentioned in Article 5(8) of the Decision, in order to provide solid and reliable references for the calculation of reasonable profit.

134. The profit safe harbour only applies to return on capital. Is there no safe harbour if, upon justification, other profit level indicators are used?

It was found not to be feasible to provide a single safe harbour for profit level indicators other than the rate of return on capital. This is because profit levels determined by other indicators, such as 'rate of return on assets' or 'rate of return on sales', have to be assessed in the light of the sector where the provider is active. For a similar risk, a certain level of return on assets would be considered reasonable in a given sector, whereas it would not be considered reasonable in another sector.

Even if a safe harbour is provided only for the rate of return on capital, this does not prevent Member States from assessing what the reasonable profit should be on the basis of profit level indicators other than the rate of return on capital, if duly justified.

135. Is there any practical means of knowing the level of the relevant swap rate?

Swap rates will soon be published on the Commission's DG Competition website. They will be provided for different EU currencies and maturities.

136. Would it be acceptable to add to the costs 20% overheads, and take that as reasonable profit?

No, it would not be acceptable to add 20% overheads to the costs and take that as reasonable profit. This is because the calculation of the profit would not be linked to the risk incurred in providing the service and could therefore exceed what should be considered as a reasonable profit.

An appropriate contribution to the overhead costs can be taken into account to determine the net cost incurred in providing an SGEI.

A reasonable profit can then be added to this net cost to determine the appropriate compensation. But this reasonable profit should be linked with the risk incurred by the provider.

137. Is there a need to keep separate accounts for an undertaking providing an SGEI, while also carrying out other, commercial, activities?

Yes, pursuant to Article 5(9) of the Decision, undertakings carrying out activities falling both inside and outside the scope of an SGEI must keep accounts that show separately the SGEI's costs and receipts, and those linked to other services.

It is the best way for such undertakings to prove that the compensation allocated does not exceed the net cost of the SGEI and thus involves no overcompensation. At the same time separate accounting for activities falling inside and outside the scope of the SGEI enables the Commission and the Member State to assess whether the criteria laid down by the Decision are indeed fulfilled.[121]

138. Is there a need to keep separate accounts for a body which is entrusted with the provision of an SGEI and also engages in non-economic activities?

The internal accounts should enable the costs linked to provision of the SGEI to be identified; otherwise, the amount of compensation cannot be established. Moreover, in case of a complaint, the undertaking to which the SGEI is attributed should be able to demonstrate the absence of overcompensation. Therefore, it is in practice necessary to keep separate accounts in such situations.

139. Which costs can be compensated when an undertaking uses the same infrastructure to provide both SGEIs and economic activities which are not characterised as SGEIs?

The undertaking must allocate costs to the two types of activities. Costs allocated to an SGEI may cover all the variable costs incurred in providing the SGEI, a proportionate contribution to fixed costs common to both the SGEI and non-SGEI operations.

3.4.2.4
Overcompensation and recovery

140. The Decision allows for the payment of public service compensation but prohibits overcompensation; what does the term 'overcompensation' mean?
Overcompensation should be understood as compensation that the undertaking receives in excess of what is necessary to cover the net cost incurred in discharging the public service obligations, including a reasonable profit.
Article 5 of the Decision provides guidance on how to determine the net cost incurred in discharging the public service obligations, including a reasonable profit.

141. There should be a control every three years. Is it possible to carry over overcompensation to the following period beyond the 10% if there will be no overcompensation over the whole period of entrustment? Or should there be recovery?
With a view to increasing flexibility, the 2011 Decision takes a multi-annual approach, rather than an annual approach as under the 2005 Decision. This means that a provider can receive compensation in excess of the net cost incurred in discharging the public service obligations for a certain year, as long as there is no overcompensation for the whole duration of the contract.
However, with a view to avoiding cases where the beneficiary would receive overcompensation over the whole duration of the contract, Article (6) of the Decision provides that Member States must carry out regular intermediate checks (at least every three years) during the period of entrustment and at the end of it. Where an undertaking has received overcompensation in excess of 10% of the amount of the average annual compensation, the Member State must intervene to ensure that the compensation mechanism is in line with what had been provided in the entrustment act. The Member State must ensure that the undertaking concerned repays the overcompensation and the parameters for calculating the compensation have to be updated for the future. Where the amount of overcompensation does not exceed 10% of the amount of the average annual compensation, such overcompensation may be carried forward to the next period and deducted from the amount of compensation payable in respect of that period.

142. What effect would the establishment of a mechanism designed to avoid any overcompensation have on the public authority's obligation to carry out checks on overcompensation?
Given how important it is to ensure that compensation does not exceed what is necessary to cover the costs incurred by an undertaking in discharging its public service obligations, taking into account relevant revenue and a reasonable profit, a mechanism designed to avoid such overcompensation might prove beneficial. Nevertheless, the existence of any such mechanism could not relieve Member States of their obligation to ensure that the undertaking does not in fact benefit from overcompensation, in accordance with Article 6 of the Decision.

143. In the event that an SGEI is jointly financed by two or more public authorities (e.g. by central government and/or a region and/or a province and/or a lower-level local authority), how should the control of overcompensation be carried out?
The entrustment acts should be designed in such a way as to ensure that the total compensation received by the SGEI provider from the different public authorities does not exceed what is necessary to cover the net cost incurred in discharging the public service obligations, including a reasonable profit.
In particular, when a public authority determines the amount of compensation to grant to an undertaking for discharging public service obligations, the said authority should include in the revenues of the undertaking the compensation that the undertaking will receive from other public authorities. If the amount of compensation received from other authorities is not known in advance, the public authority can include this amount as a parameter for calculating the compensation.
Checks for any overcompensation are based on the same principles as if the SGEI were financed by just one public authority. Public authorities should carry out regular checks, or ensure that such checks are carried out, at least every three years during the period of entrustment and at the end of such period, to ensure that the compensation actually granted is in line with the entrustment act and does not lead to overcompensation. It is for the Member State concerned to decide which public authority should carry out those checks.

144. In the event of overcompensation related to the joint financing of an SGEI by several levels of public authorities, how should the repayment of overcompensation be carried out between the various levels involved?
The way in which the repayment of any overcompensation should be shared among the various public bodies involved is not a matter for the EU but for the Member State concerned; with respect to State Aid, only the elimination of such overcompensation and of the undue advantage to which it gave rise is of any relevance.

3.4.2.5
Undercompensation

145. Do the State Aid rules forbid the undercompensation of an SSGI/SGEI provider, i.e. paying a level of compensation which is lower than the costs related to provision of the SSGI/SGEI? Does not the undercompensation of a provider give rise to an economic advantage for its competitor, which does not have to bear the financial burden of such undercompensation?
According to the rules on State Aid, providers of SGEIs/SSGIs must not be paid any overcompensation, that is to say compensation going beyond what is necessary to discharge the tasks assigned to them. These rules do not prohibit undercompensation or a lack of compensation for SGEI/SSGI providers. It is for the Member States to decide on the manner and level of financing of the SGEIs/SSGIs that they implement in accordance with the EU rules.

146. Can an undertaking entrusted with an SGEI which is undercompensated be paid provisional compensation before the end of the financial year if, after that year, it will be paid the compensation necessary for discharging its task?

It is only overcompensation which is prohibited under the State Aid rules. In the event of undercompensation, it is for the Member States to decide on the methods to be used for any revision of the amount of compensation, provided that such revision does not give rise to overcompensation. As regards the possibilities for revising the act of entrustment and the parameters for calculating compensation, see the answers to questions 58 and 117.

3.4.3 Transparency and reporting

147. Does the additional transparency requirement set out in Article 7 of the Decision apply if the compensation for one SGEI exceeds EUR 15 million or also if all SGEIs entrusted to one undertaking exceed EUR 15 million?

Article 7 applies if the compensation for one SGEI exceeds EUR 15 million. This article needs to be seen in conjunction with Article 2(1)(b) and (c) in particular, and is intended for large social services that benefit from the application of the Decision regardless of any thresholds. For these cases, the Decision sets out additional transparency requirements in Article 7. It is not intended to apply to undertakings that provide several SGEIs, each of which is individually compensated with an aid amount not exceeding EUR 15 million, as can also be understood from the reference in Article 7(a) to 'the entrustment act', in the singular.

148. Is the publication required by Article 7 of the Decision for amounts exceeding EUR 15 million needed every year or is it permissible to publish the yearly amounts at the end of the entrustment period?

Although the timing of the publication is not mentioned in Article 7 of the Decision, the objective of this article is to ensure transparency, by informing public service providers that an SGEI has been entrusted, to whom, what it covers, and what the annual compensation is. This also allows a possible competitor or a citizen to bring to the attention of a judge or of the Commission a case of illegal or incompatible aid. It would therefore appear to result from the objective of this provision that this information should be published at the time of the entrustment or in the course of that year. If one were to wait until the end of the entrustment period, the transparency objective could no longer be fully achieved.

149. Where aid in the form of public service compensation can be exempted from notification on the basis of the Decision, is there an obligation to send the Commission an information sheet?

No. When applying the Decision, national authorities are not under any obligation to send the Commission an information sheet. The only procedural obligations that the Decision imposes on Member States are that the Member States must keep available for the Commission, for a period of at least ten years, all the elements necessary to establish whether the compensation granted is compatible with the Decision,[122] and that they must submit periodic reports, every two years, on the implementation of the Decision.[123]

150. Who should provide the reports on the implementation of the Decision — the Member States or the regional / local authorities?

The reports on the implementation of the Decision must be submitted by the Member States to the Commission every two years.[124] For this purpose, the Member States should organise the reporting exercise in advance, allocating sufficient time for collecting the necessary information from the relevant regional and local authorities.

3.4.4 Entry into force and transitional provisions

151. Since when has the Decision been applied? Is it retroactive?

The Decision applies since 31 January 2012, the date of its entry into force.

It applies also to any aid put into effect before the entry into force of the Decision which was not compatible or exempted from notification under the 2005 Decision (i.e. unlawful aid), but which fulfils the conditions laid down in the (2011) Decision (Article 10(b)). This provision applies also to aid schemes that were put into effect before the entry into force of the new Decision; for those schemes it is irrelevant whether the individual provider was already entrusted with an SGEI before the entry into force of this decision or only after that. 'Aid put into effect' means that the undertaking has been granted the legal right to receive the aid; it is not relevant whether the aid has actually been paid or not.

152. Do the Member States have to bring existing individual aid, legally implemented under the 2005 Decision, into line with the new Decision?

No. Under the transitional provisions set out in Article 10 of the Decision, aid schemes that were compatible with the 2005 Decision will continue to be compatible with the internal market and exempt from notification for two years. The Decision does not mention individual aid granted in compliance with the 2005 Decision. Therefore the legal situation of those instances of individual aid is unaltered by the new Decision. The concepts of 'aid scheme' and 'individual aid' are defined in Article 1(d) and (e) of Council Regulation 659/1999 (the Procedural Regulation).

153. Can Member States that have in place SGEI schemes which were legally implemented under the 2005 Decision, still grant new entrustments under the 2005 Decision during the transitional period of two years?

As aid schemes compatible with the 2005 Decision continue to be compatible and exempt from notification for two years, the Member States can grant new entrustments under such existing schemes. However, at the end of the transitional period, aid schemes have to be brought into line with the revised Decision or terminated.

3.5 COMPENSATION UNDER THE SGEI FRAMEWORK

3.5.1 Scope of application

154. Does the Framework apply to public service compensation for the transport sector?

The Framework does not apply to the land transport sector,[125] but it applies to air and maritime transport. The Framework applies without prejudice to additional requirements laid down in:

- Regulation (EC) No 1008/2008 of the European Parliament and of the Council of 24 September 2008 on common rules for the operation of air services in the Community,[126]
- Regulation (EEC) No 3577/92 of 7 December 1992 applying the principle of freedom to provide services to maritime transport within Member States (maritime cabotage).[127]

155. Does the Framework apply to compensation for the public service broadcasting?

The Framework does not apply to the public service broadcasting.[128] This sector is covered by the Communication from the Commission on the application of State Aid rules to public service broadcasting.[129]

156. What are the rules for applying the Framework to firms in difficulty?

Aid to SGEI providers in difficulty[130] will be assessed under the Community guidelines on State Aid for rescuing and restructuring firms in difficulty.[131]

157. Is it necessary for aid exceeding the threshold laid down in Article 2(a) of the Decision to be notified to the Commission?

The Decision applies to public service compensation not exceeding EUR 15 million per year. As regards hospitals and certain social services, there is no limitation on the amounts which are exempted from notification.

If the compensation for services other than hospitals and social services exceeds the threshold of EUR 15 million per year, prior notification to the Commission is required. Such compensation will then be assessed in accordance with the provisions of the Framework. Notification does not mean that the compensation is automatically incompatible with the Treaty, but because of the high amount of aid concerned and the higher risk of distortion of competition, the aid must be assessed by the Commission in order to ensure that all the compatibility conditions are met.[132]

158. Where a Member State refuses the request of a region or of other local communities to notify aid in the form of public service compensation, is it possible for the public communities to act on their own? Could the Commission take action against this Member State?

The notification procedure is initiated by the Member State concerned.[133] The procedure primarily involves the Commission and the national authorities of the Member State concerned. Consequently, from the point of view of the EU rules on State Aid, the decision to notify an aid scheme or an individual aid award is up to the Member State and not the local or regional communities.[134]

Where aid that should be notified to the Commission in accordance with the existing rules is implemented without prior notification, it constitutes illegal State Aid. The implication is that the matter could be brought before a national court, for example by competitors of the aid recipient. In such a case, the national court would have to note this illegality and order that the aid be recovered, regardless of whether it may be compatible with the internal market, which only the Commission has the competence to establish. At the same time, the Commission could act *ex officio* or following a complaint and examine the measure concerned. The examination concludes with a decision which, in the event that the aid is incompatible, will demand its recovery.

3.5.2 Compatibility conditions (Please note that the replies to the following questions relating to the Decision are also applicable mutatis mutandis to the Framework: 117, 119, 124 to 138, 140 to 147)

159. What are the main changes compared to the 2005 Framework as regards the compatibility conditions?

The revised Framework introduces a proportionate approach by subjecting large aid cases, with more significant cross-border effects, to closer scrutiny.

The following table summarises the main changes in the 2011 Framework as compared to the 2005 Framework:

Framework 2005	**Framework 2011**
Compatibility conditions:	Compatibility conditions:
– Genuine SGEI	– Genuine SGEI
– Entrustment act	– Entrustment act
– Overcompensation test (annual check)	– Duration of the entrustment period
	– Compliance with Transparency Directive
	– Compliance with EU public procurement rules
	– Absence of discrimination
	– Overcompensation test based on ex ante multi-annual approach, efficiency incentives and the net avoided cost methodology
	– Strengthened transparency
	– Possible additional requirements for particularly distortive aid

160. What is the purpose of the requirement, mentioned in paragraph 14, for prior public consultation before an SGEI is entrusted?

Under the revised Framework, Member States have to carry out a public consultation or use any other appropriate instrument to take the interests of users and providers into account, before entrusting a public service obligation to a certain provider. This can help the public authorities to determine whether the service concerned is or could be provided by the market and increases transparency of the process. It also helps to identify the precise needs of users, and thus to draw up the entrustment act more accurately. This requirement does not apply where it is clear that a new consultation will not bring any significant added value to a recently held consultation on the same issue.

161. What should be the content of the public consultation mentioned in paragraph 14? Can such a consultation also take the form of a public hearing?

The public consultation should enable the public authority to improve its knowledge of the users' needs and interests and of the market offers with a view to defining the public service obligations in an appropriate and proportionate manner. The content could cover for instance questions relating to the users' needs in terms of accessibility, quality of service, affordability and whether/ to what extent those needs are not met by services already provided on the market in the absence of a public service provider. If there is already a public service provider entrusted with an SGEI, and the public authorities are considering a new entrustment of this or another provider, the consultation could examine whether the public service obligations of this provider are still in line with the current or future users' needs.

A consultation can also take the form of a public hearing, if users are sufficiently well informed about the hearing and able to express their views on the public needs during this hearing.

162. Is it possible for a public authority to establish in the act of entrustment that it will cover the operating losses incurred for each set period without defining any other parameters for calculating compensation?

As provided in paragraph 38 of the Framework, compensation mechanisms whereby the net cost incurred in providing the SGEI is essentially compensated ex post in full provides no efficiency incentives for the public service provider. Hence the use of such a compensation mechanism is strictly limited to cases where the Member State is able to justify that it is not feasible or appropriate to take into account productive efficiency and to have a contract which gives incentives to achieve efficiency gains. In this case, the reasonable profit may not exceed the level that corresponds to the level specified in paragraph 36 of the Framework.

163. What are non-transferable fixed assets, as referred to in paragraph 17? Can you give examples?

Non-transferable fixed assets designate assets which cannot easily be sold and/or converted into cash. For instance, capital equipment of a manufacturing company which is specific to the production methods of that company may constitute a non-transferable fixed asset.

164. What is meant by 'the most significant assets', as mentioned in paragraph 17?

In the context of paragraph 17, the most significant assets required to provide an SGEI are the assets which are necessary to provide the SGEI and whose value is sufficiently high — compared to the total value of the assets necessary for provision of the SGEI — to justify a certain period of duration for the entrustment. For instance, sorting equipment/centres could be considered to be significant assets for postal operators.

165. Would a duration of 10 years always be acceptable under the Framework? Or would even a shorter period of e.g. 8 years need a justification based on the depreciation of significant assets?

Any duration should be justified by reference to objective criteria such as the need to amortise non-transferable fixed assets. It follows from this that a duration of 10 years or even shorter would not always be acceptable under the Framework.

166. What is the difference between the requirements in terms of duration of the entrustment period under the Decision and the Framework. Is the requirement under the Decision stricter than the one under the Framework, and if so, to what extent?

According to Article 2(2) of the Decision, the Decision only applies where the entrustment period does not exceed 10 years or where a significant investment is required which needs to be amortised over a longer period.

According to paragraph 17 of the Framework, the duration of the period of entrustment should be justified by reference to objective criteria such as the need to amortise nontransferable fixed assets. In principle, the duration of the period of entrustment should not exceed the period required for the depreciation of the most significant assets required to provide the SGEI.

The Framework (paragraph 55) also provides that where the entrustment has a duration which cannot be justified by reference to objective criteria (such as the need to amortise non-transferable fixed assets), serious competition problems may arise. In such a case, the Commission would examine whether the same public service could equally well be provided in a less distortive manner, for instance by way of a more limited duration of entrustment.

The Framework is thus stricter than the Decision as any period of entrustment – including a duration not exceeding 10 years – must be justified by reference to objective criteria.

If the duration of the entrustment period exceeds 10 years without justification based on the need to amortise significant assets, the Decision does not apply and, in principle, the aid will not be found compatible under the Framework.

167. Why did the Commission introduce a new provision in paragraph 18 on compliance with the Transparency Directive?

The objective is to increase transparency and more effectively ensure proportionality of the compensation – in particular by requiring a separation of accounts between activities receiving public service compensation and other activities – so as to make it easier to quantify the net costs of the SGEI. It should be underlined that paragraph 18 does not widen the scope of application of the Transparency Directive beyond what is already set out in the Directive itself. Therefore it does not create any new obligations for undertakings entrusted with SGEIs.

168. Does paragraph 19 of the Framework require selection of the service provider by means of public procurement procedures?

The new SGEI package does not create any additional public procurement obligations. Nevertheless, whenever EU public procurement rules, including both public procurement Directives and Treaty principles, apply, in the event of non-compliance with such rules, the aid would not be considered compatible with the internal market. Paragraph 19 of the Framework therefore explicitly refers to existing public procurement requirements. Although State Aid law does not create any tendering obligations, tendering out the service can facilitate compliance with the Altmark criteria so that the compensation is considered not to constitute State Aid under Article 107 (1) TFEU (see the SGEI Communication).

169. What is the link between the fourth condition of the Altmark judgment and paragraph 19 of the Framework?

Altmark concerns the existence of State Aid, whereas the Framework deals with the compatibility of the aid.

Pursuant to the Altmark judgment, public service compensation does not constitute State Aid if four conditions are fulfilled (see question 61).

The fourth condition of the Altmark judgment provides that the compensation offered must either be the result of a public procurement procedure which allows for the selection of the tenderer capable of providing the service at the least cost to the community, or the result of a bench-marking exercise with a typical undertaking, well run and adequately provided with the necessary means.

If a public procurement procedure in line with the fourth Altmark criterion has been carried out and the other Altmark criteria are fulfilled, there is no State Aid and therefore there is no scope for applying the Framework.

If no public procurement in line with the fourth condition of Altmark has been carried out and if the measure can be classified as State Aid under Article 107(1), then the Decision or the Framework is applicable. Even if no public procurement in compliance with Altmark has been carried out, it might well be the case that the aid is in line with paragraph 19 of the Framework. This is true for instance if a selection procedure (e.g. a negotiated procedure) which complies with the requirements of the applicable EU public procurement rules, but which is not considered to be sufficient to fulfil the fourth Altmark criterion, has been carried out (see, for instance, question 67).

170. Why did the Commission introduce a provision in paragraph 20 about the absence of discrimination? Why was it not introduced in the Decision as well?

This is an important provision aiming to deal more effectively with competition distortions which may occur when public authorities entrust the same SGEI to several undertakings and compensate them on the basis of different methods. The Commission has received a number of complaints about such occurrences. It is no longer appropriate to accept such discrimination, considering that the Framework now takes better account of competition aspects.

The Decision does not include a non-discrimination clause. This is because it was felt that under the diversified and proportionate approach, competition considerations should target the large cases, with potentially more significant competition distortions, i.e. the cases covered by the Framework, while small-scale and social services should benefit from simplified treatment.

171. Why was a new methodology introduced in paragraph 24 (the net avoided cost methodology) to determine the amount of compensation?

The revised Framework encourages Member States to use the net avoided cost methodology (NACM) for calculating the net cost of a public service obligation. The choice of this methodology was an important element of the reform. The primary reason for introducing it is to better estimate the economic cost of the public service obligation and to fix the amount of compensation at a level which ensures the best allocation of resources.

Under the NACM, the cost of the public service obligation is calculated as the difference between the net cost to a company of operating an SGEI and the net cost to the same company operating without a public service obligation. The NACM is already used in the telecommunication and postal sectors to calculate the net cost of providing the universal service. Annex IV to Directive 2002/22/EC of the European Parliament and of the Council of 7 March 2002 (as amended by Directive 2009/136/EC)[135] on universal service and users' rights relating to electronic communications networks and services, and Annex I to Directive 97/67/EC of the European Parliament and of the Council of 15 December 1997 on common rules for the development of the internal market of Community postal services and the improvement of quality of service, contain more detailed guidance on how to apply the net avoided cost methodology.

The new Framework also allows for alternative methodologies when the NACM is not feasible or appropriate.

172. Why do the new rules require Member States to include efficiency incentives in their compensation mechanisms?

In devising the method of compensation, Member States must introduce incentives for the efficient provision of SGEIs, unless the use of such incentives is not feasible or appropriate. Efficiency gains have to be achieved without prejudice to the quality of the service provided. The Commission has introduced this new requirement to foster the provision of services of better quality at a lower cost for taxpayers and users and to limit distortions of competition that could arise from the ongoing subsidisation of seriously inefficient service providers.

The inclusion of efficiency incentives in the compensation mechanism has to be distinguished from the efficiency test under *Altmark*. Contrary to the *Altmark* test, there is no requirement for the provider to be as efficient as a typical well-run undertaking; there is only a requirement to introduce efficiency incentives into the compensation mechanism, so as to make providers more efficient for the benefit of both users and public authorities.

Member States have a wide margin of discretion in devising their method for compensation and determining the efficiency targets. However the mechanism should be based on objective and measurable criteria set out in the entrustment act and subject to transparent ex post assessment carried out by an entity independent of the SGEI provider.

173. Can you give examples of compensation mechanisms which would provide efficiency incentives?

The Framework gives two examples of such compensation mechanisms:

- Upfront definition of compensation level: the Member State defines a fixed compensation level which incorporates the efficiency gains that the undertaking can be expected to make over the lifetime of the entrustment act;
- payment dependent upon the extent to which efficiency targets have been met: Member States define productive efficiency targets in the entrustment act whereby the level of compensation is made dependent upon the extent to which the targets have been met. If the undertaking does not meet the objectives, the profit should be reduced. In contrast, if the undertaking exceeds the objectives, the profit should be increased.

In any event, the compensation should in principle no longer be based on incurred costs only. To preserve the incentive for the provider to become efficient, the compensation should be based on the expected costs (upfront definition of compensation level) or on a combination of expected and incurred costs (payment depending upon whether the efficiency targets have been met). The compensation mechanism has to be specified in advance in the entrustment act.

The following two graphics illustrate cases where the compensation is based on a combination of expected and incurred costs:

Case 1: efficiency gains are higher than expected, so incurred costs are below expected costs.

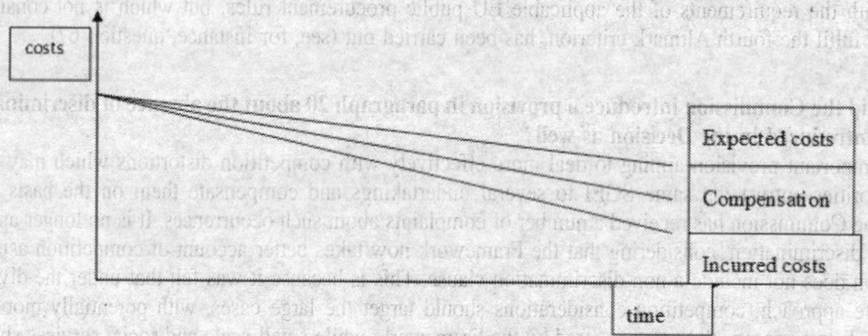

In the event that incurred costs are below expected costs, the compensation can exceed the incurred costs, thus increasing the profit of the undertaking. The compensation should however in no case exceed the expected costs (plus reasonable profit).

Case 2: efficiency gains are lower than expected, so incurred costs are above expected costs.

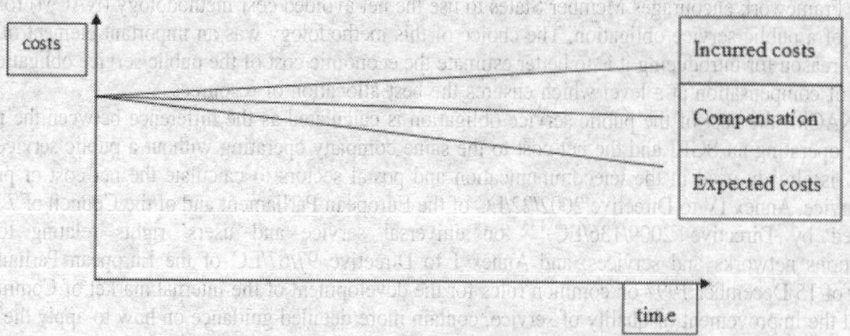

In the event that incurred costs are above expected costs, the compensation cannot cover the total incurred costs. So the undertaking has to bear part of the loss due to the fact that it was less efficient than expected.

174. If the amount of compensation is fixed following a negotiated procedure, does the Commission consider that the condition regarding efficiency incentives is fulfilled?

The negotiated procedure confers wide discretion upon the contracting authority and may restrict the participation of interested operators (see paragraph 66 of the Communication). This is the reason why the Commission considers that the negotiated procedure is not always sufficient to ensure that the amount of compensation corresponds to the least cost for the community. For the same reason, the Commission does not consider that the fixing of the compensation following a negotiated procedure is automatically sufficient to ensure that the compensation level incorporates any efficiency gains. This can only be assessed by carefully analysing all details of the individual case.

Therefore, the Member State should ensure that, if a fixed amount of compensation is determined following a negotiated procedure, this amount takes account of expected efficiency gains.

In any event, the Member State should notify the aid so as to get the Commission's clearance before entering into a contractual agreement with the public service provider.

175. In the case of an upfront payment, how can the risk of the provider overstating the expenses or underestimating the revenue be avoided?

As indicated in paragraph 23 of the Framework, where the compensation is based on expected costs and revenues, those costs and revenues must be based on plausible and observable parameters concerning the economic environment in which the SGEI is being provided. They must rely, where appropriate, on the expertise of sector regulators or of other entities independent from the undertaking.

In the absence of plausible and observable parameters and where the Member State has little means of verifying whether the expected costs and revenues are plausible, it might be appropriate to define a compensation mechanism other than an upfront payment.

For instance, Member States can design a compensation mechanism that takes into account of certain parameters, such as the number of users of the service. Those parameters should be defined in the entrustment act.

176. The Framework permits the payment of public service compensation but prohibits overcompensation; what does the term 'overcompensation' mean?

Paragraph 47 of the Framework defines overcompensation as compensation that the undertaking receives in excess of the amount necessary to cover the net cost of discharging the public service obligations including a reasonable profit for the whole duration of the contract.

This amount of compensation – or the mechanism for calculating this amount – should be specified in the entrustment act.

A surplus that results from higher than expected efficiency gains may be retained by an undertaking as specified in the entrustment act. This is not considered as overcompensation but as an additional reasonable profit.

177. Why should a 2-year or 3-year control be provided in case the compensation has been defined ex ante as a lump sum (and is therefore independent of the costs and revenues which are actually incurred)?

As provided by paragraph 50 of the Framework, where the Member State has defined upfront a fixed compensation level which adequately anticipates and incorporates the efficiency gains that the public service provider can be expected to make over the period of entrustment, on the basis of a correct allocation of costs and revenues and of reasonable expectations, the overcompensation check is in principle confined to verifying that the level of profit to which the provider is entitled in accordance with the entrustment act is indeed reasonable from an ex ante perspective.

However, if the upfront payment has not been determined on the basis of a correct allocation of costs and revenues and of reasonable expectations, the compensation mechanism should be reviewed to the extent that is legally possible. In such a case, the Member State should ensure that the efficiency incentives are maintained in the compensation mechanism.

178. Should the regular checks be limited to the issue of overcompensation or should they also look at the question of whether an SGEI is still justified or whether in the meantime the service could be provided by the market?

The check whether the service could be provided by the market should be made before the entrustment (see questions 11 and 12 above). The Framework does not require national authorities to examine during the entrustment period whether the SGEI is still justified. However, Member States are free to do so if they wish, in order to ensure that the SGEI continues to reflect actual users' needs or could be provided by other means that cause less distortion of competition or are less expensive for the public purse.

179. Is it possible to carry overcompensation over to the following period if there will be no overcompensation over the whole period of entrustment? Or should recovery take place?

Yes, carry-over is possible if it is in line with the entrustment act and there is no overcompensation over the whole period of entrustment.

180. For the purposes of the Framework, in the event that an undertaking entrusted with an SGEI is undercompensated, can it transfer any overcompensation that it might have received over the same period with respect to another SGEI entrusted to it?

As provided by paragraph 46 of the Framework, the Member State concerned may decide that profits accruing from other activities outside the scope of an SGEI (coming from another SGEI or from non-SGEI activities) will be allocated in whole or in part to the financing of the SGEI.

However this should be decided when the SGEI is entrusted to the provider and reflected in the entrustment act.

Where incentives for the efficient provision of SGEIs have been introduced in the compensation mechanism, deficits resulting from lower than expected efficiency gains should not be covered by the public authorities.
The transfer of profits accruing from other non-SGEI activities must be shown in the accounts of the undertaking in question, be carried out in accordance with the rules and principles set out in the Framework, notably as regards prior notification, and be subject to proper control. In addition, overcompensation cannot remain available to an undertaking on the grounds that it would constitute aid compatible with the TFEU; such aid should be notified to and authorised by the Commission or be exempted from notification under the relevant rules.

181. Why has the Commission introduced additional requirements for particularly serious competition distortions in section 2.9 and what are they?
The Commission has to ensure that trade and competition in the internal market are not affected to an extent contrary to the interests of the EU (Article 106(2) of the TFEU). In some exceptional circumstances, an SGEI measure has the potential to create serious distortions of competition that could affect trade to such an extent as would be contrary to the interests of the EU. In such cases, the Commission will therefore carry out an indepth assessment of its impact on competition and assess whether the distortions can be remedied through conditions applicable to or commitments obtained from Member States.

182. An example of serious distortions given in paragraph 55 of the Framework is that of unnecessary bundling. Could there also be cases of unnecessary unbundling, i.e. where bundling would be better from a competition perspective (e.g. because more profitable services would be bundled with loss-making services)?
Bundling a series of tasks can result in operators being prevented from competing for the provision of an SGEI, if those operators are not able to provide all the services included in the SGEI. Unbundling would normally not have the same effect of preventing operators from competing for the provision of the SGEI.
It is, however, correct to say that the bundling of profitable services with loss-making services would lead to lower compensation under the methodology based on cost allocation. When bundling is considered, it would also have to be examined whether the profitable services can qualify as genuine SGEIs which are not or could not be provided by the market.

183. Pursuant to paragraph 61, certain compatibility conditions do not apply to services that would have fallen within the scope of the Decision but do not comply with the Decision's compatibility conditions. Could you explain why and give an example?
The Framework contains compatibility conditions which might be considered too burdensome or not appropriate for small-scale services and social services. Cases where aid falling under Article 2(1) of the Decision – i.e. in particular compensation not exceeding €15 million and compensation to hospitals and social services – is not covered by the Decision because it fails to meet all its compatibility conditions will be assessed on the basis of the Framework (and therefore have to be notified). Such aid will escape the application of certain compatibility conditions provided for in the Framework, such as the obligation to carry out a public consultation on public needs to define the SGEI, the absence of discrimination between providers, the use of the net avoided cost methodology, the obligation to introduce efficiency incentives, etc.
For instance, if aid falls under Article 2(1) of the Decision but does not meet one of the compatibility criteria under the Decision (e.g. the entrustment act does not specify all the elements required under Article 4 of the Decision), its compatibility would be assessed on the basis of the Framework. Pursuant to paragraph 61, certain conditions of compatibility will not be applicable.

3.5.3 Entry into force and transitional provisions

184. Since when has the Framework been applied? Is it retroactive?
The Framework applies to all notified aid measures, even if these were notified before 31 January 2012, the date of its entry into force.[136]
It also applies to unlawful aid on which a decision is taken by the Commission after 31 January 2012, even if the aid was granted before this date. However, where the aid was granted before 31 January 2012, certain requirements[137] which did not exist in the previous Framework, and would therefore have been difficult to anticipate, do not apply.[138]

185. If individual aid has been legally granted on the basis of the 2005 SGEI Framework, is it necessary to ensure that such aid now complies with the new Framework? Is a new notification necessary?
No. Individual aid granted before the entry into force of the revised Framework and declared compatible by the Commission under the 2005 Framework is not affected by the revision, and does not have to comply with the revised Framework. When a new entrustment is granted, this has to be compatible with the new SGEI package and (unless the new SGEI compensation complies with the Decision) a new notification is required.

186. What are the rules for the existing schemes?
According to the appropriate measures set out in the Framework,[139] Member States have to publish a list of all existing aid schemes concerning public service compensation that are not in line with the revised Framework by 31 January 2013. This can be done on the internet, in an official journal or by other appropriate means. These aid schemes have to be brought into line with the revised Framework by 31 January 2014. All Member States have accepted those appropriate measures. As a consequence, the existing aid schemes in question can no longer be lawfully applied after 31 January 2014.

3.6 THE SGEI PACKAGE AND OTHER RULES

187. Do SGEIs concerning the social and work integration of unemployed people and the vocational training come within the scope of the Decision or the General block exemption Regulation (EC) No 800/2008[140]?

An SGEI concerning social and work integration or vocational training, defined as such by the State and entrusted to an undertaking by it, may come within the scope of the Decision, provided that the conditions laid down therein are fulfilled. Therefore, compensation paid to an undertaking which has a public service remit in the field of social and work integration or training may be exempted from notification in so far as the undertaking concerned has genuinely been entrusted with this public service task (see more specifically the conditions for entrustment in Articles 2, 4 and 6 of the Decision and section 3.4.2 of this guide).

Moreover, aid for undertakings which recruit disadvantaged persons within the meaning of Article 2(18) of Regulation (EC) No 800/2008 may benefit from the notification exemption laid down in the Regulation, provided it fulfils the conditions established in Chapter I of the Regulation and those laid down in Article 40 of the same Regulation.

As far as aid for undertakings which invest in training of workers within the meaning of Article 38 of Regulation (EC) No 800/2008 is concerned, it may benefit from the notification exemption laid down in the Regulation, provided it fulfils the conditions established in Chapter I of the Regulation and those laid down in Article 39 of the same Regulation.

188. Does compliance with the SGEI package mean that public procurement rules do not have to be applied?

No. The SGEI package only deals with EU State Aid law. It does not limit by any means the application of EU public procurement rules (see recital 29 of the Decision; para. 10 (b) of the Framework; recital 21 of the SGEI *de minimis* Regulation). It also does not limit the application of national public procurement rules.

189. Is financing of SGEIs by the ESF and the ERDF State Aid? Is this the responsibility of the Member States or the Commission?

As far as the application of the State Aid rules is concerned, financing granted by Member States using resources from the ESF and the ERDF constitutes state resources. The rules on State Aid therefore apply to financing granted by Member States using such resources in the same way as if the financing was granted directly out of a Member State's own budget.

190. Does SGEI funding via resources originating from the ESF and the ERDF have to be granted in accordance with the SGEI package? Is this the responsibility of the Member States or the Commission?

Public subsidies granted by Member States using ESF and ERDF resources are included, like any other public funding intended to enable a company to provide services of general economic interest, in the calculation of compensation for the provision of such services, and must be granted in accordance with the SGEI package. Responsibility for defining the parameters for calculating, controlling and reviewing the compensation specified in the act of entrustment rests with the national, regional or local authority setting up the service of general economic interest, regardless of the origin of the public funding allocated by that authority to the service. The fact that resources stem from the ESF or the ERDF has no bearing whatsoever on the establishment of public service remits by the Member States, which is always under their responsibility.

191. Is financing of SGEIs by the EAFRD state aid?

State aid rules apply to the financing within the framework of the Rural Development Regulation whenever MS exercise discretion as regards the allocation of the funds (cf. Article 88 of Regulation (EC) No 1698/2005). However, the Rural Development Regulation stipulates that for Annex I products the State aid rules apply neither to the Union support nor to the national contributions of the Member States.

For the support of rural development for non Annex I products, under the conditions just mentioned, the State aid rules fully apply to all parts of payments: the Union part, the financial contribution provided for by the Member State (co-financing) and the additional national part (top-ups). The specific rules on SGEI can therefore be applied if the general State aid rules do apply.

192. Does an SGEI funding via EAFRD resources for non Annex I products have to be granted in accordance with the SGEI package?

Rural development measures concerning non-agricultural products have to be covered either by *de minimis* (Regulation (EC) No 1998/2006) or by a state aid block exemption regulation or an already approved state aid decision. In the latter case, whenever an SGEI is concerned, the conditions of the SGEI package would have to be fulfilled.

Support granted from EAFRD resources is included, like any other public funding intended to enable a company to provide services of general economic interest, in the calculation of compensation for the provision of such services. The total amount of support (i.e. Union part, co-financing and top ups) must be granted in accordance with the SGEI Package.

Responsibility for defining the parameters for calculating, controlling and reviewing the compensation in the act of entrustment rests with the national, regional or local authority setting up the service of general economic interest, regardless of the origin of the public funding allocated by that authority to the service.

193. What is the interplay between the State Aid rules on regional aid that set out specific aid intensities and the SGEI rules?

If the contribution from the ERDF fulfils all the requirements of the Decision or the Framework, it is compatible with the internal market based on Article 106(2) TFEU. The aid intensities laid down in the regional aid guidelines (based on Article 107(3)(a) and (c)) do not apply in this case.

If the undertaking performs other activities in addition to its public service tasks, it can receive regional aid for those other activities. In this case, separate accounting is necessary to ensure that the respective compatibility conditions for the two sets of activities are fulfilled.

194. Are State Aid controls compatible with controls on ESF funding?

State Aid controls and controls on ESF funding serve different purposes: to prevent Member States from awarding aid that would distort competition, on the one hand, and to ensure that EU funding awarded to certain projects is used in accordance with the conditions governing the award on the other.

The funding for a single project may have to be examined from both of these angles. The ESF controls will, where applicable, also include the respect of State Aid rules. This is due to the fact that operations co-financed by the ESF have to comply with the provisions of the Treaty and with the acts adopted under it.[141]

195. According to the rules on managing ESF funds, only items of expenditure and receipts strictly devoted to the project being co-financed are eligible, i.e. excluding reasonable profit. In the case of an SSGI funded from ESF resources, can reasonable profit be included, as provided for in the Decision?

The rules on State Aid do indeed allow the public authority financing a project to cover 100% of the service provider's costs plus 'a reasonable profit'. But reasonable profit is not included in the eligible amount under the ESF. In practice, the interaction between these two sets of rules is not really a problem, because under the SGEI package the public authority is still allowed to cover the reasonable profit with its own resources, if it so wishes.

196. What is the relationship between the control mechanism for projects co-financed by the ESF and the control of overcompensation imposed by the SGEI package?

Projects funded by the ESF are subject to systematic control by the authorities responsible for managing ESF operational programmes. Regulation (EC) No 1083/2006 contains detailed provisions on the control systems to be put in place by the authorities in charge of the ESF operational programmes. ESF managing authorities have to verify whether the co-financed products and services are delivered and whether the expenditure declared by beneficiaries for operations has actually been incurred and complies with Union and national rules. Before expenditure can be declared to the Commission, the certifying authority has, inter alia, to certify that the statement of expenditure is accurate and that the expenditure declared complies with applicable Union and national rules.

The SGEI package, on the other hand, requires that a control mechanism be put in place, but leaves it up to the Member States to decide on the detailed arrangements. The aim of this mechanism is to ensure that there has been no overcompensation, which the ESF checks will not necessarily establish, since they will focus on eligible costs under the ESF (the question of reasonable profit, for example, will not be examined). Although these two control mechanisms may overlap in certain areas and could even, if necessary, be combined, each has its own logic, which should be respected.

197. If a Member State confers an advantage on an undertaking entrusted with public service obligations in the area of electronic communications which go beyond the scope of Directive 2002/22/EC[142] as amended by Directive 2009/136/EC, is it still possible to assess the compensation in question in the light of the State Aid rules?

Directive 2002/22/EC states that Member States are still free to introduce additional measures in their territory which are not covered by the universal service obligations provided for by the Directive, and to fund them in accordance with EU law (see Article 32 and recitals 25 and 46 of Directive 2002/22/EC).

Consequently, when a Member State confers an advantage on an entity responsible for providing telephone services accessible to the public which are not covered by the universal service obligations, as defined in Chapter II of the Directive, it should always assess the applicability of the *Altmark* criteria and the other State Aid conditions (i.e. transfer of state resources and imputability, distortion of competition and effect on trade between Member States, selectivity of the measure in question), in order to determine whether or not State Aid is involved.

NOTES

44 Joined Cases C-180/98 to C-184/98 *Pavlov and Others* [2000] ECR I-6451.

45 Case 118/85 *Commission* v *Italy* [1987] ECR 2599, paragraph 7; Case C-35/96 *Commission* v *Italy* [1998] ECR I-3851, paragraph 36; and *Pavlov*.

46 *Pavlov*, paragraph 118; Case C-218/00 *INAIL* [2002] ECR I-691, paragraph 37; and Case C-355/00 *Freskot* [2003] ECR I-5263.

47 Case C-41/90 *Höffner and Elser* [1991] ECR I-1979, paragraph 21.

48 Case C-244/94 *FFSA* [1995] ECR I-4013, paragraphs 17-22; Case C-67/96 *Albany* [1999] ECR I-5751, paragraphs 80-87.

49 Case C-475/99 *Glöckner* [2001] ECR I-8089, paragraph 20.

50 Case C-35/96 *Commission* v *Italy* [1998] ECR I-3851, paragraph 37.

51 Case C-451/03 *Servizi Ausiliari Dottori Commercialisti* [2006] ECR I-2941, paragraph 63.

52 Case C-82/01 P *Aéroports de Paris* v *Commission* [2002] ECR I-9297.

53 Case C-157/99 *Smits* [2001] ECR I-5473, paragraph 53; Joined Cases 286/82 and 26/83 *Luisi and Carbone* [1984] ECR 377, paragraph 16; Case C-159/90 *Society for the Protection of unborn children* [1999] ECR I-4685,

paragraph 18; Case C-368/98 *Abdon Vanbraekel* [2001] ECR I-5363, paragraph 43; Case T-167/04 *Asklepios Kliniken* [2007] ECR II-2379, paragraphs 49-55.

54 Commission Decision on state aid No N 89/2004 – Ireland – Guarantee in favour of the Housing Financing Agency, Social housing schemes funded by the HFA, OJ C131, 28.5.2005, ec.europa.eu/competition/elojade/isef/case_details.cfm?proc_code=3_N89_2004

55 Commission Decision in case N 395/05 – Ireland – Loan guarantee for social infrastructure schemes funded by the Housing Finance Agency (HFA), OJ C77, 5.4.2007, ec.europa.eu/competition/elojade/isef/case_details.cfm?proc_code=3_N395_2005

56 Joined Cases C-180/98 to C-184/98 *Pavlov and Others* [2000] ECR I-6451.

57 Case 118/85 *Commission* v *Italian Republic* [1987] ECR 2599, paragraphs 7 and 8.

58 Case C-364/92 *SAT/Eurocontrol* [1994] ECR I-43, paragraph 27; Case C-113/07 P *Selex Sistemi Integrati* v *Commission* [2009] ECR I-2207, paragraph 71.

59 Commission Decisions in case N 309/2002 of 19 March 2003, Aviation security – compensation for costs incurred following the attacks of 11 September 2001, OJ C148, 25.6.2003, and in case N 438/2002 of 16 October 2002, Aid in support of public authority functions in the Belgian sector, OJ C284, 21.11.2002.

60 Commission Decision in case N 438/02 of 16 October 2002, Belgium – Aid to port authorities, OJ C284, 21.11.2002.

61 Case C-343/95 *Calì & Figli* [1997] ECR I-1547, paragraph 22.

62 Commission Decision in case N140/2006 – Lithuania – Allotment of subsidies to the State Enterprises at the Correction Houses, OJ C244, 11.10.2006, ec.europa.eu/comm/competition/state_aid/register/ii/doc/N-140-2006-WLWL-en-19.7.2006.pdf.

63 Case C-159/91 *Poucet et Pistre* [1993] ECR I-637; Case C-218/00 *Cisal and INAIL* [2002] ECR I-691, paragraphs 43-48; Joined Cases C-264/01, C-306/01, C-354/01 and C-355/01 *AOK Bundesverband* [2004] ECR I-2493, paragraphs 51-55.

64 Case 263/86 *Humbel* [1988] ECR 5365, paragraph 18; Case C-318/05 *Commission* v *Germany* [2007], ECR I-06957, paragraphs 74-75, and Commission Decisions concerning state aid Nos N 118/00 – Public grants to professional sports clubs, OJ C333, 28.11.2001, p 6, NN 54/2006 – Prerov Logistics College, OJ C291, 30.11.2006, p 18; Judgment of the EFTA Court of 21 February 2008 in Case E-5/07.

65 Case T-319/99, *FENIN*.

66 Joined Cases 209/78 to 215/78 and 218/79 *Van Landewyck* [1980] ECR 3125 and Case C-244/94 *FFSA and Others* [1995] ECR I-4013, paragraph 21.

67 Case C-475/99 *Glöckner* [2001] ECR I-8089, paragraph 21.

68 Cases T-214/95 *Vlaams Gewest* v *Commission* [1998] ECR II-717, paragraphs 48 to 50, C-280/00, *Altmark Trans and Regierungspräsidium Magdeburg* [2003] ECR I-7747, paragraphs 81-82 and C-172/03 *Heiser* [2005] ECR I-1627, paragraphs 32-33.

69 Commission Regulation (EC) No 1998/2006 of 15 December 2006 on the application of Articles 87 and 88 of the Treaty to *de minimis* aid.

70 Commission Decision N 258/00, OJ C172, 16.6.2001, p 16.

71 Commission Decision N 630/03, OJ C275, 8.12.2005, p 3.

72 Commission Decision 1999/705/EC of 20 July 1999, OJ L280, 30.10.1999, p 87 confirmed by ECJ Case C-382/99 *Netherlands* v *Commission* [2002] ECR I-5163.

73 ECJ, *Altmark trans and Regierungspräsidium Magdeburg*, cited above, paragraph 77.

74 ECJ, *Altmark trans and Regierungspräsidium Magdeburg*, cited above, paragraph 78 et seq.

75 Commission Decision in case N 258/2000 – Germany – Leisure Pool Dorsten, IP/001509 of 21.12.2000, OJ C172, 16.6.2001, p 16 ec.europa.eu/competition/elojade/isef/case_details.cfm?proc_code=3_N258_2000

76 Commission Decision in case N 543/2001 – Ireland – Capital allowances for hospitals, OJ C154, 28.6.2002, p 4 ec.europa.eu/competition/elojade/isef/case_details.cfm?proc_code=3_N543_2001

77 Commission Decision in case NN 29/02 – Spain – Aid for installation of service areas in Tenerife, OJ C110, 8.5.2003, p 13, ec.europa.eu/competition/elojade/isef/case_details.cfm?proc_code=3_NN29_2002

78 Commission Decision in Case N 630/2003 – Italy – Local museums – Sardinia, OJ C275, 8.12.2005, p 3, ec.europa.eu/competition/elojade/isef/case_details.cfm?proc_code=3_N630_2003

79 Commission Decision in case N 257/2007 – Spain – Grants for theatrical productions in the Basque country, OJ C173, 26.7.2007, p 2.

80 Commission Decision in case SA.34466 – Cyprus – Centre for Visual Arts and Research, decision of 7.11.2012 (not yet published).

81 Commission Decision in case SA.34576 – Portugal – Jean Piaget / Northeast medium- and long-term continuing care unit, decision of 7.11.2012 (not yet published).

82 Commission Decision in case SA.33243 – Portugal – Jornal de Madeira, decision of 7.11.2012 (not yet published).

83 Commission Decision in case SA.34404 – The Netherlands – Purchase of land for relocating riding school, decision of 7.11.2012, OJ C370, 30.11.2012, p 2.

84 Cases C-320/91 *Corbeau* [1993] ECR I-2533, paragraphs 14-16, C-67/96 *Albany* [1999] ECR I-5751, paragraph 107.

85 That is, 1) the transfer of resources and imputability to the State, 2) effect on trade between Member States and distortion of competition, and 3) the selective nature of the measure in question.

86 That is, 1) economic advantage 2) effect on trade between Member States and distortion of competition, and 3) the selective nature of the measure in question.

87 Commission Decision of 20 December 2011 on the application of Article 106(2) of the Treaty on the Functioning of the European Union to State aid in the form of public service compensation granted to certain undertakings entrusted with the operation of services of general economic interest.

88 Communication from the Commission: European Union framework for State aid in the form of public service compensation (2011), OJ C8, 11.1.2012, p 15.

89 In the land transport sector this compatibility is governed by Regulation 1370/2007. As regards air and maritime transport, this compatibility can be assessed on the basis of the Community Guidelines on financing of airports and start-up aid to

airlines departing from regional airports, Commission Communication 94/C 350/07 on the application of Articles 92 and 93 of the Treaty in the aviation sector, OJ C350, 10.12.1994, p 5, or the Community guidelines on state aid to maritime transport, OJ C13, 17.1.2004. The SGEI Decision and Framework also apply to air and maritime transport.

90 Commission Decision in case N 562/05 – Italy – *Proroga della durata della concessione della Società Italiana del Traforo del Monte Bianco (SITMN)*, OJ C90, 25.4.2007, ec.europa.eu/competition/elojade/isef/case_details.cfm?proc_code=3_N562_2005

91 Commission Decision in case NN 51/06 – Italy – *Poste Italiane SpA*: compensation by the Member State for universal postal service obligations 2000-2005, OJ C291, 30.11.2006, ec.europa.eu/competition/elojade/isef/case_details.cfm?proc_code=3_NN51_2006

92 Commission Decision in case N 166/05 – UK – Government rural network support funding to Post Office Limited, OJ C141, 16.6.2006, ec.europa.eu/competition/elojade/isef/case_details.cfm?proc_code=3_N166_2005

93 Judgment of the Court of First Instance in Case T-289/03 *BUPA and Others* v *Commission* [2008] ECR II-741, paragraphs 182 and 183. Commission Decision in case NN 8/07 – Spain – *Financiamento de las medidas de reducción de plantilla de RTVE*, OJ C109, 15.5.2007, ec.europa.eu/comm/competition/state_aid/register/ii/doc/NN-8-2007-WLWL-7.3.2007.pdf.

94 Commission Decision in case N 395/05 – Ireland – Loan guarantees for social infrastructure schemes funded by the Housing Finance Agency (HFA), OJ C77, 5.4.2007, ec.europa.eu/competition/elojade/isef/case_details.cfm?proc_code=3_N395_2005

95 Commission Decision in case C 24/2005 – France – *Laboratoire national de métrologie et d'essais*, OJ L95, 5.4.2007, p 25.

96 See the judgment of the Court (Third Chamber) in Case C-451/03 *Servizi Ausiliari Dottori Commercialisti* v *Giuseppe Calafiori* [2006] ECR I-2941.

97 It should be noted that the wide margin of discretion Member States have in defining their public service tasks is always subject to control for manifest error by the Commission and the Court of Justice (see in detail questions 6 and 7 above).

98 On this point see the Commission Decision in cases N 541/04 and N 542/04 – The Netherlands – Risk equalisation system and retention of reserves, OJ C324, 21.12.2005, ec.europa.eu/competition/elojade/isef/case_details.cfm?proc_code=3_N541_2004 ec.europa.eu/competition/elojade/isef/case_details.cfm?proc_code=3_N542_2004

99 Commission Decision in case N 475/2003 – Ireland – Public service obligation in respect of new electricity generation capacity for security of supply, OJ C34, 7.2.2004, p 8.

100 Commission Decision in case N 381/2004 – France – Setting up of a high speed infrastructure in Pyrénées-Atlantiques, OJ C162, 2.7.2005, p 5 and the Commission Decision on aid N 331/2008 – France – High-speed broadband in the Hauts-de-Seine Department, ec.europa.eu/eu_law/state_aids/comp-2008/n331-08.pdf.

101 Commission Decision in case N 382/2004 – France – Setting up of a high-speed infrastructure in the Limousin region (Dorsal), OJ C230, 2.7.2005, p 5, ec.europa.eu/competition/state_aid/cases/164637/164637_509484_51_2.pdf.

102 Commission Decision in case C 49/06 – Poste Italiane – Banco Posta – Remuneration paid for the distribution of postal savings financial products, OJ C31, 13.2.2007.

103 See Commission Decision N 381/04 — France, Projet de réseau de télécommunications haut débit des Pyrénées-Atlantiques, and Commission Decision 382/04 — France, Mise en place d'une infrastructure haut débit sur le territoire de la région Limousin (DORSAL).

104 See Commission Decision on aid C 49/06, cited above, paragraphs 85–93.

105 Commission Decision on state aid C 3/2008 (ex NN 102/2005) – Czech Republic concerning public service compensations for Southern Moravia Bus Companies, OJ L97, 16.4.2009, paragraphs 82-83.

106 That is, (1) transfer of state resources and imputability to the state, (2) an effect on trade between the Member States and distortion of competition, and (3) the selective nature of the measure concerned.

107 *Ibid*.

108 OJ C244, 1.10.2004, p 2.

109 Parenting support services encompass different types of interventions (e.g. information, training, counselling, etc.) directly linked to rearing children from disadvantaged families. The ultimate goals of parenting support is helping parents raise their children and having a positive impact on the physical, emotional and cognitive development of children from disadvantaged families.

110 Commission Regulation (EC) No 800/2008 of 6 August 2008 declaring certain categories of aid compatible with the common market in application of Article 87 and 88 of the Treaty (General block exemption Regulation).

111 Commission Regulation (EC) No 1998/2006 of 15 December 2006 on the application of Articles 87 and 88 of the Treaty to *de minimis* aid, OJ L379 of 28.12.2006.

112 As long as the other three criteria of the *Altmark* judgment are met (see question 61).

113 As long as the other conditions laid down in the Decision are met.

114 See Article 6(1) of the Decision.

115 See Article 5(7) of the Decision.

116 See Article 4(f) of the Decision.

117 See Article 7 of the Decision.

118 See Article 5 of the Decision.

119 Commission Directive 2006/111/EC of 16 November 2006 on the transparency of financial relations between Member States and public undertakings as well as on financial transparency within certain undertakings, OJ L318, 17.11.2006, p 17.

120 Judgment of the Court of Justice in Case C-379/98 *Preussen Elektra AG* [2001] ECR I-2009, paragraph 58.

121 See Article 5(9) of the Decision.

122 See Article 8 of the Decision.

123 See Article 9 of the Decision.

124 See Article 9 of the Decision.

125 See paragraph 8 of the Framework.

126 OJ L293, 31.10.2008, p 3.

127 OJ L364, 12.12.1992, p 7.

128 See paragraph 8 of the Framework.

129 OJ C257, 27.10.2009, p 1.

130 See paragraph 9 of the Framework.

131 OJ C244, 1.10.2004, p 2.

132 For more details on the compatibility conditions of the Framework, see section 3.5.2.

133 See Article 108 TFEU and Article 2 of Regulation (EC) No 659/1999 of 22 March 1999 laying down implementing rules for Article 93 of the EC Treaty, OJ L83, 27.3.1999, p 1.

134 See Article 108 TFEU.

135 OJ L337, 18.12.2009.

136 See Paragraph 68 of the Framework.

137 The consultation on the public service needs, compliance with EU public procurement rules, the absence of discrimination, use of the net avoided cost methodology, introduction of efficiency incentives in the compensation mechanism and publication of information including the amounts of aid granted.

138 See Paragraph 69 of the Framework.

139 See Paragraph 70 of the Framework.

140 OJ L214, 9.8.2008, p 3.

141 Cf. Article 9(5) Regulation (EC) No 1083/2006.

142 Directive 2002/22/EC of the European Parliament and of the Council of 7 March 2002 on universal service and users' rights relating to electronic communications networks and services (Universal Service Directive), OJ L108, 24.4.2002, p 51.

4 QUESTIONS RELATING TO THE APPLICATION TO SSGI OF THE RULES ON PUBLIC PROCUREMENT

4.1 THE SSGI IS PROVIDED BY THE PUBLIC AUTHORITY ITSELF

[5.677]

198. To what extent can a public authority decide to provide an SSGI directly itself? In other words, what room for manoeuvre do the public authorities have when deciding whether to provide a service directly or to externalise it? Is the decision left entirely to their discretion?

It is entirely up to the public authorities to decide whether to provide a service themselves or to entrust it to a third party (externalisation). The public procurement rules only apply if the public authority decides to externalise the service provision by entrusting it to a third party against remuneration.

199. The EU rules on the selection of the provider do not normally apply when public authorities provide the service directly themselves or through an internal provider (this is referred to as an 'in-house provider' situation). What are the scope and limits of the 'in-house' exception?

The 'in-house' exception is meant to cover a situation where a public authority decides to provide a service itself, albeit acting through a legally distinct entity. In this case the public authority and the entity providing the service are effectively regarded as one. Such a relationship is covered neither by the principles of transparency, equal treatment and non-discrimination derived from the Treaty, nor by the Public Procurement Directive 2004/18/EC (hereinafter 'the Directive').[143]

The conditions for applying the principle of the in-house exception are as follows:

A) The control exercised by the public authority, alone or with other public authorities, over the legally distinct entity must be similar to that which it exercises over its own departments.

The question whether or not a public authority exercises similar control over a legally distinct entity as it does over its own departments can only be settled case by case, taking into account all the relevant legislative provisions and circumstances (legislation, articles of association of the entity in question, shareholders' agreement, etc.). The public authority must, in any case, exercise a degree of control over the entity that allows it to have a decisive influence on both the strategic objectives and the major decisions of that entity.

The Court of Justice has made it clear that if a private undertaking holds even a minority share in the capital of that third entity this will exclude the possibility of a public authority exercising over that entity a control similar to that which it exercises over its own departments.[144]

and

B) The essential part of the activities of the legally distinct entity is carried out with the controlling public authority or authorities.[145]

In house-exception and similar joint control: As regards the first criterion (similar control), the Court has recognised that it is not essential for the similar control to be individual and that it can therefore be exercised jointly by several public authorities.[146] It has also confirmed that, if several public authorities control a legally distinct entity, the second criterion (essential activity) may also be met by taking into account the activity which the legally distinct entity carries out with all of the public authorities together.[147] Consequently, public procurement procedures do not have to be applied if several public authorities cooperate within a separate public entity which is subject to joint control by the public entities which own it and which carries out its essential activity with those same public entities. For further information on cooperation between public authorities see the answer to question 211.

For information about compliance with the rules on State Aid in cases where the SSGI provider is linked to the public authority ('in-house provider'), see the answer to question 220.

4.2 PROVISION OF THE SSGI IS ENTRUSTED TO A THIRD PARTY AGAINST REMUNERATION

200. What is the applicable legal framework when a public authority decides to externalise the provision of an SSGI against remuneration?

If the public authority decides to externalise a service against remuneration it is bound by the provisions of EU law on the award of public service contracts or service concessions.

Two cases must be distinguished:

A) The public authority concludes a public service contract. In this case the public authority pays the service provider a fixed remuneration. There are two possible situations:

(a) the value of the contract exceeds the thresholds for application of Directive 2004/18/EC.

If the relevant thresholds are reached[148] the public service contracts will fall within the scope of the Directive. However, under Article 21 of the Directive, health and social services contracts are not subject to all of the detailed rules of the Directive;[149] only a very small number of its articles apply. These require, in particular, that the technical specifications[150] must be laid down in accordance with the Directive at the start of the procurement process (see the answer to question 203) and the results of the award procedure[151] must be published. Moreover, when awarding health and social services contracts, the public authorities must also comply with the basic principles of the TFEU, such as the transparency requirement and the obligation to treat economic operators equally, without discrimination, if and in so far as the services in question are of cross-border interest.[152] For further information about the concept of cross-border interest see the answer to question 201.

These principles, however, require only observance of the basic standards developed by the Court of Justice of the European Union and not compliance with the full set of provisions of Directive 2004/18/EC. Therefore, when externalising social services via a public service contract, public authorities already benefit from a greater margin of discretion than in other sectors.

It should be noted, however, that in the case of mixed service contracts that comprise social services and other services that are fully covered by the Public Procurement Directive,[153] such as transport, scientific research, consulting or maintenance, the Directive will apply to a limited extent only – as explained above – if the value of the social service[154] is greater than the value of the other service. For example, ambulance services have both a health service component and a transport service component. If the transport service exceeds the health service in value, all the provisions of the Directive will apply. If the value of the health service is higher, the Directive will apply only partially, as explained above.[155]

(b) the value of the contract is less than the thresholds for application of Directive 2004/18/EC.

If the value of the contract to be awarded is less than the threshold for applying the Directive, the public authority must nevertheless comply with the basic rules and principles of EU law, such as the principles of equal treatment, non-discrimination and transparency, if the contract in question is of cross-border interest. For further information about the exact nature of these principles, see the answer to question 201.

B) The public authority grants a service concession. In this case the remuneration consists mainly of the right to exploit the service economically.[156] The concessionaire assumes the substantial operating risk resulting from the exploitation of the service in question.[157] Public authorities granting service concessions must, where they have a cross-border interest comply with the basic rules and principles of EU law, particularly the principles of transparency, equal treatment and nondiscrimination.[158] For further information about the exact nature of these principles see the answer to question 202.

201. What is meant by the concept of cross-border interest?

A public contract or concession has a cross-border interest if it is of interest to economic operators situated in other Member States of the European Economic Area.[159]

It is up to the public authority to evaluate the potential interest of the contract for economic operators located in other Member States on a case by case basis, unless national law provides specific guidance.

If a public contract or concession is of cross-border interest, the public authority must comply with the principles of the TFEU (non-discrimination, transparency, etc.)[160] during the procedure for awarding it. Public contracts and concessions that have no cross-border interest are not bound by the principles of the TFEU.

Thus, under certain conditions, small, local service contracts may be awarded without complying with the above principles, if the services in question have no cross-border interest for operators from other Member States and therefore have no impact on the functioning of the internal market. This might be the case if, in view of the very modest value of the contract[161] (well below the threshold for application of the Directive 2004/18/EC which currently stands at EUR 200,000)[162] and the nature of the social service and market segment involved, it is unlikely that economic operators from other Member States will be potentially interested in providing the services in question.[163] For instance, in cases involving contracts for legal services worth an average of around EUR 5000 EUR[164] or town planning services worth between EUR 6000 and EUR 26500[165] the Commission considered that, in view of their low value (around 10% or less of the threshold for application of the Directive) and the individual circumstances of the cases, the contracts in question were not relevant to the internal market.

Nor is the existence of a complaint relating to the contract in question sufficient evidence that it is of cross-border interest.[166]

When evaluating the relevance of the contract to the internal market, public authorities can refer to the Commission interpretative communication[167] on EU law applicable to contract awards not or not fully subject to the provisions of the Public Procurement Directives.[168] This communication encompasses contracts only partially covered by the Public Procurement Directives, such as contracts for health and social services.[169] Since the communication contains a general interpretation of the concept of internal market relevance under the Treaty, it can also be used as a guide for concessions.

202. What are the obligations deriving from the principles of transparency and nondiscrimination?

According to the case law of the Court of Justice of the European Union, the principles of transparency, equal treatment and non-discrimination require that the public authority's intention to conclude a public contract or a concession be adequately publicised. The advertisement may be limited to a short description of the essential details of the contract to be awarded and of the award method together with an invitation to contact the public authority. It is essential that all EU potentially interested service providers have the possibility to express their interest in bidding for the contract.

The public authority may then select, in a non-discriminatory and impartial way, the applicants to be invited to submit an offer and, where relevant, to negotiate the terms of the contract or of the concession. During such negotiations all economic operators should be on an equal footing and receive the same information from the public authority.

Court of Justice case law on effective judicial protection[170] requires, at a minimum, that decisions adversely affecting a person who has or had an interest in obtaining the contract, such as a decision to eliminate a bidder, should be subject to review for possible violations of the basic standards derived from EU primary law.

When applying these principles, the public authorities can draw on the Commission interpretative communication on the EU law applicable to contract awards not or not fully subject to the provisions of the Public Procurement Directives. As mentioned above, this communication also deals with contracts that are only partially covered by the Public Procurement Directives ('the Directives'),[171] such as contracts for the services listed in Annex II B to Directive 2004/18/EC, which include health and social services.[172] As stated at question 200 and pursuant to Article 21 of Directive 2004/18/EC, public contracts for these services are subject to certain rules of Directive 2004/18/EC only (namely the obligation to define the technical specifications in the contract documents and to publish the result at the end of the procedure) and are otherwise governed by the general principles of the TFEU (non-discrimination, transparency, etc.) if they are of a certain cross-border interest.

Since the communication contains a general interpretation of the principles of transparency, equal treatment and non-discrimination, it can also be used as guidance for concessions, bearing in mind that these contracts usually represent a value well above the thresholds of the Public Procurement Directives and therefore, even though these Directives do not apply to service concessions, these are likely to have a cross border interest and thus do still have to be advertised in a medium with Europe-wide coverage in accordance with the principles of the TFEU.

203. How to draft specifications suitable for awarding a service contract in such a way as (i) to respond holistically to the different requirements of the users and (ii) to enable the service to be adapted to changing circumstances in terms of intensity, number of users, etc.

The Directive offers a wide range of possibilities for drawing up specifications.[173] It is up to the public authorities to make full use of these possibilities by requiring bidders to develop tailor-made service concepts in order to provide the best possible services of the requisite quality standard. They may, for instance, specify that bidders have to address the particular needs of certain groups of users or insist that the proposed service concept must be compatible with existing structures that are already in place. It is also conceivable that a public authority might insist that the service be operated and evaluated in a way that involves the users.

However, the bottom line is that the specifications must be drafted in a way that does not discriminate or prejudge the tender procedure at the outset.

204. What other quality requirements can be included in the award of a public contract or concession for an SSGI?

When awarding a public contract or concession for an SSGI the public authorities may include any quality requirements linked to the subject-matter of the contract that they consider necessary, in order to offer users a high-quality service and the best value for money. Depending on the nature of these requirements, they may come into play at different stages of the procedure:

When **setting out the technical specifications**,[174] for example, the public authority may specify all the characteristics of the service which it considers useful to ensure high quality provision (e.g. requirements to ensure continuity of service, the satisfaction of the specific needs of different categories of user, accessibility of infrastructure for people with reduced mobility, and more generally requirements relating to the quality of this infrastructure). The technical specifications of the service may be defined in the form of very detailed characteristics (which may in some cases contribute to over-standardisation of the services offered), or in terms of requirements for functional performance. The second approach usually leaves candidates a greater margin of discretion, allowing them the opportunity to suggest to the public authority more innovative solutions/working methods for achieving the quality targets that have been set.

The experience and standard of the service provider's staff are also decisive factors contributing to the quality of the service provided. When setting out the **selection criteria**,[175] the public authority may specify particular requirements for professional ability (e.g. professional experience, staff qualifications, technical infrastructure available) to ensure that the selected contractor has sufficient capacity to perform the service to the quality standards laid down by the contract.

Quality requirements may also be included in the **award criteria**.[176] The public authority is not compelled to award the contract on the basis of the lowest price, but may award it to the most economically advantageous tender. This allows it to include in the award criteria all the qualitative factors it considers important and which are linked to the subject matter of the contract. The public authority may also use the weighting of the different award criteria to reflect the importance it attaches to the various qualitative aspects of the service.

The **conditions for performance of the contract**[177] are another way of focusing on the quality of the service. The public authority may, for example, include in the performance criteria[178] clauses requiring the contractor to ensure a proper level of training and remuneration for the staff involved in implementing the contract, provided that these are compatible with the relevant provisions of EU law. Such clauses ensure that the contractor is not tempted to cut staff costs, which might demoralise the employees in question, increase staff turnover and ultimately undermine the quality of the service delivered.

Finally, when awarding a public contract/concession for an SSGI the public authorities may adopt an integrated approach for the performance of complex services which do not have to be divided into a number of contracts but may be awarded as a single lot, to enable the user, if it so wishes, to deal with a single service provider taking responsibility for multiple related needs. They are also free to choose a suitable duration for the contract in question, to ensure the stability and continuity of the relevant service(s).

205. Is it possible to amend the contract during implementation?

Amendments during the lifetime of the contract are possible provided they do not substantially change the terms of the original tender.[179]

According to the Court of Justice, an amendment to a public contract during its currency may be regarded as being substantial in the following cases:

- when it introduces conditions which, had they been part of the initial award procedure, would have allowed for the admission of tenderers other than those initially admitted or would have allowed for the acceptance of a tender other than the one initially accepted;
- when it extends the scope of the contract considerably to encompass services not initially covered;
- when it changes the economic balance of the contract in favour of the contractor in a manner which was not provided for in the terms of the initial contract.[180]

206. How to avoid placing too heavy a burden on small service providers, who are often the best equipped to understand the specific features of SSGIs in situations which have a strong local dimension?

It is up to the public authority to structure the tender in a way that gives small economic operators a chance to participate and succeed. The wider the scope of the service required and consequently the more exacting the economic and financial requirements, the more difficult it will be for small service providers to participate. In the case of bigger contracts (for instance for a range of services or for services to be performed in several places), the awarding authority might consider dividing the contract into different lots that are more accessible to SMEs. However, an artificial splitting of contracts into separate contracts of a value under the thresholds with the effect of circumventing the application of the relevant provisions of the Public Procurement Directives is not permitted by the Directives. In general, it is advisable for public authorities to draw up tender specifications with SMEs in mind, keeping formalities to a strict minimum.

207. How to reconcile public procurement procedures which limit the number of providers selected with the preservation of a sufficient degree of freedom of choice for SSGI users?

Public procurement procedures do not aim to limit the number of service providers selected. Contracting authorities are entirely free to choose one or several operators to satisfy their needs. Public authorities can, for example, entrust the same service concession to several operators, if this is practically feasible, thereby guaranteeing a larger choice for users of the service.

208. Is it possible to make familiarity with the local context a criterion for the selection of a service provider, this aspect often being essential for the successful provision of an SSGI?

EU public procurement rules aim to ensure fair competition between operators across Europe in order to provide better value for money to the public authorities. A requirement of familiarity with the local context might lead to unlawful discrimination against foreign service providers. At the same time, it risks restricting the public authority's choice to a small number of local operators and consequently diminishing the beneficial effect of Europe-wide competition.

Nevertheless, certain requirements related to the local context may be acceptable if they can be justified by the particularities of the service to be provided (type of service and/or categories of user) and are strictly related to the performance of the contract.

Examples:

- A public authority may, for instance, require as part of the performance criteria that the successful tenderer establish a local infrastructure such as an office or a workshop or deploy specific equipment at the place of performance, if this is necessary for the provision of the service.
- A municipal authority intending to set up a women's shelter, intended particularly for women from a specific cultural minority, may specify in the call for tenders that the service provider must have prior experience of this kind of service in an environment with similar social and economic characteristics, and that the employees who will be in contact with and/or address the needs of the women facing problems must be sufficiently familiar with the relevant cultural and linguistic context.
- A public authority that intends to put in place a job placement service targeting young unemployed adults from disadvantaged areas and addressing in an integrated way the specific difficulties encountered by the users (e.g. mental health problems, drug addiction or alcohol abuse, social housing and debt) might specify that the service provider must have prior experience with this kind of service for similar target groups. It may also indicate that the service provider must ensure that from the outset the employees dealing with the users of the service have a knowledge of the networks of social actors that already exist, with whom they will need to liaise in order to address the needs of the young unemployed adults in an integrated way.

In any event, a restriction of this kind must not go beyond what is strictly necessary to ensure adequate service provision. The Court of Justice decided, for example, that when awarding a public contract for health services providing home respiratory treatments a public authority cannot require the potential tenderer to have, at the time when the tender is submitted, an office open to the public in the capital of the province where the service is to be provided.[181]

It is the responsibility of the public authority to make sure that such conditions are objectively justified and do not result in discriminatory treatment by unduly favouring certain groups of bidders, in particular local undertakings or incumbent service providers.

The issue of the direct award of low-value contracts to small local service providers has already been addressed in the answer to question 206.

209. Is it possible to limit the tender to non-profit service providers only?

Two situations have to be distinguished:

- Individual contracting authorities cannot decide themselves to limit a tender procedure to non-profit service providers. The Public Procurement Directive is based on the principles of equal treatment and non-discrimination of economic operators.[182] The Directive does not, therefore, allow contracts to be reserved for specific categories of undertaking,[183] such as non-profit organisations, regardless of the type of services involved – whether listed in Annex II A or Annex II B to the Directive (e.g. social services).[184]
- However, national law[185] regulating a particular activity might, in exceptional cases, provide for restricted access to certain services for the benefit of non-profit organisations. In this case public authorities would be authorised to limit participation in a tender procedure to such non-profit organisations, if the national law is compatible with European law. Nevertheless, such a national law would restrict the working of Articles 49 and 56 of the TFEU, on the freedom of establishment and the free movement of services, and would have to be justified on a case-by-case basis. On the basis of the case law of the Court of Justice, such a restriction could be justified, in particular, if it is necessary and proportionate in view of the attainment of certain social objectives pursued by the national social welfare system.[186]

210. Do public authorities still have the possibility of negotiating with service providers during the selection phase? This is particularly important for SSGIs given that the public authorities are not always in a position to define their needs precisely at the start of the process. It is sometimes necessary for the public authorities to have a discussion with the potential service providers.

As mentioned in the answer to question 202, the public authorities may use negotiated procedures in order to purchase health or social services through public contracts or concessions. The public authorities in question will not be subject to the specific rules on negotiated procedures laid down in Directive 2004/18/EC, since this Directive does not apply to service concessions and contains only a few rules applicable to the services listed in Annex II B to the Directive (such as SSGIs).[187] For this reason, when awarding a public contract or an SSGI concession, public authorities are free to organise an *ad hoc* negotiated procedure provided national law does not lay down specific rules. In any case, the general principles of transparency and non-discrimination laid down by the TFEU, in accordance with which equal treatment must be given to all the economic operators invited to participate in the negotiated procedure, are applicable to services with a crossborder interest.

211. To what extent do the public procurement rules apply to inter-municipal cooperation? This cooperation can take various forms, e.g. one municipality purchasing a service from another, or two municipalities jointly launching a public procurement procedure or creating an entity for the purpose of providing an SSGI, etc.

The public procurement rules apply when a public authority intends to award a public service contract to a third party[188] in return for payment. It makes no difference whether the third party is a private operator or public authority. However, as is shown by the examples below, there are situations in which public authorities entrust economic activities to other public authorities or carry out these activities jointly with other public authorities without being obliged to apply the EU public procurement rules.

- Thus, the Court of Justice recently found that public authorities could carry out the public service activities for which they were responsible by using their own resources, in cooperation with other public authorities, without the need for any particular form of organisation or the need to provide for application of European public procurement legislation to the implementation of these organisational practices.
  - (a) Cooperation between public authorities can be organised within the framework of a separate public body that meets the in-house criteria.[189] Concerning this point, see question 199.
  - (b) The Court of Justice has also stated[190] that public/public cooperation does not necessarily require the creation of new jointly-controlled entities. According to the Court, such cooperation can be based simply on cooperation between public bodies with the sole purpose of jointly ensure the execution of a public task which the bodies concerned have to perform, for the pursuit of public interest objectives. This does not necessarily mean that each public authority cooperates in an equal measure in carrying out the public interest tasks, since the cooperation can be based on sharing tasks and on specialisation. However, there must be genuine cooperation, with mutual rights and obligations between the participants, as opposed to a public contract where one party carries out a task in return for payment. There must not be any financial transfers between the public authorities other than reimbursements of costs. The cooperation must be based solely on considerations and requirements linked to the pursuit of public interest objectives, which excludes the pursuit of profit and the participation of any private or mixed capital entities. Finally, the cooperation agreement cannot be artificially used as a means to circumvent the application of the relevant rules of the Public Procurement Directives.
- Public authorities such as municipalities can of course jointly organise public procurement procedures. Thus, a public authority can launch a procedure for itself and for another public authority[191] provided it announces this at the start of the procedure. The public procurement rules will thus apply to a procedure launched by the public authority for itself and for the other public authority/ies, but will not apply to cooperation between public authorities.

- Several public authorities can create a new entity and fully transfer to it a specific task. In this case, the public authorities do not retain any control over the service performed, which is provided by the new entity acting in full independence and under its own responsibility. In this case, no service is provided and consequently neither the Treaty nor the directives apply.[192]
- When public authorities put in place structures involving mutual assistance and cooperation for no remuneration, there is no provision of services within the meaning of the Treaty and EU law is not applicable.

212. To what extent do the public procurement rules apply to public-private partnerships (PPPs)?

Generally speaking, the creation of a PPP constitutes the award of a public contract or of a concession. This award is subject to the public procurement rules applicable in the case at hand, according to the type of contract involved and the value of the contract.

With regard to institutionalised PPPs (implying the existence of a mixed capital entity), it should be pointed out that, as indicated in the answer to question 199, there cannot be an 'in-house' relationship between a public authority and a public-private entity in which a public authority participates jointly with a private entity. Consequently, it follows that services entrusted to a public-private entity must be awarded in accordance with the public procurement rules laid down in the Treaty or in the Public Procurement Directives. It also follows that the acquisition by a private operator of a share in the capital of an entity that performs public tasks awarded under an arrangement involving an in-house relationship puts an end to this relationship and makes it necessary to retender the contract or concession in question, unless the private operator has been selected in accordance with the public procurement rules.

If a public authority follows an award procedure in accordance with European public procurement law in order to select a private partner who is to perform the service contract or benefit from the service concession jointly with a public authority within the framework of a mixed public-private entity, it is no longer necessary to organise a second award procedure for provision of the service. However, if there is any substantial change in the parameters concerning the provision of the service not envisaged in the original public procurement procedure, a new procedure must be launched. For further information, refer to the Commission communication on institutionalised PPPs,[193] which explains in detail how to organise such a procedure.

213. To what extent is it possible, in the award of a public contract or of a concession for a social service of general interest, to lay down an obligation to comply with certain corporate governance rules (e.g. equal control of the enterprise by employers' representatives and trade union representatives, or inclusion of user representatives on the board of directors)?

The Public Procurement Directives enable public purchasers to take account at the different stages of a public procurement procedure of specific requirements (which may also be of a social nature) provided that these considerations are compatible with EU law (particularly in terms of observing the principles of the Treaty – non-discrimination, transparency, etc.) and that they are indicated in the contract notice or tender documents. Furthermore, according to the above-mentioned Directives, the requirements laid down in the technical specifications, the selection criteria or the award criteria must be related to the subject matter of the contract (i.e. must serve to define the products/services sought). However, the requirements included in the performance clauses need not necessarily be linked to the subject matter of the contract, but only to the contract performance (i.e. to the tasks enabling the production of the goods or the provision of the services purchased).

If the contract in question is not covered by the above-mentioned Directives, as is the case, for example, with service concessions or public contracts whose value is lower than the thresholds for application of those Directives, the rules and principles of the TFEU, as interpreted by the Court of Justice, still apply if the contracts are of certain crossborder interest.[194] In this respect, the obligation to observe the principles laid down by the TFEU, in particular the principle of non-discrimination, also prevents the authority awarding the contract from imposing conditions not linked to the subject of the contract or to its performance, when awarding contracts not covered by the Public Procurement Directives.

Corporate governance obligations, however, particularly as regards the control of the enterprise or the presence of certain groups of persons on the board of directors of the service provider, concern the organisation of the enterprise in general, and therefore cannot be deemed either to be linked to the subject matter of the contract in question (since they are not appropriate for defining the services sought, in terms of technical features or better value for money) or to the performance of the contract (since they are not linked to the tasks needed to provide the services in question). However, as mentioned in the answer to question 203, the public authority may require the specific service to be performed and assessed in a way involving the participation of the users, provided that this does not lead to discrimination of any kind or prejudge the award of the contract.

There are various ways of involving users to a greater or lesser extent (polls, inviting suggestions, etc.). The public authority may have precise ideas about what degree of user participation it wants. It might, for example, require the service provider that obtains the contract to have or to put in place a structure or mechanism allowing user representatives to be involved in decision-making at the contract performance stage, provided that these decisions do not change the contract and are not discriminatory. If the public authority does not have any precise ideas on this point, it may also ask the candidates to suggest approaches to ensure such participation.

214. How can the public procurement rules be reconciled with the public authorities' need to encourage innovative solutions that meet the complex needs of the users of SSGIs?

The public procurement rules offer public authorities a wide range of tools for encouraging innovation.

For example, public authorities are free to define the technical specifications,[195] either by drawing up detailed technical characteristics or by performance or functional requirements.[196] In the latter case, the public authorities may indicate the results sought without specifying in detail the means. This encourages the creativity of the candidates, who can identify and propose more innovative solutions in order to meet users' complex needs.

The use of variants[197] is another means of encouraging innovation. Public authorities which authorise variants can thus compare the advantages and disadvantages of a more innovative alternative to the standard solution.

Given that SSGIs are subject only to a few of the rules in Directive 2004/18/EC, the public authorities may choose the procedure they consider the most appropriate for the specific service in question, provided that the procedure chosen is in line with the TFEU principles (transparency, non-discrimination). For example, in the case of complex SSGIs for which the public authority is not in a position to identify the best way of meeting users' specific needs, it can use a procedure similar to that of the competitive dialogue.[198]

215. What are the advertising requirements for SSGI concessions? Is publication in the EU's Official Journal possible?

Service concessions, unlike public works concessions and public contracts, are not subject to Directive 2004/18/EC, including in particular the obligation to publish a notice in the Official Journal of the European Union. This is why until now no specific form has been available for the publication of service concessions in the Official Journal. However, service concessions are governed by the principles of the TFEU, including transparency and equal treatment. In accordance with these principles and the interpretation of the European Court of Justice in its judgment in Case C-324/98 *Telaustria*, the contracting authorities (or the contracting bodies) must guarantee potential bidders 'a degree of advertising sufficient to enable the services market to be opened up to competition and the impartiality of the procedures to be reviewed' and hence must publish an appropriate notice having regard, among other things, to the subject and economic value of the concession in question.

- It follows that within the limits laid down by ECJ case law, Member States/contracting authorities are free to define appropriate advertising rules to ensure the transparency of service concessions. Contracting authorities may, of course, publish notices of service concessions in the Official Journal, even if this is not required by European law.

216. Are there any arrangements for outsourcing SSGIs other than public contracts and concessions that would be compatible with the principles of transparency and nondiscrimination and would offer a wide choice of providers?

Yes. The competent public authority may, for example, establish in advance the conditions for provision of a social service and, after sufficient advertising and in accordance with the principles of transparency and non-discrimination (see the answer to question 202), grant licences or authorisations to all providers meeting these conditions. Such a system does not specify any limits or quotas concerning the number of service providers; all those meeting the conditions can participate.

Providers which have obtained a licence/authorisation must provide the service at the request of the user, who will thus have the choice of several providers, at a price set beforehand by the public authority.

NOTES

143 Directive 2004/18/EC of the European Parliament and of the Council of 31 March 2004 on the coordination procedures for the award of public works contracts, public supply contracts and public service contracts, OJ L134, 30.4.2004, p 114.

144 Case C-26/03 *Stadt Halle* [2005] ECR I-0001, paragraphs 49-50.

145 Case C-107/98 *Teckal* [1999] ECR I-8121, paragraph 50.

146 Case C-324/07 *Coditel Brabant* [2008] ECR I-8457 and Case C-573/07 *Sea* [2009] ECR I-8127.

147 Case C-340/04 *Carbotermo* [2006] ECR-I-4137, paragraph 70, and Case C-295/05 *Asemfo* [2007] ECR I-2999, paragraph 62.

148 Article 7 of Directive 2004/18/EC.

149 Social services and health services are among the services listed in Annex II B to Directive 2004/18/EC. Contracts for such services are subject only to a limited number of provisions of the Directive (on the distinction between the services listed in Annexes II A and II B, see Articles 20 and 21 of Directive 2004/18/EC). The codes referred to may be consulted on the DG Internal Market website at www.simap.europa.eu.

150 Article 21 read in conjunction with Article 23 of Directive 2004/18/EC.

151 Article 21 read in conjunction with Article 35(4) of Directive 2004/18/EC.

152 In other words, they are of interest to economic operators situated in other Member States of the European Economic Area. See Case C-507/03 *Commission* v *Ireland* [2007] ECR I-9777, paragraphs 29 *et seq.*

153 The services listed in Annex II A to Directive 2004/18/EC.

154 Article 22 of Directive 2004/18/EC.

155 See Case C-76/97 *Tögel* [1998] ECR I-5357, paragraphs 29-40.

156 See Article 1(4) of Directive 2004/18/EC.

157 See Article 17 of Directive 2004/18/EC and Court of Justice case law, particularly the judgment of 25 March 2010 in Case C-451/08 *Helmut Mueller* [2010] ECR I-2673.

158 See the following judgments: Case C-324/98 *Telaustria* [2000] REC I-10745, paragraph 62; Case C-231/03 *Coname* [2005] ECR I-7287, paragraphs 16-19 and Case C-458/03 *Parking Brixen* [2005] ECR I-8585, paragraph 49.

159 See Case C-507/03 *Commission* v *Ireland* [2007] ECR I-9777, paragraphs 29 *et seq.*

160 Case C-59/00 *Bent Mousten Vestergaard* [2001] ECR I-9505, paragraph 20, Case C-264/03 *Commission* v *France* [2005] ECR I-8831, paragraphs 32-33, Case C-6/05 *Commission* v *Greece* [2007] ECR I-4557, paragraph 3.

161 The criterion of value alone is not sufficient to indicate that a market has no cross-border interest. As the Court of Justice ruled in Joined Cases C-147/2006 and C-148/2006 *Secap* [2008] ECR I-3565, paragraph 31 'in certain cases, account must be taken of the fact that the borders straddle conurbations which are situated in the territory of different Member States and that, in those circumstances, even low-value contracts may be of certain cross-border interest.'.

162 After indexation under Commission Regulation (EU) No 1251/2011 of 30 November 2011 amending Directives 2004/17/EC, 2004/18/EC and 2009/81/EC of the European Parliament and of the Council in respect of their application thresholds for the procedures for the awards of contract.

163 See Case C-231/03 *Coname* [2005] ECR I-7287, paragraph 20, which related to service concessions.

164 See press release IP/07/357, 21 March 2007.

165 See press release IP/06/1786, 13 December 2006.

166 See Case C-507/03 *Commission* v *Ireland* [2007] ECR I-9777, paragraph 34.

167 This Communication has been analysed by the Court case T-258/06, *Germany v Commission* who concluded, in general, that the Communication does not contain new rules for the award of public contracts which go beyond the obligations under Union law as it currently stands.

168 OJ C179, 1.8.2006, p 2.

169 As referred to in Annex II B to Directive 2004/18/EC.

170 See Case C-50/00 P *Union de Pequeños Agricultores* [2002] ECR I-6677, paragraph 39, and Case 222/86 *Heylens* [1987] ECR 4097, paragraph 14.

171 Directive 2004/18/EC of the European Parliament and of the Council of 31 March 2004 on the coordination of procedures for the award of public works contracts, public supply contracts and public service contracts and Directive 2004/17/EC of the European Parliament and of the Council of 31 March 2004 coordinating the procurement procedures of entities operating in the water, energy, transport and postal services sectors.

172 As referred to in Annex II B to Directive 2004/18/EC.

173 Article 23 of Directive 2004/18/EC, which also applies to the services listed in Annex II B to the Directive, including social services.

174 See Article 23 of Directive 2004/18/EC.

175 See Articles 44 and 48 of Directive 2004/18/EC.

176 See Article 53 of Directive 2004/18/EC.

177 See Article 26 of Directive 2004/18/EC.

178 For reasons of transparency, the performance criteria must be published in advance in the contract documentation. Compliance with the performance criteria cannot be verified before the contract is awarded; verification will only be possible during implementation. To ensure compliance the public authority may make provision for deterrent contractual penalties.

179 Case C-496/99 *Commission* v *CAS Succhi di Frutta SpA* [2004] ECR I-3801, paragraph 116 and Case C-454/06 *Pressetext*, 2008 I-04401, paragraphs 35 to 37.

180 Case C-454/06 *Pressetext*, 2008 I-04401, paragraphs 35 to 37.

181 Case C-234/03 *Contse* [2005] ECR I-9315, paragraph 79.

182 Article 2 of Directive 2004/18/EC.

183 This is why a specific exception had to be included in the Directive to allow Member States to reserve the right to participate in certain contracts to a particular category of organisations, i.e. sheltered workshops where most of the employees concerned are disabled (see Article 19 of Directive 2004/18/EC).

184 The distinction between the services in Annex II A and those in Annex II B is relevant only from Article 20 of the Directive onwards.

185 The term 'national law' refers to general, abstract national rules, as opposed to a decision by an awarding authority in the context of a specific contract. On the other hand, the level of legislation (national or regional) is not crucial here, provided that the rules are abstract and generally applicable.

186 See Case C-70/95 *Sodemare SA* v *Regione Lombardia* [1997] ECR I-3395.

187 As stated in answer 199 and pursuant to Article 21 of Directive 2004/18/EC, public contracts for these services are subject only to certain rules of Directive 2004/18/EC (namely the obligation to define the technical specifications in the contract documents and to publish ex-post the result of the procedure) and are otherwise governed by the general principles of the TFEU (non-discrimination, transparency, etc.).

188 See the judgments in Cases C-107/98 *Teckal* [1999] ECR I-8121, paragraph 51, C-94/99 *ARGE* [2000] ECR I-11037, paragraph 40, and C-220/05 *Auroux* [2007] ECR I-385, paragraph 62.

189 See the judgment in Case C-324/07 *Coditel Brabant* [2008] ECR I-8457.

190 See the judgment in Case C-480/06 *Commission* v *Germany* [2009] ECR I-4747.

191 See Article 11 of Directive 2004/18/EC on central purchasing bodies.

192 See Commission press release IP/07/357 of 21.3.2007, which states that the complete transfer of a public task from one public entity to another does not imply the provision of services for remuneration within the meaning of Article 49 of the EC Treaty, if the public entity to which the task has been transferred performs this task in full independence and under its own responsibility. Such a transfer of public tasks constitutes an act of internal organisation of the public administration of the Member State in question. As such, it is not subject to the Treaty and its fundamental freedoms.

193 Commission interpretative communication C(2007) 6661 on the application of Community law on public procurement and concessions to institutionalised public-private partnerships (IPPPs), OJ 2008 C 91, p 4.

194 See the judgment in Case C-324/98 *Telaustria* [2000] ECR I-10745.

195 Article 23 of Directive 2004/18/EC.

196 As stated in Article 23(3) of Directive 2004/18/EC, when technical specifications are defined in terms of performance or functional requirements, 'However, such parameters must be sufficiently precise to allow tenderers to determine the subject-matter of the contract and to allow contracting authorities to award the contract'.

197 See Article 24 of Directive 2004/18/EC. Even if the social services of general interest are subject only to a limited number of the rules laid down in Directive 2004/18/EC, the public authorities may of course use the optional provisions of the Directive if they consider them useful.

198 Provided for in Article 29 of Directive 2004/18/EC for contracts subject to all the Directive's rules.

5 SIMULTANEOUS APPLICATION OF THE STATE AID RULES AND THE RULES ON PUBLIC CONTRACTS AND SERVICE CONCESSIONS TO SGEIS

[5.678]

217. Does EU law impose a specific form of management of SGEIs?

According to settled case law, Member States have broad discretion concerning the definition of what they consider to be SGEIs and the organisation of these services. Consequently, the public authorities are free to choose how to manage the SGEIs they set up.

In accordance with the State Aid rules, public authorities can organise and finance their SGEIs as they wish, provided that the compensation granted does not exceed the amount necessary to enable the SGEI tasks to be performed under economically acceptable conditions, in line with Article 106(2) of the TFEU.

When the establishment of an SGEI gives rise to the award of a public contract or a concession (i.e. when a service is provided in return for remuneration in the form of payment of a price or by granting the right to exploit the service notably remunerated by a fee payable by users), the public authorities must comply not only with the State Aid rules but also with the rules on public contracts and concessions. For more information see the answer to question 200.

If management of an SGEI is awarded as part of a public procurement procedure allowing selection of the candidate able to provide the service at the least cost to the community, and if the other conditions of the *Altmark* judgment are complied with (for these conditions, see question 61), the compensation awarded does not constitute State Aid within the meaning of the *Altmark* judgment.

218. When a public authority finances the provider of an SGEI in accordance with the State Aid rules, must it also apply the EU rules on the award of public service contracts or service concessions?

The State Aid rules and the rules on public contracts and concessions have different aims and scope. The State Aid rules relate to the conditions for financing SGEIs and consequently economic SSGIs and are aimed at preventing distortions of competition caused by financing or similar benefits granted by the State and its emanations. The rules on public contracts and concessions, on the other hand, concern the conditions for awarding these services to operators. One of their main aims is to ensure equal treatment and transparency and prevent distortions of competition that may arise from the management of public funds by the contracting authorities when awarding these services. Other aims are to maximise competition in Europe and value for money, particularly for service users.

Public authorities wishing to set up an SGEI must therefore comply not only with the State Aid rules but also with the rules on the award of public contracts or concessions.

The rules on public contracts apply from the time when there is an obligation to provide a specific service in return for remuneration, irrespective of the general interest objective of the service. The mere financing of an activity, however, which is usually linked to the obligation to reimburse the amounts received if they are not used for the purposes intended, does not usually come under the public procurement rules.

The legal classification of a contract as a public contract or as a concession under EU law must be based on the concept of a public contract and concession as defined in the relevant Directives (particularly Directive 2004/18/EC), irrespective of the legal classification of the contract under national law.

A contract can be covered by the definitions of public service contract or concession if:

a) the aim of the contract is to meet needs previously defined by the public authority within the framework of its competences;
b) the nature of the service and the way in which it is to be provided are specified in detail by the public authority;
c) the contract provides for remuneration of the service (payment of a price or granting of the right to operate the service in return for a fee payable by users);
d) the public authority takes the initiative of finding a provider to whom to entrust the service
e) the contract lays down penalties for failure to meet contractual obligations, in order to guarantee that the service entrusted to the third party is provided properly in such a way as to meet the public authority's requirements (penalties, compensation for damages, etc.).

The above criteria serve to establish whether the subject matter of the contract is indeed an obligation to provide a service in return for remuneration.

219. Is it possible for the concessionaire of an SGEI to receive State Aid in the form of public service compensation in order to cover the effective costs of the public service task it is entrusted with?

Under Articles 106, 107 and 108 of the TFEU, it is up to the Member States to designate their SGEI services in accordance with the conditions laid down in the Decision. If a Member State decides that an entity is responsible for a service of general economic interest, the entity may receive public service compensation if the income from providing the SGEI does not cover the costs incurred. This compensation must not exceed the net costs actually incurred and a reasonable profit.

With regard to the rules on public contracts and concessions, the concept of service concession does not preclude granting of State Aid if the concessionaire continues to assume the substantial operating risk involved in providing the service. However, if the aid removes the risk involved in providing the service or renders it negligible, the contract in question might qualify as a public service contract. In this case, the detailed provisions of the Directive are applicable in principle.

However, with regard to the services indicated in Annex II B to the Directive, such as social services, only certain provisions of the Directive are applicable (see the answer to questions 200 and 202).

220. Does the exception whereby the public procurement rules do not apply to in-house operations mean that the State Aid rules do not apply either?

If a situation is not covered by EU public procurement law, this does not automatically mean that it is also excluded from the State Aid rules. For information on the State Aid rules, see the answer to question 44. For information on the EU rules on public procurement, see the answer to question 199.

221. What are the objective criteria for determining that a certain level of compensation neutralises the operating risk?

The concept of risk is an essential element of the concept of concession. According to the definitions of works concession and service concession in Article 1(3) and (4) of Directive 2004/18/EC, a concession is a contract with the same characteristics as a public contract, except for the fact that the consideration for the works/the provision of the services consists either solely in the right to exploit the work/service or in this right together with payment.

The concept of exploitation, implying the existence of a risk, is therefore essential in order to determine whether a service is a concession. Thus, in accordance with Court of Justice case law (in particular the judgments in Cases C-300/07 *Oymanns* and C-206/08 *Eurawasser*), a concession exists only if a substantial or significant operating risk is transferred to the operator.

The existence of a significant risk can only be verified on a case-by-case basis. The risks to be taken into account are those involved in providing the service or making available or using the work, particularly the risk associated with demand. In principle, the operator can be deemed to assume substantial operating risks if there is uncertainty as to the return on the investment made for providing the service.

The absence of significant risk, where the compensation is sufficient to neutralise or render negligible the operating risk, entails re-classifying the service concession contract as a service contract, with the resulting legal consequences (i.e. the contract can be annulled in the event of a breach of the public procurement rules).

6 GENERAL QUESTIONS RELATING TO THE APPLICATION TO SGEIS, AND SSGIS IN PARTICULAR, OF THE TREATY RULES ON THE INTERNAL MARKET (FREEDOM OF ESTABLISHMENT AND FREEDOM TO PROVIDE SERVICES)

[5.679]

The 'Treaty rules on the internal market' here refer to the provisions of the Treaty on the Functioning of the European Union (TFEU) on the freedom of establishment (Article 49 of the Treaty) and the freedom to provide services (Article 56 of the Treaty). With regard to the rules on public procurement, see the part of the document dealing with public procurement (section 4).

222. When do the Treaty rules on the internal market (Articles 49 and 56 TFEU) apply to SSGIs?

SSGIs are covered by the internal market rules in the TFEU (Articles 49 and 56) where they constitute an 'economic activity' within the meaning of the Court's case law on the interpretation of those Articles. Certain SSGIs may also be covered by the Services Directive. However, 'non-economic' activities are not covered by any of these rules.

The concept of 'economic activity' is a concept in EU law which has been progressively developed by the Court on the basis of Articles 49 and 56 of the TFEU. Since this concept defines the field of application of two of the fundamental freedoms guaranteed by the Treaty, it may not, as such, be interpreted restrictively[199]. For more information on the concept of 'economic activity' within the meaning of the Treaty rules on the internal market, see question 223.

223. When is an activity classified as 'economic' within the meaning of the Treaty rules on the internal market (Articles 49 and 56 TFEU) and of the Services Directive?

Generally speaking, only services constituting 'economic activities' are covered by the Treaty rules on the internal market (Articles 49 and 56 TFEU) and the Services Directive.

In accordance with the Treaty rules on the internal market, all services provided for remuneration must be classified as economic activities. According to Court of Justice case law, the service does not necessarily have to be paid for by those for whom it is performed,[200] but there must be a consideration for the service in question.

The Court has also stated that the 'economic' nature of an activity does not depend on the legal status of the operator or of the organisation (which may be a public body or not-for-profit),[201] nor on the nature of the service (e.g. the fact that the service provided is a social security or health service does not in itself exclude it from application of the Treaty rules).[202] The activities performed by members of a religious community or amateur sports association could thus be deemed to constitute an economic activity.[203] Furthermore, the 'economic' nature of an activity does not depend on how it is classified in national law. A service deemed in domestic law to be of the 'non-market sector' can be deemed to be an 'economic activity' under the Treaty rules referred to above. The fact that a service is provided in the general interest does not necessarily affect the economic nature of the activity.

In order to determine whether a given service constitutes an economic activity subject to the Treaty rules on the internal market and, where relevant, to the Services Directive, a case-by-case examination must be made of all the characteristics of the activity in question, particularly of the way the service is provided, organised and financed in the Member State concerned.

The Services Directive applies to all the services that are not explicitly excluded from its scope (certain social services are excluded: for more information on the application of the Services Directive to social services, see the answer to question 229). Only activities of an economic nature as defined above are covered by the concept of 'service' as defined in the Directive.

For more information on the implications, for the social services concerned, of being qualified as an 'economic activity' within the meaning of the Treaty rules on the internal market, see also the answers to questions 226 and 227.

224. When is an activity qualified as 'non-economic' within the meaning of the Treaty rules on the internal market (Articles 49 and 56 TFEU) and of the Services Directive?

According to Court of Justice case law, activities that are performed without any consideration, by the State or on behalf of the State, as part of its duties in the social field, for example, do not constitute an economic activity under the Treaty rules on the internal market and the Services Directive.[204]

Examples:

- services provided by an organisation as part of an obligatory insurance scheme (e.g. the payment of compensation in the event of damage from natural risks).[205]
- courses provided under the national education system[206] or at an institute of higher education financed essentially out of state funds.[207]

225. Are the social services not covered by the Services Directive nevertheless subject to the Treaty rules on the internal market?

The exclusion in Article 2(2)(j) of the Services Directive covers social services relating to social housing, childcare and support of families and persons permanently or temporarily in need which are provided by the State itself (at national, regional or local level), by providers mandated by the State or by charities recognised as such by the State. Services excluded from the scope of the Services Directive which constitute economic activities continue to be covered by the Treaty rules, in particular those on freedom of establishment and freedom to provide services (Articles 49 and 56 of the TFEU). National measures regulating the services excluded from the Services Directive are therefore still liable to be assessed for their compatibility with EU law by a national court or by the Court of Justice, in particular in the light of the above-mentioned Articles 49 and 56. Measures aimed at regulating the social services sector may be justified on the grounds of social policy objectives provided these measures are proportionate to the objectives pursued. See also the answers to questions 226 and 227.

226. Can social policy objectives justify the application of measures aimed at regulating the social services sector?

According to the Court of Justice, Member States are free to set social policy objectives and, where appropriate, to define precisely the level of protection sought. However, the rules that they impose must satisfy the conditions laid down in the case law of the Court case law as regards their justification and proportionality. Restrictions on the freedoms of the internal market must be assessed by reference to the objectives pursued by the competent authorities of the Member State concerned and the level of protection which they seek to ensure.

Case law has identified a number of 'overriding reasons of general interest' which constitute objectives allowing the Member States to justify restrictions on the freedoms of the internal market (e.g. objectives relating to social policy, protection of the recipients of the services, consumer protection, etc.). Generally speaking, current Court case law shows that social considerations may justify restrictions on the fundamental freedoms, for example in so far as it may be considered unacceptable to allow private profit to be drawn from the weakness of recipients of services.[208] Any measure must, however, be suitable for guaranteeing the achievement of one or more legitimate objectives invoked by that Member State and must not go beyond what is necessary to achieve those objectives.

Thus, for example, in accordance with the Treaty and (for the services included in it) the Services Directive, prior authorisation regimes for carrying out an activity can be maintained provided they are non-discriminatory, pursue an objective of general interest and are appropriate for achieving this objective and, lastly, provided the objective pursued cannot be achieved by other less restrictive measures. In the social sector, the Court has held that social policy objectives constitute 'overriding reasons of general interest' that may justify applying an authorisation regime or other measures aimed at regulating the markets provided that these systems or measures are proportionate to the objectives pursued.

227. Can Member States decide to restrict the provision of certain social services to non-profit-making service providers?

The Court of Justice has held that, according to the scale of values held by each of the Member States and having regard to the discretion available to them, a Member State may restrict the operation of certain activities by entrusting them to public or charitable bodies.[209] Any measure of this kind must, however, be suitable for guaranteeing the achievement of one or more legitimate objectives invoked by that Member State and must not go beyond what is necessary to achieve those objectives. National legislation is appropriate for ensuring attainment of the objective pursued only if it genuinely reflects a concern to attain it in a consistent and systematic manner. In any event, such restrictions must be applied without discrimination.

NOTES

199 Joined Cases 51/96 and C-191/97 *Deliège* [2000] ECR I-2549, paragraph 52.

200 For example, the Court has considered that hospital services provided free of charge under the applicable health insurance scheme could constitute an economic activity within the meaning of the Treaty.

201 Case C-172/98 *Commission* v *Belgium*. In Case C-157/99 *Smits and Peerbooms* (paragraph 50), the Court threw out the argument that an additional condition for considering the provision of a service to constitute an economic activity within the meaning of Article 60 of the Treaty is that the service provider must seek to make a profit.

202 Judgment in *Smits and Peerbooms*, cited above.

203 Case C-196/87 *Steymann* and Joined Cases C-51/96 and C-191/97 *Deliège*.

204 Case C-109/92 *Wirth*.

205 In its judgment in Case C-355/00 *Freskot*, the Court considered that contributions paid to this body did not constitute economic consideration if, in particular, they were essentially imposed by the legislator and the level of the benefits provided by the insurer and the system for payment of these benefits were fixed by the legislator.

206 In its judgment in Case C-263/86 *Humbel*, the Court stresses that, in establishing and maintaining a national education system, the State is not seeking to engage in gainful activity, but is fulfilling its duties towards its own population in the social, cultural and educational fields. Secondly, the system in question is, as a general rule, funded from the public purse and not by pupils or their parents. The Court added that the nature of the activity is not affected by the fact that pupils or their parents must sometimes pay teaching or enrolment fees in order to make a certain contribution to the operating expenses of the system.

207 In the *Wirth* judgment referred to earlier, the Court in fact ruled that the considerations set forth in the aforementioned

Humbel judgment applied equally to courses provided at an establishment of higher education which is financed essentially out of public funds.

[208] See the judgment in Joined Cases C-447/08 and C-448/08 on gambling via the internet.

[209] See judgment in Joined Cases C-447/08 and 448/08, paragraph 43, cited above. See also the previously cited Case C-70/95 *Sodemare SA* v *Regione Lombardia* [1997] ECR I-3395.

7 QUESTIONS CONCERNING THE APPLICABILITY OF THE SERVICES DIRECTIVE TO SGEIS AND, IN PARTICULAR, TO SSGIS

[5.680]

228. Which services of general economic interest fall within the scope of the Services Directive?

Services of general economic interest (SGEIs) are covered by the Services Directive if they are not specifically excluded from its scope (as are, for instance, transport services, healthcare services, certain social services, electronic communications networks and services and audio-visual services). Social services have been partially excluded: they are covered by the Directive when they are provided by private operators not mandated by the State, but they are excluded when they are provided by the State, by providers mandated by the State or by charities recognised as such by the State.

For those SGEIs that have not been excluded from the scope of the Services Directive, the latter contains a whole series of 'safeguards' aimed at allowing Member States to take full account of the special features of these sectors when implementing the Directive into national law. Member States will thus be able to maintain in force the national rules governing these sectors, for instance in order to guarantee high-quality services.

First, the provisions in the Directive on freedom of establishment allow Member States to take account of the special features of SGEIs. In particular, the review and assessment of certain requirements under national law, which Member States had to carry out in accordance with the Directive, 'should not obstruct the performance of the particular task assigned to SGEIs' (Article 15(4)). Moreover, pursuant to Articles 9 to 13, Member States are entitled to maintain in force authorisation schemes governing access to or the exercise of a service activity (including SGEIs) in all cases in which such authorisations are not discriminatory, are justified by an overriding reason relating to the public interest and are proportionate.

Second, the Directive provides that the freedom to provide services clause, set out in Article 16, does not apply to SGEIs (pursuant to an explicit derogation in Article 17).

Generally speaking, the implementation work carried out by the Member States shows that the Directive is beneficial for the modernisation of our economies and benefits both service providers and consumers. During the implementation phase, the Commission was not made aware of any particular problems arising from the application of the Directive to SGEIs.

Information on the laws adopted by the Member States to implement the Services Directive and links to the various legislative texts once available can be found at:

ec.europa.eu/internal_market/services/services-dir/implementing_legislation_en.htm

229. Which social services have been excluded from the Services Directive and when do the Directive's provisions apply to these social services?

Some social services have been excluded from the scope of the Services Directive. The exclusion set out in Article 2(2)(j) of the Services Directive does not cover all social services but only those relating to social housing, childcare and support of families and persons permanently or temporarily in need which are provided by the State (at national, regional or local level), by providers mandated by the State or by charities recognised as such by the State. Since this provision derogates from a general rule, the exclusion must, according to the settled case law of the European Court of Justice, be strictly interpreted.

On the other hand, the social services not covered by Article 2(2)(j) of the Directive (for instance, childcare services which are not provided by the above-mentioned providers) are subject to the regulatory framework established by the Services Directive.

It is worth mentioning that there is a whole series of provisions in the Directive which recognise and take account of the special features of the social services that have not been excluded from the Directive's scope. For instance, the Directive does not question the possibility of Member States to regulate access to and the exercise of these services in order to guarantee their quality. Under Articles 9 to 13 of the Directive, Member States may keep their authorisation schemes governing access to a service activity and the exercise thereof such an activity provided that such schemes are not discriminatory and are justified and proportionate. Social services which are covered by the Directive, and which are SGEIs, are excluded (under Article 17 of the Directive) from the freedom to provide services clause set out in Article 16 of the Directive. Lastly, the Directive does not deal with the funding of social services. It does not deal with aid granted by Member States, which comes under the rules of competition (see section on State Aid). In particular, it does not concern requirements governing access to public funding or the quality standards which need to be observed for receiving public funding (see recitals 10, 17 and 28 of the Directive).

230. When implementing the Services Directive, can Member States keep authorisation schemes for social services?

Article 9 of the Services Directive imposes on Member States the obligation to review their legislation in order to identify authorisation schemes governing access to and the exercise of a service activity. Where a law requires a decision by a competent authority before a service provider can have access to or exercise an activity falling within the scope of the Directive, this is in effect an authorisation scheme that should be assessed in the light of the Directive. For each scheme (and its procedures) identified, the Member State had to carry out an evaluation during the implementation period based on the rules laid down in Articles 9 to 13 of the Directive. Thus all authorisation schemes relating to access to or the exercise of a service activity falling within the scope of the Services Directive had to be evaluated, as part of the implementation of the Directive, in the light of the principle of non-discrimination, the existence or not of overriding reasons of general interest and, where appropriate, the proportionality of the measures concerned.

Depending on the outcome of the evaluation, Member States were required to abolish the authorisation schemes that are incompatible with Article 9 or replace them with less restrictive measures that were compatible with the Directive. Moreover, it should be noted that the authorisation schemes excluded from the Services Directive still come under the Treaty rules, in particular those concerning freedom of establishment and freedom to provide services (Articles 49 and 56 of the TFEU). They are thus still liable to be assessed for compatibility with EU law by a national court or by the Court of Justice, in particular in the light of the above-mentioned Articles 49 and 56 TFEU. See also the answers to questions 225 and 230.

231. Where the same authorisation scheme applies to services both excluded from and included in the scope of the Directive, does this scheme come under the provisions of the Directive? If so, must the Member State set up separate authorisation schemes for the excluded and included services?

Where the same authorisation scheme applies to services both excluded from and included in the scope of the Directive, this scheme does indeed come under the provisions of the Directive.

However, the Directive does not require the Member State to set up separate authorisation schemes depending on whether or not a service comes within the scope of the Directive, nor does it prohibit a Member State from establishing separate schemes. The main thing, from the point of view of the Directive, is that the Member State must ensure that the authorisation schemes relating to services under the scope of the Directive are brought into line with the Directive (for further details, see the answer to question 230).

232. Does Article 2(2)(j) of the Services Directive apply to social services relating to nurseries and day care centres for children furnished by providers mandated by the State or the local authorities or by any other body mandated for this purpose?

Social services relating to nurseries and day care centres are covered by the exclusion in Article 2(2)(j) of the Services Directive if they are provided by the State itself (at national, regional or local level), by providers mandated by the State or by charities recognised as such by the State.

Social services relating to nurseries and day care centres provided by operators not mandated by the State are not excluded from the scope of the Directive. See also the answer to question 229.

233. Article 2(2)(j) of the Services Directive states that the social services must be provided by the 'State' or by 'providers mandated by the State'. What does the concept of 'State' cover in this context?

First, it must be pointed out that the purpose of this Article is to define the scope of the exclusion from the Directive of certain social services. Since this provision derogates from a general rule, the exclusion must, according to the settled case law of the European Court of Justice, be strictly interpreted.

Pursuant to Article 2(2)(j) some social services (both those furnished by the 'State' and those provided by 'providers mandated by the State') have been excluded from the scope of the Directive. In accordance with recital 27 of the Directive, the concept of State within the meaning of Article 2(2)(j) covers not only the central state administration but also all regional and local authorities. A provider mandated by the State within the meaning of the Directive is a natural or legal person, in the public or private sector, to whom the State, as defined above, has entrusted the obligation to provide a certain service instead of providing it directly itself. Thus to benefit from the exception laid down in the Directive, the question whether it is a social service provided by the State or by a public body entrusted with the obligation, explicitly by and on behalf of the State, to provide this service, for instance by means of a law, is not decisive.

234. What does the concept of 'providers mandated by the State' (Article 2(2)(j)) cover?

The Commission takes the view that, for a provider to be regarded as 'mandated by the State' within the meaning of Article 2(2)(j), it must be under an obligation to provide the service entrusted to it by the State. A provider under an obligation to provide a service, for instance as a result of a tendering procedure or service concession, can be regarded as a provider 'mandated by the State' within the meaning of the Services Directive. This also applies to any other type of measure taken by the State provided that it involves an obligation for the provider in question to provide the service.

235. Is the concept of 'provider mandated by the State' set out in the Services Directive (Article 2(2)(j)) the same as the concept of 'act of entrustment' within the meaning of Article 106(2) TFEU and of the SGEI package?

See the answer to question 51.

236. Does the following constitute an act of entrustment within the meaning of the Services Directive: an official decision by a regional public authority defining a vocational training social service of general interest and entrusting management of this to one or more training undertakings by means of a service concession, with the granting of public service compensation?

Where an official decision by a regional public authority entrusts to a training undertaking a service concession involving the management of a vocational training social service of general interest, the undertaking cannot be regarded as a 'mandated provider' within the meaning of Article 2(2)(j) unless it is under an obligation to provide the service. Each individual case must be examined in the light of the specific circumstances.

In addition, under Article 2(2)(j) of the Directive, read in conjunction with recital 27 of the Directive, the vocational training service provided by a provider mandated by the State cannot be regarded as excluded from the scope of the Directive unless it fulfils the conditions of recital 27, being aimed at people 'who are permanently or temporarily in a particular state of need because of their insufficient family income or total or partial lack of independence' and for those 'who risk being marginalised', for instance the unemployed.

Lastly, it must be pointed out that the services excluded from the scope of the Services Directive still come under the TFEU rules, in particular those on freedom of establishment and freedom to provide services (Articles 49 and 56 TFEU). See also the answer to question 226. As regards the application of the rules on State Aid to this type of measure, see the answer to question 52.

237. What does the concept of 'charities recognised as such by the State' (Article 2(2)(j)) cover?

The concept is specific to the Services Directive, hence its interpretation does not depend directly on concepts existing in the national laws of Member States or in other EU instruments. It is intended only to identify certain operators whose services can be excluded from the scope of the Directive by virtue of Article 2(2)(j), namely social services relating to social housing, childcare and support of families and persons permanently or temporarily in need which are provided by charities recognised as such by the State.

Thus in accordance with the Services Directive, the concept of 'charities recognised as such by the State' means not only that the providers of the services in question must be non-profit-making but also that they must perform activities of a charitable nature (specifically recognised as such by the authorities) for third parties (in other words, not their members) in need. It follows from this *inter alia* that mere recognition as a non-profit-making organisation (for instance for tax purposes) or the general interest nature of the activities performed are not enough in themselves for an organisation to be regarded as coming under the heading of 'charities recognised as such by the State'. Nor can mere approval by the State be regarded as a sufficient criterion in itself for an organisation to be regarded as coming under this heading (and for its activities to then be excluded from the scope of the Services Directive).

Referring to this concept in its implementation handbook,[210] the Commission quoted the following as examples of charities within the meaning of the Directive: 'churches and church organisations which serve charitable and benevolent purposes'. Whether or not such an organisation is religious or lay is not decisive, however, for the purposes of defining the scope of the exclusion of social services from the Services Directive. It follows that the services provided by an organisation whose charitable nature has been recognised by the State are excluded from the Services Directive pursuant to Article 2(2)(j) irrespective of whether the organisation concerned is lay or religious.

NOTES

210 Handbook on implementation of the Services Directive, available at the following website: ec.europa.eu/internal_market/services/services-dir/documents_en.htm.

PART 6
UK AND EU COURT MATERIALS

A. UK COURTS

COMPETITION APPEAL TRIBUNAL RULES 2003 (NOTE)

(SI 2003/1372)

[6.1]

NOTES

These Rules have been omitted from this edition due to constraints on the amount of available space. Customers who wish to refer to these Rules are advised to retain the 24th edition (2018) of this Handbook.

These Rules were revoked and replaced by the Competition Appeal Tribunal Rules 2015, SI 2015/1648, as from 1 October 2015, subject to savings in r 119 of the 2015 Rules at **[6.126]**. These Rules now only apply to proceedings commenced before 1 October 2015. The 2015 Rules are at **[6.8]**.

Previously, these Rules replaced the Competition Commission Appeal Tribunal Rules 2000, SI 2000/261 which were revoked, as from 20 June 2003, except in relation to proceedings commenced before the Tribunal before that date.

COMPETITION APPEAL TRIBUNAL GUIDE TO PROCEEDINGS (2005) (NOTE)

(October 2005)

[6.2]

NOTES

This Guide has been omitted from this edition due to constraints on the amount of available space. Customers who wish to refer to this Guide are advised to retain the 24th edition (2018) of this Handbook.

Note that this Guide is relevant for cases commenced before 1 October 2015. For cases commenced after that date, see the 2015 Guide to Proceedings at **[6.128]**.

PRACTICE DIRECTION COMPETITION LAW CLAIMS RELATING TO THE APPLICATION OF . . . CHAPTERS I AND II OF PART I OF THE COMPETITION ACT 1998

[6.3]

NOTES

This Practice direction is available on the Ministry of Justice's website at: www.justice.gov.uk/courts/procedure-rules/civil/rules/competitionlaw_pd. It is reproduced as amended by the 107th Update – Practice Direction Amendments (March 2019) at **[7.90]** (as from IP completion day, as defined in the European Union (Withdrawal Agreement) Act 2020, s 39).

The words omitted from the title were revoked by the 107th Update – Practice Direction Amendments (March 2019) at **[7.90]** (as from IP completion day (as defined in the European Union (Withdrawal Agreement) Act 2020, s 39)).

SCOPE AND INTERPRETATION

1.1 This practice direction applies to any claim relating to the application of—

(a) . . .

(b) Chapter I or Chapter II of Part I of the Competition Act 1998.

1.2 In this practice direction—

(a) 'the Act' means the Competition Act 1998;

(b) . . .

(c) . . .

(d) ["competition authority" means—

(i) the Competition and Markets Authority; or

(ii) a regulator as defined in section 54 of the Act;]

(e) . . .

NOTES

The words omitted were revoked, and the words in square brackets were substituted, by the 107th Update – Practice Direction Amendments (March 2019) at **[7.90]** (as from IP completion day).

VENUE

2.1 A claim to which this Practice Direction applies—

(a) must be commenced in the High Court at the Royal Courts of Justice; and

(b) will be assigned to the Chancery Division, unless it comes within the scope of rule 58.1(2), in which case it will be assigned to the Commercial Court of the Queen's Bench Division.

2.2 Any party whose statement of case raises an issue relating to the application of *Article 81 or 82 of the Treaty, or* Chapter I or II of Part I of the Act, must—

(a) state that fact in his statement of case; and
(b) apply for the proceedings to be transferred to the Chancery Division at the Royal Courts of Justice, if they have not been commenced there, or in the Commercial or Admiralty Courts; or
(c) apply for the transfer of the proceedings to the Commercial Court, in accordance with rules 58.4(2) and 30.5(3). If such application is refused, the proceedings must be transferred to the Chancery Division of the High Court at the Royal Courts of Justice.

2.3 Rule 30.8 provides that where proceedings are taking place in the Queen's Bench Division (other than proceedings in the Commercial or Admiralty Courts), a district registry of the High Court or a county court, the court must transfer the proceedings to the Chancery Division at the Royal Courts of Justice if the statement of case raises an issue relating to the application of *Article 81 or 82, or* Chapter I or II. However, if any such proceedings which have been commenced in the Queen's Bench Division or a Mercantile Court fall within the scope of rule 58.1(2), any party to those proceedings may apply for the transfer of the proceedings to the Commercial Court, in accordance with rules 58.4(2) and 30.5(3). If the application is refused, the proceedings must be transferred to the Chancery Division of the High Court at the Royal Courts of Justice.

2.4 Where proceedings are commenced in or transferred to the Chancery Division at the Royal Courts of Justice in accordance with this paragraph, that court may transfer the proceedings or any part of the proceedings to another court if—

(a) the issue relating to the application of *Article 81 or 82, or* Chapter I or II, has been resolved; or
(b) the judge considers that the proceedings or part of the proceedings to be transferred does not involve any issue relating to the application of *Article 81 or 82, or* Chapter I or II.

(Rule 30.3 sets out the matters to which the court must have regard when considering whether to make a transfer order.)

NOTES

The words in italics were revoked by the 107th Update – Practice Direction Amendments (March 2019) at **[7.90]** (as from IP completion day). For transitional provisions see para 6 of the 107th Update which provides that the amendments to paragraph 2 of this Practice Direction do not apply in relation to proceedings relating to competition described in paragraph 14(2) of Schedule 4 to the Competition (Amendment etc) (EU Exit) Regulations 2019. Paragraph 14(2) of Schedule 4 to the 2019 Regulations is at **[7.74]**.

Note: with effect from 1 December 2009, the EC Treaty was replaced by the Treaty on the Functioning of the European Union. References in this document to provisions of the EC Treaty should be construed accordingly. As to Articles 81 and 82 of the EC Treaty, see now Articles 101 and 102 of the Treaty on the Functioning of the European Union.

NOTICE OF PROCEEDINGS

3. Any party whose statement of case raises or deals with an issue relating to the application of . . . Chapter I or II, must serve a copy of the statement of case on the [the Competition and Markets Authority] at the same time as it is served on the other parties to the claim [(addressed to the General Counsel,, the Competition and Markets Authority, Victoria House, Southampton Row, London WC1B 4AD)].

NOTES

Words omitted revoked, and words in square brackets substituted, by the 107th Update – Practice Direction Amendments (March 2019) at **[7.90]** (as from IP completion day).

CASE MANAGEMENT

4.1 . . .

4.1A A . . . competition authority may . . . make written observations to the court, or apply for permission to make oral observations, on issues relating to the application of Chapter I or II.

4.2 If a [competition authority] intends to make written observations to the court, it must give notice of its intention to do so by letter to Chancery Chambers at the Royal Courts of Justice (including the claim number and addressed to the Court Manager, Room TM 6.06, Royal Courts of Justice, Strand, London WC2A 2LL) at the earliest reasonable opportunity.

4.3 An application by a [competition authority] for permission to make oral representations at the hearing of a claim must be made by letter to Chancery Chambers (including the claim number and addressed to the Court Manager, Room TM 6.06, Royal Courts of Justice, Strand, London WC2A 2LL) at the earliest reasonable opportunity, identifying the claim and indicating why the applicant wishes to make oral representations.

4.4 If a [competition authority] files a notice under paragraph 4.2 or an application under paragraph 4.3, it must at the same time serve a copy of the notice or application on every party to the claim.

4.5 Any request by a [competition authority] for the court to send it any documents relating to a claim should be made at the same time as filing a notice under paragraph 4.2 or an application under paragraph 4.3.

4.6 Where the court receives a notice under paragraph 4.2 it may give case management directions to the [competition authority], including directions about the date by which any written observations are to be filed.

4.7 The court will serve on every party to the claim a copy of any directions given or order made—
(a) on an application under paragraph 4.3; or
(b) under paragraph 4.6.

4.8 In any claim to which this practice direction applies, the court shall direct a pre-trial review to take place shortly before the trial, if possible before the judge who will be conducting the trial.

NOTES

Words omitted revoked, and words in square brackets substituted, by the 107th Update – Practice Direction Amendments (March 2019) at **[7.90]** (as from IP completion day).

AVOIDANCE OF CONFLICT WITH COMMISSION DECISIONS

5 . . .

NOTES

Revoked by the 107th Update – Practice Direction Amendments (March 2019) at **[7.90]** (as from IP completion day).

JUDGMENTS

6. . . .

NOTES

Revoked by the 107th Update – Practice Direction Amendments (March 2019) at **[7.90]** (as from IP completion day).

PRACTICE DIRECTION 52D STATUTORY APPEALS AND APPEALS SUBJECT TO SPECIAL PROVISION

[6.4]

NOTES

This Practice direction is available on the Ministry of Justice's website at: www.justice.gov.uk/courts/procedure-rules/civil/rules/part52/practice-direction-52d-statutory-appeals-and-appeals-subject-to-special-provision.

It is reproduced as amended by the 107th Update – Practice Direction Amendments (March 2019) at **[7.90]** (as from IP completion day, as defined in the European Union (Withdrawal Agreement) Act 2020, s 39).

Only paragraphs 7 and 8 are reproduced here. Other paragraphs are outside the scope of this work.

APPEALS TO THE COURT OF APPEAL

Appeals relating to the application of *Articles 101 and 102 of the Treaty on the Functioning of the European Union and* Chapters I and II of Part I of the Competition Act 1998

[6.5]

7.1 (1) This paragraph applies to any appeal to the Court of Appeal relating to the application [Chapter I or Chapter II of Part I of the Competition Act 1998].

(2) In this paragraph—
(a) 'the Act' means the Competition Act 1998;
(b) . . .
(c) . . .
(d) ["competition "authority" means—
(i) the Competition and Markets Authority; or
(ii) a regulator as defined in section 54 of the Act;]
(e) . . .

(3) Any party whose appeal notice raises an issue relating to the application of *Article 101 or 102 of the Treaty, or* Chapter I or II of Part I of the Act, must—
(a) state that fact in the appeal notice; and
(b) serve a copy of the appeal notice on [the Competition and Markets Authority] at the same time as it is served on the other party to the appeal [(addressed to the General Counsel, the Competition and Markets Authority, Victoria House, Southampton Row, London WC1B 4AD)].

(4) . . .

(5) A . . . competition authority may . . . make written observations to the Court of Appeal, or apply for permission to make oral observations, on issues relating to the application of Chapter I or II.

(6) If a [competition authority] intends to make written observations to the Court of Appeal, it must give notice of its intention to do so by letter to the Civil Appeals Office at the earliest opportunity.

(7) An application by a [competition authority] for permission to make oral representations at the hearing of an appeal must be made by letter to the Civil Appeals Office at the earliest opportunity, identifying the appeal and indicating why the applicant wishes to make oral representations.

(8) If a [competition authority] files a notice under sub-paragraph (6) or an application under sub-paragraph (7), it must at the same time serve a copy of the notice or application on every party to the appeal.

(9) Any request by a [competition authority] for the court to send it any documents relating to an appeal should be made at the same time as filing a notice under sub-paragraph (6) or an application under sub-paragraph (7).

(10) When the Court of Appeal receives a notice under sub-paragraph (6) it may give case management directions to the [competition authority], including directions about the date by which any written observations are to be filed.

(11) The Court of Appeal will serve on every party to the appeal a copy of any directions given or order made
(a) on an application under sub-paragraph (7); or
(b) under sub-paragraph (10).

(12)–(14) . . .

NOTES

The words omitted were revoked, and the words in square brackets were substituted by the 107th Update – Practice Direction Amendments (March 2019) at **[7.90]** (as from IP completion day). Note also that the words in italics in paragraph 7.1(3) were also revoked by the 107th Update, subject to transitional provisions in para 5 of the 107th Update which provides that the amendments to that paragraph do not apply in relation to proceedings relating to competition described in paragraph 14(2) of Schedule 4 to the Competition (Amendment etc) (EU Exit) Regulations 2019. Paragraph 14(2) of Schedule 4 to the 2019 Regulations is at **[7.74]**.

Appeal from Competition Appeal Tribunal

[6.6]

8.1 (1) Where the appellant applies for permission to appeal at the hearing at which the decision is delivered by the tribunal and—
(a) permission is given; or
(b) permission is refused and the appellant wishes to make an application to the Court of Appeal for permission to appeal,

the appellant's notice must be filed at the Court of Appeal within 14 days after the date of that hearing.

(2) Where the appellant applies in writing to the Registrar of the tribunal for permission to appeal and—
(a) permission is given; or
(b) permission is refused and the appellant wishes to make an application to the Court of Appeal for permission to appeal,

the appellant's notice must be filed at the Court of Appeal within 14 days after the date of receipt of the tribunal's decision on permission.

(3) Where the appellant does not make an application to the tribunal for permission to appeal, but wishes to make an application to the Court of Appeal for permission, the appellant's notice must be filed at the Court of Appeal within 14 days after the end of the period within which the appellant may make a written application to the Registrar of the tribunal.

COMPETITION APPEAL TRIBUNAL RULES 2015

(SI 2015/1648)

[6.7]

NOTES

Made: 7 September 2015.
Authority: Enterprise Act 2002, s 15(1)–(3), Sch 4, Pt 2; Communications Act 2003, ss 192(3), (4), 193(1), (2)(b), (3).
Commencement: 1 October 2015.
Note: these Rules replace the Competition Appeal Tribunal Rules 2003, SI 2003/1372 which were revoked, as from 1 October 2015, except in relation to proceedings commenced before the Tribunal before that date (see rr 118, 119 at **[6.125]**, **[6.126]**). These Rules apply to cases commenced on or after 1 October 2015.

ARRANGEMENT OF RULES

PART 1
INTRODUCTION

PART 1 INTRODUCTION

[6.8]
1 Citation and commencement

These Rules may be cited as the Competition Appeal Tribunal Rules 2015 and come into force on 1st October 2015.

[6.9]
2 Interpretation

(1) In these Rules—

"the 1998 Act" means the Competition Act 1998;

"the 2002 Act" means the Enterprise Act 2002;

"the 2003 Act" means the Communications Act 2003;
"additional claim" has the meaning given in rule 39(1);
"a chairman" means a person who falls within one of the categories of persons specified in section 12(2)(aa) to (ac) or (b) of the 2002 Act (constitution of the Competition Appeal Tribunal);
"the chairman" means the chairman of the Tribunal as constituted for particular proceedings;
"class representative" has the meaning given for representative in section 59(1) of the 1998 Act (interpretation) or means a representative of a sub-class who is specified in a collective proceedings order;
"CMA" means the Competition and Markets Authority;
"collective proceedings" means proceedings under section 47B(1) of the 1998 Act (collective proceedings before the Tribunal);
"collective settlement" means settlement under section 49A (collective settlements: where a collective proceedings order has been made) or 49B (collective settlements: where a collective proceedings order has not been made) of the 1998 Act;
"collective settlement order" means an order authorising the settlement representative to act in relation to the collective settlement;
"confidentiality ring" means an arrangement set up in accordance with a direction by the Tribunal under which documents are treated as confidential and disclosed only on such terms as the Tribunal thinks fit;
"costs" has the meaning given by rule 104;
"CPR" means the Civil Procedure Rules 1998;
"damages" means any sum of money (other than costs or expenses) which may be awarded in respect of a claim under section 47A (claims for damages etc) or 47B (collective proceedings) of the 1998 Act;
"disclose", in rules 60 to 65, has the meaning given in rule 60;
"document" means anything in which information of any description is recorded, in whatever form; and "copy", in relation to a document, means anything onto which information recorded in the document has been copied, by whatever means and whether directly or indirectly;
"filing", in relation to a document, means sending it to the Registrar in accordance with rule 111(1);
"foreign defendant" means a defendant domiciled outside the United Kingdom;
"infringement decision" has the meaning given by section 47A(6) of the 1998 Act;
"President" means the person appointed to be President of the Tribunal;
"Registrar" means the person appointed to be Registrar of the Tribunal;
"relevant period", in rules 47 to 49, has the meaning given in rule 45(1);
"Rule 45 Offer" in rules 45 to 49, has the meaning given in rule 45(1);
"settlement representative" means a person who is authorised by a collective settlement order to act in relation to a collective settlement;
"specified price control matter" means a price control matter specified in rule 116(1);
"statement of truth" means a statement that the party putting forward a document, or in the case of a witness statement, the maker of the witness statement, believes the facts stated in the document or witness statement are true;
"sub-class" means a member of a distinct class of class members, described in the collective proceedings order or a collective settlement order, as the case may be;
"TFEU" means the Treaty on the Functioning of the European Union;
"Tribunal" means (a) the Competition Appeal Tribunal or (b) in relation to any proceedings, the tribunal as constituted for the purposes of those proceedings, as the context requires; and
"undertaking as to damages" means an undertaking to pay damages which a person sustains as a result of an interim injunction or other interim order and which the Tribunal considers the person in whose favour the injunction or other order is granted should pay.

(2) These Rules are to be applied by the Tribunal and interpreted in accordance with the governing principles set out in rule 4.

NOTES

Para (1): definition "TFEU" in italics revoked by the Competition (Amendment etc) (EU Exit) Regulations 2019, SI 2019/93, reg 61, Sch 2, Pt 2, para 8, as from IP completion day (as defined in the European Union (Withdrawal Agreement) Act 2020, s 39) (for transitional provisions and savings in relation to the operation of the 2019 Regulations, see Sch 4 to those Regulations at **[7.69]** et seq and, in particular, Sch 4, Pts 3 and 7 to the 2019 Regulations at **[7.71]** and **[7.76]**).

[6.10]
3 Application of Rules

These Rules apply as follows—
(a) Parts 1 and 6 apply to all proceedings before the Tribunal;
(b) Part 2 applies to all proceedings before the Tribunal save as otherwise provided in Parts 3, 4, 5 and 7;
(c) Part 3 applies to proceedings for a review or an appeal against penalties under the 2002 Act;
(d) Part 4 applies to claims under section 47A of the 1998 Act and, subject to rule 74, to collective proceedings;
(e) Part 5 applies to collective proceedings and collective settlements;
(f) Part 7 applies to appeals under section 192(2) of the 2003 Act relating to price control.

[6.11]
4 Governing principles

(1) The Tribunal shall seek to ensure that each case is dealt with justly and at proportionate cost.

(2) Dealing with a case justly and at proportionate cost includes, so far as is practicable—
(a) ensuring that the parties are on an equal footing;
(b) saving expense;
(c) dealing with the case in ways which are proportionate—

(i) to the amount of money involved;
(ii) to the importance of the case;
(iii) to the complexity of the issues; and
(iv) to the financial position of each party;

(d) ensuring that it is dealt with expeditiously and fairly;
(e) allotting to it an appropriate share of the Tribunal's resources, while taking into account the need to allot resources to other cases; and
(f) enforcing compliance with these Rules, any practice direction issued under rule 115, and any order or direction of the Tribunal.

(3) Each party's case shall be fully set out in writing as early as possible.

(4) The Tribunal shall actively manage cases.

(5) Active case management includes—

(a) encouraging the parties to co-operate with each other in the conduct of the proceedings;
(b) identification of and concentration on the main issues as early as possible;
(c) fixing a target date for the main hearing as early as possible together with a timetable for the proceedings up to the main hearing, taking into account the nature of the case;
(d) adopting fact-finding procedures that are most effective and appropriate for the case;
(e) planning the structure of the main hearing in advance with a view to avoiding unnecessary oral evidence and argument; and
(f) ensuring that the main hearing is conducted within defined time-limits.

(6) The Tribunal may—

(a) encourage and facilitate the use of an alternative dispute resolution procedure if the Tribunal considers that appropriate;
(b) dispense with the need for the parties to attend any hearing; and
(c) use technology actively to manage cases.

(7) The parties (together with their representatives and any experts) are required to co-operate with the Tribunal to give effect to the principles in this rule.

[6.12]

5 The Registrar

(1) Any person appointed to be the Registrar under section 12(3) of the 2002 Act (constitution of the Competition Appeal Tribunal) shall—

(a) have a seven year general qualification within the meaning of section 71 of the Courts and Legal Services Act 1990 (qualification for judicial and certain other appointments), or
(b) be an advocate or solicitor in Scotland of at least seven years' standing, or
(c) be—
(i) a member of the Bar of Northern Ireland of at least seven years' standing, or
(ii) a solicitor of the Court of Judicature of Northern Ireland of at least seven years' standing.

(2) The Registrar shall act in accordance with the instructions of the President and is, in particular, to be responsible for—

(a) the establishment and maintenance of a register in which all pleadings and supporting documents and all orders and decisions of the Tribunal are to be registered;
(b) the acceptance, transmission, service and custody of documents in accordance with these Rules;
(c) the enforcement of decisions of the Tribunal under paragraphs 4 and 5 of Schedule 4 to the 2002 Act (procedure of the Tribunal) and certification for the purposes of paragraph 1A of that Schedule;
(d) certifying that any order, direction or decision is an order, direction or decision of the Tribunal, the President or a chairman, as the case may be.

(3) Any function of the Registrar may be performed by any member of staff of the Competition Service whom the President or Registrar may authorise for the purpose.

[6.13]

6 Tribunal address for service

The address for the filing or service of documents at or on the Tribunal (referred to in these Rules as "the Tribunal address for service") is: The Registrar of the Competition Appeal Tribunal, Victoria House, Bloomsbury Place, London WC1A 2EB or such other address as may be notified on the Tribunal website from time to time.

NOTES

See further the notice given by the CAT under this rule with regard to the change to the Tribunal's address for the filing or service of documents at or on the Tribunal at **[6.252]**. The new address (with effect from 8 November 2019) is:
The Registrar of the Competition Appeal Tribunal
Salisbury Square House
8 Salisbury Square
London EC4Y 8AP.

[6.14]

7 Tribunal website

The location of the Tribunal website is: www.catribunal.org.uk or such other location as may be notified from time to time in such manner as the President may direct.

[6.15]
8 Representation

(1) In proceedings before the Tribunal, a party may be represented by—

(a) a qualified lawyer having a right of audience before a court in the United Kingdom; or

(b) any other person allowed by the Tribunal to appear on behalf of the party.

(2) A party shall notify the Tribunal where—

(a) the party changes its legal representative;

(b) the party, having conducted the proceedings in person, appoints a legal representative to act on its behalf; or

(c) the party, having conducted the proceedings by a legal representative, intends to act in person.

(3) The notice referred to in paragraph (2) shall state the party's new address for service and be served on—

(a) every other party to the proceedings; and

(b) where paragraph (2)(a) or (c) applies, the former legal representative.

(4) Until service of the notice referred to in paragraph (2), service of any document at the existing address for service is valid.

PART 2 APPEALS

COMMENCING APPEAL PROCEEDINGS

[6.16]
9 Time and manner of commencing appeals

(1) An appeal to the Tribunal shall be made by filing a notice of appeal within two months of the date upon which the appellant was notified of the disputed decision or the date of publication of the decision, whichever is the earlier.

(2) The Tribunal may not extend the time limit provided under paragraph (1) unless it is satisfied that the circumstances are exceptional.

(3) The notice of appeal shall state—

(a) the name and address of the appellant;

(b) the name and address of the appellant's legal representative, if any;

(c) an address for service in the United Kingdom;

(d) the name and address of the respondent to the proceedings,

and shall be signed and dated by the appellant, or on its behalf by its duly authorised officer or legal representative.

(4) The notice of appeal shall contain—

(a) a concise statement of the facts;

(b) details of the decision to which the proceedings relate;

(c) observations on the question in which part of the United Kingdom the proceedings of the Tribunal are to be treated as taking place under rule 18;

(d) a summary of the grounds for contesting the decision, identifying in particular—

(i) under which statutory provision the appeal is brought;

(ii) to what extent (if any) the appellant contends that the disputed decision was based on an error of fact or was wrong in law;

(iii) to what extent (if any) the appellant is appealing against the respondent's exercise of its discretion in making the disputed decision;

(e) a succinct presentation of the arguments supporting each of the grounds of appeal;

(f) the relief sought by the appellant, and any directions sought in accordance with rule 19;

(g) a schedule listing all the documents annexed to the notice of appeal; and

(h) a statement identifying the evidence (whether witness statements or other documents annexed to the notice of appeal) the substance of which, so far as the appellant is aware, was not before the maker of the disputed decision.

(5) In proceedings under the 2003 Act, the notice of appeal shall include a statement indicating the extent to which the appeal relates to price control or a specified price control matter arises in the appeal.

(6) There shall be annexed to the notice of appeal—

(a) a copy of the disputed decision; and

(b) as far as practicable, a copy of every document (or part of a document) on which the appellant relies, including the written statements of all witnesses of fact and expert witnesses, if any.

(7) Unless the Tribunal otherwise directs, the signed original of the notice of appeal shall be accompanied by ten copies of the notice of appeal and its annexes certified by the appellant or its legal representative as conforming to the original.

[6.17]
10 Defective notices of appeal

(1) If the Tribunal considers that a notice of appeal does not comply with rule 9, or is materially incomplete, or is unduly prolix or lacking in clarity, the Tribunal may give such directions as may be necessary to ensure that those defects are remedied.

(2) The Tribunal may, if satisfied that the efficient conduct of the proceedings so requires, instruct the Registrar to defer service of the notice of appeal on the respondent until after the directions referred to in paragraph (1) have been complied with.

[6.18]
11 Power to strike out

(1) The Tribunal may, after giving the parties an opportunity to be heard, strike out an appeal in whole or in part at any stage in the proceedings if—

(a) it considers that the Tribunal has no jurisdiction to hear or determine the appeal;
(b) it considers that the notice of appeal, or part of it, discloses no valid ground of appeal;
(c) it considers that the appellant does not have (or represent those who have) a sufficient interest in the decision in respect of which the appeal is made;
(d) it is satisfied that the appellant has habitually and persistently and without any reasonable ground—
 (i) instituted vexatious proceedings, whether against the same person or different persons; or
 (ii) made vexatious applications in any proceedings; or
(e) the appellant fails to comply with any rule, practice direction issued under rule 115, or order or direction of the Tribunal.

(2) When the Tribunal strikes out an appeal it may make any consequential order it considers appropriate.

[6.19]
12 Amendments to notice of appeal

(1) The appellant may amend the notice of appeal only with the permission of the Tribunal.

(2) Where the Tribunal grants permission under paragraph (1) it may do so on such terms as it thinks fit, and may give any further or consequential directions it considers necessary.

(3) In deciding whether to grant permission under paragraph (1), the Tribunal shall take into account all the circumstances including whether the proposed amendment—
(a) involves a substantial change or addition to the appellant's case;
(b) is based on matters of law or fact which have come to light since the appeal was made; or
(c) for any other reason could not practicably have been included in the notice of appeal.

[6.20]
13 Withdrawal of the appeal

(1) The appellant may withdraw its appeal only with the permission of the Tribunal, or if no Tribunal has been constituted, the President.

(2) Where permission is granted under paragraph (1), the Tribunal or the President, as the case may be, ("the grantor") may—
(a) do so on such terms as the grantor thinks fit;
(b) instruct the Registrar to publish notice of the withdrawal on the Tribunal website or in such other manner as the grantor may direct; and
(c) publish any decision which the grantor would have made had the appeal not been withdrawn.

(3) Where an appeal is withdrawn—
(a) any interim order of the Tribunal, other than an order made in respect of costs, immediately ceases to have effect; and
(b) no fresh appeal may be brought by the appellant in relation to the decision which was the subject of the appeal without the permission of the Tribunal.

RESPONSE TO APPEAL PROCEEDINGS

[6.21]
14 Acknowledgment and notification

(1) On receiving a notice of appeal the Registrar shall—
(a) send an acknowledgement of its receipt to the appellant; and
(b) subject to rules 10(2) and 11, send a copy of the notice of appeal to the respondent who made the disputed decision.

(2) Subject to rules 10 and 11, the Registrar shall as soon as practicable upon receipt of a notice of appeal publish a summary on the Tribunal website and in any other manner the President may direct.

(3) The summary referred to in paragraph (2) shall—
(a) state that a notice of appeal has been received;
(b) contain the name and address of the appellant and its legal representative (if any);
(c) specify the disputed decision to which the appeal relates and the person by whom it was made;
(d) specify particulars of the relief sought by the appellant;
(e) contain a summary of the principal grounds relied on; and
(f) contain a statement indicating that any person with sufficient interest may apply to intervene in the proceedings, in accordance with rule 16, within three weeks of publication of the summary or within any other period the President may direct.

[6.22]
15 Defence

(1) The respondent shall file a defence in the form required by this rule within six weeks (or such further time as the Tribunal may allow) of the date on which the respondent received a copy of the notice of appeal in accordance with rule 14(1)(b).

(2) The defence shall state—
(a) the name and address of the respondent;
(b) the name and address of the respondent's legal representative, if any;
(c) an address for service in the United Kingdom,

and shall be signed and dated by the respondent, or on its behalf by its duly authorised officer or legal representative.

(3) The defence shall contain—
(a) observations on the question in which part of the United Kingdom the proceedings of the Tribunal are to be treated as taking place under rule 18;

- (b) a succinct presentation of the arguments of fact and law upon which the respondent will rely;
- (c) details of any objection to the admission of evidence put forward by the appellant;
- (d) the relief sought by the respondent and any directions sought under rule 19;
- (e) a schedule listing all the documents annexed to the defence; and
- (f) a statement identifying the evidence (whether witness statements or other documents annexed to the defence) the substance of which, so far as the respondent is aware, was not referred to in the disputed decision or disclosed to the appellant before that decision was made.

(4) In proceedings under the 2003 Act, the defence shall include a statement indicating the extent to which the appeal relates to price control or a specified price control matter arises in the appeal, including (where applicable) a statement in rebuttal of a statement under rule 9(5).

(5) As far as practicable, there shall be annexed to the defence a copy of every document (or part of a document) upon which the respondent relies including the written statements of all witnesses of fact and expert witnesses, if any, but excluding any document (or part of a document) annexed to the notice of appeal.

(6) The signed original of the defence shall be accompanied by ten copies of the defence and its annexes certified by the respondent or its duly authorised officer or legal representative as conforming to the original.

(7) Rules 10(1), 11 (except paragraph (1)(a), (c) and (d)) and 12 apply to a defence as if—

- (a) references to "notice of appeal" were references to "defence";
- (b) references to "an appeal" or "the appeal" were references to "a defence" or "the defence";
- (c) references to "ground of appeal" were references to "ground of defence";
- (d) references to "the appellant" were references to "the respondent"; and
- (e) in rule 10(1), the reference to rule 9 were a reference to rule 15.

(8) The respondent shall send a copy of the defence and any accompanying documents to each other party at the same time as it files the defence.

INTERVENTION, CONSOLIDATION AND FORUM

[6.23]

16 Intervention

(1) Any person with sufficient interest in the outcome may make a request to the Tribunal for permission to intervene in the proceedings.

(2) The request shall be filed within the period referred to in rule 14(3)(f).

(3) The Registrar shall give notice of the request for permission to intervene to all the other parties to the proceedings and invite their observations on that request within a specified period.

(4) A request for permission to intervene shall state—

- (a) the title of the proceedings to which that request relates;
- (b) the name and address of the person wishing to intervene;
- (c) the name and address of its legal representative, if any; and
- (d) an address for service in the United Kingdom.

(5) The request shall contain—

- (a) a concise statement of the matters in issue in the proceedings which affect the person making the request;
- (b) the name of any party whose position the person making the request intends to support; and
- (c) a succinct presentation of the reasons for making the request.

(6) If the Tribunal is satisfied, having taken into account the observations of the parties, that the intervening party has a sufficient interest, it may permit the intervention on such terms and conditions as it thinks fit.

(7) On granting permission under paragraph (6), the Tribunal may any consequential directions it considers necessary with regard, in particular, to the service on the intervener of the documents lodged with the Registrar, the filing by the intervener of a statement of intervention and, if appropriate, the filing by the principal parties of a response to the statement of intervention and any objections to the admission of evidence put forward by the intervener.

(8) The statement of intervention shall contain—

- (a) a succinct presentation of the facts and arguments supporting the intervention;
- (b) the relief sought by the intervener;
- (c) a schedule listing all the documents annexed to the intervention; and
- (d) a statement identifying the evidence (whether witness statements or other documents annexed to the statement of intervention) the substance of which, so far as the intervener is aware, was not before the maker of the disputed decision.

(9) As far as practicable, there shall be annexed to the statement of intervention, a copy of every document (or part of a document) on which the intervener relies including the written statements of witnesses of fact and expert witnesses, if any, but excluding any document (or part of a document) annexed to the notice of appeal or defence.

(10) Rules 10(1), 11 (except paragraph (1)(a), (c) and (d)) and 12 apply to a statement of intervention as if—

- (a) references to "notice of appeal" were references to "statement of intervention";
- (b) references to "an appeal" or "the appeal" were references to "a statement of intervention" or "the statement of intervention";
- (c) references to "ground of appeal" were references to "ground of intervention";
- (d) references to "the appellant" were references to "the intervener"; and
- (e) in rule 10(1), the reference to rule 9 were a reference to rule 16.

(11) The intervener shall send a copy of the statement of intervention and any accompanying documents to each other party at the same time as it files the statement of intervention.

[6.24]
17 Consolidation

(1) Where two or more proceedings are pending in respect of the same decision, or which involve the same or similar issues, the Tribunal may, on the request of a party or of its own initiative, order that the proceedings or any particular issue or matter raised in the proceedings be consolidated.

(2) Before making an order under this rule, the Tribunal shall invite the parties to the relevant proceedings to submit their observations.

[6.25]
18 Forum

(1) The Tribunal, after taking into account the observations of the parties, may at any time determine whether any proceedings, or part of any proceedings, before it are to be treated, for all or for any purpose (including a purpose connected with any appeal from a decision of the Tribunal made in those proceedings) as proceedings in England and Wales, in Scotland or in Northern Ireland.

(2) Despite any determination under paragraph (1), the Tribunal may hold any meeting, case management conference, pre-hearing review or hearing, or give any directions, in such place and in such manner as it thinks fit having regard to the just, expeditious and economical conduct of the proceedings.

(3) In making a determination under paragraph (1), the Tribunal may have regard to all matters which appear to it to be relevant and in particular the part of the United Kingdom where—

(a) any individual party to the proceedings is habitually resident or has its head office or principal place of business;
(b) the majority of the parties are habitually resident or have their head offices or principal places of business;
(c) any agreement, decision or concerted practice to which the proceedings relate was made or implemented or intended to be implemented;
(d) any conduct to which the proceedings relate took place;
(e) in collective proceedings or proceedings concerning a collective settlement, the place where the class representative or settlement representative is habitually resident or has its head office or principal place of business.

(4) Without prejudice to paragraph (3), in making a determination under paragraph (1) for the purposes of a claim under section 47A (claims for damages etc) or section 47B (collective proceedings) of the 1998 Act, the Tribunal may have regard to the law which is applicable to the claim.

CASE MANAGEMENT

[6.26]
19 Directions

(1) The Tribunal may at any time, on the request of a party or of its own initiative, at a case management conference, pre-hearing review or otherwise, give such directions as are provided for in paragraph (2) or such other directions as it thinks fit to secure that the proceedings are dealt with justly and at proportionate cost.

(2) The Tribunal may give directions—

(a) as to the manner in which the proceedings are to be conducted, including any time limits to be observed in the conduct of the oral hearing;
(b) that the parties file a reply, rejoinder or other additional pleadings or particulars;
(c) for the preparation and exchange of skeleton arguments;
(d) requiring persons to attend and give evidence or to produce documents;
(e) requiring clarification of any matter in dispute or additional information in relation to any such matter;
(f) as to the evidence which may be required or admitted in proceedings before the Tribunal and the extent to which it must be oral or written;
(g) as to the submission in advance of a hearing of any witness statements or expert reports;
(h) as to the examination or cross-examination of witnesses;
(i) for the filing of a list of issues;
(j) for the production of bundles for any hearing;
(k) for the creation of a confidentiality ring;
(l) as to the fixing of time limits with respect to any aspect of the proceedings;
(m) as to the abridgement or extension of any time limits, whether or not expired;
(n) that the whole or part of any proceedings or judgment be stayed either generally or until a specified date or event;
(o) to enable a disputed decision to be referred back in whole or in part to the person by whom it was taken;
(p) for the disclosure and the production by a party or third party of documents or classes of documents;
(q) for the appointment and instruction of experts, whether by the Tribunal or by the parties and as to the manner in which expert evidence is to be given;
(r) for the costs management of proceedings, including for the provision of such schedules of incurred and estimated costs as the Tribunal thinks fit;
(s) for the award of costs or expenses, including any allowances payable to persons in connection with their attendance before the Tribunal;
(t) for the hearing of any issues as preliminary issues prior to the main substantive hearing; and
(u) for hearing a person who is not a party where, in any proceedings, it is proposed to make an order or give a direction in relation to that person.

(3) The Tribunal may also, of its own initiative—

(a) put questions to the parties;
(b) invite the parties to make written or oral submissions on certain aspects of the proceedings;

(c) ask the parties or third parties for information or particulars;
(d) ask for documents relating to the case to be produced;
(e) summon the parties' representatives or the parties in person to meetings.

(4) A request by a party for directions shall—
(a) be made in writing as soon as practicable;
(b) be supported by reasons and indicate whether it is agreed or contested by the other parties;
(c) be served on any other party who might be affected by such directions; and
(d) be determined by the Tribunal taking into account the observations of the parties.

[6.27]
20 Case management conference etc

(1) Where it appears to the Tribunal that any proceedings would be facilitated by holding a case management conference or pre-hearing review the Tribunal may, on the request of a party or of its own initiative, give directions for such a conference or review to be held.

(2) Unless the Tribunal otherwise directs, a case management conference is to be held as soon as practicable after the filing of an appeal, whether or not the time for service of the defence has expired.

(3) The purpose of a case management conference or pre-hearing review is—
(a) to ensure the efficient conduct of the proceedings;
(b) to determine the points on which the parties must present further argument or which call for further evidence to be produced;
(c) to set a timetable up to an oral hearing in the proceedings, and, if appropriate, fix a date for that hearing;
(d) to clarify the forms of order sought by the parties, their arguments of fact and law and the points at issue between them;
(e) to hear and determine any submissions in relation to the admission of evidence;
(f) to determine any issues relating to confidentiality;
(g) to ensure that all agreements that can be reached between the parties about the matters in issue and the conduct of the proceedings are made and recorded;
(h) to facilitate the settlement of the proceedings.

(4) The Tribunal may authorise the President or a chairman to carry out on its behalf a case management conference, pre-hearing review or any other preparatory measure relating to the organisation or disposal of the proceedings.

[6.28]
21 Evidence

(1) The Tribunal may give directions as to—
(a) the provision by the parties of statements of agreed matters;
(b) the issues on which it requires evidence, and the admission or exclusion from the proceedings of particular evidence;
(c) the nature of the evidence which it requires to decide those issues;
(d) whether the parties are permitted to provide expert evidence;
(e) any limit on the number of witnesses whose evidence a party may put forward, whether in relation to a particular issue or generally; and
(f) the way in which evidence is to be placed before the Tribunal.

(2) In deciding whether to admit or exclude evidence, the Tribunal shall have regard to whether it would be just and proportionate to admit or exclude the evidence, including by reference to the following factors—
(a) the statutory provision under which the appeal is brought and the applicable standard of review being applied by the Tribunal;
(b) whether or not the substance of the evidence was available to the respondent before the disputed decision was taken;
(c) where the substance of the evidence was not available to the respondent before the disputed decision was taken, the reason why the party seeking to adduce the evidence had not made it available to the respondent at that time;
(d) the prejudice that may be suffered by one or more parties if the evidence is admitted or excluded;
(e) whether the evidence is necessary for the Tribunal to determine the case.

(3) Unless the Tribunal otherwise directs, no witness of fact or expert witness maybe heard unless the relevant witness statement or expert report has been submitted in advance of the hearing and in accordance with any directions of the Tribunal.

(4) The Tribunal may require any witness to give evidence on oath or affirmation or if in writing by way of affidavit.

(5) The Tribunal may allow a witness to give evidence through a video link or by other means.

(6) The Tribunal may dispense with the need to call a witness to give oral evidence if a witness statement or expert report has been submitted in respect of that witness.

(7) The Tribunal may limit cross-examination of witnesses to any extent or in any manner it considers appropriate.

[6.29]
22 Summoning or citing of witnesses

(1) Subject to paragraphs (2) and (3), the Tribunal may, at any time, either of its own initiative or at the request of any party, issue a summons (or in relation to proceedings taking place in Scotland, a citation) in any form authorised by the Tribunal, requiring any person wherever that person may be in the United Kingdom to do one or both of the following—
(a) attend as a witness before the Tribunal, at the time and place set out in the summons or citation;

(b) answer any questions or produce any documents or other material in the possession or under the control of that person which relate to any matter in question in the proceedings.

(2) A request by a party for the issue of a summons or citation under this rule shall state with reasons—

(a) upon which facts the witness is to be questioned;

(b) the documents or material required to be produced.

(3) No person may be required to attend in compliance with a summons or citation under this rule unless that person—

(a) has been given at least seven days' notice of the hearing; and

(b) is offered or paid such sum as would be recoverable by that witness in respect of attendance in proceedings before the Senior Courts of England and Wales, the Court of Session or the Court of Judicature of Northern Ireland, as appropriate according to any determination of the Tribunal under rule 18.

(4) The Tribunal may make the summoning or citation of a witness in accordance with paragraph (1) conditional upon the deposit with the Registrar of a sum determined by the Tribunal as sufficient to cover—

(a) the costs of the summons or citation;

(b) the sum referred to in paragraph (3)(b).

(5) The Registrar shall advance the funds necessary in connection with the examination of any witness summoned by the Tribunal of its own initiative.

(6) The Tribunal may direct a party to serve on its behalf a summons issued under this rule and to pay the sum referred to in paragraph (3)(b).

[6.30]

23 Failure to comply with directions

(1) If any party fails to comply with any direction given in accordance with these Rules, the Tribunal may if it considers that the justice of the case so requires, order that—

(a) the requirements of the direction be waived;

(b) the failure be remedied;

(c) the party be debarred from taking any further part in the proceedings without the permission of the Tribunal;

(d) the party (or its representative) be subject to an order for any costs the Tribunal sees fit.

(2) Before making an order under paragraph (1)(c) or (d), the Tribunal shall give the party (or its representative) the opportunity to make submissions as to why the order should not be made.

INTERIM ORDERS AND MEASURES

[6.31]

24 Power to make interim orders and to take interim measures

(1) The Tribunal may make an order on an interim basis—

(a) suspending in whole or part the effect of any decision which is the subject matter of proceedings before it;

(b) in the case of an appeal under section 46 (appealable decisions) or 47 (third party appeals) of the 1998 Act, varying the conditions or obligations attached to an exemption;

(c) granting any remedy which the Tribunal would have the power to grant in its final decision.

(2) Without prejudice to the generality of paragraph (1), if the Tribunal considers that it is necessary as a matter of urgency for the purpose of—

(a) preventing significant damage to a particular person or category of person, or

(b) protecting the public interest,

the Tribunal may give such directions as it considers appropriate for that purpose.

(3) The Tribunal shall exercise its power under this rule taking into account all the relevant circumstances, including—

(a) the urgency of the matter;

(b) the effect on the party making the request if the relief sought is not granted;

(c) the effect on competition if the relief is granted; and

(d) the existence and adequacy of any offer of an undertaking as to damages.

(4) Any order or direction under this rule is subject to the Tribunal's further order, direction or final decision.

(5) A party shall apply for an order or a direction under paragraph (1) or (2) by filing a request for interim relief in the form required by paragraph (6).

(6) The request for interim relief shall state—

(a) the subject matter of the proceedings;

(b) in the case of a request for a direction under paragraph (2), the circumstances giving rise to the urgency;

(c) the factual and legal grounds establishing a prima facie case for the granting of interim relief by the Tribunal;

(d) the relief sought;

(e) where no appeal or application has been made in accordance with rule 9 in respect of the decision which is the subject of the request for interim relief, an outline of the information required by rule 9(4).

(7) The request for interim relief shall be verified by a statement of truth, signed and dated by the applicant or on its behalf by its duly authorised officer or legal representative.

(8) On receiving a request for interim relief the Registrar shall send a copy to all the other parties to the proceedings (or where no appeal or application has been made in accordance with rule 9, to the person who made the decision to which the request for interim relief relates) and shall inform them of the date by which they may submit written or oral observations to the Tribunal.

(9) Subject to paragraph (10), an order or direction for interim relief may be made against a person who is not a party to the proceedings, provided that no such order may be made unless that person has been given an opportunity to be heard.

(10) If the urgency of the case so requires, the Tribunal may grant the request for interim relief before the observations of the other parties have been submitted or the person referred to in paragraph (9) has been heard.

PART 3 PROCEEDINGS UNDER THE 2002 ACT

[6.32]

25 Time for commencing proceedings for a review under the 2002 Act

(1) An application under section 120(1) of the 2002 Act for the review of a decision in connection with a reference or possible reference in relation to a relevant merger situation or a special merger situation shall be made by filing a notice of application within four weeks of the date on which the applicant was notified of the disputed decision, or the date of publication of the decision, whichever is the earlier.

(2) An application under section 179(1) of the 2002 Act for review of a decision in connection with a reference or possible reference under Part 4 of that Act (market investigations) shall be made by filing a notice of application within two months of the date on which the applicant was notified of the disputed decision, or the date of publication of the decision, whichever is the earlier.

(3) The Tribunal may not extend the time limit provided under paragraph (1) or (2) unless it is satisfied that the circumstances are exceptional.

[6.33]

26 Supplementary provisions concerning reviews

(1) In proceedings for a review under section 120 or 179 of the 2002 Act rules 9 to 16 are to be construed and applied as if—

(a) references to "appeal" were references to "application";
(b) references to "the notice of appeal" were references to "the notice of application";
(c) references to the "appellant" were references to the "applicant";
(d) references to the "grounds of appeal" were references to the "grounds of review"; and
(e) the words "or expert witnesses" in rule 9(6)(b) were omitted.

(2) In proceedings for a review under section 120 of the 2002 Act, rule 15(1) applies with the substitution of "four weeks" for "six weeks".

(3) The Tribunal's power to strike out an appeal under rule 11 includes a power to strike out an application for review if it considers that the applicant is not a person aggrieved by the decision in respect of which the review is sought.

[6.34]

27 Expert evidence

If the applicant in proceedings for a review under section 120 or section 179 of the 2002 Act wishes to rely upon expert evidence that was not before the decision maker whose decision is the subject of the application, it shall serve with its application for review an application to adduce that evidence, attaching either the statement of expert evidence on which it wishes to rely or a detailed explanation of the nature of the expert evidence that it wishes to adduce.

[6.35]

28 Appeals in relation to penalties under section 114 of the 2002 Act

(1) An appeal against a penalty brought under section 114 of the 2002 Act (appeals in relation to penalties) shall be made by filing a notice of appeal within the period of 28 days starting with—

(a) in the case of an appeal against a penalty imposed under section 110(1) or (3) (enforcement of investigation powers under Part 3) or 174A(1) or (3) (enforcement of investigation powers under Part 4) of the 2002 Act, the day on which a copy of the notice of the penalty was served on the person concerned under section 112(1) of that Act (penalties: main procedural requirements);
(b) in the case of an appeal against a decision on an application under section 112(3) of the 2002 Act, the day on which the person concerned was notified of the decision.

(2) In an appeal against a penalty brought under section 114 of the 2002 Act, rule 15(1) applies with the substitution of "three weeks" for "six weeks".

(3) Rules 14(2) and 16 do not apply to appeals against penalties under section 114 of the 2002 Act.

PART 4 CLAIMS UNDER SECTION 47A OF THE 1998 ACT

[6.36]

29 Application of Rules to proceedings in Scotland

In respect of proceedings in Scotland, references in this Part to "claimant" and "defendant" are to be read respectively as references to "pursuer" and "defender".

COMMENCEMENT OF PROCEEDINGS

[6.37]

30 Manner of commencing proceedings under section 47A of the 1998 Act

(1) A claim under section 47A of the 1998 Act (proceedings before the Tribunal: claims for damages etc) shall be made by filing a claim form.

(2) The claim form shall state—

(a) the full name and address of the claimant;
(b) the full name and address of the claimant's legal representative, if any;

(c) an address for service in the United Kingdom; and
(d) the name and address of the defendant to the proceedings.

(3) The claim form shall contain—
(a) a statement as to whether the claim is in respect of an infringement decision, and if so, whether that decision has become final within the meaning of section 58A of the 1998 Act (infringement decisions);
(b) observations on the question in which part of the United Kingdom the proceedings of the Tribunal are to be treated as taking place under rule 18;
(c) a concise statement of the relevant facts, identifying, where applicable, any relevant findings in an infringement decision;
(d) a concise statement of any contentions of law which are relied on;
(e) the relief sought in the proceedings, including (where applicable)—
(i) an estimate of the amount claimed in damages, supported by an explanation of how that amount has been calculated;
(ii) details of any other claim for a sum of money;
(iii) in proceedings in England and Wales or Northern Ireland, a statement that the claimant is making a claim for an injunction;
(f) such other matters as may be specified by practice direction.

(4) The contents of the claim form shall be verified by a statement of truth signed and dated by the claimant or on its behalf by its duly authorised officer or legal representative.

(5) There shall be annexed to the claim form—
(a) a copy of any infringement decision referred to in paragraph (3)(a);
(b) copies of any documents referred to in the claim form;
(c) any application for the claim to be subject to the fast-track procedure under rule 58 supported by reasons for the application and cross-referenced to the claim form; and
(d) such other documents or annexes as may be specified by practice direction.

(6) Unless the Tribunal otherwise directs, the signed original of the claim form shall be accompanied by five copies of the form and its annexes certified by the claimant or its legal representative as conforming to the original.

(7) When filing the claim form the claimant shall also indicate the method by which the claimant (or the claimant's representative) proposes to effect service on the defendant and provide any other information with regard to service of the claim form as may be specified by practice direction.

[6.38]

31 Service out of the jurisdiction

(1) Where the claim form is to be served on one or more foreign defendants and the permission of the Tribunal is not required for service out of the jurisdiction, the claimant shall file with the claim form a notice verified by a statement of truth signed and dated by the claimant or on its behalf by its duly authorised officer or legal representative, setting out—
(a) the grounds on which the claimant is entitled to serve the claim form out of the jurisdiction; and
(b) any material facts relied on.

(2) Where the permission of the Tribunal is required for service of the claim form on one or more foreign defendants out of the jurisdiction, the claimant shall make an application for permission verified by a statement of truth setting out—
(a) the address of such foreign defendant or, if not known, in what place that defendant is, or is likely, to be found; and
(b) that the claimant believes that the claim against any such foreign defendant has a reasonable prospect of success; and
(c) if under rule 30(3)(b), the claimant contends that the proceedings are to be treated as taking place in England and Wales, which ground set out in paragraph 3.1 of Practice Direction 6B of the CPR is relied on; or
(d) if under rule 30(3)(b), the claimant contends that the proceedings are to be treated as taking place in Scotland, which ground set out in Schedule 8 of the Civil Jurisdiction and Judgments Act 1982 is relied on; or
(e) if under rule 30(3)(b), the claimant contends that the proceedings are to be treated as taking place in Northern Ireland, which ground set out in rule 1(1) of Order 11 of the Rules of the Court of Judicature (Northern Ireland) 1980 is relied on; and
(f) any material facts relied on.

(3) Where paragraph (2) applies, the Tribunal shall not give permission for service out of the jurisdiction unless satisfied that the Tribunal is the proper place in which to bring the claim.

[6.39]

32 Amendments to claim form

(1) A claim form may only be amended—
(a) with the written consent of all the parties; or
(b) with the permission of the Tribunal.

(2) Where any relevant period of limitation has expired, the Tribunal may permit an amendment—
(a) to add or substitute a new claim, but only if the new claim arises out of the same facts or substantially the same facts as a claim in respect of which the party applying for permission has already claimed a remedy in the proceedings;
(b) to correct a mistake as to the name of a party, but only where the mistake was genuine and not one which would cause reasonable doubt as to the identity of the party in question; or
(c) to alter the capacity in which a party claims, but only if the new capacity is one which that party had when the proceedings started or has since acquired.

RESPONSE TO A CLAIM

[6.40]

33 Acknowledgment, service and notification

(1) On receiving a claim the Registrar shall send an acknowledgment of receipt to the claimant and, except where paragraph (2) applies, shall direct that the claimant or its representative serve the claim form on the defendant.

(2) Where service of the claim form outside the jurisdiction requires the permission of the Tribunal in accordance with rule 31, the claim form shall be served on the defendant only if permission is granted.

(3) The Registrar's direction for service under paragraph (1) may specify any matter the Registrar may consider appropriate with regard to the service of the claim form, including—

- (a) the time within and the method by which service of the claim form is to be effected;
- (b) the documents that are to accompany the claim form, including an acknowledgment of service in the form required by the Tribunal;
- (c) the information to be provided to the Registrar by the claimant concerning the date of service and the calculation of the time limit for acknowledging service and filing a defence;
- (d) the provision of any other information that may be required by the Registrar (whether by way of certificate of service verified by a statement of truth, witness statement or otherwise) regarding the service of the claim form; and
- (e) the time within which any information required by the Registrar is to be provided.

(4) The defendant shall within seven days of receipt of the copy of the claim form file an acknowledgment of service of the claim in the form required by the Tribunal.

(5) Where the claim form is served on a foreign defendant, the period for acknowledging service set out in paragraph (4) is varied so as to accord with the period applicable under Part 6 of the CPR in relation to proceedings in England and Wales or the equivalent provisions in the equivalent procedural rules for Scotland or Northern Ireland in relation to proceedings taking place in Scotland or Northern Ireland respectively.

(6) The Registrar shall, as soon as practicable, notify the claimant of the receipt of an acknowledgment of service from a defendant.

(7) The claimant shall send a copy of the claim form to the CMA at the same time as it is served on the other parties to the claim.

(8) The Registrar shall publish a summary of the claim on the Tribunal website and in any other manner the President may direct.

[6.41]

34 Disputing the Tribunal's jurisdiction

(1) A defendant who wishes to—

- (a) dispute the Tribunal's jurisdiction to hear the claim; or
- (b) argue that the Tribunal should not exercise its jurisdiction,

may apply to the Tribunal for an order declaring that it has no such jurisdiction or should not exercise any jurisdiction which it might have.

(2) A defendant who wishes to make such an application shall first file an acknowledgment of service in accordance with rule 33.

(3) A defendant who files an acknowledgment of service does not by doing so lose any right it may have to dispute the Tribunal's jurisdiction and does not need to file a defence before the hearing of its application under this rule.

(4) An application under this rule shall—

- (a) be made within 14 days after filing an acknowledgment of service; and
- (b) be supported by evidence.

(5) If the defendant—

- (a) files an acknowledgment of service; and
- (b) does not make an application within the period specified in paragraph (4),

the defendant is to be treated as having accepted that the Tribunal has jurisdiction to hear the claim.

(6) An order containing a declaration that the Tribunal has no jurisdiction or will not exercise its jurisdiction may also make further provision as to the disposal or stay of the proceedings.

(7) If on an application under this rule the Tribunal does not make a declaration under paragraph (6), the Tribunal shall give directions regarding the future conduct of the proceedings.

[6.42]

35 Defence to a claim

(1) Subject to rule 34, within 28 days of service of the copy of the claim form the defendant shall file a defence—

- (a) setting out in sufficient detail which of the facts and contentions of law in the claim form the defendant admits or denies, on what grounds and on what other facts or contentions of law the defendant relies; and
- (b) containing observations on the question in which part of the United Kingdom the proceedings of the Tribunal are to be treated as taking place under rule 18.

(2) The contents of the defence shall be verified by a statement of truth signed and dated by the defendant or on its behalf by its duly authorised officer or legal representative.

(3) As far as practicable, there shall be annexed to the defence a copy of every document referred to in the defence (except where such documents have been annexed to the claim form).

(4) Unless the Tribunal otherwise directs, the signed original of the defence shall be accompanied by five copies of the defence and its annexes certified by the defendant or its legal representative as conforming to the original.

(5) The defendant shall serve a copy of the defence and any accompanying documents on each other party at the same time as it files the defence.

(6) The defendant shall send a copy of the defence to the CMA at the same time as it is served on the other parties to the claim.

(7) Where the claim form is served on a foreign defendant, the period for filing a defence set out in paragraph (1) is varied so as to accord with the period applicable under Part 6 of the CPR in relation to proceedings in England and Wales or the equivalent provisions in the equivalent procedural rules for Scotland or Northern Ireland in relation to proceedings taking place in Scotland or Northern Ireland respectively.

[6.43]
36 Reply to defence

(1) Within 21 days of receipt of the copy of the defence, the claimant may file a reply to the defence.

(2) The contents of the reply shall be verified by a statement of truth signed and dated by the claimant or on its behalf by its duly authorised officer or legal representative.

(3) If the claimant files a reply to the defence, it shall send a copy of the reply and any accompanying documents to each other party at the same time as it files the reply.

(4) The claimant shall send a copy of the reply to the CMA at the same time as it is served on the other parties to the claim.

[6.44]
37 Further pleadings

No further pleadings may be filed without the permission of the Tribunal.

ADDITIONAL PARTIES AND ADDITIONAL CLAIMS

[6.45]
38 Additional parties

(1) The Tribunal may grant permission to remove, add or substitute a party in the proceedings.

(2) An application for permission under this rule shall be served on the parties to the proceedings and may be made by—

(a) an existing party; or
(b) a person who wishes to become a party.

(3) The Tribunal may order any person to cease to be a party if it is not desirable for that person to be a party to the proceedings.

(4) Before the expiry of a relevant period of limitation, the Tribunal may order a person to be added as a new party if—

(a) it is desirable to add or substitute the new party so that the Tribunal can resolve the matters in dispute in the proceedings; or
(b) there is an issue involving the new party and an existing party that is connected to the matters in dispute in the proceedings, and it is desirable to add the new party so as to resolve that issue.

(5) Before the expiry of a relevant period of limitation, the Tribunal may order a new party to be substituted for an existing one if—

(a) the existing party's interest or liability has passed to the new party; and
(b) it is desirable to substitute the new party so that the court can resolve the matters in dispute in the proceedings.

(6) After the expiry of a relevant period of limitation, the Tribunal may add or substitute a party only if—

(a) that limitation period was current when the proceedings were started; and
(b) the addition or substitution is necessary.

(7) The addition or substitution of a new party, as the case may be, is necessary for the purpose of paragraph (6)(b) only if the Tribunal is satisfied that—

(a) the new party is to be substituted for a party who was named in the claim form by mistake;
(b) the claim cannot properly be carried on by or against the original party unless the new party is added or substituted as claimant or defendant; or
(c) the original party has died or had a bankruptcy order made against it and its interest or liability has passed to the new party.

[6.46]
39 Additional claims

(1) In this rule and rule 40 an "additional claim" means—

(a) a counterclaim by a defendant against the claimant or against the claimant and some other person;
(b) a claim by a defendant against any person (whether or not already a party) for contribution or indemnity or some other remedy; or
(c) where an additional claim has been made against a person who is not already a party, any claim made by that person against any other person (whether or not already a party).

(2) An additional claim is to be treated as if it were a claim for the purpose of these Rules.

(3) A defendant may make an additional claim under section 47A of the 1998 Act (other than a claim for contribution or indemnity falling within paragraph (4))—

(a) without the Tribunal's permission, if it files that claim with its defence; or
(b) at any other time, with the permission of the Tribunal.

(4) A defendant who has filed an acknowledgment of service or a defence, may make an additional claim for a contribution or indemnity against an existing party to the proceedings—

(a) without the Tribunal's permission, if it files that claim with its defence, or, if the additional claim is a claim against a party added to the claim later, within 28 days after that party files its defence; or
(b) at any other time, with the permission of the Tribunal.

[6.47]
40 Powers on receipt of an additional claim

(1) The Tribunal may—
(a) permit an additional claim to be made;
(b) dismiss an additional claim;
(c) require an additional claim to be dealt with separately from the claim by the claimant against the defendant;
(d) direct that the additional claim is transferred in accordance with rule 71.

(2) The matters to which the Tribunal may have regard in deciding whether to exercise any of its powers under paragraph (1) include—
(a) the connection between the additional claim and the claim made by the claimant against the defendant;
(b) whether the additional claimant is seeking substantially the same remedy which some other party is claiming from it;
(c) whether the additional claimant wants the Tribunal to decide any question connected with the subject matter of the proceedings—
(i) not only between existing parties but also between existing parties and a person not already a party; or
(ii) against an existing party not only in a capacity in which it is already a party but also in some further capacity.

(3) Where the Tribunal exercises any of its powers under paragraph (1), it may make further orders or give further directions as it thinks appropriate.

SUMMARY DISPOSAL

[6.48]
41 Power to strike out

(1) The Tribunal may, of its own initiative or on the application of a party, after giving the parties an opportunity to be heard, strike out in whole or in part a claim at any stage of the proceedings if—
(a) it considers that the Tribunal has no jurisdiction to hear or determine the claim;
(b) it considers that there are no reasonable grounds for making the claim;
(c) it is satisfied that the claimant has habitually and persistently and without any reasonable ground—
(i) instituted vexatious proceedings, whether against the same person or different persons; or
(ii) made vexatious applications in any proceedings; or
(d) the claimant fails to comply with any rule, practice direction issued under rule 115, or any order or direction of the Tribunal.

(2) When the Tribunal strikes out a claim it may make any other consequential order it considers appropriate.

[6.49]
42 Default judgment

(1) The Tribunal may of its own initiative or on the application of a party give default judgment without a hearing of the claim where—
(a) the defendant has not filed an acknowledgment of service;
(b) the defendant has not filed a defence to the claim or any part of the claim; or
(c) a counterclaim has been made under rule 39 and a defence to the counterclaim has not been filed,
and, in any of those cases, the relevant time for filing has expired.

(2) A default judgment may not be given if the defendant has made an application—
(a) disputing the Tribunal's jurisdiction under rule 34;
(b) to have the claim struck out under rule 41; or
(c) for summary judgment under rule 43,
and that application has not been disposed of.

(3) Where the claim form has been served on the defendant in accordance with the directions of the Registrar, the claimant may not obtain default judgment unless the claimant has complied with any directions concerning proof of service.

(4) A default judgment given under this rule shall be—
(a) such judgment as it appears to the Tribunal that the claimant is entitled to on the claim form;
(b) for an amount to be decided by the Tribunal as to damages, costs and interest or for such other relief to be decided by the Tribunal in accordance with any directions it may give for the determination of those matters.

(5) A default judgment may be given against one of two or more defendants and the claimant may proceed against the other defendants.

(6) The Tribunal may only give a default judgment against one of two or more defendants in accordance with paragraph (5) if it is satisfied that the claim against that defendant can be dealt with separately from the claim against the other defendants.

(7) The Tribunal shall set aside a default judgment if the judgment was wrongly entered because any of the conditions set out in paragraph (1) were not satisfied.

(8) In any other case, the Tribunal may set aside or vary a default judgment (and attach any conditions it may think fit) if—
(a) the defendant has a real prospect of defending the claim; or

(b) it appears to the Tribunal that there is some other good reason why—
(i) the judgment should be set aside or varied; or
(ii) the defendant should be allowed to defend the claim;

(9) In considering whether to set aside or vary a default judgment under paragraph (8)(b), the matters to which the Tribunal shall have regard include whether the person seeking to set aside the judgment made an application to do so promptly.

(10) Where—
(a) the claimant claimed a remedy in addition to damages;
(b) the claimant has abandoned its claim for that remedy in order to apply for default judgment; and
(c) the default judgment is set aside,
the abandoned claim is restored when the default judgment is set aside.

[6.50]
43 Summary judgment

(1) The Tribunal may of its own initiative or on the application of a party, after giving the parties an opportunity to be heard, give summary judgment against a claimant or defendant on the whole of a claim or on a particular issue if—
(a) it considers that—
(i) the claimant has no real prospect of succeeding on the claim or issue; or
(ii) the defendant has no real prospect of successfully defending the claim or issue; and
(b) there is no other compelling reason why the case or issue should be disposed of at a substantive hearing.

(2) The Tribunal may give any directions it considers appropriate for dealing with an application under this rule.

(3) Upon giving summary judgment, the Tribunal may make any consequential order it considers appropriate.

[6.51]
44 Withdrawal of the claim

(1) The claimant may withdraw its claim only—
(a) with the consent of the defendant; or
(b) with the permission of the Tribunal or, if no Tribunal has been constituted, the President.

(2) Where a claim is withdrawn, the Tribunal may make any consequential order it thinks fit.

OFFERS TO SETTLE

[6.52]
45 Settlement offers

(1) For the purposes of this rule and rules 46 to 49—
"Rule 45 Offer" means an offer to settle which is made in accordance with this rule; and
"relevant period" means—
(a) in the case of an offer made not less than 21 days before the main substantive hearing of the claim, the period specified under paragraph (3)(c) or such longer period as the parties agree; or
(b) in any other case, the period up to the end of the main substantive hearing of the claim.

(2) A Rule 45 Offer may be made at any time, including before the commencement of proceedings.

(3) A Rule 45 Offer shall—
(a) be in writing;
(b) state on its face that it is intended to be a Rule 45 Offer under these Rules;
(c) except where the Rule 45 Offer is made less than 21 days before the start of the substantive hearing of the claim, specify a period of not less than 21 days within which the defendant will be liable for the claimant's costs in accordance with rule 48 if the offer is accepted;
(d) state whether it relates to the whole of the claim, to part of it or to an issue that arises in it and, if so, to which part or issue;
(e) state whether it takes into account any counterclaim; and
(f) where it is made by some, but not all, of a number of defendants, state whether or not it is made in satisfaction of the claim against all defendants.

(4) A Rule 45 Offer which offers to pay or offers to accept a sum of money is to be treated as inclusive of all interest until—
(a) the date on which the period specified under paragraph (3)(c) expires; or
(b) where paragraph (3)(c) does not apply, a date 21 days after the date the Rule 45 Offer was made.

(5) A defendant's offer that includes an offer to pay all or part of the sum at a date later than 14 days following the date of acceptance is not to be treated as a Rule 45 Offer unless the claimant accepts the offer.

(6) A Rule 45 Offer is accepted by serving written notice of acceptance on the offeror.

(7) A Rule 45 Offer may—
(a) be accepted any time before the substantive hearing of the claim, unless it has already been withdrawn;
(b) only be accepted after the substantive hearing of the claim has started with the permission of the Tribunal.

(8) The fact that a Rule 45 Offer has been made shall not be communicated to the members of the Tribunal deciding the case until all questions of liability and the amount of money to be awarded have been agreed between the parties or determined by the Tribunal.

(9) Paragraph (8) does not apply where—
(a) the offeror and offeree agree in writing to that effect; or
(b) although the case has not been decided—
(i) any part of, or issue in, the case has been decided; and
(ii) the Rule 45 Offer relates only to parts or issues that have been decided.

(10) In a case to which paragraph (9)(b)(i) applies, the members of the Tribunal deciding the case may be told whether or not there are Rule 45 Offers other than those referred to in paragraph (9)(b)(ii), but must not be told the terms of any such other offers unless the offeror and offeree agree in writing to that effect.

(11) Where the claimant wishes to accept a Rule 45 Offer made by one or more, but not all, of a number of defendants—

(a) if the claimant alleges that the defendants are jointly and severally liable and the Rule 45 Offer states that it is in satisfaction of the claim against all defendants, the claimant may accept the Rule 45 Offer and the Tribunal shall then direct that the claim against the defendants who did not make the Rule 45 Offer be discontinued;

(b) if the claimant alleges that the defendants are jointly and severally liable and the Rule 45 Offer states that it is in satisfaction of the claim against those defendants making it, the claimant may—

(i) serve notice on the defendants making the Rule 45 Offer agreeing not to continue its claims against them in return for payment of the sum offered; and

(ii) continue with the claims against the other defendants;

(c) if the claimant alleges that the defendants are severally but not jointly liable, the claimant may—

(i) accept the Rule 45 Offer; and

(ii) continue with its claims against the other defendants;

(d) if the defendants are sued only jointly or in the alternative, the claimant may accept the Rule 45 Offer if—

(i) the claimant discontinues the claim against those defendants who have not made the Rule 45 Offer; and

(ii) those defendants give written consent to the acceptance of the Rule 45 Offer.

(12) Service of a notice under paragraph (11)(b)(i) is to be treated as acceptance of the Rule 45 Offer for the purposes of rules 47 to 49 and references in those rules to notice of acceptance are to be construed as including a reference to notice under paragraph (11)(b)(i).

(13) A Rule 45 Offer is to be treated as "without prejudice except as to costs".

(14) This rule does not preclude a party from making an offer to settle at any time or by any other means but, if not made in accordance with this rule, it shall not have the consequences specified in rules 48 and 49.

[6.53]

46 Clarification of a Rule 45 Offer

(1) The offeree may, within seven days of a Rule 45 Offer being made, request the offeror to clarify the offer.

(2) If the offeror does not give the clarification requested under paragraph (1) within seven days of receiving the request, the offeree may, unless the substantive hearing of the claim has started, apply for an order that the offeror do so.

(3) If the Tribunal makes an order under paragraph (2), it shall specify the date when the Rule 45 Offer is to be treated as having been made.

[6.54]

47 Withdrawing or changing a Rule 45 Offer

(1) A Rule 45 Offer may only be withdrawn, or its terms changed, if the offeree has not previously served notice of acceptance.

(2) The offeror withdraws the offer or changes its terms by serving written notice of the withdrawal or change of terms on the offeree.

(3) Subject to paragraph (1), after the expiry of the relevant period—

(a) the offeror may withdraw the Rule 45 Offer or change its terms without the permission of the Tribunal; or

(b) the Rule 45 Offer may be automatically withdrawn in accordance with its terms.

(4) Where the offeror changes the terms of a Rule 45 Offer to make it more advantageous to the offeree, such improved offer is to be treated, not as the withdrawal of the original Rule 45 Offer, but as the making of a new Rule 45 Offer on improved terms.

(5) Subject to paragraphs (1) and (6), if the offeror serves notice, before the expiry of the relevant period, of withdrawal of the Rule 45 Offer or change of its terms to be less advantageous to the offeree, that notice has effect on the expiry of the relevant period.

(6) If the offeree serves notice of acceptance of the original Rule 45 Offer before expiry of the relevant period but after the offeror has served a notice of withdrawal of that offer or change of its terms to be less advantageous to the offeree, that acceptance has effect unless the Tribunal gives permission for the original Rule 45 Offer to be withdrawn or its terms changed.

(7) The offeror shall apply for such permission—

(a) within seven days of the offeree's notice of acceptance; or

(b) if earlier, before the first day of the substantive hearing.

(8) On an application under paragraph (7), the Tribunal may give permission for the original Rule 45 Offer to be withdrawn or its terms changed if satisfied that there has been a change of circumstances since the making of the original Rule 45 Offer and that it is in the interests of justice to give permission.

[6.55]

48 Costs consequences of acceptance of a Rule 45 Offer

(1) Subject to paragraphs (4) and (5), where a Rule 45 Offer is accepted within the relevant period, the claimant is entitled to the relevant costs of the proceedings up to the date on which notice of acceptance of the Rule 45 Offer was served on the offeror.

(2) Subject to paragraph (4), where a Rule 45 Offer is accepted after the expiry of the relevant period, unless the parties have agreed the liability for costs or the Tribunal otherwise directs—

(a) the claimant is entitled to the relevant costs of the proceedings up to the date on which the relevant period expired; and

(b) the offeree is liable for the offeror's relevant costs for the period from the date of expiry of the relevant period to the date on which notice of acceptance was served on the offeror.

(3) The relevant costs for the purposes of paragraphs (1) and (2) are the costs related to the proceedings against the defendants making or accepting the Rule 45 Offer, except where rule 45(11)(a) applies when they are the costs of the proceedings against all defendants.

(4) Where—

(a) a Rule 45 Offer made less than 21 days before the start of the substantive hearing of the claim is accepted, or

(b) subject to paragraph (5), a Rule 45 Offer which does not relate to the whole of the claim is accepted at any time,

the Tribunal shall make an order as to costs unless the parties have agreed the liability for costs.

(5) Where—

(a) a defendant's Rule 45 Offer relates to part only of the claim; and

(b) at the time of serving notice of acceptance within the relevant period the claimant abandons the balance of the claim,

the claimant is only entitled to the costs of such part of the claim unless the Tribunal otherwise directs.

[6.56]

49 Costs consequences following judgment

(1) This rule applies where a Rule 45 Offer is not accepted and upon judgment being handed down—

(a) a claimant fails to obtain a judgment more advantageous than a defendant's Rule 45 Offer; or

(b) judgment against the defendant is at least as advantageous to the claimant as the proposals contained in a claimant's Rule 45 Offer.

(2) Where paragraph (1)(a) applies, the Tribunal shall, unless it considers it unjust to do so, order that any defendant who made the Rule 45 Offer, either alone or jointly with any other defendant, is entitled to—

(a) costs from the date on which the relevant period expired; and

(b) interest on those costs.

(3) Where paragraph (1)(b) applies, the Tribunal shall, unless it considers it unjust to do so, order that the claimant is entitled to—

(a) interest on the whole or part of any sum of money (excluding interest) awarded, at a rate not exceeding 10% above base rate for some or all of the period starting with the date on which the relevant period expired;

(b) costs on the indemnity basis from the date on which the relevant period expired;

(c) interest on those costs at a rate not exceeding 10% above base rate; and

(d) an additional amount to be determined by the Tribunal in accordance with CPR Rule 36.17(4)(d).

(4) In considering whether it would be unjust to make the orders referred to in paragraphs (1) and (2), the Tribunal shall take into account all the circumstances of the case including—

(a) the terms of any Rule 45 Offer;

(b) the stage in the proceedings when any Rule 45 Offer was made, including in particular how long before the substantive hearing of the claim started the offer was made;

(c) the information available to the parties to the Rule 45 Offer at the time when the Rule 45 Offer was made;

(d) the conduct of the parties to the Rule 45 Offer with regard to the giving or refusal to give information for the purposes of enabling the Rule 45 Offer to be made or evaluated; and

(e) whether the offer was a genuine attempt to settle the proceedings.

(5) Paragraphs (2) and (3) do not apply to a Rule 45 Offer—

(a) which has been withdrawn;

(b) which has been changed so that its terms are less advantageous to the offeree, where the offeree has beaten the less advantageous offer; or

(c) made less than 21 days before the substantive hearing of the claim, unless the Tribunal has abridged the relevant period.

INTERVENTION, CONSOLIDATION AND FORUM

[6.57]

50 Intervention

(1) Rule 16 (except paragraphs (2) and (8) to (10)) applies to claims falling within this Part.

(2) The CMA may submit written observations to the Tribunal on issues relating to the application of *Article 101 or 102 of the TFEU or* Chapter I or II of Part 1 of the 1998 Act and, with the permission of the Tribunal, submit oral observations to the Tribunal.

NOTES

Para (2): words in italics revoked by the Competition (Amendment etc) (EU Exit) Regulations 2019, SI 2019/93, reg 61, Sch 2, Pt 2, para 8, as from IP completion day (as defined in the European Union (Withdrawal Agreement) Act 2020, s 39) (for transitional provisions and savings in relation to the operation of the 2019 Regulations, see Sch 4 to those Regulations at **[7.69]** et seq and, in particular, Sch 4, Pts 3 and 7 to the 2019 Regulations at **[7.71]** and **[7.76]**).

[6.58]

51 Consolidation

Rule 17 applies to claims falling within this Part.

[6.59]
52 Forum

Rule 18 applies to claims falling within this Part.

CASE MANAGEMENT

[6.60]
53 Directions

(1) The Tribunal may at any time, on the request of a party or of its own initiative, at a case management conference, pre-hearing review or otherwise, give such directions as are provided for in paragraph (2) or such other directions as it thinks fit to secure that the proceedings are dealt with justly and at proportionate cost.

(2) The Tribunal may give directions—
- (a) as to the manner in which the proceedings are to be conducted, including any time limits to be observed in the conduct of the oral hearing;
- (b) that the parties file a rejoinder or other additional pleadings or particulars;
- (c) for the preparation and exchange of skeleton arguments;
- (d) requiring clarification of any matter in dispute or additional information in relation to any such matter;
- (e) for the appointment and instruction of experts, whether by the Tribunal or by the parties;
- (f) for the filing of a list of issues;
- (g) for the production of bundles for any hearing;
- (h) for the creation of a confidentiality ring;
- (i) as to the fixing of time limits with respect to any aspect of the proceedings;
- (j) as to the abridgement or extension of any time limits, whether or not expired;
- (k) that the whole or part of any proceedings or judgment be stayed either generally or until a specified date or event;
- (l) for the disclosure and the production by a party or third party of documents or classes of documents;
- (m) for the costs management of proceedings, including for the provision of such schedules of incurred and estimated costs as the Tribunal thinks fit;
- (n) for the award of costs or expenses, including any allowances payable to persons in connection with their attendance before the Tribunal;
- (o) for the hearing of any issues as preliminary issues prior to the main substantive hearing; and
- (p) for hearing a person who is not a party where, in any proceedings, it is proposed to make an order or give a direction in relation to that person.

(3) The Tribunal may also, of its own initiative—
- (a) put questions to the parties;
- (b) invite the parties to make written or oral submissions on certain aspects of the proceedings;
- (c) ask the parties or third parties for information or particulars;
- (d) ask for documents or any papers relating to the case to be produced;
- (e) summon the parties' representatives or the parties in person to meetings.

(4) A request by a party for directions shall—
- (a) be made in writing as soon as practicable;
- (b) be supported by reasons and indicate whether it is agreed or contested by the other parties;
- (c) be served on any other party who might be affected by such directions; and
- (d) be determined by the Tribunal taking into account the observations of the parties.

[6.61]
54 Case management conference etc

(1) Where it appears to the Tribunal that any proceedings would be facilitated by holding a case management conference or pre-hearing review the Tribunal may, on the request of a party or of its own initiative, give directions for such a conference or review to be held.

(2) Unless the Tribunal otherwise directs, a case management conference is to be held as soon as practicable after the service of the reply or the expiry of the time for the filing of the reply if none is served.

(3) The purpose of a first case management conference or pre-hearing review is to give directions for the efficient conduct of the proceedings including—
- (a) to set a timetable up to an oral hearing in the proceedings, and if appropriate fix a date for that hearing;
- (b) to clarify the forms of order sought by the parties, their arguments of fact and law and the points at issue between them;
- (c) to determine any issues relating to confidentiality;
- (d) to ensure that all agreements that can be reached between the parties about the matters in issue and the conduct of the proceedings are made and recorded;
- (e) to consider any issues relating to disclosure and the provision of a disclosure report and completed Electronic Documents Questionnaire in accordance with rule 60;
- (f) to facilitate the settlement of the proceedings; and
- (g) to determine whether the parties should be given permission to adduce expert evidence and, if so, to what extent.

(4) Where it appears to the Tribunal that any proceedings would be facilitated by holding a subsequent case management conference, the Tribunal may, on the request of a party or of its own initiative, give directions for such a conference to be held.

(5) The Tribunal may authorise the President or a chairman to carry out on its behalf a case management conference, pre-hearing review or any other preparatory measure relating to the organisation or disposal of the proceedings.

[6.62]

55 Evidence

(1) The Tribunal may give directions as to—

(a) the provision by the parties of statements of agreed matters;

(b) the issues on which it requires evidence, and the admission or exclusion from the proceedings of evidence;

(c) the nature of the evidence which it requires to decide those issues;

(d) whether the parties are permitted to provide expert evidence;

(e) any limit on the number of witnesses whose evidence a party may put forward, whether in relation to a particular issue or generally;

(f) the way in which evidence is to be placed before the Tribunal;

(g) the submission in advance of a hearing of any witness statements or expert reports;

(h) the examination or cross-examination of witnesses.

(2) Unless the Tribunal otherwise directs, no witness of fact or expert witness may be heard unless the relevant witness statement or expert report has been submitted in advance of the hearing and in accordance with any directions of the Tribunal under paragraph (1).

(3) The Tribunal may require any witness to give evidence on oath or affirmation or, if in writing, by way of affidavit.

(4) The Tribunal may allow a witness to give evidence through a video link or by other means.

(5) The Tribunal may dispense with the need to call a witness to give oral evidence if a witness statement or expert report has been submitted in respect of that witness.

(6) The Tribunal may limit cross-examination of witnesses to any extent or in any manner it considers appropriate.

[6.63]

56 Summoning or citing of witnesses

(1) Subject to paragraphs (2) and (3), the Tribunal may, at any time, at the request of any party, issue a summons (or in relation to proceedings taking place in Scotland, a citation) in any form, requiring any person wherever that person may be in the United Kingdom to do one or both of the following—

(a) attend as a witness before the Tribunal, at the time and place set out in the summons or citation;

(b) answer any questions or produce any documents or other material in the possession or under the control of that person which relate to any matter in question in the proceedings.

(2) A request by a party for the issue of a summons or citation under this rule shall state with reasons—

(a) upon which facts the witness is to be questioned; and

(b) the documents or material required to be produced.

(3) No person may be required to attend in compliance with a summons or citation under this rule unless the person—

(a) has been given at least seven days' notice of the hearing; and

(b) is offered or paid such sum as would be recoverable by that witness in respect of attendance in proceedings before the Senior Courts of England and Wales, the Court of Session or the Court of Judicature of Northern Ireland, as appropriate according to any determination of the Tribunal under rule 18.

(4) The Tribunal may make the summoning or citation of a witness in accordance with paragraph (1) conditional upon the deposit with the Registrar of a sum determined by the Tribunal as sufficient to cover—

(a) the costs of the summons or citation;

(b) the sum referred to in paragraph (3)(b).

(5) The Tribunal may direct a party to serve on its behalf a summons issued under this rule and pay the sum referred to in paragraph (3)(b).

[6.64]

57 Failure to comply with directions

(1) If any party fails to comply with any direction given in accordance with these Rules, the Tribunal may, if it considers that the justice of the case so requires, order that—

(a) the requirements of the direction be waived;

(b) the failure be remedied;

(c) such party be debarred from taking any further part in the proceedings without the permission of the Tribunal;

(d) such party (or its representative) be subject to an order for any costs the Tribunal sees fit.

(2) Before making an order under paragraph (1)(c) or (d), the Tribunal shall give the party (or its representative) the opportunity to make submissions as to why the order should not be made.

FAST-TRACK PROCEDURE

[6.65]

58 Fast-track procedure

(1) The Tribunal may, at any time, either of its own initiative or on the application of a party, make an order that particular proceedings be, or cease to be, subject to the fast-track procedure.

(2) Where the Tribunal has ordered that particular proceedings be subject to the fast-track procedure—

(a) the main substantive hearing is to be fixed to commence as soon as practicable and in any event within six months of an order of the Tribunal stating that the particular proceedings are to be subject to the fast-track procedure; and

(b) the amount of recoverable costs is to be capped at a level to be determined by the Tribunal.

(3) In deciding whether to make particular proceedings subject to the fast-track procedure the Tribunal shall take into account all matters it thinks fit, including—

(a) whether one or more of the parties is an individual or a micro, small or medium-sized enterprise within the meaning of Commission Recommendation No 361 (EC) of 2003 concerning the definition of micro, small and medium-sized enterprises;
(b) whether the time estimate for the main substantive hearing is three days or less;
(c) the complexity and novelty of the issues involved;
(d) whether any additional claims have been or will be made in accordance with rule 39;
(e) the number of witnesses involved (including expert witnesses, if any);
(f) the scale and nature of the documentary evidence involved;
(g) whether any disclosure is required and, if so, the likely extent of such disclosure; and
(h) the nature of the remedy being sought and, in respect of any claim for damages, the amount of any damages claimed.

SECURITY FOR COSTS

[6.66]
59 Security for costs

(1) A defendant to a claim may seek security for its costs of the proceedings.

(2) A request for security for costs shall be supported by written evidence.

(3) Where the Tribunal makes an order for security for costs, it shall—
(a) determine the amount of security; and
(b) direct—
(i) the manner in which, and
(ii) the time within which,
the security must be given.

(4) The Tribunal may make an order for security for costs under this rule if it is satisfied, having regard to all the circumstances of the case, that it is just to make such an order, and—
(a) one or more of the conditions in paragraph (5) or, as the case may be, paragraph (6) applies; or
(b) an enactment permits the Tribunal to require security for costs.

(5) Where a defendant seeks security for costs against the claimant, the conditions are that—
(a) the claimant is—
(i) resident out of the jurisdiction; *but*
(ii) not resident in a Brussels Contracting State, a State bound by the Lugano Convention or a Regulation State, as defined in section 1(3) of the Civil Jurisdiction and Judgments Act 1982;
(b) the claimant is a company or other body (whether incorporated in or outside the United Kingdom) and there is reason to believe that it will be unable to pay the defendant's costs if ordered to do so;
(c) the claimant has changed its address since the claim was commenced with a view to evading the consequences of the litigation;
(d) the claimant failed to give its address in the claim form, or gave an incorrect address in that form;
(e) the claimant is acting as a nominal claimant, other than under section 47B of the 1998 Act (collective proceedings), and there is reason to believe that it will be unable to pay the defendant's costs if ordered to do so;
(f) the claimant has been authorised to act as the class representative in collective proceedings under rule 78 and there is reason to believe that the claimant will be unable to pay the defendant's costs if ordered to do so;
(g) the claimant has taken steps in relation to its assets that would make it difficult to enforce an order for costs against it.

(6) Where a defendant seeks security for costs against someone other than the claimant, the conditions are that the person—
(a) has assigned the right to the claim to the claimant with a view to avoiding the possibility of a costs order being made against the person; or
(b) has contributed or agreed to contribute to the claimant's costs in return for a share of any money or property which the claimant may recover in the proceedings,
and is a person against whom a costs order may be made.

NOTES

Para (5): sub-para (a)(ii) and the preceding word were revoked by the Competition (Amendment etc) (EU Exit) Regulations 2019, SI 2019/93, reg 61, Sch 2, Pt 2, para 8, as from IP completion day (as defined in the European Union (Withdrawal Agreement) Act 2020, s 39) (for transitional provisions and savings in relation to the operation of the 2019 Regulations, see Sch 4 to those Regulations at **[7.69]** et seq and, in particular, Sch 4, Pts 3 and 7 to the 2019 Regulations at **[7.71]** and **[7.76]**).

DISCLOSURE

[6.67]
60 Disclosure by parties to the proceedings

(1) In this rule, and in rules 61 to 65—
(a) a party discloses a document by stating that the document exists or has existed;
(b) a "disclosure report" means a report verified by a statement of truth, which—
(i) describes briefly what documents exist or may exist that are or may be relevant to the matters in issue in the case;
(ii) describes where and with whom those documents are or may be located;
(iii) in the case of electronic documents, describes how those documents are stored;
(iv) estimates the broad range of costs that could be involved in giving disclosure in the case, including the costs of searching for and disclosing any electronically stored documents; and

(v) states which directions are to be sought regarding disclosure;

(c) an "Electronic Documents Questionnaire" means a questionnaire in the form of the questionnaire in the Schedule to Practice Direction 31B of the CPR.

(2) Subject to paragraph (3) and unless the Tribunal otherwise thinks fit—

(a) at the first case management conference, the Tribunal shall decide whether and when the disclosure report and a completed Electronic Documents Questionnaire should be filed; and

(b) at a subsequent case management conference, the Tribunal shall decide, having regard to the governing principles and the need to limit disclosure to that which is necessary to deal with the case justly, what orders to make in relation to disclosure.

(3) The Tribunal may at any point give directions as to how disclosure is to be given, and in particular—

(a) what searches are to be undertaken, of where, for what, in respect of which time periods and by whom and the extent of any search for electronically stored documents;

(b) whether lists of documents are required;

(c) in what format documents are to be disclosed (and whether any identification is required);

(d) what is required in relation to documents that once existed but no longer exist; and

(e) whether disclosure is to take place in stages.

(4) A party's duty to disclose documents is limited to documents which are or have been in its control; and for this purpose, a party has or has had a document in its control if—

(a) the document is or was in its physical possession;

(b) it has or has had a right to possession of the document; or

(c) it has or has had a right to inspect or take copies of the document.

(5) A party need not disclose more than one copy of a document, and for that purpose a copy of a document that contains a modification, obliteration or other marking or feature is to be treated as a separate document.

(6) Any duty of disclosure continues until the proceedings are concluded.

(7) If documents to which such a duty extends come to a party's notice at any time during the proceedings, it shall immediately notify every other party.

[6.68]

61 Documents referred to in statements of case etc

A party may request disclosure of any document mentioned in—

(a) a claim form, defence, or reply to a defence;

(b) a witness statement or affidavit; or

(c) an expert report, except that any instructions referred to in an expert's report shall not (unless the party serving the report consents) be disclosed without an order of the Tribunal.

[6.69]

62 Disclosure before proceedings start

(1) This rule applies where an application is made to the Tribunal for disclosure before proceedings have started.

(2) The application shall be supported by evidence.

(3) The Tribunal may make an order under this rule only where—

(a) the respondent, or an associated body corporate (as defined in section 256 of the Companies Act 2006), is likely to be a party to subsequent proceedings;

(b) the applicant is also likely to be a party to those proceedings;

(c) disclosure before proceedings have started is desirable in order to—

(i) dispose fairly of the anticipated proceedings;

(ii) assist the dispute to be resolved without proceedings; or

(iii) save costs; and

(d) the Tribunal would, if proceedings had started, have ordered disclosure under rule 60.

(4) An order under this rule shall—

(a) specify the documents or the classes of documents which the respondent shall disclose; and

(b) require the respondent, when making disclosure, to specify any of those documents—

(i) which are no longer in its control; or

(ii) in respect of which it claims a right or duty to withhold disclosure.

(5) Such an order may—

(a) require the respondent to indicate what has happened to any documents which are no longer in its control; and

(b) specify the time and place for disclosure.

[6.70]

63 Orders for disclosure against a person not a party

(1) This rule applies where an application is made to the Tribunal by a party for disclosure by a person who is not a party to the proceedings.

(2) The application shall be supported by evidence.

(3) The Tribunal may make an order under this rule only where—

(a) the documents of which disclosure is sought are likely to support the case of the applicant or adversely affect the case of one of the other parties to the proceedings; and

(b) disclosure is necessary in order to dispose fairly of the claim or to save costs.

(4) An order under this rule shall—

(a) specify the documents or the classes of documents which the respondent must disclose; and

(b) require the respondent, when making disclosure, to specify any of those documents—

(i) which are no longer in its control; or
(ii) in respect of which it claims a right or duty to withhold inspection.

(5) Such an order may—
(a) require the respondent to indicate what has happened to any documents which are no longer in its control; and
(b) specify the time and place for disclosure.

[6.71]
64 Claim to withhold inspection or disclosure of a document

(1) A person may apply, without notice, for an order permitting that person to withhold disclosure of a document on the ground that disclosure would damage the public interest.

(2) Unless the Tribunal orders otherwise, an order of the Tribunal under paragraph (1)—
(a) shall not be served on any other person; and
(b) shall not be open to inspection by any person.

(3) A person who wishes to claim a right or a duty to withhold inspection of a document, or part of a document, shall state in writing—
(a) that that person is claiming such a right or duty; and
(b) the grounds on which that person claims that right or duty.

(4) The statement referred to in paragraph (3) shall be made—
(a) in the list in which the document is disclosed; or
(b) if there is no list, to the person wishing to inspect the document.

(5) A party may apply to the Tribunal to decide whether a claim made under paragraph (3) should be upheld.

(6) For the purpose of deciding an application under paragraph (1) or paragraph (5) the Tribunal may—
(a) require the person seeking to withhold disclosure or inspection of a document to produce that document to the Tribunal;
(b) invite any person, whether or not a party, to make representations; and
(c) give any directions it considers appropriate.

(7) An application under paragraph (1) or paragraph (5) shall be supported by evidence.

(8) This rule does not affect any rule of law which permits or requires a document to be withheld from disclosure or inspection on the ground that its disclosure or inspection would damage the public interest.

[6.72]
65 Restriction on use of a privileged document inspection of which has been inadvertently allowed

Where a party inadvertently discloses a privileged document, the party who has seen the document may use it or its contents only with the permission of the Tribunal.

INTERIM PAYMENTS

[6.73]
66 Interim payments on claims

(1) An interim payment is an order for payment by the defendant (in one sum or in instalments) on account of any damages or other sum of money (except costs) which the Tribunal may hold the defendant liable to pay.

(2) The claimant may not apply for an order for an interim payment before the end of the period for filing a defence by the defendant against whom the claim is made.

(3) The claimant may make more than one application for an order for an interim payment.

(4) The Tribunal may make an interim payment order if—
(a) the defendant against whom the order is sought has admitted liability to pay damages to the claimant;
(b) the claimant has obtained judgment against that defendant for damages to be assessed or for a sum of money (other than costs) to be assessed; or
(c) it is satisfied that, if the claim were to be heard, the claimant would obtain judgment for a substantial amount of money (other than costs) against that defendant.

(5) The Tribunal shall not order an interim payment of more than a reasonable proportion of the likely amount of the final judgment.

(6) An application for an interim payment shall be supported by evidence and include—
(a) the grounds on which an interim payment is sought; and
(b) any directions necessary in the opinion of the claimant for the determination of the application.

(7) On receiving an application for an interim payment the Registrar shall send a copy to all the other parties to the proceedings and shall inform them of the date by which they may submit written or oral observations to the Tribunal.

INJUNCTIONS

[6.74]
67 Injunctions generally

(1) This rule and rules 68 to 70 do not apply to proceedings in Scotland.

(2) The Tribunal may by order (whether interim or final) grant an injunction in all cases in which it appears to the Tribunal to be just and convenient to do so.

(3) Any such order may be made either unconditionally or on such terms and conditions as the Tribunal thinks just.

[6.75]
68 Interim injunctions

(1) An order for an interim injunction may be made at any time, including—

(a) before proceedings are started; and
(b) after judgment has been given.

(2) The Tribunal may grant an interim remedy whether or not there has been a claim for a final remedy of that kind.

(3) The Tribunal may grant an interim injunction before proceedings are started only if—
(a) the matter is urgent; or
(b) it is otherwise necessary to do so in the interests of justice.

(4) Where it grants an interim remedy before proceedings are started, the Tribunal may give directions requiring a claim to be commenced.

(5) In proceedings subject to the fast-track procedure in accordance with rule 58, the Tribunal may grant an interim injunction—
(a) without requiring the applicant to provide an undertaking as to damages; or
(b) subject to a cap on the amount of the undertaking as to damages.

[6.76]
69 How to apply for an interim remedy

(1) The Tribunal may grant an interim remedy on an application made without notice if it appears to the Tribunal that there are good reasons for not giving notice.

(2) An application for an interim remedy shall be supported by evidence, unless the Tribunal orders otherwise.

(3) The evidence in support of the application shall—
(a) include all material information regarding the applicant's ability to pay under any undertaking as to damages that the Tribunal may require to be given; and
(b) if the application is made without notice, state the reasons why notice has not been given.

[6.77]
70 Enforcement

(1) After the granting of an injunction by the Tribunal, if a party contends that the party subject to the injunction has failed to comply, the party so contending may apply to the Tribunal for certification of the matter to the High Court in accordance with paragraph 1A of Schedule 4 to the 2002 Act (Tribunal: procedure).

(2) Any evidence relied on in an application made under paragraph (1) shall be served on all other parties to the proceedings.

(3) The Tribunal may, after giving the parties an opportunity to be heard, make any directions as it thinks fit for determining whether to certify the matter to the High Court.

TRANSFERS

[6.78]
71 Transfer of claims from the Tribunal

The Tribunal may, at any stage of the proceedings, on the request of a party or of its own initiative, and after considering any observations of the parties, direct that all or part of a claim made in proceedings brought under section 47A of the 1998 Act (proceedings before the Tribunal: claims for damages etc) be transferred to—
(a) the High Court or the county court in England and Wales or Northern Ireland; or
(b) the Court of Session or the Sheriff Court in Scotland.

[6.79]
72 Transfer of claims to the Tribunal

(1) This rule applies where any court has ordered the transfer to the Tribunal of all or part of any proceedings.

(2) The person bringing the claim shall within seven days of the order of the court transferring the claim or such other period directed by that court, file—
(a) a certified copy of the order of the court transferring the claim to the Tribunal;
(b) any pleadings and documents in support of the claim filed with the court in which the claim was begun; and
(c) any directions sought for the further progress of the claim.

(3) As soon as practicable after receipt of the documents referred to in paragraph (2) a case management conference shall be held in accordance with rule 54.

PART 5 COLLECTIVE PROCEEDINGS AND COLLECTIVE SETTLEMENTS

[6.80]
73 Scope and interpretation

(1) The rules in this Part apply to collective proceedings and collective settlement.

(2) In this Part—

"aggregate award of damages" means an award of damages made by the Tribunal in collective proceedings without undertaking an assessment of the amount of damages recoverable in respect of each represented person;

"class member" means a person falling within the class described in the collective proceedings order, or a collective settlement order, as the case may be;

"collective proceedings order" means an order made by the Tribunal authorising the continuance of collective proceedings;

"collective settlement approval order" means an order of the Tribunal approving a proposed collective settlement;

"common issues" means the same, similar or related issues of fact or law;

"domicile date" means the date specified in a collective proceedings order or collective settlement order for the purposes of determining whether a person is domiciled in the United Kingdom;

"opt-in collective proceedings" has the meaning given in section 47B(10) of the 1998 Act;

Part 6 UK and EU Court Materials

"opt-out collective proceedings" has the meaning given in section 47B(11) of the 1998 Act; "proposed class representative" means a person who proposes to be a class representative by applying to the Tribunal to be a class representative; and

"represented person" means a class member who, in accordance with rule 82—

(a) has opted in to opt-in collective proceedings;

(b) was domiciled in the United Kingdom on the domicile date and has not opted out of opt-out collective proceedings; or

(c) has opted in to opt-out collective proceedings.

[6.81]

74 General

(1) Part 4 of these Rules applies to collective proceedings in accordance with this rule—

(2) References in Part 4 to "claim form" and "claimant" are to be read respectively as "collective proceedings claim form" and "class representative".

(3) The following rules do not apply to collective proceedings—

(a) rule 30 (manner of commencing proceedings under section 47A of the 1998 Act);

(b) rule 33 (acknowledgment, service and notification);

(c) rule 45 (settlement offers);

(d) rule 58 (fast-track procedure);

(e) rule 71 (transfer of claims from the Tribunal);

(f) rule 72 (transfer of claims to the Tribunal).

(4) The following rules apply to collective proceedings with the following modifications—

(a) rule 35 (defence to a claim): the time limit for the filing of the defence in rule 35(1) does not apply;

(b) rule 36 (reply to defence): the time limit for the filing of the reply in rule 36(1) does not apply;

(c) rule 42 (default judgment): default judgment may only be given in collective proceedings after the Tribunal has made a collective proceedings order in accordance with rule 80;

(d) rule 54 (case management conference): references to the first case management conference are to be read as referring to the first case management conference after the Tribunal has made a collective proceedings order in accordance with rule 80;

(e) rule 60 (disclosure by parties to the proceedings): references to the first case management conference are to be read as referring to the first case management conference after the Tribunal has made a collective proceedings order in accordance with rule 80;

(5) Rule 44 (withdrawal) applies to collective proceedings, in accordance with rules 86 (individual settlement by the class representative) and 87 (applications for withdrawal by the class representative);

(6) A collective proceedings order and a collective settlement order may be limited to only some parts or issues in the claims to which it relates.

COLLECTIVE PROCEEDINGS

[6.82]

75 Manner of commencing proceedings under section 47B of the 1998 Act

(1) An application to commence collective proceedings shall be made by the proposed class representative filing a collective proceedings claim form.

(2) The collective proceedings claim form shall state—

(a) the full name and address of the proposed class representative;

(b) the full name and address of the proposed class representative's legal representative;

(c) an address for service in the United Kingdom;

(d) the name and address of each defendant to the proceedings;

(e) that the proposed class representative is making an application for a collective proceedings order;

(f) whether the application relates to proposed opt-in collective proceedings or opt-out collective proceedings;

(g) whether the parties have used an alternative dispute resolution procedure; and

(h) that the proposed class representative believes that the claims which it is sought to combine in the collective proceedings have a real prospect of success.

(3) The collective proceedings claim form shall contain—

(a) description of the proposed class;

(b) a description of any possible sub-class and how it is proposed that their interests may be represented;

(c) an estimate of the number of class and any sub-class members and the basis for that estimate;

(d) a summary of the basis on which the proposed class representative seeks to be authorised to act in that capacity in accordance with rule 78;

(e) a summary of the basis on which it is contended that the criteria for certification and approval in rule 79 are satisfied;

(f) a statement as to whether the claims are in respect of an infringement decision, and if so whether that decision has become final within the meaning of section 58A of the 1998 Act (infringement decisions);

(g) a concise statement of the relevant facts, identifying, where applicable, any relevant findings in an infringement decision;

(h) a concise statement of any contentions of law which are relied on;

(i) the relief sought in the proceedings including—

(i) where applicable, an estimate of the amount claimed in damages, including whether an aggregate award of damages is sought, supported by an explanation of how that amount has been calculated;

(ii) details of any other claim for a sum of money;

(iii) in proceedings in England and Wales or Northern Ireland, whether the proposed class representative is making an application for an injunction;

(j) observations on the question in which part of the United Kingdom the proceedings are to be treated as taking place under rule 18; and

such other matters as may be specified by practice direction.

(4) The contents of the collective proceedings claim form shall be verified by a statement of truth signed and dated by the proposed class representative or on its behalf by its duly authorised officer or legal representative.

(5) There shall be annexed to the collective proceedings claim form—

(a) a copy of any infringement decision referred to in paragraph (4)(f) and any other document referred to in the collective proceedings claim form;

(b) a draft collective proceedings order; and

(c) a draft of the notice referred to in rule 81.

(6) Unless the Tribunal otherwise directs, the signed original of the collective proceedings claim form shall be accompanied by five copies of the form and its annexes certified by the proposed class representative or its legal representative as conforming to the originals.

(7) When filing the collective proceedings claim form, the proposed class representative shall also indicate the method by which it proposes to effect service on the defendant and provide any other information with regard to service of the collective proceedings claim form as may be specified by practice direction.

[6.83]

76 Response to a collective proceedings claim form

(1) On receiving a collective proceedings claim form, the Registrar shall send an acknowledgment of receipt to the proposed class representative and, except where paragraph (2) applies, direct that the proposed class representative serve the collective proceedings claim form on the defendant.

(2) Where service of the collective proceedings claim form outside the jurisdiction requires the permission of the Tribunal in accordance with rule 31, the collective proceedings claim form may be served on the defendant only if permission is granted.

(3) The Registrar's direction for service under paragraph (1) may specify any matter the Registrar may consider appropriate with regard to the service of the collective proceedings claim form, including—

(a) the time within and the method by which service of the collective proceedings claim form is to be effected;

(b) the documents that are to accompany the collective proceedings claim form including the acknowledgment of service in the form required by the Tribunal;

(c) the information to be provided to the Registrar by the proposed class representative concerning the date of service and the calculation of the time limit for acknowledging service; and

(d) the provision of any other information that may be required by the Registrar (whether by way of certificate of service, verified by a statement of truth, witness statement or otherwise) regarding the service of the collective proceedings claim form and;

(e) the time within which any information required by the Registrar is to be provided.

(4) Where the collective proceedings claim form is served on a defendant domiciled in the United Kingdom, the defendant shall within seven days of receipt of the copy of the collective proceedings claim form file an acknowledgment of service of the claim in the form provided by the Registrar.

(5) Where the collective proceedings claim form is served on a foreign defendant, the period for acknowledging service set out in paragraph (4) shall be varied so as to accord with the period applicable under Part 6 of the CPR in relation to proceedings in England and Wales or the equivalent provisions in the equivalent procedural rules for Scotland or Northern Ireland in relation to proceedings taking place in Scotland or Northern Ireland respectively.

(6) The proposed class representative shall send a copy of the collective proceedings claim form to the CMA at the same time as it is served on the other parties to the claim.

(7) The Registrar shall as soon as practicable notify the proposed class representative of the receipt of an acknowledgment of service from the defendant.

(8) The Registrar shall publish a summary of the collective proceedings claim form on the Tribunal website and in any other manner the President may direct.

(9) As soon as practicable, the Tribunal shall hold a case management conference to give directions in relation to the application for a collective proceedings order.

(10) The Tribunal may give directions—

(a) as regards any question concerning service out of the jurisdiction;

(b) as to the time by which the defendant shall respond to the application for a collective proceedings order;

(c) as to the time by which any person with an interest (including any class member) may object to the application for a collective proceedings order or the authorisation of the proposed class representative;

(d) regarding the hearing of the application; or

(e) as to a stay of proceedings while the parties attempt to compromise the proceedings by alternative dispute resolution or other means.

(11) Subject to any directions of the Tribunal, the defendant does not need to file a defence before the hearing of the application for a collective proceedings order.

(12) A defendant who opposes an application for a collective proceedings order does not, by doing so, lose any right that the defendant may have to dispute the Tribunal's jurisdiction.

[6.84]

77 Determination of the application for a collective proceedings order

(1) The Tribunal may make a collective proceedings order, after hearing the parties, only—

(a) if it considers that the proposed class representative is a person who, if the order were made, the Tribunal could authorise to act as the class representative in those proceedings in accordance with rule 78; and
(b) in respect of claims or specified parts of claims which are eligible for inclusion in collective proceedings in accordance with rule 79.

(2) If the Tribunal makes a collective proceedings order it may attach such conditions to the order or give such directions as it thinks fit, including—
(a) directions for filing and service of the order, pleadings and any other document in relation to the collective proceedings; and
(b) directions regarding any class member who is a child or person who lacks capacity.

[6.85]
78 Authorisation of the class representative

(1) The Tribunal may authorise an applicant to act as the class representative—
(a) whether or not the applicant is a class member, but
(b) only if the Tribunal considers that it is just and reasonable for the applicant to act as a class representative in the collective proceedings.

(2) In determining whether it is just and reasonable for the applicant to act as the class representative, the Tribunal shall consider whether that person—
(a) would fairly and adequately act in the interests of the class members;
(b) does not have, in relation to the common issues for the class members, a material interest that is in conflict with the interests of class members;
(c) if there is more than one applicant seeking approval to act as the class representative in respect of the same claims, would be the most suitable;
(d) will be able to pay the defendant's recoverable costs if ordered to do so; and
(e) where an interim injunction is sought, will be able to satisfy any undertaking as to damages required by the Tribunal.

(3) In determining whether the proposed class representative would act fairly and adequately in the interests of the class members for the purposes of paragraph (2)(a), the Tribunal shall take into account all the circumstances, including—
(a) whether the proposed class representative is a member of the class, and if so, its suitability to manage the proceedings;
(b) if the proposed class representative is not a member of the class, whether it is a pre-existing body and the nature and functions of that body;
(c) whether the proposed class representative has prepared a plan for the collective proceedings that satisfactorily includes—
 (i) a method for bringing the proceedings on behalf of represented persons and for notifying represented persons of the progress of the proceedings; and
 (ii) a procedure for governance and consultation which takes into account the size and nature of the class; and
 (iii) any estimate of and details of arrangements as to costs, fees or disbursements which the Tribunal orders that the proposed class representative shall provide.

(4) If the represented persons include a sub-class of persons whose claims raise common issues that are not shared by all the represented persons, the Tribunal may authorise a person who satisfies the criteria for approval in paragraph (1) to act as the class representative for that sub-class.

[6.86]
79 Certification of the claims as eligible for inclusion in collective proceedings

(1) The Tribunal may certify claims as eligible for inclusion in collective proceedings where, having regard to all the circumstances, it is satisfied by the proposed class representative that the claims sought to be included in the collective proceedings—
(a) are brought on behalf of an identifiable class of persons;
(b) raise common issues; and
(c) are suitable to be brought in collective proceedings.

(2) In determining whether the claims are suitable to be brought in collective proceedings for the purposes of paragraph (1)(c), the Tribunal shall take into account all matters it thinks fit, including—
(a) whether collective proceedings are an appropriate means for the fair and efficient resolution of the common issues;
(b) the costs and the benefits of continuing the collective proceedings;
(c) whether any separate proceedings making claims of the same or a similar nature have already been commenced by members of the class;
(d) the size and the nature of the class;
(e) whether it is possible to determine in respect of any person whether that person is or is not a member of the class;
(f) whether the claims are suitable for an aggregate award of damages; and
(g) the availability of alternative dispute resolution and any other means of resolving the dispute, including the availability of redress through voluntary schemes whether approved by the CMA under section 49C of the 1998 Act or otherwise.

(3) In determining whether collective proceedings should be opt-in or opt-out proceedings, the Tribunal may take into account all matters it thinks fit, including the following matters additional to those set out in paragraph (2)—
(a) the strength of the claims; and

(b) whether it is practicable for the proceedings to be brought as opt-in collective proceedings, having regard to all the circumstances, including the estimated amount of damages that individual class members may recover.

(4) At the hearing of the application for a collective proceedings order, the Tribunal may hear any application by the defendant—

(a) under rule 41(1), to strike out in whole or part any or all of the claims sought to be included in the collective proceedings; or

(b) under rule 43(1), for summary judgment.

(5) Any member of the proposed class may apply to make submissions either in writing or orally at the hearing of the application for a collective proceedings order.

[6.87]

80 The collective proceedings order

(1) A collective proceedings order shall authorise the class representative to act as such in continuing the collective proceedings and shall—

(a) state the name and address for service of the class representative or, where there are sub-classes, representatives;

(b) state the name of each defendant;

(c) describe or otherwise identify the class and any sub-classes;

(d) describe or otherwise identify the claims certified for inclusion in the collective proceedings;

(e) state the remedy sought;

(f) state whether the collective proceedings are opt-in or opt-out collective proceedings;

(g) specify the domicile date;

(h) specify the time and the manner by which—

(i) in the case of opt-in collective proceedings, a class member may opt in;

(ii) in the case of opt-out collective proceedings, a class member who is domiciled in the United Kingdom on the domicile date may opt out; and

(iii) in the case of opt-out collective proceedings, a class member who is not domiciled in the United Kingdom on the domicile date may opt in;

(i) order the publication of a notice to class members in accordance with rule 81; and

(j) specify the part of the United Kingdom in which the collective proceedings are to be treated as taking place.

(2) In describing or otherwise identifying the class for the purposes of paragraph (1)(c), it is not necessary for the order to name or specify the number of the class members.

[6.88]

81 Notice of the collective proceedings order

(1) The class representative shall give notice of the collective proceedings order to class members in a form and manner approved by the Tribunal.

(2) The notice referred to in paragraph (1) shall—

(a) incorporate or have annexed to it the collective proceedings order;

(b) identify each defendant;

(c) contain a summary in easily understood language of the collective proceedings claim form and the common issues;

(d) include a statement explaining that any judgment on the common issues for the class members or any sub-class will bind represented persons in the class, or those within the sub-class;

(e) draw attention to the provisions of the order setting out what a class member is required to do and by what date so as to opt into or opt out of the collective proceedings and

(f) give such other information as the Tribunal directs.

[6.89]

82 Opting in and opting out of collective proceedings

(1) A class member may on or before the time and in the manner specified in the collective proceedings order—

(a) in the case of opt-in collective proceedings, opt into the collective proceedings; or

(b) in the case of opt-out collective proceedings, either—

(i) opt out of the collective proceedings; or

(ii) if not domiciled in the United Kingdom at the domicile date, opt into the collective proceedings.

(2) A class member who does not opt in or opt out in accordance with paragraph (1) may not do so without the permission of the Tribunal.

(3) In considering whether to grant permission under paragraph (2), the Tribunal shall consider all of the circumstances, including in particular—

(a) whether the delay was caused by the fault of that class member; and

(b) whether the defendant would suffer substantial prejudice if permission were granted.

(4) A class member who has already brought a claim that raises one or more of the common issues set out in the collective proceedings order may not be a represented person unless the class member:

(a) discontinues the claim, or;

(b) for claims brought in England, Wales or Northern Ireland, applies to stay that claim, or;

(c) for claims brought in Scotland, applies to sist that claim before the time specified in the collective proceedings order under rule 80(1)(h) to opt into or out of the collective proceedings.

[6.90]
83 Class records

(1) After a collective proceedings order has been made, the class representative shall establish a register on which it shall record the names of those class members who, in accordance with rule 82, opt in to or opt out of the collective proceedings.

(2) The class representative shall, on request, make such register available for inspection by the Tribunal and any defendant and by such other person as the Tribunal may direct.

[6.91]
84 Scope of the collective proceedings

A class representative may not in collective proceedings bring different claims or bring claims against different defendants to those specified in the collective proceedings order.

[6.92]
85 Stay of proceedings and variation or revocation of the collective proceedings order

(1) The Tribunal may at any time, either of its own initiative or on the application of the class representative, a represented person or a defendant, make an order for the variation or revocation of the collective proceedings order, or for the stay or sist of collective proceedings.

(2) In deciding whether to vary or revoke a collective proceedings order, the Tribunal shall take account of all the relevant circumstances, including in particular—

- (a) whether the criteria for certification of claims set out in rule 79 still apply or apply in the same way as when the order was made; and
- (b) whether the class representative continues to satisfy the criteria for authorisation set out in rule 78 and if not, whether a suitable alternative class representative can be authorised;
- (c) whether the Tribunal has granted the class representative permission to withdraw in accordance with rule 87 and it will not be substituted.

(3) If the Tribunal makes an order under paragraph (1), the order may also make further provision including—

- (a) that the proceedings should be discontinued in whole or in part or continue between different parties and, for that purpose, the Tribunal may—
  - (i) order the addition, removal or substitution of parties; or
  - (ii) order the amendment of the collective proceedings claim form;
- (b) that there be substituted as the class representative another person who satisfies the criteria for approval in rule 78;
- (c) as regards costs.

(4) If the Tribunal varies the collective proceedings order so as to alter the description or identification of class members, it may also make any other orders that it considers appropriate, including an order relating to the specified time for the purposes of rules 80 and 82.

[6.93]
86 Individual settlement by the class representative in opt-in proceedings

If the class representative in opt-in collective proceedings is a member of the class and settles in whole or part its personal claim included within the collective proceedings, it shall promptly give notice of that fact—

- (a) to all represented persons; and
- (b) to the Tribunal.

[6.94]
87 Applications for withdrawal by the class representative

(1) A class representative may only withdraw from acting in that capacity in the collective proceedings if the Tribunal gives permission for the withdrawal.

(2) The Tribunal may only give permission for the withdrawal under paragraph (1)—

- (a) if it is satisfied that the class representative has given notice of the application to withdraw to represented persons in a form and manner approved by the Tribunal; and
- (b) on conditions as to costs, if any, that the Tribunal considers just.

(3) If the Tribunal gives permission for the class representative to withdraw from acting in that capacity and no substitute class representative is approved, the Tribunal may give directions for the future conduct of the proceedings which may include provision that the proceedings should continue as one or more proceedings between different parties or be discontinued.

[6.95]
88 Case management of the collective proceedings

(1) The Tribunal may, at any time, give any directions it thinks appropriate for the case management of the collective proceedings.

(2) Without limitation to the generality of paragraph (1), such directions may order that—

- (a) the common issues for the class be determined together;
- (b) the common issues for a sub-class be determined together;
- (c) issues that are relevant only to certain represented persons ("individual issues") be determined in further hearings either separately or at the same time;
- (d) the class representative give notice in such manner as the Tribunal directs to represented persons of any step taken by the class representative.

(3) If the Tribunal directs that the participation of any represented persons is necessary in order to determine individual issues, the class representative shall give notice of the further hearings to those persons in a form and manner approved by the Tribunal.

[6.96]
89 Disclosure

(1) In addition to the Tribunal's general powers under these Rules to order disclosure, the Tribunal may order, on any terms it thinks fit, disclosure to be given—

(a) by any party to the collective proceedings to any other party;
(b) by the class representative to any or all represented persons; and
(c) by any represented person to any other represented person (including a person within a different sub-class), the class representative or the defendant.

NOTES

Note: there is no para (2) in this rule.

[6.97]
90 Notices

If a class member or represented person does not receive, or fails to respond to, a notice, this does not affect a step taken, order made or judgment given, in the collective proceedings, unless the Tribunal orders otherwise.

[6.98]
91 Judgments and orders

(1) A judgment or order of the Tribunal made in collective proceedings may specify the sub-class of represented persons or individual represented persons to whom it shall not apply.

(2) The class representative shall give notice of any judgment or order to all represented persons in a form and manner approved by the Tribunal.

(3) Unless ordered otherwise by the Tribunal, the notice referred to in paragraph (2) shall—

(a) incorporate or have annexed to it the judgment or order;
(b) if it relates to a judgment on common issues in favour of represented persons, include a statement in easily understood language—
   (i) explaining that represented persons may be entitled to individual remedies;
   (ii) stating the steps that shall be taken to claim that remedy; and
   (iii) stating the consequences of failing to take those steps;
(c) if it relates to a judgment on common issues against represented persons, include a statement—
   (i) informing them that an appeal may be brought only by the class representative; and
   (ii) stating the date by which the class representative would have to serve a notice of appeal or application for permission to appeal;
(d) if the Tribunal has specified under paragraph (1) that some represented persons are not bound by the judgment or order, a statement to that effect; and
(e) give such other information as the Tribunal directs.

[6.99]
92 Assessment of damages

(1) Where the Tribunal makes an aggregate award of damages, it shall give directions for assessment of the amount that may be claimed by individual represented persons out of that award.

(2) Directions given may include—

(a) a method or formula by which such amounts are to be quantified;
(b) provision for making an interim payment before the final amount which a represented person may receive is determined;
(c) the appointment of an independent third party to determine a claim or dispute by any represented person regarding the quantification of the amount which that person will receive, and provision for payment of the costs of that independent third party; and
(d) a requirement that the apportionment of the aggregate award as between represented persons is approved by the Tribunal.

(3) The class representative shall give notice to represented persons, in such manner as the Tribunal directs, of any hearing to determine what directions should be given in accordance with paragraph (1), and any represented person may apply to the Tribunal to make submissions either in writing or orally at that hearing.

[6.100]
93 Distribution of award

(1) Where the Tribunal makes an award of damages in opt-out collective proceedings, it shall make an order providing for the damages to be paid on behalf of the represented persons to—

(a) the class representative; or
(b) such person other than a represented person as the Tribunal thinks fit.

(2) Where the Tribunal makes an award of damages in opt-in collective proceedings, it may make an order as described in paragraph (1).

(3) An order made in collective proceedings in accordance with paragraphs (1) and (2), may specify—

(a) the date by which represented persons shall claim their entitlement to a share of that aggregate award;
(b) the date by which the class representative or person specified in accordance with paragraph (1)(b) shall notify the Tribunal of any undistributed damages which have not been claimed;
(c) any other matters as the Tribunal thinks fit.

(4) Where the Tribunal is notified that there are undistributed damages in accordance with paragraph (3)(b), it may make an order directing that all or part of any undistributed damages is paid to the class representative in respect of all or part of any costs, fees or disbursements incurred by the class representative in connection with the collective proceedings.

(5) In exercising its discretion under paragraph (4), the Tribunal may itself determine the amounts to be paid in respect of costs, fees or disbursements or may direct that any such amounts be determined by a costs judge of the High Court or a taxing officer of the Supreme Court of Northern Ireland or the Auditor of the Court of Session.

(6) Subject to any order made under paragraph (4), the Tribunal shall order that all or part of any undistributed damages is paid to the charity designated in accordance with section 47C(5) of the 1998 Act and a copy of that order shall be sent to that charity.

COLLECTIVE SETTLEMENTS

[6.101]

94 Collective settlement where a collective proceedings order has been made: opt-out collective proceedings

(1) Where a collective proceedings order has been made and the Tribunal has specified that the proceedings are opt-out collective proceedings, the claims which are the subject of the collective proceedings, may not be settled other than by a collective settlement approval order issued in accordance with this rule.

(2) Any offer to settle by a defendant in the collective proceedings shall be made to the class representative.

(3) An application for a collective settlement approval order shall be made to the Tribunal by—

(a) the class representative; and

(b) the defendant in the collective proceedings, or if there is more than one defendant, such of them as wish to be bound by the proposed collective settlement.

(4) The application referred to in paragraph (3) shall—

(a) provide details of the claims to be settled by the proposed collective settlement;

(b) set out the terms of the proposed collective settlement, including any related provisions as to the payment of costs, fees and disbursements;

(c) contain a statement that the applicants believe that the terms of the proposed settlement are just and reasonable, supported by evidence which may include any report by an independent expert or any opinion of the applicants' legal representatives as to the merits of the collective settlement;

(d) specify how any sums received under the collective settlement are to be paid and distributed;

(e) have annexed to it a draft collective settlement approval order; and

(f) set out the form and manner by which the class representative proposes to give notice of the application to—

(i) represented persons, in a case where it is expected that paragraph (11) will apply; or

(ii) class members, in a case where it is expected that paragraph (12) will apply.

(5) Unless the Tribunal otherwise directs, the signed original of the application for a collective settlement approval order shall be accompanied by five copies of the application and its annexes certified by the class representative or its legal representative as conforming to the original.

(6) On receiving an application for a collective settlement approval order, the Tribunal may give any directions it thinks fit, including—

(a) for the confidential treatment of any part of an application for a collective settlement approval order;

(b) for the giving of or dispensing with the notice referred to in paragraph (4)(f);

(c) for further evidence to be filed on the merits of the proposed collective settlement;

(d) for the hearing of the application.

(7) Any represented person or, in a case where paragraph (12) applies, any class member may apply to make submissions either in writing or orally at the hearing of the application for a collective settlement approval order.

(8) At the hearing of the application, the Tribunal may make a collective settlement approval order where it is satisfied that the terms of the collective settlement are just and reasonable.

(9) In determining whether the terms are just and reasonable, the Tribunal shall take account of all relevant circumstances, including—

(a) the amount and terms of the settlement, including any related provisions as to the payment of costs, fees and disbursements;

(b) the number or estimated number of persons likely to be entitled to a share of the settlement;

(c) the likelihood of judgment being obtained in the collective proceedings for an amount significantly in excess of the amount of the settlement;

(d) the likely duration and cost of the collective proceedings if they proceeded to trial;

(e) any opinion by an independent expert and any legal representative of the applicants;

(f) the views of any represented person in a case to which paragraph (11) applies, or of any class member in a case to which paragraph (12) applies; and

(g) the provisions regarding the disposition of any unclaimed balance of the settlement, but a provision that any unclaimed balance of the settlement amount reverts to the defendants shall not of itself be considered unreasonable.

(10) A collective settlement approval order may specify the time and manner by which—

(a) a represented person or class member, as the case may be, who is domiciled in the United Kingdom on the domicile date may opt out of the collective settlement; and

(b) a represented person or class member, as the case may be, who is not domiciled in the United Kingdom on the domicile date may opt in to the collective settlement.

(11) Where the Tribunal approves the collective settlement after the expiry of the period specified in the collective proceedings order in accordance with rule 80(1)(h)(ii) or (iii) within which persons may opt out or (if not domiciled in the United Kingdom) opt in to the collective proceedings, the collective settlement approval order binds all represented persons except—

(a) a person who opts out of the collective settlement by notifying the class representative in a manner and by a time specified in the collective settlement approval order; and

(b) a person who is not domiciled in the United Kingdom on the domicile date and does not opt in to the collective settlement by notifying the class representative in a manner and by a time specified in the collective settlement approval order.

(12) Where the Tribunal approves the collective settlement before the expiry of the period referred to in paragraph (11), the collective settlement approval order binds all class members except—

(a) a person who opts out of the collective settlement by notifying the class representative in a manner and by a time specified in the collective settlement approval order; and

(b) a person who is not domiciled in the United Kingdom on the domicile date and does not opt in to the collective settlement by notifying the class representative in a manner and by a time specified in the collective settlement approval order.

(13) If the Tribunal approves the proposed collective settlement, the class representative shall give notice of the terms of the settlement and its approval, in a form and manner approved by the Tribunal, to the represented persons in a case to which paragraph (11) applies, or to the class members in a case to which paragraph (12) applies, and to any other persons as the Tribunal may direct.

(14) If one or more of the represented persons or class members are to be omitted from the collective settlement, the Tribunal may permit the proceedings to continue as one or more claims between different parties and for that purpose—

(a) order the addition, removal or substitution of parties;

(b) order the amendment of the collective proceedings claim form; or

(c) make any other order that it considers appropriate.

(15) If the Tribunal does not approve the proposed collective settlement, the application for a collective settlement approval order and the terms of the proposed collective settlement may not be relied on at the trial of the collective proceedings, unless all the parties to that application agree in writing.

[6.102]

95 Collective settlements where a collective proceedings order has been made: opt-in proceedings

Where a collective proceedings order has been made and the Tribunal has specified that the proceedings are opt-in collective proceedings, the class representative may not without the permission of the Tribunal settle those proceedings before the expiry of the time specified in the collective proceedings order as the time by which a class member may without the permission of the Tribunal opt in to those proceedings.

[6.103]

96 Collective settlements where a collective proceedings order has not been made

(1) An application for a collective settlement order shall be made to the Tribunal by—

(a) a person who proposes to be the settlement representative in relation to the collective settlement; and

(b) the person who, if collective proceedings were brought in respect of the claims would be a defendant in those proceedings (or where more than one person would be a defendant in those proceedings, such of those persons as wish to be bound by the proposed collective settlement).

(2) The application for a collective settlement order referred to in paragraph (1) shall—

(a) identify the proposed settlement representative;

(b) provide a summary of the basis on which the proposed settlement representative seeks to be authorised to act in that capacity in accordance with paragraphs (9) to (11);

(c) identify the person or persons who would be a defendant or defendants in collective proceedings and who it is proposed will be parties to the collective settlement;

(d) provide a description of the proposed settlement class;

(e) provide an estimate of the number of class members and the basis for that estimate;

(f) provide details of the claims to be settled by the proposed collective settlement;

(g) provide a summary of the basis on which the claims, if they had been made in collective proceedings, would satisfy the requirements of rule 79; and

(h) annex—

(i) a draft collective settlement order;

(ii) a draft of the summary referred to in paragraph (5); and

(iii) a draft of the notice referred to in paragraph (15).

(3) Unless the Tribunal otherwise directs, the signed original of the application for a collective settlement order shall be accompanied by five copies of the application and its annexes certified by the proposed settlement representative or its legal representative as conforming to the original.

Response to an application for a collective settlement order

(4) On receiving an application for a collective settlement order, the Tribunal may give any directions it thinks fit, including for the hearing of the application.

(5) The Registrar shall publish a summary of the application for a collective settlement order on the Tribunal website.

Determination of the application for a collective settlement order

(6) The Tribunal may make a collective settlement order only—

(a) if it considers that the person who proposes to be the settlement representative is a person who, if the order were made, the Tribunal could authorise to act as the settlement representative in relation to the collective settlement in accordance with paragraphs (9) to (11); and
(b) in respect of claims which, if collective proceedings were brought, would be eligible for inclusion in such proceedings in accordance with rule 79.

(7) At the hearing of the application for a collective settlement order, the Tribunal may make—
(a) a collective settlement order; and
(b) any other order or give any other directions as it considers appropriate.

(8) Any member of the proposed settlement class may apply to make submissions either in writing or orally at the hearing of the application for a collective settlement order.

(9) The Tribunal may authorise a person to act as the settlement representative only if it considers that it is just and reasonable.

(10) In determining whether it is just and reasonable for a person to act as the settlement representative, the Tribunal shall consider whether that person—
(a) would fairly and adequately act in the interests of the class members; and
(b) does not have, in relation to the common issues for the class members, a material interest that is in conflict with the interests of the class members.

(11) In determining whether the proposed settlement representative would act fairly and adequately in the interests of the class members for the purposes of paragraph (10)(a), the Tribunal may take into account all the circumstances, including—
(a) whether the proposed settlement representative is a member of the settlement class, and if so, its suitability to manage the settlement;
(b) if the proposed representative is not a member of the settlement class, whether it is a pre-existing body and the nature and functions of that body; and
(c) whether the proposed settlement representative has prepared a plan for the collective settlement that satisfactorily includes—
(i) a method for notifying the class members of the fact and progress of the collective settlement; and
(ii) where the proposed collective settlement involves payment of an aggregate amount, a procedure for determination of claims by class members to be paid out of that amount that takes into account the size and nature of the settlement class.

The collective settlement order

(12) A collective settlement order shall authorise the settlement representative to continue to act in relation to the collective settlement and shall—
(a) state the name and address of the settlement representative;
(b) state the name of each party to the collective settlement who would be a defendant had collective proceedings been brought;
(c) describe or otherwise identify the settlement class;
(d) describe or otherwise identify the claims to be settled by the collective settlement;
(e) specify the domicile date; and
(f) order the publication of a notice to class members in accordance with paragraph (15).

(13) A collective settlement order may include any other provision the Tribunal considers appropriate.

(14) In describing or otherwise identifying the settlement class for the purposes of paragraph (12)(c), it is not necessary for the order to name or specify the number of the class members.

Notice of the collective settlement order

(15) The settlement representative shall give notice of the collective settlement order to class members in a form and manner approved by the Tribunal.

(16) The notice referred to in paragraph (15) shall—
(a) incorporate or have annexed to it the collective settlement order;
(b) contain a summary in easily understood language of the claims to be settled by the collective settlement;
(c) include a statement explaining that the subsequent making of a collective settlement approval order will bind—
(i) a class member domiciled in the United Kingdom on the domicile date who does not opt out of the collective settlement; and
(ii) a class member who is not domiciled in the United Kingdom on the domicile date who opts in to the collective settlement; and
(d) give such other information as the Tribunal directs.

Variation or revocation of the collective settlement order

(17) The Tribunal may, either of its own initiative or on the application of a class member or party, make an order for the variation or revocation of the collective settlement order.

[6.104]

97 Collective settlement approval order

(1) Where the Tribunal has made a collective settlement order, an application for a collective settlement approval order shall be made to the Tribunal by—
(a) the settlement representative; and
(b) the person who, if collective proceedings were brought in respect of the claims, would be a defendant in those proceedings or, where more than one person would be a defendant in those proceedings, such of those persons as wish to be bound by the proposed collective settlement.

(2) The application referred to in paragraph (1) shall—
 (a) provide details of the claims to be settled by the proposed collective settlement;
 (b) set out the terms of the proposed collective settlement, including any related provisions as to the payment of costs, fees and disbursements;
 (c) contain a statement that the applicants believe that the terms of the proposed settlement are just and reasonable, supported by evidence which may include any report by an independent expert or any opinion of the applicants' legal representatives as to the merits of the collective settlement;
 (d) specify how any sums received under the collective settlement are to be paid and distributed;
 (e) have annexed to it a draft collective settlement approval order; and
 (f) set out the form and manner by which the settlement representative proposes to give notice of the application to members of the settlement class.

(3) Unless the Tribunal otherwise directs, the signed original of the application for a collective settlement approval order shall be accompanied by five copies of the order and its annexes certified by the class representative or its legal representative as conforming to the original.

(4) On receiving an application for a collective settlement approval order, the Tribunal may give any directions it thinks fit, including—
 (a) for the confidential treatment of any part of an application for a collective settlement approval order;
 (b) for the giving of or dispensing with the notice referred to in paragraph (2)(f);
 (c) for further evidence to be filed on the merits of the proposed collective settlement; and
 (d) for the hearing of the application.

(5) Any member of the proposed settlement class may apply to make submissions in writing or orally at the hearing of the application for a collective settlement approval order.

(6) At the hearing of the application, the Tribunal may make a collective settlement approval order where it is satisfied that terms of the collective settlement are just and reasonable.

(7) In determining whether the terms are just and reasonable, the Tribunal may take account of all relevant circumstances, including—
 (a) the amount and terms of the settlement, including any related provisions as to the payment of costs, fees and disbursements;
 (b) the number or estimated number of persons likely to be entitled to a share of the settlement;
 (c) the likelihood of judgment being obtained if the claims were made in collective proceedings for an amount significantly in excess of the amount of the settlement;
 (d) the likely duration and cost of proceedings if the claims were made in collective proceedings which proceeded to trial;
 (e) any opinion by an independent expert and any legal representative of the applicants;
 (f) the views of any member of the settlement class; and
 (g) the provisions regarding the disposition of any unclaimed balance of the settlement, but a provision that any unclaimed balance of the settlement amount reverts to the parties paying or contributing to the settlement amount shall not of itself be considered unreasonable.

(8) A collective settlement approval order may specify the time and manner by which—
 (a) a class member who is domiciled in the United Kingdom on the domicile date may opt out of the collective settlement; and
 (b) a class member who is not domiciled in the United Kingdom on the domicile date may opt in to the collective settlement.

(9) A collective settlement approval order binds all class members except—
 (a) a person who opts out of the collective settlement by notifying the class representative in a manner and by a time specified in the collective settlement approval order; and
 (b) a person who is not domiciled in the United Kingdom on the domicile date and does not opt in to the collective settlement by notifying the class representative in a manner and by a time specified in the collective settlement approval order.

(10) If the Tribunal approves the proposed collective settlement, the settlement representative shall give notice of the terms of the settlement and its approval, in a form and manner approved by the Tribunal, to the class members and to any other persons as the Tribunal may direct.

(11) An application for a collective settlement approval order may be made at the same time as an application for a collective settlement order.

(12) If the Tribunal does not approve the proposed collective settlement, the application for a collective settlement approval order and the terms of the proposed collective settlement may not be relied on at the trial of the claims that are the subject of the proposed collective settlement, unless all the parties to that application agree in writing.

COSTS AND FEES

[6.105]
98 Costs

(1) Subject to paragraph (2), costs may be awarded to or against the class representative, but may not be awarded to or against a represented person who is not the class representative, save that—
 (a) if the Tribunal has approved the appointment of a class representative for a sub-class, costs associated with the determination of the common issues for the sub-class may be awarded to or against that person, and not the class representative for the whole class; and
 (b) costs associated with the determination of individual issues in accordance with rule 88(2)(c) may be awarded to or against the relevant individual represented persons.

(2) Costs relating to an application made by a class member, whether or not that class member is a represented person under a collective proceedings order, may be awarded to or against that class member.

PART 6 GENERAL AND SUPPLEMENTARY

THE HEARING

[6.106]

99 Hearing to be in public

(1) Every hearing is to be in public except that a hearing or part of a hearing may be in private if the Tribunal is satisfied that it will be considering information which is, in the opinion of the Tribunal, information of the kind referred to in paragraph 1(2) of Schedule 4 to the 2002 Act.

(2) Where a hearing, or part of it, is to be held in private, the Tribunal may determine who is entitled to attend the hearing or part of it.

[6.107]

100 Quorum

(1) If, after the commencement of any hearing, the chairman is unable to continue, the President may appoint either of the remaining two members to chair the Tribunal; and in that case the Tribunal is to consist of the remaining two members for the rest of the proceedings.

(2) If the person appointed under paragraph (1) is not a member of the panel of chairmen, the President may attend the proceedings and advise the remaining members on any questions of law arising, or appoint some other suitably qualified person to do so.

(3) For the purposes of paragraph (2), a person is "suitably qualified" if that person is, or is qualified for appointment as, a member of the panel of chairmen.

(4) If, after the commencement of any hearing, a member of the Tribunal (other than its chairman) is unable to continue, the President may decide that the Tribunal is to consist of the remaining two members for the rest of the proceedings.

(5) Where in accordance with this rule the Tribunal consists of two members, a decision of the Tribunal shall be unanimous.

CONFIDENTIALITY

[6.108]

101 Requests for confidential treatment

(1) A request for the confidential treatment of any document or part of a document provided in the course of proceedings before the Tribunal shall—

- (a) be made in writing indicating the relevant words, figures or passages for which confidentiality is claimed; and
- (b) be supported in each case by specific reasons,

and, if so directed by the Registrar, the person making the request shall supply a non-confidential version of the relevant document.

(2) In the event of a dispute as to whether confidential treatment should be accorded, the Tribunal shall decide the matter after hearing the parties and having regard to the need to exclude information of the kind referred to in paragraph 1(2) of Schedule 4 to the 2002 Act.

(3) The Tribunal may direct that documents, or parts of a document, containing confidential information are disclosed within a confidentiality ring.

[6.109]

102 Subsequent use of documents provided in proceedings

(1) Subject to paragraphs (2) to (4), a party to whom a document has been provided in the course of proceedings—

- (a) by the Tribunal;
- (b) by another party; or
- (c) in accordance with an order under rule 63,

may use that document only for the purpose of those proceedings.

(2) Except where a document or a part of a document has been provided within a confidentiality ring, the restriction in paragraph (1) does not apply to a document if—

- (a) subject to paragraph (5), the document has been read to or by the Tribunal, or referred to, at a hearing which has been held in public;
- (b) the Tribunal gives permission; or
- (c) the party who produced or disclosed the document and the person to whom the document belongs agree.

(3) Where a document or part of a document has been provided within a confidentiality ring, the restriction in paragraph (1) applies unless the Tribunal gives permission for further use of that document or the information contained in the document or part of a document.

(4) The restriction in paragraph (1) does not prevent the CMA or any statutory body which is the maker of a disputed decision that is remitted to it by the Tribunal from using such documents for the purposes of determining the remitted issue.

(5) The Tribunal may, either of its own initiative or on the application of a party under paragraph (6), make an order restricting or prohibiting the use of any document provided in the course of proceedings, even where the document has been read to or by the Tribunal, or referred to, at a hearing which has been held in public.

(6) An application for such an order may be made—

- (a) by a party;

(b) by any person to whom the document belongs; or
(c) by any person who claims that the document contains confidential information relating to them.

DECISION OF THE TRIBUNAL

[6.110]
103 Delivery of the decision

(1) The decision of the Tribunal shall be delivered—
(a) by handing down the decision in public on a date fixed for that purpose;
(b) by publishing the decision on the Tribunal's website; or
(c) in such other manner as may be specified by practice direction.

(2) The Registrar shall send a copy of the document recording the decision to each party and shall enter it on the register.

(3) The decision of the Tribunal is to be treated as having been notified on the date on which a copy of the document recording it is sent to the parties under paragraph (2).

(4) The decision of the Tribunal be published in such manner as the President considers appropriate.

[6.111]
104 Costs

(1) For the purposes of these rules "costs" means costs and expenses recoverable before the Senior Courts of England and Wales, the Court of Session or the Court of Judicature of Northern Ireland, as appropriate, and include payments in respect of the representation of a party to proceedings under section 47A (claims for damages) or 47B (collective proceedings) of the 1998 Act, where the representation by a legal representative was provided free of charge.

(2) The Tribunal may at its discretion, subject to rules 48 and 49, at any stage of the proceedings make any order it thinks fit in relation to the payment of costs in respect of the whole or part of the proceedings.

(3) For the purposes of paragraph (2), applications made under rule 62 or 63 are considered to be proceedings of the Tribunal.

(4) In making an order under paragraph (2) and determining the amount of costs, the Tribunal may take account of—
(a) the conduct of all parties in relation to the proceedings;
(b) any schedule of incurred or estimated costs filed by the parties;
(c) whether a party has succeeded on part of its case, even if that party has not been wholly successful;
(d) any admissible offer to settle made by a party which is drawn to the Tribunal's attention, and which is not a Rule 45 Offer to which costs consequences under rules 48 and 49 apply;
(e) whether costs were proportionately and reasonably incurred; and
(f) whether costs are proportionate and reasonable in amount.

(5) The Tribunal may assess the sum to be paid under any order under paragraph (2) or may direct that it be—
(a) assessed by the President, a chairman or the Registrar; or
(b) dealt with by the detailed assessment of a costs officer of the Senior Courts of England and Wales or a taxing officer of the Court of Judicature of Northern Ireland or by the Auditor of the Court of Session, as appropriate.

(6) The power to award costs under paragraphs (1) to (5) includes the power to direct any party to pay to the Tribunal such sum as may be appropriate in reimbursement of any costs incurred by the Tribunal in connection with the summoning or citation of witnesses or the instruction of experts on the Tribunal's behalf; and any sum due as a result of such a direction may be recovered by the Tribunal as a civil debt due to the Tribunal.

[6.112]
105 Interest

(1) If it imposes, confirms or varies any penalty under Part 1 of the 1998 Act, the Tribunal may, in addition, order that interest is to be payable on the amount of any such penalty from such date, not being a date earlier than the date of the notice of appeal, and at such rate, as the Tribunal considers appropriate.

(2) Interest ordered to be paid under paragraph (1) is to form part of the penalty and be recoverable as a civil debt in addition to the amount recoverable under section 36 of the 1998 Act.

(3) If it makes an award of damages the Tribunal may include in any sum awarded interest on all or any part of the damages in respect of which the award is made, for all or any part of the period between the date when the cause of action arose and—
(a) in the case of any sum paid before the decision making the award, the date of the payment; and
(b) in the case of the sum awarded, the date of that decision.

(4) Unless the Tribunal otherwise directs, the rate of interest ordered to be paid or included in an award in accordance with this rule shall not exceed the rate specified in any Order made under section 44 of the Administration of Justice Act 1970.

[6.113]
106 Consent orders

(1) If all the parties agree the terms of an order, the Tribunal may, if it thinks fit, make the order, in which case it shall be identified as having been made by consent.

(2) If the Tribunal considers that a draft consent order may have a significant effect on competition, it may—
(a) require the parties to file a consent order impact statement; and
(b) direct the Registrar to publish a notice on the Tribunal website or in such other manner as the Tribunal may direct.

(3) A consent order impact statement shall provide an explanation of the draft consent order, including an explanation of the circumstances giving rise to the draft order, the relief to be obtained if the order is made and the anticipated effects on competition of that relief.

APPEALS FROM THE TRIBUNAL

[6.114]
107 Permission to appeal

(1) A request to the Tribunal for permission to appeal from a decision of the Tribunal shall be made in writing and sent to the Registrar within three weeks of the notification of that decision.

(2) A request for permission to appeal shall be signed and dated by the party or its representative and shall—

(a) state the name and address of the party and of any representative of the party;
(b) identify the Tribunal decision to which the request relates;
(c) state the grounds on which the party intends to rely in its appeal; and
(d) state whether the party requests a hearing of its request and any special circumstances relied on.

[6.115]
108 Decision of the Tribunal on request for permission to appeal

(1) On receipt of a request for permission to appeal, the Tribunal may decide without a hearing whether or not to grant such permission, unless it considers that special circumstances render a hearing desirable.

(2) The decision of the Tribunal on a request for permission to appeal shall be recorded in writing and the Registrar shall notify the parties of the decision.

REFERENCES TO THE EUROPEAN COURT

[6.116]
109 References to the European Court

(1) A reference may be made by the Tribunal of its own initiative at any stage in the proceedings or on application by a party before or at the oral hearing.

(2) A reference shall include a schedule setting out the request for the preliminary ruling of the European Court and the Tribunal may give directions as to the manner and form in which the schedule is to be prepared.

(3) The proceedings in relation to which a reference is made shall, unless the Tribunal otherwise directs, be stayed (or in Scotland, sisted) until the European Court has given a preliminary ruling on the question referred to it.

(4) When a reference has been made, the Registrar shall send a copy of it to the Registrar of the European Court.

(5) In this rule—

"European Court" means the Court of Justice of the European Union;

"reference" means an order referring a question to the European Court for a preliminary ruling under Article 267 of the TFEU or as provided for under any agreement to which the European Union or the Member States of the European Union are parties.

NOTES

Revoked by the Competition (Amendment etc) (EU Exit) Regulations 2019, SI 2019/93, reg 61, Sch 2, Pt 2, para 8, as from IP completion day (as defined in the European Union (Withdrawal Agreement) Act 2020, s 39) (for transitional provisions and savings in relation to the operation of the 2019 Regulations, see Sch 4 to those Regulations at **[7.69]** et seq and, in particular, Sch 4, Pts 3 and 7 to the 2019 Regulations at **[7.71]** and **[7.76]**).

SUPPLEMENTARY

[6.117]
110 Power of President, chairman and Registrar to exercise powers of Tribunal

(1) Any act required or authorised by these Rules, other than one required or authorised by the following rules—

(a) rules 11 and 26(3) (power to strike out);
(b) rule 13 (withdrawal of the appeal), in the case of a withdrawal during or after the hearing;
(c) rule 41 (power to strike out);
(d) rule 42 (default judgment);
(e) rule 43 (summary judgment);
(f) rule 44 (withdrawal of the claim), in the case of a withdrawal during or after the hearing;
(g) rule 77 (determination of the application for a collective proceedings order);
(h) rule 85 (stay, variation or revocation of the collective proceedings order), in the case of revocation of the collective proceedings order;
(i) rule 87 (applications for withdrawal by the class representative);
(j) rules 94(8) and 97(6) (making of a collective settlement approval order);
(k) rule 96(6) (determination of the application for a collective settlement order);
(l) rule 108 (decision of the Tribunal on request for permission to appeal);
(m) rule 109 (references to the European Court),

may be done by the President or a chairman acting alone.

(2) If so authorised by the President, the Registrar may, subject to paragraph (3) and without prejudice to rule 104(5)—

(a) make any order by consent (except where rule 106(2) applies);
(b) make a direction under rule 9(7);
(c) deal with extensions or abridgments of time limits under rule 19(2)(m), except a request for an extension of time for filing an appeal or application under Part 2 or Part 3 of these Rules;

(d) deal with requests for confidential treatment under rule 101;
(e) exercise the Tribunal's powers in respect of the service of documents under rule 111.

(3) A party may within five days of any decision by the Registrar in accordance with paragraph (2) request in writing that the decision be reviewed by the President, and the President may determine the matter acting alone or refer the matter to a chairman or to the Tribunal.

NOTES

Para (1): sub-para (m) was revoked by the Competition (Amendment etc) (EU Exit) Regulations 2019, SI 2019/93, reg 61, Sch 2, Pt 2, para 8, as from IP completion day (as defined in the European Union (Withdrawal Agreement) Act 2020, s 39) (for transitional provisions and savings in relation to the operation of the 2019 Regulations, see Sch 4 to those Regulations at **[7.69]** et seq and, in particular, Sch 4, Pts 3 and 7 to the 2019 Regulations at **[7.71]** and **[7.76]**).

[6.118]

111 Documents etc

(1) Subject to paragraph (16), any document required to be sent to or served on any person for the purposes of proceedings under these Rules (including documents required to be sent to the Registrar for filing) may be—
(a) delivered personally at the appropriate address;
(b) sent to that person at the appropriate address by first class post;
(c) served through a document exchange or by any other service which provides for delivery on the next business day;
(d) where authorised by the Tribunal, sent to that person by fax or other means of electronic communication; or
(e) sent or served in such other manner as may be specified by practice direction.

(2) Where it appears to the Tribunal that there is a good reason to authorise service by a method or at a place not otherwise permitted by these Rules, the Tribunal may of its own initiative or on the request of a party make an order permitting and specifying an alternative method of service or place, and specifying when the document is to be deemed to be served.

(3) The Tribunal may dispense with service of a document if the interests of justice so require.

(4) A document which is filed, sent to or served on a person in accordance with these Rules is to be treated as if it had been filed, received by or served on that person—
(a) in the case of personal delivery, on the day of delivery;
(b) when sent by first class post, through a document exchange or any other service in accordance with paragraph (1)(c), on the second day after it was posted or left at the document exchange or delivered to or collected by the relevant service provider; and
(c) in the case of a fax or other electronic communication sent on a business day before 5pm, on that day, or in any other case, on the next business day.

(5) If a document (other than a fax or other electronic communication) is filed, sent or served or is treated in accordance with paragraph (4) as having been filed, sent or served at or after 5pm on a business day, or at any time on a Saturday, Sunday or a Bank Holiday, the document is to be treated as having been filed, sent or served on the next business day.

(6) For the purposes of these Rules "business day" means any day except Saturday, Sunday or a Bank Holiday and "Bank Holiday" includes Christmas Day and Good Friday.

(7) With regard to an appeal or application made under Part 2 or 3 of these Rules, the appropriate address for a person for the purposes of paragraph (1) is—
(a) in the case of a document directed to the appellant or applicant (or to its representative), the address stated in the notice of appeal or notice of application , or such other address as may be subsequently notified to the Tribunal;
(b) in the case of a document addressed to the respondent, the address stated in the defence, or such other address as may be subsequently notified to the Tribunal;
(c) in the case of an intervener, the address stated in the request to intervene, or such other address as may be subsequently notified to the Tribunal.

(8) With regard to a claim made or collective proceedings brought under Part 4 or 5 of these Rules, the appropriate address for a person for the purposes of paragraph (1) is—
(a) in the case of a document directed to the claimant or the person applying for a collective proceedings order, the address stated in the claim form or the collective proceedings claim form or such other address as may be notified by the Tribunal;
(b) in the case of a claim form to be served on the defendant, subject to paragraph (9), the address of the defendant stated in the claim form or the collective proceedings claim form;
(c) in the case of any other document addressed to the defendant, the address stated in that defendant's acknowledgment of service filed with the Tribunal or such other address as may be subsequently notified to the Tribunal.

(9) Where—
(a) the defendant has given in writing the business address within the jurisdiction of a legal representative as an address at which the defendant may be served with the claim form or collective proceedings claim form; or
(b) a legal representative acting for the defendant has notified the claimant or person applying for a collective proceedings order in writing that the legal representative is instructed by the defendant to accept service of the claim form or collective proceedings claim form on behalf of the defendant at a business address within the jurisdiction,

the claim form or collective proceedings claim form shall be served at the business address of that legal representative.

(10) The appropriate address for the Registrar and Tribunal for the purposes of paragraph (1) is the Tribunal's address for service in accordance with rule 6.

(11) Where the address for service of a party changes, that party shall give notice in writing of the change as soon as it has taken place to the Tribunal and every other party.

(12) Anything required to be sent to or served on a company or other corporation is duly sent or served if it is sent to or served on a person holding a senior position within the company or corporation; and for that purpose, each of the following persons is a person holding a senior position—

(a) in respect of a registered company or corporation, a director, the treasurer, the secretary of the company or corporation, the chief executive or other officer of the company or corporation; and

(b) in respect of a company or corporation which is not registered, in addition to any of the persons set out in paragraph (a), the mayor, the chairman, the president, a town clerk or similar officer of the company or corporation.

(13) Anything required to be sent or delivered to or served on a partnership is duly sent or served if it is sent to or served on any one of the partners for the time being or a person who, at the time of service, has the control or management of the partnership business at its principal place of business.

(14) Where—

(a) a document is to be served by the Tribunal; and

(b) the Tribunal is unable to serve it,

the Tribunal shall send a notice of non-service, stating the method attempted, to the other parties to the proceedings.

(15) The Registrar shall, at the request of the Tribunal, or any party, certify the steps taken to serve a document in accordance with this rule, including the date and manner of service.

(16) With regard to a claim form or collective proceedings claim form to be served on a defendant outside the jurisdiction (and subject to rules 31, 33(2) and 76(2)), the claimant or person applying for a collective proceedings order shall serve the claim form or collective proceedings claim form by any method permissible under Part 6 of the CPR in relation to proceedings in England and Wales or the equivalent provisions in the equivalent procedural rules for Scotland or Northern Ireland in relation to proceedings taking place in Scotland or Northern Ireland respectively.

[6.119]
112 Time

(1) Unless otherwise specified, an act required by the Tribunal, the President, a chairman or the Registrar, or by these Rules, to be done on or by a particular day shall be done before 5pm on that day.

(2) Where a period expressed in days, weeks or months is to be calculated from the moment at which an event occurs or an action takes place, the day during which that event occurs or that action takes place is not to be counted as falling within the period in question.

(3) A period expressed in weeks or months ends with the expiry of whichever day in the last week or month is the same day of the week or falls on the same date in the month, as the day during which the event or action from which the period is to be calculated occurred or took place; and if, in a period expressed in months, the day on which it should expire does not occur in the last month, the period ends with the expiry of the last day of that month.

(4) "Month" means calendar month.

(5) Where the time prescribed for doing any act expires on a Saturday, Sunday or Bank Holiday, the act is in time if done on the next following day which is not a Saturday, Sunday or Bank Holiday.

[6.120]
113 Funding Arrangements

Subject to section 47C(8) of the 1998 Act and rule 93(4), the rules on funding arrangements made under Part 2 of the Courts and Legal Services Act 1990 apply to proceedings before the Tribunal.

[6.121]
114 Irregularities

(1) Any irregularity resulting from failure to comply with any provision of these Rules before the Tribunal has reached its decision does not of itself render the proceedings void.

(2) Where any such irregularity comes to the attention of the Tribunal, the Tribunal may, and shall if it considers any person may have been prejudiced by the irregularity, give such directions as it thinks just, to cure or waive the irregularity before reaching its decision.

(3) Clerical mistakes in any document recording a direction, order or decision of the Tribunal, the President, a chairman or the Registrar, or errors arising in such a document from an accidental slip or omission, may be corrected by the President, that chairman or the Registrar, as the case may be, by—

(a) sending notification of the amended direction, order or decision, or a copy of the amended document, to each party; and

(b) making the necessary amendment to any information published on the Tribunal website in relation to the direction, order or decision.

[6.122]
115 General power of the Tribunal

(1) Subject to the provisions of these Rules, the Tribunal may regulate its own procedure.

(2) A power of the Tribunal under these Rules to make an order or direction includes a power to vary or revoke the order or direction.

(3) The President may issue practice directions in relation to the procedures provided for by these Rules.

PART 7 REFERENCE OF PRICE CONTROL MATTERS TO THE CMA UNDER THE 2003 ACT

[6.123]

116 Reference of price control matters to the CMA

(1) For the purposes of subsection (1) of section 193 of the 2003 Act (reference of price control matters to the CMA), there is specified every price control matter falling within subsection (10) of that section which is disputed between the parties and which relates to—

(a) the principles applied in setting the condition which imposes the price control in question,
(b) the methods applied or calculations used or data used in determining that price control, or
(c) what the provisions imposing the price control which are contained in that condition should be (including at what level the price control should be set).

(2) The Tribunal shall refer to the CMA for determination in accordance with section 193 of the 2003 Act and rule 117 every matter which, either upon consideration of any statement provided for in rules 9(5) or 15(4) or in the subsequent course of the appeal, the Tribunal decides is a specified price control matter.

(3) The Tribunal may make a reference to the CMA under paragraph (2) at any time before it delivers its decision.

[6.124]

117 Determination by the CMA of price control matters

(1) Subject to any directions given by the Tribunal (which may be given at any time before the CMA has made its determination), the CMA shall determine every price control matter within four months of receipt by it of the reference.

(2) The Tribunal may give directions as to the procedure in accordance with which the CMA is to make its determination.

(3) The Tribunal may give directions under this rule of its own motion or upon the application of the CMA or of any party.

PART 8 REVOCATION AND SAVINGS

[6.125]

118 Revocation

The following Rules are revoked—

(a) the Competition Appeal Tribunal Rules 2003
(b) the Competition Appeal Tribunal (Amendment and Communications Act Appeals) Rules 2004.

[6.126]

119 Savings

(1) Proceedings commenced before the Tribunal before 1st October 2015 continue to be governed by the Competition Appeal Tribunal Rules 2003 (the "2003 Rules") as if they had not been revoked.

(2) Rule 31(1) to (3) of the 2003 Rules (time limit for making a claim) continues to apply in respect of a claim which falls within paragraph (3) for the purposes of determining the limitation or prescriptive period which would apply in respect of the claim if it were to be made on or after 1st October 2015 in—

(a) proceedings under section 47A of the 1998 Act, or
(b) collective proceedings.

(3) A claim falls within this paragraph if—

(a) it is a claim to which section 47A of the 1998 Act applies; and
(b) the claim arose before 1st October 2015.

(4) Section 47A(7) and (8) of the 1998 Act as they had effect before they were substituted by paragraph 4 of Schedule 8 to the Consumer Rights Act 2015 continue to apply to the extent necessary for the purposes of paragraph (2).

PART 9 REVIEW

[6.127]

120 Review

(1) The Secretary of State shall from time to time—

(a) carry out a review of these Rules,
(b) set out the conclusions of the review in a report, and
(c) publish the report.

(2) The report shall in particular—

(a) set out the objectives intended to be achieved by the regulatory system established by these Rules,
(b) assess the extent to which those objectives are achieved, and
(c) assess whether those objectives remain appropriate and, if so, the extent to which they could be achieved with a system that imposes less regulation.

(3) The first report under this rule is to be published before 1st October 2020.

(4) Reports under this rule are afterwards to be published at intervals not exceeding five years.

COMPETITION APPEAL TRIBUNAL GUIDE TO PROCEEDINGS (2015)

(October 2015)

[6.128]

NOTES

Note that for cases commenced before 1 October 2015 the previous Guide is still relevant (the 2005 Guide).

This Guide to Proceedings is available on the rules and guidance section of the Competition Appeal Tribunal website at www.catribunal.org.uk/rules-and-guidance.

GLOSSARY

[6.129]

"the 1998 Act" the Competition Act 1998 (as amended)

"the 2002 Act" the Enterprise Act 2002 (as amended)

"the 2003 Act" the Communications Act 2003 (as amended)

"the 2003 Act" the Civil Aviation Authority

"the 2011 Act" the Postal Services Act 2011

"the 2012 Act" the Civil Aviation Act 2012

"the 2013 Act" the Financial Services (Banking Reform) Act 2013

"the 2015 Act" the Consumer Rights Act 2015

"CAA" the Civil Aviation Authority

"CC" the Competition Commission (see also CMA)

"CMA" the Competition and Markets Authority, which assumed certain functions of the Office of Fair Trading and the Competition Commission on 1 April 2014 pursuant to the Enterprise and Regulatory Reform Act 2013

"CMC" case management conference

"CPO" collective proceedings order

"CPR" Civil Procedure Rules

"CSAO" collective settlement approval order

"CSO" collective settlement order

"the Chapter I prohibition" the prohibition contained in section 2 of the 1998 Act

"the Chapter II prohibition" the prohibition contained in section 18 of the 1998 Act

"the EC Treaty" the Treaty establishing the European Community (as amended)

"Regulation 1/2003" Council Regulation (EC) No 1/2003 of 16 December 2002 on the implementation of the rules on competition laid down in Articles 81 and 82 of the EC Treaty (now Articles 101 and 102 TFEU) OJ 2003 L 1/1

"the CJEU" the Court of Justice of the European Union

"FCA" the Financial Conduct Authority

"FTP" fast-track procedure

"General Court" the General Court of the European Union, a constituent court of the Court of Justice of the European Union

"GEMA" the Gas and Electricity Markets Authority

"Guide to Proceedings" "the Guide" this Guide to Proceedings

"Monitor" the regulator for the National Health Service in England

"NIAUR" Northern Ireland Authority for Utility Regulation

"OFCOM" Office of Communications

"ORR" Office of Rail and Road

"PSR" the Payment Systems Regulator

"the 2001 Regulations" EC Competition Law (Articles 84 and 85) Enforcement Regulations 2001 (SI 2001/2916)

"the 2004 Regulations" the Competition Act 1998 and Other Enactments (Amendment) Regulations 2004 (SI 2004/1261)

"the Regulators" CAA, FCA, GEMA, Monitor, NIAUR, OFCOM, ORR, PSR and WSRA

"the 2003 Rules" the Competition Appeal Tribunal Rules 2003 (SI 2003/1372), revoked (save as provided by Rule 119) pursuant to Rule 118 of the 2015 Rules

"the 2004 Rules" the Competition Appeal Tribunal (Amendment and Communications Act Appeals) Rules 2004 (SI 2004/2068), revoked (save as provided by Rule 119) pursuant to Rule 118 of the 2015 Rules

"the 2015 Rules" "the Rules" the Competition Appeal Tribunal Rules 2015 (SI 2015/1648)

"TFEU" the Treaty on the Functioning of the European Union

"the Tribunal" the Competition Appeal Tribunal

"a Tribunal" a tribunal of three persons, drawn from the membership of the Competition Appeal Tribunal and including at least one member from the panel of Chairmen, to hear a particular case

"The Tribunal website" www.catribunal.org.uk

"WSRA" the Water Services Regulation Authority

PRACTICE DIRECTION

[6.130]
The requirements of this Guide to Proceedings in the Competition Appeal Tribunal (and any supplements that may be issued from time to time) constitute a Practice Direction issued by the President pursuant to Rule 115(3) of The Competition Appeal Tribunal Rules 2015 (SI 2015 No 1648).

The Hon. Mr Justice Roth
President
1 October 2015

PREFACE

[6.131]
This Guide to Proceedings applies to the conduct of proceedings before the Tribunal commenced on or after 1 October 2015 in accordance with The Competition Appeal Tribunal Rules 2015, which came into force on that date and which revoked the 2003 Rules and the 2004 Rules.

The new rules of procedure follow an independent review carried out by Sir John Mummery in 2014. He was appointed by the Secretary of State for Business Innovation and Skills (BIS) following the Government's commitment to undertake a review of the 2003 Rules in its consultation entitled *'Streamlining Regulatory and Competition Appeals'* in June 2013. Sir John Mummery's Report was published on 5 February 2015.[1]

BIS consulted on proposed changes to the rules in February 2015.[2] The statutory instrument containing the 2015 Rules was laid before Parliament on 8 September 2015 and came into force on 1 October 2015.

As well as updating the previous rules, the revised rules reflect the Tribunal's new jurisdiction, as a result of major changes brought about by the Consumer Rights Act 2015, in the sphere of private actions. Under its expanded remit, the Tribunal may hear stand-alone claims in competition cases, including by way of collective proceedings, approve collective settlements of such claims, and (except for proceedings in Scotland) grant injunctions.

As regards collective proceedings and collective settlements, the jurisdiction of the Tribunal is novel. In prescribing directions and providing guidance for such proceedings and settlements, the Tribunal therefore has no prior practice from any part of the United Kingdom on which to draw. While the Guide seeks to provide as much assistance as possible, it is expected that the Tribunal will further develop its approach on a case-by-case basis, and the Guide is likely to need revision accordingly in the light of experience.

Charles Dhanowa OBE, QC (Hon)
Registrar
1 October 2015

NOTES

1 *Independent report: review of the rules of procedure of the Competition Appeal Tribunal (CAT)*, BIS/15/73.

2 BIS, *Competition Appeal Tribunal (CAT) Rules of Procedure: Review by the Rt Honourable Sir John Mummery, Consultation* (February 2015).

INTRODUCTION TO THE GUIDE

(1) This Guide to Proceedings applies to the conduct of proceedings before the Tribunal commenced on or after 1 October 2015 in accordance with The Competition Appeal Tribunal Rules 2015 (the "2015 Rules"), which came into force on that date.[3] Proceedings commenced before the Tribunal prior to 1 October 2015 are governed by the Competition Appeal Tribunal Rules 2003 (the "2003 Rules") and the Competition Appeal Tribunal (Amendment and Communications Act Appeals) Rules 2004 (the "2004 Rules")[4].

(2) The Guide describes the Tribunal's procedures chronologically, differentiating where relevant between different types of proceedings. To avoid undue repetition, aspects of the Tribunal's procedure and practice that are common to different types of proceedings are considered separately, in Sections 7 and 8. This means that it is important to consult different

sections of the Guide in order to obtain a full overview of the Tribunal's approach to a particular type of case. Moreover, the relevant statutory provisions, including the 2015 Rules, should always be consulted in addition to the Guide. In the event of any conflict between the Rules and the Guide, the Rules prevail.

(3) The most up to date version of the Guide can be found on the Tribunal website, www.catribunal.org.uk, which also contains the judgments, orders and other documents relating to proceedings before the Tribunal. New editions and revisions of, and supplements to, the Guide may be issued from time to time and these will be published on the Tribunal website.

(4) In respect of matters not addressed by the Rules or the Guide, parties and their representatives are expected to act reasonably and in accordance with the governing principles in Rule 4.

(5) The Registry may be consulted on any points of procedure that arise, either before or during proceedings. See Section 9 for details of how to contact the Registry.

(6) The Guide is structured as follows:

- **Section 1** summarises the statutory functions of the Tribunal, describes its constitution and gives an overview of the office of the Registrar.
- **Section 2** describes the Tribunal's statutory functions and the context in which they arise in more detail.
- **Section 3** addresses the governing principles enshrined in the 2015 Rules.
- **Section 4** deals with statutory appeals and applications for review, including those under the Competition Act 1998 (the "1998 Act"), the Enterprise Act 2002 (the "2002 Act") and the Communications Act 2003 (the "2003 Act"). It sets out the time limits for bringing a legal challenge and the requirements relating to notices of appeal/applications, the defence and the intervention procedure; it also outlines the steps immediately following commencement of proceedings. Further steps in these proceedings, such as the first case management conference ("CMC"), adducing evidence and hearings are set out in Section 7. Section 4 also covers applications for interim measures.
- **Section 5** deals with private actions, namely claims for damages and injunctions. It also deals with the fast-track procedure ("FTP") under Rule 58 and settlement offers under Rule 45.
- **Section 6** deals with collective actions, including collective settlements.
- **Section 7** addresses procedural elements that are common to some or all of the proceedings dealt with in the preceding sections, for example: case management conferences, forum, consolidation, amendment of pleadings, confidentiality, evidence, hearings and the Tribunal's decision.
- **Section 8** details aspects of the Tribunal's procedure that typically occur after the Tribunal issues its final judgment, namely costs applications and appeals.
- Section 9 provides some general information about contacting and visiting the Tribunal, filing documents at the Tribunal, legal representation, arrangements for hearings and practical matters such as labelling of files, use of electronic signatures and citation of authorities.
- The Glossary at the start of the Guide sets out the meaning of frequently used defined terms and the full form of any abbreviations not defined in the body of the text.

NOTES

3 See The Competition Appeal Tribunal Rules 2015 (SI 2015/1648), Rule 1.

4 Rule 118 and Rule 119 of the 2015 Rules.

SECTION 1: THE TRIBUNAL

[6.133]

1.1 The Tribunal was created by section 12(1) and Schedule 2 of the 2002 Act and came into existence on 1 April 2003.[5]

1.2 The Tribunal is an entirely independent judicial body.

1.3 The Tribunal is supported by the Competition Service, an executive non-departmental public body established by section 13 of the 2002 Act to provide the administrative staff, finance and accommodation required by the Tribunal to carry out its functions. Although the Tribunal and the Competition Service are, in formal terms, separate bodies, in practice they are different aspects of one integrated organisation; a single body of staff multi-tasks across case-handling and administrative roles using a common pool of resources.

1.4 The principal functions of the Tribunal may be summarised as follows.

- Firstly, the Tribunal may hear *appeals on the merits* in respect of decisions applying the competition rules found in Article 101 TFEU (formerly Article 81 EC) and Article 102 TFEU (formerly Article 82 EC) and Chapters I and II of the 1998 Act, decisions imposing penalties pursuant to sections 114 or 176(1) of the 2002 Act, and decisions applying the relevant provisions of the 2003 Act.
- Secondly, it may entertain *applications for review* of merger and market investigation decisions under the 2002 Act, decisions to accept or release binding commitments under section 31A of the 1998 Act and determinations concerning a price control matter under section 193(7) of the 2003 Act.
- Thirdly, it may determine *claims for damages or other sums of money* brought by claimants who have suffered loss or damage as a result of an infringement of one of the relevant prohibitions contained in the TFEU or the 1998 Act; these are also referred to as "private actions". Such claims may be by way of follow-on action (in which case the claim is based on an infringement decision

of the CMA or European Commission and the claimant does not have to prove that the infringement has incurred) or stand-alone action (in which case the claimant also has to establish that there has been an infringement of the relevant competition law provisions). Furthermore, a claim may be made by an individual claimant under section 47A of the 1998 Act or be brought by way of a collective action under section 47B of the 1998 Act. Collective actions may be opt-in or opt-out.

– Finally the Tribunal may entertain applications for interim measures under the 1998 Act. The Tribunal also has the power to issue injunctions in private actions.

1.5 These functions and the context in which they arise are described in more detail in Section 2 of the Guide.

THE CONSTITUTION OF THE TRIBUNAL

[6.134]

1.6 The constitution of the Tribunal is governed by section 12(2)–(5) and Schedule 2 of the 2002 Act. The Tribunal consists of the President, the Chairmen and the Ordinary Members. The Tribunal is supported by the Registrar. Details of the current post holders can be found on the Tribunal website (www.catribunal.org.uk).

1.7 The President and Chairmen are appointed by the Lord Chancellor for a fixed term upon the recommendation of the Judicial Appointments Commission and following an open competition as appropriate. Chairmen must be legally qualified and appear to the Lord Chancellor to have appropriate experience and knowledge (either of competition law and practice or any other relevant law and practice).[6] The Registrar is appointed by the Secretary of State.

1.8 In addition, the Lord Chief Justice of England and Wales, the Lord President of the Court of Session and the Lord Chief Justice of Northern Ireland may nominate any suitably qualified judge who is already sitting, respectively, in the High Court of England and Wales, the Court of Session in Scotland or the High Court of Northern Ireland to be deployed as a Chairman of the Tribunal.[7]

1.9 Ordinary Members are recruited in open competition according to the guidelines of the Office of the Commissioner for Public Appointments and are appointed by the Secretary of State for Business Innovation and Skills for a period of eight years. They must have appropriate experience and expertise. Some are professionally qualified economists, lawyers or accountants, while others have backgrounds in business, the public service or other relevant experience.

1.10 Biographical details of the President, Chairmen and the Ordinary Members can be found on the Tribunal website.

1.11 Cases are typically heard by a Tribunal of three persons and chaired by either the President or a Chairman.[8] The other two members are drawn from the Chairmen or the Ordinary Members.

1.12 However, pursuant to Rule 110 the President, or a Chairman, may exercise the powers of the Tribunal acting alone, save in relation to:

– Rules 11 and 26(3) (power to strike out);
– Rule 13 (withdrawal of the appeal, in the case of a withdrawal during or after the hearing);
– Rule 41 (power to strike out);
– Rule 42 (default judgment);
– Rule 43 (summary judgment);
– Rule 44 (withdrawal of the claim, in the case of a withdrawal during or after the hearing);
– Rule 77 (determination of the application for a collective proceedings order);
– Rule 85 (stay, variation or revocation of the collective proceedings order, in the case of revocation of the collective proceedings order);
– Rule 87 (applications for withdrawal by the class representative);
– Rules 94(8) and 97(6) (making of a collective settlement approval order);
– Rule 96(6) (determination of the application for a collective settlement order);
– Rule 108 (decision of the Tribunal on request for permission to appeal); and
– Rule 109 (references to the CJEU).

THE REGISTRAR

[6.135]

1.13 The day to day operation of the Tribunal is managed by the Registrar who is the main point of contact for the public.

1.14 Under Rule 5 the Registrar is responsible for the establishment and maintenance of a register in which all pleadings and supporting documents and all orders and decisions of the Tribunal shall be registered; the acceptance, transmission and custody of documents in accordance with the rules of procedure; the enforcement of Tribunal decisions pursuant to paragraphs 4 and 5 of Schedule 4 to the 2002 Act; and certifying that any order, direction or decision is an order, direction or decision of the Tribunal, the President or Chairman as the case may be.

1.15 The Registrar must act in accordance with the instructions of the President (Rule 5(2)). Pursuant to Rule 110(2) (and the practice direction that this Guide constitutes) the Registrar is authorised by the President to:

– make any order by consent, except where Rule 106(2) applies (which concerns cases where the order may have a significant effect on competition);

- make a direction under Rule 9(7) (which stipulates that unless the Tribunal directs otherwise, the signed original of the notice of appeal (and its annexes) must be accompanied by ten certified copies by the appellant or the appellant's legal representative);
- deal with extensions or abridgments of time limits under Rule 19(2)(m), except a request for an extension of time for filing an appeal or application under Part 2 or Part 3 of the 2015 Rules;
- deal with requests for confidential treatment under Rule 101;
- exercise the Tribunal's powers in respect of the service of documents under Rule 111; and
- deliver the Tribunal's decision by handing down in public pursuant to Rule 103(1)(a), where the parties have been informed in advance and there is no other business to conduct on that occasion.

1.16 A party dissatisfied with any exercise by the Registrar of his functions may request in writing a review of that direction by the President. Any request for review of any exercise by the Registrar of his functions must be received by the Tribunal within five days of the exercise of such functions. The President may determine the matter acting alone or refer the matter to a Chairman or to the Tribunal: Rule 110(3).

NOTES

5 The Tribunal replaced the Competition Commission Appeal Tribunals established under the 1998 Act.

6 Section 12(2) and Schedule 2, paragraph 1 to the 2002 Act.

7 Section 12(2) of the 2002 Act (as amended by section 82 of the Consumer Rights Act 2015 which came into force on 27 May 2015 pursuant to SI 2015/1333).

8 Section 14 of the 2002 Act.

SECTION 2: TYPES OF PROCEEDINGS BEFORE THE TRIBUNAL

[6.136]

2.1 A number of different proceedings may be commenced before and heard by the Tribunal, including:

- Private actions by persons who have suffered loss or damage in respect of an infringement decision or alleged infringement: sections 47A and 47B of the 1998 Act.
- Applications for approval of collective settlements of such private actions brought, or which could have been brought, by way of collective proceedings: sections 49A and 49B of the 1998 Act.
- Appeals on the merits by parties or third parties against decisions, including interim measures decisions, made under the 1998 Act by the CMA or a Regulator: sections 46 and 47 of the 1998 Act.
- Appeals on judicial review principles by parties or third parties of decisions by the CMA or a Regulator to accept, vary, release, or not release binding commitments under section 31A of the 1998 Act: sections 46 and 47 of the 1998 Act.
- Applications to review, as the case may be, the decisions of the CMA, a Regulator or the Secretary of State in connection with a reference or possible reference in relation to a relevant or special merger situation, or a market investigation: sections 120 and 179 of the 2002 Act.
- Appeals against a penalty imposed by the CMA for failure to comply with a notice requiring the production of documents and information and the attendance of witnesses: sections 114 and 176(1) of the 2002 Act.
- Appeals against certain decisions made by OFCOM or the Secretary of State under the 2003 Act. Those decisions principally concern the exercise by OFCOM of its powers to regulate electronic communications networks and services under Part 2 of the 2003 Act, the use of the radio spectrum under the Wireless Telegraphy Acts 1949 and 2006 and the exercise of Broadcasting Act 1990 powers for a competition purpose: sections 192 and 317(6) of the 2003 Act. The competition aspects of certain decisions concerning the Channel 3 networking arrangements may also be appealed to the Tribunal: Schedule 11, paragraph 9 of the 2003 Act.
- The Postal Services Act 2011 provides for an appeal to the Tribunal in respect of certain decisions taken by OFCOM in relation to the regulation of postal services: section 57 of the 2011 Act.
- Appeals by parties against the decisions of OFCOM under the Mobile Roaming (European Communities) Regulations 2007 (SI 2007/1933) and the Authorisation of Frequency Use for the Provision of Mobile Satellite Services (European Union) Regulations 2010 (SI 2010/672).
- Applications by affected parties for a review of a determination made by GEMA in relation to certain property schemes: Schedule 2A of the Electricity Act 1989 and Schedule 18 of the Energy Act 2004.
- Applications by affected parties for a review of decisions of GEMA in respect of: (i) the application of a market power licence condition to particular types of exploitative behaviour in electricity markets; and (ii) the imposition and amount of any penalty imposed by the Authority: sections 20 and 21 of the Energy Act 2010.
- Appeals against a market power determination or operator determination by the CAA: Schedule 1 of the Civil Aviation Act 2012 (the "2012 Act").
- Appeals against enforcement orders and penalties, and licence revocation decisions, of the CAA: Schedules 3, 4, 5 and 13 of the Civil Aviation Act 2012.
- Applications by persons to review decisions of the Payment Systems Regulator ("PSR") pursuant to the Payment Services Regulations 2009 (SI 209/2009) (as amended) to give a direction under regulation 104(1) to that person or to impose a penalty under regulation 105 on that person.
- Appeals against certain decisions of the PSR: sections 76 and 78 of the Financial Services (Banking Reform) Act 2013 (the "2013 Act").

2.2 Unless specific provision is made in the relevant legislation, the procedures to be followed in respect of the above proceedings before the Tribunal are set out in the Tribunal's 2015 Rules which may be supplemented by practice directions, such as this Guide, issued by the President under Rule 115(3).

2.3 Parts 1 and 6 of the Rules apply to all proceedings before the Tribunal. Part 2 of the Rules applies to all proceedings before the Tribunal save as otherwise provided in Parts 3, 4, 5 and 7. Part 3 applies to proceedings under the 2002 Act, Part 4 applies to claims made pursuant to section 47A of the 1998 Act and, subject to Rule 74 to collective proceedings, Part 5 applies to collective proceedings and collective settlements and Part 7 applies to appeals relating to price control matters: Rule 3.

2.4 In this Guide, unless the context otherwise requires, references to the CMA include reference to the other Regulators competent to apply the relevant provisions of the 1998 Act and the 2002 Act.

PRIVATE ACTIONS UNDER THE COMPETITION ACT 1998

[6.137]

2.5 Under section 47A of the 1998 Act any person who has suffered loss or damage as a result of an infringement or an alleged infringement of either UK or EU competition law (i.e. breaches of the Chapter I or Chapter II prohibitions contained in the 1998 Act and breaches of the prohibitions in Article 101(1) or Article 102 TFEU) may bring a claim for damages or for a sum of money before the Tribunal in respect of that loss or damage.

2.6 Consequently, the Tribunal is able to hear any claim for damages (whether brought on a stand-alone basis or following on from a decision of the CMA finding an infringement).

2.7 Pursuant to section 47A(3)(c), in proceedings in England and Wales or Northern Ireland "claims" includes claims for an injunction.

Collective proceedings

2.8 In addition, under section 47B of the 1998 Act collective actions for damages (including both follow-on and stand-alone claims) may be brought in the Tribunal on an "opt-in" or "opt-out" basis.

2.9 Collective proceedings must be commenced by a representative of the claimants, and that person must be authorised by the Tribunal to act as a representative. Claims are eligible for inclusion in collective proceedings only if the Tribunal considers that they raise the same, similar or related issues and are suitable to be brought in collective proceedings.

2.10 The Tribunal is also able to approve the settlement of claims in collective proceedings: see sections 49A and 49B of the 1998 Act.

PROCEEDINGS UNDER THE COMPETITION ACT 1998

[6.138]

2.11 The 1998 Act prohibits:

- certain agreements or concerted practices which have as their object or effect the prevention, restriction or distortion of competition within the United Kingdom (section 2 of the 1998 Act, referred to as 'the Chapter I prohibition'); and
- the abuse of a dominant position in a market if it may affect trade within the United Kingdom (section 18 of the 1998 Act, referred to as 'the Chapter II prohibition').

2.12 Those provisions are enforceable by the CMA and Regulators who may, by decision, give directions for bringing the infringement to an end and impose penalties of up to 10 per cent of the turnover of the undertaking concerned.[9] Similar powers are exercisable by the Regulators with concurrent powers within their respective spheres of activity (communications, electricity, gas, water, railways, health, financial services, retail payment systems and air traffic services).

2.13 Under section 46 of the 1998 Act, any party to an agreement in respect of which, or any person in respect of whose conduct the CMA has made a decision, may appeal to the Tribunal against, or with respect to, that decision. Under section 46(3), an appealable decision is:

(i) a decision as to whether the Chapter I or the Chapter II prohibition has been infringed;
(ii) a decision as to whether the prohibitions contained in Article 101(1) or Article 102 TFEU have been infringed;
(iii) a decision to impose a penalty for infringement of the competition provisions under section 36 of the 1998 Act or as to the amount of such penalty;
(iv) a decision giving directions under sections 32 or 33 of the 1998 Act with a view to bringing an infringement to an end;
(v) a decision cancelling a block or parallel exemption from the Chapter I prohibition;
(vi) a decision withdrawing the benefit of a regulation of the European Commission pursuant to Article 29(2) of Regulation 1/2003;
(vii) a decision imposing interim measures under section 35 of the 1998 Act; and
(viii) a decision relating to the release or non-release of commitments pursuant to section 31A(4)(b) of the 1998 Act.

2.14 Under section 49D(3) of the 1998 Act, a person required by the CMA to pay an amount of the CMA's costs relating to that person's application for approval of a redress scheme under section 49C of the 1998 Act may appeal to the Tribunal against the amount.

2.15 Most appealable decisions may also be appealed by a third party whom the Tribunal considers has a sufficient interest in the decision: section 47 of the 1998 Act.

2.16 The Secretary of State has the power to add to the list of decisions that may be appealed pursuant to sections 46 and 47.[10]

2.17 Appealable decisions, other than those relating to commitments, must be determined by the Tribunal on the merits by reference to the grounds of appeal set out in the notice of appeal: Schedule 8, paragraph 3 of the 1998 Act.[11] Under paragraph 3(2) the power of the Tribunal on such an appeal includes the power to:
– confirm or set aside the decision in question;
– remit the matter to the CMA;
– impose or revoke or vary the amount of any penalty;
– give such directions, or take such other steps, as the CMA itself could have given or taken; and
– make any other decision which the CMA could itself have made.

2.18 In respect of appeals concerning the acceptance, release, non-release or variation of commitments, the Tribunal must determine such appeals in accordance with judicial review principles and may:
– dismiss the appeal or quash the whole or part of the decision to which it relates; and
– where it quashes the whole or part of that decision, remit the matter back to the CMA with a direction to reconsider and make a new decision in accordance with the ruling of the Tribunal: Schedule 8, paragraph 3A of the 1998 Act.

2.19 Except in the case of an appeal against the imposition, or the amount, of a penalty, the making of an appeal to the Tribunal does not suspend the effect of the decision to which the appeal relates, unless the Tribunal orders otherwise: section 46(4) and section 47(3) of the 1998 Act.

PROCEEDINGS UNDER THE ENTERPRISE ACT 2002

[6.139]
2.20 Parts 3 and 4 of the 2002 Act set out the UK competition law regime for the supervision of mergers and markets.

Part 3 — Mergers

2.21 Part 3 of the 2002 Act provides, subject to a number of exceptions, that where the CMA believes that:
– a relevant merger situation has been created or believes that arrangements in progress or contemplation will result in such a situation if carried into effect; and
– it is or may be the case that that situation may be expected to result in a substantial lessening of competition within any market or markets in the United Kingdom for goods or services; it must make a reference to the CMA Panel Chair: sections 22 and 23.

2.22 Once a reference has been made in respect of a completed or anticipated merger, the CMA must decide whether a relevant merger situation has been, or would be created, and if so whether that situation has resulted, or may be expected to result, in a substantial lessening of competition within any market or markets in the United Kingdom for goods or services. Where this is the case, the CMA must decide whether any action should be taken by it for the purpose of remedying, mitigating or preventing the substantial lessening of competition and/or any adverse effects which arise from the substantial lessening of competition: sections 35 to 41.

2.23 Although the CMA is the principal decision maker under Part 3 of the 2002 Act, the Secretary of State may in certain prescribed circumstances intervene in the decision-making process in relation to certain public interest cases: sections 42 to 68.

Part 4 — Market investigations

2.24 Part 4 of the 2002 Act provides that market investigation references may be made to the CMA Panel Chair where the CMA (or a Regulator with concurrent powers) has reasonable grounds for suspecting that any feature, or combination of features, of a market in the United Kingdom for goods or services prevents restricts or distorts competition in connection with the supply or acquisition of any goods or services in the United Kingdom or a part of the United Kingdom: see section 131. The CMA must then determine whether any feature, or combination of features, of each relevant market prevents, restricts, or distorts competition in the United Kingdom or a part of the United Kingdom: section 134.

Applications to the Tribunal for review of decisions adopted under Parts 3 and 4

2.25 Any person aggrieved by a decision of the CMA or the Secretary of State in connection with a reference or possible reference in relation to a merger situation or market investigation may make an application for a review under section 120 (mergers) or section 179 (market investigations) of the 2002 Act. A "decision" includes a failure to take a decision permitted or required by the 2002 Act. The 2002 Act (unlike the 1998 Act) does not set out a list of decisions which may be challenged on a review.

2.26 In determining an application for a review the Tribunal must apply the same principles as would be applied by a court on an application for judicial review: section 120(4) (mergers) and section 179(4) (market investigations). The standard of review was considered by the Court of Appeal in *British Sky Broadcasting v CC* [2010] EWCA Civ 2.

2.27 Under section 120(5) (mergers) and section 179(5) (market investigations) the Tribunal may dismiss the application or quash the whole or part of the decision to which it relates and, where it quashes the whole or part of that decision, refer the matter back to the original decision maker with a direction to reconsider and make a new decision in accordance with the ruling of the Tribunal.

Appeals against penalties in merger and market investigations

2.28 Where the CMA imposes a penalty for failure to comply with a notice issued by it requiring the production of documents or information or the attendance of witnesses in a merger or market investigation under the 2002 Act, the person on whom the penalty is imposed may appeal to the Tribunal against the imposition of the penalty, the amount of a penalty or the date by which the penalty is required to be paid: section 114 (mergers) and section 176(1)(f) (market investigations).

PROCEEDINGS UNDER THE COMMUNICATIONS ACT 2003

[6.140]
2.29 In February 2002 the European Parliament and Council of Ministers enacted a number of measures designed to create a common regulatory framework for electronic communications networks and services.[12] A significant number of the obligations imposed by those measures on the United Kingdom are implemented by Part 2 of the 2003 Act.

2.30 Part 2 of the 2003 Act confers power on OFCOM to regulate the provision of electronic communications networks and services by the setting, modification or revocation of general or specific conditions of entitlement to provide such networks or services in accordance with section 45 of that Act.

2.31 Part 2 of the 2003 Act also confers power on OFCOM relating to the use of the radio spectrum under the Wireless Telegraphy Acts. The decisions under Part 2 of the 2003 Act or under the Wireless Telegraphy Acts that may be appealed to the Tribunal are set out in section 192 of the 2003 Act.

2.32 A person affected by any such decision may appeal to the Tribunal: section 192(2).

2.33 Certain appeals may also be brought by a Channel 3 licence holder against a decision made by OFCOM pursuant to sections 290 to 294 and Schedule 11, paragraphs 9 and 10, concerning the competition aspects of networking arrangements.

2.34 Appeals may also be made against decisions of OFCOM using powers under the Broadcasting Act 1990 for a competition purpose: section 317.

2.35 The Tribunal must decide an appeal under the 2003 Act on the merits and by reference to the grounds of appeal set out in the notice of appeal: section 195(2). If the Tribunal allows the appeal, its decision must include a decision as to what (if any) is the appropriate action for OFCOM to take in relation to the subject-matter of the decision under appeal, and the Tribunal shall then remit the decision under appeal to OFCOM with such directions (if any) as the Tribunal considers appropriate for giving effect to its decision: section 195(3) and (4).

2.36 In the case of an appeal against a decision given effect to by a restriction or condition set by regulations under section 109 of the 2003 Act, the Tribunal must take only such steps as it considers are not detrimental to good administration: section 195(7).

Specified price control matters

2.37 If an appeal raises a price control matter (as specified in Rule 116(1)), the Tribunal must, before reaching its decision, refer the matter to the CMA for determination in accordance with section 193 of the 2003 Act and Rule 116. Subject to the Tribunal's direction, the CMA shall then determine the specified price control matter within four months of receipt of the reference: Rule 117(1). The Tribunal may give directions as to the procedure in accordance with which the CMA is to make its determination: Rule 117(2).

2.38 In its final decision the Tribunal must follow the CMA's determination concerning the specified price control matter unless the Tribunal decides, applying the principles applicable on an application for judicial review, that the determination of the CMA would fall to be set aside on such an application: section 193(7) of the 2003 Act.

PROCEEDINGS UNDER THE POSTAL SERVICES ACT 2011

[6.141]
2.39 Section 57 of the 2011 Act stipulates that where OFCOM takes a decision to: (i) impose or modify a regulatory condition; (ii) give, modify or withdraw a direction, consent or approval; (iii) impose a penalty, or give or modify a direction; (iv) give or modify a direction under section 89A or 116(2A) of the Postal Services Act 2000; or (v) give a direction under section 25(5) of the Consumers, Estate Agents and Redress Act 2007, a person affected by such a decision may appeal against it to the Tribunal.

2.40 In determining the appeal, the Tribunal must apply the same principles as would be applied by a court on an application for judicial review. The Tribunal must either dismiss the appeal, or quash the whole or part of the decision to which the appeal relates.

PROCEEDINGS UNDER THE ELECTRICITY ACT 1989 AND THE ENERGY ACTS OF 2004 AND 2010

[6.142]
2.41 Under Schedule 2A of the Electricity Act 1989 (inserted by section 44(4) of the Energy Act 2008) GEMA may, on application, make a property scheme in the context of tenders in relation to offshore electricity transmission licences so that property, rights and liabilities can be transferred from the existing owner to the successful bidder. Any person aggrieved by such a decision may apply to the Tribunal for a review: paragraph 23 of Schedule 2A to the 1989 Act.

2.42 Under Schedule 18 of the Energy Act 2004 GEMA may, on application, make a property arrangements scheme which provides for the transfer of property, rights or liabilities from an existing transmission licence holder to a new system operator. Any person aggrieved by such a decision may apply to the Tribunal for a review: paragraph 10 of Schedule 18 to the Energy Act 2004.

2.43 The Tribunal is able to hear appeals in relation to decisions taken by GEMA in respect of: (i) orders made to secure compliance with a licence condition pursuant to section 25 of the 1989 Act; and (ii) the imposition and amount of any penalty imposed by GEMA under section 27A of the 1989 Act: sections 20 and 21, of the Energy Act 2010.

PROCEEDINGS UNDER THE CIVIL AVIATION ACT 2012

[6.143]

2.44 Under the regime introduced by the 2012 Act, the CAA grants licences to operators of "dominant areas" located at "dominant airports" which enable those operators to levy charges for airport operation services. These licences may contain price control conditions. In order to determine whether an airport area is dominant within the meaning of the 2012 Act, the CAA conducts a market power test.

2.45 The Tribunal's jurisdiction includes the hearing of appeals in respect of certain decisions of the CAA taken pursuant to the 2012 Act, namely:

– Section 13 and Schedule 1 of the 2012 Act (determinations): market power determinations and operator determinations by the CAA.
– Section 47 and Schedule 3 of the 2012 Act (orders and penalties): where the CAA takes action to enforce licence conditions by making an enforcement order or imposing a penalty for contravention of a licence condition.
– Section 49 and Schedule 4 to the 2012 Act (licence revocations): where the CAA gives a notice revoking a licence, or a further notice withdrawing a licence revocation notice.
– Section 55 and Schedule 5 of the 2012 Act (penalties: information): where the CAA imposes a penalty for failure to provide information, or for provision of false or misleading information, under section 51 or section 52 of the 2012 Act.
– Section 90 and Schedule 13 of the 2012 Act (penalties): where the CAA imposes a penalty under section 86 or section 87 of the 2012 Act for failure to provide information requested, or for provision of false or misleading information, in relation to the CAA's duty to publish information for the benefit of users of air transport services and environmental information.

2.46 The Tribunal's powers in respect of appeals under the 2012 Act are set out in the relevant Schedules. In particular, the Tribunal may only allow an appeal to the extent that it is satisfied that the decision being challenged is based on an error of fact, was wrong in law, or an error was made in the exercise of discretion. The Tribunal may then confirm or set aside the decision and give the CAA such other directions as it considers appropriate. In the case of market power determinations and operator determinations, the Tribunal also has the power to direct the CAA to make a further determination and, if the CAA fails to do so, to make the determination itself. The Tribunal is required to have regard to the CAA's duties under section 1 in any appeal under the 2012 Act.

PROCEEDINGS UNDER THE FINANCIAL SERVICES (BANKING REFORM) ACT 2013

[6.144]

2.47 The 2013 Act created a new statutory regulator for retail payments systems, the Payment Systems Regulator ("PSR").

2.48 The Tribunal has jurisdiction to hear appeals against certain enforcement decisions of the PSR pursuant to section 77 of the 2013 Act. Other enforcement decisions are appealable to the CMA (subject to a permission requirement). In essence, an affected party will be able to challenge before the Tribunal any "CAT-appealable decisions" and decisions to impose a penalty in respect of a compliance failure:

– CAT-appealable decisions are defined by section 76(4) of the 2013 Act as a decision to: (i) give a direction under section 54; (ii) impose a requirement under section 55; or (iii) publish details under section 72(1). In such an appeal, the Tribunal must apply the same principles as would be applied by a court on an application for judicial review. The Tribunal must either dismiss the appeal or quash the whole or part of the decision to which it relates. Where the Tribunal quashes the whole or part of a decision, it may refer the matter back to the PSR.
– Section 76(5) of the 2013 Act provides that decisions to impose a penalty taken under section 73 can be appealed to the Tribunal in accordance with section 78. An appellant may challenge the imposition of the penalty, its amount or the date for payment. The Tribunal has the power to uphold the penalty, set it aside and/or vary the amount or the date for payment.

PROCEEDINGS UNDER THE PAYMENT SERVICES REGULATIONS 2009

[6.145]

2.49 Under the Payment Services Regulations 2009 (as amended), the PSR supervises and enforces the prohibition of restrictive rules on access to payment systems. Pursuant to regulation 106, a person affected by a decision of the PSR under regulation 104(1) or 105 may appeal to the Tribunal. In determining the appeal, the Tribunal must apply the same principles as would be applied by a court on an application for judicial review.

NOTES

[9] Determined in accordance with the provisions of the Competition Act 1998 (Determination of Turnover for Penalties) Order 2000 (SI 2000/309) (as amended by the Competition Act 1998 (Determination of Turnover for Penalties) (Amendment) Order 2004 (SI 2004 No 1259)).

10 See for example the Competition Act 1998 (Appealable Decisions and Revocation of Notification of Excluded Agreements) Regulations 2004 (SI 2004/1078), which adds as decisions for the purposes of sections 46 and 47 of the 1998 Act decisions imposing, varying or removing conditions or obligations subject to which a parallel exemption is to have effect.

11 See also the analogous paragraph 3B concerning an appeal under section 49D(3) of the 1998 Act.

12 Those measures are: Directive 2002/19/EC on access to, and interconnection of, electronic communications networks and associated facilities (2002 OJ L108/7; the "Access Directive"); Directive 2002/20/EC on the authorisation of electronic communications networks and services (2002 OJ L108/21; the "Authorisation Directive"); Directive 2002/21/EC on a common regulatory framework for electronic communications networks and services (2002 OJ L108/33; the "Framework Directive"); Directive 2002/22/EC on universal service and users' rights relating to electronic communications networks and services (2002 OJ L108/51; the "Universal Service Directive"); Directive 2002/58/EC on the processing of personal data and the protection of privacy in the electronic communications sector (2002 OJ L201/37; the "Privacy Directive"); and EU Decision No 676/2002/EC of the European Parliament and the Council of 7 March 2002 on a regulatory framework for radio spectrum policy on the European Community (2002 OJ L108/1; the "Radio Spectrum Decision").

SECTION 3: THE GENERAL APPROACH OF THE RULES

[6.146]

3.1 The 2015 Rules seek to achieve the general objective of enabling the Tribunal to deal with cases justly and at proportionate cost, in particular by ensuring that the parties are on an equal footing, that expense is saved and that appeals are dealt with expeditiously and fairly. This is set out in the **governing principles** in Rule 4. The Rules will be interpreted in accordance with those principles: Rule 2(2).

3.2 The Rules pursue the same philosophy as the CPR of the High Court and many of the rules are modelled on the CPR. Where, in particular as regards private actions, a rule mirrors the CPR, the Tribunal would generally expect to interpret that rule in the same way as the High Court or Court of Appeal. However, the Tribunal's Rules are different in various respects and parties should not assume that the approach of the CPR applies to a particular procedural issue. Furthermore, the Tribunal is a United Kingdom, not an English, tribunal and it may therefore also have regard to the procedural rules that apply in Scotland or Northern Ireland, in particular in a case where the proceedings are to be treated as proceedings in either of those jurisdictions: see Rule 18.

3.3 A particular feature of all proceedings before the Tribunal is **active case management**: Rule 4(4). Rule 4(5) sets out what is meant by active case management. Essentially the concept involves the Tribunal and the parties working together to ensure that the case proceeds in the quickest and most efficient manner possible. Rule 4(1) places a duty on the parties to co-operate with the Tribunal to give effect to that aim and the governing principles as a whole.

3.4 As part of the process of active case management, the Tribunal constituted to deal with the case will generally handle it from inception through to the final hearing, dealing with all procedural points as they arise. However, the Chairman may be appointed first and may deal with preparatory matters before being joined by the other two Ordinary Members to concentrate on the substantive issues in the case. Collective proceedings, for the reasons explained in Section 6, may be conducted on a different basis.

3.5 In all cases, the Tribunal will seek to identify and concentrate on the main issues at as early a stage as possible, to avoid undue prolixity or delay and to ensure the efficient preparation of the case for a final hearing and that evidence is presented in an efficient manner. Four general features of the Tribunal's procedure should be noted:

– *Early disclosure in writing*

Each party's case must be fully set out in writing as early as possible, with supporting documents produced at the outset so far as practicable: (Rule 4(3). The Tribunal's proceedings rely more on written argument than traditional court pleadings. However, it is recognised that in private actions, it may not be possible to set out in full a party's case prior to disclosure.

– *Strict timetables*

The Tribunal will generally indicate, as early as possible, a target date for the main hearing: Rule 4(5)(c). The main stages of the case, and the planning of the Tribunal's work, will then be geared to meeting this timetable. In general, the Tribunal will aim to complete straightforward appeals or judicial review applications within six to nine months. Private claims assigned to the Fast-track (see Rule 58) should be completed within six months of that designation. In urgent cases, and where appropriate, the Tribunal will pursue an expedited procedure, giving case management directions as appropriate. However, it is recognised that many private actions may take longer to get to a main hearing for various reasons, for example due to the time required to conduct disclosure. Where a claim concerns an actual or contemplated infringement decision by a competition authority, a final hearing may not be possible before the infringement decision becomes final: see section 58A of the 1998 Act and Article 16 of Regulation 1/2003.

– *Effective fact-finding procedures*

The Tribunal will pay close attention to the probative value of documentary evidence. Where there are essential evidential issues that cannot be satisfactorily resolved without cross-examination, the Tribunal will permit the oral examination of witnesses. As regards expert evidence, the Tribunal expects the parties to make every effort to narrow the points at issue and to reach agreement where possible: Rule 4(5)(a).

– *Structured oral hearings*

The structure of the main oral hearings of the Tribunal will be planned in advance, in consultation with the parties, and will be fixed with a defined time limit: Rule 4(5)(e)-(f). Since the written arguments of the parties will already have been fully set out and since the main issues will have been identified prior to the main oral hearing, lengthy oral argument can normally be avoided.

3.6 At the conclusion of the main hearing, the Tribunal will normally inform the parties when judgment is likely to be given. In the event of unexpected delay, the parties will be kept informed.

SECTION 4: STATUTORY APPEALS AND APPLICATIONS FOR REVIEW

[6.147]

4.1 This part of the Guide outlines the procedures for statutory appeals from and applications for review of decisions of the CMA or a Regulator listed at paragraphs 2.11–2.48 above. It also deals with applications for interim measures.

4.2 The structure of this section mirrors the typical sequence of procedural steps in proceedings before the Tribunal, including:

– commencing proceedings: time limits for filing the notice of appeal/application and its form and content;
– steps immediately following receipt by the Tribunal of the notice of appeal or application: acknowledgment, defective notices of appeal/applications, service on the respondent, publication of the web summary, constitution of the Tribunal and preparation for the first CMC;
– the defence: the time limits for filing, its form and content; and
– the intervention procedure.

4.3 Other and subsequent procedural steps, including case management, evidence, hearings and the Tribunal's decision, are dealt with in Section 7.

4.4 Generally, the word "appeal" is used where the jurisdiction of the Tribunal extends to "the merits". The party appealing is referred to as the "appellant" and the claim is commenced by filing a "notice of appeal". Where the jurisdiction of the Tribunal is one applying the standard of judicial review, for example in merger and market investigation cases, the person applying for review is referred to as "the applicant", and proceedings are commenced by filing an "application". The term "applicant" is also used in connection with applications for interim measures. The party defending the decision that is being challenged, usually the CMA or a Regulator, is referred to as "the respondent". However, in certain contexts (for example commitment decisions under the 1998 Act) the relevant legislation provides for an appeal on judicial review grounds. The terminology is therefore not determinative of the standard of review, and where this Guide refers to an appeal, the comment will often apply equally to applications for review unless the context indicates otherwise.

TIME LIMITS FOR COMMENCING PROCEEDINGS UNDER THE 1998, 2002 AND 2003 ACTS

[6.148]

4.5 The following paragraphs set out the time limits for commencing proceedings and the manner of calculating them. The time limits vary according to the decision in respect of which a legal challenge is raised. As well as consulting this Guide, advisers must ensure they have taken into account the relevant statutory provisions.

4.6 It is useful if parties intending to commence proceedings contact the Registry as early as possible in order to indicate, on an informal and confidential basis, that an appeal or application is imminent. That will enable the Registry to make preparations for an efficient start to the proceedings. Until such time as the relevant notice of appeal or application has been served on the respondent and, if relevant, the summary of the appeal or application has been published on the Tribunal website. Generally, Tribunal staff will not be at liberty to disclose whether the Tribunal has received a notice of appeal or application before publication of the summary on the website, but where a time limit has clearly expired they may disclose the fact that a notice of appeal or application was not received before the expiry of the time limit.

4.7 Parties are also strongly advised not to wait until the last possible moment to commence proceedings. The Tribunal is only permitted to extend the relevant time limits if it is satisfied that the circumstances are exceptional.

Proceedings under the 1998 Act and the 2003 Act

4.8 The filing of an appeal under the 1998 Act or the 2003 Act is governed by Rule 9 of the Rules. Under Rule 9(1) an appeal must be made by filing a notice of appeal **within two months** of the date on which the appellant was notified of the disputed decision or the date of publication of the decision, whichever is the earlier.[13]

4.9 The Tribunal may not extend this time limit unless it is satisfied that the circumstances are exceptional: Rule 9(2).

Applications for review under the 2002 Act: Market investigations

4.10 Applications pursuant to section 179 of the 2002 Act for review of a decision in connection with a reference or possible reference under Part 4 of the 2002 Act must be filed within the same timescale as that applicable to appeals under the 1998 and 2003 Acts, that is by filing a notice of application within two months of the date on which the applicant was notified of the disputed decision, or the date of publication of the decision, whichever is the earlier: Rule 25(2).

4.11 The Tribunal may not extend this time limit unless it is satisfied that the circumstances are exceptional: Rule 25(3).

Applications for review under the 2002 Act: Mergers

4.12 These applications must be made within a much shorter time period than other types of proceedings.

4.13 An application for a review under section 120 of the 2002 Act must be made by filing a notice of application **within four weeks** of the date on which the applicant was notified of the disputed decision, or the date of publication of the decision, whichever is the earlier: Rule 25(1).

4.14 The Tribunal may not extend this time limit unless it is satisfied that the circumstances are exceptional: Rule 25(3).

CALCULATION OF TIME LIMITS FOR COMMENCING PROCEEDINGS GOVERNED BY RULES 9 AND 25

[6.149]
4.15 The combined effect of Rule 112(2) and (3) is that the last day for filing a notice of appeal under the 1998 Act, the 2003 Act, or an application pursuant to section 179 of the 2002 Act in respect of market investigations (but *not* mergers: see paragraph 4.17 below), is normally the day which falls on the same date in the month which occurs two months after the date on which the appellant/applicant was notified of the disputed decision. Thus, if the appellant/applicant was notified of the decision on 10 June, the last date for filing proceedings is 10 August. Time is not suspended during legal vacations. The Tribunal considered the time for filing an appeal in *Casting Book v OFT* [2006] CAT 16.

4.16 If the decision is notified on a date that does not exist in the month in which the time for making the appeal expires, time expires on the last day of that month. Thus for a decision notified on 31 July (and assuming that the two month time limit for commencing proceedings is applicable) the last day for filing the notice of appeal is 30 September. For a decision notified on 31 December, the last day for filing the notice of appeal is 28 February (29 February in a leap year).

4.17 In respect of applications pursuant to section 120 of the 2002 Act (mergers), the last day for filing the application is normally the day which falls on the same day in the fourth week after the date on which the applicant was notified of the disputed decision. In *Federation of Wholesale Distributors v OFT* [2004] CAT 11, the Tribunal indicated that for the purpose of Rule 25(1)[14] time starts to run from the date on which the reasoned decision is notified to the applicant or published (and not from the date of the press announcement of the fact of the decision).

4.18 The effect of Rule 112(3) is that if the last day for filing proceedings falls on a Saturday, Sunday or Bank Holiday, time expires on the following day which is not a Saturday, Sunday or Bank Holiday. Thus for a decision under the 1998 Act notified on 28 March, the last day for filing the appeal would normally be 28 May. Suppose, however, that 28 May is a Saturday and that 30 May is the Spring Bank Holiday Monday: in this hypothetical example the last day for filing the notice of appeal would be Tuesday, 31 May.

4.19 In accordance with Rules 111(4)(a) and 111(5), the latest time for personally delivering a notice of appeal to the Registry is 5.00 pm on the last day for filing an appeal. A notice of appeal sent by first class post is deemed to be received on the second day after posting: Rule 111(4)(b).

LIMITED POWER TO EXTEND THE TIME LIMIT FOR COMMENCING PROCEEDINGS

[6.150]
4.20 As noted above, under Rule 9(2) and Rule 25(3), the Tribunal may not extend the time limit for commencing proceedings ß¢unless it is satisfied that the circumstances are exceptional'. Any application for an extension of time must be made a reasonable time before the prescribed period has expired and reasons for the application must be given.

4.21 In *Hasbro v DGFT* [2003] CAT 1, the President indicated that respect for the deadline for commencing proceedings is, in many ways, the keystone of the whole procedure. The possibilities of obtaining an extension of the time limit for commencing proceedings are thus extremely limited. In order to demonstrate the existence of unforeseen circumstances, the party concerned may have to point to an excusable error or a situation of force majeure which prevented it from complying with the time limit. For examples of cases where the Tribunal has considered the concept of exceptional circumstances see orders of the President in: *Prater v OFT* [2006] CAT 11; *Fish Holdings v OFT* [2009] CAT 34; and *Somerfield Stores & others v OFT* [2013] CAT 5 (and the Court of Appeal judgment [2014] EWCA Civ 400). In the context of an application for review under section 120 of the 2002 Act, see *British Sky Broadcasting v CC & the Secretary of State* [2008] CAT 1.

TIME LIMITS FOR COMMENCING APPEALS UNDER OTHER LEGISLATION

Where the time limit in Rule 9 applies

[6.151]
4.22 The **two month** time period set out in Rule 9 of the Rules also applies when commencing proceedings in the Tribunal under certain other legislation by virtue of the following provisions in that legislation:

– Appeals against certain decisions of the PSR: see sections 77(3) and 78(4) of the 2013 Act.
– Applications for review of certain decisions of GEMA: see section 20(6) of the Energy Act 2010.
– Applications for review of certain decisions of the PSR: see Regulation 106(3) of the Payment Services Regulations 2009 (as amended).
– Appeals against certain decisions of OFCOM: Regulation 10 of the Authorisation of Frequency Use for the Provision of Mobile Satellite Services (European Union) Regulations 2010.
– Appeals against certain decisions of OFCOM: Regulation 14(3) of the Mobile Roaming (European Communities) Regulations 2007.

Where the time limit in Rule 28 applies

4.23 The time for filing an appeal under sections 114 or 176(1)(f) of the 2002 Act is governed by Rule 28.[15] Such an appeal must be made by sending a notice of appeal to the Registrar so that it is received within the period of **28 days** from:

– in the case of an appeal against a penalty imposed by a notice under section 112(1) of the 2002 Act, the day on which a copy of the notice was served on the person concerned;
– in the case of an appeal against a decision on an application under section 112(3), the day on which the person concerned was notified of the decision.[16]

Where a different time limit is set by legislation

4.24 Some statutory appeals that fall within the jurisdiction of the Tribunal are governed by different time limits which are set out in the relevant legislation rather than the Rules:

– Schedule 18 of the Energy Act 2004 empowers the Tribunal to review determinations made by GEMA in relation to certain property schemes. Paragraph 10(3) of that schedule states that an application may be made at any time before the end of the period of **seven days** beginning with the day on which the scheme is made.
– Schedule 2 of the Energy Act 2008 also enables the Tribunal to review determinations made by GEMA in relation to certain property schemes. Paragraph 23(3) of that schedule states that an application must be made either: **21 days** beginning with the day on which a notice in respect of the scheme is published or in any other case, 21 days beginning with the day on which the determination was made.
– Schedule 1 (paragraph 2) of the 2012 Act states that an appeal against a market power determination made by the CAA must be made by sending a notice of appeal to the Tribunal, to be received by the Registrar before the end of the period of **60 days** beginning with the relevant day.[17] The "relevant day" means the later of: (a) the day on which the CAA publishes the notice of the determination; or (b) the day on which the CAA publishes the reasons for the determination.
– Schedule 4 (paragraph 2) of the 2012 Act provides for a **30 day** limitation period for bringing an appeal against a decision of the CAA to revoke a licence.[18]

THE NOTICE OF APPEAL: REQUIREMENTS

[6.152]

4.25 There is no prescribed form that must be used to commence proceedings in the Tribunal. However, the 2015 Rules set out a number of requirements relating to the content of notices of appeal/applications: see Rules 9(3)–(7) and the guidance given below. This guidance should also be borne in mind when commencing proceedings under any of the statutory provisions not specifically covered here.

Formal requirements: Rule 9(3)

4.26 Under Rule 9(3), the notice of appeal must be signed and dated by the appellant, or on its behalf by a duly authorised officer or by its legal representative, and must state:

– the appellant's name and address;
– the name and address of the appellant's legal representative, if any;
– an address for service in the United Kingdom; and
– the name and address of the respondent.

Substantive requirements

4.27 The notice of appeal must be clear, concise and complete. The notice of appeal is intended to be a fully pleaded statement of the appellant's case, and the Tribunal should be able, on a single reading, to apprehend all the essential matters of fact and law that are in issue.

4.28 Rule 9(4) sets out a list of substantive requirements for the notice of appeal. Those requirements are:

– a concise statement of the facts;
– details of the decision to which the proceedings relate;
– observations on which part of the UK the proceedings are to be treated as taking place under Rule 18;
– a summary of the grounds for contesting the decision, including: (i) the statutory provisions under which the appeal is brought; and (ii) to what extent (if any) the appellant contends that the disputed decision was based on an error of fact or was wrong in law or is an appeal against the respondent's exercise of its discretion;
– a succinct presentation of the arguments supporting each ground of appeal;
– the relief sought and any directions in accordance with Rule 19;
– a schedule listing all documents annexed to the notice of appeal; and
– a statement identifying the evidence (witness statements or other documents annexed to the notice of appeal) the substance of which, so far as the appellant is aware, was not before the maker of the disputed decision.

4.29 It is a key feature of the above requirements that the notice of appeal should contain not only *all* the grounds relied on for the appeal, but also a succinct presentation of *each* of the arguments supporting those grounds. The notice of appeal will therefore contain a written development of each of the factual, legal or other grounds of appeal relied on, so that the Tribunal is seized in writing, from the outset, with the substance of the case advanced on appeal.

4.30 To achieve that aim, it will normally be appropriate to set out first the factual context in which the appeal arises, with a brief mention of the course of events leading to the decision that is being challenged. If the primary facts are not themselves in dispute, for example where the appeal turns largely on questions of law, reference may be made to the facts as summarised in the contested decision. There will be other cases where the primary facts are themselves contested, and the appeal will turn largely on questions of fact and evidence. Parties should pay careful attention to distinguishing in the notice of appeal between disputes about primary facts and disagreements which are more appropriately characterised as ones of appraisal or assessment of those primary facts. **The application should clearly identify which of the primary facts found by the respondent authority are contested by the appellant and upon what grounds.**

4.31 Having briefly set out the factual context, the notice of appeal should clearly identify each principal ground of appeal relied on ßž for example that the facts found in the decision are not supported by the evidence; that the respondent has defined the relevant market incorrectly; that the decision is insufficiently reasoned; that the penalty imposed for an infringement of competition law is excessive; and so on. The extent to which the appellant contends that the relevant decision was based on an error of fact, or was wrong in law, or that the respondent wrongly exercised its discretion, should be specifically stated (Schedule 8, paragraph 2(2)(b) and (c) of the 1998 Act and section 192(5)(b) of the 2003 Act). Each main ground of appeal should then be developed by a succinct presentation of the arguments in support of that ground, avoiding repetition. Where grounds overlap, it is sufficient to refer back to the arguments already developed.

4.32 When dealing with the arguments in support of each ground, it is unnecessary to set out lengthy extracts from decided cases: short citations, accompanied by the case reference and paragraph number, will normally suffice.

4.33 In setting out the grounds, arguments and details of the relief sought, appellants should bear in mind that the Registrar will draw on those details when drafting the summary of the notice of appeal required for the Tribunal website pursuant to Rule 14(2). If it is possible to provide a brief encapsulation of any part of more extensive sections dealing with the grounds, arguments and relief sought that would be of assistance in the production of the website summary.

The documents to be annexed

4.34 The following should be annexed to the notice of appeal:

– a copy of the disputed decision: Rule 9(6)(a); and
– as far as practicable, a copy of every document (or part of a document) on which the appellant relies, including the written statements of all witnesses of fact or expert witnesses, if any: Rule 9(6)(a).

4.35 The notice of appeal should clearly explain the relevance of each of the annexed documents and which passages of the document are relied on.

4.36 Documents that might be annexed to a notice of appeal include: (i) pertinent documents relating to the administrative procedure prior to the adoption of the contested decision; (ii) documents relating to primary facts; (iii) witness statements relating to primary facts; (iv) documents related to market characteristics and other economic issues; and (v) expert opinion and other evidence directed to economic or technical issues. **Documents of only peripheral relevance to the case should not be annexed.**

4.37 It is important that a common sense approach is taken to these requirements. If a document is voluminous (or might, as in the case of the disputed decision, be produced by several appellants) it might be preferable for the appellant to annex extracts (provided such extracts are not taken out of context) or perhaps rely on the fact that the document is being produced by another appellant. Where complications of this kind are likely to occur, appellants should liaise with the Registrar on the most efficient approach.

4.38 As regards witness statements on issues of primary fact (for example as to whether a particular agreement was entered into, or whether conduct took place or not), statements by witnesses on whose evidence the appellant will rely must be provided with the notice of appeal.

4.39 Similarly, any experts' reports (see Section 7 (Evidence)) or other documents relied on relating to market characteristics and information such as market surveys, consumer research, trade statistics, price studies, etc. or going to technical matters, must be annexed to the notice of appeal. The Tribunal may request certain documents and any underlying calculations (spreadsheets for example) to be supplied in electronic form.

4.40 In proceedings where a confidentiality ring is established, the Tribunal may find it appropriate to order disclosure of all annexed documents into the ring. In the event that this is likely to be problematic (for example because the document contains information that is confidential to a third party), appellants ought to consider if they can rely on, and annex, non-confidential versions of the relevant document.

New evidence

4.41 Rule 9(4)(h) provides that any new evidence (that is, material the substance of which ßž to the knowledge of the appellant — was not before the maker of the challenged decision) relied must be identified in a statement. See further paragraphs 7.71–7.78 below.

Confidential treatment

4.42 If an appellant wishes to request confidential treatment over any information included in the notice of appeal, the notice should be accompanied by a written request indicating the relevant words, figures or passages for which confidentiality is claimed, and supported in each case by specific reasons: see Rule 101(1) and Section 7 (Confidentiality) which deal with the procedure to be followed with regard to such a request.

The relief sought

4.43 The relief sought — for example, that the decision be set aside, or the penalty be reduced, or the matter be remitted to the respondent, etc. — must be set out in the concluding section of the notice of appeal. If an order is sought that the respondent pay the appellant's costs, this should be specifically mentioned. If the appellant wishes to invite the Tribunal to 'give such directions, or take such other steps, as the CMA could itself have given or taken' or 'make any other decision which the CMA could itself have made' (Schedule 8, paragraphs 3(2)(d) and (e) of the 1998 Act), this should be made clear in the notice of appeal, providing an appropriate level of detail as to the particular relief sought.

4.44 If the appellant wishes to seek any directions in the context of the Tribunal's case management powers under Rule 19, for example, as to the disclosure of documents, or the presentation of evidence (Rule 21), these should be requested in the notice of appeal: Rule 9(4)(f). The early identification of case management issues will facilitate the first CMC which will normally be held around four weeks after the appeal has been filed. See Section 7 (Case management conferences: planning the case).

The length and format of the notice of appeal

4.45 Modern technology and the understandable desire of parties' representatives to leave no stone unturned may lead to the notice of appeal (and other pleadings) being longer than is necessary or useful. However, this is a matter that requires a common sense approach. In general, a notice of appeal which is too long or badly organised is likely to be counterproductive, especially if it contains repetition, irrelevant information or padding.

4.46 In the interest of ensuring that cases are dealt with expeditiously and at proportionate costs, appellants and their legal representatives are requested to make every effort to express themselves logically and concisely and to limit the length of pleadings as much as possible. In general, in a case of no particular difficulty or complexity a short notice of appeal will suffice, and a length of 20 to 30 pages should not normally be exceeded. Even in complex and difficult cases, a notice of appeal of more than 75 pages should be regarded as highly exceptional.

4.47 The notice should have a table of contents, and pages and paragraphs should be numbered. The notice and all annexed documents should be printed on both sides of A4 paper. All materials should be hole-punched and placed in two or four-hole ring binders that are clearly indexed and labelled on the spine, the front cover and the inside front cover.

4.48 Every notice of appeal must include a schedule listing the documents annexed in a numbered sequence: Rule 9(4)(g). It is preferable if the disputed decision is put as the first document in the list.

Number of copies

4.49 Rule 9(7) requires the appellant/applicant to provide the Tribunal with the signed original of the notice of appeal/application and the annexes and ten copies, certified by the appellant or the appellant's legal representative as conforming to the original. Like the original, copies should be double-sided and placed in appropriately indexed and labelled ring binders.

Amendment, striking out and defective notices of appeal/applications

4.50 The Tribunal's permission is required to amend the notice of appeal: Rule 12(1). The Tribunal may grant permission on such terms as it thinks fit: Rule 12(2). Rule 12(3) provides that the Tribunal, in deciding whether or not to grant permission to amend, shall take into account all the circumstances including whether: (i) the proposed amendment involves a substantial change or addition to the appellant's case; (ii) is based on matters of law or fact which have come to light since the appeal was made; or (iii) could not otherwise practicably have been included in the notice of appeal; see for example *Carphone Warehouse v OFCOM (Local Loop Unbundling)* [2009] CAT 30 (decided under the 2003 Rules).

4.51 The Tribunal may refuse to hear argument on a matter that has not been set out as a ground of appeal, but has been raised subsequently in the appellant's skeleton argument.[19]

4.52 Under Rule 11 (Power to strike out), the Tribunal has power to strike out an appeal in whole or in part at any stage in the proceedings if it considers that the Tribunal has no jurisdiction to hear or determine the appeal, or it considers that the notice of appeal, or part of it, discloses no valid ground of appeal. See further paragraph 7.110 of Section 7 (Power to strike out).

4.53 Under Rule 10 (Defective notices of appeal), the Tribunal has power to give directions for putting a notice of appeal in order if it considers that it 'is materially incomplete, or is unduly prolix or lacking in clarity', and — if satisfied that the efficient conduct of the proceedings so requires - to defer service of the notice of appeal on the respondent until any defect has been remedied. The exercise of this power may be appropriate in cases where the notice of appeal is excessively long or confused.[20]

THE NOTICE OF APPLICATION: REQUIREMENTS

[6.153]
4.54 By virtue of Rule 3, Rule 9 applies to proceedings for review under section 120 or section 179 of

the 2002 Act. This means that the requirements mentioned in sub-paragraphs (2), (3), (4), (6) and (7) of Rule 9 and the guidance outlined above at paragraphs 4.25–4.49 applies equally to applications for review.

4.55 In addition, Rule 27 provides that if the applicant in proceedings for a review under section 120 or section 179 of the 2002 Act wishes to rely on expert evidence that was not before the decision maker whose decision is the subject of the application, it must serve with its application for review an application to adduce that evidence, attaching either the statement of expert evidence on which it wishes to rely or a detailed explanation of the nature of the expert evidence that it wishes to adduce. See further paragraph 7.78(a) below.

4.56 The Tribunal's power to strike out an appeal under Rule 11 includes a power to reject an application for review under sections 120 or 179 of the 2002 Act if it considers that the applicant is not a "person aggrieved" by the decision in respect of which the review is sought: see Rule 26(3). As to the meaning of "person aggrieved", see *Merger Action Group v Secretary of State* [2008] CAT 36 at [38]–[48] and *Stagecoach v CC* [2010] CAT 1 at [10]–[18].

FILING THE PROCEEDINGS

[6.154]
4.57 See Section 9 of the Guide for information about how to file documents at the Tribunal. Unlike claims for damages (where the responsibility for service of the proceedings rests with the party commencing proceedings) service on the respondent authority will be carried out by the Registrar. However, in relation to applications for review pursuant to section 120 of the 2002 Act the applicant should provide any likely interveners with copies of the notice of application at the same time as filing it with the Tribunal.

THE INITIAL PROCEDURE AFTER THE PROCEEDINGS ARE FILED

Checking the notice

[6.155]
4.58 Once the notice of appeal or application has been filed with the Registrar, it will be checked by the Registry to ensure that the various requirements of the Rules and this Guide have been complied with. Documents that do not constitute appeals or applications, or which are out of time, will not be registered.

4.59 Where a notice of appeal or application does not comply with one of the requirements of Rule 9, is materially incomplete, or is unduly prolix or lacking in clarity, the Tribunal may give directions for putting the document in order (Rule 10(1)) and may defer service on the respondent until this has been done: Rule 10(2). Failure to comply with such a direction may lead to the notice of appeal or application being struck out under Rule 11(1)(e).

Acknowledgment and notification

4.60 If the notice of appeal or application is in order, the Registrar will send an acknowledgment of receipt to the appellant or applicant and send a copy of the notice to the respondent: Rule 14(1)(a)–(b).

4.61 A summary of the notice of appeal or application will be published on the Tribunal's website in accordance with Rule 14(2) to notify the fact that a notice of appeal or application has been received and to invite those who consider that they have a sufficient interest in the outcome of the proceedings to seek permission to intervene (see paragraph 4.92 et seq. for further details of the intervention procedure).

Constitution of the Tribunal

4.62 Following receipt of a notice of appeal or application, a Tribunal will be constituted to hear the matter and the Registrar will write to the parties informing them which Tribunal members will hear the case. If there are no immediate steps to be taken (because, for example, the case has been immediately stayed on request of the parties) the constitution of a Tribunal may be deferred until the case becomes active. Alternatively, if the only immediate steps in the case relate to case management, a Chairman may be appointed to the case and the other members of the Tribunal appointed at a later date when substantive issues have come to the fore.

Setting the date for the first case management conference

4.63 The Registrar's letter notifying the constitution of a Tribunal will, usually, also state the date for the first CMC. Unless the case is urgent, this will usually take place around four weeks after the proceedings have commenced and approximately two weeks **before** the defence is due to be filed. Once set, the date of the first CMC will seldom be changed. For further information with regard to the first CMC, see Section 7 of this Guide.

Correspondence on the case

4.64 The Registrar's letter will also set out the usual principle on the basis of which correspondence in respect of the proceedings ought to be conducted, namely that all correspondence to the Tribunal should be copied by the originator to all other parties, save where it is clear that only one of the parties has an interest in the correspondence, or where considerations of confidentiality or possible settlement prevail. Where several cases are being managed together it may also be expedient for correspondence to be copied to all parties in the other cases.

4.65 The Tribunal will generally address correspondence in proceedings to the appellant/applicant, copied to all other parties, including (proposed) interveners, unless there is good reason to do otherwise.

Special points on applications for review under section 120 of the 2002 Act

4.66 Parties should be prepared for the fact that the Tribunal will adapt its procedures to the individual circumstances of the case.

4.67 The Tribunal will normally regard applications for review of a decision relating to a merger as meriting a high degree of urgency.[21] As a result it is quite likely that the parties will be expected to assemble and present their respective cases within demanding timescales.[22] It is therefore important that the Registry is contacted as soon as it becomes likely that such an application will be made. It is also imperative that the applicant takes steps at an early stage to make all interested parties aware of the applicant's intention to make an application and to provide their contact details to the Registry.[23] Where possible, the applicant should provide a copy of the application to the respondent (and any known interested parties who are likely to wish to apply to intervene in the proceedings) at the same time as filing the application with the Registry, although the Registrar will still formally serve a copy of the application on the respondent.

4.68 The first CMC in an application for review under section 120 of the 2002 Act is likely to take place quite quickly after the application is filed. The precise timing of the CMC will depend on the urgency of the application[24] but it may well be listed to take place within a few days of the application being filed. For example, in *Sports Direct v CC* (Case 1116/4/8/09) a CMC was held two working days following the receipt of the notice of application. The Tribunal Registry will liaise with the parties on such matters. If urgency so requires, the Tribunal may dispense with the CMC altogether and proceed directly to a substantive hearing (subject to directions contained in an order of the President or Chairman — see below).

4.69 In urgent cases it is usual for the President (or Chairman, if appointed) to make an order as soon as the application is filed setting out whatever abridgment of the timetable is deemed necessary in the circumstances.

4.70 It is likely that the order will abridge the time for submitting a request for permission to intervene. By way of illustration, in the case of *CTS Eventim v CC* (Case 1150/4/8/10) the normal period of three weeks was abridged to ten days. In *Ryanair Holdings Plc v CMA*, the period for intervention requests was abridged to three days.[25]

4.71 In appropriate cases the order may also set a timetable for preparatory steps leading up to the hearing and dispense with the need to file a defence, instead ordering that skeleton arguments are to stand as pleadings in the matter.

Applications for review under section 179 of the 2002 Act

4.72 In general, an application for review under section 179 of the 2002 Act will be dealt with, at this initial stage of the proceedings, in the same way as an appeal under the 1998 Act.

Special points on appeals against a penalty under sections 114 and 176 of the 2002 Act

4.73 In the case of appeals pursuant to sections 114 and 176(1)(f) of the 2002 Act, the Registrar will not publish a summary of the appeal, and interventions are not permitted: Rule 28(3).

THE DEFENCE

[6.156]
4.74 In most types of proceedings before the Tribunal (the exception being claims for damages) the first CMC generally takes place before the service of the defence. At that CMC the Tribunal may have taken the opportunity to establish in outline what will be the areas covered by the defence and other related questions, such as witness statements and expert evidence.

4.75 The formal requirements applicable to the defence (Rule 15(2)) are broadly similar to those applicable to the notice of appeal.

4.76 Rule 15(3)(a) stipulates that the defence must contain observations on forum. Rule 15(3)(c) stipulates that the defence should contain details of any objections to the admission of evidence put forward by the appellant. In this regard it should also be noted that the respondent must also include a statement identifying the evidence (witness statements or documents annexed to the defence) the substance of which, so far as the respondent is aware, was not referred to in the disputed decision or disclosed to the appellant before that decision was made: Rule 15(3)(f). See further paragraph 7.71 et seq. of Section 7 (Evidence).

4.77 The defence is intended to respond, in a reasoned manner, to the grounds contained in the notice of appeal or application. It must contain a succinct presentation of the arguments of fact and law upon which the respondent relies: Rule 15(3)(b). Where the respondent's position in fact and law has already been set out in the decision under appeal, it may be sufficient to refer to the passages in the decision which deal with the arguments advanced, rather than rehearsing the contents of the decision.

4.78 The defence should set out the relief sought by the respondent and any directions sought under Rule 19.

4.79 The powers of the Tribunal in relation to a defective notice of appeal, mentioned at paragraph 4.53 above, apply equally to the defence: see Rule 15(7).

4.80 Rule 15(5) requires the respondent, as far as practicable, to annex to the defence a copy of every document (or part of a document) upon which the respondent relies. However, where a large number of those documents have already been annexed to the notice of appeal, it may well be more convenient to cross refer to them rather than duplicating documents that are already in the Tribunal's file. The practical application of Rule 15(5) as regards documents may be one of the matters to be discussed at the first CMC, before the defence is served.

4.81 Rule 15(5) further requires the respondent to annex to the defence 'the written statements of all witnesses of fact, and expert witnesses, if any'. In so far as the respondent's case depends on findings of primary fact, for example whether a particular concerted practice took place or not, the evidence relied on by the respondent will normally be already referred to in the contested decision. In so far as that evidence consists of statements of witnesses, the production of those statements should present no difficulty. Similarly, in so far as the respondent relies on expert evidence, it is important, for the expeditious conduct of proceedings, that such evidence is annexed to the defence.

4.82 Pursuant to Rule 3, the requirements of Rule 15 will also apply to a defence to a notice of application pursuant to the 2002 Act (except in relation to the time limit for filing the defence in merger cases — see further below). Rule 15 also applies to a defence to a penalty appeal under section 114 of the 2002 Act (again subject to a variation of the time limit for filing the defence — see further below).

Time for filing the defence in appeals under the 1998 and 2003 Acts

4.83 The respondent must file the defence and its annexes, together with ten copies certified as conforming to the original, within **six weeks** (or such further time as the Tribunal may allow) of the date on which the respondent received a copy of the notice of appeal: Rule 15(1) and Rule 15(6).

4.84 In principle the Tribunal will treat requests for extensions of time to file the defence in the same way as requests to extend the time for the filing of the notice of appeal, that is to say an extension of time will only be granted if the circumstances are exceptional: see *Napp v DGFT* [2001] CAT 2; *Freeserve v DGT* [2002] CAT 9; and *Vodafone v OFCOM* [2008] CAT 4.

4.85 It should be noted that the Tribunal may enquire at the first CMC (which, as already noted, will generally take place before service of the defence) whether it is possible for the defence to be served before the time calculated in accordance with Rule 15(1).

Time for filing the defence to an application for a review under section 120

4.86 The respondent to an application for a review under section 120 of the 2002 Act must file the defence within **four weeks** of the date on which the respondent received a copy of the notice of application (Rule 26(2) read with Rule 15(1)), unless the Tribunal directs otherwise.

4.87 In practice, the notice of application should indicate the urgency of the proceedings: see paragraph 4.68 of this Guide. In particularly urgent cases, the Tribunal will be prepared to abridge the time limit for filing the defence, or indeed order that the respondent's skeleton argument stand as the defence (see, for example: the Order of the President of 24 November 2003 in *IBA Health v OFT*; the Order of the Tribunal of 3 December 2008 in *Merger Action Group v Secretary of State*; the Order of the President dated 19 November 2009 in *Sports Direct v CC*; and the Order of the Chairman of 24 June 2015 in *Ryanair Holdings PLC v CMA*).

Time for filing the defence to an application for a review under section 179

4.88 The respondent to an application for a review under section 179 must send its defence to the Registrar so that it is received within **six weeks** of the date upon which the respondent received a copy of the notice of application: Rule 15(1).

Time for filing the defence to an appeal against a penalty imposed under sections 114 or 176(1)(f)

4.89 The respondent must file a defence within **three weeks** of the date on which it received a copy of the notice of appeal: Rule 28(2), read with Rule 15(1). The reason for this shorter period is that in most cases the CMA will have set out its case in the notice required to be served on the person in respect of whom the penalty has been imposed.

Service of the defence on the other parties

4.90 Rule 15(8) provides that the respondent must provide a copy of the defence and any accompanying documents to each other party to the proceedings at the same time as it files the defence.

FURTHER PLEADINGS AFTER THE DEFENCE

[6.157]
4.91 Rule 19(2)(b) provides that the Tribunal may give directions that the parties file a reply, rejoinder or other additional pleadings or particulars; see for example, the Order of 21 September 2004 in *Albion Water (Dŵr Cymru/ Shotton Paper) v DGWS*. However, the filing of a reply and a rejoinder is not standard practice in the Tribunal, and will only be permitted where the Tribunal considers that they are appropriate.

THE INTERVENTION PROCEDURE

[6.158]
4.92 The Tribunal's decisions may have far-reaching consequences for third parties and the wider

public interest. Interventions give those who are sufficiently interested in the outcome of proceedings the right to be heard and assist the Tribunal to consider the issues fully.

Publication of a summary of the proceedings

4.93 As mentioned above, pursuant to Rule 14(2) the Registrar must publish a summary on the Tribunal website (and in any other manner as the President may think fit) indicating that an appeal or application has been received and containing the information referred to in Rule 14(3) (the "notice"). The notice will be based on the appellant's summary of the principal grounds of appeal as it appears in the notice of appeal. For this reason it is helpful if the appellant does not include confidential information in the summary of its grounds.

Requesting permission to intervene

4.94 Persons wishing to intervene in the proceedings and who have 'sufficient interest in the outcome' have **three weeks** from the date of publication of the notice, **or such other period as directed by the President**, in which to make a request for permission to intervene: Rule 16(2) read with Rule 14(3)(f). The period within which such a request must be filed will be set out in the notice. The request must be sent to the Registrar.

4.95 If the circumstances require it, the President or the Tribunal may abridge the three week period in order to ensure the swift conduct of the proceedings. This is highly likely in applications for review pursuant to section 120 of the 2002 Act (mergers) . see, for example: Order of the President of 20 January 2005 in *Unichem v OFT* (Case 1049/4/1/05) and Order of the President of 19 June 2015 in *Ryanair Holdings PLC v CMA* (Case 1239/4/12/15); see paragraph 4.70 above.

4.96 Parties who wish to request permission to intervene should do so at the earliest moment without waiting until the end of the period allowed (see, for example *T-Mobile & Ors v OFCOM (Truphone's intervention)* [2007] CAT 31). The earlier a request to intervene is made, the greater the possibility for the intervener to participate in the development of the case (particularly at the first CMC which is the key planning stage in the Tribunal's procedure) and the more efficiently the Tribunal will be able to carry out its case management functions. Under Rule 19(2)(m), the Tribunal may extend the time period for making applications for permission to intervene: see, for example: *Cityhook v OFT (Interventions)* [2006] CAT 26; and *Tesco v CC (ACS's intervention)* [2008] CAT 20.

4.97 Persons should not make a request for permission to intervene unless they have a sufficient interest in the outcome of the particular case before the Tribunal.

4.98 The request for permission to intervene must contain the information set out in Rule 16(4). It must also show a 'sufficient interest' by including 'a concise statement of the matters at issue in the proceedings which affect the person making the request': Rule 16(5)(a). It should state the name of the party whose position the person making the request intends to support and include a succinct presentation of the reasons for making the request: Rule 16(5)(b) and (c). The request to intervene should be as clear and concise as possible.

4.99 The request for permission to intervene will be sent to the other parties by the Registrar and their observations will be invited, usually within a fairly short time frame (Rule 16(3)), for example one to three days. At this stage the main issue is whether the potential intervener has 'a sufficient interest'.

Considering the request for permission to intervene

4.100 If the Tribunal is satisfied, having taken into account the observations of the parties, that the proposed intervener has a sufficient interest, it may permit the intervention on such terms and conditions as it sees fit: Rule 16(6). Often, requests for permission to intervene will be considered by the Tribunal before or at the first CMC, so if permission is granted the intervener will be able to participate in the proceedings (to the extent allowed by the Tribunal) from that point onwards.

4.101 With regard to the criterion of sufficient interest, see: *BT v DGT (O2's intervention)* [2003] CAT 20; *Umbro v OFT (Sports World's intervention)* [2003] CAT 25; *Floe Telecom v OFCOM (Intervention)* [2004] CAT 2; *Albion Water v DGWS* [2004] CAT 19; *Umbro v OFT (Sports World's intervention on costs)* [2005] CAT 26; and *Barclays v CC (permission to intervene)* [2009] CAT 15. A party with a more general interest in the proceedings, such as a consumer body, may have a sufficient interest, depending on the circumstances: Order of the Tribunal of 7 September 2004 granting the Consumers' Association permission to intervene in *Burgess v OFT* (Case 1044/2/1/04). Conversely, there is no need for an interested party to intervene if the interests of that party are already adequately protected by the position taken by one or other of the principal parties (see *Umbro v OFT (Sportsworld's intervention)* [2003] CAT 25).

4.102 Interventions may sometimes be permitted at a later stage of a case where a specific issue arises, for example as to remedy, as in *Genzyme v OFT* [2005] CAT 32.

4.103 If the Tribunal gives permission, the Tribunal will give any necessary directions with regard, for example, to the service on the intervener of the documents filed with the Tribunal, admission to any confidentiality ring, the time limit for filing of the statement of intervention and, if appropriate, the submission by the main parties of a response to the statement of intervention and any objections to the admission of evidence put forward by the intervener: Rule 16(7). The nature and form of the directions for the conduct of the intervention will depend on the particular circumstances of the case, and may need to be determined after hearing the parties, for example at the first CMC.

4.104 Since the proceedings are primarily between the appellant/applicant and the respondent, the role of the intervener is by its nature an ancillary one.[26] Moreover, there is a risk that the arguments put forward by the intervener will, in practice, largely duplicate the arguments already advanced by the principal parties (see *National Grid v GEMA* [2008] CAT 26 and [2008] CAT 30). Particularly in cases where multiple interventions are made in support of one party, the Tribunal will generally order the interveners to liaise with each other and the party they support in order to avoid unnecessary duplication (see: Order of the Tribunal of 28 April 2009 in *Barclays v CC*; and Order of the Tribunal of 26 January 2010 in *Carphone Warehouse v OFCOM (Wholesale Line Rental)*).

4.105 In some circumstances the Tribunal may give directions as to the scope of the intervention (see Ruling of the Tribunal in *Albion Water v DGWS* [2004] CAT 19) or the admissibility of evidence filed by an intervener. Where it is appropriate to do so, the Tribunal may direct that the intervention be limited to the filing of a statement of intervention, without the scope for further oral or written submissions.

4.106 However, in appeals pursuant to section 192(2) of the 2003 Act against the determination by OFCOM under section 190 of a dispute resolution between private parties, although OFCOM will be the respondent to the appeal, the party in whose favour OFCOM resolved the dispute is generally permitted to intervene in support of OFCOM. OFCOM is not obliged to take an active part in the proceedings and may leave it to the intervener to resist the appeal.[27] In those circumstances, the intervener plays a much more prominent role, akin to that of a respondent in other appeals, and the Tribunal will give directions accordingly.

The statement of intervention

4.107 When directing the intervener to file a statement of intervention the Tribunal will also stipulate the deadline by which it should be filed. The statement of intervention must comply with the requirements of Rule 16(8) and Rule 16(9): it must contain a succinct presentation of the facts and arguments supporting the intervention; the relief sought by the intervener; a schedule listing all documents annexed to the intervention and, as far as practicable; a copy of every document or part of a document on which the intervener relies, including written statements of fact and expert witnesses, if any. It is not necessary to annex documents on which the intervener relies if these have been annexed to the notice of appeal or defence.

4.108 The statement of intervention must also contain a statement identifying the evidence (witness statements or documents annexed) the substance of which — to the best of the intervener's knowledge — was not before the maker of the disputed decision: Rule 16(8)(d). See further Section 7 (Evidence).

4.109 As mentioned above, duplication of material contained in statements of intervention filed by other interveners and the pleadings of the party in support of whom the intervention is made should be avoided.

4.110 The statement of intervention and any accompanying documents must be served by the intervener on all parties at the same time as it is filed with the Tribunal: Rule 16(11).

Defective statements of intervention and amendment

4.111 If the Tribunal considers that a statement of intervention is defective, it may give directions to ensure that the defects are remedied: Rule 16(10) and Rule 10(1). The intervener may amend the statement of intervention only with the Tribunal's permission: Rule 16(10) and Rule 12.

Intervention in applications for review

4.112 The intervention procedure in applications for review is similar to that in appeals save that in applications under section 120 of the 2002 Act where the matter is usually urgent, the President or Chairman will often direct that any request to intervene be made earlier than within three weeks of publication of the notice and/or order that the intervener's skeleton argument stand as the statement of intervention: see Order of the President of 24 November 2003 in *IBA Health v OFT*; and Order of the President of 20 January 2005 in *Unichem v OFT*.

4.113 For examples of circumstances in which the Tribunal granted or refused permission to intervene in applications for review, see: *Somerfield v CC (Vue's intervention)* [2005] CAT 37; *Tesco v CC (ACS's intervention)* [2008] CAT 20; *Barclays Bank v CC (Permission to intervene)* [2009] CAT 15; and *BAA v CC* [2009] CAT 22.

Intervention in appeals against penalties under the 2002 Act

4.114 Rule 16 (Intervention) does not apply to appeals against penalties under sections 114 or 176(1)(f) of the 2002 Act.

Intervention in private actions

4.115 For information concerning intervention in private actions, see paragraph 5.92 below.

REFERENCES OF PRICE CONTROL MATTERS UNDER THE 2003 ACT

[6.159]
4.116 There are specific arrangements under Rule 116 and Rule 117 for the reference to the CMA of certain "price control matters" arising in appeals under section 192 of the 2003 Act in respect of decisions made by OFCOM.

Specified price control matters

4.117 Identifying an issue as a specified price control matter is a two-stage process. First the issue must relate to a form of price control set by a significant market power ("SMP") condition within the meaning

Part 6 UK and EU Court Materials

of section 193(10) of the 2003 Act. If that test is satisfied, the second stage is to consider whether it is a "specified" price control matter for the purpose of the Rules. Under Rule 116(1), a specified "price control matter" is a matter relating to the imposition of any form of price control by way of an SMP condition imposed by OFCOM under sections 87(9), 91 or 93(3) of the 2003 Act which is disputed between the parties and which relates to:

– the principles applied in setting the condition imposing the price control in question;
– the methods applied, calculations used or data used in determining the price control; or
– what the provisions imposing the price control contained in the condition should be (including at what level the price control should be set).

4.118 To the extent that matters in an appeal under section 192 of the 2003 Act are specified price control matters, those matters must be referred by the Tribunal to the CMA: section 193(1) of the 2003 Act.

4.119 Price control matters raised by the appeal which are not specified price control matters are to be decided by the Tribunal on the merits: section 195(2) of the 2003 Act.

4.120 The notice of appeal must include a statement indicating the extent to which the appeal relates to price control, or a specified price control matter arises in the appeal: Rule 9(5). The defence must also include such a statement, as well as a statement in rebuttal of the appellant's statement under Rule 9(5): Rule 15(4).

4.121 Appellants are expected to develop in full all the grounds of appeal relied on in relation to both specified and non-specified price control matters, together with any supporting documents, in the notice of appeal as it may be difficult to amend the notice of appeal at a later date: Rule 12.

4.122 In appeals that raise both specified price control matters and non-specified price control matters it is particularly important that all pleadings indicate clearly which section(s) of the pleadings (and which evidence or parts of evidence) relate to each.

4.123 If there appears to be a dispute about whether matters raised in an appeal are specified price control matters to be determined by the CMA or non-specified price control matters to be determined by the Tribunal, it is likely that this will be considered in the context of the first CMC and the matter listed to be heard and decided as a preliminary issue. In light of this, parties should set out their reasoned position on the issue (and how it should be addressed) in any written observations submitted in advance of the first CMC.

4.124 The Tribunal has previously considered the scope of specified price control matters in *Hutchison 3G v OFCOM* [2007] CAT 26 and [2007] CAT 27. See also *TalkTalk Telecom Group v OFCOM and BT v OFCOM* [2015] CAT 13.

4.125 Given the role of the CMA in determining specified price control matters, it is likely to be expedient, in the context of appeals that raise such matters, to provide the CMA with copies of pleadings and to copy the CMA in on relevant correspondence in the proceedings.

Procedure for the reference of specified price control matters to the CMA

4.126 Once the issues in the appeal have been divided into specified price control matters and non-specified price control matters and any dispute over that subject has been dealt with, the Tribunal must decide whether it will deal with the non-specified matters first, postponing any reference to the CMA until after the Tribunal has come to a conclusion on those matters; whether the Tribunal should refer the price control matters to the CMA without delay and allow the CMA investigation to run in parallel to the Tribunal's proceedings; or whether the Tribunal should stay the part of the proceedings before it pending the determination by the CMA.

4.127 The Tribunal will formulate the questions to be referred to the CMA on the basis of the pleadings. This is normally done in consultation with the parties. It may be helpful if the parties provide drafts of how they think the questions might be formulated.

4.128 The reference may be made by the Tribunal at any time prior to delivery of its decision on the substance of the appeal: see Rule 116(3) and *H3G v OFCOM and BT v OFCOM (Mobile Call Termination)* [2008] CAT 5.

4.129 Subject to any directions by the Tribunal to the contrary, the CMA must determine the matter within four months of receipt of the terms of reference. The Tribunal may give directions, either of its own motion or upon the application of the CMA or any party, as to the procedure which the CMA must follow in making its determination: Rule 117(2) and (3); see, for example: Orders of the Tribunal of 15 September 2008 and 7 January 2009 in *Hutchison 3G v OFCOM and BT v OFCOM (Mobile Call Termination)* extending time for the CMA's determination of the referred price control matters referred in those appeals; see also the Orders of the Tribunal dated 27 November 2009 and 18 February 2010 in *Carphone Warehouse v OFCOM (Local Loop Unbundling)*; and the Order of the Tribunal dated 16 December 2009 in *Cable & Wireless UK v OFCOM (Leased Lines Charge Control)*.

4.130 Once the CMA has determined the issues set out in the reference, it is required to notify the Tribunal of its determination as soon as practicable under sections 193(4) and (5) of the 2003 Act. The Tribunal must, when deciding the appeal on the merits under section 195 of the 2003 Act, decide any specified price control matters raised in the appeal in accordance with the determination made by the CMA: section 193(6) of the 2003 Act. The sole exception is where the Tribunal, applying the principles applicable on an application for judicial review, decides that the determination of the CMA would fall to be set aside on such an application: in such circumstances the Tribunal is not obliged to determine the price control matter in accordance with the CMA's determination: section 193(7) of the 2003 Act. Generally the Tribunal is unlikely to take this course of its own motion. It will be for the parties to raise any challenge to the CMA's determination in a reasoned application to the Tribunal; see *Hutchison 3G v OFCOM and BT v OFCOM (Mobile Call Termination)* [2009] CAT 11.

Interim orders and interim measures

4.131 The powers of the Tribunal (or, as the case may be, the President or a Chairman acting alone) to make interim orders or take interim measures, and the procedures to be followed, are set out in Rule 24. These powers will be exercised flexibly, according to the particular circumstances of the case. Where the interests of justice so require, an application for interim measures may be made before a notice of appeal or application has been filed and may seek an order against third parties as well as the maker of the decision founding the right to commence proceedings in the Tribunal.

4.132 Under Rule 24, the Tribunal may, with regard to a decision that is being challenged in proceedings before it, make an order on an interim basis that: (i) suspends the effect of the decision in whole or in part; (ii) in the case of an appeal under section 46 or 47 of the 1998 Act, varies the conditions or obligations attached to an exemption; or (iii) grants any remedy which the Tribunal would have the power to grant in its final decision. Moreover, where this is necessary as a matter of urgency, the Tribunal may give any directions it considers appropriate for the purpose of preventing significant damage to a particular person or category of person, or to protect the public interest: Rule 24(2).

4.133 The requirements which a request for an order or direction under Rule 24 must satisfy are set out in Rule 24(6): the request must state the subject matter of the proceedings; the circumstances giving rise to urgency (in relation to a request under Rule 24(2)); the factual and legal background establishing a prima facie case for the granting of interim relief; and the relief sought. Where no substantive appeal or application for review has yet been made to the Tribunal, the application must also provide an outline of the information required by Rule 9(4) (see paragraph 4.28 above). In such cases the Tribunal would normally require from the person making the request for interim relief a firm indication of the date on which the substantive appeal or application for review would be lodged as well as an undertaking to pursue that appeal or application with due expedition.

4.134 The request for interim relief must be verified by a statement of truth, signed and dated by the applicant or on the applicant's behalf: Rule 24(7).

4.135 The Registry should be consulted on how many copies of the request should be provided to the Tribunal.

4.136 The request, when received, will be sent by the Registrar to the respondent (or the person who made the decision if no substantive proceedings have yet been commenced) and any other parties, and a timetable will be set for the submission of written and/or oral observations: Rule 24(8). A request for interim relief may be decided on paper or following a hearing.

4.137 If the urgency of the case so requires, the Tribunal may grant a request for interim relief before the observations of the other parties have been submitted: Rule 24(10). However, that is an exceptional course and if the applicant seeks an order in those circumstances it has a duty of full and frank disclosure in respect of all relevant matters, including those adverse to the grant of the order that might reasonably be put forward by those other parties.

4.138 An order or direction for interim relief may be sought against a person who is not a party to the proceedings but that person must first be given an opportunity to be heard: Rule 24(9). Only if the urgency of the case so requires may the request be granted before that person has been heard: Rule 24(10) (see also above).

4.139 In accordance with Rule 24(3), the Tribunal must take into account all the relevant circumstances, including: the urgency of the matter; the effect on the party making the request if the interim order or direction is not made; the effect on competition if the order is made; and the existence and adequacy of any offer of an undertaking as to damages.

4.140 Any interim order made by the Tribunal may be subject to such conditions as the Tribunal thinks fit.

4.141 The Tribunal has adjudicated on requests for interim relief that were decided under the 2003 Rules in: *Napp v DGFT* [2001] CAT 1; *Genzyme v OFT* [2003] CAT 8; *VIP v OFCOM* [2007] CAT 12; and *Wm Morrison v CC* [2009] CAT 33. Agreed orders were made in *Albion Water v DGWS* (Order made on 2 June 2005 and mentioned in [2005] CAT 19); *Burgess v OFT* (Order made on 6 July 2005 in case 1037/2/1/04(IR)); *National Grid v GEMA* (Order of 14 March 2008) and *BskyB v OFCOM (Pay TV)* (Order of 29 April 2010 in case 1152/8/3/10(IR)). The President considered an application to vary an interim relief order in *BskyB v OFCOM* [2014] CAT 17.

4.142 The Tribunal considered an application for interim relief in the context of a decision taken by the CC in the exercise of its remedial powers under Part 3 of the 2002 Act in *Wm Morrison v CC* [2009] CAT 33.

NOTES

13 As to what may constitute notification see *Federation of Wholesale Distributors v OFT* [2004] AT 11 at [22].

14 This decision was made in respect of the Tribunal Rules 2003; the equivalent rule was Rule 26.

15 See also section 114(3)–(4) of the 2002 Act.

16 The requirements mentioned in sub-paragraphs (2), (3), (4), (6) and (7) of Rule 9 apply also to notices of appeal against a penalty made under sections 114 or 176(1)(f) of the 2002 Act: Rule 3(b).

17 Schedule 1, paragraph 2(4)(b) provides that the 60 day time limit stipulated in paragraph 2(2) of that Schedule applies subject to provisions in rules made under section 15 of the 2002 Act that provide that a notice of appeal must be received within a longer or shorter period.

18 Schedule 4, paragraph 2(5)(b) provides that the 30 day time limit stipulated in paragraph 2(2) of that Schedule applies subject to provisions in rules made under section 15 of the 2002 Act that provide that a notice of appeal must be received within a longer or shorter period.

19 See *Albion Water v DGWS (Thames Water / Bath House)* [2005] CAT 23 at [8] and *Independent Media v OFCOM* [2008] CAT 13 at [82]–[83].

20 See *Brannigan v OFT* [2006] CAT 28 at [81]–[82]. The Tribunal made critical comments about a notice of appeal in *National Grid Plc v GEMA* [2009] CAT 14 at [228]; see also the ruling on costs in that case: [2009] CAT 24 at [12].

21 See *Co-operative Group v OFT*, Transcript of first CMC, 11 May 2007, page 1, lines 4–8.

22 See *Merger Action Group v Secretary of State* [2008] CAT 36 at [5].

23 See *British Sky Broadcasting v CC & Secretary of State* [2008] CAT 1 at [16], *Merger Action Group v Secretary of State* [2009] CAT 19 at [33] and *Wm Morrison Supermarkets plc v CC (Interim Relief)* [2009] CAT 33 at [23].

24 The notice of application should explain whether, and why, the matter is urgent.

25 Order of the President dated 19 June 2015 in Case 1239/4/12/15.

26 However, note the comments made by the Tribunal when proposing to take its own decision in *Burgess v OFT* [2005] CAT 25 at [138].

27 *BT v OFCOM ("08 Numbers (Preliminary Issues)")* 2011 EWCA Civ 245 at [87].

SECTION 5: DAMAGES CLAIMS AND INJUNCTIONS UNDER SECTION 47A OF THE 1998 ACT

INTRODUCTION

[6.160]
5.1 This part of the Guide deals with all civil proceedings in the Tribunal apart from collective proceedings and collective settlements which are dealt with in Section 6 of the Guide. However, where a provision in Part 4 of the Rules applies to collective proceedings, the guidance in this section concerning that provision may be relevant to those collective proceedings.

THE CLAIMS THAT MAY BE MADE IN THE TRIBUNAL

[6.161]
5.2 The following claims may be made in the Tribunal pursuant to section 47A of the 1998 Act: (i) a claim for damages; (ii) any other claim for a sum of money; and (iii) a claim for an injunction.

5.3 The claim must be in respect of:

(a) an infringement of the Chapter I and/or Chapter II prohibitions or Articles 101 and/or 102 TFEU established by a decision of a UK competition authority, the Tribunal itself, or the European Commission; and/or

(b) an alleged infringement of the above provisions.

5.4 A claim made in respect of (i) above is sometimes referred to as a "follow-on" claim since it follows on from a prior infringement decision made by a competition authority. A claim made in respect of (ii) above, since it is not made in the wake of a competition authority's infringement decision, is sometimes referred to as a "stand-alone" claim. An action may combine both follow-on and stand-alone claims.

5.5 Generally, if the claim for damages or a sum of money (whether follow-on or stand-alone) could be made in civil proceedings in any part of the United Kingdom then it can be made in proceedings before the Tribunal.

5.6 However, a claim for an injunction can be made in the Tribunal only if it could be made in proceedings in England and Wales or Northern Ireland.[28] The Tribunal does not have jurisdiction to grant an injunction in relation to Scotland, and such a claim has to be brought before the Scottish Courts.

THE RULES APPLICABLE TO CLAIMS

[6.162]
5.7 The rules applicable to claims under section 47A of the 1998 Act are principally those set out in Part 4 of the 2015 Rules. However Parts 1 and 6 of the Rules also apply to claims, and Part 2 of the Rules will also apply unless otherwise provided for in Part 4: Rule 3.

TIME FOR FILING A CLAIM FOR DAMAGES: LIMITATION

[6.163]
5.8 Claimants do not have an indefinite time within which to make claims in the Tribunal. Whether a claim can be made to the Tribunal depends, crucially, on whether it is brought within a period of time usually known as a limitation period. Claims made outside the applicable limitation period are "time barred" and cannot proceed.

5.9 Section 47E of the 1998 Act establishes that claims made in the Tribunal under section 47A are subject to the law on limitation periods applicable in the part of the UK in which the proceedings arise.[29]

5.10 Therefore, in the case of claims arising in England and Wales, the Limitation Act 1980 applies to a claim under section 47A as if the claim were an action in the High Court.[30] Usually that means that a claimant has six years from the date on which the cause of action accrued in which to make a claim in the Tribunal.[31] A similar position applies in respect of claims arising in Northern Ireland.[32] Since claims made pursuant to section 47A are essentially claims for breach of statutory duty, the cause of action will generally accrue once the breach has caused damage to the claimant.

5.11 In relation to proceedings in Scotland, the position is different.[33] Section 6 of the Prescription and Limitation (Scotland) Act 1973 applies, and the limitation period in respect of such claims will generally be five years.

5.12 Section 47E of the 1998 Act sets out limitation rules that apply both to claims under section 47A and to collective proceedings brought pursuant to section 47B. However, those limitation rules do not apply to claims which arose before 1 October 2015.[34]

5.13 Where a claim arose prior to 1 October 2015, the limitation periods set out in Rule 31(1) to (3) of the 2003 Rules continue to apply: Rule 119. Although the permission of the Tribunal is required under rule 31(3) for a follow-on claim to be made before the end of the period specified in section 47A(7) or (8) of the 1998 Act as it was prior to the amendments made by the 2015 Act,[35] the decision on whether to grant such permission will be made in the context of the new regime for private actions before the Tribunal introduced by the 2015 Act and the implementation of section 16(1) of the 2002 Act. The approach adopted by the Tribunal prior to 1 October 2015 will therefore not govern its exercise of this discretion.

5.14 These limitation rules apply only to claims commenced in the Tribunal and have no effect on claims commenced in any other court in the United Kingdom.

5.15 It should be stressed that these are merely general guidelines, and it is beyond the scope of this Guide to provide definitive advice. Determining whether a particular claim is still in time can be a complex matter, and potential claimants should seek legal advice at the earliest available opportunity.

COMMENCING A CLAIM UNDER SECTION 47A OF THE 1998 ACT

[6.164]

5.16 A claim for damages under section 47A of the 1998 Act should be made by sending a claim form to the Registrar.

5.17 The claim form is a document which sets out the nature of the cause of action alleged against the defendant together with details of the relief being sought (for example damages in respect of an overcharge and/or an injunction).

5.18 The required contents of the claim form are set out in Rule 30 and may be divided into formal requirements and substantive requirements.

Formal requirements of the claim form

5.19 A claim form must contain:
- the claimant's full name and address;
- the full name and address of its legal representative, if any;
- an address for service in the United Kingdom; and
- the name and address of the defendant.

5.20 The contents of the claim form must be verified by a statement of truth signed and dated by the claimant, or on the claimant's behalf by its duly authorised officer or legal representative. However, a claim form will remain effective even if not verified by a statement of truth unless it is struck out.

Substantive requirements of the claim form

5.21 The claim form should:
- State whether the claim is following on from an infringement decision and if so, whether that infringement decision has become final within the meaning of section 58A of the 1998 Act (that is, whether it is a final decision which will bind the Tribunal or whether it is still open to appeal and therefore possible reversal or modification).
- Make observations on the question in which part of the United Kingdom the proceedings of the Tribunal are to be treated as taking place pursuant to Rule 18. This will assist the Tribunal in determining whether the case is to be treated as an English and Welsh case, a Scottish case or a Northern Irish case. This can be important since it will affect questions such as which limitation period applies to the claim (see above).
- Contain a concise statement of the relevant facts, identifying, in a follow-on claim, any relevant findings in the decision on the basis of which the claim is being made.
- Set out a concise statement of any contentions of law which are relied on.
- State the relief which the claimant is requesting from the Tribunal.[36] Where applicable, this should include:
    - a statement of the amount claimed in damages, supported by an explanation of how that amount has been calculated;
    - details of any other claim for a sum of money;
    - a statement that the claimant is making a claim for an injunction (the Tribunal only has power to grant injunctions in cases arising in England and Wales and Northern Ireland. It does not have this power with regard to Scottish cases (see above);
    - any matters that may from time to time be specified by a practice direction.

The structure of the claim form

5.22 Whilst the Rules do not prescribe a structure for the presentation of the claim, it is vital that the Tribunal is able fully to understand the claim from the moment of its receipt. Clarity, concision and common sense should underpin the drafting and presentation of the claim form.

5.23 It is useful to have the names and contact details of the parties set out at the beginning of the document so that the Tribunal does not have to search through the document for that information.

5.24 After that, it is helpful to have a brief summary of the factual and legal nature of the claim (in no more than a few paragraphs). This might form the basis of the summary which the Registrar will, at a later stage, place on the Tribunal website in accordance with Rule 33(8).

5.25 Next, it will normally be appropriate to set out fully the factual background to the claim, how it has arisen and how those facts are alleged to have caused loss to the claimant. If the claim is following on from an infringement decision, the claimant should be particularly careful to identify concisely the facts found in the relevant infringement decision that are relied on. Whilst extensive quotations from the infringement decision should be avoided, the claim form should cross-refer to the relevant parts of that decision.

5.26 Having identified the facts on which the claim is based, the claim form should identify the grounds which entitle the claimant to recover the sums claimed. The arguments supporting those grounds should then be developed in a concise manner. Where grounds overlap, it is sufficient to refer back to the arguments already developed. Any calculations relied on as to the amounts claimed and any interest thereon should be clearly set out, either in the body of the claim form or, if lengthy in nature, in a document annexed to the claim form.

5.27 In setting out the arguments in support of each ground, it is unnecessary to set out lengthy extracts from decided cases: short citations, accompanied by the case reference and paragraph number, will normally suffice.

Documents to be annexed

5.28 The claimant should annex to the claim form:

- a copy of any infringement decision on the basis of which the claim is being made;
- copies of any documents that are referred to in the claim form;
- any application for the claim to be subject to the fast-track procedure (see paragraphs 5.139–5.149 below).

5.29 At this stage it is not necessary to produce every document on which the claimant will rely; it suffices to include any relevant infringement decision forming the basis of the claim and any document to which reference is made in the claim form. In this regard, the claim form should only refer to documents of central importance and should not include material of a peripheral nature.

5.30 If a particular document is very lengthy and production of the full document would serve no purpose, the claimant need only annex the relevant extracts in between the first and the last pages of the document. Where this is done, the claimant should of course be ready to produce full copies of the document if requested by the Tribunal or another party to the proceedings.

5.31 The claimant is not required to annex the statements of any witnesses (whether factual or expert), unless the witness evidence is fundamental to a proper understanding of the claim. If witness evidence is not annexed, the claimant should indicate in the claim form the nature of the evidence that will be relied on and, where possible, identify the witness, or witnesses, concerned. See also Section 7 of the Guide (Evidence).

Copies

5.32 Unless the Tribunal otherwise directs, the signed original of the claim form and any annexes should be accompanied by five copies certified by the claimant or its legal representative as conforming to the original: Rule 30(6).

Other practical points concerning the preparation of the claim form and annexes

5.33 The claim form and its annexes should be hole-punched on the left hand side and bound in ring binders or lever arch files. All documents in the claim form bundle should be printed on both sides of A4 paper unless there are common sense reasons for doing otherwise. See also Section 9 of the Guide (Files and labelling).

5.34 A schedule of annexes should be included with the claim form.

Indication of method of service

5.35 When sending the claim form to the Registrar, the claimant must also provide details of how the claimant proposes to serve the claim form on the defendant: Rule 30(7). This is to enable the Registrar to provide suitable directions for service in accordance with Rule 33(1). The claimant must not proceed with service before receiving the Registrar's directions.

CLAIMS AGAINST DEFENDANTS OUTSIDE THE JURISDICTION: ADDITIONAL REQUIREMENTS

[6.165]

5.36 There are very important additional considerations to be taken into account when assembling a claim against a defendant outside the jurisdiction (a "foreign defendant"). These flow from the provisions concerning service of a claim form on a foreign defendant set out in Rule 31. However, since the Tribunal has UK-wide jurisdiction, these provisions do not apply as regards service in another part of the United Kingdom.

5.37 The position is fundamentally different according to whether or not the permission of the Tribunal is required for service of the claim form out of the jurisdiction.

Where permission is not required

5.38 In a case where permission is not required, the claimant **must**, when sending the claim form to the Registrar, also file with the Tribunal a notice verified by a statement of truth setting out the grounds on which the claimant is entitled to serve the claim form out of the jurisdiction and any material facts relied on: Rule 31(1). This notice must be a self-contained document, separate from the claim form.

5.39 In summary, permission for service of the claim form on a foreign defendant is not required if:

(i) the defendant is domiciled in any Member State of the European Union and each claim made against that defendant is a claim which the Tribunal has power to determine under Regulation (EU) No 1215/2012 of the European Parliament and the Council ("the Judgments Regulation"); *and/or*

(ii) the defendant is domiciled in any territory to which the Lugano Convention or the Brussels Convention, as defined in section 1(1) of the Civil Jurisdiction and Judgments Act 1982, applies (in either case, a "Convention territory")[37] and the claim made against that defendant is a claim which the Tribunal has power to determine under the respective Convention; *and in either case*

(iii) no proceedings between the parties concerning the same claim are pending in the courts of any other Member State or Convention territory, as the case may be.

But where the conditions in (i) apply, then if the defendant is party to an agreement within Article 25 of the Judgments Regulation that confers exclusive jurisdiction as regards the claim on the courts of any part of the United Kingdom, then condition (iii) does not apply.

5.40 In general, apart from the case where there is an agreement between the parties conferring jurisdiction on the courts of any part of the United Kingdom, the Tribunal will have power under the Judgments Regulation, the Lugano Convention or the Brussels Convention to determine a claim under section 47A of the 1998 Act:

- if the United Kingdom is the place where the harmful event occurred (or in the case of an injunction application, may occur): see Article 7(2) of the Judgments Regulation, Article 5(3) of the Lugano Convention and the Brussels Convention; and/or
- if the foreign defendant is one of a number of defendants at least one of whom is domiciled in the United Kingdom: see Article 8(1) of the Judgments Regulation, Article 6(1) of the Lugano Convention and the Brussels Convention.

5.41 For ground (i), the place where the harmful event occurred means the place where the event giving rise to the damage occurred or the place where the damage occurred: Case C-189/08 *Zuid-Chemie* [2009] ECR I-6917 at 19 and 23. See generally *Deutsche Bahn AG v Morgan Advanced Materials* [2013] CAT 18.

Where permission is required

5.42 Where a claimant requires permission to serve out of the jurisdiction, it **must** make an application to the Tribunal verified by a statement of truth setting out the matters specified in Rule 31(2). The application must be a self-contained document, completely separate from the claim form.

5.43 The claim form will include observations as to which part of the United Kingdom in which the proceedings should be treated as taking place pursuant to Rule 18: see paragraph 5.21 above. The Tribunal will determine the application for permission to serve out of the jurisdiction according to the relevant principles that apply under the law of that part of the United Kingdom: for example, if the claimant states that the proceedings should be treated as taking place in England and Wales, the Tribunal will apply the approach of the High Court and the grounds for service out of the jurisdiction must satisfy one of the 'gateways' under paragraph 3.1 of CPR Practice Direction 6B. See *DSG Retail Ltd v MasterCard, Inc* [2015] CAT 7.

5.44 Applications for permission need not be served on the defendants and will usually be determined on the papers. Since the Tribunal will not at that stage generally hear submissions from the defendants, the claimant is under duty to make full and frank disclosure of matters material to the application: see *DSG Retail* at [44]–[45.

5.45 If permission is granted, the Tribunal will normally give directions as to service on the foreign defendant.

THE INITIAL PROCEDURE AFTER THE CLAIM FORM HAS BEEN SENT TO THE REGISTRAR

[6.166]

5.46 Upon receipt of the claim form and annexes, the Tribunal Registry will check to see that the claim form is in order. Claim forms that clearly fail to meet the requirements of the Rules or which are clearly out of time will not be registered and will be returned to the claimant.

5.47 Claimants should note that, pursuant to Rule 3(b), the provisions of Rule 10 (Defective notices of appeal) will also apply to claim forms. Therefore if a claim form does not comply with the requirements of the Rules, or is materially incomplete, or is unduly prolix or lacking in clarity, the Tribunal may give directions for putting the document in order: Rule 10(1).

5.48 Once satisfied that the claim form is in order, the Registrar will register it and write to the claimant to acknowledge receipt.

5.49 The Registrar's letter of acknowledgement will usually contain directions allowing the claimant to proceed with service of the claim form on the defendant: Rule 33(1) and (3). Where the claimant is seeking permission to serve the claim form on a defendant outside the jurisdiction, any directions for service must await the Tribunal's determination of that application and, if the application is granted, will be notified to the claimant thereafter.

5.50 Where the claim is ready to proceed to the service stage, the Registrar will provide the claimant with the Tribunal's form of acknowledgment of service (bearing the Tribunal's official stamp) which the claimant will need to include with the claim form when serving it on the defendant.

SERVICE OF THE CLAIM FORM

[6.167]
5.51 When the claimant has received directions allowing service of the claim form from either the Registrar (or, in the case of permission to serve outside the jurisdiction, the Tribunal), the claimant should promptly comply with those directions and proceed to serve on the defendant:
– the claim form and annexes; and
– the acknowledgement of service form provided by the Registrar.

5.52 In addition, where service is taking place outside the jurisdiction, the claimant must at the same time serve on the defendant:
– a copy of the claimant's notice pursuant to Rule 31(1), indicating that the permission of the Tribunal is not required to serve the claim form on the defendant; or
– a copy of the claimant's application, pursuant to Rule 31(2), for permission to serve the claim form on the defendant; and
– a copy of the Tribunal's order granting permission and giving directions for service outside the jurisdiction.

5.53 The claimant must provide a copy of the claim form to the CMA at the same time as serving it on the defendant: Rule 33(7). The relevant address for this purpose is:
The Director of Competition Policy
Competition and Markets Authority
Victoria House
37 Southampton Row
London
WC1B 4AD

Documents can also be sent to the CMA electronically at the following address: privateactions@cma.gsi.gov.uk

5.54 Further guidance may be found on the CMA website.

ACKNOWLEDGMENT OF SERVICE

[6.168]
5.55 Where the claim form is served on a defendant within the United Kingdom, the defendant should ensure that the acknowledgment of service form is completed and filed with the Registrar within seven days of the date on which the defendant received the claim form: Rule 33(4).

5.56 Where the claim form is served on a defendant outside the jurisdiction, the period of seven days for filing the acknowledgment of service form with the Registrar is extended so as to accord with the period applicable under the CPR (or equivalent provisions in Scotland or Northern Ireland): Rule 33(5). Usually this period will be specified in the directions of the Tribunal regarding service out of the jurisdiction. Rule 34(3) provides that the filing of an acknowledgment of service does not deprive a defendant of any right to dispute the jurisdiction of the Tribunal; on the contrary, it is a pre-condition for the making of an application to challenge the jurisdiction: Rule 34(2).

5.57 Failure by a defendant to ensure that the acknowledgment of service form is filed with the Registrar within the specified period may result in judgment being entered against it: Rule 42(1)(a).

DISPUTING THE JURISDICTION

[6.169]
5.58 Where after service upon it of the claim form a defendant wishes to challenge the jurisdiction, it must:
– file an acknowledgment of service to the Registrar in accordance with Rule 33(4) or (5); and
– within 14 days thereafter, make an application, supported by evidence, for an order declaring that the Tribunal has no jurisdiction: Rule 34(4).

5.59 Any application to dispute the jurisdiction will usually be set down for oral hearing by a Chairman sitting alone. The defendant need not serve a defence until the application has been heard: Rule 34(3).

GETTING THE CASE UNDERWAY

Constitution of the Tribunal

[6.170]
5.60 After the Registrar has received the acknowledgment of service, the President will allocate the case to a Chairman who will normally sit alone during most of the preparatory and intermediate stages of the proceedings. The President will constitute a full Tribunal for the case as and when appropriate in the circumstances, for example if there is a particular need for wider expertise in relation to any particular aspect of the case or if there is a matter which the Chairman cannot deal with sitting alone (see Rule 110(1) — which essentially deals with situations in which the case is being brought to an end before a final hearing). In many cases, the allocation of the other members of the Tribunal will take place nearer the time fixed for the final hearing.

Correspondence on the case

5.61 The Registrar's letter to the parties informing them of the constitution of the Tribunal will also set out the usual principle on which correspondence in respect of proceedings is to be conducted, namely that all correspondence to or from the Tribunal will be copied to all other parties save where it is clear that only one of the parties has an interest in the correspondence or where considerations of confidentiality or possible settlement prevail.

Summary of proceedings

5.62 Following acknowledgment of service, the Registrar will publish a summary of the claim form on the Tribunal website in accordance with Rule 33(8). In a case where there are several defendants, this will be done after the last defendant has acknowledged service.

The first case management conference

5.63 In the case of claims pursuant to section 47A, the first CMC will not generally take place until after the filing of the defence and reply. The Tribunal will be in a better position to understand how the case should proceed having reviewed the pleadings (see paragraph 5.83 below).

5.64 However a different approach may be taken if there is an early application requiring judicial determination, for example an application to contest the jurisdiction, move the case to the fast track or for injunctive relief. In such cases, a consideration of the future shape of the case, such as would occur at the first CMC, may be brought forward.

5.65 See Section 7 (Case Management) for further information about CMCs.

THE DEFENCE

[6.171]
5.66 Within 28 days of service of the claim form, the defendant should file a defence setting out in sufficient detail which of the facts and contentions of law in the claim form it admits or denies and on what grounds, and on what other facts or contentions of law it relies: Rule 35(1). If the defendant is outside the jurisdiction then the period for filing the defence will be extended so as to accord with the period applicable under the CPR (or equivalent provisions in Scotland or Northern Ireland) in such circumstances: Rule 35(7). Usually this period will be specified in the directions of the Tribunal regarding service out of the jurisdiction: see paragraph 5.56 above.

5.67 The defence should also make observations on the question in which part of the United Kingdom the proceedings are to be treated as taking place under Rule 18. If there is no dispute between the parties concerning that issue, a simple statement that the defendant agrees with the observations in the claim form will suffice. Failure to make any observations on this aspect will mean the agreement of the defendant will be presumed by the Tribunal.

5.68 The contents of the defence must be verified by a statement of truth signed and dated by the defendant or on its behalf by its duly authorised officer or legal representative: Rule 35(2).

5.69 The defence should contain the same level of detail as required in respect of the claim form and, as far as practicable, annex a copy of every document referred to in the defence.

5.70 Unless the context requires otherwise, the guidance given above in respect of the claim form applies equally to the preparation and presentation of the defence. Overall, the defendant should ensure that there is no unnecessary duplication of material between the claim form and the defence. Rule 35(3) makes clear that it is not necessary to annex to the defence any document which has already been annexed to the claim form.

5.71 The defendant must serve a copy of the defence and annexes on each party at the same time as it files the defence with the Tribunal. The defendant should at the same time send a copy of the defence to the CMA: see paragraph 5.53 above for the CMA's address for this purpose.

REPLY TO THE DEFENCE AND FURTHER PLEADINGS

[6.172]
5.72 Rule 36(1) allows the claimant, within 21 days of receipt of the defence, to file a reply. However, this is not a requirement. If the claimant does not wish to file a reply, it should inform the Registrar and

the other parties of that fact as soon as possible rather than let the 21 day period expire. Similar considerations to those mentioned above in respect of the claim form and defence apply to the preparation and presentation of the reply.

5.73 Following the reply, no further pleadings may be filed by any party without the permission of the Tribunal: Rule 37.

AMENDMENT OF PLEADINGS

[6.173]
5.74 Amendment of the claim form can only be made with the written consent of all the parties or with the permission of the Tribunal: Rule 32(1). Rule 32(2) makes provision for certain types of amendment outside the limitation period.

5.75 Amendments of other pleadings may only be made if the Tribunal gives permission in exercise of its general power of case management under Rule 53.

ADDITIONAL PARTIES AND ADDITIONAL CLAIMS

[6.174]
5.76 Rule 38 governs the removal, addition or substitution of parties in the proceedings. These changes require the permission of the Tribunal and it will therefore be necessary for any party (whether an existing party or a person seeking to become a party) wanting to make such a change to make an application to the Tribunal. The application should be served on the other parties and any new person whom it is sought to introduce to the proceedings. Rules 38(6) and (7) make clear that the scope for adding or substituting parties is more restricted when a relevant limitation period has expired.

5.77 Rule 39 allows for the possibility of additional claims. The Rule covers both a counterclaim by a defendant against a claimant and claims made by a defendant against a third party (and by that third party against another third party). Any such additional claim has to fall within the ambit of section 47A of the 1998 Act (Rule 39(3)).

5.78 An additional claim will require the permission of the Tribunal unless filed at the same time as the defence (Rule 39(3) and (4)) and will be treated as if it were a claim for the purposes of the Rules: Rule 39(2). Therefore, in respect of an additional claim against a third party, the procedures in respect of the filing and service of a claim have to be observed by the person making the additional claim; and the third party recipient of the additional claim has to file an acknowledgement of service and defence in accordance with the Rules and will become a party to the proceedings. Where the additional claim is a counterclaim by the defendant against the claimant, the claimant has to comply with Rule 35 regarding the filing of a defence.

5.79 Rule 40 sets out the powers of the Tribunal upon receipt of an additional claim. Whether or not the permission of the Tribunal is required to make the additional claim, the Tribunal has power to decide whether the additional claim may be dealt with alongside the main claim or dismissed, or whether it should proceed separately or be transferred to another court: see Rule 40(1)(c) and (d). In deciding whether to exercise its powers under Rule 40(1) with regard to the additional claim, the Tribunal will consider the matters set out Rule 40(2) so as to ensure the whole case is dealt with justly and at proportionate cost in accordance with the governing principle set out in Rule 4(1).

CASE MANAGEMENT

[6.175]
5.80 Rules 53 to 57 contain case management powers for the Tribunal when dealing with claims for damages. These rules also apply to cases proceeding under the fast-track procedure and to collective proceedings.[38]

5.81 The Tribunal may at any time, on the request of a party or of its own initiative, at a CMC, pre-hearing review or otherwise, give such directions as are provided for in Rule 53(2) or such other directions as it thinks fit to secure that the proceedings are dealt with justly and at proportionate cost: Rule 53(1).

5.82 Although Rule 53(2) contains a list of types of directions the Tribunal may make, this should be regarded as indicative. As Rule 53(1) makes clear, the Tribunal may make other types of directions if that is necessary or appropriate for the just and proportionate determination of the case. It should be noted that the Tribunal may be pro-active in seeking further information, submissions or documents: Rule 53(3).

5.83 In general, a CMC will be held as soon as practicable after the reply is served (or the time for service of a reply has expired). This will be an opportunity for the Tribunal to consider with the parties and their legal representatives the future conduct of the case, having regard to the governing principles set out in Rule 4. The matters usually addressed at the first CMC are set out in Rule 54(3). For more information about CMCs, see Section 7 (Case management conferences).

5.84 Where a party wishes to ask the Tribunal to make a direction, it should make a reasoned application supported by any evidence on which it wishes to rely: Rule 53(4)

5.85 Rule 57 sets out the Tribunal's powers to deal with a failure to comply with its directions. These include the power to debar a party from taking any further part in the proceedings without the permission of the Tribunal and power to make a costs order against a party or its representative.

DISCLOSURE

[6.176]
5.86 Disclosure in proceedings before the Tribunal is not automatic and proceeds on the order or

direction of the Tribunal. The only exception is that a party may request disclosure of any document referred to in the pleadings or in witness statements or affidavits or in an expert report: Rule 61.

5.87 In general, the Tribunal will consider at the first CMC whether and when each party should file a disclosure report and, where appropriate, an electronic documents questionnaire, in the form set out in the schedule to CPR Practice Direction 31B. On consideration of these reports and questionnaires, at a further CMC the Tribunal will determine what disclosure should be provided, having regard to the governing principles as set out in Rule 4. This is an area in which the Tribunal will expect the parties to pay close attention to the requirement of co-operation in Rule 4(7) and to the need to devise a sensible and practical approach to the conduct of the proceedings. The purpose of disclosure is to obtain documentary material that assists in determination of the issues raised by the pleadings and it is not to be used as a weapon in a war of attrition.

5.88 The ambit of the duty to disclose documents is set out in Rule 60(4) to (7). Basically a party has a duty to disclose documents which are or have been in its "control" (a wider term than physical possession). That duty continues until the proceedings are concluded and extends to any documents which come to a party's notice at any time during the proceedings.

Pre-action disclosure

5.89 An application may be made to the Tribunal for disclosure before any proceedings have started, where the applicant is likely to be a party to such subsequent proceedings and the respondent from whom disclosure is sought is likely to be a defendant: Rule 62. However, such disclosure will only be ordered if it is desirable to dispose fairly of those anticipated proceedings, assist in avoiding them altogether or otherwise to save costs. Any such application must be supported by evidence. The Tribunal is likely to order pre-action disclosure only of specific documents or a very limited category of documents, and it will be alert to reject any purely speculative disclosure requests. The applicant must satisfy the Tribunal that there is good reason why the disclosure requested should not come in the usual way after proceedings have started and the applicant has set out its full case.

Disclosure against non-parties

5.90 A party to proceedings before the Tribunal may apply for an order of disclosure by someone who is not a party of documents likely to support the applicant's case or adversely affect the case of another party: Rule 63. Such an application must be supported by evidence. As with pre-action disclosure, the Tribunal is only likely to order disclosure of clearly defined documents or a very limited category of documents, and it will have regard to the fact that the person from whom disclosure is sought is not involved in the proceedings. Any such application must be served on the person from whom disclosure is sought, as well as on the other parties. If the Tribunal makes such an order, it may include provision for the payment of the costs incurred by the non-party in making disclosure.

5.91 Rule 64 governs both the procedure for seeking an order to withhold disclosure of a document on the ground of damage to the public interest (Rule 64(1) and (2)) and privilege claims: Rule 64(3). Rule 64(6) indicates how the Tribunal may proceed to decide such matters.

INTERVENTION, CONSOLIDATION AND FORUM

[6.177]
5.92 Whilst Rule 50 indicates that the intervention procedure can (with modifications) be invoked in the context of a claim under section 47A, it is likely to be confined to cases where a third party can make useful observations to the Tribunal on the broader policy context in which a particular case arises.

5.93 Rule 50(2) makes specific provision for the CMA to make written observations to the Tribunal on issues relating to the application of European competition law and the Chapter I and Chapter II prohibitions. Further, the CMA may, with the permission of the Tribunal, make oral observations on those matters at a hearing. This rule follows Article 15(3) of Regulation 1/2003 and applies the same approach to the relevant provision of national competition law.

5.94 Rules 51 and 52 apply Rules 17 (Tribunal's power to consolidate proceedings) and 18 (Determination of which part of the UK is to be treated as the forum of the proceedings) to claims under section 47A. See also Section 7 of this Guide.

SUMMARY DISPOSAL

[6.178]
5.95 Rules 41 to 44 set out a number of ways in which a claim may be terminated without a settlement or proceeding to a full hearing.

Power to strike out

5.96 Rule 41 provides that the Tribunal may strike out in whole or part a claim at any stage of the proceedings if it considers that: (a) it does not have jurisdiction; (b) there were no reasonable grounds for making the claim; (c) the claim is vexatious; or (d) the claimant has failed to comply with any rule, practice direction, order or direction of the Tribunal.

5.97 This is a severe sanction which the Tribunal will not invoke without hearing the parties. Any application for the Tribunal to exercise its power under Rule 41 should be fully reasoned and supported by evidence. The application should be made when it becomes apparent that grounds for the application exist, which should normally be well before the substantive hearing of the claim.

5.98 Where a claimant fails to comply with a rule, practice direction or order, the Tribunal will not usually exercise its power to strike out the claim without making a further 'unless' order giving the claimant an opportunity to remedy the default and thereby avoid the claim being struck out.

5.99 Although Rule 41 applies only to claims (and additional claims: Rule 39(2)), the Tribunal also has power to debar any party that has failed to comply with a direction of the Tribunal from taking any further part in the proceedings: Rule 57(1)(c).

Default judgment

5.100 Rule 42 provides that the Tribunal may of its own initiative or on the application of a party give default judgment (without consideration of the merits) where the defendant has not filed an acknowledgment of service or a defence to the claim or where the claimant has not filed a defence to a counterclaim within the time required by the Rules.

5.101 In most cases, it will be for a party to make an application to the Tribunal for a default judgment. That application should provide proof of service (Rule 42(3)) and should indicate the amount as to damages, costs and interest and any other relief in respect of which the default judgment is sought. If the application relates to only some of the defendants, it should also set out the basis on which the applicant contends that the claim against those defendants can be dealt with separately from the claim against the other defendants: Rule 42(6).

5.102 A default judgment cannot be given where the defendant has made one of the applications listed in Rule 42(2) that has not yet been determined, i.e. where the defendant is disputing the jurisdiction or has applied to strike out the claim or for summary judgment. For Rule 42(2) to apply, the defendant must have filed and served such an application. Mere mention of the intention to make an application in correspondence with the Tribunal or the claimant will not be sufficient.

5.103 If a defendant seeks to set aside a default judgment, it should make a reasoned application supported by evidence.

Summary judgment

5.104 Summary judgment may be given against a claimant or a defendant on the whole of a claim or a particular issue if the Tribunal considers that the relevant party has no real prospect of success in relation to the claim or that issue and if there is no other compelling reason why the case or issue should await determination at a substantive hearing: Rule 43.

5.105 The broad purpose of summary judgment is to allow a claim or an issue as to which there is a clear and unanswerable case to be disposed of without the need to devote further resources to the proceedings through to a final substantive hearing. It is a mechanism for ensuring that the case is handled in a proportionate way in order to satisfy the governing principles set out in Rule 4(1).

5.106 Ordinarily, the Tribunal would not expect to receive an application by a claimant for summary judgment until the defendant has filed an acknowledgment of service. If the defendant intends to apply for summary judgment against the claimant then that application should be filed after filing an acknowledgment of service and preferably at the same time as the defence. An application for summary judgment should be filed with the Tribunal and served on the other party at the same time. The application should append a draft of the order being sought and state the reasons for the application. It should include a statement of belief that the other party has no real prospect of succeeding and that the applicant knows of no other reason why the matter should proceed to a final hearing. The application may be supported by one or more witness statements, but the Tribunal would not ordinarily expect oral evidence to be given at the hearing of the application.

Withdrawal of the claim

5.107 A claimant can only withdraw its claim with the consent of the defendant or with the permission of the Tribunal: Rule 44. If the parties agree that the claim should be withdrawn, they should submit an agreed draft order to the Tribunal for its consideration.

SETTLEMENT OFFERS

[6.179]

5.108 Any party to proceedings may make an offer to one or more other parties to settle the case as between them in whatever way it chooses. As noted above, the parties may by consent seek an order for withdrawal of the claim pursuant to Rule 44. Alternatively, they may by consent apply for an order that the proceedings are stayed except for the purpose of giving effect to agreed terms of settlement: Rule 53(2)(k).[39]

5.109 However, Rule 45 introduces a special regime which carries potentially significant implications for costs if an offer of settlement that complies with its requirements is either accepted or not accepted. Such an offer is referred to as a "Rule 45 Offer".

5.110 A Rule 45 Offer may be made by either a claimant or a defendant. However, the regime does **not** apply to collective proceedings and it is accordingly not possible to make a Rule 45 Offer in those proceedings. It will be possible to make an offer to settle such proceedings by way of a *Calderbank* letter (i.e. a written offer made "without prejudice save as to costs").

5.111 The regime is modelled on CPR Part 36 and will be interpreted accordingly, but there are some important differences which are highlighted below.

5.112 To constitute a Rule 45 Offer, the offer must comply with the provisions of Rule 45(3). In particular, the offer must be in writing and state expressly that it is intended to be a Rule 45 Offer. If the terms of the offer are unclear, the offeree may within seven days ask for clarification; and if that is not provided the offeree may apply to the Tribunal for an order to that effect: Rule 46.

5.113 There are particular provisions and restrictions regarding the withdrawal or amendment of a Rule 45 Offer: see Rule 47.

If the Rule 45 Offer is accepted

5.114 The costs consequences of acceptance of a Rule 45 Offer are set out in Rule 48.

5.115 For the costs implications of a Rule 45 Offer when the offer is accepted, it is necessary to distinguish between: (i) offers made at least 21 days before trial; and (ii) offers made less than 21 days before trial.

(i) Offers made at least 21 days before trial
 (a) Offer is accepted within the Relevant Period:[40] the claimant is entitled to its costs up to the date of acceptance (or Rule 45(11)(b)(i) notice);
 (b) Offer is accepted after the expiry of the Relevant Period: if the parties cannot agree liability for costs, the claimant is entitled to its costs up to the expiry of the Relevant Period and the offeree shall pay the offeror's costs incurred between the expiry of the Relevant Period and the date of acceptance (or Rule 45(11)(b)(i) notice), unless the Tribunal otherwise directs.

(ii) Offers made less than 21 days before trial. The Tribunal will make an order as to costs unless the parties agree liability for costs.

5.116 There are particular provisions (which differ from the CPR in certain respects) concerning the situation where a claim is brought against a number of defendants and only one or more, but not all, of those defendants make a Rule 45 Offer: Rules 45(11) and 48. Such an offer must state whether it is made in satisfaction of the claim against all defendants or only against those making the offer: Rule 45(3)(f). It is then necessary to distinguish the position according to whether: (i) the claimant alleges that the defendants are jointly and severally liable; (ii) the claimant alleges that the defendants are liable severally but not jointly; or (iii) the claimant alleges that the defendants are liable only jointly or in the alternative:

(i) *Defendants' alleged liability is joint and several.* If the offer is to settle the claim against all defendants and the claimant accepts the offer, the Tribunal will direct that the claim against the other defendants is discontinued: Rule 45(11)(a). The costs which the claimant is entitled to recover under Rule 48(1) will then be its costs of the proceedings against all defendants: Rule 48(3). On the other hand, if the offer is to settle the claim only against those defendants making the offer, the claimant may serve notice on them agreeing not to continue with its claims against them in return for payment, and continue its claim against the other defendants: Rule 45(11)(b). Such a notice means that the resulting agreement is to be interpreted as a covenant not to proceed against the offerors and not as a release of liability that might discharge the other defendants.[41] The costs to which the claimant is entitled under Rule 48(1) will then be its costs related to the proceedings against only those defendants: Rule 48(3).

(ii) *Defendants' alleged liability is several but not joint*: The claimant may accept the offer and continue with its claims against the other defendants: Rule 45(11)(c). The costs to which the claimant is entitled under Rule 48(1) will then be its costs related to the proceedings against only those defendants: Rule 48(3).

(iii) *Defendants' alleged liability is only joint or in the alternative*. The claimant may only accept the offer if the claimant also discontinues its claim against the other defendants and those defendants give their written consent: Rule 45(11)(d). The costs to which the claimant is entitled under Rule 48(1) will then be its costs related to the proceedings against only those defendants: Rule 48(3).

If the Rule 45 Offer is not accepted

5.117 The costs consequences of a Rule 45 Offer which is not accepted are set out in Rule 49.

5.118 For the costs implications of a Rule 45 Offer following judgment, it is necessary to distinguish between: (i) a defendant's Rule 45 Offer: and (ii) a claimant's Rule 45 Offer:

(i) *Defendant's offer*. If the claimant fails to obtain a judgment more advantageous than the offer, then — subject to (iii) below - any defendant who made the offer is entitled to its costs from the date on which the Relevant Period (as defined in Rule 45(1)) expired, and interest on those costs: Rules 49(1)(a) and 49(2).

(ii) *Claimant's offer*. If the claimant obtains a judgment against a defendant at least as advantageous as the offer, then — subject to (iii) below — the claimant will receive interest on the sum recovered (excluding interest) at a rate not exceeding 10% above base rate for some or all of the period starting from the expiry of the Relevant Period; costs on the indemnity basis from the expiry of the Relevant Period; interest on those costs at a rate no more than base rate + 10%; and an additional amount determined by the Tribunal in accordance with CPR rule 36.17(4)(d) (as amended from time to time): Rules 49(1)(b) and 49(3). The 'additional amounts' currently prescribed are:

Amount awarded	Prescribed percentage
Up to £500,000	10% of the amount awarded
Above £500,000	10% of the first £500,000 and (subject to a cap of £75,000) 5% of any amount above.

(iii) However, where the Tribunal considers that it would be unjust to make an order in terms of (i) and (ii) above, it will not make such an order. It is impossible to set out all the possible circumstances which may render such an order unjust, but guidance is given in Rule 49(4). It is to be noted that the circumstances include the information available to the parties at the time the Rule 45 Offer was made and the conduct of the parties with regard to the provision of information in order for the Rule 45 Offer to be evaluated.[42] The Tribunal will also have regard to whether the offer was a genuine attempt to settle the proceedings or a cynical attempt to benefit from the costs rules, although the latter is unlikely to apply to a claim for damages as opposed to a fixed sum.[43] Further, the Rules deliberately do not contain a definition of "advantageous" corresponding to CPR rule 36.17(2), and the Tribunal may not adopt the same approach.

INJUNCTIONS

[6.180]
5.119 The Tribunal has power to grant an injunction on both an interim or final basis: Rule 67(2). However that power is confined to proceedings in England and Wales or Northern Ireland. The Tribunal has no jurisdiction to grant an injunction (whether final or interim) in connection with proceedings before it (or likely to come before it) in Scotland. Any application for injunctive relief in such cases must be made to the Court of Session.

5.120 An injunction granted by the Tribunal has the same effect as an injunction granted by the High Court and is enforceable as if it were an injunction granted by the High Court.[44]

INTERIM OR INTERLOCUTORY INJUNCTIONS

[6.181]
5.121 Applications for interim injunctions in proceedings before the Tribunal in England and Wales and Northern Ireland are governed by Rules 67 to 70.

When may an application be made?

5.122 An order for an interim injunction may be made at any time including before proceedings are started and after judgment has been given: Rule 68(1).

5.123 The Tribunal will, however, grant an interim injunction before a claim has been made only if the matter is urgent or it is otherwise necessary to do so in the interests of justice: Rule 68(3).

Making the application

5.124 In order to ensure that an application for an interim injunction can be served on the defendant ahead of the formal service of the claim form, it should not be included in a claim form but should be made in a separate document.

5.125 Such an application should, as far as possible, follow the format and requirements of the claim form. Therefore, the application should start with the names and contact details of the parties; provide a brief summary; describe the factual background insofar as it relates to the application for an interim injunction; and set out the grounds on which the application is made and the arguments in support of those grounds. The contents of the application must be verified by a statement of truth.

5.126 The Tribunal is required to apply the principles which the High Court would apply in deciding whether to grant an injunction.[45] Although there are no fixed rules governing the grant of an interim injunction, the application should address the guidelines developed by the courts following *American Cyanamid v Ethicon Ltd* [1975] AC 396,[46] namely whether:

– there is a serious question to be tried (the applicant has to show a real prospect of success but an in-depth analysis of the merits of the case is not required and resolution of contested evidence or complex questions of law will be inappropriate);
– damages would be an inadequate remedy for the applicant;
– if an injunction were granted, compensation under the applicant's cross-undertaking in damages would be an adequate remedy for the respondent;
– the balance of convenience is in favour of the grant of an injunction (or which course carries the least risk of injustice as between the parties);[47] and
– there are any special factors applicable in the case (e.g. whether the grant or refusal of the injunction will effectively determine the case;[48] or whether the injunction would have an effect on third parties, and if so, whether a cross-undertaking is offered to those parties as well as to the respondent[49]).

Evidence in support

5.127 The application must be supported by evidence of the facts relied on in support of the application and must contain all material information regarding the applicant's ability to pay under any undertaking as to damages that the Tribunal may require the applicant to give.

5.128 If the application is made without notice (see paragraphs 5.134–5.137):

– the applicant has a duty to the Tribunal to give full and frank disclosure of all relevant facts that both support and undermine its case (and to carry out proper enquiries to ensure this duty is met) and these must be included in a witness statement. Failure to give full and frank disclosure may lead to the injunction being refused or discharged (if already granted); and

– the application must set out why notice was not given.

Draft order

5.129 The applicant should also provide with the application a draft order the terms of which should contain:

– the relief being sought by the applicant by indicating clearly what the respondent must not do;
– the undertaking as to damages to be provided by the applicant to the Tribunal (see below);
– if the application is made without notice to the respondent, an undertaking by the applicant to the Tribunal to serve on the respondent, as soon as practicable, the application, evidence in support, a note of the hearing (which took place without the respondent being present) and any order made by the Tribunal; and
– a penal notice (so that the injunction can be enforced in any subsequent committal proceedings). This is a warning to the person subject to the injunction that disobeying the order may be a contempt of court punishable by imprisonment, a fine or sequestration of assets.

5.130 The applicant should also be prepared to provide the Tribunal with the order in electronic form.

Undertaking as to damages

5.131 In cases that are not subject to the fast-track procedure (Rule 58), the provision by the applicant of an undertaking as to damages will normally be a prerequisite to the grant of an interim injunction by the Tribunal. The purpose of the undertaking is to provide a means of compensating the respondent in the event that it subsequently emerges that the injunction should not have been granted.

5.132 Where the applicant for an injunction is not able to show sufficient assets within the jurisdiction of the Tribunal to provide substance to the undertaking as to damages (and any other financial undertakings the applicant may be required to provide), the applicant may be required to reinforce its obligation by providing security. Security will be ordered in such form as the Tribunal decides is appropriate but may, for example, take the form of a payment to be held by the Tribunal, a bond issued by an insurance company or a first demand guarantee or standby credit issued by a first-class bank.

5.133 In proceedings which are subject to the fast-track procedure, the Tribunal may grant an interim injunction without requiring the applicant to provide an undertaking or subject to a cap on the amount of the undertaking as to damages: see paragraph 5.147 below.

On or without notice

5.134 Generally, the Tribunal would expect an application for an interim injunction to be made on notice and the applicant should serve a copy of the application on the respondent at the same time as filing it with the Tribunal. The applicant should inform the Registrar of the steps that have been taken to serve the respondent with the application. Even where urgency prevents formal service being carried out, modern communications should enable the applicant to give at least informal notice to the respondent.

5.135 In cases of extreme urgency, or where giving notice would frustrate the purpose of the order, the Tribunal may be prepared to proceed to hear the applicant and make an order for an interim injunction without the respondent having been given notice of the application. The applicant should state the reasons why the application is being made without notice.

5.136 Without notice applications in competition cases will be wholly exceptional. If the Tribunal is persuaded to make an interim order without notice, that order will only cover the period pending the full hearing of all the parties. When the Tribunal makes an order on a without notice application, it will generally give directions for bringing the application and the Tribunal's Order to the immediate attention of the defendant and for the fixing of a further hearing to fully consider the application in the light of observations from all parties.

5.137 Certain applications may be heard in private if the President or Chairman thinks it appropriate to do so.

Enforcement

5.138 Failure to comply with an injunction granted by the Tribunal may be treated as a contempt of court, with the consequent sanction of imprisonment, a fine or sequestration of assets. In cases where the Tribunal considers that an injunction has not been complied with, it will certify the matter to the High Court which will then carry out its own inquiry before making any appropriate contempt order.[50]

FAST-TRACK PROCEDURE

[6.182]

5.139 Rule 58 makes provision for a fast-track procedure ("FTP").[51] A claim brought pursuant to Section 47A of the 1998 Act may be subject to the FTP. The FTP cannot be used in collective proceedings: Rule 74(3)(d).

5.140 The FTP is a particular procedure intended to enable less complex claims to be brought, in particular by individuals and small businesses, and decided quickly with limited risk as to costs. The Tribunal has power to expedite any proceedings before it, and the fact that proceedings are not subject to the FTP does not preclude the Tribunal from treating a case as urgent and directing a short time-frame to a hearing when the circumstances of the case justify this.

5.141 In any case subject to the FTP, the final hearing will be fixed to take place as soon as practicable and *in any* event within six months, and the recoverable costs will be capped at a level to be determined by the Tribunal: Rule 58(2)

5.142 In general, the Tribunal will only assign a claim to the FTP on application by one or more of the parties, although it has the right to do so on its own initiative; if an interim injunction is applied for, it may in an appropriate case raise with the parties the possibility of the case being handled under the FTP. Equally, the fact that an application for the case to be subject to the FTP is not opposed does not mean that the Tribunal will necessarily grant it.

5.143 The application for the assignment of the claim to the FTP should be made at the earliest possible time. Normally the application will be annexed to the claim form: see Rule 30(5)(c). In order to allow the Tribunal to consider the costs position as fully as possible, the applicant should provide a budget setting out the costs and disbursements likely to be incurred by the applicant in the future conduct of the proceedings.

5.144 Where an application for FTP designation is made, as soon as practicable after receipt of the defendant's acknowledgement of service, the Tribunal will direct the defendant to file a response to the application and fix a date for an early CMC. Whether the CMC should take place before or after service of the defence will be determined by the Tribunal in the light of its assessment at that stage of the proceedings.

5.145 In determining whether it should be subject to the FTP, the Tribunal will consider all the circumstances of the case. However, it will have particular regard to those matters set out in Rule 58(3), namely:

- Whether one or more of the parties is an individual or a micro, small or medium-sized enterprise ("SME") as defined in Commission Recommendation No 361 (EC) of 2003.[52] In essence, an SME is an entity engaged in economic activity which employs fewer than 250 people and has annual turnover of no more than €50 million or an annual balance sheet total of no more than €43 million. For further details, see the Recommendation and the Commission's guide, available at: ec.europa.eu/enterprise/policies/sme/files/sme_definition/sme_user_guide_en.pdf
- Whether the time estimate for the final hearing is no more than three days. This criterion is aligned to the purpose of the FTP as designed for less complex or 'heavy' cases. However, this is not an absolute limit and in appropriate circumstances the Tribunal may direct that the case is subject to the FTP if the estimate is a little longer.
- The complexity and novelty of the issues involved. As stated above, the FTP is designed for less complex cases.
- Whether any additional claims have been or will be made.
- The number of witnesses involved (including expert witnesses, if any).
- The scale and nature of the documentary evidence involved.
- Whether any disclosure is required and if so, the likely extent of such disclosure.
- The nature of the remedy being sought and the amount of any damages claimed.

5.146 Given that competition cases generally tend to be heavy, complex and often involve consideration of novel issues, it is unlikely that the Tribunal will designate a case as suitable for the FTP unless it is a clear-cut candidate for such an approach. Generally, such a case is likely to arise or be linked to a scenario where injunctive relief is being sought, or, in the case of a claim for damages, where all the parties are clearly committed to a tightly constrained and exceptionally focused approach to the litigation. Cases where interlocutory issues involving major points of principle are anticipated are unlikely to be suitable for the FTP procedure.

5.147 Where the Tribunal grants an interim injunction in an FTP case, it may do so without requiring the applicant to provide an undertaking as to damages or impose a cap on the amount covered by the undertaking: Rule 68(5).[53] The Tribunal will only dispense with or cap the undertaking as to damages where in all the circumstances this is necessary or appropriate in the interests of justice. In that regard, the Tribunal will in particular consider the following:

- the strength of the claimant's case (however, this will not involve a 'mini-trial' on the merits);
- the loss which the respondent is likely to suffer from the grant of the injunction in the event that it subsequently emerges that it should not have been granted; and
- the financial resources of, or available to, the claimant.

5.148 FTP cases will be closely case-managed, in particular as regards the extent of any disclosure and the evidence which the parties can adduce at trial. Any disclosure ordered will be specific: there will be no standard disclosure in cases subject to the FTP.

5.149 The Tribunal may, at any time, order that a case cease to be subject to the FTP: Rule 58(1). However, before doing so, the Tribunal will raise the matter with the parties and consider what changes might be made to the conduct of the case so as to preserve it in the FTP. The Tribunal will further have regard to the prejudice that may be caused to the parties if the case ceases to be subject to the FTP, and in particular may maintain a cap on the recoverable costs either in the same or in an adjusted amount.

INTERIM PAYMENTS

[6.183]

5.150 The Tribunal may order a defendant to make an interim payment of damages: Rule 66. An interim payment is a payment on account of any damages or other sum or money (except costs) which the Tribunal may hold the defendant liable to pay.

5.151 The Tribunal may make an interim payment order if the defendant against whom the order is sought has admitted liability to pay damages to the claimant or where the claimant has obtained judgment against the defendant for damages or a sum to be assessed: Rule 66(4)(a) and (b).

5.152 The Tribunal may also order an interim payment where satisfied that if the claim were to be heard, the claimant would obtain judgment for a substantial amount of money (other than costs) against that defendant: Rule 66(4)(c). It is unlikely that a case under the FTP would meet this criterion.

5.153 The Tribunal must not order an interim payment of more than a reasonable proportion of the likely amount of the final judgment: Rule 66(5).

5.154 An application for an interim payment may not be made before the time for filing the defence has expired: Rule 66(2). A claimant may make more than one application for an order for an interim payment: Rule 66(3). The application must set out the grounds on which the interim payment is sought and any directions necessary in the opinion of the claimant for the determination of the application: Rule 66(6).

5.155 Rule 66(7) indicates that on receiving an application for an interim payment, the Registrar shall send a copy to all the other parties to the proceedings (Rule 66(7)), but the claimant should nonetheless serve the other parties with copies of the application at the same time as filing it at the Tribunal. Upon receipt of the application the Registrar will write to the other parties informing them of the date by which they may submit observations to the Tribunal.

5.156 Rule 66 applies to collective proceedings as well as claims under section 47A of the 1998 Act.

Security for costs

[6.184]
5.157 A defendant to a claim for damages may apply for security for its costs of the proceedings: Rule 59. That application should be supported by written evidence setting out the basis on which security is sought: Rule 59(2). The defendant's written evidence shall address the question of why it would be just for the Tribunal to make an order for security for costs and either refer to any enactment that permits the Tribunal to require security for costs or establish that one or more of the conditions contained in Rule 59(5) or (6) applies. Those conditions are all essentially matters which make it difficult for the defendant to recover any costs to which it might be held entitled following a successful defence of the claim.

5.158 The Tribunal will only order security for costs if it is just to do so in the circumstances of the case. Amongst the circumstances to which the Tribunal will have regard are: (a) whether it appears that the application is made in order to stifle a genuine claim, or would have that effect; (b) the stage of the proceedings at which the application is made and the amount of costs which the claimant has incurred to the date of the application; (c) the claimant's financial position, whether it is impecunious and if so why it is impecunious and particularly, whether the impecuniosity can be attributed to the defendant's infringement; (d) the likely outcome of the proceedings and the relative strengths of the parties' cases if that can be discerned without prolonged examination or voluminous evidence; (e) any admissions by the defendant and, for example open offers - but the defendant should not be adversely affected in seeking security because it had attempted to resolve the matter using alternative dispute resolution; and (f) the provisions in the Tribunal's rules as to orders for costs: see *BCL Old Co v Aventis* [2005] CAT 2, at 27.

5.159 Security for costs is unlikely to be ordered in respect of a case that is subject to the FTP.

5.160 It is possible to apply for security of costs in collective proceedings.

TRANSFER OF PROCEEDINGS

[6.185]
5.161 Rules 71 and 72 govern the transfer of claims to and from the Tribunal.

Transfer of claims from the Tribunal

5.162 If at any stage of the proceedings the Tribunal considers, whether upon the application of a party or on its own initiative, that the claim or any part of it could be more appropriately dealt with by another court, it may direct that a claim made in proceedings under section 47A of the 1998 Act be transferred to the High Court in England and Wales or Northern Ireland, or to the Court of Session or the Sheriff Court in Scotland: Rule 71.[54] In England and Wales, such a transfer will generally be to the Chancery Division of the High Court.

5.163 Where the Tribunal makes an order transferring proceedings to another court it shall direct one of or all the parties to file with that court a bundle of all documents filed with the Tribunal up to the date of the Tribunal's order. Usually it will be the claimant who bears this responsibility. The Tribunal shall send a copy of its order to the court receiving the case.

Transfer of claims to the Tribunal

5.164 The Section 16 Enterprise Act 2002 Regulations 2015[55] enable the High Court in England and Wales[56], the Court of Session or a Sheriff Court in Scotland[57] and the High Court or the county court in Northern Ireland to transfer to the Tribunal for its determination so much of any proceedings as relates to "an infringement issue".

5.165 Section 16(6) of the 2002 Act defines an infringement issue as any question relating to whether or not an infringement of the Chapter I or Chapter II prohibition or Article 101 or 102 TFEU has been or is being committed.

5.166 Within seven days of the order of the court transferring the proceedings, the claimant must file with the Registrar the documents specified in Rule 72(2). The claimant should also be prepared to provide these documents to the Tribunal in electronic form.

5.167 Following such a transfer, the Tribunal will usually convene a CMC at which it will discuss the future conduct of the case with the parties. It would therefore assist the Tribunal if the parties could work together on a plan for the future conduct of the case that can be submitted to the Tribunal in advance of the CMC.

Part 6 UK and EU Court Materials

NOTES

28 Section 47A(3)(c) of the 1998 Act.

29 If it is not obvious from the outset, the Tribunal will, at an early stage, need to determine the forum of the proceedings in accordance with Rules 52 and 18.

30 Section 47E(2)(a) of the 1998 Act.

31 See section 9(1) of the Limitation Act 1980.

32 Section 47E(2)(c) of the 1998 Act and the Limitation (Northern Ireland) Order 1989.

33 Section 47E(2)(b) of the 1998 Act.

34 Paragraph 8(2) of Schedule 8 of the 2015 Act.

35 In effect, when the infringement decision on which the claim is based becomes final.

36 See paragraphs 5.119–5.138 for specific guidance in relation to claims for injunctions.

37 The Lugano Convention will apply where the defendant is domiciled in Iceland, Norway or Switzerland. The Brussels Convention will apply where the defendant is domiciled in the territory of a Member State which falls within the territorial scope of that Convention but is excluded from the Judgments Regulation pursuant to Article 355 TFEU.

38 See also Rule 88 (Case management of the collective proceedings).

39 Referred to in England and Wales as a "Tomlin order": see CPR, Vol. 1, para 40.6.2.

40 The Relevant Period is defined in Rule 45(1).

41 See *Watts v Aldington* (1993) [1999] L&TR 578.

42 See the observations of Lord Woolf MR in *Ford v GKR Construction Ltd* [2000] 1 WLR 1397.

43 *Cp Huck v Robson* [2002] EWCA Civ 398.

44 Section 47D(1) of the 1998 Act.

45 Section 47D(2) of the 1998 Act.

46 See also *Series 5 Software Ltd v Clarke* [1996] 1 All ER 853.

47 *National Commercial Bank Jamaica Ltd v Olint Corpn Ltd* [2009] UKPC 16.

48 *NWL Ltd v Woods* [1979] 1 WLR 1294.

49 See e.g., *Adidas-Salomon AG v Draper and Howorth and ors.* [2006] EWHC 1318 (Ch) at [54].

50 See paragraph 1A of Schedule 4 to the 2002 Act.

51 Pursuant to paragraph 15A of Schedule 4 to the 2002 Act.

52 OJ 2003 L124/36.

53 Following paragraph 15A(3) of Schedule 4 to the 2002 Act.

54 Rule 71 also provides for transfer to the County Court, but in practice this is unlikely since the County Court is obliged to transfer competition cases to the High Court: CPR Rule 30.8.

55 SI 2015/1643.

56 For transfers from the High Court in England and Wales see CPR Part 30, Practice Direction 8.1 to 8.8.

57 For transfers from Scotland see Chapter 32A of the Rules of the Court of Session and Chapter 42 of the Ordinary Cause Rules.

SECTION 6: COLLECTIVE PROCEEDINGS, COLLECTIVE SETTLEMENTS

INTRODUCTION

[6.186]

6.1 Collective proceedings filed in accordance with section 47B of the 1998 Act and collective settlements made under sections 49A or 49B are governed by Rules 73–98. The legislative background to these provisions is explained in Section 2 of the Guide.

6.2 Collective proceedings are proceedings brought on behalf of a defined class of persons by a representative. Such proceedings can be 'opt-in' (where each class member actively signs up to participate in the proceedings) or 'opt-out' where, in broad terms, each person within the class is automatically included in the proceedings unless they actively choose not to be).

6.3 However, collective proceedings are a form of procedure and do not establish a new cause of action. The claims of the class members brought together in collective proceedings, or subject to collective settlement, must each be claims to which section 47A of the 1998 Act applies. They may indeed include claims that have already been started on an individual basis under section 47A, provided that the individual claimant consents.[58] Part 4 of the Rules (Claims pursuant to section 47A of the 1998 Act) also applies to collective proceedings and collective settlements, save as set out in Rule 74.

6.4 Collective proceedings are governed by Rules 75–93. They have four main stages: (i) making a collective proceedings order ("CPO"); (ii) trial of the common issues; (iii) determination of any individual issues; and (iv) distribution of any damages.

6.5 A collective settlement is a specific procedure whereby the Tribunal authorises a settlement reached between the class representative, on behalf of the class, and the defendant(s) such that the terms of the settlement bind the entire class. The parties may apply to have a collective settlement approved by the Tribunal:

– after an "opt-out" collective proceedings order has been made: Rule 94; or
– by commencing the settlement process directly, where no collective proceedings order has been made: Rules 96–97.

6.6 The collective settlement procedure does not apply to opt-in collective proceedings, although the Tribunal's permission is required to settle opt-in collective proceedings in certain circumstances: Rule 95.

6.7 Collective proceedings, and in particular opt-out collective proceedings, require intensive case management by the Tribunal, so as to ensure that the interests of the class are adequately protected.

Furthermore, an application for approval of a collective settlement will often involve a Tribunal being shown material which, in the event that the settlement is not approved and the case continues to trial, should not be placed before a Tribunal hearing the trial and deciding the merits. Accordingly, if the proceedings are certified as opt-out collective proceedings, the panel conducting the case management (the "case management tribunal") will at an appropriate stage prior to the trial determine that the proceedings should thereafter be heard by a separate panel (the "trial tribunal"). If at any stage (including after the commencement of the trial) the parties come to terms and seek approval of a settlement, the application for a collective settlement order will be determined by the case management tribunal.

6.8 Where a class member opts in to opt-in proceedings, or (if he or she is domiciled in the UK on the domicile date) does not opt out of opt-out proceedings, that member becomes a "represented person". Similarly, a foreign class member who opts in to opt-out proceedings becomes a "represented person".[59]

COMMENCING COLLECTIVE PROCEEDINGS

[6.187]

6.9 Unlike ordinary civil proceedings under section 47A, the bringing of collective proceedings must be approved by the Tribunal. This approval involves two aspects: (a) authorisation of the class representative; and (b) certification of the claims as eligible for inclusion in collective proceedings: Rule 77(1).[60] The approval process is governed by Rules 75–81. The Tribunal approves collective proceedings by issuing a CPO; only then can the claims proceed.[61]

Applying for a collective proceedings order

6.10 To commence collective proceedings, the proposed class representative must first apply to the Tribunal for a CPO by sending a collective proceedings claim form to the Tribunal's Registrar in accordance with Rule 75. The collective proceedings claim form must contain the information required by Rule 75(2)–(3). Many of the formal and substantive requirements for the collective proceedings claim form mirror those of an ordinary claim form, save that the contact information relates to the proposed class representative rather than the claimant. In addition, a collective proceedings claim form must:

- state that the proposed class representative is making an application for a CPO;
- state whether the order is sought for opt-in or opt-out proceedings;
- state whether the parties have used an alternative dispute resolution procedure;
- state that the proposed class representative believes that the claims which it seeks to combine in the collective proceedings have a real prospect of success;
- describe the proposed class and any sub-classes;
- estimate the number of class (or sub-class) members and explain the basis for that estimate;
- summarise how the proposed class representative satisfies the requirements of Rule 78; and
- summarise how the claims meet the eligibility criteria for collective proceedings in Rule 79. The claim form should accordingly identify the common issues which are raised by the claims and which it is proposed should be determined in the collective proceedings.

6.11 The claim form should accordingly be in three parts:

- Part 1 should set out the information and statements to comply with Rule 75(2);
- Part 2 should set out the information and statements to comply with Rule 75(3)(a)–(e); and
- Part 3 should set out the information and statements to comply with Rule 75(3)(f)–(j).

6.12 The proposed class representative is required to annex certain documents to the collective proceedings claim form pursuant to Rule 75(5). As for ordinary claims before the Tribunal, this includes a copy of any infringement decision and any other document referred to in the collective proceedings claim form. The proposed class representative must also annex the following draft documents:

- *Collective proceedings order*
  The content requirements for a CPO are set out in Rule 80 and discussed further at paragraphs 6.46–6.52 below. The main functions of a CPO are to authorise the class representative to act as such in continuing the collective proceedings and to set out the basic details of the collective proceedings, such as the parties' names, the definition of the class (and any sub-classes), the common issues to be determined and the remedy sought.
- *Notice of the collective proceedings order*
  The content requirements for the notice of the CPO are set out in Rule 81(2) and discussed further at paragraphs 6.58–6.59 below. The purpose of the notice is to inform the class members of the nature of the proceedings in plain and easily understood language, explain the potential effect of a judgment on the common issues for the class members and set out how the class member can opt in or out of the proceedings and the deadlines for doing so.
  While the proposed class representative may have had contact with some or all class members prior to the filing of the collective proceedings claim form, this is the first formal notice and will be carefully scrutinised by the Tribunal.

6.13 The proposed class representative should send with the collective proceedings claim form any evidence relied on in support of the application for a CPO. That may include, for example, a witness statement by or on behalf of the proposed class representative addressing the considerations raised by Rules 78 and 79; and an expert's report regarding the way in which the common issues identified in the claim form may suitably be determined on a collective basis.

6.14 Unless the Tribunal otherwise directs, the signed original of the collective proceedings claim form should be accompanied by five copies certified by the proposed class representative or its lawyer as conforming to the original: Rule 75(6). Five copies of any evidence submitted should also be provided.

Part 6 UK and EU Court Materials

Response to a collective proceedings claim form: checking and acknowledgment

6.15 Once the collective proceedings claim form has been filed, the Registrar will check it and send an acknowledgment of receipt to the proposed class representative pursuant to Rule 76(1).

Service of the collective proceedings claim form

6.16 The Registrar will direct the proposed class representative to serve on the defendant the collective proceedings claim form and any evidence relied on, save where the Tribunal's permission is required to serve out of the jurisdiction (see Rules 76(1)–(2)). The Registrar's direction in relation to service may specify the time and method by which service must be carried out, as well as any other matter, including those set out in Rule 76(3). The Tribunal will provide the claimant with the acknowledgment of service form, which is to be included with the claim form when it is served on the defendant.

6.17 The proposed class representative must also send a copy of the collective proceedings claim form to the CMA: Rule 76(6).

6.18 Sending the collective proceedings claim form to the defendant constitutes service of the application for the CPO and of the claim form itself.

6.19 Upon receipt of the collective proceedings claim form, the defendant must send the acknowledgment of service to the Registrar. Defendants domiciled in the UK must file the acknowledgment of service within seven days of receipt of the claim form: Rule 76(4); for foreign defendants, the period for acknowledging service will be varied in accordance with CPR Part 6, or the equivalent provisions in the procedural rules for Scotland or Northern Ireland: Rule 76(5). The filing of an acknowledgment of service does not constitute agreement by the defendant that the proposed collective proceedings should be allowed to continue.

6.20 The Registrar will notify the proposed class representative that the acknowledgment of service has been received: Rule 76(7).

6.21 Unlike in an ordinary private action, the defendant is not required to file its defence before the hearing of the application for the CPO: Rule 76(11).

Service out of the jurisdiction

6.22 If one or more defendants are domiciled outside the Tribunal's jurisdiction, the Tribunal's permission may be required for service. The position is analogous to that which applies for a claim under section 47A (see paragraphs 5.36–5.45 above), except that the obligations here rest on the class representative, not on the claimant. In summary:

– *Where permission is not required for service out of the jurisdiction*

  The proposed class representative must file a notice verified by a statement of truth with the collective proceedings claim form: (Rules 31(1) and 74(1). As in an ordinary section 47A claim, this notice must set out the grounds on which the proposed class representative is entitled to serve the claim form out of the jurisdiction and any material facts relied on. The Tribunal will then direct that the proposed class representative serve the collective proceedings claim form on each foreign defendant named in the collective proceedings claim form.

– *Where the permission of the Tribunal is required to serve the collective proceedings claim form out of the jurisdiction*

  The proposed class representative should file its application for permission at the same time as the collective proceedings claim form. The application for permission must contain the information required by Rule 31(2). The Tribunal will address the application for permission to serve out of the jurisdiction prior to the application for a CPO, unless the circumstances make an alternative course more appropriate.

  When considering the application for permission to serve out, the Tribunal may make such directions as it thinks fit: Rule 76(10)(a). However, it will generally apply the provisions of the CPR, or the equivalent rules applicable in Scotland and Northern Ireland, with regard to service out of the jurisdiction (as if the references to "claim form" read "collective proceedings claim form").

Summary of the collective proceedings claim form

6.23 A summary of the collective proceedings claim form will be published on the Tribunal website: Rule 76(8). The summary will ordinarily be published after the collective proceedings claim form has been served or otherwise notified to the proposed defendant(s) and the acknowledgment of service has been filed.

6.24 The web summary performs an important function in publicising the existence of the claim to any other potential class representative who may be contemplating bringing collective proceedings on behalf of the same or a similar class. If a CPO is made, wider publication of the proceedings will then be required: see paragraphs 6.58–6.59 below.

THE FIRST CASE MANAGEMENT CONFERENCE: PRE-APPROVAL

[6.188]

6.25 The first CMC will generally take place as soon as practicable (Rule 76(9)), unlike in an ordinary claim (where the CMC would normally take place after the filing and service of the defence: see paragraph 5.63 above).

6.26 The purpose of the first CMC is to determine directions in relation to the application for a CPO and the two aspects to be decided: (i) authorisation of the class representative; and (ii) certification of the claims: see paragraph 6.9 above.

6.27 Typically, the Tribunal's directions will provide for the manner in which the application should be publicised (which will depend on the nature of the proposed class) and will fix a timetable for the filing of any written submissions and evidence in relation to the application for a CPO by the prospective defendant and any other relevant party (such as potential class members or a potential competing proposed class representative), and for the hearing of the application: Rule 76(10). A defendant who opposes the application for a CPO does not lose any right to dispute jurisdiction: Rule 76(12).

6.28 The Tribunal does not encourage requests for disclosure as part of the application for a CPO. However, where it appears that specific and limited disclosure or the supply of information (cf Rule 53(2)(d)) is necessary in order to determine whether the claims are suitable to be brought in collective proceedings (see Rule 79(1)), the Tribunal may direct that such disclosure or information be supplied prior to the approval hearing.

AUTHORISATION OF CLASS REPRESENTATIVE

[6.189]

6.29 The class representative need not be a member of the class and is not required to have a personal claim against the proposed defendant: Rule 78(1).[62] However, the Tribunal must consider that it is "just and reasonable" for that person to act as the class representative in the proceedings: Rule 78(1)(b).[63] The central purpose of this assessment is to ensure that class members are adequately and appropriately represented. This is particularly important in opt-out proceedings, where the class representative and its lawyers will not be in contact with many members of the class or be subject to their instructions, but must act in the interests of the class as a whole. Hence, being a class representative involves significant and serious obligations, and is not a responsibility to be taken on lightly.

6.30 The factors the Tribunal will take into account when considering whether it would be just and reasonable for the proposed class representative to act in that capacity are set out in Rule 78(2). The first of these factors is whether the proposed representative would fairly and adequately act in the interests of the class members. The fairness and adequacy test is further elaborated on in Rule 78(3), which lists the circumstances the Tribunal will take into account:

– *Where the proposed class representative is a class member, the Tribunal will consider its suitability to manage the proceedings (Rule 78(3)(a))*

  As part of this analysis, the Tribunal will consider whether the proposed class representative is competent to manage what is likely to be a large and complex piece of litigation, while also adequately representing the class members' interests. Recognising the inevitable complexity of collective proceedings, the Tribunal is also likely to consider the suitability of the proposed class representative's lawyers. The proposed class representative would usually be expected to have the ability to provide proper instructions to its lawyers and be capable of exerting sufficient control over the legal work conducted and costs incurred. Indeed, the Tribunal may require the proposed class representative to demonstrate at least a basic understanding of the facts relevant to the claim, and the nature of the claims themselves, so as to satisfy the Tribunal that it is capable of instructing its lawyers.

– *Where the proposed class representative is not a class member, the Tribunal will consider whether it is a pre-existing body and the nature and functions of that body (Rule 78(3)(b))*

  There is a range of pre-existing bodies which could potentially seek to carry out the role of class representative, such as consumers' organisations, trade associations, law firms, third party funders or special purpose vehicles ("SPV"). While there is no blanket prohibition against certain types of organisation taking on the role of class representative, the Tribunal will closely consider the nature of that body, its motivations for being involved and, crucially, whether there is an actual or potential conflict between that body and the interests of the class members. The potential conflict between the interests of a law firm or third party funder and the interests of the class member may mean that such a body is unsuitable to act as a class representative. Where the proposed class representative is a SPV, the Tribunal will expect to be given details of the constitution and management of the SPV and the reason why it was established. The Tribunal will consider each application in its individual circumstances and proposed class representatives should be prepared to explain why they are suitable to carry out that role. As in the case of class members seeking to act as the class representative, the Tribunal will also consider the body's ability to manage the proceedings and instruct its lawyers.

– *Any plan for the collective proceedings (Rule 78(3)(c))*

  The Tribunal will expect the proposed class representative to have prepared a plan for the collective proceedings which addresses the matters set out in the relevant sub-rule. Such a plan should be sufficiently detailed and comprehensive to correspond to the nature of the particular case. It should explain how the proposed class representative and its lawyers intend to ensure that the collective proceedings will be effectively and efficiently pursued in the interests of the class, referring to the issues likely to arise in the particular case. Matters that may appropriately be set out in the plan include:

  - the way the class representative intends to publicise the proceedings to class members, including a sample notice;
  - the method proposed for communicating with and reporting to class members going forward;
  - how inquiries from class members will be dealt with;
  - the degree of disclosure likely to be required in the proceedings;
  - whether disclosure from individual class members is likely, and if so, the intended process for collection of relevant documents from class members;
  - how exchange of documents will be managed, including any issues of e-disclosure;

- how necessary witnesses will be identified and what steps will be taken to obtain their evidence;
- whether experts will be needed, and if so of what kind and how appropriate experts will be identified and retained;
- where only part of the claims are proposed to be covered by the CPO, if the collective proceedings are decided in favour of the class, what it is proposed should happen to the balance of the claims;
- if it is proposed that the collective proceedings should result in an aggregate award of damages, how that award would be distributed as between members of the class; and
- proposed timetable for the litigation.

There should be appended to the litigation plan a costs budget to the end of trial. The purpose of the plan is to assist the Tribunal in deciding whether to make a CPO. It does not constrain the jurisdiction of the Tribunal to determine the appropriate procedures and, if a CPO is made, the plan may be subject to revision as the litigation proceeds.

6.31 The second factor the Tribunal is required to consider is whether the proposed class representative has a material interest that is in conflict with the interests of the class members, so far as concerns the common issues to be decided in the collective proceedings: Rule 78(2)(b). It is not possible to set out the myriad of ways in which a conflict may arise between the class representative and the class members. However, examples include where the class representative has a stake in the legal fees incurred on behalf of the class, or where the class representative represents the class in a separate but related collective action which might affect the class recovery in the instant proceedings. As made clear by Rule 78(2)(b), a conflict which does not pertain to the common issues will not usually be relevant.

6.32 The third factor relevant to the assessment of the proposed class representative applies where more than one applicant is seeking approval to act as the class representative for opt-out proceedings in respect of the same or overlapping claims. In such a scenario, the Tribunal will consider who would be the most suitable representative: Rule 78(2)(c). The Tribunal will seek to arrive at a decision which is in the best interests of all class members and is fair to the defendants. The factors that are likely to be relevant to this assessment include: the proposed class definition and scope of the claims; the quality of the litigation plan referred to above; and the experience of the lawyers of the competing proposed class representatives.

6.33 The fourth factor the Tribunal is required to consider relates to the proposed class representative's financial resources: would the proposed class representative be able to pay the defendant's recoverable costs if ordered to do so? (Rule 78(2)(d)) By extension, the proposed class representative's ability to fund its own costs of bringing the collective proceedings is also relevant. In considering this aspect, the Tribunal will have regard to the proposed class representative's financial resources, including any relevant fee arrangements with its lawyers, third party funders or insurers. The costs budget appended to the collective proceedings plan referred to above is likely to assist the Tribunal's assessment in this regard.

6.34 Finally, where an interim injunction is sought, the proposed class representative must demonstrate that it would be able to satisfy any undertaking as to damages required by the Tribunal (Rule 78(2)(e)). However, such interim remedies will rarely be suitable for collective proceedings.

6.35 Where the claim covers a sub-class of persons, the Tribunal may authorise a separate class representative for that sub-class pursuant to Rule 78(4). The use of sub-classes may be appropriate where there is a potential conflict between the interests of members of the broader class. For example in cartel damages claims, different categories of purchasers may have conflicting interests that require separate representation.

6.36 Although the Tribunal is formally required to consider the suitability of the proposed class representative only at the stage of making a CPO, the Tribunal will continue to have regard to the requirements throughout the proceedings. Where it appears that the class representative no longer meets the requirements set out in Rule 78, the Tribunal may on its own initiative, or following an application, vary or revoke the CPO authorising the class representative to act in that capacity: Rule 85. Such an order may provide for the substitution of the class representative by another person who satisfies the criteria for approval: Rule 85(3)(b).

CERTIFICATION OF ELIGIBLE CLAIMS

[6.190]

6.37 To make a CPO, the Tribunal must be satisfied that the claims are eligible to be included in collective proceedings. The three requirements for determining eligibility are set out in Rule 79(1):

– *The claims must be brought on behalf of an identifiable class of persons*

It must be possible to say for any particular person, using an objective definition of the class, whether that person falls within the class. The need for an identifiable class of persons serves several purposes. It sets the parameters of the claim by clearly delineating who is within the class and who is not, thus determining who will be bound by any resulting judgment. It affects the scope of the common issues raised by the collective proceedings. And it has practical implications, such as in relation to the requirements to give notice. Indeed, it is the class definition which potential class members will read when considering whether to opt in or out of the proceedings. However, although the claim form must give an evidence based estimate of the size of the class, it is not necessary to identify each class member (in an opt-out claim) or specify exactly how many persons are within the class.

Accordingly, class definitions based on subjective or merits-based criteria (for example "persons having suffered loss as a result of the defendant's conduct") should be avoided. Further, the class should be defined as narrowly as possible without arbitrarily excluding some people entitled to claim. If the class is too broad, the proposed collective proceedings may raise too few common issues and accordingly not be worthwhile.

– *The claims must raise "common issues"*

The core notion of collective proceedings is that they group together similar claims which raise common issues. Common issues are defined in Rule 73(2) as the same, similar or related issues of fact or law, mirroring section 47B(6) of the 1998 Act. It is accordingly important that the claim form identifies the common issues which it is contended can suitably be determined on a collective basis.

Although the claims must raise common issues to satisfy the criteria for approval, the final resolution of the claims will often require the assessment of individual issues. The existence of such individual issues is not fatal to an application for a CPO. For example, the determination of liability for an infringement may raise common issues of fact and law which justify a CPO, while causation and the quantification of any damages may not be common to the class. In such circumstances, the Tribunal may decide to approve collective proceedings in relation to only part of the claims (Rule 74(6)). Once a judgment in those proceedings on the common issues is given, if an aggregate award of damages is inappropriate the claims will continue thereafter on an individual basis.

– *The claims must be "suitable" to be brought in collective proceedings*

When determining whether the claims are suitable to be brought in collective proceedings, the Tribunal will take into account all matters it thinks fit. Specific factors the Tribunal will consider are set out in Rule 79(2). Most of these are self-explanatory and there is considerable overlap between them.

By way of illustration, the Tribunal may consider the costs and benefits of continuing the collective proceedings in various ways (Rule 79(2)(b)) having regard to the likely loss incurred, any potential damages award and the financial cost of continuing proceedings collectively. Where the estimated legal fees and expenses appear disproportionate compared to the likely damages award, the costs of pursuing collective proceedings may outweigh the benefits. The Tribunal may also consider whether collective proceedings should be preferred, in the circumstances, to ordinary individual proceedings, or other ways of resolving the dispute. In this respect, the size and nature of the class may be relevant (see Rule 79(2)(d) ßž it may be that where the class is small, but each individual member's loss is significant, redress would be more effectively obtained by an ordinary individual action).

Where only certain issues in the claims constitute common issues, there is no requirement that those must predominate over the remaining individual issues in order for it to be suitable for the part of the claims covering the common issues to be brought in collective proceedings. However, the common issues must be significant such that resolution of those issues will significantly advance the claims of the members of the class.

Whether proceedings should be opt-in or opt-out

6.38 As mentioned above, a judgment in opt-out proceedings binds all persons within the class, save for those who have opted out (or foreign class members who have not opted in), whereas a judgment in opt-in proceedings binds only those class members who have opted in to the proceedings. Where the class representative seeks approval to bring opt-out proceedings, it will need to make submissions as to why that form of proceedings is more appropriate than opt-in proceedings.

6.39 The Tribunal will consider all matters it thinks fit in determining whether proceedings should be opt-in or opt-out. Rule 79(3) lists two specific factors the Tribunal will consider:

– *Strength of the claims (Rule 79(3)(a))*

Given the greater complexity, cost and risks of opt-out proceedings, the Tribunal will usually expect the strength of the claims to be more immediately perceptible in an opt-out than an opt-in case, since in the latter case, the class members have chosen to be part of the proceedings and may be presumed to have conducted their own assessment of the strength of their claim. However, the reference to the "strength of the claims" does not require the Tribunal to conduct a full merits assessment, and the Tribunal does not expect the parties to make detailed submissions as if that were the case. Rather, the Tribunal will form a high level view of the strength of the claims based on the collective proceedings claim form. For example, where the claims seek damages for the consequence of an infringement which is covered by a decision of a competition authority (follow-on claims), they will generally be of sufficient strength for the purpose of this criterion.

– *Whether it is practicable for the proceedings to be brought as opt-in proceedings (Rule 79(3)(b))*

The Tribunal will consider all the circumstances, including the estimated amount of damages that individual class members may recover in determining whether it is practicable for the proceedings to be certified as opt-in. There is a general preference for proceedings to be opt-in where practicable. Indicators that an opt-in approach could be both workable and in the interests of justice might include the fact that the class is small but the loss suffered by each class member is high, or the fact that it is straightforward to identify and contact the class members.

Approval hearing

6.40 At the hearing, the proposed class representative will make its application for a CPO. The Tribunal will also hear any submissions in response from the proposed defendant(s). Typically, the Tribunal will have directed at the first CMC that written submissions and any evidence relied on be filed at a suitable time prior to the approval hearing, together with any bundles of documents and authorities.

6.41 Where putative class members intend to make oral submissions at the hearing, they must apply to the Tribunal for permission to do so pursuant to Rule 79(5). Such applications should be made in writing in advance of the hearing and be copied to the other parties. The same approach is to be followed in the event that the Tribunal directs that the issue of the authorisation of the class representative is to be determined at a preliminary hearing.

6.42 In determining whether to make a CPO, the Tribunal will sit as a panel of three. As well as the parties' legal representatives, it will usually be appropriate for the proposed class representative to attend the hearing. Where the proposed class representative does not intend to attend the hearing, the Tribunal should be notified in advance.

6.43 Where the defendant makes an application for strike out or summary judgment prior to the approval hearing, it will ordinarily be appropriate to hear those applications at the approval hearing: Rule 79(4). Similarly, any application for security for costs pursuant to Rule 59 will usually be heard at the approval hearing.

6.44 The Tribunal may invite the parties to make submissions on the future conduct of the case at the approval hearing, as if the claims had been made the subject of a CPO. Therefore, the parties should be prepared to assist the Tribunal in drawing up a timetable for the next steps in the proceedings, such as the time for filing the defence and any reply. In this sense, there is an overlap between the approval hearing and what would be considered at the first CMC in an ordinary section 47A claim.

6.45 The Tribunal will generally reserve judgment on the question of whether to make a CPO.

Collective proceedings order

6.46 The CPO authorises the claims to continue as collective proceedings and authorises the proposed class representative to act in that capacity. Where the Tribunal considers, after hearing the parties at the approval hearing, that the requirements in Rules 78 and 79 have been met it will issue such an order.

6.47 The content of the CPO is set out in Rule 80(1). This includes details of the parties, a description of the class and claims, whether the proceedings are to be opt-in or opt-out, the procedure for opting in or out of the proceedings and the arrangements for giving notice to the class members. The class representative is required to file a draft CPO for the Tribunal's consideration with the collective proceedings claim form.

6.48 It is important that detailed consideration is given to the wording of the CPO, particularly in describing the class and the claims certified for inclusion. Although the identification of the class must be clear and objective, it is not necessary to name or specify the number of class members: Rule 80(2). As regards the specification of the claims, the class representative may not bring different claims, or bring claims against different defendants, to those specified in the CPO: Rule 84. However, where the circumstances so require, the Tribunal may subsequently vary the CPO on its own initiative or the application of a party: Rule 85.

6.49 The process for opting in or out of the collective proceedings will be set out in the CPO: Rule 80(1)(h).

6.50 In opt-in proceedings, the CPO will specify the time and manner by which a class member may opt-in. After that date, the class is closed and other class members can no longer opt-in.

6.51 In opt-out proceedings, the CPO will specify a "domicile date", which is the date for determining whether a person is domiciled in the UK. Class members domiciled in the UK on the domicile date are automatically included in the class unless they opt out by the date specified in the CPO. By contrast, class members not domiciled in the UK need to opt in by the specified date in order to be included.

6.52 In addition to the content requirements specified in Rule 80(1), the CPO may also contain directions as to the future conduct of the case: Rule 77(2). For example, it may set the date for the filing of a defence and reply.

6.53 Where a class member does not opt in to opt-in proceedings or opts out of opt-out proceedings (or, in the case of a foreign class member, does not opt in to opt-out proceedings), he or she will not be bound by any subsequent judgment in the proceedings. That person may also be entitled to commence their own proceedings. Where they have failed to opt in or opt out within the specified time, a class member may apply to the Tribunal for permission to opt in or out of the proceedings: Rule 82(2). In determining such an application, the Tribunal will consider all the circumstances, including whether the delay was the fault of the class member and whether the defendant would suffer substantial prejudice if permission were granted: Rule 82(3).

6.54 Where opt-out proceedings lead to a collective settlement, there is a further opportunity for represented persons to opt out. Non-UK domiciled persons who opted in to the collective proceedings need separately to opt in to the collective settlement if they are to be bound (see further paragraphs 6.145–6.146 below).

NOTICES

[6.191]
6.55 The Rules require the class representative to provide the class members with information about the proceedings at the following stages of the litigation:

- when the Tribunal makes a CPO: Rule 81;
- in opt-in proceedings, if the class representative is a member of the class and settles its personal claim included in the collective proceedings: Rule 86;
- if the class representative intends to withdraw from the role: Rule 87(2);
- when the Tribunal issues a judgment or order in the proceedings: Rule 91(2); and
- when the Tribunal intends to have a hearing to determine how to quantify individual represented persons' claims from an aggregate award of damages: Rule 92(3).

6.56 The Tribunal may also require the class representative to give notice to class members at other stages of the proceedings: Rule 88(2)(d). These notice requirements perform an important role in making the class members aware of the proceedings and updating them throughout. The class representative may of course wish to provide additional information to class members beyond these requirements.

6.57 Additional notice requirements apply to collective settlements (see paragraph 6.94 et seq. below).

Notice of the collective proceedings order

6.58 The class representative must notify the class members when the Tribunal makes a CPO: Rule 81. The Tribunal will attach particular importance to the content of this notice and the method by which it will be given, since for many class members this will be the first they hear of the proceedings. Therefore, the class representative is required to annex a draft notice of the CPO to its collective proceedings claim form (Rule 75(4)(c)), which the Tribunal will consider and approve, subject to any changes it considers appropriate.

6.59 The content requirements of this first formal notice are set out in Rule 81(2). As well as annexing the CPO and identifying the defendant(s), the notice must set out in plain and easily understood language a summary of the collective proceedings claim form and common issues. It must also set out in a straightforward manner how class members opt in or out of the proceedings, the deadlines which apply, and explain the consequences of doing so. The Tribunal may require the class representative to include additional information in the notice: Rule 81(2)(f).

Notice of judgment or order

6.60 The class representative must give notice of any judgment or order to all class members in a form and manner approved by the Tribunal: Rule 91(2). The content requirements of such notices are set out in Rule 91(3).

6.61 The notice should incorporate or annex the judgment or order, or give a reference to the copy of the judgment available online. Where the judgment deals with the common issues, the notice must contain specific information depending on whether the judgment is for or against the represented persons. For example, where the judgment is in the class members' favour, the notice must explain in plain and easily understood language that they may be entitled to individual remedies, how they claim those remedies and the consequences of failing to do so: Rule 91(3)(b).

Failure to receive a notice

6.62 The fact that a class member represented person does not receive or fails to respond to a notice does not affect a step taken, order made or judgment given in the collective proceedings, unless the Tribunal orders otherwise: Rule 90.

Method of giving notice

6.63 The method of giving notice will vary depending on the class characteristics. In each case, the aim is to adopt a method which ensures the greatest proportion of class members receives the notice. It may be appropriate to alter the method of giving notice within the same case, depending on what is being notified. For example, individual notices by post may be necessary where the notice concerns the making of a CPO, whereas a less intensive method — such as social media updates, or notice to a sample group within the class — may be sufficient for Tribunal orders dealing with other aspects of the proceedings. In determining the appropriate method, the Tribunal is likely to consider the practicability and expense of giving notice, as well as the relative importance of the particular notice.

6.64 At every stage at which the Tribunal considers how notice should be given, the class representative should be prepared to assist the Tribunal as to the most appropriate method.

CLASS RECORDS

[6.192]

6.65 The class representative is required to maintain a register of all class members who have opted in or out of the collective proceedings: Rule 83. The Tribunal and the defendant(s) are entitled to see the class register on request. Other persons may apply to the Tribunal to see the class register: Rule 83(2).

CASE MANAGEMENT

[6.193]

6.66 The general provisions dealing with case management in private actions in Rules 53–57 apply to collective proceedings, save that the references to the first CMC shall be read as referring to the first CMC after the Tribunal has made a CPO: Rule 74(4)(d). Further provisions on the case management of collective proceedings are set out in Rule 88.

6.67 The Tribunal has broad powers to give any directions it thinks fit for the case management of the collective proceedings (Rule 88(1)), and it is likely to use those powers actively.

DISCLOSURE

[6.194]
6.68 The general provisions dealing with disclosure in Rules 60–65 apply to collective proceedings, save that the references to the first CMC shall be read as referring to the first CMC after the Tribunal has made a CPO: Rule 74(4)(e). The Tribunal may order disclosure to be given by any party to the collective proceedings, by the class representative to represented persons or by any represented person: Rule 89.

STAY, VARIATION OR REVOCATION OF THE COLLECTIVE PROCEEDINGS ORDER

[6.195]
6.69 The Tribunal may vary or revoke a CPO, or stay or sist the collective proceedings: Rule 85(1).

6.70 When deciding whether to vary or revoke a CPO, the Tribunal will take into account all the relevant circumstances. Rule 85(2) requires the Tribunal to consider whether the claims certification criteria continue to be met, whether the class representative continues to satisfy the criteria for authorisation and whether the Tribunal has given the class representative permission to withdraw. If the class representative no longer meets the requirements, the Tribunal will consider whether a suitable alternative can be authorised: Rule 85(2)(b) and Rule 85(3)(b).

OFFERS OF SETTLEMENT

[6.196]
6.71 The only parties to collective proceedings are the class representative (or representatives if there are sub-classes) and the defendants. Accordingly, any offer of settlement must be made to one of those parties. Represented persons cannot accept a settlement offer in relation to the common issues as they are not a party to the proceedings.

6.72 The regime for formal settlement offers under Rule 45 does not apply to collective proceedings: Rule 74(3)(c). Collective proceedings are a novel procedure with unique features and it was considered that to apply a regime with automatic cost shifting consequences could potentially create conflicts between members of the class and give rise to unreasonable pressure on the class representative. However, parties will be able to make '*Calderbank*' offers "without prejudice save as to costs". The Tribunal will take such an offer into account if subsequently asked to make an order for costs. Although such an offer does not give rise to any presumption as to how the Tribunal's discretion regarding costs will be exercised, rejection of a reasonable offer that was more favourable to the offeree than the eventual judgment may lead to adverse cost consequences.

INDIVIDUAL SETTLEMENT BY THE CLASS REPRESENTATIVE IN OPT-IN PROCEEDINGS

[6.197]
6.73 In opt-in proceedings, if the class representative is also a class member it must notify the class and the Tribunal if it settles in whole or in part its personal claim included within the collective proceedings: Rule 86. This is because such a settlement may affect whether that person continues to satisfy the criteria for acting as a class representative. For example, settlement may give rise to a conflict of interest between the class representative and the rest of the class, particularly where only the class representative's claim has been settled. In opt-out proceedings, the only form of permissible settlement is by a collective settlement order, so if the class representative is a class member it may not reach an individual settlement: Rule 94(1).

WITHDRAWAL BY THE CLASS REPRESENTATIVE

[6.198]
6.74 The class representative may withdraw from acting in that capacity with the permission of the Tribunal, which will only be granted if the class representative has given appropriate notice to the class, and on conditions which the Tribunal thinks just: Rule 87.

JUDGMENT IN COLLECTIVE PROCEEDINGS

[6.199]
6.75 A judgment of the Tribunal in collective proceedings is binding on all represented persons unless otherwise specified.[64] The judgment therefore binds all persons who have opted in to or not opted out of the proceedings in accordance with Rule 82, depending on whether those proceedings are opt-in or opt-out. Therefore, a UK domiciled class member who has not opted out of opt-out proceedings will be bound by the judgment, whether it is favourable or unfavourable to that class member's interests. The class member cannot subsequently bring separate proceedings in respect of the same claim. Nor can it appeal the Tribunal's judgment: an appeal can be brought only by the class representative or the defendant (see paragraph 6.91 below in relation to appeals).

6.76 Where appropriate, however, the Tribunal's judgment may expressly limit who is bound by it: Rule 91(1).

AWARD OF DAMAGES AND COSTS

[6.200]
6.77 The Tribunal may not award exemplary damages in collective proceedings.[65] Damages awards will usually be limited to the loss suffered, including interest if appropriate.

6.78 In awarding damages in collective proceedings, the Tribunal is not required to assess how much each represented person may recover in respect of their claim.[66] Rather, the Tribunal may make an "aggregate" award of damages as defined in Rule 73(2). An aggregate award determines the amount the class as a whole is entitled to and is designed to be a practical and proportionate method of assessing damages in collective proceedings. For example, the Tribunal may calculate the damages on a class-wide basis; this could be way of a lump sum award against the defendant, or by using a formula to determine each represented person's claim without requiring individual proof. This type of award is likely to be more suitable where its calculation can be made without information from the class members, such as where the defendant's records are sufficient, or where there is a large class with largely identical individual claims.

6.79 If it is not appropriate to make an aggregate award of damages for the entire class, it may be possible to proceed to determine the entitlement of sub-classes on a group basis, amending the CPO as appropriate to authorise the appointment of class representatives for those sub-classes. If that is not possible, the Tribunal may direct that the quantification of damages proceed as individual issues: Rule 88(2)(c).

Costs

6.80 Costs may be awarded to or against the class representative in the same way as in proceedings under section 47A but they may not be awarded to or against a represented person (unless that person is the class representative) save in the following circumstances:

– if the Tribunal has approved the appointment of a class representative for a sub-class, costs associated with the determination of the common issues for that sub-class may be awarded to or against that person: Rule 98(1)(a);
– costs associated with the determination of individual issues in accordance with Rule 88(2)(c) may be awarded to or against the relevant individual represented person: Rule 98(1)(c).

There is also provision for costs in respect of any individual application made by a class member in the course of the collective proceedings to be awarded to or against that class member: Rule 98(2).

6.81 A damages-based agreement ("DBA") for the payment of legal fees is unenforceable if it relates to opt-out collective proceedings.[67] The same restriction does not apply to opt-in collective proceedings. DBAs are defined in section 58AA(3) of the Courts and Legal Services Act 1990. In essence, a DBA provides that the fees payable by the client to its legal or other representative are determined as a percentage of the damages awarded to the client.

DISTRIBUTION OF DAMAGES

[6.201]
6.82 Where an aggregate award of damages has been made, the Tribunal will give directions as to how each class member or represented person's entitlement is to be calculated: Rule 92(1). Rule 92(2) gives examples of the types of directions the Tribunal may wish to make, such as specifying a formula to quantify an individual's entitlement, the provision of an interim payment or the appointment of an independent third party to determine the claims or any disputes regarding quantification. The Tribunal will expect the class representative to assist the Tribunal by proposing appropriate directions. The Tribunal may also require the apportionment to be placed before the Tribunal for approval.

6.83 If the question of the distribution of damages is to be considered at a hearing, the class representative must notify the class members that such a hearing is to take place: Rule 92(3). Any class member may then apply to the Tribunal to make submissions either in writing or orally at the hearing. Typically, the defendant will not be involved in the process of determining how the award is to be distributed among the class. Accordingly, subject to submissions from any members of the class, the determination by the Tribunal as to the entitlement of the individual class members will not follow adversarial argument. The Tribunal will be concerned to ensure that the method proposed by the class representative is fair to the interests of all class members.

6.84 In most cases, the Tribunal will order that the damages be paid to the class representative so that the representative manages the distribution to the class or the represented persons. In opt-out proceedings, the Tribunal is required to order that any damages be paid to the class representative or another person the Tribunal thinks fit: Rule 93(1).[68] In opt-in proceedings, the Tribunal may make such an order, although it has a wider discretion as regards who the damages are paid to: Rule 93(2).[69] The Tribunal may, for example, order that the damages be paid directly to the represented persons.

6.85 Where the Tribunal orders that the damages be paid to the class representative, or such other person as the Tribunal thinks fit, it must also specify a time within which individual represented persons may claim their entitlement: Rule 93(3)(a). The class representative must make it clear to the represented persons dealing with the distribution of the damages award that there is a limited time period for them to claim their entitlements in the notice of the judgment or order: Rule 91(3)(b). Where the damages are to be paid to the class representative, the Tribunal will need to be satisfied that suitable arrangements for holding the funds are in place.

6.86 The class representative is required to notify the Tribunal by a particular date of any damages which have not been claimed ("undistributed damages"); the same applies to any other person to whom the damages were paid: Rule 93(3)(b).

Undistributed damages

6.87 Undistributed damages are those damages which have not been claimed by the represented persons within the time period set by the Tribunal. The class representative is required to notify the

Tribunal of the existence of any undistributed damages. There may be some delay following the expiry of the time set by the Tribunal for submission of claims before the amount of the undistributed damages can be determined, for example where there are disputes as to whether a claimant falls within the class or regarding the quantification of individual claims. Once the amount has been ascertained, or largely ascertained, the Tribunal may order that the undistributed damages be used in the following ways under Rules 93(4)–(6):

- the undistributed damages may be used to cover any costs, fees or disbursements incurred by the class representative in respect of the collective proceedings; or
- the undistributed damages may be paid to the charity designated by the Lord Chancellor pursuant to section 47C(5) of the 1998 Act.

6.88 Undistributed damages cannot be returned to the defendants in collective proceedings.[70]

6.89 The default position is that undistributed damages will be paid to charity.[71] The charity currently designated[72] is the Access to Justice Foundation, whose stated aim is to facilitate access to pro-bono legal assistance for those who need it most. Where the class representative seeks an order that the undistributed damages be used instead to cover all or part of its costs, fees and disbursements, the class representative must make an application to the Tribunal. This application must specify how much is being claimed and how those costs, fees and/or disbursements were incurred (where appropriate by way of a costs schedule). Obviously, the class representative will only be able to make such a claim out of the undistributed damages insofar as it has not recovered its costs from the defendant.

6.90 The Tribunal may determine the amounts to be paid to the class representative itself, or direct that they be determined by a costs judge of the High Court, a taxing officer of the Supreme Court of Northern Ireland or the Auditor of the Court of Session: Rule 93(5). Where only part of the undistributed damages is paid to the class representative, the Tribunal will direct that the remainder is paid to the Access to Justice Foundation: Rule 93(6). Since the defendant has no interest in the amount to be paid on account of the class representative's costs, fees and disbursements, it does not have a right to be heard on this question. However, the Tribunal will give the Access to Justice Foundation permission to address it on the determination, and a copy of the application should accordingly be sent to the Foundation.[73]

APPEALS IN COLLECTIVE PROCEEDINGS

[6.202]

6.91 Section 49 of the 1998 Act deals with appeals against Tribunal decisions in collective proceedings. Such appeals are limited to:

- points of law arising from a decision of the Tribunal as to:
  - (i) an award of damages or other sum (other than a decision on costs or expenses);
  - (ii) the grant of an injunction; or
  - (iii) infringement findings in stand-alone claims; and
- decisions as to the amount of an award of damages or other sum.

6.92 However, there is no statutory provision for appeals against the Tribunal's decision on an application for a CPO. Therefore, any challenge to such decisions can only be brought by way of judicial review.

6.93 Appeals may only be brought by the class representative or the defendant. Class members have no right to appeal decisions made in respect of the claims included in the collective proceedings.[74]

COLLECTIVE SETTLEMENTS

[6.203]

6.94 The 1998 Act makes provision for two forms of collective settlement which require the approval of the Tribunal:

- collective settlement after a CPO has been made for opt-out collective proceedings;[75]
- collective settlement where no collective proceedings have started or before a CPO has been made.[76]

These two forms of settlement are discussed in more detail below.

6.95 There is no statutory provision governing collective settlement of opt-in collective proceedings after a CPO has been made, and such a settlement does not require the Tribunal's approval. The only restriction which applies is that the class representative may not, without the permission of the Tribunal, settle the collective proceedings before the time for opting-in specified in the CPO has expired: Rule 95. This ensures that there are no "absent" class members: all represented persons are identified and the class representative is able to take instructions or consult with them before reaching a settlement. It also prevents a defendant undermining the effect of a CPO by settling the proceedings before the class of represented persons has been fully constituted.

APPLYING FOR APPROVAL OF A SETTLEMENT OF OPT-OUT COLLECTIVE PROCEEDINGS (I.E. WHERE A COLLECTIVE PROCEEDINGS ORDER HAS BEEN MADE)

[6.204]

6.96 A collective settlement of opt-out collective proceedings will only bind the parties and the class if it has been approved by the Tribunal. The Tribunal's approval is necessary because such a collective settlement affects the interests of all class members (or represented persons), although many of those persons are unidentified and have not been involved in the proceedings in any way. The Tribunal's approval of the collective settlement is intended to ensure that the interests of all class members or represented persons are protected.

6.97 Rule 94 sets out the procedure for seeking approval of a collective settlement where a CPO has been made specifying that the proceedings are opt-out proceedings. In such a scenario, the Tribunal has already considered whether the class representative is suitable to act in that capacity and whether the claims are eligible to be included in collective proceedings. The Tribunal need not reconsider those issues. The essential question for the Tribunal's consideration is whether the terms of the settlement are "just and reasonable" in accordance with section 49A(5) of the 1998 Act. If the Tribunal approves a collective settlement, it will issue a "collective settlement approval order" ("CSAO").

6.98 The class representative and the settling defendant must make a joint application for a CSAO: Rule 94(3).[77] Rule 94(4) requires the application for a CSAO to contain the following information:

– *Details of the claims to be settled*
  The application should make clear whether the proposed settlement relates to all or part of the common issues which are the subject of the collective proceedings, where appropriate by reference to the CPO.
– *The terms of the proposed collective settlement*
  The application must detail the terms of the settlement, including the overall settlement sum and any related provisions as to the payment of costs, fees and disbursements. It should also set out what has been agreed in relation to any undistributed settlement funds.
– *A statement that the applicants believe that the terms of the proposed settlement are just and reasonable*
  Such a statement should be made by both the class representative and the settling defendant and must be supported by evidence. It is expected that such evidence would be served separately by the class representative and the settling defendant. The types of evidence which may be filed include a report by an independent expert (such as an economist) or an opinion by Counsel as to the merits of the settlement.
  The supporting evidence should explain how the represented persons' losses have been calculated and the amount of the settlement arrived at. It may also be appropriate for the lawyers to provide their assessment of the chances of success at trial. Where appropriate, arrangements may be made to protect the confidentiality of such supporting evidence.
– *How the settlement sums are to be paid and distributed*
  The application should explain how the defendant proposes to pay the settlement sums and how they are to be distributed. For example, the defendant and class representative may agree that the settlement sums will be paid to the class representative who will then administer the settlement pursuant to a distribution plan. Details of the distribution plan should be included with the application. The application should also explain how represented persons are to claim their entitlement, the evidence they must supply to support their claim, how the class representative proposes to manage the distribution process and how the costs of that process are to be funded.
  Where the class representative and/or defendants propose to appoint a third party to administer the distribution of the settlement sums, the application should identify that third party (or explain how it will be selected), explain its proposed role and how it will be paid. The Tribunal will consider the third party's ability, experience and resources to carry out that role and may require the third party to give evidence to the Tribunal.
– *A draft of the collective settlement approval order*
  The class representative and settling defendant must annex a draft CSAO to the application. The contents of the CSAO are discussed at paragraphs 6.132–6.133 below.
– *How the class representative proposes to give notice of the application*
  The Tribunal will usually require the class representative to give notice that it has applied for approval of a collective settlement. This notice ensures that class members or represented persons are given an opportunity to support or oppose the proposed settlement.
  Typically, notice will be given to the entire class or the represented persons, depending on whether it is expected that the time for opting in or out of the proceedings, as set out in the CPO, will have passed at the time the Tribunal approves the settlement. The application must explain how this notice will be given. However, the Tribunal may dispense with this notice where it thinks fit: Rule 94(6)(b).

6.99 The class representative and settling defendant (or their lawyers) must both sign the application for a CSAO. The original and five certified copies of this application and of any supporting evidence must then be filed with the Tribunal: Rule 94(5).

6.100 When the Tribunal receives an application for a CSAO, it has a broad discretion to give any directions it thinks fit: Rule 94(6). For example, the Tribunal may direct that part of the application receives confidential treatment. This may be necessary where the public availability of certain parts of the application — such as the defendant's estimate of the likely damage or legal advice as to the prospects of success — could be harmful to a party's interests, particularly if the settlement is not ultimately approved. At this stage, the Tribunal will usually fix a date for a hearing of the application and for any deadlines prior to the hearing (for example for class members to apply to make submissions).

6.101 The role of class members in the approval process and the criteria for approval of a collective settlement are discussed below.

APPLYING FOR APPROVAL OF A COLLECTIVE SETTLEMENT DIRECTLY (I.E. WHERE A COLLECTIVE PROCEEDINGS ORDER HAS NOT BEEN MADE)

[6.205]
6.102 There are three main stages to such a "direct" settlement: (i) approval of the collective form of

process; (ii) approval of the terms of the proposed settlement as just and reasonable; and (iii) administration of the settlement. The main difference between direct settlements and settlements of collective proceedings is that in a direct settlement the parties must apply for a "collective settlement order" or "CSO" prior to, or at the same time as, making an application for approval of the proposed collective settlement, i.e. a CSAO.

Applying for a collective settlement order

6.103 Rule 96 governs collective settlement orders. In summary, a CSO is analogous to a CPO and the criteria for approval are broadly the same. However, unless a potential class member objects, since it is made only for the purpose of settlement the application for a CSO will be uncontested.

6.104 Unlike an application for a CPO (which is made only by the proposed class representative), the application for a CSO must be made by the proposed settlement representative and the would-be defendant: Rule 96(1).[78] Rule 96(2) requires the application to:

- identify the proposed settlement representative;
- explain how the proposed settlement representative satisfies the requirements of Rule 96(9)–(11);
- identify the would-be defendant;
- describe the proposed settlement class;
- estimate the number of class members and explain the basis for that estimate;
- provide details of the claims to be settled by the proposed collective settlement;
- explain how the claims would meet the eligibility criteria for collective proceedings in Rule 79, if they had been brought in collective proceedings; and
- annex a draft: (i) CSO; (ii) summary of the CSO application for the Tribunal's website; and (iii) notice of the CSO.

6.105 Unless the Tribunal otherwise directs, the signed original of the CSO application (and its annexes) should be accompanied by five copies certified by the proposed settlement representative or its lawyer as conforming to the original: Rule 96(3).

Determination of the application for a collective settlement order

6.106 As these cases will normally be complex, the Tribunal will ordinarily list a hearing to consider the application for a CSO. However, in some cases, where the circumstances are relatively straightforward, it may be possible to determine the application on the papers.

6.107 Members of the proposed settlement class may apply to make submissions either in writing or orally at the hearing of the application for a CSO: Rule 96(8). Such applications should be made in writing in advance of any hearing and be copied to the other parties.

6.108 There is considerable overlap between the conditions for granting a CSO and a CPO. In summary, to make a CSO, the Tribunal must be satisfied that: (i) the proposed settlement representative meets the criteria for acting in that capacity; and (ii) the claims would be eligible to be brought in collective proceedings: Rule 96(6).[79]

- *Suitable settlement representative*

  The settlement representative need not be a member of the class and is not required to have his or her own claim against the would-be defendant.[80] The Tribunal will only authorise the proposed settlement representative to act in that capacity where it is satisfied that it is just and reasonable: Rule 96(9).[81] When determining whether it would be just and reasonable for the proposed settlement representative to act in that capacity, the Tribunal will consider:

  - whether the proposed representative would fairly and adequately act in the interests of the class members: Rule 96(10)(a). The fairness and adequacy test is further elaborated on in Rule 96(11), which lists the circumstances the Tribunal will take into account: (i) where the proposed settlement representative is a class member, the Tribunal will consider its suitability to manage the proceedings (Rule 96(11)(a)); (ii) where the proposed settlement representative is not a class member, the Tribunal will consider whether it is a pre-existing body and the nature and functions of that body (Rule 96(11)(b)); and (iii) any plan for the collective settlement (Rule 96(11)(c)); and
  - whether the proposed settlement representative has a material interest that is in conflict with the interests of the class members, so far as the common issues are concerned: Rule 96(10)(b).

  The Tribunal's approach to these factors is likely to be similar to the approach it would take in collective proceedings, as discussed at paragraphs 6.30–6.31 above.

- *Eligible claims*

  Certification for settlement purposes requires the Tribunal to be satisfied that the claims would be eligible to be included in collective proceedings, if collective proceedings were brought. The three requirements for determining eligibility for collective proceedings are set out in Rule 79(1), each of which is considered at paragraph 6.37 above. However, there will inevitably be less concern about the suitability of the collective handling of common issues when the parties are coming to the Tribunal only for the purpose of approving a settlement and not in order to pursue legal proceedings.

Collective settlement order

6.109 The CSO must authorise the settlement representative to act in that capacity and describe the class.[82] Further content requirements are set out in Rule 96(12). These requirements are broadly the same as for a CPO, save that there is no need to identify the remedy sought, the time for opting in or out of proceedings, or the part of the UK in which proceedings are to be treated as taking place.

Notice of the collective settlement order

6.110 The settlement representative must notify the class members that the Tribunal has made a CSO: Rule 96(15). This notice must be approved by the Tribunal.

6.111 The content requirements for the notice of the CSO are set out in Rule 96(16). The purpose of the notice is to inform the class members of the proposed collective settlement in plain and easily understood language, and to explain who will be bound by the proposed settlement if it is approved by the Tribunal.

Variation or revocation of the collective settlement order

6.112 The Tribunal may vary or revoke the CSO on its own initiative or on the application of a class member or party: Rule 96(17). The Tribunal will ordinarily seek observations from the parties on the proposed variation or revocation request.

Applying for a collective settlement approval order

6.113 Once the Tribunal has made a CSO, the parties may apply for approval of the collective settlement. This application is made in much the same way as an application for settlement of collective proceedings. The settlement representative and the would-be defendant must make a joint application for a CSAO (Rule 97(1)),[83] and provide the information required by Rule 97(2).

6.114 The discussion at paragraph 6.98 above regarding an application for approval of a settlement of collective proceedings pursuant to Rule 94(4) applies equally to an application for approval of a direct collective settlement pursuant to Rule 97(2), save that:

– it is the settlement representative and would-be defendant that apply, rather than the class representative and defendant; and
– the applicants are required to explain how they propose to give notice to the settlement class, rather than to represented persons or class members.

6.115 The settlement representative and would-be defendant (or their legal representatives) must both sign the application for a CSAO. The original and five certified copies of the application and any evidence in support must be filed with the Tribunal: Rule 97(3).

6.116 Upon receipt of an application for a CSAO, the Tribunal has a broad discretion to give any directions it thinks fit: Rule 97(4). Usually, those directions will include listing a hearing to determine the application.

ROLE OF CLASS MEMBERS IN THE APPROVAL PROCESS

[6.206]
6.117 Broadly, the class members who will be bound by the proposed settlement may participate in the approval process with the Tribunal's permission: Rules 94(7) and 97(5). Who this includes depends on whether a CPO or CSO has been issued, and whether the time for opting out of any collective proceedings has passed, as set out in the table below.

Stage of collective proceedings or collective settlement		Who may apply to make submissions
Collective proceedings order	Time for opting out has expired	Represented persons
	Time for opting out has not expired	Class members
Collective settlement order		Any member of the proposed settlement class

6.118 Persons wishing to make submissions must apply for permission within the time period fixed by the Tribunal. If the Tribunal has not set a deadline, applications must be filed with the Tribunal before the collective settlement approval hearing. In either case, applications should be made without waiting until the end of the period allowed.

6.119 There is no set form for the request to make submissions, although the Tribunal will generally expect the application to include the following:

– the title of the settlement proceedings to which the application relates;
– the name and address of the person wishing to make submissions;
– the name and address of their legal representative if appropriate;
– an address for service in the United Kingdom;
– whether the person wishes to make submissions orally or in writing;
– a concise statement of whether the person supports or objects to the proposed settlement; and
– a succinct presentation of the reasons for making the request.

6.120 The request for permission to make submissions will be served on the other parties by the Registrar, giving them an opportunity to respond within a short time limit.

6.121 The Tribunal may permit one or more class members to make submissions, either orally or in writing and will take those submissions into account when determining whether the proposed settlement is just and reasonable: Rules 94(9)(f) and 97(7)(f).

6.122 It should be noted that class members or represented persons (as the case may be) will have an opportunity to opt out of the collective settlement after it has been approved, even if they did not opt out of any collective proceedings or did not object to the settlement terms at the approval hearing: Rules 94(10) and 97(8).

SETTLEMENT APPROVAL CRITERIA

[6.207]
6.123 The Tribunal may approve a collective settlement only if it is satisfied that its terms are "just and reasonable".[84]

6.124 Unless a class member objects to the settlement, the Tribunal will not have the benefit of adversarial argument in considering whether to approve the terms proposed. However, an application for a CSAO is markedly different from the presentation to the Tribunal or a court of a consent order in ordinary civil proceedings. If approved, the settlement will bind all members of the defined class who do not opt out and bring to an end the (or preclude the commencement of) proceedings brought on behalf of the class, although many class members will not have given instructions to the class representative (or settlement representative) agreeing to the settlement. In these circumstances, the Tribunal will closely scrutinise the proposed collective settlement. However, the Tribunal will not require the settlement to be perfect and there is likely to be a range of reasonable settlements which could be approved by the Tribunal.

6.125 In considering whether a collective settlement is just and reasonable, the Tribunal will take into account all relevant circumstances, including the specific factors listed in Rules 94(9) and 97(7). While Rule 94(9) applies to settlements of collective proceedings and Rule 97(7) applies to direct collective settlements, the factors are broadly the same in both scenarios. These factors are as follows:

– *The amount and terms of the settlement*
The Tribunal's consideration of the amount and terms of the settlement will include the monetary and non-monetary benefits offered by the settling defendant, as well as any related provisions as to the payment of costs, fees and disbursements. In particular, the Tribunal may consider the amount allocated to costs, fees and disbursements as a proportion of the overall settlement. Where legal costs make up a significant proportion of the settlement funds, the Tribunal will scrutinise whether this allocation is appropriate and will be alert to any potential conflict of interest between the class (or settlement) representative and its lawyers on the one hand and the class members on the other hand.
The Tribunal will also consider carefully the terms of any waiver or release contained in the proposed settlement agreement.

– *The number or estimated number of persons likely to be entitled to a share of the settlement*
The number of persons who may be able to claim a share of the settlement will influence the Tribunal's overall assessment of the settlement amount and terms. A settlement may incorporate a provision whereby either party has a right to cancel the settlement in the event that a specified opt-out threshold is exceeded.
The Tribunal may also consider how class members will be required to claim their entitlement in order to ensure that the applicable conditions or procedures are not overly onerous or complicated so as to discourage or hinder legitimate claims.

– *The likelihood of judgment being obtained in collective proceedings for an amount significantly in excess of the amount of the settlement*
When considering the likelihood of judgment being obtained in collective proceedings for more than the amount of the settlement, the Tribunal need not conduct a detailed analysis of the claims to determine what it would have awarded in damages (if anything) following a trial. Rather, the Tribunal will adopt a broad brush assessment of the position, having regard to the prospect of success and estimated quantum of damages.

– *The likely duration and costs of the collective proceedings if they proceeded to trial*
This factor is intended to reflect the often costly and time consuming nature of legal proceedings. In light of the additional time and cost of taking a case to trial, it may be preferable to approve a settlement even though a somewhat higher damages award might be granted after trial.

– *Any opinion by an independent expert and any legal representative of the applicants*
As well as considering the written opinion of an independent expert and/or the lawyers advising the class (or settlement) representative and the settling defendant(s), the Tribunal may require that person to attend the settlement approval hearing and be questioned in relation to their opinion (in a closed hearing if necessary). In giving their opinion to the Tribunal, experts and legal representatives are reminded of their professional duties to the Tribunal. Their role is of particular importance where a CSAO is sought for a direct collective settlement: when there are no collective proceedings, the difficulty for the Tribunal is all the greater in assessing whether the proposed terms are just and reasonable.

– *The views of any represented person / class member / settlement class member (as appropriate)*
As the principal parties to the collective settlement approval application are agreed on the settlement, class objectors provide the closest thing to an adversarial testing of the settlement terms. Therefore, the Tribunal will consider carefully what any objectors have to say about the settlement to ensure that the class members' interests are served by the settlement. The Tribunal will not, however, infer from a lack of objectors that the settlement is likely to be just and reasonable.

– *The provisions relating to the disposition of any unclaimed balance*

The Tribunal will consider what will happen to any unclaimed settlement sums. Unlike damages awards in collective proceedings, unclaimed sums may revert to the defendant: Rules 94(9)(g) and 97(7)(g). Reversion to the defendant will not *of itself* be considered unreasonable, but where a settlement includes provision for reversion, the Tribunal may be concerned to see whether this is conditional upon a threshold of take-up of the settlement fund. For example, a settlement that could result in substantial fees being paid to the lawyers of the class (or settlement) representative and a significant part of the settlement sums being paid back to the defendants, while future claims by class members are barred, is unlikely to be viewed as just and reasonable. A settlement may include provision for all or part of the unclaimed balance be paid to the Access to Justice Foundation, as in the case of a judgment in opt-out collective proceedings: paragraph 6.89 above.

6.126 A collective settlement does not have to be reached in respect of the entire class as defined in the CPO. However, where a defined group within the class is excluded from the terms of the settlement, the Tribunal will wish to be satisfied that the exclusion of the claims of the excluded class members is based on objective grounds that are just and reasonable. Further, in that event the Tribunal will consider whether the terms of the CPO should be varied so as to define as a sub-class the members excluded from the collective settlement and enable the collective proceedings to continue for their benefit, possibly with the substitution of a new class representative, or whether the collective proceedings should be stayed on the terms of the settlement: see Rule 85.

6.127 The Tribunal will wish to be satisfied that the class (or settlement) representative and its lawyers had sufficient information in order to assess the reasonableness of the settlement to the class members. Accordingly, it may be relevant to ascertain whether and to what extent the class (or settlement) representative has received disclosure from the settling defendant(s), either voluntarily as part of the negotiations or in the course of the collective proceedings.

6.128 The applicants should have regard to these factors when applying for a CSAO, as should any class member making submissions in relation to the proposed collective settlement.

6.129 In most cases, the application for a CSAO will be heard by the full Tribunal panel (being the case management tribunal where the application follows the making of a CPO: paragraph 6.7 above). In the event that the Tribunal does not approve the settlement and the claims proceed to trial, the trial will be heard by a differently constituted panel.

COLLECTIVE SETTLEMENT WITH ONE OR MORE, BUT NOT ALL, DEFENDANTS

[6.208]
6.130 The class (or settlement) representative may reach a collective partial settlement, i.e. agree terms with only one, or several, of a larger number of defendants (or would-be defendants), and that collective partial settlement may be the subject of an application for a CSAO.

6.131 If the defendants are subject to joint and several liability, for example where they were participants in a cartel, achieving such a partial settlement may present difficulties if the settling defendant(s) are concerned about their potential liability to the non-settling defendant(s) in subsequent contribution proceedings. In those circumstances, the Tribunal may consider incorporating in the approval order a barring provision that prevents the non-settling defendant(s) from claiming contribution from the settling defendant(s), on the basis that if it were subsequently determined that there was such a right of contribution, the class (or settlement) representative will be limited to recover from the non-settling defendant(s) only damages for which those defendants would be proportionally liable.[85] If the settling parties apply for such a provision to be included in the Tribunal's order, the Tribunal will permit any non-settling defendant (or potential defendant) to make submissions as to whether an order on those terms should be made.

COLLECTIVE SETTLEMENT APPROVAL ORDER

[6.209]
6.132 The only formal requirement for the CSAO is that it must specify the time and manner by which a represented person or class member, as the case may be, must opt out (for UK-domiciled persons) or opt in (for non-UK-domiciled persons): Rules 94(10) and 97(8).

6.133 The CSAO will also typically contain the following:

- the collective settlement agreement as an annex or schedule to the order;
- a statement that the settlement agreement is just and reasonable, and that it is therefore approved pursuant to either section 49A(5) or 49B(8) of the 1998 Act; and
- a statement that any other action commenced in the Tribunal by a UK-domiciled class member who has not opted out of the collective settlement (or collective proceedings) or a non-UK-domiciled class member who has opted in to the collective settlement is dismissed.

6.134 As mentioned above, the class representative and settling defendant are required to annex a draft CSAO to their application for approval of the collective settlement.

TRIBUNAL CONCERNS ABOUT THE PROPOSED COLLECTIVE SETTLEMENT

[6.210]
6.135 If the Tribunal is not satisfied that the proposed collective settlement is just and reasonable, it will refuse to make a CSAO and issue a reasoned decision in writing rejecting the application.

6.136 Following the Tribunal's rejection of the approval application, the applicants may:

- apply for approval of a revised collective settlement;

– if the collective settlement was applied for in collective proceedings, those proceedings will continue;
– if the collective settlement was applied for directly, the settlement representative may initiate collective proceedings and apply for a CPO.

6.137 If the Tribunal rejects the proposed collective settlement, the application for a CSAO or the terms of the proposed settlement cannot be relied on at the trial of the collective proceedings (Rule 94(15)) or the trial of the claims that are the subject of the proposed collective settlement in direct settlements (Rule 97(12)), unless all parties to the CSAO application agree in writing.

6.138 Where the Tribunal has concerns about the proposed collective settlement, but considers that those concerns could be alleviated by certain modifications to the settlement terms, it may suggest changes to the applicants. If the class (or settlement) representative and settling defendant agree to make the suggested changes, the Tribunal may permit the approval application to be amended and fix another approval hearing. The revised application and new hearing date may then have to be notified to the relevant class members so that they have an opportunity to make submissions on the revised agreement.

WHO IS BOUND BY THE COLLECTIVE SETTLEMENT APPROVAL ORDER?

[6.211]
6.139 Broadly speaking, the CSAO binds all UK-domiciled class members who have not opted out. Class members who are not domiciled in the UK must actively opt in to the collective settlement.

6.140 Rules 94(11)–(12) set out who is bound by the collective settlement where there is a CPO; Rule 97(9) sets out who is bound where there is a CSO. These Rules are reflected in the following diagram:

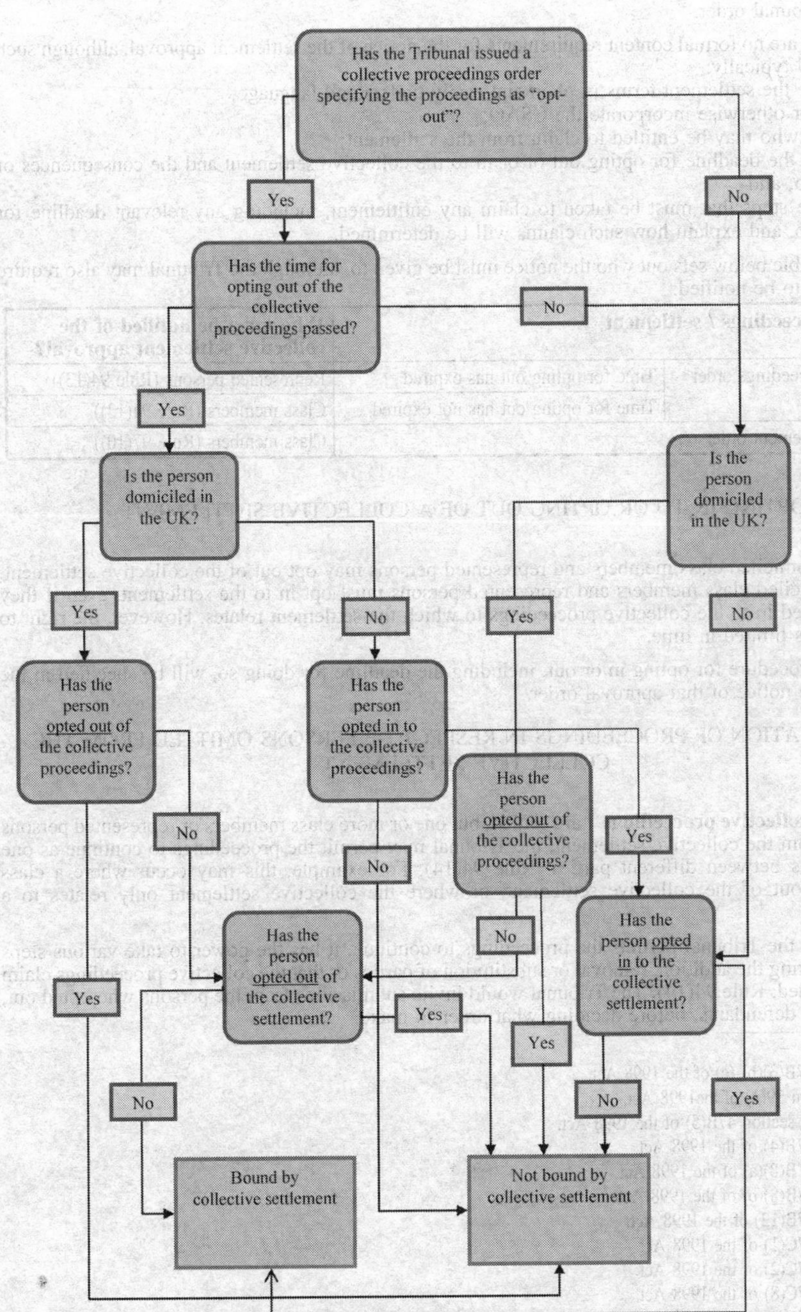

NOTICE OF THE COLLECTIVE SETTLEMENT APPROVAL ORDER

[6.212]

6.141 The class (or settlement) representative must give notice of the terms of the settlement and its approval, pursuant to Rule 94(13) where there is a CPO, or Rule 97(10) where there is a CSO. In either case, the form of the notice, and the manner in which it will be given, must be approved by the Tribunal. This notice is particularly important as it informs the represented persons or class members (as appropriate) that they may be entitled to recover and how to go about doing so, or how to opt out of the settlement if they do not wish to be bound. Therefore, the Tribunal will closely scrutinise the drafting of the notice and the way in which it will be disseminated to ensure that it will be received and understood by as many persons who are entitled to claim as possible.

6.142 In most cases, it will be appropriate for the parties to file a draft notice of the collective settlement at the same time as filing their application for a CSAO. Alternatively, the Tribunal may direct the parties to file a draft notice after it has approved the collective settlement and the notice will be the subject of a separate Tribunal order.

6.143 There are no formal content requirements for the notice of the settlement approval, although such notices should typically:

- describe the settlement terms in plain and easily understood language;
- annex or otherwise incorporate the CSAO;
- explain who may be entitled to claim from the settlement;
- identify the deadline for opting out of or in to the collective settlement and the consequences of doing so; and
- state the steps that must be taken to claim any entitlement, including any relevant deadline for doing so, and explain how such claims will be determined.

6.144 The table below sets out who the notice must be given to, although the Tribunal may also require other persons to be notified:

Stage of proceedings / settlement		Who must be notified of the collective settlement approval?
Collective proceedings order	Time for opting out has expired	Represented persons (Rule 94(13))
	Time for opting out has not expired	Class members (Rule 94(13))
Collective settlement order		Class members (Rule 97(10))

OPTING IN TO OR OPTING OUT OF A COLLECTIVE SETTLEMENT

[6.213]

6.145 UK-domiciled class members and represented persons may opt out of the collective settlement. Non-UK-domiciled class members and represented persons must opt in to the settlement, even if they previously opted in to the collective proceedings to which the settlement relates. However, the right to opt in or out is limited in time.

6.146 The procedure for opting in or out, including the deadline for doing so, will be specified in the CSAO and the notice of that approval order.

CONTINUATION OF PROCEEDINGS IN RESPECT OF PERSONS OMITTED FROM THE COLLECTIVE SETTLEMENT

[6.214]

6.147 Where collective proceedings are settled, but one or more class members or represented persons are omitted from the collective settlement, the Tribunal may permit the proceedings to continue as one or more claims between different parties: Rule 94(14). For example, this may occur where a class member opts out of the collective settlement, or where the collective settlement only relates to a sub-class.

6.148 Where the Tribunal permits the proceedings to continue, it has the power to take various steps including ordering the addition, removal or substitution of parties or that the collective proceedings claim form be amended: Rule 94(14). The Tribunal would invite submissions from the persons who opted out, along with the defendants, before deciding what order to make.

NOTES

58 Section 47B(3)(b)-(c) of the 1998 Act.
59 See section 59(1) of the1998 Act.
60 Following section 47B(5) of the 1998 Act.
61 Section 47B(4) of the 1998 Act.
62 Section 47B(8)(a) of the 1998 Act.
63 Section 47B(8)(b) of the 1998 Act.
64 Section 47B(12) of the 1998 Act.
65 Section 47C(1) of the 1998 Act.
66 Section 47C(2) of the 1998 Act.
67 Section 47C(8) of the 1998 Act.
68 Section 47C(3) of the 1998 Act.
69 Section 47C(4) of the 1998 Act.
70 The position differs in collective settlements, where the settlement representative and the defendant may agree that any undistributed settlement sums revert back the defendant.
71 Sections 47C(5)–(7) of the 1998 Act.
72 See Legal Services Act 2007 (Prescribed Charity) Order 2008, SI 2008/2680.
73 At PO Box 64162, London WC2A 9AN.
74 Section 49(2A) of the 1998 Act.
75 Section 49A of the 1998 Act.
76 Section 49B of the 1998 Act.
77 Section 49A(2) of the 1998 Act.
78 Section 49B(2) of the 1998 Act.
79 Section 49B(5) of the 1998 Act.
80 Section 49B(7)(a) of the 1998 Act.
81 Section 49B(7)(b) of the 1998 Act.

82 Section 49B(6) of the 1998 Act.

83 Section 49B(2) of the 1998 Act.

84 Sections 49A(5) and 49B(8) of the 1998 Act.

85 Cf the approach of the Canadian courts: *Osmun v Cadbury Adams Canada, Inc* [2010] OJ No 1877, (2010) 5 CPC (7th) 341 (Ont. SCJ); appeal dismissed, [2010] OJ No 5304, (2010) 5 CPC (7th) 368

SECTION 7: CASE MANAGEMENT

INTRODUCTION

[6.215]

7.1 Proceedings before the Tribunal are characterised by active case management with a view to ensuring cases are dealt with justly and at proportionate cost.[86]

7.2 Rule 4(5) states that active case management includes:

– encouraging the parties to co-operate with each other in the conduct of the proceedings;
– identification of and concentration on the main issues as early as possible;
– fixing a target date for the main hearing as early as possible together with a timetable for the proceedings up to the main hearing, taking into account the nature of the case;
– planning the structure of the main hearing in advance with a view to avoiding unnecessary oral evidence and argument; and
– ensuring that the main hearing is conducted within defined time limits.

7.3 It is a fundamental feature of the Rules that they require the parties (together with their representatives and experts) to co-operate with the Tribunal in its task of ensuring cases are dealt with justly and at proportionate cost through the use of active case management: Rule 4(7).

7.4 The Rules provide the Tribunal with powers to give a wide range of case management directions, but the procedure adopted will depend on the circumstances of each case in light of, for example, the urgency of the matter, the issues arising out of the pleadings and the submissions of the parties.

7.5 The first CMC is viewed by the Tribunal as a particularly important part of the active case management regime; its main purpose is to set a timetable to an oral hearing and to fix a date for that hearing (see, more generally, Rules 20(3) and 54(3)).

7.6 In many cases, the Tribunal will proceed from the first CMC to the main hearing of the case, possibly giving further written directions in that regard. In other cases it will be convenient to proceed either to a further CMC or a pre-hearing review envisaged by Rules 20(1) and 54(4).

7.7 Other case management steps which may be taken, depending on the specific circumstances of the case, include:

– the arrangement of a site visit[87] and/or inspection, if this is considered to be beneficial for the Tribunal's understanding of the issues in the proceedings; and
– the making of a request to the CJEU for a preliminary ruling pursuant to Article 267 TFEU: see Rule 109.[88]

7.8 Matters that typically may be dealt with at a preliminary stage (i.e. prior to the hearing of the main issues in the case)[89] are:

– objections to the jurisdiction of the Tribunal (see for example: *T-Mobile v OFCOM* [2008] CAT 15);
– objections to the admissibility of the appeal (see for example: *BetterCare v DGFT* [2001] CAT 6 and [2002] CAT 6; *Freeserve v DGT* [2002] CAT 8; *Claymore Dairies and Arla Foods v DGFT* [2003] CAT 3; *Aquavitae v DGWS* [2003] CAT 17; *Cityhook v OFT* [2007] CAT 18; *Independent Media v OFCOM* [2007] CAT 29; and note in particular *Pernod Ricard v OFT* [2003] CAT 19 and [2004] CAT 10);
– strike out applications (see for example: *Allsports v OFT* [2004] CAT 1; *Albion Water (Thames Water / Bath House) v DGWS* [2005] CAT 23; *Floe Telecom v OFCOM* [2005] CAT 35; *VIP Communications v OFCOM* [2009] CAT 28; *Stagecoach v CC* [2010] CAT 1 and, in the context of claims for damages, *Emerson Electric & Ors v Morgan Crucible* [2007] CAT 30 and *Enron v English Welsh & Scottish Railway* [2009] CAT 7);
– amendments to pleadings (see for example: *Floe Telecom v OFCOM* [2004] CAT 7; *Rapture v OFCOM* [2007] CAT 34 and *BT v OFCOM* [2007] CAT 35); in the context of applications for review of merger decisions see *Federation of Wholesale Distributors v OFT* [2004] CAT 11 at [30] and *Co-operative Group v OFT* [2007] CAT 24 at [95]–[98]);
– applications for disclosure (see for example: *Aquavitae v DGWS* [2003] CAT 4 and [2003] CAT 17 at [219]; *Argos and Littlewoods v OFT* [2004] CAT 5; *Claymore v OFT (recovery and inspection)* [2004] CAT 16; *Albion Water v WSRA* [2008] CAT 3; *British Sky Broadcasting v CC & the Secretary of State* [2008] CAT 7); and *Carphone Warehouse Group v OFCOM (Local Loop Unbundling)* [2009] CAT 37);
– further and better particulars *(Brannigan v OFT* [2006] CAT 28 at [98]);
– filing of further evidence,[90] as occurred in *Claymore v OFT* (see the Order of 27 March 2003) and *Rapture v OFCOM* [2007] CAT 34. Filing further evidence may also be a feature of the respondent's defence in a merger case (see, for example *UniChem v OFT* [2005] CAT 8 and *Co-operative Group v OFT* [2007] CAT 24).
– admissibility of evidence (*BT v OFCOM* [2015] CAT 6); and
– timetable, hearing dates and timing of skeleton arguments.

CASE MANAGEMENT CONFERENCES: PLANNING THE CASE

Timing of the first CMC

[6.216]
7.9 The timing of the first CMC will depend on the nature of the proceedings. In relation to appeals, Rule 20(2) provides that a CMC will be held as soon as practicable after the filing of an appeal, whether or not the time for service of the defence has expired. The Tribunal generally aims to summon the parties or their representatives to the first CMC **approximately four weeks after the appeal has been filed**. Very often the defence will not have been served at that point and the timing of the service of the defence will probably be one of matters to be dealt with at the CMC. It will depend on the circumstances of the case whether the Tribunal maintains the default setting of six weeks from service of the notice of appeal on the respondent or whether a longer time will be set.

7.10 In claims for damages under section 47A of the 1998 Act, the first CMC will normally be scheduled to take place **after the defence and reply have been filed**.

7.11 In collective actions pursuant to section 47B of the 1998 Act, the first CMC will usually take place **as soon as practicable** (before service of the defence); see paragraph 6.25 above and Rule 76(3).

7.12 In relation to an application for review pursuant to section 120 of the 2002 Act, the first CMC **may take place at a very early point in the proceedings**, perhaps within a few days of the filing of the application, depending on the urgency of the matter.

7.13 It is important to note that, in the case of appeals and applications for review, the date of the first CMC will be set according to the needs of the case and the Tribunal's diary. No account will be taken of the availability of the parties' legal representatives. There will be more flexibility in this regard for claims for damages, but again the needs of the case and the Tribunal's diary will be paramount.

7.14 Under Rule 20(4) the Tribunal may authorise a member of the Tribunal's panel of Chairmen to carry out on its behalf a CMC, pre-hearing review or any other preparatory measure relating to the organisation or disposal of the proceedings.

The agenda for the first CMC

7.15 About seven to ten days before the date fixed for the first CMC, the Tribunal will normally send the parties and any proposed interveners an agenda setting out the principal issues which it wishes to address. Matters that commonly feature in the agenda include:

- applications for permission to intervene; see Section 4 (The intervention procedure) for further detail;
- preliminary issues, for example in respect of jurisdiction or the admissibility of the proceedings;
- disclosure of documents: Rule 19(2)(p) and Rule 20(3)(b); in respect of claims for damages: Rule 53(2)(b) and Rule 54(3)(e);
- whether the proceedings should be consolidated or heard together with other proceedings: Rule 17; Rule 51;
- the treatment of confidential information, including the establishment of a confidentiality ring: Rule 19(2)(k) and Rule 20(3)(f) and, in respect of claims for damages Rule 53(2)(h) and Rule 54(3)(c);
- admissibility of evidence: Rule 19(2)(f) and Rule 20(3)(e);
- preliminary identification of the main issues in the case and of the evidence likely to be relevant (particularly whether any witnesses are likely to be called);
- clarification of the forms of order sought by the parties, their arguments of fact and law and the points at issue between them;
- the timetable for the case, including the date for service of the defence (if not already served) and (if applicable) the statement(s) of intervention and any further pleadings, and the date and estimated length of the main hearing;
- any other issue regarding the preparation of the proceedings which can be conveniently and fairly disposed of;
- to determine the question of forum: Rule 18; and
- any further issues raised or directions sought by the parties: this provides the parties with an opportunity to make requests to the Tribunal in respect of a matters not raised previously.

Written submissions in advance of the first CMC

7.16 The agenda will normally state a date and time by which any written submissions of the parties (and proposed interveners) should be submitted to the Tribunal. Provided they are brief, the Tribunal has found that such written submissions are useful in outlining the positions of the parties on matters mentioned in the agenda in advance of the CMC. Any written submissions must be copied to the other parties and to any proposed interveners.

7.17 Parties are encouraged to reach agreement on procedural issues and to indicate in their written submissions the extent of any agreement and the matters which remain in dispute, so that the CMC can be conducted as efficiently as possible. If there is agreement amongst the parties it may be possible to dispense with the need to hold the CMC, and the Tribunal can proceed to make an order embodying agreed directions.

7.18 The parties may also be asked to indicate in advance their availability for the main hearing so that this can be factored into the Tribunal's deliberations regarding the appropriate timetable for the proceedings.

Procedure at and following the CMC

7.19 The etiquette at the first CMC and at all other CMCs is similar to that at the hearing: see paragraphs 7.95–7.102 (Conduct of the hearing) below.

7.20 The first CMC and all following hearings will be held in public except where confidential matters are considered.

7.21 A transcript of the CMC will be made by the Tribunal's shorthand writer, and copies sent to the parties shortly after the CMC so that any transcription errors and inaccuracies, for example in relation to document references and authorities, can be identified and corrected. Generally transcripts are not proof-read or corrected for accuracy down to the finest detail because they are merely working tools for use by the Tribunal in considering the case and preparing its decision or directions. In due course, a copy of the transcript will be placed on the Tribunal's website.

7.22 Any directions made by the Tribunal will be incorporated in an order drawn up by the Registrar. If the directions are relatively straightforward the order will be signed by the President, Chairman, or Registrar and stamped by the Registry before being sent to the parties. In cases involving more complex directions, the Tribunal may ask the parties to submit a draft order, if possible in terms that are agreed.

7.23 Once finalised, a copy of the order will be placed on the Tribunal website.

7.24 Sometimes the Tribunal will wish to give a ruling or short judgment on a particular aspect of the proceedings and that too will be placed on the Tribunal website.

Subsequent case management conferences / preliminary hearings

7.25 In so far as not already dealt with at the first CMC, any subsequent CMC and/or pre-hearing review will deal primarily with the organisation of the hearing of the case, including: any outstanding matters concerning witnesses, expert evidence or disclosure of documents (see Rule 19(2)(d) to (j) and (l), Rules 21 to 22 and equivalent rules in relation to claims for damages). If there is any question of a decision being remitted to the respondent prior to the main hearing (Rule 19(2)(o))[91] or of the Tribunal being invited to deal with any preliminary points of law, or of a possible reference to the CJEU under Article 267 TFEU (Rule 109), those matters will also be addressed. If there is a substantial issue to be addressed (for example a strike out application or an application to contest the jurisdiction), the CMC will assume the character of a hearing with skeleton arguments being filed in advance.

FORUM

[6.217]
7.26 Rule 18 provides that the Tribunal may, after taking into account the observations of the parties, at any time determine whether its proceedings are to be treated as proceedings in England and Wales, in Scotland or in Northern Ireland.[92]

7.27 Under Rule 9(4)(c), a notice of appeal/application must contain observations on the question in which part of the United Kingdom the proceedings are to be treated as taking place pursuant to Rule 18. The respondent is required to include observations on this question in the defence: Rule 15(3)(a).

7.28 Rule 30(3)(c) states that the claim form in proceedings pursuant to section 47A of the 1998 Act should contain observations on the forum of the proceedings. The equivalent provision in respect of collective proceedings is Rule 75(3)(j). The defendant is required to include observations on this question in the defence: Rule 35(1)(b).

7.29 The matter of forum, if in dispute, is likely to be considered at an early stage in the proceedings, possibly at the first CMC. In determining the forum, the Tribunal may have regard to all matters that appear relevant, including where a party to the proceedings is usually resident or has its head office or place of business as well as other factors enumerated in Rule 18(3).

7.30 The determination of forum may affect certain procedural issues arising in the proceedings before the Tribunal and costs, and will determine whether any subsequent appeal from the Tribunal's decision lies, under section 49 of the 1998 Act and section 196 of the 2003 Act, to the Court of Appeal in England and Wales, to the Court of Session in Scotland or to the Court of Appeal in Northern Ireland.

7.31 It should be noted that the question of forum does not necessarily determine where the Tribunal will physically sit for the purpose of CMCs, pre-hearing reviews or hearings. Regardless of whether the forum for proceedings is England and Wales, Scotland or Northern Ireland, the Tribunal may hold meetings, CMCs, pre-hearing reviews or hearings or give directions in any location that it considers appropriate having regard to the just, expeditious and economical conduct of the proceedings.[93]

CONSOLIDATION

[6.218]
7.32 Rules 17 and 51 provide that two or more proceedings which challenge the same decision or which involve the same or similar issues may be consolidated, either at the request of a party or on the Tribunal's own initiative. Before making an order consolidating proceedings, the Tribunal will invite the parties to the proceedings to submit observations.

CONFIDENTIALITY

General principles

[6.219]
7.33 The general restrictions on disclosure of information contained in Part 9 of the 2002 Act do not

apply to the Tribunal: section 237(5) of the 2002 Act. However, the importance placed on protecting confidential information is apparent from the powers conferred on the Tribunal to protect such information, as regards documents: under Rule 101; hearings: Rule 99; and the Tribunal's decisions: paragraphs 1(2) and (3) of Schedule 4 to the 2002 Act.

7.34 Since documents filed with the Tribunal are not available for public inspection, in practice requests for confidential treatment mainly relate to the possible disclosure of confidential information to third parties in the context of the intervention procedure, in case management conferences or hearings, and in the decision of the Tribunal.

7.35 In broad terms, confidential information is information the disclosure of which would be contrary to the public interest; commercial information the disclosure of which could significantly harm the legitimate business interest of the undertaking to which it relates; or information relating to the private affairs of an individual the disclosure of which could significantly harm his or her interests: paragraph 1(2) of Schedule 4 to the 2002 Act.

7.36 In the event of a dispute, the Tribunal will decide whether information should be treated as confidential after hearing the parties and taking into account the matters set out in paragraph 1(2) of Schedule 4 to the 2002 Act: Rule 101(2).

7.37 As envisaged by Rule 101(3), the need for disclosure in the interest of fairness, on the one hand, and legitimate claims to the confidentiality of commercially sensitive information, on the other, may be accommodated by way of disclosure of the information into a confidentiality ring established pursuant to an order of the Tribunal. Under the terms of such an order, the confidential information will only be disclosed to named individuals forming "the ring" who have given appropriate protective undertakings in the form prescribed by the order.

7.38 Individuals admitted to the ring will normally be the parties' named legal representatives and possibly other external advisers or experts such as accountants and economists: see *Claymore Dairies v OFT* [2003] CAT 12 and the Order of the Tribunal of 9 June 2003 in those proceedings; *Genzyme v OFT* — see the transcript of 27 May 2004; Order of the Tribunal of 31 March 2008 in *British Sky Broadcasting v CC & the Secretary of State; National Grid v GEMA* — see the transcript of 23 May 2008. It may sometimes be necessary to add employees of the parties, such as in-house counsel, to the confidentiality ring subject to them giving suitable undertakings; these may be more onerous than those given by individuals external to the parties (see the Order of 8 October 2008 in *National Grid v GEMA*; cf. the Ruling in *Carphone Warehouse v OFCOM (Local Loop Unbundling)* [2009] CAT 37).

7.39 The Tribunal will sit in private for any part of a public hearing where it is satisfied that it will be considering confidential information: Rule 99.

7.40 If confidential information is included in the Tribunal's decision, the Tribunal will take into account the extent to which its disclosure is necessary for the purpose of explaining the reasons for its decision: paragraph 1(3) of Schedule 4 to the 2002 Act.

7.41 Parties should bear in mind that the question of confidentiality will be considered by the Tribunal not only with regard to their own interests but also with regard to the wider public interest, given that Tribunal hearings should normally be held in public, and rulings and judgments are to be publicly available. The Tribunal will therefore be alert to reject excessive claims to confidentiality, even if they are agreed between the parties.

7.42 For cases considering the principles relating to confidentiality and, where relevant, countervailing considerations of transparency and fairness of the proceedings before the Tribunal see: *Genzyme v OFT* [2003] CAT 7; *Aberdeen Journals v DGFT* [2003] CAT 14; *Umbro v OFT* [2003] CAT 26 and [2003] CAT 29; *Argos and Littlewoods v OFT* [2004] CAT 5; *Pernod-Ricard v OFT* [2004] CAT 10 (with regard to without prejudice communications and disclosure of the OFT Rule 14 notice to third parties); *Makers v OFT* [2006] CAT 13; *Albion Water v WSRA* [2008] CAT 3; *Unichem v OFT* [2005] CAT 3 and *British Sky Broadcasting v CC & the Secretary of State* [2008] CAT 7 (in the context of merger review proceedings); and *Carphone Warehouse v OFCOM (Local Loop Unbundling)* [2009] CAT 37 (in the context of an appeal under the 2003 Act). See also paragraphs 7.117–7.120 below, concerning the Tribunal's decisions.

Practical guidelines for making a request for confidential treatment

7.43 Under Rule 101(1) requests for confidential treatment of any document or part of a document filed in proceedings must be made in writing indicating the relevant words, figures or passages over which confidentiality is claimed, supported in each case by reasons.

7.44 Parties should pay close attention to the following guidelines when making a request for confidential treatment of information.

7.45 If at all possible, requests for confidential treatment should be made at the time when the document containing the confidential information is filed. It is important for the Tribunal to see at the earliest point what is claimed to be confidential and what information is not regarded as confidential.

7.46 When making the request, each document containing information in respect of which confidential treatment is sought must be marked up as follows: (i) square brackets must be inserted around the confidential information; (ii) the information itself must be highlighted in yellow or some other prominent colour (that does not obscure the information underneath it); and (iii) each page of the document must include the header 'CONTAINS CONFIDENTIAL INFORMATION'.

7.47 A schedule listing the information in respect of which confidential treatment is requested and the reasons for the request in each instance must also be provided to the Tribunal. The schedule should contain two columns: the first giving the relevant page and paragraph reference (a line number should be added if there are a number of pieces of confidential information in one paragraph in the document concerned); and the second setting out the reasons for requesting confidential treatment.

Document title	
Location in document	**Reason for requesting confidential treatment**
Page 15, paragraph 4.2	The deleted material relates to ABC Limited's key customers and confidential costs and prices The information is in the nature of a business secret

Non-confidential versions

7.48 If so directed by the Registrar, the person requesting confidential treatment must provide a non-confidential version of the relevant document: Rule 101(1).

7.49 It may be necessary to file and serve a non-confidential version of a document containing information in respect of which confidentiality has been requested, for example for the use of interveners or persons involved in the proceedings who have not been admitted to the confidentiality ring. The Registry may be consulted on how many copies of this non-confidential version of the document should be filed for the use of the Tribunal.

7.50 The non-confidential version should be prepared in such a way that the person reading the document is able to see how much material has been redacted and so that the paragraph numbering is unaffected. An indication of the nature of the information which has been redacted should be provided — for example "[customer name excised]". Each page of the document must include the header 'CONFIDENTIAL INFORMATION REDACTED'.

EVIDENCE

[6.220]

7.51 The Tribunal may control the evidence in particular cases by giving directions as to the issues on which it requires evidence; the nature of the evidence which it requires to decide those issues; the admission or exclusion of evidence from the proceedings; permission to provide expert evidence; and the way in which the evidence is to be placed before the Tribunal. The Tribunal may also give directions as to the provision by parties of statements of agreed matters: Rule 21 and Rule 55.

Witnesses

7.52 In respect of appeals and applications for review, Rule 21(3) provides that unless the Tribunal directs otherwise, no witness of fact or expert will be heard unless the relevant witness statement or expert report has been submitted in advance of the hearing and in accordance with any directions of the Tribunal. The Tribunal may dispense with the need to call a witness to give oral evidence if a witness statement has been submitted.

7.53 Where a party has filed a witness statement of one of its witnesses and neither the Tribunal nor any other party requires that witness to give oral evidence, that witness statement should be treated as evidence as if the witness had been called and confirmed the statement on oath. The Tribunal is entitled to rely on that statement as to its factual content if the Tribunal considers that it is material to the issues in the case. The other parties are entitled to make submissions to the Tribunal to the effect that the evidence is inadmissible or irrelevant without challenging the truth of the statement. Further, insofar as the witness statement contains inferences and submissions, these, too, can be contested by another party without cross-examining the witness in question.

7.54 If a party intends to submit to the Tribunal that something stated by another party's witness is not true, the Tribunal can only decide whether to accept that submission if the witness has had an opportunity in the witness box to respond to the allegation, unless the witness is deceased or too ill to give evidence. A party seeking to challenge anything in the statement of a witness put forward by another party must therefore give reasonable notice to that other party that it intends to contest that statement or identified passages in that statement. If the party putting forward the witness does not call the witness to give oral evidence, the Tribunal will determine, after hearing submissions from the parties, what weight, if any, should be given to the statement. A very significant factor for this determination is the reason why the witness is not available for cross-examination, either in person or by video-link. Normally, where a witness whose evidence is contested is in the United Kingdom, the Tribunal would expect him or her to attend the hearing.

7.55 Witnesses may be required to give evidence on oath or affirmation or, if in writing, by way of affidavit: Rule 21(4). The Tribunal may limit the cross-examination of witnesses in any way it deems appropriate: Rule 21(7).

7.56 Equivalent provisions in respect of claims under sections 47A and 47B of the 1998 Act can be found in Rule 55.

Witness statements

7.57 The function of a witness statement is to set out in writing the evidence in chief of the maker of the statement. Accordingly witness statements should, so far as possible, be expressed in the witnesses' own words.

7.58 Witness statements should be as concise as the circumstances of the case allow. They should be written in consecutively numbered paragraphs. They should present the evidence of the witness in an orderly and readily comprehensible manner. They must be signed by the witness and contain a statement that he or she believes that the facts set out in the statement are true. They must indicate which of the statements made are made from the witness's own knowledge and which are made on knowledge and belief, giving the source of the information or basis for the belief.

7.59 Lawyers should not allow the costs of the preparation of witness statements to be unnecessarily increased by over-elaboration of the statements. Any unnecessary elaboration will be borne in mind when the Tribunal comes to exercise its discretion as to costs.

7.60 Witness statements must contain the truth, the whole truth and nothing but the truth on the issues covered. Great care must be taken in the preparation of witness statements. No pressure of any kind should be placed on a witness to give other than a true and complete account of his or her evidence. It is improper to serve a witness statement which is known to be false or which the maker does not in all respects actually believe to be true. In addition, a professional adviser may be under an obligation to check where practicable the truth of facts stated in a witness statement if he or she is put on enquiry as to their truth. If a party discovers that a witness statement which has been served on its behalf is incorrect, that party must inform the Tribunal and the other parties immediately. Any correction to the witness statement should normally come from the witness (in the form of a supplementary witness statement) or, at the very least, one of the party's legal advisers should confirm in writing to the Tribunal (by means of a further witness statement) that they have raised the point with the witness and satisfied themselves that the witness has agreed to the change being made.

7.61 As regards witnesses of fact, a witness statement should simply cover those issues, but only those issues, on which the party serving the statement wishes that witness to give evidence in chief. Thus it is not, for example, the function of a witness statement to provide a commentary on the documents in the case files, to set out quotations from such documents or to engage in matters of argument.[94]

7.62 If the witness statement refers to documents, their location in the case files should be clearly indicated or alternatively the documents should be exhibited to the witness statement.

7.63 Parties must be alert to the possibility that the process of preparing witness statements, relevant documents and other material may lead to new issues of fact or law being identified. This may particularly be the case in appeals where the evidence in the witness statement covers areas which were not explored by the respondent in the decision under challenge and which did not form part of the respondent's reasoning; see *JJB Sports and Allsports v OFT* [2004] CAT 17.

7.64 Where a party intends to call a witness for examination or cross-examination at a particular hearing, it should take all possible steps to secure the attendance of that witness in person. However, the Tribunal may be prepared to hear evidence from that witness by means of video-conferencing equipment or facilities: Rule 21(5). Where the parties intend to call a witness in this way, they should contact the Registrar well in advance of the hearing to allow appropriate arrangements to be made.

Expert evidence

7.65 As regards expert evidence, the Tribunal will take into account the principles and procedures envisaged by Part 35 of the CPR, notably that expert evidence should be restricted to that which is reasonably required to resolve the proceedings.[95] It is for the party seeking to call expert evidence to satisfy the Tribunal that expert evidence is properly admissible and relevant to the issues which the Tribunal has to decide and would be helpful to the Tribunal in reaching a conclusion on those issues.

7.66 It may sometimes be appropriate to organise, prior to or during the hearing, a structured discussion, in the presence of the Tribunal, between the parties and their experts in an endeavour to focus on the main points of dispute — see for example *Genzyme v OFT* [2005] CAT 32 and the transcript of the hearing on 13 October 2004. Informal statements by experts may sometimes be permitted: see *Claymore v OFT* [2005] CAT 30 and the transcript of the final hearing on 14 January 2005. Other procedures, including putting written questions to the experts, directing "without prejudice" discussions between experts, the appointment of a single joint expert or of the Tribunal's own expert, can equally be envisaged.

7.67 As under Part 35 of the CPR, it is the duty of the expert to help the Tribunal on matters within his or her expertise: that duty overrides any obligation to the person from whom the expert has received instructions or by whom he or she is paid: see *Aberdeen Journals v OFT* [2003] CAT 11 at [288]. Expert evidence presented to the Tribunal should be, and should be seen to be, the independent product of the expert uninfluenced by the pressures of the proceedings. An expert witness should never assume the role of an advocate and should not omit to consider material facts which could detract from the expert's concluded opinion.[96] Where necessary, the expert must make it clear if a particular question or issue falls outside his or her expertise. The Tribunal considered the admissibility of expert evidence in *Enron v English Welsh & Scottish Railway* [2009] CAT 36 at [74]–[80].

7.68 An expert's report should be addressed to the Tribunal and not to the party from whom the expert has received his or her instructions. An expert's report should, in particular, set out the material facts, and the substance of all material instructions on the basis of which it was written. The expert should make it clear which, if any, of the facts stated are within his or her own direct knowledge. If a stated assumption is, in the opinion of the expert witness, unreasonable or unlikely that should be stated clearly. If an expert's opinion is not properly researched because the expert considers that insufficient data is available, this must be stated in the report with an indication that the opinion is no more than a provisional one. An expert's report should contain, at the end:

– a statement that the expert understands his or her duty to the Tribunal as set out in paragraph 7.67 of this Guide and has complied with that duty; and

– a statement that the expert believes that the facts stated in the report are true, and that the opinions expressed are correct.

7.69 If the expert wishes, at any stage, to ask the Tribunal for directions, this should be mentioned to the Registrar who will raise the matter with the Tribunal.

7.70 In proceedings for review under section 120 or section 179 of the 2002 Act, if the applicant wishes to rely on expert evidence that was not before the maker of the decision under challenge, it must serve with its application for review an application to adduce that evidence: see paragraph 7.78 below.

New evidence in appeals and applications for review

7.71 In appeals or applications for review of a decision taken by the CMA or a Regulator (both referred to as "Regulator" in the paragraphs below), it is expected that much of the factual material relied on by the appellant/applicant will have been before the Regulator at the administrative stage.

7.72 The Rules require each pleaded case, be it the notice of appeal/application or statement of intervention, to include a statement identifying the evidence annexed to the pleading the substance of which, so far as that party is aware, was not before the maker of the disputed decision at the time the decision was taken: Rule 9(4)(h) and Rule 16(8)(d). Similarly, the respondent for its part is required to include with its defence a statement identifying any evidence annexed to the defence the substance of which was neither referred to in the decision nor disclosed to the appellant before the decision was made: Rule 15(3)(f).

7.73 The Rules refer to "the substance" to reflect the fact that matters are often put forward at the administrative stage less formally, for example in correspondence or at meetings. The requirement to identify evidence as "new" therefore does not apply where the substantive material was placed before the Regulator although it was not in the form of a witness statement or expert report that is produced for the purpose of the proceedings in the Tribunal.

7.74 The qualification in these Rules "so far as [it] is aware" recognises the fact that a party may not always know all the material that was before the decision-maker, for example a Regulator may have obtained information from third parties or another addressee of the decision that was not disclosed to the appellant; if the appellant is a third party appealing pursuant to section 47 of the 1998 Act it may not know what information was before the Regulator save as disclosed in the decision document itself; similarly, an intervener may not have taken part in the administrative stage at all.

7.75 There is no prohibition on the introduction of new evidence on an appeal, but the Tribunal has power under Rule 21 to rule that evidence should not be admitted. "Evidence" here refers to documentary evidence as well as witness and expert evidence. However, different rules apply as regards expert evidence on an application for review: admission of such evidence requires the prior permission of the Tribunal: see paragraph 7.70 above.

7.76 It is in the interests of all parties and the efficient conduct of the proceedings that objections to the admissibility of evidence are raised as early as practicable. Although the Tribunal may exclude or limit evidence on the basis of relevance or proportionality, it will not normally exclude evidence of its own motion simply because it is new evidence which was not before the Regulator if none of the other parties objects: indeed, the Tribunal generally will not know if the evidence is new. As noted above, the Rules therefore require each pleaded case to include a statement identifying new evidence. The purpose of this is to enable early objection to the admission of evidence to be made. The Rules are party neutral: a respondent Regulator may choose to object to evidence adduced by an appellant or an intervener (Rule 15(3)(c)); an appellant may choose to object to evidence adduced by the Regulator or an intervener supporting the Regulator. Where the Tribunal grants a third party permission to intervene, it may give directions for the submission by the principal parties of objections to the admission of evidence put forward by the intervener: Rule 16(7).

7.77 The failure to identify evidence as being "new" does not of itself render the evidence inadmissible. However, if a party does not make a timely objection to evidence that has been identified, that will be relevant to the Tribunal's exercise of its discretion over admission of that evidence if an objection is raised only later in the proceedings. Equally, if a party has failed to identify a part of its evidence as "new", that may serve to justify another party raising an objection to the admission of that evidence later than would otherwise have been the case.

7.78 Objections to the admission of evidence will normally be considered at a CMC: Rule 20(3)(e). The Tribunal has a broad discretion over the admission of evidence, according to the justice of the case and proportionality. The Tribunal will consider all the circumstances, including the criteria set out in Rule 21(2):

(a) *"the statutory provision under which the appeal is brought and the applicable standard of review being applied by the Tribunal"*

The considerations may be very different on an appeal by an appellant who has been subjected to a penalty from those applicable on an appeal against a dispute determination by OFCOM under the 2003 Act.

– *An appeal against an infringement decision under the 1998 Act.* The Tribunal will have regard to the fact that an infringement decision is of a criminal nature for the purpose of Article 6 of the European Convention on Human Rights and that the appeal constitutes the first judicial consideration of the allegations made against the appellant. An appellant in such proceedings therefore is in general allowed to present a new case supported by new

Part 6 UK and EU Court Materials

evidence. The Regulator by contrast will generally be expected to defend an infringement decision on the basis of the material before it when the decision was taken and not by elaboration or extension of its evidence. See: *Napp v DGFT* [2001] CAT 3, and [2002] CAT 1 at [114]–[126]; *Aberdeen Journals v DGFT* [2002] CAT 4; *Argos and Littlewoods v OFT* [2003] CAT 10; and *MasterCard UK Members Forum v OFT* [2006] CAT 14. An appellant challenging a non-infringement decision on the grounds that the decision was incorrect or insufficient on an issue of fact or appraisal may also seek to rely on evidence that was not necessarily before the decision-maker: see *Freeserve.com plc v DGFT* [2003] CAT 5 at [114]–[116].

– *An appeal against a decision or determination under the 2003 Act.* By contrast, such a decision or determination does not concern a matter of a criminal nature. In general, addressees of such decisions have extensive opportunity to submit comments during the administrative stage, often including on a draft decision or determination. In those circumstances, if objection is taken the party seeking to rely on the evidence will be expected to explain why it was not put forward to OFCOM: see (c) below. In some cases, it may be appropriate for the Tribunal to hear evidence in verification or amplification of matters placed before OFCOM.

– *An application for review.* Such an application raises different considerations altogether. In an application under sections 120 or 179 of the 2002 Act, or any other proceedings by way of review, the Tribunal will apply the same principles as apply on a judicial review in the Administrative Court. Accordingly, evidence is generally limited to that which is required to show what material was before the decision-maker, to demonstrate a jurisdictional or procedural error or to show misconduct by the decision-maker: see *R v Secretary of State for the Environment, ex p. Powis* [1981] 1 WLR 584. The Regulator may respond to such evidence and seek to clarify its decision, but it will not normally be appropriate for it to supplement its reasoning: see *Tesco v CC* [2009] CAT 6 at [125]. If the applicant wishes to rely on expert evidence that was not before the Regulator, it must apply to the Tribunal for permission. That application should attach either the expert report which the party seeks to put forward or a detailed explanation of the nature of the expert evidence that it wishes to adduce: Rule 27. The Tribunal is unlikely to admit new expert evidence in a judicial review save in exceptional cases: see *BAA v Competition Commission* [2012] CAT 3 at [80].

(b) *"whether or not the substance of the evidence was available to the respondent before the decision was taken"*
For the reference to the "substance of the evidence", see paragraph 7.73 above. The concept of availability means that either the respondent had possession of the evidence or it was aware of that evidence and could reasonably have obtained it. The criterion refers to availability to the respondent: it will apply where an appellant relies on evidence which it had not placed before the Regulator before the disputed decision was taken; and where the Regulator relies on evidence in resisting an appeal which it had not referred to in its disputed decision;

(c) *"where the evidence was not available to the respondent before the disputed decision was taken, the reason why the party seeking to adduce the evidence had not made it available to the respondent at that time"*
The party seeking to put the evidence forward will be expected to explain why that material was not put forward in the administrative stage. For example, the evidence may concern events since the decision was taken; or it may address a point which only emerged in the decision and was not apparent to the party seeking to adduce the evidence during the administrative proceedings. The approach in the Tribunal does not correspond to the principle in *Ladd v Marshall* ([1954] 1WLR 1489) that applies in the Court of Appeal to new evidence on an appeal from a decision of a judicial tribunal following a trial.[97] However, the Tribunal will wish to avoid any gaming of the system where a party holds back material evidence during the administrative stage in order to deploy it only on appeal.

(d) *"the prejudice that may be suffered by one or more parties if the evidence is admitted or excluded"*
The degree of prejudice whether in costs, delay or otherwise that may result from the decision is always relevant but is not in itself determinative. Where evidence was identified as "new" in accordance with the Rules but is objected to only very late, exclusion of the evidence at that stage could in itself prejudice the party that had been relying on it.

(e) *"whether the evidence is necessary for the Tribunal to determine the case"*
This goes directly to the fundamental considerations of justice and proportionality. The Tribunal is always more likely to exclude challenged evidence if it is of only doubtful relevance or unlikely to make a material difference.

Summoning of witnesses

7.79 The Tribunal may, at the request of a party (in respect of appeals or applications for review) or on its own initiative, issue a summons requiring a person to attend as a witness at a time and place specified and to answer questions or produce documents or materials relevant to the proceedings. The requirements for the summoning of witnesses are set out in Rules 22 and 56: they must be given at least seven days' notice and are entitled to be reimbursed in the same way as witnesses who attend in proceedings before the Senior Courts of England and Wales and their equivalents in Scotland and Northern Ireland. The Tribunal may make the summoning of a witness conditional on the deposit with the Registrar of a sum sufficient to cover the cost of the summons and the reimbursement of the witness.

HEARINGS

[6.221]

7.80 Although this section primarily deals with the main hearing, most of the comments are equally applicable to other hearings before the Tribunal, unless the context otherwise requires.

Location

7.81 Usually the main hearing will take place at the Tribunal's premises at Victoria House in London.

7.82 Where the Tribunal has determined under Rule 18(1) that the proceedings are proceedings in Scotland, the main hearing will usually take place in one of the central courts in Edinburgh, unless, in the interests of extreme expediency, it is necessary to hold the main hearing in London (see, for example, *Merger Action Group v Secretary of State* [2008] CAT 34 at [1]). CMCs and other interlocutory hearings are usually held in London.

7.83 Similarly, where the Tribunal has determined that the proceedings are proceedings in Northern Ireland the main hearing will generally take place in Belfast (see, for example, *BetterCare v DGFT*).

7.84 However, the Tribunal may hold hearings in any part of the United Kingdom when it considers it appropriate to do so having regard to the just, expeditious and economical conduct of the proceedings: Rule 18(2).[98]

7.85 Notice of all hearings is given to the parties and published on the Tribunal's website.

Listing the hearing

7.86 The Tribunal will endeavour to list the main hearing as early in the course of the proceedings as possible, in accordance with the timetable for the case. Usually the first CMC is the point in the procedure at which the path to the hearing will be mapped out and timetabled.

Skeleton arguments

7.87 It is the usual practice of the Tribunal to direct that skeleton arguments are filed in preparation for a hearing.

7.88 A skeleton argument is not intended to be a substitute for oral argument but rather to assist in identifying those points which are, and those which are not, in issue and the nature of the argument in relation to the points that are in issue.

7.89 Every skeleton argument should:

– identify concisely:
  - the nature of the case generally and the background facts insofar as they are relevant to the matter before the Tribunal;
  - the propositions of law relied on with references to the relevant authorities (observing the guidance on the citation of authorities at paragraphs 9.57–9.62 below);
  - the submissions of fact to be made with reference to the evidence;

– be as brief as the nature of the issues allows **it should not normally exceed 20 pages of double spaced A4 paper** (in point 12 font) and in many cases should be much shorter than this; and

– be set out in numbered paragraphs and state the name of the advocate(s) who prepared it.

7.90 These requirements also apply to any written summaries (or "speaking notes") of opening speeches and closing speeches handed up to the Tribunal at the hearing.

Hearing bundles

7.91 In many cases, at least in the opening stages, the Tribunal will try to work with the pleadings and other documents in the form in which they have been filed with the Tribunal.

7.92 However, in particularly voluminous cases and matters where it may be important to see documents in a particular order, the Tribunal may direct one or more of the parties to prepare a set of documents drawn from the various files and assembled according to the Tribunal's requirements. The Registry will liaise closely with the parties on the detail of how this is to be done.

7.93 In particularly heavy cases it will be necessary for the parties to work with the Tribunal in devising a solution, possibly involving information technology, to ensure the material is accessible and clearly presented.

7.94 Unsolicited bundles sent to the Tribunal without any prior explanation will normally be returned: see *Napp v DGFT* [2002] CAT 1 at [76].

Conduct of the hearing

7.95 The hearing will take place in public, under the direction of the President or Chairman (Rule 99), except for any part of the proceedings where the Tribunal is considering confidential information (see paragraph 7.33 et seq.); in that event, the Tribunal may determine who is entitled to attend (that part of) the hearing: Rule 99(2).

7.96 Hearings will usually take place during normal court hours (10:30am to 4:30pm) although they may start earlier or run later depending on the demands of the timetable.

7.97 Hearings will be conducted in such a manner as to ensure the just, expeditious and economical handling of proceedings.

7.98 Lawyers appearing for the parties are not required to be robed. The President, Chairman and individual members should be addressed as 'Sir' or 'Madam' as the case may be.

7.99 Any person addressing the Tribunal and should stand and remember to push the button on their microphone before speaking. After speaking, they should remember to turn their microphone off as there is a risk that any private conversation they may have will be heard by others in the courtroom.

7.100 If the hearing involves witnesses or expert evidence, any necessary examination or cross-examination, on oath, should normally take place after brief opening statements by the parties.

7.101 **Those attending the hearing should ensure that mobile phones and wireless devices are switched off or set to silent during the hearing**. This is both as a courtesy to the Tribunal and other parties and to minimise interference with transcription equipment.

7.102 Where documents are handed up during a hearing sufficient copies should be made available for the members of the Tribunal, the Registrar, the Référendaire and the transcript writer. Six copies should normally suffice.

Time limits at the hearing

7.103 Since the parties will already have set out their case in full in the pleadings and skeleton arguments, oral submissions before the Tribunal can normally be kept short, within time limits set by the Tribunal, and structured so as to focus on the main points of the written argument.

7.104 Main hearings will generally be conducted in accordance with a timetable: Rule 19(2)(a) and Rule 53(2)(a). The Tribunal will usually invite the parties to agree a timetable and a running order for submissions in advance of the hearing. All hearings are "fixed length": i.e. they may not run on beyond the final fixed date.

REFERENCES TO THE CJEU

[6.222]

7.105 Rule 109 provides that the Tribunal make a reference to the CJEU of its own initiative at any stage in the proceedings or on application by a party before or at the oral hearing.

7.106 Parties should highlight at as early a stage as possible any question of European law which, in their opinion, should be the subject of such a reference, giving reasons for that opinion.

7.107 If the Tribunal considers it necessary to make a reference to the CJEU for a preliminary ruling on a question of European law, it will likely stay proceedings pending receipt of that ruling.

CONSENT ORDERS

[6.223]

7.108 The parties may invite the Tribunal to make a consent order in accordance with Rule 106. A request for a consent order should be made by sending the Registrar a draft consent order accompanied by a statement signed by all of the parties to the proceedings, or their legal advisers, requesting that an order be made in the form of the draft.

7.109 Where a proposed consent order may have a significant effect on competition, the Tribunal may require the parties to file a consent order impact statement dealing with the matters set out in Rule 106(3). If the Tribunal requires a consent order impact statement to be filed, it will also direct the Registrar to publish a notice of the application for a consent order on the Tribunal website or in such other manner as the Tribunal shall direct: Rule 106(2)(b).

POWER TO STRIKE OUT

[6.224]

7.110 Rule 11(1) gives the Tribunal the power, after giving the parties an opportunity to be heard, to reject an appeal, or any part of it, if it considers that the Tribunal has no jurisdiction to hear or determine the appeal; it discloses no valid ground of appeal; the appellant does not have a sufficient interest in the decision that is being challenged; the appellant is a vexatious litigant within the meaning of Rule 11(1)(d); or the appellant fails to comply with any rule, practice direction, order or direction of the Tribunal.

7.111 These provisions (apart from Rules 11(1)(c)–(d)) also apply to the defence: Rule 14(7).

7.112 A request to the Tribunal to reject a pleading on the ground that it discloses no valid ground of appeal or defence, or that the appellant is a vexatious litigant, should not be made unless there are clear grounds. For cases considering the application of this rule see: *Brannigan v OFT* [2006] CAT 28; the Order of the Tribunal of 18 September 2007 in *Bracken Bay v OFCOM; VIP Communications v OFCOM* [2009] CAT 28; and *Stagecoach v CC* [2010] CAT 1.

7.113 In the event that a party does not comply with a Tribunal direction, the Tribunal may, instead of rejecting the pleading in question, order that the party in question be debarred from taking any further part in the proceedings without the permission of the Tribunal: Rule 23.

7.114 By virtue of Rule 3, the Tribunal's power under Rule 11 to strike out also applies to applications for a review under the 2002 Act. Rule 26(3) provides in such cases that the power includes a power to strike out an application for review if it considers that the applicant is not a person aggrieved by the decision being challenged.

7.115 For the power to strike out a claim under section 47A or 47B of the 1998 Act, see Rule 41 (and Rule 74) and Section 5 of the Guide.

COMPLIANCE WITH DIRECTIONS

[6.225]
7.116 If a party fails to comply with a direction of the Tribunal, the Tribunal may, if it considers that the justice of the case so requires, order that the requirements of the direction be waived, the failure be remedied, or the relevant party be prohibited from taking further part in the proceedings without the Tribunal's permission and may make an appropriate costs order against that party. In any event, the party who is in default will be given an opportunity to make submissions as to why the Tribunal should not make such an order: Rule 23 (Rules 57 and 74 in respect of claims under section 47A or 47B of the 1998 Act).

THE TRIBUNAL'S DECISION

[6.226]
7.117 As a matter of practice, decisions of the Tribunal are referred to as "judgments" where the decision deals with the substantive issues in the case; where predominantly procedural or ancillary issues such as disclosure, costs, or permission to appeal are involved, the Tribunal's decisions may also be referred to as "rulings", "decisions" or "reasoned orders".

7.118 There are two ways in which a decision of the Tribunal may be delivered: (i) by handing down in public on a date fixed in advance for that purpose; and (ii) by publication on the Tribunal's website: Rule 103(1)(a)-(b).

7.119 The hearing at which the judgment is handed down will usually, unless the Tribunal directs otherwise, take place in London, even if the main hearing took place elsewhere. Notice of the handing down is given to the parties and published on the Tribunal's website.

7.120 Each party will receive a copy of the document recording the decision: Rule 103(2). The decision shall be treated as having been notified on the date on which a copy of the document recording it is sent to the parties: Rule 103(3).

CONFIDENTIALITY CONSIDERATIONS

[6.227]
7.121 As already noted, pursuant to the requirements of paragraph 1(2) of Schedule 4 to the 2002 Act the Tribunal will, in preparing its judgment, have regard to the need for excluding so far as practicable:

– information the disclosure of which would in its opinion be contrary to the public interest;
– commercial information the disclosure of which would or might in its opinion significantly harm the legitimate business interests of the undertaking to which it relates;
– information relating to the private affairs of an individual the disclosure of which would or might, in its opinion, significantly harm his or her interests.

7.122 Such information will have already formed the subject matter of a request for confidential treatment made to the Tribunal pursuant to Rule 101. See paragraph 7.33 et seq. with regard to confidentiality generally in proceedings before the Tribunal.

7.123 Paragraph 1(3) of Schedule 4 to the 2002 Act states that the Tribunal shall also have regard to the extent to which any disclosure of such information is necessary for the purpose of explaining the reasons for the decision. This may result in information which was accorded confidential treatment during the proceedings (either in a passive sense, because this was uncontested by the parties, or because the Tribunal had ruled on the matter during the proceedings) being subsequently disclosed in the Tribunal's judgment: see for example *Aberdeen Journals v OFT* [2003] CAT 14. However, prior to or immediately upon handing down, the Tribunal will consult the parties with regard to the treatment in the judgment of information in respect of which confidentiality has been requested, or which otherwise raises confidentiality concerns.

7.124 Where applicable, a non-confidential version of the judgment will be prepared. In such circumstances the judgment will contain a statement that excisions in the judgment relate to confidential information protected by paragraph 1 of Schedule 4 to the 2002 Act; see, for example *Hutchison 3G v OFCOM* [2008] CAT 11 at [43].

DRAFT JUDGMENTS ISSUED UNDER EMBARGO

[6.228]
7.125 In certain circumstances, the Tribunal **may** supply the judgment in draft to the parties' legal representatives a short time in advance of the handing down hearing under the terms of an embargo.

7.126 Provision of the judgment in draft unapproved form is **not** an entitlement. The terms of the embargo can vary according to the circumstances. The Tribunal takes very seriously compliance with the terms of an embargo. It may require evidence of compliance on the part of the parties and their legal representatives.

7.127 The primary purpose of an embargo arrangement is to enable the parties' legal representatives to assist in identifying any confidentiality issues and correcting any misprints, inadvertent errors of fact or ambiguities of expression contained in the draft judgment.

7.128 An embargo arrangement is not intended to assist the parties for any collateral purpose, such as the preparation of press releases. On occasion it appears that parties have issued press releases (formulated on the basis of the embargoed draft judgment), precipitately, even whilst the handing down hearing was still in progress. This can give rise to a perception of unfairness as between parties. Furthermore, it is difficult for the Registry to deal with queries about the judgment before it has been placed on the Tribunal website, which usually occurs shortly after the handing down hearing. Therefore it is both prudent and courteous to wait until the handing down hearing has been concluded before making any public announcement.

7.129 The Tribunal will not make any public comment on its decision outside the handing down hearing. Media representatives wishing to know more about the background to the judgment and its effect should contact the parties or their representatives.

ISSUES DEALT WITH ON HANDING DOWN

[6.229]

7.130 On the occasion of the handing down the Tribunal may wish to deal with such issues as costs or permission to appeal, or may wish to adjourn such issues to a later date, to be dealt with either in writing or orally. If the Tribunal intends to deal with such issues on handing down the judgment, it will usually inform the parties in advance. Otherwise, the parties may assume that the handing down hearing will be purely formal in nature, with the President or Chairman sitting alone for the purpose of handing down the Tribunal's decision, or with the Registrar conducting the hearing. It is not normally necessary for the parties or their representatives to attend a formal handing down of this nature.

PUBLICATION

[6.230]

7.131 The judgment will be published on the Tribunal website shortly after the hearing at which it is handed down, subject to supervening technical issues, or unresolved issues of confidentiality. The Tribunal website contains a section where the text of all the judgments, rulings and decisions of the Tribunal can be found, subject to excisions for confidentiality. An unofficial summary prepared by the Tribunal Registry will also be available on the Tribunal website, although the parties should note that by its very nature the summary is intended to be a very brief overview of the Tribunal's decision.

NOTES

86 Rule 4(1); see Rule 4(2) for what is meant by dealing with a case justly and at proportionate cost.

87 This occurred, for example, in *BT v Director General of Telecommunications (RBS backhaul circuits)* [2004] CAT 8 at [75]; *Albion Water (Dwr Cymru/Shotton Paper) v WSRA* (Case 1046/2/4/04) and *Albion Water (Thames Water / Bath House) v DGWS* (Case 1042/2/4/04).

88 Making such a reference was considered in *The Number v OFCOM* [2008] CAT 33 at [159]-[173] and was subsequently made by the Court of Appeal: *BT v The Number* [2009] EWCA Civ 1360.

89 Due to considerations of expediency, the Tribunal may direct that certain matters that may be considered preliminary in nature be rolled-up with the substantive hearing (see, for example, *Merger Action Group*, Transcript of CMC, 3 December 2008).

90 Note that under Rule 19(3) the Tribunal may of its own initiative make enquiries of the parties, for example, see *Aberdeen Journals v DGFT* [2003] CAT 11 (where the Tribunal requested certain information) and *Napp v DGFT* [2002] CAT 1 (where the Tribunal required the production of internal strategy documents). See also Rule 53(3) in relation to claims for damages.

91 For example, see *Argos and Littlewoods v OFT* [2003] CAT 16 and *Albion Water v WSRA* [2008] CAT 31.

92 See *Aberdeen Journals v DGFT* [2001] CAT 5, *BetterCare v DGFT* [2001] CAT 6 and *Merger Action Group v Secretary of State* [2008] CAT 34.

93 See *Merger Action Group v Secretary of State* [2008] CAT 34 at [1].

94 See, for example, comments of the Chairman (Lord Carlile) in the transcript of the hearing on 4 December 2009 (page 27, lines 19 to 23) with regard to a witness statement in *Sports Direct v*. CC.

95 For observations on the use of expert evidence see: *Napp v DGFT* [2002] CAT 1 at [254]; *Aberdeen Journals v DGFT* [2003] CAT 11 at [288]; see also *Leeds City Council v Watkins* [2003] UKCLR 467 at [88]; *Hendry v WPBSA* [2002] UKCLR 5; and *Chester City Council v Arriva* [2007] UKCLR 1582 at [141]-[149].

96 As to the proper bounds of expert evidence, see: *Hutchison 3G v OFCOM* [2008] CAT 11 at [174]-[175]; and *Bookmakers Afternoon Greyhound Services v Amalgamated Racing* [2008] EWHC 1978 (Ch) at [287]-[288].

97 See *BT v OFCOM* [2011] EWCA Civ 245.

98 For example, the claim for damages in 2 *Travel Group PLC (in liquidation) v Cardiff City Transport Services Ltd* was heard at the Civil Justice Centre in Cardiff.

SECTION 8: AFTER THE TRIBUNAL'S DECISION

COSTS

[6.231]

8.1 Rule 104(2), which covers all proceedings before the Tribunal, provides that the Tribunal has discretion, at any stage of the proceedings, to make any order it thinks fit in relation to the payment of costs by one party to another in respect of the whole or part of the proceedings. In the normal course, costs orders are made shortly after the delivery of the decision.

8.2 'Costs' means costs and expenses recoverable in civil proceedings before the Senior Courts of England and Wales, the Court of Session in Scotland or the Court of Judicature of Northern Ireland. It also includes payments in respect of the representation of a party to proceedings under section 47A or 47B of the 1998 Act, where the representation by a legal representative was provided free of charge.

8.3 The Tribunal will encourage the parties to agree costs, but if no agreement can be reached the Tribunal may either assess the sum to be paid pursuant to any costs order itself, or direct that it be assessed by the President, a Chairman or the Registrar, or that it be dealt with by way of the detailed assessment of a costs officer of the Senior Courts of England and Wales or a taxing officer of the Court of Judicature of Northern Ireland or by the Auditor of the Court of Session, as appropriate: Rule 104(5).

8.4 Rule 104(4) sets out the factors that the Tribunal may take into account in making a costs order, including: the conduct of all the parties; any schedule of incurred or estimated costs filed by the parties; whether a party has succeeded in part of its case, even if that party was not wholly successful; whether costs were proportionately and reasonably incurred; and whether costs are proportionate and reasonable in amount.

8.5 A costs order may also include directions to a party to pay to the Tribunal an appropriate sum in reimbursement of any costs incurred by the Tribunal in connection with the summoning or citation of witnesses or the instruction of experts on the Tribunal's behalf: Rule 104(6).

8.6 The following cases provide a useful overview of the Tribunal's approach to costs applications in different contexts; note, however, that these decisions were made under the 2003 Rules: *Tesco v Competition Commission* [2009] CAT 26; *Stagecoach v Competition Commission* [2010] CAT 20; *Skyscanner Ltd v CMA* [2014] CAT 19; and *Federation of Independent Practitioner Organisations v CMA* [2015] CAT 10. Costs orders of the Tribunal were considered by the Court of Appeal in *Quarmby Construction Co Limited v OFT* [2012] EWCA Civ 1552.

8.7 Costs in respect of proceedings under the 2003 Act, again under the 2003 Rules, were considered, for example, in: *BT v OFCOM* (CPS save activity) [2005] CAT 21; *The Number (UK) Ltd v OFCOM* [2009] CAT 5; *T-Mobile (UK) Ltd v OFCOM* [2009] CAT 8; *Sky and others v OFCOM (Pay TV)* [2013] CAT 9; and *BT and others v OFCOM (Ethernet Determinations)* [2014] CAT 20.

8.8 For the cost implications of Rule 45 Offers and specific rules relating to costs in the context of collective proceedings, see Sections 5 and 6 of this Guide.

8.9 The Tribunal considered costs in relation to interim relief applications in: *Genzyme v OFT* [2003] CAT 9; and *VIP v OFCOM* [2007] CAT 19.

Interveners' costs

8.10 The general position is that interveners are neither liable for other parties' costs, nor able to recover their own costs: see, for example, *Ryanair Holding plc v Competition Commission* [2012] CAT 29 at [7]. However, the matter remains in the discretion of the Tribunal and that approach may be departed from in appropriate circumstances: *National Grid v GEMA* [2009] CAT 24. For an example of a case where an intervener recovered part of its costs see: *Independent Media Support v OFCOM* [2008] CAT 27. For an example of a case where an intervener was ordered to pay another party's costs see: *BT v OFCOM (Ethernet Determinations)* [2014] CAT 20; note, however, that this concerned an appeal in the context of OFCOM's dispute resolution role under the 2003 Act.

INTEREST

[6.232]

8.11 Rule 105(1) provides that if the Tribunal imposes, confirms or varies any penalty under Part 1 of the 1998 Act, the Tribunal may, in addition, order that interest is to be payable on the amount of any such penalty from such date, not being a date earlier than the date of the notice of appeal, and at such rate as the Tribunal considers appropriate.

8.12 Unless the Tribunal otherwise directs, the rate of interest shall not exceed the rate specified in any order made under section 44 of the Administration of Justice Act 1970. Such interest is to form part of the penalty and be recoverable as a civil debt in addition to the amount recoverable under section 36 of the 1998 Act.

8.13 The Tribunal considers that appeals under the 1998 Act should not be brought merely to delay payment: an undertaking upon which a penalty has been imposed in respect of an infringement of the 1998 Act and which obtains the automatic suspension of the obligation to pay the penalty by appealing to the Tribunal, should not obtain any benefit from the delay inherent in the appeal process.

8.14 The rate of interest should therefore reflect the benefit derived by the appellant from the suspension of the obligation to pay the penalty. The normal measure of that benefit will represent the cost saved by the appellant in not borrowing the amount of the penalty during the appeal period, and the Tribunal will calculate interest by reference to borrowing rather than deposit rates. The Tribunal will apply the rate at which appellants in general can borrow money and will not look at the special position of a particular appellant. The rate of interest which the Tribunal will normally apply is the Bank of England base rate plus 1%, although that presumption can be displaced in an appropriate case where evidence is adduced showing that such a rate would be unfair to one party or the other.

8.15 For cases where the Tribunal has considered the issue of interest see: *Napp v DGFT* [2002] CAT 3; *Aberdeen Journals v DGFT* [2003] CAT 13; *Apex Asphalt and Paving Co. Ltd v OFT* [2005] CAT 11; *Richard W. Price v OFT* [2005] CAT 12; *Genzyme v OFT*, Order of the Tribunal of 29 September 2005; and *National Grid v GEMA* [2009] CAT 14.

8.16 Rule 105(3) provides that if the Tribunal makes an award of damages following a claim under section 47A or 47B of the 1998 Act, it may include in any sum awarded interest on all or any part of the damages in respect of which the award is made. For examples see: *2 Travel Group plc (in liquidation) v Cardiff City Transport Services Ltd* [2012] CAT 19; and *Albion Water Limited v Dŵr Cymru Cyfyngedig* [2013] CAT 6.

ENFORCEMENT OF DECISIONS

[6.233]

8.17 A decision of the Tribunal containing a direction or ordering the payment of damages or costs or expenses is enforceable in accordance with Part 1 of Schedule 4 to the 2002 Act.

8.18 Slightly different arrangements apply in respect of England and Wales and Scotland but essentially the process involves the registration of the decision with the High Court in England and Wales or, in the case of proceedings in Scotland, recording the decision in the Books of Council and Session. In Northern Ireland it will be necessary to seek the leave of the High Court.

8.19 Once registered or recorded or once leave is granted, the decision may be enforced using the procedures available in the relevant court.

8.20 In relation to the enforcement of a Tribunal direction, the enforcement procedure can be initiated by the Registrar or a party to the proceedings. In the case of an award of damages or costs or expenses the enforcement procedure will be initiated by the person in whose favour the award was made. In the case of collective proceedings, enforcement can be carried out by the class representative.

8.21 Where a person fails to comply with an injunction granted by the Tribunal in proceedings in England and Wales or Northern Ireland under section 47A or 47B of the 1998 Act, the Tribunal may certify the matter to the High Court which will then carry out its own inquiry before making any necessary contempt order.[99] For more information concerning injunctions, see Section 5 of this Guide.

APPEALS FROM THE TRIBUNAL

[6.234]

8.22 An appeal lies from the Tribunal to the appropriate court:[100]

– on a point of law arising from a decision on an appeal from a Regulator under section 46 or 47 of the 1998 Act (concerning the Chapter I or Chapter II prohibitions or Articles 101 or 102 TFEU: see paragraph 2.13 above);
– from a decision as to the amount of a penalty imposed in respect of such an infringement of the Chapter I or Chapter II prohibition or Articles 101 or 102 TFEU;
– on a point of law arising from a decision under section 47A of the 1998 Act or in collective proceedings (a) as to the award of damages or other sum (other than costs or expenses, or (b) as to the grant of an injunction;
– from a decision under section 47A of the 1998 Act or in collective proceedings as the amount of an award of damages or other sum (other than costs or expenses);
– on a point of law arising from a decision on appeal or review under the 2002 Act;
– on a point of law arising from a decision on appeal or review under any other statute.

8.23 Any appeal requires the permission of either the Tribunal or the appropriate court. The appropriate court means the Court of Appeal in England and Wales or in the case of proceedings in Scotland the Court of Session, or in the case of proceedings in Northern Ireland the Court of Appeal of Northern Ireland.

8.24 A request to the Tribunal for permission to appeal from a decision of the Tribunal must be made in writing and sent to the Registrar, within **three weeks** of the notification of that decision: Rule 107(1).

8.25 The written request must be signed and dated by the party making the request, or its representative, and must set out:

– the name and address of the party and of any representative of the party;
– the Tribunal decision to which the request relates;
– the grounds on which the party intends to rely in its appeal; and
– whether the party requests a hearing of its request and any special circumstances relied on.

8.26 On receipt of a request for permission to appeal, the Tribunal may invite observations from the other parties to the proceedings. The application may be decided without a hearing, unless there are special circumstances which mean that a hearing would be desirable: Rule 108(1). The Tribunal will give its decision in writing and notify the parties: Rule 108(2).

8.27 Where permission to appeal is sought on a point of law, it is important that the parties seeking permission identify where in the criticised judgment the error of law was made and why the Tribunal's approach is erroneous; see *Napp v DGFT* [2002] EWCA Civ 796; *T-Mobile & Ors v OFCOM* [2008] CAT 17 and *National Grid v GEMA* [2009] CAT 21. The Court of Appeal in *Napp* noted in particular (per Buxton LJ) that an applicant should:

– identify in precise terms the rule of law said to have been infringed;
– demonstrate where in the jurisprudence (of the EU or UK courts or otherwise) that rule is to be found, by specific reference to the authorities; and
– demonstrate briefly from the Tribunal's judgment the nature of the error, by reference to the Tribunal's handling of the issue in question.

8.28 In considering whether to grant permission to appeal to the Court of Appeal in England and Wales, the Tribunal applies the test in CPR Rule 52.3(6). Permission to appeal may only be granted where: (a) the Tribunal considers that the appeal would have a real prospect of success; or (b) there is some other compelling reason why the appeal should be heard; see for example *Hutchison 3G and BT v OFCOM* [2009] CAT 17.

8.29 Unless the Court of Appeal or the Tribunal orders otherwise, an appeal shall not operate as a stay of any order or decision of the Tribunal: CPR Rule 52.7.

8.30 For examples of decisions on permission to appeal see:
Napp v DGFT [2002] CAT 5
Argos and Littlewoods v OFT [2005] CAT 16
JJB Sports v OFT [2005] CAT 27
Floe Telecom v OFCOM [2005] CAT 28
Tesco v CC [2009] CAT 13
Enron v English Welsh & Scottish Railway [2010] CAT 4
BT and another v OFCOM [2011] CAT 39
Quarmby and another v OFT [2011] CAT 43
TalkTalk v OFCOM [2012] CAT 8
BT v OFCOM [2013] CAT 2
Ryanair Holdings plc v CMA [2014] CAT 6
Federation of Independent Practitioner Organisations v CMA [2015] CAT 11
Ryanair Holdings plc v CMA [2015] CAT 15

Renewed applications for permission to appeal

8.31 The procedures for appeal vary depending on the appellate court. In relation to proceedings in England and Wales, where the Tribunal refuses permission to appeal, a party may file a further application for permission directly with the Court of Appeal within **14 days** after the date of receipt of the Tribunal's decision on permission: paragraph 8.1(2)(b) of CPR Practice Direction 52D - Statutory appeals and appeals subject to special provision.

8.32 Parties are requested to inform the Registrar when they apply to an appellate court for permission to appeal a decision of the Tribunal and when any application for permission to appeal is refused or granted by the appellate court. The relevant appellate court case reference and case name should also be communicated to the Registrar.

NOTES

[99] See paragraph 1A of Schedule 4 to the 2002 Act, Rule 70 and paragraph 5.138 above.

[100] In relation to proceedings under the 1998 Act, see section 49 of that Act. In relation to review proceedings under the 2002 Act, see sections 120(6) to (8) and sections 179(6) to (8) of that Act. In relation to appeals against penalties under sections 114 or 176(1)(f) of the 2002 Act, see sub-sections 114(10) to (12) and section 176(1)(f) of that Act. In relation to proceedings under the 2003 Act, see section 196 of that Act.

SECTION 9: GENERAL INFORMATION

THE TRIBUNAL WEBSITE

[6.235]
9.1 The address of the Tribunal website is: www.catribunal.org.uk, or such other location as may be notified from time to time in such manner as the President may direct: Rule 7.

9.2 The website contains general information about the Tribunal and the current status of cases. It also has a diary of future hearings and a searchable database containing all the judgments of the Tribunal. It should be the first port of call for those with general queries about the role and functions of the Tribunal or those wanting to know the current position on cases and the dates of forthcoming hearings.

THE TRIBUNAL'S CONTACT DETAILS

[6.236]
9.3 Contact details for the Tribunal are as follows:
Personal delivery/post:
The Registrar
The Competition Appeal Tribunal
Victoria House
Bloomsbury Place
London
WC1A 2EB
+44 (0)20 7979 7979
+44 (0)20 7979 7978
registry@catribunal.org.uk

SENDING DOCUMENTS TO THE TRIBUNAL: PROTOCOL

[6.237]
9.4 The following protocol should be strictly observed when sending documents to the Tribunal.

General requirements

9.5 Any documents required under the Rules to be sent to the Registrar for filing should be sent to the address stated in paragraph 9.3, which is the Tribunal's address for service for the purposes of these Rules: see Rules 111(1) and (10) and Rule 6.

9.6 Any document required to be filed under the Rules as a signed original document and accompanied by a specified number of copies of that document **must** be filed by personal delivery or by post. The use of fax or email for filing these documents is not permissible and no authorisation has been given by the Tribunal pursuant to Rule 111(1)(d). The table below summarises the documents falling within this category.

Rule(s)	Document	Requirement
	Appeals and applications[101]	
Rule 9(7)	*Notice of appeal*	The signed original of the notice of appeal shall be accompanied by **ten copies** of the notice of appeal and its annexes certified by the appellant or its legal representative as conforming to the original
Rule 15(6)	*Defence*	The signed original of the defence shall be accompanied by **ten copies** of the defence and its annexes certified by the respondent or its legal representative as conforming to the original
	Claims made under section 47A of the 1998 Act	
Rule 30(6)	*Claim form*	Unless the Tribunal otherwise directs, the signed original of the claim form shall be accompanied by **five copies** of the form and its annexes certified by the claimant or its legal representative as conforming to the original
Rule 35(4)	*Defence*	Unless the Tribunal otherwise directs, the signed original of the defence shall be accompanied by **five copies** of the form and its annexes certified by the defendant or its legal representative as conforming to the original
	Collective proceedings and collective settlements	
Rule 75(6)	*Collective proceedings claim form*	Unless the Tribunal otherwise directs, the signed original of the collective proceedings claim form shall be accompanied by **five copies** of the form and its annexes certified by the proposed class representative or its legal representative as conforming to the original
Rule 96(3)	*Collective settlement order*	Unless the Tribunal otherwise directs, the signed original of the application for a collective settlement approval order shall be accompanied by **five copies** of the application and its annexes certified by the proposed settlement representative or its legal representative as conforming to the original
Rules 94(5) and 97(3)	*Collective settlement approval order*	Unless the Tribunal otherwise directs, the signed original of the application for a collective settlement approval order shall be accompanied by **five copies** of the application and its annexes certified by the class representative or its legal representative as conforming to the original

9.7 Any other document (for example, correspondence on the case, submissions for case management conferences, skeleton arguments, etc.) may (unless the Tribunal otherwise directs) be sent to the Tribunal by fax or email as an alternative to personal delivery or post: see the more detailed requirements with regard to electronic communications set out below. However, pleadings not referred to in the above table, such as statements of intervention, replies, expert reports or witness statements, should still be personally filed or sent by post if they are large documents with annexes.

9.8 If a document sent to the Tribunal by electronic means turns out to be voluminous, the party sending the document may be required to provide the Tribunal with hard copies.

9.9 The Tribunal may at any time request that the parties provide any pleading or other document previously submitted in hard copy, in electronic form.

9.10 It is often the case that the Tribunal directs parties to *"file and serve"* pleadings. This is a shorthand way of stipulating that the relevant party is responsible for both filing the relevant pleading or other documents, for example skeleton arguments, with the Registrar and simultaneously serving copies on the other parties.

9.11 Bundles for hearings (including bundles of authorities) will usually be the subject of specific directions given by the Tribunal in the circumstances of the particular case.

Personal delivery

9.12 A document which is delivered in person at Victoria House may be deposited in the Registry between **10.00 am and 5.00 pm Monday to Friday**. During those hours, documents should **not** be left at the reception desk on the ground floor of Victoria House. On arrival at the entrance to Victoria House in Bloomsbury Square contact should be made, via the central reception on the ground floor of Victoria House, with a member of the Registry's staff who will take delivery of the document.

9.13 Documents delivered after 5.00 pm may be received by a member of the Registry staff, if the Registry is manned at the time of delivery. Parties should be aware that there is no guarantee that this will be the case. Documents should **not** be left at the main Victoria House reception if it has not been possible to contact the Registry after 5.00 pm.

9.14 The person delivering the document will be given a receipt by the Registry indicating the date and time of receipt.

Electronic communications

9.15 Generally, email is only a suitable means of communicating with the Tribunal if:

– the material being transmitted does not exceed a reasonable volume; if it does, the sender may be asked to provide hard copies in accordance with paragraph 9.8 above; and
– the sender considers that email is a secure enough method of communication given the sensitivity of the information that is being communicated.

9.16 The Tribunal does not guarantee the confidentiality of any information communicated to or from the parties by electronic means (which for this purpose includes fax). Nor does it guarantee the availability of its electronic communications systems, which may, from time to time be unavailable because of routine maintenance or other technical issues. This should be taken into account when using email or fax for time-critical communications.

9.17 If a party or their legal representative initiates email correspondence with the Tribunal then they will be taken as giving their consent for the Tribunal to contact them by email.

9.18 Emails concerning cases before the Tribunal must **always** be addressed to: registry@catribunal.org.uk.

9.19 Occasionally, it may be convenient for a party to communicate via email directly with a member of the Tribunal's staff. This may only be done if that member of staff has agreed and any emails sent to that person are also copied to the registry email address. If this requirement is not observed there is a danger that emails sent to an individual member of staff may not end up on the Tribunal file and the information contained in them may be overlooked. Avoiding errors of this type is the sole responsibility of the sender.

9.20 Correspondence on the case from legal representatives and businesses intended for consideration by the Tribunal, the President, a Chairman, or the Registrar **must** always be in the form of a letter attached to the email as a pdf attachment ("the pdf letter"). It should not be in the form of an informal message in the body of an email. This is required in order to observe the traditional formal dialogue between courts and legal representatives and to allow the Tribunal to maintain an orderly file. The Tribunal will only allow some latitude in respect of this requirement to litigants in person.

9.21 The subject line of the email **must** start with the word "Case" then state the first four digits from the case number and short form case name and indicate the subject (for example 'Observations by [Party] on permission application') in enough detail for the recipient immediately to apprehend the purpose of the email. Examples of this approach would be:

– Case 1732: Telco v OFCOM: CMC submissions
– Case 1827: B Ltd v A Plc: Disclosure directions
– Case 1953: Victoria Plc v CMA: Expert's report

9.22 Any email sent to the Tribunal must be a fresh message and not one that is tacked onto a stream of previous messages. If the sender wishes to refer to an email received from another party then that should be included, either as part of the pdf letter or as an attachment.

9.23 The body of the email must indicate the number of attachments and contain a brief description of each attachment. It should also set out the name, address, telephone number and email address of the sender as well as the name of the party for whom the sender is acting.

9.24 If other parties are copied in to the email, the email should set out the names and email addresses of the copy recipients in the body of the email in a way that makes their identities and contact details immediately apparent. Using a cryptic list of addresses in the "cc" box will not be acceptable.

9.25 Attachments must generally be in one of the following formats: Microsoft Word (.doc or .docx) or Adobe Acrobat (.pdf). If there is a need to use another format the sender should liaise with the Registry to see whether the Tribunal would be able to receive it in that format.

9.26 Any failure to adhere to these guidelines may result in an email being rejected by the Registry.

SENDING DOCUMENTS TO THE TRIBUNAL: TIMING CONSIDERATIONS

[6.238]

9.27 There are important considerations arising out of the provisions of Rule 111 (concerning the service of documents) which parties should bear in mind when filing at or sending documents to the Tribunal.

9.28 A document delivered personally to the Tribunal or sent by fax or email **must be received the Registry before 5.00 pm** if it is to be treated as having been filed or sent on that day: Rule 111.

9.29 A document that is sent to the Tribunal by first class post will be treated as if it had been received on the **second** day after it was posted: Rule 111(4)(b).

9.30 If the Tribunal receives a document by personal delivery, fax or email **at or after 5.00 pm** on a business day, or it receives a document by post on a **Saturday, Sunday or Bank Holiday,** that document will be treated as having been being filed or sent on the **next business day:** Rule 111(4) and Rule 111(5).

9.31 "Business day" means any day except Saturday, Sunday or a Bank Holiday and "Bank Holiday" includes Christmas Day and Good Friday: Rule 111(6).

9.32 **It is crucial to take account of these requirements when filing a notice of appeal/application or claim form as failure to file on a particular day may prove fatal if, as a result, a limitation period has expired.**

9.33 Those sending their notice of appeal/application or claim form by post are also advised to use recorded delivery or, at the least, to obtain a certificate of posting.[102]

Examples

9.34 Therefore if a decision is notified on 10 June, and the last day for filing the appeal is 10 August, a Friday, the effect of the above Rules is illustrated by the following examples:

– the notice of appeal is sent to the Registrar by first class post on 8 August: the appeal is in time, 10 August being the second day after posting;
– the notice of appeal is sent by first class post on 9 August and arrives on Saturday, 11 August: the appeal is out of time, and is to be treated as served on Monday 13 August;
– the notice of appeal is personally delivered to the Registry at 4.30 pm on 10 August: the appeal is in time;
– the notice of appeal is personally delivered to the Registry at 5.15 pm on 10 August: the appeal is out of time, and is to be treated as served on Monday 13 August.

ELECTRONIC SIGNATURES

[6.239]

9.35 Where any of the Rules requires a document to be signed, the Tribunal will generally be content that the requirement is satisfied by a signature printed by computer or other mechanical or electronic means provided it is accompanied by a statement that this has been done with the consent of the person whose signature is reproduced.

REPRESENTATION

[6.240]

9.36 Under Rule 8, a party may be represented before the Tribunal by a qualified lawyer having rights of audience before a court in the United Kingdom, or 'by any other person allowed by the Tribunal to appear on behalf of the party'.

9.37 Parties may thus be represented before the Tribunal by barristers, advocates or solicitors qualified in the United Kingdom, whether in private practice or employed lawyers, or by certain lawyers qualified to practice in other Member States of the EU, if the lawyer concerned has a right of audience before a court in the United Kingdom. The question whether the lawyer concerned has such a right of audience will be determined by the relevant statutory provisions, including the Courts and Legal Services Act 1990, as amended by the Access to Justice Act 1999, and the rules governing the profession in question.

9.38 Legal representatives must be in a position to establish both their status and their authority to act for the client, if so requested by the Registrar. Barristers in employment should ensure that they are entitled to exercise rights of audience under the applicable professional regulations and code of conduct.

9.39 Rule 8 does not preclude a litigant from acting in person, but a body corporate would require the formal permission of the Tribunal under Rule 8(b) if it wished to be represented by someone other than a qualified lawyer having rights of audience before a court in the United Kingdom.

9.40 The Tribunal is sympathetic to small businesses that wish to pursue a case before the Tribunal but lack the means to obtain legal representation. In certain cases free legal advice and representation may be available from solicitor members of the Solicitors Pro Bono Group or from barrister members of the Bar Pro Bono Unit or other pro bono schemes. Details of pro bono schemes can be found on the following websites: www.probonogroup.org.uk/competition (provides initial free advice on competition law issues in suitable cases), www.lawworks.org.uk (Solicitors Pro Bono Group) and www.barprobono.org.uk (Bar Pro Bono Unit).

9.41 Advice from a barrister without the intervention of a solicitor may be available to businesses and individuals through the licensed and public access schemes, details of which can also be found on the Bar Council website: www.barcouncil.org.uk.

9.42 The Tribunal will consider each case on its merits when deciding whether to exercise its power under Rule 8(b) to admit a person other than a qualified lawyer to represent a party: see *Emerson Electric & Ors v Morgan Crucible*, Transcript, 13 March 2007, page 39, lines 1–20. Any person who wishes to commence proceedings without being represented by a qualified lawyer having rights of audience before a court in the United Kingdom should inform the Registry of their intentions as soon as possible.

9.43 Any change in a party's legal representation should also be notified to the Registry as soon as possible: Rule 8(2). The notification must state the party's new address for service. It must also be served on every other party to the proceedings and, where relevant, the former legal representative: Rule 8(3).

VISITING THE TRIBUNAL AT VICTORIA HOUSE

[6.241]

9.44 A map showing the Tribunal's location can be found on the Tribunal's website.

9.45 Please note that the entrance in Bloomsbury Place is not the public entrance to the Tribunal. If you are visiting the Tribunal to attend a hearing or personally deliver documents for a hearing or for filing you should enter Victoria House by the entrance located on the eastern side of Bloomsbury Square.

9.46 There is a short flight of stairs leading from the Bloomsbury Square entrance up to the Victoria House reception; there is also a lift on the left side of the entrance hall which can be used for taking hearing documents up to the reception level. If you ask the Victoria House reception staff to telephone the Tribunal Registry, a member of the Registry staff will usually be able to come to meet you and guide you to the Tribunal's own reception area if that is necessary. Otherwise, take the northern lifts, by the clock, up to the second floor where there will be signs directing you to the Tribunal's reception area and court rooms. If you are bringing documents to file at the Registry, you will be given a receipt indicating the date and time on which the Registry received the documents.

FACILITIES AT VICTORIA HOUSE

[6.242]

9.47 There are two courtrooms at Victoria House. Court 1 is a large room capable of seating 48 at desks with 20 to 40 additional seats in the "public gallery". Court 2 is about half the size of Court 1. Both courts have some portable shelving that can be used to accommodate documents. In addition there is enough space in between the desks to position files in cardboard shelving boxes of the type commonly used in courts. It is not possible for the parties' legal representatives to bring their own document carousels into the courtrooms, unless this has been agreed and arranged with the Registry in advance.

9.48 Both courts are equipped with microphones which are operated by pressing the red button. The parties' legal representatives should try to ensure, when addressing the Tribunal, that the microphone is operational (a red light will appear at the top of the microphone) as otherwise the transcript writers may be unable to hear the speaker. The courts and associated public areas have a wireless system for access to the internet. The Tribunal does not guarantee its availability or its security for transmitting or receiving confidential information.

9.49 There are also facilities for simultaneous transcription services (in substitution for the Tribunal's usual arrangements with regard to transcripts — see paragraph 9.55 below) and the visual display of material. If these facilities are required this should be mentioned well in advance to the Registrar so that appropriate arrangements can be made without disruption to the other arrangements for the hearing. The parties will be expected to make the necessary arrangements with the service provider and to bear the costs amongst themselves. Close liaison will be needed with the Registry in order to ensure that all the technical requirements of such a service are anticipated and dealt with. The Tribunal will expect the parties when making their arrangements to make adequate provision for the members of the Tribunal and the Tribunal staff involved in the hearing to access and use the contracted transcription service.

9.50 Each court has three modestly sized consultation rooms nearby which will ordinarily be made available, on a first come first served basis, for the use of the principal parties and, where possible, the interveners. The consultation rooms will be available one hour before the commencement of the hearing and half an hour after the hearing on each day of the hearing. They may also be used over the lunch hour when usually the courtroom will be locked. Use of the consultation rooms is a privilege and not an entitlement. A room may be withdrawn from use if circumstances require it. Ordinarily, consultation rooms will be limited to one room for each party. The parties should bear this in mind when determining the number of persons attending the hearing on their behalf.

9.51 In the foyer outside each courtroom are coin operated coffee and tea facilities and water points, although **no food or drink (other than water) may be taken into the courtrooms**. The lavatories are in the lift lobby area.

ARRANGEMENTS FOR HEARINGS AT VICTORIA HOUSE

[6.243]

9.52 One hour before the commencement of the hearing, a member of the Registry will be present at the Tribunal's reception point outside the court room. Those attending will be asked to sign a register and will then be provided with a one-day visitor pass, which should be returned when leaving at the end of the day. For hearings listed for more than one day a new pass will be issued each day.

9.53 The consultation rooms will be available one hour before the commencement of the hearing and the half an hour after the hearing on each day of the hearing, and may also be used over the lunch hour.

9.54 The parties and their representatives are solely responsible for transporting documents to and from the relevant courtroom and arranging these for use by counsel.

9.55 Unless the parties have made their own arrangements (see paragraph 9.49 above), a transcript of the hearing will be made by the Tribunal's shorthand writer. Copies will be sent to the parties shortly after the hearing so that any transcription errors and inaccuracies, for example in relation to document references and authorities, can be identified and corrected. Generally this is not a same-day service. If a same-day service is necessary the parties may be requested to pay any extra costs incurred. Transcripts are not proof-read or corrected for accuracy down to the finest detail because they are merely working tools for use by the Tribunal in considering the case and preparing its decision or directions. In due course, a copy of the transcript will be placed on the Tribunal's website.

FILES AND LABELLING

[6.244]
9.56 In submitting documents to the Tribunal at any stage of the proceedings, they need to be in sturdy files that are able to withstand being taken to and from the courtroom. The files should also be capable of being stood up properly on a bookshelf and should be labelled properly to allow for easy identification. The label on the spine of the file should be legible from a distance, and the front cover of the file should be labelled. There should be a label (indicating the file number and contents) on the front inside cover of the file positioned in the top left hand corner. If files provided for the use of the Tribunal do not meet these requirements, they may be returned to the party providing them for them to be put in order.

CITATION OF AUTHORITIES

[6.245]
9.57 Regard should be had to the *Practice Direction (Citation of Authorities)* [2012] 1 WLR 780 which governs the citation of authorities in the Senior Courts of England and Wales. Those requirements should be observed by the legal representatives in proceedings before the Tribunal.

9.58 The Tribunal reports all cases by reference to a neutral citation: the neutral citation allocated to each judgment, ruling and reasoned order issued by the Tribunal is a unique number that can be used to search for the relevant decision electronically, including on the Tribunal website.

9.59 Tribunal judgments and rulings are numbered in the following way:
[2014] CAT 1, 2, 3 etc.
[2015] CAT 1, 2, 3 etc.

9.60 For example, under this scheme, paragraph 49 in *Ryanair Holdings plc v CMA*, the fourteenth numbered judgment issued by the Tribunal in 2015, should be cited as follows: [2015] CAT 14 at [49]. The neutral citation will be the official number attributed to the judgment by the Tribunal and will always be used on at least one occasion when the judgment is cited in a later Tribunal decision.

9.61 In all future references to the judgment the paragraph numbering must follow the paragraph numbering of the original. To cite successive paragraphs of a judgment, the following format should be used: *Ryanair Holdings plc v CMA* [2015] CAT 14 at [10]-[11].

9.62 The neutral citation for each of the judgments issued by the Tribunal can be found in the judgments section of the Tribunal website. It is also included on the first page of the decision.

PUBLIC ACCESS TO CORRESPONDENCE AND PLEADINGS

Correspondence

[6.246]
9.63 Generally, correspondence between the Tribunal and the parties to the proceedings is treated as private. The Tribunal generally does not disclose such correspondence to non-parties.

9.64 As well as protecting from disclosure any commercially sensitive information contained in the correspondence, this approach contributes to a constructive and cooperative approach to proceedings before the Tribunal, which is of the utmost importance to the effective functioning of the Tribunal's active case management procedures, whereby the Tribunal and the parties work together in the swift and efficient preparation of the proceedings.

Pleadings and other documents referred to during public hearings

9.65 For this purpose, "pleading" includes a notice of appeal, application, claim form, defence, statement of intervention and any reply/rejoinder.

9.66 Where a pleading, skeleton argument, witness statement or expert report is referred to or quoted in open court, the party who produced that document or for whom that document was produced, should be prepared to make a non-confidential version of that document available to a non-party upon request. The non-party should approach the party in question directly to seek access to the relevant document. In the event that access is refused, the non-party may make a formal application to the Tribunal.

9.67 The Tribunal's website provides a thorough and searchable record of proceedings before it (see paragraphs 9.1–9.2 above). This includes: (i) a summary of the notice of appeal, application or claim; (ii) the transcript of any case management conferences and hearings; (iii) copies of orders and rulings; (iv) the decision(s) of the Tribunal; and (v) to the extent available, information relating to any appeals. The page for each case includes a case status which is updated regularly. This provides a much fuller public record of proceedings before the Tribunal, than is generally available in relation to cases pending before other tribunals and courts.

CLERICAL MISTAKES AND ACCIDENTAL SLIPS AND OMISSIONS

[6.247]

9.68 Rule 114(3) provides that clerical mistakes, including those arising from an accidental slip or omission, in directions, orders or decisions may be corrected by sending a notification (or a copy of the amended document) to each party and making the necessary amendment to any information published on the Tribunal website.

9.69 Parties are requested to bring any such mistakes to the Tribunal's attention without delay.

SEEKING GUIDANCE FROM THE REGISTRY

[6.248]

9.70 A list of answers to "Frequently asked questions" is available on the Tribunal website: www. catribunal.org.uk. If a query relates to a particular case or potential proceedings, the Registry may be contacted by telephone, letter or via email.

9.71 Whilst the Registry is always prepared to answer queries of a general nature and provide guidance on the practice and procedure of the Tribunal, it is the responsibility of the parties and their representatives to ensure that they have complied with the requirements of relevant legislation, the Rules and any directions of the Tribunal.

NOTES

101 Rules 9(7) and 15(6) apply to both appeals and applications brought under the 2002 Act: see Rule 3(b) and Part 3 of the Rules.

102 See *Fish Holdings Limited v OFT* [2009] CAT 34 at [18]–[19].

GUIDANCE – SERVICE OF DOCUMENTS ON THE CMA IN COURT PROCEEDINGS RELATING TO COMPETITION LAW

[6.249]

NOTES

Published 17 November 2015.

Note that this guidance has been updated since originally published in November 2015.

Court rules require parties in cases that raise competition issues to provide certain court documents to the CMA. This requirement applies in the High Court, Court of Session and Competition Appeal Tribunal (CAT).

The CMA took over the competition functions of the Office of Fair Trading on 1 April 2014. The relevant competition law provisions are:

— Articles 101 and 102 of the Treaty on the Functioning of the European Union (formerly Articles 81 and 82 of the Treaty establishing the European Community)

— Chapters I and II of the Competition Act 1998.

PROCEEDINGS IN THE HIGH COURT AND THE COURT OF SESSION

The documents to be served on the CMA in High Court cases are set out in paragraph 3 of the Competition Law Practice Direction.[1] Similar provisions apply on subsequent appeal to the Court of Appeal, with the documents to be served on the CMA set out in paragraph 7.1(3) of the Appeals Practice Direction.[2]

In Scotland, the documents to be served on the CMA are set out in Chapter 87 of the Court of Session Rules.[3]

COMPETITION APPEAL TRIBUNAL PROCEEDINGS

In the CAT, the documents to be served on the CMA are set out in Rules 33(7), 35(6), 36(4), and 76(6) of the CAT Rules and in paragraphs 5.53 and 6.17 of the CAT's Guide to Proceedings. Both documents are available on the CAT website.[4]

Part 6 UK and EU Court Materials

Parties should send the relevant documents – at the same time they are served on other parties to the proceedings and in the form they were served on the Court/CAT – to the CMA at the following address:

Director of Competition Policy
Competition and Markets Authority
The Cabot
25 Cabot Square
London
E14 4QZ
United Kingdom

Documents can also be sent to the CMA at the following email address: privateactions@cma.gov.uk

Electronic documents should be in PDF, Word, or Excel format.

The CMA will treat all documents received from parties under the obligations above in line with applicable confidentiality laws, including the Data Protection Act 1998 and the restrictions on disclosure in part 9 of the Enterprise Act 2002.

NOTES

1 See https://www.justice.gov.uk/courts/procedure-rules/civil/rules/competitionlaw_pd.

2 See www.justice.gov.uk/courts/procedure-rules/civil/rules/part52/practice-direction-52d-statutory-appeals-and-appeals-subject-to-special-provision.

3 See https://www.scotcourts.gov.uk/rules-and-practice/rules-of-court/court-of-session-rules.

4 See www.catribunal.org.uk/rules-and-guidance.

PRACTICE DIRECTION 31C – DISCLOSURE AND INSPECTION IN RELATION TO COMPETITION CLAIMS (JANUARY 2017)

[6.250]

NOTES

This is available at www.justice.gov.uk/courts/procedure-rules/civil/rules/part31/practice-direction-31c-disclosure-and-inspection-in-relation-to-competition-claims.

It is reproduced as amended by the 107th Update – Practice Direction Amendments (March 2019) at **[7.90]** (as from IP completion day, as defined in the European Union (Withdrawal Agreement) Act 2020, s 39).

DISCLOSURE AND INSPECTION OF EVIDENCE IN RELATION TO A COMPETITION CLAIM

1.1 In this Practice Direction—

(a) "the 1998 Act" means the Competition Act 1998;

(b) "competition claim" has the same meaning as in paragraph 2(2) of Schedule 8A to the 1998 Act. [(The Competition (Amendment etc.) (EU Exit) Regulations 2019 (SI 2019/93), Schedule 4 ('saving and transitional provision'), Part 6 ('court and tribunal proceedings relating to competition') makes transitional provision relating to pre-exit day competition infringements. Modifications to paragraph 2(2) of Schedule 8A to the 1998 Act by Part 2 of those Regulations are disapplied in relation to claims described in paragraph 14(2) by paragraph 15 (in conjunction with paragraph 7(3)–(8)) of Schedule 4 to those Regulations)];

(c) . . .

(d) "reasoned justification" means a statement containing reasonably available facts and evidence sufficient to support the plausibility of the claim for damages to which the relevant evidence relates;

(e) "relevant evidence" means evidence that a person is seeking to have disclosed or is seeking to inspect that relates to a competition claim.

1.2 Where a person seeks disclosure or inspection of relevant evidence, that person must apply in accordance with Part 23.

1.3 The person who has control of the relevant evidence must be named as a respondent to the application and must be served with a copy of the application notice.

1.4 The application must include a description of the evidence that is sought that is as precise and narrow as possible on the basis of the reasoned justification.

1.5 The court may only permit disclosure or inspection that is proportionate.

1.6 [In order to determine proportionality, the court must in particular consider—

(a) the extent to which the claim or defence is supported by available facts and evidence justifying the request to disclose evidence;
(b) the scope and cost of disclosure, especially for any third parties concerned, including preventing non-specific searches for information which is unlikely to be of relevance for the parties in the procedure;
(c) whether the evidence the disclosure of which is sought contains confidential information, especially concerning any third parties, and what arrangements are in place for protecting such confidential information.]

1.7 Where this paragraph applies, Part 31 applies to the extent that it is consistent with this paragraph.

NOTES

Words in square brackets in para 1.1 inserted, words omitted revoked, and para 1.6 substituted, by the 107th Update – Practice Direction Amendments (March 2019) at **[7.90]** (as from IP completion day).

DISCLOSURE AND INSPECTION OF EVIDENCE IN RELATION TO A COMPETITION CLAIM – EVIDENCE IN THE FILE OF THE COMPETITION AUTHORITY

2.1 In this paragraph—
(a) "cartel leniency statement" has the same meaning as in paragraph 4(4) of Schedule 8A to the 1998 Act;
(b) "competition authority" has the same meaning as in paragraph 3(1) of Schedule 8A to the 1998 Act;
(c) "competition authority evidence" means evidence in the file of a competition authority;
(d) "investigation materials" has the same meaning as in paragraph 3(3) of Schedule 8A to the 1998 Act;
(e) "settlement submission" has the same meaning as in paragraph 5(1) of Schedule 8A to the 1998 Act.

2.2 This paragraph applies where the application for disclosure or inspection made under paragraph 1 relates to relevant evidence that includes competition authority evidence.

2.3 This paragraph applies to the competition authority evidence in addition to paragraph 1.

2.4 Where the competition authority would not otherwise be named as a respondent under paragraph 1, the competition authority must be named as a respondent and served with a copy of the application notice.

2.5 If, after the application has been made, the applicant or respondent becomes aware that the application for disclosure or inspection made under paragraph 1 relates to evidence that includes competition authority evidence, the applicant or respondent (as appropriate) must—
(a) notify the court and the other parties of that fact as soon as practicable; and
(b) if the competition authority has not otherwise been named as a respondent—
(i) apply for the competition authority to be joined as a respondent; and
(ii) serve the competition authority with a copy of the application for disclosure, within 7 days after the date of the application to the court.

2.6 Where the court receives notification under paragraph 2.5, the court may give such other directions as it considers appropriate.

2.7 [In order to determine the proportionality of disclosure or inspection, in addition to the requirements of paragraph 1.6 the court must consider—
(a) whether the request has been formulated specifically with regard to the nature, subject matter or contents of documents submitted to a competition authority or held in the file of that authority, rather than by a non-specific application concerning documents submitted to a competition authority;
(b) whether the party requesting disclosure is doing so in relation to an action for damages before a court;
(c) in a case where—
(i) a competition authority has closed the investigation to which the request for its investigation materials relates; and
(ii) the court is satisfied that no-one other than the competition authority is reasonably able to provide the documents or information,
the need to safeguard the effectiveness of the public enforcement of competition law;
(d) in a case where a competition authority submits written or oral representations to the court, the need to safeguard the effectiveness of the public enforcement of competition law.]

2.8 Where the competition authority evidence includes a competition authority's investigation materials, the application for disclosure or inspection must be supported by evidence that the competition authority has closed the investigation to which those materials relate.

2.9 Where the application is for an order requiring the competition authority to disclose or allow inspection of competition authority evidence, the application for disclosure must be supported by evidence that no other person is reasonably able to provide that evidence.

2.10 Any application under paragraph 4(7) or 5(3) of Schedule 8A to the 1998 Act for the inspection by the court of an alleged cartel leniency statement or settlement submission must be made in accordance with Part 23.

(Paragraph 28 of Schedule 8A to the 1998 Act provides that the court must not make a disclosure order in respect of a settlement submission which has not been withdrawn or a cartel leniency statement, whether or not it has been withdrawn.)

2.11 Where an application is made under paragraph 2.10 and the competition authority or the author of the alleged cartel leniency statement or settlement submission would not otherwise be a party, they must be named as respondents to the application and must be served with a copy of the application notice.

2.12 Copies of the alleged cartel leniency statement or settlement submission and the content of the alleged statements or submissions must not be served on any parties other than the competition authority and the author of the alleged cartel leniency settlement or settlement submission.

(Paragraphs 4(8) and 5(4) of Schedule 8A place restrictions on the courts' ability to seek assistance to help determine whether information is a cartel leniency statement or whether a document is a settlement submission.)

2.13 Any hearings held in relation to the application under paragraph 2.10 must be in private and may only be attended by—

(a) the competition authority;

(b) the author of the statement or submission in question.

2.14 Rules 5.4B and 5.4C do not apply in relation to cartel leniency settlements and settlement submissions.

NOTES

Para 2.7 substituted by the 107th Update – Practice Direction Amendments (March 2019) at **[7.90]** (as from IP completion day).

COMPETITION APPEAL TRIBUNAL — PRACTICE DIRECTION RELATING TO DISCLOSURE AND INSPECTION OF EVIDENCE IN CLAIMS MADE PURSUANT TO PARTS 4 AND 5 OF THE COMPETITION APPEAL TRIBUNAL RULES 2015 (MARCH 2017)

[6.251]

NOTES

This PD relates to the disclosure and inspection of evidence in claims made pursuant to Parts 4 and 5 of the Competition Appeal Tribunal Rules 2015 (ie, claims under section 47A of the Competition Act 1998, and collective proceedings and collective settlements). It is available on the rules and guidance section of the Competition Appeal Tribunal website at www.catribunal.org.uk/rules-and-guidance.

INTRODUCTION

This Practice Direction is issued pursuant to Rule 115 (3) of the Competition Appeal Tribunal Rules 2015[1] (the "Rules") in relation to the procedures provided for by the Rules.

The Rules (notably Rules 60 to 65 and 89) provide for disclosure and inspection of evidence in proceedings under Parts 4 and 5 of the Rules. As mentioned in paragraph 5.86 of the Tribunal's Guide to Proceedings (2015), disclosure in such proceedings is not automatic and will only proceed on the order or direction of the Tribunal. Generally in making an order for disclosure or inspection, the Tribunal will have regard not only to the specific requirements of the Rules concerning disclosure but also to the governing principles contained in Rule 4 to ensure that disclosure or inspection is limited to that which is proportionate in the circumstances to deal with the case justly and to minimise costs. Where appropriate to do so (for example where evidence is disclosed by third parties), the Tribunal will exercise its powers under the Rules to preserve the confidentiality of information disclosed in the proceedings.

The purpose of this Practice Direction is to ensure that the practice and procedure of the Tribunal with regard to the disclosure or inspection of evidence is aligned with the relevant requirements of the Damages Directive (defined in paragraph 1 of the Practice Direction) as transposed by Schedule 8A of the Competition Act 1998 (inserted by The Claims in respect of Loss or Damage arising from Competition Infringements (Competition Act 1998 and Other Enactments (Amendment)) Regulations 2017).[2]

The Hon. Mr Justice Roth; President

14 March 2017

NOTES

[1] 2015 No 1648

[2] 2017 No 385.

1. INTERPRETATION

In this Practice Direction—

"the 1998 Act" means the Competition Act 1998;

"cartel leniency statement" has the same meaning as in paragraph 4(4) of Schedule 8A to the 1998 Act;

"competition authority" has the same meaning as in paragraph 3(1) of Schedule 8A to the 1998 Act;

"competition authority evidence" means evidence in the file of a competition authority;

"Damages Directive" means Directive 2014/104/EU of the European Parliament and of the Council of 26 November 2014 on certain rules governing actions for damages under national law for infringements of the competition law provisions of the Member States and of the European Union;

"investigation materials" has the same meaning as in paragraph 3(3) of Schedule 8A to the 1998 Act;

"reasoned justification" means a statement containing reasonably available facts and evidence to support the plausibility of the claim for damages to which the relevant evidence relates;

"relevant evidence" means evidence that a person is seeking to have disclosed or is seeking to inspect that relates to a claim made pursuant to parts 4 and 5 of the Rules;

"the Rules" means the Competition Appeal Tribunal Rules 2015 (2015 No 1648);

"settlement submission" has the same meaning as in paragraph 5(1) of Schedule 8A to the 1998 Act.

2. GENERAL APPROACH OF THE TRIBUNAL WITH REGARD TO DISCLOSURE OR INSPECTION OF EVIDENCE

2.1 This Practice Direction applies in addition to other requirements of the Rules (and other practice directions issued pursuant to Rule 115(3) of the Rules) relating to applications for disclosure or inspection of evidence.

2.2 The application must include a description of the evidence that is sought that is as precise and narrow as possible on the basis of a reasoned justification.

2.3 The Tribunal will limit disclosure or inspection of evidence to that which is proportionate.

2.4 In determining whether any application for disclosure or inspection of evidence is proportionate, the Tribunal will consider the legitimate interests of all parties and third parties concerned and will, in particular, consider the factors set out in article 5(3) of the Damages Directive.[3]

NOTES

[3] Those factors are: (a) the extent to which the claim or defence is supported by available facts and evidence justifying the request to disclose evidence; (b) the scope and cost of disclosure, especially for any third parties concerned, including preventing non-specific searches for information which is unlikely to be of relevance for the parties in the procedure; (c) whether the evidence the disclosure of which is sought contains confidential information, especially concerning any third parties, and what arrangements are in place for protecting such confidential information.

3. MAKING AN APPLICATION FOR DISCLOSURE OR INSPECTION OF COMPETITION AUTHORITY EVIDENCE

3.1 Where an application is made for an order requiring the competition authority to disclose or allow inspection of competition authority evidence, the application must be supported by evidence that no other person is reasonably able to provide that evidence. Where an application is made for an order requiring the competition authority to disclose or allow inspection of competition authority evidence, the application must be supported by evidence that no other person is reasonably able to provide that evidence.

3.2 Where an application for disclosure or inspection of competition authority evidence includes investigation materials, the application must be supported by evidence that the competition authority has closed the investigation to which those materials relate.[4]

3.3 Where relevant, the application must specify that the applicant is applying for the Tribunal to determine whether any document is a cartel leniency statement or a settlement submission[5] in accordance with paragraphs 4(7) or 5(3) of Schedule 8A of the 1998 Act.

NOTES

4 Paragraph 29 of Schedule 8A to the 1998 Act provides that the Tribunal must not make a disclosure order in respect of a competition authority's investigation materials before the day on which the competition authority closes the investigation to which those materials relate.

5 Paragraph 28 of Schedule 8A to the 1998 Act provides that the Tribunal must not make a disclosure order in respect of—

(a) A settlement submission which has not been withdrawn, or

(b) A cartel leniency statement (whether or not it has been withdrawn). A cartel leniency statement (whether or not it has been withdrawn).

4. INFORMING THE COMPETITION AUTHORITY AND OTHER INTERESTED PERSONS OF THE APPLICATION FOR DISCLOSURE OR INSPECTION OF COMPETITION AUTHORITY EVIDENCE

4.1 Where the applicant is applying for the Tribunal to determine whether a document is a cartel leniency statement or settlement submission, the applicant must serve a copy of the application on—

(a) the competition authority; and

(b) the author of the document;

at the same time as the application is filed with the Tribunal.

4.2 In determining whether a document is a cartel leniency statement or settlement submission, the Tribunal may take evidence from the author of the document and obtain assistance from the competition authority.[6]

4.3 Copies of alleged cartel leniency statements or settlement submissions and information concerning the content of the alleged statements or submissions must not be served on any parties other than the competition authority and the author of any such alleged statement or submission.

NOTES

6 Paragraphs 4(8) and 5(4) of Schedule 8A to the 1998 Act stipulate that the Tribunal may not obtain assistance from anyone else when making such a determination.

5. DETERMINING AN APPLICATION FOR DISCLOSURE OR INSPECTION OF COMPETITION AUTHORITY EVIDENCE

5.1 The Tribunal may give such directions in accordance with the Rules as it considers appropriate for hearing and determining an application for disclosure or inspection of competition authority evidence.

5.2 In determining the application the Tribunal will have regard to:

(a) the Rules (including but not limited to Rules 60 (disclosure by parties to the proceedings, 61 (documents referred to in statements of case etc.), 62 (disclosure before proceedings start), and 63 (Orders for disclosure against a person not a party);

(b) the factors set out in Article 6(4) of the Damages Directive;[7] and

(c) any observations of the competition authority (made on its own initiative or at the request of the Tribunal) in respect of the proportionality of the application.

NOTES

7 Those matters are: (a) whether the request has been formulated specifically with regard to the nature, subject matter or contents of documents submitted to a competition authority or held in the file thereof, rather than by a non-specific application concerning documents submitted to a competition authority; (b) whether the party requesting disclosure is doing so in relation to an action for damages before a national court; and (c) the need to safeguard the effectiveness of the public enforcement of competition law.

6. ENTRY INTO FORCE

6.1 This Practice Direction comes into force on the same day as the coming into force of The Claims in respect of Loss or Damage arising from Competition Infringements (Competition Act 1998 and Other Enactments (Amendment)) Regulations 2017.

7. TRANSITIONAL PROVISION

7.1 This Practice Direction applies to applications for disclosure or inspection of evidence made in relation to a claim where the first proceedings in relation to that claim were brought before the Tribunal on or after the date on which the Practice Direction came into force.

COMPETITION APPEAL TRIBUNAL CHANGE TO TRIBUNAL ADDRESS FOR SERVICE

[6.252]

NOTES

This notice is available on the rules and guidance section of the Competition Appeal Tribunal website at www.catribunal.org.uk/rules-and-guidance.

NOTICE UNDER RULE 6 OF THE COMPETITION APPEAL TRIBUNAL RULES 2015

The Registrar of the Competition Appeal Tribunal gives notice, in accordance with Rule 6 of the Competition Appeal Tribunal Rules 2015 (SI 2015 No 1648), of a change to the Tribunal's address for the filing or service of documents at or on the Tribunal ("the Tribunal address for service").

With effect from Monday 18 November 2019, the Tribunal address for service is:

The Registrar of the Competition Appeal Tribunal
Salisbury Square House
8 Salisbury Square
London EC4Y 8AP

No documents will be accepted at Victoria House after 5pm on Friday 15 November 2019.

Should you have any queries regarding the filing or service of original and/or hard copy documents at the Tribunal in this period, please contact the Registry in advance on 020 7979 7979.

The address for electronic communications to the Tribunal (registry@catribunal.org.uk) remains unchanged.

Charles Dhanowa OBE, QC (Hon)
Registrar

Published 11 November 2019

COMPETITION APPEAL TRIBUNAL — PRACTICE DIRECTION 1/2021: SKELETON ARGUMENTS AND BUNDLES FOR HEARING (FEBRUARY 2021)

[6.253]

NOTES

This PD is available on the rules and guidance section of the Competition Appeal Tribunal website at www.catribunal.org.uk/rules-and-guidance.

1. This Direction sets out mandatory requirements regarding skeleton arguments and bundles of documents provided in proceedings in the Competition Appeal Tribunal.

SKELETON ARGUMENTS

2. All skeleton arguments shall be supplied in hard copy and electronically in Word. They shall be typed in 12-point font with 1.5 line spacing.

3. Skeleton arguments submitted by an appellant, applicant or claimant shall not exceed 20 pages. Skeleton arguments by a respondent or defendant shall not exceed 20 pages, save that if there is more than one separately represented opposing party, the skeleton may extend to 25 pages.

4. The Tribunal may, on its own motion or on the written application of a party, dispense with the requirement for the provision of hard copies in paragraph 2 above and/or vary the page limits in paragraph 3.

BUNDLES FOR HEARING

5. Paragraph 9.56 of the Competition Appeal Tribunal Guide to Proceedings 2015 contains requirements concerning the provision of bundles containing hard copy documents for use in hearings. It is imperative that those requirements are observed. In particular, the labelling on the spine of each bundle must be in large, bold writing or typeface and the label required to be affixed to the top left hand corner of the inside cover of the bundle must be visible when the bundle is open.

6. In addition, all pages within each separate tab of a bundle shall be printed double sided except where they comprise a spreadsheet or table for which two or more pages need to be viewed together.

7. Failure to observe all requirements in respect of bundles may result in them being returned to the relevant party for them to be put in order and there may be consequences with regard to costs should any delay occur in the proceedings as a result.

The Hon. Mr Justice Roth

President

25 February 2021

B. EU COURTS

ADVICE TO COUNSEL APPEARING BEFORE THE COURT

[6.254]

NOTES

This document is available on the Court of Justice website at https://curia.europa.eu/jcms/jcms/Jo2_7031/en/.

The task of simultaneous interpreters in the multilingual environment of the Court of Justice of the European Union is to help you to communicate easily and fluently with the Judges and the other participants in the hearing. The interpreters prepare in advance for every hearing by studying the case-file in depth. However, it may be helpful to bear the following points in mind when pleading:

— Reading out a written text at speed makes simultaneous interpretation into another language particularly difficult. The interpreters will be able to work much more effectively if you speak freely, at a natural and calm pace.

— If you do decide to read out a written text which you have prepared, please send it if possible in advance to the Interpretation Directorate* by email. This will help the interpreters to prepare for the hearing. It goes without saying that:

  — your text will be used only by the interpreters and will not be communicated or disclosed to anyone else;

  — at the hearing, only what you actually say when addressing the Court will be interpreted.

— Even handwritten notes with references are helpful. You can always give a copy to the interpreters just before the hearing.

— Please remember to quote citations, references, figures, names and acronyms clearly and slowly.

— Before you speak, please remove your earphone, lower the volume, and place it away from the microphone in order to avoid any interference.

— Turn off your mobile phone / PDA completely.

For more information please see the Practice directions to parties, available on the Court of Justice's 'Procedure' page.

NOTES

* Interpretation Directorate
Email: interpret@curia.europa.eu
Fax: +352/4303-3697
Telephone: +352/4303-1

DECISION OF THE GENERAL COURT

of 11 July 2018

on the lodging and service of procedural documents by means of e-Curia

[6.255]

NOTES

Date of publication in OJ: OJ L240, 25.9.2018, p 72.

THE GENERAL COURT

Having regard to the Rules of Procedure and, in particular, Article 56a(1), (2) and (5) thereof

Whereas:

(1) In order to take account of developments in communication technology, an information technology application has been developed to allow the lodging and service of procedural documents by electronic means.

(2) This application, which is based on an electronic authentication system using a combination of a user identification and a password, meets the requirements of authenticity, integrity and confidentiality of documents exchanged.

(3) Having regard to the advantages of the immediacy of paperless communication offered by this application, its use has become mandatory for the lodging and service of procedural documents in proceedings before the General Court,

HAS DECIDED AS FOLLOWS:

Article 1

The information technology application known as 'e-Curia', common to the constituent courts of the Court of Justice of the European Union, allows the lodging and service of procedural documents by electronic means under the conditions laid down by this Decision.

Article 2

Use of this application shall require the opening of an access account and use of a personal user identification and password.

Article 3

A procedural document shall be lodged by e-Curia where the representative's user identification and password have been used to effect the lodging. Use of the representative's personal user identification and password for the lodging of a procedural document shall constitute the signature of the document concerned.

Article 4

A procedural document lodged by means of e-Curia must be accompanied by the annexes referred to therein and a schedule listing such annexes.

Article 5

A procedural document shall be deemed to have been lodged for the purposes of Article 72(2) of the Rules of Procedure at the time of the representative's validation of lodging of that document.

The relevant time shall be the time in the Grand Duchy of Luxembourg.

Article 6

Procedural documents, including judgments and orders, shall be served by e-Curia on the holders of access accounts in the cases which concern them.

The intended recipients of the documents served referred to in the preceding paragraph shall be notified by email of any document served on them by means of e-Curia.

A procedural document shall be served at the time when the intended recipient (representative or assistant) requests access to that document. In the absence of any request for access, the document shall be deemed to have been served on the expiry of the seventh day following the day on which the notification email was sent.

Where a party is represented by more than one agent or lawyer, the time to be taken into account in the reckoning of time limits shall be the time when the first request for access was made.

The relevant time shall be the time in the Grand Duchy of Luxembourg.

Article 7

Where it is technically impossible to lodge a procedural document by e-Curia, the user must notify immediately the Registry of the General Court by email (GC.Registry@curia.europa.eu) or by fax (+352 43032100), indicating:

— the type of document the user wishes to lodge,

— where appropriate, the relevant time limit for the lodging of that document,

— the nature of the technical impossibility identified, for verification by the staff of the institution if it is due to the unavailability of e-Curia.

If the representative is bound to comply with a time limit, he shall transmit a copy of the document to the Registry of the General Court by any appropriate means (lodging of a paper version or transmission by post, email or fax). That transmission must be followed by the lodging of the document by e-Curia as soon as it is again technically possible to use that application.

The General Court or the President of the General Court will if necessary give a ruling on the acceptance of a document lodged by e-Curia after the prescribed time limit, taking into consideration information provided by the party lodging that document to prove that it was technically impossible to lodge that document by e-Curia before the prescribed time limit.

Where the use of e-Curia is technically impossible and if urgency requires, the Registrar shall transmit the procedural documents by any means appropriate. That transmission must be followed by service by e-Curia as soon as it is again technically possible to use that application.

Article 8

The Registrar shall draw up the conditions of use of e-Curia and ensure that they are observed. Any use of e-Curia contrary to those conditions may result in the deactivation of the access account concerned.

The General Court shall take the necessary steps to protect e-Curia from any abuse or malicious use.

Users shall be notified by email of any action taken pursuant to this Article that prevents them from using their access account.

Article 9

This decision shall replace the decision of the General Court of 14 September 2011 on the lodging and service of procedural documents by means of e-Curia.[1]

NOTES

[1] OJ C289, 1.10.2011, p 9.

Article 10

This decision shall enter into force on the first day of the third month following that of its publication in the *Official Journal of the European Union*.

DECISION OF THE COURT OF JUSTICE

of 16 October 2018

on the lodging and service of procedural documents by means of e-Curia

[6.256]

NOTES

Date of publication in OJ: OJ L293, 20.11.2018, p 36.

THE COURT OF JUSTICE,

Having regard to the Rules of Procedure and, in particular, Articles 48(4) and 57(8) thereof,

Whereas:

(1) In order to take account of developments in communication technology, an information technology application has been developed to allow the lodging and service of procedural documents by electronic means.

(2) This application, which is based on an electronic authentication system using a combination of a personal user identification and password, meets the requirements of authenticity, integrity and confidentiality of documents exchanged.

(3) In view of the success of this application and the advantages it offers, notably in terms of the rapidity with which documents are exchanged, it is appropriate to widen the circle of its beneficiaries and to give the courts and tribunals of the Member States the opportunity to lodge or to receive procedural documents using this application when the Court is dealing with requests for a preliminary ruling.

(4) In the interests of the proper administration of justice — and for the purposes of dealing with references for a preliminary ruling only — the same opportunity must be given to persons who are not agents or lawyers but who are nevertheless authorised, under national procedural rules, to represent a party before the courts or tribunals of their own State,

HAS DECIDED AS FOLLOWS:

Article 1 Definition

The information technology application known as 'e-Curia', common to the constituent courts of the Court of Justice of the European Union, allows the lodging and service of procedural documents by electronic means under the conditions laid down by this Decision.

Article 2 Access to the application

Use of this application shall require the opening of an access account and use of a personal user identification and password.

Article 3 Lodging of a procedural document

A procedural document lodged by means of e-Curia shall be deemed to be the original of that document for the purposes of Article 57(1) of the Rules of Procedure where the personal user identification and password of a party's representative or of a person acting on behalf of a court or tribunal of a Member State have been used to effect the lodging. Use of that user identification and of that password shall constitute the signature of the document concerned.

Article 4 Annexes and copies

A procedural document lodged by means of e-Curia must be accompanied by the annexes referred to therein and a schedule listing such annexes.

It shall not be necessary to lodge certified copies of a document lodged by means of e-Curia or of any annexes thereto.

Article 5 Date and time of lodging

A procedural document shall be deemed to have been lodged for the purposes of Article 57(7) of the Rules of Procedure at the time of validation of the lodging of that document by the party's representative or by the person acting on behalf of the court or tribunal concerned.

The relevant time shall be the time in the Grand Duchy of Luxembourg.

Article 6 Service of procedural documents

Procedural documents, including judgments and orders, shall be served by means of e-Curia on the holders of e-Curia accounts who, in a case, represent a party or act on behalf of a court or tribunal of a Member State, as well as on their assistants, if any.

Procedural documents shall also be served by means of e-Curia on Member States, other States which are parties to the Agreement on the European Economic Area and institutions, bodies, offices or agencies of the Union that have accepted this method of service.

Procedural documents may also be served in accordance with the other methods of transmission provided for by the Rules of Procedure if required because of the size or nature of the item or where the use of e-Curia is not possible for technical reasons.

Article 7 Date and time of service

The intended recipients of the documents served referred to in Article 6 shall be notified by email of any document served on them by means of e-Curia.

A procedural document shall be served at the time when the intended recipient requests access to that document. In the absence of any request for access, the document shall be deemed to have been served on the expiry of the seventh day following the day on which the notification email was sent.

Where a party is represented by more than one person or where several persons are authorised to act on behalf of a court or tribunal of a Member State, the time to be taken into account in the reckoning of time limits shall be the time when the first request for access was made.

The relevant time shall be the time in the Grand Duchy of Luxembourg.

Article 8 Conditions of use of the application

The Registrar shall draw up the conditions of use of e-Curia and ensure that they are observed. Any use of e-Curia contrary to those conditions may result in the deactivation of the access account concerned.

The Court shall take the necessary steps to protect e-Curia from any abuse or malicious use.

Users shall be notified by email of any action taken pursuant to this Article that prevents them from using their access account.

Article 9 Repeal

This decision repeals and replaces the decision of the Court of Justice of 13 September 2011 on the lodging and service of procedural documents by means of e-Curia.[1]

NOTES

[1] OJ C289, 1.10.2011, p 7.

Article 10 Entry into force

This decision shall enter into force on the first day of the month following that of its publication in the *Official Journal of the European Union.*

RULES OF PROCEDURE OF THE GENERAL COURT (CONSOLIDATED VERSION, DECEMBER 2018)

[6.257]

NOTES

Date of original publication in Official Journal: OJ L105, 23.4.2015, p 1.

A consolidated version of these Rules is available on the General Court website at https://curia.europa.eu/jcms/jcms/Jo2_7040/en/. It includes the following amendments:

— amendments published in OJ L217, 12.8.2016, p 71 (with effect from 12 July 2016);
— amendments published in OJ L217, 12.8.2016, p 72 (with effect from 12 July 2016);
— amendments published in OJ L217, 12.8.2016, p 73–77 (with effect from 1 September 2016);
— amendments published in OJ L240, 25.9.2018, p 67 (with effect from 1 October 2018);
— amendments published in OJ L240, 25.9.2018, p 68–71 (with effect from 1 December 2018).

THE GENERAL COURT,

Having regard to the Treaty on European Union, and in particular Article 19 thereof,

Having regard to the Treaty on the Functioning of the European Union, and in particular the fifth paragraph of Article 254 thereof,

Having regard to the Treaty establishing the European Atomic Energy Community, and in particular Article 106a(1) thereof,

Having regard to the Protocol on the Statute of the Court of Justice of the European Union, and in particular the sixth paragraph of Article 19, Article 63 and the second paragraph of Article 64 thereof,

Whereas:

(1) The Rules of Procedure of 2 May 1991 have been amended numerous times in order to equip the General Court gradually with provisions enabling it to deal under the best possible conditions with different kinds of cases falling within increasingly varied areas.

(2) Full revision of the text is necessary in order to give this set of rules a new coherence, to promote consistency in the procedural provisions governing proceedings brought before the Courts of the European Union, to preserve the capacity of the General Court to rule on cases within a reasonable time, to clarify parties' rights, to specify the General Court's expectations regarding the parties' representatives and to adjust a certain number of provisions to take account of certain changes, including technological changes, in relation to the lodging and service of procedural documents, and of difficulties encountered in their implementation.

(3) Actions brought in the field of intellectual property and appeals lodged against decisions of the European Union Civil Service Tribunal must, on account of their specific nature, be subject to particular procedural rules set out in special titles, while being otherwise governed by the procedural provisions applicable to direct actions. The rules relating to direct actions, actions in the field of intellectual property and appeals therefore constitute the framework of these Rules.

(4) In the light of experience, it is also necessary to supplement or to clarify for the benefit of litigants the

rules that apply to each procedure. The rules in question concern, in particular, the extent of the rights conferred on the main parties and that of the rights afforded to interveners or, in intellectual property cases, the acquisition of the status of intervener and the extent of his rights. Observance of the adversarial principle and the need, in certain situations, to preserve the confidentiality of sensitive information which is relevant to the outcome of the proceedings are the subject of specific provisions. With regard to appeals against decisions of the Civil Service Tribunal, a clearer distinction must in addition be drawn between appeals and cross-appeals following the service of an appeal. A similar distinction must be drawn, with regard to cases in the field of intellectual property, between the original action and the cross-claim brought by an intervener, following service of the application initiating proceedings.

(5) The excessive complexity of certain procedures has come to light on their implementation. It is appropriate, therefore, to simplify them. On that basis, the rules for determining the language of the case in intellectual property cases ensure greater predictability of situations for the benefit of those concerned and a 'light touch' by the General Court. The rules relating to the default procedure are intended to enable cases to be disposed of more promptly, in the interests of the applicant, who, if successful, is exposed to the risk of the defendant applying for the judgment in default to be set aside.

(6) In the interests of making the Rules easier to understand, all requests and applications relating to judgments and orders, currently to be found in a number of separate titles and chapters of the Rules of Procedure, should be brought together in the title relating to direct actions. Similarly, to assist the reader, the procedures following referral by the Court of Justice, either after a decision has been set aside, or after review, are set out in a single title.

(7) Although required to deal with an ever-increasing caseload, the General Court must continue to deliver its rulings within a reasonable time. It is therefore essential to continue the efforts undertaken to reduce the duration of proceedings before the General Court, in particular by providing for the written part of the procedure in intellectual property cases to be limited to a single exchange of pleadings, managing applications to modify the form of order sought in the application, reducing certain legal time limits, simplifying the rules on intervention by removing as a category of intervention those which may be allowed after expiry of the legal time limit following publication in the *Official Journal of the European Union*, making provision for the General Court to be able to rule without an oral part of the procedure in direct actions if none of the main parties has requested a hearing and if it considers that it has sufficient information available to it from the material in the file in the case, and to be able to rule without an oral part of the procedure in appeals, increasing the decision-making powers of the Presidents of Chambers and, lastly, increasing the circumstances in which a ruling is to be given by means of a simple decision.

(8) With the same objective, provisions have been added to the title relating to the organisation of the General Court with a view, in particular, to specifying the circumstances in which a case may be reassigned and extending the powers of a single Judge so as to enable him to hear and determine intellectual property cases.

(9) The fact that proceedings are to be conducted in accordance with the adversarial principle is confirmed by the affirmation of that principle in a specific article and by a strict set of rules governing the circumstances in which preservation of the confidentiality of certain information provided by a main party which is necessary in order for the General Court to rule in the case justifies, exceptionally, the non-communication of that information to the other main party. New provisions also provide the General Court with a formal framework in the event of a Judge's withdrawal from a case or of his being excused. The reform is also intended to elevate to the status of rules of procedure provisions which were previously contained in practice directions to parties, such as that relating to the length of pleadings, or in instructions to the registrar of the General Court, such as the provision concerning anonymity and that specifying the circumstances in which a third party may be given access to the file in the case.

(10) Lastly, the text has been made easier to read by the removal of certain rules which are outdated or not applied, the numbering of every paragraph of the articles in these Rules, the addition of a specific heading for each article and the harmonisation of terminology,

With the agreement of the Court of Justice,

With the approval of the Council given on 10 February 2015,

HAS ADOPTED THESE RULES OF PROCEDURE:

INTRODUCTORY PROVISIONS

[6.258]

Article 1 Definitions

1. In these Rules:
   (a) provisions of the Treaty on European Union are referred to by the number of the article concerned followed by 'TEU';
   (b) provisions of the Treaty on the Functioning of the European Union are referred to by the number of the article concerned followed by 'TFEU';
   (c) provisions of the Treaty establishing the European Atomic Energy Community are referred to by the number of the article concerned followed by 'TEAEC';
   (d) 'Statute' means the Protocol on the Statute of the Court of Justice of the European Union;
   (e) 'EEA Agreement' means the Agreement on the European Economic Area;[1]
   (f) 'Council Regulation No 1' means Council Regulation No 1 of 15 April 1958 determining the languages to be used by the European Economic Community.[2]
2. For the purposes of these Rules:
   (a) 'General Court' means, in cases assigned or referred to a Chamber, that Chamber, and, in cases delegated or assigned to a single Judge, that Judge;
   (b) 'President', unless otherwise specified, means:
      — in cases not yet assigned to a formation of the Court, the President of the General Court,
      — in cases assigned to Chambers, the President of the Chamber to which the case is assigned,
      — in cases delegated or assigned to a single Judge, that Judge;
   (c) 'party' and 'parties', unless otherwise specified, means any party to the proceedings, including interveners;

(d) 'main party' and 'main parties' means the applicant or the defendant or both of them, as the case may be;
(e) 'representatives of the parties' means the lawyers and agents, the latter assisted, where appropriate, by an adviser or lawyer, representing the parties before the General Court in accordance with Article 19 of the Statute;
(f) 'institution' and 'institutions' means the institutions of the European Union referred to in Article 13(1) TEU and the bodies, offices or agencies established by the Treaties, or by an act adopted in implementation thereof, which may be parties before the General Court;
(g) 'Office' means the [the European Union Intellectual Property Office] or the Community Plant Variety Office, as the case may be;
(h) 'EFTA Surveillance Authority' means the European Free Trade Association surveillance authority referred to in the EEA Agreement;
[(i) 'direct actions' means actions brought on the basis of Articles 263 TFEU, 265 TFEU, 268 TFEU, 270 TFEU and 272 TFEU;]
[(j) 'Staff Regulations' means the Regulation laying down the Staff Regulations of Officials of the European Union and the Conditions of Employment of other servants of the European Union];
[(k) 'e-Curia' means the computer application of the Court of Justice of the European Union that enables procedural documents to be lodged and served electronically.]

NOTES

The words in square brackets in sub-para 2(g) were substituted by the Amendment to the Rules of Procedure of the General Court, Article 1 (OJ L217, 12.8.2016, p 71).

Sub-para 2(i) was substituted, and sub-para 2(j) was added, by the Amendment to the Rules of Procedure of the General Court, Article 1(1) (OJ L217, 12.8.2016, p 73).

Sub-para 2(k) was added by the Amendments to the Rules of Procedure of the General Court, Article 1(1) (OJ L240, 25.9.2018, p 68).

[1] OJ L1, 3.1.1994, p 3.

[2] OJ, English special edition 1952-1958 (I), p 59.

[6.259]
Article 2 Purport of these Rules

These Rules implement and supplement, so far as necessary, the relevant provisions of the EU, FEU and EAEC Treaties, and the Statute.

TITLE I ORGANISATION OF THE GENERAL COURT

CHAPTER 1 MEMBERS OF THE GENERAL COURT

[6.260]
Article 3 Duties of Judge and Advocate General

1. Every Member of the General Court shall, as a rule, perform the duties of a Judge.
2. Members of the General Court are hereinafter referred to as 'Judges'.
3. Every Judge, with the exception of the President . . . and the Presidents of Chambers of the General Court, may, in the circumstances defined in Articles 30 and 31, perform the duties of an Advocate General in a particular case.
4. References to the Advocate General in these Rules shall apply only where a Judge has been designated as Advocate General.

NOTES

Para 3: words omitted repealed by the Amendments to the Rules of Procedure of the General Court, Article 1(1) (OJ L240, 25.9.2018, p 67).

[6.261]
Article 4 Commencement of the term of office of Judges

The term of office of a Judge shall begin on the date fixed for that purpose in the instrument of appointment. In the absence of any provision in that instrument regarding the date of commencement of the term of office, that term shall begin on the date of publication of the instrument in the *Official Journal of the European Union*.

[6.262]
Article 5 Taking of the oath

Before taking up his duties, a Judge shall take the following oath before the Court of Justice, provided for in Article 2 of the Statute:

'I swear that I will perform my duties impartially and conscientiously; I swear that I will preserve the secrecy of the deliberations of the Court.'

[6.263]
Article 6 Solemn undertaking

Immediately after taking the oath, a Judge shall sign a declaration by which he gives the solemn undertaking provided for in the third paragraph of Article 4 of the Statute.

[6.264]
Article 7 Depriving a Judge of his office

1. Where the Court of Justice is called upon, pursuant to Article 6 of the Statute, to decide, after consulting the General Court, whether a Judge of the General Court no longer fulfils the requisite conditions or no longer meets the obligations arising from his office, the President of the General Court shall invite the Judge concerned to make representations to the General Court, in the absence of the Registrar.
2. The General Court shall state the reasons for its opinion.

3. An opinion to the effect that a Judge of the General Court no longer fulfils the requisite conditions or no longer meets the obligations arising from his office must receive the votes of a majority of the Judges composing the General Court according to Article 48 of the Statute. In that event, particulars of the voting shall be communicated to the Court of Justice.
4. Voting shall be by secret ballot in the absence of the Registrar; the Judge concerned shall not take part in the deliberations.

[6.265]
Article 8 Order of seniority
1. The seniority of Judges shall be calculated according to the date on which they took up their duties.
2. Where there is equal seniority on that basis, the order shall be determined by age.
3. Judges whose terms of office are renewed shall retain their former seniority.

CHAPTER 2 PRESIDENCY OF THE GENERAL COURT

[6.266]
Article 9 Election of the President and of the Vice-President of the General Court
1. The Judges shall, immediately after the partial replacement provided for in the second paragraph of Article 254 TFEU, elect one of their number as President of the General Court for a term of three years.
2. If the office of President of the General Court falls vacant before the normal date of expiry of the term thereof, the General Court shall elect a successor for the remainder of the term.
3. The elections provided for in this Article shall be by secret ballot. The Judge obtaining the votes of more than half the Judges composing the General Court according to Article 48 of the Statute shall be elected. If no Judge obtains that majority, further ballots shall be held until that majority is attained.
4. The Judges shall then elect one of their number as Vice-President of the General Court for a term of three years, in accordance with the procedures laid down in paragraph 3. Paragraph 2 shall apply if the office of the Vice-President of the General Court falls vacant before the normal date of expiry of the term thereof.
5. The names of the President and Vice-President of the General Court elected in accordance with this Article shall be published in the *Official Journal of the European Union*.

[6.267]
Article 10 Responsibilities of the President of the General Court
1. The President of the General Court shall represent the General Court.
2. The President of the General Court shall direct the judicial business and the administration of the General Court.
3. The President of the General Court shall preside at the plenum referred to in Article 42.
4. The President of the General Court shall preside over the Grand Chamber. In that case Article 19 shall apply.
5. If the President of the General Court is attached to a Chamber, he shall preside over that Chamber. In that case Article 19 shall apply.
6. In cases not yet assigned to a formation of the Court, the President of the General Court may adopt the measures of organisation of procedure provided for in Article 89.

[6.268]
Article 11 Responsibilities of the Vice-President of the General Court
1. The Vice-President of the General Court shall assist the President of the General Court in the performance of his duties and shall take the President's place when the latter is prevented from acting.
2. He shall take the President's place, at the latter's request, in performing the duties referred to in Article 10(1) and (2).
3. The General Court shall, by decision, specify the conditions under which the Vice-President of the General Court shall take the place of the President of the General Court in the performance of his judicial duties. That decision shall be published in the *Official Journal of the European Union*.
4. Subject to Article 10(5), if the Vice-President of the General Court is attached to a Chamber, he shall preside over that Chamber. In that case Article 19 shall apply.

[6.269]
Article 12 Where the President and Vice-President of the General Court are prevented from acting
When the President and the Vice-President of the General Court are simultaneously prevented from acting, the functions of President shall be exercised by a President of a Chamber or, failing that, by one of the other Judges, according to the order of seniority laid down in Article 8.

CHAPTER 3 CHAMBERS AND FORMATIONS OF THE COURT

SECTION 1 CONSTITUTION OF THE CHAMBERS AND COMPOSITION OF THE FORMATIONS OF THE COURT

[6.270]
Article 13 Constitution of Chambers
1. The General Court shall set up Chambers sitting with three and with five Judges.
2. The General Court shall decide, on a proposal from the President of the General Court, which Judges shall be attached to the Chambers.
3. The decisions taken in accordance with this Article shall be published in the *Official Journal of the European Union*.

[6.271]
Article 14 Competent formation of the Court
1. Cases before the General Court shall be heard and determined by Chambers sitting with three or with five Judges in accordance with Article 13.
2. Cases may be heard and determined by the Grand Chamber under the conditions laid down in Article 28.

3. Cases may be heard and determined by a single Judge where they are delegated to him under the conditions laid down in Article 29.

[6.272]
Article 15 Composition of the Grand Chamber
1. The Grand Chamber shall be composed of 15 Judges.
2. The General Court shall decide how to designate the Judges composing the Grand Chamber. The decision shall be published in the *Official Journal of the European Union*.

[6.273]
Article 16 Withdrawal and excusing of a Judge
1. Where a Judge considers, in accordance with the first and second paragraphs of Article 18 of the Statute, that he should not take part in the disposal of a case, he shall so inform the President of the General Court who shall exempt him from sitting.
2. Where the President of the General Court considers that a Judge should not, in accordance with the first and second paragraphs of Article 18 of the Statute, take part in the disposal of a case, he shall notify the Judge concerned and shall hear that Judge before giving his decision.
3. In accordance with the third paragraph of Article 18 of the Statute, in the event of any difficulty arising as to the application of this Article, the President of the General Court shall refer the matters referred to in paragraphs 1 and 2 to the plenum. In that case, voting shall be by secret ballot in the absence of the Registrar after the Judge concerned has been heard; the latter shall not take part in the deliberations.

[6.274]
Article 17 Where a member of the formation of the Court is prevented from acting
1. If in the Grand Chamber the number of Judges provided for by Article 15 is not attained as a result of a Judge's being prevented from acting before the deliberations have begun or before the case is pleaded, the President of the General Court shall designate a Judge to complete that Chamber in order to restore the requisite number of Judges.
2. If in a Chamber sitting with three or five Judges the number of Judges provided for is not attained as a result of a Judge's being prevented from acting before the deliberations have begun or before the case is pleaded, the President of that Chamber shall designate another Judge of that Chamber to replace the Judge prevented from acting. If it is not possible to replace the Judge prevented from acting with a Judge of the same Chamber, the President of that Chamber shall notify the President of the General Court, who shall designate, according to the criteria determined by the General Court, another Judge in order to restore the requisite number of Judges. The decision containing those criteria shall be published in the *Official Journal of the European Union*.
3. If the Judge to whom the case has been delegated or assigned as a single Judge is prevented from acting, the President of the General Court shall designate another Judge to replace that Judge.

SECTION 2 PRESIDENTS OF CHAMBERS

[6.275]
Article 18 Election of Presidents of Chambers
1. The Judges shall elect from among their number, in accordance with Article 9(3), the Presidents of the Chambers sitting with three and with five Judges.
2. The Presidents of Chambers sitting with five Judges shall be elected for a term of three years. They may be re-elected once.
3. The Presidents of Chambers sitting with three Judges shall be elected for a defined term.
4. The election of the Presidents of Chambers sitting with five Judges shall take place immediately after the elections of the President and the Vice-President of the General Court provided for in Article 9.
5. If the office of the President of a Chamber falls vacant before the normal date of expiry of the term thereof, the Judges shall elect a successor for the remainder of the term.
6. The names of the Presidents of Chambers elected in accordance with this Article shall be published in the *Official Journal of the European Union*.

[6.276]
Article 19 Powers of the President of a Chamber
1. The President of a Chamber shall exercise the powers conferred on him by these Rules after hearing the Judge-Rapporteur.
2. The President of a Chamber may refer any decision falling within his remit to the Chamber.

[6.277]
Article 20 Where the President of a Chamber is prevented from acting
Without prejudice to Article 10(5) and Article 11(4), when the President of a Chamber is prevented from acting, his functions shall be exercised by a Judge of that formation of the Court according to the order laid down in Article 8.

SECTION 3 DELIBERATIONS

[6.278]
Article 21 Procedures concerning deliberations
1. The deliberations of the General Court shall be and shall remain secret.
2. When a hearing has taken place, only those Judges who participated in that hearing shall take part in the deliberations.
3. Every Judge taking part in the deliberations shall state his opinion and the reasons for it.
4. The conclusions reached by the majority of the Judges after final discussion shall determine the decision of the General Court. Votes shall be cast in reverse order to the order laid down in Article 8, with the exception of the Judge-Rapporteur who shall vote first and the President who shall vote last.

[6.279]

Article 22 Number of Judges taking part in the deliberations

Where, as a result of a Judge's being prevented from acting, there is an even number of Judges, the most junior Judge for the purposes of Article 8 shall abstain from taking part in the deliberations unless he is the President or the Judge-Rapporteur. In the latter case, the Judge immediately senior to him shall abstain from taking part in the deliberations.

[6.280]

Article 23 Quorum of the Grand Chamber

1. Decisions of the Grand Chamber shall be valid only if 11 Judges are sitting.
2. If, as a result of a Judge's being prevented from acting, that quorum has not been attained, the President of the General Court shall designate another Judge in order to attain the quorum of the Grand Chamber.
3. If the quorum is no longer attained but the hearing has taken place, the Judge prevented from acting shall be replaced as provided in paragraph 2 and a new hearing shall be organised at the request of a main party. It may also be organised by the General Court of its own motion. A new hearing must be held if measures of inquiry have been adopted in accordance with Article 91(a) and (d) and Article 96(2). If no new hearing is organised, Article 21(2) shall not apply.

[6.281]

Article 24 Quorum of the Chambers sitting with three or with five Judges

1. Decisions of the Chambers sitting with three or with five Judges shall be valid only if three Judges are sitting.
2. If, as a result of a Judge's being prevented from acting, the quorum has not been attained in a Chamber sitting with three or with five Judges, the President of that Chamber shall designate another Judge of the same Chamber to replace the Judge prevented from acting. If it is not possible to replace the Judge prevented from acting with a Judge of the same Chamber, the President of the Chamber concerned shall notify the President of the General Court, who shall designate, according to the criteria determined by the General Court, another Judge in order to attain the quorum of the Chamber. The decision containing those criteria shall be published in the *Official Journal of the European Union.*
3. If the quorum is no longer attained but the hearing has taken place, the Judge prevented from acting shall be replaced as provided in paragraph 2 and a new hearing shall be organised at the request of a main party. It may also be organised by the General Court of its own motion. A new hearing must be held if measures of inquiry have been adopted in accordance with Article 91(a) and (d) and Article 96(2). A new hearing must be held if more than one Judge who took part in the original hearing has to be replaced. If no new hearing is organised, Article 21(2) shall not apply.

CHAPTER 4 ASSIGNMENT AND REASSIGNMENT OF CASES, DESIGNATION OF JUDGE-RAPPORTEURS, REFERRAL TO FORMATIONS OF THE COURT AND DELEGATION TO A SINGLE JUDGE

[6.282]

Article 25 Assignment criteria

1. The General Court shall lay down criteria by which cases are to be allocated among the Chambers. The General Court may make one or more Chambers responsible for hearing and determining cases in specific matters.
2. The decision shall be published in the *Official Journal of the European Union.*

[6.283]

Article 26 First assignment of a case and designation of the Judge-Rapporteur

1. As soon as possible after the document initiating proceedings has been lodged, the President of the General Court shall assign the case to a Chamber according to the criteria laid down by the General Court in accordance with Article 25.
2. The President of the Chamber shall propose to the President of the General Court, in respect of each case assigned to the Chamber, the designation of a Judge to act as Rapporteur. The President of the General Court shall decide on the proposal.
3. If in any Chamber sitting with three or with five Judges the number of Judges assigned to that Chamber is higher than three or five respectively, the President of the Chamber shall decide which of the Judges will be called upon to take part in the judgment of the case.

[6.284]

Article 27 Designation of a new Judge-Rapporteur and reassignment of a case

1. If the Judge-Rapporteur is prevented from acting, the President of the competent formation of the Court shall notify the President of the General Court, who shall designate a new Judge-Rapporteur. If the new Judge-Rapporteur is not attached to the Chamber to which the case was first assigned, the case shall be heard and determined by the Chamber in which the new Judge-Rapporteur sits.
2. In order to take account of a connection between cases on the basis of their subject-matter, the President of the General Court may, by reasoned decision and after consulting the Judge-Rapporteurs concerned, reassign the cases to enable the same Judge-Rapporteur to conduct preparatory inquiries in all the cases concerned. If the Judge-Rapporteur to whom the cases have been reassigned does not belong to the Chamber to which the cases were first assigned, the cases shall be heard and determined by the Chamber in which the new Judge-Rapporteur sits.
3. In the interests of the proper administration of justice, and by way of exception, the President of the General Court may, before the presentation of the preliminary report referred to in Article 87, by reasoned decision and after consulting the Judges concerned, designate another Judge-Rapporteur. If that Judge-Rapporteur is not attached to the Chamber to which the case was first assigned, the case shall be heard and determined by the Chamber in which the new Judge-Rapporteur sits.
4. Before designating the Judge-Rapporteur as provided in paragraphs 1 to 3, the President of the General Court shall seek the views of the Presidents of the Chambers concerned.

5. Where the composition of the Chambers has changed as a result of a decision of the General Court on the assignment of Judges to Chambers, a case shall be heard and determined by the Chamber in which the Judge-Rapporteur sits following that decision, unless the deliberations have commenced or the oral part of the procedure has been opened.

[6.285]
Article 28 Referral to a Chamber sitting with a different number of Judges

1. Whenever the legal difficulty or the importance of the case or special circumstances so justify, a case may be referred to the Grand Chamber or to a Chamber sitting with a different number of Judges.
2. The Chamber seised of the case[, the Vice-President of the General Court'] or the President of the General Court may, at any stage in the proceedings, either of its or his own motion or at the request of a main party, propose to the plenum that the case be referred as provided for in paragraph 1.
3. The decision to refer a case to a formation sitting with a greater number of Judges shall be taken by the plenum.
4. The decision to refer a case to a formation sitting with a lesser number of Judges shall be taken by the plenum, after the main parties have been heard.
5. The case shall be heard and determined by a Chamber sitting with at least five Judges where a Member State or an institution of the Union which is a party to the proceedings so requests.

NOTES

Para 2: words in square brackets inserted by the Amendments to the Rules of Procedure of the General Court, Article 1(2) (OJ L240, 25.9.2018, p 67).

[6.286]
Article 29 Delegation to a single Judge

1. The following cases assigned to a Chamber sitting with three Judges may be heard and determined by the Judge-Rapporteur sitting as a single Judge where, having regard to the lack of difficulty of the questions of law or fact raised, to the limited importance of those cases and to the absence of other special circumstances, they are suitable for being so heard and determined and have been delegated under the conditions laid down in this Article:
   (a) cases referred to in Article 171 below;
   (b) [cases brought pursuant to the fourth paragraph of Article 263 TFEU, the third paragraph of Article 265 TFEU, Article 268 TFEU and Article 270 TFEU] that raise only questions already clarified by established case-law or that form part of a series of cases in which the same relief is sought and of which one has already been finally decided;
   (c) cases brought pursuant to Article 272 TFEU.
2. Delegation to the single Judge shall not be possible:
   (a) in an action for annulment against an act of general application or in cases in which a plea of illegality is expressly raised against an act of general application;
   [(b) in an action brought pursuant to Article 270 TFEU in which a plea of illegality is expressly raised against an act of general application, unless the Court of Justice or the General Court has already given a ruling on the issues raised by that plea;]
   [(c)] in cases concerning the implementation of the rules:
      — on competition and on control of concentrations,
      — relating to aid granted by States,
      — relating to measures to protect trade,
      — relating to the common organisation of the agricultural markets, with the exception of cases that form part of a series of cases in which the same relief is sought and of which one has already been finally decided.
3. The decision relating to the delegation of a case to the single Judge shall be taken, after the main parties have been heard, by the Chamber sitting with three Judges before which the case is pending. Where a Member State or an institution of the Union which is a party to the proceedings objects to the case being heard and determined by the single Judge the case shall be maintained before the Chamber to which the Judge-Rapporteur belongs.
4. The single Judge shall refer the case back to the Chamber if he finds that the conditions justifying its delegation are no longer satisfied.

NOTES

The words in square brackets in sub-para 1(b) were substituted, sub-para 2(c) was designated as such (it was formerly sub-para 2(b)), and a new sub-para 2(b) was inserted, by the Amendment to the Rules of Procedure of the General Court, Article 1(2) (OJ L217, 12.8.2016, p 73).

CHAPTER 5 DESIGNATION OF ADVOCATES GENERAL

[6.287]
Article 30 Circumstances in which an Advocate General may be designated

The General Court may be assisted by an Advocate General if it is considered that the legal difficulty or the factual complexity of the case so requires.

[6.288]
Article 31 Procedures concerning the designation of an Advocate General

1. The decision to designate an Advocate General in a particular case shall be taken by the plenum at the request of the Chamber to which the case has been assigned or referred.
2. The President of the General Court shall designate the Judge called upon to perform the function of Advocate General in that case.
3. After being so designated, the Advocate General shall be heard before the decisions provided for in Articles 16, 28, 45, 68, 70, 83, 87, 90, 92, 98, 103, 105, 106, 113, 126 to 132, 144, 151, 165, 168, 169 and 207 to 209 are taken.

CHAPTER 6 REGISTRY

SECTION 1 THE REGISTRAR

[6.289]

Article 32 Appointment of the Registrar

1. The General Court shall appoint the Registrar.
2. When the post of Registrar is vacant, an advertisement shall be published in the *Official Journal of the European Union*. Interested persons shall be invited to submit their applications within a period of not less than three weeks, accompanied by full details of their nationality, university degrees, knowledge of languages, present and past professional activities, and experience, if any, in judicial and international fields.
3. Voting shall take place in accordance with the procedure laid down in Article 9(3).
4. The Registrar shall be appointed for a term of six years. He may be reappointed. The General Court may decide to renew the term of office of the incumbent Registrar without availing itself of the procedure laid down in paragraph 2. In that case paragraph 3 shall apply.
5. The Registrar shall take the oath set out in Article 5 and sign the declaration provided for in Article 6.
6. The Registrar may be deprived of his office only if he no longer fulfils the requisite conditions or no longer meets the obligations arising from his office. The General Court shall take its decision, in the absence of the Registrar, after giving him an opportunity to make representations.
7. If the office of Registrar falls vacant before the normal date of expiry of the term thereof, the General Court shall appoint a new Registrar for a term of six years.
8. The name of the Registrar elected in accordance with this Article shall be published in the *Official Journal of the European Union*.

[6.290]

Article 33 Deputy Registrar

The General Court may, in accordance with the procedure laid down in respect of the Registrar, appoint one or more Deputy Registrars to assist the Registrar and to take his place if he is prevented from acting.

[6.291]

Article 34 Where the Registrar and Deputy Registrar are prevented from acting

Where the Registrar is prevented from acting and, if necessary, where the Deputy Registrar is so prevented, the President of the General Court shall designate an official or servant to carry out the duties of Registrar.

[6.292]

Article 35 Responsibilities of the Registrar

1. The Registrar shall be responsible, under the authority of the President of the General Court, for the acceptance, transmission and custody of all documents and for effecting service as provided for by these Rules.
2. The Registrar shall assist the Members of the General Court in all their official functions.
3. The Registrar shall have custody of the seals and shall be responsible for the records. He shall be in charge of the publications of the General Court, in particular, the European Court Reports, and of the dissemination on the internet of documents concerning the General Court.
4. The Registrar shall be responsible, under the authority of the President of the General Court, for the administration of the General Court, its financial management and its accounts, and shall be assisted in this by the departments of the Court of Justice of the European Union.
5. Save as otherwise provided in these Rules, the Registrar shall attend the sittings of the General Court.

[6.293]

Article 36 Keeping of the register

1. There shall be kept in the Registry, under the responsibility of the Registrar, a register in which all procedural documents shall be entered in the order in which they are lodged.
[2. When a procedural document has been registered, the Registrar shall make a note to that effect on the procedural document included in the file in the case and, if a party so requests, on any copy submitted for the purpose.]
3. Entries in the register and the notes provided for in paragraph 2 shall be authentic.

NOTES

Para 2 substituted by the Amendments to the Rules of Procedure of the General Court, Article 1(2) (OJ L240, 25.9.2018, p 68).

[6.294]

Article 37 Consultation of the register

Anyone may consult the register at the Registry and obtain copies or extracts on payment of a charge on a scale fixed by the General Court on a proposal from the Registrar.

[6.295]

Article 38 Access to the file in the case

1. Subject to the provisions of Article 68(4), Articles 103 to 105 and of Article 144(7), any party to the proceedings may have access to the file in the case and, on payment of the appropriate charge referred to in Article 37, may obtain copies of procedural documents and authenticated copies of orders and judgments.
2. No third party, private or public, may have access to the file in a case without the express authorisation of the President of the General Court, once the parties have been heard. That authorisation may be granted, in whole or in part, only upon written request accompanied by a detailed explanation of the third party's legitimate interest in having access to the file.

SECTION 2 OTHER DEPARTMENTS

[6.296]
Article 39 Officials and other servants

1. [The officials and other servants whose task is to assist directly the President, the Judges and the Registrar shall be appointed under the conditions laid down by the Staff Regulations]. They shall be responsible to the Registrar, under the authority of the President of the General Court.

2. They shall take one of the following two oaths before the President of the General Court in the presence of the Registrar:

'I swear that I will perform loyally, discreetly and conscientiously the duties assigned to me by the General Court.'

or

'I solemnly and sincerely affirm that I will perform loyally, discreetly and conscientiously the duties assigned to me by the General Court.'

NOTES

Para 1: words in square brackets substituted by the Amendment to the Rules of Procedure of the General Court, Article 1(3) (OJ L217, 12.8.2016, p 73).

CHAPTER 7 THE WORKING OF THE GENERAL COURT

[6.297]
Article 40 Location of the sittings of the General Court

The General Court may choose to hold one or more specific sittings in a place other than that in which the General Court has its seat.

[6.298]
Article 41 Calendar of the General Court's judicial business

1. The judicial year shall begin on 1 September of each calendar year and end on 31 August of the following year.
2. The judicial vacations shall be determined by the General Court.
3. In a case of urgency, the President of the General Court and the Presidents of Chambers may convene the Judges and, if necessary, the Advocate General during the judicial vacations.
4. The General Court shall observe the official holidays of the place where it has its seat.
5. The General Court may, in proper circumstances, grant leave of absence to any Judge.
6. The dates of the judicial vacations shall be published annually in the *Official Journal of the European Union*.

[6.299]
Article 42 Plenum

1. Decisions concerning administrative issues and the decisions referred to in [Articles 7, 9, 11, 13, 15, 16, 18, 25, 28, 31 to 33, 41, 56a and 224] shall be taken by the General Court at the plenum in which all the Judges shall take part and have a vote, save as otherwise provided in these Rules. The Registrar shall be present, unless the General Court decides to the contrary.

2. If, after the plenum has been convened, it is found that the quorum referred to in the fourth paragraph of Article 17 of the Statute has not been attained, the President of the General Court shall adjourn the sitting until there is a quorum.

NOTES

Para 1: words in square brackets substituted by the Amendments to the Rules of Procedure of the General Court, Article 1(3) (OJ L240, 25.9.2018, p 68).

[6.300]
Article 43 Drawing-up of minutes

1. Where the General Court sits in the presence of the Registrar, the Registrar shall, if necessary, draw up minutes which shall be signed by the President of the General Court or by the President of the Chamber, as the case may be, and by the Registrar.

2. Where the General Court sits without the Registrar being present it shall, if necessary, instruct the most junior Judge for the purposes of Article 8 to draw up minutes which shall be signed by the President of the General Court or by the President of the Chamber, as the case may be, and by that Judge.

TITLE II LANGUAGES

[6.301]
Article 44 Language of a case

The language of a case shall be Bulgarian, Croatian, Czech, Danish, Dutch, English, Estonian, Finnish, French, German, Greek, Hungarian, Irish, Italian, Latvian, Lithuanian, Maltese, Polish, Portuguese, Romanian, Slovak, Slovenian, Spanish or Swedish.

[6.302]
Article 45 Determination of the language of a case

1. In direct actions within the meaning of Article 1, the language of a case shall be chosen by the applicant, except that:

(a) where the defendant is a Member State or a natural or legal person having the nationality of a Member State, the language of the case shall be the official language of that State; where that State has more than one official language, the applicant may choose between them;

(b) at the joint request of the main parties, the use of another of the languages mentioned in Article 44 for all or part of the proceedings may be authorised;

(c) at the request of one of the parties, and after the other parties have been heard, the use of another of the languages mentioned in Article 44 as the language of the case for all or part of the proceedings may be authorised by way of derogation from subparagraph (b); such a request may not be submitted by an institution.

2. Requests as above shall be decided on by the President; where the latter proposes to accede to a request without the agreement of all the parties, he must refer the request to the General Court.

3. Without prejudice to the provisions of paragraph 1(b) and (c):

(a) in appeals against decisions of the Civil Service Tribunal as referred to in Articles 9 and 10 of Annex I to the Statute, the language of the case shall be the language of the decision of the Civil Service Tribunal against which the appeal is brought;

(b) in the case of applications for rectification, applications for the General Court to remedy a failure to adjudicate or for it to set aside judgments by default, third-party proceedings and applications for interpretation or revision of a judgment or in the case of disputes concerning the costs to be recovered, the language of the case shall be the language of the decision to which those applications or disputes relate.

4. Without prejudice to the provisions in paragraph 1(b) and (c), in proceedings brought against decisions of the Boards of Appeal of the Office, referred to in Article 1, with respect to the application of the rules relating to an intellectual property regime:

(a) the language of the case shall be chosen by the applicant if the applicant was the only party to the proceedings before the Board of Appeal of the Office;

(b) the language of the application, chosen by the applicant from among the languages referred to in Article 44, shall be the language of the case if another party to the proceedings before the Board of Appeal of the Office does not object to this within the time limit laid down for that purpose by the Registrar after the application has been lodged;

(c) in the event of an objection to the language of the application by a party to the proceedings before the Board of Appeal of the Office other than the applicant, the language of the decision that is contested before the General Court shall become the language of the case; in such cases, the Registrar shall ensure the translation of the application into the language of the case.

[6.303]

Article 46 Use of the language of the case

1. The language of the case shall in particular be used in the written and oral pleadings of the parties, including the material annexed to them, and also in the minutes and decisions of the General Court.

2. Any material produced or annexed that is expressed in another language must be accompanied by a translation into the language of the case.

3. However, in the case of substantial material, translations may be confined to extracts. At any time the President may, of his own motion or at the request of one of the parties, call for a complete or fuller translation.

4. Notwithstanding the foregoing provisions, a Member State shall be entitled to use its official language when intervening in a case before the General Court. This provision shall apply both to written documents and to oral statements. The Registrar shall arrange in each instance for translation into the language of the case.

5. The States, other than the Member States, which are parties to the EEA Agreement, and also the EFTA Surveillance Authority, may be authorised to use one of the languages mentioned in Article 44, other than the language of the case, when they intervene in a case before the General Court. This provision shall apply both to written documents and to oral statements. The Registrar shall arrange in each instance for translation into the language of the case.

6. Where a witness or expert states that he is unable adequately to express himself in one of the languages referred to in Article 44, the President may authorise him to give his evidence in another language. The Registrar shall arrange for translation into the language of the case.

7. The President in conducting oral proceedings, Judges and, where appropriate, the Advocate General in putting questions and the Advocate General in delivering his Opinion may use one of the languages referred to in Article 44 other than the language of the case. The Registrar shall arrange for translation into the language of the case.

[6.304]

Article 47 Responsibility of the Registrar concerning language arrangements

The Registrar shall, at the request of any Judge, of the Advocate General or of a party, arrange for anything said or written in the course of the proceedings before the General Court to be translated into the languages chosen from those referred to in Article 44.

[6.305]

Article 48 Languages of the publications of the General Court

Publications of the General Court shall be issued in the languages referred to in Article 1 of Council Regulation No 1.

[6.306]

Article 49 Authentic texts

The texts of documents drawn up in the language of the case or, where applicable, in another language authorised pursuant to Articles 45 and 46 of these Rules shall be authentic.

TITLE III DIRECT ACTIONS

[6.307]

Article 50 Scope

The provisions of this Title shall apply to direct actions within the meaning of Article 1.

CHAPTER 1 GENERAL PROVISIONS

SECTION 1 REPRESENTATION OF THE PARTIES

[6.308]
Article 51 Obligation to be represented

1. A party must be represented by an agent or a lawyer in accordance with the provisions of Article 19 of the Statute.
2. The lawyer representing or assisting a party must lodge at the Registry a certificate that he is authorised to practise before a court of a Member State or of another State which is a party to the EEA Agreement.
3. Where the party represented by the lawyer is a legal person governed by private law, the lawyer must lodge at the Registry an authority to act given by that person.
4. If the documents referred to in paragraphs 2 and 3 are not lodged, the Registrar shall prescribe a reasonable time limit within which the party concerned is to produce them. If the party concerned fails to produce the required documents within the time limit prescribed, the General Court shall decide whether the non-compliance with that procedural requirement renders the application or written pleadings formally inadmissible.

SECTION 2 RIGHTS AND OBLIGATIONS OF PARTIES' REPRESENTATIVES

[6.309]
Article 52 Privileges, immunities and facilities

1. Agents, advisers and lawyers who appear before the General Court or before any judicial authority to which it has addressed letters rogatory shall enjoy immunity in respect of words spoken or written by them concerning the case or the parties.
2. Agents, advisers and lawyers shall also enjoy the following privileges and facilities:
   (a) any papers and documents relating to the proceedings shall be exempt from both search and seizure; in the event of a dispute, the customs officials or police may seal those papers and documents; they shall then be immediately forwarded to the General Court for inspection in the presence of the Registrar and of the person concerned;
   (b) agents, advisers and lawyers shall be entitled to travel in the course of duty without hindrance.

[6.310]
Article 53 Status of the parties' representatives

1. In order to qualify for the privileges, immunities and facilities specified in Article 52, persons entitled to them shall furnish proof of their status as follows:
   (a) agents shall produce an official document issued by the party for whom they act, who shall immediately serve a copy thereof on the Registrar;
   (b) lawyers shall produce a certificate that they are authorised to practise before a court of a Member State or of another State which is a party to the EEA Agreement, and, where the party which they represent is a legal person governed by private law, an authority to act issued by that person;
   (c) advisers shall produce an authority to act issued by the party whom they are assisting.
2. The Registrar shall issue them with a certificate, as required. The validity of this certificate shall be limited to a specified period, which may be extended or curtailed according to the duration of the proceedings.

[6.311]
Article 54 Waiver of immunity

1. The privileges, immunities and facilities specified in Article 52 are granted exclusively in the interests of the proper conduct of proceedings.
2. The General Court may waive immunity where it considers that the proper conduct of proceedings will not be hindered thereby.

[6.312]
Article 55 Exclusion from the proceedings

1. If the General Court considers that the conduct of an agent, adviser or lawyer before the General Court, the President, a Judge or the Registrar is incompatible with the dignity of the General Court or with the requirements of the proper administration of justice, or that such agent, adviser or lawyer is using his rights for purposes other than those for which they were granted, it shall inform the person concerned. The General Court may inform the competent authorities to whom the person concerned is answerable. A copy of the letter sent to those authorities shall be forwarded to the person concerned.
2. On the same grounds, the General Court may at any time, having heard the person concerned, decide to exclude an agent, adviser or lawyer from the proceedings by reasoned order. That order shall have immediate effect.
3. Where an agent, adviser or lawyer is excluded from the proceedings, the proceedings shall be suspended for a period fixed by the President in order to allow the party concerned to appoint another agent, adviser or lawyer.
4. Decisions taken under this Article may be rescinded.

[6.313]
Article 56 University teachers

The provisions of this Section shall apply to the university teachers referred to in the seventh paragraph of Article 19 of the Statute.

[SECTION 2A COMMUNICATION WITH PARTIES' REPRESENTATIVES VIA E-CURIA

[6.314]
Article 56a e-Curia

1. Without prejudice to the cases referred to in Article 57(2), Article 72(4), Article 80(1), Article 105(1) and (2), Article 147(6), Article 148(9) and Article 178(2) and (3), all procedural documents shall be lodged and served via e-Curia.

2. The conditions for the lodging and service of procedural documents via e-Curia shall be specified in a decision adopted by the General Court. That decision shall be published in the *Official Journal of the European Union*.
3. Use of e-Curia shall require an access account to have been opened under the conditions laid down in the decision referred to in paragraph 2.
4. If a procedural document is lodged via e-Curia before the supporting documents required for validation of the access account have been produced, those supporting documents must be received in paper format at the Registry of the General Court within 10 days of the procedural document being lodged. This time limit may not be extended and Article 60 shall not apply. If the supporting documents are not received within the prescribed time limit, the Court shall declare the procedural document lodged via e-Curia to be inadmissible.
5. Where the use of e-Curia is technically impossible and without prejudice to the application of the second paragraph of Article 45 of the Statute, a procedural document may be lodged or served by any appropriate means available. The procedure to be followed in such circumstances shall be specified in the decision referred to in paragraph 2.]

NOTES

Section 2a inserted by the Amendments to the Rules of Procedure of the General Court, Article 1(4) (OJ L240, 25.9.2018, p 68).

SECTION 3 SERVICE

[6.315]
Article 57 Methods of service

[1. Without prejudice to Article 80(1), Article 148(9) and Article 178(2) and (3), where the Statute or these Rules require a document to be served on a person the Registrar shall ensure that service is effected via e-Curia.]
2. [Where, on account of the nature of the document,] service of the document in accordance with the procedures laid down in paragraph 1 is impossible or impracticable, the document shall be served at the address of the representative of the party concerned by registered post with a form for acknowledgement of receipt or by personal delivery of the copy against a receipt. The addressee shall be so informed [via e-Curia]. Service shall then be deemed to have been effected on the addressee by registered post on the tenth day following the lodging of the registered letter at the post office of the place in which the General Court has its seat, unless it is shown by the acknowledgement of receipt that the letter was received on a different date or the addressee informs the Registrar, within three weeks of being informed [via e-Curia], that the document to be served has not reached him.
[3. Without prejudice to Article 72(4), the Registrar shall prepare and certify the copies of documents to be served pursuant to paragraph 2.]
4. . . .

NOTES

Paras 1, 3: substituted by the Amendments to the Rules of Procedure of the General Court, Article 1(5)(a), (c) (OJ L240, 25.9.2018, p 68).

Para 2: words in square brackets substituted by the Amendments to the Rules of Procedure of the General Court, Article 1(5)(b) (OJ L240, 25.9.2018, p 68).

Para 4: repealed by the Amendments to the Rules of Procedure of the General Court, Article 1(5)(d) (OJ L240, 25.9.2018, p 68).

SECTION 4 TIME LIMITS

[6.316]
Article 58 Calculation of time limits

1. Any procedural time limit prescribed by the Treaties, the Statute or these Rules shall be calculated as follows:
   (a) where a time limit expressed in days, weeks, months or years is to be calculated from the moment at which an event occurs or an action takes place, the day during which that event occurs or that action takes place shall not be counted as falling within the time limit in question;
   (b) a time limit expressed in weeks, months or years shall end with the expiry of whichever day in the last week, month or year is the same day of the week, or falls on the same date, as the day during which the event or action from which the time limit is to be calculated occurred or took place; if, in a time limit expressed in months or years, the day on which it should expire does not occur in the last month, the time limit shall end with the expiry of the last day of that month;
   (c) where a time limit is expressed in months and days, it shall first be calculated in whole months, then in days;
   (d) time limits shall include Saturdays, Sundays and official holidays;
   (e) time limits shall not be suspended during the judicial vacations.
2. If the time limit would otherwise end on a Saturday, Sunday or an official holiday, it shall be extended until the end of the next working day.
3. The list of official holidays drawn up by the Court of Justice and published in the *Official Journal of the European Union* shall apply to the General Court.

[6.317]
Article 59 Proceedings against a measure adopted by an institution and published in the Official Journal of the European Union

Where the time limit allowed for initiating proceedings against a measure adopted by an institution runs from the publication of that measure in the *Official Journal of the European Union*, that time limit shall be calculated, for the purposes of Article 58(1)(a), from the end of the fourteenth day after such publication.

[6.318]
Article 60 Extension on account of distance

The procedural time limits shall be extended on account of distance by a single period of 10 days.

[6.319]
Article 61 Setting and extension of time limits
1. Any time limit prescribed pursuant to these Rules may be extended by whoever prescribed it.
2. The President may delegate to the Registrar power of signature for the purposes of setting certain time limits which, pursuant to these Rules, it falls to the President to prescribe, or of extending such time limits.

[6.320]
Article 62 Procedural documents lodged out of time
A procedural document lodged at the Registry after expiry of the time limit set by the President or by the Registrar pursuant to these Rules may be accepted only pursuant to a decision of the President to that effect.

SECTION 5 CONDUCT OF THE PROCEEDINGS AND PROCEDURES FOR DEALING WITH CASES

[6.321]
Article 63 Conduct of the proceedings
Without prejudice to the special provisions laid down in the Statute or in these Rules, the procedure before the General Court shall consist of a written part and an oral part.

[6.322]
Article 64 Adversarial nature of the proceedings
Subject to the provisions of Article 68(4), Article 104, Article 105(8) and Article 144(7), the General Court shall take into consideration only those procedural documents and items which have been made available to the representatives of the parties and on which they have been given an opportunity of expressing their views.

[6.323]
Article 65 Service of procedural documents and of decisions taken in the course of proceedings
1. Subject to the provisions of Article 68(4), Articles 103 to 105 and Article 144(7), procedural documents and items included in the file in the case shall be served on the parties.
2. The Registrar shall ensure that decisions taken in the course of the proceedings and included in the file in the case are brought to the attention of the parties.

[6.324]
Article 66 Anonymity and omission of certain information vis-à-vis the public
On a reasoned application by a party, made by a separate document, or of its own motion, the General Court may omit the name of a party to the dispute or of other persons mentioned in connection with the proceedings, or certain information, from those documents relating to a case to which the public has access if there are legitimate reasons for keeping the identity of a person or the information confidential.

[6.325]
Article 67 Order in which cases are dealt with
1. The General Court shall deal with the cases before it in the order in which they become ready for examination.
2. The President may in special circumstances decide that a case be given priority over others.

[6.326]
Article 68 Joinder
1. Two or more cases concerning the same subject-matter may at any time, either of the General Court's own motion or on application by a main party, be joined, on account of the connection between them, for the purposes, alternatively or cumulatively, of the written or oral part of the procedure or of the decision which closes the proceedings.
2. A decision on whether cases should be joined shall be taken by the President. Before taking that decision, the President shall prescribe a time limit within which the main parties may submit their observations on any joinder, if they have not already expressed their views in that regard.
3. Joined cases may be disjoined, in accordance with the provisions of paragraph 2.
[4. Procedural documents included in the files of the joined cases shall be served via e-Curia on the parties who request this. The President may, however, on application by a party, order that certain information from the case file which it is claimed is confidential be excluded from such service.]
5. . . .

NOTES

Para 4: substituted by the Amendments to the Rules of Procedure of the General Court, Article 1(6)(a) (OJ L240, 25.9.2018, p 68).

Para 5: repealed by the Amendments to the Rules of Procedure of the General Court, Article 1(6)(b) (OJ L240, 25.9.2018, p 68).

[6.327]
Article 69 Circumstances in which proceedings may be stayed
Without prejudice to Article 163, proceedings may be stayed:
(a) in the circumstances specified in the third paragraph of Article 54 of the Statute;
(b) where an appeal is brought before the Court of Justice against a decision of the General Court disposing of the substantive issues in part only, disposing of a procedural issue concerning a plea of lack of competence or inadmissibility or dismissing an application to intervene;
(c) at the request of a main party with the agreement of the other main party;
(d) in other particular cases where the proper administration of justice so requires.

[6.328]

Article 70 Decisions to stay and to resume proceedings

1. The decision to stay the proceedings shall be taken by the President. Before taking that decision, the President shall prescribe a time limit within which the main parties may submit their observations on any stay of the proceedings, if they have not already expressed their views in that regard.

2. A decision ordering that the proceedings be resumed before the end of the stay, or as referred to in Article 71(3), shall be taken in accordance with the procedures laid down in paragraph 1.

[6.329]

Article 71 Length and effects of a stay

1. The stay of proceedings shall take effect on the date indicated in the decision to stay or, in the absence of such indication, on the date of that decision.

2. During the period in which proceedings are stayed all procedural time limits shall be suspended, except for the time limit prescribed in Article 143(1) for an application to intervene.

3. Where the decision to stay the proceedings does not fix the length of stay, it shall end on the date indicated in the decision to resume the proceedings or, in the absence of such indication, on the date of the latter decision.

4. From the date of the resumption of proceedings following a stay, any suspended procedural time limits shall be replaced by new time limits and time shall begin to run from the date of that resumption.

CHAPTER 2 PROCEDURAL DOCUMENTS

[6.330]

Article 72 [Rules for the lodging of procedural documents via e-Curia]

[1. With the exception of documents lodged pursuant to Article 105(1) and (2) and Article 147(6), all procedural documents shall be lodged at the Registry via e-Curia.]

2. All procedural documents shall bear a date. In the calculation of procedural time limits, only the date and time in the Grand Duchy of Luxembourg of lodgement at the Registry shall be taken into account.

3. To every procedural document there shall be annexed the material relied on in support of it, together with a schedule listing each item.

[4. Where, on account of its nature, an annex to a procedural document cannot be lodged via e-Curia, the relevant annex shall be sent separately by post or shall be delivered to the Registry. The annex shall be submitted together with a copy for the General Court and a copy for every other party to the proceedings. Copies shall be certified as being identical by the party lodging them.]

[5]. Where, in view of the length of the material, only extracts from it are annexed to the procedural document, the whole item or a full copy of it shall be lodged at the Registry.

[6]. The institutions shall produce, within time limits laid down by the President, translations of any procedural document into the other languages provided for by Article 1 of Council Regulation No 1.

NOTES

Article heading: substituted by the Amendments to the Rules of Procedure of the General Court, Article 1(7)(a) (OJ L240, 25.9.2018, p 68).

Para 1: substituted by the Amendments to the Rules of Procedure of the General Court, Article 1(7)(b) (OJ L240, 25.9.2018, p 68).

Para 4 was inserted, and the original paras 4 and 5 were renumbered as paras 5 and 6 respectively, by the Amendments to the Rules of Procedure of the General Court, Article 1(7)(c), (d) (OJ L240, 25.9.2018, p 68).

Articles 73, 74 (*Articles 73, 74 repealed by the Amendments to the Rules of Procedure of the General Court, Article 1(8), (9) (OJ L240, 25.9.2018, p 68).*)

[6.331]

Article 75 Length of written pleadings

1. The General Court shall set, in accordance with Article 224, the maximum length of written pleadings lodged pursuant to this Title.

2. Authorisation to exceed the maximum length of written pleadings may be given by the President only in cases involving particularly complex legal or factual issues.

CHAPTER 3 WRITTEN PART OF THE PROCEDURE

[6.332]

Article 76 Content of the application

An application of the kind referred to in Article 21 of the Statute shall contain:

(a) the name and address of the applicant;
(b) particulars of the status and address of the applicant's representative;
(c) the name of the main party against whom the action is brought;
(d) the subject-matter of the proceedings, the pleas in law and arguments relied on and a summary of those pleas in law;
(e) the form of order sought by the applicant;
(f) where appropriate, any evidence produced or offered.

Article 77 (*Repealed by the Amendments to the Rules of Procedure of the General Court, Article 1(10) (OJ L240, 25.9.2018, p 68).*)

[6.333]

Article 78 Annexes to the application

1. The application shall be accompanied, where appropriate, by the documents specified in the second paragraph of Article 21 of the Statute.

[2. An application submitted pursuant to Article 270 TFEU shall be accompanied, where appropriate, by the complaint within the meaning of Article 90(2) of the Staff Regulations and the decision responding to the complaint, together with an indication of the dates on which the complaint was submitted and the decision notified.]

[3]. An application submitted under Article 272 TFEU pursuant to an arbitration clause in a contract governed by public or private law, entered into by the Union or on its behalf, shall be accompanied by a copy of the contract which contains that clause.

[4]. An application made by a legal person governed by private law shall be accompanied by recent proof of that person's existence in law (extract from the register of companies, firms or associations or any other official document).

[5]. The application shall be accompanied by the documents referred to in Article 51(2) and (3).

[6]. If the application does not comply with the requirements set out in [paragraphs 1 to 5], the Registrar shall prescribe a reasonable time limit within which the applicant is to produce the abovementioned documents. If the applicant fails to put the application in order within the time limit prescribed, the General Court shall decide whether the non-compliance with these conditions renders the application formally inadmissible.

NOTES

The original paras 2–5 were renumbered as paras 3–6, a new para 2 was inserted, and the words in square brackets in para 6 (as so renumbered) were substituted, by the Amendment to the Rules of Procedure of the General Court, Article 1(4) (OJ L217, 12.8.2016, p 73).

[6.334]

Article 79 Notice in the Official Journal of the European Union

A notice shall be published in the *Official Journal of the European Union* indicating the date of lodging of an application initiating proceedings, the names of the main parties, the form of order sought by the applicant and a summary of the pleas in law and of the main supporting arguments.

[6.335]

Article 80 Service of the application

[1. The application shall be served on the defendant via e-Curia if he has an e-Curia account. Where the defendant has no such account, the application shall be served on him in the form of a certified copy sent by registered post with a form for acknowledgement of receipt or by delivery of the copy against receipt.]

2. In cases where [Article 78(6)] applies, service shall be effected as soon as the application has been put in order or the General Court has declared it admissible notwithstanding the failure to observe the requirements set out in that Article.

NOTES

Para 1: substituted by the Amendments to the Rules of Procedure of the General Court, Article 1(11) (OJ L240, 25.9.2018, p 68).

Para 2: words in square brackets substituted by the Amendment to the Rules of Procedure of the General Court, Article 1(5) (OJ L217, 12.8.2016, p 73).

[6.336]

Article 81 Defence

1. Within two months after service on him of the application, the defendant shall lodge a defence, containing:
   (a) the name and address of the defendant;
   (b) particulars of the status and address of the applicant's representative;
   (c) the pleas in law and arguments relied on;
   (d) the form of order sought by the defendant;
   (e) where appropriate, any evidence produced or offered.

[2. Article 78(4) to (6) shall apply to the defence.]

3. The time limit laid down in paragraph 1 of this Article may, in exceptional circumstances, be extended by the President at the reasoned request of the defendant.

NOTES

Para 2: substituted by the Amendments to the Rules of Procedure of the General Court, Article 1(12) (OJ L240, 25.9.2018, p 68).

[6.337]

Article 82 Transmission of documents

Where the European Parliament, the Council or the European Commission is not a party to a case, the General Court shall send to them copies of the application and of the defence, without the annexes thereto, to enable them to assess whether the inapplicability of one of their acts is being invoked under Article 277 TFEU.

[6.338]

Article 83 Reply and rejoinder

1. The application initiating proceedings and the defence may be supplemented by a reply from the applicant and by a rejoinder from the defendant unless the General Court decides that a second exchange of pleadings is unnecessary because the contents of the file in the case are sufficiently comprehensive.

2. Where the General Court decides that a second exchange of pleadings is unnecessary it may authorise the main parties to supplement the file in the case if the applicant presents a reasoned request to that effect within two weeks from the service of that decision.

3. The President shall prescribe the time limits within which those procedural documents are to be produced. He may specify the matters to which the reply or the rejoinder should relate.

CHAPTER 4 PLEAS IN LAW, EVIDENCE AND MODIFICATION OF THE APPLICATION

[6.339]

Article 84 New pleas in law

1. No new plea in law may be introduced in the course of proceedings unless it is based on matters of law or of fact which come to light in the course of the procedure.
2. Any new pleas in law shall be introduced in the second exchange of pleadings and identified as such. Where the matters of law or of fact justifying the introduction of new pleas in law are known after the second exchange of pleadings or after it has been decided not to authorise a second exchange of pleadings, the main party concerned shall introduce the new pleas in law as soon as those matters come to his knowledge.
3. Without prejudice to the decision to be taken by the General Court on the admissibility of the new pleas in law, the President shall give the other parties an opportunity to respond to those pleas.

[6.340]

Article 85 Evidence produced or offered

1. Evidence produced or offered shall be submitted in the first exchange of pleadings.
2. In reply or rejoinder a main party may produce or offer further evidence in support of his arguments, provided that the delay in the submission of such evidence is justified.
3. The main parties may, exceptionally, produce or offer further evidence before the oral part of the procedure is closed or before the decision of the General Court to rule without an oral part of the procedure, provided that the delay in the submission of such evidence is justified.
4. Without prejudice to the decision to be taken by the General Court on the admissibility of the evidence produced or offered pursuant to paragraphs 2 and 3, the President shall give the other parties an opportunity to comment on such evidence.

[6.341]

Article 86 Modification of the application

1. Where a measure the annulment of which is sought is replaced or amended by another measure with the same subject-matter, the applicant may, before the oral part of the procedure is closed, or before the decision of the General Court to rule without an oral part of the procedure, modify the application to take account of that new factor.
2. The modification of the application must be made by a separate document within the time limit laid down in the sixth paragraph of Article 263 TFEU within which the annulment of the measure justifying the modification of the application may be sought.

[3. In cases brought pursuant to Article 270 TFEU, the modification of the application must be made by a separate document and, by way of derogation from paragraph 2, within the time limit laid down in Article 91(3) of the Staff Regulations within which the annulment of the measure justifying the modification of the application may be sought.]

[4]. The statement of modification shall contain:

(a) the modified form of order sought;
(b) where appropriate, the modified pleas in law and arguments;
(c) where appropriate, the evidence produced and offered in connection with the modification of the form of order sought.

[5]. The statement of modification must be accompanied by the measure justifying the modification of the application. If that measure is not produced, the Registrar shall prescribe a reasonable time limit within which the applicant is to produce it. If the applicant fails to produce the measure within the time limit prescribed, the General Court shall decide whether the non-compliance with that requirement renders the statement modifying the application inadmissible.

[6]. Without prejudice to the decision to be taken by the General Court on the admissibility of the statement modifying the application, the President shall prescribe a time limit within which the defendant may respond to the statement of modification.

[7]. The President shall, where appropriate, prescribe a time limit within which any interveners may supplement their statements in intervention in the light of the statement modifying the application and the statement in response. Those statements shall be served simultaneously on the interveners for that purpose.

NOTES

The original paras 3–6 were renumbered as paras 4–7, and a new para 3 was inserted, by the Amendment to the Rules of Procedure of the General Court, Article 1(7) (OJ L217, 12.8.2016, p 73).

CHAPTER 5 THE PRELIMINARY REPORT

[6.342]

Article 87 Preliminary report

1. When the written part of the procedure is closed, the President shall fix a date on which the Judge-Rapporteur is to present a preliminary report to the General Court.
2. The preliminary report shall contain an analysis of the relevant issues of fact and of law raised by the action, proposals as to whether measures of organisation of procedure or measures of inquiry should be undertaken, whether there should be an oral part of the procedure and whether the case should be referred to the Grand Chamber or to a Chamber sitting with a different number of Judges, and whether the case should be delegated to a single Judge.
3. The General Court shall decide what action to take on the proposals of the Judge-Rapporteur and, where appropriate, whether to open the oral part of the procedure.

CHAPTER 6 MEASURES OF ORGANISATION OF PROCEDURE AND MEASURES OF INQUIRY

[6.343]
Article 88 General

1. Measures of organisation of procedure and measures of inquiry may be taken or modified at any stage of the proceedings either of the General Court's own motion or on the application of a main party.
2. The application referred to in paragraph 1 must state precisely the purpose of the measures sought and the reasons for them. Where the application is made after the first exchange of pleadings, the party submitting that application must state the reasons for which he was unable to submit it earlier.
3. Where an application for measures of organisation of procedure or for measures of inquiry is made, the President shall give the other parties an opportunity to comment on that application.

SECTION 1 MEASURES OF ORGANISATION OF PROCEDURE

[6.344]
Article 89 Purpose

1. The purpose of measures of organisation of procedure shall be to ensure that cases are prepared for hearing, procedures carried out and disputes resolved under the best possible conditions.
2. Measures of organisation of procedure shall, in particular, have as their purpose:
   (a) to ensure the efficient conduct of the written or oral part of the procedure and to facilitate the taking of evidence;
   (b) to determine the points on which the parties must present further argument or which call for measures of inquiry;
   (c) to clarify the forms of order sought by the parties, their pleas in law and arguments and the points at issue between them;
   (d) to facilitate the amicable settlement of proceedings.
3. Measures of organisation of procedure may, in particular, consist of:
   (a) putting questions to the parties;
   (b) inviting the parties to make written or oral submissions on certain aspects of the proceedings;
   (c) asking the parties or third parties for the information referred to in the second paragraph of Article 24 of the Statute;
   (d) asking the parties to produce any material relating to the case;
   (e) summoning the parties to meetings.
4. Where a hearing is organised, the General Court shall, in so far as possible, invite the parties to concentrate in their oral pleadings on one or more specified issues.

[6.345]
Article 90 Procedure

1. Measures of organisation of procedure shall be prescribed by the General Court.
2. If the General Court decides to adopt measures of organisation of procedure and does not undertake such measures itself, it shall entrust the task of so doing to the Judge-Rapporteur.

SECTION 2 MEASURES OF INQUIRY

[6.346]
Article 91 Purpose

Without prejudice to Articles 24 and 25 of the Statute, the following measures of inquiry may be adopted:
   (a) the personal appearance of the parties;
   (b) a request to a party for information or for production of any material relating to the case;
   (c) a request for production of documents to which access has been denied by an institution in proceedings relating to the legality of that denial;
   (d) oral testimony;
   (e) the commissioning of an expert's report;
   (f) an inspection of the place or thing in question.

[6.347]
Article 92 Procedure

1. The General Court shall prescribe the measures of inquiry that it considers appropriate by means of an order setting out the facts to be proved.
2. Before the General Court decides on the measures of inquiry referred to in Article 91(d) to (f), the parties shall be heard.
3. A measure of inquiry referred to in Article 91(b) may be ordered only where the party concerned by the measure has not complied with a measure of organisation of procedure previously adopted to that end, or where expressly requested by the party concerned by the measure and that party explains the need for such a measure to be in the form of an order for a measure of inquiry. The order prescribing the measure of inquiry may provide that inspection by the parties' representatives of information and material obtained by the General Court in consequence of that order may take place only at the Registry and that no copies may be made.
4. If the General Court orders a preparatory inquiry and does not undertake such an inquiry itself, it shall entrust the task of so doing to the Judge-Rapporteur.
5. The Advocate General shall take part in the measures of inquiry.
6. The parties shall be entitled to attend the measures of inquiry.
7. Evidence may be submitted in rebuttal and previous evidence may be amplified.

[6.348]

Article 93 Summoning of witnesses

1. Witnesses whose examination is deemed necessary shall be summoned by an order, referred to in Article 92(1), containing the following information:

(a) the name, description and address of the witness;

(b) the date and place of the examination;

(c) an indication of the facts to be established and which witnesses are to be heard in respect of each of those facts.

2. Witnesses shall be summoned by the General Court, where appropriate after lodgement of the security provided for in Article 100(1).

[6.349]

Article 94 Examination of witnesses

1. After the identity of the witness has been established, the President shall inform him that he will be required to vouch the truth of his evidence in the manner laid down in paragraph 5 and in Article 97.

2. The witness shall give his evidence to the General Court, the parties having been given notice to attend. After the witness has given his evidence the President may, at the request of one of the parties or of his own motion, put questions to him.

3. The other Judges and the Advocate General may do likewise.

4. Subject to the control of the President, questions may be put to witnesses by the representatives of the parties.

5. Subject to the provisions of Article 97, the witness shall, after giving his evidence, take the following oath:

'I swear that I have spoken the truth, the whole truth and nothing but the truth.'

6. The General Court may, after hearing the main parties, exempt a witness from taking the oath.

[6.350]

Article 95 Duties of witnesses

1. Witnesses who have been duly summoned shall obey the summons and attend for examination.

2. If, without good reason, a witness who has been duly summoned fails to appear before the General Court, the General Court may impose upon him a pecuniary penalty not exceeding EUR 5,000 and may order that a further summons be served on the witness at his own expense.

3. The same penalty may be imposed upon a witness who, without good reason, refuses to give evidence or to take the oath.

[6.351]

Article 96 Expert's report

1. The order appointing the expert shall define his task and set a time limit within which he is to submit his report.

2. After the expert has submitted his report and that report has been served on the parties, the General Court may order that the expert be examined, the parties having been given notice to attend. At the request of one of the parties or of his own motion, the President may put questions to the expert.

3. The other Judges and the Advocate General may do likewise.

4. Subject to the control of the President, questions may be put to the expert by the representatives of the parties.

5. Subject to the provisions of Article 97, the expert shall, after making his report, take the following oath before the General Court:

'I swear that I have conscientiously and impartially carried out my task.'

6. The General Court may, after hearing the main parties, exempt the expert from taking the oath.

[6.352]

Article 97 Witnesses' and experts' oath

1. The President shall instruct any person who is required to take an oath before the General Court, as witness or expert, to tell the truth or to carry out his task conscientiously and impartially, as the case may be, and shall warn him of the criminal liability provided for in his national law in the event of any breach of this duty.

2. Witnesses and experts shall take the oath either in accordance with Article 94(5) and Article 96(5) or in the manner laid down by their national law.

[6.353]

Article 98 Perjury by witnesses or experts

1. The General Court may decide to report to the competent authority referred to in the Rules supplementing the Rules of Procedure of the Court of Justice of the Member State whose courts have penal jurisdiction any case of perjury on the part of a witness or expert before the General Court.

2. The Registrar shall be responsible for communicating the decision of the General Court. The decision shall set out the facts and circumstances on which the report is based.

[6.354]

Article 99 Objection to a witness or expert

1. If one of the parties objects to a witness or an expert on the ground that he is not a competent or proper person to act as a witness or expert or for any other reason, or if a witness or expert refuses to give evidence or to take the oath, the matter shall be resolved by the General Court.

2. An objection to a witness or an expert shall be raised within two weeks after service of the order summoning the witness or appointing the expert; the statement of objection must set out the grounds of objection and indicate the nature of any evidence offered.

[6.355]

Article 100 Witnesses' and experts' costs

1. Where the General Court orders the examination of witnesses or an expert's report, it may request the main parties or one of them to lodge security for the witnesses' costs or the costs of the expert's report.

2. Witnesses and experts shall be entitled to reimbursement of their travel and subsistence expenses. The cashier of the General Court may make an advance payment towards these expenses.
3. Witnesses shall be entitled to compensation for loss of earnings, and experts to fees for their services. The cashier of the General Court shall pay witnesses and experts these sums after they have carried out their respective duties or tasks.

[6.356]
Article 101 Letters rogatory
1. The General Court may, on application by a main party or of its own motion, issue letters rogatory for the examination of witnesses or experts.
2. Letters rogatory shall be issued in the form of an order. The order shall contain the name, description and address of the witness or expert, set out the facts on which the witness or expert is to be examined, name the parties, their representatives, indicate their addresses and briefly describe the subject-matter of the proceedings.
3. The Registrar shall send the order to the competent authority named in the Rules supplementing the Rules of Procedure of the Court of Justice of the Member State in whose territory the witness or expert is to be examined. Where necessary, the order shall be accompanied by a translation into the official language or languages of the Member State to which it is addressed.
4. The authority named pursuant to paragraph 3 shall transmit the order to the judicial authority which is competent according to its national law.
5. The competent judicial authority shall give effect to the letters rogatory in accordance with its national law. After implementation the competent judicial authority shall transmit to the authority named pursuant to paragraph 3 the order embodying the letters rogatory, any documents arising from the implementation and a detailed statement of costs. These documents shall be sent to the Registrar.
6. The Registrar shall be responsible for the translation of the documents into the language of the case.
7. The General Court shall defray the expenses occasioned by the letters rogatory without prejudice to the right to charge them, where appropriate, to the main parties.

[6.357]
Article 102 Minutes of inquiry hearings
1. The Registrar shall draw up minutes of every inquiry hearing. The minutes shall be signed by the President and by the Registrar. They shall constitute an official record.
2. In the case of the examination of witnesses or experts, the minutes shall be signed by the President or by the Judge-Rapporteur responsible for conducting the examination of the witness or expert, and by the Registrar. Before the minutes are thus signed, the witness or expert must be given an opportunity to check the content of the minutes and to sign them.
3. The minutes shall be served on the parties.

SECTION 3 TREATMENT OF CONFIDENTIAL INFORMATION, ITEMS AND DOCUMENTS PRODUCED IN THE CONTEXT OF MEASURES OF INQUIRY

[6.358]
Article 103 Treatment of confidential information and material
1. Where it is necessary for the General Court to examine, on the basis of the matters of law and of fact relied on by a main party, the confidentiality, vis-à-vis the other main party, of certain information or material produced before the General Court following a measure of inquiry referred to in Article 91(b) that may be relevant in order for the General Court to rule in a case, that information or material shall not be communicated to that other party at the stage of such examination.
2. Where the General Court concludes in the examination provided for in paragraph 1 that certain information or material produced before it is relevant in order for it to rule in the case and is confidential vis-à-vis the other main party, it shall weigh that confidentiality against the requirements linked to the right to effective judicial protection, particularly observance of the adversarial principle.
3. After weighing up the matters referred to in paragraph 2, the General Court may decide to bring the confidential information or material to the attention of the other main party, making its disclosure subject, if necessary, to the giving of specific undertakings, or it may decide not to communicate such information or material, specifying, by reasoned order, the procedures enabling the other main party, to the greatest extent possible, to make his views known, including ordering the production of a non-confidential version or a non-confidential summary of the information or material, containing the essential content thereof.
4. The procedural regime in this Article shall not apply to the cases referred to in Article 105.

[6.359]
Article 104 Documents to which access has been denied by an institution
Where, following a measure of inquiry referred to in Article 91(c), a document to which access has been denied by an institution has been produced before the General Court in proceedings relating to the legality of that denial, that document shall not be communicated to the other parties.

CHAPTER 7 INFORMATION OR MATERIAL PERTAINING TO THE SECURITY OF THE UNION OR THAT OF ONE OR MORE OF ITS MEMBER STATES OR TO THE CONDUCT OF THEIR INTERNATIONAL RELATIONS

[6.360]
Article 105 Treatment of information or material pertaining to the security of the Union or that of one or more of its Member States or to the conduct of their international relations
1. Where, contrary to the adversarial principle set out in Article 64 under which all information and material must be fully communicated between the parties, a main party intends to base his claims on certain information or material but submits that its communication would harm the security of the Union or that of one or more of its Member States or

the conduct of their international relations, he shall produce that information or material by a separate document. The information or material thus produced shall be accompanied by an application for confidential treatment thereof, setting out the overriding reasons which, to the extent strictly required by the exigencies of the situation, justify the confidentiality of that information or material being preserved and which militate against its communication to the other main party. The application for confidential treatment shall also be submitted by a separate document and shall not contain anything which is confidential. Where the information or material in respect of which confidential treatment is sought has been transmitted to the main party by one or more Member States, the overriding reasons put forward by the main party to justify the confidential treatment of that information or material may include those provided by the Member State(s) concerned.

2. The production of information or material the confidential nature of which is based on the overriding reasons referred to in paragraph 1 may be requested by the General Court in the form of a measure of inquiry. Formal note shall be taken of any refusal. By way of derogation from Article 103, the procedural regime applicable to such information or material produced following a measure of inquiry shall be that of the present Article.

3. While the information or material produced by a main party in accordance with paragraph 1 or 2 is being examined as to its relevance to the General Court's ruling in the case and as to its confidential nature vis-à-vis the other main party, that information or material shall not be communicated to the other main party.

4. Where the General Court decides, after the examination provided for in paragraph 3, that the information or material produced before it is relevant in order for it to rule in the case and is not confidential for the purposes of the proceedings before the General Court, it shall ask the party concerned to authorise the communication of that information or material to the other main party. If the first party objects to such communication within a period prescribed by the President, or fails to reply by the end of that period, that information or material shall not be taken into account in the determination of the case and shall be returned to that party.

5. Where the General Court decides, after the examination provided for in paragraph 3, that certain information or material produced before it is relevant in order for it to rule in the case and is confidential vis-à-vis the other main party, it shall not communicate that information or material to that main party. It shall then weigh the requirements linked to the right to effective judicial protection, particularly observance of the adversarial principle, against the requirements flowing from the security of the Union or of one or more of its Member States or the conduct of their international relations.

6. After weighing up the matters referred to in paragraph 5, the General Court shall make a reasoned order specifying the procedures to be adopted to accommodate the requirements referred to in paragraph 5, such as the production by the party concerned, for subsequent communication to the other main party, of a non-confidential version or a non-confidential summary of the information or material, containing the essential content thereof and enabling the other main party, to the greatest extent possible, to make its views known.

7. The information or material that is confidential vis-à-vis the other main party may be withdrawn, wholly or in part, by the main party who produced it in accordance with paragraph 1 or 2, within two weeks after service of the decision taken pursuant to paragraph 5. The information or material withdrawn shall not be taken into account in the determination of the case and shall be returned to the main party concerned.

8. Where the General Court considers that information or material which, owing to its confidential nature, has not been communicated to the other main party in accordance with the procedures referred to in paragraph 6 is essential in order for it to rule in the case, it may, by way of derogation from Article 64 and confining itself to what is strictly necessary, base its judgment on such information or material. When assessing that information or material, the General Court shall take account of the fact that a main party has not been able to make his views on it known.

9. The General Court shall ensure that confidential matters contained in the information or material produced by a main party in accordance with paragraph 1 or 2 which have not been communicated to the other main party are not disclosed in the order made pursuant to paragraph 6 or in the decision which closes the proceedings.

[10. The information or material referred to in paragraph 5, which has not been withdrawn pursuant to paragraph 7 by the main party that produced it, shall be returned to the party concerned as soon as the period referred to in the first paragraph of Article 56 of the Statute has expired, unless, within that period, an appeal has been brought against the decision of the General Court. Where such an appeal is brought, the abovementioned information or material shall be made available to the Court of Justice on the conditions laid down in the decision referred to in paragraph 11.]

11. The General Court shall determine, by decision, the security rules for protecting the information or material produced in accordance with paragraph 1 or paragraph 2, as the case may be. That decision shall be published in the *Official Journal of the European Union*.

NOTES

Para 10: substituted by the Amendment to the Rules of Procedure of the General Court, Article 1 (OJ L217, 12.8.2016, p 72).

CHAPTER 8 ORAL PART OF THE PROCEDURE

[6.361]

Article 106 Oral part of the procedure

1. The procedure before the General Court shall include, in the oral part, a hearing arranged either of the General Court's own motion or at the request of a main party.

2. Any request for a hearing made by a main party must state the reasons for which that party wishes to be heard. It must be submitted within three weeks after service on the parties of notification of the close of the written part of the procedure. That time limit may be extended by the President.

3. If there is no request as referred to in paragraph 2, the General Court may, if it considers that it has sufficient information available to it from the material in the file, decide to rule on the action without an oral part of the procedure. In that case, it may nevertheless later decide to open the oral part of the procedure.

[6.362]

Article 107 Date of the hearing

1. If the General Court decides to open the oral part of the procedure, the President shall fix the date of the hearing.

2. The President may, in exceptional circumstances, of his own motion or at the reasoned request of a main party, adjourn the hearing to another date.

[6.363]
Article 108 Absence of the parties from the hearing

1. Where a party informs the General Court that he will not be present at the hearing or where the General Court finds at the hearing that a party who has been duly given notice to attend is absent without excuse, the hearing shall proceed in the absence of the party concerned.
2. Where the main parties indicate to the General Court that they will not be present at the hearing, the President shall decide whether the oral part of the procedure may be closed.

[6.364]
Article 109 Cases heard in camera

1. After hearing the parties, the General Court may, in accordance with Article 31 of the Statute, decide to hear a case *in camera.*
2. The request by a party for a case to be heard *in camera* must include reasons and specify whether it concerns all or part of the hearing.
3. The oral proceedings in cases heard *in camera* shall not be published.

[6.365]
Article 110 Conduct of the hearing

1. The oral proceedings shall be opened and directed by the President, who shall be responsible for the proper conduct of the hearing.
2. A party may address the General Court only through his representative.
3. The members of the formation of the Court and the Advocate General may in the course of the hearing put questions to the representatives of the parties.
[4. In cases brought pursuant to Article 270 TFEU, the members of the formation of the Court and the Advocate General may in the course of the hearing invite the parties themselves to express their views on certain aspects of the case.]

NOTES

Para 4: added by the Amendment to the Rules of Procedure of the General Court, Article 1(8) (OJ L217, 12.8.2016, p 73).

[6.366]
Article 111 Close of the oral part of the procedure

Where an Advocate General has not been designated in a case, the President shall declare the oral part of the procedure closed at the end of the hearing.

[6.367]
Article 112 Delivery of the Opinion of the Advocate General

1. Where an Advocate General has been designated in a case and delivers his Opinion in writing, he shall lodge it at the Registry, which shall communicate it to the parties.
2. The President shall declare the oral part of the procedure closed after the delivery, orally or in writing, of the Opinion of the Advocate General.

[6.368]
Article 113 Reopening of the oral part of the procedure

1. The General Court shall order the reopening of the oral part of the procedure when the conditions set out in Article 23(3) or Article 24(3) are satisfied.
2. The General Court may order the reopening of the oral part of the procedure:
(a) if it considers that it lacks sufficient information;
(b) where the case must be decided on the basis of an argument which has not been debated between the parties;
(c) where requested by a main party who is relying on facts which are of such a nature as to be a decisive factor for the decision of the General Court but which it was unable to put forward before the oral part of the procedure was closed.

[6.369]
Article 114 Minutes of the hearing

1. The Registrar shall draw up minutes of every hearing. The minutes shall be signed by the President and by the Registrar. They shall constitute an official record.
2. The minutes shall be served on the parties.

[6.370]
Article 115 Recording of the hearing

The President of the General Court may, on a duly substantiated request, authorise a party who has participated in the written part or the oral part of the proceedings to listen, on the General Court's premises, to the sound recording of the hearing in the language used by the speakers during that hearing.

CHAPTER 9 JUDGMENTS AND ORDERS

[6.371]
Article 116 Date of delivery of a judgment

The parties shall be informed of the date of delivery of a judgment.

[6.372]
Article 117 Content of a judgment

A judgment shall contain:

(a) a statement that it is the judgment of the General Court;
(b) an indication as to the formation of the Court;
(c) the date of delivery;
(d) the names of the President and of the Judges who took part in the deliberations, with an indication as to the name of the Judge-Rapporteur;
(e) the name of the Advocate General, if designated;
(f) the name of the Registrar;
(g) a description of the parties;
(h) the names of their representatives;
(i) a statement of the forms of order sought by the parties;
(j) where applicable, the date of the hearing;
(k) a statement, where appropriate, that the Advocate General has been heard and, where applicable, the date of his Opinion;
(l) a summary of the facts;
(m) the grounds for the decision;
(n) the operative part of the judgment, including the decision as to costs.

[6.373]
Article 118 Delivery and service of the judgment
1. The judgment shall be delivered in open court.
2. The original of the judgment, signed by the President, by the Judges who took part in the deliberations and by the Registrar, shall be sealed and deposited at the Registry. A copy of the judgment shall be served on each of the parties.

[6.374]
Article 119 Content of an order
Any order from which an appeal may lie under Article 56 or Article 57 of the Statute shall contain:
(a) a statement that it is the order of the General Court, the President or the Judge hearing applications for interim measures, as the case may be;
(b) where applicable, an indication as to the formation of the Court;
(c) the date of its adoption;
(d) an indication as to the legal basis of the order;
(e) the names of the President and, where applicable, the Judges who took part in the deliberations, with an indication as to the name of the Judge-Rapporteur;
(f) the name of the Advocate General, if designated;
(g) the name of the Registrar;
(h) a description of the parties;
(i) the names of their representatives;
(j) a statement of the forms of order sought by the parties;
(k) a statement, where appropriate, that the Advocate General has been heard;
(l) a summary of the facts;
(m) the grounds for the decision;
(n) the operative part of the order, including, where appropriate, the decision as to costs.

[6.375]
Article 120 Signature and service of the order
The original of every order, signed by the President and by the Registrar, shall be sealed and deposited at the Registry. A copy of the order shall be served on each of the parties and, if necessary, on the Court of Justice . . .

NOTES
Words omitted repealed by the Amendment to the Rules of Procedure of the General Court, Article 1(9) (OJ L217, 12.8.2016, p 73).

[6.376]
Article 121 Binding nature of judgments and orders
1. Subject to the provisions of Article 60 of the Statute, a judgment shall be binding from the date of its delivery.
2. Subject to the provisions of Article 60 of the Statute, an order shall be binding from the date of its service.

[6.377]
Article 122 Publication in the Official Journal of the European Union
A notice containing the date and the operative part of the judgment or order of the General Court which closes the proceedings shall be published in the *Official Journal of the European Union*, save in the case of decisions adopted before the application has been served on the defendant.

CHAPTER 10 JUDGMENTS BY DEFAULT

[6.378]
Article 123 Judgments by default
1. Where the General Court finds that a defendant on whom an application initiating proceedings has been duly served has failed to respond to the application in the proper form or within the time limit prescribed in Article 81, without prejudice to the application of the provisions of the second paragraph of Article 45 of the Statute, the applicant may, within a time limit prescribed by the President, apply to the General Court for judgment by default.
2. A defendant in default shall not intervene in the default procedure and, with the exception of the decision which closes the proceedings, no procedural document shall be served on him.

3. The General Court shall give judgment in favour of the applicant in the judgment by default, unless it is clear that the General Court has no jurisdiction to hear and determine the action or that the action is manifestly inadmissible or manifestly lacking any foundation in law.
4. A judgment by default shall be enforceable. The General Court may, however, grant a stay of execution until it has given its decision on any application under Article 166 to set aside the judgment, or it may make execution subject to the provision of security of an amount and nature to be fixed in the light of the circumstances. This security shall be released if no such application is made or if the application fails.

CHAPTER 11 AMICABLE SETTLEMENT AND DISCONTINUANCE

[6.379]
Article 124 Amicable settlement
1. [If, before the General Court has given its decision, the main parties reach an out-of-court settlement of their dispute] and inform the General Court of the abandonment of their claims, the President shall order the case to be removed from the register and shall give a decision as to costs in accordance with Articles 136 and 138, having regard to any proposals made by the parties on the matter.
2. This provision shall not apply to proceedings under Articles 263 TFEU and 265 TFEU.

NOTES

Para 1: words in square brackets substituted by the Amendment to the Rules of Procedure of the General Court, Article 1(10) (OJ L217, 12.8.2016, p 73).

[6.380]
Article 125 Discontinuance
If the applicant informs the General Court in writing or at the hearing that he wishes to discontinue the proceedings, the President shall order the case to be removed from the register and shall give a decision as to costs in accordance with Articles 136 and 138.

[CHAPTER 11A PROCEDURE IN RELATION TO AMICABLE SETTLEMENTS INITIATED BY THE GENERAL COURT IN CASES BROUGHT PURSUANT TO ARTICLE 270 TFEU

[6.381]
Article 125a Procedure
1. The General Court may, at all stages of the procedure, examine the possibilities of an amicable settlement of all or part of the dispute between the main parties.
2. The General Court shall instruct the Judge-Rapporteur, assisted by the Registrar, to seek the amicable settlement of a dispute.
3. The Judge-Rapporteur may propose one or more solutions capable of putting an end to the dispute, adopt appropriate measures with a view to facilitating its amicable settlement and implement the measures which he has adopted to that end. He may, in particular:
(a) invite the main parties to supply information or particulars;
(b) invite the main parties to produce documents;
(c) invite to meetings the main parties' representatives, the main parties themselves or any official or servant of the institution empowered to negotiate an agreement;
(d) on the occasion of the meetings referred to in point (c), have contact with each of the main parties separately, if they consent to that.
4. Paragraphs 1 to 3 shall apply to proceedings for interim measures also.]

NOTES

Chapter 11a (Articles 125a–125d) inserted by the Amendment to the Rules of Procedure of the General Court, Article 1(11) (OJ L217, 12.8.2016, p 73).

[6.382]
[Article 125b Effect of the main parties' agreement
1. Where the main parties come to an agreement before the Judge-Rapporteur on a solution which brings the dispute to an end, they may request that the terms of that agreement be recorded in a document signed by the Judge-Rapporteur and by the Registrar. That document shall be served on the main parties and shall constitute an official record.
2. The case shall be removed from the register by reasoned order of the President. At the request of a main party with the agreement of the other main party, the terms of the agreement reached by the main parties shall be recorded in the order removing the case from the register.
3. The President shall give a decision as to costs in accordance with the agreement or, failing that, at his discretion. Where appropriate, he shall give a decision as to the costs of an intervener in accordance with Article 138.]

NOTES

Inserted as noted to Article 125a at **[6.381]**.

[6.383]
[Article 125c Specific register and file
1. Material produced in the context of the amicable settlement procedure as provided for in Article 125a:
— shall be entered in a specific register which shall not be subject to the rules laid down in Articles 36 and 37,
— shall be placed in a file separate from the case file.
2. Material produced in the context of the amicable settlement procedure as provided for in Article 125a shall be brought to the attention of the main parties, with the exception of material which either of them has communicated to the Judge-Rapporteur in the separate meetings provided for in Article 125a(3)(d).

3. The main parties may have access to the material in the file separate from the case file as referred to in paragraph 1, with the exception of material which either of the main parties has communicated to the Judge-Rapporteur in the separate meetings provided for in Article 125a(3)(d).

4. An intervener may not have access to material in the file separate from the case file as referred to in paragraph 1.

5. The parties may examine the specific register referred to in paragraph 1 at the Registry.]

NOTES

Inserted as noted to Article 125a at **[6.381]**.

[6.384]

[Article 125d Amicable settlement and judicial proceedings

No opinion expressed, suggestion made, proposal put forward, concession made or document drawn up for the purposes of the amicable settlement may be relied upon as evidence by the General Court or the main parties in the judicial proceedings.]

NOTES

Inserted as noted to Article 125a at **[6.381]**.

CHAPTER 12 ACTIONS AND ISSUES DETERMINED BY ORDER

[6.385]

Article 126 Action manifestly bound to fail

Where it is clear that the General Court has no jurisdiction to hear and determine an action or where the action is manifestly inadmissible or manifestly lacking any foundation in law, the General Court may, on a proposal from the Judge-Rapporteur, at any time decide to give a decision by reasoned order without taking further steps in the proceedings.

[6.386]

Article 127 [Referral of a case to the Court of Justice]

Decisions referring an action in the circumstances specified in the second paragraph of Article 54 of the Statute . . . shall be made by the General Court by reasoned order on a proposal from the Judge-Rapporteur.

NOTES

Article heading substituted, and words omitted repealed, by the Amendment to the Rules of Procedure of the General Court, Article 1(12) (OJ L217, 12.8.2016, p 73).

[6.387]

Article 128 Declining of jurisdiction

Decisions declining jurisdiction in the circumstances specified in the third paragraph of Article 54 of the Statute shall be made by the General Court by reasoned order on a proposal from the Judge-Rapporteur.

[6.388]

Article 129 Absolute bar to proceeding with a case

On a proposal from the Judge-Rapporteur, the General Court may at any time of its own motion, after hearing the main parties, decide to rule by reasoned order on whether there exists any absolute bar to proceeding with a case.

[6.389]

Article 130 Preliminary objections and issues

1. A defendant applying to the General Court for a decision on inadmissibility or lack of competence without going to the substance of the case shall submit the application by a separate document within the time limit referred to in Article 81.

2. A party applying to the General Court for a declaration that the action has become devoid of purpose and that there is no longer any need to adjudicate on it or for a decision on another preliminary issue shall submit the application by a separate document.

3. The applications referred to in paragraphs 1 and 2 must state the pleas of law and arguments relied on and the form of order sought; any supporting material must be annexed to the applications.

4. As soon as the application referred to in paragraph 1 has been submitted, the President shall prescribe a time limit within which the applicant in the action may submit in writing his pleas in law and the form of order which he seeks.

5. As soon as the application referred to in paragraph 2 has been submitted, the President shall prescribe a time limit within which the other parties may submit in writing their observations on that application.

6. The General Court may decide to open the oral part of the procedure in respect of the applications referred to in paragraphs 1 and 2. Article 106 shall not apply.

7. The General Court shall decide on the application as soon as possible or, where special circumstances so justify, reserve its decision until it rules on the substance of the case. [It shall refer the case to the Court of Justice if the case falls within the latter's jurisdiction].

8. If the General Court refuses the application or reserves its decision, the President shall prescribe new time limits for further steps in the proceedings.

NOTES

Para 7: words in square brackets substituted by the Amendment to the Rules of Procedure of the General Court, Article 1(13) (OJ L217, 12.8.2016, p 73).

[6.390]
Article 131 Cases that, of the General Court's own motion, do not proceed to judgment
1. If the General Court declares that the action has become devoid of purpose and that there is no longer any need to adjudicate on it, it may at any time, of its own motion, on a proposal from the Judge-Rapporteur and after hearing the parties, decide to rule by reasoned order.
2. If the applicant ceases to reply to the General Court's requests, the General Court may, on a proposal from the Judge-Rapporteur and after hearing the parties, declare of its own motion, by reasoned order, that there is no longer any need to adjudicate.

[6.391]
Article 132 Actions that are manifestly well founded
Where the Court of Justice or the General Court has already ruled on one or more questions of law identical to those raised by the pleas in law of the action and the General Court finds that the facts have been established, it may, after the written part of the procedure has been closed, on a proposal from the Judge-Rapporteur and after hearing the parties, decide by reasoned order in which reference is made to the relevant case-law to declare the action manifestly well founded.

CHAPTER 13 COSTS

[6.392]
Article 133 Decision as to costs
A decision as to costs shall be given in the judgment or order which closes the proceedings.

[6.393]
Article 134 General rules as to allocation of costs
1. The unsuccessful party shall be ordered to pay the costs if they have been applied for in the successful party's pleadings.
2. Where there is more than one unsuccessful party the General Court shall decide how the costs are to be shared.
3. Where each party succeeds on some and fails on other heads, the parties shall bear their own costs. However, if it appears justified in the circumstances of the case, the General Court may order that one party, in addition to bearing his own costs, pay a proportion of the costs of the other party.

[6.394]
Article 135 Equity and unreasonable or vexatious costs
1. . . . if equity so requires, the General Court may decide that an unsuccessful party is to pay only a proportion of the costs of the other party in addition to bearing his own, or even that he is not to be ordered to pay any.
2. The General Court may order a party, even if successful, to pay some or all of the costs, if this appears justified by the conduct of that party, including before the proceedings were brought, especially if he has made the opposite party incur costs which the General Court holds to be unreasonable or vexatious.

NOTES
Para 1: word omitted repealed by the Amendment to the Rules of Procedure of the General Court, Article 1(14) (OJ L217, 12.8.2016, p 73).

[6.395]
Article 136 Costs in the event of discontinuance or withdrawal
1. A party who discontinues or withdraws from proceedings shall be ordered to pay the costs if they have been applied for in the other party's observations on the discontinuance.
2. However, at the request of the party who discontinues or withdraws from proceedings, the costs shall be borne by the other party if this appears justified by the conduct of that party.
3. Where the parties have come to an agreement on costs, the decision as to costs shall be in accordance with that agreement.
4. If costs are not claimed, the parties shall bear their own costs.

[6.396]
Article 137 Costs where a case does not proceed to judgment
Where a case does not proceed to judgment, the costs shall be in the discretion of the General Court.

[6.397]
Article 138 Costs of interveners
1. The Member States and institutions which have intervened in the proceedings shall bear their own costs.
2. The States other than the Member States, which are parties to the EEA Agreement, and also the EFTA Surveillance Authority, shall similarly bear their own costs if they have intervened in the proceedings.
3. The General Court may order an intervener other than those referred to in paragraphs 1 and 2 to bear his own costs.

[6.398]
Article 139 Costs of proceedings
Proceedings before the General Court shall be free of charge, except that:
(a) where a party has caused the General Court to incur avoidable costs, in particular where the action is manifestly an abuse of process, the General Court may order that party to refund them;
(b) where copying or translation work is carried out at the request of a party, the cost shall, in so far as the Registrar considers it excessive, be paid for by that party on the Registry's scale of charges referred to in Article 37;

(c) in the event of any repeated failure to comply with the requirements of these Rules or of the practice rules referred to in Article 224, requiring regularisation to be sought, the costs involved in the requisite processing thereof by the General Court shall, at the request of the Registrar, be paid for by the party concerned on the Registry's scale of charges referred to in Article 37.

[6.399]
Article 140 Recoverable costs

Without prejudice to Article 139, the following shall be regarded as recoverable costs:

(a) sums payable to witnesses and experts under Article 100;
(b) expenses necessarily incurred by the parties for the purpose of the proceedings, in particular the travel and subsistence expenses and the remuneration of agents, advisers or lawyers.

[6.400]
Article 141 Procedure for payment

1. Sums due from the cashier of the General Court and from its debtors shall be paid in euros.
2. Where costs to be recovered have been incurred in a currency other than the euro or where the steps in respect of which payment is due were taken in a country of which the euro is not the currency, the conversion shall be effected at the European Central Bank's official rates of exchange on the day of payment.

CHAPTER 14 INTERVENTION

[6.401]
Article 142 Object and effects of the intervention

1. The intervention shall be limited to supporting, in whole or in part, the form of order sought by one of the main parties. It shall not confer the same procedural rights as those conferred on the main parties and, in particular, shall not give rise to any right to request that a hearing be held.
2. The intervention shall be ancillary to the main proceedings. It shall become devoid of purpose if the case is removed from the register of the General Court as a result of a main party's discontinuance or withdrawal from the proceedings or of an agreement between the main parties, or where the application is declared inadmissible.
3. The intervener must accept the case as he finds it at the time of his intervention.

[6.402]
Article 143 Application to intervene

1. An application to intervene must be submitted within six weeks of the publication of the notice referred to in Article 79.
2. The application to intervene shall contain:
(a) a description of the case;
(b) a description of the main parties;
(c) the name and address of the applicant for leave to intervene;
(d) particulars of the status and address of the representative of the applicant for leave to intervene;
(e) the form of order sought in support of which the applicant for leave to intervene is applying for leave to intervene;
(f) a statement of the circumstances establishing the right to intervene, where the application is submitted pursuant to the second or third paragraph of Article 40 of the Statute.
3. The applicant for leave to intervene shall be represented in accordance with Article 19 of the Statute.
[4. Article 78(4) to (6) and Article 139 shall apply to the application to intervene.]

NOTES

Para 4: substituted by the Amendments to the Rules of Procedure of the General Court, Article 1(13) (OJ L240, 25.9.2018, p 68).

[6.403]
Article 144 Decision on applications to intervene

1. The application to intervene shall be served on the main parties.
2. The President shall give the main parties an opportunity to submit their written or oral observations on the application to intervene and to apply, if necessary, for certain confidential information in the file in the case not to be communicated to an intervener.
3. Where the defendant lodges a plea of inadmissibility or of lack of competence, as provided in Article 130(1), a decision on the application to intervene shall not be given until after the plea has been rejected or the decision on the plea reserved.
4. Where the application is submitted pursuant to the first paragraph of Article 40 of the Statute and the main parties have not identified information in the file in the case that is confidential and which they claim would be prejudicial to them if communicated to the intervener, the intervention shall be allowed by decision of the President.
5. In any other case the President shall decide on the application to intervene as soon as possible, by order, and, where applicable, on the communication to the intervener of information which it is claimed is confidential.
6. If the application to intervene is refused, the order referred to in paragraph 5 must state the reasons on which it is based and include a decision as to the costs relating to the application to intervene, including the costs of the applicant for leave to intervene, pursuant to Articles 134 and 135.
7. If the application to intervene is granted, the intervener shall receive a copy of every procedural document served on the main parties, save, where applicable, for the confidential information excluded from such communication pursuant to paragraph 5.
8. In the event that the application to intervene is withdrawn, the President shall order that the applicant for leave to intervene be removed from the case and shall give a decision as to costs, including the costs of the applicant for leave to intervene, pursuant to Article 136.

9. In the event that the intervention is withdrawn, the President shall order that the intervener be removed from the case and shall give a decision as to costs pursuant to Articles 136 and 138. 10.If the proceedings in the main case are concluded before the application to intervene has been decided, the applicant for leave to intervene and the main parties shall each bear their own costs relating to the application to intervene. A copy of the order closing the proceedings shall be transmitted to the applicant for leave to intervene.

[6.404]
Article 145 Submission of statements
1. The intervener may submit a statement in intervention within the time limit prescribed by the President.
2. The statement in intervention shall contain:
 (a) the form of order sought by the intervener in support, in whole or in part, of the form of order sought by one of the main parties;
 (b) the pleas in law and arguments relied on by the intervener;
 (c) where appropriate, any evidence produced or offered.
3. After the statement in intervention has been lodged, the President shall prescribe a time limit within which the main parties may reply to that statement.

CHAPTER 15 LEGAL AID

[6.405]
Article 146 General
1. Any person who, because of his financial situation, is wholly or partly unable to meet the costs of the proceedings shall be entitled to legal aid.
2. Legal aid shall be refused if it is clear that the General Court has no jurisdiction to hear and determine the action in respect of which the application for legal aid is made or if that action appears to be manifestly inadmissible or manifestly lacking any foundation in law.

[6.406]
Article 147 Application for legal aid
1. An application for legal aid may be made before the action has been brought or while it is pending.
2. The application for legal aid must be made using a form which is published in the Official Journal of the European Union and available on the internet site of the Court of Justice of the European Union. . . . An application for legal aid submitted without the application form will not be taken into consideration.
3. The application for legal aid must be accompanied by all information and supporting documents making it possible to assess the applicant's financial situation, such as a certificate issued by a competent national authority attesting to his financial situation.
4. If the application for legal aid is made before the action has been brought, the applicant must briefly state the subject-matter of the proposed action, the facts of the case and the arguments in support of the action. The application must be accompanied by supporting documents in that regard.
5. Where applicable, the application for legal aid shall be accompanied by the documents referred to in Article 51(2) and (3) and [Article 78(4)]. In that case Article 51(4) and [Article 78(6)] shall apply.
[6. Where the applicant for legal aid is not represented by a lawyer, the original of the application for legal aid shall be lodged at the Registry in paper form. The original of the application for legal aid must bear the handwritten signature of the applicant for legal aid.]
7. The introduction of an application for legal aid shall, for the person who made it, suspend the time limit prescribed for the bringing of an action until the date of service of the order making a decision on that application or, in the cases referred to in Article 148(6), of the order designating the lawyer instructed to represent the applicant.

NOTES

Para 2: words omitted repealed by the Amendments to the Rules of Procedure of the General Court, Article 1(14)(a) (OJ L240, 25.9.2018, p 68).

Para 5: words in square brackets substituted by the Amendment to the Rules of Procedure of the General Court, Article 1(16) (OJ L217, 12.8.2016, p 73).

Para 6: substituted by the Amendments to the Rules of Procedure of the General Court, Article 1(14)(b) (OJ L240, 25.9.2018, p 68).

[6.407]
Article 148 Decision on the application for legal aid
1. Before giving his decision on an application for legal aid, the President shall prescribe a time limit within which the other main party may submit his written observations unless it is already apparent from the information produced that the conditions laid down in Article 146(1) have not been satisfied or that those laid down in Article 146(2) have been satisfied.
2. The decision on the application for legal aid shall be taken by the President by way of an order.
3. An order refusing legal aid shall state the reasons on which it is based.
4. Any order granting legal aid may designate a lawyer to represent the person concerned if that lawyer has been proposed by the applicant in the application for legal aid and has agreed to represent the applicant before the General Court.
5. If the person concerned has not indicated his choice of lawyer in the application for legal aid or following an order granting legal aid or if his choice is unacceptable, the Registrar shall send a copy of the order granting legal aid and a copy of the application to the competent authority of the Member State concerned mentioned in the Rules supplementing the Rules of Procedure of the Court of Justice. If the person concerned is not resident in the Union, the Registrar shall send a copy of the order granting legal aid and a copy of the application to the competent authority of the State in which the Court of Justice of the European Union has its seat.

6. Without prejudice to paragraph 4, the lawyer instructed to represent the applicant shall be designated by way of an order, having regard to the suggestions made by the person concerned or to the suggestions made by the authority referred to in paragraph 5, as the case may be.
7. An order granting legal aid may specify the amount to be paid to the lawyer instructed to represent the person concerned or fix a limit which the lawyer's disbursements and fees may not, in principle, exceed. It may provide for a contribution to be made by the person concerned to the costs referred to in Article 149(1), having regard to his financial situation.
8. No appeal shall lie from orders made under this Article.
[9. Where the applicant for legal aid is not represented by a lawyer, a copy of the document to be served shall be served on him by registered post with a form for acknowledgement of receipt or by delivery of the copy against receipt. Service on other parties shall be effected as provided for in Article 80(1).]

NOTES

Para 9: substituted by the Amendments to the Rules of Procedure of the General Court, Article 1(15) (OJ L240, 25.9.2018, p 68).

[6.408]
Article 149 Advances and responsibility for costs
1. Where legal aid is granted, the cashier of the General Court shall be responsible, where applicable within the limits fixed, for costs involved in the assistance and representation of the applicant before the General Court. At the request of the lawyer designated in accordance with Article 148, the President may decide that an amount by way of advance should be paid to that lawyer.
2. Where, by virtue of the decision closing the proceedings, the recipient of legal aid has to bear his own costs, the President shall fix the lawyer's disbursements and fees which are to be paid by the cashier of the General Court by way of a reasoned order from which no appeal shall lie.
3. Where, in the decision closing the proceedings, the General Court has ordered another party to pay the costs of the recipient of legal aid, that other party shall be required to refund to the cashier of the General Court any sums advanced by way of aid.
4. The Registrar shall take steps to obtain the recovery of the sums referred to in paragraph 3 from the party ordered to pay them.
5. Where the recipient of the legal aid is unsuccessful, the General Court may, in ruling as to costs in the decision closing the proceedings, if equity so requires, order that one or more parties should bear their own costs or that those costs should be borne, in whole or in part, by the cashier of the General Court by way of legal aid.

[6.409]
Article 150 Withdrawal of legal aid
1. If the circumstances which led to the grant of legal aid alter during the proceedings, the President may, of his own motion or on request, withdraw that legal aid, having heard the person concerned.
2. An order withdrawing legal aid shall contain a statement of reasons and no appeal shall lie from it.

CHAPTER 16 URGENT PROCEDURES

SECTION 1 EXPEDITED PROCEDURE

[6.410]
Article 151 Decision relating to the expedited procedure
1. The General Court may, at the request of the applicant or the defendant, after hearing the other main party, decide, having regard to the particular urgency and the circumstances of the case, to adjudicate under an expedited procedure. That decision shall be taken as soon as possible.
2. On a proposal from the Judge-Rapporteur, the General Court may, in exceptional circumstances, of its own motion and after hearing the main parties, decide to adjudicate under an expedited procedure.
3. The decision of the General Court to adjudicate under an expedited procedure may prescribe conditions as to the volume and presentation of the pleadings of the main parties; the subsequent conduct of the proceedings or as to the pleas in law and arguments on which the General Court will be called upon to decide.
4. If one of the main parties does not comply with any one of the conditions referred to in paragraph 3, the decision to adjudicate under an expedited procedure may be revoked. The proceedings shall then continue in accordance with the ordinary procedure.

[6.411]
Article 152 Request for an expedited procedure
1. A request for an expedited procedure shall be made by a separate document lodged at the same time as the application initiating the proceedings or the defence, and shall contain a statement of reasons specifying the particular urgency of the case and any other relevant circumstances.
2. The request for an expedited procedure may state that certain pleas in law or arguments or certain passages of the application initiating the proceedings or the defence are raised only in the event that the case is not decided under an expedited procedure, in particular by enclosing with the request an abridged version of the application initiating the proceedings and a schedule of annexes and only the annexes which are to be taken into consideration if the case is decided under an expedited procedure.

[6.412]
Article 153 Priority treatment
By way of derogation from Article 67(1), cases on which the General Court has decided to adjudicate under an expedited procedure shall be given priority.

[6.413]
Article 154 Written part of the procedure

1. By way of derogation from Article 81(1), where the applicant has requested that the case be decided under an expedited procedure, the period prescribed for the lodging of the defence shall be one month. That period may be extended pursuant to Article 81(3).
2. If the General Court decides not to allow a request for an expedited procedure, the defendant shall be granted an additional period of one month in order to lodge or, as the case may be, supplement the defence.
3. Under the expedited procedure, the pleadings referred to in Articles 83(1) and 145(1) and (3) may be lodged only if the General Court, by way of measures of organisation of procedure adopted in accordance with Articles 88 to 90, so allows.
4. Under the expedited procedure, the President shall take account, when setting the time limits provided for by these Rules, of the particular urgency in adjudicating on the action.

[6.414]
Article 155 Oral part of the procedure

1. Where the General Court has approved an expedited procedure, it shall decide to open the oral part of the procedure as soon as possible after the presentation of the preliminary report by the Judge-Rapporteur. The General Court may nevertheless decide to rule without an oral part of the procedure where the main parties decide not to participate in a hearing and the General Court considers that it has sufficient information available to it from the material in the file in the case.
2. Without prejudice to Articles 84 and 85, the main parties may supplement their arguments and offer further evidence during the oral part of the procedure, provided that the delay in submission is justified.

SECTION 2 SUSPENSION OF OPERATION OR ENFORCEMENT AND OTHER INTERIM MEASURES

[6.415]
Article 156 Application for suspension or other interim measures

1. An application to suspend the operation of any measure adopted by an institution, made pursuant to Article 278 TFEU or Article 157 TEAEC, shall be admissible only if the applicant has challenged that measure in an action before the General Court.
2. An application for the adoption of one of the other interim measures referred to in Article 279 TFEU shall be admissible only if it is made by a main party to a case before the General Court and relates to that case.
[3. In cases brought pursuant to Article 270 TFEU, an application of a kind referred to in paragraphs 1 and 2 may be presented as soon as the complaint under Article 90(2) of the Staff Regulations has been submitted, on the conditions laid down in Article 91(4) of those Regulations.]
[4]. An application of a kind referred to in paragraphs 1 and 2 shall state the subject-matter of the proceedings, the circumstances giving rise to urgency and the pleas of fact and law establishing a prima facie case for the interim measure applied for. It shall contain all the evidence and offers of evidence available to justify the grant of interim measures.
[5]. The application shall be made by a separate document and in accordance with the provisions of [Articles 76 and 78].

NOTES

The original paras 3 and 4 were renumbered as paras 4 and 5, and a new para 3 was inserted, by the Amendment to the Rules of Procedure of the General Court, Article 1(17) (OJ L217, 12.8.2016, p 73).

Para 5: words in square brackets substituted by the Amendments to the Rules of Procedure of the General Court, Article 1(16) (OJ L240, 25.9.2018, p 68).

[6.416]
Article 157 Procedure

1. The application shall be served on the opposite party, and the President of the General Court shall prescribe a short time limit within which that party may submit written or oral observations.
2. The President of the General Court may grant the application even before the observations of the opposite party have been submitted. This decision may be varied or cancelled even without any application being made by any party.
3. The President of the General Court shall prescribe, where appropriate, measures of organisation of procedure and measures of inquiry.
4. In the event that the President of the General Court is prevented from acting, Articles 11 and 12 shall apply.

[6.417]
Article 158 Decision on the application

1. The President of the General Court shall decide on the application by way of a reasoned order. The order shall be served on the parties forthwith.
2. The execution of the order may be made conditional on the lodging by the applicant of security, of an amount and nature to be fixed in the light of the circumstances.
3. Unless the order fixes the date on which the interim measure is to lapse, the measure shall lapse upon delivery of the final judgment.
4. The order shall have only an interim effect, and shall be without prejudice to the decision of the General Court on the substance of the case.
5. In the order closing the proceedings for interim relief, costs shall be reserved until the decision of the General Court on the substance of the case. However, if it appears justified in the light of the circumstances of the case, a decision as to the costs relating to the proceedings for interim relief shall be given in the order, pursuant to Articles 134 to 138.

[6.418]

Article 159 Change in circumstances

On application by a party, the order may at any time be varied or cancelled on account of a change in circumstances.

[6.419]

Article 160 New application

Refusal of an application for an interim measure shall not bar the main party who made it from making a further application on the basis of new facts.

[6.420]

Article 161 Applications pursuant to Articles 280 TFEU, 299 TFEU and 164 TEAEC

1. The provisions of this Section shall apply to applications to suspend the enforcement of a decision of the General Court or of any measure adopted by the Council, the European Commission or the European Central Bank, submitted pursuant to Articles 280 TFEU, 299 TFEU or 164 TEAEC.

2. The order granting the application shall fix, where appropriate, a date on which the interim measure is to lapse.

CHAPTER 17 APPLICATIONS RELATING TO JUDGMENTS AND ORDERS

[6.421]

Article 162 Assignment of the application

1. The applications referred to in this Chapter shall be assigned to the formation of the Court which delivered the decision to which the application relates.

2. If the quorum referred to in Articles 23 and 24 can no longer be attained, the application shall be assigned to another formation of the Court sitting with the same number of Judges. If the decision was delivered by a Judge ruling as a single Judge who is prevented from acting, the application shall be assigned to another Judge.

[6.422]

Article 163 Stay of proceedings

Where an appeal before the Court of Justice and one of the applications referred to in this Chapter, with the exception of the applications referred to in Articles 164 and 165, concern the same decision of the General Court, the President, after hearing the parties, may decide to stay the proceedings until the Court of Justice has delivered its ruling on the appeal.

[6.423]

Article 164 Rectification of judgments and orders

1. Without prejudice to the provisions relating to the interpretation of judgments and orders, the General Court may, of its own motion or on application by a party, rectify clerical mistakes, errors in calculation and obvious inaccuracies.

2. The application for rectification shall be made within two weeks after delivery of the judgment or service of the order.

3. Where the rectification concerns the operative part or one of the grounds constituting the necessary support for the operative part, the parties may submit written observations within the time limit prescribed by the President.

4. The General Court shall give its decision by way of an order.

5. The original of the rectification order shall be annexed to the original of the rectified decision. A note of this order shall be made in the margin of the original of the rectified decision.

[6.424]

Article 165 Failure to adjudicate

1. If the General Court has failed to adjudicate on a specific head of claim or on costs, any party wishing to rely on that may apply to the General Court to supplement its decision.

2. The application shall be made within one month after delivery of the judgment or service of the order.

3. The application shall be served on the other parties, who may submit written observations within the time limit prescribed by the President.

4. After giving the parties an opportunity to submit their observations, the General Court shall decide, by way of an order, both on the admissibility and on the substance of the application.

[6.425]

Article 166 Application to set aside a judgment by default

1. Application may be made pursuant to Article 41 of the Statute to set aside a judgment given by default.

2. The application to set aside the judgment must be made by the defendant in default within one month from the date of service of the judgment given by default. It must be submitted in the form prescribed by [Articles 76 and 78].

3. After the application has been served, the President shall prescribe a time limit within which the other party may submit his written observations.

4. The proceedings shall be conducted in accordance with the provisions of Title III or of Title IV, as the case may be.

5. The General Court shall decide by way of a judgment which may not be set aside.

6. The original of this judgment shall be annexed to the original of the judgment by default. A note of the judgment on the application to set aside shall be made in the margin of the original of the judgment by default.

NOTES

Para 2: words in square brackets substituted by the Amendments to the Rules of Procedure of the General Court, Article 1(17) (OJ L240, 25.9.2018, p 68).

[6.426]

Article 167 Third-party proceedings

1. The provisions of [Articles 76 and 78] shall apply to an application initiating third-party proceedings made pursuant to Article 42 of the Statute. In addition such an application shall:

(a) specify the judgment or order contested;
(b) state how the contested judgment or order is prejudicial to the rights of the third party;
(c) indicate the reasons for which the third party was unable to take part in the case before the General Court.

2. The application initiating third-party proceedings must be submitted within two months of the publication referred to in Article 122.
3. The General Court may, on application by the third party, order a stay of execution of the contested judgment or order. The provisions of Articles 156 to 161 shall apply.
4. The application shall be served on the parties, who may submit written observations within the time limit prescribed by the President.
5. After giving the parties an opportunity to submit their observations, the General Court shall decide on the application.
6. The contested judgment or order shall be varied on the points on which the submissions of the third party are upheld.
7. The original of the decision in the third-party proceedings shall be annexed to the original of the contested judgment or order. A note of the decision in the third-party proceedings shall be made in the margin of the original of the contested judgment or order.

NOTES

Para 1: words in square brackets substituted by the Amendments to the Rules of Procedure of the General Court, Article 1(18) (OJ L240, 25.9.2018, p 68).

[6.427]
Article 168 Interpretation of judgments and orders

1. In accordance with Article 43 of the Statute, if the meaning or scope of a judgment or order is in doubt, the General Court shall construe it on application by any party or any institution of the Union establishing an interest therein.
2. An application for interpretation must be submitted within two years after the date of delivery of the judgment or service of the order.
3. An application for interpretation shall be submitted in the form prescribed by [Articles 76 and 78]. In addition it shall specify:
(a) the judgment or order in question;
(b) the passages of which interpretation is sought.

4. The application for interpretation shall be served on the other parties, who may submit written observations within the time limit prescribed by the President.
5. After giving the parties an opportunity to submit their observations, the General Court shall decide on the application.
6. The original of the interpreting decision shall be annexed to the original of the decision interpreted. A note of the interpreting decision shall be made in the margin of the original of the decision interpreted.

NOTES

Para 3: words in square brackets substituted by the Amendments to the Rules of Procedure of the General Court, Article 1(19) (OJ L240, 25.9.2018, p 68).

[6.428]
Article 169 Revision

1. In accordance with Article 44 of the Statute, an application for revision of a decision of the General Court may be made only on discovery of a fact which is of such a nature as to be a decisive factor and which, when the judgment was delivered or the order served, was unknown to the General Court and to the party claiming revision.
2. Without prejudice to the time limit of 10 years prescribed in the third paragraph of Article 44 of the Statute, an application for revision shall be made within three months of the date on which the facts on which the application is founded came to the applicant's knowledge.
3. [Articles 76 and 78] shall apply to an application for revision. In addition the application shall:
(a) specify the judgment or order contested;
(b) indicate the points on which the judgment or order is contested;
(c) set out the facts on which the application is founded;
(d) indicate the nature of the evidence to show that there are facts justifying revision, and that the time limits laid down in paragraph 2 have been observed.

4. The application for revision shall be served on the other parties, who may submit written observations within the time limit prescribed by the President.
5. After giving the parties an opportunity to submit their observations, the General Court shall, without prejudice to its decision on the substance, give its decision on the admissibility of the application by way of an order.
6. If the General Court declares the application admissible, it shall give its decision on the substance of the case, in accordance with the provisions of these Rules.
7. The original of the revising decision shall be annexed to the original of the decision revised. A note of the revising decision shall be made in the margin of the original of the decision revised.

NOTES

Para 3: words in square brackets substituted by the Amendments to the Rules of Procedure of the General Court, Article 1(20) (OJ L240, 25.9.2018, p 68).

[6.429]
Article 170 Dispute concerning the costs to be recovered

1. If there is a dispute concerning the costs to be recovered, the party concerned may apply to the General Court to determine the dispute. The application shall be submitted in the form prescribed in [Articles 76 and 78].

2. The application shall be served on the party concerned by the application, who may submit written observations within the time limit prescribed by the President.
3. After giving the party concerned by the application an opportunity to submit his observations, the General Court shall give its decision by way of an order from which no appeal shall lie.
4. The parties may, for the purposes of enforcement, request an authenticated copy of the order.

NOTES

Para 1: words in square brackets substituted by the Amendments to the Rules of Procedure of the General Court, Article 1(20) (OJ L240, 25.9.2018, p 68).

TITLE IV PROCEEDINGS RELATING TO INTELLECTUAL PROPERTY RIGHTS

[6.430]
Article 171 Scope
The provisions of this Title shall apply to actions brought against decisions of the Boards of Appeal of the Office, as referred to in Article 1, and concerning the application of the rules relating to an intellectual property regime.

CHAPTER 1 THE PARTIES TO THE PROCEEDINGS

[6.431]
Article 172 Defendant
The application shall be made against the Office to which the Board of Appeal which adopted the contested decision belongs, as defendant.

[6.432]
Article 173 Status before the General Court of the other parties to the proceedings before the Board of Appeal
1. A party to the proceedings before the Board of Appeal other than the applicant may participate, as intervener, in the proceedings before the General Court by responding to the application in the manner and within the time limit prescribed.
2. Before the expiry of the time limit prescribed for the lodging of a response, a party to the proceedings before the Board of Appeal other than the applicant shall become a party to the proceedings before the General Court, as intervener, on lodging a procedural document. He shall lose the status of intervener before the General Court if he fails to respond to the application in the manner and within the time limit prescribed. In that case, the intervener shall bear his own costs in relation to the procedural documents lodged by him.
3. The intervener referred to in paragraphs 1 and 2 shall have the same procedural rights as the main parties. He may support the form of order sought by a main party and may apply for a form of order and put forward pleas in law independently of those applied for and put forward by the main parties.
4. A party to the proceedings before the Board of Appeal other than the applicant, who becomes a party before the General Court in accordance with paragraphs 1 and 2, shall be represented in accordance with the provisions of Article 19 of the Statute.
[5. Article 78(4) to (6) shall apply to the procedural document referred to in paragraph 2.]
6. By way of derogation from Article 123, the default procedure shall not apply where an intervener, as referred to in paragraphs 1 and 2, has responded to the application in the manner and within the time limit prescribed.

NOTES

Para 5: substituted by the Amendments to the Rules of Procedure of the General Court, Article 1(22) (OJ L240, 25.9.2018, p 68).

[6.433]
Article 174 Replacement of a party
Where an intellectual property right affected by the proceedings has been transferred to a third party by a party to the proceedings before the Board of Appeal of the Office, the successor to that right may apply to replace the original party in the proceedings before the General Court.

[6.434]
Article 175 Application for replacement of a party
1. An application for replacement shall be made by a separate document. It may be lodged at any stage of the proceedings.
2. The application shall contain:
(a) a description of the case;
(b) a description of the parties to the case and of the party whom the applicant for replacement proposes to replace;
(c) the name and address of the applicant for replacement;
(d) particulars of the status and address of the representative of the applicant for replacement;
(e) a statement of the circumstances justifying replacement, together with supporting evidence.
3. The applicant for replacement shall be represented in accordance with the provisions of Article 19 of the Statute.
[4. Article 78(4) to (6) and Article 139 shall apply to the application for replacement.]

NOTES

Para 4: substituted by the Amendments to the Rules of Procedure of the General Court, Article 1(23) (OJ L240, 25.9.2018, p 68).

[6.435]
Article 176 Decision on the application for replacement of a party
1. The application for replacement shall be served on the parties.

2. The President shall give the parties an opportunity to submit their written or oral observations on the application for replacement.
3. The decision on the application for replacement shall take the form of a reasoned order of the President or shall be included in the decision closing the proceedings.
4. If the application for replacement is refused, a decision shall be given as to the costs relating to that application, including the costs of the applicant for replacement, pursuant to the provisions of Articles 134 and 135.
5. If the application for replacement is granted, the successor to the party who is replaced must accept the case as he finds it at the time of that replacement. He shall be bound by the procedural documents lodged by the party whom he replaces.

CHAPTER 2 THE APPLICATION AND RESPONSES

[6.436]
Article 177 Application
1. An application shall contain:
 (a) the name and address of the applicant;
 (b) particulars of the status and address of the applicant's representative;
 (c) the name of the Office against which the action is brought;
 (d) the subject-matter of the proceedings, the pleas in law and arguments relied on and a summary of those pleas in law;
 (e) the form of order sought by the applicant.
2. Where the applicant was not the only party to the proceedings before the Board of Appeal of the Office, the application shall also contain the names of all the parties to those proceedings and the addresses which they had given for the purposes of notifications.
3. The contested decision of the Board of Appeal shall be appended to the application. The date on which the applicant was notified of that decision must be indicated.
4. An application made by a legal person governed by private law shall be accompanied by recent proof of that person's existence in law (extract from the register of companies, firms or associations or any other official document).
5. The application shall be accompanied by the documents referred to in Article 51(2) and (3).
[6]. If an application does not comply with paragraphs 2 to 5, the Registrar shall prescribe a reasonable time limit within which the applicant is to put the application in order. If the applicant fails to put the application in order within the time limit prescribed, the General Court shall decide whether the non-compliance with that procedural requirement renders the application formally inadmissible.

NOTES
The original para 6 was repealed, and the original para 7 was renumbered as para 6, by the Amendments to the Rules of Procedure of the General Court, Article 1(24) (OJ L240, 25.9.2018, p 68).

[6.437]
Article 178 Service of the application
1. The Registrar shall inform the defendant and all the parties to the proceedings before the Board of Appeal of the lodging of the application as provided for in Article 80(1). He shall arrange for service of the application after determining the language of the case in accordance with Article 45(4) and, where appropriate, for service of the translation of the application into the language of the case.
[2. The application shall be served on the defendant via e-Curia if he has an e-Curia account. Where the defendant has no such account, the application shall be served on him in the form of a certified copy sent by registered post with a form for acknowledgement of receipt or by delivery of the copy against receipt.]
[3. The application shall be served on a party to the proceedings before the Board of Appeal via e-Curia where that party has become a party to the proceedings before the General Court in accordance with Article 173(2). If the party to the proceedings before the Board of Appeal is an institution that has an account giving access to e-Curia, service of the application shall be made by e-Curia. Otherwise, the application shall be served by registered post with a form for acknowledgement of receipt at the address given by the party concerned for the purposes of the notifications to be effected in the course of the proceedings before the Board of Appeal.]
4. In cases where [Article 177(6)] applies, service shall be effected as soon as the application has been put in order or the General Court has declared it admissible notwithstanding the failure to observe the requirements set out in that Article.
5. Once the application has been served, the defendant shall forward to the General Court the file relating to the proceedings before the Board of Appeal.

NOTES
Paras 2, 3: substituted by the Amendments to the Rules of Procedure of the General Court, Article 1(25)(a), (b) (OJ L240, 25.9.2018, p 68).
Para 4: words in square brackets substituted by the Amendments to the Rules of Procedure of the General Court, Article 1(25)(c) (OJ L240, 25.9.2018, p 68).

[6.438]
Article 179 Parties authorised to lodge a response
The defendant and the parties to the proceedings before the Board of Appeal other than the applicant shall submit their responses to the application within a time limit of two months from the service of the application. That time limit may, in exceptional circumstances, be extended by the President at the reasoned request of the party concerned.

[6.439]
Article 180 Response
1. A response shall contain:
 (a) the name and address of the party lodging it;

(b) particulars of the status and address of the party's representative;
(c) the pleas in law and arguments relied on;
(d) the form of order sought by the party lodging it.

2. [Article 177(4) to (6)] shall apply to the response.

NOTES

Para 2: words in square brackets substituted by the Amendments to the Rules of Procedure of the General Court, Article 1(26) (OJ L240, 25.9.2018, p 68).

[6.440]
Article 181 Close of the written part of the procedure

Without prejudice to the provisions of Chapter 3, the written part of the procedure shall be closed after the submission of the response of the defendant and, where applicable, of the intervener within the meaning of Article 173.

CHAPTER 3 CROSS-CLAIMS

[6.441]
Article 182 Cross-claim

1. The parties to the proceedings before the Board of Appeal other than the applicant may submit a cross-claim within the same time limit as that prescribed for the submission of a response.
2. A cross-claim must be submitted by a document separate from the response.

[6.442]
Article 183 Content of the cross-claim

A cross-claim shall contain:
(a) the name and address of the party lodging it;
(b) particulars of the status and address of the party's representative;
(c) the pleas in law and arguments relied on;
(d) the form of order sought.

[6.443]
Article 184 Form of order sought, pleas in law and arguments contained in the cross-claim

1. The cross-claim shall seek an order annulling or altering the decision of the Board of Appeal on a point not raised in the application.
2. The pleas in law and arguments relied on shall identify precisely the points in the grounds of the decision being challenged that are contested.

[6.444]
Article 185 Response to the cross-claim

Where a cross-claim is lodged, the other parties may submit a pleading confined to responding to the form of order sought, the pleas in law and arguments relied on in the cross-claim, within two months of its being served on them. That time limit may, in exceptional circumstances, be extended by the President at the reasoned request of the party concerned.

[6.445]
Article 186 Close of the written part of the procedure

When a cross-claim has been lodged, the written part of the procedure shall be closed after the submission of the last response to that cross-claim.

[6.446]
Article 187 Relationship between the main action and the cross-claim

A cross-claim shall be deemed to be devoid of purpose:
(a) if the applicant discontinues the main action;
(b) if the main action is declared manifestly inadmissible.

CHAPTER 4 OTHER ASPECTS OF THE PROCEDURE

[6.447]
Article 188 Subject-matter of the proceedings before the General Court

The pleadings lodged by the parties in proceedings before the General Court may not change the subject-matter of the proceedings before the Board of Appeal.

[6.448]
Article 189 Length of written pleadings

1. The General Court shall set, in accordance with Article 224, the maximum length of written pleadings lodged pursuant to this Title.
2. Authorisation to exceed the maximum length of written pleadings may be given by the President only in cases involving particularly complex legal or factual issues.

[6.449]
Article 190 Provisions relating to costs

1. Where an action against a decision of a Board of Appeal is successful, the General Court may order the defendant to bear only its own costs.
2. Costs necessarily incurred by the parties for the purposes of the proceedings before the Board of Appeal shall be regarded as recoverable costs.

[6.450]

Article 191 Other provisions applicable

Subject to the special provisions of this Title, the provisions of Title III shall apply to the proceedings referred to in this Title.

TITLE V APPEALS AGAINST DECISIONS OF THE CIVIL SERVICE TRIBUNAL

[6.451]

Article 192 Scope

The provisions of this Title shall apply to appeals against decisions of the Civil Service Tribunal as referred to in Articles 9 and 10 of Annex I to the Statute.

CHAPTER 1 THE APPEAL

[6.452]

Article 193 Lodging of the appeal

. . . An appeal shall be brought by lodging an application at the Registry of the General Court . . .

2. . . .

NOTES

Number and words omitted repealed by the Amendment to the Rules of Procedure of the General Court, Article 1(20) (OJ L217, 12.8.2016, p 73).

[6.453]

Article 194 Content of the appeal

1. An appeal shall contain:
   (a) the name and address of the appellant;
   (b) particulars of the status and address of the appellant's representative;
   (c) a reference to the decision of the Civil Service Tribunal appealed against;
   (d) the names of the other parties to the relevant case before the Civil Service Tribunal;
   (e) the pleas in law and legal arguments relied on, and a summary of those pleas in law;
   (f) the form of order sought by the appellant.
2. The appeal shall state the date on which the decision appealed against was served on the appellant.
3. An appeal brought by a legal person governed by private law shall be accompanied by recent proof of that person's existence in law (extract from the register of companies, firms or associations or any other official document).
4. The appeal shall be accompanied by the documents referred to in Article 51(2) and (3).

[5.] If an appeal does not comply with paragraphs 2 to 4, the Registrar shall prescribe a reasonable time limit within which the appellant is to put the appeal in order. If the appellant fails to put the appeal in order within the time limit prescribed, the General Court shall decide whether the non-compliance with that procedural requirement renders the appeal formally inadmissible.

NOTES

The original para 5 was repealed, and the original para 6 was renumbered as para 5, by the Amendments to the Rules of Procedure of the General Court, Article 1(27) (OJ L240, 25.9.2018, p 68).

[6.454]

Article 195 Form of order sought, pleas in law and arguments contained in the appeal

1. An appeal shall seek to have set aside, in whole or in part, the decision of the Civil Service Tribunal as set out in the operative part of that decision.
2. The pleas in law and legal arguments relied on shall identify precisely those points in the grounds of the decision of the Civil Service Tribunal that are contested.

[6.455]

Article 196 Form of order sought in the event that the appeal is allowed

1. An appeal shall seek, in the event that it is declared well founded, the same form of order, in whole or in part, as that sought at first instance and shall not seek a different form of order. The subject-matter of the proceedings before the Civil Service Tribunal may not be changed in the appeal.
2. Where the appellant requests that the case be referred back to the [General Court ruling as a court of first instance] in the event of the decision appealed against being set aside, he shall set out the reasons why the state of the proceedings does not permit a decision by the General Court [ruling as a court of appeal].

NOTES

Para 2: words in first pair of square brackets substituted, and words in second pair of square brackets inserted, by the Amendment to the Rules of Procedure of the General Court, Article 1(21) (OJ L217, 12.8.2016, p 73).

CHAPTER 2 THE RESPONSE, THE REPLY AND THE REJOINDER

[6.456]

Article 197 Service of the appeal

1. The appeal shall be served on the other parties to the relevant case before the Civil Service Tribunal. Article 80(1) shall apply.
2. Where [Article 194(5)] applies, service shall be effected as soon as the appeal has been put in order or the General Court has declared it admissible notwithstanding the failure to observe the formal requirements laid down by that Article.

NOTES

Para 2: words in square brackets substituted by the Amendments to the Rules of Procedure of the General Court, Article 1(28) (OJ L240, 25.9.2018, p 68).

[6.457]

Article 198 Parties authorised to lodge a response

Any party to the relevant case before the Civil Service Tribunal having an interest in the appeal being allowed or dismissed may submit a response within two months after service on him of the appeal. The time limit for submitting a response shall not be extended.

[6.458]

Article 199 Content of the response

1. A response shall contain:
   (a) the name and address of the party submitting it;
   (b) particulars of the status and address of that party's representative;
   (c) the date on which the appeal was served on him;
   (d) the pleas in law and legal arguments relied on;
   (e) the form of order sought.
2. [Article 194(3) to (5)] shall apply to responses.

NOTES

Para 2: words in square brackets substituted by the Amendments to the Rules of Procedure of the General Court, Article 1(29) (OJ L240, 25.9.2018, p 68).

[6.459]

Article 200 Form of order sought in the response

A response shall seek to have the appeal allowed or dismissed, in whole or in part.

[6.460]

Article 201 Reply and rejoinder

1. The appeal and the response may be supplemented by a reply and a rejoinder only where the President, on a reasoned application submitted by the appellant within seven days of service of the response, considers it necessary, in particular to enable the appellant to present his views on a plea of inadmissibility or on new matters relied on in the response.

2. The President shall fix the date by which the reply is to be produced and, upon service of that pleading, the date by which the rejoinder is to be produced. He may limit the number of pages and the subject-matter of those pleadings.

CHAPTER 3 THE CROSS-APPEAL

[6.461]

Article 202 Cross-appeal

1. The parties referred to in Article 198 may submit a cross-appeal within the same time limit as that prescribed for the submission of a response.

2. A cross-appeal must be introduced by a document separate from the response.

[6.462]

Article 203 Content of the cross-appeal

A cross-appeal shall contain:
   (a) the name and address of the party bringing the cross-appeal;
   (b) particulars of the status and address of that party's representative;
   (c) the date on which the appeal was served on him;
   (d) the pleas in law and legal arguments relied on;
   (e) the form of order sought.

[6.463]

Article 204 Form of order sought, pleas in law and arguments contained in the cross-appeal

1. A cross-appeal shall seek to have set aside, in whole or in part, the decision of the Civil Service Tribunal.

2. It may also seek to have set aside an express or implied decision relating to the admissibility of the action before the Civil Service Tribunal.

3. The pleas in law and legal arguments relied on shall identify precisely those points in the grounds of the decision of the Civil Service Tribunal which are contested. The pleas in law and arguments must be separate from those relied on in the response.

CHAPTER 4 PLEADINGS CONSEQUENT ON THE CROSS-APPEAL

[6.464]

Article 205 Response to the cross-appeal

Where a cross-appeal is brought, the appellant or any other party to the relevant case before the Civil Service Tribunal having an interest in the cross-appeal being allowed or dismissed may submit a response, which must be limited to the pleas in law relied on in that cross-appeal, within two months after its being served on him. That time limit shall not be extended.

[6.465]
Article 206 Reply and rejoinder following a cross-appeal
1. The cross-appeal and the response thereto may be supplemented by a reply and a rejoinder only where the President, on a reasoned application submitted by the party who brought the cross-appeal within seven days of service of the response to the cross-appeal, considers it necessary, in particular to enable that party to present his views on a plea of inadmissibility or on new matters relied on in the response to the cross-appeal.
2. The President shall fix the date by which that reply is to be produced and, upon service of that pleading, the date by which the rejoinder is to be produced. He may limit the number of pages and the subject-matter of those pleadings.

CHAPTER 5 THE ORAL PART OF THE PROCEDURE

[6.466]
Article 207 Oral part of the procedure
1. The parties to the appeal proceedings may request an opportunity to state their case in a hearing. Any such request must be reasoned and be submitted within three weeks after service on the parties of notification of the close of the written part of the procedure. That time limit may be extended by the President.
2. On a proposal from the Judge-Rapporteur, the General Court may, if it considers that it has sufficient information available to it from the material in the file, decide to rule on the appeal without an oral part of the procedure. It may nevertheless later decide to open the oral part of the procedure.

CHAPTER 6 APPEALS DETERMINED BY ORDER

[6.467]
Article 208 Manifestly inadmissible or manifestly unfounded appeal or cross-appeal
Where the appeal or cross-appeal is, in whole or in part, manifestly inadmissible or manifestly unfounded, the General Court may at any time, acting on a proposal from the Judge-Rapporteur, decide by reasoned order to dismiss that appeal or cross-appeal in whole or in part.

[6.468]
Article 209 Manifestly well-founded appeal or cross-appeal
Where the Court of Justice or the General Court has already ruled on one or more questions of law identical to those raised by the pleas in law of the appeal or cross-appeal, and the General Court considers the appeal or cross-appeal to be manifestly well founded, it may, acting on a proposal from the Judge-Rapporteur and after hearing the parties, decide by reasoned order in which reference is made to the relevant case-law to declare the appeal or cross-appeal manifestly well founded.

CHAPTER 7 EFFECT ON A CROSS-APPEAL OF THE REMOVAL OF THE APPEAL FROM THE REGISTER

[6.469]
Article 210 Effect on a cross-appeal of the discontinuance or manifest inadmissibility of the appeal
A cross-appeal shall be deemed to be devoid of purpose:
(a) if the appellant discontinues his appeal;
(b) if the appeal is declared manifestly inadmissible for non-compliance with the time limit for lodging an appeal;
(c) if the appeal is declared manifestly inadmissible on the sole ground that it is not directed against a final decision of the Civil Service Tribunal or against a decision disposing of the substantive issues in part only or disposing of a procedural issue concerning a plea of lack of jurisdiction or inadmissibility within the meaning of the first paragraph of Article 9 of Annex I to the Statute.

CHAPTER 8 COSTS IN APPEALS

[6.470]
Article 211 Provisions relating to costs in appeals
1. Subject to the following provisions, Articles 133 to 141 shall apply, *mutatis mutandis*, to the procedure before the General Court on appeal from a decision of the Civil Service Tribunal.
2. Where the appeal is unfounded or where the appeal is well founded and the General Court itself gives final judgment in the case, the General Court shall make a decision as to costs.
3. In appeals brought by institutions, the institutions shall bear their own costs, without prejudice to Article 135(2).
4. By way of derogation from Article 134(1) and (2), the General Court may, in appeals brought by officials or other servants of an institution, decide to apportion the costs between the parties where equity so requires.
5. Where he has not brought the appeal, an intervener at first instance may not be ordered to pay costs in the appeal proceedings unless he participated in the written or oral part of the proceedings before the General Court. Where an intervener at first instance takes part in the proceedings, the General Court may decide that he shall bear his own costs.

CHAPTER 9 OTHER PROVISIONS APPLICABLE TO APPEALS

[6.471]
Article 212 Length of written pleadings
1. The General Court shall set, in accordance with Article 224, the maximum length of written pleadings lodged pursuant to this Title.
2. Authorisation to exceed the maximum length of written pleadings may be given by the President only in cases involving particularly complex issues.

[6.472]
Article 213 Other provisions applicable to appeals
1. [Articles 51 to 58, 60 to 72, 79, 84, 87, 89, 90, 107 to 122, 124, 125, 129, 131, 142 to 162, 164, 165 and 167 to 170] shall apply to the procedure before the General Court on appeal from a decision of the Civil Service Tribunal.

2. By way of derogation from Article 143(1), an application to intervene must be submitted within one month of the publication of the notice referred to in Article 79.
3. Decisions given pursuant to Article 256(2) TFEU shall be communicated to the Court of Justice . . .

NOTES

Para 1: words in square brackets substituted by the Amendments to the Rules of Procedure of the General Court, Article 1(30) (OJ L240, 25.9.2018, p 68).

Para 3: words omitted repealed by the Amendment to the Rules of Procedure of the General Court, Article 1(22) (OJ L217, 12.8.2016, p 73).

CHAPTER 10 APPEALS AGAINST DECISIONS DISMISSING AN APPLICATION TO INTERVENE AND AGAINST DECISIONS ON INTERIM MEASURES

[6.473]
Article 214 Appeals against decisions dismissing an application to intervene and against decisions on interim measures
By way of derogation from the provisions of this Title, the President of the General Court shall adjudicate upon the appeals referred to in Article 10(1) and (2) of Annex I to the Statute in accordance with the procedure laid down in Article 157(1) and (3) and Article 158(1).

TITLE VI PROCEDURES AFTER A CASE IS REFERRED BACK TO THE GENERAL COURT

CHAPTER 1 DECISIONS OF THE GENERAL COURT GIVEN AFTER ITS DECISION HAS BEEN SET ASIDE AND THE CASE REFERRED BACK TO IT

[6.474]
Article 215 Setting aside and referral back by the Court of Justice
Where the Court of Justice sets aside a judgment or an order of the General Court and refers the case back to that Court, the latter shall be seised of the case by the decision so referring it.

[6.475]
Article 216 Assignment of the case
1. Where the Court of Justice sets aside a judgment or an order of a Chamber, the President of the General Court may assign the case to another Chamber sitting with the same number of Judges.
2. Where the Court of Justice sets aside a judgment delivered or an order made by the Grand Chamber of the General Court, the case shall be assigned to that Chamber.
3. Where the Court of Justice sets aside a judgment delivered or an order made by a Judge ruling as a single Judge, the President of the General Court may assign the case to a single Judge, without prejudice to the referral of the case by that single Judge to the Chamber in which he sits.

[6.476]
Article 217 Conduct of the proceedings
1. Where the decision later set aside by the Court of Justice was made after the written procedure before the General Court on the substance of the case had been closed, the parties to the proceedings before the General Court may lodge their written observations on the conclusions to be drawn from the decision of the Court of Justice for the outcome of the proceedings within two months of the service on them of the decision of the Court of Justice. This time limit may not be extended.
2. Where the decision later set aside by the Court of Justice was made when the written procedure before the General Court on the substance of the case had not yet been closed, it shall be resumed at the stage which it had reached.
3. The President may, if the circumstances so justify, allow supplementary statements of written observations to be lodged.

[6.477]
Article 218 Rules applicable to the procedure
Subject to the provisions of Article 217, the procedure shall be conducted in accordance with the provisions of Title III or of Title IV, as the case may be.

[6.478]
Article 219 Costs
The General Court shall decide on the costs relating to the proceedings instituted before it and to the proceedings on the appeal before the Court of Justice.

CHAPTER 2 DECISIONS OF THE GENERAL COURT GIVEN AFTER ITS DECISION HAS BEEN REVIEWED AND THE CASE REFERRED BACK TO IT

[6.479]
Article 220 Review and referral back by the Court of Justice
Where the Court of Justice reviews a judgment or an order of the General Court and refers the case back to that Court, the latter shall be seised of the case by the judgment so referring it.

[6.480]
Article 221 Assignment of the case
1. Where the Court of Justice refers back to the General Court a case that was originally heard by a Chamber, the President of the General Court may assign the case to another Chamber sitting with the same number of Judges.
2. Where the Court of Justice refers back to the General Court a case that was originally heard by the Grand Chamber of the General Court, the case shall be assigned to that Chamber.

[6.481]

Article 222 Conduct of the proceedings

1. Within one month of the service of the judgment of the Court of Justice, the parties to the proceedings before the General Court may lodge their written observations on the conclusions to be drawn from that judgment for the outcome of the proceedings. This time limit may not be extended.

2. The General Court may, by way of measures of organisation of procedure, invite the parties to the proceedings before it to lodge written submissions and may decide to hear the parties' submissions in a hearing.

[6.482]

Article 223 Costs

The General Court shall decide on the costs relating to the proceedings instituted before it following the review of its decision by the Court of Justice.

FINAL PROVISIONS

[6.483]

Article 224 Implementing rules

The General Court shall, by a separate act, adopt practice rules for the implementation of these Rules.

[6.484]

Article 225 Enforcement

Penalties imposed and other measures ordered under these Rules shall be enforced in accordance with Articles 280 TFEU, 299 TFEU and 164 TEAEC.

[6.485]

Article 226 Repeal

These Rules replace the Rules of Procedure of the General Court of 2 May 1991, as last amended on 19 June 2013.

[6.486]

Article 227 Publication and entry into force of these Rules

1. These Rules, which are authentic in the languages referred to in Article 44, shall be published in the *Official Journal of the European Union*.

2. These Rules shall enter into force on the first day of the third month following their publication.

3. The provisions of Article 105 shall apply only from the entry into force of the decision referred to in Article 105(11).

4. The provisions of Article 45(4), Article 139(c) and Article 181 shall apply only to actions brought before the General Court after the entry into force of these Rules.

5. The provisions of Articles 106 and 207 shall apply only to cases in which the written part of the procedure has not yet been closed on the date on which these Rules enter into force.

6. The provisions of Article 115(1), Article 116(6), Article 131 and Article 135(2) of the Rules of Procedure of the General Court of 2 May 1991, as last amended on 19 June 2013, shall continue to apply to actions brought before the General Court before the entry into force of these Rules.

7. The provisions of Articles 135a and 146 of the Rules of Procedure of the General Court of 2 May 1991, as last amended on 19 June 2013, shall continue to apply to actions pending before the General Court in which the written part of the procedure was closed before the entry into force of these Rules.

PRACTICE RULES FOR THE IMPLEMENTATION OF THE RULES OF PROCEDURE OF THE GENERAL COURT (CONSOLIDATED VERSION)

(December 2018)

[6.487]

NOTES

Date of publication in the OJ: OJ L152, 18.6.2015, p 1.

A consolidated version of these Rules is available on the General Court website at https://curia.europa.eu/jcms/jcms/Jo2_7040/en/. It consolidates the original Practice Rules adopted by the General Court on 20 May 2015, as amended by OJ L217, 12.8.2016, p 78 (with effect from 1 September 2016), and by OJ L294, 21.11.2018, p 23 (with effect from 1 December 2018). Note that the 2018 amendments substitute, inter alia, new points 14 to 229 for the original points 14 to 270, and substitute Annexes 1 to 3. These amendments supersede the amendments made by OJ L217, 12.8.2016, p 78, and the corrigendum published in OJ L196, 21.7.2016, p 56. The amendments made by OJ L294, 21.11.2018, p 23 were corrected in the corrigendum published in OJ L296, 22.11.2018, p 40.

TABLE OF CONTENTS

THE GENERAL COURT,

Having regard to Article 224 of its Rules of Procedure (OJ 2015 L105, p 1);

Whereas in the interests of transparency, legal certainty and the proper implementation of the Rules of Procedure, implementing rules must be laid down in respect of the responsibilities of the Registrar, in particular those relating to the maintenance of the register and case files, the regularisation and service of procedural documents and items and the Registry's scale of charges;

Whereas in accordance with Article 37 of the Rules of Procedure, it is appropriate to fix the Registry's scale of charges;

Whereas in the interests of the proper administration of justice, parties' representatives, whether lawyers or agents within the meaning of Article 19 of the Protocol on the Statute of the Court of Justice of the European Union ('the Statute'), should be given practice directions on the presentation of procedural documents and items and as to how best to prepare for hearings before the General Court;

Whereas these Practice Rules explain, detail and supplement certain provisions of the Rules of Procedure and are intended to enable the parties' representatives to take account of matters which the General Court must take into consideration, particularly those relating to the lodging of procedural documents and items, to their presentation and translation and to interpretation at hearings;

Whereas there are particular features relating to the confidential treatment of procedural documents and items;

Whereas the Registrar is required to ensure that procedural documents and items placed on the case file are in conformity with the provisions of the Statute, the Rules of Procedure and these Practice Rules;

Whereas the lodging of procedural documents and items that do not comply with the provisions of the Statute, the Rules of Procedure or these Practice Rules contributes, sometimes significantly, to an increase in the duration of proceedings and in the costs;

Whereas by complying with these Practice Rules, the parties' representatives, acting in their capacity as officers of the court, contribute through their adherence to procedural fairness to the efficiency of justice by enabling the General Court to deal effectively with the procedural documents and items which they lodge, thereby avoiding the risk of Article 139(a) of the Rules of Procedure being applied with regard to the points covered in these Practice Rules;

Whereas any repeated failure to comply with the requirements of the Rules of Procedure or of these Practice Rules, requiring regularisation to be sought, may result in the costs involved in the requisite processing thereof by the General Court having to be repaid pursuant to Article 139(c) of the Rules of Procedure;

Whereas the treatment of information or material produced pursuant to Article 105(1) or (2) of the Rules of Procedure is to be governed by the decision adopted by the General Court under Article 105(11) of the Rules of Procedure;[1]

[Whereas the rules on the lodging and service of procedural documents by means of e-Curia are contained in the decision adopted by the Court under Article 56a(2) of the Rules of Procedure;[2]]

After consulting the agents of the Member States, the institutions intervening in proceedings before the General Court, the Office for Harmonisation in the Internal Market (Trade Marks and Designs) (OHIM), [now the European Union Intellectual Property Office (EUIPO), and the Council of Bars and Law Societies of Europe (CCBE)];

NOTES

The words in square brackets (and the footnotes below) were inserted by Amendments to the Practice Rules for the Implementation of the Rules of Procedure of the General Court, Article 1 (OJ L294, 21.11.2018, p 23).

1 Decision (EU) 2016/2387 of the General Court of 14 September 2016 concerning the security rules applicable to information or material produced in accordance with Article 105(1) or (2) of the Rules of Procedure (OJ 2016 L355, p 18) ('decision of the Court of 14 September 2016').

2 Decision of the General Court of 11 July 2018 on the lodging and service of procedural documents by means of e-Curia (OJ 2018 L240, p 72) ('decision of the Court of 11 July 2018').

HAS ADOPTED THESE PRACTICE RULES:

I. THE REGISTRY

A. TASKS OF THE REGISTRAR

[6.488]

1. The Registrar shall be responsible for the maintenance of the register of the General Court ('the Court') and the files of pending cases, for the acceptance, transmission, service and custody of documents, for correspondence with the parties, applicants for leave to intervene and applicants for legal aid, and for the custody of the seals of the Court. He shall ensure that Registry charges are collected and that sums due to the cashier of the Court are recovered. He shall be in charge of the publications of the Court and of the dissemination on the Internet site of the Court of Justice of the European Union of documents concerning the Court.

2. In carrying out the duties specified in point 1 above, the Registrar shall be assisted by one or more Deputy Registrars. If the Registrar is prevented from acting, those duties shall be performed by one of the Deputy Registrars, according to seniority, who shall take the decisions reserved to the Registrar by the Rules of Procedure of the General Court or these Practice Rules, or delegated to him pursuant to these Practice Rules.

B. OPENING HOURS OF THE REGISTRY

3. The offices of the Registry shall be open every working day. All days other than Saturdays, Sundays and the official holidays on the list referred to in Article 58(3)of the Rules of Procedure shall be working days.

4. If a working day as referred to in point 3 above is a holiday for the officials and servants of the institution, arrangements shall be made for a skeleton staff to be on duty at the Registry during the hours in which it is normally open.

5. The Registry shall be open at the following times:
— in the morning, from Monday to Friday, from 9.30 a.m. to 12 noon,
— in the afternoon, from Monday to Thursday, from 2.30 p.m. to 5.30 p.m. and on Fridays from 2.30 p.m. to 4.30 p.m.

6. The Registry shall be open half an hour before the commencement of a hearing to the representatives of the parties who have been given notice to attend that hearing.

7. [Outside the Registry's opening hours, the annex referred to in Article 72(4) of the Rules of Procedure and the procedural document referred to in Article 147(6) of the Rules of Procedure may] be validly lodged with the janitor at the entrances to the buildings of the Court of Justice of the European Union at any time of the day or night. The janitor shall make a record, which shall constitute good evidence, of the date and time of such lodgment and shall issue a receipt upon request.

C. REGISTER

8. All documents placed on the file in cases brought before the Court shall be entered in the register.

9. Information or material produced pursuant to Article 105(1) or (2) of the Rules of Procedure, the treatment of which shall be governed by [the decision of the Court of 14 September 2016], shall also be entered in the register.

10. Entries in the register shall be numbered consecutively. They shall be made in the language of the case and contain the information necessary for identifying the document, in particular the date of lodgment, the date of registration, the number of the case and the nature of the document.

11. The register kept in electronic form shall be set up and maintained in such a way that no registration can be deleted therefrom and that following any amendment the original entry is preserved.

12. The registration number of every document issued by the Court shall be noted on its first page.

13. The note of the registration, including the registration number, the date of lodgment and the date of entry in the register, shall be [made on the procedural document placed on the case file, as well as on every copy which is served on the parties]. This note shall be made in the language of the case.

[14. The date of lodgment referred to in point 13 above shall be, depending on the circumstances: the date referred to in Article 5 of the decision of the Court of 11 July 2018, the date on which the document was received by the Registry, the date referred to in point 7 above, or the date referred to in the second paragraph of Article 3 of the decision of the Court of 14 September 2016. In the cases provided for by the first paragraph of Article 54 of the Statute, the date of lodgment referred to in point 13 above shall be the date on which the procedural document was lodged, via e-Curia, with the Registrar of the Court of Justice or, in the case of a document lodged as referred to in Article 147(6) of the Rules of Procedure, the date on which the document was lodged with the Registrar of the Court of Justice.

15. In accordance with Article 125c of the Rules of Procedure, material produced in the context of the amicable settlement procedure referred to in Articles 125a to 125d of the Rules of Procedure shall be entered in a specific register which shall not be subject to the rules set out in Articles 36 and 37 of those Rules.

D. CASE NUMBER

16. When an application initiating proceedings is registered, the case shall be given a serial number preceded by 'T-' and followed by an indication of the year.

17. Applications for interim measures, applications to intervene, applications for rectification or interpretation, applications for the Court to remedy a failure to adjudicate, applications for revision, applications for the Court to set aside judgments by default or initiating third-party proceedings, applications for the taxation of costs and applications for legal aid relating to pending cases shall be given the same serial number as the principal action, followed by a reference to indicate that the proceedings concerned are separate special forms of procedure.

18. An application for legal aid made with a view to bringing an action shall be given a serial number preceded by 'T-', followed by an indication of the year and a specific reference.

19. An action which is preceded by an application for legal aid in connection therewith shall be given the same case number as the latter.

20. Where the Court of Justice refers a case back to the Court following the setting aside or review of a decision, that case shall be given the number previously allocated to it when it was before the Court, followed by a specific reference.

21. The serial number of the case together with the names of the parties shall be indicated on the procedural documents, in correspondence relating to the case and, without prejudice to Article 66 of the Rules of Procedure, in the publications of the Court and in the documents of the Court on the internet site of the Court of Justice of the European Union.

E. CASE FILE AND INSPECTION OF THE CASE FILE

E.1. Maintenance of the Case File

22. The case file shall contain: the procedural documents (where applicable together with the annexes thereto) which will be taken into account in the determination of the case, bearing the note referred to in point 13 above, signed by the Registrar; the correspondence with the parties; where applicable, the minutes of the meeting with the parties, the report for the hearing, minutes of the hearing and minutes of the inquiry hearing, and the decisions taken in the case.

23. The documents placed on the case file shall be given a serial number.

24. The confidential and non-confidential versions of procedural documents and of the annexes thereto shall be filed separately in the case file.

25. Documents relating to the special forms of procedure referred to in point 17 above shall be filed separately in the case file.

26. Material produced in the context of the amicable settlement procedure as provided for in Article 125a of the Rules of Procedure shall be placed in a file separate from the case file.

27. A procedural document and annexes thereto which are produced in a case and placed on the file of that case may not be taken into account for the purpose of preparing another case for hearing.

28. At the close of the proceedings before the Court, the Registry shall arrange for the case file and the file referred to in Article 125c(1) of the Rules of Procedure to be closed and archived. The closed file shall contain a list of all the documents on the case file, an indication of their number, and a cover page showing the serial number of the case, the parties and the date on which the case was closed.

29. The treatment of information or material produced pursuant to Article 105(1) or (2)of the Rules of Procedure shall be governed by the decision of the Court of 14 September 2016.

E.2. Inspection of the Case File

30. The representatives of the main parties to a case before the Court may inspect the case file, including administrative files produced before the Court, at the Registry and may request copies of procedural documents or extracts of the case file and of the register.

31. The representatives of the parties granted leave to intervene pursuant to Article 144 of the Rules of Procedure shall have the same right of inspection of the case file as the main parties, subject to Article 144(5) and (7) of the Rules of Procedure.

32. In joined cases, the representatives of all parties shall have the right to inspect the files in the cases concerned by the joinder, subject to Article 68(4) of the Rules of Procedure.

33. Any person having made an application for legal aid pursuant to Article 147 of the Rules of Procedure without the assistance of a lawyer shall have the right to inspect the file relating to the legal aid.

34. Authorisation to inspect the confidential version of procedural documents and of any annexes thereto shall be granted only to the parties in respect of whom no confidential treatment has been ordered.

35. As regards information or material produced pursuant to Article 105(1) or (2) of the Rules of Procedure, reference is made to point 29 above.

36. The requirements of points 30 to 35 above do not apply to access to the file referred to in Article 125c(1) of the Rules of Procedure. Access to that specific file is governed by Article 125c of the Rules of Procedure.

F. ORIGINALS OF JUDGMENTS AND ORDERS

37. Originals of judgments and orders of the Court shall be kept in chronological order in the archives of the Registry. A certified copy shall be placed on the case file.

38. At the parties' request, the Registrar shall supply them with a copy of the original of a judgment or of an order, if necessary in a non-confidential version.

39. The Registrar may supply uncertified copies of judgments and orders to third parties who so request, provided that those decisions are not already publicly accessible and do not contain confidential information.

40. Orders rectifying a judgment or an order, judgments or orders interpreting a judgment or an order, judgments given on applications to set aside judgments by default, judgments given and orders made in third-party proceedings or on applications for revision and judgments or orders of the Court of Justice in appeals or in reviews of decisions shall be mentioned in the margin of the judgment or order concerned. The original or a certified copy shall be appended to the original of the judgment or order.

G. TRANSLATIONS

41. The Registrar shall, in accordance with Article 47 of the Rules of Procedure, arrange for everything said or written in the course of the proceedings to be translated, at the request of a Judge, an Advocate General or a party, into the language of the case or, where necessary, into another language as provided for in Article 45(1) of the Rules of Procedure. Where, for the purposes of the efficient conduct of the proceedings, a translation into another language, as provided for in Article 44 of the Rules of Procedure, is necessary, the Registrar shall also arrange for such a translation to be made.

H. WITNESSES AND EXPERTS

42. The Registrar shall take the measures necessary for giving effect to orders requiring the taking of expert opinion or the examination of witnesses.

43. The Registrar shall obtain from witnesses evidence of their expenses and loss of earnings and from experts a fee note accounting for their expenses and services.

44. The Registrar shall cause sums due to witnesses and experts under the Rules of Procedure to be paid by the cashier of the Court. In the event of a dispute concerning such sums, the Registrar shall refer the matter to the President in order for a decision to be taken.

I. REGISTRY'S SCALE OF CHARGES

45. Where an extract from the register is supplied in accordance with Article 37 of the Rules of Procedure, the Registrar shall impose a Registry charge of EUR 3.50 per page for a certified copy and EUR 2.50 per page for an uncertified copy.

46. Where a copy of a procedural document or an extract from the case file is supplied to a party on paper at his request in accordance with Article 38(1) of the Rules of Procedure, the Registrar shall impose a Registry charge of EUR 3.50 per page for a certified copy and EUR 2.50 per page for an uncertified copy.

47. Where an authenticated copy of an order or of a judgment is, for the purposes of enforcement, supplied to a party at his request in accordance with Article 38(1) or Article 170 of the Rules of Procedure, the Registrar shall impose a Registry charge of EUR 3.50 per page.

48. Where an uncertified copy of a judgment or of an order is supplied in accordance with point 39 above to a third party at his request, the Registrar shall impose a Registry charge of EUR 2.50 per page.

49. Where, at the request of a party, the Registrar arranges for a translation to be produced of a procedural document or an extract from the case file, the size of which is considered in accordance with Article 139(b) of the Rules of Procedure to be excessive, a Registry charge of EUR 1.25 per line shall be imposed.

50. Where a party or an applicant for leave to intervene has repeatedly failed to comply with the requirements of the Rules of Procedure or of these Practice Rules, the Registrar shall impose a Registry charge, in accordance with Article 139(c) of the Rules of Procedure, which may not exceed EUR 7,000 (2,000 times the charge of EUR 3.50 referred to in points 45 to 47 above).

J. RECOVERY OF SUMS

51. Where sums paid out by way of legal aid, sums paid to witnesses or experts, or avoidable costs, within the meaning of Article 139(a) of the Rules of Procedure, incurred by the Court are recoverable by the cashier of the Court, the Registrar shall demand payment of those sums from the party who is to bear them.

52. If the sums referred to in point 51 above are not paid within the period prescribed by the Registrar, he may request the Court to make an enforceable order and, if necessary, require its enforcement.

53. Where Registry charges are recoverable by the cashier of the Court, the Registrar shall demand payment of those sums from the party or the third party who is to bear them.

54. If the sums referred to in point 53 above are not paid within the period prescribed by the Registrar, he may adopt an enforceable decision under Article 35(4) of the Rules of Procedure and, if necessary, require its enforcement.

K. PUBLICATIONS AND POSTING OF DOCUMENTS ON THE INTERNET

55. The Registrar shall cause to be published in the *Official Journal of the European Union* the names of the President and of the Vice-President of the Court and of the Presidents of Chambers who have been elected by the Court, the composition of the Chambers and the criteria applied in the allocation of cases to them, the criteria applied in order to complete the formation of the Court or to attain the quorum, as the case may be, where a member of the formation of the Court is prevented from acting, the name of the Registrar and of any Deputy Registrar(s) elected by the Court, and the dates of the judicial vacations.

56. The Registrar shall cause to be published in the *Official Journal of the European Union* the decisions referred to in Article 11(3), Article 56a(2) and Article 105(11) of the Rules of Procedure.

57. The Registrar shall cause to be published in the *Official Journal of the European Union* the legal aid form.

58. The Registrar shall cause to be published in the *Official Journal of the European Union* notices of proceedings brought and of decisions closing proceedings, save in the case of decisions closing proceedings adopted before the application has been served on the defendant.

59. The Registrar shall ensure that the case-law of the Court is made public in accordance with arrangements adopted by the Court. Information concerning those arrangements shall be available on the internet site of the Court of Justice of the European Union.]

NOTES

The words in square brackets in points 7, 9 and 13 were substituted by Amendments to the Practice Rules for the Implementation of the Rules of Procedure of the General Court, Article 1 (OJ L294, 21.11.2018, p 23).

Points 14 to 229 and the associated headings were substituted (for the original points 14 to 270) by Amendments to the Practice Rules for the Implementation of the Rules of Procedure of the General Court, Article 1 (OJ L294, 21.11.2018, p 23).

[II. GENERAL PROVISIONS ON PROCEDURES FOR DEALING WITH CASES

A. SERVICE

[6.489]

60. Service shall be effected by the Registry in accordance with Article 57 of the Rules of Procedure.

61. The copy of the document to be served shall be accompanied by a letter specifying the case number, the register number and a brief indication of the nature of the document.

62. Where a document is served in accordance with Article 57(2) of the Rules of Procedure, the addressee shall be informed of such service by the transmission by e-Curia of a copy of the letter accompanying the document to be served and drawing his attention to the provisions of Article 57(2) of the Rules of Procedure.

63. The proof of service shall be kept on the case file.

64. If service of the application on the defendant is attempted unsuccessfully, the Registrar shall prescribe a time limit within which the applicant is to supply additional information for service or to ask whether the applicant will agree to use, at his own expense, the services of a judicial officer for the purpose of re-serving the application.

B. TIME LIMITS

65. As regards Article 58(1)(a) and (b) of the Rules of Procedure, where a time limit is expressed in weeks, months or years, it shall expire at the end of the day which, in the last week, month or year indicated in the time limit, is the same day of the week, or falls on the same date, as the day on which the time limit began to run, that is the day on which the event which started time running occurred, or the action which started time running took place, and not the following day.

66. Article 58(2) of the Rules of Procedure, according to which a time limit which would otherwise end on a Saturday, Sunday or an official holiday is to be extended until the end of the next working day, shall be applicable only where the entire time limit, including the extension on account of distance, ends on a Saturday, Sunday or official holiday.

67. The Registrar shall prescribe the time limits provided for in the Rules of Procedure, in accordance with the authority accorded to him by the President.

68. In accordance with Article 62 of the Rules of Procedure, procedural documents or items received at the Registry after the time limit prescribed for their lodgment has expired may be accepted only with the authorisation of the President.

69. The Registrar may extend the time limits prescribed, in accordance with the authority accorded to him by the President. When necessary, he shall submit to the President proposals for the extension of time limits. Applications for extensions of time limits must be duly reasoned and be submitted in good time before the expiry of the time limit prescribed.

70. A time limit may not be extended more than once save for exceptional reasons.

C. ANONYMITY

71. Where a party considers that his identity should not be made public in a case brought before the Court, he must request, pursuant to Article 66 of the Rules of Procedure, that the Court 'anonymise' the relevant case, in whole or in part.

72. The application for anonymity must be made by a separate document stating appropriate reasons.

73. In order to ensure that anonymity is preserved, the application must be made at the outset of the proceedings. On account of the dissemination of information concerning the case on the internet, the practical effect of anonymisation is jeopardised if the case concerned has been referred to in the list of cases brought before the Court that is published on the internet site of the Court of Justice of the European Union or if the notice of the case concerned has already been published in the *Official Journal of the European Union*.

D. OMISSION OF INFORMATION VIS-À-VIS THE PUBLIC

74. In accordance with Article 66 of the Rules of Procedure, a party may submit an application for the identity of third parties mentioned in connection with the proceedings or certain confidential information to be omitted from those documents relating to the case to which the public has access.

75. The application for omission must be made by a separate document. It must accurately identify the information concerned and state the reasons for which each item of information is regarded as confidential.

76. In order to ensure that the information concerned is not disclosed to the public, it is recommended that the application be made at the outset of the proceedings, or when lodging the procedural document containing the information concerned, or immediately after becoming aware of that procedural document, as the case may be. On account of the dissemination of information concerning the case on the internet, omitting information vis-à-vis the public becomes much more difficult if the notice of the case concerned has already been published in the *Official Journal of the European Union*, or where the decision of the Court taken in the course of proceedings or closing them has been made available on the internet site of the Court of Justice of the European Union.]

NOTES

Points 14 to 229 and the associated headings were substituted (for the original points 14 to 270) by Amendments to the Practice Rules for the Implementation of the Rules of Procedure of the General Court, Article 1 (OJ L294, 21.11.2018, p 23).

[III. PROCEDURAL DOCUMENTS AND THE ANNEXES THERETO

A. LODGING OF PROCEDURAL DOCUMENTS AND ANNEXES VIA E-CURIA

[6.490]

77. All procedural documents must be lodged at the Registry by exclusively electronic means using the e-Curia application (https://curia.europa.eu/e-Curia) in compliance with the decision of the Court of 11 July 2018 and the Conditions of use of e-Curia, save for those cases referred to in points 89 to 91 below. The latter two documents shall be available on the internet site of the Court of Justice of the European Union.

78. The representative lodging a document via e-Curia must satisfy all the requirements laid down in Article 19 of the Statute and must, if he is a lawyer, have the requisite independence from the party he represents.

79. The use of the representative's personal username and password shall be equivalent to his signature on the procedural document lodged in accordance with Article 3 of the decision of the Court of 11 July 2018, and is intended to guarantee the authenticity of that document. By the use of his personal username and password, the representative shall accept responsibility for the content of the document lodged.

B. PRESENTATION OF PROCEDURAL DOCUMENTS AND ANNEXES

B.1. PROCEDURAL DOCUMENTS

80. The following information must appear on the first page of each procedural document:
   (a) the case number (T- . . . /..), where it has already been notified by the Registry;
   (b) the title of the procedural document (application, defence, response, reply, rejoinder, application to intervene, statement in intervention, plea of inadmissibility, observations on . . . , replies to questions, etc.);
   (c) the names of the applicant, of the defendant, of the intervener, if any, and of any other party to the proceedings in intellectual property cases;
   (d) the name of the party on whose behalf the procedural document is lodged.

81. In order to facilitate the electronic consultation of procedural documents, these must be submitted:
   (a) in A4 format;
   (b) with a commonly used font (such as Times New Roman, Courier or Arial) in at least 12 point in the body of the text and at least 10 point in the footnotes, with single line spacing, and upper, lower, left and right margins of at least 2.5 cm;
   (c) with each paragraph numbered consecutively;
   (d) with each page numbered consecutively.

B.2. SCHEDULE OF ANNEXES

82. The schedule of annexes must appear at the end of the procedural document. Annexes submitted without a schedule of annexes will not be accepted.

83. The schedule of annexes must indicate, for each item annexed:
   (a) the number of the annex (by reference to the procedural document to which the items are annexed, using a letter and a number: for example, Annex A.1, A.2, . . . for annexes to the application; B.1, B.2, . . . for annexes to the defence or to the response; C.1, C.2, . . . for annexes to the reply; D.1, D.2, . . . for annexes to the rejoinder);
   (b) a short description of the annex (for example: 'letter', followed by its date, author and addressee and the number of pages);
   (c) the page numbers of the first and last pages of each annex, according to the consecutive page numbering of the annexes (for example: pages 43 to 49 of the annexes);
   (d) the number of the paragraph in which the item is first mentioned and its relevance described.

84. In order to ensure optimal handling by the Registry, any annexes that are in colour must be clearly indicated as such in the schedule of annexes.

B.3. ANNEXES

85. Only those items mentioned in the actual text of a procedural document which are referred to in the schedule of annexes and which are necessary in order to prove or illustrate its contents may be submitted as annexes to a procedural document.

86. Items annexed to a procedural document must be submitted in such a way as to facilitate the electronic inspection of documents by the Court and to avoid any possibility of confusion. Accordingly, the following requirements must be complied with:
   (a) each annex must be numbered in accordance with point 83(a) above;
   (b) it is recommended that each annex be introduced by means of a specific coverpage;
   (c) where annexes are documents which themselves contain annexes, they must be arranged and numbered in such a way as to avoid any possibility of confusion;
   (d) items annexed to a procedural document must be paginated in the top right-hand corner, in ascending order. Those items must be paginated consecutively but separately from the procedural document to which they are annexed;
   (e) the annexes must be easily legible.

87. Each reference to an item lodged must state the relevant annex number as given in the schedule of annexes and indicate the procedural document with which the annex has been lodged (for example: Annex A.1 to the application).

C. PRESENTATION OF FILES LODGED BY E-CURIA

88. Procedural documents and annexes thereto lodged by means of the e-Curia application shall be presented in the form of files. In order to assist the Registry in handling them, it is recommended to follow the practical guidance given in the e-Curia User Guide available online on the internet site of the Court of Justice of the European Union, namely:

- files must include names identifying the procedural document (Pleading, Annexes Part 1, Annexes Part 2, Covering letter, etc.);
- the text of the procedural document can be saved in PDF directly from the word-processing software without the need for scanning;
- the procedural document must include the schedule of annexes;
- the annexes must be contained in one or more files separate from the file containing the procedural document. A file may contain several annexes. It is not obligatory to create one file per annex. It is recommended that annexes be added in ascending order when they are lodged, and that they be sufficiently clearly named (for example: Annexes 1 to 3, Annexes 4 to 6, etc.).

D. LODGING OF DOCUMENTS OTHERWISE THAN BY E-CURIA

89. The general rule according to which all procedural documents must be lodged at the Registry by means of e-Curia shall be without prejudice to those cases referred to in Article 105(1) and (2) and Article 147(6) of the Rules of Procedure.

90. In addition, annexes to a procedural document, which are mentioned in the body of that document and which by their nature cannot be lodged by e-Curia, may be sent separately by post or delivered to the Registry in accordance with Article 72(4) of the Rules of Procedure, provided that they are mentioned in the schedule of annexes to the document lodged by e-Curia. The schedule of annexes must identify which annexes are to be lodged separately. Those annexes must reach the Registry no later than 10 days after the lodging of the procedural document by e-Curia. They must be lodged at the following address:

Registry of the General Court of the European Union
Rue du Fort Niedergrünewald
L-2925 Luxembourg

91. Where it is technically impossible to lodge a procedural document by e-Curia, the representative must follow the procedure laid down in Article 7 of the decision of the Court of 11 July 2018. The copy of the document lodged otherwise than by e-Curia in accordance with the second paragraph of Article 7 of the decision of the Court of 11 July 2018 must include the schedule of annexes and all the annexes referred to therein. It is not necessary for the copy of the procedural document thus lodged to be signed by hand.

E. NON-ACCEPTANCE OF PROCEDURAL DOCUMENTS AND ITEMS

92. The Registrar shall refuse to enter in the register and to place on the case file procedural documents and, where appropriate, items which are not provided for by the Rules of Procedure. If in doubt, the Registrar shall refer the matter to the President in order for a decision to be taken.

93. Save in the cases expressly provided for by the Rules of Procedure and subject to points 99 and 100 below, the Registrar shall refuse to enter in the register and to place on the case file procedural documents or items drawn up in a language other than the language of the case.

94. Where a party challenges the Registrar's refusal to enter a procedural document or an item in the register and to place it on the case file, the Registrar shall submit that issue to the President for a decision on whether the document or item in question is to be accepted.

F. REGULARISATION OF PROCEDURAL DOCUMENTS AND ANNEXES

F.1. GENERAL

95. The Registrar shall ensure that procedural documents placed on the case file and the annexes thereto are in conformity with the provisions of the Statute and the Rules of Procedure, and with these Practice Rules.

96. If necessary, he shall allow the parties a period of time for making good any formal irregularities in the procedural documents lodged.

97. In the event of any repeated failure to comply with the requirements of the Rules of Procedure or of these Practice Rules, requiring regularisation to be sought, the Registrar will request the party or applicant for leave to intervene to pay the costs involved in the requisite processing thereof by the Court, in accordance with Article 139(c) of the Rules of Procedure.

98. Where annexes are still not submitted in accordance with the provisions of the Rules of Procedure or of these Practice Rules despite requests for regularisation, the Registrar shall refer the matter to the President for a decision on whether to refuse to accept those annexes.

99. Where material annexed to a procedural document is not accompanied by a translation into the language of the case, the Registrar shall require the party concerned to make good the irregularity if such a translation appears necessary for the purposes of the efficient conduct of the proceedings. If the irregularity is not made good, the annexes in question shall be removed from the case file.

100. Where an application to intervene originating from a third party other than a Member State is not drawn up in the language of the case, the Registrar shall require the application to be put in order before it is served on the parties. If a version of such an application drawn up in the language of the case is lodged within the time limit prescribed for this purpose by the Registrar, the date on which the first version, not in the language of the case, was lodged shall be taken as the date on which the procedural document was lodged.

F.2. REGULARISATION OF APPLICATIONS

101. If an application does not comply with the requirements specified in Annex 1 to these Practice Rules, the Registry shall not serve it and a reasonable time limit shall be prescribed for the purposes of putting it in order. Failure to put the application in order may result in the action being dismissed as inadmissible, in accordance with Article 78(6), Article 177(6) and Article 194(5) of the Rules of Procedure.

102. If an application does not comply with the procedural rules specified in Annex 2 to these Practice Rules, service of the application shall be delayed and a reasonable time limit shall be prescribed for the purposes of putting the application in order.

103. If an application does not comply with the procedural rules specified in Annex 3 to these Practice Rules, the application shall be served and a reasonable time limit shall be prescribed for the purposes of putting it in order.

F.3. REGULARISATION OF OTHER PROCEDURAL DOCUMENTS

104. The instances of regularisation referred to in points 101 to 103 above shall apply as necessary to procedural documents other than the application.]

NOTES

Points 14 to 229 and the associated headings were substituted (for the original points 14 to 270) by Amendments to the Practice Rules for the Implementation of the Rules of Procedure of the General Court, Article 1 (OJ L294, 21.11.2018, p 23).

[IV. THE WRITTEN PART OF THE PROCEDURE

A. LENGTH OF WRITTEN PLEADINGS

A.1. DIRECT ACTIONS

[6.491]

105. In direct actions within the meaning of Article 1 of the Rules of Procedure, the maximum number of pages[1] shall be as follows.

In direct actions other than those brought pursuant to Article 270 TFEU:

— 50 pages for the application and for the defence;
— 25 pages for the reply and for the rejoinder;
— 20 pages for a plea of inadmissibility and for observations thereon;
— 20 pages for a statement in intervention and 15 pages for observations thereon.

In direct actions brought pursuant to Article 270 TFEU:

— 30 pages for the application and for the defence;
— 15 pages for the reply and for the rejoinder;
— 10 pages for a plea of inadmissibility and for observations thereon;
— 10 pages for a statement in intervention and 5 pages for observations thereon.]

106. Authorisation to exceed those maximum lengths will be given only in cases involving particularly complex legal or factual issues.

A.2. INTELLECTUAL PROPERTY CASES

107. In intellectual property cases, the maximum number of pages[2] shall be as follows:

— 20 pages for the application and for responses;
— 15 pages for the cross-claim and for responses thereto;
— 10 pages for a plea of inadmissibility and for observations thereon;
— 10 pages for a statement in intervention and 5 pages for observations thereon.

108. Authorisation to exceed those maximum lengths will be given only in cases involving particularly complex legal or factual issues.

A.3. REGULARISATION OF EXCESSIVELY LONG PLEADINGS

109. A pleading comprising a number of pages which exceeds by 40% or more the maximum number of pages prescribed in points 105 and 107 above, as the case may be, shall require regularisation, unless otherwise directed by the President.

110. A pleading comprising a number of pages which exceeds by less than 40% the maximum number of pages prescribed in points 105 and 107 above, as the case may be, may require regularisation if so directed by the President.

111. Where a party is requested to put his pleading in order on account of its excessive length, service of the pleading which requires regularisation on account of its length shall be delayed.

B. STRUCTURE AND CONTENT OF WRITTEN PLEADINGS

B.1. DIRECT ACTIONS

1)
Application initiating proceedings

112. The mandatory information to be included in the application initiating proceedings is prescribed by Article 76 of the Rules of Procedure.

113. The introductory part of the application should be followed by a brief account of the facts giving rise to the dispute.

114. The precise wording of the form of order sought by the applicant must be stated either at the beginning or at the end of the application.

115. Legal arguments should be set out and grouped by reference to the particular pleas in law to which they relate. Each argument or group of arguments should generally be preceded by a summary statement of the relevant plea. In addition, the pleas in law put forward should ideally each be given a heading to enable them to be identified easily.

116. The documents referred to in Article 51(2) and (3) and Article 78 of the Rules of Procedure must be produced together with the application.

117. For the purposes of the production of the document required by Article 51(2) of the Rules of Procedure certifying that the lawyer representing a party or assisting the party's agent is authorised to practise before a court of a Member State or of another State which is a party to the Agreement on the European Economic Area, reference may be made to a document previously lodged in a case before the Court.

118. Each application must be accompanied by a summary of the pleas in law and main arguments relied on, designed to facilitate the drafting of the notice required to be published in the *Official Journal of the European Union* in accordance with Article 79 of the Rules of Procedure.

119. In order to assist the Court in processing the summary of pleas in law and main arguments relied on, it is requested that the summary:

– be produced separately from the body of the application and the annexes mentioned in the application;
– not exceed two pages;
– be prepared in the language of the case in accordance with the model available online on the internet site of the Court of Justice of the European Union;

– be transmitted by email, as an ordinary electronic file produced using word-processing software, to GC.Registry@curia.europa.eu, indicating the case to which it relates.

120. If the application is lodged after the submission of an application for legal aid, the effect of which, under Article 147(7) of the Rules of Procedure, is to suspend the time limit prescribed for the bringing of an action, this must be stated at the beginning of the application initiating proceedings.

121. If the application is lodged after service of the order making a decision on an application for legal aid or, where no lawyer is designated in that order to represent the applicant for legal aid, after service of the order designating the lawyer instructed to represent the applicant for legal aid, reference must also be made in the application to the date on which the order was served on the applicant.

122. In order to facilitate formal preparation of the application, the parties' representatives are invited to consult the document entitled 'Aide-mémoire: Application', which is available on the internet site of the Court of Justice of the European Union.

2)
Defence

123. The mandatory information to be included in the defence is prescribed by Article 81(1) of the Rules of Procedure.

124. The precise wording of the form of order sought by the defendant must be stated either at the beginning or at the end of the defence.

125. Any fact alleged by the applicant which is contested must be specified and the basis on which it is contested expressly stated.

126. Since the legal framework of the proceedings is fixed by the application, the legal arguments developed in the defence must, so far as is possible, be set out and grouped by reference to the pleas in law or complaints put forward in the application.

127. Points 116 and 117 above shall apply to the defence.

128. In cases brought pursuant to Article 270 TFEU, the institutions should preferably annex to the defence any acts of general application cited which have not been published in the *Official Journal of the European Union*, together with details of the dates of their adoption, their entry into force and, where applicable, their repeal.

3)
Reply and rejoinder

129. Where there is a second exchange of pleadings, the main parties may supplement their legal arguments with a reply or a rejoinder, as the case may be.

130. The framework and the pleas in law or complaints at the heart of the dispute having been set out (or disputed) in depth in the application and the defence, the purpose of the reply and the rejoinder shall be to allow the applicant and the defendant to make clear their position or to refine their arguments on an important issue, and to respond to new matters raised in the defence and in the reply. The President may also, pursuant to Article 83(3) of the Rules of Procedure, himself specify the matters to which those procedural documents should relate.

B.2. Intellectual Property Cases

1)
Application initiating proceedings

131. The mandatory information to be included in the application initiating proceedings is prescribed by Article 177(1) of the Rules of Procedure.

132. The application must also contain the information referred to in Article 177(2) and (3) of the Rules of Procedure.

133. The documents referred to in Article 177(3) to (5) of the Rules of Procedure must be produced together with the application.

134. Points 113 to 115, 117 and 120 to 122 above shall apply to applications in intellectual property cases.

2)
Response

135. The mandatory information to be included in the response is prescribed by Article 180(1) of the Rules of Procedure.

136. The precise wording of the form of order sought by the defendant or by the intervener must be stated either at the beginning or at the end of the response.

137. The documents referred to in Article 177(4) and (5) of the Rules of Procedure must be produced together with the response lodged by the intervener, in so far as those documents have not already been lodged in accordance with Article 173(5) of the Rules of Procedure.

138. Points 117, 125 and 126 above shall apply to the response.

3)
Cross-claim and responses to the cross-claim

139. If, when the application has been served on him, a party to the proceedings before the Board of Appeal other than the applicant intends to challenge the contested decision on a point not raised in the application, that party must introduce a cross-claim when lodging his response. That cross-claim must be introduced by a separate document and meet the requirements set out in Articles 183 and 184 of the Rules of Procedure.

140. Where such a cross-claim is made, the other parties to the proceedings may submit a pleading in response confined to the form of order sought, the pleas in law and the arguments relied on in the cross-claim.]

NOTES

Points 14 to 229 and the associated headings were substituted (for the original points 14 to 270) by Amendments to the Practice Rules for the Implementation of the Rules of Procedure of the General Court, Article 1 (OJ L294, 21.11.2018, p 23).

1 The text must be presented in accordance with the requirements set out in point 81(b) of these Practice Rules.

2 The text must be presented in accordance with the requirements set out in point 81(b) of these Practice Rules.

[V. THE ORAL PART OF THE PROCEDURE

A. REQUESTS FOR A HEARING

[6.492]

141. As is apparent from Article 106 of the Rules of Procedure, the Court shall arrange a hearing either of its own motion or at the request of a main party.

142. A main party who wishes to present oral argument must submit a reasoned request for a hearing, within three weeks after service on the parties of notification of the close of the written part of the procedure. That reasoning — which is not to be confused with written pleadings or observations and should not exceed three pages — must be based on a real assessment of the benefit of a hearing to the party in question and must indicate the elements of the case file or arguments which that party considers it necessary to develop or refute more fully at a hearing. In order better to ensure that the arguments remain focused at the hearing, the statement of reasons should preferably not be in general terms merely referring, for example, to the importance of the case.

143. If no reasoned request is submitted by a main party within the prescribed time limit, the Court may decide to rule on the action without an oral part of the procedure.

B. PREPARATION FOR THE HEARING

144. The parties shall be given notice to attend the hearing by the Registry at least one month before it takes place, provided always that, where the circumstances so require, a shorter period of notice may apply.

145. In accordance with Article 107(2) of the Rules of Procedure, requests for an adjournment of the hearing shall be granted only in exceptional circumstances. Such requests may be lodged only by the main parties, must state adequate reasons, be accompanied by appropriate supporting documents, and be submitted to the Court as soon as possible after notice to attend has been given.

146. If the representative of a party intends not to be present at the hearing, he is requested to inform the Court as soon as possible after notice to attend has been given.

147. The Court will make every effort to ensure that the parties' representatives receive a summary report for the hearing three weeks before the hearing. The purpose of the summary report for the hearing is to enable the parties to prepare for the hearing.

148. The summary report for the hearing, drawn up by the Judge-Rapporteur, shall be confined to setting out the pleas in law and a succinct summary of the parties' arguments.

149. Any observations the parties may wish to make on the summary report for the hearing may be made at the hearing. In such cases, a reference to such observations shall be recorded in the minutes of the hearing.

150. The summary report for the hearing shall be made available to the public outside the courtroom on the day of the hearing, unless the case is to be entirely heard in camera.

151. Before every public hearing the Registrar shall cause the following information to be displayed outside the courtroom in the language of the case: the date and time of the hearing, the competent formation of the Court, the case(s) which will be called and the names of the parties.

152. A request to use particular technical means for the purposes of a presentation must be made at least two weeks before the date of the hearing. If the request is approved by the President, the arrangements for such use of technology should be made with the Registry, so that any technical or practical constraints can be taken into account. The sole object of the presentation shall be to illustrate the information contained in the case file and it must not, therefore, contain new pleas in law or new evidence. Supporting material for such presentations shall not be placed on the case file, nor, therefore, shall it be served on the other parties, unless the President otherwise decides.

153. In view of the security measures in place to control access to the buildings of the Court of Justice of the European Union, it is recommended that the parties' representatives take the necessary steps to ensure that they are present in the courtroom at least 15 minutes before the hearing is due to start, as the members of the formation of the Court will normally wish to discuss the organisation of the hearing with them.

154. In order to prepare for their participation in a hearing, the parties' representatives are invited to consult the following document, which is available on the internet site of the Court of Justice of the European Union: 'Aide-mémoire: Hearing of oral argument'.

C. CONDUCT OF THE HEARING

155. The parties' representatives shall be required to appear before the Court in their gowns.

156. The purpose of the hearing shall be:

- where necessary, to reiterate in condensed form the position taken by the parties, emphasising the key submissions advanced in writing;
- to clarify, if necessary, certain arguments advanced during the written part of the procedure and to submit any new material arising from events occurring after the close of the written part of the procedure and which therefore could not have been set out in the pleadings;
- to reply to any questions put by the Court.

157. It will be for each party to assess, in the light of the purpose of the hearing, as defined in point 156 above, whether oral argument is really necessary or whether it would be sufficient simply to refer to the written observations or pleadings. The hearing can then concentrate on the replies to questions put by the Court. If the representative does consider it necessary to address the Court, it is recommended that he confine himself to making specific points and referring to the pleadings in relation to other points.

158. Where, before the hearing, the Court has invited the parties, in accordance with Article 89(4) of the Rules of Procedure, to concentrate in their oral pleadings on one or more specified issues, those issues must be addressed as a matter of priority in the oral submissions.

159. If a party refrains from presenting oral argument, this shall not constitute acquiescence in the oral argument presented by another party where the arguments in question have already been refuted in writing. Such silence shall not preclude that party from responding to the other party's submission.

160. In the interests of clarity and in order to enable the Members of the Court to understand oral submissions better, it will generally be preferable for Counsel to speak freely on the basis of notes rather than to read out a written text. The parties' representatives are also requested to simplify their presentation of the case as far as possible and to use short sentences. It would also assist the Court if representatives could structure their oral argument and indicate, before developing it, the structure they intend to adopt.

161. In order to assist the Court in relation to certain technical issues, the President of the formation may authorise the parties' representatives to give the floor to individuals who, despite not having the status of representative, are best placed to comment. Those individuals shall intervene only in the presence of the representative of the party concerned and responsibility for them shall lie with him. Before addressing the Court, those individuals must identify themselves.

162. The time taken in presenting oral submissions may vary, depending on the complexity of the case and on whether or not new facts have arisen. Each of the main parties will be allowed 15 minutes and each intervener will be allowed 10 minutes to present oral submissions (in joined cases, each of the main parties will be allowed 15 minutes for each case and each intervener will be allowed 10 minutes for each case), unless the Registry has indicated otherwise. These limitations shall apply only to the oral submissions themselves and not to the time required to answer questions put at the hearing or for final replies.

163. If circumstances so require, a request for leave to exceed the speaking time normally allowed, giving reasons and indicating the speaking time considered necessary, may be made to the Registry at least two weeks (or less, in duly substantiated exceptional circumstances) before the date fixed for the hearing. When such requests are made, representatives will be informed of the time which they will have for presenting their oral submissions.

164. When several representatives act for a party, only two of them may normally present oral argument, and their combined speaking time must not exceed the time limits indicated in point 162 above. However, representatives other than those who addressed the Court may answer questions from Members of the Court and make final replies.

165. Where two or more parties are advancing the same argument before the Court (a situation which may arise where, in particular, there are interventions or where cases are joined), their representatives are requested to confer with each other before the hearing in order to avoid any repetition.

166. When citing a decision of the Court of Justice, the General Court or the Civil Service Tribunal, representatives are requested to refer to it by the usual name of the case and the case number, and, where relevant, to specify the relevant paragraph(s).

167. In accordance with Article 85(3) of the Rules of Procedure, the main parties may, exceptionally, produce further evidence at the hearing. In such cases, the other parties will be heard on the admissibility and content thereof. It would be prudent to bring sufficient copies where appropriate.

D. INTERPRETATION

168. In order to facilitate interpretation, parties' representatives are requested to send any text or written notes for their submissions to the Interpretation Directorate in advance by email (interpret@curia.europa.eu).

169. Any notes for submissions thus transmitted will be treated in the strictest confidence. In order to avoid any misunderstanding, the name of the party must be stated. Notes for submissions will not be placed on the case file.

170. Representatives are reminded that, depending on the case being heard, only some of the Members of the bench may be following the oral argument in the language in which it is being presented; the other Members will be listening to the simultaneous interpretation. In the interests of the better conduct of the hearing and of maintaining the quality of the simultaneous interpretation, representatives are strongly advised to speak slowly and directly into the microphone.

171. Where representatives intend to cite verbatim passages from certain texts or documents, particularly passages not appearing in the case file, it would be helpful if they would indicate the passages concerned to the interpreters before the hearing. Similarly, it may be helpful to draw the interpreters' attention to any terms which may be difficult to translate.

E. MINUTES OF THE HEARING

172. The Registrar shall draw up in the respective language of each case the minutes of every hearing. Those minutes shall contain: an indication of the case; the date, time and place of the hearing; an indication, where applicable, that the case was heard in camera; the names of the Judges and the Registrar present; the names and status of the parties' representatives present; a reference to any observations on the summary report for the hearing; the surnames, forenames, status and permanent addresses of any witnesses or experts examined; an indication, where applicable, of the procedural documents or items produced at the hearing; and, in so far as is necessary, the statements made at the hearing and the decisions pronounced at the hearing by the Court or the President.]

NOTES

Points 14 to 229 and the associated headings were substituted (for the original points 14 to 270) by Amendments to the Practice Rules for the Implementation of the Rules of Procedure of the General Court, Article 1 (OJ L294, 21.11.2018, p 23).

VI. CONFIDENTIAL TREATMENT

A. GENERAL

[6.493]

173. In accordance with Article 64 and subject to the provisions of Article 68(4), Article 104, Article 105(8) and Article 144(7) of the Rules of Procedure, the Court shall take into consideration only those procedural documents and items which have been made available to the representatives of the parties and on which they have been given an opportunity of expressing their views.

174. It follows that, without prejudice to the provisions of Articles 103 to 105 of the Rules of Procedure, no consideration may be given to an application by the applicant for certain information on the case file to be treated as confidential in relation to the defendant. Likewise, no such application may be made by the defendant in relation to the applicant.

175. Nevertheless, a main party may apply for confidential information on the case file to be excluded from the documents to be communicated to an intervener in accordance with Article 144(7) of the Rules of Procedure.

176. Each party may also request that a party to joined cases not be given access to certain information in the files concerned by the joinder on account of its alleged confidentiality, in accordance with Article 68(4) of the Rules of Procedure.

B. CONFIDENTIAL TREATMENT WHERE AN APPLICATION TO INTERVENE HAS BEEN MADE

177. Where an application to intervene is made in a case, the main parties are requested to state, within the time limit prescribed by the Registrar to that effect, whether they wish to seek confidential treatment in respect of certain information included in the procedural documents already placed on the case file.

178. The main parties must submit simultaneously with any procedural document or item that they may lodge subsequently any application for confidential treatment that may be required in respect of the procedural document or item concerned. In the absence of such an application, the procedural documents and items lodged will be communicated to the intervener.

179. Any application for confidential treatment must be made by a separate document. It may not be lodged as a confidential version and must not, therefore, contain confidential information.

180. An application for confidential treatment must specify the party in relation to whom confidentiality is requested.

181. An application for confidential treatment must be limited to what is strictly necessary and may not in any event cover the entirety of a procedural document; only exceptionally may it extend to the entirety of an annexed document. It should usually be possible to furnish a non-confidential version of a procedural document and items in which certain passages, words or figures have been deleted without affecting the interests it is sought to protect.

182. An application for confidential treatment must accurately identify the particulars or passages to be excluded and state the reasons for which each of those particulars or passages is regarded as confidential. Failure to provide such information may result in the application being refused by the Court.

183. On lodging an application for confidential treatment in respect of one or more procedural documents, a party must produce a full non-confidential version of each procedural document and item concerned, with the confidential particulars or passages removed.

184. Where an application for confidential treatment does not comply with points 179, 180 and 183 above, the Registrar shall request the party concerned to put the application in order. If, despite such a request, the application for confidential treatment is not made to comply with the requirements of these Practice Rules, it will not be possible for it to be properly processed, and a copy of every procedural document and item concerned will be communicated to the intervener.

C. CONFIDENTIAL TREATMENT WHERE CASES ARE JOINED

185. Where it is envisaged that several cases will be joined, the parties are requested to state, within the time limit prescribed by the Registrar to that effect, whether they wish to seek confidential treatment in respect of certain information included in the procedural documents and material already placed on the files of the cases concerned by the joinder.

186. The parties must submit simultaneously with any procedural document or item that they may lodge subsequently any application for confidential treatment that may be required in respect of the procedural document or item concerned. In the absence of such an application, the procedural documents and items lodged will be made available to the other parties in the joined cases.

187. Points 179 to 184 above shall apply to applications for confidential treatment submitted where cases are joined.

D. CONFIDENTIAL TREATMENT UNDER ARTICLE 103 OF THE RULES OF PROCEDURE

188. The Court may, pursuant to the measures of inquiry referred to in Article 91 of the Rules of Procedure, order a party to produce information or material relating to the case. In accordance with Article 92(3) of the Rules of Procedure, such production may be ordered only where the party concerned has not complied with a measure of organisation of procedure previously adopted to that end, or where expressly requested by the party concerned by the measure and that party explains the need for such a measure to be in the form of an order for a measure of inquiry.

189. Where a main party submits in his response to an application for a measure of organisation of procedure that certain information or material is confidential and he therefore objects to its transmission or proposes that a measure of inquiry be adopted, the Court shall, if it considers that that information or material may be relevant in order for it to rule in the case, order its production by means of an order for a measure of inquiry under Article 91(b) of the Rules of Procedure. The treatment of confidential information or material thus produced before the Court shall be governed by Article 103 of the Rules of Procedure. The regime in question does not provide for any derogation from the principle of the adversarial nature of the proceedings, but lays down the rules for the implementation of that principle.

190. In accordance with that provision, the Court shall examine the relevance of the information or material to the outcome of the proceedings and verify the confidential nature of that information or material. If it considers that the information concerned is both relevant to the outcome of the proceedings and confidential, the Court shall weigh that confidentiality against the requirements linked to the right to effective judicial protection, particularly observance of the adversarial principle, and, after weighing up those matters, will have two options.

191. The Court may decide that the information or material must be brought to the attention of the other main party, notwithstanding its confidential nature. In that respect, the Court may, by way of a measure of organisation of procedure, request the representatives of the parties other than the party who produced the confidential information to give an undertaking to preserve the confidentiality of the document or item by not communicating to their respective clients or to a third party the information that is to be disclosed to them. Any breach of that undertaking may result in Article 55 of the Rules of Procedure being applied.

192. Alternatively, the Court may decide not to communicate the confidential information, whilst nevertheless ensuring that the other main party is provided with non-confidential information so that he can, to the greatest extent possible, make his views known in compliance with the adversarial principle. The Court shall then order the main party who produced the confidential information to communicate certain particulars in such a way as to enable the preservation of the confidentiality of the information to be reconciled with the adversarial nature of the proceedings. It will, for example, be possible for the information to be transmitted in summarised form. If the Court considers that the other main party cannot properly exercise his rights of defence, it may make one or more orders, until it considers that the proceedings can properly be continued on an adversarial basis.

193. Where the Court considers that the communication of information to the other main party in accordance with the procedures prescribed by the order made under Article 103(3) of the Rules of Procedure has enabled that party to present his views effectively, the confidential information or material which has not been brought to the attention of that party shall not be taken into consideration by the Court. The confidential information or material shall be removed from the file, and the parties informed accordingly.

E. CONFIDENTIAL TREATMENT UNDER ARTICLE 104 OF THE RULES OF PROCEDURE

194. In the context of its review of the legality of a measure adopted by an institution denying access to a document, the Court may order, by way of a measure of inquiry under Article 91(c) of the Rules of Procedure, that the document be produced.

195. The document produced by the institution shall not be communicated to the other parties, as the action would otherwise be devoid of purpose.

F. CONFIDENTIAL TREATMENT UNDER ARTICLE 105 OF THE RULES OF PROCEDURE

196. In accordance with Article 105(1) and (2) of the Rules of Procedure, a main party to the proceedings may, on his own initiative or following a measure of inquiry ordered by the Court, produce information or material pertaining to the security of the European Union or to that of one or more of its Member States or to the conduct of their international relations. Article 105(3) to (10) lays down the procedural rules applicable to such information or material.

197. In view of the sensitive, confidential nature of information or material pertaining to the security of the Union or to that of one or more of its Member States or to the conduct of their international relations, the application of the body of rules established by Article 105 of the Rules of Procedure requires a suitable security framework to be set up in order to ensure a high level of protection for that information or material. That framework is documented in the decision of the Court of 14 September 2016.]

NOTES

Points 14 to 229 and the associated headings were substituted (for the original points 14 to 270) by Amendments to the Practice Rules for the Implementation of the Rules of Procedure of the General Court, Article 1 (OJ L294, 21.11.2018, p 23).

[VII. LEGAL AID

[6.494]

198. In accordance with Article 147(2) of the Rules of Procedure, the use of a form in making an application for legal aid shall be compulsory. The form is available on the internet site of the Court of Justice of the European Union.

199. An applicant for legal aid who is not represented by a lawyer when the legal aid form is lodged may, in accordance with Article 147(6) of the Rules of Procedure, lodge the duly completed and signed paper form at the Registry by post or physically deliver it to the address indicated in point 90 above. Forms not bearing a handwritten signature will not be processed.

200. Where the applicant for legal aid is represented by a lawyer when the legal aid form is lodged, the form shall be lodged in accordance with Article 72(1) of the Rules of Procedure, taking into account the requirements of points 77 to 79 above.

201. The legal aid form is intended to provide the Court, in accordance with Article 147(3) and (4) of the Rules of Procedure, with the information required to give an effective decision on the application for legal aid. The information required concerns:

– the legal aid applicant's financial situation

and,

– where the action has not yet been brought, the subject matter of that action, the facts of the case and the arguments relating thereto.

202. The legal aid applicant shall be required to produce, together with the legal aid form, documentary evidence to support the information referred to in point 201 above.

203. Where applicable, the documents referred to in Article 51(2) and (3) and Article 78(4) of the Rules of Procedure must be produced together with the legal aid form.

204. The duly completed legal aid form and supporting documents must be intelligible in themselves.

205. Without prejudice to the Court's power to request information or the production of further documents under Articles 89 and 90 of the Rules of Procedure, the application for legal aid may not be supplemented by the subsequent filing of additional material. Such material shall be rejected, unless it has been lodged at the request of the Court. In exceptional cases, supporting documents intended to establish the applicant's lack of means may nevertheless be accepted subsequently, subject to the delay in their production being adequately explained.

206. Under Article 147(7) of the Rules of Procedure, the introduction of an application for legal aid shall suspend the time limit prescribed for the bringing of the action to which the application refers until the date of service of the order making a decision on that application or, where no lawyer is designated in that order to represent the applicant for legal aid, until the date of service of the order designating the lawyer instructed to represent him.

207. Since the lodging of an application for legal aid has the effect of suspending the time limit prescribed for bringing an action until service of the order referred to in point 206 above, the remaining period within which the application initiating proceedings may be lodged may be very short. Recipients of legal aid who are duly represented by a lawyer are therefore advised to pay particular attention to compliance with the legal time limit.]

NOTES

Points 14 to 229 and the associated headings were substituted (for the original points 14 to 270) by Amendments to the Practice Rules for the Implementation of the Rules of Procedure of the General Court, Article 1 (OJ L294, 21.11.2018, p 23).

[VIII. URGENT PROCEDURES

A. EXPEDITED PROCEDURE

A.1. Request for an expedited procedure

[6.495]

208. In accordance with Article 152(1) of the Rules of Procedure, a request for an expedited procedure must be made by a separate document lodged simultaneously with the application initiating the proceedings or the defence, as the case may be, and contain a statement of reasons specifying the particular urgency of the case and any other relevant circumstances.

209. In order to facilitate immediate processing by the Registry, the request for an expedited procedure must state on the first page that it is lodged under Articles 151 and 152 of the Rules of Procedure.

210. The application in respect of which the expedited procedure is requested must not in principle exceed 25 pages. Such an application must be submitted in accordance with the requirements set out in points 112 to 121 above.

211. It is recommended that the party applying for the expedited procedure specify in his request the pleas in law, arguments or passages of the pleading in question (application or defence) which are put forward only in the event that the case is not decided under the expedited procedure. That information, referred to in Article 152(2) of the Rules of Procedure, must be clearly specified in the request, indicating the numbers of the paragraphs concerned.

A.2. Abridged version

212. It is recommended that an abridged version of the relevant pleading be annexed to any request for an expedited procedure which contains the information referred to in point 211 above.

213. Where an abridged version is annexed, it must comply with the following directions:

(a) the abridged version shall be in the same format as the original version of the pleading in question, with omitted passages being identified by the word 'omissis' in square brackets;

(b) paragraphs which are retained in the abridged version shall keep the same numbering as in the original version of the pleading in question;

(c) if the abridged version does not refer to all the annexes to the original version of the pleading in question, the schedule of annexes accompanying the abridged version shall identify each annex omitted by the word 'omissis';

(d) annexes which are retained in the abridged version must keep the same numbering as in the schedule of annexes in the original version of the pleading in question;

(e) the annexes referred to in the schedule accompanying the abridged version must be attached to that version.

214. In order to ensure that it is dealt with as expeditiously as possible, the abridged version must comply with the above directions.

215. Where the production of an abridged version of the pleading is requested by the Court under Article 151(3) of the Rules of Procedure, the abridged version must be prepared in accordance with the above directions, unless otherwise specified.

A.3. DEFENCE

216. If the applicant has not specified in his request for an expedited procedure the pleas in law, arguments or passages of the application initiating the proceedings which are to be taken into consideration only in the event that the case is not decided under the expedited procedure, the defendant must respond to the application initiating the proceedings within a period of one month.

217. If the applicant has specified in his request for an expedited procedure the pleas in law, arguments or passages of the application initiating the proceedings which are to be taken into consideration only in the event that the case is not decided under the expedited procedure, the defendant must respond, within a period of one month, to the pleas in law and arguments advanced in the application, in the light of the information provided in the request for the expedited procedure.

218. If the applicant has attached an abridged version of the application initiating proceedings to his request for an expedited procedure, the defendant must respond, within a period of one month, to the pleas in law and arguments contained in that abridged version of the application.

219. If the Court decides to refuse the request for an expedited procedure before the defendant has lodged his defence, the period of one month for the lodging of the defence prescribed by Article 154(1) of the Rules of Procedure shall be extended by a further month.

220. If the Court decides to refuse the request for an expedited procedure after the defendant has lodged his defence within the period of one month prescribed by Article 154(1) of the Rules of Procedure, the defendant shall be allowed a further period of one month from the date of service of the decision refusing the request for an expedited procedure, in order to supplement his defence.

A.4. ORAL PART OF THE PROCEDURE

221. Under the expedited procedure, since the written part of the procedure is in principle limited to one exchange of pleadings, the emphasis shall be on the oral part of the procedure and a hearing shall be organised promptly after the written part of the procedure has been closed. The Court may nevertheless decide to rule without an oral part of the procedure where the main parties indicate, within a period prescribed by the President, that they have decided not to participate in a hearing and the Court considers that it has sufficient information available to it from the material in the file in the case.

222. Where the Court has not authorised the lodging of a statement in intervention, the intervener may submit his observations only orally, if a hearing is organised.

B. SUSPENSION OF OPERATION OR ENFORCEMENT AND OTHER INTERIM MEASURES

223. In accordance with Article 156(5) of the Rules of Procedure, an application for suspension of operation or enforcement or other interim measures must be made by a separate document. It must be intelligible in itself, without necessitating reference to the application lodged in the main proceedings, including the annexes thereto.

224. In order to facilitate immediate processing by the Registry, the application for suspension of operation or enforcement or other interim measures must state on the first page that it is lodged under Article 156 of the Rules of Procedure and, where appropriate, that it contains an application based on Article 157(2) of the Rules of Procedure.

225. The application for suspension of operation or enforcement or other interim measures must state, with the utmost concision, the subject matter of the proceedings, the pleas of fact and of law on which the main action is based (establishing a prima facie case on the merits in that action) and the circumstances giving rise to urgency. It must specify the measure(s) applied for. It must also contain all the evidence and offers of evidence available to justify the grant of interim measures.

226. Since an application for interim measures requires the existence of a prima facie case to be assessed for the purposes of a summary procedure, it need not set out in full the text of the application in the main proceedings.

227. In order that an application for interim measures may be dealt with urgently, the number of pages it contains must not in principle (depending on the subject matter and the circumstances of the case) exceed a maximum of 25 pages.]

NOTES

Points 14 to 229 and the associated headings were substituted (for the original points 14 to 270) by Amendments to the Practice Rules for the Implementation of the Rules of Procedure of the General Court, Article 1 (OJ L294, 21.11.2018, p 23).

Part 6 UK and EU Court Materials

[IX. ENTRY INTO FORCE OF THESE PRACTICE RULES

[6.496]

228. The Instructions to the Registrar of 5 July 2007 (OJ 2007 L232, p 1), as amended on 17 May 2010 (OJ 2010 L170, p 53) and on 24 January 2012 (OJ 2012 L68, p 20), and the Practice Directions to parties before the General Court of 24 January 2012 (OJ 2012 L68, p 23) are hereby repealed and replaced by these Practice Rules.

229. These Practice Rules shall be published in the *Official Journal of the European Union*. They shall enter into force on the first day of the first month following their publication.

NOTES

Points 14 to 229 and the associated headings were substituted (for the original points 14 to 270) by Amendments to the Practice Rules for the Implementation of the Rules of Procedure of the General Court, Article 1 (OJ L294, 21.11.2018, p 23).

ANNEXES

[ANNEX 1: REQUIREMENTS NON-COMPLIANCE WITH WHICH IS GROUNDS FOR NOT SERVING THE APPLICATION (POINT 101 OF THESE PRACTICE RULES)

[6.497]

Failure to put the following points in order may result in the action being dismissed as inadmissible, in accordance with Article 78(6), Article 177(6) and Article 194(5) of the Rules of Procedure.

	Direct actions	*Intellectual property cases*
a)	production of the certificate of the lawyer's authorisation to practise (Article 51(2) of the Rules of Procedure)	production of the certificate of the lawyer's authorisation to practise (Article 51(2) of the Rules of Procedure)
b)	production of recent proof of the existence in law of a legal person governed by private law (Article 78(4) of the Rules of Procedure)	production of recent proof of the existence in law of a legal person governed by private law (Article 177(4) of the Rules of Procedure)
c)	production of authority to act if the party represented is a legal person governed by private law (Article 51(3) of the Rules of Procedure)	production of authority to act if the party represented is a legal person governed by private law (Article 51(3) of the Rules of Procedure)
d)	production of the contested measure(action for annulment) or of the documentary evidence of the date on which the institution was requested to act (action for failure to act) (second paragraph of Article 21 of the Statute; Article 78(1) of the Rules of Procedure)	production of the contested decision of the Board of Appeal (Article 177(3) of the Rules of Procedure)
e)	production of the complaint within the meaning of Article 90(2) of the Staff Regulations and the decision responding to the complaint (Article 78(2) of the Rules of Procedure)	
f)	production of a copy of the contract containing the arbitration clause (Article 78(3) of the Rules of Procedure)	
g)		indication of the names of all the parties to the proceedings before the Board of Appeal and the addresses which they had given for the purposes of notifications (Article 177(2) of the Rules of Procedure)
h)	indication of the dates on which the complaint within the meaning of Article 90(2) of the Staff Regulations was submitted and the decision responding to the complaint notified (Article 78(2) of the Rules of Procedure)	indication of the date on which the decision of the Board of Appeal was notified (Article 177(3) of the Rules of Procedure)]

NOTES

Annex 1 substituted by Amendments to the Practice Rules for the Implementation of the Rules of Procedure of the General Court, Article 1 (OJ L294, 21.11.2018, p 23).

[ANNEX 2: PROCEDURAL RULES NON-COMPLIANCE WITH WHICH JUSTIFIES DELAYING SERVICE (POINT 102 OF THESE PRACTICE RULES)

[6.498]

a)	indication of the applicant's permanent address (first paragraph of Article 21 of the Statute; Article 76(a), Article 177(1)(a) and Article 194(1)(a) of the Rules of Procedure)
b)	indication of the address of the applicant's representative (Article 76(b), Article 177(1)(b) and Article 194(1)(b) of the Rules of Procedure)

c)	new original of the application the length of which will have been reduced(points 109 and 110 of these Practice Rules)
d)	new original of the application with identical content but with numbered paragraphs (point 81(c) of these Practice Rules)
e)	new, paginated original of the application with identical content (point 81(d) of these Practice Rules)
f)	production of a schedule of annexes containing the mandatory information(Article 72(3) of the Rules of Procedure; point 83 of these Practice Rules)
g)	production of the annexes mentioned in the application but not produced(Article 72(3) of the Rules of Procedure)
h)	production of paginated annexes (point 86(d) of these Practice Rules)
i)	production of numbered annexes (point 86(a) of these Practice Rules)]

NOTES

Annex 2 substituted by Amendments to the Practice Rules for the Implementation of the Rules of Procedure of the General Court, Article 1 (OJ L294, 21.11.2018, p 23).

[ANNEX 3: PROCEDURAL RULES NON-COMPLIANCE WITH WHICH DOES NOT PREVENT SERVICE (POINT 103 OF THESE PRACTICE RULES)

[6.499]

a)	production of the certificate of any additional lawyer's authorisation to practise (Article 51(2) of the Rules of Procedure)
b)	in cases other than intellectual property cases, production of the summary of pleas in law and main arguments (points 118 and 119 of these Practice Rules)
c)	production of a translation into the language of the case of material drawn up in a language other than the language of the case (Article 46(2) of the Rules of Procedure; point 99 of these Practice Rules)]

NOTES

Annex 3 substituted by Amendments to the Practice Rules for the Implementation of the Rules of Procedure of the General Court, Article 1 (OJ L294, 21.11.2018, p 23).

CONDITIONS OF USE OF E-CURIA

(December 2018)

[6.500]

NOTES

This document is available on the Court of Justice website at https://curia.europa.eu/jcms/jcms/Jo2_7031/en/, and the General Court website at https://curia.europa.eu/jcms/jcms/Jo2_7040/en/.

1. E-Curia is a computer application common to both Courts of the Court of Justice of the European Union. This application allows procedural documents to be lodged and served electronically, and makes them available for consultation.

2. Users are asked to read the following information carefully and to give the undertakings set out at the end of this document.

3. The rules relating to the use of e-Curia are contained in a number of documents.

At the Court of Justice, those rules are contained in:

– the Rules of Procedure of the Court of Justice;
– the decision of the Court of Justice of 16 October 2018 on the lodging and service of procedural documents by means of e-Curia.

At the General Court, those rules are contained in:

– the Rules of Procedure of the General Court;
– the decision of the General Court of 11 July 2018 on the lodging and service of procedural documents by means of e-Curia;
– the Practice Rules for the Implementation of the Rules of Procedure of the General Court.

Those documents, and the e-Curia User Guide which is common to both courts, are available online on the website of the Court of Justice of the European Union.

4. The display screens in e-Curia include information about the steps to be followed and a link to the e-Curia User Guide.

ACCESS TO E-CURIA

5. Access to e-Curia is free of charge.

6. In both the General Court and the Court of Justice, a request to open an account maybe submitted by:
   – an agent or a lawyer authorised to practise before a court of a Member State or of another State party to the Agreement on the European Economic Area;
   – a university teacher being a national of a Member State whose law accords him or her a right of audience.

7. In the Court of Justice — and for the purposes of preliminary ruling proceedings only — a request to open an account may also be submitted by:
   – a person acting on behalf of a court or tribunal of a Member State;
   – a person who does not have the status of agent or lawyer but who, under national procedural rules, is nevertheless authorised to represent a party before the court or tribunal of a Member State.

PROCEDURE FOR OPENING AN ACCOUNT

8. In order to use e-Curia, users must submit a request to open an account in accordance with the procedure set out below.

9. The procedure for opening an account varies depending on whether the user follows the standard procedure or the special procedure. The standard procedure enables an account to be opened in order for procedural documents to be exchanged with the Court of Justice or the General Court. The special procedure is intended for urgent situations and enables an account to be opened provisionally in order for procedural documents to be lodged with the General Court only.

STANDARD PROCEDURE, APPLICABLE TO BOTH COURTS

10. The account request form is available on the website of the Court of Justice of the European Union via the e-Curia login page. The form must be completed, printed, dated, signed by hand, and then sent by post or physically delivered (Rue du Fort Niedergrünewald, L-2925 Luxembourg) to the Registry of the Court of Justice or the Registry of the General Court (in the case of requests referred to in point 6 of these conditions), or to the Registry of the Court of Justice (in the case of requests referred to in point 7 of these conditions), together with the necessary supporting documents.

11. Once the request to open an account has been validated by the Registry of the Court concerned, two separate emails are sent to the user. The first confirms the user's user ID, the second, his or her personal password. The user is required to change that password when first logging on to e-Curia, and subsequently at least once every six months.

12. Representatives may additionally request the opening of an account for every assistant they designate by name. That account allows the assistant to receive documents served, to consult procedural documents lodged or served via e-Curia and to prepare the lodging of a document, such lodging, once prepared, then requiring validation by the representative. The representative is responsible for the use of that account and is required to update the list of assistants regularly and, in particular, in the event of a change in professional responsibilities or termination of activity, to cancel any account assigned to his or her assistant(s).

SPECIAL PROCEDURE, APPLICABLE ONLY TO THE GENERAL COURT

13. Where a representative referred to in point 6 of these conditions has not taken the requisite steps to open an account under the standard procedure in good time before the expiry of a time limit for lodging a procedural document with the General Court, that representative may open an account on a provisional basis in order to lodge that document under the special procedure. In order for the creation of that account to be validated by the Registry of the General Court, the representative must complete the account request form online, print it, date it, sign it by hand and send the paper version by registered post or have it physically delivered to the Registry of the General Court(Rue du Fort Niedergrünewald, L-2925 Luxembourg), together with the necessary supporting documents. If the paper version of the form, duly completed, dated, signed by hand and accompanied by the necessary supporting documents, does not reach the Registry of the General Court within 10 days of the date on which the procedural document was lodged via e-Curia, the General Court will declare the procedural document lodged via e-Curia inadmissible. That time limit cannot be extended and the extension on account of distance provided for in Article 60 of the Rules of Procedure of the General Court shall not apply.

DEACTIVATION OF AN ACCOUNT

14. Accounts that remain unused for a period of three years will be deactivated automatically. In that case, a new request to open an account will have to be submitted.

THE FUNCTIONALITIES OF E-CURIA

LODGING OF PROCEDURAL DOCUMENTS

15. Procedural documents lodged by means of e-Curia must be transmitted as PDF files (image and text).

16. Documents transmitted to the Court of Justice and to the General Court are checked to ensure that transmission is secure. If such checks reveal an anomaly, the lodging of the document will be refused.

17. Confirmation of lodging stating, inter alia, the date and time of lodging is sent to the user. The point in time taken into account for the lodging of a procedural document is that of the representative's validation of the lodging of that document. The relevant time is the time in the Grand Duchy of Luxembourg.

18. Since the time involved in preparing the lodging of documents and in the uploading of files can vary, users are advised not to wait until the very last moment before the expiry of a time limit before lodging a document.

19. Confirmation of lodging is generated by e-Curia and is without prejudice to the procedural admissibility of the documents transmitted.

20. The transmission of procedural documents is automatically encrypted. Every procedural document lodged is given a unique digital signature, in accordance with a standard procedure (SHA-512). That digital signature appears in the confirmation of lodging which users are advised to retain electronically for the duration of the case. It is possible at any time to check that a procedural document has not been altered or amended; any change to that document will result in the allocation of a new digital signature.

SERVICE OF PROCEDURAL DOCUMENTS

21. The user is notified by email when a procedural document awaiting service is available in e-Curia.

22. Where a party is represented by more than one person holding an e-Curia account, an email confirming that a procedural document is awaiting service is sent to each of them and, if applicable, to any assistants designated by them.

23. The date and time of service is the point in time at which the user requests access to the procedural document. The relevant time is the time in the Grand Duchy of Luxembourg. Where a party is represented by more than one person, the point in time taken into account in the reckoning of time limits is the time when the first request for access was made.

24. A procedural document is, however, deemed to have been served on the expiry of the seventh day following the day on which an email was sent to the user to notify him or her of the availability of the document in e-Curia. Users are advised to log on to e-Curia at least once a week.

25. The date of actual or presumed service of a procedural document is stated in e-Curia. In the event of service being presumed to have been effected, an email is sent to the user to notify him or her of the date of service.

CONSULTATION OF PROCEDURAL DOCUMENTS

26. E-Curia allows users to consult the documents which they have lodged or which have been served on them via e-Curia.

27. The procedural documents in a case may be consulted until the expiry of a period of three months from the date of the decision closing that case in the Court concerned.

TECHNICAL IMPOSSIBILITY OF USING E-CURIA

28. If e-Curia cannot be used for technical reasons, users are invited to inform the Registry of the Court of Justice or of the General Court immediately and, where appropriate, to take all necessary steps in compliance with the procedural rules applicable in the Court concerned, as referred to in point 3 of these conditions.

UNDERTAKINGS TO BE GIVEN BY THE REPRESENTATIVE

You are requested to give the following undertakings, breach of which may result in the deactivation of your account:

I have taken note of the Conditions of Use of e-Curia and I expressly undertake:

- not to communicate my personal password to third parties, any process carried out using my user ID and my password being deemed to have been carried out by me;
- to communicate without delay any change of my email address as entered in e-Curia and any termination of my professional activity or change in my responsibilities;
- to log on to e-Curia regularly and to consult the procedural documents awaiting service of which I am the intended recipient, accepting that any such procedural document will, if not consulted, be deemed to have been served on me on the expiry of the seventh day following the day on which an email was sent to notify me of the availability of that document in e-Curia;
- to update regularly the list of any assistants I may have and, in particular, in the event of a change in professional responsibilities or termination of activity to cancel any account that I have assigned to them.

UNDERTAKING TO BE GIVEN BY THE ASSISTANT

You are requested give the following undertaking, breach of which may result in the deactivation of your account:

I have taken note of the Conditions of Use of e-Curia, and I expressly undertake not to communicate my personal password to third parties, any process carried out using my user ID and my password being deemed to have been carried out by me.

Luxembourg, 17 October 2018.

A. Calot Escobar
E. Coulon

STATUTE OF THE COURT OF JUSTICE OF THE EUROPEAN UNION (CONSOLIDATED VERSION MAY 2019)

[6.501]

NOTES

Date of original publication in OJ: C83, 30.3.2010, p 210.

A consolidated version of this Statute is available on the Court of Justice website at https://curia.europa.eu/jcms/jcms/Jo2_7031/en/.

The consolidated version includes the amendments made by: Regulation (EU, Euratom) No 741/2012 of the European Parliament and of the Council of 11 August 2012 (OJ L228, 23.8.2012, p 1); Article 9 of the Act concerning the conditions of accession to the EU of the Republic of Croatia and the adjustments to the Treaty on European Union, the Treaty on the Functioning of the European Union and the Treaty establishing the European Atomic Energy Community (OJ L112, 24.4.2012, p 21); Regulation (EU, Euratom) 2015/2422 of the European Parliament and of the Council of 16 December 2015 (OJ L341, 24.12.2015, p 14); Regulation (EU, Euratom) 2016/1192 of the European Parliament and of the Council of 6 July 2016 on the transfer to the General Court of jurisdiction at first instance in disputes between the European Union and its servants (OJ L200, 26.7.2016, p 137); and Regulation (EU, Euratom) 2019/629 of the European Parliament and of the Council of 17 April 2019 (OJ L111, 25.4.2019, p 1).

THE HIGH CONTRACTING PARTIES,

DESIRING to lay down the Statute of the Court of Justice of the European Union provided for in Article 281 of the Treaty on the Functioning of the European Union,

HAVE AGREED UPON the following provisions, which shall be annexed to the Treaty on European Union, the Treaty on the Functioning of the European Union and the Treaty establishing the European Atomic Energy Community:

[6.502]
Article 1
The Court of Justice of the European Union shall be constituted and shall function in accordance with the provisions of the Treaties, of the Treaty establishing the European Atomic Energy Community (EAEC Treaty) and of this Statute.

TITLE I JUDGES AND ADVOCATES-GENERAL

[6.503]
Article 2
Before taking up his duties each Judge shall, before the Court of Justice sitting in open court, take an oath to perform his duties impartially and conscientiously and to preserve the secrecy of the deliberations of the Court.

[6.504]
Article 3
The Judges shall be immune from legal proceedings. After they have ceased to hold office, they shall continue to enjoy immunity in respect of acts performed by them in their official capacity, including words spoken or written.
The Court of Justice, sitting as a full Court, may waive the immunity. If the decision concerns a member of the General Court or of a specialised court, the Court shall decide after consulting the court concerned.
Where immunity has been waived and criminal proceedings are instituted against a Judge, he shall be tried, in any of the Member States, only by the court competent to judge the members of the highest national judiciary.
Articles 11 to 14 and Article 17 of the Protocol on the privileges and immunities of the European Union shall apply to the Judges, Advocates-General, Registrar and Assistant Rapporteurs of the Court of Justice of the European Union, without prejudice to the provisions relating to immunity from legal proceedings of Judges which are set out in the preceding paragraphs.

[6.505]
Article 4
The Judges may not hold any political or administrative office.
They may not engage in any occupation, whether gainful or not, unless exemption is exceptionally granted by the Council, acting by a simple majority.
When taking up their duties, they shall give a solemn undertaking that, both during and after their term of office, they will respect the obligations arising therefrom, in particular the duty to behave with integrity and discretion as regards the acceptance, after they have ceased to hold office, of certain appointments or benefits.
Any doubt on this point shall be settled by decision of the Court of Justice. If the decision concerns a member of the General Court or of a specialised court, the Court shall decide after consulting the court concerned.

[6.506]
Article 5
Apart from normal replacement, or death, the duties of a Judge shall end when he resigns.
Where a Judge resigns, his letter of resignation shall be addressed to the President of the Court of Justice for transmission to the President of the Council. Upon this notification a vacancy shall arise on the bench.
Save where Article 6 applies, a Judge shall continue to hold office until his successor takes up his duties.

[6.507]
Article 6
A Judge may be deprived of his office or of his right to a pension or other benefits in its stead only if, in the unanimous opinion of the Judges and Advocates-General of the Court of Justice, he no longer fulfils the requisite conditions or meets the obligations arising from his office. The Judge concerned shall not take part in any such deliberations. If the person concerned is a member of the General Court or of a specialised court, the Court shall decide after consulting the court concerned.
The Registrar of the Court shall communicate the decision of the Court to the President of the European Parliament and to the President of the Commission and shall notify it to the President of the Council.
In the case of a decision depriving a Judge of his office, a vacancy shall arise on the bench upon this latter notification.

[6.508]
Article 7
A Judge who is to replace a member of the Court whose term of office has not expired shall be appointed for the remainder of his predecessor's term.

[6.509]
Article 8
The provisions of Articles 2 to 7 shall apply to the Advocates-General.

TITLE II ORGANISATION OF THE COURT OF JUSTICE

[6.510]
[Article 9
When, every three years, the Judges are partially replaced, one half of the number of Judges shall be replaced. If the number of Judges is an uneven number, the number of Judges who shall be replaced shall alternately be the number which is the next above one half of the number of Judges and the number which is next below one half.

The first paragraph shall also apply when the Advocates-General are partially replaced, every three years.]

NOTES

Substituted by Regulation (EU, Euratom) 2015/2422 of the European Parliament and of the Council of 16 December 2015 amending Protocol No 3 on the Statute of the Court of Justice of the European Union, Article 1(1).

[6.511]
[Article 9a
The Judges shall elect the President and the Vice-President of the Court of Justice from among their number for a term of three years. They may be re-elected.

The Vice-President shall assist the President in accordance with the conditions laid down in the Rules of Procedure. He shall take the President's place when the latter is prevented from attending or when the office of President is vacant.]

NOTES

Inserted by Regulation (EU, Euratom) No 741/2012 of the European Parliament and of the Council of 11 August 2012 amending the Protocol on the Statute of the Court of Justice of the European Union and Annex I thereto, Article 1(1). Note that this amendment applies from the first occasion when the Judges are partially replaced, as provided for in the first paragraph of Article 9 (see Article 3 of the 2012 Regulation).

[6.512]
Article 10
The Registrar shall take an oath before the Court of Justice to perform his duties impartially and conscientiously and to preserve the secrecy of the deliberations of the Court of Justice.

[6.513]
Article 11
The Court of Justice shall arrange for replacement of the Registrar on occasions when he is prevented from attending the Court of Justice.

[6.514]
Article 12
Officials and other servants shall be attached to the Court of Justice to enable it to function. They shall be responsible to the Registrar under the authority of the President.

[6.515]
Article 13
At the request of the Court of Justice, the European Parliament and the Council may, acting in accordance with the ordinary legislative procedure, provide for the appointment of Assistant Rapporteurs and lay down the rules governing their service. The Assistant Rapporteurs may be required, under conditions laid down in the Rules of Procedure, to participate in preparatory inquiries in cases pending before the Court and to cooperate with the Judge who acts as Rapporteur.

The Assistant Rapporteurs shall be chosen from persons whose independence is beyond doubt and who possess the necessary legal qualifications; they shall be appointed by the Council, acting by a simple majority. They shall take an oath before the Court to perform their duties impartially and conscientiously and to preserve the secrecy of the deliberations of the Court.

[6.516]
Article 14
The Judges, the Advocates-General and the Registrar shall be required to reside at the place where the Court of Justice has its seat.

[6.517]
Article 15
The Court of Justice shall remain permanently in session. The duration of the judicial vacations shall be determined by the Court with due regard to the needs of its business.

[6.518]
Article 16
The Court of Justice shall form chambers consisting of three and five Judges. The Judges shall elect the Presidents of the chambers from among their number. The Presidents of the chambers of five Judges shall be elected for three years. They may be re-elected once.

[The Grand Chamber shall consist of 15 Judges. It shall be presided over by the President of the Court. The Vice-President of the Court and, in accordance with the conditions laid down in the Rules of Procedure, three of the Presidents of the chambers of five Judges and other Judges shall also form part of the Grand Chamber.]

The Court shall sit in a Grand Chamber when a Member State or an institution of the Union that is party to the proceedings so requests.

The Court shall sit as a full Court where cases are brought before it pursuant to Article 228(2), Article 245(2), Article 247 or Article 286(6) of the Treaty on the Functioning of the European Union.

Moreover, where it considers that a case before it is of exceptional importance, the Court may decide, after hearing the Advocate-General, to refer the case to the full Court.

NOTES

Words in square brackets substituted by Regulation (EU, Euratom) No 741/2012 of the European Parliament and of the Council of 11 August 2012 amending the Protocol on the Statute of the Court of Justice of the European Union and Annex I thereto, Article 1(2). Note that this amendment applies from the first occasion when the Judges are partially replaced, as provided for in the first paragraph of Article 9 (see Article 3 of the 2012 Regulation).

[6.519]
Article 17
Decisions of the Court of Justice shall be valid only when an uneven number of its members is sitting in the deliberations.

Decisions of the chambers consisting of either three or five Judges shall be valid only if they are taken by three Judges.

[Decisions of the Grand Chamber shall be valid only if 11 Judges are sitting.

Decisions of the full Court shall be valid only if 17 Judges are sitting.]

In the event of one of the Judges of a chamber being prevented from attending, a Judge of another chamber may be called upon to sit in accordance with conditions laid down in the Rules of Procedure.

NOTES

Words in square brackets substituted by Regulation (EU, Euratom) No 741/2012 of the European Parliament and of the Council of 11 August 2012 amending the Protocol on the Statute of the Court of Justice of the European Union and Annex I thereto, Article 1(3). Note that this amendment applies from the first occasion when the Judges are partially replaced, as provided for in the first paragraph of Article 9 (see Article 3 of the 2012 Regulation).

[6.520]
Article 18
No Judge or Advocate-General may take part in the disposal of any case in which he has previously taken part as agent or adviser or has acted for one of the parties, or in which he has been called upon to pronounce as a member of a court or tribunal, of a commission of inquiry or in any other capacity.

If, for some special reason, any Judge or Advocate-General considers that he should not take part in the judgment or examination of a particular case, he shall so inform the President. If, for some special reason, the President considers that any Judge or Advocate-General should not sit or make submissions in a particular case, he shall notify him accordingly.

Any difficulty arising as to the application of this Article shall be settled by decision of the Court of Justice.

A party may not apply for a change in the composition of the Court or of one of its chambers on the grounds of either the nationality of a Judge or the absence from the Court or from the chamber of a Judge of the nationality of that party.

TITLE III PROCEDURE BEFORE THE COURT OF JUSTICE

[6.521]
Article 19
The Member States and the institutions of the Union shall be represented before the Court of Justice by an agent appointed for each case; the agent may be assisted by an adviser or by a lawyer.

The States, other than the Member States, which are parties to the Agreement on the European Economic Area and also the EFTA Surveillance Authority referred to in that Agreement shall be represented in same manner.

Other parties must be represented by a lawyer.

Only a lawyer authorised to practise before a court of a Member State or of another State which is a party to the Agreement on the European Economic Area may represent or assist a party before the Court.

Such agents, advisers and lawyers shall, when they appear before the Court, enjoy the rights and immunities necessary to the independent exercise of their duties, under conditions laid down in the Rules of Procedure.

As regards such advisers and lawyers who appear before it, the Court shall have the powers normally accorded to courts of law, under conditions laid down in the Rules of Procedure.

University teachers being nationals of a Member State whose law accords them a right of audience shall have the same rights before the Court as are accorded by this Article to lawyers.

[6.522]
Article 20
The procedure before the Court of Justice shall consist of two parts: written and oral.

The written procedure shall consist of the communication to the parties and to the institutions of the Union whose decisions are in dispute, of applications, statements of case, defences and observations, and of replies, if any, as well as of all papers and documents in support or of certified copies of them.

Communications shall be made by the Registrar in the order and within the time laid down in the Rules of Procedure. [The oral procedure shall consist of the hearing by the Court of agents, advisers and lawyers and of the submissions of the Advocate-General, as well as the hearing, if any, of witnesses and experts.]
Where it considers that the case raises no new point of law, the Court may decide, after hearing the Advocate-General, that the case shall be determined without a submission from the Advocate-General.

NOTES

Words in square brackets substituted by Regulation (EU, Euratom) No 741/2012 of the European Parliament and of the Council of 11 August 2012 amending the Protocol on the Statute of the Court of Justice of the European Union and Annex I thereto, Article 1(4).

[6.523]
Article 21

A case shall be brought before the Court of Justice by a written application addressed to the Registrar. The application shall contain the applicant's name and permanent address and the description of the signatory, the name of the party or names of the parties against whom the application is made, the subject-matter of the dispute, the form of order sought and a brief statement of the pleas in law on which the application is based.
The application shall be accompanied, where appropriate, by the measure the annulment of which is sought or, in the circumstances referred to in Article 265 of the Treaty on the Functioning of the European Union, by documentary evidence of the date on which an institution was, in accordance with those Articles, requested to act. If the documents are not submitted with the application, the Registrar shall ask the party concerned to produce them within a reasonable period, but in that event the rights of the party shall not lapse even if such documents are produced after the time limit for bringing proceedings.

[6.524]
Article 22

A case governed by Article 18 of the EAEC Treaty shall be brought before the Court of Justice by an appeal addressed to the Registrar. The appeal shall contain the name and permanent address of the applicant and the description of the signatory, a reference to the decision against which the appeal is brought, the names of the respondents, the subject-matter of the dispute, the submissions and a brief statement of the grounds on which the appeal is based.
The appeal shall be accompanied by a certified copy of the decision of the Arbitration Committee which is contested.
If the Court rejects the appeal, the decision of the Arbitration Committee shall become final.
If the Court annuls the decision of the Arbitration Committee, the matter may be re-opened, where appropriate, on the initiative of one of the parties in the case, before the Arbitration Committee. The latter shall conform to any decisions on points of law given by the Court.

[6.525]
Article 23

In the cases governed by Article 267 of the Treaty on the Functioning of the European Union, the decision of the court or tribunal of a Member State which suspends its proceedings and refers a case to the Court of Justice shall be notified to the Court by the court or tribunal concerned. The decision shall then be notified by the Registrar of the Court to the parties, to the Member States and to the Commission, and to the institution, body, office or agency of the Union which adopted the act the validity or interpretation of which is in dispute.
Within two months of this notification, the parties, the Member States, the Commission and, where appropriate, the institution, body, office or agency which adopted the act the validity or interpretation of which is in dispute, shall be entitled to submit statements of case or written observations to the Court.
In the cases governed by Article 267 of the Treaty on the Functioning of the European Union, the decision of the national court or tribunal shall, moreover, be notified by the Registrar of the Court to the States, other than the Member States, which are parties to the Agreement on the European Economic Area and also to the EFTA Surveillance Authority referred to in that Agreement which may, within two months of notification, where one of the fields of application of that Agreement is concerned, submit statements of case or written observations to the Court.
Where an agreement relating to a specific subject matter, concluded by the Council and one or more non-member States, provides that those States are to be entitled to submit statements of case or written observations where a court or tribunal of a Member State refers to the Court of Justice for a preliminary ruling a question falling within the scope of the agreement, the decision of the national court or tribunal containing that question shall also be notified to the non-member States concerned. Within two months from such notification, those States may lodge at the Court statements of case or written observations.

[6.526]
[Article 23a

The Rules of Procedure may provide for an expedited or accelerated procedure and, for references for a preliminary ruling relating to the area of freedom, security and justice, an urgent procedure.
Those procedures may provide, in respect of the submission of statements of case or written observations, for a shorter period than that provided for by Article 23, and, in derogation from the fourth paragraph of Article 20, for the case to be determined without a submission from the Advocate General.
In addition, the urgent procedure may provide for restriction of the parties and other interested persons mentioned in Article 23, authorised to submit statements of case or written observations and, in cases of extreme urgency, for the written stage of the procedure to be omitted.][1]

NOTES

[1] Article inserted by Decision 2008/79/EC, Euratom (OJ L24, 29.1.2008, p 42).

[6.527]
Article 24
The Court of Justice may require the parties to produce all documents and to supply all information which the Court considers desirable. Formal note shall be taken of any refusal.
The Court may also require the Member States and institutions, bodies, offices and agencies not being parties to the case to supply all information which the Court considers necessary for the proceedings.

[6.528]
Article 25
The Court of Justice may at any time entrust any individual, body, authority, committee or other organisation it chooses with the task of giving an expert opinion.

[6.529]
Article 26
Witnesses may be heard under conditions laid down in the Rules of Procedure.

[6.530]
Article 27
With respect to defaulting witnesses the Court of Justice shall have the powers generally granted to courts and tribunals and may impose pecuniary penalties under conditions laid down in the Rules of Procedure.

[6.531]
Article 28
Witnesses and experts may be heard on oath taken in the form laid down in the Rules of Procedure or in the manner laid down by the law of the country of the witness or expert.

[6.532]
Article 29
The Court of Justice may order that a witness or expert be heard by the judicial authority of his place of permanent residence.
The order shall be sent for implementation to the competent judicial authority under conditions laid down in the Rules of Procedure. The documents drawn up in compliance with the letters rogatory shall be returned to the Court under the same conditions.
The Court shall defray the expenses, without prejudice to the right to charge them, where appropriate, to the parties.

[6.533]
Article 30
A Member State shall treat any violation of an oath by a witness or expert in the same manner as if the offence had been committed before one of its courts with jurisdiction in civil proceedings. At the instance of the Court of Justice, the Member State concerned shall prosecute the offender before its competent court.

[6.534]
Article 31
The hearing in court shall be public, unless the Court of Justice, of its own motion or on application by the parties, decides otherwise for serious reasons.

[6.535]
Article 32
During the hearings the Court of Justice may examine the experts, the witnesses and the parties themselves. The latter, however, may address the Court of Justice only through their representatives.

[6.536]
Article 33
Minutes shall be made of each hearing and signed by the President and the Registrar.

[6.537]
Article 34
The case list shall be established by the President.

[6.538]
Article 35
The deliberations of the Court of Justice shall be and shall remain secret.

[6.539]
Article 36
Judgments shall state the reasons on which they are based. They shall contain the names of the Judges who took part in the deliberations.

[6.540]
Article 37
Judgments shall be signed by the President and the Registrar. They shall be read in open court.

[6.541]
Article 38
The Court of Justice shall adjudicate upon costs.

[6.542]
Article 39

The President of the Court of Justice may, by way of summary procedure, which may, in so far as necessary, differ from some of the rules contained in this Statute and which shall be laid down in the Rules of Procedure, adjudicate upon applications to suspend execution, as provided for in Article 278 of the Treaty on the Functioning of the European Union and Article 157 of the EAEC Treaty, or to prescribe interim measures pursuant to Article 279 of the Treaty on the Functioning of the European Union, or to suspend enforcement in accordance with the fourth paragraph of Article 299 of the Treaty on the Functioning of the European Union or the third paragraph of Article 164 of the EAEC Treaty.

[The powers referred to in the first paragraph may, under the conditions laid down in the Rules of Procedure, be exercised by the Vice-President of the Court of Justice.

Should the President and the Vice-President be prevented from attending, another Judge shall take their place under the conditions laid down in the Rules of Procedure.]

The ruling of the President or of the Judge replacing him shall be provisional and shall in no way prejudice the decision of the Court on the substance of the case.

NOTES

Words in square brackets substituted by Regulation (EU, Euratom) No 741/2012 of the European Parliament and of the Council of 11 August 2012 amending the Protocol on the Statute of the Court of Justice of the European Union and Annex I thereto, Article 1(5). Note that this amendment applies from the first occasion when the Judges are partially replaced, as provided for in the first paragraph of Article 9 (see Article 3 of the 2012 Regulation).

[6.543]
Article 40

Member States and institutions of the Union may intervene in cases before the Court of Justice.

The same right shall be open to the bodies, offices and agencies of the Union and to any other person which can establish an interest in the result of a case submitted to the Court. Natural or legal persons shall not intervene in cases between Member States, between institutions of the Union or between Member States and institutions of the Union.

Without prejudice to the second paragraph, the States, other than the Member States, which are parties to the Agreement on the European Economic Area, and also the EFTA Surveillance Authority referred to in that Agreement, may intervene in cases before the Court where one of the fields of application of that Agreement is concerned.

An application to intervene shall be limited to supporting the form of order sought by one of the parties.

[6.544]
Article 41

Where the defending party, after having been duly summoned, fails to file written submissions in defence, judgment shall be given against that party by default. An objection may be lodged against the judgment within one month of it being notified. The objection shall not have the effect of staying enforcement of the judgment by default unless the Court of Justice decides otherwise.

[6.545]
Article 42

Member States, institutions, bodies, offices and agencies of the Union and any other natural or legal persons may, in cases and under conditions to be determined by the Rules of Procedure, institute third-party proceedings to contest a judgment rendered without their being heard, where the judgment is prejudicial to their rights.

[6.546]
Article 43

If the meaning or scope of a judgment is in doubt, the Court of Justice shall construe it on application by any party or any institution of the Union establishing an interest therein.

[6.547]
Article 44

An application for revision of a judgment may be made to the Court of Justice only on discovery of a fact which is of such a nature as to be a decisive factor, and which, when the judgment was given, was unknown to the Court and to the party claiming the revision.

The revision shall be opened by a judgment of the Court expressly recording the existence of a new fact, recognising that it is of such a character as to lay the case open to revision and declaring the application admissible on this ground.

No application for revision may be made after the lapse of 10 years from the date of the judgment.

[6.548]
Article 45

Periods of grace based on considerations of distance shall be determined by the Rules of Procedure.

No right shall be prejudiced in consequence of the expiry of a time limit if the party concerned proves the existence of unforeseeable circumstances or of *force majeure*.

[6.549]
Article 46

Proceedings against the Union in matters arising from non-contractual liability shall be barred after a period of five years from the occurrence of the event giving rise thereto. The period of limitation shall be interrupted if proceedings are instituted before the Court of Justice or if prior to such proceedings an application is made by the aggrieved party to the relevant institution of the Union. In the latter event the proceedings must be instituted within the period of two months provided for in Article 263 of the Treaty on the Functioning of the European Union; the provisions of the second paragraph of Article 265 of the Treaty on the Functioning of the European Union shall apply where appropriate.

This Article shall also apply to proceedings against the European Central Bank regarding non-contractual liability.

TITLE IV GENERAL COURT

[6.550]

Article 47

[The first paragraph of Article 9, Article 9a, Articles 14 and 15, the first, second, fourth and fifth paragraphs of Article 17 and Article 18 shall apply to the General Court and its members.]

The fourth paragraph of Article 3 and Articles 10, 11 and 14 shall apply to the Registrar of the General Court *mutatis mutandis*.

NOTES

Words in square brackets substituted by Regulation (EU, Euratom) No 741/2012 of the European Parliament and of the Council of 11 August 2012 amending the Protocol on the Statute of the Court of Justice of the European Union and Annex I thereto, Article 1(6). Note that this amendment applies from the first occasion when the Judges are partially replaced, as provided for in the first paragraph of Article 9 (see Article 3 of the 2012 Regulation).

[6.551]

[Article 48

The General Court shall consist of:

(a) 40 Judges as from 25 December 2015;

(b) 47 Judges as from 1 September 2016;

(c) two Judges per Member State as from 1 September 2019.]

NOTES

Substituted by Regulation (EU, Euratom) 2015/2422 of the European Parliament and of the Council of 16 December 2015 amending Protocol No 3 on the Statute of the Court of Justice of the European Union, Article 1(2).

Article 2 of Regulation (EU, Euratom) 2015/2422 of the European Parliament and of the Council of 16 December 2015 amending Protocol No 3 on the Statute of the Court of Justice of the European Union provides as follows—

"The term of office of the additional Judges of the General Court to be appointed pursuant to Article 48 of Protocol No 3 on the Statute of the Court of Justice of the European Union shall be as follows:

(a) The term of office of six of the twelve additional Judges to be appointed as from 25 December 2015 shall end on 31 August 2016. Those six Judges shall be chosen in such a way that the governments of six Member States nominate two Judges for the partial replacement of the General Court in 2016. The term of office of the other six Judges shall end on 31 August 2019;

(b) The term of office of three of the seven additional Judges to be appointed as from 1 September 2016 shall end on 31 August 2019. Those three Judges shall be chosen in such a way that the governments of three Member States nominate two Judges for the partial replacement of the General Court in 2019. The term of office of the other four Judges shall end on 31 August 2022;

(c) The term of office of four of the nine additional Judges to be appointed as from 1 September 2019 shall end on 31 August 2022. Those four Judges shall be chosen in such a way that the governments of four Member States nominate two Judges for the partial replacement of the General Court in 2022. The term of office of the other five Judges shall end on 31 August 2025.".

Note also that Article 3 of the 2015 Regulation provides that, by 26 December 2020, the Court of Justice shall draw up a report, using an external consultant, for the European Parliament, the Council and the Commission on the functioning of the General Court. In particular, that report shall focus on the efficiency of the General Court, the necessity and effectiveness of the increase to 56 Judges, the use and effectiveness of resources and the further establishment of specialised chambers and/or other structural changes.

[6.552]

Article 49

The Members of the General Court may be called upon to perform the task of an Advocate-General.

It shall be the duty of the Advocate-General, acting with complete impartiality and independence, to make, in open court, reasoned submissions on certain cases brought before the General Court in order to assist the General Court in the performance of its task.

The criteria for selecting such cases, as well as the procedures for designating the Advocates-General, shall be laid down in the Rules of Procedure of the General Court.

A Member called upon to perform the task of Advocate-General in a case may not take part in the judgment of the case.

[6.553]

Article 50

The General Court shall sit in chambers of three or five Judges. The Judges shall elect the Presidents of the chambers from among their number. The Presidents of the chambers of five Judges shall be elected for three years. They may be re-elected once.

The composition of the chambers and the assignment of cases to them shall be governed by the Rules of Procedure. In certain cases governed by the Rules of Procedure, the General Court may sit as a full court or be constituted by a single Judge.

The Rules of Procedure may also provide that the General Court may sit in a Grand Chamber in cases and under the conditions specified therein.

[6.554]

[Article 50a

1. The General Court shall exercise at first instance jurisdiction in disputes between the Union and its servants as referred to in Article 270 of the Treaty on the Functioning of the European Union, including disputes between all institutions, bodies, offices or agencies, on the one hand, and their servants, on the other, in respect of which jurisdiction is conferred on the Court of Justice of the European Union.

2. At all stages of the procedure, including the time when the application is filed, the General Court may examine the possibilities of an amicable settlement of the dispute and may try to facilitate such settlement.]

NOTES

Inserted by Regulation (EU, Euratom) 2016/1192 of the European Parliament and of the Council, Art 2(1).

[6.555]

[Article 51

By way of derogation from the rule laid down in Article 256(1) of the Treaty on the Functioning of the European Union, jurisdiction shall be reserved to the Court of Justice:

(a) in actions referred to in Articles 263 and 265 of the Treaty on the Functioning of the European Union which are brought by a Member State against:

(i) a legislative act, an act of the European Parliament, of the European Council or of the Council, or against a failure to act by one or more of those institutions, except for:

— decisions taken by the Council under the third subparagraph of Article 108(2) of the Treaty on the Functioning of the European Union,

— acts of the Council adopted pursuant to a Council regulation concerning measures to protect trade within the meaning of Article 207 of the Treaty on the Functioning of the European Union,

— acts of the Council by which the Council exercises implementing powers in accordance with Article 291(2) of the Treaty on the Functioning of the European Union;

(ii) an act of, or a failure to act by, the Commission under Article 331(1) of the Treaty on the Functioning of the European Union;

(b) in actions referred to in Articles 263 and 265 of the Treaty on the Functioning of the European Union which are brought by an institution of the Union against a legislative act, an act of the European Parliament, of the European Council, of the Council, of the Commission or of the European Central Bank, or against a failure to act by one or more of those institutions;

(c) in actions referred to in Article 263 of the Treaty on the Functioning of the European Union which are brought by a Member State against an act of the Commission relating to a failure to comply with a judgment delivered by the Court under the second subparagraph of Article 260(2), or the second subparagraph of Article 260(3), of the Treaty on the Functioning of the European Union.]

NOTES

Substituted by Regulation (EU, Euratom) 2019/629 of the European Parliament and of the Council of 17 April 2019, Article 1(1).

[6.556]

Article 52

The President of the Court of Justice and the President of the General Court shall determine, by common accord, the conditions under which officials and other servants attached to the Court of Justice shall render their services to the General Court to enable it to function. Certain officials or other servants shall be responsible to the Registrar of the General Court under the authority of the President of the General Court.

[6.557]

Article 53

The procedure before the General Court shall be governed by Title III.

Such further and more detailed provisions as may be necessary shall be laid down in its Rules of Procedure. The Rules of Procedure may derogate from the fourth paragraph of Article 40 and from Article 41 in order to take account of the specific features of litigation in the field of intellectual property.

Notwithstanding the fourth paragraph of Article 20, the Advocate-General may make his reasoned submissions in writing.

[6.558]

Article 54

Where an application or other procedural document addressed to the General Court is lodged by mistake with the Registrar of the Court of Justice, it shall be transmitted immediately by that Registrar to the Registrar of the General Court; likewise, where an application or other procedural document addressed to the Court of Justice is lodged by mistake with the Registrar of the General Court, it shall be transmitted immediately by that Registrar to the Registrar of the Court of Justice.

Where the General Court finds that it does not have jurisdiction to hear and determine an action in respect of which the Court of Justice has jurisdiction, it shall refer that action to the Court of Justice; likewise, where the Court of Justice finds that an action falls within the jurisdiction of the General Court, it shall refer that action to the General Court, whereupon that Court may not decline jurisdiction.

Where the Court of Justice and the General Court are seised of cases in which the same relief is sought, the same issue of interpretation is raised or the validity of the same act is called in question, the General Court may, after hearing the parties, stay the proceedings before it until such time as the Court of Justice has delivered judgment or, where the action is one brought pursuant to Article 263 of the Treaty on the Functioning of the European Union, may decline jurisdiction so as to allow the Court of Justice to rule on such actions. In the same circumstances, the Court of Justice may also decide to stay the proceedings before it; in that event, the proceedings before the General Court shall continue.

Where a Member State and an institution of the Union are challenging the same act, the General Court shall decline jurisdiction so that the Court of Justice may rule on those applications.

[6.559]
Article 55

Final decisions of the General Court, decisions disposing of the substantive issues in part only or disposing of a procedural issue concerning a plea of lack of competence or inadmissibility, shall be notified by the Registrar of the General Court to all parties as well as all Member States and the institutions of the Union even if they did not intervene in the case before the General Court.

[6.560]
Article 56

An appeal may be brought before the Court of Justice, within two months of the notification of the decision appealed against, against final decisions of the General Court and decisions of that Court disposing of the substantive issues in part only or disposing of a procedural issue concerning a plea of lack of competence or inadmissibility.

Such an appeal may be brought by any party which has been unsuccessful, in whole or in part, in its submissions. However, interveners other than the Member States and the institutions of the Union may bring such an appeal only where the decision of the General Court directly affects them.

With the exception of cases relating to disputes between the Union and its servants, an appeal may also be brought by Member States and institutions of the Union which did not intervene in the proceedings before the General Court. Such Member States and institutions shall be in the same position as Member States or institutions which intervened at first instance.

[6.561]
Article 57

Any person whose application to intervene has been dismissed by the General Court may appeal to the Court of Justice within two weeks from the notification of the decision dismissing the application.

The parties to the proceedings may appeal to the Court of Justice against any decision of the General Court made pursuant to Article 278 or Article 279 or the fourth paragraph of Article 299 of the Treaty on the Functioning of the European Union or Article 157 or the third paragraph of Article 164 of the EAEC Treaty within two months from their notification.

The appeal referred to in the first two paragraphs of this Article shall be heard and determined under the procedure referred to in Article 39.

[6.562]
Article 58

An appeal to the Court of Justice shall be limited to points of law. It shall lie on the grounds of lack of competence of the General Court, a breach of procedure before it which adversely affects the interests of the appellant as well as the infringement of Union law by the General Court.

No appeal shall lie regarding only the amount of the costs or the party ordered to pay them.

[6.563]
[Article 58a

An appeal brought against a decision of the General Court concerning a decision of an independent board of appeal of one of the following offices and agencies of the Union shall not proceed unless the Court of Justice first decides that it should be allowed to do so:

(a) the European Union Intellectual Property Office;
(b) the Community Plant Variety Office;
(c) the European Chemicals Agency;
(d) the European Union Aviation Safety Agency.

The procedure referred to in the first paragraph shall also apply to appeals brought against decisions of the General Court concerning a decision of an independent board of appeal, set up after 1 May 2019 within any other office or agency of the Union, which has to be seised before an action can be brought before the General Court.

An appeal shall be allowed to proceed, wholly or in part, in accordance with the detailed rules set out in the Rules of Procedure, where it raises an issue that is significant with respect to the unity, consistency or development of Union law.

The decision as to whether the appeal should be allowed to proceed or not shall be reasoned, and it shall be published.]

NOTES

Inserted by Regulation (EU, Euratom) 2019/629 of the European Parliament and of the Council of 17 April 2019, Article 1(2).

[6.564]
Article 59

Where an appeal is brought against a decision of the General Court, the procedure before the Court of Justice shall consist of a written part and an oral part. In accordance with conditions laid down in the Rules of Procedure, the Court of Justice, having heard the Advocate-General and the parties, may dispense with the oral procedure.

[6.565]
Article 60

Without prejudice to Articles 278 and 279 of the Treaty on the Functioning of the European Union or Article 157 of the EAEC Treaty, an appeal shall not have suspensory effect.

By way of derogation from Article 280 of the Treaty on the Functioning of the European Union, decisions of the General Court declaring a regulation to be void shall take effect only as from the date of expiry of the period referred to in the first paragraph of Article 56 of this Statute or, if an appeal shall have been brought within that period, as from the date of dismissal of the appeal, without prejudice, however, to the right of a party to apply to the Court of Justice, pursuant to Articles 278 and 279 of the Treaty on the Functioning of the European Union or Article 157 of the EAEC Treaty, for the suspension of the effects of the regulation which has been declared void or for the prescription of any other interim measure.

[6.566]
Article 61

If the appeal is well founded, the Court of Justice shall quash the decision of the General Court. It may itself give final judgment in the matter, where the state of the proceedings so permits, or refer the case back to the General Court for judgment.

Where a case is referred back to the General Court, that Court shall be bound by the decision of the Court of Justice on points of law.

When an appeal brought by a Member State or an institution of the Union, which did not intervene in the proceedings before the General Court, is well founded, the Court of Justice may, if it considers this necessary, state which of the effects of the decision of the General Court which has been quashed shall be considered as definitive in respect of the parties to the litigation.

[6.567]
Article 62

In the cases provided for in Article 256(2) and (3) of the Treaty on the Functioning of the European Union, where the First Advocate-General considers that there is a serious risk of the unity or consistency of Union law being affected, he may propose that the Court of Justice review the decision of the General Court.

The proposal must be made within one month of delivery of the decision by the General Court. Within one month of receiving the proposal made by the First Advocate-General, the Court of Justice shall decide whether or not the decision should be reviewed.

[6.568]
Article 62a

The Court of Justice shall give a ruling on the questions which are subject to review by means of an urgent procedure on the basis of the file forwarded to it by the General Court.

Those referred to in Article 23 of this Statute and, in the cases provided for in Article 256(2) of the EC Treaty, the parties to the proceedings before the General Court shall be entitled to lodge statements or written observations with the Court of Justice relating to questions which are subject to review within a period prescribed for that purpose.

The Court of Justice may decide to open the oral procedure before giving a ruling.

[6.569]
Article 62b

In the cases provided for in Article 256(2) of the Treaty on the Functioning of the European Union, without prejudice to Articles 278 and 279 of the Treaty on the Functioning of the European Union, proposals for review and decisions to open the review procedure shall not have suspensory effect. If the Court of Justice finds that the decision of the General Court affects the unity or consistency of Union law, it shall refer the case back to the General Court which shall be bound by the points of law decided by the Court of Justice; the Court of Justice may state which of the effects of the decision of the General Court are to be considered as definitive in respect of the parties to the litigation. If, however, having regard to the result of the review, the outcome of the proceedings flows from the findings of fact on which the decision of the General Court was based, the Court of Justice shall give final judgment.

In the cases provided for in Article 256(3) of the Treaty on the Functioning of the European Union, in the absence of proposals for review or decisions to open the review procedure, the answer(s) given by the General Court to the questions submitted to it shall take effect upon expiry of the periods prescribed for that purpose in the second paragraph of Article 62. Should a review procedure be opened, the answer(s) subject to review shall take effect following that procedure, unless the Court of Justice decides otherwise. If the Court of Justice finds that the decision of the General Court affects the unity or consistency of Union law, the answer given by the Court of Justice to the questions subject to review shall be substituted for that given by the General Court.

TITLE IVA SPECIALISED COURTS

[6.570]
[Article 62c

The provisions relating to the jurisdiction, composition, organisation and procedure of any specialised court established under Article 257 of the Treaty on the Functioning of the European Union shall be contained in an Annex to this Statute.]

NOTES

Substituted by Regulation (EU, Euratom) 2016/1192 of the European Parliament and of the Council, Art 2(2).

TITLE V FINAL PROVISIONS

[6.571]
Article 63
The Rules of Procedure of the Court of Justice and of the General Court shall contain any provisions necessary for applying and, where required, supplementing this Statute.

[6.572]
Article 64
The rules governing the language arrangements applicable at the Court of Justice of the European Union shall be laid down by a regulation of the Council acting unanimously. This regulation shall be adopted either at the request of the Court of Justice and after consultation of the Commission and the European Parliament, or on a proposal from the Commission and after consultation of the Court of Justice and of the European Parliament.

Until those rules have been adopted, the provisions of the Rules of Procedure of the Court of Justice and of the Rules of Procedure of the General Court governing language arrangements shall continue to apply. By way of derogation from Articles 253 and 254 of the Treaty on the Functioning of the European Union, those provisions may only be amended or repealed with the unanimous consent of the Council.

ANNEX I
THE EUROPEAN UNION CIVIL SERVICE TRIBUNAL

(Annex I (the only Annex) was repealed by Regulation (EU, Euratom) 2016/1192 of the European Parliament and of the Council, Art 2(3). Note that Articles 3 and 4 of the 2016 Regulation provide for the following transitional provisions. Cases pending before the Civil Service Tribunal on 31 August 2016 shall be transferred to the General Court. The General Court shall continue dealing with those cases as it finds them at that date and in accordance with its Rules of Procedure. In the event of a case being transferred to the General Court after the oral part of the procedure has been closed, that part of the procedure shall be reopened (Article 3). Notwithstanding point (3) of Article 2 of this Regulation, Articles 9 to 12 of Annex I to Protocol No 3 shall continue to apply to the appeals against decisions of the Civil Service Tribunal of which the General Court is seised as at 31 August 2016 or which are brought after that date. If the General Court sets aside a decision of the Civil Service Tribunal but considers that the state of the proceedings does not permit a decision, it shall refer the case to a chamber other than that which ruled on the appeal (Article 4). Note also that this Protocol does not contain an Annex II even though this Annex is numbered as Annex I.)

COURT OF JUSTICE OF THE EUROPEAN UNION

(2019/C380/01)

Recommendations to national courts and tribunals, in relation to the initiation of preliminary ruling proceedings

[6.573]

NOTES

Date of publication in the OJ: OJ C380, 8.11.2019, p 1.

These Recommendations are available on the Court of Justice website at https://curia.europa.eu/jcms/jcms/Jo2_7031/en/.

Note from the Official Journal: These recommendations have been drawn up for the attention of the courts and tribunals of the Member States of the European Union and echo the provisions of Title III of the Rules of Procedure of the Court of Justice.[1] They serve as a reminder of the essential characteristics of the preliminary ruling procedure and the matters to be taken into account by the national courts and tribunals before a reference for a preliminary ruling is made to the Court of Justice, while providing practical guidance as to the form and content of requests for a preliminary ruling. Since such requests will be served, after having been translated, on all the interested persons referred to in Article 23 of the Protocol on the Statute of the Court of Justice of the European Union and the decisions of the Court closing the proceedings will in principle be published in all the official languages of the European Union, close attention must be paid to the presentation of requests for a preliminary ruling and, in particular, to the protection of the personal data which they contain.

[1] OJ L265, 29.9.2012, p 1.

INTRODUCTION

[6.574]
1. The reference for a preliminary ruling, provided for in Article 19(3)(b) of the Treaty on European Union ('TEU') and Article 267 of the Treaty on the Functioning of the European Union ('TFEU'), is a fundamental mechanism of EU law. It is designed to ensure the uniform interpretation and application of EU law within the European Union, by offering the courts and tribunals of the Member States a means of bringing before the Court of Justice of the European Union ('the Court') for a preliminary ruling questions concerning the interpretation of EU law or the validity of acts adopted by the institutions, bodies, offices or agencies of the Union.

2. The preliminary ruling procedure is based on close cooperation between the Court and the courts and tribunals of the Member States. In order to ensure that that procedure is fully effective, it is necessary to recall its essential characteristics and to provide further information to clarify the provisions of the rules of procedure relating, in particular, to the originator, subject matter and scope of a request for a preliminary ruling, as well as to the form and

content of such a request. That information — which applies to all requests for a preliminary ruling (I) — is supplemented by provisions concerning requests for a preliminary ruling requiring particularly expeditious handling (II) and by an annex which summarises, by way of a reminder, all the elements that must be included in a request for a preliminary ruling.

I. PROVISIONS WHICH APPLY TO ALL REQUESTS FOR A PRELIMINARY RULING

THE ORIGINATOR OF THE REQUEST FOR A PRELIMINARY RULING

[6.575]

3. The jurisdiction of the Court to give a preliminary ruling on the interpretation or validity of EU law is exercised exclusively on the initiative of the national courts and tribunals, whether or not the parties to the main proceedings have expressed the wish that a question be referred to the Court. In so far as it is called upon to assume responsibility for the subsequent judicial decision, it is for the national court or tribunal before which a dispute has been brought — and for that court or tribunal alone — to determine, in the light of the particular circumstances of each case, both the need for a request for a preliminary

4. Status as a court or tribunal is interpreted by the Court as an autonomous concept of EU law. The Court takes account of a number of factors such as whether the body making the reference is established by law, whether it is permanent, whether its jurisdiction is compulsory, whether its procedure is *inter partes*, whether it applies rules of law and whether it is independent.

5. The courts and tribunals of the Member States may refer a question to the Court on the interpretation or validity of EU law where they consider that a decision of the Court on the question is necessary to enable them to give judgment (see second paragraph of Article 267 TFEU). A reference for a preliminary ruling may, inter alia, prove particularly useful when a question of interpretation is raised before the national court or tribunal that is new and of general interest for the uniform application of EU law, or where the existing case-law does not appear to provide the necessary guidance in a new legal context or set of facts.

6. Where a question is raised in the context of a case that is pending before a court or tribunal against whose decisions there is no judicial remedy under national law, that court or tribunal is nonetheless required to bring a request for a preliminary ruling before the Court (see third paragraph of Article 267 TFEU), unless there is already well-established case-law on the point or unless the correct interpretation of the rule of law in question admits of no reasonable doubt.

7. It follows, moreover, from settled case-law that although national courts and tribunals may reject pleas raised before them challenging the validity of acts of an institution, body, office or agency of the Union, the Court has exclusive jurisdiction to declare such acts invalid. When it has doubts about the validity of such an act, a court or tribunal of a Member State must therefore refer the matter to the Court, stating the reasons why it has such doubts.

THE SUBJECT MATTER AND SCOPE OF THE REQUEST FOR A PRELIMINARY RULING

8. A request for a preliminary ruling must concern the interpretation or validity of EU law, not the interpretation of rules of national law or issues of fact raised in the main proceedings.

9. *The Court can give a preliminary ruling only if EU law applies to the case in the main proceedings.* It is essential, in that respect, that the referring court or tribunal set out all the relevant matters of fact and of law that have prompted it to consider that any provisions of EU law may be applicable in the case.

10. With regard to references for a preliminary ruling concerning the interpretation of the Charter of Fundamental Rights of the European Union, it must be noted that, under Article 51(1) of the Charter, the provisions of the Charter are addressed to the Member States only when they are implementing EU law. While the circumstances of such implementation can vary, it must nevertheless be clearly and unequivocally apparent from the request for a preliminary ruling that a rule of EU law other than the Charter is applicable to the case in the main proceedings. Since the Court has no jurisdiction to give a preliminary ruling where a legal situation does not come within the scope of EU law, any provisions of the Charter that may be relied upon by the referring court or tribunal *cannot, of themselves, form the basis for such jurisdiction.*

11. Lastly, although, in order to deliver its decision, the Court necessarily takes into account the legal and factual context of the dispute in the main proceedings, as defined by the referring court or tribunal in its request for a preliminary ruling, it does not itself apply EU law to that dispute. When ruling on the interpretation or validity of EU law, the Court makes every effort to give a reply which will be of assistance in resolving the dispute in the main proceedings, but it is for the referring court or tribunal to draw case-specific conclusions, if necessary by disapplying the rule of national law that has been held to be incompatible with EU law.

THE APPROPRIATE STAGE AT WHICH TO MAKE A REFERENCE FOR A PRELIMINARY RULING

12. A national court or tribunal may submit a request for a preliminary ruling to the Court as soon as it finds that a ruling on the interpretation or validity of EU law is necessary to enable it to give judgment. It is that court or tribunal which is in fact in the best position to decide at what stage of the national proceedings such a request should be made.

13. Since, however, that request will serve as the basis of the proceedings before the Court and the Court must therefore have available to it all the information that will enable it both to assess whether it has jurisdiction to give a reply to the questions raised and, if so, to give a useful reply to those questions, it is necessary that a decision to make a reference for a preliminary ruling be taken when the national proceedings have reached a stage at which the referring court or tribunal is able to *define, in sufficient detail, the legal and factual context of the case in the main proceedings, and the legal issues which it raises.* In the interests of the proper administration of justice, it may also be appropriate for the reference to be made only after both sides have been heard.

THE FORM AND CONTENT OF THE REQUEST FOR A PRELIMINARY RULING

14. The request for a preliminary ruling may be in any form allowed by national law, but it should be borne in mind that that request serves as the basis of the proceedings before the Court and is served on all the interested persons referred to in Article 23 of the Protocol on the Statute of the Court of Justice of the European Union ('the Statute') and, in particular, on all the Member States, with a view to obtaining any observations they may wish to make. Owing to the consequential need to translate it into all the official languages of the European Union, the request for a preliminary ruling should therefore be drafted simply, clearly and precisely by the referring court or tribunal, avoiding superfluous detail. As experience has shown, about 10 pages are often sufficient to set out adequately the legal and factual context of a request for a preliminary ruling and the grounds for making the reference to the Court.

15. The content of any request for a preliminary ruling is prescribed by Article 94 of the Rules of Procedure of the Court and is summarised, by way of a reminder, in the annex hereto. In addition to the text of the questions referred to the Court for a preliminary ruling, *the request for a preliminary ruling must contain*:

— a summary of the subject matter of the dispute in the main proceedings and the relevant findings of fact as determined by the referring court or tribunal, or, at the very least, an account of the facts on which the questions referred are based,

— the tenor of any national provisions applicable in the case and, where appropriate, the relevant national case-law, and

— a statement of the reasons which prompted the referring court or tribunal to inquire about the interpretation or validity of certain provisions of EU law, and the relationship between those provisions and the national legislation applicable to the main proceedings.

In the absence of one or more of the above, the Court may find it necessary, notably on the basis of Article 53(2) of the Rules of Procedure, to decline jurisdiction to give a preliminary ruling on the questions referred or dismiss the request for a preliminary ruling as inadmissible.

16. In its request for a preliminary ruling, the referring court or tribunal must provide the *precise references for the national provisions applicable to the facts of the dispute in the main proceedings and for the provisions of EU law* whose interpretation is sought or whose validity is challenged. Those references must, as far as possible, include both the exact title and date of adoption of the acts containing the provisions concerned and the publication references for those acts. When referring to case-law, the referring court or tribunal is also requested to mention the European Case Law Identifier (ECLI) of the decision concerned.

17. If it considers it necessary for the purpose of understanding the case, the referring court or tribunal may briefly set out the *main arguments of the parties to the main proceedings*. It should be borne in mind in that context that only the request for a preliminary ruling will be translated, not any annexes to that request.

18. The referring court or tribunal may also briefly state *its view on the answer to be given to the questions referred for a preliminary ruling*. That information may be useful to the Court, particularly where it is called upon to give a preliminary ruling in an expedited or urgent procedure.

19. Lastly, *the questions referred to* the Court for a preliminary ruling must appear *in a separate and clearly identified section of the order for reference*, preferably at the beginning or the end. It must be possible to understand them on their own terms, without it being necessary to refer to the statement of the grounds for the request.

20. In order to make the request for a preliminary ruling easier to read, it is essential that the Court receive it in typewritten form and that the pages and paragraphs of the order for reference be numbered. Handwritten requests for a preliminary ruling will not be processed by the Court.

PROTECTION OF PERSONAL DATA AND ANONYMISATION OF THE REQUEST FOR A PRELIMINARY RULING

21. In order to ensure optimal protection of personal data in the Court's handling of the case, service of the request for a preliminary ruling on the interested persons referred to in Article 23 of the Statute and the subsequent dissemination, in all official languages of the European Union, of the decision closing the proceedings, *the referring court or tribunal* — which alone has full knowledge of the file submitted to the Court — *is invited to anonymise the case by replacing, for example using initials or a combination of letters, the names of individuals* referred to in the request *and by redacting information that might enable them to be identified*. Given the increasing use of new information technologies and, in particular, the use of search engines, any anonymisation effected after the request for a preliminary ruling has been served on the interested persons referred to in Article 23 of the Statute and publication of the notice relating to the case in the *Official Journal of the European Union* is likely to be less effective.

22. If the referring court or tribunal has a nominative version of the request for a preliminary ruling, containing the full names and contact details of the parties to the main proceedings, and an anonymised version of that request, it is requested to send both versions to the Court to facilitate the Court's handling of the case.

TRANSMISSION TO THE COURT OF THE REQUEST FOR A PRELIMINARY RULING AND OF THE CASE FILE IN THE NATIONAL PROCEEDINGS

23. The request for a preliminary ruling must be dated and signed, then sent to the Court Registry electronically or by post (Registry of the Court of Justice, Rue du Fort Niedergrünewald, L-2925 Luxembourg). For reasons connected, in particular, with the need to ensure expeditious handling of the case and optimal communication with the referring court or tribunal, the Court recommends that national courts and tribunals use the e-Curia application. The rules on access to that application, which enables procedural documents to be lodged and served electronically, and the conditions of use of e-Curia may be viewed on the institution's website (https://curia.europa.eu/jcms/jcms/P_78957/en/). In order to facilitate the Court's processing of requests for a preliminary ruling and, in particular, their translation into

all the official languages of the European Union, national courts and tribunals are requested, in addition to sending the original version of the request for a preliminary ruling via e-Curia, to send an editable version (word processing software such as 'Word', 'OpenOffice' or 'LibreOffice') of that request to the following address: DDP-GreffeCour@curia.europa.eu.

24. The request for a preliminary ruling must reach the Registry together with all the relevant documents and documents useful for the Court's handling of the case and, in particular, the precise contact details for the parties to the main proceedings and their representatives, if any, as well as the file of the case in the main proceedings or a copy of it. The file (or copy file) — which may be sent electronically or by post — will be retained at the Registry throughout the proceedings before the Court where, unless otherwise indicated by the referring court or tribunal, it may be consulted by the interested persons referred to in Article 23 of the Statute.

INTERACTION BETWEEN THE REFERENCE FOR A PRELIMINARY RULING AND THE NATIONAL PROCEEDINGS

25. Although the referring court or tribunal may still order protective measures, particularly in connection with a reference on determination of validity, the lodging of a request for a preliminary ruling nevertheless calls for the national proceedings to be stayed until the Court has given its ruling.

26. While the Court, in principle, remains seised of a request for a preliminary ruling for so long as that request is not withdrawn by the referring court or tribunal, it must nevertheless be borne in mind that the Court's role in the preliminary ruling procedure is to contribute to the effective administration of justice in the Member States, and not to give opinions on general or hypothetical questions. Since the preliminary ruling procedure is predicated on there being proceedings actually pending before the referring court or tribunal, it is incumbent on that court or tribunal to inform the Court of any procedural step that may affect the referral and, in particular, of any discontinuance or withdrawal or of any amicable settlement of the dispute in the main proceedings, and of any other event leading to the termination of the proceedings. The referring court or tribunal must also inform the Court of any decision delivered in the context of an appeal against the order for reference and of the consequences of that decision for the request for a preliminary ruling. In the interests of the proper conduct of the preliminary ruling proceedings before the Court and, in particular, to ensure that the Court does not devote time and resources to a case that is likely to be withdrawn or become devoid of purpose, it is important that such information is communicated to the Court with the minimum of delay.

27. National courts and tribunals should also note that the withdrawal of a request for a preliminary ruling may have an impact on the management of similar cases by the referring court or tribunal. Where the outcome of a number of cases pending before the referring court or tribunal depends on the reply to be given by the Court to the questions submitted by that court or tribunal, it is appropriate for that court or tribunal to join those cases before submitting to the Court its request for a preliminary ruling in order to enable the Court to reply to the questions referred notwithstanding any withdrawal of one or more cases.

COSTS AND LEGAL AID

28. Preliminary ruling proceedings before the Court are free of charge and the Court does not rule on the costs of the parties to the proceedings pending before the referring court or tribunal. It is for the referring court or tribunal to rule on those costs.

29. If a party to the main proceedings has insufficient means, the Court may grant that party legal aid to cover the costs, particularly those in respect of its representation, which it incurs before the Court. That aid can, however, be granted only if the party in question is not already in receipt of aid under national rules or to the extent to which that aid does not cover, or covers only partly, costs incurred before the Court. That party is requested in any event to send to the Court all information and supporting documents that will enable his or her true financial situation to be assessed.

CONDUCT OF THE PROCEEDINGS BEFORE THE COURT AND THE ACTION TAKEN BY THE REFERRING COURT OR TRIBUNAL UPON THE COURT'S DECISION

30. The Court Registry will remain in contact with the referring court or tribunal throughout the proceedings, and will send it copies of all procedural documents and any requests for information or clarification deemed necessary in order for a useful reply to be given to the questions referred by that court or tribunal.

31. At the end of the proceedings which, as a rule, comprise a written part and an oral part, the Court gives its ruling in the form of a judgment on the questions put by the referring court or tribunal. In some cases, however, the Court may find it necessary to rule on those questions without an oral part of the procedure, or even without seeking the written observations of the interested persons referred to in Article 23 of the Statute. That is the case, in particular, when the question referred for a preliminary ruling is identical to a question on which the Court has already ruled, or where the answer to such a question may be clearly deduced from existing case-law or admits of no reasonable doubt. In such cases, the Court will, on the basis of Article 99 of its Rules of Procedure, rule expeditiously on the question put, by a reasoned order which has the same scope and the same binding force as a judgment.

32. After the judgment has been delivered or the order closing the proceedings has been signed, the Registry will send the Court's decision to the referring court or tribunal, which is requested to inform the Court of the action taken upon that decision in the case in the main proceedings. The final decision of the referring court or tribunal must be sent, with an express reference to the case number of the case before the Court, to the following address: Follow-up-DDP@curia.europa.eu.

II. PROVISIONS APPLICABLE TO REQUESTS FOR A PRELIMINARY RULING REQUIRING PARTICULARLY EXPEDITIOUS HANDLING

[6.576]

33. As provided in Article 23a of the Statute and Articles 105 to 114 of the Rules of Procedure, a reference for a preliminary ruling may, in certain circumstances, be determined pursuant to an expedited procedure or an urgent procedure. The Court will decide whether these procedures are to be applied, either on submission by the referring court or tribunal of a separate, duly reasoned, request setting out the matters of fact or of law which justify the application of such procedure(s), or, exceptionally, of its own motion, where that appears to be required by the nature or the particular circumstances of the case.

CONDITIONS FOR THE APPLICATION OF THE EXPEDITED PROCEDURE AND THE URGENT PROCEDURE

34. Article 105 of the Rules of Procedure provides that a reference for a preliminary ruling may thus be determined pursuant to *an expedited procedure*, derogating from the provisions of those rules, where the nature of the case requires that it be dealt with within a short time. Since that procedure imposes significant constraints on all those involved in it, and, in particular, on all the Member States called upon to lodge observations, whether written or oral, within much shorter time limits than would ordinarily apply, its application must be sought only when particular circumstances create an emergency that warrants the Court ruling quickly on the questions referred. That may be the case, inter alia, if there is a serious and immediate danger to public health or to the environment which a prompt decision by the Court might help to avert, or if particular circumstances require uncertainties concerning fundamental issues of national constitutional law and of EU law to be resolved within a very short time. According to settled case-law, the large number of persons or legal situations potentially affected by the decision that the referring court or tribunal has to deliver after bringing the matter before the Court for a preliminary ruling, the fact that there may be important economic issues at stake or that the referring court or tribunal is obliged to rule expeditiously do not, however, in themselves constitute exceptional circumstances that would justify the use of the expedited procedure.

35. The same applies *a fortiori* to *the urgent preliminary ruling procedure*, provided for in Article 107 of the Rules of Procedure. That procedure, which applies only in the areas covered by Title V of Part Three of the TFEU, relating to the area of freedom, security and justice, imposes even greater constraints on those concerned, since it limits the number of parties authorised to lodge written observations and, in cases of extreme urgency, allows the written part of the procedure before the Court to be omitted altogether. The application of the urgent procedure must therefore be requested only where it is absolutely necessary for the Court to give its ruling very quickly on the questions submitted by the referring court or tribunal.

36. Although it is not possible to provide an exhaustive list of such circumstances, particularly because of the varied and evolving nature of the rules of EU law governing the area of freedom, security and justice, a national court or tribunal may, for example, consider submitting a request for the urgent preliminary ruling procedure to be applied in the case, referred to in the fourth paragraph of Article 267 TFEU, of a person in custody or deprived of his or her liberty, where the answer to the question raised is decisive as to the assessment of that person's legal situation, or in proceedings concerning parental authority or custody of young children, in so far, in particular, as the outcome of the dispute in the main proceedings depends on the answer to the question referred for a preliminary ruling and the use of the ordinary procedure could cause serious, and perhaps irreparable, harm to the relationship between a child and (one of) that child's parents or to the child's development and integration into his or her family and social environment. By contrast, mere economic interests, however substantial and legitimate they may be, the legal uncertainty affecting the parties to the main proceedings or other parties to similar disputes, the large number of persons or legal situations potentially affected by the decision that a referring court has to deliver after bringing a matter before the Court for a preliminary ruling, or the large number of cases that may be affected by the decision of the Court do not constitute, as such, circumstances that would justify the application of the urgent preliminary ruling procedure.

THE REQUEST FOR APPLICATION OF THE EXPEDITED PROCEDURE OR THE URGENT PROCEDURE

37. To enable the Court to decide quickly whether the expedited procedure or the urgent preliminary ruling procedure should be applied, the request must *set out precisely the matters of fact and law which establish the urgency* and, in particular, the risks involved in following the ordinary procedure. In so far as it is possible to do so, the referring court or tribunal must also briefly state its view on the answer to be given to the questions referred. Such a statement makes it easier for the parties to the main proceedings and the other interested persons participating in the procedure to define their positions, and therefore contributes to the rapidity of the procedure.

38. The request for the application of the expedited procedure or the urgent procedure must in any event be submitted in an unambiguous form that enables the Registry to establish immediately that the file has to be dealt with in a particular way. Accordingly, the referring court or tribunal is requested to specify which of the two procedures is required in the particular case, and to mention in its request the relevant article of the Rules of Procedure (Article 105 for the expedited procedure or Article 107 for the urgent procedure). That mention must be included in a clearly identifiable place in its order for reference or in a separate letter from the referring court or tribunal.

39. As regards the order for reference itself, it is particularly important that it should be concise where the matter is urgent, as this will help to ensure the rapidity of the procedure.

COMMUNICATION BETWEEN THE COURT, THE REFERRING COURT OR TRIBUNAL AND THE PARTIES TO THE MAIN PROCEEDINGS

40. A court or tribunal submitting a request for the expedited procedure or the urgent procedure to be applied is requested to send that request and the order for reference itself — together with the text of the latter in an editable format (word processing software such as 'Word', 'Open Office' or 'LibreOffice') — by means of the e-Curia application or by email (DDP-GreffeCour@curia.europa.eu).

41. In order to facilitate subsequent communication by the Court with the referring court or tribunal and with the parties to the main proceedings, the referring court or tribunal is also requested to state its email address and any fax number which may be used by the Court, together with the email addresses and any fax numbers of the representatives of the parties to the main proceedings.

ANNEX

THE ESSENTIAL ELEMENTS OF A REQUEST FOR A PRELIMINARY RULING

[6.577]

This annex summarises, by way of a reminder, the main elements that must be included in a request for a preliminary ruling. These are followed by an indication of the paragraphs in the present recommendations in which those elements are discussed in more detail.

Whether transmitted electronically or by post, all requests for a preliminary ruling must mention:

1. the identity of the court or tribunal making the reference and, where appropriate, the chamber or formation of the court or tribunal having jurisdiction (see, in that respect, paragraphs 3 to 7);
2. the precise identity of the parties to the main proceedings and of anyone representing them before the referring court or tribunal (with regard to the parties to the main proceedings, see, however, paragraphs 21 and 22 of the present recommendations, in relation to the protection of personal data);
3. the subject matter of the dispute in the main proceedings and the relevant facts (see paragraph 15);
4. the relevant provisions of national law and of EU law (see paragraphs 15 and 16);
5. the reasons that prompted the referring court or tribunal to inquire about the interpretation or validity of EU law (see paragraphs 8 to 11 and 15 to 18);
6. the questions referred for a preliminary ruling (see paragraph 19) and, if applicable,
7. the possible need for specific treatment of the request, related, for example, to the need to preserve the anonymity of individuals concerned by the dispute or to the particularly expeditious way in which the request should be dealt with by the Court (see paragraph 33 et seq).

As regards form, requests for a preliminary ruling must be typewritten, dated and signed and must be received at the Court Registry, preferably electronically, together with all the documents that are relevant and useful for the handling of the case (see, in that respect, paragraphs 20 to 24 of the present recommendations and, with regard to requests requiring particularly expeditious treatment, paragraphs 40 and 41).

TRANSMISSION CHANNELS RECOMMENDED BY THE COURT

In order to ensure the best possible communication with courts and tribunals that have referred questions to the Court for a preliminary ruling, the Court recommends the use of the following transmission channels:

(1) Lodging of the request for a preliminary ruling (or of other relevant documents linked to that request):
- Signed original of the request for a preliminary ruling (or of the other documents linked to that request): to be sent via the e-Curia application. The rules on access to that application, which is free of charge and secure, and the conditions of use of e-Curia, are available here: https://curia.europa.eu/jcms/jcms/P_78957/en
- Editable version of the request for a preliminary ruling (or of the other documents linked to it): DDP-GreffeCour@curia.europa.eu

(2) Transmission of the final decision of the referring court or tribunal (anonymised, if necessary, including for the purposes of being placed online), following the Court's decision on the request for a preliminary ruling: Follow-up-DDP@curia.europa.eu.

RULES OF PROCEDURE OF THE COURT OF JUSTICE (CONSOLIDATED VERSION JANUARY 2020)

[6.578]

NOTES

Date of original publication in OJ: OJ L265, 29.9.2012, p 1.

A consolidated version of these Rules is available on the Court of Justice website at https://curia.europa.eu/jcms/jcms/Jo2_7031/en/. It includes the following amendments:

— amendments published in OJ L173, 26.6.2013, p 65 (with effect from 1 July 2013);
— amendments published in OJ L217, 12.8.2016, p 69 (with effect from 12 August 2016);
— amendments published in OJ L111, 25.4.2019, p 73 (with effect from 1 May 2019);
— amendments published in OJ L316, 6.12.2019, p 103 (with effect from 1 January 2020).

THE COURT OF JUSTICE

Having regard to the Treaty on European Union, and in particular Article 19 thereof,

Having regard to the Treaty on the Functioning of the European Union, and in particular the sixth paragraph of Article 253 thereof,

Having regard to the Treaty establishing the European Atomic Energy Community, and in particular Article 106a(1) thereof,

Having regard to the Protocol on the Statute of the Court of Justice of the European Union, and in particular Article 63 and the second paragraph of Article 64 thereof,

Whereas:

(1) Despite having been amended on several occasions over the years, the Rules of Procedure of the Court of Justice have remained fundamentally unchanged in structure since their original adoption on 4 March 1953. The Rules of Procedure of 19 June 1991, which are currently in force, still reflect the initial preponderance of direct actions, whereas in fact the majority of such actions now fall within the jurisdiction of the General Court, and references for a preliminary ruling from the courts and tribunals of the Member States represent, quantitatively, the primary category of cases brought before the Court. That fact should be taken into account and the structure and content of the Rules of Procedure of the Court adapted, in consequence, to changes in its caseload.

(2) While references for a preliminary ruling should be given their proper place in the Rules of Procedure, it is also appropriate to draw a clearer distinction between the rules that apply to all types of action and those that are specific to each type, to be contained in separate titles. In the interests of clarification, procedural provisions common to all cases brought before the Court should, therefore, all be contained in an initial title.

(3) In the light of experience gained in the course of implementing the various procedures, it is also necessary to supplement or to clarify, for the benefit of litigants as well as of national courts and tribunals, the rules that apply to each procedure. The rules in question concern, in particular, the concepts of party to the main proceedings, intervener and party to the proceedings before the General Court, or, in preliminary rulings, the rules governing the bringing of matters before the Court and the content of the order for reference. With regard to appeals against decisions of the General Court, a clearer distinction must also be drawn between appeals and cross-appeals in consequence of the service of an appeal on the cross-appellant.

(4) Conversely, the excessive complexity of certain procedures, such as the review procedure, has come to light on their implementation. Accordingly, they should be simplified by providing, inter alia, for a Chamber of five Judges to be designated for a period of one year to be responsible for ruling both on the First Advocate General's proposal to review and on the questions to be reviewed.

(5) Similarly, the procedural arrangements for dealing with requests for Opinions should be eased by aligning them with those that apply to other cases and by providing, in consequence, for a single Advocate General to be involved in dealing with the request for an Opinion. In the interests of making the Rules easier to understand, all the particular procedures currently to be found in a number of separate titles and chapters of the Rules of Procedure should also be brought together in a single title.

(6) In order to maintain the Court's capacity, in the face of an ever-increasing caseload, to dispose within a reasonable period of time of the cases brought before it, it is also necessary to continue the efforts made to reduce the duration of proceedings before the Court, in particular by extending the opportunities for the Court to rule by reasoned order, simplifying the rules relating to the intervention of the States and institutions referred to in the first and third paragraphs of Article 40 of the Statute and providing for the Court to be able to rule without a hearing if it considers that it has sufficient information on the basis of all the written observations lodged in a case.

(7) In the interests of making the Rules applied by the Court easier to understand, lastly, certain rules which are outdated or not applied should be deleted, every paragraph of the present Rules numbered, each article given a specific heading summarising its content and the terminology harmonised.

With the Council's approval given on 24 September 2012.

HAS ADOPTED THESE RULES OF PROCEDURE:

INTRODUCTORY PROVISIONS

[6.579]

Article 1 Definitions

1. In these Rules:
   (a) provisions of the Treaty on European Union are referred to by the number of the article concerned followed by 'TEU',
   (b) provisions of the Treaty on the Functioning of the European Union are referred to by the number of the article concerned followed by 'TFEU',
   (c) provisions of the Treaty establishing the European Atomic Energy Community are referred to by the number of the article concerned followed by 'TEAEC',
   (d) 'Statute' means the Protocol on the Statute of the Court of Justice of the European Union,
   (e) 'EEA Agreement' means the Agreement on the European Economic Area,[1]
   (f) 'Council Regulation No 1' means Council Regulation No 1 of 15 April 1958 determining the languages to be used by the European Economic Community.[2]
2. For the purposes of these Rules:
   (a) 'institutions' means the institutions of the European Union referred to in Article 13(1) TEU and bodies, offices and agencies established by the Treaties, or by an act adopted in implementation thereof, which may be parties before the Court,
   (b) 'EFTA Surveillance Authority' means the surveillance authority referred to in the EEA Agreement,
   (c) 'interested persons referred to in Article 23 of the Statute' means all the parties, States, institutions, bodies, offices and agencies authorised, pursuant to that Article, to submit statements of case or observations in the context of a reference for a preliminary ruling.

NOTES

[1] OJ L1, 3.1.1994, p 27.

[2] OJ, English Special Edition 1952-1958 (I), p 59.

[6.580]

Article 2 Purport of these Rules

These Rules implement and supplement, so far as necessary, the relevant provisions of the EU, FEU and EAEC Treaties, and the Statute.

TITLE I ORGANISATION OF THE COURT

CHAPTER 1 JUDGES AND ADVOCATES GENERAL

[6.581]

Article 3 Commencement of the term of office of Judges and Advocates General

The term of office of a Judge or Advocate General shall begin on the date fixed for that purpose in the instrument of appointment. In the absence of any provisions in that instrument regarding the date of commencement of the term of office, that term shall begin on the date of publication of the instrument in the *Official Journal of the European Union*.

[6.582]

Article 4 Taking of the oath

Before taking up his duties, a Judge or Advocate General shall, at the first public sitting of the Court which he attends after his appointment, take the following oath provided for in Article 2 of the Statute:

> 'I swear that I will perform my duties impartially and conscientiously; I swear that I will preserve the secrecy of the deliberations of the Court.'

[6.583]

Article 5 Solemn undertaking

Immediately after taking the oath, a Judge or Advocate General shall sign a declaration by which he gives the solemn undertaking provided for in the third paragraph of Article 4 of the Statute.

[6.584]

Article 6 Depriving a Judge or Advocate General of his office

1. Where the Court is called upon, pursuant to Article 6 of the Statute, to decide whether a Judge or Advocate General no longer fulfils the requisite conditions or no longer meets the obligations arising from his office, the President shall invite the Judge or Advocate General concerned to make representations.
2. The Court shall give a decision in the absence of the Registrar.

[6.585]

Article 7 Order of seniority

1. The seniority of Judges and Advocates General shall be calculated without distinction according to the date on which they took up their duties.
2. Where there is equal seniority on that basis, the order of seniority shall be determined by age.
3. Judges and Advocates General whose terms of office are renewed shall retain their former seniority.

CHAPTER 2 [PRESIDENCY OF THE COURT, CONSTITUTION OF THE CHAMBERS AND ELECTION OF THE FIRST ADVOCATE GENERAL]

NOTES

The Chapter 2 heading was substituted by the Amendments of the Rules of Procedure of the Court of Justice, Article 1(1) (OJ L316, 6.12.2019, p 103).

[6.586]

Article 8 Election of the President and of the Vice-President of the Court

1. The Judges shall, immediately after the partial replacement provided for in the second paragraph of Article 253 TFEU, elect one of their number as President of the Court for a term of three years.
2. If the office of the President falls vacant before the normal date of expiry of the term thereof, the Court shall elect a successor for the remainder of the term.
3. The elections provided for in this Article shall be by secret ballot. The Judge obtaining the votes of more than half the Judges of the Court shall be elected. If no Judge obtains that majority, further ballots shall be held until that majority is attained.
4. The Judges shall then elect one of their number as Vice-President of the Court for a term of three years, in accordance with the procedures laid down in the preceding paragraph. Paragraph 2 shall apply if the office of the Vice-President of the Court falls vacant before the normal date of expiry of the term thereof.
5. The names of the President and Vice-President elected in accordance with this Article shall be published in the *Official Journal of the European Union*.

[6.587]

Article 9 Responsibilities of the President of the Court

1. The President shall represent the Court.
2. The President shall direct the judicial business of the Court. He shall preside at general meetings of the Members of the Court and at hearings before and deliberations of the full Court and the Grand Chamber.
3. The President shall ensure the proper functioning of the services of the Court.

[6.588]

Article 10 Responsibilities of the Vice-President of the Court

1. The Vice-President shall assist the President of the Court in the performance of his duties and shall take the President's place when the latter is prevented from acting.

2. He shall take the President's place, at his request, in performing the duties referred to in Article 9(1) and (3) of these Rules.

3. The Court shall, by decision, specify the conditions under which the Vice-President shall take the place of the President of the Court in the performance of his judicial duties. That decision shall be published in the *Official Journal of the European Union*.

[6.589]

Article 11 Constitution of Chambers

1. The Court shall set up Chambers of five and three Judges in accordance with Article 16 of the Statute and shall decide which Judges shall be attached to them.

2. The Court shall designate the Chambers of five Judges which, for a period of one year, shall be responsible for cases of the kind referred to in Article 107 and Articles 193 and 194.

3. In respect of cases assigned to a formation of the Court in accordance with Article 60, the word 'Court' in these Rules shall mean that formation.

4. In respect of cases assigned to a Chamber of five or three Judges, the powers of the President of the Court shall be exercised by the President of the Chamber.

5. The composition of the Chambers and the designation of the Chambers responsible for cases of the kind referred to in Article 107 and Articles 193 and 194 shall be published in the *Official Journal of the European Union*.

[6.590]

Article 12 Election of Presidents of Chambers

1. The Judges shall, immediately after the election of the President and Vice-President of the Court, elect the Presidents of the Chambers of five Judges for a term of three years.

2. The Judges shall then elect the Presidents of the Chambers of three Judges for a term of one year.

3. The provisions of Article 8(2) and (3) shall apply.

4. The names of the Presidents of Chambers elected in accordance with this Article shall be published in the *Official Journal of the European Union*.

[6.591]

Article 13 Where the President and Vice-President of the Court are prevented from acting

When the President and the Vice-President of the Court are prevented from acting, the functions of President shall be exercised by one of the Presidents of the Chambers of five Judges or, failing that, by one of the Presidents of the Chambers of three Judges or, failing that, by one of the other Judges, according to the order of seniority laid down in Article 7.

[6.592]

[Article 14 Election of the First Advocate General

1. The Advocates General shall, immediately after the partial replacement provided for in the second paragraph of Article 253 TFEU, elect one of their number as First Advocate General for a term of three years.

2. If the office of the First Advocate General falls vacant before the normal date of expiry of the term thereof, he shall be replaced for the remainder of the term.

3. The elections provided for in this Article shall be by secret ballot. The Advocate General obtaining the votes of more than half of the Advocates General of the Court shall be elected. If no Advocate General obtains that majority, further ballots shall be held until that majority is attained.

4. The name of the First Advocate General elected in accordance with this Article shall be published in the *Official Journal of the European Union*.]

NOTES

Substituted by the Amendments of the Rules of Procedure of the Court of Justice, Article 1(2) (OJ L316, 6.12.2019, p 103). This amendment applies from the first partial replacement of Judges and Advocates General (provided for in the second paragraph of Article 253 of the Treaty on the Functioning of the European Union) following this amendment.

CHAPTER 3 ASSIGNMENT OF CASES TO JUDGE-RAPPORTEURS AND ADVOCATES GENERAL

[6.593]

Article 15 Designation of the Judge-Rapporteur

1. As soon as possible after the document initiating proceedings has been lodged, the President of the Court shall designate a Judge to act as Rapporteur in the case.

2. For cases of the kind referred to in Article 107 and Articles 193 and 194, the Judge-Rapporteur shall be selected from among the Judges of the Chamber designated in accordance with Article 11(2), on a proposal from the President of that Chamber. If, pursuant to Article 109, the Chamber decides that the reference is not to be dealt with under the urgent procedure, the President of the Court may reassign the case to a Judge-Rapporteur attached to another Chamber.

3. The President of the Court shall take the necessary steps if a Judge-Rapporteur is prevented from acting.

[6.594]

Article 16 Designation of the Advocate General

1. The First Advocate General shall assign each case to an Advocate General.

2. The First Advocate General shall take the necessary steps if an Advocate General is prevented from acting.

CHAPTER 4 ASSISTANT RAPPORTEURS

[6.595]

Article 17 Assistant Rapporteurs

1. Where the Court is of the opinion that the consideration of and preparatory inquiries in cases before it so require, it shall, pursuant to Article 13 of the Statute, propose the appointment of Assistant Rapporteurs.
2. Assistant Rapporteurs shall in particular:
   (a) assist the President of the Court in interim proceedings and
   (b) assist the Judge-Rapporteurs in their work.
3. In the performance of their duties the Assistant Rapporteurs shall be responsible to the President of the Court, the President of a Chamber or a Judge-Rapporteur, as the case may be.
4. Before taking up his duties, an Assistant Rapporteur shall take before the Court the oath set out in Article 4 of these Rules.

CHAPTER 5 REGISTRY

[6.596]

Article 18 Appointment of the Registrar

1. The Court shall appoint the Registrar.
2. When the post of Registrar is vacant, an advertisement shall be published in the *Official Journal of the European Union*. Interested persons shall be invited to submit their applications within a time-limit of not less than three weeks, accompanied by full details of their nationality, university degrees, knowledge of languages, present and past occupations, and experience, if any, in judicial and international fields.
3. The vote, in which the Judges and the Advocates General shall take part, shall take place in accordance with the procedure laid down in Article 8(3) of these Rules.
4. The Registrar shall be appointed for a term of six years. He may be reappointed. The Court may decide to renew the term of office of the incumbent Registrar without availing itself of the procedure laid down in paragraph 2 of this Article.
5. The Registrar shall take the oath set out in Article 4 and sign the declaration provided for in Article 5.
6. The Registrar may be deprived of his office only if he no longer fulfils the requisite conditions or no longer meets the obligations arising from his office. The Court shall take its decision after giving the Registrar an opportunity to make representations.
7. If the office of Registrar falls vacant before the normal date of expiry of the term thereof, the Court shall appoint a new Registrar for a term of six years.
8. The name of the Registrar elected in accordance with this Article shall be published in the *Official Journal of the European Union*.

[6.597]

Article 19 Deputy Registrar

The Court may, in accordance with the procedure laid down in respect of the Registrar, appoint a Deputy Registrar to assist the Registrar and to take his place if he is prevented from acting.

[6.598]

Article 20 Responsibilities of the Registrar

1. The Registrar shall be responsible, under the authority of the President of the Court, for the acceptance, transmission and custody of all documents and for effecting service as provided for by these Rules.
2. The Registrar shall assist the Members of the Court in all their official functions.
3. The Registrar shall have custody of the seals and shall be responsible for the records. He shall be in charge of the publications of the Court and, in particular, the European Court Reports.
4. The Registrar shall direct the services of the Court under the authority of the President of the Court. He shall be responsible for the management of the staff and the administration, and for the preparation and implementation of the budget.

[6.599]

Article 21 Keeping of the register

1. There shall be kept in the Registry, under the responsibility of the Registrar, a register in which all procedural documents and supporting items and documents lodged shall be entered in the order in which they are submitted.
2. When a document has been registered, the Registrar shall make a note to that effect on the original and, if a party so requests, on any copy submitted for the purpose.
3. Entries in the register and the notes provided for in the preceding paragraph shall be authentic.

[4. A notice shall be published in the *Official Journal of the European Union* indicating the date of registration of an application initiating proceedings, the names of the parties or, as the case may be, initials replacing a name, the form of order sought by the applicant and a summary of the pleas in law and of the main supporting arguments.

5. In the cases referred to in Title III of these Rules, the notice published in the *Official Journal of the European Union* shall indicate the date of lodging of a request for a preliminary ruling, the referring court or tribunal, the names of the parties to the main proceedings or, as the case may be, initials replacing a name, as well as the questions referred to the Court.]

NOTES

Paras 4, 5: substituted (for the original para 4) by the Amendments of the Rules of Procedure of the Court of Justice, Article 1(3) (OJ L316, 6.12.2019, p 103).

[6.600]
Article 22 Consultation of the register and of judgments and orders
1. Anyone may consult the register at the Registry and may obtain copies or extracts on payment of a charge on a scale fixed by the Court on a proposal from the Registrar.
2. The parties to a case may, on payment of the appropriate charge, obtain certified copies of procedural documents.
3. Anyone may, on payment of the appropriate charge, also obtain certified copies of judgments and orders.

CHAPTER 6 THE WORKING OF THE COURT

[6.601]
Article 23 Location of the sittings of the Court
The Court may choose to hold one or more specific sittings in a place other than that in which it has its seat.

[6.602]
Article 24 Calendar of the Court's judicial business
1. The judicial year shall begin on 7 October of each calendar year and end on 6 October of the following year.
2. The judicial vacations shall be determined by the Court.
3. In a case of urgency, the President may convene the Judges and the Advocates General during the judicial vacations.
4. The Court shall observe the official holidays of the place in which it has its seat.
5. The Court may, in proper circumstances, grant leave of absence to any Judge or Advocate General.
6. The dates of the judicial vacations and the list of official holidays shall be published annually in the *Official Journal of the European Union.*

[6.603]
Article 25 General meeting
Decisions concerning administrative issues or the action to be taken upon the proposals contained in the preliminary report referred to in Article 59 of these Rules shall be taken by the Court at the general meeting in which all the Judges and Advocates General shall take part and have a vote. The Registrar shall be present, unless the Court decides to the contrary.

[6.604]
Article 26 Drawing-up of minutes
Where the Court sits without the Registrar being present it shall, if necessary, instruct the most junior Judge for the purposes of Article 7 of these Rules to draw up minutes, which shall be signed by that Judge and by the President.

CHAPTER 7 FORMATIONS OF THE COURT

SECTION 1. COMPOSITION OF THE FORMATIONS OF THE COURT

[6.605]
Article 27 Composition of the Grand Chamber
1. The Grand Chamber shall, for each case, be composed of the President and the Vice-President of the Court, three Presidents of Chambers of five Judges, the Judge-Rapporteur and the number of Judges necessary to reach 15. The last-mentioned Judges and the three Presidents of Chambers of five Judges shall be designated from the lists referred to in paragraphs 3 and 4 of this Article, following the order laid down therein. The starting-point on each of those lists, in every case assigned to the Grand Chamber, shall be the name of the Judge immediately following the last Judge designated from the list concerned for the preceding case assigned to that formation of the Court.
2. After the election of the President and the Vice-President of the Court, and then of the Presidents of the Chambers of five Judges, a list of the Presidents of Chambers of five Judges and a list of the other Judges shall be drawn up for the purposes of determining the composition of the Grand Chamber.
3. The list of the Presidents of Chambers of five Judges shall be drawn up according to the order laid down in Article 7 of these Rules.
4. The list of the other Judges shall be drawn up according to the order laid down in Article 7 of these Rules, alternating with the reverse order: the first Judge on that list shall be the first according to the order laid down in that Article, the second Judge shall be the last according to that order, the third Judge shall be the second according to that order, the fourth Judge the penultimate according to that order, and so on.
5. The lists referred to in paragraphs 3 and 4 shall be published in the *Official Journal of the European Union*.
6. In cases which are assigned to the Grand Chamber between the beginning of a calendar year in which there is a partial replacement of Judges and the moment when that replacement has taken place, two substitute Judges may be designated to complete the formation of the Court for so long as the attainment of the quorum referred to in the third paragraph of Article 17 of the Statute is in doubt. Those substitute Judges shall be the two Judges appearing on the list referred to in paragraph 4 immediately after the last Judge designated for the composition of the Grand Chamber in the case.
7. The substitute Judges shall replace, in the order of the list referred to in paragraph 4, such Judges as are unable to take part in the determination of the case.

[6.606]
Article 28 Composition of the Chambers of five and of three Judges
1. The Chambers of five Judges and of three Judges shall, for each case, be composed of the President of the Chamber, the Judge-Rapporteur and the number of Judges required to attain the number of five and three Judges respectively. Those last-mentioned Judges shall be designated from the lists referred to in paragraphs 2 and 3, following the order laid down therein. The starting-point on those lists, in every case assigned to a Chamber, shall be the name of the Judge immediately following the last Judge designated from the list for the preceding case assigned to the Chamber concerned.

2. For the composition of the Chambers of five Judges, after the election of the Presidents of those Chambers lists shall be drawn up including all the Judges attached to the Chamber concerned, with the exception of its President. The lists shall be drawn up in the same way as the list referred to in Article 27(4).
3. For the composition of the Chambers of three Judges, after the election of the Presidents of those Chambers lists shall be drawn up including all the Judges attached to the Chamber concerned, with the exception of its President. The lists shall be drawn up according to the order laid down in Article 7.
4. The lists referred to in paragraphs 2 and 3 shall be published in the *Official Journal of the European Union*.

[6.607]
Article 29 Composition of Chambers where cases are related or referred back
1. Where the Court considers that a number of cases must be heard and determined together by one and the same formation of the Court, the composition of that formation shall be that fixed for the case in respect of which the preliminary report was examined first.
2. Where a Chamber to which a case has been assigned requests the Court, pursuant to Article 60(3) of these Rules, to assign the case to a formation composed of a greater number of Judges, that formation shall include the members of the Chamber which has referred the case back.

[6.608]
Article 30 Where a President of a Chamber is prevented from acting
1. When the President of a Chamber of five Judges is prevented from acting, the functions of President of the Chamber shall be exercised by a President of a Chamber of three Judges, where necessary according to the order laid down in Article 7 of these Rules, or, if that formation of the Court does not include a President of a Chamber of three Judges, by one of the other Judges according to the order laid down in Article 7.
2. When the President of a Chamber of three Judges is prevented from acting, the functions of President of the Chamber shall be exercised by a Judge of that formation of the Court according to the order laid down in Article 7.

[6.609]
Article 31 Where a member of the formation of the Court is prevented from acting
1. When a member of the Grand Chamber is prevented from acting, he shall be replaced by another Judge according to the order of the list referred to in Article 27(4).
2. When a member of a Chamber of five Judges is prevented from acting, he shall be replaced by another Judge of that Chamber, according to the order of the list referred to in Article 28(2). If it is not possible to replace the Judge prevented from acting by a Judge of the same Chamber, the President of that Chamber shall so inform the President of the Court who may designate another Judge to complete the Chamber.
3. When a member of a Chamber of three Judges is prevented from acting, he shall be replaced by another Judge of that Chamber, according to the order of the list referred to in Article 28(3). If it is not possible to replace the Judge prevented from acting by a Judge of the same Chamber, the President of that Chamber shall so inform the President of the Court who may designate another Judge to complete the Chamber.

SECTION 2. DELIBERATIONS

[6.610]
Article 32 Procedures concerning deliberations
1. The deliberations of the Court shall be and shall remain secret.
2. When a hearing has taken place, only those Judges who participated in that hearing and, where relevant, the Assistant Rapporteur responsible for the consideration of the case shall take part in the deliberations.
3. Every Judge taking part in the deliberations shall state his opinion and the reasons for it.
4. The conclusions reached by the majority of the Judges after final discussion shall determine the decision of the Court.

[6.611]
Article 33 Number of Judges taking part in the deliberations
Where, by reason of a Judge being prevented from acting, there is an even number of Judges, the most junior Judge for the purposes of Article 7 of these Rules shall abstain from taking part in the deliberations unless he is the Judge-Rapporteur. In that case the Judge immediately senior to him shall abstain from taking part in the deliberations.

[6.612]
Article 34 Quorum of the Grand Chamber
1. If, for a case assigned to the Grand Chamber, it is not possible to attain the quorum referred to in the third paragraph of Article 17 of the Statute, the President of the Court shall designate one or more other Judges according to the order of the list referred to in Article 27(4) of these Rules.
2. If a hearing has taken place before that designation, the Court shall re-hear oral argument from the parties and the Opinion of the Advocate General.

[6.613]
Article 35 Quorum of the Chambers of five and of three Judges
1. If, for a case assigned to a Chamber of five or of three Judges, it is not possible to attain the quorum referred to in the second paragraph of Article 17 of the Statute, the President of the Court shall designate one or more other Judges according to the order of the list referred to in Article 28(2) or (3), respectively, of these Rules. If it is not possible to replace the Judge prevented from acting by a Judge of the same Chamber, the President of that Chamber shall so inform the President of the Court forthwith who shall designate another Judge to complete the Chamber.
2. Article 34(2) shall apply, *mutatis mutandis*, to the Chambers of five and of three Judges.

CHAPTER 8 LANGUAGES

[6.614]

[Article 36 Language of a case

The language of a case shall be Bulgarian, Croatian, Czech, Danish, Dutch, English, Estonian, Finnish, French, German, Greek, Hungarian, Irish, Italian, Latvian, Lithuanian, Maltese, Polish, Portuguese, Romanian, Slovak, Slovenian, Spanish or Swedish.]

NOTES

Substituted by the Amendment of the Rules of Procedure of the Court of Justice, Article 1 (OJ L173, 26.6.2013, p 65).

[6.615]

Article 37 Determination of the language of a case

1. In direct actions, the language of a case shall be chosen by the applicant, except that:
   (a) where the defendant is a Member State, the language of the case shall be the official language of that State; where that State has more than one official language, the applicant may choose between them;
   (b) at the joint request of the parties, the use of another of the languages mentioned in Article 36 for all or part of the proceedings may be authorised;
   (c) at the request of one of the parties, and after the opposite party and the Advocate General have been heard, the use of another of the languages mentioned in Article 36 may be authorised as the language of the case for all or part of the proceedings by way of derogation from subparagraphs (a) and (b); such a request may not be submitted by one of the institutions of the European Union.
2. Without prejudice to the provisions of paragraph 1(b) and (c), and of Article 38(4) and (5) of these Rules,
   (a) in appeals against decisions of the General Court as referred to in Articles 56 and 57 of the Statute, the language of the case shall be the language of the decision of the General Court against which the appeal is brought;
   (b) where, in accordance with the second paragraph of Article 62 of the Statute, the Court decides to review a decision of the General Court, the language of the case shall be the language of the decision of the General Court which is the subject of review;
   (c) in the case of challenges concerning the costs to be recovered, applications to set aside judgments by default, third-party proceedings and applications for interpretation or revision of a judgment or for the Court to remedy a failure to adjudicate, the language of the case shall be the language of the decision to which those applications or challenges relate.

[3. In preliminary ruling proceedings, the language of the case shall be the language of the referring court or tribunal. At the duly substantiated request of one of the parties to the main proceedings, and after the other party to the main proceedings and the Advocate General have been heard, the use of another of the languages mentioned in Article 36 may be authorised for the oral part of the procedure. Where granted, the authorisation to use that other language shall apply in respect of all the interested persons referred to in Article 23 of the Statute.]

4. Requests as above may be decided on by the President; the latter may, and where he wishes to accede to a request without the agreement of all the parties must, refer the request to the Court.

NOTES

Para 3: substituted by the Amendments of the Rules of Procedure of the Court of Justice, Article 1(4) (OJ L316, 6.12.2019, p 103).

[6.616]

Article 38 Use of the language of the case

1. The language of the case shall in particular be used in the written and oral pleadings of the parties, including the items and documents produced or annexed to them, and also in the minutes and decisions of the Court.

2. Any item or document produced or annexed that is expressed in another language must be accompanied by a translation into the language of the case.

3. However, in the case of substantial items or lengthy documents, translations may be confined to extracts. At any time the Court may, of its own motion or at the request of one of the parties, call for a complete or fuller translation.

4. Notwithstanding the foregoing provisions, a Member State shall be entitled to use its official language when taking part in preliminary ruling proceedings, when intervening in a case before the Court or when bringing a matter before the Court pursuant to Article 259 TFEU. This provision shall apply both to written documents and to oral statements. The Registrar shall arrange in each instance for translation into the language of the case.

[5. The States, other than the Member States, which are parties to the EEA Agreement, and also the EFTA Surveillance Authority, shall be entitled to use one of the languages mentioned in Article 36, other than the language of the case, when they take part in preliminary ruling proceedings or intervene in a case before the Court. This provision shall apply both to written documents and to oral statements. The Registrar shall arrange in each instance for translation into the language of the case.]

[6. Non-Member States taking part in preliminary ruling proceedings pursuant to the fourth paragraph of Article 23 of the Statute shall be entitled to use one of the languages mentioned in Article 36 other than the language of the case. This provision shall apply both to written documents and to oral statements. The Registrar shall arrange in each instance for translation into the language of the case.]

7. Where a witness or expert states that he is unable adequately to express himself in one of the languages referred to in Article 36, the Court may authorise him to give his evidence in another language. The Registrar shall arrange for translation into the language of the case.

8. The President and the Vice-President of the Court and also the Presidents of Chambers in conducting oral proceedings, Judges and Advocates General in putting questions and Advocates General in delivering their Opinions may use one of the languages referred to in Article 36 other than the language of the case. The Registrar shall arrange for translation into the language of the case.

NOTES

Paras 5, 6: substituted by the Amendments of the Rules of Procedure of the Court of Justice, Article 1(5), (6) (OJ L316, 6.12.2019, p 103).

[6.617]

[Article 39 Responsibility of the Registrar concerning language arrangements

1. The Registrar shall arrange for procedural documents lodged during the written part of the procedure to be translated into the language of the case and, as the case may be, into another language mentioned in Article 36.

2. The Registrar shall also ensure that what is said at the hearing is interpreted into the language of the case and into the other languages that are mentioned in Article 36 and are used by the parties present at the hearing or considered necessary for the efficient conduct of that hearing.]

NOTES

Substituted by the Amendments of the Rules of Procedure of the Court of Justice, Article 1(7) (OJ L316, 6.12.2019, p 103).

[6.618]

Article 40 Languages of the publications of the Court

Publications of the Court shall be issued in the languages referred to in Article 1 of Council Regulation No 1.

[6.619]

Article 41 Authentic texts

The texts of documents drawn up in the language of the case or, where applicable, in another language authorised pursuant to Articles 37 or 38 of these Rules shall be authentic.

[6.620]

Article 42 Language service of the Court

The Court shall set up a language service staffed by experts with adequate legal training and a thorough knowledge of several official languages of the European Union.

TITLE II COMMON PROCEDURAL PROVISIONS

CHAPTER 1 RIGHTS AND OBLIGATIONS OF AGENTS, ADVISERS AND LAWYERS

[6.621]

Article 43 Privileges, immunities and facilities

1. Agents, advisers and lawyers who appear before the Court or before any judicial authority to which the Court has addressed letters rogatory shall enjoy immunity in respect of words spoken or written by them concerning the case or the parties.

2. Agents, advisers and lawyers shall also enjoy the following privileges and facilities:

(a) any papers and documents relating to the proceedings shall be exempt from both search and seizure. In the event of a dispute, the customs officials or police may seal those papers and documents; they shall then be immediately forwarded to the Court for inspection in the presence of the Registrar and of the person concerned;

(b) agents, advisers and lawyers shall be entitled to travel in the course of duty without hindrance.

[6.622]

Article 44 Status of the parties' representatives

1. In order to qualify for the privileges, immunities and facilities specified in Article 43, persons entitled to them shall furnish proof of their status as follows:

(a) agents shall produce an official document issued by the party for whom they act, who shall immediately serve a copy thereof on the Registrar;

(b) lawyers shall produce a certificate that they are authorised to practise before a court of a Member State or of another State which is a party to the EEA Agreement, and, where the party which they represent is a legal person governed by private law, an authority to act issued by that person;

(c) advisers shall produce an authority to act issued by the party whom they are assisting.

2. The Registrar of the Court shall issue them with a certificate, as required. The validity of this certificate shall be limited to a specified period, which may be extended or curtailed according to the duration of the proceedings.

[6.623]

Article 45 Waiver of immunity

1. The privileges, immunities and facilities specified in Article 43 of these Rules are granted exclusively in the interests of the proper conduct of proceedings.

2. The Court may waive immunity where it considers that the proper conduct of proceedings will not be hindered thereby.

[6.624]

Article 46 Exclusion from the proceedings

1. If the Court considers that the conduct of an agent, adviser or lawyer before the Court is incompatible with the dignity of the Court or with the requirements of the proper administration of justice, or that such agent, adviser or lawyer is using his rights for purposes other than those for which they were granted, it shall inform the person concerned. If the Court informs the competent authorities to whom the person concerned is answerable, a copy of the letter sent to those authorities shall be forwarded to the person concerned.

2. On the same grounds, the Court may at any time, having heard the person concerned and the Advocate General, decide to exclude an agent, adviser or lawyer from the proceedings by reasoned order. That order shall have immediate effect.

3. Where an agent, adviser or lawyer is excluded from the proceedings, the proceedings shall be suspended for a period fixed by the President in order to allow the party concerned to appoint another agent, adviser or lawyer.
4. Decisions taken under this Article may be rescinded.

[6.625]
Article 47 University teachers and parties to the main proceedings
1. The provisions of this Chapter shall apply to university teachers who have a right of audience before the Court in accordance with Article 19 of the Statute.
2. They shall also apply, in the context of references for a preliminary ruling, to the parties to the main proceedings where, in accordance with the national rules of procedure applicable, those parties are permitted to bring or defend court proceedings without being represented by a lawyer, and to persons authorised under those rules to represent them.

CHAPTER 2 SERVICE

[6.626]
Article 48 Methods of service
1. Where these Rules require that a document be served on a person, the Registrar shall ensure that service is effected at that person's address for service either by the dispatch of a copy of the document by registered post with a form for acknowledgement of receipt or by personal delivery of the copy against a receipt. The Registrar shall prepare and certify the copies of documents to be served, save where the parties themselves supply the copies in accordance with Article 57(2) of these Rules.
2. Where the addressee has agreed that service is to be effected on him by telefax or any other technical means of communication, any procedural document, including a judgment or order of the Court, may be served by the transmission of a copy of the document by such means.
3. Where, for technical reasons or on account of the nature or length of the document, such transmission is impossible or impracticable, the document shall be served, if the addressee has not specified an address for service, at his address in accordance with the procedures laid down in paragraph 1 of this Article. The addressee shall be so informed by telefax or any other technical means of communication. Service shall then be deemed to have been effected on the addressee by registered post on the 10th day following the lodging of the registered letter at the post office of the place in which the Court has its seat, unless it is shown by the acknowledgement of receipt that the letter was received on a different date or the addressee informs the Registrar, within three weeks of being informed by telefax or any other technical means of communication, that the document to be served has not reached him.
4. The Court may, by decision, determine the criteria for a procedural document to be served by electronic means. That decision shall be published in the *Official Journal of the European Union*.

CHAPTER 3 TIME-LIMITS

[6.627]
Article 49 Calculation of time-limits
1. Any procedural time-limit prescribed by the Treaties, the Statute or these Rules shall be calculated as follows:
   (a) where a time-limit expressed in days, weeks, months or years is to be calculated from the moment at which an event occurs or an action takes place, the day during which that event occurs or that action takes place shall not be counted as falling within the time-limit in question;
   (b) a time-limit expressed in weeks, months or years shall end with the expiry of whichever day in the last week, month or year is the same day of the week, or falls on the same date, as the day during which the event or action from which the time-limit is to be calculated occurred or took place. If, in a time-limit expressed in months or years, the day on which it should expire does not occur in the last month, the time-limit shall end with the expiry of the last day of that month;
   (c) where a time-limit is expressed in months and days, it shall first be calculated in whole months, then in days;
   (d) time-limits shall include Saturdays, Sundays and the official holidays referred to in Article 24(6) of these Rules;
   (e) time-limits shall not be suspended during the judicial vacations.
2. If the time-limit would otherwise end on a Saturday, Sunday or an official holiday, it shall be extended until the end of the first subsequent working day.

[6.628]
Article 50 Proceedings against a measure adopted by an institution
Where the time-limit allowed for initiating proceedings against a measure adopted by an institution runs from the publication of that measure, that time-limit shall be calculated, for the purposes of Article 49(1)(a), from the end of the 14th day after publication of the measure in the *Official Journal of the European Union*.

[6.629]
Article 51 Extension on account of distance
The procedural time-limits shall be extended on account of distance by a single period of 10 days.

[6.630]
Article 52 Setting and extension of time-limits
1. Any time-limit prescribed by the Court pursuant to these Rules may be extended.
2. The President and the Presidents of Chambers may delegate to the Registrar power of signature for the purposes of setting certain time-limits which, pursuant to these Rules, it falls to them to prescribe, or of extending such time-limits.

CHAPTER 4 DIFFERENT PROCEDURES FOR DEALING WITH CASES

[6.631]

Article 53 Procedures for dealing with cases

1. Without prejudice to the special provisions laid down in the Statute or in these Rules, the procedure before the Court shall consist of a written part and an oral part.
2. Where it is clear that the Court has no jurisdiction to hear and determine a case or where a request or an application is manifestly inadmissible, the Court may, after hearing the Advocate General, at any time decide to give a decision by reasoned order without taking further steps in the proceedings.
3. The President may in special circumstances decide that a case be given priority over others.
4. A case may be dealt with under an expedited procedure in accordance with the conditions provided by these Rules.
5. A reference for a preliminary ruling may be dealt with under an urgent procedure in accordance with the conditions provided by these Rules.

[6.632]

Article 54 Joinder

1. Two or more cases of the same type concerning the same subject-matter may at any time be joined, on account of the connection between them, for the purposes of the written or oral part of the procedure or of the judgment which closes the proceedings.
2. A decision on whether cases should be joined shall be taken by the President after hearing the Judge-Rapporteur and the Advocate General, if the cases concerned have already been assigned, and, save in the case of references for a preliminary ruling, after also hearing the parties. The President may refer the decision on this matter to the Court.
3. Joined cases may be disjoined, in accordance with the provisions of paragraph 2.

[6.633]

Article 55 Stay of proceedings

1. The proceedings may be stayed:
   (a) in the circumstances specified in the third paragraph of Article 54 of the Statute, by order of the Court, made after hearing the Advocate General;
   (b) in all other cases, by decision of the President adopted after hearing the Judge-Rapporteur and the Advocate General and, save in the case of references for a preliminary ruling, the parties.
2. The proceedings may be resumed by order or decision, following the same procedure.
3. The orders or decisions referred to in paragraphs 1 and 2 shall be served on the parties or interested persons referred to in Article 23 of the Statute.
4. The stay of proceedings shall take effect on the date indicated in the order or decision of stay or, in the absence of such indication, on the date of that order or decision.
5. While proceedings are stayed time shall cease to run for the parties or interested persons referred to in Article 23 of the Statute for the purposes of procedural time-limits.
6. Where the order or decision of stay does not fix the length of stay, it shall end on the date indicated in the order or decision of resumption or, in the absence of such indication, on the date of the order or decision of resumption.
7. From the date of resumption of proceedings following a stay, the suspended procedural time-limits shall be replaced by new time-limits and time shall begin to run from the date of that resumption.

[6.634]

Article 56 Deferment of the determination of a case

After hearing the Judge-Rapporteur, the Advocate General and the parties, the President may in special circumstances, either of his own motion or at the request of one of the parties, defer a case to be dealt with at a later date.

CHAPTER 5 WRITTEN PART OF THE PROCEDURE

[6.635]

Article 57 Lodging of procedural documents

1. The original of every procedural document must bear the handwritten signature of the party's agent or lawyer or, in the case of observations submitted in the context of preliminary ruling proceedings, that of the party to the main proceedings or his representative, if the national rules of procedure applicable to those main proceedings so permit.
2. The original, accompanied by all annexes referred to therein, shall be submitted together with five copies for the Court and, in the case of proceedings other than preliminary ruling proceedings, a copy for every other party to the proceedings. Copies shall be certified by the party lodging them.
3. The institutions shall in addition produce, within time-limits laid down by the Court, translations of any procedural document into the other languages provided for by Article 1 of Council Regulation No 1. The preceding paragraph of this Article shall apply.
4. To every procedural document there shall be annexed a file containing the items and documents relied on in support of it, together with a schedule listing them.
5. Where in view of the length of an item or document only extracts from it are annexed to the procedural document, the whole item or document or a full copy of it shall be lodged at the Registry.
6. All procedural documents shall bear a date. In the calculation of procedural time-limits, only the date and time of lodgment of the original at the Registry shall be taken into account.
7. Without prejudice to the provisions of paragraphs 1 to 6, the date on and time at which a copy of the signed original of a procedural document, including the schedule of items and documents referred to in paragraph 4, is received at the Registry by telefax or any other technical means of communication available to the Court shall be deemed to be the date and time of lodgment for the purposes of compliance with the procedural time-limits, provided that the signed original of the procedural document, accompanied by the annexes and copies referred to in paragraph 2, is lodged at the Registry no later than 10 days thereafter. [Article 51 of these Rules shall not apply to the latter time limit.]

8. Without prejudice to paragraphs 3 to 6, the Court may, by decision, determine the criteria for a procedural document sent to the Registry by electronic means to be deemed to be the original of that document. That decision shall be published in the *Official Journal of the European Union*.

NOTES

Para 7: words in square brackets inserted by the Amendments of the Rules of Procedure of the Court of Justice, Article 1(8) (OJ L316, 6.12.2019, p 103).

[6.636]

Article 58 Length of procedural documents

Without prejudice to any special provisions laid down in these Rules, the Court may, by decision, set the maximum length of written pleadings or observations lodged before it. That decision shall be published in the *Official Journal of the European Union*.

CHAPTER 6 THE PRELIMINARY REPORT AND ASSIGNMENT OF CASES TO FORMATIONS OF THE COURT

[6.637]

Article 59 Preliminary report

1. When the written part of the procedure is closed, the President shall fix a date on which the Judge-Rapporteur is to present a preliminary report to the general meeting of the Court.
2. The preliminary report shall contain proposals as to whether particular measures of organisation of procedure, measures of inquiry or, if appropriate, requests to the referring court or tribunal for clarification should be undertaken, and as to the formation to which the case should be assigned. It shall also contain the Judge-Rapporteur's proposals, if any, as to whether to dispense with a hearing and as to whether to dispense with an Opinion of the Advocate General pursuant to the fifth paragraph of Article 20 of the Statute.
3. The Court shall decide, after hearing the Advocate General, what action to take on the proposals of the Judge-Rapporteur.

[6.638]

Article 60 Assignment of cases to formations of the Court

1. The Court shall assign to the Chambers of five and of three Judges any case brought before it in so far as the difficulty or importance of the case or particular circumstances are not such as to require that it should be assigned to the Grand Chamber, unless a Member State or an institution of the European Union participating in the proceedings has requested that the case be assigned to the Grand Chamber, pursuant to the third paragraph of Article 16 of the Statute.
2. The Court shall sit as a full Court where cases are brought before it pursuant to the provisions referred to in the fourth paragraph of Article 16 of the Statute. It may assign a case to the full Court where, in accordance with the fifth paragraph of Article 16 of the Statute, it considers that the case is of exceptional importance.
3. The formation to which a case has been assigned may, at any stage of the proceedings, request the Court to assign the case to a formation composed of a greater number of Judges.
4. Where the oral part of the procedure is opened without an inquiry, the President of the formation determining the case shall fix the opening date.

CHAPTER 7 MEASURES OF ORGANISATION OF PROCEDURE AND MEASURES OF INQUIRY

SECTION 1. MEASURES OF ORGANISATION OF PROCEDURE

[6.639]

Article 61 Measures of organisation prescribed by the Court

1. In addition to the measures which may be prescribed in accordance with Article 24 of the Statute, the Court may invite the parties or the interested persons referred to in Article 23 of the Statute to answer certain questions in writing, within the time-limit laid down by the Court, or at the hearing. The written replies shall be communicated to the other parties or the interested persons referred to in Article 23 of the Statute.
2. Where a hearing is organised, the Court shall, in so far as possible, invite the participants in that hearing to concentrate in their oral pleadings on one or more specified issues.

[6.640]

Article 62 Measures of organisation prescribed by the Judge-Rapporteur or the Advocate General

1. The Judge-Rapporteur or the Advocate General may request the parties or the interested persons referred to in Article 23 of the Statute to submit within a specified time-limit all such information relating to the facts, and all such documents or other particulars, as they may consider relevant. The replies and documents provided shall be communicated to the other parties or the interested persons referred to in Article 23 of the Statute.
2. The Judge-Rapporteur or the Advocate General may also send to the parties or the interested persons referred to in Article 23 of the Statute questions to be answered at the hearing.

SECTION 2. MEASURES OF INQUIRY

[6.641]

Article 63 Decision on measures of inquiry

1. The Court shall decide in its general meeting whether a measure of inquiry is necessary.
2. Where the case has already been assigned to a formation of the Court, the decision shall be taken by that formation.

[6.642]
Article 64 Determination of measures of inquiry
1. The Court, after hearing the Advocate General, shall prescribe the measures of inquiry that it considers appropriate by means of an order setting out the facts to be proved.
2. Without prejudice to Articles 24 and 25 of the Statute, the following measures of inquiry may be adopted:
(a) the personal appearance of the parties;
(b) a request for information and production of documents;
(c) oral testimony;
(d) the commissioning of an expert's report;
(e) an inspection of the place or thing in question.
3. Evidence may be submitted in rebuttal and previous evidence may be amplified.

[6.643]
Article 65 Participation in measures of inquiry
1. Where the formation of the Court does not undertake the inquiry itself, it shall entrust the task of so doing to the Judge-Rapporteur.
2. The Advocate General shall take part in the measures of inquiry.
3. The parties shall be entitled to attend the measures of inquiry.

[6.644]
Article 66 Oral testimony
1. The Court may, either of its own motion or at the request of one of the parties, and after hearing the Advocate General, order that certain facts be proved by witnesses.
2. A request by a party for the examination of a witness shall state precisely about what facts and for what reasons the witness should be examined.
3. The Court shall rule by reasoned order on the request referred to in the preceding paragraph. If the request is granted, the order shall set out the facts to be established and state which witnesses are to be heard in respect of each of those facts.
4. Witnesses shall be summoned by the Court, where appropriate after lodgment of the security provided for in Article 73(1) of these Rules.

[6.645]
Article 67 Examination of witnesses
1. After the identity of the witness has been established, the President shall inform him that he will be required to vouch the truth of his evidence in the manner laid down in these Rules.
2. The witness shall give his evidence to the Court, the parties having been given notice to attend. After the witness has given his evidence the President may, at the request of one of the parties or of his own motion, put questions to him.
3. The other Judges and the Advocate General may do likewise.
4. Subject to the control of the President, questions may be put to witnesses by the representatives of the parties.

[6.646]
Article 68 Witnesses' oath
1. After giving his evidence, the witness shall take the following oath:
'I swear that I have spoken the truth, the whole truth and nothing but the truth.'
2. The Court may, after hearing the parties, exempt a witness from taking the oath.

[6.647]
Article 69 Pecuniary penalties
1. Witnesses who have been duly summoned shall obey the summons and attend for examination.
2. If, without good reason, a witness who has been duly summoned fails to appear before the Court, the Court may impose upon him a pecuniary penalty not exceeding EUR 5,000 and may order that a further summons be served on the witness at his own expense.
3. The same penalty may be imposed upon a witness who, without good reason, refuses to give evidence or to take the oath.

[6.648]
Article 70 Expert's report
1. The Court may order that an expert's report be obtained. The order appointing the expert shall define his task and set a time-limit within which he is to submit his report.
2. After the expert has submitted his report and that report has been served on the parties, the Court may order that the expert be examined, the parties having been given notice to attend. At the request of one of the parties or of his own motion, the President may put questions to the expert.
3. The other Judges and the Advocate General may do likewise.
4. Subject to the control of the President, questions may be put to the expert by the representatives of the parties.

[6.649]
Article 71 Expert's oath
1. After making his report, the expert shall take the following oath:
'I swear that I have conscientiously and impartially carried out my task.'
2. The Court may, after hearing the parties, exempt the expert from taking the oath.

[6.650]

Article 72 Objection to a witness or expert

1. If one of the parties objects to a witness or an expert on the ground that he is not a competent or proper person to act as a witness or expert or for any other reason, or if a witness or expert refuses to give evidence or to take the oath, the matter shall be resolved by the Court.

2. An objection to a witness or an expert shall be raised within two weeks after service of the order summoning the witness or appointing the expert; the statement of objection must set out the grounds of objection and indicate the nature of any evidence offered.

[6.651]

Article 73 Witnesses' and experts' costs

1. Where the Court orders the examination of witnesses or an expert's report, it may request the parties or one of them to lodge security for the witnesses' costs or the costs of the expert's report.

2. Witnesses and experts shall be entitled to reimbursement of their travel and subsistence expenses. The cashier of the Court may make an advance payment towards these expenses.

3. Witnesses shall be entitled to compensation for loss of earnings, and experts to fees for their services. The cashier of the Court shall pay witnesses and experts these sums after they have carried out their respective duties or tasks.

[6.652]

Article 74 Minutes of inquiry hearings

1. The Registrar shall draw up minutes of every inquiry hearing. The minutes shall be signed by the President and by the Registrar. They shall constitute an official record.

2. In the case of the examination of witnesses or experts, the minutes shall be signed by the President or by the Judge-Rapporteur responsible for conducting the examination of the witness or expert, and by the Registrar. Before the minutes are thus signed, the witness or expert must be given an opportunity to check the content of the minutes and to sign them.

3. The minutes shall be served on the parties.

[6.653]

Article 75 Opening of the oral part of the procedure after the inquiry

1. Unless the Court decides to prescribe a time-limit within which the parties may submit written observations, the President shall fix the date for the opening of the oral part of the procedure after the measures of inquiry have been completed.

2. Where a time-limit has been prescribed for the submission of written observations, the President shall fix the date for the opening of the oral part of the procedure after that time-limit has expired.

CHAPTER 8 ORAL PART OF THE PROCEDURE

[6.654]

Article 76 Hearing

1. Any reasoned requests for a hearing shall be submitted within three weeks after service on the parties or the interested persons referred to in Article 23 of the Statute of notification of the close of the written part of the procedure. That time-limit may be extended by the President.

2. On a proposal from the Judge-Rapporteur and after hearing the Advocate General, the Court may decide not to hold a hearing if it considers, on reading the written pleadings or observations lodged during the written part of the procedure, that it has sufficient information to give a ruling.

3. The preceding paragraph shall not apply where a request for a hearing, stating reasons, has been submitted by an interested person referred to in Article 23 of the Statute who did not participate in the written part of the procedure.

[6.655]

Article 77 Joint hearing

If the similarities between two or more cases of the same type so permit, the Court may decide to organise a joint hearing of those cases.

[6.656]

Article 78 Conduct of oral proceedings

Oral proceedings shall be opened and directed by the President, who shall be responsible for the proper conduct of the hearing.

[6.657]

Article 79 Cases heard in camera

1. For serious reasons related, in particular, to the security of the Member States or to the protection of minors, the Court may decide to hear a case *in camera*.

2. The oral proceedings in cases heard *in camera* shall not be published.

[6.658]

Article 80 Questions

The members of the formation of the Court and the Advocate General may in the course of the hearing put questions to the agents, advisers or lawyers of the parties and, in the circumstances referred to in Article 47(2) of these Rules, to the parties to the main proceedings or to their representatives.

[6.659]

Article 81 Close of the hearing

After the parties or the interested persons referred to in Article 23 of the Statute have presented oral argument, the President shall declare the hearing closed.

[6.660]

Article 82 Delivery of the Opinion of the Advocate General

1. Where a hearing takes place, the Opinion of the Advocate General shall be delivered after the close of that hearing.
2. The President shall declare the oral part of the procedure closed after the Advocate General has delivered his Opinion.

[6.661]

Article 83 Opening or reopening of the oral part of the procedure

The Court may at any time, after hearing the Advocate General, order the opening or reopening of the oral part of the procedure, in particular if it considers that it lacks sufficient information or where a party has, after the close of that part of the procedure, submitted a new fact which is of such a nature as to be a decisive factor for the decision of the Court, or where the case must be decided on the basis of an argument which has not been debated between the parties or the interested persons referred to in Article 23 of the Statute.

[6.662]

Article 84 Minutes of hearings

1. The Registrar shall draw up minutes of every hearing. The minutes shall be signed by the President and by the Registrar. They shall constitute an official record.
2. The parties and interested persons referred to in Article 23 of the Statute may inspect the minutes at the Registry and obtain copies.

[6.663]

Article 85 Recording of the hearing

The President may, on a duly substantiated request, authorise a party or an interested person referred to in Article 23 of the Statute who has participated in the written or oral part of the proceedings to listen, on the Court's premises, to the soundtrack of the hearing in the language used by the speaker during that hearing.

CHAPTER 9 JUDGMENTS AND ORDERS

[6.664]

Article 86 Date of delivery of a judgment

The parties or interested persons referred to in Article 23 of the Statute shall be informed of the date of delivery of a judgment.

[6.665]

Article 87 Content of a judgment

A judgment shall contain:

(a) a statement that it is the judgment of the Court,
(b) an indication as to the formation of the Court,
(c) the date of delivery,
(d) the names of the President and of the Judges who took part in the deliberations, with an indication as to the name of the Judge-Rapporteur,
(e) the name of the Advocate General,
(f) the name of the Registrar,
(g) a description of the parties or of the interested persons referred to in Article 23 of the Statute who participated in the proceedings,
(h) the names of their representatives,
(i) in the case of direct actions and appeals, a statement of the forms of order sought by the parties,
(j) where applicable, the date of the hearing,
(k) a statement that the Advocate General has been heard and, where applicable, the date of his Opinion,
(l) a summary of the facts,
(m) the grounds for the decision,
(n) the operative part of the judgment, including, where appropriate, the decision as to costs.

[6.666]

Article 88 Delivery and service of the judgment

1. The judgment shall be delivered in open court.
2. The original of the judgment, signed by the President, by the Judges who took part in the deliberations and by the Registrar, shall be sealed and deposited at the Registry; certified copies of the judgment shall be served on the parties and, where applicable, the referring court or tribunal, the interested persons referred to in Article 23 of the Statute and the General Court.

[6.667]

Article 89 Content of an order

1. An order shall contain:

(a) a statement that it is the order of the Court,
(b) an indication as to the formation of the Court,
(c) the date of its adoption,
(d) an indication as to the legal basis of the order,
(e) the names of the President and, where applicable, the Judges who took part in the deliberations, with an indication as to the name of the Judge-Rapporteur,
(f) the name of the Advocate General,
(g) the name of the Registrar,
[(h) a description of the parties or of the interested persons referred to in Article 23 of the Statute who participated in the proceedings,]

(i) the names of their representatives,
(j) a statement that the Advocate General has been heard,
(k) the operative part of the order, including, where appropriate, the decision as to costs.

2. Where, in accordance with these Rules, an order must be reasoned, it shall in addition contain:
(a) in the case of direct actions and appeals, a statement of the forms of order sought by the parties,
(b) a summary of the facts,
(c) the grounds for the decision.

NOTES

Para 1: point (h) substituted by the Amendments of the Rules of Procedure of the Court of Justice, Article 1(9) (OJ L316, 6.12.2019, p 103).

[6.668]
Article 90 Signature and service of the order

The original of the order, signed by the President and by the Registrar, shall be sealed and deposited at the Registry; certified copies of the order shall be served on the parties and, where applicable, the referring court or tribunal, the interested persons referred to in Article 23 of the Statute and the General Court.

[6.669]
Article 91 Binding nature of judgments and orders

1. A judgment shall be binding from the date of its delivery.
2. An order shall be binding from the date of its service.

[6.670]
Article 92 Publication in the Official Journal of the European Union

A notice containing the date and the operative part of the judgment or order of the Court which closes the proceedings shall be published in the *Official Journal of the European Union*.

TITLE III REFERENCES FOR A PRELIMINARY RULING

CHAPTER 1 GENERAL PROVISIONS

[6.671]
Article 93 Scope

The procedure shall be governed by the provisions of this Title:
(a) in the cases covered by Article 23 of the Statute,
(b) as regards references for interpretation which may be provided for by agreements to which the European Union or the Member States are parties.

[6.672]
Article 94 Content of the request for a preliminary ruling

In addition to the text of the questions referred to the Court for a preliminary ruling, the request for a preliminary ruling shall contain:
(a) a summary of the subject-matter of the dispute and the relevant findings of fact as determined by the referring court or tribunal, or, at least, an account of the facts on which the questions are based;
(b) the tenor of any national provisions applicable in the case and, where appropriate, the relevant national case-law;
(c) a statement of the reasons which prompted the referring court or tribunal to inquire about the interpretation or validity of certain provisions of European Union law, and the relationship between those provisions and the national legislation applicable to the main proceedings.

[6.673]
Article 95 Anonymity

1. Where anonymity has been granted by the referring court or tribunal, the Court shall respect that anonymity in the proceedings pending before it.
[2. At the request of the referring court or tribunal, of a party to the main proceedings or of its own motion, the Court may also render anonymous one or more persons or entities concerned by the case.]

NOTES

Para 2: substituted by the Amendments of the Rules of Procedure of the Court of Justice, Article 1(10) (OJ L316, 6.12.2019, p 103).

[6.674]
Article 96 Participation in preliminary ruling proceedings

1. Pursuant to Article 23 of the Statute, the following shall be authorised to submit observations to the Court:
(a) the parties to the main proceedings,
(b) the Member States,
(c) the European Commission,
(d) the institution which adopted the act the validity or interpretation of which is in dispute,
(e) the States, other than the Member States, which are parties to the EEA Agreement, and also the EFTA Surveillance Authority, where a question concerning one of the fields of application of that Agreement is referred to the Court for a preliminary ruling,
(f) non-Member States which are parties to an agreement relating to a specific subject-matter, concluded with the Council, where the agreement so provides and where a court or tribunal of a Member State refers to the Court of Justice for a preliminary ruling a question falling within the scope of that agreement.

2. Non-participation in the written part of the procedure does not preclude participation in the oral part of the procedure.

[6.675]
Article 97 Parties to the main proceedings

1. The parties to the main proceedings are those who are determined as such by the referring court or tribunal in accordance with national rules of procedure.
2. Where the referring court or tribunal informs the Court that a new party has been admitted to the main proceedings, when the proceedings before the Court are already pending, that party must accept the case as he finds it at the time when the Court was so informed. That party shall receive a copy of every procedural document already served on the interested persons referred to in Article 23 of the Statute.
3. As regards the representation and attendance of the parties to the main proceedings, the Court shall take account of the rules of procedure in force before the court or tribunal which made the reference. In the event of any doubt as to whether a person may under national law represent a party to the main proceedings, the Court may obtain information from the referring court or tribunal on the rules of procedure applicable.

[6.676]
Article 98 Translation and service of the request for a preliminary ruling

1. The requests for a preliminary ruling referred to in this Title shall be served on the Member States in the original version, accompanied by a translation into the official language of the State to which they are being addressed. Where appropriate, on account of the length of the request, such translation shall be replaced by the translation into the official language of the State to which it is addressed of a summary of that request, which will serve as a basis for the position to be adopted by that State. The summary shall include the full text of the question or questions referred for a preliminary ruling. That summary shall contain, in particular, in so far as that information appears in the request for a preliminary ruling, the subject-matter of the main proceedings, the essential arguments of the parties to those proceedings, a succinct presentation of the reasons for the reference for a preliminary ruling and the case-law and the provisions of national law and European Union law relied on.
2. In the cases covered by the third paragraph of Article 23 of the Statute, the requests for a preliminary ruling shall be served on the States, other than the Member States, which are parties to the EEA Agreement and also on the EFTA Surveillance Authority in the original version, accompanied by a translation of the request, or where appropriate of a summary, into one of the languages referred to in Article 36, to be chosen by the addressee.
3. Where a non-Member State has the right to take part in preliminary ruling proceedings pursuant to the fourth paragraph of Article 23 of the Statute, the original version of the request for a preliminary ruling shall be served on it accompanied by a translation of the request, or where appropriate of a summary, into one of the languages referred to in Article 36, to be chosen by the non-Member State concerned.

[6.677]
Article 99 Reply by reasoned order

Where a question referred to the Court for a preliminary ruling is identical to a question on which the Court has already ruled, where the reply to such a question may be clearly deduced from existing case-law or where the answer to the question referred for a preliminary ruling admits of no reasonable doubt, the Court may at any time, on a proposal from the Judge-Rapporteur and after hearing the Advocate General, decide to rule by reasoned order.

[6.678]
Article 100 Circumstances in which the Court remains seised

1. The Court shall remain seised of a request for a preliminary ruling for as long as it is not withdrawn by the court or tribunal which made that request to the Court. The withdrawal of a request may be taken into account until notice of the date of delivery of the judgment has been served on the interested persons referred to in Article 23 of the Statute.
2. However, the Court may at any time declare that the conditions of its jurisdiction are no longer fulfilled.

[6.679]
Article 101 Request for clarification

1. Without prejudice to the measures of organisation of procedure and measures of inquiry provided for in these Rules, the Court may, after hearing the Advocate General, request clarification from the referring court or tribunal within a time-limit prescribed by the Court.
2. The reply of the referring court or tribunal to that request shall be served on the interested persons referred to in Article 23 of the Statute.

[6.680]
Article 102 Costs of the preliminary ruling proceedings

It shall be for the referring court or tribunal to decide as to the costs of the preliminary ruling proceedings.

[6.681]
Article 103 Rectification of judgments and orders

1. Clerical mistakes, errors in calculation and obvious inaccuracies affecting judgments or orders may be rectified by the Court, of its own motion or at the request of an interested person referred to in Article 23 of the Statute made within two weeks after delivery of the judgment or service of the order.
2. The Court shall take its decision after hearing the Advocate General.
3. The original of the rectification order shall be annexed to the original of the rectified decision. A note of this order shall be made in the margin of the original of the rectified decision.

[6.682]

Article 104 Interpretation of preliminary rulings

1. Article 158 of these Rules relating to the interpretation of judgments and orders shall not apply to decisions given in reply to a request for a preliminary ruling.

2. It shall be for the national courts or tribunals to assess whether they consider that sufficient guidance is given by a preliminary ruling, or whether it appears to them that a further reference to the Court is required.

CHAPTER 2 EXPEDITED PRELIMINARY RULING PROCEDURE

[6.683]

Article 105 Expedited procedure

1. At the request of the referring court or tribunal or, exceptionally, of his own motion, the President of the Court may, where the nature of the case requires that it be dealt with within a short time, after hearing the Judge-Rapporteur and the Advocate General, decide that a reference for a preliminary ruling is to be determined pursuant to an expedited procedure derogating from the provisions of these Rules.

2. In that event, the President shall immediately fix the date for the hearing, which shall be communicated to the interested persons referred to in Article 23 of the Statute when the request for a preliminary ruling is served.

3. The interested persons referred to in the preceding paragraph may lodge statements of case or written observations within a time-limit prescribed by the President, which shall not be less than 15 days. The President may request those interested persons to restrict the matters addressed in their statement of case or written observations to the essential points of law raised by the request for a preliminary ruling.

4. The statements of case or written observations, if any, shall be communicated to all the interested persons referred to in Article 23 of the Statute prior to the hearing.

5. The Court shall rule after hearing the Advocate General.

[6.684]

Article 106 Transmission of procedural documents

1. The procedural documents referred to in the preceding Article shall be deemed to have been lodged on the transmission to the Registry, by telefax or any other technical means of communication available to the Court, of a copy of the signed original and the items and documents relied on in support of it, together with the schedule referred to in Article 57(4). The original of the document and the annexes referred to above shall be sent to the Registry immediately.

2. Where the preceding Article requires that a document be served on or communicated to a person, such service or communication may be effected by transmission of a copy of the document by telefax or any other technical means of communication available to the Court and the addressee.

CHAPTER 3 URGENT PRELIMINARY RULING PROCEDURE

[6.685]

Article 107 Scope of the urgent preliminary ruling procedure

1. A reference for a preliminary ruling which raises one or more questions in the areas covered by Title V of Part Three of the Treaty on the Functioning of the European Union may, at the request of the referring court or tribunal or, exceptionally, of the Court's own motion, be dealt with under an urgent procedure derogating from the provisions of these Rules.

2. The referring court or tribunal shall set out the matters of fact and law which establish the urgency and justify the application of that exceptional procedure and shall, in so far as possible, indicate the answer that it proposes to the questions referred.

3. If the referring court or tribunal has not submitted a request for the urgent procedure to be applied, the President of the Court may, if the application of that procedure appears, prima facie, to be required, ask the Chamber referred to in Article 108 to consider whether it is necessary to deal with the reference under that procedure.

[6.686]

Article 108 Decision as to urgency

1. The decision to deal with a reference for a preliminary ruling under the urgent procedure shall be taken by the designated Chamber, acting on a proposal from the Judge-Rapporteur and after hearing the Advocate General. The composition of that Chamber shall be determined in accordance with Article 28(2) on the day on which the case is assigned to the Judge-Rapporteur if the application of the urgent procedure is requested by the referring court or tribunal, or, if the application of that procedure is considered at the request of the President of the Court, on the day on which that request is made.

2. If the case is connected with a pending case assigned to a Judge-Rapporteur who is not a member of the designated Chamber, that Chamber may propose to the President of the Court that the case be assigned to that Judge-Rapporteur. Where the case is reassigned to that Judge-Rapporteur, the Chamber of five Judges which includes him shall carry out the duties of the designated Chamber in respect of that case. Article 29(1) shall apply.

[6.687]

Article 109 Written part of the urgent procedure

1. A request for a preliminary ruling shall, where the referring court or tribunal has requested the application of the urgent procedure or where the President has requested the designated Chamber to consider whether it is necessary to deal with the reference under that procedure, be served forthwith by the Registrar on the parties to the main proceedings, on the Member State from which the reference is made, on the European Commission and on the institution which adopted the act the validity or interpretation of which is in dispute.

2. The decision as to whether or not to deal with the reference for a preliminary ruling under the urgent procedure shall be served immediately on the referring court or tribunal and on the parties, Member State and institutions referred to in the preceding paragraph. The decision to deal with the reference under the urgent procedure shall

prescribe the time-limit within which those parties or entities may lodge statements of case or written observations. The decision may specify the matters of law to which such statements of case or written observations must relate and may specify the maximum length of those documents.

3. Where a request for a preliminary ruling refers to an administrative procedure or judicial proceedings conducted in a Member State other than that from which the reference is made, the Court may invite that first Member State to provide all relevant information in writing or at the hearing.

4. As soon as the service referred to in paragraph 1 above has been effected, the request for a preliminary ruling shall also be communicated to the interested persons referred to in Article 23 of the Statute, other than the persons served, and the decision whether or not to deal with the reference for a preliminary ruling under the urgent procedure shall be communicated to those interested persons as soon as the service referred to in paragraph 2 has been effected.

5. The interested persons referred to in Article 23 of the Statute shall be informed as soon as possible of the likely date of the hearing.

6. Where the reference is not to be dealt with under the urgent procedure, the proceedings shall continue in accordance with the provisions of Article 23 of the Statute and the applicable provisions of these Rules.

[6.688]

Article 110 Service and information following the close of the written part of the procedure

1. Where a reference for a preliminary ruling is to be dealt with under the urgent procedure, the request for a preliminary ruling and the statements of case or written observations which have been lodged shall be served on the interested persons referred to in Article 23 of the Statute other than the parties and entities referred to in Article 109(1). The request for a preliminary ruling shall be accompanied by a translation, where appropriate of a summary, in accordance with Article 98.

2. The statements of case or written observations which have been lodged shall also be served on the parties and other interested persons referred to in Article 109(1).

3. The date of the hearing shall be communicated to the interested persons referred to in Article 23 of the Statute at the same time as the documents referred to in the preceding paragraphs are served.

[6.689]

Article 111 Omission of the written part of the procedure

The designated Chamber may, in cases of extreme urgency, decide to omit the written part of the procedure referred to in Article 109(2).

[6.690]

Article 112 Decision on the substance

The designated Chamber shall rule after hearing the Advocate General.

[6.691]

Article 113 Formation of the Court

1. The designated Chamber may decide to sit in a formation of three Judges. In that event, it shall be composed of the President of the designated Chamber, the Judge-Rapporteur and the first Judge or, as the case may be, the first two Judges designated from the list referred to in Article 28(2) on the date on which the composition of the designated Chamber is determined in accordance with Article 108(1).

2. The designated Chamber may also request the Court to assign the case to a formation composed of a greater number of Judges. The urgent procedure shall continue before the new formation of the Court, where necessary after the reopening of the oral part of the procedure.

[6.692]

Article 114 Transmission of procedural documents

Procedural documents shall be transmitted in accordance with Article 106.

CHAPTER 4 LEGAL AID

[6.693]

Article 115 Application for legal aid

1. A party to the main proceedings who is wholly or in part unable to meet the costs of the proceedings before the Court may at any time apply for legal aid.

2. The application shall be accompanied by all information and supporting documents making it possible to assess the applicant's financial situation, such as a certificate issued by a competent national authority attesting to his financial situation.

3. If the applicant has already obtained legal aid before the referring court or tribunal, he shall produce the decision of that court or tribunal and specify what is covered by the sums already granted.

[6.694]

Article 116 Decision on the application for legal aid

1. As soon as the application for legal aid has been lodged it shall be assigned by the President to the Judge-Rapporteur responsible for the case in the context of which the application has been made.

2. The decision to grant legal aid, in full or in part, or to refuse it shall be taken, on a proposal from the Judge-Rapporteur and after hearing the Advocate General, by the Chamber of three Judges to which the Judge-Rapporteur is assigned. The formation of the Court shall, in that event, be composed of the President of that Chamber, the Judge-Rapporteur and the first Judge or, as the case may be, the first two Judges designated from the list referred to in Article 28(3) on the date on which the application for legal aid is brought before that Chamber by the Judge-Rapporteur.

3. If the Judge-Rapporteur is not a member of a Chamber of three Judges, the decision shall be taken, under the same conditions, by the Chamber of five Judges to which he is assigned. In addition to the Judge-Rapporteur, the formation of the Court shall be composed of four Judges designated from the list referred to in Article 28(2) on the date on which the application for legal aid is brought before that Chamber by the Judge-Rapporteur.
4. The formation of the Court shall give its decision by way of order. Where the application for legal aid is refused in whole or in part, the order shall state the reasons for that refusal.

[6.695]
Article 117 Sums to be advanced as legal aid
Where legal aid is granted, the cashier of the Court shall be responsible, where applicable within the limits set by the formation of the Court, for costs involved in the assistance and representation of the applicant before the Court. At the request of the applicant or his representative, an advance on those costs may be paid.

[6.696]
Article 118 Withdrawal of legal aid
The formation of the Court which gave a decision on the application for legal aid may at any time, either of its own motion or on request, withdraw that legal aid if the circumstances which led to its being granted alter during the proceedings.

TITLE IV DIRECT ACTIONS

CHAPTER 1 REPRESENTATION OF THE PARTIES

[6.697]
Article 119 Obligation to be represented
1. A party may be represented only by his agent or lawyer.
2. Agents and lawyers must lodge at the Registry an official document or an authority to act issued by the party whom they represent.
3. The lawyer acting for a party must also lodge at the Registry a certificate that he is authorised to practise before a court of a Member State or of another State which is a party to the EEA Agreement.
[4. If those documents are not lodged, the Registrar shall prescribe a reasonable time limit within which the party concerned is to produce them. If the party concerned fails to produce the required documents within the time limit prescribed, the President shall, after hearing the Judge-Rapporteur and the Advocate General, decide whether the non-compliance with that procedural requirement renders the application or written pleading formally inadmissible. If he considers it necessary, the President may refer that question to the Court of Justice.]

NOTES
Para 4: substituted by the Amendments of the Rules of Procedure of the Court of Justice, Article 1(11) (OJ L316, 6.12.2019, p 103).

CHAPTER 2 WRITTEN PART OF THE PROCEDURE

[6.698]
Article 120 Content of the application
An application of the kind referred to in Article 21 of the Statute shall state:
(a) the name and address of the applicant;
(b) the name of the party against whom the application is made;
(c) the subject-matter of the proceedings, the pleas in law and arguments relied on and a summary of those pleas in law;
(d) the form of order sought by the applicant;
(e) where appropriate, any evidence produced or offered.

[6.699]
Article 121 Information relating to service
1. For the purpose of the proceedings, the application shall state an address for service. It shall indicate the name of the person who is authorised and has expressed willingness to accept service.
2. In addition to, or instead of, specifying an address for service as referred to in paragraph 1, the application may state that the lawyer or agent agrees that service is to be effected on him by telefax or any other technical means of communication.
3. If the application does not comply with the requirements referred to in paragraphs 1 or 2, all service on the party concerned for the purpose of the proceedings shall be effected, for so long as the defect has not been cured, by registered letter addressed to the agent or lawyer of that party. By way of derogation from Article 48, service shall then be deemed to be duly effected by the lodging of the registered letter at the post office of the place in which the Court has its seat.

[6.700]
Article 122 Annexes to the application
1. The application shall be accompanied, where appropriate, by the documents specified in the second paragraph of Article 21 of the Statute.
2. An application submitted under Article 273 TFEU shall be accompanied by a copy of the special agreement concluded between the Member States concerned.
[3. If an application does not comply with the requirements set out in paragraphs 1 or 2 of this Article, the Registrar shall prescribe a reasonable time limit within which the applicant is to produce the abovementioned documents. If the applicant fails to put the application in order, the President shall, after hearing the Judge-Rapporteur and the Advocate General, decide whether the non-compliance with these conditions renders the application formally inadmissible. If he considers it necessary, the President may refer that question to the Court of Justice.]

NOTES

Para 3: substituted by the Amendments of the Rules of Procedure of the Court of Justice, Article 1(12) (OJ L316, 6.12.2019, p 103).

[6.701]

[Article 123 Service of the application

The application shall be served on the defendant. In cases where Article 119(4) or Article 122(3) applies, service shall be effected as soon as the application has been put in order or the President or the Court has declared it admissible notwithstanding the failure to observe the requirements set out in those two Articles.]

NOTES

Substituted by the Amendments of the Rules of Procedure of the Court of Justice, Article 1(13) (OJ L316, 6.12.2019, p 103).

[6.702]

Article 124 Content of the defence

1. Within two months after service on him of the application, the defendant shall lodge a defence, stating:
 (a) the name and address of the defendant;
 (b) the pleas in law and arguments relied on;
 (c) the form of order sought by the defendant;
 (d) where appropriate, any evidence produced or offered.
2. Article 121 shall apply to the defence.
3. The time-limit laid down in paragraph 1 may exceptionally be extended by the President at the duly reasoned request of the defendant.

[6.703]

Article 125 Transmission of documents

Where the European Parliament, the Council or the European Commission is not a party to a case, the Court shall send to them copies of the application and of the defence, without the annexes thereto, to enable them to assess whether the inapplicability of one of their acts is being invoked under Article 277 TFEU.

[6.704]

Article 126 Reply and rejoinder

1. The application initiating proceedings and the defence may be supplemented by a reply from the applicant and by a rejoinder from the defendant.
2. The President shall prescribe the time-limits within which those procedural documents are to be produced. He may specify the matters to which the reply or the rejoinder should relate.

CHAPTER 3 PLEAS IN LAW AND EVIDENCE

[6.705]

Article 127 New pleas in law

1. No new plea in law may be introduced in the course of proceedings unless it is based on matters of law or of fact which come to light in the course of the procedure.
2. Without prejudice to the decision to be taken on the admissibility of the plea in law, the President may, on a proposal from the Judge-Rapporteur and after hearing the Advocate General, prescribe a time-limit within which the other party may respond to that plea.

[6.706]

Article 128 Evidence produced or offered

1. In reply or rejoinder a party may produce or offer further evidence in support of his arguments. The party must give reasons for the delay in submitting such evidence.
2. The parties may, exceptionally, produce or offer further evidence after the close of the written part of the procedure. They must give reasons for the delay in submitting such evidence. The President may, on a proposal from the Judge-Rapporteur and after hearing the Advocate General, prescribe a time-limit within which the other party may comment on such evidence.

CHAPTER 4 INTERVENTION

[6.707]

Article 129 Object and effects of the intervention

1. The intervention shall be limited to supporting, in whole or in part, the form of order sought by one of the parties. It shall not confer the same procedural rights as those conferred on the parties and, in particular, shall not give rise to any right to request that a hearing be held.
2. The intervention shall be ancillary to the main proceedings. It shall become devoid of purpose if the case is removed from the register of the Court as a result of a party's discontinuance or withdrawal from the proceedings or of an agreement between the parties, or where the application is declared inadmissible.
3. The intervener must accept the case as he finds it at the time of his intervention.
4. Consideration may be given to an application to intervene which is made after the expiry of the time-limit prescribed in Article 130 but before the decision to open the oral part of the procedure provided for in Article 60(4). In that event, if the President allows the intervention, the intervener may submit his observations during the hearing, if it takes place.

[6.708]

Article 130 Application to intervene

1. An application to intervene must be submitted within six weeks of the publication of the notice referred to in Article 21(4).

2. The application to intervene shall contain:

(a) a description of the case;

(b) a description of the main parties;

(c) the name and address of the intervener;

(d) the form of order sought, in support of which the intervener is applying for leave to intervene;

(e) a statement of the circumstances establishing the right to intervene, where the application is submitted pursuant to the second or third paragraph of Article 40 of the Statute.

3. The intervener shall be represented in accordance with Article 19 of the Statute.

4. Articles 119, 121 and 122 of these Rules shall apply.

[6.709]

[Article 131 Decision on applications to intervene

1. The application to intervene shall be served on the parties in order to obtain any written or oral observations they may wish to make on that application.

2. Where the application is submitted pursuant to the first paragraph of Article 40 of the Statute, the intervention shall be allowed by decision of the President and the intervener shall receive a copy of every procedural document served on the parties, unless the parties have, within 10 days after the service referred to in paragraph 1 has been effected, identified secret or confidential items or documents which, if communicated to the intervener, the parties claim would be prejudicial to them. In that case, the President shall decide on the application to intervene by order, after hearing the Judge-Rapporteur and the Advocate General, and the intervener shall receive a copy of every procedural document served on the parties, save, where applicable, for the secret or confidential items or documents excluded from such communication.

3. Where the application is submitted pursuant to the second paragraph of Article 40 of the Statute, the President shall decide on the application to intervene by order, after hearing the Judge-Rapporteur and the Advocate General, or shall refer the application to the Court. If the application to intervene is granted, the intervener shall receive a copy of every procedural document served on the parties, save, where applicable, for the secret or confidential items or documents excluded from such communication.

4. Where the application is submitted pursuant to the third paragraph of Article 40 of the Statute, the intervention shall be allowed by decision of the President and the intervener shall receive a copy of every procedural document served on the parties unless those parties have, within 10 days after the service referred to in paragraph 1 has been effected, put forward observations on the application to intervene or identified secret or confidential items or documents which, if communicated to the intervener, the parties claim would be prejudicial to them. In such cases, the President shall decide on the application to intervene by order, after hearing the Judge-Rapporteur and the Advocate General, and the intervener shall receive a copy of every procedural document served on the parties, save, where applicable, for the secret or confidential items or documents excluded from such communication.]

NOTES

Substituted by the Amendments of the Rules of Procedure of the Court of Justice, Article 1(14) (OJ L316, 6.12.2019, p 103).

[6.710]

Article 132 Submission of statements

1. The intervener may submit a statement in intervention within one month after communication of the procedural documents referred to in the preceding Article. That time-limit may be extended by the President at the duly reasoned request of the intervener.

2. The statement in intervention shall contain:

(a) the form of order sought by the intervener in support, in whole or in part, of the form of order sought by one of the parties;

(b) the pleas in law and arguments relied on by the intervener;

(c) where appropriate, any evidence produced or offered.

3. After the statement in intervention has been lodged, the President shall, where necessary, prescribe a time-limit within which the parties may reply to that statement.

CHAPTER 5 EXPEDITED PROCEDURE

[6.711]

Article 133 Decision relating to the expedited procedure

1. At the request of the applicant or the defendant, the President of the Court may, where the nature of the case requires that it be dealt with within a short time, after hearing the other party, the Judge-Rapporteur and the Advocate General, decide that a case is to be determined pursuant to an expedited procedure derogating from the provisions of these Rules.

2. The request for a case to be determined pursuant to an expedited procedure must be made by a separate document submitted at the same time as the application initiating proceedings or the defence, as the case may be, is lodged.

3. Exceptionally the President may also take such a decision of his own motion, after hearing the parties, the Judge-Rapporteur and the Advocate General.

[6.712]

Article 134 Written part of the procedure

1. Under the expedited procedure, the application initiating proceedings and the defence may be supplemented by a reply and a rejoinder only if the President, after hearing the Judge-Rapporteur and the Advocate General, considers this to be necessary.

2. An intervener may submit a statement in intervention only if the President, after hearing the Judge-Rapporteur and the Advocate General, considers this to be necessary.

[6.713]

Article 135 Oral part of the procedure

1. Once the defence has been submitted or, if the decision to determine the case pursuant to an expedited procedure is not made until after that pleading has been lodged, once that decision has been taken, the President shall fix a date for the hearing, which shall be communicated forthwith to the parties. He may postpone the date of the hearing where it is necessary to undertake measures of inquiry or where measures of organisation of procedure so require.
2. Without prejudice to Articles 127 and 128, a party may supplement his arguments and produce or offer evidence during the oral part of the procedure. The party must, however, give reasons for the delay in producing such further arguments or evidence.

[6.714]

Article 136 Decision on the substance

The Court shall give its ruling after hearing the Advocate General.

CHAPTER 6 COSTS

[6.715]

Article 137 Decision as to costs

A decision as to costs shall be given in the judgment or order which closes the proceedings.

[6.716]

Article 138 General rules as to allocation of costs

1. The unsuccessful party shall be ordered to pay the costs if they have been applied for in the successful party's pleadings.
2. Where there is more than one unsuccessful party the Court shall decide how the costs are to be shared.
3. Where each party succeeds on some and fails on other heads, the parties shall bear their own costs. However, if it appears justified in the circumstances of the case, the Court may order that one party, in addition to bearing its own costs, pay a proportion of the costs of the other party.

[6.717]

Article 139 Unreasonable or vexatious costs

The Court may order a party, even if successful, to pay costs which the Court considers that party to have unreasonably or vexatiously caused the opposite party to incur.

[6.718]

Article 140 Costs of interveners

1. The Member States and institutions which have intervened in the proceedings shall bear their own costs.
2. The States, other than the Member States, which are parties to the EEA Agreement, and also the EFTA Surveillance Authority, shall similarly bear their own costs if they have intervened in the proceedings.
3. The Court may order an intervener other than those referred to in the preceding paragraphs to bear his own costs.

[6.719]

Article 141 Costs in the event of discontinuance or withdrawal

1. A party who discontinues or withdraws from proceedings shall be ordered to pay the costs if they have been applied for in the other party's observations on the discontinuance.
2. However, at the request of the party who discontinues or withdraws from proceedings, the costs shall be borne by the other party if this appears justified by the conduct of that party.
3. Where the parties have come to an agreement on costs, the decision as to costs shall be in accordance with that agreement.
4. If costs are not claimed, the parties shall bear their own costs.

[6.720]

Article 142 Costs where a case does not proceed to judgment

Where a case does not proceed to judgment the costs shall be in the discretion of the Court.

[6.721]

Article 143 Costs of proceedings

Proceedings before the Court shall be free of charge, except that:

(a) where a party has caused the Court to incur avoidable costs the Court may, after hearing the Advocate General, order that party to refund them;
(b) where copying or translation work is carried out at the request of a party, the cost shall, in so far as the Registrar considers it excessive, be paid for by that party on the Registry's scale of charges referred to in Article 22.

[6.722]

Article 144 Recoverable costs

Without prejudice to the preceding Article, the following shall be regarded as recoverable costs:

(a) sums payable to witnesses and experts under Article 73 of these Rules;
(b) expenses necessarily incurred by the parties for the purpose of the proceedings, in particular the travel and subsistence expenses and the remuneration of agents, advisers or lawyers.

[6.723]
Article 145 Dispute concerning the costs to be recovered
1. If there is a dispute concerning the costs to be recovered, the Chamber of three Judges to which the Judge-Rapporteur who dealt with the case is assigned shall, on application by the party concerned and after hearing the opposite party and the Advocate General, make an order. In that event, the formation of the Court shall be composed of the President of that Chamber, the Judge-Rapporteur and the first Judge or, as the case may be, the first two Judges designated from the list referred to in Article 28(3) on the date on which the dispute is brought before that Chamber by the Judge-Rapporteur.
2. If the Judge-Rapporteur is not a member of a Chamber of three Judges, the decision shall be taken, under the same conditions, by the Chamber of five Judges to which he is assigned. In addition to the Judge-Rapporteur, the formation of the Court shall be composed of four Judges designated from the list referred to in Article 28(2) on the date on which the dispute is brought before that Chamber by the Judge-Rapporteur.
3. The parties may, for the purposes of enforcement, apply for an authenticated copy of the order.

[6.724]
Article 146 Procedure for payment
1. Sums due from the cashier of the Court and from its debtors shall be paid in euro.
2. Where costs to be recovered have been incurred in a currency other than the euro or where the steps in respect of which payment is due were taken in a country of which the euro is not the currency, the conversion shall be effected at the European Central Bank's official rates of exchange on the day of payment.

CHAPTER 7 AMICABLE SETTLEMENT, DISCONTINUANCE, CASES THAT DO NOT PROCEED TO JUDGMENT AND PRELIMINARY ISSUES

[6.725]
Article 147 Amicable settlement
1. If, before the Court has given its decision, the parties reach a settlement of their dispute and inform the Court of the abandonment of their claims, the President shall order the case to be removed from the register and shall give a decision as to costs in accordance with Article 141, having regard to any proposals made by the parties on the matter.
2. This provision shall not apply to proceedings under Articles 263 TFEU and 265 TFEU.

[6.726]
Article 148 Discontinuance
If the applicant informs the Court in writing or at the hearing that he wishes to discontinue the proceedings, the President shall order the case to be removed from the register and shall give a decision as to costs in accordance with Article 141.

[6.727]
Article 149 Cases that do not proceed to judgment
If the Court declares that the action has become devoid of purpose and that there is no longer any need to adjudicate on it, the Court may at any time of its own motion, on a proposal from the Judge-Rapporteur and after hearing the parties and the Advocate General, decide to rule by reasoned order. It shall give a decision as to costs.

[6.728]
Article 150 Absolute bar to proceeding with a case
On a proposal from the Judge-Rapporteur, the Court may at any time of its own motion, after hearing the parties and the Advocate General, decide to rule by reasoned order on whether there exists any absolute bar to proceeding with a case.

[6.729]
Article 151 Preliminary objections and issues
1. A party applying to the Court for a decision on a preliminary objection or issue not going to the substance of the case shall submit the application by a separate document.
2. The application must state the pleas of law and arguments relied on and the form of order sought by the applicant; any supporting items and documents must be annexed to it.
3. As soon as the application has been submitted, the President shall prescribe a time-limit within which the opposite party may submit in writing his pleas in law and the form of order which he seeks.
4. Unless the Court decides otherwise, the remainder of the proceedings on the application shall be oral.
5. The Court shall, after hearing the Advocate General, decide on the application as soon as possible or, where special circumstances so justify, reserve its decision until it rules on the substance of the case.
6. If the Court refuses the application or reserves its decision, the President shall prescribe new time-limits for the further steps in the proceedings.

CHAPTER 8 JUDGMENTS BY DEFAULT

[6.730]
Article 152 Judgments by default
1. If a defendant on whom an application initiating proceedings has been duly served fails to respond to the application in the proper form and within the time-limit prescribed, the applicant may apply to the Court for judgment by default.
2. The application for judgment by default shall be served on the defendant. The Court may decide to open the oral part of the procedure on the application.
3. Before giving judgment by default the Court shall, after hearing the Advocate General, consider whether the application initiating proceedings is admissible, whether the appropriate formalities have been complied with, and whether the applicant's claims appear well founded. The Court may adopt measures of organisation of procedure or order measures of inquiry.

4. A judgment by default shall be enforceable. The Court may, however, grant a stay of execution until the Court has given its decision on any application under Article 156 to set aside the judgment, or it may make execution subject to the provision of security of an amount and nature to be fixed in the light of the circumstances; this security shall be released if no such application is made or if the application fails.

CHAPTER 9 REQUESTS AND APPLICATIONS RELATING TO JUDGMENTS AND ORDERS

[6.731]
Article 153 Competent formation of the Court

1. With the exception of applications referred to in Article 159, the requests and applications referred to in this Chapter shall be assigned to the Judge-Rapporteur who was responsible for the case to which the request or application relates, and shall be assigned to the formation of the Court which gave a decision in that case.
2. If the Judge-Rapporteur is prevented from acting, the President of the Court shall assign the request or application referred to in this Chapter to a Judge who was a member of the formation of the Court which gave a decision in the case to which that request or application relates.
3. If the quorum referred to in Article 17 of the Statute can no longer be attained, the Court shall, on a proposal from the Judge-Rapporteur and after hearing the Advocate General, assign the request or application to a new formation of the Court.

[6.732]
Article 154 Rectification

1. Without prejudice to the provisions relating to the interpretation of judgments and orders, clerical mistakes, errors in calculation and obvious inaccuracies may be rectified by the Court, of its own motion or at the request of a party made within two weeks after delivery of the judgment or service of the order.
2. Where the request for rectification concerns the operative part or one of the grounds constituting the necessary support for the operative part, the parties, whom the Registrar shall duly inform, may submit written observations within a time-limit prescribed by the President.
3. The Court shall take its decision after hearing the Advocate General.
4. The original of the rectification order shall be annexed to the original of the rectified decision. A note of this order shall be made in the margin of the original of the rectified decision.

[6.733]
Article 155 Failure to adjudicate

1. If the Court has failed to adjudicate on a specific head of claim or on costs, any party wishing to rely on that may, within a month after service of the decision, apply to the Court to supplement its decision.
2. The application shall be served on the opposite party and the President shall prescribe a time-limit within which that party may submit written observations.
3. After these observations have been submitted, the Court shall, after hearing the Advocate General, decide both on the admissibility and on the substance of the application.

[6.734]
Article 156 Application to set aside

1. Application may be made pursuant to Article 41 of the Statute to set aside a judgment delivered by default.
2. The application to set aside the judgment must be made within one month from the date of service of the judgment and must be submitted in the form prescribed by Articles 120 to 122 of these Rules.
3. After the application has been served, the President shall prescribe a time-limit within which the other party may submit his written observations.
4. The proceedings shall be conducted in accordance with Articles 59 to 92 of these Rules.
5. The Court shall decide by way of a judgment which may not be set aside.
6. The original of this judgment shall be annexed to the original of the judgment by default. A note of the judgment on the application to set aside shall be made in the margin of the original of the judgment by default.

[6.735]
Article 157 Third-party proceedings

1. Articles 120 to 122 of these Rules shall apply to an application initiating third-party proceedings made pursuant to Article 42 of the Statute. In addition such an application shall:
   (a) specify the judgment or order contested;
   (b) state how the contested decision is prejudicial to the rights of the third party;
   (c) indicate the reasons for which the third party was unable to take part in the original case.
2. The application must be made against all the parties to the original case.
3. The application must be submitted within two months of publication of the decision in the *Official Journal of the European Union*.
4. The Court may, on application by the third party, order a stay of execution of the contested decision. The provisions of Chapter 10 of this Title shall apply.
5. The contested decision shall be varied on the points on which the submissions of the third party are upheld.
6. The original of the judgment in the third-party proceedings shall be annexed to the original of the contested decision. A note of the judgment in the third-party proceedings shall be made in the margin of the original of the contested decision.

[6.736]
Article 158 Interpretation

1. In accordance with Article 43 of the Statute, if the meaning or scope of a judgment or order is in doubt, the Court shall construe it on application by any party or any institution of the European Union establishing an interest therein.
2. An application for interpretation must be made within two years after the date of delivery of the judgment or service of the order.

3. An application for interpretation shall be made in accordance with Articles 120 to 122 of these Rules. In addition it shall specify:
   (a) the decision in question;
   (b) the passages of which interpretation is sought.

4. The application must be made against all the parties to the case in which the decision of which interpretation is sought was given.
5. The Court shall give its decision after having given the parties an opportunity to submit their observations and after hearing the Advocate General.
6. The original of the interpreting decision shall be annexed to the original of the decision interpreted. A note of the interpreting decision shall be made in the margin of the original of the decision interpreted.

[6.737]
Article 159 Revision

1. In accordance with Article 44 of the Statute, an application for revision of a decision of the Court may be made only on discovery of a fact which is of such a nature as to be a decisive factor and which, when the judgment was delivered or the order served, was unknown to the Court and to the party claiming the revision.
2. Without prejudice to the time-limit of 10 years prescribed in the third paragraph of Article 44 of the Statute, an application for revision shall be made within three months of the date on which the facts on which the application is founded came to the applicant's knowledge.
3. Articles 120 to 122 of these Rules shall apply to an application for revision. In addition such an application shall:
   (a) specify the judgment or order contested;
   (b) indicate the points on which the decision is contested;
   (c) set out the facts on which the application is founded;
   (d) indicate the nature of the evidence to show that there are facts justifying revision, and that the time-limits laid down in paragraph 2 have been observed.
4. The application for revision must be made against all parties to the case in which the contested decision was given.
5. Without prejudice to its decision on the substance, the Court shall, after hearing the Advocate General, give in the form of an order its decision on the admissibility of the application, having regard to the written observations of the parties.
6. If the Court declares the application admissible, it shall proceed to consider the substance of the application and shall give its decision in the form of a judgment in accordance with these Rules.
7. The original of the revising judgment shall be annexed to the original of the decision revised. A note of the revising judgment shall be made in the margin of the original of the decision revised.

[6.738]
[Article 159a Manifestly inadmissible or manifestly unfounded requests and applications

Where a request or an application referred to in this Chapter is, in whole or in part, manifestly inadmissible or manifestly unfounded, the Court may, having heard the Judge-Rapporteur and the Advocate General, at any time decide to dismiss it, in whole or in part, by reasoned order.]

NOTES

Inserted by the Amendments of the Rules of Procedure of the Court of Justice, Article 1(15) (OJ L316, 6.12.2019, p 103).

CHAPTER 10 SUSPENSION OF OPERATION OR ENFORCEMENT AND OTHER INTERIM MEASURES

[6.739]
Article 160 Application for suspension or for interim measures

1. An application to suspend the operation of any measure adopted by an institution, made pursuant to Article 278 TFEU or Article 157 TEAEC, shall be admissible only if the applicant has challenged that measure in an action before the Court.
2. An application for the adoption of one of the other interim measures referred to in Article 279 TFEU shall be admissible only if it is made by a party to a case before the Court and relates to that case.
3. An application of a kind referred to in the preceding paragraphs shall state the subject-matter of the proceedings, the circumstances giving rise to urgency and the pleas of fact and law establishing a prima facie case for the interim measure applied for.
4. The application shall be made by a separate document and in accordance with the provisions of Articles 120 to 122 of these Rules.
5. The application shall be served on the opposite party, and the President shall prescribe a short time-limit within which that party may submit written or oral observations.
6. The President may order a preparatory inquiry.
7. The President may grant the application even before the observations of the opposite party have been submitted. This decision may be varied or cancelled even without any application being made by any party.

[6.740]
Article 161 Decision on the application

1. The President shall either decide on the application himself or refer it immediately to the Court.
2. If the President is prevented from acting, Articles 10 and 13 of these Rules shall apply.
3. Where the application is referred to it, the Court shall give a decision immediately, after hearing the Advocate General.

[6.741]
Article 162 Order for suspension of operation or for interim measures

1. The decision on the application shall take the form of a reasoned order, from which no appeal shall lie. The order shall be served on the parties forthwith.

2. The execution of the order may be made conditional on the lodging by the applicant of security, of an amount and nature to be fixed in the light of the circumstances.
3. Unless the order fixes the date on which the interim measure is to lapse, the measure shall lapse when the judgment which closes the proceedings is delivered.
4. The order shall have only an interim effect, and shall be without prejudice to the decision of the Court on the substance of the case.

[6.742]

Article 163 Change in circumstances

On application by a party, the order may at any time be varied or cancelled on account of a change in circumstances.

[6.743]

Article 164 New application

Rejection of an application for an interim measure shall not bar the party who made it from making a further application on the basis of new facts.

[6.744]

Article 165 Applications pursuant to Articles 280 TFEU and 299 TFEU and Article 164 TEAEC

1. The provisions of this Chapter shall apply to applications to suspend the enforcement of a decision of the Court or of any measure adopted by the Council, the European Commission or the European Central Bank, submitted pursuant to Articles 280 TFEU and 299 TFEU or Article 164 TEAEC.
2. The order granting the application shall fix, where appropriate, a date on which the interim measure is to lapse.

[6.745]

Article 166 Application pursuant to Article 81 TEAEC

1. An application of a kind referred to in the third and fourth paragraphs of Article 81 TEAEC shall contain:
   (a) the names and addresses of the persons or undertakings to be inspected;
   (b) an indication of what is to be inspected and of the purpose of the inspection.
2. The President shall give his decision in the form of an order. Article 162 of these Rules shall apply.
3. If the President is prevented from acting, Articles 10 and 13 of these Rules shall apply.

TITLE V APPEALS AGAINST DECISIONS OF THE GENERAL COURT

CHAPTER 1 FORM AND CONTENT OF THE APPEAL, AND FORM OF ORDER SOUGHT

[6.746]

[Article 167 Lodging of the appeal

1. An appeal shall be brought by lodging an application at the Registry of the Court of Justice or of the General Court. When that application is lodged at the Registry of the General Court, it shall be transmitted forthwith to the Registry of the Court of Justice.
2. As soon as it is informed of the existence of an appeal, the Registry of the General Court shall forthwith transmit to the Registry of the Court of Justice the file in the case at first instance and any procedural file of the Board of Appeal transmitted to the General Court to the provisions of the Rules of Procedure of the General Court concerning proceedings relating to intellectual property rights.]

NOTES

Substituted by the Amendments of the Rules of Procedure of the Court of Justice, Article 1(16) (OJ L316, 6.12.2019, p 103).

[6.747]

Article 168 Content of the appeal

1. An appeal shall contain:
   (a) the name and address of the appellant;
   (b) a reference to the decision of the General Court appealed against;
   (c) the names of the other parties to the relevant case before the General Court;
   (d) the pleas in law and legal arguments relied on, and a summary of those pleas in law;
   (e) the form of order sought by the appellant.
2. Articles 119, 121 and 122(1) of these Rules shall apply to appeals.
3. The appeal shall state the date on which the decision appealed against was served on the appellant.

[4. If an appeal does not comply with paragraphs 1 to 3 of this Article, the Registrar shall prescribe a reasonable time limit within which the appellant is to put the appeal in order. If the appellant fails to put the appeal in order within the time limit prescribed, the President shall, after hearing the Judge-Rapporteur and the Advocate General, decide whether the non-compliance with that formal requirement renders the appeal formally inadmissible. If he considers it necessary, the President may refer that question to the Court of Justice.]

NOTES

Para 4: substituted by the Amendments of the Rules of Procedure of the Court of Justice, Article 1(17) (OJ L316, 6.12.2019, p 103).

[6.748]

Article 169 Form of order sought, pleas in law and arguments of the appeal

1. An appeal shall seek to have set aside, in whole or in part, the decision of the General Court as set out in the operative part of that decision.
2. The pleas in law and legal arguments relied on shall identify precisely those points in the grounds of the decision of the General Court which are contested.

[6.749]
Article 170 Form of order sought in the event that the appeal is allowed

1. An appeal shall seek, in the event that it is declared well founded, the same form of order, in whole or in part, as that sought at first instance and shall not seek a different form of order. The subject-matter of the proceedings before the General Court may not be changed in the appeal.
2. Where the appellant requests that the case be referred back to the General Court if the decision appealed against is set aside, he shall set out the reasons why the state of the proceedings does not permit a decision by the Court of Justice.

[CHAPTER 1A PRIOR DETERMINATION AS TO WHETHER APPEALS UNDER ARTICLE 58A OF THE STATUTE SHOULD BE ALLOWED TO PROCEED

[6.750]
Article 170a Request that the appeal be allowed to proceed

1. In the situations referred to in the first and second paragraphs of Article 58a of the Statute, the appellant shall annex to the appeal a request that the appeal be allowed to proceed, setting out the issue raised by the appeal that is significant with respect to the unity, consistency or development of European Union law and containing all the information necessary to enable the Court of Justice to rule on that request. If there is no such request, the Vice President of the Court shall declare the appeal inadmissible.
2. The request that the appeal be allowed to proceed shall not exceed seven pages and shall be drawn up taking into account all the formal requirements contained in the Practice Directions to parties concerning cases brought before the Court, adopted on the basis of these Rules.
3. If the request that the appeal be allowed to proceed does not comply with the requirements set out in the preceding paragraph, the Registrar shall prescribe a reasonable time-limit within which the appellant is to put the request in order. If the appellant fails to put the request in order within the time-limit prescribed, the Vice-President of the Court shall decide, on a proposal from the Judge-Rapporteur and after hearing the Advocate General, whether the non-compliance with that formal requirement renders the appeal formally inadmissible.]

NOTES

Chapter 1a (Articles 170a, 170b) inserted by the Amendment of the Rules of Procedure of the Court of Justice, Article 1 (OJ L111, 25.4.2019, p 73).

[6.751]
[Article 170b Decision on the request that the appeal be allowed to proceed

1. The Court of Justice shall rule as soon as possible on the request that the appeal be allowed to proceed.
2. The decision on that request shall be taken, on a proposal from the Judge-Rapporteur and after hearing the Advocate General, by a Chamber specially established for that purpose, presided over by the Vice-President of the Court and including also the Judge-Rapporteur and the President of the Chamber of three Judges to which the Judge-Rapporteur is attached on the date on which the request is made.
3. The decision on the request that the appeal be allowed to proceed shall take the form of a reasoned order.
4. Where the Court of Justice decides that the appeal should be allowed to proceed, wholly or in part, having regard to the criteria set out in the third paragraph of Article 58a of the Statute, the proceedings shall continue in accordance with Articles 171 to 190a of these Rules. The order referred to in the preceding paragraph shall be served, together with the appeal, on the parties to the relevant case before the General Court and shall specify, where the appeal is to be allowed to proceed in part, the pleas in law or parts of the appeal to which the response must relate.
5. The General Court and, if they were not parties to the proceedings before it, the Member States, the European Parliament, the Council and the European Commission shall forthwith be informed by the Registrar of the decision that the appeal should be allowed to proceed.]

NOTES

Chapter 1a (Articles 170a, 170b) inserted by the Amendment of the Rules of Procedure of the Court of Justice, Article 1 (OJ L111, 25.4.2019, p 73).

CHAPTER 2 RESPONSES, REPLIES AND REJOINDERS

[6.752]
Article 171 Service of the appeal

1. The appeal shall be served on the other parties to the relevant case before the General Court.
[2. In a case where Article 168(4) of these Rules applies, service shall be effected as soon as the appeal has been put in order or the President or the Court of Justice has declared it admissible notwithstanding the failure to observe the formal requirements laid down by that Article.]

NOTES

Para 2: substituted by the Amendments of the Rules of Procedure of the Court of Justice, Article 1(18) (OJ L316, 6.12.2019, p 103).

[6.753]
Article 172 Parties authorised to lodge a response

Any party to the relevant case before the General Court having an interest in the appeal being allowed or dismissed may submit a response within two months after service on him of the appeal. The time-limit for submitting a response shall not be extended.

[6.754]
Article 173 Content of the response

1. A response shall contain:
   (a) the name and address of the party submitting it;

(b) the date on which the appeal was served on him;
(c) the pleas in law and legal arguments relied on;
(d) the form of order sought.

2. Articles 119 and 121 of these Rules shall apply to responses.

[6.755]
Article 174 Form of order sought in the response
A response shall seek to have the appeal allowed or dismissed, in whole or in part.

[6.756]
Article 175 Reply and rejoinder
1. The appeal and the response may be supplemented by a reply and a rejoinder only where the President, on a duly reasoned application submitted by the appellant within seven days of service of the response, considers it necessary, after hearing the Judge-Rapporteur and the Advocate General, in particular to enable the appellant to present his views on a plea of inadmissibility or on new matters relied on in the response.
2. The President shall fix the date by which the reply is to be produced and, upon service of that pleading, the date by which the rejoinder is to be produced. He may limit the number of pages and the subject-matter of those pleadings.

CHAPTER 3 FORM AND CONTENT OF THE CROSS-APPEAL, AND FORM OF ORDER SOUGHT

[6.757]
Article 176 Cross-appeal
1. The parties referred to in Article 172 of these Rules may submit a cross-appeal within the same time-limit as that prescribed for the submission of a response.
2. A cross-appeal must be introduced by a document separate from the response.

[6.758]
Article 177 Content of the cross-appeal
1. A cross-appeal shall contain:
(a) the name and address of the party bringing the cross-appeal;
(b) the date on which the appeal was served on him;
(c) the pleas in law and legal arguments relied on;
(d) the form of order sought.

2. Articles 119, 121 and 122(1) and (3) of these Rules shall apply to cross-appeals.

[6.759]
Article 178 Form of order sought, pleas in law and arguments of the cross-appeal
1. A cross-appeal shall seek to have set aside, in whole or in part, the decision of the General Court.
2. It may also seek to have set aside an express or implied decision relating to the admissibility of the action before the General Court.
3. The pleas in law and legal arguments relied on shall identify precisely those points in the grounds of the decision of the General Court which are contested. The pleas in law and arguments must be separate from those relied on in the response.

CHAPTER 4 PLEADINGS CONSEQUENT ON THE CROSS-APPEAL

[6.760]
Article 179 Response to the cross-appeal
Where a cross-appeal is brought, the applicant at first instance or any other party to the relevant case before the General Court having an interest in the cross-appeal being allowed or dismissed may submit a response, which must be limited to the pleas in law relied on in that cross-appeal, within two months after its being served on him. That time-limit shall not be extended.

[6.761]
Article 180 Reply and rejoinder on a cross-appeal
1. The cross-appeal and the response thereto may be supplemented by a reply and a rejoinder only where the President, on a duly reasoned application submitted by the party who brought the cross-appeal within seven days of service of the response to the cross-appeal, considers it necessary, after hearing the Judge-Rapporteur and the Advocate General, in particular to enable that party to present his views on a plea of inadmissibility or on new matters relied on in the response to the cross-appeal.
2. The President shall fix the date by which that reply is to be produced and, upon service of that pleading, the date by which the rejoinder is to be produced. He may limit the number of pages and the subject-matter of those pleadings.

CHAPTER 5 APPEALS DETERMINED BY ORDER

[6.762]
Article 181 Manifestly inadmissible or manifestly unfounded appeal or cross-appeal
Where the appeal or cross-appeal is, in whole or in part, manifestly inadmissible or manifestly unfounded, the Court may at any time, acting on a proposal from the Judge-Rapporteur and after hearing the Advocate General, decide by reasoned order to dismiss that appeal or cross-appeal in whole or in part.

[6.763]

Article 182 Manifestly well-founded appeal or cross-appeal

Where the Court has already ruled on one or more questions of law identical to those raised by the pleas in law of the appeal or cross-appeal and considers the appeal or cross-appeal to be manifestly well founded, it may, acting on a proposal from the Judge-Rapporteur and after hearing the parties and the Advocate General, decide by reasoned order in which reference is made to the relevant case-law to declare the appeal or cross-appeal manifestly well founded.

CHAPTER 6 EFFECT ON A CROSS-APPEAL OF THE REMOVAL OF THE APPEAL FROM THE REGISTER

[6.764]

Article 183 Effect on a cross-appeal of the discontinuance or manifest inadmissibility of the appeal

A cross-appeal shall be deemed to be devoid of purpose:

(a) if the appellant discontinues his appeal;

(b) if the appeal is declared manifestly inadmissible for non-compliance with the time-limit for lodging an appeal;

(c) if the appeal is declared manifestly inadmissible on the sole ground that it is not directed against a final decision of the General Court or against a decision disposing of the substantive issues in part only or disposing of a procedural issue concerning a plea of lack of competence or inadmissibility within the meaning of the first paragraph of Article 56 of the Statute.

CHAPTER 7 COSTS AND LEGAL AID IN APPEALS

[6.765]

Article 184 Costs in appeals

1. Subject to the following provisions, Articles 137 to 146 of these Rules shall apply, *mutatis mutandis*, to the procedure before the Court of Justice on an appeal against a decision of the General Court.
2. Where the appeal is unfounded or where the appeal is well founded and the Court itself gives final judgment in the case, the Court shall make a decision as to the costs.
3. When an appeal brought by a Member State or an institution of the European Union which did not intervene in the proceedings before the General Court is well founded, the Court of Justice may order that the parties share the costs or that the successful appellant pay the costs which the appeal has caused an unsuccessful party to incur.
4. Where the appeal has not been brought by an intervener at first instance, he may not be ordered to pay costs in the appeal proceedings unless he participated in the written or oral part of the proceedings before the Court of Justice. Where an intervener at first instance takes part in the proceedings, the Court may decide that he shall bear his own costs.

[6.766]

Article 185 Legal aid

1. A party who is wholly or in part unable to meet the costs of the proceedings may at any time apply for legal aid.
2. The application shall be accompanied by all information and supporting documents making it possible to assess the applicant's financial situation, such as a certificate issued by a competent national authority attesting to his financial situation.

[6.767]

Article 186 Prior application for legal aid

1. If the application is made prior to the appeal which the applicant for legal aid intends to commence, it shall briefly state the subject of the appeal.
2. The application for legal aid need not be made through a lawyer.
3. The introduction of an application for legal aid shall, with regard to the person who made that application, suspend the time-limit prescribed for the bringing of the appeal until the date of service of the order making a decision on that application.
4. The President shall assign the application for legal aid, as soon as it is lodged, to a Judge-Rapporteur who shall put forward, promptly, a proposal as to the action to be taken on it.

[6.768]

Article 187 Decision on the application for legal aid

1. The decision to grant legal aid, in whole or in part, or to refuse it shall be taken, on a proposal from the Judge-Rapporteur and after hearing the Advocate General, by the Chamber of three Judges to which the Judge-Rapporteur is assigned. In that event, the formation of the Court shall be composed of the President of that Chamber, the Judge-Rapporteur and the first Judge or, as the case may be, the first two Judges designated from the list referred to in Article 28(3) on the date on which the application for legal aid is brought before that Chamber by the Judge-Rapporteur. It shall consider, if appropriate, whether the appeal is manifestly unfounded.
2. If the Judge-Rapporteur is not a member of a Chamber of three Judges, the decision shall be taken, under the same conditions, by the Chamber of five Judges to which he is assigned. In addition to the Judge-Rapporteur, the formation of the Court shall be composed of four Judges designated from the list referred to in Article 28(2) on the date on which the application for legal aid is brought before that Chamber by the Judge-Rapporteur.
3. The formation of the Court shall give its decision by way of order. Where the application for legal aid is refused in whole or in part, the order shall state the reasons for that refusal.

[6.769]

Article 188 Sums to be advanced as legal aid

1. Where legal aid is granted, the cashier of the Court shall be responsible, where applicable within the limits set by the formation of the Court, for costs involved in the assistance and representation of the applicant before the Court. At the request of the applicant or his representative, an advance on those costs may be paid.

2. In its decision as to costs the Court may order the payment to the cashier of the Court of sums advanced as legal aid.
3. The Registrar shall take steps to obtain the recovery of these sums from the party ordered to pay them.

[6.770]
Article 189 Withdrawal of legal aid
The formation of the Court which gave a decision on the application for legal aid may at any time, either of its own motion or on request, withdraw that legal aid if the circumstances which led to its being granted alter during the proceedings.

CHAPTER 8 OTHER PROVISIONS APPLICABLE TO APPEALS

[6.771]
Article 190 Other provisions applicable to appeals
1. Articles 127, 129 to 136, 147 to 150, 153 to 155 and 157 to 166 of these Rules shall apply to the procedure before the Court of Justice on an appeal against decisions of the General Court.
2. By way of derogation from Article 130(1), an application to intervene shall, however, be made within one month of the publication of the notice referred to in Article 21(4).
3. Article 95 shall apply, *mutatis mutandis*, to the procedure before the Court of Justice on an appeal against decisions of the General Court.

[6.772]
[Article 190a Treatment of information or material produced before the General Court in accordance with Article 105 of its Rules of Procedure
1. Where an appeal is brought against a decision of the General Court adopted in proceedings in which information or material has been produced by a main party in accordance with Article 105 of the Rules of Procedure of the General Court and has not been communicated to the other main party, the Registry of the General Court shall make that information or material available to the Court of Justice, on the conditions laid down in the decision referred to in paragraph 11 of that Article.
2. The information or material referred to in paragraph 1 shall not be communicated to the parties to the proceedings before the Court of Justice.
3. The Court of Justice shall ensure that the confidential matters contained in the information or material referred to in paragraph 1 are not disclosed in the decision which closes the proceedings or in any Opinion of the Advocate General.
4. The information or material referred to in paragraph 1 shall be returned to the party that produced it before the General Court as soon as the decision closing the proceedings before the Court of Justice has been served, save where the case is referred back to the General Court. In the latter case, the information or material concerned shall again be made available to the General Court, on the conditions laid down in the decision referred to in paragraph 5.
5. The Court of Justice shall adopt, by decision, the security rules for protecting the information or material referred to in paragraph 1. That decision shall be published in the *Official Journal of the European Union*.]

NOTES
Inserted by the Amendment of the Rules of Procedure of the Court of Justice, Article 1 (OJ L217, 12.8.2016, p 69). Note that Article 2 provides that provisions this Article apply only from the entry into force of the decision referred to in Article 190a(5).

TITLE VI REVIEW OF DECISIONS OF THE GENERAL COURT

[6.773]
Article 191 Reviewing Chamber
A Chamber of five Judges shall be designated for a period of one year for the purpose of deciding, in accordance with Articles 193 and 194 of these Rules, whether a decision of the General Court is to be reviewed in accordance with Article 62 of the Statute.

[6.774]
Article 192 Information and communication of decisions which may be reviewed
1. As soon as the date for the delivery or signature of a decision to be given under Article 256(2) or (3) TFEU is fixed, the Registry of the General Court shall inform the Registry of the Court of Justice.
2. The decision shall be communicated to the Registry of the Court of Justice immediately upon its delivery or signature, as shall the file in the case, which shall be made available forthwith to the First Advocate General.

[6.775]
Article 193 Review of decisions given on appeal
1. The proposal of the First Advocate General to review a decision of the General Court given under Article 256(2) TFEU shall be forwarded to the President of the Court of Justice and to the President of the reviewing Chamber. Notice of that transmission shall be given to the Registrar at the same time.
2. As soon as he is informed of the existence of a proposal, the Registrar shall communicate the file in the case before the General Court to the members of the reviewing Chamber.
3. As soon as the proposal to review has been received, the President of the Court shall designate the Judge-Rapporteur from among the Judges of the reviewing Chamber on a proposal from the President of that Chamber. The composition of the formation of the Court shall be determined in accordance with Article 28(2) of these Rules on the day on which the case is assigned to the Judge-Rapporteur.
4. That Chamber, acting on a proposal from the Judge-Rapporteur, shall decide whether the decision of the General Court is to be reviewed. The decision to review the decision of the General Court shall indicate only the questions which are to be reviewed.

5. The General Court, the parties to the proceedings before it and the other interested persons referred to in the second paragraph of Article 62a of the Statute shall forthwith be informed by the Registrar of the decision of the Court of Justice to review the decision of the General Court.
6. Notice of the date of the decision to review the decision of the General Court and of the questions which are to be reviewed shall be published in the *Official Journal of the European Union*.

[6.776]
Article 194 Review of preliminary rulings
1. The proposal of the First Advocate General to review a decision of the General Court given under Article 256(3) TFEU shall be forwarded to the President of the Court of Justice and to the President of the reviewing Chamber. Notice of that transmission shall be given to the Registrar at the same time.
2. As soon as he is informed of the existence of a proposal, the Registrar shall communicate the file in the case before the General Court to the members of the reviewing Chamber.
3. The Registrar shall also inform the General Court, the referring court or tribunal, the parties to the main proceedings and the other interested persons referred to in the second paragraph of Article 62a of the Statute of the existence of a proposal to review.
4. As soon as the proposal to review has been received, the President of the Court shall designate the Judge-Rapporteur from among the Judges of the reviewing Chamber on a proposal from the President of that Chamber. The composition of the formation of the Court shall be determined in accordance with Article 28(2) of these Rules on the day on which the case is assigned to the Judge-Rapporteur.
5. That Chamber, acting on a proposal from the Judge-Rapporteur, shall decide whether the decision of the General Court is to be reviewed. The decision to review the decision of the General Court shall indicate only the questions which are to be reviewed.
6. The General Court, the referring court or tribunal, the parties to the main proceedings and the other interested persons referred to in the second paragraph of Article 62a of the Statute shall forthwith be informed by the Registrar of the decision of the Court of Justice as to whether or not the decision of the General Court is to be reviewed.
7. Notice of the date of the decision to review the decision of the General Court and of the questions which are to be reviewed shall be published in the *Official Journal of the European Union*.

[6.777]
Article 195 Judgment on the substance of the case after a decision to review
1. The decision to review a decision of the General Court shall be served on the parties and other interested persons referred to in the second paragraph of Article 62a of the Statute. The decision served on the Member States, and the States, other than the Member States, which are parties to the EEA Agreement, as well as the EFTA Surveillance Authority, shall be accompanied by a translation of the decision of the Court of Justice in accordance with the provisions of Article 98 of these Rules. The decision of the Court of Justice shall also be communicated to the General Court and, if applicable, to the referring court or tribunal.
2. Within one month of the date of service referred to in paragraph 1, the parties and other interested persons on whom the decision of the Court of Justice has been served may lodge statements or written observations on the questions which are subject to review.
3. As soon as a decision to review a decision of the General Court has been taken, the First Advocate General shall assign the review to an Advocate General.
4. The reviewing Chamber shall rule on the substance of the case, after hearing the Advocate General.
5. It may, however, request the Court of Justice to assign the case to a formation of the Court composed of a greater number of Judges.
6. Where the decision of the General Court which is subject to review was given under Article 256(2) TFEU, the Court of Justice shall make a decision as to costs.

TITLE VII [REQUESTS FOR OPINIONS]

NOTES

Title VII heading substituted by the Amendments of the Rules of Procedure of the Court of Justice, Article 1(19) (OJ L316, 6.12.2019, p 103).

[6.778]
Article 196 Written part of the procedure
1. In accordance with Article 218(11) TFEU, a request for an Opinion may be made by a Member State, by the European Parliament, by the Council or by the European Commission.
2. A request for an Opinion may relate both to whether the envisaged agreement is compatible with the provisions of the Treaties and to whether the European Union or any institution of the European Union has the power to enter into that agreement.
3. It shall be served on the Member States and on the institutions referred to in paragraph 1, and the President shall prescribe a time-limit within which they may submit written observations.

[6.779]
Article 197 Designation of the Judge-Rapporteur and of the Advocate General
As soon as the request for an Opinion has been submitted, the President shall designate a Judge-Rapporteur and the First Advocate General shall assign the case to an Advocate General.

[6.780]
Article 198 Hearing
The Court may decide that the procedure before it shall also include a hearing.

[6.781]
Article 199 Time-limit for delivering the Opinion
The Court shall deliver its Opinion as soon as possible, after hearing the Advocate General.

[6.782]
[Article 200 Delivery of the Opinion
1. The Opinion, signed by the President, the Judges who took part in the deliberations and the Registrar, shall be delivered in open court.
2. It shall be served on all the Member States and on the institutions referred to in Article 196(1).]

NOTES
Substituted by the Amendments of the Rules of Procedure of the Court of Justice, Article 1(20) (OJ L316, 6.12.2019, p 103).

TITLE VIII PARTICULAR FORMS OF PROCEDURE

[6.783]
Article 201 Appeals against decisions of the arbitration committee
1. An application initiating an appeal under the second paragraph of Article 18 TEAEC shall state:
(a) the name and permanent address of the applicant;
(b) the description of the signatory;
(c) a reference to the arbitration committee's decision against which the appeal is made;
(d) the names of the respondents;
(e) a summary of the facts;
(f) the grounds on which the appeal is based and arguments relied on, and a brief statement of those grounds;
(g) the form of order sought by the applicant.
2. Articles 119 and 121 of these Rules shall apply to the application.
3. A certified copy of the contested decision shall be annexed to the application.
4. As soon as the application has been lodged, the Registrar of the Court shall request the arbitration committee registry to transmit to the Court the file in the case.
5. Articles 123 and 124 of these Rules shall apply to this procedure. The Court may decide that the procedure before it shall also include a hearing.
6. The Court shall give its decision in the form of a judgment. Where the Court sets aside the decision of the arbitration committee it may refer the case back to the committee.

[6.784]
Article 202 Procedure under Article 103 TEAEC
1. Four certified copies shall be lodged of an application under the third paragraph of Article 103 TEAEC. The application shall be accompanied by the draft of the agreement or contract concerned, by the observations of the European Commission addressed to the State concerned and by all other supporting documents.
2. The application and annexes thereto shall be served on the European Commission, which shall have a time-limit of 10 days from such service to submit its written observations. This time-limit may be extended by the President after the State concerned has been heard.
3. Following the lodging of such observations, which shall be served on the State concerned, the Court shall give its decision promptly, after hearing the Advocate General and, if they so request, the State concerned and the European Commission.

[6.785]
Article 203 Procedures under Articles 104 TEAEC and 105 TEAEC
Applications under the third paragraph of Article 104 TEAEC and the second paragraph of Article 105 TEAEC shall be governed by the provisions of Titles II and IV of these Rules. Such applications shall also be served on the State to which the respondent person or undertaking belongs.

[6.786]
Article 204 Procedure provided for by Article 111(3) of the EEA Agreement
1. In the case governed by Article 111(3) of the EEA Agreement, the matter shall be brought before the Court by a request submitted by the Contracting Parties which are parties to the dispute. The request shall be served on the other Contracting Parties, on the European Commission, on the EFTA Surveillance Authority and, where appropriate, on the other interested persons on whom a request for a preliminary ruling raising the same question of interpretation of European Union legislation would be served.
2. The President shall prescribe a time-limit within which the Contracting Parties and the other interested persons on whom the request has been served may submit written observations.
3. The request shall be made in one of the languages referred to in Article 36 of these Rules. Article 38 shall apply. The provisions of Article 98 shall apply *mutatis mutandis*.
4. As soon as the request referred to in paragraph 1 of this Article has been submitted, the President shall designate a Judge-Rapporteur. The First Advocate General shall, immediately afterwards, assign the request to an Advocate General.
5. The Court shall, after hearing the Advocate General, give a reasoned decision on the request.
6. The decision of the Court, signed by the President, the Judges who took part in the deliberations and the Registrar, shall be served on the Contracting Parties and on the other interested persons referred to in paragraphs 1 and 2.

205 *(Repealed by the Amendments of the Rules of Procedure of the Court of Justice, Article 1(21) (OJ L316, 6.12.2019, p 103).)*

[6.787]
Article 206 Requests under Article 269 TFEU
1. Four certified copies shall be submitted of a request under Article 269 TFEU. The request shall be accompanied by any relevant document and, in particular, any observations and recommendations made pursuant to Article 7 TEU.
[2. The request and annexes thereto shall be served on the European Council or on the Council, as appropriate, each of which shall have a non-extendible time limit of 10 days from such service to submit its written observations. Article 51 shall not apply to that time limit.]
3. The request and annexes thereto shall also be communicated to the Member States other than the State in question, to the European Parliament and to the European Commission.
4. Following the lodging of the observations referred to in paragraph 2, which shall be served on the Member State concerned and on the States and institutions referred to in paragraph 3, the Court shall give its decision within a time-limit of one month from the lodging of the request and after hearing the Advocate General. At the request of the Member State concerned, the European Council or the Council, or of its own motion, the Court may decide that the procedure before it shall also include a hearing, which all the States and institutions referred to in this Article shall be given notice to attend.

NOTES
Para 2: substituted by the Amendments of the Rules of Procedure of the Court of Justice, Article 1(22) (OJ L316, 6.12.2019, p 103).

FINAL PROVISIONS

[6.788]
Article 207 Supplementary rules
Subject to the provisions of Article 253 TFEU and after consultation with the Governments concerned, the Court shall adopt supplementary rules concerning its practice in relation to:
(a) letters rogatory;
(b) applications for legal aid;
(c) reports by the Court of perjury by witnesses or experts, delivered pursuant to Article 30 of the Statute.

[6.789]
Article 208 Implementing rules
The Court may, by a separate act, adopt practice rules for the implementation of these Rules.

[6.790]
Article 209 Repeal
These Rules replace the Rules of Procedure of the Court of Justice of the European Communities adopted on 19 June 1991, as last amended on 24 May 2011 (*Official Journal of the European Union*, L162 of 22 June 2011, p 17).

[6.791]
Article 210 Publication and entry into force of these Rules
These Rules, which are authentic in the languages referred to in Article 36 of these Rules, shall be published in the *Official Journal of the European Union* and shall enter into force on the first day of the second month following their publication.

PRACTICE DIRECTIONS TO PARTIES CONCERNING CASES BROUGHT BEFORE THE COURT

(February 2020)

[6.792]

NOTES
Date of publication in Official Journal: OJ L42I, 14.2.2020, p 1.
These Practice Directions are available on the Court of Justice website at: https://curia.europa.eu/jcms/jcms/Jo2_7031/en/.

THE COURT OF JUSTICE,

Having regard to the Rules of Procedure and, in particular, Article 208 thereof,

Whereas:

(1) On 25 November 2013, the Court of Justice adopted, on the basis of Article 208 of its Rules of Procedure, new Practice directions to parties concerning cases brought before the Court.[1] Those directions were intended to give the parties and their representatives specific guidance based on the new Rules of Procedure adopted on 25 September 2012,[2] that took account, in particular, of the experience gained in the course of the first year of their implementation.

(2) Since the entry into force of those directions, on 1 February 2014, there have, however, been a number of important technical and legislative developments.

(3) First, parties are increasingly using electronic methods of communication for the transmission of their procedural documents, which helps to speed up case handling but, at the same time, requires further details to be provided of the procedures for such transmission and of the steps to be taken to facilitate the processing and translation of the document lodged and, if necessary, to preserve the confidentiality of the information it contains.

(4) Second, the Rules of Procedure of the Court have been amended several times since 2012, as much in order to clarify or specify the rules on parties' interventions before the Court as to reflect the changes made by the Union legislature in areas such as the protection of personal data or the handling of appeals referred to in Article 58a of the

Protocol on the Statute of the Court of Justice of the European Union.

(5) In the interests of the proper administration of justice and for the purposes of greater clarity, it is appropriate, therefore, to adopt new practice directions that take these developments into account.

(6) These new directions, which apply to all categories of cases brought before the Court, are not intended to replace the relevant provisions of the Statute and of the Rules of Procedure. Their purpose is to afford the parties and their representatives a better understanding of the implications of those provisions and to outline in greater detail the conduct of proceedings before the Court and, in particular, the constraints on the Court, particularly those associated with the processing and translation of procedural documents or the simultaneous interpretation of the observations submitted in the course of a hearing. Observing and taking into account these directions constitutes, both for the parties and for the Court, the best guarantee that the latter will be able to deal with cases with the greatest efficiency,

NOTES

[1] OJ L31, 31.1.2014, p 1.

[2] OJ L265, 29.9.2012, p 1, as last amended on 26 November 2019 (OJ L316, 6.12.2019, p 103).

HEREBY ADOPTS THESE PRACTICE DIRECTIONS:

I. GENERAL PROVISIONS

THE STAGES IN THE PROCEDURE BEFORE THE COURT AND THEIR ESSENTIAL CHARACTERISTICS

[6.793]

1. Subject to special provisions laid down in the Protocol on the Statute of the Court of Justice of the European Union ('the Statute') or in the Rules of Procedure, the procedure before the Court is to consist, as a general rule, of a written part and an oral part. The purpose of the written part of the procedure is to put before the Court the claims, pleas and arguments of the parties to the proceedings or, in preliminary rulings, the observations which the interested persons referred to in Article 23 of the Statute intend to submit concerning the questions put by the courts and tribunals of the Member States of the European Union. The oral part, which follows it, is intended for its part to allow the Court to complete its knowledge of the case by the possible hearing of submissions from those parties or interested persons at a hearing and, if appropriate, by hearing the Opinion of the Advocate General.

REPRESENTATION OF THE PARTIES BEFORE THE COURT

2. In accordance with Article 19 of the Statute, parties to proceedings before the Court must be represented by a person who is duly authorised to represent them. With the exception of the Member States, other States which are parties to the Agreement on the European Economic Area ('the EEA Agreement'), the European Free Trade Association ('EFTA') Surveillance Authority and the institutions of the European Union, which are generally to be represented by an agent appointed for each case, other parties to the proceedings must be represented by a lawyer authorised to practise before a court of a Member State or of another State which is a party to the EEA Agreement. The evidence of that capacity must be capable of being produced, on request, at any stage of the proceedings. University teachers who are nationals of a Member State whose law accords them a right of audience are treated as lawyers by virtue of the seventh paragraph of Article 19 of the Statute.

3. In preliminary ruling proceedings, the Court is to take account, so far as concerns the representation of the parties to the main proceedings, of the procedural rules applicable in the court or tribunal which made the reference. Any person empowered to represent a party before that court or tribunal may therefore also represent that party before the Court of Justice and, if permitted under national procedural rules, the parties to the main proceedings are entitled to submit their own written and oral observations. In the event of uncertainty in this respect, the Court may, at any time, request those parties, their representatives or the court or tribunal which made the reference to provide the relevant information.

COSTS OF PROCEEDINGS BEFORE THE COURT AND LEGAL AID

4. Subject to the provisions set out in Article 143 of the Rules of Procedure, proceedings before the Court are to be free of charge, no charge or tax being payable to the Court on account of the initiation of proceedings or the lodging of a procedural document. The costs referred to in Article 137 et seq. of the Rules of Procedure include only 'recoverable' costs, that is, any sums payable to witnesses and experts, and expenses necessarily incurred by the parties for the purpose of the proceedings before the Court, in connection with the remuneration of their representative and the expenses of his or her travel to and subsistence in Luxembourg, if a hearing is organised. The Court rules on the amount of those costs and the party ordered to pay them in the judgment or order which closes the proceedings, whereas in preliminary rulings it is for the referring court or tribunal to rule on the costs of the proceedings.

5. A party or, in preliminary ruling proceedings, a party to the main proceedings who is wholly or in part unable to meet of the costs of the proceedings before the Court may, at any time, apply for legal aid under the conditions provided for, respectively, in Articles 115 to 118 and 185 to 189 of the Rules of Procedure. In order for it to be possible for such applications to be considered, they must, however, be accompanied by all the information and supporting documents necessary to enable the Court to assess the legal aid applicant's true financial situation. Since, in preliminary rulings, the Court gives its ruling at the request of a court or tribunal of a Member State, the parties to the main proceedings must, first of all, apply for any legal aid from that court or tribunal or the competent authorities of the Member State concerned, the aid granted by the Court being only subsidiary to the aid granted at national level.

6. It is worth noting that, where it grants the application for legal aid, the Court is responsible, where applicable within the limits set by the formation of the Court, solely for costs involved in the assistance and representation before the Court of the applicant for legal aid. In accordance with the rules set out in the Rules of Procedure, those costs can be recovered subsequently by the Court in the decision ending the proceedings and ruling on costs, and the formation of the Court which gave a decision on the application for legal aid may, moreover, withdraw that legal aid at any time if the circumstances which led to its being granted change during the proceedings.

PROTECTION OF PERSONAL DATA

7. In order to ensure optimal protection of personal data, in particular in connection with material published by the Court concerning the cases that are brought before it, the Court as a general rule deals with preliminary ruling cases in anonymised form. This approach means in practice that, unless there are special circumstances, the Court will redact the names of individuals mentioned in the request for a preliminary ruling and, if necessary, other information that may enable them to be identified, if the referring court or tribunal did not do so before submitting its request. All interested persons referred to in Article 23 of the Statute are requested to respect, in their written observations or oral submissions, the anonymity thus conferred.

8. The same applies in relation to appeals. Unless there are special circumstances, the Court will respect the anonymity granted by the General Court, and the parties to the proceedings are requested also to respect that anonymity in the proceedings before the Court of Justice.

9. In any event, where a party to proceedings before the Court does not wish his or her identity or certain details concerning him or her to be disclosed in a case brought before the Court — or, conversely, where that party does wish his or her identity and those details to be disclosed in the context of that case — it is open to that party to contact the Court so that the Court may decide whether or not to anonymise the relevant case, in whole or in part, or to maintain the anonymity previously conferred. To be effective, such an application must, however, be made at as early a stage as possible. On account of the increasing use of new information and communication technologies, granting anonymity becomes much more difficult if the notice of the case concerned has already been published in the *Official Journal of the European Union* or, in preliminary ruling proceedings, if the request for a preliminary ruling has already been served on the interested persons referred to in Article 23 of the Statute, about one month after the request has been lodged at the Court.

II. THE WRITTEN PART OF THE PROCEDURE

THE PURPOSE OF THE WRITTEN PART OF THE PROCEDURE

[6.794]

10. The written part of the procedure plays an essential role in the Court's understanding of the case. It must allow the Court, by reading the written pleadings or observations lodged, to acquire a detailed and accurate idea of the subject matter of the case before it and the issues raised by that case. Although this is the Court's objective when dealing with any case brought before it, the conduct and the pattern of the written part of the procedure differ depending on the nature of the action. Whereas in direct actions or appeals the parties are requested to adopt a position on the written pleadings lodged by the other parties to the proceedings, the written part of the procedure in references for a preliminary ruling is characterised by the absence of adversarial proceedings, the interested persons referred to in Article 23 of the Statute being merely requested to submit any observations they may make on the questions referred by a national court or tribunal, without as a general rule knowing the position adopted by the other interested persons on those questions. This gives rise to different requirements as regards both the form and content of those observations and also the subsequent conduct of the procedure, although it must be borne in mind that most of the written pleadings or observations lodged during the written part of the procedure will have to be translated. Short and simple sentences should always be used, therefore, and the parties' arguments must appear in their written pleadings or observations and not in any annexes thereto, which are generally not translated.

THE WRITTEN PART OF THE PROCEDURE IN REFERENCES FOR A PRELIMINARY RULING

11. On account of the non-adversarial nature of preliminary ruling proceedings, the lodging of written observations by the interested persons referred to in Article 23 of the Statute does not involve any specific formalities. Where a request for a preliminary ruling is served on them by the Court, those persons may thus submit, if they wish, written observations in which they set out their point of view on the request made by the referring court or tribunal. The purpose of those observations — which must be lodged within a time limit of two months from service of the request for a preliminary ruling (extended on account of distance by a single period of 10 days) that cannot otherwise be extended — is to help clarify for the Court the scope of that request, and above all the answers to be provided to the questions referred by the referring court or tribunal.

12. Although the statement must be complete and include, in particular, the arguments on which the Court may base its answer to the questions referred, it is not necessary, on the other hand, to repeat the factual and legal background of the dispute set out in the order for reference, unless it requires further comment. Subject to special circumstances or specific provisions of the Rules of Procedure providing for a restriction of the length of the documents because of the urgency of the case, written observations lodged in a preliminary ruling should not exceed 20 pages.

THE WRITTEN PART OF THE PROCEDURE IN DIRECT ACTIONS

THE APPLICATION

13. On account of its adversarial nature, the written part of the procedure in direct actions follows stricter rules. These are set out in Article 119 et seq. (Title IV) of the Rules of Procedure and concern both the obligation for the parties to be represented by an agent or lawyer and the formal requirements linked to the content and the submission of written pleadings. It is apparent, in particular, from Article 120 of the Rules of Procedure, that the application initiating proceedings must, in addition to stating the name and address of the applicant and the name of the party against whom the application is made, state accurately the subject matter of the proceedings, the pleas in law and arguments relied upon supported, as appropriate, by any evidence produced or offered, and the form of order sought by the applicant. Failure to comply with those requirements renders the application inadmissible. Unless there are special circumstances, the application should not exceed 30 pages.

14. As is apparent from Article 120(c) of the Rules of Procedure, the application must also include a summary of the pleas in law relied upon. That summary — which must not exceed two pages — is intended to facilitate the drafting of the notice, of each case brought before the Court, which must be published in the *Official Journal of the European Union* in accordance with Article 21(4) of the Rules of Procedure.

THE DEFENCE

15. The defence, to which Article 124 of the Rules of Procedure relates, is essentially subject to the same formal requirements as the application and must be lodged within two months of service of the latter. That time limit — extended on account of distance by a single period of 10 days — may otherwise be extended only exceptionally and where a duly reasoned request setting out the circumstances capable of justifying such an extension has been submitted within the prescribed time limit.

16. Since the legal framework of the proceedings is fixed by the application, the structure of the legal argument developed in the defence must, so far as is possible, reflect that of the pleas in law or complaints put forward in the application. No new plea in law may be introduced in the course of the proceedings unless it is based on matters of law or of fact which come to light in the course of the procedure. The factual and legal background is to be recapitulated in the defence only in so far as its presentation in the application is disputed or calls for further particulars. As in the case of the application, unless there are special circumstances the defence should not exceed 30 pages.

THE REPLY AND REJOINDER

17. If they consider it necessary, the applicant and the defendant may supplement their arguments, the former by a reply and the latter by a rejoinder. Those written pleadings are subject to the same formal rules as the application and the defence but, since they are optional and supplementary, they must necessarily be shorter than those documents. The framework and the pleas in law or claims at the heart of the dispute having been set out (or disputed) in depth in the application and the defence, the only purpose of the reply and the rejoinder is to allow the applicant and the defendant to make clear their position or to refine their arguments on an important issue, the President also being able, pursuant to Article 126 of the Rules of Procedure, to specify the matters to which those documents should relate. Except in special circumstances, a reply or a rejoinder should therefore be no more than approximately 10 pages long. Those documents must be lodged with the Registry within the time limits set by the Court, an extension of those time limits being granted by the President only in exceptional circumstances and on a duly reasoned request.

REQUEST FOR AN EXPEDITED PROCEDURE

18. Where the nature of the case requires it to be dealt with within a short time, the applicant or defendant may request the Court to deal with the case under an expedited procedure derogating from the provisions of the Rules of Procedure. Provided for in Article 133 of those Rules, that possibility is nevertheless subject to the lodging, by a separate document, of an express request to that effect setting out in detail the circumstances capable of justifying the use of such a procedure and involves, where such a request is granted, an adjustment to the written part of the procedure. The ordinary time limits for the lodging of written pleadings are reduced, as is the length of those pleadings and, pursuant to Article 134 of the Rules of Procedure, a reply, a rejoinder or a statement in intervention can be submitted only if the President considers this to be necessary.

APPLICATIONS FOR SUSPENSION OF OPERATION OR FOR INTERIM MEASURES (INTERIM PROCEEDINGS)

19. A direct action may also be accompanied by an application for suspension of operation of the contested measure or by an application for interim measures, as referred to in Articles 278 and 279 respectively of the Treaty on the Functioning of the European Union (TFEU). In accordance with the provisions of Article 160 of the Rules of Procedure, such an application is, however, admissible only if it is made by the applicant who has challenged the measure at issue before the Court or a party to the case before the Court and it must be made by a separate document stating the subject matter of the proceedings and the circumstances giving rise to urgency as well as the pleas of fact and law establishing a prima facie case for the measure applied for. As a general rule, the application is then served on the other party to the proceedings, and the President prescribes a short period within which that other party may submit written or oral observations. In cases of extreme urgency, the President may grant the application provisionally even before such observations have been submitted. In such a case, the decision closing the interim proceedings can, however, be adopted only after that other party has been heard.

THE WRITTEN PART OF THE PROCEDURE IN APPEALS

20. The written part of the procedure in an appeal is similar in many respects to the conduct of that part of the procedure in direct actions. The relevant rules are in Article 167 et seq. (Title V) of the Rules of Procedure, which state both the mandatory content of the appeal and of the response and the scope of the forms of order sought.

THE APPEAL

21. As is apparent from Articles 168 and 169 of the Rules of Procedure (which supplement, in this respect, Articles 56 to 58 of the Statute), an appeal cannot be brought against a measure of an institution, a body, an office or an agency of the European Union, but must be directed against the decision of the General Court ruling on the action brought against that measure. It is apparent from that point that the form of order sought in the appeal must necessarily seek to have set aside, in whole or in part, the decision of the General Court as set out in the operative part of that decision, and not the annulment of the measure challenged before the General Court. If they are not to be held inadmissible, the pleas in law and legal arguments relied upon in the appeal — which, unless there are special circumstances, should not exceed 25 pages — must moreover identify precisely those points in the grounds of that decision that are contested and set out in detail the reasons for which that decision is alleged to be vitiated by an error of law.

22. In order to facilitate the drawing up of the notice published in the *Official Journal of the European Union*, in accordance with Article 21(4) of the Rules of Procedure, the appellant must also attach to the appeal a summary of those pleas in law, no more than two pages long, and lodge at the Registry the necessary items and documents attesting that the requirements set out in Article 19 of the Statute and reiterated in Article 119 of the Rules of Procedure are met.

23. In the situations referred to in Article 58a of the Statute, the appellant must also annex to the appeal a request that the appeal be allowed to proceed, which should be no more than seven pages long and must contain all the information necessary to enable the Court to rule on whether the appeal should be allowed to proceed and to determine, where the appeal is to be allowed to proceed in part, the pleas in law of the appeal to which the response must relate.

24. The request that the appeal be allowed to proceed must, in any event, set out clearly and in detail the grounds on which the appeal is based, identify with equal clarity and detail the issue of law raised by each ground of appeal and state, specifically, how that issue is significant with respect to the unity, consistency or development of European Union law.

25. In accordance with Article 170a(1) of the Rules of Procedure, the absence of such a request renders the appeal as a whole inadmissible.

The response

26. Within a time limit of two months from the service of the appeal (extended on account of distance by a single period of 10 days), which may not otherwise be extended, any party to the case at issue before the General Court may submit a response. The content of the written pleadings is subject to the requirements fixed in Article 173 of the Rules of Procedure and, in accordance with Article 174 of those Rules, the form of order must seek to have the appeal allowed or dismissed, in whole or in part. The structure of the legal arguments in the response must, so far as is possible, reflect the pleas in law put forward by the appellant but it is not necessary to reiterate in those pleadings the factual and legal background to the proceedings, unless its presentation in the appeal is disputed or calls for further particulars. On the other hand, any challenge to the admissibility, in whole or in part, of that appeal must be included in the actual body of the response, since the possibility — provided for in Article 151 of the Rules of Procedure — of raising a plea of inadmissibility in relation to the proceedings by a separate document is not applicable to appeals. Like the appeal, and subject to special circumstances, the response should not exceed 25 pages.

The cross-appeal

27. If, when the appeal has been served on him or her, one of the parties to the relevant case before the General Court intends to dispute that court's decision on an aspect which was not mentioned in the appeal, that party must bring a cross-appeal against the General Court's decision. That appeal must be introduced by a separate document, within the same time limit —which may not be extended — as the time limit for submission of the response and meet the requirements set out in Articles 177 and 178 of the Rules of Procedure. The pleas in law and legal arguments which it contains must be separate from those relied on in the response.

The response to the cross-appeal

28. Where such a cross-appeal is brought, the applicant, or any other party to the relevant case before the General Court having an interest in the cross-appeal being allowed or dismissed, may submit a response, which must be limited to the pleas in law relied on in that cross-appeal. In accordance with Article 179 of the Rules of Procedure, those written pleadings must be submitted within a time limit — which may not be extended — of two months from service of the cross-appeal (extended on account of distance by a single period of 10 days).

The reply and rejoinder

29. Whether in the case of a main appeal or a cross-appeal, the appeal and the response may be supplemented by a reply and a rejoinder, in particular in order to allow the parties to adopt a position on a plea of inadmissibility or new matters raised in the response. Unlike the rules applicable to direct actions, that possibility is, however, made subject to the express authorisation of the President of the Court. To that effect, the appellant (or the party having brought the cross-appeal) is requested to submit, within a time limit of seven days from service of the response (or of the response to the cross-appeal), extended on account of distance by a single period of 10 days, a duly reasoned application setting out the reasons for which, in that party's opinion, a reply is necessary. That application — which should not exceed three pages — must be intelligible in itself, without necessitating reference to the appeal or to the response.

30. Due to the special nature of appeals, which are restricted to the examination of questions of law, the President may also, if granting the application to lodge a reply, limit the number of pages and the subject matter of that reply and of the rejoinder submitted subsequently. The observance of those instructions is an essential condition for the proper conduct of the procedure, and exceeding the number of pages authorised or referring to other questions in the reply or the rejoinder will lead to the pleadings being sent back to their author.

Appeals brought under Article 57 of the Statute

31. The rules set out in points 20 to 30 of these directions are nevertheless not applicable in their entirety to appeals brought against decisions of the General Court dismissing an application to intervene or adopted following an application for interim measures submitted under Articles 278 or 279 TFEU. Pursuant to the third paragraph of Article 57 of the Statute, such appeals are subject to the same procedure as an application for interim measures made directly to the Court. The parties are therefore set a short period for the submission of any observations on the appeal and the Court rules on that appeal without any additional written part of the procedure, or even without an oral part of the procedure.

CONFIDENTIALITY IN APPEALS

32. As is apparent from the foregoing provisions, the appeal and the pleadings lodged subsequently are to be served on all the parties to the relevant case before the General Court, irrespective of their procedural status before that court (main party or intervener). Since appeals are, in accordance with Article 58 of the Statute, to be limited to points of law, the parties must in principle refrain from mentioning secret or confidential matters in their written pleadings. If, exceptionally, they nevertheless do so, the party relying on the confidentiality of certain matters in its written pleading is requested to submit, by a separate document, a duly reasoned request for confidential treatment (specifying both the scope of the confidentiality requested and the parties to the proceedings to whom that request relates), together with a non-confidential version of the pleading that can be served on those other parties. In the event that that request for confidentiality — the scope of which cannot, in any event, go beyond the confidential treatment already approved by the General Court in relation to an intervener — is approved in part, the party claiming that confidentiality is requested to produce, without delay, a new non-confidential version of its written pleading that can be served on the other parties to the proceedings.

INTERVENTION IN DIRECT ACTIONS AND APPEALS

THE APPLICATION TO INTERVENE

33. In accordance with Article 40 of the Statute, the Member States and institutions of the European Union, on the one hand, and, in the circumstances provided for in the second and third paragraphs of that article, non-Member States party to the Agreement on the EEA, the EFTA Surveillance Authority, the bodies, offices and agencies of the European Union and any other natural or legal person, on the other hand, may intervene in cases before the Court for the purposes of supporting, in whole or in part, the form of order sought by one of the parties. To be taken into account, the application to intervene must be submitted within the time limit referred to in Article 130(1) (direct actions), or Article 190(2) (appeals) of the Rules of Procedure and meet the conditions set out in Article 130(2) to (4) of those Rules.

THE STATEMENT IN INTERVENTION

34. If the application to intervene is granted, the intervener receives a copy of every procedural document served on the parties except, where applicable, for secret or confidential items or documents, and has one month from receipt of those items or documents to submit a statement in intervention. Although that statement must meet the requirements in Article 132(2) of the Rules of Procedure, its content is necessarily more succinct than the written pleadings of the party supported and it should not exceed 10 pages in length. Since the intervention is ancillary to the main proceedings, the intervener must refrain from repeating in that statement the pleas in law and arguments in the written pleadings of the party which the intervener is supporting and must set out only additional pleas in law or arguments which bear out that party's submissions. Recapitulation of the factual or legal background to the case is not necessary, except in so far as its presentation in the written pleadings of the main parties is disputed or calls for further particulars.

OBSERVATIONS ON THE STATEMENT IN INTERVENTION

35. After the statement in intervention has been lodged, the President may, if it is considered necessary, prescribe a time limit for the submission of brief observations on that statement. The lodging of those observations, the length of which should not exceed five pages, is nevertheless optional. The purpose of such observations is merely to enable the main parties to respond to certain claims made by the intervener or to adopt a position on new pleas in law or arguments raised by the intervener. Where there are no such matters, it is recommended that the parties desist from lodging such observations in order to avoid unnecessarily prolonging the written part of the procedure.

APPLICATIONS TO INTERVENE MADE OUT OF TIME

36. In so far as it meets the conditions set out in Article 130(2) to (4) of the Rules of Procedure, the Court may also give consideration to an application to intervene made after the passing of the time limit prescribed in Article 130(1) or 190(2) of the Rules of Procedure, provided, however, that that application reaches it before the decision to open the oral part of the procedure provided for in Article 60(4) of those Rules is adopted. In that case, the intervener will be able to submit observations during the hearing, if it takes place.

INTERVENTION IN THE CONTEXT OF AN APPLICATION FOR INTERIM MEASURES OR AN EXPEDITED PROCEDURE

37. The same is true in general in the context of an application for interim measures or where a case is to be dealt with under an expedited procedure. If there are no special circumstances warranting the lodging of written observations, the person or entity authorised to intervene in the context of such a procedure may submit observations only orally, if a hearing is organised.

NO INTERVENTION IN REFERENCES FOR A PRELIMINARY RULING

38. The above rules on intervention are, in contrast, not applicable to references for a preliminary ruling. Due to the non- adversarial nature of that category of case and the special function of the Court when it is called upon to give a preliminary ruling on the interpretation or validity of European Union law, only the interested persons referred to in Article 23 of the Statute — and any institutions, bodies, offices and agencies of the European Union called upon under the second paragraph of Article 24 of the Statute — are authorised to submit observations, written or oral, on the questions submitted to the Court by the courts and tribunals of the Member States.

THE FORM AND STRUCTURE OF PROCEDURAL DOCUMENTS

39. Irrespective of the foregoing matters and the prerequisites relating to the content of procedural documents resulting from the provisions of the Statute and the Rules of Procedure, the written pleadings and observations lodged before the Court must meet certain additional requirements intended to facilitate the reading and processing of those documents by the Court, in particular by electronic means. Those requirements concern the form and the presentation of procedural documents as well as their structure or their length.

40. As to the formal conditions, first of all, it is essential that the written pleadings or observations lodged by the parties are presented in a form in which they can be processed electronically by the Court. To that end, the following requirements must be taken into account:

— the written pleadings or observations are to be drafted on white, unlined and A4-size paper, with text on one side of the page only (recto), and not on both sides of the page (recto-verso);
— the text is to be in a commonly used font (such as Times New Roman, Courier or Arial), in at least 12 point in the body of the text and at least 10 point in the footnotes, with 1,5 line spacing and horizontal and vertical margins of at least 2,5 cm (above, below, at the left and at the right of the page);
— all the paragraphs of the written pleadings or observations are to be numbered consecutively;
— the same is true for the pages of the written pleadings or observations, including any annexes to them and their schedule, which are to be numbered consecutively, in the top right-hand corner;
— the pages of the written pleadings or observations are not to exceed 1 500 characters per page, excluding spaces;
— lastly, where they are not sent to the Court by electronic means, pages of written pleadings or observations are to be assembled in such a way as to be easily separable and not permanently attached by, for example, glue or staples.

41. In addition to these formal requirements, the procedural documents lodged before the Court must be drafted in a form which allows their structure and scope to be grasped from the first few pages. Besides stating, on the first page of the written pleadings or observations concerned, the title of the document, the case number (if it has already been notified by the Registry) and the parties concerned or their initials (if the case has been anonymised), the written pleadings or observations are to begin with a brief summary of the schema adopted by the author or with a table of contents. Those written pleadings or observations must end with the forms of order sought by the author or, in preliminary ruling proceedings, with the author's proposed answers to the questions put by the referring court or tribunal.

42. Although the documents which are sent to the Court are not subject, as regards their content, to any requirement other than those resulting from the Statute and the Rules of Procedure, it must nevertheless be borne in mind that such documents constitute the basis for the Court's study of the file and that they must, as a general rule, be translated by the Court or the institution which produced them. In the interests of the proper conduct of the procedure and in the interests of the parties themselves, *the written pleadings or observations must therefore be drafted in clear, concise language*, without the use of technical terms specific to a national legal system. Repetition must be avoided and short sentences must, as far as possible, be used in preference to long and complex sentences that include parenthetical and subordinate clauses.

43. When, in their written pleadings or observations, the parties refer to a specific text or piece of legislation, of national or European Union law, *the references to that text or legislation must be accurately cited*, both so far as concerns the date of adoption and, where possible, the date of publication of that document and so far as concerns its temporal applicability. Likewise, when citing an extract or a passage of a judicial decision or of an Advocate General's Opinion, the parties are requested to specify both the name and number of the case concerned and the ECLI (European Case Law Identifier) of the decision or Opinion and the exact references of the extract or the passage at issue.

44. Lastly, it must be pointed out that *the legal argument of the parties or the interested persons referred to in Article 23 of the Statute must appear in the written pleadings or observations, and not in any attached annexes*, which are generally not translated. Only documents mentioned in the actual body of written pleadings or observations and necessary in order to prove or illustrate its contents may be submitted as annexes. Annexes are furthermore not accepted, pursuant to Article 57(4) of the Rules of Procedure, unless they are accompanied by a schedule of annexes. That schedule is to indicate, for each document annexed, the number of the annex, a short description of the document and the page or paragraph of the written pleadings or observations in which the document is cited and which justifies its production.

45. If a procedural document manifestly does not comply with the above requirements and, in particular, the instructions relating to the length of that document, the Registry may request the author of the document lodged to put it in order within a short period of time.

THE LODGING AND TRANSMISSION OF PROCEDURAL DOCUMENTS

46. Only the documents expressly provided for by the procedural rules may be lodged at the Registry. Those documents must be lodged within the prescribed time limits and observing the requirements set out in Article 57 of the Rules of Procedure.

47. The Court's recommended method of lodging a procedural document is via the *e-Curia application*. This allows the lodging and service of procedural documents by exclusively electronic means, without it being necessary to provide certified copies of the document transmitted to the Court or to duplicate that transmission by sending the document by post. The procedure for access to the e-Curia application and its conditions of use are described in detail in the Decision of the Court of 16 October 2018 on the lodging and service of procedural documents by means of e-Curia, and in the conditions of use to which that decision refers. Those documents are available on the Court's website (https://curia.europa.eu/jcms/jcms/P_78957/en/).

48. If it is not transmitted to the Court by means of the abovementioned application, a procedural document may also be sent to the Court *by post*. The envelope containing that document must be sent to the Court Registry at the following address: Rue du Fort Niedergrünewald — L-2925 Luxembourg. In this connection, it is appropriate to mention that, pursuant to Article 57(7) of the Rules of Procedure, only the date and time of lodging of the original at the Registry are taken into consideration in the calculation of procedural time limits. To prevent any time-barring, it is therefore strongly recommended that the document be sent by registered post or by express delivery, several days before the passing of the time limit prescribed for its lodgement, or that the relevant document be lodged in person at the Court Registry or, outside the opening hours of the Registry, at the reception of the Court buildings where the janitor will acknowledge receipt of the document by recording on it the date and time of lodgement.

49. Finally, at present, a copy of the signed original of a procedural document may also be transmitted to the Registry as an attachment to an *email* (ecj.registry@curia.europa.eu) or *by fax* ((+ 352) 433766). In addition to the technical limitations inherent in those two means of transmission, it should be noted that a document lodged by email or fax will be treated as complying with the relevant time limit only if the signed original itself, together with the annexes and copies referred to in Article 57(2) of the Rules of Procedure, reaches the Registry at the latest 10 days after the copy of that signed original was sent by email or fax That original must therefore be sent or delivered without delay, immediately after the dispatch of the copy, without any corrections or amendments, even of a minor nature. In the event of any discrepancies between the signed original and the copy previously transmitted, only the date on which the signed original was lodged will be taken into consideration.

50. In order to facilitate the Court's processing of the written pleadings or observations lodged and, in particular, their translation into one or more official languages of the European Union, the parties are requested — in addition to sending, within the prescribed time limits, the original of their written pleading or of their observations, that version alone being authentic — to send an editable version (word processing software such as Word, Open Office or LibreOffice) of that pleading or of those observations to the following address: editable-versions@curia.europa.eu.

III. THE ORAL PART OF THE PROCEDURE

[6.795]
51. As is apparent from the fourth paragraph of Article 20 of the Statute, the oral part of the procedure essentially consists of two distinct stages: the hearing of the parties or interested persons referred to in Article 23 of the Statute and the presentation of the Advocate General's Opinion. Under the fifth paragraph of Article 20 of the Statute, the Court may nevertheless decide, where it considers that the case raises no new point of law, that the case is to be determined without hearing the Advocate General's Opinion. A hearing will not automatically be arranged.

THE PURPOSE OF THE HEARING

52. Having regard to the importance of the written part of the procedure in cases brought before the Court, and subject to the application of Article 76(3) of the Rules of Procedure, in the case of references for a preliminary ruling, the decisive criterion for holding a hearing is not so much whether an express request has been made to that effect as the assessment made by the Court itself as to the added value of that hearing and its potential contribution to the outcome of the dispute or to determining the answers which the Court could provide to the questions referred by a court or tribunal of a Member State. *A hearing is therefore arranged by the Court whenever it is likely to contribute to a better understanding of the case and the issues raised by it, whether or not a request to that effect has been submitted by the parties or the interested persons referred to in Article 23 of the Statute.*

THE REQUEST FOR A HEARING

53. Where those parties or those interested persons consider that a hearing must be arranged in a case, the onus is on them, in any event, as soon as they have received notification of the end of the written part of the procedure, to *inform the Court by letter of the precise reasons why they wish to be heard by the Court*. That reasoning — which is not to be confused with written pleadings or observations and must not exceed three pages — must be based on a real assessment of the benefit of a hearing to the party in question and must indicate the documentary elements or arguments which that party considers it necessary to develop or disprove more fully at the hearing. It is not sufficient to provide a general statement of reasons referring, for example, to the importance of the case or of the questions to be decided by the Court.

THE NOTICE TO ATTEND THE HEARING AND THE NEED FOR A PROMPT RESPONSE TO THAT NOTICE

54. When the Court decides to arrange a hearing in a particular case, it fixes the exact date and time and the parties or interested persons referred to in Article 23 of the Statute are immediately sent a letter of notice to attend by the Registry, which also notifies them of the composition of the formation to which the case has been assigned, of any measures of organisation of procedure decided on by the Court and, where applicable, that there is to be no Advocate General's Opinion. In order to enable the Court to arrange that hearing in the best possible conditions, *the parties or the abovementioned interested persons are requested to reply to the Registry's letter within a short period* stating, in particular, whether they intend actually to attend the hearing and the name of the lawyer or agent who will represent them at it. A late reply to the Registry's letter of notice to attend jeopardises the proper organisation of the hearing, both from the point of view of the speaking time allocated by the Court to the party concerned and with regard to the constraints on the operation of the interpretation service.

THE STEPS TO BE TAKEN WITH A VIEW TO THE HEARING

55. The persons called upon to present oral argument before the Court, irrespective of their qualifications or the capacity in which they are called upon, are required to wear gowns. Agents and lawyers taking part in a hearing are therefore requested to provide their own gowns. Should the parties or their representatives not have a gown, a number

of plain gowns may be made available by the Court but, since these are limited in number and in the sizes available, the parties and representatives concerned are requested to inform the Court of any such requirement in advance, in their response to the letter of notice to attend the hearing.

56. In the context of that response, and with a view to ensuring the best possible organisation of the hearing, the parties and their representatives are also requested to inform the Court of any particular measures that would facilitate their actual participation in the hearing, in particular in cases of disability or reduced mobility.

57. On account of the traffic conditions in Luxembourg and the security measures applicable to access to the Court buildings, it is advisable to take the steps necessary to be present in the room where the hearing will take place on the day of the hearing well before it is due to start. Before the hearing begins, the members of the formation of the Court usually hold a short meeting with the representatives of the parties or interested persons referred to in Article 23 of the Statute about the organisation of the hearing. At that meeting the Judge-Rapporteur and the Advocate General may invite those representatives to provide, at the hearing, further information on certain questions or to develop one or more specific aspects of the case at issue.

THE NORMAL PROCEDURE AT A HEARING

58. While the procedure at a hearing before the Court may vary depending on the circumstances of each case, in general it consists of three separate parts: the oral submissions proper, questions from the members of the Court and replies.

THE FIRST STAGE OF THE HEARING: ORAL SUBMISSIONS

THE PURPOSE OF THE ORAL SUBMISSIONS

59. Subject to any special circumstances, the hearing usually starts with the oral submissions of the parties or the interested persons referred to in Article 23 of the Statute. In the light of the knowledge which the Court already has of the case following the written part of the procedure, it is not the purpose of those submissions to recall the content of the written pleadings or observations. They are intended to enable the parties or the above mentioned interested persons to respond to any requests to concentrate on specified issues in the submissions, or to answer the questions which the Court put to them before the hearing. As far as possible, participants in the hearing who are advocating the same line of argument or adopting the same position are, moreover, requested to liaise before the hearing in order to avoid unnecessary repetition.

SPEAKING TIME AND ITS POSSIBLE EXTENSION

60. The speaking time is fixed by the President of the formation of the Court, after consulting the Judge-Rapporteur and, if applicable, the Advocate General responsible for the case. As a general rule, the speaking time is fixed at 15 minutes, irrespective of the formation of the Court to which the case has been assigned. However, that time may be made longer or shorter depending on the nature or the specific complexity of the case, the number and procedural status of the participants in the hearing and any measures of organisation of procedure. An extension of the speaking time allocated may, exceptionally, be granted by the President of the formation of the Court on the duly reasoned application of a party or one of the interested persons referred to in Article 23 of the Statute. To be taken into account, such an application must nevertheless be made by the party or interested person concerned in the reply to the letter of notice to attend the hearing.

THE NUMBER OF PERSONS PRESENTING ORAL ARGUMENT

61. For reasons connected with the proper conduct of the hearing, the oral submissions of the parties or of the interested persons present at the hearing must, for each of them, be made by a single person. In exceptional circumstances, a second person may nevertheless be authorised to present oral argument where this is warranted by the nature or particular complexity of the case, provided a duly reasoned application to this effect has been submitted in the reply of the party or interested person concerned to the letter of notice to attend the hearing. If it is granted, that authorisation does not, however, include any extension of the speaking time, and the two persons presenting oral argument must share the speaking time allocated to the party concerned.

THE LANGUAGE OF ORAL SUBMISSIONS

62. Without prejudice to the possibility, for a Member State, of using its own official language when taking part in a hearing and the possibility, for third States, of using one of the languages mentioned in Article 36 of the Rules of Procedure when taking part in preliminary ruling proceedings or intervening in a case before the Court, the other parties to the proceedings are required to present oral argument in the language of the case, as determined in accordance with the rules laid down in Article 37 of the Rules of Procedure.

63. In preliminary ruling proceedings, the parties to the main proceedings may, exceptionally, request that the Court authorise the use of a language other than that of the referring court or tribunal for the oral part of the procedure. That request — which must be submitted in the response of the party concerned to the letter of notice to attend the hearing — must be duly substantiated and explain the reasons why the use of another language is sought and those militating in favour of that other language, of those mentioned in Article 36 of the Rules of Procedure. Under Article 37(4) of those Rules, the decision on that request is, depending on the circumstances, a matter for the President of the formation of the Court to which the case was referred or for the Court, after the other party or parties to the main proceedings and the Advocate General have been heard with respect to the request. If the request is granted, the requested language may be used by all the interested persons referred to in Article 23 of the Statute.

64. The exception referred to in the preceding point is, however, applicable only to preliminary ruling proceedings. Except in the cases referred to in point 62 of these Practice Directions, the parties to the proceedings in a direct action or an appeal are obliged to present oral argument, to make submissions in reply and to answer any questions put by the Court in the language of the case.[3]

THE SECOND STAGE OF THE HEARING: QUESTIONS FROM MEMBERS OF THE COURT

65. Without prejudice to the questions which may be asked by the members of the Court before or during the oral submissions, the persons presenting oral argument may be requested, at the end of the oral submissions, to answer additional questions from the members of the Court. The purpose of those questions is to supplement the members' knowledge of the file and to allow the persons presenting oral argument to explain or elaborate on certain points on which additional information may still be required.

THE THIRD STAGE OF THE HEARING: REPLIES

66. After that exchange, the representatives of the parties or the interested persons referred to in Article 23 of the Statute finally have the opportunity, if they consider it necessary, of replying briefly. Those replies, of a maximum duration of five minutes each, do not constitute a second round of oral submissions. They are designed only to enable the persons presenting oral argument to react succinctly to observations made or questions put during the hearing by the other participants or by the members of the Court. If two persons have been authorised to speak for a party, only one of them is authorised to reply.

THE IMPLICATIONS AND CONSTRAINTS OF SIMULTANEOUS INTERPRETATION

67. Whether in their oral submissions, their replies or their responses to questions from the Court, the persons presenting oral argument must bear in mind that very frequently the members of the formation of the Court, the Advocate General and the interested persons referred to in Article 23 of the Statute will listen to their argument by means of simultaneous interpretation. In the interests of the proper conduct of the hearing and in order to guarantee the quality of the interpretation provided, the representatives of the parties or the interested persons referred to in Article 23 of the Statute are therefore requested, if they have a text available, however short, of notes for the oral submissions or an outline of their argument, to send it as soon as possible before the hearing to the interpretation directorate, either by email (Interpretation@curia.europa.eu) or by fax ((+ 352) 43033697). That text or those notes for the oral submissions are intended solely for the interpreters and are destroyed after the hearing. They are neither transmitted to the members of the formation of the Court and the Advocate General responsible for the case nor included in the case file.

68. To facilitate interpretation and, therefore, comprehension of the oral submissions both by the members of the formation of the Court and the Advocate General responsible for the case and by the other parties present at the hearing, it is essential, during the hearing, to speak directly into the microphone, at a natural and unforced pace. It is helpful for the purposes of the interpretation if the person presenting oral argument states in advance the outline of his or her argument and uses short and simple sentences as a matter of course. When referring in his or her oral submissions to a decision of the Court of Justice or of the General Court, the person presenting oral argument is also requested to specify the date of that decision and the number and name of the case concerned.

THE PROCEDURE FOLLOWING THE HEARING

69. The active participation of the parties or interested persons referred to in Article 23 of the Statute comes to an end at the end of the hearing. Subject to the exceptional situation in which the oral part of the procedure is reopened, pursuant to Article 83 of the Rules of Procedure, the parties or abovementioned interested persons are no longer authorised to put forward written or oral observations, in particular in response to the Advocate General's Opinion, once the President of the formation of the Court has declared the hearing closed.

NOTES

[3] In the case of infringement proceedings, the defendant Member State is entitled to use, during the oral part of the procedure, a language other than that used during the written part, provided, however, that that other language is one of the official languages of that State and that a request to that effect has been submitted in good time, if possible in the response to the letter of notice to attend the hearing. If the request is granted, the requested language may be used by all the parties to the proceedings.

IV. FINAL PROVISIONS

[6.796]

70. The Practice directions to parties concerning cases before the Court of 25 November 2013 are hereby repealed and replaced by these Practice Directions.

71. These Practice Directions shall be published in the *Official Journal of the European Union*. They shall enter into force on the first day of the month following that of their publication.

Adopted at Luxembourg, 10 December 2019.

PART 7
BREXIT-RELATED MATERIALS

A. UK LEGISLATION

EUROPEAN UNION (WITHDRAWAL) ACT 2018

(2018 c 16)

ARRANGEMENT OF SECTIONS

SCHEDULES

An Act to repeal the European Communities Act 1972 and make other provision in connection with the withdrawal of the United Kingdom from the EU.

[26 June 2018]

Repeal of the ECA

[7.1]

1 Repeal of the European Communities Act 1972

The European Communities Act 1972 is repealed on exit day.

NOTES

Commencement: 17 August 2019.

[Savings for implementation period

[7.2]

1A Saving for ECA for implementation period

(1)–(4) . . .

(5) Subsections (1) to (4) are repealed on IP completion day.

(6) In this Act—

"the implementation period" means the transition or implementation period provided for by Part 4 of the withdrawal agreement and beginning with exit day and ending on IP completion day;

"IP completion day" (and related expressions) have the same meaning as in the European Union (Withdrawal Agreement) Act 2020 (see section 39(1) to (5) of that Act);

"withdrawal agreement" has the same meaning as in that Act (see section 39(1) and (6) of that Act).

(7) In this Act—

(a) references to the European Communities Act 1972 are to be read, so far as the context permits or requires, as being or (as the case may be) including references to that Act as it continues to have effect by virtue of subsections (2) to (4) above, and

(b) references to any Part of the withdrawal agreement or the EEA EFTA separation agreement include references to any other provisions of that agreement so far as applying to that Part.]

NOTES

Commencement: exit day (31 January 2020 at 11pm).

Inserted, together with the previous heading, by the European Union (Withdrawal Agreement) Act 2020, s 1.

Sub-ss (1)–(4): repealed by subsection (5) above, as from IP completion day (as defined in the European Union (Withdrawal Agreement) Act 2020, s 39).

[7.3]

[1B Saving for EU-derived domestic legislation for implementation period

(1)–(5) . . .

(6) Subsections (1) to (5) are repealed on IP completion day.

(7) In this Act "EU-derived domestic legislation" means any enactment so far as—

(a) made under section 2(2) of, or paragraph 1A of Schedule 2 to, the European Communities Act 1972,

(b) passed or made, or operating, for a purpose mentioned in section 2(2)(a) or (b) of that Act,

(c) relating to—

(i) anything which falls within paragraph (a) or (b), or

(ii) any rights, powers, liabilities, obligations, restrictions, remedies or procedures which are recognised and available in domestic law by virtue of section 2(1) of the European Communities Act 1972, or

(d) relating otherwise to the EU or the EEA,

but does not include any enactment contained in the European Communities Act 1972 or any enactment contained in this Act or the European Union (Withdrawal Agreement) Act 2020 or in regulations made under this Act or the Act of 2020.]

NOTES

Commencement: exit day (31 January 2020 at 11pm).

Inserted by the European Union (Withdrawal Agreement) Act 2020, s 2.

Sub-ss (1)–(5): repealed by subsection (6) above, as from IP completion day (as defined in the European Union (Withdrawal Agreement) Act 2020, s 39).

Retention of [saved EU law at end of implementation period]

NOTES

Words in square brackets in the above heading substituted by the European Union (Withdrawal Agreement) Act 2020, s 41(4), Sch 5, Pt 2, paras 38, 39, as from IP completion day (as defined in the European Union (Withdrawal Agreement) Act 2020, s 39).

[7.4]

2 Saving for EU-derived domestic legislation

(1) EU-derived domestic legislation, as it has effect in domestic law immediately before [IP completion day], continues to have effect in domestic law on and after [IP completion day].

(2) . . .

(3) This section is subject to section 5 and Schedule 1 (exceptions to savings and incorporation) [and section 5A (savings and incorporation: supplementary)].

NOTES

Commencement: IP completion day (as defined in the European Union (Withdrawal Agreement) Act 2020, s 39).

Words in square brackets in sub-s (1) substituted, sub-s (2) repealed, and words in square brackets in sub-s (3) inserted, by the European Union (Withdrawal Agreement) Act 2020, s 25(1), as from IP completion day (as defined in the European Union (Withdrawal Agreement) Act 2020, s 39).

[7.5]

3 Incorporation of direct EU legislation

(1) Direct EU legislation, so far as operative immediately before [IP completion day], forms part of domestic law on and after [IP completion day].

(2) In this Act "direct EU legislation" means—

(a) any EU regulation, EU decision or EU tertiary legislation, as it has effect in EU law immediately before [IP completion day] and so far as—

[(ai) it is applicable to and in the United Kingdom by virtue of Part 4 of the withdrawal agreement,

(bi) it neither has effect nor is to have effect by virtue of section 7A or 7B,]

(i) it is not an exempt EU instrument (for which see section 20(1) and Schedule 6), [and]

(ii) . . .

(iii) its effect is not reproduced in an enactment to which section 2(1) applies,

(b) any Annex to the EEA agreement, as it has effect in EU law immediately before [IP completion day] and so far as—

[(ai) it is applicable to and in the United Kingdom by virtue of Part 4 of the withdrawal agreement,

(bi) it neither has effect nor is to have effect by virtue of section 7A or 7B,]

(i) it refers to, or contains adaptations of, anything falling within paragraph (a), and

(ii) its effect is not reproduced in an enactment to which section 2(1) applies, or

(c) Protocol 1 to the EEA agreement (which contains horizontal adaptations that apply in relation to EU instruments referred to in the Annexes to that agreement), as it has effect in EU law immediately before [IP completion day and so far as—

(i) it is applicable to and in the United Kingdom by virtue of Part 4 of the withdrawal agreement, and

(ii) it neither has effect nor is to have effect by virtue of section 7A or 7B,]

(3) For the purposes of this Act, any direct EU legislation is operative immediately before [IP completion day] if—

(a) in the case of anything which comes into force at a particular time and is stated to apply from a later time, it is in force and applies immediately before [IP completion day],

(b) in the case of a decision which specifies to whom it is addressed, it has been notified to that person before [IP completion day], and

(c) in any other case, it is in force immediately before [IP completion day].

(4) This section—

(a) brings into domestic law any direct EU legislation only in the form of the English language version of that legislation, and

(b) does not apply to any such legislation for which there is no such version,

but paragraph (a) does not affect the use of the other language versions of that legislation for the purposes of interpreting it.

(5) This section is subject to section 5 and Schedule 1 (exceptions to savings and incorporation) [and section 5A (savings and incorporation: supplementary)].

NOTES

Commencement: IP completion day (as defined in the European Union (Withdrawal Agreement) Act 2020, s 39).

All amendments to this section were made by the European Union (Withdrawal Agreement) Act 2020, s 25(2), as from IP completion day (as defined in the European Union (Withdrawal Agreement) Act 2020, s 39).

[7.6]

4 Saving for rights etc under section 2(1) of the ECA

(1) Any rights, powers, liabilities, obligations, restrictions, remedies and procedures which, immediately before [IP completion day]—

(a) are recognised and available in domestic law by virtue of section 2(1) of the European Communities Act 1972, and

(b) are enforced, allowed and followed accordingly,

continue on and after [IP completion day] to be recognised and available in domestic law (and to be enforced, allowed and followed accordingly).

(2) Subsection (1) does not apply to any rights, powers, liabilities, obligations, restrictions, remedies or procedures so far as they—

(a) form part of domestic law by virtue of section 3,

[(aa) are, or are to be, recognised and available in domestic law (and enforced, allowed and followed accordingly) by virtue of section 7A or 7B,] or

(b) arise under an EU directive (including as applied by the EEA agreement) and are not of a kind recognised by the European Court or any court or tribunal in the United Kingdom in a case decided before [IP completion day] (whether or not as an essential part of the decision in the case).

(3) This section is subject to section 5 and Schedule 1 (exceptions to savings and incorporation) [and section 5A (savings and incorporation: supplementary)].

NOTES

Commencement: IP completion day (as defined in the European Union (Withdrawal Agreement) Act 2020, s 39).

All amendments to this section were made by the European Union (Withdrawal Agreement) Act 2020, s 25(3), as from IP completion day (as defined in the European Union (Withdrawal Agreement) Act 2020, s 39).

[7.7]

5 Exceptions to savings and incorporation

(1) The principle of the supremacy of EU law does not apply to any enactment or rule of law passed or made on or after [IP completion day].

(2) Accordingly, the principle of the supremacy of EU law continues to apply on or after [IP completion day] so far as relevant to the interpretation, disapplication or quashing of any enactment or rule of law passed or made before [IP completion day].

(3) Subsection (1) does not prevent the principle of the supremacy of EU law from applying to a modification made on or after [IP completion day] of any enactment or rule of law passed or made before [IP completion day] if the application of the principle is consistent with the intention of the modification.

(4) The Charter of Fundamental Rights is not part of domestic law on or after [IP completion day].

(5) Subsection (4) does not affect the retention in domestic law on or after [IP completion day] in accordance with this Act of any fundamental rights or principles which exist irrespective of the Charter (and references to the Charter in any case law are, so far as necessary for this purpose, to be read as if they were references to any corresponding retained fundamental rights or principles).

(6) Schedule 1 (which makes further provision about exceptions to savings and incorporation) has effect.

[(7) Subsections (1) to (6) and Schedule 1 are subject to relevant separation agreement law (for which see section 7C).]

NOTES

Commencement: 4 July 2018 (sub-s (6) certain purposes); IP completion day (as defined in the European Union (Withdrawal Agreement) Act 2020, s 39) (otherwise).

Sub-ss (1)–(5): words in square brackets substituted by the European Union (Withdrawal Agreement) Act 2020, s 25(4)(a), as from IP completion day (as defined in the European Union (Withdrawal Agreement) Act 2020, s 39).

Sub-s (7): added by the European Union (Withdrawal Agreement) Act 2020, s 25(4)(b), as from exit day (as defined in s 20 of this Act) (for the purposes of sub-s (6) above, and Sch 1 *post*, so far as they are in force on exit day), and as from IP completion day (as defined in the European Union (Withdrawal Agreement) Act 2020, s 39) (otherwise).

[7.8]

[5A Savings and incorporation: supplementary

The fact that anything which continues to be, or forms part of, domestic law on or after IP completion day by virtue of section 2, 3 or 4 has an effect immediately before IP completion day which is time-limited by reference to the implementation period does not prevent it from having an indefinite effect on and after IP completion day by virtue of section 2, 3 or 4.]

NOTES

Commencement: IP completion day (as defined in the European Union (Withdrawal Agreement) Act 2020, s 39).

Inserted by the European Union (Withdrawal Agreement) Act 2020, s 25(5), as from IP completion day (as defined in the European Union (Withdrawal Agreement) Act 2020, s 39).

Transitional provisions: nothing in this section prevents the modification on or after IP completion day of Retained EU law by an enactment passed or made before IP completion day and coming into force or otherwise having effect on or after IP completion day (whether or not that enactment is itself retained EU law). See the European Union (Withdrawal) Act 2018 and European Union (Withdrawal Agreement) Act 2020 (Commencement, Transitional and Savings Provisions) Regulations 2020, SI 2020/1622, reg 17.

[7.9]

6 Interpretation of retained EU law

(1) A court or tribunal—

(a) is not bound by any principles laid down, or any decisions made, on or after [IP completion day] by the European Court, and

(b) cannot refer any matter to the European Court on or after [IP completion day].

(2) Subject to this and subsections (3) to (6), a court or tribunal may have regard to anything done on or after [IP completion day] by the European Court, another EU entity or the EU so far as it is relevant to any matter before the court or tribunal.

(3) Any question as to the validity, meaning or effect of any retained EU law is to be decided, so far as that law is unmodified on or after [IP completion day] and so far as they are relevant to it—

(a) in accordance with any retained case law and any retained general principles of EU law, and

(b) having regard (among other things) to the limits, immediately before [IP completion day], of EU competences.

(4) But—

(a) the Supreme Court is not bound by any retained EU case law,

(b) the High Court of Justiciary is not bound by any retained EU case law when—

(i) sitting as a court of appeal otherwise than in relation to a compatibility issue (within the meaning given by section 288ZA(2) of the Criminal Procedure (Scotland) Act 1995) or a devolution issue (within the meaning given by paragraph 1 of Schedule 6 to the Scotland Act 1998), or

(ii) sitting on a reference under section 123(1) of the Criminal Procedure (Scotland) Act 1995,

[(ba) a relevant court or relevant tribunal is not bound by any retained EU case law so far as is provided for by regulations under subsection (5A),] and

(c) no court or tribunal is bound by any retained domestic case law that it would not otherwise be bound by.

(5) In deciding whether to depart from any retained EU case law [by virtue of subsection (4)(a) or (b)], the Supreme Court or the High Court of Justiciary must apply the same test as it would apply in deciding whether to depart from its own case law.

[(5A) A Minister of the Crown may by regulations provide for—

(a) a court or tribunal to be a relevant court or (as the case may be) a relevant tribunal for the purposes of this section,

(b) the extent to which, or circumstances in which, a relevant court or relevant tribunal is not to be bound by retained EU case law,

(c) the test which a relevant court or relevant tribunal must apply in deciding whether to depart from any retained EU case law, or

(d) considerations which are to be relevant to—

(i) the Supreme Court or the High Court of Justiciary in applying the test mentioned in subsection (5), or

(ii) a relevant court or relevant tribunal in applying any test provided for by virtue of paragraph (c) above.

(5B) Regulations under subsection (5A) may (among other things) provide for—

(a) the High Court of Justiciary to be a relevant court when sitting otherwise than as mentioned in subsection (4)(b)(i) and (ii),

(b) the extent to which, or circumstances in which, a relevant court or relevant tribunal not being bound by retained EU case law includes (or does not include) that court or tribunal not being bound by retained domestic case law which relates to retained EU case law,

(c) other matters arising in relation to retained domestic case law which relates to retained EU case law (including by making provision of a kind which could be made in relation to retained EU case law), or

(d) the test mentioned in paragraph (c) of subsection (5A) or the considerations mentioned in paragraph (d) of that subsection to be determined (whether with or without the consent of a Minister of the Crown) by a person mentioned in subsection (5C)(a) to (e) or by more than one of those persons acting jointly.

(5C) Before making regulations under subsection (5A), a Minister of the Crown must consult—

(a) the President of the Supreme Court,

(b) the Lord Chief Justice of England and Wales,

(c) the Lord President of the Court of Session,

(d) the Lord Chief Justice of Northern Ireland,

(e) the Senior President of Tribunals, and

(f) such other persons as the Minister of the Crown considers appropriate.

(5D) No regulations may be made under subsection (5A) after IP completion day.]

(6) Subsection (3) does not prevent the validity, meaning or effect of any retained EU law which has been modified on or after [IP completion day] from being decided as provided for in that subsection if doing so is consistent with the intention of the modifications.

[(6A) Subsections (1) to (6) are subject to relevant separation agreement law (for which see section 7C).]

(7) In this Act—

"retained case law" means—

(a) retained domestic case law, and

(b) retained EU case law;

"retained domestic case law" means any principles laid down by, and any decisions of, a court or tribunal in the United Kingdom, as they have effect immediately before [IP completion day] and so far as they—

(a) relate to anything to which section 2, 3 or 4 applies, and

(b) are not excluded by section 5 or Schedule 1,

(as those principles and decisions are modified by or under this Act or by other domestic law from time to time);

"retained EU case law" means any principles laid down by, and any decisions of, the European Court, as they have effect in EU law immediately before [IP completion day] and so far as they—

(a) relate to anything to which section 2, 3 or 4 applies, and

(b) are not excluded by section 5 or Schedule 1,

(as those principles and decisions are modified by or under this Act or by other domestic law from time to time);

"retained EU law" means anything which, on or after [IP completion day], continues to be, or forms part of, domestic law by virtue of section 2, 3 or 4 or subsection (3) or (6) above (as that body of law is added to or otherwise modified by or under this Act or by other domestic law from time to time);

"retained general principles of EU law" means the general principles of EU law, as they have effect in EU law immediately before [IP completion day] and so far as they—

(a) relate to anything to which section 2, 3 or 4 applies, and

(b) are not excluded by section 5 or Schedule 1,

(as those principles are modified by or under this Act or by other domestic law from time to time).

NOTES

Commencement: 4 July 2018 (sub-s (7)); IP completion day (as defined in the European Union (Withdrawal Agreement) Act 2020, s 39) (otherwise).

The words "IP completion day" in square brackets were substituted, sub-s (4)(ba) was inserted, the words "by virtue of subsection (4)(a) or (b)" in square brackets in sub-s (5) were inserted, and sub-s (6A) was inserted, by the European Union (Withdrawal Agreement) Act 2020, s 26(1)(a)–(c), (e), as from IP completion day (as defined in the European Union (Withdrawal Agreement) Act 2020, s 39).

Sub-ss (5A)–(5D) were inserted by the European Union (Withdrawal Agreement) Act 2020, s 26(1)(d).

The words "IP completion day" in square brackets in sub-s (7) (in each place that they occur) were substituted by the European Union (Withdrawal Agreement) Act 2020, s 26(1)(a).

[7.10]

7 Status of retained EU law

(1) Anything which—

(a) was, immediately before exit day, primary legislation of a particular kind, subordinate legislation of a particular kind or another enactment of a particular kind, and

(b) continues to be domestic law on and after exit day by virtue of [section 1A(2) or 1B(2)],

continues to be domestic law as an enactment of the same kind.

[(1A) Anything which—

(a) was, immediately before IP completion day, primary legislation of a particular kind, subordinate legislation of a particular kind or another enactment of a particular kind, and

(b) continues to be domestic law on and after IP completion day by virtue of section 2,

continues to be domestic law as an enactment of the same kind.]

(2) Retained direct principal EU legislation cannot be modified by any primary or subordinate legislation other than—

(a) an Act of Parliament,

(b) any other primary legislation (so far as it has the power to make such a modification), or

(c) any subordinate legislation so far as it is made under a power which permits such a modification by virtue of—

(i) paragraph 3, 5(3)(a) or (4)(a), 8(3), 10(3)(a) or (4)(a), 11(2)(a) or 12(3) of Schedule 8,

(ii) any other provision made by or under this Act,

(iii) any provision made by or under an Act of Parliament passed before, and in the same Session as, this Act, or

(iv) any provision made on or after the passing of this Act by or under primary legislation.

(3) Retained direct minor EU legislation cannot be modified by any primary or subordinate legislation other than—

(a) an Act of Parliament,

(b) any other primary legislation (so far as it has the power to make such a modification), or

(c) any subordinate legislation so far as it is made under a power which permits such a modification by virtue of—

(i) paragraph 3, 5(2) or (4)(a), 8(3), 10(2) or (4)(a) or 12(3) of Schedule 8,

(ii) any other provision made by or under this Act,

(iii) any provision made by or under an Act of Parliament passed before, and in the same Session as, this Act, or

(iv) any provision made on or after the passing of this Act by or under primary legislation.

(4) Anything which is retained EU law by virtue of section 4 cannot be modified by any primary or subordinate legislation other than—

(a) an Act of Parliament,

(b) any other primary legislation (so far as it has the power to make such a modification), or

(c) any subordinate legislation so far as it is made under a power which permits such a modification by virtue of—

(i) paragraph 3, 5(3)(b) or (4)(b), 8(3), 10(3)(b) or (4)(b), 11(2)(b) or 12(3) of Schedule 8,

(ii) any other provision made by or under this Act,

(iii) any provision made by or under an Act of Parliament passed before, and in the same Session as, this Act, or

(iv) any provision made on or after the passing of this Act by or under primary legislation.

(5) For other provisions about the status of retained EU law, see—

(a) section 5(1) to (3) [and (7)] (status of retained EU law in relation to other enactments or rules of law),

(b) section 6 (status of retained case law and retained general principles of EU law),

[(ba) section 7C (status of case law of European Court etc in relation to retained EU law which is relevant separation agreement law),]

(c) section 15(2) and Part 2 of Schedule 5 (status of retained EU law for the purposes of the rules of evidence),

(d) paragraphs 13 to 16 of Schedule 8 (affirmative and enhanced scrutiny procedure for, and information about, instruments which amend or revoke subordinate legislation under section 2(2) of the European Communities Act 1972 including subordinate legislation implementing EU directives),

(e) paragraphs 19 and 20 of that Schedule (status of certain retained direct EU legislation for the purposes of the Interpretation Act 1978), and

(f) paragraph 30 of that Schedule (status of retained direct EU legislation for the purposes of the Human Rights Act 1998).

(6) In this Act—

"retained direct minor EU legislation" means any retained direct EU legislation which is not retained direct principal EU legislation;

"retained direct principal EU legislation" means—

(a) any EU regulation so far as it—

(i) forms part of domestic law on and after [IP completion day] by virtue of section 3, and

(ii) was not EU tertiary legislation immediately before [IP completion day], or

(b) any Annex to the EEA agreement so far as it—

(as modified by or under this Act or by other domestic law from time to time).

(i) forms part of domestic law on and after [IP completion day] by virtue of section 3, and

(ii) refers to, or contains adaptations of, any EU regulation so far as it falls within paragraph (a),

NOTES

Commencement: exit day (as defined in s 20 of this Act) (sub-ss (1) and (6)); IP completion day (as defined in the European Union (Withdrawal Agreement) Act 2020, s 39) (otherwise).

Sub-s (1): words in square brackets substituted by the European Union (Withdrawal Agreement) Act 2020, s 41(4), Sch 5, Pt 2, paras 38, 40(1), (2).

Sub-s (1A): inserted by the European Union (Withdrawal Agreement) Act 2020, s 41(4), Sch 5, Pt 2, paras 38, 40(1), (3), as from IP completion day (as defined in the European Union (Withdrawal Agreement) Act 2020, s 39).

Sub-s (5): words in square brackets inserted by the European Union (Withdrawal Agreement) Act 2020, s 41(4), Sch 5, Pt 2, paras 38, 40(1), (4), as from IP completion day (as defined in the European Union (Withdrawal Agreement) Act 2020, s 39).

Sub-s (6): words in square brackets substituted by the European Union (Withdrawal Agreement) Act 2020, s 41(4), Sch 5, Pt 2, paras 38, 40(1), (5).

[Further aspects of withdrawal

[7.11]

7A General implementation of remainder of withdrawal agreement

(1) Subsection (2) applies to—

(a) all such rights, powers, liabilities, obligations and restrictions from time to time created or arising by or under the withdrawal agreement, and

(b) all such remedies and procedures from time to time provided for by or under the withdrawal agreement,

as in accordance with the withdrawal agreement are without further enactment to be given legal effect or used in the United Kingdom.

(2) The rights, powers, liabilities, obligations, restrictions, remedies and procedures concerned are to be—

(a) recognised and available in domestic law, and

(b) enforced, allowed and followed accordingly.

(3) Every enactment (including an enactment contained in this Act) is to be read and has effect subject to subsection (2).

(4) This section does not apply in relation to Part 4 of the withdrawal agreement so far as section 2(1) of the European Communities Act 1972 applies in relation to that Part.

(5) See also (among other things)—

(a) Part 3 of the European Union (Withdrawal Agreement) Act 2020 (further provision about citizens' rights),

(b) section 20 of that Act (financial provision),

(c) section 7C of this Act (interpretation of law relating to withdrawal agreement etc),

(d) section 8B of this Act (power in connection with certain other separation issues),

(e) section 8C of this Act (power in connection with the Protocol on Ireland/Northern Ireland in withdrawal agreement), and

(f) Parts 1B and 1C of Schedule 2 to this Act (powers involving devolved authorities in connection with certain other separation issues and the Ireland/Northern Ireland Protocol).]

NOTES

Commencement: exit day (as defined in s 20 of this Act).

Inserted by the European Union (Withdrawal Agreement) Act 2020, s 5.

[7.12]

[7B General implementation of EEA EFTA and Swiss agreements

(1) Subsection (2) applies to all such rights, powers, liabilities, obligations, restrictions, remedies and procedures as—

(a) would from time to time be created or arise, or (in the case of remedies or procedures) be provided for, by or under the EEA EFTA separation agreement or the Swiss citizens' rights agreement, and

(b) would, in accordance with Article 4(1) of the withdrawal agreement, be required to be given legal effect or used in the United Kingdom without further enactment,

if that Article were to apply in relation to the EEA EFTA separation agreement and the Swiss citizens' rights agreement, those agreements were part of EU law and the relevant EEA states and Switzerland were member States.

(2) The rights, powers, liabilities, obligations, restrictions, remedies and procedures concerned are to be—

(a) recognised and available in domestic law, and

(b) enforced, allowed and followed accordingly.

(3) Every enactment (other than section 7A but otherwise including an enactment contained in this Act) is to be read and has effect subject to subsection (2).

(4) See also (among other things)—

(a) Part 3 of the European Union (Withdrawal Agreement) Act 2020 (further provision about citizens' rights),

(b) section 7C of this Act (interpretation of law relating to the EEA EFTA separation agreement and the Swiss citizens' rights agreement etc),

(c) section 8B of this Act (power in connection with certain other separation issues), and

(d) Part 1B of Schedule 2 to this Act (powers involving devolved authorities in connection with certain other separation issues).

(5) In this section "the relevant EEA states" means Norway, Iceland and Liechtenstein.
(6) In this Act "EEA EFTA separation agreement" and "Swiss citizens' rights agreement" have the same meanings as in the European Union (Withdrawal Agreement) Act 2020 (see section 39(1) of that Act).]

NOTES

Commencement: exit day (as defined in s 20 of this Act).
Inserted by the European Union (Withdrawal Agreement) Act 2020, s 5.

[7.13]

[7C Interpretation of relevant separation agreement law

(1) Any question as to the validity, meaning or effect of any relevant separation agreement law is to be decided, so far as they are applicable—
(a) in accordance with the withdrawal agreement, the EEA EFTA separation agreement and the Swiss citizens' rights agreement, and
(b) having regard (among other things) to the desirability of ensuring that, where one of those agreements makes provision which corresponds to provision made by another of those agreements, the effect of relevant separation agreement law in relation to the matters dealt with by the corresponding provision in each agreement is consistent.

(2) See (among other things)—
(a) Article 4 of the withdrawal agreement (methods and principles relating to the effect, the implementation and the application of the agreement),
(b) Articles 158 and 160 of the withdrawal agreement (jurisdiction of the European Court in relation to Part 2 and certain provisions of Part 5 of the agreement),
(c) Articles 12 and 13 of the Protocol on Ireland/Northern Ireland in the withdrawal agreement (implementation, application, supervision and enforcement of the Protocol and common provisions),
(d) Article 4 of the EEA EFTA separation agreement (methods and principles relating to the effect, the implementation and the application of the agreement), and
(e) Article 4 of the Swiss citizens' rights agreement (methods and principles relating to the effect, the implementation and the application of the agreement).

(3) In this Act "relevant separation agreement law" means—
(a) any of the following provisions or anything which is domestic law by virtue of any of them—
(i) section 7A, 7B, 8B or 8C or Part 1B or 1C of Schedule 2 or this section, or
(ii) Part 3, or section 20, of the European Union (Withdrawal Agreement) Act 2020 (citizens' rights and financial provision), or
(b) anything not falling within paragraph (a) so far as it is domestic law for the purposes of, or otherwise within the scope of—
(i) the withdrawal agreement (other than Part 4 of that agreement),
(ii) the EEA EFTA separation agreement, or
(iii) the Swiss citizens' rights agreement,
as that body of law is added to or otherwise modified by or under this Act or by other domestic law from time to time.]

NOTES

Commencement: exit day (as defined in s 20 of this Act).
Inserted by the European Union (Withdrawal Agreement) Act 2020, s 26(2).

Main powers in connection with withdrawal

[7.14]

8 Dealing with deficiencies arising from withdrawal

(1) A Minister of the Crown may by regulations make such provision as the Minister considers appropriate to prevent, remedy or mitigate—
(a) any failure of retained EU law to operate effectively, or
(b) any other deficiency in retained EU law,
arising from the withdrawal of the United Kingdom from the EU.

(2) Deficiencies in retained EU law are where the Minister considers that retained EU law—
(a) contains anything which has no practical application in relation to the United Kingdom or any part of it or is otherwise redundant or substantially redundant,
(b) confers functions on, or in relation to, EU entities which no longer have functions in that respect under EU law in relation to the United Kingdom or any part of it,
(c) makes provision for, or in connection with, reciprocal arrangements between—
(i) the United Kingdom or any part of it or a public authority in the United Kingdom, and
(ii) the EU, an EU entity, a member State or a public authority in a member State,
which no longer exist or are no longer appropriate,
(d) makes provision for, or in connection with, other arrangements which—
(i) involve the EU, an EU entity, a member State or a public authority in a member State, or
(ii) are otherwise dependent upon the United Kingdom's membership of the EU [or Part 4 of the withdrawal agreement],
and which no longer exist or are no longer appropriate,
(e) makes provision for, or in connection with, any reciprocal or other arrangements not falling within paragraph (c) or (d) which no longer exist, or are no longer appropriate, as a result of the United Kingdom ceasing to be a party to any of the EU Treaties [or as a result of either the end of the implementation period or any other effect of the withdrawal agreement],
[(ea) is not clear in its effect as a result of the operation of any provision of sections 2 to 6 or Schedule 1,]
(f) does not contain any functions or restrictions which—

(i) were in an EU directive and in force immediately before [IP completion day] (including any power to make EU tertiary legislation), and

(ii) it is appropriate to retain, or

(g) contains EU references which are no longer appropriate.

(3) There is also a deficiency in retained EU law where the Minister considers that there is—

(a) anything in retained EU law which is of a similar kind to any deficiency which falls within subsection (2), or

(b) a deficiency in retained EU law of a kind described, or provided for, in regulations made by a Minister of the Crown.

(4) But retained EU law is not deficient merely because it does not contain any modification of EU law which is adopted or notified, comes into force or only applies on or after [IP completion day].

(5) Regulations under subsection (1) may make any provision that could be made by an Act of Parliament.

(6) Regulations under subsection (1) may (among other things) provide for functions of EU entities or public authorities in member States (including making an instrument of a legislative character or providing funding) to be—

(a) exercisable instead by a public authority (whether or not established for the purpose) in the United Kingdom, or

(b) replaced, abolished or otherwise modified.

(7) But regulations under subsection (1) may not—

(a) impose or increase taxation or fees,

(b) make retrospective provision,

(c) create a relevant criminal offence,

(d) establish a public authority,

(e) . . .

(f) amend, repeal or revoke the Human Rights Act 1998 or any subordinate legislation made under it, or

(g) amend or repeal the Scotland Act 1998, the Government of Wales Act 2006 or the Northern Ireland Act 1998 (unless the regulations are made by virtue of paragraph 21(b) of Schedule 7 to this Act or are amending or repealing any provision of those Acts which modifies another enactment).

(8) No regulations may be made under this section after the end of the period of two years beginning with [IP completion day].

(9) The reference in subsection (1) to a failure or other deficiency arising from the withdrawal of the United Kingdom from the EU includes a reference to any failure or other deficiency arising from[—

(a) any aspect of that withdrawal, including (among other things)—

(i) the end of the implementation period, or

(ii) any other effect of the withdrawal agreement, or

(b) that withdrawal, or any such aspect of it, taken together] with the operation of any provision, or the interaction between any provisions, made by or under this Act [or the European Union (Withdrawal Agreement) Act 2020].

NOTES

Commencement: 26 June 2018.

All amendments to this section were made by the European Union (Withdrawal Agreement) Act 2020, s 27(1).

Regulations: the Competition (Amendment etc) (EU Exit) Regulations 2019, SI 2019/93 at **[7.61]**; the Competition (Amendment etc) (EU Exit) Regulations 2020, SI 2020/1343; the State Aid (Revocations and Amendments) (EU Exit) Regulations 2020, SI 2020/1470 at **[7.79]**. Note that only Regulations relevant to this Handbook are listed; the numerous other Regulations made under this section are considered outside the scope of this work. See also the note below.

Note that the Competition (Amendment etc) (EU Exit) (No 2) Regulations 2019, SI 2019/1245 were made under this section on 9 September 2019. They were made under the urgent made affirmative procedure of this Act (see Sch 7, para 5 *post*) and sought to address a potential enforcement gap that could arise in the circumstances of a no-deal exit, in respect of merger and antitrust commitments provided to the European Commission insofar as they relate to the UK. However, the Regulations were subsequently found to contain drafting errors and, as a result, the government decided not to bring them forward for debate by Parliament within the required 28 days for their approval by the House. Consequently, the Regulations have ceased to have effect.

[7.15]

[8A Supplementary power in connection with implementation period

(1) A Minister of the Crown may by regulations—

(a) provide for other modifications for the purposes of section 1B(3)(f)(i) (whether applying in all cases or particular cases or descriptions of case),

(b) provide for subsection (3) or (4) of section 1B not to apply to any extent in particular cases or descriptions of case,

(c) make different provision in particular cases or descriptions of case to that made by subsection (3) or (4) of that section,

(d) modify any enactment contained in this Act in consequence of any repeal made by section 1A(5) or 1B(6), or

(e) make such provision not falling within paragraph (a), (b), (c) or (d) as the Minister considers appropriate for any purpose of, or otherwise in connection with, Part 4 of the withdrawal agreement.

(2) The power to make regulations under subsection (1) may (among other things) be exercised by modifying any provision made by or under an enactment.

(3) In subsection (2) "enactment" does not include primary legislation passed or made after IP completion day.

(4) No regulations may be made under subsection (1) after the end of the period of two years beginning with IP completion day.]

NOTES

Commencement: 23 January 2020.

Inserted by the European Union (Withdrawal Agreement) Act 2020, s 3.

[7.16]

[8B Power in connection with certain other separation issues

(1) A Minister of the Crown may by regulations make such provision as the Minister considers appropriate—

(a) to implement Part 3 of the withdrawal agreement (separation provisions),

(b) to supplement the effect of section 7A in relation to that Part, or

(c) otherwise for the purposes of dealing with matters arising out of, or related to, that Part (including matters arising by virtue of section 7A and that Part).

(2) A Minister of the Crown may by regulations make such provision as the Minister considers appropriate—

(a) to implement Part 3 of the EEA EFTA separation agreement (separation provisions),

(b) to supplement the effect of section 7B in relation to that Part, or

(c) otherwise for the purposes of dealing with matters arising out of, or related to, that Part (including matters arising by virtue of section 7B and that Part).

(3) Regulations under this section may make any provision that could be made by an Act of Parliament.

(4) Regulations under this section may (among other things) restate, for the purposes of making the law clearer or more accessible, anything that forms part of domestic law by virtue of—

(a) section 7A above and Part 3 of the withdrawal agreement, or

(b) section 7B above and Part 3 of the EEA EFTA separation agreement.

(5) But regulations under this section may not—

(a) impose or increase taxation or fees,

(b) make retrospective provision,

(c) create a relevant criminal offence,

(d) establish a public authority,

(e) amend, repeal or revoke the Human Rights Act 1998 or any subordinate legislation made under it, or

(f) amend or repeal the Scotland Act 1998, the Government of Wales Act 2006 or the Northern Ireland Act 1998 (unless the regulations are made by virtue of paragraph 21(b) of Schedule 7 to this Act or are amending or repealing any provision of those Acts which modifies another enactment).

(6) In this section references to Part 3 of the withdrawal agreement or of the EEA EFTA separation agreement include references to any provision of EU law which is applied by, or referred to in, that Part (to the extent of the application or reference).]

NOTES

Commencement: 19 May 2020.

Inserted by the European Union (Withdrawal Agreement) Act 2020, s 18.

Regulations: the Insolvency (Amendment) (EU Exit) Regulations 2020, SI 2020/647.

[7.17]

[8C Power in connection with Ireland/Northern Ireland Protocol in withdrawal agreement

(1) A Minister of the Crown may by regulations make such provision as the Minister considers appropriate—

(a) to implement the Protocol on Ireland/Northern Ireland in the withdrawal agreement,

(b) to supplement the effect of section 7A in relation to the Protocol, or

(c) otherwise for the purposes of dealing with matters arising out of, or related to, the Protocol (including matters arising by virtue of section 7A and the Protocol).

(2) Regulations under subsection (1) may make any provision that could be made by an Act of Parliament (including modifying this Act).

(3) Regulations under subsection (1) may (among other things) make provision facilitating the access to the market within Great Britain of qualifying Northern Ireland goods.

(4) Such provision may (among other things) include provision about the recognition within Great Britain of technical regulations, assessments, registrations, certificates, approvals and authorisations issued by—

(a) the authorities of a member State, or

(b) bodies established in a member State,

in respect of qualifying Northern Ireland goods.

(5) Regulations under subsection (1) may (among other things) restate, for the purposes of making the law clearer or more accessible, anything that forms part of domestic law by virtue of section 7A and the Protocol.

[(5A) Regulations under subsection (1) may not amend, repeal or otherwise modify the operation of section 47 of the United Kingdom Internal Market Act 2020 ("the 2020 Act"), except by making—

(a) provision of the sort that is contemplated by section 47(2) of the 2020 Act (permitted checks);

(b) provision under subsection (6);

(c) provision of the sort described in paragraph 21(b) of Schedule 7 (supplementary and transitional provision etc) in connection with—

(i) provision within either of the preceding paragraphs;

(ii) Articles 5 to 10 of the Northern Ireland Protocol ceasing to apply (and the resulting operation of section 55(1) of the 2020 Act).]

(6) A Minister of the Crown may by regulations define "qualifying Northern Ireland goods" for the purposes of this Act.

(7) In this section any reference to the Protocol on Ireland/Northern Ireland includes a reference to—

(a) any other provision of the withdrawal agreement so far as applying to the Protocol, and

(b) any provision of EU law which is applied by, or referred to in, the Protocol (to the extent of the application or reference),

but does not include the second sentence of Article 11(1) of the Protocol (which provides that the United Kingdom and the Republic of Ireland may continue to make new arrangements that build on the provisions of the Belfast Agreement in other areas of North-South cooperation on the island of Ireland).]

NOTES

Commencement: 19 May 2020.

Inserted by the European Union (Withdrawal Agreement) Act 2020, s 21.

Sub-s (5A): inserted by the United Kingdom Internal Market Act 2020, s 55(3), as from IP completion day (as defined in the European Union (Withdrawal Agreement) Act 2020, s 39). See also s 55(1) of that Act which provides that this subsection ceases to have effect when Articles 5 to 10 of the Northern Ireland Protocol cease to apply.

Regulations: the State Aid (Revocations and Amendments) (EU Exit) Regulations 2020, SI 2020/1470 at **[7.79]**. Other Regulations made under this section are considered to be outside the scope of this work.

9 (*Repealed by the European Union (Withdrawal Agreement) Act 2020, s 36.*)

Devolution

[7.18]

10 [Protection for] North-South co-operation and . . . prevention of new border arrangements

(1) In exercising any of the powers under this Act, a Minister of the Crown or devolved authority must—

(a) act in a way that is compatible with the terms of the Northern Ireland Act 1998, and

(b) have due regard to the joint report from the negotiators of the EU and the United Kingdom Government on progress during phase 1 of negotiations under Article 50 of the Treaty on European Union.

(2) Nothing in section 8 . . . or 23(1) or (6) of this Act authorises regulations which—

(a) diminish any form of North-South cooperation provided for by the Belfast Agreement . . . , or

(b) create or facilitate border arrangements between Northern Ireland and the Republic of Ireland after exit day which feature physical infrastructure, including border posts, or checks and controls, that did not exist before exit day and are not in accordance with an agreement between the United Kingdom and the EU.

[(3) A Minister of the Crown may not agree to the making of a recommendation by the Joint Committee under Article 11(2) of the Protocol on Ireland/Northern Ireland in the withdrawal agreement (recommendations as to North-South cooperation) to—

(a) alter the arrangements for North-South co-operation as provided for by the Belfast Agreement,

(b) establish a new implementation body, or

(c) alter the functions of an existing implementation body.

(4) In this section—

"the Belfast Agreement" has the meaning given by section 98 of the Northern Ireland Act 1998;

"implementation body" has the meaning given by section 55(3) of that Act.]

NOTES

Commencement: 26 June 2018.

Section heading: words in square brackets substituted, and word omitted repealed, by the European Union (Withdrawal Agreement) Act 2020, s 41(4), Sch 5, Pt 2, paras 38, 41(1), (2), as from IP completion day (as defined in the European Union (Withdrawal Agreement) Act 2020, s 39).

Sub-s (2) is amended as follows:

Figure omitted repealed by the European Union (Withdrawal Agreement) Act 2020, s 41(4), Sch 5, Pt 2, paras 38, 41(1), (3)(a).

Words omitted from para (a) repealed by the European Union (Withdrawal Agreement) Act 2020, s 41(4), Sch 5, Pt 2, paras 38, 41(1), (3)(b), as from IP completion day (as defined in the European Union (Withdrawal Agreement) Act 2020, s 39).

Sub-ss (3), (4): added by the European Union (Withdrawal Agreement) Act 2020, s 24, as from IP completion day (as defined in the European Union (Withdrawal Agreement) Act 2020, s 39).

[7.19]

11 Powers involving devolved authorities corresponding to sections 8 [to 8C]

Schedule 2 (which confers powers to make regulations involving devolved authorities which correspond to the powers conferred by sections 8 [to 8C] has effect.

NOTES

Commencement: 26 June 2018.

Words in square brackets substituted by the European Union (Withdrawal Agreement) Act 2020, s 41(4), Sch 5, Pt 2, paras 38, 42.

[7.20]

12 Retaining EU restrictions in devolution legislation etc

(1)–(6) (*Amend the Scotland Act 1998, the Government of Wales Act 2006, and the Northern Ireland Act 1998.*)

(7) Part 1 of Schedule 3 (which makes corresponding provision in relation to executive competence to that made by subsections (1) to (6) in relation to legislative competence) has effect.

(8) Part 2 of Schedule 3 (which imposes reporting obligations on a Minister of the Crown in recognition of the fact that the powers to make regulations conferred by subsections (1) to (6) and Part 1 of Schedule 3, and any restrictions arising by virtue of them, are intended to be temporary) has effect.

(9) A Minister of the Crown may by regulations—

(a) repeal any of the following provisions—

(i) section 30A or 57(4) to (15) of the Scotland Act 1998,

(ii) section 80(8) to (8L) or 109A of the Government of Wales Act 2006, or

(iii) section 6A or 24(3) to (15) of the Northern Ireland Act 1998, or

(b) modify any enactment in consequence of any such repeal.

(10) Until all of the provisions mentioned in subsection (9)(a) have been repealed, a Minister of the Crown must, after the end of each review period, consider whether it is appropriate—

(a) to repeal each of those provisions so far as it has not been repealed, or

(b) to revoke any regulations made under any of those provisions so far as they have not been revoked.

(11) In considering whether to exercise the power to make regulations under subsection (9), a Minister of the Crown must have regard (among other things) to—

(a) the fact that the powers to make regulations conferred by the provisions mentioned in subsection (9)(a), and any restrictions arising by virtue of them, are intended to be temporary and, where appropriate, replaced with other arrangements, and

(b) any progress which has been made in implementing those other arrangements.

(12) Part 3 of Schedule 3 (which contains amendments of devolution legislation not dealt with elsewhere) has effect.

(13) In this section—

"arrangement" means any enactment or other arrangement (whether or not legally enforceable);

"review period" means—

(a) the period of three months beginning with the day on which subsection (10) comes into force, and

(b) after that, each successive period of three months.

NOTES

Commencement: this section has been brought into force as follows:
Sub-s (2): 26 June 2018 (for the purposes of making regulations under the Scotland Act 1998, s 30A).
Sub-s (4): 26 June 2018 (for the purposes of making regulations under the Government of Wales Act 2006, s 109A).
Sub-s (6): 26 June 2018 (for the purposes of making regulations under the Northern Ireland Act 1998, s 6A).
Sub-ss (7), (8), (12): 26 June 2018 (certain purposes).
Sub-ss (9)–(11), (13): 4 July 2018.
IP completion day (as defined in the European Union (Withdrawal Agreement) Act 2020, s 39) for all other purposes.

Parliamentary [oversight of withdrawal]

NOTES

Words in square brackets in the heading above substituted by the European Union (Withdrawal Agreement) Act 2020, s 41(4), Sch 5, Pt 2, paras 38, 43.

13 *(S 13 (Parliamentary approval of the outcome of negotiations with the EU) repealed by the European Union (Withdrawal Agreement) Act 2020, s 31(1). S 31(2) further provides that accordingly, none of the conditions set out in paras (a)–(d) of sub-s (1) of s 13 apply in relation to the ratification of the withdrawal agreement.)*

[7.21]

[13A Review of EU legislation during implementation period

(1) Subsection (2) applies where the European Scrutiny Select Committee of the House of Commons ("the ESC") publishes a report in respect of any EU legislation made, or which may be made, during the implementation period and the report—

(a) states that, in the opinion of the ESC, the EU legislation raises a matter of vital national interest to the United Kingdom,

(b) confirms that the ESC has taken such evidence as it considers appropriate as to the effect of the EU legislation and has consulted any Departmental Select Committee of the House of Commons which the ESC considers also has an interest in the EU legislation, and

(c) sets out the wording of a motion to be moved in the House of Commons in accordance with subsection (2).

(2) A Minister of the Crown must, within the period of 14 Commons sitting days beginning with the day on which the report is published, make arrangements for the motion mentioned in subsection (1)(c) to be debated and voted on by the House of Commons.

(3) Subsection (4) applies where the EU Select Committee of the House of Lords ("the EUC") publishes a report in respect of any EU legislation made, or which may be made, during the implementation period and the report—

(a) states that, in the opinion of the EUC, the EU legislation raises a matter of vital national interest to the United Kingdom,

(b) confirms that the EUC has taken such evidence as it considers appropriate as to the effect of the EU legislation, and

(c) sets out the wording of a motion to be moved in the House of Lords in accordance with subsection (4).

(4) A Minister of the Crown must, within the period of 14 Lords sitting days beginning with the day on which the report is published, make arrangements for the motion mentioned in subsection (3)(c) to be debated and voted on by the House of Lords.

(5) In this section—

"EU legislation" means—

(a) any amendment to the Treaty on European Union, the Treaty on the Functioning of the European Union, the Euratom Treaty or the EEA agreement,

(b) any EU directive, or

(c) any EU regulation or EU decision which is not EU tertiary legislation;

"the European Scrutiny Select Committee of the House of Commons" means the Select Committee of the House of Commons known as the European Scrutiny Select Committee or any successor of that committee;

"the EU Select Committee of the House of Lords" means the Select Committee of the House of Lords known as the EU Select Committee or any successor of that committee.]

NOTES

Commencement: 23 January 2020.
Inserted by the European Union (Withdrawal Agreement) Act 2020, s 29.

[7.22]

[13B Certain dispute procedures under withdrawal agreement

(1) Subsection (2) applies if a request has been made under Article 170 of the withdrawal agreement to the other party in a dispute (request to establish an arbitration panel in relation to a dispute between the EU and the United Kingdom).

(2) A Minister of the Crown must, within the 14 day period beginning with the day on which the request is made, make a statement in writing to each House of Parliament that the request has been made and setting out the details of it.

(3) Subsection (4) applies if the European Court has given a ruling in response to a request by an arbitration panel under Article 174(1) of the withdrawal agreement (request for ruling by European Court on certain questions arising in a dispute submitted to arbitration).

(4) A Minister of the Crown must, within the 14 day period beginning with the publication in the Official Journal of the European Union of the ruling of the European Court, make a statement in writing to each House of Parliament that the ruling has been made and setting out the details of it contained in the Official Journal.

(5) After the end of each reporting period, a Minister of the Crown must lay before each House of Parliament a report setting out the number of times within the reporting period that the Joint Committee has been provided with notice under Article 169(1) of the withdrawal agreement (notice concerning the commencement of consultations in the Joint Committee to resolve a dispute between the EU and the United Kingdom about the interpretation and application of the withdrawal agreement).

(6) In this section—

"reporting period" means—

(a) the period of one year beginning with the day on which IP completion day falls, and

(b) each subsequent year;

"the 14 day period" means—

(a) in relation to the House of Commons, the period of 14 Commons sitting days, and

(b) in relation to the House of Lords, the period of 14 Lords sitting days.]

NOTES

Commencement: IP completion day (as defined in the European Union (Withdrawal Agreement) Act 2020, s 39).

Inserted by the European Union (Withdrawal Agreement) Act 2020, s 30, as from IP completion day (as defined in the European Union (Withdrawal Agreement) Act 2020, s 39).

Financial and other matters

[7.23]

14 Financial provision

(1) Schedule 4 (which contains powers in connection with fees and charges) has effect.

(2) A Minister of the Crown, government department or devolved authority may incur expenditure, for the purpose of, or in connection with, preparing for anything about which provision may be made under a power to make subordinate legislation conferred or modified by or under this Act, before any such provision is made.

(3) There is to be paid out of money provided by Parliament—

(a) any expenditure incurred by a Minister of the Crown, government department or other public authority by virtue of this Act, and

(b) any increase attributable to this Act in the sums payable by virtue of any other Act out of money so provided.

(4) Subsection (3) is subject to any other provision made by or under this Act or any other enactment.

NOTES

Commencement: 26 June 2018.

[7.24]

15 Publication and rules of evidence

(1) Part 1 of Schedule 5 (which makes provision for the publication by the Queen's Printer of copies of retained direct EU legislation and related information) has effect.

(2) Part 2 of Schedule 5 (which makes provision about rules of evidence) has effect.

NOTES

Commencement: this section has been brought into force as follows:

Sub-s (1): 4 July 2018 (in so far as relating to Sch 5, para 2); 3 July 2019 (in so far as relating to Sch 5, para 1).

Sub-s (2): 4 July 2018 (in so far as relating to Sch 5, para 4); IP completion day (as defined in the European Union (Withdrawal Agreement) Act 2020, s 39) (otherwise).

[7.25]

[15A Prohibition on extending implementation period

A Minister of the Crown may not agree in the Joint Committee to an extension of the implementation period.]

NOTES

Commencement: 23 January 2020.

Inserted by the European Union (Withdrawal Agreement) Act 2020, s 33.

[7.26]

[15B Ministerial co-chairs of the Joint Committee

The functions of the United Kingdom's co-chair of the Joint Committee, under Annex VIII of the withdrawal agreement (rules of procedure of the Joint Committee and specialised committees), are to be exercised personally by a Minister of the Crown (and, accordingly, only a Minister of the Crown may be designated as a replacement under Rule 1(3)).]

NOTES

Commencement: 23 January 2020.

Inserted by the European Union (Withdrawal Agreement) Act 2020, s 34.

[7.27]

[15C No use of written procedure in the Joint Committee

(1) The United Kingdom's co-chair of the Joint Committee may not consent to the Joint Committee using the written procedure provided for in Rule 9(1) of Annex VIII of the withdrawal agreement.

(2) In subsection (1) the reference to the United Kingdom's co-chair of the Joint Committee includes a reference to any designee of the co-chair designated under Rule 1(3) of Annex VIII of the withdrawal agreement.]

NOTES

Commencement: 23 January 2020.

Inserted by the European Union (Withdrawal Agreement) Act 2020, s 35.

16–19 *(Ss 16, 18, 19 repealed by the European Union (Withdrawal Agreement) Act 2020, s 36. S 17 (Family unity for those seeking asylum or other protection in Europe) outside the scope of this work)*

General and final provision

[7.28]

20 Interpretation

(1) In this Act—

"Charter of Fundamental Rights" means the Charter of Fundamental Rights of the European Union of 7 December 2000, as adapted at Strasbourg on 12 December 2007;

["Commons sitting day" means a day on which the House of Commons is sitting (and a day is only a day on which the House of Commons is sitting if the House begins to sit on that day);"]

"devolved authority" means—

(a) the Scottish Ministers,

(b) the Welsh Ministers, or

(c) a Northern Ireland department;

"domestic law" means—

(a) in [sections 3, 7A and 7B], the law of England and Wales, Scotland and Northern Ireland, and

(b) in any other case, the law of England and Wales, Scotland or Northern Ireland;

"the EEA" means the European Economic Area;

"enactment" means an enactment whenever passed or made and includes—

(a) an enactment contained in any Order in Council, order, rules, regulations, scheme, warrant, byelaw or other instrument made under an Act,

(b) an enactment contained in any Order in Council made in exercise of Her Majesty's Prerogative,

(c) an enactment contained in, or in an instrument made under, an Act of the Scottish Parliament,

(d) an enactment contained in, or in an instrument made under, a Measure or Act of the National Assembly for Wales,

(e) an enactment contained in, or in an instrument made under, Northern Ireland legislation,

(f) an enactment contained in any instrument made by a member of the Scottish Government, the Welsh Ministers, the First Minister for Wales, the Counsel General to the Welsh Government, a Northern Ireland Minister, the First Minister in Northern Ireland, the deputy First Minister in Northern Ireland or a Northern Ireland department in exercise of prerogative or other executive functions of Her Majesty which are exercisable by such a person on behalf of Her Majesty,

(g) an enactment contained in, or in an instrument made under, a Measure of the Church Assembly or of the General Synod of the Church of England, and

(h) except in sections [1B] and 7 or where there is otherwise a contrary intention, any retained direct EU legislation;

"EU decision" means—

(a) a decision within the meaning of Article 288 of the Treaty on the Functioning of the European Union, or

(b) a decision under former Article 34(2)(c) of the Treaty on European Union;

"EU directive" means a directive within the meaning of Article 288 of the Treaty on the Functioning of the European Union;

"EU entity" means an EU institution or any office, body or agency of the EU;

"EU reference" means—

(a) any reference to the EU, an EU entity or a member State,

(b) any reference to an EU directive or any other EU law, or

(c) any other reference which relates to the EU;

"EU regulation" means a regulation within the meaning of Article 288 of the Treaty on the Functioning of the European Union;

"EU tertiary legislation" means—

(a) any provision made under—

(i) an EU regulation,

(ii) a decision within the meaning of Article 288 of the Treaty on the Functioning of the European Union, or

(iii) an EU directive,

by virtue of Article 290 or 291(2) of the Treaty on the Functioning of the European Union or former Article 202 of the Treaty establishing the European Community, or

(b) any measure adopted in accordance with former Article 34(2)(c) of the Treaty on European Union to implement decisions under former Article 34(2)(c),

but does not include any such provision or measure which is an EU directive;

"exempt EU instrument" means anything which is an exempt EU instrument by virtue of Schedule 6;

"exit day" [means [31 January 2020] at 11.00 pm (and] see subsections (2) to (5));

["future relationship agreement" has the same meaning as in the European Union (Future Relationship) Act 2020 (see section 37 of that Act);]

["Joint Committee" means the Joint Committee established by Article 164(1) of the withdrawal agreement;]

["Lords sitting day" means a day on which the House of Lords is sitting (and a day is only a day on which the House of Lords is sitting if the House begins to sit on that day);]

"member State" (except in the definitions of "direct EU legislation" and "EU reference") does not include the United Kingdom;

"Minister of the Crown" has the same meaning as in the Ministers of the Crown Act 1975 and also includes the Commissioners for Her Majesty's Revenue and Customs;

"modify" includes amend, repeal or revoke (and related expressions are to be read accordingly);

"Northern Ireland devolved authority" means the First Minister and deputy First Minister in Northern Ireland acting jointly, a Northern Ireland Minister or a Northern Ireland department;

"primary legislation" means—

(a) an Act of Parliament,

(b) an Act of the Scottish Parliament,

(c) a Measure or Act of the National Assembly for Wales, or

(d) Northern Ireland legislation;

"public authority" means a public authority within the meaning of section 6 of the Human Rights Act 1998;

["ratify", whether in relation to the withdrawal agreement or otherwise, has the same meaning as it does for the purposes of Part 2 of the Constitutional Reform and Governance Act 2010 in relation to a treaty (see section 25 of that Act);]

"relevant criminal offence" means an offence for which an individual who has reached the age of 18 (or, in relation to Scotland or Northern Ireland, 21) is capable of being sentenced to imprisonment for a term of more than 2 years (ignoring any enactment prohibiting or restricting the imprisonment of individuals who have no previous convictions);

"retained direct EU legislation" means any direct EU legislation which forms part of domestic law by virtue of section 3 (as modified by or under this Act or by other domestic law from time to time, and including any instruments made under it on or after [IP completion day]);

"retrospective provision", in relation to provision made by regulations, means provision taking effect from a date earlier than the date on which the regulations are made;

"subordinate legislation" means—

(a) any Order in Council, order, rules, regulations, scheme, warrant, byelaw or other instrument made under any Act, or

(b) any instrument made under an Act of the Scottish Parliament, Northern Ireland legislation or a Measure or Act of the National Assembly for Wales,

and (except in section 7 or Schedule 2 or where there is a contrary intention) includes any Order in Council, order, rules, regulations, scheme, warrant, byelaw or other instrument made on or after [IP completion day] under any retained direct EU legislation;

"tribunal" means any tribunal in which legal proceedings may be brought;

"Wales" and "Welsh zone" have the same meaning as in the Government of Wales Act 2006 (see section 158 of that Act);

. . .

(2) In this [Act references to before, after or on exit day, or to beginning with exit day, are to be read as references to before, after or at 11.00 pm on [31 January 2020] or (as the case may be) to beginning with 11.00 pm on that day].

(3) Subsection (4) applies if the day or time on or at which the Treaties are to cease to apply to the United Kingdom in accordance with Article 50(3) of the Treaty on European Union is different from that specified in the definition of "exit day" in subsection (1).

(4) A Minister of the Crown [must] by regulations—

(a) amend the definition of "exit day" in subsection (1) to ensure that the day and time specified in the definition are the day and time that the Treaties are to cease to apply to the United Kingdom, and

(b) amend subsection (2) in consequence of any such amendment.

(5) In subsections (3) and (4) "the Treaties" means the Treaty on European Union and the Treaty on the Functioning of the European Union.

[(5A) In this Act references to anything which continues to be domestic law by virtue of section 1B(2) include—

(a) references to anything to which section 1B(2) applies which continues to be domestic law on or after exit day (whether or not it would have done so irrespective of that provision), and

(b) references to anything which continues to be domestic law on or after exit day by virtue of section 1B(2) (as that body of law is added to or otherwise modified by or under this Act or by other domestic law from time to time).]

(6) In this Act references to anything which continues to be domestic law by virtue of section 2 include references to anything to which subsection (1) of that section applies which continues to be domestic law on or after [IP completion day] (whether or not it would have done so irrespective of that section).

(7) In this Act references to anything which is retained EU law by virtue of section 4 include references to any modifications, made by or under this Act or by other domestic law from time to time, of the rights, powers, liabilities, obligations, restrictions, remedies or procedures concerned.

(8) References in this Act (however expressed) to a public authority in the United Kingdom include references to a public authority in any part of the United Kingdom.

(9) References in this Act to former Article 34(2)(c) of the Treaty on European Union are references to that Article as it had effect at any time before the coming into force of the Treaty of Lisbon.

(10) Any other reference in this Act to—

(a) an Article of the Treaty on European Union or the Treaty on the Functioning of the European Union, or

(b) Article 10 of Title VII of Protocol 36 to those treaties,

includes a reference to that Article as applied by Article 106a of the Euratom Treaty.

NOTES

Commencement: 26 June 2018.

Sub-s (1) is amended as follows:

Definition "Commons sitting day" inserted by the European Union (Withdrawal Agreement) Act 2020, s 41(4), Sch 5, Pt 2, paras 38, 44(1), (2)(a).

Words in square brackets in the definition "domestic law" substituted by the European Union (Withdrawal Agreement) Act 2020, s 41(4), Sch 5, Pt 2, paras 38, 44(1), (2)(b).

Figure in square brackets in para (h) of the definition "enactment" substituted by the European Union (Withdrawal Agreement) Act 2020, s 41(4), Sch 5, Pt 2, paras 38, 44(1), (2)(c).

Words in first (outer) pair of square brackets in the definition "exit day" substituted by the European Union (Withdrawal) Act 2018 (Exit Day) (Amendment) (No 2) Regulations 2019, SI 2019/859, reg 2(1), (2). Words "31 January 2020" in square brackets substituted by the European Union (Withdrawal) Act 2018 (Exit Day) (Amendment) (No 3) Regulations 2019, SI 2019/1423, reg 2(1), (2).

Definition "future relationship agreement" inserted by the European Union (Future Relationship) Act 2020, s 39(3), (5), Sch 6, Pt 1, para 6, as from IP completion day (as defined in the European Union (Withdrawal Agreement) Act 2020, s 39).

Definitions "Joint Committee", "Lords sitting day" and "ratify" inserted by the European Union (Withdrawal Agreement) Act 2020, s 41(4), Sch 5, Pt 2, paras 38, 44(1), (2)(d), (e).

Words in square brackets in the definitions "retained direct EU legislation" and "subordinate legislation" substituted by the European Union (Withdrawal Agreement) Act 2020, s 41(4), Sch 5, Pt 2, paras 38, 44(1), (2)(f), (g).

Definition "withdrawal agreement" (omitted) repealed by the European Union (Withdrawal Agreement) Act 2020, s 41(4), Sch 5, Pt 2, paras 38, 44(1), (2)(h).

Sub-s (2): words first (outer) pair of in square brackets substituted by SI 2019/859, reg 2(1), (3). Words "31 January 2020" in square brackets substituted by SI 2019/1423, reg 2(1), (3).

Sub-s (4): word in square brackets substituted the European Union (Withdrawal) (No 2) Act 2019, s 4(1).

Sub-s (5A): inserted by the European Union (Withdrawal Agreement) Act 2020, s 41(4), Sch 5, Pt 2, paras 38, 44(1), (3).

Sub-s (6): words in square brackets substituted by the European Union (Withdrawal Agreement) Act 2020, s 41(4), Sch 5, Pt 2, paras 38, 44(1), (4).

National Assembly for Wales: see further, in relation to the renaming of the National Assembly for Wales as the Senedd Cymru or the Welsh Parliament, the Senedd and Elections (Wales) Act 2020, s 2 (with effect from 6 May 2020). See also ss 3–9 of the 2020 Act in relation to the renaming of Acts of the National Assembly for Wales, Members of the National Assembly for Wales, etc.

Regulations: the European Union (Withdrawal) Act 2018 (Exit Day) (Amendment) Regulations 2019, SI 2019/718; the European Union (Withdrawal) Act 2018 (Exit Day) (Amendment) (No 2) Regulations 2019, SI 2019/859; the European Union (Withdrawal) Act 2018 (Exit Day) (Amendment) (No 3) Regulations 2019, SI 2019/1423. Note that the amendments made by the European Union (Withdrawal) Act 2018 (Exit Day) (Amendment) (No 2) Regulations 2019 supersede the amendments made by the European Union (Withdrawal) Act 2018 (Exit Day) (Amendment) Regulations 2019, SI 2019/718.

[7.29]

21 Index of defined expressions

(1) In this Act, the expressions listed in the left-hand column have the meaning given by, or are to be interpreted in accordance with, the provisions listed in the right-hand column.

Expression	*Provision*
[Anything which continues to be domestic law by virtue of section 1B(2)	Section 20(5A)]
Anything which continues to be domestic law by virtue of section 2	Section 20(6)
Anything which is retained EU law by virtue of section 4	Section 20(7)
Article (in relation to the Treaty on European Union or the Treaty on the Functioning of the European Union)	Section 20(10)
Charter of Fundamental Rights	Section 20(1)
[Commons sitting day	Section 20(1)]
Devolved authority	Section 20(1)
Direct EU legislation	Section 3(2)
Domestic law	Section 20(1)
The EEA	Section 20(1)
EEA agreement	Schedule 1 to the Interpretation Act 1978
[EEA EFTA separation agreement	Section 7B(6)]
Enactment	Section 20(1)
The EU	Schedule 1 to the Interpretation Act 1978
EU decision	Section 20(1)
[EU-derived domestic legislation	Section 1B(7)]

Expression	*Provision*
EU directive	Section 20(1)
EU entity	Section 20(1)
EU institution	Schedule 1 to the Interpretation Act 1978
EU instrument	Schedule 1 to the Interpretation Act 1978
Euratom Treaty	Schedule 1 to the Interpretation Act 1978
EU reference	Section 20(1)
EU regulation	Section 20(1)
[European Communities Act 1972	Section 1A(7)(a)]
European Court	Schedule 1 to the Interpretation Act 1978
EU tertiary legislation	Section 20(1)
EU Treaties	Schedule 1 to the Interpretation Act 1978
Exempt EU instrument	Section 20(1)
Exit day (and related expressions)	Section 20(1) to (5)
Former Article 34(2)(c) of Treaty on European Union	Section 20(9)
[Future relationship agreement	Section 20(1)]
[Implementation period	Section 1A(6)]
[IP completion day (and related expressions)	Section 1A(6)]
[Joint Committee	Section 20(1)]
[Lords sitting day	Section 20(1)]
Member State	Section 20(1) and Schedule 1 to the Interpretation Act 1978
Minister of the Crown	Section 20(1)
Modify (and related expressions)	Section 20(1)
Northern Ireland devolved authority	Section 20(1)
Operative (in relation to direct EU legislation)	Section 3(3)
[Part (of withdrawal agreement or EEA EFTA separation agreement)	Section 1A(7)(b)]
Primary legislation	Section 20(1)
Public authority	Section 20(1)
Public authority in the United Kingdom (however expressed)	Section 20(8)
[Qualifying Northern Ireland goods	Section 8C(6)]
[Ratify	Section 20(1)]
Relevant criminal offence	Section 20(1) (and paragraph 44 of Schedule 8)
[Relevant separation agreement law	Section 7C(3)]
Retained case law	Section 6(7)
Retained direct EU legislation	Section 20(1)
Retained direct minor EU legislation	Section 7(6)
Retained direct principal EU legislation	Section 7(6)
Retained domestic case law	Section 6(7)
Retained EU case law	Section 6(7)
Retained EU law	Section 6(7)
Retained general principles of EU law	Section 6(7)
Retrospective provision	Section 20(1)
Subordinate legislation	Section 20(1)
[Swiss citizens' rights agreement	Section 7B(6)]
Tribunal	Section 20(1)
Wales	Section 20(1)
Welsh zone	Section 20(1)
Withdrawal agreement	[Section 1A(6)]

(2) See paragraph 22 of Schedule 8 for amendments made by this Act to Schedule 1 to the Interpretation Act 1978.

NOTES

Commencement: 26 June 2018.

Part 7 Brexit-related Materials

Entry "Future relationship agreement" inserted by the European Union (Future Relationship) Act 2020, s 39(3), (5), Sch 6, Pt 1, para 7, as from IP completion day (as defined in the European Union (Withdrawal Agreement) Act 2020, s 39).

All other amendments to this section were made by the European Union (Withdrawal Agreement) Act 2020, s 41(4), Sch 5, Pt 2, paras 38, 45.

[7.30]

22 Regulations

Schedule 7 (which makes provision about the scrutiny by Parliament and the devolved legislatures of regulations under this Act and contains other general provision about such regulations) has effect.

NOTES

Commencement: 26 June 2018.

[7.31]

23 Consequential and transitional provision

(1) A Minister of the Crown may by regulations make such provision as the Minister considers appropriate in consequence of this Act.

(2) The power to make regulations under subsection (1) may (among other things) be exercised by modifying any provision made by or under an enactment.

(3) In subsection (2) "enactment" does not include primary legislation passed or made after [IP completion day].

(4) No regulations may be made under subsection (1) after the end of the period of 10 years beginning with [IP completion day].

(5) Parts 1 and 2 of Schedule 8 (which contain consequential provision) have effect.

(6) A Minister of the Crown may by regulations make such transitional, transitory or saving provision as the Minister considers appropriate in connection with the coming into force of any provision of this Act (including its operation in connection with exit day [or IP completion day]).

(7) Parts 3 and 4 of Schedule 8 (which contain transitional, transitory and saving provision) have effect.

(8) The enactments mentioned in Schedule 9 (which contains repeals not made elsewhere in this Act) are repealed to the extent specified.

NOTES

Commencement: 26 June 2018 (sub-ss (1)–(4), (6), and sub-s (7) for certain purposes); 4 July 2018 (sub-ss (5), (7), (8) for certain purposes); 1 March 2019 (sub-s (7) for certain purposes); exit day (as defined in s 20 of this Act) (sub-s (5) for certain purposes); 31 December 2020 (sub-s (8) for certain purposes); IP completion day (as defined in the European Union (Withdrawal Agreement) Act 2020, s 39) (sub-ss (5), (7), and sub-s (8) for certain purposes); to be appointed (otherwise).

All amendments to this section were made by the European Union (Withdrawal Agreement) Act 2020, s 41(4), Sch 5, Pt 2, paras 38, 46.

Regulations: the European Union (Withdrawal) Act 2018 (Commencement and Transitional Provisions) Regulations 2018, SI 2018/808; the European Communities (Designation Orders) (Revocation) (EU Exit) Regulations 2018, SI 2018/1011; the European Union (Definition of Treaties Orders) (Revocation) (EU Exit) Regulations 2018, SI 2018/1012; the European Union (Withdrawal) Act 2018 (Commencement No 5, Transitional Provisions and Amendment) Regulations 2020, SI 2020/74. Other Regulations made under this section are considered to be outside the scope of this work.

[7.32]

24 Extent

(1) Subject to subsections (2) and (3), this Act extends to England and Wales, Scotland and Northern Ireland.

(2) Any provision of this Act which amends or repeals an enactment has the same extent as the enactment amended or repealed.

(3) Regulations under section 8(1) or 23 may make provision which extends to Gibraltar—

- (a) modifying any enactment which—
  - (i) extends to Gibraltar and relates to European Parliamentary elections, or
  - (ii) extends to Gibraltar for any purpose which is connected with Gibraltar forming part of an electoral region, under the European Parliamentary Elections Act 2002, for the purposes of such elections, or
- (b) which is supplementary, incidental, consequential, transitional, transitory or saving provision in connection with a modification within paragraph (a).

NOTES

Commencement: 26 June 2018.

Regulations: made under this section are considered outside the scope of this work.

[7.33]

25 Commencement and short title

(1) The following provisions—

- (a) sections 8 to 11 (including Schedule 2),
- (b) paragraphs 4, 5, 21(2)(b), 48(b), 51(2)(c) and (d) and (4) of Schedule 3 (and section 12(8) and (12) so far as relating to those paragraphs),
- (c) sections 13 and 14 (including Schedule 4),
- (d) sections 16 to 18,
- (e) sections 20 to 22 (including Schedules 6 and 7),
- (f) section 23(1) to (4) and (6),
- (g) paragraph 41(10), 43 and 44 of Schedule 8 (and section 23(7) so far as relating to those paragraphs),
- (h) section 24, and
- (i) this section,

come into force on the day on which this Act is passed.

(2) In section 12—

(a) subsection (2) comes into force on the day on which this Act is passed for the purposes of making regulations under section 30A of the Scotland Act 1998,

(b) subsection (4) comes into force on that day for the purposes of making regulations under section 109A of the Government of Wales Act 2006, and

(c) subsection (6) comes into force on that day for the purposes of making regulations under section 6A of the Northern Ireland Act 1998.

(3) In Schedule 3—

(a) paragraph 1(b) comes into force on the day on which this Act is passed for the purposes of making regulations under section 57(4) of the Scotland Act 1998,

(b) paragraph 2 comes into force on that day for the purposes of making regulations under section 80(8) of the Government of Wales Act 2006,

(c) paragraph 3(b) comes into force on that day for the purposes of making regulations under section 24(3) of the Northern Ireland Act 1998,

(d) paragraph 24(2) comes into force on that day for the purposes of making regulations under section 30A of the Scotland Act 1998,

(e) paragraph 24(3) comes into force on that day for the purposes of making regulations under section 57(4) of the Scotland Act 1998,

(f) paragraph 25 comes into force on that day for the purposes of making regulations under section 30A or 57(4) of the Scotland Act 1998,

(g) paragraph 43 comes into force on that day for the purposes of making regulations under section 80(8) or 109A of the Government of Wales Act 2006, and

(h) paragraphs 57 and 58 come into force on that day for the purposes of making regulations under section 6A or 24(3) of the Northern Ireland Act 1998;

and section 12(7) and (12), so far as relating to each of those paragraphs, comes into force on that day for the purposes of making the regulations mentioned above in relation to that paragraph.

(4) The provisions of this Act, so far as they are not brought into force by subsections (1) to (3), come into force on such day as a Minister of the Crown may by regulations appoint; and different days may be appointed for different purposes.

(5) This Act may be cited as the European Union (Withdrawal) Act 2018.

NOTES

Commencement: 26 June 2018.

Regulations: the European Union (Withdrawal) Act 2018 (Commencement and Transitional Provisions) Regulations 2018, SI 2018/808; the European Union (Withdrawal) Act 2018 (Commencement No 2) Regulations 2019, SI 2019/399; the European Union (Withdrawal) Act 2018 (Commencement No 3) Regulations 2019, SI 2019/1077; the European Union (Withdrawal) Act 2018 (Commencement No 4) Regulations 2019, SI 2019/1198; the European Union (Withdrawal) Act 2018 (Commencement No 5, Transitional Provisions and Amendment) Regulations 2020, SI 2020/74; the European Union (Withdrawal) Act 2018 and European Union (Withdrawal Agreement) Act 2020 (Commencement, Transitional and Savings Provisions) Regulations 2020, SI 2020/1622.

SCHEDULES

SCHEDULE 1
FURTHER PROVISION ABOUT EXCEPTIONS TO SAVINGS AND INCORPORATION

Section 5(6)

Challenges to validity of retained EU law

[7.34]

1. (1) There is no right in domestic law on or after [IP completion day] to challenge any retained EU law on the basis that, immediately before [IP completion day], an EU instrument was invalid.

(2) Sub-paragraph (1) does not apply so far as—

(a) the European Court has decided before [IP completion day] that the instrument is invalid, or

(b) the challenge is of a kind described, or provided for, in regulations made by a Minister of the Crown.

(3) Regulations under sub-paragraph (2)(b) may (among other things) provide for a challenge which would otherwise have been against an EU institution to be against a public authority in the United Kingdom.

General principles of EU law

2. No general principle of EU law is part of domestic law on or after [IP completion day] if it was not recognised as a general principle of EU law by the European Court in a case decided before [IP completion day] (whether or not as an essential part of the decision in the case).

3. (1) There is no right of action in domestic law on or after [IP completion day] based on a failure to comply with any of the general principles of EU law.

(2) No court or tribunal or other public authority may, on or after [IP completion day]—

(a) disapply or quash any enactment or other rule of law, or

(b) quash any conduct or otherwise decide that it is unlawful,

because it is incompatible with any of the general principles of EU law.

Rule in Francovich

4. There is no right in domestic law on or after [IP completion day] to damages in accordance with the rule in *Francovich*.

Interpretation

5. (1) References in section 5 and this Schedule to the principle of the supremacy of EU law, the Charter of Fundamental Rights, any general principle of EU law or the rule in *Francovich* are to be read as references to that principle, Charter or rule so far as it would otherwise continue to be, or form part of, domestic law on or after [IP completion day] [by virtue of section 2, 3, 4 or 6(3) or (6) and otherwise in accordance with this Act].

(2) Accordingly (among other things) the references to the principle of the supremacy of EU law in section 5(2) and (3) do not include anything which would bring into domestic law any modification of EU law which is adopted or notified, comes into force or only applies on or after [IP completion day].

NOTES

Commencement: 4 July 2018 (para 1(2)(b) for the purpose of making regulations, and para 1(3)); IP completion day (as defined in the European Union (Withdrawal Agreement) Act 2020, s 39) (otherwise).

The words "IP completion day" in square brackets were substituted by the European Union (Withdrawal Agreement) Act 2020, s 25(6)(a), as from exit day (as defined in s 20 of this Act) (for the purposes of s 5(6) above, and this Schedule, so far as they are in force on exit day), and as from IP completion day (as defined in the European Union (Withdrawal Agreement) Act 2020, s 39) (otherwise).

The words "by virtue of section 2, 3, 4 or 6(3) or (6) and otherwise in accordance with this Act" in square brackets were substituted by the European Union (Withdrawal Agreement) Act 2020, s 25(6)(b), as from IP completion day (as defined in the European Union (Withdrawal Agreement) Act 2020, s 39).

Regulations: the Challenges to Validity of EU Instruments (EU Exit) Regulations 2019, SI 2019/673. These Regulations make provision about the exceptions to the saving and incorporation of EU law set out in paragraph 1, which provides that, on or after IP completion day, no challenge can be brought in the UK courts to retained EU law on the basis that immediately before IP completion day, an EU instrument was invalid. Regulations 1 and 2 provide for citation, commencement and interpretation. Regulation 3 provides that this exception for claims in respect of validity will not apply in respect of a certain class of claims. They must be based on whether an EU instrument was invalid immediately before IP completion day under the grounds in Article 263 TFEU and relate to proceedings which have begun before IP completion day but are not yet decided. Regulation 4 gives jurisdiction to courts and tribunals in the UK to declare an EU instrument invalid in these cases. Regulation 5 makes provision for notice to be given to a Minister of the Crown or the devolved administrations about any proceedings under these Regulations. Regulation 6 allows for a Minister of the Crown or the devolved administrations to be able to intervene in proceedings under these Regulations.

SCHEDULE 2
CORRESPONDING POWERS INVOLVING DEVOLVED AUTHORITIES

Section 11

PART 1 DEALING WITH DEFICIENCIES ARISING FROM WITHDRAWAL

Power to deal with deficiencies

[7.35]

1. (1) A devolved authority may by regulations make such provision as the devolved authority considers appropriate to prevent, remedy or mitigate—

(a) any failure of retained EU law to operate effectively, or
(b) any other deficiency in retained EU law,

arising from the withdrawal of the United Kingdom from the EU.

(2) A Minister of the Crown acting jointly with a devolved authority may by regulations make such provision as they consider appropriate to prevent, remedy or mitigate—

(a) any failure of retained EU law to operate effectively, or
(b) any other deficiency in retained EU law,

arising from the withdrawal of the United Kingdom from the EU.

(3) Section 8(2) to (9) apply for the purposes of this Part as they apply for the purposes of section 8 (including the references to the Minister in section 8(2) and (3) (but not the reference to a Minister of the Crown in section 8(3)(b)) being read as references to the devolved authority or (as the case may be) the Minister acting jointly with the devolved authority and the references to section 8(1) being read as references to sub-paragraph (1) or (2) above).

(4) Regulations under sub-paragraph (1) above are subject to paragraphs 2 to 7.

No power to make provision outside devolved competence

2. (1) No provision may be made by a devolved authority acting alone in regulations under this Part unless the provision is within the devolved competence of the devolved authority.

(2) See paragraphs 8 to 11 for the meaning of "devolved competence" for the purposes of this Part.

No power to modify retained direct EU legislation or confer certain functions

3. (1) No provision may be made by the Scottish Ministers acting alone in regulations under this Part so far as the provision—

(a) modifies any retained direct EU legislation or anything which is retained EU law by virtue of section 4 or confers functions which correspond to functions to make EU tertiary legislation, and
(b) would, when made, be in breach of—
  (i) the restriction in section 30A(1) of the Scotland Act 1998 if the provision were made in an Act of the Scottish Parliament, or
  (ii) the restriction in section 57(4) of the Act of 1998 if section 57(5)(b) of that Act so far as relating to this Schedule were ignored.

(2) No provision may be made by the Welsh Ministers acting alone in regulations under this Part so far as the provision—

(a) modifies any retained direct EU legislation or anything which is retained EU law by virtue of section 4 or confers functions which correspond to functions to make EU tertiary legislation, and

(b) would, when made, be in breach of—

(i) the restriction in section 80(8) of the Government of Wales Act 2006 if section 80(8A)(b) of that Act so far as relating to this Schedule were ignored, or

(ii) the restriction in section 109A(1) of that Act if the provision were made in an Act of the National Assembly for Wales.

(3) No provision may be made by a Northern Ireland department acting alone in regulations under this Part so far as the provision—

(a) modifies any retained direct EU legislation or anything which is retained EU law by virtue of section 4 or confers functions which correspond to functions to make EU tertiary legislation, and

(b) would, when made, be in breach of—

(i) the restriction in section 6A(1) of the Northern Ireland Act 1998 if the provision were made in an Act of the Northern Ireland Assembly, or

(ii) the restriction in section 24(3) of the Act of 1998 if section 24(4)(b) of that Act so far as relating to this Schedule were ignored.

(4) No provision may be made by a devolved authority acting alone in regulations under this Part so far as, when made, the provision is inconsistent with any modification (whether or not in force) which—

(a) is a modification of any retained direct EU legislation or anything which is retained EU law by virtue of section 4,

(b) is made by this Act or a Minister of the Crown under this Act, and

(c) could not be made by the devolved authority by virtue of sub-paragraph (1), (2) or (as the case may be) (3).

(5) For the purposes of sub-paragraphs (1)(b), (2)(b) and (3)(b), sections 30A and 57(4) to (15) of the Scotland Act 1998, sections 80(8) to (8L) and 109A of the Government of Wales Act 2006 and sections 6A and 24(3) to (15) of the Northern Ireland Act 1998, and any regulations made under them and any related provision, are to be assumed to be wholly in force so far as that is not otherwise the case.

(6) References in this paragraph to section 80(8) of the Government of Wales Act 2006 are to be read as references to the new section 80(8) of that Act provided for by paragraph 2 of Schedule 3 to this Act.

Requirement for consultation in certain circumstances

4. No regulations may be made under this Part by a devolved authority acting alone so far as the regulations—

(a) are to come into force before [IP completion day], or

(b) remove (whether wholly or partly) reciprocal arrangements of the kind mentioned in section 8(2)(c) or (e),

unless the regulations are, to that extent, made after consulting with the Secretary of State.

Requirement for consent where it would otherwise be required

5. (1) The consent of a Minister of the Crown is required before any provision is made by the Welsh Ministers acting alone in regulations under this Part so far as that provision, if contained in an Act of the National Assembly for Wales, would require the consent of a Minister of the Crown.

(2) The consent of the Secretary of State is required before any provision is made by a Northern Ireland department acting alone in regulations under this Part so far as that provision, if contained in an Act of the Northern Ireland Assembly, would require the consent of the Secretary of State.

(3) Sub-paragraph (1) or (2) does not apply if—

(a) the provision could be contained in subordinate legislation made otherwise than under this Act by the Welsh Ministers acting alone or (as the case may be) a Northern Ireland devolved authority acting alone, and

(b) no such consent would be required in that case.

(4) The consent of a Minister of the Crown is required before any provision is made by a devolved authority acting alone in regulations under this Part so far as that provision, if contained in—

(a) subordinate legislation made otherwise than under this Act by the devolved authority, or

(b) subordinate legislation not falling within paragraph (a) and made otherwise than under this Act by (in the case of Scotland) the First Minister or Lord Advocate acting alone or (in the case of Northern Ireland) a Northern Ireland devolved authority acting alone,

would require the consent of a Minister of the Crown.

(5) Sub-paragraph (4) does not apply if—

(a) the provision could be contained in—

(i) an Act of the Scottish Parliament, an Act of the National Assembly for Wales or (as the case may be) an Act of the Northern Ireland Assembly, or

(ii) different subordinate legislation of the kind mentioned in sub-paragraph (4)(a) or (b) and of a devolved authority acting alone or (as the case may be) other person acting alone, and

(b) no such consent would be required in that case.

Requirement for joint exercise where it would otherwise be required

6. (1) No regulations may be made under this Part by the Scottish Ministers, so far as they contain provision which relates to a matter in respect of which a power to make subordinate legislation otherwise than under this Act is exercisable by—

(a) the Scottish Ministers acting jointly with a Minister of the Crown, or

(b) the First Minister or Lord Advocate acting jointly with a Minister of the Crown,

unless the regulations are, to that extent, made jointly with the Minister of the Crown.

(2) No regulations may be made under this Part by the Welsh Ministers, so far as they contain provision which relates to a matter in respect of which a power to make subordinate legislation otherwise than under this Act is exercisable by the Welsh Ministers acting jointly with a Minister of the Crown, unless the regulations are, to that extent, made jointly with the Minister of the Crown.

(3) No regulations may be made under this Part by a Northern Ireland department, so far as they contain provision which relates to a matter in respect of which a power to make subordinate legislation otherwise than under this Act is exercisable by—

(a) a Northern Ireland department acting jointly with a Minister of the Crown, or
(b) another Northern Ireland devolved authority acting jointly with a Minister of the Crown,

unless the regulations are, to that extent, made jointly with the Minister of the Crown.

(4) Sub-paragraph (1), (2) or (3) does not apply if the provision could be contained in—

(a) an Act of the Scottish Parliament, an Act of the National Assembly for Wales or (as the case may be) an Act of the Northern Ireland Assembly without the need for the consent of a Minister of the Crown, or
(b) different subordinate legislation made otherwise than under this Act by—
  (i) the Scottish Ministers, the First Minister or the Lord Advocate acting alone,
  (ii) the Welsh Ministers acting alone, or
  (iii) (as the case may be), a Northern Ireland devolved authority acting alone.

Requirement for consultation where it would otherwise be required

7. (1) No regulations may be made under this Part by the Welsh Ministers acting alone, so far as they contain provision which, if contained in an Act of the National Assembly for Wales, would require consultation with a Minister of the Crown, unless the regulations are, to that extent, made after consulting with the Minister of the Crown.

(2) No regulations may be made under this Part by the Scottish Ministers acting alone, so far as they contain provision which relates to a matter in respect of which a power to make subordinate legislation otherwise than under this Act is exercisable by the Scottish Ministers, the First Minister or the Lord Advocate after consulting with a Minister of the Crown, unless the regulations are, to that extent, made after consulting with the Minister of the Crown.

(3) No regulations may be made under this Part by the Welsh Ministers acting alone, so far as they contain provision which relates to a matter in respect of which a power to make subordinate legislation otherwise than under this Act is exercisable by the Welsh Ministers after consulting with a Minister of the Crown, unless the regulations are, to that extent, made after consulting with the Minister of the Crown.

(4) No regulations may be made under this Part by a Northern Ireland department acting alone, so far as they contain provision which relates to a matter in respect of which a power to make subordinate legislation otherwise than under this Act is exercisable by a Northern Ireland department after consulting with a Minister of the Crown, unless the regulations are, to that extent, made after consulting with the Minister of the Crown.

(5) Sub-paragraph (2), (3) or (4) does not apply if—

(a) the provision could be contained in an Act of the Scottish Parliament, an Act of the National Assembly for Wales or (as the case may be) an Act of the Northern Ireland Assembly, and
(b) there would be no requirement for the consent of a Minister of the Crown, or for consultation with a Minister of the Crown, in that case.

(6) Sub-paragraph (2), (3) or (4) does not apply if—

(a) the provision could be contained in different subordinate legislation made otherwise than under this Act by—
  (i) the Scottish Ministers, the First Minister or the Lord Advocate acting alone,
  (ii) the Welsh Ministers acting alone, or
  (iii) (as the case may be), a Northern Ireland devolved authority acting alone, and
(b) there would be no requirement for the consent of a Minister of the Crown, or for consultation with a Minister of the Crown, in that case.

Meaning of devolved competence: Part 1

8. (1) A provision is within the devolved competence of the Scottish Ministers for the purposes of this Part if—

(a) it would be within the legislative competence of the Scottish Parliament if it were contained in an Act of that Parliament (ignoring section 29(2)(d) of the Scotland Act 1998 so far as relating to EU law and retained EU law), or
(b) it meets the conditions in sub-paragraph (2).

(2) The conditions are—

(a) the provision—
  (i) amends or revokes subordinate legislation made before [IP completion day] by the Scottish Ministers, the First Minister or the Lord Advocate acting alone, or
  (ii) makes supplementary, incidental, consequential, transitional, transitory or saving provision in connection with any such amendment or revocation,
(b) the subject-matter of the provision does not go beyond the subject-matter of the subordinate legislation concerned,
(c) the provision only forms part of the law of Scotland,
(d) the provision does not confer or remove functions exercisable otherwise than in or as regards Scotland, and
(e) the provision does not modify any enactment so far as the enactment cannot, by virtue of paragraph 1, 4 or 5 of Schedule 4 to the Scotland Act 1998, be modified by an Act of the Scottish Parliament.

9. (1) A provision is within the devolved competence of the Welsh Ministers for the purposes of this Part if—

(a) it would be within the legislative competence of the National Assembly for Wales if it were contained in an Act of the Assembly (ignoring section 108A(2)(e) of the Government of Wales Act 2006 so far as relating to EU law and retained EU law but including any provision that could be made only with the consent of a Minister of the Crown), or

(b) it meets the conditions in sub-paragraph (2).

(2) The conditions are—

(a) the provision—

(i) amends or revokes subordinate legislation made before [IP completion day] by the Welsh Ministers acting alone or the National Assembly for Wales constituted by the Government of Wales Act 1998, or

(ii) makes supplementary, incidental, consequential, transitional, transitory or saving provision in connection with any such amendment or revocation,

(b) the subject-matter of the provision does not go beyond the subject-matter of the subordinate legislation concerned,

(c) the provision only forms part of the law of England and Wales,

(d) the provision does not confer or remove functions exercisable otherwise than in relation to Wales or the Welsh zone, and

(e) the provision does not modify any enactment so far as the enactment cannot, by virtue of paragraph 5, 6 or 7 of Schedule 7B to the Government of Wales Act 2006, be modified by an Act of the National Assembly for Wales.

10. (1) A provision is within the devolved competence of a Northern Ireland department for the purposes of this Part if—

(a) the provision, if it were contained in an Act of the Northern Ireland Assembly—

(i) would be within the legislative competence of the Assembly (ignoring section 6(2)(d) of the Northern Ireland Act 1998), and

(ii) would not require the consent of the Secretary of State,

(b) the provision—

(i) amends or repeals Northern Ireland legislation, and

(ii) would, if it were contained in an Act of the Northern Ireland Assembly, be within the legislative competence of the Assembly (ignoring section 6(2)(d) of the Northern Ireland Act 1998) and require the consent of the Secretary of State, or

(c) the provision meets the conditions in sub-paragraph (2).

(2) The conditions are—

(a) the provision—

(i) amends or revokes subordinate legislation made before [IP completion day] by a Northern Ireland devolved authority acting alone, or

(ii) makes supplementary, incidental, consequential, transitional, transitory or saving provision in connection with any such amendment or revocation,

(b) the subject-matter of the provision does not go beyond the subject-matter of the subordinate legislation concerned,

(c) the provision only forms part of the law of Northern Ireland,

(d) the provision does not confer or remove functions exercisable otherwise than in or as regards Northern Ireland,

(e) the provision does not modify any enactment so far as the enactment cannot, by virtue of section 7 of the Northern Ireland Act 1998, be modified by an Act of the Northern Ireland Assembly, and

(f) the provision does not deal with, or otherwise relate to, a matter to which paragraph 22 of Schedule 2, or paragraph 42 of Schedule 3, to the Northern Ireland Act 1998 applies.

11. References in paragraphs 8 to 10, in connection with the making of regulations under this Part, to the subject-matter of any provision or subordinate legislation are to be read as references to the subject-matter of the provision or subordinate legislation when the regulations concerned are made.

NOTES

Commencement: 26 June 2018.

Paras 4, 8–10: words in square brackets substituted by the European Union (Withdrawal Agreement) Act 2020, s 27(7).

National Assembly for Wales: as to the renaming of the National Assembly for Wales, etc, see the note at **[7.28]**.

Regulations: many Regulations have been made under this Part and they are not listed here for reasons of space.

[PART 1A PROVISION IN CONNECTION WITH IMPLEMENTATION PERIOD

Supplementary power in connection with implementation period

[7.36]

11A. (1) A devolved authority may by regulations—

(a) provide for other modifications for the purposes of section 1B(3)(f)(i) (whether applying in all cases or particular cases or descriptions of case),

(b) provide for subsection (3) or (4) of section 1B not to apply to any extent in particular cases or descriptions of case,

(c) make different provision in particular cases or descriptions of case to that made by subsection (3) or (4) of that section, or

(d) make such provision not falling within paragraph (a), (b) or (c) as the devolved authority considers appropriate for any purpose of, or otherwise in connection with, Part 4 of the withdrawal agreement.

(2) A Minister of the Crown acting jointly with a devolved authority may by regulations—

(a) provide for other modifications for the purposes of section 1B(3)(f)(i) (whether applying in all cases or particular cases or descriptions of case),

(b) provide for subsection (3) or (4) of section 1B not to apply to any extent in particular cases or descriptions of case,

(c) make different provision in particular cases or descriptions of case to that made by subsection (3) or (4) of that section, or

(d) make such provision not falling within paragraph (a), (b) or (c) as they consider appropriate for any purpose of, or otherwise in connection with, Part 4 of the withdrawal agreement.

(3) The power to make regulations under this Part may (among other things) be exercised by modifying any provision made by or under an enactment.

(4) In sub-paragraph (3) "enactment" does not include primary legislation passed or made after IP completion day.

(5) No regulations may be made under this Part after the end of the period of two years beginning with IP completion day.

(6) Regulations under sub-paragraph (1) are also subject to paragraphs 11B and 11C.

No power to make provision outside devolved competence

11B. (1) No provision may be made by a devolved authority acting alone in regulations under this Part unless the provision is within the devolved competence of the devolved authority.

(2) See paragraphs 11D to 11F for the meaning of "devolved competence" for the purposes of this Part.

Certain requirements for consent, joint exercise or consultation

11C. Paragraphs 5 to 7 apply for the purposes of this Part as they apply for the purposes of Part 1.

Meaning of devolved competence: Part 1A

11D. A provision is within the devolved competence of the Scottish Ministers for the purposes of this Part if—

(a) it would be within the legislative competence of the Scottish Parliament if it were contained in an Act of that Parliament (ignoring, in the case of regulations made under this Part before exit day, section 29(2)(d) of the Scotland Act 1998 so far as relating to EU law), or

(b) it is provision which could be made in other subordinate legislation by the Scottish Ministers, the First Minister or the Lord Advocate acting alone (ignoring, in the case of regulations made under this Part before exit day, section 57(2) of the Scotland Act 1998 so far as relating to EU law).

11E. A provision is within the devolved competence of the Welsh Ministers for the purposes of this Part if—

(a) it would be within the legislative competence of the National Assembly for Wales if it were contained in an Act of the Assembly (ignoring, in the case of regulations made under this Part before exit day, section 108A(2)(e) of the Government of Wales Act 2006 so far as relating to EU law but including any provision that could be made only with the consent of a Minister of the Crown), or

(b) it is provision which could be made in other subordinate legislation by the Welsh Ministers acting alone (ignoring, in the case of regulations made under this Part before exit day, section 80(8) of the Government of Wales Act 2006 so far as relating to EU law).

11F. A provision is within the devolved competence of a Northern Ireland department for the purposes of this Part if—

(a) the provision, if it were contained in an Act of the Northern Ireland Assembly—

(i) would be within the legislative competence of the Assembly (ignoring, in the case of regulations made under this Part before exit day, section 6(2)(d) of the Northern Ireland Act 1998 so far as relating to EU law), and

(ii) would not require the consent of the Secretary of State,

(b) the provision—

(i) amends or repeals Northern Ireland legislation, and

(ii) would, if it were contained in an Act of the Northern Ireland Assembly, be within the legislative competence of the Assembly (ignoring, in the case of regulations made under this Part before exit day, section 6(2)(d) of the Northern Ireland Act 1998 so far as relating to EU law) and require the consent of the Secretary of State, or

(c) the provision is provision which could be made in other subordinate legislation by any Northern Ireland devolved authority acting alone (ignoring, in the case of regulations made under this Part before exit day, section 24(1)(b) of the Northern Ireland Act 1998).]

NOTES

Commencement: 23 January 2020.

Inserted by the European Union (Withdrawal Agreement) Act 2020, s 4,.

National Assembly for Wales: as to the renaming of the National Assembly for Wales, etc, see the note at **[7.28]**.

[PART 1B PROVISION IN CONNECTION WITH CERTAIN OTHER SEPARATION ISSUES

Powers in connection with Part 3 of withdrawal agreement and EEA EFTA separation agreement

[7.37]

11G. (1) A devolved authority may by regulations make such provision as the devolved authority considers appropriate—

(a) to implement Part 3 of the withdrawal agreement (separation provisions),

(b) to supplement the effect of section 7A in relation to that Part, or

(c) otherwise for the purposes of dealing with matters arising out of, or related to, that Part (including matters arising by virtue of section 7A and that Part).

(2) A Minister of the Crown acting jointly with a devolved authority may by regulations make such provision as they consider appropriate—

(a) to implement Part 3 of the withdrawal agreement (separation provisions),

(b) to supplement the effect of section 7A in relation to that Part, or

(c) otherwise for the purposes of dealing with matters arising out of, or related to, that Part (including matters arising by virtue of section 7A and that Part).

(3) A devolved authority may by regulations make such provision as the devolved authority considers appropriate—

(a) to implement Part 3 of the EEA EFTA separation agreement (separation provisions),

(b) to supplement the effect of section 7B in relation to that Part, or

(c) otherwise for the purposes of dealing with matters arising out of, or related to, that Part (including matters arising by virtue of section 7B and that Part).

(4) A Minister of the Crown acting jointly with a devolved authority may by regulations make such provision as they consider appropriate—

(a) to implement Part 3 of the EEA EFTA separation agreement (separation provisions),

(b) to supplement the effect of section 7B in relation to that Part, or

(c) otherwise for the purposes of dealing with matters arising out of, or related to, that Part (including matters arising by virtue of section 7B and that Part).

(5) Regulations under this Part may make any provision that could be made by an Act of Parliament.

(6) Regulations under this Part may (among other things) restate, for the purposes of making the law clearer or more accessible, anything that forms part of domestic law by virtue of—

(a) section 7A above and Part 3 of the withdrawal agreement, or

(b) section 7B above and Part 3 of the EEA EFTA separation agreement.

(7) But regulations under this Part may not—

(a) impose or increase taxation or fees,

(b) make retrospective provision,

(c) create a relevant criminal offence,

(d) establish a public authority,

(e) amend, repeal or revoke the Human Rights Act 1998 or any subordinate legislation made under it, or

(f) amend or repeal the Scotland Act 1998, the Government of Wales Act 2006 or the Northern Ireland Act 1998 (unless the regulations are made by virtue of paragraph 21(b) of Schedule 7 to this Act or are amending or repealing any provision of those Acts which modifies another enactment).

(8) Regulations under sub-paragraph (1) or (3) are also subject to paragraphs 11H and 11I.

(9) In this paragraph references to Part 3 of the withdrawal agreement or of the EEA EFTA separation agreement include references to any provision of EU law which is applied by, or referred to in, that Part (to the extent of the application or reference).

No power to make provision outside devolved competence

11H. (1) No provision may be made by a devolved authority acting alone in regulations under this Part unless the provision is within the devolved competence of the devolved authority.

(2) See paragraphs 11J to 11L for the meaning of "devolved competence" for the purposes of this Part.

Certain requirements for consent, joint exercise or consultation

11I. Paragraphs 5 to 7 apply for the purposes of this Part as they apply for the purposes of Part 1.

Meaning of devolved competence: Part 1B

11J. A provision is within the devolved competence of the Scottish Ministers for the purposes of this Part if—

(a) it would be within the legislative competence of the Scottish Parliament if it were contained in an Act of that Parliament (ignoring section 29(2)(d) of the Scotland Act 1998 so far as relating to EU law and retained EU law), or

(b) it is provision which could be made in other subordinate legislation by the Scottish Ministers, the First Minister or the Lord Advocate acting alone (ignoring section 57(2) of the Scotland Act 1998 so far as relating to EU law and section 57(4) of that Act).

11K. A provision is within the devolved competence of the Welsh Ministers for the purposes of this Part if—

(a) it would be within the legislative competence of the National Assembly for Wales if it were contained in an Act of the Assembly (ignoring section 108A(2)(e) of the Government of Wales Act 2006 so far as relating to EU law and retained EU law but including any provision that could be made only with the consent of a Minister of the Crown), or

(b) it is provision which could be made in other subordinate legislation by the Welsh Ministers acting alone (ignoring section 80(8) of the Government of Wales Act 2006).

11L. A provision is within the devolved competence of a Northern Ireland department for the purposes of this Part if—

(a) the provision, if it were contained in an Act of the Northern Ireland Assembly—

(i) would be within the legislative competence of the Assembly (ignoring section 6(2)(d) of the Northern Ireland Act 1998), and

(ii) would not require the consent of the Secretary of State,

(b) the provision—

(i) amends or repeals Northern Ireland legislation, and

(ii) would, if it were contained in an Act of the Northern Ireland Assembly, be within the legislative competence of the Assembly (ignoring section 6(2)(d) of the Northern Ireland Act 1998) and require the consent of the Secretary of State, or

(c) the provision is provision which could be made in other subordinate legislation by any Northern Ireland devolved authority acting alone (ignoring section 24(1)(b) and (3) of the Northern Ireland Act 1998).]

NOTES

Commencement: 19 May 2020.

Inserted by the European Union (Withdrawal Agreement) Act 2020, s 19.

National Assembly for Wales: as to the renaming of the National Assembly for Wales, etc, see the note at **[7.28]**.

Regulations: Regulations made under this Part are outside the scope of this work.

[PART 1C PROVISION IN CONNECTION WITH PROTOCOL ON IRELAND/NORTHERN IRELAND

Power in connection with Protocol on Ireland/Northern Ireland

[7.38]

11M. (1) A devolved authority may by regulations make such provision as the devolved authority considers appropriate—

(a) to implement the Protocol on Ireland/Northern Ireland in the withdrawal agreement,
(b) to supplement the effect of section 7A in relation to the Protocol, or
(c) otherwise for the purposes of dealing with matters arising out of, or related to, the Protocol (including matters arising by virtue of section 7A and the Protocol).

(2) A Minister of the Crown acting jointly with a devolved authority may by regulations make such provision as they consider appropriate—

(a) to implement the Protocol on Ireland/Northern Ireland in the withdrawal agreement,
(b) to supplement the effect of section 7A in relation to the Protocol, or
(c) otherwise for the purposes of dealing with matters arising out of, or related to, the Protocol (including matters arising by virtue of section 7A and the Protocol).

(3) Regulations under this Part may make any provision that could be made by an Act of Parliament.

(4) Regulations under this Part may (among other things) make provision facilitating the access to the market within Great Britain of qualifying Northern Ireland goods.

(5) Such provision may (among other things) include provision about the recognition within Great Britain of technical regulations, assessments, registrations, certificates, approvals and authorisations issued by—

(a) the authorities of a member State, or
(b) bodies established in a member State,

in respect of qualifying Northern Ireland goods.

(6) Regulations under this Part may (among other things) restate, for the purposes of making the law clearer or more accessible, anything that forms part of domestic law by virtue of section 7A and the Protocol.

(7) Regulations under sub-paragraph (1) are also subject to paragraphs 11N and 11O.

(8) In this paragraph any reference to the Protocol on Ireland/Northern Ireland includes a reference to—

(a) any other provision of the withdrawal agreement so far as applying to the Protocol, and
(b) any provision of EU law which is applied by, or referred to in, the Protocol (to the extent of the application or reference),

but does not include the second sentence of Article 11(1) of the Protocol (which provides that the United Kingdom and the Republic of Ireland may continue to make new arrangements that build on the provisions of the Belfast Agreement in other areas of North-South cooperation on the island of Ireland).

No power to make provision outside devolved competence

11N. (1) No provision may be made by a devolved authority acting alone in regulations under this Part unless the provision is within the devolved competence of the devolved authority.

(2) See paragraphs 11P to 11R for the meaning of "devolved competence" for the purposes of this Part.

Certain requirements for consent, joint exercise or consultation

11O. Paragraphs 5 to 7 apply for the purposes of this Part as they apply for the purposes of Part 1.

Meaning of devolved competence: Part 1C

11P. A provision is within the devolved competence of the Scottish Ministers for the purposes of this Part if—

(a) it would be within the legislative competence of the Scottish Parliament if it were contained in an Act of that Parliament (ignoring section 29(2)(d) of the Scotland Act 1998 so far as relating to EU law), or
(b) it is provision which could be made in other subordinate legislation by the Scottish Ministers, the First Minister or the Lord Advocate acting alone (ignoring section 57(2) of the Scotland Act 1998 so far as relating to EU law).

11Q. A provision is within the devolved competence of the Welsh Ministers for the purposes of this Part if—

(a) it would be within the legislative competence of the National Assembly for Wales if it were contained in an Act of the Assembly (ignoring section 108A(2)(e) of the Government of Wales Act 2006 so far as relating to EU law but including any provision that could be made only with the consent of a Minister of the Crown), or
(b) it is provision which could be made in other subordinate legislation by the Welsh Ministers acting alone (ignoring section 80(8) of the Government of Wales Act 2006 so far as relating to EU law).

11R. A provision is within the devolved competence of a Northern Ireland department for the purposes of this Part if—

(a) the provision, if it were contained in an Act of the Northern Ireland Assembly—
  (i) would be within the legislative competence of the Assembly (ignoring section 6(2)(d) of the Northern Ireland Act 1998 so far as relating to EU law), and
  (ii) would not require the consent of the Secretary of State,
(b) the provision—
  (i) amends or repeals Northern Ireland legislation, and

(ii) would, if it were contained in an Act of the Northern Ireland Assembly, be within the legislative competence of the Assembly (ignoring section 6(2)(d) of the Northern Ireland Act 1998 so far as relating to EU law) and require the consent of the Secretary of State, or

(c) the provision is provision which could be made in other subordinate legislation by any Northern Ireland devolved authority acting alone (ignoring section 24(1)(b) of the Northern Ireland Act 1998).]

NOTES

Commencement: 19 May 2020.

Inserted by the European Union (Withdrawal Agreement) Act 2020, s 22.

National Assembly for Wales: as to the renaming of the National Assembly for Wales, etc, see the note at **[7.28]**.

Regulations: Regulations made under this Part are outside the scope of this work.

(Sch 2, Pt 2 (Implementing the Withdrawal Agreement) repealed by the European Union (Withdrawal Agreement) Act 2020, s 36.)

SCHEDULE 3
FURTHER AMENDMENTS OF DEVOLUTION LEGISLATION AND REPORTING REQUIREMENT

Section 12(7), (8) and (12)

PART 1 CORRESPONDING PROVISION IN RELATION TO EXECUTIVE COMPETENCE

(Amends the Scotland Act 1998, the Government of Wales Act 2006, and the Northern Ireland Act 1998.)

PART 2 REPORTS IN CONNECTION WITH RETAINED EU LAW RESTRICTIONS

Reports on progress towards removing retained EU law restrictions

[7.39]

4. (1) After the end of each reporting period, a Minister of the Crown must lay before each House of Parliament a report which—

(a) contains details of any steps which have been taken in the reporting period by Her Majesty's Government (whether or not in conjunction with any of the appropriate authorities) towards implementing any arrangements which are to replace any relevant powers or retained EU law restrictions,

(b) explains how principles—

(i) agreed between Her Majesty's Government and any of the appropriate authorities, and

(ii) relating to implementing any arrangements which are to replace any relevant powers or retained EU law restrictions,

have been taken into account during the reporting period,

(c) specifies any relevant regulations, or regulations under section 12(9), which have been made in the reporting period,

(d) in relation to any retained EU law restriction which has effect at the end of the reporting period, sets out the Minister's assessment of the progress which still needs to be made before it can be removed,

(e) in relation to any relevant power that has not been repealed before the end of the reporting period, sets out the Minister's assessment of the progress which still needs to be made before it can be repealed, and

(f) contains any other information relating to any relevant powers or retained EU law restrictions, or the arrangements which are to replace them, that the Minister considers appropriate.

(2) The first reporting period is the period of three months beginning with the day on which this Act is passed.

(3) Each successive period of three months after the first reporting period is a reporting period.

(4) A Minister of the Crown must provide a copy of every report laid before Parliament under this paragraph—

(a) to the Scottish Ministers,

(b) to the Welsh Ministers, and

(c) either to the First Minister in Northern Ireland and the deputy First Minister in Northern Ireland or to the relevant Northern Ireland department and its Northern Ireland Minister.

(5) In sub-paragraph (4) "the relevant Northern Ireland department" means such Northern Ireland department as the Minister of the Crown concerned considers appropriate.

(6) This paragraph ceases to apply when no retained EU law restrictions have effect and all the relevant powers have been repealed.

Interpretation

5. In this Part—

"appropriate authority" means—

(a) the Scottish Ministers,

(b) the Welsh Ministers, or

(c) a Northern Ireland devolved authority;

"arrangement" means any enactment or other arrangement (whether or not legally enforceable);

"relevant power" means a power to make regulations conferred by—

(a) section 30A or 57(4) of the Scotland Act 1998,

(b) section 80(8) or 109A of the Government of Wales Act 2006, or

(c) section 6A or 24(3) of the Northern Ireland Act 1998;

"relevant regulations" means regulations made under a relevant power;

"retained EU law restriction" means any restriction which arises by virtue of relevant regulations.

NOTES

Commencement: 26 June 2018.

PART 3 OTHER AMENDMENTS OF DEVOLUTION LEGISLATION

(Contains further amendments to the Scotland Act 1998, the Government of Wales Act 2006, and the Northern Ireland Act 1998.)

SCHEDULE 4
POWERS IN CONNECTION WITH FEES AND CHARGES

Section 14(1)

PART 1 CHARGING IN CONNECTION WITH CERTAIN NEW FUNCTIONS

Power to provide for fees or charges

[7.40]

1. (1) An appropriate authority may by regulations make provision for, or in connection with, the charging of fees or other charges in connection with the exercise of a function ("the relevant function") which a public authority has by virtue of provision made under—

(a) section 8 or Part 1 of Schedule 2 (powers to deal with deficiencies arising from withdrawal),

[(aa) section 8B or Part 1B of Schedule 2 (powers in connection with Part 3 of the withdrawal agreement and Part 3 of the EEA EFTA separation agreement),

(ab) section 8C or Part 1C of Schedule 2 (powers in connection with the Ireland/Northern Ireland Protocol in the withdrawal agreement)], . . .

(b) . . .

(2) Where there is more than one appropriate authority in relation to the relevant function, two or more of the appropriate authorities may make regulations under this paragraph jointly.

(3) Regulations under this paragraph may (among other things)—

(a) prescribe the fees or charges or make provision as to how they are to be determined;

(b) provide for the recovery or disposal of any sums payable under the regulations;

(c) confer power on the public authority to make, by subordinate legislation, any provision that the appropriate authority may make under this paragraph in relation to the relevant function.

Meaning of "appropriate authority"

2. (1) A Minister of the Crown is an "appropriate authority" for the purposes of paragraph 1.

(2) The Scottish Ministers are an "appropriate authority" for the purposes of paragraph 1—

(a) if the Scottish Ministers (whether acting jointly or alone) made the provision, as mentioned in paragraph 1(1), by virtue of which the public authority has the relevant function,

(b) if the relevant function is a function of the Scottish Ministers, the First Minister or the Lord Advocate, or

(c) if the provision by virtue of which the public authority has the relevant function, if it were included in an Act of the Scottish Parliament, would be within the legislative competence of that Parliament (ignoring section 29(2)(d) of the Scotland Act 1998 so far as relating to EU law and retained EU law).

(3) The Welsh Ministers are an "appropriate authority" for the purposes of paragraph 1—

(a) if the Welsh Ministers (whether acting jointly or alone) made the provision, as mentioned in paragraph 1(1), by virtue of which the public authority has the relevant function,

(b) if the relevant function is a function of the Welsh Ministers, or

(c) if the provision by virtue of which the public authority has the relevant function, if it were included in an Act of the National Assembly for Wales, would be within the legislative competence of that Assembly (ignoring section 108A(2)(e) of the Government of Wales Act 2006 so far as relating to EU law and retained EU law but including any provision that could be made only with consent of a Minister of the Crown).

(4) A Northern Ireland department is an "appropriate authority" for the purposes of paragraph 1—

(a) if a Northern Ireland department (whether acting jointly or alone) made the provision, as mentioned in paragraph 1(1), by virtue of which the public authority has the relevant function,

(b) if the relevant function is a function of a Northern Ireland devolved authority, or

(c) if the provision by virtue of which the public authority has the relevant function, if it were included in an Act of the Northern Ireland Assembly—

(i) would be within the legislative competence of that Assembly (ignoring section 6(2)(d) of the Northern Ireland Act 1998), and

(ii) would not require the consent of the Secretary of State.

Requirements for consent

3. (1) A Minister of the Crown may only make regulations under paragraph 1 with the consent of the Treasury.

(2) A devolved authority may only make regulations under paragraph 1 with the consent of a Minister of the Crown if—

(a) the relevant function is a function of a Minister of the Crown, or

(b) the public authority that has the relevant function—

(i) in the case of the Scottish Ministers, has any functions that can be exercised otherwise than in or as regards Scotland,

(ii) in the case of the Welsh Ministers, has any functions that can be exercised otherwise than in relation to Wales or the Welsh zone, or

(iii) in the case of a Northern Ireland department, has any functions that can be exercised otherwise than in or as regards Northern Ireland and is not an implementation body.

(3) In sub-paragraph (2)(b)(iii) "implementation body" has the same meaning as in section 55 of the Northern Ireland Act 1998 (see subsection (3) of that section).

Minister of the Crown power in relation to devolved authorities

4. A Minister of the Crown may by regulations—
(a) prescribe circumstances in which, or functions in relation to which, a devolved authority is to be regarded as being an appropriate authority for the purposes of paragraph 1;
(b) provide that a devolved authority that is regarded as being an appropriate authority under regulations made under paragraph (a) may only make regulations under paragraph 1, by virtue of being so regarded, with the consent of a Minister of the Crown;
(c) prescribe circumstances in which, or functions in relation to which, a devolved authority may, despite paragraph 3(2), make regulations under paragraph 1 without the consent of a Minister of the Crown.

Time limit for making certain provision

5. (1) Subject to [sub-paragraphs (2) and (2A)], no regulations may be made under paragraph 1 after the end of the period of two years beginning with [IP completion day].

(2) After the end of that period, regulations may be made under paragraph 1 for the purposes of—
(a) revoking any provision made under that paragraph,
(b) altering the amount of any of the fees or charges that are to be charged under any provision made under that paragraph,
(c) altering how any of the fees or charges that are to be charged under any provision made under that paragraph are to be determined, or
(d) otherwise altering the fees or charges that may be charged in relation to anything in respect of which fees or charges may be charged under any provision made under that paragraph.

[(2A) This paragraph does not apply in relation to regulations made under paragraph 1(1)(aa) or (ab).]

(3) This paragraph does not affect the continuation in force of any regulations made at or before the end of the period mentioned in sub-paragraph (1) (including the exercise after the end of that period of any power conferred by regulations made under that paragraph at or before the end of that period).

Relationship to other powers

6. This Part does not affect the powers under [sections 8 to 8C] or Schedule 2, or any other power exercisable apart from this Part, to require the payment of, or to make other provision in relation to, fees or other charges.

NOTES

Commencement: 26 June 2018.

Para 1: sub-paras (aa), (ab) were inserted by the European Union (Withdrawal Agreement) Act 2020, s 28. Sub-para (1)(b) and the preceding word were repealed by the European Union (Withdrawal Agreement) Act 2020, s 41(4), Sch 5, Pt 2, paras 38, 47(1), (2).

Para 5: the words in the first pair of square brackets in sub-para (1) were substituted, and sub-para (2A) was inserted, by the European Union (Withdrawal Agreement) Act 2020, s 28. The words in the second pair of square brackets in sub-para (1) were substituted by the European Union (Withdrawal Agreement) Act 2020, s 41(4), Sch 5, Pt 2, paras 38, 47(1), (3).

Para 6: words in square brackets substituted by the European Union (Withdrawal Agreement) Act 2020, s 41(4), Sch 5, Pt 2, paras 38, 47(1), (4).

National Assembly for Wales: as to the renaming of the National Assembly for Wales, etc, see the note at **[7.28]**.

Regulations: the Competition (Amendment etc) (EU Exit) Regulations 2019, SI 2019/93 at **[7.61]**; the Competition (Amendment etc) (EU Exit) Regulations 2020, SI 2020/1343. Other Regulations made under this Part are considered to be outside the scope of this work.

PART 2 MODIFYING PRE-EXIT FEES OR CHARGES

Power to modify pre-exit fees or charges

[7.41]

7. (1) Sub-paragraph (2) applies where any subordinate legislation contains provision ("the charging provision") for, or in connection with, the charging of fees or other charges that—
(a) was made under section 2(2) of the European Communities Act 1972, section 56 of the Finance Act 1973 or this Part, and
(b) forms part of retained EU law.

(2) Any appropriate authority may by regulations make provision ("the proposed modification") modifying the subordinate legislation for the purposes of—
(a) revoking the charging provision,
(b) altering the amount of any of the fees or charges that are to be charged,
(c) altering how any of the fees or charges are to be determined, or
(d) otherwise altering the fees or charges that may be charged in relation to anything in respect of which fees or charges may be charged under the charging provision.

Meaning of "appropriate authority"

8. In this Part an "appropriate authority" means a Minister of the Crown, or devolved authority, that could have made the proposed modification—
(a) under section 2(2) of the European Communities Act 1972 immediately before [IP completion day], or
(b) under section 56 of the Finance Act 1973 immediately before the amendment of that section by paragraph 17 of Schedule 8.

Restriction on exercise of power

9. (1) Where the charging provision consists solely of 1972 Act provision, regulations under this Part may not impose or increase taxation.

(2) In sub-paragraph (1) "1972 Act provision" means—

(a) provision that is made under section 2(2) of the European Communities Act 1972 and not under section 56 of the Finance Act 1973, including such provision as modified under this Part, or
(b) provision that is made under this Part and is incidental to, or supplements or replaces, provision within paragraph (a).

Requirement for consent

10. If a Minister of the Crown—
(a) is an appropriate authority, and
(b) immediately before the amendment of section 56 of the Finance Act 1973 by paragraph 17 of Schedule 8 could only have made the proposed modification under that section,

the Minister may only make that modification under this Part with the consent of the Treasury.

Relationship to other powers

11. This Part does not affect the powers under [sections 8 to 8C] or Schedule 2, or any other power exercisable apart from this Part, to require the payment of, or to make other provision in relation to, fees or other charges.

NOTES

Commencement: 26 June 2018.

Para 8: words in square brackets substituted by the European Union (Withdrawal Agreement) Act 2020, s 41(4), Sch 5, Pt 2, paras 38, 47(1), (5).

Para 11: words in square brackets substituted by the European Union (Withdrawal Agreement) Act 2020, s 41(4), Sch 5, Pt 2, paras 38, 47(1), (6).

Regulations: Regulations made under this Part are considered to be outside the scope of this work.

SCHEDULE 5
PUBLICATION AND RULES OF EVIDENCE

Section 15(1) and (2)

PART 1 PUBLICATION OF RETAINED DIRECT EU LEGISLATION ETC

Things that must or may be published

[7.42]

1. (1) The Queen's Printer must make arrangements for the publication of—
(a) each relevant instrument that has been published before [IP completion day] by an EU entity, and
(b) the relevant international agreements.

(2) In this paragraph—

"relevant instrument" means—
(a) an EU regulation,
(b) an EU decision, and
(c) EU tertiary legislation;

"relevant international agreements" means—
(a) the Treaty on European Union,
(b) the Treaty on the Functioning of the European Union,
(c) the Euratom Treaty, and
(d) the EEA agreement.

(3) The Queen's Printer may make arrangements for the publication of—
(a) any decision of, or expression of opinion by, the European Court, or
(b) any other document published by an EU entity.

(4) The Queen's Printer may make arrangements for the publication of anything which the Queen's Printer considers may be useful in connection with anything published under this paragraph.

(5) This paragraph does not require the publication of—
(a) anything repealed before [IP completion day], or
(b) any modifications made on or after [IP completion day].

Exceptions from duty to publish

2. (1) A Minister of the Crown may create an exception from the duty under paragraph 1(1) in respect of a relevant instrument if satisfied that it has not become (or will not become, on [IP completion day]) retained direct EU legislation.

(2) An exception is created by giving a direction to the Queen's Printer specifying the instrument or category of instruments that are excepted.

(3) A Minister of the Crown must publish any direction under this paragraph.

(4) In this paragraph—

"instrument" includes part of an instrument;

"relevant instrument" has the meaning given by paragraph 1(2).

NOTES

Commencement: 4 July 2018 (para 2); 3 July 2019 (para 1).

All amendments to this Part were made by the European Union (Withdrawal Agreement) Act 2020, s 41(4), Sch 5, Pt 2, paras 38, 48(1), (2).

PART 2 RULES OF EVIDENCE

Questions as to meaning of EU law

[7.43]

3. (1) Where it is necessary [in legal proceedings] to decide a question as to—

(a) the meaning or effect in EU law of any of the EU Treaties or any other treaty relating to the EU, or

(b) the validity, meaning or effect in EU law of any EU instrument,

the question is to be treated . . . as a question of law.

(2) In this paragraph—

. . .

"treaty" includes—

(a) any international agreement, and

(b) any protocol or annex to a treaty or international agreement.

Power to make provision about judicial notice and admissibility

4. (1) A Minister of the Crown may by regulations—

(a) make provision enabling or requiring judicial notice to be taken of a relevant matter, or

(b) provide for the admissibility in any legal proceedings of specified evidence of—

(i) a relevant matter, or

(ii) instruments or documents issued by or in the custody of an EU entity.

(2) Regulations under sub-paragraph (1)(b) may provide that evidence is admissible only where specified conditions are met (for example, conditions as to certification of documents).

(3) Regulations under this paragraph may modify any provision made by or under an enactment.

(4) In sub-paragraph (3) "enactment" does not include primary legislation passed or made after [IP completion day].

(5) For the purposes of this paragraph each of the following is a "relevant matter"—

(a) retained EU law,

(b) EU law,

(c) the EEA agreement,

[(ca) the EEA EFTA separation agreement,

(cb) the Swiss citizens' rights agreement,

(cc) the withdrawal agreement,] and

(d) anything which is specified in the regulations and which relates to a matter mentioned in paragraph (a), (b)[, (c), (ca), (cb) or (cc)].

NOTES

Commencement: 4 July 2018 (para 4); IP completion day (as defined in the European Union (Withdrawal Agreement) Act 2020 (para 3).

Para 3: words in square brackets substituted, and words omitted repealed, by the European Union (Withdrawal Agreement) Act 2020, s 41(4), Sch 5, Pt 2, paras 38, 48(1), (3), as from IP completion day (as defined in the European Union (Withdrawal Agreement) Act 2020, s 39).

Para 4: all amendments to this paragraph were made by the European Union (Withdrawal Agreement) Act 2020, s 41(4), Sch 5, Pt 2, paras 38, 48(1), (4).

SCHEDULE 6
INSTRUMENTS WHICH ARE EXEMPT EU INSTRUMENTS

Section 20(1)

EU decisions

[7.44]

1. (1) . . .

(2) If any decision under Title V or former Title V of the Treaty on European Union is a decision within the meaning of Article 288 of the Treaty on the Functioning of the European Union (and accordingly falls within the definition of "EU decision" in section 20(1)), it is "an exempt EU instrument".

(3) In sub-paragraph (2), the reference to former Title V of the Treaty on European Union is a reference to that Title as it had effect at any time before the coming into force of the Treaty of Lisbon.

EU regulations

2. . . .

EU tertiary legislation

3. EU tertiary legislation is "an exempt EU instrument" so far as it is made under—

(a) an EU decision . . . which is an exempt EU instrument, . . .

(b) . . .

Interpretation

4. . . .

NOTES

Commencement: 26 June 2018.

All words omitted were repealed by the European Union (Withdrawal Agreement) Act 2020, s 41(4), Sch 5, Pt 2, paras 38, 49.

SCHEDULE 7
REGULATIONS

Section 22

PART 1 SCRUTINY OF POWERS TO DEAL WITH DEFICIENCIES

Scrutiny of regulations made by Minister of the Crown or devolved authority acting alone

[7.45]

1. (1) A statutory instrument containing regulations under section 8(1) which contain provision falling within sub-paragraph (2) may not be made unless a draft of the instrument has been laid before, and approved by a resolution of, each House of Parliament.

(2) Provision falls within this sub-paragraph if it—

(a) provides for any function of an EU entity or public authority in a member State of making an instrument of a legislative character to be exercisable instead by a public authority in the United Kingdom,

(b) relates to a fee in respect of a function exercisable by a public authority in the United Kingdom,

(c) creates, or widens the scope of, a criminal offence, or

(d) creates or amends a power to legislate.

(3) Any other statutory instrument containing regulations under section 8(1) is (if a draft of the instrument has not been laid before, and approved by a resolution of, each House of Parliament) subject to annulment in pursuance of a resolution of either House of Parliament.

(4) See paragraph 3 for restrictions on the choice of procedure under sub-paragraph (3).

(5) A statutory instrument containing regulations under section 8(3)(b) (including as applied by paragraph 1(3) of Schedule 2) may not be made unless a draft of the instrument has been laid before, and approved by a resolution of, each House of Parliament.

(6) Regulations under Part 1 of Schedule 2 of the Scottish Ministers which contain provision falling within sub-paragraph (2) are subject to the affirmative procedure (see section 29 of the Interpretation and Legislative Reform (Scotland) Act 2010 (asp 10)).

(7) Any other regulations under Part 1 of Schedule 2 of the Scottish Ministers are (if they have not been subject to the affirmative procedure) subject to the negative procedure (see section 28 of the Interpretation and Legislative Reform (Scotland) Act 2010).

(8) A statutory instrument containing regulations under Part 1 of Schedule 2 of the Welsh Ministers which contain provision falling within sub-paragraph (2) may not be made unless a draft of the instrument has been laid before, and approved by a resolution of, the National Assembly for Wales.

(9) Any other statutory instrument containing regulations under Part 1 of Schedule 2 of the Welsh Ministers is (if a draft of the instrument has not been laid before, and approved by a resolution of, the National Assembly for Wales) subject to annulment in pursuance of a resolution of the Assembly.

(10) See paragraph 4 for restrictions on the choice of procedure under sub-paragraph (9).

(11) Regulations under Part 1 of Schedule 2 of a Northern Ireland department which contain provision falling within sub-paragraph (2) may not be made unless a draft of the regulations has been laid before, and approved by a resolution of, the Northern Ireland Assembly.

(12) Any other regulations under Part 1 of Schedule 2 of a Northern Ireland department are (if a draft of the regulations has not been laid before, and approved by a resolution of, the Northern Ireland Assembly) subject to negative resolution within the meaning of section 41(6) of the Interpretation Act (Northern Ireland) 1954 as if they were a statutory instrument within the meaning of that Act.

(13) This paragraph—

(a) does not apply to regulations to which paragraph 2 applies, and

(b) is subject to paragraphs 5 to 8.

Scrutiny of regulations made by Minister of the Crown and devolved authority acting jointly

2. (1) This paragraph applies to regulations under Part 1 of Schedule 2 of a Minister of the Crown acting jointly with a devolved authority.

(2) The procedure provided for by sub-paragraph (3) or (4) applies in relation to regulations to which this paragraph applies as well as any other procedure provided for by this paragraph which is applicable in relation to the regulations concerned.

(3) A statutory instrument containing regulations to which this paragraph applies which contain provision falling within paragraph 1(2) may not be made unless a draft of the instrument has been laid before, and approved by a resolution of, each House of Parliament.

(4) Any other statutory instrument containing regulations to which this paragraph applies is (if a draft of the instrument has not been laid before, and approved by a resolution of, each House of Parliament) subject to annulment in pursuance of a resolution of either House of Parliament.

(5) Regulations to which this paragraph applies which are made jointly with the Scottish Ministers and contain provision falling within paragraph 1(2) are subject to the affirmative procedure.

(6) Any other regulations to which this paragraph applies which are made jointly with the Scottish Ministers are (if they have not been subject to the affirmative procedure) subject to the negative procedure.

(7) Section 29 of the Interpretation and Legislative Reform (Scotland) Act 2010 (asp 10) (affirmative procedure) applies in relation to regulations to which sub-paragraph (5) or (6) applies and which are subject to the affirmative procedure as it applies in relation to devolved subordinate legislation (within the meaning of Part 2 of that Act) which is subject to the affirmative procedure (but as if references to a Scottish statutory instrument were references to a statutory instrument).

(8) Sections 28(2), (3) and (8) and 31 of the Interpretation and Legislative Reform (Scotland) Act 2010 (negative procedure etc) apply in relation to regulations to which sub-paragraph (6) applies and which are subject to the negative procedure as they apply in relation to devolved subordinate legislation (within the meaning of Part 2 of that Act) which is subject to the negative procedure (but as if references to a Scottish statutory instrument were references to a statutory instrument).

(9) Section 32 of the Interpretation and Legislative Reform (Scotland) Act 2010 (laying) applies in relation to the laying before the Scottish Parliament of a statutory instrument containing regulations to which sub-paragraph (5) or (6) applies as it applies in relation to the laying before that Parliament of a Scottish statutory instrument (within the meaning of Part 2 of that Act).

(10) A statutory instrument containing regulations to which this paragraph applies which are made jointly with the Welsh Ministers and contain provision falling within paragraph 1(2) may not be made unless a draft of the instrument has been laid before, and approved by a resolution of, the National Assembly for Wales.

(11) Any other statutory instrument containing regulations to which this paragraph applies which are made jointly with the Welsh Ministers is (if a draft of the instrument has not been laid before, and approved by a resolution of, the National Assembly for Wales) subject to annulment in pursuance of a resolution of the Assembly.

(12) Regulations to which this paragraph applies which are made jointly with a Northern Ireland department and contain provision falling within paragraph 1(2) may not be made unless a draft of the regulations has been laid before, and approved by a resolution of, the Northern Ireland Assembly.

(13) Any other regulations to which this paragraph applies which are made jointly with a Northern Ireland department are (if a draft of the regulations has not been laid before, and approved by a resolution of, the Northern Ireland Assembly) subject to negative resolution within the meaning of section 41(6) of the Interpretation Act (Northern Ireland) 1954 as if they were a statutory instrument within the meaning of that Act.

(14) If in accordance with sub-paragraph (4), (6), (11) or (13)—

(a) either House of Parliament resolves that an address be presented to Her Majesty praying that an instrument be annulled, or

(b) a relevant devolved legislature resolves that an instrument be annulled,

nothing further is to be done under the instrument after the date of the resolution and Her Majesty may by Order in Council revoke the instrument.

(15) In sub-paragraph (14) "relevant devolved legislature" means—

(a) in the case of regulations made jointly with the Scottish Ministers, the Scottish Parliament,

(b) in the case of regulations made jointly with the Welsh Ministers, the National Assembly for Wales, and

(c) in the case of regulations made jointly with a Northern Ireland department, the Northern Ireland Assembly.

(16) Sub-paragraph (14) does not affect the validity of anything previously done under the instrument or prevent the making of a new instrument.

(17) Sub-paragraphs (14) [to (16)] apply in place of provision made by any other enactment about the effect of such a resolution.

Parliamentary committee to sift certain deficiencies regulations of a Minister of the Crown

3. (1) Sub-paragraph (2) applies if a Minister of the Crown who is to make a statutory instrument to which paragraph 1(3) applies is of the opinion that the appropriate procedure for the instrument is for it to be subject to annulment in pursuance of a resolution of either House of Parliament.

(2) The Minister may not make the instrument so that it is subject to that procedure unless—

(a) condition 1 is met, and

(b) either condition 2 or 3 is met.

(3) Condition 1 is that a Minister of the Crown—

(a) has made a statement in writing to the effect that in the Minister's opinion the instrument should be subject to annulment in pursuance of a resolution of either House of Parliament, and

(b) has laid before each House of Parliament—

(i) a draft of the instrument, and

(ii) a memorandum setting out the statement and the reasons for the Minister's opinion.

(4) Condition 2 is that a committee of the House of Commons charged with doing so and a committee of the House of Lords charged with doing so have, within the relevant period, each made a recommendation as to the appropriate procedure for the instrument.

(5) Condition 3 is that the relevant period has ended without condition 2 being met.

(6) Sub-paragraph (7) applies if—

(a) a committee makes a recommendation as mentioned in sub-paragraph (4) within the relevant period,

(b) the recommendation is that the appropriate procedure for the instrument is for a draft of it to be laid before, and approved by a resolution of, each House of Parliament before it is made, and

(c) the Minister who is to make the instrument is nevertheless of the opinion that the appropriate procedure for the instrument is for it to be subject to annulment in pursuance of a resolution of either House of Parliament.

(7) Before the instrument is made, the Minister must make a statement explaining why the Minister does not agree with the recommendation of the committee.

(8) If the Minister fails to make a statement required by sub-paragraph (7) before the instrument is made, a Minister of the Crown must make a statement explaining why the Minister has failed to do so.

(9) A statement under sub-paragraph (7) or (8) must be made in writing and be published in such manner as the Minister making it considers appropriate.

(10) In this paragraph "the relevant period" means the period—

(a) beginning with the first day on which both Houses of Parliament are sitting after the day on which the draft instrument was laid before each House as mentioned in sub-paragraph (3)(b)(i), and
(b) ending with whichever of the following is the later—
(i) the end of the period of 10 Commons sitting days beginning with that first day, and
(ii) the end of the period of 10 Lords sitting days beginning with that first day.

(11) For the purposes of sub-paragraph (10)—
(a) where a draft of an instrument is laid before each House of Parliament on different days, the later day is to be taken as the day on which it is laid before both Houses,
(b), (c) . . .

(12) Nothing in this paragraph prevents a Minister of the Crown from deciding at any time before a statutory instrument to which paragraph 1(3) applies is made that another procedure should apply in relation to the instrument (whether under paragraph 1(3) or 5).

(13) Section 6(1) of the Statutory Instruments Act 1946 (alternative procedure for certain instruments laid in draft before Parliament) does not apply in relation to any statutory instrument to which this paragraph applies.

Committee of the National Assembly for Wales to sift certain deficiencies regulations of Welsh Ministers

4. (1) Sub-paragraph (2) applies if the Welsh Ministers are to make a statutory instrument to which paragraph 1(9) applies and are of the opinion that the appropriate procedure for the instrument is for it to be subject to annulment in pursuance of a resolution of the National Assembly for Wales.

(2) The Welsh Ministers may not make the instrument so that it is subject to that procedure unless—
(a) condition 1 is met, and
(b) either condition 2 or 3 is met.

(3) Condition 1 is that the Welsh Ministers—
(a) have made a statement in writing to the effect that in their opinion the instrument should be subject to annulment in pursuance of a resolution of the National Assembly for Wales, and
(b) have laid before the Assembly—
(i) a draft of the instrument, and
(ii) a memorandum setting out the statement and the reasons for the Welsh Ministers' opinion.

(4) Condition 2 is that a committee of the National Assembly for Wales charged with doing so has made a recommendation as to the appropriate procedure for the instrument.

(5) Condition 3 is that the period of 14 days beginning with the first day after the day on which the draft instrument was laid before the National Assembly for Wales as mentioned in sub-paragraph (3) has ended without any recommendation being made as mentioned in sub-paragraph (4).

(6) In calculating the period of 14 days, no account is to be taken of any time during which the National Assembly for Wales is—
(a) dissolved, or
(b) in recess for more than four days.

(7) Nothing in this paragraph prevents the Welsh Ministers from deciding at any time before a statutory instrument to which paragraph 1(9) applies is made that another procedure should apply to the instrument (whether under paragraph 1(9) or 7).

(8) Section 6(1) of the Statutory Instruments Act 1946 as applied by section 11A of that Act (alternative procedure for certain instruments laid in draft before the Assembly) does not apply in relation to any statutory instrument to which this paragraph applies.

(9) . . .

Scrutiny procedure in certain urgent deficiencies cases: Ministers of the Crown

5. (1) Sub-paragraph (2) applies to—
(a) a statutory instrument to which paragraph 1(1) applies, or
(b) a statutory instrument to which paragraph 1(3) applies which would not otherwise be made without a draft of the instrument being laid before, and approved by a resolution of, each House of Parliament.

(2) The instrument may be made without a draft of the instrument being laid before, and approved by a resolution of, each House of Parliament if it contains a declaration that the Minister of the Crown concerned is of the opinion that, by reason of urgency, it is necessary to make the regulations without a draft being so laid and approved.

(3) After an instrument is made in accordance with sub-paragraph (2), it must be laid before each House of Parliament.

(4) Regulations contained in an instrument made in accordance with sub-paragraph (2) cease to have effect at the end of the period of 28 days beginning with the day on which the instrument is made unless, during that period, the instrument is approved by a resolution of each House of Parliament.

(5) In calculating the period of 28 days, no account is to be taken of any time during which—
(a) Parliament is dissolved or prorogued, or
(b) either House of Parliament is adjourned for more than four days.

(6) If regulations cease to have effect as a result of sub-paragraph (4), that does not—
(a) affect the validity of anything previously done under the regulations, or
(b) prevent the making of new regulations.

(7) Sub-paragraph (8) applies to a statutory instrument to which paragraph 1(3) applies where the Minister of the Crown who is to make the instrument is of the opinion that the appropriate procedure for the instrument is for it to be subject to annulment in pursuance of a resolution of either House of Parliament.

(8) Paragraph 3 does not apply in relation to the instrument if the instrument contains a declaration that the Minister is of the opinion that, by reason of urgency, it is necessary to make the regulations without meeting the requirements of that paragraph.

Scrutiny procedure in certain urgent deficiencies cases: devolved authorities

6. (1) This paragraph applies to—

(a) regulations to which paragraph 1(6) applies, or

(b) regulations to which paragraph 1(7) applies which would not otherwise be made without being subject to the affirmative procedure.

(2) The regulations may be made without being subject to the affirmative procedure if the regulations contain a declaration that the Scottish Ministers are of the opinion that, by reason of urgency, it is necessary to make the regulations without them being subject to that procedure.

(3) After regulations are made in accordance with sub-paragraph (2), they must be laid before the Scottish Parliament.

(4) Regulations made in accordance with sub-paragraph (2) cease to have effect at the end of the period of 28 days beginning with the day on which they are made unless, during that period, the regulations are approved by resolution of the Scottish Parliament.

(5) In calculating the period of 28 days, no account is to be taken of any time during which the Scottish Parliament is—

(a) dissolved, or

(b) in recess for more than four days.

(6) If regulations cease to have effect as a result of sub-paragraph (4), that does not—

(a) affect the validity of anything previously done under the regulations, or

(b) prevent the making of new regulations.

(7) . . .

7. (1) Sub-paragraph (2) applies to—

(a) a statutory instrument to which paragraph 1(8) applies, or

(b) a statutory instrument to which paragraph 1(9) applies which would not otherwise be made without a draft of the instrument being laid before, and approved by a resolution of, the National Assembly for Wales.

(2) The instrument may be made without a draft of the instrument being laid before, and approved by a resolution of, the National Assembly for Wales if it contains a declaration that the Welsh Ministers are of the opinion that, by reason of urgency, it is necessary to make the regulations without a draft being so laid and approved.

(3) After an instrument is made in accordance with sub-paragraph (2), it must be laid before the National Assembly for Wales.

(4) Regulations contained in an instrument made in accordance with sub-paragraph (2) cease to have effect at the end of the period of 28 days beginning with the day on which the instrument is made unless, during that period, the instrument is approved by a resolution of the National Assembly for Wales.

(5) In calculating the period of 28 days, no account is to be taken of any time during which the National Assembly for Wales is—

(a) dissolved, or

(b) in recess for more than four days.

(6) If regulations cease to have effect as a result of sub-paragraph (4), that does not—

(a) affect the validity of anything previously done under the regulations, or

(b) prevent the making of new regulations.

(7) Sub-paragraph (8) applies to a statutory instrument to which paragraph 1(9) applies where the Welsh Ministers are of the opinion that the appropriate procedure for the instrument is for it to be subject to annulment in pursuance of a resolution of the National Assembly for Wales.

(8) Paragraph 4 does not apply in relation to the instrument if the instrument contains a declaration that the Welsh Ministers are of the opinion that, by reason of urgency, it is necessary to make the regulations without meeting the requirements of that paragraph.

(9) . . .

8. (1) This paragraph applies to—

(a) regulations to which paragraph 1(11) applies, or

(b) regulations to which paragraph 1(12) applies which would not otherwise be made without a draft of the regulations being laid before, and approved by a resolution of, the Northern Ireland Assembly.

(2) The regulations may be made without a draft of the regulations being laid before, and approved by a resolution of, the Northern Ireland Assembly if they contain a declaration that the Northern Ireland department concerned is of the opinion that, by reason of urgency, it is necessary to make the regulations without a draft being so laid and approved.

(3) After regulations are made in accordance with sub-paragraph (2), they must be laid before the Northern Ireland Assembly.

(4) Regulations made in accordance with sub-paragraph (2) cease to have effect at the end of the period of 28 days beginning with the day on which they are made unless, during that period, the regulations are approved by a resolution of the Northern Ireland Assembly.

(5) In calculating the period of 28 days, no account is to be taken of any time during which the Northern Ireland Assembly is—

(a) dissolved,

(b) in recess for more than four days, or
(c) adjourned for more than six days.

(6) If regulations cease to have effect as a result of sub-paragraph (4), that does not—
(a) affect the validity of anything previously done under the regulations, or
(b) prevent the making of new regulations.

(7) . . .

NOTES

Commencement: 26 June 2018.

All amendments to this Part were made by the European Union (Withdrawal Agreement) Act 2020, s 41(4), Sch 5, Pt 2, paras 38, 50.

National Assembly for Wales: as to the renaming of the National Assembly for Wales, etc, see the note at **[7.28]**.

[PART 1A SCRUTINY OF SPECIFIC POWERS RELATING TO WITHDRAWAL AGREEMENT ETC

Powers in connection with Part 4 of the withdrawal agreement

[7.46]

8A. A statutory instrument containing regulations under section 1A(3)(a)(ii) may not be made unless a draft of the instrument has been laid before, and approved by a resolution of, each House of Parliament.

8B. (1) A statutory instrument containing regulations under section 8A which amend, repeal or revoke—
(a) primary legislation, or
(b) retained direct principal EU legislation,
may not be made unless a draft of the instrument has been laid before, and approved by a resolution of, each House of Parliament.

(2) Any other statutory instrument containing regulations under section 8A is subject to annulment in pursuance of a resolution of either House of Parliament.

(3) Regulations under Part 1A of Schedule 2 of the Scottish Ministers acting alone which amend, repeal or revoke—
(a) primary legislation, or
(b) retained direct principal EU legislation,
are subject to the affirmative procedure (see section 29 of the Interpretation and Legislative Reform (Scotland) Act 2010 (asp 10)).

(4) Any other regulations under Part 1A of Schedule 2 of the Scottish Ministers acting alone are subject to the negative procedure (see section 28 of the Interpretation and Legislative Reform (Scotland) Act 2010).

(5) A statutory instrument containing regulations under Part 1A of Schedule 2 of the Welsh Ministers acting alone which amend, repeal or revoke—
(a) primary legislation, or
(b) retained direct principal EU legislation,
may not be made unless a draft of the instrument has been laid before, and approved by a resolution of, the National Assembly for Wales.

(6) Any other statutory instrument containing regulations under Part 1A of Schedule 2 of the Welsh Ministers acting alone is subject to annulment in pursuance of a resolution of the National Assembly for Wales.

(7) Regulations under Part 1A of Schedule 2 of a Northern Ireland department acting alone which amend, repeal or revoke—
(a) primary legislation, or
(b) retained direct principal EU legislation,
may not be made unless a draft of the regulations has been laid before, and approved by a resolution of, the Northern Ireland Assembly.

(8) Any other regulations under Part 1A of Schedule 2 of a Northern Ireland department acting alone are subject to negative resolution within the meaning of section 41(6) of the Interpretation Act (Northern Ireland) 1954 as if they were a statutory instrument within the meaning of that Act.

8C. (1) This paragraph applies to regulations under Part 1A of Schedule 2 of a Minister of the Crown acting jointly with a devolved authority.

(2) The procedure provided for by sub-paragraph (3) or (4) applies in relation to regulations to which this paragraph applies as well as any other procedure provided for by this paragraph which is applicable in relation to the regulations concerned.

(3) A statutory instrument containing regulations to which this paragraph applies which amend, repeal or revoke—
(a) primary legislation, or
(b) retained direct principal EU legislation,
may not be made unless a draft of the instrument has been laid before, and approved by a resolution of, each House of Parliament.

(4) Any other statutory instrument containing regulations to which this paragraph applies is subject to annulment in pursuance of a resolution of either House of Parliament.

(5) Regulations to which this paragraph applies which are made jointly with the Scottish Ministers and amend, repeal or revoke—
(a) primary legislation, or
(b) retained direct principal EU legislation,
are subject to the affirmative procedure.

(6) Any other regulations to which this paragraph applies which are made jointly with the Scottish Ministers are subject to the negative procedure.

(7) Section 29 of the Interpretation and Legislative Reform (Scotland) Act 2010 (affirmative procedure) applies in relation to regulations to which sub-paragraph (5) applies as it applies in relation to devolved subordinate legislation (within the meaning of Part 2 of that Act) which is subject to the affirmative procedure (but as if references to a Scottish statutory instrument were references to a statutory instrument).

(8) Sections 28(2), (3) and (8) and 31 of the Interpretation and Legislative Reform (Scotland) Act 2010 (negative procedure etc) apply in relation to regulations to which sub-paragraph (6) applies as they apply in relation to devolved subordinate legislation (within the meaning of Part 2 of that Act) which is subject to the negative procedure (but as if references to a Scottish statutory instrument were references to a statutory instrument).

(9) Section 32 of the Interpretation and Legislative Reform (Scotland) Act 2010 (laying) applies in relation to the laying before the Scottish Parliament of a statutory instrument containing regulations to which sub-paragraph (5) or (6) applies as it applies in relation to the laying before that Parliament of a Scottish statutory instrument (within the meaning of Part 2 of that Act).

(10) A statutory instrument containing regulations to which this paragraph applies which are made jointly with the Welsh Ministers and amend, repeal or revoke—

(a) primary legislation, or

(b) retained direct principal EU legislation,

may not be made unless a draft of the instrument has been laid before, and approved by a resolution of, the National Assembly for Wales.

(11) Any other statutory instrument containing regulations to which this paragraph applies which are made jointly with the Welsh Ministers is subject to annulment in pursuance of a resolution of the National Assembly for Wales.

(12) Regulations to which this paragraph applies which are made jointly with a Northern Ireland department and amend, repeal or revoke—

(a) primary legislation, or

(b) retained direct principal EU legislation,

may not be made unless a draft of the regulations has been laid before, and approved by a resolution of, the Northern Ireland Assembly.

(13) Any other regulations to which this paragraph applies which are made jointly with a Northern Ireland department are subject to negative resolution within the meaning of section 41(6) of the Interpretation Act (Northern Ireland) 1954 as if they were a statutory instrument within the meaning of that Act.

(14) If in accordance with sub-paragraph (4), (6), (11) or (13)—

(a) either House of Parliament resolves that an address be presented to Her Majesty praying that an instrument be annulled, or

(b) a relevant devolved legislature resolves that an instrument be annulled,

nothing further is to be done under the instrument after the date of the resolution and Her Majesty may by Order in Council revoke the instrument.

(15) In sub-paragraph (14) "relevant devolved legislature" means—

(a) in the case of regulations made jointly with the Scottish Ministers, the Scottish Parliament,

(b) in the case of regulations made jointly with the Welsh Ministers, the National Assembly for Wales, and

(c) in the case of regulations made jointly with a Northern Ireland department, the Northern Ireland Assembly.

(16) Sub-paragraph (14) does not affect the validity of anything previously done under the instrument or prevent the making of a new instrument.

(17) Sub-paragraphs (14) to (16) apply in place of provision made by any other enactment about the effect of such a resolution.

Powers in connection with other separation issues in the withdrawal agreement etc

8D. (1) A statutory instrument containing regulations under section 8B which amend, repeal or revoke—

(a) primary legislation, or

(b) retained direct principal EU legislation,

may not be made unless a draft of the instrument has been laid before, and approved by a resolution of, each House of Parliament.

(2) Any other statutory instrument containing regulations under section 8B is subject to annulment in pursuance of a resolution of either House of Parliament.

(3) Regulations under Part 1B of Schedule 2 of the Scottish Ministers acting alone which amend, repeal or revoke—

(a) primary legislation, or

(b) retained direct principal EU legislation,

are subject to the affirmative procedure (see section 29 of the Interpretation and Legislative Reform (Scotland) Act 2010).

(4) Any other regulations under Part 1B of Schedule 2 of the Scottish Ministers acting alone are subject to the negative procedure (see section 28 of the Interpretation and Legislative Reform (Scotland) Act 2010).

(5) A statutory instrument containing regulations under Part 1B of Schedule 2 of the Welsh Ministers acting alone which amend, repeal or revoke—

(a) primary legislation, or

(b) retained direct principal EU legislation,

may not be made unless a draft of the instrument has been laid before, and approved by a resolution of, the National Assembly for Wales.

(6) Any other statutory instrument containing regulations under Part 1B of Schedule 2 of the Welsh Ministers acting alone is subject to annulment in pursuance of a resolution of the National Assembly for Wales.

(7) Regulations under Part 1B of Schedule 2 of a Northern Ireland department acting alone which amend, repeal or revoke—

(a) primary legislation, or

(b) retained direct principal EU legislation,

may not be made unless a draft of the regulations has been laid before, and approved by a resolution of, the Northern Ireland Assembly.

(8) Any other regulations under Part 1B of Schedule 2 of a Northern Ireland department acting alone are subject to negative resolution within the meaning of section 41(6) of the Interpretation Act (Northern Ireland) 1954 as if they were a statutory instrument within the meaning of that Act.

8E. (1) This paragraph applies to regulations under Part 1B of Schedule 2 of a Minister of the Crown acting jointly with a devolved authority.

(2) The procedure provided for by sub-paragraph (3) or (4) applies in relation to regulations to which this paragraph applies as well as any other procedure provided for by this paragraph which is applicable in relation to the regulations concerned.

(3) A statutory instrument containing regulations to which this paragraph applies which amend, repeal or revoke—

(a) primary legislation, or

(b) retained direct principal EU legislation,

may not be made unless a draft of the instrument has been laid before, and approved by a resolution of, each House of Parliament.

(4) Any other statutory instrument containing regulations to which this paragraph applies is subject to annulment in pursuance of a resolution of either House of Parliament.

(5) Regulations to which this paragraph applies which are made jointly with the Scottish Ministers and amend, repeal or revoke—

(a) primary legislation, or

(b) retained direct principal EU legislation,

are subject to the affirmative procedure.

(6) Any other regulations to which this paragraph applies which are made jointly with the Scottish Ministers are subject to the negative procedure.

(7) Section 29 of the Interpretation and Legislative Reform (Scotland) Act 2010 (affirmative procedure) applies in relation to regulations to which sub-paragraph (5) applies as it applies in relation to devolved subordinate legislation (within the meaning of Part 2 of that Act) which is subject to the affirmative procedure (but as if references to a Scottish statutory instrument were references to a statutory instrument).

(8) Sections 28(2), (3) and (8) and 31 of the Interpretation and Legislative Reform (Scotland) Act 2010 (negative procedure etc) apply in relation to regulations to which sub-paragraph (6) applies as they apply in relation to devolved subordinate legislation (within the meaning of Part 2 of that Act) which is subject to the negative procedure (but as if references to a Scottish statutory instrument were references to a statutory instrument).

(9) Section 32 of the Interpretation and Legislative Reform (Scotland) Act 2010 (laying) applies in relation to the laying before the Scottish Parliament of a statutory instrument containing regulations to which sub-paragraph (5) or (6) applies as it applies in relation to the laying before that Parliament of a Scottish statutory instrument (within the meaning of Part 2 of that Act).

(10) A statutory instrument containing regulations to which this paragraph applies which are made jointly with the Welsh Ministers and amend, repeal or revoke—

(a) primary legislation, or

(b) retained direct principal EU legislation,

may not be made unless a draft of the instrument has been laid before, and approved by a resolution of, the National Assembly for Wales.

(11) Any other statutory instrument containing regulations to which this paragraph applies which are made jointly with the Welsh Ministers is subject to annulment in pursuance of a resolution of the National Assembly for Wales.

(12) Regulations to which this paragraph applies which are made jointly with a Northern Ireland department and amend, repeal or revoke—

(a) primary legislation, or

(b) retained direct principal EU legislation,

may not be made unless a draft of the regulations has been laid before, and approved by a resolution of, the Northern Ireland Assembly.

(13) Any other regulations to which this paragraph applies which are made jointly with a Northern Ireland department are subject to negative resolution within the meaning of section 41(6) of the Interpretation Act (Northern Ireland) 1954 as if they were a statutory instrument within the meaning of that Act.

(14) If in accordance with sub-paragraph (4), (6), (11) or (13)—

(a) either House of Parliament resolves that an address be presented to Her Majesty praying that an instrument be annulled, or

(b) a relevant devolved legislature resolves that an instrument be annulled,

nothing further is to be done under the instrument after the date of the resolution and Her Majesty may by Order in Council revoke the instrument.

(15) In sub-paragraph (14) "relevant devolved legislature" means—

(a) in the case of regulations made jointly with the Scottish Ministers, the Scottish Parliament,

(b) in the case of regulations made jointly with the Welsh Ministers, the National Assembly for Wales, and

(c) in the case of regulations made jointly with a Northern Ireland department, the Northern Ireland Assembly.

(16) Sub-paragraph (14) does not affect the validity of anything previously done under the instrument or prevent the making of a new instrument.

(17) Sub-paragraphs (14) to (16) apply in place of provision made by any other enactment about the effect of such a resolution.

Powers in connection with the Ireland/Northern Ireland Protocol in the withdrawal agreement

8F. (1) A statutory instrument containing regulations under section 8C(1) which contain provision falling within sub-paragraph (2) may not be made unless a draft of the instrument has been laid before, and approved by a resolution of, each House of Parliament.

(2) Provision falls within this sub-paragraph if it—

(a) amends, repeals or revokes primary legislation or retained direct principal EU legislation,
(b) establishes a public authority,
(c) relates to a fee in respect of a function exercisable by a public authority in the United Kingdom,
(d) creates, or widens the scope of, a criminal offence,
(e) creates or amends a power to legislate, or
(f) facilitates the access to the market within Great Britain of qualifying Northern Ireland goods.

(3) Any other statutory instrument containing regulations under section 8C(1) is subject to annulment in pursuance of a resolution of either House of Parliament.

(4) A statutory instrument containing regulations under section 8C(6) may not be made unless a draft of the instrument has been laid before, and approved by a resolution of, each House of Parliament.

(5) Regulations under Part 1C of Schedule 2 of the Scottish Ministers acting alone which contain provision falling within sub-paragraph (2) are subject to the affirmative procedure (see section 29 of the Interpretation and Legislative Reform (Scotland) Act 2010).

(6) Any other regulations under Part 1C of Schedule 2 of the Scottish Ministers acting alone are subject to the negative procedure (see section 28 of the Interpretation and Legislative Reform (Scotland) Act 2010).

(7) A statutory instrument containing regulations under Part 1C of Schedule 2 of the Welsh Ministers acting alone which contain provision falling within sub-paragraph (2) may not be made unless a draft of the instrument has been laid before, and approved by a resolution of, the National Assembly for Wales.

(8) Any other statutory instrument containing regulations under Part 1C of Schedule 2 of the Welsh Ministers acting alone is subject to annulment in pursuance of a resolution of the National Assembly for Wales.

(9) Regulations under Part 1C of Schedule 2 of a Northern Ireland department acting alone which contain provision falling within sub-paragraph (2) may not be made unless a draft of the regulations has been laid before, and approved by a resolution of, the Northern Ireland Assembly.

(10) Any other regulations under Part 1C of Schedule 2 of a Northern Ireland department acting alone are subject to negative resolution within the meaning of section 41(6) of the Interpretation Act (Northern Ireland) 1954 as if they were a statutory instrument within the meaning of that Act.

8G. (1) This paragraph applies to regulations under Part 1C of Schedule 2 of a Minister of the Crown acting jointly with a devolved authority.

(2) The procedure provided for by sub-paragraph (3) or (4) applies in relation to regulations to which this paragraph applies as well as any other procedure provided for by this paragraph which is applicable in relation to the regulations concerned.

(3) A statutory instrument containing regulations to which this paragraph applies which contain provision falling within paragraph 8F(2) may not be made unless a draft of the instrument has been laid before, and approved by a resolution of, each House of Parliament.

(4) Any other statutory instrument containing regulations to which this paragraph applies is subject to annulment in pursuance of a resolution of either House of Parliament.

(5) Regulations to which this paragraph applies which are made jointly with the Scottish Ministers and contain provision falling within paragraph 8F(2) are subject to the affirmative procedure.

(6) Any other regulations to which this paragraph applies which are made jointly with the Scottish Ministers are subject to the negative procedure.

(7) Section 29 of the Interpretation and Legislative Reform (Scotland) Act 2010 (affirmative procedure) applies in relation to regulations to which sub-paragraph (5) applies as it applies in relation to devolved subordinate legislation (within the meaning of Part 2 of that Act) which is subject to the affirmative procedure (but as if references to a Scottish statutory instrument were references to a statutory instrument).

(8) Sections 28(2), (3) and (8) and 31 of the Interpretation and Legislative Reform (Scotland) Act 2010 (negative procedure etc) apply in relation to regulations to which sub-paragraph (6) applies as they apply in relation to devolved subordinate legislation (within the meaning of Part 2 of that Act) which is subject to the negative procedure (but as if references to a Scottish statutory instrument were references to a statutory instrument).

(9) Section 32 of the Interpretation and Legislative Reform (Scotland) Act 2010 (laying) applies in relation to the laying before the Scottish Parliament of a statutory instrument containing regulations to which sub-paragraph (5) or (6) applies as it applies in relation to the laying before that Parliament of a Scottish statutory instrument (within the meaning of Part 2 of that Act).

(10) A statutory instrument containing regulations to which this paragraph applies which are made jointly with the Welsh Ministers and contain provision falling within paragraph 8F(2) may not be made unless a draft of the instrument has been laid before, and approved by a resolution of, the National Assembly for Wales.

(11) Any other statutory instrument containing regulations to which this paragraph applies which are made jointly with the Welsh Ministers is subject to annulment in pursuance of a resolution of the National Assembly for Wales.

(12) Regulations to which this paragraph applies which are made jointly with a Northern Ireland department and contain provision falling within paragraph 8F(2) may not be made unless a draft of the regulations has been laid before, and approved by a resolution of, the Northern Ireland Assembly.

(13) Any other regulations to which this paragraph applies which are made jointly with a Northern Ireland department are subject to negative resolution within the meaning of section 41(6) of the Interpretation Act (Northern Ireland) 1954 as if they were a statutory instrument within the meaning of that Act.

(14) If in accordance with sub-paragraph (4), (6), (11) or (13)—

(a) either House of Parliament resolves that an address be presented to Her Majesty praying that an instrument be annulled, or

(b) a relevant devolved legislature resolves that an instrument be annulled,

nothing further is to be done under the instrument after the date of the resolution and Her Majesty may by Order in Council revoke the instrument.

(15) In sub-paragraph (14) "relevant devolved legislature" means—

(a) in the case of regulations made jointly with the Scottish Ministers, the Scottish Parliament,

(b) in the case of regulations made jointly with the Welsh Ministers, the National Assembly for Wales, and

(c) in the case of regulations made jointly with a Northern Ireland department, the Northern Ireland Assembly.

(16) Sub-paragraph (14) does not affect the validity of anything previously done under the instrument or prevent the making of a new instrument.

(17) Sub-paragraphs (14) to (16) apply in place of provision made by any other enactment about the effect of such a resolution.]

NOTES

Commencement: 23 January 2020 (for the purposes of making regulations under s 8A, or Part 1A of Schedule 2); exit day (31 January 2020 at 11pm) (for the purposes of making regulations under s 1A(3)(a)(ii)); this Part came into force on 19 May 2020 for all other purposes..

Inserted by the European Union (Withdrawal Agreement) Act 2020, s 41(4), Sch 5, Pt 2, paras 38, 51.

National Assembly for Wales: as to the renaming of the National Assembly for Wales, etc, see the note at **[7.28]**.

PART 2 SCRUTINY OF OTHER POWERS UNDER ACT

Power to enable challenges to validity of retained EU law

[7.47]

9. (1) A statutory instrument containing regulations under paragraph 1(2)(b) of Schedule 1 may not be made unless a draft of the instrument has been laid before, and approved by a resolution of, each House of Parliament.

(2) This paragraph is subject to paragraph 19.

[Power in relation to interpretation of retained EU law

9A. A statutory instrument containing regulations under section 6(5A) may not be made unless a draft of the instrument has been laid before, and approved by a resolution of, each House of Parliament.]

. . .

10. . . .

Power to repeal provisions relating to retained EU law restrictions

11. A statutory instrument containing regulations under section 12(9) may not be made unless a draft of the instrument has been laid before, and approved by a resolution of, each House of Parliament.

Powers in connection with fees and charges

12. (1) A statutory instrument containing regulations of a Minister of the Crown under Schedule 4 which contain provision which does not relate to altering the amount of a fee or charge to reflect changes in the value of money may not be made unless a draft of the instrument has been laid before, and approved by a resolution of, each House of Parliament.

(2) Any other statutory instrument containing regulations under Schedule 4 of a Minister of the Crown is (if a draft of the instrument has not been laid before, and approved by a resolution of, each House of Parliament) subject to annulment in pursuance of a resolution of either House of Parliament.

(3) Paragraphs 1(6) to (13)(a) and 2 apply to regulations under Schedule 4 as they apply to regulations under Part 1 of Schedule 2 except that any reference to provision falling within paragraph 1(2) is to be read as a reference to any provision made under Schedule 4 which does not relate to altering the amount of a fee or charge to reflect changes in the value of money.

(4) This paragraph is subject to paragraph 19.

Power to make provision about judicial notice and admissibility

13. A statutory instrument containing regulations under paragraph 4 of Schedule 5 may not be made unless a draft of the instrument has been laid before, and approved by a resolution of, each House of Parliament.

Power to amend the definition of "exit day"

14. A statutory instrument containing regulations under section 20(4) [is subject to annulment in pursuance of a resolution of either] House of Parliament.

Power to make consequential provision

15. (1) A statutory instrument containing regulations under section 23(1) is (if a draft of the instrument has not been laid before, and approved by a resolution of, each House of Parliament) subject to annulment in pursuance of a resolution of either House of Parliament.

(2) See paragraph 17 for restrictions on the choice of procedure under sub-paragraph (1).

Power to make transitional, transitory or saving provision

16. (1) Sub-paragraph (2) applies if a Minister of the Crown who is to make regulations under section 23(6) considers that—

- (a) it is not appropriate for the statutory instrument containing them to be subject to no parliamentary procedure, and
- (b) it is appropriate for that statutory instrument to be subject to the parliamentary procedure in sub-paragraph (2).

(2) The statutory instrument containing the regulations may not be made unless a draft of the instrument has been laid before, and approved by a resolution of, each House of Parliament.

(3) Sub-paragraph (4) applies if a Minister of the Crown who is to make regulations under section 23(6) considers that—

- (a) it is not appropriate for the statutory instrument containing them to be subject to no parliamentary procedure, and
- (b) it is appropriate for that statutory instrument to be subject to the parliamentary procedure in sub-paragraph (4).

(4) The statutory instrument containing the regulations is subject to annulment in pursuance of a resolution of either House of Parliament.

Parliamentary committee to sift . . . consequential regulations of a Minister of the Crown

17. (1) Sub-paragraph (2) applies if a Minister of the Crown who is to make a statutory instrument to which paragraph . . . 15 applies is of the opinion that the appropriate procedure for the instrument is for it to be subject to annulment in pursuance of a resolution of either House of Parliament.

(2) The Minister may not make the instrument so that it is subject to that procedure unless—

- (a) condition 1 is met, and
- (b) either condition 2 or 3 is met.

(3) Condition 1 is that a Minister of the Crown—

- (a) has made a statement in writing to the effect that in the Minister's opinion the instrument should be subject to annulment in pursuance of a resolution of either House of Parliament, and
- (b) has laid before each House of Parliament—
  - (i) a draft of the instrument, and
  - (ii) a memorandum setting out the statement and the reasons for the Minister's opinion.

(4) Condition 2 is that a committee of the House of Commons charged with doing so and a committee of the House of Lords charged with doing so have, within the relevant period, each made a recommendation as to the appropriate procedure for the instrument.

(5) Condition 3 is that the relevant period has ended without condition 2 being met.

(6) Sub-paragraph (7) applies if—

- (a) a committee makes a recommendation as mentioned in sub-paragraph (4) within the relevant period,
- (b) the recommendation is that the appropriate procedure for the instrument is for a draft of it to be laid before, and approved by a resolution of, each House of Parliament before it is made, and
- (c) the Minister who is to make the instrument is nevertheless of the opinion that the appropriate procedure for the instrument is for it to be subject to annulment in pursuance of a resolution of either House of Parliament.

(7) Before the instrument is made, the Minister must make a statement explaining why the Minister does not agree with the recommendation of the committee.

(8) If the Minister fails to make a statement required by sub-paragraph (7) before the instrument is made, a Minister of the Crown must make a statement explaining why the Minister has failed to do so.

(9) A statement under sub-paragraph (7) or (8) must be made in writing and be published in such manner as the Minister making it considers appropriate.

(10) In this paragraph "the relevant period" means the period—

- (a) beginning with the first day on which both Houses of Parliament are sitting after the day on which the draft instrument was laid before each House of Parliament as mentioned in sub-paragraph (3)(b)(i), and
- (b) ending with whichever of the following is the later—
  - (i) the end of the period of 10 Commons sitting days beginning with that first day, and
  - (ii) the end of the period of 10 Lords sitting days beginning with that first day.

(11) For the purposes of sub-paragraph (10)—

- (a) where a draft of an instrument is laid before each House of Parliament on different days, the later day is to be taken as the day on which it is laid before both Houses,

(b), (c) . . .

(12) Nothing in this paragraph prevents a Minister of the Crown from deciding at any time before a statutory instrument to which paragraph . . . 15 applies is made that another procedure should apply in relation to the instrument (whether under that paragraph or paragraph 19).

(13) Section 6(1) of the Statutory Instruments Act 1946 (alternative procedure for certain instruments laid in draft before Parliament) does not apply in relation to any statutory instrument to which this paragraph applies.

18. . . .

Scrutiny procedure for certain powers to which this Part applies in urgent cases

19. (1) Sub-paragraph (2) applies to—

- (a) a statutory instrument to which paragraph 9(1) . . . or 12(1) applies, or

(b) a statutory instrument to which paragraph . . . , 12(2) or 15 applies which would not otherwise be made without a draft of the instrument being laid before, and approved by a resolution of, each House of Parliament.

(2) The instrument may be made without a draft of the instrument being laid before, and approved by a resolution of, each House of Parliament if it contains a declaration that the Minister of the Crown concerned is of the opinion that, by reason of urgency, it is necessary to make the regulations without a draft being so laid and approved.

(3) After an instrument is made in accordance with sub-paragraph (2), it must be laid before each House of Parliament.

(4) Regulations contained in an instrument made in accordance with sub-paragraph (2) cease to have effect at the end of the period of 28 days beginning with the day on which the instrument is made unless, during that period, the instrument is approved by a resolution of each House of Parliament.

(5) In calculating the period of 28 days, no account is to be taken of any time during which—

(a) Parliament is dissolved or prorogued, or

(b) either House of Parliament is adjourned for more than four days.

(6) If regulations cease to have effect as a result of sub-paragraph (4), that does not—

(a) affect the validity of anything previously done under the regulations, or

(b) prevent the making of new regulations.

(7) . . .

(8) Sub-paragraph (9) applies to a statutory instrument to which paragraph . . . 15 applies where the Minister of the Crown who is to make the instrument is of the opinion that the appropriate procedure for the instrument is for it to be subject to annulment in pursuance of a resolution of either House of Parliament.

(9) Paragraph 17 does not apply in relation to the instrument if the instrument contains a declaration that the Minister is of the opinion that, by reason of urgency, it is necessary to make the regulations without meeting the requirements of that paragraph.

NOTES

Commencement: 26 June 2018.

Para 9A: inserted by the European Union (Withdrawal Agreement) Act 2020, s 41(4), Sch 5, Pt 2, paras 38, 52(1), (2).

Para 14: words in square brackets substituted by the European Union (Withdrawal) Act 2019, s 2.

All words omitted were repealed by the European Union (Withdrawal Agreement) Act 2020, s 41(4), Sch 5, Pt 2, paras 38, 52(1)–(7).

PART 3 GENERAL PROVISION ABOUT POWERS UNDER ACT

Scope and nature of powers: general

[7.48]

20. (1) Any power to make regulations under this Act—

(a) so far as exercisable by a Minister of the Crown or by a Minister of the Crown acting jointly with a devolved authority, is exercisable by statutory instrument,

(b) so far as exercisable by the Welsh Ministers or by the Welsh Ministers acting jointly with a Minister of the Crown, is exercisable by statutory instrument, and

(c) so far as exercisable by a Northern Ireland department (other than when acting jointly with a Minister of the Crown), is exercisable by statutory rule for the purposes of the Statutory Rules (Northern Ireland) Order 1979 (SI 1979/1573 (NI 12)) (and not by statutory instrument).

(2) For regulations made under this Act by the Scottish Ministers, see also section 27 of the Interpretation and Legislative Reform (Scotland) Act 2010 (asp 10) (Scottish statutory instruments).

21. Any power to make regulations under this Act—

(a) may be exercised so as to—

(i) modify [anything which continues to be domestic law by virtue of section 1B(2) or any] retained EU law, or

(ii) make different provision for different cases or descriptions of case, different circumstances, different purposes or different areas, and

(b) includes power to make supplementary, incidental, consequential, transitional, transitory or saving provision (including provision re-stating [anything which continues to be domestic law by virtue of section 1B(2), or any retained EU law,] in a clearer or more accessible way).

22. The fact that a power to make regulations is conferred by this Act does not affect the extent of any other power to make regulations under this Act.

Scope of consequential and transitional powers

23. (1) The fact that anything continues to be, or forms part of, domestic law by virtue of any provision of [sections 1A] to 6 or Schedule 1 does not prevent it from being modified by regulations made under section 23(1) in consequence of any other provision made by or under this Act.

(2) Accordingly, [anything which continues to be domestic law by virtue of section 1B(2) or] any retained EU law may, for example, be modified by regulations made under section 23(1) in consequence of the repeal of any enactment contained in the European Communities Act 1972.

(3) The power to make regulations under section 23(6) includes the power to make transitional, transitory or saving provision in connection with—

(a) the repeal of any enactment contained in the European Communities Act 1972, or

(b) the withdrawal of the United Kingdom from the EU,

which is additional to that made by any provision of [sections 1A] to 6 or Schedule 1 or alters its effect in particular cases or descriptions of case.

(4) The power to make regulations under section 23(1) includes the power to make transitional, transitory or saving provision which—

(a) is in connection with any repeal or revocation made by any such regulations of an enactment in consequence of—

(i) the repeal of any enactment contained in the European Communities Act 1972, or

(ii) the withdrawal of the United Kingdom from the EU, and

(b) is additional to that made by any provision of [sections 1A] to 6 or Schedule 1 or alters its effect in particular cases or descriptions of case.

(5) Provision of the kind mentioned in sub-paragraph (3) or (4) may (among other things) include further provision treating any provision of that kind as [anything which continues to be domestic law by virtue of section 1B(2), or as retained EU law,] for particular purposes or all purposes.

[Anticipatory exercise of powers in relation to section 1B(2) saved law

23A. Any power to make regulations under this Act which modify anything which continues to be domestic law by virtue of section 1B(2) is capable of being exercised before exit day so that the regulations come into force on or after exit day.]

Anticipatory exercise of powers in relation to retained EU law

24. Any power to make regulations under this Act which modify retained direct EU legislation, anything which is retained EU law by virtue of section 4 or any other retained EU law is capable of being exercised before [IP completion day] so that the regulations come into force on or after [IP completion day].

[Anticipatory exercise of powers in relation to the withdrawal agreement etc

24A. Any power to make regulations under this Act in relation to the withdrawal agreement, the EEA EFTA separation agreement or the Swiss citizens' rights agreement, or any modification of any of them which requires ratification, is capable of being exercised before the agreement or (as the case may be) modification concerned is ratified.]

Scope of appointed day powers

25. Any power of a Minister of the Crown under this Act to appoint a day includes a power to appoint a time on that day if the Minister considers it appropriate to do so.

Effect of certain provisions in Schedule 8 on scope of powers

26. The modifications made by Part 1 of Schedule 8 and paragraphs 18 to 22 and 31 to 35 of that Schedule do not prevent or otherwise limit the making of different provision, in particular cases or descriptions of case, in regulations under section 23(1) or in any other regulations under this Act.

Disapplication of certain review provisions

27. Section 28 of the Small Business, Enterprise and Employment Act 2015 (duty to review regulatory provisions in secondary legislation) does not apply in relation to any power to make regulations conferred by this Act.

Explanatory statements for certain powers: appropriateness, equalities etc

28. (1) This paragraph applies where—

(a) a statutory instrument containing regulations under section 8(1) . . . or 23(1) or paragraph 1(2) or 12(2) of Schedule 2, or

(b) a draft of such an instrument,

is to be laid before each House of Parliament.

(2) Before the instrument or draft is laid, the relevant Minister must make a statement to the effect that in the Minister's opinion the instrument or draft does no more than is appropriate.

(3) Before the instrument or draft is laid, the relevant Minister must make a statement as to why, in the Minister's opinion—

(a) there are good reasons for the instrument or draft, and

(b) the provision made by the instrument or draft is a reasonable course of action.

(4) Before the instrument or draft is laid, the relevant Minister must make a statement—

(a) as to whether the instrument or draft amends, repeals or revokes any provision of equalities legislation, and

(b) if it does, explaining the effect of each such amendment, repeal or revocation.

(5) Before the instrument or draft is laid, the relevant Minister must make a statement to the effect that, in relation to the instrument or draft, the Minister has, so far as required to do so by equalities legislation, had due regard to the need to eliminate discrimination, harassment, victimisation and any other conduct that is prohibited by or under the Equality Act 2010.

(6) Before the instrument or draft is laid, the relevant Minister must make a statement otherwise explaining—

(a) the instrument or draft,

(b) its purpose,

(c) the law before [IP completion day] which is relevant to it, and

(d) its effect (if any) on retained EU law.

(7) Where an instrument or draft creates a criminal offence, the statement required by sub-paragraph (3) must (among other things) include an explanation of why, in the relevant Minister's opinion, there are good reasons for creating the offence and for the penalty provided in respect of it.

(8) If the relevant Minister fails to make a statement required by sub-paragraph (2), (3), (4), (5) or (6) before the instrument or draft is laid, a Minister of the Crown must make a statement explaining why the relevant Minister has failed to do so.

(9) A statement under sub-paragraph (2), (3), (4), (5), (6) or (8) must be made in writing and be published in such manner as the Minister making it considers appropriate.

(10) For the purposes of this paragraph, where an instrument or draft is laid before each House of Parliament on different days, the earlier day is to be taken as the day on which it is laid before both Houses.

(11) This paragraph does not apply in relation to any laying before each House of Parliament of an instrument or draft instrument where an equivalent draft instrument (ignoring any differences relating to procedure) has previously been laid before both Houses.

(12) In this paragraph—

"equalities legislation" means the Equality Act 2006, the Equality Act 2010 or any subordinate legislation made under either of those Acts;

"the relevant Minister" means the Minister of the Crown who makes, or is to make, the instrument.

29. (1) This paragraph applies where—

(a) a Scottish statutory instrument containing regulations under Part 1 . . . of Schedule 2, or

(b) a draft of such an instrument,

is to be laid before the Scottish Parliament.

(2) Before the instrument or draft is laid, the Scottish Ministers must make a statement to the effect that in the Scottish Ministers' opinion the instrument or draft does no more than is appropriate.

(3) Before the instrument or draft is laid, the Scottish Ministers must make a statement as to why, in the Scottish Ministers' opinion—

(a) there are good reasons for the instrument or draft, and

(b) the provision made by the instrument or draft is a reasonable course of action.

(4) Before the instrument or draft is laid, the Scottish Ministers must make a statement—

(a) as to whether the instrument or draft amends, repeals or revokes any provision of equalities legislation, and

(b) if it does, explaining the effect of each such amendment, repeal or revocation.

(5) Before the instrument or draft is laid, the Scottish Ministers must make a statement to the effect that, in relation to the instrument or draft, the Scottish Ministers have, so far as required to do so by equalities legislation, had due regard to the need to eliminate discrimination, harassment, victimisation and any other conduct that is prohibited by or under the Equality Act 2010.

(6) Before the instrument or draft is laid, the Scottish Ministers must make a statement otherwise explaining—

(a) the instrument or draft,

(b) its purpose,

(c) the law before [IP completion day] which is relevant to it, and

(d) its effect (if any) on retained EU law.

(7) Where an instrument or draft creates a criminal offence, the statement required by sub-paragraph (3) must (among other things) include an explanation of why, in the Scottish Ministers' opinion, there are good reasons for creating the offence and for the penalty provided in respect of it.

(8) If the Scottish Ministers fail to make a statement required by sub-paragraph (2), (3), (4), (5) or (6) before the instrument or draft is laid, the Scottish Ministers must make a statement explaining why they have failed to do so.

(9) A statement under sub-paragraph (2), (3), (4), (5), (6) or (8) must be made in writing and be published in such manner as the Scottish Ministers consider appropriate.

(10) In this paragraph "equalities legislation" means the Equality Act 2006, the Equality Act 2010 or any subordinate legislation made under either of those Acts.

Further explanatory statements in certain sub-delegation cases

30. (1) This paragraph applies where—

(a) a statutory instrument containing regulations under section 8(1) . . . or paragraph 1 of Schedule 4 which create a relevant sub-delegated power, or

(b) a draft of such an instrument,

is to be laid before each House of Parliament.

(2) Before the instrument or draft is laid, the relevant Minister must make a statement explaining why it is appropriate to create a relevant sub-delegated power.

(3) If the relevant Minister fails to make a statement required by sub-paragraph (2) before the instrument or draft is laid, a Minister of the Crown must make a statement explaining why the relevant Minister has failed to do so.

(4) A statement under sub-paragraph (2) or (3) must be made in writing and be published in such manner as the Minister making it considers appropriate.

(5) Sub-paragraphs (10) and (11) of paragraph 28 apply for the purposes of this paragraph as they apply for the purposes of that paragraph.

(6) For the purposes of this paragraph references to creating a relevant sub-delegated power include (among other things) references to—

(a) amending a power to legislate which is exercisable by statutory instrument by a relevant UK authority so that it becomes a relevant sub-delegated power, or

(b) providing for any function of an EU entity or public authority in a member State of making an instrument of a legislative character to be exercisable instead as a relevant sub-delegated power by a public authority in the United Kingdom.

(7) In this paragraph—

"the relevant Minister" means the Minister of the Crown who makes, or is to make, the instrument;

"relevant sub-delegated power" means a power to legislate which—

(a) is not exercisable by any of the following—

(i) statutory instrument,
(ii) Scottish statutory instrument, or
(iii) statutory rule, or

(b) is so exercisable by a public authority other than a relevant UK authority;

"relevant UK authority" means a Minister of the Crown, a member of the Scottish Government, the Welsh Ministers, the First Minister for Wales, the Counsel General to the Welsh Government or a Northern Ireland devolved authority.

31. (1) This paragraph applies where—

(a) a Scottish statutory instrument containing regulations under Part 1 . . . of Schedule 2 or paragraph 1 of Schedule 4 which create a relevant sub-delegated power, or

(b) a draft of such an instrument,

is to be laid before the Scottish Parliament.

(2) Before the instrument or draft is laid, the Scottish Ministers must make a statement explaining why it is appropriate to create a relevant sub-delegated power.

(3) If the Scottish Ministers fail to make a statement required by sub-paragraph (2) before the instrument or draft is laid, the Scottish Ministers must make a statement explaining why they have failed to do so.

(4) A statement under sub-paragraph (2) or (3) must be made in writing and be published in such manner as the Scottish Ministers consider appropriate.

(5) For the purposes of this paragraph references to creating a relevant sub-delegated power include (among other things) references to—

(a) amending a power to legislate which is exercisable by Scottish statutory instrument by a member of the Scottish Government so that it becomes a relevant sub-delegated power, or

(b) providing for any function of an EU entity or public authority in a member State of making an instrument of a legislative character to be exercisable instead as a relevant sub-delegated power by a public authority in the United Kingdom.

(6) In this paragraph "relevant sub-delegated power" means a power to legislate which—

(a) is not exercisable by Scottish statutory instrument, or

(b) is so exercisable by a public authority other than a member of the Scottish Government.

Annual reports in certain sub-delegation cases

32. (1) Each person by whom a relevant sub-delegated power is exercisable by virtue of regulations made by a Minister of the Crown under section 8(1) . . . or paragraph 1 of Schedule 4 must—

(a) if the power has been exercised during a relevant year, and

(b) as soon as practicable after the end of the year,

prepare a report on how the power has been exercised during the year.

(2) The person must—

(a) lay the report before each House of Parliament, and

(b) once laid—

(i) provide a copy of it to a Minister of the Crown, and
(ii) publish it in such manner as the person considers appropriate.

(3) In this paragraph—

"relevant sub-delegated power" has the same meaning as in paragraph 30;

"relevant year" means—

(a) in the case of a person who prepares an annual report, the year by reference to which the report is prepared, and

(b) in any other case, the calendar year.

33. (1) Each person by whom a relevant sub-delegated power is exercisable by virtue of regulations made by the Scottish Ministers by Scottish statutory instrument under Part 1 . . . of Schedule 2 or paragraph 1 of Schedule 4 must—

(a) if the power has been exercised during a relevant year, and

(b) as soon as practicable after the end of the year,

prepare a report on how the power has been exercised during the year.

(2) The person must—

(a) lay the report before the Scottish Parliament, and

(b) once laid—

(i) send a copy of it to the Scottish Ministers, and
(ii) publish it in such manner as the person considers appropriate.

(3) In this paragraph—

"relevant sub-delegated power" has the same meaning as in paragraph 31;

"relevant year" means—

(a) in the case of a person who prepares an annual report, the year by reference to which the report is prepared, and

(b) in any other case, the calendar year.

Further explanatory statements in urgency cases

34. (1) This paragraph applies where a statutory instrument containing regulations under this Act is to be made by virtue of paragraph 5(2) or 19(2).

Part 7 Brexit-related Materials

(2) The Minister of the Crown who is to make the instrument must make a statement in writing explaining the reasons for the Minister's opinion that, by reason of urgency, it is necessary to make the regulations without a draft of the instrument containing them being laid before, and approved by a resolution of, each House of Parliament.

(3) A statement under sub-paragraph (2) must be published before, or at the same time as, the instrument as made is laid before each House of Parliament.

(4) If the Minister—

(a) fails to make the statement required by sub-paragraph (2) before the instrument is made, or
(b) fails to publish it as required by sub-paragraph (3),

a Minister of the Crown must make a statement explaining the failure.

(5) A statement under sub-paragraph (4) must be made in writing and be published in such manner as the Minister making it considers appropriate.

(6) For the purposes of this paragraph, where an instrument is laid before each House of Parliament on different days, the earlier day is to be taken as the day on which it is laid before both Houses.

35. (1) This paragraph applies where regulations are to be made by the Scottish Ministers under this Act by virtue of paragraph 6(2)

(2) The Scottish Ministers must make a statement in writing explaining the reasons for the Scottish Ministers' opinion that, by reason of urgency, it is necessary to make the regulations without them being subject to the affirmative procedure.

(3) A statement under sub-paragraph (2) must be published before, or at the same time as, the regulations as made are laid before the Scottish Parliament.

(4) If the Scottish Ministers—

(a) fail to make the statement required by sub-paragraph (2) before the regulations are made, or
(b) fail to publish it as required by sub-paragraph (3),

they must make a statement explaining the failure.

(5) A statement under sub-paragraph (4) must be made in writing and be published in such manner as the Scottish Ministers consider appropriate.

Hybrid instruments

36. If an instrument, or a draft of an instrument, containing regulations under this Act would, apart from this paragraph, be treated as a hybrid instrument for the purposes of the standing orders of either House of Parliament, it is to proceed in that House as if it were not a hybrid instrument.

Procedure on re-exercise of certain powers

37. (1) A power to make regulations which, under this Schedule, is capable of being exercised subject to different procedures may (in spite of section 14 of the Interpretation Act 1978) be exercised, when revoking, amending or re-enacting an instrument made under the power, subject to a different procedure from the procedure to which the instrument was subject.

(2) For the purposes of sub-paragraph (1) in its application to regulations under section 23(6) no procedure is also a procedure.

Combinations of instruments

38. (1) Sub-paragraph (2) applies to a statutory instrument containing regulations under this Act which is subject to a procedure before Parliament for the approval of the instrument in draft before it is made or its approval after it is made.

(2) The statutory instrument may also include regulations under this Act or another enactment which are made by statutory instrument which is subject to a procedure before Parliament that provides for the annulment of the instrument after it has been made.

(3) Where regulations are included as mentioned in sub-paragraph (2), the procedure applicable to the statutory instrument is the procedure mentioned in sub-paragraph (1) and not the procedure mentioned in sub-paragraph (2).

(4) Sub-paragraphs (1) to (3) apply in relation to a statutory instrument containing regulations under this Act which is subject to a procedure before the National Assembly for Wales as they apply in relation to a statutory instrument containing regulations under this Act which is subject to a procedure before Parliament but as if the references to Parliament were references to the National Assembly for Wales.

(5) Sub-paragraphs (1) to (3) apply in relation to a statutory rule as they apply in relation to a statutory instrument but as if the references to Parliament were references to the Northern Ireland Assembly.

(6) Sub-paragraphs (1) to (3) apply in relation to a statutory instrument containing regulations under this Act which is subject to a procedure before the Scottish Parliament, the National Assembly for Wales or the Northern Ireland Assembly as well as a procedure before Parliament as they apply to a statutory instrument containing regulations under this Act which is subject to a procedure before Parliament but as if the references to Parliament were references to Parliament and the Scottish Parliament, the National Assembly for Wales or (as the case may be) the Northern Ireland Assembly.

(7) This paragraph does not prevent the inclusion of other regulations in a statutory instrument or statutory rule which contains regulations under this Act (and, accordingly, references in this Schedule to an instrument containing regulations are to be read as references to an instrument containing (whether alone or with other provision) regulations).

NOTES

Commencement: 26 June 2018.

All amendment to this Part were made by the European Union (Withdrawal Agreement) Act 2020, s 41(4), Sch 5, Pt 2, paras 38, 53.

National Assembly for Wales: as to the renaming of the National Assembly for Wales, etc, see the note at **[7.28]**.

SCHEDULE 8
CONSEQUENTIAL, TRANSITIONAL, TRANSITORY AND SAVING PROVISION

Section 23(5) and (7)

PART 1 GENERAL CONSEQUENTIAL PROVISION

Existing ambulatory references to retained direct EU legislation

[7.49]

1. (1) Any reference [so far as it], immediately before [IP completion day]—

(a) exists in—

(i) any enactment,

(ii) any EU regulation, EU decision, EU tertiary legislation or provision of the EEA agreement which is to form part of domestic law by virtue of section 3, or

(iii) any document relating to anything falling within sub-paragraph (i) or (ii), and

(b) is a reference to (as it has effect from time to time) any EU regulation, EU decision, EU tertiary legislation or provision of the EEA agreement which is to form part of domestic law by virtue of section 3,

is to be read, on or after [IP completion day], as a reference to the EU regulation, EU decision, EU tertiary legislation or provision of the EEA agreement as it forms part of domestic law by virtue of section 3 and, unless the contrary intention appears, as modified by domestic law from time to time.

(2) Sub-paragraph (1) does not apply to any reference [so far as it] forms part of a power to make, confirm or approve subordinate legislation so far as the power to make the subordinate legislation—

(a) continues to be part of domestic law by virtue of section 2, and

(b) is subject to a procedure before Parliament, the Scottish Parliament, the National Assembly for Wales or the Northern Ireland Assembly.

(3) Sub-paragraphs (1) and (2) are subject to any other provision made by or under this Act or any other enactment.

[Existing ambulatory references to relevant separation agreement law

1A. (1) Any reference which, immediately before IP completion day—

(a) exists in—

(i) any enactment,

(ii) any EU regulation, EU decision, EU tertiary legislation or provision of the EEA agreement which is to form part of domestic law by virtue of section 3, or

(iii) any document relating to anything falling within sub-paragraph (i) or (ii), and

(b) is a reference to (as it has effect from time to time) any of the EU Treaties, any EU instrument or any other document of an EU entity,

is, if the treaty, instrument or document has effect on or after IP completion day by virtue of section 7A or 7B and so far as required for the purposes of relevant separation agreement law, to be read on or after that day as, or including, a reference to the treaty, instrument or document as it so has effect (including, so far as so required, as it has effect from time to time). .

(2) In sub-paragraph (1) "treaty" includes any international agreement (and any protocol or annex to a treaty or international agreement).

(3) Sub-paragraphs (1) and (2) are subject to any other provision made by or under this Act or any other enactment.]

Other existing ambulatory references

2. (1) Any reference [so far as it]—

(a) exists, immediately before [IP completion day], in—

(i) any enactment,

(ii) any EU regulation, EU decision, EU tertiary legislation or provision of the EEA agreement which is to form part of domestic law by virtue of section 3, or

(iii) any document relating to anything falling within sub-paragraph (i) or (ii),

(b) is not a reference to which paragraph 1(1) applies, and

(c) is, immediately before [IP completion day], a reference to (as it has effect from time to time) any of the EU Treaties, any EU instrument or any other document of an EU entity,

is to be read, on or after [IP completion day], as a reference to the EU Treaty, instrument or document as it has effect immediately before [IP completion day].

(2) Sub-paragraph (1) does not apply to any reference [so far as it] forms part of a power to make, confirm or approve subordinate legislation so far as the power to make the subordinate legislation—

(a) continues to be part of domestic law by virtue of section 2, and

(b) is subject to a procedure before Parliament, the Scottish Parliament, the National Assembly for Wales or the Northern Ireland Assembly.

[(2A) Sub-paragraph (1) does not apply so far as any reference forms part of relevant separation agreement law.]

(3) Sub-paragraphs (1) [to (2A)] are subject to any other provision made by or under this Act or any other enactment.

[Existing non-ambulatory references

2A. (1) Any reference which, immediately before IP completion day—

(a) exists in—

(i) any enactment,

(ii) any EU regulation, EU decision, EU tertiary legislation or provision of the EEA agreement which is to form part of domestic law by virtue of section 3, and

(b) is a reference to any of the EU Treaties, any EU instrument or any other document of an EU entity as it has effect at a particular time which is earlier than IP completion day,

is to be read, on or after IP completion day, in accordance with one or more of subparagraphs (2) to (4).

(2) If the treaty, instrument or document has effect by virtue of section 7A or 7B on or after IP completion day and so far as required for the purposes of relevant separation agreement law, the reference is to be read on or after that day as, or as including, a reference to the treaty, instrument or document as it so has effect (including, so far as so required, as it has effect from time to time).

(3) So far as—

(a) the reference is a reference to—

(i) any EU regulation, EU decision or EU tertiary legislation,

(ii) any provision of the EEA agreement, or

(iii) any part of anything falling within sub-paragraph (i) or (ii),

(b) what has been referred to ("the subject law") is to form part of domestic law by virtue of section 3 or forms part of domestic law by virtue of section 1 of the Direct Payments to Farmers (Legislative Continuity) Act 2020, and

(c) there has been no relevant modification of the subject law after the particular time and before IP completion day (or, where the subject law forms part of domestic law by virtue of section 1 of the Direct Payments to Farmers (Legislative Continuity) Act 2020, before exit day),

the reference is to be read, on or after IP completion day, as a reference to the subject law as it forms part of domestic law by virtue of section 3 or (as the case may be) section 1 of the Direct Payments to Farmers (Legislative Continuity) Act 2020.

(4) So far as the reference is not to be read in accordance with sub-paragraphs (2) and (3), the reference is to be read, on or after IP completion day, as a reference to the treaty, instrument or document as it had effect in EU law at the particular time.

(5) Sub-paragraph (3) does not determine whether, where the subject law is modified by domestic law on or after IP completion day, the reference is to be read as a reference to the subject law as modified; but, where the subject law forms part of domestic law by virtue of section 1 of the Direct Payments to Farmers (Legislative Continuity) Act 2020 and is modified by domestic law before IP completion day, the reference is to be read by virtue of sub-paragraph (3) as a reference to the subject law as so modified.

(6) This paragraph is subject to any provision made by or under this Act or any other enactment.

(6A) This paragraph does not apply to a reference in—

(a) the Direct Payments to Farmers (Legislative Continuity) Act 2020 or any subordinate legislation made under that Act, or

(b) any retained direct EU CAP legislation (within the meaning given by section 2(10) of that Act).

(7) In this paragraph—

"relevant modification" means any modification in EU law which—

(a) is to form part of domestic law by virtue of section 3 or forms part of domestic law by virtue of section 1 of the Direct Payments to Farmers (Legislative Continuity) Act 2020, and

(b) would, if the reference were to the subject law as modified, result in an alteration to the effect of the reference (ignoring any alteration which is irrelevant in the context concerned);

"the subject law" has the meaning given by sub-paragraph (3)(b);

"treaty" includes any international agreement (and any protocol or annex to a treaty or international agreement).]

Existing powers to make subordinate legislation etc

3. (1) Any power to make, confirm or approve subordinate legislation which—

(a) was conferred before the day on which this Act is passed, and

(b) is capable of being exercised to amend or repeal (or, as the case may be, result in the amendment or repeal of) an enactment contained in primary legislation,

is to be read, so far as the context permits or requires, as being capable of being exercised to modify (or, as the case may be, result in the modification of) any retained direct EU legislation or anything which is retained EU law by virtue of section 4.

(2) But sub-paragraph (1) does not apply if the power to make, confirm or approve subordinate legislation is only capable of being exercised to amend or repeal (or, as the case may be, result in the amendment or repeal of) an enactment contained in Northern Ireland legislation which is an Order in Council.

4. (1) Any subordinate legislation which—

(a) is, or is to be, made, confirmed or approved by virtue of paragraph 3, and

(b) amends or revokes any retained direct principal EU legislation,

is to be subject to the same procedure (if any) before Parliament, the Scottish Parliament, the National Assembly for Wales or the Northern Ireland Assembly as would apply to that legislation if it were amending or repealing an enactment contained in primary legislation.

(2) Any subordinate legislation which—

(a) is, or is to be, made, confirmed or approved by virtue of paragraph 3, and

(b) either—

(i) modifies (otherwise than as a connected modification and otherwise than by way of amending or revoking it) any retained direct principal EU legislation, or

(ii) modifies (otherwise than as a connected modification) anything which is retained EU law by virtue of section 4,

is to be subject to the same procedure (if any) before Parliament, the Scottish Parliament, the National Assembly for Wales or the Northern Ireland Assembly as would apply to that legislation if it were amending or repealing an enactment contained in primary legislation.

(3) Any subordinate legislation which—

(a) is, or is to be, made, confirmed or approved by virtue of paragraph 3, and

(b) amends or revokes any retained direct minor EU legislation,

is to be subject to the same procedure (if any) before Parliament, the Scottish Parliament, the National Assembly for Wales or the Northern Ireland Assembly as would apply to that legislation if it were amending or revoking an enactment contained in subordinate legislation made under a different power.

(4) Any subordinate legislation which—

(a) is, or is to be, made, confirmed or approved by virtue of paragraph 3, and

(b) modifies (otherwise than as a connected modification and otherwise than by way of amending or revoking it) any retained direct minor EU legislation,

is to be subject to the same procedure (if any) before Parliament, the Scottish Parliament, the National Assembly for Wales or the Northern Ireland Assembly as would apply to that legislation if it were amending or revoking an enactment contained in subordinate legislation made under a different power.

(5) Any subordinate legislation which—

(a) is, or is to be, made, confirmed or approved by virtue of paragraph 3, and

(b) modifies as a connected modification any retained direct EU legislation or anything which is retained EU law by virtue of section 4,

is to be subject to the same procedure (if any) before Parliament, the Scottish Parliament, the National Assembly for Wales or the Northern Ireland Assembly as would apply to the modification to which it is connected.

(6) Any provision which may be made, confirmed or approved by virtue of paragraph 3 may be included in the same instrument as any other provision which may be so made, confirmed or approved.

(7) Where more than one procedure of a kind falling within sub-paragraph (8) would otherwise apply in the same legislature for an instrument falling within sub-paragraph (6), the higher procedure is to apply in the legislature concerned.

(8) The order of procedures is as follows (the highest first)—

(a) a procedure which requires a statement of urgency before the instrument is made and the approval of the instrument after it is made to enable it to remain in force,

(b) a procedure which requires the approval of the instrument in draft before it is made,

(c) a procedure not falling within paragraph (a) which requires the approval of the instrument after it is made to enable it to come into, or remain in, force,

(d) a procedure which provides for the annulment of the instrument after it is made,

(e) a procedure not falling within any of the above paragraphs which provides for the laying of the instrument after it is made,

(f) no procedure.

(9) The references in this paragraph to amending or repealing an enactment contained in primary legislation or amending or revoking an enactment contained in subordinate legislation do not include references to amending or repealing or (as the case may be) amending or revoking an enactment contained in any Northern Ireland legislation which is an Order in Council.

(10) In this paragraph "connected modification" means a modification which is supplementary, incidental, consequential, transitional or transitory, or a saving, in connection with—

(a) another modification under the power of retained direct EU legislation or anything which is retained EU law by virtue of section 4, or

(b) anything else done under the power.

5. (1) This paragraph applies to any power to make, confirm or approve subordinate legislation—

(a) which was conferred before the day on which this Act is passed, and

(b) is not capable of being exercised as mentioned in paragraph 3(1)(b) or is only capable of being so exercised in relation to Northern Ireland legislation which is an Order in Council.

(2) Any power to which this paragraph applies (other than a power to which sub-paragraph (4) applies) is to be read—

(a) so far as is consistent with any retained direct principal EU legislation or anything which is retained EU law by virtue of section 4, and

(b) so far as the context permits or requires,

as being capable of being exercised to modify (or, as the case may be, result in the modification of) any retained direct minor EU legislation.

(3) Any power to which this paragraph applies (other than a power to which sub-paragraph (4) applies) is to be read, so far as the context permits or requires, as being capable of being exercised to modify (or, as the case may be, result in the modification of)—

(a) any retained direct principal EU legislation, or

(b) anything which is retained EU law by virtue of section 4,

so far as the modification is supplementary, incidental or consequential in connection with any modification of any retained direct minor EU legislation by virtue of sub-paragraph (2).

(4) Any power to which this paragraph applies so far as it is a power to make, confirm or approve transitional, transitory or saving provision is to be read, so far as the context permits or requires, as being capable of being exercised to modify (or, as the case may be, result in the modification of)—

(a) any retained direct EU legislation, or

(b) anything which is retained EU law by virtue of section 4.

6. Any subordinate legislation which is, or is to be, made, confirmed or approved by virtue of paragraph 5(2), (3) or (4) is to be subject to the same procedure (if any) before Parliament, the Scottish Parliament, the National Assembly for Wales or the Northern Ireland Assembly as would apply to that legislation if it were doing anything else under the power.

[**7.** Any power to make, confirm or approve subordinate legislation which, immediately before exit day, is subject to an implied restriction that it is exercisable only compatibly with EU law is to be read—

(a) on or after exit day, without that restriction, and

(b) on or after IP completion day, without any corresponding restriction in relation to compatibility with retained EU law,

so far as the restriction concerned is not applicable to and in the United Kingdom by virtue of the withdrawal agreement.]

8. (1) Paragraphs 3 to 7 and this paragraph—

(a) do not prevent the conferral of wider powers,

(b) do not apply so far as section 57(4) of the Scotland Act 1998, section 80(8) of the Government of Wales Act 2006 or section 24(3) of the Northern Ireland Act 1998 applies (or would apply when in force on and after [IP completion day]), and

(c) are subject to any other provision made by or under this Act or any other enactment.

(2) For the purposes of paragraphs 3 and 5—

(a) a power is conferred whether or not it is in force, and

(b) a power in retained direct EU legislation is not conferred before the day on which this Act is passed.

(3) A power which, by virtue of paragraph 3 or 5 or any Act of Parliament passed before, and in the same Session as, this Act, is capable of being exercised to modify any retained EU law is capable of being so exercised before [IP completion day] so as to come into force on or after [IP completion day].

Review provisions in existing subordinate legislation

9. (1) In carrying out a review of a provision of subordinate legislation on or after [IP completion day] (whether under provision made in accordance with section 28 of the Small Business, Enterprise and Employment Act 2015 or otherwise), a person is not required, by any [pre-IP completion day] enactment, to have regard to how any former EU obligation is implemented elsewhere than in the United Kingdom.

(2) In this paragraph—

"former EU obligation" means an obligation by which the United Kingdom is, as a result of the United Kingdom's withdrawal from the EU, no longer bound at the time of the review;

"[pre-IP completion day] enactment" means an Act passed, or subordinate legislation made, before [IP completion day];

"subordinate legislation" does not include an instrument made under an Act of the Scottish Parliament, Northern Ireland legislation or a Measure or Act of the National Assembly for Wales.

Future powers to make subordinate legislation

10. (1) This paragraph applies to any power to make, confirm or approve subordinate legislation which is conferred on or after the day on which this Act is passed.

(2) Any power to which this paragraph applies (other than a power to which sub-paragraph (4) applies) may—

(a) so far as is consistent with any retained direct principal EU legislation or anything which is retained EU law by virtue of section 4, and

(b) so far as applicable and unless the contrary intention appears,

be exercised to modify (or, as the case may be, result in the modification of) any retained direct minor EU legislation.

(3) Any power to which this paragraph applies (other than a power to which sub-paragraph (4) applies) may, so far as applicable and unless the contrary intention appears, be exercised to modify (or, as the case may be, result in the modification of)—

(a) any retained direct principal EU legislation, or

(b) anything which is retained EU law by virtue of section 4,

so far as the modification is supplementary, incidental or consequential in connection with any modification of any retained direct minor EU legislation by virtue of sub-paragraph (2).

(4) Any power to which this paragraph applies so far as it is a power to make, confirm or approve transitional, transitory or saving provision may, so far as applicable and unless the contrary intention appears, be exercised to modify (or, as the case may be, result in the modification of)—

(a) any retained direct EU legislation, or

(b) anything which is retained EU law by virtue of section 4.

11. (1) Sub-paragraph (2) applies to any power to make, confirm or approve subordinate legislation which—

(a) is conferred on or after the day on which this Act is passed, and

(b) is capable of being exercised to amend or revoke (or, as the case may be, result in the amendment or revocation of) any retained direct principal EU legislation.

(2) The power may, so far as applicable and unless the contrary intention appears, be exercised—

(a) to modify otherwise than by way of amendment or revocation (or, as the case may be, result in such modification of) any retained direct principal EU legislation, or

(b) to modify (or, as the case may be, result in the modification of) anything which is retained EU law by virtue of section 4.

12. (1) Paragraphs 10 and 11 and this paragraph—

(a) do not prevent the conferral of wider powers,

(b) do not apply so far as section 57(4) of the Scotland Act 1998, section 80(8) of the Government of Wales Act 2006 or section 24(3) of the Northern Ireland Act 1998 applies (or would apply when in force on and after [IP completion day]), and

(c) are subject to any other provision made by or under this Act or any other enactment.

(2) For the purposes of paragraphs 10 and 11—

(a) a power is conferred whether or not it is in force,

(b) a power in retained direct EU legislation is conferred on or after the day on which this Act is passed, and

(c) the references to powers conferred include powers conferred by regulations under this Act (but not powers conferred by this Act).

(3) A power which, by virtue of paragraph 10 or 11 or any Act of Parliament passed after [this Act and before IP completion day], is capable of being exercised to modify any retained EU law is capable of being so exercised before [IP completion day] so as to come into force on or after [IP completion day].

Affirmative procedure for instruments which amend or revoke subordinate legislation made under section 2(2) of the ECA (including subordinate legislation implementing EU directives)

13. (1) A statutory instrument which—

(a) is to be made on or after [IP completion day] by a Minister of the Crown under a power conferred before the beginning of the Session in which this Act is passed,

(b) is not to be made jointly with any person who is not a Minister of the Crown,

(c) amends or revokes any subordinate legislation made under section 2(2) of the European Communities Act 1972, and

(d) would otherwise be subject to a lower procedure before each House of Parliament and no procedure before any other legislature,

may not be made unless a draft of the instrument has been laid before, and approved by a resolution of, each House of Parliament.

(2) Sub-paragraph (1) has effect instead of any other provision which would otherwise apply in relation to the procedure for such an instrument before each House of Parliament but does not affect any other requirements which apply in relation to making, confirming or approving the instrument.

(3) Any provision which—

(a) may be made under the power mentioned in sub-paragraph (1)(a),

(b) is not provision which falls within sub-paragraph (1)(c), and

(c) is subject to a lower procedure than the procedure provided for by sub-paragraph (1),

may be included in an instrument to which sub-paragraph (1) applies (and is accordingly subject to the procedure provided for by that sub-paragraph instead of the lower procedure).

(4) If a draft of a statutory instrument which—

(a) is to be made on or after [IP completion day] by a Minister of the Crown under a power conferred before the beginning of the Session in which this Act is passed,

(b) is not to be made jointly with any person who is not a Minister of the Crown,

(c) amends or revokes any provision, made otherwise than under section 2(2) of the European Communities Act 1972 (whether or not by way of amendment), of subordinate legislation made under that section, and

(d) would otherwise be subject to a lower procedure before each House of Parliament and no procedure before any other legislature,

is laid before, and approved by a resolution of, each House of Parliament, then the instrument is not subject to the lower procedure.

(5) This paragraph applies to an instrument which is subject to a procedure before the House of Commons only as it applies to an instrument which is subject to a procedure before each House of Parliament but as if the references to each House of Parliament were references to the House of Commons only.

(6) For the purposes of this paragraph, the order of procedures is as follows (the highest first)—

(a) a procedure which requires a statement of urgency before the instrument is made and the approval of the instrument after it is made to enable it to remain in force,

(b) a procedure which requires the approval of the instrument in draft before it is made,

(c) a procedure not falling within paragraph (a) which requires the approval of the instrument after it is made to enable it to come into, or remain in, force,

(d) a procedure which provides for the annulment of the instrument after it is made,

(e) a procedure not falling within any of the above paragraphs which provides for the laying of the instrument after it is made,

(f) no procedure.

(7) For the purposes of this paragraph a power is conferred whether or not it is in force.

(8) References in this paragraph, other than in sub-paragraph (4), to subordinate legislation made under section 2(2) of the European Communities Act 1972—

(a) do not include references to any provision of such legislation which is made (whether or not by way of amendment) otherwise than under section 2(2) of that Act, and

(b) do include references to subordinate legislation made otherwise than under section 2(2) of that Act so far as that legislation is amended by provision made under that section (but do not include references to any primary legislation so far as so amended).

[(8A) This paragraph does not apply where the amendment or revocation of subordinate legislation is for the purposes of—

(a) the withdrawal agreement (other than Part 4 of that agreement),

(b) the EEA EFTA separation agreement, . . .

(c) the Swiss citizens' rights agreement[, or

(d) a future relationship agreement.]]

(9) This paragraph is subject to any other provision made by or under this Act or any other enactment.

Enhanced scrutiny procedure for instruments which amend or revoke subordinate legislation under section 2(2) of the ECA (including subordinate legislation implementing EU directives)

14. (1) This paragraph applies where, on or after [IP completion day]—

(a) a statutory instrument which—

(i) amends or revokes subordinate legislation made under section 2(2) of the European Communities Act 1972, and

(ii) is made under a power conferred before the beginning of the Session in which this Act is passed, or

(b) a draft of such an instrument,

is to be laid before each House of Parliament and subject to no procedure before any other legislature.

(2) The relevant authority must publish, in such manner as the relevant authority considers appropriate, a draft of the instrument at least 28 days before the instrument or draft is laid.

(3) The relevant authority must make a scrutiny statement before the instrument or draft is laid.

(4) A scrutiny statement is a statement—

(a) setting out the steps which the relevant authority has taken to make the draft instrument published in accordance with sub-paragraph (2) available to each House of Parliament,

(b) containing information about the relevant authority's response to—

(i) any recommendations made by a committee of either House of Parliament about the published draft instrument, and

(ii) any other representations made to the relevant authority about the published draft instrument, and

(c) containing any other information that the relevant authority considers appropriate in relation to the scrutiny of the instrument or draft instrument which is to be laid.

(5) A scrutiny statement must be in writing and must be published in such manner as the relevant authority considers appropriate.

(6) Sub-paragraphs (2) to (5) do not apply if the relevant authority—

(a) makes a statement in writing to the effect that the relevant authority is of the opinion that, by reason of urgency, sub-paragraphs (2) to (5) should not apply, and

(b) publishes the statement in such manner as the relevant authority considers appropriate.

(7) This paragraph does not apply in relation to any laying before each House of Parliament of an instrument or draft instrument where an equivalent draft instrument (ignoring any differences relating to procedure) has previously been laid before both Houses.

(8) This paragraph applies to an instrument which is subject to a procedure before the House of Commons only as it applies to an instrument which is subject to a procedure before each House of Parliament but as if references to each or either House of Parliament, or both Houses, were references to the House of Commons only.

(9) For the purposes of this paragraph—

(a) a power is conferred whether or not it is in force,

(b) the draft instrument published under sub-paragraph (2) need not be identical to the final version of the instrument or draft instrument as laid,

(c) where an instrument or draft is laid before each House of Parliament on different days, the earlier day is to be taken as the day on which it is laid before both Houses, and

(d) in calculating the period of 28 days, no account is to be taken of any time during which—

(i) Parliament is dissolved or prorogued, or

(ii) either House of Parliament is adjourned for more than four days.

(10) Sub-paragraph (8) of paragraph 13 applies for the purposes of this paragraph as it applies for the purposes of sub-paragraph (1) of that paragraph.

(11) In this paragraph "the relevant authority" means—

(a) in the case of an Order in Council or Order of Council, the Minister of the Crown who has responsibility in relation to the instrument,

(b) in the case of any other statutory instrument which is not to be made by a Minister of the Crown, the person who is to make the instrument, and

(c) in any other case, the Minister of the Crown who is to make the instrument.

[(11A) This paragraph does not apply where the amendment or revocation of subordinate legislation is for the purposes of—

(a) the withdrawal agreement (other than Part 4 of that agreement),

(b) the EEA EFTA separation agreement, . . .

(c) the Swiss citizens' rights agreement[, or

(d) a future relationship agreement.]]

(12) This paragraph is subject to any other provision made by or under this Act or any other enactment.

Explanatory statements for instruments amending or revoking regulations etc under section 2(2) of the ECA

15. (1) This paragraph applies where, on or after [IP completion day]—

(a) a statutory instrument which amends or revokes any subordinate legislation made under section 2(2) of the European Communities Act 1972, or

(b) a draft of such an instrument,

is to be laid before each House of Parliament or before the House of Commons only.

(2) Before the instrument or draft is laid, the relevant authority must make a statement as to why, in the opinion of the relevant authority, there are good reasons for the amendment or revocation.

(3) Before the instrument or draft is laid, the relevant authority must make a statement otherwise explaining—

(a) the law which is relevant to the amendment or revocation, and

(b) the effect of the amendment or revocation on retained EU law.

(4) If the relevant authority fails to make a statement required by sub-paragraph (2) or (3) before the instrument or draft is laid—

(a) a Minister of the Crown, or

(b) where the relevant authority is not a Minister of the Crown, the relevant authority,

must make a statement explaining why the relevant authority has failed to make the statement as so required.

(5) A statement under sub-paragraph (2), (3) or (4) must be made in writing and be published in such manner as the person making it considers appropriate.

(6) For the purposes of this paragraph, where an instrument or draft is laid before each House of Parliament on different days, the earlier day is to be taken as the day on which it is laid before both Houses.

(7) This paragraph applies in relation to instruments whether the power to make them is conferred before, on or after [IP completion day] including where the power is conferred by regulations under this Act (but not where it is conferred by this Act).

(8) This paragraph does not apply in relation to any laying before each House of Parliament, or before the House of Commons only, of an instrument or draft instrument where an equivalent draft instrument (ignoring any differences relating to procedure) has previously been laid before both Houses or before the House of Commons only.

(9) Sub-paragraph (8) of paragraph 13 applies for the purposes of this paragraph as it applies for the purposes of sub-paragraph (1) of that paragraph.

(10) In this paragraph "the relevant authority" means—

(a) in the case of an Order in Council or Order of Council, the Minister of the Crown who has responsibility in relation to the instrument,

(b) in the case of any other statutory instrument which is not made by a Minister of the Crown, the person who makes, or is to make, the instrument, and

(c) in any other case, the Minister of the Crown who makes, or is to make, the instrument.

[(11) This paragraph does not apply where the amendment or revocation of subordinate legislation is for the purposes of—

(a) the withdrawal agreement (other than Part 4 of that agreement),

(b) the EEA EFTA separation agreement, . . .

(c) the Swiss citizens' rights agreement[, or

(d) a future relationship agreement.]]

16. (1) This paragraph applies where, on or after [IP completion day]—

(a) a Scottish statutory instrument which amends or revokes any subordinate legislation made under section 2(2) of the European Communities Act 1972, or

(b) a draft of such an instrument,

is to be laid before the Scottish Parliament.

(2) Before the instrument or draft is laid, the relevant authority must make a statement as to why, in the opinion of the relevant authority, there are good reasons for the amendment or revocation.

(3) Before the instrument or draft is laid, the relevant authority must make a statement otherwise explaining—

(a) the law which is relevant to the amendment or revocation, and

(b) the effect of the amendment or revocation on retained EU law.

(4) If the relevant authority fails to make a statement required by sub-paragraph (2) or (3) before the instrument or draft is laid, the relevant authority must make a statement explaining why the relevant authority has failed to make the statement as so required.

(5) A statement under sub-paragraph (2), (3) or (4) must be made in writing and be published in such manner as the relevant authority considers appropriate.

(6) This paragraph applies in relation to instruments whether the power to make them is conferred before, on or after [IP completion day] including where the power is conferred by regulations under this Act (but not where it is conferred by this Act).

(7) Sub-paragraph (8) of paragraph 13 applies for the purposes of this paragraph as it applies for the purposes of sub-paragraph (1) of that paragraph.

(8) In this paragraph "the relevant authority" means—

(a) in the case of a Scottish statutory instrument which is not made by the Scottish Ministers, other than an Order in Council, the person who makes, or is to make, the instrument, and

(b) in any other case, the Scottish Ministers.

[(9) This paragraph does not apply where the amendment or revocation of subordinate legislation is for the purposes of—

(a) the withdrawal agreement (other than Part 4 of that agreement),

(b) the EEA EFTA separation agreement, . . .

(c) the Swiss citizens' rights agreement[, or

(d) a future relationship agreement.]]

NOTES

Commencement: exit day (as defined in s 20 of this Act) (paras 7, 8, 10–12); IP completion day (as defined in the European Union (Withdrawal Agreement) Act 2020, s 39) (otherwise).

Para 1: words "so far as it" in square brackets substituted by the European Union Withdrawal (Consequential Modifications) (EU Exit) Regulations 2020, SI 2020/1447, reg 3(2)(a), as from IP completion day (as defined in the European Union

(Withdrawal Agreement) Act 2020, s 39). Words "IP completion day" in square brackets substituted by the European Union (Withdrawal Agreement) Act 2020, s 41(4), Sch 5, Pt 2, paras 38, 54(1), (2), as from IP completion day (as defined in the European Union (Withdrawal Agreement) Act 2020, s 39).

Para 1A: inserted by SI 2020/1447, reg 3(2)(b), as from IP completion day (as defined in the European Union (Withdrawal Agreement) Act 2020, s 39).

Para 2: words "so far as it" in square brackets in sub-paras (1) and (2) substituted by SI 2020/1447, reg 3(2)(c), as from IP completion day (as defined in the European Union (Withdrawal Agreement) Act 2020, s 39). All other amendments to this paragraph were made by the European Union (Withdrawal Agreement) Act 2020, s 41(4), Sch 5, Pt 2, paras 38, 54(1), (3), as from IP completion day (as defined in the European Union (Withdrawal Agreement) Act 2020, s 39).

Para 2A: inserted by SI 2020/1447, reg 3(2)(d), as from IP completion day (as defined in the European Union (Withdrawal Agreement) Act 2020, s 39). Note that reg 3(2)(d) of the 2020 Regulations was amended by the Spirit Drinks, Wine and European Union Withdrawal (Consequential Modifications) (Amendment) (EU Exit) Regulations 2020, SI 2020/1636, reg 4, as from 30 December 2020 (and the effect of the amendment has been incorporated in the text set out above).

Para 7: substituted by the European Union (Withdrawal Agreement) Act 2020, s 41(4), Sch 5, Pt 2, paras 38, 54(1), (4).

Para 8: words in square brackets substituted by the European Union (Withdrawal Agreement) Act 2020, s 41(4), Sch 5, Pt 2, paras 38, 54(1), (5).

Para 9: word in square brackets substituted by the European Union (Withdrawal Agreement) Act 2020, s 41(4), Sch 5, Pt 2, paras 38, 54(1), (6), as from IP completion day (as defined in the European Union (Withdrawal Agreement) Act 2020, s 39).

Para 12: words in square brackets substituted by the European Union (Withdrawal Agreement) Act 2020, s 41(4), Sch 5, Pt 2, paras 38, 54(1), (7).

Para 13: words in square brackets in sub-paras (1)(a) and (4)(a) substituted, and sub-para (8A) inserted, by the European Union (Withdrawal Agreement) Act 2020, s 41(4), Sch 5, Pt 2, paras 38, 54(1), (8), as from IP completion day (as defined in the European Union (Withdrawal Agreement) Act 2020, s 39). Word omitted from sub-para (8A)(b) repealed, and sub-para (8A)(d) and the preceding word inserted, by the European Union (Future Relationship) Act 2020, s 39(3), (5), Sch 6, Pt 1, para 8, as from IP completion day (as defined in the European Union (Withdrawal Agreement) Act 2020, s 39).

Para 14: words in square brackets in sub-para (1) substituted, and sub-para (11A) inserted, by the European Union (Withdrawal Agreement) Act 2020, s 41(4), Sch 5, Pt 2, paras 38, 54(1), (9), as from IP completion day (as defined in the European Union (Withdrawal Agreement) Act 2020, s 39). Word omitted from sub-para (11A)(b) repealed, and sub-para (11A)(d) and the preceding word inserted, by the European Union (Future Relationship) Act 2020, s 39(3), (5), Sch 6, Pt 1, para 8, as from IP completion day (as defined in the European Union (Withdrawal Agreement) Act 2020, s 39).

Para 15: words in square brackets in sub-paras (1) and (7) substituted, and sub-para (11) added, by the European Union (Withdrawal Agreement) Act 2020, s 41(4), Sch 5, Pt 2, paras 38, 54(1), (10), as from IP completion day (as defined in the European Union (Withdrawal Agreement) Act 2020, s 39). Word omitted from sub-para (11)(b) repealed, and sub-para (11)(d) and the preceding word inserted, by the European Union (Future Relationship) Act 2020, s 39(3), (5), Sch 6, Pt 1, para 8, as from IP completion day (as defined in the European Union (Withdrawal Agreement) Act 2020, s 39).

Para 16: words in square brackets in sub-paras (1) and (6) substituted, and sub-para (9) added, by the European Union (Withdrawal Agreement) Act 2020, s 41(4), Sch 5, Pt 2, paras 38, 54(1), (11), as from IP completion day (as defined in the European Union (Withdrawal Agreement) Act 2020, s 39). Word omitted from sub-para (9)(b) repealed, and sub-para (9)(d) and the preceding word inserted, by the European Union (Future Relationship) Act 2020, s 39(3), (5), Sch 6, Pt 1, para 8, as from IP completion day (as defined in the European Union (Withdrawal Agreement) Act 2020, s 39).

National Assembly for Wales: as to the renaming of the National Assembly for Wales, etc, see the note at **[7.28]**.

PART 2 SPECIFIC CONSEQUENTIAL PROVISION

(*This Part contains various amendments that are outside the scope of this work.*)

PART 3 GENERAL TRANSITIONAL, TRANSITORY OR SAVING PROVISION

Continuation of existing acts etc

[7.50]

[36A. (1) Anything done—

(a) in connection with anything which continues to be domestic law by virtue of section 1A(2) or 1B(2), or

(b) for a purpose mentioned in section 2(2)(a) or (b) of the European Communities Act 1972 or otherwise related to the EU or the EEA,

if in force or effective immediately before exit day, continues to be in force or effective on and after exit day.

(2) Anything done—

(a) in connection with anything which continues to be domestic law by virtue of section 1A(2) or 1B(2), or

(b) for a purpose mentioned in section 2(2)(a) or (b) of the European Communities Act 1972 or otherwise related to the EU or the EEA,

which, immediately before exit day, is in the process of being done continues to be done on and after exit day.

(3) Sub-paragraphs (1) and (2) are subject to—

(a) sections 1 to 1B and the withdrawal of the United Kingdom from the EU,

(b) any provision made under section 23(6) of this Act or section 41(5) of the European Union (Withdrawal Agreement) Act 2020, and

(c) any other provision made by or under this Act, the European Union (Withdrawal Agreement) Act 2020 or any other enactment.

(4) References in this paragraph to anything done include references to anything omitted to be done.]

37. (1) Anything done—

(a) in connection with anything which continues to be, or forms part of, domestic law by virtue of section 2, 3, 4 or 6(3) or (6), or

(b) for a purpose mentioned in section 2(2)(a) or (b) of the European Communities Act 1972 or otherwise related to the EU or the EEA,

if in force or effective immediately before [IP completion day], continues to be in force or effective on and after [IP completion day].

(2) Anything done—

(a) in connection with anything which continues to be, or forms part of, domestic law by virtue of section 2, 3, 4 or 6(3) or (6), or

(b) for a purpose mentioned in section 2(2)(a) or (b) of the European Communities Act 1972 or otherwise related to the EU or the EEA,

which, immediately before [IP completion day], is in the process of being done continues to be done on and after [IP completion day].

(3) Sub-paragraphs (1) and (2) are subject to—

(a) [sections 1 to 1B] and the withdrawal of the United Kingdom from the EU,

(b) sections 2 to [7C] and Schedule 1,

(c) any provision made under section 23(6) [of this Act or section 41(5) of the European Union (Withdrawal Agreement) Act 2020], and

(d) any other provision made by or under this Act[, the European Union (Withdrawal Agreement) Act 2020] or any other enactment.

(4) References in this paragraph to anything done include references to anything omitted to be done.

NOTES

Commencement: IP completion day (as defined in the European Union (Withdrawal Agreement) Act 2020.

Para 36A: inserted by the European Union (Withdrawal Agreement) Act 2020, s 41(4), Sch 5, Pt 2, paras 38, 55(1), (2).

Para 37: all amendment to this paragraph were made by the European Union (Withdrawal Agreement) Act 2020, s 41(4), Sch 5, Pt 2, paras 38, 55(1), (3), as from IP completion day (as defined in the European Union (Withdrawal Agreement) Act 2020, s 39).

PART 4 SPECIFIC TRANSITIONAL, TRANSITORY AND SAVING PROVISION

Retention of [saved EU law at end of implementation period]

[7.51]

[37A. The repeal of section 1A(1) to (4) by section 1A(5) and the repeal of section 1B(1) to (5) by section 1B(6) do not prevent an enactment to which section 2 applies from continuing to be read, on and after IP completion day and by virtue of section 2, in accordance with section 1B(3) or (4).]"

38. Section 4(2)(b) does not apply in relation to any rights, powers, liabilities, obligations, restrictions, remedies or procedures so far as they are of a kind recognised by a court or tribunal in the United Kingdom in a case decided on or after [IP completion day] but begun before [IP completion day] (whether or not as an essential part of the decision in the case).

39. (1) Subject as follows and subject to [relevant separation agreement law (for which see section 7C) and] any provision made by regulations under section 23(6) [of this Act or section 41(5) of the European Union (Withdrawal Agreement) Act 2020], section 5(4) and paragraphs 1 to 4 of Schedule 1 apply in relation to anything occurring before [IP completion day] (as well as anything occurring on or after [IP completion day]).

(2) Section 5(4) and paragraphs 1 to 4 of Schedule 1 do not affect any decision of a court or tribunal made before [IP completion day].

(3) Section 5(4) and paragraphs 3 and 4 of Schedule 1 do not apply in relation to any proceedings begun, but not finally decided, before a court or tribunal in the United Kingdom before [IP completion day].

(4) Paragraphs 1 to 4 of Schedule 1 do not apply in relation to any conduct which occurred before [IP completion day] which gives rise to any criminal liability.

(5) Paragraph 3 of Schedule 1 does not apply in relation to any proceedings begun within the period of three years beginning with [IP completion day] so far as—

(a) the proceedings involve a challenge to anything which occurred before [IP completion day], and

(b) the challenge is not for the disapplication or quashing of—

(i) an Act of Parliament or a rule of law which is not an enactment, or

(ii) any enactment, or anything else, not falling within sub-paragraph (i) which, as a result of anything falling within that sub-paragraph, could not have been different or which gives effect to, or enforces, anything falling within that sub-paragraph.

(6) Paragraph 3(2) of Schedule 1 does not apply in relation to any decision of a court or tribunal, or other public authority, on or after [IP completion day] which is a necessary consequence of any decision of a court or tribunal made before [IP completion day] or made on or after that day by virtue of this paragraph.

(7) Paragraph 4 of Schedule 1 does not apply in relation to any proceedings begun within the period of two years beginning with [IP completion day] so far as the proceedings relate to anything which occurred before [IP completion day].

Main powers in connection with withdrawal

40. The prohibition on making regulations under section [6(5A),] 8, [8A] . . . or 23(1) or [Part 1 or 1A of] Schedule 2 after a particular time does not affect the continuation in force of regulations made at or before that time (including the exercise after that time of any power conferred by regulations made at or before that time).

Devolution

41. (1) The amendments made by section 12 and Part 1 of Schedule 3 do not affect the validity of—

(a) any provision of an Act of the Scottish Parliament, Act of the National Assembly for Wales or Act of the Northern Ireland Assembly made before [IP completion day],

(b) any subordinate legislation which is subject to confirmation or approval and is made and confirmed or approved before [IP completion day], or

(c) any other subordinate legislation made before [IP completion day].

(2) Accordingly and subject to sub-paragraphs (3) to (10), the validity of anything falling within sub-paragraph (1)(a), (b) or (c) is to be decided by reference to the law before [IP completion day].

(3) Section 29(2)(d) of the Scotland Act 1998, so far as relating to EU law, does not apply to any provision of an Act of the Scottish Parliament made before [IP completion day] if the provision—

(a) comes into force on or after [IP completion day] or comes into force before that day and is a power to make, confirm or approve subordinate legislation, and

(b) is made when there are no regulations under section 30A of the Scotland Act 1998 by virtue of which the provision would be in breach of the restriction in subsection (1) of that section when the provision comes into force (or, in the case of a provision which comes into force before [IP completion day], on or after [IP completion day]) if the provision were made and the regulations were in force at that time.

(4) Section 108A(2)(e) of the Government of Wales Act 2006, so far as relating to EU law, does not apply to any provision of an Act of the National Assembly for Wales made before [IP completion day] if the provision—

(a) comes into force on or after [IP completion day] or comes into force before that day and is a power to make, confirm or approve subordinate legislation, and

(b) is made when there are no regulations under section 109A of the Government of Wales Act 2006 by virtue of which the provision would be in breach of the restriction in subsection (1) of that section when the provision comes into force (or, in the case of a provision which comes into force before [IP completion day], on or after [IP completion day]) if the provision were made and the regulations were in force at that time.

(5) Section 6(2)(d) of the Northern Ireland Act 1998, so far as relating to EU law, does not apply to any provision of an Act of the Northern Ireland Assembly made before [IP completion day] if the provision—

(a) comes into force on or after [IP completion day] or comes into force before that day and is a power to make, confirm or approve subordinate legislation, and

(b) is made when there are no regulations under section 6A of the Northern Ireland Act 1998 by virtue of which the provision would be in breach of the restriction in subsection (1) of that section when the provision comes into force (or, in the case of a provision which comes into force before [IP completion day], on or after [IP completion day]) if the provision were made and the regulations were in force at that time.

(6) Section 57(2) of the Scotland Act 1998, so far as relating to EU law, does not apply to the making, confirming or approving before [IP completion day] of any subordinate legislation if the legislation—

(a) comes into force on or after [IP completion day], and

(b) is made, confirmed or approved when there are no regulations under subsection (4) of section 57 of the Scotland Act 1998 by virtue of which the making, confirming or approving would be in breach of the restriction in that subsection when the legislation comes into force if—

(i) the making, confirming or approving had occurred at that time,

(ii) in the case of legislation confirmed or approved, the legislation was made at that time, and

(iii) the regulations were in force at that time.

(7) Section 80(8) of the Government of Wales Act 2006, so far as relating to EU law, does not apply to the making, confirming or approving before [IP completion day] of any subordinate legislation if the legislation—

(a) comes into force on or after [IP completion day], and

(b) is made, confirmed or approved when there are no regulations under subsection (8) of section 80 of the Government of Wales Act 2006 by virtue of which the making, confirming or approving would be in breach of the restriction in that subsection, so far as relating to retained EU law, when the legislation comes into force if—

(i) the making, confirming or approving had occurred at that time,

(ii) in the case of legislation confirmed or approved, the legislation was made at that time, and

(iii) the regulations were in force at that time.

(8) Section 24(1)(b) of the Northern Ireland Act 1998, so far as relating to EU law, does not apply to the making, confirming or approving before [IP completion day] of any subordinate legislation if the legislation—

(a) comes into force on or after [IP completion day], and

(b) is made, confirmed or approved when there are no regulations under subsection (3) of section 24 of the Northern Ireland Act 1998 by virtue of which the making, confirming or approving would be in breach of the restriction in that subsection when the legislation comes into force if—

(i) the making, confirming or approving had occurred at that time,

(ii) in the case of legislation confirmed or approved, the legislation was made at that time, and

(iii) the regulations were in force at that time.

(9) For the purposes of sub-paragraphs (3) to (8) assume that the restrictions relating to retained EU law in—

(a) sections 30A(1) and 57(4) of the Scotland Act 1998,

(b) sections 80(8) and 109A(1) of the Government of Wales Act 2006, and

(c) sections 6A(1) and 24(3) of the Northern Ireland Act 1998,

come into force on [IP completion day].

(10) Section 57(2) of the Scotland Act 1998, section 80(8) of the Government of Wales Act 2006 and section 24(1)(b) of the Northern Ireland Act 1998, so far as relating to EU law, do not apply to[—

(a) the making of regulations before exit day under Part 1A of Schedule 2, or

(b) the making of regulations under—

(i) Part 1B or 1C of Schedule 2, or

(ii) Schedule 4.]

42. The amendments made by Part 1 of Schedule 3 do not affect the validity of any act (other than the making, confirming or approving of subordinate legislation) done before [IP completion day] by a member of the Scottish Government, the Welsh Ministers, the First Minister for Wales, the Counsel General to the Welsh Government, a Northern Ireland Minister, the First Minister in Northern Ireland, the deputy First Minister in Northern Ireland or a Northern Ireland department.

43. A consent decision of the Scottish Parliament, the National Assembly for Wales or the Northern Ireland Assembly made before the day on which this Act is passed, or the commencement of the 40-day period before the day on which this Act is passed, is as effective for the purposes of—

(a) section 30A(3) or 57(6) of the Scotland Act 1998,

(b) section 80(8C) or 109A(4) of the Government of Wales Act 2006, or

(c) section 6A(3) or 24(5) of the Northern Ireland Act 1998,

as a consent decision made, or (as the case may be) the commencement of that period, on or after that day.

Other provision

44. (1) The definition of "relevant criminal offence" in section 20(1) is to be read, until the appointed day, as if for the words "the age of 18 (or, in relation to Scotland or Northern Ireland, 21)" there were substituted "the age of 21".

(2) In sub-paragraph (1), "the appointed day" means the day on which the amendment made to section 81(3)(a) of the Regulation of Investigatory Powers Act 2000 by paragraph 211 of Schedule 7 to the Criminal Justice and Court Services Act 2000 comes into force.

45. (1) The amendment made by paragraph 17 does not affect whether the payment of any fees or other charges may be required under section 56 of the Finance Act 1973 in connection with a service or facilities provided, or an authorisation, certificate or other document issued, before that amendment comes into force.

(2) Sub-paragraph (3) applies where—

(a) immediately before the amendment made by paragraph 17 comes into force, the payment of fees or other charges could be required, under section 56 of the Finance Act 1973, in connection with the provision of a service or facilities, or issuing an authorisation, certificate or other document, in pursuance of an EU obligation, and

(b) after the amendment made by paragraph 17 comes into force—

(i) regulations made under that section (whether or not modified under Part 2 of Schedule 4 or otherwise) prescribing the fees or charges, or under which the fees or charges are to be determined, form part of retained EU law, and

(ii) the service or facilities are provided, or the authorisation, certificate or other document is issued, under or in connection with retained EU law.

(3) Despite the amendment made by paragraph 17, the payment of fees or other charges may be required, under that section and in accordance with the regulations, in connection with the provision of the service or facilities, or the issuing of the authorisation, certificate or other document.

NOTES

Commencement: 26 June 2018 (paras 41(10), 43, 44); 4 July 2018 (para 40); 1 March 2019 para 41(3)–(9)); IP completion day (as defined in the European Union (Withdrawal Agreement) Act 2020, s 39) (otherwise).

Words in square brackets in the heading preceding para 37A substituted by the European Union (Withdrawal Agreement) Act 2020, s 41(4), Sch 5, Pt 2, paras 38, 56(1), (2), as from IP completion day (as defined in the European Union (Withdrawal Agreement) Act 2020, s 39).

Para 37A: inserted by the European Union (Withdrawal Agreement) Act 2020, s 41(4), Sch 5, Pt 2, paras 38, 56(1), (3), as from IP completion day (as defined in the European Union (Withdrawal Agreement) Act 2020, s 39).

Para 38: words in square brackets substituted by the European Union (Withdrawal Agreement) Act 2020, s 41(4), Sch 5, Pt 2, paras 38, 56(1), (4), as from IP completion day (as defined in the European Union (Withdrawal Agreement) Act 2020, s 39).

Para 39: words "IP completion day" in square brackets substituted, and other words in square brackets inserted, by the European Union (Withdrawal Agreement) Act 2020, s 41(4), Sch 5, Pt 2, paras 38, 56(1), (5), as from IP completion day (as defined in the European Union (Withdrawal Agreement) Act 2020, s 39).

Para 40: the figure "6(5A)," in square brackets was inserted by the European Union (Withdrawal Agreement) Act 2020, s 41(4), Sch 5, Pt 2, paras 38. All other amendments to this paragraph were made by the European Union (Withdrawal Agreement) Act 2020, s 41(4), Sch 5, Pt 2, paras 38, 56(1), (6)(b)–(d).

Para 41 is amended as follows:

The words "IP completion day" in square brackets were substituted by the European Union (Withdrawal Agreement) Act 2020, s 41(4), Sch 5, Pt 2, paras 38, 56(1), (7)(a), as from 23 January 2020 (in so far as the words occur in sub-paras (3)–(9)), and as from IP completion day (as defined in the European Union (Withdrawal Agreement) Act 2020, s 39) (otherwise).

Words in square brackets in sub-para (10) substituted by the European Union (Withdrawal Agreement) Act 2020, s 41(4), Sch 5, Pt 2, paras 38, 56(1), (7)(b), as from exit day (as defined in s 20 of this Act) (for the purposes of making regulations under s 8A, or Part 1A of Sch 2), as from 19 May 2020 (for all other purposes except in so far as relating to the making of regulations under Part 1 of Sch 2), and as from IP completion day (otherwise).

Para 42: words in square brackets substituted by the European Union (Withdrawal Agreement) Act 2020, s 41(4), Sch 5, Pt 2, paras 38, 56(1), (8), as from IP completion day (as defined in the European Union (Withdrawal Agreement) Act 2020, s 39).

National Assembly for Wales: as to the renaming of the National Assembly for Wales, etc, see the note at **[7.28]**.

SCHEDULE 9
ADDITIONAL REPEALS

(Repeals the European Parliamentary Elections Act 2002, the European Parliament (Representation) Act 2003, the European Union (Amendment) Act 2008, the European Union Act 2011, the European Union (Approval of Treaty Amendment Decision) Act 2012, the European Union (Approvals) Act 2013, the European Union (Approvals) Act 2014, the European Union (Finance) Act 2015, the European Union (Approvals) Act 2015, and ss 82, 88(5)(c) of the Serious Crime Act 2015.)

EUROPEAN UNION (WITHDRAWAL AGREEMENT) ACT 2020

(2020 c 1)

NOTES

The EU-UK Withdrawal Agreement has not been included in this edition due to its size. It is available on the European Commission's website at: ec.europa.eu/info/european-union-and-united-kingdom-forging-new-partnership/eu-uk-withdrawal-agreement_en.

An Act to implement, and make other provision in connection with, the agreement between the United Kingdom and the EU under Article 50(2) of the Treaty on European Union which sets out the arrangements for the United Kingdom's withdrawal from the EU

[23 January 2020]

ARRANGEMENT OF SECTIONS

PART 5
GENERAL AND FINAL PROVISION

PART 1 IMPLEMENTATION PERIOD

1–4 (*Ss 1–4 insert the European Union (Withdrawal) Act 2018, ss 1A, 1B, 8A, Sch 2, Pt 1A ante.*)

PART 2 REMAINING IMPLEMENTATION OF WITHDRAWAL AGREEMENT ETC: GENERAL

5, 6 (*Ss 5, 6 insert the European Union (Withdrawal) Act 2018, ss 7A, 7B ante.*)

PART 3 CITIZENS' RIGHTS

7–17 (*Outside the scope of this work.*)

PART 4 OTHER SUBJECT AREAS

18–37 (*Ss 18–37 amend the European Union (Withdrawal) Act 2018 ante, and are otherwise outside the scope of this work.*)

PART 5 GENERAL AND FINAL PROVISION

Parliamentary sovereignty

[7.52]

38 Parliamentary sovereignty

(1) It is recognised that the Parliament of the United Kingdom is sovereign.

(2) In particular, its sovereignty subsists notwithstanding—

(a) directly applicable or directly effective EU law continuing to be recognised and available in domestic law by virtue of section 1A or 1B of the European Union (Withdrawal) Act 2018 (savings of existing law for the implementation period),

(b) section 7A of that Act (other directly applicable or directly effective aspects of the withdrawal agreement),

(c) section 7B of that Act (deemed direct applicability or direct effect in relation to the EEA EFTA separation agreement and the Swiss citizens' rights agreement), and

(d) section 7C of that Act (interpretation of law relating to the withdrawal agreement (other than the implementation period), the EEA EFTA separation agreement and the Swiss citizens' rights agreement).

(3) Accordingly, nothing in this Act derogates from the sovereignty of the Parliament of the United Kingdom.

NOTES

Commencement: 23 January 2020.

Interpretation

[7.53]

39 Interpretation

(1) In this Act—

"devolved authority" means—

(a) the Scottish Ministers,

(b) the Welsh Ministers, or

(c) a Northern Ireland department;

"EEA EFTA separation agreement" means (as modified from time to time in accordance with any provision of it) the Agreement on arrangements between Iceland, the Principality of Liechtenstein, the Kingdom of Norway and the United Kingdom of Great Britain and Northern Ireland following the withdrawal of the United Kingdom from the European Union, the EEA Agreement and other agreements applicable between the United Kingdom and the EEA EFTA States by virtue of the United Kingdom's membership of the European Union;

"enactment" means an enactment whenever passed or made and includes—

(a) an enactment contained in any Order in Council, order, rules, regulations, scheme, warrant, byelaw or other instrument made under an Act of Parliament,

(b) an enactment contained in any Order in Council made in exercise of Her Majesty's Prerogative,

(c) an enactment contained in, or in an instrument made under, an Act of the Scottish Parliament,

(d) an enactment contained in, or in an instrument made under, a Measure or Act of the National Assembly for Wales,

(e) an enactment contained in, or in an instrument made under, Northern Ireland legislation,

(f) an enactment contained in any instrument made by a member of the Scottish Government, the Welsh Ministers, the First Minister for Wales, the Counsel General to the Welsh Government, a Northern Ireland Minister, the First Minister in Northern Ireland, the deputy First Minister in Northern Ireland or a Northern Ireland department in exercise of prerogative or other executive functions of Her Majesty which are exercisable by such a person on behalf of Her Majesty,

(g) an enactment contained in, or in an instrument made under, a Measure of the Church Assembly or of the General Synod of the Church of England, and

(h) any retained direct EU legislation;

"IP completion day" means 31 December 2020 at 11.00 p.m (and see subsections (2) to (5));

"Minister of the Crown" has the same meaning as in the Ministers of the Crown Act 1975 and also includes the Commissioners for Her Majesty's Revenue and Customs;

"modify" includes amend, repeal or revoke (and related expressions are to be read accordingly);

"primary legislation" means—

(a) an Act of Parliament,

(b) an Act of the Scottish Parliament,

(c) a Measure or Act of the National Assembly for Wales, or

(d) Northern Ireland legislation;

"subordinate legislation" means any Order in Council, order, rules, regulations, scheme, warrant, byelaw or other instrument made under any primary legislation;

"Swiss citizens' rights agreement" means (as modified from time to time in accordance with any provision of it) the Agreement signed at Bern on 25 February 2019 between the United Kingdom of Great Britain and Northern Ireland and the Swiss Confederation on citizens' rights following the withdrawal of the United Kingdom from—

(a) the European Union, and

(b) the free movement of persons agreement,

so far as the Agreement operates for the purposes of the case where "specified date" for the purposes of that Agreement has the meaning given in Article 2(b)(ii) of that Agreement;

"withdrawal agreement" means the agreement between the United Kingdom and the EU under Article 50(2) of the Treaty on European Union which sets out the arrangements for the United Kingdom's withdrawal from the EU (as that agreement is modified from time to time in accordance with any provision of it).

(2) In this Act references to before, after or on IP completion day, or to beginning with IP completion day, are to be read as references to before, after or at 11.00 pm on 31 December 2020 or (as the case may be) to beginning with 11.00 pm on that day.

(3) Subsection (4) applies if, by virtue of any change to EU summer-time arrangements, the transition or implementation period provided for by Part 4 of the withdrawal agreement is to end on a day or time which is different from that specified in the definition of "IP completion day" in subsection (1).

(4) A Minister of the Crown may by regulations—

(a) amend the definition of "IP completion day" in subsection (1) to ensure that the day and time specified in the definition are the day and time that the transition or implementation period provided for by Part 4 of the withdrawal agreement is to end, and

(b) amend subsection (2) in consequence of any such amendment.

(5) In subsection (3) "EU summer-time arrangements" means the arrangements provided for by Directive 2000/84/EC of the European Parliament and of the Council of 19 January 2001 on summer-time arrangements.

(6) In this Act any reference to an Article of the Treaty on European Union includes a reference to that Article as applied by Article 106a of the Euratom Treaty.

NOTES

Commencement: 23 January 2020.

National Assembly for Wales: as to the renaming of the National Assembly for Wales, etc, see the note at **[7.28]**.

Supplementary and final

[7.54]

40 Regulations

Schedule 4 contains provision about regulations under this Act (including provision about procedure).

NOTES

Commencement: 23 January 2020.

[7.55]

41 Consequential and transitional provision etc

(1) A Minister of the Crown may by regulations make such provision as the Minister considers appropriate in consequence of this Act.

(2) The power to make regulations under subsection (1) may (among other things) be exercised by modifying any provision made by or under an enactment.

(3) In subsection (2) "enactment" does not include primary legislation passed or made after IP completion day.

(4) Parts 1 and 2 of Schedule 5 contain minor and consequential provision.

(5) A Minister of the Crown may by regulations make such transitional, transitory or saving provision as the Minister considers appropriate in connection with the coming into force of any provision of this Act (including its operation in connection with exit day or IP completion day).

(6) Part 3 of Schedule 5 contains transitional, transitory and saving provision.

NOTES

Commencement: 23 January 2020 (sub-ss (1), (3), (5), and sub-ss (4) and (6) for certain purposes); immediately before exit day (31 January 2020 at 11pm) (sub-s (4) for certain purposes); exit day (sub-ss (4) and (6) for certain purposes); 19 May 2020 (sub-ss (4) and (6) for certain purposes); to be appointed (otherwise).

Regulations: the Competition (Amendment etc) (EU Exit) Regulations 2020, SI 2020/1343; the European Union Withdrawal (Consequential Modifications) (EU Exit) Regulations 2020, SI 2020/1447; the Challenges to Validity of EU Instruments (Amendment) (EU Exit) Regulations 2020, SI 2020/1503; the European Union (Withdrawal) Act 2018 and European Union (Withdrawal Agreement) Act 2020 (Commencement, Transitional and Savings Provisions) Regulations 2020, SI 2020/1622. Note that only Regulations relevant to this Handbook are listed; the other Regulations made under this section are considered to be outside the scope of this work.

[7.56]

42 Extent, commencement and short title

(1) Subject to subsections (2) to (5), this Act extends to England and Wales, Scotland and Northern Ireland.

(2) Any provision of this Act which amends or repeals an enactment has the same extent as the enactment amended or repealed.

(3) Accordingly, section 1 (but not section 2) also extends to the Isle of Man, the Channel Islands and Gibraltar.

(4) The power in section 36 of the Immigration Act 1971 or (as the case may be) section 60(4) of the UK Borders Act 2007 may be exercised so as to extend (with or without modifications) to the Isle of Man or any of the Channel Islands the modifications made to that Act by section 10 above.

(5) Paragraphs 1 and 2 of Schedule 5, so far as they relate to the modification of any provision in subordinate legislation which extends outside England and Wales, Scotland and Northern Ireland, also extend there.

(6) The following provisions—

- (a) sections 3 and 4,
- (b) sections 11, 16 and 17,
- (c) sections 20, 29 and 31 to 40 (including Schedule 4),
- (d) section 41(1) to (3) and (5),
- (e) the following provisions of Schedule 5—
  - (i) paragraphs 1(3) to (6) and 2,
  - (ii) paragraph 3(2) to (8),
  - (iii) paragraph 4,
  - (iv) paragraphs 5 and 7(a) and (b),
  - (v) paragraphs 8 and 12(a) and (b),
  - (vi) paragraphs 17, 20, 22, 24, 27 and 31,
  - (vii) paragraphs 32, 36(a) and (b) and 37(b) and (c),
  - (viii) paragraphs 38, 41(1) and (3)(a), 42, 44(1), (2)(a), (d) and (e) and (3), 47(1), (2), (4) and (6) and 50,
  - (ix) paragraphs 51 and 56(1) and (7)(b) for the purposes of making regulations under section 8A of, or Part 1A of Schedule 2 to, the European Union (Withdrawal) Act 2018,
  - (x) paragraphs 52(1) and (3) to (7) and 53(1) to (4), (6), (7)(a), (8)(a) and (9) to (13),
  - (xi) paragraph 56(1) and (6)(b) to (d), and
  - (xii) paragraphs 65 to 68,

  (and section 41(4) and (6) so far as relating to any provision so far as it falls within any of sub-paragraphs (i) to (xii)), and
- (f) this section,

come into force on the day on which this Act is passed.

(7) The provisions of this Act, so far as they are not brought into force by subsection (6), come into force on such day as a Minister of the Crown may by regulations appoint; and different days may be appointed for different purposes.

(8) This Act may be cited as the European Union (Withdrawal Agreement) Act 2020.

NOTES

Commencement: 23 January 2020.

Regulations: the European Union (Withdrawal Agreement) Act 2020 (Commencement No 1) Regulations 2020, SI 2020/75; the European Union (Withdrawal Agreement) Act 2020 (Commencement No 2) Regulations 2020, SI 2020/317 (note that these

Regulations commence certain provisions in s 15 and Schs 2 and 3 which are outside the scope of this work); the European Union (Withdrawal Agreement) Act 2020 (Commencement No 3) Regulations 2020, SI 2020/518; the European Union (Withdrawal) Act 2018 and European Union (Withdrawal Agreement) Act 2020 (Commencement, Transitional and Savings Provisions) Regulations 2020, SI 2020/1622.

SCHEDULES

SCHEDULES 1–3

(Schedule 1 (Powers of Devolved Authorities under Sections 12, 13 and 14); Schedule 2 (Independent Monitoring Authority for the Citizens' Rights Agreements); Schedule 3 (Protection for Certain Rights, Safeguards etc in Belfast Agreement) outside the scope of this work.)

SCHEDULE 4
REGULATIONS UNDER THIS ACT

Section 40

PART 1 PROCEDURE

Rights in relation to entry and residence

[7.57]

1. (1) A statutory instrument containing—

(a) the first regulations under section 7(1)(b), (c), (d), (e), (f) or (g), 8(1) or 9, or

(b) regulations under section 7, 8 or 9 which amend, repeal or revoke primary legislation or retained direct principal EU legislation,

may not be made unless a draft of the instrument has been laid before, and approved by a resolution of, each House of Parliament.

(2) Any other statutory instrument containing regulations under section 7, 8 or 9 is subject to annulment in pursuance of a resolution of either House of Parliament.

2. (1) A statutory instrument containing the first regulations under section 11—

(a) must be laid before Parliament after being made, and

(b) ceases to have effect at the end of the period of 40 days beginning with the day on which the instrument is made unless, during that period, the instrument is approved by a resolution of each House of Parliament.

(2) Any other statutory instrument containing regulations under section 11 which amend, repeal or revoke—

(a) primary legislation, or

(b) retained direct principal EU legislation,

may not be made unless a draft of the instrument has been laid before, and approved by a resolution of, each House of Parliament.

(3) A statutory instrument containing regulations under section 11, other than a statutory instrument to which sub-paragraph (1) or (2) applies, is subject to annulment in pursuance of a resolution of either House of Parliament.

(4) In calculating the period of 40 days for the purposes of sub-paragraph (1) no account is to be taken of any time during which—

(a) Parliament is dissolved or prorogued, or

(b) either House of Parliament is adjourned for more than four days.

(5) If regulations cease to have effect as a result of sub-paragraph (1) that—

(a) does not affect the validity of anything previously done under the regulations, and

(b) does not prevent the making of new regulations.

Powers under sections 12, 13 and 14: sole exercise

3. (1) A statutory instrument containing regulations under section 12, 13 or 14 of a Minister of the Crown acting alone which amend, repeal or revoke—

(a) primary legislation, or

(b) retained direct principal EU legislation,

may not be made unless a draft of the instrument has been laid before, and approved by a resolution of, each House of Parliament.

(2) Any other statutory instrument containing regulations under section 12, 13 or 14 of a Minister of the Crown acting alone is subject to annulment in pursuance of a resolution of either House of Parliament.

(3) Regulations under section 12, 13 or 14 of the Scottish Ministers acting alone which amend, repeal or revoke—

(a) primary legislation, or

(b) retained direct principal EU legislation,

are subject to the affirmative procedure (see section 29 of the Interpretation and Legislative Reform (Scotland) Act 2010 (asp 10)).

(4) Any other regulations under section 12, 13 or 14 of the Scottish Ministers acting alone are subject to the negative procedure (see section 28 of the Interpretation and Legislative Reform (Scotland) Act 2010).

(5) A statutory instrument containing regulations under section 12, 13 or 14 of the Welsh Ministers acting alone which amend, repeal or revoke—

(a) primary legislation, or

(b) retained direct principal EU legislation,

may not be made unless a draft of the instrument has been laid before, and approved by a resolution of, the National Assembly for Wales.

(6) Any other statutory instrument containing regulations under section 12, 13 or 14 of the Welsh Ministers acting alone is subject to annulment in pursuance of a resolution of the National Assembly for Wales.

(7) Regulations under section 12, 13 or 14 of a Northern Ireland department acting alone which amend, repeal or revoke—

(a) primary legislation, or

(b) retained direct principal EU legislation,

may not be made unless a draft of the regulations has been laid before, and approved by a resolution of, the Northern Ireland Assembly.

(8) Any other regulations under section 12, 13 or 14 of a Northern Ireland department acting alone are subject to negative resolution within the meaning of section 41(6) of the Interpretation Act (Northern Ireland) 1954 as if they were a statutory instrument within the meaning of that Act.

Powers under sections 12, 13 and 14: joint exercise

4. (1) This paragraph applies to regulations under section 12, 13 or 14 of a Minister of the Crown acting jointly with a devolved authority.

(2) The procedure provided for by sub-paragraph (3) or (4) applies in relation to regulations to which this paragraph applies as well as any other procedure provided for by this paragraph which is applicable in relation to the regulations concerned.

(3) A statutory instrument containing regulations to which this paragraph applies which amend, repeal or revoke—

(a) primary legislation, or

(b) retained direct principal EU legislation,

may not be made unless a draft of the instrument has been laid before, and approved by a resolution of, each House of Parliament.

(4) Any other statutory instrument containing regulations to which this paragraph applies is subject to annulment in pursuance of a resolution of either House of Parliament.

(5) Regulations to which this paragraph applies which are made jointly with the Scottish Ministers and amend, repeal or revoke—

(a) primary legislation, or

(b) retained direct principal EU legislation,

are subject to the affirmative procedure.

(6) Any other regulations to which this paragraph applies which are made jointly with the Scottish Ministers are subject to the negative procedure.

(7) Section 29 of the Interpretation and Legislative Reform (Scotland) Act 2010 (affirmative procedure) applies in relation to regulations to which sub-paragraph (5) applies as it applies in relation to devolved subordinate legislation (within the meaning of Part 2 of that Act) which is subject to the affirmative procedure (but as if references to a Scottish statutory instrument were references to a statutory instrument).

(8) Sections 28(2), (3) and (8) and 31 of the Interpretation and Legislative Reform (Scotland) Act 2010 (negative procedure etc) apply in relation to regulations to which sub-paragraph (6) applies as they apply in relation to devolved subordinate legislation (within the meaning of Part 2 of that Act) which is subject to the negative procedure (but as if references to a Scottish statutory instrument were references to a statutory instrument).

(9) Section 32 of the Interpretation and Legislative Reform (Scotland) Act 2010 (laying) applies in relation to the laying before the Scottish Parliament of a statutory instrument containing regulations to which sub-paragraph (5) or (6) applies as it applies in relation to the laying before that Parliament of a Scottish statutory instrument (within the meaning of Part 2 of that Act).

(10) A statutory instrument containing regulations to which this paragraph applies which are made jointly with the Welsh Ministers and amend, repeal or revoke—

(a) primary legislation, or

(b) retained direct principal EU legislation,

may not be made unless a draft of the instrument has been laid before, and approved by a resolution of, the National Assembly for Wales.

(11) Any other statutory instrument containing regulations to which this paragraph applies which are made jointly with the Welsh Ministers is subject to annulment in pursuance of a resolution of the National Assembly for Wales.

(12) Regulations to which this paragraph applies which are made jointly with a Northern Ireland department and amend, repeal or revoke—

(a) primary legislation, or

(b) retained direct principal EU legislation,

may not be made unless a draft of the regulations has been laid before, and approved by a resolution of, the Northern Ireland Assembly.

(13) Any other regulations to which this paragraph applies which are made jointly with a Northern Ireland department are subject to negative resolution within the meaning of section 41(6) of the Interpretation Act (Northern Ireland) 1954 as if they were a statutory instrument within the meaning of that Act.

(14) If in accordance with sub-paragraph (4), (6), (11) or (13)—

(a) either House of Parliament resolves that an address be presented to Her Majesty praying that an instrument be annulled, or

(b) a relevant devolved legislature resolves that an instrument be annulled,

nothing further is to be done under the instrument after the date of the resolution and Her Majesty may by Order in Council revoke the instrument.

(15) In sub-paragraph (14) "relevant devolved legislature" means—

(a) in the case of regulations made jointly with the Scottish Ministers, the Scottish Parliament,

(b) in the case of regulations made jointly with the Welsh Ministers, the National Assembly for Wales, and

(c) in the case of regulations made jointly with a Northern Ireland department, the Northern Ireland Assembly.

(16) Sub-paragraph (14) does not affect the validity of anything previously done under the instrument or prevent the making of a new instrument.

(17) Sub-paragraphs (14) to (16) apply in place of provision made by any other enactment about the effect of such a resolution.

Power to amend definition of "IP completion day"

5. A statutory instrument containing regulations under section 39(4) is subject to annulment in pursuance of a resolution of either House of Parliament.

Consequential provision

6. A statutory instrument containing regulations under section 41(1) is subject to annulment in pursuance of a resolution of either House of Parliament.

The IMA

7. A statutory instrument containing regulations under paragraph 39 or 40 of Schedule 2 may not be made unless a draft of the instrument has been laid before, and approved by a resolution of, each House of Parliament.

Power under paragraph 1(3) of Schedule 5: sole exercise

8. (1) A statutory instrument containing regulations made by a Minister of the Crown acting alone under paragraph 1(3) of Schedule 5 on or after exit day is subject to annulment in pursuance of a resolution of either House of Parliament.

(2) Regulations made by the Scottish Ministers acting alone under paragraph 1(3) of Schedule 5 on or after exit day are subject to the negative procedure (see section 28 of the Interpretation and Legislative Reform (Scotland) Act 2010).

(3) A statutory instrument containing regulations made by the Welsh Ministers acting alone under paragraph 1(3) of Schedule 5 on or after exit day is subject to annulment in pursuance of a resolution of the National Assembly for Wales.

(4) Regulations made by a Northern Ireland department acting alone under paragraph 1(3) of Schedule 5 on or after exit day are subject to negative resolution within the meaning of section 41(6) of the Interpretation Act (Northern Ireland) 1954 as if they were a statutory instrument within the meaning of that Act.

Power under paragraph 1(3) of Schedule 5: joint exercise

9. (1) This paragraph applies to regulations under paragraph 1(3) of Schedule 5 of a Minister of the Crown acting jointly with a devolved authority.

(2) The procedure provided for by sub-paragraph (3) applies in relation to regulations to which this paragraph applies as well as any other procedure provided for by this paragraph which is applicable in relation to the regulations concerned.

(3) A statutory instrument containing regulations to which this paragraph applies which are made on or after exit day is subject to annulment in pursuance of a resolution of either House of Parliament.

(4) Regulations to which this paragraph applies which are made jointly with the Scottish Ministers on or after exit day are subject to the negative procedure.

(5) Sections 28(2), (3) and (8) and 31 of the Interpretation and Legislative Reform (Scotland) Act 2010 (negative procedure etc) apply in relation to regulations to which sub-paragraph (4) applies as they apply in relation to devolved subordinate legislation (within the meaning of Part 2 of that Act) which is subject to the negative procedure (but as if references to a Scottish statutory instrument were references to a statutory instrument).

(6) Section 32 of the Interpretation and Legislative Reform (Scotland) Act 2010 (laying) applies in relation to the laying before the Scottish Parliament of a statutory instrument containing regulations to which sub-paragraph (4) applies as it applies in relation to the laying before that Parliament of a Scottish statutory instrument (within the meaning of Part 2 of that Act).

(7) A statutory instrument containing regulations to which this paragraph applies which are made jointly with the Welsh Ministers on or after exit day is subject to annulment in pursuance of a resolution of the National Assembly for Wales.

(8) Regulations to which this paragraph applies which are made jointly with a Northern Ireland department on or after exit day are subject to negative resolution within the meaning of section 41(6) of the Interpretation Act (Northern Ireland) 1954 as if they were a statutory instrument within the meaning of that Act.

(9) If in accordance with this paragraph—

(a) either House of Parliament resolves that an address be presented to Her Majesty praying that an instrument be annulled, or

(b) a relevant devolved legislature resolves that an instrument be annulled,

nothing further is to be done under the instrument after the date of the resolution and Her Majesty may by Order in Council revoke the instrument.

(10) In sub-paragraph (9) "relevant devolved legislature" means—

(a) in the case of regulations made jointly with the Scottish Ministers, the Scottish Parliament,

(b) in the case of regulations made jointly with the Welsh Ministers, the National Assembly for Wales, and

(c) in the case of regulations made jointly with a Northern Ireland department, the Northern Ireland Assembly.

(11) Sub-paragraph (9) does not affect the validity of anything previously done under the instrument or prevent the making of a new instrument.

(12) Sub-paragraphs (9) to (11) apply in place of provision made by any other enactment about the effect of such a resolution.

Power under paragraph 3(2) of Schedule 5

10. (1) Regulations made by the Scottish Ministers under paragraph 3(2) of Schedule 5 on or after exit day are subject to the negative procedure (see section 28 of the Interpretation and Legislative Reform (Scotland) Act 2010).

(2) A statutory instrument containing regulations made by the Welsh Ministers under paragraph 3(2) of Schedule 5 on or after exit day is subject to annulment in pursuance of a resolution of the National Assembly for Wales.

(3) Regulations made by a Northern Ireland department under paragraph 3(2) of Schedule 5 on or after exit day are subject to negative resolution within the meaning of section 41(6) of the Interpretation Act (Northern Ireland) 1954 as if they were a statutory instrument within the meaning of that Act.

NOTES

Commencement: 23 January 2020.

National Assembly for Wales: as to the renaming of the National Assembly for Wales, etc, see the note at **[7.28]**.

PART 2 GENERAL PROVISION ABOUT POWERS UNDER ACT

Scope and nature of powers: general

[7.58]

11. (1) Any power to make regulations under this Act—

(a) so far as exercisable by a Minister of the Crown or by a Minister of the Crown acting jointly with a devolved authority, is exercisable by statutory instrument,

(b) so far as exercisable by the Welsh Ministers or by the Welsh Ministers acting jointly with a Minister of the Crown, is exercisable by statutory instrument, and

(c) so far as exercisable by a Northern Ireland department (other than when acting jointly with a Minister of the Crown), is exercisable by statutory rule for the purposes of the Statutory Rules (Northern Ireland) Order 1979 (SI 1979/1573 (NI 12)) (and not by statutory instrument).

(2) For regulations made under this Act by the Scottish Ministers, see also section 27 of the Interpretation and Legislative Reform (Scotland) Act 2010 (asp 10) (Scottish statutory instruments).

12. Any power to make regulations under this Act—

(a) may be exercised so as to make different provision for different cases or descriptions of case, different circumstances, different purposes or different areas, and

(b) includes power to make supplementary, incidental, consequential, transitional, transitory or saving provision.

13. The fact that a power to make regulations is conferred by this Act does not affect the extent of any other power to make regulations under this Act.

Anticipatory exercise of powers in relation to withdrawal agreement etc

14. Any power to make regulations under this Act in relation to the withdrawal agreement, the EEA EFTA separation agreement or the Swiss citizens' rights agreement, or any modification of any of them which requires ratification, is capable of being exercised before the agreement or (as the case may be) modification concerned is ratified.

Scope of appointed day power

15. The power of a Minister of the Crown under section 42(7) to appoint a day includes a power to appoint a time on that day if the Minister considers it appropriate to do so.

Hybrid instruments

16. If an instrument, or a draft of an instrument, containing regulations under this Act would, apart from this paragraph, be treated as a hybrid instrument for the purposes of the standing orders of either House of Parliament, it is to proceed in that House as if it were not a hybrid instrument.

Combinations of instruments

17. (1) Sub-paragraph (2) applies to a statutory instrument containing regulations under this Act which is subject to a procedure before Parliament for the approval of the instrument in draft before it is made or its approval after it is made.

(2) The statutory instrument may also include regulations under this Act or another enactment which are made by statutory instrument which is subject to a procedure before Parliament that provides for the annulment of the instrument after it has been made.

(3) Where regulations are included as mentioned in sub-paragraph (2), the procedure applicable to the statutory instrument is the procedure mentioned in sub-paragraph (1) and not the procedure mentioned in sub-paragraph (2).

(4) Sub-paragraphs (1) to (3) apply in relation to a statutory instrument containing regulations under this Act which is subject to a procedure before the National Assembly for Wales as they apply in relation to a statutory instrument containing regulations under this Act which is subject to a procedure before Parliament but as if the references to Parliament were references to the National Assembly for Wales.

(5) Sub-paragraphs (1) to (3) apply in relation to a statutory rule as they apply in relation to a statutory instrument but as if the references to Parliament were references to the Northern Ireland Assembly.

(6) Sub-paragraphs (1) to (3) apply in relation to a statutory instrument containing regulations under this Act which is subject to a procedure before the Scottish Parliament, the National Assembly for Wales or the Northern Ireland Assembly as well as a procedure before Parliament as they apply to a statutory instrument containing regulations

under this Act which is subject to a procedure before Parliament but as if the references to Parliament were references to Parliament and the Scottish Parliament, the National Assembly for Wales or (as the case may be) the Northern Ireland Assembly.

(7) This paragraph does not prevent the inclusion of other regulations in a statutory instrument or statutory rule which contains regulations under this Act (and, accordingly, references in this Schedule to an instrument containing regulations are to be read as references to an instrument containing (whether alone or with other provision) regulations).

NOTES

Commencement: 23 January 2020.

National Assembly for Wales: as to the renaming of the National Assembly for Wales, etc, see the note at **[7.28]**.

SCHEDULE 5
CONSEQUENTIAL AND TRANSITIONAL PROVISION ETC

Section 41(4) and (6)

PART 1 GENERAL CONSEQUENTIAL PROVISION

Subordinate legislation with commencement by reference to exit day

[7.59]

1. (1) Any provision in subordinate legislation made before exit day under—

(a) any provision of the European Union (Withdrawal) Act 2018 (or any provision made under any such provision), or

(b) any other enactment,

which provides, by reference to exit day (however expressed), for all or part of that or any other subordinate legislation to come into force immediately before exit day, on exit day or at any time after exit day is to be read instead as providing for the subordinate legislation or (as the case may be) the part to come into force immediately before IP completion day, on IP completion day or (as the case may be) at the time concerned after IP completion day.

(2) Sub-paragraph (1) does not apply so far as it is expressly disapplied by the subordinate legislation that provides as mentioned in that sub-paragraph.

(3) An appropriate authority may by regulations—

(a) provide for sub-paragraph (1) not to apply to any extent in particular cases or descriptions of case, or

(b) make different provision in particular cases or descriptions of case to that made by sub-paragraph (1).

(4) But see paragraph 2 for further provision about the power of a devolved authority acting alone to make regulations under sub-paragraph (3).

(5) No regulations may be made under sub-paragraph (3) after the end of the period of one year beginning with IP completion day.

(6) In this paragraph "appropriate authority" means—

(a) a Minister of the Crown,

(b) a devolved authority, or

(c) a Minister of the Crown acting jointly with a devolved authority.

2. (1) No provision may be made by a devolved authority acting alone in regulations under paragraph 1(3) so far as those regulations relate to the coming into force of regulations under section 23(1) or (6) of, or paragraph 1(2)(b) of Schedule 1 to, the European Union (Withdrawal) Act 2018.

(2) Subject to this, no provision may be made by a devolved authority acting alone in regulations under paragraph 1(3) relating to the coming into force of all or part of any subordinate legislation unless—

(a) the devolved authority acting alone otherwise than under paragraph 1(3) made the provision for the coming into force of the subordinate legislation or part and either—

(i) the regulations provide for paragraph 1(1) not to apply to the subordinate legislation or part, or

(ii) the devolved authority acting alone otherwise than under paragraph 1(3) could provide for the subordinate legislation or part to come into force at the same time as is provided for by virtue of the regulations, or

(b) the devolved authority acting alone could make provision corresponding to that made by the subordinate legislation or part and could provide for that provision to come into force at the same time as is provided for by virtue of the regulations.

(3) Where the test in sub-paragraph (2)(a) or (b) is (to any extent) only met by a devolved authority acting alone with the consent of a Minister of the Crown, the consent of a Minister of the Crown is required before the regulations under paragraph 1(3) may be made by the devolved authority acting alone.

(4) Except where sub-paragraph (3) applies, no provision may be made under paragraph 1(3) by a devolved authority acting alone unless the devolved authority has consulted a Minister of the Crown.

Devolved preparatory legislation of a kind mentioned in paragraph 41(3) to (5) of Schedule 8 to EUWA 2018

3. (1) Any provision of primary legislation which—

(a) is made before exit day by virtue of any of sub-paragraphs (3) to (5) of paragraph 41 of Schedule 8 to the European Union (Withdrawal) Act 2018, and

(b) provides, by reference to exit day (however expressed), for itself or any other provision so made to come into force on exit day or at any time after exit day,

is to be read instead as providing for the provision to come into force on IP completion day or (as the case may be) at that time after IP completion day.

(2) But a relevant devolved authority may, by regulations and subject to sub-paragraphs (4) to (7)—

(a) provide for sub-paragraph (1) not to apply to any extent in particular cases or descriptions of case,

(b) make different provision in particular cases or descriptions of case to that made by sub-paragraph (1), or
(c) make such provision as the relevant devolved authority considers appropriate in consequence of sub-paragraph (1) (including provision restating the effect of that sub-paragraph).

(3) The power to make regulations under sub-paragraph (2) may (among other things) be exercised by modifying any provision made by or under an enactment.

(4) No provision may be made by the Scottish Ministers in regulations under sub-paragraph (2) unless it would be within the legislative competence of the Scottish Parliament if it were contained in an Act of that Parliament.

(5) No provision may be made by the Welsh Ministers in regulations under sub-paragraph (2) unless it would be within the legislative competence of the National Assembly for Wales if it were contained in an Act of the Assembly (including any provision that could be made only with the consent of a Minister of the Crown).

(6) No provision may be made by a Northern Ireland department in regulations under sub-paragraph (2) unless it would be within the legislative competence of the Northern Ireland Assembly if it were contained in an Act of the Assembly (including any provision that could be made only with the consent of the Secretary of State).

(7) No regulations may be made under sub-paragraph (2) after the end of the period of one year beginning with IP completion day.

(8) In this paragraph "relevant devolved authority" means—
(a) in relation to any provision of an Act of the Scottish Parliament, the Scottish Ministers,
(b) in relation to any provision of an Act of the National Assembly for Wales, the Welsh Ministers, and
(c) in relation to any provision of an Act of the Northern Ireland Assembly, a Northern Ireland department.

Power to make consequential regulations under EUWA 2018

4. (1) The power of a Minister of the Crown under section 23(1) of the European Union (Withdrawal) Act 2018 to make such provision as the Minister considers appropriate in consequence of that Act includes the power to make such provision as the Minister considers appropriate in consequence of that Act as modified, or to be modified, by or under this Act (and references in the Act of 2018 to the power under section 23(1) of that Act are to be read accordingly).

(2) Sub-paragraph (1) does not limit the power conferred by section 41(1) above.

(3) The reference in sub-paragraph (1) to any modification by or under this Act of the European Union (Withdrawal) Act 2018 includes a reference to any modification made by or under this Act of a provision of another Act which was inserted into that other Act or otherwise modified by the Act of 2018.

NOTES

Commencement: 23 January 2020 (paras 1(3)–(6), 2, 3(2)–(8), 4); immediately before exit day (as defined in the European Union (Withdrawal) Act 2018, s 20) (para 1(1), (2)); exit day (as defined in the European Union (Withdrawal) Act 2018, s 20) (para 3(1)).

National Assembly for Wales: as to the renaming of the National Assembly for Wales, etc, see the note at **[7.28]**.

Regulations: the Financial Services (Consequential Amendments) Regulations 2020, SI 2020/56; the European Union (Withdrawal Agreement) Act 2020 (Disapplication of the Deferral of Subordinate Legislation) (Wales) (EU Exit) Regulations 2020, SI 2020/93.

(Sch 5, Pt 2 (Specific Consequential Provision etc) amends the European Union (Withdrawal) Act 2018 ante, and other enactments that are outside the scope of this work.)

PART 3 TRANSITIONAL, TRANSITORY AND SAVING PROVISION

Retention of existing grounds for deportation

[7.60]

63. (*Outside the scope of this work.*)

Certain powers of devolved authorities in relation to EU law

64. Section 57(2) of the Scotland Act 1998, section 80(8) of the Government of Wales Act 2006 and section 24(1)(b) of the Northern Ireland Act 1998, so far as relating to EU law, do not apply to the making of regulations under section 12, 13 or 14.

Savings in connection with section 36

65. Section 36(e) and (f) do not affect the continued operation of the amendments made by section 2 of the European Union (Withdrawal) Act 2019 and section 4 of the European Union (Withdrawal) (No 2) Act 2019.

Regulations under EUWA 2018 etc

66. (1) The fact that a power to make regulations is conferred by this Act in the European Union (Withdrawal) Act 2018 does not affect the extent of any other power to make regulations under that Act.

(2) The modifications made by this Act to any power to make regulations conferred by the European Union (Withdrawal) Act 2018 do not affect the validity of any regulations made under that power before the coming into force of the modifications.

(3) Sub-paragraph (2) is subject to any provision made by regulations under section 41(5) above or section 23(6) of the Act of 2018.

Time-limited powers

67. The prohibition on making regulations under paragraph 1(3) or 3(2) of this Schedule after the end of the period of one year beginning with IP completion day does not affect the continuation in force of regulations made at or before that time.

Power to make transitional, transitory or saving regulations under EUWA 2018

68. (1) The power of a Minister of the Crown under section 23(6) of the European Union (Withdrawal) Act 2018 to make such transitional, transitory or saving provision as the Minister considers appropriate in connection with the coming into force of any provision of that Act includes the power to make such transitional, transitory or saving provision as the Minister considers appropriate in connection with the coming into force (whether by virtue of this Act, this Act and that Act, or otherwise) of any provision of that Act as inserted into that Act, or modified, by or under this Act (and references in the Act of 2018 to the power under section 23(6) of that Act are to be read accordingly).

(2) Sub-paragraph (1) does not limit the power conferred by section 41(5) above; and the power of a Minister of the Crown under section 25(4) of the European Union (Withdrawal) Act 2018 does not apply to any insertions into, or other modifications of, that Act made by this Act (for which see section 42(6) and (7) above).

(3) References in this paragraph to any modification made by or under this Act of any provision of the European Union (Withdrawal) Act 2018 include references to any modification made by or under this Act of a provision of another Act which was inserted into that other Act or otherwise modified by the Act of 2018.

NOTES

Commencement: 23 January 2020 (paras 65–68); exit day (as defined in the European Union (Withdrawal) Act 2018, s 20) (para 63); 19 May 2020 (para 64).

COMPETITION (AMENDMENT ETC) (EU EXIT) REGULATIONS 2019

(SI 2019/93)

NOTES

Made: 22 January 2019.

Authority: European Union (Withdrawal) Act 2018, s 8)1), Sch 4, para 1(1), Sch 7, para 21.

Commencement: IP completion day (as defined in the European Union (Withdrawal Agreement) Act 2020, s 39).

Note that these Regulations are reproduced as amended by the Competition (Amendment etc) (EU Exit) Regulations 2020, SI 2020/1343. The 2020 Regulations come into force immediately before IP completion day. The amendments made by the 2020 Regulations to these Regulations include amendments to provisions that amend other Acts and statutory instruments – and those amendments have been incorporated at the appropriate place in Parts 1 and 2 of this Handbook *ante*.

Note (the Competition (Amendment etc) (EU Exit) (No 2) Regulations 2019): these Regulations were amended by the Competition (Amendment etc) (EU Exit) (No 2) Regulations 2019, SI 2019/1245 (the No 2 Regulations). The No 2 Regulations were due to come into force immediately before exit day. Note that the No 2 Regulations were made under the urgent made affirmative procedure of the European Union (Withdrawal) Act 2018. They sought to address a potential enforcement gap that could arise in the circumstances of a no-deal exit, in respect of merger and antitrust commitments provided to the European Commission insofar as they relate to the UK. However, the Regulations were subsequently found to contain drafting errors and, as a result, the government decided not to bring them forward for debate by Parliament within the required 28 days for their approval by the House. Consequently, the No 2 Regulations have ceased to have effect. Amendments made to these Regulations by the No 2 Regulation have, therefore, not been reproduced below.

ARRANGEMENT OF REGULATIONS

Part 7 Brexit-related Materials

PART 1 INTRODUCTION

[7.61]
1 Citation, commencement and extent

(1) These Regulations may be cited as the Competition (Amendment etc) (EU Exit) Regulations 2019 and come into force on exit day.

(2) An amendment, repeal or revocation made by these Regulations has the same extent as the provision to which it relates.

(3) Transitional or saving provision made by these Regulations has the same extent as the provision to which it relates.

NOTES

Commencement: IP completion day (as defined in the European Union (Withdrawal Agreement) Act 2020, s 39).

As to the commencement of these Regulations, see the European Union (Withdrawal Agreement) Act 2020, Sch 5, para 1 (at **[7.59]**) which gives legal effect to the implementation period by 'non-textually amending' the coming into force dates of subordinate legislation which comes into force immediately before exit day, on exit day or at any time after exit day. This subordinate legislation will instead come into force immediately before the end of the implementation period (IP completion day), on IP completion day or (as the case may be) at the time concerned after IP completion day.

PART 2 AMENDMENT OF THE COMPETITION ACT 1998

2–31 *(This Part (as amended by the Competition (Amendment etc) (EU Exit) Regulations 2020, SI 2020/1343) amends the Competition Act 1998 at* **[1.41]**.)

PART 3 AMENDMENT OF THE ENTERPRISE ACT 2002

32–59 *(This Part (as amended by the Competition (Amendment etc) (EU Exit) Regulations 2020, SI 2020/1343) amends the Enterprise Act 2002 at* **[1.184]**.)

PART 4 AMENDMENT OF OTHER PRIMARY LEGISLATION

[7.62]
60

Schedule 1 (which amends other primary legislation) has effect.

NOTES

Commencement: IP completion day (as defined in the European Union (Withdrawal Agreement) Act 2020, s 39).

PART 5 AMENDMENT OF SUBORDINATE LEGISLATION

[7.63]
61

Schedule 2 (which amends subordinate legislation) has effect.

NOTES

Commencement: IP completion day (as defined in the European Union (Withdrawal Agreement) Act 2020, s 39).

PART 6 AMENDMENT OF RETAINED EU LAW

[7.64]
62 Cessation of Treaty Rights and Obligations

Any rights, powers, liabilities, obligations, restrictions, remedies and procedures which—

(a) continue by virtue of section 4(1) of the European Union (Withdrawal) Act 2018; and
(b) are derived from Articles 101, 102, 106(1) or 106(2) of the Treaty of the Functioning of the European Union or from Articles 53, 54, 57(1), 59(1) or 59(2) of the EEA Agreement

cease to be recognised and available in domestic law (and to be enforced, allowed and followed accordingly) on the coming into force of these Regulations.

NOTES

Commencement: IP completion day (as defined in the European Union (Withdrawal Agreement) Act 2020, s 39).

[7.65]
63 Amendment of retained direct EU legislation

In Schedule 3—

(a) Part 1 revokes certain retained direct EU legislation;
(b) Part 2 amends certain retained EU Regulations.

NOTES

Commencement: IP completion day (as defined in the European Union (Withdrawal Agreement) Act 2020, s 39).

PART 7 SAVING AND TRANSITIONAL PROVISION

[7.66]
64

Schedule 4 (which makes saving and transitional provision) has effect.

NOTES

Commencement: IP completion day (as defined in the European Union (Withdrawal Agreement) Act 2020, s 39).

SCHEDULES

SCHEDULES 1 AND 2

(Schedule 1 (Amendment of other Primary Legislation) amends the Competition Act 1980, the Company Directors Disqualification Act 1986, the Water Industry Act 1991, the Financial Services and Markets Act 2000, the Financial Services (Banking Reform) Act 2013, and a variety of other Acts that are outside the scope of this work. In so far as relevant, the amendments have been incorporated in Part 1 of this Handbook ante. Schedule 2 (Amendment of Subordinate Legislation) amends Competition Act 1998 (Small Agreements and Conduct of Minor Significance) Regulations 2000, SI 2000/262, the Competition Act 1998 (Determination of Turnover for Penalties) Order 2000, SI 2000/309, the Competition Act 1998 (Appealable Decisions and Revocation of Notification of Excluded Agreements) Regulations 2004, SI 2004/1078, the Competition Act 1998 (Competition and Markets Authority's Rules) Order 2014, SI 2014/458, the Competition Act 1998 (Concurrency) Regulations 2014, SI 2014/536, the Enterprise Act 2002 (Anticipated Mergers) Order 2003, SI 2003/1595, the Enterprise Act 2002 (Mergers) (Interim Measures: Financial Penalties) (Determination of Control and Turnover) Order 2014, SI 2014/533, the Competition Appeal Tribunal Rules 2015, SI 2015/1648, the Competition Act 1998 and other Enactments (Amendment) Regulations 2004, SI 2004/1261, and the Water Mergers (Modification of Enactments) Regulations 2004, SI 2004/3202. Schedule 2 also amends other statutory instruments that are outside the scope of this work, and revokes the EEC Merger Control (Distinct Market Investigations) Regulations 1990, SI 1990/1715, and the Designation of the Competition and Markets Authority as a National Competition Authority Regulations 2014, SI 2014/537. In so far as relevant, the amendments have been incorporated in Part 2 of this Handbook ante. Note also that Schs 1 and 2 are amended by the Competition (Amendment etc) (EU Exit) Regulations 2020, SI 2020/1343.)

SCHEDULE 3
AMENDMENT OF RETAINED DIRECT EU LEGISLATION

Regulation 63

PART 1 REVOCATION OF RETAINED DIRECT EU LEGISLATION

[7.67]
1. The following instruments are revoked—

(a) Council Regulation (EEC) 17/62: First Regulation implementing Articles 85 and 86 of the Treaty;
(b) Council Regulation (EEC) 19/65 on the application of Article 85(3) of the Treaty to certain categories of agreements and concerted practices;
(c) Council Regulation (EEC) 2821/71 on the application of Article 85(3) of the Treaty to categories of agreements, decisions and concerted practices;
(d) Council Regulation (EEC) No 2988/74 concerning limitation periods in proceedings and the enforcement of sanctions under the rules of the European Economic Community relating to transport and competition;
(e) Council Regulation (EEC) 1534/91 on the application of Article 85(3) of the Treaty to certain categories of agreements, decisions and concerted practices in the insurance sector;
(f) Council Regulation (EC) 1/2003 on the implementation of the rules on competition laid down in Articles 81 and 82 of the Treaty;
(g) Council Regulation (EC) No 139/2004 on the control of concentrations between undertakings;
(h) Council Regulation (EC) 246/2009 on the application of Article 81(3) of the Treaty to certain categories of agreements, decisions and concerted practices between liner shipping companies (consortia);
(i) Council Regulation (EC) 487/2009 on the application of Article 81(3) of the Treaty to certain categories of agreements and concerted practices in the air transport sector;
(j) Annex 14 to the EEA Agreement insofar as it forms part of domestic law on and after [IP completion day] by virtue of section 3(1) of the European Union (Withdrawal) Act 2018;
[(k) Regulation (EU) 2019/452 of the European Parliament and of the Council of 19 March 2019 establishing a framework for the screening of foreign direct investments into the Union].

2. EU decisions and EU regulations made by the European Commission under the instruments revoked by paragraph 1 (as they form part of domestic law on and after [IP completion day] by virtue of section 3(1) of the European Union (Withdrawal) Act 2018) are revoked, with the exception of EU regulations made by the European Commission under the EU regulations specified in paragraph 1(b), (c) and (h).

NOTES

Commencement: IP completion day (as defined in the European Union (Withdrawal Agreement) Act 2020, s 39).

The words "IP completion day" in square brackets in sub-para (j) of para 1 and in para 2 were substituted, and sub-para (k) of para 1 was added, by the Competition (Amendment etc) (EU Exit) Regulations 2020, SI 2020/1343, reg 34, with effect from immediately before IP completion day.

Note that the following EU Regulations which are included in this Handbook are repealed by para 2 above:

— Commission Regulation 773/2004/EC relating to the conduct of proceedings by the Commission pursuant to Articles 81 and 82 of the EC Treaty at **[4.83]**;

— Commission Regulation 622/2008/EC amending Regulation (EC) No 773/2004, as regards the conduct of settlement procedures in cartel cases at **[4.405]**;

— Commission Regulation 802/2004/EC implementing Council Regulation (EC) No 139/2004 on the control of concentrations between undertakings at **[4.567]**.

Note that the following EU Regulations which are included in this Handbook are not repealed by para 2 above (ie, they are EU Regulations made by the European Commission under the EU Regulations specified in sub-paragraphs 1(b), (c) and (h)):

— Commission Regulation 1217/2010/EU on the application of Article 101(3) of the Treaty on the Functioning of the European Union to certain categories of research and development agreements at **[4.201]**;

— Commission Regulation 1218/2010/EU on the application of Article 101(3) of the Treaty on the Functioning of the European Union to certain categories of specialisation agreements at **[4.211]**;

— Commission Regulation 330/2010/EU on the application of Article 101(3) of the Treaty on the Functioning of the European Union to categories of vertical agreements and concerted practices at **[4.237]**;

— Commission Regulation 461/2010/EU on the application of Article 101(3) of the Treaty on the Functioning of the European Union to categories of vertical agreements and concerted practices in the motor vehicle sector at **[4.255]**;

— Commission Regulation 316/2014/EU on the application of Article 101(3) of the Treaty on the Functioning of the European Union to categories of technology transfer agreements at **[4.277]**;

— Commission Regulation 906/2009/EU on the application of Article 81(3) of the Treaty to certain categories of agreements, decisions and concerted practices between liner shipping companies (consortia) at **[4.325]**.

PART 2 AMENDMENT OF RETAINED EU REGULATIONS

[7.68]

3–9 *(Para 3 amends Council Regulation (EC) No 169/2009 applying rules of competition to transport by rail, road and inland waterway. Para 4 amends Commission Regulation (EC) 906/2009 on the application of Article 81(3) of the Treaty to certain categories of agreements, decisions and concerted practices between liner shipping companies (consortia). Para 5 amends Commission Regulation (EU) 330/2010 on the application of Article 101(3) of the Treaty on the Functioning of the European Union to categories of vertical agreements and concerted practices. Para 6 amends Commission Regulation (EU) 461/2010 on the application of Article 101(3) of the Treaty on the Functioning of the European Union to categories of vertical agreements and concerted practices in the motor vehicle sector. Para 7 amends Commission Regulation (EU) 1217/2010 on the application of Article 101(3) of the Treaty on the Functioning of the European Union to certain categories of research and development agreements. Para 8 amends Commission Regulation (EU) 1218/2010 on the application of Article 101(3) of the Treaty on the Functioning of the European Union to certain categories of specialisation agreements. Para 9 amends Commission Regulation (EU) 316/2014 on the application of Article 101(3) of the Treaty on the Functioning of the European Union to categories of technology transfer agreements.)*

Effect of certain revocations

10. (1) The revocation of the provisions of Commission Regulations listed in sub-paragraph (2) is not to be read as—

(a) preventing the Secretary of State from exercising the power under section 10A(1) of the Competition Act 1998 to disapply those Regulations as described in those provisions, or

(b) limiting that power in any other way.

(2) Those provisions are—

(a) Article 6 of Commission Regulation (EU) 330/2010 on the application of Article 101(3) of the Treaty on the Functioning of the European Union to categories of vertical agreements and concerted practices;

(b) Article 6 of Commission Regulation (EU) 461/2010 on the application of Article 101(3) of the Treaty on the Functioning of the European Union to categories of vertical agreements and concerted practices in the motor vehicle sector;

(c) Article 7 of Commission Regulation (EU) 316/2014 on the application of Article 101(3) of the Treaty on the Functioning of the European Union to categories of technology transfer agreements.

(3) The revocation of Article 6 of Commission Regulation (EU) 316/2014 on the application of Article 101(3) of the Treaty on the Functioning of the European Union to categories of technology transfer agreements is not to be read as—

(a) preventing the Competition and Markets Authority from exercising its power under section 10(5) of the Competition Act 1998 to impose conditions or obligations subject to which an exemption is to have effect or to cancel the exemption for an agreement in the circumstances described in that Article, or

(b) limiting that power in any other way.

NOTES

Commencement: IP completion day (as defined in the European Union (Withdrawal Agreement) Act 2020, s 39).

SCHEDULE 4
SAVING AND TRANSITIONAL PROVISION

Regulation 64

PART 1 INTERPRETATION

Interpretation

[7.69]

1. In this Schedule—

"the 1998 Act" means the Competition Act 1998;

"the 2002 Act" means the Enterprise Act 2002;

"the CMA" means the Competition and Markets Authority.

NOTES

Commencement: IP completion day (as defined in the European Union (Withdrawal Agreement) Act 2020, s 39).

PART 2 EXEMPTIONS FROM THE CHAPTER 1 PROHIBITION

Pre-existing agreements exempt by virtue of an EU decision

[7.70]

2. (1) This paragraph applies if—

(a) immediately before [IP completion day], an agreement is exempt from the Chapter 1 prohibition under section 10 of the 1998 Act by virtue of an EU decision; and

(b) the decision (as it has effect in EU law) has not expired or been revoked under EU law.

(2) On and after [IP completion day], section 10 of the 1998 Act has effect in relation to the agreement without the modifications made by regulation 3(3), (4), (6)(c) and (8) of these Regulations.

(3) In this paragraph—

(a) "the Chapter 1 prohibition" means the prohibition imposed by section 2(1) of the 1998 Act;

(b) references to an agreement include a reference to a decision by an association of undertakings and a concerted practice.

(4) For the purposes of section 10 of the 1998 Act as it has effect by virtue of this paragraph, section 59 of that Act (interpretation) has effect without the modifications made by regulation 21(2).

Pre-existing research and development agreements

3. (1) Sub-paragraph (2) applies if—

(a) a research and development agreement is entered into before [IP completion day], and

(b) in relation to the agreement, the 7 year period specified in Article 4(1) of the EU R&D block exemption regulation begins before [IP completion day].

(2) On and after [IP completion day], Article 4(1) of the retained R&D block exemption regulation has effect in relation to the agreement without the modification made by paragraph 7(4) of Schedule 3 to these Regulations.

(3) Sub-paragraph (4) applies if—

(a) a research and development agreement is entered into before [IP completion day], and

(b) immediately before [IP completion day], the agreement contains an obligation described in Article 6(b) of the EU R&D block exemption regulation.

(4) On and after [IP completion day], Article 6(b) of the retained R&D block exemption regulation has effect in relation to the agreement without the modification made by paragraph 7(6)(b) of Schedule 3 to these Regulations.

(5) In this paragraph—

"research and development agreement" has the same meaning as in the EU R&D block exemption regulation;

"the R&D block exemption regulation" means Commission Regulation (EU) 1217/2010 on the application of Article 101(3) of the Treaty on the Functioning of the European Union to certain categories of research and development agreements;

"the EU R&D block exemption regulation" means the R&D block exemption regulation as it has effect as part of EU law immediately before [IP completion day];

"the retained R&D block exemption regulation" means the R&D block exemption regulation as it has effect as part of domestic law on and after [IP completion day].

NOTES

Commencement: IP completion day (as defined in the European Union (Withdrawal Agreement) Act 2020, s 39).

Paras 1, 2: words "IP completion day" in square brackets substituted by the Competition (Amendment etc) (EU Exit) Regulations 2020, SI 2020/1343, reg 35, with effect from immediately before IP completion day.

PART 3 CMA INVESTIGATIONS UNDER PART 1 OF THE 1998 ACT

Interpretation

[7.71]

4. (1) In this Part of this Schedule—

"investigation" means an investigation under section 25 of the 1998 Act;

"domestic element", in relation to an investigation, means any part of the investigation conducted by virtue of section 25(2), (4) or (6) of the 1998 Act;

"EU element", in relation to an investigation, means any part of the investigation conducted by virtue of section 25(3), (5) or (7) of the 1998 Act.

(2) References in this Part of this Schedule to cases in which the CMA is conducting an investigation at a particular time include cases in which the CMA would be conducting such an investigation but for section 31B(2) of the 1998 Act (suspension of investigation where commitments given under section 31A of that Act).

(3) References in this Part of this Schedule to the CMA are to be read as including a reference to a regulator (as defined in section 54 of the 1998 Act).

Termination of EU elements of on-going investigations

5. Where the CMA is conducting an investigation immediately before [IP completion day], it may not continue any EU elements of the investigation on and after [IP completion day].

6. (1) This paragraph applies where, immediately before [IP completion day], the CMA is conducting an investigation which has both domestic elements and EU elements.

(2) Anything done before [IP completion day] for the purposes of, or in connection with, the EU elements of the investigation is to be treated, on and after [IP completion day], as done for the purposes of, or in connection with, the domestic elements of the investigation.

(3) The reference in sub-paragraph (2) to anything done includes anything omitted to be done.

(4) On and after [IP completion day]—

- (a) a notice validly issued before [IP completion day] under section 26, 26A, or 27 of the 1998 Act for the purposes of the EU elements of the investigation is to be treated as validly issued for the purposes of the domestic elements of the investigation;
- (b) a warrant validly issued, or an application for a warrant made, before [IP completion day] under section 28 or 28A of the 1998 Act for the purposes of the EU elements of the investigation is to be treated as validly issued or made in connection with the domestic elements of the investigation;
- (c) documents and other information obtained, and representations made, before [IP completion day] for the purposes of, or in connection with, the EU elements of the investigation are to be treated as obtained or made for the purposes of, or in connection with, the domestic elements of the investigation; and
- (d) a commitment accepted under section 31A of the 1998 Act before [IP completion day] for the purposes of addressing a competition concern identified during the course of the EU elements of the investigation, and not released before [IP completion day], continues in force until released.

(5) Sub-paragraph (4) is without prejudice to the generality of sub-paragraph (2).

(6) On and after [IP completion day] a notice given before [IP completion day] under section 31(1) of the 1998 Act is to be treated as if any reference to a proposed decision described in section 31(2)(c) or (d) of the 1998 Act were omitted.

Completed investigations terminated by decisions under section 31(2)(c) or (d) of the 1998 Act

7. (1) This paragraph applies where, before [IP completion day], the CMA has made a decision within the meaning of section 31(2)(c) or (d) of the 1998 Act.

(2) On and after [IP completion day], in connection with the decision, the enactments mentioned in sub-paragraphs (3) to (8) have effect as described there.

(3) Part 1 of the 1998 Act has effect—

- (a) without the modifications made by Part 2 of these Regulations, other than the modifications made by regulations 21(3), 22 and 23 (principles to be applied in determining questions), and
- (b) [except in relation to cases in which the European Commission has continued competence after IP completion day in accordance with Article 92 of the EU withdrawal agreement,] with the further modifications set out in sub-paragraph (4).

(4) The further modifications mentioned in sub-paragraph (3)(b) are as follows—

- (a) references (however expressed) to a decision of the European Commission or a Member State competition authority that there has been an infringement of the prohibition in Article 101(1) or 102 of the Treaty on the Functioning of the European Union do not include a decision made on or after [IP completion day];
- (b) paragraph 21(3) of Schedule 8A to the 1998 Act has effect as if—
  - (i) in [paragraph] (a), after "if the competition authority makes a decision" there were inserted "before [IP completion day]";
  - (ii) the "and" at the end of [paragraph] (a) were omitted;
  - (iii) in [paragraph] (b), for "otherwise" there were substituted "if the competition authority closes the investigation before [IP completion day] without making such a decision"; and
  - (iv) after [paragraph] (b) there were inserted—

  "; and

  (c) otherwise, at the end of the period of one year beginning with [IP completion day].".

(5) Section 16 of the 2002 Act has effect without the modification made by regulation 33 of these Regulations.

(6) The enactments listed in paragraphs [paragraphs 2 to 9 and 12 to 15] of Schedule 1 to these Regulations and in paragraphs 11 and 13 of Part 3 of Schedule 2 to these Regulations have effect without the modifications made in those paragraphs.

[(6A) The Communications Act 2003 applies without the modifications made by paragraph 11 of Schedule 1 to these Regulations, except for the modifications made by sub-paragraphs (3) to (7) of that paragraph.]

(7) Subordinate legislation made under Part 1 of the 1998 Act has effect without the modifications made by Part 1 of Schedule 2 to these Regulations, except for the modifications made by paragraph 4(4) of that Schedule (amendments to the Competition Act 1998 (Competition and Market Authority's Rules) Order 2014).

(8) The Competition Appeal Tribunal Rules 2015 have effect without the modifications made by paragraph 8 of Schedule 2 to these Regulations, except for the modifications made by subparagraphs (4), (5) and (6) of that paragraph.

(9) References in sub-paragraph (4)(a) to a decision by a Member State competition authority are to be interpreted in accordance with paragraph 3(6) of Schedule 8A to the 1998 Act (see paragraph (c) of that provision).

[Appropriate level of a penalty

7A. (1) This paragraph applies where—

(a) before IP completion day, a penalty or a fine has been imposed by the European Commission, or a court or other body in another Member State, in respect of an agreement or conduct; or

(b) on or after IP completion day, a penalty or fine has been imposed by the European Commission in respect of an agreement or conduct in relation to which it has continued competence in accordance with Article 92 of the EU withdrawal agreement.

(2) The CMA, the Tribunal or the appropriate court must take that penalty or fine into account when setting the amount of penalty under Part 1 of the 1998 Act in relation to that agreement or conduct.

(3) In sub-paragraph (2), "the appropriate court" means—

(a) in relation to England and Wales, the Court of Appeal;

(b) in relation to Scotland, the Court of Session;

(c) in relation to Northern Ireland, the Court of Appeal in Northern Ireland;

(d) the Supreme Court.]

[Cases subject to relevant separation agreement law]

[8. (1) In this paragraph and paragraphs 8A and 8B—

"Regulation 1/2003" means Council Regulation (EC) No 1/2003 of 16th December 2002 on the implementation of the rules on competition laid down in Articles 81 and 82 of the Treaty as it has effect from time to time for the purposes of relevant separation agreement law; and

"relevant decision" means—

a decision adopted by the European Commission pursuant to article 7(1) of Regulation 1/2003; or

a decision adopted by the European Commission pursuant to article 9(1) of Regulation 1/2003.

(2) This paragraph applies where before IP completion day—

(a) under article 11(6) of Regulation 1/2003, the CMA was relieved of competence to apply one or both of articles 101 (in relation to an agreement) or 102 (in relation to conduct), by the European Commission initiating proceedings in relation to that agreement or conduct;

(b) the European Commission had made a relevant decision; and

(c) the relevant decision has not been annulled in full or in part by the European Court insofar as it related to—

(i) the finding of an infringement or making of any directions in a decision adopted pursuant to article 7(1) of Regulation 1/2003; or

(ii) commitments accepted under a decision adopted pursuant to article 9(1) of Regulation 1/2003.

(3) On and after IP completion day the CMA must not—

(a) accept a commitment under section 31A of the 1998 Act in relation to the agreement or conduct to which the relevant decision relates;

(b) give a direction under section 32 of the 1998 Act in relation to the agreement to which the relevant decision relates; or

(c) give a direction under section 33 of the 1998 Act in relation to the conduct to which the relevant decision relates;

which conflicts with any remedial directions given or commitments made binding by the relevant decision.

8A. (1) This paragraph applies where on and after IP completion day the European Commission has continued competence in relation to an investigation into an agreement, decision, concerted practice or abuse of a dominant position under Regulation 1/2003 in accordance with article 92 of the EU withdrawal agreement.

(2) While the Commission's investigation is ongoing, the CMA must not open or re-open any investigation by virtue of section 25(2), (4) or (6) of the 1998 Act into the competition concerns with which the Commission's investigation is concerned.

(3) Nothing in sub-paragraph (2) prevents the CMA from opening an investigation by virtue of section 25(2), (4) or (6) into competition concerns relating to an agreement, decision, concerted practice or abuse of a dominant position insofar as those concerns relate to the effects arising from the agreement, decision, concerted practice or abuse of a dominant position on and after IP completion day.

8B. (1) This paragraph applies where on and after IP completion day the European Commission has continued competence in relation to an investigation under regulation 1/2003 in accordance with article 92 of the EU withdrawal agreement and—

(a) the European Commission has made a relevant decision;

(b) the relevant decision has not been annulled in full or in part by the European Court insofar as it related to—

(i) the finding of an infringement or making of any directions in a decision adopted pursuant to article 7(1) of Regulation 1/2003; or

(ii) commitments accepted under a decision adopted pursuant to article 9(1) of Regulation 1/2003.

(2) On and after IP completion day the CMA must not—

(a) accept a commitment under section 31A of the 1998 Act in relation to the agreement or conduct to which the relevant decision relates;

(b) give a direction under section 32 of the 1998 Act in relation to the agreement to which the relevant decision relates; or

(c) give a direction under section 33 of the 1998 Act in relation to the conduct to which the relevant decision relates;

which conflicts with any directions given or commitments made binding by the relevant decision.]

NOTES

Commencement: IP completion day (as defined in the European Union (Withdrawal Agreement) Act 2020, s 39).

All amendments to this Part were made by the Competition (Amendment etc) (EU Exit) Regulations 2020, SI 2020/1343, reg 36, with effect from immediately before IP completion day.

PART 4 INSPECTIONS AND INVESTIGATIONS UNDER PARTS 2 AND 2A OF THE 1998 ACT

[7.72]

[8C. (1) This paragraph applies where, on or after IP completion day, the European Commission has ordered an Article 20 inspection, an Article 21 inspection, or an Article 22(2) inspection (as defined in section 61 of the 1998 Act) in relation to a case in which it has continued competence in accordance with Article 92 of the EU withdrawal agreement.

(2) Despite its repeal by these Regulations, Part 2 of the 1998 Act continues to have effect on and after IP completion day.

(3) Part 4 of the 1998 Act has effect—

(a) as if, in subsection 72(1), after "sections 42 to 44" there were inserted "or 65";
(b) without the modifications made by regulations 26(3) and (4) of these Regulations;
(c) as if section 73(8)(b) read "that may be conferred by a warrant under section 28, 28A, 62, 62A or 63";
(d) without the modification made by regulation 27 of these Regulations.

(4) The Schedule to the Competition Act 1998 (Competition and Markets Authority's Rules) Order 2014 has effect—

(a) as if, in rule 2, paragraph (1) read—

"These Regulations apply when the CMA takes investigation or enforcement action under the Act in relation to the Chapter I prohibition or the Chapter II prohibition, or investigation action under Part 2 of the Act in relation to the prohibition in Article 101(1) or Article 102"; and

(b) without the modifications made by paragraph 4(4) of Schedule 2 to these Regulations.]

9. [On and after IP completion day]—

(a) [except in relation to cases in which the European Commission has continued competence in accordance with Article 92 of the EU withdrawal agreement,] the CMA and other persons may not take or continue any action for the purposes of, or in connection with, an Article 20 inspection, an Article 21 inspection or an Article 22(2) inspection (as defined in section 61 of the 1998 Act) in reliance on Part 2 of the 1998 Act; and
(b) the CMA may not continue an Article 22(1) investigation (as defined in section 65C(1) of the 1998 Act).

10. A warrant issued and in force under section 62(1), 62A(1), 63(1), 65G(1) or 65H(1) of the 1998 Act ceases to have effect on [IP completion day, except where the warrant relates to a case in which the European Commission has continued competence in accordance with article 92 of the EU withdrawal agreement].

11. A notice given under section 65E(2) or 65F(2) of the 1998 Act ceases to have effect on [IP completion day].

12. Despite their repeal by these Regulations, sections 65B and 65K of the 1998 Act (use of statements in prosecution) continue to have effect on and after [IP completion day] in relation to statements made before [IP completion day].

NOTES

Commencement: IP completion day (as defined in the European Union (Withdrawal Agreement) Act 2020, s 39).

All amendments to this Part were made by the Competition (Amendment etc) (EU Exit) Regulations 2020, SI 2020/1343, reg 37, with effect from immediately before IP completion day.

PART 5 REDRESS SCHEMES FURTHER TO EUROPEAN COMMISSION DECISIONS

[7.73]

13. [(1) This paragraph applies where—

(a) before IP completion day, the European Commission has made a decision that the prohibition in Article 101(1) or Article 102 has been infringed; or
(b) the European Commission has made a decision that the prohibition in Article 101(1) or Article 102 has been infringed after IP completion day in a case in which it had continued competence in accordance with article 92 of the EU withdrawal agreement.]

(2) In relation to schemes offering compensation in consequence of the decision, and applications for the approval of such schemes, on and after [IP completion day], in connection with the decision, the enactments mentioned in paragraph 7(3) to (8) have effect as described there.

NOTES

Commencement: IP completion day (as defined in the European Union (Withdrawal Agreement) Act 2020, s 39).

Para 13: sub-para (1) and the words "IP completion day" in square brackets in sub-para (2) were substituted by the Competition (Amendment etc) (EU Exit) Regulations 2020, SI 2020/1343, reg 38, with effect from immediately before IP completion day.

PART 6 COURT AND TRIBUNAL PROCEEDINGS RELATING TO COMPETITION

[Interpretation

[7.74]

13A. In this Part of this Schedule—

"domestic competition infringement" means an infringement or alleged infringement of the Chapter I prohibition or the Chapter II prohibition (in each case as defined in section 59 of the 1998 Act);

"EU competition infringement" means an infringement or alleged infringement of—

(a) the prohibition in Article 101(1) of the Treaty on the Functioning of the European Union,
(b) the prohibition in Article 102 of that Treaty,

(c) the prohibition in Article 53 of the European Economic Area Agreement, or
(d) the prohibition in Article 54 of that Agreement.]

Claims before a court or tribunal relating to [pre-IP completion day] EU competition infringements

14. (1) . . .

(2) Where an EU competition infringement occurs before [IP completion day], on and after [IP completion day] a person may—

(a) continue any claim (or defence to a claim) in relation to that infringement in proceedings before a court or tribunal in the United Kingdom, and
(b) make any claim (or defence to a claim) in relation to that infringement in proceedings before a court or tribunal in the United Kingdom which the person could have made before [IP completion day].

(3) The reference in sub-paragraph (2)(b) to a claim which a person could have made before [IP completion day] includes a claim which the person could have made if any loss or damage to which the claim relates had arisen before [IP completion day] (whether or not it did so).

(4) Where a person has acquired the right to make a claim from another person (whether by operation of law or otherwise), the reference in sub-paragraph (2)(b) to a claim which a person could have made before [IP completion day] includes a claim which that other person could have made before [IP completion day].

15. [(1)] In relation to claims (and defences to claims) described in paragraph 14(2) the enactments mentioned in paragraph 7(3) to (8) have effect as described there.

[(2) Sub-paragraph (1) continues to apply if the claim (or defence to a claim) includes a claim (or defence to a claim) in respect of loss or damage arising from a domestic competition infringement that occurred before IP completion day including if that domestic competition infringement continues on or after IP completion day.]

16. Where, before [IP completion day], a reference has been made in proceedings by the Competition Appeal Tribunal to the European Court under rule 109 of the Competition Appeal Tribunal Rules 2015 and no preliminary ruling has been made, any stay (or in Scotland, sist) under rule 109(3) is to continue on and after [IP completion day] unless or until the Tribunal otherwise directs.

Claims before a court or tribunal relating to [pre-IP completion day] domestic competition infringements

17. (1) . . .

[(2) This paragraph applies to a claim (or defence to a claim)—

(a) which is in respect of loss or damage arising from a domestic competition infringement that occurred before IP completion day including if that infringement continues on or after IP completion day;
(b) which is not included in a claim (or defence to a claim) described in paragraph 14(2).]

[(3) On and after IP completion day, in relation to proceedings before a court or tribunal relating to a claim (or defence to a claim) to which this paragraph applies, the enactments mentioned in paragraphs 7(3) to (8) have effect as described there.]

NOTES

Commencement: IP completion day (as defined in the European Union (Withdrawal Agreement) Act 2020, s 39).

All amendments to this Part were made by the Competition (Amendment etc) (EU Exit) Regulations 2020, SI 2020/1343, reg 39, with effect from immediately before IP completion day.

[PART 6A CONCENTRATIONS SUBJECT TO EU CONTROLS IN ACCORDANCE WITH THE EU WITHDRAWAL AGREEMENT

[7.75]

17A. (1) On and after IP completion day, to the extent to which an agreement (either on its own or when taken together with another agreement) gives rise to, or would if carried out give rise to, a concentration, the prohibition in section 2 of the 1998 Act does not apply to the agreement if the European Commission has exclusive jurisdiction in the matter in accordance with Article 92 of the EU withdrawal agreement.

(2) On and after IP completion day, to the extent to which conduct (either on its own or when taken together with other conduct) gives rise to, or would if pursued give rise to, a concentration, the prohibition in section 18 of the 1998 Act does not apply to the conduct if the European Commission has exclusive jurisdiction in the matter in accordance with Article 92 of the EU withdrawal agreement.

(3) In this paragraph, "concentration" means a concentration with a Community dimension within the meaning of Articles 1 and 3 of Council Regulation (EC) No 139/2004 of 20th January 2004.]

NOTES

Commencement: IP completion day (as defined in the European Union (Withdrawal Agreement) Act 2020, s 39).

This Part was inserted by the Competition (Amendment etc) (EU Exit) Regulations 2020, SI 2020/1343, reg 40, with effect from immediately before IP completion day.

PART 7 ENTERPRISE ACT 2002 [AND OTHER MERGER CONTROL LEGISLATION]

Interpretation

[7.76]

18. (1) In this Part of this Schedule—

"the 2003 Order" means the Enterprise Act 2002 (Protection of Legitimate Interests) Order 2003;

"EC Merger Regulation" means Council Regulation (EC) 139/2004 on the control of concentrations between undertakings as it has effect in EU law [from time to time];

"enterprise" has the meaning given by section 129 of the 2002 Act;

"European relevant merger situation" has the meaning given by section 68(2) of the 2002 Act.

(2) For the purposes of this Part of this Schedule the EU merger decision has been taken in relation to a concentration if—

(a) the European Commission has made a decision in relation to the concentration under Article 6(1)(b) or 8(1), (2) or (3) of the EC Merger Regulation; or

(b) the concentration is deemed to have been declared compatible with the internal market under Article 10(6) of that Regulation.

19. . . .

[EU merger decisions annulled in full or in part

19A (1) This paragraph applies if, on or after IP completion day, a decision by the European Commission in relation to a continued competence concentration is annulled in full or in part by the European Court and European Commission or the European Court makes a binding decision that the European Commission is not competent—

(a) to re-examine the concentration concerned under Article 10(5) of the EC Merger Regulation; or

(b) to consider as part of such a re-examination any effects of the concentration concerned on competition within a market or markets in the United Kingdom.

(2) Nothing in the EU withdrawal agreement is to be taken as preventing the following in relation to the concentration concerned—

(a) a reference being made under section 22 or 33 of the 2002 Act;

(b) an intervention notice being given under section 42 of the 2002 Act;

(c) a reference being made under section 45 of the 2002 Act.

(3) The European Commission and the European Court are to be treated as having made a binding decision for the purposes of sub-paragraph (1)(a) or (b) when—

(a) the decision or other document containing a decision to that effect or from which a decision to that effect may reasonably be inferred is published; and

(b) the decision becomes final.

(4) A decision of the European Commission becomes final—

(a) when the time for appealing against it in the European Court expires without an appeal having been brought; or

(b) where an appeal has been brought against the decision, when—

(i) the appeal and any further appeal in the European Court in relation to the decision has been decided or has otherwise ended; and

(ii) the time for appealing against the result of the appeal or further appeal in the European Court has expired without another appeal having been brought.

(5) A decision by the European Court becomes final—

(a) when the time for appealing against it expires without an appeal having been brought; or

(b) where an appeal has been brought against the decision, when the appeal in relation to the decision has been decided or has otherwise ended.

(6) On and after IP completion day, despite their repeal by these Regulations, subsections (3) to (5) of section 122 of the 2002 Act continue to have effect in relation to the concentration concerned except that the condition mentioned in section 122(4) is to be treated as being satisfied during the period starting on IP completion day and ending on the day the binding decision referred to in sub-paragraph (1)(a) or (b) is made by the European Commission or the European Court (as the case may be).

(7) In this paragraph, "continued competence concentration" means a concentration—

(a) in relation to which the EU merger decision was taken before IP completion day; or

(b) in relation to which the European Commission has continued competence as regards the United Kingdom on and after IP completion day in accordance with Article 92 of the EU withdrawal agreement.]

Article 22 cases referred to but not decided by the European Commission before [IP completion day]

20. (1) This paragraph applies in a case in which immediately before [IP completion day] the CMA—

(a) has given a notice under section 25(6) of the 2002 Act to persons carrying on enterprises which have or may have ceased to be distinct extending the four month period mentioned in section 24(1)(a) or (2)(b) of that Act following a request made to the European Commission by the United Kingdom under Article 22(1) of the EC Merger Regulation, but

(b) has not given a notice under section 25(8) of that Act ending that extension.

(2) Subsections (6) to (8) of section 25 of the 2002 Act continue to have effect in relation to the extension under section 25(6) of that Act, despite their repeal by regulation 35(a).

(3) Section 25(10) of that Act continues to have effect in relation to that extension without the modification made by regulation 35(b).

(4) If, immediately before [IP completion day], the European Commission has not completed its consideration of the request of the United Kingdom, section 25(8) of that Act, as it continues to have effect by virtue of this paragraph, has effect as if for "of the completion by the European Commission of its consideration of" there were substituted "that the EC Merger Regulation has ceased to apply to".

21. . . .

22. (1) This paragraph applies in a case in which immediately before [IP completion day] the CMA—

(a) has given a notice under section 34ZB(5) of the 2002 Act, extending the initial period mentioned in section 34ZA(1) of that Act, following a request made to the European Commission by the United Kingdom under Article 22(1) of the EC Merger Regulation, but

(b) has not given notice as mentioned in section 34ZB(8)(b) of that Act ending that extension.

(2) Subsections (5) and (8) of section 34ZB of the 2002 Act continue to have effect in relation to the extension under section 34ZB(5) of that Act, despite their repeal by regulation 39.

(3) Section 34ZC(1), (3) and (4) of that Act continues to have effect in relation to that extension without the modifications made by regulation 40.

(4) If, immediately before [IP completion day], the European Commission has not completed its consideration of the request of the United Kingdom, section 34ZB(8)(b) of that Act, as it continues to have effect by virtue of this paragraph, has effect as if for "of the completion by the European Commission of its consideration of" there were substituted "that the EC Merger Regulation has ceased to apply to".

23. . . .

Cases referred by the European Commission to the CMA . . .

24. (1) This paragraph applies [if]—

(a) the European Commission has by a decision referred the whole or part of a case to the CMA under Article 4(4) or 9 of the EC Merger Regulation, or is deemed to have taken such a decision; and

(b) [in a case in which the decision to refer was taken, or is deemed to have been taken, before IP completion day,] the preliminary assessment period in relation to the case has not ended.

(2) In relation to the case—

(a) sections 34A, 46A, 46B and 122(3) to (5) of the 2002 Act continue to have effect despite their repeal by Part 3 of these Regulations, and

(b) sections 34ZA, 73A, 107 and 110B continue to have effect without the modifications made by regulations 38, 48, 50 and 51.

(3) References to the EC Merger Regulation in any provision which continues to have effect by virtue of sub-paragraph (2) have the meaning given by paragraph 18.

(4) In sub-paragraph (1), "the preliminary assessment period" has the meaning given by—

(a) section 46A(4) of the 2002 Act, in any case where an intervention notice (as defined in section 42(2) of the 2002 Act) is in force; and

(b) section 34A(4) of that Act, in any other case.

Intervention to protect legitimate interests: no European intervention notice before [IP completion day]

25. (1) This paragraph applies in a case in which immediately before [IP completion day]—

(a) a concentration has been examined by the European Commission under the EC Merger Regulation and the EU merger decision has been taken in relation to the concentration;

(b) the conditions specified in section 67(1) of the 2002 Act are met in relation to the concentration concerned; and

(c) the Secretary of State has not made a decision to give an intervention notice under [section 67(2) of the 2002 Act].

(2) The old legitimate interests law continues to have effect on and after [IP completion day] in relation to the concentration concerned except that the conditions in section [67(1)(a)(ii), (b) and (c)] are treated as being met on and after [IP completion day].

(3) In this paragraph "the old legitimate interests law" means—

(a) sections 67 and 68 of the 2002 Act;

(b) the Enterprise Act 2002 (Anticipated Mergers) Order 2003 without the modification made by paragraph 6(2) of Schedule 2 to these Regulations; and

(c) the 2003 Order.

[25A. (1) This paragraph applies in a case where immediately before IP completion day—

(a) a concentration is being examined by the European Commission but the EU merger decision has not been taken in relation to the concentration, and

(b) the Secretary of State has not made a decision to give an intervention notice under section 67(2) of the 2002 Act in relation to the concentration concerned.

(2) The old legitimate interests law continues to have effect on and after IP completion day in relation to the case concerned except that—

(a) the references to "EU law" in sections 67(1)(b) and 68(2)(c) of the 2002 Act are to be read as references to "relevant separation agreement law" within the meaning of section 7C of the European Union (Withdrawal Agreement) Act 2020; and

(b) references to the EC Merger Regulation in sections 67 and 68 of the 2002 Act have the meaning given by paragraph 18.

(3) In this paragraph—

(a) "the old legitimate interests law" has the same meaning as in paragraph 25; and

(b) a concentration is being examined by the European Commission if proceedings under the EC Merger Regulation in relation to the concentration have been initiated for the purposes of Article 92 of the EU withdrawal agreement.]

Intervention to protect legitimate interests: European intervention notice before [IP completion day]

26. (1) This paragraph applies in a case in which immediately before [IP completion day]—

(a) the Secretary of State has given a notice to the CMA under section 67(2) of the 2002 Act in relation to a European relevant merger situation; and

(b) the matter to which the notice relates has been finally determined in accordance with article 3 of the 2003 Order.

(2) The old legitimate interests law continues to have effect on and after [IP completion day in connection with the matter to which the notice relates].

(3) In this paragraph, "the old legitimate interests law" has the same meaning as in paragraph 25.

27. (1) This paragraph applies in a case in which immediately before [IP completion day]—

(a) the Secretary of State has given a notice to the CMA under section 67(2) of the 2002 Act in relation to a European relevant merger situation; [and]

(b) the matter to which the notice relates has not been finally determined in accordance with article 3 of the 2003 Order; . . .

(c) . . . .

(2) The old legitimate interests law continues to have effect on and after [IP completion day] in connection with the matter to which the notice relates [except that in section 68(2) of the 2002 Act—

(a) the reference to "EU law" includes a reference to "relevant separation agreement law" within the meaning of section 7C of the European Union (Withdrawal Agreement) Act 2020; and

(b) the reference to the EC Merger Regulation has the meaning given by paragraph 18.]

(3) In this paragraph, "the old legitimate interests law" has the same meaning as in paragraph 25.

28. (1) This paragraph applies in a case in which immediately before [IP completion day]—

(a) the Secretary of State has given a notice to the CMA under section 67(2) of the 2002 Act in relation to a European relevant merger situation;

(b) the matter to which the notice relates has not been finally determined in accordance with article 3 of the 2003 Order; and

[(c) proceedings under the EC Merger Regulation in relation to the concentration concerned have not been initiated for the purposes of Article 92 of the EU withdrawal agreement].

(2) On and after [IP completion day]—

(a) the notice under section 67(2) of the 2002 Act has effect as if it were a notice under section 42(2) of that Act, and

(b) Part 3 of the 2002 Act has effect in relation to the case . . .

(3) In sub-paragraph (2), the reference to Part 3 of the 2002 Act—

(a) includes provision made under that Part; and

(b) is a reference to that Part and provision made under it as modified by these Regulations.

29–33. . . .

General savings

34. (1) On and after [IP completion day], despite their repeal by these Regulations, subsections (3) to (5) of section 122 of the 2002 Act continue to have effect in relation to any case where enterprises ceased to be distinct before [IP completion day], other than in a case falling within paragraph 19(1) in relation to which sub-paragraph (2) of that paragraph has effect.

(2) In its continued application by virtue of sub-paragraph (1), section 122(4) has effect as if the reference in that subsection to the "EC Merger Regulation or anything done under or in accordance with them" were a reference to Council Regulation (EC) 139/2004 on the control of concentrations between undertakings as it has effect in EU law before [IP completion day] or anything done under or in accordance with that instrument before [IP completion day].

35. The repeal of section 209 of the 2002 Act does not affect the validity of any provision made under that section before [IP completion day].

[35A. (1) Section 240 of the 2002 Act continues to have effect in respect of continued competence cases despite its repeal by regulation 59.

(2) In any case where section 240 of the 2002 Act continues to have effect by virtue of this paragraph, the reference in that section to an EU obligation is to be treated as a reference to an obligation which arises by virtue of relevant separation agreement law.

(3) In this paragraph—

"continued competence cases" means proceedings for the application of Article 101 or 102 TFEU conducted by the European Commission under Regulation 1/2003 and proceedings in connection with the control of concentrations between undertakings governed by Regulation 139/2004, for which the European Commission has competence on and after IP completion day by virtue of Part 3 of the EU withdrawal agreement;

"Regulation 1/2003" means Council Regulation (EC) No 1/2003 of 16 December 2002 on the implementation of the rules on competition laid down in Articles 81 and 82 of the Treaty, as it has effect from time to time for the purposes of relevant separation agreement law;

"Regulation 139/2004" means Council Regulation (EC) No 139/2004 of 20 January 2004 on the control of concentrations between undertakings as it has effect from time to time for the purposes of relevant separation agreement law.

35B. EEC Merger Control (Distinct Market Investigations) Regulations 1990

(1) This paragraph applies where, on or after IP completion day, the European Commission has requested information under the second sentence of Article 19(2) of the EC Merger Regulation in relation to a case for which it has continued competence in accordance with Article 92 of the EU withdrawal agreement.

(2) The EEC Merger Control (Distinct Market Investigations) Regulations 1990 continue to have effect on and after IP completion day in relation to the case despite their repeal by these Regulations.]

NOTES

Commencement: IP completion day (as defined in the European Union (Withdrawal Agreement) Act 2020, s 39).

All amendments to this Part were made by the Competition (Amendment etc) (EU Exit) Regulations 2020, SI 2020/1343, regs 41–58, with effect from immediately before IP completion day.

PART 8 COMPANY DIRECTORS DISQUALIFICATION LEGISLATION

[7.77]

36. (1) This paragraph applies where an undertaking engages in conduct which infringes Article 101 or 102 of the Treaty of the Functioning of the European Union before [IP completion day].

(2) On and after [IP completion day]—

(a) section 9A of the Company Directors Disqualification Act 1986 has effect without the modifications made by paragraph 1(1) to (3) of Schedule 1 to these Regulations; and

(b) Article 13A of the Company Directors Disqualification (Northern Ireland) Order 2002 has effect without the modifications made by paragraph 10(1) to (3) of Schedule 1 to these Regulations.

NOTES

Commencement: IP completion day (as defined in the European Union (Withdrawal Agreement) Act 2020, s 39).

The words "IP completion day" in square brackets were substituted by the Competition (Amendment etc) (EU Exit) Regulations 2020, SI 2020/1343, reg 59, with effect from immediately before IP completion day.

COMPETITION (AMENDMENT ETC) (EU EXIT) REGULATIONS 2020 (NOTE)

(SI 2020/1343)

[7.78]

NOTES

Made: 19 November 2020.

Authority: European Union (Withdrawal) Act 2018, ss 8(1), 8B, Sch 7, para 21; European Union (Withdrawal Agreement) Act 2020, s 41(1).

Commencement: immediately before IP completion day.

These Regulations are made in exercise of the powers noted above in order to address deficiencies arising from the withdrawal of the United Kingdom from the European Union, and to give effect to measures in Title X of Part 3 of the Withdrawal Agreement as they relate to the field of competition law.

These Regulations amend the Competition (Amendment etc) (EU Exit) Regulations 2019, SI 2019/93 (at **[7.61]**) ("the principal Regulations"). The principal Regulations originally were due to come into force on exit day. However, paragraph 1(1) of Schedule 5 to the European Union (Withdrawal Agreement) Act 2020 provides that references to subordinate legislation coming into force on exit day are to be read, instead, as references to coming into force on IP completion day.

These Regulations amend the principal Regulations to—

— replace references to exit day with references to IP completion day where appropriate;

— make transitional provision in relation to cases in which the European Commission will continue to have competence in accordance with Article 92 of the Withdrawal Agreement;

— make provision in relation to cases in which responsibility for the monitoring and enforcement of remedies imposed by the European Commission is transferred to a national competition authority in accordance with Article 95 of the Withdrawal Agreement, empowering the Competition and Markets Authority and concurrent regulators to monitor and enforce transferred EU anti-trust commitments, transferred EU anti-trust directions and transferred EU merger commitments;

— make clarifications to the transitional provisions that apply in relation to claims for damages for loss arising out of competition infringements;

— revoke Regulation (EU) No 2019/452 of the European Parliament and of the Council of 19 March 2019 establishing a framework for the screening of foreign direct investments into the Union, which would otherwise be retained EU law.

Part 2 amends the principal Regulations to amend the Competition Act 1998. Part 3 amends the principal Regulations to amend the Enterprise Act 2002). Part 4 makes amendments to the principal Regulations to amend other primary legislation. Part 5 makes amendments to the principal Regulations to amend subordinate legislation. Part 6 makes amendments to the principal Regulations to make further amendments and provisions relating to the revocation of retained EU law. Part 7 amends the transitional and savings provisions in the principal Regulations, in particular, to clarify the transitional provisions which apply in relation to claims for damages for loss arising out of competition infringements and make some amendments in relation to the transitional provisions that apply in respect of certain merger cases which are ongoing at the end of the transition period to ensure that they implement the Withdrawal Agreement.

STATE AID (REVOCATIONS AND AMENDMENTS) (EU EXIT) REGULATIONS 2020

(SI 2020/1470)

NOTES

Made: 4 December 2020.

Authority: European Union (Withdrawal) Act 2018, ss 8(1), 8C(1), Sch 7, para 21.

Commencement: IP completion day (as defined in the European Union (Withdrawal Agreement) Act 2020, s 39) (subject to the exceptions listed in reg 1(3) and (4) at **[7.79]**).

ARRANGEMENT OF REGULATIONS

SCHEDULES

[7.79]

1 Citation, commencement and extent

(1) These Regulations may be cited as the State Aid (Revocations and Amendments) (EU Exit) Regulations 2020.

(2) Subject to paragraphs (3) and (4), these Regulations come into force on IP completion day.

(3) Paragraphs 3(3), 7(8)(b) and (c), 7(9) and 8 of Schedule 1 come into force immediately after IP completion day.

(4) Paragraphs 17 and 18 of Schedule 2 come into force immediately before IP completion day.

(5) Paragraph 2 of Schedule 1 does not extend to Northern Ireland.

NOTES

Commencement: IP completion day (as defined in the European Union (Withdrawal Agreement) Act 2020, s 39).

[7.80]

2 Interpretation

In these Regulations—

"TFEU" means the Treaty on the Functioning of the European Union;

"Withdrawal Act" means the European Union (Withdrawal) Act 2018.

NOTES

Commencement: IP completion day (as defined in the European Union (Withdrawal Agreement) Act 2020, s 39).

[7.81]

3 Cessation of Treaty rights

Any rights, powers, liabilities, obligations, restrictions, remedies and procedures which—

(a) continue to be recognised and available in domestic law by virtue of section 4(1) of the Withdrawal Act; and

(b) are derived from—

(i) Article 107(1) or 108(3) of the TFEU;

(ii) Article 346(1) of the TFEU, so far as Article 346(1) relates to Article 107(1) or Article 108(3) of the TFEU;

(iii) Article 61(1) or 62(1) of the EEA agreement; or

(iv) Article 123 of the EEA agreement, so far as Article 123 relates to Article 61(1) or 62(1) of the EEA agreement;

cease to be recognised and available in domestic law (and to be enforced, allowed and followed accordingly).

NOTES

Commencement: IP completion day (as defined in the European Union (Withdrawal Agreement) Act 2020, s 39).

[7.82]

4 Revocation of Annex to the EEA Agreement

Annex 15 of the EEA agreement, so far as it forms part of domestic law by virtue of section 3(1) of the Withdrawal Act, is omitted.

NOTES

Commencement: IP completion day (as defined in the European Union (Withdrawal Agreement) Act 2020, s 39).

[7.83]

5 Revocation of EU regulations

The following Regulations, so far as they form part of domestic law by virtue of section 3(1) of the Withdrawal Act, are revoked—

(a) Commission Regulation (EC) No 794/2004 of 21 April 2004 implementing Council Regulation (EC) No 659/1999 laying down detailed rules for the application of Article 93 of the EC Treaty;

(b) Commission Regulation (EC) No 1627/2006 of 24 October 2006 amending Regulation (EC) No 794/2004 as regards the standard forms for notification of aid;

(c) Commission Regulation (EC) No 1935/2006 of 20 December 2006 amending Regulation (EC) No 794/2004 implementing Council Regulation (EC) No 659/1999 laying down detailed rules for the application of Article 93 of the EC Treaty;

(d) Commission Regulation (EC) No 271/2008 of 30 January 2008 amending Regulation (EC) No 794/2004 implementing Council Regulation (EC) No 659/1999 laying down detailed rules for the application of Article 93 of the EC Treaty;

(e) Commission Regulation (EC) No 1147/2008 of 31 October 2008 amending Regulation (EC) No 794/2004 of 21 April 2004 implementing Council Regulation (EC) No 659/1999 laying down detailed rules for the application of Article 93 of the EC Treaty, as regards Part III.10 of its Annex 1;

(f) Commission Regulation (EC) No 257/2009 of 24 March 2009 amending Regulation (EC) No 794/2004 as regards the supplementary information sheet for notification of aid to fisheries and aquaculture;

(g) Commission Regulation (EC) No 1125/2009 of 23 November 2009 amending Regulation (EC) No 794/2004 implementing Council Regulation (EC) No 659/1999 laying down detailed rules for the application of Article 93 of the EC Treaty, as regards Part III.2, Part III.3 and Part III.7 of its Annex I;

(h) Commission Regulation (EU) No 360/2012 of 25 April 2012 on the application of Articles 107 and 108 of the Treaty on the Functioning of the European Union to de minimis aid granted to undertakings providing services of general economic interest;

(i) Commission Regulation (EU) No 1407/2013 of 18 December 2013 on the application of Articles 107 and 108 of the Treaty on the Functioning of the European Union to de minimis aid;

(j) Commission Regulation (EU) No 1408/2013 of 18 December 2013 on the application of Articles 107 and 108 of the Treaty on the Functioning of the European Union to de minimis aid in the agriculture sector;

(k) Commission Regulation (EU) No 372/2014 of 9 April 2014 amending Regulation (EC) No 794/2004 as regards the calculation of certain time limits, the handling of complaints, and the identification and protection of confidential information;

(l) Commission Regulation (EU) No 651/2014 of 17 June 2014 declaring certain categories of aid compatible with the internal market in application of Articles 107 and 108 of the Treaty;

(m) Commission Regulation (EU) No 702/2014 of 25 June 2014 declaring certain categories of aid in the agricultural and forestry sectors and in rural areas compatible with the internal market in application of Articles 107 and 108 of the Treaty on the Functioning of the European Union;

(n) Commission Regulation (EU) No 717/2014 of 27 June 2014 on the application of Articles 107 and 108 of the Treaty on the Functioning of the European Union to de minimis aid in the fishery and aquaculture sector;

(o) Commission Regulation (EU) No 1388/2014 of 16 December 2014 declaring certain categories of aid to undertakings active in the production, processing and marketing of fishery and aquaculture products compatible with the internal market in application of Articles 107 and 108 of the Treaty on the Functioning of the European Union;

(p) Council Regulation (EU) 2015/1588 of 13 July 2015 on the application of Articles 107 and 108 of the Treaty on the Functioning of the European Union to certain categories of horizontal State aid;

(q) Council Regulation (EU) 2015/1589 of 13 July 2015 laying down detailed rules for the application of Article 108 of the Treaty on the Functioning of the European Union;

(r) Commission Regulation (EU) 2015/2282 of 27 November 2015 amending Regulation (EC) No 794/2004 as regards the notification forms and information sheets;

(s) Commission Regulation (EU) 2016/246 of 3 February 2016 amending Annex I to Regulation (EC) No 794/2004 as regards the forms to be used for the notification of State aid in the agricultural and forestry sectors and in rural areas;

(t) Commission Regulation (EU) 2016/2105 of 1 December 2016 amending Annex I to Regulation (EC) No 794/2004 as regards the form to be used for the notification of State aid to the fishery and aquaculture sector;

(u) Commission Regulation (EU) 2017/1084 of 14 June 2017 amending Regulation (EU) No 651/2014 as regards aid for port and airport infrastructure, notification thresholds for aid for culture and heritage conservation and for aid for sport and multifunctional recreational infrastructures, and regional operating aid schemes for outermost regions and amending Regulation (EU) No 702/2014 as regards the calculation of eligible costs;

(v) Council Regulation (EU) 2018/1911 of 26 November 2018 amending Regulation (EU) 2015/1588 on the application of Articles 107 and 108 of the Treaty on the Functioning of the European Union to certain categories of horizontal State aid;

(w) Commission Regulation (EU) 2018/1923 of 7 December 2018 amending Regulation (EU) No 360/2012 as regards its period of application;

(x) Commission Regulation (EU) 2019/289 of 19 February 2019 amending Regulation (EU) No 702/2014 declaring certain categories of aid in the agricultural and forestry sectors and in rural areas compatible with the internal market in application of Articles 107 and 108 of the Treaty on the Functioning of the European Union; and

(y) Commission Regulation (EU) 2020/972 of 2 July 2020 amending Regulation (EU) No 1407/2013 as regards its prolongation and amending Regulation (EU) No 651/2014 as regards its prolongation and relevant adjustments.

NOTES

Commencement: IP completion day (as defined in the European Union (Withdrawal Agreement) Act 2020, s 39).

[7.84]

6 Revocation of EU decisions

(1) The following decisions, so far as they form part of domestic law by virtue of section 3(1) of the Withdrawal Act, are revoked—

(a) Council Decision (2010/787/EU) of 10 December 2010 on State aid to facilitate the closure of uncompetitive coal mines;

(b) Commission Decision 2012/21/EU of 20 December 2011 on the application of Article 106(2) of the Treaty on the Functioning of the European Union to State aid in the form of public service compensation granted to certain undertakings entrusted with the operation of services of general economic interest; and

(c) any other EU decision which forms part of domestic law on and after IP completion day by virtue of section 3(1) of the European Union (Withdrawal) Act 2018 and is made under—

  (i) the procedural regulation or predecessor legislation; or

  (ii) Article 108(2) of the TFEU or Article 88(2) of the Treaty establishing the European Community.

(2) In this regulation—

"predecessor legislation" means—

  (a) Council Regulation (EC) No 994/98 of 7 May 1998 on the application of Articles 92 and 93 of the Treaty establishing the European Community to certain categories of horizontal State aid; and

  (b) Council Regulation (EC) No 659/1999 of 22 March 1999 laying down detailed rules for the application of Article 93 of the EC Treaty;

"procedural regulation" means Council Regulation (EU) 2015/1589 of 13 July 2015 laying down detailed rules for the application of Article 108 of the Treaty on the Functioning of the European Union.

NOTES

Commencement: IP completion day (as defined in the European Union (Withdrawal Agreement) Act 2020, s 39).

[7.85]

7 Amendments to legislation

(1) Schedule 1, which makes amendments to retained EU law, has effect.

(2) Schedule 2, which makes amendments to other legislation, has effect.

NOTES

Commencement: IP completion day (as defined in the European Union (Withdrawal Agreement) Act 2020, s 39).

[7.86]

8 Transitional and savings provisions

Schedule 3, which contains transitional and savings provisions, has effect.

NOTES

Commencement: IP completion day (as defined in the European Union (Withdrawal Agreement) Act 2020, s 39).

SCHEDULES

SCHEDULE 1
AMENDMENTS TO RETAINED EU LAW

[7.87]

This Schedule amends the following and, in so far as relevant to this Handbook, the amendments have been incorporated at the appropriate place:

— Council Regulation (EC) No 1184/2006 of 24 July 2006 applying certain rules of competition to the production of and trade in certain agricultural products

— Regulation (EC) No 1370/2007 of the European Parliament and of the Council of 23 October 2007 on public passenger transport services by rail and by road and repealing Council Regulations (EEC) No 1191/69 and 1107/70

— Regulation (EU) No 575/2013 of the European Parliament and of the Council of 26 June 2013 on prudential requirements for credit institutions and investment firms and amending Regulation (EU) No 648/2012

— Regulation (EU) No 1305/2013 of the European Parliament and of the Council of 17 December 2013 on support for rural development by the European Agricultural Fund for Rural Development (EAFRD) and repealing Council Regulation (EC) No 1698/2005

— Regulation (EU) No 1307/2013 of the European Parliament and of the Council of 17 December 2013 establishing rules for direct payments to farmers under support schemes within the framework of the common agricultural policy and repealing Council Regulation (EC) No 637/2008 and Council Regulation (EC) No 73/2009

— Regulation 1308/2013 of the European Parliament and of the Council of 17 December 2013 establishing a common organisation of the markets in agricultural products and repealing Council Regulations (EEC) No 922/72, (EEC) No 234/79, (EC) No 1037/2001 and (EC) No 1234/2007

— Regulation (EU) No 1303/2013 of the European Parliament and of the Council of 17 December 2013 laying down common provisions on the European Regional Development Fund, the European Social Fund, the Cohesion Fund, the European Agricultural Fund for Rural Development and the European Maritime and Fisheries Fund and laying down general provisions on the European Regional Development Fund, the European Social Fund, the Cohesion Fund and the European Maritime and Fisheries Fund and repealing Council Regulation (EC) No 1083/2006

— Commission Implementing Regulation (EU) No 808/2014 of 17 July 2014 laying down rules for the application of Regulation (EU) No 1305/2013 of the European Parliament and of the Council on support for rural development by the European Agricultural Fund for Rural Development (EAFRD)

— Regulation (EU) No 1144/2014 of the European Parliament and of the Council of 22 October 2014 on information provision and promotion measures concerning agricultural products implemented in the internal market and in third countries and repealing Council Regulation (EC) No 3/2008

— Regulation (EU) 2019/943 of the European Parliament and of the Council of 5 June 2019 on the internal market for electricity (recast)

— Financial Transparency (EC Directive) Regulations 2009, SI 2009/2331.

NOTES

Commencement: IP completion day (as defined in the European Union (Withdrawal Agreement) Act 2020, s 39) (subject to the exceptions listed in reg 1(3) at **[7.79]**).

SCHEDULE 2
AMENDMENTS TO OTHER LEGISLATION

[7.88]

This Schedule amends the following and, in so far as relevant to this Handbook, the amendments have been incorporated at the appropriate place:

— Banking Act 2009

— Financial Services Act 2012

— Financial Services (Banking Reform) Act 2013

— Enterprise Act 2002 (Merger Fees and Determination of Turnover) Order 2003, SI 2003/1370

— Electronic Communications (Networks and Services) (Penalties) (Rules for Calculation of Turnover) Order 2003, SI 2003/2712

— Water Mergers (Determination of Turnover) Regulations 2004, SI 2004/3206

— Pension Protection Fund (Partially Guaranteed Schemes) (Modification) Regulations 2005, SI 2005/277

— Water Industry (Determination of Turnover for Penalties) Order 2005, SI 2005/477

— Pension Protection Fund (Entry Rules) Regulations 2005, SI 2005/590

— Mobile Roaming (European Communities) Regulations 2007, SI 2007/1933

— Community Infrastructure Levy Regulations 2010, SI 2010/948

— Climate Change Agreements (Administration) Regulations 2012, SI 2012/1976

— Electricity Capacity Regulations 2014, SI 2014/2043

— Payment of Pension Levies for Past Periods Regulations 2014, SI 2014/2939

— Bank Recovery and Resolution (No 2) Order 2014, SI 2014/3348

— Open Internet Access (EU Regulation) Regulations 2016, SI 2016/607

— Capital Requirements (Amendment) (EU Exit) Regulations 2018, SI 2018/1401

— Common Organisation of the Markets in Agricultural Products Framework (Miscellaneous Amendments, etc) (EU Exit) Regulations 2019, SI 2019/821

— Intra-EU Communications (EU Regulation) Regulations 2019, SI 2019/980.

NOTES

Commencement: IP completion day (as defined in the European Union (Withdrawal Agreement) Act 2020, s 39) (subject to the exceptions listed in reg 1(4) at **[7.79]**).

SCHEDULE 3
TRANSITIONAL AND SAVINGS PROVISIONS

Regulation 8

Claims before a court or tribunal relating to State aid infringement before IP completion day

[7.89]

1 (1) In this paragraph, “State aid breach” means a breach or alleged breach of—

(a) the prohibition in Article 107(1) of the TFEU; and

(b) the obligation in Article 108(3) of the TFEU.

(2) The cessation of the rights, powers, liabilities, obligations, restrictions, remedies and procedures provided for by regulation 4 and the revocations provided for by regulations 5, 6 and 7 do not affect the ability of any person on or after IP completion day—

(a) to continue any existing claim (or defence to such a claim) in relation to a State aid breach which occurred before IP completion day in proceedings before a court or tribunal in the United Kingdom; or

(b) to begin any new claim (or defence to such a claim) in relation to a State aid breach which occurred before IP completion day in proceedings before a court or tribunal in the United Kingdom which the person could have made before IP completion day.

(3) If a person has acquired a right to begin proceedings from another person (whether by operation of law or otherwise), the reference in subparagraph (2)(b) to proceedings which a person could have made before IP completion day includes proceedings which that other person could have begun before IP completion day.

NOTES

Commencement: IP completion day (as defined in the European Union (Withdrawal Agreement) Act 2020, s 39).

Note that this Schedule only contains a paragraph 1.

— Regulation (EU) 2019/943 of the European Parliament and of the Council of 5 June 2019 on the internal market for electricity (recast);

— Financial Transparency (EC Directive) Regulations 2009, SI 2009/2331.

NOTES

Commencement: IP completion day (as defined in the European Union (Withdrawal Agreement) Act 2020, s 39) (subject to the exceptions listed in reg 1(3) at [7.79]).

SCHEDULE 2
AMENDMENTS TO OTHER LEGISLATION

[7.88]

This Schedule amends the following and, in so far as relevant to this Handbook, the amendments have been incorporated at the appropriate place:

— Banking Act 2009

— Financial Services Act 2012

— Financial Services (Banking Reform) Act 2013

— Enterprise Act 2002 (Merger Fees and Determination of Turnover) Order 2003, SI 2003/1370

— Electronic Communications (Networks and Services) (Penalties) (Rules for Calculation of Turnover) Order 2003, SI 2003/2712

— Water Mergers (Determination of Turnover) Regulations 2004, SI 2004/3206

— Pension Protection Fund (Partially Guaranteed Schemes) (Modification) Regulations 2005, SI 2005/277

— Water Industry (Determination of Turnover for Penalties) Order 2005, SI 2005/477

— Pension Protection Fund (Entry Rules) Regulations 2005, SI 2005/590

— Mobile Roaming (European Communities) Regulations 2007, SI 2007/1933

— Community Infrastructure Levy Regulations 2010, SI 2010/948

— Climate Change Agreements (Administration) Regulations 2012, SI 2012/1976

— Electricity Capacity Regulations 2014, SI 2014/2043

— Payment of Pension Levies for Past Periods Regulations 2014, SI 2014/2935

— Bank Recovery and Resolution (No 2) Order 2014, SI 2014/3348

— Open Internet Access (EU Regulation) Regulations 2016, SI 2016/607

— Capital Requirements (Amendment) (EU Exit) Regulations 2018, SI 2018/1401

— Common Organisation of the Markets in Agricultural Products Framework (Miscellaneous Amendments etc) (EU Exit) Regulations 2019, SI 2019/821

— Intra-EU Communications (EU Regulation) Regulations 2019, SI 2019/780.

NOTES

Commencement: IP completion day (as defined in the European Union (Withdrawal Agreement) Act 2020, s 39) (subject to the exceptions listed in reg 1(3) at [7.79]).

SCHEDULE 3
TRANSITIONAL AND SAVINGS PROVISIONS

Regulation 9

Claims before a court or tribunal relating to State aid infringements before IP completion day

[7.89]

1. (1) In this paragraph, "State aid breach" means a breach or alleged breach of—

(a) the prohibition in Article 107(1) of the TFEU; and

(b) the obligation in Article 108(3) of the TFEU.

(2) The cessation of the rights, powers, liabilities, obligations, restrictions, remedies and procedures provided for by regulation 4 and the revocations provided for by regulations 5, 6 and 7 do not affect the ability of any person on or after IP completion day—

(a) to continue any existing claim (or defence to such a claim) in relation to a State aid breach which occurred before IP completion day in proceedings before a court or tribunal in the United Kingdom; or

(b) to begin any new claim (or defence to such a claim) in relation to a State aid breach which occurred before IP completion day in proceedings before a court or tribunal in the United Kingdom which the person could have made before IP completion day.

(3) If a person has acquired a right to begin proceedings from another person (whether by operation of law or otherwise), the reference in sub-paragraph (2)(b) to proceedings which a person could have made before IP completion day includes proceedings which that other person could have begun before IP completion day.

NOTES

Commencement: IP completion day (as defined in the European Union (Withdrawal Agreement) Act 2020, s 39).

Note that this Schedule only contains a paragraph.

B. OTHER MATERIALS

107TH UPDATE – PRACTICE DIRECTION AMENDMENTS (MARCH 2019)

[7.90]

NOTES

Note that this Practice Direction amends various PDs that are not included in this Handbook. The relevant amendments to material that is included in this work are to:

— Practice Direction: Competition Law: Claims Relating to the Application of Articles 81 And 82 of the EC Treaty and Chapters I and II of Part I of the Competition Act 1998 at **[6.3]**;

— Practice Direction 52D: Statutory Appeals and Appeals Subject to Special Provision at **[6.4]**; and

— Practice Direction 31C: disclosure and inspection in relation to competition claims **[6.250]**.

The amendments to those PDs have been incorporated at the appropriate place *ante*. The transitional provisions associated with the amendments are reproduced below. Amendments to PDs that are outside the scope of this Handbook are not annotated.

Note also that the Civil Procedure Rules 1998 (Amendment) (EU Exit) Regulations 2019 (SI 2019/521) come into force on IP completion day in accordance with Sch 5, para 1 to the European Union (Withdrawal Agreement) Act 2020 at **[7.59]**.

[7.91]

The amendments to the Practice Directions, supplementing the Civil Procedure Rules 1998, are made by the Master of the Rolls under the powers delegated to him by the Lord Chief Justice under Schedule 2, Part 1, paragraph 2(2) of the Constitutional Reform Act 2005, and are approved by Lucy Frazer QC MP, Parliamentary Under-Secretary of State for Justice, by the authority of the Lord Chancellor.

The amendments to the Practice Directions come into force on at the same time as the Civil Procedure Rules 1998 (Amendment) (EU Exit) Regulations 2019 (SI 2019/521).

The Right Honourable Sir Terence Etherton

Master of the Rolls and Head of Civil Justice

Signed by authority of the Lord Chancellor:

Lucy Frazer QC MP

Parliamentary Under-Secretary of State for Justice

Ministry of Justice

Date: 29th March 2019

TRANSITIONAL PROVISION

1) This transitional provision relates to the amendments made by this Update to Practice Directions 34A, 52D, 63A and Practice Direction – Competition Law – Claims relating to the application of Articles 81 and 82 of the EC Treaty and Chapters I and II of Part I of the Competition Act 1998.

2) In this transitional provision, "exit day" means the coming into force of the Civil Procedure Rules 1998 (Amendment) (EU Exit) Regulations 2019 (SI 2019/521).

3) (*Outside the scope of this work.*)

4) PRACTICE DIRECTION 52D – STATUTORY APPEALS AND APPEALS SUBJECT TO SPECIAL PROVISIONS

(a) The amendments made by this Update to paragraph 7.1(3) of Practice Direction 52D do not apply in relation to proceedings relating to competition described in paragraph 14(2) of Schedule 4 to the Competition (Amendment etc.) (EU Exit) Regulations 2019.

5) (*Outside the scope of this work.*)

6) PRACTICE DIRECTION – COMPETITION LAW – CLAIMS RELATING TO THE APPLICATION OF ARTICLES 81 AND 82 OF THE EC TREATY AND CHAPTERS I AND II OF PART I OF THE COMPETITION ACT 1998

(a) The amendments made by this Update to paragraph 2 of Practice Direction – Competition Law – Claims Relating to the Application of Articles 81 and 82 of the EC Treaty and Chapters I and II of Part I of the Competition Act 1998 do not apply in relation to proceedings relating to competition described in paragraph 14(2) of Schedule 4 to the Competition (Amendment etc.) (EU Exit) Regulations 2019.

UK EXIT FROM THE EU: GUIDANCE ON THE FUNCTIONS OF THE CMA UNDER THE WITHDRAWAL AGREEMENT (CMA113, 28 JANUARY 2020)

[7.92]

NOTES

See also the Explanatory Note to this Guidance at: https://www.gov.uk/government/publications/uk-exit-from-the-eu-guidance-on-the-functions-of-the-cma-under-the-withdrawal-agreement.

CONTENTS

1. PREFACE

[7.93]

1.1 The United Kingdom's exit from the European Union (EU Exit) is effective in the UK from 11 p.m. on 31 January 2020 (Exit Day).[1] Pursuant to Article 126 of the Agreement on the Withdrawal of the United Kingdom of Great Britain and Northern Ireland from the European Union and the European Atomic Energy Community (the Withdrawal Agreement),[2] a transition period runs from Exit Day until 11 p.m. on the 31 December 2020 (the Transition Period).[3] During the Transition Period, existing arrangements for the discharge of the functions of the Competition and Markets Authority (CMA) will be largely unaffected.

1.2 This guidance is designed to explain how EU Exit affects the CMA's powers and processes for competition law enforcement ('antitrust', including cartels), merger control and consumer protection law enforcement during the Transition Period, towards the end of that period, and after it ends.[4] The guidance also explains the treatment of 'live' cases, which are those cases that are being reviewed by the European Commission or the CMA during and at the end of the Transition Period.

1.3 This guidance applies to the CMA's ongoing and future:

- merger cases under the Enterprise Act 2002 (EA02);
- antitrust cases, including cartels, under the Competition Act 1998 (CA98) — i.e. relating to the competition law prohibitions on anti-competitive agreements, and on abuse of a dominant position; and
- enforcement of consumer protection legislation, in particular under Part 8of the EA02.

1.4 This guidance cross-refers to, and should be read alongside, the CMA's existing guidance, which continues to apply. In case of conflict between this guidance and any other CMA guidance document, the most recent guidance should prevail.[5]

WHAT IS NOT SPECIFICALLY COVERED BY THIS GUIDANCE?

The UK's future relationship with the EU

1.5 At the time of publishing this guidance, the UK's relationship with the EU after the end of the Transition Period (referred to as the Future Relationship)[6] remains subject to negotiation with the EU.

1.6 The CMA may issue further guidance in due course to clarify or amend elements of this guidance and explain any differences to the UK regime which will take effect at the end of the Transition Period.

'No deal' Statutory Instruments and guidance

1.7 On 22 January 2019, the Government made the Competition (Amendment etc) (EU Exit) Regulations 2019.[7] These were designed to apply from Exit Day and give effect to EU Exit in the event of 'no deal' – i.e. in the absence of a ratified Withdrawal Agreement (and therefore no Transition Period).[8] A number of 'no deal' statutory instruments in the field of consumer protection were also made, in particular the Consumer Protection (Enforcement) (Amendment etc.) (EU Exit) Regulations 2019 relating to enforcement of consumer legislation.[9] Since there is now a ratified Withdrawal Agreement and a Transition Period, the present guidance does not cover those 'no deal' Statutory Instruments in detail.[10]

CMA's functions

1.8 Some of the CMA's functions which are less materially affected by EU Exit are not specifically covered by this guidance, including regulatory appeals, market studies, market investigations and the criminal cartel offence. The CMA guidance on these functions may, however, refer to concepts under EU law.[11] These references will continue to have effect in the UK for as long as, and in so far as, EU law has legal effect in the UK.[12] For example, the cartel offence regime is governed exclusively by UK domestic law and will therefore not be directly affected by EU Exit, but the Cartel Offence Prosecution Guidance (CMA9) refers to exclusions from the cartel offence, which are based on EU law.[13] During the Transition Period, those exclusions will continue to apply.

1.9 The CMA's prioritisation principles[14] are also not materially affected by this guidance. More generally, unless otherwise stated in this guidance, the CMA's existing guidance will continue to apply to the exercise of each of its functions.

1.10 This guidance offers an explanation of the legal changes expected to result from EU Exit but it is not a definitive statement of, or a substitute for, the law itself. The legal tests which the CMA applies in carrying out its functions are not addressed in this guidance. A range of publications on how the CMA carries out this substantive assessment is available at www.gov.uk/cma. Any person who considers that they or their business may be affected by an investigation into suspected anti-competitive practices or a breach of consumer protection law or may have an interest in it,[15] or that they or their business may be involved in a transaction which may trigger the UK merger control thresholds in the EA02, should consider seeking independent legal advice.

GUIDANCE STRUCTURE

1.11 The remainder of this guidance is split into four sections:

- **Section 2: Legal framework** – this section presents and explains the impact of the Withdrawal Agreement and consequential domestic legislation on the UK legal framework in relation to merger control, competition and consumer protection;
- **Section 3: Merger control** – this section explains the rules and procedures that will apply to merger control during the Transition Period and how it is envisaged that mergers with an EU element will be treated at the end of the Transition Period;
- **Section 4: Competition law enforcement (antitrust, including cartels)** – this section focuses on the rules and procedures that will apply to cases under the competition law prohibitions during the Transition Period and on how it is envisaged that competition cases with an EU cross-border element will be treated at the end of the Transition Period;
- **Section 5: Consumer protection law enforcement** – this section focuses on the rules and procedures that will apply to consumer cases during the Transition Period and on how it is envisaged that consumer cases with an EU element will be treated at the end of the Transition Period;
- **Annex:** this annex provides a table listing the EU block exemptions in force under EU law.

NOTES

1 Article 185, Agreement on the Withdrawal of the United Kingdom of Great Britain and Northern Ireland from the European Union and the European Atomic Energy Community; and section 20(1), European Union (Withdrawal) Act 2018.

2 Agreement on the withdrawal of the United Kingdom of Great Britain and Northern Ireland from the European Union and the European Atomic Energy Community, as endorsed by leaders at a special meeting of the European Council on 13 December 2019.

3 Article 132 of the Withdrawal Agreement provides for the possibility to extend the Transition Period by up to one or two years if such an extension is agreed by the 'Joint Committee' before 1 July 2020. However, under UK law, section 15A of the European Union (Withdrawal Act) 2018 (as introduced by section 33 of the European Union (Withdrawal Agreement) Act 2020) prohibits UK ministers from agreeing an extension. Any reference to the Transition Period in this document includes any extension.

4 So far as they relate to competition law under the Competition Act 1998 and Enterprise Act 2002, as amended by the Enterprise and Regulatory Reform Act 2013, and the CMA's enforcement powers under consumer protection legislation, in particular Part 8 of the Enterprise Act 2002.

5 All CMA guidance documents are available at: www.gov.uk/cma.

6 See the 'Political declaration setting out the framework for the future relationship between the European Union and the United Kingdom'.

7 As amended by section 22, The International Accounting Standards and European Public Limited-Liability Company (Amendment etc.) (EU Exit) Regulations 2019.

8 As explained in paragraph 2.20, the European Union (Withdrawal Agreement) Act 2020 delays the effect of the Withdrawal Act SIs (the 'no deal' statutory instruments) until the end of the Transition Period and grants powers to make statutory instruments where provisions of the Withdrawal Agreement need further implementation. The Withdrawal Act SIs will be amended using these powers, where appropriate, to give effect to the Withdrawal Agreement.

9 Other 'no deal' statutory instruments in the field of consumer protection are Package Travel and Linked Travel Arrangements (Amendment) (EU Exit) Regulations 2018 and Timeshare, Holiday Products, Resale and Exchange Contracts (Amendment etc.) (EU Exit) Regulations 2018.

10 The CMA has published guidance which describes the effects of EU Exit on the CMA's functions in a 'no deal' scenario (the No Deal Guidance). For the avoidance of doubt, the No Deal Guidance will not apply during the Transition Period. Guidance on the functions of the CMA after a 'no deal' exit from the EU, 18 March 2019.

11 See the following existing guidance in respect of these areas: Regulatory appeals and references, Market studies and investigations: CMA3; Guidelines for market investigations: CC3 (revised); and Cartel offence prosecution: CMA9.

12 The CMA will conduct market studies and market investigation, as it currently does, under domestic legislation. When relevant, the CMA will take into consideration the relationship between domestic legislation and Articles 101 and 102 Treaty on the Functioning of the European Union, in compliance with Article 3 of Council Regulation (EC) No 1/2003 of 16 December 2002 on the implementation of the rules on competition laid down in Article 81 and 82 of the Treaty (Regulation 1/2003).

13 The exclusions to the offence are also contained in the EA02, as amended by Enterprise and Regulatory Reform Act 2013 (Section 188A). Under paragraph 4.17 of Cartel Offence Prosecution Guidance (CMA9), an individual will not commit

Part 7 Brexit-related Materials

an offence if the agreement is made in order to comply with a legal requirement, and a legal requirement includes a requirement: "[. . .] *(b) imposed by or under TFEU or the European Economic Area Agreement and having legal effect in the United Kingdom without further enactment, or (c) imposed by or under the law in force in another European Union Member State and having legal effect in the United Kingdom*."

[14] Prioritisation principles for the CMA: CMA16.

[15] For example, complainants or customers.

2. THE LEGAL FRAMEWORK

PART 1: THE WITHDRAWAL AGREEMENT

Key provisions of the Withdrawal Agreement

[7.94]

2.1 During the Transition Period, EU law (with the exception of certain specified provisions) applies in the UK.[16] EU law must also be interpreted and applied in the UK in accordance with the same methods and general principles as those applicable within the EU.[17]

2.2 Provisions of the Treaty on the Functioning of the European Union (TFEU), the Treaty on European Union, EU regulations and other legislation which deal with European competition and consumer law therefore continue to apply in and to the UK during the Transition Period.[18]

2.3 The European Commission and the Court of Justice of the European Union (CJEU) shall also continue to have the powers conferred upon them by EU law in relation to the UK and natural and legal persons residing or established in the UK during the Transition Period.[19]

2.4 The jurisdiction of the European Commission and the CJEU in the UK during the Transition Period, and for certain types of cases after the end of the Transition Period, accordingly remains the same as it did before EU Exit.[20]

2.5 Further detail on what this means in practice for merger control, competition and consumer law enforcement in the UK during the Transition Period is set out in this guidance.

PART 2: THE UK DOMESTIC LEGISLATION GIVING EFFECT TO EU EXIT AND THE TRANSITION PERIOD

2.6 The UK Parliament has passed two key pieces of primary legislation which give legal effect in UK law to EU Exit and to the Withdrawal Agreement:

- the European Union (Withdrawal) Act 2018 (referred to in this guidance as the 'Withdrawal Act') which essentially repeals the European Communities Act 1972 with effect from Exit Day and brings across certain EU legislation to form part of the UK's domestic law (see below from paragraph 2.7 onwards); and
- the European Union (Withdrawal Agreement) Act 2020 (referred to in this guidance as the 'Withdrawal Agreement Act') which postpones the effects of the Withdrawal Act from Exit Day until the end of the Transition Period, gives effect to the Withdrawal Agreement and amends the Withdrawal Act (see below, paragraph 2.15 onwards).

Key provisions of the Withdrawal Act

2.7 Set out below are the key provisions of the Withdrawal Act. However, the effect of these provisions is altered by the Withdrawal Agreement Act, and therefore should be read in conjunction with paragraph 2.15 onwards.

2.8 On 26 June 2018, the Withdrawal Act received Royal Assent. The Withdrawal Act repeals the European Communities Act 1972 on Exit Day.[21] The European Communities Act 1972 was the principal piece of legislation passed by the UK Parliament that gave effect to EU law in the UK.[22]

2.9 Pursuant to section 3 of the Withdrawal Act (although subject to the exceptions contained in section 5 of the Withdrawal Act), directly effective EU legislation, including EU regulations, decisions and EU treaty articles,[23] so far as operative immediately before EU Exit, are brought across and form part of the UK's domestic law on and after EU Exit.

2.10 Furthermore, under section 2 of the Withdrawal Act, UK domestic legislation which is EU-derived — including that enacted under section 2(2) of the European Communities Act in order to implement an EU directive — also continues to have effect in UK domestic law on and after Exit Day.

2.11 Following EU Exit, anything which continues to be, or forms part of, UK domestic legislation by virtue of sections 2 or 3 of the Withdrawal Act (see the two preceding paragraphs of this guidance) constitutes '**retained EU law**'. For further information on the concept of 'retained EU law' under the Withdrawal Act, please refer to the following public papers:

House of Commons Library — The European Union (Withdrawal) Bill: Retained EU law; and
House of Commons Library — The status of 'retained EU Law'.

2.12 Under section 8 of the Withdrawal Act, UK Ministers have the power to make statutory instruments to amend retained EU law with a view to preventing, remedying or mitigating (a) any failure of retained EU law to operate effectively, or (b) any other deficiency in retained EU law.[24] The Government used this power when it made the Competition (Amendment etc.) (EU Exit) Regulations 2019 on 22 January 2019 and the Consumer Protection (Enforcement) (Amendment etc.) (EU Exit) Regulations 2019 on 6 February 2019 (together, the Withdrawal Act SIs),[25] which were designed to apply from Exit Day in the event a withdrawal agreement was not concluded. As noted below (paragraphs 2.20 and 2.21), the Withdrawal Agreement Act provides for additional powers for Ministers to make statutory instruments.

2.13 Under the Withdrawal Act, any question as to the validity, meaning or effect of unmodified retained EU law is to be decided, so far as they are relevant to it, in accordance with any case law or general principles of the CJEU laid down up until Exit Day.[26]

2.14 As a final point, it is important to note that under the Withdrawal Act, the UK Supreme Court and Scotland's High Court of Justiciary[27] are not bound by any retained EU case law.[28] As a result, after Exit Day, CJEU case law relating to unmodified retained EU law will have the same status in domestic courts and tribunals as existing decisions of the UK Supreme Court or High Court of Justiciary. However, the Withdrawal Agreement Act has amended section 6 of the Withdrawal Act in order to enable the Government to alter, and set out in regulations (after consultation), the circumstances in which specified UK courts and tribunals would not be bound by retained EU case law.[29] The status of CJEU case law after Exit Day could, therefore, be subject to change and it is possible that it might not, in certain circumstances, bind courts lower than the UK Supreme Court and Scotland's High Court of Justiciary.

Key provisions of the Withdrawal Agreement Act

2.15 The Withdrawal Agreement Act gives effect to the Withdrawal Agreement[30] and amends the Withdrawal Act in a number of ways, including those set out further below.

2.16 As mentioned above (paragraph 2.6 (ii)), despite the fact that the Withdrawal Act repeals the European Communities Act 1972, the Withdrawal Agreement Act modifies the Withdrawal Act to include a saving provision that preserves the effect of the repealed European Communities Act 1972 until the end of the Transition Period.[31] The Withdrawal Agreement Act also modifies certain parts of the European Communities Act 1972 to reflect the fact that the UK has left the EU, and that the UK's relationship with EU law during the Transition Period is determined by the UK's commitments in the Withdrawal Agreement, rather than as a Member State.[32]

2.17 This means that directly applicable EU law, including the main treaty articles relevant for competition purposes (Articles 101 and 102 TFEU) and the main relevant EU regulations (such as Regulation 1/2003,[33] EU block exemption Regulations[34] and the EU Merger Regulation)[35] will continue to apply in the UK during the Transition Period, through the saved effect of section 2(1) of the European Communities Act 1972.[36]

2.18 In addition, the Withdrawal Agreement Act ensures that domestic legislation implementing or referring to EU law still has effect in the UK in accordance with the Withdrawal Agreement.[37] For example, where there are references to the obligations on 'Member States' in CA98 and EA02, as a result of a provision in the Withdrawal Agreement Act, these references are to be read as though the UK were still a Member State during the Transition Period.

2.19 The Withdrawal Agreement Act also amends the Withdrawal Act so that the directly effective EU legislation brought across to form part of UK's domestic law as retained EU law,[38] is that which is operative immediately before the end of the Transition Period rather than immediately before Exit Day.

2.20 The Withdrawal Agreement Act delays the effect of the Withdrawal Act SIs until the end of the Transition Period. The Withdrawal Agreement Act also amends the powers granted to Ministers under section 8 of the Withdrawal Act (to make statutory instruments to amend retained EU law) to allow for the correction of any deficiencies arising as a result of or in connection with the end of the Transition Period or any other effect of the Withdrawal Agreement.[39]

2.21 Moreover, the Withdrawal Agreement Act gives domestic legal effect to the provisions of the Withdrawal Agreement relating to matters other than the Transition Period. Where provisions of the Withdrawal Agreement need further implementation, it grants powers which can be used to make statutory instruments for this purpose. This will allow, for example, for specific provision to be made in relation to competition cases ongoing at the end of the Transition Period.[40] The Withdrawal Act SIs will be amended using these powers, where appropriate, to give effect to the Withdrawal Agreement.

NOTES

16 Articles 127(1) and (3), Withdrawal Agreement.

17 Article 127(3), Withdrawal Agreement.

18 Including, but not limited to, Articles 101, 102 and 106 of the TFEU, the EU Merger Regulation, Council Regulation (EC) No 1/2003, Regulation (EC) No 2006/2004 on Consumer Protection Cooperation Regulation and Council Directive 93/13/EEC on unfair terms in consumer contracts.

19 Article 131, Withdrawal Agreement.

20 Article 95(1), Withdrawal Agreement provides that decisions adopted by EU institutions before the end of the Transition Period which are addressed to the UK, or to its natural and legal persons, will be fully binding on and in the UK. Article 86(1), Withdrawal Agreement provides that the CJEU will have exclusive jurisdiction to hear issues relating to the legality of such decisions and the compliance of the UK with such decisions. Article 86(2), Withdrawal Agreement provides that the CJEU shall continue to have jurisdiction to give preliminary rulings on requests from courts and tribunals of the UK made before the end of the Transition Period.

Articles 95(1), 92 and 93, Withdrawal Agreement provide that decisions made by EU institutions after the end of the Transition Period which are addressed to the UK, or to its natural and legal persons will be fully binding on and in the UK if the procedures that led to the adoption of these decisions were initiated before the end of the Transition Period and concern compliance with EU law of the United Kingdom or compliance with EU competition law in the United Kingdom. Article 95(3), Withdrawal Agreement provides that the CJEU shall have exclusive jurisdiction to review the legality of these decisions.

21 Section 1, Withdrawal Act.
22 See further paragraph 2.16.
23 Including articles of the Treaty on European Union and articles of the TFEU.
24 Section 8(1), Withdrawal Act.
25 Mentioned also in paragraph 1.7 above. A number of other consumer protection statutory instruments were also made.
26 Pursuant to section 6 of the Withdrawal Act, this applies so far as retained EU law remains "unmodified". Where retained EU law has been modified on or after Exit Day it can be interpreted in accordance with CJEU case law and the general principles of EU law where that accords with the intention of the amendments (s.6(6) Withdrawal Act). Retained EU law can be modified only in a way prescribed under section 7, Withdrawal Act, as amended by Schedule 5(40), Withdrawal Agreement Act.
27 The highest criminal court in Scotland.
28 Section 6(4), Withdrawal Act and Withdrawal Act, Explanatory Notes, Section 6: Interpretation of retained EU law.
29 Sections 5A, 5B, 5C and 5D, Withdrawal Act (as introduced by section 26, Withdrawal Agreement Act).
30 See in particular Parts 1, 2 and 3 of the Withdrawal Agreement Act.
31 Section 1A, Withdrawal Act (as introduced by section 1, Withdrawal Agreement Act).
32 Sections 1A and 1B, Withdrawal Act (as introduced by sections 1 and 2, Withdrawal Agreement Act).
33 Council Regulation (EC) No 1/2003 of 16 December 2002 on the implementation of the rules on competition laid down in Articles 81 and 82 of the Treaty, Official Journal L 1, 4.1.2003, p 1–25.
34 See Annex.
35 Council Regulation (EC) No 139/2004 of 20 January 2004 on the control of concentrations between undertakings, Official Journal L 24, 29.01.2004, p 1–22.
36 Note that UK consumer protection legislation enacted under section 2(2) of the European Communities Act 1972, which implements EU consumer law directives, remains in force notwithstanding the repeal of the European Communities Act 1972.
37 Section 1B, Withdrawal Act (as introduced by section 2, Withdrawal Agreement Act).
38 See paragraph 2.8.
39 Section 8, Withdrawal Act (as amended by section 27, Withdrawal Agreement Act).
40 Section 7A, Withdrawal Act (as introduced by section 5, Withdrawal Agreement Act) and section 8B, Withdrawal Act (as introduced by section 18, Withdrawal Agreement Act).

3. MERGER CONTROL

PART 1: DURING THE TRANSITION PERIOD

'One-stop-shop'

[7.95]

3.1 During the Transition Period, pursuant to the Withdrawal Agreement[41] and the Withdrawal Agreement Act, the UK will broadly continue to be treated as if it were a Member State under the EU Merger Regulation (EUMR),[42] such that the 'one-stop shop' principle under the EUMR continues to apply.[43] The division of jurisdiction between the European Commission and the CMA over mergers which are notifiable under the EUMR or the EA02 will therefore remain the same during the Transition Period.

3.2 Accordingly, the UK turnover generated by merging parties[44] will still need to be taken into account when establishing whether a merger[45] satisfies the EUMR jurisdictional thresholds.[46] Relevant UK turnover of merging parties will be included within the 'Union-wide' turnover and the UK will be regarded as a Member State for the purposes of the alternative turnover thresholds under Article 1(3) EUMR.

3.3 Where a merger satisfies the EUMR jurisdictional thresholds, the European Commission will continue to retain exclusive competence for the investigation of that merger, including with respect to any effects on any UK market (or market that includes all or a part of the UK).[47] In such a situation, the CMA will not open an investigation, unless jurisdiction is transferred under the referral mechanisms set out in the EUMR (described further in paragraph 3.4). The CMA will continue to work with the European Commission in relation to any issues raised by such mergers that are relevant to the UK, including through attendance at Advisory Committee meetings (subject to the rules governing the UK's invitation to meetings of EU bodies during the Transition Period, set out in the Withdrawal Agreement).[48]

Case referrals

3.4 During the Transition Period, the UK will continue to be treated as if it were a Member State for the purposes of referrals of merger control cases from the European Commission to the national competition authorities of the Member States (NCAs) and vice versa under the following provisions:

- Article 4(4), EUMR — a request by the merging parties that a merger be reviewed by an NCA even though it satisfies the EUMR jurisdictional thresholds;[49]
- Article 4(5), EUMR — a request by the merging parties for a merger to be reviewed by the European Commission, even though it does not have a Community dimension, if it is capable of being reviewed under the national merger control laws of at least three Member States;[50]
- Article 9, EUMR — a request by an NCA for the European Commission to refer a merger to an NCA where the conditions of Article 9 are met;[51]
- Article 22, EUMR — a request by one or more NCAs that a merger be examined by the European Commission rather than the NCA(s), even if that merger does not satisfy the EUMR jurisdictional thresholds.[52]

3.5 Where a request for a referral to the CMA (under Article 9 or Article 4(4), EUMR) is accepted by the European Commission prior to the end of the Transition Period, the CMA will retain jurisdiction to review the merger after EU Exit.[53]

Public interest interventions

3.6 The Secretary of State will continue to be able to intervene on certain limited public interest grounds in mergers being reviewed by the European Commission under Article 21(4), EUMR.[54]

Review of decisions by the European Commission

3.7 The CJEU retains full jurisdiction to review decisions of the European Commission under the EUMR that were either adopted before the end of the Transition Period or for mergers in which the administrative procedure has been initiated before the end of the Transition Period (as described below in paragraph 3.9).[55] The jurisdiction of the CJEU covers the effects of these mergers within any UK market.

3.8 The UK courts and the Competition Appeal Tribunal do not have jurisdiction to review decisions of the European Commission (or the UK-related aspects of these decisions) and this is not affected by EU Exit.

PART 2: TOWARDS THE END OF THE TRANSITION PERIOD

Cases where the European Commission retains jurisdiction

3.9 At the end of the Transition Period there will be some merger cases which are under review by the European Commission where a final decision has not yet been taken (which are referred to as 'live' cases for the purposes of this guidance). The Withdrawal Agreement makes provision for how live cases are to be dealt with in terms of jurisdiction between the UK and the EU.[56] It sets out three scenarios where the European Commission will retain exclusive jurisdiction to review a merger (including in relation to any effects on any UK market) and the CMA will therefore not have jurisdiction over the case.[57] These are:

- Where a merger has been formally notified to the European Commission before the end of the Transition Period. This requires that the "*date of notification*"[58] falls before the end of the Transition Period.
- Where the European Commission has, before the end of the Transition Period, accepted (or is deemed to have accepted)[59] an Article 22 EUMR referral request in which the CMA participated.
- Where the European Commission has, before the end of the Transition Period, accepted an Article 4(5) referral request (or the deadline for Member States to disagree to the request has expired).[60]

3.10 The European Commission will retain jurisdiction over these cases until it reaches a final decision, whether at Phase 1 (after an initial phase) or Phase 2 (after an in-depth investigation). For these cases, the CMA will continue sharing and receiving case-related information until the European Commission reaches a final decision. The CMA expects to be included in Advisory Committee meetings for these cases, on the basis that the criteria for invitation set out in the Withdrawal Agreement will be met, although it will no longer have the formal right to vote at such meetings.[61]

3.11 For mergers where the European Commission has accepted commitments from the merging parties, the European Commission will continue to be responsible for monitoring and enforcing all aspects of these commitments, including any UK elements, after the end of the Transition Period. This will also be the case when the commitments have not been agreed before the end of the Transition Period, but the European Commission has exclusive jurisdiction to review the merger (i.e. in the circumstances set out in paragraph 3.9 above).[62] The Withdrawal Agreement provides that the European Commission and the CMA may agree to transfer responsibility for monitoring and enforcing the UK elements of such commitments from the European Commission to the CMA.[63] As set out in Section 2 above, secondary legislation will be necessary to make corresponding amendments to domestic legislation.

Cases where the European Commission does not retain jurisdiction at the end of the Transition Period

3.12 The CMA may have jurisdiction to review a merger that has not been formally notified or subject to referral to the European Commission before the end of the Transition Period.[64]

3.13 If there is a material likelihood that the merger will not have been formally notified or referred to the European Commission before the end of the Transition Period, merging parties may wish to consider the possibility that the CMA will ultimately have jurisdiction to review the merger (and consider engaging with the CMA significantly in advance of the end of the Transition Period).

Engagement with the CMA and pre-notification discussions

3.14 Merging parties are encouraged to approach the CMA to discuss whether it might be useful to begin pre-notification discussions in particular where:

- the merger might not be formally notified to the European Commission before the end of the Transition Period; and
- the merger is likely to meet the conditions set out in the EA02 such that the CMA would have jurisdiction and may raise the possibility of competition concerns.[65]

3.15 The CMA considers that early and constructive engagement on mergers that may fall under the jurisdiction of the CMA at the end of the Transition Period is likely to help with the expedient investigation of the case. Where merging parties choose not to engage with the CMA until after the end of the Transition Period (and therefore substantive pre-notification discussions can only begin at this point), this is, in practice, likely to result in the final outcome of any investigation being reached later than would otherwise be the case.

3.16 In considering how to approach the CMA to commence pre-notification discussions, merging parties should follow the guidance set out in Chapter 6 of CMA2.

3.17 Where there is some uncertainty about whether the CMA will obtain jurisdiction over a case before the end of the Transition Period, merging parties may wish, in the interests of clarity and certainty, to consider requesting an earlier referral of a case to the CMA under Article 4(4) EUMR.[66] The CMA may also consider whether to request that a case should be referred to the CMA under Article 9 EUMR.

The CMA's mergers monitoring during the Transition Period

3.18 The UK merger control regime is voluntary and therefore there is no obligation to notify a merger. The CMA will only open an investigation on its own initiative where there is a reasonable chance that the transactions may give rise to a relevant merger situation and to a realistic prospect of a substantial lessening of competition.[67]

3.19 As noted above, merging parties are encouraged to engage with the CMA at an early stage, particularly where a merger may raise potential competition concerns in the UK.[68] Not notifying a qualifying merger to the CMA raises certain risks for parties (described in more detail in paragraphs 6.20 and 6.21 of Mergers: Guidance on the CMA's jurisdiction and procedure: CMA2). The risks apply equally in cases that fall under CMA jurisdiction because they have not been formally notified or referred to the European Commission by the end of the Transition Period.

3.20 The CMA retains the ability to refer a merger for a Phase 2 investigation for a period of four months after completion.[69] Following the end of the Transition Period, this statutory four-month period will apply for completed mergers from the latest of: (i) the end of the Transition Period;[70] (ii) the date of completion; or (iii) the point at which the CMA is considered to have been provided with notice of material facts about the merger.[71]

3.21 Prior to the end of the Transition Period, the CMA will monitor cases which may be the subject of pre-notification discussions with the European Commission but may fall under UK jurisdiction at the end of the Transition Period.

3.22 Although the CMA would not start a formal investigation until after the end of the Transition Period,[72] the CMA may take certain preparatory steps during the Transition Period to assess whether a formal investigation is likely to be necessary. In particular, the CMA may approach parties (or third parties) to request information about a merger which is in pre-notification with the European Commission. The CMA may also decide to issue an invitation to comment before the end of the Transition Period to invite third party comments about a merger. The CMA may conduct its own preliminary analysis, or contact other competition authorities, to advance its understanding of the competition issues that might be raised by a merger in preparation for a formal investigation.

3.23 In practice, merging parties providing the CMA with information that they have already shared with the European Commission and which is relevant to the UK aspects of the case is likely to facilitate the CMA's initial assessment of whether a formal investigation is likely to be necessary (and, if so, to enable the CMA to progress the case expediently).

Cases being reviewed by the CMA prior to the end of the Transition Period

3.24 The CMA's powers to review a merger under Part 3 of the EA02 are independent of those of the European Commission under the EUMR. Therefore the CMA does not envisage that there will be any change to the procedure followed for cases where the CMA has started its review prior to the end of the Transition Period. In particular, if a merger was referred to the CMA by the European Commission under the EUMR before the end of the Transition Period, the CMA anticipates that it will progress according to a 45 EU working day timetable.[73]

'Public interest' cases

3.25 As explained in paragraphs 16.16 to 16.22 of CMA2, the Secretary of State may also intervene on certain 'legitimate interest' grounds in cases falling under the EUMR through Article 21(4) EUMR. If the Secretary of State has issued or issues a European Intervention Notice in relation to a case which has already been formally notified or referred to the European Commission before the end of the Transition Period, the review will proceed as set out in existing guidance. The European Commission will review the competition aspects of the case and the CMA will review the 'legitimate interest' aspects as defined in Article 21(4) of the EUMR.

3.26 In relation to mergers which may raise public interest concerns, but which have not been formally notified or referred to the European Commission before the end of the Transition Period, the standard procedure for public interest mergers set out in paragraphs 16.7 to 16.15 of CMA2 will apply.

PART 3: AFTER THE END OF THE TRANSITION PERIOD

3.27 After the end of the Transition Period, mergers will no longer be subject to the EU one-stop shop principle in relation to the UK.

3.28 Pursuant to the Withdrawal Agreement, the turnover of parties in the UK will no longer be relevant for determining whether a merger satisfies the EUMR jurisdictional thresholds. The CMA will also cease to be a competent authority of a Member State for the purposes of the EUMR and may therefore investigate mergers which satisfy the EUMR jurisdictional thresholds.

3.29 With the exception of mergers over which the European Commission retains jurisdiction, as described above in paragraph 3.9, the European Commission will no longer have jurisdiction to investigate the effects within the UK of any mergers, with the CMA instead having jurisdiction (to the extent that a merger triggers the thresholds under the EA02).

3.30 Where a merger satisfies the jurisdictional thresholds of the EUMR and the EA02, the CMA and the European Commission may conduct parallel assessments of the same merger in their respective jurisdictions.

3.31 It will remain important for the CMA to be informed about whether mergers being reviewed in the UK are also subject to investigation in other jurisdictions (as explained in paragraph 19.1 of CMA2). Where possible and appropriate, the CMA will endeavour to coordinate merger reviews relating to the same or related cases with the European Commission (and other competition authorities). Merging parties (and third parties) are encouraged to facilitate cooperation with the European Commission and other competition authorities wherever possible.

NOTES

41 Article 127(6), Withdrawal Agreement.

42 Council Regulation (EC) No 139/2004 of 20 January 2004 on the control of concentrations between undertakings (EUMR).

43 Chapter 18 of Mergers: Guidance on the CMA's jurisdiction and procedure, January 2014 (CMA2) which should be read in light of this guidance and the changes mentioned in paragraphs 3.27 to 3.31.

44 The 'merging parties' are referred to as 'the undertakings concerned' under the EUMR. This concept is defined in the Commission Consolidated Jurisdictional Notice under Council Regulation (EC) No 139/2004 on the control of concentrations between undertakings.

45 The EUMR only applies to 'concentrations' as defined in Article 3 EUMR. Where this guidance refers to mergers in the context of the EUMR, it is to be understood to mean a transaction which would meet the definition of a concentration under the EUMR and the Commission Consolidated Jurisdictional Notice under Council Regulation (EC) No 139/2004 on the control of concentrations between undertakings.

46 Article 1(2) and (3), EUMR.

47 Article 21(3), EUMR.

48 Article 128(5), Withdrawal Agreement.

49 See paragraphs 18.16 to 18.25 and 18.32 to 18.35 of CMA2 for further information on these types of referrals.

50 See paragraphs 18.41 to 18.47 of CMA2 for further information on these types of referrals.

51 See paragraphs 18.26 to 18.35 of CMA2 for further information on the CMA's procedure in relation to Article 9 referral requests.

52 See paragraphs 18.48 to 18.58 of CMA2 for further information on this procedure.

53 The CMA has, under section 34A of the Enterprise Act 2002, a maximum of 45 working days beginning on the working day after receipt of the European Commission's referral decision to inform the merger parties of the result of its preliminary competition assessment. Subject to any changes in future legislation, the CMA expects that this timetable will remain unchanged for mergers referred to the CMA where the 45 working day deadline expires after the end of the Transition Period. If a request for a referral to the CMA is not accepted by the European Commission, then the European Commission will retain jurisdiction to review the case.

54 See paragraphs 16.16 to 16.22 of CMA2 for further information.

55 Article 21(2), EUMR. Article 95 and Article 131, Withdrawal Agreement.

56 Article 92, Withdrawal Agreement.

57 Except where the case has been referred to the CMA pursuant to a request under Article 9 EUMR or in a situation where the CMA may ultimately take responsibility for monitoring and enforcing any commitments on behalf of the European Commission subject to agreement between the European Commission and the CMA (see paragraph 3.11).

58 Articles 1, 3, 4 and 10 EUMR.

59 Under Article 22(3) EUMR, if the European Commission does not take a decision within 25 working days from the date on which all Member States have been informed by the European Commission of the initial referral request, then it shall be deemed to have adopted a decision to review the merger in accordance with the request.

60 If the European Commission has not expressly accepted the request, then the time limit of 15 working days referred to in Article 4(5) EUMR has expired without any of the Member States competent to examine the concentration under their national competition laws having expressed any disagreement as regards the request to refer the case to the European Commission.

61 Under Article 128(5), Withdrawal Agreement, UK representatives may be invited to meetings of the institutions of the EU during the Transition Period when:

- the discussion concerns individual acts to be addressed during the Transition Period to the UK or to natural or legal persons residing or established in the UK; or
- the presence of the UK is necessary and in the interest of the EU, in particular for the effective implementation of EU law during the Transition Period.

The Withdrawal Agreement adds that the UK representative shall have no voting rights during such meetings. Pursuant to Article 94(4) of the Withdrawal Agreement, Article 128(5) shall apply to the extent necessary for any procedures where the European Commission retains jurisdiction after the end of the Transition Period.

62 Article 92(2), Withdrawal Agreement.

63 Article 95(2), Withdrawal Agreement.

64 If merging parties are in pre-notification discussions with the European Commission prior to the end of the Transition Period, or considering a merger which meets the EUMR jurisdictional thresholds, it will be necessary to carefully consider whether the merger is likely to be formally notified or referred to the European Commission prior to 31 December 2020. See Commission Decision of 28 January 2019 on public holidays for 2020 for the institutions of the European Union (2019/C 38/05).

65 Section 23, EA02.

66 Such a referral is available if the merger may significantly affect competition in a market in the UK which presents all the characteristics of a distinct market. Such effects on competition need not be adverse for the purpose of Article 4(4). Paragraph 18.18 of CMA2 lists additional factors in support of a referral to the UK which would also be relevant in this situation.

67 CMA2, paragraph 4.38.

68 The CMA case team will be able to advise, among other matters, on steps that could potentially be taken to expedite the preparation of a draft Merger Notice in anticipation of the CMA gaining jurisdiction after the end of the Transition Period. This may include discussion and review of the Form CO or other submissions made to the European Commission, for which purpose the parties may wish to share such information with the CMA and consent to its use by the CMA in the event of the CMA opening an investigation.

69 As currently set out in section 24 of the Enterprise Act 2002. This section might be amended according to any guidance on the functions of the CMA after a 'deal' exit from the EU.

70 The CMA will only obtain jurisdiction over mergers that would otherwise fall under the jurisdiction of the European Commission at the end of the Transition Period. For mergers meeting the EUMR thresholds where EU proceedings have not been initiated but the transaction has completed before the end of the Transition Period (which are likely to be rare in practice), the statutory four-month clock will not commence before the end of the Transition Period.

71 CMA2, paragraph 4.44.

72 As mentioned above, until the end of the Transition Period, the UK and the CMA remain subject to the EUMR which provides that national merger control rules cannot be applied to a merger with a "Community dimension" (Article 21(3), EUMR).

73 The CMA has, under section 34A of the Enterprise Act 2002, a maximum of 45 working days beginning on the working day after receipt of the European Commission's referral decision to inform the merger parties of the result of its preliminary competition assessment. Subject to any changes in future legislation, the CMA expects that this timetable will remain unchanged for mergers referred to the CMA where the 45 working day deadline expires after the end of the Interim Period.

4. ENFORCEMENT OF THE COMPETITION LAW PROHIBITIONS ('ANTITRUST', INCLUDING CARTELS)

PART 1: DURING THE TRANSITION PERIOD

[7.96]

4.1 As explained in paragraph 2.17 of this guidance, Article 101 (the EU law prohibition on anti-competitive agreements) and Article 102 (the EU law prohibition on abuse of a dominant position) TFEU will have full force and effect in the UK during the Transition Period. This is in addition to the equivalent UK domestic law prohibitions in CA98. Regulation 1/2003 and the EU block exemption Regulations and EU Guidance will also continue to apply.[74]

European Commission's enforcement of Article 101 and Article 102 TFEU in relation to the UK

4.2 The European Commission will continue to have the power to enforce Article 101 and Article 102 TFEU in relation to the UK and natural and legal persons residing or established in the UK in the same way as it did before Exit Day. The European Commission may investigate suspected infringements of Article 101 or Article 102 TFEU in the UK or which have effects on a UK market, in the same way as if the UK continued to be a Member State.[75] Appeals related to a decision of the European Commission addressed to natural or legal persons residing or established in the UK will continue to be heard exclusively by the CJEU.[76]

4.3 During the Transition Period, the UK and the CMA continue to be subject to the provisions of Regulation 1/2003 which governs the coordination of enforcement of the competition law prohibitions across the EU. Accordingly, where the European Commission has initiated an investigation into a suspected breach of either Article 101 or Article 102, the CMA and the UK concurrent regulators[77] will be relieved of their competence to launch or continue their own parallel investigation into the same UK conduct.[78]

Commitments and remedies accepted by the European Commission

4.4 For those cases where the European Commission has, before or during the Transition Period, accepted commitments or remedies from parties in order to address concerns, the European Commission will continue to have responsibility for the monitoring and enforcement of any UK elements of these during the Transition Period (see paragraph 4.23 below for the treatment of commitments and remedies which are due to expire after the end of the Transition Period).

CMA's enforcement of the EU competition law prohibitions – Article 101 and Article 102 TFEU

4.5 Regulation 1/2003 will also continue to apply to the CMA and the UK concurrent regulators during the Transition Period. This means that, as well as having the power to apply the domestic UK competition law prohibition – the Chapter I prohibition (anti-competitive agreements) and the Chapter II prohibition (abuse of dominance) in CA98, the CMA and the UK concurrent regulators also have the power,[79] and are obliged,[80] to apply Article 101 and Article 102 TFEU, to the extent that those provisions are also engaged by the subject matter of the investigation.

4.6 During the Transition Period the CMA will also continue to be able to assist the European Commission and national competition authorities of the Member States with their investigations,[81] and in turn will expect the CMA and concurrent regulators to receive equivalent assistance.

4.7 In addition, pursuant to Regulation 1/2003, the CMA and the UK concurrent regulators may exchange relevant information (including confidential information) with the European Commission or a national competition authority of a Member State during the Transition Period. The CMA and the UK concurrent regulators will also continue to have access to information shared amongst the European Competition Network as if the UK were still a Member State.[82] However, pursuant to the Withdrawal Agreement, the participation and attendance of the CMA or UK concurrent regulators in European Competition Network meetings, oral hearings and Advisory Committee meetings during the Transition Period will be by invitation only and in circumstances where cases involving the UK are under discussion or the presence of the UK is necessary and in the interest of the European Union.[83]

4.8 During the Transition Period, section 60 of CA98 will continue to apply. Section 60 CA98 incorporates into UK law a governing principle that UK competition law relating to the Chapter I prohibition and the Chapter II prohibition in CA98 should not diverge in its substantive application from equivalent EU law. In particular, it imposes an obligation on the CMA, the UK concurrent regulators and national courts to ensure the consistent interpretation of the CA98 with the TFEU and established and future EU case law; and a general duty to have regard to any *"relevant decision or statement"* of the European Commission when determining any matter. This means that the CMA, the UK concurrent regulators, and the UK courts must continue to ensure that, so far as is possible, questions arising under the Chapter I prohibition and the Chapter II prohibition in CA98 are dealt with in a way that is consistent with the treatment of corresponding questions arising in EU law in relation to competition within the European Union.

Application of EU block exemption Regulations

4.9 All existing EU block exemption Regulations will continue to apply in the UK during the Transition Period, as they did before Exit Day. The EU block exemption Regulations currently in force (and their corresponding expiry dates) are listed in the Annex. In addition, existing agreements between companies that benefit from a 'parallel exemption" under s10 CA98 will continue to have that benefit during the Transition Period (see paragraph 4.22 onwards below for the situation post-Transition Period).

Application of the CMA guidance relevant to antitrust (including cartel) cases

4.10 As stated in paragraph 1.4, the CMA's existing guidance will continue to apply and in case of conflict between existing guidance and this document, the most recent guidance should prevail.

4.11 In addition, the UK regime for competition law redress (i.e. private action for breaches of competition law) remains the same during the Transition Period. Parties therefore will be able to bring private UK court action on the basis of suspected infringements of EU and UK competition law or follow-on damages claims on the basis of EU and UK competition law infringement decisions of the CMA, the UK concurrent regulators, the European Commission or Member State national competition law authorities.[84]

Guidance on Competition Disqualification Orders (CMA102)

4.12 The disqualification of directors for infringements of competition law is set out under domestic legislation, and for the most part will not be affected by the UK exiting the EU. However, under the current legislation, infringements of EU competition law are relevant to disqualification and the guidance on Competition Disqualification Orders (CMA102) contains references to EU law, which will continue to apply during the Transition Period.[85]

CMA leniency regime in cartel cases

4.13 The leniency regime applicable in the UK remains the same during the Transition Period, subject to any future amendment unrelated to EU Exit.

4.14 The leniency regimes of the European Commission, the CMA and the national competition authorities of the Member States will remain separate and each jurisdiction should be considered individually. The fact that a party has made a leniency application to the European Commission whether before or after the end of the Transition Period will not provide it with any protection from fines with respect to any UK investigation under the CA98. Nor will such an application provide its employees or directors with any protection from prosecution for the criminal cartel offence in relation to that cartel activity in the UK or from director disqualification proceedings.

4.15 As was the case before EU Exit, when considering whether to make a leniency application to the European Commission, parties are encouraged to consider whether it would also be appropriate to make such an application to the CMA[86] and *vice versa*.

PART 2: TOWARDS THE END OF THE TRANSITION PERIOD

European Commission's enforcement of Article 101 and Article 102 TFEU in relation to the UK

4.16 Where the European Commission has formally initiated an investigation under Article 101 or Article 102 TFEU but is yet to reach a decision in respect of that prior to the end of the Transition Period (a 'live' case), the Withdrawal Agreement makes provisions for how the UK elements of these cases are to be dealt with in terms of jurisdiction between the UK and the EU.[87]

(i) Cases where the European Commission retains jurisdiction

4.17 Where the European Commission has formally initiated proceedings before the end of the Transition Period,[88] the European Commission will continue to be competent for the proceedings after the end of the Transition Period. During the Transition Period, Regulation 1/2003 and Regulation (EC) 773/2004 continue to apply to the CMA and the UK concurrent regulators.

4.18 For these cases, the CMA and the UK concurrent regulators will continue to have access to relevant information shared amongst the European Competition Network and to be included in the corresponding Advisory Committee meetings (subject to the rules governing the UK's invitation to meetings of EU bodies set out in the Withdrawal Agreement, see paragraph 4.7 above).[89]

(ii) Cases where the CMA and the UK concurrent regulators may obtain jurisdiction

4.19 After the Transition Period ends, the CMA and UK concurrent regulators may obtain jurisdiction over elements of proceedings which have already been formally initiated by the European Commission. For example, if the agreements or conduct under investigation may affect trade within the UK and are ongoing as at the end of the Transition Period, the CMA or concurrent regulators may investigate facts postdating the Transition Period. The precise scope of the jurisdiction of the CMA and UK concurrent regulators with respect to such future cases may be the subject of future legislation. The CMA will consider issuing further guidance in due course.

4.20 Where the CMA and the UK concurrent regulators consider that they may have jurisdiction to review the UK elements of a 'live' European Commission case after the end of the Transition Period, the CMA and the UK concurrent regulators may approach the parties to begin gathering information before the end of the Transition Period. Any such first approach does not necessarily imply that the CMA will take enforcement action. The CMA will follow existing principles and procedures, in particular as set out in its guidance on prioritisation principles (CMA16), taking into account the circumstances of EU Exit.

'Live' CMA antitrust investigations, including cartel investigations

4.21 When the CMA and the UK concurrent regulators are investigating conduct that may affect trade between EU Member States and have not issued a decision before the end of the Transition Period and the case proceeds, they will no longer apply the EU prohibitions after the end of the Transition Period. The CMA expects that all actions taken by the CMA and the UK concurrent regulators in relation to an investigation prior to the end of the Transition Period will remain valid for the purposes of the continuing domestic investigation (in particular with respect to information gathered through notices, interviews or inspections).

PART 3: AFTER THE END OF THE TRANSITION PERIOD

4.22 After the end of the Transition Period, the CMA and the UK concurrent regulators will only investigate suspected infringements of UK domestic competition law (i.e. the Chapter I and Chapter II prohibitions in CA98) and **not** Articles 101 and 102 TFEU.[90]

Commitments accepted and remedies imposed by the European Commission before the end of the Transition Period

4.23 The Withdrawal Agreement provides that, after the end of the Transition Period, the European Commission will continue to have responsibility for the monitoring and enforcement of any UK elements of commitments given or remedies imposed in connection with any European Commission proceedings for the application of Article 101 or 102 TFEU. However, the Withdrawal Agreement provides an option to transfer responsibility for enforcing the UK elements of the commitments or remedies to the CMA and the concurrent regulators by mutual agreement between the Commission and the CMA.[91] As noted in paragraph 4.4 above, the CMA will consider whether to issue further guidance in due course on the procedure that would be followed in such cases.

Leniency regime

4.24 After the end of the Transition Period, the separate leniency regime applicable in the UK will remain, subject to any future amendment.

Company director disqualification orders (CDOs) in competition cases

4.25 It is expected that the Competition (Amendment etc.) (EU Exit) Regulations 2019 will be amended so that the CMA and UK concurrent regulators will be able to rely on conduct found to have infringed Article 101 or 102 TFEU (in addition to the Chapter I and Chapter II prohibitions in CA98) during the Transition Period for the purposes of making an application for a director disqualification order under s.9A of the Company Directors Disqualification Act 1986 (CDDA).

EU block exemption Regulations

4.26 The Withdrawal Act and the Competition (Amendment etc.) (EU Exit) Regulations 2019 made under the Withdrawal Act preserve the EU block exemption Regulations in the UK as 'retained exemptions'.[92]

4.27 This means that, after the Transition Period, the retained exemptions will operate as exemptions from domestic prohibitions (as covered by s.10 CA98). Beneficiaries of the EU block exemption Regulations and the 'parallel exemption' pre-Exit will continue to benefit from the EU block exemption Regulations as incorporated into domestic law after the end of the Transition Period (and so long as they continue to comply with the retained exemptions). The power to vary (including to extend) or revoke the application of the retained exemptions to the domestic prohibitions will lie with the Secretary of State, acting in consultation with the CMA.

4.28 In addition, going forward, companies entering into new agreements after the end of the Transition Period will also be able to benefit from the retained exemptions provided they meet the relevant criteria.

NOTES

[74] See also CMA guidance based on EU law, including Guidance on Modernisation: OFT 442, and other guidance such as Guidance on Agreements and concerted practices: Understanding competition law: OFT 401 and Vertical agreements: Understanding competition law: OFT419.

[75] Further to Article 94(1) of the Withdrawal Agreement, EU law will continue to apply to such investigations. This means for example that in carrying out its investigations with respect to agreements or conduct in the UK, or affecting the UK, the European Commission may use its powers as set out under Council Regulation (EC) No 1/2003 on the implementation of the rules on competition laid down in Articles 81 and 82 of the Treaty (Regulation 1/2003).

[76] Article 95(3), Withdrawal Agreement.

[77] The term 'concurrent regulators' refers to the sector regulators in the UK which have been conferred with legal powers to apply competition law in their sectors concurrently with the CMA. The concurrent regulators are the Civil Aviation Authority (air traffic control and airport operations), the Financial Conduct Authority (provision of financial services), NHS Improvement (health care England), Ofcom (telecoms, broadcasting, post and spectrum), Office of Rail and Road (rail), Ofgem (gas and electricity), Ofwat (water and sewerage), Payment Systems Regulator (participation in payment systems) and NIAUR (gas, electricity, water in Northern Ireland). However, NHS Improvement is not a designated competition authority for the purposes of Regulation 1/2003. For further information, please refer to Regulated Industries: Guidance on concurrent application of competition law to regulated industries: CMA10.

[78] Article 11(6), Council Regulation (EC) No 1/2003. The power of the CMA to investigate is restored once the proceeding initiated by the European Commission has concluded. The Withdrawal Agreement does not change the existing EU rules relating to the competence of national competition authorities following a commitments decision by the European Commission.

[79] Article 5, Council Regulation (EC) No 1/2003.

[80] Article 3(1), Council Regulation (EC) No 1/2003.

[81] The UK concurrent regulators are not designated as national competition authorities for Article 20 and Article 22 of Regulation 1/2003. The CMA's powers in UK law to carry out inspections in the UK on behalf of the European Commission and Member State national competition authorities are set out in Part II and Part IIA of the CA98. Guidance on the CMA's investigation procedures in CA98 cases 18 January 2019: CMA8.

[82] Competition law modernisation: OFT442, paragraph 8.2, referring to the European Commission's *Notice on Cooperation within the Network of Competition Authority*.

[83] Article 128(5), Withdrawal Agreement.

[84] Competition law redress: CMA55. As mentioned in CMA55, a final infringement decision of any national competition authority or review court of any EU Member State is treated as 'at least prima facie evidence that an infringement of competition law has occurred and, as appropriate, may be assessed along with any other evidence adduced by the parties'. Decisions of the CMA, UK concurrent regulators and the European Commission are binding on the Courts.

[85] Guidance on Competition Disqualification Orders: CMA102.

[86] The CMA receives leniency applications, including in relation to regulated sectors. See Information Note — Arrangements for the handling of leniency applications in the regulated sectors.

[87] Article 92, Withdrawal Agreement.

[88] Article 92(3)(b), Withdrawal Agreement. The European Commission can initiate proceedings at any point in time, but not later than the date:

– it issues a preliminary assessment (a Statement of Objections), or a request for parties to express their interest in engaging in settlement discussions, or
– on which the European Commission publishes the summary of the case and main content of the commitments or the notice of inapplicability of Article 101 or 102, but cases can be formally initiated early in the European Commission's investigatory process.

Formal initiation of proceedings is pursuant to Article 2(1) of Commission Regulation (EC) No 773/2004. Pursuant to Article 2(2) of Regulation (EC) 773/2004, the European Commission may make public the initiation of proceedings, but shall inform the parties concerned before doing so.

[89] Pursuant to Article 94(4) of the Withdrawal Agreement, Article 128(5) shall apply to the extent necessary for any procedures referred to in Articles 92 and 93 after the end of the transition period. For the criteria of the UK's invitation to meetings of EU bodies under Article 128(5) see footnote 61 of this guidance.

[90] Leaving aside proceedings formally initiated by the European Commission before the end of the Transition Period (which are discussed at paragraph 4.17 above), this may mean that after the Transition Period there will be parallel UK and EU investigations into the same both pre and post Transition Period conduct.

[91] Article 95(2) of the Withdrawal Agreement. Domestic legislation will need to provide for the CMA being able to monitor and enforce these commitments and remedies.

[92] The EU block exemption Regulation applicable to consortium agreements between liner shipping companies will expire on 25 April 2020. At the time of writing, the European Commission is recommending extending the duration of the existing block exemption for another four years. If, in line with the recommendation, the EU block exemption Regulation applicable to consortium agreements between liner shipping companies is extended, this new block exemption will become the retained exemption applicable in the UK for its duration, unless it is varied or revoked before that by the Secretary of State.

5. CONSUMER PROTECTION LAW ENFORCEMENT

PART 1: DURING THE TRANSITION PERIOD

[7.97]

5.1 As explained in section 2, under the Withdrawal Agreement EU law will continue to apply to, and in, the UK during the Transition Period. The practical implications in the area of consumer protection are that, in general, immediately after Exit Day UK businesses will be subject to the same requirements as applied beforehand. Similarly, UK consumers will benefit from the same rights, and the CMA will have the same consumer enforcement powers and obligations.

Consumer protection law

5.2 Consumer protection law is, to a great extent, harmonised within the EU. It therefore follows that much of the UK's existing consumer protection law reflects EU consumer protection law.

5.3 During the Transition Period, businesses based in the UK or elsewhere that trade with UK consumers must continue to comply with UK, including EU-derived, consumer protection laws.[93]

5.4 In addition, new EU consumer protection laws which come into effect during the Transition Period will apply to, and in, the UK.[94]

5.5 Both during and after the Transition Period, UK traders directing their business activities to consumers in the EU must continue to comply with those consumers' local national consumer law which will largely reflect EU law.

Consumer protection law enforcement in EU cross-border cases

5.6 Currently, Part 8 of the EA02 (Part 8) sets out the principal UK regime for the civil enforcement of a wide range of consumer protection law by the CMA[95] and by other UK enforcers.[96] As well as covering purely domestic cases, it also allows EU enforcers to bring proceedings against UK businesses in the UK courts to protect consumers in their jurisdiction,[97] and also allows the CMA and other UK enforcers to bring proceedings in the UK against EU businesses that are harming UK consumers.[98]

5.7 Alternatively, UK businesses directing trade activities to EU consumers and breaching EU or local national consumer law could be subject to enforcement action by national enforcers in the courts of that Member State.[99]

5.8 During the Transition Period, the Injunctions Directive and Brussels la Regulation[100] will continue to apply to the UK and the Part 8 regime will remain unchanged. If UK consumers are affected by breaches of UK consumer law by EU firms targeting their business activities at UK consumers, the CMA and other UK enforcers will continue to have the power to take action in the firms' local courts and in the UK courts. Similarly, EU enforcers will continue to have the same powers to take action against UK businesses harming EU consumers.

5.9 Where a case is commenced during the Transition Period, the same rules on jurisdiction and applicable law will continue to apply to it until the final conclusion of the court case.

Consumer protection law enforcement cooperation with EU enforcers

5.10 The 2006 Consumer Protection Cooperation (CPC) Regulation[101] established a regime for EU cross-border consumer enforcement cooperation and assistance, by prescribing reciprocal powers and duties for Member States' competent authorities to respectively request and provide assistance. As of 17 January 2020, this regulation has been repealed and replaced by the 2017 CPC Regulation.[102] The 2017 CPC Regulation preserves the main features of the 2006 CPC Regulation, but strengthens the cooperation mechanisms and provides for a wider range of investigation and enforcement powers for national authorities to better equip them to meet the challenges of the European digital economy.[103] Collectively we refer to the scheme created by these Regulations as the CPC system.

5.11 Under the CPC system, competent authorities can ask a cross-border authority for information on a business based in the requested authority's jurisdiction and can require it to take enforcement action against that local business to stop it committing infringements which are harming consumers in the other member state.

5.12 The CMA is a UK competent authority under the CPC system and the UK's Single Liaison Office responsible for co-ordinating requests coming to, and from, the UK. The CMA sends requests for assistance to other EU enforcers, including ones referred through it from other UK competent authorities. It also receives requests for assistance from other Member States and refers them to the most appropriate UK competent authority (including itself) or other designated body, such as a Local Authority Trading Standards Service.

5.13 In addition, the CPC system provides for Member States' competent authorities, or the European Commission, to co-ordinate common consumer protection law enforcement activities to tackle businesses or infringements that span multiple Member States. The CMA has been involved in a number of these common activities.[104]

5.14 Throughout the Transition Period, the legal rights and obligations created under the CPC system, which apply to UK competent authorities, and the CMA's role as the Single Liaison Office, will remain.[105] Therefore, during that period, the CMA will liaise and co-ordinate with the European Commission and other EU competent authorities in the same way as it did before Exit Day.

CMA consumer protection law enforcement guidance

5.15 Information on the CMA's consumer enforcement powers and approach is set out in CMA58 which covers cases involving businesses or consumers in other Member States.[106] The information in CMA58 will continue to apply during the Transition Period.[107]

5.16 During the Transition Period, for cases involving businesses or consumers in Member States, the CMA will continue to exercise its consumer enforcement powers in the way indicated in the guidance.

PART 2: TOWARDS THE END OF THE TRANSITION PERIOD

5.17 In the event that consumer enforcement proceedings being brought by the CMA in the UK courts result in a reference to the CJEU for a preliminary ruling on a point of interpretation of European consumer law, it is possible that any such reference may not be determined by the end of the Transition Period. If so, and as explained above in paragraphs 2.3 and 2.4, the CJEU would continue to have jurisdiction to give preliminary rulings on requests from UK courts referred to it before the end of the Transition Period.[108]

Cross-border enforcement cases

5.17 The Withdrawal Agreement provides no specific rules on how ongoing cases or requests for assistance which have been referred by, or to, the UK through the CPC regime should be dealt with after the end of the Transition Period. In the case of referrals which have been made to the UK for enforcement action for which the CMA is responsible, the CMA will determine whether and how to take the case forward in accordance with its published prioritisation principles.

PART 3: AFTER THE END OF THE TRANSITION PERIOD

5.19 After the end of the Transition Period, businesses based in the UK or elsewhere that trade with UK consumers must comply with UK consumer protection laws.

5.20 The CMA has taken an active role in co-ordinated enforcement projects and knowhow-sharing within the CPC network, and a leading role in the development of wider partnership working in international fora. The CMA will continue to develop relationships and work with all our international counterparts, including, for example, through the International Consumer Protection and Enforcement Network (ICPEN).

5.21 The exact nature of consumer protection law enforcement cooperation to be agreed with the EU as part of the Future Relationship is not known at the time of publishing this document.

NOTES

93 This includes both consumer protection laws that implement EU directives and any EU consumer laws that are embodied in EU regulations, which are directly applicable to EU-based traders, (e.g. Council Regulation (EC) No 261/2004 of 11 February 2004 establishing common rules on compensation and assistance to passengers in the event of denied boarding and of cancellation or long delay of flights).

94 For example, the new Consumer Cooperation Regulation (Reg (EU) 2017/2394) which will apply from January 2020.

95 The CMA has additional enforcement powers under some specific consumer protection legislation, in particular the power to bring criminal enforcement proceedings under the Consumer Protection from Unfair Trading Regulations 2008 (Trading Standards Services and the Department of Enterprise, Trade and Investment in Northern Ireland (DETINI) have the primary duty to enforce these Regulations).

96 Other UK enforcers include Trading Standards Services and DETINI, the Advertising Standards Authority and sectoral regulators such as the Financial Conduct Authority and the Civil Aviation Authority.

97 Section 215(4) of the EA02 giving effect to Directive (98/27/EC) on injunctions for the protection of consumers' interests (Injunctions Directive).

98 By virtue of Regulation (EU) No 1215/2012 on jurisdiction and the recognition and enforcement of judgments in civil and commercial matters (Brussels la Regulation) the UK courts may have jurisdiction to hear enforcement proceedings for infringements affecting UK consumers and emanating from traders established elsewhere in the EU.

99 By virtue of the Brussels la Regulation.

100 Article 67(1), Withdrawal Agreement.

101 Regulation (EC) No 2006/2004 of the European Parliament and of the Council on cooperation between national authorities responsible for the enforcement of consumer protection laws.

102 Regulation (EU) 2017/2394 on cooperation between national authorities responsible for the enforcement of consumer protection laws and repealing Regulation (EC) No 2006/2004.

103 For example, these include new powers to order website take-downs and the power to impose penalties.

104 For example, common activities on children's online games, social media and car hire.

105 Article 127, Withdrawal Agreement.

106 Consumer protection: Enforcement Guidance: CMA58, paragraph 2.7 and Annex C.

107 Note that after Exit Day, paragraph 2.7, the last entry in the table under Annex A (Consumer legislation under which the CMA has enforcement powers) and Annex C (Wider international working) of CMA58 should be read as referring to the UK's participation in EU consumer cooperation arrangements on the basis that it is no longer a Member State of the EU.

108 Article 86(2), Withdrawal Agreement.

ANNEX A: EU BLOCK EXEMPTIONS IN FORCE UNDER EU LAW

[7.98]

Regulation	Expiry date	Guidance[109]	Date
Commission Regulation 316/2014 of 21 March 2014 on the application of Article 101(3) of the TFEU to categories of technology transfer agreements.	30/04/2026	Guidelines on the application of Article 101 of the TFEU to technology transfer agreements 2014/C 89/03	28/03/2014
Commission Regulation 330/2010 of 20 April 2010 on the application of Article 101(3) TFEU to categories of vertical agreements and concerted practices	31/05/2022	Guidelines on Vertical Restraints 2010/C 130/01 See also CMA Antitrust Vertical agreements: Understanding competition law (OFT419) (Dec 2004)	19/05/2010
Commission Regulation 461/2010 on the application of Article 101(3) TFEU to categories of vertical agreements and concerted practices in the motor vehicle sector	31/05/2023	Supplementary guidelines on vertical restraints in agreements for the sale and repair of motor vehicles and for the distribution of spare parts for motor vehicles 2010/C 138/05	28/05/2010
Commission Regulation No 1217/2010 of 14 December 2010 on the application of Article 101(3) of the TFEU to categories of research and development agreements	31/12/2022	Guidelines on the applicability of Article 101 of the TFEU to horizontal co-operation agreements Text 2011/C 11/01 NOTE: Corrigendum to Communication from the Commission, Guidelines on the applicability of Article 101 of the TFEU to horizontal co-operation agreements 2011/C 33/08 (2/2/2011)	14/01/2011
Commission Regulation No 1218/2010 of 14 December 2010 on the application of Article 101(3) of the TFEU to categories of specialisation agreements	31/12/2022		
Commission Regulation (EC) No 906/2009 of 28 September 2009 on the application of Article 81(3) of the TFEU to certain categories of agreements, decisions and concerted practices between liner shipping companies (consortia).[110] At the time of writing this guidance, the European Commission has recommended extending the duration of the liner shipping block exemption for another four years. This has been extended until 25 April 2020 by Commission Regulation (EU) No 697/2014 of 24 June 2014 amending Regulation (EC) No 906/2009 as regards its period of application.	25/04/2020	N/A	
Council Regulation (EC) No 169/2009 of 26 February 2009 applying rules of competition to transport by rail, road and inland waterway (Codified version). There are no Commission Regulations granting block exemption under Regulation 169/2009.	N/A	N/A	
Council Regulation (EC) 487/2009 of 25 May 2009 on the application of Article 81(3) of the Treaty to certain categories of agreements and concerted practices in the air transport sector.[111] There are no Commission regulations currently in force under Regulation 487/2009.	N/A	N/A	

NOTES

[109] These guidance documents remain relevant in interpreting the relevant EU block exemption Regulations.

[110] At the time of writing, the European Commission is recommending extending the duration of the existing block exemption for another four years.

[111] Subject to the Future Relationship and subsequent legislation, paragraph 1 of Schedule 3 of the Competition (Amendments etc.) (EU Exit) Regulations 2019 made under the Withdrawal Act revoke this Regulation and thus would not preserve it as a Retained BER after the Transition Period.

GUIDANCE ON THE FUNCTIONS OF THE CMA AFTER THE END OF THE TRANSITION PERIOD (CMA125, 1 DECEMBER 2020)

[7.99]

NOTES

CONTENTS

1. PREFACE

[7.100]

1.1 The United Kingdom's exit from the European Union (**EU Exit**) took place at 11pm UK time on 31 January 2020 (**Exit Day**).[1] Article 126 of the Agreement on the Withdrawal of the United Kingdom of Great Britain and Northern Ireland from the European Union and the European Atomic Energy Community (the **Withdrawal Agreement**)[2] provides for a 'transition period' which will end at 11pm UK time on 31 December 2020 (the **Transition Period**).[3]

1.2 As explained in the CMA's Guidance on the functions of the CMA under the terms of the Withdrawal Agreement, during the Transition Period, existing arrangements for the discharge of the functions of the Competition and Markets Authority (**CMA**) have been – and continue until the end of the Transition Period to be - largely unaffected. This guidance explains how EU Exit will affect the powers and processes of the CMA for antitrust and cartel enforcement, merger control and consumer protection law enforcement after the end of the Transition Period.[4] The guidance also explains how the CMA will approach the 'transitional provisions' contained in the Withdrawal Agreement, insofar as they relate to the UK competition regime.

1.3 This guidance will come into effect at 11pm UK time on 31 December 2020 when the Competition (Amendment etc.) (EU Exit) Regulations 2019 (the **Competition SI**); the Competition (Amendment etc.) (EU Exit) Regulations 2020 (the **Implementation SI**); the Consumer Protection (Enforcement) (Amendment etc.) (EU Exit) Regulations 2019 (the **Consumer Protection SI**); and the Consumer Protection (Enforcement) (Amendment etc) (EU Exit) Regulations 2020 (together with the Consumer Protection SI, the **Consumer Protection EU Exit SIs**), come into effect. Further detail in respect of these pieces of legislation are provided in Section 2 below.

1.4 This guidance applies to the CMA's ongoing and future:

- merger cases under the Enterprise Act 2002 (**EA02**);
- 'antitrust' cases, including cartels, under the Competition Act 1998 (**CA98**)–ie relating to the competition law prohibitions on anti-competitive agreements and on abuse of a dominant position; and
- enforcement of consumer protection legislation, in particular under Part 8of the EA02.

1.5 This guidance also applies to cases over which the European Commission has 'continued competence' under the terms of the Withdrawal Agreement (as explained in paragraphs 2.4, 3.4 to 3.6, and 4.1 to 4.5 below).

1.6 This guidance cross-refers to, and should be read alongside, existing CMA guidance and in case of conflict between an existing guidance document and the present guidance, the most recent guidance should prevail.[5] The CMA may issue further guidance in due course to clarify or amend elements of this guidance and explain any future cooperation arrangements agreed with the European Commission after EU Exit. The CMA expects to remove references to EU legislation and processes over time as guidance is re-issued.

WHAT IS NOT COVERED BY THIS GUIDANCE?

The UK's future relationship with the EU

1.7 At the time of publishing this guidance, the UK's relationship with the EU after the end of the Transition Period (referred to as the Future Relationship)[6] remains subject to negotiation with the EU. Negotiations with the EU in respect of a possible free trade agreement are ongoing.

1.8 The CMA may issue further guidance in due course to clarify or amend elements of this guidance and explain any differences to the UK regime which take effect after 31 December 2020 as a result of the outcome of Future Relationship negotiations.

CMA's functions

1.9 Some of the CMA's functions which are less materially affected by EU Exit are not specifically covered by this guidance, including regulatory appeals, market studies, market investigations and the criminal cartel offence. The CMA guidance on these functions may, however, refer to concepts under EU law.[7] These references will continue to have effect in the UK for as long as, and in so far as, EU law has legal effect in the UK (that is, unless and until the EU law to which these concepts relate is superseded, whether through the application of section 60A CA98 or by the ruling of any Court or Tribunal with the power to disapply or overrule these references).[8]

1.10 This guidance offers an explanation of the legal changes resulting from EU Exit but it is not a definitive statement of, or a substitute for, the law itself. The legal tests which the CMA applies in carrying out its functions are not addressed in this guidance. A range of publications on how the CMA carries out this substantive assessment is available at www.gov.uk/cma. Any person who considers that they or their business may be affected by an investigation into suspected anti-competitive practices or a breach of consumer protection law or may have an interest in it,[9] or that they or their business may be involved in a transaction which may trigger the UK merger control thresholds in the EA02, should consider seeking independent legal advice.

GUIDANCE STRUCTURE

1.11 The remainder of this guidance is split into four further sections:

- **Section 2: Legal framework** – this section presents and explains the impact of the European Union (Withdrawal) Act 2018 (referred to in this guidance as the **Withdrawal Act**) and consequential domestic legislation on the UK legal framework in relation to merger control, competition and consumer protection;
- **Section 3: Merger control** – this section explains how the rules and procedures will apply to merger control after 31 December 2020, and how merger control in the UK will be affected by the relevant provisions of the Withdrawal Agreement;
- **Section 4: Competition law enforcement (antitrust, including cartels)**–this section focuses on the rules and procedures that will apply to cases with an EU cross-border element under the competition law prohibitions on anti-competitive agreements and on abuse of a dominant position after 31 December 2020. This section will also cover the way in which the CMA will approach the relevant provisions of the Withdrawal Agreement insofar as they relate to competition law enforcement;
- **Section 5: Consumer protection law enforcement** – this section focuses on the rules and procedures that will apply to consumer cases with an EU element after 31 December 2020;
- **Annex A:** this annex sets out a list of CMA guidance which is not impacted by EU Exit;
- **Annex B:** this annex provides a table listing the EU block exemptions in force at the end of the Transition Period under EU law and being retained under national law.

NOTES

1 Article 185, Agreement on the Withdrawal of the United Kingdom of Great Britain and Northern Ireland from the European Union and the European Atomic Energy Community; and section 20(1), European Union (Withdrawal) Act 2018.

2 Agreement on the withdrawal of the United Kingdom of Great Britain and Northern Ireland from the European Union and the European Atomic Energy Community, as endorsed by leaders at a special meeting of theEuropean Council on 13 December 2019. It is important to note that the Northern Ireland Protocol, included in the Withdrawal Agreement, does not include provisions affecting the CMA's antitrust, merger control or consumer functions, and its application is therefore beyond the scope of this guidance.

3 In the remainder of this document, we refer to the end of the Transition Period and 31 December 2020 interchangeably. References to 31 December 2020 should be taken to mean **11pm UK time** on 31 December 2020, when the Transition Period ends under the terms of the Withdrawal Agreement.

4 So far as they relate to competition law under the Competition Act 1998 and Enterprise Act 2002, as amended by the Enterprise and Regulatory Reform Act 2013, and the CMA's enforcement powers under consumer protection legislation, in particular Part 8 of the Enterprise Act 2002. Where sector regulators hold competition powers concurrently with the CMA, the legal framework described in this guidance applies equally to them.

5 All CMA guidance documents are available at: www.gov.uk/cma.

6 See the Political declaration setting out the framework for the future relationship between the European Union and the United Kingdom.

7 See the following existing guidance in respect of these areas: Regulatory appeals and references, Market studies and investigations: CMA3; Guidelines for market investigations: CC3 (revised); and Cartel offence prosecution: CMA9.

8 The CMA will conduct market studies and market investigation, as it currently does, under domestic legislation. When relevant, until the end of the Transition Period the CMA will take into consideration the relationship between domestic legislation and Articles 101 and 102 Treaty on the Functioning of the European Union, in compliance with Article 3 of Council Regulation (EC) No 1/2003 of 16 December 2002 on the implementation of the rules on competition laid down in Article 81 and 82 of the Treaty (EU Regulation 1/2003).

9 For example, complainants or customers.

2. THE LEGAL FRAMEWORK

THE WITHDRAWAL AGREEMENT

Key provisions of the Withdrawal Agreement

[7.101]

2.1 The Withdrawal Agreement introduced the Transition Period, during which EU law (with the exception of certain specified provisions) continues to apply in the UK until 31 December 2020.[10] During the Transition Period, EU law must also be interpreted and applied in the UK in accordance with the same methods and general principles as those applicable within the EU.[11]

2.2 Provisions of the Treaty on the Functioning of the European Union (**TFEU**), the Treaty on European Union, EU regulations and other legislation which deal with EU competition and consumer law therefore continue to apply in and to the UK until the end of the Transition Period.[12]

2.3 The European Commission and the Court of Justice of the European Union (**CJEU**) shall also continue to have the powers conferred upon them by EU law in relation to the UK and natural and legal persons residing or established in the UK until the end of the Transition Period.[13]

2.4 The Withdrawal Agreement also has certain direct implications for 'ongoing administrative procedures' (including competition and consumer cases), in some cases **beyond** 31 December 2020. For example:

(i) EU institutions bodies, offices and agencies will continue to be competent for certain administrative procedures (including merger, antitrust or cartel cases) initiated before the end of the Transition Period.[14] The CMA will continue to provide assistance to the European Commission for these particular cases in the same way it would have before 31 December 2020;[15]

(ii) Decisions adopted by EU institutions, bodies, offices and agencies before 31 December 2020 (or after 31 December 2020 for the types of cases described at sub-paragraph 2.4i) above), and addressed to the UK or to natural or legal persons residing in the UK, shall be binding on and in the UK. The legality of such a decision shall be reviewed exclusively by the CJEU;[16] and

(iii) The European Commission will continue to be responsible to monitor and enforce commitments given or remedies imposed in, or in relation to, the UK in connection with competition or merger proceedings. By mutual agreement the European Commission can transfer responsibility for the monitoring and enforcement of any such commitments or remedies to the CMA.[17]

THE UK DOMESTIC LEGISLATION GIVING EFFECT TO EU EXIT AND THE TRANSITION PERIOD

2.5 The UK Parliament has passed two key pieces of primary legislation which give legal effect in UK law to EU Exit and to the Withdrawal Agreement:

- the Withdrawal Act, which essentially repealed the European Communities Act 1972 with effect from Exit Day and brought across certain EU legislation to form part of the UK's domestic law (see below from paragraph 2.7 onwards); and
- the European Union (Withdrawal Agreement) Act 2020 (referred to in this guidance as the **Withdrawal Agreement Act**) which postponed the effects of the Withdrawal Act from Exit Day until 31 December 2020, gave effect to the Withdrawal Agreement and amended the Withdrawal Act.[18]

2.6 Using its powers under the Withdrawal Act and the Withdrawal Agreement Act, the Government has made the following statutory instruments:

- The Competition SI (see paragraph 2.16 for further detail);
- The Implementation SI (see paragraph 2.17 for further detail); and
- the Consumer Protection EU Exit SIs (see paragraph 0 for further detail).

Key provisions of the Withdrawal Act (as amended by the Withdrawal Agreement Act)

2.7 The Withdrawal Act repealed the European Communities Act 1972 on Exit Day. However, the Withdrawal Agreement Act inserted a savings provision into the Withdrawal Act which preserves the effects of that Act for the duration of the Transition Period.[19] This means that directly applicable EU law, including the main treaty articles relevant for competition purposes (Articles 101 and 102 TFEU) and the main relevant EU regulations (such as EU Regulation 1/2003, EU block exemption Regulations[20] and the EU Merger Regulation (**EUMR**))[21] continue to apply in the UK until 31 December 2020.[22] After this date, as explained further in Sections 3 and 4 of this guidance, all such directly applicable EU law will no longer apply in the UK (except as specified in the Withdrawal Agreement).

2.8 Pursuant to section 3 of the Withdrawal Act (although subject to the exceptions contained in section 5 of the Withdrawal Act), directly effective EU legislation, including EU regulations, decisions and EU treaty articles,[23] so far as operative immediately before the end of the Transition Period, are brought across and will form part of the UK's domestic law.

2.9 Furthermore, under section 2 of the Withdrawal Act, UK domestic legislation which is EU-derived – including that enacted under section 2(2) of the European Communities Act in order to implement an EU directive – also continues to have effect in UK domestic law.

2.10 Following the end of the Transition Period, anything which continues to be, or forms part of, UK domestic legislation by virtue of sections 2 or 3 of the Withdrawal Act (see the two preceding paragraphs of this guidance) constitutes **'retained EU law'**.[24] Under section 8 of the Withdrawal Act, UK Ministers have the power to make statutory instruments to amend retained EU law with a view to preventing, remedying or mitigating (a) any failure of retained EU law to operate effectively, or (b) any other deficiency in retained EU law.[25] The Government used this power when it made the Competition SI on 22 January 2019 and the Consumer Protection SI on 6 February 2019,[26] which would have applied from Exit Day in the event that a withdrawal agreement had not been concluded.[27]

2.11 Under the Withdrawal Act, any question as to the validity, meaning or effect of unmodified retained EU law is to be decided, so far as they are relevant to it, in accordance with any case law or general principles of the CJEU laid down up until 31 December 2020.[28]

2.12 It is important to note that, under the Withdrawal Act, the UK Supreme Court and Scotland's High Court of Justiciary[29] are not bound by any retained EU case law.[30] As a result, after 31 December 2020, CJEU case law relating to unmodified retained EU law will have the same status in domestic courts and tribunals as existing decisions of the UK Supreme Court or High Court of Justiciary. However, the Withdrawal Agreement Act also amended section 6 of the Withdrawal Act in order to enable the Government to alter, and set out in regulations (after consultation), the circumstances in which specified UK courts and tribunals would not be bound by retained EU case law.[31] Subsequently, the Government laid before Parliament on 15 October 2020, the European Union (Withdrawal) Act 2018 (Relevant Court) (Retained EU Case Law) Regulations 2020, together with a draft explanatory memorandum. These regulations, once made, will extend the power to depart from retained EU case law after 31 December 2020, in the interpretation of retained EU law, to specified appellate domestic courts including the Court of Appeal.

2.13 With respect to Competition Act 1998 cases specifically, a new section 60A of the Competition Act 1998 provides that the CMA and UK Courts will be bound by an obligation to ensure consistency with EU competition case law that pre-dates the end of the Transition Period (see paragraphs 4.18 to 4.24 for further detail).[32] However, the CMA and UK courts may depart from this case law where it is considered appropriate in the light of certain specific circumstances as further discussed below.[33]

Key provisions of the Withdrawal Agreement Act

2.14 The Withdrawal Agreement Act ensures that domestic legislation implementing or referring to EU law still has effect in the UK for the duration of the Transition Period, in accordance with the Withdrawal Agreement.[34] For example, where there are references to the obligations on 'Member States' in CA98 and EA02, as a result of a provision in the Withdrawal Agreement Act, these references are to be read until the end of the Transition Period as though the UK were still a Member State.

2.15 In addition, the Withdrawal Agreement Act gives domestic legal effect to the provisions of the Withdrawal Agreement relating to matters other than the Transition Period. Where provisions of the Withdrawal Agreement need further implementation, it grants powers which can be used to make statutory instruments for this purpose. This allows, for example, for specific provision to be made in relation to competition cases ongoing at the end of the Transition Period.[35] The Government used this power to make the Implementation SI on 19 November 2020, which is designed to apply from 31 December 2020 and is further discussed below.

The Competition (Amendment etc.) (EU Exit) Regulations 2019

2.16 The Competition SI separates the UK and EU antitrust enforcement and merger control systems and makes provision for transition to a standalone UK competition regime. In particular, the Competition SI revokes EU competition regulations, certain European Commission decisions made under EU regulations and treaty rights that will be incorporated into UK law at the end of the Transition Period. It also amends the CA98, EA02, European block exemption Regulations and other legislation containing competition provisions, as appropriate. Further explanation of the Competition SI can be found in the Explanatory Memorandum accompanying the legislation.

The Competition (Amendment etc.) (EU Exit) Regulations 2020

2.17 The Implementation SI amends the Competition SI in order to give effect to the provisions in the Withdrawal Agreement that relate to competition law.[36] In particular, it gives effect in domestic legislation to the European Commission's continued competence over competition cases that were initiated but not concluded before the end of the Transition Period (**Continued Competence Cases**)[37]; and empowers the CMA (and concurrent regulators)[38] to monitor and enforce EU commitments or remedies that relate to the UK in cases where, after 31 December 2020, it is agreed between the EU and the UK that responsibility for these functions in respect of such commitments or remedies should be 'transferred' to the CMA or a concurrent regulator.[39] Further explanation of the Implementation SI can be found in Section 4 below, and in the Explanatory Memorandum accompanying the legislation.

The Consumer Protection EU Exit SIs

2.18 The Consumer Protection EU Exit SIs together amend the enforcement provisions in Part 8 of the EA02 (Part 8), and the investigatory powers in Schedule 5 to the Consumer Rights Act 2015 (**CRA**), to make them appropriate for a purely domestic consumer protection enforcement regime. In particular they revoke the Consumer Protection Co-operation (**CPC**) Regulation[40] and remove related powers in Part 8 and the CRA, to reflect the end of the UK's formal role in the EU consumer enforcement co-operation regime. They also change the nomenclature of certain infringements.

2.19 Further detail on what this new domestic legislation means in practice for merger control, competition and consumer law enforcement in the UK after 31 December 2020 is set out in this guidance.

NOTES

10 Articles 127(1) and (3), Withdrawal Agreement.

11 Article 127(3), Withdrawal Agreement.

12 Including, but not limited to, Articles 101, 102 and 106 of the TFEU, the EUMR, EU Regulation 1/2003, Regulation (EC) No 2006/2004 on Consumer Protection Cooperation and Council Directive 93/13/EEC on unfair terms in consumer contracts.

13 Article 131, Withdrawal Agreement.

14 Article 92(1), Withdrawal Agreement. For antitrust or cartel cases, as per Article 92(3)(b), Withdrawal Agreement, the European Commission can initiate proceedings at any point in time, but not later than the date:

- it issues a preliminary assessment (a Statement of Objections), or a request for parties to express their interest in engaging in settlement discussions, or
- on which the European Commission publishes the summary of the case and main content of the commitments or the notice of inapplicability of the EU prohibitions, but cases can be formally initiated early in the European Commission's investigatory process.

Formal initiation of proceedings is pursuant to Article 2(1) of Commission Regulation (EC) No 773/2004. Pursuant to Article 2(2) of Regulation (EC) 773/2004, the European Commission may make public the initiation of proceedings, but shall inform the parties concerned before doing so.

For merger cases, as per Article 92(3)(c) the European Commission is deemed to have initiated proceedings before the Transition Period in three circumstances:

- the merger has been notified to the European Commission in accordance with Article 1, 3 or 4 EUMR(subject to any initiated mergers referred to Member States after notification pursuant to Article 9 EUMR);
- the notifying parties have asked for the European Commission to examine a transaction that is capable of review under the national competition laws of at least three Member States and the 15 working day limit has expired without any of the Member States expressing an objection to their jurisdiction (pursuant to Article 4(5) EUMR); or
- the European Commission has accepted a reference from a Member State to examine the merger(pursuant to Article 22(3) EUMR).

15 Article 92, Withdrawal Agreement.

16 Articles 95(1) and 95(3), Withdrawal Agreement. It is important also to note that Article 86(1), Withdrawal Agreement provides that the CJEU will have exclusive jurisdiction in any proceedings brought by or against the UK before 31 December 2020, and Article 86(2), Withdrawal Agreement provides that the CJEU shall continue to have jurisdiction to give preliminary rulings on requests from courts and tribunals of the UK made before the end of the Transition Period.

17 Article 95(2), Withdrawal Agreement. Antitrust commitments can also be transferred to the concurrent regulators. Further details regarding the possible 'transfer' of commitments or remedies is set out in paragraphs 3.33 to 3.36 and 4.13 to 4.17 below.

18 Note that references in this guidance to the Withdrawal Act are to that Act as amended by the Withdrawal Agreement Act.

19 Section 1, Withdrawal Act. The European Communities Act 1972 was the principal piece of legislation passed by Parliament that gave effect to EU law in the UK. The Withdrawal Agreement Act modified the Withdrawal Act to include a saving provision that preserves the effect of the repealed European Communities Act 1972 until 31 December 2020. The Withdrawal Agreement Act also modifies certain parts of the European Communities Act 1972 to reflect the fact that the UK has left the EU, and that the UK's relationship with EU law during the Transition Period is determined by the UK's commitments in the Withdrawal Agreement, rather than as a Member State (see sections 1 and 2, Withdrawal Agreement Act).

20 See Annex B.

21 Council Regulation (EC) No 139/2004 of 20 January 2004 on the control of concentrations between undertakings, Official Journal L 24, 29.01.2004, p 1-22.

22 Note that UK consumer protection legislation enacted under section 2(2) of the European Communities Act 1972, which implements EU consumer law directives, remains in force notwithstanding the repeal of the European Communities Act 1972.

23 Including articles of the Treaty on European Union and articles of the TFEU.

24 For further information on the concept of 'retained EU law' under the Withdrawal Act, please refer to the public paper prepared by the House of Commons Library: <u>*The status of 'retained EU Law'*</u>

25 Section 8(1), Withdrawal Act.

26 Mentioned also in paragraph 2.6 above. A number of other consumer protection statutory instruments were also made.

27 It is important to note that the Withdrawal Agreement Act delayed the effect of these SIs until 31 December 2020. The Withdrawal Agreement Act also amended the powers granted to Ministers under section 8 of the Withdrawal Act (to make statutory instruments to amend retained EU law) to allow for the correction of any deficiencies arising as a result of or in connection with the end of the Transition Period or any other effect of the Withdrawal Agreement.

28 Pursuant to section 6 of the Withdrawal Act, this applies so far as retained EU law remains 'unmodified'. Where retained EU law has been modified on or after Exit Day it can be interpreted in accordance with CJEU case law and the general principles of EU law where that accords with the intention of the amendments (section 6(6) Withdrawal Act). Retained EU law can be modified only in a way prescribed under section 7, Withdrawal Act, as amended by Schedule 5(40), Withdrawal Agreement Act.

29 The highest criminal court in Scotland.

30 Section 6(4), Withdrawal Act and Withdrawal Act, Explanatory Notes, Section 6: Interpretation of retained EU law.

31 Sections 5A, 5B, 5C and 5D, Withdrawal Act (as introduced by section 26, Withdrawal Agreement Act).

32 Previously, section 60 of the Competition Act 1998 provided that the UK competition authorities and courts must, in as far as possible, interpret UK competition law in a manner that is consistent with EU competition law and must have regard to any decision or statement of the European Commission. Section 60 was amended to correct a deficiency pursuant to s.6(3) Withdrawal Act, in line with the position set out in s.6(6) Withdrawal Act. See the <u>Explanatory Memorandum</u> to the Competition SI for further detail.

33 Section 60A(7) CA98.

34 Section 1B, Withdrawal Act (as introduced by section 2, Withdrawal Agreement Act).

35 Section 7A, Withdrawal Act (as introduced by section 5, Withdrawal Agreement Act) and section 8B, Withdrawal Act (as introduced by section 18, Withdrawal Agreement Act).

36 The Implementation SI also replaces references in the Competition SI to 'exit day' with 'IP completion day' and amends savings and transitional provisions in the Competition SI so that they can operate from the end of the Transition Period.

37 As per Article 92 of the Withdrawal Agreement.

38 These are sectoral regulators with concurrent competition powers. They include the Civil Aviation Authority (air traffic control and airport operations), the Financial Conduct Authority (provision of financial services), NHS Improvement (health care England), Ofcom (telecoms, broadcasting, post and spectrum), Office of Rail and Road (rail), Ofgem (gas and electricity), Ofwat (water and sewerage), Payment Systems Regulator (participation in payment systems) and the Northern Ireland Authority for Utility Regulation (gas, electricity, water in Northern Ireland). For further information, please refer to Regulated Industries: Guidance on concurrent application of competition law to regulated industries: CMA10. References in the remainder of this guidance to the CMA should be read, where appropriate, as including concurrent regulators.

39 As per Article 95(2) of the Withdrawal Agreement.

40 The CPC Regulation having been converted to UK law under the Withdrawal Act.

3. MERGER CONTROL

[7.102]

3.1 Prior to EU Exit (and during the Transition Period), where a merger had a Community dimension, the European Commission had exclusive competence to review that merger within the EU, including with respect to its effects on any UK market or markets.[41] In such a situation, the CMA did not undertake its own competition assessment, except where all or part of the case was transferred under the referral provisions of the EUMR.

3.2 Save for cases subject to the terms of the Withdrawal Agreement (described in further detail in this section), following the end of the Transition Period, the European Commission's review of a merger will no longer cover the merger's effects within any UK market and mergers may be subject to review by both the CMA and the European Commission.

3.3 This section of the guidance explains how cases which are 'live' at the end of the Transition Period are to be treated under the terms of the Withdrawal Agreement and how existing CMA guidance should be read in the light of EU Exit.

CASE ALLOCATION AROUND 31 DECEMBER 2020

Cases where EUMR merger proceedings are initiated on or before 31 December 2020

3.4 Under the Withdrawal Agreement, the European Commission remains responsible for **EUMR merger proceedings** (ie mergers that meet the applicable thresholds to qualify for investigation by the European Commission) that have been initiated before the end of the Transition Period.[42] Consequently, the CMA, like other Member States, is not entitled to examine the merger (subject to a referral request to the CMA under Article 9 EUMR). An EUMR merger proceeding will be considered to have been **initiated** before the end of the Transition Period, where any of the following three steps occurred before the end of the Transition Period:[43]

- the merger has been notified to the European Commission in accordance with Article 1, 3 and 4 EUMR (subject to any initiated mergers referred to Member States after notification pursuant to Article 9 EUMR, as discussed in relation to the UK further below);
- the notifying parties have asked for the European Commission to examine a transaction that is capable of review under the national competition laws of at least three Member States and the 15 working day[44] limit has expired without any of the Member States expressing an objection to their jurisdiction (pursuant to Article 4(5) EUMR); or
- the European Commission has accepted a reference from a Member State to examine the merger (pursuant to Article 22 EUMR).

3.5 For cases where EUMR merger proceedings have been initiated before the end of the Transition Period, the CMA will continue to have access to relevant information and may be included in the corresponding Advisory Committee meetings (subject to the rules governing the UK's invitation to meetings of EU bodies set out in the Withdrawal Agreement).

3.6 Where a merger decision of the European Commission over a case initiated before the end of the Transition Period is annulled, in full or in part following an appeal, the CMA could assert jurisdiction from when it becomes clear that the UK elements of the merger would not be re-examined by the European Commission pursuant to Article 10(5) EUMR.[45] This is deemed to become clear when the European Commission publishes a decision or other document containing a decision to that effect, or from which a decision to that effect may reasonably be inferred, and the decision becomes final (ie is not capable of being appealed).

Cases where EUMR merger proceedings are not initiated prior to 31 December 2020

3.7 For mergers where EUMR merger proceedings are not initiated before the end of the Transition Period, the CMA is no longer prohibited by the EUMR from taking jurisdiction over the merger and UK national merger control law will apply.[46] This means that the CMA has jurisdiction to review the merger and its effects within the UK, if the UK jurisdictional requirements are met (see section 4 in the CMA's guidance on jurisdiction and procedure (CMA2)[47] and the CMA's guidance on changes to jurisdictional thresholds for UK merger control (CMA90)).

3.8 After 31 December 2020, therefore, the CMA may formally investigate mergers notified to the CMA by merging parties or identified by the CMA's mergers intelligence function, where EUMR merger proceedings have not been initiated by 31 December 2020. The CMA's standard approach to calling in cases as described in the Guidance on the CMA's mergers intelligence function (CMA56) will apply to such cases.[48]

3.9 Although the UK merger control regime is voluntary (and therefore there is no obligation to notify a merger), merging parties involved in a transaction that could be subject to review around the end of the Transition Period are encouraged to engage with the CMA at an early stage, particularly where the transaction may raise potential competition concerns in the UK.[49] Not notifying a merger to the CMA raises certain risks for merging parties (described in more detail in CMA2), which will apply equally to cases where EUMR merger proceedings are not initiated before the end of the Transition Period. In particular, the CMA may issue initial enforcement orders in relation to completed mergers (including completed mergers which were notified to the European Commission after the end of the Transition Period and were subsequently cleared and completed).[50]

3.10 If merging parties decide to complete such mergers without notifying the CMA, there is a risk that the CMA could subsequently investigate and ultimately prohibit the merger or require other remedies to resolve competition concerns that could arise.

Pre-notification referral to the CMA from the European Commission (Article 4(4) EUMR)

3.11 Article 4(4) EUMR allows merging parties to inform the European Commission by means of a reasoned submission (**Form RS**) prior to notification that they consider the whole or part of an EU merger proceeding (and would therefore otherwise be reviewed by the European Commission under the EUMR) should be referred to a Member State (or Member States) that is better placed to review the transaction.

3.12 Where the European Commission receives a Form RS that such a merger should be reviewed by a Member State, the European Commission shall transmit that submission to the Member State's National Competition Authorities (**NCAs**). Pursuant to Article 4(4) EUMR, the NCAs have 15 working days to express their agreement or disagreement with the request. The European Commission must take a final decision within 25 working days of receiving the Form RS as to whether the conditions for the request are met and whether it is willing to relinquish jurisdiction over the case. The European Commission will thereafter inform the Member States and the merging parties of its decision.[51]

3.13 Where, before 31 December 2020, such a request is made for the CMA to review the merger and the CMA does not disagree with the request, the European Commission may decide to refer whole or part of the case to the CMA.

3.14 After 31 December 2020, merging parties are not able to make a reasoned submission under Article 4(4) EUMR that a merger that meets the EUMR thresholds should be referred to the CMA.

Post-notification referral from the European Commission to the CMA (Article 9 EUMR)

3.15 Where a merger is notified to the European Commission before 31 December 2020, the European Commission is required, under Article 4(5) EUMR, to provide a copy of the Form CO notifying the merger to the CMA. Under Article 9 EUMR, the CMA may, within 15 working days of receipt of the Form CO, request that the whole or part of a merger be referred to the CMA for consideration under the EA02, if the merger:

- threatens to affect significantly competition in a market within the UK which presents all the characteristics of a distinct market (Article 9(2)(a)); or
- affects competition in a market within the UK which presents all the characteristics of a distinct market and which does not constitute a substantial part of the common market (Article 9(2)(b)).

3.16 As the EUMR will continue to apply to cases notified to the European Commission before 31 December 2020, the CMA is able to make an Article 9 request after 31 December 2020 for such cases (subject to the 15 working day limit after the CMA's receipt of the Form CO).

3.17 The European Commission will inform the CMA and the notifying parties of its decision within 35 working days from notification of the merger or within 65 working days of such notification if the European Commission considers the merger raises serious doubts as to its compatibility with the internal market.[52]

3.18 If the request under Article 9 EUMR is accepted by the European Commission, the CMA will gain jurisdiction to review the merger. Section 34A EA02 requires that the CMA make its decision on whether or not to refer the merger for a phase 2 investigation (absent undertakings in lieu of a reference) within 45 working days beginning on the working day after the Article 9 referral decision is taken by the European Commission. If a request for a referral to the CMA is rejected by the European Commission, then the European Commission will retain jurisdiction to review the case.

Pre-notification referral from the CMA to the European Commission (Article 4(5) EUMR)

3.19 Under Article 4(5) of the EUMR, parties to a concentration that does not meet the EUMR thresholds but is capable of being reviewed under the national merger control laws of at least three Member States may, prior to notification, request that the transaction be examined by the European Commission under the 'one stop shop' principle. Transactions are deemed 'capable of being reviewed' in the UK if they meet either the share of supply or turnover test under the EA02.

3.20 Under the terms of the EUMR, any Member State competent to examine the concentration under its national competition law may, within 15 working days of receiving the request, express its

Part 7 Brexit-related Materials

disagreement to the European Commission taking jurisdiction over the merger. Where one Member State disagrees, the European Commission will not gain jurisdiction.

3.21 Where the time limit of 15 working days expires before 31 December 2020 without any Member State competent to examine the concentration under its national competition law expressing its disagreement, the European Commission will gain exclusive jurisdiction over the merger. Where that time limit has not expired before 31 December 2020 or a competent Member State has indicated it does not agree with the request, the CMA will be able to assert jurisdiction over that merger. After 31 December 2020, merging parties cannot make an Article 4(5) request to the European Commission on the basis of the CMA having jurisdiction over the merger (ie that the merger would otherwise be capable of review in the UK).

Post-notification referral from the CMA to the European Commission (Article 22 EUMR)

3.22 Under Article 22 of the EUMR, the CMA may singularly or jointly with other NCAs make a request that the European Commission review a merger that does not meet the EUMR thresholds where it affects trade between Member States and threatens to significantly affect competition within the territory of the Member State or States making the request.

3.23 Article 22 of the EUMR stipulates that the European Commission must inform Member States without delay of the receipt of the initial request. Member States have 15 working days to decide whether to join the request. The European Commission has 25 working days after all the Member States have received the initial request from the European Commission to make its decision on referral. If the European Commission has not adopted a decision with that 25-working day period, then the European Commission is deemed to have accepted jurisdiction.

3.24 Where the European Commission has, by 31 December 2020, accepted or can be deemed to have accepted a referral request from the CMA (whether that request is initiated or subsequently joined by the CMA) under Article 22 EUMR, the European Commission will retain exclusive jurisdiction to review the effects of that merger in the UK until it reaches a final decision. However, if the European Commission has not accepted, or cannot be deemed to have accepted, a referral request initiated or joined by the CMA under Article 22 EUMR by 31 December 2020, the CMA will be able to exert jurisdiction in respect of that merger after 31 December 2020 (assuming that the UK jurisdictional thresholds are met). Further, if the CMA did not join a referral request made by one or more Member States, the CMA would retain jurisdiction over the case (assuming that the UK jurisdictional thresholds are met).

3.25 After 31 December 2020, the CMA is not able to make or join a request under Article 22 EUMR that a case that does not meet the EUMR thresholds should be referred to the European Commission.

Cases being reviewed by the CMA after 31 December 2020

3.26 The CMA does not envisage that there will be any change in the procedure followed for cases that fall under UK jurisdiction in which investigations are opened before 31 December 2020. In particular, if a merger was referred to the CMA by the European Commission under the EUMR before 31 December 2020, it will progress according to a 45 EU working day timetable.[53]

'Public interest' cases

3.27 For cases where EUMR merger proceedings are initiated before 31 December 2020, the Secretary of State may intervene on public interest grounds[54] in cases falling for consideration under the EUMR through the use of Article 21(4) EUMR.[55]

3.28 Article 21 is invoked by means of the Secretary of State giving the CMA a European Intervention Notice (**EIN**) under section 67 EA02.[56] In this situation, the European Commission will examine, or continue to examine, the merger on competition grounds in the normal way, but the Secretary of State is able to make a decision on public interest grounds.[57] There is no competition assessment by the CMA in such cases.

3.29 The EIN requires the CMA to advise the Secretary of State on the considerations relevant to the making of a reference under section 22 or 33 EA02 which are relevant to the decision on whether to make a reference to phase 2.

3.30 When an EIN has been issued, the CMA will publish an invitation to comment seeking third party views on the public interest issues (but not on competition issues). The CMA's advice must contain a summary of any representations received from third parties that relate to the public interest considerations specified in the EIN.

3.31 The Secretary of State may make a reference for a phase 2 investigation if he or she believes that it is or may be the case that, taking account only of the public interest consideration, the creation of the European relevant merger situation operates or may be expected to operate against the public interest.

3.32 If the Secretary of State issues an EIN for a case where an EUMR merger proceeding is not initiated before 31 December 2020, the EIN shall be treated as a public interest intervention notice (**PIIN**) issued under section 42 EA02 after 31 December 2020. PIINs are described in more detail in CMA2. The Secretary of State is unable to issue EINs for a case where an EUMR merger proceeding is initiated after 31 December 2020, but instead would issue a PIIN provided the grounds for doing so were met.

TRANSFER OF EU MERGER COMMITMENTS

Commitments accepted by the European Commission before 31 December 2020

3.33 The Withdrawal Agreement provides that, after 31 December 2020, the European Commission will continue to be competent for the monitoring and enforcement of any UK elements of commitments given in connection with decided EU merger cases. This includes commitments given after 31 December 2020 in Continued Competence Cases. However, the Withdrawal Agreement provides an option to transfer responsibility for monitoring and enforcing the UK elements of the commitments to the CMA by mutual agreement between the European Commission and the CMA.[58]

3.34 Where the CMA and the European Commission agree to such a transfer of commitments, the CMA will be responsible for the monitoring and enforcement of those commitments (**transferred EU merger commitments**).[59]

3.35 The CMA must monitor whether transferred EU merger commitments are being, or have been, complied with by the addressees of those commitments. The CMA has the power to issue a notice requiring a person to provide information or documents, or to give evidence as a witness (under section 109 EA02) to assist the CMA with monitoring and enforcing transferred EU merger commitments.[60] The notice may specify or describe the documents and/or information that the CMA requires, and set out the offences and/or sanctions that may apply if the recipient does not comply.[61]

3.36 The CMA can enforce transferred EU merger commitments by bringing civil proceedings for an injunction or issuing directions (as discussed below). The rights of the CMA are not affected by any provisions of a transferred EU merger commitment which requires disputes to be resolved by arbitration.[62]

CMA's powers to issue directions

3.37 The CMA may issue directions in relation to the transferred EU merger commitments to:[63]

- take such action as may be specified or described in the directions for the purpose of carrying out, or ensuring compliance with, the transferred EU merger commitment concerned; or
- do, or refrain from doing, anything so specified or described which the relevant party is required by that commitment to do or refrain from doing.

3.38 The CMA has the power to vary or revoke any directions that it has issued.[64]

3.39 The CMA assesses the nature of breaches to assess the appropriate response, including whether to issue directions, by reference to a number of factors including:

- the significance of the breach;
- the actions taken by the firm to address the breach;
- recidivism and previous conduct;
- the need for the CMA to take action to address the breach; and
- contextual factors, such as the status and age of the remedy.

3.40 Where a person has failed to comply with a transferred EU merger commitment or any directions given by the CMA, the CMA may apply to the court[65] for an order requiring compliance with the direction or otherwise remedying the failure, within such a time as may be specified in the order.[66]

EUMR MERGER PROCEEDINGS INITIATED AFTER 31 DECEMBER 2020

3.41 The CMA will cease to be a competent authority of a Member State for the purposes of the EUMR in respect of EUMR merger proceedings that are initiated after 31 December 2020. Therefore, the CMA will no longer be prohibited from investigating a merger that is being reviewed by the European Commission under the provisions of the EA02.

3.42 As noted above, mergers may be subject to review by both the CMA and the European Commission after 31 December 2020.

3.43 The CMA and the European Commission (and/or any Member State(s) which may have jurisdiction where a merger does not trigger the EUMR thresholds) may therefore conduct parallel reviews of the same merger in their respective jurisdictions.

3.44 Where mergers are subject to investigation in more than one country, there can be substantial benefits to the parties and to the competition authorities in those jurisdictions from encouraging communication and cooperation between the competition authorities. This will be particularly important after 31 December 2020, as a significant proportion of mergers that will fall under UK jurisdiction will be investigated in parallel by the European Commission and other jurisdictions. Where possible and appropriate, the CMA will endeavour to coordinate merger reviews relating to the same or related cases with the European Commission as with other competition authorities.[67] Where national legislation prevents the exchange of confidential information, the CMA and other competition authorities may seek permission from the parties to exchange confidential information.

CMA MERGER CONTROL GUIDANCE AFTER 31 DECEMBER 2020

3.45 A number of CMA merger guidance documents do not contain any references to EU law or bodies and will thus be largely or wholly unaffected by EU Exit. Such guidance documents are listed at Annex A to this guidance. Some CMA merger guidance documents, published before this guidance, that contain references to EU law or bodies may remain in force after EU Exit. Where there is any difference between this guidance and the earlier documents, this guidance will take precedence. By way of illustration, at the time of this guidance being published, the following general clarifications should be considered when reading such guidance (until such time that it is updated):[68]

- References to referral mechanisms no longer apply (see e.g. 6.45 and 6.64 of CMA2[69] and 2.2 in a Quick guide to UK merger assessment: CMA18).
- References to the public interest intervention in cases under the EUMR should be read with this guidance in mind (see e.g. 16.16 to 16.22 of CMA2[70] and the section in Merger assessment guidelines: CC2/OFT1254).[71]

- Descriptions of the EUMR process should be read with this guidance in mind (see e.g. 2.12 to 2.15 and Chapter 18 of CMA2[72] and references in Water and sewerage mergers: CMA49).

NOTES

41 Article 21(3), EUMR.

42 Article 92(1), Withdrawal Agreement.

43 Before restructuring the transaction after EUMR merger proceedings have been initiated, parties should consider the potential effect on jurisdiction and are encouraged to discuss this with the CMA.

44 References to 'working days' under EUMR procedure means all days other than Saturdays, Sundays and European Commission holidays as published in the Official Journal of the European Union.

45 Regulation 45 of the Implementation SI inserting paragraph 19A to Part 7 of Schedule 4 to the Competition SI.

46 Where a merger is not notified to the European Commission before the end of the Transition Period, but the relevant date for establishing European Union jurisdiction (in accordance with EU law) has arisen before the end of the Transition Period, the merger parties should consult the European Commission as regards the treatment of UK turnover in determining whether the EUMR jurisdictional thresholds are met.

47 Please note that at the time of publishing this guidance a revised version of CMA2 is under consultation (see consultation page for further details) and is expected to be adopted before 31 December 2020.

48 Please note that at the time of publishing this guidance a revised version of CMA56 is under consultation (see consultation page for further details) and is expected to be adopted before 31 December 2020.

49 The CMA's case team will be able to advise, among other matters, on steps that could potentially be taken to expedite the preparation of a draft Merger Notice in anticipation of the CMA gaining jurisdiction after 31 December 2020. This may include discussion and review of the Form CO or other submissions made to the European Commission, for which purpose the parties may wish to share such information with the CMA and consent to its use by the CMA in the event of the CMA opening an investigation after 31 December 2020.

50 An initial enforcement order is binding on the parties and is intended to prevent any action which might prejudice the CMA's inquiry or impede the taking of any remedial action by the CMA. The CMA's standard practice is set out in the Guidance on initial enforcement orders and derogations in merger investigations (CMA60).

51 If the European Commission does not take a decision within this period, it is deemed to have adopted a decision to refer the case in accordance with the Form RS.

52 If the European Commission does not take a decision within this 65 working day period following a request despite a reminder from the CMA, nor taken such preparatory steps, it is deemed to have adopted a decision to refer the case to the UK (Article 9(5) EUMR).

53 The CMA has, under section 34A EA02, a maximum of 45 working days beginning on the working day after receipt of the European Commission's referral decision to inform the merging parties of the result of its preliminary competition assessment.

54 See sections 58(2) and 67 EA02.

55 See also *The Enterprise Act 2002 (Protection of Legitimate Interests) Order* SI 2003/1592.

56 See also *The Enterprise Act 2002 (Protection of Legitimate Interests)* Order SI 2003/1592.

57 See, for example, the EINs issued in relation to the Anticipated acquisition by The General Electric Company of Smiths Aerospace (2007); the Anticipated acquisition of British Sky Broadcasting PLC by News Corporation (2010–2011); and the Anticipated acquisition by Twenty-First Century Fox, Inc of Sky PLC (2017–2018); Anticipated acquisition by Advent International Corporation of Cobham Plc (2019).

58 Article 95(2), Withdrawal Agreement.

59 Regulation 8 of the Implementation SI inserting section 95A EA02.

60 Regulation 9 of the Implementation SI inserting section 109A EA02.

61 The penalties for failure to comply with a section 109 request are set out in Administrative penalties: Statement of Policy on the CMA's approach (CMA4).

62 Regulation 8 of the Implementation SI inserting section 95A(4) EA02.

63 Regulation 8 of the Implementation SI inserting section 95B EA02

64 Regulation 8 of the Implementation SI inserting section 95B(3) EA02.

65 From the High Court of England and Wales or Northern Ireland, the Court of Session in Scotland.

66 Regulation 8 of the Implementation SI inserting sections 95B(5), 95B(6) and 95A(7) EA02.

67 See paragraph 3.56 of the CMA Merger remedies guidance (CMA87).

68 Note that these are examples of general principles to assist with reading CMA guidance considering the UK's Exit from the EU and may not apply in all instances. This list is not exhaustive and must be read considering this guidance in its entirety and any updates made to CMA guidance.

69 Please note that at the time of publishing this guidance a revised version of CMA2 is under consultation (see consultation page for further details) and is expected to be adopted before 31 December 2020. It is proposed to remove the references to the EU law or bodies that are contained in the current guidance.

70 See FN69 above.

71 Please note that at the time of publishing this guidance a revised version of the CMA's Merger assessment guidelines (CC2/OFT1254) is under consultation (see consultation page for further details). It is proposed to remove the references to the EU law or bodies that are contained in the current guidance

72 See FN69 above.

4. ENFORCEMENT OF THE COMPETITION LAW PROHIBITIONS ('ANTITRUST', INCLUDING CARTELS)

CASES INITIATED BY THE EUROPEAN COMMISSION BEFORE 31 DECEMBER 2020

[7.103]

4.1 Under the Withdrawal Agreement, the European Commission continues to be competent for antitrust cases in the UK which it has initiated under EU Regulation 1/2003 before 31 December 2020, also referred to as Continued Competence Cases.[73]

4.2 After 31 December 2020, EU Regulation 1/2003, which deals with parallel jurisdiction over competition cases between the European Commission and the competition authorities of the Member States of the EU, ceases to apply to the UK as a result of the Transition Period coming to an end, except as specified in the Withdrawal Agreement. The Withdrawal Agreement and the Implementation SI make provision for how the UK elements of Continued Competence Cases are to be dealt with in terms of jurisdiction between the UK and the EU.[74]

4.3 For Continued Competence Cases, the CMA will continue to have access to relevant information from the European Commission and will continue to be able to assist the European Commission with its UK-specific expertise, including when invited to the corresponding Advisory Committee meetings (subject to the rules governing the UK's invitation to meetings of EU bodies set out in the Withdrawal Agreement).[75] After the end of the Transition Period, where the European Commission has ordered an Article 20 inspection, an Article 21 inspection, or an Article 22(2) inspection,[76] Part 2 of CA98 (which makes provision for the CMA to assist, or act on behalf of, the European Commission in connection with European Commission investigations relating to Articles 101 and 102 TFEU) continues to have effect despite its repeal by the Competition SI.[77]

4.4 Pursuant to the Competition SI (as amended by the Implementation SI), the CMA may not open or re-open an investigation into competition concerns which are the subject of a Continued Competence Case. Therefore, the position with respect to Continued Competence Cases is essentially the same as when the UK was still an EU Member State: the CMA may not investigate the same conduct or agreement that is already the subject of a formally initiated investigation by the European Commission until the European Commission has concluded that investigation.

4.5 Once the European Commission has concluded its investigation and issued a decision in relation to a Continued Competence Case (ie after the end of the Transition Period), and the decision has not been annulled in full or in part, the CMA may not accept commitments or give directions in relation to conduct which is the subject of the European Commission decision which conflict with any commitments or directions made binding under the European Commission's decision.[78] The same applies to investigations concluded by the European Commission in respect of which it issued its decision before 31 December 2020.[79]

CMA'S ENFORCEMENT IN RELATION TO CONTINUED COMPETENCE CASES

4.6 After 31 December 2020, the CMA may open an investigation into competition concerns which are the subject of a European Commission Continued Competence Case in so far as those concerns relate to effects arising from conduct **after** 31 December 2020.[80] In such circumstances, if the agreements or conduct under investigation may affect trade within the UK and are ongoing as at 31 December 2020, the CMA may investigate facts from that date onwards. Therefore, businesses that are participating in alleged infringements that are being investigated by the European Commission and that have not been brought to an end by 31 December 2020 are at risk of the CMA opening a parallel investigation into the effects of such alleged infringements as they exist following that date.

4.7 In deciding whether or not to open or continue with such a case, the CMA will have regard to its published prioritisation principles as applicable at the relevant time and, in doing so, will have regard to the consideration of whether a separate CMA investigation is needed to protect consumers, businesses or the economy in the United Kingdom. The CMA would also typically expect to liaise with the European Commission as it would with other competition authorities in the context of parallel investigations.

'LIVE' CMA ANTITRUST INVESTIGATIONS

4.8 When the CMA is investigating conduct that may affect trade between the UK and one or more EU Member States and has not issued a decision before 31 December 2020 and the case proceeds, it will no longer apply the EU prohibitions after 31 December 2020. All actions taken before 31 December 2020 in connection with the EU elements of the investigation – such as information gathering through notices, interviews or inspections – will be treated, after that date, as having been done for the purposes of the domestic elements of the investigation.[81] Such actions therefore remain valid for such purposes.

NEW CMA ANTITRUST INVESTIGATIONS AFTER 31 DECEMBER 2020

4.9 After 31 December 2020, the CMA will only investigate suspected infringements of UK domestic competition law (ie the Chapter I and Chapter II prohibitions in CA98 (the **UK Prohibitions**)) in relation to conduct from both before and after 31 December 2020.

4.10 The CMA will no longer be subject to EU Regulation 1/2003. Therefore, anti-competitive behaviour may be subject to separate investigations by the CMA and the European Commission where it may affect both trade within the UK and trade between EU Member States, respectively.[82] The factors discussed in paragraph 4.7 above are equally relevant to the question of whether to commence such a separate investigation in parallel with a European Commission investigation started after the end of the Transition Period.

4.11 Except in relation to Continued Competence Cases (as discussed above in paragraph 4.2), Part 2 of CA98 ceases to have effect.

4.12 As explained below, the CMA, concurrent regulators and the UK courts will still be required to ensure consistency between the interpretation of the UK Prohibitions and CJEU case law pre-dating 31 December 2020, but they may depart from such case law where appropriate in certain specified circumstances.

TRANSFER OF EU ANTITRUST COMMITMENTS AND REMEDIES

4.13 The Withdrawal Agreement provides that, after 31 December 2020, the European Commission will continue to be competent to monitor and enforce commitments given or remedies imposed in or in relation to the UK in connection with EU antitrust cases. This includes commitments given or remedies imposed after 31 December 2020 in Continued Competence Cases. However, under the Withdrawal Agreement, the European Commission may transfer responsibility for monitoring and enforcing such commitments or remedies in the UK to the CMA and the concurrent regulators by mutual agreement between the European Commission and the CMA (or the relevant concurrent regulator, where applicable).[83]

4.14 Where the CMA and the European Commission agree to such a transfer of commitments or remedies, the CMA will obtain responsibility for the monitoring and enforcement of the transferred EU antitrust commitments and/or transferred EU antitrust directions.[84]

4.15 For the purposes of monitoring compliance with transferred EU antitrust commitments and/or transferred EU antitrust directions and deciding whether to make an application to enforce such commitments and/or directions, the CMA has the power to require any person to provide specified information and documents[85].[86] The CMA may exercise this by a notice in writing, which will set out the commitments and/or directions to which the notice relates, specify or describe the documents and/or information that the CMA requires, and set out the sanctions that may apply if the recipient does not comply. The request may also give details of where and when the documents and/or information must be produced.[87]

4.16 The CMA can fine any person who fails, without reasonable excuse, to comply with a formal information request.[88]

4.17 In the event of non-compliance with transferred commitments or directions, the CMA may apply to court for an order requiring the defaulter to rectify the default, including taking any action necessary to ensure compliance.[89] Depending on the circumstances of the case, non-compliance may also give rise to a potential new infringement of the UK Prohibitions. The CMA may therefore also consider opening a new antitrust investigation under section 25 of CA98 in case of such non-compliance.

CONSIDERATION OF EU LAW PRINCIPLES

Section 60A CA98

4.18 Before 31 December 2020, section 60 of the CA98 provided that, so far as possible, the CMA, concurrent regulators and the UK courts are to interpret the UK Prohibitions in a manner that is consistent with the principles of the TFEU and the decisions and principles laid down by the CJEU in relation to the EU prohibitions. Regard was also to be had to any 'relevant decision or statement' of the European Commission.

4.19 The Competition SI repeals section 60 CA98 and replaces it with a new provision, section 60A.

4.20 Under section 60A, the default position will remain that the CMA, concurrent regulators and the UK courts[90] must act with a view to securing that there is no inconsistency between:

(i) the principles that they apply, and the decisions they reach, in determining a question arising under Part 1 of CA98 in relation to competition within the UK; and

(ii) the principles laid down by the TFEU and the CJEU before the end of the Transition Period, and any relevant decision made by that Court before the end of the Transition Period, so far as applicable immediately before the end of the Transition Period in determining any corresponding question arising in EU law.[91]

4.21 In determining any such question, they must also have regard to any relevant decision or statement of the European Commission made before the end of the Transition Period and not withdrawn.

4.22 However, section 60A allows the CMA, concurrent regulators and the UK courts to depart from the principles of the TFEU and CJEU case law pre-dating the end of the Transition Period where they consider it 'appropriate' to do so, in light of one of the following prescribed factors:

(i) differences between the provisions of Part I of the CA98 (including the UK Prohibitions) and the corresponding provisions of EU law as those provisions of EU law had effect immediately before the end of the Transition Period;

(ii) differences between markets in the United Kingdom and markets in the European Union;

(iii) developments in forms of economic activity since the time the principle or decision was laid down or made;

(iv) generally accepted principles of competition analysis or a generally accepted application of such principles;

(v) a principle laid down or a decision made by the CJEU after the end of the Transition Period; and

(vi) the particular circumstances under consideration.[92]

4.23 In addition, the CMA, concurrent regulators and the UK courts will not be required to act with a view to securing that there is no inconsistency between the principles they apply or decisions they reach and TFEU or CJEU principles or decisions pre-dating the end of the Transition Period where they are bound by a principle or decision of a court or tribunal in England and Wales, Scotland or Northern Ireland that requires them to act otherwise.[93]

4.24 Section 60A applies to all cases from 31 December 2020 onwards, ie it will apply to any CMA or concurrent regulator investigations or UK court cases which are 'live' on 31 December 2020 and in relation to facts pre-dating that date.[94]

CONTINUED APPLICATION OF OTHER DOMESTIC LEGISLATION AND PROCEDURE

CMA leniency regime

4.25 The leniency regimes of the European Commission, the CMA and the national competition authorities of the Member States will remain separate and each jurisdiction should be considered individually. The fact that a party has made a leniency application to the European Commission whether before or after the end of the Transition Period will not provide it with any protection from fines with respect to any UK investigation under the CA98. Nor will such an application provide its employees or directors with any protection from prosecution for the criminal cartel offence and/or director disqualification proceedings in relation to that cartel activity in the UK. As was the case before EU Exit and during the Transition Period, when considering whether to make a leniency application to the European Commission, parties are encouraged to consider whether it would also be appropriate to make such an application to the CMA[95] and vice versa. Following the end of the Transition Period, this will be even more important than before given the possibility of parallel investigations by the European Commission and the CMA or a concurrent regulator.

4.26 Before the end of the Transition Period, and as set out in the CMA's Applications for leniency and no action in cartel cases guidance (OFT1495), it has been possible for parties applying for leniency to the European Commission to obtain a marker from the CMA on a 'no names' basis pending confirmation from the European Commission as to the availability of immunity under the European Commission's leniency policy.[96] However, following the end of the Transition Period 'Commission immunity application' cases will be treated in the same way as other cases, meaning that a strong justification will be needed for obtaining a 'no names' marker.[97]

4.27 As the CMA will no longer be a member of the European Competition Network (**ECN**), the ECN Model Leniency Programme will no longer apply and thus summary applications to the CMA in 'European Commission immunity application' cases will also no longer be available.[98] Similarly, where an undertaking has qualified for immunity under the European Commission Leniency Notice after the end of the Transition Period but has not also qualified for Type A immunity in the UK, for example because another undertaking has already qualified for Type A leniency in the UK, it will no longer be the case that the CMA can be expected 'normally' to grant no action letters to the implicated employees and directors of that undertaking.[99] In addition, references in the CMA's Applications for leniency and no action in cartel cases guidance (OFT1495) to the European Commission Notice on cooperation within the Network of Competition Authorities will no longer be relevant.

Company director disqualification orders (CDOs) in competition cases

4.28 The disqualification of directors for infringements of competition law is set out under domestic legislation – namely, under section 9A of the Company Directors Disqualification Act 1986 (**CDDA**) – and for the most part will not be affected by EU Exit. The main change to the provisions dealing with director disqualification for competition law infringements is that references to breaches of the EU prohibitions are removed from the meaning of a breach of competition law for which a director can be disqualified.[100] The CMA guidance on director disqualification (Guidance on Competition Disqualification Orders (CMA102)) also contains references to EU law which will no longer be relevant to competition law infringements following the end of the Transition Period.

4.29 The CMA and concurrent regulators will continue to be able to rely on conduct found to have infringed the EU prohibitions (in addition to the UK Prohibitions) before the end of the Transition Period for the purposes of making an application for a director disqualification order under section 9A of the CDDA.[101]

4.30 For conduct which occurs after the end of the Transition Period, the CMA and concurrent regulators can continue to make applications for director disqualification orders under section 9A of the CDDA. However, they will be able to do so on the basis of an infringement of the UK Prohibitions only.

RETAINED EU LAW

EU block exemption Regulations

4.31 The Withdrawal Act and the Competition SI preserve the EU block exemption Regulations in the UK as 'retained exemptions'.[102]

4.32 This means that, after 31 December 2020, the retained exemptions will operate as exemptions from UK Prohibitions (as covered by section 10 CA98). Beneficiaries of the EU block exemption Regulations and the 'parallel exemptions' before 31 December 2020 will continue to benefit from the EU block exemption Regulations as incorporated into domestic law after that date (and so long as they continue to comply with the retained exemptions).[103] The power to vary (including to extend) or revoke the application of the retained exemptions to the UK Prohibitions will lie with the Secretary of State, acting in consultation with the CMA.[104]

4.33 In addition, going forward, companies entering into new agreements after 31 December 2020 will also be able to benefit from the retained exemptions provided they meet the relevant criteria.

4.34 There are seven EU block exemption Regulations which will become retained exemptions when the Transition Period comes to an end (**Retained Block Exemption Regulations**).[105] These relate to vertical agreements, motor vehicles, research and development, technology transfers, specialisation, liner shipping consortia, and road, rail and inland waterway transport. Details of these Retained Block Exemption Regulations can be found at Annex B to this guidance. The Competition SI however makes various amendments to the Retained Block Exemption Regulations to correct deficiencies resulting from the UK ceasing to be a Member State of the EU.[106] For example, references to EU Treaties and institutions will change to references to domestic legislation and references to Euros will be changed to Pounds Sterling. References to the internal market will also be changed to references to the UK, which will impact the geographic scope of these Regulations, e.g. the liner shipping Retained Block Exemption Regulation will apply to consortia only in so far as they provide international liner shipping services from or to one or more ports *in the UK*.[107]

4.35 Geographic scope is also relevant to certain provisions of some of the Retained Block Exemption Regulations, and in particular the concept of the restriction of 'passive sales'. For example, under the EU Vertical Block Exemption Regulation,[108] vertical agreements which have as their object the restriction of passive sales into an exclusive territory or customer group reserved to the supplier or allocated to another buyer are regarded as hardcore restrictions and are likely to infringe Article 101(1) (and the Chapter I prohibition) since such restrictions confer 'absolute territorial protection'.[109] In certain circumstances, passive sales bans affecting sales to a UK market or UK customer are capable of falling within the scope of the Chapter I prohibition. They may not satisfy the requirements of the Retained Vertical Agreements Block Exemption Regulation and may be treated as hardcore restrictions of competition.[110]

4.36 The guidance issued by the European Commission in relation to the EU block exemption Regulations which will become Retained Block Exemption Regulations will be relevant to interpreting the latter. Details of this guidance can be found at Annex B. Such guidance constitutes relevant statements of the European Commission to which the CMA, concurrent regulators and UK courts must have regard after 31 December 2020.[111] However, the guidance should be read with EU Exit and the amendments made by the Competition SI in mind.

APPLICATION OF OTHER GUIDANCE RELEVANT TO ANTITRUST CASES

4.37 A large body of CMA antitrust guidance documents do not contain any references to EU law or bodies and will thus be largely or wholly unaffected by EU Exit. Such guidance documents are listed at Annex A to this guidance. In relation to CMA antitrust guidance published before this guidance which is impacted by EU Exit, this guidance should prevail in relation to the specific references to EU law or bodies. By way of illustration, the following general clarifications should be considered when reading such guidance following the end of the Transition Period (until such time that it is updated):[112]

- As a result of EU Exit, certain changes will be needed to the CMA's guidance as to the appropriate amount of a penalty (CMA73). Amendments to this guidance will be consulted upon in due course and, once finalised, will be published subject to Secretary of State approval. Until such time as the CMA has published revised CMA73 guidance, we will interpret it within the appropriate context of the UK having left the European Union.
- Unless stated otherwise, references to the EU prohibitions throughout the CMA's antitrust guidance will no longer be relevant to the UK's competition enforcement regime after the end of the Transition Period. Where CMA guidance refers to either or both of the EU prohibitions together with the UK Prohibitions, after the end of the Transition Period it should be read as only referring to either or both of the UK Prohibitions as applicable.[113] Similarly, references to Article 101(3) should be read as references to section 9(1) of CA98 (or ignored where they are duplicative of references to section 9(1) CA98).
- References to the Block Exemption Regulations should be read as references to the relevant Retained Block Exemption Regulations, as amended by the Competition SI and any future amendments.
- References to section 60 CA98 and to the primacy of EU law should be read with the new section 60A CA98 in mind.
- Sections in CMA's antitrust guidance on the CMA's relationship and/or co-operation with the European Commission and other NCAs, such as those in OFT401 Part 4, OFT402 Part 3 and OFT442, among others, will generally no longer be relevant. Similarly, references to the Modernisation Regime, throughout the CMA's antitrust guidance and in particular in OFT442, will generally no longer be relevant, given the CMA (and concurrent regulators) will no longer be enforcing the EU prohibitions. However, this is not to say such guidance ought to be ignored in its entirety; for example, discussion of the exemption regime may still be informative in relation to the UK exemption regime under section 9(1)CA98.
- References to the ability to bring standalone actions and actions for damages, such as in OFT401 Part 7, OFT402 Part 2, OFT408 Part 8 and others, and in particular in CMA55, will no longer be entirely accurate. Decisions by the European Commission reached before 31 December 2020, as well as decisions by the European Commission in respect of Continued Competence Cases, can still form the basis of follow-on damages claims, including cases that have not exhausted the appeals process. However, claimants who wish to pursue follow-on damages claims in UK courts will no longer be able to rely on an infringement decision under EU law reached by the European Commission in respect of cases which are either:
  - initiated, but not decided, **before** 31 December 2020 but are **not** 'Continued Competence Cases' for the purposes of Article 92 of the Withdrawal Agreement; or
  - cases which are initiated **after** 31 December 2020,

  as a binding finding of an infringement under the CA98.[114] Claimants will continue to be able to rely on infringement decisions of the CMA and concurrent regulators in pursuing follow-on damages claims in the UK. In relation to standalone actions, these can still be brought after

31 December 2020 in relation to infringements of the EU prohibitions (either on their own or in parallel with the UK Prohibitions) where these infringements occurred before 31 December 2020.[115] The ability to bring standalone actions in relation to infringements of the UK Prohibitions will remain unchanged.

- As set out above, the CMA is required (subject to specified exceptions) to interpret questions under Part 1 of the CA98 in a manner which is consistent with the principles laid down by the TFEU and the CJEU before the end of the Transition Period and any relevant decision made by the CJEU before the end of the Transition Period, so far as applicable immediately before that date in determining any corresponding question arising in EU law. Therefore, references to such EU case law in CMA guidance will continue to be relevant to the interpretation of the UK Prohibitions and other questions under Part 1 of the CA98 (as may be applicable) unless and until such case law is departed from under section 60A CA98 (as explained at paragraphs 4.18 to 4.24 above). For example, several CMA guidance documents refer to the definition of 'undertaking' as set out in EU law, which will remain relevant to the interpretation of this concept under domestic law unless and until it is departed from.

4.38 Section 60A CA98 will require regard to be had to any relevant decision or statement of the European Commission made before the end of the Transition Period and not withdrawn. However, differences between the EU and domestic competition enforcement regimes from the end of the Transition Period onwards must be borne in mind, and European Commission decisions and guidance may contain concepts and references which are no longer relevant to the UK competition enforcement regime. An example of this is the European Commission's Block Exemption Regulation guidance, as cited in Annex B, which has interpretative value for the Retained Block Exemption Regulation, but which refers to concepts which are not relevant for the UK regime, such as the objective of achieving an integrated internal market in the EU.

NOTES

73 Article 92(3)(b), Withdrawal Agreement. See Footnote 14 above for more detail as to the circumstances in which the European Commission will be considered to have 'initiated' proceedings.

74 Article 92, Withdrawal Agreement.

75 Pursuant to Article 94(3) of the Withdrawal Agreement, Article 128(5) shall apply to the extent necessary for any procedures referred to in Articles 92 and 93 after the end of the Transition Period. The criteria for the UK's invitation to meetings of EU bodies is set out in Article 128(5). By way of example, the UK may be invited where it is considered necessary for the effective implementation of EU law.

76 As defined in section 61 of CA98.

77 Regulation 37 of the Implementation SI, inserting paragraph 8C of Part 4 of Schedule 4 to the Competition SI.

78 Regulation 36 of the Implementation SI, inserting paragraphs 8(3) and 8B(2) of Part 3 of Schedule 4 of the Competition SI.

79 The requirement to avoid such conflict falls away in the event that the relevant European Commission decision is annulled in full or in part, provided that the annulment is substantial rather than procedural in nature. See Regulation 36 of the Implementation SI, inserting paragraph 8(2)(c) of Part 3 of Schedule 4 of the Competition SI.

80 Regulation 36 of the Implementation SI, inserting paragraph 8A(3) of Part 3 of Schedule 4 of the Competition SI.

81 Paragraph 6(2) of Schedule 4 of the Competition SI.

82 The conduct of UK businesses could still be caught by Articles 101 and 102 TFEU after 31 December 2020 and investigated by the European Commission where it has effects in the EU. Under the 'qualified effects doctrine', conduct occurring outside of the EU falls within the European Commission's jurisdiction when it has economic effects within the EU and such effects are immediate, substantial and foreseeable (*Intel Corporation Inc. v European Commission*, C-413/14 P EU:C:2017:632, judgment of the Grand Chamber of the CJEU, 6 September 2017, paragraphs 40-65).

83 Article 95(2), Withdrawal Agreement.

84 Article 95(2), Withdrawal Agreement, as reflected in Regulation 4 of the Implementation SI inserting sections 40ZB and 40ZC CA98.

85 Specified information is such information as the CMA considers relevant for the purposes of monitoring compliance with the transferred commitments and/or directions.

86 Regulation 4 of the Implementation SI inserting section 40ZD CA98.

87 The CMA will have regard to Chapter 6 of CMA8 which provides further details of the CMA's formal investigation powers.

88 Section 40A CA98. Failure to comply includes failures to answer questions asked by the CMA, failures to produce documents required by the CMA, or failures to provide adequate or accurate information in response to any requirement imposed on a person under section 40ZD CA98 (as inserted by the Implementation SI). See CMA guideline Administrative Penalties: Statement of policy on the CMA's approach (CMA4).

89 Regulation 4 of the Implementation SI inserting sections 40ZB and 40ZC CA98.

90 Including the Competition Appeal Tribunal.

91 Section 60A(8) makes clear this means principles as they have effect in EU law immediately before the end of the Transition Period, disregarding the effect of principles laid down, and decisions made, by the CJEU on or after the end of the Transition Period.

92 In the CMA's interpretation, sub-section 60A(7)(f) should not be regarded as a 'catch-all': as the CMA understands it, sub-sections 60A(7)(a) to (e) represent a limited and specified set of circumstances, and although sub-section 60A(7)(f) permits departure in further limited and potentially unforeseen circumstances, it should not be interpreted expansively such that divergence from the 'no inconsistency' principle would be permitted under any particular circumstance in addition to those in sub-sections 60A(7)(a) to (e); on the CMA's interpretation, that would be at odds with the specific wording and nature of sub-sections 60A(7)(a) to (e).

93 Section 60A(6) CA98.

94 Paragraph 7 of Schedule 4 of the Competition SI.

95 The CMA receives leniency applications, including in relation to regulated sectors. See Information Note –

Arrangements for the handling of leniency applications in the regulated sectors.

96 Paragraphs 4.36-4.39 of OFT1495.

97 Based on its experience to date, the CMA would expect this to arise only rarely.

98 Paragraphs 4.41-4.42 of OFT1495 should be read accordingly. Although the UK will no longer participate in the ECN Model Leniency Programme after the end of the Transition Period, any summary applications received before the end of the Transition Period will not automatically need to be replaced by a full application to the CMA after the end of the Transition Period. Rather, the CMA will assess any such applications, and the need for further information from the applicants, on a case-by-case basis, and contact applicants should it need to be provided with further information in relation to summary applications.

99 Paragraph 8.4 of OFT1495 should be read accordingly.

100 Section 9A Company Directors Disqualification Act 1986, as amended by the Competition SI.

101 Paragraph 36 of Schedule 4 of the Competition SI.

102 Before its expiry on 25 April 2020, the application period of the EU block exemption Regulation applicable to consortium agreements between liner shipping companies was extended by the Commission Regulation (EU) 2020/436 until 25 April 2024. This renewed block exemption will become the retained exemption applicable in the UK for its duration, unless it is varied or revoked before that by the Secretary of State.

103 The Competition SI amends section 10 CA98 by substituting 'parallel exemptions' by 'retained exemptions'. This means that following the end of the Transition Period, the parallel exemptions regime ceases to exist but as explained in paragraph 4.32 of the present guidance, beneficiaries of parallel exemptions before the end of the Transition Period continue to benefit from the EU block exemptions Regulations via the retained exemptions.

104 Regulation 4 of the Competition SI, inserting section 10A CA98.

105 Regulation 3(9) of the Competition SI.

106 For the amendments see Competition SI, Schedule 3, Part 2.

107 Article 1 of Commission Regulation (EC) 906/2009 on the application of Article 81(3) of the Treaty to certain categories of agreements, decisions and concerted practices between liner shipping companies (consortia), as amended by the Competition SI.

108 Commission Regulation 330/2010 of 20 April 2010 on the application of Article 101(3) TFEU to categories of vertical agreements and concerted practices.

109 See further Articles 4(b) and 4(c) Commission Regulation (EU) No 330/2010.

110 This guidance is not meant exhaustively to cover all scenarios in relation to passive sales (or indeed other types of vertical agreements) but rather to provide an example of how geographic scope is relevant to certain provisions of the Retained Block Exemption Regulations. The CMA is currently considering its approach to the Retained Block Exemption Regulations.

111 Under section 60A CA98, to the extent such decisions or statements pre-dating the end of the Transition Period are made and not withdrawn. See paragraph 4.18 to 4.24 of the present guidance.

112 Note that these are examples of general principles to assist with reading CMA guidance considering EU Exit and may not apply in all instances. This list is not exhaustive.

113 Unless the context clearly requires otherwise, such as where reference is made to CJEU case law.

114 UK courts will also no longer be required to treat infringement decisions of an EU Member State national competition authority as 'prima facie' evidence of an infringement.

115 Paragraph 14 of Schedule 4 of the Competition SI (as amended by Regulation 39 of the Implementation SI).

5. CONSUMER PROTECTION LAW ENFORCEMENT

IMPACT OF UK'S EU EXIT LEGISLATION

[7.104]

5.1 As explained in section 2 of this guidance, the effect of the Withdrawal Act is that, from 31 December 2020, EU law will be converted to UK law and EU-derived UK law will be maintained. This covers both directly effective EU legislation such as Regulations, and EU directives that have been implemented into UK domestic legislation.

5.2 A number of consumer protection statutory instruments were made to implement some amendments to the UK's consumer protection legislation deemed necessary for it to operate effectively after the UK's Exit from the EU. These largely leave transactions between UK businesses and UK consumers unaffected but make some changes to the law applying to UK/EU cross-border trading.

5.3 In the area of consumer protection, the broad effect of the EU Exit legislation is that immediately after 31 December 2020 UK businesses dealing with UK consumers will be largely subject to the same consumer protection law requirements as applied beforehand. Similarly, UK consumers buying from UK businesses will benefit from the same rights, and the CMA will have the same consumer enforcement powers regarding these domestic transactions.

5.4 The position will change in some respects for UK businesses selling to EU consumers, and for UK consumers buying from EU traders. For detailed explanation of these changes, see the consumer protection statutory instruments made under section 8 of the Withdrawal Act including their Explanatory Notes.[116]

Consumer protection law after 31 December 2020

5.5 Consumer protection law is, to a great extent, harmonised within the EU. It therefore follows that much of the UK's existing consumer protection law reflects EU consumer law. As the effect of the EU Exit legislation is to confirm that law's status in UK law, from 31 December 2020, businesses trading with UK consumers must continue to comply with these EU-derived consumer protection laws[117] unless and until they are repealed or amended by the UK Parliament.

5.6 To a large extent the Withdrawal Act maintains the status in UK law of CJEU judgments made up to the end of the Transition Period. Most UK courts and authorities applying UK consumer protection law which derives from EU law will continue to be bound by judgments of the CJEU which pre-date the end of the Transition Period on the meaning and interpretation of the underlying EU consumer directives and regulations.[118] However, the UK Supreme Court, the High Court of Justiciary[119] and other UK courts[120] may depart from existing CJEU judgments having applied the same respective tests as they would when considering whether to depart from their own previous decisions.

5.7 UK traders directing their business activities to consumers in the EU must continue to comply with UK law, since otherwise they may face enforcement action under Part 8 EA02 for example. However, they may also face enforcement locally if they fail to comply with those consumers' local national consumer laws which will largely reflect EU law.[121]

Consumer protection law enforcement after 31 December 2020

5.8 Part 8 EA02 sets out the principal UK regime for the civil enforcement of a wide range of consumer protection law by the CMA[122] and by other UK enforcers.[123] Under Part 8, before 31 December 2020, the CMA could take action against infringements of a wide range of UK consumer protection law implementing European laws – known as Community infringements[124] - as well as taking action against infringements of purely domestic laws (known as domestic infringements). As well as covering purely domestic cases, it also allowed EU enforcers to bring proceedings against UK businesses in the UK courts to protect consumers in their jurisdiction, and UK enforcers to take proceedings against EU businesses in their local courts.[125]

5.9 By virtue of the changes to Part 8 and Schedule 5 to the CRA made by the Consumer Protection EU Exit SIs, these cross-border proceedings will no longer be provided for in Part 8, and the related investigatory powers will be removed.

5.10 However, the CMA and other UK enforcers will still generally be able to bring Part 8 proceedings in the UK against EU businesses that are directing their trading activities towards UK consumers and breaching UK consumer protection law.[126] Similarly, UK businesses directing trade activities to EU consumers and breaching EU or local national consumer law, may still find themselves subject to enforcement action by national enforcers in the courts of that Member State.

Consumer enforcement co-operation with EU enforcers after 31 December 2020

5.11 Until 31 December 2020, the UK is covered by the CPC Regulation.[127] The CPC Regulation establishes a regime for EU cross-border consumer enforcement co-operation and assistance, by prescribing reciprocal powers and duties for Member States' Competent Authorities to request and provide each other with assistance. Under the CPC Regulation, Competent Authorities can ask a cross-border authority for information on a business based in the requested authority's jurisdiction and can require it to take enforcement action against that local business to stop it committing infringements which are harming consumers in the other Member State.

5.12 In addition, the CPC Regulation provides for Member States' Competent Authorities (sometimes with the assistance of the European Commission) to co-ordinate common consumer enforcement activities to tackle businesses or infringements that span multiple Member States.

5.13 Until the end of the Transition Period, the CMA remains a UK Competent Authority under the CPC Regulation and the UK's Single Liaison Office responsible for co-ordinating requests coming to, and from, the UK. It has also been involved in a number of CPC common activities.[128]

5.14 After the end of the Transition Period, the CPC Regulation no longer applies to the UK and the CMA's formal role under it ceases. As noted above, the CMA's related powers under Part 8 and Schedule 5 to the CRA to assist EU enforcers with investigations of UK businesses harming EU consumers, also no longer apply.

5.15 However, the CMA has taken an active role in co-ordinated enforcement projects and knowhow-sharing within the CPC network, and a leading role in the development of wider partnership working in international fora. For example, the CMA's active role in CPC Joint Actions has resulted in binding commitments from businesses which UK consumers will continue to benefit from after the transition period.

5.16 Following the end of the Transition Period the CMA will seek to continue to work with EU enforcers as far as possible, while developing relationships and working with all our other international counterparts, including, for example, through ICPEN. This could include sharing evidence and intelligence, for example, as provided for under Part 9 of the EA02. It could also include co-ordinating investigations. There is also scope for co-operation arrangements between the EU and the UK as a third country, to be agreed under the CPC Regulation. The extent to which the CMA is able to assist EU enforcers using its formal powers will be considered further in the context of any future agreement on cross border co-operation.

CMA consumer protection law enforcement guidance

5.17 Information on the CMA's consumer enforcement powers and approach is set out in CMA58[129] which includes a section on cases involving businesses or consumers in other Member States.[130] The CMA proposes to make appropriate updates to CMA58 to reflect EU exit and other recent legal developments in due course. However, in the meantime CMA 58 will continue to apply with the exception of those parts of the guidance dealing with the CPC Regulation and the CMA's role under it.[131]

Cross-border enforcement cases in progress on 31 December 2020

5.18 The Consumer Protection EU Exit SIs provide that, in general, the changes to Part 8 and to Schedule 5 to the CRA do not apply in the case of Community infringements of consumer protection law occurring before 31 December 2020. Therefore, any Part 8 cases started by the CMA before 31 December 2020, and which relate to one or more Community infringements, will continue to be covered by this legislation as it was before it was amended. This is equally true for any Part 8 cases which the CMA may open after 31 December 2020 but which relate to Community infringements occurring before that date.[132]

NOTES

116 The following SIs can be found on www.legislation.gov.uk: the Consumer Protection SI, Consumer Protection (Amendment etc) (EU Exit Regulations 2019, Consumer Protection (Amendment etc.) (EU Exit) Regulations 2020, Package Travel and Linked Travel Arrangements (Amendment) (EU Exit) Regulations 2018 and Timeshare, Holiday Products, Resale and Exchange Contracts (Amendment etc.) (EU Exit) Regulations 2018. In addition to these, the UK has continued to implement EU law during the Transition Period, for example by passing the Consumer Protection (Enforcement) (Amendment etc) Regulation 2020, which implement the UK's obligations under the revised CPC Regulation (EU) 2017/2394.

117 This includes both consumer protection laws that implement EU directives (e.g. Part 2 of the CRA implementing Council Directive 93/13/EEC on unfair terms in consumer contracts), and any EU consumer laws that are embodied in EU regulations, which were directly applicable to EU-based traders, and which will be converted to UK legislation (e.g. Council Regulation (EC) No 261/2004 of 11 February 2004 establishing common rules on compensation and assistance to passengers in the event of denied boarding and of cancellation or long delay of flights).

118 They will not have to follow post-Exit CJEU judgments but may have regard to them where relevant.

119 In cases before it where there is no further right of appeal to the Supreme Court.

120 The European Union (Withdrawal) Act 2018 (Relevant Court) (Retained EU Case Law) Regulations 2020 allows the Court of Appeal and a range of other UK courts to depart from CJEU judgments.

121 EU consumers' local law will follow EU law. Differences between EU Member States' domestic consumer protection laws and the UK's consumer protection laws will open up from the end of the Transition Period and may increase over time.

122 The CMA has additional enforcement powers under some specific consumer protection legislation, in particular the power to bring criminal enforcement proceedings under the Consumer Protection from Unfair Trading Regulations 2008. (Trading Standards Services and the Department for the Economy have the primary duty to enforce these Regulations).

123 Other UK enforcers include Trading Standards Services and Department for the Economy, the Advertising Standards Authority and sectoral regulators such as the Financial Conduct Authority and the Civil Aviation Authority.

124 Community infringements will be called Schedule 13 infringements after the end of the Transition Period under the Consumer Protection EU Exit SIs.

125 Former section 215(4) of the EA02 giving effect to Directive (98/27/EC) on injunctions for the protection of consumers' interests.

126 While Regulation (EU) No 1215/2012 on jurisdiction and the recognition and enforcement of judgments in civil and commercial matters (Brussels Ia Regulation) will no longer apply to the UK, the UK courts may accept jurisdiction to hear such enforcement proceedings having applied existing UK common law and statutory rules in this area.

127 Regulation (EC) No 2017/2394 of the European Parliament and of the Council on cooperation between national authorities responsible for the enforcement of consumer protection laws.

128 For example, common activities on children's apps, social media and on car hire.

129 Consumer protection: Enforcement Guidance

130 See paragraph 2.7, the last entry in the table under Annex A (Consumer legislation under which the CMA has enforcement powers) and Annex C (Wider international working) of CMA58.

131 These parts include, in particular, the first two bullets in paragraph 2.7, the last entry in the table under Annex A (Consumer legislation under which the CMA has enforcement powers) and the paragraphs 1 to 6 of Annex C (Wider international working).

132 The Consumer Protection SI makes provision for proceedings brought in the UK under Part 8 by an EU enforcer before the end of the Transition Period. However, no such proceedings had been brought as at the date of this guidance.

ANNEX A: CMA GUIDANCE

[7.105]

CMA guidance unaffected by EU Exit:

MERGERS GUIDANCE UNAFFECTED BY EU EXIT:

- Merger: Exception to the duty to refer (CMA64)
- Disclosure of information in CMA work (CC7)
- Review of NHS mergers (CMA29)
- Good practice in the design and presentation of consumer survey evidencein merger cases (CMA78)
- Retail mergers commentary (CMA62)
- Guidance on the CMA's mergers intelligence function (CMA56)
- Suggested best practice for submissions of technical economic analysisfrom parties to the Competition Commission (CC2com3)
- Guidance on requests for internal documents in merger investigations (CMA100)

ANTITRUST (INCLUDING CARTELS) GUIDANCE UNAFFECTED BY EU EXIT:

- The OFT and the bus industry (OFT397)
- Street furniture advertising: Recommendations to local authorities (OFT1415)

- Competition impact assessment: Part 1: overview (CMA50)
- Competing fairly: short guide to competition law
- Leniency: information for businesses and individuals
- Competition law: advice for company secretaries
- Competition law: information for accountants in practice[133]
- Competition law: advice for internal auditors[134]
- Avoiding disqualification: advice for company directors[135]
- Price-fixing: guidance for online sellers[136]
- Resale price maintenance: advice for retailers[137]
- High-strength alcohol schemes: competition law issues for retailers
- Local authority initiatives: advice on competition law
- Private medical practitioners: information on competition law[138]
- Private medical practitioners: information about fees
- Competition law for private medical practitioners: cans, can'ts and maybes
- Competition law: dos and dont's for trade associations
- Four-step process to competition law compliance

CONSUMER PROTECTION GUIDANCE UNAFFECTED BY EU EXIT:

- Secondary ticket websites: information for consumers
- Unit pricing: information for consumers[139]
- Children's app and online games: advice for parents and carers
- Higher education providers: consumer law
- Undergraduate Students: Your Consumer Rights
- Reporting possible non-compliance with consumer law
- Online reviews: letting your customers see the true picture[140]
- Giving a balanced picture: do's and don'ts for online review sites[141]
- Online endorsements: being open and honest with your audience[142]
- Pyramid selling: advice for the public and communities
- Higher education: Undergraduate students: Your rights under consumer law (CMA33(a))
- Principle on food pricing display and promotional practices (OFT1527)

NOTES

133 https://www.gov.uk/government/publications/competition-law-information-for-charteredaccountants/competition-law-information-for-accountants-in-practice

134 https://www.gov.uk/government/publications/internal-auditors-advice-on-competition-law/competition-law-advicefor-internal-auditors#why-do-i-need-to-know-about-competition-law

135 https://www.gov.uk/government/publications/advice-for-company-directors-on-avoiding-cartel-infringements/avoiding-disqualification-advice-for-company-directors

136 https://www.gov.uk/government/publications/price-fixing-guidance-for-online-sellers/price-fixing-guidance-for-onlinesellers

137 https://www.gov.uk/government/publications/resale-price-maintenance-advice-for-retailers/resale-price-maintenanceadvice-for-retailers

138 https://www.gov.uk/government/publications/medical-practitioners-advice-on-competition-law/private-medicalpractitioners-information-on-competition-law

139 https://www.gov.uk/government/publications/unit-pricinginformation-for-consumers/unit-pricing-information-forconsumers

140 https://www.gov.uk/government/publications/online-reviews-andendorsements-advice-for-businesses/online-reviews-giving-consumersthe-full-picture

141 https://www.gov.uk/government/publications/online-reviews-and-endorsementsadvice-for-businesses/giving-a-balanced-picture-dos-and-donts-for-onlinereview-sites

142 https://www.gov.uk/government/publications/online-reviews-and-endorsements-advice-forbusinesses/online-endorsements-being-open-and-honest-with-your-audience

ANNEX B: EU BLOCK EXEMPTIONS IN FORCE UNDER EU LAW, BECOMING RETAINED BLOCK EXEMPTION REGULATIONS[143]

[7.106]

Regulation	Expiry date	Guidance[144]	Date
Commission Regulation 316/2014 of 21 March 2014 on the application of Article 101(3) of the TFEU to categories of technology transfer agreements.	30/04/2026	Guidelines on the application of Article 101 of the TFEU to technology transfer agreements 2014/C 89/03	28/03/2014
Commission Regulation 330/2010 of 20 April 2010 on the application of Article 101(3) TFEU to categories of vertical agreements and concerted practices	31/05/2022	Guidelines on Vertical Restraints 2010/C 130/01	19/05/2010

Part 7 Brexit-related Materials

Regulation	Expiry date	Guidance[144]	Date
Commission Regulation 461/2010 on the application of Article 101(3) TFEU to categories of vertical agreements and concerted practices in the motor vehicle sector	31/05/2023	Supplementary guidelines on vertical restraints in agreements for the sale and repair of motor vehicles and for the distribution of spare parts for motor vehicles 2010/C 138/05	28/05/2010
Commission Regulation No 1217/2010 of 14 December 2010 on the application of Article 101(3) of the TFEU to categories of research and development agreements	31/12/2022	Guidelines on the applicability of Article 101 of the TFEU to horizontal co-operation agreements Text 2011/C 11/01	14/01/2011
Commission Regulation No 1218/2010 of 14 December 2010 on the application of Article 101(3) of the TFEU to categories of specialisation agreements	31/12/2022	NOTE: Corrigendum to Communication from the Commission, Guidelines on the applicability of Article 101 of the TFEU to horizontal co-operation agreements 2011/C 33/08 (2/2/2011)	
Commission Regulation (EC) No 906/2009 of 28 September 2009 on the application of Article 81(3) of the TFEU to certain categories of agreements, decisions and concerted practices between liner shipping companies (consortia). This has been extended in force until 25 April 2024 by Commission Regulation (EU) No 2020/436 of 24 March 2020 amending Regulation (EC) No 906/2009 as regards its period of application.	25/04/2024	N/A	
Council Regulation (EC) No 169/2009 of 26 February 2009 applying rules of competition to transport by rail, road and inland waterway (Codified version). There are no Commission Regulations granting block exemption under Regulation 169/2009.	N/A	N/A	

NOTES

143 Under section 10 CA98.

144 These guidelines remain relevant in interpreting the relevant Retained Block Exemption Regulations.

EUROPEAN COMMISSION NOTICE TO STAKEHOLDERS WITHDRAWAL OF THE UNITED KINGDOM AND EU RULES IN THE FIELD OF COMPETITION (BRUSSELS, 2 DECEMBER 2020)

[7.107]

NOTES

Since 1 February 2020, the United Kingdom has withdrawn from the European Union and has become a "third country".[1] The Withdrawal Agreement[2] provides for a transition period ending on 31 December 2020. Until that date, EU law in its entirety applies to and in the United Kingdom.[3]

However, after the end of the transition period the United Kingdom will no longer apply EU law.

Therefore, all interested parties, and especially economic operators, are reminded of the legal situation applicable after the end of the transition period. This notice notably explains the relevant legal situation in the fields of antitrust (Part A below) and merger control (Part B below).

Please note:

This notice does not address:

— EU rules on cross-border mergers set in Directive (EU) 2017/1132;[4]

— EU rules on conflict of laws and jurisdictions.

For these aspects, other notices have been published.[5]

NOTES

1 A third country is a country not member of the EU.

2 Agreement on the withdrawal of the United Kingdom of Great Britain and Northern Ireland from the European Union and the European Atomic Energy Community, OJ L29, 31.1.2020, p 7 ("Withdrawal Agreement").

3 Subject to certain exceptions provided for in Article 127 of the Withdrawal Agreement, none of which is relevant in the context of this notice.

4 Directive (EU) 2017/1132 of the European Parliament and of the Council of 14 June 2017 relating to certain aspects of company law, OJ L169, 30.6.2017, p 46.

5 https://ec.europa.eu/info/european-union-and-united-kingdom-forging-new-partnership/future-partnership/getting-ready-end-transition-period_en

A. EU ANTITRUST ENFORCEMENT

1. GENERAL FRAMEWORK

[7.108]

EU antitrust enforcement is governed by Articles 101 and 102 of the Treaty on the Functioning of the European Union ("TFEU"), Regulation (EC) No 1/2003,[6] and Regulation (EC) No 773/2004.[7] This legal framework is complemented by other Regulations dealing with particular types of conduct or with specific sectors, as well as the guidance provided in various decisions,[8] notices and guidelines adopted by the European Commission ("Commission") and in the case law of the Union Courts.[9]

The territorial application of EU antitrust rules is defined in Articles 101 and 102 TFEU, as interpreted by the Court of Justice of the European Union ("Court of Justice"). They apply regardless of the nationality of the undertaking or its country of incorporation or where its headquarters are located, and may also cover conduct occurring outside of the EU. The Court of Justice has held that the fact that an undertaking participating in an agreement is situated in a third country does not prevent the application of the TFEU, if that agreement is operative on the territory of the internal market.[10] For conduct occurring outside the EU, the Commission's jurisdiction can be justified under public international law either on the basis of the implementation of conduct in the EU[11] or on the basis of the qualified effects doctrine in the EU.[12]

Hence, the fact that the United Kingdom has become a third country following its withdrawal, will not have as such an impact on the applicability of the EU antitrust rules to UK undertakings, even after the end of the transition period. As any other undertaking registered or headquartered in a third country, a UK undertaking will be subject to EU antitrust rules if its anticompetitive conduct is implemented or produces effects in the EU. This also applies to public undertakings and undertakings enjoying special or exclusive rights located or established in the United Kingdom.

The Commission will thus continue to exercise its jurisdiction on agreements or conduct affecting competition within the internal market, including with regard to UK undertakings. The jurisdiction of the United Kingdom over such practices pursuant to its own national antitrust rules may also be applicable in parallel, subject to the limitations stemming from the provisions of the Withdrawal Agreement concerning the proceedings initiated by the Commission before the end of the transition period (see section 2 below).

In carrying out its investigations, the Commission will still be able to obtain information under Article 18 of Regulation (EC) No 1/2003 from UK undertakings. Conversely, after the end of the transition period, the Commission will no longer be able to carry out inspections in the United Kingdom on the basis of Articles 20 or 21 of Regulation (EC) No 1/2003 (with the exception of the inspections carried out in the context of proceedings initiated before the end of the transition period; see section 2 below).

2. SPECIFIC PROVISIONS OF THE WITHDRAWAL AGREEMENT CONCERNING PROCEEDINGS INITIATED BY THE COMMISSION BEFORE THE END OF THE TRANSITION PERIOD

Article 92 of the Withdrawal Agreement provides that the Commission remains competent for administrative procedures concerning compliance with Union law relating to competition in the United Kingdom that have been 'initiated' before the end of the transition period. In particular, the same provision clarifies that proceedings for the application of Article 101 or 102 TFEU conducted by the Commission under Regulation (EC) No 1/2003 shall be considered as having been initiated at the moment at which the Commission has decided to initiate proceedings in accordance with Article 2(1) of Regulation (EC) No 773/2004. In such instances, the Commission remains competent to investigate the facts occurring until the end of the transition period, whereas the relevant authorities of the United Kingdom can investigate the same conduct pursuant to UK antitrust rules only for the facts occurring after the end of the transition period.

Pursuant to Article 94 of the Withdrawal Agreement, Regulation (EC) No 1/2003 and Regulation (EC) No 773/2004 shall apply to the proceedings initiated by the Commission before the end of the transition period, including in the United Kingdom. As regards investigative powers, this means that, in the context of such proceedings, the Commission will not only be able to obtain information under Article 18 of Regulation (EC) No 1/2003 from UK undertakings, but it also retains the power to carry out inspections in the United Kingdom.

Like all decisions adopted by the Commission, decisions adopted by the Commission in the procedures referred to in Articles 92 of the Withdrawal Agreement, even if adopted after the end of the transition period, shall be binding, including on and in the United Kingdom, and their legality shall be reviewed exclusively by the Court of Justice in accordance with Article 263 TFEU.

The Commission remains competent to monitor and enforce commitments given or remedies imposed in, or in relation to, the United Kingdom in connection with any proceedings for the application of Articles 101 or 102 TFEU conducted by the Commission under Regulation (EC) No 1/2003.[13] If so agreed between the Commission and the designated national competition authority of the United Kingdom, the Commission can transfer the monitoring and enforcement of such commitments or remedies in the United Kingdom to the designated national competition authority of the United Kingdom. The possibility of any such transfer will be subject to a case-by-case assessment, where appropriate, and agreed with the designated national competition authority of the United Kingdom on an *ad hoc* basis.

NOTES

6 Council Regulation (EC) No 1/2003, of 16 December 2002 on the implementation of the rules on competition laid down in Articles [101] and [102] of the Treaty, OJ L1, 4.1.2003, p 1.

7 Commission Regulation (EC) No 773/2004 of 7 April 2004 relating to the conduct of proceedings by the Commission pursuant to Articles [101] and [102] of the Treaty, OJ L123, 27.4.2004, p 18.

8 E.g. Decision 2011/695/EU of the President of the European Commission of 13 October 2011 on the function and terms of reference of the hearing officer in certain competition proceedings, OJ L275, 20.10.2011, p 29.

9 For an overview of the legislation and the various notices and guidelines, see http://ec.europa.eu/competition/antitrust/legislation/legislation.html.

10 See for example judgment of the Court of Justice of 25 November 1971, *Béguelin Import*, 22/71, ECLI-:EU:C:1971:113, paragraph 11.

11 Judgment of the Court of Justice of 27 September 1988, *Ahlström Osakeyhtiö and Others v Commission*, joined cases 89/85, 104/85, 114/85, 116/85, 117/85 and 125/85 to 129/85, ECLI:EU:C:1988:447, paragraph 16.

12 Judgment of the Court of Justice of 6 September 2017, *Intel Corp. v Commission*, C-413/14 P, ECLI:EU:C:2017:632, paragraphs 43-47.

13 Article 95(2) of the Withdrawal Agreement.

B. EU MERGER CONTROL

1. GENERAL FRAMEWORK

[7.109]

EU merger control is governed by the EU Merger Regulation (EC) No 139/2004 ("EUMR")[14] and its Implementing Regulation.[15] This legal framework is complemented by guidance provided in various Commission notices and guidelines and in the Union Courts' case law.[16]

The EUMR establishes an *ex ante* control system, in which certain types of transactions with specific turnover thresholds have to obtain the Commission's approval before the parties involved are allowed to implement them. If the Commission has jurisdiction over a transaction under the EUMR, Member States are no longer allowed to apply their national competition laws to the transaction. They may, however, take appropriate measures to protect legitimate interests other than those taken into consideration by the EUMR, under the conditions provided for in Article 21 thereof. The exclusive jurisdiction of the Commission in the EU under the EUMR is also referred to as the "one-stop-shop principle".

As for antitrust rules, the EU merger control system applies regardless of the nationality or country of incorporation or where the headquarters of an undertaking are located. Hence, the fact that the United Kingdom has become a third country following its withdrawal from the EU, has no impact on the applicability of the EUMR to UK undertakings when the jurisdictional criteria of the EUMR are fulfilled.

The Withdrawal Agreement provides that the EU merger control system continues to apply to and in the United Kingdom during the transition period. After the end of the transition period, it is possible that both the Commission and the UK national competition authority will be competent to review in parallel a planned concentration but under their respective substantive and jurisdictional rules on merger control.[17] Therefore, undertakings will no longer benefit from the one-stop-shop principle in that regard

2. SPECIFIC ISSUES CONCERNING THE ASSESSMENT OF THE COMMISSION'S JURISDICTION

2.1. Turnover calculations under EUMR

The relevant date for establishing EU jurisdiction over a concentration pursuant to Articles 1 and 3 EUMR is the date of the conclusion of the binding legal agreement, the announcement of a public bid or the acquisition of a controlling interest or the date of the first merger notification, whichever date is earlier.[18] These rules are not altered by the Withdrawal Agreement or otherwise by the United Kingdom's withdrawal from the EU. If any of the relevant events takes place prior to the end of the transition period, the Commission will assess whether the jurisdictional test of the EUMR is met on the date of that event and will take into account the turnover that the parties to the concentration realise in the United Kingdom to establish the turnover of the undertakings concerned at the EU and individual Member State level.

If the relevant date for establishing EU jurisdiction takes place after the end of the transition period, the Commission will no longer take into account the turnover that the parties to the concentration realise in the United Kingdom.[19]

2.2. Cases 'initiated' before the end of the transition period

Article 92 of the Withdrawal Agreement provides that the Commission remains competent for administrative procedures that have been 'initiated' before the end of the transition period. For those cases, the Commission has the sole competence to assess the effects of a concentration on the UK territory, including assessing and accepting commitments in the UK, even after the end of the transition period. Pursuant to Article 94 of the Withdrawal Agreement, the investigative and procedural framework of the EUMR and its Implementing Regulation shall apply to the proceedings initiated before the end of the transition period, including in the United Kingdom.

For a concentration that meets the turnover thresholds laid down in Art 1 EUMR and that thus has Union dimension, a case is considered to have been initiated on the day of notification to the Commission of a Form CO (or short Form CO), or Form RS with a view of initiating a referral procedure under Article 4(4) EUMR.

As regards the Commission's jurisdiction following a referral of a concentration without Union dimension, a distinction needs to be drawn between pre-notification referrals pursuant to Article 4(5) EUMR and post-notification referrals pursuant to Article 22 EUMR.

2.2.1.
Pre-notification referrals pursuant to Article 4(5) EUMR

Under Article 4(5) EUMR, the notifying party or parties may make a reasoned submission that a concentration without a Union dimension be reviewed by the Commission, provided that the concentration is capable of being reviewed under the national competition laws of at least three Member States. Any competent Member State may object within 15 working days.

In instances where an Article 4(5) submission has been made and where a concentration without Union dimension is capable of being reviewed in three Member States, amongst which the United Kingdom, the Commission will acquire jurisdiction under Article 4(5) EUMR if, prior to the end of the transition period, the period of 15 working days has elapsed without any competent Member State expressing its disagreement.

2.2.2.
Post-notification referrals pursuant to Article 22 EUMR

After the end of the transition period, the United Kingdom will no longer be empowered to refer cases to the Commission or to join referral requests by other Member States under Article 22 EUMR.

If the United Kingdom has requested a referral or joined a referral request by another Member State, and the Commission has decided (or is deemed to have decided) to examine the concentration in accordance with Article 22(3) EUMR before the end of the transition period, the case will be considered to be referred also with respect to the United Kingdom. If the United Kingdom has not made or joined such a referral request, or if the Commission has not decided (or is not deemed to have decided) to examine the concentration before the end of the transition period, the case will not be considered to be referred in relation to the United Kingdom.

3. SUBSTANTIVE ASSESSMENT

The Commission will have to take account of the fact that the United Kingdom will, after the end of the transition period, no longer be part of the internal market. This implies that the Commission will after the end of the transition period no longer be competent to find that a planned concentration would (or would not) significantly impede effective competition in UK national or sub-national markets (save in cases initiated before the end of the transition period).[20] Moreover, the modalities of trade between the EU and the United Kingdom may have a bearing on the Commission's competitive assessment including the suitability and viability of remedies where a concentration leads to competition concerns. The consequences will have to be assessed individually for each case concerned and merging parties are invited to discuss those aspects with the services of the Commission's Directorate-General for Competition

4. CONTINUED VALIDITY OF COMMISSION DECISIONS UNDER THE EUMR AFTER THE END OF THE TRANSITION PERIOD

All Commission decisions under the EUMR (including decisions imposing conditions and obligations) remain valid after the end of the transition period. The decisions will remain valid also in instances where commitments address a competition issue only affecting a UK national or sub-national market.[21]

The Commission remains competent to monitor and enforce commitments in its merger cases after the end of the transition period. This also applies to remedies in a UK national or sub-national market or a wider market that includes the United Kingdom. Nonetheless, the Commission and the designated national competition authority of the United Kingdom can agree that the monitoring and enforcement of commitments is transferred to the designated national competition authority of the United Kingdom. Such transfer is not automatic but requires the explicit agreement of both the Commission and the relevant UK authority.[22]

The website of the Commission on EU rules on competition (http://ec.europa.eu/competition/index_en.html) provides general information concerning EU Competition law. These pages will be updated with further information, where necessary.

European Commission
Directorate-General for Competition

NOTES

[14] Council Regulation (EC) No 139/2004 of 20 January 2004 on the control of concentrations between undertakings, OJ L24, 29.1.2004, p 1.

[15] Commission Regulation (EC) No 802/2004 of 21 April 2004 implementing Council Regulation (EC) No 139/2004 on the control of concentrations between undertakings and its annexes (Form CO, Short Form CO, Form RS and Form RM) (OJ L133, 30.4.2004, p 1), as amended by Commission Regulation (EC) No 1033/2008 (OJ L279, 22.10.2008, p 3), and by Commission Implementing Regulation (EU) No 1269/2013 (OJ L336, 14.12.2013, p 1).

[16] For an overview of the various notices and guidelines, see http://ec.europa.eu/competition/mergers/legislation/legislation.html.

[17] As is the case now for transactions which are reviewed by the Commission and third-country competition agencies.

[18] See paragraph 156 of the Consolidated Jurisdictional Notice under Council Regulation (EC) No 139/2004 on the control of concentrations between undertakings, OJ C95 of 16.4.2008, p 1.

[19] This may result in some transactions that would have met the EUMR thresholds, if the UK turnover of the undertakings concerned were to be included, not being notifiable; for example where the target undertaking does not realise a turnover of at least EUR 250 million in the EU without counting its turnover in the United Kingdom.

[20] Cf. section B.2.2 of this notice.

[21] At the time of taking the decision, the Commission had jurisdiction and therefore the obligation to seek a remedy to address

a competition concerns in the United Kingdom, while the UK national competition authority did not have jurisdiction to do so.

22 Article 95(2) of the Withdrawal Agreement.

EUROPEAN COMMISSION NOTICE TO STAKEHOLDERS WITHDRAWAL OF THE UNITED KINGDOM AND EU RULES IN THE FIELD OF STATE AID (BRUSSELS, 18 JANUARY 2021)

[7.110]

NOTES

Since 1 February 2020, the United Kingdom has withdrawn from the European Union and has become a "third country".[1] The Withdrawal Agreement[2] provided for a transition period which ended on 31 December 2020. The Withdrawal Agreement provided also, in some cases, for separation provisions at the end of the transition period.

All interested parties are reminded of the legal situation applicable since the end of the transition period (Part A below). This notice also explains the rules applicable to Northern Ireland after the end of the transition period (Part B below).

NOTES

1 A third country is a country not member of the EU.

2 Agreement on the withdrawal of the United Kingdom of Great Britain and Northern Ireland from the European Union and the European Atomic Energy Community, OJ L29, 31.1.2020, p 7 ("Withdrawal Agreement").

A. LEGAL SITUATION SINCE THE END OF THE TRANSITION PERIOD

1. STATE AID PROCEDURES

[7.111]

As from the end of the transition period, EU State aid control will cease to apply to any State aid granted by the United Kingdom as from that date, unless it affects trade between Northern Ireland and the European Union that is subject to the Protocol on Ireland/Northern Ireland.[3] The European Commission will therefore no longer have the power to investigate, and take decisions on, potential State aid measures granted by the United Kingdom after that date. Consequently, stakeholders will not be able to make formal complaints to the European Commission about such measures.

As regards State aid granted by the United Kingdom before the end of the transition period, the following rules will apply:

Pursuant to Article 92(1) of the Withdrawal Agreement, the European Commission will remain competent to continue any ongoing procedures[4] concerning State aid granted by the United Kingdom.

Pursuant to Article 93(1) of the Withdrawal Agreement, the European Commission will also remain competent to initiate new administrative proceedings concerning State aid granted by the United Kingdom before the end of the transitional period, if such proceedings are started within four years of the end of the transitional period.

Pursuant to Article 95(1) of the Withdrawal Agreement, the European Commission's decisions are binding and enforceable on the United Kingdom in these cases.

Furthermore, the European Commission retains the right to bring an action before the Court of Justice of the European Union ("CJEU") for non-compliance with such decisions for a period of 4 years after the end of the transition period or the date of the decision concerned, whichever is later.[5] The Court's judgments on these matters remain binding and enforceable on the United Kingdom.

As a result, stakeholders can continue to inform the European Commission – by way of formal complaints or otherwise – of any potentially illegal State aid granted by the United Kingdom before the end of the transition period. This includes cases where such aid is only paid out or otherwise disbursed at a later stage, provided that the legal right to receive the aid was conferred on the beneficiary before the end of the transition period.

2. SUBSTANTIVE STATE AID PROVISIONS

Exceptionally, certain compatibility criteria set out in the European Commission's State aid guidelines refer to cooperation between EU Member States and/or a certain EU or EEA dimension.[6] After the end of the transition period, the United Kingdom will no longer be counted towards such criteria, and Member States will have to take due account of this for any new aid granted under the relevant provisions.

As regards the effect on undertakings benefitting from existing aid schemes, there is an immediate effect on certain stakeholders in the maritime sector. With the end of the transition period, vessels registered in the United Kingdom will no longer qualify as "EEA flagged". This may have the following consequences for operators:

Operators may become ineligible under national tonnage tax schemes that require them to increase or at least maintain a certain share of their fleet under an EEA flag and/or to meet minimum EEA flag requirements, including for ship management companies to be eligible (where applicable).[7]

Operators may become ineligible under national schemes that foresee a (partial) exemption from non-wage labour costs for employing seafarers on vessels registered in a Member State. After the end of the transition period, seafarers on vessels registered in the United Kingdom will no longer be eligible under such schemes. In addition, in certain cases (e.g. seafarers working on board vessels providing scheduled passenger services between ports of the Union), United Kingdom nationals employed as seafarers on vessels registered in a Member State will no longer be eligible.[8]

Therefore, stakeholders in the maritime sector are advised to verify their situation against the background of these changes.

NOTES

3 For further details on the State aid provisions of the Protocol on Ireland/Northern Ireland, see Part B of this notice.

4 The term "ongoing procedures" refers to procedures that have been allocated an internal case number before the end of the transitional period (see Article 92(3)(a) of the Withdrawal Agreement).

5 See respectively Articles 87(1) and (2) of the Withdrawal Agreement.

6 For example, certain instruments foresee increased aid intensities in case of cross-border cooperation between EU Member States and/or with Contracting Parties to the EEA.

7 See Section 3.1 of Commission communication C(2004) 43 — Community guidelines on State aid to maritime transport OJ C13, 17.1.2004, p 3 ("Maritime Guidelines").

8 See Section 3.2 of the Maritime Guidelines.

B. APPLICABLE RULES FOR AID AFFECTING TRADE BETWEEN NORTHERN IRELAND AND THE EUROPEAN UNION

[7.112]
Since the end of the transition period, the Protocol on Ireland/Northern Ireland ("IE/NI Protocol") applies.[9] The IE/NI Protocol is subject to periodic consent of the Northern Ireland Legislative Assembly, the initial period of application extending to 4 years after the end of the transition period.[10]

The IE/NI Protocol makes certain provisions of EU law applicable also to and in the United Kingdom in respect of Northern Ireland.

Article 10 of the IE/NI Protocol provides that "*the provisions of Union law listed in Annex 5 to this Protocol shall apply to the United Kingdom, including with regard to measures supporting the production of and trade in agricultural products in Northern Ireland, in respect of measures which affect that trade between Northern Ireland and the Union which is subject to this Protocol*".[11]

This means that EU State aid rules will continue to apply to the EU Member States, as well as to the United Kingdom in respect of aid that has an effect on the trade between Northern Ireland and the European Union that is subject to the IE/NI Protocol. In this context, the Protocol foresees that these rules shall apply to trade in goods and to the wholesale electricity market.[12] The European Commission, as well as the CJEU and the General Court ("the Union Courts"), will remain competent as regards such aid.[13]

This section will first address the scope of Article 10 of the IE/NI Protocol and clarify the notion of effect on trade, based on the principles developed by the Union Courts. Section 2 of this part of the notice will give some explanations as regards Article 5(6) of the IE/NI Protocol. The explanations provided herein do not intend to be exhaustive. Their purpose is to give in particular guidance on the application of the notion of effect on trade between Northern Ireland and the Union to the courts and granting authorities of the EU Member States and of the United Kingdom.

1. ARTICLE 10 OF THE IE/NI PROTOCOL

The application of Article 10 of the IE/NI Protocol is limited to measures that affect that trade between Northern Ireland and the Union, which is subject to the IE/NI Protocol, i.e. trade in goods and the Single Electricity Market.[14]

This does not mean, however, that only State aid measures relating to the production of and/or trade in goods (including agricultural and fisheries, see below), or relating to the Single Electricity Market, would have to be considered. Rather, any public support for any economic activity can fall within the scope of Article 10 of the IE/NI Protocol, as long as it can be established that the public support is liable to affect the relevant trade between Northern Ireland and the Union. For example, public support to a service provider – wherever located – whose customers engage in trade subject to the IE/NI Protocol might fall within the scope of Article 10 of IE/NI Protocol.

Furthermore, Article 10 of the IE/NI Protocol also subjects any measures supporting the production of and trade in agricultural and fisheries products in Northern Ireland to the application of the Union's State aid rules listed in Annex 5 to the IE/NI Protocol if those measures affect the relevant trade between Northern Ireland and the Union. At the same time, Article 10(2) of the IE/NI Protocol provides for an exemption from the application of Union law up to a determined maximum overall annual level of support, provided that a determined minimum percentage of that exempted support complies with the provisions of Annex 2 to the WTO Agreement on Agriculture. The said maximum level and minimum percentage have been determined by the Joint Committee (European Union and United Kingdom) with Decision No 05/2020 of 17 December 2020.[15] All measures taken to support the production of and trade in agricultural and fisheries products in Northern Ireland which do not fall within the scope of the exemption and that have an effect on the relevant trade between Northern Ireland and the Union fall within the scope of Article 10(1) of the IE/NI Protocol.

For the purposes of applying Article 10 of the IE/NI Protocol, the notion of "effect on trade" in that provision has to be read in light of the same notion in Article 107(1) of the Treaty on the Functioning of the European Union.

On 17 December 2020, the EU released the following unilateral declaration in the Joint Committee established under Article 164 of the Withdrawal Agreement: "*When applying Art. 107 TFEU to situations referred to in Art. 10(1) of the Protocol, the European Commission will have due regard to Northern Ireland's integral place in the United Kingdom's internal market. The European Union underlines that, in any event, an effect on trade between Northern Ireland and the Union which is subject to this Protocol cannot be merely hypothetical, presumed, or without a genuine and direct link to Northern Ireland. It must be established why the measure is liable to have such an effect on trade between Northern Ireland and the Union, based on the real foreseeable effects of the measure.*"[16]

This declaration clarifies the scope of Article 10(1) of the IE/NI Protocol. It is, however, without prejudice to the interpretation of the notion of "effect on trade" by the Union Courts, which will be explained below.

In this context, it should be noted that the sentence stating: "*[. . .] cannot be merely hypothetical, presumed, or without a genuine and direct link to Northern Ireland*" as well as the explanation that such finding must be "*based on the real and quantifiable effects of the measure*" qualify the earlier phrase "*effect on trade between Northern Ireland and the Union which is subject to this Protocol*". This qualification is fully in line with the case law of the Union Courts (see below) that an effect on trade cannot be merely hypothetical or presumed, but has to be demonstrated, and needs to extend to the relevant trade, i.e. between Northern Ireland and the Union in the case of Article 10(1) of the IE/NI Protocol.

The declaration therefore clarifies, but does not alter, the notion of "effect on trade" as interpreted by the Union Courts.

1.1. The notion of State aid

According to the European Commission Notice on the notion of State aid as referred to in Article 107(1) of the Treaty,[17], for the "effect on trade" threshold to be met, "*it is not necessary to establish that the aid has an actual effect on trade (. . .) but only whether the aid is liable to affect such trade. In particular, the Union Courts have ruled that 'where State financial aid strengthens the position of an undertaking as compared with other undertakings competing in [such] trade, the latter must be regarded as affected by the aid'.*"[18]

The case law thus creates a presumption that an effect on trade exists as soon as a financial support from State resources strengthens the position of an undertaking compared with other undertakings in a market subject to trade.[19] Alternatively, an effect on trade exists where it is at least conceivable that the beneficiary of the support is in competition with operators established in other Member States. The Courts observe that, "*aid distorts competition in so far as it strengthens the financial position and opportunities of the recipient firms with respect to competitors who do not receive the aid. Whenever this effect extends to intra-[Union] trade, the latter is impaired by the aid*".[20]

Aid may also affect trade within the Union even if the undertaking receiving the aid exports almost all of its production outside the Union.[21] This is because it would place the undertaking receiving the aid at a competitive advantage compared to other undertakings of the Union. Moreover, the Court has clarified that, with the exception of situations covered by the *de minimis* rules, the effect on trade does not need to meet any significance test.[22] That is to say that even a very small, or indeed, even merely potential effect on trade suffices.[23] However, an effect on trade cannot be merely hypothetical or presumed, but has to be demonstrated.[24] This excludes for example measures with a purely local impact from the scope of the State aid rules.[25] Finally, the fact that aid is granted to all the operators in a given economic sector does not exclude an effect on trade, as the beneficiaries would for example be compensated for costs that they would otherwise had to face.

1.2. The notion of effect on trade between Northern Ireland and the Union

For aid to have an effect on trade between Northern Ireland and the Union, the beneficiary does not necessarily need to be located in the EU Member States or in Northern Ireland, nor does the beneficiary necessarily need to be directly involved in trade between Northern Ireland and the Union.

Rather, any aid granted to an undertaking by the Member States or the United Kingdom may be found to affect trade between Northern Ireland and the Union if it affects the possibilities for undertakings located in the other market to engage in such trade, or strengthens the ability of the beneficiary to enter the Union or Northern Irish markets, should it wish to do so.[26] In particular, aid granted by the United Kingdom to undertakings that are not located in Northern Ireland may also fall under Article 10 of the IE/NI Protocol if the potential of an effect on the relevant trade between Northern Ireland and the Union can be demonstrated. This might notably be the case if the undertaking operates in, or trades with, Northern Ireland, as the aid might reduce the possibilities of Union competitors to be active in that market.

To clarify the above by means of examples, the following measures would likely be considered to affect trade between Northern Ireland and the Union:

— A tax scheme granting a direct or indirect benefit to any firm trading with Northern Ireland;

— Incentives to the financial services industry that would allow manufacturers or electricity companies engaged in trade between Northern Ireland and the Union to access cheaper credit, thus gaining an advantage over their trading partners;

— Aid to a manufacturer in difficulty if its goods are available for sale in Northern Ireland.

2. ARTICLE 5(6) OF THE IE/NI PROTOCOL

Article 5(6) of the IE/NI Protocol identifies specific measures in relation to the IE/NI Protocol.[27] These measures, in so far as they affect the relevant trade between Northern Ireland and the Union (i.e. trade in goods and trade in wholesale energy), are subject to the provisions of Article 10 of the IE/NI Protocol on State aid.

As a result, the United Kingdom will be able to waive tariff debt or reimburse traders as foreseen in Article 5(6) of the IE/NI Protocol, but only in accordance with the EU State aid rules. To that end, reimbursements of more than 200 000 EUR over three years (i.e. above the de minimis threshold) would be subject to notification to the European Commission, unless an exemption applies.

When assessing the compatibility of such aid measures, the European Commission will take the circumstances in Northern Ireland into account as appropriate.[28]

The website of the European Commission on EU rules on State aid (https://ec.europa.eu/competition/state_aid/overview/index_en.html) provides general information concerning Union legislation on State aid. These pages will be updated with further information, where necessary.

European Commission
Directorate-General Competition

NOTES

9 Article 185 of the Withdrawal Agreement.

10 Article 18 of the IE/NI Protocol.

11 Article 10 of the IE/NI Protocol

12 Articles 5 to 9 of the IE/NI Protocol.

13 See Article 12(4) of the IE/NI Protocol.

14 See Articles 5 to 9 of the IE/NI Protocol.

15 Decision No 5/2020 of the Joint Committee established by the Agreement on the Withdrawal of the United Kingdom of Great Britain and Northern Ireland from the European Union and the European Atomic Energy Community of 17 December 2020. Determining the initial maximum exempted overall annual level of support and the initial minimum percentage referred to in Article 10(2) of the Protocol on Ireland/Northern Ireland to the Agreement on the withdrawal of the United Kingdom of Great Britain and Northern Ireland from the European Union and the European Atomic Energy Community, OJ L443, 30.12.2020, p 13.

16 https://ec.europa.eu/info/publications/
unilateral-declarations-eu-and-uk-application-unions-state-aidrules-under-article-10-ie-ni-protocol_en.

17 Commission Notice on the notion of State aid as referred to in Article 107(1) of the Treaty on the Functioning of the European Union ("NoA"), OJ C262, 19.07.2016, p 1.

18 NoA, paragraph 190 (footnotes not reproduced).

19 *Case 730/79 Philip Morris v Commission, ECLI:EU:C:1980:209, paragraph 11.*

20 *Case C-310/99 Italy v Commission, ECLI:EU:C:2002:143; Case T-291/11 Portovesme v Commission, ECLI-:EU:T:2014:896 and in Case T-308/11 Eurallumina v Commission, ECLI:EU:T:2014:894.*

21 *Case C-142/87 Belgium v Commission ("Tubemeuse"), ECLI:EU:C:1990:125.*

22 *Case T-55/99 CETM v Commission, ECLI:EU:T:2000:223, paragraph 6.*

23 *Case C-518/13 Eventech, ECLI:EU:C:2015:9; Case C-706/17 Achema and others, ECLI:EU:C:2019:407; Case C-659/17 Azienda Napoletana Mobilità, ECLI:EU:C:2019:633; Case T-578/17 A&O hostel and hotel Berlin v Commission, ECLI:EU:T:2019:437.*

24 *Case T-728/17 Marinvest and Porting v Commission, ECLI:EU:T:2019:325, paragraph 81.*

25 NoA, paragraph 196.

26 *Joined Cases C-197/11 and 203/11 Libert and others, ECLI:EU:C:2013:288.*

27 The United Kingdom reimbursing duties on goods brought into Northern Ireland; the waiving (by the United Kingdom) of customs debts for goods brought into Northern Ireland; the establishment (by the United Kingdom) of conditions under which customs duties are reimbursed on goods "shown not to have entered the Union"; and to "compensate undertakings to offset" the application of these provisions (by the United Kingdom).

28 Article 5(6) of the IE/NI Protocol.

PART 8
COVID-19-RELATED MATERIALS

A. UK LEGISLATION

COMPETITION APPEAL TRIBUNAL (CORONAVIRUS) (RECORDING AND BROADCASTING) ORDER 2020

(SI 2020/801)

NOTES

Made: 23 July 2020.
Authority: Crime and Courts Act 2013, s 32(1).
Commencement: 24 July 2020.

ARRANGEMENT OF ARTICLES

[8.1]

1 Citation and commencement

This Order may be cited as the Competition Appeal Tribunal (Coronavirus) (Recording and Broadcasting) Order 2020 and comes into force on the day after the day on which it is made.

NOTES

Commencement: 24 July 2020.
This Order expires on 25 March 2022 in accordance with art 9 at **[8.9]**.

[8.2]

2 Definitions

In this Order—

"broadcast" means the transmission to members of the public of a recording of proceedings of the Tribunal;

"chairman" has the meaning given in Rule 2(1) of the Rules;

"President" has the meaning given in Rule 2(1) of the Rules;

"proceedings" means a hearing before the Tribunal conducted in accordance with the Rules;

"recording" includes a visual or sound recording on any medium from which a single image, a moving image or any sound may be produced or reproduced, or the making of any such recording, and "record" and "recorded" shall be construed accordingly;

"representative" means a person within Rule 8(1)(a) or (b) of the Rules who represents a party in proceedings;

"Registrar" has the meaning given in Rule 2(1) of the Rules;

"Rules" means the Competition Appeal Tribunal Rules 2015; and

"Tribunal" means the Competition Appeal Tribunal established by section 12 of the Enterprise Act 2002 however constituted in accordance with section 14 of that Act.

NOTES

Commencement: 24 July 2020.
This Order expires on 25 March 2022 in accordance with art 9 at **[8.9]**.

[8.3]

3 The Tribunal

This Order applies to the recording of and broadcast of proceedings in England and Wales.

NOTES

Commencement: 24 July 2020.
This Order expires on 25 March 2022 in accordance with art 9 at **[8.9]**.

[8.4]

4 Recording and broadcasting proceedings

Section 41 of the Criminal Justice Act 1925 and section 9 of the Contempt of Court Act 1981 do not apply where proceedings are—

(a) recorded in accordance with the conditions in articles 5 to 7; or

(b) broadcast in accordance with the condition in article 8.

NOTES

Commencement: 24 July 2020.
This Order expires on 25 March 2022 in accordance with art 9 at **[8.9]**.

[8.5]
5 Recording

Recording is only permitted by a person who—

(a) is permitted in writing by the President or Registrar of the Tribunal to record proceedings; and

(b) assigns copyright in the recording of proceedings to the Registrar on behalf of the Tribunal.

NOTES

Commencement: 24 July 2020.

This Order expires on 25 March 2022 in accordance with art 9 at **[8.9]**.

[8.6]
6

Recording is only of—

(a) submissions of a representative;

(b) exchanges between a representative and the Tribunal;

(c) exchanges between a representative or the Tribunal and a witness of fact or expert witness; and

(d) the Tribunal giving an order, direction or decision, including interim decisions or interim orders.

NOTES

Commencement: 24 July 2020.

This Order expires on 25 March 2022 in accordance with art 9 at **[8.9]**.

[8.7]
7

Recording of proceedings is only with the permission of the chairman, which permission may be limited to part of parts of the proceedings.

NOTES

Commencement: 24 July 2020.

This Order expires on 25 March 2022 in accordance with art 9 at **[8.9]**.

[8.8]
8 Broadcast

Only recordings made in accordance with articles 5 to 7 may be broadcast.

NOTES

Commencement: 24 July 2020.

This Order expires on 25 March 2022 in accordance with art 9 at **[8.9]**.

[8.9]
9 Expiry

This Order expires at the end of 25th March 2022.

NOTES

Commencement: 24 July 2020.

This Order expires on 25 March 2022 in accordance with this article.

COMPETITION ACT 1998 (CORONAVIRUS) (PUBLIC POLICY EXCLUSIONS) (AMENDMENT AND REVOCATION) ORDER 2020 (NOTE)

(SI 2020/933)

[8.10]

NOTES

Made: 2 September 2020.

Authority: Competition Act 1998, s 71(3), Sch 3, para 7(1)–(3).

Commencement: 25 September 2020 (arts 1–3, Schedule); 8 October 2020 (art 4).

Article 1 provides for citation and commencement.

Article 2 introduces the Schedule to this Order.

Article 3 revokes the Competition Act 1998 (Dairy Produce) (Coronavirus) (Public Policy Exclusion) Order, SI 2020/481.

Article 4 revokes the Competition Act 1998 (Groceries) (Public Policy Exclusion) Order 2020, SI 2020/1568.

The Schedule contains amendments to:

— the Competition Act 1998 (Health Services for Patients in England) (Coronavirus) (Public Policy Exclusion) Order 2020, SI 2020/368 (note that this Order was subsequently revoked by the Competition Act 1998 (Coronavirus) (Public Policy Exclusions) (Revocations) Order, SI 2021/773, as from 29 July 2021);

— the Competition Act 1998 (Groceries) (Coronavirus) (Public Policy Exclusion) Order 2020, SI 2020/369 (note that this Order was subsequently revoked by the Competition Act 1998 (Coronavirus) (Public Policy Exclusions) (Amendment and Revocation) Order, SI 2020/933, as from 8 October 2020);

— the Competition Act 1998 (Solent Maritime Crossings) (Coronavirus) (Public Policy Exclusion) Order 2020, SI 2020/370 (note that this Order was subsequently revoked by the Competition Act 1998 (Coronavirus) (Public Policy Exclusions) (Revocations) Order, SI 2021/773, as from 29 July 2021);

— the Competition Act 1998 (Health Services for Patients in Wales) (Coronavirus) (Public Policy Exclusion) Order 2020, SI 2020/435 (note that this Order was subsequently revoked by the Competition Act 1998 (Coronavirus) (Public Policy Exclusions) (Revocations) Order, SI 2021/773, as from 29 July 2021).

COMPETITION ACT 1998 (CORONAVIRUS) (PUBLIC POLICY EXCLUSIONS) (REVOCATIONS) ORDER 2021 (NOTE)

(SI 2021/773)

[8.11]

NOTES

Made: 24 June 2021.
Authority: Competition Act 1998, s 71(3), Sch 3, para 7(1)–(3).
Commencement: 29 July 2021.
Article 1 provides for citation and commencement.
Article 2 introduces the Schedule to this Order.
The Schedule revokes the following Orders:
— the Competition Act 1998 (Health Services for Patients in England) (Coronavirus) (Public Policy Exclusion) Order 2020, SI 2020/368;
— the Competition Act 1998 (Solent Maritime Crossings) (Coronavirus) (Public Policy Exclusion) Order 2020, SI 2020/370;
— the Competition Act 1998 (Health Services for Patients in Wales) (Coronavirus) (Public Policy Exclusion) Order 2020, SI 2020/435;
— the Competition Act 1998 (Groceries) (Public Policy Exclusion) Order 2020, SI 2020/1568.

COMPETITION ACT 1998 (FOOTBALL BROADCASTING RIGHTS) (PUBLIC POLICY EXCLUSION) ORDER 2021

(SI 2021/1148)

NOTES

Made: 14 October 2021.
Authority: Competition Act 1998, s 71(3), Sch 3, para 7(1)–(5).
Commencement: 7 November 2021.

[8.12]

1 Citation, commencement and extent

(1) This Order may be cited as the Competition Act 1998 (Football Broadcasting Rights) (Public Policy Exclusion) Order 2021 and comes into force on 7th November 2021.

(2) This Order extends to England and Wales, Scotland and Northern Ireland.

NOTES

Commencement: 7 November 2021.
As to the expiry of this Order, see art 5 at **[8.16]**.

[8.13]

2 Interpretation

In this Order—

"2022 to 2025 football broadcasting rights" means rights to exploit in the United Kingdom the broadcasting of association football matches played as part of the 2022 to 2023, 2023 to 2024 and 2024 to 2025 Premier League football seasons;

"broadcast rights holder" means any of the following—

(a) Amazon Media EU SARL, a company registered in Luxembourg (company number 112767) or Amazon Digital UK Limited, a company incorporated in England and Wales (company number 06528297);
(b) the British Broadcasting Corporation, a Royal Charter company (company number RC000057);
(c) British Telecommunications Public Limited Company, a company incorporated in England and Wales (company number 01800000);
(d) Sky UK Limited, a company incorporated in England and Wales (company number 02906991);

"the Football Association Premier League" means the Football Association Premier League Limited, a company incorporated in England and Wales (company number 02719699);

"football broadcasting rights agreement" means any of the following—

(a) the agreement dated 6th June 2018 between the Football Association Premier League and the British Broadcasting Corporation in relation to the Free-to-Air Highlights Package for exploitation in the United Kingdom during the 2019 to 2020, 2020 to 2021 and 2021 to 2022 Premier League football seasons;
(b) the agreement dated 14th June 2018 between the Football Association Premier League and Sky UK Limited in relation to Live Packages B, C, D and E for exploitation in the United Kingdom during the 2019 to 2020, 2020 to 2021 and 2021 to 2022 Premier League football seasons;

(c) the agreement dated 14th June 2018 between the Football Association Premier League and Amazon Media EU SARL in relation to Live Package F for exploitation in the United Kingdom during the 2019 to 2020, 2020 to 2021 and 2021 to 2022 Premier League football seasons;

(d) the agreement dated 19th June 2018 between the Football Association Premier League and British Telecommunications Public Limited Company in relation to Live Package A and Live Package G for exploitation in the United Kingdom during the 2019 to 2020, 2020 to 2021 and 2021 to 2022 Premier League football seasons;

(e) the agreement dated 19th February 2019 between the Football Association Premier League and Sky UK Limited in relation to the Near Live Package for exploitation in the United Kingdom during the 2019 to 2020, 2020 to 2021 and 2021 to 2022 Premier League football seasons;

"Free-to-Air Highlights Package" means the package of audio-visual rights to association football matches played as part of a Premier League football season which principally includes the right to broadcast and make available on a free-to-air basis programmes featuring edited highlights of association football matches;

"Live Package A" means the package of live and associated audio-visual rights to 32 association football matches each Premier League football season played at weekends as part of the season and selected by the licensee using the pick priorities in the package;

"Live Packages B, C, D and E" means the packages of live and associated audio-visual rights, each of which includes rights to broadcast 32 association football matches each Premier League football season played at weekends or on Friday or Monday evenings as part of the season and selected by the licensee using the pick priorities in each of those packages;

"Live Package F" means the package of live and associated audio-visual rights to 20 association football matches each Premier League football season played as part of one midweek and one bank holiday fixture programme included in the season;

"Live Package G" means the package of live and associated audio-visual rights to 20 association football matches each Premier League football season, at least 15 of which are played as part of two midweek fixture programmes included in the season;

"Near Live Package" means the package of audio-visual rights which principally includes—

(a) the right to make delayed and on-demand long-form transmission of 180 association football matches played as part of each Premier League football season which are not included in any of Live Package A, Live Packages B, C, D and E, Live Package F or Live Package G, and

(b) the right to make available clips of all 380 association football matches played as part of each Premier League football season by means of the internet;

"Premier League club" means a football club which is for the time being a member of the Football Association Premier League;

"Premier League football season" means an association football competition, generally running from August in one year to May in the next, in which each Premier League club usually plays each other Premier League club twice, once at their own home ground and once at the home ground of the other Premier League club.

NOTES

Commencement: 7 November 2021.

As to the expiry of this Order, see art 5 at **[8.16]**.

[8.14]

3 Chapter I prohibition

(1) The Chapter I prohibition does not apply to an agreement or decision to the extent that it is—

(a) an agreement between two or more Premier League clubs or between one or more Premier League clubs and the Football Association Premier League,

(b) a decision by the Football Association Premier League as an association of undertakings, or

(c) an agreement between the Football Association Premier League and any one or more broadcast rights holders,

to renew a football broadcasting rights agreement so that it applies on the same or substantially the same terms to 2022 to 2025 football broadcasting rights without the Football Association Premier League carrying out a competitive tender process or auction for the sale of those rights.

(2) The Chapter I prohibition is to be deemed never to have applied in relation to an agreement or decision to the extent that it was an agreement or decision referred to in paragraph (1) which was entered into or made during the period beginning with 13th May 2021 and ending with the day before the day on which this Order comes into force.

NOTES

Commencement: 7 November 2021.

As to the expiry of this Order, see art 5 at **[8.16]**.

[8.15]

4 Chapter II prohibition

(1) The Chapter II prohibition does not apply to the renewal of a football broadcasting rights agreement so that it applies on the same or substantially the same terms to 2022 to 2025 football broadcasting rights without the Football Association Premier League carrying out a competitive tender process or auction for sale of those rights.

(2) The Chapter II prohibition is to be deemed never to have applied in relation to conduct referred to in paragraph (1) which was engaged in during the period beginning with 13th May 2021 and ending with the day before the day on which this Order comes into force.

NOTES

Commencement: 7 November 2021.

As to the expiry of this Order, see art 5 at **[8.16]**.

[8.16]

5 Expiry

This Order expires at the earlier of the end of—

(a) the period of fourteen days beginning with the day after the last association football match played in the 2024 to 2025 Premier League football season, or

(b) July 2025.

NOTES

Commencement: 7 November 2021.

As to the expiry of this Order, see above.

COMPETITION ACT 1998 (CARBON DIOXIDE) (PUBLIC POLICY EXCLUSION) ORDER 2021

(SI 2021/1169)

NOTES

Made: 20 October 2021.

Authority: Competition Act 1998, s 71(3), Sch 3, para 7(1)–(3).

Commencement: 15 November 2021.

ARRANGEMENT OF ARTICLES

[8.17]

1 Citation and commencement and extent

(1) This Order may be cited as the Competition Act 1998 (Carbon Dioxide) (Public Policy Exclusion) Order 2021 and comes into force on 15th November 2021.

(2) This Order extends to England and Wales, Scotland and Northern Ireland.

NOTES

Commencement: 15 November 2021.

This Order expires at the end of 31 January 2022 in accordance with art 7 at **[8.23]**.

[8.18]

2 Interpretation

In this Order—

"CF" means CF Fertilisers UK Limited, a company incorporated in England and Wales (company number 03455690), and any company which is a group undertaking in relation to CF Fertilisers UK Limited;

"the Chapter I exclusion period" means the period beginning with 30th September 2021 and ending with whichever is the earlier of—

(a) the revocation of this Order; or

(b) the expiry of this Order in accordance with article 7;

"CO_2" means carbon dioxide produced at—

(a) the plant at Billingham, Cleveland operated by CF; or

(b) the plant at Wilton, Teesside operated by Ensus UK Limited, a company incorporated in England and Wales (company number 05816694);

"the CO_2 negotiation period" means the period beginning with 30th September 2021 and ending with 12th October 2021;

"consumer" means a person who is, or seeks to be, supplied with CO_2 by a distributor;

"distributor" means any of the following—

(a) Air Liquide UK Limited, a company incorporated in England and Wales (company number 00232592);

(b) BOC Limited, a company incorporated in England and Wales (company number 00337663);

(c) Nippon Gases UK Limited, a company incorporated in England and Wales (company number 09938383);

(d) any company which is a group undertaking in relation to any of the companies referred to in paragraphs (a) to (c);

"essential user" means a consumer who requires CO_2 for the purpose of maintaining the supply of essential goods or services, such as goods or services relating to animal welfare, energy, food, water or health;

"group undertaking" has the meaning given by section 1161(5) of the Companies Act 2006;

"qualifying activities" has the meaning given by article 3.

NOTES

Commencement: 15 November 2021.

This Order expires at the end of 31 January 2022 in accordance with art 7 at **[8.23]**.

[8.19]

3 Qualifying activities

(1) For the purposes of this Order a qualifying activity is any activity specified in paragraph (2) insofar as it—

(a) is for the purpose referred to in article 4(4)(a); and

(b) in the case of a qualifying activity specified in paragraph (2)(b) or (c), does not involve the sharing between distributors of any information regarding costs or pricing.

(2) The activities specified in this paragraph are—

(a) sharing information during the CO_2 negotiation period in relation to—

(i) the price payable by a distributor for the purchase of CO_2;

(ii) the quantity of CO_2 purchased or to be purchased by a distributor;

(iii) the term of any contract relating to the purchase by a distributor of CO_2; and

(iv) the names of consumers;

(b) sharing information and coordination as regards the allocation, movement and distribution of CO_2 to consumers and, in particular, essential users during the Chapter I exclusion period; and

(c) sharing information on the day to day stock position and shortages of CO_2 within any part of the United Kingdom during the Chapter I exclusion period.

NOTES

Commencement: 15 November 2021.

This Order expires at the end of 31 January 2022 in accordance with art 7 at **[8.23]**.

[8.20]

4 Exclusion from the Chapter I prohibition

(1) The Chapter I prohibition does not apply to agreements between two or more distributors which—

(a) relate to a qualifying activity specified in article 3(2)(b) or (c);

(b) are notified to the Secretary of State in accordance with article 5(1); and

(c) meet the conditions set out in paragraph (4).

(2) The Chapter I prohibition is to be deemed never to have applied in relation to an agreement referred to in paragraph (1) which was entered into in the period beginning with 30th September 2021 and ending with the day before the day on which this Order comes into force.

(3) The Chapter I prohibition is to be deemed never to have applied in relation to agreements entered into during the CO_2 negotiation period which—

(a) are between CF and any distributor or between two or more distributors;

(b) relate to a qualifying activity specified in article 3(2)(a);

(c) are notified to the Secretary of State in accordance with article 5(1); and

(d) meet the conditions set out in paragraph (4).

(4) The conditions referred to in paragraphs (1)(c) and (3)(d) are that—

(a) the purpose of the agreement is to prevent or mitigate disruption to the supply of CO_2 to distributors, consumers and, in particular, essential users in any part of the United Kingdom during the Chapter I exclusion period;

(b) the agreement does not have as its object or effect the prevention, restriction or distortion of competition within the United Kingdom, except in relation to qualifying activities specified in article 3 in a market for the provision of CO_2 to distributors, consumers and, in particular, essential users in any part of the United Kingdom; and

(c) in the case of an agreement relating to a qualifying activity referred to in article 3(2)(a), the term of any contract for the purchase by a distributor of CO_2 that arises out of or in connection with the qualifying activity expires no later than the end of 31st January 2022.

NOTES

Commencement: 15 November 2021.

This Order expires at the end of 31 January 2022 in accordance with art 7 at **[8.23]**.

[8.21]

5 Notification to the Secretary of State

(1) An agreement is notified to the Secretary of State in accordance with this paragraph if the following details of the agreement are given to the Secretary of State in writing within 14 days of the relevant date—

(a) the names of the undertakings which are parties to the agreement;

(b) a description of the nature of the agreement; and

(c) the date the agreement was entered into.

(2) In this article the "relevant date", in relation to an agreement, means—

(a) in the case of an agreement entered into before the coming into force of this Order, the date this Order comes into force;

(b) in any other case, the date on which the agreement is entered into.

NOTES

Commencement: 15 November 2021.

This Order expires at the end of 31 January 2022 in accordance with art 7 at **[8.23]**.

[8.22]

6 Register of agreements

(1) The Secretary of State must compile and maintain a register of agreements notified under this Order.

(2) The register must be kept in such form as the Secretary of State considers appropriate.

(3) The Secretary of State must publish the register when it is first compiled and each time it is revised.

NOTES

Commencement: 15 November 2021.

This Order expires at the end of 31 January 2022 in accordance with art 7 at **[8.23]**.

[8.23]

7 Expiry

This Order expires at the end of 31st January 2022.

NOTES

Commencement: 15 November 2021.

This Order expires at the end of 31 January 2022; see above.

B. OTHER UK MATERIALS

GUIDANCE: CMA COVID-19 TASKFORCE

(20 March 2020)

[8.24]

NOTES

This is available at: www.gov.uk/government/publications/covid-19-cma-taskforce/cma-covid-19-taskforce.

BACKGROUND

The outbreak of coronavirus (COVID-19) is an unprecedented and rapidly evolving challenge that has prompted many concerns that businesses might exploit the situation to take advantage of people, for example by charging excessive prices or making misleading claims about their products.

Coronavirus, and the measures taken to suppress its impact on public health, are likely to have a substantial impact on competition, with the risk of an increase in consumer detriment.

That is why the Competition and Markets Authority (CMA) is establishing a dedicated COVID-19 Taskforce (the 'Taskforce').

KEY AREAS OF FOCUS

The taskforce will:

— Scrutinise market developments to identify harmful sales and pricing practices as they emerge.

— Warn firms suspected of exploiting these exceptional circumstances – and people's vulnerability – through unjustifiable prices or misleading claims.

— Take enforcement action if there is evidence that firms may have breached competition or consumer protection law and fail to respond to warnings.

— Equip the CMA to advise government on emergency legislation if there are negative impacts for people which cannot be addressed through existing powers.

— Advise government on how to ensure competition law does not stand in the way of legitimate measures that protect public health and support the supply of essential goods and services. It will also advise on further policy and legislative measures to ensure markets function as well as possible in the coming months.

The COVID-19 Taskforce is monitoring market developments to enable us to intervene as quickly as possible, where required. The CMA has a range of options at our disposal, including warnings, enforcement action and seeking emergency powers.

We will do whatever is required to stop a small minority of businesses that may seek to exploit the present situation.

CONTACTING THE TASKFORCE

The CMA will use any information you provide in facilitating its statutory functions. Initially the information you provide will help us develop our understanding of potential issues arising in connection with the coronavirus outbreak, though it may also be used to help us in considering or taking competition or consumer enforcement action should that be appropriate.

The information you provide will be treated in accordance with the restrictions on disclosure in Part 9 Enterprise Act 2002.

When handling personal data (like your contact details), we follow data protection law as set out in the General Data Protection Regulation 2016 and the Data Protection Act 2018 and other law designed to protect sensitive information. 'Personal data' is information which relates to you or someone else from which you can be identified. The CMA will be the data controller for any personal information you provide.

We may use any personal information you provide to facilitate our statutory functions, as set out above. For example, we may contact you again for further information that might help us with our work or, where necessary, we may share information with other law enforcement, consumer or regulatory bodies (nationally and internationally).

Please use our form to report concerns about business practices during the coronavirus (COVID-19) outbreak (www.coronavirus-business-complaint.service.gov.uk/).

For more information about the CMA's statutory functions, how the CMA processes personal data and your rights relating to that personal data, including your right to complain, please see the CMA personal information charter (www.gov.uk/government/organisations/competition-and-markets-authority/about/personal-information-charter).

CMA APPROACH TO BUSINESS COOPERATION IN RESPONSE TO COVID-19 (CMA118, 25 MARCH 2020)

[8.25]

NOTES

CONTENTS

1. INTRODUCTION

[8.26]

1.1 The focus of the CMA in the next few months will be to protect UK consumers from the adverse consequences of the COVID-19 pandemic to the greatest extent possible.

1.2 The CMA is conscious of concerns that competition law enforcement could impede necessary cooperation between businesses to deal with the current crisis and ensure security of supplies of essential products and services.[1]

1.3 Competition typically benefits consumers by spurring businesses to offer lower prices, better service and higher quality. Competition law exists to make sure that businesses do not limit competition to the detriment of consumers. For example, there is a **prohibition in competition law on agreements and arrangements between businesses that restrict competition.**[2] This prohibits businesses from colluding or cooperating to limit competition - for example by agreeing to increase prices or to divide up markets or customers amongst themselves.

1.4 Throughout the UK, businesses are assisting in national and local efforts to tackle the consequences of the COVID-19 pandemic, from providing essential goods and services to consumers, to ensuring key workers can carry out their important tasks in getting the country through this crisis.

1.5 The CMA understands that this may involve coordination between competing businesses. It wants to provide reassurance that, provided that any such coordination is undertaken solely to address concerns arising from the current crisis and does not go further or last longer than what is necessary, the CMA will not take action against it.[3]

1.6 This guidance sets out:

(a) details of the CMA's approach to the **prioritisation** of its work; and

(b) the CMA's views on how, in the unprecedented context of the COVID-19 pandemic, it will apply the criteria for **exemption** from the competition law prohibition on agreements and arrangements restricting competition.[4]

1.7 At the same time, the CMA will not tolerate conduct which opportunistically seeks to exploit the crisis. Therefore, this guidance also explains when the CMA will take enforcement action to prevent consumer detriment.

1.8 The impact of the COVID-19 pandemic continues to evolve. So too may the issues faced by businesses as they participate in efforts to mitigate the effects of the pandemic, and also the types of exploitative behaviour that cause consumer detriment. The CMA will continue to monitor the current situation and may update this guidance as and when it becomes necessary to do so in order to provide maximum clarity and certainty for businesses.

1.9 This guidance should not be interpreted as applying to any matter other than those relating strictly to, or arising directly out of, the COVID-19 pandemic. The CMA will give notice on its webpage withdrawing this guidance when it considers that it is no longer necessary.

NOTES

1 See also the CMA's 19 March 2020 press notice: https://www.gov.uk/government/news/covid-19-cma-approach-to-essential-business-cooperation; and the 23 March 2020 joint statement by the European Competition Network on the 'application of competition law during the Corona crisis': https://ec.europa.eu/competition/ecn/202003_joint-statement_ecn_corona-crisis.pdf.

2 The prohibition is set out in section 2 of the Competition Act 1998 and is known as the 'Chapter I prohibition'. There is an EU law equivalent, in Article 101 of the Treaty on the Functioning of the EU.

3 A joint statement issued by the European Competition Network on the 'application of competition law during the Corona crisis', on 23 March 2020, says that '*necessary and temporary measures put in place in order to avoid a shortage of supply . . . are unlikely to be problematic, since they would either not amount to a restriction of competition under Article 101 TFEU . . . or generate efficiencies that would most likely outweigh any such restriction.*'

4 Under the UK Competition Act 1998 section 9 and, in so far as it applies, the EU law equivalent in Article 101(3) of the Treaty on the Functioning of the EU. The full text of section 9 of the Competition Act 1998 is set out in the **Annex** to this guidance. Forms of cooperation not discussed in this guidance may still benefit from individual exemption under sec-

tion 9, provided they meet the criteria specified. Certain agreements may also be block exempted by application of one of the block exemption regulations adopted by the European Commission which continue to be in force in the UK during the Transition Period (as set out in the UK/EU Withdrawal Agreement (i.e., up until and including 31 December 2020)). Other agreements may benefit from exclusion orders issued by the Government under paragraph 7 of Schedule 3 to the Competition Act 1998. This guidance does not apply to such block exempted or excluded agreements.

2. HOW THE CMA WILL PRIORITISE CASES DURING THE COVID-19 OUTBREAK

[8.27]

2.1 The CMA's Annual Plan for 2020 / 2021 is clear that the CMA intends to '*sharpen* [its] *focus on what matters to consumers*' so that its '*interventions deliver impact where it is most needed*'. The CMA has also pledged to '*improve how* [it] *choose*[s] *which problems to take on*' with '[p]*rotecting consumers, including in particular those in vulnerable circumstances*' a key strategic objective for the organisation.

2.2 These principles apply equally in a crisis such as the present one: the CMA's work should be focussed on what matters most to consumers.

2.3 The current extraordinary situation may trigger the need for companies to cooperate in order to ensure the supply and fair distribution of scarce products and/or services affected by the crisis to all consumers. Where **temporary** measures to coordinate action taken by businesses:

(a) are **appropriate** and **necessary** in order to avoid a shortage, or ensure security, of supply;
(b) are clearly in the **public interest**;
(c) contribute to the **benefit or wellbeing of consumers**;
(d) deal with **critical issues** that arise **as a result of the COVID-19 pandemic**; and
(e) last **no longer than is necessary** to deal with these critical issues,

the CMA will **not** take enforcement action.

2.4 This does not give a 'free pass' to businesses to engage in conduct that could lead to harm to consumers in other ways. The CMA will not tolerate unscrupulous businesses exploiting the crisis as a 'cover' for non-essential collusion. This could include, for example:

(a) businesses exchanging with their competitors commercially sensitive information on future pricing or business strategies, where this is not necessary to meet the needs of the current situation;
(b) retailers excluding smaller rivals from any efforts to cooperate or collaborate in order to achieve security of supply, or denying rivals access to supplies or services;
(c) a business abusing its dominant position in a market (which might be a dominant position conferred by the particular circumstances of this crisis) to raise prices significantly above normal competitive levels;[5]
(d) collusion between businesses that seeks to mitigate the commercial consequences of a fall in demand by artificially keeping prices high to the detriment of consumers; or
(e) coordination between businesses that is wider in scope than what is actually needed to address the critical issue in question (for example, if the coordination extends to the distribution or provision of goods or services that are **not** affected by the COVID-19 pandemic).

2.5 In applying this approach to enforcement during the current crisis, the key factor for the CMA will be the potential for the coordination to cause harm to consumers or to the wider economy. Where the coordination is necessary, for example, to ensure that essential supplies find their way to consumers or that key workers can travel safely to their place of work it is highly unlikely that it would cause harm to consumers. This applies even if the coordination leads to a reduction in the range of products available to consumers, provided that reduction is necessary to avoid supply shortages of the relevant product in the first place.

2.6 It is of the utmost importance to ensure that the prices of products or services considered essential to protect the health of consumers in the current situation (for example, face masks and sanitising gel) are not artificially inflated by unscrupulous businesses seeking to take advantage of the current situation by colluding to keep prices high[6] or, if they have a dominant position in a market,[7] by unilaterally exploiting that position.[8]

2.7 Manufacturers can also take steps themselves to help combat 'price gouging' or excessive pricing. Manufacturers setting **maximum** prices at which retailers may sell their products is **not** unlawful.[9] Manufacturers may therefore directly address price gouging by setting maximum prices for the retail of their products.

NOTES

5 Unilateral conduct by a business with a dominant position in a market might be prohibited under the competition law prohibition on the abuse of a dominant position. This is in section 18 of the Competition Act 1998 and is known as the 'Chapter II prohibition'. There is an EU law equivalent, in Article 102 of the Treaty on the Functioning of the EU.

6 In breach of the prohibition on agreements or arrangements between businesses restricting competition.

7 Including a dominant position conferred by the current circumstances.

8 In breach of the prohibition on abuse of a dominant position.

9 Under the EU Vertical Agreements Block Exemption, a supplier can impose maximum prices above which its retailers or distributors may not resell the products, provided that the maximum price does not amount to a **fixed** or **minimum** resale price as a result of pressure or incentives and provided the supplier and retailers remain below the market share thresholds in the Block Exemption.

3. OUR APPROACH TO THE EXEMPTION CRITERIA DURING THECOVID-19 OUTBREAK

[8.28]

3.1 The CMA wishes to offer additional information in this guidance to businesses about how the CMA will apply the legal criteria for **exemption** from the prohibition on agreements and arrangements restrictive of competition[10] **in the specific circumstances of this crisis**.

3.2 Under section 9 of the Competition Act 1998 (set out in the Annex to this guidance), an agreement that restricts competition is exempt from the prohibition on agreements and arrangements restricting competition if it meets **all** the following criteria:

(a) it contributes to improving production or distribution, or promoting technical or economic progress (the first criterion);

(b) it allows consumers a fair share of the resulting benefit (the second criterion);

(c) it does not impose on the undertakings concerned restrictions which are not indispensable to the attainment of those objectives (the third criterion); and

(d) it does not afford the undertakings concerned the possibility of eliminating competition in respect of a substantial part of the products or services in question (the fourth criterion).

3.3 Agreements are automatically exempt from the prohibition on agreements and arrangements between businesses restricting competition if all these criteria are fulfilled. Businesses need to assess for themselves whether these exemption criteria apply: the CMA does not have the power to make a formal 'clearance' decision to that effect.

3.4 To assist businesses in more confidently making their own assessment in the **specific circumstances** of the COVID-19 pandemic, the CMA offers the following guidance:

(a) Cooperation that ensures essential goods and services can be made available to the public or an important sub-set of the public such as key workers or vulnerable consumers will be considered efficiency-enhancing (i.e. meeting the first criterion).

(b) If without the cooperation there would have been significant shortages of a product, the cooperation will be likely to give consumers a fair share of the benefits if it avoids or mitigates those shortages (i.e. the second criterion).

(c) In determining whether the cooperation is indispensable to achieve the efficiency, the key factor will be whether in the circumstances and limited time available to consider alternatives, the cooperation can reasonably be considered necessary (i.e. the third criterion). A further factor that will be important is the extent to which the cooperation is temporary in nature. Businesses should not restrict competition in any area where such a restriction would be unnecessary for the achievement of the benefits or efficiencies for which the agreement is entered into in the first place.

(d) In applying the fourth criterion, the CMA considers that it is important that competition remains wherever possible. For example, if it is necessary to share capacity information there may still be room for competition on price. Similarly, where the scope of a restriction can be limited to particular goods or geographical areas in order to address a particular issue, businesses should make efforts to limit the restriction in this way.

3.5 Overall, the types of coordinated actions that, in the exceptional circumstances of the COVID-19 pandemic:

(a) avoid a shortage, or ensure security, of supply;

(b) ensure a fair distribution of scarce products;

(c) continue essential services; or

(d) provide new services such as food delivery to vulnerable consumers,

are most likely to be unproblematic from a competition law perspective based on the exemption criteria – **provided that** they do not go further than what can reasonably be considered necessary.

NOTES

[10] This exemption is not available in respect of infringements of the Chapter II prohibition.

4. ADDITIONAL POINTS

[8.29]

4.1 This guidance covers only the approach the CMA intends to adopt to public competition law enforcement during the COVID-19 pandemic. It does not bind the European Commission[11] in its application of EU competition law in the UK. The CMA cannot offer protection against private litigation brought by third party litigants for perceived breaches of UK competition law.[12] Businesses may wish to seek legal advice as to any potential exposure they might face in this regard.

4.2 The CMA hopes that this guidance will answer most questions that businesses and stakeholders might have in respect of the CMA's competition law enforcement activities during the crisis. However, in certain cases where businesses and their legal advisers remain genuinely uncertain about the legality of the actions they propose to take, and the matter is of critical importance, the CMA will be prepared to offer additional, informal guidance about our enforcement priorities on a case-by-case basis, to the extent that this is possible given current CMA staffing constraints.

NOTES

[11] As noted above in footnote 1, on 23 March 2020 the European Competition Network issued a joint statement on the 'application of competition law during the Corona crisis', which provides guidance for businesses as to the ECN's approach to cooperation between businesses in the context of the COVID-19 pandemic.

[12] Although UK Courts may take this guidance into account when deciding any corresponding competition law cases.

ANNEX
COMPETITION ACT 1998, SECTION 9

EXEMPT AGREEMENTS

[8.30]

(1) An agreement is exempt from the Chapter I prohibition if it—

(a) contributes to—

(i) improving production or distribution, or

(ii) promoting technical or economic progress,

while allowing consumers a fair share of the resulting benefit; and

(b) does not—

(i) impose on the undertakings concerned restrictions which are not indispensable to the attainment of those objectives; or

(ii) afford the undertakings concerned the possibility of eliminating competition in respect of a substantial part of the products in question.

(2) In any proceedings in which it is alleged that the Chapter I prohibition is being or has been infringed by an agreement, any undertaking or association of undertakings claiming the benefit of subsection (1) shall bear the burden of proving that the conditions of that subsection are satisfied.

COMPETITION APPEAL TRIBUNAL — PRACTICE DIRECTION 1/2020: COVID-19 – FILING AND HEARING ARRANGEMENTS

(20 March 2020)

[8.31]

NOTES

1. This Direction is issued in response to the current situation concerning Covid-19. Since the situation is changing rapidly, amendment to this Direction may become necessary at short notice.

Filing or service of documents

2. The Tribunal Registry remains open. However, it is directed that in place of the requirement to file a signed original accompanied by a specified number of copies in rules 9(7), 15(6), 30(6), 35(4) and 75(6) of the Competition Appeal Tribunal Rules 2015 ("the Rules") the relevant document should be filed electronically by email to registry@catribunal.org.uk. The time for filing of a specified number of copies as set out in those Rules is extended generally, to be subject to further direction on a case-by-case basis. The parties are encouraged to file all other documents electronically and any party wishing to file or serve hard copy documents at the Tribunal should contact the Registry in advance.

Time limits

3. The Tribunal has general power to extend any time limits set by the Rules: rules 19(2)(l) and 53(2)(j), subject to the requirement that for certain time limits under Parts 2 and 3 of the Rules, concerning decisions of public authorities, this may be done only where the Tribunal is satisfied that the circumstances are exceptional.

4. No general extension of time is granted but the Tribunal recognises that the constraints resulting from the current situation are exceptional. Any party should endeavour to give advance notice to the Tribunal as soon as it anticipates that it may need to request an extension to a time limit as a result of, or to take account of, particular circumstances related to Covid-19. Such notice should also be given to all other parties or intended parties to the proceedings. The parties and intended parties are encouraged to reach agreement as to the terms of any extension to be requested from the Tribunal.

5. Any resulting requests for extensions of time in this context will then be considered on a case-by-case basis.

6. The Tribunal has power to permit amendments to a notice of appeal or an application for review: rules 12 and 26. Parties should seek to file their notice of appeal or application in as final form as possible. However if circumstances related to Covid-19 make that difficult to achieve, the Tribunal will be sympathetic to a subsequent application to amend as soon as practicable, provided that any delay is kept to a minimum and that this is consistent with the interests of justice.

Hearing arrangements

7. It may be expected that anticipated timescales in cases pending before the Tribunal may be disrupted or lengthened. Accordingly, any hearings listed by the Tribunal will be subject to confirmation closer to the time. The Tribunal is currently considering how routine case management conferences and hearings with relatively few parties can be held by videolink and telephone. Pursuant to rule 4(7), the parties should cooperate with the Tribunal in this regard.

The Hon. Mr Justice Roth
President
20 March 2020

MERGER ASSESSMENTS DURING THE CORONAVIRUS (COVID-19) PANDEMIC (CMA120, 22 APRIL 2020)

[8.32]

NOTES

See also *CMA120 – Annex A: Summary of CMA's position on mergers involving 'failing firms' (April 2020)* which follows this document.

MERGER ASSESSMENTS DURING THE CORONAVIRUS (COVID-19) PANDEMIC

[8.33]

1. The CMA is aware of the pressures which the current crisis is causing for a number of businesses and the economy as a whole. The CMA has been working closely with government to relax competition law where appropriate and to provide guidance on the CMA's approach to essential business cooperation during the current crisis. The CMA has also already published some guidance on its own working arrangements during the pandemic.

2. The CMA is also conscious that the pressures brought about by Coronavirus (Covid-19) could have a material impact on its merger control work. The information set out below is intended to provide further detail on the CMA's expected approach over the coming weeks and months.

OVERALL APPROACH

[8.34]

3. The CMA's merger control investigations follow established processes, set out in its published guidance, and are subject to binding statutory deadlines. The timescales under which the CMA is required to operate have not been altered.

4. The CMA has made a number of adjustments to its own working arrangements, in particular through increased remote working and the internal reallocation of staff, to ensure that it is able to continue progressing cases in as close to the usual way as possible, and to continue making decisions and meeting deadlines. It remains possible, however, that some aspects of investigations, in particular, the pre-notification process, may be subject to some delay, as described further below.

5. On the substance of the cases that come before us, the CMA's overall approach to assessing whether a merger gives rise to competition concerns remains unchanged. It will continue to investigate potential competitive concerns fully and take appropriate action where necessary.

INFORMATION-GATHERING

[8.35]

6. It is already clear that some businesses (whether merging parties or third parties) are facing challenges, as a result of Coronavirus, that make it difficult to engage with the CMA's merger investigations.

7. In particular, the CMA understands that businesses may encounter difficulties in responding to statutory information requests during this period because of conflicting priorities or staff availability. Substantiated claims that a business is facing difficulties brought about by Coronavirus will generally constitute a reasonable excuse for not providing certain information by a specified deadline in response to a statutory information request, i.e. under the CMA's information-gathering powers set out in section 109 of the Enterprise Act.

8. The CMA is therefore unlikely to impose penalties where businesses are unable to comply with statutory requests for information by the specified deadline in such circumstances. In keeping with its usual practice, the CMA may 'stop the clock' where merging parties are unable to provide information by a specified deadline in a statutory information request.

THE TIMING OF INVESTIGATIONS

[8.36]

9. The statutory deadlines that apply to the CMA's work have not been altered. The CMA remains keen to ensure that its investigations can be completed as quickly and efficiently as possible, given that merger control is critical to the competitive functioning of markets in the longer term. The Coronavirus pandemic is, however, likely to raise some challenges to the expedient running of investigations, in particular because of the difficulties, as noted above, that may arise in obtaining the information that the CMA requires to carry out its statutory duties.

10. Within individual cases, it is possible that the pre-notification process will take longer than it otherwise would because of difficulties in obtaining information from the merging parties and third parties. In particular, the CMA may not be able to start the 40-working day clock where third parties are unable to meaningfully engage with the CMA's investigation. It will take steps where possible to mitigate any delays in third party engagement, for example by publishing Invitations to Comment during the pre-notification process. The timing of individual cases should be discussed with the relevant case team.

11. Unlike a number of other competition authorities, the CMA is not currently asking merging parties to delay merger notifications, because we do not see this working well with the UK's voluntary system of merger control. The CMA would, however, encourage merging parties to consider whether some filings could be postponed (e.g. where a merger is not particularly well-advanced and may not ultimately proceed).

12. When submitting a case team allocation form to the CMA, merging parties are asked to provide as much information as possible (and to be realistic) about the likely timing of the case. Merging parties are then asked to update the CMA on a regular basis regarding any changes in the timing of mergers under consideration or changes in the likelihood that these mergers will proceed under current market conditions.

MEETINGS AND HEARINGS

[8.37]
13. All meetings are being conducted remotely via videoconferencing or telephone. It is no longer necessary or appropriate, given the official UK government guidance, to hold face-to-face external meetings.

14. The same principle applies equally to all meetings and hearings that make up part of the formal investigation process, (i.e. issues meetings, main party hearings and remedies hearings). A number of these meetings have already been held remotely and have worked well. Arrangements for these meetings in ongoing and future cases should be discussed with the relevant case team.

15. The 'site visits' that typically occur during the early weeks of a Phase 2 investigation will not take place at present. The CMA will arrange an alternative opportunity to gain a greater understanding of the Parties' businesses and meet (remotely) key operational staff during the early stages of the Phase 2 investigation.

16. Site visits will not be rearranged at a later stage of a Phase 2 investigation in the event that the restrictions on in-person meetings brought about by Coronavirus are relaxed in the coming weeks or months.

INTERIM MEASURES

[8.38]
17. The CMA has already received a high volume of requests from merging parties for changes to interim measures in completed mergers (i.e. initial enforcement orders (IEO) and interim orders (IO)) in order to address operational challenges brought about by Coronavirus.

18. The CMA will assess each request on a case by case basis. If the CMA decides to investigate a merger, it is essential to the functioning of the UK merger regime that the pre-merger competitive structure of the market is preserved during its review. The CMA will therefore continue to impose interim measures in line with its policy pre-Coronavirus, and is unlikely to lift interim measures that are already in place, during the course of its review.

19. Derogations can be, and have been, granted rapidly where merging parties demonstrate that such steps are necessary to ensure the viability of their businesses, and appropriate safeguards are put in place to protect the CMA's ability to take appropriate action to protect UK consumers as part of the merger review process.

20. The CMA encourages merging parties to engage with the relevant case team as early as possible after they conclude that such derogations may be necessary. As ever, derogations can be granted more quickly where they are fully specified, reasoned and evidenced.

SUBSTANTIVE ASSESSMENT

[8.39]
21. The Coronavirus pandemic has not brought about any relaxation of the standards by which mergers are assessed or the CMA's investigational standards. It remains critical to preserve competition in markets through rigorous merger investigations in order to protect the interests of consumers in the longer term.

22. The CMA's merger investigations are forward-looking and evidence-led, and the impacts of Coronavirus will be factored into the substantive assessment of a merger where appropriate. It is clear that, at least in the short-term, there will be a substantial impact across the UK as a result of changes in market conditions. There remains considerable uncertainty about the extent and duration of this impact. A merger control investigation typically looks beyond the short-term and considers what lasting structural impacts a merger might have on the markets at issue. Even significant short-term industry-wide economic shocks may not be sufficient, in themselves, to override competition concerns that a permanent structural change in the market brought about by a merger could raise. The CMA needs to ensure its decisions are based on evidence and not speculation, and will carefully consider the available evidence in relation to the possible impacts of Coronavirus on competition in each case.

23. Finally, the CMA is aware that the current market environment may lead to additional submissions that firms involved in mergers are failing financially and would have exited the market absent the merger in question. It is important that these submissions are treated in a fair and transparent way that

Part 8 COVID-19-Related Materials

appropriately protects the interests of consumers. While these submissions are carefully considered on a case-by-case basis, the CMA has issued a general 'refresher' on how it is likely to approach 'failing firm' claims.

NEXT STEPS

[8.40]
24. The CMA's case teams are working very hard in challenging circumstances to ensure that UK consumers continue to be protected. The CMA will continue to assess the conduct of its investigations and may be required to make further changes to its practice in light of the impact of Coronavirus.

CMA120 – ANNEX A
SUMMARY OF CMA'S POSITION ON MERGERS INVOLVING 'FAILING FIRMS'

(April 2020)

[8.41]

NOTES

INTRODUCTION

[8.42]
1. This summary is an Annex to the CMA's guidance on merger assessments during the Coronavirus (COVID-19) pandemic and it should be read in conjunction with that document. It is intended to act as a short reference guide for how the CMA will assess mergers involving 'failing firm' claims. The CMA is aware that the current market environment may lead to additional submissions that firms involved in mergers are failing financially and would have exited the market absent the merger in question. It is important that these submissions are treated in a fair and transparent way that appropriately protects the interests of consumers. Such an approach is also the best means of ensuring that businesses can continue to assess regulatory risk whatever the economic and market conditions.

2. 2.Accordingly, while 'failing firm' scenarios will be carefully considered on a case-by-case basis, this summary reiterates the principles, outlined in the CMA's existing guidance and decisional practice, that govern how the CMA will assess mergers in which such 'failing firm' claims are raised.

THE CMA'S APPROACH TO THE ANALYSIS OF 'FAILING FIRM' CLAIMS

FRAMEWORK FOR ASSESSMENT

[8.43]
3. 'Failing firm' claims are typically considered as part of the CMA's assessment of the counterfactual. The counterfactual is an analytical tool used to help answer the question of whether a merger has or may be expected to result in a substantial lessening of competition (**SLC**).[1] It does this by providing the basis for a comparison of the competitive situation on the market with the merger against the future competitive situation on the market without the merger.[2] The latter is the counterfactual.[3] The CMA may examine several possible scenarios to determine the appropriate counterfactual, one of which may be the continuation of the pre-merger situation (ie, the prevailing conditions of competition).

4. One example of a situation where the CMA may select a counterfactual different from the prevailing conditions of competition is where one of the merging parties is likely to exit the market absent the transaction under review. The exiting firm scenario is most commonly considered when one of the firms is said to be failing financially,[4] and would have exited the market without the merger because of financial failure.[5] This is commonly referred to as a 'failing firm' scenario.

5. The CMA seeks to avoid importing into the assessment of the appropriate counterfactual any spurious claims to accurate prediction or foresight. Given that the counterfactual incorporates only those elements of scenarios that are foreseeable, it will not in general be necessary to make finely balanced judgements about what is and what is not included in the counterfactual.[6]

6. Events which occur during the CMA's review of a transaction (such as the business impact of Coronavirus (COVID-19)), but which are not a result of the merger, can be incorporated into the counterfactual.[7] Where future events or circumstances are not certain or foreseeable enough to include in the counterfactual, the analysis of such events can take place in the assessment of competitive effects.[8] Accordingly, where a business's financial difficulties do not meet the conditions of the exiting firm counterfactual (as described further below), the implications of those financial difficulties (where appropriately evidenced) could still be considered within the CMA's competitive assessment.

7. As the SLC test requires that the merger be the cause of competitive harm, the CMA has previously found that mergers should, on the basis of sufficiently evidenced 'failing firm' arguments, be unconditionally cleared after rigorous assessment. The conditions for the failing firm scenario (as described further below) are stringent, however, and the CMA's experience to date (consistent with the experience of other competition authorities, such as the European Commission) has been that relatively few cases have met the criteria to be cleared on the basis of the failing firm counterfactual.

8. The CMA's approach to 'failing firm' claims is set out in detail in its Merger Assessment Guidelines and decisional practice in this area.[9] The Merger Assessment Guidelines set out a three-limb framework for assessing the exiting firm scenario, requiring the CMA to consider:

(a) **Limb 1:** Whether the firm would have exited (through failure or otherwise)absent the transaction;
(b) **Limb 2:** Whether there would have been an alternative purchaser for the firm or its assets; and
(c) **Limb 3:** What the impact of exit would be on competition compared to the competitive outcome that would arise from the acquisition.

9. The CMA's assessment of the relevant counterfactual, and its application of the three limbs of the exiting firm test described above are, however, determined by the specific facts of each case. There may be specific features of some cases that mean that the wording set out in the Merger Assessment Guidelines is not always directly applicable. In such circumstances, the CMA will seek to apply the broader principles that underpin those tests.

NOTES

1 *Merger Assessment Guidelines* (OFT1254/CC2), September 2010, paragraph 4.3.1. The Merger Assessment Guidelines have been adopted by the CMA.

2 Merger Assessment Guidelines, paragraphs 4.3.1 and 4.3.6.

3 Merger Assessment Guidelines, paragraph 4.3.1.

4 'Failing firm' arguments may alternatively apply to the acquiring business (see, for example, *A report on the completed acquisition by Sonoco Products Company of Weidenhammer Packaging Group GmbH*, 3 July 2015, in which 'failing firm' claims were made by both the acquirer and the target). Whether referring to the target or the acquiring business, 'failing firm' arguments may apply to an entire business or to divisions or stand-alone business units (for example, individual retail stores).

5 An exiting firm scenario can also apply where a firm will exit the market for reasons other than financial failure, for example as a result of a (pre-merger) change in corporate strategy by the selling firm. The focus of this statement is on failing firm scenarios (although many of the principles set out would be applicable in the extent of exit as a result of changes in corporate strategy).

6 Merger Assessment Guidelines, paragraphs 4.3.2 and 4.3.6.

7 See, in this regard, *British Sky Broadcasting plc v Competition Commission e.a.* [2008] CAT 25, paragraph 91.

8 Merger Assessment Guidelines, paragraph 4.3.2.

9 Merger Assessment Guidelines, paragraphs 4.3.8 to 4.3.18. Since the formation of the CMA in April 2014, the CMA has applied the 'failing firm' defence under the Enterprise Act 2002 in: (i) ME/6642-16 *Completed acquisition by East Coast Buses Limited of the east coast operations of First Scotland East Limited* (***East Coast buses***) (23 Jan 2017) ('failing firm' defence met at Phase 1 in respect of certain bus operations); and (ii) completed acquisition by Alliance Medical Group Limited of the assets of IBA Molecular UK Limited used to manufacture 18F-Fluorodeoxyglucose (***Alliance/IBA***) (see Final Report, 15 August 2014) ('failing firm' defence met after an in-depth Phase 2 investigation in respect of the target IBA business). In the anticipated acquisition by Poundland Group plc of 99p Stores Limited, the CMA rejected the 'failing firm' defence after an in-depth Phase 2 investigation and following a detailed assessment of the financial and operational performance of the target 99p (while going on to ultimately clear the transaction) (see Final Report, 18 September 2015, Section 5). In the completed acquisition by Sonoco Products Company of Weidenhammer Packaging Group GmbH, the CMA rejected the 'failing firm' claims made by both merging parties after an in-depth Phase 2 investigation (while going on to ultimately clear the transaction) – see Final Report, 3 July 2015, Section 5.

Limb 1: Would the firm would have exited absent the transaction?

[8.44]

10. The first question the CMA will consider is whether one of the firms would have exited the market absent the Merger.

11. Where a firm may be exiting because of financial failure, consideration is given both to whether the firm is unable to meet its financial obligations in the near future and to whether it is unable to restructure itself successfully. In practice, the CMA will carefully examine the firm's profitability over time, cash flows and its balance sheet in order to determine the profile of assets and liabilities. It will also consider the action the management has taken to address the firm's position and will review contemporaneous internal documents such as board minutes, management accounts and strategic plans. The CMA will also typically request and consider contemporaneous analysis provided by external legal, financial and insolvency advisers, as well as external auditors, in relation to the position of the company.[10] The CMA may also request evidence from the company's debt or equity providers, such as the banks that provide its financial facilities or existing shareholders.

12. If the firm is part of a larger corporate group, the CMA will also consider the parent company's ability to provide continued financial support. In previous cases, the CMA has found that limb 1 has not been met where a parent company would be able to provide continued financial support to a business experiencing financial difficulties.[11] An exiting firm scenario may, however, still exist in such circumstances if the CMA were satisfied that the business would have ultimately exited for strategic reasons unrelated to the transaction in question.

NOTES

10 In relation to the materials produced by these advisers, the CMA notes that, under section 117(2) of the Enterprise Act 2002, it is an offence to provide information that is false or misleading in a material respect to another person knowing that information is to be used for the purposes of supplying information to the CMA.

11 ME/6523/15 *Anticipated acquisition by Chemring Group plc of the air countermeasures and pyrotechnics business and certain assets of Wallop Defence Systems Limited* (2016), paragraph 51.

Limb 2: Would there have been an alternative purchaser for the firm or its assets?

[8.45]

13. The second question the CMA will consider is whether there was any substantially less anti-competitive purchaser for the business or its assets.

14. Even if the CMA believes that the firm would have exited, there may be other buyers whose acquisition of the firm as a going concern, or of its assets, would produce a better outcome for competition than the merger under consideration. These buyers may be interested in acquiring the firm or its assets as a means of entering the market.

15. When considering the prospects for an alternative purchaser, the CMA will look at available evidence supporting any claims that there was genuinely only one possible purchaser and will consider the prospects of alternative offers for the business above liquidation value. In particular, the CMA is likely to conduct a stringent assessment of the marketing process through which a business has been sold, and to consider whether other realistic prospective purchasers would have had sufficient opportunity to advance a purchase. The fact that no other bids were ultimately received for a business may not, by itself, support the position that there were no alternative purchasers for a firm or its assets.

16. Similarly, the possible unwillingness of alternative purchasers to pay the seller's asking price (or to pay as much as the purchaser ultimately chosen)would not rule out a counterfactual in which there is a merger with an alternative purchaser, so long as any alternative offer would have been above liquidation value.[12]

17. The CMA notes that the management of struggling businesses may wish to maximise shareholder value by selling for the highest price possible (and that, for obvious reasons, a close competitor active in the same market may value the business being sold more highly than other bidders). The CMA notes, in this regard, that businesses wishing to exit the market should carefully consider the implications of choosing to try to sell to a close competitor and, in particular, that execution risks (including those relating to merger control proceedings) should be carefully considered in conjunction with other commercial considerations (including not only what price might be achieved but also how quickly the seller might be able to complete the sales process).

18. As a voluntary merger control regime, merging parties are not required to notify the CMA of any merger, and the CMA would not call a merger in for investigation unless there was a reasonable chance that the test for a reference to an in-depth phase 2 investigation will be met.[13] Sellers seeking to minimise execution risk may therefore prefer to pursue a sale to a purchaser that raises no competition issues, if such a purchaser exists, even if the price that purchaser offers is lower than that which was offered by a close competitor. In this regard, sellers should note that (as explained elsewhere in this document) establishing that a 'failing firm' scenario exists will require a significant amount of information to be provided to the CMA to establish financial failure and the absence of any realistic and substantially less anti-competitive alternative purchaser.

NOTES

12 Merger Assessment Guidelines, paragraphs 4.3.13-4.3.17.

13 *Guidance on the CMA's mergers intelligence function* (CMA56), September 2015, paragraph 2.

Limb 3: What would the impact of exit be on competition compared to the competitive outcome that would arise from the acquisition?

[8.46]

19. The third question the CMA will consider is what the impact of exit be on competition compared to the competitive outcome that would arise from the acquisition.

20. The wording in the Merger Assessment Guidelines for this limb focuses on the sales of the exiting firm. If its sales were likely to have been dispersed across several firms, the merger, by transferring most or all sales to the acquirer, may have a significant impact on competition. If, on the other hand, the majority of sales were expected to have switched to the acquiring firm in the absence of the merger, the merger may be expected to have little effect on competition.

21. In practice, the CMA has applied this test less mechanistically than is suggested in the wording of the Merger Assessment Guidelines (given the undue emphasis that this wording places on the redistribution of sales for the purposes of competitive assessment). Depending on the nature of the markets at issue, the CMA will not only consider what might happen to the sales of the merging party but will also consider the impact that the merger is likely to have on competition more broadly. More specifically, the CMA is likely to consider the impact that the exit of the failing firm would have on competition within the markets at issue (looking at the overall market structure and taking all relevant parameters of competition into account) compared to the competitive outcome that would arise from the acquisition.

Application in completed transactions

[8.47]

22. In keeping with its established practice, the CMA will not, for the purposes of substantive assessment, treat completed acquisitions any differently to anticipated transactions. Accordingly, the fact that a merger is a 'done deal' will not be taken into account by the CMA when considering whether to call in a transaction that has not been notified for investigation or in its substantive assessment (including in considering whether a failing firm scenario applies).Previous cases show that completed mergers can be referred for a Phase 2investigation and have remedies imposed by the CMA in appropriate circumstances.[14]

23. Moreover, as noted above, only events that are not a result of the merger under review can be incorporated into the counterfactual. Accordingly, a 'failing firm' scenario is unlikely to exist where the merger under review is a contributing factor to the target firm's exit. Similarly, the fact that a merger may have served to reduce the interest of alternative purchasers in a business or its assets (for example, because of the access that the acquirer might have had to proprietary business information during the intervening period) is also unlikely to be taken into account by the CMA, which will typically look at whether there were alternative purchasers for the business around the time that the merger agreement was entered into.

24. Finally, as the Guidance on the CMA's jurisdiction and procedure makes clear, merging parties that choose to complete a merger without prior CMA approval necessarily accept certain costs and risks.[15] In particular, the CMA will typically impose interim measures in completed mergers, which will require the acquiring business to preserve the viability and competitive capability of the acquired business during the CMA's investigation.[16] This is likely to include making sufficient resources available to the target business to ensure that it is able to continue to operate on the basis of its pre-merger business plan.[17] The CMA may also use its powers to unwind integration that took place prior to interim measures coming into force. It is therefore the case that the investigation of a completed transaction is likely to result in the acquirer incurring significant additional transaction-related costs, even if the acquisition is ultimately cleared.

25. In addition, completing a merger without first obtaining clearance from the CMA carries the risk that the completed transaction may be terminated by disposal of the acquired business (or otherwise remedied by disposal of other businesses or assets) following an investigation. Where this is the case, the CMA will not normally consider the cost of divestiture to the merger parties in selecting appropriate remedies.[18]

NOTES

14 *Completed acquisition by Euro Car Parts of the assets of the Andrew Page business* (see Final Report, 31 Oct 2017). 'Failing firm' claims have been made at Phase 1 in a number of completed acquisitions that were then referred by the CMA for an in-depth Phase 2 investigation, but ultimately cleared: for example (i) *Alliance/IBA* (see Final Report, 15 Aug 2014); and (ii) *Completed acquisition by VTech Holdings Limited of LeapFrog Enterprises, Inc* (see Final Report, 12 Jan 2017).

15 *Mergers: Guidance on the CMA's jurisdiction and procedure* (CMA2) (**Guidance on the CMA's jurisdiction and procedure**), January 2014, paragraphs 6.20-6.21.

16 *Interim measures in merger investigations* (CMA108) (**Interim Measures Guidance**), 28 June 2019,paragraph 1.7.

17 See *Template Initial Enforcement Order (Completed Merger)*, clause 5(b) which requires the acquiring business to ensure, *inter alia*, that the acquired business (as well as the acquiring business) is maintained as a going concern and sufficient resources are made available for the development of the business on the basis of its pre-merger business plans. The CMA's guidance notes that, in circumstances where the acquired business is in severe financial difficulty, the CMA may permit the acquiring business to exercise direct control over the commercial policy of the acquired business or to appoint an independent manager to run that business, subject to appropriate safeguards (Interim Measures Guidance, paragraph 3.67). This will, however, depend on the specific circumstances of a given case (including, in particular, the reasons for the acquired business's severe financial difficulties).Where, for example, the available evidence indicates that the target business was well-run and its financial difficulties are primarily attributable to changes in market conditions brought about by Covid-19, a derogation to replace the target's existing management team would be unlikely to be granted.

18 *Merger remedies* (CMA87), December 2018, paragraph 4.80.

Evidential standards

[8.48]

26. The Coronavirus (COVID-19) pandemic has not brought about any relaxation of the standards by which mergers are assessed or the CMA's investigational standards. It remains critical to preserve competition in markets through rigorous merger investigations in order to protect the interests of consumers in the longer term

27. The CMA needs to ensure its decisions are based on evidence and not speculation, and will carefully consider the available evidence in relation to the possible impacts of Coronavirus (COVID-19) on competition in each case.

28. At Phase 1, the CMA will select the most competitive counterfactual, provided that situation is a realistic prospect. At Phase 2, the CMA will ultimately select the counterfactual it considers would be the most likely scenario to have arisen absent the merger.[19] Merging parties, giving proper consideration to execution risks (as noted above), should therefore note that there is a higher evidential bar to establish that a 'failing firm' scenario exists in Phase 1 proceedings (where, as the Merger Assessment Guidelines make clear, the CMA requires 'compelling evidence' to satisfy that the test is met). Given the implications of a 'failing firm' scenario (the clearance of a transaction that could otherwise raise significant competition concerns), 'failing firm' claims are only likely to be accepted, whether at Phase 1 or Phase 2, where supported by a material body of probative evidence, which the merging parties can expect the CMA to test thoroughly with both the merging parties and their advisers, as well as third parties. Unsupported assertions in relation to the financial health of a business or the absence of alternative purchasers are highly unlikely to be sufficient to establish a failing firm scenario.

NOTES

19 Merger Assessment Guidelines, paragraph 4.3.6.

Engagement with the CMA

[8.49]

29. Where the CMA has opened (or will open) a merger investigation, the CMA recommends early engagement with the case team to discuss what information is likely to be required to inform the CMA's assessment of a firm's financial position and the existence of alternative purchasers for a business or its assets. In particular, merging parties are advised to make clear that they consider that a 'failing firm' scenario exists when submitting a case team allocation form.

30. The CMA notes that its Guidance on the CMA's jurisdiction and procedure states that the CMA may be willing to give informal advice in relation to whether one of the merging businesses can be regarded as a 'failing firm'.[20] The CMA notes that informal advice is only available for good faith confidential transactions,[21] and where there is a 'genuine issue.'[22] The CMA's guidance makes clear that informal advice is not available as a substitute for external legal advice or as a tool to seek endorsement of external legal advice.

31. A considerable amount of information to inform merging parties' own analysis of the exiting firm test is available in the Merger Assessment Guidelines, in this guidance and in the CMA's decisional practice. Moreover, the CMA would not, within the context of informal advice, be able to carry out a fact-intensive investigation (likely, as noted above, to require the use of formal evidence-gathering powers and evidence from third parties) to assess whether the first two limbs of the test are met in a given case. Accordingly, while the CMA is aware of the pressures which the current crisis is causing for a number of businesses and the economy as a whole, and is keen to provide guidance to merging businesses where appropriate, it notes that informal advice is, in practice, only likely to be available where a genuinely 'novel' query arises.

NOTES

20 Guidance on the CMA's jurisdiction and procedure, paragraph 6.25 and footnote 103.

21 Guidance on the CMA's jurisdiction and procedure, paragraph 6.27.

22 Guidance on the CMA's jurisdiction and procedure, paragraph 6.28.

C. EU MATERIALS

EUROPEAN COMMISSION: ANTITRUST RULES AND CORONAVIRUS (MARCH 2020)

[8.50]

NOTES

This document is available on the European Commission website at https://ec.europa.eu/competition-policy/antitrust/coronavirus_en. Note that the footnotes below were not part of the original document, but have been added in place of the hypertext links that were part of that document. Note also that the document has been updated since it was originally published in March 2020.

Businesses are facing particular challenges due to the coronavirus crisis and they can play a crucial role in overcoming the effects of such a crisis. The exceptional circumstances of this time and its related challenges may trigger the need for companies to cooperate with each other in order to overcome the crisis to the ultimate benefit of consumers. This would include, for example, cooperation in order to ensure the supply and fair distribution of essential scarce products and services to all consumers. In response to this need, the European Commission, the EFTA Surveillance Authority and the National Competition Authorities that together form the European Competition Network have issued a joint statement on the application of the antitrust rules during the current coronavirus crisis[1], explaining how competition authorities can help companies deal with these unprecedented times. A similar statement by the International Competition Network[2] was published on 8 April 2020.

NOTES

1 See paragraph **[8.51]** *post*.

2 See www.internationalcompetitionnetwork.org/wp-content/uploads/2020/04/SG-Covid19Statement-April2020.pdf.

The Commission has already issued several sets of guidelines that can help companies assess the compatibility of their business arrangements with EU competition law (see notably Commission's Guidelines on Article 101(3)[3], the Horizontal and the Vertical Guidelines[4]). However, for specific cooperation initiatives with an EU dimension, that need to be swiftly implemented in order to effectively tackle the coronavirus pandemic, and where there is still uncertainty about whether such initiatives are compatible with EU competition law, DG Competition is ready to guide companies, associations and their legal advisors.

NOTES

3 See paragraph **[4.112]** *ante*.

4 See paragraphs **[4.219]** and **[4.248]** respectively *ante*.

On 8 April 2020, the Commission adopted a Temporary Framework Communication[5], setting out the main criteria that the Commission will follow when assessing cooperation projects aimed at addressing a shortage of supply of essential products and services during the coronavirus outbreak. The document also foresees the possibility of providing companies with written comfort (via ad hoc "comfort letters") on specific cooperation projects falling within the scope of the Temporary Framework. Please also see the press release[6]. On the basis of this Temporary Framework, the Commission has issued on 8 April 2020 a comfort letter[7] addressed to co-organisers of a pan-European matchmaking event, which aims at addressing bottlenecks in current production of COVID-19 vaccines and accelerating the use of additional available capacities across Europe. The comfort letter identifies the conditions under which the matchmaking and exchanges between participating companies, including direct competitors, can take place at this matchmaking event in compliance with the EU competition rules.

NOTES

5 See paragraph **[8.52]** *post*.

6 See ec.europa.eu/commission/presscorner/detail/en/IP_20_618.

7 See ec.europa.eu/competition/antitrust/medicines_for_europe_comfort_letter.pdf.

In order for businesses to request guidance (within and outside the scope of the Temporary Framework), we have set up a dedicated mailbox COMP-COVID-ANTITRUST@ec.europa.eu that can be used to seek informal guidance on specific initiatives. In order to facilitate a swift follow-up, companies are asked to provide upfront as much detail as possible on the initiative, including: (i) the firm(s), product(s) or service(s) concerned; (ii) the scope and set-up of the cooperation; (iii) the aspects that may raise concerns under EU antitrust law; and (iv) the benefits that the cooperation seeks to achieve, and an explanation of why the cooperation is necessary and proportionate to achieve those benefits in the current circumstances.

Please note that DG Competition can only provide guidance on the compatibility of such cooperation initiatives with EU antitrust law. Individual queries relating to consumer protection or unfair commercial practices should be directed via the Online Dispute Resolution platform[8] (for online purchases), the European Consumer Centres Network[9] (for cross-border issues), national out-of-court dispute resolution bodies[10], or other means[11] when the direct contact with the trader does not solve your consumer problem. Further information on consumer protection aspects, including the common position of the consumer protection authorities[12] of the EU Member States to stop scams and unfair practices amidst the ongoing coronavirus pandemic can be found here[13].

NOTES

8 See ec.europa.eu/consumers/odr/main/index.cfm?event=main.home2.show&lng=EN.

9 See ec.europa.eu/info/live-work-travel-eu/consumers/resolve-your-consumer-complaint/european-consumer-centres-network-ecc-net_en.

10 See ec.europa.eu/consumers/odr/main/?event=main.adr.show2.

11 See ec.europa.eu/info/live-work-travel-eu/consumers/resolve-your-consumer-complaint_en.

12 See ec.europa.eu/info/live-work-travel-eu/consumers/enforcement-consumer-protection/scams-related-covid-19_en.

13 See ec.europa.eu/info/live-work-travel-eu/consumers/enforcement-consumer-protection_en.

Please also note that the competition authorities of the EU Member States are also competent to apply the EU competition rules in their respective territory. They are therefore well placed to deal with specific antitrust issues that primarily concern their particular Member State. For local or national cooperation issues, we recommend that companies, associations or their legal advisers contact directly the competent National Competition Authority[14].

NOTES

14 See ec.europa.eu/competition/ecn/competition_authorities.html.

The information provided in any submission to the mailbox will be treated with utmost confidentiality. We invite any interested company or legal adviser to read our e-services privacy policy[15] before contacting us. Please also note that this information may be shared with National Competition Authorities in the context of the working arrangements of the European Competition Network.

NOTES

15 See europa.eu/european-union/abouteuropa/privacy-policy_en.

Finally, the Commission wishes to underline that under these exceptional circumstances, it is more important than ever that businesses and consumers receive protection under competition law. The European Commission will therefore continue to closely and actively monitor relevant market developments to detect companies which take advantage of the current situation to breach EU antitrust law. The European Commission also encourages businesses and citizens to continue reporting any cartels and other antitrust violations, including abuses of dominant positions, that may come to their attention.

In addition to the usual channels for contacting the European Commission or submitting an antitrust complaint[16], individuals can help anonymously in the fight against cartels and other anti-competitive practices through the Commission's whistleblower tool[17].

The Commission's leniency programme,[18] which allows businesses to report their own involvement in a cartel in exchange for a reduction of the fine imposed on them, also remains fully applicable during these exceptional times.

Please note that individual messages sent to the address COMP-COVID-ANTITRUST@ec.europa.eu should not exceed 30MBs

NOTES

16 See ec.europa.eu/competition/contacts/electronic_documents_en.html.

17 See ec.europa.eu/competition/cartels/whistleblower/index.html.

18 See ec.europa.eu/competition-policy/cartels/leniency_en.

ANTITRUST: JOINT STATEMENT BY THE EUROPEAN COMPETITION NETWORK (ECN) ON APPLICATION OF COMPETITION LAW DURING THE CORONA CRISIS (MARCH 2020)

[8.51]

NOTES

This document is available at ec.europa.eu/competition/ecn/202003_joint-statement_ecn_corona-crisis.pdf.

The ECN is fully aware of the social and economic consequences triggered by the COVID-19 outbreak in the EU/EEA.

The different EU/EEA competition instruments have mechanisms to take into account, where appropriate and necessary, market and economic developments. Competition rules ensure a level playing field between companies. This objective remains relevant also in a period when companies and the economy as a whole suffer from crisis conditions.

The ECN understands that this extraordinary situation may trigger the need for companies to cooperate in order to ensure the supply and fair distribution of scarce products to all consumers. In the current circumstances, the ECN will not actively intervene against necessary and temporary measures put in place in order to avoid a shortage of supply. Considering the current circumstances, such measures are unlikely to be problematic, since they would either not amount to a restriction of competition under Article 101 TFEU/53 EEA or generate efficiencies that would most likely outweigh any such restriction. If companies have doubts about the compatibility of such cooperation initiatives with

EU/EEA competition law, they can reach out to the Commission, the EFTA Surveillance Authority or the national competition authority concerned any time for informal guidance.

At the same time, it is of utmost importance to ensure that products considered essential to protect the health of consumers in the current situation (e.g. face masks and sanitising gel) remain available at competitive prices. The ECN will therefore not hesitate to take action against companies taking advantage of the current situation by cartelising or abusing their dominant position.

In this context, the ECN would like to point out that the existing rules allow manufacturers to set maximum prices for their products. The latter could prove useful to limit unjustified price increase at the distribution level.

COMMUNICATION FROM THE COMMISSION

(2020/C116I/02)

Temporary Framework for assessing antitrust issues related to business cooperation in response to situations of urgency stemming from the current COVID-19 outbreak

[8.52]

NOTES

Date of publication in OJ: OJ C116I, 8.4.2020, p 7.

1. THE COVID-19 OUTBREAK, ITS IMPACT ON THE ECONOMY, AND POSSIBLE ANTITRUST IMPLICATIONS

[8.53]

(1) The COVID-19 outbreak is a severe public health emergency for citizens and societies. It is also a major and unprecedented shock to the global and Union economies.

(2) This shock affects the whole economy through different channels and in different ways. There is a general supply shock resulting from the disruption of supply chains, combined with an asymmetric demand shock caused by either an abrupt decline in consumer demand for certain products and services or a steep rise in demand for other products and services, notably those related to the health sector (including e.g. pharmaceutical companies, medical equipment producers, and their distributors). There is also uncertainty at this stage on both the duration and intensity of the shock, which mainly rest on factors that are not all in the control of undertakings, but rather on decisions by public authorities, driven inter alia by public health considerations.

(3) Undertakings are thus facing exceptional challenges due to the COVID-19 crisis and they can play a crucial role in overcoming the effects of the crisis. The exceptional circumstances of this time and its related challenges may trigger the need for undertakings to cooperate with each other in order to overcome or at least to mitigate the effects of the crisis to the ultimate benefit of citizens. In light of the multi-faceted and asymmetric nature of the crisis, undertakings might face different challenges and thus might need to resort to different forms of cooperation.

(4) The present Communication covers possible forms of cooperation between undertakings in order to ensure the supply and adequate distribution of essential scarce products and services during the COVID-19 outbreak and thus address the shortages of such essential products and services resulting first and foremost from the rapid and exponential growth of demand.[1] This includes notably medicines and medical equipment[2] that are used to test and treat COVID-19 patients or are necessary to mitigate and possibly overcome the outbreak. Such cooperation could take place among undertakings active within the relevant sector to overcome this shortage, as well as between undertakings active in other sectors (e.g. certain undertakings converting part of their production lines to start producing scarce products). Depending on the evolution of the crisis, the Commission might amend or supplement this Communication in order to cover other forms of cooperation.

(5) The purpose of this Communication is to explain:

a. the main criteria that the Commission will follow in assessing these possible cooperation projects aimed at addressing the shortage of essential products and services during the COVID-19 outbreak, and in setting its enforcement priorities during this crisis; and

b. a temporary process that the Commissions has exceptionally set up to provide, where appropriate, ad hoc written comfort to undertakings in relation to specific and well-defined cooperation projects in this context.

NOTES

1 Other factors exacerbating shortages include massive precautionary stockpiling throughout the distribution chain, the lockdown in factories due to quarantine or confinement measures, logistical issues caused by border closures, export bans, lockdowns in third countries supplying the EU.

2 Unless otherwise specified, references to medicines in the present Communication also cover medical equipment.

2. MAIN CRITERIA FOR THE ANTITRUST ASSESSMENT OF BUSINESS COOPERATION PROJECTS AIMED AT ADDRESSING THE SHORTAGE OF ESSENTIAL PRODUCTS AND SERVICES DURING THE COVID-19 OUTBREAK

[8.54]

(6) Since the entry into force of Council Regulation (EC) No 1/2003,[3] undertakings can no longer notify their agreements to the Commission in order to receive an individual exemption from Article 101 TFEU, but are themselves responsible for assessing the legality of their agreements and practices. This system of self-assessment framed by the extensive guidance[4] provided by the Commission is now consolidated.

(7) The Commission understands that cooperation between undertakings might help in more efficiently addressing the shortage of essential products and services during the COVID-19 outbreak and, in this context, undertakings might need specific guidance on their cooperation initiatives in order to facilitate their self-assessment. It may even be appropriate to provide undertakings with ad hoc feedback or comfort on the legality of specific cooperation initiatives. The Commission is therefore ready to provide such guidance and comfort to undertakings or associations of undertakings in order to facilitate initiatives that need to be swiftly implemented in order to effectively tackle the COVID-19 outbreak, notably where there may still be uncertainty about whether such initiatives are compatible with EU competition law.[5] To this end, the Commission's Directorate General for Competition has already set up a dedicated webpage (https://ec.europa.eu/competition/antitrust/coronavirus.html) and a dedicated mailbox (COMP-COVID-ANTITRUST@ec.europa.eu) that can be used to seek informal guidance on specific initiatives.

(8) Many EU Member States have indicated that they are already experiencing shortages of medicines used to treat patients with COVID-19 or are expecting such shortages to occur very soon.[6] Over the last weeks, the Commission has received several requests from undertakings and trade associations asking for guidance about their envisaged cooperation, notably in the health sector and in view of the risk of shortages of critical hospital medicines used to treat COVID-19 patients.

(9) These requests provide a useful example of the types of cooperation that might be required to address emergency situations related to the current COVID-19 outbreak and their assessment under Article 101 TFEU, along the lines outlined below.

(10) Different measures may contribute to bridging the gap between demand and supply. It might require a very significant, rapid increase of production for products that are needed but are in short supply. This may lead to a reduction in the production of other products. It might also require the reallocation of stocks, which would require that undertakings agree to exchange/communicate information on sales and stocks. To increase production, undertakings might need to switch their production lines for some non-essential/non-shortage medicines (or other products) to medicines (or other products) necessary to address the outbreak. In addition, output could be increased further and more efficiently if, at a certain site, only one medicine was produced (as opposed to switching production between different products, which requires time-consuming cleaning of machinery, etc.), balancing economies of scale with the need to avoid excessive reliance on any particular production site.

(11) This shows that the response to emergency situations related to the COVID-19 outbreak might require different degrees of cooperation, with a varying scale of potential antitrust concerns.

(12) Based on recent experience, the Commission understands that cooperation in the health sector might for instance be limited to entrusting a trade association (or an independent advisor, or independent service provider, or a public body), to e.g:

a. Coordinate joint transport for input materials;
b. Contribute to identifying those essential medicines for which, in view of forecasted production, there are risks of shortages;
c. Aggregate production and capacity information, without exchanging individual company information;
d. Work on a model to predict demand on a Member State level, and identifying supply gaps;
e. Share aggregate supply gap information, and request participating undertakings, on an individual basis and without sharing that information with competitors, to indicate whether they can fill the supply gap to meet demand (either through existing stocks or increase of production).

(13) Such activities do not raise antitrust concerns, provided that they are subject to sufficient safeguards (such as no flow of individualised company information back to competitors), as indicated in the Commission's Guidelines on the applicability of Article 101 of TFEU to horizontal co-operation agreements.[7]

(14) Cooperation in the health sector might even need to go further to overcome critical supply shortages. It may, for instance, need to extend to coordinating the re-organisation of production with a view to increasing and optimising output so that not all firms focus on one or a few medicines, and other medicines remain in under-production, where such re-organisation would allow producers to satisfy demand for urgently needed medicines across Member States.

(15) Measures to adapt production, stock management and, potentially, distribution in the industry may require exchanges of commercially sensitive information and a certain coordination of which site produces which medicines, so that not all undertakings focus on one or a few medicines, while others remain in under-production. Such exchanges and coordination between undertakings are in normal circumstances problematic under EU competition rules. Nevertheless, in the current exceptional circumstances, such measures would not be problematic under EU competition law or – in view of the emergency situation and temporary nature – they would not give rise to an enforcement priority for the Commission, to the extent that such measures would be: (i) designed and objectively necessary to actually increase output in the most efficient way to address or avoid a shortage of supply of essential products or services, such as those that are used to treat COVID-19 patients; (ii) temporary in nature (i.e. to be applied only as long there is a risk of shortage or in any event during the COVID-19 outbreak); and (iii) not exceeding what is strictly necessary to achieve the objective of addressing or avoiding the shortage of supply. Undertakings should document all exchanges, and agreements between them and make them available to the Commission on request. The fact that a cooperation is encouraged and/or coordinated by a public authority (or carried out within a framework set up by the latter) is also a relevant factor to be taken into account to conclude that such cooperation would not be problematic under EU competition law or would not be an enforcement priority for the Commission.

(16) In the context of an imperative request from public authorities to undertakings to temporarily cooperate in response to urgency situations related to the current COVID-19 outbreak (e.g. to organise production and delivery to meet an urgent need to keep up the functioning of health care for COVID-19 patients), such cooperation is allowed.

NOTES

[3] Council Regulation (EC) No 1/2003 of 16 December 2002 on the implementation of the rules on competition laid down in Articles 81 and 82 of the Treaty (OJ L1, 4.1.2003, p 1)

4 The Commission has issued several sets of guidelines that can help undertakings assess the compatibility of their business arrangements with EU competition law (see notably Communication from the Commission — Notice — Guidelines on the application of Article 81(3) of the Treaty (OJ C101, 27.4.2004, p 97) ("Guidelines on Article 101(3)"), the Communication from the Commission — Guidelines on the applicability of Article 101 of the Treaty on the Functioning of the European Union to horizontal co-operation agreements (OJ C11, 14.1.2011, p 1) ("Horizontal Guidelines") and Commission Notice – Guidelines on Vertical Restraints (OJ C130, 19.5.2010, p 1) ("Vertical Guidelines"). See also Commission Regulation (EU) No 1217/2010 of 14 December 2010 on the application of Article 101(3) of the Treaty on the Functioning of the European Union to certain categories of research and development agreements (OJ L335, 18.12.2010, p 36) ("R&D Block Exemption Regulation"), Commission Regulation (EU) No 1218/2010 of 14 December 2010 on the application of Article 101(3) of the Treaty on the Functioning of the European Union to certain categories of specialisation agreements, (OJ L335, 18.12.2010, p 43) ("Specialisation Block Exemption Regulation"), Commission Regulation (EU) No 316/2014 of 21 March 2014 on the application of Article 101(3) of the Treaty on the Functioning of the European Union to categories of technology transfer agreements (OJ L93, 28.3.2014, p 17) ("Technology Transfer Block Exemption Regulation"), Commission Regulation (EU) No 330/2010 of 20 April 2010 on the application of Article 101(3)of the Treaty on the Functioning of the European Union to categories of vertical agreements and concerted practices (OJ L102, 23.4.2010, p 1) ("Vertical Block Exemption Regulation").

5 See also the joint statement on the application of the antitrust rules during the COVID-19 crisis, issued jointly by the European Commission, the EFTA Surveillance Authority and the National Competition Authorities that together form the European Competition Network (https://ec.europa.eu/competition/ecn/202003_joint-statement_ecn_corona-crisis.pdf).

6 See also the Commission Guidelines on the optimal and rational supply of medicines to avoid shortages during the COVID-19 adopted on 8 April 2020.

7 Communication from the Commission — Guidelines on the applicability of Article 101 of the Treaty on the Functioning of the European Union to horizontal co-operation agreements (OJ C11, 14.1.2011, p 1).

3. AN EXCEPTIONAL PROCEDURE TO PROVIDE AD HOC GUIDANCE ON SPECIFIC COOPERATION PROJECTS AIMED AT ADDRESSING THE SHORTAGE OF ESSENTIAL PRODUCTS AND SERVICES DURING THE COVID-19 OUTBREAK

[8.55]

(17) The Commission, through its Directorate General for Competition, will continue to provide guidance to undertakings and trade associations with respect to specific cooperation initiatives with an EU dimension, that need to be swiftly implemented in order to effectively tackle the COVID-19 outbreak, especially where there is still uncertainty about whether such initiatives are compatible with EU competition law.

(18) With a view to increasing the degree of legal certainty as regards antitrust guidance within a timeframe that is compatible with the urgency of certain situations related to the current COVID-19 outbreak, the Commission, through its Directorate General for Competition, stands ready, exceptionally and at its own discretion, to provide such guidance by means of an ad hoc "comfort" letter.

4. CONCLUSION

[8.56]

(19) The Commission is aware of the exceptional challenges that undertakings are facing due to the COVID-19 outbreak and of their crucial role in overcoming the effects of such a crisis. The Commission encourages pro-competitive cooperation aimed at addressing these challenges, notably in response to urgent situations related to the current COVID-19 outbreak, and it is committed to provide antitrust guidance and support to facilitate the proper and swift implementation of cooperation that is needed to overcome the crisis to the ultimate benefit of citizens.

(20) At the same time, the Commission underlines that in these exceptional circumstances, it is more important than ever that undertakings and consumers receive protection under competition law. It will therefore continue to closely and actively monitor relevant market developments to detect instances of undertakings taking advantage of the current situation to breach EU antitrust law, either by engaging in anti-competitive agreements or abusing their dominant position. Notably, the Commission will not tolerate conduct by undertakings that opportunistically seek to exploit the crisis as a cover for anti-competitive collusion or abuses of their dominant position (including dominant positions conferred by the particular circumstances of this crisis) by, for example, exploiting customers and consumers (e.g. by charging prices above normal competitive levels) or limiting production to the ultimate prejudice of consumers (e.g. by obstructing attempts to scale up production to face shortages of supply). The Commission thus encourages undertakings and citizens to continue reporting any cartels and other antitrust violations, including abuses of dominant positions, that may come to their attention through the usual tools at their disposal.[8]

(21) The Commission will apply this Communication as of 8 April, having regard to the impact of the COVID-19 outbreak, which requires immediate action. The Commission may review the Communication on the basis of the evolution of the COVID-19 outbreak. The Communication shall remain applicable until the Commission withdraws it (once it considers that the underlying exceptional circumstances are no longer present).

NOTES

8 In addition to the usual channels for contacting the European Commission or submitting an antitrust complaint (https://ec.europa.eu/competition/contacts/electronic_documents_en.html), individuals can help anonymously in the fight against cartels and other anti-competitive practices through the Commission's whistle blower tool (https://ec.europa.eu/competition/cartels/whistleblower/index.html). The Commission's leniency programme, which allows businesses to report their own involvement in a cartel in exchange for a reduction of the fine imposed on them, also remains fully applicable during these exceptional times (https://ec.europa.eu/competition/cartels/leniency/leniency.html).

EUROPEAN COMMISSION: MERGER RULES AND CORONAVIRUS: SPECIAL MEASURES DUE TO CORONAVIRUS/ COVID-19 (APRIL 2020)

[8.57]

NOTES

This document is available on the European Commission website at https://ec.europa.eu/competition-policy/mergers/coronavirus_en. Note that the footnotes below were not part of the original document, but have been added in place of the hypertext links that were part of that document. Note also that it has been update since it was first published in April 2020.

MERGER NOTIFICATIONS

DG COMP has put in place a number of measures to ensure business continuity and has continued to ensure the implementation of the EU Merger Regulation. The Commission has adopted a number of merger decisions and processed the notifications filed by companies.

In the current situation, DG COMP faces difficulties in some cases in collecting information from the notifying parties and third parties, such as their customers, competitors and suppliers, given the disturbances caused by the coronavirus outbreak.

Consequently, DG COMP encourages parties to discuss the timing of notifications of transactions with the relevant case team and to use electronic means to notify their transactions.

DG COMP is committed to helping and supporting businesses at this difficult time. It will deal with notifications to the best of its ability.

DG COMP stands ready to deal with cases where firms can show very compelling reasons to proceed with a merger notification without delay.

DG COMP will provide updated information as the situation evolves.

TEMPORARY ACCEPTANCE OF ELECTRONIC SUBMISSIONS

Hand deliveries to DG COMP premises will remain possible but may become difficult due to a reduced presence of staff. As before, according to the general rules, the delivering law firm or company must call the Merger Registry prior to making a hand delivery.

However, DG Competition will temporarily accept and in fact, encourages all submissions in digital format, either:

— electronically by email to the functional mailbox of the merger registry (comp-merger-registry@ec.europa.eu), putting the case team in copy if one has been assigned, or

— electronically through eTrustEx.[1]

— **Merger notifications and reasoned submissions filed electronically on Mondays to Thursdays before 17h and on Fridays and days preceding Commission holidays before 16h will be processed on the same day and will thus have the date of receipt as the notification date, in line with previous practice regarding paper filings. Submissions arriving after 17h or 16 h respectively will be dealt with the following working day, which will accordingly be considered the notification date.**

The delivery of paper originals will then be arranged at a later time. Further information on delivery of merger-related documents can be found here.[2]

See also: Organisation of and participation in Advisory Committee meetings by video-link.[3]

NOTES

1 See https://ec.europa.eu/competition-policy/index/etrustex_en.

2 See https://ec.europa.eu/competition-policy/mergers/contact_en.

3 See https://ec.europa.eu/competition-policy/system/files/2021-04/advisory_committee_modalities_videoconferencing.pdf.

COMMUNICATION FROM THE COMMISSION

(2020/C112I/01)

Amendment to the Temporary Framework for State aid measures to support the economy in the current COVID-19 outbreak

[8.58]

NOTES

Date of publication in OJ: OJ C112I, 4.4.2020, p 1.

1. INTRODUCTION

1. On 19 March 2020, the Commission adopted its Communication 'Temporary Framework for State aid measures to support the economy in the current COVID-19 outbreak'[1] ('the Temporary Framework'), which, inter alia, sets out the possibilities Member States have under Union rules to ensure liquidity and access to finance for undertakings, especially small and medium-sized undertakings ('SMEs') that face a sudden shortage in this period in order to allow them to recover from the current situation. The aim is to lay down a framework that enables Member States to support undertakings experiencing difficulties due to the current COVID-19 outbreak, whilst maintaining the integrity of the EU Internal Market, ensuring a level playing field.

2. Targeted and proportionate application of EU State aid control serves to make sure that national support measures are effective in helping the affected undertakings during the COVID-19 outbreak but also that they allow them to bounce back from the current situation, keeping in mind the importance of meeting the green and digital twin transitions in accordance with EU objectives.

3. The aim of this Communication is to identify additional temporary State aid measures that the Commission considers compatible under Article 107(3) TFEU in light of the COVID-19 outbreak.

4. The Commission considers that beyond ensuring access to liquidity and finance, it is also essential to facilitate COVID-19 relevant research and development, to support the construction and upgrade of testing facilities of COVID-19 relevant products, as well as the setting up of additional capacities for the production for products needed to respond to outbreak. This includes relevant medicinal products (including vaccines) and treatments, their intermediates, active pharmaceutical ingredients and raw materials; medical devices, hospital and medical equipment (including ventilators and protective clothing and equipment as well as diagnostic tools) and necessary raw materials; disinfectants and their intermediary products and raw chemical materials necessary for their production and data collection and processing tools.

5. Furthermore, under the current circumstances it is also crucial to preserve employment. Deferrals of payment of taxes and social security contributions can be a valuable tool to reduce the liquidity constraints of undertakings and preserve employment. If such deferrals apply to the whole economy, they fall outside the scope of State aid control. If they provide undertakings with a selective advantage, which can happen if they are restricted to certain sectors (e.g. transport, tourism, health), regions or types of undertakings, they involve aid within the meaning of Article 107(1) TFEU.

6. In the same way, in order to preserve employment, Member States may envisage contributing to the wage costs of undertakings, which, due to the COVID-19 outbreak, would otherwise lay off personnel. If such support schemes apply to the whole economy, they fall outside the scope of State aid control. If they are restricted, for example, to certain sectors (e.g. transport, tourism, health), regions or types of undertakings, they involve aid within the meaning of Article 107(1) TFEU.

7. The Commission has a positive view vis-à-vis measures taken by Member States in order to increase flex-security and avoid massive layoffs. Temporary lay-off schemes of general application, which aim at providing employees with total or partial compensation for the loss of their remuneration while they are on furlough from their employment, would usually not be selective.

8. Moreover, the application of the Temporary Framework has shown the need to introduce additional clarifications and amendments as regards certain provisions, especially in section 3.1, section 3.2, section 3.3 and section 3.5.

NOTES

[1] Communication from the Commission of 19 March 2020, C(2020)1863 (OJ C91I, 20.3.2020, p 1).

2. AMENDMENTS TO THE TEMPORARY FRAMEWORK

9. The following amendments to the Temporary Framework for State aid measures to support the economy in the current COVID-19 outbreak will take effect as of 3 April 2020.

10–24. (*Amend the Commission Communication on the Temporary Framework for State aid measures to support the economy in the current COVID-19 outbreak at* **[8.63]**.)

COMMUNICATION FROM THE COMMISSION

(2020/C164/03)

Amendment to the Temporary Framework for State aid measures to support the economy in the current COVID-19 outbreak (No 2)

[8.59]

NOTES

Date of publication in OJ: OJ C164I, 13.5.2020, p 3.

1. INTRODUCTION

1. On 19 March 2020, the Commission adopted its Communication 'Temporary Framework for State aid measures to support the economy in the current COVID-19 outbreak'[1] (the 'Temporary Framework'). On 3 April 2020, it adopted a first amendment to enable aid to accelerate research, testing and production of COVID-19 relevant products, to protect jobs and to further support the economy during the current crisis.[2]

2. A targeted and proportionate application of EU State aid control ensures that national support measures effectively help affected undertakings during the COVID-19 outbreak, whilst limiting undue distortions to the Internal Market, maintaining the integrity of the Internal Market and ensuring a level playing field. This will contribute to the continuity of economic activity during the COVID-19 outbreak and provide the economy with a strong platform to recover from the crisis, keeping in mind the importance of meeting the green and digital transitions, in line with EU law and objectives.

3. The aim of this Communication is to identify additional temporary State aid measures that the Commission considers compatible under Article 107(3)(b) of the Treaty on the Functioning of the European Union (TFEU) in light of the COVID-19 outbreak.

4. First, the Commission considers that otherwise viable non-financial undertakings subject to a temporary liquidity crisis due to the COVID-19 outbreak may face longer-term solvency issues. For a large number of these undertakings, the emergency measures put in place to control the spread of the COVID-19 outbreak have resulted in a decrease or even suspension of their production of goods and/or the provision of services, as well as a significant demand shock. The resulting losses will be reflected in a decrease of undertakings' equity and will negatively affect their ability to take on loans from financial institutions.

5. Reduced equity for undertakings in markets with low demand and disrupted supply aggravates the risk of a serious economic downturn affecting potentially the whole EU economy for a longer period. Well-targeted public interventions providing equity and/or hybrid capital instruments to undertakings could reduce the risk for the EU economy of a significant number of insolvencies. They could thereby contribute to preserving the continuity of economic activity during the COVID-19 outbreak and to supporting subsequent economic recovery.

6. This Communication therefore sets out the criteria under EU State aid rules, based on which Member States may provide public support in the form of equity and/or hybrid capital instruments to undertakings facing financial difficulties due to the COVID-19 outbreak. It aims at ensuring that the disruption of the economy does not result in the unnecessary exit from the market of undertakings that were viable before the COVID-19 outbreak. Recapitalisations must therefore not exceed the minimum needed to ensure the viability of the beneficiary, and should not go beyond restoring the capital structure of the beneficiary to the one predating the COVID-19 outbreak.

7. The Commission underlines that providing national public support in the form of equity and/or hybrid capital instruments to undertakings facing financial difficulties due to the COVID-19 outbreak, as part of schemes or in specific individual cases, should only be considered if no other appropriate solution can be found and be subject to stringent conditions. This is because such instruments are highly distortive for competition between undertakings. Such interventions should therefore also be subject to clear conditions as regards the State's entry, remuneration and exit from the undertakings concerned, governance provisions and appropriate measures to limit distortions of competition.

8. If support were to be granted at EU level, taking into account the EU common interest, the risk of distortion to the Internal Market could be lower, and may therefore require less stringent conditions to be imposed. The Commission considers that additional EU level support and funds are necessary to make sure that this global symmetric crisis does not transform into an asymmetric shock to the detriment of Member States with less possibility to support their economy and the EU's competitiveness as a whole.

9. The green transition and the digital transformation will play a central and priority role in ensuring a successful recovery. The Commission welcomes steps taken by Member States to take these challenges into account when designing national support measures, and recalls their responsibility in ensuring that such measures do not hinder the achievement of EU climate and digital objectives. Furthermore, the Commission notes that designing national support measures in a way that meets the EU's policy objectives related to green and digital transformation of their economies will allow for a more sustainable long term growth, and promote the transformation to the agreed EU's objective of climate neutrality by 2050. In this context of aid to remedy a serious disturbance in the economy of Member States, it is primarily the responsibility of Member States to design national support measures in a way that meets their policy objectives. For aid under this Communication, large undertakings shall report on how the aid received supports their activities in line with EU objectives and national obligations linked to the green and digital transformation.

10. Furthermore, a number of Member States are considering taking an equity stake in strategic companies, to ensure that their contribution to the proper functioning of the EU economy is not jeopardised. The Commission recalls that the TFEU is neutral as regards public versus private ownership (Article 345 TFEU). If Member States purchase

existing shares of undertakings at market price or invest *pari passu* with private shareholders, this normally does not constitute State aid.[3] Similarly, if Member States decide to purchase newly issued shares and/or provide undertakings with other types of equity support or hybrid capital instruments on market terms, i.e. under conditions complying with the Market Economy Operator Principle, this also does not constitute State aid.

11. The Commission also recalls that there are a number of additional tools to deal with acquisitions of strategic companies. In its Communication issued on 25 March 2020,[4] the Commission called upon Member States that already have an existing foreign direct investment screening mechanism in place to make full use of such tools to prevent capital flows from non-EU countries that could undermine EU's security or public order. The Commission also called on Member States that currently do not have a screening mechanism, or whose screening mechanisms do not cover all relevant transaction to set up a fully-fledged screening mechanism, in full compliance with Union law, including the FDI Screening Regulation[5] and free movement of capital (Article 63 TFEU), and international obligations.

12. Second, the Commission considers that subordinated debt can also be an appropriate means to support undertakings facing financial difficulties due to the COVID-19 outbreak. In particular, it is a less distortive instrument than equity or hybrid capital, given that it cannot be converted into equity when the company is a going concern. This Communication therefore introduces the possibility for Member States to grant aid in this additional form in section 3.3 of the Temporary Framework, which concerns debt instruments, subject to additional safeguards to protect the level playing field in the Internal Market. However, if subordinated debt goes beyond the ceilings set out in section 3.3, such subordinated debt measure should be assessed in line with the conditions for COVID-19 recapitalisation measures set out in section 3.11 to ensure equal treatment.

13. Third, the application of the Temporary Framework has shown the need to introduce clerical modifications as well as additional clarifications and amendments as regards certain provisions in section 3.1, section 3.2, section 3.3, section 3.4, section 3.7, section 4 and section 5.

14. Finally, the Commission recognises that to ensure a successful recovery, additional large-scale private and public investments will be needed to meet the challenges and seize the opportunities of the green and digital twin transitions. In this context, the Commission recalls that this amendment to the Temporary Framework complements rather than replaces existing possibilities under EU State aid rules for Member States to provide support. For example, as regards capital support, in particular to innovative companies, the Commission's Risk Finance Guidelines[6] and the General Block Exemption Regulation[7] provide ample possibilities for Member States.

15. Similarly, Member States can decide to grant State aid to support green and digital innovation and investment, and increase the level of environmental protection in line with existing State aid rules.[8] As already announced in the Commission's Communication of 14 January 2020, relevant State aid rules, in particular the Environmental and Energy State aid guidelines, will be revised by 2021 in light of the policy objectives of the European Green Deal and support a cost-effective and socially-inclusive transition to climate neutrality by 2050. This will contribute to a recovery strategy for the European economy that meets the important green and digital twin transitions in line with EU and national objectives.

NOTES

1 Communication from the Commission of 19 March 2020, C(2020)1863 (OJ C91 I, 20.3.2020, p 1).

2 Communication from the Commission of 3 April 2020, C(2020) 2215 (OJ C112 I, 4.4.2020, p 1).

3 See section 4.2.3 of the Commission Notice on the notion of State aid as referred to in Article 107(1) of the Treaty on the Functioning of the European Union, C/2016/2946 (OJ C262, 19.7.2016, p 1).

4 Communication from the Commission – Guidance to the Member States concerning foreign direct investment and free movement of capital from third countries, and the protection of Europe's strategic assets, ahead of the application of Regulation (EU) 2019/452 (FDI Screening Regulation), C(2020) 1981 final of 25.3.2020.

5 Regulation (EU) 2019/452 of the European Parliament and of the Council of 19 March 2019 establishing a framework for the screening of foreign direct investments into the Union (OJ L79 I, 21.3.2019, p 1).

6 Communication from the Commission — Guidelines on State aid to promote risk finance investments (OJ C19, 22.1.2014, p 4).

7 Commission Regulation (EU) No 651/2014 of 17 June 2014 declaring certain categories of aid compatible with the internal market in application of Articles 107 and 108 of the Treaty (OJ L187, 26.6.2014, p 1).

8 For example, Guidelines on State aid for environmental protection and energy 2014-2020 (OJ C200, 28.6.2014, p 1), Guidelines for the application of state aid rules in relation to the rapid deployment of broadband networks (OJ C25, 26.1.2013, p 1), Guidelines on regional State aid for 2014-2020 (OJ C209, 23.7.2013, p 1), Framework for State aid for research and development and innovation (OJ C198, 27.6.2014, p 1) and Criteria for the analysis of the compatibility with the internal market of State aid to promote the execution of important projects of common European interest (OJ C188, 20.6.2014, p 4).

2. AMENDMENTS TO THE TEMPORARY FRAMEWORK

16. The following amendments to the Temporary Framework for State aid measures to support the economy in the current COVID-19 outbreak will take effect as of 8 May 2020.

17–40. (*Amend the Commission Communication on the Temporary Framework for State aid measures to support the economy in the current COVID-19 outbreak at* **[8.63]**.)

COMMUNICATION FROM THE COMMISSION

(2020/C218/03)

Third amendment to the Temporary Framework for State aid measures to support the economy in the current COVID-19 outbreak

[8.60]

NOTES

Date of publication in OJ: OJ C218, 2.7.2020, p 3.

1. INTRODUCTION

1. On 19 March 2020, the Commission adopted its Communication 'Temporary Framework for State aid measures to support the economy in the current COVID-19 outbreak'[1] (the 'Temporary Framework'). On 3 April 2020, it adopted a first amendment to include aid to accelerate research, testing and the production of COVID-19 relevant products, to protect jobs and to further support the economy during the current crisis.[2] On 8 May 2020, it adopted a second amendment to ease further the access to capital and liquidity for undertakings affected by the crisis.[3]

2. A targeted and proportionate application of EU State aid control ensures that national support measures effectively help affected undertakings during the COVID-19 outbreak, whilst limiting undue distortions to the Internal Market, maintaining the integrity of the Internal Market and ensuring a level playing field. This will contribute to the continuity of economic activity during the COVID-19 outbreak and provide the economy with a strong platform to recover from the crisis, keeping in mind the importance of meeting the green and digital transitions, in line with Union law and objectives.

3. The aim of this Communication is to clarify and amend conditions for temporary State aid measures that the Commission considers compatible under Article 107(3)(b) and (c) of the Treaty on the Functioning of the European Union (TFEU) in light of the COVID-19 outbreak.

4. First, the main purpose of the Temporary Framework is to provide targeted support to otherwise viable companies that have entered into financial difficulty as a result of the COVID-19 outbreak. This is an important principle to avoid undue distortions of competition. In that context, the Temporary Framework complements rather than replaces existing possibilities for Member States to provide support. For example, as regards undertakings that were already in financial difficulty before the COVID-19 outbreak, the Commission's Rescue and Restructuring Guidelines[4] set clear conditions on the basis of which such undertakings must work out sound restructuring plans that allow them to achieve long-term viability. Those conditions aim to ensure that such undertakings do not continue to seek State aid instead of competing in the market on their own merits.

5. Micro and small companies (*i.e.* undertakings with less than 50 employees and less than EUR 10 million of annual turnover and/or annual balance sheet) contribute heavily to jobs and growth in the Union in aggregate terms: they generate more than 37% of value added and almost 50% of employment in the non-financial business sector. During the current crisis, micro and small undertakings have been particularly affected by the liquidity shortage caused by the economic impact of the COVID-19 outbreak. The unprecedented supply and demand shock due to the crisis has also exacerbated the difficulties such undertakings face to access financing on the market in general, as compared to medium-sized and large enterprises. If left unaddressed, those difficulties could lead to a large number of bankruptcies of micro and small undertakings causing serious disturbances to the whole Union economy.

6. The Commission, therefore, considers it appropriate to include under the Temporary Framework State aid to all micro and small undertakings, even if they would fall under the category of an undertaking in financial difficulty[5] on 31 December 2019, provided that they are not subject to collective insolvency procedure under national law and that they have not received rescue aid (which has not been repaid) or restructuring aid (and are still subject to a restructuring plan). Given their limited size and limited involvement in cross-border transactions, the Commission considers that State aid to micro and small undertakings is less likely to distort competition in the Internal Market and affect intra-EU trade than State aid to medium-sized and large companies.

7. Such aid is also intended to increase support possibilities to innovative start-up companies, which are in their high-growth phase and are therefore crucial for the economic recovery of the Union. Whilst there is no EU definition for start-ups, it appears that the vast majority of such start-up companies fall within the micro and small companies cluster of the definition of small and medium-sized enterprises (SMEs) in Annex I of the General Block Exemption Regulation. The Commission recalls further that, even prior to this amendment, all SMEs that were in existence for less than three years on 31 December 2019 already benefit from the aid measures laid down in the Temporary Framework, since they could not qualify as undertakings in difficulty on 31 December 2019 according to the General Block Exemption Regulation, apart from exceptional cases of insolvency procedure or rescue or restructuring aid.[6]

8. Member States may envisage modifying existing schemes approved by the Commission under the Temporary Framework in order to include as beneficiaries within their scope micro and small companies that were already in difficulty on 31 December 2019, provided that they correspond to the circumstances described in points 6 and 7 above. Member States which plan to do so are invited to notify a list of all existing schemes they envisage modifying and to provide the necessary information listed in the annex of this Communication. This will allow the Commission to adopt one decision covering the list of schemes.

9. Second, the Temporary Framework as amended on 8 May 2020 sets out the criteria under EU State aid rules, on the basis of which Member States may provide public support in the form of equity and/or hybrid capital instruments to undertakings facing financial difficulties due to the COVID-19 outbreak. In this context, the Commission recalls that the TFEU is neutral as regards public versus private ownership (Article 345 TFEU). The conditions applicable to

undertakings that are fully or partially State-owned to raise capital from public and private shareholders should be aligned with those applicable to private undertakings, whilst maintaining the same safeguards to preserve effective competition with the appropriate adjustments. In particular, in view of the need to limit State aid to the minimum necessary, the conditions should encourage capital injections with significant private participation.

10. Third, the Commission considers that aid should not be conditioned on the relocation of a production activity or of another activity of the beneficiary from another country within the European Economic Area (EEA) to the territory of the Member State granting the aid, since such condition would appear to be particularly harmful for the internal market.

11. Finally, the application of the Temporary Framework has also shown the need to introduce additional clarifications and amendments to other points of the framework, especially in section 3.3, section 3.10 and section 3.11.

NOTES

1 Communication from the Commission of 19 March 2020, C(2020)1863 (OJ C91I, 20.3.2020, p 1).

2 Communication from the Commission of 3 April 2020, C(2020) 2215 (OJ C112I, 4.4.2020, p 1).

3 Communication from the Commission of 8 May 2020, C(2020) 3156 (OJ C164, 13.5.2020, p 3).

4 Communication from the Commission – Guidelines on State aid for rescuing and restructuring non-financial undertakings in difficulty (OJ C249, 31.7.2014, p 1).

5 As defined in the General Block Exemption Regulation, i.e. Article 2(18) of the Commission Regulation (EU) No 651/2014 of 17 June 2014 declaring certain categories of aid compatible with the internal market in application of Articles 107 and 108 of the Treaty (OJ L187, 26.6.2014, p 1).

6 According to Article 2(18) of the General Block Exemption Regulation, SMEs that have been in existence for less than three years do not qualify as undertakings in difficulty, except if: (i) they are subject to collective insolvency proceedings or fulfil the criteria under domestic law for being placed in collective insolvency proceedings at the request of creditors, (ii) they have received rescue aid and have not yet reimbursed the loan or terminated the guarantee, or (iii) they have received restructuring aid and are still subject to a restructuring plan.

2. AMENDMENTS TO THE TEMPORARY FRAMEWORK

12. The following amendments to the Temporary Framework for State aid measures to support the economy in the current COVID-19 outbreak will take effect as of 29 June 2020.

13–22. (*Amend the Commission Communication on the Temporary Framework for State aid measures to support the economy in the current COVID-19 outbreak at* **[8.63]**.)

ANNEX

INFORMATION TO BE PROVIDED IN THE LIST OF EXISTING SCHEMES AUTHORISED UNDER THE TEMPORARY FRAMEWORK FOR STATE AID MEASURES TO SUPPORT THE ECONOMY IN THE CURRENT COVID-19 OUTBREAK, FOR WHICH AN EXTENSION OF THE SCOPE OF ELIGIBLE BENEFICIARIES IS NOTIFIED TO THE COMMISSION

List of existing schemes and envisaged modification

State aid number of the authorised scheme[1]	Title	Notified amendment	Confirm that there are no other changes to the existing scheme

NOTES

1 If the scheme has been amended, please indicate the State aid number of the initial authorising decision.

COMMUNICATION FROM THE COMMISSION

(2020/C340I/01)

Fourth Amendment to the Temporary Framework for State aid measures to support the economy in the current COVID-19 outbreak and amendment to the Annex to the Communication from the Commission to the Member States on the application of Articles 107 and 108 of the Treaty on the Functioning of the European Union to short-term export-credit insurance

[8.61]

NOTES

Date of publication in OJ: OJ C340I, 13.10.2020, p 1.

Part 8 COVID-19-Related Materials

1. INTRODUCTION

1. On 19 March 2020, the Commission adopted its Communication "Temporary Framework for State aid measures to support the economy in the current COVID-19 outbreak"[1] (the 'Temporary Framework'). On 3 April 2020, it adopted a first amendment to enable aid to accelerate research, testing and production of COVID-19 relevant products, to protect jobs and to further support the economy during the current crisis.[2] On 8 May 2020, it adopted a second amendment to further ease the access to capital and liquidity for undertakings affected by the crisis.[3] On 29 June2020, it adopted a third amendment to further support micro, small and start-up companies and incentivise private investments.[4]

2. The aid measures covered by the Temporary Framework ensure an appropriate balance between their positive effects in assisting undertakings and any potential negative effects on competition and trade in the Internal Market. A targeted and proportionate application of EU State aid control ensures that national support measures effectively help affected undertakings during the COVID-19 outbreak, whilst limiting undue distortions to the Internal Market, maintaining the integrity of the Internal Market and ensuring a level playing field. This will contribute to the continuity of economic activity during the COVID-19 outbreak and provide the economy with a strong platform to recover from the crisis, keeping in mind the importance of meeting the green and digital transitions, in line with EU law and objectives.

3. The aim of this Communication is to prolong the measures set out in the Temporary Framework until 30 June 2021 and, for section 3.11, until 30 September 2021; identify additional temporary State aid measures (aid in the form of support for uncovered fixed costs); and clarify and amend conditions for certain temporary State aid measures that the Commission considers compatible under Article 107(3)(b) of the Treaty on the Functioning of the European Union (TFEU) in light of the COVID-19 outbreak. This Communication also aims to amend the list of marketable risk countries set out in the Annex to the Communication from the Commission to the Member States on the application of Articles 107 and 108 of the Treaty on the Functioning of the European Union to short-term export-credit insurance ("STEC").[5]

4. First, the Commission recalls that the Temporary Framework was initially set to expire after 31 December 2020, except for section 3.11, which would expire after 30 June 2021. The Temporary Framework also envisaged that the Commission could review the Temporary Framework before 31 December 2020 on the basis of important competition policy or economic considerations.

5. In that context, the Commission assessed the continued need for aid under the Temporary Framework, with a view to deciding whether it was necessary to maintain it after 31 December 2020. In particular, the Commission considered the following factors: on the one hand, the evolution of the economic situation in the exceptional circumstances created by the COVID-19 outbreak; on the other hand, the appropriateness of the Temporary Framework as an instrument to ensure that national support measures effectively help affected undertakings during the outbreak, whilst limiting undue distortions to the Internal Market and ensuring a level playing field.

6. According to the Summer 2020 Economic Forecast,[6] the EU economy is projected to contract by 8.3% in 2020, a deeper contraction than the 7.4% envisaged in spring. As the lifting of restrictive measures is proceeding more gradually than initially envisaged, the impact of the COVID-19 outbreak on economic activity may be more significant than anticipated. GDP for the euro area at the end of 2021 is expected to be about 2% lower than it was at the end of 2019, before the crisis, and about 4.5%below the GDP level estimated in the winter forecast.[7] Due to the gradual lifting of restrictions, but also the more permanent effects of the outbreak (*e.g.*, widespread employment destructions and corporate insolvencies), there could be a slower, incomplete recovery.

7. Member States have made substantial use of the possibilities under the Temporary Framework as an instrument to address the economic consequences of the outbreak. On 16 September 2020, the Commission sent a questionnaire to Member States focusing on the impact and the effectiveness of the Temporary Framework. Evidence being collected by the Commission shows that it constituted a useful additional instrument to support the economy during the crisis.

8. While the Temporary Framework has been useful as an instrument to address the economic consequences of the outbreak, the use of the Temporary Framework has also highlighted disparities in the Internal Market, mainly due to the differences in economic size and budgets of Member States. The Commission therefore considers that a limited prolongation of the measures set out in the Temporary Framework until 30 June 2021 and, for section 3.11, until 30 September 2021 is appropriate to ensure that national support measures effectively help affected undertakings during the outbreak, but also to maintain the integrity of the Internal Market and to ensure a level playing field. With a view to ensuring legal certainty, the Commission will assess before 30 June 2021 if the Temporary Framework needs to be further extended.

9. In addition, the Commission clarifies that for the purpose of section 3.1, section 3.2 and section 3.3 of the Temporary Framework, the actual advantage at a given moment in time must be considered and must be always within the overall limits of the Temporary Framework. That means that if, for example, a repayable advance of EUR 800,000 is granted to an undertaking under section 3.1, where such repayable advance has been reimbursed before the end of validity of the Temporary Framework, that undertaking would be eligible again for limited amounts of aid under section 3.1, provided the conditions set out therein are fulfilled. Furthermore, the Commission clarifies that where an aid measure has been granted under section 3.2 or section 3.3 and its terms have been adjusted before the end of validity of the Temporary Framework, the aid already received and the new aid must overall remain in conformity and within the limits set out in section 3.2 and section 3.3 for the entire duration of the measure.

10. Member States may envisage modifying existing aid measures approved by the Commission under the Temporary Framework in order to prolong their period of application until 30 June 2021 and, for section 3.11, until 30 September 2021. Member States which plan to do so are invited to notify a list of all existing aid measures they envisage modifying and to provide the necessary information listed in the annex of this Communication. This will allow the Commission to adopt one decision covering the list of schemes.

11. Second, as a result of the COVID-19 outbreak, many undertakings temporarily face lower demand that does not allow them to cover part of their fixed costs. In many instances, demand is expected to recover over the coming months, while it may not be efficient for those undertakings to downsize if doing so entails significant restructuring costs. Supporting those undertakings by contributing to part of their fixed costs on a temporary basis may be an efficient way of bridging the gap, thereby avoiding the deterioration of their capital, maintaining their business activity and providing them with a strong platform from which to recover.

12. The Commission therefore considers that Member States may envisage contributing to the uncovered fixed costs of those undertakings for which the COVID-19 outbreak resulted in the suspension or reduction of their business activity. The Commission considers that aid granted under such measures is justified and can be declared compatible with the internal market on the basis of Article 107(3)(b) TFEU, for a limited period, to addresses the wider negative economic effects of the economic disturbance caused by the COVID-19 outbreak.

13. Third, the Temporary Framework sets out the criteria, on the basis of which Member States may provide compatible aid in the form of equity and/or hybrid capital instruments to undertakings facing financial difficulties due to the COVID-19 outbreak. In that regard, the Commission clarifies that priority rights to existing shareholders under point 64 of the Temporary Framework should not cause the existing shareholders to exceed their stake in the equity of the beneficiary prior to the COVID-19 recapitalisation. The Commission also clarifies that the exit of the State from beneficiaries of COVID-19 recapitalisation through the mechanism of point 64 of the Temporary Framework requires a sale of the State's equity stake at market prices to third-party purchasers, meaning entities other than the beneficiary that are neither public authorities nor public undertakings within the meaning of Article 2 of Directive 2006/111/EC.[8]

14. Nevertheless, because that mechanism should respect the principle of neutrality laid down in the TFEU as regards public versus private ownership (Article 345 TFEU), the Commission adds certain adjustments to that mechanism in order to ensure that the exit of the State from undertakings in which the State is an existing shareholder, *i.e.*, before the COVID-19 recapitalisation, takes place at conditions that can reasonably be considered equivalent to those applicable to private undertakings.

15. Member States that have already committed to the possibility of exiting from beneficiaries of COVID-19 recapitalisation through the mechanism of point 64 of the Temporary Framework, *i.e.*, by selling their equity stake to third-party purchasers other than the beneficiary, may envisage modifying existing aid measures approved by the Commission under the Temporary Framework in order to include the additional possibilities added by this Communication. Member States which plan to do so are invited to notify a list of all existing aid measures they envisage modifying and to provide the necessary information listed in the annex of this Communication. This will allow the Commission to adopt one decision covering the list of measures.

16. Fourth, the application of the Temporary Framework has shown the need to introduce additional clarifications and amendments to other points of the framework, especially in section 3.1 and section 3.11.

17. Finally, this Communication provides for an amendment to the list of marketable risk countries set out in the Annex to STEC as well as for an amendment of the relevant provisions of the Temporary Framework concerning short-term export credit insurance.

18. STEC provides that marketable risks shall not be covered by export-credit insurance with the support of Member States. As a consequence of the COVID-19 outbreak, the Commission found in March 2020 that there is a lack of sufficient private insurance capacity for short-term export-credits in general and considered all commercial and political risks associated with exports to the countries listed in the Annex to STEC as temporarily non-marketable until 31 December 2020.[9]

19. In the context of the continuing difficulties due to the COVID-19 outbreak and in accordance with points 35 and 36 of STEC, the Commission conducted a public consultation to assess the availability of short-term export-credit insurance in order to determine whether the current market situation might justify the prolongation of the removal of all countries from the list of marketable risk countries in the Annex to STEC beyond 31 December 2020. The Commission received a significant number of replies from Member States, private insurers, exporters, and trade associations, which pointed to the continuing rapid contraction of private credit insurance capacity for exports in general. Most State insurers registered a significant increase in the number of requests for credit insurance policy for exports to marketable risk countries. The majority of respondents expect the insurance coverage to remain scarce, implying that an insufficient availability of private insurance for those countries can be expected in 2021.

20. Taking into account the outcome of the public consultation, as well as the overall signs of continuing disruptive impact of COVID-19 on the economy of the Union as a whole, the Commission considers that there is still a general lack of sufficient private capacity to cover all economically justifiable risks for exports to countries from the list of marketable risk countries in the Annex to STEC. In those circumstances, the Commission will consider all commercial and political risks associated with exports to the countries listed in the Annex to STEC as temporarily on-marketable until 30 June 2021, in line with the duration of the Temporary Framework. In accordance with point 36 of STEC, the Commission will assess whether to prolong the temporary exception before its expiration.

NOTES

1 Communication from the Commission of 19 March 2020, C(2020)1863, OJ C091I of 20.3.2020, p 1.

2 Communication from the Commission of 3 April 2020, C(2020) 2215, OJ C112I of 4.4.2020, p 1.

3 Communication from the Commission of 8 May 2020, C(2020) 3156, OJ C164, 13.5.2020, p 3.

4 Communication from the Commission of 29 June 2020, C(2020) 4509, OJ C218, 2.7.2020, p 3.

5 OJ C392, 19.12.2012, p 1.

6 European Commission, Economic and Financial Affairs: *Summer Forecast 2020* (Interim) (July 2020).

7 European Commission, Economic and Financial Affairs: *Winter Forecast 2020* (Interim) (February 2020).

8 Commission Directive 2006/111/EC of 16 November 2006 on the transparency of financial relations between Member States and public undertakings as well as on financial transparency within certain undertakings, OJ L318, 17.11.2006, p 17.

[9] Communication from the Commission amending the Annex to the Communication from the Commission to the Member States on the application of Articles 107 and 108 of the Treaty on the Functioning of the European Union to short-term export-credit insurance, OJ C101I, 28.3.2020, p 1.

2. AMENDMENTS TO THE TEMPORARY FRAMEWORK

21. The following amendments to the Temporary Framework for State aid measures to support the economy in the current COVID-19 outbreak will take effect as of 13 October 2020.

22–44. (*Amend the Commission Communication on the Temporary Framework for State aid measures to support the economy in the current COVID-19 outbreak at* **[8.63]**.)

3. AMENDMENT TO STEC

45. (*Substitutes the Annex to the Communication from the Commission to the Member States on the application of Articles 107 and 108 of the Treaty on the Functioning of the European Union to short-term export-credit insurance at* **[5.630]**. *The paragraph also provides that the amendment will apply until 30 June 2021.*)

ANNEX

INFORMATION TO BE PROVIDED IN THE LIST OF EXISTING AID MEASURES AUTHORISED UNDER THE TEMPORARY FRAMEWORK FOR STATE AID MEASURES TO SUPPORT THE ECONOMY IN THE CURRENT COVID-19 OUTBREAK, FOR WHICH A PROLONGATION OF THE PERIOD OF APPLICATION AND/OR AN EXTENSION OF THE POSSIBILITIES FOR THE EXIT OF THE STATE FROM UNDERTAKINGS UNDER SECTION 3.11 IS NOTIFIED TO THE COMMISSION

List of existing measures and envisaged modification			
State aid number of the authorised measure[10]	**Title**	**Notified amendment**	**Confirm that there are no other changes to the existing measure**

NOTES

[10] If the measure has been amended, please indicate the State aid number of the initial authorising decision.

COMMUNICATION FROM THE COMMISSION

(2021/C34/06)

Fifth Amendment to the Temporary Framework for State aid measures to support the economy in the current COVID-19 outbreak and amendment to the Annex to the Communication from the Commission to the Member States on the application of Articles 107 and 108 of the Treaty on the Functioning of the European Union to short-term export-credit insurance

[8.62]

NOTES

Date of publication in OJ: OJ C34, 1.2.2021, p 6.

1. INTRODUCTION

1. On 19 March 2020, the Commission adopted its Communication 'Temporary Framework for State aid measures to support the economy in the current COVID-19 outbreak'[1] (the 'Temporary Framework'). On 3 April 2020, it adopted a first amendment to enable aid to accelerate research, testing and production of COVID-19 relevant products, to protect jobs and to further support the economy during the current crisis).[2] On 8 May 2020, it adopted a second amendment to further ease the access to capital and liquidity for undertakings affected by the crisis.[3] On 29 June 2020, it adopted a third amendment to further support micro, small and start-up companies and incentivise private investments.[4] On 13 October 2020, it adopted a fourth amendment to prolong the Temporary Framework and to enable aid covering part of the uncovered fixed costs of undertakings affected by the crisis.[5]

2. The Temporary Framework seeks to ensure an appropriate balance between the positive effects of the aid measures covered in assisting undertakings and any potential negative effects on competition and trade in the Internal Market. A targeted and proportionate application of EU State aid control ensures that national support measures effectively help affected undertakings during the COVID-19 outbreak, whilst limiting undue distortions to the Internal Market, maintaining the integrity of the Internal Market and ensuring a level playing field. This will contribute to the continuity of economic activity during the COVID-19 outbreak and provide the economy with a strong platform to recover from the crisis, keeping in mind the importance of meeting the green and digital transitions, in line with EU law and the Union's objectives.

3. The aim of this Communication is to prolong the measures set out in the Temporary Framework until 31 December 2021; to adapt the aid ceilings of certain measures in order to address the prolonged economic effects of the ongoing crisis; and to clarify and amend the conditions for certain temporary State aid measures that

the Commission considers compatible under Article 107(3)(b) of the Treaty on the Functioning of the European Union ('TFEU') in light of the COVID-19 outbreak. This Communication also aims to amend the list of marketable risk countries set out in the Annex to the Communication from the Commission to the Member States on the application of Articles 107 and 108 of the Treaty on the Functioning of the European Union to short-term export-credit insurance ('STEC').[6]

4. First, the Commission recalls that the Temporary Framework was set to expire on 30 June 2021, except for section 3.11, which would expire on 30 September 2021. The Temporary Framework also envisaged that the Commission would review that framework before 30 June 2021 on the basis of important competition or economic considerations.

5. In that context, the Commission assessed the continued need for aid under the Temporary Framework, with a view to deciding whether it was necessary to maintain it after 30 June 2021. In particular, the Commission considered the following factors: on the one hand, the evolution of the economic situation in the exceptional circumstances created by the COVID-19 outbreak; on the other hand, the appropriateness of the Temporary Framework as an instrument to ensure that national support measures effectively help affected undertakings during the outbreak, whilst limiting undue distortions to the Internal Market and ensuring a level playing field.

6. According to the Autumn 2020 Economic Forecast,[7] the introduction of new and/or the tightening of existing restrictive measures taken to contain the virus ('second wave') is expected to slow down economic activity and to threaten many small businesses in the most affected sectors. EU GDP was projected to contract by about 7.5% in 2020 before rebounding by 4% in 2021, which is less than previously forecast, and by 3 % in 2022. This implies that the expected recovery has been interrupted, as the output in the European economy would barely return to pre-pandemic levels in 2022.

7. Member States have made substantial use of the possibilities under the Temporary Framework as an instrument to address the economic consequences of the COVID-19 outbreak. On 7 December 2020, the Commission sent a questionnaire to Member States focusing on the impact and the effectiveness of the Temporary Framework. Evidence collected by the Commission shows that it constitutes a useful additional instrument to support the economy during the crisis.

8. Taking into account that the Temporary Framework has been useful as an instrument to address the economic consequences of the outbreak, the Commission considers that a limited prolongation of the measures set out in that framework until 31 December 2021 is appropriate to ensure that national support measures effectively help affected undertakings during the outbreak, but also to maintain the integrity of the Internal Market and to ensure a level playing field. With a view to ensuring legal certainty, the Commission will assess before 31 December 2021 whether the Temporary Framework needs to be further extended and/or adapted.

9. Second, taking into consideration the continued impact of the COVID-19 outbreak and the lapse of time since the adoption of the Temporary Framework, the Commission considers that it is necessary to increase the aid ceilings set out in section 3.1 and section 3.12 of that framework. This is confirmed by the data submitted by Member States in response to the Commission's questionnaire on the application of the Temporary Framework, which indicate that the respective ceilings have been or are about to be exhausted in relation to a number of undertakings active in certain sectors or appear to be insufficient to address the impact of the measures taken by Member States aimed to contain the second wave of the outbreak.

10. Third, in order to provide an incentive to initially choose repayable forms of aid, the Commission considers that it is necessary to provide for the possibility for Member States, upon notification of this possibility to the Commission prior to the expiry of the Temporary Framework, to convert repayable forms of aid granted under that framework such as repayable advances, guarantees and loans into other forms of aid such as grants. That conversion should respect the conditions set out in section 3.1 and should take place by 31 December 2022 at the latest. The Commission invites Member States to provide for such a conversion based on transparent and non-discriminatory conditions. Furthermore, upon notification prior to the expiry of the Temporary Framework, Member States may convert certain forms of aid granted under that framework provided the conditions set out in the relevant sections of that framework are complied with.

11. Fourth, the application of the Temporary Framework has shown the need to introduce additional clarifications and amendments to other points of the framework, especially in section 1.3, section 3.1, section 3.2, section 3.3, section 3.10, section 3.12 and section 4.

12. In view of the above, Member States may envisage modifying existing aid measures approved by the Commission under the Temporary Framework in order to prolong their period of application until 31 December 2021. Member States may also envisage increasing the budget of existing measures or introducing other amendments to align those measures with the Temporary Framework, as amended by this Communication. Member States which plan to do so are invited to notify a list of all existing aid measures they envisage modifying and to provide the necessary information listed in the annex of this Communication. This will allow the Commission to adopt one decision covering the list of notified measures.

13. Finally, this Communication provides for an amendment to the list of marketable risk countries set out in the Annex to the STEC as well as for an amendment of the relevant provisions of the Temporary Framework concerning short-term export credit insurance.

14. The STEC provides that marketable risks shall not be covered by export-credit insurance with the support of Member States. As a consequence of the COVID-19 outbreak, the Commission found in March 2020 that there is a lack of sufficient private insurance capacity for short-term export-credits in general and considered all commercial and political risks associated with exports to the countries listed in the Annex to the STEC as temporarily non-marketable until 31 December 2020.[8] By its Communication of 13 October 2020, the Commission prolonged that temporary exception until 30 June 2021.

15. In the context of the continuing difficulties due to the COVID-19 outbreak and in accordance with points 35 and 36 of the STEC, the Commission conducted a public consultation to assess the availability of short-term export-credit insurance in order to determine whether the current market situation might justify the prolongation of the removal of all countries from the list of marketable risk countries in the Annex to the STEC beyond 30 June 2021. The Commission received a significant number of replies from Member States, private insurers, exporters, and trade associations, which point to the continuing rapid contraction of private credit insurance capacity for exports in general. Most State insurers registered a significant increase in the number of requests for credit insurance policy for exports to marketable risk countries. The majority of respondents expect the insurance coverage to remain scarce, implying that an insufficient availability of private insurance for those countries can be expected in 2021.

16. Taking into account the outcome of the public consultation, as well as the global signs of continuing disruptive impact of COVID-19 on the economy of the Union as a whole, the Commission considers that there is still a general lack of sufficient private capacity to cover all economically justifiable risks for exports to countries from the list of marketable risk countries in the Annex to the STEC. In those circumstances, the Commission will consider all commercial and political risks associated with exports to the countries listed in the Annex to the STEC as temporarily non-marketable until 31 December 2021, in line with the duration of the Temporary Framework. In accordance with point 36 of the STEC, the Commission will assess whether to prolong the temporary exception before its expiration.

NOTES

[1] Communication from the Commission of 19 March 2020, C(2020)1863, OJ C091I of 20.3.2020, p 1.

[2] Communication from the Commission of 3 April 2020, C(2020)2215, OJ C112I of 4.4.2020, p 1.

[3] Communication from the Commission of 8 May 2020, C(2020)3156, OJ C164, 13.5.2020, p 3.

[4] Communication from the Commission of 29 June 2020, C(2020)4509, OJ C218, 2.7.2020, p 3.

[5] Communication from the Commission of 13 October 2020, C(2020)7127 (OJ C340 I, 13.10.2020, p 1).

[6] OJ C392, 19.12.2012, p 1.

[7] European Commission, Economic and Financial Affairs: *Autumn Forecast 2020* (Interim) (November 2020).

[8] Communication from the Commission amending the Annex to the Communication from the Commission to the Member States on the application of Articles 107 and 108 of the Treaty on the Functioning of the European Union to short-term export-credit insurance, OJ C101I, 28.3.2020, p 1.

2. AMENDMENTS TO THE TEMPORARY FRAMEWORK

17. The following amendments to the Temporary Framework for State aid measures to support the economy in the current COVID-19 outbreak will take effect as of 28 January 2021.

18–48. (*Amend the Commission Communication on the Temporary Framework for State aid measures to support the economy in the current COVID-19 outbreak at* **[8.63]**.)

3. AMENDMENT TO STEC

49. (*Substitutes the Annex to the Communication from the Commission to the Member States on the application of Articles 107 and 108 of the Treaty on the Functioning of the European Union to short-term export-credit insurance at* **[5.630]**. *The paragraph also provides that the amendment will apply until 31 December 2021.*)

ANNEX

INFORMATION TO BE PROVIDED IN THE LIST OF EXISTING AID MEASURES AUTHORISED UNDER THE TEMPORARY FRAMEWORK FOR STATE AID MEASURES TO SUPPORT THE ECONOMY IN THE CURRENT COVID-19 OUTBREAK, FOR WHICH A PROLONGATION OF THE PERIOD OF APPLICATION, AN INCREASE OF THE BUDGET AND/OR OTHER AMENDMENTS TO ALIGN THOSE MEASURES WITH THE TEMPORARY FRAMEWORK, AS AMENDED BY THIS COMMUNICATION, IS NOTIFIED TO THE COMMISSION

List of existing measures and envisaged modification					
State aid number of the authorised measure[9]	**Title**	**Notified amendment (potentially to be sub-divided into modifications 1, 2, 3 etc.)**	**Relevant point in the Temporary Framework for the planned modifications**	**Confirm that there are no other changes to the existing measure**	**National legal basis for the amendment**

NOTES

[9] If the measure has been amended, please indicate the State aid number of the initial authorising decision.

COMMUNICATION FROM THE COMMISSION

(C(2021)8442 final)

Sixth Amendment to the Temporary Framework for State aid measures to support the economy in the current COVID-19 outbreak and amendment to the Annex to the Communication from the Commission to the Member States on the application of Articles 107 and 108 of the Treaty on the Functioning of the European Union to short-term export-credit insurance

[8.62A]

NOTES

Date of publication in OJ: OJ C473, 24.11.2021, p 1.

1. INTRODUCTION

1. On 19 March 2020, the Commission adopted its Communication "Temporary Framework for State aid measures to support the economy in the current COVID-19 outbreak"[1] (the 'Temporary Framework'). On 3 April 2020, it adopted a first amendment to enable aid to accelerate research, testing and production of COVID-19 relevant products, to protect jobs and to further support the economy during the current crisis[2]. On 8 May 2020, it adopted a second amendment to further ease the access to capital and liquidity for undertakings affected by the crisis[3]. On 29 June 2020, it adopted a third amendment to further support micro, small and start-up companies and incentivise private investments[4]. On 13 October 2020, it adopted a fourth amendment to prolong the Temporary Framework and to enable aid covering part of the uncovered fixed costs of undertakings affected by the crisis[5]. On 28 January 2021, it adopted a fifth amendment to further prolong the Temporary Framework, to adapt the aid ceilings set out therein and to enable the conversion of repayable instruments into direct grants under certain conditions[6].

2. The Temporary Framework seeks to ensure an appropriate balance between the positive effects of the aid measures granted to undertakings and any potential negative effects on competition and trade in the internal market. A targeted and proportionate application of State aid control ensures that national support measures effectively help affected undertakings during the COVID-19 pandemic, whilst limiting undue distortions to the internal market, maintaining the integrity of the internal market and ensuring a level playing field. This will contribute to the continuity of economic activity during the COVID-19 pandemic and provide the economy with a strong platform to recover from the crisis, and accelerate the necessary green and digital transitions, in line with EU law and the Union's objectives.

3. It is necessary to prolong the measures set out in the Temporary Framework until 30 June 2022; to adapt the aid ceilings of the uncovered fixed cost measure in order to address the prolonged economic effects of the ongoing crisis; to enable investment support towards a sustainable recovery and solvency support; and to clarify and amend the conditions for certain temporary State aid measures that the Commission considers compatible under Article 107(3)(b) of the Treaty on the Functioning of the European Union ('TFEU') in light of the serious economic disturbance caused to the economies of all the Member States by the COVID-19 pandemic. In addition, the removal of the list of marketable risk countries set out in the Annex to the Communication from the Commission to the Member States on the application of Articles 107 and 108 of the Treaty on the Functioning of the European Union to short-term export-credit insurance ("STEC")[7] should be prolonged.

4. First, the Commission recalls that the Temporary Framework was set to expire on 31 December 2021. The Temporary Framework also envisaged that the Commission would review that framework before 31 December 2021 on the basis of important competition or economic considerations.

5. In that context, the Commission has assessed the continued need for aid under the Temporary Framework, with a view to deciding whether it was necessary to maintain it after 31 December 2021. In particular, the Commission considered the following factors: on the one hand, the evolution of the economic situation in the exceptional circumstances created by the COVID-19 pandemic; on the other hand, the appropriateness of the Temporary Framework as an instrument to ensure that national support measures effectively help affected undertakings during the outbreak, whilst limiting undue distortions to the Internal Market and ensuring a level playing field.

6. According to the Autumn 2021 Economic Forecast[8], GDP is forecast to grow by 5.0 % in 2021 and 4.3 % in 2022 in both the Union and the euro area. The volume of output is projected to return to pre-crisis level (2019-Q4) by the end of 2021. However, uncertainty and risks surrounding the growth outlook remain high taking into account the resurgence in COVID-19 infections across certain Member States, increasing tensions in the supply chains and the rise of energy prices.

7. Member States have made substantial use of the possibilities under the Temporary Framework as an instrument to address the serious economic disturbance affecting their economies, as well as to facilitate the development of certain economic activities required to tackle the COVID-19 pandemic.

8. Given that the Temporary Framework has been useful as an instrument to address the economic consequences of the pandemic and also in light of the feedback received from Member States, the Commission considers that a limited prolongation of existing measures set out in that framework until 30 June 2022 is appropriate to ensure that national support measures effectively help affected undertakings during the outbreak while maintaining the integrity of the internal market and to ensure a level playing field. This limited prolongation will also ensure that undertakings still affected by the crisis need not be cut off suddenly from necessary support. Rather, it will enable a coordinated phase-out of the level of support in light of the observed economic recovery. That phase-out has to be seen in light of the heterogeneity of the recovery, with specific sectors and regions in different Member States still lagging behind others. Based on currently available information, the Commission considers it likely that no additional prolongation of the existing types of measures covered under sections 3.1 to 3.12 may be necessary beyond 30 June 2022. This is

especially the case as regards existing liquidity measures, where the new forward-looking possibilities for investment support towards a sustainable recovery and solvency support should be better suited in the recovery phase to address business needs and policy objectives, including to limit undue distortions in the internal market. The Commission will nevertheless continue to closely monitor the situation and assess whether any measures need to be further extended and/or adapted on the basis of important competition or economic considerations.

9. The Commission also considers it necessary to adjust the aid ceilings provided under section 3.1 in line with this prolongation.

10. Second, taking into consideration the continued impact of the COVID-19 pandemic and the lapse of time since the adoption of the Temporary Framework, the Commission considers that it is necessary to increase the aid ceilings set out in section 3.12 of that framework, which enables targeted support to companies that experienced significant turnover losses.

11. Third, several Member States have underlined the need to mitigate the risk of corporate insolvencies through additional possibilities for debt restructuring and conversion of repayable aid instruments into other forms of aid (e.g, direct grants)[9]. In order to address those concerns and mitigate the risk of corporate insolvencies, the Commission considers that it is necessary to enable the conversion of repayable aid instruments into other forms of aid under section 3.1 and section 3.12 of the Temporary Framework until 30 June 2023 provided that the conditions of the applicable sections are complied with[10]. Furthermore, the Commission also considers that repayable instruments under section 3.1, section 3.3, and section 3.12 may require restructuring in line with ordinary prudential practices of the financial intermediaries involved. Such a restructuring will be considered compatible, if completed at the latest by 30 June 2023 and under the conditions specified in this Communication. In particular, such restructuring must respect the conditions laid down in the applicable sections and may not lead to an increase of the initially granted amounts[11].

12. In addition, this Communication clarifies that Member States may extend the duration of guarantees granted under section 3.1, section 3.2, and section 3.12 of the Temporary Framework also after the expiry of that framework, provided the conditions in those sections and section 3.4 are respected. The terms and conditions of such an extension should be stipulated in the initial guarantee contracts between the State and the credit or financial institutions. Those conditions should not leave any discretion to the Member State's authorities when the duration of the guarantee is extended. Final beneficiaries must be informed at the time of the financing being initially granted that they can request an extension of the maturity of that financing, without prejudice to the fact that the credit or financial institutions may accept or refuse that request in accordance with their standard policies and procedures[12].

13. Fourth, the Commission considers that the recovery of the Union's economy will be largely determined by the speed of vaccination programmes and the progression of possible variants of the virus, but also by other unknown factors such as the state of the international economy and the spending and investment behaviours of companies and households.

14. The Commission recalls that the risk of a post-crisis investment drop actually materialised in the Union in the years following the 2008 crisis, because of increased indebtedness of the private sector. When the present crisis comes to an end, financial difficulties, risk aversion and spare capacity in some sectors could also hold back corporate investment and therefore long-term growth.

15. It is appropriate to provide further options for Member States based on Article 107(3)(c) TFEU to directly support investments in assets as well as provide an instrument to improve the equity position of European companies, by introducing a new section on investment support towards a sustainable recovery, as well as a new section on solvency support. In parallel, the Commission also considers it to be necessary to apply the individual notification requirements for schemes under specific existing guidelines with particular importance for the recovery in a more flexible manner for a limited amount of time.

16. On the one hand, investment support should facilitate the development of economic activities required for the return to a sustainable long-term growth, overcoming the negative economic effects of the crisis including a widening of the investment gap. It should also support a more resilient economy for the future, while effectively limiting potential negative effects on competition and trade.

17. Support of that kind may also help Member States to particularly develop those economic activities required to achieve the objectives of the green and digital transitions and support recovery towards a greener and more digital future while strengthening resilience and preserving a level playing field. It is also relevant as part of a phase-out of immediate short-term crisis response measures, predominantly in terms of liquidity support, and a shift towards fostering a more long-term recovery of the economy. In order to achieve the intended effect of accelerated investment spending, the application of this measure should be limited until 31 December 2022.

18. The pandemic and the measures taken by the Member States to combat the spread of the COVID-19 virus induced an immediate fall in economic activity on an unprecedented scale, in particular as regards investment. In light of these exceptional circumstances created by this crisis, the Commission considers that the provisions of section 3.13 of the present amendment may be applied to aid granted after 1 February 2020, provided all conditions are met and in particular an incentive effect can be demonstrated. Such measures need to pursue the same objective as the one laid down in section 3.13, namely provide a stimulus to overcome an investment gap accumulated in the economy due to the crisis.

19. On the other hand, solvency support is an important element for the development of economic activities in a wide range of sectors in situations where undertakings are suffering from increased debt ratios due to the crisis. Given the overall macroeconomic increase of indebtedness, Member States may seek to provide undertakings with easier access to private investments in the form of equity while limiting potential negative effects on the internal market. Such support can be an important element to strengthen the economic recovery. A longer application period for this type of solvency support measure is appropriate given the complexity and time needed to set up such schemes. Against that background, the period of application of this type of measure should extend to 31 December 2023.

20. Through the Technical Support Instrument[13], the Commission supports Member States in designing and implementing reforms aimed at overcoming the investment gap and accelerating the green and digital transitions. Member States can ask for support through the Technical Support Instrument to design and put in place solvency support measures.

21. Fifth, the application of the Temporary Framework has shown the need to introduce additional clarifications and amendments to other points of that framework, especially in section 1.3, section 3.11 and section 4, and add new tools under sections 3.13 and 3.14.

22. Therefore, Member States may envisage modifying existing aid measures approved by the Commission under the Temporary Framework in order to prolong their period of application until 30 June 2022, allow restructuring or conversion of certain instruments up to 30 June 2023, introduce new measures supporting investments towards a sustainable recovery until 31 December 2022, or new measures providing solvency support until 31 December 2023. Member States may also envisage increasing the budget of existing measures approved in light of section 3.12 or introducing other amendments to align those measures with the Temporary Framework, as amended by this Communication. This may also include a dedicated tailoring of new or existing aid measures to sectors that are particularly affected by the crisis in specific Member States within the limits of the amended Framework.

23. Member States that plan to prolong or modify existing schemes are invited to notify a list of all existing aid measures they envisage modifying and to provide the necessary information listed in the Annex of this Communication. This will allow the Commission to adopt one decision covering the list of notified measures.

24. Finally, the Commission considers that it should continue applying the provisions of the communication on the short-term export-credit insurance ("STEC") beyond 2021 to allow for a coordinated transition to normal market practice or the adoption of specific schemes under the applicable rules where necessary. It accordingly prolongs the temporary removal of all countries on the list of marketable risk countries set out in the Annex of STEC until 31 March 2022.

25. The STEC provides that marketable risks shall not be covered by export-credit insurance with the support of Member States. As a consequence of the COVID-19 pandemic, the Commission found in March 2020 that there is a lack of sufficient private insurance capacity for short-term export-credits in general and considered all commercial and political risks associated with exports to the countries listed in the Annex to the STEC as temporarily non-marketable until 31 December 2020[14]. By its Communications of 13 October 2020 and 28 January 2021, the Commission prolonged that temporary exception until 30 June 2021 and 31 December 2021, respectively. The current STEC will expire on 31.12.2021 and will be replaced by a new communication, which will still consider the criterion of non-marketable risk.

26. In the context of the continuing difficulties due to the COVID-19 pandemic and in accordance with points 35 and 36 of the STEC, the Commission conducted a public consultation to assess the availability of short-term export-credit insurance in order to determine whether the current market situation might justify the prolongation of the removal of all countries from the list of marketable risk countries in the Annex to the STEC beyond 31 December 2021.

27. Taking into account the outcome of the public consultation, as well as the global signs of continuing disruptive impact of COVID-19 on the economy of the Union as a whole, the Commission considers that a prolongation of that removal for a period of three months is an adequate solution to allow for a smooth transition before all countries listed in the Annex are considered marketable again as from 1 April 2022. Evidence submitted in the consultation by private insurers and a number of Member States indicates that private insurers started to provide coverage to serve the exporters active in most relevant markets. At the same time, further feedback received points towards a situation where market capacity is still insufficient to cover all economically justifiable risks for exports to countries from the list of marketable risk countries in the Annex to the STEC. In those circumstances, the Commission will therefore continue to consider all commercial and political risks associated with exports to the countries listed in the Annex to the STEC as temporarily non-marketable until 31 March 2022 as a prolongation to ensure a smooth transition towards normal market practice or the adoption of specific schemes under the applicable rules where needed.

NOTES

1 Communication from the Commission of 19 March 2020, C(2020)1863, OJ C091I of 20.3.2020, p 1.

2 Communication from the Commission of 3 April 2020, C(2020)2215, OJ C112I of 4.4.2020, p 1.

3 Communication from the Commission of 8 May 2020, C(2020)3156, OJ C164, 13.5.2020, p 3.

4 Communication from the Commission of 29 June 2020, C(2020)4509, OJ C218, 2.7.2020, p 3.

5 Communication from the Commission of 13 October 2020, C(2020)7127 (OJ C340 I, 13.10.2020, p 1).

6 Communication from the Commission of 28 January 2021, C(2021)564, OJ C 34, 1.2.2021, p. 6

7 OJ C 392, 19.12.2012, p. 1.

8 European Commission, Economic and Financial Affairs: *Autumn Forecast 2021* (Interim) (November 2021).

9 See, also, European Systemic Risk Board: *Prevention and management of a large number of corporate insolvencies* (April 2021).

10 The Commission clarifies that point 9 of the Communication of 13 October 2020 (C(2020)7127, OJ C 340I, 13.10.2020, p. 1) applies also to aid granted under section 3.12 of the Temporary Framework.

11 This is without prejudice to the existing possibilities of granting new aid under the Temporary Framework, which may be used to repay existing instruments, provided that the relevant conditions set out in that framework are fulfilled. Aid which has been reimbursed before or at the same time as granting new aid shall not be taken into account in determining whether the relevant ceiling is exceeded.

12 The extension should not result in an increase in the interest rate or fee rates applicable to the underlying instrument (including due to a downgrade of the final beneficiary's rating even if that downgrade happens before the extension request is decided).

13 Regulation (EU) 2021/240 of the European Parliament and of the Council of 10 February 2021 establishing a Technical Support Instrument, OJ L 57, 18.2.2021, p. 1.

14 Communication from the Commission amending the Annex to the Communication from the Commission to the

Member States on the application of Articles 107 and 108 of the Treaty on the Functioning of the European Union to short-term export-credit insurance, OJ C 101I, 28.3.2020, p. 1.

2. AMENDMENTS TO THE TEMPORARY FRAMEWORK

28. The following amendments to the Temporary Framework for State aid measures to support the economy in the current COVID-19 outbreak will take effect as of 18 November 2021.

29–61. (*Amend the Commission Communication on the Temporary Framework for State aid measures to support the economy in the current COVID-19 outbreak at* **[8.63]**.)

3. PROLONGATION OF THE REMOVAL OF THE LIST OF MARKETABLE RISK COUNTRIES FROM STEC

62. (*Sets out the Annex to the Communication from the Commission to the Member States on the application of Articles 107 and 108 of the Treaty on the Functioning of the European Union to short-term export-credit insurance . The paragraph also provides that it will apply until 31 March 2022.*)

ANNEX
INFORMATION TO BE PROVIDED IN THE LIST OF EXISTING AID MEASURES AUTHORISED UNDER THE TEMPORARY FRAMEWORK FOR STATE AID MEASURES TO SUPPORT THE ECONOMY IN THE CURRENT COVID-19 OUTBREAK, FOR WHICH A PROLONGATION OF THE PERIOD OF APPLICATION, AN INCREASE OF THE BUDGET AND/OR OTHER AMENDMENTS TO ALIGN THOSE MEASURES WITH THE TEMPORARY FRAMEWORK, AS AMENDED BY THIS COMMUNICATION, IS NOTIFIED TO THE COMMISSION

List of existing measures and envisaged modification					
State aid number of the authorised measure[15]	**Title**	**Notified amendment (potentially to be sub-divided into modifications 1, 2, 3 etc)**	**Relevant point in the Temporary Framework for the planned modifications**	**Confirm that there are no other changes to the existing measure**	**National legal basis for the amendment**

NOTES

[15] If the measure has been amended, please indicate the State aid number of the initial authorising decision.

COMMUNICATION FROM THE COMMISSION

(2020/C91I/01)

Temporary Framework for State aid measures to support the economy in the current COVID-19 outbreak (Consolidated version as last amended on 18 November 2021)

[8.63]

NOTES

Date of publication in OJ: OJ C91I, 20.3.2020, p 1.

Editorial note: this Communication is reproduced as amended by the following:

— Commission Communication: Amendment to the Temporary Framework for State aid measures to support the economy in the current COVID-19 outbreak (2020/C112I/01) at **[8.58]** ("the First Amending Communication").

— Commission Communication: Amendment to the Temporary Framework for State aid measures to support the economy in the current COVID-19 outbreak (No 2) (2020/C164/03) at **[8.59]** ("the Second Amending Communication").

— Commission Communication: Third amendment to the Temporary Framework for State aid measures to support the economy in the current COVID-19 outbreak (2020/C218/03) at **[8.60]** ("the Third Amending Communication").

— Commission Communication: Fourth Amendment to the Temporary Framework for State aid measures to support the economy in the current COVID-19 outbreak and amendment to the Annex to the Communication from the Commission to the Member States on the application of Articles 107 and 108 of the Treaty on the Functioning of the European Union to short-term export-credit insurance (2020/C340I/01) at **[8.61]** ("the Fourth Amending Communication").

— Commission Communication: Fifth Amendment to the Temporary Framework for State aid measures to support the economy in the current COVID-19 outbreak and amendment to the Annex to the Communication from the Commission to the Member States on the application of Articles 107 and 108 of the Treaty on the Functioning of the European Union to short-term export-credit insurance (2021/C34/06) at **[8.62]** ("the Fifth Amending Communication").

— Commission Communication: Sixth Amendment to the Temporary Framework for State aid measures to support the economy in the current COVID-19 outbreak and amendment to the Annex to the Communication from the Commission to the Member States on the application of Articles 107 and 108 of the Treaty on the Functioning of the European Union to short-term export-credit insurance (2021/C34/06) at **[8.62A]** ("the Sixth Amending Communication").

See further the press release of 18 November 2021 (https://ec.europa.eu/commission/presscorner/detail/en/ip_21_6092) in which the Commission announced that it has decided to prolong this Temporary Framework until 30 June 2022.

Note also that various footnotes reproduced below have been inserted or amended. For the sake of convenience, they have been renumbered in order to keep them sequential. The footnotes reproduced below, therefore, may not be numbered in the same way as in the original document.

1. THE COVID-19 OUTBREAK, ITS IMPACT ON THE ECONOMY AND THE NEED FOR TEMPORARY MEASURES

1.1. THE COVID-19 OUTBREAK AND ITS IMPACT ON THE ECONOMY

[8.64]

1. The COVID-19 outbreak is a severe public health emergency for citizens and societies, with infections in all the Union's Member States. It is also a major shock to the global and Union's economies and a coordinated economic response of Member States and EU institutions is crucial to mitigate these negative repercussions on the EU economy.

2. This shock is affecting the economy through different channels. There is a supply shock resulting from the disruption of supply chains, there is a demand shock caused by lower consumer demand and there is the negative effect of uncertainty on investment plans and the impact of liquidity constraints for undertakings.

3. The various containment measures adopted by the Member States, such as social distancing measures, travel restrictions, quarantines and lock downs are intended to ensure that the shock is as short and limited as possible. These measures have an immediate impact on both demand and supply, and hit undertakings and employees, especially in the health, tourism, culture, retail and transport sectors. Beyond the immediate effects on mobility and trade, the COVID-19 outbreak is also increasingly affecting undertakings in all sectors and of all kinds, small and medium enterprises ('SMEs') as well as large undertakings. The impact is also felt on global financial markets, in particular with concerns for liquidity. These effects will not be contained to one particular Member State and they will have a disruptive impact on the economy of the Union as a whole.

4. In the exceptional circumstances created by the COVID-19 outbreak, undertakings of all kinds may face a severe lack of liquidity. Solvent or less solvent undertakings alike may face a sudden shortage or even unavailability of liquidity. SMEs are at particular risk. This can therefore seriously affect the economic situation of many healthy undertakings and their employees in the short and medium term, while having also longer-lasting effects by endangering their survival.

5. Banks and other financial intermediaries have a key role to play in dealing with the effects of the COVID-19 outbreak, by maintaining the flow of credit to the economy. If the flow of credit is severely constrained, economic activity will decelerate sharply, as undertakings struggle to pay their suppliers and employees. Against this background, it is appropriate that Member States can take measures to incentivise credit institutions and other financial intermediaries to continue to play their role in continuing supporting economic activity in the EU.

6. Aid granted by Member States under Article 107(3)(b) TFEU under this Communication to undertakings, which is channelled through banks as financial intermediaries, benefits those undertakings directly. Such aid does not have the objective to preserve or restore the viability, liquidity or solvency of banks. Similarly, aid granted by Member States to banks under Article 107(2)(b) TFEU to compensate for direct damage suffered as a result of the COVID-19 outbreak[1] does not have the objective to preserve or restore the viability, liquidity or solvency of an institution or entity. As a result, such aid would not be qualified as extraordinary public financial support under the Directive 2014/59/EU of the European Parliament and of the Council (the BRRD)[2] nor under the Regulation 806/2014 of the European Parliament and of the Council (the SRM Regulation)[3], and would also not be assessed under the State aid rules[4] applicable to the banking sector.[5]

[7. If due to the COVID-19 outbreak, banks would need extraordinary public financial support (see Article 2(1) (28) BRRD and Article 3(1)(29) SRMR) in the form of liquidity, recapitalisation or impaired asset measure, it will have to be assessed whether the measure meets the conditions of Article 32(4)(d)(i), (ii) or (iii) of the BRRD and Article 18(4)(d)(i), (ii) or (iii) of the SRMR. Where the latter conditions are fulfilled, the bank receiving such extraordinary public financial support would not be deemed to be failing-or-likely-to-fail. To the extent such measures address problems linked to the COVID-19 outbreak, they would be deemed to fall under point 45 of the 2013 Banking Communication,[6] which sets out an exception to the requirement of burden-sharing by shareholders and subordinated creditors.]

8. Undertakings may not only face insufficient liquidity, but they may also suffer significant damage because of the COVID-19 outbreak. The exceptional nature of the COVID-19 outbreak means that such damages could not have been foreseen, are of a significant scale and hence put undertakings in conditions that sharply differ from the market conditions in which they normally operate. Even healthy undertakings, well prepared for the risks inherent to the normal course of business, can struggle in these exceptional circumstances, to such an extent that their viability may be undermined.

[9. The COVID-19 outbreak poses the risk of a serious downturn affecting the whole economy of the EU, hitting businesses, jobs and households. Well-targeted public support is needed to ensure that sufficient liquidity remains available in the markets, to counter the damage inflicted on healthy undertakings and to preserve the continuity of economic activity during and after the COVID-19 outbreak. Furthermore, Member States can decide support to operators in the travel and tourism industry to ensure that reimbursement claims caused by the COVID-19 outbreak are satisfied with a view to ensuring the protection of passenger and consumer rights, and equal treatment of passengers and travellers. Given the limited size of the EU budget, the main response will come from Member States' national budgets. EU State aid rules enable Member States to take swift and effective action to support citizens and undertakings, in particular SMEs, facing economic difficulties due to the COVID-19 outbreak.]

1.2. THE NEED FOR CLOSE EUROPEAN COORDINATION OF NATIONAL AID MEASURES

10. Targeted and proportionate application of EU State aid control serves to make sure that national support measures are effective in helping the affected undertakings during the COVID-19 outbreak but also that they allow them to bounce back from the current situation, keeping in mind the importance of meeting the green and digital twin transitions in accordance with EU objectives. Likewise, EU State aid control ensures that the EU Internal Market is

not fragmented and that the level playing field stays intact. The integrity of the Internal Market will also lead to a faster recovery. It also avoids harmful subsidy races, where Member States with deeper pockets can outspend neighbours to the detriment of cohesion within the Union.

1.3. THE NEED FOR APPROPRIATE STATE AID MEASURES

11. In the overall effort of Member States to tackle the effects of the COVID-19 outbreak on their economy, this Communication sets out the possibilities Member States have under EU rules to ensure liquidity and access to finance for undertakings, especially SMEs that face a sudden shortage in this period in order to allow them to recover from the current situation.

12. The Commission set out in the Communication on a Coordinated economic response to the COVID-19 outbreak of 13 March 2020[7] the various options available to Member States outside the scope of EU State aid control and which they may put in place without the involvement of the Commission. These include measures applicable to all undertakings regarding wage subsidies, suspension of payments of corporate and value added taxes or social welfare contributions, or financial support directly to consumers for cancelled services or tickets not reimbursed by the concerned operators.

[13. Member States may also design support measures in line with Block Exemption Regulations[8] without the involvement of the Commission.]

14. In addition, on the basis of Article 107(3)(c) TFEU and as further specified in the Rescue and Restructuring State aid Guidelines, Member States can notify to the Commission aid schemes to meet acute liquidity needs and support undertakings facing financial difficulties, also due to or aggravated by the COVID-19 outbreak.[9]

[14*bis*. The Commission acknowledges that the COVID-19 pandemic and the measures taken to contain it have created exceptional circumstances for many undertakings. In that unique situation, and depending on the individual case, the Commission clarifies that it may be justified that own contributions within the meaning of points (62) to (64) of the Guidelines on State aid for rescuing and restructuring non-financial undertakings in difficulty[9a] (the "Rescue and Restructuring Guidelines") remain below 50 % of the restructuring costs, as long as they remain significant and include additional fresh funding at market conditions. The exceptional and unforeseeable nature of the current situation may also allow for exceptions from the 'one time last time' principle, pursuant to point (72)(c) of the Rescue and Restructuring Guidelines, if the renewed difficulties arise from the COVID-19 pandemic and the economic downturn generated by it, i.e., if the undertaking concerned has become an undertaking in difficulty due to the COVID-19 pandemic and the following economic downturn. For the avoidance of doubt it should be noted that the remaining provisions of the Rescue and Restructuring Guidelines, and in particular the need for a restructuring plan, the return to long-term viability, and burden-sharing, continue to apply.]

15. Furthermore, on the basis of Article 107(2)(b) TFEU Member States can also compensate undertakings in sectors that have been particularly hit by the outbreak (e.g. transport, tourism, culture, hospitality and retail) and/or organisers of cancelled events for damages suffered due to and directly caused by the outbreak. Member States can notify such damage compensation measures and the Commission will assess them directly under Article 107(2)(b) TFEU.[10] The principle of 'one time last time'[11] of the Rescue and Restructuring Guidelines does not cover aid that the Commission declares compatible under Article 107(2)(b) TFEU, since the latter type of aid is not '*rescue aid, restructuring aid or temporary restructuring support*' within the meaning of point 71 of the Rescue and Restructuring Guidelines. Therefore, Member States may compensate under Article 107(2)(b) TFEU the damages directly caused by the COVID-19 outbreak to undertakings that have received aid under the Rescue and Restructuring Guidelines.

[15*bis*. Nevertheless, aid on the basis of Article 107(2)(b) TFEU must compensate for damage directly caused by the COVID-19 outbreak, such as damage directly caused by restrictive measures precluding the beneficiary, de jure or de facto, from operating its economic activity or a specific and severable part of its activity.[11a]

Such measures can include measures which require the complete cessation of an economic activity (e.g. closure of bars, restaurants or non-essential shops), or its cessation in certain areas (e.g. restrictions of flights or other transport to or from certain points of origin or destination)[11b]. The exclusion of certain highly material categories of clients (e.g. leisure travellers as far as concerns hotels, school trips as far as concerns dedicated youth accommodation) also constitutes measures that create a direct link between the exceptional occurrence and damage resulting from the exclusion of those client categories. Restrictive measures allowing the award of compensation under Article 107(2)(b) TFEU can also include measures capping attendance for specific sectors or activities (e.g. entertainment, trade fairs, sports events) at levels demonstrably and materially below those that would be dictated, in that specific setting, by generally applicable social distancing rules or rules on capacity in commercial spaces (e.g. because it does not appear sufficiently certain that protocols can be devised and successfully applied to ensure respect for the generally applicable measures in such settings). Such caps on attendance may amount to a de facto restriction where economic mitigation measures entail cessation of all or a sufficiently substantial part of the affected activity.[11c]

By contrast, other restrictive measures (for instance, general social distancing measures or general sanitary constraints, including measures merely translating such general requirements in terms specific to the characteristics of certain sectors or types of venues) would not seem to meet the requirements of Article 107(2)(b) TFEU. In the same vein, other kinds of aid addressing more generally the economic downturn from the COVID-19 outbreak are to be assessed under the different compatibility basis of Article 107(3)(b) TFEU, and therefore in principle on the basis of this Temporary Framework.]

[15*ter*. Article 107(2)(b) TFEU requires also that there is no overcompensation. Only the damage resulting directly from the restrictive measures can be compensated and a rigorous quantification of such damage must take place. Therefore, it is important to demonstrate that the aid compensates only for the damage directly caused by the measure, up to the level of profits which could have been credibly generated by the beneficiary in the absence of the measure, for the part of its activity which is curtailed. In view of the prolonged crisis, economic effects of declines in demand or in attendance due to lower aggregate demand; or due to greater customer reluctance to gather in public places, transport means or other venues; or due to generally applicable restrictions on capacity, social distancing measures, etc. cannot be taken into account in the calculation of damage attributable to the restrictive measure which can be compensated under Article 107(2)(b) TFEU.]

16. To complement the above mentioned possibilities, the Commission sets out in this Communication additional temporary State aid measures that it considers compatible under Article 107 (3)(b) TFEU, which can be approved very rapidly upon notification by the Member State concerned. Moreover, notification of alternative approaches – both aid schemes and individual measures – remains possible. The aim of this Communication is to lay down a framework that allows Member States to tackle the difficulties undertakings are currently encountering whilst maintaining the integrity of the EU Internal Market and ensuring a level playing field.

[16*bis*. Furthermore, the Commission considers that beyond aid measures allowed under Article 107(3)(b) TFEU and existing possibilities under Article 107(3)(c) TFEU, it is also essential to accelerate COVID-19 relevant research and development, to support testing and upscaling infrastructures that contribute to develop COVID-19 relevant products, as well as to support the production of products needed to respond to the outbreak. Therefore, this Communication lays down the conditions under which the Commission will consider such measures compatible with the internal market under Article 107(3)(c) TFEU. The Commission took due consideration of the common objective pursued by such aid measures and their positive effects on tackling the health emergency crisis provoked by the COVID-19 outbreak when balancing them against the potential negative effects of such measures on the internal market.]

[16*ter*. Aid granted under this Communication on the basis of Article 107(3)(b) or (c) TFEU shall not be conditioned on the relocation of a production activity or of another activity of the beneficiary from another country within the EEA to the territory of the Member State granting the aid. Such condition would appear to be harmful to the internal market. This is irrespective of the number of job losses actually occurred in the initial establishment of the beneficiary in the EEA.]

NOTES

Points 7, 9, 13: substituted by the Second Amending Communication, points 17–19.

Point 14*bis*: inserted by the Sixth Amending Communication, point 29, as from 18 November 2021.

Point 15*bis*: inserted by the Third Amending Communication, point 13. Subsequently substituted by the Fifth Amending Communication, point 18, as from 28 January 2021.

Point 15*ter*: inserted by the Fifth Amending Communication, point 19, as from 28 January 2021.

Point 16*bis*: inserted by the First Amending Communication, point 10.

Point 16*ter*: inserted by the Third Amending Communication, point 14.

[1] Such aid must be notified by Member States and the Commission will assess it under Article 107(2)(b) TFEU.

[2] OJ L173, 12.6.2014, p 190.

[3] OJ L225, 30.7.2014, Article 3 (1)(29) of the SRM Regulation.

[4] Communication on the recapitalisation of financial institutions in the current financial crisis: limitation of aid to the minimum necessary and safeguards against undue distortions of competition ('Recapitalisation Communication') (OJ C10, 15.1.2009, p 2), Communication from the Commission on the treatment of impaired assets in the Community financial sector ('Impaired Assets Communication') (OJ C72, 26.3.2009, p 1), Communication on the return to viability and the assessment of restructuring measures in the financial sector in the current crisis under the State aid rules ('Restructuring Communication') (OJ C195, 19.8.2009, p 9), Communication from the Commission on the application, from 1 January 2011, of State aid rules to support measures in favour of financial institutions in the context of the financial crisis ('2010 Prolongation Communication') (OJ C329, 7.12.2010, p 7), Communication from the Commission on the application, from 1 January 2012, of State aid rules to support measures in favour of financial institutions in the context of the financial crisis ('2011 Prolongation Communication') (OJ C356, 6.12.2011, p 7), Communication from the Commission on the application, from 1 August 2013, of State aid rules to support measures in favour of banks in the context of the financial crisis ('2013 Banking Communication') (OJ C216, 30.7.2013, p 1).

[5] Any measures to support credit institutions or other financial institutions that constitute State aid in the meaning of Article 107(1) TFEU, which fall outside the present Communication or are not covered by Article 107(2)(b) TFEU must be notified to the Commission and shall be assessed under the State aid rules applicable to the banking sector.

[6] Communication from the Commission on the application, from 1 August 2013 , of State aid rules to support measures in favour of banks in the context of the financial crisis (OJ C216, 30.7.2013, p 1).

[7] Communication from the Commission to the European Parliament, the European Council, the Council, the European Central Bank, the European Investment Bank and the Eurogroup on Coordinated economic response to the COVID-19 Outbreak, COM(2020) 112 final of 13. 3.2020.

[8] Commission Regulation (EU) No 651/2014 of 17 June 2014 declaring certain categories of aid compatible with the internal market in application of Articles 107 and 108 of the Treaty (OJ L187, 26.6.2014, p 1), Commission Regulation (EC) No 702/2014 of 25 June 2014 declaring certain categories of aid in the agricultural and forestry sectors and in rural areas compatible with the internal market in application of Articles 107 and 108 of the Treaty on the Functioning of the European Union (OJ L193, 1.7.2014, p 1) and Commission Regulation (EU) No 1388/2014 of 16 December 2014 declaring certain categories of aid to undertakings active in the production, processing and marketing of fishery and aquaculture products compatible with the internal market in application of Articles 107 and 108 of the Treaty on the Functioning of the European Union (OJ L369, 24.12.2014, p 37).

[9] Guidelines on State aid for rescuing and restructuring non-financial undertakings in difficulty (OJ C249, 31.7.2014, p 1). The Commission has authorised various schemes in nine different Member States.

[9a] Communication from the Commission (OJ C 249, 31.7.2014, p. 1).

[10] See for example, Commission decision SA. 56685, Denmark - Compensation scheme for cancellation of events related to COVID-19, https://ec.europa.eu/competition/state_aid/cases1/202011/285054_2139535_70_2.pdf.

[11] See section 3.6.1 of the Rescue and Restructuring Guidelines.

[11a] An indicative, non-exhaustive list of Commission decisions concerning aid measures authorised under Article 107(2)(b) TFEU is available at https://ec.europa.eu/competition/state_aid/what_is_new/covid_19.html.

[11b] See, e.g., the Commission's proposal for a Regulation of the European Parliament and of the Council amending Council

Regulation (EEC) No 95/93 as regards temporary relief from the slot utilisation rules at Community airports due to the COVID-19 pandemic, COM/2020/818 final.

11c This assessment may be qualified where the undertaking is under a legal obligation to continue providing the service or goods in question.

2. APPLICABILITY OF ARTICLE 107(3)(B) OF THE TREATY ON THE FUNCTIONING OF THE EUROPEAN UNION

[8.65]

17. Pursuant to Article 107(3)(b) TFEU the Commission may declare compatible with the internal market aid 'to remedy a serious disturbance in the economy of a Member State'. In this context, the Union courts have ruled that the disturbance must affect the whole or an important part of the economy of the Member State concerned, and not merely that of one of its regions or parts of its territory. This, moreover, is in line with the need to make a strict interpretation of any exceptional provision such as Article 107(3)(b) TFEU.[12] This interpretation has been consistently applied by the Commission in its decision-making.[13]

18. Considering that the COVID-19 outbreak affects all Member States and that the containment measures taken by Member States impact undertakings, the Commission considers that State aid is justified and can be declared compatible with the internal market on the basis of Article 107(3)(b) TFEU, for a limited period, to remedy the liquidity shortage faced by undertakings and ensure that the disruptions caused by the COVID-19 outbreak do not undermine their viability, especially of SMEs.

19. The Commission sets out in this Communication the compatibility conditions it will apply in principle to the aid granted by Member States under Article 107(3)(b) TFEU. Member States must therefore show that the State aid measures notified to the Commission under this Communication are necessary, appropriate and proportionate to remedy a serious disturbance in the economy of the Member State concerned and that all the conditions of this Communication are fully respected.

[20. Temporary aid measures covered by this Communication may be cumulated with one another in line with the provisions in the specific sections of this Communication. Temporary aid measures covered by this Communication may be cumulated with aid under de minimis Regulations[14] or with aid under Block Exemption Regulations[14a] provided the provisions and cumulation rules of those Regulations are respected.]

[20*bis*. Aid to credit and financial institutions is not to be assessed under this Communication except for: (i) indirect advantages to credit or financial institutions channelling aid in the form of loans or guarantees under sections 3.1 to 3.3 pursuant to the safeguards of section 3.4, and (ii) aid under section 3.10 provided the scheme is not targeting exclusively employees from the financial sector.]

NOTES

Point 20: substituted by the Second Amending Communication, point 20.

Point 20*bis*: inserted by the Second Amending Communication, point 21.

12 Joined Cases T-132/96 and T-143/96 *Freistaat Sachsen, Volkswagen AG and Volkswagen Sachsen GmbH v Commission*, ECLI:EU: T:1999:326, paragraph 167.

13 Commission Decision 98/490/EC in Case C 47/96 *Crédit Lyonnais* (OJ L221, 8.8.1998, p 28), point 10.1; Commission Decision 2005/345/EC in Case C 28/02 *Bankgesellschaft Berlin* (OJ L116, 4.5.2005, p 1), points 153 et seq.; and Commission Decision 2008/263/EC in Case C 50/06 *BAWAG* (OJ L83, 26.3.2008, p 7), point 166. See Commission Decision in Case NN 70/07 *Northern Rock* (OJ C43, 16.2.2008, p 1), Commission Decision in Case NN 25/08 *Rescue aid to Risikoabschirmung WestLB* (OJ C189, 26.7.2008, p 3) and Commission Decision of 4 June 2008 in State aid C 9/08 *SachsenLB* (OJ L104, 24.4.2009, p 34), and Commission Decision of 16 June 2017 in case .SA.32544 (2011/C) *Restructuring of TRAINOSE S.A* (OJ L186, 24.7.2018, p 25).

14 Commission Regulation (EU) No 1407/2013 of 18 December 2013 on the application of Articles 107 and 108 of the Treaty on the Functioning of the European Union to de minimis aid (OJ L352, 24.12.2013, p 1), Commission Regulation (EU) No 1408/2013 of 18 December 2013 on the application of Articles 107 and 108 of the Treaty on the Functioning of the European Union to de minimis aid in the agriculture sector (OJ L352, 24.12.2013, p 9), Commission Regulation (EU) No 717/2014 of 27 June 2014 on the application of Articles 107 and 108 of the Treaty on the Functioning of the European Union to de minimis aid in the fishery and aquaculture sector (OJ L190, 28.6.2014, p 45) and Commission Regulation (EU) No 360/2012 of 25 April 2012 on the application of Articles 107 and 108 of the Treaty on the Functioning of the European Union to de minimis aid granted to undertakings providing services of general economic interest (OJ L114, 26.4.2012, p 8).

14a Commission Regulation (EU) No 651/2014 of 17 June 2014 declaring certain categories of aid compatible with the internal market in application of Articles 107 and 108 of the Treaty (General Block Exemption Regulation), Commission Regulation (EC) No 702/2014 of 25 June 2014 declaring certain categories of aid in the agricultural and forestry sectors and in rural areas compatible with the internal market in application of Articles 107 and 108 of the Treaty on the Functioning of the European Union (OJ L193, 1.7.2014, p 1) and Commission Regulation (EU) No 1388/2014 of 16 December 2014 declaring certain categories of aid to undertakings active in the production, processing and marketing of fishery and aquaculture products compatible with the internal market in application of Articles 107 and 108 of the Treaty on the Functioning of the European Union (OJ L369, 24.12.2014, p 37).

3. TEMPORARY STATE AID MEASURES

3.1. [LIMITED AMOUNTS OF AID]

[8.66]

21. Beyond the existing possibilities based on Article 107(3)(c) TFEU, temporary limited amounts of aid to undertakings that find themselves facing a sudden shortage or even unavailability of liquidity can be an appropriate, necessary and targeted solution during the current circumstances.

[22. The Commission will consider such State aid compatible with the internal market on the basis of Article 107(3)(b) TFEU, provided that all the following conditions are met (the specific provisions for the primary agriculture, the fishery and aquaculture sectors are set out in point 23):]

[a. The overall aid does not exceed EUR 2.3 million per undertaking at any given point in time.[14b] The aid may be granted in the form of direct grants, tax and payment advantages or other forms such as repayable advances, guarantees, loans and equity provided the total nominal value of such measures remains below the overall cap of EUR 2.3 million per undertaking;]

b. the aid is granted on the basis of a scheme with an estimated budget;

[c. Aid may not be granted to undertakings that were already in difficulty (within the meaning of the General Block Exemption Regulation)[15] on 31 December 2019.]

[*cbis*. In derogation to the above, aid can be granted to micro or small enterprises (within the meaning of Annex I of the General Block Exemption Regulation) that were already in difficulty on 31 December 2019 provided that they are not subject to collective insolvency procedure under national law, and that they have not received rescue aid* or restructuring aid.**]

[d. the aid is granted no later than 30 June 2022;[16]]

[e. the aid granted to undertakings active in the processing and marketing of agricultural products[17] is conditional on not being partly or entirely passed on to primary producers and is not fixed on the basis of the price or quantity of products put on the market by the undertakings concerned or purchased from primary producers, unless, in the latter case, the products were either not put on the market or were used for non-food purposes such as distillation, methanization or composting by the undertakings concerned.]

[23. By way of derogation from point 22(a), the following specific conditions shall apply to aid granted to undertakings in the agriculture, fishery and aquaculture sectors, in addition to the conditions of point 22 (b) to (e):

[a. the overall aid does not at any point in time exceed EUR 345 000 per undertaking active in the fishery and aquaculture sector[19] or EUR 290 000 per undertaking active in the primary production of agricultural products[19a];[19b] the aid may be granted in the form of direct grants, tax and payment advantages or other forms such as repayable advances, guarantees, loans and equity provided the total nominal value of such measures does not exceed the overall cap of EUR 345 000 or EUR 290 000 per undertaking; all figures used must be gross, that is, before any deduction of tax or other charge;]

b. aid to undertakings active in the primary production of agricultural products must not be fixed on the basis of the price or quantity of products put on the market;

c. aid to undertakings active in the fishery and aquaculture does not concern any of the categories of aid referred to in Article 1, paragraph (1) (a) to (k), of Commission Regulation (EU) No 717/2014.[20]]

[23*bis*. Where an undertaking is active in several sectors to which different maximum amounts apply in accordance with points 22(a) and 23(a), the Member State concerned shall ensure, by appropriate means, such as separation of accounts, that the relevant ceiling is respected for each of those activities and that the overall maximum amount of EUR 2.3 million is not exceeded per undertaking. Where an undertaking is active in the sectors covered by point 23(a), the overall maximum amount of EUR 345 000 should not be exceeded per undertaking.]

[23*ter*. Measures granted under this Communication in the form of repayable advances, guarantees, loans or other repayable instruments may be converted into other forms of aid such as grants, provided the conversion takes place by 30 June 2023 at the latest and the conditions in this section are complied with.]

3.2. AID IN THE FORM OF GUARANTEES ON LOANS

[24. In order to ensure access to liquidity to undertakings facing a sudden shortage, public guarantees on loans[20a] for a limited period and loan amount can be an appropriate, necessary and targeted solution during the current circumstances.]

[24*bis*. Aid granted under section 3.2 shall not be cumulated with aid granted for the same underlying loan principal under section 3.3 and vice versa. Aid granted under section 3.2 and section 3.3 may be cumulated for different loans provided the overall amount of loans per beneficiary does not exceed the ceilings set out in point 25(d) or in point 27(d). A beneficiary may benefit in parallel from multiple measures under section 3.2 provided the overall amount of loans per beneficiary does not exceed the ceilings set out in point 25(d) and (e).]

[25. The Commission will consider such State aid granted in the form of new public guarantees on individual loans in response to the COVID-19 outbreak as compatible with the internal market on the basis of Article 107(3)(b) TFEU provided:

a. Guarantee premiums are set per individual loans at a minimum level, which shall increase progressively as the duration of the guaranteed loan increases, as set out in the following table:

Type of recipient	For 1st year	For 2nd – 3rd year	For 4th – 6th year
SMEs	25bps	50bps	100bps
Large enterprises	50bps	100bps	200bps

b. As an alternative, Member States may notify schemes, considering the above table as a basis, but whereby guarantee duration, guarantee premiums and guarantee coverage may be modulated for each underlying individual loan principal, such as lower guarantee coverage could offset a longer duration or could allow lower guarantee premiums; a flat premium may be used for the entire duration of the guarantee, if it is higher than the minimum premiums for the 1st year set out in the table above for each type of beneficiary, as adjusted according to guarantee duration and guarantee coverage under this paragraph;

[c. The guarantee is granted by 30 June 2022 at the latest;]

[d. For loans with a maturity beyond 30 June 2022, the overall amount of loans per beneficiary shall not exceed:]

i. double the annual wage bill of the beneficiary (including social charges as well as the cost of personnel working on the undertaking's site but formally in the payroll of subcontractors) for 2019, or for the last year available. In the case of undertakings created on or after 1 January 2019, the maximum loan must not exceed the estimated annual wage bill for the first two years in operation; or

ii. 25% of the beneficiary's total turnover in 2019; or

[iii. with appropriate justification provided by the Member State to the Commission (for example in connection with the characteristics of certain type of undertakings), the amount of the loan may be increased to cover the liquidity needs from the moment of granting for the coming 18 months for SMEs[21] and for the coming 12 months for large enterprises. The liquidity needs should be established through self-certification by the beneficiary.[22]]

[e. For loans with a maturity until 30 June 2022, the amount of the loan principal may be higher than under point 25(d) with appropriate justification provided by the Member State to the Commission, and provided that the proportionality of the aid remains assured and is demonstrated by the Member State to the Commission;]

f. The duration of the guarantee is limited to maximum six years, unless modulated according to point 25 (b), and the public guarantee may not exceed:

i. 90% of the loan principal where losses are sustained proportionally and under the same conditions by the credit institution and the State; or

ii. 35% of the loan principal, where losses are first attributed to the State and only then to the credit institutions (*i.e.* a first-loss guarantee); and

iii. in both of the above cases, when the size of the loan decreases over time, for instance because the loan starts to be reimbursed, the guaranteed amount must decrease proportionally;

g. The guarantee shall relate to investment and/or working capital loans;

h. The guarantee may not be granted to undertakings that were already in difficulty (within the meaning of the General Block Exemption Regulation)[23] on 31 December 2019.

[h*bis*. In derogation to the above, aid can be granted to micro or small enterprises (within the meaning of Annex I of the General Block Exemption Regulation) that were already in difficulty on 31 December 2019 provided that they are not subject to collective insolvency procedure under national law, and that they have not received rescue aid[*] or restructuring aid.]][**]

[25*bis*. Guarantees on newly issued debt instruments which are subordinated to ordinary senior creditors in the case of insolvency proceedings, may be granted with guarantee premiums which are at least equal to the guarantee premiums referred to in the table of point 25(a) plus 200 bps for large enterprises and 150 bps for SMEs. The alternative possibility of point 25(b) applies to such guarantees on debt instruments. Points 25(c), 25(f)(i) and (iii), 25(g), 25(h) and 25(h)bis shall also be complied with.[23a] The amount of the guaranteed subordinated debt shall not exceed both of the following ceilings:[23b]

i. Two thirds of the annual wage bill of the beneficiary for large enterprises and the annual wage bill of the beneficiary for SMEs, as defined in point 25(d)(i); and

ii. 8.4 % of the beneficiary's total turnover in 2019 for large enterprise and 12.5 % of the beneficiary's total turnover in 2019 for SMEs.]

3.3. AID IN THE FORM OF SUBSIDISED INTEREST RATES FOR LOANS

[26. In order to ensure access to liquidity to undertakings facing a sudden shortage, subsidized interest rates for a limited period and loan amount may be an appropriate, necessary and targeted solution during the current circumstances. In addition, subordinated debt, which is subordinated to ordinary senior creditors in the case of insolvency proceedings, may also be an appropriate, necessary and targeted solution during the current circumstances. Such debt is a less distortive instrument than equity or hybrid capital, since it cannot be converted automatically into equity when the company is a going concern. Therefore, aid in form of subordinated debt[23c] must fulfil the respective conditions under section 3.3, which concerns debt instruments. However, as it increases the ability of companies to take on senior debt in a way similar to capital support, a credit risk mark-up and a further limitation as to the amount compared to senior debt (one third for large enterprises and half the amount for SMEs, as defined in point 27(d) (i) or (ii)), shall apply in addition. Beyond these ceilings, subordinated debt should be assessed in line with the conditions for COVID-19 recapitalisation measures set out in section 3.11 to ensure equal treatment.]

[26*bis*. Aid granted under section 3.3 shall not be cumulated with aid granted for the same underlying loan principal under section 3.2 and vice versa. Aid granted under section 3.2 and section 3.3 may be cumulated for different loans provided the overall amount of loans per beneficiary does not exceed the thresholds set out in point 25(d) or in point 27(d). A beneficiary may benefit in parallel from multiple measures under section 3.3 provided the overall amount of loans per beneficiary does not exceed the ceilings set out in points 27(d) and (e).]

[27. The Commission will consider State aid in the form of subsidies to public loans in response to the COVID-19 outbreak as compatible with the internal market on the basis of Article 107(3)(b) TFEU provided the following conditions are met:

[a. The loans may be granted at reduced interest rates which are at least equal to the base rate (1 year IBOR or equivalent as published by the Commission[24] available either on 1 January 2020 or at the moment of notification, plus the credit risk margins as set-out in the table below:[25]

Type of recipient	**Credit risk margin for 1st year**	**Credit risk margin for 2nd – 3rd year**	**Credit risk margin for 4th – 6th year**
SMEs	25bps	50bps	100bps
Large enterprises	50bps	100bps	200bps

b. As an alternative, Member States may notify schemes, considering the above table as a basis, but whereby the loan maturity and the level of credit risk margins may be modulated, such as a flat credit risk margin may be used for the entire duration of the loan, if it is higher than the minimum credit risk margin for the 1st year for each type of beneficiary, as adjusted according to the loan maturity under this paragraph;[26]

[c. The loan contracts are signed by 30 June 2022 at the latest and are limited to maximum six years, unless modulated according to point 27(b);]

[d. For loans with a maturity beyond 30 June 2022, the overall amount of the loans per beneficiary shall not exceed:]

i. double the annual wage bill of the beneficiary (including social charges as well as the cost of personnel working on the undertaking's site but formally in the payroll of subcontractors) for 2019 or for the last year available. In the case of undertakings created on or after 1 January 2019, the maximum loan must not exceed the estimated annual wage bill for the first two years in operation; or

ii. 25% of the beneficiary's total turnover in 2019; or

[iii. with appropriate justification provided by the Member State to the Commission (for example in connection with the characteristics of certain type of undertakings), the amount of the loan may be increased to cover the liquidity needs from the moment of granting for the coming 18 months for SMEs[27] and for the coming 12 months for large enterprises. The liquidity needs should be established through self-certification by the beneficiary.[28]]

[e. For loans with a maturity until 30 June 2022, the amount of the loan principal may be higher than under point 27(d) with appropriate justification provided by the Member State to the Commission, and provided that the proportionality of the aid remains assured and is demonstrated by the Member State to the Commission;]

f. The loan shall relate to investment and/or working capital needs;

g. The loan may not be granted to undertakings that were already in difficulty (within the meaning of the General Block Exemption Regulation)[28a] on 31 December 2019.

[*gbis*. In derogation to the above, aid can be granted to micro or small enterprises (within the meaning of Annex I of the General Block Exemption Regulation) that were already in difficulty on 31 December 2019 provided that they are not subject to collective insolvency procedure under national law, and that they have not received rescue aid[*] or restructuring aid.[**]]

[27*bis*. Debt instruments, which are subordinated to ordinary senior creditors in the case of insolvency proceedings may be granted at reduced interest rates, which are at least equal to the base rate and the credit risk margins referred to in the table of point 27(a) plus 200 bps for large enterprises and 150 bps for SMEs. The alternative possibility of point 27(b) applies to such debt instruments. Points 27(c), 27(f), 27(g) and 27(g)bis shall also be complied with. If the amount of subordinated debt exceeds both of the following ceilings,[28b] the compatibility of the instrument with the Internal Market is determined pursuant to section 3.11:

i. Two thirds of the annual wage bill of the beneficiary for large enterprises and the annual wage bill of the beneficiary for SMEs, as defined in point 27(d)(i); and

ii. 8.4 % of the beneficiary's total turnover in 2019 for large enterprise and 12.5 % of the beneficiary's total turnover in 2019 for SMEs.]

[27*ter*. The Commission considers that in case repayable instruments granted under this section, section 3.1, or section 3.12 require restructuring, this will be compatible provided that: (i) it is based on sound economic analysis of the specific situation of the individual case as part of the ordinary prudential practices; (ii) it respects the conditions of the applicable section especially in terms of minimum credit risk margins and maximum duration, as well as the requirements of section 3.4 (where applicable); (iii) it does not lead to an increase in the initially granted loan amount; and (iv) such restructuring takes place at the latest by 30 June 2023.]

3.4. AID IN THE FORM OF GUARANTEES AND LOANS CHANNELLED THROUGH CREDIT INSTITUTIONS OR OTHER FINANCIAL INSTITUTIONS

[28. Aid in the form of guarantees and loans pursuant to section 3.1, section 3.2, section 3.3 and section 3.12 of this Communication may be provided to undertakings facing a sudden liquidity shortage directly or through credit institutions and other financial institutions as financial intermediaries. In the latter case, the conditions set out below must be complied with.]

29. While such aid is directly targeting undertakings facing a sudden liquidity shortage and not credit institutions or other financial institutions, it may also constitute an indirect advantage to the latter. Nevertheless, such indirect aid does not have the objective to preserve or restore the viability, liquidity or solvency of the credit institutions. As a result, the Commission considers that such aid should not be qualified as extraordinary public financial support according to Article 2(1) No 28 BRRD and Article 3(1) No 29 SRMR, and should not be assessed under the State aid rules applicable to the banking sector.[29]

30. In any event, it is appropriate to introduce certain safeguards in relation to the possible indirect aid in favour of the credit institutions or other financial institutions to limit undue distortions to competition.

[31. The credit institutions or other financial institutions should, to the largest extent possible, pass on the advantages of the public guarantee or subsidised interest rates on loans to the final beneficiaries. The financial intermediary must be able to demonstrate that it operates a mechanism that ensures that the advantages are passed on to the largest extent possible to the final beneficiaries in the form of higher volumes of financing, riskier portfolios, lower collateral requirements, lower guarantee premiums or lower interest rates than without such public guarantees or loans.]

[3.5. SHORT-TERM EXPORT CREDIT INSURANCE

32. The Communication from the Commission on short-term export-credit insurance ("STEC")[30] provides that marketable risks shall not be covered by export-credit insurance with the support of Member States. As a consequence of the current COVID-19 outbreak and after having conducted the public consultation on the availability of short-term export-credit insurance for exports to all currently marketable risk countries, the Commission found that there is a lack of sufficient private insurance capacity for short-term export credits in general and that the cover for marketable risks is temporarily unavailable.

[33. In that context, the Commission considers all commercial and political risks associated with exports to the countries listed in the Annex to the STEC as temporarily non-marketable until 31 March 2022.]

[3.6. AID FOR COVID-19 RELEVANT RESEARCH AND DEVELOPMENT

34. Beyond the existing possibilities based on Article 107(3)(c) TFEU, it is essential to facilitate COVID-19 relevant research and development (R&D) to address the current emergency health crisis.

35. The Commission will consider compatible with the internal market aid for R&D projects carrying out COVID-19 and other antiviral relevant research[31] including projects having received a COVID-19-specific Seal of Excellence quality label under the Horizon 2020 SME-instrument, provided that all the following conditions are met:

[a. The aid is granted in the form of direct grants, repayable advances or tax advantages by 30 June 2022;]

b. For R&D projects started as of 1 February 2020 or for projects having received a COVID-19-specific Seal of Excellence,, the aid is deemed to have an incentive effect; for projects started before 1 February 2020, the aid is deemed to have an incentive effect, if the aid is necessary to accelerate or widen the scope of the project. In such cases, only the additional costs in relation to the acceleration efforts or the widened scope shall be eligible for aid;

c. Eligible costs may refer to all the costs necessary for the R&D project during its duration, including amongst others, personnel costs, costs for digital and computing equipment, for diagnostic tools, for data collection and processing tools, for R&D services, for pre-clinical and clinical trials (trial phases I-IV), for obtaining, validating and defending patents and other intangible assets, for obtaining the conformity assessments and/or authorisations necessary for the marketing of new and improved vaccines and medicinal products, medical devices, hospital and medical equipment, disinfectants, and personal protective equipment; phase-IV trials are eligible as long as they allow further scientific or technological advance;

d. The aid intensity for each beneficiary may cover 100% of eligible costs for fundamental research and shall not exceed 80% of eligible costs for industrial research and experimental development;[32]

e. The aid intensity for industrial research and experimental development may be increased by 15 percentage points, if more than one Member State supports the research project, or it is carried out in cross-border collaboration with research organisations or other undertakings;

f. Aid under this measure may be combined with support from other sources for the same eligible costs, provided the combined aid does not exceed the ceilings defined under points (d) and (e) above;

g. The aid beneficiary shall commit to grant non-exclusive licences under non-discriminatory market conditions to third parties in the EEA;

h. Aid may not be granted to undertakings that were already in difficulty (within the meaning of the General Block Exemption Regulation)[32a] on 31 December 2019.

[h*bis*. In derogation to the above, aid can be granted to micro or small enterprises (within the meaning of Annex I of the General Block Exemption Regulation) that were already in difficulty on 31 December 2019 provided that they are not subject to collective insolvency procedure under national law, and that they have not received rescue aid[*] or restructuring aid.]][**]

[3.7. INVESTMENT AID FOR TESTING AND UPSCALING INFRASTRUCTURES

36. Beyond the existing possibilities based on Article 107(3)(c) TFEU, it is essential to support testing and upscaling infrastructures that contribute to develop COVID-19 relevant products.

37. The Commission will therefore consider investment aid for the construction or upgrade of testing and upscaling infrastructures required to develop, test and upscale, up to first industrial deployment prior to mass production, COVID-19 relevant products as outlined in section 3.8 compatible with the internal market provided the following conditions are met:

a. The aid is granted for the construction or upgrade of testing and upscaling infrastructures required to develop, test and upscale, up to first industrial deployment prior to mass production, COVID-19 relevant medicinal products (including vaccines) and treatments, their intermediates, active pharmaceutical ingredients and raw materials; medical devices, hospital and medical equipment (including ventilators and protective clothing and equipment as well as diagnostic tools) and necessary raw materials; disinfectants and their intermediary products and raw chemical materials necessary for their production; as well as data collection/processing tools;

[b. The aid is granted in the form of direct grants, tax advantages or repayable advances by 30 June 2022;]

c. For projects started as of 1 February 2020, the aid is deemed to have an incentive effect; for projects started before 1 February 2020, the aid is deemed to have an incentive effect, if the aid is necessary to accelerate or widen the scope of the project. In such cases, only the additional costs in relation to the acceleration efforts or the widened scope shall be eligible for aid;

d. The investment project shall be completed within six months after the date of granting the aid. An investment project is considered completed when it is accepted by the national authorities as completed. Where the six-month deadline is not met, per month of delay, 25% of the amount of aid awarded in form of direct grants or tax advantages shall be reimbursed, unless the delay is due to factors outside the control of the aid beneficiary. Where the deadline is respected, aid in the form of repayable advances is transformed into grants; if not, the repayable advance is reimbursed in equal annual instalments within five years after the date of granting the aid;

e. Eligible costs are the investment costs necessary for setting up the testing and upscaling infrastructures required to develop the products listed in point (a) above. The aid intensity shall not exceed 75% of the eligible costs;

f. The maximum allowable aid intensity of the direct grant or tax advantage may be increased by an additional 15 percentage points, either if the investment is concluded within two months after the date of aid granting or date of application of the tax advantage, or if the support comes from more than one Member State. If the aid is granted in form of a repayable advance, and the investment is completed within two months, or if the support comes from more than one Member State, an additional 15 percentage points may be granted;

g. The aid under this measure shall not be combined with other investment aid for the same eligible costs;

h. A loss cover guarantee may be granted in addition to a direct grant, tax advantage or repayable advance, or as an independent aid measure. The loss cover guarantee is issued within one month after the undertaking applied for it; the amount of loss to be compensated is established five years after completion of the investment. The compensation amount is calculated as the difference between sum of investment costs, reasonable profit of 10% p. a. on the investment cost over five years, and operating cost on the one hand, and the sum of the direct grant received, revenues over the five year period, and the terminal value of the project;

i. The price charged for the services provided by the testing and upscaling infrastructure shall correspond to the market price;

[j. The testing and upscaling infrastructures shall be open to several users and access shall be granted on a transparent and non-discriminatory basis. Undertakings, which have financed at least 10% of the investment costs may be granted preferential access under more favourable conditions.]

k. Aid may not be granted to undertakings that were already in difficulty (within the meaning of the General Block Exemption Regulation)[32b] on 31 December 2019.

[k*bis*. In derogation to the above, aid can be granted to micro or small enterprises (within the meaning of Annex I of the General Block Exemption Regulation) that were already in difficulty on 31 December 2019 provided that they are not subject to collective insolvency procedure under national law, and that they have not received rescue aid[*] or restructuring aid.]][**]

[3.8. INVESTMENT AID FOR THE PRODUCTION OF COVID-19 RELEVANT PRODUCTS

38. Beyond the existing possibilities based on Article 107(3)(c) TFEU, it is essential to facilitate the production of COVID-19 relevant products. This includes: relevant medicinal products (including vaccines) and treatments, their intermediates, active pharmaceutical ingredients and raw materials; medical devices, hospital and medical equipment (including ventilators, protective clothing and equipment as well as diagnostic tools) and necessary raw materials; disinfectants and their intermediary products and raw chemical materials necessary for their production; data collection/processing tools.

39. The Commission will consider investment aid for the production of COVID-19 relevant products compatible with the internal market provided the following conditions are met:

a. The investment aid is granted for the production of COVID-19 relevant products, such as medicinal products (including vaccines) and treatments, their intermediates, active pharmaceutical ingredients and raw materials; medical devices, hospital and medical equipment (including ventilators, protective clothing and equipment as well as diagnostic tools) and necessary raw materials; disinfectants and their intermediary products and raw chemical materials necessary for their production; data collection/processing tools;

[b. The aid is granted in the form of direct grants, tax advantages or repayable advances by 30 June 2022;]

c. For projects started as of 1 February 2020, the aid is deemed to have an incentive effect; for projects started before 1 February 2020, the aid is deemed to have an incentive effect, if the aid is necessary to accelerate or widen the scope of the project. In such cases, only the additional costs in relation to the acceleration efforts or the widened scope shall be eligible for aid;

d. The investment project is completed within six months after the date of granting the aid. An investment project is considered completed when it is accepted by the national authorities as completed. Where the six-month deadline is not met, per month of delay, 25% of the amount of aid awarded in form of direct grants or tax advantages is to be reimbursed, unless the delay is due to factors outside the control of the aid beneficiary. Where the deadline is respected, aid in the form of repayable advances is transformed into grants; if not, the repayable advance is reimbursed in equal annual instalments within five years after the date of granting the aid;

e. Eligible costs relate to all investment costs necessary for the production of the products listed in point (a) and to the costs of trial runs of the new production facilities. The aid intensity shall not exceed 80% of the eligible costs;

f. The maximum allowable aid intensity of the direct grant or tax advantage may be increased by an additional 15 percentage points, either if the investment is concluded within two months after the date of the aid granting or the date of application of the tax advantage, or if the support comes from more than one Member State. If the aid is granted in the form of a repayable advance and the investment is completed within two months or if the support comes from more than one Member State an additional 15 percentage points may be granted;

g. Aid under this measure shall not be combined with other investment aid for the same eligible costs;

h. A loss cover guarantee may be granted in addition to a direct grant, tax advantage or repayable advance or as an independent aid measure. The loss cover guarantee is issued within one month after the undertaking applied for it; the amount of loss to be compensated is established five years after completion of the investment. The compensation amount is calculated as the difference between sum of investment costs, reasonable profit of 10% p.a. on the investment cost over five years, and operating cost on the one hand, and the sum of the direct grant received, revenues over the five year period, and the terminal value of the project;

i. Aid may not be granted to undertakings that were already in difficulty (within the meaning of the General Block Exemption Regulation)[32c] on 31 December 2019.

[i*bis*. In derogation to the above, aid can be granted to micro or small enterprises (within the meaning of Annex I of the General Block Exemption Regulation) that were already in difficulty on 31 December 2019 provided that they are not subject to collective insolvency procedure under national law, and that they have not received rescue aid[*] or restructuring aid.[**]]]

[3.9. AID IN FORM OF DEFERRALS OF TAX AND/OR OF SOCIAL SECURITY CONTRIBUTIONS

40. Deferrals of payment of taxes and/or of social security contributions may be a valuable tool to reduce the liquidity constraints of undertakings (including self-employed individuals) and preserve employment. Where such deferrals are of a general application and do not favour certain undertakings, or the production of certain goods, they do not fall within the scope of Article 107(1) TFEU. If they are restricted for example to certain sectors, regions or types of undertakings, they involve aid within the meaning of Article 107(1) TFEU.[32d]

[41. The Commission will consider compatible with the internal market on the basis of Article 107(3)(b) TFEU aid schemes that consist in temporary deferrals of taxes or of social security contributions which apply to undertakings (including self-employed individuals) that are particularly affected by the COVID-19 pandemic, for example in specific sectors, regions or of a certain size. This applies also to measures provided for in relation to fiscal and social security obligations intended to ease the liquidity constraints faced by the beneficiaries, including but not limited to the deferral of payments due in instalments, easier access to tax debt payment plans and of the granting of interest free periods, suspension of tax debt recovery, and expedited tax refunds. The aid shall be granted before 30 June 2022 and the end date for the deferral shall not be later than 30 June 2023.]

[3.10. AID IN FORM OF WAGE SUBSIDIES FOR EMPLOYEES TO AVOID LAY-OFFS DURING THE COVID-19 OUTBREAK

[42. In order to preserve employment, Member States may envisage contributing to the wage costs of undertakings, which, due to the COVID-19 outbreak, would otherwise lay off personnel or to the wage equivalent income of self-employed individuals for whom the adoption of national measures in response to the COVID-19 outbreak resulted in the suspension or reduction of their business activity. If such support schemes apply to the whole economy, they fall outside the scope of Union State aid control, since they are not selective. In contrast, those schemes shall be considered to provide undertakings with a selective advantage, if they are restricted to certain sectors, regions or types of undertakings.]

43. If such measures constitute aid, the Commission will consider them compatible with the internal market on the basis of Article 107(3)(b) TFEU provided the following conditions are met:

[a. The aid is aimed at avoiding lay-offs during the COVID-19 outbreak (and to ensure the continuation of business activities of self-employed individuals);]

b. The aid is granted in the form of schemes to undertakings in specific sectors, regions or of a certain size that are particularly affected by the COVID-19 outbreak;

[c. The individual aid awards of the wage subsidy scheme are granted no later than 30 June 2022, for employees that would otherwise have been laid off as a consequence of the suspension or reduction of business activities due to the COVID-19 pandemic (or for self-employed individuals whose business activity has been negatively affected by the COVID-19 pandemic), and subject to the condition that the benefitting personnel is maintained in continuous employment for the entire period for which the aid is granted (or subject to the condition that the relevant business activity of the self-employed individual is maintained for the entire period for which the aid is granted);]

[d. The monthly wage subsidy shall not exceed 80 % of the monthly gross salary (including employer's social security contributions) of the benefitting personnel (or 80 % of the average monthly wage equivalent income of the self-employed individual). Member States may also notify, in particular in the interest of low wage categories, alternative calculation methods of the aid intensity, such as using the national wage average, minimum wage or the monthly gross wage cost of the employees concerned (or the monthly wage equivalent income of self-employed individuals) before the COVID-19 outbreak, provided the proportionality of the aid is maintained;]

e. The wage subsidy may be combined with other generally available or selective employment support measures, provided the combined support does not lead to overcompensation of the wage costs of the personnel concerned. Wage subsidies may further be combined with tax deferrals and deferrals of social security payments.]

[43*bis*. To the extent that such a scheme includes also employees of credit or financial institutions, any aid to those institutions does not have the objective to preserve or restore their viability, liquidity or solvency, given the predominantly social objective of such aid.[32e] As a result, the Commission considers that such aid should not be qualified as extraordinary public financial support according to Article 2(1) (28) BRRD and Article 3(1) (29) SRMR, and should not be assessed under the State aid rules applicable to the banking sector.[32f]]

[3.11. RECAPITALISATION MEASURES

44. This Temporary Framework sets out the criteria under EU State aid rules, based on which Member States may provide public support in the form of equity and/or hybrid capital instruments to undertakings facing financial difficulties due to the COVID-19 outbreak.[32g] It aims at ensuring that the disruption of the economy does not result in the unnecessary exit from the market of undertakings that were viable before the COVID-19 outbreak. Recapitalisations must therefore not exceed the minimum needed to ensure the viability of the beneficiary, and should not go beyond restoring the capital structure of the beneficiary to the one predating the COVID-19 outbreak. Large undertakings must report on how the aid received supports their activities in line with EU objectives and national obligations linked to the green and digital transformation, including the EU objective of climate neutrality by 2050.

45. At the same time, the Commission underlines that providing national public support in the form of equity and/or hybrid capital instruments, as part of schemes or in individual cases, should only be considered if no other appropriate solution can be found. Moreover, the issuing of such instruments should be subject to stringent conditions because they are highly distortive for competition between undertakings. Such interventions must therefore be subject to clear conditions as regards the State's entry, remuneration and exit from the equity of the undertakings concerned, governance provisions and appropriate measures to limit distortions of competition. Against this background,

the Commission notes that designing national support measures in a way that meets the EU's policy objectives related to green and digital transformation of their economies will allow for a more sustainable long-term growth, and promote the transformation to the agreed EU objective of climate neutrality by 2050.

3.11.1. Applicability

46. The following conditions shall apply to recapitalisation schemes and individual recapitalisation measures of Member States for non-financial undertakings (collectively referred to as 'COVID-19 recapitalisation' measures) under this Communication, which are not covered by section 3.1 of this Communication. They apply to COVID-19 recapitalisation measures for large undertakings and SMEs.[32h]

47. The following conditions shall also apply to subordinated debt instruments that exceed both of the ceilings referred to in point 27*bis* (i) and (ii) in section 3.3 of this Communication.

[48. COVID-19 recapitalisation measures shall not be granted later than 30 June 2022.]

3.11.2 Eligibility and entry conditions

49. The COVID-19 recapitalisation measure must fulfil the following conditions:

a. without the State intervention the beneficiary would go out of business or would face serious difficulties to maintain its operations. Such difficulties may be shown by the deterioration of, in particular, the beneficiary's debt to equity ratio or similar indicators;

b. it is in the common interest to intervene. This may relate to avoiding social hardship and market failure due to significant loss of employment, the exit of an innovative company, the exit of a systemically important company, the risk of disruption to an important service, or similar situations duly substantiated by the Member State concerned;

c. the beneficiary is not able to find financing on the markets at affordable terms and the horizontal measures existing in the Member State concerned to cover liquidity needs are insufficient to ensure its viability; and

d. the beneficiary is not an undertaking that was already in difficulty on 31 December 2019 (within the meaning of the General Block Exemption Regulation.)[32i]

[d*bis*. In derogation to the above, aid can be granted to micro or small enterprises (within the meaning of Annex I of the General Block Exemption Regulation) that were already in difficulty on 31 December 2019 provided that they are not subject to collective insolvency procedure under national law, and that they have not received rescue aid* or restructuring aid.**]]

50. Member States shall grant COVID-19 recapitalisation measures under an aid scheme approved by the Commission only following a written request for such aid by the prospective beneficiary undertakings. As regards individually notifiable aid, Member States shall provide evidence of such a written request as part of the notification of the individual aid measure to the Commission.

51. The requirements of this section and sections 3.11.4, 3.11.5, 3.11.6 and 3.11.7 apply to both COVID-19 recapitalisation schemes and individual aid measures. When approving a scheme, the Commission will request the separate notification of individual aid above the threshold of EUR 250 million. In relation to such notifications the Commission will assess whether existing financing in the market or horizontal measures to cover liquidity needs are insufficient to ensure the viability of the beneficiary; that the selected recapitalisation instruments and the conditions attached to them are appropriate to address the beneficiary's serious difficulties; that the aid is proportionate; and that the conditions in this section and sections 3.11.4, 3.11.5, 3.11.6 and 3.11.7 are complied with.

3.11.3. Types of recapitalisation measures

52. Member States can provide COVID-19 recapitalisation measures using two distinct sets of recapitalisation instruments:

a. equity instruments, in particular, the issuance of new common or preferred shares; and/or

b. instruments with an equity component (referred to as 'hybrid capital instruments'),[32j] in particular profit participation rights, silent participations and convertible secured or unsecured bonds.

53. The State intervention can take the form of any variation of the above instruments, or a combination of equity and hybrid capital instruments. Member States may also underwrite the above instruments in the context of a market offering, under the condition that any resulting State intervention in a beneficiary meets the conditions set out in this section 3.11 of the Communication. The Member State must ensure that the selected recapitalisation instruments and the conditions attached thereto are appropriate to address the beneficiary's recapitalisation needs, while at the same time being the least distortive to competition.

3.11.4. Amount of the recapitalisation

[54. In order to ensure proportionality of the aid, the amount of the COVID-19 recapitalisation must not exceed the minimum needed to ensure the viability of the beneficiary, and should not go beyond restoring the capital structure of the beneficiary to the one predating the COVID-19 outbreak, i.e. the situation on 31 December 2019. In assessing the proportionality of the aid, State aid received or planned in the context of the COVID-19 outbreak shall be taken into account.[32k]]

3.11.5. Remuneration and exit of the State

General principles

55. The State shall receive appropriate remuneration for the investment. The closer the remuneration is to market terms, the lower the potential competition distortion caused by the State intervention.

56. The COVID-19 recapitalisation should be redeemed when the economy stabilises. The Commission considers it appropriate to give the beneficiary sufficient time to redeem the recapitalisation. The Member State must put a mechanism in place to gradually incentivise redemption.

57. The remuneration of the COVID-19 recapitalisation measure should be increased in order to converge with market prices to provide an incentive to the beneficiary and to the other shareholders to redeem the State recapitalisation measure and to minimise the risk of distortions of competition.

58. It follows that COVID-19 recapitalisation measures need to contain appropriate incentives for undertakings to redeem the recapitalisation and look for alternative capital when market conditions permit, by requiring a sufficiently high remuneration for the recapitalisation.

59. As an alternative to the remuneration methodologies set out below, Member States may notify schemes or individual measures where the remuneration methodology is adapted in accordance with the features and seniority of the capital instrument provided they overall lead to a similar outcome with regard to the incentive effects on the exit of the State and a similar overall impact on the State's remuneration.

Remuneration of equity instruments

60. A capital injection by the State, or an equivalent intervention, shall be conducted at a price that does not exceed the average share price of the beneficiary over the 15 days preceding the request for the capital injection. If the beneficiary is not a publicly listed company, an estimate of its market value should be established by an independent expert or by other proportionate means.

61. Any recapitalisation measure shall include a step-up mechanism increasing the remuneration of the State, to incentivise the beneficiary to buy back the State capital injections. This increase in remuneration can take the form of additional shares[32l] granted to the State or other mechanisms, and should correspond to a minimum of 10% increase in the remuneration of the State (for the participation resulting from the State's COVID-19 equity injection that has not been repaid), for each of the step-up steps:

a. Four years after the COVID-19 equity injection, if the State has not sold at least 40 percent of its equity participation resulting from the COVID-19 equity injection, the step-up mechanism will be activated.
b. Six years after the COVID-19 equity injection, if the State has not sold in full its equity participation resulting from the State's COVID-19 equity injection, the step-up mechanism will again be activated.[32m]

If the beneficiary is not a publicly listed company, Member States may decide to implement each of the two steps one year later, i.e. five years and seven years after granting of the COVID-19 equity injection, respectively.

62. The Commission may accept alternative mechanisms, provided they overall lead to a similar outcome with regard to the incentive effects on the exit of the State and a similar overall impact on the State's remuneration.

63. The beneficiary should, have at any time, the possibility to buy back the equity stake that the State has acquired. To ensure that the State receives appropriate remuneration for the investment, the buy-back price should be the higher amount of (i) the nominal investment by the State increased by an annual interest remuneration 200 basis points higher than presented in the table below;[32n] or (ii) the market price at the moment of the buy-back.

[64. As an alternative, the State may sell at any time its equity stake at market prices to purchasers other than the beneficiary. Such a sale requires, in principle, an open and non-discriminatory consultation of potential purchasers or a sale on the stock exchange. The State may give existing shareholders, *i.e.* shareholders before the COVID-19 recapitalisation, priority rights to buy at the price resulting from the public consultation. If the State sells its equity stake at a price below the minimum price laid down in point 63, the governance rules laid down in section 3.11.6 shall continue to apply at least until four years after the COVID-19 equity injection measure was granted.]

[64*bis* If the State is the only existing shareholder, the redemption of COVID-19 recapitalisation may take the following form, notwithstanding point 64. Provided two years have passed since the granting of COVID-19 recapitalisation:

a. the sales process referred to in point 64 is not required, and
b. the open and non-discriminatory consultation referred to in point 64 may be replaced by a valuation of the beneficiary performed by an entity independent from that beneficiary and from the State. If that independent valuation establishes a positive market value, the State is deemed to have exited from the COVID-19 recapitalisation, even if the beneficiary remains State-owned. Nevertheless, if the positive market value is less than the minimum price laid down in point 63, the governance rules laid down in section 3.11.6 shall continue to apply until four years after the grant of the COVID-19 recapitalisation measure. For COVID-19 recapitalisation measures that exceed EUR 250 million, the Member State shall submit that independent valuation to the Commission. The Commission may in any case on its own initiative request the submission of the independent valuation and may evaluate it to ensure that it complies with the standard set to ensure transactions that are in line with market conduct.]

[64*ter.* If the State is one of several existing shareholders, the redemption of the COVID-19 recapitalisation may take the following form, alternatively to point 64. Provided two years have passed since the granting of the COVID-19 recapitalisation:

a. For the part of the COVID-19 equity that the State would need to retain in order to restore its shareholding to that before the COVID-19 recapitalisation, the possibility of point 64*bis* is applicable. If the State sells a significant fraction of the shares of the beneficiary undertaking to private investors via a competitive process as referred to in point 64, that process can be considered as an independent valuation for the purposes of point 64*bis*.
b. For the rest of the COVID-19 equity, point 64 applies. This includes in particular the need to conduct a competitive process. The State does not have the priority rights mentioned in point 64 as it already exercised that right under application of letter (a) above.[32o]

When the redemption of the COVID-19 recapitalisation concerns only a fraction of the COVID-19 equity, letters (a) and (b) above apply to that fraction of the COVID-19 equity.]

Remuneration of hybrid capital instruments

65. The overall remuneration of hybrid capital instruments must adequately factor in the following elements:

a. the characteristics of the instrument chosen, including its level of subordination, risk and all modalities of payment;
b. built-in incentives for exit (such as step-up and redemption clauses); and
c. an appropriate benchmark interest rate.

66. The minimum remuneration of hybrid capital instruments until they are converted into equity-like instruments shall be at least equal to the base rate (1 year IBOR or equivalent as published by the Commission),[32p] plus the premium as set out below.

Remuneration of hybrid capital instruments: 1-year IBOR +

Type of recipient	1st year	2nd and 3rd year	4th and 5th year	6th and 7th year	8th year and after
SMEs	225 bps	325 bps	450 bps	600 bps	800 bps
Large enterprises	250 bps	350 bps	500 bps	700 bps	950 bps

67. The conversion of hybrid capital instruments into equity shall be conducted at 5 percent or more below TERP (Theoretical Ex-Rights Price) at the time of the conversion.

68. After conversion into equity, a step-up mechanism must be included to increase the remuneration of the State, to incentivise the beneficiaries to buy back the State capital injections. If the equity resulting from the State's COVID-19 intervention is still owned by the State two years after the conversion into equity the State shall receive an additional share of ownership of the beneficiary in addition to its remaining participation resulting from the State's conversion of the COVID-19 hybrid capital instruments. This additional share of ownership shall be at a minimum 10 percent of the remaining participation resulting from the State's conversion of the COVID-19 hybrid capital instruments. The Commission may accept alternative step-up mechanisms provided they have the same incentive effect and a similar overall impact on the State's remuneration.

69. Member States may choose a pricing formula that includes additional step-up or payback clauses. Such features should be designed so that they encourage an early end to the State's recapitalisation support of the beneficiary. The Commission may also accept alternative pricing methodologies, provided they lead to remunerations that are higher than or similar to those resulting from the above methodology.

70. Since the nature of hybrid instruments varies significantly, the Commission does not provide guidance for all types of instruments. Hybrid instruments shall in any event follow the principles mentioned above, with remuneration reflecting the risk of the particular instruments.

3.11.6. Governance and prevention of undue distortions of competition

71. In order to prevent undue distortions of competition beneficiaries must not engage in aggressive commercial expansion financed by State aid or beneficiaries taking excessive risks. As a general principle, the smaller the equity stake of the Member State and the higher the remuneration, the less there is a need for safeguards.

72. If the beneficiary of a COVID-19 recapitalisation measure above EUR 250 million is an undertaking with significant market power on at least one of the relevant markets in which it operates, Member States must propose additional measures to preserve effective competition in those markets. In proposing such measures, Member States may in particular offer structural or behavioural commitments foreseen in Commission Notice on remedies acceptable under the Council Regulation (EC) No 139/2004 and under Commission Regulation (EC) No 802/2004.

73. Beneficiaries receiving a COVID-19 recapitalisation measures are prohibited from advertising it for commercial purposes.

74. As long as at least 75% of the COVID-19 recapitalisation measures have not been redeemed, beneficiaries other than SMEs shall be prevented from acquiring a more than 10% stake in competitors or other operators in the same line of business, including upstream and downstream operations.

75. In exceptional circumstances, and without prejudice to merger control, such beneficiaries may acquire a more than 10% stake in operators upstream or downstream in their area of operation, only if the acquisition is necessary to maintain the beneficiary's viability. The Commission may authorise the acquisition if it is necessary to maintain the beneficiary's viability. The acquisition may not be implemented before the Commission has taken a decision on this issue.

76. State aid shall not be used to cross-subsidise economic activities of integrated undertakings that were in economic difficulties already on 31 December 2019. A clear account separation shall be put in place in integrated companies to ensure that the recapitalisation measure does not benefit those activities.

77. As long as the COVID-19 recapitalisation measures have not been fully redeemed, beneficiaries cannot make dividend payments, nor non-mandatory coupon payments, nor buy back shares, other than in relation to the State.

[77*bis*. In derogation from the above, the ban on non-mandatory coupon payments does not apply to:

a) hybrid capital instruments issued at the same time[32p1] as, with the same level of subordination as, and with a coupon no more than 150 bps higher than the coupon on the COVID-19 hybrid capital instruments. Moreover, the COVID-19 hybrid capital instruments should correspond to more than 20 % of the overall hybrid issuance[32p2];
b) hybrid capital instruments issued after any COVID-19 recapitalisation, provided that the proceeds from those instruments are used exclusively to redeem the COVID-19 recapitalisation instruments and/or hybrid capital instruments issued in accordance with the present point 77bis; and
c) COVID-19 hybrid capital instruments whenever they are sold by the State to private investors (i.e. not public authorities) at a price equal to or greater than the par value of the hybrid instrument plus any accrued unpaid coupons including compound interest.

In any event, non-mandatory coupon payments on COVID-19 hybrid capital instruments shall take place before or at the same time as any respective coupon payments on hybrid capital instruments that benefit from the lifting of the ban on non-mandatory coupon payments pursuant to this point.

Without prejudice to the redemption options set out in letter b., in the case of a partial or full redemption of hybrid capital instruments that benefit from the lifting of the ban on non-mandatory coupon payments pursuant to this point, the beneficiary shall: (i) redeem at least the same amount of COVID-19 hybrid capital instruments[32p3]; or (ii) issue at least the same amount of new hybrid capital instruments; or (iii) if neither (i) nor (ii) are fulfilled within six months from the partial or full redemption of the hybrid capital instruments, increase, retroactively from the date of the redemption of the hybrid capital instrument, the remuneration on the outstanding COVID-19 hybrid capital instruments. In this latter case, the increase of the remuneration is calculated as the maximum step-up[32p4]) that may be applied over the life of the redeemed hybrid capital instruments on the nominal amount of such instrument[32p5], with a minimum of 100 bps. Moreover, in case of a partial redemption of COVID-19 hybrid capital instruments or in case of the issuance of new hybrid capital instruments, the nominal amount on which this remuneration increase is applied is reduced accordingly.

The present derogation will apply to all hybrid capital instruments mentioned above issued as of 18 November 2021, including in the context of COVID-19 recapitalisation measures already granted, as authorised by the Commission, prior to this date.]

[78. As long as at least 75% of the COVID-19 recapitalisation measures has not been redeemed, the remuneration of each member of the beneficiaries' management must not go beyond the fixed part of his/her remuneration on 31 December 2019. For persons becoming members of the management on or after the recapitalisation, the applicable limit is the fixed remuneration of the members of the management with the same level of responsibility on 31 December 2019. Under no circumstances, shall bonuses or other variable or comparable remuneration elements be paid.]

[78*bis* Where the State is an existing shareholder, *i.e.* before the COVID-19 equity injection, and:

a) the State injects new equity under the same conditions as private investors and pro rata to its existing shareholding (or below), and
b) the private participation is significant (in principle at least 30% of the new equity injected), and
c) the State's new equity injection constitutes State aid because of its particular circumstances, for instance because of another measure benefitting the company,

it is not necessary to impose specific conditions as regards the State's exit and the following shall apply:

i. points 61 and 62 do not apply to such a COVID-19 equity injection measure;
ii. in derogation from points 74, 75 and 78, the acquisition ban and the cap on the remuneration of the management are limited to three years;
iii. in derogation from point 77, the dividend ban is lifted for the holders of the new shares. For existing shares, the dividend ban is lifted, provided the holders of those existing shares are altogether diluted to below 10% in the company. If holders of existing shares are not altogether diluted to a share in the company below 10%, the dividend ban applies to existing shareholders for three years. In any event, the remuneration due for COVID-19 hybrid capital and subordinated debt instruments held by the State shall be paid before any dividends are paid to shareholders in a given year;
iv. the requirements in section 3.11.7 do not apply except for the reporting obligations under point 83 that shall apply for three years; and
v. all the other conditions laid down in section 3.11 apply *mutatis mutandis*.'

78*ter* Where the State injects equity into a company in which it is not an existing shareholder (*i.e.* before the COVID-19 equity injection measure), and

a) it injects new equity under the same conditions as private investors, and
b) the private participation is significant (in principle at least 30% of the new equity injected), and
c) where the State's equity injection constitutes State aid because of its particular circumstances, for instance because of another measure benefiting the company,

the following shall apply:

i. in derogation from point 77, the dividend ban is lifted for all holders of new shares. For existing shares, the dividend ban is lifted, provided the holders of such existing shares are altogether diluted to a share in the company below 10%. In any event, the remuneration due for COVID-19 hybrid capital and subordinated debt instruments held by the State shall be paid before any dividends are paid to shareholders in given a year; and
ii. all the other conditions laid down in section 3.11 apply *mutatis mutandis*.]

3.11.7. Exit strategy of the State from the participation resulting from the recapitalisation and reporting obligations

79. Beneficiaries other than SMEs that have received a COVID-19 recapitalisation of more than 25% of equity at the moment of intervention must demonstrate a credible exit strategy for the participation of the Member State, unless the State's intervention is reduced below the level of 25% of equity within 12 months from the date of the granting of the aid.[32q]

80. The exit strategy shall lay out:

a. the plan of the beneficiary on the continuation of its activity and the use of the funds invested by the State, including a payment schedule of the remuneration and of the redemption of the State investment (together 'the repayment schedule'); and
b. the measures that the beneficiary and the State will take to abide by the repayment schedule.

81. The exit strategy should be prepared and submitted to the Member State within 12 months after aid is granted and must to be endorsed by the Member State.

82. Beyond the obligation set out in points 79 to 81, beneficiaries must report to the Member State on the progress in the implementation of the repayment schedule and the compliance with the conditions in section 3.11.6 within 12 months of the schedule's presentation, and thereafter periodically every 12 months.

83. As long as the COVID-19 recapitalisation measures has not been fully redeemed, beneficiaries of a COVID-19 recapitalisation, other than SMEs, shall, within 12 months from the date of the granting of the aid and thereafter periodically every 12 months, publish information on the use of the aid received. In particular, this should include information on how their use of the aid received supports their activities in line with EU objectives and national obligations linked to the green and digital transformation, including the EU objective of climate neutrality by 2050.

84. The Member State should report to the Commission annually on the implementation of the repayment schedule and compliance with the conditions in section 3.11.6. Where the beneficiary received a COVID-19 recapitalisation above EUR 250 million, the report shall include information on compliance with the conditions set in point 54.

85. If six years after the COVID-19 recapitalisation the State's intervention has not been reduced below 15% of beneficiary's equity, a restructuring plan in accordance with the Rescue and Restructuring Guidelines must be notified to the Commission for approval. The Commission will assess whether the actions contemplated in the restructuring plan ensure the beneficiary's viability, also with a view of EU objectives and national obligations linked to the green and digital transformation, and the exit of the State without adversely affecting trade to an extent contrary to the common interest. If the beneficiary is not a publicly listed company, or is an SME, the Member State may decide to notify a restructuring plan only if the State's intervention has not been reduced below the level of 15% of equity seven years after the COVID-19 recapitalisation.]

[3.12 AID IN THE FORM OF SUPPORT FOR UNCOVERED FIXED COSTS

86. Member States may envisage contributing to the uncovered fixed costs of those undertakings for which the COVID-19 outbreak resulted in the suspension or reduction of their business activity.

87. If such measures constitute aid, the Commission will consider them compatible with the internal market on the basis of Article 107(3)(b) TFEU provided the following conditions are met:

[a. The aid is granted no later than 30 June 2022 and covers uncovered fixed costs incurred during the period between 1 March 2020 and 30 June 2022, including such costs incurred in part of that period ('eligible period');]

b. The aid is granted on the basis of a scheme to undertakings that suffer a decline in turnover during the eligible period of at least 30% compared to the same period in 2019;[32r]

c. Uncovered fixed costs are the fixed costs incurred by undertakings during the eligible period which are not covered by the profit contribution (i.e. revenues minus variable costs) during the same period and which are not covered by other sources, such as insurance, temporary aid measures covered by this Communication or support from other sources.[32s] The aid intensity shall not exceed 70% of the uncovered fixed costs, except for micro and small companies(within the meaning of Annex I of the General Block Exemption Regulation), where the aid intensity shall not exceed 90% of the uncovered fixed costs. For the purpose of this point, the losses of undertakings from their profit and loss statements during the eligible period[32t] are considered to constitute uncovered fixed costs. The aid under this measure may be granted based on forecasted losses, while the final amount of aid shall be determined after realisation of the losses on the basis of audited accounts or, with appropriate justification provided by the Member State to the Commission (for example in connection with the characteristics or size of certain type of undertakings) on the basis of tax accounts. Any payment exceeding the final amount of the aid shall be recovered;

[d. The overall aid shall not exceed EUR 12 million per undertaking.[32t1] The aid may be granted in the form of direct grants, tax and payment advantages or other forms such as repayable advances, guarantees, loans and equity provided the total nominal value of such measures remains below the overall cap of EUR 12 million per undertaking; all figures used must be gross, that is, before any deduction of tax or other charge;]

e. The aid under this measure shall not be cumulated with other aid for the same eligible costs;

f. Aid may not be granted to undertakings that were already in difficulty (within the meaning of the General Block Exemption Regulation)[32u] on 31 December2019. In derogation to the above, aid can be granted to micro or small enterprises (within the meaning of Annex I of the General Block Exemption Regulation) that were already in difficulty on 31 December 2019 provided that they are not subject to collective insolvency procedure under national law, and that they have not received rescue aid[*] or restructuring aid.[**]

[87*bis*. Measures granted under this Communication in the form of repayable advances, guarantees, loans or other repayable instruments may be converted into other forms of aid such as grants, provided the conversion takes place by 30 June 2023 at the latest and the conditions in this section are complied with.]

[3.13 INVESTMENT SUPPORT TOWARDS A SUSTAINABLE RECOVERY

88. Member States may envisage supporting private investment as a stimulus to overcome an investment gap accumulated in the economy due to the crisis. Such a stimulus could facilitate the development of certain economic activities or of certain economic areas.

89. The Commission will consider such measures compatible with the internal market under Article 107(3)(c) TFEU provided the following conditions are met:

a. The aid is granted on the basis of a scheme. The maximum individual aid amount that may be granted per undertaking shall in principle not exceed 1 % of the total budget available for such a scheme except in situations that will have to be duly justified by the Member State.

b. Eligible costs may include only the costs of investments in tangible and intangible assets. Costs related to purchasing land may be included only in as far as they are part of an investment for production of goods or provision of services. Financial investments are not eligible.

c. Member States may limit the aid to investments that support specific economic areas of particular importance for the economic recovery. However, such limits need to be designed broadly and not lead to an artificial limitation of eligible investments or potential beneficiaries that would result in targeting only a small number of undertakings.

d. The aid intensity may not exceed 15 % of the eligible costs. However,
   i. for investments made by small enterprises[32u1], the aid intensity may be increased by 20 percentage points;
   ii. for investments made by other SMEs[32u2], the aid intensity may be increased by 10 percentage points; or
   iii. for investments in assisted areas that comply with the conditions of Article 14 of the General Block Exemption Regulation, excluding Article 14(14) of the General Block Exemption Regulation, the aid intensity may be increased by the aid intensity established in the regional aid map, which is in force at the time the aid is granted in the area concerned.

e. The overall aid granted under this section may not exceed EUR 10 million per undertaking in nominal terms, regardless of the specific aid instrument. However, in assisted areas, the overall aid granted under this section per undertaking may not exceed the maximum aid amount calculated in accordance with Article 14 of the General Block Exemption Regulation, with the exception of Article 14(14) of the General Block Exemption Regulation and based on the applicable regional aid map, increased by EUR 10 million, in nominal terms, regardless of the specific aid instrument.

f. The aid may be granted in different forms, including non-repayable grants, tax grants or deferrals, subsidised interest rates on loans, or guarantees. In case of repayable instruments, Member States may provide for a possibility for conversion into grants under predefined conditions and on the basis of predefined criteria that must be laid down in the scheme and specified in the individual granting decisions. Repayable instruments such as loans as well as guarantees must be limited to a maximum duration of eight years.

90. In weighing the positive effects of the aid against its negative effects on competition and trade, the Commission will pay particular attention to Article 3 of the EU Taxonomy Regulation (EU) 2020/852, including the 'Do no significant harm' principle or other comparable methodologies. The Commission considers that investments that do significant harm to environmental objectives[32u3] are unlikely to have sufficient positive effects to outweigh their negative effects on competition and trade.[32u4]

91. Aid under this section may be added to notifiable regional investment aid and cumulated with other types of aid under the conditions specified in point 20 of this Temporary Framework. Under no circumstances may the total aid amount exceed 100 % of eligible costs. As a result, cumulation with other aid instruments that allow the coverage of a funding gap is excluded.

92. Aid under this section may not be granted to undertakings that were already in difficulty (within the meaning of the General Block Exemption Regulation[32u5]) on 31 December 2019. This does not apply to micro and small enterprises (within the meaning of Annex I to the General Block Exemption Regulation) that were already in difficulty on 31 December 2019 provided that they are not subject to collective insolvency procedure under national law and that they have not received rescue aid* or restructuring aid**.

93. Aid under this section may be granted until 31 December 2022. Aid for investments that predate 1 February 2020 is excluded.

94. Aid granted under this section shall be considered to have an incentive effect if the beneficiary has submitted a written application for the aid to the Member State concerned before works on the investment have started.

95. By way of derogation from point 94, measures in the form of tax advantages shall be deemed to have an incentive effect if the following conditions are fulfilled:

a. the measure establishes a right to aid in accordance with objective criteria and without further exercise of discretion by the Member State; and

b. the measure has been adopted and is in force before works on the investment have started.

96. Where investment support schemes exclusively provide aid in the form of guarantees or loans or similar repayable instruments, in derogation of point 89(e) the overall aid may not exceed EUR 15 million per undertaking in nominal terms and in derogation of point 89(d) aid intensities may not exceed 30 % of the eligible costs. Where the conditions of 89(d) (i), (ii), or (iii) apply, this limit may be increased in line with these provisions. Schemes under this point shall comply with points 25(a), 25(b), 25bis first and second sentence, or 27(a), 27(b), and 27bis first and second sentence respectively. Cumulation with other aid under this section is excluded. Furthermore, points 29, 30, and 31 must be respected. In case of guarantees, these may not exceed:

i. 90% of the loan principal where losses are sustained proportionally and under same conditions by the credit institution and the State; or

ii. 35% of the loan principal, where losses are first attributed to the State and only then to the credit institutions (i.e. a first-loss guarantee); and

iii. in both of the above cases, when the size of the loan decreases over time, for instance because the loan starts to be reimbursed, the guaranteed amount must decrease proportionally.

97. Member States may also consider setting up or amending existing schemes under the rules applicable to environmental or research projects, namely the Environmental and Energy Aid Guidelines[32u6] or the Research, Development and Innovation Aid Framework[32u7] to support the sustainable recovery of the economy. The Commission considers that, in light of the objectives to facilitate the speedy recovery of the European economy, Member States may temporarily envisage setting up or amending existing schemes that would also allow to cover larger individual aid under those guidelines, without requiring individual notification of measures. The Commission

will consider such aid schemes or amendments of existing schemes to be compatible where the applicable thresholds for individual notifications are exceeded by up to 50 %, provided all other provisions of the applicable guidelines are complied with, the Commission decision authorising the measure is taken before 1 January 2023, and the individual aid concerned is granted before 1 January 2024.]

[3.14 SOLVENCY SUPPORT

98. Member States may envisage supporting economic recovery by strengthening the solvency of undertakings. This may be especially the case where debt levels of companies have risen due to the economic crisis, which may hamper further investment and long-term growth. Such measures should be designed in a way that incentivises private investments into undertakings with growth potential.

99. The Commission will consider such measures compatible with the internal market under Article 107(3)(c) TFEU provided the following conditions are met:

a. Solvency support is provided as an incentive for private investments into equity, subordinated debt, or quasi-equity, including silent participations or participative loans.
b. The aid is granted on the basis of a scheme, in the form of public guarantees or similar measures for dedicated investment funds as an incentive to invest in final beneficiaries. Such investment shall be made via financial intermediaries in the form of such investment funds that are in principle selected in an open, transparent, and non-discriminatory procedure. The remuneration of the managers of those funds should in principle be based on the performance of the entire portfolio of the fund.
c. Eligible final beneficiaries are limited to SMEs and small mid-caps.[32u8]
d. In as far as credit institutions act as financial intermediaries in relation to measures taken under this section, for example by securitising such investments in order to make them available to other investors, they must share an appropriate part of the risk. Keeping at least 10 % of the volume of such instruments on the balance sheet of the institution would likely be considered appropriate risk-sharing.
e. Eligible schemes leverage additional new investments from private investors. Investments decisions need to be taken in a profit-oriented manner based on business or investment plans demonstrating that eligible final beneficiaries are long-term viable undertakings.
f. All institutional investors, irrespective of their nature or geographical location, may invest on equal terms in the investment funds to be set up.
g. The aid ensures that an appropriate share of the risk is borne by investors to ensure profit-driven investments. In case of first losses covered by the State, such risk sharing can be achieved by limiting the value of such a guarantee or similar measure to no more than 30 % of the underlying portfolio, including only the principal amounts without interest or any ancillary liabilities.
h. The duration of the guarantee does not exceed eight years in total, regardless of the underlying instrument. In case of guarantees on debt, it must not exceed the maturity of the underlying debt instrument. For equity investments, the guarantee may not cover investments made by the financial intermediary after the date specified in point 101.
i. The mobilisation of the guarantee is contractually linked to specific conditions ("guarantee events") which may go as far as the compulsory declaration of bankruptcy of the beneficiary undertaking, or any similar procedure. These conditions will have to be agreed between the parties when the guarantee is initially granted. In case of guarantees provided for equity investments, eligible losses may only be covered by the guarantee at the moment when the fund is dissolved and all portfolio investments have been divested on market terms.
j. The risk taken by the State is reflected in an adequate, market-oriented return. Such return can take the form of direct remuneration in form of a guarantee premium or rights to participate in profits to be accumulated by such funds, depending also on the nature of the instrument (be it subordinated loans or equity). It must be calibrated considering the investment grade of the final beneficiaries, the types of instruments covered, and the duration of the protection granted.
k. Effective safeguards are implemented to ensure that the advantage is passed on to the final beneficiaries to the maximum extent possible.
l. The total amount of finance provided does not exceed for EUR 10 million per undertaking.
m. With appropriate justification provided by the Member State to the Commission and additional conditions to limit competition distortions, the Commission may accept alternative selection and remuneration methods, higher amounts of finance and/or intermediate size enterprises.

100. Financial institutions are excluded as final beneficiaries.

101. Aid under this section may be granted no later than 31 December 2023.

102. Aid under this section may be cumulated with other aid, provided the respective thresholds and other conditions for such other aid are complied with. However, aid under this section may not be granted to undertakings receiving support under section 3.11 of this Communication.]

NOTES

Section 3.1 heading: substituted by the Second Amending Communication, point 22.

Point 22 is amended as follows:

The words in the first pair of square brackets and sub-para (c) were substituted by the First Amending Communication, point 12.

Sub-paras (a), (d) substituted by the Sixth Amending Communication, points 31–33, as from 18 November 2021.

Sub-para (d) substituted by the Fifth Amending Communication, point 21, as from 28 January 2021.

Sub-para (*cbis*) inserted by the Third Amending Communication, point 15.

Sub-para substituted by the Fourth Amending Communication, point 23.

Point 23: substituted by the First Amending Communication, point 13. Sub-para (a) substituted by the by the Sixth Amending Communication, point 34, as from 18 November 2021.

Point 23*bis*: originally inserted by the First Amending Communication), point 14. Subsequently substituted by the Sixth Amending Communication, point 35, as from 18 November 2021.

Point 23*ter*: originally inserted by the Fifth Amending Communication, point 25, as from 28 January 2021. Subsequently substituted by the Sixth Amending Communication, point 37, as from 18 November 2021.

Point 24: substituted by the Fifth Amending Communication, point 26, as from 28 January 2021.

Point 24*bis*: inserted by the Second Amending Communication, point 25.

Point 25 is amended as follows:

Substituted by the First Amending Communication, point 15.

Sub-paras (c) and (e), and the opening words of sub-para (d), were substituted by the Sixth Amending Communication, points 38–41, as from 18 November 2021.

Sub-para (d)(iii) substituted by the Second Amending Communication, point 26.

Sub-para (h*bis*) inserted by the Third Amending Communication, point 15.

Point 25*bis*: inserted by the Fifth Amending Communication, point 30, as from 28 January 2021.

Point 26: substituted by the Second Amending Communication, point 28.

Point 26*bis*: inserted by the Second Amending Communication, point 29.

Point 27 is amended as follows:

Substituted by the First Amending Communication, point 16.

Sub-para was substituted by the Fifth Amending Communication, point 314, as from 28 January 2021.

Sub-paras (c) and (e), and the opening words of sub-para (d), were substituted by the Sixth Amending Communication, points 41–43, as from 18 November 2021.

Sub-para (d)(iii) substituted by the Second Amending Communication, point 30.

Sub-para (g*bis*) inserted by the Third Amending Communication, point 15.

Point 27*bis*: originally inserted by the Second Amending Communication, point 32. Subsequently substituted by the Fifth Amending Communication, point 35, as from 28 January 2021.

Point 27*ter*: inserted by the Sixth Amending Communication, point 44, as from 18 November 2021.

Point 28: substituted by the Fourth Amending Communication, point 31.

Point 31: substituted by the Second Amending Communication, point 34.

Section 3.5: substituted by the First Amending Communication, point 17. Subsequently amended as follows—

Point 33: substituted by the Sixth Amending Communication, point 45, as from 18 November 2021.

Sections 3.6–3.10: inserted by the First Amending Communication, points 18–22. Subsequently amended as follows—

Point 35: sub-para (a) substituted by the Sixth Amending Communication, point 46, as from 18 November 2021. Sub-para (h*bis*) inserted by the Third Amending Communication, point 15.

Point 37: sub-para (b) substituted by the Sixth Amending Communication, point 47, as from 18 November 2021. Sub-para (j) substituted by the Second Amending Communication, point 35. Sub-para (k*bis*) inserted by the Third Amending Communication, point 15.

Point 39: sub-para (b) substituted by the Sixth Amending Communication, point 48, as from 18 November 2021. Sub-para (l*bis*) inserted by the Third Amending Communication, point 15.

Point 41: substituted by the Sixth Amending Communication, point 49, as from 18 November 2021.

Point 42: substituted by the Third Amending Communication, point 17.

Point 43: sub-para (a) substituted by the Third Amending Communication, point 18. Sub-para (c) substituted by the Sixth Amending Communication, point 50, as from 18 November 2021. Sub-para (d) substituted by the Fifth Amending Communication, point 42, as from 28 January 2021.

Point 43*bis*: inserted by the Second Amending Communication, point 36.

Section 3.11: inserted by the Second Amending Communication, point 37. Subsequently amended as follows—

Point 48: substituted by the Sixth Amending Communication, point 51, as from 18 November 2021.

Point 49: sub-para (d*bis*) inserted by the Third Amending Communication, point 15.

Point 54: substituted by the Fourth Amending Communication, point 37.

Points 64, 78: substituted by the Third Amending Communication, points 19, 20.

Points 64*bis*, 64*ter*: inserted by the Fourth Amending Communication, points 39, 40.

Point 77*bis*: inserted by the Sixth Amending Communication, point 52, as from 18 November 2021.

Points 78*bis*, 78*ter*: inserted by the Third Amending Communication, point 21.

Section 3.12: inserted by the Fourth Amending Communication, point 41. Subsequently amended as follows—

Point 87: sub-paras (a), (d) substituted by the Sixth Amending Communication, points 53–55, as from 18 November 2021. Sub-para (d) substituted by the Fifth Amending Communication, point 45, as from 28 January 2021.

Point 87*bis*: inserted by the Sixth Amending Communication, point 56, as from 18 November 2021.

Sections 3.13, 3.14: inserted by the Sixth Amending Communication, points 57, 58, as from 18 November 2021.

[14b] Aid granted on the basis of schemes approved under this section which has been reimbursed before granting new aid shall not be taken into account in determining whether the relevant ceiling is exceeded.

[15] As defined in Article 2 (18) of the Commission Regulation (EU) No 651/2014 of 17 June 2014 declaring certain categories of aid compatible with the internal market in application of Articles 107 and 108 of the Treaty (OJ L187, 26.6.2014, p 1). Wherever reference is made in this Temporary Framework to the definition of "undertaking in difficulty" as contained in Article 2(18) of Regulation (EU) No 651/2014, it shall be read as also referring to the definitions contained in Article 2(14) of Regulation (EU) No 702/2014 and Article 3(5) of Regulation 1388/2014 respectively.

[16] If the aid is granted in the form of a tax advantage, the tax liability in relation to which that advantage is granted must have arisen no later than 30 June 2022.

[17] As defined in Article 2(6) and Article 2(7) of Commission Regulation (EC) No 702/2014 of 25 June 2014 declaring certain categories of aid in the agricultural and forestry sectors and in rural areas compatible with the internal market in application of Articles 107 and 108 of the Treaty on the Functioning of the European Union (OJ L193, 1.7.2014, p 1).

[18] As defined in Article 2(1) of Commission Regulation (EU) No 717/2014 of 27 June 2014 on the application of Articles 107 and 108 of the Treaty on the Functioning of the European Union to de minimis aid in the fishery and aquaculture sector (OJ L190, 28.6.2014, p 45).

[19] As defined in Article 2(1) of Commission Regulation (EU) No 717/2014 of 27 June 2014 on the application of Articles 107 and 108 of the Treaty on the Functioning of the European Union to de minimis aid in the fishery and aquaculture sector, OJ L 190, 28.6.2014, p. 45.

[19a] As defined in Article 2(5) of Commission Regulation (EC) No 702/2014 of 25 June 2014 declaring certain categories of aid in the agricultural and forestry sectors and in rural areas compatible with the internal market in application of Articles 107 and 108 of the Treaty on the Functioning of the European Union, OJ L 193, 1.7.2014, p. 1.

[19b] Aid granted on the basis of schemes approved under this section which has been reimbursed before granting of new aid

shall not be taken into account in determining whether the relevant ceiling is exceeded.

20 Commission Regulation (EC) No (EU) No 717/2014 of 27 June 2014 on the application of Articles 107 and 108 of the Treaty on the Functioning of the European Union to de minimis aid in the fishery and aquaculture sector (OJ L190, 28.6.2014, p 45).

20a For the purposes of this section, the term 'public guarantees on loans' covers also guarantees on certain factoring products, namely guarantees on recourse and reverse factoring where the factor has the right of recourse to the factoree. Eligible reverse factoring products shall be limited to products that are used only after the seller has already provided its part of the transaction, i.e. the product or service has been delivered.

21 As defined in Annex I of Commission Regulation (EU) No 651/2014 of 17 June 2014 declaring certain categories of aid compatible with the internal market in application of Articles 107 and 108 of the Treaty (General Block Exemption Regulation).

22 The liquidity plan may include both working capital and investment costs.

23 As defined in Article 2(18) of the Commission Regulation (EU) No 651/2014 of 17 June 2014 declaring certain categories of aid compatible with the internal market in application of Articles 107 and 108 of the Treaty (OJ L187 of 26.6.2014, p 1).

23a For the avoidance of doubt, the omission of point 25(f)(ii) means that first-loss guarantees on debt instruments, which are subordinated to ordinary senior creditors in the case of insolvency proceedings, are not covered by this point..

23b If coupon payments are capitalised this must be taken into account when determining these ceilings, provided that such capitalisation was planned or foreseeable at the time of notification of the measure. Also any other State aid measure in the form of subordinated debt granted in the context of the COVID-19 outbreak, even outside this Communication, must be included in such calculation. However, subordinated debt granted in compliance with section 3.1 of this Communication does not count for these ceilings..

23c Except if such aid complies with the conditions of section 3.1 of this Communication.

24 Base rates calculated in accordance with the Communication from the Commission on the revision of the method for setting the reference and discount rates (OJ C14, 19.01.2008, p 6.) and published on the website of DG Competition at https://ec.europa.eu/competition/state_aid/legislation/reference_rates.html.

25 The minimum all in interest rate (base rate plus the credit risk margins) for SMEs and large enterprises should be at least 10bps per year.

26 The minimum all in interest rate (base rate plus the credit risk margins) should be at least 10bps per year.

27 As defined in Annex I of the General Block Exemption Regulation.

28 The liquidity plan may include both working capital and investment costs.

28a As defined in Article 2(18) of the Commission Regulation (EU) No 651/2014 of 17 June 2014 declaring certain categories of aid compatible with the internal market in application of Articles 107 and 108 of the Treaty (OJ L187, 26.6.2014, p 1).

28b If coupon payments are capitalised this must be taken into account when determining these ceilings, provided that such capitalisation was planned or foreseeable at the time of notification of the measure. Also any other State aid measure in the form of subordinated debt granted in the context of the COVID-19 outbreak, even outside this Communication, must be included in such calculation. However, subordinated debt granted in compliance with section 3.1 of this Communication does not count for these ceilings.

29 See point 6 of this Temporary Framework.

30 OJ C392, 19.12.2012, p 1.

31 COVID-19 and other antiviral relevant research includes research into vaccines, medicinal products and treatments, medical devices and hospital and medical equipment, disinfectants, and protective clothing and equipment, and into relevant process innovations for an efficient production of the required products.

32 As defined in paragraph (84), (85) and (86) of Article 2 of the Commission Regulation (EU) No 651/2014 of 17 June 2014 declaring certain categories of aid compatible with the internal market in application of Articles 107 and 108 of the Treaty (OJ L187, 26.6.2014, p 1).

32a As defined in Article 2 (18) of the Commission Regulation (EU) No 651/2014 of 17 June 2014 declaring certain categories of aid compatible with the internal market in application of Articles 107 and 108 of the Treaty (OJ L187, 26.6.2014, p 1).

32b As defined in Article 2 (18) of the Commission Regulation (EU) No 651/2014 of 17 June 2014 declaring certain categories of aid compatible with the internal market in application of Articles 107 and 108 of the Treaty (OJ L187, 26.6.2014, p 1).

32c As defined in Article 2 (18) of the Commission Regulation (EU) No 651/2014 of 17 June 2014 declaring certain categories of aid compatible with the internal market in application of Articles 107 and 108 of the Treaty, (OJ L187, 26.6.2014, p 1).

32d See also point 118 of the Commission Notice on the notion of State aid as referred to in Article 107(1) of the Treaty on the Functioning of the European Union C/2016/2946 (OJ C262, 19.7.2016, p 1).

32e See by analogy Commission decision SA.49554- CY- Cypriot scheme for non-performing loans collateralized with primary residences (Estia), recital 73 and Commission decision SA.53520-EL- Primary Residence Protection Scheme, recital 71.

32f See point 6 of this Communication.

32g The possibility of offering aid in the form of equity and/or hybrid capital instruments, but for much lower nominal amounts, is already provided under the conditions of section 3.1 of this Communication.

32h As set out in point 16 of the Communication, notification of alternative approaches remains possible in line with Article 107(3)(b) TFEU.

32i As defined in Article 2(18) of the Commission Regulation (EU) No 651/2014 of 17 June 2014 declaring certain categories of aid compatible with the internal market in application of Articles 107 and 108 of the Treaty (OJ L187, 26.6.2014, p 1).

32j Hybrid capital instruments are instruments that have characteristics of debt as well as of equity. For instance, convertible bonds are remunerated like bonds until they are converted into equity. The assessment of the overall remuneration of hybrid capital instruments thus depends on the one hand on their remuneration while they are debt-like instruments and on the other hand on the conditions for conversion into equity-like instruments.

32k For the purpose of this subsection 3.11.4, hybrid instruments granted by the State should be counted as equity.

32l Additional shares can, for instance, be granted via the issuance of convertible bonds at the date of the recapitalisation, which will be converted into equity at the date of trigger of the step-up mechanism.

32m For instance, if the step-up takes the form of the grant to the State of additional shares. If the State's participation in a beneficiary is 40% as a result of its capital injection, and if the State does not sell its participation before the requested date, the State's participation should increase by at least 0,1 x 40% = 4% to reach 44% four years after the COVID-19 equity injection, and to reach 48% six years after COVID-19 equity injection, resulting in a corresponding dilution of the stakes of other shareholders.

32n The 200 bps increase does not apply in year 8 and onwards.

32o Example: Pre-recapitalisation, the State owns 50% of the beneficiary undertaking. Following the COVID-19 recapitalisation, the State owns 90% of the undertaking (10% shareholding concerns pre-COVID-19 State-owned shares and 80% shareholding concerns COVID-19 shares). Two years after the COVID-19 recapitalisation, the State sells 40% of the undertaking (corresponding to 50% of the COVID-19 shares) via a competitive process to private investors (for a positive market value), in application of point 64ter, letter (b). The State retains the remaining part in application of point 64ter, letter (a). The sale is akin to an independent valuation of the company. The State is deemed to have redeemed the COVID-19 recapitalisation since the part of COVID-19 shares it retains restores its shareholding to pre-COVID-19 levels, i.e., 50%, and is equivalent to the State exercising its priority right under point 64. If the market price of the COVID-19 equity is less than the minimum price laid down in point 63, the governance rules laid down in section 3.11.6 continue to apply for two more years.'

32p Base rates calculated in accordance with the Communication from the Commission on the revision of the method for setting the reference and discount rates (OJ C14, 19.1.2008, p 6), published on the website of DG Competition at https://ec.europa.eu/competition/state_aid/legislation/reference_rates.html

32p1 For the purpose of this point, hybrid capital instruments issued up to six months after the issuance of the COVID-19 hybrid capital instruments are considered to have been issued at the same time as those instruments.

32p2 Such hybrid capital instruments shall be taken into account in the assessment under point 54.

32p3 Up to the total amount of existing COVID-19 hybrid capital instruments.

32p4 Difference between the contractually agreed maximum and minimum coupon rates over the lifetime of the hybrid instruments.

32p5 If the beneficiary redeems several tranches of hybrid capital instruments with different interest rates, this condition must be applied to each tranche independently.'

32q For the purpose of this subsection 3.11.7, hybrid instruments granted by the State should be counted as equity.

32r The reference period is a period in 2019 irrespective of whether the eligible period is in 2020, 2021 or 2022.

32s For the purpose of this point, costs refer to fixed and variable costs: the former are incurred independently of the level of output, while the latter are incurred depending on the level of output.

32t One-off impairment losses are not included in the calculation of the losses under this provision.

32t1 Aid granted on the basis of schemes approved under this section that has been reimbursed before granting new aid under this section shall not be taken into account in determining whether the relevant ceiling is exceeded.

32u As defined in Article 2(18) of the Commission Regulation (EU) No 651/2014 of 17 June 2014 declaring certain categories of aid compatible with the internal market in application of Articles 107 and 108 of the Treaty, OJ L187, 26.6.2014, p 1.

32u1 Within the meaning of Annex I of the General Block Exemption Regulation.

32u2 Within the meaning of Annex I of the General Block Exemption Regulation.

32u3 Within the meaning of Article 17 of Regulation (EU) 2020/852, OJ L 198, 22.6.2020, p. 13.

32u4 For measures which are identical to measures within Recovery and Resilience Plans as approved by the Council, compliance with the 'Do no significant harm' principle is considered fulfilled, since this has already been verified.

32u5 As defined in Article 2(18) of the General Block Exemption Regulation.

32u6 Guidelines on State aid for environmental protection and energy 2014-2020, OJ C 200, 28.6.2014, p. 1.

32u7 Framework for State aid for research and development and innovation, OJ C 198, 27.6.2014, p. 1.

32u8 As defined in point 52 (xxvii) of the Guidelines on State aid to promote risk finance investments, OJ C 19, 22.1.2014, p. 4.

* Alternatively, if they have received rescue aid, they have reimbursed the loan or terminated the guarantee at the moment of granting of the aid under this Communication.

** Alternatively, if they have received restructuring aid, they are no longer subject to a restructuring plan at the moment of granting of the aid under this Communication.'

---

4. MONITORING AND REPORTING

[[103]. Apart from aid granted under sections 3.9, 3.10 and 3.11, Member States must publish relevant information on each individual aid above EUR 100 000[33] granted under this Communication, and above EUR 10 000[33a] in the primary agriculture and in the fisheries sectors, on the comprehensive State aid website or Commission's IT tool[33b] within 12 months from the moment of granting. Member States must publish relevant information[33c] on each individual recapitalisation granted under section 3.11 on the comprehensive State aid website or Commission's IT tool within 3 months from the moment of the recapitalisation. The nominal value of the recapitalisation shall be included per beneficiary.]

[104]. Member States must submit annual reports to the Commission.[34]

[105]. By 30 June 2022, Member States must provide the Commission with a list of measures put in place on the basis of schemes approved based on this Communication.]

[106]. Member States must ensure that detailed records regarding the granting of aid provided for by this Communication are maintained. Such records, which must contain all information necessary to establish that the necessary conditions have been observed, must be maintained for 10 years upon granting of the aid and be provided to the Commission upon request.

[107]. The Commission may request additional information regarding the aid granted, to verify whether the conditions laid down in the Commission decision approving the aid measure have been met.

NOTES

Points 103–107: renumbered as such by the Sixth Amending Communication, point 59, as from 18 November 2021.

Point 103 (as so renumbered) was previously substituted by the Fifth Amending Communication, point 46, as from 28 January 2021.

Point 105 (as so renumbered) was substituted by the Sixth Amending Communication, point 60, as from 18 November 2021.

[33] Referring to information required in Annex III to Commission Regulation (EU) No 651/2014 of 17 June 2014 and of Annex III to Commission Regulation (EU) No 702/2014. For repayable advances, guarantees, loans, subordinated loans and other forms the nominal value of the underlying instrument shall be inserted per beneficiary. For tax and payment advantages, the aid amount of the individual aid may be indicated in ranges.

[33a] Referring to information required in Annex III to Commission Regulation (EU) No 702/2014 and Annex III to Commission Regulation (EU) No 1388/2014 of 16 December 2014. For repayable advances, guarantees, loans, subordinated loans and other forms the nominal value of the underlying instrument shall be inserted per beneficiary. For tax and payment advantages, the aid amount of the individual aid may be indicated in ranges.

[33b] The State aid transparency public search gives access to State aid individual award data provided by Member States in compliance with the European transparency requirements for State aid and can be found at https://webgate.ec.europa.eu/competition/transparency/public?lang=en.

[33c] Referring to information required in Annex III to Commission Regulation (EU) No 651/2014 of 17 June 2014 and of Annex III to Commission Regulation (EU) No 702/2014 and Annex III to Commission Regulation (EU) No 1388/2014 of 16 December 2014.

[34] OJ L140, 30.4.2004, p 1.

5. FINAL PROVISIONS

[[108]. The Commission applies this Communication from 19 March 2020, having regard to the economic impact of the COVID-19 pandemic, which required immediate action. This Communication is justified by the current exceptional circumstances and will not be applied after the dates specified herein. The Commission will review all sections under this Communication before 30 June 2022 on the basis of important competition or economic considerations. Where helpful, the Commission may also provide further clarifications on its approach to particular issues.]

[109]. The Commission applies the provisions of this Communication to all relevant notified measures as of 19 March 2020 even if the measures were notified prior to that date.

[110]. In accordance with the Commission notice on the determination of the applicable rules for the assessment of unlawful State aid[35] the Commission applies the following in respect of non-notified aid:

a. this Communication, if the aid was granted after 1 February 2020;
b. the rules applicable when the aid was granted in all other cases.

[111]. The Commission, in close cooperation with the Member States concerned, ensures swift adoption of decisions upon clear and complete notification of measures covered by this Communication. Member States should inform the Commission of their intentions and notify plans to introduce such measures as early and comprehensively as possible. The Commission will provide guidance and assistance to Member States in this process.

NOTES

Points 108–111: renumbered as such by the Sixth Amending Communication, point 59, as from 18 November 2021.

Point 108 (as so renumbered) was substituted by the Sixth Amending Communication, point 61, as from 18 November 2021.

[35] OJ C119, 22.5.2002, p 22.

COVID-19 – INFORMATION – PARTIES BEFORE THE GENERAL COURT CHANGE TO JUDICIAL ACTIVITIES (JUNE 2021)

[8.67]

NOTES

This document is available on the General Court section of the Curia website at curia.europa.eu/jcms/jcms/p1_3012067/en/. It was originally published on 19 November 2020, and was updated on 15 June 2021.

Owing to the current health crisis, the General Court has been obliged, since March 2020, to make changes to its working arrangements.

The aim of this communication is to summarise certain important information for parties and their representatives. As this information is subject to frequent changes depending on how the health crisis evolves, parties and their representatives are asked to consult this website regularly.

Time limits

Time limits continue to run and parties are required to comply with those time limits, without prejudice to the possibility of invoking the second paragraph of Article 45 of the Protocol on the Statute of the Court of Justice of the European Union. **Where it is possible for time limits to be extended, it is for a party seeking an extension to make a request in good time, so that the Court may give a ruling on that request.**

Hearings

Request for a hearing

Article 106 of the Rules of Procedure provides that any request for a hearing made by a main party 'must state the reasons for which that party wishes to be heard'. Paragraph 142 of the Practice Rules for the implementation of the Rules of Procedure makes clear that the request for a hearing must contain a statement of reasons.

Since the organisation of hearings is made more difficult by the health crisis, a main party seeking a hearing is encouraged to consider whether that hearing is appropriate in the circumstances and, if a request for a hearing is submitted, ensure that that request genuinely meets the requirements laid down by the Rules of Procedure.

Travel to Luxembourg for a hearing

To facilitate travel to Luxembourg, the Registry can, on request, issue representatives with a document certifying that a hearing is being held before the General Court.

If it is not possible for a party's representative to travel to Luxembourg to attend a hearing before the General Court owing to the health crisis and measures taken by the national authorities, he or she may lodge, by way of a specific emergency measure, a reasoned request to participate in the hearing via video conference link. That request must be lodged as early as possible prior to the hearing date. Before lodging such a request, the representative must familiarise himself or herself with the documents attached to the notification of the hearing sent by the Registry ('Technical requirements' and 'Best practice' guidance for parties making submissions remotely) and check that the requirements described can be met. These requirements (including the technical equipment to be used) are intended to ensure the highest quality of image, sound and interpretation for everyone participating in the hearing. The use of video conferencing will be decided by the General Court, subject to a series of technical and interpreting tests to be taken by the representative and within the limits of the resources available to the Court.

Sanitary measures adopted in order to ensure the efficient conduct of hearings (applicable to the Court of Justice and the General Court)

The strictest sanitary measures are adopted, in accordance with the laws adopted by the Luxembourgish authorities, in order to allow hearings of the Court of Justice and of the General Court to proceed efficiently.

Those measures concern both (I) access to the institution's buildings and the rules that must be complied with while moving around within them, and (II) the arrangements for the hearing itself, which have been adapted in response to the current exceptional circumstances.

I. Access to the institution's buildings and the essential rules of conduct within them

Access by parties' representatives to the institution's buildings is exclusively through the entrance to the Erasmus building (rue du fort Niedergrünewald, L-2925 Luxembourg).

The reception procedure for parties' representatives is similar to the usual procedure, subject to a temperature check, which is carried out at a distance (persons with a temperature higher than 37.5°C are not permitted to enter the buildings).

If parties' representatives do not possess appropriate masks upon arrival at the institution's buildings, a mask will be provided by the security service. The mask must be worn at all times while moving around the institution's buildings and wherever it is not possible to maintain a distance of two meters between two individuals.

In the same way as the institution's staff, parties' representatives are asked to read carefully the information given on notice boards and to observe strictly the instructions given. Those notices are repeated, where appropriate, by relevant markings on the floor and walls.

Finally, it should be noted that new procedures for restaurant services have been put in place. The parties' representatives may dine inside the institution's buildings, in the same way as the institution's staff, provided the applicable sanitary rules are complied with.

II. Arrangements for hearings

In order to provide a high level of sanitary protection, tables, microphones and earphones are disinfected after each hearing.

The institution will not be making gowns available for use by parties' representatives. Agents and lawyers are therefore asked to bring their own gown for use at hearings but, if that is not possible, the Court of Justice and the General Court will, by way of derogation from the applicable rules, allow representatives to plead without a gown.

Contrary to the usual practice, the members of the formation of the Court hearing the case will not be meeting with parties' representatives before the start of hearings. The registrar for the hearing and the court usher will check, before the start of the hearing, that the parties' representatives are present.

The necessary arrangements have also been made in order to ensure compliance with physical distancing rules within each hearing room. The parties' representatives will be positioned in such a way as to maintain a distance of two meters between each person in the room.

A mask must be worn in the hearing room. Parties' representatives are to make their oral submissions from the place that will have been indicated to them. In cases where one microphone must be used by several people, it will be cleaned and disinfected after each use.

Those representatives who wish to provide a text or written outline for their oral submissions for the benefit of the interpretation services are asked to send them, where possible, before midday (local time of the Grand Duchy of Luxembourg) on the working day before the day of the hearing, to the following address: Interpretation@curia.europa.eu.

COVID-19 – INFORMATION -- PARTIES BEFORE THE COURT OF JUSTICE CHANGE TO JUDICIAL ACTIVITIES (JUNE 2021)

[8.68]

NOTES

This document is available on the Court of Justice section of the Curia website at curia.europa.eu/jcms/jcms/p1_3012066/en/. It was originally published on 16 November 2020, and was updated on 15 June 2021.

Owing to the current health crisis, the Court of Justice has been obliged, since March 2020, to make changes to its working arrangements. Those changes concern the conduct of the written phase of proceedings – and, in particular, the extension of certain time limits for the filing of parties' statements or observations – as well as the conduct of the oral phase of proceedings.

The aim of this communication is to summarise all of those measures for the parties and their representatives. As these measures remain subject to frequent modifications depending on how the health crisis evolves, parties and their representatives are asked to consult this website regularly.

Procedural time limits

Procedural time limits continue to run despite the health crisis and parties are required to comply with those time limits, without prejudice to the possible application of the second paragraph of Article 45 of the Protocol on the Statute of the Court of Justice of the European Union ('the Statute').

In order to take into account the particular circumstances of the present time and in order to allow the interested parties referred to in Article 23 of the Statute to have available to them, in those circumstances, an amount of time that is sufficient for the submission of their observations in requests for preliminary rulings referred to the Court of Justice, the time limit for submitting written observations in requests for preliminary rulings – except in the case of requests subject to the accelerated procedure or the urgent procedure – is currently extended by one month. That additional month is to be added to the time limit of two months and ten days that flows from the combined application of Article 23 of the Statute and Article 51 of the Rules of Procedure of the Court of Justice.

Given the evolving improvement in the health crisis, the above-mentioned time limit will, however, not be extended again beyond the month of August. **From 1 September 2021, the ordinary procedural time limits shall, therefore, apply to all procedural documents served by the registry as from that date**. Interested parties referred to in Article 23 of the Statute of the Court of Justice will, therefore, once more be subject to the usual time limit, which cannot be extended, of two months and ten days, in which to submit any written observations in requests for a preliminary ruling served by the Court.

Hearings

All necessary measures are being taken to ensure that hearings take place under optimal conditions from both a logistical and sanitary perspective, but the holding and conduct of hearings evidently remain dependent on the decisions taken by the national authorities in order to combat transmission of the virus. If a party is entirely unable to travel to Luxembourg, they may, under certain conditions, be permitted to attend a hearing by videoconference. Furthermore, it cannot be ruled out that some hearings may have to be replaced with questions to the parties for a written response owing to the difficulties caused by Covid-19.

In order to ensure the efficient conduct of hearings, particularly from a linguistic perspective, **parties' representatives are asked to inform the registry as soon as possible whether they will be attending a hearing, or whether they are prevented from attending**.

Communication with the parties - Importance of the e-Curia application

In order to facilitate communication with the parties in this period of crisis, the courts of the Member States and parties' representatives who do not yet have an e-Curia account are strongly encouraged to become familiar with e-Curia, which is a secure application and allows procedural documents to be filed and served electronically in cases brought before the Court. All details as to the application's functions and the method for opening an account can be found here: e-Curia. (curia.europa.eu/jcms/jcms/P_78957/en/).

Due to the circumstances, application forms for opening accounts sent to the registry by email will be accepted, exceptionally, provided that they are accompanied by the necessary supporting documents, which are duly signed and scanned.

Sanitary measures adopted in order to ensure the efficient conduct of hearings (applicable to the Court of Justice and the General Court)

The strictest sanitary measures are adopted, in accordance with the laws adopted by the Luxembourgish authorities, in order to allow hearings of the Court of Justice and of the General Court to proceed efficiently.

Those measures concern both (I) access to the institution's buildings and the rules that must be complied with while moving around within them, and (II) the arrangements for the hearing itself, which have been adapted in response to the current exceptional circumstances.

I. Access to the institution's buildings and the essential rules of conduct within them

Access by parties' representatives to the institution's buildings is exclusively through the entrance to the Erasmus building (rue du fort Niedergrünewald, L-2925 Luxembourg).

The reception procedure for parties' representatives is similar to the usual procedure, subject to a temperature check, which is carried out at a distance (persons with a temperature higher than 37.5°C are not permitted to enter the buildings).

If parties' representatives do not possess appropriate masks upon arrival at the institution's buildings, a mask will be provided by the security service. The mask must be worn at all times while moving around the institution's buildings and wherever it is not possible to maintain a distance of two meters between two individuals.

In the same way as the institution's staff, parties' representatives are asked to read carefully the information given on notice boards and to observe strictly the instructions given. Those notices are repeated, where appropriate, by relevant markings on the floor and walls.

Finally, it should be noted that new procedures for restaurant services have been put in place. The parties' representatives may dine inside the institution's buildings, in the same way as the institution's staff, provided the applicable sanitary rules are complied with.

II. Arrangements for hearings

In order to provide a high level of sanitary protection, tables, microphones and earphones are disinfected after each hearing.

The institution will not be making gowns available for use by parties' representatives. Agents and lawyers are therefore asked to bring their own gown for use at hearings but, if that is not possible, the Court of Justice and the General Court will, by way of derogation from the applicable rules, allow representatives to plead without a gown.

Contrary to the usual practice, the members of the formation of the Court hearing the case will not be meeting with parties' representatives before the start of hearings. The registrar for the hearing and the court usher will check, before the start of the hearing, that the parties' representatives are present.

The necessary arrangements have also been made in order to ensure compliance with physical distancing rules within each hearing room. The parties' representatives will be positioned in such a way as to maintain a distance of two meters between each person in the room.

A mask must be worn in the hearing room. Parties' representatives are to make their oral submissions from the place that will have been indicated to them. In cases where one microphone must be used by several people, it will be cleaned and disinfected after each use.

Those representatives who wish to provide a text or written outline of their oral submissions for the benefit of the interpretation services are asked to send them, where possible, before midday (local time of the Grand Duchy of Luxembourg) on the working day prior to the day of the hearing, to the following address: Interpretation@curia.europa.eu.

APPENDIX

Appendix: List of Consultations & Draft Documents

[A1]

NOTES

This Appendix lists the titles of UK and EU consultations and draft documents and gives the internet address where these can be found.

PART 3 CMA GUIDELINES ETC

NHS Long term plan: legislative proposals inquiry (June 2019)

https://publications.parliament.uk/pa/cm201719/cmselect/cmhealth/2000/200002.htm

Algorithms, competition and consumer harm: call for information (January 2021)

https://www.gov.uk/government/consultations/algorithms-competition-and-consumer-harm-call-for-information

Retained Vertical Agreements Block Exemption Regulation (February 2021)

https://www.gov.uk/government/consultations/retained-vertical-block-exemption-regulation?utm_medium=email&utm_campaign=govuk-notifications&utm_source=097d5375-a86e-42cf-b37a-ac4d1c61df15&utm_content=daily

Interim measures in merger cases (April 2021)

https://www.gov.uk/government/consultations/interim-measures-in-merger-cases

Ofcom: the future of media plurality in the UK (June 2021)

https://www.ofcom.org.uk/consultations-and-statements/category-2/future-media-plurality-uk

CMA's guidance on the appropriate amount of a penalty – Draft for consultation (July 2021)

https://www.gov.uk/government/consultations/consultation-on-draft-ca98-penalties-guidance

BEIS: Reforming competition and consumer policy (July 2021)

https://www.gov.uk/government/consultations/reforming-competition-and-consumer-policy

DCMS and BEIS: A new pro-competition regime for digital markets (July 2021)

https://www.gov.uk/government/consultations/a-new-pro-competition-regime-for-digital-markets

Consultation on draft Competition Act 1998 procedures guidance (August 2021)

https://www.gov.uk/government/consultations/consultation-on-draft-ca98-procedures-guidance

Environmental sustainability advice to government: Call for inputs (September 2021)

https://www.gov.uk/government/consultations/environmental-sustainability-advice-to-government-call-for-inputs

PART 4 EU MATERIALS (EXCLUDING STATE AID)

Timeline for Mergers and Antitrust policy reviews 2019–2022

https://ec.europa.eu/competition/antitrust/legislation/timeline_table_M_AT_final.pdf

Single Market: new complementary tool to strengthen competition enforcement (June 2020)

https://ec.europa.eu/info/law/better-regulation/have-your-say/initiatives/12416-New-competition-tool/public-consultation_en

Digital Services Act package – ex ante regulatory instrument of very large online platforms acting as gatekeepers (June 2020)

https://ec.europa.eu/info/law/better-regulation/have-your-say/initiatives/12418-Digital-Services-Act-package-ex-ante-regulatory-instrument-of-very-large-online-platforms-acting-as-gatekeepers_en

White Paper on Foreign Subsidies (June 2020)

https://ec.europa.eu/info/law/better-regulation/have-your-say/initiatives/12452-White-Paper-on-Foreign-Subsidies_en

EU competition law – market definition notice (evaluation) (June 2020)

https://ec.europa.eu/info/law/better-regulation/have-your-say/initiatives/12325-Evaluation-of-the-Commission-Notice-on-market-definition-in-EU-competition-law/public-consultation_en

Proposal for a Regulation of the European Parliament and of the Council on contestable and fair markets in the digital sector (Digital Markets Act)

https://content.mlex.com/Attachments/2021-11-23_O5L8G1T4MWKN7S3Q/DMA_Comrpomise_AMs_EN.pdf

Review of the Motor Vehicle Block Exemption Regulation (January 2021)

https://ec.europa.eu/competition-policy/sectors/motor-vehicles/review-motor-vehicle-block-exemption-regulation_en

Collective bargaining agreements for self-employed – assessing the scope of application of Article 101 TFEU (March 2021)

https://ec.europa.eu/competition-policy/public-consultations/2021-collective-bargaining_en

Merger control in the EU – further simplification of procedures (March 2021)

https://ec.europa.eu/info/law/better-regulation/have-your-say/initiatives/12957-Merger-control-in-the-EU-further-simplification-of-procedures_en

Proposal for a Regulation of the European Parliament and of the Council on foreign subsidies distorting the internal market (May 2021)

https://ec.europa.eu/competition/international/overview/proposal_for_regulation.pdf

Draft revised Regulation on vertical agreements and vertical guidelines – for consultation (July 2021)

https://ec.europa.eu/competition-policy/public-consultations/2021-vber_en

Horizontal agreements between companies – revision of EU competition rules (July 2021)

https://ec.europa.eu/info/law/better-regulation/have-your-say/initiatives/13058-Horizontal-agreements-between-companies-revision-of-EU-competition-rules/public-consultation_en

PART 5 STATE AID

Agriculture – simplified EU approval scheme (block exemption) for state subsidies (review) (January 2019)

https://ec.europa.eu/info/law/better-regulation/have-your-say/initiatives/11548-Agriculture-simplified-EU-approval-scheme-block-exemption-for-state-subsidies-review-_en

2012 State aid modernisation package, railways guidelines and short-term export credit insurance – fitness check (April 2019)

https://ec.europa.eu/info/law/better-regulation/have-your-say/initiatives/2044-Fitness-check-of-2012-State-aid-modernisation-package-railways-guidelines-and-short-term-%20export-credit-insurance/public-consultation_en

Review of agricultural State aid guidelines (April 2019)

https://ec.europa.eu/info/law/better-regulation/have-your-say/initiatives/2089-Agricultural-State- aid-guidelines-review_en

Targeted consultation on the ex-post evaluation of the 2014 Aviation Guidelines (May 2019)

https://ec.europa.eu/competition-policy/public-consultations/2019-aviation-guidelines_et

Block-exempted state aid – fishing and fish farming sector (2021–27) (May 2019)

https://ec.europa.eu/info/law/better-regulation/have-your-say/initiatives/11545-Block-exempted-state-aid-fishing-and-fish-farming-sector-2021-27-_en

State aid (small amounts) – fishing and fish farming sector (2021–27) (May 2019)

https://ec.europa.eu/info/law/better-regulation/have-your-say/initiatives/11543-State-aid-small-amounts-fishing-and-fish-farming-sector-2021-27-_en

Public consultation on state aid guidelines for fisheries – amendment (June 2019)

https://ec.europa.eu/info/law/better-regulation/have-your-say/initiatives/11544-Amendment-to-the-State-aid-Guidelines-for-fisheries/public-consultation_en

Targeted review of the General Block Exemption Regulation (State aid): extension to national funds combined with certain Union programmes (June 2019)

https://ec.europa.eu/competition-policy/public-consultations/2019-gber_en

State subsidy rules for health and social services of general economic interest (evaluation) (July 2019)

https://ec.europa.eu/info/law/better-regulation/have-your-say/initiatives/11835-State-subsidy-rules-for-health-and-social-services-of-general-economic-interest-evaluation-_en

Timeline for State aid policy reviews 2020–2024

https://ec.europa.eu/competition-policy/system/files/2021-11/timeline_policy_review_state-aid.pdf

Targeted review of the General Block Exemption Regulation (State aid): extended scope for national funds to be combined with certain Union programmes (2nd consultation) (May 2020)

https://ec.europa.eu/competition-policy/public-consultations/2020-gber_en

State aid for environmental protection and energy – revised guidelines (November 2020)

https://ec.europa.eu/info/law/better-regulation/have-your-say/initiatives/12616-State-aid-for-environmental-protection-and-energy-revised-guidelines_en

Consultation on the Notice on the enforcement of State aid rules by national courts (January 2021)

https://ec.europa.eu/competition-policy/public-consultations/2021-sa-enforecement-notice_en

Communication on the Framework for State aid for research and development and innovation – draft for consultation (April 2021)

https://ec.europa.eu/competition-policy/public-consultations/2021-rdi_en

Revised Guidelines on State aid to promote risk finance investments – draft for consultation (May 2021)

https://ec.europa.eu/competition-policy/public-consultations/2021-risk-finance_en

Regulation amending the Agriculture and Fishery De minimis regulations – draft for consultation (May 2021)

https://ec.europa.eu/competition-policy/public-consultations/2021-deminimis-agri_en

Revised Climate, Energy and Environmental Aid Guidelines - draft for consultation (June 2021)

https://ec.europa.eu/competition-policy/public-consultations/2021-ceeag_en

Revision of the Short-term export credit insurance Communication (September 2021)

https://ec.europa.eu/competition-policy/public-consultations/2021-revision-stec_en

Information request: Availability of short-term export-credit insurance for exports to all countries in the Annex of the Short-term export-credit insurance Communication (October 2021)

https://ec.europa.eu/competition-policy/public-consultations/2021-availability-stec_en

Targeted review of the General Block Exemption Regulation (State aid): revised rules for State aid promoting the green and digital transition (October 2021)

https://ec.europa.eu/competition-policy/public-consultations/2021-gber_en

Revised Guidelines on State aid for broadband networks – draft for consultation (November 2021)

https://ec.europa.eu/competition-policy/public-consultations/2021-broadband_en

Index

NOTES

The Competition and Markets Authority (references to the OFT and Competition Commission etc)

On 1 April 2014 the Competition and Markets Authority replaced the Office of Fair Trading and the Competition Commission as part of the wider reform to the UK competition regime. As a consequence, many of the OFT and Competition Commission guidance documents reproduced in previous editions of this Handbook have been replaced or rendered obsolete. Others have been adopted by the CMA Board. See further the introductory notes to Part 3 *ante*. In cases where this index contains a reference to a paragraph number contained in an OFT or Competition Commission document adopted by the CMA, the index entry will contain a reference to the CMA, and not the OFT or Competition Commission.

O

P

V